S0-AAG-919

NAVE'S TOPICAL LIVING BIBLE

NAVE'S TOPICAL LIVING BIBLE

Topically Arranged Selections from Scripture

using the text of

The Living Bible, Paraphrased

More Than Twenty Thousand
Topics and Subtopics
Over One Hundred Thousand
References to the Scriptures

by Orville J. Nave
Edited by Suellen Sinclair Wenz

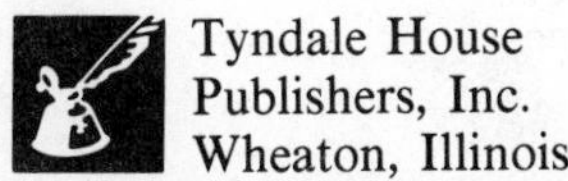

Tyndale House
Publishers, Inc.
Wheaton, Illinois

First printing, March 1982
Nave's Topical Living Bible
Library of Congress Catalog Card Number 82–80155
ISBN 0–8423–4669–4, cloth

Printed in the United States of America

Editor's Preface

Nave's Topical Bible has the distinction of having been an important resource work for at least three generations. It was the work of Orville J. Nave, A.M., D.D., LL.D., who was a U. S. Army chaplain during the latter part of the nineteenth century. Based originally upon the King James Version, this reference work has served thousand of serious Bible students, beginning with its first appearance in 1896.

The Living Bible, Paraphrased is the work of Kenneth N. Taylor, Th.M., Litt.D., L.H.D., and appeared in seven component volumes between 1962 and 1970. The complete, one-volume edition was released in 1971. *The Living Bible* is known throughout the world for its easy readability and contemporary clarity of vocabulary. In his preface to the earliest edition of *The Living Bible*, Dr. Taylor explained a paraphrase in this way: "To paraphrase is to say something in different words than the author used. It is a restatement of an author's thoughts, using different words than he did. This book is a paraphrase of the Old and New Testaments. Its purpose is to say as exactly as possilbe what the writers of the Scriptures meant, and to say it simply, expanding where necessary for a clear understanding by the modern reader."

Most editions of *Nave's Topical Bible* contain the compiler's preface, in which Dr. Nave outlined his purpose for the book and offered suggestions for its effective use. We quote from that preface:

"The object of this book is to bring together in cyclopedic form and under familiar headings all that the Bible contains on particular subjects. The subjects formulated are of practical value to every profession and to all who desire to consult the Bible.

"Verses, parts of verses, series of verses, and chapters are cited or quoted as often as they contain distinct subjects. Numerous verses are repeated from one to thirty times each, according to the number of subjects they contain and their position in extensive citations or extracts. . . . Passages variously interpreted by different religious schools or accepted authorities are cited under the subjects they are claimed to support, without reference to the personal views of the author.

"Some subjects abound in the Scriptures to such an extent, and are used so frequently by religious teachers and others, that, were references only given in this work to the books, chapters, and verses containing them, the student would stagger at the thought of developing the topics. In order to make this class of subjects quickly and easily available, the verses, or parts of verses, themselves are printed. This method of treatment might have been extended, but the size of a convenient volume had to be taken into consideration. Minor topics are made almost equally available by brief sub-topical divisions followed by references.

"One of the most important, and it is believed valuable, features of this book is its elaborate system of cross references to kindred and antithetical subjects. Wide scope is thus given each subject by connecting it with those to which it is related.

"Under the sub-topic, INSTANCES OF, are grouped all the illustrative facts that occur in the Scriptures relating to each subject. As a book of illustrations this book should prove valuable. It also contains numerous and elaborate Bible readings, with a wide range of subjects.

"It was not the object of the author in preparing this Digest to develop religious subjects only, but to note and classify everything found in the Scriptures. It is believed that it is approximately exhaustive."

By combining the topical organization of *Nave's Topical Bible* with the fresh, up-to-the-minute vernacular of *The Living Bible*, Tyndale House Publishers has produced a book which will be cherished for research and reference as well as for devotional and inspirational reading.

Suellen Sinclair Wenz
Editor

AARON Lineage of, Ex 6:16–20; Josh 21:4, 9–16; 1 Chron 6:2,3; 23:13. Marriage of, Ex 6:23. Children of, Ex 6:23,25; 1 Chron 6:3; 24:1,2. Descendants of, Ex 6:23,25; 1 Chron 6:3–15,50–53; 24.

Meets Moses in the wilderness and is made spokesman for Moses, Ex 4:14–16,27–31; 7:1,2. Inspiration of, Ex 12:1; Lev 10:8,9; 11:1; 13:1; 15:1; Num 2:1; 4:1,17–19; 18:1; 19:1; 20:12. Commissioned as a deliverer of Israel, Ex 6:13,26,27; Josh 24:5; 1 Sam 12:8; Ps 77:20; 105:26; Mic 6:4. Summoned to Sinai with Nadab, Abihu, and 70 elders, Ex 19:24; 24:1,9,10.

Priesthood of, Ex 28:1; 29:9; Num 17; 18:1; Ps 99:6; Heb 5:4. Consecration of, to the priesthood, Ex 28; 29; Lev 8. Enters the priestly office, Lev 9. See *Priest, High.* Descendants of, ordained priests forever, Ex 28:40–43; 29:9; Num 3:3; 18:1; 1 Chron 23:13; 2 Chron 26:17,18.

Judges Israel in the absence of Moses, Ex 24:14. Makes the golden calf-idol, Ex 32; Deut 9:20,21; Acts 7:40. Rod of, buds, Num 17; Heb 9:4; preserved, Num 17; Heb 9:4. Murmured against, by the people, Ex 5:20,21; 16:2–10; Num 14:2–5,10, 11; 16:3–12,41; 20:2; Ps 106:16. Places container of manna in the ark, Ex 16:34. With Hur supports the hands of Moses during battle, Ex 17:12. His blessings on the people, Lev 9:22; Num 6:22,23. Forbidden to mourn the death of his sons, Nadab and Abihu, Lev 10:6,19. Intercedes for Miriam, Num 12:11,12. Stops the plague by priestly intercession, Num 16:46–48. Jealous of Moses, Num 12:11. His presumption, when the rock is struck, Num 20:10–12. Not permitted to enter Canaan, Num 20:12,23–29. Age of, at death, Num 33:38,39. Death and burial of, Num 20:27,28; Deut 10:6; 32:50.

Character of, Ps 106:16.

AB See *Calendar.*

ABADDON The Prince of the bottomless pit, Rev 9:11.

See *Apollyon.*

ABAGTHA A Persian eunuch, Esther 1:10.

ABANA River of Damascus, 2 Kgs 5:12.

ABARIM A mountain range east of the Jordan, Num 27:12; 33:47; Deut 32:49.

See *Nebo, 2.*

ABDA Father of Adoniram, 1 Kgs 4:1–6.

ABDEEL Father of Shelemiah, Jer 36:26.

ABDI 1. A Levite, son of Malluch, 1 Chron 6:44–47.

2. Father of Kish, 2 Chron 29:12–14. Possibly identical to 1, above.

3. An Israelite who divorced his heathen wife, Ezra 10:26.

ABDI-EL A Gadite, 1 Chron 5:15.

ABDON 1. A judge of Israel, in the time of the judges, Judg 12:13–15.

2. A Levitical city, Josh 21:30; 1 Chron 6:74.

3. A Benjaminite chief, 1 Chron 8:22–25.

4. Son of Je-iel, 1 Chron 8:30–32; 9:35–37.

5. Son of Micah, 2 Chron 34:20. Called also *Achbor,* 2 Kgs 22:12.

ABEDNEGO Called also *Azariah,* a Jewish captive in Babylon, Dan 1:6–20; 2:17,49; 3:12–30; Heb 11:34.

ABEL 1. Son of Adam. History of, Gen 4:1–15,25. References to the death of, Mt 23:35; Lk 11:51; Heb 11:4; 12:24; 1 Jn 3:12.

2. See *Abel-beth-maacah.*

ABEL-BETH-MAACAH Called also *Abel* and *Abel-Maim.* A city in the north of Palestine. Sheba killed in, 2 Sam 20:14–22. Taken by Ben-hadad, 1 Kgs 15:20; 2 Chron 16:4; by Tiglath, 2 Kgs 15:29.

ABEL-MAIN See *Abel-beth-maacah.*

ABEL-MEHOLAH A city near the Jordan, Judg 7:22; 1 Kgs 4:8–19. Elisha's birthplace, 1 Kgs 19:16.

ABEL-MIZRAIM The place where the Israelites mourned for Jacob, Gen 50:11.

ABEL-SHITTIM See *Acacia, 1.*

ABETTING See *Complicity.*

ABI Mother of Hezekiah, 2 Kgs 18:2. Called *Abijah,* 2 Chron 29:1.

ABI-ALBON Called also *Abiel.* One of David's heroes, 2 Sam 23:24–39; 1 Chron 11:26–47.

ABIASAPH Son of Korah, Ex 6:24.

ABIATHAR High priest, son of Ahimelech, 1 Sam 22:20. Escapes to David from the vengeance of Saul, who killed the priests in the city of Nob, 1 Sam 22:20–23, with *vs.* 6–19. Consults the ephod for David, 1 Sam 22:9,10; 23:9; 30:7. Associate high priest with Zadok during the reign of David, 2 Sam 15:35,36; 20:25; 1 Kgs 4:1–6; 1 Chron 15:11. Loyal to David when Absalom rebelled; leaves

Jerusalem with the Ark of the Covenant, but is directed by David to return with the Ark, 2 Sam 15:24–29. Aids David by sending his son from Jerusalem to David with secret information concerning the counsel of Ahithophel, 2 Sam 15:35,36; 17:15–22; 1 Kgs 2:26. Supports Adonijah's pretensions to the throne, 1 Kgs 1:7. Thrown out of office by Solomon, 1 Kgs 2:26,27, with 1 Sam 2:31–35.

It is not certain whether Abiathar had a son named Ahimelech or whether the names have been transposed, 2 Sam 8:17; 1 Chron 18:16; 24:3,6,31. See *Ahimelech.*

ABIB See *Calendar.*

ABIDA Son of Midian, Gen 25:4; 1 Chron 1:33.

ABIEL 1. Saul's grandfather, 1 Sam 9:1; 14:51.

2. See *Abi-Albon.*

ABIEZER 1. Called also *Jezer,* progenitor of the Abiezrites, Num 26:28–37; Josh 17:2; Judg 6:34; 8:2,3.

2. One of David's heroes, 2 Sam 23:24–39; 1 Chron 27:12.

ABIGAIL 1. Nabal's wife. Her wisdom and tact, and marriage to David, 1 Sam 25; 27:2,3; 2 Sam 2:2. Mother of Chileab (or Daniel) by David, 2 Sam 3:3; 1 Chron 3:1. Taken captive and rescued by David, 1 Sam 30:1–19.

2. David's sister, and mother of Amasa, 2 Sam 17:25; 1 Chron 2:16,17.

ABIHAIL 1. Father of Esther, Esther 2:15.

2. Mother of Mahalath, Rehoboam's wife, 2 Chron 11:18,19.

3. A Levite and father of Zuriel, Num 3:31–35.

4. Wife of Abishur, 1 Chron 2:29.

5. A Gadite living in Gilead (in Bashan), 1 Chron 5:14.

ABIHU Son of Aaron, Ex 6:23; Num 3:2. Summoned by God to Sinai, Ex 24:9. Called to the priesthood, Ex 28:1. Death of, Lev 10:1,2; Num 26:61. Died childless, Num 3:4.

ABIHUD Son of Bela, 1 Chron 8:3–5.

ABIJAH 1. Son of Samuel, 1 Sam 8:1–5; 1 Chron 6:28.

2. Son of Jeroboam, 1 Kgs 14:1–18.

3. Leader of one of the temple service corps divisions, Lk 1:55. Called also *Ahijah,* 1 Chron 24:10.

4. King of Judah. See *Abijam.*

5. Son of Becher, 1 Chron 7:8.

6. A priest who signed the covenant with Nehemiah, Neh 10:1–8.

7. A priest who returned from exile with Zerubbabel, Neh 12:1–7.

8. A priestly clan, Neh 12:12–21.

9. See *Abi.*

ABIJAM King of Judah, 1 Kgs 14:31; 15:1. History of, 1 Kgs 15:1–8. Succeeded by Asa, 1 Kgs 15:8. Called also *Abijah,* 1 Chron 3:10; 2 Chron 11:22; 12:16; 13; 14:1.

ABILENE A Roman province in Palestine, Lk 3:1.

ABIMA-EL Son of Joktan, Gen 10:6–30; 1 Chron 1:20–23.

ABIMELECH 1. King of Gerar, Gen 20; 21:22–32.

2. Another king of Gerar, Gen 26.

3. Son of Gideon, Judg 8:31; 9; 2 Sam 11:19–21.

4. See *Achish.*

5. See *Ahimelech.*

ABINADAB 1. A Levite, in whose house the ark of God remained 20 years, 1 Sam 7:1,2; 2 Sam 6:3; 1 Chron 13:7.

2. Son of Jesse, 1 Sam 16:8; 17:13.

3. Called also *Ishvi,* son of Saul, 1 Sam 14:49; 31:2.

4. Father of one of Solomon's court officials, Ben-abinadab, 1 Kgs 4:8–19.

ABINOAM Father of Barak, Judg 4:6.

ABIRAM 1. An Israelite who conspired with Dathan against Moses and Aaron, Num 16; 26:5–11; Deut 11:6; Ps 106:17.

2. Son of Hiel, 1 Kgs 16:34.

ABISHAG David's nurse, 1 Kgs 1:1–4; 2:13–25.

ABISHAI Son of Zeruiah, David's sister, 1 Chron 2:16. One of David's chief officers, 2 Sam 23:18. Seeks Saul's life, 1 Sam 26:5–8. Pursues and kills Abner, 2 Sam 2:24; 3:30. Defeats the Edomites, 1 Chron 18:12; the Ammonites, 2 Sam 10:10,14. Seeks the life of Shime-i, 2 Sam 16:9; 19:21. Leads a division of David's army against Absalom, 2 Sam 18:2,5. Overthrows Sheba, 2 Sam 20:1–22. Saves David from being killed by a Philistine, 2 Sam 21:17. Obtains water from the well of Bethlehem for David, 1 Chron 11:15–20.

ABISHALOM See *Absalom, 2.*

ABISHUA 1. A high priest, 1 Chron 6:4–15, 50–53.

2. A son of Bela, 1 Chron 8:4.

ABISHUR Son of Shammai, 1 Chron 2:28,29.

ABITAL Wife of David, 2 Sam 3:4; 1 Chron 3:3.

ABITUB A Benjaminite, 1 Chron 8:11.

ABIUD Ancestor of Jesus, Mt 1:13.

ABLUTION Ceremonial washing, Ex 19:10, 14; Mt 15:2; Mk 7:1–5,8,9; Lk 11:37,38; Heb 9:10. Of priests, Ex 29:3,4; 30:17–21; 40:12,31,32; Lev 8:6; 16:4,24,26,28; Num 19:7–10,19; 2 Chron 4:6.

Of burnt offerings, Lev 1:9,13; 9:14; 2 Chron 4:6. Of the dead, Acts 9:37. Of infants, Ezk 16:4. Of the feet, Gen 18:3,4; 24:32; 43:24; Ex 30:19; 40:31; Song 5:3; Lk 7:38,44; Jn 13:5. Of the hands, Ex 30:17–21; 40:30–32. Of the hands, as a token of innocency, Deut 21:6; Ps 26:6; Mt 27:24.

For defilement: Of lepers, Lev 14:3,9; those having genital discharge, Lev 15:5–13; those having eaten a dead animal, Lev 17:15,16.

Traditional forms of, not observed by Jesus, Lk 11:37–39.

See *Purification; Defilement.*

FIGURATIVE. Ps 51:2. Oh, wash me, cleanse me from this guilt. Let me be pure again. [7]Sprinkle me with the cleansing blood and I shall be clean again. Wash me and I shall be whiter than snow.

Ps 73:13. Have I been wasting my time? Why take the trouble to be pure?

Prov 20:9. Who can ever say, "I have cleansed my heart; I am sinless"?

Isa 1:16. Oh, wash yourselves, be clean! *v.* 18.

Isa 4:2–4. Those whose names are written down to escape the destruction of Jerusalem will be washed and rinsed of all their moral filth by the horrors and the fire. They will be God's holy people. And the land will produce for them its lushest bounty and its richest fruit.

Isa 52:11. You are the holy people of the Lord; purify yourselves, all you who carry home the vessels of the Lord.

Jer 33:8. And I will cleanse away all their sins against me, and pardon them.

Ezk 36:25. Then it will be as though I had sprinkled clean water on you, for you will be clean—your filthiness will be washed away, your idol worship gone. [33]The Lord God says: When I cleanse you from your sins, I will bring you home again to Israel, and rebuild the ruins.

Dan 12:10. Many shall be purified by great trials and persecutions. Zech 13:1; Jn 13:8.

Acts 22:16. And now, why delay? Go and be baptized, and be cleansed from your sins, calling on the name of the Lord.

1 Cor 5:7. Remove this evil cancer—this wicked person—from among you, so that you can stay pure.

1 Cor 6:11. There was a time when some of you were just like that but now your sins are washed away, and you are set apart for God, and he has accepted you because of what the Lord Jesus Christ and the Spirit of our God have done for you. 2 Cor 7:1; Eph 5:26.

Tit 3:5. Then he saved us—not because we were good enough to be saved, but because of his kindness and pity—by washing away our sins and giving us the new joy of the indwelling Holy Spirit [6]whom he poured out upon us with wonderful fullness—and all because of what Jesus Christ our Savior did.

Heb 1:3. He is the one who died to cleanse us and clear our record of all sin, and then sat down in highest honor beside the great God of Heaven.

Heb 9:14. Just think how much more surely the blood of Christ will transform our lives and hearts. His sacrifice frees us from the worry of having to obey the old rules, and makes us want to serve the living God.

Heb 10:22. Let us go right in, to God himself, with true hearts fully trusting him to receive us, because we have been sprinkled with Christ's blood to make us clean, and because our bodies have been washed with pure water.

Jas 4:8. Wash your hands, you sinners, and let your hearts be filled with God alone to make them pure and true to Him.

1 Jn 1:7. But if we are living in the light of God's presence, just as Christ does, then we have wonderful fellowship and joy with each other, and the blood of Jesus his Son cleanses us from every sin. [9]But if we confess our sins to him, he can be depended on to forgive us and to cleanse us from all wrong.

Rev 7:14. "These are the ones coming out of the Great Tribulation," he said; "they washed their robes and whitened them by the blood of the Lamb." Rev 22:14.

See *Regeneration.*

ABNER Son of Ner. Cousin of Saul, 1 Sam 14:50, 51, with 1 Sam 9:1. General of the army, 1 Sam 14:50; 17:55; 26:5, 14. Dedicated spoils of war to the Tabernacle, 1 Chron 26:27, 28. Loyalty of, to the house of Saul, 2 Sam 2:8–32. Alienation of, from the house of Saul, 2 Sam 3:6–21. Murdered by Joab, David's sorrow from, 2 Sam 3:27–39.

ABOMINATION Detestable act or characteristic. Things that are, to God: Idolatry, Deut 7:25; 12:30,31; 27:15; 32:16; Jer 13:27; 32:34; unjust weights and measures, Deut 25:13–16; Prov 11:1; 20:10,23; homosexuality, Lev 18:22; 20:13; remarriage to previous wife, Deut 24:4; incest, Lev 18:6–18; sexual relation with a woman during menstruation, Lev 18:19; adultery, Lev 18:20; sodomy, Lev 18:23; offering children in sacrifice, Lev 18:21; Deut 18:10; sorcery and necromancy, Deut 18:10,11; the earnings of a prostitute or homosexual as an offering, Deut 23:18. See also Lev 18:24–30.

UNCLASSIFIED SCRIPTURES RELATING TO. Deut 22:5. A woman must not wear men's clothing, and a man must not wear women's clothing. This is abhorrent to the Lord your God.

Prov 3:31. Don't envy violent men. Don't copy their ways. [32]For such men are an abomination to the Lord, but he gives his friendship to the godly.

Prov 6:16–19. For there are six things the Lord hates—no seven: haughtiness, lying, murdering, plotting evil, eagerness to do wrong, a false witness, sowing discord among brothers.

Prov 8:7. For I hate lies and every kind of deception.

Prov 11:20. The Lord hates the stubborn but delights in those who are good.

Prov 12:22. God delights in those who keep their promises, and abhors those who don't.

Prov 15:8. The Lord hates the gifts of the wicked, but delights in the prayers of his people. [9]The Lord despises the deeds of the wicked, but loves those who try to be good. [26]The Lord hates the thoughts of the wicked but delights in kind words.

Prov 16:5. Pride disgusts the Lord. Take my word for it—*proud men shall be punished.*

Prov 17:15. The Lord despises those who say that bad is good, and good is bad.

Prov 20:10. The Lord despises every kind of cheating. *v.* 23

Prov 21:27. God loathes the gifts of evil men, especially if they are trying to bribe him!

Prov 24:9. The rebel's schemes are sinful, and the mocker is the scourge of all mankind.

Prov 28:9. God doesn't listen to the prayers of men who flout the law.

Prov 29:27. The good hate the badness of the wicked. The wicked hate the goodness of the good.

Lk 16:15. Then he said to them [Pharisees], "You

wear a noble, pious expression in public, but God knows your evil hearts. Your pretense brings you honor from the people, but it is an abomination in the sight of God."

ABOMINATION OF DESOLATION An act of sacrilege by which the Temple of God would be defiled. It is first mentioned in the prophecy of Daniel, Dan 9:27; 12:11, and is thought by some to have been fulfilled by Antiochus IV in 169 B.C. when he took treasures from the Holy of Holies. Later references to it by Jesus suggest a different fulfillment. In the Olivet Discourse, Jesus notes that it is the sign to warn the inhabitants of Judea to escape because the great tribulation is about to begin, Mt 24:15–22; Mk 13:14–23. Some think it was fulfilled in 70 A.D. when Jerusalem was destroyed by the Roman Titus. The premillennial or literal view is that the abomination will probably be an image set up in the Temple by the Antichrist as part of the still future great tribulation, 2 Kgs 23:13,14; Rev 13:14.

See *Tribulation, The Great.*

ABORTION Ex 21:22. If two men are fighting, and in the process hurt a pregnant woman so that she has a miscarriage, but she lives, then the man who injured her shall be fined whatever amount the woman's husband shall demand, and as the judges approve. [23]But if any harm comes to the woman and she dies, he shall be executed.

As a judgment, Hos 9:14. Of animals, caused by thunder, Ps 29:9.

ABRAHAM Called also *Abram.* Son of Terah, Gen 11:26. Marries Sarai, Gen 11:29. Lives in Ur, but moves to Haran, Gen 11:31; Neh 9:7; Acts 7:5, and Canaan, Gen 12:4–6; Acts 7:4.

Divine call of, Gen 12:1–3; Josh 24:3; Neh 9:7; Isa 51:1,2; Acts 7:2,3; Heb 11:8. Canaan given to, Gen 12:1,7; 15:7–21; Ezk 33:24. Lives in Bethel, Gen 12:8. Lives in Egypt, Gen 12:10–20; 26:1. Deferring to Lot, chooses Hebron, Gen 13; 14:13; 35:27. Lives in Gerar, Gen 20; 21:22–34.

Defeats Ched-or-laomer, Gen 14:5–24; Heb 7:1. Is blessed by Melchizedek, Gen 14:18–20; Heb 7:1–10.

God's covenant with, Gen 15; 17:1–22; Mic 7:20; Lk 1:72,73; Rom 4:13; 15:8; Gal 3:6–18,29; 4:22–31; Heb 6:13,14. Called *Abraham,* Gen 17:5; Neh 9:7. Circumcision, Gen 17:9–14,23–27. Angels appear to, Gen 18:1–16; 22:11,15; 24:7. His questions about the destruction of the godly and wicked in Sodom, Gen 18:23–32. Witnesses the destruction of Sodom, Gen 19:27,28. Ishmael born to, Gen 16:2,3,15. Lives in Gerar; deceives Abimelech concerning Sarah, his wife, Gen 20. Isaac born to, Gen 21:1–3; Gal 4:22–30. Sends Hagar and Ishmael away, Gen 21:10–14; Gal 4:22–30.

Test of his faith in the offering of Isaac, Gen 22:1–19; Heb 11:17; Jas 2:21. Sarah, his wife, dies, Gen 23:1,2. He purchases a place for her burial, and buries her in a cave, Gen 23:3–20. Marries Keturah, Gen 25:1. Provides a wife for Isaac, Gen 24.

Children of, Gen 16:15; 21:1–3; 25:1–4; 1 Chron 1:32–34. Testament of, Gen 25:5,6. Wealth of, Gen 13:1,2; 24:35; Isa 51:1,2. Age of, at different periods, Gen 12:4; 16:16; 21:4,5; 25:7,8. Death, Gen 15:15; 25:7–10. In Paradise, Mt 8:11; Lk 13:28; 16:22–31.

Friend of God, 2 Chron 20:7; Isa 41:8; Jas 2:23. Piety of, Gen 12:7,8; 13:3,4,18; 18:19; 20:7; 21:33; 22:3–13; 26:5; 2 Chron 20:7; Neh 9:7,8; Isa 41:8; Rom 4:16–18; Jas 2:23. A prophet, Gen 20:7. Faith of, Gen 15:6; Rom 4:1–22; Gal 3:6–9; Heb 11:8–10, 17–19; Jas 2:21–24. Unselfishness of, Gen 13:9; 21:25–30. Independence of, in character, Gen 14:23; 23:5–16.

Ancestors of, idolatrous, Josh 24:2. How regarded by his descendants, Mt 3:9; Lk 13:28; 19:9,10; Jn 8:33–40, 52–59.

ABRONAH A camping place of the Israelites, Num 33:34,35.

ABSALOM 1. Son of David by Maacah, 2 Sam 3:3; 1 Chron 3:2. Beauty of, 2 Sam 14:25. Kills Amnon, 2 Sam 13:21–30. Flees to Geshur, 2 Sam 13:37–39. Is permitted by David to return to Jerusalem, 2 Sam 14:1–24. His demagogism, 2 Sam 15:2–6,13; conspiracy, 2 Sam chapters 15–17; death and burial, 2 Sam 18:9–17. David's mourning for, 2 Sam 18:33; 19:1–7. Children of, 2 Sam 14:27; 18:18; 1 Kgs 15:1,2; 2 Chron 11:20. Monument of, 2 Sam 18:18.

2. Father of Maacah, wife of Rehoboam, 2 Chron 11:20. Called *Abishalom* in 1 Kgs 15:1,2,10.

ABSTINENCE, TOTAL FROM INTOXICATING BEVERAGES. Lev 10:8,9. Now the Lord instructed Aaron, "Never drink wine or strong drink when you go into the Tabernacle, lest you die; and this rule applies to your sons and to all your descendants from generation to generation. [10]Your duties will be to arbitrate for the people, to teach them the difference between what is holy and what is ordinary, what is pure and what is impure."

Num 6:3,4. He must not thereafter, during the entire period of his special consecration to the Lord, taste strong drink or wine or even fresh wine, grape juice, grapes or raisins! He may eat nothing that comes from grape vines, not even the seeds or skins!

Judg 13:4. Don't drink any wine or beer, and don't eat any food that isn't kosher. [13,14]And the Angel replied, "Be sure that your wife follows the instructions I gave her. She must not eat grapes or raisins, or drink any wine or beer, or eat anything that isn't kosher."

Esther 1:8. The only restriction on the drinking was that no one should be compelled to take more than he wanted, but those who wished could have as much as they pleased. For the king had instructed his officers to let everyone decide this matter for himself.

Prov 23:19,20. Oh my son, be wise and stay in God's paths; don't carouse with drunkards and gluttons. [31]Don't let the sparkle and the smooth taste of strong wine deceive you. [32]For in the end it bites like a poisonous serpent; it stings like an adder.

Prov 31:4. And it is not for kings, O Lemuel, to

drink wine and whiskey. Chapter 20:1; Isa 5:22.

Jer 35:6. "No," they said. "We don't drink, for Jonadab our father (son of Rechab) commanded that none of us should ever drink, neither we nor our children forever. [7]He also told us not to build houses or plant crops or vineyards and not to own farms, but always to live in tents; and that if we obeyed we would live long, good lives in our own land. [8]And we have obeyed him in all these things. We have never had a drink of wine since then, nor our wives or our sons or daughters either." [14]They don't drink, because their father told them not to. But I have spoken to you again and again and you won't listen or obey.

Lk 1:15. For he will be one of the Lord's great men. He must never touch wine or hard liquor—and he will be filled with the Holy Spirit, even from before his birth!

See *Temperance.*

INSTANCES OF. Israelites in the wilderness, Deut 29:6. Samson, Judg 16:16,17, with 13:2–5,13,14; Num 6:3,4. Daniel and his Hebrew companions, Dan 1:8–16. Rechabites, Jer 35:6–14. John the Baptist, Mt 11:18; Lk 1:15; 7:33.

ACACIA 1. Called also *Abel-shittim,* Num 33:49. A camping place of Israel, Num 25:1; 33:49. Joshua sends spies from, Josh 2:1. Valley of, Joel 3:18. Balaam prophesies in, Mic 6:5.

2. A tree, the wood of which is fragrant. The Ark of the Covenant made of, Ex 25:10; poles of the Ark, Ex 25:13,14; 38:6; framework of the Tabernacle, Ex 26:15–37; the altar of burnt offering, Ex 38:1.

ACCAD A city conquered by Nimrod, Gen 10:10.

ACCESSORY See *Complicity.*

ACCO Called also *Ptolemais,* a Phoenician seaport, Judg 1:31,32; Acts 21:7.

ACCOMPLICE See *Complicity.*

ACCOUNTABILITY See *Responsibility.*

ACCUSATION, FALSE Ex 23:1. Do not pass along untrue reports. Do not cooperate with an evil man by affirming on the witness stand something you know is false. [7]Keep far away from falsely charging anyone with evil; never let an innocent person be put to death. I will not stand for this.

Lev 19:16. Don't gossip. Don't falsely accuse your neighbor of some crime, for I am Jehovah.

Ps 41:5. But my enemies say, "May he soon die and be forgotten!" [6]They act so friendly when they come to visit me while I am sick; but all the time they hate me and are glad that I am lying there upon my bed of pain. And when they leave, they laugh and mock. [7]They whisper together about what they will do when I am dead. [8]"It's fatal, whatever it is," they say. "He'll never get out of that bed!" [9]Even my best friend has turned against me—a man I completely trusted; how often we ate together.

Mt 5:11. When you are reviled and persecuted and lied about because you are my followers—wonderful!

Lk 3:14. "And us," asked some soldiers, "What about us?" John replied, "Don't extort money by threats and violence; don't accuse anyone of what you know he didn't do; and be content with your pay!"

2 Tim 3:3. They will be constant liars and troublemakers and will think nothing of immorality.

1 Pet 4:14. Be happy if you are cursed and insulted for being a Christian, for when that happens the Spirit of God will come upon you with great glory.

See *Conspiracy; Evidence; False Witness; Gossip; Persecution; Speaking, Evil.*

INCIDENTS ILLUSTRATIVE OF. Against Joseph by Potiphar's wife, Gen 39:7–20; against Joseph's brothers by Joseph, Gen 42:8–14; against Moses by Korah, Num 16:3,13; against the prophet Ahimelech by Saul, 1 Sam 22:11–16; against Abner by Joab, 2 Sam 3:24–27; against David by the princes of Ammon, 2 Sam 10:3; against Elijah by Ahab, 1 Kgs 18:17,18; against Naboth by Jezebel, 1 Kgs 21:9,10,13; against Jews, returned under Ezra, Ezra 4:6–16; Neh 6:5–8; against Jeremiah, Jer 26:7,8,11; 37:13,14; 43:2,3; against Amos, Amos 7:10,11; against Mary, Mt 1:19; against Jesus, Mt 9:34; 10:25; 12:2–14; 26:59–61; 27:12; Mk 3:22; 15:3,4; 14:53–65; Lk 23:2; Jn 18:30; against Stephen, Acts 6:11,13; against Paul, Acts 17:7; 21:28; 24:5,6,13; 25:2,7; Rom 3:8; against Paul and Silas, Acts 16:20,21. Satan falsely accuses Job, Job 1:9,10; 2:4,5.

ACHAIA A region of Greece. Paul visits, Acts 18; 19:21; 1 Cor 16:15; 2 Cor 1:1. Benevolence of the Christians in, Rom 15:26; 2 Cor 11:10.

ACHAICUS A citizen of Corinth, 1 Cor 16:17, 18.

ACHAN The son of Carmi, sin and punishment of, Josh 7; 22:20; 1 Chron 2:7.

ACHBOR 1. Father of King Baal-hanan, Gen 36:39; 1 Chron 1:49.

2. One of Josiah's courtiers, 2 Kgs 22:14. Called also *Abdon,* 2 Chron 34:20.

3. Father of Elnathan, Jer 26:22; 36:12.

ACHIM Ancestor of Jesus, Mt 1:14.

ACHISH King of the Philistines, called also *Abimelech.* David escapes to, 1 Sam 21:10–15; 27; 28:1,2; 29; 1 Kgs 2:39,40.

ACHOR A valley near Jericho, Josh 7:26; 15:7; Isa 65:10; Hos 2:15.

ACHSAH Caleb's daughter, Josh 15:16–19; Judg 1:9–13; 1 Chron 2:49.

ACHSHAPH An ancient city in north Palestine, Josh 11:1; 12:20; 19:25.

ACHZIB 1. A city of Asher, Josh 19:29; Judg 1:31,32.

2. A city of Judah, Josh 15:44, Mic 1:14. Called also *Chezib,* Gen 38:3,4,5.

ACKNOWLEDGMENT Of Christ, see *Confession, of Christ.*

ACRE The indefinite quantity of land a yoke of oxen could plow in a day with the kinds of plows, and modes of plowing, used in the times referred to, 1 Sam 14:14; Isa 5:10.

ACROSTIC POETRY See *Poetry.*

ACTIONS AT LAW Duty of defendant, Mt 5:40.

See *Adjudication; Arbitration.*

ADADAH A city of Judah, Josh 15:22.

ADAH 1. Wife of Lamech, Gen 4:19–23.

2. Wife of Esau, Gen 36:10–12.

ADAIAH 1. Grandfather of Josiah, 2 Kgs 22:1,2.

2. A musician, 1 Chron 6:41.

3. A priest, 1 Chron 9:12; Neh 11:12.

4. A Benjaminite, 1 Chron 8:21.

5. Father of Maaseiah, 2 Chron 23:1

6. Two sons of Bani, Ezra 10:29,39.

7. Son of Joiarib, Neh 11:5.

ADALIA Son of Haman, Esther 9:8.

ADAM 1. The first man. Creation of, Gen 1:26–28; 2:7; 1 Cor 15:45; 1 Tim 2:13. History of, before he sinned, Gen 1:26–30; 2:16–25. Temptation and sin of, Gen 3; Job 31:33; Isa 43:27; Hos 6:7 (see R.V.); Rom 5:14–21; 1 Tim 2:14. Subsequent history of, Gen 3:20–24; 4:1,2,25; 5:1–5. His death, Gen 5:3,4,5.

Progenitor of the human race, Acts 17:26. Brought sin into the world, 1 Cor 15:22,45. Type of Christ, Rom 5:14.

2. A name of Christ, 1 Cor 15:45,47.

3. A city near the Jordan, Josh 3:15,16.

ADAMAH Called also *Adami-nekeb,* a city of Naphtali, Josh 19:33,36.

ADAMI-NEKEB See *Adamah.*

ADAR See *Calendar.*

ADBEEL Son of Ishmael, Gen 25:13; 1 Chron 1:29.

ADDAN A Persian city, Ezra 2:59. Called also *Addon,* Neh 7:61.

ADDAR Son of Bela, 1 Chron 8:3–5.

ADDER A venomous snake, Prov 23:32.

FIGURATIVE. Isa 11:81; 14:29.

ADDON See *Addan.*

ADI-EL 1. A prince of the tribe of Simeon, 1 Chron 4:36.

2. A priest, 1 Chron 9:12.

3. Father of Azmaveth, 1 Chron 27:25.

ADIN A Jewish captive, Ezra 2:15; 8:6; Neh 7:20; 10:16.

ADINA One of David's heroes, 1 Chron 11:42.

ADINO One of David's valiant men, 2 Sam 23:8. Called also *Joshebbasshebeth* and *Jashobeam.* See *Jashobeam, 1.*

ADITHAIM A city of Judah, Josh 15:36.

ADJUDICATION AT LAW TO BE AVOIDED. Prov 17:14. It is hard to stop a quarrel once it starts, so don't let it begin.

Prov 20:3. It is an honor for a man to stay out of a fight. Only fools insist on quarreling.

Prov 25:8, 9, 10. Don't be hot-headed and rush to court! You may start something you can't finish and go down before your neighbor in shameful defeat. So discuss the matter with him privately. Don't tell anyone else, lest he accuse you of slander and you can't withdraw what you said.

Mt 5:25. Come to terms quickly with your enemy before it is too late and he drags you into court, and you are thrown into a debtor's cell.

See *Actions at Law; Arbitration; Compromise; Court; Justice.*

ADLAI Father of Shaphat, 1 Chron 27:29.

ADMAH A city in the Valley of Siddim, Gen 10:15–19; 14:2; Deut 29:23; Hos 11:8.

ADMATHA A Persian prince, Esther 1:13–15.

ADMONITION See *Wicked, Warned.*

ADNA 1. A son of Pahath-moab, Ezra 10:30.

2. A priest, Neh 12:15.

ADNAH 1. One of David's captains, 1 Chron 12:20.

2. A military chief, 2 Chron 17:14,15.

ADONI-BEZEK King of Bezek, Judg 1:4–7.

ADONIJAH 1. Son of David and Haggith, 2 Sam 3:4; 1 Kgs 1:5,6; 1 Chron 3:2. Usurpation of, and downfall, 1 Kgs 1. Executed by Solomon, 1 Kgs 2:13,25.

2. A Levite, 2 Chron 17:7–9.

3. See *Adonikam.*

ADONIKAM Called also *Adonijah,* a Jew who returned with Ezra from Babylon, Ezra 2:13; 8:13; Neh 7:18; 10:16.

ADONIRAM Called also *Adoram,* official in charge of forced labor, 2 Sam 20:24; 1 Kgs 4:6; 5:14; 12:18.

See *Hadoram, 3.*

ADONI-ZEDEK A king of Jerusalem, Josh 10:1–27.

ADOPTION Gen 15:3.

INDIVIDUAL. Instances of: Of Joseph's sons, Gen 48:5,14,16,22. Of Moses, Ex 2:5–10; Acts 7:21; Heb 11:24,25. Of Esther, Esther 2:7.

NATIONAL. Ex 4:22. Then you are to tell him, "Jehovah says, 'Israel is my eldest son, [23]and I have commanded you to let him go away and worship me, but you have refused: and now see, I will slay your eldest son.' "

Num 6:27. This is how Aaron and his sons shall call down my blessings upon the people of Israel; and I myself will personally bless them. Deut 28:10; 2 Chron 7:14; Isa 43:7.

Deut 14:1. . . . you are the people of God.

Deut 26:18. And the Lord has declared today that you are his very own people, just as he promised, and that you must obey all his laws.

Deut 27:9. Then Moses and the Levite-priests addressed all Israel as follows: "O Israel, listen! Today you have become the people of the Lord your God."

Deut 32:5. But Israel has become corrupt, smeared with sin. They are no longer his; they are a stubborn, twisted generation. [6]Is this the way you treat Jehovah? O foolish people, is not God your Father? Has he not created you? Has he not established you and made you strong?

2 Sam 7:14. I will be his father, and he shall be my son.

1 Chron 22:10. He shall build my temple, and he shall be as my own son, and I will be his father. 1 Chron 28:6.

Prov 14:26. His children have a place of refuge and security.

Isa 8:18. I and the children God has given me.

Isa 43:6. I will bring my sons and daughters back to Israel from the farthest corners of the earth.

Isa 63:16. Surely you are still our Father! Even if Abraham and Jacob would disown us, still you would be our Father, our Redeemer from ages past. *v.* 8

Jer 3:19. And I thought how wonderful it would be for you to be here among my children. I planned to give you part of this beautiful land, the finest in the world. I looked forward to your calling me "Father," and thought that you would never turn away from me again.

Jer 31:9. For I am a Father to Israel, and Ephraim is my oldest child. [20]And the Lord replies; Ephraim is still my son, my darling child.

Hos 1:9. And God said, "Call him Lo-ammi (meaning 'Not mine'), for Israel is not mine and I am not her God. [10]Yet the time will come when Israel shall prosper and become a great nation; in that day her people will be too numerous to count —like sand along a seashore! Then, instead of saying to them, 'You are not my people', I will tell them, 'You are my sons, children of the living God.' "

Hos 11:1. When Israel was a child I loved him as a son and brought him out of Egypt.

Rom 9:4. God has given you so much, but still you will not listen to him. He took you as his own special, chosen people.

POSITIONAL. The word adoption (adopt) means the placing of a child by admitting him or her to a family, as an heir, with the same privileges and responsibilities as a natural child. When used of believers in this age, adoption means that they have become sons, or children, of God. While all Christians are to grow in grace, the adoption is total, and is not gained by degrees. Only the full inheritance awaits God's children in the coming age, Rom 8:15,23; 9:4; Gal 4:5; Eph 1:5; 1 Pet 2:1–5; 2 Pet 3:18.

Mt 5:9. Happy are those who strive for peace, for they shall be called sons of God. [45]In that way you will be acting as true sons of God.

Mt 13:43. Then the godly shall shine as the sun in their Father's Kingdom.

Lk 6:35. . . . you will be truly acting as sons of God.

Jn 1:12. But to all who received him, he gave the right to become children of God. All they needed to do was to trust him to save them. [13]All those who believe this are reborn!—not a physical rebirth resulting from human passion and plan—but from the will of God.

Jn 11:52. It was a prediction that Jesus' death would not be for Israel only, but for all the children of God scattered around the world.

Rom 8:14. For all who are led by the Spirit of God are the sons of God. [15]And so we should not be like cringing, fearful slaves, but we should behave like God's very own children, adopted into the bosom of his family, and calling to him, "Father, Father." [16]For his Holy Spirit speaks to us deep in our hearts, and tells us that we really are God's children. [17]And since we are his children, we will share his treasures—for all God gives to his Son Jesus is now ours too. But if we are to share his glory, we must also share his suffering. [19]For all creation is waiting patiently and hopefully for that future day when God will resurrect his children. [20,21]For on that day— . . . the things that overcame the world against its will at God's command—will all disappear, and the world around us will share in the glorious freedom from sin which God's children enjoy. [29]For from the very beginning God decided that those who came to him—and all along he knew who would—should become like his Son, so that his Son would be the First, with many brothers.

Rom 9:8. This means that not all of Abraham's children are children of God, but only those who believe the promise of salvation which he made to Abraham. *v.* 26; 2 Sam 7:14; Heb 1:5,6.

2 Cor 6:17. That is why the Lord has said, "Leave them; separate yourselves from them; don't touch their filthy things, and I will welcome you, [18]and be a Father to you, and you will be my sons and daughters."

Gal 3:26. For now we are all children of God by faith in Christ Jesus. [29]And now that we are Christ's we are the true descendants of Abraham, and all of God's promises to him belong to us.

Gal 4:5. To buy freedom for us who were slaves to the law so that he could adopt us as his very own sons. [6]And because we are his sons God has sent the Spirit of his Son into our hearts, so now we can rightly speak of God as our dear Father. [7]Now we are no longer slaves, but God's own sons. And since we are his sons, everything he has belongs to us, for that is the way God planned.

Eph 1:5. His unchanging plan has always been to adopt us into his own family by sending Jesus Christ to die for us. And he did this because he wanted to!

Eph 2:19. Now you are no longer strangers to God and foreigners to heaven, but you are members of God's very own family, citizens of God's country, and you belong in God's household with every other Christian.

Eph 3:6. And this is the secret: that the Gentiles will have their full share with the Jews in all the riches inherited by God's sons; both are invited to belong to his church, and all of God's promises of mighty blessings through Christ apply to them both when they accept the Good News about Christ and what he has done for them. [15]I fall down on my knees and pray to the Father of all the great family of God.

Phil 2:15. You are to live clean, innocent lives as children of God in a dark world full of people who are crooked and stubborn. Shine out among them like beacon lights.

Heb 2:10. And it was right and proper that God, who made everything for his own glory, should allow Jesus to suffer, for in doing this he was bringing vast multitudes of God's people to heaven; for his suffering made Jesus a perfect leader, one fit to bring them into their salvation. [11]We who have been made holy by Jesus, now have the same Father he has. That is why Jesus is not ashamed to call us his brothers. [13]At another time he said . . . "See here I am and the children God gave me."

Heb 12:6. For when he punishes you, it proves that he loves you. When he whips you it proves you are really his child. [7]Let God train you, for he is doing what any loving father does for his children. Whoever heard of a son who was never corrected? [9]Since we respect our fathers here on earth, though they punish us, should we not all the more cheerfully submit to God's training so that we can begin really to live?

1 Jn 3:1. See how very much our heavenly Father loves us, for he allows us to be called his children —think of it—and we really are! But since most people don't know God, naturally they don't understand that we are his children. [2]Yes, dear friends, we are already God's children, right now, and we can't even imagine what it is going to be like later on. But we do know this, that when he comes we will be like him, as a result of seeing him as he really is. [10]So now we can tell who is a child of God and who belongs to Satan. Whoever is living a life of sin and doesn't love his brother shows that he is not in God's family.

1 Jn 4:4. Dear young friends, you belong to God and have already won your fight with those who are against Christ, because there is someone in your hearts who is stronger than any evil teacher in this wicked world.

Rev 21:7. Everyone who conquers will inherit all these blessings, and I will be his God and he will be my son.

FORMAL OR CEREMONIAL. When believers receive their new bodies, adoption will be consummated in the public acknowledgment of his children by God as he places on them the *toga virilis,* evidently before all created intelligences, and they enter into their inheritance, Rom 8:15–17; 1 Pet 1: 3–5.

Rom 8:23. And even we Christians, although we have the Holy Spirit within us as a foretaste of future glory, also groan to be released from pain and suffering. We, too, wait anxiously for that day when God will give us our full rights as his children, including the new bodies he has promised us —bodies that will never be sick again and will never die.

Rev. 21:7. Everyone who conquers will inherit all these blessings, and I will be his God and he will be my son.

TYPIFIED. In Israel, Ex 4:22; Hos 11:1; Rom 9: 4.

See *God, Fatherhood of; Righteous, Unity of, with Christ.*

ADORAIM A city of Judah, 2 Chron 11:9.

ADORAM See *Adoniram.*

ADRAMMELECH 1. An Assyrian idol, 2 Kgs 17:31.

2. Son of Sennacherib, 2 Kgs 19:37; Isa 37:38.

ADRAMYTTIUM A city of Mysia, Acts 27:2.

ADRIATIC SEA Acts 27:27.

ADRIEL Saul's son-in-law, 1 Sam 18:19; 2 Sam 21:8,9.

ADULLAM 1. A cave near the Dead Sea. David hides in, 1 Sam 22:1; 2 Sam 23:13; 1 Chron 11: 15. Psalms 57 and 142 written here.

2. An ancient city of Canaan, Gen 38:1; Josh 12: 15; 15:35; 2 Chron 11:7; Neh 11:30; Mic 1:15.

ADULTERY AND FORNICATION Gen 20:3. But that night God came to him in a dream and told him, "You are a dead man, for that woman you took is married."

2 Sam 12:14. But you have given great opportunity to the enemies of the Lord to despise and blaspheme him, so your child shall die.

Job 24:15. They are murderers who rise in the early dawn to kill the poor and needy; at night they are thieves and adulterers, waiting for the twilight "when no one will see me," they say. They mask their faces so no one will know them. [16]They break into houses at night and sleep in the daytime—they are not acquainted with the light. [17]The black night is their morning; they ally themselves with the terrors of the darkness. *v.* 18

Job 31:1. I made a covenant with my eyes not to look with lust upon a girl. [9]Or if I have longed for another man's wife, [10]then may I die, and may my wife be in another man's home, and someone else become her husband. [11]For lust is a shameful sin, a crime that should be punished. [12]It is a devastating fire that destroys to hell, and would root out all I have planted.

Prov 2:16,17. Only wisdom from the Lord can save a man from the flattery of prostitutes; these girls have abandoned their husbands and flouted the laws of God. [18]Their houses lie along the road to death and hell. [19]The men who enter them are doomed. None of these men will ever be the same again.

Prov 5:3. For the lips of a prostitute are as sweet as honey, and smooth flattery is her stock in trade. [4]But afterwards only a bitter conscience is left to you, sharp as a double-edged sword. *vs.* 5–22

Prov 6:24. Their counsel will keep you far away from prostitutes with all their flatteries. [25]Don't lust for their beauty. Don't let their coyness seduce you. [26]For a prostitute will bring a man to poverty, and an adulteress may cost him his very life. [27]Can a man hold fire against his chest and not be burned? [28]Can he walk on hot coals and not blister his feet? [29]So it is with the man who commits adultery with another's wife. He shall not go unpunished for this sin. [32]But the man who commits adultery is an utter fool, for he destroys his own soul. [33]Wounds and constant disgrace are his lot, [34]for the woman's husband will be furious in his jealousy, and he will have no mercy on you in his day of vengeance.

Prov 7:5. Let her hold you back from visiting a prostitute, from listening to her flattery. [6]I was looking out the window of my house one day, [7]and saw a simple-minded lad, a young man lacking common sense, [8,9]walking at twilight down the street to the house of this wayward girl, a prostitute. [10]She approached him, saucy and pert, and dressed seductively. [11,12]She was the brash, coarse type, seen often in the streets and markets, soliciting at every corner for men to be her lovers. [13]She put her arms around him and kissed him, and with a saucy look she said, [14]"I've decided to forget our quarrel! [15]I was just coming to look for you and here you are! [16,17]My bed is spread with lovely colored sheets of finest linen imported from Egypt, perfumed with myrrh, aloes and cinnamon. [18]Come on, let's take our fill of love until morning, [19]for my husband is away on a long trip. [20]He has taken a wallet full of money with him, and won't return for several days." [21]So she seduced him with her pretty speech, her coaxing and her wheedling, until he yielded to her. He couldn't resist her flattery. [22]He followed her as an ox going to the butcher, or as a stag that is trapped, [23]waiting to be killed with an arrow through its heart. He was as a bird flying into a snare, not knowing the fate awaiting there.

Prov 9:13. A prostitute is loud and brash, and never has enough of lust and shame. [14]She sits at the door of her house or stands at the street corners of the city, [15]whispering to men going by, and to those minding their own business. [16]"Come home with me," she urges simpletons. [17]"Stolen melons are the sweetest; stolen apples taste the best!" [18]But they don't realize that her former guests are now citizens of hell.

Prov 22:14. A prostitute is a dangerous trap; those cursed of God are caught in it.

Prov 23:26–28. O my son, trust my advice—stay away from prostitutes. For a prostitute is a deep and narrow grave. Like a robber, she waits for her victims as one after another become unfaithful to their wives.

Prov 29:3. A wise son makes his father happy, but a lad who hangs around with prostitutes disgraces him.

Prov 30:18–19. There are three things too wonderful for me to understand—no, four! How an eagle glides through the sky. How a serpent crawls upon a rock. How a ship finds its way across the heaving ocean. The growth of love between a man and a girl. [20]There is another thing too: how a prostitute can sin and then say, "What's wrong with that?"

Prov 31:3. Do not spend your time with women —the royal pathway to destruction.

Isa 57:3. But you—come here, you witches' sons, you offspring of adulterers and harlots! [4]Who is it you mock, making faces and sticking out your tongues? You children of sinners and liars!

Jer 3:1. There is a law that if a man divorces a woman who then remarries, he is not to take her back again, for she has become corrupted.

Jer 5:7. How can I pardon you? For even your children have turned away, and worship gods that are not gods at all. I fed my people until they were fully satisfied, and their thanks was to commit adultery wholesale and to gang up at the city's brothels. [8]They are well-fed, lusty stallions, each neighing for his neighbor's mate.

Jer 7:9. Do you really think that you can steal, murder, commit adultery, lie, and worship Baal and all of those new gods of yours, [10]and then come here and stand before me in my Temple and chant, "We are saved!"—only to go right back to all these evil things again?

Jer 23:10. For the land is full of adultery and the curse of God is on it.

Ezk 18:5. But if a man is just and does what is lawful and right, [6]and has not gone out to the mountains to feast before the idols of Israel and worship them, and does not commit adultery, nor lie with any woman during the time of her menstruation, [9]and obeys my laws—that man is just, says the Lord, and he shall surely live.

Hos 4:1. Hear the word of the Lord, O people of Israel. The Lord has filed a lawsuit against you listing the following charges: There is no faithfulness, no kindness, no knowledge of God in your land. [2]You swear and lie and kill and steal and commit adultery. There is violence everywhere, with one murder after another. [11]Wine, women, and song have robbed my people of their brains.

Mt 5:28. But I say: Anyone who even looks at a woman with lust in his eye has already committed adultery with her in his heart. [32]But I say that a man who divorces his wife, except for fornication, causes her to commit adultery if she marries again. And he who marries her commits adultery. Mk 10: 11,12; Lk 16:18.

Mt 15:19. For from the heart come evil thoughts, murder, adultery, fornication, theft, lying and slander. Mk 7:21.

Mt 19:9. And I tell you this, that anyone who divorces his wife, except for fornication, and marries another, commits adultery. Mk 10:11

Mk 10:19. But as for your question—you know the commandments: don't kill, don't commit adultery, don't steal, don't lie, don't cheat, respect your father and mother. Jas 2:11.

Acts 15:20. Except that we should write to them to refrain from eating meat sacrificed to idols, from all fornication. *v.* 27–29.

Rom 1:28. So it was that when they gave God up and would not even acknowledge him, God gave them up to doing everything their evil minds could think of. [29]Their lives became full of every kind of wickedness and sin, of greed and hate, envy, murder, fighting, lying, bitterness, and gossip. [32]They were fully aware of God's death penalty for these crimes, yet they went right ahead and did them anyway, and encouraged others to do them, too.

Rom 7:3. Then she can marry someone else if she wants to. That would be wrong while he was alive, but it is perfectly all right after he dies.

1 Cor 5:9. When I wrote to you before I said not to mix with evil people. [10]But when I said that I wasn't talking about unbelievers who live in sexual sin, or are greedy cheats and thieves and idol wor-

shipers. For you can't live in this world without being with people like that.

1 Cor 6:15. Don't you realize that your bodies are actually parts and members of Christ? So should I take part of Christ and join him to a prostitute? Never! [16]And don't you know that if a man joins himself to a prostitute she becomes a part of him and he becomes a part of her? For God tells us in the Scriptures that in his sight the two become one person. [18]That is why I say to run from sex sin. No other sin affects the body as this one does. When you sin this sin it is against your own body.

1 Cor 10:8. Another lesson for us is what happened when some of them sinned with other men's wives, and 23,000 fell dead in one day.

2 Cor 12:21. Yes, I am afraid that when I come God will humble me before you and I will be sad and mourn because many of you who have sinned became sinners and don't even care about the wicked, impure things you have done: your lust and immorality, and the taking of other men's wives.

Gal 5:19. But when you follow your own wrong inclinations your lives will produce these evil results: impure thoughts, eagerness for lustful pleasure. [21]Let me tell you again as I have before, that anyone living that sort of life will not inherit the kingdom of God.

1 Tim 1:9. But they were not made for us, whom God has saved; . . . [10]these laws are made to identify as sinners all who are immoral and impure: homosexuals, kidnappers, liars, and all others who do things that contradict the glorious Good News of our blessed God, whose messenger I am.

2 Tim 3:6. They are the kind who craftily sneak into other people's homes and make friendships with silly, sin-burdened women and teach them their new doctrines.

1 Pet 4:3. You have had enough in the past of the evil things the godless enjoy—sex sin, lust, getting drunk, wild parties, drinking bouts, and the worship of idols, and other terrible sins. [4]Of course your former friends will be very surprised when you don't eagerly join them any more in the wicked things they do, and they will laugh at you in contempt and scorn.

2 Pet 2:9. So also the Lord can rescue you and me from the temptations that surround us, and continue to punish the ungodly until the day of final judgment comes. [10]He is especially hard on those who follow their own evil, lustful thoughts, and those who are proud and willful, daring even to scoff at the Glorious Ones without so much as trembling. [14]No woman can escape their sinful stare, and of adultery they never have enough. They make a game of luring unstable women.

Jude 1:7. And don't forget the cities of Sodom and Gomorrah and their neighboring towns, all full of lust of every kind including lust of men for other men. Those cities were destroyed by fire and continue to be a warning to us that there is a hell in which sinners are punished.

Rev 2:20. Yet I have this against you: You are permitting that woman Jezebel, who calls herself a prophetess, to teach my servants that sex sin is not a serious matter; she urges them to practice immorality and to eat meat that has been sacrificed to idols. [21]I gave her time to change her mind and attitude, but she refused. [22]Pay attention now to what I am saying: I will lay her upon a sickbed of intense affliction, along with all her immoral followers, unless they turn again to me, repenting of their sin with her.

Rev 9:21. Neither did they change their mind and attitude about all their murders and witchcraft, their immorality and theft.

See *Homosexuality; Lasciviousness; Prostitute; Prostitution; Rape; Sensuality; Sodomites.*

FORBIDDEN. Ex 20:14. You must not commit adultery. Deut 5:18; Mt 5:27; 19:18; Lk 18:20; Rom 13:9; Jas 2:11.

Lev 18:19. . . . There must be no sexual relationship . . . [20]with anyone else's wife, to defile yourself with her.

Lev 19:29. Do not violate your daughter's sanctity by making her a prostitute, lest the land become full of enormous wickedness.

Deut 23:17. No prostitutes are permitted in Israel, either men or women; you must not bring to the Lord any offering from the earnings of a prostitute or a homosexual, for both are detestable to the Lord your God.

Acts 15:20. . . . We should write to them to refrain . . . from all fornication.

Rom 13:13. So quit the evil deeds of darkness and put on the armor of right living, as we who live in the daylight should! Be decent and true in everything you do so that all can approve your behavior. Don't spend your time in wild parties and getting drunk or in adultery and lust.

1 Cor 5:11. What I meant was that you are not to keep company with anyone who claims to be a brother Christian but indulges in sexual sins . . . Don't even eat lunch with such a person. *vs.* 9,10.

1 Cor 6:13. But sexual sin is never right: our bodies are not made for that, but for the Lord, and the Lord wants to fill our bodies with himself. [15]Don't you realize that your bodies are actually parts and members of Christ? So should I take part of Christ and join him to a prostitute? Never! [18]That is why I say to run from sex sin. No other sin affects the body as this one does. When you sin this sin it is against your own body.

1 Cor 10:8. Another lesson for us is what happened when some of them sinned with other men's wives, and 23,000 fell dead in one day.

Eph 4:17,18. Let me say this, then, speaking for the Lord: Live no longer as the unsaved do, for they are blinded and confused. Their closed hearts are full of darkness; they are far away from the life of God because they have shut their minds against him, and they cannot understand his ways. [19]They don't care anymore about right and wrong and have given themselves over to impure ways. They stop at nothing, being driven by their evil minds and reckless lusts. [20]But that isn't the way Christ taught you!

Eph 5:3. Let there be no sex sin, impurity or greed among you. Let no one be able to accuse you of any such things. [11]Take no part in the worthless pleasures of evil and darkness, but instead rebuke and expose them. [12]It would be shameful even to mention here those pleasures of darkness which the ungodly do.

Col 3:5. Away then with sinful, earthly things; deaden the evil desires lurking within you; have nothing to do with sexual sin, impurity, lust and shameful desires; don't worship the good things of life, for that is idolatry.

1 Thess 4:3,4. For God wants you to be holy and pure, and to keep clear of all sexual sin so that each of you will marry in holiness and honor— [5]not in lustful passion as the heathen do, in their ignorance of God and his ways. [7]For God has not called us to be dirty-minded and full of lust, but to be holy and clean.

FORGIVENESS OF. Instances of; Judg 19:1–4.

Jn 8:10. Then Jesus stood up again and said to her, "Where are your accusers? Didn't even one of them condemn you?" [11]"No, sir," she said. And Jesus said, "Neither do I. Go and sin no more."

PENALTIES FOR. Gen 20:7. Now restore her to her husband, and he will pray for you (for he is a prophet) and you shall live. But if you don't return her to him, you are doomed to death along with all your household.

Gen 26:11. Then Abimelech made a public proclamation: "Anyone harming this man or his wife shall die."

Gen 38:24. About three months later word reached Judah that Tamar, his daughter-in-law, was pregnant, obviously as a result of prostitution. "Bring her out and burn her," Judah shouted.

Ex 22:16. If a man seduces a girl who is not engaged to anyone, and sleeps with her, he must pay the usual dowry and accept her as his wife. [17]But if her father utterly refuses to let her marry him, then he shall pay the money anyway.

Lev 19:20. If a man seduces a slave girl who is engaged to be married, they shall be tried in a court but not put to death, because she is not free. [21]The man involved shall bring his guilt offering to the Lord at the entrance of the Tabernacle; the offering shall be a ram. [22]The priest shall make atonement with the ram for the sin the man has committed, and it shall be forgiven him.

Lev 20:10. If a man commits adultery with another man's wife, both the man and woman shall be put to death. [11]If a man sleeps with his father's wife, he has defiled what is his father's; for both the man and the woman must die, for it is their own fault. [12]And if a man has sexual intercourse with his daughter-in-law, both shall be executed: they have brought it upon themselves by defiling each other.

Lev 21:9. The daughter of any priest who becomes a prostitute, thus violating her father's holiness as well as her own, shall be burned alive.

Num 5:11,12. And the Lord said to Moses, "Tell the people of Israel that if a man's wife commits adultery, [13]but there is no proof, there being no witness, [14]and he is jealous and suspicious, [15]the man shall bring his wife to the priest with an offering for her of a tenth of a bushel of barley meal without oil or frankincense mingled with it—for it is a suspicion offering—to bring out the truth as to whether or not she is guilty. [16]The priest shall bring her before the Lord, [17]and take holy water in a clay jar and mix into it dust from the floor of the Tabernacle. [18]He shall unbind her hair and place the suspicion offering in her hands to determine whether or not her husband's suspicions are justified. The priest shall stand before her holding the jar of bitter water that brings a curse. [19]He shall require her to swear that she is innocent, and then he shall say to her, "If no man has slept with you except your husband, be free from the effects of this bitter water that causes the curse. [20]But if you have committed adultery, [21,22]then Jehovah shall make you a curse among your people, for he will make your thigh rot away and your body swell." And the woman shall be required to say, "Yes, let it be so." [23]Then the priest shall write these curses in a book and wash them off into the bitter water. [24](When he requires the woman to drink the water, it becomes bitter within her if she is guilty). [25]Then the priest shall take the suspicion offering from the woman's hand and wave it before Jehovah, and carry it to the altar. [26]He shall take a handful, representing all of it, and burn the handful upon the altar, and then require the woman to drink the water. [27]If she has been defiled, having committed adultery against her husband, the water will become bitter within her, and her body shall swell and her thigh will rot, and she shall be a curse among her people. [28]But if she is pure and has not committed adultery, she shall be unharmed and will soon become pregnant. [29]This, then, is the law concerning a wayward wife —or a husband's suspicions against his wife— [30]to determine whether or not she has been unfaithful to him. He shall bring her before the Lord and the priest shall handle the situation as outlined above.

Deut 22:13,14. If a man marries a girl, then after sleeping with her accuses her of having had premarital intercourse with another man, saying, "She was not a virgin when I married her," [15]then the girl's father and mother shall bring the proof of her virginity to the city judges. [16]Her father shall tell them, "I gave my daughter to this man to be his wife, and now he despises her, [17,18]and has accused her of shameful things, claiming that she was not a virgin when she married; yet here is the proof." And they shall spread the garment before the judges. The judges shall sentence the man to be whipped, [19]and fine him one hundred dollars to be given to the girl's father, for he has falsely accused a virgin of Israel. She shall remain his wife and he may never divorce her. [20]But if the man's accusations are true, and she was not a virgin, [21]the judges shall take the girl to the door of her father's home where the men of the city shall stone her to death. She has defiled Israel by flagrant crime, being a prostitute while living at home with her parents;

and such evil must be cleansed from among you. [22]If a man is discovered committing adultery, both he and the other man's wife must be killed; in this way evil will be cleansed from Israel. [23,24]If a girl who is engaged is seduced within the walls of a city, both she and the man who seduced her shall be taken outside the gates and stoned to death—the girl because she didn't scream for help, and the man because he has violated the virginity of another man's fiancée. [25,26,27]In this way you will reduce crime among you. But if this deed takes place out in the country only the man shall die. The girl is as innocent as the murder victim; for it must be assumed that she screamed, but there was no one to hear and rescue her out in the field. [28,29]If a man rapes a girl who is not engaged, and is caught in the act, he must pay a fine to the girl's father and marry her; he may never divorce her. A man shall not sleep with his father's widow since she belonged to his father.

Deut 27:20. Cursed is he who commits adultery with one of his father's wives, for she belongs to his father. And all the people shall reply, "Amen." [22]Cursed is he who has sexual intercourse with his sister, whether she be a full sister or a half-sister. And all the people shall reply, "Amen." [23]Cursed is he who has sexual intercourse with his widowed mother-in-law. And all the people shall reply, "Amen."

2 Sam 12:10. Therefore murder shall be a constant threat in your family from this time on, because you have insulted me by taking Uriah's wife. [11]I vow that because of what you have done I will cause your own household to rebel against you. I will give your wives to another man, and he will go to bed with them in public view. [12]You did it secretly, but I will do this to you openly, in the sight of all Israel.

Jer 29:22. Their fate shall become proverbial of all evil, so that whenever anyone wants to curse someone he will say, "The Lord make you like Zedekiah and Ahab whom the king of Babylon burned alive!" [23]For these men have done a terrible thing among my people. They have committed adultery with their neighbor's wives and have lied in my name. I know, for I have seen everything they do, says the Lord.

Ezk 16:38. I will punish you as a murderess is punished and as a woman breaking wedlock living with other men. [40,41]They will burn your homes, punishing you before the eyes of many women. And I will see to it that you stop your adulteries with other gods and end your payments to your allies for their love.

Ezk 23:45. But just persons everywhere will judge them for what they really are—adulteresses and murderers. They will mete out to them the sentences the law demands. [47]For their enemies will stone them and kill them with swords; they will butcher their sons and daughters and burn their homes. [48]Thus will I make lewdness and idolatry to cease from the land.

Mal 3:5. "At that time my punishments will be quick and certain; I will move swiftly against wicked men who trick the innocent, against adulterers, and liars, against all those who cheat their hired hands, or oppress widows and orphans, or defraud strangers, and do not fear me," says the Lord of Hosts.

Jn 8:4. "Teacher," they said to Jesus, "this woman was caught in adultery. [5]Moses' law says to kill her. What about it?"

1 Cor 5:1. Everyone is talking about the terrible thing that has happened among you, something so evil that even the heathen don't do it: you have a man in your church who is living in sin with his father's wife. [2]And are you still so conceited, so "spiritual"? Why aren't you mourning in sorrow and shame, and seeing to it that this man is removed from your membership? [3,4]Although I am not there with you, I have been thinking a lot about this, and in the name of the Lord Jesus Christ I have already decided what to do, just as though I were there. You are to call a meeting of the church —and the power of the Lord Jesus will be with you as you meet, and I will be there in spirit—[5]and cast out this man from the fellowship of the church and into Satan's hands, to punish him, in the hope that his soul will be saved when our Lord Jesus Christ returns. [6]What a terrible thing it is that you are boasting about your purity, and yet you let this sort of evil go on. Don't you realize that if even one person is allowed to go on sinning, soon all will be affected? [7]Remove this evil cancer—this wicked person—from among you, so that you can stay pure. Christ, God's Lamb, has been slain for us. [8]So let us feast upon him and grow strong in the Christian life, leaving entirely behind us the cancerous old life with all its hatreds and wickedness. Let us feast instead upon the pure bread of honor and sincerity and truth. [9]When I wrote to you before I said not to mix with evil people. [10]But when I said that I wasn't talking about unbelievers who live in sexual sin, or are greedy cheats and thieves and idol worshipers. For you can't live in this world without being with people like that. [11]What I meant was that you are not to keep company with anyone who claims to be a brother Christian but indulges in sexual sins, or is greedy, or is a swindler, or worships idols, or is a drunkard, or abusive. Don't even eat lunch with such a person. [12]It isn't our job to judge outsiders. But it certainly is our job to judge and deal strongly with those who are members of the church, and who are sinning in these ways. [13]God alone is the Judge of those on the outside. But you yourselves must deal with this man and put him out of your church.

1 Cor 6:9,10. Don't you know that those doing such things have no share in the Kingdom of God? Don't fool yourselves. Those who live immoral lives, who are idol worshipers, adulterers or homosexuals—will have no share in his kingdom.

1 Cor 10:8. Another lesson for us is what happened when some of them sinned with other men's wives, and 23,000 fell dead in one day.

Gal 5:19. But when you follow your own wrong

inclinations your lives will produce these evil results: impure thoughts, eagerness for lustful pleasure. [21]Let me tell you again as I have before, that anyone living that sort of life will not inherit the kingdom of God.

Eph 5:5. You can be sure of this: The kingdom of Christ and of God will never belong to anyone who is impure or greedy, for a greedy person is really an idol worshiper—he loves and worships the good things of this life more than God. [6]Don't be fooled by those who try to excuse these sins, for the terrible wrath of God is upon all those who do them.

Heb 13:4. Honor your marriage and its vows, and be pure; for God will surely punish all those who are immoral or commit adultery.

Rev 18:9. And the world leaders, who took part in her immoral acts and enjoyed her favors, will mourn for her as they see the smoke rising from her charred remains. [10]They will stand off, trembling with fear and crying out, "Alas, Babylon, that mighty city! In one moment her judgment fell."

Rev 21:8. But cowards who turn back from following me, and those who are unfaithful to me, and the corrupt, and murderers, and the immoral and those conversing with demons, and idol worshipers and all liars—their doom is in the Lake that burns with fire and sulphur. This is the Second Death.

Rev 22:15. Outside the city are those who have strayed away from God, and the sorcerers and the immoral and murderers and idolaters, and all who love to lie, and do so.

FIGURATIVE. Jer 3:2; Ezk 16:15,16; Hos 1. See *Prostitution; Idolatry.*

INSTANCES OF. Sodomites, Gen 19:4–8. Lot, Gen 19:31–38. Shechem, Gen 34:2. Reuben, Gen 35:22. Judah, Gen 38:1–24. Potiphar's wife, Gen 39:7–12. The Gibeahites, Judg 19:22–25. Gilead, Judg 11:1. Samson, Judg 16:1. Sons of Eli, 1 Sam 2:22. David, 2 Sam 11:1–5. Amnon, 2 Sam 13:1–20. Absalom, 2 Sam 16:22. Israelites, Ex 32:6,25; Jer 29:23; Ezk 22:9–11; 33:26; Hos 7:4. Herod, Mt 14:3,4; Mk 6:17,18; Lk 3:19,20. Samaritan woman, Jn 4:17,18. The woman brought to Jesus in the temple, Jn 8:4–11. Corinthians, 1 Cor 5:1–5. Heathen, Eph 4:17–19; 1 Pet 4:3.

ADUMMIM A pass on the road between the fords of the Jordan and Jerusalem, Josh 15:7; 18:17.

ADVENT See *Jesus, Second Coming of; Millennium.*

ADVERSITY See *Afflictions and Adversities.*

ADVERSARY An enemy, Ps 89:23.

ADVICE See *Counsel.*

ADVOCATE One who pleads the cause of another.

1. Evil, representing the Jews against Paul, Acts 24:1–9.

2. The Holy Spirit. Jn 14:15,16. If you love me, obey me; and I will ask the Father and he will give you another Comforter, and he will never leave you. [26]But when the Father sends the Comforter instead of me—and by the Comforter I mean the Holy Spirit—he will teach you much, as well as remind you of everything I myself have told you.

Jn 15:26. But I will send you the Comforter—the Holy Spirit, the source of all truth. He will come to you from the Father and will tell you all about me.

Jn 16:7. But the fact of the matter is that it is best for you that I go away, for if I don't, the Comforter won't come. If I do, he will—for I will send him to you.

3. The Lord Jesus Christ. Job 16:19. Yet even now the Witness to my innocence is there in heaven; my Advocate is there on high.

Heb 7:25. He is able to save completely all who come to God through him. Since he will live forever, he will always be there to remind God that he has paid for their sins with his blood.

1 Jn 2:1. My little children, I am telling you this so that you will stay away from sin. But if you sin, there is someone to plead for you before the Father. His name is Jesus Christ, the one who is all that is good and who pleases God completely.

AENEAS Healed, Acts 9:33,34.

AENON A place west of the Jordan where John baptized, Jn 3:23,24.

AFFECTIONS Should be supremely set on God, Deut 6:5; Mk 12:30. Should be set on the commandments of God, Ps 19:7–10; 119:20,97,102,103,167; on the house and worship of God, 1 Chron 29:3; Ps 26:8; 27:4; 84:1,2; on the people of God, Ps 16:3; Rom 12:10; 2 Cor 7:13–16; 1 Thess 2:8; on heavenly things, Col 3:1,2. Should be zealously engaged for God, Ps 69:9; 119:139; Gal 4:18. Christ claims the first place in, Mt 10:37; Lk 14:26. Kindled by communion with Christ, Lk 24:32. Blessedness of making God the object of, Ps 91:14. Should not grow cold, Ps 106:12,13; Mt 24:12; Gal 4:15; Rev 2:4. Of saints, supremely set on God, Ps 42:1; 73:25; 119:10. Of the wicked, not sincerely set on God, Isa 58:1,2; Ezk 33:31,32; Lk 8:13. Carnal, should be disciplined, Rom 8:13; 13:14; 1 Cor 9:27; Col 3:5; 1 Thess 4:5. Carnal affections crucified in saints, Rom 6:6; Gal 5:24. False teachers seek to captivate, Gal 1:10; 4:17; 2 Tim 3:6; 2 Pet 2:3,18; Rev 2:14,30. Of the wicked, are unnatural and perverted, Rom 1:29–31; 2 Tim 3:3; 2 Pet 2:10.

See *Love.*

AFFLICTED DUTY TO THE. Job 6:14. One should be kind to a fainting friend.

Job 22:29. If you are attacked and knocked down, you will know that there is someone who will lift you up again. Yes, he will save the humble.

Isa 58:6. No, the kind of fast I want is that you stop oppressing those who work for you and treat them fairly and give them what they earn. [7]I want you to share your food with the hungry and bring right into your own home those who are helpless, poor and destitute. Clothe those who are cold and don't hide from relatives who need your help. [10]Feed the hungry! Help those in trouble! Then your light will shine out from the darkness, and the darkness around you shall be as bright as day.

Mt 25:34. Then I, the King, shall say to those at my right, "Come, blessed of my Father, into the

Kingdom prepared for you from the founding of the world. [35]For I was hungry and you fed me; I was thirsty and you gave me water; I was a stranger and you invited me into your homes; [36]naked and you clothed me; sick and in prison and you visited me." [37]Then these righteous ones will reply "Sir, when did we ever see you hungry and feed you? Or thirsty and give you anything to drink? [38]Or a stranger, and help you? Or naked, and clothe you? [39]When did we ever see you sick or in prison, and visit you?" [40]And I, the King, will tell them, "When you did it to these my brothers you were doing it to me!" [41]Then I will turn to those on my left and say, "Away with you, you cursed ones, into the eternal fire prepared for the devil and his demons. [42]For I was hungry and you wouldn't feed me; thirsty, and you wouldn't give me anything to drink; [43]a stranger, and you refused me hospitality; naked, and you wouldn't clothe me; sick, and in prison, and you didn't visit me." [44]Then they will reply, "Lord, when did we ever see you hungry or thirsty or a stranger or naked or sick or in prison and not help you?" [45]And I will answer, "When you refused to help the least of these my brothers, you were refusing to help me."

Lk 10:30. Jesus replied with an illustration: "A Jew going on a trip from Jerusalem to Jericho was attacked by bandits. They stripped him of his clothes and money and beat him up and left him lying half dead beside the road. [31]By chance a Jewish priest came along; and when he saw the man lying there, he crossed to the other side of the road and passed him by. [32]A Jewish Temple-assistant walked over and looked at him lying there, but then went on. [33]But a despised Samaritan came along, and when he saw him, he felt deep pity. [34]Kneeling beside him the Samaritan soothed his wounds with medicine and bandaged them. Then he put the man on his donkey and walked along beside him till they came to an inn, where he nursed him through the night. [35]The next day he handed the innkeeper two twenty-dollar bills and told him to take care of the man. 'If his bill runs higher than that,' he said, 'I'll pay the difference the next time I am here.' [36]Now which of these three would you say was a neighbor to the bandits' victim?" [37]The man replied, "The one who showed him some pity." Then Jesus said, "Yes, now go and do the same."

Phil 2:1. Is there any such thing as Christians cheering each other up? Do you love me enough to want to help me? Does it mean anything to you that we are brothers in the Lord, sharing the same Spirit? Are your hearts tender and sympathetic at all? [2]Then make me truly happy by loving each other and agreeing wholeheartedly with each other, working together with one heart and mind and purpose.

1 Tim 5:10. She must be well thought of by everyone because of the good she has done. Has she brought up her children well? Has she been kind to strangers as well as to other Christians? Has she helped those who are sick and hurt? Is she always ready to show kindness?

Jas 5:13. Is anyone among you suffering? He should keep on praying about it. And those who have reason to be thankful should continually be singing praises to the Lord. [14]Is anyone sick? He should call for the elders of the church and they should pray over him and pour a little oil upon him, calling on the Lord to heal him. [15]And their prayer, if offered in faith, will heal him, for the Lord will make him well; and if his sickness was caused by some sin, the Lord will forgive him.

AFFLICTIONS AND ADVERSITIES

LIST OF SUB-TOPICS. *Miscellany of Minor Sub-topics, Unclassified Scriptures Relating to, Benefits of, Benefits of, Illustrated, Consolation in, Deliverance from, Design of, Despondency in, Dispensation of God, From Satan, Impenitence in, Mocking at, Murmuring in, Penitence in, Prayer in, Prayer in, Answered, Prayer for the Afflicted, Resignation in, Resignation in, Exemplified, Instances of Resignation in.*

MISCELLANY OF MINOR SUB-TOPICS. God regulates the measure of afflictions, Ps 80:5; Isa 9:1; Jer 46:28; determines the continuance of, Gen 15:13,14; Num 14:33; Isa 10:25; Jer 29:10; does not willingly send, Lam 3:33. Man is born to, Job 5:6,7; 14:1. Saints appointed to, 1 Thess 3:2,3. Result of the fall, Gen 3:16–19. Sin produces, Job 4:7,8; Prov 1:31. Sinners corrected by, 2 Sam 12:14; Ps 89:30–32; Isa 57:17; Acts 13:10,11. Often severe, Job 16:7–16; Ps 42:7; 66:12; Jon 2:3; Rev 7:14. Always less than deserved, Ezra 9:13; Ps 103:10. Results of, good, Gen 50:20; Ex 1:11,12; Deut 8:15,16; Jer 24:4–6; Ezk 20:37. Tempered with mercy, Ps 78:38,39; 106:43–46; Isa 30:18–21; Lam 3:32; Mic 7:7–9; Nah 1:12.

Of Believers. To be expected, Jn 16:33; Acts 14:22. Comparatively light, Acts 20:23,24; Rom 8:18; 2 Cor 4:17. Temporary, Ps 30:5; 103:9; Isa 54:7,8; Jn 16:20; 1 Pet 1:6; 5:10. Joy under, Job 5:17; Jas 5:11. End in joy and blessedness, Ps 126:5,6; Isa 61:2,3; Mt 5:4; 1 Pet 4:13,14. Often arise from the profession of the gospel, Mt 24:9; Jn 15:21; 2 Tim 3:11,12. Exhibit the love and faithfulness of God, Deut 8:5; Ps 119:75–77; Prov 3:11–12; 1 Cor 11:32; Heb 12:6,7; Rev 3:19.

Of the Wicked. God is glorified in, Ex 14:4; Ezk 38:22,23. God holds in derision, Ps 37:12,13; Prov 1:26,27. Are multiplied, Deut 31:17; Job 20:4,5; Ps 32:10; continual, Job 15:20; Eccl 2:20–23; Isa 32:10; often sudden, Ps 73:19; Prov 6:15; Isa 30:13; Rev 18:10. Are often judicially sent, Ps 107:17; Jer 30:15. Are for examples to others, Ps 64:7–9; Zeph 3:6,7; 1 Cor 10:5,11; 2 Pet 2:6. Are ineffectual for their conversion, Ex 9:30; Isa 9:13; Jer 2:30; Hag 2:16,17. Their persecution of the saints, a cause of, Deut 30:7,8; Ps 55:19; Zech 2:9; 2 Thess 1:6. Impenitence is a cause of, Prov 1:29–31; Ezk 24:13; Amos 4:6–12; Zech 7:11,12; Rev 2:21,22. Sometimes humble them, 1 Kgs 21:27. Frequently harden, Neh 9:28,29; Jer 5:3. Produce slavish fear, Job 15:23,24; Ps 73:19; Jer 49:3,5. Saints should not be alarmed at, Prov 3:24–26.

Exemplified: in Pharaoh and the Egyptians, Ex 9:14; 14:24,25; Ahaziah, 2 Kgs 1:1–5; Gehazi,

2 Kgs 5:27; Jehoram, 2 Chron 21:12–19; Uzziah, 2 Chron 26:19–21; Ahaz, etc., 2 Chron 28:5–8,22.

Forsaken by Friends in. Instances of: Job 2:9; 19: 13–19. David, Ps 31:11,12; 41:9; 88:8,18. Jesus, Mt 26: 56. Paul, 2 Tim 4:16. National lessons from, Joel 1; 2.

UNCLASSIFIED SCRIPTURES RELATING TO. Gen 3:16. Then God said to the woman, "You shall bear children in intense pain and suffering; yet even so, you shall welcome your husband's affections, and he shall be your master." [17]And to Adam, God said, "Because you listened to your wife and ate the fruit when I told you not to, I have placed a curse upon the soil. All your life you will struggle to extract a living from it."

Deut 8:5. So you should realize that, as a man punishes his son, the Lord punishes you to help you.

2 Sam 7:14. I will be his father and he shall be my son. If he sins, I will use other nations to punish him.

Job 3:1. At last Job spoke, and cursed the day of his birth. [2,3]"Let the day of my birth be cursed," he said, "and the night when I was conceived. [4]Let that day be forever forgotten. Let it be lost even to God, shrouded in eternal darkness. [5]Yes, let the darkness claim it for its own, and may a black cloud overshadow it. [6]May it be blotted off the calendar, never again to be counted among the days of the month of that year. [7]Let that night be bleak and joyless. [8]Let those who are experts at cursing curse it. [9]Let the stars of the night disappear. Let it long for light, but never see it, never see the morning light. [10]Curse it, for its failure to shut my mother's womb, for letting me be born to come to all this trouble. [11]Why didn't I die at birth? [12]Why did the midwife let me live? Why did she nurse me at her breasts? [13]For if only I had died at birth, then I would be quiet now, asleep and at rest, [14,15]along with prime ministers and kings with all their pomp, and wealthy princes whose castles are full of rich treasures. [16]Oh, to have been stillborn! —to have never breathed or seen the light. [17]For there in death the wicked cease from troubling, and there the weary are at rest. [18]There even prisoners are at ease, with no brutal jailer to curse them. [19]Both rich and poor alike are there, and the slave is free at last from his master. [20,21]Oh, why should light and life be given to those in misery and bitterness, who long for death, and it won't come; who search for death as others search for food or money? [22]What blessed relief when at last they die! [23]Why is a man allowed to be born if God is only going to give him a hopeless life of uselessness and frustration? [24]I cannot eat for sighing; my groans pour out like water. [25]What I always feared has happened to me. I was not fat and lazy, yet trouble struck me down."

Job 5:6. Misery comes upon them to punish them for sowing seeds of sin. [7]Mankind heads for sin and misery as predictably as flames shoot upward from a fire. [17]How enviable the man whom God corrects! Oh, do not despise the chastening of the Lord when you sin. [18]For though he wounds, he binds and heals again.

Job 6:1. *Job's reply:* [2]"Oh, that my sadness and troubles were weighed. [3]For they are heavier than the sand of a thousand seashores. That is why I spoke so rashly. [4]For the Lord has struck me down with his arrows; he has sent his poisoned arrows deep within my heart. All God's terrors are arrayed against me. [5,6,7]When wild donkeys bray, it is because their grass is gone; oxen do not low when they have food; a man complains when there is no salt in his food. And how tasteless is the uncooked white of an egg—my appetite is gone when I look at it; I gag at the thought of eating it! [8,9]Oh, that God would grant the thing I long for most—to die beneath his hand, and be freed from his painful grip. [10]This, at least, gives me comfort despite all the pain—that I have not denied the words of the holy God. [11]Oh, why does my strength sustain me? How can I be patient till I die? [12]Am I unfeeling, like stone? Is my flesh made of brass? [13]For I am utterly helpless, without any hope. [14]One should be kind to a fainting friend, but you have accused me without the slightest fear of God. [15-18]My brother, you have proved as unreliable as a brook; it floods when there is ice and snow, but in hot weather, disappears. The caravans turn aside to be refreshed, but there is nothing there to drink, and so they perish. [19-21]When caravans from Tema and from Sheba stop for water there, their hopes are dashed. And so my hopes in you are dashed—you turn away from me in terror and refuse to help. [22]But why? Have I ever asked you for one slightest thing? Have I begged you for a present? [23]Have I ever asked your help? All I want is a reasonable answer—then I will keep quiet. Tell me, what have I done wrong? [25,26]It is wonderful to speak the truth, but your criticisms are not based on fact. Are you going to condemn me just because I impulsively cried out in desperation? [27]That would be like injuring a helpless orphan, or selling a friend. [28]Look at me! Would I lie to your face? [29]Stop assuming my guilt, for I am righteous. Don't be so unjust. [30]Don't I know the difference between right and wrong? Would I not admit it if I had sinned?

Job 7:2. How he longs for the day to end. How he grinds on to the end of the week and his wages. [3]And so to me also have been allotted months of frustration, these long and weary nights. [4]When I go to bed I think, "Oh, that it were morning," and then I toss till dawn. [5]My skin is filled with worms and blackness. My flesh breaks open, full of pus. [6]My life flies by—day after hopeless day.

Job 9:18. He will not let me breathe, but fills me with bitter sorrows.

Job 12:5. Meanwhile, the rich mock those in trouble and are quick to despise all those in need.

Job 14:1. How frail is man, how few his days, how full of trouble! [22]For him there is only sorrow and pain.

Job 16:6. But now my grief remains no matter how I defend myself; nor does it help if I refuse to speak. [7]For God has ground me down, and taken away my family. [8]O God, you have turned me to skin and bones—as a proof, they say, of my sins. [9]God hates me and angrily tears at my flesh; he has gnashed upon me with his teeth, and watched to snuff out any sign of life. [10]These "comforters" have gaping jaws to swallow me; they slap my cheek. My enemies gather themselves against me. [11]And God has delivered me over to sinners, into the hands of the wicked. [12]I was living quietly until he broke me apart. He has taken me by the neck and dashed me to pieces, then hung me up as his target. [13]His archers surround me, letting fly their arrows, so that the ground is wet from my wounds. [14]Again and again he attacks me, running upon me like a giant.

Job 17:7. My eyes are dim with weeping and I am but a shadow of my former self. [8]Fair-minded men are astonished when they see me. Yet, finally, the innocent shall come out on top, above the godless; [9]the righteous shall move onward and forward; those with pure hearts shall become stronger and stronger. [10]As for you—all of you please go away; for I do not find a wise man among you. [11]My good days are in the past. My hopes have disappeared. My heart's desires are broken. [12]They say that night is day and day is night; how they pervert the truth! [13,14]If I die, I go out into darkness, and call the grave my father, and the worm my mother and my sister. Where then is my hope? Can anyone find any? [16]No, my hope will go down to the grave. We shall rest together in the dust!

Job 19:7. I scream for help and no one hears me. I shriek, but get no justice. [8]God has blocked my path and turned my light to darkness. [9]He has stripped me of my glory and removed the crown from my head. [10]He has broken me down on every side, and I am done for. He has destroyed all hope. [11]His fury burns against me; he counts me as an enemy. [12]He sends his troops to surround my tent. [13]He has sent away my brothers, and my friends. [14]My relatives have failed me, my friends have all forsaken me. [15]Those living in my home, even my servants, regard me as a stranger. I am like a foreigner to them. [16]I call my servant, but he doesn't come; I even beg him! [17]My own wife and brothers refuse to recognize me. [18]Even young children despise me. When I stand to speak, they mock. [19]My best friends abhor me. Those I loved have turned against me. [20]I am skin and bones and have escaped death by the skin of my teeth.

Job 23:10. But he knows every detail of what is happening to me; and when he has examined me, he will pronounce me completely innocent—as pure as solid gold!

Job 30:15. I live in terror now. They hold me in contempt and my prosperity has vanished as a cloud before a strong wind. [16]My heart is broken. Depression haunts my days. [17]My weary nights are filled with pain as though something were relentlessly gnawing at my bones. [18]All night long I toss and turn, and my garments bind about me. [19]God has thrown me into the mud. I have become as dust and ashes.

Job 33:19. Or, God sends sickness and pain, even though no bone is broken, [20]so that a man loses all taste and appetite for food and doesn't care for even the daintiest dessert. [21]He becomes thin, mere skin and bones, [22]and draws near to death.

Job 36:8. If troubles come upon them, and they are enslaved and afflicted, [9]then he takes the trouble to point out to them the reason, what they have done that is wrong, or how they have behaved proudly. [10]He helps them hear his instruction to turn away from their sin. [11]If they listen and obey him, then they will be blessed with prosperity throughout their lives. [12]If they won't listen to him, they shall perish in battle and die because of their lack of good sense. [15]He delivers by distress! This makes them listen to him!

Ps 6:6. I am worn out with pain; every night my pillow is wet with tears. [7]My eyes are growing old and dim with grief because of all my enemies.

Ps 18:4. Death bound me with chains, and the floods of ungodliness mounted a massive attack against me. [5]Trapped and helpless, I struggled against the ropes that drew me on to death. [6]In my distress I screamed to the Lord for his help. And he heard me from heaven; my cry reached his ears.

Ps 31:9,10. O Lord, have mercy on me in my anguish. My eyes are red from weeping; my health is broken from sorrow. I am pining away with grief; my years are shortened, drained away because of sadness. My sins have sapped my strength; I stoop with sorrow and with shame. [11]I am scorned by all my enemies and even more by my neighbors and friends. They dread meeting me and look the other way when I go by. [12]I am forgotten like a dead man, like a broken and discarded pot. [13]I heard the lies about me, the slanders of my enemies. Everywhere I looked I was afraid, for they were plotting against my life.

Ps 32:3. There was a time when I wouldn't admit what a sinner I was. But my dishonesty made me miserable and filled my days with frustration. [4]All day and all night your hand was heavy on me. My strength evaporated like water on a sunny day until I finally admitted all my sins to you and stopped trying to hide them.

Ps 39:1. I said to myself, I'm going to quit complaining! I'll keep quiet, especially when the ungodly are around me. [2,3]But as I stood there silently the turmoil within me grew to the bursting point. The more I mused, the hotter the fires inside. Then at last I spoke, and pled with God: [4]Lord, help me to realize how brief my time on earth will be. Help me to know that I am here for but a moment more.

Ps 42:6. Yet I am standing here depressed and gloomy, but I will meditate upon your kindness to this lovely land where the Jordan River flows and where Mount Hermon and Mount Mizar stand. [7]All your waves and billows have gone over me, and floods of sorrow pour upon me like a thundering cataract.

Ps 55:4. My heart is in anguish within me. Stark fear overpowers me. [5]Trembling and horror overwhelm me. [6]Oh, for wings like a dove, to fly away and rest! [7]I would fly to the far off deserts and stay there. [8]I would flee to some refuge from all this storm.

Ps 66:10. You have purified us with fire, O Lord, like silver in a crucible. [11]You captured us in your net and laid great burdens on our backs. [12]You sent troops to ride across our broken bodies. We went through fire and flood. But in the end, you brought us into wealth and great abundance.

Ps 69:1,2. Save me, O my God. The floods have risen. Deeper and deeper I sink in the mire; the waters rise around me. [3]I have wept until I am exhausted; my throat is dry and hoarse; my eyes are swollen with weeping, waiting for my God to act. [20]Their contempt has broken my heart; my spirit is heavy within me. If even one would show some pity, if even one would comfort me!

Ps 73:10. And so God's people are dismayed and confused, and drink it all in.

Ps 77:2. I am in deep trouble and I need his help so badly. All night long I pray, lifting my hands to heaven, pleading. There can be no joy for me until he acts. [3]I think of God and moan, overwhelmed with longing for his help. [4]I cannot sleep until you act. I am too distressed even to pray!

Ps 80:5 You have fed us with sorrow and tears, [6]and have made us the scorn of the neighboring nations. They laugh among themselves.

Ps 88:3. For my life is full of troubles, and death draws near. [4]They say my life is ebbing out—a hopeless case. [5]They have left me here to die, like those slain on battlefields, from whom your mercies are removed. [6]You have thrust me down to the darkest depths. [7]Your wrath lies heavy on me; wave after wave engulfs me. [8]You have made my friends to loathe me, and they have gone away. I am in a trap with no way out. [9]My eyes grow dim with weeping. Each day I beg your help; O Lord, I reach my pleading hands to you for mercy. [10]Soon it will be too late! Of what use are your miracles when I am in the grave? How can I praise you then? [11]Can those in the grave declare your loving-kindness? Can they proclaim your faithfulness? [12]Can the darkness speak of your miracles? Can anyone in the Land of Forgetfulness talk about your help? [13]O Lord, I plead for my life and will keep on pleading day by day. [14]O Jehovah, why have you thrown my life away? Why are you turning your face from me, and looking the other way? [15]From my youth I have been sickly and ready to die. I stand helpless before your terrors. [16]Your fierce wrath has overwhelmed me. Your terrors have cut me off. [17]They flow around me all day long. [18]Lover, friend, acquaintance—all are gone. There is only darkness everywhere.

Ps 89:30–32. If his children forsake my laws and don't obey them, then I will punish them.

Ps 90:10. Seventy years are given us! And some may even live to eighty. But even the best of these years are often emptiness and pain; soon they disappear, and we are gone.

Ps 102:3,4. For my days disappear like smoke. My health is broken and my heart is sick; it is trampled like grass and is withered. My food is tasteless, and I have lost my appetite. [5]I am reduced to skin and bones because of all my groaning and despair. [6]I am like a vulture in a far-off wilderness, or like an owl alone in the desert. [7]I lie awake, lonely as a solitary sparrow on the roof. [8]My enemies taunt me day after day and curse at me. [9,10]I eat ashes instead of bread. My tears run down into my drink because of your anger against me, because of your wrath. For you have rejected me and thrown me out. [11]My life is passing swiftly as the evening shadows. I am withering like grass.

Ps 107:4. They were wandering homeless in the desert, [5]hungry and thirsty and faint. [10]Who are those who sit in darkness, in the shadow of death, crushed by misery and slavery? [17]Others, the fools, were ill because of their sinful ways. [18]Their appetites were gone and death was near. [19]Then they cried to the Lord in their troubles, and he helped them and delivered them.

Ps 109:22,23. I am slipping down the hill to death; I am shaken off from life as easily as a man brushes a grasshopper from his arm. [24]My knees are weak from fasting and I am skin and bones.

Ps 116:3. Death stared me in the face—I was frightened and sad.

Ps 141:6,7 When their leaders are condemned and their bones are strewn across the ground, then these men will finally listen to me and know that I am trying to help them.

Ps 143:3. My enemies chased and caught me. They have knocked me to the ground. They force me to live in the darkness like those in the grave. [4]I am losing all hope; I am paralyzed with fear.

Prov 3:11,12. Young man, do not resent it when God chastens and corrects you, for his punishment is proof of his love. Just as a father punishes a son he delights in to make him better, so the Lord corrects you.

Prov 12:25. Anxious hearts are very heavy but a word of encouragement does wonders!

Prov 13:12. Hope deferred makes the heart sick; but when dreams come true at last, there is life and joy.

Prov 14:10. Only the person involved can know his own bitterness or joy—no one else can really share it. [13]Laughter cannot mask a heavy heart. When the laughter ends, the grief remains.

Prov 15:13. A happy face means a glad heart; a sad face means a breaking heart. [15]When a man is gloomy, everything seems to go wrong; when he is cheerful, everything seems right!

Prov 17:3. Silver and gold are purified by fire, but God purifies hearts. [22]A cheerful heart does good like medicine, but a broken spirit makes one sick.

Prov 18:14. A man's courage can sustain his broken body, but when courage dies, what hope is left?

Eccl 2:22,23. So what does a man get for all his hard work? Days full of sorrow and grief, and restless, bitter nights. It is all utterly ridiculous.

Eccl 7:2. It is better to spend your time at funerals than at festivals. For you are going to die and it is a good thing to think about it while there is still time. [3]Sorrow is better than laughter, for sadness has a refining influence on us. [4]Yes, a wise man thinks much of death, while the fool thinks only of having a good time now.

Isa 1:5,6 Oh, my people, haven't you had enough of punishment? Why will you force me to whip you again and again? Must you forever rebel? From head to foot you are sick and weak and faint, covered with bruises and welts and infected wounds, unanointed and unbound.

Isa 24:1. Look! The Lord is overturning the land of Judah and making it a vast wasteland of destruction. See how he is emptying out all its people and scattering them over the face of the earth. [2]Priests and people, servants and masters, slave girls and mistresses, buyers and sellers, lenders and borrowers, bankers and debtors—none will be spared. [3]The land will be completely emptied and looted. The Lord has spoken. [4,5]The land suffers for the sins of its people. The earth languishes, the crops wither, the skies refuse their rain. The land is defiled by crime; the people have twisted the laws of God and broken his everlasting commands. [6]Therefore the curse of God is upon them; they are left desolate, destroyed by the drought. Few will be left alive. [7]All the joys of life will go: the grape harvest will fail, the wine will be gone, the merrymakers will sigh and mourn. [8]The melodious chords of the harp and timbrel are heard no more; the happy days are ended. [9]No more are the joys of wine and song; strong drink turns bitter in the mouth. [10]The city lies in chaos; every home and shop is locked up tight to keep out looters. [11]Mobs form in the streets, crying for wine; joy has reached its lowest ebb; gladness has been banished from the land. [12]The city is left in ruins; its gates are battered down. [13]Throughout the land the story is the same —only a remnant is left. [14]But all who are left will shout and sing for joy; those in the west will praise the majesty of God, [15,16]and those in the east will respond with praise. Hear them singing to the Lord from the ends of the earth, singing glory to the Righteous One!

Isa 26:16. Lord, in their distress they sought for you. When your punishment was on them, they poured forth a whispered prayer. [17]How we missed your presence, Lord! We suffered as a woman giving birth, who cries and writhes in pain.

Isa 48:10. I refined you in the furnace of affliction, but found no silver there. You are worthless, with nothing good in you at all.

Lam 1:7. And now in the midst of all Jerusalem's sadness she remembers happy bygone days. She thinks of all the precious joys she had before her mocking enemy struck her down—and there was no one to give her aid. [12]Is it nothing to you, all you who pass by? Look and see if there is any sorrow like my sorrow, because of all the Lord has done to me in the day of his fierce wrath.

Lam 3:1. I am the man who has seen the afflictions that come from the rod of God's wrath. [2]He has brought me into deepest darkness, shutting out all light. [3]He has turned against me. Day and night his hand is heavy on me. [4]He has made me old and has broken my bones. [5]He has built forts against me and surrounded me with anguish and distress. [6]He buried me in dark places, like those long dead. [7]He has walled me in; I cannot escape; he has fastened me with heavy chains. [8]And though I cry and shout, he will not hear my prayers! [9]He has shut me into a place of high, smooth walls; he has filled my path with detours. [10]He lurks like a bear, like a lion, waiting to attack me. [11]He has dragged me into the underbrush and torn me with his claws, and left me bleeding and desolate. [12]He has bent his bow and aimed it squarely at me, [13]and sent his arrows deep within my heart. [14]My own people laugh at me; all day long they sing their ribald songs. [15]He has filled me with bitterness, and given me a cup of deepest sorrows to drink. [16]He has made me eat gravel and broken my teeth; he has rolled me in ashes and dirt. [17]O Lord, all peace and all prosperity have long since gone, for you have taken them away. I have forgotten what enjoyment is. [18]All hope is gone; my strength has turned to water, for the Lord has left me. [19]Oh, remember the bitterness and suffering you have dealt to me! [20]For I can never forget these awful years; always my soul will live in utter shame. [21]*Yet there is one ray of hope:* [22]*his compassion never ends!* It is only the Lord's mercies that have kept us from complete destruction. [23]Great is his faithfulness; his lovingkindness begins afresh each day. [24]My soul claims the Lord as my inheritance; therefore will I hope in him. [25]The Lord is wonderfully good to those who wait for him, to those who seek for him. It is good both to hope and wait quietly for the salvation of the Lord. [27]It is good for a young man to be under discipline, [28]for it causes him to sit apart in silence beneath the Lord's demands, [29]to lie face downward in the dust; then at last there is hope for him. [30]Let him turn the other cheek to those who strike him, and accept their awful insults, [31]for the Lord will not abandon him forever. [32]Although God gives him grief, yet he will show compassion too, according to the greatness of his lovingkindness. [33]For he does not enjoy afflicting men and causing sorrow. [34,35,36]But you have trampled and crushed beneath your feet the lowly of the world, and deprived men of their God-given rights, and refused them justice. No wonder the Lord has had to deal with you!

Zech 13:9. I will bring the third that remain through the fire and make them pure, as gold and silver are refined and purified by fire.

Mk 9:48. Where the worm never dies, and the fire never goes out—[49]where all are salted with fire.

Jn 15:2. He lops off every branch that doesn't produce. And he prunes those branches that bear fruit for even larger crops.

Jn 16:33. Here on earth you will have many trials and sorrows.

2 Cor 1:8. I think you ought to know, dear brothers, about the hard time we went through in Asia. We were really crushed and overwhelmed, and feared we would never live through it. [9]We felt we

were doomed to die and saw how powerless we were to help ourselves; but that was good, for then we put everything into the hands of God, who alone could save us, for he can even raise the dead.

2 Cor 4:7. But this precious treasure—this light and power that now shine within us—is held in a perishable container, that is, in our weak bodies. Everyone can see that the glorious power within must be from God and is not our own. [8]We are pressed on every side by troubles, but not crushed and broken. We are perplexed because we don't know why things happen as they do, but we don't give up and quit. [9]We are hunted down, but God never abandons us. We get knocked down but we get up again and keep going. [10]These bodies of ours are constantly facing death just as Jesus did; so it is clear to all that it is only the living Christ within [who keeps us safe]. [11]Yes, we live under constant danger to our lives because we serve the Lord, but this gives us constant opportunities to show forth the power of Jesus Christ within our dying bodies. [12]Because of our preaching we face death, but it has resulted in eternal life for you. [16]That is why we never give up. Though our bodies are dying, our inner strength in the Lord is growing every day. [17]These troubles and sufferings of ours are, after all, quite small and won't last very long. Yet this short time of distress will result in God's richest blessing upon us forever and ever!

2 Cor 6:4. In fact, in everything we do we try to show that we are true ministers of God. We patiently endure suffering and hardship and trouble of every kind. [5]We have been beaten, put in jail, faced angry mobs, worked to exhaustion, stayed awake through sleepless nights of watching, and gone without food. [6]We have proved ourselves to be what we claim by our wholesome lives and by our understanding of the Gospel and by our patience. We have been kind and truly loving and filled with the Holy Spirit. [7]We have been truthful, with God's power helping us in all we do. All of the godly man's arsenal—weapons of defense, and weapons of attack—have been ours. [8]We stand true to the Lord whether others honor us or despise us, whether they criticize us or commend us. We are honest, but they call us liars. [9]The world ignores us, but we are known to God; we live close to death, but here we are, still very much alive. We have been injured but kept from death. Our hearts ache, but at the same time, we have the joy of the Lord. We are poor, but we give rich spiritual gifts to others. We own nothing, and yet we enjoy everything.

2 Cor 11:23. They say they serve Christ? But I have served him far more! (Have I gone mad to boast like this?) I have worked harder, been put in jail oftener, been whipped times without number, and faced death again and again and again. [24]Five different times the Jews gave me their terrible thirty-nine lashes. [25]Three times I was beaten with rods. Once I was stoned. Three times I was shipwrecked. Once I was in the open sea all night and the whole next day. [26]I have traveled many weary miles and have been often in great danger from flooded rivers, and from robbers, and from my own people, the Jews, as well as from the hands of the Gentiles. I have faced grave dangers from mobs in the cities and from death in the deserts and in the stormy seas and from men who claim to be brothers in Christ but are not. [27]I have lived with weariness and pain and sleepless nights. Often I have been hungry and thirsty and have gone without food; often I have shivered with cold, without enough clothing to keep me warm. [28]Then, besides all this, I have the constant worry of how the churches are getting along: [29]Who makes a mistake and I do not feel his sadness? Who falls without my longing to help him? Who is spiritually hurt without my fury rising against the one who hurt him? [30]But if I must brag, I would rather brag about the things that show how weak I am.

Heb 12:6. For when he punishes you, it proves that he loves you. When he whips you it proves you are really his child. [7]Let God train you, for he is doing what any loving father does for his children. Whoever heard of a son who was never corrected? [9]Since we respect our fathers here on earth, though they punish us, should we not all the more cheerfully submit to God's training so that we can begin really to live?

1 Pet 5:9. Stand firm when he attacks. Trust the Lord; and remember that other Christians all around the world are going through these sufferings too.

Rev 3:19. I continually discipline and punish everyone I love; so I must punish you, unless you turn from your indifference and become enthusiastic about the things of God.

See *Penitent; Persecution; Poor; Sorrow; Temptation.*

BENEFITS OF. 1 Kgs 8:33. And when your people sin, and their enemies defeat them, hear them from heaven and forgive them if they turn to you again and confess that you are their God. [47]And they come to their senses and turn to you and cry to you saying, "We have sinned, we have done wrong"; [48]if they honestly return to you and pray toward this land which you have given their fathers, and toward this city of Jerusalem which you have chosen, and toward this Temple, which I have built for your name, [49]hear their prayers, and pleadings from heaven where you live, and come to their assistance. *vs.* 35,36,49–53; Deut 4:30,31; 30:1,2; 2 Chron 6:28–31.

Job 5:6. Misery comes upon them to punish them for sowing seeds of sin. [7]Mankind heads for sin and misery as predictably as flames shoot upwards from a fire. [8]My advice to you is this; Go to God and confess your sins to him. [9]For he does wonderful miracles, marvels without number. [10]He sends the rain on the earth to water the fields, [11]and gives prosperity to the poor and humble, and takes sufferers to safety. [17]How enviable the man whom God corrects! Oh, do not despise the chastening of the Lord when you sin.

Job 23:10. But he knows every detail of what is

happening to me; and when he has examined me, he will pronounce me completely innocent—as pure as solid gold!

Ps 94:12,13. So he helps us by punishing us. This makes us follow his paths, and gives us respite from our enemies while God traps them and destroys them.

Prov 3:11,12. Young man, do not resent it when God chastens and corrects you, for his punishment is proof of his love. Just as a father punishes his son in whom he delights, to make him better, so the Lord corrects you. Heb 12:5.

Eccl 7:2. It is better to spend your time at funerals than festivals. For you are going to die and it is a good thing to think about it while there is still time. [3]Sorrow is better than laughter, for sadness has a refining influence on us.

Isa 19:20. This will be for a sign of loyalty to the Lord of Hosts; then when they cry to the Lord for help against those who oppress them, he will send them a Savior—and he shall deliver them. [22]The Lord will smite Egypt and then restore her! For the Egyptians will turn to the Lord and he will listen to their plea and heal them.

Isa 26:9. All night long I search for you; earnestly I seek for God; for only when you come in judgment on the earth to punish it will people turn away from wickedness and do what is right.

Isa 27:9. And why did God do it? It was to purge away her sins, to rid her of all her idol altars and her idols.

Jer 2:26,27. Like a thief, the only shame that Israel knows is getting caught. . . . Yet in time of trouble they cry to me to save them!

Jer 22:22. And now all your allies have disappeared with a puff of wind; all your friends are taken off as slaves. Surely at last you will see your wickedness and be ashamed. [23]It's very nice to live graciously in a beautiful palace, among the cedars of Lebanon, but soon you will cry and groan in anguish—anguish as of a woman in labor.

Jer 31:19. I turned away from God, but I was sorry afterwards. I kicked myself for my stupidity. I was thoroughly ashamed of all I did in younger days.

Lam 3:27. It is good for a young man to be under discipline, [28]for it causes him to sit apart in silence beneath the Lord's demands.

Ezk 20:37. I will count you carefully and let only a small quota return. [43]Then you will look back at all your sins and loathe yourselves because of the evil you have done. Ezk 6:9.

Hos 2:6. But I will fence her in with briars and thornbushes; I'll block the road before her to make her lose her way, so that [7]when she runs after her lovers she will not catch up with them. She will search for them but not find them. Then she will think, "I might as well return to my husband, for I was better off with him than I am now."

Hos 5:15. I will abandon them and return to my home until they admit their guilt and look to me for help again.

Rom 5:3. We can rejoice, too, when we run into problems and trials for we know that they are good for us—they help us learn to be patient. [4]And patience develops strength of character in us and helps us trust God more each time we use it until finally our hope and faith are strong and steady.

Rom 8:17. And since we are his children, we will share his treasures—for all God gives to his Son Jesus is now ours too. But if we are to share his glory, we must also share his suffering. [28]And we know that all that happens to us is working for our good if we love God and are fitting into his plans.

2 Cor 4:17. These troubles and sufferings of ours are, after all, quite small and won't last very long. Yet this short time of distress will result in God's richest blessing upon us forever and ever!

Phil 1:12. And I want you to know this, dear brothers: Everything that has happened to me here has been a great boost in getting out the Good News concerning Christ. [13]For everyone around here, including all the soldiers over at the barracks, knows that I am in chains simply because I am a Christian. [14]And because of my imprisonment many of the Christians here seem to have lost their fear of chains! Somehow my patience has encouraged them and they have become more and more bold in telling others about Christ. [19]I am going to keep on being glad, for I know that as you pray for me, and as the Holy Spirit helps me, this is all going to turn out for my good.

Jas 1:2. Dear brothers, is your life full of difficulties and temptations? Then be happy, [3]for when the way is rough, your patience has a chance to grow. [4]So let it grow. And don't try to squirm out of your problems. For when your patience is finally in full bloom, then you will be ready for anything, strong in character, full and complete. [12]Happy is the man who doesn't give in and do wrong when he is tempted, for afterwards he will get as his reward the crown of life that God has promised those who love him.

1 Pet 1:7. These trials are only to test your faith, to see whether or not it is strong and pure. It is being tested as fire tests gold and purifies it—and your faith is far more precious to God than mere gold; so if your faith remains strong after being tried in the test tube of fiery trials, it will bring you much praise and glory and honor on the day of his return.

1 Pet 4:14. Be happy if you are cursed and insulted for being a Christian, for when that happens the Spirit of God will come upon you with great glory.

BENEFITS OF, ILLUSTRATED. Gen 22:12. "Lay down the knife; don't hurt the lad in any way," the Angel said, "for I know that God is first in your life—you have not withheld even your beloved son from me. [16]I, the Lord, have sworn by myself that because you have obeyed me and have not withheld even your beloved son from me, [17]I will bless you with incredible blessings and multiply your descendants into countless thousands and millions, like the stars above you in the sky, and like the sands along the seashore. These descendants of yours will conquer their enemies, [18]and be a blessing to all the nations of the earth—all because you have obeyed me."

Gen 32:11. O Lord, please deliver me from destruction at the hand of my brother Esau, for I am frightened—terribly afraid that he is coming to kill me and these mothers and my children. With *vs.* 9–31.

Gen 42:21. Speaking among themselves, they said, "This has all happened because of what we did to Joseph long ago. We saw his terror and anguish and heard his pleadings, but we wouldn't listen."

Ex 9:27. Then Pharaoh sent for Moses and Aaron. "I finally see my fault," he confessed. "Jehovah is right, and I and my people have been wrong all along. [28]Beg God to end this terrifying thunder and hail, and I will let you go at once."

Ex 10:7. The court officials now came to Pharaoh, and asked him, "Are you going to destroy us completely? Don't you know even yet that all Egypt lies in ruins? Let the *men* go and serve Jehovah their God!" [16]Then Pharaoh sent an urgent call for Moses and Aaron and said to them, "I confess my sin against Jehovah your God and against you. [17]Forgive my sin only this once, and beg Jehovah your God to take away this death. I promise not to refuse afterwards to let you go." Ex 12:31–33.

Num 21:7. Then the people came to Moses and cried out, "We have sinned, for we have spoken against Jehovah and against you. Pray to him to take away the snakes." Moses prayed for the people.

Judg 10:6. Then the people of Israel turned away from the Lord again, and worshiped the heathen gods Baal and Ashtaroth, and the gods of Syria, Sidon, Moab, Ammon and Philistia. Not only this, but they no longer worshiped Jehovah at all. [7,8]This made Jehovah very angry with his people, so he immediately permitted the Philistines and the Ammonites to begin tormenting them. [10]Finally the Israelis turned to Jehovah again and begged him to save them.

1 Sam 12:9. But they soon forgot about the Lord their God, so he let them be conquered by Sisera, the general of King Hazor's army, and by the Philistines and the king of Moab. [10]Then they cried to the Lord again and confessed that they had sinned by turning away from him and worshipping the Baal and Ashtaroth idols. And they pleaded, "We will worship you and you alone if you will only rescue us from our enemies."

1 Kgs 13:6. "Oh, please, please," the king cried out to the prophet, "beg the Lord your God to restore my arm again." So he prayed to the Lord, and the king's arm became normal again. With *vs.* 1–10.

2 Chron 15:4. But whenever they have turned again to the Lord God of Israel in their distress, and searched for him, he has helped them.

2 Chron 33:12. Then at last he came to his senses and cried out humbly to God for help. [13]And the Lord listened, and answered his plea by returning him to Jerusalem and to his kingdom! At that point Manasseh finally realized that the Lord was really God!

Ezra 9:13. And now, even after our punishment in exile because of our wickedness (and we have been punished far less than we deserved), and even though you have let some of us return. With *vs.* 5–15.

Neh 9:32. And now, O great and awesome God, you who keep your promises of love and kindness —do not let all the hardships we have gone through become as nothing to you. Great trouble has come upon us and upon our kings and princes and priests and prophets and ancestors from the days when the kings of Assyria first triumphed over us until now. With *vs.* 4–38

Job 34:31. Why don't people exclaim to their God, "We have sinned, but we will stop"? [32]Or, "We know not what evil we have done; only tell us, and we will cease at once."

Job 40:1. *The Lord went on:* [2]"Do you still want to argue with the Almighty? Or will you yield? Do you—God's critic—have the answers?" [3]*Then Job replied to God:* [4]"I am nothing—how could I ever find the answers? I lay my hand upon my mouth in silence. [5]I have said too much already."

Ps 18:4. Death bound me with chains, and the floods of ungodliness mounted a massive attack against me. [5]Trapped and helpless, I struggled against the ropes that drew me on to death. [6]In my distress I screamed to the Lord for his help. And he heard me from heaven; my cry reached his ears.

Ps 66:10. You have purified us with fire, O Lord, like silver in a crucible. [11]You captured us in your net and laid great burdens on our backs. [12]You sent troops to ride across our broken bodies. We went through fire and flood. But in the end, you brought us into wealth and great abundance.

Ps 78:34. Then at last, when he had ruined them, they walked awhile behind him; how earnestly they turned around and followed him! [35]Then they remembered that God was their Rock—that their Savior was the God above all gods.

Ps 119:67. I used to wander off until you punished me; now I closely follow all you say. [71]The punishment you gave me was the best thing that could have happened to me, for it taught me to pay attention to your laws.

Isa 26:16. Lord, in their distress they sought for you. When your punishment was on them, they poured forth a whispered prayer.

Jer 31:18. I have heard Ephraim's groans: "You have punished me greatly; but I needed it all, as a calf must be trained for the yoke. Turn me again to you and restore me, for you alone are the Lord, my God. [19]I turned away from God but I was sorry afterwards. I kicked myself for my stupidity. I was thoroughly ashamed of all I did in younger days."

Lam 3:19. Oh, remember the bitterness and suffering you have dealt to me! [20]For I can never forget these awful years; always my soul will live in utter shame.

Hos 6:1. Come, let us return to the Lord; it is he who has torn us—he will heal us. He has wounded—he will bind us up.

Jon 2:1. Then Jonah prayed to the Lord his God from inside the fish: [2]"In my great trouble I cried to the Lord and he answered me; from the depths of death I called, and Lord, you heard me! [3]You threw me into the ocean depths; I sank down into the floods of waters and was covered by your wild and stormy waves. [4]Then I said, 'O Lord, you have rejected me and cast me away. How shall I ever again see your holy Temple?' [5]I sank beneath the waves, and death was very near. The waters closed above me; the seaweed wrapped itself around my head. [6]I went down to the bottoms of the mountains that rise from off the ocean floor. I was locked out of life and imprisoned in the land of death. But, O Lord my God, you have snatched me from the yawning jaws of death! [7]When I had lost all hope, I turned my thoughts once more to the Lord. And my earnest prayer went to you in your holy Temple. [8](Those who worship false gods have turned their backs on all the mercies waiting for them from the Lord!) [9]I will never worship anyone but you! For how can I thank you enough for all you have done? I will surely fulfill my promises. For my deliverance comes from the Lord alone." [10]And the Lord ordered the fish to spit up Jonah on the beach, and it did.

Lk 15:17. When he finally came to his senses, he said to himself, "At home even the hired men have food enough and to spare, and here I am, dying of hunger!" With *vs.* 11–24.

Acts 8:24. "Pray for me," Simon exclaimed, "that these terrible things won't happen to me."

Exemplified. Joseph's brothers, Gen 42:21. Joseph, Gen 45:5,7,8. Israel, Deut 8:3,5. Josiah, 2 Kgs 22:18,19. Hezekiah, 2 Chron 32:25,26. Manasseh, 2 Chron 33:12. Jonah, Jon 2:7. Prodigal son, Lk 15:21.

CONSOLATION IN. Gen 21:17. Then God answered the lad's cries, and the Angel of God called to Hagar from the sky, "Hagar, what's wrong? Don't be afraid! For God has heard the lad's cries as he is lying there." *vs.* 12–21. Gen 16:7–13.

Gen 26:24. Jehovah appeared to him on the night of his arrival. "I am the God of Abraham your father," he said. "Fear not, for I am with you and will bless you, and will give you so many descendants that they will become a great nation—because of my promise to Abraham, who obeyed me." With *vs.* 17–33.

Gen 31:42. In fact, except for the grace of God—the God of my grandfather Abraham, even the glorious God of Isaac, my father—you would have sent me off without a penny to my name. But God has seen your cruelty and my hard work, and that is why he appeared to you last night.

Ex 3:7. Then the Lord told him, "I have seen the deep sorrows of my people in Egypt, and have heard their pleas for freedom from their harsh taskmasters. [8]I have come to deliver them from the Egyptians and to take them out of Egypt into a good land, a large land, a land 'flowing with milk and honey.' " *vs.* 16,17

Ex 14:13. But Moses told the people, "Don't be afraid. Just stand where you are and watch, and you will see the wonderful way the Lord will rescue you today. The Egyptians you are looking at—you will never see them again. [14]The Lord will fight for you, and you won't need to lift a finger!"

Deut 33:27. The eternal God is your Refuge, and underneath are the everlasting arms. He thrusts out your enemies before you; it is he who cries, "Destroy them!"

2 Sam 22:28. You will save those in trouble, but you bring down the haughty; for you watch their every move.

Job 5:6. Misery comes upon them to punish them for sowing seeds of sin. [7]Mankind heads for sin and misery as predictably as flames shoot upwards from a fire. [8]My advice to you is this: Go to God and confess your sins to him. [9]For he does wonderful miracles, marvels without number. [10]He sends the rain upon the earth to water the fields, [11]and gives prosperity to the poor and humble, and takes sufferers to safety. [12]He frustrates the plans of crafty men. [13]They are caught in their own traps; he thwarts their schemes. [14]They grope like blind men in the daylight; they see no better in the daytime than at night. [15]God saves the fatherless and the poor from the grasp of these oppressors. [16]And so at last the poor have hope, and the fangs of the wicked are broken. [17]How enviable the man whom God corrects! Oh, do not despise the chastening of the Lord when you sin. [18]For though he wounds, he binds and heals again. [19]He will deliver you again and again, so that no evil can touch you. [20]He will keep you from death in famine, and from the power of the sword in time of war. [21]You will be safe from slander; no need to fear the future. [22]You shall laugh at war and famine; wild animals will leave you alone. [23]Dangerous animals will be at peace with you. [24]You need not worry about your home while you are gone; nothing shall be stolen from your barns. [25]Your sons shall become important men; your descendants shall be as numerous as grass. [26]You shall live a long, good life; like standing grain, you'll not be harvested until it's time! [27]I have found from experience that all of this is true. For your own good, listen to my counsel.

Job 11:16. Only then can you forget your misery. It will all be in the past. [17]And your life will be cloudless; any darkness will be as bright as morning! [18]You will have courage because you will have hope. You will take your time, and rest in safety. [19]You will lie down unafraid and many will look to you for help.

Job 16:5. But no! I would speak in such a way that it would help you. I would try to take away your grief.

Job 29:25. I told them what they should do, and corrected them as their chief, or as a king instructs his army, and as one who comforts those who mourn.

Job 31:19,20. If I have seen anyone freezing and

not given him clothing, or fleece from my sheep to keep him warm, [21]or if I have taken advantage of an orphan because I thought I could get away with it—[22]if I have done any of these things, then let my arm be torn from its socket! Let my shoulder be wrenched out of place!

Job 35:10. Yet none of them cry to God, asking, "Where is God my Maker who gives songs in the night?"

Ps 9:9. All who are oppressed may come to him. He is a refuge for them in their times of trouble. [10]All those who know your mercy, Lord, will count on you for help. For you have never yet forsaken those who trust in you.

Ps 23:4. Even when walking through the dark valley of death I will not be afraid, for you are close beside me, guarding, guiding all the way.

Ps 27:5. There I'll be when troubles come. He will hide me. He will set me on a high rock [6]out of reach of all my enemies. Then I will bring him sacrifices and sing his praises with much joy.

Ps 30:5. His anger lasts a moment; his favor lasts for life! Weeping may go on all night, but in the morning there is joy!

Ps 31:7. I am radiant with joy because of your mercy, for you have listened to my troubles and have seen the crisis in my soul.

Ps 34:4. For I cried to him and he answered me! He freed me from all my fears. [19]The good man does not escape all troubles—he has them too. But the Lord helps him in each and every one. [20]God even protects him from accidents.

Ps 37:23. The steps of good men are directed by the Lord. He delights in each step they take. [24]If they fall it isn't fatal, for the Lord holds them with his hand. [32]Evil men spy on the godly, waiting for an excuse to accuse them and then demanding their death. [33]But the Lord will not let these evil men succeed, nor let the godly be condemned when they are brought before the judge.

Ps 41:3. He nurses them when they are sick, and soothes their pains and worries.

Ps 42:5. Why then be downcast? Why be discouraged and sad? Hope in God! I shall yet praise him again. Yes, I shall again praise him for his help.

Ps 46:1. God is our refuge and strength, a tested help in times of trouble.

Ps 50:15. I want you to trust me in your times of trouble, so I can rescue you, and you can give me glory.

Ps 55:22. Give your burdens to the Lord. He will carry them. He will not permit the godly to slip or fall.

Ps 56:8. You have seen me tossing and turning through the night. You have collected all my tears and preserved them in your bottle! You have recorded every one in your book. [9]The very day I call for help, the tide of battle turns. My enemies flee! This one thing I *know: God is for me!* [10,11]I am trusting God—oh, praise his promises! I am not afraid of anything mere man can do to me! Yes, praise his promises.

Ps 62:1. I stand silently before the Lord, waiting for him to rescue me. For salvation comes from him alone. [2]Yes, he alone is my Rock, my rescuer, defense and fortress. Why then should I be tense with fear when troubles come? [5]But I stand silently before the Lord, waiting for him to rescue me. For salvation comes from him alone. [6]Yes, he alone is my Rock, my rescuer, defense and fortress—why then should I be tense with fear when troubles come? [7]My protection and success come from God alone. He is my refuge, a Rock where no enemy can reach me. [8]O my people, trust him all the time. Pour out your longings before him, for he can help! [11]Don't let the rich men be proud. [12]He is loving and kind and rewards each one of us according to the work we do for him.

Ps 68:6. He gives families to the lonely, and releases prisoners from jail, singing with joy! But for rebels there is famine and distress.

Ps 69:20. Their contempt has broken my heart; my spirit is heavy within me. If even one would show some pity, if even one would comfort me! [33]For Jehovah hears the cries of his needy ones, and does not look the other way.

Ps 71:20. You have let me sink down deep in desperate problems. But you will bring me back to life again, up from the depths of the earth.

Ps 73:26. My health fails; my spirits droop, yet God remains! He is the strength of my heart; he is mine forever!

Ps 94:17. I would have died unless the Lord had helped me. [18]I screamed, "I'm slipping, Lord!" and he was kind and saved me. [19]Lord, when doubts fill my mind, when my heart is in turmoil, quiet me and give me renewed hope and cheer.

Ps 103:13. He is like a father to us, tender and sympathetic to those who reverence him. [14]For he knows we are but dust.

Ps 112:4. When darkness overtakes him, light will come bursting in. He is kind and merciful.

Ps 119:49,50. Never forget your promises to me your servant, for they are my only hope. They give me strength in all my troubles; how they refresh and revive me! [52]From my earliest youth I have tried to obey you; your word has been my comfort. [54]For these laws of yours have been my source of joy and singing through all these years of my earthly pilgrimage. [92]I would have despaired and perished unless your laws had been my deepest delight. [143]In my distress and anguish, your commandments comfort me.

Ps 138:3. When I pray, you answer me, and encourage me by giving me the strength I need. [7]Though I am surrounded by troubles, you will bring me safely through them. You will clench your fist against my angry enemies! Your power will save me. [8]The Lord will work out his plans for my life—for your lovingkindness, Lord, continues forever. Don't abandon me, for you made me.

Ps 140:12. But the Lord will surely help those they persecute; he will maintain the rights of the poor.

Ps 145:14. The Lord lifts the fallen and those bent beneath their loads.

Ps 147:3. He heals the brokenhearted, binding up their wounds.

Prov 12:13. Lies will get any man into trouble, but honesty is its own defense.

Eccl 4:1. Next I observed all the oppression and sadness throughout the earth—the tears of the oppressed, and no one helping them, while on the side of their oppressors were powerful allies.

Isa 4:6. The Lord will provide shade on all Jerusalem—over every home and all its public grounds—a canopy of smoke and cloud throughout the day, and clouds of fire at night, covering the Glorious Land, [6]protecting it from daytime heat and from rains and storms.

Isa 14:31. Weep, Philistine cities—you are doomed. All your nation is doomed. For a perfectly trained army is coming down from the north against you. [32]What then shall we tell the reporters? Tell them that the Lord has founded Jerusalem and is determined that the poor of his people will find a refuge within her walls.

Isa 25:4. But to the poor, O Lord, you are a refuge from the storm, a shadow from the heat, a shelter from merciless men who are like a driving rain that melts down an earthen wall.

Isa 30:19. O my people in Jerusalem, you shall weep no more, for he will surely be gracious to you at the sound of your cry. He will answer you. [20]Though he give you the bread of adversity and water of affliction, yet he will be with you to teach you—with your own eyes you will see your Teacher.

Isa 40:1. Comfort, oh, comfort my people, says your God. [2]Speak tenderly to Jerusalem and tell her that her sad days are gone. Her sins are pardoned, and the Lord will give her twice as many blessings as he gave her punishment before. [29]He gives power to the tired and worn out, and strength to the weak.

Isa 41:10. Fear not, for I am with you. Do not be dismayed. I am your God. I will strengthen you; I will help you; I will uphold you with my victorious right hand. [13]I am holding you by your right hand—I, the Lord your God—and I say to you, Don't be afraid; I am here to help you. [14]Despised though you are, fear not, O Israel; for I will help you. I am the Lord, your Redeemer; I am the Holy One of Israel. [17]When the poor and needy seek water and there is none and their tongues are parched from thirst, then I will answer when they cry to me. I, Israel's God, will not ever forsake them.

Isa 42:3. He will not break the bruised reed, nor quench the dimly burning flame. He will encourage the fainthearted, those tempted to despair. He will see full justice given to all who have been wronged.

Isa 43:2. When you go through deep waters and great trouble, I will be with you. When you go through rivers of difficulty, you will not drown! When you walk through the fire of oppression, you will not be burned up—the flames will not consume you.

Isa 49:13. Sing for joy, O heavens; shout, O earth. Break forth with a song, O mountains, for the Lord has comforted his people, and will have compassion upon them in their sorrow.

Isa 50:4. The Lord God has given me his words of wisdom so that I may know what I should say to all these weary ones. Morning by morning he wakens me and opens my understanding to his will. [7]Because the Lord God helps me, I will not be dismayed; therefore, I have set my face like flint to do his will, and I know that I will triumph. [8]He who gives me justice is near. Who will dare to fight against me now? Where are my enemies? Let them appear! [9]See, the Lord God is for me! Who shall declare me guilty! All my enemies shall be destroyed like old clothes eaten up by moths! [10]Who among you fears the Lord and obeys his Servant? If such men walk in darkness, without one ray of light, let them trust the Lord, let them rely upon their God.

Isa 51:3. And the Lord will bless Israel again, and make her deserts blossom; her barren wilderness will become as beautiful as the Garden of Eden. Joy and gladness will be found there, thanksgiving and lovely songs. [12]I, even I, am he who comforts you and gives you all this joy. So what right have you to fear mere mortal men, who wither like the grass and disappear? With *vs.* 3–13.

Isa 54:4. Fear not; you will no longer live in shame. The shame of your youth and the sorrows of widowhood will be remembered no more. [11]O my afflicted people, tempest-tossed and troubled, I will rebuild you on a foundation of sapphires and make the walls of your houses from precious jewels.

Isa 58:10. Feed the hungry! Help those in trouble! Then your light will shine out from the darkness, and the darkness around you shall be as bright as day.

Isa 61:1. The Spirit of the Lord God is upon me, because the Lord has anointed me to bring good news to the suffering and afflicted. He has sent me to comfort the broken-hearted, to announce liberty to captives and to open the eyes of the blind. [2]He has sent me to tell those who mourn that the time of God's favor to them has come, and the day of his wrath to their enemies. [3]To all who mourn in Israel will he give: Beauty for ashes; joy instead of mourning; praise instead of heaviness. For God has planted them like strong and graceful oaks for his own glory.

Isa 63:9. In all their affliction he was afflicted, and he personally saved them. In his love and pity he redeemed them and lifted them up and carried them through all the years.

Isa 66:5. Hear the words of God, all you who fear him, and tremble at his words: Your brethren hate you and cast you out for being loyal to my name. "Glory to God," they scoff. "Be happy in the Lord!" But they shall be put to shame. [13]I will comfort you there as a little one is comforted by its mother. [14]When you see Jerusalem, your heart will rejoice; vigorous health will be yours. All the world will see the good hand of God upon his people, and his wrath upon his enemies.

Jer 31:13. The young girls will dance for joy, and men folk—old and young—will take their part in all the fun; for I will turn their mourning into joy and I will comfort them and make them rejoice, for their captivity with all its sorrows will be behind them. [25]For I have given rest to the weary and joy to all the sorrowing.

Jer 39:17. But I will deliver you. You shall not be killed by those you fear so much. [18]As a reward for trusting me, I will preserve your life and keep you safe.

Lam 3:31. For the Lord will not abandon him forever. [32]Although God gives him grief, yet he will show compassion too, according to the greatness of his lovingkindness. [33]For he does not enjoy afflicting men and causing sorrow. [57]Yes, you came at my despairing cry and told me not to fear.

Ezk 11:16. But tell the exiles that the Lord God says: Although I have scattered you in the countries of the world, yet I will be a sanctuary to you for the time that you are there.

Hos 2:14. But I will court her again, and bring her into the wilderness, and speak to her tenderly there. [15]There I will give back her vineyeards to her, and transform her Valley of Troubles into a Door of Hope. She will respond to me there, singing with joy as in days long ago in her youth, after I had freed her from captivity in Egypt.

Hos 6:1. Come, let us return to the Lord; it is he who has torn us—he will heal us. He has wounded —he will bind us up. [2]In just a couple of days, or three at the most, he will set us on our feet again, to live in his kindness! [3]Oh, that we might know the Lord! Let us press on to know him, and he will respond to us as surely as the coming of dawn or the rain of early spring.

Nah 1:7. The Lord is good. When trouble comes, he is the place to go! And he knows everyone who trusts in him!

Zeph 3:18. "I have gathered your wounded and taken away your reproach."

Mt 5:4. Those who mourn are fortunate! for they shall be comforted. [10]Happy are those who are persecuted because they are good, for the Kingdom of Heaven is theirs. [11]When you are reviled and persecuted and lied about because you are my followers—wonderful! [12]Be *happy* about it! Be *very glad!* For a *tremendous reward* awaits you up in heaven. And remember, the ancient prophets were persecuted too.

Mt 10:29. Not one sparrow (What do they cost? Two for a penny?) can fall to the ground without your Father knowing it. [30]And the very hairs of your head all are numbered. [Luke 21:18] [31]So don't worry! You are more valuable to him than many sparrows. Lk 12:6,7

Mt 11:28. Come to me and I will give you rest—all of you who work so hard beneath a heavy yoke.

Mt 14:27. But Jesus immediately spoke to them, reassuring them. "Don't be afraid!" he said. Mk 6:50

Mt 25:34. Then I, the King, shall say to those at my right, "Come, blessed of my Father, into the Kingdom prepared for you from the founding of the world. [35]For I was hungry and you fed me; I was thirsty and you gave me water; I was a stranger and you invited me into your homes; [36]naked and you clothed me; sick and in prison, and you visited me." [40]And I, the King, will tell them, "When you did it to these my brothers you were doing it to me!"

Mt 28:5. Then the angel spoke to the women. "Don't be frightened!" he said. "I know you are looking for Jesus, who was crucified." [9]And as they were running, suddenly Jesus was there in front of them! "Good morning!" he said. And they fell to the ground before him, holding his feet and worshiping him. [10]Then Jesus said to them, "Don't be frightened! Go tell my brothers to leave at once for Galilee, to meet me there."

Lk 6:21. What happiness there is for you who are now hungry, for you are going to be satisfied! What happiness there is for you who weep, for the time will come when you shall laugh with joy! [22]What happiness it is when others hate you and exclude you and insult you and smear your name because you are mine! [23]When that happens, rejoice! Yes, leap for joy! For you will have a great reward awaiting you in heaven. And you will be in good company—the ancient prophets were treated that way too!

Lk 7:13. When the Lord saw her, his heart overflowed with sympathy. "Don't cry!" he said.

Jn 14:1. Let not your heart be troubled. You are trusting God, now trust in me. [15,16]If you love me, obey me; and I will ask the Father and he will give you another Comforter, and he will never leave you. [18]No, I will not abandon you or leave you as orphans in the storm—I will come to you. [27]I am leaving you with a gift—peace of mind and heart! And the peace I give isn't fragile like the peace the world gives. So don't be troubled or afraid.

Jn 15:18. You get enough hate from the world! But then, it hated me before it hated you. [20]Do you remember what I told you? "A slave isn't greater than his master!" So since they persecuted me, naturally they will persecute you. And if they had listened to me, they would listen to you.

Jn 16:20. The world will greatly rejoice over what is going to happen to me, and you will weep. But your weeping shall suddenly be turned to wonderful joy [when you see me again]. [22]You have sorrow now, but I will see you again and then you will rejoice; and no one can rob you of that joy. [33]I have told you all this so that you will have peace of heart and mind. Here on earth you will have many trials and sorrows; but cheer up, for I have overcome the world.

Acts 12:5. But earnest prayer was going up to God from the Church for his safety all the time he was in prison.

Acts 23:11. That night the Lord stood beside Paul and said, "Don't worry, Paul; just as you have told the people about me here in Jerusalem, so you must also in Rome."

Rom 8:28. And we know that all that happens to us is working for our good if we love God and are fitting into his plans. [35]Who then can ever keep Christ's love from us? When we have trouble or calamity, when we are hunted down or destroyed, is it because he doesn't love us anymore? And if we are hungry, or penniless, or in danger, or threatened with death, has God deserted us? [36]No, for the Scriptures tell us that for his sake we must be ready to face death at every moment of the day—we are like sheep awaiting slaughter; [37]but despite all this, overwhelming victory is ours through Christ who loved us enough to die for us. [38]For I am convinced that nothing can ever separate us from his love. Death can't, and life can't. The angels won't, and all the powers of hell itself cannot keep God's love away. Our fears for today, our worries about tomorrow, [39]or where we are—high above the sky, or in the deepest ocean—nothing will ever be able to separate us from the love of God demonstrated by our Lord Jesus Christ when he died for us.

Rom 12:12. Be glad for all God is planning for you. Be patient in trouble, and prayerful always. [15]When others are happy, be happy with them. If they are sad, share their sorrow.

Rom 15:4. These things that were written in the Scriptures so long ago are to teach us patience and to encourage us, so that we will look forward expectantly to the time when God will conquer sin and death.

2 Cor 1:3,4. What a wonderful God we have—he is the Father of our Lord Jesus Christ, the source of every mercy, and the one who so wonderfully comforts and strengthens us in our hardships and trials. And why does he do this? So that when others are troubled, needing our sympathy and encouragement, we can pass on to them this same help and comfort God has given us. [5]You can be sure that the more we undergo sufferings for Christ, the more he will shower us with his comfort and encouragement. [6,7]We are in deep trouble for bringing you God's comfort and salvation. But in our trouble God has comforted us—and this, too, to help you: to show you from our personal experience how God will tenderly comfort you when you undergo these same sufferings. He will give you the strength to endure.

2 Cor 4:8. We are pressed on every side by troubles, but not crushed and broken. We are perplexed because we don't know why things happen as they do, but we don't give up and quit. [9]We are hunted down, but God never abandons us. We get knocked down, but we get up again and keep going. [10]These bodies of ours are constantly facing death just as Jesus did; so it is clear to all that it is only the living Christ within (who keeps us safe). [16]That is why we never give up. Though our bodies are dying, our inner strength in the Lord is growing every day. [17]These troubles and sufferings of ours are, after all, quite small and won't last very long. Yet this short time of distress will result in God's richest blessing upon us forever and ever!

2 Cor 7:6. Then God who cheers those who are discouraged refreshed us by the arrival of Titus.

2 Cor 12:9. Each time he said, "No. But I am with you; that is all you need. My power shows up best in weak people." Now I am glad to boast about how weak I am; I am glad to be a living demonstration of Christ's power, instead of showing off my own power and abilities.

Gal 6:2. Share each other's troubles and problems, and so obey our Lord's command.

Phil 1:19. I am going to keep on being glad, for I know that as you pray for me, and as the Holy Spirit helps me, this is all going to turn out for my good.

1 Thess. 4:13. And now, dear brothers, I want you to know what happens to a Christian when he dies so that when it happens, you will not be full of sorrow, as those who have no hope. [16]For the Lord Himself will come down from heaven with a mighty shout and with the soul-stirring cry of the archangel and the great trumpet-call of God. And the believers who are dead will be the first to rise to meet the Lord. [17]Then we who are still alive and remain on the earth will be caught up with them in the clouds to meet the Lord in the air and remain with him forever. [18]So comfort and encourage each other with this news.

2 Thess 1:7. And so I would say to you who are suffering, God will give you rest along with us when the Lord Jesus appears suddenly from heaven in flaming fire with his mighty angels.

2 Thess 2:16. May our Lord Jesus Christ himself and God our Father, who has loved us and given us everlasting comfort and hope which we don't deserve, [17]comfort your hearts with all comfort, and help you in every good thing you say and do.

2 Tim 2:12. And if we think that our present service for him is hard, just remember that some day we are going to sit with him and rule with him.

2 Tim 4:17. But the Lord stood with me and gave me the opportunity to boldly preach a whole sermon for all the world to hear. And he saved me from being thrown to the lions.

Heb 2:14. Since we, God's children, are human beings—made of flesh and blood—he became flesh and blood too by being born in human form; for only as a human being could he die and in dying break the power of the devil who had the power of death. [15]Only in that way could he deliver those who through fear of death have been living all their lives as slaves to constant dread. [18]For since he himself has now been through suffering and temptation, he knows what it is like when we suffer and are tempted, and he is wonderfully able to help us.

Heb 4:15. This High Priest of ours understands our weaknesses, since he had the same temptations we do, though he never once gave way to them and sinned. [16]So let us come boldly to the very throne of God and stay there to receive his mercy and to find grace to help us in our times of need.

Heb 6:18. He has given us both his promise and his oath, two things we can completely count on, for it is impossible for God to tell a lie. Now all those who flee to him to save them can take new courage when they hear such assurances from God; now they can know without doubt that he will give them the salvation he has promised them.

Heb 12:1. Since we have such a huge crowd of men of faith watching us from the grandstands, let us strip off anything that slows us down or holds us back, and especially those sins that wrap themselves so tightly around our feet and trip us up; and let us run with patience the particular race that God has set before us. [2]Keep your eyes on Jesus, our leader and instructor. He was willing to die a shameful death on the cross because of the joy he knew would be his afterwards; and now he sits in the place of honor by the throne of God. [3]If you want to keep from becoming fainthearted and weary, think about his patience as sinful men did such terrible things to him. [4]After all, you have never yet struggled against sin and temptation until you sweat great drops of blood.

Heb 13:3. Don't forget about those in jail. Suffer with them as though you were there yourself. Share the sorrow of those being mistreated, for you know what they are going through. [5]Stay away from the love of money; be satisfied with what you have. For God has said, "I will never, *never* fail you nor forsake you." [6]That is why we can say without any doubt or fear, "The Lord is my Helper and I am not afraid of anything that mere man can do to me."

Jas 1:12. Happy is the man who doesn't give in and do wrong when he is tempted, for afterwards he will get as his reward the crown of life that God has promised those who love him. [27]The Christian who is pure and without fault, from God the Father's point of view, is the one who takes care of orphans and widows, and who remains true to the Lord—not soiled and dirtied by his contacts with the world.

Jas 5:8. Yes, be patient. And take courage, for the coming of the Lord is near. [10]For examples of patience in suffering, look at the Lord's prophets.

1 Pet 2:21. This suffering is all part of the work God has given you. Christ, who suffered for you, is your example. Follow in his steps: [22]He never sinned, never told a lie, [23]never answered back when insulted; when he suffered he did not threaten to get even; he left his case in the hands of God who always judges fairly. [24]He personally carried the load of our sins in his own body when he died on the cross, so that we can be finished with sin and live a good life from now on. For his wounds have healed ours!

1 Pet 4:12. Dear friends, don't be bewildered or surprised when you go through the fiery trials ahead, for this is no strange, unusual thing that is going to happen to you. [13]Instead, be really glad—because these trials will make you partners with Christ in his suffering and afterwards you will have the wonderful joy of sharing his glory in that coming day when it will be displayed. [14]Be happy if you are cursed and insulted for being a Christian, for when that happens the Spirit of God will come upon you with great glory.

1 Pet 5:7. Let him have all your worries and cares, for he is always thinking about you and watching everything that concerns you. [9]Stand firm when he attacks. Trust the Lord; and remember that other Christians all around the world are going through these sufferings too.

Rev 2:9. I know how much you suffer for the Lord, and I know all about your poverty (but you have heavenly riches!). I know the slander of those opposing you, who say that they are Jews—the children of God—but they aren't, for they support the cause of Satan. [10]Stop being afraid of what you are about to suffer—for the devil will soon throw some of you into prison to test you. You will be persecuted for "ten days." Remain faithful even when facing death and I will give you the crown of life—an unending, glorious future.

Rev 3:2. Now wake up! Strengthen what little remains—for even what is left is at the point of death. Your deeds are far from right in the sight of God. [10]Because you have patiently obeyed me despite the persecution, therefore I will protect you from the time of Great Tribulation and temptation, which will come upon the world to test everyone alive.

Rev 7:14. "No sir," I replied. "Please tell me." "These are the ones coming out of the Great Tribulation," he said; "they washed their robes and whitened them by the blood of the Lamb. [15]That is why they are here before the throne of God, serving him day and night in his temple. The one sitting on the throne will shelter them; [16]they will never be hungry again, nor thirsty, and they will be fully protected from the scorching noontime heat. [17]For the Lamb standing in front of the throne will feed them and be their Shepherd and lead them to the springs of the Water of Life. And God will wipe their tears away."

DELIVERANCE FROM. See *Prayer, Answered.*

DESIGN OF. Deut 8:2. Do you remember how the Lord led you through the wilderness for all those forty years, humbling you and testing you to find out how you would respond, and whether or not you would really obey him? [16]He fed you with manna in the wilderness (it was a kind of bread unknown before) so that you would become humble and so that your trust in him would grow, and he could do you good.

Deut 30:1. When all these things have happened to you—the blessings and the curses I have listed—you will meditate upon them as you are living among the nations where the Lord your God will have driven you. [2]If at that time you want to return to the Lord your God, and you and your children have begun wholeheartedly to obey all of the commandments I have given you today, [3]then the Lord your God will rescue you from your captivity! He will have mercy upon you and come and gather you out of all the nations where he will have scattered you.

Deut 31:17. Then my anger will flame out against them and I will abandon them, hiding my face from them, and they shall be destroyed. Terrible trouble will come upon them, so that they will say, "God is no longer among us!"

Judg 2:21. I will no longer drive out the nations left unconquered by Joshua when he died. [22]Instead, I will use these nations to test my people, to see whether or not they will obey the Lord as their ancestors did.

1 Kgs 8:33,34. And when your people sin and their enemies defeat them, hear them from heaven and forgive them if they turn to you again and confess that you are their God. Bring them back again to this land which you have given to their fathers. With *vs.* 35–48; 2 Chron 6:24–31.

2 Chron 7:13. If I shut up the heavens so that there is no rain, or if I command the locust swarms to eat up all of your crops, or if I send an epidemic among you, [14]then if my people will humble themselves and pray, and search for me, and turn from their wicked ways, I will hear them from heaven and forgive their sins and heal their land.

Job 33:11. "And he puts my feet in the stocks," you say, "and watches every move I make." [16]He opens their ears in times like that, and gives them wisdom and instruction, [17,18] causing them to change their minds, and keeping them from pride, and warning them of the penalties of sin, and keeping them from falling into some trap. [19]Or, God sends sickness and pain, even though no bone is broken, [20]so that a man loses all taste and appetite for food and doesn't care for even the daintiest dessert. [21]He becomes thin, mere skin and bones, [22]and draws near to death. [23,24]But if a messenger from heaven is there to intercede for him as a friend, to show him what is right, then God pities him and says, "Set him free. Do not make him die, for I have found a substitute." [25]Then his body will become as healthy as a child's, firm and youthful again. [26]And when he prays to God, God will hear and answer and receive him with joy, and return him to his duties. [27]And he will declare to his friends, "I sinned, but God let me go. [28]He did not let me die. I will go on living in the realm of light." [29]Yes, God often does these things for man—[30]brings back his soul from the pit, so that he may live in the light of the living.

Job 36:8. If troubles come upon them, and they are enslaved and afflicted, [9]then he takes the trouble to point out to them the reason, what they have done that is wrong, or how they have behaved proudly. [10]He helps them hear his instruction to turn away from their sin.

Ps 66:10. You have purified us with fire, O Lord, like silver in a crucible.

Ps 106:43. Again and again he delivered them from their slavery, but they continued to rebel against him, and were finally destroyed by their sin. [44]Yet, even so, he listened to their cries and heeded their distress.

Ps 107:10. Who are these who sit in darkness, in the shadow of death, crushed by misery and slavery? [11]They rebelled against the Lord, scorning him who is the God above all gods. [12]That is why he broke them with hard labor; they fell and none could help them rise again. [13]Then they cried to the Lord in their troubles, and he rescued them! [14]He led them from the darkness and shadow of death and snapped their chains. [17]Others, the fools, were ill because of their sinful ways. [18]Their appetites were gone and death was near. [19]Then they cried to the Lord in their troubles, and he helped them and delivered them. [20]He spoke, and they were healed—snatched from the door of death. [21]Oh, that these men would praise the Lord for his lovingkindness and for all of his wonderful deeds! [23]And then there are the sailors sailing the seven seas, plying the trade routes of the world. [24]They too, observe the power of God in action. [25]He calls to the storm winds; the waves rise high. [26]Their ships are tossed to the heavens and sink again to the depths; the sailors cringe in terror. [27]They reel and stagger like drunkards and are at their wit's end. [28]Then they cry to the Lord in their trouble, and he saves them. [29]He calms the storm and stills the waves. [30]What a blessing is that stillness as he brings them safely into harbor! [31]Oh, that these men would praise the Lord for his lovingkindness and for all of his wonderful deeds!

Ps 119:71. The punishment you gave me was the best thing that could have happened to me, for it taught me to pay attention to your laws.

Eccl 7:14. Enjoy prosperity whenever you can, and when hard times strike, realize that God gives one as well as the other—so that everyone will realize that nothing is certain in this life.

Isa 1:25. I myself will melt you in a smelting pot, and skim off your slag. [26]And afterwards I will give you good judges and wise counselors like those you used to have. Then your city shall again be called "The City of Justice," and "The Faithful Town." [27]Those who return to the Lord, who are just and good, shall be redeemed.

Isa 4:2–4. Those whose names are written down to escape the destruction of Jerusalem will be washed and rinsed of all their moral filth by the horrors and the fire. They will be God's holy people. And the land will produce for them its lushest bounty and its richest fruit.

Isa 9:13. For after all this punishment you will not repent and turn to him, the Lord of heaven's armies. [14,15]Therefore the Lord, in one day, will destroy the leaders of Israel and the lying prophets.

Isa 52:5. And now, what is this? asks the Lord. Why are my people enslaved again, and oppressed without excuse? Those who rule them shout in exultation, and my name is constantly blasphemed, day by day. [6]Therefore I will reveal my name to my people and they shall know the power in that name. Then at last they will recognize that it is I, yes, I, who speaks to them.

Jer 24:4,5 Then the Lord said: "The good figs represent the exiles sent to Babylon. I have done it for their good."

Lam 1:5. Her enemies prosper, for the Lord has punished Jerusalem for all her many sins; her young children are captured and taken far away as slaves.

Ezk 6:10. They will realize that I alone am God, and that I wasn't fooling when I told them that all this would happen to them.

Ezk 14:10. False prophets and hypocrites—evil people who say they want my words—all will be punished for their sins, [11]so that the people of Israel will learn not to desert me and not to be polluted any longer with sin, but to be my people and I their God. So says the Lord.

Dan 4:25. That your people will chase you from your palace, and you will live in the fields like an animal, eating grass like a cow, your back wet with dew from heaven. For seven years this will be your life, until you learn that the Most High God dominates the kingdoms of men, and gives power to anyone he chooses. [26]But the stump and the roots were left in the ground! This means that you will get your kingdom back again, when you have learned that heaven rules. [27]O King Nebuchadnezzar, listen to me—stop sinning; do what you know is right; be merciful to the poor. Perhaps even yet God will spare you. [34]"At the end of seven years I, Nebuchadnezzar, looked up to heaven, and my sanity returned, and I praised and worshiped the Most High God and honored him who lives forever, whose rule is everlasting, his kingdom evermore."

Hos 5:15. I will abandon them and return to my home until they admit their guilt and look to me for help again, for as soon as trouble comes, they will search for me.

Amos 4:6. "I sent you hunger," says the Lord, "but it did no good; you still would not return to me."

Mic 6:9. The Lord's voice calls out to all Jerusalem—listen to the Lord if you are wise! The armies of destruction are coming; the Lord is sending them.

Mal 3:3. Like a refiner of silver he will sit and closely watch as the dross is burned away. He will purify the Levites, the ministers of God, refining them like gold or silver, so that they will do their work for God with pure hearts.

Jn 9:2. "Master," his disciples asked him, "why was this man born blind? Was it a result of his own sins or those of his parents?" [3]"Neither," Jesus answered. "But to demonstrate the power of God."

Jn 11:4. But when Jesus heard about it he said, "The purpose of his illness is not death, but for the glory of God. I, the Son of God, will receive glory from this situation."

Jn 15:2. He lops off every branch that doesn't produce. And he prunes those branches that bear fruit for even larger crops.

Jn 21:19. Jesus said this to let him know what kind of death he would die to glorify God. Then Jesus told him, "Follow me."

1 Cor 11:32. Yet, when we are judged and punished by the Lord, it is so that we will not be condemned with the rest of the world.

2 Cor 1:3,4. What a wonderful God we have—he is the Father of our Lord Jesus Christ, the source of every mercy, and the one who so wonderfully comforts and strengthens us in our hardships and trials. And why does he do this? So that when others are troubled, needing our sympathy and encouragement, we can pass on to them this same help and comfort God has given us. [5]You can be sure that the more we undergo sufferings for Christ, the more he will shower us with his comfort and encouragement. [6,7]We are in deep trouble for bringing you God's comfort and salvation. But in our trouble God had comforted us—and this, too, to help you: to show you from our personal experience how God will tenderly comfort you when you undergo these same sufferings. He will give you the strength to endure.

2 Cor 4:11. Yes, we live under constant danger to our lives because we serve the Lord, but this gives us constant opportunities to show forth the power of Jesus Christ within our dying bodies. [17]These troubles and sufferings of ours are, after all, quite small and won't last very long. Yet this short time of distress will result in God's richest blessing upon us forever and ever!

2 Cor 12:7. I will say this: because these experiences I had were so tremendous, God was afraid I might be puffed up by them; so I was given a physical condition which has been a thorn in my flesh, a messenger from Satan to hurt and bother me, and prick my pride.

Phil 1:29. For to you has been given the privilege of not only trusting him but also of suffering for him. [30]We are in this fight together. You have seen me suffer for him in the past; and I am still in the midst of a great and terrible struggle now, as you know so well.

2 Thess 1:4. We are happy to tell other churches about your patience and complete faith in God, in spite of all the crushing troubles and hardships you are going through. [5]This is only one example of the fair, just way God does things, for he is using your sufferings to make you ready for his kingdom.

Heb 2:10. And it was right and proper that God, who made everything for his own glory, should allow Jesus to suffer, for in doing this he was bringing vast multitudes of God's people to heaven; for his suffering made Jesus a perfect Leader, one fit to bring them into their salvation. [11]We who have been made holy by Jesus, now have the same Father he has. That is why Jesus is not ashamed to call us brothers. [12]For he says in the book of Psalms, "I will talk to my brothers about God my Father, and together we will sing his praises." [13]At another time he said, "I will put my trust in God along with my brothers." And at still another time, "See, here I am and the children God gave me." [14]Since we, God's children, are human beings—made of flesh and blood—he became flesh and blood too by being born in human form; for only as a human being could he die and in dying break the power of the devil who had the power of death. [15]Only in that way could he deliver those who through fear of death have been living all their lives as slaves to constant dread. [16]We all know he did not come as an angel but as a human being—yes, a Jew. [17]And it was necessary for Jesus to be like us, his brothers, so that he could be our merciful and faithful High Priest before God, a Priest who would be both merciful to us and faithful to God in dealing with the sins of the people. [18]For since he himself has now been through suffering and temptation, he knows what it is like when we suffer and are tempted, and he is wonderfully able to help us.

Heb 5:8. And even though Jesus was God's Son, he had to learn from experience what it was like to obey, when obeying meant suffering. [9]It was after he had proved himself perfect in this experience that Jesus became the Giver of eternal salvation to all those who obey him.

Heb 12:5. And have you quite forgotten the encouraging words God spoke to you, his child? He said, "My son, don't be angry when the Lord punishes you. Don't be discouraged when he has to show you where you are wrong. [6]For when he punishes you, it proves that he loves you. When he whips you it proves you are really his child." [7]Let God train you, for he is doing what any loving father does for his children. Whoever heard of a son who was never corrected? [8]If God doesn't punish you when you need it, as other fathers punish their sons, then it means that you aren't really God's son at all—that you don't really belong in his family. [9]Since we respect our fathers here on earth, though they punish us, should we not all the more cheerfully submit to God's training so that we can begin really to live? [10]Our earthly fathers trained us for a few brief years, doing the best for us that they knew how, but God's correction is always right and for our best good, that we may share his holiness. [11]Being punished isn't enjoyable while it is happening—it hurts! But afterwards we can see the result, a quiet growth in grace and character.

1 Pet 1:6. So be truly glad! There is wonderful joy ahead, even though the going is rough for a while down here. [7]These trials are only to test your faith, to see whether or not it is strong and pure. It is being tested as fire tests gold and purifies it—and your faith is far more precious to God than mere gold; so if your faith remains strong after being tried in the test tube of fiery trials, it will bring you much praise and glory and honor on the day of his return.

1 Pet 5:10. After you have suffered a little while, our God, who is full of kindness through Christ, will give you his eternal glory. He personally will come and pick you up, and set you firmly in place, and make you stronger than ever.

Rev. 2:10. Stop being afraid of what you are about to suffer—for the devil will soon throw some of you into prison to test you. You will be persecuted for 'ten days.' Remain faithful even when facing death and I will give you the crown of life—an unending, glorious future.

See *Benefits of,* above.

DESPONDENCY IN. Job 4:5. But now, when trouble strikes, you faint and are broken.

Job 9:16. And even if my prayers were answered I could scarce believe that he had heard my cry. [17]For he is the one who destroys, and multiplies my wounds without a cause. [18]He will not let me breathe, but fills me with bitter sorrows. [19]He alone is strong and just. [20]But I? Am I righteous? My own mouth says no. Even if I were perfect, God would prove me wicked. [21]And even if I am utterly innocent, I dare not think of it. I despise what I am. [22]Innocent or evil, it is all the same to him, for he destroys both kinds. [23]He will laugh when calamity crushes the innocent. [24]The whole earth is in the hands of the wicked. God blinds the eyes of the judges and lets them be unfair. If not he, then who? [25]My life passes swiftly away, filled with tragedy. [26]My years disappear like swift ships, like the eagle that swoops upon its prey. [27]If I decided to forget my complaints against God, to end my sadness and be cheerful, [28]then he would pour even greater sorrows upon me. For I know that you will not hold me innocent, O God, [29]but will condemn me. So what's the use of trying? [30]Even if I were to wash myself with purest water and cleanse my hands with lye to make them utterly clean, [31]even so you would plunge me into the ditch and mud; and even my clothing would be less filthy than you consider me to be! [32,33]And I cannot defend myself, for you are no mere man as I am. If you were, then we could discuss it fairly, but there is no umpire between us, no middle man, no mediator to bring us together. [34]Oh, let him stop beating me, so that I need no longer live in terror of his punishment. [35]Then I could speak without fear to him, and tell him boldly that I am not guilty.

Ps 22:1. My God, my God, why have you forsaken me? Why do you refuse to help me or even to listen to my groans? [2]Day and night I keep on weeping, crying for your help, but there is no reply.

Prov 24:10. You are a poor specimen if you can't stand the pressure of adversity.

Lam 3:39. Why then should we, mere humans as we are, murmur and complain when punished for our sins?

Mk 15:34. Then Jesus called out with a loud voice, "Eli, Eli, lama sabachthani?" ("My God, my God, why have you deserted me?") Mt 27:46

Lk 18:1. One day Jesus told his disciples a story to illustrate their need for constant prayer and to show them that they must keep praying until the answer comes.

DISPENSATION OF GOD. Ex 4:11. "Who makes mouths?" Jehovah asked him. "Isn't it I, the Lord? Who makes a man so that he can speak or not speak, see or not see, hear or not hear?"

Deut 28:20. For the Lord himself will send his personal curse upon you. You will be confused and a failure in everything you do, until at last you are destroyed because of the sin of forsaking him. With *vs.* 15–68.

Deut 32:39. Don't you see that I alone am God? I kill and make live. I wound and heal—no one delivers from my power.

Ruth 1:20. But she told them, "Don't call me Naomi. Call me Mara," (Naomi means "pleasant"; Mara means "bitter") "for Almighty God has dealt me bitter blows. [21]I went out full and the Lord has brought me home empty; why should you call me Naomi when the Lord has turned his back on me and sent such calamity!"

1 Sam 2:6. The Lord kills, the Lord gives life. [7]Some he causes to be poor and others to be rich. He cuts one down and lifts another up.

2 Sam 16:10. "No!" the king said. "If the Lord has told him to curse me, who am I to say no?"

2 Kgs 6:33. "The Lord has caused this mess," the king stormed. "Why should I expect any help from him?"

2 Kgs 15:5. Because of this the Lord struck him with leprosy, which lasted until the day of his death.

2 Chron 7:13. If I shut up the heavens so that there is no rain, or if I command the locust swarms to eat up all of your crops, or if I send an epidemic among you. With vs. 12–22.

Job 1:21. "I came naked from my mother's womb," he said, "and I shall have nothing when I die. The Lord gave me everything I had, and they were his to take away. Blessed be the name of the Lord."

Job 5:17. How enviable the man whom God corrects! Oh, do not despise the chastening of the Lord when you sin. [v. 6] [18]For though he wounds, he binds and heals again.

Job 6:4. For the Lord has struck me down with his arrows; he has sent his poisoned arrows deep within my heart. All God's terrors are arrayed against me.

Job 9:12. When he sends death to snatch a man away, who can stop him? Who dares to ask him, "What are you doing?" [22]Innocent or evil, it is all the same to him, for he destroys both kinds.

Job 10:8. You have made me, and yet you destroy me.

Job 11:10. If he rushes in and makes an arrest, and calls the court to order, who is going to stop him?

Job 12:14. And how great is his might! What he destroys can't be rebuilt. When he closes in on a man, there is no escape. [15]He withholds the rain, and the earth becomes a desert; he sends the storms, and floods the ground. [16]Yes, with him is strength and wisdom. Deceivers and deceived are both his slaves. [17]He makes fools of counselors and judges. [18]He reduces kings to slaves and frees their servants. [19]Priests are led away as slaves. He overthrows the mighty. [20]He takes away the voice of orators, and the insight of the elders. [21]He pours contempt upon princes, and weakens the strong. [22]He floods the darkness with light, even the dark shadow of death. [23]He raises up a nation and then destroys it. He makes it great, and then reduces it to nothing. [24,25]He takes away the understanding of presidents and kings, and leaves them wandering, lost and groping, without a guiding light.

Job 19:6. The fact of the matter is that God has overthrown me and caught me in his net. [21]Oh, my friends, pity me, for the angry hand of God has touched me.

Job 21:17. Yet the wicked get away with it every time. They never have trouble, and God skips them when he distributes his sorrows and anger.

Job 23:16,17. God has given me a fainting heart; he, the Almighty, has terrified me with darkness all around me, thick, impenetrable darkness everywhere.

Job 27:2. I vow by the living God, who has taken away my rights, even the Almighty God who has embittered my soul.

Job 30:11. For God has placed my life in jeopardy. These young men, having humbled me, now cast off all restraint before me.

Job 34:29,30. Yet when he chooses not to speak, who can criticize? Again, he may prevent a vile man from ruling, thus saving a nation from ruin, and he can depose an entire nation just as easily.

Ps 38:3,4. Because of your anger my body is sick, my health is broken beneath my sins. They are like a flood, higher than my head; they are a burden too heavy to bear.

Ps 66:11. You captured us in your net and laid great burdens on our backs.

Ps 71:20. You have let me sink down deep in desperate problems. But you will bring me back to life again, up from the depths of the earth.

Ps 78:31. The anger of the Lord rose against them and killed the finest of Israel's young men. [32]Yet even so the people kept on sinning and refused to believe in miracles. [33]So he cut their lives short and gave them years of terror and disaster. [34]Then at last, when he had ruined them, they walked awhile behind him; how earnestly they turned around and followed him!

Ps 88:6. You have thrust me down to the darkest depths. [7]Your wrath lies heavy on me; wave after wave engulfs me. [16]Your fierce wrath has overwhelmed me. Your terrors have cut me off.

Ps 89:38. Then why cast me off, rejected? Why be so angry with the one you chose as king? [39]Have you renounced your covenant with him? For you have thrown his crown in the dust. [40]You have broken down the walls protecting him and laid in ruins every fort defending him. [41]Everyone who comes along has robbed him while his neighbors mock. [42]You have strengthened his enemies against him and made them rejoice. [43]You have struck down his sword and refused to help him in battle. [44]You have ended his splendor and overturned his throne. [45]You have made him old before his time and publicly disgraced him.

Ps 90:7. We die beneath your anger; we are overwhelmed by your wrath. [15]Give us gladness in proportion to our former misery! Replace the evil years with good.

Ps 102:9,10. I eat ashes instead of bread. My tears run down into my drink because of your anger against me, because of your wrath. For you have rejected me and thrown me out. [23]He has cut me down in middle life, shortening my days.

Isa 30:20. Though he give you the bread of adversity and the water of affliction, yet he will be with you to teach you—with your own eyes you will see your Teacher.

Isa 45:7. I form the light and make the dark. I send good times and bad. I, Jehovah, am he who does these things.

Jer 45:3. You have said, Woe is me! Don't I have troubles enough already? And now the Lord has added more! I am weary of my own sighing and I find no rest.

Lam 1:5. Her enemies prosper, for the Lord has punished Jerusalem for all her many sins.

Lam 3:1. I am the man who has seen the afflictions that come from the rod of God's wrath.

Dan 4:24. Your Majesty, the Most High God has decreed—and it will surely happen—[25]that your people will chase you from your palace, and you will live in the fields like an animal, eating grass like a cow, your back wet with dew from heaven. For seven years this will be your life, until you learn that the Most High God dominates the kingdoms of men, and gives power to anyone he chooses. [26]But the stump and the roots were left in the ground! This means that you will get your kingdom back again, when you have learned that heaven rules.

Amos 3:6. The alarm has sounded—listen and fear! For I, the Lord, am sending disaster into your land.

Jon 2:3. You threw me into the ocean depths; I sank down into the floods of waters and was covered by your wild and stormy waves.

Mic 1:12. The people of Maroth vainly hope for better days, but only bitterness awaits them as the Lord stands poised against Jerusalem.

Rom 8:20,21. For on that day thorns and thistles, sin, death, and decay—the things that overcame the world against its will at God's command—will all disappear, and the world around us will share in the glorious freedom from sin which God's children enjoy.

1 Cor 11:32. Yet, when we are judged and punished by the Lord, it is so that we will not be condemned with the rest of the world.

Heb 12:10. Our earthly fathers trained us for a few brief years, doing the best for us that they knew how, but God's correction is always right and for our best good, that we may share his holiness.

Rev 3:19. I continually discipline and punish everyone I love; so I must punish you, unless you turn from your indifference and become enthusiastic about the things of God.

FROM SATAN. Job 1; 2; 2 Cor 12:7. See *Temptation.*

IMPENITENCE IN. Lev 26:23. And if even this will not reform you, but you continue to walk against my wishes, [24]then I will walk against your wishes, and I, even I, will personally smite you seven times for your sin. *vs.* 27,28.

Job 36:12. If they won't listen to him, they shall perish in battle and die because of their lack of good sense. [13]But the godless reap his anger. They do not even return to him when he punishes them.

Ps 78:31. The anger of the Lord rose against them and killed the finest of Israel's young men. [32]Yet even so the people kept on sinning and refused to believe in miracles.

Isa 8:21. My people will be led away captive, stumbling, weary and hungry. And because they are hungry they will rave and shake their fists at heaven and curse their King and their God.

Isa 9:13. For after all this punishment you will not repent and turn to him, the Lord of heaven's armies.

Isa 22:12. The Lord God of Hosts called you to repent, to weep and mourn and shave your heads in sorrow for your sins, and to wear clothes made of sackcloth to show your remorse. [13]But instead, you sing and dance and play, and feast and drink. "Let us eat, drink, and be merry," you say: "What's the difference, for tomorrow we die."

Isa 26:11. They do not listen when you threaten; they will not look to see your upraised fist. Show them how much you love your people. Perhaps they will be ashamed! Yes, let them be burned up by the fire reserved for your enemies.

Isa 42:25. That is why God poured out such fury and wrath on his people and destroyed them in battle. Yet, though set on fire and burned, they will not understand the reason why—that it is God, wanting them to repent.

Isa 57:17. I was angry and smote these greedy men. But they went right on sinning, doing everything their evil hearts desired.

Jer 2:30. I have punished your children but it did them no good; they still will not obey. [35]And yet you say, "I haven't done a thing to anger God. I'm sure he isn't angry!" I will punish you severely because you say, "I haven't sinned!"

Jer 3:3. That is why even the springtime rains have failed. For you are a prostitute, and completely unashamed.

Jer 5:3. O Lord, you will take naught but truth. You have tried to get them to be honest, for you have punished them, but they won't change! You have destroyed them but they refuse to turn from their sins. They are determined, with faces hard as rock, not to repent.

Jer 7:28. Say to them: This is the nation that refuses to obey the Lord its God, and refuses to be taught. She continues to live a lie.

Dan 9:13. Every curse against us written in the law of Moses has come true; all the evils he predicted—all have come. But even so we still refuse to satisfy the Lord our God by turning from our sins and doing right.

Hos 7:9. Worshiping foreign gods has sapped their strength, but they won't know it. Ephraim's hair is turning gray, and he doesn't even realize how weak and old he is. [10]His pride in other gods has openly condemned him; yet he doesn't return to his God, nor even try to find him. [14]They lie there sleepless with anxiety, but won't ask my help. Instead, they worship heathen gods, asking them for crops and for prosperity.

Hos 9:17. My God will destroy the people of Israel because they will not listen or obey.

Amos 4:6. "I sent you hunger," says the Lord, "but it did no good; you still would not return to me." [vs. 7–10] [11]"I destroyed some of your cities, as I did Sodom and Gomorrah; those left are like half-burned firebrands snatched away from fire. And still you won't return to me," says the Lord.

Zeph 3:2. In her pride she won't listen even to the voice of God. No one can tell her anything; she refuses all correction. She does not trust the Lord, nor seek for God. [7]I thought, "Surely they will listen to me now—surely they will heed my warnings, so that I'll not need to strike again." But no, however much I punish them, they continue all their evil ways from dawn to dusk and dusk to dawn.

Hag 2:17. "I rewarded all your labor with rust and mildew and hail. Yet, even so, you refused to return to me," says the Lord.

Rev 9:20. But the men left alive after these plagues *still refused to worship God!* They would not renounce their demon-worship, nor their idols made of gold and silver, brass, stone, and wood—which neither see nor hear nor walk! [21]Neither did they change their mind and attitude about all their murders and witchcraft, their immorality and theft.

Rev 16:9. Everyone was burned by this blast of heat, and they cursed the name of God who sent the plagues—they did not change their mind and attitude to give him glory. [10]Then the fifth angel poured out his flask upon the throne of the Creature from the sea, and his kingdom was plunged into darkness. And his subjects gnawed their tongues in anguish, [11]and cursed the God of heaven for their pains and sores, but they refused to repent of all their evil deeds. *v.* 21.

As a judgment. See *Judgment of God.*

See *Impenitence.*

Instances of. Pharaoh, Ex 8:19; 9:30–34; 14:5–9. Asa, 2 Chron 16:12. Ahaz, 2 Chron 28:22,23.

MOCKING AT. Job 12:5. Meanwhile, the rich mock those in trouble and are quick to despise all those in need.

Prov 17:5. Mocking the poor is mocking the God who made them. He will punish those who rejoice at other's misfortunes.

MURMURING IN. See *Murmuring.*

PENITENCE IN.

Instances of. Pharaoh, Ex 8:8; 9:27–30; 12:30,31. David, 2 Sam 12:15,16,23. Nebuchadnezzar, Dan 4:28–37. Levites, Neh 9:33.

PRAYER IN. Gen 32:11. O Lord, please deliver me from destruction at the hand of my brother Esau, for I am frightened—terribly afraid that he is coming to kill me and these mothers and my children.

Gen 43:14. May God Almighty give you mercy before the man, so that he will release Simeon and return Benjamin. And if I must bear the anguish of their deaths, then so be it.

Ex 17:4. Then Moses pleaded with Jehovah. "What shall I do? For they are almost ready to stone me."

Num 20:16. But when we cried to the Lord he heard us and sent an Angel who brought us out of Egypt, and now we are here at Kadesh, encamped on the borders of your land.

2 Sam 12:22. David replied, "I fasted and wept while the child was alive, for I said, 'Perhaps the Lord will be gracious to me and let the child live.' " 1 Sam 1:10,11.

2 Sam 15:31. When someone told David that Ahithophel, his advisor, was backing Absalom, David prayed, "O Lord, please make Ahithophel give Absalom foolish advice!"

2 Sam 22:7. But I called upon the Lord in my distress, and he heard me from his Temple. My cry reached his ears.

1 Kgs 8:35. And when the skies are shut up and there is no rain because of their sin, hear them from heaven and forgive them when they pray toward this place and confess your name. With *vs.* 36–50; 2 Chron 6:24–39.

2 Kgs 19:16. Bend low, O Lord, and listen. Open your eyes, O Lord, and see. Listen to this man's defiance of the living God. [19]O Lord our God, we plead with you to save us from his power; then all the kingdoms of the earth will know that you alone are God.

1 Chron 5:20. They cried out to God to help them, and he did, for they trusted in him.

2 Chron 14:11. "O Lord," he cried out to God, "no one else can help us! Here we are, powerless against this mighty army. Oh, help us, Lord our God! For we trust in you alone to rescue us, and in your name we attack this vast horde. Don't let mere men defeat you!"

2 Chron 20:12. O our God, won't you stop them? We have no way to protect ourselves against this mighty army. We don't know what to do, but we are looking to you. *vs.* 4–13.

2 Chron 33:12. Then at last he came to his senses and cried out humbly to God for help. [13]And the Lord listened, and answered his plea by returning him to Jerusalem and to his kingdom! At that point Manasseh finally realized that the Lord was really God!

Neh 4:4. Then I prayed, "Hear us, O Lord God, for we are being mocked. May their scoffing fall back upon their own heads, and may they themselves become captives in a foreign land!" *vs.* 5,9; Neh 6:9,14.

Neh 9:32. And now, O great and awesome God, you who keep your promises of love and kindness—do not let all the hardships we have gone through become as nothing to you. Great trouble has come upon us and upon our kings and princes and priests and prophets and ancestors from the days when the kings of Assyria first triumphed over us until now.

Job 10:2. "I will say to God, 'Don't just condemn me—tell me why you are doing it.' [9]Oh, please remember that I'm made of dust—will you change me back again to dust so soon?" *v.* 15

Job 13:21. Don't abandon me. And don't terrify me with your awesome presence.

Job 16:20. My friends scoff at me, but I pour out my tears to God.

Ps 3:1. O Lord, so many are against me. So many seek to harm me. I have so many enemies. [2]So many say that God will never help me. [7]I will cry to him, "Arise, O Lord! Save me, O my God!"

Ps 4:1. O God, you have declared me perfect in your eyes; you have always cared for me in my distress; now hear me as I call again. Have mercy on me. Hear my prayer.

Ps 5:8. Lord, lead me as you promised me you would; otherwise my enemies will conquer me. Tell me clearly what to do, which way to turn.

Ps 6:1. No, Lord! Don't punish me in the heat of your anger. [2]Pity me, O Lord, for I am weak. Heal me, for my body is sick, [3]and I am upset and disturbed. My mind is filled with apprehension and with gloom. Oh, restore me soon. [4]Come, O Lord, and make me well. In your kindness save me. *vs.* 5–7.

Ps 7:1. I am depending on you, O Lord my God, to save me from my persecutors. [2]Don't let them pounce upon me as a lion would and maul me and drag me away with no one to rescue me. *vs.* 6–8.

Ps 9:13. And now, O Lord, have mercy on me; see how I suffer at the hands of those who hate me. Lord, snatch me back from the jaws of death. *v.* 14.

Ps 10:1. Lord, why are you standing aloof and far away? Why do you hide when I need you the most? [12]O Lord, arise! O God, crush them! Don't forget the poor or anyone else in need. *vs.* 13–15

Ps 13:1. How long will you forget me, Lord? Forever? How long will you look the other way when I am in need? [2]How long must I be hiding daily anguish in my heart? How long shall my enemy have the upper hand? [3]Answer me, O Lord my God; give me light in my darkness lest I die. *v.* 4.

Ps 16:1. Save me, O God, because I have come to you for refuge.

Ps 17:1. I am pleading for your help, O Lord; for I have been honest and have done what is right, and you must listen to my earnest cry! [6]Why am I praying like this? Because I know you will answer me, God! Yes, listen as I pray. [7]Show me your strong love in wonderful ways, O Savior of all those seeking your help against their foes. [8]Protect me as you would the pupil of your eye; hide me in the shadow of your wings as you hover over me. [9]My enemies encircle me with murder in their eyes. [13]Lord, arise and stand against them. Push them back! Come and save me from these men of the world whose only concern is earthly gain. *vs.* 2,14.

Ps 20:1. In your day of trouble, may the Lord be with you! May the God of Jacob keep you from all harm. [2]May he send you aid from his sanctuary in Zion.

Ps 22:1. My God, my God, why have you forsaken me? Why do you refuse to help me or even to listen to my groans? [11]Don't leave me now, for trouble is near and no one else can possibly help. [19]O Lord, don't stay away. O God my Strength, hurry to my aid. [20]Rescue me from death; spare my precious life from all these evil men. [21]Save me from these lion's jaws and from the horns of these wild oxen. *vs.* 1–21.

Ps 25:2. Don't fail me, Lord, for I am trusting you. Don't let my enemies succeed. Don't give them victory over me. [16]Come, Lord, and show me your mercy, for I am helpless, overwhelmed, in deep distress; [17]my problems go from bad to worse. Oh, save me from them all! [18]See my sorrows; feel my pain; forgive my sins. [19]See how many enemies I have and how viciously they hate me! [22]Ransom Israel from all her troubles.

Ps 27:11. Tell me what to do, O Lord, and make it plain because I am surrounded by waiting enemies. [12]Don't let them get me, Lord! Don't let me fall into their hands! For they accuse me of things I never did, and all the while are plotting cruelty.

Ps 28:1. I plead with you to help me, Lord, for you are my Rock of safety. If you refuse to answer me, I might as well give up and die.

Ps 30:9. What will you gain, O Lord, from killing me? How can I praise you then to all my friends? How can my dust in the grave speak out and tell the world about your faithfulness? [10]Hear me, Lord; oh, have pity and help me.

Ps 31:1. Lord, I trust in you alone. Don't let my enemies defeat me. Rescue me because you are the God who always does what is right. [2]Answer quickly when I cry to you; bend low and hear my whispered plea. Be for me a great Rock of safety from my foes. [3]Yes, you are my Rock and my fortress; honor your name by leading me out of this peril. [4]Pull me from the trap my enemies have set for me. For you alone are strong enough. (*vs.* 15–18) [9]O Lord, have mercy on me in my anguish. My eyes are red from weeping; my health is broken from sorrow. I am pining away with grief; my years are shortened, drained away because of sadness. [14,15]But I was trusting you, O Lord. I said, "You alone are my God; my times are in your hands. Rescue me from those who hunt me down relentlessly. [16]Let your favor shine again upon your servant; save me just because you are so kind! [17]Don't disgrace me, Lord, by not replying when I call to you for aid.

Ps 35:1. O Lord, fight those fighting me; declare war on them for their attacks on me. [2]Put on your armor, take your shield and protect me by standing in front. [3]Lift your spear in my defense, for my pursuers are getting very close. Let me hear you say that you will save me from them. [17]Lord, how long will you stand there, doing nothing? Act now and rescue me, for I have but one life and these young lions are out to get it. [19]Don't give victory to those who fight me without any reason! Don't let them rejoice at my fall—let them die. [22]Lord, you know all about it. Don't stay silent! Don't desert me now! [23]Rise up, O Lord my God; vindicate me. [24]Declare me "not guilty," for you are just. Don't let my enemies rejoice over me in my troubles. [25]Don't let them say, "Aha! Our dearest wish against him will soon be fulfilled!" and "At last we have him!"

Ps 38:1. O Lord, don't punish me while you are angry! [2]Your arrows have struck deep; your blows are crushing me. [9]Lord, you know how I long for my health once more. You hear my every sigh. [10]My heart beats wildly, my strength fails, and I am going blind. [16]Put an end to their arrogance, these who gloat when I am cast down! [21]Don't leave me, Lord; don't go away! [22]Come quickly! Help me, O my Savior. *vs.* 1–22

Ps 39:10. Lord, don't hit me anymore—I am exhausted beneath your hand. [12]Hear my prayer, O Lord; listen to my cry! Don't sit back, unmindful of my tears. For I am your guest. I am a traveler passing through the earth, as all my fathers were. [13]Spare me, Lord! Let me recover and be filled with happiness again before my death.

Ps 40:13. Please, Lord, rescue me! Quick! Come and help me! [17]I am poor and needy, yet the Lord is thinking about me right now! O my God, you are my helper. You are my Savior; come quickly, and save me. Please don't delay. Ps 70:5

Ps 42:9. "O God my Rock," I cry, "why have you forsaken me? Why must I suffer these attacks from my enemies?"

Ps 43:1. O God, defend me from the charges of these merciless deceitful men. [2]For you are God, my only place of refuge. Why have you tossed me aside? Why must I mourn at the oppression of my enemies? *vs.* 3–5

Ps 44:4. You are my King and my God. Decree victories for your people. [23]Waken! Rouse yourself! Don't sleep, O Lord! Are we cast off forever? [24]Why do you look the other way? Why do you ignore our sorrows and oppression? [25]We lie face downward in the dust. [26]Rise up, O Lord, and come and help us. Save us by your constant love.

Ps 50:15. I want you to trust me in your times of trouble, so I can rescue you, and you can give me glory.

Ps 54:1. Come with great power, O God, and save me! Defend me with your might! [2]Oh, listen to my prayer. [3]For violent men have risen against me —ruthless men who care nothing for God are seeking my life.

Ps 55:1. Listen to my prayer, O God; don't hide yourself when I cry to you. [2]Hear me, Lord! Listen to me! For I groan and weep beneath my burden of woe. [3]My enemies shout against me and threaten me with death. They surround me with terror and plot to kill me. Their fury and hatred rise to engulf me. *vs.* 1–17.

Ps 56:1,2. Lord have mercy on me; all day long the enemy troops press in. So many are proud to fight against me; how they long to conquer me. *vs.* 1–13

Ps 57:1. O God, have pity, for I am trusting you! I will hide beneath the shadow of your wings until this storm is past. [2]I will cry to God of heaven who does such wonders for me.

Ps 59:1. O my God, save me from my enemies. Protect me from these who have come to destroy me. [2]Preserve me from these criminals, these murderers. [4]Yet they prepare to kill me. Lord, waken! See what is happening! Help me! *vs.* 1–17.

Ps 60:1. O God, you have rejected us and broken our defenses; you have become angry and deserted us. Lord, restore us again to your favor. [2]You have caused this nation to tremble in fear; you have torn it apart. Lord, heal it now, for it is shaken to its depths. [3]You have been very hard on us and made us reel beneath your blows. [11]Yes, Lord, help us against our enemies, for man's help is useless.

Ps 61:1. O God, listen to me! Hear my prayer! [2]For wherever I am, though far away at the ends of the earth, I will cry to you for help. When my heart is faint and overwhelmed, lead me to the mighty, towering Rock of safety.

Ps 64:1,2. Lord, listen to my complaint: Oh, preserve my life from the conspiracy of these wicked men, these gangs of criminals.

Ps 69:1. Save me, O my God. The floods have risen. Deeper and deeper I sink in the mire; the waters rise around me. [13]But I keep right on praying to you, Lord. For now is the time—you are bending down to hear! You are ready with a plentiful supply of love and kindness. Now answer my prayer and rescue me as you promised. [14]Pull me out of this mire. Don't let me sink in. Rescue me from those who hate me, and from these deep waters I am in. [15]Don't let the floods overwhelm me, or the ocean swallow me; save me from the pit that threatens me. [17]Don't hide from me, for I am in deep trouble. Quick! Come and save me. [18]Come, Lord, and rescue me. Ransom me from all my enemies. [19]You know how they talk about me, and how they so shamefully dishonor me. You see them all and know what each has said. [29]But rescue me, O God, from my poverty and pain. *vs.* 1–36.

Ps 70:1. Rescue me, O God! Lord, hurry to my aid! [2,3]They are after my life, and delight in hurting me. Confuse them! Shame them! Stop them! Don't let them keep on mocking me! *vs.* 4–5.

Ps 71:1. Lord, you are my refuge! Don't let me down! [2]Save me from my enemies, for you are just! Rescue me! Bend down your ear and listen to my plea and save me. [4]Rescue me, O God, from these unjust and cruel men. *vs.* 1–24.

Ps 71:9. And now, in my old age, don't set me aside. Don't forsake me now when my strength is failing. [12]O God, don't stay away! Come quickly! Help!

Ps 74:1. O God, why have you cast us away forever? Why is your anger hot against us—the sheep of your own pasture? [3]Walk through the awful ruins of the city, and see what the enemy has done to your sanctuary.

Ps 74:10. How long, O God, will you allow your enemies to dishonor your name? Will you let them get away with this forever? [11]Why do you delay? Why hold back your power? Unleash your fist and give them a final blow. [19]O Lord, save me! Protect your turtledoves from the hawks. Save your beloved people from these beasts. [21]O Lord, don't let your downtrodden people be constantly insulted.

Give cause for these poor and needy ones to praise your name! [22]Arise, O God, and state your case against our enemies. Remember the insults these rebels have hurled against you all day long. [23]Don't overlook the cursing of these enemies of yours; it grows louder and louder. *vs.* 1–23.

Ps 77:1. I cry to the Lord; I call and call to him. Oh, that he would listen. [2]I am in deep trouble and I need his help so badly. All night long I pray, lifting my hands to heaven, pleading. There can be no joy for me until he acts. [7]Has the Lord rejected me forever? Will he never again be favorable? [8]Is his lovingkindness gone forever? Has his promise failed? [9]Has he forgotten to be kind to one so undeserving? Has he slammed the door in anger on his love? *vs.* 1–20.

Ps 79:1. O God, your land has been conquered by the heathen nations. Your Temple is defiled and Jerusalem is a heap of ruins. [5]O Jehovah, how long will you be angry with us? Forever? Will your jealousy burn till every hope is gone?

Ps 79:8. Oh, do not hold us guilty for our former sins! Let your tenderhearted mercies meet our needs, for we are brought low to the dust. [9]Help us, God of our salvation! Help us for the honor of your name. Oh, save us and forgive us our sins. *vs.* 1–13.

Ps 79:11. Listen to the sighing of the prisoners and those condemned to die. Demonstrate the greatness of your power by saving them. *vs.* 1–11.

Ps 80:1. O Shepherd of Israel who leads Israel like a flock; O God enthroned above the cherubim; bend down your ear and listen as I plead. Display your power and radiant glory.

Ps 80:3. Turn us again to yourself, O God. Look down on us in joy and love, only then shall we be saved. [4]O Jehovah, God of heaven's armies, how long will you be angry and reject our prayers? [5]You have fed us with sorrow and tears. [14]Come back, we beg of you, O God of the armies of heaven and bless us. Look down from heaven and see our plight and care for this your vine! *vs.* 1–16.

Ps 83:1. O God, don't sit idly by, silent and inactive when we pray. Answer us! Deliver us! [2]Don't you hear the tumult and commotion of your enemies? Don't you see what they are doing, these proud men who hate the Lord? *vs.* 1–18.

Ps 85:5. (Or will you be always angry—on and on to distant generations?) [6]Oh, revive us! Then your people can rejoice in you again. [7]Pour out your love and kindness on us, Lord, and grant us your salvation.

Ps 86:1. Bend down and hear my prayer, O Lord, and answer me, for I am deep in trouble. [2]Protect me from death, for I try to follow all your laws. Save me, for I am serving you and trusting you. [3]Be merciful, O Lord, for I am looking up to you in constant hope. [4]Give me happiness, O Lord, for I worship only you. *vs.* 1–17.

Ps 86:16. So look down in pity and grant strength to your servant and save me. [17]Send me a sign of your favor. When those who hate me see it they will lose face because you help and comfort me.

Ps 88:9. My eyes grow dim with weeping. Each day I beg your help; O Lord, I reach my pleading hands to you for mercy. [13]O Lord, I plead for my life and will keep on pleading day by day. [14]O Jehovah, why have you thrown my life away? Why are you turning your face from me, and looking the other way? *vs.* 10–12.

Ps 89:46. O Jehovah, how long will this go on? Will you hide yourself from me forever? How long will your wrath burn like fire? [47]Oh, remember how short you have made man's lifespan. Is it an empty, futile life you give the sons of men? [49]Lord, where is the love you used to have for me? Where is your kindness that you promised to David with a faithful pledge?

Ps 89:50. Lord, see how all the people are despising me. [51]Your enemies joke about me, the one you anointed as their king. *vs.* 39–51.

Ps 90:15. Give us gladness in proportion to our former misery! Replace the evil years with good.

Ps 94:1–2. Lord God, to whom vengeance belongs, let your glory shine out. Arise and judge the earth; sentence the proud to the penalties they deserve. *vs.* 1–23.

Ps 102:2. Don't turn away from me in this time of my distress. Bend down your ear and give me speedy answers. [24]But I cried to him, "O God, you live forever and forever! Don't let me die half through my years!"

Ps 106:47. O Lord God, save us! Regather us from the nations so we can thank your holy name and rejoice and praise you.

Ps 108:6. Hear the cry of your beloved child—come with mighty power and rescue me. [12]Oh, help us fight against our enemies, for men are useless allies.

Ps 109:1. O God of my praise, don't stand silent and aloof [2]while the wicked slander me and tell their lies. [21]But as for me, O Lord, deal with me as your child, as one who bears your name! Because you are so kind, O Lord, deliver me. [26]Help me, O Lord my God! Save me because you are loving and kind. [27]Do it publicly, so all will see that you yourself have done it. [28]Then let them curse me if they like—I won't mind that if you are blessing me! *vs.* 1–31.

Ps 116:4. Then I cried, "Lord, save me!"

Ps 119:22. Don't let them scorn me for obeying you. [28]I weep with grief; my heart is heavy with sorrow; encourage and cheer me with your words. [39]How I dread being mocked for obeying, for your laws are right and good. [40,41,42]I long to obey them! Therefore in fairness renew my life, for this was your promise—yes, Lord, to save me! Now spare me by your kindness and love. Then I will have an answer for those who taunt me, for I trust your promises. [75,76,77]I know, O Lord, that your decisions are right and that your punishment was right and did me good. Now let your lovingkindness comfort me, just as you promised. Surround me with your tender mercies, that I may live. For your law is my delight. [82]My eyes are straining to see your promises come true. When will you comfort me with your help? [84]How long must I wait before you punish those who persecute me? [107]I am close to death at the hands of my enemies; oh, give me back my life again, just as you promised me. [121]Don't leave me to the mercy of my enemies, for I have done what is right; I've been perfectly fair. [122]Commit yourself to bless me! Don't let the proud oppress me! [123]My eyes grow dim with longing for you to fulfill your wonderful promise to rescue me. [134]Rescue me from the oppression of evil men; then I can obey you. [145]I am praying with great earnestness; answer me, O Lord, and I will obey your laws. [146]"Save me," I cry, "for I am obeying." [147]Early in the morning, before the sun is up, I was praying and pointing out how much I trust you. [148]I stay awake through the night to think about your promises. [149]Because you are so loving and kind, listen to me and make me well again. [153]Look down upon my sorrows and rescue me, for I am obeying your commands. [154]Yes, rescue me and give me back my life again just as you have promised. [170]Hear my prayers; rescue me as you said you would. [173]Stand ready to help me because I have chosen to follow your will.

Ps 120:2. Deliver me, O Lord, from liars.

Ps 123:3,4. Have mercy on us, Lord, have mercy. For we have had our fill of contempt and of the scoffing of the rich and proud.

Ps 126:4. May we be refreshed as by streams in the desert.

Ps 130:1. O Lord, from the depths of despair I cry for your help: [2]"Hear me! Answer! Help me!" *vs.* 1–8

Ps 140:4. Keep me out of their power. Preserve me from their violence, for they are plotting against me. [6,7,8]O Jehovah, my Lord and Savior, my God and my shield—hear me as I pray! Don't let these wicked men succeed. Don't let them prosper and be proud. *vs.* 1–13.

Ps 141:8. I look to you for help, O Lord God. You are my refuge. Don't let them slay me. [9]Keep me out of their traps. Let them fall into their own snares, while I escape. *vs.* 1–10.

Ps 142:1,2. How I plead with God, how I implore his mercy, pouring out my troubles before him. [5]Then I prayed to Jehovah. "Lord," I pled, "you are my only place of refuge. Only you can keep me safe. [6]Hear my cry, for I am very low. Rescue me from my persecutors, for they are too strong for me. [7]Bring me out of prison, so that I can thank you. The godly will rejoice with me for all your help."

Ps 143:7. Come quickly, Lord, and answer me, for my depression deepens; don't turn away from me or I shall die. [8]Let me see your kindness to me in the morning, for I am trusting you. Show me where to walk, for my prayer is sincere. [9]Save me from my enemies, O Lord, I run to you to hide me. [11]Lord, saving me will bring glory to your name. Bring me out of all this trouble because you are true to your promises. *vs.* 1–12.

Isa 33:2. But to us, O Lord, be merciful, for we have waited for you. Be our strength each day and our salvation in the time of trouble.

Isa 38:2. When Hezekiah heard this, he turned his face to the wall and prayed: [3]"O Lord, don't you remember how true I've been to you and how I've always tried to obey you in everything you said?" Then he broke down with great sobs. [2 Kgs 20:3] [14]"Delirious, I chattered like a swallow and mourned like a dove; my eyes grew weary of looking up for help. 'O God,' I cried, 'I am in trouble—help me.' [15]But what can I say? For he himself has sent this sickness. All my sleep has fled because of my soul's bitterness. [16]O Lord, your discipline is good and leads to life and health. Oh, heal me and make me live! [17]Yes, now I see it all —it was good for me to undergo this bitterness, for you have lovingly delivered me from death; you have forgiven all my sins. [18]For dead men cannot praise you. They cannot be filled with hope and joy. [19]The living, only the living, can praise you as I do today. One generation makes known your faithfulness to the next."

Isa 51:9. Awake, O Lord! Rise up and robe yourself with strength. Rouse yourself as in the days of old when you slew Egypt, the dragon of the Nile.

Isa 63:15. O Lord, look down from heaven and see us from your holy, glorious home; where is the love for us you used to show—your power, your mercy and your compassion? Where are they now? [16]Surely you are still our Father! Even if Abraham and Jacob would disown us, still you would be our Father, our Redeemer from ages past. [17]O Lord, why have you hardened our hearts and made us sin and turn against you? Return and help us, for we who belong to you need you so.

Isa 64:1. Oh, that you would burst forth from the skies and come down! How the mountains would quake in your presence. [9]Oh, be not so angry with us, Lord, nor forever remember our sins. Oh, look and see that we are all your people. [10]Your holy cities are destroyed; Jerusalem is a desolate wilderness. [11]Our holy, beautiful Temple where our fathers praised you is burned down, and all the things of beauty are destroyed. [12]After all of this, must you still refuse to help us, Lord? Will you stand silent and still punish us?

Jer 10:24. So you correct me, Lord; but please be gentle. Don't do it in your anger, for I would die.

Jer 14:8. O Hope of Israel, our Savior in times of trouble, why are you as a stranger to us, as one passing through the land who is merely stopping for the night? [9]Are you also baffled? Are you helpless to save us? O Lord, you are right here among us, and we carry your name; we are known as your people. O Lord, don't desert us now! [19]"O Lord," the people will cry, "have you completely rejected Judah? Do you abhor Jerusalem? Even after punishment, will there be no peace? We thought, Now at last he will heal us and bind our wounds. But no peace has come and there is only trouble and terror everywhere. [20]O Lord, we confess our wickedness, and that of our fathers too. [21]Do not hate us, Lord, for the sake of your own name. Do not disgrace yourself and the throne of your glory by forsaking your promises to bless us!" Jer 32:16–25.

Jer 15:15. Then Jeremiah replied, "Lord, you know it is for your sake that I am suffering. They are persecuting me because I have proclaimed your word to them. Don't let them kill me! Rescue me from their clutches, and give them what they deserve!"

Jer 16:19. O Lord, my Strength and Fortress, my Refuge in the day of trouble, nations from around the world will come to you saying, "Our fathers have been foolish, for they have worshiped worthless idols!"

Jer 17:17. Lord, don't desert me now! You alone are my hope. [18]Bring confusion and trouble on all who persecute me, but give me peace. Yes, bring double destruction upon them!

Jer 18:19. *O Lord, help me! See what they are planning to do to me!* Jer 20:7,8.

Lam 1:9. She indulged herself in immorality, and refused to face the fact that punishment was sure to come. Now she lies in the gutter with no one left to lift her out. "O Lord," she cries, "see my plight. The enemy has triumphed." [10]Her enemies have plundered her completely, taking everything precious she owns. She has seen foreign nations violate her sacred Temple—foreigners you had forbidden even to enter. [11]Her people groan and cry for bread; they have sold all they have for food to give a little strength. "Look, O Lord," she prays, "and see how I'm despised." [20]*See, O Lord, my anguish;* my heart is broken and my soul despairs, for I have terribly rebelled. In the streets the sword awaits me; at home, disease and death.

Lam 2:18. Then the people wept before the Lord. O walls of Jerusalem, let tears fall down upon you like a river; give yourselves no rest from weeping day or night. [19]Rise in the night and cry to your God. Pour out your hearts like water to the Lord; lift up your hands to him; plead for your children as they faint with hunger in the streets.

Lam 5:1. O Lord, remember all that has befallen us; see what sorrows we must bear! [16]Our glory is gone. The crown is fallen from our head. Woe upon us for our sins. [17]Our hearts are faint and weary; our eyes grow dim. [19]O Lord, forever you remain the same! Your throne continues from generation to generation. [20]Why do you forget us forever? Why do you forsake us for so long? [21]Turn us around and bring us back to you again! That is our only hope. Give us back the joys we used to have! [22]*Or have you utterly rejected us? Are you angry with us still?* chapters 1–5.

Dan 6:10. But though Daniel knew about the law, he went home and knelt down as usual in his upstairs bedroom, with its window open toward Jerusalem, and prayed three times a day, just as he always had, giving thanks to his God.

Joel 1:19. Lord, help us! For the heat has withered the pastures and burned up all the trees.

Jon 1:14. Then they shouted out a prayer to Jehovah, Jonah's God. "O Jehovah," they pleaded, "don't make us die for this man's sin, and don't hold us responsible for his death, for it is not our fault—you have sent this storm upon him for your own good reasons."

Jon 2:1. Then Jonah prayed to the Lord his God from inside the fish: [2]"In my great trouble I cried to the Lord and he answered me; from the depths of death I called, and Lord, you heard me! [3]You threw me into the ocean depths; I sank down into the floods of waters and was covered by your wild and stormy waves. [4]Then I said, 'O Lord, you have rejected me and cast me away. How shall I ever again see your holy Temple?' [5]I sank beneath the waves, and death was very near. The waters closed above me; the seaweed wrapped itself around my head. [6]I went down to the bottoms of the mountains that rise from off the ocean floor. I was locked out of life and imprisoned in the land of death. But, O Lord my God, you have snatched me from the yawning jaws of death! [7]When I had lost all hope, I turned my thoughts once more to the Lord. And my earnest prayer went to you in your holy Temple. [8](Those who worship false gods have turned their backs on all the mercies waiting for them from the Lord!) [9]I will never worship anyone but you! For how can I thank you enough for all you have done? I will surely fulfill my promises. For my deliverance comes from the Lord alone." [10]And the Lord ordered the fish to spit up Jonah on the beach, and it did.

Hab 1:12. O Lord my God, my Holy One, you who are eternal—is not your plan in all of this to wipe us out? Surely not! O God our Rock, you have decreed the rise of these Chaldeans to chasten and correct us for our awful sins. [13]We are wicked, but they far more! Will you, who cannot allow sin in any form, stand idly by while they swallow us up? Should you be silent while the wicked destroy those who are better than they?

Mt 8:25. The disciples went to him and wakened him, shouting, "Lord, save us! We're sinking!"

Mt 14:30. But when he looked around at the high waves, he was terrified and began to sink. "Save me, Lord!" he shouted.

Mt 15:22. A woman from Canaan who was living there came to him, pleading, "Have mercy on me, O Lord, King David's Son! For my daughter has a demon within her, and it torments her constantly." [23]But Jesus gave her no reply—not even a word. Then his disciples urged him to send her away. "Tell her to get going," they said, "for she is bothering us with all her begging." [24]Then he said to the woman, "I was sent to help the Jews—the lost sheep of Israel—not the Gentiles." [25]But she came and worshiped him and pled again, "Sir, help me!" [26]"It doesn't seem right to take bread from the children and throw it to the dogs," he said. [27]"Yes, it is!" she replied, "for even the puppies beneath the table are permitted to eat the crumbs that fall." [28]"Woman," Jesus told her, "your faith is large, and your request is granted." And her daughter was healed right then.

Mt 26:39. He went forward a little, and fell face downward on the ground, and prayed, "My Father! If it is possible, let this cup be taken away from me. But I want your will, not mine." [42]Again he left them and prayed, "My Father! If this cup cannot go away until I drink it all, your will be done." *v.* 44, Mk 14:36; Lk 22:41,42.

Mt 27:46. About three o'clock, Jesus shouted, "Eli, Eli, lama sabachthani," which means, "My God, my God, why have you forsaken me?" Mk 15: 34; Lk 23:46.

Lk 18:1. One day Jesus told his disciples a story to illustrate their need for constant prayer and to show them that they must keep praying until the answer comes.

Jn 11:3. So the two sisters sent a message to Jesus telling him, "Sir, your good friend is very, very sick."

Acts 4:29. And now, O Lord, hear their threats, and grant to your servants great boldness in their preaching, [30]and send your healing power, and may miracles and wonders be done by the name of your holy servant Jesus.

Acts 7:59. And as the murderous stones came hurtling at him, Stephen prayed, "Lord Jesus, receive my spirit." [60]And he fell to his knees, shouting, "Lord, don't charge them with this sin!" and with that, he died.

2 Cor 12:8. Three different times I begged God to make me well again.

Jas 5:13. Is anyone among you suffering? He should keep on praying about it. And those who have reason to be thankful should continually be singing praises to the Lord. [14]Is anyone sick? He should call for the elders of the church and they should pray over him and pour a little oil upon him, calling on the Lord to heal him. [15]And their prayer, if offered in faith, will heal him, for the Lord will make him well; and if his sickness was caused by some sin, the Lord will forgive him. [16]Admit your faults to one another and pray for each other so that you may be healed. The earnest prayer of a righteous man has great power and wonderful results.

See *Prayer.*

PRAYER IN, ANSWERED. See *Prayer, Answered.*

PRAYER FOR THE AFFLICTED. See *Intercession.*

RESIGNATION IN. Job 5:17. How enviable the man whom God corrects! Oh, do not despise the chastening of the Lord when you sin.

Job 13:15. God may kill me for saying this—in fact, I expect him to. Nevertheless I am going to argue my case with him.

Job 34:31. Why don't people exclaim to their God, "We have sinned, but we will stop"? [32]Or, "We know not what evil we have done; only tell us, and we will cease at once." *v.* 34

Ps 46:10. Stand silent! Know that I am God! Ps 4:4.

Prov 3:11. Young man, do not resent it when God chastens and corrects you.

Lam 3:22. His compassion never ends. It is only the Lord's mercies that have kept us from complete destruction. [23]Great is his faithfulness; his lovingkindness begins afresh each day. [24]My soul claims the Lord as my inheritance; therefore I will hope in him. [25]The Lord is wonderfully good to those who wait for him, to those who seek him. It is good both to hope and wait quietly for the salvation of the Lord. [27]It is good for a young man to be under discipline, [28]for it causes him to sit apart in silence beneath the Lord's demands, [29]to lie face downward in the dust; then at last there is hope for him. [30]Let him turn the other cheek to those who strike him, and accept their awful insults, [31]for the Lord will not abandon him forever. [32]Although God gives him grief, yet he will show compassion too, according to the greatness of his lovingkindness. [33]For he does not enjoy afflicting men and causing sorrow. [34,35,36]But you have trampled and crushed beneath your feet the lowly of the world, and deprived men of their God-given rights, and refused them justice. No wonder the Lord has had to deal with you! [39]Why then should we, mere humans as we are, murmur and complain when punished for our sins?

Mic 6:9. The Lord's voice calls out to all Jerusalem—listen to the Lord if you are wise! The armies of destruction are coming; the Lord is sending them.

Mt 26:39. He went forward a little, and fell face downward on the ground, and prayed, "My Father! If it is possible, let this cup be taken away from me. But I want your will, not mine." Mk 14: 36; Luke 22:41,42; Jn 18:11.

Lk 21:19. For if you stand firm, you will win your souls.

Rom 5:3. We can rejoice too, when we run into problems and trials for we know that they are good for us—they help us learn to be patient.

Rom 12:12. Be glad for all God is planning for you. Be patient in trouble and prayerful always.

2 Cor 12:9. Each time he said, "No. But I am with you; that is all you need. My power shows up best in weak people." Now I am glad to boast about how weak I am; I am glad to be a living demonstration of Christ's power, instead of showing off my own power and abilities.

Phil 2:14. In everything you do, stay away from complaining and arguing.

Col 1:11. We are praying too, that you will be filled with his mighty, glorious strength so that you can keep going no matter what happens—always full of the joy of the Lord.

1 Thess 3:3. To keep you from becoming fainthearted in all the troubles you were going through. (But of course you know that such troubles are a part of God's plan for us Christians.) *v.* 4.

2 Thess 1:4. We are happy to tell other churches about your patience and complete faith in God, in spite of all the crushing troubles and hardships you are going through.

2 Tim 2:3. Take your share of suffering as a good soldier of Jesus Christ.

2 Tim 4:5. Stand steady, and don't be afraid of suffering for the Lord.

Heb 10:34. You suffered with those thrown into

jail, and you were actually joyful when all you owned was taken from you, knowing that better things were awaiting you in heaven, things that would be yours forever.

Heb 12:3. If you want to keep from becoming fainthearted and weary, think about his patience as sinful men did such terrible things to him. [4]After all, you have never yet struggled against sin and temptation until you sweat great drops of blood. [5]And have you quite forgotten the encouraging words God spoke to you, his child? He said, "My son, don't be angry when the Lord punishes you. Don't be discouraged when he has to show you where you are wrong." [9]Since we respect our fathers here on earth, though they punish us, should we not all the more cheerfully submit to God's training so that we can begin really to live? *vs.* 6–12.

Jas 1:10. But a rich man should be glad that his riches mean nothing to the Lord, for he will soon be gone, like a flower that has lost its beauty and fades away, withered—killed by the scorching summer sun.

Jas 4:7. So give yourselves humbly to God.

1 Pet 1:6. So be truly glad! There is wonderful joy ahead, even though the going is rough for a while down here.

1 Pet 2:20. Of course, you get no credit for being patient if you are beaten for doing wrong; but if you do right and suffer for it, and are patient beneath the blows, God is well pleased.

1 Pet 4:12. Dear friends, don't be bewildered or surprised when you go through the fiery trials ahead, for this is no strange, unusual thing that is going to happen to you. [13]Instead, be really glad—because these trials will make you partners with Christ in his suffering and afterwards you will have the wonderful joy of sharing his glory in that coming day when it will be displayed. [19]So if you are suffering according to God's will, keep on doing what is right and trust yourself to the God who made you, for he will never fail you.

1 Pet 5:6. If you will humble yourselves under the mighty hand of God, in his good time he will lift you up. [7]Let him have all your worries and cares, for he is always thinking about you and watching everything that concerns you.

See *Resignation.*

RESIGNATION IN, EXEMPLIFIED. Judg 10:15. But they pleaded with him again and said, "We have sinned. Punish us in any way you think best, only save us once more from our enemies."

1 Sam 3:18. So Samuel told him what the Lord had said. "It is the Lord's will," Eli replied; "let him do what he thinks best."

2 Sam 12:23. But why should I fast when he is dead? Can I bring him back again? I shall go to him, but he shall not return to me.

2 Sam 15:26. "If the Lord sees fit," David said, "he will bring me back to see the Ark and the Tabernacle again. But if he is through with me, well, let him do what seems best to him."

2 Sam 16:10. "No!" the king said. "If the Lord has told him to curse me, who am I to say no? [12]And perhaps the Lord will see that I am being wronged and will bless me because of these curses."

2 Sam 24:14. "This is a hard decision," David replied, "but it is better to fall into the hand of the Lord (for his mercy is great) than into the hands of men."

2 Kgs 4:26. "Run and meet her and ask her what the trouble is. See if her husband is all right and the child is well." "Yes," she told Gehazi, "everything is fine."

2 Kgs 20:19. "All right," Hezekiah replied, "if this is what the Lord wants, it is good." But he was really thinking, "at least there will be peace and security during the remainder of my own life!" Isa 39:8.

Neh 9:33. Every time you punished us you were being perfectly fair; we have sinned so greatly that you gave us only what we deserved.

Esther 4:16. Though it is strictly forbidden, I will go in to see the king, and if I perish, I perish.

Job 1:21. "I came naked from my mother's womb," he said, "and I shall have nothing when I die. The Lord gave me everything I had, and they were his to take away. Blessed be the name of the Lord." [22]In all of this, Job did not sin or revile God.

Job 2:10. But he replied, "You talk like some heathen woman. What? Shall we receive only pleasant things from the hand of God and never anything unpleasant?" So in all this Job said nothing wrong.

Job 13:15. God may kill me for saying this—in fact, I expect him to. Nevertheless I am going to argue my case with him.

Job 14:14. If a man dies, shall he live again? This thought gives me hope, so that in all my anguish I eagerly wait sweet death!"

Ps 39:9. Lord I am speechless before you. I will not open my mouth to speak one word of complaint, for my punishment is from you.

Ps 71:20. You have let me sink down deep in desperate problems. But you will bring me back to life again, up from the depths of the earth.

Ps 119:75. I know, O Lord, that your decisions are right and that your punishment was right and did me good.

Jer 10:19. Desperate is my wound. My grief is great. My sickness is incurable, but I must bear it.

Lam 1:18. And the Lord is right, for we rebelled.

Lam 3:39. Why then should we, mere humans as we are, murmur and complain when punished for our sins?

Dan 9:14. And so the Lord deliberately crushed us with the calamity he prepared; he is fair in everything he does, but we would not obey.

Mic 7:9. I will be patient while the Lord punishes me, for I have sinned against him; then he will defend me from my enemies and punish them for all the evil they have done to me. God will bring me out of my darkness into the light, and I will see his goodness.

Lk 23:40,41. But the other criminal protested. "Don't you even fear God when you are dying? We deserve to die for our evil deeds, but this man hasn't done one thing wrong."

Acts 21:14. When it was clear that he wouldn't be dissuaded, we gave up and said, "The will of the Lord be done."

Rom 5:3. We can rejoice, too, when we run into problems and trials for we know that they are good for us—they help us learn to be patient. [4]And patience develops strength of character in us and helps us trust God more each time we use it until finally our hope and faith are strong and steady.

2 Cor 6:4. In fact, in everything we do we try to show that we are true ministers of God. We patiently endure suffering and hardship and trouble of every kind. [5]We have been beaten, put in jail, faced angry mobs, worked to exhaustion, stayed awake through sleepless nights of watching and gone without food. [6]We have proved ourselves to be what we claim by our wholesome lives and by our understanding of the Gospel and by our patience. We have been kind and truly loving and filled with the Holy Spirit. [7]We have been truthful, with God's power helping us in all we do. All of the godly man's arsenal—weapons of defense, and weapons of attack—have been ours. [8]We stand true to the Lord whether others honor us or despise us, whether they criticize or commend us. We are honest, but they call us liars. [9]The world ignores us, but we are known to God; we live close to death, but here we are, still very much alive. We have been injured but kept from death. [10]Our hearts ache, but at the same time we have the joy of the Lord. We are poor, but we give rich spiritual gifts to others. We own nothing, and yet we enjoy everything.

2 Cor 7:4. I have the highest confidence in you, and my pride in you is great. You have greatly encouraged me; you have made me so happy in spite of all my suffering.

2 Thess 1:4. We are happy to tell other churches about your patience and complete faith in God, in spite of all the crushing troubles and hardships you are going through.

Jas 5:11. We know how happy they are now because they stayed true to him then, even though they suffered greatly for it. Job is an example of a man who continued to trust the Lord in sorrow; from his experiences we can see how the Lord's plan finally ended in good, for he is full of tenderness and mercy.

See *Resignation.*

INSTANCES OF RESIGNATION IN. Aaron, at the death of Nadab and Abihu, Lev 10:1–3. Eli, when judgments against his house were predicted, 1 Sam 3:15–18. David, at the death of his child, 2 Sam 12:23. The Shunammite, 2 Kgs 4:18–37. Jesus, in Gethsemane, Mt 26:39; Mk 14:36; Lk 22:41,42; Jn 18:11. Paul and Silas in prison, Acts 16:23–25.

AGABUS A prophet, Acts 11:28; 21:10.

AGAG 1. A king of the Amalekites, Num 24:3–9.

2. A king of the Amalekites, taken prisoner by Saul, and killed by Samuel, 1 Sam 15:8,31–33.

AGAGITE See *Hammedatha.*

AGATE A precious stone, Ex 28:19; 39:12; Isa 54:12; Ezk 27:16.

AGE, AGES The end of the age, Mt 13:39,40; 24:3; 28:20, Heb 9:26. Endless, Eph 3:21. Secret kept for, Col 1:26,27.

AGE, OLD See *Old Age.*

AGED See *Old Age.*

AGEE Father of Shammah, 2 Sam 23:11,12.

AGENCY IN SALVATION OF MEN. Job 33:14. For God speaks again and again, [15]in dreams, in visions of the night when deep sleep falls on men as they lie on their beds. [16]He opens their ears in times like that and gives them wisdom and instruction, [17,18]causing them to change their minds, and keeping them from pride, and warning them of the penalties of sin, and keeping them from falling into some trap. [19]Or, God sends sickness and pain, even though no bone is broken, [20]so that a man loses all taste and appetite for food and doesn't care for even the daintiest dessert. [21]He becomes thin, mere skin and bones, and draws near to death. [23,24]But if a messenger from heaven is there to intercede for him as a friend, to show him what is right, then God pities him and says, "Set him free. Do not make him die, for I have found a substitute." [25]Then his body will become as healthy as a child's, firm and youthful again. [26]And when he prays to God, God will hear and answer him and receive him with joy, and return him to his duties. [27]And he will declare to his friends, "I sinned, but God let me go. [28]He did not let me die. I will go on living in the realm of light." [29]Yes, God often does these things for man—[30]brings back his soul from the pit, so that he may live in the light of the living.

Ps 8:2. You have taught the little children to praise you perfectly. May their example shame and silence your enemies!

Mt 4:19. Jesus called out, "Come along with me and I will show you how to fish for the souls of men!" Lk 5:10.

Mt 5:13. You are the world's seasoning, to make it tolerable. If you lose your flavor, what will happen to the world? And you yourselves will be thrown out and trampled underfoot as worthless. [14]You are the world's light—a city on a hill, glowing in the night for all to see. [15,16]Don't hide your light! Let it shine for all; let your good deeds glow for all to see, so that they will praise your heavenly Father.

Lk 1:17. He will be a man of rugged spirit and power like Elijah, the prophet of old; and he will precede the coming of the Messiah, preparing the people for his arrival. He will soften adult hearts to become like little children's and will change disobedient minds to the wisdom of faith.

Lk 10:17. When the seventy disciples returned, they joyfully reported to him, "Even the demons obey us when we use your name." [21]Then he was filled with the joy of the Holy Spirit and said, "I praise you, O Father, Lord of heaven and earth, for hiding these things from the intellectuals and worldly wise and for revealing them to those who are as trusting as little children. Yes, thank you, Father, for that is the way you wanted it."

Jn 15:16. You didn't choose me! I chose you! I appointed you to go and produce lovely fruit always, so that no matter what you ask for from the Father, using my name, he will give it to you.

1 Cor 1:26. Notice among yourselves, dear brothers, that few of you who follow Christ have big names or power or wealth. [27]Instead, God has deliberately chosen to use ideas the world considers foolish and of little worth in order to shame those people considered by the world as wise and great. [28]He has chosen a plan despised by the world, counted as nothing at all, and used it to bring down to nothing those the world considers great, [29]so that no one anywhere can ever brag in the presence of God.

1 Thess 2:4. For we speak as messengers from God, trusted by him to tell the truth; we change his message not one bit to suit the taste of those who hear it; for we serve God alone, who examines our hearts' deepest thoughts.

1 Tim 6:20. Oh, Timothy, don't fail to do these things that God entrusted to you. Keep out of foolish arguments with those who boast of their "knowledge" and thus prove their lack of it.

Jas 5:20. That person who brings him back to God will have saved a wandering soul from death, bringing about the forgiveness of many sins.

See *Preaching.*

IN EXECUTING JUDGMENTS. Gen 3:15. From now on you and the woman will be enemies, as will all of your offspring and hers. And I will put the fear of you into the woman, and between your offspring and hers. He shall strike you on your head, while you will strike at his heel.

1 Sam 15:18. And he sent you on an errand and told you, "Go and completely destroy the sinners, the Amalekites, until they are all dead." With *vs.* 1–19.

2 Sam 7:14. I will be his father and he shall be my son. If he sins, I will use other nations to punish him.

2 Kgs 9:6. The Lord God of Israel says, "I anoint you king of the Lord's people, Israel. [7]You are to destroy the family of Ahab; you will avenge the murder of my prophets and of all my other people who were killed by Jezebel."

2 Kgs 19:25. Why haven't you realized long before this that it is I, the Lord, who lets you do these things? I decreed your conquest of all those fortified lands! [26]So of course the nations you conquered had no power against you!

2 Chron 22:7. God had decided to punish Ahaziah for his alliance with Jehoram. It was during this visit that Ahaziah went out with Jehoram to challenge Jehu (son of Nimshi), whom the Lord had appointed to end the dynasty of Ahab.

Ps 17:13,14. Lord, arise and stand against them. Push them back! Come and save me from these men of the world whose only concern is earthly gain—these men whom you have filled with your treasures so that their children and grandchildren are rich and prosperous.

Isa 10:5,6. Assyria is the whip of my anger; his military strength is my weapon upon this godless nation, doomed and damned; he will enslave them and plunder them and trample them like dirt beneath his feet.

Isa 13:5. They are his weapons against you, O Babylon. They carry his anger with them and will destroy your whole land.

Jer 27:8. Submit to him and serve him—put your neck under Babylon's yoke! I will punish any nation refusing to be his slave; I will send war, famine and disease upon that nation until he has conquered it.

Jer 51:20. Cyrus is God's battleaxe and sword. I will use you, says the Lord, to break nations in pieces and to destroy many kingdoms. [21]With you I will crush armies, destroying the horse and his rider, the chariot and the charioteer—[22]yes, and the civilians too, both old and young, young men and maidens, [23]shepherds and flocks, farmers and oxen, captains and rulers. Isa 41:15.

AGENCY, FREE MORAL See *Contingencies.*

AGONY Christ in agony, Lk 22:44; cf. Mt 26:36–46; Mk 14:32–42; Heb 5:7,8.

See *Afflictions; Suffering.*

AGREEMENT See *Contracts; Covenant.*

AGRICULTURE Divine institution of, Gen 2:15; 3:19,23. Practiced by Cain, Gen 4:2; Noah, Gen 9:20,21; Elisha, 1 Kgs 19:19; David, 1 Chron 27:26–28; Uzziah, 2 Chron 26:10; Solomon, Eccl 2:4–6.

God to be acknowledged in, Jer 5:23,24; Hos 2:9. Requires wisdom, Isa 28:26; diligence, Prov 27:23–27; Eccl 11:6; patience, Jas 5:7; toil, 2 Tim 2:6. Persons engaged in, called workers, Mt 9:37; 20:1; farmers, Gen 4:2. Planters of vineyards exempted from military service, Deut 20:6. Fruits blasted because of sin, Isa 5:10; 7:23; Jer 12:13; Joel 1:10,11.

LAWS CONCERNING. Ex 22:5. If someone deliberately lets his animal loose and it gets into another man's vineyard; or if he turns it into another man's field to graze, he must pay for all damages by giving the owner of the field or vineyard an equal amount of the best of his own crop.

6. If the field is being burned off and the fire gets out of control and goes into another field so that the shocks of grain, or the standing wheat are destroyed, the one who started the fire shall make full restitution.

Ex 34:21. Even during plowing and harvest times, work only six days, and rest on the seventh. Ex 20:9; 23:12; Deut 5:13,14.

22. And you must remember to celebrate these three annual religious festivals: the Festival of Weeks, the Festival of the First Wheat, and the Harvest Festival.

Lev 19:9. When you harvest your crops, don't reap the corners of your fields, and don't pick up stray grains of wheat from the ground. [10]It is the same with your grape crop—don't strip every last piece of fruit from the vines, and don't pick up the grapes that fall to the ground. Leave them for the poor and for those traveling through, for I am Jehovah your God.

19. Obey my laws: Do not mate your cattle with a different kind; don't sow your field with two kinds of seed; don't wear clothes made of half wool and half linen.

23. When you enter the land and have planted all kinds of fruit trees, do not eat the first three crops, for they are considered ceremonially defiled. [24]And the fourth year the entire crop shall be devoted to the Lord, and shall be given to the Lord in praise to Him. [25]Finally, in the fifth year, the crop is yours.

Lev 25:2. When you come into the land I am going to give you, you must let the land rest before the Lord every seventh year. [3]For six years you may sow your field and prune your vineyards and harvest your crops, [4]but during the seventh year the land is to lie fallow before the Lord, uncultivated. Don't sow your crops and don't prune your vineyards during that entire year. [Ex 23:10, 11.] [5]Don't even reap for yourself the volunteer crops that come up, and don't gather the grapes for yourself; for it is a year of rest for the land. [6,7]Any crops that do grow that year shall be free to all—for you, your servants, your slaves, and any foreigners living among you. Cattle and wild animals alike shall be allowed to graze there.

8. Every fiftieth year, [9]on the Day of Atonement, let the trumpets blow loud and long throughout the land. [10]For the fiftieth year shall be holy, a time to proclaim liberty throughout the land to all enslaved debtors, and a time for the canceling of all public and private debts. It shall be a year when all the family estates sold to others shall be returned to the original owners or their heirs. [11]What a happy year it will be! In it you shall not sow, nor gather crops nor grapes; for it is a holy Year of Jubilee for you. That year your food shall be the volunteer crops that grow wild in the fields. [15,16]If the Jubilee is many years away, the price will be high; if few years, the price will be low; for what you are really doing is selling the number of crops the new owner will get from the land before it is returned to you. [19]When you obey the land will yield bumper crops and you can eat your fill in safety. [20]But you will ask, "What shall we eat the seventh year, since we are not allowed to plant or harvest crops that year?" [21,22]The answer is, "I will bless you with bumper crops the sixth year that will last you until the crops of the eighth year are harvested!"

23. And remember, the land is mine, so you may not sell it permanently. You are merely my tenants and sharecroppers! [24]In every contract of sale there must be a stipulation that the land can be redeemed at any time by the seller.

25. If anyone becomes poor and sells some of his land, then his nearest relatives may redeem it. [26]If there is no one else to redeem it, and he himself gets together enough money, [27]then he may always buy it back at a price proportionate to the number of harvests until the Jubilee, and the owner must accept the money and return the land to him. [28]But if the original owner is not able to redeem it, then it shall belong to the new owner until the Year of Jubilee; but at the Jubilee year it must be returned again.

Deut 22:9. Do not sow other crops in the rows of your vineyard. If you do, both the crops and the grapes shall be confiscated by the priests.

10. Don't plow with an ox and a donkey harnessed together.

Deut 23:24. You may eat your fill of the grapes from another man's vineyard, but do not take any away in a container. [25]It is the same with someone else's grain—you may eat a few handfuls of it, but don't use a sickle. Mt 12:1.

Deut 24:19. If, when reaping your harvest, you forget to bring in a sheaf from the field, don't go back after it. Leave it for the migrants, orphans, and widows; then the Lord your God will bless and prosper all you do. [20]When you beat the olives from your olive trees, don't go over the boughs twice; leave anything remaining for the migrants, orphans, and widows. [21]It is the same for the grapes in your vineyard, don't glean the vines after they are picked, but leave what's left for those in need.

Prov 3:9,10. Honor the Lord by giving him the first part of all your income, and he will fill your barns with wheat and barley and overflow your wine vats with the finest wines.

Prov 27:23,24. Riches can disappear fast. And the king's crown doesn't stay in his family forever—so watch your business interests closely. Know the state of your flocks and your herds; [25,26,27]then there will be lamb's wool enough for clothing, and goat's milk enough for food for all your household after the hay is harvested, and the new crop appears, and the mountain grasses are gathered in.

FACTS ABOUT. Gen 8:22. As long as the earth remains, there will be springtime and harvest, cold and heat, winter and summer, day and night.

1 Sam 13:19. There were no blacksmiths at all in the land of Israel in those days, for the Philistines wouldn't allow them for fear of their making swords and spears for the Hebrews. [20]So whenever the Israelites needed to sharpen their plowshares, discs, axes, or sickles, they had to take them to a Philistine blacksmith. [21](The schedule of charges was as follows: For sharpening a plow point, 60¢; for sharpening a disc, 60¢; for sharpening an axe, 30¢; for sharpening a sickle, 30¢; for sharpening an ox goad, 30¢.)

Isa 28:24. Does a farmer always plow and never sow? Is he forever harrowing the soil and never planting it? [25]Does he not finally plant his many kinds of grain, each in its own section of his land? [26]He knows just what to do, for God has made him see and understand. [27]He doesn't thresh all grains the same. A sledge is never used on dill, but it is beaten with a stick. A threshing wheel is never rolled on cummin, but it is beaten softly with a flail.

[28]Bread grain is easily crushed, so he doesn't keep on pounding it.

Mt 13:3. He used many illustrations such as this one in his sermon: "A farmer was sowing grain in his fields. [4]As he scattered the seed across the ground, some fell beside a path, the birds came and ate it. [5]And some fell on rocky soil where there was little depth of earth; the plants sprang up quickly enough in the shallow soil, but the hot sun soon scorched them and they withered and died, for they had so little root. [7]Other seeds fell among thorns, and the thorns choked out the tender blades. [8]But some fell on good soil, and produced a crop that was thirty, sixty, and even a hundred times as much as he had planted."

2 Cor 9:6. But remember this—if you give little, you will get little. A farmer who plants just a few seeds will get only a small crop, but if he plants much, he will reap much.

Gal 6:7. Don't be misled; remember that you can't ignore God and get away with it: a man will always reap just the kind of crop he sows!

See *Husbandman.*

FIGURATIVE. Fallow ground, Jer 4:3. Sowing wheat, but reaping thorns, Jer 12:13. Parable of the farmer sowing grain, Mt 13:3–8, 19–23; Luke 8:5–15; of the thistles, Mt 13:24–30,36–43.

OPERATIONS IN. See *Churning; Fertilizer; Gleaning; Grafting; Irrigation; Manure; Mowing; Pruning; Reaping; Sower; Threshing; Winnowing.*

IMPLEMENTS OF. *See Axe; Cart; Flail; Goad; Harrow; Mill; Plow; Pruning Hook; Sickle; Sieve; Sifter.*

PRODUCTS OF. See *Apple; Barley; Butter; Chaff; Corn; Cucumber; Date; Dill; Emmer; Fig; Garlic; Grain; Grape; Grass; Honey; Leek; Melon; Milk; Oil; Onion; Pomegranate; Spelt; Straw; Wheat; Wine.*

ANIMALS OF. See *Camel; Cattle; Donkey; Goat; Horse; Mule; Sheep; Swine.*

See also *Barn; Fence; Vineyard.*

AGRIPPA A king, son of Herod Agrippa I, Acts 25:13–26:32.

See *Herod.*

AGUR Son of Jakeh, Prov 30:1.

AHAB 1. King of Israel, 1 Kgs 16:29. Marries Jezebel, 1 Kgs 16:31. Idolatry of, 1 Kgs 16:30–33; 18:18,19; 21:25,26; other evilness of, 2 Kgs 3:2; 2 Chron 21:6; 22:3,4; Mic 6:16. Reproved by Elijah; assembles the prophets of Baal, 1 Kgs 18:17–46. Fraudulently confiscates Naboth's vineyard, 1 Kgs 21. Defeats Ben-hadad, 1 Kgs 20. Closing history and death of, 1 Kgs 22; 2 Chron 18. Succeeded by his son, Ahaziah, 1 Kgs 22:40. Prophecies against, 1 Kgs 20:42; 21:19–24; 22:19–28; 2 Kgs 9:8,25,26. Sons of, murdered, 2 Kgs 10:1–8.

2. A false prophet, Jer 29:21,22.

AHARAH Called also *Ehi,* and *Ahiram,* and *Aher,* son of Benjamin, Gen 46:19–22; Num 26:38–41; 1 Chron 7:12; 8:1.

AHARHEL Son of Harum, 1 Chron 4:8.

AHASBAI Father of Eliphelet, 2 Sam 23:24–39. See *Ur,* 1 Chron 11:26–47.

AHASUERUS 1. King of Persia, Ezra 4:6. History of, see the book of Esther. Father of Artaxerxes, which see.

2. Father of Darius the Mede, Dan 9:1.

AHAVA A river of Babylon, Ezra 8:15,21,31.

AHAZ 1. King of Judah, son and successor of Jotham, 2 Kgs 15:38; 16:1; 2 Chron 27:9; 28:1. Idolatrous abominations of, 2 Kgs 16:2–4; 2 Chron 28:2–4,22–25. Kingdom of, invaded by the kings of Syria and Samaria, 2 Kgs 16:5,6; 2 Chron 28:5–8. Robs the temple to purchase aid from the king of Assyria, 2 Kgs 16:7–9,17,18; 2 Chron 28:21. Visits Damascus, obtains a novel design of an altar, which he substitutes for the altar in the temple in Jerusalem, and otherwise perverts the forms of worship, 2 Kgs 16:10–16. Sundial of, 2 Kgs 20:11; Isa 38:8. Prophets in the reign of, Isa 1:1; Hos 1:1; Mic 1:1. Prophecies concerning, Isa 7:13–25. Succeeded by Hezekiah, 2 Kgs 16:20.

2. Son of Micah, 1 Chron 8:35; 9:41,42.

AHAZIAH 1. King of Judah. Called *Jehoahaz,* 2 Chron 21:17. History of, 2 Kgs 8:25–29; 9:16–29. Gifts of, to the temple, 2 Kgs 12:18. Brothers of, killed, 2 Kgs 10:13,14. Succeeded by Athaliah, 2 Chron 22:10–12.

2. King of Israel. History of, 1 Kgs 22:40,49,51–53; 2 Chron 20:35–37; 2 Kgs 1. Succeeded by Jehoram, 2 Kgs 3:1.

AHBAN Son of Abishur, 1 Chron 2:29.

AHER See *Aharah.*

AHI Son of Abdi-el, 1 Chron 5:15.

AHIAH An Israelite leader who signed the covenant of Nehemiah, Neh 10:14–27.

AHIAM One of David's heroes, 2 Sam 23:24–39; 1 Chron 11:26–47.

AHIAN Son of Shemida, 1 Chron 7:19.

AHIEZER 1. Captain of the tribe of Dan, Num 1:2–15; 2:23–31. Contributes to the Tabernacle, Num 7:66–71.

2. One of David's warriors, 1 Chron 12:3–7.

AHIHUD 1. A leader of the tribe of Asher, assists in dividing the land of Canaan among the tribes, Num 34:16–28.

2. Son of Ehud, 1 Chron 8:7.

AHIJAH 1. A Benjaminite, 1 Chron 8:7.

2. Son of Jerahmeel, 1 Chron 2:25.

3. A priest in Shiloh, probably identical with Ahimelech, mentioned in 1 Sam 22:11,12. Was priest in Saul's reign, 1 Sam 14:3,18. Killed, 1 Sam 22:11–19.

4. One of David's heroes, 1 Chron 11:26–47. Called also *Eliam,* 2 Sam 23:34.

5. A Levite who was treasurer in the Tabernacle, 1 Chron 26:20–22.

6. One of Solomon's secretaries and son of Shisha, 1 Kgs 4:1–6.

7. A prophet in Shiloh, 1 Kgs 11:29–39.

8. Father of Baasha, 1 Kgs 15:27; 2 Kgs 9:9.

9. See *Abijah, 3.*

AHIKAM Son of Shaphan, 2 Kgs 22:12–14; 25:22; 2 Chron 34:20; Jer 26:24; 39:14.

AHILUD Father of Baana, 1 Kgs 4:8–19; and of Jehoshaphat, 2 Sam 8:16; 1 Kgs 4:1–6; 1 Chron 18:15.

AHIMA-AZ 1. Father-in-law of King Saul, 1 Sam 14:50,51.

2. Son of Zadok, the high priest. Loyal to David, 2 Sam 15:35,36; 17:17–20; 18:19–33; 1 Chron 6:4–15, 50–53.

3. Solomon's son-in-law, 1 Kgs 4:8–19.

AHIMAN 1. A giant of Hebron, Josh 15:14. Also the name of a clan or group of clans, Num 13: 22; Judg 1:10.

2. A Levite, 1 Chron 9:17,18.

AHIMELECH 1. A high priest during the reign of David. Gives holy bread and the sword of Goliath to David, 1 Sam 21. Killed by command of Saul, 1 Sam 22:9–22.

2. A Hittite, and friend of David, 1 Sam 26:5–7.

3. Possible son of Abiathar and grandson of Ahimelech (see 1, above), 2 Sam 8:17; 1 Chron 18: 16; 24:3,6,31. See *Abiathar.*

AHIMOTH A Levite, 1 Chron 6:25–27.

AHINADAB Son of Iddo, 1 Kgs 4:8–19.

AHINO-AM 1. Wife of King Saul, 1 Sam 14: 50,51.

2. Wife of King David, 1 Sam 25:43; 27:2, 3; 30: 5; 2 Sam 2:2; 3:2; 1 Chron 3:1.

AHIO 1. A Levite, who drove the cart bearing the ark, 2 Sam 6:3,4; 1 Chron 13:7.

2. A Benjaminite, 1 Chron 8:14.

3. Son of Je-iel, 1 Chron 8:31; 9:35–37.

AHIRA Leader of the tribe of Naphtali, Num 1:2–15; 2:3–31; 7:78–83; 10:27.

AHIRAM See *Aharah.*

AHISAMACH Father of Oholiab, Ex 31:6; 35:34; 38:23.

AHISHAHAR Son of Bilhan, 1 Chron 7:10.

AHISHAR One of Solomon's cabinet members, 1 Kgs 4:1–6.

AHITHOPHEL One of David's counselors, 2 Sam 15:12; 1 Chron 27:33. Joins Absalom, 2 Sam 15:31,33,34; 16:15,20–23; 17:1–23. Probably referred to by David in Ps 55:12–14. Suicide of, 2 Sam 17:1–14,23.

AHITUB 1. High priest, father of Ahijah (Ahimelech), 1 Sam 14:3; 22:11,12.

2. Father of Zadok, 2 Sam 8:17; 1 Chron 6:4–15, 50–53; 18:16; Ezra 7:1–5.

3. Chief priest, 1 Chron 9:10,11; Neh 11:10–14.

4. The second Ahitub mentioned in 1 Chron 6: 4–15 is probably identical with the last described above, or else he is confused with Azariah, 2 Chron 31:10.

AHLAB A city of Asher, the original inhabitants of which were not expelled, Judg 1:31,32.

AHLAI 1. Son or daughter of Sheshan, 1 Chron 2:31, 34,35.

2. Father of Zabad, 1 Chron 11:26–47.

AHOAH Son of Bela, 1 Chron 8:3–4. Called also *Ahijah,* 1 Chron 8:6,7, and *Iri,* 1 Chron 7:7.

AHUMAI Son of Jahath, 1 Chron 4:2.

AHUZZAM Son of Ashhur, 1 Chron 4:6.

AHUZZATH An advisor to Abimelech, Gen 26:26.

AHZAI A priest, grandson of Immer, Neh 11: 10–14.

AI 1. A royal city of the Canaanites. Conquest and destruction of, Josh 7; 8. Rebuilt, Ezra 2:3–35. Called also *Aija,* Neh 11:31–35, and *Aiath,* Isa 10:28, 29. Population of, Josh 8:25.

2. A city of the Ammonites, Jer 49:3.

AIAH 1. A Horite, Gen 36:24; 1 Chron 1:40.

2. Father of Rizpah, 2 Sam 21:8–11.

AIATH See *Ai.*

AIJA See *Ai.*

AIJALON 1. A city of Dan, Josh 19:42. Assigned to the Levites, Josh 21:23,24; 1 Sam 14:31; 1 Chron 6:66–69. Amorites of, made slaves, Judg 1: 35. Overlooking the valley of Aijalon, see 4, below.

2. A city of Zebulun, Judg 12:11,12.

3. A city of Judah, 2 Chron 11:5–10; 28:17,18. Probably the same as 1, above.

4. A valley between Jericho and the Mediterranean Sea, Josh 10:12.

AIJELETH SHAHAR A musical term which probably indicated the sprightly movement of the music set to Psalm 22.

AILMENT PHYSICAL. Moses exempt from, Deut 34:7; Caleb, Josh 14:11.

See *Afflictions; Blindness; Deafness; Lameness; Old Age.*

AIN 1. A city of Simeon, Josh 15:21–32; 21:9–16; 1 Chron 4:32,33. Called also *Ashan,* Josh 19:7; 1 Chron 6:59. Possibly identical with *En-rimmon,* Neh 11:25–30.

2. A landmark on the northern boundary of Palestine, Num 34:10,11.

AKAN A Horite, Gen 36:27. Called also *Jaakan,* 1 Chron 1:42.

AKKUB 1. Son of Eli-o-enai, 1 Chron 3:24.

2. A returned exile and gatekeeper, 1 Chron 9:17. Descendant of 3, below.

3. Ancestor of a family of Levite gatekeepers, Ezra 2:40–42.

4. One of the Temple assistants, Ezra 2:45.

5. An assistant to Ezra, Neh 8:7,8. Possibly the same as 6, below.

6. Leader of the gatekeepers, Neh 11:19; 12:25.

AKRABBIM A mountain pass in southern Palestine, Josh 15:2–4. Called also *Scorpion Pass,* Num 34:4; Judg 1:36.

ALAMOTH A musical term, 1 Chron 15:20. See *Music.*

ALARM The sound of a silver trumpet, used as a signal by the Jews on a journey or when faced with war, Lev 23:23,24; 25:9; Num 10:5–7; 29:1; Judg 6:34; 2 Chron 13:12; Jer 4:19; Joel 2:1,15; Zeph 1:16; 1 Cor 14:8.

ALEMETH 1. A Levitical city, 1 Chron 6:60. See *Almon.*

2. Son of Jehoaddah, 1 Chron 8:36; or of Jarah, 1 Chron 9:42.

3. Son of Becher, 1 Chron 7:8.

ALEXANDER 1. Son of Simon who carried the cross of Jesus, Mk 15:21.

2. A relative of the high priest, present at the defense of Peter and John, Acts 4:6.

3. A Jew of Ephesus, Acts 19:33.

4. A coppersmith, 1 Tim 1:20; 2 Tim 4:14.

ALEXANDRIA A city of Egypt, Acts 6:9. Ships of, Acts 27:6; 28:11. Apollos born in, Acts 18: 24.

ALGUM Trees of Ophir and Lebanon, 1 Kgs 10:11,12; 2 Chron 2:8.

ALIAH See *Alvah.*

ALIAN See *Alvan.*

ALIENS Strangers, heathen. To be treated with justice, Ex 22:21; 23:9; Lev 19:33,34; Deut 1:16; 10:19; 24:14,15,17; 27:19; Jer 7:6; 22:3; Ezk 22:29; Mal 3:5. Religious privileges of, Ex 12:24,29; Num 9:14; 15:13–16. Kindness to Edomites, commanded, Deut 23:7. Jews authorized to purchase, as slaves, Lev 25:44,45; and to take interest from, Deut 15:3; 23:20; not permitted to make kings of, Deut 17:15. Forbidden to eat the passover, Ex 12:45. Partially exempt from Jewish law, Deut 14:21. Numerous in time of David and Solomon, 2 Sam 22:44–46; 2 Chron 2:17; 15:9. Oppressed, Ezk 22:29. Rights of, Num 35:15; Josh 20:9; Ezk 47:22,23. David's kindness to, 2 Sam 15:19,20. Hospitality to, required by Jesus, Mt 25:35, 38, 43.

See *Gleaning; Heathen; Hospitality; Inhospitableness; Strangers.*

ALKALI In Palestine, Deut 29:23.

ALLAMMELECH A town of Asher, Josh 19:24–26.

ALLEGORY Of the trees seeking a king, Judg 9:8–15. Messiah's kingdom represented under, of the wolf and the lamb living together, Isa 11:6–8. Wilderness to blossom as flowers, Isa 35. The two covenants, Gal 4:24, 25.

See *Parable; Symbols.*

ALLIANCES POLITICAL. With idolaters forbidden, Ex 23:32, 33; 34:12–15; Deut 7:2; Judg 2: 2,; 2 Chron 19:21; 20:37; Isa 30:2; 31:1; Hos 4:17; 5: 13; 12:1; Ezk 17:15. Ratification of: By oaths, Gen 21: 23; 26:28–31; Josh 9:14–20; 1 Sam 20:16,17.

See *Covenants; Treaty.*

INSTANCES OF. Between Abraham and Mamre, Eshcol, and Aner, Gen 14:13. Abraham and Abimelech, Gen 21:22–32. Isaac and Abimelech, Gen 26:26–31. Canaanite nations against Israel, Josh 9:1,2. Joshua and the Gibeonites, Josh 9. Moabites, Amalekites, and Ammonites, Judg 3:12, 13. Solomon and Hiram, 1 Kgs 5:12; Amos 1:9. Asa and Ben-hadad, 1 Kgs 15:18,19; 2 Chron 16:3. Jehoshaphat and Ahab, 1 Kgs 22; 2 Chron 18:1. Jehoshaphat and Ahaziah, 2 Chron 20:35. Ahaz and Tiglath-pileser, 2 Kgs 16:7,8; 2 Chron 28:16,21. Rezin and Pekah, 2 Kgs 16:5. Zedekiah and Pharaoh, Jer 37:1–8; Ezk 17:15–17.

ALLON Son of Jedaiah, 1 Chron 4:34–39.

ALLOY Of metals, Isa 1:22.

ALMODAD Son of Joktan, Gen 10:26–30; 1 Chron 1:20.

ALMON Levitical city of Benjamin, Josh 21: 17,18. Called *Alemeth,* 1 Chron 6:60.

ALMOND A tree, Gen 30:37. Fruit of, Gen 43:11. Aaron's rod of the, Num 17:8. Lampstand in the Tabernacle fashioned after, Ex 25:31–35; 37: 19–21.

FIGURATIVE. Jer 1:11,12.

ALMON-DIBIATHAIM Camping place of the Israelites, Num 33:46. Probably identical with *Beth-diblathaim,* Jer 48:22; and with *Riblah,* Ezk 6:14.

ALMS See *Charity.*

ALOES A drug made from the plant. Used as perfume, Num 24:6; Ps 45:8; Prov 7:16,17; Song 4: 13,14. In embalming the dead, Jn 19:39.

ALPHA AND OMEGA The first and last letters of the Greek alphabet. A title of Christ, Rev 1:8,11; 21:6; 22:13. Compare Isa 41:4; 44:6; 48:12.

ALPHAEUS 1. Father of James, Mt 10:2–4; Mk 3:16–19; Lk 6:14–16; Acts 1:14.

2. Father of Levi, Mk 2:14.

ALTAR Built by Noah, Gen 8:20; Abraham, Gen 12:7,8; 13:18; 22:9; Isaac, Gen 26:25; Jacob, Gen 33:20; 35:1–7; Moses, Ex 17:15; 24:4; Balaam, Num 23:1,14,29; Joshua, Deut 27:2–7; Josh 8:30–32; Reubenites and Gadites, Josh 22:10,34; Gideon, Judg 6:26,27; Samuel, 1 Sam 7:17; Saul, 1 Sam 14:35; David, 2 Sam 24:18,19; Elijah, 1 Kgs 18:31,32.

Mosaic commandments prescribing the construction of, Ex 20:24–26; Deut 27:5–7; Josh 8:30, 31. See Ezk 43:13.

Used in idolatrous worship, Judg 6:25; 1 Kgs 12: 32,33; 16:32; 18:26; 2 Kgs 16:10; 23:12,15; Isa 27:9; 65: 3; Hos 8:11; Acts 17:23.

OF BURNT OFFERINGS. Called *Bronze Altar,* Ex 39:39; 1 Kgs 8:64; *Altar of God,* Ps 43:4.

In the Tabernacle. Pattern of, Ex 27:1–8. Constructed by Bezalel, Ex 38:1–7, with 37:1. Location of, Ex 40:6,29; Ezk 8:16; Mt 23:35. Furniture of, Ex 27:3–7; 38:3–7; 1 Sam 2:13,14. Horns of, Ex 27:2.

How sanctified, Ex 29:36,37,44; 30:26–28; 40:10; Lev 8:10,11; Num 7. See Ezk 43:18–27. See *Blood.* Sanctified everything that touched it, Ex 29:37; 30: 29; Mt 23:18,19. A place of refuge, Ex 21:14; 1 Kgs 1:49,50; 2:28.

In Solomon's Temple. Description of, 2 Chron 4: 1. Renewed by Asa, 2 Chron 15:8. Removed by Ahaz, and one of idolatrous fashion substituted, 2 Kgs 16:14–17. Cleansed by Hezekiah, 2 Chron 29: 18–24. Rebuilt by Manasseh, 2 Chron 33:16. Furniture of, taken to Babylon, 2 Kgs 25:14,15.

In Second Temple. Ezra 3:1–6.

Ezekiel's Vision of. Ezk 43:13–27.

See *Tabernacle; Temple.*

OF INCENSE. Called the *Golden Altar,* Ex 39: 33–40; Num 4:11; *Incense Altar,* Lev 4:7; *Altar Before the Lord,* Lev 16:18.

Pattern of, Ex 30:1–5. Constructed, Ex 37:25–28. Location of, Ex 30:6; 40:5,26. A cover made for, of the censers of Korah, Num 16:36–40. Uses of, Ex 30:7–10,26,27; 40:27; Lev 4:7,18; 8:15,16; 9:9; 16:12, 18. How prepared for carrying, Num 4:4–15. Cared for by the Kohathites, Num 3:31. In Solomon's temple, 1 Kgs 6:19,20; 7:48; 1 Chron 28:18. Seen in John's vision, Rev 8:3; 9:13.

ALTRUISM Benevolent practices. Mt. 20: 26. But among you it is quite different. Anyone wanting to be a leader among you must be your servant. [27]And if you want to be right at the top, you must serve like a slave. [Mt 23:11] [28]Your attitude must be like my own, for I, the Messiah, did not come to be served, but to serve, and to give my life as a ransom for many. Mk 10:43–45; Lk 22:26, 27.

Mk 9:35. He sat down and called them around him and said, "Anyone wanting to be the greatest must be the least—the servant of all!"

Jn 13:12. After washing their feet he put on his robe again and sat down and asked, "Do you understand what I was doing? [13]You call me 'Master' and 'Lord,' and you do well to say it, for it is true. [14]And since I, the Lord and Teacher, have washed your feet, you ought to wash each other's feet. [15]I have given you an example to follow: do as I have done to you." *vs.* 4–17.

Acts 20:33. I have never been hungry for money or fine clothing—[34]you know that these hands of mine worked to pay my own way and even to supply the needs of those who were with me. [35]And I was a constant example to you in helping the poor; for I remembered the words of the Lord Jesus, "It is more blessed to give than to receive."

Rom 15:1,2. Even if we believe that it makes no difference to the Lord whether we do these things, still we cannot just go ahead and do them to please ourselves; for we must bear the "burden" of being considerate of the doubts and fears of others—of those who feel these things are wrong. Let's please the other fellow, not ourselves, and do what is for his good and thus build him up in the Lord. [3]Christ didn't please himself. As the Psalmist said, "He came for the very purpose of suffering under the insults of those who were against the Lord."

1 Cor 9:18. Under this circumstance, what is my pay? It is the special joy I get from preaching the Good News without expense to anyone, never demanding my rights. [19]And this has a real advantage: I am not bound to obey anyone just because he pays my salary; yet I have freely and happily become a servant of any and all so that I can win them to Christ. [20]When I am with the Jews I seem as one of them so that they will listen to the Gospel and I can win them to Christ. When I am with Gentiles who follow Jewish customs and ceremonies I don't argue, even though I don't agree, because I want to help them. [21]When with the heathen I agree with them as much as I can, except of course that I must always do what is right as a Christian. And so, by agreeing, I can win their confidence and help them too. [22]When I am with those whose consciences bother them easily, I don't act as though I know it all and don't say they are foolish; the result is that they are willing to let me help them. Yes, whatever a person is like, I try to find common ground with him so that he will let me tell him about Christ and let Christ save him.

1 Cor 10:24. Don't think only of yourself. Try to think of the other fellow, too, and what is best for him. [31]Well, I'll tell you why. It is because you must do everything for the glory of God, even your eating and drinking. [32]So don't be a stumbling block to anyone, whether they are Jews or Gentiles or Christians. [33]That is the plan I follow, too. I try to please everyone in everything I do, not doing what I like or what is best for me, but what is best for them, so that they may be saved.

2 Cor 4:5. We don't go around preaching about ourselves, but about Christ Jesus as Lord. All we say of ourselves is that we are your slaves because of what Jesus has done for us.

2 Cor 6:10. Our hearts ache, but at the same time we have the joy of the Lord. We are poor, but we give rich spiritual gifts to others. We own nothing, and yet we enjoy everything.

2 Cor 8:9. You know how full of love and kindness our Lord Jesus was: though he was so very rich, yet to help you he became so very poor, so that by being poor he could make you rich.

Gal 6:10. That's why whenever we can we should always be kind to everyone, and especially to our Christian brothers.

Phil 2:3. Don't be selfish; don't live to make a good impression on others. Be humble, thinking of others as better than yourself. [4]Don't just think about your own affairs, but be interested in others, too, and in what they are doing. [5]Your attitude should be the kind that was shown us by Jesus Christ, [6]who, though he was God, did not demand and cling to his rights as God, [7]but laid aside his mighty power and glory, taking the disguise of a slave and becoming like men. [8]And he humbled himself even further, going as far as actually to die a criminal's death on a cross.

See *Benevolence; Charitableness; Charity; Duty, of Man to Man; Liberality; Love.*

ALUSH Camping place of the Israelites, Num 33:13.

ALVAH Edomite chief, Gen 36:40–43. Called *Aliah,* 1 Chron 1:51–54.

ALVAN Son of Shobal, Gen 36:23. Called *Alian,* 1 Chron 1:40.

AMAD A town of Asher, Josh 19:24–26.

AMAL Son of Helem, 1 Chron 7:35.

AMALEK Son of Eliphaz, Gen 36:12; 1 Chron 1:36. Probably not the ancestor of the Amalekites mentioned in time of Abraham, Gen 14:7.

AMALEKITES A people inhabiting the country south of Idumea and east of the Red Sea, Num 13:29; 14:25; 1 Sam 15:7; 27:8. Defeated by Ched-or-laomer, Gen 14:7; by Joshua, Ex 17:8,13; by Gideon, Judg 7; by Saul, 1 Sam 14:47,48; 15:1–33; by David, 1 Sam 27:8,9; 30:1–20; by the Simeonites, 1 Chron 4:42,43. Defeat the Israelites, Num 14:45; Judg 3:13. Israel commanded to destroy, Deut 25:17–19; 1 Sam 28:18. Prophecies against, Ex 17:14–16; Num 24:20.

AMAM A city of Judah, Josh 15:21–32. Probably situated within the district assigned afterward to Simeon, Josh 19:1–9.

AMANA A mountain mentioned in Song 4:8.

AMARIAH 1. Two Levites, 1 Chron 6:4–15, 50–53 and 1 Chron 23:19; 24:23.

2. Chief priest in the reign of Jehoshaphat, 2 Chron 19:11.

3. A high priest, father of Ahitub, 1 Chron 6:4–15; Ezra 7:1–6.

4. A Levite, who assisted in distributing temple gifts, 2 Chron 31:14–19.

5. Son of Hezekiah, Zeph 1:1.

6. Father of Zechariah, Neh 11:4–6.

7. A priest, returned from exile, Neh 10:1–8; 12:1–7. Probably identical with one mentioned in Neh 12:12–21.

8. A returned exile. Divorces his heathen wife, Ezra 10:34–42.

AMASA 1. Nephew of David, 2 Sam 17:25; 1 Chron 2:17. Joins Absalom, 2 Sam 17:25. Returns to David, and is made commander-in-chief of the army, 2 Sam 19:13. Killed, 2 Sam 20:8–12; 1 Kgs 2:5,32.

2. Son of Hadlai, 2 Chron 28:12.

AMASAI 1. A Levite and ancestor of Samuel, 1 Chron 6:25,35.

2. Leader of a body of men discontented with Saul, who joined David, 1 Chron 12:18.

3. A priest and bugler, 1 Chron 15:24.

4. A Levite of the Kohathites, 2 Chron 29:12–14.

AMASHSAI A leader of Judah, Neh 11:10–14.

AMASIAH A commander of the army of Judah, 2 Chron 17:16.

AMAZIAH 1. A Levite, 1 Chron 6:44–47.

2. King of Judah. History of, 2 Kgs 14; 2 Chron 25.

3. An idolatrous priest at Bethel, Amos 7:10–17.

4. Father of Joshah mentioned in 1 Chron 4:34–39.

AMBASSADORS Sent by Moses to Edom, Num 20:14; to the Amorites, Num 21:21; Deut 2:26; by Gibeonites to the Israelites, Josh 9:3–5; Israelites to various nations, Judg 11:12–28; David to Hanun, 2 Sam 10:2; 1 Chron 19:2,3; Hiram to Solomon, 1 Kgs 5:1; Ben-hadad to Ahab, 1 Kgs 20:2–6; Amaziah to Jehoash, 2 Kgs 14:8; Ahaz to Tiglath-pileser, 2 Kgs 16:7; Sennacherib through Rabshakeh to Hezekiah, 2 Kgs 18:19,28; Merodach-baladan to Hezekiah, 2 Kgs 20:12; 2 Chron 32:31; Zedekiah to Egypt, Ezk 17:15.

Other references to, Prov 13:17; Isa 18:2; 33:7; 36:11; 39:1,2; Lk 14:32.

FIGURATIVE. Job 33:23,24; Obd 1; Jn 12:13; 2 Cor 5:20; Eph 6:20.

AMBER A yellowish resin and precious stone, Ex 28:19; Ezk 1:16; 8:2.

AMBITION Falsely charged against Moses, Num 16:13. Parable of the thistle, illustrating, 2 Kgs 14:9.

WRONG. Job 20:6. Though the godless be proud as the heavens, and walk with his nose in the air,
[7]yet he shall perish forever, cast away like his own dung. Those who knew him will wonder where he is gone.

Ps 49:11. You name your estates after yourselves as though your lands could be forever yours, and you could live on them eternally.
[12]But man with all his pomp must die like any animal.
[13]Such is the folly of these men, though after they die they will be quoted as having great wisdom.

Prov 27:20. Ambition and death are alike in this; neither is ever satisfied.

Isa 5:8. You buy up property so that others have no place to live. Your homes are built on great estates so you can be alone in the midst of the earth!

Hab 2:5. What's more, these arrogant Chaldeans are betrayed by all their wine, for it is treacherous. In their greed they have collected many nations, but like death and hell, they are never satisfied.
[6]The time is coming when all their captives will taunt them, saying: "You robbers! At last justice has caught up with you! Now you will get your just deserts for your oppression and extortion!"
[9]Woe to you for getting rich by evil means, attempting to live beyond the reach of danger.

Mt 4:8. Next Satan took him to the peak of a very high mountain and showed him the nations of the world and all their glory.
[9]"I'll give it all to you," he said, "if you will only kneel and worship me."
[10]"Get out of here, Satan," Jesus told him. "The Scriptures say, 'Worship only the Lord God. Obey only him.' " Lk 4:5–8.

Mt 16:26. What profit is there if you gain the whole world—and lose eternal life? What can be compared with the value of eternal life? Lk 9:25.

Mt 23:5. Everything they do is done for show. They act holy by wearing on their arms little prayer boxes with Scripture verses inside, and by lengthening the memorial fringes of their robes.
[6]And how they love to sit at the head table at banquets, and in the reserved pews in the synagogue! [Mk 12:38,39; Lk 11:43.]
[7]How they enjoy the deference paid them on the streets, and to be called "Rabbi" and "Master"!
[12]But those who think themselves great shall be disappointed and humbled; and those who humble themselves shall be exalted.

Mk 9:33. And so they arrived at Capernaum. When they were settled in the house where they were to stay he asked them, "What were you discussing out on the road?" [Lk 22:24.]
[34]But they were ashamed to answer, for they had been arguing about which of them was the greatest!
[35]He sat down and called them around him and said to them, "Anyone wanting to be the greatest must be the least—the servant of all!"
[36]Then he placed a little child among them; and taking the child in his arms he said to them,
[37]"Anyone who welcomes a little child like this in my name is welcoming me, and anyone who welcomes me is welcoming my Father who sent me!" Mt 18:1; Lk 9:46.

Mk 10:35. Then James and John, the sons of Zebedee, came over and spoke to him in a low voice. "Master," they said, "we want you to do us a favor." [Mt 20:20]
[36]"What is it?" he asked.
[37]"We want to sit on the thrones next to yours in your kingdom," they said, "one at your right and the other at your left!"
[38]But Jesus answered, "You don't know what you are asking! Are you able to drink from the bitter cup of sorrow I must drink from? Or to be baptized with the baptism of suffering I must be baptized with?"
[39]"Oh, yes," they

said, "we are!" And Jesus said, "You shall indeed drink from my cup and be baptized with my baptism, [40]but I do not have the right to place you on thrones next to mine. Those appointments have already been made." [41]When the other disciples discovered what James and John had asked, they were very indignant. [42]So Jesus called them to him and said, "As you know, the kings and great men of the earth lord it over the people; [43]but among you it is different. Whoever wants to be great among you must be your servant. [44]And whoever wants to be greatest of all must be the slave of all. [Lk 22:26.] [45]For even I, the Messiah, am not here to be served, but to help others, and to give my life as a ransom for many."

Jn 5:44. No wonder you can't believe! For you gladly honor each other, but you don't care about the honor that comes from the only God!

Jas 4:1. What is causing the quarrels and fights among you? Isn't it because there is a whole army of evil desires within you? [2]You want what you don't have, so you kill to get it. You long for what others have, and can't afford it, so you start a fight to take it away from them. And yet the reason you don't have what you want is that you don't ask God for it. Jas 3:16.

1 Jn 2:16. For all these worldly things, these evil desires—the craze for sex, the ambition to buy everything that appeals to you, and the pride that comes from wealth and importance—these are not from God. They are from this evil world itself.

See *Pride.*

INSTANCES OF. Lucifer, Isa 14:12–15. Eve, Gen 3:5,6. The builders of Babel, Gen 11:3,4. Aaron and Miriam, Num 12:2–10. Korah and his co-conspirators, Num 16:3–35. Abimelech, Judg 9:1–6. Absalom, 2 Sam 15:1–13; 18:18. Ahithophel, 2 Sam 17:23. Adonijah, 1 Kgs 1:5. Sennacherib, 2 Kgs 19:21–23. Haman, Esther 5:9–13; 6:6–9. Mother of James and John, Mt 20:20,21. Diotrephes, 3 Jn 1:9, 10.

RIGHT. Deut 4:29. But you will also begin to search again for Jehovah your God, and you shall find him when you search for him with all your hearts and souls.

Ps 14:2. The Lord looks down from heaven on all mankind to see if there are any who are wise, who want to please God.

Prov 28:5. Evil men don't understand the importance of justice, but those who follow the Lord are much concerned about it.

Mt 16:24. Then Jesus said to the disciples, "If anyone wants to be a follower of mine, let him deny himself and take up his cross and follow me."

Lk 11:9. And so it is with prayer—keep on asking and you will keep on getting; keep on looking and you will keep on finding; knock and the door will be opened.

Lk 12:31. He will always give you all you need from day to day if you will make the Kingdom of God your primary concern. Chapter 13:24,25.

1 Cor 9:24. In a race, everyone runs but only one person gets first prize. So run your race to win. Phil 3:14.

1 Cor 14:12. Since you are so anxious to have special gifts from the Holy Spirit, ask him for the very best, for those that will be of real help to the whole church. Chapter 12:31.

1 Thess 4:11. This should be your ambition: to live a quiet life, minding your own business and doing your own work, just as we told you before.

1 Tim 3:1. It is a true saying that if a man wants to be a pastor he has a good ambition.

2 Tim 2:22. Run from anything that gives you the evil thoughts that young men often have, but stay close to anything that makes you want to do right. Have faith and love, and enjoy the companionship of those who love the Lord and have pure hearts.

AMBUSH INSTANCES OF. At Ai, Josh 8:2–22; Shechem, Judg 9:25,34; Gibe-ah, Judg 20:29–41; Gilead, Hos 6:9. Near Zemaraim, 2 Chron 13:13.

By Jehoshaphat, 2 Chron 20:22.

David's prayer for protection from, Ps 11:2; 59:3; 64:4; 140:5.

See *Armies.*

FIGURATIVE. Job 18:8,9; Ps 11:2; 59:3; 64:5; Jer 51:12.

AMEN A word used to reinforce a statement, Deut 27:12–26; Neh 5:13; Rev 22:20. Used in prayer and praise, 1 Kgs 1:36; 1 Chron 16:36; Neh 8:6; Ps 41:13; 72:19; 89:52; 106:48; Jer 28:6; Mt 6:13; Rev 5:14; 19:4. A title of Christ, Rev 3:14.

AMETHYST A precious stone, Ex 28:19; 39:12; Rev 21:19,20.

AMI See *Amon, 3.*

AMITTAI Father of Jonah, 2 Kgs 14:25; Jon 1:1.

AMMAH A hill, 2 Sam 2:24.

AMMI A figurative name given to Israel, Hos 2:1.

AMMIEL 1. One of the 12 spies, Num 13:3–15.

2. Father of Machir, 2 Sam 17:27.

3. Father of Bathsheba, 1 Chron 3:5. Called also *Eliam,* 2 Sam 11:3.

4. Son of Obed-edom, 1 Chron 26:5.

AMMIHUD 1. Son of Laadan, 1 Chron 7:25–27, and father of Elishama, Num 1:2–15; 2:3–31.

2. Father of Shemuel, Num 34:16–28.

3. Father of Pedahel, Num 34:16–28.

4. Father of the king of Geshur, 2 Sam 13:37–39.

5. Son of Omri, 1 Chron 9:4.

AMMINADAB 1. Father-in-law of Aaron, Ex 6:23. Father of Nahshon, Num 1:2–15; 2:3–31. Lineage of, Ruth 4:18–22; 1 Chron 2:10; Mt 1:4; Lk 3:33.

2. A son of Kohath, 1 Chron 6:22–24.

3. A son of Uzziel, 1 Chron 15:4–11.

AMMISHADDAI Father of Ahiezer, Num 1:2–15.

AMMIZABAD Son of Benaiah, 1 Chron 27:6.

AMMON See *Benammi.*

AMMONITES Descendants of Benammi, one of the sons of Lot, Gen 19:38. Character of, Judg 10:6; 2 Kgs 23:13; 2 Chron 20:25; Jer 27:3,9;

Ezk 25:3,6; Amos 1:13; Zeph 2:10. Territory of, Num 21:24; Deut 2:19; Josh 12:2; 13:10,25; Judg 11:13.

Israelites forbidden to disturb, Deut 2:19,37. Excluded from the congregation of Israel, Deut 23:3–6. Confederate with Moabites and Amalekites against Israel, Judg 3:12,13. Defeated by the Israelites, Judg 10:7–18; 11:32,33; 12:1–3; 1 Sam 11; 2 Sam 8:12; 10; 11:1; 12:26–31; 17:27; 1 Chron 18:11; 20:1–3; 2 Chron 20; 26:7,8; 27:5. Conspire against the Jews, Neh 4:7,8.

Solomon takes wives from, 1 Kgs 11:1; 2 Chron 12:13; Neh 13:26. Jews intermarry with, Ezra 9:12; 10:10–44; Neh 13:23.

Kings of: Baalis, Jer 40:14; Hanun, 2 Sam 10; 1 Chron 19; Nahash, 1 Sam 11; 2 Sam 10:1,2; 1 Chron 19:1.

Idols of: Milcom, 2 Kgs 23:13; Molech, see *Molech.* Prophecies concerning, Isa 11:14; Jer 9:25,26; 25:15–21; 27:1–11; 49:1–6; Ezk 21:19,20,28–32; 25:1–6; Dan 11:41; Amos 1:13–15; Zeph 2:8–11.

AMNESTY For political offenses: To Shime-i, 2 Sam 19:16–23; to Amasa, 2 Sam 19:13, with 17:25.

AMNON 1. Son of David, 2 Sam 3:2; 1 Chron 3:1. Incest of, and death, 2 Sam 13.

2. Son of Shimon, 1 Chron 4:20.

AMOK A priest, Neh 12:1–7, 12–21.

AMON 1. Governor of the city of Samaria, 1 Kgs 22:26; 2 Chron 18:25.

2. King of Judah, 2 Kgs 21:18–26; 2 Chron 33:20–25; Zeph 1:1; Mt 1:10.

3. Ancestor of one of the families of the Nethinim, Neh 7:57–59. Called *Ami,* Ezra 2:55–57.

4. An Egyptian god, Jer 46:25.

AMORITES Descendants of Canaan, Gen 10:15–19; 1 Chron 1:13–16. Were giants, Amos 2:9. Defeated by Ched-or-laomer and rescued by Abraham, Gen 14.

Territory of, Gen 14:7; Num 13:29; 21:13; Deut 1:1–5,7,19–21; 3:8,9; Josh 5:1; 10:1–5; 12:2,3; Judg 1:35,36; 11:21,22; given to descendants of Abraham, Gen 15:19–21; 48:22; Deut 1:19–21; 2:26–36; Josh 3:10; Judg 11:23; Amos 2:10; allotted to Reuben, Gad, and Manasseh, Num 32:33–42; Josh 13:15–21; conquest of, Num 21:21–30; Josh 10:11; Judg 1:34–36.

Chiefs of, Josh 13:21. Wickedness of, Gen 15:16; 2 Kgs 21:11; Ezra 9:1. Idolatry of, Judg 6:10; 1 Kgs 21:26. Judgments pronounced against, Ex 23:24; 33:2; 34:10,11; Deut 20:17,18. Hornets sent among, Josh 24:12. Not exterminated, Judg 1:34–36; 3:1–3,5–8; 1 Sam 7:14; 2 Sam 21:2; 1 Kgs 9:20,21; 2 Chron 8:7,8. Intermarry with Jews, Ezra 9:1,2; 10:16–44. Kings of, Josh 10:3–26.

AMOS A prophet, Amos 1:1,2. Forbidden to prophesy in Israel, Amos 7:10–17. Vision of, Amos 8:2.

AMOZ Father of Isaiah, 2 Kgs 19:2; Isa 1:1; 13:1.

AMPHIPOLIS A city of Macedonia, Acts 17:1.

AMPHITHEATER Acts 19:29.

AMPLIATUS A disciple, Paul sends greeting to, Rom 16:8.

AMRAM 1. Father of Moses, Ex 6:18,20; Num 26:58,59; 1 Chron 6:2,18; 23:12,13. Head of one of the branches of Levites, Num 3:25–30; 1 Chron 26:23,24. Age of, at death, Ex 6:20.

2. Son of Bani, Ezra 10:34–42.

AMRAPHEL King of Shinar, Gen 14:1,2.

AMUSEMENTS, WORLDLY Produce evil results, Gal 5:19,21; are transitory, Heb 11:24,25; useless, Eccl 2:11; choke the word of God in the heart, Lk 8:14; formed a part of idolatrous worship, Ex 32:4,6,19, with 1 Cor 10:7; Judg 16:23–26.

Lead to rejection of God, Job 21:12–15; poverty, Prov 21:17; disregard of the judgments and works of God, Isa 5:12; Amos 6:1–6; end in sorrow, Prov 14:13; lead to greater evil, Job 1:5; Mt. 14:6–8; the wicked seek for happiness in, Eccl 2:1,2,7,8.

Indulgence in, a proof of folly, Eccl 7:4; a characteristic of the wicked, Isa 47:8; Eph 4:17–19; 2 Tim 3:4; Tit 3:3; 1 Pet 4:3; a proof of spiritual death, 1 Tim 5:6; an abuse of riches, Jas 5:1,5; wisdom of abstaining from, Eccl 7:2,3; shunned by the primitive saints, 1 Pet 4:3.

Abstinence from, seems strange to the wicked, 1 Pet 4:4; denounced by God, Isa 5:11,12; exclude from the kingdom of God, Gal 5:21; punishment of, Eccl 11:9; 2 Pet 2:12,13; renunciation of, exemplified by Moses, Heb 11:24,25.

See *Dancing; Games; Pleasure, Worldly; Worldliness.*

AMZI 1. A Levite, 1 Chron 6:44–47.

2. A priest, Neh 11:10–14.

ANAB A city of Canaan, Josh 11:21; 15:48–62.

ANAH 1. Son of Seir, Gen 36:20,21,25; 1 Chron 1:38,39,41.

2. Son of Zibeon the Hivite, and father of Oholibamah, Gen 36:2,3,18,19.

3. Son of a different Zibeon, Gen 36:24. This Zibeon's brother was Anah, 1.

ANAHARATH City on the border of Issachar, Josh 19:17–23.

ANAIAH 1. A priest who stood by Ezra while reading the law, Neh 8:1–5.

2. One who signed the covenant with Nehemiah, Neh 10:14–27. Possibly the same as 1, above.

ANAK Father of three giants, Num 13:22; Josh 15:13,14; 21:9–16.

ANAKIM A race of giants, Num 13:28–33; Deut 1:28; 2:10; 9:1,2. Defeated: By Joshua, Josh 11:21,22; Caleb, Josh 14:12,15; 15:13,14; Judg 1:20.

See *Hebron, 1.*

ANAMIM A tribe descended from Mizraim, Gen 10:13,14; 1 Chron 1:11,12.

ANAMMELECH An Assyrian idol, 2 Kgs 17:31.

ANAN A Jew, returned from Babylonian captivity, Neh 10:14–27.

ANANI A descendant of David, 1 Chron 3:24.

ANANIAH 1. Son of Ma-aseiah, Neh 3:23.

2. Town of Benjamin, Neh 11:31–35.

ANANIAS 1. High priest, before whom Paul was tried, Acts 23:2–5; 24:1.

2. A covetous member of the church at Jerusalem. Falsehood and death of, Acts 5:1–11.

3. A Christian in Damascus, Acts 9:10–18; 22:12–16.

ANARCHY Isa 3:5. And the worst sort of anarchy will prevail—everyone stepping on someone else, neighbors fighting neighbors, youths revolting against authority, criminals sneering at honorable men. [6]In those days a man will say to his brother, "You have extra clothing, so you be our king and take care of this mess." [7]"No!" he will reply. "I cannot be of any help! I have no extra food or clothes. Don't get me involved!" [8]Israel's civil government will be in utter ruin because the Jews have spoken out against their Lord and will not worship him; they offend his glory.

Ezk 30:13. And I will smash the idols of Egypt and the images of Memphis, and there will be no king in Egypt; anarchy shall reign!

Gal 5:13. For, dear brothers, you have been given freedom: not freedom to do wrong, but freedom to love and serve each other. [14]For the whole Law can be summed up in this one command: "Love others as you love yourself."

2 Pet 2:10. He is especially hard on those who follow their own evil, lustful thoughts, and those who are proud and willful, daring even to scoff at the Glorious Ones without so much as trembling, [11]although the angels in heaven who stand in the very presence of the Lord, and are far greater in power and strength than these false teachers, never speak out disrespectfully against these evil Mighty Ones. [12]But false teachers are fools—no better than animals. They do whatever they feel like; born only to be caught and killed, they laugh at the terrifying powers of the underworld which they know so little about; and they will be destroyed along with all the demons and powers of hell. [13]That is the pay these teachers will have for their sin. For they live in evil pleasures day after day. They are a disgrace and a stain among you, deceiving you by living in foul sin on the side while they join your love feasts as though they were honest men. [14]No woman can escape their sinful stare, and of adultery they never have enough. They make a game of luring unstable women. They train themselves to be greedy; and are doomed and cursed. [15]They have gone off the road and become lost like Balaam, the son of Beor, who fell in love with the money he could make by doing wrong; [16]but Balaam was stopped from his mad course when his donkey spoke to him with a human voice, scolding and rebuking him. [17]These men are as useless as dried-up springs of water, promising much and delivering nothing; they are as unstable as clouds driven by the storm winds. They are doomed to the eternal pits of darkness. [18]They proudly boast about their sins and conquests, and, using lust as their bait, they lure back into sin those who have just escaped from such wicked living. [19]"You aren't saved by being good," they say, "so you might as well be bad. Do what you like, be free." But these very teachers who offer this "freedom" from law are themselves slaves to sin and destruction. For a man is a slave to whatever controls him.

Jude 1:8. Yet these false teachers carelessly go right on living their evil, immoral lives, degrading their bodies and laughing at those in authority over them, even scoffing at the Glorious Ones. [9]Yet Michael, one of the mightiest of the angels, when he was arguing with Satan about Moses' body, did not dare to accuse even Satan, or jeer at him, but simply said, "The Lord rebuke you." [10]But these men mock and curse at anything they do not understand, and, like animals, they do whatever they feel like, thereby ruining their souls. [11]Woe upon them! For they follow the example of Cain who killed his brother; and, like Balaam, they will do anything for money; and like Korah, they have disobeyed God and will die under his curse. [12]When these men join you at the love feasts of the church, they are evil smears among you, laughing and carrying on, gorging and stuffing themselves without a thought for others. They are like clouds blowing over dry land without giving rain, promising much, but producing nothing. They are like fruit trees without any fruit at picking time. They are not only dead, but doubly dead, for they have been pulled out, roots and all, to be burned. [13]All they leave behind them is shame and disgrace like the dirty foam left along the beach by the wild waves. They wander around looking as bright as stars, but ahead of them is the everlasting gloom and darkness that God has prepared for them.

Rev 6:4. This time a red horse rode out. Its rider was given a long sword and the authority to banish peace and bring anarchy to the earth; war and killing broke out everywhere.

ANATH Father of Shamgar, Judg 3:31.

ANATHOTH 1. A Levitical city in Benjamin, Josh 21:18; 1 Chron 6:60. Abiathar confined in, 1 Kgs 2:26. Birthplace of Jeremiah, Jer 1:1,2; 32:7–12; of Abi-ezer, 2 Sam 23:24–39; of Jehu, 1 Chron 12:3–7. Prophecies against, Jer 11:21–23. Population of, after Babylonian captivity, Ezra 2:3–35; Neh 7:27.

2. Son of Becher, 1 Chron 7:8.

3. A Jew, who returned from Babylon, Neh 10:14–27.

ANATOMY Human, Job 10:11.

ANCHOR Acts 27:29,30,40.

FIGURATIVE. Ps 119:61; Prov 10:25. Heb 6:19.

ANCIENT OF DAYS A name of Jehovah, Dan 7:9,13,22,26.

ANDREW An apostle. A fisherman, Mt 4:18. From Bethsaida, Jn 1:44. A disciple of John, Jn 1:35–40. Finds Peter, his brother, and brings him to Jesus, Jn 1:41–42. Call of, Mt 4:19–20; Mk 1:16, 17. His name appears in the list of the apostles in Mt 10:2–4; Mk 3:16–19; Lk 6:14–16. Asks the Master privately about the destruction of the temple, Mk 13:3,4. Tells Jesus of the Greeks who want to meet him, Jn 12:20–22. Reports the number of loaves and fish at the feeding of the 5,000, Jn 6:8. Meets with the disciples after the Lord's ascension, Acts 1:14.

ANDRONICUS A relative of Paul, Rom 16:7.

ANEM A Levitical city of Issachar, 1 Chron 6:73.

ANER 1. A Canaanite chief, Gen 14:13,24.

2. A Levitical city of Manasseh, 1 Chron 6:70.

ANGEL ONE OF THE HOLY TRINITY. Some authorities consider that certain Biblical references to angels are theophanies, or appearances of the pre-incarnate Christ. Though there is a lack of agreement among these authorities, several Old Testament passages (and New Testament references to Old Testament passages) appear to refer not merely to a messenger of God, but to an appearance of God, especially where it seems impossible to distinguish between the Angel of the Lord and the Lord himself, Gen 16:7–13; 48:16. Probable references include, but are not limited to: *Angel,* Acts 7:30,38; *Angel of God,* Gen 21:17; 22:11; 31:11; Ex 14:19; 2 Sam 14:17,20; *Angel of his Presence,* Isa 63:9; *Angel of Jehovah,* Ex 3:2; *Angel of the Lord,* Judg 2:1; 6:11,12; 13:6; *Commander-in-Chief of the Lord's army,* Josh 5:14.

A CELESTIAL BEING OR MESSENGER. Angels are created spiritual beings, some of whom have rebelled and are classified as fallen angels (see *Angel, Fallen,* below). Some passages refer to the Angel of the Lord, but are *not* appearances of one of the Holy Trinity (see above): Mt 2:19; Acts 5:19; 8:26; 12:7,23.

Created, Gen 2:1; Neh 9:6; Col 1:16. Of different orders, Isa 6:2; 1 Thess 4:16; 1 Pet 3:22; Jude 1:9; Rev 12:7. Immortal, Lk 20:36. Worship God, Neh 9:6; Phil 2:9–11; Heb 1:5,6. Not to be worshipped, Col 2:18; Rev 19:10; 22:8,9. Do not marry, Mt 22:30; Mk 12:25; Lk 20:35. Are obedient, Ps 103:20; Mt 6:10; 1 Pet 3:22; 2 Pet 2:11; Judg 1:6. Have knowledge of, and interest in, earthly affairs, Mt 24:36; Lk 15:7, 10; 1 Tim 5:21; 1 Pet 1:12. To be judged by men, 1 Cor 6:3. Called rulers, Eph 3:10; Col 1:16.

David called an, 2 Sam 19:27. Are examples of meekness, 2 Pet 2:11; Jude 1:9. Are mighty, Ps 103:20; 2 Pet 2:11; holy, Mk 8:38; 1 Tim 5:21; innumerable, Deut 33:2; Job 25:3; Heb 12:22; Jude 1:14.

Aspects of, Isa 6:2; Dan 10:5,6; Mt 28:3. See *Unclassified Scriptures Relating to,* below.

FUNCTIONS OF. Guard the entrance to the Tree of Life, Gen 3:24. Law given by, Acts 7:53; Gal 3:19; Heb 2:2. Vehicle of revelation to prophets, 2 Kgs 1:15; Dan 4:13–17; 8:17–19; 9:21–27; 10:10–21; Zech 1:9–11; Acts 8:26; Gal 3:19; Heb 2:2; Rev 1:1; 5:2–14; 7:1–3,11–17; 8:2–13; chapters 9 to 20; 22:6,7,16.

Remonstrates Balaam, Num 22:22–35. Announces the birth of John the Baptist, Lk 1:11–20; of Jesus, Mt 1:20,21; Lk 1:28–38; 2:7–15. Warns Joseph to escape to Egypt, Mt 2:13. Care for Jesus after the temptation, Mt 4:11; Mk 1:12,13; Jn 1:51; during his passion, Lk 22:43. Present at the tomb of Jesus, Mt 28:2–7; the ascension, Acts 1:10,11. Will be with Christ at his second coming, Mt 25:31; Mk 8:38; 2 Thess 1:7; Jude 1:14,15; at the judgment, Mt 13:39,41,49; 16:27; 24:31; 25:31; Mk 13:27.

Minister to the Righteous. Gen 24:7. He will send his angel on ahead of you. [Ex 33:2.] [40]For my Lord, in whose presence I have walked, will send his angel with you and make your mission successful.

Ex 23:20. See, I am sending an Angel before you to lead you safely to the land I have prepared for you. [23]For my Angel shall go before you and bring you into the land of the Amorites, Hittites, Perizzites, Canaanites, Hivites, and Jebusites, to live there. And I will destroy those people before you. Ex 33:2.

Num 20:16. But when we cried to the Lord he heard us and sent an Angel who brought us out of Egypt.

1 Kgs 19:5. Then he lay down and slept beneath the broom bush. But as he was sleeping, an angel touched him and told him to get up and eat! [6]He looked around and saw some bread baking on hot stones, and a jar of water! So he ate and drank and lay down again. [7]Then the angel of the Lord came again and touched him and said, "Get up and eat some more, for there is a long journey ahead of you." [8]So he got up and ate and drank, and the food gave him enough strength to travel forty days and forty nights to Mount Horeb, the mountain of God.

2 Chron 18:18. "Listen to what else the Lord has told me," Micaiah continued. "I saw him upon the throne surrounded by vast throngs of angels."

Ps 34:7. For the Angel of the Lord guards and rescues all who reverence him.

Ps 91:11. For he orders his angels to protect you wherever you go. [12]They will steady you with their hands to keep you from stumbling against the rocks on the trail. Mt 4:6; Lk 4:9–11.

Ps 104:4. The angels are his messengers—his servants of fire!

Eccl 5:6. In that case, your mouth is making you sin. Don't try to defend yourself by telling the messenger from God that it was all a mistake (to make a vow).

Dan 6:22. "My God has sent his angel," he said, "to shut the lions' mouths so that they can't touch me; for I am innocent before God, nor, sir, have I wronged you."

Dan 7:10. A river of fire flowed from before him. Millions of angels ministered to him and hundreds of millions of people stood before him, waiting to be judged. Then the court began its session and The Books were opened.

Lk 16:22. Finally the beggar died and was carried by the angels to be with Abraham in the place of the righteous dead.

Jn 1:51. You will even see heaven open and the angels of God coming back and forth to me, the Messiah.

Jn 5:4. For an angel of the Lord came from time to time and disturbed the water, and the first person to step down into it afterwards was healed.

Acts 5:19. But an angel of the Lord came at night, opened the gates of the jail and brought them out. Then he told them, [20]"Go over to the Temple and preach about this Life!"

Acts 10:3. While wide awake one afternoon he

had a vision—it was about three o'clock—and in this vision he saw an angel of God coming toward him. "Cornelius!" the angel said. [4]Cornelius stared at him in terror. "What do you want, sir?" he asked the angel. And the angel replied, "Your prayers and charities have not gone unnoticed by God! [5,6]Now send some men to Joppa to find a man named Simon Peter, who is staying with Simon, the tanner, down by the shore, and ask him to come and visit you."

Acts 12:7. When suddenly there was a light in the cell and an angel of the Lord stood beside Peter! The angel slapped him on the side to awaken him and said, "Quick! Get up!" And the chains fell off his wrists! [8]Then the angel told him, "Get dressed and put on your shoes." And he did. "Now put on your coat and follow me!" the angel ordered. [9]So Peter left the cell, following the angel. But all the time he thought it was a dream or vision, and didn't believe it was really happening. [10]They passed the first and second cell blocks and came to the iron gate to the street, and this opened to them of its own accord! So they passed through and walked along together for a block, and then the angel left him.

Heb 1:7. God speaks of his angels as messengers swift as the wind and as servants made of flaming fire; [14]No, for the angels are only spirit messengers sent out to help and care for those who are to receive his salvation.

Heb 13:2. Don't forget to be kind to strangers, for some who have done this have entertained angels without realizing it!

Execute Judgments on the Wicked. Gen 19:1. That evening the two angels came to the entrance of the city of Sodom, and Lot was sitting there as they arrived. When he saw them he stood up to meet them, and welcomed them. [13]"For we will destroy the city completely. The stench of the place has reached to heaven and God has sent us to destroy it." *vs.* 1–25.

2 Sam 24:16. But as the death angel was preparing to destroy Jerusalem, the Lord was sorry for what was happening and told him to stop. He was by the threshing floor of Araunah the Jebusite at the time. [17]When David saw the angel, he said to the Lord, "Look, I am the one who has sinned! What have these sheep done? Let your anger be only against me and my family." 1 Chron 21:15,16.

2 Kgs 19:35. That very night the angel of the Lord killed 185,000 Assyrian troops, and dead bodies were seen all across the landscape in the morning.

2 Chron 32:21. And the Lord sent an angel who destroyed the Assyrian army with all its officers and generals! Isa 37:36.

Ps 35:5. Blow them away like chaff in the wind —wind sent by the Angel of the Lord. [6]Make their path dark and slippery before them, with the Angel of the Lord pursuing them.

Ps 78:49. He loosed on them the fierceness of his anger, sending sorrow and trouble. He dispatched against them a band of destroying angels.

Mt 13:41. I will send my angels and they will separate out of the Kingdom every temptation and all who are evil, [42]and throw them into the furnace and burn them. There shall be weeping and gnashing of teeth. *vs.* 49,50.

Acts 12:23. Instantly, an angel of the Lord struck Herod with a sickness so that he was filled with maggots and died—because he accepted the people's worship instead of giving the glory to God.

Acts 27:23. For last night an angel of the God to whom I belong and whom I serve stood beside me, [24]and said, "Don't be afraid, Paul—for you will surely stand trial before Caesar! What's more, God has granted your request and will save the lives of all those sailing with you."

Jude 1:14. Enoch, who lived seven generations after Adam, knew about these men and said this about them: "See, the Lord is coming with millions of his holy ones. [15]He will bring the people of the world before him in judgment, to receive just punishment, and to prove the terrible things they have done in rebellion against God, revealing all they have said against him."

Rev 7:1. Then I saw four angels standing at the four corners of the earth, holding back the four winds from blowing, so that not a leaf rustled in the trees, and the ocean became as smooth as glass. [2]And I saw another angel coming from the east, carrying the Great Seal of the Living God. And he shouted out to those four angels who had been given power to injure earth and sea.

Rev 9:14. Saying to the sixth angel, "Release the four mighty demons held bound at the great River Euphrates." [15]They had been kept in readiness for that year and month and day and hour, and now they were turned loose to kill a third of all mankind.

Rev 15:1. And I saw in heaven another mighty pageant showing things to come: Seven angels were assigned to carry down to earth the seven last plagues—and then at last God's anger will be finished.

UNCLASSIFIED SCRIPTURES RELATING TO. Num 22:35. But the angel told him, "Go with the men, but say only what I tell you to say." So Balaam went on with them.

Deut 33:2. The Lord came to us at Mount Sinai, and dawned upon us from Mount Seir; he shone from Mount Paran, surrounded by ten thousands of holy angels, and with flaming fire at his right hand.

Job 4:15. As a spirit passed before my face—my hair stood up on end. [16]I felt the spirit's presence, but couldn't see it standing there. Then out of the dreadful silence came this voice: [17]"Is mere man more just than God? More pure than his creator? [18,19]If God cannot trust his own messengers (for even angels make mistakes), how much less men made of dust, who are crushed to death as easily as moths!"

Job 38:6,7. What supports its foundations, and who laid its cornerstone, as the morning stars sang together and all the angels shouted for joy?

Ps 103:20. Bless the Lord, you mighty angels of his who carry out his orders, listening for each of his commands. [21]Yes, bless the Lord, you armies of his angels who serve him constantly.

Ps 104:4 The angels are his messengers—his servants of fire! Heb 1:7.

Ps 148:2. Praise him, all his angels, all the armies of heaven.

Isa 6:2. Hovering about him were mighty, six-winged seraphs. With two of their wings they covered their faces; with two others they covered their feet, and with two they flew. [5]Then I said, "My doom is sealed, for I am a foul-mouthed sinner, a member of a sinful, foul-mouthed race; and I have looked upon the King, the Lord of heaven's armies." [6]Then one of the seraphs flew over to the altar and with a pair of tongs picked out a burning coal. [7]He touched my lips with it and said, "Now you are pronounced 'Not guilty' because this coal has touched your lips. Your sins are all forgiven."

Ezk 1:13. Going up and down among them were other forms that glowed like bright coals of fire or brilliant torches, and it was from these the lightning flashed. [14]The living beings darted to and fro, swift as lightning. [24]And as they flew, their wings roared like waves against the shore, or like the voice of God, or like the shouting of a mighty army. When they stopped they let down their wings. *vs.* 4–25; Ezk 10.

Dan 4:13. Then as I lay there dreaming, I saw one of God's angels coming down from heaven.

17. For this has been decreed by the Watchers, demanded by the Holy Ones. The purpose of this decree is that all the world may understand that the Most High dominates the kingdoms of the world, and gives them to anyone he wants to, even the lowliest of men!

Dan 8:13. Then I heard two of the holy angels talking to each other. One of them said, "How long will it be until the daily sacrifice is restored again? How long until the destruction of the Temple is avenged and God's people triumph?" [14]The other replied, "Twenty-three hundred days must first go by."

Dan 9:21. Gabriel, whom I had seen in the earlier vision, flew swiftly to me at the time of the evening sacrifice, [22]and said to me, "Daniel, I am here to help you understand God's plans. [23]The moment you began praying a command was given. I am here to tell you what it was, for God loves you very much. Listen, and try to understand the meaning of the vision that you saw!"

Zech 1:12. Upon hearing this, the Angel of the Lord prayed this prayer: "O Lord of Hosts, for seventy years your anger has raged against Jerusalem and the cities of Judah. How long will it be until you again show mercy to them?" [13]And the Lord answered the angel who stood beside me, speaking words of comfort and assurance. [14]Then the angel said, "Shout out this message from the Lord of Hosts: Don't you think I care about what has happened to Judah and Jerusalem? I am as jealous as a husband for his captive wife."

Zech 6:5. He replied, "These are the four heavenly spirits who stand before the Lord of all the earth; they are going out to do His work."

Mt 4:6. "Jump off," he said, "and prove you are the Son of God; for the Scriptures declare, 'God will send his angels to keep you from harm,' . . . they will prevent you from smashing on the rocks below." [11]Then Satan went away, and angels came and cared for Jesus. Mk 1:12,13.

Mt 13:41. I will send my angels and they will separate out of the Kingdom every temptation and all who are evil, [42]and throw them into the furnace and burn them. There shall be weeping and gnashing of teeth.

Mt 18:10. Beware that you don't look down upon a single one of these little children. For I tell you that in heaven their angels have constant access to my Father.

Mt 24:31. And I shall send forth my angels with the sound of a mighty trumpet blast, and they shall gather my chosen ones from the farthest ends of the earth and heaven. [36]But no one knows the date and hour when the end will be—not even the angels. No, nor even God's Son. Only the Father knows.

Mt 25:31. But when I, the Messiah, shall come in my glory, and all the angels with me, then I shall sit upon my throne of glory.

Mt 26:53. Don't you realize that I could ask my Father for thousands of angels to protect us, and he would send them instantly?

Lk 9:30. Then two men appeared and began talking with him—Moses and Elijah! [31]They were splendid in appearance, glorious to see; and they were speaking of his death at Jerusalem, to be carried out in accordance with God's plan. Mt 17:3; Mk 9:4.

Lk 12:8. And I assure you of this: I, the Messiah, will publicly honor you in the presence of God's angels if you publicly acknowledge me here on earth as your Friend. [9]But I will deny before the angels those who deny me here among men. Mk 8:38.

Lk 15:10. In the same way there is joy in the presence of the angels of God when one sinner repents. *v.* 7.

Jn 1:51. You will see greater proofs than this. [51]You will even see heaven open and the angels of God coming back and forth to me, the Messiah.

Acts 7:53. Yes, and you deliberately destroyed God's laws, though you received them from the hands of angels.

Acts 8:26. But as for Philip, an angel of the Lord said to him, "Go over to the road that runs from Jerusalem through the Gaza Desert, arriving around noon."

Gal 3:19. Well then, why were the laws given? They were added after the promise was given, to show men how guilty they are of breaking God's laws. But this system of law was to last only until the coming of Christ, the Child to whom God's promise was made. (And there is this further difference. God gave his laws to angels to give to Moses, who then gave them to the people; [20]but when God gave his promise to Abraham, he did it by himself alone, without angels or Moses as go-betweens.)

Eph 1:20. That raised Christ from the dead and seated him in the place of honor at God's right hand in heaven, [21]far, far above any other king or ruler or dictator or leader. Yes, his honor is far more glorious than that of anyone else either in this world or in the world to come.

Eph 3:10. And his reason? To show to all the rulers in heaven how perfectly wise he is when all of his family—Jews and Gentiles alike—are seen to be joined together in his church.

Col 1:16. Christ himself is the Creator who made everything in heaven and earth, the things we can see and the things we can't; the spirit world with its kings and kingdoms, its rulers and authorities; all were made by Christ for his own use and glory.

Col 2:10. *So you have everything when you have Christ,* and you are filled with God through your union with Christ. He is the highest Ruler, with authority over every other power.

2 Thess 1:7. And so I would say to you who are suffering, God will give you rest along with us when the Lord Jesus appears suddenly from heaven in flaming fire with his mighty angels.

1 Tim 3:16. It is quite true that the way to live a godly life is not an easy matter. But the answer lies in Christ, who came to earth as a man, was proved spotless and pure in his Spirit, was served by angels.

1 Tim 5:21. I solemnly command you in the presence of God and the Lord Jesus Christ and of the holy angels to do this whether the pastor is a special friend of yours or not. All must be treated exactly the same.

Heb 1:4. Thus he became far greater than the angels, as proved by the fact that his name, "Son of God," which was passed on to him by his Father, is far greater than the names and titles of the angels. [5]For God never said to any angel, "You are my Son, and today I have given you the honor that goes with that name." [13]And did God ever say to an angel, as he does to his Son, "Sit here beside me in honor until I crush all your enemies beneath your feet"?

Heb 2:2. For since the messages from angels have always proved true and people have always been punished for disobeying them.

7. For though you made Him lower than the angels for a little while, now you have crowned him with glory and honor. with *v.* 5. Ps 8:5.

16. We all know he did not come as an angel but as a human being—yes, a Jew.

Heb 12:22. But you have come right up into Mt. Zion, to the city of the Living God, the heavenly Jerusalem, and to the gathering of countless happy angels.

Heb 13:2. Don't forget to be kind to strangers, for some who have done this have entertained angels without realizing it!

1 Pet 1:12. They were finally told that these things would not occur during their lifetime, but long years later, during yours. And now at last this good news has been plainly announced to all of us. It was preached to us in the power of the same heaven-sent Holy Spirit who spoke to them; and it is all so strange and wonderful that even the angels in heaven would give a great deal to know more about it.

1 Pet 3:22. And now Christ is in heaven, sitting in the place of honor next to God the Father, with all the angels and powers of heaven bowing before him and obeying him.

2 Pet 2:11. Although the angels in heaven who stand in the very presence of the Lord, and are far greater in power and strength than these false teachers, never speak out disrespectfully against these evil Mighty Ones.

Rev 5:11. Then in my vision I heard the singing of millions of angels surrounding the throne and the Living Beings and the Elders.

Rev 10:1. Then I saw another mighty angel coming down from heaven, surrounded by a cloud, with a rainbow over his head; his face shone like the sun and his feet flashed with fire. [2]And he held open in his hand a small scroll. He set his right foot on the sea and his left foot on the earth, [3]and gave a great shout—it was like the roar of a lion—and the seven thunders crashed their reply. [4]I was about to write what the thunders said when a voice from heaven called to me, "Don't do it. Their words are not to be revealed." [5]Then the mighty angel standing on the sea and land lifted his right hand to heaven and [6]swore by him who lives forever and ever, who created heaven and everything in it and the earth and all that it contains and the sea and its inhabitants, that there should be no more delay.

Rev 14:10. And they will be tormented with fire and burning sulphur in the presence of the holy angels and the Lamb.

Rev 18:1. After all this I saw another angel come down from heaven with great authority, and the earth grew bright with his splendor. [2]He gave a mighty shout, "Babylon the Great is fallen, she has become a den of demons, a haunt of devils and every kind of evil spirit. [3]For all the nations have drunk the fatal wine of her intense immorality. The rulers of earth have enjoyed themselves with her, and businessmen throughout the world have grown rich from all her luxurious living."

Rev 19:10. Then I fell down at his feet to worship him, but he said, "No! Don't! For I am a servant of God just as you are, and as your brother Christians are, who testify of their faith in Jesus. The purpose of all prophecy and of all I have shown you is to tell about Jesus."

Rev 22:8. I, John, saw and heard all these things, and fell down to worship the angel who showed them to me; [9]but again he said, "No, don't do anything like that. I, too, am a servant of Jesus as you are, and as your brothers the prophets are, as well as all those who heed the truth stated in this Book. Worship God alone."

APPEARANCES OF. To Abraham, Gen 18:2;

Lot, in Sodom, Gen 19:1–17; Jacob, in his various visions, Gen 28:12; Moses, Ex 3:2; Balaam, Num 22:31; David, at the threshing floor of Araunah, 2 Sam 24:16,17; 1 Chron 21:15,16; Elijah, while he slept beneath the broom bush, 1 Kgs 19:5–11; Daniel, in the lion's den, Dan 6:22; 8:16; 9:21; 10:5–10, 16, 18; 12:5–7; Shadrach, Meshach, and Abednego, in the fiery furnace, Dan 3:25,28; Zechariah, in a vision, Zech 2:3; 3:1,2; 4:1; Joseph, in a dream, Mt 1:20; 2:13,19. At the transfiguration of Jesus, Mt 17:3; Lk 9:30,31. To Mary, concerning Jesus, Lk 1:26–38; Zacharias, Lk 1:11–20, 26–38; the shepherds, Lk 2:9–11, 13,14; Jesus after his temptation, Mt 4:11; in Gethsemane, Lk 22:43. At the tomb, Mt 28:2–7; Mk 16:5–7; Lk 24:22,23; Jn 20:12; the ascension, Acts 1:10,11. To Peter and John, while in prison, Acts 5:19; Philip, Acts 8:26; Cornelius, in a dream, Acts 10:3, 30–32; Peter, in prison, Acts 12:7–11; Paul, on the way to Rome, Acts 27:23; John, in Patmos, Rev 1:1; 5:2; 7:11; 10:1; 9; 17:7; 19:10; 22:8.

See *Cherubim.*

FALLEN. Job 4:18,19; Isa 14:12–17; Ezk 28:12–19; Mt 25:41; 2 Pet 2:4; Jude 1:6; cf. Gen 6:1–4; Rev 12:7–9.

OF THE CHURCHES. Rev 1:20; 2:1,8,12,18; 3:1, 7,14.

ANGER Gen 4:6. "Why are you angry?" the Lord asked him. "Why is your face so dark with rage?"

Gen 49:7. Cursed be their anger, for it is fierce and cruel. Therefore, I will scatter their descendants throughout Israel.

2 Chron 28:9. But Oded, a prophet of the Lord, was there in Samaria and he went out to meet the returning army. "Look!" he exclaimed. "The Lord God of your fathers was angry with Judah and let you capture them, but you have butchered them without mercy, and all heaven is disturbed."

Job 5:2. They die in helpless frustration, overcome by their own anger.

Ps 37:8. Stop your anger! Turn off your wrath. Don't fret and worry—it only leads to harm.

Ps 55:3. My enemies shout against me and threaten me with death. They surround me with terror and plot to kill me. Their fury and hatred rise to engulf me.

Ps 76:10. Man's futile wrath will bring you glory. You will use it as an ornament!

Prov 6:34. For the woman's husband will be furious in his jealousy, and he will have no mercy on you in his day of vengeance.

Prov 12:16. A fool is quick-tempered; a wise man stays cool when insulted.

Prov 14:17. A short-tempered man is a fool. He hates the man who is patient. [29]A wise man controls his temper. He knows that anger causes mistakes.

Prov 15:1. A soft answer turns away wrath, but harsh words cause quarrels. [18]A quick-tempered man starts fights; a cool-tempered man tries to stop them.

Prov 16:14. The anger of the king is a messenger of death and a wise man will appease it. [32]It is better to be slow-tempered than famous; it is better to have self-control than to control an army.

Prov 17:14. It is hard to stop a quarrel once it starts, so don't let it begin.

Prov 19:11. A wise man restrains his anger and overlooks insults. This is to his credit. [12]The king's anger is as dangerous as a lion's. But his approval is as refreshing as the dew on grass. [19]A short-tempered man must bear his own penalty; you can't do much to help him. If you try once you must try a dozen times!

Prov 22:24,25. Keep away from angry, short-tempered men, lest you learn to be like them and endanger your soul.

Prov 25:28. A man without self-control is as defenseless as a city with broken-down walls.

Prov 27:3. A rebel's frustrations are heavier than sand and rocks. Jealousy is more dangerous and cruel than anger.

Prov 29:8. Fools start fights everywhere while wise men try to keep peace. [9]There's no use arguing with a fool. He only rages and scoffs, and tempers flare. [22]A hot-tempered man starts fights and gets into all kinds of trouble.

Prov 30:33. As the churning of cream yields butter, and a blow to the nose causes bleeding, so anger causes quarrels.

Eccl 7:9. Don't be quick-tempered—that is being a fool!

Hos 7:16. Their leaders will perish by the sword of the enemy for their insolence to me.

Amos 1:11. The Lord says, "Edom has sinned again and again, and I will not forget it. I will not leave him unpunished any more. For he chased his brother, Israel, with the sword; he was pitiless in unrelenting anger."

Jon 4:4. Then the Lord said, "Is it right to be *angry* about *this*?"

Mt 5:22. But I have added to that rule, and tell you that if you are only *angry,* even in your own home, you are in danger of judgment! If you call your friend an idiot, you are in danger of being brought before the court. And if you curse him, you are in danger of the fires of hell.

2 Cor 12:20. For I am afraid that when I come to visit you I won't like what I find, and then you won't like the way I will have to act. I am afraid that I will find you quarreling, and envying each other, and being angry with each other, and acting big, and saying wicked things about each other and whispering behind each other's backs, filled with conceit and disunity.

Gal 5:19. But when you follow your own wrong inclinations your lives will produce these evil results: . . . [20]idolatry, spiritism (that is, encouraging the activity of demons), hatred and fighting, jealousy and anger, constant effort to get the best for yourself, complaints and criticisms, the feeling that everyone else is wrong except those in your own little group—and there will be wrong doctrine, [21]envy, murder, drunkenness, wild parties, and all that sort of thing. Let me tell you again as I have before, that anyone living that sort of life will not inherit the kingdom of God.

Eph 4:26. If you are angry, don't sin by nursing your grudge. Don't let the sun go down while you are still angry—get over it quickly. [31]Stop being mean, bad-tempered and angry. Quarreling, harsh words, and dislike of others should have no place in your lives.

Col 3:8. But now is the time to cast off and throw away all these rotten garments of anger, hatred, cursing, and dirty language.

1 Tim 2:8. So I want men everywhere to pray with holy hands lifted up to God, free from sin and anger and resentment.

Tit 1:7. These pastors must be men of blameless lives because they are God's ministers. They must not be proud or impatient; they must not be drunkards or fighters or greedy for money.

Jas 1:19. Dear brothers, don't ever forget that it is best to listen much, speak little, and not become angry; [20]for anger doesn't make us good, as God demands that we must be.

See *Hatred; Jealousy; Malice; Speaking, Evil; Strife; Kindness; Meekness; Patience.*

INSTANCES OF. Of Cain killing Abel, Gen 4:5–8; Simeon and Levi on account of the rape of their sister, Dinah, Gen 49:5–7; Pharaoh, toward Moses, Ex 10:11,28; Moses, toward Israel, Ex 32:19; Num 20:10,11; Balaam, toward his donkey, Num 22:27,29; Balak, toward Balaam, Num 24:10,11; Ephraimites, toward Gideon, for not soliciting their help against the Midianites, Judg 8:1; Jonathan, on account of Saul's persecution of David, 1 Sam 20:34; Saul, toward Jonathan, 1 Sam 20:30–34; Ahab, because Naboth would not sell his vineyard, 1 Kgs 21:4; Naaman, because Elisha directed him to wash in the Jordan, 2 Kgs 5:12; Asa, because the prophet reproved him, 2 Chron 16:10; Ephraimites, toward Judah, 2 Chron 25:10; Uzziah, toward Azariah, the priest, because of his reproof of, 2 Chron 26:19; Ahasuerus, toward Vashti, Esther 1:12; Haman, because Mordecai did not bow to him, Esther 3:5; Ahasuerus, toward Haman, Esther 7:7,8; Elihu, because Job had beaten his friends in argument, Job 32:3; Moab, Isa 16:6; Nebuchadnezzar, on account of the insubordination of the three Hebrews, who refused to worship his statue, Dan 3:13,19; Jonah, because the plant died, Jon 4:1,2,4,9; Herod, toward the astrologers who disobeyed him, Mt 2:16; people of Nazareth, toward Jesus, Lk 4:28; Paul, toward Ananias, Acts 23:3; Jews, against Stephen, Acts 7:54–58.

OF GOD. Ex 22:24. And my anger shall flame out against you, and I will kill you with enemy armies, so that your wives will be widows and your children fatherless.

Ex 33:5. For the Lord had told Moses to tell them, "You are an unruly, stubborn people. If I were there among you for even a moment, I would exterminate you. Remove your jewelry and ornaments until I decide what to do with you."

Num 11:1. The people were soon complaining about all their misfortunes, and the Lord heard them. His anger flared out against them because of their complaints, so the fire of the Lord began destroying those at the far end of the camp. [10]Moses heard all the families standing around their tent doors weeping, and the anger of the Lord grew hot; Moses too was highly displeased. [33]But as everyone began eating the meat, the anger of the Lord rose against the people and he killed large numbers of them with a plague.

Num 12:9. The anger of the Lord grew hot against them, and he departed.

Num 14:11. The Lord said to Moses, "How long will these people despise me? Will they *never* believe me, even after all the miracles I have done among them?"

Num 16:20. And Jehovah said to Moses and Aaron, [21]"Get away from these people so that I may instantly destroy them." *v.* 45.

Num 25:3. Before long all Israel was joining freely in the worship of Baal, the god of Moab; and the anger of the Lord was hot against his people. [4]He issued the following command to Moses: "Execute all the tribal leaders of Israel. Hang them up before the Lord in broad daylight, so that his fierce anger will turn away from the people. [11]Phineas (son of Eleazar and grandson of Aaron the priest) has turned away my anger, for he was as angry as I, concerning my honor; so I have stopped destroying all Israel as I had intended."

Num 32:10, 11. And the Lord's anger was hot against them, and he swore that of all those he had rescued from Egypt, no one over twenty years of age would ever see the land he promised Abraham, Isaac, and Jacob, for they had refused to do what he wanted them to. [13]The Lord made us wander back and forth in the wilderness for forty years until all that evil generation died.

Deut 6:14. You must not worship the gods of the neighboring nations, [15]for Jehovah your God who lives among you is a jealous God, and his anger may rise quickly against you, and wipe you off the face of the earth.

Deut 9:13,14. "Let me alone that I may destroy this evil, stubborn people!" the Lord told me, "and I will blot out their name from under heaven, and I will make a mighty nation of you, mightier than and greater than they are." [Ex 32:10.] [18]Then, for another forty days and nights I lay before the Lord, neither eating bread nor drinking water, for you had done what the Lord hated most, thus provoking him to great anger. [19]How I feared for you—for the Lord was ready to destroy you. But that time, too, he listened to me. [20]Aaron was in great danger because the Lord was so angry with him; but I prayed, and the Lord spared him.

Deut 32:21. They have made me very jealous of their idols, which are not gods at all. Now I, in turn, will make them jealous by giving my affections to the foolish Gentile nations of the world. [22]For my anger has kindled a fire that burns to the depths of the underworld, consuming the earth and all of its crops, and setting its mountains on fire.

Josh 7:1. But there was sin among the Israelis.

God's command to destroy everything except that which was reserved for the Lord's treasury was disobeyed. For Achan (the son of Carmi, grandson of Zabdi, and great-grandson of Zerah, of the tribe of Judah) took some loot for himself, and the Lord was very angry with the entire nation of Israel because of this. [26]And so the fierce anger of the Lord was ended.

Josh 23:15. But as certainly as the Lord has given you the good things he promised, just as certainly he will bring evil upon you if you disobey him. [16]For if you worship other gods he will completely wipe you out from this good land which the Lord has given you. His anger will rise hot against you, and you will quickly perish.

Judg 2:12–14. They abandoned Jehovah, the God loved and worshiped by their ancestors—the God who had brought them out of Egypt. Instead they were worshiping and bowing low before the idols of the neighboring nations. So the anger of the Lord flamed out against all Israel. He left them to the mercy of their enemies, for they had departed from Jehovah and were worshiping Baal and the Ashtaroth idols.

Judg 3:8. Then the anger of the Lord flamed out against Israel, and he let King Cushan-rishathaim of eastern Syria conquer them. Judg 10:7.

1 Sam 28:18. All this has come upon you because you did not obey the Lord's instructions when he was so angry with Amalek.

2 Sam 6:7. Then the anger of the Lord flared out against Uzzah and he killed him for doing this, so he died there beside the Ark.

2 Sam 22:8. Then the earth shook and trembled; the foundations of the heavens quaked because of his wrath. [9]Smoke poured from his nostrils; fire leaped from his mouth and burned up all before him, setting the world on fire.

1 Kgs 11:9,10. Jehovah was very angry with Solomon about this, for now Solomon was no longer interested in the Lord God of Israel who had appeared to him twice to warn him specifically against worshiping other gods. But he hadn't listened.

1 Kgs 16:7. This message was sent to Baasha and his family because he had angered the Lord by all his evil deeds. *vs.* 2–13.

2 Kgs 13:3. So the Lord was very angry with Israel, and he continually allowed King Hazael of Syria and his son Ben-hadad to conquer them.

2 Kgs 17:17. So the Lord was very angry. [18]He swept them from his sight until only the tribe of Judah remained in the land.

2 Kgs 22:13. What shall we do? For we have not been following the instructions of this book: you must be very angry with us, for neither we nor our ancestors have followed your commands.

2 Kgs 23:26. But the Lord still did not hold back his great anger against Judah, caused by the evils of King Manasseh.

Ps 7:11. God is a judge who is perfectly fair, and he is angry with the wicked every day.

Ps 69:24. Pour out your fury upon them; consume them with the fierceness of your anger.

Ps 74:1. O God, why have you cast us away forever? Why is your anger hot against us—the sheep of your own pasture?

Ps 76:7. No wonder you are greatly feared! Who can stand before an angry God?

Ps 78:21. Jehovah heard them and was angry; the fire of his wrath burned against Israel. [38]Yet he was merciful and forgave their sins and didn't destroy them all. Many and many a time he held back his anger. [49]He loosed on them the fierceness of his anger, sending sorrow and trouble. He dispatched against them a band of destroying angels. [50]He gave free course to his anger and did not spare the Egyptians' lives, but handed them over to plagues and sickness.

Ps 85:3. So that all your wrath, your blazing anger, is now ended.

Ps 90:11. Who can realize the terrors of your anger? Which of us can fear you as he should?

Ps 103:8. He is merciful and tender toward those who don't deserve it; he is slow to get angry and full of kindness and love. [9]He never bears a grudge, nor remains angry forever.

Ps 106:23. So the Lord declared he would destroy them. But Moses, his chosen one, stepped into the breach between the people and their God and begged him to turn from his wrath, and not destroy them. [29]With all these things they angered him—and so a plague broke out among them. [32]At Meribah, too, Israel angered God, causing Moses serious trouble.

Ps 110:5. God stands beside you to protect you. He will strike down many kings in the day of his anger.

Isa 5:25. That is why the anger of the Lord is hot against his people; that is why he has reached out his hand to smash them. The hills will tremble, and the rotting bodies of his people will be thrown as refuse in the streets. But even so, his anger is not ended; his hand is heavy on them still. Isa 9:17, 19-21.

Isa 12:1. On that day you will say, "Praise the Lord! He was angry with me, but now he comforts me."

Isa 13:9. For see, the day of the Lord is coming, the terrible day of his wrath and fierce anger. The land shall be destroyed and all the sinners with it. [13]For I will shake the heavens in my wrath and fierce anger, and the earth will move from its place in the skies.

Isa 30:27. See, the Lord comes from afar, aflame with wrath, surrounded by thick rising smoke. His lips are filled with fury; his words consume like fire.

Isa 42:25. That is why God poured out such fury and wrath on his people and destroyed them in battle. Yet though set on fire and burned, they will not understand the reason why—that it is God, wanting them to repent.

Isa 48:9. Yet for my own sake and for the honor of my name I will hold back my anger and not wipe you out.

Isa 57:16. For I will not fight against you forever,

nor always show my wrath; if I did, mankind would perish—the very souls that I have made. [17]I was angry and smote these greedy men. But they went right on sinning, doing everything their evil hearts desired.

Isa 63:3. I have trodden the winepress alone. No one was there to help me. In my wrath I have trodden my enemies like grapes. In my fury I trampled my foes. It is their blood you see upon my clothes. [4]For the time has come for me to avenge my people, to redeem them from the hands of their oppressors. [5]I looked but no one came to help them; I was amazed and appalled. So I executed vengeance alone; unaided, I meted out judgment. [6]I crushed the heathen nations in my anger and made them stagger and fall to the ground.

Isa 66:15. For see, the Lord will come with fire and with swift chariots of doom to pour out the fury of his anger and his hot rebuke with flames of fire.

Jer 3:12. Therefore go and say to Israel, O Israel, my sinful people, come home to me again, for I am merciful; I will not be forever angry with you.

Jer 4:4. Cleanse your minds and hearts, not just your bodies, or else my anger will burn you to a crisp because of all your sins. And no one will be able to put the fire out. [8]Put on clothes of mourning and weep with broken hearts, for the fierce anger of the Lord has not stopped yet.

Jer 7:20. So the Lord God says, I will pour out my anger, yes, my fury on this place—people, animals, trees and plants will be consumed by the unquenchable fire of my anger.

Jer 10:10. But the Lord is the only true God, the living God, the everlasting King. The whole earth shall tremble at his anger; the world shall hide before his displeasure.

Jer 17:4. And the wonderful heritage I reserved for you will slip out of your hand, and I will send you away as slaves to your enemies in distant lands. For you have kindled a fire of my anger that shall burn forever.

Jer 21:5. And I myself will fight against you, for I am very angry. [6]And I will send a terrible plague on this city, both men and animals shall die.

Jer 23:20. The terrible anger of the Lord will not abate until it has carried out the full penalty he decrees against them. Later, when Jerusalem has fallen, you will see what I mean. Jer 30:24.

Jer 25:15. For the Lord God said to me, "Take from my hand this wine cup filled to the brim with my fury, and make all the nations to whom I send you drink from it. [16]They shall drink from it and reel, crazed by the death blows I rain upon them." [17]So I took the cup of fury from the Lord and made all the nations drink from it—every nation God had sent me to. [3]People now living undisturbed will be cut down by the fierceness of the anger of the Lord. [38]He has left his lair like a lion seeking prey; their land has been laid waste by warring armies—because of the fierce anger of the Lord.

Jer 32:37. But I will bring my people back again from all the countries where in my fury I will scatter them. I will bring them back to this very city, and make them live in peace and safety.

Jer 33:5. Yet the Babylonians will enter, and the men of this city are already as good as dead, for I have determined to destroy them in my furious anger. I have abandoned them because of all their wickedness, and I will not pity them when they cry for help.

Jer 36:7. Perhaps even yet they will turn from their evil ways and ask the Lord to forgive them before it is too late, even though these curses of God have been pronounced upon them.

Jer 42:18. For the Lord of Hosts, the God of Israel, says: Just as my anger and fury were poured out upon the people of Jerusalem, so it will be poured out on you when you enter Egypt. You will be received with disgust and with hatred—you will be cursed and reviled. And you will never again see your own land.

Jer 44:6. And so my fury and anger boiled forth and fell as fire upon the cities of Judah and into the streets of Jerusalem, and there is desolation until this day.

Jer 51:45. O my people, flee from Babylon; save yourselves from the fierce anger of the Lord.

Lam 2:1. A cloud of anger from the Lord has overcast Jerusalem; the fairest city of Israel lies in the dust of the earth, cast from the heights of heaven at his command. In his day of awesome fury he has shown no mercy even to his Temple. [3]All the strength of Israel vanishes beneath his wrath. He has withdrawn his protection as the enemy attacks. God burns across the land of Israel like a raging fire. [6]He has violently broken down his Temple as though it were a booth of leaves and branches in a garden! No longer can the people celebrate their holy feasts and Sabbaths. Kings and priests together fall before his wrath.

Lam 4:11. But now at last the anger of the Lord is satisfied; his fiercest anger has been poured out. He started a fire in Jerusalem that burned it down to its foundations.

Ezk 5:13. Then at last my anger will be appeased. And all Israel will know that what I threaten, I do. [15]You will become a laughingstock to the world and an awesome example to everyone for all to see what happens when the Lord turns against an entire nation in furious rebuke. I, the Lord, have spoken it!

Ezk 25:14. By the hand of my people Israel, this shall be done. They will carry out my furious vengeance. [15]And the Lord God says: Because the Philistines have acted against Judah out of revenge and long-standing hatred, [16]I will shake my fist over the land of the Philistines, and I will wipe out the Cherithites and utterly destroy those along the sea coast. [17]I will execute terrible vengeance upon them to rebuke them for what they have done. And when all this happens, then they shall know I am the Lord.

Dan 9:16. Yet because of all your faithful mercies, Lord, please turn away your furious anger from Jerusalem, your own city, your holy mountain. For the heathen mock at you because your city lies in ruins for our sins.

Hos 11:9. No, I will not punish you as much as my fierce anger tells me to. This is the last time I will destroy Ephraim. For I am God and not man; I am the Holy One living among you, and I did not come to destroy.

Hos 13:11. I gave you kings in my anger, and I took them away in my wrath.

Hos 14:4. Then I will cure you of idolatry and faithlessness, and my love will know no bounds, for my anger will be forever gone!

Nah 1:2. God is jealous over those he loves; that is why he takes vengeance on those who hurt them. He furiously destroys their enemies. [3]He is slow in getting angry, but when aroused, his power is incredible, and he does not easily forgive. He shows his power in the terrors of the cyclone and the raging storms; clouds are billowing dust beneath his feet! [6]Who can stand before an angry God? His fury is like fire; the mountains tumble down before his anger.

Mt 22:7. Then the angry king sent out his army and destroyed the murderers and burned their city. [13]Then the king said to his aides, "Bind him hand and foot and throw him out into the outer darkness where there is weeping and gnashing of teeth."

Rom 1:18. But God shows his anger from heaven against all sinful, evil men who push away the truth from them.

Rom 2:5. But no, you won't listen; and so you are saving up terrible punishment for yourselves because of your stubbornness in refusing to turn from your sin; for there is going to come a day of wrath when God will be the just Judge of all the world.

Eph 5:6. Don't be fooled by those who try to excuse these sins, for the terrible wrath of God is upon all those who do them.

Col 3:6. God's terrible anger is upon those who do such things. *v.* 5.

Heb 3:11. Then God, full of this anger against them, bound himself with an oath that he would never let them come to his place of rest. Heb 4:3.

Rev 6:16. And cried to the mountains to crush them. "Fall on us," they pleaded, "and hide us from the face of the one sitting on the throne, and from the anger of the Lamb, [17]because the great day of their anger has come, and who can survive it?"

Rev 14:10. Must drink the wine of the anger of God; it is poured out undiluted into God's cup of wrath. And they will be tormented with fire and burning sulphur in the presence of the holy angels and the Lamb. [11]The smoke of their torture rises forever and ever, and they will have no relief day or night, for they have worshiped the Creature and his statue, and have been tattooed with the code of his name.

Rev 15:1. And I saw in heaven another mighty pageant showing things to come: Seven angels were assigned to carry down to earth the seven last plagues—and then at last God's anger will be finished. [7]And one of the four Living Beings handed each of them a golden flask filled with the terrible wrath of the Living God who lives forever and forever.

Rev 16:19. The great city of "Babylon" split into three sections, and cities around the world fell in heaps of rubble; and so all of "Babylon's" sins were remembered in God's thoughts, and she was punished to the last drop of anger in the cup of the wine of the fierceness of his wrath.

Rev 19:15. In his mouth he held a sharp sword to strike down the nations; he ruled them with an iron grip; and he trod the winepress of the fierceness of the wrath of Almighty God.

ANIAM Son of Shemida, 1 Chron 7:19.

ANIM A city of Judah, Josh 15:48–62.

ANIMALS Creation of, Gen 1:24,25; 2:19,20; Jer 27:5. Food of, Gen 1:30. Named, Gen 2:19,20. Ordained as food for man, Gen 9:2,3; Lev 11:2,3,9, 21,22; Deut 14:3–6,9,11–18. God's care of, Gen 9: 9-11; Deut 25:4; Job 38:41; Ps 36:6; 104:11,12,21; 147: 9; Jon 4:11; Mt 6:26; 10:29; Lk 12:6,24; 1 Cor 9:9. Under the curse, Gen 6:7,17. Suffer under God's judgments, Jer 7:20; 12:4; 21:6; Ezk 14:13,17,19–21; Joel 1:18–20. Two of every kind preserved in the ark, Gen 6:19,20; 7:2,3,5,8,9,14,15; 8:18,19. Suffered the plagues of Egypt, Ex 8:17; 9:9,10,19; 11:5. Perish at death, Eccl 3:21; 12:7. Possessed by demons, Mt 8:31,32; Mk 5:13; Lk 8:33. Clean and unclean, Gen 8:20; Lev 7:21; 11; 20:25; Deut 14:3–20; Acts 10:11–15; 1 Tim 4:3–5. Offered in sacrifice, Gen 4:4; 7:2–9; 8: 20. See *Offerings.*

God's control of, Ps 91:13; Isa 11:6–8; 35:9; Lk 10: 19. Instruments of God's will, Ex chapters 8, 9 and 10:1–20; Num 21:6; 22:28; Josh 24:12; Jer 8:17; Joel 1:4. Belong to God, Ps 50:10–12. Sent in judgment, Lev 26:22; Num 21:6,7; Deut 8:15; 28:26; Ezk 5:17; 14:15; 32:4; Rev 6:8. Paul contends with, 1 Cor 15: 32. Nature of, Job 39; Ps 32:9; 49:12; Eccl 3:18–21. Habits of, Job 12:7,8; 37:8; 39; 40:20; Ps 29:9; 104: 20–25; Isa 13:21,22; 34:14; Jas 3:7. Menstruation of, Jer 2:24. Facts about breeding, Gen 30:35–43; 31:8, 9. Instincts of, Deut 32:11; Job 35:11; 39; 40; 41; Ps 59:6; 104; Prov 6:6–8; 30:24–28; Jer 2:24; 8:7; Mt 24: 28. Homes of, Job 24:5; 37:8; 39; Ps 104:20–25; Isa 34:14; 50:39; Mk 1:12,13.

See *Birds; Cattle; Fish.*

BEASTS, SYMBOLICAL. Isa 30:6; Dan 7:3–7,11,- 17,19; 8:3,4; Acts 10:12; Rev 4:6–9; 5:6–14; 6:1–8; 7: 11; 13; 14:3,9,11; 15:2; 16:2,10–13; 17; 19:4,19,20; 20:4, 10.

CRUELTY TO. Instances of: Balaam, Num 22: 22–33. Hamstringing horses, 2 Sam 8:4; 1 Chron 18: 4.

See *Laming.*

KINDNESS TO.

Instances of. Jacob, in building pens for his flocks and herds, Gen 33:17. People of Gerar, in providing tents for cattle, 2 Chron 14:15.

LAWS CONCERNING. Ex 20:10. But the seventh day is the day of Sabbath rest before the Lord your God. On that day you are to do no work of any kind, nor shall your son, daughter, or slaves—

whether men or women—or your cattle or your house guests. Deut 5:14.

Ex 21:28. If an ox gores a man or woman to death, the ox shall be stoned and its flesh not eaten, but the owner shall not be held—[29]unless the ox was known to gore people in the past, and the owner had been notified and still the ox was not kept under control; in that case, if it kills someone, the ox shall be stoned and the owner also shall be killed. [30]But the dead man's relatives may accept a fine instead, if they wish. The judges will determine the amount. [31]The same law holds if the ox gores a boy or a girl. [32]But if the ox gores a slave, whether male or female, the slave's master shall be given thirty pieces of silver, and the ox shall be stoned. [33]If a man digs a well and doesn't cover it, and an ox or a donkey falls into it, [34]the owner of the well shall pay full damages to the owner of the animal, and the dead animal shall belong to him. [35]If a man's ox injures another, and it dies, then the two owners shall sell the live ox and divide the price between them—and each shall also own half of the dead ox. [36]But if the ox was known from past experience to gore, and its owner has not kept it under control, then there will not be a division of the income; but the owner of the living ox shall pay in full for the dead ox, and the dead one shall be his.

Ex 22:1. If a man steals an ox or sheep and then kills or sells it, he shall pay a fine of five to one—five oxen shall be returned for each stolen ox. For sheep, the fine shall be four to one—four sheep returned for one sheep stolen. [2]If a thief is caught in the act of breaking into a house and is killed, the one who killed him is not guilty. [3]But if it happens in the daylight, it must be presumed to be murder and the man who kills him is guilty. If a thief is captured, he must make full restitution; if he can't, then he must be sold as a slave for his debt. [4]If he is caught in the act of stealing a live ox or donkey or sheep or whatever it is, he shall pay double values as his fine.

19. Anyone having sexual relations with an animal shall certainly be executed.

Ex 23:5. If you see your enemy trying to get his donkey onto its feet beneath a heavy load, you must not go on by, but must help him. Deut 22:4.

12. Work six days only, and rest the seventh; this is to give your oxen and donkeys a rest, as well as the people of your household, your slaves and visitors.

Lev 19:19. Obey my laws: Do not mate your cattle with a different kind.

Deut 22:6. If a bird's nest is lying on the ground, or if you spy one in a tree, and there are young ones or eggs in it with the mother sitting in the nest, don't take the mother with the young. [7]Let her go, and take only the young. The Lord will bless you for it.

10. Don't plow with an ox and a donkey harnessed together.

Deut 25:4. Don't muzzle an ox as it treads out the grain. 1 Tim 5:18.

Prov 12:10 A good man is concerned for the welfare of his animals, but even the kindness of godless men is cruel.

Firstborn of. See *Firstborn.*

Man's dominion over. See *Man, Dominion of.*

See *Adder; Ant; Antelope; Ape; Bat; Bear; Behemoth; Birds; Boar; Camel; Cattle; Chameleon; Chickens; Cliff Badger; Coney; Deer; Dog; Dolphin; Donkey; Dragon; Dromedary; Fish; Fox; Frogs; Goat; Hare; Hind; Hornet; Horse; Leopard; Leviathan; Lion; Lizard; Mole; Mouse; Panther; Peacock; Ram; Rat; Rock Badger; Roe; Scorpion; Serpent; Sheep; Snake; Swine; Viper; Whale; Wild Ox; Wolf; Worm.*

See *Insects.*

ANKLET Num 31:50.

See *Chains.*

ANNA A prophetess and widow, Lk 2:36, 37.

ANNALS See *Book.*

ANNAS Associate high priest with Caiaphas, Lk 3:2; Jn 18:13, 19, 24; Acts 4:6.

ANOINTING Of the body, Deut 28:40; Ruth 3:3; Esther 2:12; Ps 92:10; 104:15; Prov 27:9, 16; Eccl 9:8; Song 1:3; Amos 6:6; Mic 6:15. Of guests, Lk 7:46; the sick, Lev 14:18; Isa 1:5, 6; Mk 6:13; Lk 10:34; Jas 5:14; Rev 3:18; the dead, Mt 26:12; Mk 14: 8; 16:1; Lk 23:56. Of Jesus, as a token of love, Mt 14:3; Lk 7:37, 38, 46; Jn 11:1,2; 12:3. Omitted in mourning, 2 Sam 12:20; 14:2, 3; Isa 61:3; Dan 10:3. God preserves those who receive, Ps 89:20–23.

IN CONSECRATION.

Of High Priests. Ex 29:7, 29; 40:13; Lev 6:19, 20; 8:12; 16:32; Ps 133:2.

Of Priests. Ex 28:41; 30:30; 40:15; Lev 8:30; 10:7; Num 3:3.

Of Kings. Saul, 1 Sam 9:16; 10:1; 12:3, 5; David, 1 Sam 16:3, 12, 13; 1 Chron 11:3; Ps 89:20; Solomon, 1 Kgs 1:39; 1 Chron 29:22; Jehu, 1 Kgs 19:16; 2 Kgs 9:1–3, 6, 12; Hazael, 1 Kgs 19:15; Joash, 2 Kgs 11:12; Cyrus, Isa 45.1.

Of Prophets. 1 Kgs 19:16.

Of the Tabernacle. Ex 30:26, 27; 40:9; Lev 8:10; Num 7:1; altars of, Ex 30:26–28; 40:10; Lev 8:11; Num 7:1; utensils of, Ex 30:26–28; 40:9–11; Lev 8: 10,11; Num 7:1.

Jacob's Pillar. At Bethel, Gen 28:18; 31:13; 35:13, 14.

See *Dedication.*

FIGURATIVE. Of Christ's kingly and priestly office, Ps 89:20; Isa 61:1; Dan 9:25; Acts 4:27; 10:38.

Typified. Ex 40:13–15; Lev 8:12; 1 Sam 16:13; 1 Kgs 19:16.

Symbolical. Of Jesus, Mt 26:7–12; Jn 12:3–7.

ANOINTING OIL Formula of, given by Moses, Ex 30:22–25, 31–33.

See *Oil; Ointment.*

ANT Prov 6:6–8; 30:24–28.

ANTEDILUVIANS Worship God, Gen 4: 3, 4, 26. Occupations of, Gen 4:2,3,20–22. Arts of, Gen 4:2,3,20–22; 6:14–22. Enoch prophesies to, Jude 1:14,15. Noah preaches to, 2 Pet 2:5. Wickedness of, Gen 6:5-7. Destruction of, Gen 7:1,21–23; Job 22:15–17; Mt 24:37–39; Lk 17:26,27; 2 Pet 2:5.

See *Flood.*

Longevity of, see *Longevity.*
Giants among, see *Giants.*

ANTELOPE Deut 14:3,4,5. See *Deer.*

ANTHOTHIJAH A Benjaminite, 1 Chron 8:22–25.

ANTHROPOMORPHISMS Figures of speech, which attribute human forms, acts and affections to God.

MISCELLANEOUS FIGURES. Gen 2:2. So on the seventh day, having finished his task, God ceased from this work he had been doing, [3]and God blessed the seventh day and declared it holy, because it was the day when he ceased this work of creation. [Ex 31:17.] [19]So the Lord God formed from the soil every kind of animal and bird, and brought them to the man to see what he would call them; and whatever he called them, that was their name.

Gen 6:6. He was sorry he had made them. It broke his heart. Ex 32:14; Judg 2:18; 1 Sam 15:35; 2 Sam 24:16; 1 Chron 21:15; Ps 106:45.

Gen 9:16, 17. For I will see the rainbow in the cloud and remember my promise to every living being on the earth.

Gen 11:5. God came down to see the city and the tower mankind was making, [7]"Come, let us go down and give them different languages, so that they won't understand each other's words!" Num 11:25.

Gen 18:17. "Should I hide my plan from Abraham?" God asked. [18]"For Abraham shall become a mighty nation, and he will be a source of blessing for all the nations of the earth. [19]And I have picked him out to have godly descendants and a godly household—men who are just and good—so that I can do for them all I have promised. [21]I am going down to see whether these reports are true or not. Then I will know." [33]And the Lord went on his way when he had finished his conversation with Abraham. And Abraham returned to his tent.

Gen 19:29. So God heeded Abraham's plea and kept Lot safe, removing him from the maelstrom of death that engulfed the cities.

Gen 22:12. "Lay down the knife; don't hurt the lad in any way," the Angel said, "for I know that God is first in your life—you have not withheld even your beloved son from me."

Gen 28:13. At the top of the stairs stood the Lord. "I am Jehovah," he said, "the God of Abraham, and of your father Isaac."

Gen 35:13. Afterwards Jacob built a stone pillar at the place where God had appeared to him; and he poured wine over it as an offering to God, and then anointed the pillar with olive oil.

Ex 2:23. He heard their cries from heaven, [24]and remembered his promise to Abraham, Isaac, and Jacob (to bring their descendants back into the land of Canaan).

Ex 3:8. I have come to deliver them from the Egyptians.

Ex 14:24. But in the early morning Jehovah looked down from the cloud of fire upon the array of the Egyptians, and began to harass them.

Ex 20:5. You must never bow to an image or worship in any way; for I, the Lord your God, am very possessive. I will not share your affections with any other god!

Ps 31:2. Answer quickly when I cry to you; bend low and hear my whispered plea.

Ps 33:6. He merely spoke, and the heavens were formed, and all the galaxies of stars.

Ps 35:1. O Lord, fight those fighting me; declare war on them for their attacks on me. [2]Put on your armor, take your shield and protect me by standing in front of me. [3]Lift your spear in my defense for my pursuers are getting very close. Let me hear you say that you will save me from them.

Ps 36:7. How precious is your constant love, O God! All humanity takes refuge in the shadow of your wings.

Ps 57:1. O God, have pity, for I am trusting you! I will hide beneath the shadow of your wings until this storm is past.

Ps 68:17. Surrounded by unnumbered chariots, the Lord moves on from Mount Sinai and comes to his holy temple high upon Mount Zion.

Ps 94:9. Is God deaf and blind—he who makes ears and eyes?

Ps 121:4. He is always watching, never sleeping.

Isa 1:15. From now on when you pray with your hands stretched out to heaven, I won't look or listen. Even though you make many prayers, I will not hear.

Ezk 1:24. And as they flew, their wings roared like waves against the shore, or like the voice of God, or like the shouting of a mighty army. When they stopped they let down their wings. [28]That was the way the glory of the Lord appeared to me. And when I saw it, I fell face downward on the ground, and heard the voice of someone speaking to me.

Hab 1:13. We are wicked, but they far more! Will you, who cannot allow sin in any form, stand idly by while they swallow us up? Should you be silent while the wicked destroy those who are better than they?

1 Pet 3:12. For the Lord is watching his children, listening to their prayers; but the Lord's face is hard against those who do evil. Lev 17:10; Deut 31:17; Isa 59:2; Ezk 39:23.

INTELLECTUAL FACULTIES ATTRIBUTED TO GOD. Memory, Isa 43:26; 63:11; assisted by tokens, Gen 9:16, 17. Reason, Isa 1:18. Understanding, Ps 147:5. Will, Rom 9:19.

MISCELLANEOUS ACTS AND STATES OF MIND ATTRIBUTED TO. Walking, Gen 3:8; Deut 23:14; Job 22:14; resting, Gen 2:2,3; Ex 20:11; 31:17; Deut 5:14; Heb 4:4,10; never tires, Isa 40:28; amazement, Isa 59:16; 63:5; Mk 6:6; laughing, Ps 2:4; 37:12,13; 59:8; Prov 1:26; sleeping, Ps 44:23; 78:65; grieved, Gen 6:6; Judg 10:16; angry, Ps 95:10; Heb 3:10, 17.

Oaths, Isa 62:8; Heb 6:16,17; 7:21,28.

See *Oath.* See also *Anger of God.*

ANTICHRIST Dan 7:24–26; 8:23–25; 9:26–27; Mt 24:5,23,24,26; Mk 13:6,21,22; Lk 21:8;

2 Thess 2:3–12; 1 Jn 2:18,22; 4:3; 2 Jn 7; Rev 13; 17: 8–14. To be destroyed, Rev 19:20; 20:10, 15.

See *Man of Rebellion.*

ANTIOCH 1. A city of Syria. Disciples first called Christians in, Acts 11:19–30. Church in, Acts 13:1; 14:26,27. Barnabas and Paul make second visit to, Acts 14:26–28. Dissension in church of, Acts 15: 22, with *vs.* 1–35. Paul and Peter's controversy at, Gal 2:11–15.

2. A city of Pisidia. Persecutes Paul, Acts 13: 14–52; 2 Tim 3:11; Acts 14:19–22; 18:22.

ANTIPAS A martyr, Rev 2:13.

ANTIPATRIS A city in Samaria, Acts 23:31.

ANUB Son of Koz, 1 Chron 4:8.

ANVIL Isa 41:7; Zech 1:21.

ANXIETY See *Care.*

APE In Solomon's zoological collections, 1 Kgs 10:22; 2 Chron 9:21.

APELLES A disciple in Rome, Rom 16:10.

APHEK 1. A site in Canaanite territory, Josh 13:2–7.

2. A city of the tribe of Asher, Josh 19:30,31. Called *Aphik,* Judg 1:31.

3. A city of the tribe of Issachar. Philistines defeat Israelites at, 1 Sam 4:1–11. Saul slain at, 1 Sam 29:1, with chapter 31. Probably the same mentioned in Josh 12:8–24 as a royal city of the Canaanites.

4. A city between Damascus and Palestine. Benhadad defeated at, 1 Kgs 20:26–30.

APHEKAH A city in the hill country of Judah, Josh 15:48–62.

APHIAH A Benjaminite, 1 Sam 9:1.

APHIK See *Aphek,* 2.

APOLLONIA A city of Macedonia, Acts 17: 1.

APOLLOS An eloquent Christian convert at Corinth, Acts 18:24–28; 19:1; 1 Cor 1:12; 3:4–7. Refuses to return to Rome, 1 Cor 16:12. Paul writes Titus about, Tit 3:13.

APOLLYON The Prince of the bottomless pit, Rev 9:11.

See *Abaddon.*

APOSTASY Described, Deut 13:12–14; Heb 3:12. Caused by persecution, Mt 24:9,10; Lk 8:13; by worldliness, 2 Tim 4:10. Guilt and punishment of, Zeph 1:4–6; Heb 10:25–31,39; 2 Pet 2:17,20–22. Cautions against, Heb 3:12; 2 Pet 3:17. Will be prevalent in the last days, Mt 24:12; 2 Thess 2:3; 1 Tim 4:1–3.

See *Antichrist.*

UNCLASSIFIED SCRIPTURES RELATING TO. Deut 32:15. Then, in plenty, they forsook their God. They shrugged away the Rock of their salvation.

1 Chron 28:9. If you seek him, you will find him; but if you forsake him, he will permanently throw you aside.

Isa 1:28. But all sinners shall utterly perish, for they refuse to come to me.

Isa 65:11. But because the rest of you have forsaken the Lord and his Temple and worship gods of "Fate" and "Destiny," [12]therefore I will "destine" you to the sword, and your "fate" shall be a dark one; for when I called, you didn't answer; when I spoke, you wouldn't listen. You deliberately sinned before my eyes, choosing to do what you know I despise. [13]Therefore the Lord God says, You shall starve, but my servants shall eat; you shall be thirsty while they drink; you shall be sad and ashamed, but they shall rejoice. [14]You shall cry in sorrow and vexation and despair, while they sing for joy. [15]Your name shall be a curse word among my people, for the Lord God will slay you and call his true servants by another name. [16]And yet, the days will come when all who invoke a blessing or take an oath shall swear by the God of Truth; for I will put aside my anger and forget the evil that you did.

Jer 17:5. The Lord says: Cursed is the man who puts his trust in mortal man and turns his heart away from God. [6]He is like a stunted shrub in the desert, with no hope for the future; he lives on the salt-encrusted plains in the barren wilderness; good times pass him by forever.

Ezk 3:20. And if a good man becomes bad, and you refuse to warn him of the consequences, and the Lord destroys him, his previous good deeds won't help him—he shall die in his sin. But I will hold you responsible for his death, and punish you.

Ezk 18:24. However, if a righteous person turns to sinning and acts like any other sinner, should he be allowed to live? No, of course not. All his previous goodness will be forgotten and he shall die for his sins. [26]When a good man turns away from being good, and begins sinning and dies in his sins, he dies for the evil he has done.

Ezk 33:12. For the good works of a righteous man will not save him if he turns to sin; and the sins of an evil man will not destroy him if he repents and turns from his sins. [13]I have said the good man will live. But if he sins, expecting his past goodness to save him, then none of his good deeds will be remembered. I will destroy him for his sins. [18]For again I say, when the good man turns to evil, he shall die.

Mt 13:20. The shallow, rocky soil represents the heart of a man who hears the message and receives it with real joy, [21]but he doesn't have much depth in his life, and the seeds don't root very deeply, and after a while when trouble comes, or persecution begins because of his beliefs, his enthusiasm fades, and he drops out. Mk 4:5–17; Lk 8:13.

Mt 24:10. And many of you shall fall back into sin and betray and hate each other. *v.* 12.

Lk 11:24. When a demon is cast out of a man, it goes to the deserts, searching there for rest; but finding none, it returns to the person it left, [25]and finds that its former home is all swept and clean. [26]Then it goes and gets seven other demons more evil than itself, and they all enter the man. And so the poor fellow is seven times worse off than he was before.

Jn 15:6. If anyone separates from me, he is thrown away like a useless branch, withers, and is gathered into a pile with all the others and burned.

Acts 7:39. But our fathers rejected Moses and

wanted to return to Egypt. 40They told Aaron, "Make idols for us, so that we will have gods to lead us back; for we don't know what has become of this Moses, who brought us out of Egypt." 41So they made a calf-idol and sacrificed to it, and rejoiced in this thing they had made. 42Then God turned away from them and gave them up, and let them serve the sun, moon and stars as their gods! In the book of Amos' prophecies the Lord God asks, "Was it to me you were sacrificing during those forty years in the desert, Israel? 43No, your real interest was in your heathen gods—Sakkuth, and the star god, Kaiway, and in all the images you made. So I will send you into captivity far away beyond Babylon."

2 Thess 2:3. Don't be carried away and deceived regardless of what they say. For that day will not come until two things happen: first, there will be a time of great rebellion against God, and then the man of rebellion will come—the son of hell. 11So God will allow them to believe lies with all their hearts, 12and all of them will be justly judged for believing falsehood, refusing the Truth, and enjoying their sins.

I Tim 4:1. But the Holy Spirit tells us clearly that in the last times some in the church will turn away from Christ and become eager followers of teachers with devil-inspired ideas. 2These teachers will tell lies with straight faces and do it so often that their consciences won't even bother them.

2 Tim 3:1. You may as well know this too, Timothy, that in the last days it is going to be very difficult to be a Christian. 2For people will love only themselves and their money; they will be proud and boastful, sneering at God, disobedient to their parents, ungrateful to them, and thoroughly bad. 3They will be hardheaded and never give in to others; they will be constant liars and troublemakers and will think nothing of immorality. They will be rough and cruel, and sneer at those who try to be good. 4They will betray their friends; they will be hotheaded, puffed up with pride, and prefer good times to worshiping God. 5They will go to church, yes, but they won't really believe anything they hear. Don't be taken in by people like that. 6They are the kind who craftily sneak into other people's homes and make friendships with silly, sin-burdened women and teach them their new doctrines. 7Women of that kind are forever following new teachers, but they never understand the truth. 8And these teachers fight truth just as Jannes and Jambres fought against Moses. They have dirty minds, warped and twisted, and have turned against the Christian faith. 9But they won't get away with all this forever. Some day their deceit will be well known to everyone, as was the sin of Jannes and Jambres.

2 Tim 4:3. For there is going to come a time when people won't listen to the truth, but will go around looking for teachers who will tell them just what they want to hear. 4They won't listen to what the Bible says but will blithely follow their own misguided ideas.

Heb 6:4. There is no use trying to bring you back to the Lord again if you have once understood the Good News and tasted for yourself the good things of heaven and shared in the Holy Spirit, 5and know how good the Word of God is, and felt the mighty powers of the world to come, and then have turned against God. You cannot bring yourself to repent again if you have nailed the Son of God to the cross again by rejecting him, holding him up to mocking and to public shame. 7When a farmer's land has had many showers upon it and good crops come up, that land has experienced God's blessing upon it. 8But if it keeps on having crops of thistles and thorns, the land is considered no good and is ready for condemnation and burning off. Lk 9:62.

Heb 10:26. If anyone sins deliberately by rejecting the Savior after knowing the truth of forgiveness, this sin is not covered by Christ's death; there is no way to get rid of it. 27There will be nothing to look forward to but the terrible punishment of God's awful anger which will consume all his enemies. 28A man who refused to obey the laws given by Moses was killed without mercy if there were two or three witnesses to his sin. 29Think how much more terrible the punishment will be for those who have trampled underfoot the Son of God and treated his cleansing blood as though it were common and unhallowed, and insulted and outraged the Holy Spirit who brings God's mercy to his people.

2 Pet 2:1. But there were false prophets, too, in those days, just as there will be false teachers among you. They will cleverly tell their lies about God, turning against even their Master who bought them; but theirs will be a swift and terrible end. 15They have gone off the road and become lost like Balaam, the son of Beor, who fell in love with the money he could make by doing wrong. 17These men are as useless as dried-up springs of water, promising much and delivering nothing; they are as unstable as clouds driven by the storm winds. They are doomed to the eternal pits of darkness. 20And when a person has escaped from the wicked ways of the world by learning about our Lord and Savior Jesus Christ, and then gets tangled up with sin and becomes its slave again, he is worse off than he was before. 21It would be better if he had never known about Christ at all than to learn of him and then afterwards turn his back on the holy commandments that were given to him. 22There is an old saying that "A dog comes back to what he has vomited, and a pig is washed only to come back and wallow in the mud again." That is the way it is with those who turn again to their sin.

2 Jn 1:9. For if you wander beyond the teaching of Christ, you will leave God behind.

Jude 1:4. I say this because some godless teachers have wormed their way in among you, saying that after we become Christians we can do just as we like without fear of God's punishment. The fate of such people was written long ago, for they have turned against our only Master and Lord, Jesus

Christ. [5]My answer to them is: Remember this fact —which you know already—that the Lord saved a whole nation of people out of the land of Egypt, and then killed every one of them who did not trust and obey him. [6]And I remind you of those angels who were once pure and holy, but turned to a life of sin. Now God has them chained up in prisons of darkness, waiting for the judgment day. [11]Woe upon them! For they follow the example of Cain who killed his brother; and, like Balaam, they will do anything for money; and like Korah, they have disobeyed God and will die under his curse. [12]When these men join you at the love feasts of the church, they are evil smears among you, laughing and carrying on, gorging and stuffing themselves without a thought for others. They are like clouds blowing over dry land without giving rain, promising much, but producing nothing. They are like fruit trees without any fruit at picking time. They are not only dead, but doubly dead, for they have been pulled out, roots and all, to be burned. [13]All they leave behind them is shame and disgrace like the dirty foam left along the beach by the wild waves. They wander around looking as bright as stars, but ahead of them is the everlasting gloom and darkness that God has prepared for them. [16]These men are constant gripers, never satisfied, doing whatever evil they feel like; they are loud-mouthed "show-offs," and when they show respect for others, it is only to get something from them in return. [19]They stir up arguments; they love the evil things of the world; they do not have the Holy Spirit living in them.

See *Backslider; Reprobate.*

INSTANCES OF. Israelites, Ex 32; Num 14. Saul, 1 Sam 15:26–29; 18:12; 28:15, 18. Amaziah, 2 Chron 25:14, 27. Disciples, Jn 6:66. Judas, Mt 26:14–16; 27:3–5; Mk 14:10, 11; Lk 6:14–16; 22:3–6, 47, 48; Acts 1:16–18. Hymenaeus and Alexander, 1 Tim 1:19,20. Phygellus and Hermogenes, 2 Tim 1:15.

APOSTLES A title used of the 12 selected disciples of Jesus, and several other individuals. In the Gospels, the word refers to the original 12 disciples, but in subsequent New Testament books, the term is applied to Paul and Barnabas. Outside of the Gospels, Judas Iscariot is not referred to as an apostle.

Names of, Lk 6:14–16. Here are their names: Simon (he also called him Peter), Andrew (Simon's brother), James, John, Philip, Bartholomew, Matthew, Thomas, James (the son of Alphaeus), Simon (a member of the Zealots, a subversive political party), Judas (son of James), Judas Iscariot, who later betrayed him. Mt 10:2–4; Mk 3:16–19; Acts 1:14, 26.

Selection of, Mt 4:18–22; 9:9, 10; 10:2–4; Mk 3:13–19; Lk 6:13–16; Jn 1:43.

Commission of, Mt 10; 28:19, 20; Mk 3:14, 15; 6:7–11; 16:15; Lk 9:1–5; 22:28–30; Jn 20:23; 21:15–19; Acts 1; 2; 10:42. Unlearned, Mt 11:25; Acts 4:13. Miraculous power given to, Mt 10:1; Mk 3:15; 6:7; 16:17; Lk 9:1, 2; 10:8, 9, 17; Acts 2:4, 43; 5:12–16; 1 Cor 14:18; 2 Cor 12:12. Authority of, see *Commission of,* above, and Mt 16:19; 18:18; 19:28.

Inspiration of, Mt 10:27; 16:17–19; Lk 24:45; Acts 1:2; 13:9. Duties of, see *Commission of,* above, and Jn 15:27; Acts 1:8,21,22; 2:32; 3:15; 4:33; 5:32; 10:39–41; 13:31; 2 Pet 1:16-19; 1 Jn 1:1–3. See *Minister, New Testament.*

Moral state of, before Pentecost, Mt 17:17; 18:3; 20:20–22; Lk 9:54,55. Slow to receive Jesus, as Messiah, Mt 14:33. Forsake Jesus, Mk 14:50.

Fail to comprehend the nature and mission of Jesus, and the nature of the kingdom he came to establish, Mt 8:25–27; 15:23; 16:8–12; 19:25; Mk 4:13; 6:51,52; 8:17,18; 9:9,10,30-32; 10:13,14; Lk 9:44,45; 18:34; 24:19,21; Jn 4:32,33; 10:6; 11:12,13; 12:16; 13:6–8; 14:5–9,22; 16:6,17,18,32; 20:9; 21:12; Acts 1:6.

Title used of Paul and Barnabas, Acts 14:4; of Paul, 1 Cor 4:9; 15:9; 1 Thess 2:6.

See *Barnabas; Disciples; Matthias; Minister, New Testament; Paul.*

FALSE. 2 Cor 11:13; Rev 2:2.

See *Teachers, False.*

APOSTROPHE To death and the grave, Hos 13:14; 1 Cor 15:55,56.

APPA-IM Son of Nadab, 1 Chron 2:30,31.

APPEAL Paul makes, to Caesar, Acts 25:10, 11, 21–27; 26:32; 28:19.

See *Change of Venue; Court, Superior and Inferior.*

APPETITE Kept in subjection, Dan 1:8–16; 1 Cor 9:27.

See *Temperance.*

APPHIA A Christian at Colosse, Philemon 1:2.

APPIAN WAY First paved Roman road, Acts 28:15.

APPII FORUM A market town in Italy, Acts 28:15.

APPLE A fruit, Prov 9:17; 25:11; Eccl 9:18; Song 2:3, 5; 7:8; 8:5; Joel 1:12.

APRIL See *Calendar.*

AQUILA AND PRISCILLA Christians at Corinth, Acts 18:1–3, 18, 19, 26. Friendship of, for Paul, Rom 16:3, 4. Paul sends greetings to, 2 Tim 4:19.

AR A city of Moab, Deut 2:18, 29. Destruction of, Num 21:27–30; Isa 15:1.

ARA Son of Jether, 1 Chron 7:38.

ARAB A city of Judah, Josh 15:48–62.

ARABAH Desert steppe land which runs from the sea of Galilee south to the Gulf of Aqaba, Deut 1:1–7; 2:8; 3:17; 4:49; Josh 8:14; 11:1–3, 16; 12:8–24; 18:18; 2 Kgs 25:4, 5; Jer 52:7; Amos 6:14.

ARABIA Tributary to Solomon, 2 Chron 9:13, 14; to Jehoshaphat, 2 Chron 17:11. Exports of, Ezk 27:21. Prophecies against, Isa 21:13; Jer 25:24. Paul visits, Gal 1:17.

ARABIANS Pay tribute to Solomon, 2 Chron 9:13, 14; to Jehoshaphat, 2 Chron 17:11. Invade and defeat Judah, 2 Chron 21:16, 17; 22:1. Defeated by Uzziah, 2 Chron 26:7. Oppose Nehemiah's rebuilding the walls of Jerusalem, Neh 2:19;

4:7. Commerce of, Ezk 27:21. Gospel preached to, Acts 2:11; Gal 1:17. Prophecies concerning, Isa 21:13–17; 42:11; 60:7; Jer 25:24.

ARAD 1. A city in the south of Canaan, Num 21:1; 33:40; Judg 1:16. Destroyed by Joshua, Josh 12:8–24.

2. Son of Beriah, 1 Chron 8:15.

ARAH 1. Son of Ulla, 1 Chron 7:39.

2. An Israelite, whose descendants returned from Babylon, Ezra 2:3–35; Neh 7:8–38. Probably identical with Arah in Neh 6:18.

ARAM The name of various regions, and of several men. The word signifies highlands, and is applied in its compounds to various highland districts of Syria.

1. The region from which Balaam came at Balak's command, Num 23:7–10.

2. A region north of Canaan, 1 Chron 2:23.

3. Son of Shem, Gen 10:22, 23; 1 Chron 1:17.

4. Son of Kemuel, Gen 22:20–23.

5. Son of Shemer, 1 Chron 7:34.

ARAM-MAACAH Called also *Maacah.* A small kingdom, 1 Chron 19:6.

See *Maacah, 10.*

ARAN Son of Dishan, Gen 36:28–30; 1 Chron 1:42.

ARARAT A district of Armenia, Jer 51:27. Ark rested in mountains of, Gen 8:3, 4. Assassins of Sennacherib escape to, 2 Kgs 19:37; Isa 37:38.

ARAUNAH A Jebusite from whom David bought a site for an altar, 2 Sam 24:16, 24. Called also *Ornan,* 1 Chron 21:15–25.

ARBA 1. Father of Anak, Josh 15:13; 21:9–16.

2. See *Hebron, 1.*

ARBITRATION INSTANCES OF. The two prostitutes before Solomon, 1 Kgs 3:16–28. Urged by Paul, as a mode of action for Christians, 1 Cor 6:1–8.

See *Court.*

ARCHANGEL 1 Thess 4:16; Jude 1:9.

See *Angel.*

ARCHELAUS A ruler of Judea, Mt 2:22.

ARCHERY Practiced by Ishmael, Gen 21:20, 21; Esau, Gen 27:2–4; Jonathan, 1 Sam 20:20, 36, 37; sons of Ulam, 1 Chron 8:40; Philistines, 1 Sam 31:1–4; 1 Chron 10:3; people of Kedar, Isa 21:17; Elamites, Isa 22:6, 7; Syrians, 1 Kgs 22:31–34; Israelites, 1 Chron 5:18; 12:2; 2 Chron 14:8; 26:14; Neh 4:13; Zech 9:13; Lydians, Jer 46:9.

In war, Gen 49:23; 1 Sam 31:3, 4; Isa 22:6, 7; Jer 51:3; Zech 10:4.

See *Arrow; Armies; Bow; War.*

ARCHIPPUS A disciple at Colosse, Col 4:17; Philemon 1:2.

ARCHITECTURE Heb 3:3, 4.

FIGURATIVE. Eph 2:21, 22.

See *Art; House; Tabernacle; Temple.*

ARCHIVES Royal, Ezra 5:17; 6:1.

ARCTURUS Constellation of the Great Bear, Job 38:32.

ARD Son of Benjamin, Gen 46:19–22; Num 26:38–41.

ARDON Son of Caleb, 1 Chron 2:18.

ARELI Son of Gad, Gen 46:16, 17; Num 26:15–18.

ARETAS A ruler of Syria, 2 Cor 11:32.

ARGOB 1. A region east of the Jordan in Bashan, Deut 3:4, 13, 14; 1 Kgs 4:8–19.

2. A possible conspirator with Pekah, 2 Kgs 15:25.

ARGUMENT See *Strife.*

ARIDAI Son of Haman, Esther 9:7–10.

ARIDATHA Son of Haman, Esther 9:7–10.

ARIEH A possible conspirator with Pekah, 2 Kgs 15:25.

ARIEL 1. A Moabite, 2 Sam 23:20.

2. A messenger from Ezra to Iddo, Ezra 8:16.

3. A symbolical name for Jerusalem, Isa 29:1, 2.

ARIMATHEA Called also *Ramah.* A town 20 miles north of Jerusalem, Mt 27:57; Mk 15:42, 43; Lk 23:50–52; Jn 19:38.

ARIOCH 1. King of Ellasar, Gen 14:1.

2. Captain of Nebuchadnezzar's guard, Dan 2:14, 15, 24, 25.

ARISAI Son of Haman, Esther 9:7–10.

ARISTARCHUS A companion of Paul, Acts 19:29; 20:4; 27:2; Col 4:10; Philemon 1:24.

ARISTOBULUS A Christian at Rome, Rom 16:10.

ARK 1. Noah's. Directions for building of, Gen 6:14–16. Noah and family preserved in, Gen 6:18; 7; 8; Lk 17:27; Heb 11:7; 1 Pet 3:20. Animals saved in, Gen 6:19, 20; 7:1–16.

2. In the Tabernacle. Called *Ark of the Covenant,* 1 Sam 5:4; 6:11; 2 Sam 15:24; 1 Kgs 8:1; 1 Chron 17:1; 28:2; Jer 3:16; Heb 9:4; *Of the Lord,* Josh 7:6; 1 Sam 4:6; 2 Sam 6:1, 15; 1 Kgs 2:26; *Of God,* Josh 4:7; 1 Sam 4:11, 13, 21, 22; 5:1; 6:2; 14:18; 2 Sam 7:2; 15:29; 1 Chron 13:12; 15:1; 16:1; 2 Chron 1:4; *Of God's Strength,* 2 Chron 6:41; *Of Jehovah,* 1 Sam 5:3; 1 Chron 15:12.

Sanctification of, Ex 30:26, 27. Ceremonies connected with, on the day of atonement, Lev 16:13–15. Holy, 2 Chron 8:11; 35:3.

An oracle of God, Num 10:33; 14:44; Josh 7:6–15; Judg 20:27, 28; 1 Sam 4:3, 4, 6, 7; 1 Chron 13:3; 16:4, 37; 2 Chron 6:41; Ps 132:8.

See *Mercy Seat.*

Directions for making, Ex 25:10–15; 35:10–19. Construction of, Ex 37:1–5; Deut 10:3.

Contents of: The law, Ex 25:16, 21; 40:20; Deut 10:5; 31:26; 1 Kgs 8:9; 2 Chron 5:10. Aaron's rod, Num 17:10; Heb 9:4. Jar of manna, Ex 16:33, 34; Heb 9:4.

Place of, Ex 26:33; 40:21; 2 Sam 7:2; Heb 9:2–4.

How prepared for conveyance, Num 4:5, 6. Carried by Kohathites, Num 3:30, 31; 4:4, 15; Deut 10:8; 1 Chron 15:2, 15. On special occasions carried by priests: Crossing Jordan, Josh 3:6, 13, 14; siege of Jericho, Josh 6:6–9.

Taken to battle, Josh 6:6–20; 1 Sam 4:3–22. Captured by the Philistines, 1 Sam 4:10,11; Ps 78:61. Returned by the Philistines, 1 Sam 6. Remains at the house of Abinadab, 1 Sam 7:1,2; 2 Sam 6:4; in the house of Obed-edom, 2 Sam 6:9–11.

Set up in Shiloh, Josh 18:1; Judg 20:27,28;

1 Sam 4:3,4; in Jerusalem, 2 Sam 6:12–17; 1 Chron 6:31; 15; 16:1. Removed from Jerusalem by Zadok at the time of Absalom's revolt, but returned by command of David, 2 Sam 15:24–29. Transferred to Solomon's temple, 1 Kgs 8:6–9; 2 Chron 5:2–9; 35: 3.

Prophecy concerning, Jer 3:16. In John's vision, Rev 11:19.

ARKITES Descendants of Canaan, Gen 10: 17; 1 Chron 1:15.

ARM FIGURATIVE USE OF. Deut 9:29. They are your people and your inheritance which you brought from Egypt by your great power and your mighty arm.

Deut 33:27. The eternal God is your Refuge, and underneath are the everlasting arms. He thrusts out your enemies before you; it is he who cries, "Destroy them!"

Ps 89:13. Strong is your arm! Strong is your hand! Your right hand is lifted high in glorious strength.

Ps 136:11,12. He brought them out with mighty power and upraised fist to strike their enemies, for his lovingkindness to Israel continues forever.

Song 2:6. His left hand is under my head and with his right hand he embraces me.

Isa 40:10. Yes, the Lord God is coming with mighty power; he will rule with awesome strength. See, his reward is with him, to each as he has done. [11]He will feed his flock like a shepherd; he will carry the lambs in his arms and gently lead the ewes with young.

Isa 52:10. The Lord has bared his holy arm before the eyes of all the nations; the ends of the earth shall see the salvation of our God.

Ezk 20:33. I will rule you with an iron fist and in great anger and with power.

Lk 1:51. How powerful is his mighty arm! How he scatters the proud and haughty ones!

See *Anthropomorphisms.*

ARMAGEDDON Mountain of Megiddo, (Hebrew) on the southern edge of the plain of Esdraelon, of which the valley of Megiddo formed a part. The word occurs only in Rev 16:16. Some consider the reference to be figurative; many regard it as a literal reference to the great battleground of Palestine. There Deborah and Barak defeated Sisera and the Canaanites, Judg 4:15, 16; Gideon defeated the Midianites, Judg 7; Israel was defeated by the Philistines and Saul was killed, 1 Sam 31:1–8; Josiah died in battle with the Egyptians, 2 Kgs 23:29, 30; 2 Chron 35:22–25; Israel will mourn at Christ's return, Zech 12:10, 11. Revelation 16:16 indicates that this is the place where the armies of the world will assemble for the complex struggle called the battle of that great coming Judgment Day of God Almighty, Rev 16:14; cf. Isa 63:1–3; Dan 2:34, 35; Joel 3:1, 2, 9–12; Zech 14:1, 2.

ARMIES Who of the Israelites were subject to serve in, Num 1:2,3; 26:2; 2 Chron 25:5,6; who were exempt from service in, Num 1:47–50; 2:33; Deut 20:5–9; Judg 7:3. Enumeration of Israel's military forces, Num 1:2,3; 26:2; 1 Sam 11:8; 2 Sam 18:1,2; 24:1–9; 1 Kgs 20:15; 2 Chron 25:5,6. Levies for, Num 31:4,5; Judg 20:8–10. Cumpulsory service in, 1 Sam 14:52. See *Cowardice.*

How officered: Commander-in-chief, 1 Sam 14: 50,51; 2 Sam 2:8; 8:16; 17:25; 19:13; 20:23; generals of corps and divisions, Num 2:3–31; 1 Chron 27: 1–15; 2 Chron 17:12–19; commanders, battalion leaders, officers, Num 31:14,48, 49; 1 Sam 17:18; 2 Kgs 1:9; 1 Chron 28:1; 2 Chron 25:5; Isa 3:3. See *Cavalry; Chariots.*

Assembly of. Methods employed in effecting: Sounding of a trumpet, Num 10:9; Judg 3:27; 6:34; 1 Sam 13:3,4; cutting oxen in pieces, and sending the pieces throughout Israel, 1 Sam 11:7. Refusal to obey the summons, instance of, Judg 21:5–12, with Judg 20.

Tactics: Camp and march, Num 2. March in ranks, 1 Chron 12:33; Joel 2:7. Move, in attack, in three divisions, Judg 7:16; 9:43; 1 Sam 11:11; 13:17,18; 2 Sam 18:2; Job 1:17. See *Strategy.*

Orders delivered with trumpets, 2 Sam 2:28; 18: 16; 20:1,22; Neh 4:18,19.

Stratagems: Ambushes, at Ai, Josh 8:2–22; Shechem, Judg 9:25,34; Gibe-ah, Judg 20:29–43; Zemaraim, 2 Chron 13:13,14. By Jehoshaphat, 2 Chron 20:22. Reconnoissances: Of Jericho, Josh 2; Ai, Josh 7:2,3; Bethel, Judg 1:22-24; Laish, Judg 18:2–10. Night attacks, Gen 14:15; Judg 7:16–22. Decoy, Josh 8:4–22; Judg 20:29–43; Neh 6. Delay, 2 Sam 17:7–14. Swiftness of action: Abraham, in pursuit of Ched-or-laomer, Gen 14:14,15; Joshua, against the Amorites, Josh 10:6,9; the confederated kings, Josh 11:7. David's attack upon the Philistines, 2 Sam 5:23–25. Forced marches, Isa 5:26,27. Sieges: Jer 39:1; of Jericho, Josh 6; Samaria, 2 Kgs 6:24–33; 7; Jerusalem, 2 Kgs 25:1,2.

"Engines" used, 2 Chron 26:15; Jer 6:6; Ezk 26: 9. Fortifications, 2 Sam 5:9; 2 Chron 11:11; 26:9; Neh 3:1,2; 4:1,2; Isa 22:9–11; 25:12; 29:3; 32:14; Jer 6:6; 32: 24; 33:4; Ezk 4:1,2; 21:22; 26:8; 33:27; Dan 11:15; Nah 2:1; 3:14. Standards, Num 2:1–31,34; 10:14,18,22, 25. Uniforms of, Ezk 23:6, 12; Nah 2:3. Standing armies, 1 Sam 13:2; 1 Chron 27; 2 Chron 1:14; 17: 12–19; 26:11–15.

Religious ceremonies attending: Seeking counsel from God before battle, Num 27:21; Judg 1:1; 1 Sam 14:19,37–41; 23:2–12; 30:8; 2 Sam 2:1; 5:19, 23,24; 1 Kgs 22:7–28; 2 Kgs 3:11–19; 1 Chron 14:10, 14; Jer 37:7–10; sacrifices, 1 Sam 13:11,12; purifications, Num 31:19–24; prophets prophesy before, 2 Chron 20:14–17; holiness commanded, Deut 23: 9–14; officers consecrate themselves to God, 2 Chron 17:16. Army choir and songs, 2 Chron 20: 21,22. Ark taken to battle, Josh 6:6-11; 1 Sam 4:4–11.

Divine assistance to: When Aaron and Hur held up Moses' hands, Ex 17:11,12; in siege of Jericho, Josh 6; sun stands still, Josh 10:11–14; Gideon's victory, Judg 7; Samaria's deliverances, 1 Kgs 20; 2 Kgs 7; Jehoshaphat's victories, 2 Kgs 3; 2 Chron 20; angel of the Lord kills the Assyrians, 2 Kgs 19:35.

Determine royal succession, 2 Sam 2:8,9; 1 Kgs 16:15,16; 2 Kgs 11:4–12.

Composed of insurgents, 1 Sam 22:1,2. Mercenaries, 2 Sam 10:6; 1 Chron 19:6,7; 2 Chron 25:5,6. Confederated, Josh 10:1–5; 11:1–5; Judg 1:3; 2 Sam 10:6,15,16,19; 1 Kgs 15:18–20; 22:1–4; 2 Kgs 16:8,9; 18: 19–21; 1 Chron 19:6,7; 2 Chron 16:2–9; 18:1–5; 20:1; 22:5; 28:16, 20; Ps 83:1–12; Isa 7:1–9; 8:9–12; 54:15. Exhorted before battle, Deut 20:1–9. Battle shouts, Judg 7:18; 1 Sam 17:20,52. Triumphs of, celebrated: With songs, Judg 5; 1 Sam 18:6,7; music, 2 Chron 20:28; dancing, 1 Sam 18:6,7.

Rewards for meritorious conduct: The general offers his daughter in marriage, Josh 15:16,17; king offers his daughter, 1 Sam 17:25; 18:17–27; promotion, 2 Sam 23:8–39; 1 Chron 11:5,6,10–47; share the booty, Num 31:25–47.

Insubordination in, punished, Achan, Josh 7. Check roll-call, 1 Sam 14:17; Num 31:48,49.

Panics: Isa 30:17; among the Midianites, Judg 7: 21; Philistines, 1 Sam 14:15–19; Syrians, 2 Kgs 7: 7–15. Soldiers destroy each other to escape captivity, 1 Sam 14:20; 31:3–6.

Champions fight instead of, 1 Sam 17:8–53; 2 Sam 2:14–16; 21:15–22. Confidence in, vain, Ps 33: 16, 17; 44:6. Escort duty performed by, 2 Kgs 1:9; Acts 23:23, 24, 31–33.

Roman army: Officers of, Mt 8:5, 6, 8, 9; 27:54; Lk 7:2; 23:47; Acts 10:1, 7, 22; 21:32; 22:24–29; 23: 17, 23, 24; 27:1, 11, 43; 28:16. Divided into regiments, Acts 10:1; 27:1.

Armies of heaven, Deut 33:2; Josh 5:14; Jude 1: 14; Rev 19:14.

For other than armies of the Israelites and Romans, see *Amalekites; Assyria; Babylon; Egyptians; Midianites; Persia; Syria.*

For commissaries of, see *Commissary.*

For weapons used, see *Armor.*

See *Ambush; Cavalry; Flag; Fort; Garrison; Herald; Hostage; Navy; Reconnoissance; Siege; Signal; Spies; Strategy; Truce; War.*

FIGURATIVE. Deut 33:2; 2 Kgs 6:17; Ps 34:7; 68:17; Rev 9:16.

ARMONI Son of Rizpah, 2 Sam 21:8.

ARMOR The equipment of a soldier, 1 Sam 17:38, 39; 31:9; 1 Chron 10:9; Jer 46:3, 4; 51:3; Ezk 38:4; Lk 11:22; Eph 6:14–17.

See *Breastplate; Coat of Mail; Leggings; Shield.*

FIGURATIVE. Isa 59:17; Rom 13:12, 13; 2 Cor 6: 7; 10:4; Eph 6:11–17; 1 Thess 5:8.

ARMOR-BEARER An attendant who carried a soldier's equipment, a bodyguard. Of Abimelech, Judg 9:54; Jonathan, 1 Sam 14:6, 7, 12, 13, 17; Saul, 1 Sam 16:21; 31:6; Goliath, 1 Sam 17:4–7; Joab, 2 Sam 18:15.

ARMORY A place for the storage of armor, 2 Kgs 10:2, 3; 20:13; 2 Chron 12:11; Neh 3:19; Isa 22: 8; Mt 27:27; Acts 21:34; 23:10, 16, 32. In different parts of the kingdom, 1 Kgs 10:16, 17; 2 Chron 11: 12.

See *Castle; Fortress; Jerusalem.*

FIGURATIVE. Jer 50:25.

ARMS See *Armor; Arrow; Battering Ram; Battle-Axe; Bow; Chariot; Dagger; Dart; Engine; Javelin; Shield; Sling; Spear; Sword.*

ARNAN Patronymic of a family descended from David, 1 Chron 3:21.

ARNI See *Ram, 1.*

ARNON A river emptying into the Dead Sea from the east. Boundary between Moabites and Amorites, Num 21:13, 14; 22:36; Deut 2:24, 25, 36; 3:8, 16; Josh 12:1. Fords of, Isa 16:2.

AROD Son of Gad, Gen 46:16; Num 26:15–18.

AROER 1. A city of the Amorites in the Arnon River valley, Deut 4:48. Conquered by Israelites, Deut 2:35, 36; 3:12; Judg 11:26. Taken by Hazael, 2 Kgs 10:32, 33.

2. A city built, or probably more correctly, rebuilt, by the Gadites, Num 32:34–36; Josh 13:25. Jephthah destroys the Ammonites at, Judg 11:33.

3. A city in Judah, 1 Sam 30:27–31. Birthplace of two of David's heroes, 1 Chron 11:26–47.

ARPACHSHAD Son of Shem, Gen 10:22; 11: 10–13; 1 Chron 1:17, 18, 24–27. Called *Arphaxad* in Lk 3:23–38.

ARPAD A fortified city of Syria, perhaps identical with Arvad, 2 Kgs 18:34; 19:13. Idols of, Isa 36:19.

ARPHAXAD See *Arpachshad.*

ARREST Of Jesus, Mt 26:57; Mk 14:46; Lk 22:54; Jn 18:12; apostles, Acts 5:17, 18; 6:12; Paul and Silas, Acts 16:19; Paul, Acts 21:30. Paul authorized to arrest Christians, Acts 9:2.

See *Extradition; Prison; Prisoners.*

ARROGANCE 1 Sam 2:3 Quit acting proud and arrogant! The Lord knows what you have done, and he will judge your deeds.

Prov 8:13. If anyone respects and fears God, he will hate evil. For wisdom hates pride, arrogance, corruption and deceit of every kind.

Isa 13:11. And I will punish the world for its evil, the wicked for their sin; I will crush the arrogance of the proud man and the haughtiness of the rich.

See *Pride.*

ARROW A weapon. Used in hunting, Gen 21: 20,21; 27:2–4; in war, 1 Sam 31:3,4; 2 Sam 22:15; 1 Kgs 22:34; 2 Kgs 19:32; Ps 7:13; Jer 51:3. Divination by, Ezk 21:21. Shot by Jonathan as a sign to David, 1 Sam 20:20–42. Shot by Joash as a sign against the Syrians, 2 Kgs 13:14–19.

FIGURATIVE. Num 24:3–9; Deut 32:23,42; Job 6:4; Ps 11:2; 21:12; 38:2; 45:5; 57:4; 120:4; 144:6; Prov 25:18; Lam 3:12,13; Ezk 5:16; Hab 3:11.

ARSON Ps 74:7,8. Law concerning, Ex 22:6.

INSTANCES OF. By Samson, Judg 15:4,5; Absalom, 2 Sam 14:30; Zimri, 1 Kgs 16:18.

ART PRIMITIVE. Invention of musical instruments and instruments of iron and copper, Gen 4: 21,22. Carpentry, Gen 6:14–16; Ex 31:2–9. Of the perfumer, Ex 30:25,35; armorer, 1 Sam 8:12; baker, Gen 40:1; 1 Sam 8:13; barber, Isa 7:20; Ezk 5:1; brickmaker, Gen 11:3,4; Ex 5:7,8,18; calker, Ezk 27: 9; gardener, Jer 29:5; Jn 20:15; goldsmith, Isa 40: 19; mariner, Ezk 27:9; mason, 2 Sam 5:11; 2 Chron 24:12; musician, 1 Sam 18:6; 1 Chron 15:16; potter, Isa 64:8; Jer 18:3; Lam 4:2; refiner of metals, 1 Chron 28:18; Mal 3:2,3; ropemaker, Judg 16:11; stonemason, Ex 20:25; 1 Chron 22:15; shipbuilder,

1 Kgs 9:26; smelter of metals, Job 28:2; spinner, Ex 35:25; Prov 31:19,20; tailor, Ex 28:3; tanner, Acts 9:43; 10:5,6; tentmaker, Gen 4:20; Acts 18:2,3; weaver, Ex 35:35; Jn 19:23,24; winemaker, Neh 13:15; Isa 63:3.

Artisans, Skillful. Jubal, Gen 4:21; Tubal-cain, Gen 4:22; Bezalel and Oholiab, Ex 31:2–14; 35:30–35; Hiram, 1 Kgs 7:13–51; 2 Chron 2:13,14.

For the various arts practiced, and products manufactured, in ancient times, see *Beaten Work; Brass; Bread; Brick; Carpentry; Carving; Copper; Drawing; Dyeing; Embroidery; Engraving; Goldsmith; Jeweler; Leather; Lime; Mason; Master Workman; Molding; Music; Painting; Paper; Parchment; Perfumer; Picture; Pottery; Rope; Ship; Silk; Silversmith; Smith; Soap; Spinning; Sun Dial; Tapestry; Tailoring; Tent; Weaving; Wine.*

AR-TA-XERXES A Persian king, son of Ahasuerus. Prohibits the rebuilding of Jerusalem, Ezra 4:7–24. Decrees of, in behalf of the Jews, Ezra 7; Neh 2; 5:14.

ARTEMAS A companion of Paul, Tit 3:12.

ARTILLERY See *Arms.*

ARTISAN See *Art; Master Workman.*

ARUBBOTH A district under tribute to Solomon's commissary, 1 Kgs 4:8–19.

ARUMAH A place near Shechem, Judg 9:41.

ARVAD An island near Zidon, Ezk 27:8,11.

ARVADITES Descendants of Canaan, Gen 10:15–19; 1 Chron 1:13–16.

ARZA Steward of Elah, 1 Kgs 16:9.

ASA 1. King of Judah, 1 Kgs 15:8–24; 1 Chron 3:10–14; 2 Chron 14; 15; 16; Mt 1:7.

2. A Levite, 1 Chron 9:16.

ASAHEL 1. Nephew of David, and one of his captains, 2 Sam 2:18–24,32; 23:24; 1 Chron 2:16; 11:26; 27:7.

2. A Levite commissioned by Jehoshaphat to teach the law to Judah, 2 Chron 17:7–9.

3. A Levite, who had charge of offerings, 2 Chron 31:13.

4. Father of Jonathan, Ezra 10:15.

ASAIAH 1. An officer of King Josiah, 2 Kgs 22:12–20; 2 Chron 34:20–28.

2. A descendant of Simeon, 1 Chron 4:34–39.

3. A Levite, 1 Chron 6:29,30. Probably identical with a man of same name mentioned in 1 Chron 15:4–11.

4. A Shilonite, 1 Chron 9:5.

ASAPH 1. Father of Joah, Isa 36:3,22.

2. Son of Berachiah. One of the three leaders of music in David's organization of the tabernacle service, 1 Chron 15:16–19; 16:5–7; 25:1–8; 2 Chron 5:11,12; 35:15; Neh 12:46. Appointed to sound the cymbals in the temple choir, I Chron 15:17, 19; 16:5,7. A composer of sacred lyrics, 2 Chron 29:12–30. Descendants of, in the temple choir, 1 Chron 25:1–8; 2 Chron 20:14; 29:12–14; Ezra 2:40–42; 3:10; Neh 7:43–45; 11:22,23.

3. A Levite, whose descendants lived in Jerusalem after the exile, 1 Chron 9:15, 16.

4. A Kohath Levite, 1 Chron 26:1.

5. Keeper of forests, Neh 2:8.

ASAREL Son of Jehallelel, 1 Chron 4:16.

ASCENSION Of Elijah, 2 Kgs 2:1–18. Of Jesus, Mk 16:19,20, Lk 24:50–53; Acts 1:9–12. Of two witnesses, Rev 11:12.

ASCETICISM A philosophy that leads to severe austerities in subordinating the body to the control of the moral attributes of the mind. Extreme application of, rebuked by Jesus, Mt 11:19; Lk 7:34; by Paul, Col 2:20–23; 1 Tim 4:1–4,8.

See *Stoicism.*

INSTANCES OF THE PRACTICE OF. John the Baptist, Mt 11:18; Lk 7:33. Those who practiced celibacy "for the sake of the Kingdom of Heaven," Mt 19:12.

ASENATH Wife of Joseph, Gen 41:45, 50; 46:19–22.

ASH A tree, Isa 44:14.

ASHAN A Levitical city of Judah, later of Simeon, Josh 15:37–44; 19:7; 1 Chron 4:32; 6:58,59. See *Ain.*

ASHARELAH One of the temple choir, 1 Chron 25:2,14; probably identical with *Azarel. v.* 18.

ASHBEL Son of Benjamin, Gen 46:19–22; Num 26:38–41; 1 Chron 8:1.

ASHDOD A city of the Philistines, Josh 13:2–7; 1 Sam 6:17. Anakim inhabit, Josh 11:22. Assigned to Judah, Josh 15:47. Dagon's temple in, in which was deposited the ark, 1 Sam 5. Conquest of, by Uzziah, 2 Chron 26:6; by Tartan, Isa 20:1. People of, conspire against the Jews, Neh 4:7, 8. Jews intermarry with, Neh 13:23, 24. Prophecies concerning, Jer 25:19, 20; Amos 1:8; 3; Zeph 2:4; Zech 9:6. Called *Azotus,* Acts 8:40.

ASHER 1. Son of Jacob, by Zilpah, Gen 30:13; 35:26; 49:20; Ex 1:1–4; 1 Chron 2:1, 2. Descendants of, Gen 46:16, 17; Num 26:44–47.

2. Tribe of: Census of, by families, Num 1:20–46; 26:44–47; 1 Chron 7:40; 12:24–37. Station of, in camp, Num 2:3–31. Prophecies concerning, by Moses, Deut 33:24, 25; by John, Rev 7:4–8. Allotment to, of land in Canaan, Josh 19:24–31; Ezk 48:2. Chided by Deborah, Judg 5:17. Summoned by Gideon, Judg 6:35; 7:23. Join Hezekiah, 2 Chron 30:11.

3. A city of Shechem, Josh 17:7; 1 Kgs 4:16.

ASHERAH, ASHEROTH A Canaanite goddess. Worshiped by the Israelites, Judg 3:7; 2 Kgs 13:6; 21:3–7. Idols of, destroyed by Gideon, Judg 6:19, 25, 28; Hezekiah, 2 Kgs 18:4; Josiah, 2 Kgs 23:14; 2 Chron 34:3, 4; Asa, 2 Chron 14:3; Jehoshaphat, 2 Chron 17:6; 19:3.

ASHES Use of, in purification, Num 19:9, 10, 17; Heb 9:13. A symbol of mourning, 2 Sam 13:19; Esther 4:1, 3. Sitting in, Job 2:8; Jer 6:26; Ezk 27:30; Jon 3:6; Lk 10:13. Repenting in, Job 42:6; Isa 58:5; Dan 9:3; Jon 3:6; Lk 10:13.

ASHHUR Son of Hezron, 1 Chron 2:24; 4:5.

ASHIMA An idol, 2 Kgs 17:30.

ASHKELON One of five chief cities of the Philistines, Josh 13:2–7. Captured by the armies of Judah, Judg 1:18. Samson kills 30 men of, Judg 14:

19. Tumors of, 1 Sam 6:17. Prophecies concerning, Jer 25:19, 20; 47:5, 7; Amos 1:8; Zeph 2:4, 7; Zech 9:5.

ASHKENAZ Son of Gomer, Gen 10:3; 1 Chron 1:5–9. Descendants of, Jer 51:27.

ASHNAH Name of two cities in Judah, Josh 15:33–44.

ASHPENAZ A eunuch in Nebuchadnezzar's court, Dan 1:3, 4.

ASHTAROTH 1. Plural form of *Ashtoreth,* which see.

2. The capital city of Bashan, Deut 1:4; Josh 12:4. Giants (Rephaim) live at, Josh 12:4. Alloted to Manasseh, Josh 13:31; 1 Chron 6:71. Possibly identical with *Ashteroth-karnaim,* mentioned in Gen 14:5.

ASHTEROTH-KARNAIM An ancient city of Palestine taken by Ched-or-laomer, Gen 14:5.

ASHTORETH An idol of the Philistines, Sidonians, and Phoenicians. Probably identical with queen of heaven, Jer 7:18. Worshiped by the Israelites, Judg 2:12–14; 10:6; 1 Sam 7:3, 4; 12:10; 1 Kgs 11:5, 33; 2 Kgs 23:13. Temple of, 1 Sam 31:10. Shrines of, at Jerusalem, destroyed, 2 Kgs 23:13.

ASHURI Possibly Geshurites, 2 Sam 2:9.

ASHVATH Son of Japhlet, 1 Chron 7:33.

ASIA Called also *Turkey.* Inhabitants of, in Jerusalem, at Pentecost, Acts 2:9; 21:27; 24:18. Paul and Silas forbidden by the Holy Spirit to preach in, Acts 16:6. Gospel preached in, by Paul, Acts 19; 20:4. Paul leaves, Acts 20:13. Churches of, 1 Cor 16:19; Rev 1:4, 11.

ASNAH Family of, return to Jerusalem, Ezra 2:43–54; Neh 7:46–56.

ASPATHA Son of Haman, Esther 9:7–10.

ASPHALT Salt Sea valley full of, Gen 14:10.

See *Bitumen; Pitch; Tar.*

ASRIEL Son of Manasseh, Num 26:28–37; Josh 17:2; 1 Chron 7:14.

ASS See *Donkey.*

ASSASSINATION David's abhorrence of, 2 Sam 4:9–12. Laws prohibiting, Deut 27:24.

INSTANCES OF. Of Eglon, by Ehud, Judg 3:15–23; Abner, by Joab, 2 Sam 3:27; Ishbosheth, by the sons of Rimmon, 2 Sam 4:5–7; Amnon, by Absalom, 2 Sam 13:28, 29; Amasa, by Joab, 2 Sam 20:8–10; Joash, by his officers, 2 Kgs 12:20; Sennacherib, by his sons, 2 Kgs 19:37; Isa 37:38.

ASSAULT AND BATTERY LAWS CONCERNING. Ex 21:15. Anyone who strikes his father or mother shall surely be put to death.

18. If two men are fighting, and one hits the other with a stone or with his fist and injures him so that he must be confined to bed, but doesn't die, [19]if later he is able to walk again, even with a limp, the man who hit him will be innocent except that he must pay for the loss of his time until he is thoroughly healed, and pay any medical expenses.

22. If two men are fighting, and in the process hurt a pregnant woman so that she has a miscarriage, but she lives, then the man who injured her shall be fined whatever amount the woman's husband shall demand, and as the judges approve. [23]But if any harm comes to the woman and she dies, he shall be executed. [24]If her eye is injured, injure his; if her tooth is knocked out, knock out his; and so on—hand for hand, foot for foot, [25]burn for burn, wound for wound, lash for lash.

26. If a man hits his slave in the eye, whether man or woman, and the eye is blinded, then the slave shall go free because of his eye. [27]And if a master knocks out his slave's tooth, he shall let him go free to pay for the tooth.

Deut 17:8. If a case arises that is too hard for you to decide—for instance, whether someone is guilty of murder when there is insufficient evidence, or whether someone's rights have been violated—you shall take the case to the sanctuary of your God, [9]to the priests and Levites, and the chief judge on duty at the time will make the decision. [10]His decision is without appeal and is to be followed to the letter. [11]The sentence he imposes is to be fully executed. [12]If the defendant refuses to accept the decision of the priest or judge appointed by God for this purpose, the penalty is death. Such sinners must be purged from Israel.

Mt 5:38. The law of Moses says, "If a man gouges out another's eye, he must pay with his own eye. If a tooth gets knocked out, knock out the tooth of the one who did it." [39]But I say: Don't resist violence! If you are slapped on one cheek, turn the other too.

THE ASSAULT ON JESUS. Prophecies of, Isa 50:6; Lam 3:30. The attacks upon, Mt 26:67; 27:30; Mk 14:65; Lk 22:63, 64; Jn 19:3.

See *Beating; Stoning; Stripes; Whipping.*

ASSHUR 1. Son of Shem, and ancestor of the Assyrians, Gen 10:22; 1 Chron 1:17.

2. Capital city of Assyria, Ezk 27:23.

See *Assyria.*

ASSHURIM Descendants of Dedan, Gen 25:3.

ASSIR 1. Son of Korah, Ex 6:24; 1 Chron 6:22–24.

2. Son of Ebiasaph, 1 Chron 6:22–24, 33–38.

ASSOS A seaport in Mysia, Acts 20:13.

ASSURANCE Produced by faith, Eph 3:12; 2 Tim 1:12; Heb 10:22. Made full by hope, Heb 6:11,19. Confirmed by love, 1 Jn 3:14,19; 4:18. Is the effect of righteousness, Isa 32:17. Is abundant in the understanding of the gospel, Col 2:2; 1 Thess 1:5.

Saints privileged to have, of their election, Ps 4:3; 1 Thess 1:4; their redemption, Job 19:25; their adoption, Rom 8:16; 1 Jn 3:2; their salvation, Isa 12:2; eternal life, 1 Jn 5:13; the unalienable love of God, Rom 8:38,39; union with God and Christ, 1 Cor 6:15; 2 Cor 13:5; Eph 5:29,30; 1 Jn 2:5; 4:13; peace with God by Christ, Rom 5:1; preservation, Ps 3:6; 8; 27:3–5; 46:1–3; answers to prayer, 1 Jn 3:22; 5:14,15; comfort in suffering, Ps 73:26; Lk 4:18,19; 2 Cor 4:8–10,16–18; continuance in grace, Phil 1:6; a support in death, Ps 23:4; a glorious resurrection, Job 19:26; Ps 17:15; Phil 3:21; 1 Jn 3:2; a kingdom, Heb 12:28; Rev 5:10; a crown, 2 Tim 4:7,8; Jas 1:12. Saints work hard to attain, 2 Pet 1:10,11; strive to maintain, Heb 3:14,18. Confident hope in God restores, Ps 42:11.

Exemplified: David, Ps 23:4; 73:24–26; Paul, 2 Tim 1:12; 4:18.

See *Faith.*

ASSYRIA An empire founded by Nimrod, Gen 10:8–12; Mic 5:6. It extended from east of the Tigris, Gen 2:14; 10:11,12; possibly to Egypt, Gen 25:18. Its armies invade the land of Israel under Pul (or Tiglath-pileser), 2 Kgs 15:19,20; 1 Chron 5:6,26; Shalmaneser, 2 Kgs 17:3–6,24–28; 18:9–12; Jer 50:17; Sennacherib, 2 Kgs 18:13–37; 19; 2 Chron 32; Isa chapters 36; 37.

Army of, destroyed by the Angel of the Lord, Isa 37:36. Alliances with, sought by Judah and Israel, Hos 5:13. Israelites subject to, Lam 5:6. Israelites carried captive into, 2 Kgs 17:3–23. Jews carried captive to, 2 Kgs chapters 24; 25; 2 Chron 36:5–21. Invaded by King Neco, 2 Kgs 23:29.

Commerce of, Ezk 27:23. Productiveness of, Isa 36:17.

Prophecies concerning, Isa 7:17–25; 8:4–10; 10:5–34; 14:24–28; 19:23–25; 20; 30:27–33; 31:8,9; 37:21–35; Jer 1:15; Ezk 31; Jon 3:1–5; Nah chapters 1–3; Zeph 2:13–15; Zech 10:11.

Prophecies of captivity of Israelites in, Hos 9:3; 11:5,11.

Idols of. See *Adrammelech; Anammelech; Nisroch; Tartak.*

ASTROLOGERS See *Magi; Wise Men.*

ASTROLOGY Isa 47:13; Jer 10:1–3; Dan 1:20; 2:27; 4:7; 5:7; Mt 2:1,7,9,16.

See *Astronomy; Sorcery.*

ASTRONOMY Job 26:7. God stretches out heaven over empty space, and hangs the earth upon nothing. [13]The heavens are made beautiful by his Spirit; he pierces the swiftly gliding serpent.

Job 37:18. Can you spread out the gigantic mirror of the skies as he does?

Job 38:31. Can you hold back the stars? Can you restrain Orion or Pleiades? [32]Can you ensure the proper sequence of the seasons, or guide the constellation of the Bear with her satellites across the heavens? [33]Do you know the laws of the universe and how the heavens influence the earth?

Ps 8:3. When I look up into the night skies and see the work of your fingers—the moon and the stars you have made.

Ps 19:1. The heavens are telling the glory of God; they are a marvelous display of his craftmanship. [2]Day and night they keep on telling about God. [3,4]Without a sound or word, silent in the skies, their message reaches out to all the world. The sun lives in the heavens where God placed it and moves out across the skies as radiant as a bridegroom going to his wedding, or as joyous as an athlete looking forward to a race! [6]The sun crosses the heavens from end to end, and nothing can hide from its heat.

Ps 68:33. To him who rides upon the ancient heavens, whose mighty voice thunders from the sky.

Ps 136:5. Praise him who made the heavens, for his lovingkindness continues forever. [6]Praise him who planted the water within the earth, for his lovingkindness continues forever. [7]Praise him who made the heavenly lights, for his lovingkindness continues forever: [8]the sun to rule the day, for his lovingkindness continues forever; [9]and the moon and stars at night, for his lovingkindness endures forever.

Isa 13:10. The heavens will be black above them. No light will shine from stars or sun or moon.

Isa 40:22. It is God who sits above the circle of the earth. (The people below must seem to him like grasshoppers!) He is the one who stretches out the heavens like a curtain and makes his tent from them. [26]Look up into the heavens! Who created all these stars? As a shepherd leads his sheep, calling each by its pet name, and counts them to see that none are lost or strayed, so God does with stars and planets!

Isa 47:13. You have advisors by the ton—your astrologers and stargazers, who try to tell you what the future holds.

Jer 31:35. The Lord who gives us sunlight in the daytime and the moon and stars to light the night, and who stirs the sea to make the roaring waves—his name is Lord of Hosts—says this: [36]I am as likely to reject my people Israel as I am to do away with these laws of nature! [37]Not until the heavens can be measured and the foundations of the earth explored, will I consider casting them away forever for their sins!

Jer 33:22. And as the stars cannot be counted nor the sand upon the seashores measured, so the descendants of David my servant and the line of the Levites who minister to me will be multiplied.

Amos 5:8. Seek him who created the Seven Stars and the constellation Orion, who turns darkness into morning, and day into night, who calls forth the water from the ocean and pours it out as rain upon the land. The Lord, Jehovah, is his name.

1 Cor 15:41. The sun has one kind of glory while the moon and the stars have another kind. And the stars differ from each other in beauty and brightness.

Jude 1:13. All they leave behind them is shame and disgrace like the dirty foam left along the beach by the waves. They wander around looking as bright as stars, but ahead of them is the everlasting gloom and darkness that God has prepared for them.

SIDEREAL PHENOMENA. Josh 10:12. As the men of Israel were pursuing and harassing the foe, Joshua prayed aloud, "Let the sun stand still over Gibeon, and let the moon stand in its place over the valley of Aijalon!" [13]And the sun and the moon didn't move until the Israeli army had finished the destruction of its enemies! This is described in greater detail in *The Book of Jashar.* So the sun stopped in the heavens and stayed there for almost twenty-four hours! [14]There had never been such a day before, and there has never been another since, when the Lord stopped the sun and moon—all because of the prayer of one man.

Job 9:6. He shakes the earth to its foundations. [7]The sun won't rise, the stars won't shine, if he commands it so! [8]Only he has stretched the heavens out and stalked along the seas. [9]He made the Bear, Orion and the Pleiades, and the constellations of the southern Zodiac.

Eccl 1:5. The sun rises and sets and hurries around to rise again.

Isa 13:13. For I will shake the heavens in my wrath and fierce anger, and the earth will move from its place in the skies.

Isa 34:4. At that time the heavens above will melt away and disappear just like a rolled-up scroll, and the stars will fall as leaves, as ripe fruit from the trees.

Ezk 32:7,8 I will blot you out, and I will veil the heavens and darken the stars. I will cover the sun with a cloud, and the moon shall not give you her light. [8]Yes, darkness will be everywhere across your land—even the bright stars will be dark above you.

Mt 24:29. Immediately after the persecution of those days the sun will be darkened, and the moon will not give light, and the stars will seem to fall from the heavens, and the powers overshadowing the earth will be convulsed. [Mk 13:24,25] [35]Heaven and earth shall pass away, but my words remain forever.

Mt 27:45. That afternoon, the whole earth was covered with darkness for three hours, from noon until three o'clock.

Lk 21:25. Then there will be strange events in the skies—warnings, evil omens and portents in the sun, moon and stars; and down here on earth the nations will be in turmoil, perplexed by the roaring seas and strange tides.

Lk 23:44. By now it was noon, and darkness fell across the whole land for three hours, until three o'clock. [45]The light from the sun was gone—and suddenly the thick veil hanging in the Temple split apart.

Acts 2:19. And I will cause strange demonstrations in the heavens and on the earth—blood and fire and clouds of smoke; [20]the sun shall turn black and the moon blood-red before that awesome Day of the Lord arrives.

2 Pet 3:10. The day of the Lord is surely coming, as unexpectedly as a thief, and then the heavens will pass away with a terrible noise and the heavenly bodies will disappear in fire, and the earth and everything on it will be burned up.

Rev 6:12. I watched as he broke the sixth seal and there was a vast earthquake; and the sun became dark like black cloth, and the moon was blood-red. [13]Then the stars of heaven appeared to be falling to earth—like green fruit from fig trees buffeted by mighty winds. [14]And the starry heavens disappeared as though rolled up like a scroll and taken away; and every mountain and island shook and shifted.

Rev 8:10. The third angel blew, and a great flaming star fell from heaven upon a third of the rivers and springs. [11]The star was called "Bitterness" because it poisoned a third of all the water on the earth and many people died. [12]The fourth angel blew his trumpet and immediately a third of the sun was blighted and darkened, and a third of the moon and the stars, so that the daylight was dimmed by a third, and the nighttime darkness deepened.

Rev 9:1. Then the fifth angel blew his trumpet and I saw one who was fallen to earth from heaven, and to him was given the key to the bottomless pit. [2]When he opened it, smoke poured out as though from some huge furnace, and the sun and air were darkened by the smoke.

Rev 10:1. Then I saw another mighty angel coming down from heaven, surrounded by a cloud, with a rainbow over his head; his face shone like the sun and his feet flashed with fire. [2]And he held open in his hand a small scroll. He set his right foot on the sea and his left foot on the earth.

Rev 12:3. Suddenly a red Dragon appeared, with seven heads and ten horns, and seven crowns on his heads. [4]His tail drew along behind him a third of the stars, which he plunged to the earth.

Rev 13:13. He did unbelievable miracles such as making fire flame down to earth from the skies while everyone was watching.

Rev 16:8. Then the fourth angel poured out his flask upon the sun, causing it to scorch all men with its fire. [9]Everyone was burned by the blast of heat.

Rev 19:11. Then I saw heaven opened and a white horse standing there; and the one sitting on the horse was named "Faithful and True"—the one who justly punishes and makes war. [12]His eyes were like flames, and on his head were many crowns. A name was written on his forehead, and only he knew its meaning. [13]He was clothed with garments dipped in blood, and his title was "The Word of God." [14]The armies of heaven, dressed in finest linen, white and clean, followed him on white horses.

Rev 21:1. Then I saw a new earth (with no oceans!) and a new sky, for the present earth and sky had disappeared.

See *Constellations; Eclipse; Heaven; Meteorology; Moon; Stars; Sun.*

ASYNCRITUS A disciple at Rome, Rom 16:14.

ATAD The place where the sons of Jacob mourned for their father, Gen 50:10,11.

ATARAH Wife of Jerahmeel, 1 Chron 2:26.

ATAROTH 1. A city east of Jordan, Num 32:3, 4, 34–36.

2. A city, or possibly two different cities, of Ephraim, Josh 16:1–5,7; 18:13. Called *Ataroth-addar.*

3. A city of Judah, and the descendants of Salma who lived there, 1 Chron 2:54. Called *Atroth-beth-joab.*

4. A city of Gad, Num 32:34–36. Called *Atroth-shopan.*

ATAROTH-ADDAR See *Ataroth, 2.*

ATER 1. A descendant of Hezekiah, whose family returned from Babylon, Ezra 2:3–35; Neh 7:8–38.

2. Ancestor of a family of gatekeepers, Ezra 2:42.

3. An Israelite, who subscribed to Nehemiah's covenant, Neh 10:14–27.

ATHACH A city of Judah, 1 Sam 30:27–31.

ATHAIAH Son of Uzziah, perhaps identical with *Asaiah,* Neh 11:4.

ATHALIAH 1. Wife of Jehoram, king of Judah, 2 Kgs 8:18,26; 11:1–3,12–16,20; 2 Chron 22:10–12; 23:12–17,21.

2. Son of Jehoram, 1 Chron 8:26,27.

3. Father of Jeshaiah, Ezra 8:2–14.

ATHEISM Ps 10:4. The wicked men, so proud and haughty, seem to think that God is dead. They wouldn't think of looking for him!

Ps 14:1. That man is a fool who says to himself, "There is no God!" Anyone who talks like that is warped and evil and cannot really be a good person at all. Ps 53:1.

ARGUMENTS AGAINST. Job 12:7–9. Who doesn't know that the Lord does things like that? Ask the dumbest beast—he knows that it is so; ask the birds—they will tell you; or let the earth teach you, or the fish of the sea. [10]For the soul of every living thing is in the hand of God, and the breath of all mankind. [11]Just as my mouth can taste good food, so my mind tastes truth when I hear it. [12]And as you say, older men like me are wise. They understand. [13]But true wisdom and power are God's. He alone knows what we should do; he understands. [14]And how great is his might! What he destroys can't be rebuilt. When he closes in on a man, there is no escape. [15]He withholds the rain, and the earth becomes a desert; he sends the storms, and floods the ground. [16]Yes, with him is strength and wisdom. Deceivers and deceived are both his slaves. [17]He makes fools of counselors and judges. [18]He reduces kings to slaves and frees the servants. [19]Priests are led away as slaves. He overthrows the mighty. [20]He takes away the voice of orators, and the insight of the elders. [21]He pours contempt upon princes, and weakens the strong. [22]He floods the darkness with light, even the dark shadow of death. [23]He raises up a nation and then destroys it. He makes it great, and then reduces it to nothing. [24,25]He takes away the understanding of presidents and kings, and leaves them wandering lost and groping, without a guiding light.

Rom 1:19. For the truth about God is known to them instinctively, God has put this knowledge in their hearts. [20]Since earliest times men have seen the earth and sky and all God made, and have known of his existence and great eternal power. So they will have no excuse (when they stand before God at Judgment Day).

See *God; Faith; Unbelief.*

ATHENS A city of Greece, Acts 17:15–34; 1 Thess 3:1.

ATHLAI A son of Bebai, Ezra 10:28.

ATONEMENT For tabernacle and furniture, Lev 16:15–20,33. In consecration of the Levites, Num 8:21. For those defiled by the dead, Num 6:11. Made for houses, Lev 14:53.

For sin, see below.

By meat offerings, Lev 5:11–13; by jewels, Num 31:50; by money, Ex 30:11–16; Lev 5:15,16; 2 Kgs 12:16; by incense, Num 16:46–50; by animals, see below; by Jesus, see below.

DAY OF. Time of, Ex 30:10; Lev 23:26,27; 25:8,9; Num 29:7. How observed, Ex 30:10; Lev 16:3–34; 23:26–32; Num 29:7–11; Heb 5:1–3; 9:7.

MADE BY ANIMAL SACRIFICES. Ex 29:36. Every day you shall sacrifice a young bull as a sin offering for atonement; afterwards, purge the altar by making atonement for it; pour olive oil upon it to sanctify it.

Lev 1:4. The person bringing it is to lay his hand upon its head, and it then becomes his substitute; the death of the animal will be accepted by God instead of the death of the man who brings it, as penalty for his sins.

Lev 4:13. If the entire nation of Israel sins without realizing it, and does something that Jehovah has said not to do, all the people are guilty. [14]When they realize it, they shall offer a young bull for a sin offering, bringing it to the Tabernacle [15]where the leaders of the nation shall lay their hands upon the animal's head and kill it before the Lord. [16]Then the priest shall bring its blood into the Tabernacle, [17]and shall dip his finger in the blood and sprinkle it seven times before the Lord, in front of the veil. [18]Then he shall put blood upon the horns of the altar there in the Tabernacle before the Lord, and all the remainder of the blood shall be poured out at the base of the burnt offering altar, at the entrance to the Tabernacle.

Lev 4:20. He shall follow the same procedure as for a sin offering; in this way the priest shall make atonement for the nation, and everyone shall be forgiven.

22. If one of the leaders sins without realizing it, and is guilty of disobeying one of God's laws, [23]as soon as it is called to his attention he must bring as his sacrifice a billy goat without any physical defect. [24]He shall lay his hand upon its head and kill it at the place where the burnt offerings are killed, and present it to the Lord. This is his sin offering. [25]Then the priest shall take some of the blood of this sin offering and place it with his finger upon the horns of the altar of burnt offerings, and the rest of the blood shall be poured out at the base of the altar. [26]All the fat shall be burned upon the altar, just as if it were the fat of the sacrifice of a thank-offering; thus the priest shall make atonement for the leader concerning his sin, and he shall be forgiven. [27]If any one of the common people sins and doesn't realize it, he is guilty. [28]But as soon as he does realize it, he is to bring as his sacrifice a nanny goat without defect to atone for his sin. [29]He shall bring it to the place where the animals for burnt offerings are killed, and there lay his hand upon the head of the sin offering and kill it. [30]And the priest shall take some of the blood with his finger and smear it upon the horns of the burnt offering altar. Then the priest shall pour out the remainder of the blood at the base of the altar. [31]All

the fat shall be taken off, just as in the procedure for the thank-offering sacrifice, and the priest shall burn it upon the altar; and the Lord will appreciate it. Thus the priest shall make atonement for that man, and he shall be forgiven. [32]However, if he chooses to bring a lamb as his sin offering, it must be a female without physical defect. [33]He shall bring it to the place where the burnt offerings are killed, and lay his hand upon its head and kill it there as a sin offering. [34]The priest shall take some of the blood with his finger and smear it upon the horns of the altar, and all the rest of the blood shall be poured out at the base of the altar. [35]The fat shall be used just as in the case of a thank-offering lamb —the priest shall burn the fat on the altar as in any other sacrifice made to Jehovah by fire; and the priest shall make atonement for the man, and his sin shall be forgiven.

Lev 5:5. He shall confess his sin [6]and bring his guilt offering to the Lord, a female lamb or goat, and the priest shall make atonement for him, and he shall be freed from his sin, and need not fulfill the vow. [7]If he is too poor to bring a lamb to the Lord, then he shall bring two turtledoves or two young pigeons as his guilt offering; one of the birds shall be his sin offering and the other his burnt offering. [8]The priest shall offer as the sin sacrifice whichever bird is handed to him first, wringing its neck, but not severing its head from its body. [9]Then he shall sprinkle some of the blood at the side of the altar and the rest shall be drained out at the base of the altar; this is the sin offering. [10]He shall offer the second bird as a burnt offering, following the customary procedures that have been set forth; so the priest shall make atonement for him concerning his sin and he shall be forgiven.

Lev 6:7. And the priest shall make atonement for him before the Lord, and he shall be forgiven.

Lev 8:15. He smeared some of the blood with his finger upon the four horns of the altar, and upon the altar itself, to sanctify it, and poured out the rest of the blood at the base of the altar; thus he sanctified the altar, making atonement for it.

Lev 9:7. Moses then told Aaron to proceed to the altar and to offer the sin offering and the burnt offering, making atonement for himself first, and then for the people, as the Lord had commanded.

Lev 10:17. "Why haven't you eaten the sin offering in the sanctuary, since it is most holy, and God has given it you to take away the iniquity and guilt of the people, to make atonement for them before the Lord?" he demanded.

Lev 12:6. When these days of purification are ended (the following instructions are applicable whether her baby is a boy or girl), she must bring a yearling lamb as a burnt offering, and a young pigeon or a turtledove for a sin offering. She must take them to the door of the Tabernacle to the priest; [7]and the priest will offer them before the Lord and make atonement for her; then she will be ceremonially clean again after her bleeding at childbirth. These then, are the procedures after childbirth. [8]But if she is too poor to bring a lamb, then she must bring two turtledoves or two young pigeons. One will be for a burnt offering and the other for a sin offering. The priest will make atonement for her with these, so that she will be ceremonially pure again.

Lev 14:12. The priest shall take one of the lambs and the pint of olive oil and offer them to the Lord as a guilt offering by the gesture of waving them before the altar. [13]Then he shall kill the lamb at the place where sin offerings and burnt offerings are killed, there at the Tabernacle; this guilt offering shall then be given to the priest for food, as in the case of a sin offering. It is a most holy offering. [14]The priest shall take the blood from this guilt offering and smear some of it upon the tip of the right ear of the man being cleansed, and upon the thumb of his right hand, and upon the big toe of his right foot. [15]Then the priest shall take the olive oil and pour it into the palm of his left hand, [16]and dip his right finger into it, and sprinkle it with his finger seven times before the Lord. [17]Some of the oil remaining in his left hand shall then be placed by the priest upon the tip of the man's right ear and the thumb of his right hand and the big toe of his right foot—just as he did with the blood of the guilt offering. [18]The remainder of the oil in his hand shall be used to anoint the man's head. Thus the priest shall make atonement for him before the Lord. [19]Then the priest must offer the sin offering and again perform the rite of atonement for the person being cleansed from his leprosy; and afterwards the priest shall kill the burnt offering, [20]and offer it along with the grain offering upon the altar, making atonement for the man, who shall then be pronounced finally cleansed. [21]If he is so poor that he cannot afford two lambs, then he shall bring only one, a male lamb for the guilt offering, to be presented to the Lord in the rite of atonement by waving it before the altar; and only three quarts of fine white flour, mixed with olive oil, for a grain offering, and a pint of olive oil. [22]He shall also bring two turtledoves or two young pigeons—whichever he is able to afford—and use one of the pair for a sin offering and the other for a burnt offering. [23]He shall bring them to the priest at the entrance of the Tabernacle on the eighth day, for his ceremony of cleansing before the Lord. [24]The priest shall take the lamb for the guilt offering, and the pint of oil, and wave them before the altar as a gesture of offering to the Lord. [25]Then he shall kill the lamb for the guilt offering and smear some of its blood upon the tip of the man's right ear—the man on whose behalf the ceremony is being performed— and upon the thumb of his right hand and on the big toe of his right foot. [26]The priest shall then pour the olive oil into the palm of his own left hand, [27]and with his right finger he is to sprinkle some of it seven times before the Lord. [28]Then he must put some of the olive oil from his hand upon the tip of the man's right ear, and upon the thumb of his right hand, and upon the big toe of his right foot, just as he did with the blood of the guilt offering. [29]The remaining oil in his hand shall be placed upon the head of the man being cleansed, to make atonement for him before the Lord. [30]Then he must offer the two turtledoves or two young pigeons (whichever pair he is able to afford). [31]One of the pair is for a sin offering and the other for a burnt offering, to be sacrificed along with the grain offering; and the priest shall make atonement for the man before the Lord. [32]These, then, are the laws concerning those who are cleansed of leprosy but are not able to bring the sacrifices normally required for the ceremony of cleansing.

Lev 16:6. First he shall present to the Lord the young bull as a sin offering for himself, making atonement for himself and his family. [10]The other goat shall be kept alive and placed before the Lord. The rite of atonement shall be performed over it, and it shall then be sent out into the desert as a scapegoat. [11]After Aaron has sacrificed the young bull as a sin offering for himself and his family, [12]he shall take a censer full of live coals from the altar of the Lord, and fill his hands with sweet incense beaten into fine powder, and bring it inside the veil. [15]Then he must go out and sacrifice the people's sin offering goat, and bring its blood within the veil, and sprinkle it upon the place of mercy and in front of it, just as he did with the blood of the young bull. [16]Thus he shall make atonement for the holy place because it is defiled by the sins of the people of Israel, and for the Tabernacle, located right among them and surrounded by their defilement. [17]Not another soul shall be inside the Tabernacle when Aaron enters to make atonement in the Holy Place —not until after he comes out again and has made atonement for himself and his household and for all the people of Israel. [18]Then he shall go out to the altar before the Lord and make atonement for it. He must smear the blood of the young bull and the goat on the horns of the altar, [19]and sprinkle blood upon the altar seven times with his finger, thus cleansing it from the sinfulness of Israel, and making it holy. [24]Then he shall bathe in a sacred place, put on his clothes again, and go out and sacrifice his own burnt offering and the burnt offering for the people, making atonement for himself and for them. [25]He shall also burn upon the altar the fat for the sin offering. [26](The man who took the goat out into the desert shall afterwards wash his clothes and bathe himself and then come back into the camp.) [27]And the young bull and the goat used for the sin offering (their blood was taken into the Holy Place by Aaron, to make atonement) shall be carried outside the camp and burned, including the hides and internal organs. [28]Afterwards the person doing the burning shall wash his clothes and bathe himself and then return to camp. [29,30]This is a permanent law: You must do no work on the twenty-fifth day of September, but must spend the day in self-examination and humility. This applies whether you are born in the land or are a foreigner living among the people of Israel; for this is the day commemorating the atonement, cleansing you in the Lord's eyes from all of your sins. [31]It is a Sabbath of solemn rest for you, and you shall spend the day in quiet humility; this is a permanent law. [32]This ceremony, in later generations, shall be performed by the anointed High Priest, consecrated in place of his ancestor Aaron; he shall be the one to put on the holy linen garments, [33]and make atonement for the holy sanctuary, the Tabernacle, the altar, the priests, and the people. [34]This shall be an everlasting law for you, to make atonement for the people of Israel once each year, because of their sins.

Lev 17:11. For the life of the flesh is in the blood, and I have given you the blood to sprinkle upon the altar as an atonement for your souls; it is the blood that makes atonement, because it is the life.

Lev 19:22. The priest shall make atonement with the ram for the sin the man has committed, and it shall be forgiven him.

Num 15:22. If by mistake you or future generations fail to carry out all of these regulations which the Lord has given you over the years through Moses, [23,24]then when the people realize their error, they must offer one young bull for a burnt offering. It will be a pleasant odor before the Lord, and must be offered along with the usual grain offering and drink offering, and one male goat for a sin offering. [25]And the priest shall make atonement for all the people of Israel and they shall be forgiven; for it was an error, and they have corrected it with their sacrifice made by fire before the Lord, and by their sin offering. [26]All the people shall be forgiven, including the foreigners living among them, for the entire population is involved in such error and forgiveness. [27]If the error is made by a single individual, then he shall sacrifice a one-year-old female goat for a sin-offering, [28]and the priest shall make atonement for him before the Lord, and he shall be forgiven.

Num 28:30. Also offer one male goat to make atonement for yourselves. *v.* 22; Num 29:5, 9–11.

Heb 9:22. In fact we can say that under the old agreement almost everything was cleansed by sprinkling it with blood, and without the shedding of blood there is no forgiveness of sins.

MADE BY JESUS. Divinely ordained: Lk 2:29–31; Gal 4:4,5; Eph 1:3–12,16–22; 2:4–10; Col 1:19,20; 1 Pet 1:20; Rev 13:8. A mystery, 1 Cor 2:7, with context; 1 Pet 1:8–12. Made once for all, Heb 7:27; 9:24–28; 10:10,12,14; 1 Pet 3:18. Redemption by, Mt 20:28; Acts 20:28; Gal 3:13; 1 Tim 2:6; Heb 9:12; Rev 5:9. Typified, Gen 4:4, with Heb 11:4; Gen 22:2, with Heb 11:17,19; Ex 12:5,11,14 with 1 Cor 5:7; Ex 24:8, with Heb 9:20; Lev 16:29,30,34, with Heb 9:7,12,28; Lev 17:11 with Heb 9:22.

See *Salvation, Plan of.*

UNCLASSIFIED SCRIPTURES RELATING TO. Ps 40:6. It isn't sacrifices and offerings which you really want from your people. Burnt animals bring no special joy to your heart. But you have accepted the offer of my life-long service. [7]Then I said, "See, I have come, just as all the prophets foretold. [8]And I delight to do your will, my God, for your law is written upon my heart!" Heb 10:5–9.

Isa 53:4. Yet it was *our* grief he bore, *our* sorrows that weighed him down. And we thought his troubles were a punishment from God, for his *own* sins! [5]But he was wounded and bruised for *our* sins. He was chastised that we might have peace; he was lashed—and we were healed! [6]*We* are the ones who strayed away like sheep! *We,* who left God's path to follow our own. Yet God laid on *him* the guilt and sins of every one of us! [7]He was oppressed and he was afflicted, yet he never said a word. He was brought as a lamb to the slaughter; and as a sheep before her shearers is dumb, so he stood silent before the ones condemning him. [8]From prison and trial they led him away to his death. But who among the people of that day realized it was their sins that he was dying for—that he was suffering their punishment? [10]Yet it was the Lord's good plan to bruise him and fill him with grief. But when his soul has been made an offering for sin, then he shall have a multitude of children, many heirs. He shall live again and God's program shall prosper in his hands. [11]And when he sees that all is accomplished by the anguish of his soul, he shall be satisfied; and because of what he has experienced, my righteous Servant shall make many to be counted righteous before God, for he shall bear all their sins. [12]Therefore I will give him the honors of one who is mighty and great, because he has poured out his soul unto death. He was counted as a sinner, and he bore the sins of many, and he pled with God for sinners.

Dan 9:24. The Lord has commanded 490 years of further punishment upon Jerusalem and your people. Then at last they will learn to stay away from sin, and their guilt will be cleansed; then the kingdom of everlasting righteousness will begin, and the Most Holy Place (in the Temple) will be rededicated, as the prophets have declared. [25]Now listen! It will be forty-nine years plus 434 years from the time the command is given to rebuild Jerusalem, until the Anointed One comes! Jerusalem's streets and walls will be rebuilt despite the perilous times. [26]After this period of 434 years, the Anointed One will be killed, his kingdom still unrealized . . . and a king will arise whose armies will destroy the city and the Temple. They will be overwhelmed as with a flood, and war and its miseries are decreed from that time to the very end. [27]This king will make a seven-year treaty with the people, but after half that time, he will break his pledge and stop the Jews from all their sacrifices and their offerings; then, as a climax to all his terrible deeds, the Enemy shall utterly defile the sanctuary of God. But in God's time and plan, his judgment will be poured out upon this Evil One.

Zech 13:1. At that time a Fountain will be opened to the people of Israel and Jerusalem, a Fountain to cleanse them from all their sins and uncleanness.

Mt 26:28. For this is my blood, sealing the New Covenant. It is poured out to forgive the sins of multitudes. Lk 22:20.

Lk 24:46. And he said, "Yes, it was written long ago that the Messiah must suffer and die and rise again from the dead on the third day; [47]and that this message of salvation should be taken from Jerusalem to all the nations: *There is forgiveness of sins for all who turn to me.*"

Jn 1:29. The next day John saw Jesus coming toward him and said, "Look! There is the Lamb of God who takes away the world's sin!" *v.* 36

Jn 6:51. This Bread is my flesh given to redeem humanity.

Jn 11:49. And one of them, Caiaphas, who was High Priest that year, said, "You stupid idiots—[50]let this one man die for the people—why should the whole nation perish?" [51]This prophecy that Jesus should die for the entire nation came from Caiaphas in his position as High Priest, he didn't think of it by himself, but was inspired to say it.

Acts 17:2. As was Paul's custom, he went there to preach, and for three Sabbaths in a row he opened the Scriptures to the people, [3]explaining the prophecies about the sufferings of the Messiah and his coming back to life, and proving that Jesus is the Messiah.

Acts 20:28. And now beware! Be sure that you feed and shepherd God's flock—his church, purchased with his blood—for the Holy Spirit is holding you responsible as overseers.

Rom 3:24. Yet now God declares us "not guilty" of offending him if we trust in Jesus Christ, who in his kindness freely takes away our sins. [25]For God sent Christ Jesus to take the punishment for our sins and to end all God's anger against us. He used Christ's blood and our faith as the means of saving us from his wrath. In this way he was being entirely fair, even though he did not punish those who sinned in former times. For he was looking forward to the time when Christ would come and take away those sins. [26]And now in these days also he can receive sinners in this same way, because Jesus took away their sins.

Rom 4:25. He died for our sins and rose again to make us right with God, filling us with God's goodness.

Rom 5:1. And now, since we have been made right in God's sight by faith in his promises, we can have real peace with him because of what Jesus Christ our Lord has done for us. [2]For because of our faith, he has brought us into this place of highest privilege where we now stand, and we confidently and joyfully look forward to actually becoming all that God has had in mind for us to be. [6]When we were utterly helpless with no way of escape, Christ came at just the right time and died for us sinners who had no use for him. [7]Even if we were good, we really wouldn't expect anyone to die for us, though, of course, that might be barely possible. [8]But God showed his great love for us by sending Christ to die for us while we were still sinners. [9]And since by his blood he did all this for us as sinners, how much more will he do for us now that he has declared us not guilty? Now he will save us from all of God's wrath to come. [10]And since, when we were his enemies, we were brought back to God by the death of his Son, what blessings he must have for us now that we are his friends, and he is living within us! [11]Now we rejoice in our wonderful new relationship with God—all because of what our Lord Jesus Christ has done in dying for our sins—making us friends of God. [15]And what a difference between man's sin and God's forgiveness! For this one man, Adam, brought death to many through his *sin.* But this one man, Jesus Christ, brought forgiveness to many through God's *mercy.* [16]Adam's *one* sin brought the penalty of death to many, while Christ freely takes away *many* sins and gives glorious life instead. [17]The sin of this one man, Adam, caused *death to be king over all,* but all who will take God's gift of forgiveness and spiritual acquittal are *kings of life* because of this one man, Jesus Christ. [18]Yes, Adam's *sin* brought *punishment* to all, but Christ's *righteousness* makes men *right with God,* so that they can live. [19]Adam caused many to be sinners because he *disobeyed* God, and Christ caused many to be made acceptable to God because he *obeyed.* [20]The Ten Commandments were given so that all could see the extent of their failure to obey God's laws. But the more we see our sinfulness, the more we see God's abounding grace forgiving us. [21]Before, sin ruled over all men and brought them to death, but now God's kindness rules instead, giving us right standing with God and resulting in eternal life through Jesus Christ our Lord.

1 Cor 1:17. For Christ didn't send me to baptize, but to preach the Gospel; and even my preaching sounds poor, for I do not fill my sermons with profound words and high sounding ideas, for fear of diluting the mighty power there is in the simple message of the cross of Christ. [18]I know very well how foolish it sounds to those who are lost, when they hear that Jesus died to save them. But we who are saved recognize this message as the very power of God. [23]So when we preach about Christ dying to save them, the Jews are offended and the Gentiles say it's all nonsense. [24]But God has opened the eyes of those called to salvation, both Jews and Gentiles, to see that Christ is the mighty power of God to save them; Christ himself is the center of God's wise plan for their salvation.

1 Cor 15:3. I passed on to you right from the first what had been told to me, that Christ died for our sins just as the Scriptures said he would.

2 Cor 5:18. All these new things are from God who brought us back to himself through what Christ Jesus did. And God has given us the privilege of urging everyone to come into his favor and be reconciled to him. [19]For God was in Christ, restoring the world to himself, no longer counting men's sins against them but blotting them out. This is the wonderful message he has given us to tell others.

Gal 1:3. May peace and blessing be yours from God the Father and from our Lord Jesus Christ. [4]He died for our sins just as God our Father planned, and rescued us from this evil world in which we live.

Gal 4:4. But when the right time came, the time God decided on, he sent his Son, born of a woman, born as a Jew, [5]to buy freedom for us who were slaves to the law so that he could adopt us as his very own sons.

Eph 1:7. So overflowing is his kindness towards us that he took away all our sins through the blood of his Son, by whom we are saved.

Eph 2:13. But now you belong to Christ Jesus, and though you once were far away from God, now you have been brought very near to him because of what Jesus Christ has done for you with his blood. [14]For Christ himself is our way of peace. He has made peace between us Jews and you Gentiles by making us all one family, breaking down the wall of contempt that used to separate us. [15]By his death he ended the angry resentment between us, caused by the Jewish laws which favored the Jews and excluded the Gentiles, for he died to annul that whole system of Jewish laws. Then he took the two groups that had been opposed to each other and made them parts of himself; thus he fused us together to become one new person, and at last there was peace. [16]As parts of the same body, our anger against each other has disappeared, for both of us have been reconciled to God. And so the feud ended at last at the cross. [17]And he has brought this Good News of peace to you Gentiles who were very far away from him, and to us Jews who were near. [18]Now all of us, whether Jews or Gentiles, may come to God the Father with the Holy Spirit's help because of what Christ has done for us.

Eph 5:2. Be full of love for others, following the example of Christ who loved you and gave himself to God as a sacrifice to take away your sins. And God was pleased, for Christ's love for you was like sweet perfume to him. *v.* 25.

Col 1:14. Who bought our freedom with his blood and forgave us all our sins. [19]For God wanted all of himself to be in his Son. [20]It was through what his Son did that God cleared a path for everything to come to him—all things in heaven and on earth —for Christ's death on the cross has made peace with God for all by his blood. [21]This includes you who were once so far away from God. You were his enemies and hated him and were separated from him by your evil thoughts and actions, yet now he has brought you back as his friends. [22]He has done this through the death on the cross of his own human body, and now as a result Christ has brought you into the very presence of God, and you are standing there before him with nothing left against you—nothing left that he could even chide you for.

1 Thess 5:9. For God has not chosen to pour out his anger upon us, but to save us through our Lord Jesus Christ; [10]he died for us so that we can live with him forever, whether we are alive or dead at the time of his return.

1 Tim 2:5. That God is on one side and all the people on the other side, and Christ Jesus, himself man, is between them to bring them together, [6]by giving his life for all mankind. This is the message which at the proper time God gave to the world.

Tit 2:14. He died under God's judgment against

our sins, so that he could rescue us from constant falling into sin and make us his very own people, with cleansed hearts and real enthusiasm for doing kind things for others.

Heb 1:3. God's Son shines out with God's glory, and all that God's Son is and does marks him as God. He regulates the universe by the mighty power of his command. He is the one who died to cleanse us and clear our record of all sin, and then sat down in highest honor beside the great God of heaven.

Heb 2:9. But we do see Jesus—who for awhile was a little lower than the angels—crowned now by God with glory and honor because he suffered death for us. Yes, because of God's great kindness, Jesus tasted death for everyone in all the world.
[17]And it was necessary for Jesus to be like us, his brothers, so that he could be our merciful and faithful High Priest before God, a Priest who would be both merciful to us and faithful to God in dealing with the sins of the people.

Heb 9:12. And once for all took blood into that inner room, the Holy of Holies, and sprinkled it on the mercy seat; but it was not the blood of goats and calves. No, he took his own blood and with it he, by himself, made sure of our eternal salvation.
[13]And if under the old system the blood of bulls and goats and the ashes of young cows could cleanse men's bodies from sin, [14]just think how much more surely the blood of Christ will transform our lives and hearts. His sacrifice frees us from the worry of having to obey the old rules, and makes us want to serve the living God. For by the help of the eternal Holy Spirit, Christ willingly gave himself to God to die for our sins—he being perfect, without a single sin or fault. [15]Christ came with this new agreement so that all who are invited may come and have forever all the wonders God has promised them. For Christ died to rescue them from the penalty of the sins they had committed while still under that old system. [25]Nor has he offered himself again and again, as the high priest down here on earth offers animal blood in the Holy of Holies each year. [26]If that had been necessary, then he would have had to die again and again, ever since the world began. But no! He came once for all, at the end of the age, to put away the power of sin forever by dying for us.

Heb 10:1. The old system of the Jewish laws gave only a dim foretaste of the good things Christ would do for us. The sacrifices under the old system were repeated again and again, year after year, but even so they could never save those who lived under their rules. [2]If they could have, one offering would have been enough; the worshipers would have been cleansed once for all, and their feeling of guilt would be gone. [3]But just the opposite happened: those yearly sacrifices reminded them of their disobedience and guilt instead of relieving their minds. [4]For it is not possible for the blood of bulls and goats really to take away sins. [5]That is why Christ said, as he came into the world, "O God, the blood of bulls and goats cannot satisfy you, so you have made ready this body of mine for me to lay as a sacrifice upon your altar. [6]You were not satisfied with the animal sacrifices, slain and burnt offerings for sin. [7]Then I said, 'See, I have come to do your will, to lay down my life, just as the Scriptures said that I would.' " [8]After Christ said this, about not being satisfied with the various sacrifices and offerings required under the old system, [9]he then added, "Here I am. I have come to give my life." He cancels the first system in favor of a far better one. [10]Under this new plan we have been forgiven and made clean by Christ's dying for us once and for all. [11]Under the old agreement the priests stood before the altar day after day offering sacrifices that could never take away our sins. [12]But Christ gave himself to God for our sins as one sacrifice for all time, and then sat down in the place of highest honor at God's right hand. [18]Now, when sins have once been forever forgiven and forgotten, there is no need to offer more sacrifices to get rid of them. [19]And so, dear brothers, now we may walk right into the very Holy of Holies where God is, because of the blood of Jesus. [20]This is the fresh, new, life-giving way which Christ has opened up for us by tearing the curtain—his human body—to let us into the holy presence of God.

Heb 12:24. And to Jesus himself, who has brought us his wonderful new agreement; and to the sprinkled blood which graciously forgives instead of crying out for vengeance as the blood of Abel did.

Heb 13:12. That is why Jesus suffered and died outside the city, where his blood washed our sins away. [20,21]And now may the God of peace, who brought again from the dead our Lord Jesus, equip you with all you need for doing his will. May he who became the great Shepherd of the sheep by an everlasting agreement between God and you, signed with his blood, produce in you through the power of Christ all that is pleasing to him.

1 Pet 1:18. God paid a ransom to save you from the impossible road to heaven which your fathers tried to take, and the ransom he paid was not mere gold or silver, as you very well know. [19]But he paid for you with the precious lifeblood of Christ, the sinless, spotless Lamb of God. [20]God chose him for this purpose long before the world began, but only recently was he brought into public view, in these last days, as a blessing to you.

1 Pet 2:24. He personally carried the load of our sins in his own body when he died on the cross, so that we can be finished with sin and live a good life from now on. For his wounds have healed ours!

1 Pet 3:18. Christ also suffered. He died once for the sins of all of us guilty sinners, although he himself was innocent of any sin at any time, that he might bring us safely home to God. But though his body died, his spirit lived on.

1 Jn 1:7. But if we are living in the light of God's presence just as Christ does, then we have wonderful fellowship and joy with each other, and the blood of Jesus his Son cleanses us from every sin.

1 Jn 2:2. He is the one who took God's wrath

against our sins upon himself, and brought us into fellowship with God; and he is the forgiveness for our sins, and not only ours but all the world's.

1 Jn 3:5. And you know that he became a man so that he could take away our sins, and that there is no sin in him, no missing of God's will at any time in any way.

1 Jn 4:10. In this act we see what real love is: it is not our love for God, but his love for us when he sent his Son to satisfy God's anger against our sins.

1 Jn 5:6. And we know he is, because God said so with a voice from heaven when Jesus was baptized, and again as he was facing death—yes, not only at his baptism but also as he faced death. And the Holy Spirit, forever truthful, says it too.

Rev 1:5. And from Jesus Christ who faithfully reveals all truth to us. He was the first to rise from death, to die no more. He is far greater than any king in all the earth. All praise to him who always loves us and who set us free from our sins by pouring out his lifeblood for us.

Rev 5:9. They were singing him a new song with these words: "You are worthy to take the scroll and break its seals and open it; for you were slain, and your blood has bought people from every nation as gifts for God."

Rev 7:14. "These are the ones coming out of the Great Tribulation," he said; "they washed their robes and whitened them by the blood of the Lamb."

Rev 12:11. They defeated him by the blood of the Lamb, and by their testimony; for they did not love their lives but laid them down for him.

See *Blood; Jesus, Death of, Mission of, Sufferings of; Redemption; Salvation.*

ATROPHY Of the hand, Mt 12:10–13.

ATROTH-BETH-JOAB See *Ataroth,* 3.

ATROTH-SHOPAN See *Ataroth, 4.*

ATTAI 1. A Gadite warrior, 1 Chron 12:8–13.
2. Son of Rehoboam, 2 Chron 11:20.
3. Grandson of Sheshan, 1 Chron 2:34–36.

ATTALIA A seaport of Pamphylia, Acts 14:25.

ATTORNEY FIGURATIVE. Isa 3:13.

ATTRIBUTES OF GOD See *God.*

AUGUST See *Calendar.*

AUGUSTUS A title of Roman emperors, Lk 2:1.

AVARICE Eccl 4:7. I also observed another piece of foolishness around the earth. [8]This is the case of a man who is quite alone, without a son or brother, yet he works hard to keep gaining more riches, and to whom will he leave it all? And why is he giving up so much now? It is all so pointless and depressing.

Eccl 5:10. He who loves money shall never have enough. The foolishness of thinking that wealth brings happiness!" [11]The more you have, the more you spend, right up to the limits of your income, so what is the advantage of wealth—except perhaps to watch it as it runs through your fingers!

1 Tim 3:2. For a pastor must be a good man whose life cannot be spoken against. He must have only one wife, and he must be hard working and thoughtful, orderly, and full of good deeds. He must enjoy having guests in his home, and must be a good Bible teacher. [3]He must not be a drinker or quarrelsome, but he must be gentle and kind, and not be one who loves money. Tit 1:7.

1 Tim 6:5. These arguers—their minds warped by sin—don't know how to tell the truth; to them the Good News is just a means of making money. Keep away from them. [10]For the love of money is the first step towards all kind of sin. Some people have even turned away from God for love of it, and as a result have pierced themselves with many sorrows.

See *Covetousness; Rich; Riches.*

INSTANCES OF. The descendants of Joseph, Josh 17:14–18.

AVEN 1. "The plain of the Sun," Amos 1:5.
2. Abbreviation for *Beth-aven,* Hos 10:8.

AVENGER OF BLOOD Premosaic, Gen 9:5,6. Cain fears, Gen 4:14,15. Lamech fears, Gen 4:24. Law concerning, set aside by David, 2 Sam 14:4–11.

See *Homicide.*

FIGURATIVE. Ps 44:16; Rom 13:4; 1 Thess 4:6.

SCRIPTURES RELATING TO. Gen 9:5,6. And murder is forbidden. Man-killing animals must die, and any man who murders shall be killed; for to kill a man is to kill one made like God.

Num 35:19. The avenger of his death shall personally kill the murderer when he meets him. [20]So, if anyone kills another out of hatred by throwing something at him, or ambushing him, [21]or angrily striking him with his fist so that he dies, he is a murderer; and the murderer shall be executed by the avenger. [22,23]But if it is an accident—a case in which something is thrown unintentionally, or in which a stone is thrown without anger, without realizing it will hit anyone, and without wanting to harm an enemy—yet the man dies, [24]then the people shall judge whether or not it was an accident, and whether or not to hand the killer over to the avenger of the dead man. [25]If it is decided that it was accidental, then the people shall save the killer from the avenger; the killer shall be permitted to stay in the City of Refuge; and he must live there until the death of the High Priest. [26]If the slayer leaves the City, [27]and the avenger finds him outside and kills him, it is not murder, [28]for the man should have stayed inside the City until the death of the High Priest. But after the death of the High Priest, the man may return to his own land and home. [29]These are permanent laws for all Israel from generation to generation.

Deut 19:4. Here is an example of the purpose of these cities: [5]If a man goes into the forest with his neighbor to chop wood, and the axe head flies off the handle and kills the man's neighbor, he may flee to one of those cities and be safe. [6,7]Anyone seeking to avenge the death will not be able to. These cities must be scattered so that one of them will be reasonably close to everyone; otherwise the angry avenger might catch and kill the innocent slayer, even though he should not have died since he had not killed deliberately. [8]If the Lord enlarges your boundaries as he promised your ancestors, and gives you all the land he promised [9](whether he does this depends on your obedience to all these commandments I am giving you today—loving the Lord your God and walking his paths), then you must designate three additional Cities of Refuge. [10]In this way you will be able to avoid the death of innocent people, and you will not be held responsible for unjustified bloodshed. [11]But if anyone hates his neighbor and springs out of hiding and kills him, and then flees into one of the Cities of Refuge, [12]the elders of his home town shall send for him and shall bring him home and deliver him over to the dead man's avenger, to kill him. [13]Don't pity him! Purge all murderers from Israel! Only then will all go well with you.

Josh 20:1. The Lord said to Joshua, [2]"Tell the people of Israel to designate now the Cities of Refuge, as I instructed Moses. [3]If a man is guilty of killing someone unintentionally, he can run to one of these cities and be protected from the relatives of the dead man, who may try to kill him in revenge. [4]When the innocent killer reaches any of these cities, he will meet with the city council and explain what happened, and they must let him come in and must give him a place to live among them. [5]If a relative of the dead man comes to kill him in revenge, the innocent slayer must not be released to them, for the death was accidental. [6]The man who caused the accidental death must stay in that city until he has been tried by the judges, and must live there until the death of the High Priest who was in office at the time of the accident. But then he is free to return to his own city and home." [7]The cities chosen as Cities of Refuge were Kedesh of Galilee in the hill country of Naphtali; Shechem, in the hill country of Ephraim; and Kiriath-arba (also known as Hebron) in the hill country of Judah. [8]The Lord also instructed that three cities be set aside for this purpose on the east side of the Jordan River, across from Jericho. They were Bezer, in the wilderness of the land of the tribe of Reuben; Ramoth of Gilead, in the territory of the tribe of Gad; and Golan of Bashan, in the land of the tribe of Manasseh. [9]These Cities of Refuge were for foreigners living in Israel as well as for the Israelis themselves, so that anyone who accidentally killed another man could run to that place for a trial, and not be killed in revenge.

AVITH Capital city of the Edomites, Gen 36: 31–39; 1 Chron 1:46.

AVVA Called also *Ivvah.* A district near Babylon, 2 Kgs 17:24; 18:34; 19:13. See Ezra 4:8,9.

AVVIM 1. A city of Benjamin, Josh 18:21–28.

2. A nation in southern part of Canaan, Deut 2: 23; Josh 13:3.

AVVITES Colonists of Samaria, 2 Kgs 17:31.

AWL A tool, Ex 21:6; Deut 15:17.

AXE An implement, Deut 19:5; 1 Sam 13:20,21; 2 Sam 12:31; Ps 74:5,6. Elisha causes to float, 2 Kgs 6:5,6. A weapon, Prov 25:18. Used to make idols, Isa 44:13.

FIGURATIVE. Prov 25:18; Eccl 10:8–10; Isa 10: 34; Jer 51:20; Mt 3:10; Lk 3:9.

AXLE Part of a wheeled vehicle, 1 Kgs 7:32, 33.

AYYAH A city of Ephraim, 1 Chron 7:28.

AZALIAH Father of Shaphan, 2 Kgs 22:3, 4; 2 Chron 34:8.

AZANIAH Father of Jeshua, Neh 10:9–13.

AZAREL 1. An Aaronite of the family of Korah, 1 Chron 12:3–7.

2. A musician in the Temple, 1 Chron 25:9–31; called *Uzziel, v.* 4.

3. A Danite officer, 1 Chron 27:16–22.

4. A son of Bani, Ezra 10:34–42.

5. A priest, Neh 11:10–14.

6. A priest at the dedication of the wall, Neh 12: 35, 36.

AZARIAH 1. Son of Zadok, 1 Kgs 4:1–6; perhaps identical with 5, below.

2. Solomon's secretary of state, 1 Kgs 4:1–6.

3. Son of Ethan, 1 Chron 2:8.

4. Son of Jehu, 1 Chron 2:38, 39.

5. A high priest, 1 Chron 6:4–15. Called also *Amariah,* 2 Chron 19:11.

6. Son of Johanan, possibly identical with *Zechariah,* son of Jehoiada, 1 Chron 6:4–15; 2 Chron 24:20–22.

7. Son of Hilkiah, 1 Chron 6:4–15; 9:10, 11; Ezra 7:1–5.

8. A Levite, 1 Chron 6:33–38.

9. A prophet, son of Obed, 2 Chron 15:1.

10. Two sons of Jehoshaphat, 2 Chron 21:2.

11. King of Judah, called *Ahaziah,* 2 Chron 22: 6. See *Ahaziah.*

12. Son of Jeroham, 2 Chron 23:1.

13. Son of Obed, 2 Chron 23:1.

14. See *Uzziah,* king of Judah.

15. High priest at the time of Uzziah, 2 Chron 26: 16–20.

16. Leader of the tribe of Ephraim, 2 Chron 28: 12.

17. Father of Joel, 2 Chron 29:12–14.

18. A Levite who cleansed the Temple, 2 Chron 29:12–14.

19. High priest in Hezekiah's reign, 2 Chron 31: 10, 12, 13. Probably identical with *Ahitub* (son of Amariah and grandson of Meraioth) mentioned in 1 Chron 6:4–15.

20. Son of Ma-aseiah, Neh 3:23.

21. An exile returned from Babylon, Neh 7:7. Called also *Seraiah,* Ezra 2:2.

22. One who explained the law after Ezra read it, Neh 8:7, 8.

23. A priest who signed the covenant with Nehemiah, Neh 10:1–8; 12:33.

24. Son of Hoshaiah, Jer 43:2–7.

25. Hebrew name of *Abed-nego,* Dan 1:7, 18, 19.

AZAZ Father of Bela, 1 Chron 5:7, 8.

AZAZEL Symbolic destination and fate of the scapegoat, Lev 16:8, 10, 26.

See *Atonement, Day of.*

AZAZIAH 1. A harpist in the Temple, 1 Chron 15:21.

2. Father of Hoshea, 1 Chron 27:16–22.

3. Overseer in the Temple, 2 Chron 31:13.

AZBUK Father of Nehemiah, Neh 3:16.

AZEKAH A town of Judah, Josh 10:10, 11; 15:33–36; 1 Sam 17:1; 2 Chron 11:5–10; Neh 11:25–30; Jer 34:7.

AZEL 1. A Benjaminite, 1 Chron 8:37, 38; 9:43, 44.

2. A place near Jerusalem, Zech 14:5.

AZGAD 1. Ancestor of certain exiles who returned from Babylon, Ezra 2:3–35; 8:2–14; Neh 7:8–38.

2. A leader who signed Nehemiah's covenant, Neh 10:15.

AZIEL A Temple musician, 1 Chron 15:20.

AZIZA Son of Zattu, Ezra 10:27.

AZMAVETH 1. One of David's heroes, 2 Sam 23:24–39; 1 Chron 11:26–47.

2. A descendant of Jonathan, 1 Chron 8:36; 9:42.

3. Son of Adi-el, 1 Chron 27:25.

4. Father of two of David's warriors, 1 Chron 12:3–7.

5. A village of Judah or Benjamin, Ezra 2:3–35; Neh 12:29. Called *Beth-azmaveth,* Neh 7:8–38.

AZMON A place in the south of Canaan, Num 34:4, 5; Josh 15:2–4.

AZNOTH-TABOR A town in Naphtali, Josh 19:34.

AZOR Ancestor of Jesus, Mt 1:13, 14. Perhaps identical with *Azrikam,* 1 Chron 3:23.

AZOTUS See *Ashdod.*

AZRI-EL 1. A chief of Manasseh, 1 Chron 5:24.

2. Father of Jeremoth, 1 Chron 27:16–22.

3. Father of Seraiah, Jer 36:26.

AZRIKAM 1. Son of Nearaiah, 1 Chron 3:23.

2. Son of Azel, 1 Chron 8:38; 9:44.

3. A Levite, 1 Chron 9:14; Neh 11:15–17.

4. Administrator of the house of Ahaz, 2 Chron 28:7.

AZUBAH 1. Mother of Jehoshaphat, 1 Kgs 22:42; 2 Chron 20:31.

2. Wife of Caleb, 1 Chron 2:18, 19.

AZZAN Father of Paltiel, Num 34:16–28.

AZZUR 1. An Israelite, who signed Nehemiah's covenant, Neh 10:14–27.

2. A Gibeonite and father of Hanaiah, Jer 28:1.

3. Father of Ja-azaniah, Ezk 11:1.

B

BAAL 1. A Canaanite deity, meaning "Master." Wickedly worshiped by the Israelites in the time of the judges, Judg 2:10–23; 1 Sam 7:3, 4; by the kingdom of Israel, 2 Kgs 17:16; Jer 23:13; Hos 1; 2; 13:1; under Ahab, 1 Kgs 16:31–33; 18:18; 19:18; Jehoram, 2 Kgs 3:2, 3; by the Jews, 2 Kgs 21:3–5; 2 Chron 22:2–4; 24:7, 8; 28:2; 33:3. Jeremiah preaches against the worship of, Jer 2:8, 23; 7:9.

Altars of, destroyed by Gideon, Judg 6:25–32; by Jehoiada, 2 Kgs 11:18; by Josiah, 2 Kgs 23:4, 5.

Prophets of, killed by Elijah, 1 Kgs 18:40. All worshipers of, killed by Jehu, 2 Kgs 10:18–25.

2. A Benjaminite, 1 Chron 8:30–32; 9:35–37.

3. A Reubenite, 1 Chron 5:5.

4. A city in the tribe of Simeon, 1 Chron 4:32, 33. Called *Baalath-beer,* Josh 19:8.

BAALAH 1. A city in the south of Judah, Josh 15:21–32. Apparently identical with *Balah,* Josh 19:2–7; and *Bilhah,* 1 Chron 4:29.

2. A city in the north of Judah, called also *Kiriath-jearim,* Josh 15:9, 1 Chron 13:6. See *Kiriath-jearim.*

3. A mountain in Judah, Josh 15:10, 11. Probably identical with *Mount Jearim, vs.* 10, 11.

BAALATH A city of Dan, Josh 19:41–46; 1 Kgs 9:17, 18; 2 Chron 8:6.

BAALATH-BEER See *Baal, 4.*

BAAL-BERITH A god of the Shechemites, Judg 9:4, 46. Worshiped by Israelites, Judg 8:33.

BAAL-GAD A city of the Canaanites, Josh 11:17; 12:7; 13:2–7. Probably identical with *Baal-hermon,* Judg 3:1–3; 1 Chron 5:23.

BAAL-HAMON A place in Mount Ephraim, Song 8:11. Called *Hammon,* Josh 19:28.

BAAL-HANAN 1. A king of Edom, Gen 36:31–39; 1 Chron 1:49, 50.

2. One of David's overseers, 1 Chron 27:28.

BAAL-HAZOR The place where Amnon was murdered, 2 Sam 13:21–24.

BAAL-HERMON 1. A city near Mount Hermon, 1 Chron 5:23. Identical with *Baal-gad,* which see.

2. A mountain of Lebanon, Judg 3:1–3.

BAALIS King of the Ammonites, Jer 40:13, 14.

BAAL-JUDAH City of Judah, 2 Sam 6:1, 2. See *Kiriath-jearim.*

BAAL-MEON A city of the Reubenites, Num 32:38; 1 Chron 5:7, 8; Ezk 25:9, 10. Called *Beth-meon,* Jer 48:23; *Beth-baal-meon,* Josh 13:17; *Beon,* Num 32:3, 4.

BAAL-PEOR An idol of Moab, Deut 4:3; Ps 106:28; Hos 9:10. See also Num 31:16; Josh 22:17, 18.

BAAL-PERAZIM A place in the valley of Rephaim, 2 Sam 5:20; 1 Chron 14:11. Called *Perazim,* Isa 28:21.

BAAL-SHALISHAH A place near Gilgal, 2 Kgs 4:42.

BAAL-TAMAR A place near Gibe-ah, Judg 20:33.

BAAL-ZEBUB A god of the Philistines, 2 Kgs 1:2, 3, 6, 16.

BAANA 1. Son of Ahilud, 1 Kgs 4:8–19.

2. Father of Zadok, Neh 3:4.

3. Son of Hushai, 1 Kgs 4:8–19.

BAANAH 1. A captain of Ish-bosheth's army, 2 Sam 4:2, 3, 5, 6, 7.

2. Father of Heleb or Heled, 2 Sam 23:34–39; 1 Chron 11:26–47.

3. A chief Jew of the exile, Ezra 2:2; Neh 7:7. Called *Har Baana,* Neh 10:14–27.

BAARA Wife of Shaharaim, 1 Chron 8:8–10.

BA-ASEIAH A Levite, 1 Chron 6:39–43.

BAASHA King of Israel, 1 Kgs 15:16–22, 27–34; 16:1–7; 21:22; 2 Kgs 9:9; 2 Chron 16:1–6; Jer 41:9.

BABEL A city in the plain of Shinar. Tower built, and languages confused at, Gen 11:1–9. See *Babylon.*

BABIES Praise God, Mt 21:16. A symbol of the guileless, Mt 11:25; Lk 10:21; 1 Cor 14:20; of the children of the kingdom of heaven, Mt 18:2–6; Lk 18:15–17.

FIGURATIVE. Of weak Christians, 1 Cor 3:1; Heb 5:12, 13; 1 Pet 2:2.

See *Children; Parents.*

BABYLON 1. CITY OF. Built by Nimrod, Gen 10:8–10. In the land of Shinar, Gen 10:10; 11:2. Tower of, Gen 11:1–9. Capital of the kingdom of Babylon, Dan 4:29, 30; 2 Kgs 25:13; 2 Chron 36:6, 7, 10, 20. Gates of, Isa 45:1, 2; Jer 51:58. Walled, Jer 51:44, 58.

Peter writes from, 1 Pet 5:13.

Prophecies concerning, Ps 87:4; 137:8, 9; Isa 13;

14:4–26; 21:1–10; 46:1, 2; 47; 48:14, 20; Jer 21:4–10; 25: 12–14; 27:1–11; 28:14; 32:28; 34:2, 3; 42:11, 12; 43; 46: 13–26; 49:28–30; 50; 51; Ezk 21:19–26; 29:17–20; 30: 10; 32:11; Dan 2:21–38; 4:10–26; 5:25–29; 7; Hab 1: 5–11; Zech 2:7–9.

Figurative. Rev 14:8; 16:19; 17; 18.

2. EMPIRE OF. Founded by Nimrod, Gen 10: 8–10. Called *Land of Shinar,* Gen 10:10; 11:2; 14:1; Dan 1:2; *Merathaim,* Jer 50:21. Called also *Chaldea,* which see.

Divisions of, 2 Kgs 17:24; 24:7; Isa 23:12, 13; Dan 3:1; Acts 7:4. Extent of, at the time of Nebuchadnezzar, Dan 2:37, 38; 4:1; of Darius, Dan 6:1; of Ahasuerus, Esther 1:1; 8:9, 10; 9:29–31.

Armies of, invade ancient Canaan, Gen 14; Samaria, 2 Kgs 17:5–24; Judah, 2 Kgs 24:1–16. Jews carried to, 2 Kgs 25; 1 Chron 9:1; 2 Chron 33:11; 36: 17–21; Jer 32:2; 39; 52. Colonists from, sent to Samaria, Ezra 4:8–10, with 2 Kgs 17:29–32. Conquest of Egypt by, 2 Kgs 24:7.

Prophecies of conquests by, 2 Kgs 20:16–19; Jer 20:4–7; 21; 22; 25:1–11; 27; 28; 29; 32:28, 29; 34; 36: 29; 38:17, 18; 43:8–13; 46:13–26; Ezk 12; 17; 19; 21; 24; 26; 29:18–20; 30; 32.

Prophetic denunciations against, Ps 137:8, 9; Isa 13; 14:21; 43:14–17; 47; Jer 50; 51.

Government of. A limited monarchy, Esther 1: 13–19; 8:8; Dan 6:8, 14, 17. Tyrannical, Esther 3: 7–15; Dan 3.

Kings of. See *Belshazzar; Cyrus; Darius; Evil-merodach; Nebuchadnezzar.*

BACKBITING Ps 15:1. Lord, who may go and find refuge and shelter in your tabernacle up on your holy hill? [2]Anyone who leads a blameless life and is truly sincere. [3]Anyone who refuses to slander others, does not listen to gossip, never harms his neighbor.

Prov 25:23. As surely as a wind from the north brings cold, just as surely a retort causes anger!

Rom 1:28. So it was that when they gave God up and would not even acknowledge him, God gave them up to doing everything their evil minds could think of. [30]They were backbiters, haters of God, insolent, proud, braggarts, always thinking of new ways of sinning and continually being disobedient to their parents.

2 Cor 12:20. For I am afraid that when I come to visit you that I won't like what I find, and then you won't like the way I will have to act. I am afraid that I will find you quarreling, and envying each other, and being angry with each other, and acting big, and saying wicked things about each other and whispering behind each other's backs, filled with conceit and disunity.

See *Accusation, False; Slander; Speaking, Evil.*

BACKSLIDER In the Old Testament it usually referred to a turning back to a life of sin and idolatry. In the New Testament the word does not appear, but the term has come to be applied to believers who live a carnal or worldly life. Some of the references given here are to actual apostasy, which see. Lev 26:14. But if you will not listen to
me or obey me, [15]but reject my laws, [16]this is what
I will do to you: I will punish you with sudden terrors and panic, and with tuberculosis and burning fever; your eyes shall be consumed and your life shall ebb away; you will sow your crops in vain, for your enemies will eat them.
[17]I will set my face against you and you will flee before your attackers; those who hate you will rule you; you will even run when no one is chasing you!
[18]And if you still disobey me, I will punish you seven times more severely for your sins.
[19]I will break your proud power and make your heavens as iron, and your earth as bronze.
[20]Your strength shall be spent in vain; for your land shall not yield its crops, nor your trees their fruit.
[21]And if even then you will not obey me and listen to me, I will send you seven times more plagues because of your sins.
[22]I will send wild animals to kill your children and destroy your cattle and reduce your numbers so that your roads will be deserted.
[23]And if even this will not reform you, but you continue to walk against my wishes,
[24]then I will walk against your wishes, and I, even I, shall personally smite you seven times for your sin.
[25]I will revenge the breaking of my covenant by bringing war against you. You will flee to your cities, and I will send a plague among you there; and you will be conquered by your enemies.
[26]I will destroy your food supply so that one oven will be large enough to bake all the bread available for ten entire families; and you will still be hungry after your pittance has been doled out to you.
[27]And if you still won't listen to me or obey me,
[28]then I will let loose my great anger and send you seven times greater punishment for your sins.
[29]You shall eat your own sons and daughters,
[30]and I will destroy the altars on the hills where you worship your idols, and I will cut down your incense altars, leaving your dead bodies to rot among your idols; and I will abhor you.
[31]I will make your cities desolate, and destroy your places of worship, and will not respond to your incense offerings.
[32]Yes, I will desolate your land; your enemies shall live in it, utterly amazed at what I have done to you.
[33]I will scatter you out among the nations, destroying you with war as you go. Your land shall be desolate and your cities destroyed.
[34, 35]Then at last the land will rest and make up for the many years you refused to let it lie idle; for it will lie desolate all the years that you are captives in enemy lands. Yes, then the land will rest and enjoy its Sabbaths! It will make up for the rest you didn't give it every seventh year when you lived upon it.
[36]And for those who are left alive, I will cause them to be dragged away to distant lands as prisoners of war, and slaves. There they will live in constant fear. The sound of a leaf driven in the wind will send them fleeing as though chased by a man with a sword; they shall fall when no one is pursuing them.
[37]Yes, though none pursue they shall stumble over each other in flight, as though fleeing in battle, with no power to stand before their enemies.
[38]You shall perish among the nations and be destroyed among your enemies.
[39]Those left shall pine away in enemy lands because of their sins, the same

sins as those of their fathers. [40,41]But at last they shall confess their sins and their fathers' sins of treachery against me. (Because they were against me, I was against them, and brought them into the land of their enemies.) When at last their evil hearts are humbled and they accept the punishment I send them for their sins, [42]then I will remember again my promises to Abraham, Isaac, and Jacob, and I will remember the land (and its desolation).

Deut 4:9. But watch out! Be very careful never to forget what you have seen God doing for you. May his miracles have a deep and permanent effect upon your lives! Tell your children and your grandchildren about the glorious miracles he did.

Deut 8:11. But that is the time to be careful! Beware that in your plenty you don't forget the Lord your God and begin to disobey him. [12,13]For when you have become full and prosperous and have built fine homes to live in, and when your flocks and herds have become very large, and your silver and gold have multiplied, [14]that is the time to watch out that you don't become proud, and forget the Lord your God who brought you out of your slavery in the land of Egypt.

Deut 28:58, 59. If you refuse to obey all the laws written in this book, thus refusing reverence to the glorious and fearful name of Jehovah your God, then Jehovah will send perpetual plagues upon you and upon your children.

63. Just as the Lord has rejoiced over you and has done such wonderful things for you and has multiplied you, so the Lord at that time will rejoice in destroying you; and you shall disappear from the land. *vs.* 15–68; 1 Kgs 9:6–9.

Deut 29:18. That day that any of you—man or woman, family or tribe of Israel—begins to turn away from the Lord our God and desires to worship these gods of other nations, that day a root will be planted that will grow bitter and poisonous fruit. *vs.* 18–28.

Deut 32:15. But Israel was soon overfed; yes, fat and bloated; then, in plenty, they forsook their God. They shrugged away the Rock of their salvation. [16]Israel began to follow foreign gods, and Jehovah was very angry; he was jealous of his people. [17]They sacrificed to heathen gods, to new gods never before worshiped. [18]They spurned the Rock who had made them, forgetting it was God who had given them birth. [19]God saw what they were doing, and detested them! His sons and daughters were insulting him. [20]He said, "I will abandon them; see what happens to them then! For they are a stubborn, faithless generation. [21]They have made me very jealous of their idols, which are not gods at all. Now, I, in turn, will make them jealous by giving my affections to the foolish Gentile nations of the world. [22]For my anger has kindled a fire that burns to the depths of the underworld, consuming the earth and all of its crops, and setting its mountains on fire. [23]I will heap evils upon them and shoot them down with my arrows. [24]I will waste them with hunger, burning fever, and fatal disease. I will devour them! I will set wild beasts upon them, to rip them apart with their teeth; and deadly serpents crawling in the dust. [25]Outside, the enemies' sword—inside, the plague—shall terrorize young men and girls alike; the baby nursing at the breast, and aged men. [26]I had decided to scatter them to distant lands, so that even the memory of them would disappear. But then I thought, "My enemies will boast, 'Israel is destroyed by our own might; it was not the Lord who did it!' " [28]Israel is a stupid nation; foolish, without understanding. [29]Oh, that they were wise! Oh, that they could understand! Oh, that they would know what they are getting into! [30]How could one single enemy chase a thousand of them, and two put ten thousand to flight, unless their Rock had abandoned them, unless the Lord had destroyed them?"

Josh 24:27. Then Joshua said to all the people, "This stone has heard everything the Lord said, so it will be a witness to testify against you if you go back on your word." *vs.* 20–27.

2 Chron 15:2. He went out to meet King Asa as he was returning from the battle. "Listen to me, Asa! Listen, armies of Judah and Benjamin!" he shouted. "The Lord will stay with you as long as you stay with him! Whenever you look for him, you will find him. But if you forsake him, he will forsake you. [3]For a long time now, over in Israel, people haven't worshiped the true God, and have not had a true priest to teach them. They have lived without God's laws. [4]But whenever they have turned again to the Lord God of Israel in their distress, and searched for him, he has helped them."

Ezra 8:22. After all, we had told the king that our God would protect all those who worshiped him, and that disaster could only come to those who had forsaken him!

Job 34:26. Or openly strikes them down as wicked men. [27]For they turned aside from following him.

Ps 44:20. If we had turned away from worshiping our God, and were worshiping idols, [21]would God not know it? Yes, he knows the secrets of every heart.

Ps 73:27. But those refusing to worship God will perish, for he destroys those serving other gods.

Ps 85:8. I am listening carefully to all the Lord is saying—for he speaks peace to his people, his saints, if they will only stop their sinning.

Ps 125:4. O Lord, do good to those who are good, whose hearts are right with the Lord; [5]but lead evil men to execution.

Prov 2:16, 17. Only wisdom from the Lord can save a man from the flattery of prostitutes; these girls have abandoned their husbands and flouted the laws of God.

Prov 14:14. The backslider gets bored with himself; the godly man's life is exciting.

Prov 24:15, 16. O evil man, leave the upright man alone, and quit trying to cheat him out of his rights. Don't you know that this good man, though you trip him seven times, will each time rise again? But one calamity is enough to lay you low.

Prov 26:11. As a dog returns to his vomit, so a fool repeats his folly.

Jer 17:13. O Lord, the Hope of Israel, all who turn away from you shall be disgraced and shamed; they are registered for earth and not for glory, for they have forsaken the Lord, the Fountain of living waters.

Ezk 3:20. And if a good man becomes bad, and you refuse to warn him of the consequences, and the Lord destroys him, his previous good deeds won't help him—he shall die in his sin. But I will hold you responsible for his death, and punish you.

Ezk 18:26. When a good man turns away from being good and begins sinning and dies in his sins, he dies for the evil he has done. *v.* 24.

Ezk 23:35. Because you have forgotten me and turned your backs upon me, therefore you must bear the consequence of all your sin.

Ezk 33:12. For the good works of a righteous man will not save him if he turns to sin; and the sins of an evil man will not destroy him if he repents and turns from his sins. [13]I have said the good
man will live. But if he sins, expecting his past
goodness to save him, then none of his good deeds
will be remembered. I will destroy him for his sins.
[18]For again I say, when the good man turns to evil,
he shall die.

Hos 11:7. For my people are determined to desert
me. And so I have sentenced them to slavery, and
no one shall set them free. [8]Oh, how can I give you
up, my Ephraim? How can I let you go? How can
I forsake you like Admah and Zeboiim? My heart
cries out within me; how I long to help you!

Jon 2:4. Then I said, "Oh Lord, you have rejected me and cast me away. How shall I ever again see your holy Temple?"

Mt 5:13. You are the world's seasoning, to make it tolerable. If you lose your flavor, what will happen to the world? And you yourselves will be thrown out and trampled underfoot as worthless. Mk 9:50.

Mt 24:12. Sin will be rampant everywhere and will cool the love of many.

Mt 26:31. Then Jesus said to them, "Tonight you will all desert me. For it is written in the Scriptures that God will smite the Shepherd, and the sheep of the flock will be scattered."

Mk 4:7. Other seeds fell among thorns that shot
up and crowded the young plants so that they
produced no grain. [15]The hard pathway, where
some of the seed fell, represents the hard hearts of
some of those who hear God's message; Satan
comes at once to try to make them forget it. [16]The
rocky soil represents the hearts of those who hear
the message with joy, [17]but, like young plants in
such soil, their roots don't go very deep, and
though at first they get along fine, as soon as persecution begins, they wilt. [18]The thorny ground
represents the hearts of people who listen to the
Good News and receive it, [19]but all too quickly the
attractions of this world and the delights of wealth,
and the search for success and lure of nice things
come in and crowd out God's message from their
hearts, so that no crop is produced.

Mk 8:38. And anyone who is ashamed of me and my message in these days of unbelief and sin, I, the Messiah, will be ashamed of him when I return in the glory of my Father, with the holy angels.

Lk 9:62. But Jesus told him, "Anyone who lets himself be distracted from the work I plan for him is not fit for the Kingdom of God."

Lk 11:21. For when Satan, strong and fully
armed, guards his palace, it is safe—[22]until someone stronger and better-armed attacks and overcomes him and strips him of weapons and carries
off his belongings. [23]Anyone who is not for me is
against me; if he isn't helping me, he is hurting my
cause. [24]When a demon is cast out of a man, it goes
to the deserts, searching there for rest; but finding
none, it returns to the person it left, [25]and finds that
its former home is all swept and clean. [26]Then it
goes and gets seven other demons more evil than
itself, and they all enter the man. And so the poor
fellow is seven times worse off than he was before.
Mt 12:43–45.

Lk 17:32. Remember what happened to Lot's wife!

Jn 6:67. Then Jesus turned to the Twelve and asked, "Are you going too?"

Jn 15:6. If anyone separates from me, he is thrown away like a useless branch, withers, and is gathered into a pile with all the others and burned.

1 Cor 10:1. For we must never forget, dear brothers, what happened to our people in the wilderness
long ago. God guided them by sending a cloud that
moved along ahead of them; and he brought them
all safely through the waters of the Red Sea. [2]This
might be called their "baptism"—baptized both in
sea and cloud!—as followers of Moses—their com-
mitment to him as their leader. [3, 4]And by a miracle
God sent them food to eat and water to drink there
in the desert; they drank the water that Christ gave
them. He was there with them as a mighty Rock
of spiritual refreshment. [5]Yet after all this most of
them did not obey God, and he destroyed them in
the wilderness. [6]From this lesson we are warned
that we must not desire evil things as they did, [7]nor
worship idols as they did. (The Scriptures tell us,
"The people sat down to eat and drink and then got
up to dance" in worship of the golden calf.) [8]An-
other lesson for us is what happened when some of
them sinned with other men's wives, and 23,000
fell dead in one day. [9]And don't try the Lord's
patience—they did, and died from snake bites.
[10]And don't murmur against God and his dealings
with you, as some of them did, for that is why God
sent his Angel to destroy them. [11]All these things
happened to them as examples—as object lessons
to us—to warn us against doing the same things;
they were written down so that we could read
about them and learn from them in these last days
as the world nears its end. [12]So be careful. If you
are thinking, "Oh, I would never behave like that"
—let this be a warning to you. For you too may fall

into sin. [13]But remember this—the wrong desires that come into your life aren't anything new and different. Many others have faced exactly the same problems before you. And no temptation is irresistible. You can trust God to keep the temptation from becoming so strong that you can't stand up against it, for he has promised this and will do what he says. He will show you how to escape temptation's power so that you can bear up patiently against it.

2 Cor 12:20. For I am afraid that when I come to visit you I won't like what I find, and then you won't like the way I will have to act. I am afraid that I will find you quarreling, and envying each other, and being angry with each other, and acting big, and saying wicked things about each other and whispering about each other behind each other's backs, filled with conceit and disunity. [21]Yes, I am afraid that when I come God will humble me before you and I will be sad and mourn because many of you who have sinned became sinners and don't even care about the wicked, impure things you have done: your lust and immorality, and the taking of other men's wives.

Gal 1:6. I am amazed that you are turning away so soon from God who, in his love and mercy, invited you to share the eternal life he gives through Christ; you are already following a different "way to heaven," which really doesn't go to heaven at all. *v.* 7.

Gal 3:1. Oh, foolish Galatians! What magician has hypnotized you and cast an evil spell upon you? For you used to see the meaning of Jesus Christ's death as clearly as though I had waved a placard before you with a picture on it of Christ dying on the cross.

Gal 4:9. And now that you have found God (or I should say, now that God has found you) how can it be that you want to go back again and become slaves once more to another poor, weak, useless religion of trying to get to heaven by obeying God's laws? [10]You are trying to find favor with God by what you do or don't do on certain days or months or seasons or years. [11]I fear for you. I am afraid that all my hard work for you was worth nothing.

Gal 5:7. You were getting along so well. Who has interfered with you to hold you back from following the truth?

1 Tim 1:19. Cling tightly to your faith in Christ and always keep your conscience clear, doing what you know is right. For some people have disobeyed their consciences and have deliberately done what they knew was wrong. It isn't surprising that soon they had lost their faith in God after defying God like that.

1 Tim 5:15. For I am afraid that some of them have already turned away from the church and been led astray by Satan.

1 Tim 6:10. For the love of money is the first step toward all kinds of sin. Some people have even turned away from God because of their love for it, and as a result have pierced themselves with many sorrows. [20]Oh Timothy, don't fail to do these things that God entrusted to you. Keep out of foolish arguments with those who boast of their "knowledge" and thus prove their lack of it. [21]Some of these people have missed the most important thing in life—they don't know God.

2 Tim 1:8. If you will stir up this inner power, you will never be afraid to tell others about our Lord, or to let them know that I am your friend even though I am here in jail for Christ's sake. You will be ready to suffer with me for the Lord, for he will give you strength in suffering.

2 Tim 2:12. And if we think that our present service for him is hard, just remember that some day we are going to sit with him and rule with him. But if we give up when we are suffering, and turn against Christ, then he must turn against us.

2 Tim 4:10. For Demas has left me, he loved the good things of this life.

Heb 3:12. Beware then of your own hearts, dear brothers, lest you find that they, too, are evil and unbelieving and are leading you away from the living God. [13]Speak to each other about these things every day while there is still time, so that none of you will become hardened against God, being blinded by the glamor of sin.

Heb 4:1. Although God's promise still stands—his promise that all may enter his place of rest—we ought to tremble with fear because some of you may be on the verge of failing to get there after all. [11]Let us do our best to go into that place of rest, too, being careful not to disobey God as the children of Israel did, thus failing to get in.

Heb 5:11. There is much more I would like to say along these lines, but you don't seem to listen, so it's hard to make you understand. [12]You have been Christians a long time now, and you ought to be teaching others, but instead you have dropped back to the place where you need someone to teach you all over again the very first principles in God's Word. You are like babies who can drink only milk, not old enough for solid food.

Heb 6:4. There is no use trying to bring you back to the Lord again if you have once understood the Good News and tasted for yourself the good things of heaven and shared in the Holy Spirit, [5]and know how good the Word of God is, and felt the mighty powers of the world to come, [6]and then have turned against God. You cannot bring yourself to repent again if you have nailed the Son of God to the cross again by rejecting him, holding him up to mocking and to public shame. [7]When a farmer's land has had many showers upon it and good crops come up, that land has experienced the blessing of God upon it. [8]But if it keeps on having crops of thistles and thorns, the land is considered no good and is ready for condemnation and burning off.

Heb 10:26. If anyone sins deliberately by rejecting the Savior after knowing the truth of forgiveness, this sin is not covered by Christ's death; there is no way to get rid of it. [27]There will be nothing to look forward to but the terrible punishment of God's awful anger which will consume all his enemies. [28]A man who refused to obey the laws given by Moses was killed without mercy if there were two or three witnesses to his sin. [29]Think how much more terrible the punishment will be for those who have trampled underfoot the Son of God and treated his cleansing blood as though it were common and unhallowed, and insulted and outraged the Holy Spirit who brings God's mercy to his people. [38]And those whose faith has made them good in God's sight must live by faith, trusting him in everything. Otherwise, if they shrink back, God will have no pleasure in them. [39]But we have never turned our backs on God and sealed our fate. No, our faith in him assures our soul's salvation.

Heb 11:14. And quite obviously when they talked like that, they were looking forward to their real home in heaven. [15]If they had wanted to, they could have gone back to the good things of this world.

Heb 12:15. Look after each other so that not one of you will fail to find God's best blessings. Watch out that no bitterness takes root among you, for as it springs up it causes deep trouble, hurting many in their spiritual lives.

2 Pet 1:9. But anyone who fails to go after these additions to faith is blind indeed, or at least very shortsighted, and has forgotten that God delivered him from the old life of sin so that now he can live a strong, good life for the Lord.

2 Pet 2:20. And when a person has escaped from the wicked ways of the world by learning about our Lord and Savior Jesus Christ, and then gets tangled up with sin and becomes its slave again, he is worse off than he was before. [21]It would be better if he had never known about Christ at all than to learn of him and then afterwards turn his back on the holy commandments that were given to him.

2 Jn 1:9. For if you wander beyond the teaching of Christ, you will leave God behind; while if you are loyal to Christ's teachings, you will have God too. Then you will have both the Father and the Son.

Rev 2:4. Yet there is one thing wrong, you don't love me as at first! [5]Think about those times of your first love (how different now!) and turn back to me again and work as you did before; or else I will come and remove your candlestick from its place among the churches.

21. I gave her time to change her mind and attitude, but she refused. [22]Pay attention now to what I am saying: I will lay her upon a sickbed of intense affliction, along with all her immoral followers, unless they turn again to me, repenting of their sin with her; [23]and I will strike her children dead. And all the churches shall know that I am he who searches deep within men's hearts and minds; I will give to each of you whatever you deserve.

Rev 3:2. Now wake up! Strengthen what little remains—for even what is left is at the point of death. Your deeds are far from right in the sight of God. [3]Go back to what you believed at first; hold to if firmly and turn to me again. Unless you do, I will come suddenly upon you, unexpected as a thief, and punish you.

Rev 21:8. But cowards who turn back from following me, and those who are unfaithful to me, . . . their doom is in the Lake that burns with fire and sulphur. This is the Second Death.

See *Apostasy; Backsliding of Israel, below; Reprobate.*

INSTANCES OF. Saul, 1 Sam 15:11, 26–28. Solomon, 1 Kgs 11:4–40; Neh 13:26. Amon, 2 Kgs 21:21, 22. Rehoboam, 2 Chron 12:1, 2. Asa, 2 Chron 16:7–9. Joash, 2 Chron 24:24. Amaziah, 2 Chron 25:27. Syrians, Isa 17:10, 11. Jonah, Jon 1:3. The disciples, Mt 26:56; Jn 6:66. Peter, Mt 26:69–75. Corinthian Christians, 1 Cor 5:1–8; 2 Cor 12:20, 21. Galatians, Gal 1:6; 3:1; 4:9–11; 5:6, 7. Phygellus and Hermogenes, 2 Tim 1:15. Demas, 2 Tim 4:10. Churches of Asia, 1 Tim 5:15; Rev 2:4, 14, 15, 20; 3:2, 3, 15–18.

PROMISES TO. Lev 26:40, 41. But at last they shall confess their sins and their fathers' sins of treachery against me. (Because they were against me, I was against them, and brought them into the land of their enemies.) When at last their evil hearts are humbled and they accept the punishment I send them for their sins, [42]then I will remember again my promises to Abraham, Isaac, and Jacob, and I will remember the land (and its desolation).

Deut 4:29. But you will also begin to search again for Jehovah your God, and you shall find him when you search for him with all you hearts and souls. [30]When those bitter days have come upon you in the latter times, you will finally return to the Lord your God and listen to what he tells you. *v.* 31.

Deut 30:1. When all these things have happened to you—the blessings and the curses I have listed —you will meditate upon them as you are living among the nations where the Lord your God will have driven you. [2]If at that time you want to return to the Lord your God, and you and your children have begun wholeheartedly to obey all of the commandments I have given you today, [3]then the Lord your God will rescue you from your captivity! He will have mercy upon you and come and gather you out of all the nations where he will have scattered you. [4]Though you are at the ends of the earth, he will go and find you and bring you back again [5]to the land of your ancestors. You shall possess the land again, and he will do you good and bless you even more than he did your ancestors! [6]He will cleanse your hearts and the hearts of your children and of your children's children so that you will love the Lord your God with all your hearts and souls, and Israel shall come alive again! [7, 8]If you return to the Lord and obey all the commandments that I command you today, the Lord your God will take his curses and turn them against your enemies —against those who hate you and persecute you. [9]The Lord your God will prosper everything you do and give you many children and much cattle and wonderful crops; for the Lord will again rejoice over you as he did over your fathers. [10]He will rejoice if you but obey the commandments written in this book of the law, and if you turn to the Lord your God with all your hearts and souls.

Deut 32:26. I had decided to scatter them to distant lands, so that even the memory of them would disappear. [28]Israel is a stupid nation; foolish, without understanding. [29]Oh, that they were wise! Oh, that they could understand! Oh, that they would know what they are getting into!

1 Kgs 8:33, 34. And when your people sin and their enemies defeat them, hear them from heaven and forgive them if they turn to you again and confess that you are their God. Bring them back again to this land which you have given to their fathers. *vs.* 35–53.

2 Chron 30:9. For if you turn to the Lord again, your brothers and your children will be treated mercifully by their captors, and they will be able to return to this land. For the Lord your God is full of kindness and mercy and will not continue to turn away his face from you if you return to him.

Job 22:23. If you return to God and put right all the wrong in your home, then you will be restored. [24]If you give up your lust for money, and throw your gold away, [25]then the Almighty himself shall be your treasure; he will be your precious silver. [26]Then you will delight yourself in the Lord, and look up to God. [27]You will pray to him, and he will hear you, and you will fulfill all your promises to him. [28]Whatever you wish will happen! And the light of heaven will shine upon the road ahead of you. [29]If you are attacked and knocked down, you will know that there is someone who will lift you up again. Yes, he will save the humble, [30]and help even sinners by your pure hands.

Ps 56:13 For you have saved me from death and my feet from slipping, so that I can walk before the Lord in the land of the living.

Ps 81:13. But oh, that my people would listen to me! Oh, that Israel would follow me, walking in my paths! [14]How quickly then I would subdue her enemies! How soon my hands would be upon her foes!

Isa 42:3. He will not break the bruised reed, nor quench the dimly burning flame. He will encourage the fainthearted, those tempted to despair. He will see full justice given to all who have been wronged. [4]He won't be satisfied until truth and righteousness prevail throughout the earth, nor until even distant lands beyond the seas have put their trust in him.

Isa 57:18. I have seen what they do, but I will heal them anyway! I will lead them and comfort them, helping them to mourn and to confess their sins. [19]Peace, peace to them, both near and far, for I will heal them all.

Jer 3:4, 5. And yet you say to me, "O Father, you have always been my Friend; surely you won't be angry about such a little thing! Surely you will just forget it?" So you talk, and keep right on doing all the evil that you can. [6]This message from the Lord came to me during the reign of King Josiah: Have you seen what Israel does? Like a wanton wife who gives herself to other men at every chance, so Israel has worshiped other gods on every hill, beneath every shady tree. [7]I thought that someday she would return to me and once again be mine; but she didn't come back. And her faithless sister Judah saw the continued rebellion of Israel. [12]Therefore go and say to Israel, O Israel, my sinful people, come home to me again, for I am merciful; I will not be forever angry with you. [13]Only acknowledge your guilt; admit that you rebelled against the Lord your God and committed adultery against him by worshiping idols under every tree; confess that you refused to follow me. [14]O sinful children, come home, for I am your Master and I will bring you again to the land of Israel—one from here and two from there, wherever you are scattered. [15]And I will give you leaders after my own heart, who will guide you with wisdom and understanding. [16]Then, when your land is once more filled with people, says the Lord, you will no longer wish for "the good old days of long ago" when you possessed the Ark of God's covenant. Those days will not be missed or even thought about, and the Ark will not be reconstructed, [17]for the Lord himself will be among you, and the whole city of Jerusalem will be known as the throne of the Lord, and the nations will come to him there and no longer stubbornly follow their evil desires. [18]At that time the people of Judah and of Israel will return together from their exile in the north, to the land I gave their fathers as an inheritance forever. [19]And I thought how wonderful it would be for you to be here among my children. I planned to give you part of this beautiful land, the finest in the world. I looked forward to your calling me "Father," and thought that you would never turn away from me again. [20]But you have betrayed me; you have gone off and given yourself to a host of foreign gods; you have been like a faithless wife who leaves her husband. [21]I hear voices high upon the windswept mountains, crying, crying. It is the sons of Israel who have turned their backs on God and wandered far away. [22]O my rebellious children, come back to me again and I will heal you from your sins. And they reply, Yes, we will come, for you are the Lord our God.

Jer 4:1. O Israel, if you will truly return to me and absolutely discard your idols, [2]and if you will swear by me alone, the living God, and begin to live good, honest, clean lives, then you will be a testimony to the nations of the world and they will come to me and glorify my name. [14]O Jerusalem, cleanse your hearts while there is time. You can yet be saved by casting out your evil thoughts.

Jer 6:16. Yet the Lord pleads with you still: Ask where the good road is, the godly paths you used to walk in, in the days of long ago. Travel there, and you will find rest for your souls.

Hos 14:4. Then I will cure you of idolatry and faithlessness, and my love will know no bounds, for my anger will be forever gone!

Zech 10:6. I will strengthen Judah, yes, and Israel too; I will reestablish them because I love them. It will be as though I had never cast them all away, for I, the Lord their God, will hear their cries.

Mal 3:7. "Though you have scorned my laws from earliest time, yet you may still return to me," says the Lord of Hosts. "Come and I will forgive you. But you say, 'We have never even gone away!' "

Mt 23:37. O Jerusalem, Jerusalem, the city that kills the prophets, and stones all those God sends to her! How often I have wanted to gather your children together as a hen gathers her chicks beneath her wings, but you wouldn't let me.

Rev 3:8. I know you well; you aren't strong, but you have tried to obey and have not denied my Name. Therefore I have opened a door to you that no one can shut. [15]I know you well—you are neither hot nor cold; I wish you were one or the other! [16]But since you are merely lukewarm, I will spit you out of my mouth! [17]You say, "I am rich, with everything I want; I don't need a thing!" And you don't realize that spiritually you are wretched and miserable and poor and blind and naked. [18]My advice to you is to buy pure gold from me, gold purified by fire—only then will you truly be rich. And to purchase from me white garments, clean and pure, so you won't be naked and ashamed; and to get medicine from me to heal your eyes and give you back your sight. [19]I continually discipline and punish everyone I love; so I must punish you, unless you turn from your indifference and become enthusiastic about the things of God. [20]Look! I have been standing at the door and I am constantly knocking. If anyone hears me calling him and opens the door, I will come in and fellowship with him and he with me. [21]I will let every one who conquers sit beside me on my throne, just as I took my place with my Father on his throne when I had conquered.

See *Penitent; Repentance; Seekers.*

RETURN OF. Ps 80:3. Turn us again to yourself, O God. Look down on us in joy and love; only then shall we be saved. [4]O Jehovah, God of heaven's armies, how long will you be angry and reject our prayers? [5]You have fed us with sorrow and tears, [6]and have made us the scorn of the neighboring nations. They laugh among themselves. [7]Turn us again to yourself, O God of Hosts. Look down on us in joy and love; only then shall we be saved. [14]Come back, we beg of you, O God of the armies of heaven, and bless us. Look down from heaven and see our plight and care for this your vine! [15]Protect what you yourself have planted, this son you have raised for yourself. [16]For we are chopped and burned by our enemies. May they perish at your frown. [17]Strengthen the man you love, the son of your choice, [18]and we will never forsake you again. Revive us to trust in you. [19]Turn us again to yourself, O God of the armies of heaven. Look down on us, your face aglow with joy and love—only then shall we be saved.

Isa 17:7. Then at last they will think of God their Creator and have respect for the Holy One of Israel.

Isa 29:24. Those in error will believe the truth, and complainers will be willing to be taught!

Isa 31:6. Therefore, O my people, though you are such wicked rebels, come, return to God. [7]I know the glorious day will come when every one of you will throw away his golden idols and silver images—which in your sinfulness you have made.

Jer 50:4. Then the people of Israel and Judah shall join together, weeping and seeking the Lord their God. [5]They shall ask the way to Zion and start back home again. "Come," they will say, "let us be united to the Lord with an eternal pledge that will never be broken again." [6]My people have been lost sheep. Their shepherds led them astray and then turned them loose in the mountains. They lost their way and didn't remember how to get back to the fold.

Hos 3:5. Afterward they will return to the Lord their God, and to the Messiah, their King, and they shall come trembling, submissive to the Lord and to his blessings, in the end times.

Hos 6:1. Come, let us return to the Lord; it is he who has torn us—he will heal us. He has wounded—he will bind us up. [2]In just a couple of days, or three at the most, he will set us on our feet again, to live in his kindness! [3]Oh, that we might know the Lord! Let us press on to know him, and he will respond to us as surely as the coming of dawn or the rain of early spring.

Instances of. Jews, Ezra 6:16–22; 10. David, Ps 51. Jonah, Jon 2; 3. Peter, Mt 26:75; Mk 14:72; Lk 22:62. Thomas, Jn 20:27–29.

BACKSLIDING OF ISRAEL. Ex 17:7. Moses named the place Massah (meaning "tempting Jehovah to slay us"), and sometimes they referred to it as Meribah (meaning "argument" and "strife!")—for it was there that the people of Israel argued against God and tempted him to slay them by saying, "Is Jehovah going to take care of us or not?"

Deut 4:25. In the future, when your children and grandchildren are born and you have been in the land a long time, and you have defiled yourselves by making idols, and the Lord your God is very angry because of your sin, [26]heaven and earth are witnesses that you shall be quickly destroyed from the land. Soon, now, you will cross the Jordan River and conquer that land. But your days there will be brief; you will then be utterly destroyed. [27]Jehovah will scatter you among the nations, and you will be but few in number. [28]There, far away, you will worship idols made from wood and stone, idols that neither see nor hear nor eat nor smell. [29]But you will also begin to search again for Jehovah your God, and you shall find him when you search for him with all your hearts and souls. [30]When those bitter days have come upon you in the latter times, you will finally return to the Lord your God and listen to what he tells you. [31]For the Lord your God is merciful—he will not abandon you nor destroy you nor forget the promises he has made to your ancestors.

Deut 31:16. [The Lord] said to Moses, "You shall die and join your ancestors. After you are gone, these people will begin worshiping foreign gods in the Promised Land. They will forget about me and break the contract I have made with them. [17]Then my anger will flame out against them and I will abandon them, hiding my face from them, and they shall be destroyed. Terrible trouble will come upon them, so that they will say, 'God is no longer among us!' [18]I will turn away from them because of their sins in worshiping other gods. [19]Now write down the words of this song, and teach it to the people of Israel as my warning to them. [20]When I have brought them into the land I promised their ancestors—a land 'flowing with milk and honey'—and when they have become fat and prosperous, and worship other gods and despise me and break my contract, [21]and great disasters come upon them, then this song will remind them of the reason for their woes. (For this song will live from generation to generation.) I know now, even before they enter the land, what these people are like." [22]So, on that very day, Moses wrote down the words of the song and taught it to the Israelites. [23]Then he charged Joshua (son of Nun) to be strong and courageous, and said to him, "You must bring the people of Israel into the land the Lord promised them; for the Lord says, 'I will be with you.' " [24]When Moses had finished writing down all the laws that are recorded in this book, [25]he instructed the Levites who carried the Ark containing the Ten Commandments [26]to put this book of the law beside the Ark, as a solemn warning to the people of Israel. [27]"For I know how rebellious and stubborn you are," Moses told them. "If even today, while I am still here with you, you are defiant rebels against the Lord, how much more rebellious will you be after my death! [28]Now summon all the elders and officers of your tribes so that I can speak to them, and call heaven and earth to witness against them. [29]I know that after my death, you will utterly defile yourselves and turn away from God and his commands; and in the days to come evil will crush you for you will do what the Lord says is evil, making him very angry." [30]So Moses recited this entire song to the whole assembly of Israel.

Deut 32:5. But Israel has become corrupt, smeared with sin. They are no longer his; they are a stubborn, twisted generation. [6]Is this the way you treat Jehovah? O foolish people, is not God your Father? Has he not created you? Has he not established you and made you strong? [15]But Israel was soon overfed; yes, fat and bloated; then, in plenty, they forsook their God. They shrugged away the Rock of their salvation. *v.* 18; Num 14:43; Judg 2:12–14; 10:12–14.

2 Chron 24:20. Then the Spirit of God came upon Zechariah, Jehoiada's son. He called a meeting of all the people. Standing before them upon a platform, he said to them, "God wants to know why you are disobeying his commandments. For when you do, everything you try fails. You have forsaken the Lord, and now he has forsaken you." 2 Kgs 18:1–13; 2 Chron 13:11; 27:2; 29:6, 8.

Ezra 9:10. And now, O God, what can we say after all of this? For once again we have abandoned you and broken your laws! [13]And now, even after our punishment in exile because of our wickedness (and we have been punished far less than we deserved), and even though you have let some of us return, [14]we have broken your commandments again and intermarried with people who do these awful things. Surely your anger will destroy us now until not even this little remnant escapes.

Neh 9:26. But despite all this they were disobedient and rebelled against you. They threw away your law, killed the prophets who told them to return to you, and they did many other terrible things.

Ps 78:10. Because they didn't obey his laws, they refused to follow his ways. [11, 12]And they forgot about the wonderful miracles God had done for them, and for their fathers in Egypt. [40]Oh, how often they rebelled against him in those desert years and grieved his heart. [41]Again and again they turned away and tempted God to kill them, and limited the Holy One of Israel from giving them his blessings. [42]They forgot his power and love, and how he had rescued them from their enemies; [43]they forgot the plagues he sent upon the Egyptians in Tanis. [56]Yet though he did all this for them, they still rebelled against the God above all gods, and refused to follow his commands. [57]They turned back from entering the Promised Land and disobeyed as their fathers had. Like a crooked arrow, they missed the target of God's will. [58]They made him angry by erecting idols and altars to other gods. [59]When God saw their deeds, his wrath was strong and he despised his people. [60]Then he abandoned his Tabernacle at Shiloh, where he had lived among mankind, [61]and allowed his Ark to be captured; he surrendered his glory into enemy hands. [62]He caused his people to be butchered because his anger was intense. [63]Their young men were killed by fire and their girls died before they were old enough to sing their wedding songs. [64]The priests were slaughtered and their widows died before they could even begin their lament.

Ps 106:13. Yet how quickly they forgot again! They wouldn't wait for him to act, [14]but demanded better food, testing God's patience to the breaking point.

Isa 1:4. Oh, what a sinful nation they are! They walk bent-backed beneath their load of guilt. Their fathers before them were evil too. Born to be bad, they have turned their backs upon the Lord, and have despised the Holy One of Israel. They have cut themselves off from my help. [5, 6]Oh, my people, haven't you had enough of punishment? Why will you force me to whip you again and again? Must you forever rebel? From head to foot you are sick and weak and faint, covered with bruises and welts and infected wounds, unanointed and unbound. [7]Your country lies in ruins; your cities are burned; while you watch, foreigners are destroying and plundering everything they see. [21]Jerusalem, once my faithful wife! And now a prostitute! Running after another god! Once "The City of Fair Play," but now a gang of murderers. [22]Once like sterling silver; now mixed with worthless alloy! Once so pure, but now diluted like watered-down wine! Isa 50:1.

Isa 2:6. The Lord has rejected you because you welcome foreigners from the East who practice magic and communicate with evil spirits, as the Philistines do.

Isa 5:24. Therefore God will deal with them and burn them. They will disappear like straw on fire. Their roots will rot and their flowers wither, for they have thrown away the laws of God and despised the Word of the Holy One of Israel. *vs.* 12–30.

Isa 9:16. For the leaders of his people have led them down the paths of ruin. *vs.* 13–21.

Isa 17:10. Why? Because you have turned from the God who can save you—the Rock who can hide you; therefore, even though you plant a wonderful, rare crop of greatest value, [11]and though it grows so well that it will blossom on the very morning that you plant it, yet you will never harvest it—your only harvest will be a pile of grief and incurable pain.

Isa 24:5. The land is defiled by crime; the people have twisted the laws of God and broken his everlasting commands. [6]Therefore the curse of God is upon them; they are left desolate, destroyed by the drought. Few will be left alive.

Isa 30:9. For if you don't write it, they will claim I never warned them. "Oh, no," they'll say, "you never told us that!" For they are stubborn rebels. [15]For the Lord God, the Holy One of Israel, says: Only in returning to me and waiting for me will you be saved; in quietness and confidence is your strength; but you'll have none of this.

Isa 31:6. Therefore, O my people, though you are such wicked rebels, come, return to God.

Isa 43:22. But O my people, you won't ask my help; you have grown tired of me! [24]You have brought me no sweet-smelling incense nor pleased me with the sacrificial fat. No, you have presented me only with sins, and wearied me with all your faults.

Isa 51:17. Wake up, wake up, Jerusalem! You have drunk enough from the cup of fury of the Lord. You have drunk to the dregs the cup of terror and squeezed out the last drops. *vs.* 18–20.

Isa 63:17. O Lord, why have you hardened our hearts and made us sin and turn against you? Return and help us, for we who belong to you need you so.

Isa 65:2. But my own people—though I have been spreading out my arms to welcome them all day long—have rebelled; they follow their own evil paths and thoughts. [3]All day long they insult me to my face by worshiping idols in many gardens and burning incense on the rooftops of their homes.

Jer 2:4, 5. O Israel, says the Lord, why did your fathers desert me? What sin did they find in me that turned them away and changed them into fools who worship idols? [10, 11]Look around you and see if you can find another nation anywhere that has traded in its old gods for new ones—even though their gods are nothing. . . . And yet my people have given up their glorious God for silly idols! [12]The heavens are shocked at such a thing and shrink back in horror and dismay. [13]For my people have done two evil things: They have forsaken me, the Fountain of Life-giving Water; and they have built for themselves broken cisterns that can't hold water!

17. And you have brought this on yourselves by rebelling against the Lord your God when he wanted to lead you and show you the way! [19]Your own wickedness will punish you. You will see what an evil, bitter thing it is to rebel against the Lord your God, fearlessly forsaking him, says the Lord, the God of Hosts.

21. How could this happen? How could this be? For when I planted you, I chose my seed so carefully—the very best. Why have you become this degenerate race of evil men? [27]They call a carved-up wooden post their father, and for their mother they have an idol chiseled out from stone. Yet in time of trouble they cry to me to save them!

31. O my people, listen to the words of God: Have I been unjust to Israel? Have I been to them a land of darkness and of evil? Why then do my people say, "At last we are free from God; we won't have anything to do with him again!" [32]How can you disown your God like that? Can a girl forget her jewels? What bride will seek to hide her wedding dress? Yet for years on end my people have forgotten me—the most precious of their treasures.

Jer 3:21. I hear voices high upon the windswept mountains, crying, crying. It is the sons of Israel who have turned their backs on God and wandered far away. *vs.* 1–25.

Jer 5:19. And when your people ask, "Why is it that the Lord is doing this to us?" then you shall say, "You rejected him and gave yourselves to other gods while in your land; now you must be slaves to foreigners in their lands." [23, 24]But my people have rebellious hearts; they have turned against me and gone off into idolatry. Though I am the one who gives them rain each year in spring and fall and sends the harvest times, yet they have no respect or fear for me. *vs.* 1–31; Jer 11:9–17.

Jer 6:30. I must label them "Impure, Rejected Silver," and I have discarded them. Ezk 22:18–20.

Jer 7:12. Go to Shiloh, the city I first honored with my name, and see what I did to her because of all the wickedness of my people Israel. *vs.* 13–34.

Jer 8:4, 5. Once again give them this message from the Lord: When a person falls, he jumps up again; when he is on the wrong road and discovers his mistake, he goes back to the fork where he made the wrong turn. But these people keep on along their evil path, even though I warn them. [14]Then the people will say, "Why should we wait here to die? Come, let us go to the walled cities and perish there. For the Lord our God has decreed our doom and given us a cup of poison to drink because of all our sins. [15]We expected peace, but no peace came; we looked for health but there was only terror." *vs.* 1–22.

Jer 10:20. My home is gone; my children have been taken away and I will never see them again. There is no one left to help me rebuild my home. [21]The shepherds of my people have lost their senses; they no longer follow God nor ask his will. Therefore they perish and their flocks are scattered. *vs.* 17–22.

Jer 12:7. Then the Lord said: I have abandoned my people, my inheritance; I have surrendered my dearest ones to their enemies.

Jer 13:24, 25. Because you have put me out of your mind and put your trust in false gods, I will scatter you as chaff is scattered by fierce winds off the desert. This then is your allotment, that which is due you, which I have measured out especially for you.

Jer 14:7. O Lord, we have sinned against you grievously, yet help us for the sake of your own reputation! [10]But the Lord replies: You have loved to wander far from me and have not tried to follow in my paths. Now I will no longer accept you as my people; now I will remember all the evil you have done, and punish your sins.

Jer 15:1. Then the Lord said to me, Even if Moses and Samuel stood before me pleading for these people, even then I wouldn't help them—away with them! Get them out of my sight! *vs.* 2–14.

Jer 18:13. Then the Lord said: Even among the heathen, no one has ever heard of such a thing! My people have done something too horrible to understand. [14]The snow never melts high up in the Lebanon mountains. The cold, flowing streams from the crags of Mount Hermon never run dry. [15]These can be counted on. But not my people. They have deserted me and turned to foolish idols. They have turned away from the ancient highways of good, and walk the muddy paths of sin. Jer 19.

Jer 32:31. From the time this city was built until now it has done nothing but anger me; so I am determined to be rid of it. *v.* 30.

Jer 50:6. My people have been lost sheep. Their shepherds led them astray and then turned them loose in the mountains. They lost their way and didn't remember how to get back to the fold.

Ezk 2:3. "Son of dust," he said, "I am sending you to the nation of Israel, to a nation rebelling against me. They and their fathers have kept on sinning against me until this very hour. [4]For they are a hardhearted, stiff-necked people. But I am sending you to give them my messages—the messages of the Lord God. [5]And whether they listen or not (for remember, they are rebels), they will at least know they have had a prophet among them. [6]Son of Dust, don't be afraid of them; don't be frightened even though their threats are sharp and barbed and sting like scorpions. Don't be dismayed by their dark scowls. For remember, they are rebels! [7]You must give them my messages whether they listen or not (but they won't, for they are utter rebels). [8]Listen, son of dust, to what I say to you. Don't you be a rebel too! Open your mouth and eat what I give you."

Ezk 5:5–7. The Lord God says, "This illustrates what will happen to Jerusalem, for she has turned away from my laws and has been even more wicked than the nations surrounding her." *vs.* 1–17.

Ezk 11:21. "But as for those now in Jerusalem, who long for idols, I will repay them fully for their sins," the Lord God says. *vs.* 1–21. (See Parable of the Vine, Ezk 15.)

Ezk 16:43. But first, because you have not remembered your youth, but have angered me by all these evil things you do, I will fully repay you for all of your sins, says the Lord. For you are thankless in addition to all your other faults. (See Parable of an Unfaithful Wife, Ezk 16; 23; Hos 2; 3.)

Hos 1:6. Soon Gomer had another child—this one a daughter. And God said to Hosea, "Name her Lo-ruhamah (meaning 'No more mercy') for I will have no more mercy upon Israel, to forgive her again." [9]And God said, "Call him Lo-ammi (meaning 'Not mine'), for Israel is not mine and I am not her God." *vs.* 1–9.

Hos 4:6. My people are destroyed because they don't know me, and it is all your fault, you priests, for you yourselves refuse to know me; therefore I refuse to recognize you as my priests. Since you have forgotten my laws, I will "forget" to bless your children. [10]They will eat and still be hungry. Though they do a big business as prostitutes, they shall have no children, for they have deserted me and turned to other gods. *v.* 16.

Hos 5:11. And Ephraim will be crushed and broken by my sentence because she is determined to follow idols. [12]I will destroy her as a moth does wool; I will sap away the strength of Judah like dry rot. *vs.* 1–15.

Hos 6:4. O Ephraim and Judah, what shall I do with you? For your love vanishes like morning clouds, and disappears like dew. [7]But like Adam, you broke my covenant; you refused my love. *vs.* 4–11; Hos 8:14; 9:1–17; 13:16.

Hos 11:2. But the more I called to him, the more he rebelled, sacrificing to Baal and burning incense to idols. [7]For my people are determined to desert me. And so I have sentenced them to slavery, and no one shall set them free.

Hos 14:1. O Israel, return to the Lord, your God, for you have been crushed by your sins.

Amos 2:4. The Lord says, "The people of Judah have sinned again and again, and I will not forget it. I will not leave them unpunished any more. For they have rejected the laws of God, refusing to obey him. They have hardened their hearts and sinned as their fathers did."

Zeph 1:6. And I will destroy those who formerly worshiped the Lord, but now no longer do, and those who never loved him and never wanted to.

Mal 1:6. "A son honors his father, a servant honors his master. I am your Father and Master, yet you don't honor me, O priests, but you despise my name." "Who? Us?" you say. "When did we ever despise your name?"

Mal 3:7. "Though you have scorned my laws from earliest time, yet you may still return to me," says the Lord of Hosts. "Come and I will forgive you. But you say, 'We have never even gone away!' "

Heb 3:16. And who were those people I speak of, who heard God's voice speaking to them but then rebelled against him? They were the ones who came out of Egypt with Moses their leader. [17]And who was it who made God angry for all those forty years? These same people who sinned and as a result died in the wilderness. [18]And to whom was God speaking when he swore with an oath that they would never go into the land he had promised his people? He was speaking to all those who disobeyed him. [19]And why didn't they go in? Because they didn't trust him.

Instances of Israel's backsliding. At Massah (Meribah), Ex 17:1–7; when Aaron made the golden calf, Ex 32; after Joshua's death, Judg 2; during Asa's reign, 2 Chron 15; Hezekiah's reign, 2 Chron 30:2–12.

BAD COMPANY See *Company, Evil.*

BAHURIM A village between the fords of the Jordan and Jerusalem, 2 Sam 3:16; 16:5; 17:18; 19:16; 1 Kgs 2:8.

BAIL To keep the peace, Acts 17:9.

See *Surety; Creditor; Debt; Debtor.*

BAKBAKKAR A Levite, 1 Chron 9:15, 16.

BAKBUK An ancestor of the Nethinim, Ezra 2:43–54; Neh 7:46–56.

BAKBUKIAH Two Levites, Neh 11:15–17; 12:9 and Neh 12:25.

BAKER 1 Sam 8:13; Hos 7:4. Pharaoh's chief baker, Gen 40.

See *Bread.*

BALAAM Son of Beor. From Mesopotamia, Deut 23:4. A magician, Josh 13:22. A prophet, Num 24:2–9; 2 Pet 2:15, 16. Balak sends for, to curse Israel, Num 22:5–7; Josh 24:9; Neh 13:2; Mic 6:5. Anger of, rebuked by his donkey, Num 22:22–35; 2 Pet 2:16. Advice of, a cause of Israel's corruption with the Midianites, Num 31:16; Rev 2:14, 15. Greed of, 2 Pet 2:15; Jude 1:11. Death of, Num 31:8; Josh 13:22.

BALAH A city of Simeon, Josh 19:2–7. Called *Baalah,* Josh 15:21–32 and *Bilhah,* 1 Chron 4:29.

BALAK King of Moab, Num 22:4; Josh 24:9; Judg 11:25; Mic 6:5. Tries to bribe Balaam to curse Israel, Num 22:5–7, 15–17.

See *Balaam.*

BALANCES Used for weighing, Ezk 5:1. Must be just, Prov 16:11.

See *Measure; Scales; Dishonesty.*

FIGURATIVE. Dan 5:27; Rev 6:5.

BALDNESS Lev 13:40, 41. A judgment, Isa 3:24; Jer 48:37; Ezk 7:18. Artificial, a sign of mourning, Isa 22:12; Jer 16:6; Ezk 27:31; Amos 8:10; Mic 1:16. Artificial, as an idolatrous practice, forbidden, Lev 21:5; Deut 14:1.

INSTANCES OF. Elisha, 2 Kgs 2:23; Babylonian soldiers, Ezk 29:18.

BALL Playing at, Isa 22:18.

BALM A medicinal balsam, Gen 43:11; Ezk 27:17.

BALSAM TREE 2 Sam 5:23, 24.

BAMAH A high place, Ezk 20:29.

BAMOTH A camping place of the Israelites, Num 21:19, 20. Called *Bamoth-baal,* a city of Reuben, Josh 13:17.

BANI 1. A Gadite, 2 Sam 23:24–39.

2. A Levite, 1 Chron 6:44–47.

3. A descendant of Perez, 1 Chron 9:4.

4. Father of returned exiles, Ezra 2:3–35. Called *Binnui,* Neh 7:8–38.

5. Ancestor of Shelomith, Ezra 8:2–14.

6. Ancestor of those who had heathen wives, Ezra 10:29.

7. Another ancestor of those with heathen wives, Ezra 10:34–42.

8. Possibly up to four Levites of the returned exiles, Neh 3:17; 8:7, 8; 9:4, 5; 10:9–13; 11:22, 23.

9. A leader who signed the covenant with Nehemiah, Neh 10:14–27.

BANISHMENT Ezra 7:26. Of Adam and Eve, from Eden, Gen 3:22–24. Of Cain, to be "a fugitive and a tramp," Gen 4:14. Of Jews, from Rome, Acts 18:2. Of John, to Patmos, Rev 1:9.

See *Exile.*

BANNER Of the Lord, Ex 17:15, 16. Tribal, Num 2:1, 2, 34.

FIGURATIVE. Ps 60:4, 5; 118:10; Song 6:4, 10; Isa 11:10.

See *Flag; Signal.*

BANQUET See *Feasts.*

BAPTISM JOHN'S. Mt 3:5. People from Jerusalem and from all over the Jordan Valley, and, in fact, from every section of Judea went out to the wilderness to hear him preach, [6]and when they confessed their sins, he baptized them in the Jordan River. [7]But when he saw many Pharisees and Sadducees coming to be baptized he denounced them. "You sons of snakes!" he warned. "Who said that you could escape the coming wrath of God? [8]Before being baptized, prove that you have turned from sin by doing worthy deeds. [11]With water I baptize those who repent of their sins; but someone else is coming, far greater than I am, so great that I am not worthy to carry his shoes! He shall baptize you with the Holy Spirit and with fire." [13]Then Jesus went from Galilee to the Jordan River to be baptized there by John. [14]John didn't want to do it. "This isn't proper," he said. "I am the one who needs to be baptized by you." [15]But Jesus said, "Please do it, for I must do all that is right." So then John baptized him. [16]After his baptism, as soon as Jesus came up out of the water, the heavens were opened to him and he saw the Spirit of God coming down in the form of a dove. Mk 1:8–10; Lk 3:7, 8; Jn 10:40.

Mt 21:25. "Was John the Baptist sent from God, or not?" Mk 11:30; Lk 20:4.

Mk 1:4. This messenger was John the Baptist. He lived in the wilderness and taught that all should be baptized as a public announcement of their decision to turn their backs on sin, so that God could forgive them. [5]People from Jerusalem and from all over Judea traveled out into the Judean wasteland to see and hear John, and when they confessed their sins he baptized them in the Jordan River. Lk 3:3.

Lk 3:12. Even tax collectors—notorious for their corruption—came to be baptized and asked, "How shall we prove to you that we have abandoned our sins?" [21]Then one day, after the crowds had been baptized, Jesus himself was baptized; and as he was praying, the heavens opened.

Lk 7:29. And all who heard John preach—even the most wicked of them—agreed that God's requirements were right, and they were baptized by him. [30]All, that is, except the Pharisees and teachers of Moses' Law. They rejected God's plan for them and refused John's baptism.

Jn 1:24, 25. Then those who were sent by the Pharisees asked him, "If you aren't the Messiah or Elijah or the Prophet, what right do you have to baptize?" [26]John told them, "I merely baptize with water, but right here in the crowd is someone you have never met, [27]who will soon begin his ministry among you, and I am not even fit to be his slave." [28]This incident took place at Bethany, a village on the other side of the Jordan River where John was baptizing. [31]"I didn't know he was the one, but I am here baptizing with water in order to point him out to the nation of Israel. [33]I didn't know he was the one," John said again, "but at the time God sent me to baptize he told me, 'When you see the Holy Spirit descending and resting upon someone —he is the one you are looking for. He is the one who baptizes with the Holy Spirit.' "

Jn 3:23, 24. At this time John the Baptist was not yet in prison. He was baptizing at Aenon, near Salim, because there was plenty of water there.

Acts 1:5. "John baptized you with water," he reminded them, "but you shall be baptized with the Holy Spirit in just a few days." [22]Let us select someone who has been with us constantly from our first association with the Lord—from the time he was baptized by John until the day he was taken from us into heaven.

Acts 10:36, 37. I'm sure you have heard about the Good News for the people of Israel—that there is peace with God through Jesus the Messiah, who is Lord of all creation. This message has spread all through Judea, beginning with John the Baptist in Galilee.

Acts 11:16. Then I thought of the Lord's words when he said, "Yes, John baptized with water, but you shall be baptized with the Holy Spirit." Acts 18:25, 26.

Acts 19:3. "Then what beliefs did you acknowledge at your baptism?" he asked. And they replied, "What John the Baptist taught." [4]Then Paul pointed out to them that John's baptism was to demonstrate a desire to turn from sin to God and that those receiving his baptism must then go on to believe in Jesus, the one John said would come later.

CHRISTIAN. Mt 28:19. Therefore, go and make disciples in all the nations, baptizing them into the name of the Father, the Son and of the Holy Spirit.

Mk 16:16. Those who believe and are baptized will be saved.

Jn 3:22. Afterwards Jesus and his disciples left Jerusalem and stayed there for a while in Judea and baptized there.

Acts 2:38. And Peter replied, "Each one of you must turn from sin, return to God, and be baptized in the name of Jesus Christ for the forgiveness of your sins; then you also shall receive this gift, the Holy Spirit." [41]And those who believed Peter were baptized—about 3,000 in all!

Acts 8:12. But now they believed Philip's message that Jesus was the Messiah, and his words concerning the Kingdom of God; and many men and women were baptized. [13]Then Simon himself believed and was baptized and began following Philip wherever he went, and was amazed by the miracles he did. *v.* 16.

36. As they rode along, they came to a small body of water, and the eunuch said, "Look! Water! Why can't I be baptized?" [38]He stopped the chariot, and they went down into the water and Philip baptized him.

Acts 9:18. Instantly (it was as though scales fell from his eyes) Paul could see, and was immediately baptized.

Acts 10:46, 47. But there could be no doubt about it, for they heard them speaking in tongues and praising God. Peter asked, "Can anyone object to my baptizing them, now that they have received the Holy Spirit just as we did?" [48]So he did, baptizing them in the name of Jesus, the Messiah.

Acts 16:14. One of them was Lydia, a saleswoman from Thyatira, a merchant of purple cloth. She was already a worshiper of God and, as she listened to us, the Lord opened her heart and she accepted all that Paul was saying. [15]She was baptized along with all her household and asked us to be her guests. "If you agree that I am faithful to the Lord," she said, "come and stay at my home." And she urged us until we did. [33]That same hour he washed their stripes and he and all his family were baptized.

Acts 18:8. However, Crispus, the leader of the synagogue, and all his household believed in the Lord and were baptized—as were many others in Corinth. [25]While he was in Egypt, someone had told him about John the Baptist and what John had said about Jesus, but that is all he knew. He had never heard the rest of the story!

Acts 19:4. Then Paul pointed out to them that John's baptism was to demonstrate a desire to turn from sin to God and that those receiving his baptism must then go on to believe in Jesus, the one John said would come later. [5]As soon as they heard this, they were baptized in the name of the Lord Jesus.

Acts 22:16. And now, why delay? Go and be baptized, and be cleansed from your sins, believing on the name of the Lord.

Rom 6:3. For sin's power over us was broken

when we became Christians and were baptized to become a part of Jesus Christ; through his death the power of your sinful nature was shattered. [4]Your old sin-loving nature was buried with him by baptism when he died, and when God the Father, with glorious power, brought him back to life again, you were given this wonderful new life to enjoy.

1 Cor 1:13. And so, in effect, you have broken Christ into many pieces. But did I, Paul, die for your sins? Were any of you baptized in my name? [14]I am so thankful now that I didn't baptize any of you except Crispus and Gaius. [15]For now no one can think that I have been trying to start something new, beginning a "Church of Paul." [16]Oh, yes, and I baptized the family of Stephanas. I don't remember ever baptizing anyone else. [17]For Christ didn't send me to baptize, but to preach the Gospel.

1 Cor 15:29. If the dead will not come back to life again, then what point is there in people being baptized for those who are gone? Why do it unless you believe that the dead will some day rise again?

Gal 3:27. And we who have been baptized into union with Christ are enveloped by him.

Eph 4:5. For us there is only one Lord, one faith, one baptism.

Col 2:12. For in baptism you see how your old, evil nature died with him and was buried with him; and then you came up out of death with him into a new life because you trusted the Word of the mighty God who raised Christ from the dead.

Heb 6:2. You don't need further instruction about baptism and spiritual gifts and the resurrection of the dead and eternal judgment.

1 Pet 3:18. Christ also suffered. He died once for the sins of all us guilty sinners, although he himself was innocent of any sin at any time, that he might bring us safely home to God. But though his body died, his spirit lived on, [21]That, by the way, is what baptism pictures for us: In baptism we show that we have been saved from death and doom by the resurrection of Christ; not because our bodies are washed clean by the water, but because in being baptized we are turning to God and asking him to cleanse our *hearts* from sin.

OF THE HOLY SPIRIT. Isa 44:3. And I will pour out my Spirit and my blessings on your children.

Joel 2:28. After I have poured out my rains again, I will pour out my Spirit upon all of you! Your sons and daughters will prophesy; your old men will dream dreams, and your young men see visions. [29]And I will pour out my Spirit even on your slaves, men and women alike.

Zech 12:10. Then I will pour out the spirit of grace and prayer on all the people of Jerusalem, and they will look on him they pierced, and mourn for him as for an only son, and grieve bitterly for him as for an oldest child who died.

Mt 3:11. With water I baptize those who repent of their sins; but someone else is coming, far greater than I am, so great that I am not worthy to carry his shoes! He shall baptize you with the Holy Spirit and with fire. [Mk 1:8; Lk 3:16] [16]After his baptism, as soon as Jesus came up out of the water, the heavens were opened to him and he saw the Spirit of God coming down in the form of a dove. Lk 3:22; Jn 1:32, 33.

Lk 24:49. And now I will send the Holy Spirit upon you, just as my Father promised. Don't begin telling others yet—stay here in the city until the Holy Spirit comes and fills you with power from heaven.

Jn 3:5. Jesus replied, "What I am telling you so earnestly is this: Unless one is born of water and the Spirit, he cannot enter the Kingdom of God."

Acts 1:5. "John baptized you with water," he reminded them, "but you shall be baptized with the Holy Spirit in just a few days."

Acts 2:1. Seven weeks had gone by since Jesus' death and resurrection, and the Day of Pentecost had now arrived. As the believers met together that day, [2]suddenly there was a sound like the roaring of a mighty windstorm in the skies above them and it filled the house where they were meeting. [3]Then, what looked like flames or tongues of fire appeared and settled on their heads. [4]And everyone present was filled with the Holy Spirit and began speaking in languages they didn't know, for the Holy Spirit gave them this ability. [38]And Peter replied, "Each one of you must turn from sin, return to God, and be baptized in the name of Jesus Christ for the forgiveness of your sins; then you also shall receive this gift, the Holy Spirit." [41]And those who believed Peter were baptized—about 3,000 in all!

Acts 8:15. As soon as they arrived, they began praying for these new Christians to receive the Holy Spirit, [16]for as yet he had not come upon any of them. For they had only been baptized in the name of the Lord Jesus. [17]Then Peter and John laid their hands upon these believers, and they received the Holy Spirit.

Acts 10:38. "And you no doubt know that Jesus of Nazareth was anointed by God with the Holy Spirit and with power, and he went around doing good and healing all who were possessed by demons, for God was with him." [44]Even as Peter was saying these things, the Holy Spirit fell upon all those listening! [45]The Jews who came with Peter were amazed that the gift of the Holy Spirit would be given to Gentiles too! [46, 47]But there could be no doubt about it, for they heard them speaking in tongues and praising God. Peter asked, "Can anyone object to my baptizing them, now that they have received the Holy Spirit just as we did?"

Acts 11:15. Well, I began telling them the Good News, but just as I was getting started with my sermon, the Holy Spirit fell on them, just as he fell on us at the beginning! [16]Then I thought of the Lord's words when he said, "Yes, John baptized with water, but you shall be baptized with the Holy Spirit."

Acts 19:2. "Did you receive the Holy Spirit when you believed?" he asked them. "No," they replied, "we don't know what you mean. What is the Holy Spirit?" [6]Then, when Paul laid his hands upon their heads, the Holy Spirit came on them.

1 Cor 12:13. Each of us is a part of the one body of Christ. Some of us are Jews, some are Gentiles, some are slaves and some are free. But the Holy Spirit has fitted us all together into Christ's body by the one Spirit, and have all been given that same Holy Spirit.

Tit 3:5. Then he saved us—not because we were good enough to be saved, but because of his kindness and pity—by washing away our sins and giving us the new joy of the indwelling Holy Spirit [6]whom he poured out upon us with wonderful fullness—and all because of what Jesus Christ our Savior did.

1 Pet 3:20. Spirits of those who, long before in the days of Noah, had refused to listen to God, though he waited patiently for them while Noah was building the ark. Yet only eight persons were saved from drowning in that terrible flood. [21](That, by the way, is what baptism pictures for us: In baptism we show that we have been saved from death and doom by the resurrection of Christ; not because our bodies are washed clean by the water, but because in being baptized we are turning to God and asking him to cleanse our *hearts* from sin.)

See *Holy Spirit.*

BARABBAS A prisoner released by Pilate, Mt 27:16–26; Mk 15:7–15; Lk 23:17–25; Jn 18:40; Acts 3:14.

BARACHEL Father of Elihu, Job 32:2.

BARACHIAH Father of Zechariah, Mt 23:35. Called also *Berechiah,* Zech 1:1, 7.

BARAK A judge in Israel, Judg 4; 5; 1 Sam 12:11; Heb 11:32.

BARBER Judg 16:19; Ezk 5:1.

BARIAH Son of Shemaiah, 1 Chron 3:21, 22.

BAR-JESUS A false prophet, Acts 13:6, 7.

BARKOS A Jew whose descendants returned from exile, Ezra 2:43–54; Neh 7:46–56.

BARLEY A product of Egypt, Ex 9:31; Palestine, Deut 8:8; 1 Chron 11:13; Jer 41:8. Fed to horses, 1 Kgs 4:28. Used in offerings, Num 5:15; Ezk 45:13, 15. Traffic in, 2 Chron 2:10; Hos 3:2. Tribute in, 2 Chron 27:5. Priests estimated value of, Lev 27:16; 2 Kgs 7:1; Rev 6:6. Absalom burns Joab's field of, 2 Sam 14:30.

Loaves of, Jn 6:8, 9, 11.

BARN 1 Sam 6:7, 10; Job 5:24; Ps 144:12–15; Ps 147:14; Prov 3:9, 10; Eccl 10:11; Isa 3:14; Joel 1:17; Hab 3:17; Mt 13:30; Lk 12:17, 18, 24.

BARNABAS Called also *Joseph.* A prophet, Acts 13:1. An apostle, Acts 14:14. A Levite who gave his possessions to be owned in common with other disciples, Acts 4:36, 37. Goes to Tarsus to find Paul, brings him to Antioch, Acts 11:25, 26. Accompanies Paul to Jerusalem, Acts 11:30. Returns with Paul to Antioch, Acts 12:25. Goes with Paul to Seleucia, Acts 13; to Iconium, Acts 14:1–7. Called Jupiter, Acts 14:12–18. Goes to Derbe, Acts 14:20. Is sent as a commissioner to Jerusalem, Acts 15; Gal 2:1–9. Disagrees with Paul, Acts 15:36–39. Is reconciled to Paul, 1 Cor 9:6. Piety of, Acts 11:24. Devotion of, to Jesus, Acts 15:26.

BARRACKS Jer 51:30; Mk 15:16, 17.

BARREL 1 Kgs 18:33.

BARRENNESS Sterility of women. A disgrace, Gen 30:22; 1 Sam 1:6, 7; 2:1–11; Isa 4:1; Lk 1:25. Miraculously removed, instances of: Sarai, Gen 17:15–21; Rebekah, Gen 25:21; Manoah's wife, Judg 13; Hannah, 1 Sam 1:6–20; Elizabeth, Lk 1:5–25. Sent as a judgment, Gen 20:17, 18. See *Childlessness.*

BARSABAS 1. Nominated to replace Judas as one of the apostles, also called *Joseph Justus,* Acts 1:23.

2. Called also *Judas,* Acts 15:22.

BARTER See *Commerce.*

BARTHOLOMEW One of the apostles, Mt 10:2–4; Mk 3:16–19; Lk 6:14–16; Acts 1:14.

BARTIMAEUS A blind man, Mk 10:46–52; Mt 20:29–34; Lk 18:35–43.

BARUCH 1. Jeremiah's secretary, Jer 32:12–16; 36:4–32; 43:2–6; 45:1, 2.

2. Son of Zabbai, Neh 3:20; 10:6.

3. A descendant of Perez, Neh 11:4–6.

BARZILLAI 1. A friend of David, 2 Sam 17:27–29; 19:31–39; 1 Kgs 2:7.

2. A priest, Ezra 2:61; Neh 7:63.

BASEMATH 1. A wife, or possibly two wives, of Esau, Gen 26:34; 36:2–4, 13, 14, 17.

2. Daughter of Solomon, 1 Kgs 4:8–19.

BASHAN A region east of the Jordan and north of Gilead, Gen 14:5. Og, king of, Josh 13:12. Allotted to the two and one-half tribes, which had their possession east of the Jordan, Num 32:33; Deut 3:10–14; Josh 12:4–6; 13:29–31; 17:1. Invaded and taken by Hazael, king of Syria, 2 Kgs 10:32, 33. Retaken by Jehoash, 2 Kgs 13:25. Fertility and productiveness of, Isa 33:9; Jer 50:19; Mic 7:14; Nah 1:4. Forests of, famous, Isa 2:13; Ezk 27:6; Zech 11:2. Distinguished for its fine livestock, Deut 32:14; Ps 22:12; Ezk 39:18; Amos 4:1.

See *Argob, 1; Ashtaroth, 2; Edre-i; Jair, 1.*

BASIN Made of gold, 1 Kgs 7:50; 1 Chron 28:17; 2 Chron 4:22; of bronze, Ex 27:3; 38:3; 1 Kgs 7:45.

See *Tabernacle, Furniture of.*

BASKET Gen 40:16, 17; Ex 29:3, 4, 23, 32; Lev 8:1–3, 26; Num 6:15; Deut 26:2; 2 Kgs 10:7. Held the scraps after the miracles of the loaves, Mt 14:20; 15:37, 38; 16:9. Paul let down from the wall in, Acts 9:25; 2 Cor 11:33.

BASTARD Excluded from the congregation, Deut 23:2.

INSTANCES OF. Ishmael, Gen 16:2, 3, 15; Gal 4:22; Moab and Benammi, Gen 19:36–38; Jephthah, Judg 11:1, 2; David's child by Bath-sheba, 2 Sam 11:2–5. Blind man called, Jn 9:34.

FIGURATIVE. Heb 12:8.

BAT Lev 11:13–19; Deut 14:11–18; Isa 2:20.

BATH A Hebrew liquid measure, containing about six gallons (22 liters), Ezk 45:11. Equal to the dry measure, *ephah.*

BATHING See *Ablution; Purification.*

BATH-RABBIM A gate in the city of Heshbon, Song 7:4.

BATH-SHEBA Wife of Uriah and later wife of David. Called *Bath-shua,* 1 Chron 3:5. Adultery of, 2 Sam 11:2–5. Solomon's mother, 1 Kgs 1:11–31; 2:13–21; 1 Chron 3:5.

BATH-SHUA 1. See *Bath-sheba.*

2. Wife of Judah, 1 Chron 2:3.

BATTALION LEADER Deut 20:9; Num 31:48.

See *Armies; Captain; Commander; Officer.*

BATTERING RAM Deut 20:20; Jer 6:6; Ezk 4:1, 2; 21:22; 26:9.

BATTERY See *Assault and Battery.*

BATTLE Shouting in, Judg 7:19, 20; 1 Sam 17:20. Priests in, 2 Chron 13:12. Prayer before: By Asa, 2 Chron 14:11; by Jehoshaphat, 2 Chron 20:3–12.

See *Armies; War.*

BATTLE AXE Jer 51:20.

BATTLEMENT 2 Chron 26:15.

FIGURATIVE. Song 8:9.

BAVVAI Builds the wall of Jerusalem, Neh 3:18.

BAZLITH Called also *Bazluth,* one of the Nethinim, Ezra 2:43–54; Neh 7:54.

BDELLIUM Gen 2:12.

BEACON Rom 2:19; Phil 2:15.

See *Banner; Flag; Signal.*

BEALIAH An Israelite, who joined David at Ziklag, 1 Chron 12:3–7.

BEAM Weaver's, 2 Sam 21:19.

BEAN 2 Sam 17:28, 29; Ezk 4:9.

BEAR Ferocity of, 2 Sam 17:8; Prov 17:12; 28:15; Isa 11:7; 59:11; Lam 3:10; Hos 13:8; Amos 5:19. Killed by David, 1 Sam 17:34–37. Two destroy some children of Bethel, who mocked Elisha, 2 Kgs 2:24.

FIGURATIVE. Dan 7:5; Rev 13:2.

BEARD Worn long by Aaron, Ps 133:2; Samson, Judg 16:17; David, 1 Sam 21:13; Ezk 5:1. Shaven by Egyptians, Gen 41:14. Untrimmed in mourning, 2 Sam 19:24. Plucked, Ezra 9:3. Cut, Isa 15:2. Shaven before worship, Jer 41:5. Shaven in anguish, Jer 48:37. Lepers required to shave, Lev 13:29–33; 14:9. Idolatrous practice of clipping, forbidden, Lev 19:27; 21:5. Beards of David's ambassadors half shaven by the king of the Ammonites, 2 Sam 10:4.

BEASTS See *Animals.*

BEATEN WORK Of metals, Ex 25:18; 37:17, 22; Num 8:4; 10:1; Jer 10:9.

BEATING As a punishment, Ex 5:14; Deut 25:1–3; Mk 13:9; Acts 5:40; 16:22, 37; 18:17; 21:32; 22:19. Suffered by Paul, 2 Cor 6:5.

See *Assault; Punishment.*

BEAUTY Vanity of, Prov 6:25; 31:30; Isa 3:24; Ezk 16:14; 28:17; 1 Pet 3:3.

INSTANCES OF. Sarah, Gen 12:11–13. Rebekah, Gen 24:15, 16. Rachel, Gen 29:17. Joseph, Gen 39:6. Moses, Ex 2:1, 2. David, 1 Sam 16:12, 18. Bath-sheba, 2 Sam 11:2. Tamar, 2 Sam 13:1. Absalom, 2 Sam 14:25. Abishag, 1 Kgs 1:3, 4. Vashti, Esther 1:11. Esther, Esther 2:7.

SPIRITUAL BEAUTY. 1 Chron 16:29; Ps 27:4; 29:2; 45:10, 11; 96:9; 110:3; Isa 52:7; Ezk 16:14; Zech 9:16, 17; Rom 10:15; 1 Pet 3:4.

BEBAI The name of three Jews whose descendants came from exile, Ezra 2:3–35; 8:2–14; 10:28; Neh 7:8–38; 10:14–27.

BECHER 1. Son of Benjamin, Gen 46:19–22; 1 Chron 7:6, 8.

2. Son of Ephraim, Num 26:28–37. Called *Bered,* 1 Chron 7:20, 21.

BECHORATH Son of Aphiah, 1 Sam 9:1.

BED Made of iron, Deut 3:11; of ivory, Amos 6:4. Used at meals, Amos 6:4. Not exempt from repossession, Prov 22:26, 27. Perfumed, Prov 7:16, 17.

BEDAN Son of Ullam, 1 Chron 7:17.

BEE In Palestine, Deut 1:44; Judg 14:8; Ps 118:12; Isa 7:18.

See *Honey.*

BEELIADA Son of David, 1 Chron 14:4–7. Called *Eliada,* 2 Sam 5:14–16; 1 Chron 3:6–8.

BEELZEBUB The prince of devils, Mt 12:24; Lk 11:15.

See *Baal-zebub.*

BEER 1. A stopping place of the Israelites, Num 21:16–18.

2. A place, site unknown, to which Jotham escaped for fear of Abimelech, Judg 9:21.

BE-ERA Son of Zophah, 1 Chron 7:36, 37.

BEERAH A Reubenite, 1 Chron 5:6.

BEERI 1. A Hittite, Gen 26:34. See *Anah.*

2. Father of Hosea, Hos 1:1.

BEER-LAHAI-ROI A well near Kadesh. Hagar fled to, Gen 16:7–14; Isaac lives at, Gen 24:62; 25:11.

BE-EROTH 1. A station of the Israelites. Aaron died at, Deut 10:6. See *Bene-jaakan.*

2. A city of the Hivites, Josh 9:17; 18:21–28; 2 Sam 4:2, 3; Ezra 2:3–35; Neh 7:8–38.

BEER-SHEBA 1. The most southern city of Palestine, Judg 20:1, 2. Named by Abraham, who dwelt there, Gen 21:31–33; 22:19. Residence of Isaac, Gen 26:23. Jacob left, traveling to Haran, Gen 28:10. Sacrifices offered at, by Jacob when journeying to Egypt, Gen 46:1. In the inheritance of Judah, Josh 15:20–32; 2 Sam 24:7. Afterward assigned to Simeon, Josh 19:1–7, 9; 1 Chron 4:28. Two sons of Samuel were judges at, 1 Sam 8:2. Became a seat of idolatrous worship, Amos 5:5; 8:14.

2. Well of, belonged to Abraham and Isaac, Gen 21:25, 26.

3. Wilderness of. Hagar miraculously sees a well in, Gen 21:14–19. An angel fed Elijah in, 1 Kgs 19:3, 5, 7.

BE-ESHTERAH A Levitical city, Josh 21:27. Called *Ashtaroth,* 1 Chron 6:71.

BEGGARS The results of sin, Lk 16:3. In the parable of the great feast, Lk 14:21.

INSTANCES OF. Bartimaeus, Mk 10:46. Lazarus, Lk 16:20–22. The blind man, Jn 9:8. The lame man, Acts 3:2–5, 10.

See *Poor.*

BEHEADING Execution by: Of John, Mt 14:10; Mk 6:27; Lk 9:9; of the martyrs, Rev 20:4.

See *Punishment.*

BEHEMOTH An amphibious animal, Job 40:15.

BEL A Babylonian god, Isa 46:1; Jer 51:44. Called *Marduk,* Jer 50:2.

BELA 1. A city called also Zoar, Gen 14:2, 8, 9.

2. King of Edom, Gen 36:31–39; 1 Chron 1:43, 44.

3. Son of Benjamin, Gen 46:21; Num 26:38–41; 1 Chron 7:6, 7; 8:1–5.

4. Son of Azaz, 1 Chron 5:7, 8.

BELIEVER See *Righteous.*

BELIEVING See *Faith.*

BELL Attached to the hem of the priest's robe, Ex 28:33, 34; 39:25, 26. On horses, Zech 14:20.

BELLOWS Used with the furnace of the foundry, Jer 6:29.

BELSHAZZAR King of Babylon, Dan 5:1–30.

BELT Made of linen, Prov 31:24; of leather, 2 Kgs 1:8; Mt 3:4. Used to carry weapons, 1 Sam 18:4; 2 Sam 20:8. Traffic in, Prov 31:24.

FIGURATIVE. Eph 6:14.

Symbolical. Acts 21:11; Rev 15:6.

See *Loincloth; Sash.*

BELTESHAZZAR Name given Daniel, Dan 1:7.

See *Daniel.*

BEN-ABINADAB See *Abinadab, 4.*

BENAIAH 1. Son of Jehoiada, commander of the Cherethites and Pelethites, 2 Sam 8:18; 1 Kgs 1:38. A distinguished soldier, 2 Sam 23:20–23; 1 Chron 11:22–25; 27:5, 6. Loyal to Solomon, 1 Kgs 4:1–6.

2. An Ephraimite, and distinguished soldier, 2 Sam 23:24–39; 1 Chron 11:26–47; 27:14.

3. A Levitical musician, 1 Chron 15:18, 20; 16:5.

4. A priest and trumpeter, 1 Chron 15:24; 16:6.

5. Son of Je-iel, 2 Chron 20:14.

6. A Levite in time of Hezekiah, 2 Chron 31:12, 13.

7. A prince of the Simeonites, 1 Chron 4:34–39.

8. Father of Jehoida, Ahithopel's assistant, 1 Chron 27:34.

9. Father of Pelatiah, Ezk 11:1, 13.

10. Son of Parosh, Ezra 10:25.

11. Son of Pahath-moab, Ezra 10:30.

12. Son of Bani, Ezra 10:34–42.

13. Son of Nebo, Ezra 10:43.

BENAMMI Son of Lot, Gen 19:38.

BENCH Gold and silver, Esther 1:6; judgment, Jn 19:13.

BEN-DEKER One of Solomon's officials, 1 Kgs 4:8–19.

BENE-BERAK A city of Dan, Josh 19:41–46.

BENEDICTIONS Divinely appointed, Deut 10:8; 21:5; Num 6:22–26. By God, on creatures he had made, Gen 1:21, 22; on man, Gen 1:28; on Noah, Gen 9:1.

INSTANCES OF. By Melchizedek, on Abraham, Gen 14:19, 20; Heb 7:6, 7. By Bethuel's household, on Rebekah, Gen 24:60. By Isaac, on Jacob, Gen 27:23–29, 37; 28:1–4; on Esau, Gen 27:39, 40. By Jacob on Pharaoh, Gen 47:7–10; on Joseph's sons, Gen 48; on his own sons, Gen 49. By Moses, on the people of Israel, Deut 33. By Aaron, Lev 9:22, 23; by half the tribes, who stood at Mount Gerizim, Deut 11:29, 30; 27:11–13; Josh 8:33. By Joshua, on Caleb, Josh 14:13, 14; on the Reubenites and Gadites, and half tribe of Manasseh, Josh 22:6. By Naomi, on Ruth and Orpah, Ruth 1:8, 9. By the people, on Ruth and Boaz, Ruth 4:11, 12. By Eli, on Elkanah, 1 Sam 2:20. By David, on the people, 2 Sam 6:18; on Barzillai, 2 Sam 19:39. By Araunah, on David, 2 Sam 24:23. By Solomon, on the people, 1 Kgs 8:14, 54–58; 2 Chron 6:3. By Simeon, on Jesus, Lk 2:34, 35. By Jesus, Lk 24:50.

LEVITICAL, FORMS OF. Num 6:24–26. May the Lord bless and protect you; may the Lord's face radiate with joy because of you; may he be gracious to you, show you his favor, and give you his peace.

APOSTOLIC FORMS OF. Rom 1:7. May all God's mercies and peace be yours from God our Father and our Lord Jesus Christ. 1 Cor 1:3; 2 Cor 1:2; Gal 1:3; Eph 1:2; Phil 1:2; Col 1:2; 1 Thess 1:1; 2 Thess 1:2; 2 Tim 1:2; Philemon 1:3.

Rom 15:5. May God who gives patience, steadiness, and encouragement help you to live in complete harmony with each other—each with the attitude of Christ toward the other. [6]And then all of us can praise the Lord together with one voice, giving glory to God, the Father of our Lord Jesus Christ.

13. So I pray for you Gentiles that God who gives you hope will keep you happy and full of peace as you believe in him. I pray that God will help you overflow with hope in him through the Holy Spirit's power within you.

33. And now may our God, who gives peace, be with you all. Amen.

Rom 16:20. The blessings of our Lord Jesus Christ be upon you. *v.* 24. 1 Cor 16:23; Phil 4:23; 1 Thess 5:28; 2 Thess 3:18; Rev 22:21.

2 Cor 13:14. May the grace of our Lord Jesus Christ be with you all. May God's love and the Holy Spirit's friendship be yours.

Gal 6:16. May God's mercy and peace be upon all of you who live by this principle and upon those everywhere who are really God's own.

18. Dear brothers, may the grace of our Lord Jesus Christ be with you all. Philemon 1:25.

Eph 6:23. May God give peace to you, my Christian brothers, and love, with faith from God the Father, and the Lord Jesus Christ. [24]May God's grace and blessing be upon all who sincerely love our Lord Jesus Christ.

2 Thess 3:16. May the Lord of peace himself give you his peace no matter what happens. The Lord be with you all.

18. May the blessing of our Lord Jesus Christ be upon you all.

1 Tim 1:2. May God our Father and Jesus Christ our Lord show you his kindness and mercy and give you great peace of heart and mind.

1 Tim 6:21. May God's mercy be upon you.

2 Tim 4:22. May the Lord Jesus Christ be with your spirit.

Tit 3:15. May God's blessings be with you all.

Heb 13:20, 21. And now may the God of peace, who brought again from the dead our Lord Jesus, equip you with all you need for doing his will. May he who became the great Shepherd of the sheep by an everlasting agreement between God and you, signed with his blood, produce in you through the power of Christ all that is pleasing to him. To him be glory forever and ever. Amen.

25. God's grace be with you all.

1 Pet 1:2. May God bless you richly and grant you increasing freedom from all anxiety and fear.

1 Pet 5:10. After you have suffered a little while, our God, who is full of kindness through Christ, will give you his eternal glory. He personally will come and pick you up, and set you firmly in place, and make you stronger than ever. [11]To him be all power over all things, forever and ever. Amen.

14. Peace be to all of you who are in Christ.

2 Jn 1:3. God the Father and Jesus Christ his Son will bless us with great mercy and much peace, and with truth and love.

Jude 1:2. May you be given more and more of God's kindness, peace, and love.

BENEFACTOR Gen 44:4; Lk 22:25.

BENE-JAAKAN A camping place of the Israelites, Num 33:15–37; Deut 10:6.

See *Jaakan.*

BENEVOLENCE Deut 15:7. But if, when you arrive in the land the Lord will give you, there are any among you who are poor, you must not shut your heart or hand against them; [8]you must lend them as much as they need. [9]Beware! Don't refuse a loan because the year of debt cancellation is close at hand! If you refuse to make the loan and the needy man cries out to the Lord, it will be counted against you as a sin. [10]You must lend him what he needs, and don't moan about it either! For the Lord will prosper you in everything you do because of this! [11]There will always be some among you who are poor; that is why this commandment is necessary. You must lend to them liberally. [12]If you buy a Hebrew slave, whether a man or woman, you must free him at the end of the sixth year you have owned him, [13]and don't send him away empty-handed! [14]Give him a large farewell present from your flock, your olive press, and your wine press. Share with him in proportion as the Lord your God has blessed you. [15]Remember that you were slaves in the land of Egypt and the Lord your God rescued you! That is why I am giving you this command. [18]But when you free a slave you must not feel bad, for remember that for six years he has cost you less than half the price of a hired hand! And the Lord your God will prosper you in all you do because you have released him! Lev 25:35–43.

Ps 41:1. God blesses those who are kind to the poor. He helps them out of their troubles.

Ps 112:9. He gives generously to those in need. His deeds will never be forgotten. He shall have influence and honor.

Prov 3:27, 28. Don't withhold payment of your debts. Don't say "some other time," if you can pay now.

Prov 11:24, 25. It is possible to give away and become richer! It is also possible to hold on too tightly and lose everything. Yes, the liberal man shall be rich! By watering others, he waters himself.

Prov 22:9. Happy is the generous man, the one who feeds the poor.

Prov 25:21, 22. If your enemy is hungry, give him food! If he is thirsty, give him something to drink! This will make him feel ashamed of himself, and God will reward you.

Prov 28:27. If you give to the poor, your needs will be supplied! But a curse upon those who close their eyes to poverty.

Isa 58:6. No, the kind of fast I want is that you stop oppressing those who work for you and treat them fairly and give them what they earn. [7]I want you to share your food with the hungry and bring right into your own homes those who are helpless, poor and destitute. Clothe those who are cold and don't hide from relatives who need your help. [10]Feed the hungry! Help those in trouble! Then your light will shine out from the darkness, and the darkness around you shall be as bright as day. [11]And the Lord will guide you continually, and satisfy you with all good things, and keep you healthy too; and you will be like a well-watered garden, like an everflowing spring.

Ezk 18:5. But if a man is just and does what is lawful and right, [7]and is a merciful creditor, not holding on to the items given to him in pledge by poor debtors, and is no robber, but gives food to the hungry and clothes to those in need, [8]and grants loans without interest, and stays away from sin, and is honest and fair when judging others, [9]and obeys my laws—that man is just, says the Lord, and he shall surely live.

Mt 5:42. Give to those who ask, and don't turn away from those who want to borrow.

Mt 19:21. Jesus told him, "If you want to be perfect, go and sell everything you have and give the money to the poor, and you will have treasure in heaven; and come, follow me." Mk 10:21.

Mt 25:35. "For I was hungry and you fed me; I was thirsty and you gave me water; I was a stranger and you invited me into your homes; [36]naked and you clothed me; sick and in prison, and you visited me." [37]Then the righteous ones will reply, "Sir, when did we ever see you hungry and feed you? Or thirsty and give you anything to drink? [38]Or a stranger, and help you? Or naked, and clothe you? [39]When did we ever see you sick or in prison, and visit you?" [40]And I, the King, will tell them, "When you did it to these my brothers you were doing it to me!" [41]Then I will turn to those on my left and say, "Away with you, you cursed ones, into the eternal fire prepared for the devil and his demons. [42]For I was hungry and you wouldn't feed me; thirsty, and you wouldn't give me anything to drink; [43]a stranger, and you refused me hospitality;

naked, and you wouldn't clothe me; sick, and in prison, and you didn't visit me." 44Then they will reply, "Lord, when did we ever see you hungry or thirsty or a stranger or naked or sick or in prison, and not help you?" 45And I will answer, "When you refused to help the least of these my brothers, you were refusing to help me."

Mk 9:41. If anyone so much as gives you a cup of water because you are Christ's—I say this solemnly—he won't lose his reward.

Lk 3:11. "If you have two coats," he replied, "give one to the poor. If you have extra food, give it away to those who are hungry."

Lk 11:41. Purity is best demonstrated by generosity.

Acts 6:1. But with the believers multiplying rapidly, there were rumblings of discontent. Those who spoke only Greek complained that their widows were being discriminated against, that they were not being given as much food, in the daily distribution, as the widows who spoke Hebrew. 2So the Twelve called a meeting of all the believers. "We should spend our time preaching, not administering a feeding program," they said. 3"Now look around among yourselves, dear brothers, and select seven men, wise and full of the Holy Spirit, who are well thought of by everyone; and we will put them in charge of this business. 4Then we can spend our time in prayer, preaching, and teaching."

Acts 11:29. So the believers decided to send relief to the Christians in Judea, each giving as much as he could. 30This they did, consigning their gifts to Barnabas and Paul to take to the elders of the church in Jerusalem.

Rom 15:25. But before I come, I must go down to Jerusalem to take a gift to the Jewish Christians there. 26For you see, the Christians in Macedonia and Achaia have taken up an offering for those in Jerusalem who are going through such hard times. 27They were very glad to do this, for they feel that they owe a real debt to the Jerusalem Christians. Why? Because the news about Christ came to these Gentiles from the church in Jerusalem. And since they received this wonderful spiritual gift of the Gospel from there, they feel that the least they can do in return is to give some material aid.

1 Cor 13:3. If I gave everything I have to poor people, and if I were burned alive for preaching the Gospel but didn't love others, it would be of no value whatever.

1 Cor 16:1. Now here are the directions about the money you are collecting to send to the Christians in Jerusalem; (and, by the way, these are the same directions I gave to the churches in Galatia). 2On every Lord's Day each of you should put aside something from what you have earned during the week, and use it for this offering. The amount depends on how much the Lord has helped you earn. Don't wait until I get there and then try to collect it all at once. 3When I come I will send your loving gift with a letter to Jerusalem, to be taken there by trustworthy messengers you yourselves will choose.

2 Cor 8:1. Now I want to tell you what God in his grace has done for the churches in Macedonia. 2Though they have been going through much trouble and hard times, they have mixed their wonderful joy with their deep poverty, and the result has been an overflow of giving to others. 3They gave not only what they could afford, but far more; and I can testify that they did it because they wanted to, and not because of nagging on my part. 4They begged us to take the money so they could share in the joy of helping the Christians in Jerusalem. 5Best of all, they went beyond our highest hopes, for their first action was to dedicate themselves to the Lord and to us, for whatever directions God might give to them through us. 6They were so enthusiastic about it that we have urged Titus, who encouraged your giving in the first place, to visit you and encourage you to complete your share in this ministry of giving. 7You people there are leaders in so many ways—you have so much faith, so many good preachers, so much learning, so much enthusiasm, so much love for us. Now I want you to be leaders also in the spirit of cheerful giving. 8I am not giving you an order; I am not saying you must do it, but others are eager for it. This is one way to prove that your love is real, that it goes beyond mere words. 9You know how full of love and kindness our Lord Jesus was: though he was so very rich, yet to help you he became so very poor, so that by being poor he could make you rich. 10I want to suggest that you finish what you started to do a year ago, for you were not only the first to propose this idea, but the first to begin doing something about it. 11Having started the ball rolling so enthusiastically, you should carry this project through to completion just as gladly, giving whatever you can out of whatever you have. Let your enthusiastic idea at the start be equalled by your realistic action now. 12If you are really eager to give, then it isn't important how much you have to give. God wants you to give what you have, not what you haven't. 13Of course, I don't mean that those who receive your gifts should have an easy time of it at your expense, 14but you should divide with them. Right now you have plenty and can help them; then at some other time they can share with you when you need it. In this way each will have as much as he needs. 15Do you remember what the Scriptures say about this? "He that gathered much had nothing left over, and he that gathered little had enough." So you also should share with those in need. 24Please show your love for me to these men and do for them all that I have publicly boasted you would.

2 Cor 9:1. I realize that I really don't even need to mention this to you, about helping God's people. 2For I know how eager you are to do it, and I have boasted to the friends in Macedonia that you were ready to send an offering a year ago. In fact, it was this enthusiasm of yours that stirred up many of them to begin helping. 3But I am sending these men

just to be sure that you really are ready, as I told them you would be, with your money all collected; I don't want it to turn out that this time I was wrong in my boasting about you. [4]I would be very much ashamed—and so would you—if some of these Macedonian people come with me, only to find that you still aren't ready after all I have told them! [5]So I have asked these other brothers to arrive ahead of me to see that the gift you promised is on hand and waiting. I want it to be a real gift and not look as if it were being given under pressure. [6]But remember this—if you give little, you will get little. A farmer who plants just a few seeds will get only a small crop, but if he plants much, he will reap much. [7]Every one must make up his own mind as to how much he should give. Don't force anyone to give more than he really wants to, for cheerful givers are the ones God prizes. [8]God is able to make it up to you by giving you everything you need and more, so that there will not only be enough for your own needs, but plenty left over to give joyfully to others. [9]It is as the Scriptures say: "The godly man gives generously to the poor. His good deeds will be an honor to him forever." [10]For God, who gives seed to the farmer to plant, and later on, good crops to harvest and eat, will give you more and more seed to plant and will make it grow so that you can give away more and more fruit from your harvest. [11]Yes, God will give you much so that you can give away much, and when we take your gifts to those who need them they will break out into thanksgiving and praise to God for your help. [12]So, two good things happen as a result of your gifts—those in need are helped, and they overflow with thanks to God. [13]Those you help will be glad not only because of your generous gifts to themselves and to others, but they will praise God for this proof that your deeds are as good as your doctrine. [14]And they will pray for you with deep fervor and feeling because of the wonderful grace of God shown through you. [15]Thank God for his Son—his Gift too wonderful for words.

Gal 2:10. The only thing they did suggest was that we must always remember to help the poor, and I, too, was eager for that.

Phil 4:10. How grateful I am and how I praise the Lord that you are helping me again. I know you have always been anxious to send what you could, but for a while you didn't have the chance. [11]Not that I was ever in need, for I have learned how to get along happily whether I have much or little. [12]I know how to live on almost nothing or with everything. I have learned the secret of contentment in every situation, whether it be a full stomach or hunger, plenty or want; [13]for I can do everything God asks me to with the help of Christ who gives me the strength and power. [14]But even so, you have done right in helping me in my present difficulty. [15]As you well know, when I first brought the Gospel to you and then went on my way, leaving Macedonia, only you Philippians became my partners in giving and receiving. No other church did this. [16]Even when I was over in Thessalonica you sent help twice. [17]But though I appreciate your gifts, what makes me happiest is the well-earned reward you will have because of your kindness. [18]At the moment I have all I need—more than I need! I am generously supplied with the gifts you sent me when Epaphroditus came. They are a sweet-smelling sacrifice that pleases God well.

1 Tim 5:8. But anyone who won't care for his own relatives when they need help, especially those living in his own family, has no right to say he is a Christian. Such a person is worse than the heathen. [16]Let me remind you again that a widow's relatives must take care of her, and not leave this to the church to do. Then the church can spend its money for the care of widows who are all alone and have nowhere else to turn.

1 Tim 6:18. Tell them to use their money to do good. They should be rich in good works and should give happily to those in need, always being ready to share with others whatever God has given them.

Heb 6:10. For God is not unfair. How can he forget your hard work for him, or forget the way you used to show your love for him—and still do —by helping his children?

Heb 13:16. Don't forget to do good and to share what you have with those in need, for such sacrifices are very pleasing to him.

Jas 2:15. If you have a friend who is in need of food and clothing, [16]And you say to him, "Well, good-bye and God bless you; stay warm and eat hearty," and then don't give him clothes or food, what good does that do?

1 Jn 3:17. But if someone who is supposed to be a Christian has money enough to live well, and sees a brother in need, and won't help him—how can God's love be within *him?*

See *Charity; Liberality; Poor, Duties to; Rich; Riches.*

INSTANCES OF. The old man of Gibeah, Judg 19:16–21. Boaz, Ruth 2. The returned exiled Jews, Neh 5:8–12; 8:10, 11. Job, Job 29:11–17; 31:16–23. The Temanites, Isa 21:14. The good Samaritan, Lk 10: 33–35. Zacchaeus, Lk 19:8. The first Christians, Acts 2:44–46; 4:32–37. Cornelius, Acts 10:2, 4. Onesiphorus, 2 Tim 1:16–18.

See *Charitableness; Charity; Liberality; Love.*

BEN-GEBER One of Solomon's officers, 1 Kgs 4:8–19.

BEN-HADAD 1. King of Syria, 1 Kgs 15:18–20; 2 Chron 16:2–4.

2. A king of Syria, who reigned in the time of Ahab, son of Ben-hadad I, 1 Kgs 20; 2 Kgs 5; 6; 7; 8:7–15.

3. Son of Hazael and king of Syria, 2 Kgs 13:3, 24, 25; Amos 1:4.

BEN-HAIL A prince of Judah, 2 Chron 17: 7–9.

BEN-HANAN A son of Shimon, 1 Chron 4: 20.

BEN-HESED One of Solomon's officers, 1 Kgs 4:8–19.

BEN-HUR One of Solomon's officers, 1 Kgs 4:8–19.

BENINU A Levite, Neh 10:9–13.

BENJAMIN 1. Son of Jacob by Rachel, Gen 35:18, 24; 46:19. Taken into Egypt, Gen chapters 42–45. Prophecy concerning, Gen 49:27. Descendants of, Gen 46:19–22; Num 26:38–41.

2. TRIBE OF: Census of, at Sinai, Num 1:20–46; in the plain of Moab, Num 26:38–41. Clans of, Num 26:38–41; 1 Chron 7:6–12; 8. Position of, in camp and march, Num 2:3–31. Moses' benediction upon, Deut 33:12. Allotment in the land of Canaan, Josh 18:11–28. Reallotment, Ezk 48:23. Did not exterminate the Jebusites, Judg 1:21. Join Deborah in the war against Sisera, Judg 5:14. Territory of, invaded by the Philistines and Ammonites, Judg 10:9. Did not avenge the crime of the Gibeonites against the Levite's concubine, the war that followed, Judg 19; 20. Saul, the first king of Israel, from, 1 Sam 9:1; 10:20, 21. Its rank in the time of Samuel, 1 Sam 9:21. Jerusalem within the territory of, Jer 6:1. A company of, joins David at Ziklag, 1 Chron 12:1, 2, 16. Not included by Joab when he took a census of the military forces of Israel, 1 Chron 21:6. Loyal to Ish-bosheth, the son of Saul, 2 Sam 2:9, 15, 31; 1 Chron 12:24–37. Subsequently joins David, 2 Sam 3:19; 19:16, 17. Loyal to Rehoboam, 1 Kgs 12:21; 2 Chron 11:1. Military forces of, in the reign of Asa, 2 Chron 14:8; of Jehoshaphat, 2 Chron 17:17. Skilled archers and slingers, Judg 3:15; 20:16; 1 Chron 8:40; 12:2. Return to Palestine from the exile in Babylon, Ezra 1:5. Saints of, seen in John's vision, Rev 7:4–8. Paul, of the tribe of, Rom 11:1; Phil 3:5.

See *Israel.*

3. Great-grandson of Benjamin, 1 Chron 7:10.

4. A son of Harim, Ezra 10:32; probably identical with the man mentioned in Neh 3:23.

5. A Jew who assisted in dedicating the wall of Jerusalem, Neh 12:34.

6. A gate of Jerusalem, Jer 20:2; 37:13; 38:8; Zech 14:10.

BENO A descendant of Merari, 1 Chron 24:26, 27.

BEN-ONI Name given Benjamin by Rachel, Gen 35:18.

BEN-ZOHETH Son of Ishi, 1 Chron 4:20.

BEON A city east of the Jordan, Num 32:3, 4. Probably same as *Baal-meon,* Num 32:37, 38, which see.

BEOR 1. Father of Bela, Gen 36:31–39; 1 Chron 1:43.

2. Father of Balaam, Num 22:5, 6; 24:15–19; 31:8; Deut 13:4; Josh 13:22; 24:9; Mic 6:5; 2 Pet 2:15.

BEQUEST See *Will.*

BERA King of Sodom, Gen 14:2.

BERACAH 1. An Israelite, who joined David at Ziklag, 1 Chron 12:3–7.

2. A valley in the south of Judah, where the Israelites praised the Lord for a victory, called "the Valley of Blessing," 2 Chron 20:26.

BERAIAH Son of Shime-i, 1 Chron 8:19–21.

BEREAVEMENT From God, Ex 12:29; Hos 9:12. Mourning in, forbidden to Aaron, on account of his sons' wickedness, Lev 10:6; and to Ezekiel, for his wife, Ezk 24:16–18.

INSTANCES OF. Abraham, of Sarah, Gen 23:1, 2. Jacob, of Joseph, Gen 37:34, 35. Joseph, of his father, Gen 50:1, 4. The Egyptians, of their firstborn, Ex 12:29–33. Naomi, of her husband, Ruth 1:3–5, 20, 21. David, of his child by Bathsheba, 2 Sam 12:15–23; of Absalom, 2 Sam 18:33; 19:4.

RESIGNATION IN. 2 Sam 12:22. David replied, "I fasted and wept while the child was alive, for I said, 'Perhaps the Lord will be gracious to me and let the child live.' [23]But why should I fast when he is dead? Can I bring him back again? I shall go to him, but he shall not return to me."

Job 1:18. As he was still speaking, another arrived to say, "Your sons and daughters were feasting in their oldest brother's home, [19]when suddenly a mighty wind swept in from the desert, and engulfed the house so that the roof fell in on them and all are dead; and I alone escaped to tell you." [20]Then Job stood up and tore his robe in grief and fell down upon the ground before God. [21]"I came naked from my mother's womb," he said, "and I shall have nothing when I die. The Lord gave me everything I had, and they were his to take away. Blessed be the name of the Lord."

Eccl 7:2. It is better to spend your time at funerals than at festivals. For you are going to die and it is a good thing to think about it while there is still time. [3]Sorrow is better than laughter, for sadness has a refining influence on us. [4]Yes, a wise man thinks much of death, while the fool thinks only of having a good time now.

1 Thess 4:13. And now, dear brothers, I want you to know what happens to a Christian when he dies so that when it happens, you will not be full of sorrow, as those are who have no hope. [14]For since we believe that Jesus died and then came back to life again, we can also believe that when Jesus returns, God will bring back with him all the Christians who have died. [15]I can tell you this directly from the Lord: that we who are still living when the Lord returns will not rise to meet him ahead of those who are in their graves. [16]For the Lord himself will come down from heaven with a mighty shout and with the soul-stirring cry of the archangel and the great trumpet-call of God. And the believers who are dead will be the first to rise to meet the Lord. [17]Then we who are still alive and remain on the earth will be caught up with them in the clouds to meet the Lord in the air and remain with him forever. [18]So comfort and encourage each other with this news.

See *Affliction, Comfort in, Resignation in.* See also *Resignation.*

BERECHIAH 1. Father of Asaph, 1 Chron 6:39–43; 15:17.

2. A guard for the Ark, 1 Chron 15:23.

3. A warrior of Ephraim, 2 Chron 28:12.

4. A brother of Zerubbabel, 1 Chron 3:19, 20.

5. Son of Asa. 1 Chron 9:15, 16.
6. Son of Iddo, Zech 1:1, 7.
7. Son of Meshezabel and father of Meshullam, Neh 3:4, 30; 6:18.

BERED 1. A town in the south of Palestine, Gen 16:14.
2. A son of Ephraim, 1 Chron 7:20, 21; probably same as *Becher,* Num 26:28–37.

BERI Son of Zophah, 1 Chron 7:36, 37.

BERIAH 1. Son of Asher, Gen 46:16, 17; Num 26:44–47; 1 Chron 7:30.
2. Son of Ephraim, 1 Chron 7:20–23.
3. A Benjaminite, 1 Chron 8:13.
4. Son of Shime-i, 1 Chron 23:10, 11.

BERNICE Sister of Herod Agrippa II, Acts 25:13, 23; 26:30.

BEROEA A city in the south of Macedonia, Acts 17:10, 13; 20:4.

BEROTHAH Part of the northern boundary of Canaan, Ezk 47:16.

BEROTHAI A city of Zobah, 2 Sam 8:8.

BERYL A precious stone. Set in the chestpiece, Ex 28:20; 39:13. John saw, in the foundation of the new Jerusalem, Rev 21:18–20.

BESAI One of the Nethinim, Ezra 2:43–54; Neh 7:46–56.

BESODEIAH Father of Meshullam, Neh 3:6.

BESOR A brook near Gaza, 1 Sam 30:9, 10, 21.

BESTIALITY Ex 22:19. Anyone having sexual relations with an animal shall certainly be executed.

Lev 18:23. A man shall have no sexual intercourse with any female animal, thus defiling himself; and a woman must never give herself to a male animal, to mate with it; this is a terrible perversion.

Lev 20:15. If a man has sexual intercourse with an animal, he shall be executed and the animal killed. [16]If a woman has sexual intercourse with an animal, kill the woman and the animal, for they deserve their punishment.

Deut 27:21. "Cursed is he who has sexual intercourse with an animal." And all the people shall reply, "Amen."

BETAH A city belonging to Hadadezer, 2 Sam 8:8.

BETEN A city of Asher, Josh 19:24–26.

BETH-ANATH A fortified city of Naphtali, Josh 19:35–39; Judg 1:33.

BETH-ANOTH A city in Judah, Josh 15:48–62.

BETHANY 1. A village on the eastern slope of the Mount of Olives, Jn 11:18. Mary, Martha, and Lazarus dwell at, Lk 10:38–41. Lazarus dies and is raised to life at, Jn 11. Jesus attends a banquet in, Mt 26:6–13; Jn 12:1–9. The colt on which Jesus made his triumphal entry into Jerusalem obtained at, Mk 11:1–11. Jesus visits, Mt 21:17; Mk 11:11, 12, 19.
2. A place east of the Jordan. John testifies to Christ's messiahship, and baptizes at, Jn 1:28; Jesus at, Jn 10:39–42.

BETH-ARABAH A city in the valley of the Dead Sea, Josh 15:6, 61; 18:22. Called *Arabah,* Josh 18:18.

BETH-ARBEL A city destroyed by Shalman, Hos 10:14.

BETH-ASHBEA Home of descendants of Shelah, 1 Chron 4:21, 22.

BETH-AVEN A place on the mountains of Benjamin, Josh 18:12; 1 Sam 13:5; 14:23; Hos 5:8; 10:5.

BETH-AZMAVETH A town of Benjamin, Neh 7:8–38. Called *Azmaveth,* Ezra 2:3–35; Neh 12:29.

BETH-BAAL-MEON A place in the tribe of Reuben, Josh 13:17. Called *Baal-meon,* Num 32:37, 38; Ezk 25:9, 10; and *Beon,* Num 32:3, 4; and *Beth-meon,* Jer 48:23. Subdued by the Israelites, Num 32:3, 4. Assigned to the Reubenites, Josh 13:17.

BETH-BARAH A place east of Jordan, Judg 7:24.

BETH-BIRI A city of Simeon, 1 Chron 4:31. See *Beth-lebaoth.*

BETH-CAR A place west of Mizpah, 1 Sam 7:11.

BETH-DAGON 1. A city of Judah, Josh 15:37–44.
2. A city of Asher, Josh 19:27.

BETH-DIBLATHAIM A city of Moab, Jer 48:22. Called *Almon-diblathaim,* Num 33:46.

BETHEL 1. A city north of Jerusalem. The ancient city adjacent to, and finally embraced in, was called *Luz,* Josh 18:13; Judg 1:23–26. Abraham establishes an altar at, Gen 12:8; 13:3, 4. The place where Jacob saw the vision of the ladder, Gen 28:10–22; 31:13; Hos 12:4; and builds a pillar at, Gen 35:1–15. Deborah dies at, Gen 35:8. Conquered by Joshua, Josh 8:17, with 12:8–24; by the tribe of Joseph, Judg 1:22–26. Allotted to Benjamin, Josh 18:13, 21–28. Court of justice held at, by Deborah, Judg 4:5; by Samuel, 1 Sam 7:16.

Tabernacle at, Judg 20:26–28. Jeroboam institutes idolatrous worship at, 1 Kgs 12:25–33; 2 Kgs 10:29. Idolatry at, Jer 48:13; Amos 4:4. Shalmaneser sends a priest to, 2 Kgs 17:27, 28. Prophecies against the idolatrous altars at, 1 Kgs 13:1–6, 32; 2 Kgs 23:4, 15–20; Amos 3:14. The seminary at, 2 Kgs 2:3. Children of, mock Elisha, 2 Kgs 2:23, 24. People of, return from Babylon, Ezra 2:3–35; Neh 7:8–38. Prophecies against, Amos 5:5.
2. A city in the south of Judah, 1 Sam 30:27.
3. A mountain, 1 Sam 13:2.

BETH-EMEK A city of Asher, Josh 19:27.

BETHESDA Pool of, Jn 5:2–4.

BETH-EZEL A town of Judah, Mic 1:11.

BETH-GADER A place in Judah, 1 Chron 2:51. Probably identical with *Geder,* Josh 12:8–24; and with *Gedor* in Josh 15:58.

BETH-GAMUL A city of Moab, Jer 48:23.

BETH-HACCHEREM A city on a mountain in Judah, Neh 3:14; Jer 6:1.

BETH-HAGGAN A town of Israel, 2 Kgs 9:27. Probably identical with *En-gannim,* Josh 19:21.

BETH-HARAM See *Beth-haran.*

BETH-HARAN A fortified city of Gad, Num 32:36. Probably identical with *Beth-haram,* Josh 13:27.

BETH-HOGLAH A place on the border of Judah, Josh 15:6; 18:19, 21–28.

BETH-HORON Two ancient cities of Canaan, near which Joshua defeated the Amorites, Josh 10:10, 11; 16:1–6; 18:13; 1 Sam 13:18; 1 Chron 7:24. Solomon builds, 1 Kgs 9:17, 18; 2 Chron 8:5. Raided by the army of Israel, 2 Chron 25:13.

BETH-JESHIMOTH A city in Moab assigned to Reuben, Num 33:49; Josh 13:20; Ezk 25:9.

BETH-LE-APHRAH A place in Philistia, Mic 1:10.

BETH-LEBAOTH A town of Simeon, Josh 19:6. Called *Lebaoth,* Josh 15:32, and *Beth-biri,* 1 Chron 4:31.

BETHLEHEM A city southwest of Jerusalem, Judg 17:7, 8; 19:18. Called *Ephrathah* and *Ephrath,* Gen 35:16; 48:7; Ps 132:6; Mic 5:2; and *Bethlehem-Judah,* 1 Sam 17:12. Rachel dies and is buried at, Gen 35:16, 19; 48:7. The city of Boaz, Ruth 2:1; 4. Taken and held by the Philistines, 2 Sam 23:14. Jeroboam converts it into a military stronghold, 2 Chron 11:5–10. The city of Joseph, Lk 2:4. Birthplace of Jesus, Mic 5:2; Mt 2; Lk 2:4, 15. Herod kills the children of, Mt 2:16–18.

2. A town of Zebulun, six miles west of Nazareth, Josh 19:15. Israel judged at, Judg 12:10.

BETH-MAACAH See *Abel-beth-maacah.*

BETH-MARCABOTH A town of Simeon, Josh 19:2–7; 1 Chron 4:31. Probably identical with *Madmannah,* Josh 15:21–32.

BETH-MEON See *Baal-meon.*

BETH-MILLO A place near Shechem, Judg 9:6, 20.

BETH-NIMRAH A fenced city east of Jordan, Num 32:34–36; Josh 13:27, 28. Called *Nimrah,* Num 32:3, 4.

BETH-PAZZEZ A town of Issachar, Josh 19:17–23.

BETH-PELET A city in Judah, Josh 15:21–32; Neh 11:25–30.

BETH-PEOR A place in the territory of Reuben, Deut 3:29; 4:44–46; Josh 13:20. Near the burial place of Moses, Deut 34:6.

BETHPHAGE A town on the Mount of Olives, Mt 21:1; Mk 11:1; Lk 19:29.

BETHRAPHA Son of Eshton, 1 Chron 4:11, 12. See *Rephaim.*

BETH-REHOB A place in Dan, Judg 18:28. Called *Rehob,* 2 Sam 10:6–8.

BETHSAIDA 1. A city on the north shore of Galilee. The home of Philip, Andrew, and Peter, Jn 1:44; 12:21. Jesus visits, Mk 6:45; heals a blind man in, Mk 8:22; prophecies against, Mt 11:21; Lk 10:13.

2. Desert of, east of the sea of Galilee, Jesus feeds 5,000 people in, Mt 14:13; Mk 6:32; Lk 9:10.

BETH-SHAN See *Beth-shean.*

BETH-SHEAN A city of Manasseh, Josh 17:11; 1 Chron 7:29. Not subdued, Judg 1:27. Bodies of Saul and his sons exposed in, 1 Sam 31:10, 12. Called *Beth-shan,* 1 Sam 31:10, 12; 2 Sam 21:12–14. District of, under tribute to Solomon's commissary, 1 Kgs 4:8–19.

BETH-SHEMESH 1. A Levitical city of Dan, Josh 21:9–16; 1 Sam 6:15; 1 Chron 6:58, 59. On the northern border of Judah, Josh 15:10, 11; 1 Sam 6:9, 12. In later times transferred to Judah, 2 Kgs 14:11. Mentioned in Solomon's commissary districts, 1 Kgs 4:8–19. Amaziah taken prisoner at, 2 Kgs 14:11–13; 2 Chron 25:21–23. Retaken by the Philistines, 2 Chron 28:17, 18. Called *Ir-shemesh,* Josh 19:41–46.

2. A border city of Issachar, Josh 19:22.

3. A fortified city of Naphtali, Josh 19:35–39; Judg 1:33.

BETH-SHITTAH A place near the Jordan, Judg 7:22.

BETH-TAPPU-AH A town of Judah, Josh 15:48–62.

BETHUEL 1. Son of Nahor, father of Rebekah, Gen 22:20–23; 24:15, 16, 24; 25:20; 28:2, 5.

2. See *Bethul.*

BETHUL A city of Simeon, Josh 19:2–7. Called *Chesil,* Josh 15:21–32, and *Bethuel,* 1 Chron 4:30.

BETH-ZUR A town in Judah settled by the descendents of Caleb, Josh 15:48–62; 1 Chron 2:45; 2 Chron 11:5–10; Neh 3:16.

BETONIM A town of Gad, Josh 13:26.

BETRAYAL Of Jesus, Mt 26:14–16, 45–50; Mk 14:10, 11; Lk 22:3–6, 47, 48; Jn 13:21. Of others, foretold, Mt 20:18; 24:10. Of David, by Doeg, 1 Sam 22:9, 10, with chapter 21:1–10. Of cities, Judg 1:24, 25.

See *Confidence, Betrayed.*

BETROTHAL Song 8:6.

FIGURATIVE. Hos 2:19, 20.

See *Engagement; Marriage.*

BETTING By Samson, Judg 14:12–19; by Sennacherib, 2 Kgs 18:23; Isa 36:8, 9.

BEZAI 1. Head of a Jewish family, who returned from Babylon, Ezra 2:3–35; Neh 7:8–38.

2. A Levite who signed the covenant with Nehemiah, Neh 10:14–27.

BEZALEL 1. A divinely inspired mechanic and master workman, who built the tabernacle, Ex 31:2; 35:30–35; 36:1; 37:1; 38:1–7, 22.

2. Son of Pahath-moab, Ezra 10:30.

BEZEK Residence of Adoni-bezek, Judg 1:5. A rendezvous of Israel under Saul, 1 Sam 11:8.

BEZER 1. A city of refuge, east of the Jordan, assigned to the tribe of Reuben, Deut 4:43; Josh 20:8; 21:36, 37; 1 Chron 6:78.

2. Son of Zophah, 1 Chron 7:36, 37.

BIBLE See *Law, of Moses; Word of God.*

BICHRI A Benjaminite, 2 Sam 20:1, 14.

BIDKAR Jehu's captain, 2 Kgs 9:25.

BIER 2 Sam 3:31.

BIGAMY See *Polygamy.*

BIGOTRY Isa 65:5. Yet they say to one another, "Don't come too close, you'll defile me! For I am holier than you!" They stifle me. Day in and day out they infuriate me.

Mk 2:16. But when some of the Jewish religious leaders saw him eating with these men of ill repute, they said to his disciples, "How can he stand it, to eat with such scum?" Lk 15:2.

Lk 9:49. His disciple John came to him and said, "Master, we saw someone using your name to cast out demons. And we told him not to. After all, he isn't in our group." [50]But Jesus said, "You shouldn't have done that! For anyone who is not against you is for you."

Lk 18:9. Then he told this story to some who boasted of their virtue and scorned everyone else: [10]"Two men went to the Temple to pray. One was a proud, self-righteous Pharisee, and the other a cheating tax collector. [11]The proud Pharisee 'prayed' this prayer: 'Thank God, I am not a sinner like everyone else, especially like that tax collector over there! For I never cheat, I don't commit adultery, [12]I go without food twice a week, and I give to God a tenth of everything I earn.' [13]But the corrupt tax collector stood at a distance and dared not even lift his eyes to heaven as he prayed, but beat upon his chest in sorrow, exclaiming, 'God, be merciful to me, a sinner.' [14]I tell you, this sinner, not the Pharisee, returned home forgiven! For the proud shall be humbled, but the humble shall be honored."

Acts 10:28. Peter told them, "You know it is against the Jewish laws for me to come into a Gentile home like this. But God has shown me in a vision that I should never think of anyone as inferior. [45]The Jews who came with Peter were amazed that the gift of the Holy Spirit would be given to Gentiles too!

Acts 18:12. But when Gallio became governor of Achaia, the Jews rose in concerted action against Paul and brought him before the governor for judgment. [13]They accused Paul of "persuading men to worship God in ways that are contrary to Roman law."

PAUL'S ARGUMENT. Rom 3:1. Then what's the use of being a Jew? Are there any special benefits for them from God? Is there any value in the Jewish circumcision ceremony? [2]Yes, being a Jew has many advantages. First of all, God trusted them with his laws (so that they could know and do his will). [3]True, some of them were unfaithful, but just because they broke their promises to God, does that mean God will break his promises? [4]Of course not! Though everyone else in the world is a liar, God is not. Do you remember what the book of Psalms says about this? That God's words will always prove true and right, no matter who questions them. [5]"But," some say, "our breaking faith with God is good, our sins serve a good purpose, for people will notice how good God is when they see how bad we are. Is it fair, then, for him to punish us when our sins are helping him?" (That is the way some people talk.) [6]God forbid! Then what kind of God would he be, to overlook sin? How could he ever condemn anyone? [7]For he could not judge and condemn me as a sinner if my dishonesty brought him glory by pointing up his honesty in contrast to my lies. [8]If you follow through with that idea you come to this: the worse we are, the better God likes it! But the damnation of those who say such things is just. Yet some claim that this is what I preach! [9]Well, then, are we Jews *better* than others? No, not at all, for we have already shown that all men alike are sinners, whether Jews or Gentiles. [10]As the Scriptures say, "No one is good—no one in all the world is innocent." [11]No one has ever really followed God's paths, or even truly wanted to. [12]Every one has turned away; all have gone wrong. No one anywhere has kept on doing what is right; not one. [13]Their talk is foul and filthy like the stench from an open grave. Their tongues are loaded with lies. Everything they say has in it the sting and poison of deadly snakes. [14]Their mouths are full of cursing and bitterness. [15]They are quick to kill, hating anyone who disagrees with them. [16]Wherever they go they leave misery and trouble behind them, [17]and they have never known what it is to feel secure or enjoy God's blessing. [18]They care nothing about God nor what he thinks of them. [19]So the judgment of God lies very heavily upon the Jews, for they are responsible to keep God's laws instead of doing all these evil things; not one of them has any excuse; in fact, all the world stands hushed and guilty before Almighty God. [20]Now do you see it? No one can ever be made right in God's sight by doing what the law commands. For the more we know of God's laws, the clearer it becomes that we aren't obeying them; his laws serve only to make us see that we are sinners. [21, 22]But now God has shown us a different way to heaven—not by "being good enough" and trying to keep his laws, but by a new way (though not new, really, for the Scriptures told about it long ago). Now God says he will accept and acquit us—declare us "not guilty"—if we trust Jesus Christ to take away our sins. And we all can be saved in this same way, by coming to Christ, no matter who we are or what we have been like. [23]Yes, all have sinned; all fall short of God's glorious ideal.

INSTANCES OF. Joshua, jealously seeking to suppress Eldad and Medad, who were prophesying, Num 11:27–29. Jews with regard to the Samaritans, Jn 4:9, 27; in rejecting the teachings of Jesus at Nazareth, Lk 4:28; falsely accusing Jesus of blasphemy, Jn 5:18; of gluttony and heavy drinking, Mt 11:18, 19; of keeping company with sinners, Lk 7:39; 15:2; 19:5–7; of not conforming to the traditions, Lk 11:37–39; in their treatment of the young man who was born blind, whom Jesus restored to sight, Jn 9:28, 29, 34; with regard to Paul's preaching, Acts 21:28, 29; 22:22. Of the Samaritans in refusing to receive Jesus, Lk 9:52, 53. Of the disciples in forbidding children to be brought to Jesus, Mt 19:13; Mk 10:13; Lk 18:15. Of the early Christians: In opposing the preaching of the gospel to the Gentiles, Acts 10:45; 11:2, 3; 21:20–25; in regard to circumcision, Acts 15:1–10, 24; Gal 2:3–5.

The Jews, Rom 10:2, 3; in persecutions, 1 Thess 2:15, 16. Of John in forbidding the casting out of demons by one who did not follow Jesus, Mk 9:38–40; Lk 9:49, 50; James and John in desiring to call down fire upon the Samaritans who would not receive Jesus, Lk 9:51–56. Of Paul, in persecuting the Christians, Acts 22:3, 4, with 9:1–5; Acts 26:9; Gal 1:13, 14; Phil 3:6.

See *Intolerance, Religious; Persecution; Uncharitableness.*

BIGTHAN A conspiring Persian eunuch, Esther 2:21–23. Called *Bigthana,* Esther 6:2.

BIGTHANA See *Bigthan.*

BIGVAI 1. Head of Jewish family, Ezra 2:2; 8:2–14; Neh 7:7, 8–38.

2. A Levite who signed the covenant with Nehemiah, Neh 10:14–27.

BILDAD One of Job's friends, Job 2:11; 8:1; 18:1; 25:1; 42:9.

BILE-AM A town of Manasseh, 1 Chron 6:70. Called *Ible-am,* Josh 17:11; *Gath-rimmon,* Josh 21:25.

BILGAH 1. One of the leaders of the sacerdotal groups in the temple, 1 Chron 24:7–18.

2. A priest, Neh 12:1–5, 12–21, perhaps identical with *Bilgai,* Neh 10:1–8.

BILGAI A priest who signed the covenant with Nehemiah, Neh 10:1–8.

BILHAH 1. Rachael's servant, bears children by Jacob, Gen 29:29; 30:3, 4; 37:2. Mother of Dan and Naphtali, Gen 30:1–8; 35:25; 46:23–25. Reuben's incest with, Gen 35:22; 49:4.

2. A city in the land of Simeon, 1 Chron 4:29. Called *Balah,* Josh 19:2–7; and *Baalah,* Josh 15:21–32.

BILHAN 1. A Horite chief, Gen 36:27; 1 Chron 1:42.

2. A Benjaminite, 1 Chron 7:10.

BILL OF DIVORCE See *Divorce.*

BILSHAN A Jew of the captivity, Ezra 2:2; Neh 7:7.

BIMHAL Son of Japhlet, 1 Chron 7:33.

BINE-A A descendant of King Saul, 1 Chron 8:37; 9:43.

BINNUI 1. A Jew of the captivity, Neh 7:8–38. Called *Bani,* Ezra 2:10.

2. Two Levites of the captivity, Neh 12:8 and Neh 3:24; 10:9–13.

3. Father of Noadiah, Ezra 8:33.

4. Son of Pahath-moab, Ezra 10:30.

5. Son of Bani, Ezra 10:38.

BIOGRAPHY See *Book.*

BIRDS Creation of, on the fifth creative day, Gen 1:20–23. Man's dominion over, Gen 1:26, 28; 9:2, 3; Ps 8:5–8; Dan 2:38; Jas 3:7. Appointed for food, Gen 9:2, 3; Deut 14:11–18. What species were ceremonially defiled, Lev 11:13–19; Deut 14:12–18.

Used for sacrifice, see *Dove; Pigeon.* Divine care of, Job 38:41; Ps 147:9; Mt 10:29; Lk 12:6, 24. Songs of, Ps 104:12; Eccl 12:4; Song 2:12. Domesticated, Job 41:5; Jas 3:7. Solomon's proverbs of, 1 Kgs 4:33. Nests of, Ps 104:17; Mt 8:20; 13:31, 32. Instincts of, Prov 1:17. Habits of, Job 39:13–18, 26–30. Migrate, Jer 8:7.

Mosaic law protected the mother from being taken with the young, Deut 22:6, 7. Cages of, Jer 5:27; Rev 18:2.

See *Snare.*

FIGURATIVE. Isa 16:2; 46:11; Jer 12:9; Ezk 39:4. Symbolical, Dan 7:6.

See *Buzzard; Chicken; Cormorant; Crane; Cuckoo; Dove; Eagle; Falcon; Hawk; Hen; Heron; Hoopoe; Horned Owl; Kite; Marsh Hen; Nighthawk; Osprey; Ostrich; Owl; Partridge; Peacock; Pelican; Pigeon; Quail; Raven; Seagull; Sparrow; Stork; Swallow; Vulture.*

BIRSHA A king of Gomorrah, Gen 14:2–10.

BIRTH Pangs in giving, Ps 48:6; Isa 13:8; 21:3; Jer 4:31; 6:24; 30:6; 31:8. Giving, ordained to be in suffering, Gen 3:16.

See *Abortion; Children.*

BIRTH, NEW See *Born Again.*

BIRTHDAY Celebrated by a party, Mt 14:6. Cursed, Job 3; Jer 20:14, 18.

BIRTHRIGHT Belonged to the firstborn, Deut 21:15, 16. Entitled the firstborn to a double portion of inheritance, Deut 21:15–17; royal succession, 2 Chron 21:3, 4. An honorable title, Ex 4:22; Ps 89:27; Jer 31:9; Rom 8:29; Col 1:15; Heb 1:5, 6; Rev 1:5.

Sold by Esau, Gen 25:29–34; 27:36, with 25:33; Heb 12:16; Rom 9:12, 13. Forfeited by Reuben, 1 Chron 5:1, 2. Set aside: That of Manasseh, Gen 48:15–20; Adonijah, 1 Kgs 2:15; Hosah's son, Shimri, 1 Chron 26:10.

See *Firstborn.*

BIRZAITH A descendant of Asher, 1 Chron 7:31.

BISHLAM A Samaritan who obstructed the rebuilding of the temple at Jerusalem, Ezra 4:7–24.

BIT Part of a bridle, Ps 32:9; Isa 37:29; Jas 3:3.

BITHIAH Daughter of Pharaoh, 1 Chron 4:18.

BITHYNIA A Roman province in Asia Minor, Acts 16:7; 1 Pet 1:1.

BITTER HERBS Eaten symbolically with the passover, Ex 12:8; Num 9:11. Offered to Jesus on the cross, Mk 15:23.

BITTER WATER Jas 3:11. At Marah, Ex 15:23. A ceremonial water used by the priest, Num 5:18–27.

BITUMEN An inflammable mineral. Used at Babel, Gen 11:3, 4.

See *Asphalt; Tar.*

BIZIOTHIAH A town in Judah, Josh 15:21–32. Called *Baalath-beer,* Josh 19:8; and *Balah,* Josh 19:2–7.

BIZTHA A Persian eunuch, Esther 1:10.

BLACKNESS FIGURATIVE. Job 30:29–30; Jer 4:28; Ezk 31:15; Zeph 1:15.

See *Color, Symbolical.*

BLACKSMITH See *Smith.*

BLASPHEMY Ex 20:7. You shall not use the name of Jehovah your God irreverently, nor use it to swear to a falsehood. You will not escape punishment if you do. Deut 5:11.

Lev 19:12. You must not swear to a falsehood, thus bringing reproach upon the name of your

God, for I am Jehovah. Lev 22:32, 33.

Lev 24:10. Out in the camp one day, a young man whose mother was an Israelite and whose father was an Egyptian, got into a fight with one of the men of Israel. [11]During the fight the Egyptian man's son cursed God, and was brought to Moses for judgment. (His mother's name was Shelomith, daughter of Dibri of the tribe of Dan.) [12]He was put in jail until the Lord would indicate what to do with him. [13, 14]And the Lord said to Moses, "Take him outside the camp and tell all who heard him to lay their hands upon his head; then all the people are to execute him by stoning. [15, 16]And tell the people of Israel that anyone who curses his God must pay the penalty: he must die. All the congregation shall stone him; this law applies to the foreigner as well as to the Israelite who blasphemes the name of Jehovah. He must die. Ex 22:28.

2 Kgs 19:22. Whom have you defied and blasphemed? And toward whom have you felt so cocky? It is the Holy One of Israel! Isa 37:23.

2 Chron 32:19. These messengers talked about the God of Jerusalem just as though he were one of the heathen gods—a hand-made idol!

Job 10:2. I will say to God, "Don't just condemn me—tell me *why* you are doing it. [3]Does it really seem right to you to oppress and despise me, a man you have made; and to send joy and prosperity to the wicked? [4-7]Are you unjust like men? Is your life so short that you must hound me for sins you know full well I've not committed? Is it because you know no one can save me from your hand?"

Job 21:12, 13. They spend their time singing and dancing. They are wealthy and need deny themselves nothing; they are prosperous to the end. [14]All this despite the fact that they ordered God away and wanted no part of him and his ways.

Job 34:37. For now you have added rebellion, arrogance and blasphemy to your other sins.

Job 40:2. Do you still want to argue with the Almighty? Or will you yield? Do you—God's critic—have the answers?

Ps 10:11. "God isn't watching," they say to themselves; "he'll never know!" [13]Why do you let the wicked get away with this contempt for God? For they think that God will never call them to account.

Ps 50:21. I remained silent—you thought I didn't care—but now your time of punishment has come, and I list all the above charges against you.

Ps 73:9. They boast against the very heavens, and their words strut through the earth. [11]"Does God realize what is going on?" they ask.

Ps 74:18. Lord, see how these enemies scoff at you. O Jehovah, an arrogant nation has blasphemed your name.

Ps 78:19, 20. They even spoke against God himself. "Why can't he give us decent food as well as water?" they grumbled.

Ps 94:7. "The Lord isn't looking," they say, "and besides, he doesn't care."

Ps 139:20. They blaspheme your name and stand in arrogance against you—how silly can they be?

Prov 30:8. First, help me never to tell a lie. Second, give me neither poverty nor riches! Give me just enough to satisfy my needs! [9]For if I grow rich, I may become content without God. And if I am too poor, I may steal, and thus insult God's holy name. *v.* 7.

Isa 8:21. My people will be led away captive, stumbling, weary and hungry. And because they are hungry they will rave and shake their fists at heaven and curse their King and their God. [22]Wherever they look there will be trouble and anguish and dark despair. And they will be thrust out into the darkness.

Isa 29:15. Woe to those who try to hide their plans from God, who try to keep him in the dark concerning what they do! "God can't see us," they say to themselves. "He doesn't know what is going on!" [16]How stupid can they be! Isn't he, the Potter, greater than you, the jars he makes? Will you say to him, "He didn't make us"? Does a machine call its inventor dumb?

Isa 36:15. "Don't let him talk you into trusting in the Lord by telling you the Lord won't let you be conquered by the king of Assyria. [18]Don't let Hezekiah deprive you of all this by saying the Lord will deliver you from my armies. Have any other nation's gods ever gained victory over the armies of the king of Assyria? [20]Of all the gods of these lands, which one has ever delivered their people from my power? Name just one! And do you think this God of yours can deliver Jerusalem from me? Don't be ridiculous!" [21]But the people were silent and answered not a word, for Hezekiah had told them to say nothing in reply.

Isa 37:10. Don't let this God you trust in fool you by promising that Jerusalem will not be captured by the king of Assyria!

Isa 40:27. O Jacob, O Israel, how can you say that the Lord doesn't see your troubles and isn't being fair?

Isa 45:9. Woe to the man who fights with his Creator. Does the pot argue with its maker? Does the clay dispute with him who forms it, saying, "Stop, you're doing it wrong!" or the pot exclaim, "How clumsy can you be!"?

Isa 52:5. And now, what is this? asks the Lord. Why are my people enslaved again, and oppressed without excuse? Those who rule them shout in exultation, and my name is constantly blasphemed, day by day.

Isa 65:7. Not only for their own sins but for those of their fathers too, says the Lord, for they also burned incense on the mountains and insulted me upon the hills. I will pay them back in full.

Jer 4:10. Then I said, "But Lord, the people have been deceived by what you said, for you promised great blessings on Jerusalem. Yet the sword is even now poised to strike them dead!"

Jer 17:15. Men scoff at me and say, "What is this word of the Lord you keep talking about? If these threats of yours are really from God, why don't they come true?"

Jer 20:7. Then I said, O Lord, you deceived me when you promised me your help. I have to give them your messages because you are stronger than I am, but now I am the laughingstock of the city, mocked by all.

Ezk 8:12. Then the Lord said to me: "Son of dust, have you seen what the elders of Israel are doing in their minds? For they say, 'The Lord doesn't see us; he has gone away!' "

Ezk 9:9. But he said to me, "The sins of the people of Israel and Judah are very great and all the land is full of murder and injustice, for they say, 'The Lord doesn't see it! He has gone away!' "

Ezk 18:25. Yet you say: "The Lord isn't being fair!" Listen to me, O people of Israel. Am I the one who is unfair, or is it you?

Ezk 20:27, 28. Son of dust, tell them that the Lord God says: Your fathers continued to blaspheme and betray me when I brought them into the land I promised them, for they offered sacrifices and incense on every high hill and under every tree! They roused my fury as they offered up their sacrifices to those "gods." They brought their perfumes and incense and poured out their drink offerings to them!

Ezk 33:17. And yet your people are saying the Lord isn't fair. The trouble is *they* aren't fair. [18]For again I say, when the good man turns to evil, he shall die. [19]But if the wicked turns from his wickedness and does what's fair and just, he shall live. [20]Yet you are saying the Lord isn't fair. But I will judge each of you in accordance with his deeds.

Ezk 35:12. And you shall know that I have heard each evil word you spoke against the Lord, saying, "His people are helpless; they are food for us to eat!" [13]Saying that, you boasted great words against the Lord. And I have heard them all!

Dan 7:25. He will defy the Most High God.

Dan 11:36. The king will do exactly as he pleases, claiming to be greater than every god there is, even blaspheming the God of gods, and prospering—until his time is up. For God's plans are unshakable. [37]He will have no regard for the gods of his fathers, . . . for he will boast that he is greater than them all.

Hos 7:13. Woe to my people for deserting me; let them perish, for they have sinned against me. I wanted to redeem them but their hard hearts would not accept the truth.

Zeph 1:12. I will search with lanterns in Jerusalem's darkest corners to find and punish those who sit contented in their sins, indifferent to God, thinking he will let them alone.

Zech 5:3. "This scroll," he told me, "represents the words of God's curse going out over the entire land. It says that all who steal and lie have been judged and sentenced to death. [4]I am sending this curse into the home of every thief and everyone who swears falsely by my name," says the Lord of Hosts. "And my curse shall remain upon his home and completely destroy it."

Mal 3:13. "Your attitude toward me has been proud and arrogant," says the Lord. "But you say, 'What do you mean? What have we said that we shouldn't?' [14]Listen; you have said, 'It is foolish to worship God and obey him. What good does it do to obey his laws, and to sorrow and mourn for our sins?' "

Mt 10:25. The student shares his teacher's fate. The servant shares his master's! And since I, the master of the household, have been called "Satan," how much more will you!

Mat 12:31, 32. Even blasphemy against me or any other sin, can be forgiven—all except one: speaking against the Holy Spirit shall never be forgiven, either in this world or in the world to come. Mk 3:29, 30; Lk 12:10; 1 Jn 5:17.

Mk 7:21. For from within, out of men's hearts, come evil thoughts of lust, theft, murder, adultery, [22]wanting what belongs to others, wickedness, deceit, lewdness, envy, slander, pride, and all other folly. [23]All these vile things come from within; they are what pollute you and make you unfit for God.

Jn 19:7. They replied, "By our laws he ought to die because he called himself the Son of God."

Rom 2:24. No wonder the Scriptures say that the world speaks evil of God because of you. 2 Sam 12:14.

1 Cor 12:3. But now you are meeting people who claim to speak messages from the Spirit of God. How can you know whether they are really inspired by God or whether they are fakes? Here is the test: no one speaking by the power of the Spirit of God can curse Jesus, and no one can say, "Jesus is Lord," and really mean it, unless the Holy Spirit is helping him.

Col 3:8. But now is the time to cast off and throw away all these rotten garments of anger, hatred, cursing, and dirty language.

2 Thess 2:4. He will defy every god there is, and tear down every other object of adoration and worship. He will go in and sit as God in the temple of God, claiming that he himself is God.

2 Tim 3:2. For people will love only themselves and their money; they will be proud and boastful, sneering at God, disobedient to their parents, ungrateful to them, and thoroughly bad. Rev 16:11.

Heb 10:29. Think how much more terrible the punishment will be for those who have trampled underfoot the Son of God and treated his cleansing blood as though it were common and unhallowed, and insulted and outraged the Holy Spirit who brings God's mercy to his people.

Jas 2:7. And all too often they are the ones who laugh at Jesus Christ, whose noble name you bear.

Jas 3:10. And so blessing and cursing come pouring out of the same mouth. Dear brothers, surely this is not right!

Jas 5:12. But most of all, dear brothers, do not swear either by heaven or earth or anything else; just say a simple yes or no, so that you will not sin and be condemned for it.

2 Pet 3:3. First, I want to remind you that in the last days there will come scoffers who will do every wrong they can think of, and laugh at the truth. [4]This will be their line of argument: "So Jesus pro-

mised to come back, did he? Then where is he? He'll never come! Why, as far back as anyone can remember everything has remained exactly as it was since the first day of creation."

Rev 13:1. And now, in my vision, I saw a strange Creature rising up out of the sea. . . . And written on each head were blasphemous names, each one defying and insulting God. [6]All that time he blasphemed God's Name and his temple and all those living in heaven.

Rev 16:9. Everyone was burned by this blast of heat, and they cursed the name of God who sent the plagues—they did not change their mind and attitude to give him glory. [21]And there was an incredible hailstorm from heaven; . . . and they cursed God because of the terrible hail.

Rev 17:3. So the angel took me in spirit into the wilderness. There I saw a woman sitting on a scarlet animal that had seven heads and ten horns, written all over with blasphemies against God.

Prophecy of, Rev 13:1, 5, 6; 16:9, 11, 21; 17:3.

INSTANCES OF. The depraved son of Shelomith, who, in a fight with an Israelite, cursed God, Lev 24:10–16. Of the Israelites, in murmuring against God, Num 21:5, 6. Eli's son, 1 Sam 3:13. Infidels, who used the adultery of David as an occasion to blaspheme, 2 Sam 12:14. Shime-i, in his malice toward David, 2 Sam 16:5. Sennacherib's general, in the siege of Jerusalem, 2 Kgs 18:22; 19; Isa 36:15–20; 37:10–33. Job's wife, when she exhorted Job to curse God and die, Job 2:9. Peter, when accused of being a disciple of Jesus, Mt 26:74; Mk 14:71. The revilers of Jesus when he was crucified, Mt 27:40–44, 63. The early Christians, persecuted by Saul of Tarsus, compelled to blaspheme the name of Jesus, Acts 26:11; 1 Tim 1:13. The Jews, opposing Paul, Acts 13:45; 18:6. Two disciples, Hymenaeus and Alexander, who were delivered to Satan for punishment that they might learn not to blaspheme, 1 Tim 1:20. Man of rebellion, 2 Thess 2:3,4. Backslidden Ephesians, Rev 2:4, 5.

FALSE INDICTMENTS FOR. Of Naboth, 1 Kgs 21:13; Jesus, Mt 9:3; 26:65, 66; Mk 14:58; Lk 22:70, 71; Jn 10:33–36; 19:7; Stephen, Acts 6:11, 13. Jesus falsely accused of, previous to his trial, Mk 2:7; Lk 5:21.

BLAST Sent as a judgment, Rev 16:9.

FIGURATIVE. Ex 15:8; 2 Sam 22:16; Ps 18:15; 29:9.

BLASTUS Herod's secretary, Acts 12:20.

BLEMISH A physical deformity. Excluded descendents of Aaron from exercise of priestly offices, Lev 21:17–23. Animals with, forbidden to be used for sacrifice, Lev 5:17, 18; 22:19–25; Ezk 45:23; 46:6.

FIGURATIVE. Eph 5:27; 1 Pet 1:19.

BLESSING For blessing before eating, see *Prayer, Thanksgiving and prayer before taking food.* See also *Benedictions.*

RESPONSIVE BLESSINGS OF THE LAW. Deut 28:1. If you fully obey all these commandments of the Lord your God, the laws I am declaring to you today, God will transform you into the greatest nation in the world. [2-6]These are the blessings that will come upon you: blessings in the city, blessings in the field; many children, ample crops, large flocks and herds; blessings of fruit and bread; blessings when you come in, blessings when you go out. [7]The Lord will defeat your enemies before you; they will march out together against you but scatter before you in seven directions! [8]The Lord will bless you with good crops and healthy cattle, and prosper everything you do when you arrive in the land the Lord your God is giving you. [9]He will change you into a holy people dedicated to himself; this he has promised to do if you will only obey him and walk in his ways. [10]All the nations in the world shall see that you belong to the Lord, and they will stand in awe. [11]The Lord will give you an abundance of good things in the land, just as he promised: many children, many cattle, and abundant crops. [12]He will open to you his wonderful treasury of rain in the heavens, to give you fine crops every season. He will bless everything you do; and you shall lend to many nations, but shall not borrow from them. [13]If you will only listen and obey the commandments of the Lord your God that I am giving you today, he will make you the head and not the tail, and you shall always have the upper hand. [14]But each of these blessings depends on your not turning aside in any way from the laws I have given you; and you must never worship other gods.

For the responsive curses of the law, see *Curse.*

DIVINE, CONTINGENT ON OBEDIENCE. Ex 15:26. If you will listen to the voice of the Lord your God, and obey it, and do what is right, then I will not make you suffer the diseases I send on the Egyptians, for I am the Lord who heals you.

Ex 19:5. Now if you will obey me and keep your part of my contract with you, you shall be my own little flock from among all the nations of the earth; for all the earth is mine.

Ex 20:6. But I lavish my love upon thousands of those who love me and obey my commandments.

Ex 23:22. But if you are careful to obey him, following all my instructions, then I will be an enemy to your enemies.

Lev 26:3. If you obey all of my commandments, [4, 5]I will give you regular rains, and the land will yield bumper crops, and the trees will be loaded with fruit long after the normal time! And grapes will still be ripening when sowing time comes again. You shall eat your fill, and live safely in the land, [6]for I will give you peace, and you will go to sleep without fear. I will chase away the dangerous animals. [7]You will chase your enemies; they will die beneath your swords. [8]Five of you will chase a hundred, and a hundred of you, ten thousand! You will defeat all your enemies. [9]I will look after you, and multiply you, and fulfill my covenant with you. [10]You will have such a surplus of crops that you won't know what to do with them when the new harvest is ready! [11]And I will live among you, and not despise you. [12]I will walk among you and be your God, and you shall be my people. [13]For I am the Lord your God who brought you out of the land of Egypt, with the intention that you be slaves no longer; I have broken your chains and will make you walk with dignity. 14But if you will not listen to me or obey me, 15but reject my laws, 16this is what I will do to you: I will punish you with sudden terrors and panic, and with tuberculosis and burning fever; your eyes shall be consumed and your life shall ebb away; you will sow your crops in vain, for your enemies will eat them. 17I will set my face against you and you will flee before your attackers; those who hate you will rule you; you will even run when no one is chasing you! 18And if you still disobey me, I will punish you seven times more severely for your sins. 19I will break your proud power and make your heavens as iron, and your earth as bronze. 20Your strength shall be spent in vain; for your land shall not yield its crops, nor your trees their fruit 21And if even then you will not obey me and listen to me, I will send you seven times more plagues because of your sins. 22I will send wild animals to kill your children and destroy your cattle and reduce your numbers so that your roads will be deserted. 23And if even this will not reform you, but you continue to walk against my wishes, 24then I will walk against your wishes, and I, even I, will personally smite you seven times for your sin. 25I will revenge the breaking of my covenant by bringing war against you. You will flee to your cities, and I will send a plague among you there; and you will be conquered by your enemies. 26I will destroy your food supply so that one oven will be large enough to bake all the bread available for ten entire families; and you will still be hungry after your pittance has been doled out to you. 27And if you still won't listen to me or obey me, 28then I will let loose my great anger and send you seven times greater punishment for your sins. 29You shall eat your own sons and daughters, 30and I will destroy the altars on the hills where you worship your idols, and I will cut down your incense altars, leaving your dead bodies to rot among your idols; and I will abhor you. 31I will make your cities desolate, and destroy your places of worship, and will not respond to your incense offerings. 32Yes, I will desolate your land; your enemies shall live in it, utterly amazed at what I have done to you. 33I will scatter you out among the nations, destroying you with war as you go. Your land shall be desolate and your cities destroyed. 34, 35Then at last the land will rest and make up for the many years you refused to let it lie idle; for it will lie desolate all the years that you are captives in enemy lands. Yes, then the land will rest and enjoy its Sabbaths! It will make up for the rest you didn't give it every seventh year when you lived upon it. 36And for those who are left alive, I will cause them to be dragged away to distant lands as prisoners of war, and slaves. There they will live in constant fear. The sound of a leaf driven in the wind will send them fleeing as though chased by a man with a sword; they shall fall when no one is pursuing them. 37Yes, though none pursue they shall stumble over each other in flight, as though fleeing in battle, with no power to stand before their enemies. 38You shall perish among the nations and be destroyed among your enemies. 39Those left shall pine away in enemy lands because of their sins, the same sins as those of their fathers. 40, 41But at last they shall confess their sins of treachery against me. (Because they were against me, I was against them, and brought them into the land of their enemies.) When at last their evil hearts are humbled and they accept the punishment I send them for their sins, 42then I will remember again my promises to Abraham, Isaac, and Jacob, and I will remember the land (and its desolation). 43For the land shall enjoy its Sabbaths as it lies desolate. But then at last they shall accept their punishment for rejecting my laws and for despising my rule.

Deut 4:1. And now, O Israel, listen carefully to these laws I teach you, and obey them if you want to live and enter into and possess the land given you by the Lord God of your ancestors. 40You must obey these laws that I will tell you today, so that all will be well with you and your children, and so that you will live forever in the land the Lord your God is giving you.

Deut 5:10. But I will show kindness to a thousand generations of those who love me and keep my commandments. 29Oh, that they would always have such a heart for me, wanting to obey my commandments. Then all would go well with them in the future, and with their children throughout all generations! Deut 29:9.

Deut 7:9. Understand, therefore, that the Lord your God is the faithful God who for a thousand generations keeps his promises and constantly loves those who love him and who obey his commands. 12Because of your obedience, the Lord your God will keep his part of the contract which, in his tender love, he made with your fathers. 13And he will love you and bless you and make you into a great nation. He will make you fertile and give fertility to your ground and to your animals, so that you will have large crops of grain, grapes, and olives, and great flocks of cattle, sheep, and goats when you arrive in the land he promised your fathers to give you. 14You will be blessed above all the nations of the earth; not one of you, whether male or female, shall be barren, not even your cattle. 15And the Lord will take away all your sickness and will not let you suffer any of the diseases of Egypt you remember so well; he will give them all to your enemies!

Deut 11:26. I am giving you the choice today between God's blessing or God's curse! 27There will be blessing if you obey the commandments of the Lord your God which I am giving you today. *v.* 28.

Deut 12:28. Be careful to obey all of these commandments. If you do what is right in the eyes of the Lord you God, all will go well with you and your children forever.

Deut 15:4, 5. No one will become poor because of this, for the Lord will greatly bless you in the land he is giving you if you obey this command. The only prerequisite for his blessing is that you carefully heed all the commands of the Lord your God that I am giving you today.

Deut 28:1. If you fully obey all of these commandments of the Lord your God, the laws I am declaring to you today, God will transform you into the greatest nation in the world. [2-6]These are the blessings that will come upon you: blessings in the city, blessings in the field; many children, ample crops, large flocks and herds; blessings of fruit and bread; blessings when you come in, blessings when you go out. [7]The Lord will defeat your enemies before you; they will march out together against you but scatter before you in seven directions! [8]The Lord will bless you with good crops and healthy cattle, and prosper everything you do when you arrive in the land the Lord your God is giving you. [9]He will change you into a holy people dedicated to himself; this he has promised to do if you will only obey him and walk in his ways. [10]All the nations in the world shall see that you belong to the Lord, and they will stand in awe. [11]The Lord will give you an abundance of good things in the land, just as he promised; many children, many cattle, and abundant crops. [12]He will open to you his wonderful treasury of rain in the heavens, to give you fine crops every season. He will bless everything you do; and you shall lend to many nations, but shall not borrow from them. [13]If you will only listen and obey the commandments of the Lord your God that I am giving you today, he will make you the head and not the tail, and you shall always have the upper hand. [14]But each of these blessings depends on your not turning aside in any way from the laws I have given you; and you must never worship other gods.

Deut 30:1. When all these things have happened to you—the blessings and the curses I have listed—you will meditate upon them as you are living among the nations where the Lord your God will have driven you. [2]If at that time you want to return to the Lord your God, and you and your children have begun wholeheartedly to obey all of the commandments I have given you today, [3]then the Lord your God will rescue you from your captivity! He will have mercy upon you and come and gather you out of all the nations where he will have scattered you. [4]Though you are at the ends of the earth, he will go and find you and bring you back again [5]to the land of your ancestors. You shall possess the land again, and he will do you good and bless you even more than he did your ancestors! [6]He will cleanse your hearts and the hearts of your children and of your children's children so that you will love the Lord your God with all your hearts and souls, and Israel shall come alive again! [7, 8]If you return to the Lord and obey all the commandments that I command you today, the Lord your God will take his curses and turn them against your enemies—against those who hate you and persecute you. [9]The Lord your God will prosper everything you do and give you many children and much cattle and wonderful crops; for the Lord will again rejoice over you as he did over your fathers. [10]He will rejoice if you but obey the commandments written in this book of the law, and if you turn to the Lord your God with all your hearts and souls. [15]Look, today I have set before you life and death, depending on whether you obey or disobey. [16]I have commanded you today to love the Lord your God and to follow his paths and to keep his laws, so that you will live and become a great nation, and so that the Lord your God will bless you and the land you are about to possess. [17]But if your hearts turn away and you won't listen—if you are drawn away to worship other gods—[18]then I declare to you this day that you shall surely perish; you will not have a long, good life in the land you are going in to possess. [19]I call heaven and earth to witness against you that today I have set before you life or death, blessing or curse. Oh, that you would choose life; that you and your children might live! [20]Choose to love the Lord your God and to obey him and to cling to him, for he is your life and the length of your days. You will then be able to live safely in the land the Lord promised your ancestors, Abraham, Isaac, and Jacob.

Josh 1:8. Constantly remind the people about these laws,. . . . For only then will you succeed.

1 Kgs 2:3. Obey the laws of God and follow all his ways; keep each of his commands written in the law of Moses so that you will prosper in everything you do, wherever you turn. [4]If you do this, then the Lord will fulfill the promise he gave me, that if my children and their descendants watch their step and are faithful to God, one of them shall always be the king of Israel—my dynasty will never end.

1 Kgs 3:14. And I will give you a long life if you follow me and obey my laws as your father David did.

1 Kgs 8:23. And said, "O Lord God of Israel, there is no god like you in heaven or earth, for you are loving and kind and you keep your promises to your people if they do their best to do your will."

1 Kgs 9:3. And [the Lord] said to him, "I have heard your prayer. I have hallowed this Temple which you have built and have put my name here forever. I will constantly watch over it and rejoice in it. [4]And if you live in honesty and truth as your father David did, always obeying me, [5]then I will cause your descendants to be the kings of Israel forever, just as I promised your father David when I told him, 'One of your sons shall always be upon the throne of Israel.' [6]However, if you or your children turn away from me and worship other gods and do not obey my laws, [7]then I will take away the people of Israel from this land which I have given them. I will take them from this Temple which I have hallowed for my name and I will cast them out of my sight; and Israel will become a joke to the nations and an example and proverb of sudden disaster. [8]This Temple will become a heap of ruins, and everyone passing by will be amazed and will whistle with astonishment, asking, 'Why has the Lord done such things to this land and this Temple?' [9]And the answer will be, 'The people of Israel abandoned the Lord their God who brought

them out of the land of Egypt; they worshiped other gods instead. That is why the Lord has brought this evil upon them.' " 2 Chron 7:17–22.

1 Chron 22:13. For if you carefully obey the rules and regulations which he gave to Israel through Moses, you will prosper. Be strong and courageous, fearless and enthusiastic!

1 Chron 28:7. " 'And if he continues to obey my commandments and instructions as he has until now, I will make his kingdom last forever.' " [8]Then David turned to Solomon and said: "Here before the leaders of Israel, the people of God, and in the sight of our God, I am instructing you to search out every commandment of the Lord so that you may continue to rule this good land and leave it to your children to rule forever."

2 Chron 26:5. While Zechariah was alive Uzziah was always eager to please God. Zechariah was a man who had special revelations from God. And as long as the king followed the paths of God, he prospered, for God blessed him.

2 Chron 27:6. King Jotham became powerful because he was careful to follow the path of the Lord his God.

2 Chron 30:9. For if you turn to the Lord again, your brothers and your children will be treated mercifully by their captors, and they will be able to return to this land. For the Lord your God is full of kindness and mercy and will not continue to turn away his face from you if you return to him.

2 Chron 31:10. And Azariah the High Priest from the clan of Zadok replied, "These are tithes! We have been eating from these stores of food for many weeks, but all this is left over, for the Lord has blessed his people."

Job 36:11. If they listen and obey him, then they will be blessed with prosperity throughout their lives.

Prov 3:1, 2. My son, never forget the things I've taught you. If you want a long and satisfying life, closely follow my instructions.

Prov 16:7. When a man is trying to please God, God makes even his worst enemies to be at peace with him.

Isa 1:19. If you will only let me help you, if you will only obey, then I will make you rich!

Jer 7:3. The Lord of Hosts, the God of Israel says: Even yet, if you quit your evil ways I will let you stay in your own land. [4]But don't be fooled by those who lie to you and say that since the Temple of the Lord is here, God will never let Jerusalem be destroyed. [5]You may remain under these conditions only: If you stop your wicked thoughts and deeds, and are fair to others, [6]and stop exploiting orphans, widows and foreigners. And stop your murdering. And stop worshiping idols as you do now to your hurt. [7]Then, and only then, will I let you stay in this land that I gave to your fathers to keep forever. [23]But what I told them was: *Obey* me and I will be your God and you shall be my people; only do as I say and all shall be well!

Jer 11:1–3. Then the Lord spoke to Jeremiah once again and said: Remind the men of Judah and all the people of Jerusalem that I made a contract with their father—and cursed is the man who does not heed it! [4]For I told them at the time I brought them out of slavery in Egypt that if they would obey me and do whatever I commanded them, then they and all their children would be mine and I would be their God. [5]And now, Israel, obey me, says the Lord, so that I can do for you the wonderful things I swore I would if you obeyed. I want to give you a land that "flows with milk and honey," as it is today. Then I replied, "So be it, Lord!"

Jer 12:16. And if these heathen nations quickly learn my people's ways and claim me as their God instead of Baal (whom they taught my people to worship), then they shall be strong among my people.

Jer 15:19. The Lord replied: "Stop this foolishness and talk some sense! Only if you return to trusting me will I let you continue as my spokesman. You are to influence *them,* not let them influence *you!* [20]They will fight against you like a besieging army against a high city wall. But they will not conquer you for I am with you to protect and deliver you, says the Lord. [21]Yes, I will certainly deliver you from these wicked men and rescue you from their ruthless hands."

Jer 17:24. But if you obey me, says the Lord, and refuse to work on the Sabbath day and keep it separate, special and holy, [25]then this nation shall continue forever. There shall always be descendants of David sitting on the throne here in Jerusalem; there shall always be kings and princes riding in pomp and splendor among the people, and this city shall remain forever. [26]And from all around Jerusalem and from the cities of Judah and Benjamin, and from the Negeb and from the lowlands west of Judah, the people shall come with their burnt offerings and grain offerings and incense, bringing their sacrifices to praise the Lord in his Temple. [27]But if you will not listen to me, if you refuse to keep the Sabbath holy, if on the Sabbath you bring in loads of merchandise through these gates of Jerusalem, just as on other days, then I will set fire to these gates. The fire shall spread to the palaces and utterly destroy them, and no one shall be able to put out the raging flames.

Jer 22:4. If you put an end to all these terrible deeds you are doing, then I will deliver this nation and once more give kings to sit on David's throne, and there shall be prosperity for all. [5]But if you refuse to pay attention to this warning, I swear by my own name, says the Lord, that this palace shall become a shambles.

15. But a beautiful palace does not make a great king! Why did your father Josiah reign so long? Because he was just and fair in all his dealings. That is why God blessed him. [16]He saw to it that justice and help were given the poor and the needy and all went well for him. This is how a man lives close to God.

Zech 3:7. "The Lord of Hosts declares: 'If you will follow the paths I set for you and do all I tell you to, then I will put you in charge of my Temple, to keep it holy; and I will let you walk in and out of my presence with these angels.' "

Mal 3:10. "Bring all the tithes into the storehouse so that there will be food enough in my Temple; if you do, I will open up the windows of heaven for you and pour out a blessing so great you won't have room enough to take it in! Try it! Let me prove it to you! [11]Your crops will be large, for I will guard them from insects and plagues. Your grapes won't shrivel away before they ripen," says the Lord of Hosts. [12]"And all nations will call you blessed, for you will be a land sparkling with happiness. These are the promises of the Lord of Hosts."

Mt 10:22. But all of you who endure to the end shall be saved. Mt 24:13; Mk 13:13.

Col 1:22. He has done this through the death on the cross of his own human body, and now as a result Christ has brought you into the very presence of God, and you are standing there before him with nothing left against you—nothing left that he could even chide you for; [23]the only condition is that you fully believe the Truth, standing in it steadfast and firm, strong in the Lord, convinced of the Good News that Jesus died for you, and never shifting from trusting him to save you. This is the wonderful news that came to each of you and is now spreading all over the world.

Heb 3:6. But Christ, God's faithful Son, is in complete charge of God's house. And we Christians are God's house—he lives in us!—if we keep up our courage firm to the end, and our joy and our trust in the Lord. [14]For if we are faithful to the end, trusting God just as we did when we first became Christians, we will share in all that belongs to Christ.

Heb 6:11. And we are anxious that you keep right on loving others as long as life lasts, so that you will get your full reward. [12]Then, knowing what lies ahead for you, you won't become bored with being a Christian, nor become spiritually dull and indifferent, but you will be anxious to follow the example of those who received all that God has promised them because of their strong faith and patience.

Heb 10:36. You need to keep on patiently doing God's will if you want him to do for you all that he has promised.

Rev 1:3. If you read this prophecy aloud to the church, you will receive a special blessing from the Lord. Those who listen to it being read and do what it says will also be blessed.

Rev 2:10. Remain faithful even when facing death and I will give you the crown of life—an unending, glorious future.

See *Faithfulness; Contingencies.*

SPIRITUAL, FROM GOD. Gen 49:24. But their weapons were shattered by the Mighty One of Jacob, the Shepherd, the Rock of Israel.

Ex 15:2. The Lord is my strength, my song, and my salvation.

Ex 33:16. If you don't go with us, who will ever know that I and my people have found favor with you, and that we are different from any other people upon the face of the earth?

Lev 21:8. The priest is set apart to offer the sacrifices of your God; he is holy, for I, the Lord who sanctifies you, am holy. Ex 31:12, 13.

Deut 33:25. May you be protected with strong bolts of iron and bronze, and may your strength match the length of your days! [27]The eternal God is your Refuge, and underneath are the everlasting arms. He thrusts out your enemies before you; it is he who cries, 'Destroy them!'

1 Sam 2:4. Those who were mighty are mighty no more! Those who were weak are now strong.

Neh 8:10. It is a time to celebrate with a hearty meal, and to send presents to those in need, for the joy of the Lord is your strength. You must not be dejected and sad!

Job 23:6. Would he merely overpower me with his greatness? No, he would listen with sympathy.

Ps 18:1. Lord, how I love you! For you have done such tremendous things for me. [2]The Lord is my fort where I can enter and be safe; no one can follow me in and slay me. He is a rugged mountain where I hide; he is my Savior, a rock where none can reach me, and a tower of safety. He is my shield. He is like the strong horn of a mighty fighting bull. [28]You have turned on my light! The Lord my God has made my darkness turn to light. [32]He fills me with strength and protects me wherever I go. [36]You have made wide steps beneath my feet so that I need never slip. Ps 144:1, 2.

Ps 23:2, 3. He lets me rest in the meadow grass and leads me beside the quiet streams. He restores my failing health. He helps me do what honors him the most.

Ps 27:14. Don't be impatient. Wait for the Lord, and he will come and save you! Be brave, stouthearted and courageous. Yes, wait and he will help you.

Ps 28:8. The Lord protects his people and gives victory to his anointed king.

Ps 29:11. He will give his people strength. He will bless them with peace.

Ps 30:6, 7. In my prosperity I said, "This is forever; nothing can stop me now! The Lord has shown me his favor. He has made me steady as a mountain." Then, Lord, you turned your face away from me and cut off your river of blessings. Suddenly my courage was gone; I was terrified and panic-stricken.

Ps 31:24. So cheer up! Take courage if you are depending on the Lord.

Ps 37:6. Your innocence will be clear to everyone. He will vindicate you with the blazing light of justice shining down as from the noonday sun. [17]For the strength of evil men shall be broken, but the Lord takes care of those he has forgiven. [24]If they fall it isn't fatal, for the Lord holds them with his hand. [39]The Lord saves the godly! He is their salvation and their refuge when trouble comes.

Ps 52:8. But I am like a sheltered olive tree protected by the Lord himself. I trust in the mercy of God forever and ever.

Ps 55:22. Give your burdens to the Lord. He will carry them. He will not permit the godly to slip or fall.

Ps 61:5. For you have heard my vows, O God, to praise you every day, and you have given me the blessings you reserve for those who reverence your name.

Ps 63:8. I follow close behind you, protected by your strong right arm.

Ps 66:9. For he holds our lives in his hands. And he holds our feet to the path.

Ps 68:18. He ascends the heights, leading many captives in his train. He receives gifts for men, even those who once were rebels. God will live among us here. 28Summon your might; display your strength, O God, for you have done such mighty things for us. 35What awe we feel, kneeling here before him in the sanctuary. The God of Israel gives strength and mighty power to his people. Blessed be God!

Ps 71:16. I walk in the strength of the Lord God. I tell everyone that you alone are just and good.

Ps 72:6. May the reign of this son of mine be as gentle and fruitful as the springtime rains upon the grass—like showers that water the earth! 17His name will be honored forever; it will continue as the sun; and all will be blessed in him; all nations will praise him.

Ps 73:23. But even so, you love me! You are holding my right hand! 26My health fails; my spirits droop, yet God remains! He is the strength of my heart; he is mine forever!

Ps 81:10. For it was I, Jehovah your God, who brought you out of the land of Egypt. Only test me! Open your mouth wide and see if I won't fill it. You will receive every blessing you can use!

Ps 84:5. Happy are those who are strong in the Lord, who want above all else to follow your steps. 11For Jehovah God is our Light and our Protector. He gives us grace and glory. No good thing will he withhold from those who walk along his paths.

Ps 89:17. You are their strength. What glory! Our power is based on your favor!

Ps 92:12. But the godly shall flourish like palm trees, and grow as tall as the cedars of Lebanon. 13For they are transplanted into the Lord's own garden, and are under his personal care. 14Even in old age they will still produce fruit and be vital and green. Ps 1:3.

Ps 94:17. I would have died unless the Lord had helped me. 18I screamed, "I'm slipping, Lord!" and he was kind and saved me.

Ps 105:4. Search for him and for his strength, and keep on searching!

Ps 119:32. If you will only help me to want your will, then I will follow your laws even more closely. 102No, I haven't turned away from what you taught me; your words are sweeter than honey.

Ps 132:15. I will make this city prosperous and satisfy her poor with food. 16I will clothe her priests with salvation; her saints shall shout for joy.

Ps 138:3. When I pray, you answer me, and encourage me by giving me the strength I need. 8The Lord will work out his plans for my life—for your lovingkindness, Lord, continues forever. Don't abandon me—for you made me.

Ps 146:5. But happy is the man who has the God of Jacob as his helper, whose hope is in the Lord his God.

Prov 10:29. God protects the upright but destroys the wicked.

Prov 16:6. Iniquity is atoned for by mercy and truth; evil is avoided by reverence for God.

Isa 1:25. I myself will melt you in a smelting pot, and skim off your slag.

Isa 4:2–4. Those whose names are written down to escape the destruction of Jerusalem will be washed and rinsed of all their moral filth by the horrors and the fire. They will be God's holy people. And the land will produce for them its lushest bounty and its richest fruit.

Isa 6:6. Then one of the seraphs flew over to the altar and with a pair of tongs picked out a burning coal. 7He touched my lips with it and said, "Now you are pronounced 'Not guilty' because this coal has touched your lips. Your sins are all forgiven."

Isa 26:12. Lord, grant us peace; for all we have and are has come from you.

Isa 28:6. He will give a longing for justice to your judges and great courage to your soldiers who are battling to the last before your gates.

Isa 33:5. The Lord is very great, and lives in heaven. He will make Jerusalem the home of justice and goodness and righteousness. 6An abundance of salvation is stored up for Judah in a safe place, along with wisdom and knowledge and reverence for God.

Isa 40:11. He will feed his flock like a shepherd; he will carry the lambs in his arms and gently lead the ewes with young. 29He gives power to the tired and worn out, and strength to the weak. 31But they that wait upon the Lord shall renew their strength. They shall mount up with wings like eagles; they shall run and not be weary; they shall walk and not faint.

Isa 41:10. Fear not, for I am with you. Do not be dismayed. I am your God. I will strengthen you; I will help you; I will uphold you with my victorious right hand. 13I am holding you by your right hand—I, the Lord your God—and I say to you, Don't be afraid; I am here to help you. 14Despised though you are, fear not, O Israel; for I will help you. I am the Lord, your Redeemer; I am the Holy One of Israel. 17When the poor and needy seek water and there is none and their tongues are parched from thirst, then I will answer when they cry to me. I, Israel's God, will not ever forsake them. 18I will open up rivers for them on high plateaus! I will give them fountains of water in the valleys! In the deserts will be pools of water, and rivers fed by springs shall flow across the dry, parched ground.

Isa 44:3. For I will give you abundant water for your thirst and for your parched fields. And I will pour out my Spirit and my blessings on your children.

Isa 45:8. Open up, O heavens. Let the skies pour out their righteousness. Let salvation and righteousness sprout up together from the earth. I, Jehovah, created them. 24"In Jehovah is all my righteousness and strength," the people shall declare. And all who were angry with him shall come to him and be ashamed.

Isa 54:17. But in that coming day, no weapon turned against you shall succeed, and you will have justice against every courtroom lie. This is the heritage of the servants of the Lord. This is the blessing I have given you, says the Lord.

Isa 57:19. Peace, peace to them, both near and far, for I will heal them all.

Isa 58:8. If you do these things, God will shed his own glorious light upon you. He will heal you; your godliness will lead you forward, and goodness will be a shield before you, and the glory of the Lord will protect you from behind. 10Feed the hungry! Help those in trouble! Then your light will shine out from the darkness, and the darkness around you shall be as bright as day. 11And the Lord will guide you continually, and satisfy you with all good things, and keep you healthy too; and you will be like a well-watered garden, like an ever-flowing spring.

Jer 31:12. They shall come home and sing songs of joy upon the hills of Zion, and shall be radiant over the goodness of the Lord. . . . Their life shall be like a watered garden, and all their sorrows shall be gone. 14I will feast the priests with the abundance of offerings brought to them at the Temple; I will satisfy my people with my bounty, says the Lord. 33But this is the new contract I will make with them: I will inscribe my laws upon their hearts, so that they shall want to honor me; then they shall truly be my people and I will be their God.

Ezk 16:14. Your reputation was great among the nations for your beauty; it was perfect because of all the gifts I gave you, says the Lord God.

Dan 11:32. He will flatter those who hate the things of God, and win them over to his side. But the people who know their God shall be strong and do great things.

Hos 6:3. Oh, that we might know the Lord! Let us press on to know him, and he will respond to us as surely as the coming of dawn or the rain of early spring.

Hos 14:5. I will refresh Israel like the dew from heaven; she will blossom as the lily and root deeply in the soil like cedars in Lebanon. 8O Ephraim! Stay away from idols! I am living and strong! I look after you and care for you. I am like an evergreen tree, yielding my fruit to you throughout the year. My mercies never fail. *vs.* 6, 7.

Hab 3:19. The Lord God is my Strength, and he will give me the speed of a deer and bring me safely over the mountains.

Zech 10:12. The Lord says, "I will make my people strong with power from me! They will go wherever they wish, and wherever they go, they will be under my personal care."

Zech 12:8. The Lord will defend the people of Jerusalem; the weakest among them will be as mighty as King David! And the royal line will be as God, like the Angel of the Lord who goes before them!

Mal 3:2. For he is like a blazing fire refining precious metal and he can bleach the dirtiest garments! 3Like a refiner of silver he will sit and closely watch as the dross is burned away. He will purify the Levites, the ministers of God, refining them like gold or silver, so that they will do their work for God with pure hearts.

Mal 4:2. But for you who fear my name, the Sun of Righteousness will rise with healing in his wings.

Jn 1:16. We have all benefited from the rich blessings he brought to us—blessing upon blessing heaped upon us!

Jn 17:11. Holy Father, keep them in your own care—all those you have given me—so that they will be united just as we are, with none missing.

Acts 20:32. And now I entrust you to God and his care and to his wonderful words which are able to build your faith and give you all the inheritance of those who are set apart for himself.

Rom 9:23, 24. And he has a right to take others such as ourselves, who have been made for pouring the riches of his glory into, whether we are Jews or Gentiles, and to be king to us so that everyone can see how very great his glory is.

Rom 14:4. They are God's servants, not yours. They are responsible to him, not to you. Let him tell them whether they are right or wrong. And God is able to make them do as they should.

1 Cor 12:6. There are many ways in which God works in our lives, but it is the same God who does the work in and through all of us who are his.

1 Cor 13:10. But when we have been made perfect and complete, then the need for these inadequate special gifts will come to an end, and they will disappear. 12In the same way, we can see and understand only a little about God now, as if we were peering at his reflection in a poor mirror; but someday we are going to see him in his completeness, face to face. Now all that I know is hazy and blurred, but then I will see everything clearly, just as clearly as God sees into my heart right now.

1 Cor 15:10. But whatever I am now it is all because God poured out such kindness and grace upon me—and not without results: for I have worked harder than all the other apostles, yet actually I wasn't doing it, but God working in me, to bless me.

2 Cor 1:21. It is this God who has made you and me into faithful Christians and commissioned us apostles to preach the Good News. 22He has put his brand upon us—his mark of ownership—and given us his Holy Spirit in our hearts as guarantee that we belong to him, and as the first installment of all that he is going to give us.

2 Cor 3:5. And not because we think we can do anything of lasting value by ourselves. Our only power and success comes from God.

2 Cor 5:5. This is what God has prepared for us

and, as a guarantee, he has given us his Holy Spirit.

2 Cor 9:8. God is able to make it up to you by giving you everything you need and more, so that there will not only be enough for your own needs, but plenty left over to give joyfully to others.

2 Cor 10:4. I use God's mighty weapons, not those made by men, to knock down the devil's strongholds.

Eph 3:20. Now glory be to God who by his mighty power at work within us is able to do far more than we would ever dare to ask or even dream of—infinitely beyond our highest prayers, desires, thoughts, or hopes.

Phil 1:6. And I am sure that God who began the good work within you will keep right on helping you grow in his grace until his task within you is finally finished on that day when Jesus Christ returns.

Phil 2:13. For God is at work within you, helping you want to obey him, and then helping you do what he wants.

Phil 4:7. If you do this you will experience God's peace, which is far more wonderful than the human mind can understand. His peace will keep your thoughts and your hearts quiet and at rest as you trust in Christ Jesus. [19]And it is he who will supply all your needs from his riches in glory, because of what Jesus Christ has done for us.

Col 1:11. We are praying, too, that you will be filled with his mighty, glorious strength so that you can keep going no matter what happens—always full of the joy of the Lord, [12]and always thankful to the Father who has made us fit to share all the wonderful things that belong to those who live in the kingdom of light.

1 Thess 5:24. God, who called you to become his child, will do all this for you, just as he promised.

Heb 12:10. Our earthly fathers trained us for a few brief years, doing the best for us that they knew how, but God's correction is always right and for our best good, that we may share his holiness. [11]Being punished isn't enjoyable while it is happening—it hurts! But afterwards we can see the result, a quiet growth in grace and character.

Jas 1:17. But whatever is good and perfect comes to us from God, the Creator of all light, and he shines forever without change or shadow. *v.* 18.

1 Pet 1:5. And God, in his mighty power, will make sure that you get there safely to receive it, because you are trusting him. It will be yours in that coming last day for all to see.

2 Pet 1:2. Do you want more and more of God's kindness and peace? Then learn to know him better and better. [3]For as you know him better, he will give you, through his great power, everything you need for living a truly good life: he even shares his own glory and his own goodness with us! [4]And by that same mighty power he has given us all the other rich and wonderful blessings he promised; for instance, the promise to save us from the lust and rottenness all around us, and to give us his own character.

1 Jn 1:9. But if we confess our sins to him, he can be depended on to forgive us and to cleanse us from every wrong. (And it is perfectly proper for God to do this for us because Christ died to wash away our sins.)

1 Jn 4:4. Dear young friends, you belong to God and have already won your fight with those who are against Christ, because there is someone in your hearts who is stronger than any evil teacher in this wicked world.

Jude 1:1. *To:* Christians everywhere—beloved of God and chosen by him. [25]And he is able to keep you from slipping and falling away, and to bring you, sinless and perfect, into his glorious presence with mighty shouts of everlasting joy.

Rev 14:13. And I heard a voice in the heavens above me saying, "Write this down: At last the time has come for his martyrs to enter into their full reward. Yes, says the Spirit, they are blest indeed, for now they shall rest from all their toils and trials; for their good deeds follow them to heaven!"

Rev 19:9. And the angel dictated this sentence to me: "Blessed are those who are invited to the wedding feast of the Lamb."

Rev 20:6. Blessed and holy are those who share in the First Resurrection. For them the Second Death holds no terrors, for they will be priests of God and of Christ, and shall reign with him a thousand years.

See *Regeneration; Sanctification.*

TEMPORAL, FROM GOD. Gen 1:30. And I've given all the grass and plants to the animals and birds for their food.

Gen 8:22. As long as the earth remains, there will be springtime and harvest, cold and heat, winter and summer, day and night.

Gen 9:1. God blessed Noah and his sons and told them to have many children and to repopulate the earth. [2, 3]"All wild animals and birds and fish will be afraid of you," God told him; "for I have placed them in your power, and they are yours to use for food, in addition to grain and vegetables."

Gen 22:17. I will bless you with incredible blessings and multiply your descendants into countless thousands and millions, like the stars above you in the sky, and like the sands along the seashore. These descendants of yours will conquer their enemies. Gen 26:4, 5.

Gen 28:20. And Jacob vowed this vow to God: "If God will help and protect me on this journey and give me food and clothes, [21]and will bring me back safely to my father, then I will choose Jehovah as my God!"

Gen 49:24. But their weapons were shattered by the Mighty One of Jacob, the Shepherd, the Rock of Israel. [25]May the God of your fathers, the Almighty, bless you with blessings of heaven above and of the earth beneath—blessings of the breasts and of the womb. *vs.* 11, 12, 20.

Ex 23:22. But if you are careful to obey him, following all my instructions, then I will be an enemy to your enemies.

Ex 34:24. No one will attack and conquer your

land when you go up to appear before the Lord your God those three times each year. For I will drive out the nations from before you and enlarge your boundaries.

Lev 25:20. But you will ask, "What shall we eat the seventh year, since we are not allowed to plant or harvest crops that year?" [21, 22]The answer is, "I will bless you with bumper crops the sixth year that will last you until the crops of the eighth year are harvested!"

Lev 26:4, 5. I will give you regular rains, and the land will yield bumper crops, and the trees will be loaded with fruit long after the normal time! And grapes will still be ripening when sowing time comes again. You shall eat your fill, and live safely in the land, [6]for I will give you peace, and you will go to sleep without fear. I will chase away the dangerous animals. [7]You will chase your enemies; they will die beneath your swords. [8]Five of you will chase a hundred, and a hundred of you, ten thousand! You will defeat all of your enemies. [9]I will look after you, and multiply you, and fulfill my covenant with you. [10]You will have such a surplus of crops that you won't know what to do with them when the new harvest is ready!

Deut 1:10. For the Lord has multiplied you like stars!

Deut 2:7. The Lord your God has watched over you and blessed you every step of the way for all these forty years as you have wandered around in this great wilderness; and you have lacked nothing in all that time.

Deut 4:4. But all of you who were faithful to the Lord your God are still alive today. *v.* 40; Num 10: 29; Deut 5:33; 6:2–25; 12:28.

Deut 7:13. And he will love you and bless you and make you into a great nation. He will make you fertile and give fertility to your ground and to your animals, so that you will have large crops of grain, grapes, and olives, and great flocks of cattle, sheep, and goats when you arrive in the land he promised your fathers to give you. [14]You will be blessed above all the nations of the earth; not one of you, whether male or female, shall be barren, not even your cattle. [15]And the Lord will take away all your sickness and will not let you suffer any of the diseases of Egypt you remember so well; he will give them all to your enemies! *vs.* 16–24; Ex 15:26; 23:25, 26.

Deut 8:3. Yes, he humbled you by letting you go hungry and then feeding you with manna, a food previously unknown to both you and your ancestors. He did it to help you realize that food isn't everything, and that real life comes by obeying every command of God. [4]For all these forty years your clothes haven't grown old, and your feet haven't been blistered or swollen. [5]So you should realize that, as a man punishes his son, the Lord punishes you to help you. [6]Obey the laws of the Lord your God. Walk in his ways and fear him. [7]For the Lord your God is bringing you into a good land of brooks, pools, gushing springs, valleys, and hills; [8]it is a land of wheat and barley, of grape vines, fig trees, pomegranates, olives, and honey; [9]it is a land where food is plentiful, and nothing is lacking; it is a land where iron is as common as stone, and copper is abundant in the hills. [10]When you have eaten your fill, bless the Lord your God for the good land he has given you. [15]Beware that you don't forget the God who led you through the great and terrible wilderness with the dangerous snakes and scorpions, where it was so hot and dry. He gave you water from the rock! [16]He fed you with manna in the wilderness (it was a kind of bread unknown before) so that you would become humble and so that your trust in him would grow, and he could do you good. [17]He did it so that you would never feel that it was your own power and might that made you wealthy. [18]Always remember that it is the Lord your God who gives you power to become rich, and he does it to fulfill his promise to your ancestors. *vs.* 1, 2.

Deut 10:18. He gives justice to the fatherless and widows. He loves foreigners and gives them food and clothing.

Deut 11:12. A land that the Lord your God personally cares for! His eyes are always upon it, day after day throughout the year! *vs.* 13–15.

Deut 12:7. There you and your families shall feast before the Lord your God, and shall rejoice in all he has done for you.

Deut 15:4. No one will become poor because of this, for the Lord will greatly bless you in the land he is giving you if you obey this command. [6]He will bless you as he has promised. You shall lend money to many nations but will never need to borrow! You shall rule many nations, but they shall not rule over you! Deut 26:18, 19.

Deut 28:7. The Lord will defeat your enemies before you; they will march out together against you but scatter before you in seven directions! [8]The Lord will bless you with good crops and healthy cattle, and prosper everything you do when you arrive in the land the Lord your God is giving you.

Deut 29:5. For forty years God has led you through the wilderness, yet your clothes haven't become old, and your shoes haven't worn out! Deut 8:4.

Deut 32:13. God gave them fertile hilltops, rolling, fertile fields, honey from the rock, and olive oil from stony ground! [14]He gave them milk and meat—choice Bashan rams, and goats—and the finest of the wheat; they drank the sparkling wine.

Josh 1:8. Constantly remind the people about these laws, and you yourself must think about them every day and every night so that you will be sure to obey all of them. For only then will you succeed.

Ruth 1:6, 7. She decided to return to Israel with her daughters-in-law, for she had heard that the Lord had blessed his people by giving them good crops again.

1 Sam 2:7. Some he causes to be poor and others to be rich. He cuts one down and lifts another up. [8]He lifts the poor from the dust—yes, from a pile of ashes—and treats them as princes sitting in the

seats of honor. For all the earth is the Lord's and he has set the world in order.

2 Sam 7:8. Now go and give this message to David from the Lord of heaven: "I chose you to be the leader of my people Israel when you were a mere shepherd, tending your sheep in the pastureland. [9]I have been with you wherever you have gone and have destroyed your enemies. And I will make your name greater yet, so that you will be one of the most famous men in the world!" 1 Chron 17: 7, 8.

1 Chron 29:12. Riches and honor come from you alone, and you are the Ruler of all mankind; your hand controls power and might, and it is at your discretion that men are made great and given strength. [14]Everything we have has come from you, and we only give you what is yours already! [16]O Lord our God, all of this material that we have gathered to build a temple for your holy name comes from you! It all belongs to you!

2 Chron 1:12. Yes, I am giving you the wisdom and knowledge you asked for! And I am also giving you such riches, wealth, and honor as no other king has ever had before you! And there will never again be so great a king in all the world!

2 Chron 31:10. And Azariah the High Priest from the clan of Zadok replied, "These are tithes! We have been eating from these stores of food for many weeks, but all this is left over, for the Lord has blessed his people."

Ezra 8:22. For I was ashamed to ask the king for soldiers and cavalry to accompany us and protect us from the enemies along the way. After all, we had told the king that our God would protect all those who worshiped him, and that disaster could come only to those who had forsaken him!

Neh 8:10. It is a time to celebrate with a hearty meal, and to send presents to those in need, for the joy of the Lord is your strength. You must not be dejected and sad!

Job 5:10. He sends the rain upon the earth to water the fields.

Job 12:23. He raises up a nation and then destroys it. He makes it great, and then reduces it to nothing.

Job 22:18. Yet they forgot that he had filled their homes with good things.

Job 37:6. For he directs the snow, the showers, and storm to fall upon the earth. [10]God blows upon the rivers, and even the widest torrents freeze. [13]He sends the storms as punishment, or, in his lovingkindness, to encourage. [16, 17]Do you understand the balancing of the clouds with perfection and skill? Do you know why you become warm when the south wind is blowing and everything is still?

Job 38:25–27. Who dug the valleys for the torrents of rain? Who laid out the path for the lightning, causing the rain to fall upon the barren deserts, so that the parched and barren ground is satisfied with water, and tender grass springs up? [41]Who provides for the ravens when their young cry out to God as they try to struggle up from their nest in hunger? *vs.* 1–41

Ps 21:3. You welcomed him to the throne with success and prosperity. You set a kingly crown of purest gold upon his head. [4]He asked for a long, good life, and you have granted his request; the days of his life stretch on and on forever. [5]You have given him fame and honor. You have clothed him with splendor and majesty.

Ps 23:1. Because the Lord is my Shepherd, I have everything I need! [5]You provide delicious food for me in the presence of my enemies. You have welcomed me as your guest; blessings overflow!

Ps 34:10. Even strong young lions sometimes go hungry, but those of us who reverence the Lord will never lack any good thing.

Ps 36:6. You are concerned for men and animals alike.

Ps 44:3. They did not conquer by their own strength and skill, but by your mighty power and because you smiled upon them and favored them.

Ps 65:8. In the farthest corners of the earth the glorious acts of God shall startle everyone. The dawn and sunset shout for joy! [9]He waters the earth to make it fertile. The rivers of God will not run dry! He prepares the earth for his people and sends them rich harvests of grain. [10]He waters the furrows with abundant rain. Showers soften the earth, melting the clods and causing seeds to sprout across the land. [11, 12]Then he crowns it all with green, lush pastures in the wilderness; hillsides blossom with joy. *v.* 13.

Ps 68:6. He gives families to the lonely, and releases prisoners from jail, singing with joy! But for rebels there is famine and distress. [9, 10]You sent abundant rain upon your land, O God, to refresh it in its weariness! There your people lived, for you gave them this home when they were destitute.

19. What a glorious Lord! He who daily bears our burdens also gives us our salvation.

Ps 69:35. For God will save Jerusalem; he rebuilds the cities of Judah. His people shall live in them and not be dispossessed. [36]Their children shall inherit the land; all who love his name shall live there safely.

Ps 81:16. But he would feed you with the choicest foods. He would satisfy you with honey for the taking. *vs.* 13–15.

Ps 85:12. Yes, the Lord pours down blessings on the land and it yields its bountiful crops.

Ps 91:1. We live within the shadow of the Almighty, sheltered by the God who is above all gods. [2]This I declare, that he alone is my refuge, my place of safety; he is my God, and I am trusting him. [3]For he rescues you from every trap, and protects you from the fatal plague. [4]He will shield you with his wings! They will shelter you. His faithful promises are your armor. [5]Now you don't need to be afraid of the dark any more, nor fear the dangers of the day; [6]nor dread the plagues of darkness, nor disasters in the morning. [7]Though a thousand fall at my side, though ten thousand are dying around me, the evil will not touch me. [8]I will see how the wicked are punished but I will not share it. [9]For Jehovah is my refuge! I choose the God above all gods to shelter me. [10]How then can evil overtake me or any plague come near? [11]For he orders his angels to protect you wherever you go. [12]They will steady you with their hands to keep you from stumbling against the rocks on the trail. [13]You can safely meet a lion or step on poisonous snakes, yes, even trample them beneath your feet! [14]For the Lord says, "Because he loves me, I will rescue him; I will make him great because he trusts in my name. [15]When he calls on me I will answer; I will be with him in trouble, and rescue him and honor him. [16]I will satisfy him with a full life and give him my salvation."

Ps 103:2. Yes, I will bless the Lord and not forget the glorious things he does for me. [3]He forgives all my sins. He heals me. [4]He ransoms me from hell. He surrounds me with lovingkindness and tender mercies. [5]He fills my life with good things! My youth is renewed like the eagle's!

Ps 104:14. The tender grass grows up at his command to feed the cattle, and there are fruit trees, vegetables and grain for man to cultivate, [15]and wine to make him glad, and olive oil as lotion for his skin, and bread to give him strength. [27]Every one of these depends on you to give them daily food. [28]You supply it, and they gather it. You open wide your hand to feed them and they are satisfied with all your bountiful provision. *vs.* 1–35.

Ps 105:24. In the years that followed, the people of Israel multiplied explosively, until they were a greater nation than their rulers.

Ps 107:35. Again, he turns deserts into fertile, watered valleys. [36]He brings the hungry to settle there and build their cities, [37]to sow their fields and plant their vineyards, and reap their bumper crops! [38]How he blesses them! They raise big families there, and many cattle.

Ps 111:5. He gives food to those who trust him; he never forgets his promises.

Ps 113:9. He gives children to the childless wife, so that she becomes a happy mother.

Ps 115:16. The heavens belong to the Lord, but he has given the earth to all mankind.

Ps 127:1. Unless the Lord builds a house, the builder's work is useless. Unless the Lord protects a city, sentries do no good. [2]It is senseless for you to work so hard from early morning until late at night, fearing you will starve to death; for God wants his loved ones to get their proper rest. [3]Children are a gift from God; they are his reward. [4]Children born to a young man are like sharp arrows to defend him. [5]Happy is the man who has his quiver full of them. That man shall have the help he needs when arguing with his enemies.

Ps 135:7. He makes mists rise throughout the earth and sends the lightning to bring down the rain; and sends the winds from his treasuries.

Ps 136:25. He gives food to every living thing, for his lovingkindness continues forever. *vs.* 1–26.

Ps 144:12–15. Here is my description of a truly happy land where Jehovah is God: Sons vigorous and tall as growing plants. Daughters of graceful beauty like the pillars of a palace wall. Barns full to the brim with crops of every kind. Sheep by the thousands out in our fields. Oxen loaded down with produce. No enemy attacking the walls, but peace everywhere. No crime in our streets. Yes, happy are those whose God is Jehovah.

Ps 145:15. The eyes of all mankind look up to you for help; you give them their food as they need it. [16]You constantly satisfy the hunger and thirst of every living thing.

Ps 146:5. But happy is the man who has the God of Jacob as his helper, whose hope is in the Lord his God—[6]the God who made both earth and heaven, the seas and everything in them. He is the God who keeps every promise, [7]and gives justice to the poor and oppressed, and food to the hungry. He frees the prisoners, [8]and opens the eyes of the blind; he lifts the burdens from those bent down beneath their loads. For the Lord loves good men. [9]He protects the immigrants, and cares for the orphans and widows. But he turns topsy-turvy the plans of the wicked.

Ps 147:8. He covers the heavens with clouds, sends down the showers and makes the green grass grow in mountain pastures. [9]He feeds the wild animals and the young ravens cry to him for food. [13]For he has fortified your gates against all enemies, and blessed your children. [14]He sends peace across your nation, and fills your barns with plenty of the finest wheat.

Eccl 2:24. So I decided that there was nothing better for a man to do than to enjoy his food and drink, and his job. Then I realized that even this pleasure is from the hand of God.

Eccl 3:13. That he should eat and drink and enjoy the fruits of his labors, for these are gifts from God.

Eccl 5:19. And, of course, it is very good if a man has received wealth from the Lord, and the good health to enjoy it. To enjoy your work and to accept your lot in life—that is indeed a gift from God.

Isa 25:4. But to the poor, O Lord, you are a refuge from the storm, a shadow from the heat, a shelter from merciless men who are like a driving rain that melts down an earthen wall.

Isa 30:23. Then God will bless you with rain at planting time and with wonderful harvests and with ample pastures for your cows. [26]The moon will be as bright as the sun, and the sunlight brighter than seven days! So it will be when the Lord begins to heal his people and to cure the wounds he gave them. *vs.* 24, 25.

Isa 31:1. Woe to those who run to Egypt for help, trusting their mighty cavalry and chariots instead of looking to the Holy One of Israel and consulting him. [2]In his wisdom, he will send great evil on his people and will not change his mind. He will rise against them for the evil they have done, and crush their allies too.

Isa 33:15. I will tell you who can live here: All who are honest and fair, who reject making profit by fraud, who hold back their hands from taking bribes, who refuse to listen to those who plot murder, who shut their eyes to all enticement to do wrong. [16]Such as these shall dwell on high. The rocks of the mountains will be their fortress of safety; food will be supplied to them and they will have all the water they need.

Isa 43:20. The wild animals in the fields will thank me, the jackals and ostriches too, for giving them water in the wilderness, yes, springs in the desert, so that my people, my chosen ones, can be refreshed.

Isa 48:21. They were not thirsty when he led them through the deserts; he divided the rock, and water gushed out for them to drink.

Isa 51:2. Yes, think about your ancestors Abraham and Sarah, from whom you came. You worry at being so small and few, but Abraham was only *one* when I called him. But when I blessed him, he became a great nation.

Isa 55:10. As the rain and snow come down from heaven and stay upon the ground to water the earth, and cause the grain to grow and to produce seed for the farmer and bread for the hungry.

Jer 5:24. Though I am the one who gives them rain each year in spring and fall and sends the harvest times, yet have they no respect or fear for me.

Jer 10:13. It is his voice that echoes in the thunder of the storm clouds. He causes mist to rise upon the earth; he sends the lightning and brings the rain, and from his treasuries he brings the wind.

Jer 14:22. What heathen god can give us rain? Who but you alone, O Lord our God, can do such things as this? Therefore we will wait for you to help us.

Jer 27:4. Saying, Tell your masters that the Lord of Hosts, the God of Israel, sends you this message: [5]"By my great power I have made the earth and all mankind and every animal; and I give these things of mine to anyone I want to. [6]So now I have given all your countries to King Nebuchadnezzar of Babylon, who is my deputy. And I have handed over to him all your cattle for his use."

Jer 30:19. The cities will be filled with joy and great thanksgiving, and I will multiply my people and make of them a great and honored nation.

Jer 31:35. The Lord who gives us sunlight in the daytime and the moon and stars to light the night, who stirs the sea to make the roaring waves—his name is Lord of Hosts.

Ezk 36:30. I will give you huge harvests from your fruit trees and fields, and never again will the surrounding nations be able to scoff at your land for its famines. [36]Then the nations all around—all those still left—will know that I, the Lord, rebuilt the ruins and planted lush crops in the wilderness. For I, the Lord, have promised it, and I will do it. [37, 38]The Lord God says: I am ready to hear Israel's prayers for these blessings, and to grant them their requests. Let them but ask and I will multiply them like the flocks that fill Jerusalem's streets at time of sacrifice. The ruined cities will be crowded once more, and everyone will know I am the Lord. *vs.* 28–38.

Dan 5:18. Your Majesty, the Most High God gave Nebuchadnezzar, who long ago preceded you, a kingdom and majesty and glory and honor.

Dan 6:20. And called out in anguish, "O Daniel, servant of the Living God, was your God, whom you worship continually, able to deliver you from the lions?" [22]"My God has sent his angel," he said, "to shut the lions' mouths so that they can't touch me; for I am innocent before God, nor, sir, have I wronged you."

Hos 2:8. She doesn't realize that all she has, has come from me. It was I who gave her all the gold and silver that she used in worshiping Baal, her god!

Hos 11:3. I trained him from infancy, I taught him to walk, I held him in my arms. But he doesn't know or even care that it was I who raised him.

Joel 2:21. Fear not, my people; be glad now and rejoice, for he has done amazing things for you. [23]Rejoice, O people of Jerusalem, rejoice in the Lord your God! For the rains he sends are tokens of forgiveness. Once more the autumn rains will come, as well as those of spring. [26]Once again you will have all the food you want. Praise the Lord, who does these miracles for you. Never again will my people experience disaster such as this.

Amos 4:7. I ruined your crops by holding back the rain three months before the harvest. I sent rain on one city, but not another. While rain fell on one field, another was dry and withered.

Jon 4:6. And when the leaves of the shelter withered in the heat, the Lord arranged for a vine to grow up quickly and spread its broad leaves over Jonah's head to shade him. This made him comfortable and very grateful.

Zech 10:1. Ask the Lord for rain in the springtime, and he will answer with lightning and showers. Every field will become a lush pasture.

Mal 3:10. Bring all the tithes into the storehouse so that there will be food enough in my Temple; if you do, I will open up the windows of heaven for you and pour out a blessing so great that you won't have room enough to take it in! [12]And all nations will call you blessed, for you will be a land sparkling with happiness. These are the promises of the Lord of Hosts. *v.* 11

Mt 5:45. In that way you will be acting as true sons of your Father in heaven. For he gives his sunlight to both the evil and the good, and sends rain on the just and on the unjust too.

Mt 6:26. Look at the birds! They don't worry about what to eat—they don't need to sow or reap or store up food—for your heavenly Father feeds them. And you are far more valuable to him than they are. [30]And if God cares so wonderfully for flowers that are here today and gone tomorrow, won't he more surely care for you, O men of little faith? [31, 32]So don't worry at all about having enough food and clothing. Why be like the heathen? For they take pride in all these things and are deeply concerned about them. But your heavenly Father already knows perfectly well that you need them, [33]and he will give them to you if you give him first place in your life and live as he wants you to.

Mt 10:29. Not one sparrow (What do they cost? Two for a penny?) can fall to the ground without your Father knowing it.

Lk 12:22. Then turning to his disciples he said, "Don't worry about whether you have enough food to eat or clothes to wear. [23]For life consists of far more than food and clothes. [24]Look at the ravens—they don't plant or harvest or have barns to store away their food, and yet they get along all right—for God feeds them. And you are far more valuable to him than any birds! [25]And besides, what's the use of worrying? What good does it do? Will it add a single day to your life? Of course not! [26]And if worry can't even do such little things as that, what's the use of worrying over bigger things? [27]Look at the lilies! They don't toil and spin, and yet Solomon in all his glory was not robed as well as they are. [28]And if God provides clothing for the flowers that are here today and gone tomorrow, don't you suppose that he will provide clothing for you, you doubters? [29]And don't worry about food —what to eat and drink; don't worry at all that God will provide it for you. [30]All mankind scratches for its daily bread, but your heavenly Father knows your needs. [31]He will always give you all you need from day to day if you will make the Kingdom of God your primary concern."

Jn 6:31. Give us free bread every day, like our fathers had while they journeyed through the wilderness! As the Scriptures say, "Moses gave them bread from heaven."

Acts 14:17. But he never left himself without a witness; there were always his reminders—the kind things he did such as sending you rain and good crops and giving you food and gladness.

1 Cor 2:9. That is what is meant by the Scriptures which say that no mere man has ever seen, heard or even imagined what wonderful things God has ready for those who love the Lord.

1 Cor 16:2. On every Lord's Day each of you should put aside something from what you have earned during the week, and use it for this offering. The amount depends on how much the Lord has helped you earn.

2 Cor 7:6. Then God who cheers those who are discouraged refreshed us by the arrival of Titus.

2 Cor 9:8. God is able to make it up to you by giving you everything you need and more, so that there will not only be enough for your own needs, but plenty left over to give joyfully to others. [9]It is as the Scriptures say: "The godly man gives generously to the poor. His good deeds will be an honor to him forever." [10]For God, who gives seed to the farmer to plant, and later on, good crops to harvest and eat, will give you more and more seed to plant and will make it grow so that you can give away more and more fruit from your harvest.

Phil 4:19. And it is he who will supply all your needs from his riches in glory, because of what Christ Jesus has done for us.

2 Pet 2:7,8. But at the same time the Lord rescued Lot out of Sodom because he was a good man, sick of the terrible wickedness he saw everywhere around him day after day. [9]So also the Lord can rescue you and me from the temptations that surround us, and continue to punish the ungodly until the day of final judgment comes.

See *God, Goodness of, Providence of.*

TEMPORAL, FROM GOD, EXEMPLIFIED. To Noah, at the time of the flood, Gen 7:1; Abraham, Gen 24:1; Isaac, Gen 26:12–24, 28; Jacob, Gen 35:9–15; Israelites, in Egypt, Ex 11:3; in the wilderness, supplying water, Ex 17:1–7; Num 20:10, 11; Ps 78:15–20; 105:41; manna, Ex 16:14, 31; Num 11:7–9; Neh 9:15; Ps 78:23, 24; quails, Num 11:31–33; Ps 78:23–30; 105:40. To David, 2 Sam 5:10; 1 Chron 14:17; Obed-edom, 2 Sam 6:11; Solomon, 1 Kgs 3:13; 1 Chron 29:25; 2 Chron 1:1; Elijah, fed by ravens, 1 Kgs 17:2–7; by an angel, 1 Kgs 19:5–8. To the widow of Zarephath, 1 Kgs 17:12–16. Hezekiah prospered, 2 Kgs 18:6, 7; 2 Chron 32:28, 29; restored to health, 2 Kgs 20:1–7; Asa, 2 Chron 14:6, 7; Jehoshaphat, 2 Chron 17:3–5; 20:30; Uzziah, 2 Chron 26:5–15; Jotham, 2 Chron 27:6; Job, Job 1:10; 42:10, 12; Daniel, Dan 1:9.

TEMPORAL, PRAYER FOR. Gen 27:28, 29. May God always give you plenty of rain for your crops, and good harvest of grain, and new wine. May many nations be your slaves. Be the master of your brothers. May all your relatives bow low before you. Cursed are all who curse you, and blessed are all who bless you.

Gen 28:20. And Jacob vowed this vow to God: "If God will help and protect me on this journey and give me food and clothes, [21]and will bring me back safely to my father, then I will choose Jehovah as my God! *vs.* 3, 4.

Gen 48:16. He is the Angel who has kept me from all harm. May these boys be an honor to my name and to the names of my fathers Abraham and Isaac; and may they become a mighty nation.

Deut 1:11. And may he multiply you a thousand times more, and bless you as he promised.

Deut 26:15. Look down from your holy home in heaven and bless your people and the land you have given us, as you promised our ancestors; make it a land "flowing with milk and honey"!

Deut 33:11. "O Lord, prosper the Levites and accept the work they do for you. Crush those who are their enemies; don't let them rise again." [13]Concerning the tribe of Joseph, he said: "May his land be blessed by God with the choicest gifts of heaven and of the earth that lies below. [16]May he be blessed with the best gifts of the earth and its fullness, and with the favor of God who appeared in the burning bush. Let all these blessings come upon Joseph, the prince among his brothers." [24]Of the tribe of Asher: "Asher is a favorite son, esteemed above his brothers; he bathes his feet in soothing olive oil." *vs.* 14, 15.

1 Kgs 8:35,36. And when the skies are shut up and there is no rain because of their sin, hear them from heaven and forgive them when they pray toward this place and confess your name. And after you have punished them, help them to follow the

good ways in which they should walk, and send rain upon the land which you have given your people. *vs.* 35–50.

1 Chron 4:10. He was the one who prayed to the God of Israel, "Oh, that you would wonderfully bless me and help me in my work; please be with me in all that I do, and keep me from all evil and disaster!" And God granted him his request.

1 Chron 17:27. May this blessing rest upon my children forever, for when you grant a blessing, Lord, it is an eternal blessing!

Ps 28:9. Defend your people, Lord; defend and bless your chosen ones. Lead them like a shepherd and carry them forever in your arms.

Ps 36:11. Don't let these proud men trample me. Don't let their wicked hands push me around.

Prov 30:8. Second, give me neither poverty nor riches! Give me just enough to satisfy my needs!

Mt 6:11. Give us our food again today, as usual,

Rom 1:10. And one of the things I keep on praying for is the opportunity, God willing, to come at last to see you and, if possible, that I will have a safe trip.

1 Thess 3:11. May God our Father himself and our Lord Jesus send us back to you again.

3 Jn 1:2. Dear friend, I am praying that all is well with you and that your body is as healthy as I know your soul is.

See *Affliction, Prayer in; Prayer; Prosperity.*

Temporal Blessings, Prayer for, Instances of. Abraham, Gen 15:2–4. Abraham's servant, Gen 24: 12. Laban, Gen 24:60. Isaac, Gen 25:21. Hannah, 1 Sam 1:11. Elijah, 1 Kgs 17:20, 21; 18:42, 44; Jas 5: 17, 18. Ezra, Ezra 8:21–23. Nehemiah, Neh 1:11; 2: 4; 6:9.

BLIGHT Sent as a judgment, Deut 28:22; Amos 4:9.

BLIND Cruelty to, forbidden, Lev 19:14; Deut 27:18. Hated by David, 2 Sam 5:8.

See *Blindness.*

BLINDNESS Disqualified for priestly office, Lev 21:18. Of animals, disqualified for a sacrifice, Lev 22:22; Deut 15:21; Mal 1:8. Miraculously inflicted on the Sodomites, Gen 19:11; Syrians, 2 Kgs 6:18–23; Paul, Acts 9:8,9; Elymas, Acts 13: 11. Sent as a judgment, Deut 28:28.

Miraculous healing of, Mt 9:27–30; 11:5; 12:22; 21:14; of Bartimaeus, Mt 20:30–34; Mk 10:46–52; a man of Bethsaida, Mk 8:22–25; man born blind, Jn 9:1–7.

INSTANCES OF. Isaac, Gen 27:1. Jacob, Gen 48: 10. Eli, 1 Sam 4:15. Ahijah, 1 Kgs 14:4.

SPIRITUAL. Ex 5:2. "Is that so?" retorted Pharaoh. "And who is Jehovah, that I should listen to him, and let Israel go? I don't know Jehovah and I will not let Israel go."

Deut 29:4. But even yet the Lord hasn't given you hearts that understand or eyes that see or ears that hear!

Deut 32:28. Israel is a stupid nation; foolish, without understanding. [29]Oh that they were wise! Oh, that they could understand! Oh, that they would know what they are getting into!

Judg 16:20. But he didn't realize that the Lord had left him.

Job 21:14. All this despite the fact that they ordered God away and wanted no part of him and his ways.

Job 22:13. But you reply, "That is why he can't see what I am doing! How can he judge through the thick darkness? [14]For thick clouds swirl about him so that he cannot see us. He is way up there, walking on the vault of heaven."

Ps 10:5. Yet there is success in everything they do, and their enemies fall before them. They do not see your punishment awaiting them. [6]They boast that neither God nor man can ever keep them down—somehow they'll find a way!

Ps 14:1. That man is a fool who says to himself, "There is no God!" Anyone who talks like that is warped and evil and cannot really be a good person at all. [4]They eat my people like bread and wouldn't think of praying! Don't they really know any better?

Ps 73:22. I saw myself so stupid and so ignorant; I must seem like an animal to you, O God. *vs.* 2–28.

Ps 79:6. Pour out your wrath upon the godless nations, not on us! And on kingdoms that refuse to pray, that will not call upon your name!

Ps 82:5. But you are so foolish and so ignorant! Because you are in darkness, all the foundations of society are shaken to the core.

Ps 92:6. Unthinking people do not understand them! No fool can comprehend this.

Ps 94:6,7. They murder widows, immigrants, and orphans, for "The Lord isn't looking," they say, "and besides, he doesn't care." [8]Fools!

Ps 95:10. "For forty years I watched them in disgust," the Lord God says. "They were a nation whose thoughts and heart were far away from me. They refused to accept my laws."

Ps 119:18. Open my eyes to see wonderful things in your Word.

Prov 1:7. How does a man become wise? The first step is to trust and reverence the Lord! Only fools refuse to be taught. [22]"You simpletons!" she [Wisdom] cries. "How long will you go on being fools? How long will you scoff at wisdom and fight the facts? [29]For you closed your eyes to the facts and did not choose to reverence and trust the Lord, [30]and you turned your back on me, spurning my advice."

Prov 4:19. While the evil man gropes and stumbles in the dark. Prov 7:7–23.

Prov 10:21. A godly man gives good advice, but a rebel is destroyed by lack of common sense.

Prov 13:18. If you refuse criticism you will end in poverty and disgrace; if you accept criticism you are on the road to fame.

Prov 14:12. Before every man there lies a wide and pleasant road that seems right but ends in death.

Prov 17:16. It is senseless to pay tuition to educate a rebel who has no heart for truth.

Prov 19:2. It is dangerous and sinful to rush into the unknown. [3]A man may ruin his chances by his own foolishness and then blame it on the Lord!

Prov 28:5. Evil men don't understand the importance of justice, but those who follow the Lord are much concerned about it.

Eccl 7:25. I searched everywhere, determined to find wisdom and the reason for things, and to prove to myself the wickedness of folly, and that foolishness is madness.

Isa 1:3. Even the animals—the donkey and the ox—know their owner and appreciate his care for them, but not my people Israel. No matter what I do for them, they still don't care.

Isa 5:13. Therefore I will send you into exile far away because you neither know nor care that I have done so much for you. Your great and honored men will starve, and the common people will die of thirst. [20]They say that what is right is wrong, and what is wrong is right; that black is white and white is black; bitter is sweet and sweet is bitter.

Isa 6:9. And he said, "Yes, go. But tell my people this: 'Though you hear my words repeatedly, you won't understand them. Though you watch and watch as I perform my miracles, still you won't know what they mean.' [10]Dull their understanding, close their ears and shut their eyes. I don't want them to see or to hear or to understand, or to turn to me to heal them." Mt 13:14; Jn 12:38–41.

Isa 9:2. The people who walk in darkness shall see a great Light—a Light that will shine on those who live in the land of the shadow of death.

Isa 26:10. Your kindness to the wicked doesn't make them good; they keep on doing wrong and take no notice of your majesty. [11]They do not listen when you threaten; they will not look to see your upraised fist. Show them how much you love your people. Perhaps then they will be ashamed! Yes, let them be burned up by the fire reserved for your enemies.

Isa 27:11. My people are like the dead branches of a tree, broken off and used to burn beneath the pots. They are a foolish nation, a witless, stupid people, for they turn away from God. Therefore, he who made them will not have pity on them or show them his mercy.

Isa 28:13. So the Lord will spell it out for them again, repeating it over and over in simple words whenever he can; yet over this simple, straightforward message they will stumble and fall and be broken, trapped and captured. [15]You have struck a bargain with Death, you say, and sold yourselves to the devil in exchange for his protection against the Assyrians, "They can never touch us," you say, "for we are under the care of one who will deceive and fool them."

Isa 29:10. For the Lord has poured out upon you a spirit of deep sleep. He has closed the eyes of your prophets and seers, [11]so all of these future events are a sealed book to them. When you give it to one who can read, he says, "I can't, for it's sealed." [12]When you give it to another, he says, "Sorry, I can't read."

Isa 40:21. Are you so ignorant? Are you so deaf to the words of God—the words he gave before the worlds began? Have you never heard nor understood? [27]O Jacob, O Israel, how can you say that the Lord doesn't see your troubles and isn't being fair? [28]Don't you yet understand? Don't you know by now that the everlasting God, the Creator of the farthest parts of the earth, never grows faint or weary? No one can fathom the depths of his understanding.

Isa 42:6. "I the Lord have called you to demonstrate my righteousness. I will guard and support you, for I have given you to my people as the personal confirmation of my covenant with them. You shall also be a light to guide the nations unto me. [7]You will open the eyes of the blind, and release those who sit in prison darkness and despair." [18]Oh, how blind and deaf you are towards God! Why won't you listen? Why won't you see? [19]Who in all the world is as blind as my own people, who are designed to be my messengers of truth? Who is so blind as my "dedicated one," the "Servant of the Lord"? [20]You see and understand what is right but won't heed nor do it; you hear but you won't listen.

Isa 44:18. Such stupidity and ignorance! God has shut their eyes so that they cannot see, and closed their minds from understanding. [19]The man never stops to think or figure out, "Why, it's just a block of wood! I've burned it for heat and used it to bake my bread and roast my meat. How can the rest of it be a god? Should I fall down before a chunk of wood?" [20]The poor, deluded fool feeds on ashes; he is trusting what can never give him any help at all. Yet he cannot bring himself to ask, "Is this thing, this idol that I'm holding in my hand, a lie?"

Isa 48:8. Yes, I'll tell you things entirely new, for I know so well what traitors you are, rebels from earliest childhood, rotten through and through.

Isa 56:10. For the leaders of my people—the Lord's watchmen, his shepherds—are all blind to every danger. They are featherbrained and give no warning when danger comes. They love to lie there, love to sleep, to dream.

Isa 60:2. Darkness as black as night shall cover all the peoples of the earth, but the glory of the Lord will shine from you.

Jer 2:8. Even their priests cared nothing for the Lord, and their judges ignored me; their rulers turned against me, and their prophets worshiped Baal and wasted their time on nonsense.

Jer 4:22. Until my people leave their foolishness, for they refuse to listen to me; they are dull, retarded children who have no understanding. They are smart enough at doing wrong, but for doing right they have no talent, none at all.

Jer 5:4. Then I said, "But what can we expect from the poor and ignorant? They don't know the ways of God. How can they obey him?" [5]I will go now to their leaders, the men of importance, and speak to them, for they know the ways of the Lord and the judgment that follows sin. But they too had utterly rejected their God. [21]Listen, O foolish, senseless people—you with the eyes that do not see and the ears that do not listen.

Jer 8:7. The stork knows the time of her migration, as does the turtledove, and the crane, and the swallow. They all return at God's appointed time each year; but not my people! They don't accept the laws of God. [8]How can you say, "We understand his laws," when your teachers have twisted them up to mean a thing I never said? [9]These wise teachers of yours will be shamed by exile for this sin, for they have rejected the word of the Lord. Are they then so wise?

Jer 9:3. "They bend their tongues like bows to shoot their arrows of untruth. They care nothing for right and go from bad to worse; they care nothing for me," says the Lord. [6]"They pile evil upon evil, lie upon lie, and utterly refuse to come to me," says the Lord.

Jer 16:10. And when you tell the people all these things and they ask, "Why has the Lord decreed such terrible things against us? What have we done to merit such treatment? What is our sin against the Lord our God?"

Jer 17:9. The heart is the most deceitful thing there is, and desperately wicked. No one can really know how bad it is!

Ezk 12:2. "Son of dust," he said, "you live among rebels who could know the truth if they wanted to, but they don't want to; they could hear me if they would listen, but they won't."

Dan 12:10. Many shall be purified by great trials and persecutions. But the wicked shall continue in their wickedness, and none of them will understand. Only those who are willing to learn will know what it means.

Hos 4:1. Hear the word of the Lord, O people of Israel. The Lord has filed a lawsuit against you listing the following charges: There is no faithfulness, no kindness, no knowledge of God in your land. [6]My people are destroyed because they don't know me, and it is all your fault, you priests, for you yourselves refuse to know me; therefore I refuse to recognize you as my priests. Since you have forgotten my laws, I will "forget" to bless your children. [14]Fools! Your doom is sealed, for you refuse to understand.

Hos 5:4. Your deeds won't let you come to God again, for the spirit of adultery is deep within you, and you cannot know the Lord.

Hos 7:11. Ephraim is a silly, witless dove, calling to Egypt, flying to Assyria.

Amos 9:10. But all these sinners who say, "God will not touch us," will die by the sword.

Mic 4:12. But they do not know my thoughts nor understand my plan, for the time will come when the Lord will gather together the enemies of his people like sheaves upon the threshing floor.

Mt 5:15, 16. Don't hide your light! Let it shine for all; let your good deeds glow for all to see, so that they will praise your heavenly Father.

Mt 6:23. But if your eye is clouded with evil thoughts and desires, you are in deep spiritual darkness. And oh, how deep that darkness can be! Isa 6:9, 10.

Mt 13:13. That is why I use these illustrations, so people will hear and see but not understand. [14]This fulfills the prophecy of Isaiah: "They hear, but don't understand; they look, but don't see! [15]For their hearts are fat and heavy, and their ears are dull, and they have closed their eyes in sleep, [16]so they won't see and hear and understand and turn to God again, and let me heal them." But blessed are your eyes, for they see; and your ears, for they hear. [19]The hard path where some of the seeds fell represents the heart of a person who hears the Good News about the Kingdom and doesn't understand it; then Satan comes and snatches away the seeds from his heart. Mk 4:15; Lk 8:12.

Mt 15:14. They are blind guides leading the blind, and both will fall into a ditch.

Mt 16:2, 3. He replied, "You are good at reading the weather signs of the skies . . . but you can't read the obvious signs of the times!"

Mt 22:29. But Jesus said, "Your error is caused by your ignorance of the Scriptures and of God's power!" Mk 12:24.

Mt 23:19. Blind! For which is greater, the gift on the altar, or the altar itself that sanctifies the gift? [24]Blind guides! You strain out a gnat and swallow a camel. [26]Blind Pharisees! First cleanse the inside of the cup, and then the whole cup will be clean. *vs.* 16–24.

Mk 4:11, 12. He replied, "You are permitted to know some truths about the Kingdom of God that are hidden to those outside the Kingdom: 'Though they see and hear, they will not understand or turn to God, or be forgiven for their sins.' " Lk 8:10.

Mk 6:52. For they still didn't realize who he was, even after the miracle the evening before! For they didn't want to believe!

Mk 7:18. "Don't you understand either?" he asked. "Can't you see that what you eat won't harm your soul?"

Lk 4:18. "The Spirit of the Lord is upon me; he has appointed me to preach Good News to the poor; he has sent me to heal the brokenhearted and to announce that captives shall be released and the blind shall see, that the downtrodden shall be freed from their oppressors, and that God is ready to give blessings to all who come to him."

Lk 11:52. Woe to you experts in religion! For you hide the truth from the people. You won't accept it for yourselves, and you prevent others from having a chance to believe it.

Lk 12:48. But anyone who is not aware that he is doing wrong will be punished only lightly. Much is required from those to whom much is given, for their responsibility is greater. [57]Why do you refuse to see for yourselves what is right?

Lk 19:42. "Eternal peace was within your reach and you turned it down," he wept, "and now it is too late."

Lk 23:34. "Father, forgive these people," Jesus said, "for they don't know what they are doing."

Jn 1:5. His life is the light that shines through the darkness—and the darkness can never extinguish it. [10]But although he made the world, the world didn't recognize him when he came.

Jn 3:4. "Born again!" exclaimed Nicodemus.

"What do you mean? How can an old man go back into his mother's womb and be born again?" [7]"So don't be surprised at my statement that you must be born again! [19]Their sentence is based on this fact: that the Light from heaven came into the world, but they loved the darkness more than the Light, for their deeds were evil. [20]They hated the heavenly Light because they wanted to sin in the darkness. They stayed away from that Light for fear their sins would be exposed and they would be punished." [31]"He has come from heaven and is greater than anyone else. I am of the earth, and my understanding is limited to the things of earth." *vs.* 9–12.

Jn 4:10. He replied, "If you only knew what a wonderful gift God has for you, and who I am, you would ask me for some *living* water! [22]But you Samaritans know so little about him, worshiping blindly." *vs.* 11, 15.

Jn 6:52. Then the Jews began arguing with each other about what he meant. "How can this man give us his flesh to eat?" they asked. [60]Even his disciples said, "This is very hard to understand. Who can tell what he means?"

Jn 7:28. So Jesus, in a sermon in the Temple, called out, "Yes, you know me and where I was born and raised, but I am the representative of one you don't know, and he is Truth."

Jn 8:12. Later, in one of his talks, Jesus said to the people, "I am the Light of the world. So if you follow me, you won't be stumbling through the darkness, for living light will flood your path. [15]You pass judgment on me without knowing the facts. I am not judging you now." [19]"Where is your father?" they asked. Jesus answered, "You don't know who I am, so you don't know who my Father is. If you knew me, then you would know him too." [27]But they still didn't understand that he was talking to them about God. [33]"But we are descendants of Abraham," they said, "and have never been slaves to any man on earth! What do you mean, 'set free'?" [42]Jesus told them, "If that were so, [if God were your father, *v.* 41] then you would love me, for I have come to you from God. I am not here on my own, but he sent me. [43]Why can't you understand what I am saying? It is because you are prevented from doing so!" [52]The leaders of the Jews said, "Now we know you are possessed by a demon. Even Abraham and the mightiest prophets died, and yet you say that obeying you will keep a man from dying!" [54]Then Jesus told them this: . . . [55]"But you do not even know him. I do. If I said otherwise, I would be as great a liar as you! But it is true —I know him and fully obey him." [57]*The Jewish leaders:* "You aren't even fifty years old—sure, you've seen Abraham!"

Jn 9:29. "We know God has spoken to Moses, but as for this fellow, we don't know anything about him." [30]"Why, that's very strange!" the man replied. "He can heal blind men, and yet you don't know anything about him!" [39]Then Jesus told him, "I have come into the world to give sight to those who are spiritually blind and to show those who think they see that they are blind." *vs.* 30–38.

Jn 12:38. This is exactly what Isaiah the prophet had predicted: "Lord, who will believe us? Who will accept God's mighty miracles as proof?" Isa 53:1.

Jn 14:17. He is the Holy Spirit, the Spirit who leads into all truth. The world at large cannot receive him, for it isn't looking for him and doesn't recognize him.

Jn 15:21. The people of the world will persecute you because you belong to me, for they don't know God who sent me.

Jn 16:2. For you will be excommunicated from the synagogues, and indeed the time is coming when those who kill you will think they are doing God a service. [3]This is because they have never known the Father or me.

Jn 17:25. O righteous Father, the world doesn't know you.

Acts 3:17. Dear brothers, I realize that what you did to Jesus was done in ignorance; and the same can be said of your leaders.

Acts 13:27. The Jews in Jerusalem and their leaders fulfilled prophecy by killing Jesus; for they didn't recognize him, or realize that he is the one the prophets had written about, though they heard the prophets' words read every Sabbath.

Acts 17:23. For as I was out walking I saw your many altars, and one of them had this inscription on it—"To the Unknown God." You have been worshiping him without knowing who he is, and now I wish to tell you about him.

Acts 19:2. "Did you receive the Holy Spirit when you believed?" he asked them. "No," they replied, "we don't know what you mean. What is the Holy Spirit?"

Acts 26:18. To open their eyes to their true condition so that they may repent and live in the light of God instead of in Satan's darkness, so that they may receive forgiveness for their sins and God's inheritance along with all people everywhere whose sins are cleansed away, who are set apart by faith in me.

Rom 1:19. For the truth about God is known to them instinctively; God has put this knowledge in their hearts. [20]Since earliest times men have seen the earth and sky and all God made, and have known of his existence and great eternal power. So they will have no excuse (when they stand before God at Judgment Day). [21]Yes, they knew about him all right, but they wouldn't admit it or worship him or even thank him for all his daily care. And after awhile they began to think up silly ideas of what God was like and what he wanted them to do. The result was that their foolish minds became dark and confused. [22]Claiming themselves to be wise without God, they became utter fools instead. [28]So it was that when they gave God up and would not even acknowledge him, God gave them up to doing everything their evil minds could think of. [29]Their lives became full of every kind of wickedness and sin, of greed and hate, envy, murder, fighting, lying, bitterness, and gossip. [30]They were backbiters, haters of God, insolent, proud braggarts, always thinking of new ways of sinning and continually being disobedient to their parents. [31]They tried to misunderstand, broke their promises, and were heartless—without pity. [32]They were fully aware of God's death penalty for these crimes, yet they went right ahead and did them anyway, and encouraged others to do them, too.

Rom 2:4. Don't you realize how patient he is being with you? Or don't you care? Can't you see that he has been waiting all this time without punishing you, to give you time to turn from your sin? His kindness is meant to lead you to repentance.

Rom 11:25. Yes, it is true that some of the Jews have set themselves against the Gospel now, but this will last only until all of you Gentiles have come to Christ—those of you who will.

1 Cor 1:18. I know very well how foolish it sounds to those who are lost, when they hear that Jesus died to save them. But we who are saved recognize this message as the very power of God. [20]So what about these wise men, these scholars, these brilliant debaters of this world's great affairs? God has made them all look foolish, and shown their wisdom to be useless nonsense. [21]For God in his wisdom saw to it that the world would never find God through human brilliance.

1 Cor 2:8. But the great men of the world have not understood it; if they had, they never would have crucified the Lord of Glory. [14]But the man who isn't a Christian can't understand and can't accept these thoughts from God, which the Holy Spirit teaches us. They sound foolish to him, because only those who have the Holy Spirit within them can understand what the Holy Spirit means. Others just can't take it in. [15]But the spiritual man has insight into everything, and that bothers and baffles the man of the world, who can't understand him at all.

1 Cor 15:34. For to your shame I say it, some of you are not even Christians at all and have never really known God.

2 Cor 3:14. Not only Moses' face was veiled, but his people's minds and understanding were veiled and blinded too. Even now when the Scripture is read it seems as though Jewish hearts and minds are covered by a thick veil, because they cannot see and understand the real meaning of the Scriptures. For this veil of misunderstanding can be removed only by believing in Christ.

2 Cor 4:3. If the Good News we preach is hidden from anyone, it is hidden from the one who is on the road to eternal death. [4]Satan, who is the god of this evil world, has made him blind, unable to see the glorious light of the Gospel that is shining upon him, or to understand the amazing message we preach about the glory of Christ, who is God. [6]For God, who said, "Let there be light in the darkness," has made us understand that it is the brightness of his glory that is seen in the face of Jesus Christ.

Gal 4:8. Before you Gentiles knew God you were slaves to so-called gods that did not even exist.

Eph 4:17, 18. Let me say this, then, speaking for the Lord: Live no longer as the unsaved do, for they are blinded and confused. Their closed hearts are full of darkness; they are far away from the life of God because they have shut their minds against him, and they cannot understand his ways.

Eph 5:8. For though once your heart was full of darkness, now it is full of light from the Lord, and your behavior should show it!

Col 1:13. For he has rescued us out of the darkness and gloom of Satan's kingdom and brought us into the kingdom of his dear Son.

1 Thess 4:3, 4. For God wants you to be holy and pure, and to keep clear of all sexual sin so that each of you will marry in holiness and honor—[5]not in lustful passion as the heathen do, in their ignorance of God and his ways.

1 Thess 5:4. But, dear brothers, you are not in the dark about these things, and you won't be surprised as by a thief when that day of the Lord comes. [5]For you are all children of the light and of the day, and do not belong to darkness and night. [6]So be on your guard, not asleep like the others. Watch for his return and stay sober. [7]Night is the time for sleep and the time when people get drunk.

2 Thess 1:8. Bringing judgment on those who do not wish to know God, and who refuse to accept his plan to save them through our Lord Jesus Christ.

2 Thess 2:11. So God will allow them to believe lies with all their hearts, [12]and all of them will be justly judged for believing falsehood, refusing the Truth, and enjoying their sins.

2 Tim 3:7. Women of that kind are forever following new teachers, but they never understand the truth. [13]In fact, evil men and false teachers will become worse and worse, deceiving many, they themselves having been deceived by Satan.

Tit 1:16. Such persons claim they know God, but from seeing the way they act, one knows they don't.

Heb 5:11. There is much more I would like to say along these lines, but you don't seem to listen, so it's hard to make you understand. [12]You have been Christians a long time now, and you ought to be teaching others, but instead you have dropped back to the place where you need someone to teach you all over again the very first principles in God's Word. You are like babies who can drink only milk, not old enough for solid food.

1 Pet 1:14. Obey God because you are his children; don't slip back into your old ways—doing evil because you knew no better.

1 Pet 2:9. But you are not like that, for you have been chosen by God himself—you are priests of the King, you are holy and pure, you are God's very own—all this so that you may show to others how God called you out of the darkness into his wonderful light.

2 Pet 1:9. But anyone who fails to go after these additions to faith is blind indeed, or at least very shortsighted, and has forgotten that God delivered him from the old life of sin so that now he can live a strong, good life for the Lord.

2 Pet 3:16. Our wise and beloved brother Paul has talked about these same things in many of his letters. Some of his comments are not easy to understand, and there are people who are deliberately stupid, and always demand some unusual interpretation—they have twisted his letters around to mean something quite different from what he meant, just as they do the other parts of the Scripture—and the result is disaster for them.

1 Jn 1:6. So if we say we are his friends, but go on living in spiritual darkness and sin, we are lying. [8]If we say that we have no sin, we are only fooling ourselves, and refusing to accept the truth.

1 Jn 2:4. Someone may say, "I am a Christian; I am on my way to heaven; I belong to Christ." But if he doesn't do what Christ tells him to, he is a liar. [9]Anyone who says he is walking in the light of Christ but dislikes his fellow man, is still in darkness. [11]For he who dislikes his brother is wandering in spiritual darkness and doesn't know where he is going, for the darkness had made him blind so that he cannot see the way.

1 Jn 3:1. But since most people don't know God, naturally they don't understand that we are his children. [6]So if we stay close to him, obedient to him, we won't be sinning either; but as for those who keep on sinning, they should realize this: They sin because they have never really known him or become his.

1 Jn 4:8. But if a person isn't loving and kind, it shows that he doesn't know God—for God is love.

3 Jn 1:11. Remember that those who do what is right prove that they are God's children; and those who continue in evil prove that they are far from God.

Jude 1:10. But these men mock and curse at anything they do not understand, and, like animals, they do whatever they feel like, thereby ruining their souls.

Rev 3:17. You say, "I am rich, with everything I want; I don't need a thing!" And you don't realize that spiritually you are wretched and miserable and poor and blind and naked.

See *Affliction, Impenitence in; Man, Ignorance of; God, Providence of, Mysterious and Misinterpreted.*

INSTANCES OF. Israelites, Num chapters 16; 17. Moab, 2 Kgs 3:27. Religious leaders, Mt 9:3. See in the printed text above for other instances.

BLOOD Is the life, Gen 9:4; Lev 17:11, 14; 19:16; Deut 12:20–23; Mt 27:8, 24. Forbidden to be used as food, Gen 9:4; Lev 3:17; 7:26, 27; 17:10–14; 19:26; Deut 12:16, 20–23; 15:23; Ezk 33:25; Acts 15:20, 27–29; 21:25. Plague of, Ex 7:17–24; Ps 78:44; 105:29.

SACRIFICIAL. Without shedding of, no forgiveness, Heb 9:22. Sprinkled on altar and people, Ex 24:6–8; Ezk 43:18, 20. Sprinkled on door posts, Ex 12:7–23; Heb 11:28.

Of Sin Offering. Sprinkled seven times in front of the veil, Lev 4:5, 6, 17; on horns and at the base of the altars, Ex 30:10; Lev 4:7, 18, 25, 30; 5:9; 9:9, 12. Of bull for sin offering, put on the horns of the altar, Ex 29:12; Lev 8:15, 16. See *Offerings.*

Of Guilt Offering. Sprinkled on the altar, Lev 7:2. See *Offerings.*

Of Burnt Offering. Sprinkled around and on the altar, Ex 29:16; Lev 1:5, 11, 15; 8:19; Deut 12:26, 27. See *Offerings.* Used for cleansing of leprosy, Lev 14:6, 7, 17, 28, 51, 52. See *Offerings.*

Of Peace Offering. Sprinkled on the altar, Lev 3:2, 7, 8, 13; 9:18. Blood of the ram of consecration put on tip of right ear, thumb, and big toe of, and sprinkled on Aaron and his sons, Ex 29:19–21; Lev 8:23, 24, 30. See *Offerings.*

Of Atonement. Sprinkled on mercy place, Lev 16:14, 15, 18, 19, 27; 17:11. See *Offerings.*

Blood of the Covenant. Ex 24:5–8; Zech 9:11; Mt 26:28; Heb 9:18, 19, 22; 10:29; 13:20, 21. See *Offerings.*

FIGURATIVE. Of victories, Ps 58:10; of destruction, Ezk 35:6; of guilt, Lev 20:9; of judgments, Rev 16:6.

OF SACRIFICES, TYPICAL OF THE ATONING BLOOD OF CHRIST. Heb 9:6. Well, when all was ready the priests went in and out of the first room whenever they wanted to, doing their work. [7]But only the high priest went into the inner room, and then only once a year, all alone, and always with blood which he sprinkled on the mercy seat as an offering to God to cover his own mistakes and sins, and the mistakes and sins of all the people. [8]And the Holy Spirit uses all this to point out to us that under the old system the common people could not go into the Holy of Holies as long as the outer room and the entire system it represents were still in use. [9]This has an important lesson for us today. For under the old system, gifts and sacrifices were offered, but these failed to cleanse the hearts of the people who brought them. [10]For the old system dealt only with certain rituals—what foods to eat and drink, rules for washing themselves, and rules about this and that. The people had to keep these rules to tide them over until Christ came with God's new and better way. [11]He came as High Priest of this better system which we now have. He went into that greater, perfect tabernacle in heaven, not made by men nor part of this world, [12]and once for all took blood into that inner room, the Holy of Holies, and sprinkled it on the mercy seat; but it was not the blood of goats and calves. No, he took his own blood, and with it he, by himself, made sure of our eternal salvation. [13]And if under the old system the blood of bulls and goats and the ashes of young cows could cleanse men's bodies from sin, [14]just think how much more surely the blood of Christ will transform our lives and hearts. His sacrifice frees us from the worry of having to obey the old rules, and makes us want to serve the living God. For by the help of the eternal Holy Spirit, Christ willingly gave himself to God to die for our sins—he being perfect, without a single sin or fault. [15]Christ came with this new agreement so that all who are invited may come and have forever all the wonders God has promised them. For Christ died to rescue them from the penalty of the sins they had committed while still under the old system. [16]Now, if someone dies and leaves a will—a list of things to be given away to certain people when he dies—no one gets anything until it is proved that the person who wrote the will is dead. [17]The will goes into effect only after the death of the person who wrote it. While he is still alive no one can use it to get any of those things he has promised them. [18]That is why blood was sprinkled (as proof of Christ's death) before even the first agreement could go into effect. [19]For after Moses had given the people all of God's laws, he took the blood of calves and goats, along with water, and sprinkled the blood over the book of God's laws and over all the people, using branches of hyssop bushes and scarlet wool to sprinkle with. [20]Then he said, "This is the blood that marks the beginning of the agreement between you and God, the agreement God commanded me to make with you." [21]And in the same way he sprinkled blood on the sacred tent and on whatever instruments were used for worship. [22]In fact we can say that under the old agreement almost everything was cleansed by sprinkling it with blood, and without the shedding of blood there is no forgiveness of sins. [23]That is why the sacred tent down here on earth, and everything in it—all copied from things in heaven—all had to be made pure by Moses in this way, by being sprinkled with the blood of animals. But the real things in heaven, of which these down here are copies, were made pure with far more precious offerings. [24]For Christ has entered into heaven itself, to appear now before God as our Friend. It was not in the earthly place of worship that he did this, for that was merely a copy of the real temple in heaven. [25]Nor has he offered himself again and again, as the high priest down here on earth offers animal blood in the Holy of Holies each year. [26]If that had been necessary, then he would have had to die again and again, ever since the world began. But no! He came once for all, at the end of the age, to put away the power of sin forever by dying for us. [27]And just as it is destined that men die only once, and after that comes judgment, [28]so also Christ died only once as an offering for the sins of many people; and he will come again, but not to deal again with our sins. This time he will come bringing salvation to all those who are eagerly and patiently waiting for him.

OF CHRIST. Mt 26:28. For this is my blood, sealing the New Covenant. It is poured out to forgive the sins of multitudes. Mk 14:24; Lk 22:20.

Jn 6:53. So Jesus said it again, "With all the earnestness I possess I tell you this: Unless you eat the flesh of the Messiah and drink his blood, you cannot have eternal life within you. [54]But anyone who does eat my flesh and drink my blood has eternal life, and I will raise him at the Last Day. [55]For my flesh is the true food, and my blood is the true drink. [56]Everyone who eats my flesh and drinks my blood is in me, and I in him."

Jn 19:34. However, one of the soldiers pierced his side with a spear, and blood and water flowed out.

Acts 20:28. And now beware! Be sure that you feed and shepherd God's flock—his church, purchased with his blood—for the Holy Spirit is holding you responsible as overseers.

Rom 3:24. Yet now God declares us "not guilty" of offending him if we trust in Jesus Christ, who in his kindness freely takes away our sins. [25]For God sent Christ Jesus to take the punishment for our sins and to end all God's anger against us. He used Christ's blood and our faith as the means of saving us from his wrath. In this way he was being entirely fair, even though he did not punish those who sinned in former times. For he was looking forward to the time when Christ would come and take away those sins.

Rom 5:9. And since by his blood he did all this for us as sinners, how much more will he do for us now that he has declared us not guilty? Now he will save us from all of God's wrath to come.

1 Cor 10:16. When we ask the Lord's blessing upon our drinking from the cup of wine at the Lord's Table, this means, doesn't it, that all who drink it are sharing together the blessing of Christ's blood?

1 Cor 11:25. In the same way, he took the cup of wine after supper, saying, "This cup is the new agreement between God and you that has been established and set in motion by my blood. Do this in remembrance of me whenever you drink it."

Eph 1:7. So overflowing is his kindness towards us that he took away all our sins through the blood of his Son, by whom we are saved.

Eph 2:13. But now you belong to Christ Jesus, and though you once were far away from God, now you have been brought very near to him because of what Jesus Christ has done for you with his blood. [16]As parts of the same body, our anger against each other has disappeared, for both of us have been reconciled to God. And so the feud ended at last at the cross.

Col 1:14. Who bought our freedom with his blood and forgave us all our sins. [20]It was through what his Son did that God cleared a path for everything to come to him—all things in heaven and on earth—for Christ's death on the cross has made peace with God for all by his blood.

Heb 9:12. And once for all took blood into that inner room, the Holy of Holies, and sprinkled it on the mercy seat; but it was not the blood of goats and calves. No, he took his own blood, and with it he, by himself, made sure of our eternal salvation. [13]And if under the old system the blood of bulls and goats and the ashes of young cows could cleanse men's bodies from sin, [14]just think how much more surely the blood of Christ will transform our lives and hearts. His sacrifice frees us from the worry of having to obey the old rules, and makes us want to serve the living God. For by the help of the eternal Holy Spirit, Christ willingly gave himself to God to die for our sins—he being perfect, without a single sin or fault.

Heb 10:19. And so, dear brothers, now we may walk right into the very Holy of Holies where God is, because of the blood of Jesus. [20]This is the fresh, new, life-giving way which Christ has opened up for us by tearing the curtain—his human body—to let us into the holy presence of God. [29]Think how much more terrible the punishment will be for those who have trampled underfoot the Son of God and treated his cleansing blood as though it were common and unhallowed, and insulted and outraged the Holy Spirit who brings God's mercy to his people.

Heb 12:24. And to Jesus himself, who has brought us his wonderful new agreement; and to the sprinkled blood which graciously forgives instead of crying out for vengeance as the blood of Abel did.

Heb 13:12. This is why Jesus suffered and died outside the city, where his blood washed our sins away. [20, 21]And now may the God of peace, who brought again from the dead our Lord Jesus, equip you with all you need for doing his will. May he who became the great Shepherd of the sheep by an everlasting agreement between God and you, signed with his blood, produce in you through the power of Christ all that is pleasing to him.

1 Pet 1:2. Dear friends, God the Father chose you long ago and knew you would become his children. And the Holy Spirit has been at work in your hearts, cleansing you with the blood of Jesus Christ and making you to please him. [18]God paid a ransom to save you from the impossible road to heaven which your fathers tried to take, and the ransom he paid was not mere gold or silver, as you very well know. [19]But he paid for you with the precious lifeblood of Christ, the sinless, spotless Lamb of God.

1 Jn 1:7. But if we are living in the light of God's presence, just as Christ does, then we have wonderful fellowship and joy with each other, and the blood of Jesus his Son cleanses us from every sin.

1 Jn 5:6–8. And we know he is, because God said so with a voice from heaven when Jesus was baptized, and again as he was facing death—yes, not only at his baptism but also as he faced death. And the Holy Spirit, forever truthful, says it too. So we have these three witnesses: the voice of the Holy Spirit in our hearts, the voice from heaven at Christ's baptism, and the voice before he died. And they all say the same thing: that Jesus Christ is the Son of God.

Rev 1:5. All praise to him who always loves us and who set us free from our sins by pouring out his lifeblood for us. [6]He has gathered us into his kingdom and made us priests of God his Father. Give to him everlasting glory! He rules forever!

Rev 5:9. They were singing him a new song with these words: "You are worthy to take the scroll and break its seals and open it; for you were slain, and your blood has bought people from every nation as gifts for God."

Rev 7:14. "These are the ones coming out of the Great Tribulation," he said; "they washed their robes and whitened them by the blood of the Lamb."

Rev 12:11. They defeated him by the blood of the Lamb, and by their testimony; for they did not love their lives but laid them down for him.

See *Atonement; Jesus, Mission of, Sufferings of.*

BLOOD, FIELD OF Mt 27:8; Acts 1:19.

BLUE See *Color.*

BLUSHING With shame, Ezra 9:6; Isa 1:29; Jer 6:15; 8:12.

BOAR Ps 80:13. See *Swine.*

BOARD FIGURATIVE. Mt 7:3; Lk 6:41.

BOASTING Prov 20:14; 25:14; 27:1; Isa 10:15; Jer 9:24; Rom 1:30; Jas 3:5; 4:16. Of evil, Ps 52:1.

INSTANCES OF. Goliath, 1 Sam 17. Ben-hadad, 1 Kgs 20:10. Sennacherib, 2 Kgs 18:19; Isa 10:8–15. The disciples, Lk 10:17, with *v.* 20.

SPIRITUAL. Ps 49:6. They trust in their wealth and boast about how rich they are, [7]yet not one of them, though rich as kings, can ransom his own brother from the penalty of sin! For God's forgiveness does not come that way. [8, 9]For a soul is far too precious to be ransomed by mere earthly wealth. There is not enough of it in all the earth to buy eternal life for just one soul, to keep it out of hell.

Ps 52:1. You call yourself a *hero,* do you? You *boast* about this evil deed of yours against God's people.

Ps 94:4. Hear their insolence! See their arrogance! How these men of evil boast!

Rom 3:27. Then what can we boast about doing, to earn our salvation? Nothing at all. Why? Because our acquittal is not based on our good deeds; it is based on what Christ has done and our faith in him. *vs.* 1–31.

Rom 11:17. But some of these branches from Abraham's tree, some of the Jews, have been broken off. And you Gentiles who were branches from, we might say, a wild olive tree, were grafted in. So now you, too, receive the blessing God has promised Abraham and his children, sharing in God's rich nourishment of his own special olive tree. [18]But you must be careful not to brag about being put in to replace the branches that were broken off. Remember that you are important only because you are now a part of God's tree; you are just a branch, not a root. [19]"Well," you may be saying, "those branches were broken off to make room for me so I must be pretty good." [20]Watch out! Remember that those branches, the Jews, were broken off because they didn't believe God, and you are there only because you do. Do not be proud; be humble and grateful—and careful. [21]For if God did not spare the branches he put there in the first place, he won't spare you either.

1 Cor 1:29. So that no one anywhere can ever brag in the presence of God. *vs.* 17–31.

1 Cor 4:6. I have used Apollos and myself as examples to illustrate what I have been saying: that you must not have favorites. You must not be proud of one of God's teachers more than another. [7]What are you so puffed up about? What do you have that God hasn't given you? And if all you have is from God, why act as though you are so

great, and as though you have accomplished something on your own?

2 Cor 10:12. Oh, don't worry, I wouldn't dare say that I am as wonderful as these other men who tell you how good they are! Their trouble is that they are only comparing themselves with each other, and measuring themselves against their own little ideas. What stupidity! [13]But we will not boast of authority we do not have. Our goal is to measure up to God's plan for us, and this plan includes our working there with you. [14]We are not going too far when we claim authority over you, for we were the first to come to you with the Good News concerning Christ. [15]It is not as though we were trying to claim credit for the work someone else has done among you. Instead, we hope that your faith will grow and that, still within the limits set for us, our work among you will be greatly enlarged. [16]After that, we will be able to preach the Good News to other cities that are far beyond you, where no one else is working; then there will be no question about being in someone else's field. [17]As the Scriptures say, "If anyone is going to boast, let him boast about what the Lord has done and not about himself." [18]When someone boasts about himself and how well he has done, it doesn't count for much. But when the Lord commends him, that's different!

Eph 2:8. Because of his kindness you have been saved through trusting Christ. And even trusting is not of yourselves; it too is a gift from God. [9]Salvation is not a reward for the good we have done, so none of us can take any credit for it. [10]It is God himself who has made us what we are and given us new lives from Christ Jesus; and long ages ago he planned that we should spend these lives in helping others.

BOAT See *Ship.*

BOAZ 1. An ancestor of Jesus, Mt 1:5; Lk 3:23–38. History of, Ruth chapters 2–4.

2. One of the bronze pillars of the temple, 1 Kgs 7:16–22; 2 Chron 3:17.

BOCHERU Son of Azel, 1 Chron 8:38; 9:44.

BOCHIM A place west of Jordan, near Gilgal, Judg 2:1, 5.

BODY The material part of man. Created, Gen 1:26, 27; 2:7. Dead, defiled, Num 9:6–10. Dead, restored to life, 2 Kgs 8:5; Jn 11:44. Will decay, Job 19:26. Resurrection of, Isa 26:19; Dan 12:2; 1 Cor 15:12–57. Cast into hell (Gehenna), Mt 5:30. Destroyed in hell (Gehenna), Mt 10:28. Is weak, Mt 26:41. "This is my body," Mt 26:26; 1 Cor 11:24. Light of, is the eye, Lk 11:34. Full of darkness, Lk 11:34. Sin controls, Rom 6:12. Revived, Rom 8:11. Redemption of, Rom 8:23. Presented a living sacrifice, Rom 12:1. Not for gluttony or fornication, 1 Cor 6:13. Home of the Holy Spirit, 1 Cor 6:19. Training the body, 1 Cor 9:27. To be changed, Phil 3:21. Distinguished from soul and spirit, 1 Thess 5:23; Heb 4:12. Dead without the spirit, Jas 2:26.

See *Flesh; Resurrection; Soul; Spirit.*

BODY OF CHRIST See *Church, The True.*

BODYGUARD See *Armor-bearer.*

BOHAN A Reubenite, Josh 15:6; 18:17.

BOIL An inflamed sore or tumor. Plague of Egyptians, Ex 9:9, 10; Deut 28:27, 35; of the Philistines, 1 Sam 5:6, 9; 1 Sam 6:5. Of Hezekiah, healed, 2 Kgs 20:7; Isa 38:21. Of Job, Job 2:7, 8. Levitical ceremonies prescribed for, Lev 13:18–23.

BOILING POT Parable of, Ezk 24:3–5.

BOLDNESS OF THE RIGHTEOUS. Prov 28:1. The wicked flee when no one is chasing them! But the godly are bold as lions!

Eph 3:12. Now we can come fearlessly right into God's presence, assured of his glad welcome when we come with Christ and trust in him.

Heb 4:16. So let us come boldly to the very throne of God and stay there to receive his mercy and to find grace to help us in our times of need.

Heb 10:19. And so, dear brothers, now we may walk right into the very Holy of Holies where God is, because of the blood of Jesus.

Heb 13:6. That is why we can say without any doubt or fear, "The Lord is my Helper and I am not afraid of anything that mere man can do to me."

1 Jn 2:28. And now, my little children, stay in happy fellowship with the Lord so that when he comes you will be sure that all is well, and will not have to be ashamed and shrink back from meeting him.

1 Jn 4:17. And as we live with Christ, our love grows more perfect and complete; so we will not be ashamed and embarrassed at the day of judgment, but can face him with confidence and joy, because he loves us and we love him too.

INSTANCES OF, IN PRAYER. Abraham, Gen 18:22–32; Moses, Ex 33:12–18.

See *Courage.*

BONDAGE End of, prophesied, Isa 10:27. Of physical handicap, Lk 13:16.

See *Captivity; Emancipation; Servant; Slavery.*

BONDSERVANT See *Servant, Bond.*

BONES Vision of the dry, Ezk 37:1–14. None of Christ's broken, Jn 19:36, 37.

BOOK Law of Moses written in, Num 5:23; Deut 17:18; 31:9, 24, 26; 2 Kgs 22:8, 15, 16.

Chronicles of the times kept in: By Jasher, Josh 10:13; 2 Sam 1:17, 18; Samuel, Nathan, and Gad, 1 Sam 10:25; 1 Chron 29:29; Iddo, 2 Chron 12:15; 13:22; Isaiah, 2 Chron 26:22; 32:32. Of the kings of Judah and Israel: Of David, 1 Chron 27:24; Solomon, 1 Kgs 11:41; Jehu, 2 Chron 20:34; of other kings, 2 Chron 16:11; 24:27; 25:26; 27:7; 28:26; 35:27; 36:8; of the kings of Israel, 1 Kgs 14:19; 2 Chron 20:34; 33:18. Other records kept in, Ezra 4:15; 6:1, 2; Esther 6:1; 9:32; Jer 32:12; Acts 19:18, 19.

Prophecies written in, by Jeremiah, Jer 25:13; 30:2; 45:1; Dan 9:2. Other prophecies written in, 2 Chron 33:18, 19. Eating of, Jer 15:16. Of magic, Acts 19:19.

Paul's left at Troas, 2 Tim 4:13.

Sealed, Isa 29:11; Dan 12:4.

Debir was called Kiriath-sepher, which signifies a city of books, Josh 15:15, 16; Judg 1:11, 12.

See *Scroll.*

OF LIFE. Ex 32:32. "Yet now if you will only forgive their sin—and if not, then blot *me* out of the book you have written." [33]And the Lord replied to Moses, "Whoever has sinned against me will be blotted out of my book."

Ps 69:28. Let these men be blotted from the list of the living; do not give them the joys of life with the righteous.

Ps 87:6. When he registers her citizens he will place a checkmark beside the names of those who were born here.

Dan 12:1. At that time Michael, the mighty angelic prince who stands guard over your nation, will stand up (and fight for you in heaven against satanic forces), and there will be a time of anguish for the Jews greater than any previous suffering in Jewish history. And yet every one of your people whose names are written in the Book will endure it.

Lk 10:20. However, the important thing is not that demons obey you, but that your names are registered as citizens of heaven.

Phil 4:3. And I ask you, my true teammate, to help these women, for they worked side by side with me in telling the Good News to others; and they worked with Clement, too, and the rest of my fellow workers whose names are written in the Book of Life.

Rev 3:5. Everyone who conquers will be clothed in white, and I will not erase his name from the Book of Life, but I will announce before my Father and his angels that he is mine.

Rev 13:8. And all mankind—whose names were not written down before the founding of the world in the slain Lamb's Book of Life—worshiped the evil Creature.

Rev 17:8. He was alive but isn't now. And yet, soon he will come up out of the bottomless pit and go to eternal destruction; and the people of earth, whose names have not been written in the Book of Life before the world began, will be dumbfounded at his reappearance after being dead.

Rev 20:12. I saw the dead, great and small, standing before God; and The Books were opened, including the Book of Life. And the dead were judged according to the things written in The Books, each according to the deeds he had done. [15]And if anyone's name was not found recorded in the Book of Life, he was thrown into the Lake of Fire.

Rev 21:27. Nothing evil will be permitted in it—no one immoral or dishonest—but only those whose names are written in the Lamb's Book of Life.

OTHER BOOKS. Ps 56:8. You have seen me tossing and turning through the night. You have collected all my tears and preserved them in your bottle! You have recorded every one in your book.

Ps 139:16. You saw me before I was born and scheduled each day of my life before I began to breathe. Every day was recorded in your Book!

Dan 7:10. Millions of angels ministered to him and hundreds of millions of people stood before him, waiting to be judged. Then the court began its session and The Books were opened.

Mal 3:16. Then those who feared and loved the Lord spoke often of him to each other. And he had a Book of Remembrance drawn up in which he recorded the names of those who feared him and loved to think about him.

See *Word of God.*

BOOTH Made of leaves, Job 27:18; Lam 2:6; Jon 4:5; made for cattle, Gen 33:17; watchmen, Isa 1:8; 24:20. Prescribed for the Israelites to dwell in, during the Feast of Tabernacles, to celebrate their wanderings in the wilderness, Lev 23:40–43; Neh 8:15, 16; Zech 14:16. Tax collection, Mt 9:9; Mk 2:14; Lk 5:27.

BORASHAN A town in Judah, 1 Sam 30:27–31. Perhaps identical with *Ashan,* Josh 15:42.

BORING THE EAR A token of servitude for life, Ex 21:6.

BORN AGAIN The new state of being of individuals who have been made children of God through faith in Jesus Christ, Gal 3:26. By nature men are dead in their sins, Eph 2:1, 5, and cannot see or enter into the kingdom of God, Jn 3:3, 5. They are made new people, 2 Cor 5:17; Eph 2:10, by the will of God, Jn 1:13, through the work of the Holy Spirit, Tit 3:5, with the instrumentality of the Word, Jas 1:18; 1 Pet 1:23, to a living hope and an inheritance, 1 Pet 1:3, 4. The necessity for the new birth is stated by Christ in Jn 3:3–7; the divine means by which it is brought about, in Jas 1:18; 1 Pet 1:23–25; some of its results in 1 Jn 2:29; 3:9; 4:7; 5:1, 4, 18.

See *Regeneration.*

BORROWING Ex 22:14. If a man borrows an animal (or anything else) from a neighbor, and it is injured or killed, and the owner is not there at the time, then the man who borrowed it must pay for it. [15]But if the owner is there, he need not pay; and if it was rented, then he need not pay, because this possibility was included in the original rental fee.

Neh 5:1. About this time there was a great outcry of protest from parents against some of the rich Jews who were profiteering on them. [2, 3, 4]What was happening was that families who ran out of money for food had to sell their children or mortgage their fields, vineyards, and homes to these rich men; and some couldn't even do that for they already had borrowed to the limit to pay the taxes. [5]"We are their brothers, and our children are just like theirs," the people protested. "Yet we must sell our children into slavery to get enough money to live. We have already sold some of our daughters, and we are helpless to redeem them, for our fields, too, are mortgaged to these men." [6]I was very angry when I heard this; [7]so after thinking about it I spoke out against these rich government officials. "What is this you are doing?" I demanded. "How dare you demand a mortgage as a condition for helping another Israelite?" Then I called a public trial to deal with them. [8]At the trial I shouted at them, "The rest of us are doing all we can to *help* our Jewish brothers who have returned from exile as slaves in distant lands, but you are forcing them right back into slavery again. How often must we redeem them?" And they had nothing to say in their own defense. [9]Then I pressed further. "What you are doing is very evil," I exclaimed. "Should you not walk in the fear of our God? Don't we have enough enemies among the nations around us who are trying to destroy us? [10]The rest of us are lending money and grain to our fellow-Jews without any interest. I beg you, gentlemen, stop this business of usury. [11]Restore their fields, vineyards, oliveyards, and homes to them this very day and drop your claims against them." [12]So they agreed to do it and said that they would assist their brothers without requiring them to mortgage their lands and sell them their children. Then I summoned the priests and made these men formally vow to carry out their promises. [13]And I invoked the curse of God upon any of them who refused. "May God destroy your homes and livelihood if you fail to keep this promise," I declared. And all the people shouted, "Amen," and praised the Lord. And the rich men did as they promised.

Ps 37:21. Evil men borrow and "cannot pay it back"! But the good man returns what he owes with some extra besides.

Prov 22:7. Just as the rich rule the poor, so the borrower is servant to the lender.

Mt 5:42. Give to those who ask, and don't turn away from those who want to borrow.

Rom 13:8. Pay all your debts except the debt of love for others—never finish paying that! For if you love them, you will be obeying all of God's laws, fulfilling all his requirements.

See *Lending; Interest.*

INSTANCES OF. Israelites from the Egyptians, Ex 3:22; 11:2; 12:35.

Borrowing trouble, see *Trouble, Borrowing.*

BOTANICAL GARDEN (Park, probably), Eccl 2:4–6; with 1 Kgs 4:33; 10:22.

BOTANY Laws of nature in the vegetable kingdom uniform in action, Mt 7:16–18, 20; Lk 6:43, 44; 1 Cor 15:36–38; Gal 6:7. Lily, beauty of, Mt 6:28, 29.

2 Cor 9:6. But remember this—if you give little, you will get little. A farmer who plants just a few seeds will get only a small crop, but if he plants much, he will reap much.

See *Acacia; Algum; Almond; Aloes; Apple; Ash; Balm; Barley; Bean; Broom Bush; Calamus; Cane; Cassia; Cedar; Cinnamon; Coriander; Corn; Cucumber; Cummin; Cypress; Dill; Date; Ebony; Emmer; Fig; Fir; Flax; Frankincense; Galbanum; Gall; Garlic; Gourd; Grass; Hyssop; Leek; Lentil; Lily; Mandrake; Melon; Mint; Mulberry; Mustard; Myrrh; Myrtle; Nard; Nettle; Nut; Oak; Olive; Onion; Palm; Pine; Plane; Pomegranate; Poplar; Reed; Rose; Saffron; Spelt; Stacte; Sycamore; Tare; Terebinth; Thistle; Thorn; Vine; Wheat; Willow; Wormwood.*

BOTTLE Job 10:10; Jer 48:38. Of wine, 1 Sam 1:14; 10:3; Jer 13:12. Use as a lachrymatory, Ps 56:8. Of perfume, Eccl 10:1; Mt 26:7.

See *Canteen; Dish; Jar; Pitcher; Wine, kept in skins.*

BOUNDARY Markers, not to be moved, Deut 19:14; 27:17; Prov 22:28; 23:10, 11; Hos 5:10.

See *Landmark.*

BOW A weapon. Made of bronze, 2 Sam 22:35; Ps 18:34; of wood, Ezk 39:3. Used in war, Lam 2:4; Ezk 39:3. Used in hunting, see *Archery; Arrow.*

FIGURATIVE. Job 16:13; Lam 3:12; Hab 3:9; Rev 6:2.

BOWELS Amasa's gushed out, 2 Sam 20:8–10. Diseased, 2 Chron 21:15–20. Judas's spilled out, Acts 1:18.

FIGURATIVE. See *Heart; Love.*

BOWING In worship, see *Worship, Attitudes in.*

BOWL Made of gold: For the Tabernacle, Ex 25:29; 37:15, 16; Temple, 1 Kgs 7:50; 1 Chron 28:17; 2 Chron 4:8; Ezra 1:9, 10; 8:27; of silver, Num 4:7; 7:13, 84–86. Stamped "These are Holy Property," Zech 14:20, 21.

See *Basin.*

FIGURATIVE. Eccl 12:6.

BOX Mk 4:21.

BOXING FIGURATIVE. 1 Cor 9:26.

BOX TREE Isa 60:13.

BOZEZ A rock near Gibe-ah, 1 Sam 14:4.

BOZKATH A city of Judah, Josh 15:37–44; 2 Kgs 22:1.

BOZRAH 1. A city of Edom, Gen 36:31–39; 1 Chron 1:44. Prophecies concerning, Isa 63:1; Jer 49:13, 22; Amos 1:12.

2. A town of Moab, Jer 48:24.

BRACELET Present of, Gen 24:22. Worn by women, Gen 24:29, 30, 47; Isa 3:19. Dedicated to the Tabernacle, Num 31:50. Taken as booty, Num 31:50; 2 Sam 1:10.

FIGURATIVE. Ezk 16:11; 23:42.

BRAGGING See *Boasting.*

BRAMBLE Gen 50:10; Lk 6:44.

See *Thorn.*

BRANCH FIGURATIVE. Prov 11:28; Hos 14:6; Jn 15:2–5. Pruning of, Isa 18:5; Dan 4:14; Jn 15:6; Rom 11:17, 21. Fruitless, cut off, Jn 15:2, 6. Of the Lord, meaning God's people, Isa 4:2–4. A title of Christ, Isa 4:2–4; 11:1; Jer 23:5, 6; Zech 3:8; 6:12. Symbolic name of Christ, Zech 6:12.

BRASS Or more probably bronze (copper alloy). Smelted, Job 28:2; Ezk 22:18–20. A mineral of Canaan, Deut 8:9; Josh 22:8; of Syria, 2 Sam 8:8. Tyrians traded in, Ezk 27:13. Abundance of, for the Temple, 1 Kgs 7:41–46; 1 Chron 22:14. Articles made of: altar, utensils, and other articles of the Tabernacle and Temple, Ex 38:29; 1 Kgs 7:15–47; Ezra 8:27; cymbals, 1 Chron 15:19; armor, 1 Sam 17:4–7; 2 Chron 12:10; bows, see *Bows;* chains, Judg 16:21; gates, 1 Kgs 4:8–19; Ps 107:16; Isa 45:2; idols, Dan 5:4; Rev 9:20; mirrors, Ex 38:8.

Workers in: Tubal-cain, Gen 4:22; Hiram, 1 Kgs 7:13; Alexander, 2 Tim 4:14.

See *Bronze; Copper; Molding.*

FIGURATIVE. Lev 26:19; Deut 33:25; Isa 48:4;

Jer 1:18; Ezk 1:7; Dan 2:32, 39; 7:19; 10:5, 6; Zech 6: 1; Rev 1:15.

BRAVERY See *Boldness; Courage.*

BRAZEN SERPENT See *Bronze Serpent.*

BRAZIER A utensil used for warming houses, Jer 36:22.

BREAD

Kinds of. Bread of adversity, Isa 30:20; Hos 9:4; leavened, Lev 7:13; 23:17; Hos 7:4; Mt 13:33; unleavened, Gen 19:3; Ex 29:2; Lev 8:1; Judg 6:19; 1 Sam 28:24.

Made of wheat flour, Ex 29:2, 23; 1 Kgs 4:22; 5: 11; manna, Num 11:8; barley, Judg 7:12, 13.

How prepared. Mixed with oil, Ex 29:2, 23; honey, Ex 16:31; with leaven, or ferment, see *Leavened,* in paragraph above, also see *Yeast.* Kneaded, Gen 18:6; Ex 8:3, 4; 12:34; 1 Sam 28:24; 2 Sam 13: 8; Jer 7:18; Hos 7:4. Made into loaves, 1 Sam 10:3; 17:17; 25:18; 2 Sam 6:19; 1 Kgs 14:3; 17:13; Mk 8:14; cakes, Gen 18:6; wafers, Ex 29:2, 23; Lev 8:26; Num 6:15. Baked in ovens, Ex 8:3; Lev 2:4; 7:9; 26:26; Hos 7:4; in pans, Lev 2:5, 7; 2 Sam 13:6–9; on coals, 1 Kgs 19:6; Isa 44:19; Jn 21:9.

Made by men, Gen 40:2; women, 1 Sam 8:13; Jer 7:18. Traffic in, Jer 37:21; Mk 6:37.

Sacrificed. Lev 2:12; 7:12; 21:6, 22; 23:13; Deut 16: 3; 1 Sam 2:36; 2 Kgs 23:9. By idolaters, Jer 7:18; 44: 19.

See *Bread of the Presence; Manna; Offerings.*

FIGURATIVE. Isa 55:2; 1 Cor 5:8; 10:17. Christ, Jn 6:32–35.

Symbolical. Of the body of Christ, Mt 26:26; Acts 2:42; 1 Cor 11:23, 24.

BREAD OF THE PRESENCE Ordinance concerning, Lev 24:5–9. Required to be kept before the Lord continually, Ex 25:30; 2 Chron 2: 4. Provided by a yearly *per capita* tax, Neh 10:32, 33. Prepared by the Levites, 1 Chron 9:32; 23:29. Unlawfully eaten by David, 1 Sam 21:6; Mt 12:3, 4; Mk 2:25, 26; Lk 6:3, 4. Placed on a table, Ex 40: 22, 23. See *Table of,* below.

TABLE OF. Heb 9:2. Ordinances concerning, Ex 25:23–28; 37:10–16. Its situation in the Tabernacle, Ex 26:35; 40:22. Utensils of, Ex 25:29, 30; 37:15, 16; Num 4:7. Consecration of, Ex 30:26, 27, 29. How removed, Num 4:7, 15. For the Temple, 1 Kgs 7:48; 2 Chron 4:19.

BREASTPLATE 1. Called also *chestpiece.* For high priest, Ex 25:1–7. Directions for the making of, Ex 28:15–30. Made by Bezalel, Ex 39:3, 8–21. Freewill offering of materials for, Ex 35:5–9, 27. Worn by Aaron, Ex 29:5; Lev 8:8.

2. Armor for soldiers, 2 Chron 18:33; Rev 9:9, 17, 18.

FIGURATIVE. Eph 6:14. But to do this, you will need the strong belt of truth and the breastplate of God's approval.

BREATH Of life, Gen 2:7; 6:17; Dan 5:23; Acts 17:25. Of God, 2 Sam 22:16; Job 15:30; 33:4; 37: 10; Ps 18:15; 33:6; Isa 30:33.

FIGURATIVE. Ezk 37:9.

BRIARS FIGURATIVE. Isa 5:6; 55:13; Ezk 28:24.

BRIBERY Ex 23:8. Take no bribes, for a bribe makes you unaware of what you clearly see! A bribe hurts the cause of the person who is right. Prov 23:1.

Deut 16:18. Appoint judges and administrative officials for all the cities the Lord your God is giving you. They will administer justice in every part of the land. [19]Never twist justice to benefit a rich man, and never accept bribes. For bribes blind the eyes of the wisest and corrupt their decisions. Ex 18:21; 2 Chron 19:7.

Deut 27:25. "Cursed is he who accepts a bribe to kill an innocent person." And all the people shall reply, "Amen."

1 Sam 8:1. In his old age, Samuel retired and appointed his sons as judges in his place. [3]But they were not like their father, for they were greedy for money. They accepted bribes and were very corrupt in the administration of justice.

Ps 26:9, 10. Don't treat me as a common sinner or murderer who plots against the innocent and demands bribes.

Prov 15:27. Dishonest money brings grief to all the family, but hating bribes brings happiness. Job 17:5.

Prov 17:8. A bribe works like magic. Whoever uses it will prosper! [23]It is wrong to accept a bribe to twist justice.

Prov 18:16. A bribe does wonders; it will bring you before men of importance!

Prov 21:14. An angry man is silenced by giving him a gift!

Prov 28:21. Giving preferred treatment to rich people is a clear case of selling one's soul for a piece of bread. Prov 22:16.

Prov 29:4. A just king gives stability to his nation, but one who demands bribes destroys it.

Eccl 7:7. The wise man is turned into a fool by a bribe; it destroys his understanding.

Isa 1:23. Your leaders are rebels, companions of thieves; all of them take bribes and won't defend the widows and orphans. Hab 1:4.

Isa 5:22. Woe to those who are "heroes" when it comes to drinking, and boast about the liquor they can hold. [23]They take bribes to pervert justice, letting the wicked go free and putting innocent men in jail.

Isa 33:15. I will tell you who can live here: All who are honest and fair, who reject making profit by fraud, who hold back their hands from taking bribes, who refuse to listen to those who plot murder, who shut their eyes to all enticement to do wrong. [16]Such as these shall dwell on high. The rocks of the mountains will be their fortress of safety; food will be supplied to them and they will have all the water they need.

Ezk 13:19. For the sake of a few paltry handfuls of barley or a piece of bread will you turn away my people from me? You have led those to death who should not die! And you have promised life to those who should not live, by lying to my people—and how they love it!

Ezk 22:12. Hired murderers, loan racketeers and

extortioners are everywhere. You never even think of me and my commands, the Lord God says. [13]But now I snap my fingers and call a halt to your dishonest gain and bloodshed.

Amos 2:6. The Lord says, "The people of Israel have sinned again and again, and I will not forget it. I will not leave them unpunished any more. For they have perverted justice by accepting bribes, and sold into slavery the poor who can't repay their debts; they trade them for a pair of shoes."

Amos 5:12. For many and great are your sins. I know them all so well. You are the enemies of everything good; you take bribes; you refuse justice to the poor.

Mic 7:3. They go at their evil deeds with both hands, and how skilled they are in using them! The governor and judge alike demand bribes. The rich man pays them off and tells them whom to ruin. Justice is twisted between them. Ps 58:1.

INSTANCES OF. Delilah, Judg 16:5. Samuel's sons, see above. The false prophet, Shemaiah, Neh 6:10–13. Ben-hadad, 1 Kgs 15:19. Haman bribes Ahasuerus to destroy the Jews, Esther 3:9. Chief priests bribe Judas, Mt 26:15; 27:3–9; Mk 14:11; Lk 22:5. Soldiers bribed to say that the disciples stole the body of Jesus, Mt 28:12–15. Felix seeks a bribe from Paul, Acts 24:26.

BRICK Ezk 4:1. Used in building: Babel, Gen 11:3, 4; cities in Egypt, Ex 1:11, 13, 14; vats, Ezk 46: 23. Made by Israelites, Ex 5:7–19; 2 Sam 12:31; Nah 3:14.

BRICK KILN Captives worked in, 2 Sam 12: 31.

BRIDE Ornaments of, Isa 49:18; 61:10; Jer 2: 32. Presents to, Gen 24:53. Maids of, Gen 24:59, 61; 29:24, 29. Solomon's, Song 4:8; 5:1.

FIGURATIVE. Ps 45:10–17; Isa 62:4; Jer 2:2; Ezk 16:8–14; Rev 19:7, 8; 21:2, 9; 22:17.

See *Church, The True.*

BRIDEGROOM Clothing of, Isa 61:10. Exempt from military duty, Deut 24:5. Companions of, Judg 14:11. Joy with, Mt 9:15; Mk 2:19, 20; Lk 5:34, 35.

Parable of, Mt 25:1–13. Song of, Song 4:7–16.

FIGURATIVE. Ps 19:5; Isa 62:5; Ezk 16:8–14.

BRIDLE Prov 26:3; Rev 14:20.

FIGURATIVE. 2 Kgs 19:28; Isa 30:28.

See *Bit.*

BRIMSTONE Fire and, rained on Sodom, Gen 19:24; Lk 17:29.

FIGURATIVE. Job 18:15; Ps 11:6; Ezk 38:22.

See *Alkali; Sulphur; Volcano.*

BRONZE Bows of, 2 Sam 22:35; Ps 18:34.

See *Brass.*

BRONZE SERPENT Made by Moses for the healing of the Israelites, Num 21:9. Worshiped by Israelites, 2 Kgs 18:4. A symbol of Christ, Jn 3: 14, 15.

BROOK See *River.*

BROOK OF EGYPT See *Egypt, River of.*

BROOM BUSH 1 Kgs 19:4, 5; Ps 120:4.

BROTH Judg 6:19, 20. Symbolical, Ezk 24:5.

See *Stew.*

BROTHEL See *Prostitutes; Prostitution.*

BROTHER Signifies a neighbor, Deut 23:7; Judg 21:6; any Israelite, Jer 34:9; Obd 1:10; mankind, Mt 18:35; 1 Jn 3:15; companion, 2 Sam 1:26; 1 Kgs 13:30; 20:33. Love of, Prov 17:17; 18:24; Song 8:1. Reuben's love for Joseph, Gen 37:21, 22; Joseph's, for his brothers, Gen 43:30–34; 45:1–5; 50: 19–25.

A fraternal epithet, especially among Christians. Instituted by Christ, Mt 12:50; 25:40; Heb 2:11, 12. Used by disciples, Acts 9:17; 21:20; Rom 16:23; 2 Cor 2:13; Peter, 1 Pet 2:11. Used among the Israelites, Ex 2:13; Lev 19:17; Acts 7:23.

Brother's widow, law concerning Levirate marriage of, Deut 25:5–10; Mt 22:24; Mk 12:19; Lk 20: 28.

"The Twin Brothers," a ship of Alexandria, Acts 28:11.

See *Relative.*

BROTHERLY LOVE See *Brother; Charitableness; Fellowship; Fraternity; Friendship; Love.*

BUBASTIS A city in lower Egypt. Prophesied against by Ezekiel, Ezk 30:17.

BUCKET Ex 27:3; Isa 40:15; Amos 6:6; Jn 4: 11.

BUCKLER See *Shield.*

BUILDER Of the Tabernacle, see *Bezalel; Master Workman.*

FIGURATIVE. Ps 188:22; Mt 21:42; Acts 4:11; 1 Pet 2:7; Heb 11:10.

See *Carpentry.*

BUKKI 1. Son of Abishua, 1 Chron 6:4–15, 50–53; Ezra 7:4.

2. A leader of Dan, Num 34:16–28.

BUKKIAH A Levite, 1 Chron 25:4, 5, 9–31.

BUL See *Calendar.*

BULL, BULLOCK, OR OX Uses of: For sacrifice, Ex 29:3, 10–14, 36; Lev 4:3, 14; Num 7:87, 88; 28:11–31; 29; blood of, in sacrifice, Heb 9:13; 10: 4; plowing, 1 Kgs 19:19, 20; Jer 31:18; treading out grain, Deut 25:4; with wagons, Num 7:3–8; 2 Sam 6:3–6.

Laws concerning: Trepass by, Ex 21:28–36; theft of, Ex 22:1–10; rest for, Ex 23:12; not to be muzzled, when treading grain, Deut 25:4; 1 Cor 9:9; 1 Tim 5: 18; not to be harnessed with a donkey, Deut 22:10.

Twelve bronze, under the bronze laver in Solomon's Temple, 1 Kgs 7:25; 2 Chron 4:4; Jer 52:20.

See *Cattle; Offerings; Stable.*

Symbolical. Ezk 1:10; Rev 4:7.

BUNAH Son of Jerahmeel, 1 Chron 2:25.

BUNNI 1. A Levite, a teacher with Ezra, Neh 9:4.

2. Ancestor of Shemaiah, Neh 11:15–17.

3. A leader who signed the covenant with Nehemiah, Neh 10:14–27.

BURGLARY See *Theft.*

BURIAL Rites of, Jer 34:5. Soon after death, Deut 21:23; Josh 8:29; Jn 19:38–42; Acts 5:9, 10. With spices, 2 Chron 16:14; Mk 16:1; Lk 23:56. Bier used at, 2 Sam 3:31; Lk 7:14. Attended by relatives and friends: Of Jacob, Gen 50:5–9; Abner, 2 Sam 3:31; child of Jeroboam, 1 Kgs 14:13; the son of the widow of Nain, Lk 7:12, 13; Stephen, Acts 8:2.

Lack of, a disgrace, 2 Kgs 9:10; Prov 30:17; Jer 16:4; 22:19; Ezk 39:15. Directions given about, before death, by Jacob, Gen 49:29, 30; Joseph, Gen 50:25. Burial of Gog and his armies requiring seven months, Ezk 39:12, 13.

BURYING PLACES. Bought by Abraham, Gen 23; 25:9, 10. Prepared by Jacob, Gen 50:5; Asa, 2 Chron 16:13, 14; Joseph, Mt 27:60. On hills, Josh 24:33; 2 Kgs 23:16. In valleys, Jer 7:32.

Family, Gen 47:30; 49:29, 30; Acts 7:16. Of kings, 1 Kgs 2:10; 2 Chron 32:33; a place of honor, 2 Chron 24:16, 25; 21:20. For poor and strangers, Jer 26:23; Mt 27:7.

Tombs: Beside houses, 1 Kgs 2:34; in gardens, 2 Kgs 21:18, 26; Jn 19:41; in caves, Gen 23:9; under trees, Deborah's, Gen 35:8; King Saul's, 1 Sam 31:13.

Closed with stones, Mt 27:60, 66; Jn 11:37, 38; 20:1. Sealed, Mt 27:66. Marked with stones, Rachel's, Gen 35:20, and inscriptions, 2 Kgs 23:17. Decorated, Mt 23:27, 29, 30. Demoniacs lived in, Mt 8:28. Any who touched, were defiled, Num 19:16, 18; Isa 65:4. Refused to the dead, Rev 11:9. Robbed, Jer 8:1.

See *Cremation; Dead, The; Death; Elegy; Grave; Mourning.*

FIGURATIVE. Isa 22:16; Rom 6:4; Col 2:12.

BURNING As a punishment, see *Punishment.*

BURNING BUSH Ex 3:2–5; Acts 7:30.

BURNT OFFERING See *Offerings, Burnt.*

BUSH, BURNING See *Burning Bush.*

BUSHEL 1 Kgs 4:22; 5:11; Ezra 7:22; Lk 16:7.

BUSINESSMAN See *Merchant.*

BUSYBODY Lev 19:16. Don't gossip. Don't falsely accuse your neighbor of some crime, for I am Jehovah.

2 Thess 3:11. Yet we hear that some of you are living in laziness, refusing to work, and wasting your time in gossiping. [12]In the name of the Lord Jesus Christ we appeal to such people—we command them—to quiet down, get to work, and earn their own living.

1 Tim 5:13. Besides, they are likely to be lazy and spend their time gossiping around from house to house, getting into other people's business.

1 Pet 4:15. Don't let me hear of your suffering for murdering or stealing or making trouble or being a busybody and prying into other people's affairs.

See *Gossip; Speaking, Evil.*

BUTTER 2 Sam 17:29; Job 20:17; Isa 7:15, 22. Made by churning, Prov 30:33.

BUZ 1. Son of Nahor, Gen 22:20–23.

2. Father of Jahdo, 1 Chron 5:14.

3. A place, Jer 25:23.

BUZI Father of Ezekiel, Ezk 1:1–3.

BUZZARD Forbidden as food, Deut 14:11–18.

C

CABBON A place in Judah, Josh 15:37–44.

CABINET Heads of departments in government. David's, 2 Sam 8:15–18; 15:12; 20:23–26; 1 Chron 27:32–34; Solomon's, 1 Kgs 4:1–7; Hezekiah's, Isa 36:3; Ar-ta-xerxes,' Ezra 7:14; Ahasuerus,' Esther 1:5.

See *Counselor.*

CAESAR 1. Augustus, Lk 2:1.

2. Tiberius, Lk 3:1.

3. Claudius, Acts 11:28.

4. Nero, Phil 4:22.

CAESAREA A seaport in Palestine. Home of Philip, Acts 8:40; 21:8; Cornelius, the army captain, Acts 10:1, 24; Herod, Acts 12:19–23; Felix, Acts 23:23, 24. Paul taken to, by the disciples to save him from his enemies, Acts 9:30; by Roman soldiers to be tried by Felix, Acts 23:23–35.

CAESAREA PHILIPPI A city in the north of Palestine; visited by Jesus, Mt 16:13; Mk 8:27.

CAIAPHAS High priest, Lk 3:2; son-in-law of Annas, Jn 18:13. Prophesies concerning Jesus, Jn 11:49–51; 18:14. Jesus tried before, Mt 26:2, 3, 57, 63–66; Jn 18:24, 28. Peter and other disciples accused before, Acts 4:1–22.

CAIN Son of Adam, Gen 4:1. Jealousy and crime of, Gen 4:3–15; Heb 11:4; 1 Jn 3:12; Jude 1:11. Settle in the land of Nod, Gen 4:16. Children and descendants of, Gen 4:17, 18.

CAINAN 1. Called also *Kenan.* Son of Enosh, Gen 5:9–15; 1 Chron 1:1–4; Lk 3:23–38.

2. Son of Arphaxad, Lk 3:23–38.

CALAH An ancient city of Assyria, Gen 10:11, 12.

CALAMUS A sweet cane of Palestine, Song 4:13, 14; Ezk 27:19. An ingredient of the holy ointment, Ex 30:22, 23. Commerce in, Ezk 27:19.

CALCOL Son of Mahol, 1 Kgs 4:31; 1 Chron 2:6.

CALDRON FIGURATIVE. Ezk 11:3–11.

CALEB One of the two survivors of the Israelites permitted to enter the land of promise, Num 14:30, 36–38; 26:63–65; 32:10–13; Deut 1:34–36; Josh 14:6–15. Sent to Canaan as a spy, Num 13:3–15. Brings favorable report, Num 13:26–30; 14:6–9. Assists in dividing Canaan, Num 34:16–28. Life of, miraculously saved, Num 14:10–12. Leader of the Israelites after Joshua's death, Judg 1:11, 12. Age of, Josh 14:7–10. Inheritance of, Josh 14:6–15; 15:13–16. Descendants of, 1 Chron 4:15.

See *Chelubai.*

CALENDAR Ancient use of, Gen 7:10–12; 8:5. Twelve months made up a year, 1 Chron 27:1–15.

1. Abib (March-April). Called also *Nisan.* The Jewish calendar began with, Ex 12:2; 13:4, 5; Deut 16:1. Passover instituted and celebrated in, Ex 12:1–28; 23:15. Israelites left Egypt in, Ex 13:4, 5. Tabernacle set up in, Ex 40:2, 17. Israelites arrive at Zin in, Num 20:1. Cross Jordan in, Josh 4:19. Jordan overflows in, 1 Chron 12:15. Decree issued to put the Jews to death, Esther 3:12. The death of Jesus in, Mt 26; 27.

2. Zif (April-May). Israel numbered in, Num 1:1, 17–19. Passover to be observed in, by the defiled and others who could not observe it in the first month, Num 9:10, 11. Israel left the wilderness of Zin in, Num 10:11. Temple begun in, 1 Kgs 6:1; 2 Chron 3:2. An irregular passover celebrated in, 2 Chron 30:1–27. Rebuilding of the temple begun in, Ezra 3:8.

3. Sivan (May-June). Asa renews the covenant of himself and people in, 2 Chron 15:10.

4. Tammuz (June-July). Jerusalem taken by Nebuchadnezzar in, Jer 39:2; 52:6, 7.

5. Ab (July-August). Aaron died on the first day of, Num 33:38, 39. Temple destroyed in, 2 Kgs 25:8–10; Jer 1:3; 52:12–30. Ezra arrived at Jerusalem in, Ezra 7:7–9.

6. Elul (August-September). Wall of Jerusalem finished in, Neh 6:15. Rebuilding of Temple begun in, Hag 1:14, 15.

7. Ethanim (September-October). Feasts held in, Lev 23:23–43; 1 Kgs 8:2; Neh 8:13–15. Jubilee proclaimed in, Lev 25:9. Solomon's temple dedicated in, 1 Kgs 8:2. Altar rebuilt and offerings renewed in, Ezra 3:1, 2, 6.

8. Bul (October-November). The temple finished in, 1 Kgs 6:38. Jeroboam's idolatrous feast in, 1 Kgs 12:32, 33.

9. Kislev (November-December), Ezra 10:9; Jer 36:9, 22; Hag 2:18, 19; Zech 7:1.

10. Tebeth (December-January). Esther becomes queen, Esther 2:16. Nebuchadnezzar besieges Jerusalem in, Jer 52:4.

11. Sebat (January-February). Zechariah's vision, Zech 1:7. Moses probably died in, Deut 1:1–5.

12. Adar (February-March). Jews to be exterminated in, Esther 3:7. Second temple finished in, Ezra 6:15. Feast of Purim in, Esther 9:1–26.

Months in prophecy, Rev 11:2.

CALF Offered in sacrifice, Mic 6:6. Golden, made by Aaron, Ex 32; Deut 9:16; Neh 9:18; Ps 106:19; Acts 7:41.

Idols of, set up in Bethel and Dan by Jeroboam, 1 Kgs 12:28–33; 2 Kgs 10:29. Worshiped by Jehu, 2 Kgs 10:29. Prophecies against the golden calves at Bethel, 1 Kgs 13:1–5, 32; Jer 48:13; Hos 8:5, 6; 10:5, 6, 15; 13:2; Amos 3:14; 4:4; 8:14.

CALKERS Ezk 27:9.

CALL, PERSONAL By Christ, Isa 55:5; Rom 1:6, 7; by his Spirit, Rev 22:17; by his works, Ps 19:2–4; Rom 1:20; by his ministers, Jer 35:15; 2 Cor 5:20; by his gospel, 2 Thess 2:14. Is from darkness to light, 1 Pet 2:9. Addressed to all, Isa 45:22. Most reject, Prov 1:24. Effectual to saints, Ps 110:3; Acts 13:48; 1 Cor 1:24. Does not appear wise to the world, 1 Cor 1:26.

To saints, is of love, Gal 1:6; 2 Tim 1:9; according to the purpose of God, Rom 8:28; 9:10–13, 23, 24; never withdrawn, Rom 11:29; holy, 2 Tim 1:9; heavenly, Heb 3:1; to fellowship with Christ, 1 Cor 1:9; to holiness, 1 Thess 4:7; to a prize, Phil 3:14; to liberty, Gal 5:13; to peace, 1 Cor 7:15; Col 3:15; to glory and virtue, 2 Pet 1:3; to the eternal glory of Christ, 2 Thess 2:14; 1 Pet 5:10; to eternal life, 1 Tim 6:12.

Partakers of, justified, Rom 8:30; live worthy of, Eph 4:1; 2 Thess 1:11; blessedness of receiving, Rev 19:9; is to be made sure, 2 Pet 1:10; praise God for, 1 Pet 2:9; illustrated, Prov 8:1–5; Mt 23:3–9.

Rejection of, leads to judicial blindness, Isa 6:9, 10, with Acts 28:24–27; Rom 11:8–10; delusion, Isa 66:4; 2 Thess 2:10, 11; withdrawal of the means of grace, Jer 26:4–6; Acts 13:46; 18:6; Rev 2:5; temporal judgments, Isa 28:12; Jer 6:16, 18, 19; 35:17; Zech 7:12–14; rejection by God, Prov 1:24–32; Jer 6:18–20; condemnation, Jn 12:48; Heb 2:1–3; 12:25; destruction, Prov 29:1; Mt 22:3–7.

TO VARIOUS INDIVIDUALS.

Of Abraham. Gen 12:1. After the death of Abram's father, God told him, "Leave your own country behind you, and your own people, and go to the land I will guide you to. [2]If you do, I will cause you to become the father of a great nation; I will bless you and make your name famous, and you will be a blessing to many others. [3]I will bless those who bless you and curse those who curse you; and the entire world will be blessed because of you."

Isa 51:2. Yes, think about your ancestors Abraham and Sarah, from whom you came. You worry at being so small and few, but Abraham was only *one* when I called him. But when I blessed him, he became a great nation.

Heb 11:8. Abraham trusted God, and when God told him to leave home and go far away to another land which he promised to give him, Abraham obeyed. Away he went, not even knowing where he was going.

Moses. Ex 3:2. Suddenly the Angel of Jehovah appeared to him as a flame of fire in a bush. When Moses saw that the bush was on fire and that it didn't burn up, [3, 4]he went over to investigate. Then God called out to him, "Moses! Moses!" "Who is it?" Moses asked. [10]"Now I am going to send you to Pharaoh, to demand that he let you lead my people out of Egypt."

Ex 4:1. But Moses said, "They won't believe me! They won't do what *I* tell them to. They'll say, 'Jehovah never appeared to you!' " [2]"What do you have there in your hand?" the Lord asked him. And he replied, "A shepherd's rod." [3]"Throw it down on the ground," the Lord told him. So he threw it down—and it became a serpent, and Moses ran from it! [4]Then the Lord told him, "Grab it by the tail!" He did, and it became a rod in his hand again! [5]"Do that and they will believe you!" the Lord told him. "Then they will realize that Jehovah, the God of their ancestors Abraham, Isaac, and Jacob, has really appeared to you. [6]Now reach your hand inside your robe, next to your chest." And when he did, and took it out again, it was white with leprosy! [7]"Now put it in again," Jehovah said. And when he did, and took it out again, it was normal, just as before! [8]"If they don't believe the first miracle, they will the second," the Lord said, [9]"and if they don't accept you after these two signs, then take water from the Nile River and pour it upon the dry land, and it will turn to blood." [10]But Moses pleaded, "O Lord, I'm just not a good speaker. I never have been, and I'm not now, even after you have spoken to me, for I have a speech impediment." [11]"Who makes mouths?" Jehovah asked him. "Isn't it I, the Lord? Who makes a man so that he can speak or not speak, see or not see, hear or not hear? [12]Now go ahead and do as I tell you, for I will help you to speak well, and I will tell you what to say." [13]But Moses said, "Lord, please! Send someone else." [14]Then the Lord became angry. "All right," he said, "your brother Aaron is a good speaker. And he is coming here to look for you, and will be very happy when he finds you. [15]So I will tell you what to tell him, and I will help both of you to speak well, and I will tell you what to do. [16]He will be your spokesman to the people. And you will be as God to him, telling him what to say."

Ps 105:26. But God sent Moses as his representative, and Aaron with him.

Acts 7:34. "I have seen the anguish of my people in Egypt and have heard their cries. I have come down to deliver them. Come, I will send you to Egypt." [35]And so God sent back the same man his people had previously rejected by demanding, "Who made *you* a ruler and judge over us?" Moses was sent to be their ruler and savior.

Aaron and his Sons. Ex 4:14–16, see above, and Ps 105:26.

Ex 28:1. Consecrate Aaron your brother, and his

sons Nadab, Abihu, Eleazer, and Ithamar, to be priests, to minister to me.

Heb 5:4. Another thing to remember is that no one can be a high priest just because he wants to be. He has to be called by God for this work in the same way God chose Aaron.

Joshua. Num 27:18. The Lord replied, "Go and get Joshua (son of Nun), who has the Spirit in him, 19and take him to Eleazar the priest, and as all the people watch, charge him with the responsibility of leading the people." 22So Moses did as Jehovah commanded, and took Joshua to Eleazar the priest. As the people watched, 23Moses laid his hands upon him and dedicated him to his responsibilities, as the Lord had commanded.

Deut 31:14. Then the Lord said to Moses, "The time has come when you must die. Summon Joshua and come into the Tabernacle where I can give him his instructions." So Moses and Joshua came and stood before the Lord.

23. Then he charged Joshua (son of Nun) to be strong and courageous, and said to him, "You must bring the people of Israel into the land the Lord promised them; for the Lord says, 'I will be with you.' "

Josh 1:1. After the death of Moses, the Lord's disciple, God spoke to Moses' assistant, whose name was Joshua (the son of Nun), and said to him, 2"Now that my disciple is dead, [you are the new leader of Israel]. Lead my people across the Jordan River into the Promised Land. 3I say to you what I said to Moses: 'Wherever you go will be part of the land of Israel—4all the way from Negeb desert in the south to the Lebanon mountains in the north, and from the Mediterranean Sea in the west to the Euphrates River in the east, including all the land of the Hittites.' 5No one will be able to oppose you as long as you live, for I will be with you just as I was with Moses; I will not abandon you or fail to help you. 6Be strong and brave, for you will be a successful leader of my people; and they shall conquer all the land I promised to their ancestors. 7You need only to be strong and courageous and to obey to the letter every law Moses gave you, for if you are careful to obey every one of them you will be successful in everything you do. 8Constantly remind the people about these laws, and you yourself must think about them every day and every night so that you will be sure to obey all of them. For only then will you succeed. 9Yes, be bold and strong! Banish fear and doubt! For remember, the Lord your God is with you wherever you go."

Gideon. Judg 6:11. But one day the Angel of the Lord came and sat beneath the oak tree at Ophrah, on the farm of Joash the Abiezrite. Joash's son, Gideon, had been threshing wheat by hand in the bottom of a grape press—a pit where grapes were pressed to make wine—for he was hiding from the Midianites. 12The Angel of the Lord appeared to him and said, "Mighty soldier, the Lord is with you!" 13"Stranger," Gideon replied, "if the Lord is with us, why has all this happened to us? And where are all the miracles our ancestors have told us about—such as when God brought them out of Egypt? Now the Lord has thrown us away and has let the Midianites completely ruin us." 14Then the Lord turned to him and said, "I will make you strong! Go and save Israel from the Midianites! I am sending you!" 15But Gideon replied, "Sir, how can I save Israel? My family is the poorest in the whole tribe of Manasseh, and I am the least thought of in the entire family!" 16Whereupon the Lord said to him, "But I, Jehovah, will be with you! And you shall quickly destroy the Midianite hordes!"

Samuel. 1 Sam 3:4, 5. The Lord called out, "Samuel! Samuel!" "Yes?" Samuel replied. "What is it?" He jumped up and ran to Eli. "Here I am. What do you want?" he asked. "I didn't call you," Eli said. "Go on back to bed." So he did. 6Then the Lord called again, "Samuel!" And again Samuel jumped up and ran to Eli. "Yes?" he asked. "What do you need?" "No, I didn't call you, my son," Eli said. "Go on back to bed." 7(Samuel had never had a message from Jehovah before.) 8So now the Lord called the third time, and once more Samuel jumped up and ran to Eli. "Yes?" he asked. "What do you need?" Then Eli realized it was the Lord who had spoken to the child. 9So he said to Samuel, "Go and lie down again, and if he calls again, say, 'Yes, Lord, I'm listening.' " So Samuel went back to bed. 10And the Lord came and called as before, "Samuel! Samuel!" And Samuel replied, "Yes, I'm listening."

Solomon. 1 Chron 28:6. He has told me, "Your son Solomon shall build my temple; for I have chosen him as my son and I will be his father."

10. So be very careful, for the Lord has chosen you to build his holy temple. Be strong and do as he commands.

Jehu. 2 Kgs 9:6. So Jehu left the others and went into the house, and the young man poured the oil over his head and said, "The Lord God of Israel says, 'I anoint you king of the Lord's people, Israel. 7You are to destroy the family of Ahab; you will avenge the murder of my prophets and of all my other people who were killed by Jezebel.' "

2 Chron 22:7. But this turned out to be a fatal mistake; for God had decided to punish Ahaziah for his alliance with Jehoram. It was during this visit that Ahaziah went out with Jehoram to challenge Jehu (son of Nimshi), whom the Lord had appointed to end the dynasty of Ahab.

Cyrus. Isa 45:1. This is Jehovah's message to Cyrus, God's anointed, whom he has chosen to conquer many lands. God shall empower his right hand and he shall crush the strength of mighty kings. God shall open the gates of Babylon to him; the gates shall not be shut against him any more. 2I will go before you, Cyrus, and level the mountains and smash down the city gates of brass and iron bars. 3And I will give you treasures hidden in the darkness, secret riches; and you will know that I am doing this—I, the Lord, the God of Israel, the one who calls you by your name. 4And why have

I named you for this work? For the sake of Jacob, my servant—Israel, my chosen. I called you by name when you didn't know me.

Amos. Amos 7:14. But Amos replied, "I am not really one of the prophets. I do not come from a family of prophets. I am just a herdsman and fruit picker. [15]But the Lord took me from caring for the flocks and told me, 'Go and prophesy to my people Israel.' "

Apostles. Mt 4:18. One day as he was walking along the beach beside the Lake of Galilee, he saw two brothers—Simon, also called Peter, and Andrew—out in a boat fishing with a net, for they were commercial fishermen. [19]Jesus called out, "Come along with me and I will show you how to fish for the souls of men!" [20]And they left their nets at once and went with him. [Mk 1:16, 17.] [21]A little farther up the beach he saw two other brothers, James and John, sitting in a boat with their father Zebedee, mending their nets; and he called to them to come too. [22]At once they stopped their work and, leaving their father behind, went with him. Mk 3:13–19; Lk 6:13–16.

Mk 2:14. As he was walking up the beach he saw Levi, the son of Alphaeus, sitting at his tax collection booth. "Come with me," Jesus told him. "Come be my disciple." And Levi jumped to his feet and went along. Mt 9:9; Lk 5:27.

Jn 15:16. You didn't choose me! I chose you! I appointed you to go and produce lovely fruit always, so that no matter what you ask from the Father, using my name, he will give it to you.

The Rich Young Man. Mk 10:21. Jesus felt genuine love for this man as he looked at him. "You lack only one thing," he told him; "go and sell all you have and give the money to the poor—and you shall have treasure in heaven—and come, follow me." [22]Then the man's face fell, and he went sadly away, for he was very rich.

Paul. Acts 9:4. He fell to the ground and heard a voice saying to him, "Paul! Paul! Why are you persecuting me?" [5]"Who is speaking, sir?" Paul asked. And the voice replied, "I am Jesus, the one you are persecuting! [6]Now get up and go into the city and await my further instructions."

15. But the Lord said, "Go and do what I say. For Paul is my chosen instrument to take my message to the nations and before kings, as well as to the people of Israel. [16]And I will show him how much he must suffer for me."

Acts 13:2. One day as these men were worshiping and fasting the Holy Spirit said, "Dedicate Barnabas and Paul for a special job I have for them." [3]So after more fasting and prayer, the men laid their hands on them—and sent them on their way.

Rom 1:1. Dear friends in Rome: This letter is from Paul, Jesus Christ's slave, chosen to be a missionary, and sent out to preach God's Good News. 1 Cor 1:1; Gal 1:1, 2; Eph 1:1; Col 1:1; 1 Tim 1:1; 2 Tim 1:1.

All Who Are Called of God. Rom 8:30. And having chosen us, he called us to come to him; and when we came, he declared us "not guilty," filled us with Christ's goodness, gave us right standing with himself, and promised us his glory.

1 Cor 1:2. *To:* The Christians in Corinth, invited by God to be his people and made acceptable to him by Christ Jesus. *And to:* All Christians everywhere—whoever calls upon the name of Jesus Christ, our Lord and theirs.

9. God will surely do this for you, for he always does just what he says, and he is the one who invited you into this wonderful friendship with his Son, even Christ our Lord.

24. But God has opened the eyes of those called to salvation, both Jews and Gentiles, to see that Christ is the mighty power of God to save them; Christ himself is the center of God's wise plan for their salvation.

1 Thess 2:11. We talked to you as a father to his own children—don't you remember?—pleading with you, encouraging you and even demanding [12]that your daily lives should not embarrass God, but bring joy to him who invited you into his kingdom to share his glory.

2 Thess 2:13. But we must forever give thanks to God for you, our brothers loved by the Lord, because God chose from the very first to give you salvation, cleansing you by the work of the Holy Spirit and by your trusting in the Truth. [14]Through us he told you the Good News. Through us he called you to share in the glory of our Lord Jesus Christ.

2 Tim 1:9. It is he who saved us and chose us for his holy work, not because we deserved it but because that was his plan long before the world began—to show his love and kindness to us through Christ.

Heb 3:1. Therefore, dear brothers whom God has set apart for himself—you who are chosen for heaven—I want you to think now about this Jesus who is God's Messenger and the High Priest of our faith. [2]For Jesus was faithful to God who appointed him High Priest, just as Moses also faithfully served in God's house.

7, 8. And since Christ is so much superior, the Holy Spirit warns us to listen to him, to be careful to hear his voice today and not let our hearts become set against him, as the people of Israel did. They steeled themselves against his love and complained against him in the desert while he was testing them.

1 Pet 5:10. After you have suffered a little while, our God, who is full of kindness through Christ, will give you his eternal glory. He personally will come and pick you up, and set you firmly in place, and make you stronger than ever.

2 Pet 1:3. For as you know him better, he will give you, through his great power, everything you need for living a truly good life: he even shares his own glory and his own goodness with us! [10]So, dear brothers, work hard to prove that you really are among those God has called and chosen, and then you will never stumble or fall away.

Jude 1:1. From: Jude, a servant of Jesus Christ, and a brother of James. *To:* Christians everywhere

—beloved of God and chosen by him.

Rev 17:14. Together they will wage war against the Lamb, and the Lamb will conquer them; for he is Lord over all lords, and King of kings, and his people are the called and chosen and faithful ones.

See *Ministers, Call of; Backslider; Seeker.*

CALNEH Called also *Canneh* and *Calno,* a city of Shinar, Gen 10:10; Isa 10:9; Ezk 27:23; Amos 6:2.

CALVARY See *Golgotha.*

CAMEL Herds of, Gen 12:16; 24:35; 30:43; 1 Sam 30:17; 1 Chron 27:30; Job 1:2, 3, 17; Isa 60:6.

Docility of, Gen 24:11. Uses of: For riding, Gen 24:10, 61, 64; 31:17; carrying mail, Esther 8:9, 10, 14; for carrying burdens, Gen 24:10; 37:25; 1 Kgs 10:2; 2 Kgs 8:8, 9; 1 Chron 12:40; Isa 30:6; for cavalry, 1 Sam 30:17; Isa 21:7; for milk, Gen 32:13–15. Forbidden as food, Lev 11:4–7. Hair of, made into clothing, Mt 3:4; Mk 1:6.

Ornaments of, Judg 8:21, 26. Pastures for, Ezk 25:5.

CAMP Of the Israelites around the tabernacle, Num 2:3.

See *Itinerary.*

CANA Wedding at, Jn 2:1–11. Official's son healed at, Jn 4:46, 47. Nathanael's home at, Jn 21:2.

CANAAN 1. Son of Ham, Gen 9:18, 22, 24–27. Descendants of, Gen 10:6, 15–19; 1 Chron 1:5–9, 13–16.

2. Land of, Gen 11:31; 17:8; 23:1, 2. Called *the sanctuary,* Ex 15:17; *Philistia,* Ex 15:14; *land of Israel,* 1 Sam 13:19; *God's promised land,* Heb 11:9; *Holy Land,* Zech 2:12; *Land of God,* Hos 9:3; *of Judah,* Isa 8:8; *the Land of God's Delight,* Isa 62:4; *the Pleasant Land,* Dan 11:41; Zech 7:14; *a wonderful country,* Num 14:7; *the best of all lands,* Ezk 20:6; my land, Joel 3:2; *a land flowing with milk and honey,* Ex 3:8.

Promised to Abraham and his seed, Gen 12:1–7; 13:14–17; 15:18–21; 17:7, 8; Deut 12:9, 10; Ps 105:10, 11; renewed to Isaac, Gen 26:3. Extent of: According to the promise, Gen 15:18; Ex 23:31; Deut 11:24, Josh 1:4; 15:1; after the conquest by Joshua, Josh 12:1–8; in Solomon's time, 1 Kgs 4:21, 24; 2 Chron 7:8; 9:26. Prophecy concerning, after the restoration of Israel, Ezk 47:13–20.

Fertility of, Deut 8:7–9; 11:10–13. Fruitfulness of, Num 13:27; 14:7, 8; Jer 2:7; 32:22. Products of: Fruits and grain, Deut 8:8; Jer 40:10,12; mineral, Deut 8:9. Exports of, Ezk 27:17.

Famines in, Gen 12:10; 26:1; 47:13; Ruth 1:1, 2; 2 Sam 21:1; 1 Kgs 17. See *Famine.*

Spies sent into, by Moses, Num 13:17–29. Conquest of, by the Israelites, Num 21:21–35; Deut 3:3–6; Josh chapters 6–12; Ps 44:1–3. Divided by lot among the twelve tribes, and families, Num 26:55, 56; 33:54; 34:13; by Joshua, Eleazar and a leader from each tribe, Num 34:16–29; 35:1–8; Josh chapters 14–19. Divided into twelve provinces by Solomon, 1 Kgs 4:7–19. Into two kingdoms, Judah and Israel, 1 Kgs 11:29–36; 12:16–21. Roman provinces of, Lk 3:1; Jn 4:3, 4.

Striking facts about the holy land: The only land given by God to any people, Gen 15:18; 17:7, 8; 26:3; 28:13. Located at the center of the land surface of the earth, Ezk 38:12. There Israel became a great nation; Christ was born, lived, was crucified, ascended, will return; the Holy Spirit descended; the church was born (see *Israel; Jesus Christ; Holy Spirit; Church*). The holy land for Israel, Zech 2:12, (and for Christianity and Mohammedanism also). The land bridge connecting Europe, Asia and Africa (see *Israel*), and the geographical meeting place for the white, yellow and black races.

To become an international source of trouble in the last days, Zech 12:2, 3; the graveyard of the armies of the northern confederacy, Ezk 39:11–16; the scene of Armageddon, Rev 16:13–16; ultimately the site of the world metropolis, Jer 3:17.

Desolation prophesied: Lev 26:32; Deut 28:23, 24; because of Israel's sin, Ezk 15:8; Mic 7:13; Jer 23:10; prophecy fulfilled, Lev 18:25, 28; Jer 3:3; Deut 28:38–40; 29:22–24; Isa 32:13; Jer 44:22; Zeph 1:2; Ezk 7:24; 14:13.

Destiny: God will remember the land, Lev 26:42; His eyes are upon it, Deut 11:12; purifies it, Deut 32:43; it is blessed by the Lord, Joel 2:12, 18, 25, 26; it is transformed, Isa 51:3; 55:12, 13; Ezk 36:6–9. The mount of Olives divides at Christ's return, a great valley results, Zech 14:4; (Joel 3:2?); the land becomes a plain, Zech 14:10; Jerusalem is lifted up, Isa 2:2; Ezk 20:40; a new river flows, Zech 14:8; Joel 3:18; Ezk 47:1–12; Ps 46:4; the land is enlarged, Isa 26:15; there are showers of blessing, Ezk 34:26; new springs and streams, Isa 35:6, 7; it becomes a happy land, Mal 3:12.

CANAANITES Eleven nations, descended from Canaan, Gen 10:15–19; Deut 7:1; 1 Chron 1:13–16. Territory of, Gen 10:15–19; 12:6; 15:18–21; Ex 23:31; Num 13:29; 34:1–12; Josh 1:4; 5:1; given to the Israelites, Gen 12:6, 7; 15:18–21; 17:7, 8; Ex 23:23; Deut 7:1–3; 32:49; Ps 135:11, 12.

Wickedness of, Gen 13:12, 13; Lev 18:25, 27, 28; 20:23. To be expelled from the land, Ex 33:2; 34:11. To be destroyed, Ex 23:23, 24; Deut 19:1; 31:3–5; Not expelled, Josh 17:12–18; Judg 1:1–33; 3:1–3. Defeat the Israelites, Num 14:45; Judg 4:1–3. Defeated by the Israelites, Num 21:1–3; Josh 11:1–16; Judg 4:4–24; by the Egyptians, 1 Kgs 9:16. Chariots of, Josh 17:16–18.

Isaac forbidden by Abraham to take a wife from, Gen 28:1. Judah marries a woman of, Gen 38:2; 1 Chron 2:3. The exiled Jews take wives from, Ezra 9:2.

Prophecy concerning, Gen 9:24–27.

CANDACE Queen of Ethiopia, Acts 8:27.

CANDIDATE Refuses to make promises, 2 Chron 10:3–16. Electioneering by, instance of Absalom, 2 Sam 15:1–6.

CANDLE Symbolical, of life, Job 4:21.

See *Lamp.*

CANDLESTICK OF THE TABERNACLE. Place of, Heb 9:2.

OF THE TEMPLE. Of gold, 1 Chron 28:15. Taken with other spoils to Babylon, Jer 52:19.

Symbolical. Rev 1:12, 13, 20; 2:5; 11:4.
See *Lampstand.*

CANE Jesus struck with, Mk 15:19. See *Calamus.*

CANNEH See *Calneh.*

CANNIBALISM Lev 26:29; Deut 28:53–57; 2 Kgs 6:26–30; Jer 19:9; Lam 2:20; 4:10; Ezk 5:10.

CANTEEN Gen 21:14, 19.
See *Bottle.*

CAP See *Turban.*

CAPE Isa 3:22.

CAPERNAUM A city on the shore of the Sea of Galilee, Jesus chose as his headquarters, Mt 4:13, 14; Lk 4:31. Miracles of Jesus performed at, Mt 9:1–26; 17:24–27; Mk 1:21–45; 2; 3:1–6; Lk 7:1–10; Jn 4:46–53; 6:17–25, 59.

His prophecy against, Mt 11:23; Lk 10:15.

CAPHTOR A country now unknown, Deut 2:23; Jer 47:4; Amos 9:7.

CAPHTORIM People of Caphtor, Gen 10:14; 1 Chron 1:12.

CAPITAL Top of a pillar, Ex 36:38; 1 Kgs 7:16–46; 2 Kgs 25:17; 2 Chron 4:12–16; Jer 52:22.

CAPITAL PUNISHMENT See *Punishment.*

CAPITAL AND LABOR Strife between, Mt 21:33–41; Mk 12:1–9; Lk 20:9–16.

See *Employee; Employer; Master; Rich, The; Servant.*

CAPPADOCIA Easternmost province of Asia Minor, Acts 2:9; 1 Pet 1:1.

CAPTAIN Army, Num 31:51, 52; Josh 10:24; 1 Sam 4:2, 3; 1 Chron 12:18; Jer 42:1; 51:23; Rev 19:18. Of a thousand men, 1 Sam 17:18; 18:13. Of a hundred men, Lk 7:2; 23:47. Of fifty men, 2 Kgs 1:9, 11. Signifying any commander, as Job 39:25; Ps 60:1; Dan 3:2.

Of the guard, Gen 37:36; 2 Kgs 25:8; 1 Chron 11:24, 25; 26:1; 2 Chron 12:10; Jer 39:9. Of the Temple guard, Lk 22:4; Acts 4:1; 5:24–27. Of chariots, 1 Kgs 22:31.

Egyptian, Ex 15:4. Philistine, 1 Sam 29:2. Of mercenaries, 2 Sam 15:19, 20. Assyrian, Ezk 23:6. Roman, Mt 8:5, 6; Lk 7:2; 23:47; Acts 10:1.

Of a ship, Jon 1:6; Acts 27:11; Rev 18:17.

See *Armies; Battalion Leader; Chief; Colonel; Commander; General; Leader; Lieutenant; Officer.*

CAPTIVE Prisoner of war, Gen 14:12; 1 Sam 30:1, 2. Cruelty to: Putting to death, Num 31:9–20; Deut 20:13; 21:10; Josh 8:29; 10:15–40; 11:11; Judg 7:25; 8:21; 21:10–12; 1 Sam 15:32, 33; 2 Sam 8:2; 2 Kgs 8:12; Jer 39:6; 20,000, by Amaziah, 2 Chron 25:11, 12; ripping pregnant women, 2 Kgs 8:12; 15:16; Amos 1:13; labored with picks and axes, 2 Sam 12:31; 1 Chron 20:3; blinded, Judg 16:21; Jer 39:7; maimed, Judg 1:4–7; raped, Lam 5:11; Zech 14:1, 2; enslaved, Deut 20:14; 2 Kgs 5:2; Ps 44:12; Joel 3:6; robbed, Ezk 23:25, 26; confined in dungeons, Isa 51:14. Other indignities to, Isa 20:4.

Kindness to, 2 Kgs 25:27–30; Ps 106:46. Advanced to positions in state, Gen 41:39–45; Esther 2:5, 6; Dan 1.

CAPTIVITY Of the Israelites foretold, Lev 26:33; Deut 28:36; of the ten tribes, 2 Kgs 17:6, 23, 24; 18:9–12.

Of Judah in Babylon, prophecy of, Isa 39:6; Jer 13:19; 20:4; 25:2–11; 32:28, etc.; fulfilled, 2 Kgs 24:10–16; 25; 2 Chron 36; Jer 52:28–30. Jews return from, Ezra chapters 2; 3; 8.

Israelites in, promises to, Neh 1:9.

As a judgment, Ezra 5:12; 9:7; Isa 5:13; Jer 29:16–19; Lam 1:3–5; Ezk 39:23, 24.

Among all nations, Deut 30:1; Lk 21:24.

Jews return from, Deut 30:3–5; Jer 29:14; Ezk 11:17; 37:21; Mt 24:31; Mk 13:27.

FIGURATIVE. Judg 5:12; Ps 68:18; Isa 61:1; Rom 7:23; 2 Cor 10:5; 2 Tim 2:26.

CARBUNCLE A precious stone, Ezk 28:13. One of the precious stones set in chestpiece, Ex 39:10.

CARCHEMISH A Babylonian city on the Euphrates, against which the king of Egypt made war, 2 Chron 35:20; Isa 10:9; Jer 46:2.

CARE WORLDLY. Ps 39:6. Proud man! Frail as breath! A shadow! And all his busy rushing ends in nothing. He heaps up riches for someone else to spend.

Ps 127:2. It is senseless for you to work so hard from early morning until late at night, fearing you will starve to death; for God wants his loved ones to get their proper rest.

Eccl 4:8. This is the case of a man who is quite alone, without a son or brother, yet he works hard to keep gaining more riches, and to whom will he leave it all? And why is he giving up so much now? It is all so pointless and depressing.

Mt 6:25. So my counsel is: Don't worry about *things*—food, drink, and clothes. For you already have life and a body—and they are far more important than what to eat and wear. [26]Look at the birds! They don't worry about what to eat—they don't need to sow or reap or store up food—for your heavenly Father feeds them. And you are far more valuable to him than they are. [27]Will all your worries add a single moment to your life? [28]And why worry about your clothes? Look at the field lilies! They don't worry about theirs. [29]Yet King Solomon in all his glory was not clothed as beautifully as they. [30]And if God cares so wonderfully for flowers that are here today and gone tomorrow, won't he more surely care for you, O men of little faith? [31, 32]So don't worry at all about having enough food and clothing. Why be like the heathen? For they take pride in all these things and are deeply concerned about them. But your heavenly Father already knows perfectly well that you need them, [33]and he will give them to you if you give him first place in your life and live as he wants you to. [34]So don't be anxious about tomorrow. God will take care of your tomorrow too. Live one day at a time.

Mt 13:22. The ground covered with thistles represents a man who hears the message, but the cares of this life and his longing for money choke out God's Word, and he does less and less for God. Mk 4:19; Lk 8:14.

Lk 14:18. But they all began making excuses. One said he had just bought a field and wanted to inspect it, and asked to be excused. [19]Another said he had just bought five pair of oxen and wanted to try them out. [20]Another had just been married and for that reason couldn't come.

Lk 21:34, 35. Watch out! Don't let my sudden coming catch you unawares; don't let me find you living in careless ease, carousing and drinking, and occupied with the problems of this life, like all the rest of the world.

1 Cor 7:32. In all you do, I want you to be free from worry. An unmarried man can spend his time doing the Lord's work and thinking how to please him. [33]But a married man can't do that so well; he has to think about his earthly responsibilities and how to please his wife.

Phil 4:6. Don't worry about anything; instead, pray about everything; tell God your needs and don't forget to thank him for his answers.

2 Tim 2:4. And as Christ's soldier do not let yourself become tied up in worldly affairs, for then you cannot satisfy the one who has enlisted you in his army.

See *Carnal Mindedness; Riches; Worldliness.*

REMEDY FOR. Ps 37:5. Commit everything you do to the Lord. Trust him to help you do it and he will.

Ps 55:22. Give your burdens to the Lord. He will carry them. He will not permit the godly to slip or fall.

Prov 16:3. Commit your work to the Lord, then it will succeed.

Jer 17:7. But blessed is the man who trusts in the Lord and has made the Lord his hope and confidence. [8]He is like a tree planted along a riverbank, with its roots reaching deep into the water—a tree not bothered by the heat nor worried by long months of drought. Its leaves stay green and it goes right on producing all its luscious fruit.

Mt 6:26. Look at the birds! They don't worry about what to eat—they don't need to sow or reap or store up food—for your heavenly Father feeds them. And you are far more valuable to him than they are. [27]Will all your worries add a single moment to your life? [28]And why worry about your clothes? Look at the field lilies! They don't worry about theirs. [29]Yet King Solomon in all his glory was not clothed as beautifully as they. [30]And if God cares so wonderfully for flowers that are here today and gone tomorrow, won't he more surely care for you, O men of little faith? [31, 32]So don't worry at all about having enough food and clothing. Why be like the heathen? For they take pride in all these things and are deeply concerned about them. But your heavenly Father already knows perfectly well that you need them, [33]and he will give them to you if you give him first place in your life and live as he wants you to. [34]So don't be anxious about tomorrow. God will take care of your tomorrow too. Live one day at a time. Lk 12:22–32.

Phil 4:6. Don't worry about anything; instead, pray about everything; tell God your needs and don't forget to thank him for his answers. [7]If you do this you will experience God's peace, which is far more wonderful than the human mind can understand. His peace will keep your thoughts and your hearts quiet and at rest as you trust in Christ Jesus.

Heb 13:5. Stay away from the love of money; be satisfied with what you have. For God has said, "I will never, *never* fail you nor forsake you."

1 Pet 5:6. If you will humble yourselves under the mighty hand of God, in his good time he will lift you up. [7]Let him have all your worries and cares, for he is always thinking about you and watching everything that concerns you.

INSTANCES OF. Martha, Lk 10:40, 41. Certain persons who desired to follow Jesus, Mt 8:19–22; Lk 9:57–62.

See *Rich, The.*

CARKAS A Persian eunuch, Esther 1:10.

CARMEL 1. A fertile and picturesque mountain in Palestine, Song 7:5; Isa 33:9; 35:2; Jer 46:18; 50:19; Amos 1:2. Caves of, Amos 9:3. An idolatrous high place on; Elijah builds an altar on, and confounds the worshipers of Baal, killing 450 of its prophets, 1 Kgs 18:17–46. Elisha's home in, 2 Kgs 2:25; 4:25.

2. A city of Judah, Josh 15:48–62. Saul erects a memorial at, 1 Sam 25:2. Nabal's possessions at, 1 Sam 25:2.

CARMI 1. Son of Reuben, Gen 46:8–14; Ex 6:14; Num 26:5–11.

2. Son of Hezron, 1 Chron 4:1; 5:3. Called *Chelubai,* 1 Chron 2:9, and *Caleb,* v. 18.

3. Father of Achan, Josh 7:1; 1 Chron 2:7.

CARNAL MINDEDNESS Rom 8:6. Following after the Holy Spirit leads to life and peace, but following after the old nature leads to death, [7]because the old sinful nature within us is against God. It never did obey God's laws and it never will. [8]That's why those who are still under the control of their old sinful selves, bent on following their old evil desires, can never please God.

Gal 6:8. If he sows to please his own wrong desires, he will be planting seeds of evil and he will surely reap a harvest of spiritual decay and death; but if he plants the good things of the Spirit, he will reap the everlasting life which the Holy Spirit gives him.

Jas 4:4. You are like an unfaithful wife who loves her husband's enemies. Don't you realize that making friends with God's enemies—the evil pleasures of this world—makes you an enemy of God? I say it again, that if your aim is to enjoy the evil pleasure of the unsaved world, you cannot also be a friend of God.

See *Care, Worldly; Riches; Sin, Fruits of; Worldliness.*

CARPENTRY Building the ark, Gen 6:14–16. Tabernacle, and furniture of, Ex 31:2–9; 35:35. See *Tabernacle.* David's palace, 2 Sam 5:11; 1 Chron 14:1. Temple, 1 Chron 22:15; 2 Chron 2:14; 24:12; 34:10, 11; 2 Kgs 12:11, 12; 22:5, 6; Ezra 3:7. See *Temple.* Making idols, Isa 41:7; 44:13. Carpenters, Jer 24:1. Joseph, Mt 13:55; Jesus, Mk 6:2, 3.

See *Carving; Master Workman.*

CARPET Judg 5:10; Ezk 27:24.

CARPUS A Christian at Troas, 2 Tim 4:13.

CARSHENA A Persian official, Esther 1:13–15.

CART 1 Sam 6:7–15; 2 Sam 6:3; 1 Chron 13:7; Isa 46:1; Acts 14:13.

See *Wagon.*

CARVING Woodwork of the Temple was decorated with carvings of flowers, angels, and palm trees, 1 Kgs 6:18, 29, 32, 35; Ps 74:5, 6. Idols manufactured by, Ex 34:13; Isa 44:9–17; Jer 10:2, 3. Persons skilled in: Bezalel, Ex 31:5; Hiram, 1 Kgs 7:13–51; 2 Chron 2:13, 14.

CASIPHIA A place in the Persian empire, Ezra 8:17.

CASLUHIM A people whose progenitor was a son of Mizraim, Gen 10:13, 14; 1 Chron 1:12.

CASSIA An aromatic plant, probably cinnamon, Ps 45:8; Ezk 27:19. An ingredient of the holy oil, Ex 30:24.

CASTING See *Molding.*

CASTLE A prison, Gen 40:1; 41:10. King's, Neh 3:25, 27; 12:37; Job 3:14, 15. For the doctrine, "The house is my castle," see Deut 24:10, 11.

See *Armory; Fort; Fortress; Tower.*

CATERPILLAR Sent as a judgment, 1 Kgs 8:37; 2 Chron 6:28; Ps 78:46.

CATHOLICITY Freedom from narrowness; liberality. Mk 9:38. One of his disciples, John, told him one day, "Teacher, we saw a man using your name to cast out demons; but we told him not to, for he isn't one of our group." [39]"Don't forbid him!" Jesus said. "For no one doing miracles in my name will quickly turn against me. [40]Anyone who isn't against us is for us. [41]If anyone so much as gives you a cup of water because you are Christ's —I say this solemnly—he won't lose his reward." Luke 9:49, 50.

Acts 10:1. In Caesarea there lived a Roman army officer, Cornelius, a captain of an Italian regiment. [2]He was a godly man, deeply reverent, as was his entire household. He gave generously to charity and was a man of prayer. [3]While wide awake one afternoon he had a vision—it was about three o'clock—and in this vision he saw an angel of God coming toward him. "Cornelius!" the angel said. [4]Cornelius stared at him in terror. "What do you want, sir?" he asked the angel. And the angel replied, "Your prayers and charities have not gone unnoticed by God! [5, 6]Now send some men to Joppa to find a man named Simon Peter, who is staying with Simon, the tanner, down by the shore, and ask him to come and visit you." [7]As soon as the angel was gone, Cornelius called two of his household servants and a godly soldier, one of his personal bodyguard, [8]and told them what had happened and sent them off to Joppa. [9, 10]The next day, as they were nearing the city, Peter went up on the flat roof of his house to pray. It was noon and he was hungry, but while lunch was being prepared, he fell into a trance. [11]He saw the sky open, and a great canvas sheet, suspended by its four corners, settle to the ground. [12]In the sheet were all sorts of animals, snakes and birds (forbidden to the Jews for food). [13]Then a voice said to him, "Go kill and eat any of them you wish." [14]"Never, Lord," Peter declared, "I have never in all my life eaten such creatures, for they are forbidden by our Jewish laws." [15]The voice spoke again, "Don't contradict God! If he says something is kosher, then it is." [16]The same vision was repeated three times. Then the sheet was pulled up again to heaven. [17]Peter was very perplexed. What could the vision mean? What was he supposed to do? Just then the men sent by Cornelius had found the house and were standing outside at the gate, [18]inquiring whether this was the place where Simon Peter lived! [19]Meanwhile, as Peter was puzzling over the vision, the Holy Spirit said to him, "Three men have come to see you. [20]Go down and meet them and go with them. All is well, I have sent them." [21]So Peter went down. "I'm the man you're looking for," he said. "Now what is it you want?" [22]Then they told him about Cornelius the Roman officer, a good and godly man, well thought of by the Jews, and how an angel had instructed him to send for Peter to come and tell him what God wanted him to do. [23]So Peter invited them in and lodged them overnight. The next day he went with them, accompanied by some other believers from Joppa. [24]They arrived in Caesarea the following day, and Cornelius was waiting for him, and had called together his relatives and close friends to meet Peter. [25]As Peter entered his home, Cornelius fell to the floor before him in worship. [26]But Peter said, "Stand up! I'm not a god!" [27]So he got up and they talked together for a while and then went in where the others were assembled. [28]Peter told them, "You know it is against the Jewish laws for me to come into a Gentile home like this. But God has shown me in a vision that I should never think of anyone as inferior. [29]So I came as soon as I was sent for. Now tell me what you want." Cornelius replied, "Four days ago I was praying as usual at this time of the afternoon, when suddenly a man was standing before me clothed in a radiant robe! [31]He told me, 'Cornelius, your prayers are heard and your charities have been noticed by God! [32]Now send some men to Joppa and summon Simon Peter, who is staying in the home of Simon, a tanner, down by the shore.' [33]So I sent for you at once, and you have done well to come so soon. Now here we are, waiting before the Lord, anxious to hear what he has told you to tell us!" [34]Then Peter replied, "I see very clearly that the Jews are not God's only favorites! [35]In every nation he has those who worship him and do good deeds and are acceptable to him."

Acts 15:1. While Paul and Barnabas were at Antioch, some men from Judea arrived and began to teach the believers that unless they adhered to the ancient Jewish custom of circumcision, they could not be saved. [2]Paul and Barnabas argued and discussed this with them at length, and finally the believers sent them to Jerusalem, accompanied by some local men, to talk to the apostles and elders there about this question. [3]After the entire congregation had escorted them out of the city the delegates went on to Jerusalem, stopping along the way in the cities of Phoenicia and Samaria to visit the believers, telling them—much to everyone's joy—that the Gentiles, too, were being converted. [4]Arriving in Jerusalem, they met with the church leaders—all the apostles and elders were present—and Paul and Barnabas reported on what God had been doing through their ministry. [5]But then some of the men who had been Pharisees before their conversion stood to their feet and declared that all Gentile converts must be circumcised and required to follow all the Jewish customs and ceremonies.

6. So the apostles and church elders set a further meeting to decide this question. [7]At the meeting, after long discussion, Peter stood and addressed them as follows: "Brothers, you all know that God chose me from among you long ago to preach the Good News to the Gentiles, so that they also could believe. [8]God, who knows men's hearts, confirmed the fact that he accepts Gentiles by giving them the Holy Spirit, just as he gave him to us. [9]He made no distinction between them and us, for he cleansed their lives through faith, just as he did ours. [10]And now are you going to correct God by burdening the Gentiles with a yoke that neither we nor our fathers were able to bear? [11]Don't you believe that all are saved the same way, by the free gift of the Lord Jesus?"

12. There was no further discussion, and everyone now listened as Barnabas and Paul told about the miracles God had done through them among the Gentiles. [13]When they had finished, James took the floor. "Brothers," he said, "listen to me. [19]And so my judgment is that we should not insist that the Gentiles who turn to God must obey our Jewish laws, [20]except that we should write to them to refrain from eating meat sacrificed to idols, from all fornication, and also from eating unbled meat of strangled animals. [21]For these things have been preached against in Jewish synagogues in every city on every Sabbath for many generations." [22]Then the apostles and elders and the whole congregation voted to send delegates to Antioch with Paul and Barnabas, to report on this decision. The men chosen were two of the church leaders—Judas (also called Barsabbas) and Silas. [23]This is the letter they took along with them: *"From:* The apostles, elders and brothers at Jerusalem. *To:* The Gentile brothers in Antioch, Syria and Cilicia. Greetings! [24]We understand that some believers from here have upset you and questioned your salvation, but they had no such instructions from us. [25]So it seemed wise to us, having unanimously agreed on our decision, to send to you these two official representatives, along with our beloved Barnabas and Paul. [26]These men—Judas and Silas, who have risked their lives for the sake of our Lord Jesus Christ—will confirm orally what we have decided concerning your question. [27, 28, 29]For it seemed good to the Holy Spirit and to us to lay no greater burden of Jewish laws on you than to abstain from eating food offered to idols and from unbled meat of strangled animals, and, of course, from fornication. If you do this, it is enough. Farewell." [30]The four messengers went at once to Antioch, where they called a general meeting of the Christians and gave them the letter. [31]And there was great joy throughout the church that day as they read it.

Col 3:11. In this new life one's nationality or race or education or social position is unimportant; such things mean nothing. Whether a person has Christ is what matters, and he is equally available to all. [12]Since you have been chosen by God who has given you this new kind of life, and because of his deep love and concern for you, you should practice tenderhearted mercy and kindness to others. Don't worry about making a good impression on them but be ready to suffer quietly and patiently. [13]Be gentle and ready to forgive; never hold grudges. Remember, the Lord forgave you, so you must forgive others. [14]Most of all, let love guide your life, for then the whole church will stay together in perfect harmony. [15]Let the peace of heart which comes from Christ be always present in your hearts and lives, for this is your responsibility and privilege as members of his body. And always be thankful.

See *Heathen; Strangers.*

INSTANCES OF. Solomon, in his prayer, 1 Kgs 8:41–43. Paul, in recognizing godly Gentiles, Acts 13:16, 26, 42, 43. Peter, Acts 10:34, 35. Rulers of the synagogue at Salamis, permitting the Apostles to preach, Acts 13:5.

CATTLE Of the bovine species. Used for sacrifice, 1 Kgs 8:63. See *Heifer; Offerings.* Sheltered, Gen 33:17.

Bashan adapted to the raising of, Ps 22:12; Ezk 39:18; Amos 4:1. A symbol of wealth, Gen 12:5; Deut 30:9; Ps 107:38.

See *Animals; Bull; Cow; Heifer; Offerings.*

CAUTION See *Expediency; Prudence.*

CAVALRY Mounted on horses, Ex 14:23; 1 Sam 13:5; 2 Sam 8:4; 2 Chron 9:25; 12:3; Isa 30:16; 31:1; Rev 9:16–18; on camels, 1 Sam 30:17.

See *Armies.*

CAUSE See *Actions at Law.*

CAVE Used as a dwelling: By Lot, Gen 19:30; Elijah, 1 Kgs 19:9; Israelites, Ezk 33:27; saints, Heb 11:37, 38. Place of refuge, Josh 10:16–27; Judg 6:2; 1 Sam 13:6; 1 Kgs 18:3, 4, 13; 19:9, 13. Burial place, Gen 23:9–20; 25:9, 10; 49:29–32; 50:12, 13; Jn 11:37, 38.

Of Adullam, 1 Sam 22:1; 2 Sam 23:13; 1 Chron 11:15. En-gedi, 1 Sam 24:3–8.

In prophecy, Isa 2:19; Rev 6:15.

CEDAR Valuable for building purposes, Isa 9:8–10. David's ample provision of, in Jerusalem, for the temple, 1 Chron 22:4; 2 Chron 1:15. Furnished by Hiram, king of Tyre, for Solomon's temple, 1 Kgs 5:6–10; 9:11, 12; 2 Chron 2:16. Used in rebuilding the temple, Ezra 3:7; in David's palace, 2 Sam 5:11; 1 Chron 17:1; in Solomon's palace, 1 Kgs 7:2; for masts of ships, Ezk 27:5; in purifications, Lev 14:4, 6, 49–52; Num 19:6.

FIGURATIVE. Ps 92:12; Isa 2:13; 14:8; Jer 22:7; Ezk 31:2, 3; Zech 11:2.

CELIBACY Mt 19:10. Jesus' disciples then said to him, "If that is how it is, it is better not to marry!" [11]"Not everyone can accept this statement," Jesus said. "Only those whom God helps. [12]Some are born without the ability to marry, and some are disabled by men, and some refuse to marry for the sake of the Kingdom of Heaven. Let anyone who can, accept my statement."

1 Cor 7:1. Now about those questions you asked in your last letter: my answer is that if you do not marry, it is good. [2]But usually it is best to be married, each man having his own wife, and each woman having her own husband, because otherwise you might fall back into sin. [7]I wish everyone could get along without marrying, just as I do. But we are not all the same. God gives some the gift of a husband or wife, and others he gives the gift of being able to stay happily unmarried. [8]So I say to those who aren't married, and to widows—better to stay unmarried if you can, just as I am. [9]But if you can't control yourselves, go ahead and marry. It is better to marry than to burn with lust.

25. Now I will try to answer your other question. What about girls who are not yet married? Should they be permitted to do so? In answer to this question, I have no special command for them from the Lord. But the Lord in his kindness has given me wisdom that can be trusted, and I will be glad to tell you what I think. [26]Here is the problem: We Christians are facing great dangers to our lives at present. In times like these I think it is best for a person to remain unmarried.

32. In all you do, I want you to be free from worry. An unmarried man can spend his time doing the Lord's work and thinking how to please him. [33]But a married man can't do that so well; he has to think about his earthly responsibilities and how to please his wife. [34]His interests are divided. It is the same with a girl who marries. She faces the same problem. A girl who is not married is anxious to please the Lord in all she is and does. But a married woman must consider other things such as housekeeping and the likes and dislikes of her husband. [35]I am saying this to help you, not to try to keep you from marrying. I want you to do whatever will help you serve the Lord best, with as few other things as possible to distract your attention from him. [36]But if anyone feels he ought to marry because he has trouble controlling his passions, it is all right, it is not a sin; let him marry. [37]But if a man has the willpower not to marry and decides that he doesn't need to and won't, he has made a wise decision. [38]So the person who marries does well, and the person who doesn't marry does even better. [39]The wife is part of her husband as long as he lives; if her husband dies, then she may marry again, but only if she marries a Christian. [40]But in my opinion she will be happier if she doesn't marry again; and I think I am giving you counsel from God's Spirit when I say this.

1 Cor 9:5. If I had a wife, and if she were a believer, couldn't I bring her along on these trips just as the other disciples do, and as the Lord's brothers do, and as Peter does?

1 Tim 4:1. But the Holy Spirit tells us clearly that in the last times some in the church will turn away from Christ and become eager followers of teachers with devil-inspired ideas. [2]These teachers will tell lies with straight faces and do it so often that their consciences won't even bother them. [3]They will say it is wrong to be married and wrong to eat meat, even though God gave these things to well-taught Christians to enjoy and be thankful for.

Rev 14:1. Then I saw a Lamb standing on Mount Zion in Jerusalem, and with him were 144,000 who had his Name and his Father's Name written on their foreheads. [4]For they are spiritually undefiled, pure as virgins, following the Lamb wherever he goes. They have been purchased from among the men on the earth as a consecrated offering to God and the Lamb. with *vs.* 2–5.

CENCHREAE A harbor town near Corinth, Acts 18:18; Rom 16:1.

CENSER Used for offering incense, Lev 16:12; Num 4:14; 16:6, 7, 16–18, 46; Rev 8:3. For the temple, made of gold, 1 Kgs 7:50; 2 Chron 4:22. Those which Korah used were converted into sheets, Num 16:37–39. Of the temple, returned from Babylon, Ezra 1:9, 10. Used in idolatrous rites, Ezk 8:11.

Symbolical. Rev 8:3, 5.

CENSORIOUSNESS See *Uncharitableness; Speaking, Evil; Charitableness.*

CENSUS Numbering of Israel by Moses, Ex 38:26; Num 1; 3:14–43; 26; by David, 2 Sam 24:1–9; 1 Chron 21:1–8; 27:24.

A head tax to be levied at each, Ex 30:11–16; 38: 25, 26.

Of the Roman Empire, by Caesar, Lk 2:1–3.

CHAFF FIGURATIVE. Ps 1:4; 35:5; 83:13; Isa 17:13; 29:5; 41:15; Jer 13:24, 25; 23:28; Dan 2:35; Hos 13:3; Zeph 2:2; Mt 3:12; Lk 3:17.

See *Grass; Straw.*

CHAINS Used as ornaments. Worn by princes, Gen 41:41, 42; Dan 5:7, 29. Worn on ankles, Num 31:50; Isa 3:20; on the ephod of the high priest, Ex 28:13, 14; 39:15. As ornaments on camels, Judg 8:26. A partition of, in the Temple, 1 Kgs 6: 21, 22; 7:16–22. See *Necklace.*

Used to confine prisoners, Gen 39:20; 2 Kgs 25: 7; 2 Chron 33:11; 36:6; Ps 149:8; Jer 40:4; Mt 14:3; Acts 12:6, 7; 21:33; 28:20. Made of bronze, Judg 16: 21; 2 Chron 33:11.

See *Fetters; Handcuffs; Shackles.*

FIGURATIVE. Lev 26:13; Isa 9:14; Lam 3:7; Ezk 7:23–27; 2 Pet 2:4; Jude 1:6; Rev 20:1.

CHALCEDONY A precious stone, Rev 21: 18–20.

CHALDEA The ancient region of Mesopotamia which became part of the Babylonian empire, Gen 11:28, 31; Jer 21:3, 4; 50:1, 8, 11, 35; 51:1, 4, 5; Dan 2:10; 5:11; Hab 1:6, 12; Acts 7:4. Abraham a native of, Gen 11:28, 31; 15:7. In some of the above references, the word Chaldea is used interchangeably with Babylon.

See *Babylon; Chaldeans.*

CHALDEANS The inhabitants of Chaldea, known especially for their interest in astrology, Dan 1:3, 4; 2:2; 4:7; 5:7. Assisted in the Babylonian conquest of Judah, 2 Kgs 24:2.

See *Chaldea.*

CHAMELEON Forbidden as food, Lev 11: 29, 30.

CHAMPIONSHIP Battles were decided by.

INSTANCES OF. Goliath and David, 1 Sam 4–53. Young men of David's and Abner's armies, 2 Sam 2:14–17. Representatives of the Philistines' and David's armies, 2 Sam 21:15–22.

CHANGE OF VENUE Granted Paul, Acts 23:17–35. Declined by Paul, Acts 25:9–11.

CHARACTER OF SAINTS. Attentive to Christ's voice, Jn 10:3, 4; blameless, Ps 15:2; Phil 2: 15; bold, Prov 28:1; contrite, Isa 57:15; 66:2; devout, Lk 2:25; enthusiastic, Tit 2:14; faithful, Rev 17:14; fearing God, Mal 3:16; following Christ, Jn 10:4, 27; following God's laws, Ps 119:1; generous, Ps 37:26; Isa 32:8; 2 Cor 9:13; godly, Lk 1:6; Acts 8:2; 10:2; 22:12; 2 Pet 2:9; holy, Deut 7:6; 14:2; honest, 1 Kgs 3:6; Jn 1:47; humble, Prov 16:19; Mt 5:3; 1 Pet 5:5; led by the Spirit, Rom 8:14; loathing themselves, Ezk 20:43; loving, Col 1:4; 1 Thess 4:9; loyal, Rom 16:9; meek, Isa 29:19; Mt 5:5; merciful, Mt 5:7; Col 3:12; new creatures, 2 Cor 5:17; Eph 2: 10; obedient, 1 Pet 1:14; pure, Mt 5:8; 1 Jn 3:3; righteous, Gen 6:9; Isa 60:21; Hab 2:4; Mt 5:6; sincere, 2 Cor 1:12; 2:17; steadfast, Acts 2:42; Col 2:5; taught by God, Isa 54:13; 1 Jn 2:27; true, 2 Cor 6:8; waiting, Lk 12:37; wise, Prov 16:21.

See *Righteous, Described.*

OF THE WICKED. Alienated from God, Eph 4: 17, 18; Col 1:21; blasphemous, Lk 22:65; Rev 16:9; blinded, 2 Cor 4:4; Eph 4:17, 18; boastful, Ps 10:3; 49:6; corrupt, Rev 21:8; cruel, 2 Tim 3:3; deceitful, Ps 5:6; Rom 3:13; delighting in the sins of others, Prov 2:14; Rom 1:32; destructive, Isa 59:7; disobedient, Neh 9:26; Job 21:15; Ps 53:4; Tit 1:10, 16; 3:3; 1 Pet 2:7; encourage evil, Prov 1:10–14; 16:29; 2 Tim 3:6; envious, Neh 2:10; Tit 3:3; evil, Prov 21: 8; 24:8; Isa 57:17; Jer 13:23; Mic 7:3; Acts 2:40; fearful, Prov 28:1; Rev 21:8; foolish, Deut 32:6; Ps 14:1; forgetting God, Job 8:11–13; fraudulent, Ps 37: 21; Mic 6:11; glad for the trouble of believers, Ps 35: 15; greedy, Mic 2:2; Rom 1:29; hardheaded, 2 Tim 3:4; hardhearted, Ezk 2:4; 3:7; Rom 1:31; hating the light, Job 24:13; Jn 3:20; haughty, Ps 10: 4; hostile to God, Rom 8:7; Col 1:21; hypocritical, Isa 29:13; 2 Tim 3:5; ignorant of God, Hos 4:1; 2 Thess 1:8; immoral, 2 Tim 3:3; impure, Isa 64:6; Eph 4:19; lying, Ps 58:3; 62:3, 4; Prov 13:5; Isa 59: 4; murderous, Ps 10:8; 94:6, 7; Rom 1:29; persecuting, Ps 69:26; 109:16; plotting against believers, Neh 4:8; 6:2; Ps 38:12; prefering pleasure to worshiping God, 2 Tim 3:4; proud, Ps 5:5; 59:12; Obd 1:3; Phil 3:19; 2 Tim 3:2; rebellious, Isa 1:2; 30:9; rotten, Eph 4:22; scoffing at believers, Neh 2:19; 4:2; 2 Tim 3: 3, 4; selfish, 2 Tim 3:2; sensual, Phil 3:19; Jude 1:19; skillful, Mic 7:3; stubborn, Ex 33:5; Deut 32:5; sold to evil, 1 Kgs 21:20; 2 Kgs 17:17; stiff-necked, Ezk 2:4; Acts 7:51; thoroughly bad, 2 Tim 3:2; twisted, 2 Tim 3:8; uncircumcised in spirit, Jer 9:26; unthankful, Lk 6:35; 2 Tim 3:2; useless, Mt 25:30.

See *Wicked, Described.*

GOOD. Prov 22:1. If you must choose, take a good name rather than great riches; for to be held in loving esteem is better than silver and gold. Eccl 7:1.

DEFAMATION OF, PUNISHED. Deut 22:13, 14. If a man marries a girl, then after sleeping with her accuses her of having had premarital intercourse with another man, saying, "She was not a virgin when I married her," [15]then the girl's father and mother shall bring the proof of her virginity to the city judges. [16]Her father shall tell them, "I gave my daughter to this man to be his wife, and now he despises her, [17, 18]and has accused her of shameful things, claiming that she was not a virgin when she married; yet here is the proof." And they shall spread the garment before the judges. The judges shall sentence the man to be whipped, [19]and fine him one hundred dollars to be given to the girl's father, for he has falsely accused a virgin of Israel. She shall remain his wife and he may never divorce her.

REVEALED IN COUNTENANCE. Isa 3:9. The very look on their faces gives them away and shows their guilt. And they boast that their sin is equal to the sin of Sodom; they are not even ashamed. What a catastrophe! They have doomed themselves. See *Countenance; Face.*

FIRMNESS OF. Ps 57:7. O God, my heart is quiet and confident. No wonder I can sing your praises! Ps 108:1; 112:7.

Mt 10:22. Everyone shall hate you because you belong to me. But all of you who endure to the end shall be saved.

Mk 4:20. But the good soil represents the hearts of those who truly accept God's message and produce a plentiful harvest for God—thirty, sixty, or even a hundred times as much as was planted in their hearts.

1 Cor 7:20. Usually a person should keep on with the work he was doing when God called him.

2 Thess 2:15. With all these things in mind, dear brothers, stand firm and keep a strong grip on the truth that we taught you in our letters and during the time we were with you.

2 Thess 3:3. But the Lord is faithful; he will make you strong and guard you from satanic attacks of every kind.

Heb 10:23. Now we can look forward to the salvation God has promised us. There is no longer any room for doubt, and we can tell others that salvation is ours, for there is no question that he will do what he says.

Heb 13:9. So do not be attracted by strange, new ideas. Your spiritual strength comes as a gift from God, not from ceremonial rules about eating certain foods—a method which, by the way, hasn't helped those who have tried it!

Jas 1:25. But if anyone keeps looking steadily into God's law for free men, he will not only remember it but he will do what it says, and God will greatly bless him in everything he does.

Instances of Firmness. Joseph in resisting Potiphar's wife, Gen 39:7–12; Pilate, Jn 19:22; Paul, Acts 20:22–24; 21:13, 14.

See *Decision; Stability.*

INSTABILITY OF. Prov 24:21, 22. My son, watch your step before the Lord and the king, and don't associate with radicals. For you will go down with them to sudden disaster, and who knows where it all will end?

Prov 27:8. A man who strays from home is like a bird that wanders from its nest.

Jer 2:36. First here, then there, you flit about, going from one ally to another for their help; but it's all no good—your new friends in Egypt will forsake you as Assyria did before.

Hos 6:4. O Ephraim and Judah, what shall I do with you? For your love vanishes like morning clouds, and disappears like dew.

Hos 7:8. My people mingle with the heathen, picking up their evil ways; thus they become as good-for-nothing as a half-baked cake!

Hos 10:2. The hearts of her people are false toward God. They are guilty and must be punished. God will break down their heathen altars and smash their idols.

Mt 13:19. The hard path where some of the seeds fell represents the heart of a person who hears the Good News about the Kingdom and doesn't understand it; then Satan comes and snatches away the seeds from his heart. [20]The shallow, rocky soil represents the heart of a man who hears the message and receives it with real joy, [21]but he doesn't have much depth in his life, and the seeds don't root very deeply, and after a while when trouble comes, or persecution begins because of his beliefs, his enthusiasm fades, and he drops out. [22]The ground covered with thistles represents a man who hears the message, but the cares of this life and his longing for money choke out God's Word, and he does less and less for God. Mk 4:15–19; Lk 8:5–15.

Lk 9:59. Another time, when he invited a man to come with him and to be his disciple, the man agreed—but wanted to wait until his father's death. [60]Jesus replied, "Let those without eternal life concern themselves with things like that. Your duty is to come and preach the coming of the Kingdom of God to all the world." [61]Another said, "Yes, Lord, I will come, but first let me ask permission of those at home." [62]But Jesus told him, "Anyone who lets himself be distracted from the work I plan for him is not fit for the Kingdom of God." Mt 8:19–22.

Eph 4:14. Then we will no longer be like children, forever changing our minds about what we believe because someone has told us something different, or has cleverly lied to us and made the lie sound like the truth.

Jas 1:6. But when you ask him, be sure that you really expect him to tell you, for a doubtful mind will be as unsettled as a wave of the sea that is driven and tossed by the wind; [7, 8]and every decision you then make will be uncertain, as you turn first this way, and then that. If you don't ask with faith, don't expect the Lord to give you any solid answer.

Jas 4:8. And when you draw close to God, God will draw close to you. Wash your hands, you sinners, and let your hearts be filled with God alone to make them pure and true to him.

2 Pet 2:14. No woman can escape their sinful stare, and of adultery they never have enough. They make a game of luring unstable women. They train themselves to be greedy; and are doomed and cursed.

See *Indecision; Instability; Decision; Perseverance; Stability.*

Instances of Instability.

REUBEN: Gen 49:3. Reuben, you are my oldest son, the child of my vigorous youth. You are the head of the list in rank and in honor. [4]But you are unruly as the wild waves of the sea, and you shall be first no longer. I am demoting you, for you slept with one of my wives and thus dishonored me.

PHARAOH: Ex 8:15. But when Pharaoh saw that the frogs were gone, he hardened his heart and refused to let the people go, just as the Lord had predicted. [32]But Pharaoh hardened his heart again and did not let the people go!

Ex 9:34. When Pharaoh saw this, he and his officials sinned yet more by their stubborn refusal to do what they had promised.

Ex 14:5. When word reached the king of Egypt that the Israelis were not planning to return to Egypt after three days, but to keep on going, Pharaoh and his staff became bold again. "What is this we have done, letting all these slaves get away?" they asked.

SOLOMON: 1 Kgs 11:4. They encouraged him to worship their gods instead of trusting completely in the Lord as his father David had done. [5]Solomon worshiped Ashtoreth, the goddess of the Sidonians, and Milcom, the horrible god of the Ammonites. [6]Thus Solomon did what was clearly wrong and refused to follow the Lord as his father David did. [7]He even built a temple on the Mount of Olives, across the valley from Jerusalem, for Chemosh, the depraved god of Moab, and another for Molech, the unutterably vile god of the Ammonites. [8]Solomon built temples for these foreign wives to use for burning incense and sacrificing to their gods.

ISRAELITES: Ex 32:8. And have quickly abandoned all my laws. They have molded themselves a calf, and worshiped it, and sacrificed to it, and said, "This is your god, O Israel, that brought you out of Egypt."

Judg 2:17. Yet even then Israel would not listen to the judges, but broke faith with Jehovah by worshiping other gods instead. How quickly they turned away from the true faith of their ancestors, for they refused to obey God's commands. [19]But when the judge died, the people turned from doing right and behaved even worse than their ancestors had. They prayed to heathen gods again, throwing themselves to the ground in humble worship. They stubbornly returned to the evil customs of the nations around them.

2 Chron 11:17. This strengthened the kingdom of Judah, so King Rehoboam survived for three years without difficulty; for during those years there was an earnest effort to obey the Lord as King David and King Solomon had done.

2 Chron 12:1. But just when Rehoboam was at the height of his popularity and power he abandoned the Lord, and the people followed him in this sin.

King Saul in his treatment of David, 1 Sam chapters 18; 19.

CHARGE Delivered to ministers, see *Minister.*

CHARIOT For war, Ex 14:7, 9, 25; Josh 11:4; 1 Sam 13:5; 1 Kgs 20:1, 25; 2 Kgs 6:14; 2 Chron 12: 2, 3; Jer 46:9; 47:3; 51:21; Joel 2:5; Nah 2:3, 4; 3:2. Wheels of Pharaoh's, providentially taken off, Ex 14:25.

Commanded by captains, Ex 14:7; 1 Kgs 9:22; 22: 31–33. Made of iron, Josh 17:16–18; Judg 1:19. Introduced to Israelites by David, 2 Sam 8:4. Owned by Solomon, 1 Kgs 4:26; 2 Chron 8:6; imported from Egypt, 1 Kgs 10:26–29. Cities for, 1 Kgs 9:19; 2 Chron 1:14; 8:6; 9:25. Royal, Gen 41:43; 46:29; 2 Kgs 5:9; 2 Chron 35:24, 25; Acts 8:27–29. Made of wood, Song 3:7–9. Drawn by camels, Isa 21:7. For travel, Mic 1:13.

Traffic in, Rev 18:13. Kings ride in, 2 Chron 35: 24, 25.

See *Cavalry.*

FIGURATIVE. Chariots of God, 2 Kgs 6:17; Ps 68:17; 104:3; Isa 66:15; Hab 3:8; Rev 9:9.

Symbolical. 2 Kgs 2:11, 12; Zech 6:1–8.

CHARISMATA Gifts or abilities bestowed on the apostles and early Christians, Mt 10:1, 8; Mk 16:17, 18; Lk 10:1, 8, 9, 17, 19; Acts 2:4; 10:44–47; 19: 6; 1 Cor 12.

See *Gifts from God; Miracles; Tongues.*

CHARITABLENESS Prov 10:12. Hatred stirs old quarrels, but love overlooks insults.

Prov 17:9. Love forgets mistakes; nagging about them parts the best of friends.

Mt 5:23. So if you are standing before the altar in the Temple, offering a sacrifice to God, and suddenly remember that a friend has something against you, [24]leave your sacrifice there beside the altar and go and apologize and be reconciled to him, and then come and offer your sacrifice to God.

Mt 6:14, 15. Your heavenly Father will forgive you if you forgive those who sin against you; but if *you* refuse to forgive *them, he* will not forgive *you.*

Mt 7:1. Don't criticize, and then you won't be criticized. [2]For others will treat you as you treat them. [3]And why worry about a speck in the eye of a brother when you have a board in your own? [4]Should you say, "Friend, let me help you get that speck out of your eye," when you can't even see because of the board in your own? [5]Hypocrite! First get rid of the board. Then you can see to help your brother. Lk 6:37–42.

Mt 18:21. Then Peter came to him and asked, "Sir, how often should I forgive a brother who sins against me? Seven times?" [22]"No!" Jesus replied, "seventy times seven!"

23. The Kingdom of Heaven can be compared to a king who decided to bring his accounts up to date. [24]In the process, one of his debtors was brought in who owed him $10,000,000! [25]He couldn't pay, so the king ordered him sold for the debt, also his wife and children and everything he had. [26]But the man fell down before the king, his face in the dust, and said, "Oh, sir, be patient with me and I will pay it all." [27]Then the king was filled with pity for him and released him and forgave his debt. [28]But when the man left the king, he went to a man who owed him $2,000 and grabbed him by the throat and demanded instant payment. [29]The man fell down before him and begged him to give him a little time. "Be patient and I will pay it," he pled. [30]But his creditor wouldn't wait. He had the man arrested and jailed until the debt would be paid in full. [31]Then the man's friends went to the king and told him what had happened. [32]And the king called before him the man he had forgiven and said, "You evil-hearted wretch! Here I forgave you all that tremendous debt, just because you asked me to—[33]shouldn't you have mercy on others, just as I had mercy on you?" [34]Then the angry king sent the man to the torture chamber until he had paid every last penny due. [35]So shall my heavenly Father do to you if you refuse to truly forgive your brothers.

Lk 6:36. Try to show as much compassion as your Father does. [37]Never criticize or condemn—or it will all come back on you. Go easy on others; then they will do the same for you.

Lk 17:3. Rebuke your brother if he sins, and forgive him if he is sorry. [4]Even if he wrongs you seven times a day and each time turns again and asks forgiveness, forgive him.

Rom 14:1. Give a warm welcome to any brother who wants to join you, even though his faith is weak. Don't criticize him for having different ideas from yours about what is right and wrong. [2]For instance, don't argue with him about whether or not to eat meat that has been offered to idols. You may believe there is no harm in this, but the faith of others is weaker; they think it is wrong, and will go without any meat at all and eat vegetables rather than eat that kind of meat. [3]Those who think it is all right to eat such meat must not look down on those who won't. And if you are one of those who won't, don't find fault with those who do. For God has accepted them to be his children. [4]They are God's servants, not yours. They are responsible to him, not to you. Let him tell them whether they are right or wrong. And God is able to make them do as they should. [5]Some think that Christians should observe the Jewish holidays as special days to worship God, but others say it is wrong and foolish to go to all that trouble, for every day alike belongs to God. On questions of this kind everyone must decide for himself. [6]If you have special days for worshiping the Lord, you are trying to honor him; you are doing a good thing. So is the person who eats meat that has been offered to idols; he is thankful to the Lord for it; he is doing right. And the person who won't touch such meat, he, too, is anxious to please the Lord, and is thankful. [7]We are not our own bosses to live or die as we ourselves might choose. [8]Living or dying we follow the Lord. Either way we are his. [9]Christ died and rose again for this very purpose, so that he can be our Lord both while we live and when we die. [10]You have no right to criticize your brother or look down on him. Remember, each of us will stand personally before the Judgment Seat of God. [11]For it is written, "As I live," says the Lord, "every knee shall bow to me and every tongue confess to God." [12]Yes, each of us will give an account of himself to God. [13]So don't criticize each other any more. Try instead to live in such a way that you will never make your brother stumble by letting him see you doing something he thinks is wrong. [14]As for myself, I am perfectly sure on the authority of the Lord Jesus that there is nothing really wrong with eating meat that has been offered to idols. But if someone believes it is wrong, then he shouldn't do it because for him it is wrong. [15]And if your brother is bothered by what you eat, you are not acting in love if you go ahead and eat it. Don't let your eating ruin someone for whom Christ died. [16]Don't do anything that will cause criticism against yourself even though you know that what you do is right. [17]For, after all, the important thing for us as Christians is not what we eat or drink but stirring up goodness and peace and joy from the Holy Spirit. [18]If you let Christ be Lord in these affairs, God will be glad; and so will others. [19]In this way aim for harmony in the church and try to build each other up. [20]Don't undo the work of God for a chunk of meat. Remember, there is nothing wrong with the meat, but it is wrong to eat it if it makes another stumble. [21]The right thing to do is to quit eating meat or drinking wine or doing anything else that offends your brother or makes him sin. [22]You may know that there is nothing wrong with what you do, even from God's point of view, but keep it to yourself; don't flaunt your faith in front of others who might be hurt by it. In this situation, happy is the man who does not sin by doing what he knows is right. [23]But anyone who believes that something he wants to do is wrong shouldn't do it. He sins if he does, for he thinks it is wrong, and so for him it *is* wrong. Anything that is done apart from what he feels is right is sin.

1 Cor 4:5. So be careful not to jump to conclusions before the Lord returns as to whether someone is a good servant or not. When the Lord comes, he will turn on the light so that everyone can see exactly what each one of us is really like, deep down in our hearts. Then everyone will know why we have been doing the Lord's work. At that time, God will give to each one whatever praise is coming to him.

1 Cor 10:28. But if someone warns you that his meat has been offered to idols, then don't eat it for the sake of the man who told you, and of his conscience. [29]In this case *his* feeling about it is the important thing, not yours. But why, you may ask, must I be guided and limited by what someone else thinks? [30]If I can thank God for the food and enjoy it, why let someone spoil everything just because he thinks I am wrong? [31]Well, I'll tell you why. It is because you must do everything for the glory of God, even your eating and drinking. [32]So don't be a stumbling block to anyone, whether they are Jews or Gentiles or Christians. [33]That is the plan I follow too. I try to please everyone in everything I do, not doing what I like or what is best for me, but what is best for them, so that they may be saved.

1 Cor 13:1. If I had the gift of being able to speak in other languages without learning them, and could speak in every language there is in all of heaven and earth, but didn't love others, I would only be making noise. [2]If I had the gift of prophecy and knew all about what is going to happen in the future, knew everything about *everything,* but didn't love others, what good would it do? Even if I had the gift of faith so that I could speak to a mountain and make it move, I would still be worth nothing at all without love. [3]If I gave everything I have to poor people, and if I were burned alive for preaching the Gospel but didn't love others, it would be of no value whatever.

4. Love is very patient and kind, never jealous or envious, never boastful or proud, [5]never haughty or selfish or rude. Love does not demand its own way. It is not irritable or touchy. It does not hold grudges and will hardly even notice when others do it wrong. [6]It is never glad about injustice, but rejoices whenever truth wins out. [7]If you love someone you will be loyal to him no matter what the cost. You will always believe in him, always expect the best of him, and always stand your ground in defending him.

8. All the special gifts and powers from God will someday come to an end, but love goes on forever. Someday prophecy, and speaking in unknown languages, and special knowledge—these gifts will disappear. [9]Now we know so little, even with our special gifts, and the preaching of those most gifted is still so poor. [10]But when we have been made perfect and complete, then the need for these inadequate special gifts will come to an end, and they will disappear. [11]It's like this: when I was a child I spoke and thought and reasoned as a child does. But when I became a man my thoughts grew far beyond those of my childhood, and now I have put away the childish things. [12]In the same way, we can see and understand only a little about God now, as if we were peering at his reflection in a poor mirror; but someday we are going to see him in his completeness, face to face. Now all that I know is hazy and blurred, but then I will see everything clearly, just as clearly as God sees into my heart right now.

13. There are three things that remain—faith, hope, and love—and the greatest of these is love.

1 Cor 16:14. And whatever you do, do it with kindness and love.

Gal 6:1. Dear brothers, if a Christian is overcome by some sin, you who are godly should gently and humbly help him back onto the right path, remembering that next time it might be one of you who is in the wrong.

Eph 4:32. Instead, be kind to each other, tenderhearted, forgiving one another, just as God has forgiven you because you belong to Christ.

Col 3:13. Be gentle and ready to forgive; never hold grudges. Remember, the Lord forgave you, so you must forgive others. [14]Most of all, let love guide your life, for then the whole church will stay together in perfect harmony.

1 Tim 1:5. What I am eager for is that all the Christians there will be filled with love that comes from pure hearts, and that their minds will be clean and their faith strong.

1 Tim 4:12. Don't let anyone think little of you because you are young. Be their ideal; let them follow the way you teach and live; be a pattern for them in your love, your faith, and your clean thoughts.

2 Tim 2:22. Run from anything that gives you the evil thoughts that young men often have, but stay close to anything that makes you want to do right. Have faith and love, and enjoy the companionship of those who love the Lord and have pure hearts.

Jas 2:13. For there will be no mercy to those who have shown no mercy. But if you have been merciful, then God's mercy toward you will win out over his judgment against you.

Jas 4:11. Don't criticize and speak evil about each other, dear brothers. If you do, you will be fighting against God's law of loving one another, declaring it is wrong. But your job is not to decide whether this law is right or wrong, but to obey it. [12]Only he who made the law can rightly judge among us. He alone decides to save us or destroy. So what right do you have to judge or criticize others?

1 Pet 3:9. Don't repay evil for evil. Don't snap back at those who say unkind things about you. Instead, pray for God's help for them, for we are to be kind to others, and God will bless us for it.

1 Pet 4:8. Most important of all, continue to show deep love for each other, for love makes up for many of your faults.

See *Love; Uncharitableness.*

CHARITY Commanded, Deut 15:7–11; Mt 5:42; 19:21; Lk 12:33; 2 Cor 9:5–7; Gal 2:10; 1 Tim 6:18; Heb 13:16. To be given without ostentation, Mt 6:1–4; Rom 12:8; freely, 2 Cor 9:6, 7. Withholding not of love, 1 Jn 3:17. Solicited by the unfortunate, Jn 9:8; Acts 3:2.

See *Benevolence; Giving; Liberality; Poor; Presents.*

INSTANCES OF GIVING. Zaccheus, Lk 19:8. Dorcas, Acts 9:36. Cornelius, Acts 10:2. The early Christians, Acts 2:44, 45; 4:34–37; 6:1–3; 11:29, 30; 24:17; Rom 15:25–28; 1 Cor 16:1–4; 2 Cor 8:1–4; 9:1; Heb 6:10.

See *Benevolence; Liberality; Love.*

CHARMERS AND CHARMING Jer 8:17; Nah 3:4; Acts 19:18, 19. Prohibited, Deut 18:11; Ezk 13:18, 20. Of snakes, Eccl 10:11; Ps 58:4, 5; Jer 8:17.

See *Sorcery.*

CHASTISEMENT FROM GOD. Lev 26:28. Then I will let loose my great anger and send you seven times greater punishment for your sins.

Deut 11:2. Listen! I am not talking now to your children who have never experienced the Lord's punishments or seen his greatness and his awesome power. [3]They weren't there to see the miracles he did in Egypt against Pharaoh and all his land. [4]They didn't see what God did to the armies of Egypt and to their horses and chariots—how he drowned them in the Red Sea as they were chasing you, and how the Lord has kept them powerless against you until this very day! [5]They didn't see how the Lord cared for you time and time again through all the years you were wandering in the wilderness, until your arrival here. [6]They weren't there when Dathan and Abiram (the son of Eliab, descendants of Reuben) sinned, and the earth opened up and swallowed them, with their households and tents and all their belongings, as all Israel watched! [7]But *you* have seen these mighty miracles! [8]How carefully, then, you should obey these commandments I am going to give you today, so that you may have the strength to go in and possess the land you are about to enter. [9]If you obey the commandments, you will have a long and good life in the land the Lord promised to your ancestors and to you, their descendants—a wonderful land "flowing with milk and honey"!

2 Sam 7:14. I will be his father and he shall be my son. If he sins, I will use other nations to punish him, [15]but my love and kindness shall not leave him as I took it from Saul, your predecessor.

2 Chron 6:24. If your people Israel are destroyed before their enemies because they have sinned against you, and if they turn to you and call themselves your people, and pray to you here in this Temple, [25]then listen to them from heaven and forgive their sins and give them back this land you gave to their fathers. [26]When the skies are shut and there is no rain because of our sins, and then we pray toward this Temple and claim you as our God, and turn from our sins because you have punished us, [27]then listen from heaven and forgive the sins of your people, and teach them what is right; and send rain upon this land which you have given to your people as their own property. [28]If there is a famine in the land, or plagues, or crop disease, or attacks of locusts or caterpillars, or if your people's enemies are in the land besieging our cities—whatever the trouble is—[29]listen to every individual's prayer concerning his private sorrow, as well as all the public prayers. [30]Hear from heaven where you live, and forgive, and give each one whatever he deserves, for you know the hearts

of all mankind. [31]Then they will reverence you forever, and will continually walk where you tell them to go.

2 Chron 7:13. If I shut up the heavens so that there is no rain, or if I command the locust swarm to eat up all of your crops, or if I send an epidemic among you, [14]then if my people will humble themselves and pray, and search for me, and turn from their wicked ways, I will hear them from heaven and forgive their sins and heal their land.

Job 5:17. How enviable the man whom God corrects! Oh, do not despise the chastening of the Lord when you sin.

Job 33:19. Or, God sends sickness and pain, even though no bone is broken.

Ps 6:1. No, Lord! don't punish me in the heat of your anger. Ps 38:1.

Ps 73:14. All I get out of it is trouble and woe—every day and all day long!

Ps 89:30–32. If his children forsake my laws and don't obey them, then I will punish them.

Ps 94:12, 13. So he helps us by punishing us. This makes us follow his paths, and gives us respite from our enemies while God traps them and destroys them.

Ps 106:41, 42. That is why he let the heathen nations crush them. They were ruled by those who hated them and oppressed by their enemies. [43]Again and again he delivered them from their slavery, but they continued to rebel against him, and were finally destroyed by their sin. [44]Yet, even so, he listened to their cries and heeded their distress.

Ps 107:17. Others, the fools, were ill because of their sinful ways. [18]Their appetites were gone and death was near. [19]Then they cried to the Lord in their troubles, and he helped them and delivered them. [20]He spoke, and they were healed—snatched from the door of death. [21]Oh, that these men would praise the Lord for his lovingkindness and for all of his wonderful deeds!

23. And then there are the sailors sailing the seven seas, plying the trade routes of the world. [24]They, too, observe the power of God in action. [25]He calls to the storm winds; the waves rise high. [26]Their ships are tossed to the heavens and sink again to the depths; the sailors cringe in terror. [27]They reel and stagger like drunkards and are at their wit's end. [28]Then they cry to the Lord in their trouble, and he saves them. [29]He calms the storm and stills the waves. [30]What a blessing is that stillness, as he brings them safely into harbor! [31]Oh, that these men would praise the Lord for his lovingkindness and for all of his wonderful deeds!

Ps 118:18. The Lord has punished me, but not handed me over to death.

Ps 119:67. I used to wander off until you punished me; now I closely follow all you say. [75]I know, O Lord, that your decisions are right and that your punishment was right and did me good.

Prov 3:11, 12. Young man, do not resent it when God chastens and corrects you, for his punishment is proof of his love. Just as a father punishes a son he delights in to make him better, so the Lord corrects you.

Isa 26:16. Lord, in their distress they sought for you. When your punishment was on them, they poured forth a whispered prayer.

Isa 42:25. That is why God poured out such fury and wrath on his people and destroyed them in battle. Yet, though set on fire and burned, they will not understand the reason why—that it is God, wanting them to repent.

Isa 53:4. Yet it was *our* grief he bore, *our* sorrows that weighed him down. And we thought his troubles were a punishment from God, for his *own* sins! [5]But he was wounded and bruised for *our* sins. He was chastised that we might have peace; he was lashed—and we were healed!

Isa 57:16. For I will not fight against you forever, nor always show my wrath; if I did, all mankind would perish—the very souls that I have made. [17]I was angry and smote these greedy men. But they went right on sinning, doing everything their evil hearts desired. [18]I have seen what they do, but I will heal them anyway! I will lead them and comfort them, helping them to mourn and to confess their sins.

Jer 2:30. I have punished your children but it did them no good; they still will not obey. And you yourselves have killed my prophets as a lion kills its prey.

Jer 30:14. All your lovers have left you and don't care anything about you any more; for I have wounded you cruelly, as though I were your enemy; mercilessly, as though I were an implacable foe; for your sins are so many, your guilt is so great.

Jer 31:18. I have heard Ephraim's groans: "You have punished me greatly; but I needed it all, as a calf must be trained for the yoke. Turn me again to you and restore me, for you alone are the Lord, my God. [19]I turned away from God but I was sorry afterwards. I kicked myself for my stupidity. I was thoroughly ashamed of all I did in younger days." [20]And the Lord replies: Ephraim is still my son, my darling child. I had to punish him, but I still love him. I long for him and surely will have mercy on him.

Jer 46:28. Fear not, O Jacob, my servant, says the Lord, for I am with you. I will destroy all the nations to which I have exiled you, but I will not destroy you. I will punish you, but only enough to correct you.

Lam 1:5. Her enemies prosper, for the Lord has punished Jerusalem for all her many sins; her young children are captured and taken far away as slaves.

Hos 7:12. But as she flies, I throw my net over her and bring her down like a bird from the sky; I will punish her for all her evil ways.

Hos 10:10. I will come against you for your disobedience; I will gather the armies of the nations against you to punish you for your heaped-up sins.

Hag 2:17. "I rewarded all your labor with rust and mildew and hail. Yet, even so, you refused to return to me," says the Lord.

Heb 12:5. And have you quite forgotten the encouraging words God spoke to you, his child? He said, "My son, don't be angry when the Lord punishes you. Don't be discouraged when he has to show you where you are wrong. [6]For when he punishes you, it proves that he loves you. When he whips you it proves you are really his child." [7]Let God train you, for he is doing what any loving father does for his children. Whoever heard of a son who was never corrected? [8]If God doesn't punish you when you need it, as other fathers punish their sons, then it means that you aren't really God's son at all—that you don't really belong in his family. [9]Since we respect our fathers here on earth, though they punish us, should we not all the more cheerfully submit to God's training so that we can begin really to live? [10]Our earthly fathers trained us for a few brief years, doing the best for us that they knew how, but God's correction is always right and for our best good, that we may share his holiness. [11]Being punished isn't enjoyable while it is happening—it hurts! But afterwards we can see the result, a quiet growth in grace and character.

Rev 3:19. I continually discipline and punish everyone I love; so I must punish you, unless you turn from your indifference and become enthusiastic about the things of God.

See *Afflictions, Design of; Judgments; Punishment; Wicked, Punishment of.*

CHASTITY Ex 20:14. You must not commit adultery.

Job 31:1. I made a covenant with my eyes not to look with lust upon a girl.

Prov 2:10. For wisdom and truth will enter the very center of your being, filling your life with joy. [11-13]You will be given the sense to stay away from evil men who want you to be their partners in crime—men who turn from God's ways to walk down dark and evil paths. [16, 17]Only wisdom from the Lord can save a man from the flattery of prostitutes; these girls have abandoned their husbands and flouted the laws of God. [18]Their houses lie along the road to death and hell. [19]The men who enter them are doomed. None of these men will ever be the same again. [20]Follow the steps of the godly instead, and stay on the right path, [21]for only good men enjoy life to the full; [22]evil men lose the good things they might have had, and they themselves shall be destroyed.

Prov 5:15. Drink from your own well, my son—be faithful and true to your wife. [16]Why should you beget children with women of the street? [17]Why share your children with those outside your home? [18]Let your manhood be a blessing; rejoice in the wife of your youth. [19]Let her charms and tender embrace satisfy you. Let her love alone fill you with delight. [20]Why delight yourself with prostitutes, embracing what isn't yours? [21]*For God is closely watching you,* and he weighs carefully everything you do.

Prov 6:24. Their counsel will keep you far away from prostitutes with all their flatteries. [25]Don't lust for their beauty. Don't let their coyness seduce you.

Prov 7:1. Follow my advice, my son; always keep it in mind and stick to it. [2]Obey me and live! Guard my words as your most precious possession. [3]Write them down, and also keep them deep within your heart. [4]Love wisdom like a sweetheart; make her a beloved member of your family. [5]Let her hold you back from visiting a prostitute, from listening to her flattery.

Prov 31:3. Do not spend your time with women —the royal pathway to destruction.

Mt 5:28. But I say: Anyone who even looks at a woman with lust in his eye has already committed adultery with her in his heart.

Acts 15:20. Except that we should write to them to refrain from eating meat sacrificed to idols, from all fornication, and also from eating unbled meat of strangled animals.

Rom 13:13. Be decent and true in everything you do so that all can approve your behavior. Don't spend your time in wild parties and getting drunk or in adultery and lust, or fighting, or jealousy.

1 Cor 6:13. For instance, take the matter of eating. God has given us an appetite for food and stomachs to digest it. But that doesn't mean we should eat more than we need. Don't think of eating as important, because some day God will do away with both stomachs and food. But sexual sin is never right: our bodies were not made for that, but for the Lord, and the Lord wants to fill our bodies with himself. [14]And God is going to raise our bodies from the dead by his power just as he raised up the Lord Jesus Christ. [15]Don't you realize that your bodies are actually parts and members of Christ? So should I take part of Christ and join him to a prostitute? Never! [16]And don't you know that if a man joins himself to a prostitute she becomes a part of him and he becomes a part of her? For God tells us in the Scripture that in his sight the two become one person. [17]But if you give yourself to the Lord, you and Christ are joined together as one person. [18]That is why I say to run from sex sin. No other sin affects the body as this one does. When you sin this sin it is against your own body. [19]Haven't you yet learned that your body is the home of the Holy Spirit God gave you and that he lives within you? Your own body does not belong to you.

1 Cor 7:1. Now about those questions you asked in your last letter: my answer is that if you do not marry, it is good. [2]But usually it is best to be married, each man having his own wife, and each woman having her own husband, because otherwise you might fall back into sin.

7. I wish everyone could get along without marrying, just as I do. But we are not all the same. God gives some the gift of a husband or wife, and others he gives the gift of being able to stay happily unmarried. [8]So I say to those who aren't married, and to widows—better to stay unmarried if you can, just as I am. [9]But if you can't control yourselves, go ahead and marry. It is bet-

ter to marry than to burn with lust.

25. Now I will try to answer your other question. What about girls who are not yet married? Should they be permitted to do so? In answer to this question, I have no special command for them from the Lord. But the Lord in his kindness has given me wisdom that can be trusted, and I will be glad to tell you what I think. [26]Here is the problem: We Christians are facing great dangers to our lives at present. In times like these I think it is best for a person to remain unmarried. [36]But if anyone feels he ought to marry because he has trouble controlling his passions, it is all right, it is not a sin; let him marry. [37]But if a man has the willpower not to marry and decides that he doesn't need to and won't, he has made a wise decision.

Eph 5:3. Let there be no sex sin, impurity or greed among you. Let no one be able to accuse you of any such things.

Col 3:5. Away then with sinful, earthly things; deaden the evil desires lurking within you; have nothing to do with sexual sin, impurity, lust and shameful desires; don't worship the good things of life, for that is idolatry.

1 Thess 4:3, 4. For God wants you to be holy and pure, and to keep clear of all sexual sin so that each of you will marry in holiness and honor—[7]For God has not called us to be dirty-minded and full of lust, but to be holy and clean.

Rev 14:1. Then I saw a Lamb standing on Mount Zion in Jerusalem, and with him were 144,000 who had his Name and his Father's Name written on their foreheads. [2]And I heard a sound from heaven like the roaring of a great waterfall or the rolling of mighty thunder. It was the singing of a choir accompanied by harps. [3]This tremendous choir—144,000 strong—sang a wonderful new song in front of the throne of God and before the four Living Beings and the twenty-four Elders; and no one could sing this song except those 144,000 who had been redeemed from the earth. [4]For they are spiritually undefiled, pure as virgins, following the Lamb wherever he goes. They have been purchased from among the men on the earth as a consecrated offering to God and the Lamb. [5]No falsehood can be charged against them; they are blameless.

See *Continence.*

INSTANCES OF. Joseph, Gen 39:7–20; Boaz, Ruth 3:6–13; Paul, 1 Cor 7.

CHEATING See *Dishonesty.*

CHEBAR A canal or river in Babylonia, Ezk 1:1–3; 3:14, 15; 10:15, 16, 22; 43:3.

CHED-OR-LAOMER King of Elam, Gen 14:1–16.

CHEERFULNESS See *Contentment.*

CHEESE Gen 18:8; 1 Sam 17:18; 2 Sam 17:29; Job 10:10.

See *Butter.*

CHELAL Son of Pahath-moab, Ezra 10:30.

CHELUB 1. A descendant of Judah, 1 Chron 4:11.

2. Father of Ezri, 1 Chron 27:26.

CHELUBAI Son of Hezron, 1 Chron 2:9. Called *Caleb, vs.* 18, 42. Perhaps the same as *Caleb,* which see.

CHELUHI Son of Bani, Ezra 10:34–42.

CHEMOSH A god of the Moabites and Ammonites, Num 21:27–30; Judg 11:24; 1 Kgs 11:7, 33; 2 Kgs 23:13; Jer 48:7, 13, 46.

CHENAANAH 1. Father of the false prophet Zedekiah, 1 Kgs 22:11, 24; 2 Chron 18:10, 23.

2. A Benjaminite and son of Bilhan, 1 Chron 7:10.

CHENANI A Levite, Neh 9:4.

CHENANIAH 1. A Levite, 1 Chron 15:22, 27.

2. An Izharite, 1 Chron 26:29.

CHEPHAR-AMMONI A town of Benjamin, Josh 18:21–28.

CHEPHIRAH A city of the Hivites, assigned to the tribe of Benjamin, Josh 9:17; 18:26; Ezra 2:3–35; Neh 7:8–38.

CHERAN A Horite, Gen 36:26; 1 Chron 1:41.

CHERETHITES A Philistine (Cretan) tribe, which adhered to David, and with the Pelethites formed his bodyguard, 1 Sam 30:14, 16; 2 Sam 8:18; 15:17, 18; 20:7, 23; 1 Kgs 1:38, 44, 45; 1 Chron 18:17; Ezk 25:16; Zeph 2:5. Solomon's escort at his coronation, 1 Kgs 1:38.

CHERITH A brook near Jericho, 1 Kgs 17: 3–7.

CHERUB A Persian city, Ezra 2:59; Neh 7: 61.

CHERUBIM Angelic beings. In the Tabernacle, Ex 25:18–20; 37:7–9. Ark rested beneath the wings of, 1 Kgs 8:6, 7; 2 Chron 5:7, 8; Heb 9:5. Figures of, embroidered on walls of Tabernacle, Ex 26:1; 36:8, 9; and on the veil, Ex 26:31; 36:35.

In the Temple, 1 Kgs 6:23–29; 2 Chron 3:10–13. Figures of, on the veil, 2 Chron 3:14; walls, 1 Kgs 6:29–35; 2 Chron 3:7; lavers, 1 Kgs 7:29, 36.

In Ezekiel's vision of the Temple, Ezk 41:17–20, 25.

FIGURATIVE. Ezk 28:14, 16.

Symbolical. Ezk 1:10.

See *Angel.*

CHESALON A town in the north boundary of Judah, Josh 15:10.

CHESED Son of Nahor, Gen 22:22.

CHESIL A town in southern Palestine, Josh 15:21–32. Probably identical with *Bethul,* Josh 19: 4, and *Bethuel,* 1 Chron 4:30.

CHEST For gold rats and tumor, 1 Sam 6:8, 11, 15; for money, 2 Kgs 12:9; 2 Chron 24:7–11; 34:17.

See *Treasury.*

CHESTPIECE See *Breastplate.*

CHESULLOTH A city of Issachar, near Zebulun, Josh 19:17–23. Probably identical with *Chisloth-tabor,* of *v.* 12, and *Tabor,* 1 Chron 6:77.

CHEZIB Birthplace of Shelah, Gen 38:3–5, probably identical with *Cozeba,* 1 Chron 4:21, 22, and *Achzib,* Josh 15:44.

CHICKEN 1 Kgs 20:11; Jer 5:27; protects her young, Mt 23:37; Lk 13:34.

CHIDON Place where the Lord killed Uzza,

1 Chron 13:9. Called *Nacon's threshing floor,* 2 Sam 6:6.

CHIDING Cain chides God, Gen 4:13, 14. Pharaoh chides Abraham, for calling his wife his sister, Gen 12:18, 19. Abimelech chides Abraham for a like offense, Gen 20:9, 10. Abimelech chides Isaac for similar conduct, Gen 26:9, 10. Jacob and Laban chide each other, Gen 31:26–42. Jacob chides Simeon and Levi for killing Hamor and Shechem, Gen 34:30. Reuben chides his brethren for their treatment of Joseph, Gen 42:22. Israelites chide Moses and tempt God, Ex 17:7. Deborah chides Israel in her epic, Judg 5:16–23. David chides Joab for killing Abner, 2 Sam 3:28–31. Joab chides David for lamenting the death of Absalom, 2 Sam 19:5–7.

Jesus chides his disciples for their lack of faith, Mt 8:26; 14:31; 16:8–11; 17:17; Mk 4:40; Lk 8:25; for lack of understanding, Mt 15:16; 16:8, 9, 11; Mk 7:18; Lk 24:25; Jn 14:9; for sleeping in Gethsemane, Mt 26:40; Mk 14:37; for forbidding children to be brought to him, Mt 19:14; Mk 10:14; Lk 18:16, 17.

CHIEF Of the Thirty, 1 Chron 11:21. Title of a leader of Edom, 1 Chron 1:51–54; of Midian, Josh 13:21.

See *Armies; Captain; Officer.*

CHILDLESSNESS A reproach, Gen 16:2, 3; 29:31; 30:1–3; 1 Sam 1:6; Isa 4:1; Lk 1:25.

See *Barrenness.*

CHILDREN INDEX OF SUB-TOPICS. *Miscellany; The Gift of God; God's Care of; A Blessing; Commandments to; Counsel of Parents to; Instruction of; False Instruction of; Prayer in Behalf of; Promises and Assurances to; Of the Righteous, Blessed by God; Correction of; Punishment of; Good; Wicked; Worship, Attend Divine; Symbolical of the Regenerated.*

In answer to prayer: To Abraham, Gen 15:2–5, with Gen 21:1, 2; Isaac, Gen 25:21; Leah, Gen 30:17–21; Rachel, Gen 30:22–24; Hannah, 1 Sam 1:9–20; Zacharias, Lk 1:13.

Treatment of, at birth, Ezk 16:4, 5; Lk 2:7, 12. Circumcision of, see *circumcision.*

Dedicated to God in infancy: Samson, Judg 13:5, 7; Samuel, 1 Sam 1:24–28. Promised to the righteous, Deut 7:12, 14; Job 5:25; Ps 128:2, 3, 4, 6. Weaning of, Gen 21:8; 1 Sam 1:21, 22; Ps 131:2; Isa 7:15, 16, Hos 1:8. Nurses for, Gen 24:59; Ex 2:7–9; Ruth 4:16, 17; 2 Sam 4:4; 2 Kgs 11:2, 3. Taught to walk, Hos 11:3. Tutors and guardians for, 2 Kgs 10:1; Acts 22:3; Gal 3:24; 4:1, 2. Bastard, excluded from the privileges of the congregation, Deut 23:2; Heb 12:8.

Early piety of: Samuel, 1 Sam 2:18; 3; Jeremiah, Jer 1:5–7; John the Baptist, Lk 1:15, 80. Jesus, Lk 2:40, 46, 47, 52.

Difference made between male and female, in Mosaic law, Lev 12. Partiality of parents among: Rebekah for Jacob, Gen 27:6–17; Jacob for Joseph, Gen 37:3, 4. Partiality among, forbidden, Deut 21:15–17.

Love of, for parents: Of Ruth, Ruth 1:16–18; Jesus, Jn 19:26, 27.

Sacrificed, 2 Kgs 16:3; 17:31; Jer 32:35; Ezk 16:20, 21.

Sold for debt, 2 Kgs 4:1; Neh 5:5; Job 24:9; Mt 18:25. Sold in marriage, law concerning, Ex 21:7–11; instance of, Leah and Rachel, Gen 29:15–30.

Edict to murder: Of Pharaoh, Ex 1:22; of Jehu, 2 Kgs 10:1–8; of Herod, Mt 2:16–18. Eaten, see *Cannibalism.*

Share benefits of covenant privileges guaranteed to parents, Gen 6:18; 12:7; 13:15; 17:7, 8; 19:12; 21:13; 26:3–5, 24; Lev 26:44, 45; Isa 65:23; 1 Cor 7:14. Bound by covenants of parents, Gen 17:9–14. Involved in guilt of parents, Ex 20:5; 34:7; Lev 20:5; 26:39–42; Num 14:17, 18, 33; 1 Kgs 21:29; Job 21:19; Ps 37:28; Isa 14:20, 21; 65:6, 7; Jer 32:18; Dan 6:24. Not punished for parents' sake, Jer 31:29, 30; Ezk 18:1–30.

Death of, as a judgment upon parents: Firstborn of Egypt, Ex 12:29; sons of Eli, 1 Sam 3:13, 14; sons of Saul, 1 Sam 28:18, 19; 31:8; David's child by Uriah's wife, 2 Sam 12:14–19.

Miracles in behalf of: Raised from the dead by Elijah, 1 Kgs 17:17–23; by Elisha, 2 Kgs 4:17–36; by Jesus, Mt 9:18, 24–26; Mk 5:35–42; Lk 7:13–15; 8:49–56; healing of, Mt 15:28; 17:18; Mk 7:29, 30; 9:23–27; Lk 9:38–42; Jn 4:46–54.

Character of, known by conduct, Prov 20:11. Blessed by Jesus, Mt 19:13–15; Mk 10:13–16; Lk 18:15–17. Future state of, Mt 18:10; 19:14. Minors, Gal 4:1, 2. Of pastors, 1 Tim 3:4; Tit 1:6. Alienated, Ishmael, to gratify Sarah, Gen 21:9–14.

Amusements of, Job 21:11–13; Zech 8:5; Mt 11:16, 17; Lk 7:31, 32.

Adopted. See *Adoption.*

THE GIFT OF GOD. Gen 4:1. Then Adam had sexual intercourse with Eve his wife, and she conceived and gave birth to a son, Cain (meaning "I have created"). For, as she said, "With God's help, I have created a man!" [25]Later on Eve gave birth to another son and named him Seth (meaning "Granted"); for, as Eve put it, "God has granted me another son for the one Cain killed."

Gen 17:16. And I will bless her and give you a son from her! Yes, I will bless her richly, and make her the mother of nations! Many kings shall be among your posterity. [20]As for Ishmael, all right, I will bless him also, just as you have asked me to. I will cause him to multiply and become a great nation. Twelve princes shall be among his posterity.

Gen 28:3. God Almighty bless you and give you many children; may you become a great nation of many tribes!

Gen 29:32. So Leah became pregnant and had a son, Reuben (meaning "God has noticed my trouble"), for she said, "Jehovah has noticed my trouble—now my husband will love me." [33]She soon became pregnant again and had another son and named him Simeon (meaning "Jehovah heard"), for she said, "Jehovah heard that I was unloved, and so he has given me another son." [34]Again she became pregnant and had a son, and named him Levi (meaning "Attachment") for she said, "Surely now my husband will feel affection for me, since I have given him three sons!" [35]Once again she was pregnant and had a son and named him Judah (meaning "Praise"), for she said, "Now I will praise Jehovah!" And then she stopped having children.

Gen 30:2. Jacob flew into a rage. "Am I God?" he flared. "He is the one who is responsible for your barrenness." [6]Rachel named him Dan (meaning "Justice"), for she said, "God has given me justice, and heard my plea and given me a son." [17]And God answered her [Leah's] prayers and she became pregnant again, and gave birth to her fifth son. [18]She named him Issachar (meaning "Wages"), for she said, "God has repaid me for giving my slave-girl to my husband." [19]Then once again she became pregnant, with a sixth son. [20]She named him Zebulun (meaning "Gifts"), for she said, "God has given me good gifts for my husband. Now he will honor me, for I have given him six sons." [22]Then God remembered about Rachel's plight, and answered her prayers by giving her a child. [23, 24]For she became pregnant and gave birth to a son. "God has removed the dark slur against my name," she said. And she named him Joseph (meaning "May I also have another!"), for she said, "May Jehovah give me another son."

Ruth 4:13. So Boaz married Ruth, and when he slept with her, the Lord gave her a son.

Job 1:21. "I came naked from my mother's womb," he said, "and I shall have nothing when I die. The Lord gave me everything I had, and they were his to take away. Blessed be the name of the Lord."

Ps 107:38. How he blesses them! They raise big families there, and many cattle. [41]But he rescues the poor who are godly and gives them many children and much prosperity.

Ps 113:9. He gives children to the childless wife, so that she becomes a happy mother. Hallelujah! Praise the Lord.

Ps 127:3. Children are a gift from God; they are his reward.

GOD'S CARE OF. Ex 22:22. You must not exploit widows or orphans; [23]if you do so in any way, and they cry to me for my help, I will surely give it. [24]And my anger shall flame out against you, and I will kill you with enemy armies, so that your wives will be widows and your children fatherless.

Deut 10:18. He gives justice to the fatherless and widows. He loves foreigners and gives them food and clothing.

Deut 14:29. Give it to the Levites who have no inheritance among you, or to foreigners, or to widows and orphans within your city, so that they can eat and be satisfied; and then Jehovah your God will bless you and your work.

Job 29:12. For I, as an honest judge, helped the poor in their need, and the fatherless who had no one to help them.

Ps 10:17. Lord, you know the hopes of humble people. Surely you will hear their cries and comfort their hearts by helping them. [18]You will be with the orphans and all who are oppressed, so that mere earthly man will terrify them no longer.

Ps 27:10. For if my father and mother should abandon me, you would welcome and comfort me.

Ps 68:5. He is the father to the fatherless; he gives justice to the widows, for he is holy.

Ps 146:9. He protects the immigrants, and cares for the orphans and widows.

Jer 49:11. But I will preserve your fatherless children who remain, and let your widows depend upon me.

Hos 14:3. For in you alone, O Lord, the fatherless find mercy.

Mal 3:5. I will move swiftly against . . . all those who cheat their hired hands, or oppress widows and orphans.

A BLESSING. Gen 5:29. Lamech named him Noah (meaning "Relief") because he said, "He will bring us relief from the hard work of farming this ground which God has cursed."

Gen 30:1. Rachel, realizing she was barren, became envious of her sister. "Give me children or I'll die," she exclaimed to Jacob.

Ps 127:3. Children are a gift from God; they are his reward. [4]Children born to a young man are like sharp arrows to defend him. [5]Happy is the man who has his quiver full of them. That man shall have the help he needs when arguing with his enemies.

Prov 17:6. An old man's grandchildren are his crowning glory. A child's glory is his father.

Isa 54:1. Sing, O childless woman! Break out into loud and joyful song, Jerusalem, for she who was abandoned has more blessing now than she whose husband stayed!

Jer 20:15. Cursed be the man who brought my father the news that a son was born.

COMMANDMENTS TO. Ex 20:12. Honor your father and mother, that you may have a long, good life in the land the Lord your God will give you. Deut 5:16; Mt 15:4; 19:19; Mk 10:19; Lk 18:20; Eph 6:2, 3.

Lev 19:2. You must respect your mothers and fathers, [32]You shall give due honor and respect to the elderly, in the fear of God. I am Jehovah.

Ps 119:9. How can a young man stay pure? By reading your Word and following its rules.

Ps 148:12. Young men and maidens, old men and children—[13]all praise the Lord together. For he alone is worthy. His glory is far greater than all of earth and heaven.

Prov 1:7–9. How does a man become wise? The first step is to trust and reverence the Lord! Only fools refuse to be taught. Listen to your father and mother. What you learn from them will stand you in good stead; it will gain you many honors.

Prov 3:1, 2. My son, never forget the things I've taught you. If you want a long and satisfying life, closely follow my instructions. [3]Never forget to be truthful and kind. Hold these virtues tightly. Write them deep within your heart.

Prov 4:1, 2. Young men, listen to me as you would to your father. Listen, and grow wise, for I speak the truth—don't turn away. [3]For I, too, was once a son, tenderly loved by my mother as an only child, and the companion of my father. [4]He told me never to forget his words. "If you follow them," he said, "you will have a long and happy life. [10]My son, listen to me and do as I say, and you will have a long, good life. [11]I would have you learn this great fact: that a life of doing right is the wisest life there is. [20]Listen, son of mine, to what I say. Listen carefully. [21]Keep these thoughts ever in mind; let them penetrate deep within your heart, [22]For they will mean real life for you, and radiant health.

Prov 5:1. Listen to me, my son! I know what I am saying; *listen!* [2]Watch yourself, lest you be indiscreet and betray some vital information.

Prov 6:20. Young man, obey your father and your mother. [21]Tie their instructions around your finger so you won't forget. Take to heart all of their advice. [22]Every day and all night long their counsel will lead you and save you from harm; when you wake up in the morning, let their instructions guide you into the new day. [23]For their advice is a beam of light directed into the dark corners of your mind to warn you of danger and to give you a good life. [24]Their counsel will keep you far away from prostitutes with all their flatteries. [25]Don't lust for their beauty. Don't let their coyness seduce you.

Prov 8:32. And so, young men, listen to me, for how happy are all who follow my instructions. [33]Listen to my counsel—oh, don't refuse it—and be wise.

Prov 23:22. Listen to your father's advice and don't despise an old mother's experience. [26]O my son, trust my advice.

Prov 27:11. My son, how happy I will be if you turn out to be sensible! It will be a public honor to me.

Eccl 12:1. Don't let the excitement of being young cause you to forget about your Creator. Honor him in your youth before the evil years come—when you'll no longer enjoy living.

Lam 3:27. It is good for a young man to be under discipline.

Eph 6:1. Children, obey your parents; this is the right thing to do because God has placed them in authority over you.

Col 3:20. You children must always obey your fathers and mothers, for that pleases the Lord.

1 Tim 4:12. Don't let anyone think little of you because you are young. Be their ideal; let them follow the way you teach and live; be a pattern for them in your love, your faith, and your clean thoughts.

2 Tim 2:22. Run from anything that gives you the evil thoughts that young men often have, but stay close to anything that makes you want to do right. Have faith and love, and enjoy the companionship of those who love the Lord and have pure hearts.

Tit 2:6. In the same way, urge the young men to behave carefully, taking life seriously.

See *Young Men.*

COUNSEL OF PARENTS TO. 1 Kgs 2:1. As the time of King David's death approached, he gave this charge to his son Solomon: [2]"I am going where every man on earth must some day go. I am counting on you to be a strong and worthy successor. [3]Obey the laws of God and follow all his ways; keep each of his commands written in the law of Moses so that you will prosper in everything you do, wherever you turn. [4]If you do this, then the Lord will fulfill the promise he gave me, that if my children and their descendants watch their step and are faithful to God, one of them shall always be the king of Israel—my dynasty will never end."

1 Chron 22:6. He now commanded his son Solomon to build a temple for the Lord God of Israel. [7]"I wanted to build it myself," David told him, [8]"but the Lord said not to do it. 'You have killed too many men in great wars,' he told me. 'You have reddened the ground before me with blood: so you are not to build my Temple. [9]But I will give you a son,' he told me, 'who will be a man of peace, for I will give him peace with his enemies in the surrounding lands. His name shall be Solomon (meaning "Peaceful"), and I will give peace and quietness to Israel during his reign. [10]He shall build my temple, and he shall be as my own son and I will be his father; and I will cause his sons and his descendants to reign over every generation of Israel.' [11]So now, my son, may the Lord be with you and prosper you as you do what he told you to do and build the Temple of the Lord. [12]And may the Lord give you the good judgment to follow all his laws when he makes you king of Israel. [13]For if you carefully obey the rules and regulations which he gave to Israel through Moses, you will prosper. Be strong and courageous, fearless and enthusiastic!"

See *Parents.*

INSTRUCTION OF. Ex 13:8. During those celebration days each year you must explain to your children why you are celebrating—it is a celebration of what the Lord did for you when you left Egypt. [9]This annual memorial week will brand you as his own unique people, just as though he had branded his mark of ownership upon your hands or your forehead. [10]So celebrate the event annually in late March. [14]And in the future, when your children ask you, "What is this all about?" you shall tell them, "With mighty miracles Jehovah brought us out of Egypt from our slavery. [15]Pharaoh wouldn't let us go, so Jehovah killed all the firstborn males throughout the land of Egypt, both of men and animals; that is why we now give all the firstborn males to the Lord—except that all the eldest sons are always bought back." [16]Again I say, this celebration shall identify you as God's people, just as much as if his brand of ownership were placed upon your foreheads. It is a reminder that the Lord brought us out of Egypt with great power.

Deut 4:9. But watch out! Be very careful never to forget what you have seen God doing for you. May his miracles have a deep and permanent effect upon your lives! Tell your children and your grandchildren about the glorious miracles he did. [10]Tell them especially about the day you stood before the Lord at Mount Horeb, and he told me,

"Summon the people before me and I will instruct them, so that they will learn always to reverence me, and so that they can teach my laws to their children."

Deut 6:6. And you must think constantly about these commandments I am giving you today. [7]You must teach them to your children and talk about them when you are at home or out for a walk; at bedtime and the first thing in the morning. [8]Tie them on your finger, wear them on your forehead, [9]and write them on the doorposts of your house!

Deut 11:19. Teach them to your children. Talk about them when you are sitting at home, when you are out walking, at bedtime, and before breakfast! [20]Write them upon the doors of your houses and upon your gates.

Deut 31:12. "Call them all together," the Lord instructed, "—men, women, children, and foreigners living among you—to hear the laws of God and to learn his will, so that you will reverence the Lord your God and obey his laws. [13]Do this so that your little children who have not known these laws will hear them and learn how to revere the Lord your God as long as you live in the Promised Land."

Josh 8:35. Every commandment Moses had ever given was read before the entire assembly, including the women and children and the foreigners who lived among the Israelis.

Ps 34:11. Sons and daughters, come and listen and let me teach you the importance of trusting and fearing the Lord.

Ps 78:1. O my people, listen to my teaching. Open your ears to what I am saying. [2, 3]For I will show you lessons from our history, stories handed down to us from former generations. [4]I will reveal these truths to you so that you can describe these glorious deeds of Jehovah to your children, and tell them about the mighty miracles he did. [5]For he gave his laws to Israel, and commanded our fathers to teach them to their children, [6]so that they in turn could teach their children too. Thus his laws pass down from generation to generation. [7]In this way each generation has been able to obey his laws and to set its hope anew on God and not forget his glorious miracles. [8]Thus they did not need to be as their fathers were—stubborn, rebellious, unfaithful, refusing to give their hearts to God.

Prov 1:1. These are the proverbs of King Solomon of Israel, David's son: [4]"I want to make the simple-minded wise!" he said. "I want to warn young men about some problems they will face."

Prov 22:6. Teach a child to choose the right path, and when he is older he will remain upon it.

Isa 28:9. "Who does Isaiah think he is," the people say, "to speak to us like this! Are we little children, barely old enough to talk? [10]He tells us everything over and over again, a line at a time and in such simple words!"

Joel 1:3. In years to come, tell your children about it; pass the awful story down from generation to generation.

Jn 21:15. "Then feed my lambs," Jesus told him.

Acts 22:3. "I am a Jew," he said, "born in Tarsus, a city in Cilicia, but educated here in Jerusalem under Gamaliel, at whose feet I learned to follow our Jewish laws and customs very carefully. I became very anxious to honor God in everything I did, just as you have tried to do today."

See *Instruction.* For Solomon's instruction of young men and children, see *Young Men.*

By Tutors. See *Tutor.*

FALSE INSTRUCTION OF. Mk 7:9. You are simply rejecting God's laws and trampling them under your feet for the sake of tradition. [10]For instance, Moses gave you this law from God: "Honor your father and mother." And he said that anyone who speaks against his father or mother must die. [11]But you say it is perfectly all right for a man to disregard his needy parents, telling them, "Sorry, I can't help you! For I have given to God what I could have given to you." [12, 13]And so you break the law of God in order to protect your man-made tradition. And this is only one example. There are many, many others.

PRAYER IN BEHALF OF. Gen 17:18. And Abraham said to God, "Yes, do bless Ishmael!"

2 Sam 12:16. David begged him to spare the child, and went without food and lay all night before the Lord on the bare earth.

1 Chron 22:12. And may the Lord give you the good judgment to follow all his laws when he makes you king of Israel.

1 Chron 29:19. Give my son Solomon a good heart toward God, so that he will want to obey you in the smallest detail, and will look forward eagerly to finishing the building of your temple, for which I have made all of these preparations.

Job 1:5. When these birthday parties ended—and sometimes they lasted several days—Job would summon his children to him and sanctify them, getting up early in the morning and offering a burnt offering for each of them. For Job said, "Perhaps my sons have sinned and turned away from God in their hearts." This was Job's regular practice.

PROMISES AND ASSURANCES TO. Prov 3:1, 2. My son, never forget the things I've taught you. If you want a long and satisfying life, closely follow my instructions. [3]Never forget to be truthful and kind. Hold these virtues tightly. Write them deep within your heart. [4, 5]If you want favor with both God and man, and a reputation for good judgment and common sense, then trust the Lord completely; don't ever trust yourself. [6]In everything you do, put God first, and he will direct you and crown your efforts with success. [7, 8]Don't be conceited, sure of your own wisdom. Instead, trust and reverence the Lord, and turn your back on evil; when you do that, then you will be given renewed health and vitality. [9, 10]Honor the Lord by giving him the first part of all your income, and he will fill your barns with wheat and barley and overflow your wine vats with the finest wines.

Prov 8:17. I love all who love me. Those who

search for me shall surely find me. [32]And so, young men, listen to me, for how happy are all who follow my instructions.

Prov 23:15, 16. My son, how I will rejoice if you become a man of common sense. Yes, my heart will thrill to your thoughtful, wise words. [24, 25]The father of a godly man has cause for joy—what pleasure a wise son is! So give your parents joy!

Prov 29:3. A wise son makes his father happy, but a lad who hangs around with prostitutes disgraces him.

Isa 40:11. He will feed his flock like a shepherd; he will carry the lambs in his arms and gently lead the ewes with young.

Mt 18:4. Therefore anyone who humbles himself as this little child, is the greatest in the Kingdom of Heaven. [5]And any of you who welcomes a little child like this because you are mine, is welcoming me and caring for me. [10]Beware that you don't look down upon a single one of these little children. For I tell you that in heaven their angels have constant access to my Father. Mk 9:37; Lk 9:48.

Mt 19:14. But Jesus said, "Let the little children come to me, and don't prevent them. For of such is the Kingdom of Heaven." [15]And he put his hands on their heads and blessed them before he left. Lk 18:15–17.

Mk 10:16. Then he took the children into his arms and placed his hands on their heads and he blessed them. *vs.* 13–15.

Acts 2:39. For Christ promised him to each one of you who has been called by the Lord our God, and to your children and even to those in distant lands!

1 Jn 2:12. I am writing these things to all of you, my little children, because your sins have been forgiven in the name of Jesus our Savior. [13]I am saying these things to you older men because you really know Christ, the one who has been alive from the beginning. And you young men, I am talking to you because you have won your battle with Satan. And I am writing to you younger boys and girls because you, too, have learned to know God our Father.

See *Young Men.*

OF THE RIGHTEOUS, BLESSED BY GOD. Gen 6:18. But I promise to keep you safe in the ship, with your wife and your sons and their wives.

Gen 7:1. Finally the day came when the Lord said to Noah, "Go into the boat with all your family, for among all the people of the earth, I consider you alone to be righteous."

Gen 12:7. Then Jehovah appeared to Abram and said, "I am going to give this land to your descendants." And Abram built an altar there to commemorate Jehovah's visit.

Gen 13:15. For I am going to give it all to you and your descendants.

Gen 17:7, 8. And I will continue this agreement between us generation after generation, forever, for it shall be between me and your children as well. It is a contract that I shall be your God and the God of your posterity. And I will give all this land of Canaan to you and them, forever. And I will be your God.

Gen 19:12. "What relatives do you have here in the city?" the men asked. "Get them out of this place—sons-in-law, sons, daughters, or anyone else."

15. At dawn the next morning the angels became urgent. "Hurry," they said to Lot, "take your wife and your two daughters who are here and get out while you can, or you will be caught in the destruction of the city." [16]When Lot still hesitated, the angels seized his hand and the hands of his wife and two daughters and rushed them to safety, outside the city, for the Lord was merciful.

Gen 21:13. And I will make a nation of the descendants of the slave-girl's son, too, because he also is yours.

Gen 26:3. "Do as I say and stay here in this land. If you do, I will be with you and bless you, and I will give all this land to you and to your descendants, just as I promised Abraham your father. [4]And I will cause your descendants to become as numerous as the stars! And I will give them all of these lands; and they shall be a blessing to all the nations of the earth." [24]Jehovah appeared to him on the night of his arrival. "I am the God of Abraham your father," he said. "Fear not, for I am with you and will bless you, and will give you so many descendants that they will become a great nation—because of my promise to Abraham, who obeyed me."

Lev 26:44. But despite all they have done, I will not utterly destroy them and my covenant with them, for I am Jehovah their God. [45]For their sakes I will remember my promises to their ancestors, to be their God. For I brought their forefathers out of Egypt as all the nations watched in wonder. I am Jehovah.

Deut 4:37. It was because he loved your ancestors and chose to bless their descendants that he personally brought you out from Egypt with a great display of power.

Deut 10:15. And yet he rejoiced in your fathers and loved them so much that he chose you, their children, to be above every other nation, as is evident today.

Deut 12:28. Be careful to obey all of these commandments. If you do what is right in the eyes of the Lord your God, all will go well with you and your children forever.

1 Kgs 11:12, 13. However, for the sake of your father David, I won't do this while you are still alive. I will take the kingdom away from your son. And even so I will let him be king of one tribe, for David's sake and for the sake of Jerusalem, my chosen city.

1 Kgs 15:4. But despite Abijam's sin, the Lord remembered David's love and did not end the line of David's royal descendants.

2 Kgs 8:19. Nevertheless, because God had promised his servant David that he would watch over and guide his descendants, he did not destroy Judah.

Ps 37:26. Instead, the godly are able to be generous with their gifts and loans to others, and their children are a blessing.

Ps 102:28. But our families will continue; generation after generation will be preserved by your protection.

Ps 103:17, 18. But the lovingkindness of the Lord is from everlasting to everlasting, to those who reverence him; his salvation is to children's children of those who are faithful to his covenant and remember to obey him!

Ps 112:2. His children shall be honored everywhere, for good men's sons have a special heritage. [3]He himself shall be wealthy, and his good deeds will never be forgotten.

Prov 11:21. You can be very sure that the evil man will not go unpunished forever. And you can also be very sure that God will rescue the children of the godly.

Prov 12:7. The wicked shall perish; the godly shall stand.

Prov 13:22. When a good man dies, he leaves an inheritance to his grandchildren; but when a sinner dies, his wealth is stored up for the godly.

Prov 20:7. It is a wonderful heritage to have an honest father.

Isa 44:3. For I will give you abundant water for your thirst and for your parched fields. And I will pour out my Spirit and my blessings on your children. [4]They shall thrive like watered grass, like willows on a river bank. [5]"I am the Lord's," they'll proudly say, or, "I am a Jew," and tattoo upon their hands the name of God or the honored name of Israel.

Isa 65:23. Their harvests will not be eaten by their enemies; their children will not be born to be cannon fodder. For they are the children of those the Lord has blessed; and their children, too, shall be blessed.

Jer 32:39. And I will give them one heart and mind to worship me forever, for their own good and for the good of all their descendants.

Acts 2:39. For Christ promised him to each one of you who has been called by the Lord our God, and to your children and even to those in distant lands!

1 Cor 7:14. For perhaps the husband who isn't a Christian may become a Christian with the help of his Christian wife. And the wife who isn't a Christian may become a Christian with the help of her Christian husband. Otherwise, if the family separates, the children might never come to know the Lord; whereas a united family may, in God's plan, result in the children's salvation.

CORRECTION OF. Prov 13:24. If you refuse to discipline your son, it proves you don't love him; for if you love him you will be prompt to punish him.

Prov 19:18. Discipline your son in his early years while there is hope. If you don't you will ruin his life.

Prov 22:15. A youngster's heart is filled with rebellion, but punishment will drive it out of him.

Prov 23:13, 14. Don't fail to correct your children; discipline won't hurt them! They won't die if you use a stick on them! Punishment will keep them out of hell.

Prov 29:15. Scolding and spanking a child helps him to learn. Left to himself, he brings shame to his mother. [17]Discipline your son and he will give you happiness and peace of mind.

Eph 6:4. And now a word to you parents. Don't keep on scolding and nagging your children, making them angry and resentful. Rather, bring them up with the loving discipline the Lord himself approves, with suggestions and godly advice.

Col 3:21. Fathers, don't scold your children so much that they become discouraged and quit trying.

PUNISHMENT OF. Ex 21:15. Anyone who strikes his father or mother shall surely be put to death. [17]Anyone who reviles or curses his mother or father shall surely be put to death.

Lev 20:9. Anyone who curses his father or mother shall surely be put to death—for he has cursed his own flesh and blood.

Deut 21:18. If a man has a stubborn, rebellious son who will not obey his father or mother, even though they punish him, [19]then his father and mother shall take him before the elders of the city [20]and declare, "This son of ours is stubborn and rebellious and won't obey; he is a worthless drunkard." [21]Then the men of the city shall stone him to death. In this way you shall put away this evil from among you, and all the young men of Israel will hear about what happened and will be afraid.

Deut 27:16. "Cursed is anyone who despises his father or mother." And all the people shall reply, "Amen."

Mt 15:4. For instance, God's law is "Honor your father and mother; anyone who reviles his parents must die." Mk 7:10.

GOOD. The Lord is with, 1 Sam 3:19. Know the Scriptures, 2 Tim 3:15. Their obedience to parents pleases God, Col 3:20. Partake of the promises of God, Acts 2:39. Shall be blessed, Prov 3:1–5; Eph 6:2, 3. Show love to parents, Gen 46:29. Obey parents, Gen 28:6–8; 47:30. Accept parental teaching, Prov 13:1. Take care of parents, Gen 45:9–12; 47:12; Mt 15:5, 6. Make their parents happy, Prov 10:1; 23:24, 25; 29:17. Honor the aged, Job 32:6, 7. Character of, illustrates converson, Mt 18:3. Illustrative of a teachable spirit, Mt 18:4.

Unclassified Scriptures Relating to. Neh 12:43. Many sacrifices were offered on that joyous day, for God had given us cause for great joy. The women and children rejoiced too, and the joy of the people of Jerusalem was heard far away!

Prov 10:1. Happy is the man with a level-headed son; sad the mother of a rebel.

Prov 13:1. A wise youth accepts his father's rebuke; a young mocker doesn't.

Prov 15:5. Only a fool despises his father's advice; a wise son considers each suggestion. [20]A sensible son gladdens his father. A rebellious son saddens his mother.

Prov 28:7. Young men who are wise obey the law; a son who is a member of a lawless gang is a shame to his father.

Eccl 4:13. It is better to be a poor but wise youth than to be an old and foolish king who refuses all advice.

Mal 1:6. A son honors his father.

Mt 21:15. The chief priests . . . heard even the little children in the Temple shouting, "God bless the Son of David," . . . [16]"Yes," Jesus replied. "Didn't you ever read the Scriptures? For they say, 'Even little babies shall praise him!' "

Instances of. Shem and Japheth, Gen 9:23. Isaac, Gen 22:6–12. Esau, Gen 28:6–9. Judah, Gen 44: 18–34. Joseph, Gen 45:9–13; 46:29; 47:11, 12; 48:12, 13; 50:1–13. Moses, Ex 15:2; 18:7. Jephthah's daughter, Judg 11:36. Samson, Judg 13:24. Ruth, Ruth 1: 15–17. Samuel, 1 Sam 2:26; 3:10. Saul, 1 Sam 9:5. David, 1 Sam 22:3, 4; Ps 71:5, 17. Solomon, 1 Kgs 2:19, 20; 3:3–13. Abijah, 1 Kgs 14:13. Obadiah, 1 Kgs 18:12. Jehoshaphat, 1 Kgs 22:43; 2 Chron 17: 3. The Israelitish maid, captive in Syria, 2 Kgs 5: 2–4. Jewish children, 2 Chron 20:13; Neh 8:1–5. Josiah, 2 Chron 34:1–3. Job, Job 29:4. Elihu, Job 32: 4–7. Jeremiah, Jer 1:5–8. Children in the temple, Mt 21:15. John, Lk 1:80. Jesus, Lk 2:52. Timothy, 2 Tim 1:5; 3:15.

WICKED. Gen 8:21. Man's bent is always toward evil from his earliest youth.

Ex 21:15. Anyone who strikes his father or mother shall surely be put to death. [17]Anyone who reviles or curses his mother or father shall surely be put to death. Mk 7:10.

Num 32:14. But here you are, a brood of sinners doing exactly the same thing! Only there are more of you, so Jehovah's anger against Israel will be even fiercer this time.

Deut 21:18. If a man has a stubborn, rebellious son who will not obey his father or mother, even though they punish him, [19]then his father and mother shall take him before the elders of the city [20]and declare, "This son of ours is stubborn and rebelious and won't obey; he is a worthless drunkard." [21]Then the men of the city shall stone him to death. In this way you shall put away this evil from among you, and all the young men of Israel will hear about what happened and will be afraid.

Deut 27:16. "Cursed is anyone who despises his father or mother." And all the people shall reply, "Amen."

Job 13:26. You write bitter things against me and bring up all the follies of my youth.

Job 19:18. Even young children despise me. When I stand to speak, they mock.

Job 20:11. Though still a young man, his bones shall lie in the dust.

Job 30:1. But now those younger than I deride me. [12]This rabble trip me and lay traps in my path.

Prov 7:6. I was looking out the window of my house one day, [7]and saw a simple-minded lad, a young man lacking common sense.

Prov 10:1. *These are the proverbs of Solomon:* Happy is the man with a level-headed son; sad the mother of a rebel.

Prov 13:1. A wise youth accepts his father's rebuke; a young mocker doesn't.

Prov 15:5. Only a fool despises his father's advice; a wise son considers each suggestion. [20]A sensible son gladdens his father. A rebellious son saddens his mother.

Prov 17:2. A wise slave will rule his master's wicked sons and share their estate. [21]It's no fun to be a rebel's father. [25]A rebellious son is a grief to his father and a bitter blow to his mother. Prov 19: 13.

Prov 19:26. A son who mistreats his father or mother is a public disgrace.

Prov 20:20. God puts out the light of the man who curses his father or mother.

Prov 22:15. A youngster's heart is filled with rebellion, but punishment will drive it out of him.

Prov 23:22. Listen to your father's advice and don't despise an old mother's experience.

Prov 28:7. Young men who are wise obey the law; a son who is a member of a lawless gang is a shame to his father. [24]A man who robs his parents and says, "What's wrong with that?" is no better than a murderer.

Prov 30:11, 12. There are those who curse their father and mother, and feel themselves faultless despite their many sins. [17]A man who mocks his father and despises his mother shall have his eye plucked out by ravens and eaten by vultures.

Eccl 11:9. Young man, it's wonderful to be young! Enjoy every minute of it! Do all you want to; take in everything, but realize that you must account to God for everything you do. [10]So banish grief and pain, but remember that youth, with a whole life before it, can make serious mistakes.

Isa 3:5. And the worst sort of anarchy will prevail—everyone stepping on someone else, neighbors fighting neighbors, youths revolting against authority, criminals sneering at honorable men.

Jer 3:25. We lie in shame and in dishonor, for we and our fathers have sinned from childhood against the Lord our God; we have not obeyed him.

Jer 7:17. Don't you see what they are doing throughout the cities of Judah and in the streets of Jerusalem? [18]No wonder my anger is great! Watch how the children gather wood and the fathers build fires, and the women knead dough and make cakes to offer to "The Queen of Heaven" and to their other idol-gods!

Jer 32:30. For Israel and Judah have done nothing but wrong since their earliest days; they have infuriated me with all their evil deeds.

Ezk 22:7. Fathers and mothers are contemptuously ignored; immigrants and visitors are forced to pay you for your "protection"; orphans and widows are wronged and oppressed.

Mic 7:6. For the son despises his father; the daughter defies her mother; the bride curses her mother-in-law. Yes, a man's enemies will be found in his own home.

Mk 13:12. Brothers will betray each other to death, fathers will betray their own children, and children will betray their parents to be killed.

Rom 1:30. They were backbiters, haters of God, insolent, proud braggarts, always thinking of new ways of sinning and continually being disobedient to their parents.

2 Tim 3:2. For people will love only themselves and their money; they will be proud and boastful, sneering at God, disobedient to their parents, ungrateful to them, and thoroughly bad.

Instances of. Ham, Gen 9:25. Lot's daughters, Gen 19:14, 30–38. Ishmael, Gen 21:9. Eli's sons, 1 Sam 2:12, 22–25. Samuel's sons, 1 Sam 8:3. Absalom, 2 Sam 15. Adonijah, 1 Kgs 1:5. Abijam, 1 Kgs 15:3. Ahaziah, 1 Kgs 22:52, 53. Children at Bethel, 2 Kgs 2:23, 24. Samaritans' descendants, 2 Kgs 17:41. Adrammelech and Sharezer, 2 Kgs 19:37; 2 Chron 32:21. Amon, 2 Kgs 21:21.

WORSHIP, ATTEND DIVINE. Josh 8:35. Every commandment Moses had ever given was read before the entire assembly, including the women and children and the foreigners who lived among the Israelis.

2 Chron 20:13. As the people from every part of Judah stood before the Lord with their little ones, wives, and children.

2 Chron 31:16. However, the priests on duty at the Temple and their families were supplied directly from there, so they were not included in this distribution.

Ezra 8:21. Then I declared a fast while we were at the Ahava River so that we would humble ourselves before our God; and we prayed that he would give us a good journey and protect us, our children, and our goods as we traveled.

Neh 8:2. So Ezra the priest brought out to them the scroll of Moses' laws. He stood on a wooden stand made especially for the occasion so that everyone could see him as he read. [3]He faced the square in front of the Water Gate, and read from early morning until noon. Everyone stood up as he opened the scroll. And all who were old enough to understand paid close attention.

Neh 12:43. Many sacrifices were offered on that joyous day, for God had given us cause for great joy. The women and children rejoiced too, and the joy of the people of Jerusalem was heard far away!

Ps 8:2. You have taught the little children to praise you perfectly. May their example shame and silence your enemies!

Mt 21:15. But when the chief priests and other Jewish leaders saw these wonderful miracles, and heard even the little children in the Temple shouting, "God bless the Son of David," they were disturbed and indignant and asked him, "Do you hear what these children are saying?"

Lk 2:46, 47. Three days later they finally discovered him. He was in the Temple, sitting among the teachers of Law, discussing deep questions with them and amazing everyone with his understanding and answers.

SYMBOLICAL OF THE REGENERATED. Mt 18:2. Jesus called a small child over to him and set the little fellow down among them, [3]and said, "Unless you turn to God from your sins and become as little children, you will never get into the Kingdom of Heaven. [4]Therefore anyone who humbles himself as this little child, is the greatest in the Kingdom of Heaven. [5]And any of you who welcomes a little child like this because you are mine, is welcoming me and caring for me. [6]But if any of you causes one of these little ones who trusts in me to lose his faith, it would be better for you to have a rock tied to your neck and be thrown in the sea."

Mk 9:36. Then he placed a little child among them; and taking the child in his arms he said to them, [37]"Anyone who welcomes a little child like this in my name is welcoming me, and anyone who welcomes me is welcoming my Father who sent me!"

Mk 10:15. I tell you as seriously as I know how that anyone who refuses to come to God as a little child will never be allowed into his Kingdom.

Lk 9:46. Now came an argument among them as to which of them would be greatest [in the coming Kingdom]! [47]But Jesus knew their thoughts, so he stood a little child beside him [48]and said to them, "Anyone who takes care of a little child like this is caring for me! And whoever cares for me is caring for God who sent me. Your care for others is the measure of your greatness."

Figurative. 1 Cor 13:11. It's like this: when I was a child I spoke and thought and reasoned as a child does. But when I became a man my thoughts grew far beyond those of my childhood, and now I have put away the childish things.

1 Cor 14:20. Dear brothers, don't be childish in your understanding of these things. Be innocent babies when it comes to planning evil, but be men of intelligence in understanding matters of this kind.

1 Pet 2:2, 3. Long to grow up into the fullness of your salvation; cry for this as a baby cries for his milk.

See *Babies; Young Men.*

CHILDREN OF GOD See *Righteous.*

CHILEAB A son of David, 2 Sam 3:3. Called *Daniel,* 1 Chron 3:1.

CHILION A son of Naomi, Ruth 1:1, 2, 4, 5; 4:9.

CHILMAD Merchants of, Ezk 27:23.

CHIMHAM A Gileadite, 2 Sam 19:37, 38, 40; Jer 41:16, 17.

CHINNERETH Called also *Chinneroth.* 1. A district in the north of Palestine, Deut 3:17; Josh 11:1–3; 1 Kgs 15:20.

2. A city in Naphtali, Josh 19:35–39.

3. An old name for the Sea of Galilee mentioned in Num 34:10, 11; Josh 12:3; 13:27.

See *Galilee, Sea of.*

CHINNEROTH See *Chinnereth.*

CHIOS An island west of Smyrna, Acts 20:15.

CHISLON Father of Elidad, Num 34:16–28.

CHISLOTH-TABOR A place on the border of Zebulun, Josh 19:12. Called *Tabor,* 1 Chron

6:77. Probably same as *Chesulloth,* Josh 19:18.

CHITLISH A city of Judah, Josh 15:37–44.

CHLOE A Christian of Corinth, 1 Cor 1:11.

CHOICE Between judgments, by David, 2 Sam 24:12; 1 Chron 21:10–13.

THE SINNER'S. Deut 30:19. I call heaven and earth to witness against you that today I have set before you life or death, blessing or curse. Oh, that you would choose life; that you and your children might live! [20]Choose to love the Lord your God and to obey him and to cling to him, for he is your life and the length of your days. You will then be able to live safely in the land the Lord promised your ancestors, Abraham, Isaac, and Jacob.

Josh 24:15. "But if you are unwilling to obey the Lord, then decide today whom you will obey. Will it be the gods of your ancestors beyond the Euphrates or the gods of the Amorites here in this land? But as for me and my family, we will serve the Lord." [16]And the people replied, "We would never forsake the Lord and worship other gods! [17]For the Lord our God is the one who rescued our fathers from their slavery in the land of Egypt. He is the God who did mighty miracles before the eyes of Israel, as we traveled through the wilderness, and preserved us from our enemies when we passed through their land. [18]It was the Lord who drove out the Amorites and the other nations living here in the land. Yes, we choose the Lord, for he alone is our God."

1 Kgs 18:21. Then Elijah talked to them. "How long are you going to waver between two opinions?" he asked the people. "If the Lord is God, *follow* him! But if Baal is God, then follow *him!*"

See *Contingencies; Blessing, Contingent on Obedience.*

CHOOSING See *Choice.*

CHORAZIN A city of Galilee which was unrepentant, identified by Jesus' denunciation against, Mt 11:21; Lk 10:13.

CHORUS See *Music.*

CHOSEN, OR ELECTED The land, for Israel, Gen 12:7; Ex 20:12; Num 20:12. The people of Israel, Deut 7:6; Ps 33:12; 135:4; Isa 14:1; 41:8; 44:1; 45:4. The city of Jerusalem, Deut 12:14, 18; 1 Kgs 8:44; 11:12, 13; Zech 1:17; 2:12. Israel's priesthood, 1 Sam 2:27, 28. Moses, Ps 106:23. Aaron, Ps 105:26; Heb 5:4. Saul, 1 Sam 10:24. David, 1 Chron 28:4; 2 Chron 6:5, 6. Judah, 1 Chron 28:4. Christ, Isa 42:1; Mt 12:18. The apostles, Acts 1:1, 2. Paul, Acts 9:15. Rufus, Rom 16:13. A woman named Cyria, 2 Jn 1:1. The church, Eph 1:4; Col 3:12; 1 Thess 1:4; 2 Thess 2:13; 2 Tim 2:10; Tit 1:1, 2; 1 Pet 2:9; 5:13; Rev 17:14. Believers, Mt 24:24, 31; Mk 13:20; Jn 15:16, 19; 17:6, 11.

See *Election of Grace; God, Foreknowledge of; Predestination.*

CHRIST See *Jesus Christ.*

CHRISTIAN Believers called, in Greek New Testament, Acts 11:26; 26:28; 1 Pet 4:16. Other descriptive references are: 1 Cor 5:8; 16:15; 2 Cor 5:17; Phil 3:3; 1 Thess 4:10–14; Tit 1:10; Heb 6:12–14; Jas 1:26.

See *Righteous.*

CHRONOLOGY Jewish year instituted, Ex 12:2.

See *Time.*

CHRYSOLYTE A precious stone, Ezk 10:9–13; 28:13; Rev 21:18–20.

CHRYSOPRASE A precious stone, Rev 21:18–20.

CHURCH, THE VISIBLE The Greek word *ekklesia,* a called-out company, appears on two occasions in the Greek New Testament without referring to Christianity. (It does not occur in the Old Testament) In Acts 7:38 it is used of the people of Israel, called out of Egypt into the wilderness. In Acts 19:32, 39, 41 it is used of pagan citizens of Ephesus called together as an assembly. Most occurrences of the word refer to local assemblies of professed believers, or to professed believers in general, as distinguished from the true church (see following topic).

Local congregations. In provinces: Asia, 1 Cor 16:19; Rev 1:4. Cilicia, Acts 15:40, 41. Galatia, Gal 1:1, 2. Galilee, Acts 9:31. Judea, Acts 9:31; Gal 1:22. Macedonia, 2 Cor 8:1. Samaria, Acts 9:31. Syria, Acts 15:40, 41. In cities: Antioch, Acts 11:26; 13:1; 14:26–27. Cenchreae, Rom 16:1. Caesarea, Acts 18:22. Colosse, Col 1:2. Corinth, 1 Cor 1:2; 11:18; 2 Cor 1:1. Ephesus, Acts 20:17; Rev 2:1. Jerusalem, Acts 8:1; 11:22; 15:4. Joppa, Acts 9:36–43. Laodicea, Col 4:16; Rev 3:14. Pergamos, Rev 2:12. Philippi, Phil 1:1. Philadelphia, Rev 3:7. Rome, Rom 1:6, 7; 1 Pet 5:13. Sardis, Rev 3:1. Smyrna, Rev 2:8. Thessalonica, 1 Thess 1:1; 2 Thess 1:1. In homes: Priscilla and Aquila, Rom 16:3, 5; 1 Cor 16:19. Nymphas, Col 4:15. Philemon, Philem 1:1, 2.

Professed believers in general. Mt 18:17; Acts 2:47; 5:11; 12:1, 5; 14:23; 15:3; 20:28; Rom 16:23; 1 Cor 4:17; 6:4; 10:32; 11:22; 12:28; 14:4, 5, 12, 19, 23, 28, 35; 15:9; Gal 1:13; Phil 3:6; 4:15; 1 Tim 3:5, 15; 5:16; Jas 5:14; 3 Jn 1:6, 9, 10.

A MIXED COMPANY. The visible church includes spiritual and carnal believers, and unsaved persons:

Mt 18:15. If a brother sins against you, go to him privately and confront him with his fault. If he listens and confesses it, you have won back a brother. [16]But if not, then take one or two others with you and go back to him again, proving everything you say by these witnesses. [17]If he still refuses to listen, then take your case to the church, and if the church verdict favors you, but he won't accept it, then the church should excommunicate him.

Rom 14:1. Give a warm welcome to any brother who wants to join you, even though his faith is weak. Don't criticize him for having different ideas from yours about what is right and wrong. [2]For instance, don't argue with him about whether or not to eat meat that has been offered to idols. You may believe there is no harm in this, but the faith of others is weaker; they think it is wrong, and will go without any meat at all and eat vegetables rather than eat that kind of meat. [3]Those who think it is all right to eat such meat must not look down on those who won't. And if you are one of those who won't, don't find fault with those who do. For God has accepted them to be his children. [4]They are God's servants, not yours. They are responsible to him, not to you. Let him tell them whether they are right or wrong. And God is able to make them do as they should. [5]Some think that Christians should observe the Jewish holidays as special days to worship God, but others say it is wrong and foolish to go to all that trouble, for every day alike belongs to God. On questions of this kind everyone must decide for himself. [10]You have no right to criticize your brother or look down on him. Remember, each of us will stand personally before the Judgment Seat of God. [13]So don't criticize each other any more. Try instead to live in such a way that you will never make your brother stumble by letting him see you doing something he thinks is wrong. [15]And if your brother is bothered by what you eat, you are not acting in love if you go ahead and eat it. Don't let your eating ruin someone for whom Christ died.

Rom 15:1. Even if we believe that it makes no difference to the Lord whether we do these things, still we cannot just go ahead and do them to please ourselves; for we must bear the "burden" of being considerate of the doubts and fears of others—of those who feel these things are wrong. Let's please the other fellow, not ourselves, and do what is for his good and thus build him up in the Lord.

Rom 16:17. And now there is one more thing to say before I end this letter. Stay away from those who cause divisions and are upsetting people's faith, teaching things about Christ that are contrary to what you have been taught. [18]Such teachers are not working for our Lord Jesus, but only want gain for themselves. They are good speakers, and simple-minded people are often fooled by them.

1 Cor 1:11. For some of those who live at Chloe's house have told me of your arguments and quarrels, dear brothers. [12]Some of you are saying, "I am a follower of Paul"; and others say that they are for Apollos or for Peter; and some that they alone are the true followers of Christ.

1 Cor 3:1. Dear brothers, I have been talking to you as though you were still just babies in the Christian life, who are not following the Lord, but your own desires; I cannot talk to you as I would to healthy Christians, who are filled with the Spirit. [2]I have had to feed you with milk and not with solid food, because you couldn't digest anything stronger. And even now you still have to be fed on milk. [3]For you are still only baby Christians, controlled by your own desires, not God's. When you are jealous of one another and divide up into quarreling groups, doesn't that prove you are still babies, wanting your own way? In fact, you are acting like people who don't belong to the Lord at all. [4]There you are, quarreling about whether I am greater than Apollos, and dividing the church. Doesn't this show how little you have grown in the Lord?

1 Cor 4:18. I know that some of you will have become proud, thinking that I am afraid to come to deal with you. [19]But I will come, and soon, if the Lord will let me, and then I'll find out whether these proud men are just big talkers or whether they really have God's power.

1 Cor 5:1. Everyone is talking about the terrible thing that has happened there among you, something so evil that even the heathen don't do it: you have a man in your church who is living in sin with his father's wife. [2]And are you still so conceited, so "spiritual"? Why aren't you mourning in sorrow and shame, and seeing to it that this man is removed from your membership? [3, 4]Although I am not there with you, I have been thinking a lot about this, and in the name of the Lord Jesus Christ I have already decided what to do, just as though I were there. You are to call a meeting of the church—and the power of the Lord Jesus will be with you as you meet, and I will be there in spirit—[5]and cast out this man from the fellowship of the church and into Satan's hands, to punish him, in the hope that his soul will be saved when our Lord Jesus Christ returns. [6]What a terrible thing it is that you are boasting about your purity, and yet you let this sort of thing go on. Don't you realize that if even one person is allowed to go on sinning, soon all will be affected? [7]Remove this evil cancer—this wicked person—from among you, so that you can stay pure. Christ, God's Lamb, has been slain for us. [8]So let us feast upon him and grow strong in the Christian life, leaving entirely behind us the cancerous old life with all its hatreds and wickedness. Let us feast instead upon the pure bread of honor and sincerity and truth. [9]When I wrote to you before I said not to mix with evil people. [10]But when I said that I wasn't talking about unbelievers who live in sexual sin, or are greedy cheats and thieves and idol worshipers. For you can't live in this world without being with people like that. [11]What I meant was that you are not to keep company with anyone who claims to be a brother Christian but indulges in sexual sins, or is greedy, or is a swindler, or worships idols, or is a drunkard, or abusive. Don't even eat lunch with such a person. [12]It isn't our job to judge outsiders. But it certainly is our job to judge and deal strongly with those who are members of the church, who are sinning in these ways. [13]God alone is the Judge of those on the outside. But you yourselves must deal with this man and put him out of your church.

1 Cor 6:1. How is it that when you have something against another Christian, you "go to law" and ask a heathen court to decide the matter instead of taking it to other Christians to decide which of you is right? [6]But, instead, one Christian sues another and accuses his Christian brother in front of unbelievers. [7]To have such lawsuits at all is a real defeat for you as Christians. Why not just accept mistreatment and leave it at that? It would be far more honoring to the Lord to let yourselves be cheated. [8]But, instead, you yourselves are the

ones who do wrong, cheating others, even your own brothers.

1 Cor 8:10. You see, this is what may happen: Someone who thinks it is wrong to eat this food will see you eating at a temple restaurant, for you know there is no harm in it. Then he will become bold enough to do it too, although all the time he still feels it is wrong. [11]So because you "know it is all right to do it," you will be responsible for causing great spiritual damage to a brother with a tender conscience for whom Christ died. [12]And it is a sin against Christ to sin against your brother by encouraging him to do something he thinks is wrong.

1 Cor 11:18. Everyone keeps telling me about the arguing that goes on in these meetings, and the divisions developing among you, and I can just about believe it. [19]But I suppose you feel this is necessary so that you who are always right will become known and recognized! [20]When you come together to eat, it isn't the Lord's Supper you are eating, [21]but your own. For I am told that everyone hastily gobbles all the food he can without waiting to share with the others, so that one doesn't get enough and goes hungry while another has too much to drink and gets drunk. [22]What? Is this really true? Can't you do your eating and drinking at home, to avoid disgracing the church and shaming those who are poor and can bring no food? What am I supposed to say about these things? Do you want me to praise you? Well, I certainly do not! [27]So if anyone eats this bread and drinks from this cup of the Lord in an unworthy manner, he is guilty of sin against the body and the blood of the Lord. [28]That is why a man should examine himself carefully before eating the bread and drinking from the cup. [29]For if he eats the bread and drinks from the cup unworthily, not thinking about the body of Christ and what it means, he is eating and drinking God's judgment upon himself; for he is trifling with the death of Christ. [30]That is why many of you are weak and sick, and some have even died.

Gal 2:11. But when Peter came to Antioch I had to oppose him publicly, speaking strongly against what he was doing for it was very wrong. [12]For when he first arrived he ate with the Gentile Christians [who don't bother with circumcision and the many other Jewish laws]. But afterwards when some Jewish friends of James came, he wouldn't eat with the Gentiles anymore because he was afraid of what these Jewish legalists, who insisted that circumcision was necessary for salvation, would say; [13]and then all the other Jewish Christians and even Barnabas became hypocrites too, following Peter's example, though they certainly knew better. [14]When I saw what was happening and that they weren't being honest about what they really believed, and weren't following the truth of the Gospel, I said to Peter in front of all the others, "Though you are a Jew by birth, you have long since discarded the Jewish laws; so why, all of a sudden, are you trying to make these Gentiles obey them?"

Gal 3:1. Oh, foolish Galatians! What magician has hypnotized you and cast an evil spell upon you? For you used to see the meaning of Jesus Christ's death as clearly as though I had waved a placard before you with a picture on it of Christ dying on the cross.

Gal 4:9. And now that you have found God (or I should say, now that God has found you) how can it be that you want to go back again and become slaves once more to another poor, weak, useless religion of trying to get to heaven by obeying God's laws? [10]You are trying to find favor with God by what you do or don't do on certain days or months or seasons or years.

Gal 5:15. But if instead of showing love among yourselves you are always critical and catty, watch out! Beware of ruining each other.

Gal 6:1. Dear brothers, if a Christian is overcome by some sin, you who are godly should gently and humbly help him back onto the right path, remembering that next time it might be one of you who is in the wrong.

2 Thess 3:6. Now here is a command, dear brothers, given in the name of our Lord Jesus Christ by his authority: Stay away from any Christian who spends his days in laziness and does not follow the ideal of hard work we set up for you. [14]If anyone refuses to obey what we say in this letter, notice who he is and stay away from him, that he may be ashamed of himself. [15]Don't think of him as an enemy, but speak to him as you would to a brother who needs to be warned.

1 Tim 1:19. Cling tightly to your faith in Christ and always keep your conscience clear, doing what you know is right. For some people have disobeyed their consciences and have deliberately done what they knew was wrong. It isn't surprising that soon they lost their faith in Christ after defying God like that. [20]Hymenaeus and Alexander are two examples of this. I had to give them over to Satan to punish them until they could learn not to bring shame to the name of Christ.

1 Tim 4:1. But the Holy Spirit tells us clearly that in the last times some in the church will turn away from Christ and become eager followers of teachers with devil-inspired ideas. [6]If you explain this to the others you will be doing your duty as a worthy pastor who is fed by faith and by the true teaching you have followed.

1 Tim 5:19. Don't listen to complaints against the pastor unless there are two or three witnesses to accuse him. [20]If he has really sinned, then he should be rebuked in front of the whole church so that no one else will follow his example.

1 Tim 6:10. For the love of money is the first step toward all kinds of sin. Some people have even turned away from God because of their love for it, and as a result have pierced themselves with many sorrows.

2 Tim 2:16. Steer clear of foolish discussions which lead people into the sin of anger with each other. [17]Things will be said that will burn and hurt for a long time to come. Hymenaeus and Philetus,

in their love of argument, are men like that. [18]They have left the path of truth, preaching the lie that the resurrection of the dead has already occurred; and they have weakened the faith of some who believe them.

2 Tim 4:3. For there is going to come a time when people won't listen to the truth, but will go around looking for teachers who will tell them just what they want to hear. [4]They won't listen to what the Bible says but will blithely follow their own misguided ideas. [10]For Demas has left me. He loved the good things of this life and went to Thessalonica.

Tit 1:13. And this is true. So speak to the Christians there as sternly as necessary to make them strong in the faith, [14]and to stop them from listening to Jewish folk tales and the demands of men who have turned their backs on the truth.

Tit 3:10. If anyone is causing divisions among you, he should be given a first and second warning. After that have nothing more to do with him, [11]for such a person has a wrong sense of values. He is sinning, and he knows it.

Heb 10:38. And those whose faith has made them good in God's sight must live by faith, trusting him in everything. Otherwise, if they shrink back, God will have no pleasure in them.

Heb 12:15. Look after each other so that not one of you will fail to find God's best blessings. Watch out that no bitterness takes root among you, for as it springs up it causes deep trouble, hurting many in their spiritual lives.

Jas 3:10. And so blessing and cursing come pouring out of the same mouth. Dear brothers, surely this is not right!

Jas 4:4. You are like an unfaithful wife who loves her husband's enemies. Don't you realize that making friends with God's enemies—the evil pleasures of this world—makes you an enemy of God? I say it again, that if your aim is to enjoy the evil pleasures of the unsaved world, you cannot also be a friend of God. [8]And when you draw close to God, God will draw close to you. Wash your hands, you sinners, and let your hearts be filled with God alone to make them pure and true to him. [17]Remember, too, that knowing what is right to do and then not doing it is sin.

2 Pet 2:1. But there were false prophets, too, in those days, just as there will be false teachers among you. They will cleverly tell their lies about God, turning against even their Master who bought them; but theirs will be a swift and terrible end. [2]Many will follow their evil teaching that there is nothing wrong with sexual sin. And because of them Christ and his way will be scoffed at. [10]He is especially hard on those who follow their own evil, lustful thoughts, and those who are proud and willful, daring even to scoff at the Glorious Ones without so much as trembling. [14]No woman can escape their sinful stare, and of adultery they never have enough. They make a game of luring unstable women. They train themselves to be greedy; and are doomed and cursed. [15]They have gone off the road and become lost like Balaam, the son of Beor, who fell in love with the money he could make by doing wrong. [20]And when a person has escaped from the wicked ways of the world by learning about our Lord and Savior Jesus Christ, and then gets tangled up with sin and becomes its slave again, he is worse off than he was before.

2 Pet 3:3. First, I want to remind you that in the last days there will come scoffers who will do every wrong they can think of, and laugh at the truth. [4]This will be their line of argument: "So Jesus promised to come back, did he? Then where is he? He'll never come! Why, as far back as anyone can remember everything has remained exactly as it was since the first day of creation."

1 Jn 2:19. These "against-Christ" people used to be members of our churches, but they never really belonged with us or else they would have stayed. When they left us it proved that they were not of us at all.

1 Jn 5:16. If you see a Christian sinning in a way that does not end in death, you should ask God to forgive him and God will give him life, unless he has sinned that one fatal sin. But there is that one sin which ends in death and if he has done that, there is no use praying for him. [17]Every wrong is a sin, of course. I'm not talking about these ordinary sins; I am speaking of that one that ends in death.

3 Jn 1:9. I sent a brief letter to the church about this, but proud Diotrephes, who loves to push himself forward as the leader of the Christians there, does not admit my authority over him and refuses to listen to me. [10]When I come I will tell you some of the things he is doing and what wicked things he is saying about me and what insulting language he is using. He not only refuses to welcome the missionary travelers himself, but tells others not to, and when they do he tries to put them out of the church.

Jude 1:4. I say this because some godless teachers have wormed their way in among you, saying that after we become Christians we can do just as we like without fear of God's punishment. The fate of such people was written long ago, for they have turned against our only Master and Lord, Jesus Christ. [8]Yet these false teachers carelessly go right on living their evil, immoral lives, degrading their bodies and laughing at those in authority over them, even scoffing at the Glorious Ones. [16]These men are constant gripers, never satisfied, doing whatever evil they feel like; they are loud-mouthed "show-offs," and when they show respect for others, it is only to get something from them in return. [19]They stir up arguments; they love the evil things of the world; they do not have the Holy Spirit living in them.

Rev 2:4. Yet there is one thing wrong; you don't love me as at first! [5]Think about those times of your first love (how different now!) and turn back to me again and work as you did before; or else I will come and remove your candlestick from its place among the churches.

Rev 3:15. I know you well—you are neither hot nor cold; I wish you were one or the other! [16]But since you are merely lukewarm, I will spit you out of my mouth! [17]You say, "I am rich, with everything I want; I don't need a thing!" And you don't realize that spiritually you are wretched and miserable and poor and blind and naked.

DECREES OF. Acts 15:27–29. For it seemed good to the Holy Spirit and to us to lay no greater burden of Jewish laws on you than to abstain from eating food offered to idols and from unbled meat of strangled animals, and, of course, from fornication. If you do this, it is enough.

Acts 16:4. Then they went from city to city, making known the decision concerning the Gentiles, as decided by the apostles and elders in Jerusalem.

DISCIPLINE OF. Mt 18:15. If a brother sins against you, go to him privately and confront him with his fault. If he listens and confesses it, you have won back a brother. [16]But if not, than take one or two others with you and go back to him again, proving everything you say by these witnesses. [17]If he still refuses to listen, then take your case to the church, and if the church's verdict favors you, but he won't accept it, then the church should excommunicate him.

Rom 14:1. Give a warm welcome to any brother who wants to join you, even though his faith is weak. Don't criticize him for having different ideas from you about what is right and wrong.

Rom 15:1, 2. Even if we believe that it makes no difference to the Lord whether we do these things, still we cannot just go ahead and do them to please ourselves; for we must bear the "burden" of being considerate of the doubts and fears of others—of those who feel these things are wrong. Let's please the other fellow, not ourselves, and do what is for his good and thus build him up in the Lord. *v.* 3.

Rom 16:17. And now there is one more thing to say before I end this letter. Stay away from those who cause divisions and are upsetting people's faith, teaching things about Christ that are contrary to what you have been taught.

1 Cor 4:19. But I will come, and soon, if the Lord will let me, and then I'll find out whether these proud men are just big talkers or whether they really have God's power. [21]Which do you choose? Shall I come with punishment and scolding, or shall I come with quiet love and gentleness?

1 Cor 5:1. Everyone is talking about the terrible thing that has happened there among you, something so evil that even the heathen don't do it: you have a man in your church who is living in sin with his father's wife. [2]And are you still so conceited, so "spiritual"? Why aren't you mourning in sorrow and shame, and seeing to it that this man is removed from your membership? [4]You are to call a meeting of the church—and the power of the Lord Jesus will be with you as you meet, and I will be there in spirit— [5]And cast out this man from the fellowship of the church and into Satan's hands, to punish him, in the hope that his soul will be saved when our Lord Jesus Christ returns. [6]What a terrible thing it is that you are boasting about your purity, and yet you let this sort of thing go on. Don't you realize that if even one person is allowed to go on sinning, soon all will be affected? [7]Remove this evil cancer—this wicked person—from among you, so that you can stay pure. Christ, God's Lamb, has been slain for us. [11]What I meant was that you are not to keep company with anyone who claims to be a brother Christian but indulges in sexual sins, or is greedy, or is a swindler, or worships idols, or is a drunkard, or abusive. Don't even eat lunch with such a person. [12]It isn't our job to judge outsiders. But it certainly is our job to judge and deal strongly with those who are members of the church, and who are sinning in these ways. [13]God alone is the Judge of those on the outside. But you yourselves must deal with this man and put him out of your church.

1 Cor 16:22. If anyone does not love the Lord, that person is cursed. Lord Jesus, come!

2 Cor 2:6. I don't want to be harder on him than I should. He has been punished enough by your united disapproval. [7]Now it is time to forgive him and comfort him. Otherwise he may become so bitter and discouraged that he won't be able to recover. [8]Please do show him now that you still do love him very much. [10]When you forgive anyone, I do too. And whatever I have forgiven (to the extent that this affected me too) has been by Christ's authority, and for your good. [11]A further reason for forgiveness is to keep from being outsmarted by Satan; for we know what he is trying to do.

2 Cor 6:14. Don't be teamed with those who do not love the Lord, for what do the people of God have in common with the people of sin? How can light live with darkness? [15]And what harmony can there be between Christ and the devil? How can a Christian be a partner with one who doesn't believe?

2 Cor 7:8. I am no longer sorry that I sent that letter to you, though I was very sorry for a time, realizing how painful it would be to you. But it hurt you only for a little while. 2 Cor 10:1–11.

2 Cor 13:1. This is the third time I am coming to visit you. The Scriptures tell us that if two or three have seen a wrong, it must be punished. [Well, this is my third warning, as I come now for this visit.] [2]I have already warned those who had been sinning when I was there last; now I warn them again, and all others, just as I did then, that this time I come ready to punish severely and I will not spare them. [10]I am writing this to you now in the hope that I won't need to scold and punish when I come; for I want to use the Lord's authority which he has given me, not to punish you but to make you strong.

Gal 5:10. I am trusting the Lord to bring you back to believing as I do about these things. God will deal with that person, whoever he is, who has been troubling and confusing you. [12]I only wish these teachers who want you to cut yourselves by being circumcised would cut themselves off from you and leave you alone!

Gal 6:1. Dear brothers, if a Christian is overcome by some sin, you who are godly should gently and humbly help him back onto the right path, remembering that next time it might be one of you who is in the wrong.

1 Thess 5:14. Dear brothers, warn those who are lazy; comfort those who are frightened; take tender care of those who are weak; and be patient with everyone.

2 Thess 3:6. Now here is a command, dear brothers, given in the name of our Lord Jesus Christ by his authority: Stay away from any Christian who spends his days in laziness and does not follow the ideal of hard work we set up for you. [14]If anyone refuses to obey what we say in this letter, notice who he is and stay away from him, that he may be ashamed of himself. [15]Don't think of him as an enemy, but speak to him as you would to a brother who needs to be warned.

1 Tim 1:19. Cling tightly to your faith in Christ and always keep your conscience clear, doing what you know is right. For some people have disobeyed their consciences and have deliberately done what they knew was wrong. It isn't surprising that soon they lost their faith in Christ after defying God like that. [20]Hymenaeus and Alexander are two examples of this. I had to give them over to Satan to punish them until they could learn not to bring shame to the name of Christ.

1 Tim 5:1. Never speak sharply to an older man, but plead with him respectfully just as though he were your own father. Talk to the younger men as you would to much loved brothers. [2]Treat the older women as mothers, and the girls as your sisters, thinking only pure thoughts about them.

19. Don't listen to complaints against the pastor unless there are two or three witnesses to accuse him. [20]If he has really sinned, then he should be rebuked in front of the whole church so that no one else will follow his example.

1 Tim 6:3. Some may deny these things, but they are the sound, wholesome teachings of the Lord Jesus Christ and are the foundation for a godly life. [4]Anyone who says anything different is both proud and stupid. He is quibbling over the meaning of Christ's words and stirring up arguments ending in jealousy and anger, which only lead to name-calling, accusations, and evil suspicions. [5]These arguers—their minds warped by sin—don't know how to tell the truth; to them the Good News is just a means of making money. Keep away from them.

2 Tim 4:2. To preach the Word of God urgently at all times, whenever you get the chance, in season and out, when it is convenient and when it is not. Correct and rebuke your people when they need it, encourage them to do right, and all the time be feeding them patiently with God's Word.

Tit 1:13. And this is true. So speak to the Christians there as sternly as necessary to make them strong in the faith.

Tit 2:15. You must teach these things and encourage your people to do them, correcting them when necessary as one who has every right to do so. Don't let anyone think that what you say is not important.

Tit 3:10. If anyone is causing divisions among you, he should be given a first and second warning. After that have nothing more to do with him, [11]for such a person has a wrong sense of values. He is sinning, and he knows it.

2 Jn 1:10. If anyone comes to teach you, and he doesn't believe what Christ taught, don't even invite him into your home. Don't encourage him in any way. [11]If you do you will be a partner with him in his wickedness.

DIVISION AMONG. 1 Cor 1:11. For some of those who live at Chloe's house have told me of your arguments and quarrels, dear brothers. [12]Some of you are saying, "I am a follower of Paul"; and others say that they are for Apollos or for Peter; and some that they alone are the true followers of Christ. [13]And so, in effect, you have broken Christ into many pieces. But did I, Paul, die for your sins? Were any of you baptized in my name?

1 Cor 3:3. For you are still only baby Christians, controlled by your own desires, not God's. When you are jealous of one another and divide up into quarreling groups, doesn't that prove you are still babies, wanting your own way? In fact, you are acting like people who don't belong to the Lord at all. [4]There you are, quarreling about whether I am greater than Apollos, and dividing the church. Doesn't this show how little you have grown in the Lord?

1 Cor 11:18. Everyone keeps telling me about the arguing that goes on in these meetings, and the divisions developing among you, and I can just about believe it. [19]But I suppose you feel this is necessary so that you who are always right will become known and recognized!

2 Cor 12:20. For I am afraid that when I come to visit you I won't like what I find, and then you won't like the way I will have to act. I am afraid that I will find you quarreling, and envying each other, and acting big, and saying wicked things about each other and whispering behind each other's backs, filled with conceit and disunity.

FINANCING OF. Jn 4:36. The reapers will be paid good wages and will be gathering eternal souls into the granaries of heaven! What joys await the sower and the reaper, both together!

Acts 20:33. I have never been hungry for money or fine clothing— [34]You know that these hands of mine worked to pay my own way and even to supply the needs of those who were with me.

1 Cor 9:3. This is my answer to those who question my rights. [4]Or don't I have any rights at all? Can't I claim the same privilege the other apostles have of being a guest in your homes? [7]What soldier in the army has to pay his own expenses? And have you ever heard of a farmer who harvests his crop and doesn't have the right to eat some of it? What shepherd takes care of a flock of sheep and goats

and isn't allowed to drink some of the milk? 8And I'm not merely quoting the opinions of men as to what is right. I'm telling you what God's law says. 9For in the law God gave to Moses he said that you must not put a muzzle on an ox to keep it from eating when it is treading out the wheat. Do you suppose God was thinking only about oxen when he said this? 10Wasn't he also thinking about us? Of course he was. He said this to show us that Christian workers should be paid by those they help. Those who do the plowing and threshing should expect some share of the harvest. 11We have planted good spiritual seed in your souls. Is it too much to ask, in return, for mere food and clothing? 12You give them to others who preach to you, and you should. But shouldn't we have an even greater right to them? Yet we have *never* used this right, but supply our own needs without your help. We have never demanded payment of any kind for fear that, if we did, you might be less interested in our message to you from Christ. 13Don't you realize that God told those working in his temple to take for their own needs some of the food brought there as gifts to him? And those who work at the altar of God get a share of the food that is brought by those offering it to the Lord. 14In the same way the Lord has given orders that those who preach the Gospel should be supported by those who accept it. 15Yet I have never asked you for one penny. And I am not writing this to hint that I would like to start now. In fact, I would rather die of hunger than lose the satisfaction I get from preaching to you without charge. 16For just preaching the gospel isn't any special credit to me—I couldn't keep from preaching it if I wanted to. I would be utterly miserable. Woe unto me if I don't. 17If I were volunteering my services of my own free will, then the Lord would give me a special reward; but that is not the situation, for God has picked me out and given me this sacred trust and I have no choice. 18Under this circumstance, what is my pay? It is the special joy I get from preaching the Good News without expense to anyone, never demanding my rights. 19And this has a real advantage: I am not bound to obey anyone just because he pays my salary; yet I have freely and happily become a servant of any and all so that I can win them to Christ. 20When I am with the Jews I seem as one of them so that they will listen to the Gospel and I can win them to Christ. When I am with Gentiles who follow Jewish customs and ceremonies I don't argue, even though I don't agree, because I want to help them. 21When with the heathen I agree with them as much as I can, except of course that I must always do what is right as a Christian. And so, by agreeing, I can win their confidence and help them too. 22When I am with those whose consciences bother them easily, I don't act as though I know it all and don't say they are foolish; the result is that they are willing to let me help them. Yes, whatever a person is like, I try to find common ground with him so that he will let me tell him about Christ and let Christ save him. 23I do this to get the Gospel to them and also for the blessing I myself receive when I see them come to Christ. *vs.* 1–6.

2 Cor 11:7. Did I do wrong and cheapen myself and make you look down on me because I preached God's Good News to you without charging you anything? 8,9Instead I "robbed" other churches by taking what they sent me, and using it up while I was with you, so that I could serve you without cost. And when that was gone and I was getting hungry I still didn't ask you for anything, for the Christians from Macedonia brought me another gift. I have never yet asked you for one cent, and I never will. 10I promise this with every ounce of truth I possess—that I will tell everyone in Greece about it!

2 Cor 12:13. The only thing I didn't do for you, that I do everywhere else in all other churches, was to become a burden to you—I didn't ask you to give me food to eat and a place to stay. Please forgive me for this wrong! 14Now I am coming to you again, the third time; and it is still not going to cost you anything, for I don't want your money. I want *you!* And anyway, you are my children, and little children don't pay for their father's and mother's food—it's the other way around; parents supply food for their children. 15I am glad to give you myself and all I have for your spiritual good, even though it seems that the more I love you, the less you love me. 16Some of you are saying, "It's true that his visits didn't seem to cost us anything, but he is a sneaky fellow, that Paul, and he fooled us. As sure as anything he must have made money from us some way." 17But how? Did any of the men I sent to you take advantage of you? 18When I urged Titus to visit you, and sent our other brother with him, did they make any profit? No, of course not. For we have the same Holy Spirit, and walk in each other's steps, doing things the same way.

Gal 6:6. Those who are taught the Word of God should help their teachers by paying them.

Phil 4:10. How grateful I am and how I praise the Lord that you are helping me again. I know you have always been anxious to send what you could, but for a while you didn't have the chance. 11Not that I was ever in need, for I have learned how to get along happily whether I have much or little. 12I know how to live on almost nothing or with everything. I have learned the secret of contentment in every situation, whether it be a full stomach or hunger, plenty or want; 13for I can do everything God asks me to with the help of Christ who gives me the strength and power. 14But even so, you have done right in helping me in my present difficulty. 15As you well know, when I first brought the Gospel to you and then went on my way, leaving Macedonia, only you Philippians became my partners in giving and receiving. No other church did this. 16Even when I was over in Thessalonica you sent help twice. 17But though I appreciate your gifts, what makes me happiest is the well-earned reward you will have because of your kindness. 18At the moment I have all I need—more than I need! I am generously supplied with the gifts you sent me when Epaphroditus came. They are a sweet-smelling sacrifice that pleases God well.

1 Thess 2:5. Never once did we try to win you with flattery, as you very well know, and God knows we were not just pretending to be your friends so that you would give us money! [6]As for praise, we have never asked for it from you or anyone else, although as apostles of Christ we certainly had a right to some honor from you. [9]Don't you remember, dear brothers, how hard we worked among you? Night and day we toiled and sweated to earn enough to live on so that our expenses would not be a burden to anyone there, as we preached God's Good News among you.

2 Thess 3:7. For you well know that you ought to follow our example: you never saw us loafing; [8]we never accepted food from anyone without buying it; we worked hard day and night for the money we needed to live on, in order that we would not be a burden to any of you. [9]It wasn't that we didn't have the right to ask you to feed us, but we wanted to show you, firsthand, how you should work for your living.

1 Tim 5:18. For the Scriptures say, "Never tie up the mouth of an ox when it is treading out the grain—let him eat as he goes along!" And in another place, "Those who work deserve their pay!"

3 Jn 1:7. For they are traveling for the Lord, and take neither food, clothing, shelter, nor money from those who are not Christians, even though they have preached to them.

GOVERNMENT OF. Acts 1:15. This prayer meeting went on for several days. During this time, on a day when about 120 people were present, Peter stood up and addressed them. [23]The assembly nominated two men: Joseph Justus (also called Barsabbas) and Matthias. [24, 25]Then they all prayed for the right man to be chosen. "O Lord," they said, "you know every heart; show us which of these men you have chosen as an apostle to replace Judas the traitor, who has gone to his proper place." [26]Then they drew straws, and in this manner Matthias was chosen and became an apostle with the other eleven.

Acts 6:2. So the Twelve called a meeting of all the believers. "We should spend our time preaching, not administering a feeding program," they said. [3]"Now look around among yourselves, dear brothers, and select seven men, wise and full of the Holy Spirit, who are well thought of by everyone; and we will put them in charge of this business." [5]This sounded reasonable to the whole assembly, and they elected the following: Stephen (a man unusually full of faith and the Holy Spirit), Philip, ... [6]These seven were presented to the apostles, who prayed for them and laid their hands on them in blessing.

Acts 11:22. When the church at Jerusalem heard what had happened, they sent Barnabas to Antioch to help the new converts. [29]So the believers decided to send relief to the Christians in Judea, each giving as much as he could. [30]This they did, consigning their gifts to Barnabas and Paul to take to the elders of the church in Jerusalem.

Acts 13:1. Among the prophets and teachers of the church at Antioch were Barnabas and Symeon. . . . [3]So after more fasting and prayer, the men laid their hands on them—and sent them on their way. [5]There, in the town of Salamis, they went to the Jewish synagogue and preached. (John Mark went with them as their assistant.)

Acts 14:23. Paul and Barnabas also appointed elders in every church and prayed for them with fasting, turning them over to the care of the Lord in whom they trusted.

Acts 15:1. While Paul and Barnabas were at Antioch, some men from Judea arrived and began to teach the believers that unless they adhered to the ancient Jewish custom of circumcision, they could not be saved. [2]Paul and Barnabas argued and discussed this with them at length, and finally the believers sent them to Jerusalem, accompanied by some local men, to talk to the apostles and elders there about this question. [3]After the entire congregation had escorted them out of the city the delegates went on to Jerusalem, stopping along the way in the cities of Phoenicia and Samaria to visit the believers, telling them—much to everyone's joy—that the Gentiles, too, were being converted. [4]Arriving in Jerusalem, they met with the church leaders—all the apostles and elders were present—and Paul and Barnabas reported on what God had been doing through their ministry. [5]But then some of the men who had been Pharisees before their conversion stood to their feet and declared that all Gentile converts must be circumcised and required to follow all the Jewish customs and ceremonies. [6]So the apostles and church elders set a further meeting to decide this question. [7]At the meeting, after long discussion, Peter stood and addressed them as follows: "Brothers, you all know that God chose me from among you long ago to preach the Good News to the Gentiles, so that they also could believe. [8]God, who knows men's hearts, confirmed the fact that he accepts Gentiles by giving them the Holy Spirit, just as he gave him to us. [9]He made no distinction between them and us, for he cleansed their lives through faith, just as he did ours. [10]And now are you going to correct God by burdening the Gentiles with a yoke that neither we nor our fathers were able to bear? [11]Don't you believe that all are saved the same way, by the free gift of the Lord Jesus?" [12]There was no further discussion, and everyone now listened as Barnabas and Paul told about the miracles God had done through them among the Gentiles. [13]When they had finished, James took the floor. "Brothers," he said, "listen to me. [14]Peter has told you about the time God first visited the Gentiles to take from them a people to bring honor to his name. [15]And this fact of Gentile conversion agrees with what the prophets predicted. For instance, listen to this passage from the prophet Amos: [16]'Afterwards' [says the Lord], 'I will return and renew the broken contract with David, [17]so that Gentiles, too, will find the Lord—

all those marked with my name.' [18]That is what the Lord says, who reveals his plans made from the beginning. [19]And so my judgment is that we should not insist that the Gentiles who turn to God must obey our Jewish laws, [20]except that we should write to them to refrain from eating meat sacrificed to idols, from all fornication, and also from eating unbled meat of strangled animals. [21]For these things have been preached against in Jewish synagogues in every city on every Sabbath for many generations." [22]Then the apostles and elders and the whole congregation voted to send delegates to Antioch with Paul and Barnabas, to report on this decision. The men chosen were two of the church leaders—Judas (also called Barsabbas) and Silas. [23]This is the letter they took along with them: "*From:* The apostles, elders and brothers at Jerusalem. *To:* The Gentile brothers in Antioch, Syria and Cilicia. Greetings! [24]We understand that some believers from here have upset you and questioned your salvation, but they had no such instructions from us. [25]So it seemed wise to us, having unanimously agreed on our decision, to send to you these two official representatives, along with our beloved Barnabas and Paul. [26]These men—Judas and Silas, who have risked their lives for the sake of our Lord Jesus Christ—will confirm orally what we have decided concerning your question. [27-29]For it seemed good to the Holy Spirit and to us to lay no greater burden of Jewish laws on you than to abstain from eating food offered to idols and from unbled meat of strangled animals, and, of course, from fornication. If you do this, it is enough. Farewell." [30]The four messengers went at once to Antioch, where they called a general meeting of the Christians and gave them the letter. [31]And there was great joy throughout the church that day as they read it.

Acts 16:4. Then they went from city to city, making known the decision concerning the Gentiles, as decided by the apostles and elders in Jerusalem. [5]So the church grew daily in faith and numbers.

Acts 20:17. But when we landed at Miletus, he sent a message to the elders of the church at Ephesus asking them to come down to the boat to meet him. [28]And now beware! Be sure that you feed and shepherd God's flock—his church, purchased with his blood—for the Holy Spirit is holding you responsible as overseers.

1 Cor 7:17. But be sure in deciding these matters that you are living as God intended, marrying or not marrying in accordance with God's direction and help, and accepting whatever situation God has put you into. This is my rule for all the churches.

1 Cor 11:2. I am so glad, dear brothers, that you have been remembering and doing everything I taught you. [33]So, dear brothers, when you gather for the Lord's Supper—the communion service—wait for each other; [34]if anyone is really hungry he should eat at home so that he won't bring punishment upon himself when you meet together. I'll talk to you about the other matters after I arrive.

1 Cor 12:5. There are different kinds of service to God, but it is the same Lord we are serving. [28]Here is a list of some of the parts he has placed in his church, which is his body: Apostles, prophets—those who preach God's Word, teachers, those who do miracles, those who have the gift of healing, those who can help others, those who can get others to work together, those who speak in languages they have never learned.

1 Cor 14:26. Well, my brothers, let's add up what I am saying. When you meet together some will sing, another will teach, or tell some special information God has given him, or speak in an unknown language, or tell what someone else is saying who is speaking in the unknown language, but everything that is done must be useful to all, and build them up in the Lord. [33]God is not one who likes things to be disorderly and upset. He likes harmony, and he finds it in all the other churches. [40]However, be sure that everything is done properly in a good and orderly way.

1 Cor 16:3. When I come I will send your loving gift with a letter to Jerusalem, to be taken there by trustworthy messengers you yourselves will choose. [16]Please follow their instructions and do everything you can to help them as well as all others like them who work hard at your side with such real devotion.

2 Cor 2:6. I don't want to be harder on him than I should. He has been punished enough by your united disapproval. [7]Now it is time to forgive him and comfort him. Otherwise he may become so bitter and discouraged that he won't be able to recover. *vs.* 2–11.

Gal 2:7–9. In fact, when Peter, James, and John, who were known as the pillars of the church, saw how greatly God had used me in winning the Gentiles, just as Peter had been blessed so greatly in his preaching to the Jews—for the same God gave us each our special gifts—they shook hands with Barnabas and me and encouraged us to keep right on with our preaching to the Gentiles while they continued their work with the Jews. [10]The only thing they did suggest was that we must always remember to help the poor, and I, too, was eager for that.

Eph 4:11. Some of us have been given special ability as apostles; to others he has given the gift of being able to preach well; some have special ability in winning people to Christ, helping them to trust him as their Savior; still others have a gift for caring for God's people as a shepherd does his sheep, leading and teaching them in the ways of God. [12] . . . It is that God's people will be equipped to do better work for him, building up the church, the body of Christ, to a position of strength and maturity.

Phil 1:1. From: Paul and Timothy, slaves of Jesus Christ. *To:* The pastors and deacons and all the Christians in the city of Philippi.

1 Tim 3:1. It is a true saying that if a man wants to be a pastor he has a good ambition. [2]For a pastor must be a good man whose life cannot be spoken against. [5]For if a man can't make his own family

behave, how can he help the whole church? [8]The deacons must be the same sort of good, steady men as the pastors. They must not be heavy drinkers and must not be greedy for money. [9]They must be earnest, wholehearted followers of Christ who is the hidden Source of their faith. [10]Before they are asked to be deacons they should be given other jobs in the church as a test of their character and ability, and if they do well, then they may be chosen as deacons. [11]Their wives must be thoughtful, not heavy drinkers, not gossipers, but faithful in everything they do. [12]Deacons should have only one wife and they should have happy, obedient families. [13]Those who do well as deacons will be well rewarded both by respect from others and also by developing their own confidence and bold trust in the Lord. *vs.* 1–13.

1 Tim 4:14. Be sure to use the abilities God has given you through his prophets when the elders of the church laid their hands upon your head.

1 Tim 5:1. Never speak sharply to an older man, but plead with him respectfully just as though he were your own father. Talk to the younger men as you would to much loved brothers. [17]Pastors who do their work well should be paid well and should be highly appreciated, especially those who work hard at both preaching and teaching. [22]Never be in a hurry about choosing a pastor; you may overlook his sins and it will look as if you approve of them. Be sure that you yourself stay away from all sin.

2 Tim 1:6. This being so, I want to remind you to stir into flame the strength and boldness that is in you, that entered into you when I laid my hands upon your head and blessed you.

Tit 1:5. I left you there on the island of Crete so that you could do whatever was needed to help strengthen each of its churches, and I asked you to appoint pastors in every city who would follow the instructions I gave you.

Heb 13:17. Obey your spiritual leaders and be willing to do what they say. For their work is to watch over your souls, and God will judge them on how well they do this. Give them reason to report joyfully about you to the Lord and not with sorrow, for then you will suffer for it too. [24]Give my greetings to all your leaders and to the other believers there.

Jas 5:14. Is anyone sick? He should call for the elders of the church and they should pray over him and pour a little oil upon him, calling on the Lord to heal him. [15]And their prayer, if offered in faith, will heal him, for the Lord will make him well; and if his sickness was caused by some sin, the Lord will forgive him.

1 Pet 5:1. And now, a word to you elders of the church. I, too, am an elder. . . . [2]Feed the flock of God; care for it willingly; not for what you will get out of it, but because you are eager to serve the Lord. [3]Don't be tyrants, but lead them by your good example.

3 Jn 1:9. I sent a brief letter to the church about this, but proud Diotrephes, who loves to push himself forward as the leader of the Christians there, does not admit my authority over him and refuses to listen to me. [10]When I come I will tell you some of the things he is doing and what wicked things he is saying about me and what insulting language he is using. He not only refuses to welcome the missionary travelers himself, but tells others not to, and when they do he tries to put them out of the church.

See *Elder; Deacon; Bishop; Presbytery; Ministers, Duties of.*

LAST DAYS OF. A falling away, 2 Thess 2:3. A departure from the faith, 1 Tim 4:1–3. Perilous times to come, 2 Tim 3:1–5. Sound doctrine rejected, 2 Tim 4:3, 4. False teachers will win a large following, 2 Pet 2:1, 2. There shall come scoffers, 2 Pet 3:3, 4. Sensual mockers, Jude 1:18, 19. Lukewarmness, Rev 3:14–19. Destruction during the world-wide tribulation, Rev 3:10, 16; 17:1–18.

See following topic, *Church, The True.*

MISSION OF. Bearing witness, Mt 28:19, 20; Mk 16:15; Lk 24:46–48; Rom 10:17; Acts 1:8; 2 Cor 5:19, 20. Feeding God's sheep, Jn 21:16, 17. Setting men apart for the ministry, Acts 13:1–3. Ministering to the needy, Acts 6:1–6; Jas 1:27. Giving, Phil 4:15–17. Edifying, Rom 15:2; Eph 4:11, 12. Shining as lights, Phil 2:15. Stewards of God's grace, 1 Pet 4:10. Holding forth the Word, Phil 2:16. Being examples, 1 Thess 1:7; 1 Pet 2:12, 15. Bringing comfort, 1 Thess 4:18.

MINISTERS OF. See *Minister, New Testament.*

ORDINANCES OR SACRAMENTS OF. See *Baptism; Lord's Supper.*

RELATIONSHIP TO THE STATE. Subjection to the higher powers, Rom 13:1–7. Prayer for kings, 1 Tim 2:1, 2. Obedience to magistrates, Tit 3:1. Submission to ordinances, 1 Pet 2:13–17.

CHURCH, THE TRUE In a number of passages the word church refers to all regenerated persons, the invisible organism of saved people everywhere, baptized by the Holy Spirit into one body (1 Cor 12:13) of which Christ is the Head (Eph 1:22; 4:15, 16; Col 1:18); the temple of the Holy Spirit (1 Cor 3:16; Eph 2:19–22).

Much of the content of the epistles has to do with the true church, made up of individuals described as saints (Acts 26:10; 1 Thess 3:13; 2 Thess 1:10; Rev 14:12); brothers (Acts 11:1; Rom 7:1; Col 1:2; 2 Thess 1:3; Heb 3:1); Christians (Phil 1:1; 1 Thess 5:27); believers (Acts 5:14; 1 Cor 14:24; 1 Thess 4:16); sons or children of God (Rom 8:14–17; 1 Jn 3:2; 5:1); the saved (1 Cor 1:18; 15:2; 2 Cor 2:15; Eph 2:5, 8; 2 Tim 1:9); the called (1 Cor 1:24; Eph 4:4; 2 Thess 2:14); God's people (Rom 1:6, 7; 2 Tim 2:24); new persons (2 Cor 5:17; Eph 2:10); the people of God (2 Cor 6:16; 1 Pet 2:10); born of God (1 Jn 3:9); born again (Jn 3:5; 1 Pet 1:23; 1 Jn 3:9); the Lord's sheep (Jn 10:27, 28); servants (Rev 1:1); living building-stones (1 Pet 2:5); those who belong to Christ (Gal 5:24); made alive by Christ (Eph 2:5); made by God (Eph 2:10); fellowmembers of God's family (Eph 2:19); parts of one another (Eph 4:25); children of light (1 Thess 5:5); lights in the world (Phil 2:15); the righteous (Jas 5:16; 1 Pet 4:18);

visitors (1 Pet 2:11); holy priests (1 Pet 2:5); chosen by God, priests of the King, holy and pure, God's very own (1 Pet 2:9); friends (Eph 1:1; 1 Pet 4:12; 1 Jn 4:7); those who have been delivered from hell and given eternal life (1 Jn 3:14); those who are loyal to the teachings of Christ (Jn 15:7; 2 Jn 1:9); those who have obtained the faith of the apostles (2 Pet 1:1); priests of God the Father (Rev 1:6); good soldiers (2 Tim 2:3, 4); parts of the body (1 Cor 12: 12–27); the family of God (Eph 3:14, 15); the flock of God (1 Pet 5:2); God's garden, God's building (1 Cor 3:9); a dwelling place of God (Eph 2:22); citizens of God's country (Eph 2:19); the house of God (1 Cor 3:16, 17; Heb 3:6); church of the living God (1 Tim 3:15); a spiritual house (1 Pet 2:5); the temple of God (2 Cor 6:16); the home of the living God (2 Cor 6:16).

DISTINGUISHED FROM ISRAEL AND THE GENTILES. Rom 10:1. Dear brothers, the longing of my heart and my prayer is that the Jewish people might be saved. [2]I know what enthusiasm they have for the honor of God, but it is misdirected zeal. [3]For they don't understand that Christ has died to make them right with God. Instead they are trying to make themselves good enough to gain God's favor by keeping the Jewish laws and customs, but that is not God's way of salvation. [4]They don't understand that Christ gives to those who trust in him everything they are trying to get by keeping his laws. He ends all of that.

Rom 11:25. I want you to know about this truth from God, dear brothers, so that you will not feel proud and start bragging. Yes, it is true that some of the Jews have set themselves against the Gospel now, but this will last only until all of you Gentiles have come to Christ—those of you who will. [26]And then all Israel will be saved. Do you remember what the prophets said about this? "There shall come out of Zion a Deliverer, and he shall turn the Jews from all ungodliness. [27]At that time I will take away their sins, just as I promised." [28]Now many of the Jews are enemies of the Gospel. They hate it. But this has been a benefit to you, for it has resulted in God's giving his gifts to you Gentiles. Yet the Jews are still beloved of God because of his promises to Abraham, Isaac, and Jacob.

1 Cor 10:32. So don't be a stumbling block to anyone, whether they are Jews or Gentiles or Christians.

Eph 2:11. Never forget that once you were heathen, and that you were called godless and "unclean" by the Jews. (But their hearts, too, were still unclean, even though they were going through the ceremonies and rituals of the godly, for they circumcised themselves as a sign of godliness.) [13]But now you belong to Christ Jesus, and though you once were far away from God, now you have been brought very near to him because of what Jesus Christ has done for you with his blood.

RELATIONSHIP TO ISRAEL. Hos 1:10. Yet the time will come when Israel shall prosper and become a great nation; in that day her people will be too numerous to count—like sand along a seashore! Then, instead of saying to them, "You are not my people," I will tell them "You are my sons, children of the Living God." [11]Then the people of Judah and Israel will unite and have one leader; they will return from exile together; what a day that will be—the day when God will sow his people into the fertile soil of their own land again.

Acts 11:15. Well, I began telling them the Good News, but just as I was getting started with my sermon, the Holy Spirit fell on them, just as he fell on us at the beginning! [16]Then I thought of the Lord's words when he said, "Yet, John baptized with water, but you shall be baptized with the Holy Spirit." *v.* 12.

Rom 9:23, 24. And he has a right to take others such as ourselves, who have been made for pouring the riches of his glory into, whether we are Jews or Gentiles, and to be kind to us so that everyone can see how very great his glory is. [25]Remember what the prophecy of Hosea says? There God says that he will find other children for himself (who are not from his Jewish family) and will love them, though no one had ever loved them before. [26]And the heathen, of whom it once was said, "You are not my people," shall be called "sons of the Living God."

Rom 11:11. Does this mean that God has rejected his Jewish people forever? Of course not! His purpose was to make his salvation available to the Gentiles, and then the Jews would be jealous and begin to want God's salvation for themselves. [17]But some of these branches from Abraham's tree, some of the Jews, have been broken off. And you Gentiles who were branches from, we might say, a wild olive tree, were grafted in. So now you, too, receive the blessing God has promised Abraham and his children, sharing in God's rich nourishment of his own special olive tree.

1 Cor 12:13. Each of us is a part of the one body of Christ. Some of us are Jews, some are Gentiles, some are slaves and some are free. But the Holy Spirit has fitted us all together into one body. We have been baptized into Christ's body by the one Spirit, and have all been given that same Holy Spirit.

Eph 1:22. And God has put all things under his feet and made him the supreme Head of the church —[23]which is his body, filled with himself, the Author and Giver of everything everywhere.

Eph 3:2, 3. No doubt you already know that God has given me this special work of showing God's favor to you Gentiles, as I briefly mentioned before in one of my letters. God himself showed me this secret plan of his, that the Gentiles, too, are included in his kindness. [4]I say this to explain to you how I know about these things. [5]In olden times God did not share this plan with his people, but now he has revealed it by the Holy Spirit to his apostles and prophets. [6]And this is the secret: that the Gentiles will have their full share with the Jews in all the riches inherited by God's sons; both are invited to belong to his church, and all of God's promises of mighty blessings through Christ apply to them both when they accept the Good News about Christ and what he has done for them. [7]God has given me the wonderful privilege of telling everyone about this plan of his; and he has given me his power and special ability to do it well.

BEGINNING OF. Mt 16:18. You are Peter, a stone; and upon this rock I will build my church; and all the powers of hell shall not prevail against it.

Jn 14:15, 16. If you love me, obey me; and I will ask the Father and he will give you another Comforter, and he will never leave you. [17]He is the Holy Spirit, the Spirit who leads into all truth. The world at large cannot receive him, for it isn't looking for him and doesn't recognize him. But you do, for he lives with you now and some day shall be in you.

Acts 1:4. In one of these meetings he told them not to leave Jerusalem until the Holy Spirit came upon them in fulfillment of the Father's promise, a matter he had previously discussed with them. [5]"John baptized you with water," he reminded them, "but you shall be baptized with the Holy Spirit in just a few days."

Acts 2:1. Seven weeks had gone by since Jesus' death and resurrection, and the Day of Pentecost had now arrived. As the believers met together that day, [2]suddenly there was a sound like the roaring of a mighty windstorm in the skies above them and it filled the house where they were meeting. [3]Then, what looked like flames or tongues of fire appeared and settled on their heads. [4]And everyone present was filled with the Holy Spirit and began speaking in languages they didn't know, for the Holy Spirit gave them this ability.

CHRIST IS THE BUILDER. Mt 16:18. You are Peter, a stone; and upon this rock I will build my church; and all the powers of hell shall not prevail against it.

Acts 2:47. And each day God added to them all who were being saved.

CHRIST IS THE FOUNDATION. 1 Cor 3:9. We are only God's co-workers. You are *God's* garden, not ours; you are *God's* building, not ours. [10]God, in his kindness, has taught me how to be an expert builder. I have laid the foundation and Apollos has built on it. But he who builds on the foundation must be very careful. [11]And no one can ever lay any other real foundation than that one we already have—Jesus Christ.

Eph 2:19. Now you are no longer strangers to God and foreigners to heaven, but you are members of God's very own family, citizens of God's country, and you belong in God's household with every other Christian. [20]What a foundation you stand on now: the apostles and the prophets; and the cornerstone of the building is Jesus Christ himself! [21]We who believe are carefully joined together with Christ as parts of a beautiful, constantly growing temple for God. [22]And you also are joined with him and with each other by the Spirit, and are part of this dwelling place of God.

1 Pet 2:4. Come to Christ, who is the living Foundation of Rock upon which God builds; though men have spurned him, he is very precious to God who has chosen him above all others. [5]And now you have become living building-stones for God's use in building his house. What's more, you are his holy priests; so come to him—[you who are acceptable to him because of Jesus Christ]—and offer to God those things that please him. [6]As the Scriptures express it, "See, I am sending Christ to be the carefully chosen, precious Cornerstone of my church, and I will never disappoint those who trust in him." [7]Yes, he is very precious to you who believe; and to those who reject him, well—"The same Stone that was rejected by the builders has become the Cornerstone, the most honored and important part of the building."

CHRIST IS THE HEAD. Eph 1:22. And God has put all things under his feet and made him the supreme Head of the church—[23]which is his body, filled with himself, the Author and Giver of everything everywhere.

Eph 4:15, 16. Instead, we will lovingly follow the truth at all times—speaking truly, dealing truly, living truly—and so become more and more in every way like Christ who is the Head of his body, the church. Under his direction the whole body is fitted together perfectly, and each part in its own special way helps the other parts, so that the whole body is healthy and growing and full of love.

Eph 5:23. For a husband is in charge of his wife in the same way Christ is in charge of his body the church. (He gave his very life to take care of it and be its Savior!) [24]So you wives must willingly obey your husbands in everything, just as the church obeys Christ. [29, 30]No one hates his own body but lovingly cares for it, just as Christ cares for his body the church, of which we are parts. [31](That the husband and wife are one body is proved by the Scripture which says, "A man must leave his father and mother when he marries, so that he can be perfectly joined to his wife, and the two shall be one.") [32]I know this is hard to understand, but it is an illustration of the way we are parts of the body of Christ.

Col 1:18. He is the Head of the body made up of his people—that is, his church—which he began; and he is the Leader of all those who arise from the dead, so that he is first in everything.

Col 2:19. But they are not connected to Christ, the Head to which all of us who are his body are joined; for we are joined together by his strong sinews and we grow only as we get our nourishment and strength from God.

THE BRIDE OF CHRIST. 2 Cor 11:2. I am anxious for you with the deep concern of God himself—anxious that your love should be for Christ alone, just as a pure maiden saves her love for one man only, for the one who will be her husband.

Eph 5:25. And you husbands, show the same kind of love to your wives as Christ showed to the church when he died for her, [26]to make her holy and clean, washed by baptism and God's Word; [27]so that he could give her to himself as a glorious church without a single spot or wrinkle or any other blemish, being holy and without a single fault.

Jn 3:29. The crowds will naturally go to the main attraction—the bride will go where the bridegroom is! A bridegroom's friends rejoice with him. I am the Bridegroom's friend, and I am filled with joy at his success.

Rom 7:4. Your "husband," your master, used to be the Jewish law; but you "died," as it were, with Christ on the cross; and since you are "dead," you are no longer "married to the law," and it has no more control over you. Then you came back to life again when Christ did, and are a new person. And now you are "married," so to speak, to the one who rose from the dead, so that you can produce good fruit, that is, good deeds for God.

Rev 19:7. "Let us be glad and rejoice and honor him; for the time has come for the wedding banquet of the Lamb, and his bride has prepared herself. [8]She is permitted to wear the cleanest and whitest and finest of linens." (Fine linen represents the good deeds done by the people of God.) [9]And the angel dictated this sentence to me: "Blessed are those who are invited to the wedding feast of the lamb." And he added, "God himself has stated this."

Rev 21:9. Then one of the seven angels, who had emptied the flasks containing the seven last plagues, came and said to me, "Come with me and I will show you the bride, the Lamb's wife." [10]In a vision he took me to a towering mountain peak and from there I watched that wondrous city, the holy Jerusalem, descending out of the skies from God. [11]It was filled with the glory of God, and flashed and glowed like a precious gem, crystal clear like jasper.

Rev 22:17. The Spirit and the bride say, "Come."

Old Testament types of Christ and his Bride: Adam and Eve; Isaac and Rebekah; Joseph and Asenath; Moses and Zipporah; Boaz and Ruth; David and Abigail; Solomon and the Shulamite.

GOD'S PURPOSES FOR. Jn 17:21. My prayer for all of them is that . . . the world will believe you sent me. [23]. . . so that the world will know you sent me and will understand that you love them as much as you love me.

Acts 15:14. Peter has told you about the time God first visited the Gentiles to take from them a people to bring honor to his name. [15]And this fact of Gentile conversion agrees with what the prophets predicted. For instance, listen to this passage from the prophet Amos: [16]"Afterwards" [says the Lord], "I will return and renew the broken contract with David," [17]so that Gentiles, too, will find the Lord.

1 Cor 3:16. Don't you realize that all of you together are the house of God, and that the Spirit of God lives among you in his house?

2 Cor 5:18. All these new things are from God who brought us back to himself through what Christ Jesus did. And God has given us the privilege of urging everyone to come into his favor and be reconciled to him. [19]For God was in Christ, restoring the world to himself, no longer counting men's sins against them but blotting them out. This is the wonderful message he has given us to tell others. Jn 17:18.

Eph 2:19. Now you are no longer strangers to God and foreigners to heaven, but you are members of God's very own family, citizens of God's country, and you belong in God's household with every other Christian. [20]What a foundation you stand on now: the apostles and the prophets; and the cornerstone of the building is Jesus Christ himself! [21]We who believe are carefully joined together with Christ as parts of a beautiful, constantly growing temple for God. [22]And you also are joined with him and with each other by the Spirit, and are part of this dwelling place of God.

Eph 1:22. And God has put all things under his feet and made him the supreme Head of the church —[23]which is his body, filled with himself, the Author and Giver of everything everywhere.

Eph 2:6. And lifted us up from the grave into glory along with Christ, where we sit with him in the heavenly realms—all because of what Christ Jesus did. [7]And now God can always point to us as examples of how very, very rich his kindness is, as shown in all he has done for us through Jesus Christ.

Eph 3:10. And his reason? To show to all the rulers in heaven how perfectly wise he is when all of his family—Jews and Gentiles alike—are seen to be joined together in his church, [11]in just the way he had always planned it through Jesus Christ our Lord.

Eph 5:27. So that he could give her to himself as a glorious church without a single spot or wrinkle or any other blemish, being holy and without a single fault.

Phil 2:15. Shine out among them like beacon lights, [16]holding out to them the Word of Life.

2 Thess 1:10. When he comes to receive praise and admiration because of all he has done for his people, his saints. And you will be among those praising him, because you have believed what we told you about him.

Heb 2:10. And it was right and proper that God, who made everything for his own glory, should allow Jesus to suffer, for in doing this he was bringing vast multitudes of God's people to heaven; for his suffering made Jesus a perfect Leader, one fit to bring them into their salvation. Rom 8:29.

1 Pet 2:5. And now you have become living building-stones for God's use in building his house. What's more, you are his holy priests; so come to him—[you who are acceptable to him because of Jesus Christ]—and offer to God those things that please him.

Rev 5:10. And you have gathered them into a kingdom and made them priests of our God; they shall reign upon the earth.

Rev 20:6. Blessed and holy are those who share in the First Resurrection. For them the Second Death holds no terrors, for they will be priests of

God and of Christ, and shall reign with him a thousand years.

Rev 22:5. And they shall reign forever and ever.

HEAVENLY CALLING AND DESTINY. Rom 8:16. For his Holy Spirit speaks to us deep in our hearts, and tells us that we really are God's children. [17]And since we are his children, we will share his treasures—for all God gives to his Son Jesus is now ours too. But if we are to share his glory, we must also share his suffering.

Eph 1:3. How we praise God, the Father of our Lord Jesus Christ, who has blessed us with every blessing in heaven because we belong to Christ.

Col 3:4. And when Christ who is our real life comes back again, you will shine with him and share in all his glories.

Heb 3:1. Therefore, dear brothers whom God has set apart for himself—you who are chosen for heaven—I want you to think now about this Jesus who is God's Messenger and the High Priest of our faith.

1 Pet 1:3. All honor to God, the God and Father of our Lord Jesus Christ; for it is his boundless mercy that has given us the privilege of being born again, so that we are now members of God's own family. Now we live in the hope of eternal life because Christ rose again from the dead. [4]And God has reserved for his children the priceless gift of eternal life; it is kept in heaven for you, pure and undefiled, beyond the reach of change and decay. [5]And God, in his mighty power, will make sure that you get there safely to receive it, because you are trusting him. It will be yours in that coming last day for all to see.

Rev 3:21. I will let every one who conquers sit beside me on my throne, just as I took my place with my Father on his throne when I had conquered.

Phil 3:20. But our homeland is in heaven, where our Savior the Lord Jesus Christ is; and we are looking forward to his return from there.

Heb 12:22. But you have come right up into Mount Zion, to the city of the living God, the heavenly Jerusalem, and to the gathering of countless happy angels; [23]and to the church, composed of all those registered in heaven.

FIGURES OF CHRIST AND THE CHURCH. The Shepherd and the sheep, Jn 10:1–16. The Vine and the branches, Jn 15:1–17. The Cornerstone and the stones of the building, Eph 2:19–22; 1 Cor 3:9; 1 Pet 2:5. The High Priest and the kingdom of priests, Heb 5:1–10; 6:13–8:6; 1 Pet 2:5–9; Rev 1:6. The Head and the body, 1 Cor 12:12, 13, 27; Eph 4:4. The Last Adam and the new creation, 1 Cor 15:22, 45; 2 Cor 5:17. The bridegroom and the bride, Jn 3:29; 2 Cor 11:2; Eph 5:25–33; Rev 19:7, 8.

VARIOUS TRUTHS CONCERNING. Christ's love for the church, Jn 10:11, 15; Eph 5:25–32; Rev 3:9. Brotherly love, 1 Cor 12:25; 1 Thess 4:9. Warfare of, Phil 2:25; 1 Tim 6:12; 2 Tim 2:3; 4:7; Philemon 1:1, 2. God defends, Mt 16:18. God provides pastors and teachers, Eph 4:11, 12. Cleansing of, Eph 5:25–27. To be clothed in good deeds, Rev 19:8. Believers added by and to the Lord, Acts 2:47; 5:14; 11:24. Unity of, Rom 12:4, 5; 1 Cor 10:17; 12:12; Gal 3:28; Eph 4:4. Assembling of, to be attended, Heb 10:25. Fellowship of, Jn 13:34; Acts 2:42; 4:32; Rom 1:11, 12; Phil 1:4, 5; 2:1; 1 Jn 1:3, 7; 3:14. Divisions to be shunned, Rom 16:17; 1 Cor 1:10; 3:3. Overseers commanded to feed, Acts 20:28. The wicked persecute, Acts 8:1–3; 1 Thess 2:14, 15. To avoid disgrace, 1 Cor 11:22. Preaches the Word, Acts 6:2, 4; 8:25; 12:24; 13:5, 44, 49; 14:25; 15:34–36; 16:6, 32; 17:11, 13; 18:11; Rom 10:8; 2 Cor 5:19; Gal 6:6; Eph 1:13; Phil 1:14; 2:16; 1 Thess 1:5, 6; 1 Tim 5:17; 2 Tim 4:2; Heb 13:7; Jas 1:21; 1 Pet 1:25; 2:2, 3; 2 Pet 1:19; 1 Jn 1:1; Rev 1:9; 12:11.

RELATIONSHIP TO THE HOLY SPIRIT. Regenerates, Jn 3:3–6; Tit 3:4–7. Indwells, Jn 7:37–39; 14:17; Rom 5:5; 8:9; 1 Cor 2:12; 3:16; 6:19; 1 Jn 2:27; 3:24. Baptizes, Lk 24:49; Jn 1:33; Acts 1:5, 8; 2:1–4; 1 Cor 12:13. Seals, 2 Cor 1:22; Eph 1:13, 14; 4:30. Fills, Eph 5:18–21 (cf. Gal 5:16; Eph 4:30; 1 Thess 5:19). Teaches, Jn 16:12–15; 1 Jn 2:27. Leads, Rom 8:14; Gal 5:18; Phil 2:13. Intercedes, Rom 8:26, 27. Prayer in, Eph 6:18; Jude 1:20. Gifts of, 1 Cor 12:4–31 (cf. Eph 4:7–12). Fruit of, Jn 15:1–8; Rom 7:4; Gal 5:22, 23; Eph 5:9.

JUDGMENTS OF.

Chastening, preventative. 2 Cor 12:7. I will say this: because these experiences I had were so tremendous, God was afraid I might be puffed up by them; so I was given a physical condition which has been a thorn in my flesh, a messenger from Satan to hurt and bother me, and prick my pride. [8]Three different times I begged God to make me well again. [9]Each time he said, "No. But I am with you; that is all you need. My power shows up best in weak people." Now I am glad to boast about how weak I am; I am glad to be a living demonstration of Christ's power, instead of showing off my own power and abilities."

Chastening, corrective. 1 Cor 11:27. So if anyone eats this bread and drinks from this cup of the Lord in an unworthy manner, he is guilty of sin against the body and the blood of the Lord. [28]That is why a man should examine himself carefully before eating the bread and drinking from the cup. [29]For if he eats the bread and drinks from the cup unworthily, not thinking about the body of Christ and what it means, he is eating and drinking God's judgment upon himself; for he is trifling with the death of Christ. [30]That is why many of you are weak and sick, and some have even died. [31]But if you carefully examine yourselves before eating you will not need to be judged and punished. [32]Yet, when we are judged and punished by the Lord, it is so that we will not be condemned with the rest of the world. Heb 12:3–13.

The judgment seat of Christ. Rom 14:10. You have no right to criticize your brother or look down on him. Remember, each of us will stand personally before the Judgment Seat of God.

1 Cor 3:11. And no one can ever lay any other real foundation than that one we already have—Jesus Christ. [12]But there are various kinds of materials

that can be used to build on that foundation. Some use gold and silver and jewels; and some build with sticks, and hay, or even straw! [13]There is going to come a time of testing at Christ's Judgment Day to see what kind of material each builder has used. Everyone's work will be put through the fire so that all can see whether or not it keeps its value, and what was really accomplished. [14]Then every workman who has built on the foundation with the right materials, and whose work still stands, will get his pay. [15]But if the house he has built burns up, he will have a great loss. He himself will be saved, but like a man escaping through a wall of flames. 1 Cor 3:8.

1 Cor 9:27. Like an athlete I punish my body, treating it roughly, training it to do what it should, not what it wants to. Otherwise I fear that after enlisting others for the race, I myself might be declared unfit and ordered to stand aside.

2 Cor 5:10. For we must all stand before Christ to be judged and have our lives laid bare—before him. Each of us will receive whatever he deserves for the good or bad things he has done in his earthly body. [11]It is because of this solemn fear of the Lord, which is ever present in our minds, that we work so hard to win others.

Eph 6:8. Remember, the Lord will pay you for each good thing you do, whether you are slave or free. 1 Cor 15:58.

2 Tim 4:7. I have fought long and hard for my Lord, and through it all I have kept true to him. And now the time has come for me to stop fighting and rest. [8]In heaven a crown is waiting for me which the Lord, the righteous Judge, will give me on that great day of his return. And not just to me, but to all those whose lives show that they are eagerly looking forward to his coming back again.

Rev 22:12. See, I am coming soon, and my reward is with me, to repay everyone according to the deeds he has done. (cf. Rev 19:8).

SUFFERINGS OF. Mt 10:25. The student shares his teacher's fate. The servant shares his master's! And since I, the master of the household, have been called "Satan," how much more will you!

Jn 15:18. For you get enough hate from the world! But then, it hated me before it hated you. [19]The world would love you if you belonged to it; but you don't—for I chose you to come out of the world, and so it hates you.

Acts 9:15. But the Lord said, "Go and do what I say. For Paul is my chosen instrument to take my message to the nations and before kings, as well as to the people of Israel. [16]And I will show him how much he must suffer for me."

Rom 8:16. For his Holy Spirit speaks to us deep in our hearts, and tells us that we really are God's children. [17]And since we are his children, we will share his treasures—for all God gives to his Son Jesus is now ours too. But if we are to share his glory, we must also share his suffering. [18]Yet what we suffer now is nothing compared to the glory he will give us later. [23]And even we Christians, although we have the Holy Spirit within us as a foretaste of future glory, also groan to be released from pain and suffering. We, too, wait anxiously for that day when God will give us our full rights as his children, including the new bodies he has promised us—bodies that will never be sick again and will never die.

Rom 9:1–3. Oh, Israel, my people! Oh my Jewish brothers! How I long for you to come to Christ. My heart is heavy within me and I grieve bitterly day and night because of you. Christ knows and the Holy Spirit knows that it is no mere pretense when I say that I would be willing to be forever damned if that would save you.

Phil 2:5. Your attitude should be the kind that was shown us by Jesus Christ, [6]who, though he was God, did not demand and cling to his rights as God, [7]but laid aside his mighty power and glory, taking the disguise of a slave and becoming like men. [8]And he humbled himself even further, going so far as actually to die a criminal's death on a cross.

Col 1:24. But part of my work is to suffer for you; and I am glad, for I am helping to finish up the remainder of Christ's sufferings for his body, the church.

2 Tim 2:11. I am comforted by this truth, that when we suffer and die for Christ it only means that we will begin living with him in Heaven. [12]And if we think that our present service for him is hard, just remember that some day we are going to sit with him and rule with him. But if we give up when we suffer, and turn against Christ, then he must turn against us.

1 Pet 4:12. Dear friends, don't be bewildered or surprised when you go through the fiery trials ahead, for this is no strange, unusual thing that is going to happen to you. [13]Instead, be really glad—because these trials will make you partners with Christ in his suffering, and afterwards you will have the wonderful joy of sharing his glory in that coming day when it will be displayed. [14]Be happy if you are cursed and insulted for being a Christian, for when that happens the Spirit of God will come upon you with greater glory. [15]Don't let me hear of your suffering for murdering or stealing or making trouble or being a busybody and prying into other people's affairs. [16]But it is no shame to suffer for being a Christian. Praise God for the privilege of being in Christ's family and being called by his wonderful name! [19]So if you are suffering according to God's will, keep on doing what is right and trust yourself to the God who made you, for he will never fail you. 1 Pet 1:6, 7.

MYSTERIES OF. A New Testament mystery is a revelation of truth not fully understood at the present time, but which will be revealed when Christ returns. Rom 11:25; 16:25–27; 1 Cor 2:7; 4:1; 13:2; 14:2; 15:51; Eph 1:9; 3:2–5, 9; 6:19; Col 1:26, 27; 2:2; 4:3; 2 Thess 2:7; 1 Tim 3:9, 16; Rev 1:20; 10:7; 17:5, 7 (cf. Mt 13:11; Mark 4:11, 12; Lk 8:10).

MEMBERSHIP IN. The New Testament does not refer to membership in an organized group of believers; it speaks only of membership in the body of Christ, Eph 5:29, 30. Believers are baptized into his body by the Holy Spirit, in the moment of salvation, 1 Cor 12:13. (See *Gospel; Salvation.*) For the character of believers, see *Righteous, Described.* For the fellowship of true Christians, see *Fellowship, of the Righteous.*

MISSION OF. See *God's Purposes for,* above; *Missions.*

ORDINANCES OF. See *Church, The Visible.*

UNITY OF. Jn 10:16. I have other sheep, too, in another fold. I must bring them also, and they will heed my voice; and there will be one flock with one Shepherd.

Jn 17:11. Now I am leaving the world, and leaving them behind, and coming to you. Holy Father, keep them in your own care—all those you have given me—so that they will be united just as we are, with none missing. [21]My prayer for all of them is that they will be one heart and mind, just as you and I are, Father—that just as you are in me and I am in you, so they will be in us, and the world will believe you sent me. [22]I have given them the glory you gave me—the glorious unity of being one, as we are— [23]I in them and you in me, all being perfected into one—so that the world will know you sent me and will understand that you love them as much as you love me.

Rom 12:4, 5. Just as there are many parts to our bodies, so it is with Christ's body. We are all parts of it, and it takes every one of us to make it complete, for we each have different work to do. So we belong to each other, and each needs all the others.

1 Cor 10:17. No matter how many of us there are, we all eat from the same loaf, showing that we are all parts of the one body of Christ.

1 Cor 12:5. There are different kinds of service to God, but it is the same Lord we are serving. [12]Our bodies have many parts, but the many parts make up only one body when they are all put together. So it is with the "body" of Christ. [13]Each of us is a part of the one body of Christ. Some of us are Jews, some are Gentiles, some are slaves and some are free. But the Holy Spirit has fitted us all together into one body. We have been baptized into Christ's body by the one Spirit, and have all been given that same Holy Spirit. [26]If one part suffers, all parts suffer with it, and if one part is honored, all the parts are glad. [27]Now here is what I am trying to say: All of you together are the one body of Christ and each one of you is a separate and necessary part of it. *vs.* 12–27.

Gal 3:26. For now we are all children of God through faith in Jesus Christ, [27]and we who have been baptized into union with Christ are enveloped by him. [28]We are no longer Jews or Greeks or slaves or free men or even merely men or women, but we are all the same—we are Christians; we are one in Christ Jesus.

Eph 1:10. And this was his purpose: that when the time is ripe he will gather us all together from wherever we are—in heaven or on earth—to be with him in Christ, forever.

Eph 2:14. For Christ himself is our way of peace. He has made peace between us Jews and you Gentiles by making us all one family, breaking down the wall of contempt that used to separate us. [15]By his death he ended the angry resentment between us, caused by the Jewish laws which favored the Jews and excluded the Gentiles, for he died to annul that whole system of Jewish laws. Then he took the two groups that had been opposed to each other and made them parts of himself; thus he fused us together to become one new person, and at last there was peace. [16]As parts of the same body, our anger against each other has disappeared, for both of us have been reconciled to God. And so the feud ended at last at the cross. [17]And he has brought this Good News of peace to you Gentiles who were very far away from him, and to us Jews who were near. [18]Now all of us, whether Jews or Gentiles, may come to God the Father with the Holy Spirit's help because of what Christ has done for us. [19]Now you are no longer strangers to God and foreigners to heaven, but you are members of God's very own family, citizens of God's country, and you belong in God's household with every other Christian. [21]We who believe are carefully joined together with Christ as parts of a beautiful, constantly growing temple for God.

Eph 3:6. And this is the secret: that the Gentiles will have their full share with the Jews in all the riches inherited by God's sons; both are invited to belong to his church, and all of God's promises of mighty blessings through Christ apply to them both when they accept the Good News about Christ and what he has done for them. [14, 15]When I think of the wisdom and scope of his plan I fall down on my knees and pray to the Father of all the great family of God—some of them already in heaven and some down here on earth.

Eph 4:4. We are all parts of one body, we have the same Spirit, and we have all been called to the same glorious future. [5]For us there is only one Lord, one faith, one baptism, [6]and we all have the same God and Father who is over us all and in us all, and living through every part of us. [12]Why is it that he gives us these special abilities to do certain things best? It is that God's people will be equipped to do better work for him, building up the church, the body of Christ, to a position of strength and maturity; [13]until finally we all believe alike about our salvation and about our Savior, God's Son, and all become full-grown in the Lord—yes, to the point of being filled full with Christ. [16]Under his direction the whole body is fitted together perfectly, and each part in its own special way helps the other parts, so that the whole body is healthy and growing and full of love. [25]. . . for we are parts of each other.

Col 3:11. In this new life one's nationality or race or education or social position is unimportant; such things mean nothing. Whether a person has Christ is what matters, and he is equally available to all. [15]Let the peace of heart which comes from Christ be always present in your hearts and lives, for this is your responsibility and privilege as members of his body. And always be thankful.

SPIRITUAL GIFTS TO. See *Gifts from God.*

SPIRITUAL WARFARE OF. See *Flesh; Satan; War, Figurative.*

RELATIONSHIP TO THE END TIMES. While there are several views of the place of the church at the end of the age, the approach of the end is marked by several signs in the church: Believers will see the day approaching, Heb 10:25. Prophecy a shining light, 2 Pet 1:19. The dates not known, Acts 1:6, 7. False teachers win a large following, 2 Pet 2:1, 2. Doctrines of demons proclaimed, 1 Tim 4:1, 2. A departure from the faith, 2 Thess 2:3; 1 Tim 4:1. Evil men and false teachers become worse, 2 Tim 3:13. Perilous times come, 2 Tim 3:1–5. Scoffing at the doctrine of the Lord's return, 2 Pet 3:3, 4. Worldwide ministry of the Word, Mt 28:19, 20; Mk 16:15; Rev 5:9.

A premillenial interpretation of scripture envisions a seven-year time of tribulation followed by a literal 1000-year reign of Christ on earth, Rev 20:1–4. Various views can be delineated within premillenial theology as to the place of the church in these events: Some hold to a rapture of the church at the start of the tribulation, 1 Thess 1:10; 5:9; Rev 3:10; 5:9; others hold to the deliverance of the church at the midpoint, 1 Cor 15:52; Rev 11:11, 15; while still others believe that the church will remain on the earth until Christ returns. Varying with the premillenial view, some interpret Revelation 20:1–4 as figurative and not to be fulfilled literally.

THE DESTINY OF BELIEVERS.

After death. Acts 7:59. And as the murderous stones came hurtling at him, Stephen prayed, "Lord Jesus, receive my spirit." [60]And he fell to his knees, shouting, "Lord, don't charge them with this sin!" and with that, he died.

1 Thess 4:13. And now, dear brothers, I want you to know what happens to a Christian when he dies so that when it happens, you will not be full of sorrow, as those are who have no hope.

2 Cor 5:6. Now we look forward with confidence to our heavenly bodies, realizing that every moment we spend in these earthly bodies is time spent away from our eternal home in heaven with Jesus. [8]And we are not afraid, but are quite content to die, for then we will be at home with the Lord.

Ps 16:11. You have let me experience the joys of life and the exquisite pleasures of your own eternal presence.

Phil 1:21. For to me, living means opportunities for Christ, and dying—well, that's better yet! [23]Sometimes I want to live and at other times I don't, for I long to go and be with Christ. How much happier for *me* than being here!

Resurrection. 1 Cor 15:15. We have said that God raised Christ from the grave, and of course that isn't true if the dead do not come back to life again. [16]If they don't, then Christ is still dead, [17]and you are very foolish to keep on trusting God to save you, and you are still under condemnation for your sins; [18]in that case all Christians who have died are lost! [19]And if being a Christian is of value to us only now in this life, we are the most miserable of creatures. [20]But the fact is that Christ did actually rise from the dead, and has become the first of millions who will come back to life again some day. [21]Death came into the world because of what one man (Adam) did, and it is because of what this other man (Christ) has done that now there is the resurrection from the dead. [22]Everyone dies because all of us are related to Adam, being members of his sinful race, and wherever there is sin, death results. But all who are related to Christ will rise again. [23]Each, however, in his own turn: Christ rose first; then when Christ comes back, all his people will become alive again.

1 Cor 15:51. But I am telling you this strange and wonderful secret: we shall not all die, but we shall all be given new bodies! [52]It will all happen in a moment, in the twinkling of an eye, when the last trumpet is blown. For there will be a trumpet blast from the sky and all the Christians who have died will suddenly become alive, with new bodies that will never, never die; and then we who are still alive shall suddenly have new bodies too. [53]For our earthly bodies, the ones we have now that can die, must be transformed into heavenly bodies that cannot perish but will live forever. [54]When this happens, then at last this Scripture will come true—"Death is swallowed up in victory."

1 Cor 15:35. But someone may ask, "How will the dead be brought back to life again? What kind of bodies will they have?" [36]What a foolish question! You will find the answer in your own garden! When you put a seed into the ground it doesn't grow into a plant unless it "dies" first. [37]And when the green shoot comes up out of the seed, it is very different from the seed you first planted. For all you put into the ground is a dry little seed of wheat, or whatever it is you are planting, [38]then God gives it a beautiful new body—just the kind he wants it to have; a different kind of plant grows from each kind of seed. [39]And just as there are different kinds of seeds and plants, so also there are different kinds of flesh. Humans, animals, fish, and birds are all different. [40]The angels in heaven have bodies far different from ours, and the beauty and the glory of their bodies is different from the beauty and the glory of ours. [41]The sun has one kind of glory while the moon and stars have another kind. And the stars differ from each other in their beauty and brightness. [42]In the same way, our earthly bodies which die and decay are different from the bodies we shall have when we come back to life again, for they will never die. [43]The bodies we have now embarrass us for they become sick and die; but they will be full of glory when we come back to life again. Yes, they are weak, dying bodies now, but when we live again they will be full of strength. [44]They are just human bodies at death, but when they come back to life they will be superhuman bodies. For just as there are natural, human bodies, there are also supernatural, spiritual bodies. [49]Just as each of us now has a body like Adam's, so we

shall some day have a body like Christ's. [50]I tell you this, my brothers: an earthly body made of flesh and blood cannot get into God's kingdom. These perishable bodies of ours are not the right kind to live forever.

Phil 3:20. But our homeland is in heaven, where our Savior the Lord Jesus Christ is; and we are looking forward to his return from there. [21]When he comes back he will take these dying bodies of ours and change them into glorious bodies like his own, using the same mighty power that he will use to conquer all else everywhere.

1 Jn 3:2. Yes, dear friends, we are already God's children, right now, and we can't even imagine what it is going to be like later on. But we do know this, that when he comes we will be like him, as a result of seeing him as he really is.

1 Cor 13:12. In the same way, we can see and understand only a little about God now, as if we were peering at his reflection in a poor mirror; but someday we are going to see him in his completeness, face to face. Now all that I know is hazy and blurred, but then I will see everything clearly, just as clearly as God sees into my heart right now.

Jn 14:2, 3. There are many homes up there where my Father lives, and I am going to prepare them for your coming. When everything is ready, then I will come and get you, so that you can always be with me where I am. If this weren't so, I would tell you plainly.

1 Thess 4:14. For since we believe that Jesus died and then came back to life again, we can also believe that when Jesus returns, God will bring back with him all the Christians who have died. [15]I can tell you this directly from the Lord: that we who are still living when the Lord returns will not rise to meet him ahead of those who are in their graves. [16]For the Lord himself will come down from heaven with a mighty shout and with the soul-stirring cry of the archangel and the great trumpet-call of God. And the believers who are dead will be the first to rise to meet the Lord. [17]Then we who are still alive and remain on the earth will be caught up with them in the clouds to meet the Lord in the air and remain with him forever. [18]So comfort and encourage each other with this news.

Mt 10:32. If anyone publicly acknowledges me as his friend, I will openly acknowledge him as my friend before my father in heaven.

Rev 3:5. Everyone who conquers will be clothed in white, and I will not erase his name from the Book of Life, but I will announce before my Father and his angels that he is mine.

Judgment and Rewards. 1 Cor 15:58. So, my dear brothers, since future victory is sure, be strong and steady, always abounding in the Lord's work, for you know that nothing you do for the Lord is ever wasted as it would be if there were no resurrection.

Rom 14:10. Remember, each of us will stand personally before the Judgment Seat of God.

2 Cor 5:10. For we must all stand before Christ to be judged and have our lives laid bare—before him. Each of us will receive whatever he deserves for the good or bad things he has done in his earthly body.

1 Cor 3:11. And no one can ever lay any other real foundation than that one we already have—Jesus Christ. [12]But there are various kinds of materials that can be used to build on that foundation. Some use gold and silver and jewels; and some build with sticks, and hay, or even straw! [13]There is going to come a time of testing at Christ's Judgment Day to see what kind of material each builder has used. Everyone's work will be put through the fire so that all can see whether or not it keeps its value, and what was really accomplished. [14]Then every workman who has built on the foundation with the right materials, and whose work still stands, will get his pay. [15]But if the house he has built burns up, he will have a great loss. He himself will be saved, but like a man escaping through a wall of flames.

2 Jn 1:8. Beware of being like them, and losing the prize that you and I have been working so hard to get. See to it that you win your full reward from the Lord.

1 Jn 2:28. And now, my little children, stay in happy fellowship with the Lord so that when he comes you will be sure that all is well, and will not have to be ashamed and shrink back from meeting him.

1 Cor 9:25. To win the contest you must deny yourselves many things that would keep you from doing your best. An athlete goes to all this trouble just to win a blue ribbon or a silver cup, but we do it for a heavenly reward that never disappears.

1 Thess 2:19. For what is it we live for, that gives us hope and joy and is our proud reward and crown? It is you! Yes, you will bring us much joy as we stand together before our Lord Jesus Christ when he comes back again.

2 Tim 4:8. In heaven a crown is waiting for me which the Lord, the righteous Judge, will give me on that great day of his return. And not just to me, but to all those whose lives show that they are eagerly looking forward to his coming back again.

Jas 1:12. Happy is the man who doesn't give in and do wrong when he is tempted, for afterwards he will get as his reward the crown of life that God has promised those who love him.

1 Pet 5:4. And when the Head Shepherd comes, your reward will be a never-ending share in his glory and honor.

Jn 17:22. I have given them the glory you gave me—the glorious unity of being one—as we are. [24]Father, I want them with me—these you've given me—so that they can see my glory. You gave me the glory because you loved me before the world began!

Rev 22:12. See, I am coming soon, and my reward is with me, to repay everyone according to the deeds he has done.

Acts 26:18. To open their eyes to their true condition so that they may repent and live in the light of God instead of in Satan's darkness, so that they may receive forgiveness for their sins and God's inheritance along with all people everywhere whose sins are cleansed away, who are set apart by faith in me.

Rom 8:16. For his Holy Spirit speaks to us deep in our hearts, and tells us that we really are God's children. [17]And since we are his children, we will share his treasures—for all God gives to his Son Jesus is now ours too. But if we are to share his glory, we must also share his suffering.

1 Pet 1:3. All honor to God, the God and Father of our Lord Jesus Christ; for it is his boundless mercy that has given us the privilege of being born again, so that we are now members of God's own family. Now we live in the hope of eternal life because Christ rose again from the dead. [4]And God has reserved for his children the priceless gift of eternal life; it is kept in heaven for you, pure and undefiled, beyond the reach of change and decay. [5]And God, in his mighty power, will make sure that you get there safely to receive it, because you are trusting him. It will be yours in that coming last day for all to see.

Reigning. Col 3:4. And when Christ who is our real life comes back again, you will shine with him and share in all his glories.

1 Thess 3:13. This will result in your hearts being made strong, sinless and holy by God our Father, so that you may stand before him guiltless on that day when our Lord Jesus Christ returns with all those who belong to him.

Jude 1:14. Enoch, who lived seven generations after Adam, knew about these men and said this about them: "See, the Lord is coming with millions of his holy ones."

Rev 19:14. The armies of heaven, dressed in finest linen, white and clean, followed him on white horses.

2 Thess 1:10. When he comes to receive praise and admiration because of all he has done for his people, his saints. And you will be among those praising him, because you have believed what we told you about him.

2 Tim 2:12. And if we think that our present service for him is hard, just remember that some day we are going to sit with him and rule with him. But if we give up when we suffer, and turn against Christ, then he must turn against us.

Rev 3:21. I will let every one who conquers sit beside me on my throne, just as I took my place with my Father on his throne when I had conquered.

Rev 5:9. They were singing him a new song with these words: "You are worthy to take the scroll and break its seals and open it; for you were slain, and your blood has bought people from every nation as gifts for God. [10]And you have gathered them into a kingdom and made them priests of our God; they shall reign upon the earth."

Rev 21:9. Then one of the seven angels, who had emptied the flasks containing the seven last plagues, came and said to me, "Come with me and I will show you the bride, the Lamb's wife." [10]In a vision he took me to a towering mountain peak and from there I watched that wondrous city, the holy Jerusalem, descending out of the skies from God. [11]It was filled with the glory of God, and flashed and glowed like a precious gem, crystal clear like jasper.

Rev 22:14. Blessed forever are all who are washing their robes, to have the right to enter in through the gates of the city, and to eat the fruit from the Tree of Life. [16]I, Jesus, have sent my angel to you to tell the churches all these things. I am both David's Root and his Descendant. I am the bright Morning Star.

Eph 2:6. And lifted us up from the grave into glory along with Christ, where we sit with him in the heavenly realms—all because of what Christ Jesus did. [7]And now God can always point to us as examples of how very, very rich his kindness is, as shown in all he has done for us through Jesus Christ.

See previous topic, *Church, the Visible.*

See *Government; Tax.*

CHURNING Prov 30:33. See *Butter.*

CHUZA Herod's business manager, Lk 8:3.

CILICIA Maritime province of Asia Minor, Acts 27:5. Jews live in, Acts 6:9. Churches of, Acts 15:23, 40, 41; Gal 1:21.

CINNAMON A spice, Prov 7:16, 17; Song 4:13, 14. An ingredient of the holy oil, Ex 30:22, 23.

CIRCUMCISION Institution of, Gen 17:9–14; Lev 12:3; Jn 7:21–23; Acts 7:8; Rom 4:11. A seal of righteousness, Rom 2:25–29; 4:11. Performed on all males on the eighth day, Gen 17:12, 13; Lev 12:3; Phil 3:5. Rite of, observed on the Sabbath, Jn 7:21–23. A prerequisite of the privileges of the passover, Ex 12:48. Child named at the time of, Gen 21:3–5; Lk 1:59; 2:21. Neglect of, punished, Gen 17:14; Ex 4:24. Neglected, Josh 5:4, 5. Covenant promises of, Gen 17:2–14; Acts 7:8; Rom 3:1; 4:11; 9:7–13; Gal 5:3. Necessity of, falsely taught by Judaizing Christians, Acts 15:1. Paul's argument against the continuance of, Rom 2:25, 28; Gal 6:13. Characterized by Paul as a yoke, Acts 15:10. Abrogated, Acts 15:5–29; Rom 3:30; 4:9–11; 1 Cor 7:18, 19; Gal 2:3, 4; 5:2–11; 6:12; Eph 2:11, 15; Col 2:11.

INSTANCES OF. Abraham, Gen 17:23–27; 21:3–5. Shechemites, Gen 34:24. Moses' son, Ex 4:25, 26. Israelites at Gilgal, Josh 5:2–9. John the Baptist, Lk 1:59. Jesus, Lk 2:21. Timothy, Acts 16:3. Paul, Phil 3:5.

FIGURATIVE. Jer 4:4; 9:25, 26; Rom 2:28, 29; Phil 3:3; Col 2:11.

A designation of the Jews, Eph 2:11; of Christians, Phil 3:3.

CISTERN Lev 11:36; 1 Sam 13:6; 2 Kgs 10:14; Neh 9:25; Jer 38:6; 41:7. Broken, Jer 2:13.

FIGURATIVE. Eccl 12:6. See *Wells.*

CITIES Ancient, Gen 4:17; 10:10–12. Fortified, Num 32:34–36; Deut 9:1; Josh 10:20; 14:12; 2 Chron 8:5; 11:5–12; 17:2, 19; 21:3, 4; Isa 23:11. Gates of, see *Gates.* Designated as: Royal, Josh 10:2; 1 Sam 27:5; 2 Sam 12:26, 27; 1 Chron 11:7; supply, Gen 41:48; Ex 1:11; 1 Kgs 9:19; 2 Chron 8:4; 16:4; 17:12; chariot, 2 Chron 1:14; 8:6; 9:25; merchant, Isa 23:11; Ezk 17:3, 4; 27:3.

Prophecies concerning, see under individual cities.

Mayor of, Acts 19:35. Government of, by ruler, Neh 3:9, 12, 17, 18; 7:2. See *Government.*

Suburbs of, Num 35:3–5; Josh 14:3, 4.

Watchmen of, see *Watchman.*

FIGURATIVE. Heb 11:10, 16; 12:22; 13:13,14.

CITIES OF REFUGE See *Refuge, Cities of.*

CITIZENS DUTIES OF. Ex 22:28. You shall not blaspheme God, nor curse government officials —your judges and your rulers. Acts 23:5.

Num 27:20. Publicly give him your authority so that all the people of Israel will obey him.

Ezra 7:26. Anyone refusing to obey the law of your God and the law of the king shall be punished immediately by death, banishment, confiscation of goods, or imprisonment.

Ezra 10:7, 8. Then a proclamation was made throughout Judah and Jerusalem that everyone should appear at Jerusalem within three days and that the leaders and elders had decided that anyone who refused to come would be disinherited and excommunicated from Israel.

Prov 16:14. The anger of the king is a messenger of death and a wise man will appease it. [15]Many favors are showered on those who please the king.

Prov 24:21. My son, watch your step before the Lord and the king, and don't associate with radicals.

Prov 25:6, 7. Don't demand an audience with the king as though you were some powerful prince. It is better to wait for an invitation rather than to be sent back to the end of the line, publicly disgraced! [15]Be patient and you will finally win, for a soft tongue can break hard bones.

Eccl 8:2, 3. Obey the king as you have vowed to do. Don't always be trying to get out of doing your duty, even when it's unpleasant. For the king punishes those who disobey. [4]The king's command is backed by great power, and no one can withstand it or question it.

Eccl 10:20. Never curse the king, not even in your thoughts; nor the rich man, either; for a little bird will tell them what you've said.

Jer 29:7. And work for the peace and prosperity of Babylon. Pray for her, for if Babylon has peace, so will you.

Mt 17:24. On their arrival in Capernaum, the Temple tax collectors came to Peter and asked him, "Doesn't your master pay taxes?" [25]"Of course he does," Peter replied. Then he went into the house to talk to Jesus about it, but before he had a chance to speak, Jesus asked him, "What do you think, Peter? Do kings levy assessments against their own people, or against conquered foreigners?" [26, 27]"Against the foreigners," Peter replied. "Well, then," Jesus said, "the citizens are free! However, we don't want to offend them, so go down to the shore and throw in a line, and open the mouth of the first fish you catch. You will find a coin to cover the taxes for both of us; take it and pay them."

Mt 22:17. "Now tell us, is it right to pay taxes to the Roman government or not?" [18]But Jesus saw what they were after. "You hypocrites!" he exclaimed. "Who are you trying to fool with your trick questions? [19]Here, show me a coin." And they handed him a penny. [20]"Whose picture is stamped on it?" he asked them. "And whose name is this beneath the picture?" [21]"Caesar's," they replied. "Well, then," he said, "give it to Caesar if it is his, and give God everything that belongs to God." Mk 12:14–17; Luke 20:22–25.

Acts 19:36. Since this is an indisputable fact, you shouldn't be disturbed no matter what is said, and should do nothing rash. *vs.* 35–41.

Rom 13:1. Obey the government, for God is the one who has put it there. There is no government anywhere that God has not placed in power. [2]So those who refuse to obey the laws of the land are refusing to obey God, and punishment will follow. [3]For the policeman does not frighten people who are doing right; but those doing evil will always fear him. So if you don't want to be afraid, keep the laws and you will get along well. [5]Obey the laws, then, for two reasons: first, to keep from being punished, and second, just because you know you should. [6]Pay your taxes too, for these same two reasons. For government workers need to be paid so that they can keep on doing God's work, serving you. [7]Pay everyone whatever he ought to have: pay your taxes and import duties gladly, obey those over you, and give honor and respect to all those to whom it is due.

1 Tim 2:1. Here are my directions: Pray much for others; plead for God's mercy upon them; give thanks for all he is going to do for them. [2]Pray in this way for kings and all others who are in authority over us, or are in places of high responsibility, so that we can live in peace and quietness, spending our time in godly living and thinking much about the Lord.

Tit 3:1. Remind your people to obey the government and its officers, and always to be obedient and ready for any honest work.

1 Pet 2:13. For the Lord's sake, obey every law of your government: those of the king as head of the state, [14]and those of the king's officers, for he has sent them to punish all who do wrong, and to honor those who do right. [15]It is God's will that your good lives should silence those who foolishly condemn the Gospel without knowing what it can do for them, having never experienced its power. [16]You are free from the law, but that doesn't mean you are free to do wrong. Live as those who are free to do only God's will at all times. [17]Show respect for everyone. Love Christians everywhere. Fear God and honor the government.

RIGHTS OF. Job 34:18. Are you going to condemn this God who says to kings and nobles, "You are wicked and unjust"?

Prov 14:28. A growing population is a king's glory; a dwindling nation is his doom. [35]A king rejoices in servants who know what they are doing; he is angry with those who cause trouble.

Prov 22:11. He who values grace and truth is the king's friend.

Prov 23:1, 2, 3. When dining with a rich man [ruler], be on your guard and don't stuff yourself, though it all tastes so good; for he is trying to bribe you, and no good is going to come of his invitation.

Acts 16:37. But Paul replied, "Oh, no they don't! They have publicly beaten us without trial and jailed us—and we are Roman citizens! So now they want us to leave secretly? Never! Let them come themselves and release us!"

Acts 19:36. Since this is an indisputable fact, you shouldn't be disturbed no matter what is said, and should do nothing rash. [37]Yet you have brought these men here who have stolen nothing from her temple and have not defamed her. [38]If Demetrius and the craftsmen have a case against them, the courts are currently in session and the judges can take the case at once. Let them go through legal channels. [39]And if there are complaints about other matters, they can be settled at the regular City Council meetings.

Acts 22:25. As they tied Paul down to lash him, Paul said to an officer standing there, "Is it legal for you to whip a Roman citizen who hasn't even been tried?" [26]The officer went to the commander and asked, "What are you doing? This man is a Roman citizen!" [27]So the commander went over and asked Paul, "Tell me, are you a Roman citizen?" "Yes, I certainly am." [28]"I am too," the commander muttered, "and it cost me plenty!" "But I am a citizen by birth!" [29]The soldiers standing ready to lash him, quickly disappeared when they heard Paul was a Roman citizen, and the commander was frightened because he had ordered him bound and whipped.

Acts 25:16. Of course I quickly pointed out to them that Roman law does not convict a man before he is tried. He is given an opportunity to defend himself face to face with his accusers. *vs.* 5, 10, 11; Acts 24:18, 19.

See *Change of Venue; Court; Government; Justice.*

LOYAL. *Instances of.* Israelites, Josh 1:16–18; 2 Sam 3:35–37; 15:23, 30; 18:3; 21:17; 1 Chron 12:38. David, 1 Sam 24:6–10; 26:5–16; 2 Sam 1:14. Hushai, 2 Sam 17:15, 16. David's soldiers, 2 Sam 18:12, 13; 23:15, 16. Joab, 2 Sam 19:5, 6. Barzillai, 2 Sam 19:31, 32. Jehoiada, 2 Kgs 11:4–12. Mordecai, Esther 2:21–23.

WICKED AND TREASONABLE. Prov 17:11. The wicked live for rebellion; they shall be severely punished.

Prov 19:10. It doesn't seem right for a fool to succeed or for a slave to rule over princes! [12]The king's anger is as dangerous as a lion's. But his approval is as refreshing as the dew on grass. Prov 20:2.

2 Pet 2:10. He is especially hard on those who follow their own evil, lustful thoughts, and those who are proud and willful, daring even to scoff at the Glorious Ones without so much as trembling. 2 Tim 3:1–4.

Jude 1:8. Yet these false teachers carelessly go right on living their evil, immoral lives, degrading their bodies and laughing at those in authority over them, even scoffing at the Glorious Ones.

See *Anarchy.*

Instances of Wicked. Miriam and Aaron, Num 12:1–11. Korah, Dathan and Abiram, Num 16; 26:5–11. Shechemites, Judg 9:22, 23. Ephraimites, Judg 12:1–4. Israelites, 1 Sam 10:27; 1 Kgs 12:16–19. Absalom, 2 Sam 15:10–13. Ahithophel, 2 Sam 17:1–4. Sheba, 2 Sam 20:1, 2. Adonijah, 1 Kgs 1:5–7. Hadad and Jeroboam, 1 Kgs 11:14–26. Baasha, 1 Kgs 15:27. Zimri, 1 Kgs 16:9. Jozachar and Jehozabad, 2 Kgs 12:19–21; 14:5; of Amaziah, 2 Kgs 14:19; of Amon, 2 Kgs 21:23. Shallum, 2 Kgs 15:10. Menahem, 2 Kgs 15:14. Pekah, 2 Kgs 15:25. Hoshea, 2 Kgs 15:30. Sons, Sennacherib, 2 Kgs 19:37. Ishmael, Jer 40:13–16; 41. Bigthan and Teresh, Esther 2:21. Jews, Ezk 17:12–20. Barabbas, Mk 15:7. Theudas and four hundred seditious persons, Acts 5:36, 37. An Egyptian, Acts 21:37, 38.

See *Country, Love of; Government; Rulers; Patriotism.*

FIGURATIVE. Eph 2:19.

CIVIL DAMAGES See *Damages.*

CIVIL ENGINEERING Josh 18:9; Job 28:9–11.

CIVIL SERVICE SCHOOL FOR. Dan 1:3, 4. Then he ordered Ashpenaz, who was in charge of his palace personnel, to select some of the Jewish youths brought back as captives—young men of the royal family and nobility of Judah—and to teach them the Chaldean language and literature. "Pick strong, healthy, good-looking lads," he said; "those who have read widely in many fields, are well informed, alert and sensible and have enough poise to look good around the palace." [5]The king assigned them the best of food and wine from his own kitchen during their three-year training period, planning to make them his counselors when they graduated. [17]God gave these four youths great ability to learn and they soon mastered all the literature and science of the time, and God gave to Daniel special ability in understanding the meanings of dreams and visions. [18, 19]When the three-year training period was completed, the superintendent brought all the young men to the king for oral exams, as he had been ordered to do. King Nebuchadnezzar had long talks with each of them, and none of them impressed him as much as Daniel, Hananiah, Misha-el, and Azariah. So they were put on his regular staff of advisors. [20]And in all matters requiring information and balanced judgment, the king found these young men's advice ten times better than that of all the skilled magicians and wise astrologers in his realm. [21]Daniel held this appointment as the king's counselor until the first year of the reign of King Cyrus.

Competitive Examinations for Appointment in. See above, *School for.*

APPOINTMENT IN, ON ACCOUNT OF MERIT. Gen 39:1. When Joseph arrived in Egypt as a captive of the Ishmaelite traders, he was purchased from them by Potiphar, a member of the personal staff of Pharaoh, the king of Egypt. Now this man Potiphar was the captain of the king's bodyguard and his chief executioner. [2]The Lord greatly blessed Joseph there in the home of his master, so that everything he did succeeded. [3]Potiphar noticed this and realized that the Lord was with Joseph in a very special way. [4]So Joseph naturally became quite a favorite with him. Soon he was put in charge of the administration of Potiphar's household, and all of his business affairs. [5]At once the Lord began blessing Potiphar for Joseph's sake. All his household affairs began to run smoothly, his crops flourished and his flocks multiplied. [6]So Potiphar gave Joseph the complete administrative responsibility over everything he owned. He hadn't a worry in the world with Joseph there, except to decide what he wanted to eat! Joseph, by the way, was a very handsome young man.

Gen 41:38. As they discussed who should be appointed for the job, Pharaoh said, "Who could do it better than Joseph? For he is a man who is obviously filled with the Spirit of God." [39]Turning to Joseph, Pharaoh said to him, "Since God has revealed the meaning of the dreams to you, you are the wisest man in the country! [40]I am hereby appointing you to be in charge of this entire project. What you say goes, throughout all the land of Egypt. I alone will outrank you." [41, 42]Then Pharaoh placed his own signet ring on Joseph's finger as a token of his authority, and dressed him in beautiful clothing and placed the royal golden chain about his neck and declared, "See, I have placed you in charge of all the land of Egypt." [43]Pharaoh also gave Joseph the chariot of his second-in-command, and wherever he went the shout arose, "Kneel down!" [44]And Pharaoh declared to Joseph, "I, the king of Egypt, swear that you shall have complete charge over all the land of Egypt."

1 Kgs 11:28. Jeroboam was very able, and when Solomon saw how industrious he was, he put him in charge of his labor battalions from the tribe of Joseph.

Esther 6:1, 2. That night the king had trouble sleeping and decided to read awhile. He ordered the historical records of his kingdom from the library, and in them he came across the item telling how Mordecai had exposed the plot of Bigthana and Teresh, two of the king's eunuchs, watchmen at the palace gates, who had plotted to assassinate him. [3]"What reward did we ever give Mordecai for this?" the king asked. His courtiers replied, "Nothing!" [4]"Who is on duty in the outer court?" the king inquired. Now, as it happened, Haman had just arrived in the outer court of the palace to ask the king to hang Mordecai from the gallows he was building. [5]So the courtiers replied to the king, "Haman is out there." "Bring him in," the king ordered. [6]So Haman came in and the king said to him, "What should I do to honor a man who truly pleases me?" Haman thought to himself, "Whom would he want to honor more than me?" [7, 8]So he replied, "Bring out some of the royal robes the king himself has worn, and the king's own horse, and the royal crown, [9]and instruct one of the king's most noble princes to robe the man and to lead him through the streets on the king's own horse, shouting before him, 'This is the way the king honors those who truly please him!' " [10]"Excellent!" the king said to Haman. "Hurry and take these robes and my horse, and do just as you have said—to Mordecai the Jew, who works at the Chancellery. Follow every detail you have suggested." [11]So Haman took the robes and put them on Mordecai and mounted him on the king's own steed, and led him through the streets of the city shouting, "This is the way the king honors those he delights in."

Dan 1:17. God gave these four youths great ability to learn and they soon mastered all the literature and science of the time, and God gave to Daniel special ability in understanding the meanings of dreams and visions. [18, 19]When the three-year training period was completed, the superintendent brought all the young men to the king for oral exams, as he had been ordered to do. King Nebuchadnezzar had long talks with each of them, and none of them impressed him as much as Daniel, Hananiah, Misha-el, and Azariah. So they were put on his regular staff of advisors. [20]And in all matters requiring information and balanced judgment, the king found these young men's advice ten times better than that of all the skilled magicians and wise astrologers in his realm. [21]Daniel held this appointment as the king's counselor until the first year of the reign of King Cyrus.

Mt 25:14. Again, the Kingdom of Heaven can be illustrated by the story of a man going into another country, who called together his servants and loaned them money to invest for him while he was gone. [15]He gave $5,000 to one, $2,000 to another, and $1,000 to the last—dividing it in proportion to their abilities—and then left on his trip. [23]"Good work," his master said. "You are a good and faithful servant. You have been faithful over this small amount, so now I will give you much more." [24, 25]Then the man with the $1,000 came and said, "Sir, I knew you were a hard man, and I was afraid you would rob me of what I earned, so I hid your money in the earth and here it is!" [26]But his master replied, "Wicked man! Lazy slave! Since you knew I would demand your profit, [27]you should at least have put my money into the bank so I could have some interest. [28]Take the money from this man and give it to the man with the $10,000. [29]For the man who uses well what he is given shall be given more, and he shall have abundance. But from the man who is unfaithful, even what little responsibility he has shall be taken from him. [30]And throw the useless servant out into outer darkness: there shall be weeping and gnashing of teeth." Lk 19:12–27.

CORRUPTION IN. Neh 5:15. This was quite a contrast to the former governors who had demanded food and wine and $100 a day in cash, and had put the population at the mercy of their aides, who tyrannized them; but I obeyed God and did not act that way.

Dan 6:4. This made the other presidents and governors very jealous, and they began searching for some fault in the way Daniel was handling his affairs so that they could complain to the king about him. But they couldn't find anything to criticize! He was faithful and honest, and made no mistakes. [5]So they concluded, "Our only chance is his religion!" [6]They decided to go to the king and say, "King Darius, live forever! [7]We presidents, governors, counselors and deputies have unanimously decided that you should make a law, irrevocable under any circumstance, that for the next thirty days anyone who asks a favor of God or man—except from you, Your Majesty—shall be thrown to the lions. [8]Your Majesty, we request your signature to this law; sign it so that it cannot be canceled or changed; it will be a 'law of the Medes and Persians' that cannot be revoked." [9]So King Darius signed the law. [10]But though Daniel knew about it, he went home and knelt down as usual in his upstairs bedroom, with its windows open toward Jerusalem, and prayed three times a day, just as he always had, giving thanks to his God. [11]Then the men thronged to Daniel's house and found him praying there, asking favors of his God. [12]They rushed back to the king and reminded him about his law. "Haven't you signed a decree," they said, "that permits no petitions to any God or man—except you—for thirty days? And anyone disobeying will be thrown to the lions?" "Yes," the king replied, "it is 'a law of the Medes and Persians,' that cannot be altered or revoked." [13]Then they told the king, "That fellow Daniel, one of the Jewish captives, is paying no attention to you or your law. He is asking favors of his God three times a day." [14]Hearing this, the king was very angry with himself for signing the law, and determined to save Daniel. He spent the rest of the day trying to think of some way to get Daniel out of this predicament. [15]In the evening the men came again to the king and said, "Your Majesty, there is nothing you can do. You signed the law and it cannot be changed." [16]So at last the king gave the order for Daniel's arrest, and he was taken to the den of lions. The king said to him, "May your God, whom you worship continually, deliver you." And then they threw him in. [17]A stone was brought and placed over the mouth of the den; and the king sealed it with his own signet ring, and that of his government, so that no one could rescue Daniel from the lions.

Mk 15:15. Then Pilate, afraid of a riot and anxious to please the people, released Barabbas to them. And he ordered Jesus flogged with a leaded whip, and handed him over to be crucified.

Acts 24:26. He also hoped that Paul would bribe him, so he sent for him from time to time and talked with him.

See *Bribery*.

REFORM IN. Neh 5:14. I would like to mention that for the entire twelve years that I was governor of Judah—from the twentieth until the thirty-second year of the reign of King Ar-ta-xerxes—my aides and I accepted no salaries or other assistance from the people of Israel. [15]This was quite a contrast to the former governors who had demanded food and wine and $100 a day in cash, and had put the population at the mercy of their aides, who tyrannized them; but I obeyed God and did not act that way.

INFLUENCE IN. 1 Kgs 1:11. Then Nathan the prophet went to Bathsheba, Solomon's mother, and asked her, "Do you realize that Haggith's son, Adonijah, is now the king and that our lord David doesn't even know about it? [12]If you want to save your own life and the life of your son Solomon—do exactly as I say! [13]Go at once to King David and ask him, 'My lord, didn't you promise me that my son Solomon would be the next king and would sit upon your throne? Then why is Adonijah reigning?' [14]And while you are still talking with him, I'll come and confirm everything you've said." [15]So Bath-sheba went into the king's bedroom. He was an old, old man now, and Abishag was caring for him. [16]Bath-sheba bowed low before him. "What do you want?" he asked her. [17]She replied, "My lord, you vowed to me by the Lord your God that my son Solomon would be the next king and would sit upon your throne. [18]But instead, Adonijah is the new king, and you don't even know about it. [20]And now, my lord the king, all Israel is waiting for your decision as to whether Adonijah is the one you have chosen to succeed you. [21]If you don't act, my son Solomon and I will be arrested and executed as criminals as soon as you are dead." [29]And the king vowed, "As the Lord lives who has rescued me from every danger, [30]I decree that your son Solomon shall be the next king and shall sit upon my throne, just as I swore to you before by the Lord God of Israel." [31]Then Bath-sheba bowed low before him again and exclaimed, "Oh, thank you, sir. May my lord the king live forever!" *vs.* 5–40.

2 Kgs 4:13. He said to Gehazi, "Tell her that we appreciate her kindness to us. Now ask her what we can do for her. Does she want me to put in a good word for her to the king or to the general of the army?" "No," she replied, "I am perfectly content."

Mt 20:20. Then the mother of James and John, the sons of Zebedee, brought them to Jesus and respectfully asked a favor. [21]"What is your request?" he asked. She replied, "In your Kingdom, will you let my two sons sit on two thrones next to yours?" [22]But Jesus told her, "You don't know what you are asking!" Then he turned to James and John and asked them, "Are you able to drink from the terrible cup I am about to drink from?" "Yes," they replied, "we are able!" [23]"You shall indeed drink from it," he told them. "But I have no right to say who will sit on the thrones next to mine. Those places are reserved for the persons my Father selects." Mk 10:35–40.

CLAIRVOYANCE 1 Sam 28:13, 14; 2 Kgs 6:15–17.

See *Sorcery; Witchcraft*.

CLAUDA An island near Crete, Acts 27:16.

CLAUDIA A female disciple, 2 Tim 4:21.

CLAUDIUS Emperor of Rome, Acts 11:28; 18:2, 3.

CLAUDIUS LYSIAS A Roman military officer or "commander" mentioned in Acts 21:31–40; 22:23–30. Sends Paul to Felix, Acts 23:10–35.

CLAY Man formed from, Job 33:7. Seals made of, Mt 27:66. Used by potter, Isa 41:25; 45:9.

See *Mortar; Mud.*

FIGURATIVE. Isa 41:25; 45:9; 64:8; Jer 18:6; Rom 9:21.

See *Dust; Mire.*

Symbolical. Dan 2:33–45.

CLEAN AND UNCLEAN ANIMALS See *Animals.* Of birds, see *Birds.* Of fish, see *Fish.* Of insects, see *Insects.*

CLEANLINESS Taught by frequent ablutions.

See *Ablution; Purification.*

Regulation relating to, in camp, Deut 23:12–14.

FIGURATIVE. Ps 51:7, 10; Prov 20:9; Isa 1:16; Ezk 36:25; 1 Jn 1:7, 9.

CLEANSING See *Ablution.*

CLEMENCY Of David toward disloyal subjects: Shime-i, 2 Sam 16:5–13; 19:16–23; Amasa, 2 Sam 19:13, with 2 Sam 17:25. Of Solomon toward Adonijah, 1 Kgs 1:51–53.

Divine, see *God, Longsuffering of,* and *Mercy of.*

CLEMENT A disciple at Philippi, Phil 4:3.

CLEOPAS 1. A disciple to whom Jesus appeared after his resurrection, Lk 24:18.

2. Husband of one of the Marys, Jn 19:25.

CLERGYMAN See *Minister.*

CLIFFBADGER Prov 30:26.

See *Coney; Rock Badger.*

CLOAK Deut 22:12; Esther 8:15; Mk 11:7. As security, Deut 24:12, 13. Elijah's, 1 Kgs 19:19; 2 Kgs 2:8, 13, 14.

See *Coat; Dress.*

FIGURATIVE. Prov 30:4; Jer 43:12; Ezk 16:8.

CLOTHING Of the Israelites, did not wear out, Deut 8:4; Neh 9:21. Torn as a sign of grief, Ezra 9:3; Job 1:20; 2:12.

See *Dress.*

CLOUD PILLAR OF. Ex 13:21. The Lord guided them by a pillar of cloud during the daytime, and by a pillar of fire at night. So they could travel either by day or night. [22]The cloud and fire were never out of sight.

Ex 14:19. Then the Angel of God, who was leading the people of Israel, moved the cloud around behind them. [24]But in the early morning Jehovah looked down from the cloud of fire upon the array of the Egyptians, and began to harass them.

Ex 16:10. So Aaron called them together and suddenly, out toward the wilderness, from within the guiding cloud, there appeared the awesome glory of Jehovah.

Ex 19:9. Then he said to Moses, "I am going to come to you in the form of a dark cloud, so that the people themselves can hear me when I talk with you, and then they will always believe you. [16]On the morning of the third day there was a terrific thunder and lightning storm, and a huge cloud came down upon the mountain, and there was a long, loud blast as from a ram's horn; and all the people trembled.

Ex 24:16. And the glory of the Lord rested upon Mt. Sinai and the cloud covered it six days; the seventh day he called to Moses from the cloud. [17]Those at the bottom of the mountain saw the awesome sight: the glory of the Lord on the mountain top looked like a raging fire. [18]And Moses disappeared into the cloud-covered mountain top, and was there for forty days and forty nights.

Ex 33:9. As he entered, the pillar of cloud would come down and stand at the door while the Lord spoke with Moses. [10]Then all the people worshiped from their tent doors, bowing low to the pillar of cloud.

Ex 34:5. Then the Lord descended in the form of a pillar of cloud and stood there with him, and passed in front of him and announced the meaning of his name.

Ex 40:36. Whenever the cloud lifted and moved, the people of Israel journeyed onward, following it. [37]But if the cloud stayed, they stayed until it moved. [38]The cloud rested upon the Tabernacle during the daytime, and at night there was fire in the cloud so that all the people of Israel could see it. This continued throughout all their journeys.

Lev 16:1, 2. After Aaron's two sons died before the Lord, the Lord said to Moses, "Warn your brother Aaron not to enter into the Holy Place behind the veil, where the Ark and the place of mercy are, just whenever he chooses. The penalty for intrusion is death. For I myself am present in the cloud above the place of mercy."

Num 9:15. On the day the Tabernacle was raised, the Cloud covered it; and that evening the Cloud changed to the appearance of fire, and stayed that way throughout the night. [16]It was always so—the daytime Cloud changing to the appearance of fire at night. [17]When the Cloud lifted, the people of Israel moved on to wherever it stopped, and camped there. [18]In this way they journeyed at the command of the Lord and stopped where he told them to, then remained there as long as the Cloud stayed. [19]If it stayed a long time, then they stayed a long time. But if it stayed only a few days, then they remained only a few days; for so the Lord had instructed them. [20, 21]Sometimes the fire-cloud stayed only during the night and moved on the next morning. But day or night, when it moved, the people broke camp and followed. [22]If the Cloud stayed above the Tabernacle two days, a month, or a year, that is how long the people of Israel stayed; but as soon as it moved, they moved. [23]So it was that they camped or traveled at the commandment of the Lord; and whatever the Lord told Moses they should do, they did.

Num 10:11. The Cloud lifted from the Tabernacle on the twentieth day of the second month of the second year of Israel's leaving Egypt; [12]so the Israelites left the Sinai wilderness, and followed the

Cloud until it stopped in the wilderness of Paran.

33. They traveled for three days after leaving Mount Sinai, with the Ark at the front of the column to choose a place for them to stop. [34]It was daytime when they left, with the Cloud moving along ahead of them as they began their march. [35]As the Ark was carried forward, Moses cried out, "Arise, O Lord, and scatter your enemies; let them flee before you." [36]And when the Ark was set down he said, "Return, O Lord, to the millions of Israel."

Num 11:25. And the Lord came down in the Cloud and talked with Moses, and the Lord took of the Spirit that was upon Moses and put it upon the seventy elders; and when the Spirit rested upon them, they prophesied for some time.

Num 12:5. Then the Lord descended in the Cloud and stood at the entrance of the Tabernacle. "Aaron and Miriam, step forward," he commanded; and they did. [10]As the Cloud moved from above the Tabernacle, Miriam suddenly became white with leprosy.

Num 16:19. Meanwhile, Korah had stirred up the entire nation against Moses and Aaron, and they all assembled to watch. Then the glory of Jehovah appeared to all the people. [42]Soon a great, sullen mob formed; suddenly, as they looked toward the Tabernacle, the Cloud appeared and the awesome glory of the Lord was seen.

Deut 1:33. Who had led them all the way, and had selected the best places for them to camp, and had guided them by a pillar of fire at night and a pillar of cloud during the day.

Deut 31:15. He appeared to them in a great cloud at the Tabernacle entrance.

Neh 9:12. You led our ancestors by a pillar of cloud during the day and a pillar of fire at night so that they could find their way.

19. But in your great mercy you didn't abandon them to die in the wilderness! The pillar of cloud led them forward day by day, and the pillar of fire showed them the way through the night.

Ps 78:14. In the daytime he led them by a cloud, and at night by a pillar of fire.

Ps 105:39. He spread out a cloud above them to shield them from the burning sun, and gave them a pillar of flame at night to give them light.

Isa 4:5. Then the Lord will provide shade on all Jerusalem—over every home and all its public grounds—a canopy of smoke and cloud throughout the day, and clouds of fire at night, covering the Glorious Land, [6]protecting it from daytime heat and from rains and storms.

UNCLASSIFIED SCRIPTURES RELATING TO CLOUDS. Deut 4:11. You stood at the foot of the mountain, and the mountain burned with fire; flames shot far into the sky, surrounded by black clouds and deep darkness.

Ps 97:2. Clouds and darkness surround him. Righteousness and justice are the foundation of his throne.

Ps 104:3. The clouds are his chariots. He rides upon the wings of the wind.

Isa 19:1. This is God's message concerning Egypt: Look, the Lord is coming against Egypt, riding on a swift cloud.

Ezk 1:4. I saw, in this vision, a great storm coming toward me from the north, driving before it a huge cloud glowing with fire, with a mass of fire inside that flashed continually; and in the fire there was something that shone like polished brass.

Ezk 10:3. The cherubim were standing at the south end of the Temple when the man went in. And the cloud of glory filled the inner court. [4]Then the glory of the Lord rose from above the cherubim and went over to the door of the Temple. The Temple was filled with the cloud of glory, and the court of the Temple was filled with the brightness of the glory of the Lord. 1 Kgs 8:10.

Dan 7:13. Next I saw the arrival of a Man—or so he seemed to be—brought there on clouds from heaven; he approached the Ancient of Days and was presented to him.

Joel 2:1. Sound the alarm in Jerusalem! Let the blast of the warning trumpet be heard upon my holy mountain! Let everyone tremble in fear, for the day of the Lord's judgment approaches. [2]It is a day of darkness and gloom, of black clouds and thick darkness. What a mighty army! It covers the mountains like night!

Zeph 1:14. That terrible day is near. Swiftly it comes—a day when strong men will weep bitterly. [15]It is a day of the wrath of God poured out; it is a day of terrible distress and anguish, a day of ruin and desolation, of darkness, gloom, clouds, blackness.

Mt 17:5. But even as he said it, a bright cloud came over them, and a voice from the cloud said, "*This* is my beloved Son, and I am wonderfully pleased with him. Obey *him.*" Mk 9:7; Lk 9:34, 35.

Mt 24:30. And then at last the signal of my coming will appear in the heavens and there will be deep mourning all around the earth. And the nations of the world will see me arrive in the clouds of heaven, with power and great glory. Mk 13:26; Lk 21:27.

Mt 26:64. "Yes," Jesus said, "I am. And in the future you will see me, the Messiah, sitting at the right hand of God and returning on the clouds of heaven." Mk 14:62.

Acts 1:9. It was not long afterwards that he rose into the sky and disappeared into a cloud, leaving them staring after him.

1 Thess 4:17. Then we who are still alive and remain on the earth will be caught up with them in the clouds to meet the Lord in the air and remain with him forever.

Rev 1:7. See! He is arriving, surrounded by clouds; and every eye shall see him—yes, and those who pierced him. And the nations will weep in sorrow and in terror when he comes. Yes! Amen! Let it be so!

Rev 11:12. Then a loud voice will shout from heaven, "Come up!" And they will rise to heaven in a cloud as their enemies watch.

Rev 14:14. Then the scene changed and I saw a white cloud, and someone sitting on it who looked like Jesus, who was called "The Son of Man," with a crown of solid gold upon his head and a sharp sickle in his hand. [15]Then an angel came from the temple and called out to him, "Begin to use the sickle, for the time has come for you to reap; the harvest is ripe on the earth." [16]So the one sitting on the cloud swung his sickle over the earth, and the harvest was gathered in.

FIGURATIVE. Hos 6:4; 13:3.

See *Glory.*

CNIDUS A city in Asia Minor (Turkey), Acts 27:7, 8.

COAL FIGURATIVE. Rom 12:20.

Symbolical. Isa 6:6, 7.

COAL OIL See *Oil.*

COAT Paul's, left at Troas, 2 Tim 4:13.

See *Cloak.*

COAT OF MAIL Ex 28:32; 39:23; 1 Sam 17:4–7, 38, 39; 2 Chron 26:14; Jer 51:3.

COBRA Ps 58:45.

COCK CROWING Mt 26:34, 74, 75; Mk 14:30, 68, 72; Lk 22:34, 60, 61; Jn 13:38; 18:27.

COERCION COMPULSION IN WORSHIP. Ex 22:20. Anyone sacrificing to any other god than Jehovah shall be executed.

2 Chron 15:12. Then they entered into a contract to worship only the Lord God of their fathers, [13]and agreed that anyone who refused to do this must die—whether old or young, man or woman. [14]They shouted out their oath of loyalty to God with trumpets blaring and horns sounding. [15]All were happy for this covenant with God, for they had entered into it with all their hearts and wills, and wanted him above everything else, and they found him! And he gave them peace throughout the nation.

Dan 3:2. Then he sent messages to all the princes, governors, captains, judges, treasurers, counselors, sheriffs, and rulers of all the provinces of his empire, to come to the dedication of his statue. [3]When they had all arrived and were standing before the monument, [4]a herald shouted out, "O people of all nations and languages, this is the king's command: [5]When the band strikes up, you are to fall flat on the ground to worship King Nebuchadnezzar's golden statue; [6]anyone who refuses to obey will immediately be thrown into a flaming furnace." *vs.* 1–30.

29. Therefore, I make this decree, that any person of any nation, language, or religion who speaks a word against the God of Shadrach, Meshach, and Abednego shall be torn limb from limb and his house knocked into a heap of rubble. For no other God can do what this one does.

Dan 6:26. "Greetings! I decree that everyone shall tremble and fear before the God of Daniel in every part of my kingdom. For his God is the living, unchanging God whose kingdom shall never be destroyed and whose power shall never end. [27]He delivers his people, preserving them from harm; he does great miracles in heaven and earth; it is he who delivered Daniel from the power of the lions."

See *Intolerance.*

COFFIN Gen 50:26; Lk 7:14.

See *Burial.*

COIN See *Money.*

COL-HOZEH Father of Baruch, Neh 3:15; 11:4–6.

COLLEGE See *School.*

COLLECTION Of money, for the poor, see *Benevolence; Charity; Giving; Liberality.*

COLLUSION IN SIN. Lev 20:4. And if the people of the land pretend they do not know what the man has done, and refuse to put him to death, [5]then I myself will set my face against that man and his family and cut him off, along with all others who turn to other gods than me.

See *Complicity; Connivance.*

COLONEL Of regiments, 2 Sam 18:1.

See *Armies; Officers.*

COLONIZATION Of conquered countries and people, 2 Kgs 17:6, 24; Ezra 4:8–10.

COLORS Symbolic uses of.

BLACK, A SYMBOL OF AFFLICTION, CALAMITY OR MOURNING. Job 3:5. Yes, let the darkness claim it for its own, and may a black cloud overshadow it.

Job 10:20, 21. Can't you see how little time I have left? Oh, let me alone that I may have a little moment of comfort before I leave for the land of darkness and the shadow of death never to return —[22]a land as dark as midnight, a land of the shadow of death where only confusion reigns, and where the brightest light is dark as midnight.

Job 24:17. The black night is their morning; they ally themselves with the terrors of the darkness.

Job 30:26. I therefore looked for good to come. Evil came instead. I waited for the light. Darkness came.

Ps 107:10. Who are these who sit in darkness, in the shadow of death, crushed by misery and slavery? [11]They rebelled against the Lord, scorning him who is the God above all gods.

Ps 143:3. My enemies chased and caught me. They have knocked me to the ground. They force me to live in the darkness like those in the grave.

Isa 5:30. They growl over their victims like the roaring of the sea. Over all Israel lies a pall of darkness and sorrow and the heavens are black.

Isa 8:22. Wherever they look there will be trouble and anguish and dark despair. And they will be thrust out into the darkness.

Isa 9:19. The land is blackened by that fire, by the wrath of the Lord of heaven's armies. The people are fuel for the fire. Each fights against his brother to steal his food, but will never have enough. Finally they will even eat their own children!

Isa 13:10. The heavens will be black above them. No light will shine from stars or sun or moon.

Isa 50:3. I am the one who sends the darkness out across the skies.

Jer 4:28. The earth shall mourn, the heavens shall be draped with black, because of my decree against my people, but I have made up my mind and I will not change it.

Ezk 31:15. The Lord God says: When she fell I made the oceans mourn for her and restrained their tides. I clothed Lebanon in black and caused the trees of Lebanon to weep.

Joel 2:2. It is a day of darkness and gloom, of black clouds and thick darkness.

Joel 3:14. Multitudes, multitudes waiting in the valley for the verdict of their doom! For the Day of the Lord is near, in the Valley of Judgment.
[15]The sun and moon will be darkened and the stars withdraw their light.

Amos 5:8. Seek him who created the Seven Stars and the constellation Orion, who turns darkness into morning, and day into night, who calls forth the water from the ocean and pours it out as rain upon the land. The Lord, Jehovah, is his name.

Zeph 1:14. That terrible day is near. Swiftly it comes—a day when strong men will weep bitterly.
[15]It is a day of the wrath of God poured out; it is a day of terrible distress and anguish, a day of ruin and desolation, of darkness, gloom, clouds, blackness.

Mt 8:12. And many an Israelite—those for whom the Kingdom was prepared—shall be cast into outer darkness, into the place of weeping and torment.

Mt 22:13. Then the king said to his aides, "Bind him hand and foot and throw him out into the outer darkness where there is weeping and gnashing of teeth."

Mt 25:30. And throw the useless servant out into outer darkness: there shall be weeping and gnashing of teeth.

2 Pet 2:4. For God did not spare even the angels who sinned, but threw them into hell, chained in gloomy caves and darkness until the judgment day.

Jude 1:13. They wander around looking as bright as stars, but ahead of them is the everlasting gloom and darkness that God has prepared for them.

Rev 16:10. Then the fifth angel poured out his flask upon the throne of the Creature from the sea, and his kingdom was plunged into darkness. And his subjects gnawed their tongues in anguish.

BLUE, SYMBOL OF DEITY. Ex 24:10; Ezk 1:26; 10:1. One of the predominating symbolical colors in the drapery and furnishings of the tabernacle and temple, and vestments of priests.

Ex 25:1–4. Jehovah said to Moses, "Tell the people of Israel that everyone who wants to may bring me an offering from this list: Gold, silver, bronze, blue cloth, purple cloth, scarlet cloth, fine-twined linen, goat's hair."

Ex 26:1, 2. Make the tabernacle-tent from ten colored sheets of fine-twined linen, forty-two feet long and six feet wide, dyed blue, purple, and scarlet, with cherubim embroidered on them.

Ex 28:28. Now attach the bottom of the chestpiece to the bottom rings of the ephod by means of blue ribbons; this will prevent the chestpiece from coming loose from the ephod. *v.* 37, 38.

Ex 38:18. The drapery covering the entrance to the court was made of fine-twined linen, beautifully embroidered with blue, purple, and scarlet thread. It was thirty feet long and 7 1/2 feet wide, just the same as the drapes composing the walls of the court.

Ex 39:1. Then, for the priests, the people made beautiful garments of blue, purple, and scarlet cloth—garments to be used while ministering in the Holy Place. This same cloth was used for Aaron's sacred garments, in accordance with the
Lord's instructions to Moses. [2]The ephod was
made from this cloth too, woven from fine-twined
linen thread. [3]Bezalel beat gold into thin plates and
cut it into wire threads, to work into the blue, purple, and scarlet linen; it was a skillful and beautiful piece of workmanship when finished. [4, 5]The
ephod was held together by shoulder straps at the top, and was tied down by an elaborate one-piece woven sash made of the same gold, blue, purple, and scarlet cloth cut from fine-twined linen thread, just as God had directed Moses.

21. The chestpiece was held securely above the beautifully woven sash of the ephod by tying the rings of the chestpiece to the rings of the ephod, with a blue ribbon.

24. Pomegranates were attached to the bottom edge of the robe; these were made of linen cloth, embroidered with blue, purple, and scarlet.

29. And the linen belt was beautifully embroidered with blue, purple, and scarlet threads, just as Jehovah had commanded Moses.

31. It was tied to the turban with a blue cord, just as the Lord had instructed.

Num 4:5. When the camp moves, Aaron and his sons will enter the Tabernacle first and take down
the veil and cover the Ark with it. [6]Then they will
cover the veil with goatskin leather, cover the goatskins with a blue cloth, and place the carrying
poles of the Ark in their rings. [7]Next they must
spread a blue cloth over the table where the Bread of the Presence is displayed, and place the dishes, spoons, bowls, cups, and the Bread upon the cloth.
[8]They will spread a scarlet cloth over that, and finally a covering of goatskin leather on top of the scarlet cloth. Then they shall insert the carrying
poles into the table. [9]Next they must cover with a
blue cloth the lampstand, the lamps, snuffers,
trays, and the reservoir of olive oil. [10]This entire
group of objects shall then be covered with goatskin leather, and the bundle shall be placed upon
a carrying frame. [11]They must then spread a blue
cloth over the gold altar, cover it with a covering of goatskin leather, and insert the carrying poles
into the altar. [12]All of the remaining utensils of the
Tabernacle are to be wrapped in a blue cloth, covered with goatskin leather, and placed on the carrying frame.

Num 15:37, 38. The Lord said to Moses, "Tell the people of Israel to make tassels for the hems of their clothes (this is a permanent regulation from generation to generation) and to attach the tassels
to their clothes with a blue cord. [39]The purpose of
this regulation is to remind you, whenever you notice the tassels, of the commandments of the Lord, and that you are to obey his laws instead of

following your own desires and going your own ways, as you used to do in serving other gods. [40]It will remind you to be holy to your God."

2 Chron 2:7. So send me skilled craftsmen—goldsmiths and silversmiths, brass and iron workers; and send me weavers to make purple, crimson, and blue cloth; and skilled engravers to work beside the craftsmen of Judah and Jerusalem who were selected by my father David. *v.* 14; 3:14.

For additional reference, see passages below under *Crimson.*

CRIMSON, RED, PURPLE, AND SCARLET: SYMBOLS OF VARIOUS IDEAS. Of *sin,* Isa 1:18; Rev 17:3, 4; 18:12, 16; of *royalty,* Jer 10:9; Dan 5:7, 16, 29; Mt 27:28; *prosperity,* Prov 31:22; *conquest,* Nah 2:3; Rev 12:3.

These colors figured largely in the symbolisms of the tabernacle furnishings, and priestly vestments and functions, *as types and shadows of the atonement.*

Ex 25:1–5. Jehovah said to Moses, "Tell the people of Israel that everyone who wants to may bring me an offering from this list: Gold, silver, bronze, blue cloth, fine-twined linen, goat's hair, red-dyed ram's skins, goat-skins, acacia wood."

Ex 26:1, 2. Make the tabernacle-tent from ten colored sheets of fine-twined linen, forty-two feet long and six feet wide, dyed blue, purple, and scarlet, with cherubim embroidered on them. [14]On top of these blankets is placed a layer of rams' skins, dyed red, and over them a top layer of goatskins. This completes the roof-covering.

31. [Inside the Tabernacle], make a veil from blue, purple, and scarlet cloth, the fine-twined linen, with cherubim embroidered into the cloth. chapter 36:35, 37.

36. As a screen for the door of the sacred tent, make another curtain from skillfully embroidered blue, purple, and scarlet fine-twined linen.

Ex 27:16. The entrance to the court will be a thirty-foot wide curtain, made of beautifully embroidered blue, purple, and scarlet fine-twined linen, and attached to four posts imbedded in their four sockets. chapter 38:18, 23.

Ex 28:4. This is the wardrobe they shall make: a chestpiece, an ephod, a robe, a checkered tunic, a turban, and a sash. They shall also make special garments for Aaron's sons. chapter 39:1.

5, 6. The ephod shall be made by the most skilled of the workmen, using blue, purple, and scarlet threads of fine-twined linen. chapter 39:2–5.

8. And the sash shall be made of the same material—threads of gold, blue, purple, and scarlet fine-twined linen. Ex 39:28, 29.

15. Then, using the most careful workmanship, make a chestpiece to be used as God's oracle; use the same gold, blue, purple, and scarlet threads of fine-twined linen as you did in the ephod. Ex 39: 8.

31. The ephod shall be made of blue cloth.

33, 34. The bottom edge of the ephod shall be embroidered with blue, purple, and scarlet pomegranates.

Ex 35:5–7. All of you who wish to, all those with generous hearts, may bring these offerings to Jehovah: Gold, silver, and bronze; blue, purple, and scarlet cloth, made of fine-twined linen or of goat's hair; tanned rams' skins and specially treated goatskins. Ex 25:1–7; 35:23, 25, 35; 36:8, 9, 19; 39.

Lev 14:4. He shall require two living birds of a kind permitted for food, and shall take some cedar wood, a scarlet string, and some hyssop branches, to be used for the purification ceremony of the one who is healed. *vs.* 6, 49, 51, 52.

Num 4:7. Next they must spread a blue cloth over the table where the Bread of the Presence is displayed, and place the dishes, spoons, bowls, cups, and the Bread upon the cloth. [8]They will spread a scarlet cloth over that, and finally a covering of goatskin leather on top of the scarlet cloth. Then they shall insert the carrying poles into the table.

13. The ashes are to be removed from the altar, and the altar shall be covered with a purple cloth.

Num 19:2. Tell the people of Israel to bring you a red heifer without defect, one that has never been yoked. [5]Then someone shall burn the heifer as he watches—her hide, meat, blood, and dung. [6]Eleazar shall take cedar wood and hyssop branches and scarlet thread, and throw them into the burning pile.

Isa 63:1. Who is this who comes from Edom, from the city of Bozrah, with his magnificent garments of crimson? Who is this in kingly robes, marching in the greatness of his strength? "It is I, the Lord, announcing your salvation; I, the Lord, the one who is mighty to save!" [2]"Why are your clothes so red, as from treading out the grapes?" [3]"I have trodden the winepress alone. No one was there to help me. In my wrath I have trodden my enemies like grapes. In my fury I trampled my foes. It is their blood you see upon my clothes."

Heb 9:19. For after Moses had given the people all of God's laws, he took the blood of calves and goats, along with water, and sprinkled the blood over the book of God's laws and over all the people, using branches of hyssop bushes and scarlet wool to sprinkle with. [20]Then he said, "This is the blood that marks the beginning of the agreement between you and God, the agreement God commanded me to make with you." [21]And in the same way he sprinkled blood on the sacred tent and on whatever instruments were used for worship. [22]In fact we can say that under the old agreement almost everything was cleansed by sprinkling it with blood, and without the shedding of blood there is no forgiveness of sins. [23]That is why the sacred tent down here on earth, and everything in it—all copied from things in heaven—all had to be made pure by Moses in this way, by being sprinkled with the blood of animals. But the real things in heaven, of which these down here are copies, were made pure with far more precious offerings.

WHITE, SYMBOL OF HOLINESS. The high priest's holy garments were of white linen, Lev 16: 4, 32; 2 Chron 5:12; Ps 132:9.

Scriptures Employing the Symbol. Ps 51:7. Sprinkle me with the cleansing blood and I shall be clean again. Wash me and I shall be whiter than snow.

Isa 1:18. Come, let's talk this over! says the Lord; no matter how deep the stain of your sins, I can take it out and make you as clean as freshly fallen snow. Even if you are stained as red as crimson, I can make you white as wool!

Dan 7:9. I watched as thrones were put in place and the Ancient of Days—the Almighty God—sat down to judge. His clothing was as white as snow, his hair like whitest wool. He sat upon a fiery throne brought in on flaming wheels.

Mt 17:1. Six days later Jesus took Peter, James, and his brother John to the top of a high and lonely hill, [2]and as they watched, his appearance changed so that his face shone like the sun and his clothing became dazzling white. Mk 9:3; Lk 9:28, 29.

Mt 28:2. Suddenly there was a great earthquake; for an angel of the Lord came down from heaven and rolled aside the stone and sat on it. [3]His face shone like lightning and his clothing was a brilliant white. Mk 16:4, 5.

Rev 1:13. And standing among them was one who looked like Jesus who called himself the Son of Man, wearing a long robe circled with a golden band across his chest. [14]His hair was white as wool or snow, and his eyes penetrated like flames of fire.

Rev 2:17. And I will give to each a white stone, and on the stone will be engraved a new name that no one else knows except the one receiving it.

Rev 3:4. Yet even there in Sardis some haven't soiled their garments with the world's filth; they shall walk with me in white, for they are worthy. [5]Everyone who conquers will be clothed in white, and I will not erase his name from the Book of Life, but I will announce before my Father and his angels that he is mine. [18]My advice to you is to buy pure gold from me, gold purified by fire—only then will you truly be rich. And to purchase from me white garments, clean and pure, so you won't be naked and ashamed.

Rev 4:4. Twenty-four smaller thrones surrounded his, with twenty-four Elders sitting on them; all were clothed in white, with golden crowns upon their heads.

Rev 6:2. I looked, and there in front of me was a white horse. Its rider carried a bow, and a crown was placed upon his head; he rode out to conquer in many battles and win the war. [11]White robes were given to each of them, and they were told to rest a little longer until their other brothers, fellow servants of Jesus, had been martyred on the earth and joined them.

Rev 7:9. After this I saw a vast crowd, too great to count, from all nations and provinces and languages, standing in front of the throne and before the Lamb, clothed in white, with palm branches in their hands.

13. Then one of the twenty-four Elders asked me, "Do you know who these are, who are clothed in white, and where they come from?" [14]"No, sir," I replied. "Please tell me." "These are the ones coming out of the Great Tribulation," he said; "they washed their robes and whitened them by the blood of the Lamb."

Rev 15:6. The seven angels who were assigned to pour out the seven plagues then came from the temple, clothed in spotlessly white linen, with golden belts across their chests.

Rev 19:8. "She is permitted to wear the cleanest and whitest and finest of linens." (Fine linen represents the good deeds done by the people of God.) [11]Then I saw heaven opened and a white horse standing there; and the one sitting on the horse was named "Faithful and True"—the one who justly punishes and makes war. [14]The armies of heaven, dressed in finest linen, white and clean, followed him on white horses.

Rev 20:11. And I saw a great white throne and the one who sat upon it, from whose face the earth and sky fled away, but they found no place to hide.

COLOSSE A city of Phrygia, Col 1:2.

COLT Ridden by Jesus, Zech 9:9; Mt 21:2, 5, 7; Mk 11:2; Lk 19:30; Jn 12:15.

COMFORT See *Affliction, Consolation in; Righteous, Promises to.*

COMFORTER See *God, Grace of; Holy Spirit.*

COMMANDER Of an army, Judg 4:2; 1 Kgs 2:35; 16:15, 16; 1 Chron 27:34. Of a division, 1 Chron 27; 28:1. Of a regiment, 1 Chron 27:1. Of a company, 2 Sam 18:1.

Angel of the Lord, called, Josh 5:14. Roman, Acts 21:32; 22:24–29; 23:17, 23, 24; 24:22.

See *Armies; Officer.*

COMMANDMENTS Ex 13:8. During those celebration days each year you must explain to your children why you are celebrating—it is a celebration of what the Lord did for you when you left Egypt. [9]This annual memorial week will brand you as his own unique people, just as though he had branded his mark of ownership upon your hands or your forehead. [10]So celebrate the event annually in late March.

Ex 20:3. You may worship no other god than me.

4. You shall not make yourselves any idols: any images resembling animals, birds, or fish. [5]You must never bow to an image or worship it in any way; for I, the Lord your God, am very possessive. I will not share your affection with any other god! And when I punish people for their sins, the punishment continues upon the children, grandchildren, and greatgrandchildren of those who hate me; [6]but I lavish my love upon thousands of those who love me and obey my commandments.

7. You shall not use the name of Jehovah your God irreverently, nor use it to swear to a falsehood. You will not escape punishment if you do.

8. Remember to observe the Sabbath as a holy day. [9]Six days a week are for your daily duties and your regular work, [10]but the seventh day is a day of Sabbath rest before the Lord your God. On that day you are to do no work of any kind, nor shall your son, daughter, or slaves—whether men or

women—or your cattle or your house guests. [11]For in six days the Lord made the heaven, earth, and sea, and everything in them, and rested the seventh day; so he blessed the Sabbath day and set it aside for rest.

12. Honor your father and mother, that you may have a long, good life in the land the Lord your God will give you.

13. You must not murder.

14. You must not commit adultery.

15. You must not steal.

16. You must not lie.

17. You must not be envious of your neighbor's house, or want to sleep with his wife, or want to own his slaves, oxen, donkeys, or anything else he has. Deut 5:6–21.

Deut 4:5. These are the laws for you to obey when you arrive in the land where you will live. They are from the Lord our God. He has given them to me to pass on to you. [9]But watch out! Be very careful never to forget what you have seen God doing for you. May his miracles have a deep and permanent effect upon your lives! Tell your children and grandchildren about the glorious miracles he did. [10]Tell them especially about the day you stood before the Lord at Mount Horeb, and he told me, "Summon the people before me and I will instruct them, so that they will learn always to reverence me, and so that they can teach my laws to their children."

Deut 6:4. O Israel, listen: Jehovah is our God, Jehovah alone. [5]You must love him with *all* your heart, soul, and might. [6]And you must think constantly about these commandments I am giving you today. [7]You must teach them to your children and talk about them when you are at home or out for a walk; at bedtime and the first thing in the morning. [8]Tie them on your finger, wear them on your forehead, [9]and write them on the doorposts of your house!

Deut 11:18. So keep these commandments carefully in mind. Tie them to your hand to remind you to obey them, and tie them to your forehead between your eyes! [19]Teach them to your children. Talk about them when you are sitting at home, when you are out walking, at bedtime, and before breakfast! [20]Write them upon the doors of your houses and upon your gates, [21]so that as long as there is sky above the earth, you and your children will enjoy the good life awaiting you in the land the Lord has promised you.

Deut 32:46. Moses made these comments: "Meditate upon all the laws I have given you today, and pass them on to your children. [47]These laws are not mere words—they are your life! Through obeying them you will live long, plentiful lives in the land you are going to possess across the Jordan River."

Josh 8:30. Then Joshua built an altar to the Lord God of Israel at Mount Ebal, [31]as Moses had commanded in the book of his laws: "Make me an altar of boulders that have neither been broken nor carved," the Lord had said concerning Mount Ebal. Then the priests offered burnt sacrifices and peace offerings to the Lord on the altar. [32]And as the people of Israel watched, Joshua carved upon the stones of the altar each of the Ten Commandments. [33]Then all the people of Israel—including the elders, officers, judges, and the foreigners living among them—divided into two groups, half of them standing at the foot of Mount Gerizim and half at the foot of Mount Ebal. Between them stood the priests with the Ark, ready to pronounce their blessing. (This was all done in accordance with the instructions given long before by Moses.) [34]Joshua then read to them all of the statements of blessing and curses that Moses had written in the book of God's laws. [35]Every commandment Moses had ever given was read before the entire assembly, including the women and children and the foreigners who lived among the Israelis.

2 Chron 17:7, 8, 9. In the third year of his reign he began a nationwide religious education program. He sent out top government officials as teachers in all the cities of Judah. . . . He also used Levites for this purpose, . . . also the priests, Elishama and Jehoram. They took copies of *The Book of the Law of the Lord* to all the cities of Judah, to teach the Scriptures to the people.

Neh 8:2–5. So Ezra the priest brought out to them the scroll of Moses' laws. He stood on a wooden stand made especially for the occasion so that everyone could see him as he read. He faced the square in front of the Water Gate, and read from early morning until noon. Everyone stood up as he opened the scroll. And all who were old enough to understand paid close attention. . . . [6]Then Ezra blessed the Lord, the great God, and all the people said, "Amen," and lifted their hands toward heaven; then they bowed and worshiped the Lord with their faces toward the ground. [7, 8]As Ezra read from the scroll, Jeshua, Bani, Sherebiah, Jamin, Akkub, Shabbethai, Hodiah, Ma-aseiah, Kelita, Azariah, Jozabad, Hanan, Pelaiah, and the Levites went among the people and explained the meaning of the passage that was being read.

Ps 78:1. O my people, listen to my teaching. Open your ears to what I am saying. [2, 3]For I will show you lessons from our history, stories handed down to us from former generations. [4]I will reveal these truths to you so that you can describe these glorious deeds of Jehovah to your children, and tell them about the mighty miracles he did. [5]For he gave his laws to Israel, and commanded our fathers to teach them to their children, [6]so that they in turn could teach their children too. Thus his laws pass down from generation to generation. [7]In this way each generation has been able to obey his laws and to set its hope anew on God and not forget his glorious miracles.

Prov 3:3. Never forget to be truthful and kind. Hold these virtues tightly. Write them deep within your heart. [4, 5]If you want favor with both God and man, and a reputation for good judgment and common sense, then trust the Lord completely; don't ever trust yourself.

Prov 6:20. Young man, obey your father and your mother. [21]Tie their instructions around your finger so you won't forget. Take to heart all of their advice.

Prov 7:1. Follow my advice, my son; always keep it in mind and stick to it. [2]Obey me and live! Guard my words as your most precious possession. [3]Write them down, and also keep them deep within your heart. [4]Love wisdom like a sweetheart; make her a beloved member of your family.

Isa 57:8. Behind closed doors you set your idols up and worship someone other than me. This is adultery, for you are giving these idols your love, instead of loving me.

Jer 11:4. For I told them at the time I brought them out of slavery in Egypt that if they would obey me and do whatever I commanded them, then they and all their children would be mine and I would be their God.

Zech 7:8, 9. Then this message from the Lord came to Zechariah. "Tell them to be honest and fair—and not to take bribes—and to be merciful and kind to everyone. [10]Tell them to stop oppressing widows and orphans, foreigners and poor people, and to stop plotting evil against each other."

Zech 8:16. "Here is your part: Tell the truth. Be fair. Live at peace with everyone. [17]Don't plot harm to others; don't swear that something is true when it isn't! How I hate all that sort of thing!" says the Lord.

PRECEPTS OF JESUS.

Explicitly Stated, or Implied in Didactic Discourse. Mt 5:15, 16. Don't hide your light! Let it shine for all; let your good deeds glow for all to see, so that they will praise your heavenly Father. [22]But I have added to that rule, and tell you that if you are only *angry,* even in your own home, you are in danger of judgment! If you call your friend an idiot, you are in danger of being brought before the court. And if you curse him, you are in danger of the fires of hell. [23]So if you are standing before the altar in the Temple, offering a sacrifice to God, and suddenly remember that a friend has something against you, [24]leave your sacrifice there beside the altar and go and apologize and be reconciled to him, and then come and offer your sacrifice to God.

27. The laws of Moses said, "You shall not commit adultery." [28]But I say: Anyone who even looks at a woman with lust in his eye has already committed adultery with her in his heart. [29]So if your eye—even if it is your best eye!—causes you to lust, gouge it out and throw it away. Better for part of you to be destroyed than for all of you to be cast into hell. [30]And if your hand—even your right hand—causes you to sin, cut it off and throw it away. Better that than find yourself in hell. [31]The law of Moses says, "If anyone wants to be rid of his wife, he can divorce her merely by giving her a letter of dismissal." [32]But I say that a man who divorces his wife, except for fornication, causes her to commit adultery if she marries again. And he who marries her commits adultery.

33. Again, the law of Moses says, "You shall not break your vows to God, but must fulfill them all." [34]But I say: Don't make any vows! And even to say, "By heavens!" is a sacred vow to God, for the heavens are God's throne. [35]And if you say "By the earth!" it is a sacred vow, for the earth is his footstool. And don't swear "By Jerusalem!" for Jerusalem is the capital of the great King. [36]Don't even swear "By my head!" for you can't turn one hair white or black. [37]Say just a simple "Yes, I will" or "No, I won't." Your word is enough. To strengthen your promise with a vow shows that something is wrong.

38. The law of Moses says, "If a man gouges out another's eye, he must pay with his own eye. If a tooth gets knocked out, knock out the tooth of the one who did it." [39]But I say: Don't resist violence! If you are slapped on one cheek, turn the other too. [40]If you are ordered to court, and your shirt is taken from you, give your coat too. [41]If the military demand that you carry their gear for a mile, carry it two. [42]Give to those who ask and don't turn away from those who want to borrow.

43. There is a saying, "Love your *friends* and hate your enemies." [44]But I say: Love your *enemies!* Pray for those who persecute you! [45]In that way you will be acting as true sons of your Father in heaven. For he gives his sunlight to both the evil and the good, and sends rain on the just and on the unjust too. [46]If you love only those who love you, what good is that? Even scoundrels do that much. [47]If you are friendly only to your friends, how are you different from anyone else? Even the heathen do that. [48]But you are to be perfect, even as your Father in heaven is perfect. Lk 6:27–36.

Mt 6:1. Take care! Don't do your good deeds publicly, to be admired, for then you will lose the reward from your Father in heaven. [2]When you give a gift to a beggar, don't shout about it as the hypocrites do—blowing trumpets in the synagogues and streets to call attention to their acts of charity! I tell you in all earnestness, they have received all the reward they will ever get. [3]But when you do a kindness to someone, do it secretly —don't tell your left hand what your right hand is doing. [4]And your Father who knows all secrets will reward you.

6. But when you pray, go away by yourself, all alone, and shut the door behind you and pray to your Father secretly, and your Father, who knows your secrets, will reward you. [7, 8]Don't recite the same prayer over and over as the heathen do, who think prayers are answered only by repeating them again and again. Remember, your Father knows exactly what you need even before you ask him!

16. And now about fasting. When you fast, declining your food for a spiritual purpose, don't do it publicly, as the hypocrites do, who try to look wan and disheveled so people will feel sorry for them. Truly, that is the only reward they will ever get. [17]But when you fast, put on festive clothing, [18]so that no one will suspect you are hungry, except

your Father who knows every secret. And he will reward you.

19. Don't store up treasures here on earth where they can erode away or may be stolen. [20]Store them in heaven where they will never lose their value, and are safe from thieves. [21]If your profits are in heaven your heart will be there too.

22. If your eye is pure, there will be sunshine in your soul. [23]But if your eye is clouded with evil thoughts and desires, you are in deep spiritual darkness. And oh, how deep that darkness can be! [24]You cannot serve two masters: God and money. For you will hate one and love the other, or else the other way around. [25]So my counsel is: Don't worry about *things*—food, drink, and clothes. For you already have life and a body—and they are far more important than what to eat and wear. [31, 32]So don't worry at all about having enough food and clothing. Why be like the heathen? For they take pride in all these things and are deeply concerned about them. But your heavenly Father already knows perfectly well that you need them, [33]and he will give them to you if you give him first place in your life and live as he wants you to. [34]So don't be anxious about tomorrow. God will take care of your tomorrow too. Live one day at a time. Lk 12: 12–31.

Mt 7:1. "Don't criticize, and then you won't be criticized. [2]For others will treat you as you treat them. [3]And why worry about a speck in the eye of a brother when you have a board in your own? [4]Should you say, 'Friend, let me help you get that speck out of your eye,' when you can't even see because of the board in your own? [5]Hypocrite! First get rid of the board. Then you can see to help your brother. Lk 6:37–42.

6. "Don't give holy things to depraved men. Don't give pearls to swine! They will trample the pearls and turn and attack you. [7]Ask, and you will be given what you ask for. Seek, and you will find. Knock, and the door will be opened. [8]For everyone who asks, receives. Anyone who seeks, finds. If only you will knock, the door will open. [9]If a child asks his father for a loaf of bread, will he be given a stone instead? [10]If he asks for fish, will he be given a poisonous snake? Of course not! [11]And if you hardhearted, sinful men know how to give good gifts to your children, won't your Father in heaven even more certainly give good gifts to those who ask him for them? [12]Do for others what you want them to do for you. This is the teaching of the laws of Moses in a nutshell. [13]Heaven can be entered only through the narrow gate! The highway to hell is broad, and its gate is wide enough for all the multitudes who choose its easy way. [14]But the Gateway to Life is small, and the road is narrow, and only a few ever find it. Lk 13:24, 25.

[15]"Beware of false teachers who come disguised as harmless sheep, but are wolves and will tear you apart. [16]You can detect them by the way they act, just as you can identify a tree by its fruit. You need never confuse grapevines with thorn bushes or figs with thistles. [17]Different kinds of fruit trees can quickly be identified by examining their fruit. [18]A variety that produces delicious fruit never produces an inedible kind. And a tree producing an inedible kind can't produce what is good. [19]So the trees having the inedible fruit are chopped down and thrown on the fire. [20]Yes, the way to identify a tree or a person is by the kind of fruit produced.

21. "Not all who sound religious are really godly people. They may refer to me as 'Lord,' but still won't get to heaven. For the decisive question is whether they obey my Father in heaven. [22]At the Judgment many will tell me, 'Lord, Lord, we told others about you and used your name to cast out demons and to do many other great miracles.' [23]But I will reply, 'You have never been mine. Go away, for your deeds are evil.' [24]All who listen to my instructions and follow them are wise, like a man who builds his house on solid rock. [25]Though the rain comes in torrents, and the floods rise and the storm winds beat against his house, it won't collapse, for it is built on rock. [26]But those who hear my instructions and ignore them are foolish, like a man who builds his house on sand. [27]For when the rains and floods come, and storm winds beat against his house, it will fall with a mighty crash." [28]The crowds were amazed at Jesus' sermons, [29]for he taught as one who had great authority, and not as their Jewish leaders.

Mt 16:24. Then Jesus said to the disciples, "If anyone wants to be a follower of mine, let him deny himself and take up his cross and follow me. Mk 8:34.

Mt 18:8. So if your hand or foot causes you to sin, cut it off and throw it away. Better to enter heaven crippled than to be in hell with both of your hands and feet. [9]And if your eye causes you to sin, gouge it out and throw it away. Better to enter heaven with one eye than to be in hell with two. [10]Beware that you don't look down upon a single one of these little children. For I tell you that in heaven their angels have constant access to my Father.

15. If a brother sins against you, go to him privately and confront him with his fault. If he listens and confesses it, you have won back a brother. [16]But if not, then take one or two others with you and go back to him again, proving everything you say by these witnesses. [17]If he still refuses to listen, then take your case to the church, and if the church verdict favors you, but he won't accept it, then the church should excommunicate him.

21. Then Peter came to him and asked, "Sir, how often should I forgive a brother who sins against me? Seven times?" [22]"No!" Jesus replied, "seventy times seven!"

Mt 19:16. Someone came to Jesus with this question: "Good master, what must I do to have eternal life?" [17]"When you call me good you are calling me God," Jesus replied, "for God alone is truly good. But to answer your question, you can get to heaven if you keep the commandments." [18]"Which ones?" the man asked. And Jesus replied, "Don't kill, don't commit adultery, don't steal, don't lie, [19]honor your father and mother, and love your neighbor as yourself!" Mk 10:17–22.

Mt 20:25. But Jesus called them together and said, "Among the heathen, kings are tyrants and each minor official lords it over those beneath him. [26]But among you it is quite different. Anyone wanting to be a leader among you must be your servant. [27]And if you want to be right at the top, you must serve like a slave. [28]Your attitude must be like my own, for I, the Messiah, did not come to be served, but to serve, and to give my life as a ransom for many."

Mt 22:34, 35. But not the Pharisees! When they heard that he had routed the Sadducees with his reply, they thought up a fresh question of their own to ask him. One of them, a lawyer, spoke up: [36]"Sir, which is the most important command in the laws of Moses?" [37]Jesus replied, " 'Love the Lord your God with all your heart, soul, and mind.' [38, 39]This is the first and greatest commandment. The second most important is similar: 'Love your neighbor as much as you love yourself.' [40]All the other commandments and all the demands of the prophets stem from these two laws and are fulfilled if you obey them. Keep only these and you will find that you are obeying all the others." Lk 10:28–37.

Mt 24:42. So be prepared, for you don't know what day your Lord is coming. [43]Just as a man can prevent trouble from thieves by keeping watch for them, [44]so you can avoid trouble by always being ready for my unannounced return. [45]Are you a wise and faithful servant of the Lord? Have I given you the task of managing my household, to feed my children day by day? [46]Blessings on you if I return and find you faithfully doing your work. [47]I will put such faithful ones in charge of everything I own! [48]But if you are evil and say to yourself, "My Lord won't be coming for a while," [49]and begin oppressing your fellow servants, partying and getting drunk, [50]your Lord will arrive unannounced and unexpected, [51]and severely whip you and send you off to the judgment of the hypocrites; there will be weeping and gnashing of teeth.

Mt 25:34. Then I, the King, shall say to those at my right, "Come, blessed of my Father into the Kingdom prepared for you from the founding of the world. [35]For I was hungry and you fed me; I was thirsty and you gave me water; I was a stranger and you invited me into your homes; [36]naked and you clothed me; sick and in prison, and you visited me." [37]Then these righteous ones will reply, "Sir, when did we ever see you hungry and feed you? Or thirsty and give you anything to drink? [38]Or a stranger, and help you? Or naked, and clothe you? [39]When did we ever see you sick or in prison, and visit you?" [40]And I, the King, will tell them, "When you did it to these my brothers you were doing it to me!" [41]Then I will turn to those on my left and say, "Away with you, you cursed ones, into the eternal fire prepared for the devil and his demons. [42]For I was hungry and you wouldn't feed me; thirsty, and you wouldn't give me anything to drink; [43]a stranger, and you refused me hospitality; naked, and you wouldn't clothe me; sick, and in prison, and you didn't visit me." [44]Then they will reply, "Lord, when did we ever see you hungry or thirsty or a stranger or naked or sick or in prison, and not help you?" [45]And I will answer, "When you refused to help the least of these my brothers, you were refusing help to me." [46]And they shall go away into eternal punishment; but the righteous into everlasting life.

Mk 6:7. And he called his twelve disciples together and sent them out two by two, with power to cast out demons. [Mt 10:5–42.] [8, 9]He told them to take nothing with them except their walking sticks—no food, no knapsack, no money, not even an extra pair of shoes or a change of clothes. [10]"Stay at one home in each village—don't shift around from house to house while you are there," he said. [11]"And whenever a village won't accept you or listen to you, shake off the dust from your feet as you leave; it is a sign that you have abandoned it to its fate."

Mk 9:35. He sat down and called them around him and said, "Anyone wanting to be the greatest must be the least—the servant of all!"

38. One of his disciples, John, told him one day, "Teacher, we saw a man using your name to cast out demons; but we told him not to, for he isn't one of our group." [39]"Don't forbid him!" Jesus said. "For no one doing miracles in my name will quickly turn against me."

42. But if someone causes one of these little ones who believe in me to lose faith—it would be better for that man if a huge millstone were tied around his neck and he were thrown into the sea. [43, 44]If your hand does wrong, cut it off. Better live forever with one hand than be thrown into the unquenchable fires of hell with two! [45, 46]If your foot carries you toward evil, cut it off! Better be lame and live forever than have two feet that carry you to hell. [47]And if your eye is sinful, gouge it out. Better enter the Kingdom of God half blind than have two eyes and see the fires of hell, [48]where the worm never dies, and the fire never goes out—[49]where all are salted with fire. [50]Good salt is worthless if it loses its saltiness; it can't season anything. So don't lose your flavor! Live in peace with each other.

Mk 10:9. "And no man may separate what God has joined together." [11]He told them, "When a man divorces his wife to marry someone else, he commits adultery against her. [12]And if a wife divorces her husband and remarries, she, too, commits adultery."

Mk 11:22. In reply Jesus said to the disciples, "If you only have faith in God . . ."

Mk 12:17. "All right," he said, "if it is his, give it to him. But everything that belongs to God must be given to God!" And they scratched their heads in bafflement at his reply. Mt 22:21.

Mk 13:33. And since you don't know when it will happen, stay alert. Be on the watch [for my return]. [34]My coming can be compared with that of a man who went on a trip to another country. He laid out his employees' work for them to do while he was gone, and told the gatekeeper to watch for his return. [35, 36, 37]Keep a sharp lookout! For you do not know when I will come, at evening, at midnight, early dawn or late daybreak. Don't let me find you sleeping. *Watch for my return!* This is my message to you and to everyone else.

Lk 12:15. Beware! Don't always be wishing for what you don't have. For real life and real living are not related to how rich we are.

Jn 13:34. And so I am giving a new commandment to you now—love each other just as much as I love you. [35]Your strong love for each other will prove to the world that you are my disciples.

Jn 14:11. Just believe it—that I am in the Father and the Father is in me. Or else believe it because of the mighty miracles you have seen me do.

15. If you love me, obey me.

23. Jesus replied, "Because I will only reveal myself to those who love me and obey me. The Father will love them too, and we will come to them and live with them. [24]Anyone who doesn't obey me doesn't love me. And remember, I am not making up this answer to your question! It is the answer given by the Father who sent me."

Jn 15:2. He lops off every branch that doesn't produce. And he prunes those branches that bear fruit for even larger crops. [4]Take care to live in me, and let me live in you. For a branch can't produce fruit when severed from the vine. Nor can you be fruitful apart from me. [5]Yes, I am the Vine; you are the branches. Whoever lives in me and I in him shall produce a large crop of fruit. For apart from me you can't do a thing. [7]But if you stay in me and obey my commands, you may ask any request you like, and it will be granted! [8]My true disciples produce bountiful harvests. This brings great glory to my Father. [9]I have loved you even as the Father has loved me. Live within my love. [10]When you obey me you are living in my love, just as I obey my Father and live in his love. [11]I have told you this so that you will be filled with my joy. Yes, your cup of joy will overflow! [12]I demand that you love each other as much as I love you. [14]And you are my friends if you obey me. [17]I demand that you love each other. [20]Do you remember what I told you? "A slave isn't greater than his master!" So since they persecuted me, naturally they will persecute you. And if they had listened to me, they would listen to you! [21]The people of the world will persecute you because you belong to me, for they don't know God who sent me. [22]They would not be guilty if I had not come and spoken to them. But now they have no excuse for their sin.

See *Tablet; Ten Commandments.*

PRECEPTS OF PAUL.

Explicitly Stated or Implied in Didactic Epistles.

Rom 12:1. And so, dear brothers, I plead with you to give your bodies to God. Let them be a living sacrifice, holy—the kind he can accept. When you think of what he has done for you, is this too much to ask? [2]Don't copy the behavior and customs of this world, but be a new and different person with a fresh newness in all you do and think. Then you will learn from your own experience how his ways will really satisfy you. [3]As God's messenger I give each of you God's warning: Be honest in your estimate of yourselves, measuring your value by how much faith God has given you.

6. God has given each of us the ability to do certain things well. So if God has given you the ability to prophesy, then prophesy whenever you can—as often as your faith is strong enough to receive a message from God. [7]If your gift is that of serving others, serve them well. If you are a teacher, do a good job of teaching. [8]If you are a preacher, see to it that your sermons are strong and helpful. If God has given you money, be generous in helping others with it. If God has given you administrative ability and put you in charge of the work of others, take the responsibility seriously. Those who offer comfort to the sorrowing should do so with Christian cheer. [9]Don't just pretend that you love others: really love them. Hate what is wrong. Stand on the side of the good.

10. Love each other with brotherly affection and take delight in honoring each other. [11]Never be lazy in your work but serve the Lord enthusiastically. [12]Be glad for all God is planning for you. Be patient in trouble, and prayerful always. [13]When God's children are in need, you be the one to help them out. And get into the habit of inviting guests home for dinner or, if they need lodging, for the night. [14]If someone mistreats you because you are a Christian, don't curse him; pray that God will bless him. [15]When others are happy, be happy with them. If they are sad, share their sorrow.

16. Work happily together. Don't try to act big. Don't try to get into the good graces of important people, but enjoy the company of ordinary folks. And don't think you know it all! [17]Never pay back evil for evil. Do things in such a way that everyone can see you are honest clear through. [18]Don't quarrel with anyone. Be at peace with everyone, just as much as possible. [19]Dear friends, never avenge yourselves. Leave that to God, for he has said that he will repay those who deserve it. [Don't take the law into your own hands.] [20]Instead, feed your enemy if he is hungry. If he is thirsty give him something to drink and you will be "heaping coals of fire on his head." In other words, he will feel ashamed of himself for what he has done to you. [21]Don't let evil get the upper hand but conquer evil by doing good.

Rom 13:8. Pay all your debts except the debt of love for others—never finish paying that! For if you love them, you will be obeying all of God's laws, fulfilling all his requirements. [9]If you love your neighbor as much as you love yourself you will not want to harm or cheat him, or kill him or steal from him. And you won't sin with his wife or want what is his, or do anything else the Ten Commandments say is wrong. All ten are wrapped up in this one, to love your neighbor as you love yourself. [10]Love does no wrong to anyone. That's why it fully satisfies all of God's requirements. It is the only law you need. [11]Another reason for right living is this: you know how late it is; time is running out. Wake up, for the coming of the Lord is nearer now than when we first believed. [12, 13]The night is far gone, the day of his return will soon be here. So quit the evil deeds of darkness and put on the armor of right living, as we who live in the daylight should! Be decent and true in everything you do so that all can approve your behavior. Don't spend your time in wild parties and getting drunk or in adultery and lust, or fighting, or jealousy. [14]But ask the Lord Jesus Christ to help you live as you should, and don't make plans to enjoy evil.

Rom 14:19. In this way aim for harmony in the church and try to build each other up. [20]Don't undo the work of God for a chunk of meat. Remember, there is nothing wrong with the meat, but it is wrong to eat it if it makes another stumble. [21]The right thing to do is to quit eating meat or drinking wine or doing anything else that offends your brother or makes him sin.

Rom 15:1, 2. Even if we believe that it makes no difference to the Lord whether we do these things, still we cannot just go ahead and do them to please ourselves; for we must bear the "burden" of being considerate of the doubts and fears of others—of those who feel these things are wrong. Let's please the other fellow, not ourselves, and do what is for his good and thus build him up in the Lord.

1 Cor 8:1. Next is your question about eating food that has been sacrificed to idols. On this question everyone feels that only his answer is the right one! But although being a "know-it-all" makes us feel important, what is really needed to build the church is love. [7]However, some Christians don't realize this. All their lives they have been used to thinking of idols as alive, and have believed that food offered to the idols is really being offered to actual gods. So when they eat such food it bothers them and hurts their tender consciences. [8]Just remember that God doesn't care whether we eat it or not. We are no worse off if we don't eat it, and no better off if we do. [9]But be careful not to use your freedom to eat it, lest you cause some Christian brother to sin whose conscience is weaker than yours. [10]You see, this is what may happen: Someone who thinks it is wrong to eat this food will see you eating at a temple restaurant, for you know there is no harm in it. Then he will become bold enough to do it too, although all the time he still feels it is wrong. [11]So because you "know it is all right to do it," you will be responsible for causing great spiritual damage to a brother with a tender conscience for whom Christ died. [12]And it is a sin against Christ to sin against your brother by encouraging him to do something he thinks is wrong. [13]So if eating meat offered to idols is going to make my brother sin, I'll not eat any of it as long as I live, because I don't want to do this to him.

1 Cor 10:7. Nor worship idols as they did. (The Scriptures tell us, "The people sat down to eat and drink and then got up to dance" in worship of the golden calf.) [8]Another lesson for us is what happened when some of them sinned with other men's wives, and 23,000 fell dead in one day.

9. And don't try the Lord's patience—they did, and died from snake bites. [10]And don't murmur against God and his dealings with you, as some of them did, for that is why God sent his Angel to destroy them.

24. Don't think only of yourself. Try to think of the other fellow, too, and what is best for him. [28]But if someone warns you that this meat has been offered to idols, then don't eat it for the sake of the man who told you, and of his conscience. [29]In this case *his* feeling about it is the important thing, not yours. But why, you may ask, must I be guided and limited by what someone else thinks? [31]Well, I'll tell you why. It is because you must do everything for the glory of God, even your eating and drinking. [32]So don't be a stumbling block to anyone, whether they are Jews or Gentiles or Christians.

1 Cor 14:20. Dear brothers, don't be childish in your understanding of these things. Be innocent babies when it comes to planning evil, but be men of intelligence in understanding matters of this kind.

1 Cor 16:13. Keep your eyes open for spiritual danger; stand true to the Lord; act like men; be strong; [14]and whatever you do, do it with kindness and love.

2 Cor 13:7. I pray that you will live good lives, not because that will be a feather in our caps, proving that what we teach is right; no, for we want you to do right even if we ourselves are despised.

Gal 5:1. So Christ has made us free. Now make sure that you stay free and don't get all tied up again in the chains of slavery to Jewish laws and ceremonies. [16]I advise you to obey only the Holy Spirit's instructions. He will tell you where to go and what to do, and then you won't always be doing the wrong things your evil nature wants you to.

Gal 6:1. Dear brothers, if a Christian is overcome by some sin, you who are godly should gently and humbly help him back onto the right path, remembering that next time it might be one of you who is in the wrong. [2]Share each other's troubles and problems, and so obey our Lord's command.

Eph 4:1. I beg you—I, a prisoner here in jail for serving the Lord—to live and act in a way worthy of those who have been chosen for such wonderful blessings as these. [2]Be humble and gentle. Be patient with each other, making allowance for each other's faults because of your love. [3]Try always to be led along together by the Holy Spirit, and so be at peace with one another.

26. If you are angry, don't sin by nursing your grudge. Don't let the sun go down with you still angry—get over it quickly; [27]for when you are angry you give a mighty foothold to the devil.

28. If anyone is stealing he must stop it and begin using those hands of his for honest work so he can give to others in need.

29. Don't use bad language. Say only what is good and helpful to those you are talking to, and what will give them a blessing.

30. Don't cause the Holy Spirit sorrow by the

way you live. Remember, he is the one who marks you to be present on that day when salvation from sin will be complete.

31. Stop being mean, bad-tempered and angry. Quarreling, harsh words, and dislike of others should have no place in your lives. [32]Instead, be kind to each other, tenderhearted, forgiving one another, just as God has forgiven you because you belong to Christ.

Eph 5:1. Follow God's example in everything you do just as a much loved child imitates his father. [2]Be full of love for others, following the example of Christ who loved you and gave himself to God as a sacrifice to take away your sins. And God was pleased, for Christ's love for you was like sweet perfume to him.

3. Let there be no sex sin, impurity or greed among you. Let no one be able to accuse you of any such things. [4]Dirty stories, foul talk and coarse jokes—these are not for you. Instead, remind each other of God's goodness and be thankful. [5]You can be sure of this: The kingdom of Christ and of God will never belong to anyone who is impure or greedy, for a greedy person is really an idol worshiper—he loves and worships the good things of this life more than God. [6]Don't be fooled by those who try to excuse these sins, for the terrible wrath of God is upon all those who do them.

11. Take no part in the worthless pleasures of evil and darkness, but instead, rebuke and expose them.

15, 16. So be careful how you act; these are difficult days. Don't be fools; be wise: make the most of every opportunity you have for doing good.

17. Don't act thoughtlessly, but try to find out and do whatever the Lord wants you to.

18. Don't drink too much wine, for many evils lie along that path; be filled instead with the Holy Spirit, and controlled by him. [19]Talk with each other much about the Lord, quoting psalms and hymns and singing sacred songs, making music in your hearts to the Lord. [20]Always give thanks for everything to our God and Father in the name of our Lord Jesus Christ. [21]Honor Christ by submitting to each other.

Eph 6:10. Last of all I want to remind you that your strength must come from the Lord's mighty power within you.

11. Put on all of God's armor so that you will be able to stand safe against all strategies and tricks of Satan. [13]So use every piece of God's armor to resist the enemy whenever he attacks, and when it is all over, you will still be standing up. [14]But to do this, you will need the strong belt of truth and the breastplate of God's approval. [15]Wear shoes that are able to speed you on as you preach the Good News of peace with God. [16]In every battle you will need faith as your shield to stop the fiery arrows aimed at you by Satan. [17]And you will need the helmet of salvation and the sword of the Spirit—which is the Word of God. [18]Pray all the time. Ask God for anything in line with the Holy Spirit's wishes. Plead with him, reminding him of your needs, and keep praying earnestly for all Christians everywhere.

Phil 1:27. But whatever happens to me, remember always to live as Christians should, so that, whether I ever see you again or not, I will keep on hearing good reports that you are standing side by side with one strong purpose—to tell the Good News [28]fearlessly, no matter what your enemies may do. They will see this as a sign of their downfall, but for you it will be a clear sign from God that he is with you, and that he has given you eternal life with him.

Phil 2:2. Then make me truly happy by loving each other and agreeing wholeheartedly with each other, working together with one heart and mind and purpose.

3. Don't be selfish; don't live to make a good impression on others. Be humble, thinking of others as better than yourself.

4. Don't just think about your own affairs, but be interested in others, too, and in what they are doing.

5. Your attitude should be the kind that was shown us by Jesus Christ, [6]who, though he was God, did not demand and cling to his rights as God, [7]but laid aside his mighty power and glory, taking the disguise of a slave and becoming like men. [8]And he humbled himself even further, going so far as actually to die a criminal's death on a cross.

12. Dearest friends, when I was there with you, you were always so careful to follow my instructions. And now that I am away you must be even more careful to do the good things that result from being saved, obeying God with deep reverence, shrinking back from all that might displease him. [13]For God is at work within you, helping you do what he wants.

14. In everything you do, stay away from complaining and arguing, [15]so that no one can speak a word of blame against you. You are to live clean, innocent lives as children of God in a dark world full of people who are crooked and stubborn. Shine out among them like beacon lights, [16]holding out to them the Word of Life.

Phil 4:4. Always be full of joy in the Lord; I say it again, rejoice!

5. Let everyone see that you are unselfish and considerate in all you do. Remember that the Lord is coming soon.

6. Don't worry about anything; instead, pray about everything; tell God your needs and don't forget to thank him for his answers.

8. And now, brothers, as I close this letter let me say this one more thing: Fix your thoughts on what is true and good and right. Think about things that are pure and lovely, and dwell on the fine, good things in others. Think about all you can praise God for and be glad about.

9. Keep putting into practice all you learned from me and saw me doing, and the God of peace will be with you.

Col 2:6. And now just as you trusted Christ to

save you, trust him, too, for each day's problems; live in vital union with him.

16. So don't let anyone criticize you for what you eat or drink, or for not celebrating Jewish holidays and feasts or new moon ceremonies or Sabbaths. [20]Since you died, as it were, with Christ and this has set you free from following the world's ideas of how to be saved—by doing good and obeying various rules—why do you keep right on following them anyway, still bound by such rules as [21]not eating, tasting, or even touching certain foods? [22]Such rules are mere human teachings, for food was made to be eaten and used up. [23]These rules may seem good, for rules of this kind require strong devotion and are humiliating and hard on the body, but they have no effect when it comes to conquering a person's evil thoughts and desires. They only make him proud.

Col 3:1. Since you became alive again, so to speak, when Christ arose from the dead, now set your sights on the rich treasures and joys of heaven where he sits beside God in the place of honor and power.

2. Let heaven fill your thoughts; don't spend your time worrying about things down here.

5. Away then with sinful, earthly things; deaden the evil desires lurking within you; have nothing to do with sexual sin, impurity, lust and shameful desires; don't worship the good things of life, for that is idolatry.

8. But now is the time to cast off and throw away all these rotten garments of anger, hatred, cursing, and dirty language.

9. Don't tell lies to each other; it was your old life with all its wickedness that did that sort of thing; now it is dead and gone. [12]Since you have been chosen by God who has given you this new kind of life, and because of his deep love and concern for you, you should practice tenderhearted mercy and kindness to others. Don't worry about making a good impression on them but be ready to suffer quietly and patiently. [13]Be gentle and ready to forgive; never hold grudges. Remember, the Lord forgave you, so you must forgive others. [14]Most of all, let love guide your life, for then the whole church will stay together in perfect harmony. [15]Let the peace of heart which comes from Christ be always present in your hearts and lives, for this is your responsibility and privilege as members of his body. And always be thankful. [16]Remember what Christ taught and let his words enrich your lives and make you wise; teach them to each other and sing them out in psalms and hymns and spiritual songs, singing to the Lord with thankful hearts. [17]And whatever you do or say, let it be as a representative of the Lord Jesus, and come with him into the presence of God the Father to give him your thanks. [23]Work hard and cheerfully at all you do, just as though you were working for the Lord and not merely for your masters.

1 Thess 3:12. And may the Lord make your love to grow and overflow to each other and to everyone else, just as our love does toward you.

1 Thess 4:1, 2. Let me add this, dear brothers: You already know how to please God in your daily living, for you know the commands we gave you from the Lord Jesus himself. Now we beg you—yes, we demand of you in the name of the Lord Jesus—that you live more and more closely to that ideal.

3, 4. For God wants you to be holy and pure, and to keep clear of all sexual sin so that each of you will marry in holiness and honor—[5]not in lustful passion as the heathen do, in their ignorance of God and his ways. [6]And this also is God's will: that you never cheat in this matter by taking another man's wife, because the Lord will punish you terribly for this, as we have solemnly told you before.

9. But concerning the pure brotherly love that there should be among God's people, I don't need to say very much, I'm sure! For God himself is teaching you to love one another. [10]Indeed, your love is already strong toward all the Christian brothers throughout your whole nation. Even so, dear friends, we beg you to love them more and more. [11]This should be your ambition: to live a quiet life, minding your own business and doing your own work, just as we told you before. [12]As a result, people who are not Christians will trust and respect you, and you will not need to depend on others for enough money to pay your bills.

1 Thess 5:6. So be on your guard, not asleep like the others. Watch for his return and stay sober. [8]But let us who live in the light keep sober, protected by the armor of faith and love, and wearing as our helmet the happy hope of salvation.

12. Dear brothers, honor the officers of your church who work hard among you and warn you against all that is wrong. [13]Think highly of them and give them your wholehearted love because they are straining to help you. And remember, no quarreling among yourselves.

14. Dear brothers, warn those who are lazy; comfort those who are frightened; take tender care of those who are weak; and be patient with everyone.

15. See that no one pays back evil for evil, but always try to do good to each other and to everyone else.

16. Always be joyful.

17. Always keep on praying.

18. No matter what happens, always be thankful, for this is God's will for you who belong to Christ Jesus.

19. Do not smother the Holy Spirit.

20. Do not scoff at those who prophesy.

21. But test everything that is said to be sure it is true, and if it is, then accept it.

22. Keep away from every kind of evil.

2 Thess 2:15. With all these things in mind, dear brothers, stand firm and keep a strong grip on the truth that we taught you in our letters and during the time we were with you.

2 Thess 3:6. Now here is a command, dear brothers, given in the name of our Lord Jesus Christ by his authority: Stay away from any Christian who

spends his days in laziness and does not follow the ideal of hard work we set up for you. [7]For you well know that you ought to follow our example: you never saw us loafing; [8]we never accepted food from anyone without buying it; we worked hard day and night for the money we needed to live on, in order that we would not be a burden to any of you. [9]It wasn't that we didn't have the right to ask you to feed us, but we wanted to show you, firsthand, how you should work for your living. [10]Even while we were still there with you we gave you this rule: "He who does not work shall not eat." [11]Yet we hear that some of you are living in laziness, refusing to work, and wasting your time in gossiping. [12]In the name of the Lord Jesus Christ we appeal to such people—we command them—to quiet down, get to work, and earn their own living.

13. And to the rest of you I say, dear brothers, never be tired of doing right.

14. If anyone refuses to obey what we say in this letter, notice who he is and stay away from him, that he may be ashamed of himself. [15]Don't think of him as an enemy, but speak to him as you would to a brother who needs to be warned.

1 Tim 1:4. Put an end to their myths and fables, and their idea of being saved by finding favor with an endless chain of angels leading up to God—wild ideas that stir up questions and arguments instead of helping people accept God's plan of faith.

1 Tim 2:1. Here are my directions: Pray much for others; plead for God's mercy upon them; give thanks for all he is going to do for them. [2]Pray in this way for kings and all others who are in authority over us, or are in places of high responsibility, so that we can live in peace and quietness, spending our time in godly living and thinking much about the Lord. [8]So I want men everywhere to pray with holy hands lifted up to God, free from sin and anger and resentment.

9, 10. And the women should be the same way, quiet and sensible in manner and clothing. Christian women should be noticed for being kind and good, not for the way they fix their hair or because of their jewels or fancy clothes. [11]Women should listen and learn quietly and humbly. [12]I never let women teach men or lord it over them. Let them be silent in your church meetings.

1 Tim 3:2. For a pastor must be a good man whose life cannot be spoken against. He must have only one wife, and he must be hard working and thoughtful, orderly, and full of good deeds. He must enjoy having guests in his home, and must be a good Bible teacher. [3]He must not be a drinker or quarrelsome, but he must be gentle and kind, and not be one who loves money. [4]He must have a well-behaved family, with children who obey quickly and quietly. [5]For if a man can't make his own little family behave, how can he help the whole church? [6]The pastor must not be a new Christian, because he might be proud of being chosen so soon, and pride comes before a fall. (Satan's downfall is an example.) [7]Also, he must be well spoken of by people outside the church—those who aren't Christians—so that Satan can't trap him with many accusations, and leave him without freedom to lead his flock.

8. The deacons must be the same sort of good, steady men as the pastors. They must not be heavy drinkers and must not be greedy for money. [9]They must be earnest, wholehearted followers of Christ who is the hidden Source of their faith. [10]Before they are asked to be deacons they should be given other jobs in the church as a test of their character and ability, and if they do well, then they may be chosen as deacons.

11. Their wives must be thoughtful, not heavy drinkers, not gossipers, but faithful in everything they do.

12. Deacons should have only one wife and they should have happy, obedient families. [13]Those who do well as deacons will be well rewarded both by respect from others and also by developing their own confidence and bold trust in the Lord.

1 Tim 4:1. But the Holy Spirit tells us clearly that in the last times some in the church will turn away from Christ and become eager followers of teachers with devil-inspired ideas. [2]These teachers will tell lies with straight faces and do it so often that their consciences won't even bother them. [3]They will say it is wrong to be married and wrong to eat meat, even though God gave these things to well-taught Christians to enjoy and be thankful for. [4]For everything God made is good, and we may eat it gladly if we are thankful for it, [5]and if we ask God to bless it, for it is made good by the Word of God and prayer.

6. If you explain this to the others you will be doing your duty as a worthy pastor who is fed by faith and by the true teaching you have followed.

7. Don't waste time arguing over foolish ideas and silly myths and legends. Spend your time and energy in the exercise of keeping spiritually fit.

12. Don't let anyone think little of you because you are young. Be their ideal; let them follow the way you teach and live; be a pattern for them in your love, your faith, and your clean thoughts.

13. Until I get there, read and explain the Scriptures to the church; preach God's word.

14. Be sure to use the abilities God has given you through his prophets when the elders of the church laid their hands upon your head.

15. Put these abilities to work; throw yourself into your tasks so that everyone may notice your improvement and progress.

16. Keep a close watch on all you do and think. Stay true to what is right and God will bless you and use you to help others.

1 Tim 5:1. Never speak sharply to an older man, but plead with him respectfully just as though he were your own father. Talk to the younger men as you would to much loved brothers. [2]Treat the older women as mothers, and the girls as your sisters, thinking only pure thoughts about them.

3. The church should take loving care of women whose husbands have died, if they don't have anyone else to help them. [4]But if they have children or

grandchildren, these are the ones who should take the responsibility, for kindness should begin at home, supporting needy parents. This is something that pleases God very much. [5]The church should care for widows who are poor and alone in the world, if they are looking to God for his help and spending much time in prayer; [6]but not if they are spending their time running around gossiping, seeking only pleasure and thus ruining their souls. [7]This should be your church rule so that the Christians will know and do what is right.

8. But anyone who won't care for his own relatives when they need help, especially those living in his own family, has no right to say he is a Christian. Such a person is worse than the heathen.

9. A widow who wants to become one of the special church workers should be at least sixty years old and have been married only once. [10]She must be well thought of by everyone because of the good she has done. Has she brought up her children well? Has she been kind to strangers as well as to other Christians? Has she helped those who are sick and hurt? Is she always ready to show kindness?

11. The younger widows should not become members of this special group because after awhile they are likely to disregard their vow to Christ and marry again. [12]And so they will stand condemned because they broke their first promise. [13]Besides, they are likely to be lazy and spend their time gossiping around from house to house, getting into other people's business.

14. So I think it is better for these younger widows to marry again and have children, and take care of their own homes; then no one will be able to say anything against them. [16]Let me remind you again that a widow's relatives must take care of her, and not leave this to the church to do. Then the church can spend its money for the care of widows who are all alone and have nowhere else to turn.

17. Pastors who do their work well should be paid well and should be highly appreciated, especially those who work hard at both preaching and teaching. [18]For the Scriptures say, "Never tie up the mouth of an ox when it is treading out the grain —let him eat as he goes along!" And in another place, "Those who work deserve their pay!"

19. Don't listen to complaints against the pastor unless there are two or three witnesses to accuse him. [20]If he has really sinned, then he should be rebuked in front of the whole church so that no one else will follow his example. [21]I solemnly command you in the presence of God and the Lord Jesus Christ and of the holy angels to do this whether the pastor is a special friend of yours or not. All must be treated exactly the same.

1 Tim 6:11. Oh, Timothy, you are God's man. Run from all these evil things and work instead at what is right and good, learning to trust him and love others, and to be patient and gentle. [12]Fight on for God. Hold tightly to the eternal life which God has given you, and which you have confessed with such a ringing confession before many witnesses. [13]I command you before God who gives life to all, and before Christ Jesus who gave a fearless testimony before Pontius Pilate, [14]that you fulfill all he has told you to do, so that no one can find fault with you from now until our Lord Jesus Christ returns.

17. Tell those who are rich not to be proud and not to trust in their money, which will soon be gone, but their pride and trust should be in the living God who always richly gives us all we need for our enjoyment. [18]Tell them to use their money to do good. They should be rich in good works and should give happily to those in need, always being ready to share with others whatever God has given them. [19]By doing this they will be storing up real treasure for themselves in heaven—it is the only safe investment for eternity! And they will be living a fruitful Christian life down here as well.

20. Oh, Timothy, don't fail to do these things that God entrusted to you. Keep out of foolish arguments with those who boast of their "knowledge" and thus prove their lack of it.

2 Tim 1:13. Hold tightly to the pattern of truth I taught you, especially concerning the faith and love Christ Jesus offers you. [14]Guard well the splendid God-given ability you received as a gift from the Holy Spirit who lives within you.

2 Tim 2:19. A person who calls himself a Christian should not be doing things that are wrong.

22. Run from anything that gives you the evil thoughts that young men often have, but stay close to anything that makes you want to do right. Have faith and love, and enjoy the companionship of those who love the Lord and have pure hearts.

23. Again I say, don't get involved in foolish arguments which only upset people and make them angry.

24. God's people must not be quarrelsome; they must be gentle, patient teachers of those who are wrong. [25]Be humble when you are trying to teach those who are mixed up concerning the truth. For if you talk meekly and courteously to them they are more likely, with God's help, to turn away from their wrong ideas and believe what is true.

2 Tim 3:2. For people will love only themselves and their money; they will be proud and boastful, sneering at God, disobedient to their parents, ungrateful to them, and thoroughly bad. [3]They will be hardheaded and never give in to others; they will be constant liars and troublemakers and will think nothing of immorality. They will be rough and cruel, and sneer at those who try to be good. [4]They will betray their friends; they will be hotheaded, puffed up with pride, and prefer good times to worshiping God. [5]They will go to church, yes, but they won't really believe anything they hear. Don't be taken in by people like that.

Tit 1:5. I left you there on the island of Crete so that you could do whatever was needed to help strengthen each of its churches, and I asked you to appoint pastors in every city who would follow the instructions I gave you. [6]The men you choose must be well thought of for their good lives; they must have only one wife and their children must love the Lord and not have a reputation for being wild or disobedient to their parents. 7These pastors must be men of blameless lives because they are God's ministers. They must not be proud or impatient; they must not be drunkards or fighters or greedy for money. 8They must enjoy having guests in their homes and must love all that is good. They must be sensible men, and fair. They must be clean minded and level headed. 9Their belief in the truth which they have been taught must be strong and steadfast, so that they will be able to teach it to others and show those who disagree with them where they are wrong. 10For there are many who refuse to obey; this is especially true among those who say that all Christians must obey the Jewish laws. But this is foolish talk; it blinds people to the truth, 11and it must be stopped. Already whole families have been turned away from the grace of God. Such teachers are only after your money. 12One of their own men, a prophet from Crete, has said about them, "These men of Crete are all liars; they are like lazy animals, living only to satisfy their stomachs." 13And this is true. So speak to the Christians there as sternly as necessary to make them strong in the faith, 14and to stop them from listening to Jewish folk tales and the demands of men who have turned their backs on the truth.

Tit 2:2. Teach the older men to be serious and unruffled; they must be sensible, knowing and believing the truth and doing everything with love and patience. 3Teach the older women to be quiet and respectful in everything they do. They must not go around speaking evil of others and must not be heavy drinkers, but they should be teachers of goodness. 4These older women must train the younger women to live quietly, to love their husbands and their children, 5and to be sensible and clean minded, spending their time in their own homes, being kind and obedient to their husbands, so that the Christian faith can't be spoken against by those who know them.

9. Urge slaves to obey their masters and try their best to satisfy them. They must not talk back, 10nor steal, but must show themselves to be entirely trustworthy. In this way they will make people want to believe in our Savior and God.

11. For the free gift of eternal salvation is now being offered to everyone; 12and along with this gift comes the realization that God wants us to turn from godless living and sinful pleasures and to live good, God-fearing lives day after day.

Tit 3:1. Remind your people to obey the government and its officers, and always to be obedient and ready for any honest work. 2They must not speak evil of anyone, nor quarrel, but be gentle and truly courteous to all.

8. These things I have told you are all true. Insist on them so that Christians will be careful to do good deeds all the time, for this is not only right, but it brings results.

Heb 6:1. Let us stop going over the same old ground again and again, always teaching those first lessons about Christ. Let us go on instead to other things and become mature in our understanding, as strong Christians ought to be. Surely we don't need to speak further about the foolishness of trying to be saved by being good, or about the necessity of faith in God. 11And we are anxious that you keep right on loving others as long as life lasts, so that you will get your full reward. 12Then, knowing what lies ahead for you, you won't become bored with being a Christian, nor become spiritually dull and indifferent, but you will be anxious to follow the example of those who receive all that God has promised them because of their strong faith and patience.

Heb 10:22. Let us go right in, to God himself, with true hearts fully trusting him to receive us, because we have been sprinkled with Christ's blood to make us clean, and because our bodies have been washed with pure water.

23. Now we can look forward to the salvation God has promised us. There is no longer any room for doubt, and we can tell others that salvation is ours, for there is no question that he will do what he says. 24In response to all he has done for us, let us outdo each other in being helpful and kind to each other and in doing good. 25Let us not neglect our church meetings, as some people do, but encourage and warn each other, especially now that the day of his coming back again is drawing near.

Heb 12:1. Since we have such a huge crowd of men of faith watching us from the grandstands, let us strip off anything that slows us down or holds us back, and especially those sins that wrap themselves so tightly around our feet and trip us up; and let us run with patience the particular race that God has set before us. 2Keep your eyes on Jesus, our leader and instructor. He was willing to die a shameful death on the cross because of the joy he knew would be his afterwards; and now he sits in the place of honor by the throne of God. 3If you want to keep from becoming fainthearted and weary, think about his patience as sinful men did such terrible things to him. 4After all, you have never yet struggled against sin and temptation until you sweat great drops of blood. 5And have you quite forgotten the encouraging words God spoke to you, his child? He said, "My son, don't be angry when the Lord punishes you. Don't be discouraged when he has to show you where you are wrong."

12. So take a new grip with your tired hands, stand firm on your shaky legs, 13and mark out a straight, smooth path for your feet so that those who follow you, though weak and lame, will not fall and hurt themselves, but become strong. 14Try to stay out of all quarrels and seek to live a clean and holy life, for one who is not holy will not see the Lord. 15Look after each other so that not one of you will fail to find God's best blessings. Watch out that no bitterness takes root among you, for as it springs up it causes deep trouble, hurting many in their spiritual lives. 16Watch out that no one

becomes involved in sexual sin or becomes careless about God as Esau did: he traded his rights as the oldest son for a single meal.

Heb 13:1. Continue to love each other with true brotherly love.

2. Don't forget to be kind to strangers, for some who have done this have entertained angels without realizing it!

3. Don't forget about those in jail. Suffer with them as though you were there yourself. Share the sorrow of those being mistreated, for you know what they are going through.

5. Stay away from the love of money; be satisfied with what you have. For God has said, "I will never, *never* fail you nor forsake you."

7. Remember your leaders who have taught you the Word of God. Think of all the good that has come from their lives, and try to trust the Lord as they do.

9. So do not be attracted by strange, new ideas. Your spiritual strength comes as a gift from God, not from ceremonial rules about eating certain foods—a method which, by the way, hasn't helped those who have tried it!

15. With Jesus' help we will continually offer our sacrifice of praise to God by telling others of the glory of his name.

16. Don't forget to do good and to share what you have with those in need, for such sacrifices are very pleasing to him.

17. Obey your spiritual leaders and be willing to do what they say. For their work is to watch over your souls, and God will judge them on how well they do this. Give them reason to report joyfully about you to the Lord and not with sorrow, for then you will suffer for it too.

PRECEPTS OF OTHER APOSTLES.

Explicitly Stated or Implied in Didactic Epistles.
Jas 1:16. So don't be misled, dear brothers. [19]Dear brothers, don't ever forget that it is best to listen much, speak little, and not become angry.

21. So get rid of all that is wrong in your life, both inside and outside, and humbly be glad for the wonderful message we have received, for it is able to save our souls as it takes hold of our hearts.

22. And remember, it is a message to obey, not just to listen to. So don't fool yourselves.

Jas 2:1. Dear brothers, how can you claim that you belong to the Lord Jesus Christ, the Lord of glory, if you show favoritism to rich people and look down on poor people? [2]If a man comes into your church dressed in expensive clothes and with valuable gold rings on his fingers, and at the same moment another man comes in who is poor and dressed in threadbare clothes, [3]and you make a lot of fuss over the rich man and give him the best seat in the house and say to the poor man, "You can stand over there if you like, or else sit on the floor" —well, [4]judging a man by his wealth shows that you are guided by wrong motives.

8. Yes indeed, it is good when you truly obey our Lord's command, "You must love and help your neighbors just as much as you love and take care of yourself." [9]But you are breaking this law of our Lord's when you favor the rich and fawn over them; it is sin. [10]And the person who keeps every law of God, but makes one little slip, is just as guilty as the person who has broken every law there is. [11]For the God who said you must not marry a woman who already has a husband, also said you must not murder, so even though you have not broken the marriage laws by committing adultery, but have murdered someone, you have entirely broken God's laws and stand utterly guilty before him. [12]You will be judged on whether or not you are doing what Christ wants you to. So watch what you do and what you think.

Jas 3:1. Dear brothers, don't be too eager to tell others their faults, for we all make many mistakes; and when we teachers of religion, who should know better, do wrong, our punishment will be greater than it would be for others.

Jas 4:7. So give yourselves humbly to God. Resist the devil and he will flee from you.

8. And when you draw close to God, God will draw close to you. Wash your hands, you sinners, and let your hearts be filled with God alone to make them pure and true to him.

9. Let there be tears for the wrong things you have done. Let there be sorrow and sincere grief. Let there be sadness instead of laughter, and gloom instead of joy.

10. Then you will realize your worthlessness before the Lord, he will lift you up, encourage and help you.

11. Don't criticize and speak evil about each other, dear brothers. If you do, you will be fighting against God's law of loving one another, declaring it is wrong. But your job is not to decide whether this law is right or wrong, but to obey it.

13. Look here, you people who say, "Today or tomorrow we are going to such and such a town, stay there a year, and open up a profitable business." [14]How do you know what is going to happen tomorrow? For the length of your lives is as uncertain as the morning fog—now you see it; soon it is gone. [15]What you ought to say is, "If the Lord wants us to, we shall live and do this or that."

Jas 5:7. Now as for you, dear brothers who are waiting for the Lord's return, be patient, like a farmer who waits until the autumn for his precious harvest to ripen. [8]Yes, be patient. And take courage, for the coming of the Lord is near.

9. Don't grumble about each other, brothers. Are you yourselves above criticism? For see! The great Judge is coming. He is almost here. [Let him do whatever criticizing must be done.] [10]For examples of patience in suffering, look at the Lord's prophets. [11]We know how happy they are now because they stayed true to him then, even though they suffered greatly for it. Job is an example of a man who continued to trust the Lord in sorrow; from his experiences we can see how the Lord's plan finally ended in good, for he is full of tenderness and mercy.

12. But most of all, dear brothers, do not swear

either by heaven or earth or anything else; just say a simple yes or no, so that you will not sin and be condemned for it.

16. Admit your faults to one another and pray for each other so that you may be healed. The earnest prayer of a righteous man has great power and wonderful results.

1 Pet 1:13. So now you can look forward soberly and intelligently to more of God's kindness to you when Jesus Christ returns. [14]Obey God because you are his children; don't slip back into your old ways—doing evil because you knew no better. [15]But be holy now in everything you do, just as the Lord is holy, who invited you to be his child. [16]He himself has said, "You must be holy, for I am holy." [17]And remember that your heavenly Father to whom you pray has no favorites when he judges. He will judge you with perfect justice for everything you do; so act in reverent fear of him from now on until you get to heaven.

1 Pet 2:11. Dear brothers, you are only visitors here. Since your real home is in heaven I beg you to keep away from the evil pleasures of this world; they are not for you, for they fight against your very souls. [12]Be careful how you behave among your unsaved neighbors; for then, even if they are suspicious of you and talk against you, they will end up praising God for your good works when Christ returns.

13. For the Lord's sake obey every law of your government: those of the king as head of the state, [14]and those of the king's officers, for he has sent them to punish all who do wrong, and to honor those who do right. [15]It is God's will that your good lives should silence those who foolishly condemn the Gospel without knowing what it can do for them, having never experienced its power. [16]You are free from the law, but that doesn't mean you are free to do wrong. Live as those who are free to do only God's will at all times.

17. Show respect for everyone. Love Christians everywhere. Fear God and honor the government.

18. Servants, you must respect your masters and do whatever they tell you—not only if they are kind and reasonable, but even if they are tough and cruel. [19]Praise the Lord if you are punished for doing right! [20]Of course, you get no credit for being patient if you are beaten for doing wrong; but if you do right and suffer for it, and are patient beneath the blows, God is well pleased. [21]This suffering is all part of the work God has given you. Christ, who suffered for you, is your example. Follow in his steps: [22]He never sinned, never told a lie, [23]never answered back when insulted; when he suffered he did not threaten to get even; he left his case in the hands of God who always judges fairly. [24]He personally carried the load of our sins in his own body when he died on the cross, so that we can be finished with sin and live a good life from now on. For his wounds have healed ours! [25]Like sheep you wandered away from God, but now you have returned to your Shepherd, the Guardian of your souls who keeps you safe from all attacks.

1 Pet 3:8. And now this word to all of you: You should be like one big happy family, full of sympathy toward each other, loving one another with tender hearts and humble minds. [9]Don't repay evil for evil. Don't snap back at those who say unkind things about you. Instead, pray for God's help for them, for we are to be kind to others, and God will bless us for it.

10. If you want a happy, good life, keep control of your tongue, and guard your lips from telling lies. [11]Turn away from evil and do good. Try to live in peace even if you must run after it to catch and hold it! [12]For the Lord is watching his children, listening to their prayers; but the Lord's face is hard against those who do evil.

15. Quietly trust yourself to Christ your Lord and if anybody asks why you believe as you do, be ready to tell him, and do it in a gentle and respectful way. [16]Do what is right; then if men speak against you, calling you evil names, they will become ashamed of themselves for falsely accusing you when you have only done what is good. [17]Remember, if God wants you to suffer, it is better to suffer for doing good than for doing wrong!

1 Pet 4:1. Since Christ suffered and underwent pain, you must have the same attitude he did; you must be ready to suffer, too. For remember, when your body suffers, sin loses its power, [2]and you won't be spending the rest of your life chasing after evil desires, but will be anxious to do the will of God.

3. You have had enough in the past of the evil things the godless enjoy—sex sin, lust, getting drunk, wild parties, drinking bouts, and the worship of idols, and other terrible sins. [4]Of course, your former friends will be very surprised when you don't eagerly join them any more in the wicked things they do, and they will laugh at you in contempt and scorn. [5]But just remember that they must face the Judge of all, living and dead; they will be punished for the way they have lived. [6]That is why the Good News was preached even to those who were dead—killed by the flood—so that although their bodies were punished with death, they could still live in their spirits as God lives.

7. The end of the world is coming soon. Therefore be earnest, thoughtful men of prayer.

8. Most important of all, continue to show deep love for each other, for love makes up for many of your faults.

9. Cheerfully share your home with those who need a meal or a place to stay for the night. [10]God has given each of you some special abilities; be sure to use them to help each other, passing on to others God's many kinds of blessings.

11. Are you called to preach? Then preach as though God himself were speaking through you. Are you called to help others? Do it with all the strength and energy that God supplies, so that God will be glorified through Jesus Christ—to him be glory and power forever and ever. Amen.

12. Dear friends, don't be bewildered or surprised when you go through the fiery trials ahead,

for this is no strange, unusual thing that is going to happen to you. [13]Instead, be really glad—because these trials will make you partners with Christ in his suffering, and afterwards you will have the wonderful joy of sharing his glory in that coming day when it will be displayed.

14. Be happy if you are cursed and insulted for being a Christian, for when that happens the Spirit of God will come upon you with great glory.

15. Don't let me hear of your suffering for murdering or stealing or making trouble or being a busybody and prying into other people's affairs. [16]But it is no shame to suffer for being a Christian. Praise God for the privilege of being in Christ's family and being called by his wonderful name!

1 Pet 5:1. And now, a word to you elders of the church. I, too, am an elder; with my own eyes I saw Christ dying on the cross; and I, too, will share his glory and his honor when he returns. Fellow elders, this is my plea to you: [2]Feed the flock of God; care for it willingly, not grudgingly; not for what you will get out of it, but because you are eager to serve the Lord. [3]Don't be tyrants, but lead them by your good example.

5. You younger men, follow the leadership of those who are older. And all of you serve each other with humble spirits, for God gives special blessings to those who are humble, but sets himself against those who are proud.

6. If you will humble yourselves under the mighty hand of God, in his good time he will lift you up. [7]Let him have all your worries and cares, for he is always thinking about you and watching everything that concerns you.

8. Be careful—watch out for attacks from Satan, your great enemy. He prowls around like a hungry, roaring lion, looking for some victim to tear apart. [9]Stand firm when he attacks. Trust the Lord; and remember that other Christians all around the world are going through these sufferings too.

2 Pet 1:5. But to obtain these gifts, you need more than faith; you must also work hard to be good, and even that is not enough. For then you must learn to know God better and discover what he wants you to do. [6]Next, learn to put aside your own desires so that you will become patient and godly, gladly letting God have his way with you. [7]This will make possible the next step, which is for you to enjoy other people and to like them, and finally you will grow to love them deeply.

10. So, dear brothers, work hard to prove that you really are among those God has called and chosen, and then you will never stumble or fall away.

2 Pet 3:14. Dear friends, while you are waiting for these things to happen and for him to come, try hard to live without sinning; and be at peace with everyone so that he will be pleased with you when he returns.

18. But grow in spiritual strength and become better acquainted with our Lord and Savior Jesus Christ.

1 Jn 3:10. So now we can tell who is a child of God and who belongs to Satan. Whoever is living a life of sin and doesn't love his brother shows that he is not in God's family; [11]for the message to us from the beginning has been that we should love one another. [12]We are not to be like Cain, who belonged to Satan and killed his brother. Why did he kill him? Because Cain had been doing wrong and he knew very well that his brother's life was better than his.

13. So don't be surprised, dear friends, if the world hates you.

14. If we love other Christians it proves that we have been delivered from hell and given eternal life. But a person who doesn't have love for others is headed for eternal death. [15]Anyone who hates his Christian brother is really a murderer at heart; and you know that no one wanting to murder has eternal life within. [16]We know what real love is from Christ's example in dying for us. And so we also ought to lay down our lives for our Christian brothers.

17. But if someone who is supposed to be a Christian has money enough to live well, and sees a brother in need, and won't help him—how can God's love be within *him?*

18. Little children, let us stop just *saying* we love people; let us *really* love them, and *show it* by our actions. [19]Then we will know for sure, by our actions, that we are on God's side, and our consciences will be clear, even when we stand before the Lord. [20]But if we have bad consciences and feel that we have done wrong, the Lord will surely feel it even more, for he knows everything we do. [21]But, dearly loved friends, if our consciences are clear, we can come to the Lord with perfect assurance and trust, [22]and get whatever we ask for because we are obeying him and doing the things that please him.

23. And this is what God says we must do: Believe on the name of his Son Jesus Christ, and love one another.

1 Jn 4:1. Dearly loved friends, don't always believe everything you hear just because someone says it is a message from God: test it first to see if it really is. For there are many false teachers around.

7. Dear friends, let us practice loving each other, for love comes from God and those who are loving and kind show that they are the children of God, and that they are getting to know him better. [8]But if a person isn't loving and kind, it shows that he doesn't know God—for God is love.

11. Dear friends, since God loved us as much as that, we surely ought to love each other too.

12. For though we have never yet seen God, when we love each other God lives in us and his love within us grows ever stronger.

15. Anyone who believes and says that Jesus is the Son of God has God living in him, and he is living with God.

16. We know how much God loves us because we have felt his love and because we believe him when he tells us that he loves us dearly. God is love, and

anyone who lives in love is living with God and God is living in him.

21. And God himself has said that one must love not only God, but his brother too.

1 Jn 5:21. Dear children, keep away from anything that might take God's place in your hearts.

2 Jn 1:5. And now I want to urgently remind you, dear friends, of the old rule God gave us right from the beginning, that Christians should love one another.

6. If we love God, we will do whatever he tells us to. And he has told us from the very first to love each other.

3 Jn 1:11. Dear friend, don't let this bad example influence you. Follow only what is good. Remember that those who do what is right prove that they are God's children; and those who continue in evil prove that they are far from God.

Jude 1:3. Dearly loved friends, I have been planning to write you some thoughts about the salvation God has given us, but now I find I must write of something else instead, urging you to stoutly defend the truth which God gave, once for all, to his people to keep without change through the years. [4]I say this because some godless teachers have wormed their way in among you, saying that after we become Christians we can do just as we like without fear of God's punishment. The fate of such people was written long ago, for they turned against our only Master and Lord, Jesus Christ.

20. But you, dear friends, must build up your lives ever more strongly upon the foundation of our holy faith, learning to pray in the power and strength of the Holy Spirit. [21]Stay always within the boundaries where God's love can reach and bless you. Wait patiently for the eternal life that our Lord Jesus Christ in his mercy is going to give you.

22. Try to help those who argue against you. Be merciful to those who doubt. [23]Save some by snatching them as from the very flames of hell itself. And as for others, help them to find the Lord by being kind to them, but be careful that you yourselves aren't pulled along into their sins. Hate every trace of their sin while being merciful to them as sinners.

Rev 3:11. Look, I am coming soon! Hold tightly to the little strength you have—so that no one will take away your crown. [18]My advice to you is to buy pure gold from me, gold purified by fire—only then will you truly be rich. And to purchase from me white garments, clean and pure, so you won't be naked and ashamed; and to get medicine from me to heal your eyes and give you back your sight. [19]I continually discipline and punish everyone I love; so I must punish you, unless you turn from your indifference and become enthusiastic about the things of God.

Rev 22:17. The Spirit and the bride say, "Come." Let each one who hears them say the same, "Come." Let the thirsty one come—anyone who wants to; let him come and drink the Water of Life without charge.

See *Adultery; Children; Citizen; Homicide; Instruction; Minister; Obedience, Commanded; Servant; Theft; Wife; Woman* and other topics.

OF MEN. Isa 29:13. And so the Lord says, "Since these people say they are mine but they do not obey me, and since their worship amounts to mere words learned by rote."

Mt 15:2. "Why do your disciples disobey the ancient Jewish traditions?" they demanded. "For they ignore our ritual of ceremonial handwashing before they eat." [3]He replied, "And why do your traditions violate the direct commandments of God? [4]For instance, God's law is 'Honor your father and mother; anyone who reviles his parents must die.' [5, 6]But you say, 'Even if your parents are in need, you may give their support money to the church instead.' And so, by your man-made rule, you nullify the direct command of God to honor and care for your parents. [7]You hypocrites! Well did Isaiah prophesy of you, [8]'These people say they honor me, but their hearts are far away. [9]Their worship is worthless, for they teach their man-made laws instead of those from God.' " [10]Then Jesus called to the crowds and said, "Listen to what I say and try to understand: [11]You aren't made unholy by eating non-kosher food! It is what you *say* and *think* that makes you unclean." [12]Then the disciples came and told him, "You offended the Pharisees by that remark." [13, 14]Jesus replied, "Every plant not planted by my Father shall be rooted up, so ignore them. They are blind guides leading the blind, and both will fall into a ditch." [15]Then Peter asked Jesus to explain what he meant when he said that people are not defiled by non-kosher food. [16]"Don't you understand?" Jesus asked him. [17]"Don't you see that anything you eat passes through the digestive tract and out again? [18]But evil words come from an evil heart, and defile the man who says them. [19]For from the heart come evil thoughts, murder, adultery, fornication, theft, lying and slander. [20]These are what defile; but there is no spiritual defilement from eating without first going through the ritual of ceremonial handwashing!" Mk 7:2–23.

Rom 14:1. Give a warm welcome to any brother who wants to join you even though his faith is weak. Don't criticize him for having different ideas from yours about what is right and wrong. [2]For instance, don't argue with him about whether or not to eat meat that has been offered to idols. You may believe there is no harm in this, but the faith of others is weaker; they think it is wrong, and will go without any meat at all and eat vegetables rather than eat that kind of meat. [3]Those who think it is all right to eat such meat must not look down on those who won't. And if you are one of those who won't, don't find fault with those who do. For God has accepted them to be his children. [4]They are God's servants, not yours. They are responsible to him, not to you. Let him tell them whether they are right or wrong. And God is able to make them do as they should. [5]Some think that Christians should observe the Jewish holidays as special days to worship God, but others say it is wrong and foolish to go to all that trouble, for every day alike belongs to God. On questions of this kind everyone must decide for himself. [6]If you have special days for worshiping the Lord, you are trying to honor him; you are doing a good thing. So is the person who eats meat that has been offered to idols; he is thankful to the Lord for it; he is doing right. And the person who won't touch such meat, he, too, is anxious to please the Lord, and is thankful. [10]You have no right to criticize your brother or look down on him. Remember each of us will stand personally before the Judgment Seat of God. [11]For it is written, "As I live," says the Lord, "every knee shall bow to me and every tongue confess to God." [12]Yes, each of us will give an account of himself to God. [13]So don't criticize each other any more. Try instead to live in such a way that you will never make your brother stumble by letting him see you doing something he thinks is wrong. [14]As for myself, I am perfectly sure on the authority of the Lord Jesus that there is nothing really wrong with eating meat that has been offered to idols. But if someone believes it is wrong, then he shouldn't do it because for him it is wrong. [15]And if your brother is bothered by what you eat, you are not acting in love if you go ahead and eat it. Don't let your eating ruin someone for whom Christ died. [16]Don't do anything that will cause criticism against yourself even though you know that what you do is right. [17]For, after all, the important thing for us as Christians is not what we eat or drink but stirring up goodness and peace and joy from the Holy Spirit. [18]If you let Christ be Lord in these affairs, God will be glad; and so will others. [19]In this way aim for harmony in the church and try to build each other up. [20]Don't undo the work of God for a chunk of meat. Remember, there is nothing wrong with the meat, but it is wrong to eat it if it makes another stumble. [21]The right thing to do is to quit eating meat or drinking wine or doing anything else that offends your brother or makes him sin. [22]You may know that there is nothing wrong with what you do, even from God's point of view, but keep it to yourself; don't flaunt your faith in front of others who might be hurt by it. In this situation, happy is the man who does not sin by doing what he knows is right. [23]But anyone who believes that something he wants to do is wrong shouldn't do it. He sins if he does, for he thinks it is wrong, and so for him it *is* wrong. Anything that is done apart from what he feels is right is sin.

1 Tim 4:1. But the Holy Spirit tells us clearly that in the last times some in the church will turn away from Christ and become eager followers of teachers with devil-inspired ideas. [2]These teachers will tell lies with straight faces and do it so often that their consciences won't even bother them. [3]They will say it is wrong to be married and wrong to eat meat, even though God gave these things to well-taught Christians to enjoy and be thankful for.

COMMERCE Laws concerning, Lev 19:35–37; 25:14–18. Carried on by means of caravans, Gen 37:25; Isa 60:6; ships, 1 Kgs 9:27, 28; 10:11; 22:48; Ps 107:23–30; Prov 31:14; Rev 18:17. Conducted in markets, Ezk 27:12. Of the Arabians, Isa 60:6; Jer 6:20; Ezk 27:21–24; Egyptians, Gen 42:2–34; Ethiopians, Isa 45:14; Ishmaelites, Gen 37:25; Israelites, 1 Kgs 9:26–28; Neh 3:31, 32; Ezk 27:17; Ninevites, Nah 3:16; Syrians, Ezk 27:16, 18; Tyrians, 2 Sam 5:11; 1 Kgs 5:10; Isa 23:8; Ezk 27; Sidonians, Isa 23:2; Ezk 27:8; Babylonians, Rev 18:3, 11–13. From Tarshish, Jer 10:9, Ezk 27:25.

Evil practices connected with, Prov 11:1; Ezk 22:13; Hos 12:7.

Articles of: Apes, 1 Kgs 10:22; blue cloth, Ezk 27:24; brass, Ezk 27:13; Rev 18:12; carvings, Rev 18:12; cattle, Rev 18:13; carpets, Ezk 27:24; chariots, 1 Kgs 10:29; Rev 18:13; clothes for riding, Ezk 27:20; embroidery, Ezk 27:16, 24; goats, Ezk 27:21; gold, 1 Kgs 9:27, 28; 10:22; 2 Chron 8:17, 18; Isa 60:6; Rev 18:12; gum, Gen 37:25; herbs, Gen 37:25; honey, Ezk 27:17; horses, 1 Kgs 10:29; Ezk 27:14; Rev 18:13; incense, Jer 6:20; Rev 18:13; iron, Ezk 27:12, 19; Rev 18:12; ivory, 1 Kgs 10:22; 2 Chron 9:21; Ezk 27:15; Rev 18:12; land, Gen 23:13–16; Ruth 4:3; lead, Ezk 27:12; linen, Rev 18:12; marble, Rev 18:12; oil, 1 Kgs 5:11; Ezk 27:16; Rev 18:13; ointment, Rev 18:13; pearls, Rev 18:12; peacocks, 1 Kgs 10:22; perfumes, Rev 18:13; precious stones, Ezk 27:16, 22; 28:13; Rev 18:12; purple, Ezk 27:16; scarlet, Rev 18:12; sheep, Ezk 27:21; Rev 18:13; silk, Rev 18:12; silver, 1 Kgs 10:22; 2 Chron 9:21; Rev 18:12; slaves, Gen 37:28, 36; Deut 24:7; spices, Gen 37:25; Song 3:6; Rev 18:13; timber, 1 Kgs 5:6, 8; tin, Ezk 27:12; wheat, 1 Kgs 5:11; Ezk 27:17; Rev 18:13; white wool, Ezk 27:18; wine, 2 Chron 2:15; Ezk 27:18; Rev 18:13; wood, Rev 18:12; bodies and souls of men, Rev 18:13.

Transportation of passengers, Jon 1:3; Acts 21:2; 27:2, 6, 37.

See *Merchant; Tarshish,* and names of specific trades.

COMMISSARY For armies, cattle driven with, 2 Kgs 3:9. See *Armies.* For royal households, 1 Kgs 4:7–19, 27, 28.

COMMUNION WITH GOD. Ps 16:7. I will bless the Lord who counsels me; he gives me wisdom in the night. He tells me what to do.

Jn 14:15, 16. "If you love me, obey me; and I will ask the Father and he will give you another Comforter, and he will never leave you. [17]He is the Holy Spirit, the Spirit who leads into all truth. The world at large cannot receive him, for it isn't looking for him and doesn't recognize him. But you do, for he lives with you now and some day shall be in you. [18]No, I will not abandon you or leave you as orphans in the storm—I will come to you." [23]Jesus replied, "Because I will only reveal myself to those who love me and obey me. The Father will love them too, and we will come to them and live with them."

1 Cor 10:16. When we ask the Lord's blessing upon our drinking from the cup of wine at the Lord's Table, this means, doesn't it, that all who drink it are sharing together the blessing of Christ's blood? And when we break from the loaf to eat

there together, this shows that we are sharing together in the benefits of his body.

2 Cor 6:16. And what union can there be between God's temple and idols? For you are God's temple, the home of the living God, and God has said of you, "I will live in them and walk among them, and I will be their God and they shall be my people."

2 Cor 13:14. May the grace of our Lord Jesus Christ be with you all. May God's love and the Holy Spirit's friendship be yours.

Gal 4:6. And because we are his sons God has sent the Spirit of his Son into our hearts, so now we can rightly speak of God as our dear Father.

Phil 2:1. Is there any such thing as Christians cheering each other up? Do you love me enough to want to help me? Does it mean anything to you that we are brothers in the Lord, sharing the same Spirit? Are your hearts tender and sympathetic at all? [2]Then make me truly happy by loving each other and agreeing wholeheartedly with each other, working together with one heart and mind and purpose.

1 Jn 1:3. Again I say, we are telling you about what we ourselves have actually seen and heard, so that you may share the fellowship and the joys we have with the Father and with Jesus Christ his Son.

Rev 3:20. Look! I have been standing at the door and I am constantly knocking. If anyone hears me calling him and opens the door, I will come in and fellowship with him and he with me.

See *Fellowship.*

INSTANCES OF. Enoch, Gen 5:21–24. Noah, Gen 6:9, 10, 12–22; 8:15–17. Abraham, Gen 12:1–3, 7; 17:1–4; 18:1–33; 22:1, 2, 11, 12, 16–18. Hagar, Gen 16:8–12. Isaac, Gen 26:2–5, 24. Isaac, in dreams, Gen 28:13–15; 31:3; 35:1, 7; 46:2–4. Moses, Ex 3; 4:1–17; 33:9, 11; 34:28; Num 12:7, 8. Joshua, Josh 1:1–9; 6:2–5; 7:10–15; 8:1, 2; 20:1–6. Gideon, Judg 6:11–24. Solomon, 1 Kgs 3:5–14; 2 Chron 1:7–12.

OF SAINTS. 1 Sam 23:16. Prince Jonathan now went to find David; he met him at Horesh and encouraged him in his faith in God.

Ps 55:14. What fellowship we had, what wonderful discussions as we walked together to the Temple of the Lord on holy days.

Ps 119:63. Anyone is my brother who fears and trusts the Lord and obeys him.

Ps 133:1. How wonderful it is, how pleasant, when brothers live in harmony! [2]For harmony is as precious as the fragrant anointing oil that was poured over Aaron's head, and ran down onto his beard, and onto the border of his robe. [3]Harmony is as refreshing as the dew on Mount Hermon, on the mountains of Israel. And God has pronounced this eternal blessing on Jerusalem, even life forevermore.

Amos 3:3. For how can we walk together with your sins between us?

Mal 3:16. Then those who feared and loved the Lord spoke often of him to each other. And he had a Book of Remembrance drawn up in which he recorded the names of those who feared him and loved to think about him.

Lk 22:32. So when you have repented and turned to me again, strengthen and build up the faith of your brothers.

Lk 24:32. They began telling each other how their hearts had felt strangely warm as he talked with them and explained the Scriptures during the walk down the road. *v.* 17.

Jn 17:20. I am not praying for these alone but also for the future believers who will come to me because of the testimony of these. [21]My prayer for all of them is that they will be of one heart and mind, just as you and I are, Father—that just as you are in me and I am in you, so they will be in us, and the world will believe you sent me.

Acts 2:42. They joined with the other believers in regular attendance at the apostles' teaching sessions and at the Communion services and prayer meetings.

Rom 12:15. When others are happy, be happy with them. If they are sad, share their sorrow.

1 Cor 10:16. When we ask the Lord's blessing upon our drinking from the cup of wine at the Lord's Table, this means, doesn't it, that all who drink it are sharing together the blessing of Christ's blood? And when we break off pieces of the bread from the loaf to eat there together, this shows that we are sharing together in the benefits of his body. [17]No matter how many of us there are, we all eat from the same loaf, showing that we are all parts of the one body of Christ.

1 Cor 12:12. Our bodies have many parts, but the many parts make up only one body when they are all put together. So it is with the "body" of Christ. [13]Each of us is a part of the one body of Christ. Some of us are Jews, some are Gentiles, some are slaves and some are free. But the Holy Spirit has fitted us all together into one body. We have been baptized into Christ's body by the one Spirit, and have all been given that same Holy Spirit.

2 Cor 6:14. Don't be teamed with those who do not love the Lord, for what do the people of God have in common with the people of sin? How can light live with darkness? [15]And what harmony can there be between Christ and the devil? How can a Christian be a partner with one who doesn't believe? [16]And what union can there be between God's temple and idols? For you are God's temple, the home of the living God, and God has said of you, "I live in them and walk among them, and I will be their God and they shall be my people." [17]That is why the Lord has said, "Leave them; separate yourselves from them; don't touch their filthy things, and I will welcome you, [18]and be a Father to you, and you will be my sons and daughters.

Eph 4:1. I beg you—I, a prisoner here in jail for serving the Lord—to live and act in a way worthy of those who have been chosen for such wonderful blessings as these. [2]Be humble and gentle. Be patient with each other, making allowance for each other's faults because of your love. [3]Try always to be led along together by the Holy Spirit, and so be at peace with one another.

Col 3:16. Remember what Christ taught and let his words enrich your lives and make you wise; teach them to each other and sing them out in psalms and hymns and spiritual songs, singing to the Lord with thankful hearts.

1 Thess 4:18. So comfort and encourage each other with this news.

1 Thess 5:11. So encourage each other to build each other up, just as you are already doing. [14]Dear brothers, warn those who are lazy; comfort those who are frightened; take tender care of those who are weak; and be patient with everyone.

Heb 3:13. Speak to each other about these things every day while there is still time, so that none of you will become hardened against God, being blinded by the glamor of sin.

Heb 10:24. In response to all he has done for us, let us outdo each other in being helpful and kind to each other and in doing good. [25]Let us not neglect our church meetings, as some people do, but encourage and warn each other, especially now that the day of his coming back again is drawing near.

Jas 5:16. Admit your faults to one another and pray for each other so that you may be healed. The earnest prayer of a righteous man has great power and wonderful results.

1 Jn 1:3. Again I say, we are telling you about what we ourselves have actually seen and heard, so that you may share the fellowship and the joys we have with the Father and with Jesus Christ his Son. [7]But if we are living in the light of God's presence, just as Christ does, then we have wonderful fellowship and joy with each other, and the blood of Jesus his Son cleanses us from every sin.

See *Fellowship; Lord's Supper.*

COMPANY EVIL. Gen 19:15. At dawn the next morning the angels became urgent. "Hurry," they said to Lot, "take your wife and your two daughters who are here and get out while you can, or you will be caught in the destruction of the city."

Gen 49:6. O my soul, stay away from them. May I never be a party to their wicked plans. For in their anger they murdered a man, and maimed oxen just for fun.

Ex 23:2. Don't join mobs intent on evil. [32]You must make no covenant with them, nor have anything to do with their gods. [33]Don't let them live among you! For I know that they will infect you with their sin of worshiping false gods, and that would be an utter disaster to you. Ex 34:12–15; Deut 7:2–4; Josh 23:6–13.

Lev 18:3. So don't act like heathen—like the people of Egypt where you lived so long, or the people of Canaan where I am going to take you. Lev 20:23.

Num 16:26. "Quick!" he told the people, "get away from the tents of these wicked men, and don't touch anything that belongs to them, lest you be included in their sins [and be destroyed with them]." *vs.* 21–26.

Num 33:55. But if you refuse to drive out the people living there, those who remain will be as cinders in your eyes and thorns in your sides. Judg 2:1–3.

Deut 12:30. Don't follow their example in worshiping their gods. Do not ask, "How do these nations worship their gods?" and then go and worship as they do!

2 Sam 23:6. But the godless are as thorns to be thrown away, for they tear the hand that touches them. [7]One must be armed to chop them down; they shall be burned.

2 Chron 19:2. The prophet Jehu (son of Hanani) went out to meet him. "Should you be helping the wicked, and loving those who hate the Lord?" he asked him. "Because of what you have done, God's wrath is upon you."

Ezra 9:14. We have broken your commandments again and intermarried with people who do these awful things. Surely your anger will destroy us now until not even this little remnant escapes.

Ps 1:1. Oh, the joys of those who do not follow evil men's advice, who do not hang around with sinners, scoffing at the things of God.

Ps 6:8. Go, leave me now, you men of evil deeds, for the Lord has heard my weeping.

Ps 15:4. Speaks out against sin, criticizes those committing it, commends the faithful followers of the Lord, keeps a promise even if it ruins him,

Ps 26:4. I do not have fellowship with tricky, two-faced men; they are false and hypocritical. [5]I hate the sinners' hangouts and refuse to enter them. [9]Don't treat me as a common sinner or murderer who plots against the innocent and demands bribes.

Ps 28:3. Don't punish me with all the wicked ones who speak so sweetly to their neighbors while planning to murder them.

Ps 31:6. How you hate all those who worship idols, those imitation gods.

Ps 50:18. You see a thief and help him, and spend your time with evil and immoral men.

Ps 84:10. A single day spent in your Temple is better than a thousand anywhere else! I would rather be a doorman of the Temple of my God than live in palaces of wickedness.

Ps 101:4. I will reject all selfishness and stay away from every evil. [7]But I will not allow those who deceive and lie to stay in my house.

Ps 106:34. Nor did Israel destroy the nations in the land as God had told them to, [35]but mingled in among the heathen and learned their evil ways.

Ps 119:115. Begone, you evil-minded men. Don't try to stop me from obeying God's commands.

Ps 120:5, 6. My troubles pile high among these haters of the Lord, these men of Meshech and Kedar. I am tired of being here among these men who hate peace. [7]I am for peace, but they are for war, and my voice goes unheeded in their councils.

Ps 139:19. Surely you will slay the wicked, Lord! Away, bloodthirsty men! Begone! [21]O Lord, shouldn't I hate those who hate you? Shouldn't I be grieved with them? [22]Yes, I hate them, for your enemies are my enemies too.

Ps 141:4. Take away my lust for evil things; don't let me want to be with sinners, doing what they do, sharing their dainties.

Prov 1:10. If young toughs tell you, "Come and join us"—turn your back on them! [14]"Come on, throw in your lot with us; we'll split with you in equal shares." [15]Don't do it, son! Stay far from men like that.

Prov 2:11–13. You will be given the sense to stay away from evil men who want you to be their partners in crime—men who turn from God's ways to walk down dark and evil paths. [16]Only wisdom from the Lord can save a man from the flattery of prostitutes; [19]The men . . . are doomed. None of these men will ever be the same again.

Prov 4:14. Don't do as the wicked do. [15]Avoid their haunts—turn away, go somewhere else.

Prov 5:8. *Run from her! Don't go near her house.*

Prov 12:11. Hard work means prosperity; only a fool idles away his time. [26]The good man asks advice from friends; the wicked plunge ahead—and fall.

Prov 13:20. Be with wise men and become wise. Be with evil men and become evil.

Prov 14:7. If you are looking for advice, stay away from fools.

Prov 16:29. Wickedness loves company—and leads others into sin.

Prov 17:12. It is safer to meet a bear robbed of her cubs than a fool caught in his folly.

Prov 20:19. Don't tell your secrets to a gossip unless you want them broadcast to the world.

Prov 22:5. The rebel walks a thorny, treacherous road; the man who values his soul will stay away. [10]Throw out the mocker, and you will be rid of tension, fighting and quarrels. [24, 25]Keep away from angry, short-tempered men, lest you learn to be like them and endanger your soul.

Prov 23:6. Don't associate with evil men; don't long for their favors and gifts. [20]Don't carouse with drunkards and gluttons, for they are on their way to poverty.

Prov 24:1. Don't envy godless men; don't even enjoy their company.

Prov 28:7. Young men who are wise obey the law; a son who is a member of a lawless gang is a shame to his father. [19]Hard work brings prosperity; playing around brings poverty.

Prov 29:16. When rulers are wicked, their people are too; but good men will live to see the tyrant's downfall. [24]A man who assists a thief must really hate himself! For he knows the consequence but does it anyway.

Eccl 9:18. Wisdom is better than weapons of war, but one rotten apple can spoil a barrelful.

Isa 1:23. Your leaders are rebels, companions of thieves; all of them take bribes and won't defend the widows and orphans.

Isa 6:5. Then I said, "My doom is sealed, for I am a foul-mouthed sinner, a member of a sinful, foul-mouthed race; and I have looked upon the King, the Lord of heaven's armies."

Isa 8:11. The Lord has said in strongest terms: Do not under any circumstances, go along with the plans of Judah to surrender to Syria and Israel. [12]Don't let people call you a traitor for staying true to God. Don't you panic as so many of your neighbors are doing when they think of Syria and Israel attacking them.

Jer 2:25. Why don't you turn from all this weary running after other gods? But you say, "Don't waste your breath. I've fallen in love with these strangers and I can't stop loving them now!"

Jer 9:2. Oh, that I could go away and forget them and live in some wayside shack in the desert, for they are all adulterous, treacherous men.

Jer 15:17. I have not joined the people in their merry feasts. I sit alone beneath the hand of God.

Jer 51:6. Flee from Babylon! Save yourselves! Don't get trapped! If you stay, you will be destroyed when God takes his vengeance on all of Babylon's sins. [45]O my people, flee from Babylon; save yourselves from the fierce anger of the Lord.

Hos 4:17. Stay away from her, for she is wedded to idolatry.

Hos 7:5. On the king's birthday, the princes get him drunk; he makes a fool of himself and drinks with those who mock him. [8]My people mingle with the heathen, picking up their evil ways; thus they become as good-for-nothing as a half-baked cake! [9]Worshiping foreign gods has sapped their strength, but they don't know it. Ephraim's hair is turning gray, and he doesn't even realize how weak and old he is.

Mic 6:16. The only commands you keep are those of Omri; the only example you follow is that of Ahab! Therefore I will make an awesome example of you—I will destroy you. I will make you the laughingstock of the world; all who see you will snicker and sneer!

Mt 24:12. Sin will be rampant everywhere and will cool the love of many.

Rom 16:17. And now there is one more thing to say before I end this letter. Stay away from those who cause divisions and are upsetting people's faith, teaching things about Christ that are contrary to what you have been taught. [18]Such teachers are not working for our Lord Jesus, but only want gain for themselves. They are good speakers, and simple-minded people are often fooled by them.

1 Cor 5:6. What a terrible thing it is that you are boasting about your purity, and yet you let this sort of thing go on. Don't you realize that if even one person is allowed to go on sinning, soon all will be affected? [9]When I wrote to you before I said not to mix with evil people. [10]But when I said that I wasn't talking about unbelievers who live in sexual sin, or are greedy cheats and thieves and idol worshipers. For you can't live in this world without being with people like that. [11]What I meant was that you are not to keep company with anyone who claims to be a brother Christian but indulges in sexual sins, or is greedy, or is a swindler, or worships idols, or is a drunkard, or abusive. Don't even

eat lunch with such a person. Gal 5:9.

1 Cor 15:33. Don't be fooled by those who say such things. If you listen to them you will start acting like them.

2 Cor 6:14. Don't be teamed with those who do not love the Lord, for what do the people of God have in common with the people of sin? How can light live with darkness? [15]And what harmony can there be between Christ and the devil? How can a Christian be a partner with one who doesn't believe? [17]That is why the Lord has said, "Leave them; separate yourselves from them; don't touch their filthy things, and I will welcome you."

Eph 5:6. Don't be fooled by those who try to excuse these sins, for the terrible wrath of God is upon all those who do them. [7]Don't even associate with such people. [11]Take no part in the worthless pleasures of evil and darkness, but instead, rebuke and expose them.

2 Thess 3:6. Now here is a command, dear brothers, given in the name of our Lord Jesus Christ by his authority: Stay away from any Christian who spends his days in laziness and does not follow the ideal of hard work we set up for you.

1 Tim 5:22. Never be in a hurry about choosing a pastor; you may overlook his sins and it will look as if you approve of them. Be sure that you yourself stay away from all sin.

1 Tim 6:5. These arguers—their minds warped by sin—don't know how to tell the truth; to them the Good News is just a means of making money. Keep away from them.

2 Tim 3:4. They will betray their friends; they will be hot-headed, puffed up with pride, and prefer good times to worshiping God. [5]They will go to church, yes, but they won't really believe anything they hear. Don't be taken in by people like that.

2 Pet 2:7, 8. But at the same time the Lord rescued Lot out of Sodom because he was a good man, sick of the terrible wickedness he saw everywhere around him day after day. [18]They proudly boast about their sins and conquests, and, using lust as their bait, they lure back into sin those who have just escaped from such wicked living.

2 Jn 1:10. If anyone comes to teach you, and he doesn't believe what Christ taught, don't even invite him into your home. Don't encourage him in any way. [11]If you do you will be a partner with him in his wickedness.

Rev 2:2. I know how many good things you are doing. I have watched your hard work and your patience; I know you don't tolerate sin among your members, and you have carefully examined the claims of those who say they are apostles but aren't. You have found out how they lie.

Rev 18:4. Then I heard another voice calling from heaven, "Come away from her, my people; do not take part in her sins, or you will be punished with her."

GOOD. Prov 13:20. Be with wise men and become wise. Be with evil men and become evil.

See *Communion of Saints; Example; Fellowship; Influence.*

COMPASSION OF GOD. See *God, Mercy of.*

OF CHRIST. See *Jesus, Compassion of.*

COMPLAINT See *Murmuring.*

COMPLICITY Ps 50:18. You see a thief and help him, and spend your time with evil and immoral men.

Prov 29:24. A man who assists a thief must really hate himself! For he knows the consequence but does it anyway.

Rom 1:32. They were fully aware of God's death penalty for these crimes, yet they went right ahead and did them anyway, and encouraged others to do them, too.

2 Jn 1:10. If anyone comes to teach you, and he doesn't believe what Christ taught, don't even invite him into your home. Don't encourage him in any way.

INSTANCES OF. The daughter of Herodias, in asking for the head of John the Baptist, Mt 14:8; Mk 6:24. Pilate, in the death of Jesus, Mt 27:17–26; Mk 15:9–15; Lk 23:13–25; Jn 19:13–16. Paul, in the stoning of Stephen, Acts 7:58.

See *Collusion; Connivance; Conspiracy.*

COMPROMISE BEFORE LITIGATION, COMMANDED. Prov 25:8–10. Don't be hot-headed and rush to court! You may start something you can't finish and go down before your neighbor in shameful defeat. So discuss the matter with him privately. Don't tell anyone else, lest he accuse you of slander and you can't withdraw what you said.

Lk 12:58. If you meet your accuser on the way to court, try to settle the matter before it reaches the judge, lest he sentence you to jail; [59]for if that happens you won't be free again until the last penny is paid in full. Mt 5:25, 26.

See *Adjudication; Arbitration; Justice; Court.*

CONANIAH Name of two Levites, 2 Chron 31:12, 13; 35:9.

CONCEIT Ps 36:2. Instead, in their conceit, they think they can hide their evil deeds and not get caught.

Ps 101:5. I will not tolerate anyone who secretly slanders his neighbors; I will not permit conceit and pride.

Prov 3:5. Then trust the Lord completely; don't ever trust yourself. [7]Don't be conceited, sure of your own wisdom.

Prov 12:15. A fool thinks he needs no advice, but a wise man listens to others.

Prov 26:4, 5. When arguing with a rebel, don't use foolish arguments as he does, or you will become as foolish as he is! Prick his conceit with silly replies! [12]There is one thing worse than a fool, and that is a man who is conceited. [16]Yet in his own opinion he is smarter than seven wise men.

Prov 28:11. Rich men are conceited, but their real poverty is evident to the poor. [26]A man is a fool to trust himself! But those who use God's wisdom are safe.

Isa 5:21. Woe to those who are wise and shrewd in their own eyes!

Jer 9:23. The Lord says: Let not the wise man bask in his wisdom, nor the mighty man in his might, nor the rich man in his riches.

Lk 18:11. The proud Pharisee "prayed" this prayer: "Thank God, I am not a sinner like everyone else, especially like that tax collector over there! For I never cheat, I don't commit adultery, [12]I go without food twice a week, and I give to God a tenth of everything I earn."

Rom 1:22. Claiming themselves to be wise without God, they became utter fools instead.

Rom 11:25. I want you to know about this truth from God, dear brothers, so that you will not feel proud and start bragging. Yes, it is true that some of the Jews have set themselves against the Gospel now, but this will last only until all of you Gentiles have come to Christ—those of you who will.

Rom 12:16. Work happily together. Don't try to act big. Don't try to get into the good graces of important people, but enjoy the company of ordinary folks. And don't think you know it all! 1 Cor 5:2.

2 Cor 12:20. For I am afraid that when I come to visit you I won't like what I find, and then you won't like the way I will have to act. I am afraid that I will find you . . . filled with conceit and disunity.

See *Hypocrisy; Pride.*

CONCEPTION MIRACULOUS. By Sarah, Gen 21:1, 2; Rebekah, Gen 25:21; Rachel, Gen 30:22; Manoah's wife, Judg 13:2–24; Hannah, 1 Sam 1:19, 20; Elizabeth, Lk 1:24, 25, 36, 37, 58; Mary, Mt 1:18, 20; Lk 1:31–35.

CONCUBINAGE LAWS CONCERNING. Ex 21:7–11; Lev 19:20–22; Deut 21:10–14. Concubines might be dismissed, Gen 21:9–14. Called *wives,* Gen 37:2; Judg 19:3–5. Children of, not heirs, Gen 15:4; 21:10; 25:6.

Practiced by Abraham, Gen 16:2, 3; 25:6; 1 Chron 1:32; Nahor, Gen 22:24; Jacob, Gen 30:4; Eliphaz, Gen 36:10–12; Gideon, Judg 8:31; a Levite, Judg 19:1; Caleb, 1 Chron 2:46–49; Manasseh, 1 Chron 7:14; Saul, 2 Sam 3:7; David, 2 Sam 5:13; 15:16; Solomon, 1 Kgs 11:3; Rehoboam, 2 Chron 11:21; Abijah, 2 Chron 13:21; Belshazzar, Dan 5:2–4.

See *Marriage; Polygamy.*

CONCUPISCENCE See *Lasciviousness.*

CONDEMNATION, SELF See *Self-condemnation.*

CONDESCENSION OF GOD In reasoning with his creatures: States his reasons for sending the flood, Gen 6:11–13. Enters into covenant with Abraham, Gen 15:1–21; 18:1–21. Indulges Abraham's intercession for Sodom, Gen 18:22–33. Warns Abimelech in a dream, Gen 20:3–7. Reasons with Moses, Ex 4:2–17. Sends meat and bread to the Israelites in response to their complaints, Ex 16:12. Indulges Gideon's tests, Judg 6:36–40. Reasons with Job, Job 38; 39; 40; 41. Moses' prayer to see his glory, Ex 33:18–23. Invites sinners, saying, "Come, let's talk this over," Isa 1:18–20. Remonstrates a backsliding Israel, Isa 41:21–24; 43:1–19; 65:1–16; Jer 3:1–15; 4:1–31; 7:1–34; Ezk 18:25–32; 33:10–20; Hos 2; Mic 6:1–9; Mal 3:7–15.

SCRIPTURES RELATING TO. Ps 8:4. I cannot understand how you can bother with mere puny man, to pay any attention to him! [5]And yet you have made him only a little lower than the angels, and placed a crown of glory and honor upon his head. [6]You have put him in charge of everything you made; everything is put under his authority.

Ps 113:5. Who can be compared with God enthroned on high? [6]Far below him are the heavens and the earth; he stoops to look.

Ps 144:3. O Lord, what is man that you even notice him? Why bother at all with the human race?

Isa 45:11. Jehovah, the Holy One of Israel, Israel's Creator, says: What right have you to question what I do? Who are you to command me concerning the work of my hands?

Jn 3:16. For God loved the world so much that he gave his only Son so that anyone who believes in him shall not perish but have eternal life.

Rom 5:8. But God showed his great love for us by sending Christ to die for us while we were still sinners.

Heb 2:11. We who have been made holy by Jesus, now have the same Father he has. That is why Jesus is not ashamed to call us his brothers.

Heb 6:17. God also bound himself with an oath, so that those he promised to help would be perfectly sure and never need to wonder whether he might change his plans. [18]He has given us both his promise and his oath, two things we can completely count on, for it is impossible for God to tell a lie. Now all those who flee to him to save them can take new courage when they hear such assurances from God; now they can know without doubt that he will give them the salvation he has promised them.

1 Jn 4:10. In this act we see what real love is: it is not our love for God, but his love for us when he sent his Son to satisfy God's anger against our sins. [19]So you see, our love for him comes as a result of his loving us first.

CONDOLENCE INSTANCES OF. David, to Hanun, 2 Sam 10:2. Merodach-baladan, to Hezekiah, 2 Kgs 20:12, 13. The three friends of, to Job, Job 2:11. Jesus, to Mary and Martha, Jn 11:23–35.

See *Affliction, Comfort in; Sympathy.*

CONEY Lev 11:4–7; Deut 14:7.

See *Cliff Badger; Rock Badger.*

CONFEDERACIES INSTANCES OF. Of kings, Gen 14:1, 2; Josh 10:1–5; 11:1–5; 1 Kgs 20:1.

See *Alliances.*

CONFESSION OF CHRIST. Mt 7:21. Not all who sound religious are really godly people. They may refer to me as "Lord," but still won't get to heaven. For the decisive question is whether they obey my Father in heaven. [22]At the Judgment many will tell me, "Lord, Lord, we told others about you and used your name to cast out demons and to do many other great miracles." [23]But I will reply, "You have never been mine. Go away, for your deeds are evil."

Mt 10:32. If anyone publicly acknowledges me as his friend, I will openly acknowledge him as my friend before my father in heaven. [33]But if anyone publicly denies me, I will openly deny him before my Father in heaven. Lk 12:8.

Jn 1:15. John pointed him out to the people, telling the crowds, "This is the one I was talking about when I said, 'Someone is coming who is greater by far than I am—for he existed long before I did!' " [16]We have all benefited from the rich blessings he brought to us—blessing upon blessing heaped upon us! [17]For Moses gave us only the Law with its rigid demands and merciless justice, while Jesus Christ brought us loving forgiveness as well. [18]No one has ever actually seen God, but, of course, his only Son has, for he is the companion of the Father and has told us all about him. Mt 3:11.

Jn 9:22, 23. They said this in fear of the Jewish leaders who had announced that anyone saying Jesus was the Messiah would be excommunicated. [24]So for the second time they called in the man who had been blind and told him, "Give the glory to God, not to Jesus, for we know Jesus is an evil person." [25]"I don't know whether he is good or bad," the man replied, "but I know this: *I was blind, and now I see!*" [26]"But what did he do?" they asked. "How did he heal you?" [27]"Look!" the man exclaimed. "I told you once; didn't you listen? Why do you want to hear it again? Do you want to become his disciples too?" [28]Then they cursed him and said, "You are his disciple, but we are disciples of Moses. [29]We know God has spoken to Moses, but as for this fellow, we don't know anything about him." [30]"Why, that's very strange!" the man replied. "He can heal blind men, and yet you don't know anything about him! [31]Well, God doesn't listen to evil men, but he has open ears to those who worship him and do his will. [32]Since the world began there has never been anyone who could open the eyes of someone born blind. [33]If this man were not from God, he couldn't do it." [34]"You illegitimate bastard, you!" they shouted. "Are you trying to teach *us?*" And they threw him out. [35]When Jesus heard what had happened, he found the man and said, "Do you believe in the Messiah?" [36]The man answered, "Who is he, sir, for I want to." [37]"You have seen him," Jesus said, "and he is speaking to you!" [38]"Yes, Lord," the man said, "I believe!" And he worshiped Jesus.

Jn 12:42. However, even many of the Jewish leaders believed him to be the Messiah but wouldn't admit it to anyone because of their fear that the Pharisees would excommunicate them from the synagogue; [43]for they loved the praise of men more than the praise of God.

Acts 8:35. So Philip began with this same Scripture and then used many others to tell him about Jesus. [36]As they rode along, they came to a small body of water, and the eunuch said, "Look! Water! Why can't I be baptized?" [37]"You can," Philip answered, "if you believe with all your heart." And the eunuch replied, "I believe that Jesus Christ is the Son of God."

Acts 18:5. And after the arrival of Silas and Timothy from Macedonia, Paul spent his full time preaching and testifying to the Jews that Jesus is the Messiah.

Acts 19:4. Then Paul pointed out to them that John's baptism was to demonstrate a desire to turn from sin to God and that those receiving his baptism must then go on to believe in Jesus, the one John said would come later. [5]As soon as they heard this, they were baptized in the name of the Lord Jesus.

Rom 10:9. For if you tell others with your own mouth that Jesus Christ is your Lord, and believe in your own heart that God has raised him from the dead, you will be saved. [10]For it is by believing in his heart that a man becomes right with God; and with his mouth he tells others of his faith, confirming his salvation. [11]For the Scriptures tell us that no one who believes in Christ will ever be disappointed.

1 Cor 12:3. But now you are meeting people who claim to speak messages from the Spirit of God. How can you know whether they are really inspired by God or whether they are fakes? Here is the test: no one speaking by the power of the Spirit of God can curse Jesus, and no one can say, "Jesus is Lord," and really mean it, unless the Holy Spirit is helping him.

1 Jn 1:6. So if we say we are his friends, but go on living in spiritual darkness and sin, we are lying.

1 Jn 2:4. Someone may say, "I am a Christian; I am on my way to heaven; I belong to Christ." But if he doesn't do what Christ tells him to, he is a liar.

1 Jn 4:2. And the way to find out if their message is from the Holy Spirit is to ask: Does it really agree that Jesus Christ, God's Son, actually became man with a human body? If so, then the message is from God. [3]If not, the message is not from God but from one who is against Christ, like the "Antichrist" you have heard about who is going to come, and his attitude of enmity against Christ is already abroad in the world.

15. Anyone who believes and says that Jesus is the Son of God has God living in him, and he is living with God.

OF SIN. See *Sin, Confession of.*

CONFIDENCE BETRAYED.

Instances of. Joshua, by the Gibeonites, Josh 9:3–15. Eglon, by Ehud, Judg 3:15–23. Ahimelech, by David, 1 Sam 21:1–9. Abner, by Joab, 2 Sam 3:27. Amasa, by Joab, 2 Sam 20:8–10. The worshipers of Baal, by Jehu, 2 Kgs 10:18–28.

See *Betrayal.*

FALSE. Deut 29:18. The day that any of you—man or woman, family or tribe of Israel—begins to turn away from the Lord our God and desires to worship these gods of other nations, that day a root will be planted that will grow bitter and poisonous fruit. [19]Let no one blithely think, when he hears the warnings of this curse, "I shall prosper even though I walk in my own stubborn way!"

1 Kgs 20:11. The king of Israel retorted, "Don't count your chickens before they hatch!"

2 Kgs 18:21. If you lean on Egypt, you will find her to be a stick that breaks beneath your weight and pierces your hand. The Egyptian Pharaoh is totally unreliable! Isa 36:6.

Job 11:20. But the wicked shall find no way to escape; their only hope is death.

Job 15:31. Let him no longer trust in foolish riches; let him no longer deceive himself, for the money he trusts in will be his only reward.

Job 29:18. I thought, "Surely I shall die quietly in my nest after a long, good life."

Ps 10:6. They boast that neither God nor man can ever keep them down—somehow they'll find a way!

Ps 20:7. Some nations boast of armies and of weaponry, but our boast is in the Lord our God.
[8]Those nations will collapse and perish; we will arise to stand firm and sure!

Ps 30:6. In my prosperity I said, "This is forever; nothing can stop me now! The Lord has shown me his favor. He has made me steady as a mountain."

Ps 33:16, 17. The best-equipped army cannot save a king—for great strength is not enough to save anyone. A war horse is a poor risk for winning victories—it is strong but it cannot save.

Ps 36:2. Instead, in their conceit, they think they can hide their evil deeds and not get caught.

Ps 44:6. I do not trust my weapons. They could never save me.

Ps 49:6. They trust in their wealth and boast
about how rich they are, [7]yet not one of them, though rich as kings, can ransom his own brother from the penalty of sin! For God's forgiveness does not come that way.

Ps 52:7. See what happens to those who despise God and trust in their wealth, and become ever more bold in their wickedness.

Ps 60:11. Yes, Lord, help us against our enemies, for man's help is useless. Ps 108:12.

Prov 14:16. A wise man is cautious and avoids danger; a fool plunges ahead with great confidence.

Prov 16:25. Before every man there lies a wide and pleasant road he thinks is right, but it ends in death.

Prov 18:11. The rich man thinks of his wealth as an impregnable defense, a high wall of safety. What a dreamer!

Prov 26:12. There is one thing worse than a fool, and that is a man who is conceited.

Prov 28:26. A man is a fool to trust himself! But those who use God's wisdom are safe.

Isa 2:22. Puny man! Frail as his breath! Don't ever put your trust in him!

Isa 5:21. Woe to those who are wise and shrewd in their own eyes!

Isa 9:8–10. The Lord has spoken out against that braggart Israel who says that though our land lies in ruins now, we will rebuild it better than before. The sycamore trees are cut down, but we will replace them with cedars!

Isa 22:11. Between the city walls you build a reservoir for water from the lower pool! But all your feverish plans will not avail, for you never ask for help from God, who lets this come upon you. He is the one who planned it long ago.

Isa 28:15. You have struck a bargain with Death, you say, and sold yourselves to the devil in exchange for his protection against the Assyrians. "They can never touch us," you say, "for we are under the care of one who will deceive and fool them."

18. I will cancel your agreement of compromise with Death and the devil, so when the terrible enemy floods in, you will be trampled into the ground.

Isa 30:1. Woe to my rebellious children, says the Lord; you ask advice from everyone but me, and decide to do what I don't want you to do. You yoke yourselves with unbelievers, thus piling up your
sins. [2]For without consulting me you have gone down to Egypt to find aid and have put your trust in Pharaoh for his protection.

5. Yet it will all turn out to your shame—he
won't help one little bit! [7]For Egypt's promises are worthless! "The Reluctant Dragon," I call her! Isa 20:5, 6.

10. They tell my prophets, "Shut up—we don't want any more of your reports!" Or they say, "Don't tell us the truth; tell us nice things; tell us
lies." [15]For the Lord God, the Holy One of Israel, says: Only in returning to me and waiting for me will you be saved; in quietness and confidence is
your strength; but you'll have none of this. [16]"No," you say. "We will get our help from Egypt; they will give us swift horses for riding to battle." But the only swiftness you are going to see is the swiftness of your enemies chasing you!

Isa 31:1. Woe to those who run to Egypt for help, trusting their mighty cavalry and chariots instead of looking to the Holy One of Israel and consulting
him. [3]For these Egyptians are mere men, not God! Their horses are puny flesh, not mighty spirits! When the Lord clenches his fist against them, they will stumble and fall among those they are trying to help. All will fail together.

Isa 47:7. You thought your reign would never end, Queen Kingdom of the world. You didn't care a whit about my people or think about the fate of those who do them harm.

8. O pleasure-mad kingdom, living at ease, bragging as the greatest in the world—listen to the sentence of my court upon your sins. You say, "I alone am God! I'll never be a widow; I'll never lose
my children." [10]You felt secure in all your wickedness. "No one sees me," you said. Your "wisdom" and "knowledge" have caused you to turn away from me and claim that you yourself are Jehovah.

Isa 56:12. "Come," they say. "We'll get some wine and have a party; let's all get drunk. This is really living; let it go on and on, and tomorrow will be better yet!"

Isa 57:13. Let's see if the whole collection of your idols can help you when you cry to them to save you! They are so weak that the wind can carry them off! A breath can puff them away. But he who trusts in me shall possess the land and inherit my Holy Mountain.

Jer 2:13. For my people have done two evil things: They have forsaken me, the Fountain of Life-giving Water; and they have built for themselves broken cisterns that can't hold water!

18. What have you gained by your alliances with Egypt and with Assyria? [22]No amount of soap or lye can make you clean. You are stained with guilt that cannot ever be washed away. I see it always before me, the Lord God says. [23]You say it isn't so, that you haven't worshiped idols? How can you say a thing like that? Go and look in any valley in the land! Face the awful sins that you have done, O restless female camel, seeking for a male! [37]You will be left in despair, and cover your face with your hands, for the Lord has rejected the ones that you trust. You will not succeed despite their aid.

Jer 3:23. We are weary of worshiping idols on the hills and of having orgies on the mountains. It is all a farce. Only in the Lord our God can Israel ever find her help and her salvation.

Jer 5:17. And they shall sack your walled cities that you think are safe.

Jer 6:14. You can't heal a wound by saying it's not there! Yet the priests and prophets give assurances of peace when all is war. Jer 8:11.

Jer 7:8. You think that because the Temple is here, you will never suffer? Don't fool yourselves!

Jer 12:5. The Lord replied to me: If racing with mere men—these men of Anathoth—has wearied you, how will you race against horses, against the king, his court and all his evil priests? If you stumble and fall on open ground, what will you do in Jordan's jungles?

Jer 14:13. Then I said, O Lord God, their prophets are telling them that all is well—that no war or famine will come. They tell the people you will surely send them peace, that you will bless them.

Jer 17:5. The Lord says: Cursed is the man who puts his trust in mortal man and turns his heart away from God.

Jer 21:13. I will fight against the city of Jerusalem, which boasts, "We are safe; no one can touch us here!"

Jer 23:17. They keep saying to these rebels who despise me, "Don't worry! All is well"; and to those who live the way they want to, "The Lord has said you shall have peace!"

Jer 48:7. For you trusted in your wealth and skill; therefore you shall perish. Your god Chemosh, with his priests and princes, shall be taken away to distant lands! [11]From her earliest history Moab has lived there undisturbed from all invasions. She is like wine that has not been poured from flask to flask, and is fragrant and smooth. But now she shall have the pouring out of exile!

Jer 49:4. You are proud of your fertile valleys, but they will soon be ruined. O wicked daughter, you trusted in your wealth and thought no one could ever harm you. [5]But see, I will bring terror upon you, says the Lord God of Hosts. For all your neighbors shall drive you from your land and none shall help your exiles as they flee.

Lam 4:17. We look for our allies to come and save us, but we look in vain. The nation we expected most to help us makes no move at all.

Ezk 8:12. Then the Lord said to me: "Son of dust, have you seen what the elders of Israel are doing in their minds? For they say, 'The Lord doesn't see us; he has gone away!' "

Ezk 13:10. For these evil men deceive my people by saying, "God will send peace," when that is not my plan at all! My people build a flimsy wall and these prophets praise them for it—and cover it with whitewash! [11]Tell these evil builders that their wall will fall. A heavy rainstorm will undermine it; great hailstones and mighty winds will knock it down.

Ezk 29:6. Because of the way your might collapsed when Israel called on you for aid [instead of trusting me], all of you shall know I am the Lord. [7]Israel leaned on you but, like a cracked staff, you snapped beneath her hand and wrenched her shoulder out of joint and made her stagger with the pain.

Ezk 30:8. And they will know I am the Lord when I have set Egypt on fire and destroyed her allies.

Hos 5:13. When Ephraim and Judah see how sick they are, Ephraim will turn to Assyria, to the great king there, but he can neither help nor cure.

Hos 7:9. Worshiping foreign gods has sapped their strength, but they don't know it. Ephraim's hair is turning gray, and he doesn't even realize how weak and old he is. [11]Ephraim is a silly, witless dove, calling to Egypt, flying to Assyria. *vs.* 11–16.

Hos 10:13. But you have cultivated wickedness and raised a thriving crop of sins. You have earned the full reward of trusting in a lie—believing that military might and great armies can make a nation safe!

Hos 12:1. Israel is chasing the wind, yes, shepherding a whirlwind—a dangerous game! For she has given gifts to Egypt and Assyria to get their help, and in return she gets their worthless promises.

Hos 14:3. Assyria cannot save us, nor can our strength in battle; never again will we call the idols we have made "our gods"; for in you alone, O Lord, the fatherless find mercy.

Amos 6:1. Woe to those lounging in luxury at Jerusalem and Samaria, so famous and popular among the people of Israel. [3]You push away all thought of punishment awaiting you, but by your deeds you bring the Day of Judgment near. [*vs.* 1–7.] [13]And just as stupid is your rejoicing in how great you are, when you are less than nothing! And priding yourselves on your own tiny power!

Amos 9:10. But all these sinners who say, "God will not touch us," will die by the sword.

Obd 1:3. You are proud because you live in those high, inaccessible cliffs. "Who can ever reach us way up here!" you boast. Don't fool yourselves!

Mic 3:11. You leaders who take bribes; you priests and prophets who won't preach until you're paid. (And yet you fawn upon the Lord and say, "All is well—the Lord is here among us. No harm can come to us.")

Zeph 1:12. I will search with lanterns in Jerusalem's darkest corners to find and punish those who sit contented in their sins, indifferent to God, thinking he will let them alone.

Zeph 2:15. This is the fate of that vast, prosperous city that lived in such security, that said to herself, "In all the world there is no city as great as I." But now—see how she has become a place of utter ruins, a place for animals to live! Everyone passing that way will mock, or shake his head in disbelief.

Zech 4:6. Then he said, "This is God's message to Zerubbabel. 'Not by might, nor by power, but by my Spirit, says the Lord of Hosts—you will succeed because of my Spirit, though you are few and weak.' "

Mt 25:5. So, when the bridegroom was delayed, they lay down to rest.

Mk 10:24. This amazed them. So Jesus said it again: "Dear children, how hard it is for those who trust in riches to enter the Kingdom of God."

Mk 14:29. Peter said to him, "I will never desert you no matter what the others do!" [30]"Peter," Jesus said, "before the cock crows a second time tomorrow morning you will deny me three times." [31]"No!" Peter exploded. "Not even if I have to die with you! I'll *never* deny you!" And all the others vowed the same. Mt 26:33–35; Lk 22:33, 34; Jn 13: 37, 38.

Lk 12:19. "And I'll sit back and say to myself, 'Friend, you have enough stored away for years to come. Now take it easy! Wine, women, and song for you!' " [20]But God said to him, "Fool! Tonight you die. Then who will get it all?"

Lk 17:26. [When I return] the world will be [as indifferent to the things of God] as the people were in Noah's day. [27]They ate and drank and married —everything just as usual right up to the day when Noah went into the ark and the flood came and destroyed them all. [28]And the world will be as it was in the days of Lot: people went about their daily business—eating and drinking, buying and selling, farming and building—[29]until the morning Lot left Sodom. Then fire and brimstone rained down from heaven and destroyed them all. [30]Yes, it will be "business as usual" right up to the hour of my return.

Lk 18:9. Then he told this story to some who boasted of their virtue and scorned everyone else: [10]"Two men went to the Temple to pray. One was a proud, self-righteous Pharisee, and the other a cheating tax collector. [11]The proud Pharisee 'prayed' this prayer: 'Thank God, I am not a sinner like everyone else, especially like that tax collector over there! For I never cheat, I don't commit adultery, [12]I go without food twice a week, and I give to God a tenth of everything I earn.' [13]But the corrupt tax collector stood at a distance and dared not even lift his eyes to heaven as he prayed, but beat upon his chest in sorrow, exclaiming, 'God, be merciful to me, a sinner.' [14]I tell you, this sinner, not the Pharisee, returned home forgiven! For the proud shall be humbled, but the humble shall be honored."

Jn 5:45. Yet it is not I who will accuse you of this to the Father—Moses will! Moses, on whose laws you set your hopes of heaven.

Rom 2:3. Do you think that God will judge and condemn others for doing them and overlook you when you do them, too?

Rom 12:16. Work happily together. Don't try to act big. Don't try to get into the good graces of important people, but enjoy the company of ordinary folks. And don't think you know it all!

1 Cor 3:21. So don't be proud of following the wise men of this world. For God has already given you everything you need.

2 Cor 1:9. We felt we were doomed to die and saw how powerless we were to help ourselves; but that was good, for then we put everything into the hands of God, who alone could save us, for he can even raise the dead.

Gal 6:7. Don't be misled; remember that you can't ignore God and get away with it: a man will always reap just the kind of crop he sows! [8]If he sows to please his own wrong desires, he will be planting seeds of evil and he will surely reap a harvest of spiritual decay and death; but if he plants the good things of the Spirit, he will reap the everlasting life which the Holy Spirit gives him.

1 Thess 5:3. When people are saying, "All is well, everything is quiet and peaceful"—then, all of a sudden, disaster will fall upon them as suddenly as a woman's birth pains begin when her child is born. And these people will not be able to get away anywhere—there will be no place to hide.

1 Tim 6:17. Tell those who are rich not to be proud and not to trust in their money, which will soon be gone, but their pride and trust should be in the living God who always richly gives us all we need for our enjoyment.

Jas 4:13. Look here, you people who say, "Today or tomorrow we are going to such and such a town, stay there a year, and open up a profitable business." [14]How do you know what is going to happen tomorrow? For the length of your lives is as uncertain as the morning fog—now you see it; soon it is gone. [15]What you ought to say is, "If the Lord wants us to, we shall live and do this or that."

Rev 18:7. She has lived in luxury and pleasure—match it now with torments and with sorrows. She boasts, "I am queen upon my throne. I am no helpless widow. I will not experience sorrow." [8]Therefore the sorrows of death and mourning and famine shall overtake her in a single day, and she shall be utterly consumed by fire; for mighty is the Lord who judges her.

See *Blindness, Spiritual; Conceit.*

INSTANCES OF. Builders of Babel, Gen 11:3,4. Saul, 1 Sam 13:8–14. Sennacherib, 2 Kgs 19:23. Asa, 2 Chron 16:7–9. Hezekiah, Isa 22:9–11. Jonah, Jon 1:3–5. Peter, Mt 26:33–35; Lk 22:33,34. Paul, Phil 1:25; 2:23, 24.

CONFISCATION Of property: By David, that of Mephibosheth, 2 Sam 16:4. By Ahab, of Naboth's vineyard, 1 Kgs 21:7–16. By Ahasuerus, of Haman's estate, Esther 8:1. As a penalty, Ezra 10: 7, 8.

CONFUSION Of languages, Gen 11:1–9.

CONGREGATION Those who were excluded from, Deut 23:1–3.

See *Church; Visible, Discipline of.*

CONIAH See *Jehoiachin.*

CONNIVANCE Prov 10:10. Winking at sin leads to sorrow; bold reproof leads to peace.

1 Sam 3:11. Then the Lord said to Samuel, "I am going to do a shocking thing in Israel. [12]I am going to do all of the dreadful things I warned Eli about. [13]I have continually threatened him and his entire family with punishment because his sons are blaspheming God, and he doesn't stop them.

See *Collusion; Complicity; Conspiracy.*

CONSCIENCE Job 15:21. He is surrounded by terrors, and if there are good days they will soon be gone. [24]He lives in fear, distress, and anguish. His enemies conquer him as a king defeats his foes.

Job 27:6. I am *not* a sinner—I repeat it again and again. My conscience is clear for as long as I live.

Prov 20:27. A man's conscience is the Lord's searchlight exposing his hidden motives. 1 Cor 4:4.

Mt 6:22. If your eye is pure, there will be sunshine in your soul. [23]But if your eye is clouded with evil thoughts and desires, you are in deep spiritual darkness. And oh, how deep that darkness can be!

Lk 11:33. No one lights a lamp and hides it! Instead, he puts it on a lampstand to give light to all who enter the room. [Mt 5:15, 16.] [34]Your eyes light up your inward being. A pure eye lets sunshine into your soul. A lustful eye shuts out the light and plunges you into darkness. [Mt 6:22.] [35]So watch out that the sunshine isn't blotted out. [36]If you are filled with light within, with no dark corners, then your face will be radiant too, as though a floodlight is beamed upon you.

Acts 23:1. Gazing intently at the Council, Paul began: "Brothers, I have always lived before God in all good conscience!"

Acts 24:16. Because of this I try with all my strength to always maintain a clear conscience before God and man.

Rom 2:12–15. He will punish sin wherever it is found. He will punish the heathen when they sin, even though they never had God's written laws, for down in their hearts they know right from wrong. God's laws are written within them; their own conscience accuses them, or sometimes excuses them. And God will punish the Jews for sinning because they have his written laws but don't obey them. They know what is right but don't do it. After all, salvation is not given to those who know what to do, unless they do it.

Rom 7:15. I don't understand myself at all, for I really want to do what is right, but I can't. I do what I don't want to—what I hate. [16]I know perfectly well that what I am doing is wrong, and my bad conscience proves that I agree with these laws I am breaking. [17]But I can't help myself, because I'm no longer doing it. It is sin inside me that is stronger than I am that makes me do these evil things. [18]I know I am rotten through and through so far as my old sinful nature is concerned. No matter which way I turn I can't make myself do right. I want to but I can't. [19]When I want to do good, I don't; and when I try not to do wrong, I do it anyway. [20]Now if I am doing what I don't want to, it is plain where the trouble is: sin still has me in its evil grasp. [21]It seems to be a fact of life that when I want to do what is right, I inevitably do what is wrong. [22]I love to do God's will so far as my new nature is concerned; [23-25]but there is something else deep within me, in my lower nature, that is at war with my mind and wins the fight and makes me a slave to the sin that is still within me. In my mind I want to be God's willing servant but instead I find myself still enslaved to sin.

Rom 14:1. Give a warm welcome to any brother who wants to join you, even though his faith is weak. Don't criticize him for having different ideas from yours about what is right and wrong. [2]For instance, don't argue with him about whether or not to eat meat that has been offered to idols. You may believe there is no harm in this, but the faith of others is weaker; they think it is wrong, and will go without any meat at all and eat vegetables rather than eat that kind of meat. [3]Those who think it is all right to eat such meat must not look down on those who won't. And if you are one of those who won't, don't find fault with those who do. For God has accepted them to be his children. [4]They are God's servants not yours. They are responsible to him, not to you. Let him tell them whether they are right or wrong. And God is able to make them do as they should. [5]Some think that Christians should observe the Jewish holidays as special days to worship God, but others say it is wrong and foolish to go to all that trouble, for every day alike belongs to God. On questions of this kind everyone must decide for himself. [6]If you have special days for worshiping the Lord, you are trying to honor him; you are doing a good thing. So is the person who eats meat that has been offered to idols; he is thankful to the Lord for it; he is doing right. And the person who won't touch such meat, he, too, is anxious to please the Lord, and is thankful. [7]We are not our own bosses to live or die as we ourselves might choose. [8]Living or dying we follow the Lord. Either way we are his. [9]Christ died and rose again for this very purpose, so that he can be our Lord both while we live and when we die. [10]You have no right to criticize your brother or look down on him. Remember, each of us will stand personally before the Judgment Seat of God. [11]For it is written, "As I live," says the Lord, "every knee shall bow to me and every tongue confess to God." [12]Yes, each of us will give an account of himself to God. [13]So don't criticize each other any more. Try instead to live in such a way that you will never make your brother stumble by letting him see you doing something he thinks is wrong. [14]As for myself, I am perfectly sure on the authority of the Lord Jesus that there is nothing really wrong with eating meat that has been offered to idols. But if someone believes it is wrong, then he shouldn't do it because for him it is wrong. [15]And if your brother is bothered by what you eat, you are not acting in love if you go ahead and eat it. Don't let your eating ruin someone for whom Christ died. [16]Don't do anything that will cause criticism against yourself even though you know that what you do is right. [17]For, after all, the important thing for us as Christians is not what we eat or drink but stirring up goodness and peace and joy from the Holy Spirit. [18]If you let Christ be Lord in these affairs, God will be glad; and so will others. [19]In this way aim for harmony in the church and try to build each other up. [20]Don't undo the work of God for a chunk of meat. Remember, there is nothing wrong with the meat, but it is wrong to eat it if it makes another stumble. [21]The right thing to do is to quit eating meat or drinking wine or doing anything else that offends your brother or makes him sin. [22]You may know that there is nothing wrong with what you do, even from God's point of view, but keep it to yourself; don't flaunt your faith in front of others who might be hurt by it. In this situation, happy is the man who does not sin by doing what he knows is right. [23]But anyone who believes that something he wants to do is wrong shouldn't do it. He sins if he does, for he thinks it is wrong, and so for him it *is* wrong. Anything that is done apart from what he feels is right is sin.

1 Cor 8:7. However, some Christians don't realize this. All their lives they have been used to thinking of idols as alive, and have believed that food offered to the idols is really being offered to actual gods. So when they eat such food it bothers them and hurts their tender consciences. [9]But be careful not to use your freedom to eat it, lest you cause some Christian brother to sin whose conscience is weaker than yours. [10]You see, this is what may happen: Someone who thinks it is wrong to eat this food will see you eating at a temple restaurant, for you know there is no harm in it. Then he will become bold enough to do it too, although all the time he still feels it is wrong. [11]So because you "know it is all right to do it," you will be responsible for causing great spiritual damage to a brother with a tender conscience for whom Christ died. [12]And it is a sin against Christ to sin against your brother by encouraging him to do something he thinks is wrong. [13]So if eating meat offered to idols is going to make my brother sin, I'll not eat any of it as long as I live, because I don't want to do this to him. 1 Cor 9:22.

1 Cor 10:27. If someone who isn't a Christian asks you out to dinner, go ahead; accept the invitation if you want to. Eat whatever is on the table and don't ask any questions about it. Then you won't know whether or not it has been used as a sacrifice to idols, and you won't risk having a bad conscience over eating it. [28]But if someone warns you that this meat has been offered to idols, then don't eat it for the sake of the man who told you, and of his conscience. [29]In this case *his* feeling about it is the important thing, not yours. But why, you may ask, must I be guided and limited by what someone else thinks? [30]If I can thank God for the food and enjoy it, why let someone spoil everything just because he thinks I am wrong? [31]Well, I'll tell you why. It is because you must do everything for the glory of God, even your eating and drinking. [32]So don't be a stumbling block to anyone, whether they are Jews or Gentiles or Christians.

2 Cor 1:12. We are so glad that we can say with utter honesty that in all our dealings we have been pure and sincere, quietly depending upon the Lord for his help, and not on our own skills. And that is even more true, if possible, about the way we have acted toward you.

2 Cor 4:2. We do not try to trick people into believing—we are not interested in fooling anyone. We never try to get anyone to believe that the Bible teaches what it doesn't. All such shameful methods we forego. We stand in the presence of God as we speak and so we tell the truth, as all who know us will agree.

2 Cor 5:11. It is because of this solemn fear of the Lord, which is ever present in our minds, that we work so hard to win others. God knows our hearts, that they are pure in this matter, and I hope that, deep within, you really know it too.

1 Tim 1:5. What I am eager for is that all the Christians there will be filled with love that comes from pure hearts, and that their minds will be clean and their faith strong. [19]Cling tightly to your faith in Christ and always keep your conscience clear, doing what you know is right. For some people have disobeyed their consciences and have deliberately done what they knew was wrong. It isn't surprising that soon they lost their faith in Christ after defying God like that.

Heb 9:14. Just think how much more surely the blood of Christ will transform our lives and hearts. His sacrifice frees us from the worry of having to obey the old rules, and makes us want to serve the living God. For by the help of the eternal Holy Spirit, Christ willingly gave himself to God to die for our sins—he being perfect, without a single sin or fault.

Heb 10:22. Let us go right in, to God himself, with true hearts fully trusting him to receive us, because we have been sprinkled with Christ's blood to make us clean, and because our bodies have been washed with pure water.

Heb 13:18. Pray for us, for our conscience is clear and we want to keep it that way.

1 Pet 2:19. Praise the Lord if you are punished for doing right!

1 Pet 3:16. Do what is right; then if men speak against you, calling you evil names, they will become ashamed of themselves for falsely accusing you when you have only done what is good. [21](That, by the way, is what baptism pictures for us: In baptism we show that we have been saved from death and doom by the resurrection of Christ; not

because our bodies are washed clean by the water, but because on being baptized we are turning to God and asking him to cleanse our *hearts* from sin.)

1 Jn 3:20. But if we have bad consciences and feel that we have done wrong, the Lord will surely feel it even more, for he knows everything we do. [21]But, dearly loved friends, if our consciences are clear, we can come to the Lord with perfect assurance and trust.

FAITHFUL.

Instances of. Of Pharaoh, when he took Abraham's wife for a concubine, Gen 12:18, 19. Of Abimelech, when he took Isaac's wife for a concubine, Gen 26:9–11. Of Jacob, in his care of Laban's property, Gen 31:29. Of Joseph, when Potiphar's wife tried to seduce him, Gen 39:7–12. Of Nehemiah, in the matter of taxes, Neh 5:15. Of Daniel, in refusing to eat of the king's food and wine, Dan 1:8. Of Peter, in preaching the whole counsel of God, Acts 4:19, 20; 5:29.

See *Honesty; Integrity.*

GUILTY. Job 15:21. He is surrounded by terrors, and if there are good days they will soon be gone. [24]He lives in fear, distress, and anguish. His enemies conquer him as a king defeats his foes. Prov 5:4.

Ps 51:1. O loving and kind God, have mercy. Have pity upon me and take away the awful stain of my transgressions. [2]Oh, wash me, cleanse me from this guilt. Let me be pure again. [3]For I admit my shameful deed—it haunts me day and night. [4]It is against you and you alone I sinned, and did this terrible thing. You saw it all, and your sentence against me is just. [7]Sprinkle me with the cleansing blood and I shall be clean again. Wash me and I shall be whiter than snow. [8]And after you have punished me, give me back my joy again. [9]Don't keep looking at my sins—erase them from your sight. [10]Create in me a new, clean heart, O God, filled with clean thoughts and right desires. [11]Don't toss me aside, banished forever from your presence. Don't take your Holy Spirit from me. [12]Restore to me again the joy of your salvation, and make me willing to obey you. [13]Then I will teach your ways to other sinners, and they—guilty like me—will repent and return to you. [14, 15]Don't sentence me to death. O my God, you alone can rescue me. Then I will sing of your forgiveness, for my lips will be unsealed—oh, how I will praise you. 1 Cor 14:24.

Ps 73:21. When I saw this, what turmoil filled my heart!

Prov 28:1. The wicked flee when no one is chasing them! But the godly are bold as lions! [17]A murderer's conscience will drive him into hell. Don't stop him!

Isa 59:9. It is because of all this evil that you aren't finding God's blessings; that's why he doesn't punish those who injure you. No wonder you are in darkness when you expected light. No wonder you are walking in the gloom. [10]No wonder you grope like blind men and stumble along in broad daylight, yes, even at brightest noontime, as though it were the darkest night! No wonder you are like corpses when compared with vigorous young men! [11]You roar like hungry bears; you moan with mournful cries like doves. You look for God to keep you, but he doesn't. He has turned away. [12]For your sins keep piling up before the righteous God, and testify against you. Yes, we know what sinners we are. [13]We know our disobedience; we have denied the Lord our God. We know what rebels we are and how unfair we are, for we carefully plan our lies. [14]Our courts oppose the righteous man; fairness is unknown. Truth falls dead in the streets, and justice is outlawed.

Mt 27:3. About that time Judas, who betrayed him, when he saw that Jesus had been condemned to die, changed his mind and deeply regretted what he had done, and brought back the money to the chief priests and other Jewish leaders. [4]"I have sinned," he declared, "for I have betrayed an innocent man." "That's your problem," they retorted. [5]Then he threw the money onto the floor of the Temple and went out and hanged himself.

Mk 6:14. King Herod soon heard about Jesus, for his miracles were talked about everywhere. The king thought Jesus was John the Baptist come back to life again. So the people were saying, "No wonder he can do such miracles." [16]"No," Herod said, "it is John, the man I beheaded. He has come back from the dead." Mt 14:1, 2.

Acts 2:37. These words of Peter's moved them deeply, and they said to him and to the other apostles, "Brothers, what should we do?"

1 Tim 4:2. These teachers will tell lies with straight faces and do it so often that their consciences won't even bother them.

Tit 1:15. A person who is pure of heart sees goodness and purity in everything; but a person whose own heart is evil and untrusting finds evil in everything, for his dirty mind and rebellious heart color all he sees and hears.

Heb 9:14. Just think how much more surely the blood of Christ will transform our lives and hearts. His sacrifice frees us from the worry of having to obey the old rules, and makes us want to serve the living God. For by the help of the eternal Holy Spirit, Christ willingly gave himself to God to die for our sins—he being perfect, without a single sin or fault.

Heb 10:26. If anyone sins deliberately by rejecting the Savior after knowing the truth of forgiveness, this sin is not covered by Christ's death; there is no way to get rid of it. [27]There will be nothing to look forward to but the terrible punishment of God's awful anger which will consume all his enemies.

Instances of. Of Adam and Eve, after they sinned, Gen 3:7, 8. Of Jacob, after he defrauded Esau, Gen 33:1–12. Of Joseph's brothers, Gen 37:26, 27; 42:21; 44:16. Of Pharaoh, after the plagues, Ex 9:27. Of Micah, after stealing, Judg 17:2. Of David, for having cut off Saul's skirt, 1 Sam 24:5;

for having taken a census of Israel, 2 Sam 24:10; 1 Chron 21:1–8; for his adultery and murder of Uriah, Ps 32; 38; 40:11, 12; 51. Of the lepers of Samaria, 2 Kgs 7:8–10. Of the old prophet of Bethel, 1 Kgs 13:29–32. Of Herod, for beheading John the Baptist, Mt 14:2; Lk 9:7. Of Peter, after denying the Lord, Mt 26:75; Mk 14:72; Lk 22:62. Of Judas, after betraying the Lord, Mt 27:3–5. The accusers of the woman caught in adultery, Jn 8:9.

DEAD. Prov 16:25. Before every man there lies a wide and pleasant road he thinks is right, but it ends in death.

Prov 30:20. There is another thing too: how a prostitute can sin and then say, "What's wrong with that?"

Jer 6:15. Were my people ashamed when they worshiped idols? No, not at all—they didn't even blush. Therefore they shall lie among the slain. They shall die beneath my anger.

Amos 6:1. Woe to those lounging in luxury at Jerusalem and Samaria, so famous and popular among the people of Israel. 3You push away all thought of punishment awaiting you, but by your deeds you bring the Day of Judgment near. 4You lie on ivory beds surrounded with luxury, eating the meat of the tenderest lambs and the choicest calves. 5You sing idle songs to the sound of the harp, and fancy yourselves to be as great musicians as King David was. 6You drink wine by the bucketful and perfume yourselves with sweet ointments, caring nothing at all that your brothers need your help.

Jn 16:2. For you will be excommunicated from the synagogues, and indeed the time is coming when those who kill you will think they are doing God a service. 3This is because they have never known the Father or me.

Rom 1:21. Yes, they knew about him all right, but they wouldn't admit it or worship him or even thank him for all his daily care. And after awhile they began to think up silly ideas of what God was like and what he wanted them to do. The result was that their foolish minds became dark and confused. 22Claiming themselves to be wise without God, they became utter fools instead. 23And then, instead of worshiping the glorious, ever-living God, they took wood and stone and made idols for themselves, carving them to look like mere birds and animals and snakes and puny men. 24So God let them go ahead into every sort of sex sin, and do whatever they wanted to—yes, vile and sinful things with each other's bodies. 25Instead of believing what they knew was the truth about God, they deliberately chose to believe lies. So they prayed to the things God made, but wouldn't obey the blessed God who made these things.

Eph 4:17, 18. Let me say this, then, speaking for the Lord: Live no longer as the unsaved do, for they are blinded and confused. Their closed hearts are full of darkness; they are far away from the life of God because they have shut their minds against him, and they cannot understand his ways. 19They don't care anymore about right and wrong and have given themselves over to impure ways. They stop at nothing, being driven by their evil minds and reckless lusts.

1 Tim 4:2. These teachers will tell lies with straight faces and do it so often that their consciences won't even bother them.

Tit 1:15. A person who is pure of heart sees goodness and purity in everything; but a person whose own heart is evil and untrusting finds evil in everything, for his dirty mind and rebellious heart color all he sees and hears.

INSTANCES OF. Naboth's accusers, 1 Kgs 21:13. See *Blindness, Spiritual.*

Tree of Conscience, Gen 2:9, 16, 17.

CONSCIENCE MONEY Judg 17:2, 2 Kgs 12:16; Mt 27:3–5.

See *Money; Sin Money.*

CONSCIENTIOUSNESS See *Integrity.*

CONSCRIPTION Of soldiers, Num 31:4, 5; 1 Sam 8:11; 1 Kgs 12:18; Joel 3:9. Of laborers, 1 Kgs 9:15, 20, 21.

See *Armies.*

CONSECRATED THINGS Laws regarding, Lev 27; Num 18:8–32.

See *Firstborn; First fruits.*

CONSECRATION Of Aaron, see *Aaron.* Of priests, see *Priest.* Of the altar, see *Altar.* Of the Temple, see *Temple, Dedication of.* See also *Offerings.*

PERSONAL. Ps 51:17. It is a broken spirit you want—remorse and penitence. A broken and a contrite heart, O God, you will not ignore.

Mt 13:44. The Kingdom of Heaven is like a treasure a man discovered in a field. In his excitement, he sold everything he owned to get enough money to buy the field—and get the treasure, too!

45. Again, the Kingdom of Heaven is like a pearl merchant on the lookout for choice pearls. 46He discovered a real bargain—a pearl of great value—and sold everything he owned to purchase it!

Rom 6:13. Do not let any part of your bodies become tools of wickedness, to be used for sinning; but give yourselves completely to God—every part of you—for you are back from death and you want to be tools in the hands of God, to be used for his good purposes.

16. Don't you realize that you can choose your own master? You can choose sin (with death) or else obedience (with acquittal). The one to whom you offer yourself—he will take you and be your master and you will be his slave.

19. I speak this way, using the illustration of slaves and masters, because it is easy to understand: just as you used to be slaves to all kinds of sin, so now you must let yourselves be slaves to all that is right and holy.

Rom 12:1. And so, dear brothers, I plead with you to give your bodies to God. Let them be a living sacrifice, holy—the kind he can accept. When you think of what he has done for you, is this too much to ask?

2 Cor 8:5. Best of all, they went beyond our highest hopes, for their first action was to dedicate

themselves to the Lord and to us, for whatever directions God might give to them through us.

CONDITIONAL. Gen 28:20. And Jacob vowed this vow to God: "If God will help and protect me on this journey and give me food and clothes, [21]and will bring me back safely to my father, then I will choose Jehovah as my God! [22]And this memorial pillar shall become a place for worship; and I will give you back a tenth of everything you give me!"

2 Sam 15:7, 8. After four years, Absalom said to the king, "Let me go to Hebron to sacrifice to the Lord in fulfillment of a vow I made to him while I was at Geshur—that if he would bring me back to Jerusalem, I would sacrifice to him."

See *Dedication; Offerings.*

INSTANCES OF. Cain and Abel, Gen 4:4–7. Abraham, of Isaac, Gen 22:9–12. Jephthah, of his daughter, Judg 11:30, 31, 34–40. Hannah, of Samuel, 1 Sam 1:11, 24–28. David consecrates the water obtained by his valiant officers, 2 Sam 23:16. Amasiah, of himself, 2 Chron 17:16.

CONSISTENCY Neh 5:9. Then I pressed further. "What you are doing is very evil," I exclaimed. "Should you not walk in the fear of our God? Don't we have enough enemies among the nations around us who are trying to destroy us?"

Mt 6:24. You cannot serve two masters: God and money. For you will hate one and love the other, or else the other way around. Lk 16:13.

Rom 14:22. You may know that there is nothing wrong with what you do, even from God's point of view, but keep it to yourself; don't flaunt your faith in front of others who might be hurt by it. In this situation, happy is the man who does not sin by doing what he knows is right.

1 Cor 10:21. You cannot drink from the cup at the Lord's Table and at Satan's table, too. You cannot eat bread both at the Lord's Table and at Satan's table.

See *Deceit; Expediency; Hypocrisy; Inconsistency; Obduracy; Prudence.*

CONSOLATION See *Affliction, Consolation in; Holy Spirit.*

CONSPIRACY LAW AGAINST. Ex 23:1. Do not pass along untrue reports. Do not cooperate with an evil man by affirming on the witness stand something you know is false.

2, 3. Don't join mobs intent on evil. When on the witness stand, don't be swayed in your testimony by the mood of the majority present, and do not slant your testimony in favor of a man just because he is poor."

INSTANCES OF. Joseph's brothers, against Joseph, Gen 37:18–20. Miriam and Aaron, against Moses, Num 12; 14:4; 16:1–35. Abimelech, against Gideon's sons, Judg 9:1–6. Gaal, against Abimelech, Judg 9:22–41. Delilah, against Samson, Judg 16:4–21. Abner, against Ish-bosheth, 2 Sam 3:7–21. Of Absalom, 2 Sam 15:10–13. Of Jeroboam, 1 Kgs 14:2. Of Baasha, 1 Kgs 15:27. Of Zimri, 1 Kgs 16:9. Of Jezebel, against Naboth, 1 Kgs 21:8–13. Of Jehu, 2 Kgs 9:14–26. Of Jehoiada, 2 Kgs 11:4–16. Of servants, against Joash, 2 Kgs 12:20.

People in Jerusalem, against Amaziah, 2 Kgs 14:19; 2 Chron 25:27. Shallum, against Zechariah, 2 Kgs 15:10. Pekahiah, 2 Kgs 15:23–25. Pekah, 2 Kgs 15:30. Sennacherib, 2 Kgs 19:37. Amon, 2 Kgs 21:23. Ahasuerus, Esther 2:21–23. Jeremiah, Jer 18:18. Daniel, Dan 6:4–17. Shadrach, Meshach, and Abednego, Dan 3:8–18.

Against Jesus, Jer 11:9, 19; Mt 12:14; 21:38–41; 26:3, 4; 27:1, 2; Mk 3:6. Paul, Acts 18:12; 23:12–15.

Falsely accused of: Jonathan, 1 Sam 22:8.

CONSTANCY In obedience, Ps 119:31–34. In friendship, Prov 27:10. Under suffering, Mt 5:12; Heb 12:5; 1 Pet 4:12–16. In prayer, Lk 18:1; Rom 12:12; Eph 6:18; Col 4:2; 1 Thess 5:17. In benevolence, Gal 6:9. In profession, Heb 10:23.

INSTANCES OF. Ruth, Ruth 1:14; Jonathan, 1 Sam 18:1; 20:16; Priscilla and Aquila, Rom 16:3, 4.

See *Character; Stability.*

CONSTELLATIONS Judg 5:20; Isa 13:10. The serpent, Job 26:13; cf. Rev 12:3, 4. Orion and Pleiades, Job 9:9; 38:31; Amos 5:8.

See *Astronomy.*

CONSTITUTION PRINCIPLES OF GOVERNMENT ENUNCIATED. Deut 17:18. And when he has been crowned and sits upon his throne as king, then he must copy these laws from the book kept by the Levite-priests. [19]That copy of the law shall be his constant companion. He must read from it every day of his life so that he will learn to respect the Lord his God by obeying all of his commands. [20]This regular reading of God's laws will prevent him from feeling that he is better than his fellow citizens. It will also prevent him from turning away from God's laws in the slightest respect, and will ensure his having a long, good reign. His sons will then follow him upon the throne.

2 Sam 5:3. So David made a contract before the Lord with the leaders of Israel there at Hebron, and they crowned him king of Israel.

2 Chron 23:2, 3. These men traveled out across the nation secretly, to tell the Levites and clan leaders about his plans and to summon them to Jerusalem. On arrival they swore allegiance to the young king, who was still in hiding at the Temple. "At last the time has come for the king's son to reign!" Jehoiada exclaimed. "The Lord's promise—that a descendant of King David shall be our king—will be true again."

Jer 34:8. This is the message that came to Jeremiah from the Lord after King Zedekiah of Judah had freed all the slaves in Jerusalem—[9](for King Zedekiah had ordered everyone to free his Hebrew slaves, both men and women. He had said that no Jew should be the master of another Jew for all were brothers. [10]The princes and all the people had obeyed the king's command and freed their slaves, but the action was only temporary. [11]They changed their minds and made their servants slaves again.)

Dan 6:12. They rushed back to the king and reminded him about his law. "Haven't you signed a decree," they said, "that permits no petitions to any God or man—except you—for thirty days? And anyone disobeying will be thrown to the lions?" "Yes," the king replied, "it is 'a law of the Medes and Persians,' that cannot be altered or revoked." [13]Then they told the king, "That fellow Daniel, one of the Jewish captives, is paying no attention to you or your law. He is asking favors of his God three times a day." [14]Hearing this, the king was very angry with himself for signing the law, and determined to save Daniel. He spent the rest of the day trying to think of some way to get Daniel out of this predicament. [15]In the evening the men came again to the king and said, "Your Majesty, there is nothing you can do. You signed the law and it cannot be changed."

CONTEMPT OF COURT See *Court.*

CONTENTION See *Strife.*

CONTENTMENT Ps 16:6. He sees that I am given pleasant brooks and meadows as my share! What a wonderful inheritance!

Ps 37:7. Rest in the Lord; wait patiently for him to act. Don't be envious of evil men who prosper. [16]It is better to have little and be godly than to own an evil man's wealth.

Prov 15:13. A happy face means a glad heart; a sad face means a breaking heart. [15]When a man is gloomy, everything seems to go wrong; when he is cheerful, everything seems right! [30]Pleasant sights and good reports give happiness and health.

Prov 16:8. A little, gained honestly, is better than great wealth gotten by dishonest means.

Prov 17:1. A dry crust eaten in peace is better than steak every day along with argument and strife. [22]A cheerful heart does good like medicine, but a broken spirit makes one sick.

Prov 30:8. First, help me never to tell a lie. Second, give me neither poverty nor riches! Give me just enough to satisfy my needs!

Eccl 2:24. So I decided that there was nothing better for man to do than to enjoy his food and drink, and his job. Eccl 3:12, 13; 8:15.

Eccl 5:12. The man who works hard sleeps well whether he eats little or much, but the rich must worry and suffer insomnia.

Eccl 6:9. A bird in the hand is worth two in the bush; mere dreaming of nice things is foolish; it's chasing the wind. *vs.* 7, 8.

Eccl 9:7. So go ahead, eat, drink, and be merry, for it makes no difference to God! [8]Wear fine clothes—with a dash of cologne! [9]Live happily with the woman you love through the fleeting days of life, for the wife God gives you is your best reward down here for all your earthly toil.

Lk 3:14. "And us," asked some soldiers, "what about us?" John replied, "Don't extort money by threats and violence; don't accuse anyone of what you know he didn't do; and be content with your pay!"

1 Cor 7:17. But be sure in deciding these matters that you are living as God intended, marrying or not marrying in accordance with God's direction and help, and accepting whatever situation God has put you into. This is my rule for all the churches. [20]Usually a person should keep on with the work he was doing when God called him. [21]Are you a slave? Don't let that worry you—but of course, if you get a chance to be free, take it. [24]So, dear brothers, whatever situation a person is in when he becomes a Christian, let him stay there, for now the Lord is there to help him.

Gal 5:26. Then we won't need to look for honors and popularity, which lead to jealousy and hard feelings.

Phil 4:11. Not that I was ever in need, for I have learned how to get along happily whether I have much or little. [12]I know how to live on almost nothing or with everything. I have learned the secret of contentment in every situation, whether it be a full stomach or hunger, plenty or want.

1 Tim 6:6. Do you want to be truly rich? You already are if you are happy and good. [7]After all, we didn't bring any money with us when we came into the world, and we can't carry away a single penny when we die. [8]So we should be well satisfied without money if we have enough food and clothing.

Heb 13:5. Stay away from the love of money; be satisfied with what you have. For God has said, "I will never, *never* fail you nor forsake you."

See *Affliction, Resignation in; Resignation.*

INSTANCES OF. Esau, in refusing Jacob's present, Gen 33:9. Barzillai, in refusing to go with David to Jerusalem, 2 Sam 19:33–37. The Shunemmite, in refusing to make a request of Elisha, 2 Kgs 4:13.

CONTINENCE Self-control. Job 31:1. I made a covenant with my eyes not to look with lust upon a girl.

Mt 5:27. The laws of Moses said, "You shall not commit adultery." [28]But I say: Anyone who even looks at a woman with lust in his eye has already committed adultery with her in his heart.

Mt 19:12. Some are born without the ability to marry, and some are disabled by men, and some refuse to marry for the sake of the Kingdom of Heaven.

Rom 13:13. Be decent and true in everything you do so that all can approve your behavior. Don't spend your time in wild parties and getting drunk or in adultery and lust, or fighting, or jealousy.

1 Cor 7:1. Now about those questions you asked in your last letter: my answer is that if you do not marry, it is good. [2]But usually it is best to be married, each man having his own wife, and each woman having her own husband, because otherwise you might fall back into sin. [3]The man should give his wife all that is her right as a married woman, and the wife should do the same for her husband: [4]for a girl who marries no longer has full right to her own body, for her husband then has his rights to it, too; and in the same way the husband no longer has full right to his own body, for it belongs also to his wife. [5]So do not refuse these rights to each other. The only exception to this rule would be the agreement of both husband and wife to refrain from the rights of marriage for a limited time, so that they can give themselves more completely to prayer. Afterwards, they should come

together again so that Satan won't be able to tempt them because of their lack of self-control. [6]I'm not saying you *must* marry; but you certainly *may* if you wish. [7]I wish everyone could get along without marrying, just as I do. But we are not all the same. God gives some the gift of a husband or wife, and others he gives the gift of being able to stay happily unmarried. [8]So I say to those who aren't married, and to widows—better to stay unmarried if you can, just as I am. [9]But if you can't control yourselves, go ahead and marry. It is better to marry than to burn with lust.

25. Now I will try to answer your other question. What about girls who are not yet married? Should they be permitted to do so? In answer to this question, I have no special command for them from the Lord. But the Lord in his kindness has given me wisdom that can be trusted, and I will be glad to tell you what I think. [26]Here is the problem: We Christians are facing great dangers in our lives at present. In times like these I think it is best for a person to remain unmarried. [27]Of course, if you already are married, don't separate because of this. But if you aren't, don't rush into it at this time. [28]But if you men decide to go ahead anyway and get married now, it is all right; and if a girl gets married in times like these, it is no sin. However, marriage will bring extra problems that I wish you didn't have to face right now. [29]The important thing to remember is that our remaining time is very short, [and so are our opportunities for doing the Lord's work]. For that reason those who have wives should stay as free as possible for the Lord. [36]But if anyone feels he ought to marry because he has trouble controlling his passions, it is all right, it is not a sin; let him marry. [37]But if a man has the willpower not to marry and decides that he doesn't need to and won't, he has made a wise decision. [38]So the person who marries does well, and the person who doesn't marry does even better.

1 Cor 9:27. Like an athlete I punish my body, treating it roughly, training it to do what it should, not what it wants to. Otherwise I fear that after enlisting others for the race, I myself might be declared unfit and ordered to stand aside.

Col 3:5. Away then with sinful, earthly things; deaden the evil desires lurking within you; have nothing to do with sexual sin, impurity, lust and shameful desires; don't worship the good things of life, for that is idolatry.

1 Tim 4:12. Don't let anyone think little of you because you are young. Be their ideal; let them follow the way you teach and live; be a pattern for them in your love, your faith, and your clean thoughts.

1 Tim 5:1. Never speak sharply to an older man, but plead with him respectfully just as though he were your own father. Talk to the younger men as you would to much loved brothers. [2]Treat the older women as mothers, and the girls as your sisters, thinking only pure thoughts about them.

Rev 14:1. Then I saw a Lamb standing on Mount Zion in Jerusalem, and with him were 144,000 who had his Name and his Father's Name written on their foreheads. [4]For they are spiritually undefiled, pure as virgins, following the Lamb wherever he goes. They have been purchased from among the men on the earth as a consecrated offering to God and the Lamb. [5]No falsehood can be charged against them; they are blameless.

See *Chastity.*

INSTANCES OF. Joseph, Gen 39:7–12. Uriah, 2 Sam 11:8–13. Boaz, Ruth 3:6–13. Joseph, husband of Mary, Mt 1:24, 25. Paul, 1 Cor 7:8.

CONTINENTS Gen 1:9, 10; Job 26:7, 10; 28:8–11; 38:4–18; Ps 95:5; 104:5–9; 136:6; Prov 8:27–29.

See *Geology.*

CONTINGENCIES IN DIVINE GOVERNMENT OF MAN. Gen 2:16, 17. But the Lord God gave the man this warning: "You may eat any fruit in the garden except fruit from the Tree of Conscience—for its fruit will open your eyes to make you aware of right and wrong, good and bad. If you eat its fruit, you will be doomed to die."

Gen 3:2, 3. "Of course we may eat it," the woman told him. "It's only the fruit from the tree at the *center* of the garden that we are not to eat. God says we mustn't eat it or even touch it, or we will die."

Gen 4:7. It can be bright with joy if you will do what you should! But if you refuse to obey, watch out. Sin is waiting to attack you, longing to destroy you. But you can conquer it!

Gen 18:19. And I have picked him out to have godly descendants and a godly household—men who are just and good—so that I can do for him all I have promised.

Ex 19:5. Now if you will obey me and keep your part of my contract with you, you shall be my own little flock from among all the nations of the earth; for all the earth is mine.

Lev 26:3. If you obey all of my commandments, [4]I will give you regular rains, and the land will yield bumper crops, and the trees will be loaded with fruit long after the normal time! *vs.* 3–13.

14. But if you will not listen to me or obey me, [15]but reject my laws, [16]this is what I will do to you: I will punish you with sudden terrors and panic, and with tuberculosis and burning fever; your eyes shall be consumed and your life shall ebb away; you will sow your crops in vain, for your enemies will eat them. *vs.* 14–28.

Deut 7:12. Because of your obedience, the Lord your God will keep his part of the contract which, in his tender love, he made with your fathers. *vs.* 13–26.

Deut 11:26. I am giving you the choice today between God's blessing or God's curse! [27]There will be blessing if you obey the commandments of the Lord your God which I am giving you today, [28]and a curse if you refuse them and worship the gods of these other nations.

Deut 30:15. Look, today I have set before you life and death, depending on whether you obey or disobey. [16]I have commanded you today to love the Lord your God and to follow his paths and to keep his laws, so that you will live and become a great nation, and so that the Lord your God will bless you and the land you are about to possess. [19]I call heaven and earth to witness against you that today I have set before you life or death, blessing or curse. Oh, that you would choose life; that you and your children might live!

Josh 24:15. But if you are unwilling to obey the Lord, then decide today whom you will obey. Will it be the gods of your ancestors beyond the Euphrates or the gods of the Amorites here in this land? But as for me and my family, we will serve the Lord.

2 Sam 24:12. "Tell David that I will give him three choices." [13]So Gad came to David and asked him, "Will you choose seven years of famine across the land, or to flee for three months before your enemies, or to submit to three days of plague? Think this over and let me know what answer to give to God." [14]"This is a hard decision," David replies, "but it is better to fall into the hand of the Lord (for his mercy is great) than into the hands of men."

1 Kgs 3:14. And I will give you a long life if you follow me and obey my laws as your father David did.

1 Kgs 20:42. Then the prophet told him, "The Lord says, 'Because you have spared the man I said must die, now you must die in his place, and your people shall perish instead of his.' "

1 Chron 28:7. And if he continues to obey my commandments and instructions as he has until now, I will make his kingdom last forever.

2 Chron 26:5. While Zechariah was alive Uzziah was always eager to please God. Zechariah was a man who had special revelations from God. And as long as the king followed the paths of God, he prospered, for God blessed him.

Job 36:11. If they listen and obey him, then they will be blessed with prosperity throughout their lives. [12]If they won't listen to him, they shall perish in battle and die because of their lack of good sense.

Jer 11:4. For I told them at the time I brought them out of slavery in Egypt that if they would obey me and do whatever I commanded them, then they and all their children would be mine and I would be their God.

Jer 12:17. But any nation refusing to obey me will be expelled again and finished, says the Lord.

Jer 18:8. Then if that nation renounces its evil ways, I will not destroy it as I had planned. [9]And if I announce that I will make a certain nation strong and great, [10]but then that nation changes its mind and turns to evil and refuses to obey me, then I too will change my mind and not bless that nation as I had said I would.

Jer 22:4. If you put an end to all these terrible deeds you are doing, then I will deliver this nation and once more give kings to sit on David's throne, and there shall be prosperity for all. [5]But if you refuse to pay attention to this warning, I swear by my own name, says the Lord, that this palace shall become a shambles.

Ezk 33:14. And when I tell the wicked he will die and then he turns from his sins and does what is fair and right—[15]if he gives back the borrower's pledge and returns what he has stolen and walks along the paths of right, not doing evil—he shall surely live. He shall not die. [16]None of his past sins shall be brought up against him, for he has turned to the good and shall surely live.

Jon 3:10. And when God saw that they had put a stop to their evil ways, he abandoned his plan to destroy them, and didn't carry it through.

Mt 19:17. "When you call me good you are calling me God," Jesus replied, "for God alone is truly good. But to answer your question, you can get to heaven if you keep the commandments."

Mt. 23:37. O Jerusalem, Jerusalem, the city that kills the prophets, and stones all those God sends to her! How often I have wanted to gather your children together as a hen gathers her chicks beneath her wings, but you wouldn't let me.

Mt 26:39. He went forward a little, and fell face downward on the ground, and prayed, "My Father! If it is possible, let this cup be taken away from me. But I want your will, not mine." *v.* 42.

Jn 9:41. "If you were blind, you wouldn't be guilty," Jesus replied. "But your guilt remains because you claim to know what you are doing."

Jn 14:23. Jesus replied, "Because I will only reveal myself to those who love me and obey me. The Father will love them too, and we will come to them and live with them."

Jn 15:6. If anyone separates from me, he is thrown away like a useless branch, withers, and is gathered into a pile with all the others and burned. [7]But if you stay in me and obey my commands, you may ask any request you like, and it will be granted!

Col 1:22. He has done this through the death on the cross of his own human body, and now as a result Christ has brought you into the very presence of God, and you are standing there before him with nothing left against you—nothing left that he could even chide you for; [23]the only condition is that you fully believe the Truth, standing in it steadfast and firm, strong in the Lord, convinced of the Good News that Jesus died for you, and never shifting from trusting him to save you. This is the wonderful news that came to each of you and is now spreading all over the world. And I, Paul, have the joy of telling it to others.

2 Thess 2:8. Then this wicked one will appear, whom the Lord Jesus will burn up with the breath of his mouth and destroy by his presence when he returns. [9]This man of sin will come as Satan's tool, full of satanic power, and will trick everyone with strange demonstrations, and will do great miracles. [10]He will completely fool those who are on their way to hell because they have said "no" to the Truth; they have refused to believe it and love it, and let it save them.

Heb 3:14. For if we are faithful to the end, trusting God just as we did when we first became Christians, we will share in all that belongs to Christ.

Rev 2:22. Pay attention now to what I am saying: I will lay her upon a sickbed of intense affliction, along with all her immoral followers, unless they turn again to me, repenting of their sin with her.

Rev 3:3. Go back to what you heard and believed at first; hold to it firmly and turn to me again. Unless you do, I will come suddenly upon you, unexpected as a thief, and punish you.

Rev 22:17. The Spirit and the bride say, "Come." Let each one who hears them say the same, "Come." Let the thirsty one come—anyone who wants to; let him come and drink the Water of Life without charge.

See *Blessings, Contingent on Obedience; Predestination; Will.*

CONTRACT Between Abraham and Abimelech, concerning wells of water, Gen 21:25–32; violated, Gen 26:15. First contract between Laban and Jacob for Laban's daughters, Gen 29:15–20, 27–30; violated, Gen 29:23–27; second contract, Gen 30:28–34; violated, Gen 30:37–43; 31:7; for goats and sheep, Gen 30:27–29, 31–34. See *Fraud.*

Between Solomon and Hiram, 1 Kgs 5:9–11; 9:11, 12.

Dissolved: By mutual consent, Ex 4:18; by blotting out, Col 2:14. Modes of ratifying: By giving presents, Gen 21:25–30; 1 Sam 18:4; by consummating in the presence of the public at the city gate, Gen 23:18; Ruth 4:1,2; by erecting a heap of stones, Gen 31:44–54; by oaths, Gen 26:3, 31; Josh 9:14, 15, 20; 1 Chron 16:16; Ezk 17:18; Heb 6:17; by endorsing a note, Prov 6:1; 17:18; 22:26; with salt, Num 18:19; by taking off the shoe, Ruth 4:6–8; written instrument, Jer 32:10–15.

See *Covenants; Vows.*

SCRIPTURES ILLUSTRATING THE BINDING FORCE OF. Ex 21:2. If you buy a Hebrew slave, he shall serve only six years and be freed in the seventh year, and need pay nothing to regain his freedom. [3]If he sold himself as a slave before he married, then if he married afterwards, only he shall be free; but if he was married before he became a slave, then his wife shall be freed with him at the same time. [4]But if his master gave him a wife while he was a slave, and they have sons or daughters, the wife and children shall still belong to the master, and he shall go out by himself free. [5]But if the man shall plainly declare, 'I prefer my master, my wife, and my children, and I would rather not go free,' [6]then his master shall bring him before the judge and shall publicly bore his ear with an awl, and after that he will be a slave forever.

Lev 6:1. And the Lord said to Moses, [2]"If anyone sins against me by refusing to return a deposit on something borrowed or rented, or by refusing to return something entrusted to him, or by robbery, or by oppressing his neighbor, [4, 5]on the day he is found guilty of any such sin, he shall restore what he took, adding a twenty percent fine, and give it to the one he has harmed; and on the same day he shall bring his guilt offering to the Tabernacle. [6]His guilt offering shall be a ram without defect, and must be worth whatever value you demand. He shall bring it to the priest, [7]and the priest shall make atonement for him before the Lord, and he shall be forgiven."

Josh 9:3, 4, 5. But when the people of Gibeon heard what had happened to Jericho and Ai, they resorted to trickery to save themselves. They sent ambassadors to Joshua wearing worn-out clothing, as though from a long journey, with patched shoes, weatherworn saddlebags on their donkeys, old, patched wineskins and dry, moldy bread. [6]When they arrived at the camp of Israel at Gilgal, they told Joshua and the men of Israel, "We have come from a distant land to ask for a peace treaty with you." [7]The Israelis replied to these Hivites, "How do we know you don't live nearby? For if you do, we cannot make a treaty with you." [8]They replied, "We will be your slaves." "But who are you?" Joshua demanded. "Where do you come from?" [9]And they told him, "We are from a very distant country; we have heard of the might of the Lord your God and of all that he did in Egypt. [14, 15]Joshua and the other leaders finally believed them. They did not bother to ask the Lord, but went ahead and signed a peace treaty. And the leaders of Israel ratified the agreement with a binding oath.

16. Three days later the facts came out—these men were close neighbors. [18]But the cities were not harmed because of the vow which the leaders of Israel had made before the Lord God. The people of Israel were angry with their leaders because of the peace treaty. [19]But the leaders replied, "We have sworn before the Lord God of Israel that we will not touch them, and we won't. with *vs.* 20–27.

Mt 20:1. Here is another illustration of the Kingdom of Heaven. "The owner of an estate went out early one morning to hire workers for his harvest field. [2]He agreed to pay them $20 a day and sent them out to work. [3]A couple of hours later he was passing a hiring hall and saw some men standing around waiting for jobs, [4]so he sent them also in his fields, telling them he would pay them whatever was right at the end of the day. [5]At noon and again around three o'clock in the afternoon he did the same thing. [6]At five o'clock that evening he was in town again and saw some more men standing around and asked them, 'Why haven't you been working today?' [7]'Because no one hired us,' they replied. 'Then go on out and join the others in my fields,' he told them. [8]That evening he told the paymaster to call the men in and pay them, beginning with the last men first. [9]When the men hired at five o'clock were paid, each received $20. [10]So when the men hired earlier came to get theirs, they assumed they would receive much more. But they, too, were paid $20. [11, 12]They protested, 'Those fellows worked only one hour, and yet you've paid them just as much as those of us who worked all day in the scorching heat.' [13]'Friend,' he answered one of them, 'I did you no wrong! Didn't you agree to work all day for $20? [14]Take it and go. It is my desire to pay all the same; [15]is it against the law to give away my money if I want to? Should you be angry because I am kind? [16]And so it is that the last shall be first, and the first, last.' "

Gal 3:15. Dear brothers, even in everyday life a promise made by one man to another, if it is written down and signed, cannot be changed. He cannot decide afterward to do something else instead.

See *Covenant; Land.*

CONTRITION See *Repentance; Sin, Confession of.*

CONVENTION For counsel, Prov 15:22.

CONVERSATION Mt 5:37. Say just a simple "Yes, I will" or "No, I won't." Your word is enough. To strengthen your promise with a vow shows that something is wrong.

Mt 12:35. A good man's speech reveals the rich treasures within him. An evil-hearted man is filled with venom, and his speech reveals it. [36]And I tell you this, that you must give account on Judgment Day for every idle word you speak. [37]Your words now reflect your fate then: either you will be justified by them or you will be condemned.

Eph 4:29. Don't use bad language. Say only what is good and helpful to those you are talking to, and what will give them a blessing.

Col 3:8. But now is the time to cast off and throw away all these rotten garments of anger, hatred, cursing, and dirty language.

Col 4:6. Let your conversation be gracious as well as sensible, for then you will have the right answer for everyone.

Tit 2:8. Your conversation should be so sensible and logical that anyone who wants to argue will be ashamed of himself because there won't be anything to criticize in anything you say!

Jas 5:12. But most of all, dear brothers, do not swear either by heaven or earth or anything else; just say a simple yes or no, so that you will not sin and be condemned for it.

See *Tongue.*

CONVERSION See *Regeneration.*

INSTANCES OF. See *Converts,* below.

CONVERTS "Hard path," Mt 13:4, 19. "Rocky soil," Mt 13:5, 20, 21. "Choked," Mt 13:7, 22. "Good soil," Mt 13:8, 23; Lk 8:4–15.

See *Backslider; Revival.*

INSTANCES OF. Ruth, Ruth 1:16. Nebuchadnezzar, Dan 4. The sailors with Jonah, Jon 1: 5, 6, 9, 10,14,16. Ninevites, Jon 3. Gadarenes, Lk 8: 35–39. The Samaritans, Jn 4:28–42. The thief on the cross, Lk 23:39–43. At Pentecost, three thousand, Acts 2:41. Post-pentecostal, Acts 4:4. The eunuch, Acts 8:35–38. Saul (Paul) of Tarsus, Acts 9:3–18; 26:12–23. Sergius Paulus, Acts 13:6, 7, 12. Cornelius, Acts 10. Jews and Gentiles at Antioch, Acts 13:43. Lydia, Acts 16:14, 15. Jailer, Acts 16: 27–34. Greeks, Acts 17:4,12.

ZEALOUS, INSTANCES OF. Nebuchadnezzar, Dan 3:29; 4:1–37. Andrew, Jn 1:40, 41. Philip, Jn 1: 43–45. The woman of Samaria, Jn 4:28, 29. The man possessed by demons, Lk 8:39. The blind men, Mt 9:31; Jn 9:8–38. The deaf man, Mk 7:36.

CONVEYANCE OF LAND. See *Land.*

CONVICTION OF SIN. Gen 4:13. Cain replied to the Lord, "My punishment is greater than I can bear."

Deut 28:65. There among those nations you shall find no rest, but the Lord will give you trembling hearts, darkness, and bodies wasted from sorrow and fear. [66]Your lives will hang in doubt. You will live night and day in fear, and will have no reason to believe that you will see the morning light. [67]In the morning you will say, "Oh, that night were here!" And in the evening you will say, "Oh, that morning were here!" You will say this because of the awesome horrors surrounding you.

Job 40:4. I am nothing—how could I ever find the answers? I lay my hand upon my mouth in silence. [5]I have said too much already.

Ps 31:10. I am pining away with grief; my years are shortened, drained away because of sadness. My sins have sapped my strength; I stoop with sorrow and with shame.

Ps 38:1. O Lord, don't punish me while you are angry! [2]Your arrows have struck deep; your blows are crushing me. [3, 4]Because of your anger my body is sick, my health is broken beneath my sins. They are like a flood, higher than my head; they are a burden too heavy to bear. [5, 6]My wounds are festering and full of pus. Because of my sins I am bent and racked with pain. My days are filled with anguish. [7]My loins burn with inflammation and my whole body is diseased. [8]I am exhausted and crushed; I groan in despair. [9]Lord, you know how I long for my health once more. You hear my every sigh. [10]My heart beats wildly, my strength fails, and I am going blind. [11]My loved ones and friends stay away, fearing my disease. Even my own family stands at a distance. [12]Meanwhile my enemies are trying to kill me. They plot my ruin and spend all their waking hours planning treachery. [13, 14]But I am deaf to all their threats; I am silent before them as a man who cannot speak. I have nothing to say. [15]For I am waiting for you, O Lord my God. Come and protect me. [16]Put an end to their arrogance, these who gloat when I am cast down! [17]How constantly I find myself upon the verge of sin; this source of sorrow always stares me in the face. [18]I confess my sins; I am sorry for what I have done. [19]But my enemies persecute with vigor, and continue to hate me—though I have done nothing against them to deserve it. [20]They repay me evil for good and hate me for standing for the right. [21]Don't leave me, Lord; don't go away! [22]Come quickly! Help me, O my Savior.

Ps 51:1. O loving and kind God, have mercy. Have pity upon me and take away the awful stain of my transgressions. [2]Oh, wash me, cleanse me from this guilt. Let me be pure again. [3]For I admit my shameful deed—it haunts me day and night. [4]It is against you and you alone I sinned, and did this terrible thing. You saw it all, and your sentence against me is just. [7]Sprinkle me with the cleansing blood and I shall be clean again. Wash me and I shall be whiter than snow. [8]And after you have punished me, give me back my joy again. [9]Don't keep looking at my sins—erase them from your sight. [10]Create in me a new clean heart, O God, filled with clean thoughts and right desires. [11]Don't toss me aside, banished forever from your presence. Don't take your Holy Spirit from me. [12]Restore to me again the joy of your salvation, and make me willing to obey you. [13]Then I will teach your ways to other sinners, and they—guilty like me—will repent and return to you. [14, 15]Don't sentence me to death. O my God, you alone can rescue me. Then I will sing of your forgiveness, for my lips will be unsealed—oh, how I will praise you. [16]You don't want penance; if you did, how gladly I would do it! You aren't interested in offerings burned before you on the altar. [17]It is a broken spirit you want—remorse and penitence. A broken and contrite heart, O God, you will not ignore.

Isa 6:5. Then I said, "My doom is sealed, for I am a foul-mouthed sinner, a member of a sinful, foul-mouthed race; and I have looked upon the King, the Lord of heaven's armies."

Lam 1:20. *See, O Lord, my anguish;* my heart is broken and my soul despairs, for I have terribly rebelled. In the streets the sword awaits me; at home, disease and death.

Ezk 7:16. Any who escape will be lonely as mourning doves hiding on the mountains, each weeping for his sins. [17]All hands shall be feeble, and all knees as weak as water. [18]You shall clothe yourselves with sackcloth, and horror and shame shall cover you; you shall shave your heads in sorrow and remorse. [25]For the time has come for the cutting off of Israel. You will sue for peace, but you won't get it. [26]Calamity upon calamity will befall you; woe upon woe, disaster upon disaster! You will long for a prophet to guide you, but the priests and elders and the kings and princes will stand helpless, weeping in despair.

Ezk 33:10. O people of Israel, you are saying: "Our sins are heavy upon us; we pine away with guilt. How can we live?"

Mic 7:17. They will see what snakes they are, lowly as worms crawling from their holes. They will come trembling out from their fortresses to meet the Lord our God. They will fear him; they will stand in awe.

Lk 5:8. When Simon Peter realized what had happened, he fell to his knees before Jesus and said, "Oh, sir, please leave us—I'm too much of a sinner for you to have around."

Acts 2:37. These words of Peter's moved them deeply, and they said to him and to the other apostles, "Brothers, what should we do?"

Acts 16:29. Trembling with fear, the jailer called for lights and ran to the dungeon and fell down before Paul and Silas. [30]He brought them out and begged them, "Sirs, what must I do to be saved?"

Rom 2:12–15. He will punish sin wherever it is found. He will punish the heathen when they sin, even though they never had God's written laws, for down in their hearts they know right from wrong. God's laws are written within them; their own conscience accuses them, or sometimes excuses them. And God will punish the Jews for sinning because they have his written laws but don't obey them. They know what is right but don't do it. After all, salvation is not given to those who know what to do, unless they do it.

1 Cor 14:24. But if you prophesy, preaching God's Word, [even though such preaching is mostly for believers] and an unsaved person or a new Christian comes in who does not understand about these things, all these sermons will convince him of the fact that he is a sinner, and his conscience will be pricked by everything he hears. [25]As he listens, his secret thoughts will be laid bare and he will fall down on his knees and worship God, declaring that God is really there among you.

See *Sin, Confession of.*

INSTANCES OF. Adam and Eve, after their disobedience, Gen 3:8–10. Joseph's brothers, on account of their cruelty to Joseph, Gen 42:21, 22; 44:16; 45:3; 50:15–21. Pharaoh: After the plague of hail, Ex 9:27, 28; the plague of locusts, Ex 10:16, 17; the death of the firstborn, Ex 12:31. The Israelites: After being rebuked and punished for worshiping the golden calf, Ex 33:4; the death of the ten spies, and their being sentenced to wander forty years, Num 14:39, 40; their murmuring against God and being bitten by snakes, Num 21:7. Saul, after sparing Agag and the best of the spoils, 1 Sam 15:24. David, after the plague sent on account of his census, 1 Chron 21:30. See *Psalms, Penitential.* Widow of Zarephath, when her son died, 1 Kgs 17:18. Belshazzar, when he "saw the fingers as they wrote," Dan 5:6. Darius, when Daniel was in the lions' den, Dan 6:18. Sailors, after throwing Jonah into the sea, Jon 1:16; Ninevites, at the preaching of Jonah, Jon 3; Mt 12:41; Lk 11:32. Jonah, in the fish's belly, Jon 2. Herod, when he heard of the fame of Jesus, Mt 14:2; Mk 6:14; Lk 9:7. Jews, when Jesus commanded the guiltless man to cast the first stone at the woman caught in adultery, Jn 8:9. Judas, after his betrayal of Jesus, Mt 27:3–5. Saul (Paul) of Tarsus, when he saw Jesus on the way to Damascus, Acts 9:4–18. Felix, under the preaching of Paul, Acts 24:25. Philippian jailer, after the earthquake, Acts 16:30.

See *Wicked.*

FROM GOD. Job 33:14. For God speaks again and again, [15]in dreams, in visions of the night when deep sleep falls on men as they lie on their beds. [16]He opens their ears in times like that, and gives them wisdom and instruction, [17, 18]causing them to change their minds, and keeping them from pride, and warning them of the penalties of sin, and keeping them from falling into some trap. [19]Or, God sends sickness and pain, even though no bone is broken, [20]so that a man loses all taste and appetite for food and doesn't care for even the daintiest dessert. [21]He becomes thin, mere skin and bones, [22]and draws near to death. [23, 24]But if a messenger from heaven is there to intercede for him as a friend, to show him what is right, then God pities him and says, "Set him free. Do not make him die, for I have found a substitute." [25]Then his body will become as healthy as a child's, firm and youthful again. [26]And when he prays to God, God will hear and answer and receive him with joy, and return him to his duties. [27]And he will declare to his friends, "I sinned, but God let me go. [28]He did not let me die. I will go on living in the realm of light." [29]Yes, God often does these things for man—[30]brings back his soul from the pit, so that he may live in the light of the living.

Jn 6:44, 45. For no one can come to me unless the Father who sent me draws him to me, and at the Last Day I will cause all such to rise again from the dead. [45]As it is written in the Scriptures, "They shall all be taught of God." Those the Father speaks to, who learn the truth from him, will be attracted to me.

Jn 16:7. But the fact of the matter is that it is best for you that I go away, for if I don't, the Comforter won't come. If I do, he will—for I will send him to you. [8]And when he has come he will convince the world of its sin, and of the availability of God's goodness, and of deliverance from judgment. [9]The world's sin is unbelief in me; [10]there is righteousness available because I go to the Father and you shall see me no more; [11]there is deliverance from judgment because the prince of this world has already been judged.

Acts 16:14. One of them was Lydia, a saleswoman from Thyatira, a merchant of purple cloth. She was already a worshiper of God and, as she listened to us, the Lord opened her heart and she accepted all that Paul was saying.

See *Penitent; Remorse; Repentance; Sin, Confession of.*

UNJUST. Of innocent persons, see *Accusation, False; Indictment.*

CONVOCATION, HOLY Three held annually by the Israelites, Lev 23.

See *Feasts.*

COOKING A kid might not be boiled in the mother's milk, Deut 14:21. Of meat, Ezk 24:10. Israel, a cake half-baked, Hos 7:8. In the Temple, Ezk 46:19–24.

See *Bread; Oven.*

COOP For birds, unclean, Jer 5:27.

COPPER A mineral of Canaan, Deut 8:9. Smelted, Job 28:2. Coppersmith, 2 Tim 4:14.

See *Brass.*

COPULATION Forbidden between near relatives, Lev 18:6–16. During menses, Lev 15:19; 18:19. With animals, Lev 18:23.

See *Marriage.* See also *Adultery; Bestiality; Homosexuality; Incest; Lasciviousness.*

CORAL Job 28:18; Ezk 27:16.

CORD Ancient uses of: Priests' garments, Ex 28:22–24; 39:31; fastening tents, Ex 35:10–19; 39:33–40; Israelites' garments, Num 15:37, 38; decoration, Esther 1:6; sealing, Mt 27:66.

FIGURATIVE. Of life, Eccl 12:6. Of friendship, Eccl 4:12. Of sin, Isa 5:18.

See *Rope; Tape; Yardstick.*

CORIANDER A spice, Ex 16:31; Num 11:7.

CORINTH A city of Achaia. Visited: By Paul, Acts 18; 2 Cor 12:14; 13:1; with 1 Cor 16:5–7; and 2 Cor 1:15, 16; Apollos, Acts 19:1; Titus, 2 Cor 8:16, 17; 12:18. Erastus, a Christian of, Rom 16:23; 2 Tim 4:20.

CHURCH OF. Schism in, 1 Cor 1:12; 3:4. Immoralities in, 1 Cor 5; 11. Writes to Paul, 1 Cor 7:1. Alienation of, from Paul, 2 Cor 10. Abuse of ordinances in, 1 Cor 11:22; 14. Heresies in, 1 Cor 15:12; 2 Cor 11. Lawsuits in, 1 Cor 6. Liberality of, 2 Cor 9. Paul's letters to, 1 Cor 1:2; 16:21–24; 2 Cor 1:1, 13, 14.

CORMORANT A bird forbidden as food, Lev 11:13–19; Deut 14:11–18.

See *Hawk; Vulture.*

CORN A term applied to grains, 2 Kgs 4:42. A product of Palestine, Deut 33:28; Hos 2:9; Joel 2:19. Ground, Isa 47:2.

See *Barley; Barn; Bread; Emmer; First Fruits; Gleaning; Grain; Harvest; Reaping; Spelt; Threshing, Tithes; Wheat.*

CORNELIUS A Roman army officer, Acts 10.

CORNERSTONE Job 38:6, 7; Ps 118:22; Isa 28:6; Zech 10:4; Mt 21:42; Mk 12:10.

CORNET See *Trumpet.*

CORPORAL PUNISHMENT See *Punishment.*

CORPULENCY INSTANCES OF. Eglon, Judg 3:17–19; Eli, 1 Sam 4:18.

CORRECTION See *Afflictions, Design of; Chastisement; Children, Correction of; Parents; Punishment; Scourging.*

CORRUPTION PHYSICAL DECOMPOSITION. Ezk 24:11, 13. After death, Mt 23:27; Lk 11:44; Acts 13:34–37.

FIGURATIVE. Of sin, Ps 53:3; Ezk 24:11, 13; Mt 23:27; Lk 11:44.

JUDICIAL See *Court; Government; Judge.*

ECCLESIASTICAL. See *Church, Visible; Minister.*

POLITICAL. See *Bribery; Civil Service; Government; Politics.*

COS An island, Paul visits, in the Mediterranean, Acts 21:1.

COSMETICS 2 Kgs 9:30; Jer 4:30; Ezk 23:40.

COTTON Judg 16:9; Isa 19:9.

COUNCIL Apostolic, Acts 15:1–29. Of war, 2 Sam 16:20; 17:1–15; 2 Chron 32:3. Ar-ta-xerxes', of Seven, Ezra 7:14, 28; 8:25. City, Gen 34:20; Ex 4:29; Josh 20:4; 2 Kgs 10:1; Prov 31:23; Mt 28:14; Acts 17:5, 6, 34. At Mizpah, Judg 21:5. Of Pharisees, Lk 14:1; 22:66; 23:1; Jn 11:47; Acts 4:1–23; 5:21–41; 6:12–15; 22:5, 30; 23:1–10, 28; 24:20, 21.

See *Sanhedrin.*

COUNSEL Prov 1:5, 6. I want those already wise to become the wiser and become leaders by exploring the depths of meaning in these nuggets of truth.

Prov 9:9. Teach a wise man, and he will be the wiser; teach a good man, and he will learn more.

Prov 11:14. Without wise leadership, a nation is in trouble; but with good counselors there is safety.

Prov 12:15. A fool thinks he needs no advice, but a wise man listens to others.

Prov 15:22. Plans go wrong with too few counselors; many counselors bring success.

Prov 19:20. Get all the advice you can and be wise the rest of your life.

Prov 20:18. Don't go ahead with your plans without the advice of others; don't go to war until they agree.

Prov 24:6. Don't go to war without wise guidance; there is safety in many counselors.

Prov 27:9. Friendly suggestions are as pleasant as perfume.

See *Prudence.*

REJECTED. Prov 1:24. I have called you so often but still you won't come. I have pleaded, but all in vain. [25]For you have spurned my counsel and reproof. [26]Some day you'll be in trouble, and I'll laugh! Mock me, will you?—I'll mock you! [27]When a storm of terror surrounds you, and when you are engulfed by anguish and distress, [28]then I will not answer your cry for help. It will be too late though you search for me ever so anxiously. [29]For you closed your eyes to the facts and did not choose to reverence and trust the Lord, [30]and you turned your back on me, spurning my advice. [31]That is why you must eat the bitter fruit of having your own way, and experience the full terrors of the pathway you have chosen. [32]For you turned away from me—to death; your own complacency will kill you. Fools! [33]But all who listen to me shall live in peace and safety, unafraid.

INSTANCES OF. By Rehoboam, 1 Kgs 12:8–17. By the rich young ruler, Mt 19:22.

COUNSELOR A wise man, versed in law and diplomacy, 1 Chron 27:32, 33. Ahithophel was, to David, 1 Chron 27:33; 2 Sam 16:23; to Absalom, 2 Sam 16:23. Joseph, a member of the Sanhedrin at Jerusalem, Mk 15:42, 43; Lk 23:50–52. In general, 2 Chron 22:3; Ezra 7:14; Job 3:14; Ps 119:24; Prov 11:14; 15:22; 24:6; Isa 1:26; Dan 1:21; 3:24, 27; 4:36; 6:7; Rom 11:34. A title of Christ, Isa 9:6.

COUNTENANCE Attitude indicated in, Ps 42:4, 5; 43:5.

See *Face; Spirits.*

COUNTRY LOVE OF. Judg 5:1. Then Deborah and Barak sang this song about the wonderful victory: [2]"Praise the Lord! Israel's leaders bravely led; the people gladly followed! Yes, bless the Lord! [3]Listen, O you kings and princes, for I shall sing about the Lord, the God of Israel. [4]When you led us out from Seir, out across the fields of Edom, the earth trembled and the sky poured down its rain. [5]Yes, even Mount Sinai quaked at the presence of the God of Israel! [6]In the days of Shamgar and of Jael, the main roads were deserted. Travelers used the narrow, crooked side paths. [7]Israel's population dwindled, until Deborah became a mother to Israel. [8]When Israel chose new gods, everything collapsed. Our masters would not let us have a shield or spear. Among forty thousand men of Israel, not a weapon could be found! [9]How I rejoice in the leaders of Israel who offered themselves so willingly! Praise the Lord! [10]Let all Israel, rich and poor, join in his praises—those who ride on white donkeys and sit on rich carpets, and those who are poor and must walk. [11]The village musicians gather at the village well to sing of the triumphs of the Lord. Again and again they sing the ballad of how the Lord saved Israel with an army of peasants! The people of the Lord marched through the gates! [12]Awake, O Deborah, and sing! Arise, O Barak! O son of Abino-am, lead away your captives! [13, 14]Down from Mount Tabor marched the noble remnant. The people of the Lord marched down against great odds. They came from Ephraim and Benjamin, from Machir and from Zebulun. [15]Down into the valley went the princes of Issachar with Deborah and Barak. At God's command they rushed into the valley. (But the tribe of Reuben didn't go. [16]Why did you sit at home among the sheepfolds, playing your shepherd pipes? Yes, the tribe of Reuben has an uneasy conscience. [17]Why did Gilead remain across the Jordan, and why did Dan remain with his ships? And why did Asher sit unmoved upon the seashore, at ease beside his harbors?) [18]But the tribes of Zebulun and Naphtali dared to die upon the fields of battle. [19]The kings of Canaan fought in Taanach by Megiddo's springs, but did not win the victory. [20]The very stars of heaven fought Sisera. [21]The rushing Kishon River swept them away. March on, my soul, with strength! [22]Hear the stamping of the horsehoofs of the enemy! See the prancing of his steeds! [23]But the Angel of Jehovah put a curse on Meroz. 'Curse them bitterly,' he said, 'Because they did not come to help the Lord against his enemies.' [24]Blessed be Jael, the wife of Heber the Kenite—yes, may she be blessed above all women who live in tents. [25]He asked for water and she gave him milk in a beautiful cup! [26]Then she took a tent pin and a workman's hammer and pierced Sisera's temples, crushing his head. She pounded the tent pin through his head, [27]and he lay at her feet, dead. [28]The mother of Sisera watched through the window for his return. 'Why is his chariot so long in coming? Why don't we hear the sound of the wheels?' [29]But her ladies-in-waiting—and she herself—replied, [30]'There is much loot to be divided, and it takes time. Each man receives a girl or two; and Sisera will get gorgeous robes, and he will bring home many gifts for me.' [31]O Lord, may all your enemies perish as Sisera did, but may those who love the Lord shine as the sun!" After that there was peace in the land for forty years.

2 Sam 10:12. Courage! We must really act like men today if we are going to save our people and the cities of our God. May the Lord's will be done.

Neh 1:1. The autobiography of *Nehemiah, the son of Hecaliah:* In December of the twentieth year of the reign of King Ar-ta-xerxes of Persia, when I was at the palace at Shushan, [2]one of my fellow Jews named Hanani came to visit me with some men who had arrived from Judah. I took the opportunity to inquire about how things were going in Jerusalem. "How are they getting along?" I asked. "—the Jews who returned to Jerusalem from their exile here?" [3]"Well," they replied, "things are not good; the wall of Jerusalem is still torn down, and the gates are burned."

4. When I heard this, I sat down and cried. In fact, I refused to eat for several days, for I spent the time in prayer to the God of heaven. [5]"O Lord God," I cried out; "O great and awesome God who keeps his promises and is so loving and kind to those who love and obey him! Hear my prayer! [6, 7]Listen carefully to what I say! Look down and see me praying night and day for your people Israel. I confess that we have sinned against you; yes, I and my people have committed the horrible sin of not obeying the commandments you gave us through your servant Moses. [8]Oh, please remember what you told Moses! You said, *'If you sin, I will scatter you among the nations;* [9]*but if you return to me and obey my laws, even though you are exiled to the farthest corners of the universe, I will bring you back to Jerusalem. For Jerusalem is the place in which I have chosen to live.'* [10]We are your servants, the people you rescued by your great power. [11]O Lord, please hear my prayer! Heed the prayers of those of us who delight to honor you. Please help me now as I go in and ask the king for a great favor—put it into his heart to be kind to me." (I was the king's cupbearer.)

Neh 2:1, 2. One day in April four months later, as I was serving the king his wine he asked me, "Why so sad? You aren't sick, are you? You look like a man with deep troubles." (For until then I had always been cheerful when I was with him.) I was badly frightened, [3]but I replied, "Sir, why shouldn't I be sad? For the city where my ancestors are buried is in ruins, and the gates have been burned down." [4]"Well, what should be done?" the king asked. With a quick prayer to the God of heaven, I replied, "If it please Your Majesty and if you look upon me with your royal favor, send me to Judah to rebuild the city of my fathers!" [5, 6]The king replied, with the queen sitting beside him, "How long will you be gone? When will you return?" So it was agreed! And I set a time for my departure! [7]Then I added this to my request: "If it please the king, give me letters to the governors west of the Euphrates River instructing them to let me travel through their countries on my way to Judah; [8]also a letter to Asaph, the manager of the king's forest, instructing him to give me timber for the beams and for the gates of the fortress near the Temple, and for the city walls, and for a house for myself." And the king granted these requests, for God was being gracious to me. [9]When I arrived in the provinces west of the Euphrates River, I delivered the king's letters to the governors there. (The king, I should add, had sent along army officers and troops to protect me!) [10]But when Sanballat (the Horonite) and Tobiah (an Ammonite who was a government official) heard of my arrival, they were very angry that anyone was interested in helping Israel. [11, 12]Three days after my arrival at Jerusalem I stole out during the night, taking only a few men with me; for I hadn't told a soul about the plans for Jerusalem which God had put into my heart. I was mounted on my donkey and the others were on foot, [13]and we went out through the Valley Gate toward the Jackal's Well and over to the Dung Gate to see the broken walls and burned gates. [14, 15]Then we went to the Fountain Gate and to the King's Pool, but my donkey couldn't get through the rubble. So we circled the city, and I followed the brook, inspecting the wall, and entered again at the Valley Gate. [16]The city officials did not know I had been out there, or why, for as yet I had said nothing to anyone about my plans —not to the political or religious leaders, or even to those who would be doing the work. [17]But now I told them, "You know full well the tragedy of our city; it lies in ruins and its gates are burned. Let us rebuild the wall of Jerusalem and rid ourselves of this disgrace!" [18]Then I told them about the desire God had put into my heart, and of my conversation with the king, and the plan to which he had agreed. They replied at once, "Good! Let's rebuild the wall!" And so the work began. [19]But when Sanballat and Tobiah and Geshem the Arab heard of our plan, they scoffed and said, "What are you doing, rebelling against the king like this?" [20]But I replied, "The God of heaven will help us, and we, his servants, will rebuild this wall; but you may have no part in this affair." chapters 3–6.

Neh 5:1. About this time there was a great outcry of protest from parents against some of the rich Jews who were profiteering on them. [2, 3, 4]What was happening was that families who ran out of money for food had to sell their children or mortgage their fields, vineyards, and homes to these rich men; and some couldn't even do that, for they already had borrowed to the limit to pay their taxes. [5]"We are their brothers, and our children are just like theirs," the people protested. "Yet we must sell our children into slavery to get enough money to live. We have already sold some of our daughters, and we are helpless to redeem them, for our fields, too, are mortgaged to these men." [6]I was very angry when I heard this; [7]so after thinking about it I spoke out against these rich government officials. "What is this you are doing?" I demanded. "How dare you demand a mortgage as a condition for helping another Israelite?" Then I called a public trial to deal with them. [8]At the trial I shouted at them, "The rest of us are doing all we can to *help* our Jewish brothers who have returned from exile as slaves in distant lands, but you are forcing them right back into slavery again. How often must we redeem them?" And they had nothing to say in their own defense. [9]Then I pressed further, "What you are doing is very evil," I exclaimed. "Should you not walk in the fear of our God? Don't we have enough enemies among the nations around us who are trying to destroy us? [10]The rest of us are lending money and grain to our fellow-Jews without any interest. I beg you, gentlemen, stop this business of usury. [11]Restore their fields, vineyards, oliveyards, and homes to them this very day and drop your claims against them." [12]So they agreed to do it and said that they would assist their brothers without requiring them to mortgage their lands and sell them their children. Then I summoned the priests and made these men formally vow to carry out their promises. [13]And I invoked the curse of God upon any of them who refused. "May God destroy your homes and livelihood if you fail to keep this promise," I declared. And all the people shouted, "Amen," and praised the Lord. And the rich men did as they had promised. [14]I would like to mention that for the entire twelve years that I was governor of Judah—from the twentieth until the thirty-second year of the reign of King Ar-ta-xerxes—my aides and I accepted no salaries or other assistance from the people of Israel. [15]This was quite a contrast to the former governors who had demanded food and wine and $100 a day in cash, and had put the population at the mercy of their aides, who tyrannized them; but I obeyed God and did not act that way. [16]I stayed at work on the wall and refused to speculate in land; I also required my officials to spend time on the wall. [17]All this despite the fact that I regularly fed 150 Jewish officials at my table, besides visitors from other countries! [18]The provisions required for each day were one ox, six fat sheep, and a large number of domestic fowls; and we needed a huge supply of all kinds of wines every ten days. Yet I refused to make a special levy against the people, for they were already having a difficult time.

Ps 137:1. Weeping, we sat beside the rivers of Babylon thinking of Jerusalem. [2]We have put away our lyres, hanging them upon the branches of the willow trees, [3, 4]for how can we sing? Yet our captors, our tormentors, demand that we sing for them the happy songs of Zion! [5, 6]If I forget you, O Jerusalem, let my right hand forget its skill upon the harp. If I fail to love her more than my highest joy, let me never sing again.

See *Patriotism.*

COURAGE Joshua charged to have, Deut 31: 7, 8, 22, 23; Josh 1:1–9; the Israelites, Lev 26:6–8; 2 Chron 32:7, 8; Solomon, 1 Chron 22:13; 28:20; Asa, 2 Chron 15:1–7. Charged by Jehoshaphat on the judicial and executive officers he appointed, 2 Chron 19:11.

SCRIPTURES RELATING TO. Ps 31:24. So cheer up! Take courage if you are depending on the Lord.

Prov 28:1. The wicked flee when no one is chasing them! But the godly are bold as lions!

Ezk 2:6. Son of dust, don't be afraid of them; don't be frightened even though their threats are sharp and barbed and sting like scorpions. Don't be dismayed by their dark scowls. For remember, they are rebels!

Ezk 3:9. I have made your forehead as hard as rock. So don't be afraid of them, or fear their sullen, angry looks, even though they are such rebels.

1 Cor 16:13. Keep your eyes open for spiritual danger; stand true to the Lord; act like men; be strong.

Phil 1:27. But whatever happens to me, remember always to live as Christians should, so that, whether I ever see you again or not, I will keep on hearing good reports that you are standing side by side with one strong purpose—to tell the Good News [28]fearlessly, no matter what your enemies may do. They will see this as a sign of their downfall, but for you it will be a clear sign from God that he is with you, and that he has given you eternal life with him.

2 Tim 1:7. For the Holy Spirit, God's gift, does not want you to be afraid of people, but to be wise and strong, and to love them and enjoy being with them.

Jas 5:8. Take courage, for the coming of the Lord is near.

INSTANCES OF THE COURAGE OF CONVICTION. Abraham, in leaving his fatherland, Gen 12: 1–9; Heb 11:8; in offering Isaac, Gen 22:1–14. Gideon, in destroying the altar of Baal, Judg 6: 25–31. Ezra, in undertaking the perilous journey from Babylon to Palestine without a guard, Ezra 8: 22, 23.

The Jews, in answering Tattenai, Ezra 5:11. The three Hebrews, who refused to bow down to the image of Nebuchadnezzar, Dan 3:16–18. Daniel, in persisting in prayer, regardless of the edict against praying, Dan 6:10. Peter and John, in refusing to obey men, rather than God, Acts 4:19; 5:29.

See *Ministers, Courage of; Reproof.*

INSTANCES OF PERSONAL BRAVERY. Joshua and Caleb, in advising that Israel go at once and possess the land, Num 13:30; 14:6–12. Othni-el, in conquering Kiriath-sepher, Josh 15:16, 17. Gideon, in attacking the confederate armies of the Midianites and Amalekites with 300 men, Judg 7:7–23. Deborah, in leading Israel's armies, Judg 4. Jael, in killing Sisera, Judg 4:18–22. Agag, in the indifference with which he faced death, 1 Sam 15:32, 33. David, in killing Goliath, 1 Sam 17:32–50; in entering Saul's camp, and carrying away Saul's spear, 1 Sam 26:7–12. David's captains, 2 Sam 23. Joab, in reproving King David, 2 Sam 19:5–7. Nehemiah, in refusing to hide in the temple, Neh 6:10–13. Esther, in going to the king to save her people, Esther 4: 8, 16; chapters 5–7.

Joseph of Arimathaea, in caring for the body of Jesus, Mk 15:42, 43. Thomas, in being willing to die with Jesus, Jn 11:16. Peter and other disciples, Acts 3:12–26; 4:9–13, 19, 20, 31. The apostles, under persecution, Acts 5:21, 29–32. Paul, in going to Jerusalem, despite his impressions that jail and suffering awaited him, Acts 20:22–24; 24:14, 25.

See *Boldness, of the Righteous; Minister; Reproof, Faithfulness in; Cowardice.*

COURIER See *Messenger.*

COURT IN ISRAEL. 1 Chron 26:29. Chenaniah and his sons (from the subclan of Izhar) were appointed public adminstrators and judges. [30]Hashabiah and 1,700 of his clansmen from Hebron, all outstanding men, were placed in charge of the territory of Israel west of the Jordan River; they were responsible for the religious affairs and public administration of that area. [31, 32]Twenty-seven hundred outstanding men of the clan of the Hebronites, under the supervision of Jerijah, were appointed to control the religious and public affairs of the tribes of Reuben, Gad, and the half-tribe of Manasseh. These men, all of whom had excellent qualifications, were appointed on the basis of their ancestry and ability at Jazer in Gilead in the fortieth year of King David's reign.

2 Chron 19:8. Jehoshaphat set up courts in Jerusalem, too, with the Levites and priests and clan leaders and judges. [9]These were his instructions to them: "You are to act always in the fear of God, with honest hearts. [10]Whenever a case is referred to you by the judges out in the provinces, whether murder cases or other violations of the laws and ordinances of God, you are to clarify the evidence for them and help them to decide justly, lest the wrath of God come down upon you and them; if you do this, you will discharge your responsibility." [11]Then he appointed Amariah, the High Priest, to be the court of final appeal in cases involving violation of sacred affairs.

See *Sanhedrin.*

CHURCH. Mt 18:15. If a brother sins against you, go to him privately and confront him with his fault. If he listens and confesses it, you have won back a brother. [16]But if not, then take one or two others with you and go back to him again, proving everything you say by these witnesses. [17]If he still refuses to listen, then take your case to the church, and if the church's verdict favors you, but he won't accept it, then the church should excommunicate him. [18]And I tell you this—whatever you bind on earth is bound in heaven, and whatever you free on earth will be freed in heaven.

See *Church, Visible, Discipline of.*

CIVIL. Deut 21:19; 22:15; 25:7; Josh 20:4. Held at the tabernacle, Num 27:1, 2; the gates of cities, Ruth 4:1; under a palm tree, Judg 4:5.

Composition of, and Mode of Procedure. Ex 18:25. He chose able men from all over Israel and made them judges over the people—thousands, hundreds, fifties, and tens. [26]They were constantly available to administer justice. They brought the hard cases to Moses but judged the smaller matters themselves.

Deut 1:15. I took the men they selected, some from every tribe, and appointed them as administrative assistants in charge of thousands, hundreds, fifties, and tens to decide their quarrels and assist them in every way. [16]I instructed them to be perfectly fair at all times, even to foreigners! [17]"When giving your decisions," I told them, "never favor a man because he is rich; be fair to great and small alike. Don't fear their displeasure, for you are judging in the place of God. Bring me any cases too difficult for you, and I will handle them."

Deut 17:9. To the priests and Levites, and the chief judge on duty at the time will make the decision.

Ruth 4:2. Then Boaz called for ten of the chief men of the village, and asked them to sit as witnesses. [3]Boaz said to his relative, "You know Naomi, who came back to us from Moab. She is selling our brother Elimelech's property. [4]I felt I should speak to you about it so that you can buy it if you wish, with these respected men as witnesses. If you want it, let me know right away, for if you don't take it, I will. You have the first right to purchase it and I am next." The man replied, "All right, I'll buy it." [5]Then Boaz told him, "Your purchase of the land from Naomi requires your marriage to Ruth so that she can have children to carry on her husband's name, and to inherit the land."

1 Chron 26:29. Chenaniah and his sons (from the subclan of Izhar) were appointed public administrators and judges. *vs.* 30–32.

2 Chron 19:8. Jehoshaphat set up courts in Jerusalem, too, with the Levites and priests and clan leaders and judges. [9]These were his instructions to them: "You are to act always in the fear of God, with honest hearts. [10]Whenever a case is referred to you by the judges out in the provinces, whether murder cases or other violations of the laws and ordinances of God, you are to clarify the evidence for them and help them to decide justly, lest the wrath of God come down upon you and them; if you do this, you will discharge your responsibility." [11]Then he appointed Amariah, the High Priest, to be the court of final appeal in cases involving violation of sacred affairs; and Zebadiah (son of Ishmael), a ruler in Judah, as the court of final appeal in all civil cases.

Mk 14:53. Jesus was led to the High Priest's home where all of the chief priests and other Jewish leaders soon gathered. [55]Inside, the chief priests and the whole Jewish Supreme Court were trying to find something against Jesus that would be sufficient to condemn him to death. But their efforts were in vain. [56]Many false witnesses volunteered, but they contradicted each other. [57]Finally some men stood up to lie about him and said, [58]"We heard him say, 'I will destroy this Temple made with human hands and in three days I will build another, made without hands!' " [59]But even then they didn't get their stories straight! [60]Then the High Priest stood up before the Court and asked Jesus, "Do you refuse to answer this charge? What do you have to say for yourself?" [61]To this Jesus made no reply. Then the High Priest asked him. "Are you the Messiah, the Son of God?" [62]Jesus said, "I am, and you will see me sitting at the right hand of God, and returning to earth in the clouds of heaven." [63, 64]Then the High Priest tore at his clothes and said, "What more do we need? Why wait for witnesses? You have heard his blasphemy. What is your verdict?" And the vote for the death sentence was unanimous. [65]Then some of them began to spit at him, and they blindfolded him and began to hammer his face with their fists. "Who hit you that time, you prophet?" they jeered. And even the bailiffs were using their fists on him as they led him away.

Mk 15:1. Early in the morning the chief priests, elders and teachers of religion—the entire Supreme

Court—met to discuss their next steps. Their decision was to send Jesus under armed guard to Pilate, the Roman governor. Mt 26:54–71; Lk 22:50–71; Jn 18:13–28.

Acts 5:17. The High Priest and his relatives and friends among the Sadducees reacted with violent jealousy. [18]and arrested the apostles, and put them in the public jail. [19]But an angel of the Lord came at night, opened the gates of the jail and brought them out. Then he told them, [20]"Go over to the Temple and preach about this Life!" [21]They arrived at the Temple about daybreak, and immediately began preaching! Later that morning the High Priest and his courtiers arrived at the Temple, and, convening the Jewish Council and the entire Senate, they sent for the apostles to be brought for trial. [25]Then someone arrived with the news that the men they had jailed were out in the Temple, preaching to the people! [26, 27]The police captain went with his officers and arrested them (without violence, for they were afraid the people would kill them if they roughed up the disciples) and brought them in before the Council. [28]"Didn't we tell you never again to preach about this Jesus?" the High Priest demanded. "And instead you have filled all Jerusalem with your teaching and intend to bring the blame for this man's death on us!" [34]But one of their members, a Pharisee named Gamaliel (an expert on religious law and very popular with the people), stood up and requested that the apostles be sent outside the Council chamber while he talked. [38]"And so my advice is, leave these men alone. If what they teach and do is merely on their own, it will soon be overthrown. [39]But if it is of God, you will not be able to stop them, lest you find yourselves fighting even against God." [40]The Council accepted his advice, called in the apostles, had them beaten, and then told them never again to speak in the name of Jesus, and finally let them go. [41]They left the Council chamber rejoicing that God had counted them worthy to suffer dishonor for his name.

See *Judge; Justice; Priest, Judicial Functions of; Sanhedrin.*

CIRCUIT. 1 Sam 7:15. Samuel continued as Israel's judge for the remainder of his life. [16]He rode circuit annually, setting up his court first at Bethel, then Gilgal, and then Mizpah, and cases of dispute were brought to him in each of those three cities from all the surrounding territory. [17]Then he would come back to Ramah, for his home was there, and he would hear cases there, too. And he built an altar to the Lord at Ramah.

SUPERIOR AND INFERIOR. Ex 18:21. "Find some capable, godly, honest men who hate bribes, and appoint them as judges, one judge for each 1000 people; he in turn will have ten judges under him, each in charge of a hundred; and under each of them will be two judges, each responsible for the affairs of fifty people; and each of these will have five judges beneath him, each counseling ten persons. [22]Let these men be responsible to serve the people with justice at all times. Anything that is too important or complicated can be brought to you. But the smaller matters they can take care of themselves. That way it will be easier for you because you will share the burden with them. [23]If you follow this advice, and if the Lord agrees, you will be able to endure the pressures, and there will be peace and harmony in the camp." [24]Moses listened to his father-in-law's advice, and followed this suggestion. [25]He chose able men from all over Israel and made them judges over the people—thousands, hundreds, fifties, and tens. [26]They were constantly available to administer justice. They brought the hard cases to Moses but judged the smaller matters themselves.

Deut 1:15. I took the men they selected, some from every tribe, and appointed them as administrative assistants in charge of thousands, hundreds, fifties, and tens to decide their quarrels and assist them in every way. [16]I instructed them to be perfectly fair at all times, even to foreigners! [17]"When giving your decisions," I told them, "never favor a man because he is rich; be fair to great and small alike. Don't fear their displeasure, for you are judging in the place of God. Bring me any cases too difficult for you, and I will handle them."

Deut 17:8. If a case arises that is too hard for you to decide—for instance, whether someone is guilty of murder when there is insufficient evidence, or whether someone's rights have been violated—you shall take the case to the sanctuary of the Lord your God, [9]to the priests and Levites, and the chief judge on duty at the time will make the decision. [10]His decision is without appeal and is to be followed to the letter. [11]The sentence he imposes is to be fully executed. [12]If the defendant refuses to accept the decision of the priest or judge appointed by God for this purpose, the penalty is death. Such sinners must be purged from Israel. [13]Then everyone will hear about what happened to the man who refused God's verdict, and they will be afraid to defy the court's judgment a second time.

2 Chron 19:5. He appointed judges throughout the nation in all the larger cities, [6]and instructed them: "Watch your step—I have not appointed you—God has; and he will stand beside you and help you give justice in each case that comes before you. [7]Be very much afraid to give any other decision than what God tells you to. For there must be no injustice among God's judges, no partiality, no taking of bribes." [8]Jehoshaphat set up courts in Jerusalem, too, with the Levites and priests and clan leaders and judges. [9]These were his instructions to them: "You are to act always in the fear of God, with honest hearts. [10]Whenever a case is referred to you by the judges out in the provinces, whether murder cases or other violations of the laws and ordinances of God, you are to clarify the evidence for them and help them to decide justly, lest the wrath of God come down upon you and them; if you do this, you will discharge your responsibility."

JUSTICE REQUIRED OF. Ex 23:2, 3. Don't join mobs intent on evil. When on the witness stand, don't be swayed in your testimony by the mood of the majority present, and do not slant your testimony in favor of a man just because he is poor. [6]A man's poverty is no excuse for twisting justice against him. [7]Keep far away from falsely charging anyone with evil; never let an innocent person be put to death. I will not stand for this. [8]Take no bribes, for a bribe makes you unaware of what you clearly see! A bribe hurts the cause of the person who is right.

Deut 1:16. I instructed them to be perfectly fair at all times, even to foreigners! [17]"When giving your decisions," I told them, "never favor a man because he is rich; be fair to great and small alike. Don't fear their displeasure, for you are judging in the place of God. Bring me any cases too difficult for you, and I will handle them."

2 Chron 19:5. He appointed judges throughout the nation in all the larger cities, [6]and instructed them: "Watch your step—I have not appointed you—God has; and he will stand beside you and help you give justice in each case that comes before you. [7]Be very much afraid to give any other decision than what God tells you to. For there must be no injustice among God's judges, no partiality, no taking of bribes." [8]Jehoshaphat set up courts in Jerusalem, too, with the Levites and priests and clan leaders and judges. [9]These were his instructions to them: "You are to act always in the fear of God, with honest hearts. [10]Whenever a case is referred to you by the judges out in the provinces, whether murder cases or other violations of the laws and ordinances of God, you are to clarify the evidence for them and help them to decide justly, lest the wrath of God come down upon you and them; if you do this, you will discharge your responsibility."

See *Judge; Justice.*

SENTENCE OF, FINAL AND OBLIGATORY. Deut 17:8. If a case arises that is too hard for you to decide—for instance, whether someone is guilty of murder when there is insufficient evidence, or whether someone's rights have been violated—you shall take the case to the sanctuary of the Lord your God, [9]to the priests and Levites, and the chief judge on duty at the time will make the decision. [10]His decision is without appeal and is to be followed to the letter. [11]The sentence he imposes is to be fully executed. [12]If the defendant refuses to accept the decision of the priest or judge appointed by God for this purpose, the penalty is death. Such sinners must be purged from Israel.

CONTEMPT OF. Deut 17:8. If a case arises that is too hard for you to decide—for instance, whether someone is guilty of murder when there is insufficient evidence, or whether someone's rights have been violated—you shall take the case to the sanctuary of the Lord your God, [9]to the priests and Levites, and the chief judge on duty at the time will make the decision. [10]His decision is without appeal and is to be followed to the letter. [11]The sentence he imposes is to be fully executed. [12]If the defendant refuses to accept the decision of the priest or judge appointed by God for this purpose, the penalty is death. Such sinners must be purged from Israel. [13]Then everyone will hear about what happened to the man who refused God's verdict, and they will be afraid to defy the court's judgment a second time.

Mic 5:1. Mobilize! The enemy lays siege to Jerusalem! With a rod they shall strike the Judge of Israel on the face.

Acts 23:1. Gazing intently at the Council, Paul began: "Brothers, I have always lived before God in all good conscience!" [2]Instantly Ananias the High Priest commanded those close to Paul to slap him on the mouth. [3]Paul said to him, "God shall slap you, you whitewashed pigpen. What kind of judge are you to break the law yourself by ordering me struck like that?" [4]Those standing near Paul said to him, "Is that the way to talk to God's High Priest?" [5]"I didn't realize he was the High Priest, brothers," Paul replied, "for the Scriptures say, 'Never speak evil of any of your rulers.' "

CORRUPT. Prov 17:15. The Lord despises those who say that bad is good, and good is bad.

Prov 29:26. Do you want justice? Don't fawn on the judge, but ask the Lord for it!

Isa 1:23. Your leaders are rebels, companions of thieves; all of them take bribes and won't defend the widows and orphans.

Isa 5:23. They take bribes to pervert justice, letting the wicked go free and putting innocent men in jail.

Isa 10:1. Woe to unjust judges and to those who issue unfair laws, says the Lord, [2]so that there is no justice for the poor, the widows and orphans. Yes, it is true that they even rob the widows and fatherless children.

Mic 3:11. You leaders who take bribes; you priests and prophets who won't preach and prophesy until you're paid.

Mic 7:3. They go at their evil deeds with both hands, and how skilled they are in using them! The governor and judge alike demand bribes. The rich man pays them off and tells them whom to ruin. Justice is twisted between them.

Zeph 3:3. Her leaders are like roaring lions hunting for their victims—out for everything that they can get. Her judges are like ravenous wolves at evening time, who by dawn have left no trace of their prey.

Mt 26:59. The chief priests and, in fact, the entire Jewish Supreme Court assembled there and looked for witnesses who would lie about Jesus, in order to build a case against him that would result in a death sentence. [60, 61]But even though they found many who agreed to be false witnesses, these always contradicted each other. Finally two men were found who declared, "This man said, 'I am able to destroy the Temple of God and rebuild it in three days.' " [62]Then the High Priest stood up and said to Jesus, "Well, what about it? Did you say that, or didn't you?"

Mt 27:18. For he knew very well that the Jewish leaders had arrested Jesus out of envy because of his popularity with the people. [Mk 15:10.] [19]Just then, as he was presiding over the court, Pilate's wife sent him this message: "Leave that good man alone; for I had a terrible nightmare concerning him last night." [20]Meanwhile the chief priests and Jewish officials persuaded the crowds to ask for Barabbas' release, and for Jesus' death. [21]So when the governor asked again, "Which of these two shall I release to you?" the crowd shouted back their reply: "Barabbas!" [22]"Then what shall I do with Jesus, your Messiah?" Pilate asked. And they shouted, "Crucify him!" [23]"Why?" Pilate demanded. "What has he done wrong?" But they kept shouting, "Crucify! Crucify!" [24]When Pilate saw that he wasn't getting anywhere, and that a riot was developing, he sent for a bowl of water and washed his hands before the crowd, saying, "I am innocent of the blood of this good man. The responsibility is yours!" [25]And the mob yelled back, "His blood be on us and on our children!" [26]Then Pilate released Barabbas to them. And after he had whipped Jesus, he gave him to the Roman soldiers to take away and crucify.

Mk 14:53. Jesus was led to the High Priest's home where all of the chief priests and other Jewish leaders soon gathered. [55]Inside, the chief priests and the whole Jewish Supreme Court were trying to find something against Jesus that would be sufficient to condemn him to death. But their efforts were in vain. [56]Many false witnesses volunteered, but they contradicted each other. [57]Finally some men stood up to lie about him and said, [58]"We heard him say, 'I will destroy this Temple made with human hands and in three days I will build another, made without human hands!' " [59]But even then they didn't get their stories straight! [60]Then the High Priest stood up before the Court and asked Jesus, "Do you refuse to answer this charge? What do you have to say for yourself?" [61]To this Jesus made no reply. Then the High Priest asked him. "Are you the Messiah, the Son of God?" [62]Jesus said, "I am, and you will see me sitting at the right hand of God, and returning to earth in the clouds of heaven." [63, 64]Then the High Priest tore at his clothes and said, "What more do we need? Why wait for witnesses? You have heard his blasphemy. What is your verdict?" And the vote for the death sentence was unanimous. [65]Then some of them began to spit at him, and they blindfolded him and began to hammer his face with their fists. "Who hit you that time, you prophet?" they jeered. And even the bailiffs were using their fists on him as they led him away.

Acts 4:15. So they sent them out of the Council chamber and conferred among themselves. [16]"What shall we do with these men?" they asked each other. "We can't deny that they have done a tremendous miracle, and everybody in Jerusalem knows about it. [17]But perhaps we can stop them from spreading their propaganda. We'll tell them that if they do it again we'll really throw the book at them." [18]So they called them back in, and told them never again to speak about Jesus.

Acts 6:11. So they brought in some men to lie about him, claiming they had heard Stephen curse Moses, and even God. [12]This accusation roused the crowds to fury against Stephen, and the Jewish leaders arrested him and brought him before the Council. [13]The lying witnesses testified again that Stephen was constantly speaking against the Temple and against the laws of Moses. [14]They declared, "We have heard him say that this fellow Jesus of Nazareth will destroy the Temple, and throw out all of Moses' laws."

Acts 24:26. He also hoped that Paul would bribe him, so he sent for him from time to time and talked with him. [27]Two years went by in this way; then Felix was succeeded by Porcius Festus. And because Felix wanted to gain favor with the Jews, he left Paul in chains.

See *Bribery; Judge; Justice.*

ACCUSED SPOKE IN HIS OWN DEFENSE. Jer 26:11. Then the priests and the false prophets presented their accusations to the officials and the people. "This man should die!" they said. "You have heard with your own ears what a traitor he is, for he has prophesied against this city." [12]Then Jeremiah spoke in his defense. "The Lord sent me," he said, "to prophesy against this Temple and this city. He gave me every word of all that I have spoken. [13]But if you stop your sinning and begin obeying the Lord your God, he will cancel all the punishment he has announced against you. [14]As for me, I am helpless and in your power—do with me as you think best. [15]But there is one thing sure, if you kill me, you will be killing an innocent man and the responsibility will lie upon you and upon this city and upon every person living in it; for it is absolutely true that the Lord sent me to speak every word that you have heard from me." [16]Then the officials and people said to the priests and false prophets, "This man does not deserve the death sentence, for he has spoken to us in the name of the Lord our God."

Mk 15:3, 4. Then the chief priests accused him of many crimes, and Pilate asked him, "Why don't you say something? What about all these charges against you?" [5]But Jesus said no more, much to Pilate's amazement.

Acts 4:8. Then Peter, filled with the Holy Spirit, said to them, "Honorable leaders and elders of our nation, [9]if you mean the good deed done to the cripple, and how he was healed, [10]let me clearly state to you and to all the people of Israel that it was done in the name and power of Jesus from Nazareth, the Messiah, the man you crucified—but God raised back to life again. It is by his authority that this man stands here healed! [11]For Jesus the Messiah is (the one referred to in the Scriptures when they speak of) a 'stone discarded by the builders which became the capstone of the arch.' [12]There is salvation in no one else! Under all heaven there is no other name for men to call upon to save them." [18]So they called them back in, and told them never again to speak about Jesus. [19]But Peter and John replied, "You decide whether God wants us to obey you instead of him! [20]We cannot stop telling about the wonderful things we saw Jesus do and heard him say."

Acts 5:29. But Peter and the apostles replied, "We must obey God rather than men. [30]The God of our ancestors brought Jesus back to life again after you had killed him by hanging him on a cross. [31]Then, with mighty power, God exalted him to be a Prince and Savior, so that the people of Israel would have an opportunity for repentance, and for their sins to be forgiven. [32]And we are witnesses of these things, and so is the Holy Spirit, who is given by God to all who obey him."

Acts 7:1. Then the high Priest asked him, "Are these accusations true?" [2]This was Stephen's lengthy reply: "The glorious God appeared to our ancestor Abraham in Iraq before he moved to Syria, [3]and told him to leave his native land, to say good-bye to his relatives and to start out for a country that God would direct him to. [4]So he left the land of the Chaldeans and lived in Haran, in Syria, until his father died. Then God brought him here to the land of Israel, [5]but gave him no property of his own, not one little tract of land. However, God promised that eventually the whole country would belong to him and his descendants—though as yet he had no children! [6]But God also told him that these descendants of his would leave the land and live in a foreign country and there become slaves for 400 years. [7]'But I will punish the nation that enslaves them,' God told him, 'and afterwards my people will return to this land of Israel and worship me here.' [8]God also gave Abraham the ceremony of circumcision at that time, as evidence of the covenant between God and the people of Abraham. And so Isaac, Abraham's son, was circumcised when he was eight days old. Isaac became the father of Jacob, and Jacob was the father of the twelve patriarchs of the Jewish nation. [9]These men were very jealous of Joseph and sold him to be a slave in Egypt. But God was with him, [10]and delivered him out of all his anguish, and gave him favor before Pharaoh, king of Egypt. God also gave Joseph unusual wisdom, so that Pharaoh appointed him governor over all Egypt, as well as putting him in charge of all the affairs of the palace. [11]But a famine developed in Egypt and Canaan and there was great misery for our ancestors. When their food was gone, [12]Jacob heard that there was still grain in Egypt, so he sent his sons to buy some. [13]The second time they went, Joseph revealed his identity to his brothers, and they were introduced to Pharaoh. [14]Then Joseph sent for his father Jacob and all his brothers' families to come to Egypt, seventy-five persons in all. [15]So Jacob came to Egypt, where he died, and all his sons. [16]All of them were taken to Shechem and buried in the tomb Abraham bought from the sons of Hamor, Shechem's father. [17, 18]As the time drew near when God would fulfill his promise to Abraham to free his descendants from slavery, the Jewish people greatly multiplied in Egypt; but then a king was crowned who had no respect for Joseph's memory. [19]This king plotted against our race, forcing parents to abandon their children in the fields. [20]About that time Moses was born—a child of divine beauty. His parents hid him at home for three months, [21]and when at last they could no longer keep him hidden, and had to abandon him, Pharaoh's daughter found him and adopted him as her own son, [22]and taught him all the wisdom of the Egyptians, and he became a mighty prince and orator. [23]One day as he was nearing his fortieth birthday, it came into his mind to visit his brothers, the people of Israel. [24]During this visit he saw an Egyptian mistreating a man of Israel. So Moses killed the Egyptian. [25]Moses supposed his brothers would realize that God had sent him to help them, but they didn't. [26]The next day he visited them again and saw two men of Israel fighting. He tried to be a peacemaker. 'Gentlemen,' he said, 'you are brothers and shouldn't be fighting like this! It is wrong!' [27]But the man in the wrong told Moses to mind his own business. 'Who made *you* a ruler and judge over us?' he asked. [28]'Are you going to kill me as you killed that Egyptian yesterday?' [29]At this, Moses fled the country, and lived in the land of Midian, where his two sons were born. [30]Forty years later, in the desert near Mount Sinai, an Angel appeared to him in a flame of fire in a bush. [31]Moses saw it and wondered what it was, and as he ran to see, the voice of the Lord called out to him, [32]'I am the God of your ancestors—of Abraham, Isaac and Jacob.' Moses shook with terror and dared not look. [33]And the Lord said to him, 'Take off your shoes, for you are standing on holy ground. [34]I have seen the anguish of my people in Egypt and have heard their cries. I have come down to deliver them. Come, I will send you to Egypt.' [35]And so God sent back the same man his people had previously rejected by demanding, 'Who made *you* a ruler and judge over us?' Moses was sent to be their ruler and savior. [36]And by means of many remarkable miracles he led them out of Egypt and through the Red Sea, and back and forth through the wilderness for forty years. [37]Moses himself told the people of Israel, 'God will raise up a Prophet much like me from among your brothers,' [38]How true this proved to be, for in the wilderness, Moses was the go-between—the mediator between the people of Israel and the Angel who gave them the Law of God—the Living Word—on Mount Sinai. [39]But our fathers rejected Moses and wanted to return to Egypt. [40]They told Aaron, 'Make idols for us, so that we will have gods to lead us back; for we don't know what has become of this Moses, who brought us out of Egypt.' [41]So they made a calf-idol and sacrificed to it, and rejoiced in this thing they had made. [42]Then God turned away from them and gave them up, and let them serve the sun, moon and stars as their gods! In the book of Amos' prophecies the Lord God asks, 'Was it to me you were sacrificing during those forty years in the desert, Israel? [43]No, your real interest was in your heathen gods—Sakkuth, and the star god Kaiway, and in all the images you made. So I will send you into captivity far away beyond Babylon.' 44Our ancestors carried along with them a portable Temple, or Tabernacle, through the wilderness. In it they kept the stone tablets with the Ten Commandments written on them. This building was constructed in exact accordance with the plan shown to Moses by the Angel. 45Years later, when Joshua led the battles against the Gentile nations, this Tabernacle was taken with them into their new territory, and used until the time of King David. 46God blessed David greatly, and David asked for the privilege of building a permanent Temple for the God of Jacob. 47But it was Solomon who actually built it. 48, 49However, God doesn't live in temples made by human hands. 'The heaven is my throne,' says the Lord through his prophets, 'and earth is my footstool. What kind of home could you build?' asks the Lord. 'Would I stay in it? 50Didn't I make both heaven and earth?' 51You stiff-necked heathen! Must you forever resist the Holy Spirit? But your fathers did, and so do you! 52Name one prophet your ancestors didn't persecute! They even killed the ones who predicted the coming of the Righteous One—the Messiah whom you betrayed and murdered. 53Yes, and you deliberately destroyed God's Laws, though you received them from the hands of angels." 54The Jewish leaders were stung to fury by Stephen's accusation, and ground their teeth in rage. 55But Stephen, full of the Holy Spirit, gazed steadily upward into heaven and saw the glory of God and Jesus standing at God's right hand. 56And he told them, "Look, I see the heavens opened and Jesus the Messiah standing beside God, at his right hand!"

Acts 23:1. Gazing intently at the Council, Paul began: "Brothers, I have always lived before God in all good conscience!" 2Instantly Ananias the High Priest commanded those close to Paul to slap him on the mouth. 3Paul said to him, "God shall slap you, you whitewashed pigpen. What kind of judge are you to break the law yourself by ordering me struck like that?" 4Those standing near Paul said to him, "Is that the way to talk to God's High Priest?" 5"I didn't realize he was the High Priest, brothers," Paul replied, "for the Scriptures say, 'Never speak evil of any of your rulers.' " 6Then Paul thought of something! Part of the Council were Sadducees, and part were Pharisees! So he shouted, "Brothers, I am a Pharisee, as were all my ancestors! And I am being tried here today because I believe in the resurrection of the dead!" 7This divided the Council right down the middle—the Pharisees against the Sadducees.

Acts 26:1. Then Agrippa said to Paul, "Go ahead. Tell us your story." So Paul, with many gestures, presented his defense: 2"I am fortunate, King Agrippa," he began, "to be able to present my answer before you, 3for I know you are an expert on Jewish laws and customs. Now please listen patiently! 4As the Jews are well aware, I was given a thorough Jewish training from my earliest childhood in Tarsus and later at Jerusalem, and I lived accordingly. 5If they would admit it, they know that I have always been the strictest of Pharisees when it comes to obedience to Jewish laws and customs. 6But the real reason behind their accusations is something else—it is because I am looking forward to the fulfillment of God's promise made to our ancestors. 7The twelve tribes of Israel strive night and day to attain this same hope I have! Yet, O King, for me it is a crime, they say! 8But is it a crime to believe in the resurrection of the dead? Does it seem incredible to you that God can bring men back to life again? 9I used to believe that I ought to do many horrible things to the followers of Jesus of Nazareth. 10I imprisoned many of the saints in Jerusalem, as authorized by the High Priests; and when they were condemned to death, I cast my vote against them. 11I used torture to try to make Christians everywhere curse Christ. I was so violently opposed to them that I even hounded them in distant cities in foreign lands. 12I was on such a mission to Damascus, armed with the authority and commission of the chief priests, 13when one day about noon, sir, a light from heaven brighter than the sun shone down on me and my companions. 14We all fell down, and I heard a voice speaking to me in Hebrew, 'Saul, Saul, why are you persecuting me? You are only hurting yourself.' 15'Who are you, sir?' I asked. And the Lord replied, 'I am Jesus, the one you are persecuting. 16Now stand up! For I have appeared to you to appoint you as my servant and my witness. You are to tell the world about this experience and about the many other occasions when I shall appear to you. 17And I will protect you from both your own people and the Gentiles. Yes, I am going to send you to the Gentiles 18to open their eyes to their true condition so that they may repent and live in the light of God instead of in Satan's darkness, so that they may receive forgiveness for their sins and God's inheritance along with all people everywhere whose sins are cleansed away, who are set apart by faith in me.' 19And so, O King Agrippa, I was not disobedient to that vision from heaven! 20I preached first to those in Damascus, then in Jerusalem and through Judea, and also to the Gentiles that all must forsake their sins and turn to God—and prove their repentance by doing good deeds. 21The Jews arrested me in the Temple for preaching this, and tried to kill me, 22but God protected me so that I am still alive today to tell these facts to everyone, both great and small. I teach nothing except what the prophets and Moses said — 23that the Messiah would suffer, and be the First to rise from the dead, to bring light to Jews and Gentiles alike." 24Suddenly Festus shouted, "Paul, you are insane. Your long studying has broken your mind!" 25But Paul replied, "I am not insane, Most Excellent Festus. I speak words of sober truth. 26And King Agrippa knows about these things. I speak frankly for I am sure these events are all familiar to him, for they were not done in a corner! 27King Agrippa, do you believe the prophets? But I know you do—" 28Agrippa interrupted him. "With trivial proofs like these, you expect me to become a Christian?" [29]And Paul replied, "Would to God that whether my arguments are trivial or strong, both you and everyone here in this audience might become the same as I am, except for these chains." [30]Then the king, the governor, Bernice, and all the others stood and left. [31]As they talked it over afterwards they agreed, "This man hasn't done anything worthy of death or imprisonment." [32]And Agrippa said to Festus, "He could be free if he hadn't appealed to Caesar!"

See *Appeal; Punishment; Witness.*

COURTESY See *Manners.*

COURTSHIP Ancient customs of: Suitor visited the maid, Judg 14:7; women proposed marriage, Ruth 3:9–13.

See *Marriage.*

COVENANT Sacred, Josh 9:18–21; Gal 3:15. Binding, Josh 9:18–20; Jer 34:8–21; Ezk 17:14–18; Gal 3:15. Binding, not only on those who make them, but on those who are represented, Deut 29: 14, 15.

Blood of, Ex 24:8. Book of, Ex 24:7. The Mosaic law called a covenant, Ex 34:28.

See *Contract; Vows.*

OF MEN WITH MEN. Breach of, punished, 2 Sam 21:1–6; Jer 34:8–22; Ezk 17:12–19. National, see *Alliances.*

Ratified: removing the shoe, Ruth 4:7–11; written and sealed, Neh 9:38; Jer 32:10–12; by giving presents, Gen 21:27–30; 1 Sam 18:1–4; by preparing a feast, Gen 26:30; by a monument, Gen 31:45, 46, 49–53; by salting, Lev 2:13; Num 18:19; by offering a sacrifice, Gen 15:9–17; Ezra 10:19; Jer 34:18, 19; by oath, see *Oath.*

See *Contract.*

INSTANCES OF. Abraham and Abimelech, Gen 21:22–32. Abimelech and Isaac, Gen 26:26–31. Jacob and Laban, Gen 31:44–54. Jonathan and David, 1 Sam 18:1–4; 20:16, 42; 2 Sam 21:7. Jews with each other, to serve God, 2 Chron 15:12–15; Neh 10:28–32. King Zedekiah and his subjects, Jer 34:8. Ahab with Benhadad, 1 Kgs 20:34. Subjects with sovereign, 2 Chron 23:1–3, 15–17.

OF GOD WITH MEN. Confirmed with an oath, Gen 22:16; Ps 89:35, 36; Lk 1:72, 73; Heb 6:13, 17, 18. Binding, Lev 26; Jer 11:1–3; Gal 3:15. Everlasting, Gen 8:20–22; 9:1–17; Ps 105:8–11; Isa 54:10; 61: 8. God faithful to, Lev 26:44, 45; Deut 4:31; 7:8, 9; Judg 2:1; 1 Kgs 8:22, 23; Ps 105:8–11; 106:45; 111:5; Mic 7:20. Repudiated by God on account of Jews' idolatry, Jer 44:26, 27; Heb 8:9. Broken by the Jews, Jer 22:9; Ezk 16:59, 60; Heb 8:9. Punishments for breaking of, Lev 26:25–46.

INSTANCES OF. Of the sabbath, Ex 31:16. Of the Ten Commandments, Ex 34:28; Deut 5:2, 3; 9: 9. With Adam, Gen 2:16, 17; Noah, Gen 8:15, 16; 9: 8–17; Abraham, Gen 12:1–3; 15; 17:1–22; Ex 6:4–9; Ps 105:8–11; Rom 9:7–13; Gal 3. See *Circumcision.* With Isaac, Gen 17:19; Jacob, Gen 28:13–15. With the Israelites to deliver them from Egypt, Ex 6:4–9. With Phinehas, Num 25:12, 13. With Israel, at Horeb, Deut 5:2, 3; in Moab, Deut 29:1–15. Of the Levites, Neh 13:29; Mal 2:4, 5. With David, 2 Sam 7:12–16; 1 Chron 17:11–14; 2 Chron 6:16. With David and his house, 2 Sam 23:5; Ps 89:20–37; Jer 33:20, 21. With his people, Isa 55:3; 59:21. To be confirmed, Dan 9:27.

THE NEW COVENANT. Jer 31:31. The day will come, says the Lord, when I will make a new contract with the people of Israel and Judah. [32]It won't be like the one I made with their fathers when I took them by the hand to bring them out of the land of Egypt—a contract they broke, forcing me to reject them, says the Lord. [33]But this is the new contract I will make with them: I will inscribe my laws upon their hearts, so that they shall want to honor me; then they shall truly be my people and I will be their God. [34]At that time it will no longer be necessary to admonish one another to know the Lord. For everyone, both great and small, shall really know me then, says the Lord, and I will forgive and forget their sins.

Mt 26:27. And he took a cup of wine and gave thanks for it and gave it to them and said, "Each one drink from it, [28]for this is my blood, sealing the New Covenant. It is poured out to forgive the sins of multitudes. [29]Mark my words—I will not drink this wine again until the day I drink it new with you in my Father's Kingdom." Mk 14:24; Lk 22: 20; 1 Cor 11:25.

Heb 8:4. The sacrifice he offers is far better than those offered by the earthly priests. (But even so, if he were here on earth he wouldn't even be permitted to be a priest, because down here the priests still follow the old Jewish system of sacrifices.) [5]Their work is connected with a mere earthly model of the real tabernacle in heaven; for when Moses was getting ready to build the tabernacle, God warned him to follow exactly the pattern of the heavenly tabernacle as shown to him on Mount Sinai. [6]But Christ, as a Minister in heaven, has been rewarded with a far more important work than those who serve under the old laws, because the new agreement which he passes on to us from God contains far more wonderful promises. [7]The old agreement didn't even work. If it had, there would have been no need for another to replace it. [8]But God himself found fault with the old one, for he said, "The day will come when I will make a new agreement with the people of Israel and the people of Judah. [9]This new agreement will not be like the old one I gave to their fathers on the day when I took them by the hand to lead them out of the land of Egypt; they did not keep their part in that agreement, so I had to cancel it. [10]But this is the new agreement I will make with the people of Israel, says the Lord: I will write my laws in their minds so that they will know what I want them to do without my even telling them, and these laws will be in their hearts so that they will want to obey them, and I will be their God and they shall be my people. [11]And no one then will need to speak to his friend or neighbor or brother, saying, 'You, too, should know the Lord,' because everyone, great and small, will know me already. [12]And I will be merciful to them in their wrongdoings, and I will remember their sins no more." [13]God speaks of these new promises, of this new agreement, as taking the place of the old one; for the old one is out of date now and has been put aside forever.

Heb 12:18. You have not had to stand face to face with terror, flaming fire, gloom, darkness and a terrible storm, as the Israelites did at Mount Sinai when God gave them his laws. [19]For there was an awesome trumpet blast, and a voice with a message so terrible that the people begged God to stop speaking. [20]They staggered back under God's command that if even an animal touched the mountain it must die. [21]Moses himself was so frightened at the sight that he shook with terrible fear. [22]But you have come right up into Mount Zion, to the city of the living God, the heavenly Jerusalem, and to the gathering of countless happy angels; [23]and to the church, composed of all those registered in heaven; and to God who is Judge of all; and to the spirits of the redeemed in heaven, already made perfect; [24]and to Jesus himself, who has brought us his wonderful new agreement; and to the sprinkled blood which graciously forgives instead of crying out for vengeance as the blood of Abel did.

Heb 13:20. And now may the God of peace, who brought again from the dead our Lord Jesus, equip you will all you need for doing his will. May he who became the great Shepherd of the sheep by an everlasting agreement between God and you, signed with his blood, produce in you through the power of Christ all that is pleasing to him.

OF MAN WITH GOD. Jacob, Gen 28:20–22. Joshua, Josh 24:25, with *vs.* 19–28. Absalom, 2 Sam 15:7, 8. Jehoiada and Joash, 2 Kgs 11:17. Josiah, 2 Kgs 23:3. Asa, 2 Chron 15:12–15. Nehemiah, Neh 9:38; 10. Israelites, Jer 50:5. See *Vows.*

COVETOUSNESS Ex 20:17. You must not be envious of your neighbor's house, or want to sleep with his wife, or want to own his slaves, oxen, donkeys, or anything else he has. Deut 5:21.

Neh 5:7. So after thinking about it I spoke out against these rich government officials. "What is this you are doing?" I demanded. "How dare you demand a mortgage as a condition for helping another Israelite?"

Job 20:15. He will vomit the plunder he gorged. God won't let him keep it down.

Job 31:24. If I have put my trust in money, [25]if my happiness depends on wealth. [28]This, too, must be punished by the judges. For if I had done such things, it would mean that I denied the God of heaven.

Ps 10:3. For these men brag of all their evil lusts; they revile God and congratulate those the Lord abhors, whose only goal in life is money.

Ps 119:36. Help me to prefer obedience to making money!

Prov 11:24. It is possible to give away and become richer! It is also possible to hold on too tightly and lose everything. [26]People curse the man who holds his grain for higher prices, but they bless the man who sells it to them in their time of need.

Prov 15:27. Dishonest money brings grief to all the family, but hating bribes brings happiness.

Prov 21:25, 26. The lazy man longs for many things but his hands refuse to work. He is greedy to get, while the godly love to give!

Prov 22:16. He who gains by oppressing the poor or by bribing the rich shall end in poverty.

Prov 23:4, 5. Don't weary yourself trying to get rich. Why waste your time? For riches can disappear as though they had the wings of a bird!

Prov 24:19, 20. Don't envy the wicked. Don't covet his riches. For the evil man has no future; his light will be snuffed out.

Prov 30:8. First, help me never to tell a lie. Second, give me neither poverty nor riches! Give me just enough to satisfy my needs! [9]For if I grow rich, I may become content without God. And if I am too poor, I may steal, and thus insult God's holy name.

Eccl 1:8. Everything is unutterably weary and tiresome. No matter how much we see, we are never satisfied; no matter how much we hear, we are not content. *vs.* 2–8.

Eccl 4:8. This is the case of a man who is quite alone, without a son or brother, yet he works hard to keep gaining more riches, and to whom will he leave it all? And why is he giving up so much now? It is all so pointless and depressing.

Eccl 5:10. He who loves money shall never have enough. The foolishness of thinking that wealth brings happiness! [11]The more you have, the more you spend, right up to the limits of your income, so what is the advantage of wealth—except perhaps to watch it as it runs through your fingers!

Isa 1:23. Your leaders are rebels, companions of thieves; all of them take bribes and won't defend the widows and orphans.

Isa 5:8. You buy up property so others have no place to live. Your homes are built on great estates so you can be alone in the midst of the earth!

Isa 56:11. And they are as greedy as dogs, never satisfied; they are stupid shepherds who only look after their own interest, each trying to get as much as he can for himself from every possible source.

Isa 57:17. I was angry and smote these greedy men. But they went right on sinning, doing everything their evil hearts desired.

Jer 8:10. I will give their wives and their farms to others; for all of them, great and small, prophet and priest, have one purpose in mind—to get what isn't theirs.

Jer 17:11. Like a bird that fills her nest with young she has not hatched and which will soon desert her and fly away, so is the man who gets his wealth by unjust means. Sooner or later he will lose his riches and at the end of his life become a poor old fool.

Jer 22:17. But you! You are full of selfish greed and all dishonesty! You murder the innocent, oppress the poor and reign with ruthlessness. *v.* 18.

Ezk 22:12. Hired murderers, loan racketeers and extortioners are everywhere. You never even think of me and my commands, the Lord God says. [13]But now I snap my fingers and call a halt to your dishonest gain and bloodshed.

Ezk 33:31. So they come as though they are sincere and sit before you listening. But they have no intention of doing what I tell them to; they talk very sweetly about loving the Lord, but with their hearts they are loving their money.

Hos 10:1. How prosperous Israel is—a luxuriant vine all filled with fruit! But the more wealth I give her, the more she pours it on the altars of her heathen gods; the richer the harvests I give her, the more beautiful the statues and idols she erects.

Mic 2:2. You want a certain piece of land, or someone else's house (though it is all he has); you take it by fraud and threats and violence.

Mic 3:11. You leaders who take bribes; you priests and prophets who won't preach and prophesy until you're paid. (And yet you fawn upon the Lord and say, "All is well—the Lord is here among us. No harm can come to us.")

Mic 7:3. They go at their evil deeds with both hands, and how skilled they are in using them! The governor and judge alike demand bribes. The rich man pays them off and tells them whom to ruin. Justice is twisted between them.

Hab 1:15. Must we be strung up on their hooks and dragged out in their nets, while they rejoice?
[16]Then they will worship their nets and burn incense before them! "These are the gods who make us rich," they'll say.

Hab 2:5. What's more, these arrogant Chaldeans are betrayed by all their wine, for it is treacherous. In their greed they have collected many nations, but like death and hell, they are never satisfied.
[6]The time is coming when all their captives will taunt them, saying: "You robbers! At last justice has caught up with you! Now you will get your just deserts for your oppression and extortion!" [7]Suddenly your debtors will rise up in anger and turn on you and take all you have, while you stand trembling and helpless. [8]You have ruined many nations; now they will ruin you. You murderers! You have filled the countryside with lawlessness and all the cities too. [9]Woe to you for getting rich by evil means, attempting to live beyond the reach of danger.

Hag 1:6. You plant much but harvest little. You have scarcely enough to eat or drink, and not enough clothes to keep you warm. Your income disappears, as though you were putting it into pockets filled with holes!

Mal 1:10. "Oh, to find one priest among you who would shut the doors and refuse this kind of sacrifice. I have no pleasure in you," says the Lord of Hosts, "and I will not accept your offerings."

Mt 6:19. Don't store up treasures here on earth where they can erode away or may be stolen.
[20]Store them in heaven where they will never lose their value, and are safe from thieves. [21]If your profits are in heaven your heart will be there too.

24. You cannot serve two masters: God and money. For you will hate one and love the other, or else the other way around. [25]So my counsel is: Don't worry about *things*—food, drink, and clothes. For you already have life and a body—and they are far more important than what to eat and wear.

31, 32. So don't worry at all about having enough food and clothing. Why be like the heathen? For they take pride in all these things and are deeply concerned about them. But your heavenly Father already knows perfectly well that you need them.
[33]and he will give them to you if you give him first place in your life and live as he wants you to.

Mt 13:22. The ground covered with thistles represents a man who hears the message, but the cares of this life and his longing for money choke out God's Word, and he does less and less for God. Mk 4:19; Lk 8:14.

Mt 16:26. What profit is there if you gain the whole world—and lose eternal life? What can be compared with the value of eternal life?

Mt 19:24. I say it again—it is easier for a camel to go through the eye of a needle than for a rich man to enter the Kingdom of God! *v.* 23; Lk 18:24, 25.

Mt 22:5. But the guests he had invited merely laughed and went on about their business, one to his farm, another to his store. *vs.* 1–14.

Mk 7:21. For from within, out of men's hearts, come evil thoughts . . . [22]wanting what belongs to others. . . . [23]All these vile things come from within; they are what pollute you and make you unfit for God.

Lk 12:15. Beware! Don't always be wishing for what you don't have. For real life and real living are not related to how rich we are. [See parable of rich man, *vs.* 16–21]. [33]Sell what you have and give to those in need. This will fatten your purses in heaven! And the purses of heaven have no rips or holes in them. Your treasures there will never disappear; no thief can steal them; no moth can destroy them. [34]Wherever your treasure is, there your heart and thoughts will also be. Mt 6:21.

Lk 14:18. But they all began making excuses. One said he had just bought a field and wanted to inspect it, and asked to be excused. *vs.* 16–24.

Jn 6:26. Jesus replied, "The truth of the matter is that you want to be with me because I fed you, not because you believe in me. [27]But you shouldn't be so concerned about perishable things like food. No, spend your energy seeking the eternal life that I, the Messiah, can give you. For God the Father has sent me for this very purpose."

Rom 1:29. Their lives became full of every kind of wickedness and sin, of greed and hate, envy, murder, fighting, lying, bitterness, and gossip.

Rom 13:9. If you love your neighbor as much as you love yourself you will not want to harm or cheat him, or kill him or steal from him. And you won't sin with his wife or want what is his, or do anything else the Ten Commandments say is wrong.

1 Cor 5:11. What I meant was that you are not to keep company with anyone who claims to be a brother Christian but indulges in sexual sins, or is greedy, or is a swindler, or worships idols, or is a drunkard, or abusive. Don't even eat lunch with such a person.

Eph 5:3. Let there be no sex sin, impurity or greed among you. Let no one be able to accuse you of any such things. [5]You can be sure of this: The kingdom of Christ and of God will never belong to anyone who is impure or greedy, for a greedy person is really an idol worshiper—he loves and worships the good things of this life more than God. 1 Cor 6:9, 10.

Phil 3:18. For I have told you often before, and I say it again now with tears in my eyes, there are many who walk along the Christian road who are really enemies of the cross of Christ. [19]Their future is eternal loss, for their god is their appetite: they are proud of what they should be ashamed of; and all they think about is this life here on earth.

Col 3:2. Let heaven fill your thoughts; don't spend your time worrying about things down here. [5]Away then with sinful, earthly things; deaden the evil desires lurking within you; . . . don't worship the good things of life, for that is idolatry. [6]God's terrible anger is upon those who do such things.

1 Thess 2:5. Never once did we try to win you with flattery, as you very well know, and God knows we were not just pretending to be your friends so that you would give us money!

1 Tim 3:3. He must not be a drinker or quarrelsome, but he must be gentle and kind, and not be one who loves money. Tit 1:11.

1 Tim 6:5. These arguers—their minds warped by sin—don't know how to tell the truth; to them the Good News is just a means of making money. Keep away from them. [6]Do you want to be truly rich? You already are if you are happy and good. [7]After all, we didn't bring any money with us when we came into the world, and we can't carry away a single penny when we die. [8]So we should be well satisfied without money if we have enough food and clothing.

9. But people who long to be rich begin to do all kinds of wrong things to get money, things that hurt them and make them evil-minded and finally send them to hell itself. [10]For the love of money is the first step toward all kinds of sin. Some people have even turned away from God because of their love for it, and as a result have pierced themselves with many sorrows. [11]Oh, Timothy, you are God's man. Run from all these evil things and work instead at what is right and good, learning to trust him and love others, and to be patient and gentle.

17. Tell those who are rich not to be proud and not to trust in their money, which will soon be gone, but their pride and trust should be in the living God who always richly gives us all we need for our enjoyment.

2 Tim 3:2. For people will love only themselves and their money.

Tit 1:7. These pastors must be men of blameless lives because they are God's ministers. They must not be proud or impatient; they must not be drunkards or fighters or greedy for money.

Heb 13:5. Stay away from the love of money; be satisfied with what you have.

Jas 4:2. You want what you don't have, so you kill to get it. You long for what others have, and can't afford it, so you start a fight to take it away from them. [13]Look here, you people who say, "Today or tomorrow we are going to such and such a town, stay there a year, and open up a profitable business." [14]How do you know what is going to happen tomorrow? *vs.* 13–17.

1 Pet 5:2. Feed the flock of God; care for it willingly, not grudgingly; not for what you will get out of it, but because you are eager to serve the Lord.

2 Pet 2:3. These teachers in their greed will tell you anything to get hold of your money. But God condemned them long ago and their destruction is on the way. [14]No woman can escape their sinful stare, and of adultery they never have enough. They make a game of luring unstable women. They train themselves to be greedy; and are doomed and cursed. *vs.* 15, 16.

1 Jn 2:15. Stop loving this evil world and all that it offers you, for when you love these things you show that you do not really love God. *vs.* 16, 17.

Jude 1:11. Woe upon them! For they follow the example of Cain who killed his brother; and, like Balaam, they will do anything for money; and like Korah, they have disobeyed God and will die under his curse.

See *Avarice; Envy; Rich; Riches; Worldliness.*

INSTANCES OF. Eve, in desiring the forbidden fruit, Gen 3:6. Lot, in choosing the plain of the Jordan, Gen 13:10–13. Laban, in giving Rebekah to be Isaac's wife, Gen 24:29–51; in deceiving Jacob when he served him seven years for Rachel, Gen 29:15–30; in deceiving Jacob in wages, Gen 31:7, 15, 41, 42. Jacob, in defrauding Esau of his father's blessing, Gen 27:6–29; in defrauding Laban of his flocks and herds, Gen 30:35–43; in buying Esau's birthright, Gen 25:31. Balaam, in loving the money made by wrongdoing, 2 Pet 2:15, with Num 22. Achan, in hiding the treasure, Josh 7:21. Eli's sons, in taking the flesh of the sacrifice, 1 Sam 2:13–17. Samuel's sons, in taking the bribes, 1 Sam 8:3. Saul, in sparing Agag and the booty, 1 Sam 15:8, 9. David, of Bath-sheba, 2 Sam 11:2–5. Ahab, in desiring Naboth's vineyard, 1 Kgs 21:2–16. Gehazi, in taking a gift from Naaman, 2 Kgs 5:20–27. Jews, in exacting usury of their brothers, Neh 5:1–11; in keeping back the portion of the Levites, Neh 13:10; in building fine houses while the Temple was in ruins, Hag 1:4–9; in following Jesus for food, Jn 6:26. Money changers in the temple, Mt 21:12, 13; Lk 19:45, 46; Jn 2:14–16. The rich young ruler, Mt 19:16–22. The rich fool, Lk 12:15–21. Judas, in betraying Jesus for thirty silver coins, Mt 26:15, 16; Mk 14:10, 11; Lk 22:3–6; Jn 12:6. The dishonest accountant, Lk 16:1–8. The Pharisees, Lk 16:14. Simon, in trying to buy the power of the Holy Spirit, Acts 8:18–23. The sorcerers, in filing complaint against Paul and Silas, Acts 16:19. Demetrius, in raising a riot against Paul and Silas, Acts 19:24, 27. Felix in hoping for a bribe from Paul, Acts 24:26. Demas, in forsaking Paul for love of the world, 2 Tim 4:10.

See *Avarice; Bribery; Rich; Riches.*

COW Used for draft, 1 Sam 6:7–12; Hos 10:11. Milk of, used for food, see *Milk*. Pharoah's dream of, Gen 41:2–7, 26–30.

See *Cattle*.

FIGURATIVE. Amos 4:1.

COWARDICE Lev 26:36. And for those who are left alive, I will cause them to be dragged away to distant lands as prisoners of war, and slaves. There they will live in constant fear. The sound of a leaf driven in the wind will send them fleeing as though chased by a man with a sword; they shall fall when no one is pursuing them. [37]Yes, though none pursue they shall stumble over each other in flight, as though fleeing in battle, with no power to stand before their enemies.

Deut 20:8. And now, is anyone afraid? If you are, go home before you frighten the rest of us!

Deut 32:30. How could one single enemy chase a thousand of them, and put ten thousand to flight, unless their Rock had abandoned them?

Josh 7:5. About thirty-six of the Israelis were killed during the attack, and many others died while being chased by the men of Ai as far as the quarries. The Israeli army was paralyzed with fear at this turn of events.

Josh 23:10. Each one of you has put to flight a thousand of the enemy, for the Lord your God fights for you, just as he has promised.

Judg 7:3. "Send home any of your men who are timid and frightened." So twenty-two thousand of them left, and only ten thousand remained who were willing to fight.

Job 15:24. He lives in fear, distress, and anguish. His enemies conquer him as a king defeats his foes.

Job 18:11. He has good cause for fear—his enemy is close behind him!

Prov 28:1. The wicked flee when no one is chasing them! But the godly are bold as lions!

Prov 29:25. Fear of man is a dangerous trap, but to trust in God means safety.

Isa 51:12. I, even I, am he who comforts you and gives you all this joy. So what right have you to fear mere mortal men, who wither like the grass and disappear? [13]And yet you have no fear of God, your Maker—you have forgotten him, the one who spread the stars throughout the skies and made the earth. Will you be in constant dread of men's oppression, and fear their anger all day long?

Gal 6:12. Those teachers of yours who are trying to convince you to be circumcised are doing it for just one reason: so that they can be popular and avoid the persecution they would get if they admitted that the cross of Christ alone can save.

2 Tim 4:16. The first time I was brought before the judge no one was here to help me. Everyone had run away. I hope that they will not be blamed for it.

See *Courage*.

INSTANCES OF. Adam, in attempting to shift responsibility for his sin upon Eve, Gen 3:12. Abraham, in calling his wife his sister, Gen 12:11–19; 20:2–12. Isaac, in calling his wife his sister, Gen 26:7–9. Jacob, in running from Laban, Gen 31:31. Aaron, in yielding to the Israelites, when they demanded an idol, Ex 32:22–24. The ten spies, Num 13:28, 31–33. Israelites, in fearing to attempt the conquest of Canaan, Num 14:1–5; Deut 1:26–28; in the battle with the people of Ai, Josh 7:5; to meet Goliath, 1 Sam 17:24; to fight with the Philistines, 1 Sam 13:6, 7. Twenty thousand of Gideon's army, Judg 7:3. Ephraimites, Ps 78:9. Ephraimites and Manassehites, Josh 17:14–18. Amorite kings, Josh 10:16. Canaanites, Josh 2:11; 5:1. Samuel, fearing to obey God's command to anoint a king in Saul's place, 1 Sam 16:2. David, in fleeing from Absalom, 2 Sam 15:13–17. Nicodemus, in coming to Jesus at night, Jn 3:1, 2. Joseph of Arimathaea, secretly a disciple, Jn 19:38. Parents of the blind man, whose sight was restored, Jn 9:22. Early converts among the rulers, Jn 12:42, 43. Disciples, in the storm at sea, Mt 8:26; Mk 4:38; Lk 8:25; when they saw Jesus walking on the sea, Mt 14:25; Mk 6:50; Jn 6:18, 19; when Jesus was apprehended, Mt 26:56. Peter, in denying the Lord, Mt 26:69–74; Mk 14:66–72; Lk 22:54–60; Jn 18:16, 17, 25, 27. Pilate, in condemning Jesus, through fear of the people, Jn 19:12–16. Guards of the tomb of Jesus, Mt 28:4. The Philippian jailer, Acts 16:27. Peter and other Christians, at Antioch, Gal 2:11–14.

COZBI Daughter of Zur, Num 25:15, 18.

COZEBA A city of Judah, 1 Chron 4:21, 22. See *Chezib* and *Achzib*.

CRAFTINESS INSTANCES OF. Satan, in the temptation of Eve, Gen 3:1–5. Jacob, in purchase of Esau's birthright, Gen 25:31–33; obtaining Isaac's blessing, Gen 27:6–29; in management of Laban's flocks, Gen 30:31–43. Gibeonites, in deceiving Joshua and the Israelites into a treaty, Josh 9:3–15. Sanballat, in trying to deceive Nehemiah into a conference, Neh 6. Jews, in seeking to trap Jesus, Mt 22:15–17, 24–28; Mk 12:13, 14, 18–23; Lk 20:19–26; in seeking to kill Jesus, Mt 26:4; Mk 14:1.

CRAFTSMAN See *Art; Master Workman.*

CRAFTSMEN VALLEY OF 1 Chron 4:14; Neh 11:31–35.

CRANE An amphibious bird, Jer 8:7.

CREATION Beginning of, Gen 1:1. History of, Gen 1; 2.

See *Animals; Birds; Earth; Fish; Grass; Heaven; Man; Moon; Sea; Stars; Sun; Water; Woman.*

See *God, Creator; Jesus, Creator.*

CREATURE See *Creation; God, Creator; Man, Created.*

NEW CREATURE. 2 Cor 5:17. When someone becomes a Christian he becomes a brand new person inside. He is not the same any more. A new life has begun!

Gal 6:15. It doesn't make any difference now whether we have been circumcised or not; what counts is whether we really have been changed into new and different people.

Eph 2:10. It is God himself who has made us what we are and given us new lives from Christ Jesus; and long ages ago he planned that we should spend these lives in helping others.

Eph 4:24. Yes, you must be a new and different person, holy and good. Clothe yourself with this new nature.

Col 3:10. You are living a brand new kind of life that is continually learning more and more of what is right, and trying constantly to be more and more like Christ who created this new life within you.

Jas 1:18. And it was a happy day for him when he gave us our new lives, through the truth of his Word, and we became, as it were, the first children in his new family.

See *Regeneration.*

CREATURE, EVIL Rev 13:19, 20.

See *Antichrist.*

CREDITOR LAWS CONCERNING. Ex 21:2. If you buy a Hebrew slave, he shall serve only six years and be freed in the seventh year, and need pay nothing to regain his freedom. [3]If he sold himself as a slave before he married, then if he married afterwards, only he shall be freed; but if he was married before he became a slave, then his wife shall be freed with him at the same time. [4]But if his master gave him a wife while he was a slave, and they have sons or daughters, the wife and children shall still belong to the master, and he shall go out by himself free. [5]But if the man shall plainly declare, "I prefer my master, my wife, and my children, and I would rather not go free," [6]then his master shall bring him before the judges and shall publicly bore his ear with an awl, and after that he will be a slave forever.

Ex 22:25. If you lend money to a needy fellow-Hebrew, you are not to handle the transaction in an ordinary way, with interest. [26]If you take his clothing as a pledge of his repayment, you must let him have it back at night. [27]For it is probably his only warmth; how can he sleep without it? If you don't return it, and he cries to me for help, I will hear and be very gracious to him [at your expense], for I am very compassionate.

Lev 25:14, 15, 16. Because of this, if the land is sold or bought during the preceding forty-nine years, a fair price shall be arrived at by counting the number of years until the Jubilee. If the Jubilee is many years away, the price will be high; if few years, the price will be low; for what you are really doing is selling the number of crops the new owner will get from the land before it is returned to you. [17]You must fear your God and not overcharge! For I am Jehovah.

35. If your brother becomes poor, you are responsible to help him; invite him to live with you as a guest in your home. [36]Fear your God and let your brother live with you; and don't charge him interest on the money you lend him. [37]Remember—no interest; and give him what he needs, at your cost: don't try to make a profit!

Deut 15:2. Every creditor shall write "Paid in full" on any promissory note he holds against a fellow Israelite, for the Lord has released everyone from his obligation. [3](This release does not apply to foreigners.)

Deut 23:19. Don't demand interest on loans you make to a brother Israelite, whether it is in the form of money, food, or anything else. [20]You may take interest from a foreigner, but not from an Israeli. For if you take interest from a brother, an Israeli, the Lord your God won't bless you when you arrive in the Promised Land.

Deut 24:6. It is illegal to take a millstone as a pledge, for it is a tool by which its owner gains his livelihood. [10]If you lend anything to another man, you must not enter his house to get his security. [11]Stand outside! The owner will bring it out to you. [12, 13]If the man is poor and gives you his cloak as security, you are not to sleep in it. Take it back to him at sundown so that he can use it through the night and bless you; and the Lord your God will count it as righteousness for you.

17. Justice must be given to migrants and orphans and you must never accept a widow's garment in pledge of her debt.

Mt 5:42. Give to those who ask, and don't turn away from those who want to borrow.

Lk 6:34. And if you lend money only to those who can repay you, what good is that? Even the most wicked will lend to their own kind for full return!

OPPRESSIONS OF. 2 Kgs 4:1. One day the wife of one of the seminary students came to Elisha to tell him of her husband's death. He was a man who had loved God, she said. But he had owed some money when he died, and now the creditor was demanding it back. If she didn't pay, he said he would take her two sons as his slaves.

Neh 5:1. About this time there was a great outcry of protest from parents against some of the rich Jews who were profiteering on them. [2, 3, 4]What was happening was that families who ran out of money for food had to sell their children or mortgage their fields, vineyards, and homes to these rich men; and some couldn't even do that, for they already had borrowed to the limit to pay their taxes. [5]"We are their brothers, and our children are just like theirs," the people protested. "Yet we must sell our children into slavery to get enough money to live. We have already sold some of our daughters, and we are helpless to redeem them, for our fields, too, are mortgaged to these men." [6]I was very angry when I heard this; [7]so after thinking about it I spoke out against these rich government officials. "What is this you are doing?" I demanded. "How dare you demand a mortgage as a condition for helping another Israelite?" Then I called a public trial to deal with them. [8]At the trial I shouted at them, "The rest of us are doing all we can to *help* our Jewish brothers who have returned from exile as slaves in distant lands, but you are forcing them right back into slavery again. How often must we redeem them?" And they had nothing to say in their own defense. [9]Then I pressed further. "What you are doing is very evil," I exclaimed. "Should you not walk in the fear of our God? Don't we have enough enemies among the nations around us who are trying to destroy us? [10]The rest of us are lending money and grain to our fellow-Jews without any interest. I beg you, gentlemen, stop this business of usury. [11]Restore their fields, vineyards, oliveyards, and homes to them this very day and drop your claims against them." [12]So they agreed to do it and said that they would assist their brothers without requiring them to mortgage their lands and sell them their children. Then I summoned the priests and made these men formally vow to carry out their promises. [13]And I invoked the curse of God upon any of them who refused. "May God destroy your homes and livelihood if you fail to keep this promise," I declared. And all the people shouted, "Amen," and praised the Lord. And the rich men did as they had promised.

Job 20:18. His labors shall not be rewarded; wealth will give him no joy. [19]For he has oppressed the poor and foreclosed their homes; he will never recover. [20]Though he was always greedy, now he has nothing; of all the things he dreamed of—none remain.

Job 22:6. For instance, you must have refused to loan money to needy friends unless they gave you all their clothing as a pledge—yes, you must have stripped them to the bone.

Job 24:3. And even the donkeys of the poor and fatherless are taken. Poor widows must surrender the little they have as a pledge to get a loan. [9]The wicked snatch fatherless children from their mother's breasts, and take a poor man's baby as a pledge before they will loan him any money or grain. [10]That is why they must go about naked, without clothing, and are forced to carry food while they are starving.

Ps 109:11. May creditors seize his entire estate and strangers take all he has earned.

Prov 22:26, 27. Unless you have the extra cash on hand, don't countersign a note. Why risk everything you own? They'll even take your bed!

Mt 5:25. Come to terms quickly with your enemy before it is too late and he drags you into court and you are thrown into a debtor's cell, [26]for you will stay there until you have paid the last penny. Lk 12:58, 59.

Mt 18:28. But when the man left the king, he went to a man who owed him $2,000 and grabbed him by the throat and demanded instant payment. [29]The man fell down before him and begged him to give him a little time. "Be patient and I will pay it," he pled. [30]But his creditor wouldn't wait. He had the man arrested and jailed until the debt would be paid in full. [31]Then the man's friends went to the king and told him what had happened. [32]And the king called before him the man he had forgiven and said, "You evil-hearted wretch! Here I forgave you all that tremendous debt, just because you asked me to— [33]shouldn't you have mercy on others, just as I had mercy on you?" [34]Then the angry king sent the man to the torture chamber until he had paid every last penny due. [35]So shall my heavenly Father do to you if you refuse to truly forgive your brothers.

MERCIFUL. Ps 112:5. And all goes well for the generous man who conducts his business fairly. Ezk 18:7.

Mt 18:23. The Kingdom of Heaven can be compared to a king who decided to bring his accounts up to date. [24]In the process, one of his debtors was brought in who owed him $10,000,000! [25]He couldn't pay, so the king ordered him sold for the debt, also his wife and children and everything he had. [26]But the man fell down before the king, his face in the dust, and said, "Oh, sir, be patient with me and I will pay it all." [27]Then the king was filled with pity for him and released him and forgave his debt.

Lk 7:41. Then Jesus told him this story: "A man loaned money to two people—$5,000 to one and $500 to the other. [42]But neither of them could pay him back, so he kindly forgave them both, letting them keep the money! Which do you suppose loved him most after that?" [43]"I suppose the one who had owed him the most," Simon answered. "Correct," Jesus agreed.

See *Debt; Debtor; Jubilee; Surety.*

CREED Apostolic, 1 Tim 3:16; Tit 2:11–14. See *Decrees; Law, of Moses; Ecclesiasticism; Tradition.*

CREEPING THINGS A general term for animals.

FIGURATIVE. Hab 1:14.

CREMATION Josh 7:25; 1 Sam 31:12; 2 Kgs 23:20.

See *Burial.*

CRESCENS A disciple with Paul at Rome, 2 Tim 4:10.

CRETE An island in the Mediterranean Sea. Visited by Paul, Acts 27:7, 12, 13, 21; Titus, Tit 1:5. Character of the inhabitants of, Acts 2:11; Tit 1:12.

CRIB Used for grain, Job 39:9.

CRICKET Authorized as food, Lev 11:21, 22.

CRIME PARTIAL LISTS OF. Ezk 22:8. The things of God are all despised; my Sabbaths are ignored. [9]Prisoners are falsely accused and sent to their death. Every mountain top is filled with idols; lewdness is everywhere. [10]There are men who commit adultery with their fathers' wives and lie with menstruous women. [11]Adultery with a neighbor's wife, a daughter-in-law, a half sister—this is common. [12]Hired murderers, loan racketeers and extortioners are everywhere. You never even think of me and my commands, the Lord God says. [27]Your leaders are like wolves, who tear apart their victims, and they destroy lives for profit. [28]Your "prophets" describe false visions and speak false messages they claim are from God, when he hasn't spoken one word to them at all. Thus they repair the walls with whitewash! [29]Even the common people oppress and rob the poor and needy and cruelly extort from aliens. [30]I looked in vain for anyone who would build again the wall of righteousness that guards the land, who could stand in the gap and defend you from my just attacks, but I found not one.

Hos 4:1. Hear the word of the Lord, O people of Israel. The Lord has filed a lawsuit against you listing the following charges: There is no faithfulness, no kindness, no knowledge of God in your land. [2]You swear and lie and kill and steal and commit adultery. There is violence everywhere, with one murder after another.

Mt 15:19. For from the heart come evil thoughts, murder, adultery, fornication, theft, lying and slander. Mk 7:21, 22.

Rom 1:24. So God let them go ahead into every sort of sex sin, and do whatever they wanted to—yes, vile and sinful things with each other's bodies. [29]Their lives became full of every kind of wickedness and sin, of greed and hate, envy, murder, fighting, lying, bitterness, and gossip. [30]They were backbiters, haters of God, insolent, proud braggarts, always thinking of new ways of sinning and continually being disobedient to their parents. [31]They tried to misunderstand, broke their promises, and were heartless—without pity. [32]They were fully aware of God's death penalty for these crimes, yet they went right ahead and did them anyway, and encouraged others to do them, too.

Rom 3:14. Their mouths are full of cursing and bitterness. [15]They are quick to kill, hating anyone who disagrees with them. [16]Wherever they go they leave misery and trouble behind them, [17]and they have never known what it is to feel secure or enjoy God's blessing. [18]They care nothing about God nor what he thinks of them.

Rom 13:9. If you love your neighbor as much as you love yourself you will not want to harm or cheat him, or kill him or steal from him. And you won't sin with his wife or want what is his, or do anything else the Ten Commandments say is wrong. All ten are wrapped up in this one, to love your neighbor as you love yourself.

1 Cor 5:11. What I meant was that you are not to keep company with anyone who claims to be a brother Christian but indulges in sexual sins, or is greedy, or is a swindler, or worships idols, or is a drunkard, or abusive. Don't even eat lunch with such a person.

Gal 5:19. But when you follow your own wrong inclinations your lives will produce these evil results: impure thoughts, eagerness for lustful pleasure, [20]idolatry, spiritism (that is, encouraging the activity of demons), hatred and fighting, jealousy and anger, constant effort to get the best for yourself, complaints and criticisms, the feeling that everyone else is wrong except those in your own little group—and there will be wrong doctrine, [21]envy, murder, drunkenness, wild parties, and all that sort of thing. Let me tell you again as I have before, that anyone living that sort of life will not inherit the kingdom of God.

See under terms by which various crimes are known, *Adultery, Arson, Homicide, Theft,* and the like.

See *Punishment.*

CRIMINALS Released at feasts, Mt 27:15, 21; Mk 15:6; Lk 23:17, 18. Confined in prisons, Gen 39:20–23; Ezra 7:26; Acts 4:3; 12:4, 5; 16:19–40; in dungeons, Gen 40:15; 41:14; Ex 12:29; Isa 24:22; Jer 37:15, 16; 38:10; Lam 3:53, 55. Crucified with Jesus, Mt 27:38–44; Lk 23:32–39. See *Prisoners.*

Cruelty to. See *Scourging; Stoning; Mocking.*

Punishment of. See various crimes, such as *Adultery, Arson, Homicide,* etc. See also *Punishment.*

CRIMINATION See *Self-incrimination.*

CRIMSON See *Color.*

CRISPUS A ruler at Corinth, Acts 18:8; 1 Cor 1:14.

CRITICISM Unjust, see *Uncharitableness.*

CROCODILE Ezk 32:2. Thought by some to be the leviathan of Job 41:1.

See *Leviathan.*

CROSS Jesus crucified on, Mt 27:32; Mk 15:21; Lk 23:26; Acts 2:23, 36; 4:10; 1 Cor 2:2, 8; Eph 2:16; Phil 2:8; Col 1:20; 2:14; Heb 7:27; 12:2, 1 Pet 2:24; 5:1. Carried by Simon, Mt 27:32; Mk 15:21; Lk 23:26; by Jesus, Jn 19:17.

FIGURATIVE. Mt 10:38. If you refuse to take up your cross and follow me, you are not worthy of being mine. Lk 14:27.

Mt 16:24. Then Jesus said to the disciples, "If anyone wants to be a follower of mine, let him deny himself and take up his cross and follow me." Mk 8:34; Lk 9:23.

1 Cor 1:17. For Christ didn't send me to baptize, but to preach the Gospel; and even my preaching sounds poor, for I do not fill my sermons with profound words and high sounding ideas, for fear of diluting the mighty power there is in the simple message of the cross of Christ. [18]I know very well how foolish it sounds to those who are lost, when they hear that Jesus died to save them. But we who are saved recognize this message as the very power of God.

Gal 5:11. Some people even say that I myself am preaching that circumcision and Jewish laws are necessary to the plan of salvation. Well, if I preached that, I would be persecuted no more—for that message doesn't offend anyone. The fact that I am still being persecuted proves that I am still preaching salvation through faith in the cross of Christ alone.

Gal 6:14. As for me, God forbid that I should boast about anything except the cross of our Lord Jesus Christ. Because of that cross my interest in all the attractive things of the world was killed long ago, and the world's interest in me is also long dead.

Phil 3:18. For I have told you often before, and I say it again now with tears in my eyes, there are many who walk along the Christian road who are really enemies of the cross of Christ.

Heb 13:10. We have an altar—the cross where Christ was sacrificed—where those who continue to seek salvation by obeying Jewish laws can never be helped.

See *Crucifixion; Self-Denial.*

CROSS-EXAMINING Ps 26:2; Prov 20:5. See *Witness.*

CROWN Prescribed for priests, Lev 8:9. Worn by kings, 2 Sam 1:10; 12:30; 2 Kgs 11:12; Esther 6:7, 8; Song 3:11; Rev 6:2; by queens, Esther 1:11; 2:17.

Made of gold, Esther 8:15; Ps 21:3; Zech 6:10, 11. An ornament, Ezk 23:42; 16:12. Set with gems, 2 Sam 12:30; 1 Chron 20:2; Ezk 21:26; Zech 9:16.

Of thorns, Mt 27:29; Mk 15:16, 17; Jn 19:5.

See *Turban.*

FIGURATIVE. Isa 28:5. Then at last the Lord of Hosts himself will be their crowning glory, the diadem of beauty to his people who are left.

1 Thess 2:19. For what is it we live for, that gives us hope and joy and is our proud reward and crown? It is you. Yes, you bring us much joy as we stand together before our Lord Jesus Christ when he comes back again.

2 Tim 4:8. In heaven a crown is waiting for me which the Lord, the righteous Judge, will give me on that great day of his return. And not just to me, but to all those whose lives show that they are eagerly looking forward to his coming back again.

Jas 1:12. Happy is the man who doesn't give in and do wrong when he is tempted, for afterwards he will get as his reward the crown of life that God has promised those who love him.

Rev 2:10. Stop being afraid of what you are about to suffer—for the devil will soon throw some of you into prison to test you. You will be persecuted for "ten days." Remain faithful even when facing death and I will give you the crown of life—an unending, glorious future. Jas 1:12.

Rev 3:11. Look, I am coming soon! Hold tightly to the little strength you have—so that no one will take away your crown.

Symbolical. Rev 4:4, 10; 6:2; 9:7; 12:1, 3; 13:1; 14:14; 19:12.

CRUCIFIXION The reproach of, Gal 3:13; 5:11. Of Jesus, See *Jesus, History of.* Of two robbers, Mt 27:38. Of disciples, foretold, Mt 23:34.

See *Cross.*

FIGURATIVE. Rom 6:6. Your old evil desires were nailed to the cross with him; that part of you that loves to sin was crushed and fatally wounded, so that your sin-loving body is no longer under sin's control, no longer needs to be a slave to sin.

Gal 2:20. I have been crucified with Christ.

Gal 5:24. Those who belong to Christ have nailed their natural desires to his cross and crucified them there.

Gal 6:14. As for me, God forbid that I should boast about anything except the cross of our Lord Jesus Christ. Because of that cross my interest in all the attractive things of the world was killed long ago, and the world's interest in me is also long dead.

See *Cross, Figurative.*

CRUELTY INSTANCES OF. Of Sarah to Hagar, Gen 16:6; 21:9–14. Egyptians to the Israelites, Ex 5:6–18. Peninnah to Hannah, 1 Sam 1:4–7; 2:3. Of Jews to Jesus, Mt 26:67; 27:28–31; soldiers to Jesus, Lk 22:63, 64; Jn 19:3. In war, Isa 13:16, 18.

See *Animals, Cruelty to; Kindness; Love; Malice; Prisoners, of War.*

CRYSTAL A precious stone, Job 28:18; Ezk 1:22; Rev 4:6; 21:11; 22:1.

CUBIT A measure of distance, 2 Chron 3:11–13. The common Hebrew cubit was about 18 inches (46 centimeters) in length, 1 Kgs 7:24; Rev 21:17.

CUCUMBER Num 11:4, 5.

CUD Chewing of, was one of the facts by which clean and unclean animals were distinguished, Lev 11:2–8; Deut 14:3–8.

CUMMIN A plant bearing a small aromatic seed, Isa 28:27.

CUN A Syrian city, 1 Chron 18:8.

CUP Gen 40:11; 2 Sam 12:3; 1 Kgs 7:26; Mt 23:25. Made of silver, Gen 44:2; gold, 1 Chron 28:17; Jer 52:19. Used in the institution of the Lord's Supper, Mt 26:27; Mk 14:23; Lk 22:20; 1 Cor 10:21. Of Satan's table, 1 Cor 10:21.

FIGURATIVE. Of sorrow, Ps 73:10; 75:8; Isa 51:17, 22; Jer 25:15–28; Ezk 23:31–34; Mt 20:22; 26:39; Mk 14:36; Lk 22:41, 42; Jn 18:11; Rev 14:10. Of consolation, Jer 16:7. Of joy, Ps 23:5. Of salvation, Ps 116:13.

CUPBEARER 1 Kgs 10:5; Neh 1:11.

See *Steward; Wine Taster.*

CUPIDITY See *Avarice; Covetousness; Lust.*

CURDS Isa 7:15, 16, 22. See *Butter.*

CURES Miraculous, see *Miracles.*

See *Disease; Physician.*

CURIOSITY Eccl 7:21. Don't eavesdrop! You may hear your servant cursing you!

INSTANCES OF. Of Eve, Gen 3:6. Of Abraham, to know whether God would destroy the righteous in Sodom, Gen 18:22–32. Of Jacob, to know the name of the angel, Gen 32:29. Of the Israelites, to see God, Ex 19:21, 24; to witness the offering in the holy of holies, Num 4:17–20. Of Manoah, to know the name of an angel, Judg 13:17, 18. Of the people of Beth-shemish, to see inside the Ark, 1 Sam 6:19. Of the Babylonians, to see Hezekiah's treasures, 2 Kgs 20:13. Of Daniel, to know a vision, Dan 12:8, 9. Of Peter, to know what was being done with Jesus, Mt 26:58; to know what John would be appointed to do, Jn 21:21, 22. A disciple, to know only a few would be saved, Lk 13:23. Of Herod, to see Jesus, Lk 9:9; 23:8. Of the Jews, to see Lazarus, after he was raised from the dead, Jn 12:9; and to see Jesus, Jn 12:20, 21. Of the disciples, to know whether Jesus would restore the kingdom of the Jews, Acts 1:6, 7. Of the Athenians, to hear some new idea, Acts 17:19–21. Of angels, to look into the mysteries of salvation, 1 Pet 1:12.

CURSE Denounced against the serpent, Gen 3:14, 15; against Adam and Eve, Gen 3:15–19; against the ground, Gen 3:17, 18; against Cain, Gen 4:11–16; against Canaan, Noah's son, Gen 9:24–27; against Meroz, Judg 5:23; against Gehazi, 2 Kgs 5:27. Barak commands Balaam to curse Israel, Num 22:5, 6; 23:11.

See *Benedictions.*

CURSES OF THE MOSAIC LAW. Deut 27:1. Then Moses and the elders of Israel gave the people these further instructions to obey: [2, 3, 4] "When you cross the Jordan River and go into the Promised Land—a land 'flowing with milk and honey' —take out boulders from the river bottom and immediately pile them into a monument on the other side, at Mount Ebal. Face the stones with a coating of lime and then write the laws of God in the lime. [5, 6]And build an altar there to the Lord your God. Use uncut boulders, and on the altar offer burnt offerings to the Lord your God. [7]Sacrifice peace offerings upon it also, and feast there with great joy before the Lord your God. [8]Write all of these laws plainly [upon the monument]." [9]Then Moses and the Levite-priests addressed all Israel as follows: "O Israel, listen! Today you have become the people of the Lord your God, [10]so today you must begin to obey all of these commandments I have given you." [11]That same day Moses gave this charge to the people: [12]"When you cross into the Promised Land, the tribes of Simeon, Levi, Judah, Issachar, Joseph, and Benjamin shall stand upon Mount Gerizim to proclaim a blessing, [13]and the tribes of Reuben, Gad, Asher, Zebulun, Dan, and Naphtali shall stand upon Mount Ebal to proclaim a curse. [14]Then the Levites standing between them shall shout to all Israel, [15]'The curse of God be upon anyone who makes and worships an idol, even in secret, whether carved of wood or made from molten metal—for these handmade gods are hated by the Lord.' And all the people shall reply, 'Amen.' [16]'Cursed is anyone who despises his father or mother.' And all the people shall reply, 'Amen.' [17]'Cursed is he who moves the boundary marker between his land and his neighbor's.' And all the people shall reply, 'Amen.' [18]'Cursed is he who is unjust to the foreigner, the orphan, and the widow.' And all the people shall reply, 'Amen.' [20]'Cursed is he who commits adultery with one of his father's wives, for she belongs to his father.' And all the people shall reply, 'Amen.' [21]'Cursed is he who has sexual intercourse with an animal.' And all the people shall reply, 'Amen.' [22]'Cursed is he who has sexual intercourse with his sister, whether she be a full sister or a half-sister.' And all the people shall reply, 'Amen.' [23]'Cursed is he who has sexual intercourse with his widowed mother-in-law.' And all the people shall reply, 'Amen.' [24]'Cursed is he who secretly slays another.' And all the people shall reply, 'Amen.' [25]'Cursed is he who accepts a bribe to kill an innocent person.' And all the people shall reply, 'Amen.' [26]'Cursed is anyone who does not obey these laws.' And all the people shall reply, 'Amen.' "

Josh 8:30. Then Joshua built an altar to the Lord God of Israel at Mount Ebal, [31]as Moses had commanded in the book of his laws: "Make me an altar of boulders that have neither been broken nor carved," the Lord had said concerning Mount Ebal. Then the priests offered burnt sacrifices and peace offerings to the Lord on the altar. [32]And as the people of Israel watched, Joshua carved upon the stones of the altar each of the Ten Commandments. [33]Then all the people of Israel—including the elders, officers, judges, and the foreigners living among them—divided into two groups, half of them standing at the foot of Mount Gerizim and half at the foot of Mount Ebal. Between them stood the priests with the Ark, ready to pronounce their blessing. (This was all done in accordance with the instructions given long before by Moses.) [34]Joshua then read to them all of the statements of blessing and curses that Moses had written in the book of God's laws. Deut 28:15–19.

See *Blessing.*

CURSING Of parents, Ex 21:17; Mt 15:4; Mk 7:10. Shime-i curses David, 2 Sam 16:5–8. The precepts of Jesus concerning, Mt 5:44; Lk 6:28. Apostolic, Rom 12:14.

See *Blasphemy; God, Name of, Not to be Profaned; Oath.*

CURTAINS For the Tabernacle, Ex 26; 27: 9–18; 36:8–18.

See *Tabernacle; Tapestry.*

FIGURATIVE. Ps 104:1, 2; Isa 40:22; Heb 6:19.

CUSH 1. Son of Ham, Gen 10:6–8; 1 Chron 1: 8–10.

2. Land of, Gen 2:13; Num 12:1; 2 Sam 18:21; Isa 18:1; Jer 46:9; Ezk 30:4, 5.

See *Ethiopia.*

CUSHAN Poetic form of Cush, Hab 3:7.

See *Ethiopia.*

CUSHAN-RISHATHAIM King of Mesopotamia, Judg 3:8–10.

CUSHI 1. Father of Shelemiah, Jer 36:14, 15.

2. Father of Zephaniah, Zeph 1:1.

CUSHION See *Pillow.*

CUTH Called also *Cuthah.* A district of Asia, from which colonists were transported to Samaria, 2 Kgs 17:24–30.

CUTTING Of the flesh in sorrow, forbidden, Lev 19:28; 21:5; Deut 14:1; Jer 16:6.

CYMBAL A musical instrument. Of brass, 1 Chron 15:19, 28. Used in the Tabernacle service, 2 Sam 6:5; 1 Chron 13:8; 15:16, 19, 28; in the Temple service, 1 Chron 16:5, 42; 25:1, 6, 7; 2 Chron 5:11–14; Ps 150:5. Used on special occasions: Day of atonement, 2 Chron 29:25, 26; laying of the foundation of the second Temple, Ezra 3:10; dedication of the wall, Neh 12:27.

CYPRESS 1 Kgs 5:8, 10; 6:15, 34; 9:11, 12; 2 Kgs 19:23; 2 Chron 3:5; Isa 37:24; 41:19; 44:14; Ezk 27:6; 31:8; Zech 11:2. Wood of, used for building, 1 Kgs 6:15, 34.

CYPRUS An island, Isa 23:12; Jer 2:10; Acts 21:3; 27:4. Prophecies concerning, Num 24:23, 24; Dan 11:30, 31. Their commerce, Ezk 27:6. Barnabas born in, Acts 4:36. Persecuted Jews preached the gospel at, Acts 11:19, 20. Visited by Barnabas and Paul, Acts 13:4–12. Barnabas and Mark visit, Acts 15:39. Mnason, a disciple of, Acts 21:16.

CYRENE A city in Libya, Acts 2:10. Contained a synagogue, Acts 6:9. Simon and Lucius belonged to, Mk 15:21; Acts 11:20; 13:1.

CYRUS King of Persia. Issues a decree for the emancipation of the Jews and rebuilding the Temple, 2 Chron 36:22, 23; Ezra 1; 3:7; 4:3; 5:13, 14; 6:3. Prophecies concerning, Isa 13:17–22; 21:2; 41:2; 44:28; 45:1–4, 13; 46:11; 48:14, 15.

D

DABBASHETH A place on the boundary line of Zebulun, Josh 19:11.

DABERATH A town of Issachar, Josh 19:12; 21:28, 29. Assigned to the Levites, 1 Chron 6:72.

DAGGER A short sword, Judg 3:16–23; 2 Sam 3:27; 18:14; 20:8–10.

FIGURATIVE. Ps 55:21; Heb 4:12.

DAGON An idol of the Philistines, Judg 16: 23, 24; 1 Sam 5. Temple of, 1 Chron 10:10.

DAILY OFFERING Sacrificial, Ex 29:38–42; 30:7–9; Num 28:3–8; Ezra 3:4–6; Ezk 45:23; 46: 13–15; Dan 9:21, 27; 11:30, 31; Heb 7:27. See *Offerings.*

DALMANUTHA A town on the west coast of the Sea of Galilee, Mk 8:10.

DALMATIA A country on the eastern shore of the Adriatic, 2 Tim 4:10.

DALPHON Son of Haman, Esther 9:7–10.

DAMAGES AND COMPENSATION

Ex 21:18–19. If two men are fighting, and one hits the other with a stone or with his fist and injures him so that he must be confined to bed, but doesn't die, [19]if later he is able to walk again, even with a limp, the man who hit him will be innocent except that he must pay for the loss of his time until he is thoroughly healed, and pay any medical expenses.

[22]If two men are fighting, and in the process hurt a pregnant woman so that she has a miscarriage, but she lives, then the man who injured her shall be fined whatever amount the woman's husband shall demand, and as the judges approve.

[28]If an ox gores a man or woman to death, the ox shall be stoned and its flesh not eaten, but the owner shall not be held—[29]unless the ox was known to gore people in the past, and the owner had been notified and still the ox was not kept under control; in that case, if it kills someone, the ox shall be stoned and the owner also shall be killed. [30]But the dead man's relatives may accept a fine instead, if they wish. The judges will determine the amount. [31]The same law holds if the ox gores a boy or a girl. [32]But if the ox goes a slave, whether male or female, the slave's master shall be given thirty pieces of silver, and the ox shall be stoned.

[33]If a man digs a well and doesn't cover it, and an ox or a donkey falls into it, [34]the owner of the well shall pay full damages to the owner of the animal, and the dead animal shall belong to him.

Lev 6:1. And the Lord said to Moses, [2]"If anyone sins against me by refusing to return a deposit on something borrowed or rented, or by refusing to return something entrusted to him, or by robbery, or by oppressing his neighbor, [3]or by finding a lost article and lying about it, swearing that he doesn't have it—[4, 5]on the day he is found guilty of any such sin, he shall restore what he took, adding a twenty percent fine, and give it to the one he has harmed; and on the same day he shall bring his guilt offering to the Tabernacle."

Deut 22:13, 14. If a man marries a girl, then after sleeping with her accuses her of having had premarital intercourse with another man, saying, "She was not a virgin when I married her," [15]then the girl's father and mother shall bring the proof of her virginity to the city judges. [16]Her father shall tell them, "I gave my daughter to this man to be his wife, and now he despises her, [17, 18]and has accused her of shameful things, claiming that she was not a virgin when she married; yet here is the proof." And they shall spread the garment before the judges. The judges shall sentence the man to be whipped, [19]and fine him one hundred dollars to be given to the girl's father, for he has falsely accused a virgin of Israel. She shall remain his wife and he may never divorce her.

[28, 29]If a man rapes a girl who is not engaged, and is caught in the act, he must pay a fine to the girl's father and marry her; he may never divorce her.

DAMARIS A female convert of Athens, Acts 17:34.

DAMASCUS An ancient city, Gen 14:15; 15: 2, 3. Capital of Syria, 1 Kgs 20:34; Isa 7:8; Jer 49: 23–27; Ezk 47:16, 17. Laid under tribute to David, 2 Sam 8:5, 6. Beseiged by Rezon, 1 Kgs 11:23, 24. Recovered by Jeroboam, 2 Kgs 14:28. Taken by king of Assyria, 2 Kgs 16:9. Walled, 2 Cor 11:33. Garrisoned, 1 Chron 18:6; 2 Cor 11:32. Paul's experiences in, Acts 9; 22:5–16; 26:12–20; 2 Cor 11: 32–33; Gal 1:17.

Prophecies concerning, Isa 8:4; 17:1–6; Jer 49: 23–27; Amos 1:3, 5; Zech 9:1–2.

Wilderness of, 1 Kgs 19:15.

See *Syria.*

DAMNED See *Wicked, Punishment of.*

DAN 1. First son of Jacob and Bilhah, Gen 30:6; 35:25. Descendants of, Gen 46:23–25; Num 26:42, 43. See *Tribe of,* below. Blessed of Jacob, Gen 49:16, 17.

2. TRIBE OF: Census of, Num 1:20–46; 26:42, 43. Inheritance of, according to the allotment of Joshua, Josh 19:40–48; of Ezekiel, Ezk 48:1. Position of, in journey and camp, during the exodus, Num 2:23–31; 10:25. Blessed by Moses, Deut 33:22. Cities given by, to Levites, Josh 21:23, 24. Fails to conquer the Amorites, Judg 1:34, 35. Conquests by, Josh 19:47, 48; Judg 18:27–29. Deborah chides, for cowardice, Judg 5:17. Idolatry of, Judg 18. Commerce of, Judg 5:17. Prophecy concerning, Ezk 48:32. Recruits from, for David's army, 1 Chron 12:24–37. Missing from the list of tribes in Revelation 7:4–8.

See *Israel, Tribes of.*

3. A city of the tribe of Dan. Called also *Laish,* and *Leshem,* Gen 14:14; Deut 34:1; Judg 20:1; Jer 8:16. Captured by the people of Dan, Josh 19:47, 48. Idolatry established at, Judg 18; 1 Kgs 12:28, 29; Amos 8:14. Destroyed by Ben-hadad, 1 Kgs 15:20; 2 Chron 16:4.

DANCING Ex 15:20. Then Miriam the prophetess, the sister of Aaron, took a timbrel and led the women in dances.

Ex 32:19. When they came near the camp, Moses saw the calf and the dancing, and in terrible anger he threw the tablets to the ground and they lay broken at the foot of the mountain.

Judg 11:34. When Jephthah returned home his daughter—his only child—ran out to meet him, playing on a tambourine and dancing for joy.

Judg 21:19. Suddenly someone thought of the annual religious festival held in the fields of Shiloh, between Lebonah and Bethel, along the east of the road that goes from Bethel to Shechem. [20]They told the men of Benjamin who still needed wives, "Go and hide in the vineyards, [21]and when the girls of Shiloh come out for their dances, rush out and catch them and take them home with you to be your wives!"

1 Sam 18:6. But something had happened when the victorious Israeli army was returning home after David had killed Goliath. Women came out from all the towns along the way to celebrate and to cheer for King Saul, and were singing and dancing for joy with tambourines and cymbals. chapter 29:5.

1 Sam 21:11. But Achish's officers weren't happy about his being there. "Isn't he the top leader of Israel?" they asked. "Isn't he the one the people honor at their dances, singing, 'Saul has slain his thousands and David his ten thousands'?"

1 Sam 30:16. So he led them to the Amalekite encampment. They were spread out across the fields, eating and drinking and dancing with joy because of the vast amount of loot they had taken from the Philistines and from the men of Judah.

2 Sam 6:14. And David danced before the Lord with all his might, and was wearing priests' clothing. [15]So Israel brought home the Ark of the Lord with much shouting and blowing of trumpets. [16](But as the procession came into the city, Michal, Saul's daughter, watched from a window and saw King David leaping and dancing before the Lord; and she was filled with contempt for him.) *v.* 21; 1 Chron 13:8; 15:29.

Job 21:11. They have many happy children, [12, 13]they spend their time singing and dancing.

Ps 149:3. Praise His name with dancing, accompanied by drums and lyre.

Eccl 3:4. A time to cry; a time to laugh; a time to grieve; a time to dance.

Jer 31:4. I will rebuild your nation, O virgin of Israel. You will again be happy and dance merrily with the timbrels. [13]The young girls will dance for joy, and men folk—old and young—will take their part in all the fun; for I will turn their mourning into joy and I will comfort them and make them rejoice, for their captivity with all its sorrows will be behind them.

Lam 5:14, 15. The old men sit no longer in the city gates; the young no longer dance and sing. The joy of our hearts has ended; our dance has turned to death.

Lk 15:23. "And kill the calf we have in the fattening pen. We must celebrate with a feast, [24]for this son of mine was dead and has returned to life. He was lost and is found." So the party began. [25]Meanwhile, the older son was in the fields working; when he returned home, he heard dance music coming from the house, [26]and he asked one of the servants what was going on.

Daughter of Herodias, before Herod, Mt 14:6; Mk 6:22, 23. Idolatrous, Ex 32:19; 1 Kgs 18:26; 1 Cor 10:7. Shulammite woman, Song 6:13. Jews, instead of repenting, Isa 22:13. Figurative: Luke 7:32 (see footnote).

DANIEL 1. A Jewish captive, called also *Belteshazzar.* Educated at king's court, Dan 1. Interprets visions, Dan 2; 4; 5. Promotion and executive authority of, Dan 2:48, 49; 5:11, 29; 6:2. Conspiracy against, thrown into the lions' den, Dan 6.

Prophecies of, Dan 4:8, 9; chapters 7–12; Mt 24:15.

Abstinence of, Dan 1:8–16. Wisdom of, Dan 1:17; Ezk 28:2, 3. Devoutness of, Dan 2:18; 6; 9; 10; 12; Ezk 14:14. Courage and fidelity of, Dan 4:27; 5:17–23; 6:10–23. Honored by Nebuchadnezzar, Dan 2:6.

2. David's son; 1 Chron 3:1. Called also *Chileab,* 2 Sam 3:3.

3. A descendant of Ithamar, and a companion of Ezra, Ezra 8:2–14; Neh 10:1–8.

DAN-JAAN A place near the source of the Jordan, 2 Sam 24:6.

DANNAH A city in the mountains of Judah, Josh 15:48–62.

DARA See *Darda.*

DARDA Called also *Dara.* A famous wise man, 1 Kgs 4:31; 1 Chron 2:6.

DARIUS 1. The Mede, king of Persia, Dan 5:31; 6; 9:1; 11:1.

2. King of Persia. Emancipates the Jews, Ezra 5; 6; Hag 1:1, 14, 15; Zech 1:1; 7:1.

3. The Persian, Neh 12:22.

DARKNESS Over the earth, Gen 1:2; Job 38: 8, 9, 19; Jer 4:23. Called *Nighttime,* Gen 1:4, 5. God creates, Ps 139:11, 12; Isa 45:7; 50:3. Miraculous: In Egypt, Ex 10:21, 22; 14:20; Josh 24:7; Ps 105:28; at Sinai, Ex 20:21; Deut 5:22, 23; Heb 12:18; at the crucifixion, Mt 27:45; Mk 15:33.

FIGURATIVE. Of death, Job 3:4, 5; 10:20–22; Ps 23:4; Eccl 8:8; of judgments, 1 Sam 2:9; Prov 20:20; Isa 8:22; 13:10; Jer 4:28; 13:16; 23:12; Lam 3:2; Ezk 32:7, 8; Joel 2:2, 10, 31; Amos 4:13; 5:18, 20; 8:9; Mic 3:8; 7:8, 9; Mt 24:29; Mk 13:24; Lk 23:44, 45; 2 Pet 2:17; Jude 1:6, 13; Rev 8:12; 9:2; 18:23. Called outer darkness, Mt 8:12; 22:13; 25:30. Of powers of evil, Eph 6:12; Col 1:13; 1 Thess 5:5; Rev 16:10.

OF SPIRITUAL BLINDNESS. Isa 9:2. The people who walk in darkness shall see a great Light—a Light that will shine on all those who live in the land of the shadow of death. Mt 4:15, 16; Lk 1:79.

Isa 42:16. He will bring blind Israel along a path they have not seen before. He will make the darkness bright before them and smooth and straighten out the road ahead. He will not forsake them. Ps 91:5, 6.

Isa 50:10. Who among you fears the Lord and obeys his Servant? If such men walk in darkness, without one ray of light, let them trust the Lord, let them rely upon their God.

Mt 6:22. If your eye is pure, there will be sunshine in your soul. [23]But if your eye is clouded with evil thoughts and desires, you are in deep spiritual darkness. And oh, how deep that darkness can be!

Lk 11:34. Your eyes light up your inward being. A pure eye lets sunshine into your soul. A lustful eye shuts out the light and plunges you into darkness.

Jn 1:5. His life is the light that shines through the darkness—and the darkness can never extinguish it.

Jn 3:19. Their sentence is based on this fact: that the Light from heaven came into the world, but they loved the darkness more than the Light, for their deeds were evil. [20]They hated the heavenly Light because they wanted to sin in the darkness. They stayed away from that Light for fear their sins would be exposed and they would be punished. [21]But those doing right come gladly to the Light to let everyone see that they are doing what God wants them to do. Prov 13:9; Jn 12:46; Phil 2:15.

Jn 8:12. Later, in one of his talks, Jesus said to the people, "I am the Light of the world. So if you follow me, you won't be stumbling through the darkness, for living light will flood your path." Jn 12:35, 46.

Jn 11:9. Jesus replied, "There are twelve hours of daylight every day, and during every hour of it a man can walk safely and not stumble. [10]Only at night is there danger of a wrong step, because of the dark."

Acts 26:18. To open their eyes to their true condition so that they may repent and live in the light of God instead of in Satan's darkness, so that they may receive forgiveness for their sins and God's inheritance along with all people everywhere whose sins are cleansed away, who are set apart by faith in me.

Rom 1:21. And after awhile they began to think up silly ideas of what God was like and what he wanted them to do. The result was that their foolish minds became dark and confused. Ps 53:1.

Rom 13:12, 13. The night is far gone, the day of his return will soon be here. So quit the evil deeds of darkness and put on the armor of right living, as we who live in the daylight should! Be decent and true in everything you do so that all can approve your behavior. Don't spend your time in wild parties and getting drunk or in adultery and lust, or fighting, or jealousy.

2 Cor 4:6. For God, who said, "Let there be light in the darkness," has made us understand that it is the brightness of his glory that is seen in the face of Jesus Christ.

2 Cor 6:14. Don't be teamed with those who do not love the Lord, for what do the people of God have in common with the people of sin? How can light live with darkness?

Eph 5:8. For though once your heart was full of darkness, now it is full of light from the Lord, and your behavior should show it! [11]Take no part in the worthless pleasures of evil and darkness, but instead, rebuke and expose them. Isa 58:10.

1 Thess 5:4, 5. But, dear brothers, you are not in the dark about these things, and you won't be surprised as by a thief when that day of the Lord comes. [5]For you are all children of the light and of the day, and do not belong to darkness and night.

1 Pet 2:9. But you are not like that, for you have been chosen by God himself—you are priests of the King, you are holy and pure, you are God's very own—all this so that you may show to others how God called you out of the darkness into his wonderful light.

1 Jn 1:5–7. This is the message God has given us to pass on to you: that God is Light and in him is no darkness at all. [6]So if we say we are his friends, but go on living in spiritual darkness and sin, we are lying. [7]But if we are living in the light of God's presence, just as Christ does, then we have wonderful fellowship and joy with each other, and the blood of Jesus his Son cleanses us from every sin.

1 Jn 2:8–11. Yet it is always new, and works for you just as it did for Christ; and as we obey this commandment, to love one another, the darkness in our lives disappears and the new light of life in Christ shines in. [9]Anyone who says he is walking in the light of Christ but dislikes his fellow man, is still in darkness. [10]But whoever loves his fellow man is "walking in the light" and can see his way without stumbling around in darkness and sin. [11]For he who dislikes his brother is wandering in spiritual darkness and doesn't know where he is going, for the darkness had made him blind so that he cannot see the way.

See *Blindness, Spiritual.*

The darkness of the Holy of Holies was symbolic of the dwelling place of Jehovah. See *Most Holy Place,* under the topic *Tabernacle.* See also the following scriptures:

Ex 19:16. On the morning of the third day there was a terrific thunder and lightning storm, and a huge cloud came down upon the mountain, and there was a long, loud blast as from a ram's horn; and all the people trembled.

2 Sam 22:10. He bent the heavens down and came to earth; he walked upon dark clouds. [11]He rode upon the glorious—on the wings of the wind. [12]Darkness surrounded him, and clouds were thick around him.

2 Chron 6:1. This is the prayer prayed by Solomon on that occasion: "The Lord has said that he would live in the thick darkness, but I have made a Temple for you, O Lord, to live in forever!" 1 Kgs 8:12, 13.

Ps 18:11. He enshrouded himself with darkness, veiling his approach with dense clouds dark as murky waters.

Ps 97:2. Clouds and darkness surround him. Righteousness and justice are the foundation of his throne. Ex 19:9; Deut 4:11; Job 22:13; Ps 18:19.

Heb 12:18. You have not had to stand face to face with terror, flaming fire, gloom, darkness and a terrible storm, as the Israelites did at Mount Sinai when God gave them his laws.

DARKON A servant of Solomon, Ezra 2:55–57; Neh 7:57–59.

DART Job 41:7, 26.

DATE A fruit, Song 7:7.

DATHAN A conspirator against Moses, Num 16:1–35; 26:5–11; Deut 11:6; Ps 106:17.

DAUGHTER Forbidden to be wife of near relative, Lev 18:6–17; 20:14, 17. Sold in concubinage, Ex 21:7–10; Neh 5:5. Given in marriage by parents, Gen 29:20–28; Josh 15:16, 17; Judg 1:12, 13; 12:9, 10; 1 Sam 17:25; 18:17–27; Dan 11:6, 17. Regulations for priests', Lev 21:9; 22:12; Num 18:11. Father's responsibility, Num 30:3–5, 16; Deut 22:13–19.

Property rights of, Num 27:1–11; 36; Josh 17:3–6; Ruth 4:3.

Prophecy of, Mic 7:6; Mt 10:35; Lk 12:53.

DAUGHTER-IN-LAW Instance of, Ruth, Ruth 1:11–18; 4:15. Forbidden to marry near relative, Lev 20:12. Prophecy of, Mic 7:6; Mt 10:35; Lk 12:53.

DAVID 1. King of Israel. Genealogy of, Ruth 4:18–22; 1 Sam 16:11; 17:12; 1 Chron 2:3–15; Mt 1:1–6; Lk 3:23–38. A shepherd, 1 Sam 16:11. Kills a lion and a bear, 1 Sam 17:34–36. Anointed king, while a youth, by the prophet Samuel, and inspired, 1 Sam 16:1, 13; Ps 89:19–37. Chosen of God, Ps 78:70.

Described to Saul, 1 Sam 16:18. Detailed as bodyguard and musician at Saul's court, 1 Sam 16:21–23. Kills Goliath, 1 Sam 17. Love of Jonathan for, 1 Sam 18:1–4. Popularity and discreetness of, 1 Sam 18. Saul's jealousy of, 1 Sam 18:8–30. Is defrauded of Merab, and given Michal as his wife, 1 Sam 18:17–27. Jonathan intercedes for, 1 Sam 19:1–7. Probably writes Psalm 11 at this period of his life.

Conducts a campaign against, and defeats the Philistines, 1 Sam 19:8. Saul attempts to kill him; he escapes to Ramah, and lives at Naioth, where Saul pursues him, 1 Sam 19:9–24. About this time writes Psalm 59. Returns, and Jonathan makes covenant with him, 1 Sam 20. Escapes by way of Nob, where he obtains holy bread and Goliath's sword from Abimelech, 1 Sam 21:1–9; Mt 12:3, 4; Lk 6:3, 4; to Gath, 1 Sam 21:10–15. At this time probably writes Psalms 34, 35, 52, 56, 120. Recruits an army of insurgents, goes to Moab, returns to Hereth, 1 Sam 22. Probably writes Psalms 17, 58, 64, 109, 142. Saves Keilah, 1 Sam 23:1–13. Makes second covenant with Jonathan, 1 Sam 23:16–18. Goes to the wilderness of Ziph, is betrayed to Saul, 1 Sam 23:13–26. Writes a psalm on the betrayal, Psalm 54, and probably Psalms 22, 31, 140. Saul is diverted from pursuit of, 1 Sam 23:27, 28. At this time probably writes Psalm 12. Goes to Engedi, 1 Sam 23:29. Refrains from slaying Saul, 1 Sam 24. Writes Psalm 57. Covenants with Saul, 1 Sam 24. Marries Nabal's widow, Abigail, and Ahinoam, 1 Sam 25. Lives in the wilderness of Ziph, has opportunity to kill Saul, but takes his spear only, Saul is contrite, 1 Sam 26. Runs away to Achish and lives in Ziklag, 1 Sam 27. List of men who join him, 1 Chron 12:1–22. Conducts an expedition against Amalekites, misstates the facts to Achish, 1 Sam 27:8–12. At this time probably writes Psalm 141. Is refused permission to accompany the Philistines to battle against the Israelites, 1 Sam 28:1, 2; 29. Rescues the people of Ziklag, who had been captured by the Amalekites, 1 Sam 30. Probably writes Psalm 13. Death and burial of Saul and his sons, 1 Sam 31; 2 Sam 21:1–14. Kills the murderer of Saul, 2 Sam 1:1–16. Mourning over Saul, 2 Sam 1:17–27.

After living one year and four months at Ziklag, 1 Sam 27:7, goes to Hebron, and is anointed king by Judah, 2 Sam 2:1–4, 11; 5:4, 5; 1 Kgs 2:11; 1 Chron 3:4; 11:1–3. List of those who join him at Hebron, 1 Chron 12:23–40. Ish-bosheth, son of Saul, crowned, 2 Sam chapters 2–4. David wages war against, and defeats, Ishbosheth, 2 Sam 2:13–32. Demands the restoration of Michal, his wife, 2 Sam 3:14–16. Abner revolts from Ish-bosheth, and joins David, but is killed by Joab, 2 Sam 3. Punishes Ish-bosheth's murderers, 2 Sam 4.

Anointed king over all Israel, after reigning over Judah at Hebron seven years and six months, and reigns 33 years, 2 Sam 2:11; 5:5; 1 Chron 3:4; 11:1–3; 12:23–40; 29:25–27. Captures Jerusalem, 2 Sam 5:6, 1 Chron 11:4–8; Isa 29:1. Builds a palace, 2 Sam 5:11; 2 Chron 2:3. Friendship of, with Hiram, king of Tyre, 2 Sam 5:11; 1 Kgs 5:1. Prospered of God, 2 Sam 5:10, 12; 1 Chron 11:9. Fame of, 1 Chron 14:17. Philistines make war against, and are defeated by him, 2 Sam 5:17, 25; 1 Chron 14:8–17.

Assembles 30,000 men to escort the ark to Jerusalem with music and thanksgiving, 2 Sam 6:1–5; 1 Chron 13:1–8. Uzzah is killed when he attempts to steady the ark, 2 Sam 6:6–11; 1 Chron 13:

9,10. David is terrified, and leaves the ark at the house of Obed-edom, 2 Sam 6:9–11; 1 Chron 13:11–14. After three months brings the ark to Jerusalem with dancing and great joy, 2 Sam 6:12–16; 1 Chron 15:1–15. Organized the Tabernacle service, 1 Chron 9:22; 15:16–24; 16:4–6, 37–43. Offers sacrifice, distributes gifts, and blesses the people, 2 Sam 6:17–20. Michal chides him for his enthusiasm, 2 Sam 6:20–23. Desires to build a temple, is forbidden, but receives promise that his seed should reign forever, 2 Sam 7:12–16; 23:5; 1 Kgs 8:17–20; 1 Chron 17:11–14; 28:2–7; 2 Chron 6:7–9, 16; Ps 89:3,4; 132:10–12; Acts 15:16; Rom 15:12. Interpretation and fulfillment of this prophecy, Acts 13:22, 23. At this time, probably, writes Psalms 15, 16, 24, 101, 138. Conquers the Philistines, Moabites, and Syria, 2 Sam 8; 1 Chron 18:1–13.

Treats Mephibosheth, the lame son of Saul, with great kindness, 2 Sam 9:6; 19:24–30. Sends commissioners with a message of sympathy to Hanun, son of the king of Ammon; the message misinterpreted, and commissioners treated with indignity; David retaliates by invading his kingdom, and defeating the combined armies of the Ammonites and Syrians, 2 Sam 10; 1 Chron 19. Probably writes Psalms 18, 20, 21.

Commits adultery with Bath-sheba, 2 Sam 11:2–5. Wickedly causes the death of Uriah, 2 Sam 11:6–25. Takes Bath-sheba to be his wife, 2 Sam 11:26, 27. Is rebuked by the prophet Nathan, 2 Sam 12:1–14. Repents of his crime and confesses his guilt, Ps 6; 32; 38; 39; 40; 51. Is severely punished because of his crime Ps 38; 41; 69. Death of his infant son by Bath-sheba, 2 Sam 12:15–23. Solomon is born to, 2 Sam 12:24, 25.

Ammonites defeated and tortured, 2 Sam 12:26–31; 1 Chron 20:1–3. Amnon's crime, his murder by Absalom, and Absalom's flight, 2 Sam 13. Absalom's return, 2 Sam 14:1–24. Absalom's usurpation, 2 Sam 14; 15. David's flight from Jerusalem, 2 Sam 15:13–37. He probably writes, at this time, Psalms 5, 7, 26, 61, 63, 69, 70, 86, 143. Shime-i curses him, 2 Sam 16. Crosses the Jordan, 2 Sam 17:21–29. Absalom's defeat and death, 2 Sam 18. Mourns the death of Absalom, 2 Sam 18:33; 19:1–4. Chided by Joab, 2 Sam 19:5–7. David chides the priests for not showing loyalty while the people murmur against him, 2 Sam 19:9–15. Shime-i pleads for clemency, 2 Sam 19:16–23. Mephibosheth asks for the king's favor, 2 Sam 19:24–30. Barzillai rewarded, 2 Sam 19:31–40. Judah accused by the ten tribes of stealing him away, 2 Sam 19:41–43. Returns to Jerusalem, 2 Sam 20:1–3. At this time, probably, composes Psalms 27, 66, 122, 144.

Sheba's conspiracy against David, and his death, 2 Sam 20. Makes Amasa general, 2 Sam 19:13. Amasa is killed, 2 Sam 20:4–10. Consigns seven sons of Saul to the Gibeonites to be killed to atone for Saul's persecution of the Gibeonites, 2 Sam 21:1–14. Buries Saul's bones, and his sons', 2 Sam 21:12–14.

Defeats the Philistines, 2 Sam 21:15–22; 1 Chron 20:4–8. Takes the military strength of Israel without divine authority, and is punished, 2 Sam 24; 1 Chron 21; 27:24. Probably composes Psalms 30, 131. Marries Abishag, 1 Kgs 1:1–4. Probably composes Psalms 19, 111.

Reorganizes the Tabernacle service, 1 Chron 22–26; 2 Chron 7:6; 8:14; 23:18; 29:27–30; 35:15; Ezra 3:10; 8:20.

Adonijah usurps the throne, Solomon appointed, 1 Kgs 1; 1 Chron 23:1. Delivers his charge to Solomon, 1 Kgs 2:1–11; 1 Chron 22:6–19; 28; 29. Probably composes Psalms 23, 145.

Last words of, 2 Sam 23:1–7. Death of, 1 Kgs 2:10; 1 Chron 29:28; Acts 2:29; 30. Tomb of, Acts 2:29. Age of, at death, 2 Sam 5:4, 5; 1 Chron 29:28. Length of reign, 40 years, 1 Kgs 2:11; 1 Chron 29:27, 28.

Wives of, 2 Sam 3:2–5; 11:3, 27; 1 Chron 3:5. Children born at Hebron, 2 Sam 3:2–5; 1 Chron 3:4, at Jerusalem, 2 Sam 5:14–16; 1 Chron 3:5–8; 14:4–7. Descendants of, 1 Chron 3.

Civil and military officers of, 2 Sam 8:16–18. See *Cabinet.*

Lists of his heroes, and of their exploits, 2 Sam 23; 1 Chron 11; 12:23–40.

Devoutness of, 1 Sam 13:14; 2 Sam 6:5, 14–18; 7:18–29; 8:11, 12; 24:25; 1 Kgs 3:6, 14; 15:5; 1 Chron 17:16–27; 29:10; 2 Chron 7:17; Zech 12:8; Ps 6; 7; 11; 13; 17; 22; 26; 27:7–14; 28; 31; 35; 37; 38; 39; 40:11–17; 42; 43; 51; 54; 55; 56; 57; 59; 60; 61; 62; 64:1–6; 66; 69; 70; 71; 86; 101; 108; 120:1–2; 140; 141; 142; 143; 144; Acts 13:22.

Justice in the administration of, 2 Sam 8:15; 1 Chron 18:14. Discreetness of, 1 Sam 18:14, 30. Meekness of, 1 Sam 24:7; 26:11; 2 Sam 16:11; 19:22, 23. Merciful, 2 Sam 19:23.

David as musician, 1 Sam 16:21–23; 1 Chron 15:16; 23:4, 5; 2 Chron 7:6; 29:26; Neh 12:35, 36; Amos 6:5; poet, 2 Sam 22; see *Psalms, of David;* prophet, 2 Sam 23:2–7; 1 Chron 28:19; Mt 22:41–46; Acts 2:25–38; 4:25, 26.

Type of Christ, Ps 2; 16; 18:43; 69:7–9, 20, 21, 26, 29; 89:19–37; 132:17. Jesus called son of, Mt 9:27; 12:23; 15:22; 20:30, 31; 21:9; 22:42; Mk 10:47, 48; 12:35–37; Lk 1:69 18:37–39; 20:41–44; Jn 7:41, 42; Rom 1:3; 2 Tim 2:8; Rev 5:5; 22:16.

Prophecies concerning him and his kingdom, Num 24:15–19; 2 Sam 7:11–16; 1 Chron 17:9–14; 22; 2 Chron 6:5–17; 13:5; 21:7; Ps 89:19–37; Isa 9:7; 11:1; 16:4, 5; 22:20–25; Jer 23:5, 6; 33:15–26; Mk 11:10; Lk 1:32, 33.

Chronicles of, written by Samuel, Nathan, and Gad, 1 Chron 29:29, 30.

2. Prophecies naming David as king or prince, Jer 30:9; Ezk 34:23, 24; 37:24, 25; Hos 3:5.

DAY A creative period, Gen 1:4, 5, 7, 8, 13, 19, 23, 31; 2:2. Divided into 12 hours, Jn 11:9. Prophetic, Dan 8:14, 26; 12:11–13; Rev 9:15; 11:3; 12:6. Six working days ordained, Ex 20:9; Ezk 46:1. Sixth day of the week called preparation day, Mk 15:42, 43; Jn 19:14, 31, 42. First day of the week called the Lord's Day, Rev 1:10. With the Lord as a thousand years, 2 Pet 3:8.

Day's journey, 18 or 20 miles (about 29–32 kilometers), Ex 3:18; 1 Kgs 19:4; Jon 3:4, 5. The seventh of the week ordained as a day of rest, see *Sabbath.*

Day of Atonement, see *Atonement, Day of.*

Day of the Lord: Isa 2:12; 13:6, 9; 34:8; Jer 30:7; 46:10; Ezk 7:19; 30:2, 3; 39:8; Joel 1:15; 2:1, 11, 31; 3:14; Amos 5:18, 20; Obd 1:15; Zeph 1:7, 14, 18; 2:2; Zech 14:1; 1 Thess 5:2; 2 Thess 2:2; 2 Pet 3:10; cf. Rev 16:14.

Day of Christ, 1 Cor 1:8; 2 Cor 1:13, 14; Phil 1:6.

Day of God, 2 Pet 3:12.

DEACON An ecclesiastic charged with the temporal affairs of the church. Ordained by the apostles, Acts 6:1–6; 21:8. Qualifications of, 1 Tim 3:8–13. The Greek word translated deacon signifies servant, and is so translated in Mt 23:11; Jn 12:26. Also translated minister, 1 Thess 3:2.

DEAD Raised to life, instances of: Son of the widow of Zarephath, 1 Kgs 17:17–23; Shunemmite's son, 2 Kgs 4:32–37; young man laid in Elisha's tomb, 2 Kgs 13:20, 21; widow's son, Lk 7:12–15; Jairus' daughter, Lk 8:49–55; Lazarus, Jn 11:43, 44; Dorcas, Acts 9:37–40; Eutychus, Acts 20:9–12; see Heb 11:35. Prepared for burial by washing, Acts 9:37; anointing, Mt 26:12; wrapping in linen, Mt 27:59. Burned, see *Cremation.*

Burnings of incense made for, 2 Chron 16:13, 14; Jer 34:5.

See *Burial; Cremation; Embalming.*

UNCLASSIFIED SCRIPTURES RELATING TO: Job 3:13. For if only I had died at birth, then I would be quiet now, asleep and at rest, [14, 15]along with prime ministers and kings with all their pomp, and wealthy princes whose castles are full of rich treasures. [16]Oh, to have been still-born!—to have never breathed or seen the light. [17]For there in death the wicked cease from troubling, and there the weary are at rest. [18]There even prisoners are at ease, with no brutal jailer to curse them. [19]Both rich and poor alike are there, and the slave is free at last from his master.

Job 14:11, 12. As water evaporates from a lake, as a river disappears in drought, so a man lies down for the last time, and does not rise again until the heavens are no more; he shall not awaken, nor be roused from his sleep. [13]Oh, that you would hide me with the dead, and forget me there until your anger ends; but mark your calendar to think of me again! [14]If a man dies, shall he live again? This thought gives me hope, so that in all my anguish I eagerly await sweet death! [15]You would call and I would come, and you would reward all I do. [20, 21]Always you are against him, and then he passes off the scene. You make him old and wrinkled, then send him away. He never knows it if his sons are honored; or they may fail and face disaster, but he knows it not.

Job 17:13, 14. If I die, I go out into darkness, and call the grave my father, and the worm my mother and my sister. [15]Where then is my hope? Can anyone find any? [16]No, my hope will go down with me to the grave. We shall rest together in the dust!

Ps 6:5. For if I die I cannot give you glory by praising you before my friends.

Ps 30:9. What will you gain, O Lord, from killing me? How can I praise you then to all my friends? How can my dust in the grave speak out and tell the world about your faithfulness?

Ps 49:15. But as for me, God will redeem my soul from the power of death, for he will receive me.

Ps 88:10. Soon it will be too late! Of what use are your miracles when I am in the grave? How can I praise you then? [11]Can those in the grave declare your lovingkindness? Can they proclaim your faithfulness? [12]Can the darkness speak of your miracles? Can anyone in the Land of Forgetfulness talk about your help?

Ps 115:17. The dead cannot sing praises to Jehovah here on earth.

Prov 21:16. The man who strays away from common sense will end up dead!

Eccl. 9:5, 6. For the living at least know that they will die! But the dead know nothing; they don't even have their memories. Whatever they did in their lifetimes—loving, hating, envying—is long gone, and they have no part in anything here on earth any more.

Ezk 32:31. When Pharaoh arrives, he will be comforted to find that he is not alone in having all his army slain, says the Lord God.

Dan 12:2. And many of those whose bodies lie dead and buried will rise up, some to everlasting life and some to shame and everlasting contempt. Isa 66:24.

Lk 9:30. Then two men appeared and began talking with him—Moses and Elijah! [31]They were splendid in appearance, glorious to see; and they were speaking of his death at Jerusalem, to be carried out in accordance with God's plan.

Lk 16:19. "There was a certain rich man," Jesus said, "who was splendidly clothed and lived each day in mirth and luxury. [20]One day Lazarus, a diseased beggar, was laid at his door. [21]As he lay there longing for scraps from the rich man's table, the dogs would come and lick his open sores. [22]Finally the beggar died and was carried by the angels to be with Abraham in the place of the righteous dead. The rich man also died and was buried, [23]and his soul went into hell. There, in torment, he saw Lazarus in the far distance with Abraham. [24]'Father Abraham,' he shouted, 'have some pity! Send Lazarus over here if only to dip the tip of his finger in water and cool my tongue, for I am in anguish in these flames.' [25]But Abraham said to him, 'Son, remember that during your lifetime you had everything you wanted, and Lazarus had nothing. So now he is here being comforted and you are in anguish. [26]And besides, there is a great chasm separating us, and anyone wanting to come to you from here is stopped at its edge; and no one over there can cross to us.' [27]Then the rich man said, 'O Father Abraham, then please send him to my father's home—[28]for I have five brothers—to warn them about this place of torment lest they come here when they die.' [29]But Abraham said, 'The Scriptures have warned them again and again. Your brothers can read them any time they want to.' [30]The rich man replied, 'No, Father Abraham, they won't bother to read them. But if someone is sent to them from the dead, then they will turn from their sins.' [31]But Abraham said, 'If they won't listen to Moses and the prophets, they won't listen even though someone rises from the dead.' "

Lk 20:34, 35. Jesus replied, "Marriage is for people here on earth, but when those who are counted worthy of being raised from the dead get to heaven, they do not marry. [36]And they never die again; in these respects they are like angels, and are sons of God, for they are raised up in new life from the dead."

Lk 23:43. And Jesus replied, "Today you will be with me in Paradise. This is a solemn promise."

Jn 11:25. Jesus told her, "I am the one who raises the dead and gives them life again. Anyone who believes in me, even though he dies like anyone else, shall live again."

See *Burial; Death; Mourning; Resurrection; Righteous, Promises to; Wicked, Punishment of.*

DEAD SEA Lies southeast of Jerusalem, Num 34:12; Joel 2:20; Zech 14:8. Called *Salt Sea,* Gen 14:3; Deut 3:17; 4:49; Josh 3:16; *Sea of Arabah,* Deut 3:17.

Prophecy concerning, Ezk 47:7–10, 18.

DEAFNESS Law concerning, Lev 19:14. Inflicted by God, Ex 4:11. Miraculous cure of, Mt 11:5; Mk 7:32; 9:25; Lk 7:20–22. Of old age, Eccl 12:4.

FIGURATIVE. Of moral insensibility, Isa 6:10; 29:18; 35:5; 40:21; 42:18; 43:8; Ezk 12:2; Mt 13:15; Jn 12:40; Acts 28:26, 27.

See *Blindness, Spiritual; Conscience, Dead; Impenitence; Obduracy.*

DEATH INDEX OF SUB-TOPICS. *Miscellaneous Subjects; Unclassified Scriptures Relating to; Preparation for; Of the Righteous; Scenes of; Of the Wicked; Spiritual; Second Death; Figurative of Regeneration.*

Called *King of Terrors,* Job 18:14; *Sweet,* Job 14:14; *Going the way from which there is no return,* Job 16:22; *Turning to dust,* Psa 104:29; *Returning to the ground,* Gen 3:19; *Withering,* Job 14:2; *Disappears as a shadow,* Job 14:2; *Going,* Phil 1:23.

Called Sleep. Job 14:11, 12. As water evaporates from a lake, as a river disappears in drought, so a man lies down for the last time, and does not rise again until the heavens are no more; he shall not awaken, nor be roused from his sleep.

Jer 51:39. And while they lie inflamed with all their wine, I will prepare a different kind of feast for them, and make them drink until they fall unconscious to the floor, to sleep forever, never to waken again, says the Lord.

Jn 11:11. Then he said, "Our friend Lazarus has gone to sleep, but now I will go and waken him!"

Exemption From. Enoch, Gen 5:21–24; Heb 11:5. Elijah, 2 Kgs 2. Promised to Christians at the second coming of Christ, 1 Cor 15:51; 1 Thess 4:15, 17. No death in heaven, Lk 20:36; Rev 21:4.

Desired. Jer 8:3; Rev 9:6. By Moses, Num 11:15; Elijah, 1 Kgs 19:4; Job, Job 3; 6:8–11; 7:1–3, 15, 16; 10:1; 14:13; Jonah, Jon 4:8; Simeon, Lk 2:29–31; Paul, 2 Cor 5:2, 8; Phil 1:20–23.

As a Judgment. On Adam, Gen 2:16, 17; 3:19; the Antediluvians, Gen 6:7, 11–13; the Sodomites, Gen 19:13; Onan, Gen 38:10; Nahab and Abihu, Lev 10:2; Num 3:4; Korah, Num 16:32, 33; Uzzah, 2 Sam 6:7; Saul, 1 Chron 10:13, 14; Ananias and Sapphira, Acts 5:5, 10; unworthy believers, 1 Cor 11:30.

Symbolized. By the pale horse, Rev 6:8; King of Terrors, Job 18:14.

Apostrophe to. Hos 13:14; 1 Cor 15:55, 56.

UNCLASSIFIED SCRIPTURES RELATING TO. Gen 2:16, 17. But the Lord God gave the man this warning: "You may eat any fruit in the garden except fruit from the Tree of Conscience—for its fruit will open your eyes to make you aware of right and wrong, good and bad. If you eat its fruit, you will be doomed to die."

Gen 3:19. All you life you will sweat to master it, until your dying day. Then you will return to the ground from which you came. For you were made from the ground, and to the ground you will return.

Gen 27:2, 3, 4. *Isaac:* "I am an old man now, and expect to die 'most any day. Take your bow and arrows out into the fields and get me some venison, and prepare it just the way I like it—savory and good—and bring it here for me to eat, and I will give you the blessings that belong to you, my firstborn son, before I die."

Josh 23:14. Soon I will be going the way of all the earth—I am going to die.

1 Sam 2:6. The Lord kills, the Lord gives life.

1 Sam 20:2, 3. "That's not true!" Jonathan protested. "I'm sure he's not planning any such thing, for he always tells me everything he's going to do, even little things, and I know he wouldn't hide something like this from me. It just isn't so." "Of course you don't know about it!" David fumed. "Your father knows perfectly well about our friendship, so he has said to himself, 'I'll not tell Jonathan—why should I hurt him?' But the truth is that I am only a step away from death! I swear it by the Lord and by your own soul!"

2 Sam 1:23. How much they were loved, how wonderful they were—both Saul and Jonathan! They were together in life and in death.

2 Sam 14:14. All of us must die eventually; our lives are like water that is poured out on the ground—it can't be gathered up again.

Job 3:13. For if only I had died at birth, then I would be quiet now, asleep, and at rest. [17]For there in death the wicked cease from troubling, and there the weary are at rest. [18]There even prisoners are at ease, with no brutal jailer to curse them. [19]Both rich and poor alike are there, and the slave is free at last from his master.

Job 7:1. How mankind must struggle. A man's life is long and hard, like that of a slave. [8]You see me now, but not for long. Soon you'll look upon me dead. [9]As a cloud disperses and vanishes, so those who die shall go away forever—[10]gone forever from their family and their home—never to be seen again. [21]For all so soon I'll lie down in the dust and die, and when you look for me, I shall be gone. Job 14:6.

Job 10:20, 21. Can't you see how little time I have left? Oh, let me alone that I may have a little moment of comfort before I leave for the land of darkness and the shadow of death, never to return —[22]a land as dark as midnight, a land of the shadow of death where only confusion reigns, and where the brightest light is dark as midnight.

Job 14:2. He blossoms for a moment like a flower —and withers; as the shadow of a passing cloud, he quickly disappears. [5]You have set mankind so brief a span of life—months is all you give him! Not one bit longer may he live. [7]For there is hope for a tree—if it's cut down it sprouts again, and grows tender, new branches. [8, 9]Though its roots have grown old in the earth, and its stump decays, it may sprout and bud again at the touch of water, like a new seedling. [10]But when a man dies and is buried, where does his spirit go? [11, 12]As water evaporates from a lake, as a river disappears in drought, so a man lies down for the last time, and does not rise again until the heavens are no more; he shall not awaken, nor be roused from his sleep. [14]If a man dies, shall he live again? This thought gives me hope, so that in all my anguish I eagerly await sweet death! [18, 19]Mountains wear away and disappear. Water grinds the stones to sand. Torrents tear away the soil. So every hope of man is worn away. [20, 21]Always you are against him, and then he passes off the scene. You make him old and wrinkled, then send him away. He never knows it if his sons are honored; or they may fail and face disaster, but he knows it not.

Job 16:22. For all so soon I must go down that road from which I shall never return.

Job 17:13, 14. If I die, I go out into darkness, and call the grave my father, and the worm my mother and my sister. [16]No, my hope will go down with me to the grave. We shall rest together in the dust!

Job 21:23, 24. He destroys those who are healthy, wealthy, fat, and prosperous; [25]God also destroys those in deep and grinding poverty who have never known anything good. [26]Both alike are buried in the same dust, both eaten by the same worms. [30-32]The evil man is usually spared in the day of calamity, and allowed to escape. No one rebukes him openly. No one repays him for what he has done. And an honor guard keeps watch at his grave. [33]A great funeral procession precedes and follows him as the soft earth covers him.

Job 30:23. And I know that your purpose for me is death.

Job 34:14. If God were to withdraw his Spirit, [15]all life would disappear and mankind would turn again to dust.

Job 36:18. Watch out! Don't let your anger at others lead you into scoffing at God! Don't let your suffering embitter you at the only one who can deliver you. [19]Do you really think that if you shout loudly enough against God, he will be ashamed and repent? Will this put an end to your chastisement?

Job 38:17, 18. Has the location of the gates of Death been revealed to you? Do you realize the extent of the earth?

Ps 23:4. Even when walking through the dark valley of death I will not be afraid, for you are close beside me, guarding, guiding all the way.

Ps 30:9. What will you gain, O Lord, from killing me? How can I praise you then to all my friends? How can my dust in the grave speak out and tell the world about your faithfulness? Ps 6:5; 88:9–14; 115:17; Isa 38:18.

Ps 39:4. Lord, help me to realize how brief my time on earth will be. Help me to know that I am here for but a moment more. [13]Spare me, Lord! Let me recover and be filled with happiness again before my death.

Ps 49:7. Yet not one of them, though rich as kings, can ransom his own brother from the penalty of sin! For God's forgiveness does not come that way. [8, 9]For a soul is far too precious to be ransomed by mere earthly wealth. There is not enough of it in all the earth to buy eternal life for just one soul, to keep it out of hell. [10]Rich man! Proud man! Wise man! You must die like all the rest! You have no greater lease on life than foolish, stupid men. You must leave your wealth to others.

Ps 68:20. He frees us! He rescues us from death. Deut 32:39.

Ps 82:7. But in death you are mere men. You will fall as any prince—for all must die.

Ps 89:48. No man can live forever. All will die. Who can rescue his life from the power of the grave?

Ps 90:3. You speak, and man turns back to dust.

Ps 103:14. For he knows we are but dust, [15]and that our days are few and brief, like grass, like flowers, [16]blown by the wind and gone forever.

Ps 104:29. But if you turn away from them, then all is lost. And when you gather up their breath, they die and turn again to dust.

Ps 143:3. My enemies chased and caught me. They have knocked me to the ground. They force me to live in the darkness like those in the grave. Lam 3:6.

Ps 144:4. For man is but a breath; his days are like a passing shadow.

Ps 146:4. For every man must die. His breathing stops, life ends, and in a moment all he planned for himself is ended.

Eccl 2:13, 14. That wisdom is of more value than foolishness, just as light is better than darkness; for the wise man sees, while the fool is blind. And yet I noticed that there was one thing that happened to wise and foolish alike—[15]just as the fool will die, so will I. So of what value is all my wisdom? Then I realized that even wisdom is futile. [16]For the wise and fool both die, and in the days to come both will be long forgotten. [17]So now I hate life because it is all so irrational; all is foolishness, chasing the wind. [18]And I am disgusted about this, that I must leave the fruits of all my hard work to others.

Eccl 3:2. A time to be born, a time to die. [19]For men and animals both breathe the same air, and both die. So mankind has no real advantage over the beasts; what an absurdity! [20]All go to one place—the dust from which they came and to which they must return. [21]For who can prove that the spirit of man goes upward and the spirit of animals goes downward into dust?

Eccl 4:2. So I felt that the dead were better off than the living.

Eccl 5:15. The man who speculates is soon back to where he began—with nothing. Job 1:21.

Eccl 6:6. Though a man lives a thousand years twice over, but doesn't find contentment—well, what's the use? [10]All things are decided by fate; it was known long ago what each man would be. So there's no use arguing with God about your destiny.

Eccl 7:1. A good reputation is more valuable than the most expensive perfume. The day one dies is better than the day he is born! [2]It is better to spend your time at funerals than at festivals. For you are going to die and it is a good thing to think about it while there is still time. [15-17]In this silly life I have seen everything, including the fact that some of the good die young and some of the wicked live on and on. So don't be too good or too wise! Why destroy yourself? On the other hand, don't be too wicked either—don't be a fool! Why should you die before your time?

Eccl 8:8. No one can hold back his spirit from departing; no one has the power to prevent his day of death, for there is no discharge from that obligation and that dark battle. Certainly a man's wickedness is not going to help him then.

Eccl 9:2, 3. The same providence confronts everyone, whether good or bad, religious or irreligious, profane or godly. It seems so unfair, that one fate comes to all. That is why men are not more careful to be good, but instead choose their own mad course, for they have no hope—there is nothing but death ahead anyway. [5]For the living at least know that they will die! But the dead know nothing; they don't even have their memories. [6]Whatever they did in their lifetimes—loving, hating, envying—is long gone, and they have no part in anything here on earth any more. [10]Whatever you do, do well, for in death, where you are going, there is no working or planning, or knowing, or understanding.

Eccl 12:5. You will be afraid of heights and of falling—a white-haired, withered old man, dragging himself along; without sexual desire, standing at death's door, and nearing his everlasting home as the mourners go along the streets. [7]And the dust returns to the earth as it was, and the spirit returns to God who gave it.

Isa 25:8. He will swallow up death forever. The Lord God will wipe away all tears and take away forever all insults and mockery against his land and people.

Isa 38:1. It was just before all this that Hezekiah became deathly sick and Isaiah the prophet (Amoz' son) went to visit him and gave him this message from the Lord: "Set your affairs in order, for you are going to die; you will not recover from this illness." [9]When King Hezekiah was well again, he wrote this poem about his experience: [10]"My life is but half done and I must leave it all. I am robbed of my normal years, and now I must enter the gates of Sheol. [11]Never again will I see the Lord in the land of the living. Never again will I see my friends in this world. [12]My life is blown away like a shepherd's tent; it is cut short as when a weaver stops his working at the loom. In one short day my life hangs by a thread. [13]All night I moaned; it was like being torn apart by lions."

Isa 40:7. The grass withers, the flower fades beneath the breath of God. And so it is with fragile man. 1 Pet 1:24.

Isa 51:12. I, even I, am he who comforts you and gives you all this joy. So what right have you to fear mere mortal men, who wither like the grass and disappear?

Jer 9:21. For death has crept in through your windows into your homes. He has killed off the flower of your youth. Children no longer play in the streets; the young men gather no more in the squares.

Hos 13:14. Shall I ransom him from hell? Shall I redeem him from Death? O Death, bring forth your terrors for his tasting! O Grave, demonstrate your plagues! For I will not relent!

Zech 1:5, 6. Your fathers and their prophets are now long dead, but remember the lesson they learned, that *God's Word endures!* It caught up with them and punished them. Then at last they repented.

Mt 10:28. Don't be afraid of those who can kill only your bodies—but can't touch your souls! Fear only God who can destroy both soul and body in hell.

Lk 20:34, 35. Jesus replied, "Marriage is for people here on earth, but when those who are counted worthy of being raised from the dead get to heaven, they do not marry. [36]And they never die again; in these respects they are like angels, and are sons of God, for they are raised up in new life from the dead. [37, 38]But as to your real question—whether or not there is a resurrection—why, even the writings of Moses himself prove this. For when he describes how God appeared to him in the burning bush, he speaks of God as 'the God of Abraham, the God of Isaac, and the God of Jacob.' To say that the Lord *is* some person's God means that person is *alive,* not dead! So from God's point of view, all men are living."

Lk 23:39. One of the criminals hanging beside him scoffed, "So, you're the Messiah, are you? Prove it by saving yourself—and us, too, while you're at it!" [40, 41]But the other criminal protested. "Don't you even fear God when you are dying? We deserve to die for our evil deeds, but this man hasn't done one thing wrong." [42]Then he said, "Jesus, remember me when you come into your Kingdom." [43]And Jesus replied, "Today you will be with me in Paradise. This is a solemn promise."

Jn 9:4. All of us must quickly carry out the tasks assigned us by the one who sent me, for there is little time left before the night falls and all work comes to an end.

Rom 5:12. When Adam sinned, sin entered the entire human race. His sin spread death throughout all the world, so everything began to grow old and die, for all sinned. [14]So when their bodies died it was not for their own sins since they themselves had never disobeyed God's special law against eating the forbidden fruit, as Adam had. What a contrast between Adam and Christ who was yet to come!

1 Cor 15:21. Death came into the world because of what one man (Adam) did, and it is because of what this other man (Christ) has done that now there is the resurrection from the dead. [22]Everyone dies because all of us are related to Adam, being members of his sinful race, and wherever there is sin, death results. But all who are related to Christ will rise again. [25]For Christ will be King until he has defeated all his enemies, [26]including the last enemy—death. This too must be defeated and ended. [55, 56]O death, where then your victory? Where then your sting? For sin—the sting that causes death—will all be gone; and the law, which reveals our sins, will no longer be our judge. [57]How we thank God for all of this! It is he who makes us victorious through Jesus Christ our Lord!

1 Tim 6:7. After all, we didn't bring any money with us when we came into the world, and we can't carry away a single penny when we die.

2 Tim 1:10. And now he has made all of this plain to us by the coming of our Savior Jesus Christ, who broke the power of death and showed us the way of everlasting life through trusting him.

Heb 2:14. Since we, God's children, are human beings—made of flesh and blood—he became flesh and blood too by being born in human form; for only as a human being could he die and in dying break the power of the devil who had the power of death. [15]Only in that way could he deliver those who through fear of death have been living all their lives as slaves to constant dread.

Heb 9:27. And just as it is destined that men die only once, and after that comes judgment.

Heb 13:14. For this world is not our home; we are looking forward to our everlasting home in heaven.

Jas 1:10, 11. But a rich man should be glad that his riches mean nothing to the Lord, for he will soon be gone, like a flower that has lost its beauty and fades away, withered—killed by the scorching summer sun. So it is with rich men. They will soon die and leave behind all their busy activities.

1 Pet 1:24. Yes, our natural lives will fade as grass does when it becomes all brown and dry. All our greatness is like a flower that droops and falls.

Rev 1:17, 18. When I saw him, I fell at his feet as dead; but he laid his right hand on me and said, "Don't be afraid! Though I am the First and Last, the Living One who died, who is now alive forevermore, who has the keys of hell and death—don't be afraid!

Rev 20:12. I saw the dead, great and small, standing before God; and The Books were opened, including the Book of Life. And the dead were judged according to the things written in The Books, each according to the deeds he had done. [13]The oceans surrendered the bodies buried in them; and the earth and the underworld gave up the dead in them. Each was judged according to his deeds. [14]And Death and Hell were thrown into the Lake of Fire. This is the Second Death—the Lake of Fire.

Rev 21:4. He will wipe away all tears from their eyes, and there shall be no more death, nor sorrow, nor crying, nor pain. All of that has gone forever.

PREPARATION FOR. Deut 32:29. Oh, that they were wise! Oh, that they could understand! Oh, that they would know what they are getting into!

2 Kgs 20:1 Hezekiah now became deathly sick, and Isaiah the prophet went to visit him. "Set your affairs in order and prepare to die," Isaiah told him. "The Lord says you won't recover."

Ps 39:4. Lord, help me to realize how brief my time on earth will be. Help me to know that I am here for but a moment more. [13]Spare me, Lord! Let me recover and be filled with happiness again before my death.

Ps 90:12. Teach us to number our days and recognize how few they are; help us to spend them as we should.

Eccl 9:4. There is hope only for the living. "It is better to be a live dog than a dead lion!" [10]Whatever you do, do well, for in death, where you are going, there is no working or planning, or knowing, or understanding.

Eccl 11:7. It is a wonderful thing to be alive! [8]If a person lives to be very old, let him rejoice in every day of life, but let him also remember that eternity is far longer, and that everything down here is futile in comparison.

Isa 38:18. For dead men cannot praise you. They cannot be filled with hope and joy. [19]The living, only the living, can praise you as I do today. One generation makes known your faithfulness to the next.

Lk 12:35. Be prepared—all dressed and ready—[36]for your Lord's return from the wedding feast. Then you will be ready to open the door and let him in the moment he arrives and knocks. [37]There will be great joy for those who are ready and waiting for his return.

Jn 9:4. All of us must quickly carry out the tasks assigned us by the one who sent me, for there is little time left before the night falls and all work comes to an end.

Rom 14:8. Living or dying we follow the Lord. Either way we are his.

Phil 1:21. For to me, living means opportunities for Christ, and dying—well, that's better yet!

Heb 13:14. For this world is not our home; we are looking forward to our everlasting home in heaven.

Jas 4:15. What you ought to say is, "If the Lord wants us to, we shall live and do this or that."

1 Pet 1:17. And remember that your heavenly Father to whom you pray has no favorites when he judges. He will judge you with perfect justice for everything you do; so act in reverent fear of him from now on until you get to heaven.

OF THE RIGHTEOUS. Num 23:10. If only I could die as happy as an Israelite! Oh, that my end might be like theirs!

2 Sam 12:23. But why should I fast when he is dead? Can I bring him back again? I shall go to him, but he shall not return to me.

2 Kgs 22:18, 19. "But because you were sorry and concerned and humbled yourself before the Lord when you read the book and its warnings that this land would be cursed and become desolate, and because you have torn your clothing and wept before me in contrition, I will listen to your plea. [20]The death of this nation will not occur until after you die—you will not see the evil which I will bring upon this place." So they took the message to the king.

Ps 23:4. Even when walking through the dark valley of death I will not be afraid, for you are close beside me, guarding, guiding all the way.

Ps 31:5, 6. Into your hand I commit my spirit. You have rescued me, O God who keeps his promises.

Ps 37:37. But the good man—what a different story! For the good man—the blameless, the upright, the man of peace—he has a wonderful future ahead of him. For him there is a happy ending.

Ps 49:15. But as for me, God will redeem my soul from the power of death, for he will receive me.

Ps 73:24. You will keep on guiding me all my life with your wisdom and counsel; and afterwards receive me into the glories of heaven!

Ps 116:15. His loved ones are very precious to him, and he does not lightly let them die.

Prov. 14:32. The godly have a refuge when they die, but the wicked are crushed by their sins.

Eccl 7:1. A good reputation is more valuable than the most expensive perfume. The day one dies is better than the day he is born!

Isa 57:1. The good men perish; the godly die before their time and no one seems to care or wonder why. No one seems to realize that God is taking them away from evil days ahead. [2]For the godly who die shall rest in peace.

Dan. 12:13. But go on now to the end of your life and your rest; for you will rise again and have your full share of those last days.

Lk 2:29–31. "Lord," he said, "now I can die content! For I have seen him as you promised me I would. I have seen the Savior you have given to the world."

Lk 16:22. Finally the beggar died and was carried by the angels to be with Abraham in the place of the righteous dead.

Lk 23:43. And Jesus replied, "Today you will be with me in Paradise. This is a solemn promise."

Jn 11:11. Then he said, "Our friend Lazarus has gone to sleep, but now I will go and waken him!"

Acts 7:59. And as the murderous stones came hurtling at him, Stephen prayed, "Lord Jesus, receive my spirit."

Rom 14:7. We are not our own bosses to live or die as we ourselves might choose. [8]Living or dying we follow the Lord. Either way we are his.

1 Cor 3:21. So don't be proud of following the wise men of this world. For God has already given you everything you need. [22]He has given you Paul and Apollos and Peter as your helpers. He has given you the whole world to use, and life and even death are your servants. He has given you all of the present and all of the future. All are yours, [23]and you belong to Christ, and Christ is God's.

1 Cor 15:51. But I am telling you this strange and wonderful secret: we shall not all die, but we shall all be given new bodies! [52]It will all happen in a moment, in the twinkling of an eye, when the last trumpet is blown. For there will be a trumpet blast from the sky and all the Christians who have died will suddenly become alive, with new bodies that will never, never die; and then we who are still alive shall suddenly have new bodies too. [53]For our earthly bodies, the ones we have now that can die, must be transformed into heavenly bodies that cannot perish but will live forever. [54]When this happens, then at last this Scripture will come true—"Death is swallowed up in victory." [55, 56]O death, where then your victory? Where then your sting? For sin—the sting that causes death—will all be gone; and the law, which reveals our sins, will no longer be our judge. [57]How we thank God for all of this! It is he who makes us victorious through Jesus Christ our Lord!

2 Cor 1:9. We felt we were doomed to die and saw how powerless we were to help ourselves; but that was good, for then we put everything into the hands of God, who alone could save us, for he can raise the dead. [10]And he did help us, and saved us from a terrible death; yes, and we expect him to do it again and again.

2 Cor 5:1. For we know that when this tent we live in now is taken down—when we die and leave these bodies—we will have wonderful new bodies in heaven, homes that will be ours forevermore, made for us by God himself, and not by human hands. [4]These earthly bodies make us groan and sigh, but we wouldn't like to think of dying and having no bodies at all. We want to slip into our new bodies so that these dying bodies will, as it were, be swallowed up by everlasting life. [8]And we are not afraid, but are quite content to die, for then we will be at home with the Lord.

Phil 1:20. For I live in eager expectation and hope that I will never do anything that will cause me to be ashamed of myself but that I will always be ready to speak out boldly for Christ while I am going through all these trials here, just as I have in the past; and that I will always be an honor to Christ, whether I live or whether I must die. [21]For to me, living means opportunities for Christ, and dying—well, that's better yet! [23]Sometimes I want to live and at other times I don't, for I long to go and be with Christ. How much happier for me than being here! [24]But the fact is that I can be of more help to you by staying!

1 Thess 4:13. And now, dear brothers, I want you to know what happens to a Christian when he dies so that when it happens, you will not be full of sorrow, as those are who have no hope. [14]For since we believe that Jesus died and then came back to life again, we can also believe that when Jesus returns, God will bring back with him all the Christians who have died.

1 Thess 5:9. For God has not chosen to pour out his anger upon us, but to save us through our Lord Jesus Christ; [10]he died for us so that we can live with him forever, whether we are dead or alive at the time of his return.

2 Tim 4:6. I say this because I won't be around to help you very much longer. My time has almost run out. Very soon now I will be on my way to heaven. [7]I have fought long and hard for my Lord, and through it all I have kept true to him. And now the time has come for me to stop fighting and rest. [8]In heaven a crown is waiting for me which the Lord, the righteous Judge, will give me on that great day of his return.

Heb 2:14. Since we, God's children, are human beings—made of flesh and blood—he became flesh and blood too by being born in human form; for only as a human being could he die and in dying break the power of the devil who had the power of death. [15]Only in that way could he deliver those who through fear of death have been living all their lives as slaves to constant dread.

Heb 11:13. These men of faith I have mentioned died without ever receiving all that God had promised them; but they saw it all awaiting them on ahead and were glad, for they agreed that this earth was not their real home but that they were just strangers visiting down here.

2 Pet 1:11. And God will open wide the gates of heaven for you to enter into the eternal kingdom of our Lord and Savior Jesus Christ. [13, 14]But the Lord Jesus Christ has showed me that my days here on earth are numbered, and I am soon to die.

Rev 14:13. And I heard a voice in the heavens above me saying, "Write this down: At last the time has come for his martyrs to enter into their full reward. Yes, says the Spirit, they are blest indeed, for now they shall rest from all their toils and trials; for their good deeds follow them to heaven!"

ANTICIPATED.

By Isaac. Gen 27:1. One day, in Isaac's old age when he was half-blind, he called for Esau his oldest son.

Isaac: "My son?"

Esau: "Yes, father?"

[2, 3, 4]*Isaac:* "I am an old man now, and expect to die 'most any day. Take your bow and arrows out into the fields and get me some venison, and prepare it just the way I like it—savory and good—and bring it here for me to eat, and I will give you the blessings that belong to you, my first-born son, before I die."

[22](Jacob goes over to his father. He feels him!)

Isaac: (to himself) "The voice is Jacob's, but the hands are Esau's!"

[23](The ruse convinces Isaac and he gives Jacob his blessings):

[24]*Isaac:* "Are you really Esau?"

Jacob: "Yes, of course."

[25]*Isaac:* "Then bring me the venison, and I will eat it and bless you with all my heart," (Jacob takes it over to him and Isaac eats; he also drinks the wine Jacob brings him.)

[26]*Isaac:* "Come here and kiss me, my son!" (Jacob goes over and kisses him on the cheek. Isaac sniffs his clothes, and finally seems convinced.)

[27, 28, 29]*Isaac:* "The smell of my son is the good smell of the earth and fields that Jehovah has blessed. May God always give you plenty of rain for your crops, and good harvest of grain, and new wine. May many nations be your slaves. Be the master of your brothers. May all your relatives bow low before you. Cursed are all who curse you, and blessed are all who bless you."

[30](As soon as Isaac has blessed Jacob, and almost before Jacob leaves the room, Esau arrives, coming in from his hunting.

[31]He also has prepared his father's favorite dish and brings it to him.)

Esau: "Here I am, father, with the venison. Sit up and eat it so that you can give me your finest blessings!"

[32]*Isaac:* "Who is it?"

Esau: "Why, it's me, of course! Esau, your oldest son!"

[33](Isaac begins to tremble noticeably.)

Isaac: "Then who is it who was just here with venison, and I have already eaten it and blessed him with irrevocable blessing?"

[34](Esau begins to sob with deep and bitter sobs.)

Esau: "O my father, bless me, bless me too!"

[35]*Isaac:* "Your brother was here and tricked me and has carried away your blessing."

[36]*Esau:* (bitterly) "No wonder they call him 'The Cheater.' For he took my birthright, and now he has stolen my blessing. Oh, haven't you saved even one blessing for me?"

[37]*Isaac:* "I have made him your master, and have given him yourself and all of his relatives as his servants. I have guaranteed him abundance of grain and wine—what is there left to give?"

[38]*Esau:* "Not one blessing left for me? O my father, bless me too." (Isaac says nothing as Esau weeps.)

[39, 40]*Isaac:* "Yours will be no life of ease and luxury, but you shall hew your way with your sword. For a time you will serve your brother, but you will finally shake loose from him and be free."

SCENES OF.

Of Jacob. Gen 49:1. Then Jacob called together all his sons and said, "Gather around me and I will tell you what is going to happen to you in the days to come. [2]Listen to me, O sons of Jacob; listen to Israel your father. [3]Reuben, you are my oldest son, the child of my vigorous youth. You are the head of the list in rank and in honor. [4]But you are unruly as the wild waves of the sea, and you shall be first no longer. I am demoting you, for you slept with one of my wives and thus dishonored me. [5]Simeon and Levi are two of a kind. They are men of violence and injustice. [6]O my soul, stay away from them. May I never be a party to their wicked plans. For in their anger they murdered a man, and maimed oxen just for fun. [7]Cursed be their anger, for it is fierce and cruel. Therefore, I will scatter their descendants throughout Israel. [8]Judah, your brothers shall praise you. You shall destroy your enemies. Your father's sons shall bow before you. Judah is a young lion that has finished eating its prey. He has settled down as a lion—who will dare to rouse him? [10]The scepter shall not depart from Judah until Shiloh comes, whom all people shall obey. [11]He has chained his steed to the choicest vine, and washed his clothes in wine. [12]His eyes are darker than wine and his teeth are whiter than milk. [13]Zebulun shall dwell on the shores of the sea and shall be a harbor for ships, with his borders extending to Sidon. [14]Issachar is a strong beast of burden resting among the saddle bags. [15]When he saw how good the countryside was, how pleasant the land, he willingly bent his shoulder to the task and served his masters with vigor. [16]Dan shall govern his people like any other tribe in Israel. [17]He shall be a serpent in the path that bites the horses' heels, so that the rider falls off. [18]I trust in your salvation, Lord. [19]A marauding band shall stamp upon Gad, but he shall rob and pursue them! [20]Asher shall produce rich foods, fit for kings! [21]Naphtali is a deer let loose, producing lovely fawns. [22]Joseph is a fruitful tree beside a fountain. His branches shade the wall. [23]He has been severely injured by those who shot at him and persecuted him, [24]but their weapons were shattered by the Mighty One of Jacob, the Shepherd, the Rock of Israel. [25]May the God of your fathers, the Almighty, bless you with blessings of heaven above and of the earth beneath—blessings of the breasts and of the womb, [26]blessings of the grain and flowers, blessings reaching to the utmost bounds of the everlasting hills. These shall be the blessings upon the head of Joseph who was exiled from his brothers. [27]Benjamin is a wolf that prowls. He devours his enemies in the morning, and in the evening divides the spoil." [28]So these are the blessings that Israel their father blessed his twelve sons with. [29, 30]Then he told them, "Soon I will die. You must bury me with my fathers in the land of Canaan, in the cave in the field of Mach-pelah, facing Mamre —the field Abraham bought from Ephron the Hethite for a burial ground. [31]There they buried Abraham and Sarah his wife; there they buried Isaac and Rebekah his wife; and there I buried Leah. [32]It is the cave which my grandfather Abraham purchased from the sons of Heth." [33]Then, when Jacob had finished his prophecies to his sons, he lay back in the bed, breathed his last, and died. Heb 11:21.

Of Aaron: Num 20:23. Then the Lord said to Moses and Aaron at the border of the land of Edom, [24]"The time has come for Aaron to die—for he shall not enter the land I have given the people of Israel, for the two of you rebelled against my instructions concerning the water at Meribah. [25]Now take Aaron and his son Eleazar and lead them up onto Mount Hor. [26]There you shall remove Aaron's priestly garments from him and put them on Eleazar his son; and Aaron shall die there." [27]So Moses did as the Lord commanded him. The three of them went up together into Mount Hor as all the people watched. [28]When they reached the summit, Moses removed the priestly garments from Aaron and put them on his son Eleazar; and Aaron died on the top of the mountain.

Of Moses. Deut 31:14. Then the Lord said to Moses, "The time has come when you must die. Summon Joshua and come into the Tabernacle where I can give him his instructions." So Moses and Joshua came and stood before the Lord. [15]He appeared to them in a great cloud at the Tabernacle entrance, [16]and said to Moses, "You shall die and join your ancestors. After you are gone, these people will begin worshiping foreign gods in the Promised Land. They will forget about me and break the contract I have made with them. [19]Now write down the words of this song, and teach it to the people of Israel as my warning to them. [21]And great disasters come upon them, then this song will remind them of the reason for their woes. (For this song will live from generation to generation.) I know now, even before they enter the land, what these people are like." [22]So, on that very day, Moses wrote down the words of the song and taught it to the Israelites. [23]Then he charged Joshua (son of Nun) to be strong and courageous, and said to him, "You must bring the people of Israel into the land the Lord promised them; for the Lord says, 'I will be with you'." [24]When Moses had finished writing down all the laws that are recorded in this book, [25]he instructed the Levites who carried the Ark containing the Ten Commandments [26]to put this book of the law beside the Ark, as a solemn warning to the people of Israel. [27]"For I know how rebellious and stubborn you are," Moses told them. "If even today, while I am still here with you, you are defiant rebels against the Lord, how much more rebellious will you be after my death! [28]Now summon all the elders and officers of your tribes so that I can speak to them, and call heaven and earth to witness against them. [29]I know that after my death you will utterly defile yourselves and turn away from God and his commands; and in the days to come evil will crush you for you will do what the Lord says is evil, making him very angry." [30]So Moses recited this entire song to the whole assembly of Israel:

Deut 32:1. "Listen, O heavens and earth! Listen to what I say! [2]My words shall fall upon you like the gentle rain and dew, like rain upon the tender grass, like showers on the hillside. [3]I will proclaim the greatness of the Lord. How glorious he is! [4]He is the Rock. His work is perfect. Everything he does is just and fair. He is faithful, without sin. 5But Israel has become corrupt, smeared with sin. They are no longer his; they are a stubborn, twisted generation. 6Is this the way you treat Jehovah? O foolish people, is not God your Father? Has he not created you? Has he not established you and made you strong? 7Remember the days of long ago! (Ask your father and the aged men; they will tell you all about it.) 8When God divided up the world among the nations, he gave each of them a supervising angel! 9But he appointed none for Israel; for Israel was God's own personal possession! 10God protected them in the howling wilderness as though they were the apple of his eye. 11He spreads his wings over them, even as an eagle overspreads her young. She carries them upon her wings—as does the Lord his people! 12When the Lord alone was leading them, and they lived without foreign gods, 13God gave them fertile hilltops, rolling, fertile fields, honey from the rock, and olive oil from stony ground! 14He gave them milk and meat—choice Bashan rams, and goats—and the finest of the wheat; they drank the sparkling wine. 15But Israel was soon overfed; yes, fat and bloated; then, in plenty, they forsook their God. They shrugged away the Rock of their salvation. 16Israel began to follow foreign gods, and Jehovah was very angry; he was jealous of his people. 17They sacrificed to heathen gods, to new gods never before worshiped. 18They spurned the Rock who had made them, forgetting it was God who had given them birth. 19God saw what they were doing, and detested them! His sons and daughters were insulting him. 20He said, 'I will abandon them; see what happens to them then! For they are a stubborn, faithless generation. 21They have made me very jealous of their idols, which are not gods at all. Now I, in turn, will make them jealous by giving my affections to the foolish Gentile nations of the world. 22For my anger has kindled a fire that burns to the depths of the underworld, consuming the earth and all of its crops, and setting its mountains on fire. 23I will heap evils upon them and shoot them down with my arrows. 24I will waste them with hunger, burning fever, and fatal disease. I will devour them! I will set wild beasts upon them, to rip them apart with their teeth; and deadly serpents crawling in the dust. 25Outside, the enemies' sword—inside, the plague—shall terrorize young men and girls alike; the baby nursing at the breast, and aged men. 26I had decided to scatter them to distant lands, so that even the memory of them would disappear. 27But then I thought, 'My enemies will boast, "Israel is destroyed by our own might; it was not the Lord who did it!" ' 28Israel is a stupid nation; foolish, without understanding. 29Oh, that they were wise! Oh, that they could understand! Oh, that they would know what they are getting into! 30How could one single enemy chase a thousand of them, and two put ten thousand to flight, unless their Rock had abandoned them, unless the Lord had destroyed them? 31But the rock of other nations is not like our Rock; prayers to their gods are valueless. 32They act like men of Sodom and Gomorrah: their deeds are bitter with poison; 33they drink the wine of serpent venom. 34But Israel is my special people, sealed as jewels within my treasury. 35Vengeance is mine, and I decree the punishment of all her enemies: their doom is sealed. 36The Lord will see his people righted, and will have compassion on them when they slip. He will watch their power ebb away, both slave and free. 37Then God will ask, 'Where are their gods—the rocks they claimed to be their refuge? 38Where are these gods now, to whom they sacrificed their fat and wine? Let those gods arise, and help them! 39Don't you see that I alone am God? I kill and make live, I wound and heal—no one delivers from my power. 40, 41I raise my hand to heaven and vow by my existence, that I will whet the lightning of my sword! And hurl my punishments upon my enemies! 42My arrows shall be drunk with blood! My sword devours the flesh and blood of all the slain and captives. The heads of the enemy are gory with blood.' 43Praise his people, O Gentile nations, for he will avenge his people, taking vengeance on his enemies, purifying his land and his people." 44, 45When Moses and Joshua had recited all the words of this song to the people, 46Moses made these comments: "Meditate upon all the laws I have given you today, and pass them on to your children. 47These laws are not mere words—they are your life! Through obeying them you will live long, plentiful lives in the land you are going to possess across the Jordan River." 48That same day, the Lord said to Moses, 49"Go to Mount Nebo in the Abarim mountains, in the land of Moab across from Jericho. Climb to its heights, and look out across the land of Canaan, the land I am giving to the people of Israel. 50After you see the land you must die and join your ancestors, just as Aaron your brother died in Mount Hor and joined them. 51For you dishonored me among the people of Israel at the springs of Meribath-kadesh, in the wilderness of Zin. 52You will see spread out before you the land I am giving the people of Israel, but you will not enter it."

Deut 33:1. This is the blessing that Moses, the man of God, gave to the people of Israel before his death: 2"The Lord came to us at Mount Sinai, and dawned upon us from Mount Seir; he shone from Mount Paran, surrounded by ten thousands of holy angels; and with flaming fire at his right hand. 3How he loves his people—His holy ones are in his hands. They followed in your steps, O Lord. They have received their directions from you. 4The laws I have given are your precious possession. 5The Lord became king in Jerusalem, elected by a convocation of the leaders of the tribes! 6Let Reuben live forever and may his tribe increase!" 7And Moses said of Judah: "O Lord, hear the cry of Judah and unite him with Israel; fight for him against his enemies." 8Then Moses said concerning the tribe of Levi: "Give to godly Levi your Urim and your Thummim. You tested Levi at Massah and at Meribah; 9He obeyed your instructions [and destroyed many sinners], even his own children, brothers, fathers, and mothers. 10The Levites shall teach God's laws to Israel and shall work before you at the incense altar and the altar of burnt offering. 11O Lord, prosper the Levites and accept the work they do for you. Crush those who are their enemies; don't let them rise again." 12Concerning the tribe of Benjamin, Moses said: "He is beloved of God and lives in safety beside him. God surrounds him with his loving care, and preserves him from every harm." 13Concerning the tribe of Joseph, he said: "May his land be blessed by God with the choicest gifts of heaven and of the earth that lies below. 14May he be blessed with the best of what the sun makes grow; growing richly month by month, 15with the finest of mountain crops and of the everlasting hills. 16May he be blessed with the best gifts of the earth and its fullness, and with the favor of God who appeared in the burning bush. Let all these blessings come upon Joseph, the prince among his brothers. 17He is a young bull in strength and splendor, with the strong horns of a wild ox to push against the nations everywhere; this is my blessing on the multitudes of Ephraim and the thousands of Manasseh." 18Of the tribe of Zebulun, Moses said: "Rejoice, O Zebulun, you outdoors-men, and Issachar, you lovers of your tents; 19they shall summon the people to celebrate their sacrifices with them. Lo, they taste the riches of the sea and the treasures of the sand." 20Concerning the tribe of Gad, Moses said: "A blessing upon those who help Gad. He crouches like a lion, with savage arm and face and head. 21He chose the best of the land for himself because it is reserved for a leader. He led the people because he carried out God's penalties for Israel." 22Of the tribe of Dan, Moses said: "Dan is like a lion's cub leaping out from Bashan." 23Of the tribe of Naphtali, Moses said: "O Naphtali, you are satisfied with all the blessings of the Lord; the Mediterranean coast and the Negeb are your home." 24Of the tribe of Asher: "Asher is a favorite son, esteemed above his brothers; he bathes his feet in soothing olive oil. 25May you be protected with strong bolts of iron and bronze, and may your strength match the length of your days! 26There is none like the God of Jerusalem—he descends from the heavens in majestic splendor to help you. 27The eternal God is your Refuge, and underneath are the everlasting arms. He thrusts out your enemies before you; it is he who cries, 'Destroy them!' 28So Israel dwells safely, prospering in a land of corn and wine, while the gentle rains descend from heaven. 29What blessings are yours, O Israel! Who else has been saved by the Lord? He is your shield and your helper! He is your excellent sword! Your enemies shall bow low before you, and you shall trample on their backs!"

Deut 34:1. Then Moses climbed from the plains of Moab to Pisgah Peak in Mount Nebo, across from Jericho. And the Lord pointed out to him the Promised Land, as they gazed out across Gilead as far as Dan: 2"There is Naphtali; and there is Ephraim and Manasseh; and across there, Judah, extending to the Mediterranean Sea; 3there is Negeb; and the Jordan Valley; and Jericho, the city of palm trees; and Zoar," The Lord told him. 4"It is the Promised Land," the Lord told Moses. "I promised Abraham, Isaac, and Jacob that I would give it to their descendants. Now you have seen it, but you will not enter it." 5So Moses, the disciple of the Lord, died in the land of Moab as the Lord had said. 6The Lord buried him in a valley near Beth-Peor in Moab, but no one knows the exact place.

Of Joshua. Josh 24:1–29.

Of Samson. Judg 16:25–30.

Of Eli. 1 Sam 4:12–18.

Wife of Phinehas. 1 Sam 4:19–21.

Of David. 1 Kgs 2:1. As the time of King David's death approached, he gave this charge to his son Solomon: 2"I am going where every man on earth must some day go. I am counting on you to be a strong and worthy successor. 3Obey the laws of God and follow all his ways; keep each of his commands written in the law of Moses so that you will prosper in everything you do, wherever you turn. 4If you do this, then the Lord will fulfill the promise he gave me, that if my children and their descendants watch their step and are faithful to God, one of them shall always be the king of Israel—my dynasty will never end. 5Now listen to my instructions. You know that Joab murdered my two generals, Abner and Amasa. He pretended that it was an act of war, but it was done in a time of peace. 6You are a wise man and will know what to do—don't let him die in peace. 7But be kind to the sons of Barzillai the Gileadite. Make them permanent guests of the king, for they took care of me when I fled from your brother Absalom. 8And do you remember Shime-i, the son of Gera the Benjaminite from Bahurim? He cursed me with a terrible curse as I was going to Mahanaim; but when he came down to meet me at the Jordan River I promised I wouldn't kill him. 9But that promise doesn't bind you! You are a wise man, and you will know how to arrange a bloody death for him." 10Then David died and was buried in Jerusalem.

Of Zechariah. 2 Chron 24:22. That was how King Joash repaid Jehoiada for his love and loyalty—by killing his son. Zechariah's last words as he died were, "Lord, see what they are doing and pay them back."

Of Jesus. Mt 27:34. The soldiers gave him drugged wine to drink; but when he had tasted it, he refused. 35After the crucifixion, the soldiers threw dice to divide up his clothes among themselves. 36Then they sat around and watched him as he hung there. 37And they put a sign above his head, "This is Jesus, the King of the Jews." 38Two robbers were also crucified there that morning, one on either side of him. 39And the people passing by hurled abuse, shaking their heads at him and saying, 40"So! You can destroy the Temple and build it again in three days, can you? Well, then come on down from the cross if you are the Son of God!"

[41, 42, 43]And the chief priests and Jewish leaders also mocked him. "He saved others," they scoffed, "but he can't save himself! So you are the King of Israel, are you? Come down from the cross and we'll believe you! He trusted God—let God show his approval by delivering him! Didn't he say, 'I am God's Son'?" [44]And the robbers also threw the same in his teeth. [45]That afternoon, the whole earth was covered with darkness for three hours, from noon until three o'clock. [46]About three o'clock, Jesus shouted, "Eli, Eli, lama sabachthani," which means, "My God, my God, why have you forsaken me?" [47]Some of the bystanders misunderstood and thought he was calling for Elijah. [48]One of them ran and filled a sponge with sour wine and put it on a stick and held it up to him to drink. [49]But the rest said, "Leave him alone. Let's see whether Elijah will come and save him." [50]Then Jesus shouted out again, dismissed his spirit, and died. [51]And look! The curtain secluding the Holiest Place in the Temple was split apart from top to bottom; and the earth shook, and rocks broke, [52]and tombs opened, and many godly men and women who had died came back to life again. [53]After Jesus' resurrection, they left the cemetery and went into Jerusalem, and appeared to many people there. Mk 15:23–38; Lk 23:27–49; Jn 19:16–30.

Of Stephen. Acts 7:59. And as the murderous stones came hurtling at him, Stephen prayed, "Lord Jesus, receive my spirit." [60]And he fell to his knees, shouting, "Lord, don't charge them with this sin!" and with that, he died.

Of Paul. 2 Tim 4:6. I say this because I won't be around to help you very much longer. My time has almost run out. Very soon now I will be on my way to heaven. [7]I have fought long and hard for my Lord, and through it all I have kept true to him. And now the time has come for me to stop fighting and rest. [8]In heaven a crown is waiting for me which the Lord, the righteous Judge, will give me on that great day of his return. And not just to me, but to all those whose lives show that they are eagerly looking forward to his coming back again.

OF THE WICKED. Num 16:30. But if the Lord does a miracle and the ground opens up and swallows them and everything that belongs to them, and they go down alive into Sheol, then you will know that these men have despised the Lord.

1 Sam 25:37, 38. By that time he [Nabal] was sober, and when his wife told him what had happened, he had a stroke and lay paralyzed for about ten days, then died, for the Lord killed him.

2 Chron 21:6. But he [Jehoram] was as wicked as the kings who were over in Israel. [20]He was thirty-two years old when he began to reign and he reigned in Jerusalem eight years, and died unmourned. He was buried in Jerusalem, but not in the royal cemetery.

Job 4:21. Their candle of life is snuffed out. They die and no one cares.

Job 18:14. The wealth he trusted in shall reject him, and he shall be brought down to the King of Terrors. [18]He will be driven out from the kingdom of light into darkness, and chased out of the world.

Job 20:4. Don't you realize that ever since man was first placed upon the earth, [5]the triumph of the wicked has been short-lived, and the joy of the godless but for a moment? [8]He will fade like a dream. [11]Though still a young man, his bones shall lie in the dust.

Job 21:12, 13. They spend their time singing and dancing. They are wealthy and need deny themselves nothing; they are prosperous to the end. [17]Yet the wicked get away with it every time. They never have trouble, and God skips them when he distributes his sorrows and anger. [18]Are they driven before the wind like straw? Are they carried away by the storm? Not at all! [23, 24]He destroys those who are healthy, wealthy, fat, and prosperous, [25]God also destroys those in deep and grinding poverty who have never known anything good. [26]Both alike are buried in the same dust, both eaten by the same worms.

Job 24:20. Even the sinner's own mother shall forget him. Worms shall feed sweetly on him. No one will remember him any more. For wicked men are broken like a tree in the storm. [24]But though they are very great now, yet in a moment they shall be gone like all others, cut off like heads of grain.

Job 27:8. But what hope has the godless when God cuts him off and takes away his life? [19]He goes to bed rich, but wakes up to find that all his wealth is gone. [20]Terror overwhelms him, and he is blown away in the storms of the night. [21]The east wind carries him away, and he is gone. It sweeps him into eternity. [22]For God shall hurl at him unsparingly. He longs to flee from God. [23]Everyone will cheer at his death, and boo him into eternity.

Job 34:20. In a moment they die, and at midnight great and small shall suddenly pass away, removed by no human hand.

Job. 36:12. If they won't listen to him, they shall perish in battle and die because of their lack of good sense. [14]They die young after lives of dissipation and depravity. [18]Watch out! Don't let your anger at others lead you into scoffing at God! Don't let your suffering embitter you at the only one who can deliver you. [20]Do not desire the nighttime, with its opportunities for crime.

Ps 37:1. Never envy the wicked! [2]Soon they fade away like grass and disappear. [9]For the wicked shall be destroyed, but those who trust the Lord shall be given every blessing. [10]Only a little while and the wicked shall disappear. You will look for them in vain. [35, 36]I myself have seen it happen: a proud and evil man, towering like a cedar of Lebanon, but when I looked again, he was gone! I searched but could not find him!

Ps 49:7. Yet not one of them, though rich as kings, can ransom his own brother from the penalty of sin! For God's forgiveness does not come that way. [8, 9]For a soul is far too precious to be ransomed by mere earthly wealth. There is not enough of it in all the earth to buy eternal life for just one soul, to keep it out of hell. [10]Rich man! Proud man! Wise man! You must die like all the rest! You have no greater lease on life than foolish, stupid men. You must leave your wealth to others. 14Death is the shepherd of all mankind. And "in the morning" those who are evil will be the slaves of those who are good. For the power of their wealth is gone when they die; they cannot take it with them. 17For when they die they carry nothing with them! Their honors will not follow them. 19Yet in the end he dies like everyone else, and enters eternal darkness. 20For man with all his pomp must die like any animal.

Ps 55:15. Let death seize them and cut them down in their prime, for there is sin in their homes, and they are polluted to the depths of their souls. 23He will send my enemies to the pit of destruction. Murderers and liars will not live out half their days.

Ps 58:9. God will sweep away both old and young. He will destroy them more quickly than a cooking pot can feel the blazing fire of thorns beneath it.

Ps 73:3. For I was envious of the prosperity of the proud and wicked. 4Yes, all through life their road is smooth! They grow sleek and fat. 17Then one day I went into God's sanctuary to meditate, and thought about the future of these evil men. 18What a slippery path they are on—suddenly God will send them sliding over the edge of the cliff and down to their destruction: 19an instant end to all their happiness, an eternity of terror. 20Their present life is only a dream! They will awaken to the truth as one awakens from a dream of things that never really were!

Ps 78:50. He gave free course to his anger and did not spare the Egyptians' lives, but handed them over to plagues and sickness.

Ps 92:7. That although the wicked flourish like weeds, there is only eternal destruction ahead of them.

Prov 2:22. Evil men lose the good things they might have had, and they themselves shall be destroyed.

Prov 5:22. The wicked man is doomed by his own sins; they are ropes that catch and hold him. 23He shall die because he will not listen to the truth; he has let himself be led away into incredible folly.

Prov 10:25. Disaster strikes like a cyclone and the wicked are whirled away. But the good man has a strong anchor. 27Reverence for God adds hours to each day; so how can the wicked expect a long, good life?

Prov 11:7. When an evil man dies, his hopes all perish, for they are based upon this earthly life. 10The whole city celebrates a good man's success—and also the godless man's death.

Prov 13:9. The good man's life is full of light. The sinner's road is dark and gloomy.

Prov 14:32. The godly have a refuge when they die, but the wicked are crushed by their sins.

Prov 21:16. The man who strays away from common sense will end up dead!

Prov 24:20. For the evil man has no future; his light will be snuffed out.

Prov 29:1. The man who is often reproved but refuses to accept criticism will suddenly be broken and never have another chance. 16When rulers are wicked, their people are too; but good men will live to see the tyrant's downfall.

Eccl 8:10. I have seen wicked men buried and as their friends returned from the cemetery, having forgotten all the dead man's evil deeds, these men were praised in the very city where they had committed their many crimes! How odd!

Isa 14:11. Your might and power are gone; they are buried with you. All the pleasant music in your palace has ceased; now maggots are your sheet, worms your blanket! 15But instead, you will be brought down to the pit of hell, down to its lowest depths.

Isa 17:14. In the evening Israel waits in terror, but by dawn her enemies are dead. This is the just reward of those who plunder and destroy the people of God.

Isa 26:14. Those we served before are dead and gone; never again will they return. You came against them and destroyed them, and they are long forgotten.

Jer 16:3. For the children born in this city, and their mothers and fathers 4shall die from terrible diseases. No one shall mourn for them or bury them, but their bodies shall lie on the ground to rot and fertilize the soil. They shall die from war and famine, and their bodies shall be picked apart by vultures and wild animals.

Ezk 28:8. They will bring you to the pit of hell and you shall die as those pierced with many wounds, there on your island in the heart of the seas. 10You will die like an outcast at the hands of foreigners. For I have spoken it, the Lord God says.

Amos 9:10. But all these sinners who say, "God will not touch us," will die by the sword.

Lk 12:20. But God said to him, "Fool! Tonight you die. Then who will get it all?"

Lk 16:22. Finally the beggar died and was carried by the angels to be with Abraham in the place of the righteous dead. The rich man also died and was buried, 23and his soul went into hell. There, in torment, he saw Lazarus in the far distance with Abraham. 24"Father Abraham," he shouted, "have some pity! Send Lazarus over here if only to dip the tip of his finger in water and cool my tongue, for I am in anguish in these flames." 25But Abraham said to him, "Son, remember that during your lifetime you had everything you wanted, and Lazarus had nothing. So now he is here being comforted and you are in anguish. 26And besides, there is a great chasm separating us, and anyone wanting to come to you from here is stopped at its edge; and no one over there can cross to us." 27Then the rich man said, "O Father Abraham, then please send him to my father's home—28for I have five brothers—to warn them about this place of torment lest they come here when they die."

Acts 5:3. But Peter said, "Ananias, Satan has filled your heart. When you claimed this was the full price, you were lying to the Holy Spirit. [4]The property was yours to sell or not, as you wished. And after selling it, it was yours to decide how much to give. How could you do a thing like this? You weren't lying to us, but to God." [5]As soon as Ananias heard these words, he fell to the floor, dead! Everyone was terrified, [6]and the younger men covered him with a sheet and took him out and buried him. [7]About three hours later his wife came in, not knowing what had happened. [8]Peter asked her, "Did you people sell your land for such and such a price?" "Yes," she replied, "we did." [9]And Peter said, "How could you and your husband even think of doing a thing like this—conspiring together to test the Spirit of God's ability to know what is going on? Just outside that door are the young men who buried your husband, and they will carry you out too." [10]Instantly she fell to the floor, dead, and the young men came in and, seeing that she was dead, carried her out and buried her beside her husband.

1 Thess 5:3. When people are saying, "All is well, everything is quiet and peaceful"—then, all of a sudden, disaster will fall upon them as suddenly as a woman's birth pains begin when her child is born. And these people will not be able to get away anywhere—there will be no place to hide.

SPIRITUAL. Lk 1:79. To give light to those who sit in darkness and death's shadow, and to guide us to the path of peace.

Jn 5:24. I say emphatically that anyone who listens to my message and believes in God who sent me has eternal life, and will never be damned for his sins, but has already passed out of death into life. [1 Jn 3:14] [25]And I solemnly declare that the time is coming, in fact, it is here, when the dead shall hear my voice—the voice of the Son of God—and those who listen shall live. [26]The Father has life in himself, and has granted his Son to have life in himself.

Jn 6:48–51. "Yes, I am the Bread of Life! When your fathers in the wilderness ate bread from the skies, they all died. But the Bread from heaven gives eternal life to everyone who eats it. I am that Living Bread that came down out of heaven. Anyone eating this Bread shall live forever; this Bread is my flesh to redeem humanity." [52]Then the Jews began arguing with each other about what he meant. "How can this man give us his flesh to eat?" they asked. [53]So Jesus said it again, "With all the earnestness I possess I tell you this: Unless you eat the flesh of the Messiah and drink his blood, you cannot have eternal life within you."

Jn 11:26. He is given eternal life for believing in me and shall never perish. Do you believe this, Martha?

Rom 5:12. When Adam sinned, sin entered the entire human race. His sin spread death throughout all the world, so everything began to grow old and die, for all sinned. [15]And what a difference between man's sin and God's forgiveness! For this one man, Adam, brought death to many through his *sin.* But this one man, Jesus Christ, brought forgiveness to many through God's *mercy.*

Rom 7:11. Sin fooled me by taking the good laws of God and using them to make me guilty of death.

Rom 8:5. Those who let themselves be controlled by their lower natures live only to please themselves, but those who follow after the Holy Spirit find themselves doing those things that please God. [6]Following after the Holy Spirit leads to life and peace, but following after the old nature leads to death, [12]So, dear brothers, you have no obligations whatever to your old sinful nature to do what it begs you to do. [13]For if you keep on following it you are lost and will perish, but if through the power of the Holy Spirit you crush it and its evil deeds, you shall live.

2 Cor 5:13, 14. Are we insane (to say such things about ourselves)? If so, it is to bring glory to God. And if we are in our right minds, it is for your benefit. Whatever we do, it is certainly not for our own profit, but because Christ's love controls us now. Since we believe that Christ died for all of us, we should also believe that we have died to the old life we used to live.

Eph 2:1. Once you were under God's curse, doomed forever for your sins. [5]That even though we were spiritually dead and doomed by our sins, he gave us back our lives again when he raised Christ from the dead—only by his undeserved favor have we ever been saved—[6]and lifted us up from the grave into glory along with Christ, where we sit with him in the heavenly realms—all because of what Christ Jesus did.

Eph 4:17, 18. Let me say this, then, speaking for the Lord: Live no longer as the unsaved do, for they are blinded and confused. Their closed hearts are full of darkness; they are far away from the life of God because they have shut their minds against him, and they cannot understand his ways.

Eph 5:14. That is why God says in the Scriptures, "Awake, O sleeper, and rise up from the dead; and Christ shall give you light."

Col 2:13. You were dead in sins, and your sinful desires were not yet cut away. Then he gave you a share in the very life of Christ, for he forgave all your sins.

1 Tim 5:6. But not if they are spending their time running around gossiping, seeking only pleasure and thus ruining their souls.

1 Pet 2:24. He personally carried the load of our sins in his own body when he died on the cross, so that we can be finished with sin and live a good life from now on. For his wounds have healed ours!

1 Jn 5:12. So whoever has God's Son has life; whoever does not have his Son, does not have life.

See *Depravity; Reprobate.*

SECOND. Prov 14:12. Before every man there lies a wide and pleasant road that seems right but ends in death.

Ezk 18:4. For all souls are mine to judge—fathers and sons alike—and my rule is this: It is for a man's own sins that he will die. [10]But if that man has a son who is a robber or murderer and who fulfills none of his responsibilities, [13]and loans out his money at interest—shall that man live? No! He shall surely die, and it is his own fault. [21]But if a wicked person turns away from all his sins and begins to obey my laws and do what is just and right, he shall surely live and not die. [23]Do you think I like to see the wicked die? asks the Lord. Of course not! I only want him to turn from his wicked ways and live. [24]However, if a righteous person turns to sinning and acts like any other sinner, should he be allowed to live? No, of course not. All his previous goodness will be forgotten and he shall die for his sins.

Ezk 33:8. When I say to the wicked, "O wicked man, you will die!" and you don't tell him what I say, so that he does not repent—that wicked person will die in his sins, but I will hold you responsible for his death. [9]But if you warn him to repent and he doesn't, he will die in his sin, and you will not be responsible. [11]Tell them: As I live, says the Lord God, I have no pleasure in the death of the wicked; *I desire that the wicked turn from his evil ways and live.* Turn, turn from your wickedness, for why will you die, O Israel? [14]And when I tell the wicked he will die and then he turns from his sins and does what is fair and right—[15]if he gives back the borrower's pledge and returns what he has stolen and walks along the paths of right, not doing evil—he shall surely live. He shall not die. [16]None of his past sins shall be brought up against him, for he has turned to the good and shall surely live.

Mt 7:13. Heaven can be entered only through the narrow gate! The highway to hell is broad, and its gate is wide enough for all the multitudes who choose its easy way.

Mt 10:28. Don't be afraid of those who can kill only your bodies—but can't touch your souls! Fear only God who can destroy both soul and body in hell.

Mt 25:30. And throw the useless servant out into outer darkness: there shall be weeping and gnashing of teeth. [41]Then I will turn to those on my left and say, "Away with you, you cursed ones, into the eternal fire prepared for the devil and his demons." [46]And they shall go away into eternal punishment; but the righteous into everlasting life." Jn 5:28, 29.

Mk 9:43, 44. If your hand does wrong, cut it off. Better live forever with one hand than be thrown into the unquenchable fires of hell with two!

Rom 1:32. They were fully aware of God's death penalty for these crimes, yet they went right ahead and did them anyway, and encouraged others to do them, too.

Rom 6:16. Don't you realize that you can choose your own master? You can choose sin (with death) or else obedience (with acquittal). The one to whom you offer yourself—he will take you and be your master and you will be his slave. [21]And what was the result? Evidently not good, since you are ashamed now even to think about those things you used to do, for all of them end in eternal doom. [23]For the wages of sin is death, but the free gift of God is eternal life through Jesus Christ our Lord.

Rom 8:13. For if you keep on following it [old nature] you are lost and will perish, but if through the power of the Holy Spirit you crush it and its evil deeds, you shall live.

Rom 9:22. Does not God have a perfect right to show his fury and power against those who are fit only for destruction, those he has been patient with for all this time?

2 Thess 1:9. They will be punished in everlasting hell, forever separated from the Lord, never to see the glory of his power,

Jas 1:15. These evil thoughts lead to evil actions and afterwards to the death penalty from God.

Jas 4:12. Only he who made the law can rightly judge among us. He alone decides to save us or destroy.

2 Pet 2:12. But false teachers are fools—no better than animals. They do whatever they feel like; born only to be caught and killed, they laugh at the terrifying powers of the underworld which they know so little about; and they will be destroyed along with all the demons and powers of hell. *v.* 17.

Rev 2:11. Let everyone who can hear, listen to what the Spirit is saying to the churches: He who is victorious shall not be hurt by the Second Death.

Rev 19:20. And the Evil Creature was captured, and with him the False Prophet, who could do mighty miracles when the Evil Creature was present—miracles that deceived all who had accepted the Evil Creature's mark, and who worshiped his statue. Both of them—the Evil Creature and his False Prophet—were thrown alive into the Lake of Fire that burns with sulphur.

Rev 20:14. And Death and Hell were thrown into the Lake of Fire. This is the Second Death—the Lake of Fire.

Rev 21:8. But cowards who turn back from following me, and those who are unfaithful to me, and the corrupt, and murderers, and the immoral, and those conversing with demons, and idol worshipers and all liars—their doom is in the Lake that burns with fire and sulphur. This is the Second Death.

See *Hell; Wicked, Punishment of.*

FIGURATIVE OF REGENERATION. Rom 6:2, 3. Should we keep on sinning when we don't have to? For sin's power over us was broken when we became Christians and were baptized to become a part of Jesus Christ; through his death the power of your sinful nature was shattered. [4]Your old sin-loving nature was buried with him by baptism when he died, and when God the Father, with glorious power, brought him back to life again, you were given his wonderful new life to enjoy. [5]For you have become a part of him, and so you died with him, so to speak, when he died, and now you share his new life, and shall rise as he did. [6]Your old evil desires were nailed to the cross with him; that part of you that loves to sin was crushed and fatally wounded, so that your sin-loving body is no longer under sin's control, no longer needs to be a slave to sin; [7]for when you are deadened to sin you are freed from all its allure and its power over you. [8]And since your old sin-loving nature "died" with

Christ, we know that you will share his new life. [9]Christ rose from the dead and will never die again. Death no longer has any power over him. [10]He died once for all to end sin's power, but now he lives forever in unbroken fellowship with God. [11]So look upon your old sin nature as dead and unresponsive to sin, and instead be alive to God, alert to him, through Jesus Christ our Lord.

Rom 7:1. Don't you understand yet, dear Jewish brothers in Christ, that when a person dies the law no longer holds him in its power? [2]Let me illustrate: when a woman marries, the law binds her to her husband as long as he is alive. But if he dies, she is no longer bound to him; the laws of marriage no longer apply to her. [3]Then she can marry someone else if she wants to. That would be wrong while he was alive, but it is perfectly all right after he dies. [4]Your "husband," your master, used to be the Jewish law; but you "died," as it were, with Christ on the cross; and since you are "dead," you are no longer "married to the law," and it has no more control over you. Then you came back to life again when Christ did, and are a new person. And now you are "married," so to speak, to the one who rose from the dead, so that you can produce good fruit, that is, good deeds for God. [5]When your old nature was still active, sinful desires were at work within you, making you want to do whatever God said not to, and producing sinful deeds, the rotting fruit of death. [6]But now you need no longer worry about the Jewish laws and customs because you "died" while in their captivity, and now you can really serve God; not in the old way, mechanically obeying a set of rules, but in the new way, (with all of your hearts and minds). [7]Well then, am I suggesting that these laws of God are evil? Of course not! No, the law is not sinful but it was the law that showed me my sin. I would never have known the sin in my heart—the evil desires that are hidden there—if the law had not said, "You must not have evil desires in your heart," [8]But sin used this law against evil desires by reminding me that such desires are wrong and arousing all kinds of forbidden desires within me! Only if there were no laws to break would there be no sinning. [9]That is why I felt fine so long as I did not understand what the law really demanded. But when I learned the truth, I realized that I had broken the law and was a sinner, doomed to die. [10]So as far as I was concerned, the good law which was supposed to show me the way of life resulted instead in my being given the death penalty. Sin fooled me by taking the good laws of God and using them to make me guilty of death.

Rom 8:10. Yet, even though Christ lives within you, your body will die because of sin; but your spirit will live, for Christ has pardoned it. [11]And if the Spirit of God, who raised up Jesus from the dead, lives in you, he will make your dying bodies live again after you die, by means of this same Holy Spirit living within you.

Col 2:20. Since you died, as it were, with Christ and this has set you free from following the world's ideas of how to be saved—by doing good and obeying various rules—why do you keep right on following them anyway, still bound by such rules as [21]not eating, tasting, or even touching certain foods?

See *Dead; Regeneration.*

DEBIR 1. King of Eglon, Josh 10:3–27.

2. A town in the mountains of Judah. Called also *Kiriath-Sannah,* Josh 15:48–62, and *Kiriath-sepher,* which signifies a city of books, Josh 15:15, 16; Judg 1:11. Anakim expelled from, by Joshua, Josh 11:21. Captured by Joshua, Josh 11:38, 39; 12:8–24. Taken by Othni-el, Josh 15:15–17; Judg 1:12, 13. Allotted to the Aaronites, Josh 21:9–16; 1 Chron 6:58, 59.

3. A place near the valley of Achor, Josh 15:7.

DEBORAH 1. Nurse to Rebecca, Gen 24:59. Buried beneath an oak near Bethel, Gen 35:8.

2. The prophetess, a judge of Israel, Judg 4:4, 5; 5:7. Inspires Barak to defeat Sisera, Judg 4:6–16. Triumphant song of, Judg 5.

DEBT Rom 13:8. Pay all your debts except the debt of love for others—never finish paying that! For if you love them, you will be obeying all of God's laws, fulfilling all his requirements.

SECURITY FOR. Ex 22:25. If you lend money to a needy fellow-Hebrew, you are not to handle the transaction in an ordinary way, with interest. [26]If you take his clothing as a pledge of his repayment, you must let him have it back at night. [27]For it is probably his only warmth; how can he sleep without it? If you don't return it, and he cries to me for help, I will hear and be very gracious to him (at your expense), for I am very compassionate.

Deut 24:6. It is illegal to take a millstone as a pledge, for it is a tool by which its owner gains his livelihood.

10. If you lend anything to another man, you must not enter his house to get his security. [11]Stand outside! The owner will bring it out to you. [12, 13]If the man is poor and gives you his cloak as security, you are not to sleep in it. Take it back to him at sundown so that he can use it through the night and bless you; and the Lord your God will count it as righteousness for you.

Neh 5:2, 3, 4. What was happening was that families who ran out of money for food had to sell their children or mortgage their fields, vineyards, and homes to these rich men; and some couldn't even do that, for they already had borrowed to the limit to pay their taxes.

Job 22:6. For instance, you must have refused to loan money to needy friends unless they gave you all their clothing as a pledge—yes, you must have stripped them to the bone.

Job 24:9. The wicked snatch fatherless children from their mother's breasts, and take a poor man's baby as a pledge before they will loan him any money or grain.

Prov 11:15. Be sure you know a person well before you vouch for his credit! Better refuse than suffer later.

Prov 22:26, 27. Unless you have the extra cash on hand, don't countersign a note. Why risk everything you own? They'll even take your bed! Prov 6:1.

Amos 2:8. At their religious feasts they lounge in clothing stolen from their debtors, and in my own Temple they offer sacrifices of wine they purchased with stolen money. *v.* 6; chapter 8:6.

See *Debtor; Creditor; Surety.*

DEBTOR LAWS CONCERNING. Ex 21:2. If you buy a Hebrew slave, he shall serve only six years and be freed in the seventh year, and need pay nothing to regain his freedom. [3]If he sold himself as a slave before he married, then if he married afterwards, only he shall be freed; but if he was married before he became a slave, then his wife shall be freed with him at the same time. [4]But if his master gave him a wife while he was a slave, and they have sons or daughters, the wife and children shall still belong to the master, and he shall go out by himself free. [5]But if the man shall plainly declare, "I prefer my master, my wife, and my children, and I would rather not go free," [6]then his master shall bring him before the judges and shall publicly bore his ear with an awl, and after that he will be a slave forever.

Ex 22:10. If a man asks his neighbor to keep a donkey, ox, sheep, or any other animal for him, and it dies, or is hurt, or gets away, and there is no eyewitness to report just what happened to it, [11]then the neighbor must take an oath that he has not stolen it, and the owner must accept his word, and no restitution shall be made for it. [12]But if the animal or property has been stolen, the neighbor caring for it must repay the owner. [13]If it was attacked by some wild animal, he shall bring the torn carcass to confirm the fact, and shall not be required to make restitution. [14]If a man borrows an animal (or anything else) from a neighbor, and it is injured or killed, and the owner is not there at the time, then the man who borrowed it must pay for it. But if the owner is there, he need not pay; and if it was rented, then he need not pay, because this possibility was included in the original rental fee.

Lev 25:14–16. Because of this, if the land is sold or bought during the preceding forty-nine years, a fair price shall be arrived at by counting the number of years until the Jubilee. If the Jubilee is many years away, the price will be high; if few years, the price will be low; for what you are really doing is selling the number of crops the new owner will get from the land before it is returned to you. [17, 18]You must fear your God and not overcharge! For I am Jehovah. Obey my laws if you want to live safely in the land. [25]If anyone becomes poor and sells some of his land, then his nearest relatives may redeem it. [26]If there is no one else to redeem it, and he himself gets together enough money, [27]then he may always buy it back at a price proportionate to the number of harvests until the Jubilee, and the owner must accept the money and return the land to him. [28]But if the original owner is not able to redeem it, then it shall belong to the new owner until the Year of Jubilee; but at the Jubilee year it must be returned again. [29]If a man sells a house in the city, he has up to one year to redeem it, with full right of redemption during that time. [30]But if it is not redeemed within the year, then it will belong permanently to the new owner—it does not return to the original owner in the Year of Jubilee. [31]But village houses—a village is a settlement without fortifying walls around it—are like farmland, redeemable at any time, and are always returned to the original owner in the Year of Jubilee. [32]There is one exception: The homes of the Levites, even though in walled cities, may be redeemed at any time, [33]and must be returned to the original owners in the Year of Jubilee; for the Levites will not be given farmland like the other tribes, but will receive only houses in their cities, and the surrounding fields. [34]The Levites are not permitted to sell the fields of common land surrounding their cities, for these are their permanent possession, and they must belong to no one else.

35. If your brother becomes poor, you are responsible to help him; invite him to live with you as a guest in your home. [36]Fear your God and let your brother live with you; and don't charge him interest on the money you lend him. [37]Remember —no interest; and give him what he needs, at your cost: don't try to make a profit! [38]For I, the Lord your God, brought you out of the land of Egypt to *give* you the land of Canaan, and to be your God.

39. If a fellow Israelite becomes poor and sells himself to you, you must not treat him as an ordinary slave, [40]but rather as a hired servant or as a guest; and he shall serve you only until the Year of Jubilee. [41]At that time he can leave with his children, and return to his own family and possessions.

47. If a foreigner living among you becomes rich, and an Israelite becomes poor and sells himself to the foreigner or to the foreigner's family, [48]he may be redeemed by one of his brothers, [49]his uncle, nephew, or anyone else who is a near relative. He may also redeem himself if he can find the money. [50]The price of his freedom shall be in proportion to the number of years left before the Year of Jubilee —whatever it would cost to hire a servant for that number of years. [51]If there are still many years until the Jubilee, he shall pay almost the amount he received when he sold himself; [52]if the years have passed and only a few remain until the Jubilee, then he will repay only a small part of the amount he received when he sold himself. [53]If he sells himself to a foreigner, the foreigner must treat him as a hired servant rather than as a slave or as property. [54]If he has not been redeemed by the time the Year of Jubilee arrives, then he and his children shall be freed at that time. [55]For the people of Israel are my servants; I brought them from the land of Egypt; I am the Lord your God.

Neh 10:31. And we agreed not to do any work every seventh year and to forgive and cancel the debts of our brother Jews.

Mt 5:25. Come to terms quickly with your enemy before it is too late and he drags you into court and you are thrown into a debtor's cell, [26]for you will stay there until you have paid the last penny. [40]If you are ordered to court, and your shirt it taken from you, give your coat too.

Mt 18:25. He couldn't pay, so the king ordered him sold for the debt, also his wife and children and everything he had.

UNCLASSIFIED SCRIPTURES RELATING TO. 2 Kgs 4:1. One day the wife of one of the seminary students came to Elisha to tell him of her husband's death. He was a man who had loved God, she said. But he had owed some money when he died, and now the creditor was demanding it back. If she didn't pay, he said he would take her two sons as his slaves. [2]"What shall I do?" Elisha asked. "How much food do you have in the house?" "Nothing at all, except a jar of olive oil," she replied. [3]"Then borrow many pots and pans from your friends and neighbors!" he instructed. [4]"Go into your house with your sons and shut the door behind you. Then pour olive oil from your jar into the pots and pans, setting them aside as they are filled!" [5]So she did. Her sons brought the pots and pans to her, and she filled one after another! [6]Soon every container was full to the brim! "Bring me another jar," she said to her sons. "There aren't any more!" they told her. And then the oil stopped flowing! [7]When she told the prophet what had happened, he said to her, "Go and sell the oil and pay your debt, and there will be enough money left for you and your sons to live on!"

Neh 5:2–4. What was happening was that families who ran out of money for food had to sell their children or mortgage their fields, vineyards, and homes to these rich men; and some couldn't even do that, for they already had borrowed to the limit to pay their taxes. [5]"We are their brothers, and our children are just like theirs," the people protested. "Yet we must sell our children into slavery to get enough money to live. We have already sold some of our daughters, and we are helpless to redeem them, for our fields, too, are mortgaged to these men."

Job 20:18. His labors shall not be rewarded; wealth will give him no joy. [19]For he has oppressed the poor and foreclosed their homes; he will never recover.

Hab 2:7. Suddenly your debtors will rise up in anger and turn on you and take all you have, while you stand trembling and helpless.

Mt 18:23. The Kingdom of Heaven can be compared to a king who decided to bring his accounts up to date. [24]In the process, one of his debtors was brought in who owed him $10,000,000! [25]He couldn't pay, so the king ordered him sold for the debt, also his wife and children and everything he had. [26]But the man fell down before the king, his face in the dust, and said, "Oh, sir, be patient with me and I will pay it all." [27]Then the king was filled with pity for him and released him and forgave his debt. [28]But when the man left the king, he went to a man who owed him $2,000 and grabbed him by the throat and demanded instant payment. [29]The man fell down before him and begged him to give him a little time. "Be patient and I will pay it," he pled. [30]But his creditor wouldn't wait. He had the man arrested and jailed until the debt would be paid in full. [31]Then the man's friends went to the king and told him what had happened. [32]And the king called before him the man he had forgiven and said, "You evil-hearted wretch! Here I forgave you all that tremendous debt, just because you asked me to—[33]shouldn't you have mercy on others, just as I had mercy on you?"

Lk 20:9. Now he turned to the people again and told them this story: "A man planted a vineyard and rented it out to some farmers, and went away to a distant land to live for several years. [10]When harvest time came, he sent one of his men to the farm to collect his share of the crops. But the tenants beat him up and sent him back empty-handed. [11]Then he sent another, but the same thing happened; he was beaten up and insulted and sent away without collecting. [12]A third man was sent and the same thing happened. He, too, was wounded and chased away. [13]'What shall I do?' the owner asked himself. 'I know! I'll send my cherished son. Surely they will show respect for him.' [14]But when the tenants saw his son, they said, 'This is our chance! This fellow will inherit all the land when his father dies. Come on. Let's kill him, and then it will be ours.' [15]So they dragged him out of the vineyard and killed him. What do you think the owner will do? [16]I'll tell you—he will come and kill them and rent the vineyard to others." "But they would never do a thing like that," his listeners protested.

See *Creditor; Debt; Surety.*

DECALOGUE See *Ten Commandments.*

DECAPOLIS Ten cities situated in one district on the east of the Sea of Galilee, Mt 4:25; Mk 5:20; 7:31. Called *Ten Towns* or *Ten Cities.*

DECEIT The tongue an instrument of, Rom 3:13. Comes from the heart, Mk 7:22. Characteristic of the heart, Jer 17:9. God abhors, Job 12:16; Ps 5:6. Forbidden, Prov 8:6, 7; 24:28; 1 Pet 3:10. Christ was perfectly free from, Isa 53:9, with 1 Pet 2:22.

Saints: Free from, Ps 24:4; Zeph 3:13; Rev 14:5; purpose against, Job 27:4; avoid, Job 31:5; reject those addicted to, Ps 101:7; Prov 8:13; pray for deliverance from those who use, Ps 43:1; 120:2; should beware of those who teach, Eph 5:6; Col 2:8; should put away, in seeking truth, 1 Pet 2:1–3. Ministers should not use, 2 Cor 4:2; 1 Thess 2:3.

The wicked: Are full of, Prov 12:5, 20; Rom 1:29; plot, Ps 35:20; 38:12; Dan 11:23; speak, Ps 10:7; 36:3; increase in, 2 Tim 3:13; use, to each other, Jer 9:5; Dan 11:27; use, to themselves, Job 15:31; Jer 37:9; Obd 1:3, 7; enjoy, Prov 20:17.

False teachers: Are workers of, 2 Cor 11:13; preach, Jer 14:14; 23:26; 2 Tim 3:9; impose on others by, Ezk 13:10; Rom 16:18; Eph 4:14; sport themselves with, 2 Pet 2:13. Hypocrites devise, Job 15:35. Hypocrites practice, Hos 11:12. False witnesses use, Prov 12:17. Characteristic of antichrists, Dan 8:25; Mk 13:22; 2 Jn 1:7; of the rebellion, Mt 24:24; 2 Thess 2:10; of the False Prophet,

Rev 13:14; 19:20; of Satan, Rev 12:9; 20:8.

Evil of: Hinders knowledge of God, Jer 9:6. Keeps from turning to God, Jer 8:5. Leads to pride and oppression, Isa 28:15; Jer 5:27, 28; to treason, Prov 14:25. Often accompanied by fraud and injustice, Ps 10:7; 43:1. Hatred often concealed by, Ps 62: 3, 4; Prov 26:24–26. The folly of fools is, Prov 14: 8. Blessedness of being free from, Ps 24:4, 5; 32:2. Punishment of, Ps 55:23; Jer 9:7–9; 23:9; 42:20; Rev 18:23.

See *Confidence, False; Deception; Flattery; Hypocrisy; Lying.*

DECEMBER See *Calendar.*

DECEPTION INSTANCES OF. By Satan, Gen 3:4. Abraham, in stating that Sarah was his sister, Gen 12:11–13; 20:2. Isaac, in stating that his wife was his sister, Gen 26:7. Jacob and Rebekah, in imposing Jacob on his father, and Jacob's impersonating Esau, Gen 27:6–23. Jacob's sons, in killing the Shechemites, Gen 34:13–31; in representing to their father that Joseph had been destroyed by wild animals, Gen 37:29–35. Joseph, in his ruse with his brothers, Gen 42–44. The Gibeonites, in misrepresenting their home, Josh 9:3–15. Ehud deceives Eglon, and kills him, Judg 3:15–30. Delilah deceives Samson, Judg 16:4–20. David feigns madness, 1 Sam 21:10–15. Amon deceives Tamar by feigning sickness, 2 Sam 13:6–14. By Absalom, when he avenged his sister, 2 Sam 13:21–28; when he began his conspiracy, 2 Sam 15:7. Hushai deceives Absalom, 2 Sam 16:15–19. The old prophet, 1 Kgs 13:18. Gehazi, 2 Kgs 5:20. Sanballat tries to deceive Nehemiah, Neh 6. Job's friends, Job 6: 15–18. Doeg, Ps 52:2. Herod, Mt 2:8. Pharisees, Mt 22:16. Chief priests, Mk 14:1. Lawyer, Lk 10:25. Ananias and Sapphira, Acts 5:1.

See *Deceit; False Witness; Hypocrisy; Lying.*

SELF. See *Confidence, False; Flattery.*

DECISION Deut 30:19. I call heaven and earth to witness against you that today I have set before you life or death, blessing or curse. Oh, that you would choose life; that you and your children might live!

Josh 23:8. But follow the Lord your God just as you have until now.

Josh 24:15 But if you are unwilling to obey the Lord, then decide today whom you will obey. Will it be the gods of your ancestors beyond the Euphrates or the gods of the Amorites here in this land? But as for me and my family, we will serve the Lord.

1 Sam 12:20. "Don't be frightened," Samuel reassured them. "You have certainly done wrong, but make sure now that you worship the Lord with true enthusiasm, and that you don't turn your back on him in any way."

1 Kgs 18:21. Then Elijah talked to them. "How long are you going to waver between two opinions? he asked the people. "If the Lord is God, *follow* him! But if Baal is God, then follow *him!*"

Ps 37:34. Don't be impatient for the Lord to act! Keep traveling steadily along his pathway and in due season he will honor you with every blessing, and you will see the wicked destroyed.

Ps 69:13. But I keep right on praying to you, Lord. For now is the time—you are bending down to hear! You are ready with a plentiful supply of love and kindness. Now answer my prayer and rescue me as you promised.

Prov 4:25–27. Look straight ahead; don't even turn your head to look. [26]Watch your step. Stick to the path and be safe. [27]Don't sidetrack; pull back your foot from danger.

Isa 50:7. Because the Lord God helps me, I will not be dismayed; therefore, I have set my face like flint to do his will, and I know that I will triumph.

Mt 24:13. But those enduring to the end shall be saved. Mk 13:13; Mt 10:22.

Mt 25:23. "Good work," his master said. "You are a good and faithful servant. You have been faithful over this small amount, so now I will give you much more."

Lk 7:23. And tell him, "Blessed is the one who does not lose his faith in me." Mt 11:6.

Jn 8:30, 31. Then many of the Jewish leaders who heard him say these things began believing him to be the Messiah. Jesus said to them, "You are truly my disciples if you live as I tell you to."

Jn 15:4. Take care to live in me, and let me live in you. For a branch can't produce fruit when severed from the vine. Nor can you be fruitful apart from me. [5]Yes, I am the Vine; you are the branches. Whoever lives in me and I in him shall produce a large crop of fruit. For apart from me you can't do a thing. [7]But if you stay in me and obey my commands, you may ask any request you like, and it will be granted! [9]I have loved you even as the Father has loved me. Live within my love.

Acts 11:23. When he arrived and saw the wonderful things God was doing, he was filled with excitement and joy, and encouraged the believers to stay close to the Lord, whatever the cost.

Acts 13:43. And many Jews and godly Gentiles who worshiped at the synagogue followed Paul and Barnabas down the street as the two men urged them to accept the mercies God was offering.

Acts 14:22. Where they helped the believers to grow in love for God and each other. They encouraged them to continue in the faith in spite of all the persecution, reminding them that they must enter into the Kingdom of God through many tribulations.

Rom 2:6. He will give each one whatever his deeds deserve. [7]He will give eternal life to those who patiently do the will of God, seeking for the unseen glory and honor and eternal life that he offers.

Rom 8:38. For I am convinced that nothing can ever separate us from his love. Death can't, and life can't. The angels won't, and all the powers of hell itself cannot keep God's love away. Our fears for today, our worries about tomorrow, [39]or where we are—high above the sky, or in the deepest ocean—nothing will ever be able to separate us from the love of God demonstrated by our Lord Jesus Christ when he died for us.

Rom 11:22. Notice how God is both kind and severe. He is very hard on those who disobey, but very good to you if you continue to love and trust him. But if you don't you too will be cut off.

1 Cor 15:58. So, my dear brothers, since future victory is sure, be strong and steady, always abounding in the Lord's work, for you know that nothing you do for the Lord is ever wasted as it would be if there were no resurrection.

1 Cor 16:13. Keep your eyes open for spiritual danger; stand true to the Lord; act like men; be strong.

Gal 5:1. So Christ has made us free. Now make sure that you stay free and don't get all tied up again in the chains of slavery to Jewish laws and ceremonies. [10]I am trusting the Lord to bring you back to believing as I do about these things.

Gal 6:9. And let us not get tired of doing what is right, for after a while we will reap a harvest of blessing if we don't get discouraged and give up.

Eph 4:14. Then we will no longer be like children, forever changing our minds about what we believe because someone has told us something different, or has cleverly lied to us and made the lie sound like the truth.

Eph 6:13. So use every piece of God's armor to resist the enemy whenever he attacks, and when it is all over, you will still be standing up.

Phil 1:27. But whatever happens to me, remember always to live as Christians should, so that, whether I ever see you again or not, I will keep on hearing good reports that you are standing side by side with one strong purpose—to tell the Good News [28]fearlessly, no matter what your enemies may do.

Phil 4:1. Dear brother Christians, I love you and long to see you, for you are my joy and my reward for my work. My beloved friends, stay true to the Lord.

Col 1:23. The only condition is that you fully believe the Truth, standing in it steadfast and firm, strong in the Lord, convinced of the Good News that Jesus died for you, and never shifting from trusting him to save you. This is the wonderful news that came to each of you and is now spreading all over the world. And I, Paul, have the joy of telling it to others.

1 Thess 3:8. We can bear anything as long as we know that you remain strong in him. [13]This will result in your hearts being made strong, sinless and holy by God our Father, so that you may stand before him guiltless on that day when our Lord Jesus Christ returns with all those who belong to him.

2 Thess 2:15. With all these things in mind, dear brothers, stand firm and keep a strong grip on the truth that we taught you in our letters and during the time we were with you. [17]Comfort your hearts with all comfort, and help you in every good thing you say and do.

2 Thess 3:13. And to the rest of you I say, dear brothers, never be tired of doing right.

2 Tim 1:13. Hold tightly to the pattern of truth I taught you, especially concerning the faith and love Christ Jesus offers you. [14]Guard well the splendid, God-given ability you received as a gift from the Holy Spirit who lives within you.

2 Tim 2:1. Oh, Timothy, my son, be strong with the strength Christ Jesus gives you. [3]Take your share of suffering as a good soldier of Jesus Christ, just as I do.

2 Tim 3:14. But you must keep on believing the things you have been taught. You know they are true for you know that you can trust those of us who have taught you.

Tit 1:7. These pastors must be men of blameless lives because they are God's ministers. They must not be proud or impatient; they must not be drunkards or fighters or greedy for money. [9]Their belief in the truth which they have been taught must be strong and steadfast, so that they will be able to teach it to others and show those who disagree with them where they are wrong.

Heb 2:1. So we must listen very carefully to the truths we have heard, or we may drift away from them.

Heb 3:6. But Christ, God's faithful Son, is in complete charge of God's house. And we Christians are God's house—he lives in us!—if we keep up our courage firm to the end, and our joy and our trust in the Lord. [7, 8]And since Christ is so much superior, the Holy Spirit warns us to listen to him, to be careful to hear his voice today and not let our hearts become set against him, as the people of Israel did. They steeled themselves against his love and complained against him in the desert while he was testing them. [14]For if we are faithful to the end, trusting God just as we did when we first became Christians, we will share in all that belongs to Christ.

Heb 4:14. But Jesus the Son of God is our great High Priest who has gone to heaven itself to help us; therefore let us never stop trusting him.

Heb 10:23. Now we can look forward to the salvation God has promised us. There is no longer any room for doubt, and we can tell others that salvation is ours, for there is no question that he will do what he says. [35]Do not let this happy trust in the Lord die away, no matter what happens. Remember your reward!

Heb 12:1. Since we have such a huge crowd of men of faith watching us from the grandstands, let us strip off anything that slows us down or holds us back, and especially those sins that wrap themselves so tightly around our feet and trip us up; and let us run with patience the particular race that God has set before us.

Heb 13:9. So do not be attracted by strange, new ideas. Your spiritual strength comes as a gift from God, not from ceremonial rules about eating certain foods—a method which, by the way, hasn't helped those who have tried it! [13]So let us go out to him beyond the city walls (that is, outside the interests of this world, being willing to be despised) to suffer with him there, bearing his shame.

Jas 1:4. So let it grow, and don't try to squirm out

of your problems. For when your patience is finally in full bloom, then you will be ready for anything, strong in character, full and complete. [12]Happy is the man who doesn't give in and do wrong when he is tempted, for afterwards he will get as his reward the crown of life that God has promised those who love him. [25]But if anyone keeps looking steadily into God's law for free men, he will not only remember it but he will do what it says, and God will greatly bless him in everything he does.

1 Pet 1:13. So now you can look forward soberly and intelligently to more of God's kindness to you when Jesus Christ returns.

1 Pet 5:8. Be careful—watch out for attacks from Satan, your enemy. He prowls around like a hungry, roaring lion, looking for some victim to tear apart. [9]Stand firm when he attacks. Trust the Lord; and remember that other Christians all around the world are going through these sufferings too.

2 Pet 1:10. So, dear brothers, work hard to prove that you really are among those God has called and chosen, and then you will never stumble or fall away. [11]And God will open wide the gates of heaven for you to enter into the eternal kingdom of our Lord and Savior Jesus Christ.

2 Pet 3:17. I am warning you ahead of time, dear brothers, so that you can watch out and not be carried away by the mistakes of these wicked men, lest you yourselves become mixed up too. [18]But grow in spiritual strength and become better acquainted with our Lord and Savior Jesus Christ.

1 Jn 2:24. So keep on believing what you have been taught from the beginning. If you do, you will always be in close fellowship with both God the Father and his Son. [28]And now, my little children, stay in happy fellowship with the Lord so that when he comes you will be sure that all is well, and will not have to be ashamed and shrink back from meeting him.

2 Jn 1:8. Beware of being like them, and losing the prize that you and I have been working so hard to get. See to it that you win your full reward from the Lord.

Jude 1:20. But you, dear friends, must build up your lives ever more strongly upon the foundation of our holy faith, learning to pray in the power and strength of the Holy Spirit. [21]Stay always within the boundaries where God's love can reach and bless you. Wait patiently for the eternal life that our Lord Jesus Christ in his mercy is going to give you.

Rev 2:7. Let this message sink into the ears of anyone who listens to what the Spirit is saying to the churches: To everyone who is victorious, I will give fruit from the Tree of Life in the Paradise of God. [10]Remain faithful even when facing death and I will give you the crown of life—an unending, glorious future. [11]Let everyone who can hear, listen to what the Spirit is saying to the churches: He who is victorious shall not be hurt by the Second Death.

17. Let everyone who can hear, listen to what the Spirit is saying to the churches: Every one who is victorious shall eat of the hidden manna, the secret nourishment from heaven; and I will give to each a white stone, and on the stone will be engraved a new name that no one else knows except the one receiving it. [24, 25]As for the rest of you in Thyatira who have not followed this false teaching ("deeper truths," as they call them—depths of Satan, really), I will ask nothing further of you; only hold tightly to what you have until I come. [26]To every one who overcomes—who to the very end keeps on doing things that please me—I will give power over the nations.

Rev 3:5. Everyone who conquers will be clothed in white, and I will not erase his name from the Book of Life, but I will announce before my Father and his angels that he is mine. [11]Look, I am coming soon! Hold tightly to the little strength you have—so that no one will take away your crown. [12]As for the one who conquers, I will make him a pillar in the temple of my God; he will be secure, and will go out no more; [21]I will let every one who conquers sit beside me on my throne, just as I took my place with my Father on his throne when I had conquered.

Rev 15:2. Spread out before me was what seemed to be an ocean of fire and glass, and on it stood all those who had been victorious over the Evil Creature and his statue and his mark and number. All were holding harps of God.

Rev 21:7. Everyone who conquers will inherit all these blessings, and I will be his God and he will be my son.

Rev 22:11. And when that time comes, all doing wrong will do it more and more; the vile will become more vile; good men will be better; those who are holy will continue on in greater holiness.

See *Character; Perseverance; Stability; Indecision; Instability.*

EXHORTATION TO. Josh 1:7. You need only to be strong and courageous and to obey to the letter every law Moses gave you, for if you are careful to obey every one of them you will be successful in everything you do.

1 Chron 16:15. Remember his covenant forever—the words he commanded to a thousand generations.

2 Chron 19:11. "Be fearless in your stand for truth and honesty. And may God use you to defend the innocent," was his final word to them.

Mt 4:17. From then on, Jesus began to preach, "Turn from sin, and turn to God, for the Kingdom of heaven is near."

Mt 6:24. You cannot serve two masters: God and money. For you will hate one and love the other, or else the other way around. Lk 16:13.

Mt 10:32. If anyone publicly acknowledges me as his friend, I will openly acknowledge him as my friend before my father in heaven.

Lk 9:59. Another time, when he invited a man to come with him and to be his disciple, the man agreed—but wanted to wait until his father's death. [60]Jesus replied, "Let those without eternal life concern themselves with things like that. Your duty is to come and preach the coming of the Kingdom of God to all the world." [61]Another said, "Yes, Lord, I will come, but first let me ask permission of those at home." [62]But Jesus told him, "Anyone who lets himself be distracted from the work I plan for him is not fit for the Kingdom of God." Mt 8:21, 22.

Lk 11:23. Anyone who is not for me is against me; if he isn't helping me, he is hurting my cause. Mt 12:30.

Lk 12:8. And I assure you of this: I, the Messiah, will publicly honor you in the presence of God's angels if you publicly acknowledge me here on earth as your Friend.

Lk 17:32. Remember what happened to Lot's wife!

Col 2:6. And now just as you trusted Christ to save you, trust him, too, for each day's problems; live in vital union with him. [7]Let your roots grow down into him and draw up nourishment from him. See that you go on growing in the Lord, and become strong and vigorous in the truth you were taught. Let your lives overflow with joy and thanksgiving for all he has done.

1 Tim 6:11. Oh, Timothy, you are God's man. Run from all these evil things and work instead at what is right and good, learning to trust him and love others, and to be patient and gentle.

12. Fight on for God. Hold tightly to the eternal life which God has given you, and which you have confessed with such a ringing confession before many witnesses.

13. I command you before God who gives life to all, and before Christ Jesus who gave a fearless testimony before Pontius Pilate, [14]that you fulfill all he has told you to do, so that no one can find fault with you from now until our Lord Jesus Christ returns.

INSTANCES OF.

Abel. Heb 11:4. It was by faith that Abel obeyed God and brought an offering that pleased God more than Cain's offering did. God accepted Abel and proved it by accepting his gift; and though Abel is long dead, we can still learn lessons from him about trusting God.

Enoch. Heb 11:5. Enoch trusted God too, and that is why God took him away to heaven without dying; suddenly he was gone because God took him. Before this happened God had said how pleased he was with Enoch. [6]You can never please God without faith, without depending on him. Anyone who wants to come to God must believe that there is a God and that he rewards those who sincerely look for him.

Noah. Heb 11:7. Noah was another who trusted God. When he heard God's warning about the future, Noah believed him even though there was then no sign of a flood, and wasting no time, he built the ark and saved his family. Noah's belief in God was in direct contrast to the sin and disbelief of the rest of the world—which refused to obey—and because of his faith he became one of those whom God has accepted.

Abraham. Heb 11:8. Abraham trusted God, and when God told him to leave home and go far away to another land which he promised to give him, Abraham obeyed. Away he went, not even knowing where he was going. [17]While God was testing him, Abraham still trusted in God and his promises, and so he offered up his son Isaac, and was ready to slay him on the altar of sacrifice; [18]yes, to slay even Isaac, through whom God had promised to give Abraham a whole nation of descendants! [19]He believed that if Isaac died God would bring him back to life again; and that is just about what happened, for as far as Abraham was concerned, Isaac was doomed to death, but he came back again alive!

Jacob. Gen 28:20. And Jacob vowed this vow to God: "If God will help and protect me on this journey and give me food and clothes, [21]and will bring me back safely to my father, then I will choose Jehovah as my God!

Joseph. Gen 39:9. How can I do such a wicked thing as this? It would be a great sin against God. *vs.* 7–20.

Moses. Heb 11:24, 25. It was by faith that Moses, when he grew up, refused to be treated as the grandson of the king, but chose to share ill-treatment with God's people instead of enjoying the fleeting pleasures of sin. [26]He thought that it was better to suffer for the promised Christ than to own all the treasures of Egypt, for he was looking forward to the great reward that God would give him.

Num 12:7, 8. But that is not how I communicate with my servant Moses. He is completely at home in my house! With him I speak face to face! And he shall see the very form of God! Why then were you not afraid to criticize him? Heb 3:5.

Israelites. Ex 19:7. Moses returned from the mountain and called together the leaders of the people and told them what the Lord had said. [8]They all responded in unison, "We will certainly do everything he asks of us." Moses reported the words of the people to the Lord.

Ex 24:3. Then Moses announced to the people all the laws and regulations God had given him; and the people answered in unison, "We will obey them all." [7]And he read to the people the Book he had written—the Book of the Covenant—containing God's directions and laws. And the people said again, "We solemnly promise to obey every one of these rules."

Deut 4:4. But all of you who were faithful to the Lord your God are still alive today.

Deut 5:26, 27. What man can hear, as we have, the voice of the living God speaking from the heart of the fire, and live? You go and listen to all that God says, then come and tell us, and we will listen and obey. Ex 24:3, 7; 19:8.

Deut 26:17. You have declared today that he is your God, and you have promised to obey and keep his laws and ordinances, and to heed all he tells you to do. Deut 29:12.

Josh 22:34. The people of Reuben and Gad named the altar "The Altar of Witness," for they said, "It is a witness between us and them that Jehovah is our God, too."

Josh 24:21. But the people answered, "We choose the Lord!" [22]"You have heard yourselves say it," Joshua said—"you have chosen to obey the Lord." "Yes," they replied, "we are witnesses." [23]"All right," he said, "then you must destroy all the idols you now own, and you must obey the Lord God of Israel." [24]The people replied to Joshua, "Yes, we will worship and obey the Lord alone." [25]So Joshua made a covenant with them that day at Shechem, committing them to a permanent and binding contract between themselves and God.

1 Kgs 19:18. And incidentally, there are 7,000 men in Israel who have never bowed to Baal nor kissed him!

2 Chron 11:16. Laymen, too, from all over Israel began moving to Jerusalem where they could freely worship the Lord God of their fathers, and sacrifice to him.

2 Chron 13:10. But as for us, the Lord is our God and we have not forsaken him. Only the descendants of Aaron are our priests, and the Levites alone may help them in their work. [11]They burn sacrifices to the Lord every morning and evening—burnt offerings and sweet incense; and they place the Bread of the Presence upon the holy table. The golden lampstand is lighted every night, for we are careful to follow the instructions of the Lord our God; but you have forsaken him.

2 Chron 15:12. Then they entered into a contract to worship only the Lord God of their fathers. [15]All were happy for this covenant with God, for they had entered into it with all their hearts and wills, and wanted him above everything else, and they found him! And he gave them peace throughout the nation. 2 Chron 23:15–17; 2 Kgs 11:17; 2 Chron 29:10; Ezra 10:3–44; Neh 9:38; Jer 34:15.

Neh 10:28. These men signed on behalf of the entire nation—for the common people; the priests; the Levites; the gatekeepers; the choir members; the Temple servants; and all the rest who, with their wives and sons and daughters who were old enough to understand, had separated themselves from the heathen people of the land in order to serve God. [29]For we all heartily agreed to this oath and vowed to accept the curse of God unless we obeyed God's laws as issued by his servant Moses. *vs.* 1–39.

Ps 50:5. Gather together my own people who by their sacrifice upon my altar have promised to obey me.

Jer 42:5. Then they said to Jeremiah, "May the curse of God be on us if we refuse to obey whatever he says we should do! [6]Whether we like it or not, we will obey the Lord our God, to whom we send you with our plea. For if we obey him, everything will turn out well for us."

Jer 50:5. They shall ask the way to Zion and start back home again. "Come," they will say, "let us be united to the Lord with an eternal pledge that will never be broken again."

Hos 11:12. Israel surrounds me with lies and deceit, but Judah still trusts in God and is faithful to the Holy One.

Caleb. Num 14:24. But my servant Caleb is a different kind of man—he has obeyed me fully. I will bring him into the land he entered as a spy, and his descendants shall have their full share in it. *vs.* 6–10, 37, 38; Deut 1:36; Josh 14:13, 14.

Balaam. Num 22:15. Balak tried again. This time he sent a larger number of even more distinguished ambassadors than the former group. [16, 17]They came to Balaam with this message: "King Balak pleads with you to come. He promises you great honors plus any payment you ask. Name your own figure! Only come and curse these people for us." [18]But Balaam replied, "If he were to give me a palace filled with silver and gold, I could do nothing contrary to the command of the Lord my God."

Phinehas. Num 25:7. When Phinehas (son of Eleazar and grandson of Aaron the priest) saw this, he jumped up, grabbed a spear, [8]and rushed after the man into his tent, where he had taken the girl. He thrust the spear all the way through the man's body and into her stomach. So the plague was stopped, [9]but only after 24,000 people had already died. [10, 11]Then the Lord said to Moses, "Phinehas (son of Eleazar and grandson of Aaron the priest) has turned away my anger, for he was as angry as I, concerning my honor; so I have stopped destroying all Israel as I had intended. [12, 13]Now because of what he has done—because of his zeal for his God, and because he has made atonement for the people of Israel by what he did—I promise that he and his descendants shall be priests forever."

Joshua. Josh 24:15. "But if you are unwilling to obey the Lord, then decide today whom you will obey. Will it be the gods of your ancestors beyond the Euphrates or the gods of the Amorites here in this land? But as for me and my family, we will serve the Lord." [21]But the people answered, "We choose the Lord!" [22]"You have heard yourselves say it," Joshua said—"you have chosen to obey the Lord." *vs.* 18–24.

Gideon. Judg 6:25. That night the Lord told Gideon to hitch his father's best ox to the family altar of Baal, and pull it down, and to cut down the wooden idol of the goddess Asherah that stood nearby. [26]"Replace it with an altar for the Lord your God, built here on this hill, laying the stones carefully. Then sacrifice the ox as a burnt offering to the Lord, using the wooden idol as wood for the fire on the altar." [27]So Gideon took ten of his servants and did as the Lord had commanded. But he did it at night for fear of the other members of his father's household, and for fear of the men of the city; for he knew what would happen if they found out who did it! with *vs.* 28–40, and chapter 7.

Ruth. Ruth 1:16. But Ruth replied, "Don't make me leave you, for I want to go wherever you go, and to live wherever you live; your people shall be my people, and your God shall be my God."

Saul. 1 Sam 11:4. When a messenger came to Gibe-ah, Saul's home town, and told the people about their plight, everyone broke into tears. [5]Saul was plowing in the field, and when he returned to town he asked, "What's the matter? Why is everyone crying?" So they told him about the message from Jabesh. [6]Then the Spirit of God came strongly upon Saul and he became very angry. [7]He took two oxen and cut them into pieces and sent messengers to carry them throughout all Israel. "This is what will happen to the oxen of anyone who refuses to follow Saul and Samuel to battle!" he announced. And God caused the people to be afraid of Saul's anger, and they came to him as one man.

Abigail. 1 Sam 25:18. Then Abigail hurriedly took two hundred loaves of bread, two barrels of wine, five dressed sheep, two bushels of roasted grain, one hundred raisin cakes, and two hundred fig cakes, and packed them onto donkeys. [19]"Go on ahead," she said to her young men, "and I will follow." But she didn't tell her husband what she was doing. *vs.* 4–37.

David. 1 Sam 17:32. "Don't worry about a thing," David told him. "I'll take care of this Philistine!" [33]"Don't be ridiculous!" Saul replied. "How can a kid like you fight with a man like him? You are only a boy and he has been in the army since he was a boy!" [34]But David persisted. "When I am taking care of my father's sheep," he said, "and a lion or a bear comes and grabs a lamb from the flock, [35]I go after it with a club and take the lamb from its mouth. If it turns on me I catch it by the jaw and club it to death. [36]I have done this to both lions and bears, and I'll do it to this heathen Philistine too, for he has defied the armies of the living God! [37]The Lord who saved me from the claws and teeth of the lion and the bear will save me from this Philistine!" Saul finally consented, "All right, go ahead," he said, "and may the Lord be with you!" *vs.* 20–54.

2 Sam 22:22. And I have not departed from my God. [23]I knew his laws, and I obeyed them. [24]I was perfect in obedience and kept myself from sin.

Psalmist. Ps 17:3. You have tested me and seen that I am good. You have come even in the night and found nothing amiss and know that I have told the truth.

Ps 26:6. I wash my hands to prove my innocence and come before your altar. [11]I try to walk a straight and narrow path of doing what is right; therefore in mercy save me.

Ps 40:9. I have told everyone the Good News that you forgive men's sins. I have not been timid about it, as you well know, O Lord. [10]I have not kept this Good News hidden in my heart, but have proclaimed your loving kindness and truth to all the congregation.

Ps 56:12. I will surely do what I have promised, Lord, and thank you for your help.

Ps 66:16. Come and hear, all of you who reverence the Lord, and I will tell you what he did for me.

Ps 71:17. O God, you have helped me from my earliest childhood—and I have constantly testified to others of the wonderful things you do.

Ps 86:11. Tell me where you want me to go and I will go there. May every fiber of my being unite in reverence to your name.

Ps 101:2. I will try to walk a blameless path, but how I need your help, especially in my own home, where I long to act as I should. [3]Help me to refuse the low and vulgar things; help me to abhor all crooked deals of every kind, to have no part in them.

Ps 116:9, 13, 14, 16. I shall live! Yes, in his presence—here on earth! [13]I will bring him an offering of wine and praise his name for saving me. [14]I will publicly bring him the sacrifice I vowed I would. [16]O Lord, you have freed me from my bonds and I will serve you forever.

Ps 119:8. I *will* obey! Oh, don't forsake me and let me slip back into sin again. [30]Help me, undeserving as I am, to obey your laws, for I have chosen to do right. [31]I cling to your commands and follow them as closely as I can. Lord, don't let me make a mess of things. [38]Reassure me that your promises are for me, for I trust and revere you. [44-46]Therefore I will keep on obeying you forever and forever, free within the limits of your laws. I will speak to kings about their value, and they will listen with interest and respect. [57]Jehovah is mine! And I promise to obey! [94]I am yours! Save me! For I have tried to live according to your desires. [106]I've said it once and I'll say it again and again: I will obey these wonderful laws of yours. [115]Begone, you evil-minded men. Don't try to stop me from obeying God's commands. [125]For I am your servant; therefore give me common sense to apply your rules to everything I do. [145]I am praying with great earnestness; answer me, O Lord, and I will obey your laws. [146]"Save me," I cry, "for I am obeying." Ps 143:12.

A Prophet. 1 Kgs 13:8. But the prophet said to the king, "Even if you gave me half your palace, I wouldn't go into it; nor would I eat or drink even water in this place! [9]For the Lord has given me strict orders not to eat anything or drink any water while I'm here, and not to return to Judah by the road I came on." [10]So he went back another way.

Elijah. 1 Kgs 18:22. Then Elijah spoke again. "I am the only prophet of the Lord who is left," he told them, "but Baal has 450 prophets."

Jehoshaphat. 1 Kgs 22:7. But Jehoshaphat asked, "Isn't there a prophet of the Lord here? I'd like to ask him, too." 2 Chron 18:6.

Naaman. 2 Kgs 5:15. Then he and his entire party went back to find the prophet; they stood humbly before him and Naaman said, "I know at last that there is no God in all the world except in Israel; now please accept my gifts. [17]From now on I will never again offer any burnt offerings or sacrifices to any other Gods except the Lord."

Jehu. 2 Kgs 9:18. So a soldier rode out to meet Jehu. "The king wants to know whether you are friend or foe," he demanded. "Do you come in peace?" Jehu replied, "What do you know about peace? Get behind me!" The watchman called out to the king that the messenger had met them but was not returning. [19]So the king sent out a second rider. He rode up to them and demanded in the name of the king to know whether their intentions were friendly or not. Jehu answered, "What do you know about friendliness? Get behind me!" [20]"He isn't returning either!" the watchman exclaimed. "It must be Jehu, for he is driving so furiously." *vs.* 11–37; chapter 10.

Hezekiah. 2 Kgs 18:6. For he followed the Lord in everything, and carefully obeyed all of God's commands to Moses. 2 Chron 15:17.

Josiah. 2 Kgs 22:2. Character of his reign: good; for he followed in the steps of his ancestor King David, obeying the Lord completely.

2 Kgs 23:3. He stood beside the pillar in front of the people, and he and they made a solemn promise to the Lord to obey him at all times and to do everything the book commanded. [2 Chron 34:31.] [25]There was no other king who so completely turned to the Lord and followed all the laws of Moses; and no king since the time of Josiah has approached his record of obedience.

Nehemiah. Neh 6:11. But I replied, "Should I, the governor, run away from danger? And if I go into the Temple, not being a priest, I would forfeit my life. No, I won't do it!" chapters 2; 4; 5; 6.

Mordecai. Esther 3:2. Now all the king's officials bowed before him in deep reverence whenever he passed by, for so the king had commanded. But Mordecai refused to bow. [3]"Why are you disobeying the king's commandment?" the others demanded day after day, but he still refused.

Esther. Esther 4:16. Go and gather together all the Jews of Shushan and fast for me; do not eat or drink for three days, night or day; and I and my maids will do the same; and then, though it is strictly forbidden, I will go in to see the king; and if I perish, I perish.

Job. Job 2:3. "Well, have you noticed my servant Job?" the Lord asked. "He is the finest man in all the earth—a good man who fears God and turns away from all evil. And he has kept his faith in me despite the fact that you persuaded me to let you harm him without any cause."

Job 23:11. I have stayed in God's paths, following his steps. I have not turned aside. [12]I have not refused his commandments but have enjoyed them more than my daily food.

Matthew. Mt 9:9. As Jesus was going on down the road, he saw a tax collector, Matthew, sitting at a tax collection booth. "Come and be my disciple," Jesus said to him, and Matthew jumped up and went along with him.

Joseph. Mk 15:43. Joseph from Arimathea, . . . gathered his courage and went to Pilate and asked for Jesus' body.

Nathanael. Jn 1:49. Nathanael replied, "Sir, you are the Son of God—the King of Israel!"

Martha. Jn 11:27. "Yes, Master," she told him. "I believe you are the Messiah, the Son of God, the one we have so long awaited."

The Disciples. Lk 18:28. And Peter said, "We have left our homes and followed you."

Jn 6:68. Simon Peter replied, "Master, to whom shall we go? You alone have the words that give eternal life, [69]and we believe them and know you are the holy Son of God."

Acts 2:42. They joined with the other believers in regular attendance at the apostles' teaching sessions and at the Communion services and prayer meetings.

Paul. Acts 9:29. And preached boldly in the name of the Lord. But then some Greek-speaking Jews with whom he had argued plotted to murder him.

Acts 26:6. But the real reason behind their accusations is something else—it is because I am looking forward to the fulfillment of God's promise made to our ancestors.

Rom 1:16. For I am not ashamed of this Good News about Christ. It is God's powerful method of bringing all who believe it to heaven.

Phil 1:20. For I live in eager expectation and hope that I will never do anything that will cause me to be ashamed of myself but that I will always be ready to speak out boldly for Christ while I am going through all these trials here, just as I have in the past; and that I will always be an honor to Christ, whether I live or whether I must die. [21]For to me, living means opportunities for Christ, and dying—well, that's better yet!

Col 2:5. For though I am far away from you my heart is with you, happy because you are getting along so well, happy because of your strong faith in Christ.

2 Tim 4:7. I have fought long and hard for my Lord, and through it all I have kept true to him. And now the time has come for me to stop fighting and rest. [8]In heaven a crown is waiting for me which the Lord, the righteous Judge, will give me on that great day of his return. And not just to me, but to all those whose lives show that they are eagerly looking forward to his coming back again.

Ephesians. Rev 2:2. I know how many good things you are doing. I have watched your hard work and your patience; . . . [3]You have patiently suffered for me without quitting.

Church of Sardis. Rev 3:4. Yet even there in Sardis some haven't soiled their garments with the world's filth; they shall walk with me in white, for they are worthy. [8]I know you well; you aren't strong, but you have tried to obey and have not denied my Name. Therefore I have opened a door to you that no one can shut. [10]Because you have patiently obeyed me despite the persecution, therefore I will protect you from the time of Great Tribulation and temptation, which will come upon the world to test everyone alive.

Saints. Rev 14:4. For they are spiritually undefiled, pure as virgins, following the Lamb wherever he goes. They have been purchased from among the men on the earth as a consecrated offering to God and the Lamb.

See *Perseverance; Stability; Zeal, Religious.*

DECREES Of the Medes, irrevocable, Dan 6:12–15.

Ecclesiastical, of the church at Jerusalem, Acts 16:4, with chapter 15:27–29.

Divine, see *Predestination.*

DEDAN 1. Son of Raamah, Gen 10:7; 1 Chron 1:5–9.

2. Son of Jokshan, Gen 25:3; 1 Chron 1:32.

3. A country, probably bordering on Edom, Isa 21:13; Jer 49:8; Ezk 25:13; 27:20; 38:13.

DEDICATION Law concerning dedicated things, Lev 27; Num 18:14, 15; 1 Chron 26:26, 27. Must be without defect, Lev 22:18–23; Mal 1:14. Not redeemable, Lev 27:28, 29. Offering must be voluntary, Lev 1:2, 3; 22:17–19. See *Offerings; Sanctification; Vows.*

Of the Tabernacle, Num 7. Solomon's Temple, 1 Kgs 8; 2 Chron 7:4, 5. Second temple, Ezra 6:16, 17. Of the wall of Jerusalem, Neh 12:27–43. Of houses, Deut 20:5. Of Samuel by his mother, 1 Sam 1:11, 21, 22.

OF SELF. See *Consecration.*

For instances of liberality in dedicated things, see *Liberality.*

FEAST OF. Jn 10:22, 23. See 1 Kgs 8:65; 2 Chron 7:8–10.

DEED To land, Jer 32:12, 14, 44.

See *Land.*

DEER Called also *Hind; Roebuck.* Designated among the clean animals, to be eaten, Deut 12:15; 14:3–5. Provided for Solomon's household, 1 Kgs 4:23. Fleetness of, 2 Sam 2:18; 1 Chron 12:8; Prov 6:5; Song 8:14; Isa 35:6. Gentleness of, Prov 5:19.

DEFECT Physical, see *Blemish.*

DEFENSE An argument made before a court. Of Jeremiah, Jer 26:12–16; Peter, Acts 4:8–13; 5:23–29; Stephen, Acts 7; Paul, Acts 22; 23:1–6; 24:10–21; 26:1–23.

Military defenses, see *Fort; Armies.*

DEFILEMENT Laws relating to, Lev 7:17–21; 11:43; 22:1–7. Caused by leprosy, Lev 13:3, 44–46; 14; 22:4–7; gonorrhea, Lev 15:1–15; copulation, Lev 15:18; spermatorrhea, Lev 15:16, 17; 22:4; Deut 23:9–11; childbirth, Lev 12:2–8; Lk 2:22; menses, Lev 15:19–33; 2 Sam 11:4; touching the dead, Num 19:11–22; 31:19, 20; touching carcass of any unclean animal, Lev 11:39, 40; 17:15, 16; 22:8; touching carcass of an unclean thing, Lev 5:2–13; 11:8, 24–28, 31–38; 14:46–57; 15:5–11; killing in battle, Num 31:19, 20. Contact with sinners falsely supposed to cause, Jn 18:28. Of priests, Lev 16:26, 28; Num 19:7–10; Ezk 44:25, 26.

Egyptian usage, concerning, Gen 43:32.

See *Ablution; Purification; Uncleanness.*

DEFORMITY See *Blemish.*

DEGREES Or steps in the dial of Ahaz, 2 Kgs 20:9–11; Isa 38:8.

DEITY OF CHRIST *See Jesus Christ, Deity of.*

DELAIAH 1. Head of the twenty-third division of the priestly order, 1 Chron 24:7–18.

2. A prince of Judah, Jer 36:12, 24, 25.

3. A progenitor of certain Babylonish captives, Ezra 2:60; Neh 7:62.

4. Father of a false prophet, Neh 6:10.

5. A descendant of the royal line of Judah, 1 Chron 3:24.

DELILAH Samson's illicit lover, Judg 16:4–18.

DELIVERANCE See *Afflictions; God, Providence of; Prayer, Answered.*

DELIVERER A name of Jesus, Rom 11:26.

DELUGE See *Flood.*

DELUSION, SELF See *Self-Delusion.*

DEMAGOGISM INSTANCES OF. Absalom, 2 Sam 15:2–6. Pilate, Mt 27:17–26; Mk 15:15; Lk 23:13–24; Jn 18:38–40; 19:6–13. Felix, Acts 24:27. Herod, Acts 12:3.

DEMAS A companion of Paul, Col 4:14; Philemon 1:24. Deserts Paul, 2 Tim 4:10.

DEMETRIUS 1. A silversmith, noted for raising a riot, Acts 19:24–38.

2. A Christian mentioned in 3 Jn 1:12.

DEMONS Worship of, Lev 17:7; Ps 106:37, 38; Mt 4:9; Lk 4:6, 7; 1 Cor 10:20, 21; 1 Tim 4:1; Rev 13:4. Worship of, forbidden, Lev 17:7; Zech 13:2; Rev 9:20.

Possession by, instances of: Saul, 1 Sam 16:14–23; 18:10–12; 19:9, 10. Two men of the Gadarenes, Mt 8:28–34; Mk 5:1–20. The mute, Mt 9:32, 33. The blind and mute man, Mt 12:22; Lk 11:14. The daughter of the Syrophoenician, Mt 15:22–28; Mk 7:25–30. The deranged child, Mt 17:14–18; Mk 9:17–27; Lk 9:37–42. The man in the synagogue, Mk 1:23–26; Lk 4:33–35. Mary Magdalene, Mk 16:9; Lk 8:2. The herd of swine, Mt 8:30–32.

Cast out by Jesus, Mt 4:24; 8:16; Mk 3:22; Lk 4:41; 11:14.

Power over, given the disciples, Mt 10:1; Mk 6:7; 16:17. Cast out by the disciples, Mk 9:38; Lk 10:17; by Peter, Acts 5:16; by Paul, Acts 16:16–18; 19:12; by Philip, Acts 8:7. Disciples could not expel, Mk 9:18, 28, 29. Sceva's sons exorcise, Acts 19:13–16. Parable of the man repossessed, Mt 12:43–45.

Jesus falsely accused of being possessed by, Mk 3:22–30; Jn 8:48; 10:20.

Testify to the divinity of Jesus, Mt 8:29; Mk 1:23, 24; 3:11; 5:7, 8; Lk 8:28; Acts 19:15.

Adversaries of men, Mt 12:43–45. Sent to foment trouble between Abimelech and the Shechemites, Judg 9:23. Messages given false prophets by, 1 Kgs 22:21–23.

Believe and tremble, Jas 2:19. To be judged, Mt 8:29, with 2 Pet 2:4; Jude 1:6.

Punishment of, Mt 8:29; 25:41; Lk 8:28; 2 Pet 2:4; Jude 1:6; Rev 12:7–9.

See *Satan.*

DENARIUS A Roman coin or a unit of money, paid in any medium, equivalent to a day's wage, Mt 20:2–14; Mk 6:37; Lk 10:35; Jn 6:7; Rev 6:6.

DENS Used as places of refuge, Judg 6:2; Heb 11:37, 38.

DENYING JESUS See *Jesus, Rejected.*

DEPRAVITY OF MAN Gen 6:5. When

the Lord God saw the extent of human wickedness, and that the trend and direction of men's lives were only towards evil, [6]he was sorry he had made them. It broke his heart. [7]And he said, "I will blot out from the face of the earth all mankind that I created. Yes, and the animals too, and the reptiles and the birds. For I am sorry I made them." [8]But Noah was a pleasure to the Lord. [11]Meanwhile, the crime rate was rising rapidly across the earth, and, as seen by God the world was rotten to the core. [12, 13]As God observed how bad it was, and saw that all mankind was vicious and depraved, he said to Noah, "I have decided to destroy all mankind; for the earth is filled with crime because of man. Yes, I will destroy mankind from the earth."

Gen 8:21. And Jehovah was pleased with the sacrifice and said to himself, "I will never do it again—I will never again curse the earth, destroying all living things, even though man's bent is always toward evil from his earliest youth, and even though he does such wicked things."

1 Kgs 14:24. There was homosexuality throughout the land, and the people of Judah became as depraved as the heathen nations which the Lord drove out to make room for his people.

Job 4:17. "Is mere man more just than God? More pure than his Creator?" [18, 19]If God cannot trust his own messengers (for even angels make mistakes), how much less men made of dust, who are crushed to death as easily as moths!

Job 9:2. But how can a man be truly good in the eyes of God? [3]If God decides to argue with him, can a man answer even one question of a thousand he asks? [20]But I? Am I righteous? My own mouth says no. Even if I were perfect, God would prove me wicked. [29]So what's the use of trying? [30]Even if I were to wash myself with purest water and cleanse my hands with lye to make them utterly clean, [31]even so you would plunge me into the ditch and mud; and even my clothing would be less filthy than you consider me to be!

Job 11:12. Mere man is as likely to be wise as a wild donkey's colt is likely to be born a man!

Job 14:4. How can you demand purity in one born impure?

Job 15:14. What man in all the earth can be as pure and righteous as you claim to be? [15]Why, God doesn't even trust the angels! Even the heavens can't be absolutely pure compared with him! [16]How much less someone like you, who is corrupt and sinful, drinking in sin as a sponge soaks up water!

Job 25:4. How can mere man stand before God and claim to be righteous? Who in all the earth can boast that he is clean? [5]God is so glorious that even the moon and stars are less than nothing as compared to him. [6]How much less is man, who is but a worm in his sight?

Job 36:14. They [the godless] die young after lives of dissipation and depravity.

Ps 5:9. For they cannot speak one truthful word. Their hearts are filled to the brim with wickedness. Their suggestions are full of the stench of sin and death. Their tongues are filled with flatteries to gain their wicked ends.

Ps 14:1. That man is a fool who says to himself, "There is no God!" Anyone who talks like that is warped and evil and cannot really be a good person at all. [2]The Lord looks down from heaven on all mankind to see if there are any who are wise, who want to please God. [3]But no, all have strayed away; all are rotten with sin. Not one is good, not one! Ps 53:1–3.

Ps 51:5. But I was born a sinner, yes, from the moment my mother conceived me.

Ps 58:1, 2. Justice? You high and mighty politicians don't even know the meaning of the word! Fairness? Which of you has any left? Not one! All your dealings are crooked: you give "justice" in exchange for bribes. [3]These men are born sinners, lying from their earliest words! [4, 5]They are poisonous as deadly snakes, cobras that close their ears to the most expert of charmers.

Ps 94:11. The Lord is fully aware of how limited and futile the thoughts of mankind are.

Ps 130:3. Lord, if you keep in mind our sins then who can ever get an answer to his prayers?

Ps 143:2. Don't bring me to trial! For as compared with you, no one is perfect.

Prov 10:20. When a good man speaks, he is worth listening to, but the words of fools are a dime a dozen.

Prov 20:6. Most people will tell you what loyal friends they are, but are they telling the truth? [9]Who can ever say, "I have cleansed my heart; I am sinless"?

Prov 21:8. A man is known by his actions. An evil man lives an evil life; a good man lives a godly life.

Eccl 7:20. And there is not a single man in all the earth who is always good and never sins. [29]And I found that though God has made men upright, each has turned away to follow his own downward road. 2 Chron 6:36.

Eccl 8:11. Because God does not punish sinners instantly, people feel it is safe to do wrong.

Eccl 9:3. It seems so unfair, that one fate comes to all. That is why men are not more careful to be good, but instead choose their own mad course, for they have no hope—there is nothing but death ahead anyway.

Isa 1:5, 6. Oh, my people, haven't you had enough of punishment? Why will you force me to whip you again and again? Must you forever rebel? From head to foot you are sick and weak and faint, covered with bruises and welts and infected wounds, unanointed and unbound.

Isa 42:6. I the Lord have called you to demonstrate my righteousness. I will guard and support you, for I have given you to my people as the personal confirmation of my covenant with them. You shall also be a light to guide the nations unto me. [7]You will open the eyes of the blind, and release those who sit in prison darkness and despair.

Isa 43:8. Bring them back to me—blind as they are and deaf when I call (although they see and hear!).

Isa 48:8. Yes, I'll tell you things entirely new, for I know so well what traitors you are, rebels from earliest childhood, rotten through and through.

Isa 51:1. Listen to me, all who hope for deliverance, who seek the Lord! Consider the quarry from which you were mined, the rock from which you were cut!

Isa 53:6. *We* are the ones who strayed away like sheep! *We* who left God's paths to follow our own. Yet God laid on *him* the guilt and sins of every one of us!

Isa 64:6. We are all infected and impure with sin. When we put on our prized robes of righteousness we find they are but filthy rags. Like autumn leaves we fade, wither and fall. And our sins, like the wind, sweep us away.

Jer 2:22. No amount of soap or lye can make you clean. You are stained with guilt that cannot ever be washed away. I see it always before me, the Lord God says. [29]Don't come to me—you are all rebels, says the Lord.

Jer 6:7. She spouts evil like a fountain! Her streets echo with the sounds of violence; her sickness and wounds are ever before me.

Jer 13:23. Can the Ethiopian change the color of his skin? or a leopard take away his spots? Nor can you who are so used to doing evil now start being good.

Jer 16:12. *And you have been worse than your fathers were!* You follow evil to your hearts' content and refuse to listen to me.

Jer 17:9. The heart is the most deceitful thing there is, and desperately wicked. No one can really know how bad it is!

Jer 23:14. But the prophets of Jerusalem are even worse! The things they do are horrible; they commit adultery and love dishonesty. They encourage and compliment those who are doing evil, instead of turning them back from their sins. These prophets are as thoroughly depraved as the men of Sodom and Gomorrah were.

Ezk 16:6. But I came by and saw you there, covered with your own blood, and I said, "Live!" Ezk 37:1–3.

Ezk 36:25. Then it will be as though I had sprinkled clean water on you, for you will be clean—your filthiness will be washed away, your idol worship gone. [26]And I will give you a new heart—I will give you new and right desires—and put a new spirit within you. I will take out your stony hearts of sin and give you new hearts of love.

Hos 6:7. But like Adam, you broke my covenant; you refused my love.

Hos 14:9. Whoever is wise, let him understand these things. Whoever is intelligent, let him listen. For the paths of the Lord are true and right, and good men walk along them. But sinners trying it will fail.

Mic 7:2. The good men have disappeared from the earth; not one fairminded man is left. They are all murderers, turning against even their own brothers. [3]They go at their evil deeds with both hands, and how skilled they are in using them! The governor and judge alike demand bribes. The rich man pays them off and tells them whom to ruin. Justice is twisted between them. [4]Even the best of them are prickly as briars; the straightest is more crooked than a hedge of thorns. But your judgment day is coming swiftly now; your time of punishment is almost here; confusion, destruction, and terror will be yours.

Mt 7:6. Don't give holy things to depraved men. Don't give pearls to swine! They will trample the pearls and turn and attack you.

Mt 12:34. You brood of snakes! How could evil men like you speak what is good and right? For a man's heart determines his speech. [35]A good man's speech reveals the rich treasures within him. An evil-hearted man is filled with venom, and his speech reveals it.

Mt 15:19. For from the heart come evil thoughts, murder, adultery, fornication, theft, lying and slander. Mk 7:21–23.

Lk 1:79. To give light to those who sit in darkness and death's shadow, and to guide us to the path of peace.

Lk 6:45. A good man produces good deeds from a good heart. And an evil man produces evil deeds from his hidden wickedness.

Jn 1:10. But although he made the world, the world didn't recognize him when he came. [11]Even in his own land and among his own people, the Jews, he was not accepted. Only a few would welcome and receive him.

Jn 3:19. Their sentence is based on this fact: that the Light from heaven came into the world, but they loved the darkness more than the Light, for their deeds were evil.

Jn 8:23. Then he said to them, "You are from below; I am from above. You are of this world; I am not."

Jn 14:17. He is the Holy Spirit, the Spirit who leads into all truth. The world at large cannot receive him, for it isn't looking for him and doesn't recognize him. But you do, for he lives with you now and some day shall be in you.

Acts 8:23. For I can see that there is jealousy and sin in your heart.

Rom 2:1. "Well," you may be saying, "what terrible people you have been talking about!" But wait a minute! You are just as bad. When you say they are wicked and should be punished, you are talking about yourselves, for you do these very same things."

Rom 3:9. Well, then, are we Jews *better* than others? No, not at all, for we have already shown that all men alike are sinners, whether Jews or Gentiles. [10]As the Scriptures say, "No one is good —no one in all the world is innocent." [11]No one has ever really followed God's paths, or even truly wanted to. [12]Every one has turned away; all have gone wrong. No one anywhere has kept on doing what is right; not one. [13]Their talk is foul and filthy like the stench from an open grave. Their tongues are loaded with lies. Everything they say has in it the sting and poison of deadly snakes. [14]Their mouths are full of cursing and bitterness. [15]They are quick to kill, hating anyone who disagrees with them. [16]Wherever they go they leave misery and trouble behind them, [17]and they have never known what it is to feel secure or enjoy God's blessing. [18]They care nothing about God nor what he thinks of them. [19]So the judgment of God lies very heavily upon the Jews, for they are responsible to keep God's laws instead of doing all these evil things; not one of them has any excuse; in fact, all the world stands hushed and guilty before Almighty God. [23]Yes, all have sinned; all fall short of God's glorious ideal.

Rom 5:6. When we were utterly helpless with no way of escape, Christ came at just the right time and died for us sinners who had no use for him.

12. When Adam sinned, sin entered the entire human race. His sin spread death throughout all the world, so everything began to grow old and die, for all sinned. [13](We know that it was Adam's sin that caused this) because although, of course, people were sinning from the time of Adam until Moses, God did not in those days judge them guilty of death for breaking his laws—because he had not yet given his laws to them, nor told them what he wanted them to do. [14]So when their bodies died it was not for their own sins since they themselves had never disobeyed God's special law against eating the forbidden fruit, as Adam had.

Rom 6:6. Your old evil desires were nailed to the cross with him; that part of you that loves to sin was crushed and fatally wounded, so that your sin-loving body is no longer under sin's control, no longer needs to be a slave to sin. [19]Just as you used to be slaves to all kinds of sin, so now you must let yourselves be slaves to all that is right and holy. [20]In those days when you were slaves of sin you didn't bother much with goodness. *v.* 17.

Rom 7:5. When your old nature was still active, sinful desires were at work within you, making you want to do whatever God said not to, and producing sinful deeds, the rotting fruit of death. [11]Sin fooled me by taking the good laws of God and using them to make me guilty of death. [13]It was sin, devilish stuff that it is, that used what was good to bring about my condemnation. So you can see how cunning and deadly and damnable it is. For it uses God's good laws for its own evil purposes. [14]I am sold unto slavery with Sin as my owner. [15]I don't understand myself at all, for I really want to do what is right, but I can't. I do what I don't want to—what I hate. [18]I know I am rotten through and through so far as my old sinful nature is concerned. No matter which way I turn I can't make myself do right. I want to but I can't. [19]When I want to do good, I don't; and when I try not to do wrong, I do it anyway. [20]Now if I am doing what I don't want to, it is plain where the trouble is: sin still has me in its evil grasp. [21]It seems to be a fact of life that when I want to do what is right, I inevitably do what is wrong. [23-25]But there is something else deep within me, in my lower nature, that is at war with my mind and wins the fight and makes me a slave to the sin that is still within me. In my mind I want to be God's willing servant but instead I find myself still enslaved to sin. So you see how it is: my new life tells me to do right, but the old nature that is still inside me loves to sin. Oh, what a terrible predicament I'm in! Who will free me from my slavery to this deadly lower nature? Thank God! It has been done by Jesus Christ our Lord. He has set me free.

Rom 8:5. Those who let themselves be controlled by their lower natures live only to please themselves. . . . [6]Following after the old nature leads to death, [7]because the old sinful nature within us is against God. It never did obey God's laws and it never will. [8]That's why those who are still under the control of their old sinful selves, bent on following their old evil desires, can never please God. [13]For if you keep on following it you are lost and will perish, but if through the power of the Holy Spirit you crush it and its evil deeds, you shall live.

Rom 11:32. For God has given them all up to sin so that he could have mercy upon all alike.

1 Cor 2:14. But the man who isn't a Christian can't understand and can't accept these thoughts from God, which the Holy Spirit teaches us. They sound foolish to him, because only those who have the Holy Spirit within them can understand what the Holy Spirit means. Others just can't take it in.

1 Cor 3:3. For you are still only baby Christians, controlled by your own desires, not God's. When you are jealous of one another and divide up into quarreling groups, doesn't that prove you are still babies, wanting your own way? In fact, you are acting like people who don't belong to the Lord at all.

1 Cor 5:9. When I wrote to you before I said not to mix with evil people. [10]But when I said that I wasn't talking about unbelievers who live in sexual sin, or are greedy cheats and thieves and idol worshipers. For you can't live in this world without being with people like that.

2 Cor 3:4. We dare to say these good things about ourselves only because of our great trust in God through Christ, that he will help us to be true to what we say, [5]and not because we think we can do anything of lasting value by ourselves. Our only power and success comes from God.

2 Cor 5:14. Since we believe that Christ died for all of us, we should also believe that we have died to the old life we used to live.

Gal 3:10. Yes, and those who depend on the Jewish laws to save them are under God's curse. . . . [11]Consequently, it is clear that no one can ever win God's favor by trying to keep the Jewish laws. [22]For the Scriptures insist we are all its [sin's] prisoners.

Gal 5:17. For we naturally love to do evil things that are just the opposite from the things that the Holy Spirit tells us to do; and the good things we want to do when the Spirit has his way with us are just the opposite of our natural desires. [19]But when you follow your own wrong inclinations your lives will produce these evil results: impure thoughts, eagerness for lustful pleasure, [20]idolatry, spiritism (that is, encouraging the activity of demons), hatred and fighting, jealousy and anger, constant effort to get the best for yourself, complaints and criticisms, the feeling that everyone else is wrong except those in your own little group—and there will be wrong doctrine, [21]envy, murder, drunkenness, wild parties, and all that sort of thing.

Eph 2:1. Once you were under God's curse, doomed forever for your sins. [2]You went along with the crowd and were just like all the others, full of sin, obeying Satan, the mighty prince of the power of the air, who is at work right now in the hearts of those who are against the Lord. [3]All of us used to be just as they are, our lives expressing the evil within us, doing every wicked thing that our passions or our evil thoughts might lead us into. We started out bad, being born with evil natures, and were under God's anger just like everyone else. [12]Remember that in those days you were living utterly apart from Christ; you were enemies of God's children and he had promised you no help. You were lost, without God, without hope. *v.* 11.

Eph 4:17, 18. Let me say this, then, speaking for the Lord: Live no longer as the unsaved do, for they are blinded and confused. Their closed hearts are full of darkness; they are far away from the life of God because they have shut their minds against him, and they cannot understand his ways. [19]They don't care anymore about right and wrong and have given themselves over to impure ways. They stop at nothing, being driven by their evil minds and reckless lusts. [22]Then throw off your old evil nature—the old you that was a partner in your evil ways—rotten through and through, full of lust and sham.

Eph 5:8. For though once your heart was full of darkness, now it is full of light from the Lord. [14]Awake, O sleeper, and rise up from the dead.

Col 1:13. For he has rescued us out of the darkness and gloom of Satan's kingdom. [21]This includes you who were once so far away from God. You were his enemies and hated him and were separated from him by your evil thoughts and actions.

Col 2:13. You were dead in sins, and your sinful desires were not yet cut away. Then he gave you a share in the very life of Christ, for he forgave all your sins.

Col 3:5. Away then with sinful, earthly things; deaden the evil desires lurking within you; have nothing to do with sexual sin, impurity, lust and shameful desires; don't worship the good things of life, for that is idolatry. [7]You used to do them when your life was still part of this world.

2 Tim 2:26. Then they will come to their senses and escape from Satan's trap of slavery to sin.

Tit 3:3. Once we, too, were foolish and disobedient; we were misled by others and became slaves to many evil pleasures and wicked desires. Our lives were full of resentment and envy. We hated others and they hated us.

Jas 3:2. For we all make many mistakes.

1 Pet 1:18. God paid a ransom to save you from the impossible road to heaven which your fathers tried to take, and the ransom he paid was not mere gold or silver, as you very well know.

1 Pet 2:9. So that you may show to others how God called you out of the darkness into his wonderful light. [25]Like sheep you wandered away from God.

1 Jn 1:8. If we say that we have no sin, we are only fooling ourselves, and refusing to accept the truth. [10]If we claim we have not sinned, we are lying and calling God a liar, *for he says we have sinned.*

1 Jn 2:16. For all these worldly things, these evil desires—the craze for sex, the ambition to buy everything that appeals to you, and the pride that comes from wealth and importance—these are not from God. They are from this evil world itself.

1 Jn 3:10. So now we can tell who is a child of God and who belongs to Satan. Whoever is living a life of sin and doesn't love his brother shows that he is not in God's family.

1 Jn 5:19. All the rest of the world around us is under Satan's power and control.

Rev 3:17. You say, "I am rich, with everything I want; I don't need a thing!" And you don't realize that spiritually you are wretched and miserable and poor and blind and naked.

See *Fall of Man; Sin.*

DEPUTY An officer who administers the functions of a superior in his absence, 1 Kgs 22:47; Jer 25:8, 9; 27:6.

DERBE A city of Lycaonia. Paul flees to, Acts 14:5, 6, 20. Visited by Paul and Silas, Acts 16:1. Gaius born in, Acts 20:4.

DERISION The wicked held in, by God, Ps 2:4; Prov 1:26.

INSTANCES OF. Sarah, when the angels gave her the promise of a child, Gen 18:12. The evil children of Bethel deride Elisha, 2 Kgs 2:23. The people of Israel scoff at Hezekiah, 2 Chron 30:1–10.

See *Irony; Sarcasm; Scoffing.*

DESERT An arid region bearing only a sparse vegetation, Lev 16:22; Deut 8:15; Jer 2:2, 6; 17:6. Dangers in, 2 Cor 11:26.

FIGURATIVE. Isa 35:1.

DESIGN In nature, evidence of, Job 12:7–11; Prov 16:4.

DESIRE SPIRITUAL. Ps 17:1. I am pleading for your help, O Lord; for I have been honest and have done what is right, and you must listen to my earnest cry!

Ps 22:26. All who seek the Lord shall find him and shall praise his name. Their hearts shall rejoice with everlasting joy.

Ps 24:6. These are the ones who are allowed to stand before the Lord and worship the God of Jacob.

Ps 25:5. You are the God who gives me salvation. I have no hope except in you. [15]My eyes are ever looking to the Lord for help, for he alone can rescue me.

Ps 27:8. My heart has heard you say, "Come and talk with me, O my people." And my heart responds, "Lord I am coming." [14]Don't be impatient. Wait for the Lord, and he will come and save you!

Be brave, stouthearted and courageous. Yes, wait and he will help you.

Ps 33:20. We depend upon the Lord alone to save us. Only he can help us; he protects us like a shield.

Ps 34:10. Those of us who reverence the Lord will never lack any good thing.

Ps 37:4. Be delighted with the Lord. Then he will give you all your heart's desires. [7]Rest in the Lord; wait patiently for him to act. [9]But those who trust the Lord shall be given every blessing. [34]Don't be impatient for the Lord to act! Keep traveling steadily along his pathway and in due season he will honor you with every blessing.

Ps 39:12. Hear my prayer, O Lord; listen to my cry! Don't sit back, unmindful of my tears. For I am your guest. I am a traveler passing through the earth, as all my fathers were.

Ps 40:1. I waited patiently for God to help me. [8]And I delight to do your will, my God, for your law is written upon my heart!

Ps 42:1. As the deer pants for water, so I long for you, O God. [2]I thirst for God, the living God. Where can I find him to come and stand before him? [3]Day and night I weep for his help, and all the while my enemies taunt me. "Where is this God of yours?" [4, 5]Take courage, my soul! Do you remember those times (but how could you ever forget them!) when you led a great procession to the Temple on festival days, singing with joy, praising the Lord? Why then be downcast? Why be discouraged and sad? Hope in God! I shall yet praise him again. Yes, I shall again praise him for his help. [6]Yet I am standing here depressed and gloomy, but I will meditate upon your kindness to this lovely land where the Jordan River flows and where Mount Hermon and Mount Mizar stand. [7]All your waves and billows have gone over me, and floods of sorrow pour upon me like a thundering cataract. [8]Yet day by day the Lord also pours out his steadfast love upon me, and through the night I sing his songs and pray to God who gives me life. [9]"O God my Rock," I cry, "why have you forsaken me? Why must I suffer these attacks from my enemies?" [10]Their taunts pierce me like a fatal wound; again and again they scoff, "Where is that God of yours?" [11]But O my soul, don't be discouraged. Don't be upset. Expect God to act! For I know that I shall again have plenty of reason to praise him for all that he will do. He is my help! He is my God!

Ps 51:1. O loving and kind God, have mercy. Have pity upon me and take away the awful stain of my transgressions. [2]Oh, wash me, cleanse me from this guilt. Let me be pure again. [3]For I admit my shameful deed—it haunts me day and night. [4]It is against you and you alone I sinned, and did this terrible thing. You saw it all, and your sentence against me is just. [5]But I was born a sinner, yes, from the moment my mother conceived me. [6]You deserve honesty from the heart; yes, utter sincerity and truthfulness. Oh, give me this wisdom. [7]Sprinkle me with the cleansing blood and I shall be clean again. Wash me and I shall be whiter than snow. [8]And after you have punished me, give me back my joy again. [9]Don't keep looking at my sins—erase them from your sight. [10]Create in me a new, clean heart, O God, filled with clean thoughts and right desires. [11]Don't toss me aside, banished forever from your presence. Don't take your Holy Spirit from me. [12]Restore to me again the joy of your salvation, and make me willing to obey you. [13]Then I will teach your ways to other sinners, and they —guilty like me—will repent and return to you. [14, 15]Don't sentence me to death. O my God, you alone can rescue me. Then I will sing of your forgiveness, for my lips will be unsealed—oh, how I will praise you. [16]You don't want penance; if you did, how gladly I would do it! You aren't interested in offerings burned before you on the altar. [17]It is a broken spirit you want—remorse and penitence. A broken and a contrite heart, O God, you will not ignore.

Ps 62:1. I stand silently before the Lord, waiting for him to rescue me. For salvation comes from him alone.

Ps 63:1. O God, my God! How I search for you! How I thirst for you in this parched and weary land where there is no water. How I long to find you! [8]I follow close behind you, protected by your strong right arm.

Ps 68:28. Summon your might; display your strength, O God, for you have done such mighty things for us.

Ps 69:3. My eyes are swollen with weeping, waiting for my God to act. [32]All who seek for God shall live in joy.

Ps 70:4. But fill the followers of God with joy. Let those who love your salvation exclaim, "What a wonderful God he is!"

Ps 81:10. For it was I, Jehovah your God, who brought you out of the land of Egypt. Only test me! Open your mouth wide and see if I won't fill it. You will receive every blessing you can use!

Ps 84:2. I long, yes, faint with longing to be able to enter your courtyard and come near to the Living God.

Ps 86:11. Tell me where you want me to go and I will go there. May every fiber of my being unite in reverence to your name. [12]With all my heart I will praise you. I will give glory to your name forever. [16]So look down in pity and grant strength to your servant and save me. Ps 9:1.

Ps 94:19. Lord, when doubts fill my mind, when my heart is in turmoil, quiet me and give me renewed hope and cheer.

Ps 105:4. Search for him and for his strength, and keep on searching!

Ps 118:17. I shall not die, but live to tell of all his deeds.

Ps 119:2. Happy are all who search for God, and always do his will. [10]I have tried my best to find you —don't let me wander off from your instructions. [20]I long for your instructions more than I can tell. (v. 19.) [40]I long to obey them! Therefore in fairness renew my life. [77]Surround me with your tender mercies, that I may live. For your law is my delight. [88]In your kindness, spare my life; then I can continue to obey you. [116]Lord, you promised to let me live! Never let it be said that God failed me. [117]Hold me safe above the heads of all my enemies; then I can continue to obey your laws. [122]Commit yourself to bless me! [133]Guide me with your laws so that I will not be overcome by evil. [149]Because you are so loving and kind, listen to me and make me well again. [156]Lord, how great is your mercy; oh, give me back my life again. *vs.* 107, 154, 159.

Ps 123:1. O God enthroned in heaven, I lift my eyes to you. [2]We look to Jehovah our God for his mercy and kindness just as a servant keeps his eyes upon his master or a slave girl watches her mistress for the slightest signal.

Ps 130:5. That is why I wait expectantly, trusting God to help, for he has promised. [6]I long for him more than sentinels long for the dawn.

Ps 143:5. I remember the glorious miracles you did in days of long ago. [6]I reach out for you. I thirst for you as parched land thirsts for rain.

Prov 2:3–5. Yes, if you want better insight and discernment, and are searching for them as you would for lost money or hidden treasure, then wisdom will be given you, and knowledge of God himself; you will soon learn the importance of reverence for the Lord and of trusting him.

Prov 8:17. I love all who love me. Those who search for me shall surely find me. [34]Happy is the man who is so anxious to be with me that he watches for me daily at my gates, or waits for me outside my home!

Isa 8:17. I will wait for the Lord to help us, though he is hiding now. My only hope is in him. [19]Why not ask your God?

Isa 26:8. O Lord, we love to do your will! Our hearts' desire is to glorify your name. [9]All night long I search for you; earnestly I seek for God.

Isa 40:31. But they that wait upon the Lord shall renew their strength. They shall mount up with wings like eagles.

Isa 55:1. Say there! is anyone thirsty? Come and drink—even if you have no money! Come, take your choice of wine and milk—it's all free! [2]Why spend your money on foodstuffs that don't give you strength? Why pay for groceries that don't do you any good? Listen and I'll tell you where to get good food that fattens up the soul! [6]Seek the Lord while you can find him. Call upon him now while he is near.

Jer 29:13. You will find me when you seek me, if you look for me in earnest. Deut 4:29.

Lam 3:25. The Lord is wonderfully good to those who wait for him, to those who seek for him. [26]It is good both to hope and wait quietly for the salvation of the Lord. [41]Let us lift our hearts and hands to him in heaven.

Hos 10:12. Plant the good seeds of righteousness and you will reap a crop of my love; plow the hard ground of your hearts, for now is the time to seek the Lord, that he may come and shower salvation upon you.

Hab 3:2. In this time of our deep need, begin again to help us, as you did in years gone by. Show us your power to save us. In your wrath, remember mercy.

Mt 5:6. Happy are those who long to be just and good, for they shall be completely satisfied. Lk 6:21.

Lk 10:42. There is really only one thing worth being concerned about. Mary has discovered it—and I won't take it away from her!

Jn 12:20. Some Greeks who had come to Jerusalem . . . [21]paid a visit to Philip, . . . and said, "Sir, we want to meet Jesus."

Phil 3:12. I don't mean to say I am perfect. I haven't learned all I should even yet, but I keep working toward that day when I will finally be all that Christ saved me for and wants me to be. [13]No, dear brothers, I am still not all I should be but I am bringing all my energies to bear on this one thing: Forgetting the past and looking forward to what lies ahead, [14]I strain to reach the end of the race and receive the prize for which God is calling us up to heaven because of what Christ Jesus did for us.

Heb 11:6. Anyone who wants to come to God must believe that there is a God and that he rewards those who sincerely look for him.

See *Hunger, Spiritual; Thirst, Figurative.*

EVIL. See *Covetousness; Imagination; Lust.*

DESPAIR See *Despondency.*

DESPONDENCY Num 17:12, 13. But the people of Israel only grumbled the more. "We are as good as dead," they whined. "Everyone who even comes close to the Tabernacle dies. Must we all perish?"

Deut 28:65. There among those nations you shall find no rest, but the Lord will give you trembling hearts, darkness, and bodies wasted from sorrow and fear. [66]Your lives will hang in doubt. You will live night and day in fear, and will have no reason to believe that you will see the morning light. [67]In the morning you will say, "Oh, that night were here!" And in the evening you will say, "Oh, that morning were here!" You will say this because of the awesome horrors surrounding you.

Job 3:1. At last Job spoke, and cursed the day of his birth. [2, 3]"Let the day of my birth be cursed," he said, "and the night when I was conceived. [4]Let that day be forever forgotten. Let it be lost even to God, shrouded in eternal darkness. [5]Yes, let the darkness claim it for its own, and may a black cloud overshadow it. [6]May it be blotted off the calendar, never again to be counted among the days of the month of that year. [7]Let that night be bleak and joyless. [8]Let those who are experts at cursing curse it. [9]Let the stars of the night disappear. Let it long for light, but never see it, never see the morning light. [10]Curse it for its failure to shut my mother's womb, for letting me be born to come to all this trouble. [11]Why didn't I die at birth? [12]Why did the midwife let me live? Why did she nurse me at her breasts? [13]For if only I had died at birth, then I would be quiet now, asleep and at rest, 14, 15along with prime ministers and kings with all their pomp, and wealthy princes whose castles are full of rich treasures. 16Oh, to have been stillborn! —to have never breathed or seen the light. 17For there in death the wicked cease from troubling, and there the weary are at rest. 18There even prisoners are at ease, with no brutal jailer to curse them. 19Both rich and poor alike are there, and the slave is free at last from his master. 20, 21Oh, why should light and life be given to those in misery and bitterness, who long for death, and it won't come; who search for death as others search for food or money? 22What blessed relief when at last they die! 23Why is a man allowed to be born if God is only going to give him a hopeless life of uselessness and frustration? 24I cannot eat for sighing; my groans pour out like water. 25What I always feared has happened to me. 26I was not fat and lazy, yet trouble struck me down."

Job 17:13, 14. If I die, I go out into darkness, and call the grave my father, and the worm my mother and my sister. 15Where then is my hope? Can anyone find any? 16No, my hope will go down with me to the grave. We shall rest together in the dust!

Ps 31:22. I spoke too hastily when I said, "The Lord has deserted me," for you listened to my plea and answered me.

Ps 77:7. Has the Lord rejected me forever? Will he never again be favorable? 8Is his lovingkindness gone forever? Has his promise failed? 9Has he forgotten to be kind to one so undeserving? Has he slammed the door in anger on his love?

Prov 13:12. Hope deferred makes the heart sick; but when dreams come true at last, there is life and joy.

Isa 2:19. When the Lord stands up from his throne to shake up the earth, his enemies will crawl with fear into the holes in the rocks and into the caves because of the glory of his majesty.

Jer 2:25. Don't waste your breath. I've fallen in love with these strangers and I can't stop loving them now!

Jer 8:20. The harvest is finished; the summer is over and we are not saved.

Lam 3:1. I am the man who has seen the afflictions that come from the rod of God's wrath. 2He has brought me into deepest darkness, shutting out all light. 3He has turned against me. Day and night his hand is heavy on me. 4He has made me old and has broken my bones. 5He has built forts against me and surrounded me with anguish and distress. 6He buried me in dark places, like those long dead. 7He has walled me in; I cannot escape; he has fastened me with heavy chains. 8And though I cry and shout, he will not hear my prayers! 9He has shut me into a place of high, smooth walls; he has filled my path with detours. 10He lurks like a bear, like a lion, waiting to attack me, 11He has dragged me into the underbrush and torn me with his claws, and left me bleeding and desolate. 12He has bent his bow and aimed it squarely at me, 13and sent his arrows deep within my heart. 14My own people laugh at me; all day long they sing their ribald songs. 15He has filled me with bitterness, and given me a cup of deepest sorrows to drink. 16He has made me eat gravel and broken my teeth; he has rolled me in ashes and dirt. 17O Lord, all peace and all prosperity have long since gone, for you have taken them away. I have forgotten what enjoyment is. 18All hope is gone; my strength has turned to water, for the Lord has left me. 19Oh, remember the bitterness and suffering you have dealt to me! 20For I can never forget these awful years; always my soul will live in utter shame. 21*Yet there is one ray of hope.*

Lam 5:22. Or have you utterly rejected us? Are you angry with us still?

Hos 10:8. And the idol altars of Aven at Bethel where Israel sinned will crumble. Thorns and thistles will grow up to surround them. And the people will cry to the mountains and hills to fall upon them and crush them.

Jon 2:2. In my great trouble I cried to the Lord and he answered me; from the depths of death I called, and Lord, you heard me! 3You threw me into the ocean depths; I sank down into the floods of waters and was covered by your wild and stormy waves. 4Then I said, "O Lord, you have rejected me and cast me away. How shall I ever again see your holy Temple?"

Mic 7:1, 2. Woe is me! It is as hard to find an honest man as grapes and figs when harvest days are over. Not a cluster to eat, not a single early fig, however much I long for it! The good men have disappeared from the earth; not one fair-minded man is left. They are all murderers, turning against even their own brothers. 3They go at their evil deeds with both hands, and how skilled they are in using them! The governor and judge alike demand bribes. The rich man pays them off and tells them whom to ruin. Justice is twisted between them. 4Even the best of them are prickly as briars; the straightest is more crooked than a hedge of thorns. But your judgment day is coming swiftly now; your time of punishment is almost here; confusion, destruction, and terror will be yours. 5Don't trust anyone, not your best friend—not even your wife! 6For the son despises his father; the daughter defies her mother; the bride curses her mother-in-law. Yes, a man's enemies will be found in his own home. 7As for me, I look to the Lord for his help; I wait for God to save me; he will hear me.

Mt 24:30. And then at last the signal of my coming will appear in the heavens and there will be deep mourning all around the earth. And the nations of the world will see me arrive in the clouds of heaven, with power and great glory.

Lk 13:27. And he will reply, "I tell you, I don't know you. You can't come in here, guilty as you are. Go away." 28And there will be great weeping and gnashing of teeth as you stand outside and see Abraham, Isaac, Jacob, and all the prophets within the Kingdom of God.

Lk 23:29. For the days are coming when the women who have no children will be counted fortunate indeed. [30]Mankind will beg the mountains to fall on them and crush them, and the hills to bury them.

Rev 6:14. And the starry heavens disappeared as though rolled up like a scroll and taken away; and every mountain and island shook and shifted. [15]The kings of the earth, and world leaders and rich men, and high-ranking military officers, and all men great and small, slave and free, hid themselves in the caves and rocks of the mountains, [16]and cried to the mountains to crush them. "Fall on us," they pleaded, "and hide us from the face of the one sitting on the throne, and from the anger of the Lamb, [17]because the great day of their anger has come, and who can survive it?"

Rev 9:5. They were not to kill them, but to torture them for five months with agony like the pain of scorpion stings. [6]In those days men will try to kill themselves but won't be able to—death will not come. They will long to die—but death will flee away!

See *Afflictions; Resignation; Sorrow; Suffering.*

INSTANCES OF. Cain, when God pronounced judgment on him for the murder of Abel, Gen 4: 13, 14. Hagar, when banished from the household of Abraham on account of the jealousy of Sarah, Gen 21:15, 16. Moses, when sent on his mission to the Israelites, Ex 4:1, 10, 13; 6:12; at the Red Sea, Ex 14:15; when the people wanted meat, Num 11:15. The Israelites, on account of the cruel oppressions of the Egyptians, Ex 6:8, 9. Elijah, when he fled from Jezebel to the wilderness and sat under the broom bush, and wished to die, 1 Kgs 19:4. Jonah, after he had preached to the Ninevites, Jon 4:3, 8. The sailors with Paul, Acts 27:20.

Job, see the above extracts from the Book of Job. Jeremiah, see the above extracts from the Lamentations of Jeremiah.

COMFORT IN. Isa 35:3. With this news bring cheer to all discouraged ones. [4]Encourage those who are afraid. Tell them, "Be strong, fear not, for your God is coming to destroy your enemies. He is coming to save you."

Lk 18:1. One day Jesus told his disciples a story to illustrate their need for constant prayer and to show them that they must keep praying until the answer comes. [2]"There was a city judge," he said, "a very godless man who had great contempt for everyone. [3]A widow of that city came to him frequently to appeal for justice against a man who had harmed her. [4, 5]The judge ignored her for a while, but eventually she got on his nerves. 'I fear neither God nor man,' he said to himself, 'but this woman bothers me. I'm going to see that she gets justice, for she is wearing me out with her constant coming!" [6]Then the Lord said, "If even an evil judge can be worn down like that, [7]don't you think that God will surely give justice to his people who plead with him day and night? [8]Yes! He will answer them quickly! But the question is: When I, the Messiah, return, how many will I find who have faith (and are praying)?"

Heb 12:12. So take a new grip with your tired hands, stand firm on your shaky legs, [13]and mark out a straight, smooth path for your feet so that those who follow you, though weak and lame, will not fall and hurt themselves, but become strong.

See *Afflictions, Consolation in; Righteous, Promises to.*

DESPOTISM See *Government, Monarchical, Tyranny in.*

DESTRUCTION FIGURATIVE. Mountain of, 2 Kgs 23:13.

See *Corruption.*

DETECTIVES Lk 20:20.

See *Spies.*

DEUEL Called also *Reuel.* Father of the captain of the tribe of Gad, Num 1:2–15; 2:3–31; 7: 42–47; 10:20.

DEVIL See *Demons; Satan.*

DEVOTION TO GOD. See *Religion.* For conspicuous instances of, let the student study *Enoch, Noah, Abraham, Moses, David's later history, Solomon's earlier life, Josiah, Asa, Isaiah, Elijah, Jeremiah, Daniel, Shadrach, Meshach and Abednego.*

TO JESUS. See *Peter; John; Paul; Mary Magdalene.*

For elaborated topics covering the subject, see *Love, of Man for God; Consecration; Zeal.*

DEW A merciful providence, Hos 2:21, 22. Forms in the night, Job 29:19. Called the dew of heaven, Dan 4:15. Absence of, 1 Kgs 17:1. Miraculous profusion and absence of, Judg 6:36–40.

See *Meterology.*

FIGURATIVE. Deut 32:2; Ps 110:3; 133:3; Prov 19:12; Isa 26:19; Hos 6:4; 13:3; 14:5; Mic 5:7.

DIADEM Isa 28:5.

DIAL A contrivance for indicating time by the sun's rays, 2 Kgs 20:11; Isa 38:8.

DIAMOND Jer 17:1; Ezk 28:13. One of the jewels in the chestpiece, Ex 28:18; 39:11.

DIANA Goddess of the Ephesians, Acts 19: 24–35.

DIBLAIM Father of Gomer, Hosea's wife, Hos 1:3.

DIBON 1. Called also *Dibon-gad.* A city on the northern banks of the Arnon, Num 21:27–30. Israelites camp at, Num 33:45. Allotted to Gad and Reuben, Num 32:3, 4, 34–36; Josh 13:9, 17. Taken by Moab, Isa 15:2, 9; Jer 48:18, 22.

2. A city in the tribe of Judah, Neh 11:25–30; probably identical with *Dimonah,* Josh 15:21–32.

DIBRI Father of Shelomith, Lev 24:11.

DICE See *Lots, Lottery.*

DIKLAH Son of Joktan, and name of a district inhabited by his descendants, Gen 10:26–30; 1 Chron 1:20–23.

DILEAN A city of Judah, Josh 15:37–44.

DILIGENCE Jesus an example of, Mk 1:35; Lk 2:49.

Required by God in seeking him, Heb 11:6; obeying him, Deut 6:17; 11:13; 1 Chron 22:19; listening to him, Isa 55:2; striving after perfection, Phil 3:13, 14; cultivating Christian graces, 2 Pet 1:5; remembering his miracles, Deut 4:9; guarding the affections,

Prov 4:23; labors of love, Heb 6:10–12; doing good works, 1 Tim 3:10; guarding against bitterness, Heb 12:15; seeking to be found sinless, 2 Pet 3:14; making our calling sure, 2 Pet 1:10; self-examination, Ps 77:6; lawful business, Prov 27:23, 24; Eccl 9:10; teaching religion, Rom 12:8; 2 Tim 4:2; Jude 1:3; instructing children, Deut 6:7; 11:19; discharging official duties, Deut 19:18; believers should be filled with, 2 Cor 8:7.

Required in the service of God, Jn 9:4; Gal 6:9. Is not wasted, 1 Cor 15:58. Preserves from disease, Ex 15:26. Leads to reward, Heb 6:11. God rewards, Deut 11:14; Heb 11:6.

In temporal matters leads to favor, Prov 11:27; prosperity, Prov 10:4; 13:4; 21:5; honor, Prov 12:24; 22:29.

FIGURATIVE. Prov 6:6–8.

EXEMPLIFIED. Ruth, Ruth 2:17. Hezekiah, 2 Chron 31:21. Nehemiah and his helpers, Neh 4:6. Psalmist, Ps 119:59, 60. Apostles, Acts 5:42. Apollos, Acts 18:25, 26. Titus, 2 Cor 8:22. Paul, 1 Thess 2:9. Onesiphorus, 2 Tim 1:17.

See *Industry; Zeal; Idleness; Laziness.*

DILL Isa 28:27.

DIMNAH A Levitical city of Zebulun, Josh 21:34, 35.

DIMONAH See *Dibon, 2.*

DINAH Daughter of Jacob and Leah, Gen 30:21. Rape of, Gen 34.

DINHABAH A city of Edom, Gen 36:31–39; 1 Chron 1:43.

DINNER Eaten at noon, Gen 43:16.

See *Feasts.*

DIONYSIUS A convert of Paul, Acts 17:34.

DIOTREPHES A false teacher, 3 Jn 1:9.

DIPLOMACY 1 Cor 9:20. When I am with the Jews I seem as one of them so that they will listen to the Gospel and I can win them to Christ. When I am with Gentiles who follow Jewish customs and ceremonies I don't argue, even though I don't agree, because I want to help them. [21]When with the heathen I agree with them as much as I can, except of course that I must always do what is right as a Christian. And so, by agreeing, I can win their confidence and help them too. [22]When I am with those whose consciences bother them easily, I don't act as though I know it all and don't say they are foolish; the result is that they are willing to let me help them. Yes, whatever a person is like, I try to find common ground with him so that he will let me tell him about Christ and let Christ save him. [23]I do this to get the Gospel to them and also for the blessing I myself receive when I see them come to Christ.

See *Statesmanship; Tact.*

INSTANCES OF. Of Abimelech, Gen 21:22, 23; 26:26–31. The Gibeonites, in securing a treaty with the Israelites through deception, Josh 9:3–16. Of Jephthah, with the king of Moab, unsuccessful, Judg 11:12–28. Of Abigail, 1 Sam 25:23–31. Of Hiram, to secure the good will of David, 2 Sam 5:11. Of Toi, to promote the friendship of David, 2 Sam 8:10. David, in sending Hushai to Absalom's court, 2 Sam 15:32–37; 16:15–19; 17:1–14. The wise woman of Abel, 2 Sam 20:16–22. Absalom winning the people, 2 Sam 15:2–6. Solomon, in his alliance with Hiram, 1 Kgs 5:1–12; 9:10–14, 26–28; 10:11; by intermarriage with other nations, 1 Kgs 1:1–5. Ambassadors from Ben-hadad to Ahab, 1 Kgs 20:31–34. Jehoash purchases peace from Hazael, 2 Kgs 12:18. Ahaz purchases aid from the king of Assyria, 2 Kgs 16:7–9. Assyrian general, in trying to induce Jerusalem to capitulate, 2 Kgs 18:17–37; 19:1–13; Isa 36:11–22. Sanballat, in an attempt to prevent the rebuilding of Jerusalem by Nehemiah, Neh 6.

The people of Tyre and Sidon, in securing the favor of Herod, Acts 12:20–22. Paul, in arraying the Pharisees and Sadducees against each other at his trial, Acts 23:6–10.

Ecclesiastical: Paul, in circumcising Timothy, Acts 16:3; in performing certain temple services to placate the Jews, Acts 21:20–25, with Gal 6:12.

Corrupt practices in: The officers of Nebuchadnezzar's court to secure the destruction of Daniel, Dan 6:4–15.

DISBELIEF See *Unbelief.*

DISC An agricultural implement, 1 Sam 13:21.

DISCIPLE A name given to the followers of any teacher. Of John the Baptist, Mt 9:14; 11:2; Jn 1:37; Acts 19:3. Of Jesus, Mt 10:1; 20:17; Acts 9:26; 14:20; 2:41. (The select group of 12 disciples are also called apostles after Jesus' death. See *Apostles.*) The seventy sent out, Lk 10:1. First called Christians at Antioch, Acts 11:26.

See *Righteous.*

DISCIPLESHIP Tests of, Mt 10:32–39; Lk 14:26, 27, 33; Jn 21:15–19.

See *Commandments.*

DISCIPLINE Of armies, for disobedience of orders, Josh 7:10–26; Judg 21:5–12.

See *Armies.*

CHURCH DISCIPLINE. See *Church, Visible.*

DISCOURAGEMENT See *Despondency.*

DISEASE Sent from God, Lev 14:33, 34. As judgments, Ps 107:17; Isa 3:17.

Instances of. Upon the Egyptians, see *Plague;* upon Nabal, 1 Sam 25:37, 38; David's child, 2 Sam 12:15; Gehazi, 2 Kgs 5:27; Jeroboam, 2 Chron 13:20; Jehoram, 2 Chron 21:12–19; Uzziah, 2 Chron 26:17–20.

Threatened as judgments, Lev 26:16; Deut 7:15; 28:22, 27, 28, 35; 29:22.

Healing of, from God, Ex 15:26; 23:25; Deut 7:15; 2 Chron 16:12; Ps 103:3; 107:20. In answer to prayer: Of Hezekiah, 2 Kgs 20:1–11; Isa 38:1–8; David, Ps 21:4; 116:3–8.

New Testament believers not healed: Dorcas, Acts 9:36, 37; Paul, 2 Cor 12:7–10; Timothy, 1 Tim 5:23; Trophimus, 2 Tim 4:20. Prayer for, Jas 5:14–16. For miraculous healings by Christ, see *Miracles.*

Physicians employed for, 2 Chron 16:12; Jer 8:22; Mt 9:12; Mk 5:26; Lk 4:23. Remedies used, Prov 17:22; Isa 38:21; Jer 8:22; 30:13; 46:11; Lk 10:34; poultices, 2 Kgs 20:7; ointments, Isa 1:5, 6.

Of the sexual organs, Lev 15; 22:4; Deut 23:9, 10.

See *Circumcision; Menstruation; Gonorrhea.* Treatment of fractures, Ezk 30:21.

See *Afflictions; Healing, Divine.*

FIGURATIVE. Ps 38:7; Isa 1:5, 6; Jer 30:12.

Various kinds of: See *Abortion; Atrophy; Blemish; Blindness; Boil; Deafness; Demons; Dropsy; Dysentery; Dyspepsia; Fever; Gonorrhea; Gout; Hemorrhage; Infection; Insanity; Itch; Lameness; Leprosy; Paralysis; Pestilence; Plague; Scab; Scurvy; Stammering; Sunstroke; Tuberculosis; Tumor; Worm.*

Of the bowels, see *Bowels.*

DISHAN Son of Seir, Gen 36:20, 21; 28–30; 1 Chron 1:38, 39.

DISHON 1. Son of Seir, Gen 36:20, 21, 26; 1 Chron 1:38, 39.

2. Grandson of Seir, Gen 36:25; 1 Chron 1:41.

DISHONESTY Lev 6:2. If anyone sins against me by refusing to return a deposit on something borrowed or rented, or by refusing to return something entrusted to him, or by robbery, or by oppressing his neighbor, [3]or by finding a lost article and lying about it, swearing that he doesn't have it— [4, 5]on the day he is found guilty of any such sin, he shall restore what he took, adding a twenty percent fine, and give it to the one he has harmed; and on the same day he shall bring his guilt offering to the Tabernacle. [6]His guilt offering shall be a ram without defect, and must be worth whatever value you demand. He shall bring it to the priest, [7]and the priest shall make atonement for him before the Lord, and he shall be forgiven.

Lev 19:13. You shall not rob nor oppress anyone, and you shall pay your hired workers promptly. If something is due them, don't even keep it overnight.

35, 36. You must be impartial in judgment. Use accurate measurements—lengths, weights, and volumes—and give full measure, for I am Jehovah your God who brought you from the land of Egypt.

Deut 25:13, 14, 15. In all your transactions you must use accurate scales and honest measurements, so that you will have a long, good life in the land the Lord your God is giving you. [16]All who cheat with unjust weights and measurements are detestable to the Lord your God.

Job 24:2. For a crime wave has engulfed us—landmarks are moved, flocks of sheep are stolen, [3]and even the donkeys of the poor and fatherless are taken. Poor widows must surrender the little they have as a pledge to get a loan. [4]The needy are kicked aside; they must get out of the way. [5]Like the wild donkeys in the desert, the poor must spend all their time just getting barely enough to keep soul and body together. They are sent into the desert to search for food for their children. [6]They eat what they find that grows wild, and must even glean the vineyards of the wicked. [7]All night they lie naked in the cold, without clothing or covering. [8]They are wet with the showers of the mountains and live in caves for want of a home. [9]The wicked snatch fatherless children from their mother's breasts, and take a poor man's baby as a pledge before they will loan him any money or grain. [10]That is why they must go about naked, without clothing, and are forced to carry food while they are starving. [11]They are forced to press out the olive oil without tasting it, and to tread out the grape juice as they suffer from thirst.

Ps 37:21. Evil men borrow and "cannot pay it back"!

Ps 50:18. You see a thief and help him.

Ps 62:10, 11. Don't become rich by extortion and robbery. And don't let the rich men be proud.

Prov 3:27, 28. Don't withhold repayment of your debts. Don't say "some other time," if you can pay now.

Prov 11:1. The Lord hates cheating and delights in honesty.

Prov 20:10. The Lord despises every kind of cheating. [14]"Utterly worthless!" says the buyer as he haggles over the price. But afterwards he brags about his bargain! [17]Some men enjoy cheating, but the cake they buy with such ill-gotten gain will turn to gravel in their mouths. [23]The Lord loathes all cheating and dishonesty.

Isa 32:7. The smooth tricks of evil men will be exposed, as will all the lies they use to oppress the poor in the courts.

Jer 7:8. You think that because the Temple is here, you will never suffer? Don't fool yourselves! [9]Do you really think that you can steal, murder, commit adultery, lie, and worship Baal and all of those new gods of yours, [10]and then come here and stand before me in my Temple and chant, "We are saved!"—only to go right back to all these evil things again?

Jer 9:4. Beware of your neighbor! Beware of your brother! All take advantage of one another and spread their slanderous lies. [5]With practiced tongues they fool and defraud each other; they wear themselves out with all their sinning. [6]"They pile evil upon evil, lie upon lie, and utterly refuse to come to me," says the Lord. [8]"For their tongues aim lies like poisoned spears. They speak cleverly to their neighbors while planning to kill them."

Jer 22:13. And woe to you, King Jehoiakim, for you are building your great palace with forced labor. By not paying wages you are building injustice into its walls and oppression into its doorframes and ceilings.

Ezk 22:29. Even the common people oppress and rob the poor and needy and cruelly extort from aliens.

Hos 4:1. The Lord has filed a lawsuit against you listing the following charges: There is no faithfulness, no kindness, no knowledge of God in your land. [2]You swear and lie and kill and steal. . . . There is violence everywhere.

Hos 12:7. My people are like crafty merchants selling from dishonest scales—they love to cheat.

Amos 3:10. "My people have forgotten what it means to do right," says the Lord. "Their beautiful homes are full of the loot from their thefts and banditry."

Amos 8:5. You who long for the Sabbath to end and the religious holidays to be over, so you can get out and start cheating again—using your weighted scales and under-sized measures.

Mic 6:10. For your sins are very great—is there to be no end of getting rich by cheating? The homes of the wicked are full of ungodly treasures and lying scales. [11]Shall I say "Good!" to all your merchants with their bags of false, deceitful weights? How could God be just while saying that?

Nah 3:1. Woe to Nineveh, City of Blood, full of lies, crammed with plunder.

Zeph 1:9. Yes, I will punish those who follow heathen customs and who rob and kill to fill their masters' homes with evil gain of violence and fraud.

Zech 5:3. "This scroll," he told me, "represents the words of God's curse going out over the entire land. It says that all who steal and lie have been judged and sentenced to death." [4]"'I am sending this curse into the home of every thief and everyone who swears falsely by my name," says the Lord of Hosts. "And my curse shall remain upon his home and completely destroy it."

Lk 16:1. Jesus now told this story to his disciples: "A rich man hired an accountant to handle his affairs, but soon a rumor went around that the accountant was thoroughly dishonest. [2]So his employer called him in and said, "What's this I hear about your stealing from me? Get your report in order, for you are to be dismissed.' [3]The accountant thought to himself, 'Now what? I'm through here, and I haven't the strength to go out and dig ditches, and I'm too proud to beg. [4]I know just the thing! And then I'll have plenty of friends to take care of me when I leave!' [5]So he invited each one who owed money to his employer to come and discuss the situation. He asked the first one, 'How much do you owe him?' [6]'My debt is 850 gallons of olive oil,' the man replied. 'Yes, here is the contract you signed,' the accountant told him. 'Tear it up and write another one for half that much!' [7]'And how much do you owe him?' he asked the next man. 'A thousand bushels of wheat,' was the reply. 'Here,' the accountant said, 'take your note and replace it with one for only 800 bushels!' [8]The rich man had to admire the rascal for being so shrewd. And it is true that the citizens of this world are more clever (in dishonesty!) than the godly are."

1 Thess 4:6. And this also is God's will: that you never cheat in this matter by taking another man's wife, because the Lord will punish you terribly for this, as we have solemnly told you before.

Jas 5:4. For listen! Hear the cries of the field workers whom you have cheated of their pay. Their cries have reached the ears of the Lord of Hosts.

INSTANCES OF. Abimelech's servants seize a well of water, Gen 21:25; 26:15–22. Jacob obtains his brother's birthright by unjust advantage, Gen 25:29–33; steals his father's blessing, Gen 27:6–29; Laban's flocks by skillful manipulation, Gen 30:31–43. Rebekah's guile in Jacob's behalf, Gen 27:6–17. Laban's treatment of Jacob, Gen 29:21–30; 31:36–42. Rachel steals the household gods, Gen 31:21. Simeon and Levi deceive the Shechemites, Gen 34:15–31. Achan hides the bar of gold and the Babylonish garment, Josh 7:10–26. Micah steals 1100 pieces of silver ($1000), Judg 17:2. Micah's priest steals his images, Judg 18:14–21. Joab's guile in securing Absalom's return, 2 Sam 14:2–20. Ahab claims Naboth's vineyard, 1 Kgs 21:2–16. Judas' hypocritical sympathy for the poor, Jn 12:6.

See *Diplomacy; Hypocrisy; Injustice; Treason.*

DISOBEDIENCE TO GOD DENUNCIATIONS AGAINST. Num 14:11. And the Lord said to Moses, "How long will these people despise me? Will they *never* believe me, even after all the miracles I have done among them? [12]I will disinherit them and destroy them with a plague, and I will make you into a nation far greater and mightier than they are!" [22]So it is true that not one of the men who has seen my glory and the miracles I did both in Egypt and in the wilderness—and ten times refused to trust me and obey me— [23]shall even see the land I promised to this people's ancestors. [24]But my servant Caleb is a different kind of man—he has obeyed me fully. I will bring him into the land he entered as a spy, and his descendants shall have their full share in it."

Num 32:8. This is the same kind of thing your fathers did! I sent them from Kadish-barnea to spy out the land, [9]but when they finished their survey and returned from the valley of Eshcol, they discouraged the people from going on into the Promised Land. [10,11]And the Lord's anger was hot against them, and he swore that of all those he had rescued from Egypt, no one over twenty years of age would ever see the land he promised Abraham, Isaac, and Jacob, for they had refused to do what he wanted them to. [12]The only exceptions were Caleb (son of Jephunneh the Kenizzite) and Joshua (son of Nun)—for they wholeheartedly followed the Lord and urged the people to go on into the Promised Land. [13]The Lord made us wander back and forth in the wilderness for forty years until all that evil generation died.

Deut 18:19. I will personally deal with anyone who will not listen to him and heed his messages from me.

Deut 28:15–19. If you won't listen to the Lord your God and won't obey these laws I am giving you today, then all of these curses shall come upon you: curses in the city; curses in the fields; curses on your fruit and bread; the curse of barren wombs; curses upon your crops; curses upon the fertility of your cattle and flocks; curses when you come in; curses when you go out. [20]For the Lord himself will send his personal curse upon you. You will be confused and a failure in everything you do, until at last you are destroyed because of the sin of forsaking him. [21]He will send disease among you until you are destroyed from the face of the land which you are about to enter and possess. [22]He will send tuberculosis, fever, infections, plague, and war. He will blight your crops, covering them with mildew. All these devastations shall pursue you until you perish. [23]The heavens above you will be as unyielding as bronze, and the earth beneath will be as iron. [24]The land will become as dry as dust for lack of rain, and dust storms shall destroy you. [25]The Lord will cause you to be defeated by your enemies. You will march out to battle gloriously, but flee before your enemies in utter confusion; and you will be tossed to and fro among all the nations of the earth. [26]Your dead bodies will be food to the birds and wild animals, and no one will be there to chase them away. [27]He will send upon you Egyptian boils, tumors, scurvy, and itch, for none of which will there be a remedy. [28]He will send madness, blindness, fear, and panic upon you. [29]You shall grope in the bright sunlight just as the blind man gropes in darkness. You shall not prosper in anything you do; you will be oppressed and robbed continually, and nothing will save you. [30]Someone else will marry your fiancee; someone else will live in the house you build; someone else will eat the fruit of the vineyard you plant. [31]Your oxen shall be butchered before your eyes, but you won't get a single bite of meat. Your donkeys will be driven away as you watch, and will never return to you again. Your sheep will be given to your enemies. And there will be no one to protect you. [32]You will watch as your sons and daughters are taken away as slaves. Your heart will break with longing for them, but you will not be able to help them. [33]A foreign nation you have not even heard of will eat the crops you will have worked so hard to grow. You will always be oppressed and crushed. [34]You will go mad because of the tragedy you see around you. [35]The Lord will cover you with boils from head to foot. [36]He will exile you and the king you will choose, to a nation to whom neither you nor your ancestors gave a second thought; and while in exile you shall worship gods of wood and stone! [37]You will become an object of horror, a proverb and a byword among all the nations, for the Lord will thrust you away. [38]You will sow much but reap little, for the locusts will eat your crops. [39]You will plant vineyards and care for them, but you won't eat the grapes or drink the wine, for worms will destroy the vines. [40]Olive trees will be growing everywhere, but there won't be enough olive oil to anoint yourselves! For the trees will drop their fruit before it is matured. [41]Yours sons and daughters will be snatched away from you as slaves. [42]The locusts shall destroy your trees and vines. [43]Foreigners living among you shall become richer and richer while you become poorer and poorer. [44]They shall lend to you, not you to them! They shall be the head and you shall be the tail! [45]All these curses shall pursue and overtake you until you are destroyed—all because you refuse to listen to the Lord your God. [46]These horrors shall befall you and your descendants as a warning: [47, 48]You will become slaves to your enemies because of your failure to praise God for all that he has given you. The Lord will send your enemies against you, and you will be hungry, thirsty, naked, and in want of everything. A yoke of iron shall be placed around your neck until you are destroyed! [49]The Lord will bring a distant nation against you, swooping down upon you like an eagle; a nation whose language you don't understand— [50]a nation of fierce and angry men who will have no mercy upon young or old. [51]They will eat you out of house and home until your cattle and crops are gone. Your grain, new wine, olive oil, calves, and lambs will all disappear. [52]That nation will lay siege to your cities and knock down your highest walls—the walls you will trust to protect you. [53]You will even eat the flesh of your own sons and daughters in the terrible days of siege that lie ahead. [54]The most tenderhearted man among you will be utterly callous toward his own brother and his beloved wife and his children who are still alive. [55]He will refuse to give them a share of the flesh he is devouring—the flesh of his own children—because he is starving in the midst of the siege of your cities. [56, 57]The most tender and delicate woman among you—the one who would not so much as touch her feet to the ground—will refuse to share with her beloved husband, son, and daughter. She will hide from them the afterbirth and the new baby she has borne, so that she herself can eat them: so terrible will be the hunger during the siege and the awful distress caused by your enemies at your gates. [58,59]If you refuse to obey all the laws written in this book, thus refusing reverence to the glorious and fearful name of Jehovah your God, then Jehovah will send perpetual plagues upon you and upon your children. [60]He will bring upon you all the diseases of Egypt which you feared so much, and they shall plague the land. [61]And that is not all! The Lord will bring upon you every sickness and plague there is, even those not mentioned in this book, until you are destroyed. [62]There will be few of you left, though before you were as numerous as stars. All this if you do not listen to the Lord your God. [63]Just as the Lord has rejoiced over you and has done such wonderful things for you and has multiplied you, so the Lord at that time will rejoice in destroying you; and you shall disappear from the land. [64]For the Lord will scatter you among all the nations from one end of the earth to the other. There you will worship heathen gods that neither you nor your ancestors have known, gods made of wood and stone! [65]There among those nations you shall find no rest, but the Lord will give you trembling hearts, darkness, and bodies wasted from sorrow and fear. [66]Your lives will hang in doubt. You will live night and day in fear, and will have no reason to believe that you will see the morning light. [67]In the morning you will say, "Oh, that night were here!" And in the evening you will say, "Oh, that morning were here!" You will say this because of the awesome horrors surrounding you. [68]Then the Lord will send you back to Egypt in ships, a journey I promised you would never need to make again; and there you will offer to sell yourselves to your enemies as slaves—but no one will even want to buy you. Lev 26:14–46.

PUNISHMENT OF. Of the Egyptions by plagues, see *Plague.* See also *Sin, Punishment of.*

INSTANCES OF. Of Adam and Eve, eating the forbidden fruit, Gen 3:6–11. Of Lot, in refusing to go to the mountain, as commanded by the angels, Gen 19:18–20. Of Lot's wife, in looking back on Sodom, Gen 19:26. Of Moses, in making excuses when commissioned to deliver Israel, Ex 4:13, 14; when he smote the rock, Num 20:11, 23, 24. Of Aaron, at the striking of the rock by Moses, Num 20:23, 24. Of Pharoah, in refusing to let the children of Israel go, Ex 5:2; 7:13, 22, 23; 8:15, 19, 31, 32; 9:12, 34; 10:20, 27; 11:10; 14:8. Of the children of Israel, in gathering excessive quantities of manna, Ex 16:19, 20; in refusing to enter the promised land, Deut 1:26, with Num 14:1–11; Josh 5:6; Ps 106:24, 25. Of Nadab and Abihu, in offering unholy fire, Lev 10:1, 2. Of Balaam, in accompanying the messengers from Balak, Num 22:22, 23. Of Achan, in secreting the gold bar and the Babylonian garment, Josh 7:15–26. Of Saul, in offering a sacrifice, 1 Sam 13:13; in sparing Agag and the spoils of the Amalekites, 1 Sam 15; 28:18. Of David, in his adultery, and in the murder of Uriah, 2 Sam 12:9. Of Solomon, in building places for idolatrous worship, 1 Kgs 11:7–10. Of the prophet of Judah, in not keeping the commandment to deliver his message to Jeroboam without delay, 1 Kgs 13. Of a man of Israel, who refused to kill the prophet, 1 Kgs 20:35, 36. Of Ahab, in allowing the king of Assyria to escape out of his hands, 1 Kgs 20:42. Of priests, in not performing their functions properly, 1 Chron 15:13. Of the people of Judah, Jer 43:7; in going to live in Egypt contrary to divine command, Jer 44:12–14. Of Jonah, in refusing to deliver the message to the Ninevites, Jon 1. Of the blind men Jesus healed, and commanded not to publish their healing, Mt 9:30, 31. Of the leper whom Jesus healed, and commanded not to publish the fact, Mk 1:45. Of Paul, in going to Jerusalem contrary to repeated warnings, Acts 21:4, 10–14.

OF CHILDREN. See *Children, Commandments to.*

OF THE RIGHTEOUS. See *Commandments.*

DISPERSION Of the descendants of Noah, Gen 10. After building the tower of Babel, Gen 11:1–9; Deut 32:8. Of the Jews, foretold, Jer 16:15; 24:9; Jn 7:35.

DISPUTE About property, see *Property.*

DISSEMBLING INSTANCES OF. Joseph, Gen 42:7–20; 43:26–34. David, 1 Sam 21:13–15.
See *Deception; Hypocrisy.*

DISSENSION In churches, 1 Cor 1:10–13; 3:3, 4; 11:18, 19.

DISSIPATION Dangers of, Job 1:5.
See *Drunkenness.*

DISTINCTION See *Separation.*

DIVINATION See *Sorcery.*

DIVINE HEALING See *Healing, Divine.*

DIVINITY OF CHRIST See *Jesus, Deity of.*

DIVORCE Ex 21:7. If a man sells his daughter as a slave, she shall not be freed at the end of six years as the men are. [8]If she does not please the man who bought her, then he shall let her be bought back again; but he has no power to sell her to foreigners, since he has wronged her by no longer wanting her after marrying her. [9]And if he arranges an engagement between a Hebrew slave-girl and his son, then he may no longer treat her has a slave-girl, but must treat her as a daughter. [10]If he himself marries her and then takes another wife, he may not reduce her food or clothing, or fail to sleep with her as his wife. [11]If he fails in any of these three things, then she may leave freely without any payment.

Deut 21:10. When you go to war and the Lord your God delivers your enemies to you, [11]and you see among the captives a beautiful girl you want as your wife, [12]take her home with you. She must shave her head and pare her nails [13]and change her clothing, laying aside that which she was wearing when she was captured, then remain in your home in mourning for her father and mother for a full month. After that you may marry her. [14]However, if after marrying her you decide you don't like her, you must let her go free—you may not sell her or treat her as a slave, for you have humiliated her.

Deut 24:1. If a man doesn't like something about his wife, he may write a letter stating that he has divorced her, give her the letter, and send her away. [2]If she then remarries, [3]and the second husband also divorces her, or dies, [4]the former husband may not marry her again, for she has been defiled; this would bring guilt upon the land the Lord your God is giving you.

Ezra 10:1. As I lay on the ground in front of the Temple, weeping and praying and making this confession, a large crowd of men, women, and children gathered around and cried with me. [2]Then Shecaniah (the son of Jehiel of the clan of Elam) said to me, "We acknowledge our sin against our God, for we have married these heathen women. But there is hope for Israel in spite of this. [3]For we agree before our God to divorce our heathen wives and to send them away with our children; we will follow your commands, and the commands of the others who fear our God. We will obey the laws of God. [4]Take courage and tell us how to proceed in setting things straight, and we will fully cooperate." [5]So I stood up and demanded that the leaders of the priests and the Levites and all the people of Israel swear that they would do as Shecaniah had said; and they all agreed. [6]Then I went into the room of Jeho-hanan in the Temple and refused all food and drink; for I was mourning because of the sin of the returned exiles. [7, 8]Then a proclamation was made throughout Judah and Jerusalem that everyone should appear at Jerusalem within three days and that the leaders and elders had decided that anyone who refused to come would be disinherited and excommunicated from Israel. [9]Within three days, on the fifth day of December, all the men of Judah and Benjamin had arrived and were sitting in the open space before the Temple; and they were trembling because of the seriousness of the matter and because of the heavy rainfall. 10Then I, Ezra the priest, arose and addressed them: "You have sinned, for you have married heathen women; now we are even more deeply under God's condemnation than we were before. 11Confess your sin to the Lord God of your fathers and do what he demands: separate yourselves from the heathen people about you and from these women." 12Then all the men spoke up and said, "We will do what you have said. 13But this isn't something that can be done in a day or two, for there are many of us involved in this sinful affair. And it is raining so hard that we can't stay out here much longer. 14Let our leaders arrange trials for us. Everyone who has a heathen wife will come at the scheduled time with the elders and judges of his city; then each case will be decided and the situation will be cleared up and the fierce wrath of our God will be turned away from us." 15Only Jonathan (son of Asahel), Jahzeiah (son of Tikvah), Meshullam, and Shabbethai the Levite opposed this course of action. 16So this was the plan that was followed: Some of the clan leaders and I were designated as judges; we began our work on December 15, and finished by March 15.

Neh 13:23. About the same time I realized that some of the Jews had married women from Ashdod, Ammon, and Moab, 24and that many of their children spoke in the language of Ashdod and couldn't speak the language of Judah at all. 25So I argued with these parents and cursed them and punched a few of them and knocked them around and pulled out their hair; and they vowed before God that they would not let their children intermarry with non-Jews. 26"Wasn't this exactly King Solomon's problem?" I demanded. "There was no king who could compare with him, and God loved him and made him the king over all Israel; but even so he was led into idolatry by foreign women. 27Do you think that we will let you get away with this sinful deed?" 28One of the sons of Jehoiada (the son of Eliashib the High Priest) was a son-in-law of Sanballat the Horonite, so I chased him out of the Temple. 29Remember them, O my God, for they have defiled the priesthood and the promises and vows of the priests and Levites. 30So I purged out the foreigners, and assigned tasks to the priests and Levites, making certain that each knew his work.

Jer 3:1. There is a law that if a man divorces a woman who then remarries, he is not to take her back again, for she has become corrupted. But though you have left me and married many lovers, yet I have invited you to come to me again, the Lord says.

Mal 2:14. "Why has God abandoned us?" you cry. I'll tell you why; it is because the Lord has seen your treachery in divorcing your wives who have been faithful to you through the years, the companions you promised to care for and keep. 15You were united to your wife by the Lord. In God's wise plan, when you married, the two of you became one person in his sight. And what does he want? Godly children from your union. Therefore guard your passions! Keep faith with the wife of your youth. 16For the Lord, the God of Israel, says he hates divorce and cruel men. Therefore control your passions—let there be no divorcing of your wives.

Mt 5:31. The law of Moses says, "If anyone wants to be rid of his wife, he can divorce her merely by giving her a letter of dismissal." 32But I say that a man who divorces his wife, except for fornication, causes her to commit adultery if she marries again. And he who marries her commits adultery.

Mt 19:3. Some Pharisees came to interview him, and tried to trap him into saying something that would ruin him. "Do you permit divorce?" they asked. 4"Don't you read the Scriptures?" he replied. "In them it is written that at the beginning God created man and woman, 5, 6and that a man should leave his father and mother, and be forever united to his wife. The two shall become one—no longer two, but one! And no man may divorce what God has joined together." 7"Then, why," they asked, "did Moses say a man may divorce his wife by merely writing her a letter of dismissal?" 8Jesus replies, "Moses did that in recognition of your hard and evil hearts, but it was not what God had originally intended. 9And I tell you this, that anyone who divorces his wife, except for fornication, and marries another, commits adultery." 10Jesus' disciples then said to him, "If that is how it is, it is better not to marry!" 11"Not everyone can accept this statement," Jesus said. "Only those whom God helps. 12Some are born without the ability to marry, and some are disabled by men, and some refuse to marry for the sake of the Kingdom of Heaven. Let anyone who can, accept my statement." Mk 10:2–12.

Lk 16:18. So anyone who divorces his wife and marries someone else commits adultery, and anyone who marries a divorced woman commits adultery.

1 Cor 7:10. Now, for those who are married I have a command, not just a suggestion. And it is not a command from me, for this is what the Lord himself has said: A wife must not leave her husband. 11But if she is separated from him, let her remain single or else go back to him. And the husband must not divorce his wife. 12Here I want to add some suggestions of my own. These are not direct commands from the Lord, but they seem right to me: If a Christian has a wife who is not a Christian, but she wants to stay with him anyway, he must not leave her or divorce her. 13And if a Christian woman has a husband who isn't a Christian, and he wants her to stay with him, she must not leave him. 14For perhaps the husband who isn't a Christian may become a Christian with the help of his Christian wife. And the wife who isn't a Christian may become a Christian with the help of her Christian husband. Otherwise, if the family separates, the children might never come to know the Lord; whereas a united family may, in God's plan, result in the children's salvation. 15But if the

husband or wife who isn't a Christian is eager to leave, it is permitted. In such cases the Christian husband or wife should not insist that the other stay, for God wants his children to live in peace and harmony. [16]For, after all, there is no assurance to you wives that your husbands will be converted if they stay; and the same may be said to you husbands concerning your wives. [17]But be sure in deciding these matters that you are living as God intended, marrying or not marrying in accordance with God's direction and help, and accepting whatever situation God has put you into. This is my rule for all the churches.

Disobedience of the wife to the husband, a sufficient cause for, in the Persian empire, Esther 1: 10–22.

See *Marriage.*

FIGURATIVE. Isa 50:1; Jer 3:8.

DOCTOR See *Physician; Disease.*

DOCTRINE Jn 7:16. So Jesus told them, "I'm not teaching you my own thoughts, but those of God who sent me. [17]If any of you really determines to do God's will, then you will certainly know whether my teaching is from God or is merely my own."

Set forth by church councils, Acts 15:6–29.

FALSE. Mt 5:19. And so if anyone breaks the least commandment, and teaches others to, he shall be the least in the Kingdom of Heaven.

Mt 15:9. "Their worship is worthless, for they teach their man-made laws instead of those from God." [13]Jesus replied, "Every plant not planted by my Father shall be rooted up." Mt 16:12.

Rom 16:17. And now there is one more thing to say before I end this letter. Stay away from those who cause divisions and are upsetting people's faith, teaching things about Christ that are contrary to what you have been taught. [18]Such teachers are not working for our Lord Jesus, but only want gain for themselves. They are good speakers, and simple-minded people are often fooled by them.

1 Cor 3:11. And no one can ever lay any other real foundation than that one we already have—Jesus Christ. [21]So don't be proud of following the wise men of this world. *vs.* 1–4.

1 Cor 11:18. Everyone keeps telling me about the arguing that goes on in these meetings, and the divisions developing among you, and I can just about believe it. [19]But I suppose you feel this is necessary so that you who are always right will become known and recognized!

2 Cor 2:17. We are not like those hucksters—and there are many of them—whose idea in getting out the Gospel is to make a good living out of it.

2 Cor 11:3. But I am frightened, fearing that in some way you will be led away from your pure and simple devotion to our Lord, just as Eve was deceived by Satan in the Garden of Eden. [4]You seem so gullible: you believe whatever anyone tells you even if he is preaching about another Jesus than the one we preach, or a different spirit than the Holy Spirit you received, or shows you a different way to be saved. You swallow it all.

Gal 1:6. I am amazed that you are turning away so soon from God who, in his love and mercy, invited you to share the eternal life he gives through Christ; you are already following a different "way to heaven," which really doesn't go to heaven at all. [7]For there is no other way than the one we showed you; you are being fooled by those who twist and change the truth concerning Christ. [8]Let God's curses fall on anyone, including myself, who preaches any other way to be saved than the one we told you about; yes, if an angel comes from heaven and preaches any other message, let him be forever cursed.

Eph 4:14. Then we will no longer be like children, forever changing our minds about what we believe because someone has told us something different, or has cleverly lied to us and made the lie sound like the truth.

Col 2:4. I am saying this because I am afraid that someone may fool you with smooth talk. [8]Don't let others spoil your faith and joy with their philosophies, their wrong and shallow answers built on men's thoughts and ideas, instead of on what Christ has said. [18]Don't let anyone declare you lost when you refuse to worship angels, as they say you must. They have seen a vision, they say, and know you should. These proud men (though they claim to be so humble) have a very clever imagination. [19]But they are not connected to Christ, the Head to which all of us who are his body are joined; for we are joined together by his strong sinews and we grow only as we get our nourishment and strength from God. [20]Since you died, as it were, with Christ and this has set you free from following the world's ideas of how to be saved—by doing good and obeying various rules— why do you keep right on following them anyway, still bound by such rules as [21]not eating, tasting, or even touching certain foods? [22]Such rules are mere human teachings, for food was made to be eaten and used up. [23]These rules may seem good, for rules of this kind require strong devotion and are humiliating and hard on the body, but they have no effect when it comes to conquering a person's evil thoughts and desires. They only make him proud.

1 Tim 1:3, 4. As I said when I left for Macedonia, please stay there in Ephesus and try to stop the men who are teaching such wrong doctrine. Put an end to their myths and fables, and their idea of being saved by finding favor with an endless chain of angels leading up to God—wild ideas that stir up questions and arguments instead of helping people accept God's plan of faith. [6]But these teachers have missed this whole idea and spend their time arguing and talking foolishness. [7]They want to become famous as teachers of the laws of Moses when they haven't the slightest idea what those laws really show us. [19]Cling tightly to your faith in Christ and always keep your conscience clear, doing what you know is right. For some people have disobeyed their consciences and have deliberately done what they knew was wrong. It isn't

surprising that soon they lost their faith in Christ after defying God like that.

1 Tim 4:1. But the Holy Spirit tells us clearly that in the last times some in the church will turn away from Christ and become eager followers of teachers with devil-inspired ideas. [2]These teachers will tell lies with straight faces and do it so often that their consciences won't even bother them. [3]They will say it is wrong to be married and wrong to eat meat. [7]Don't waste time arguing over foolish ideas and silly myths and legends. Spend your time and energy in the exercise of keeping spiritually fit.

1 Tim 6:3. Some may deny these things, but they are the sound, wholesome teachings of the Lord Jesus Christ and are the foundation for a godly life. [4]Anyone who says anything different is both proud and stupid. He is quibbling over the meaning of Christ's words and stirring up arguments ending in jealousy and anger, which only lead to name-calling, accusations, and evil suspicions. [5]These arguers—their minds warped by sin—don't know how to tell the truth; to them the Good News is just a means of making money. Keep away from them. [20]Oh, Timothy, don't fail to do these things that God entrusted to you. Keep out of foolish arguments with those who boast of their "knowledge" and thus prove their lack of it. [21]Some of these people have missed the most important thing in life —they don't know God.

2 Tim 2:14. Remind your people of these great facts, and command them in the name of the Lord not to argue over unimportant things. Such arguments are confusing and useless, and even harmful. [16]Steer clear of foolish discussions which lead people into the sin of anger with each other. [17]Things will be said that will burn and hurt for a long time to come. Hymenaeus and Philetus, in their love of argument, are men like that. [18]They have left the path of truth, preaching the lie that the resurrection of the dead has already occurred; and they have weakened the faith of some who believe them.

2 Tim 3:6. They are the kind who craftily sneak into other people's homes and make friendships with silly, sin-burdened women and teach them their new doctrines. [7]Women of that kind are forever following new teachers, but they never understand the truth. [8]And these teachers fight truth just as Jannes and Jambres fought against Moses. They have dirty minds, warped and twisted, and have turned against the Christian faith. [9]But they won't get away with all this forever. Some day their deceit will be well known to everyone, as was the sin of Jannes and Jambres. [13]In fact, evil men and false teachers will become worse and worse, deceiving many, they themselves having been deceived by Satan. 2 Tim 4:3.

Tit 1:10. For there are many who refuse to obey; this is especially true among those who say that all Christians must obey the Jewish laws. But this is foolish talk; it blinds people to the truth, [11]and it must be stopped. Already whole families have been turned away from the grace of God. Such teachers are only after your money. [14]And to stop them from listening to Jewish folk tales and the demands of men who have turned their backs on the truth.

Tit 3:10. If anyone is causing divisions among you, he should be given a first and second warning. After that have nothing more to do with him, [11]for such a person has a wrong sense of values. He is sinning, and he knows it.

Heb 13:9. So do not be attracted by strange, new ideas. Your spiritual strength comes as a gift from God, not from ceremonial rules about eating certain foods—a method which, by the way, hasn't helped those who have tried it!

2 Pet 2:1. But there were false prophets, too, in those days, just as there will be false teachers among you. They will cleverly tell their lies about God, turning against even their Master who bought them; but theirs will be a swift and terrible end. [2]Many will follow their evil teaching that there is nothing wrong with sexual sin. And because of them Christ and his way will be scoffed at. [3]These teachers in their greed will tell you anything to get hold of your money. But God condemned them long ago and their destruction is on the way. [14]No woman can escape their sinful stare, and of adultery they never have enough. They make a game of luring unstable women. They train themselves to be greedy; and are doomed and cursed. [15]They have gone off the road and become lost like Balaam, the son of Beor, who fell in love with the money he could make by doing wrong; [16]but Balaam was stopped from his mad course when his donkey spoke to him with a human voice, scolding and rebuking him. [17]These men are as useless as dried-up springs of water, promising much and delivering nothing; they are as unstable as clouds driven by the storm winds. They are doomed to the eternal pits of darkness. [18]They proudly boast about their sins and conquests, and, using lust as their bait, they lure back into sin those who have just escaped from such wicked living. [19]. . . But these very teachers who offer this "freedom" from law are themselves slaves to sin and destruction. *vs.* 1–22.

1 Jn 4:3. If not, the message is not from God but from one who is against Christ, like the "Antichrist" you have heard about who is going to come, and his attitude of enmity against Christ is already abroad in the world.

2 Jn 1:7. Watch out for the false leaders—and there are many of them around—who don't believe that Jesus Christ came to earth as a human being with a body like ours. Such people are against the truth and against Christ. [9]For if you wander beyond the teaching of Christ, you will leave God behind; while if you are loyal to Christ's teachings, you will have God too. Then you will have both the Father and the Son. [10]If anyone comes to teach you, and he doesn't believe what Christ taught, don't even invite him into your home. Don't encourage him in any way. [11]If you do you will be a partner with him in his wickedness.

Jude 1:4. I say this because some godless teachers have wormed their way in among you, saying that after we become Christians we can do just as we like without fear of God's punishment. The fate of such people was written long ago, for they have turned against our only Master and Lord, Jesus Christ. [11]Woe upon them! For they follow the example of Cain who killed his brother; and like Balaam, they will do anything for money; and like Korah, they have disobeyed God and will die under his curse.

See *Minister, False; Teachers, False.*

DOCUMENT Ezra 6:1.

See *Books.*

DODAI Commander of one of David's army divisions, 1 Chron 27:4.

DODANIM Descendants of Noah, Gen 10:4. Called *Rodanim,* 1 Chron 1:5–7.

DODAVAH Father of Eliezer, 2 Chron 20: 37.

DODO 1. A descendant of Issachar, Judg 10: 1.

2. Father of Eleazer, 2 Sam 23:9; 1 Chron 11:12.

3. A Bethlehemite, 2 Sam 23:24–39; 1 Chr. 11: 26–47.

DOEG An Edomite, present when Ahimelech helped David, 1 Sam 21:7; 22:9, 10, 22; Ps 52 [title]. Slew 85 priests, 1 Sam 22:18, 19.

DOER OF THE WORD. Mt 7:21. Not all who sound religious are really godly people. They may refer to me as "Lord," but still won't get to heaven. For the decisive question is whether they obey my Father in heaven.

Mt 12:50. Then he added, "Anyone who obeys my Father in heaven is my brother, sister and mother!"

Lk 11:28. He replied, "Yes, but even more blessed are all who hear the Word of God and put it into practice."

Rom 2:12–15. He will punish sin wherever it is found. He will punish the heathen when they sin, even though they never had God's written laws, for down in their hearts they know right from wrong. God's laws are written within them; their own conscience accuses them, or sometimes excuses them. And God will punish the Jews for sinning because they have his written laws but don't obey them. They know what is right but don't do it. After all, salvation is not given to those who know what to do, unless they do it.

2 Cor 8:11. Having started the ball rolling so enthusiastically, you should carry this project through to completion just as gladly, giving whatever you can out of whatever you have. Let your enthusiastic idea at the start be equalled by your realistic action now.

Jas 1:22. And remember, it is a message to obey, not just to listen to. So don't fool yourselves. [23]For if a person just listens and doesn't obey, he is like a man looking at his face in a mirror; [24]as soon as he walks away, he can't see himself anymore or remember what he looks like. [25]But if anyone keeps looking steadily into God's law for free men, he will not only remember it but he will do what it says, and God will greatly bless him in everything he does. [26]Anyone who says he is a Christian but doesn't control his sharp tongue is just fooling himself, and his religion isn't worth much. [27]The Christian who is pure and without fault, from God the Father's point of view, is the one who takes care of orphans and widows, and who remains true to the Lord—not soiled and dirtied by his contacts with the world.

Jas 4:11. Don't criticize and speak evil about each other, dear brothers. If you do, you will be fighting against God's law of loving one another, declaring it is wrong. But your job is not to decide whether this law is right or wrong, but to obey it.

See *Hearers.*

DOG Habits of: Licking blood, 1 Kgs 21:19; 22: 38; licking sores, Lk 16:21; returns to his vomit, Prov 26:11; 2 Pet 2:22; lapping of, Judg 7:5, 6. Greedy, Isa 56:11. Epithet of contempt, 1 Sam 17:43; 24:14; 2 Sam 3:8; 9:8; 16:9; 2 Kgs 8:13; Job 30:1; Isa 56:11; Mt 15:26.

FIGURATIVE. Phil 3:2.

DOGMATISM See *Commandments, of Men.*

DOLPHIN Skins of, used for shoes, Ezk 16: 9, 10.

DOMICILE RIGHTS OF. Deut 24:10. If you lend anything to another man, you must not enter his house to get his security. [11]Stand outside! The owner will bring it out to you.

DOMINION OF MAN. See *Man, Dominion of.*

DONATIONS See *Charity; Liberality.*

DONKEY DOMESTICATED. Herds of, Gen 12:16; 24:35; 32:5; 34:28; Num 31:32–35, 42–46; 1 Chron 5:21; Ezra 2:66, 67; Neh 7:68, 69.

Used for riding, Gen 22:3; Num 22:21–33; Josh 15:18, 19; Judg 1:14; 5:10; 1 Sam 25:20; 2 Chron 28: 15; Isa 21:7; Zech 9:9; 1 Pet 2:16; by Jesus, Zech 9: 9; Mt 21:2, 5; Jn 12:14, 15; carrying burdens, Gen 42: 26; 2 Sam 16:1; Isa 30:6; for food, 2 Kgs 6:25. Not to be harnessed with an ox, Deut 22:10. Rest on Sabbath, Ex 23:12. Bridles for, Prov 26:3. Jawbone of, used by Samson to kill Philistines, Judg 15:15–17.

Firstborn of, redeemed, Ex 13:13; 34:20.

WILD. Gen 16:9–12; Job 6:5–7; 24:5; 39:5; Ps 104: 11; Isa 32:14; Jer 2:24; 14:6; Hos 8:9.

DOOR Posts of, sprinkled with the blood of the paschal lamb, Ex 12:22; the law to be written on, Deut 11:20. Hinges for, Prov 26:14; made of gold, 1 Kgs 7:50. Doors of the temple made of olive-wood, carved with cherubim, palm trees and flowers and covered with gold, 1 Kgs 6:31–35.

FIGURATIVE. Door of hope, Hos 2:15; of opportunity, 1 Cor 16:9; Rev 3:8; closed, Mt 25:10; Lk 13: 25; Rev 3:7.

DOORKEEPER Of the Temple, 2 Kgs 12:9; 1 Chron 9:22; Ps 84:10; Jer 35:4.

See *Gatekeeper.*

DOPHKAH Camping place of the Israelites, Num 33:12.

DOR A town and district of Palestine, Josh 11: 1–3. Conquered by Joshua, Josh 12:8–24; 1 Kgs 4: 11. Allotted to Manasseh, although situated in the territory of Asher, Josh 17:11; Judg 1:27.

DORCAS Called also *Tabitha.* A pious woman of Joppa, Acts 9:36–42.

DOTHAN A district and town in Palestine, Gen 37:17. Syrian army made blind at, 2 Kgs 6: 13–19.

DOUBTING Josh 1:9. Yes, be bold and strong! Banish fear and doubt! For remember, the Lord your God is with you wherever you go. Deut 1:19–21.

Job 4:3, 4. In the past you have told many a troubled soul to trust in God and have encouraged those who are weak or falling, or lie crushed upon the ground or are tempted to despair. [5]But now, when trouble strikes, you faint and are broken. [6]At such a time as this should not trust in God still be your confidence? Shouldn't you believe that God will care for those who are good?

Job 9:16. And even if my prayers were answered I could scarce believe that he had heard my cry. [17]For he is the one who destroys, and multiplies my wounds without a cause. [18]He will not let me breathe, but fills me with bitter sorrows. [19]He alone is strong and just. [20]But I? Am I righteous? My own mouth says no. Even if I were perfect, God would prove me wicked. [21]And even if I am utterly innocent, I dare not think of it. I despise what I am. [22]Innocent or evil, it is all the same to him, for he destroys both kinds.

Job 30:20. I cry to you, O God, but you don't answer me. I stand before you and you don't bother to look. [21]You have become cruel toward me, and persecute me with great power and effect. Job 3; 16; 17; 23:15–17.

Ps 22:2. Day and night I keep on weeping, crying for your help, but there is no reply—.

Ps 31:22. I spoke too hastily when I said, "The Lord has deserted me," for you listened to my plea and answered me.

Ps 42:5. Why then be downcast? Why be discouraged and sad? Hope in God! I shall yet praise him again. Yes, I shall again praise him for his help. [6]Yet I am standing here depressed and gloomy.

Ps 49:5. *There is no need to fear when times of trouble come,* even though surrounded by enemies!

Ps 73:13. Have I been wasting my time? Why take the trouble to be pure? [14]All I get out of it is trouble and woe—every day and all day long! [15]If I had really said that, I would have been a traitor to your people. [16]Yet it is so hard to explain it—this prosperity of those who hate the Lord. [17]Then one day I went into God's sanctuary to meditate, and thought about the future of these evil men.

Ps 77:3. I think of God and moan, overwhelmed with longing for his help. [7]Has the Lord rejected me forever? Will he never again be favorable? [8]Is his lovingkindness gone forever? Has his promise failed? [9]Has he forgotten to be kind to one so undeserving? Has he slammed the door in anger on his love?

Ps 94:19. Lord, when doubts fill my mind, when my heart is in turmoil, quiet me and give me renewed hope and cheer.

Prov 24:10. You are a poor specimen if you can't stand the pressure of adversity.

Isa 40:27. O Jacob, O Israel, how can you say that the Lord doesn't see your troubles and isn't being fair? [28]Don't you yet understand? Don't you know by now that the everlasting God, the Creator of the farthest parts of the earth, never grows faint or weary? No one can fathom the depths of his understanding. Isa 50:2.

Isa 49:14. Yet they say, "My Lord deserted us; he has forgotten us." [15]Never! Can a mother forget her little child and not have love for her own son? Yet even if that should be, I will not forget you.

Jer 8:18. My grief is beyond healing; my heart is broken.

Jer 15:18. You have let them keep right on with all their persecutions. Will they never stop hurting me? Your help is as uncertain as a seasonal mountain brook—sometimes a flood, sometimes as dry as a bone.

Jer 45:3. You have said, Woe is me! Don't I have troubles enough already? And now the Lord has added more! I am weary of my own sighing and I find no rest.

Lam 3:8. And though I cry and shout, he will not hear my prayers! [17]O Lord, all peace and all prosperity have long since gone, for you have taken them away. I have forgotten what enjoyment is. [18]All hope is gone; my strength has turned to water, for the Lord has left me.

Lam 5:20. Why do you forget us forever? Why do you forsake us for so long? Lam chapters 1–5.

Hos 10:3. Then they will say, "We deserted the Lord and he took away our king. But what's the difference? We don't need one anyway!"

Mt 8:26. But Jesus answered, "O you men of little faith! Why are you so frightened?" Mk 4:40; Lk 8:25.

Mt 14:31. "O man of little faith," Jesus said. "Why did you doubt me?"

Mt 17:17. Jesus replied, "Oh, you stubborn, faithless people! How long shall I bear with you?" Mk 9:19; Lk 9:40.

Mk 4:38. Frantically they wakened him, shouting, "Teacher, don't you even care that we are all about to drown?"

Heb 10:23. Now we can look forward to the salvation God has promised us. There is no longer any room for doubt, and we can tell others that salvation is ours, for there is no question that he will do what he says.

Jas 1:6. But when you ask him, be sure that you really expect him to tell you, for a doubtful mind will be as unsettled as a wave of the sea that is driven and tossed by the wind.

1 Pet 1:6. So be truly glad! There is wonderful joy ahead, even though the going is rough for a while down here.

Jude 1:22. Be merciful to those who doubt. Rom 15:1.

EXEMPLIFIED. Gen 12:11–13. But as he was approaching the borders of Egypt, he asked Sarai his wife to tell everyone that she was his sister! "You are very beautiful," he told her, "and when the Egyptians see you they will say, 'This is his wife. Let's kill him and then we can have her!' But if you say you are my sister, then the Egyptians will treat me well because of you, and spare my life!" Gen 20:2, 11, 12; 26:7.

Gen 15:8. But Abram replied, "O Lord Jehovah, how can I be sure that you will give it to me?"

Gen 18:12. So Sarah laughed silently. "A woman my age have a baby?" she scoffed to herself. "And with a husband as old as mine?" [13]Then God said to Abraham, "Why did Sarah laugh? Why did she say 'Can an old woman like me have a baby?' [14]Is anything too hard for God? Next year, just as I told you, I will certainly see to it that Sarah has a son."

Gen 19:30. Afterwards Lot left Zoar, fearful of the people there, and went to live in a cave in the mountains with his two daughters.

Ex 3:11. "But I'm not the person for a job like that!" Moses exclaimed.

Ex 4:1. But Moses said, "They won't believe me! They won't do what I tell them to. They'll say, 'Jehovah never appeared to you!'" [10]Moses pleaded, "O Lord, I'm just not a good speaker. I never have been, and I'm not now, even after you have spoken to me, for I have a speech impediment." [13]Moses said, "Lord, please! Send someone else."

Ex 5:22. Then Moses went back to the Lord. "Lord," he protested, "how can you mistreat your own people like this? Why did you ever send me, if you were going to do this to them? [23]Ever since I gave Pharaoh your message, he has only been more and more brutal to them, and you have not delivered them at all!"

Ex 6:12. "But look," Moses objected, "my own people won't even listen to me any more; how can I expect Pharaoh to? I'm no orator!"

Ex 14:10. As the Egyptian army approached, the people of Israel saw them far in the distance speeding after them, and they were terribly frightened, and cried out to the Lord to help them. [11]And they turned against Moses, whining, "Have you brought us out here to die in the desert because there were not enough graves for us in Egypt? Why did you make us leave Egypt? [12]Isn't this what we told you, while we were slaves, to leave us alone? We said it would be better to be slaves to the Egyptians than dead in the wilderness." [15]Then the Lord said to Moses, "Quit praying and get the people moving! Forward march!"

Num 11:21. But Moses said, "There are 600,000 men alone [besides all the women and children], and yet you promise them meat for a whole month! [22]If we butcher all our flocks and herds it won't be enough! We would have to catch every fish in the ocean to fulfil your promise!"

Judg 6:13. "Stranger," Gideon replied, "if the Lord is with us, why has all this happened to us? And where are all the miracles our ancestors have told us about—such as when God brought them out of Egypt? Now the Lord has thrown us away and has let the Midianites completely ruin us. [15]Sir, how can I save Israel? My family is the poorest in the whole tribe of Manasseh, and I am the least thought of in the entire family!"

1 Sam 16:1. Finally the Lord said to Samuel, "You have mourned long enough for Saul, for I have rejected him as king of Israel. Now take a vial of olive oil and go to Bethlehem and find a man named Jesse, for I have selected one of his sons to be the new king." [2]But Samuel asked, "How can I do that? If Saul hears about it, he will kill me." "Take a heifer with you," the Lord replied, "and say that you have come to make a sacrifice to the Lord."

1 Sam 17:11. When Saul and the Israeli army heard this, they were dismayed and frightened. [24]As soon as they saw him [Goliath] the Israeli army began to run away in fright.

1 Sam 22:3. Later David went to Mizpeh in Moab to ask permission of the king for his father and mother to live there under royal protection until David knew what God was going to do for him. [4]They stayed in Moab during the entire period when David was living in the cave.

1 Kgs 18:7. Suddenly Obadiah saw Elijah coming toward him! Obadiah recognized him at once and fell to the ground before him. "Is it really you, my lord Elijah?" he asked. [8]"Yes, it is," Elijah replied. "Now go and tell the king I am here." [9]"Oh, sir," Obadiah protested, "what harm have I done to you that you are sending me to my death? [10]For I swear by God that the king has searched every nation and kingdom on earth from end to end to find you. And each time when he was told 'Elijah isn't here,' King Ahab forced the king of that nation to swear to the truth of his claim. [11]And now you say, 'Go and tell him Elijah is here'! [12]But as soon as I leave you, the Spirit of the Lord will carry you away, who knows where, and when Ahab comes and can't find you, he will kill me; yet I have been a true servant of the Lord all my life. [13]Has no one told you about the time when Queen Jezebel was trying to kill the Lord's prophets, and I hid a hundred of them in two caves and fed them with bread and water? [14]And now you say, 'Go tell the king that Elijah is here'! Sir, if I do that, I'm dead!"

1 Kgs 19:13. When Elijah heard it, he wrapped his face in his scarf and went out and stood at the entrance of the cave. And a voice said, "Why are you here, Elijah?" [14]He replied again, "I have been working very hard for the Lord God of the armies of heaven, but the people have broken their covenant and have torn down your altars; they have killed every one of your prophets except me; and now they are trying to kill me, too." [15]Then the Lord told him, "Go back by the desert road to Damascus, and when you arrive, anoint Hazael to be king of Syria. [16]Then anoint Jehu (son of Himshi) to be king of Israel, and anoint Elisha (the son of Shaphat of Abel-meholah) to replace you as my prophet. [17]Anyone who escapes from Hazael shall be killed by Jehu, and those who escape Jehu shall be killed by Elisha! [18]And incidentally, there are 7,000 men in Israel who

have never bowed to Baal nor kissed him!"

2 Kgs 13:18. "Now pick up the other arrows and strike them against the floor." So the king picked them up and struck the floor three times. [19]But the prophet was angry with him. "You should have struck the floor five or six times," he exclaimed, "for then you would have beaten Syria until they were entirely destroyed; now you will be victorious only three times."

Jer 1:6. "O Lord God," I said, "I can't do that! I'm far too young! I'm only a youth!"

Jer 32:24. See how the siege mounds have been built against the city walls, and the Babylonians shall conquer the city by sword, famine and disease. Everything has happened just as you said—as you determined it should! [25]And yet you say to buy the field—paying good money for it before these witnesses—even though the city will belong to our enemies. Lam chapters 1–5.

Mt 8:23. Then he got into a boat and started across the lake with his disciples. [24]Suddenly a terrible storm came up, with waves higher than the boat. But Jesus was asleep. [25]The disciples went to him and wakened him, shouting, "Lord, save us! We're sinking!" [26]But Jesus answered, "O you men of little faith! Why are you so frightened?" Then he stood up and rebuked the wind and waves, and the storm subsided and all was calm. [27]The disciples just sat there, awed! "Who is this," they asked themselves, "that even the winds and the sea obey him?"

Mt 11:2. John the Baptist, who was now in prison, heard about all the miracles the Messiah was doing, so he sent his disciples to ask Jesus, [3]"Are you really the one we are waiting for, or shall we keep on looking?"

Mt 14:29. "All right," the Lord said, "come along!" So Peter went over the side of the boat and walked on the water towards Jesus. [30]But when he looked around at the high waves, he was terrified and began to sink. "Save me, Lord!" he shouted. [31]Instantly Jesus reached out his hand and rescued him. "O man of little faith," Jesus said. "Why did you doubt me?"

Mt 17:14. When they arrived at the bottom of the hill, a huge crowd was waiting for them. A man came and knelt before Jesus and said, [15]"Sir, have mercy on my son, for he is mentally deranged, and in great trouble, for he often falls into the fire or into the water; [16]so I brought him to your disciples, but they couldn't cure him." [17]Jesus replied, "Oh, you stubborn, faithless people! How long shall I bear with you? Bring him here to me." [18]Then Jesus rebuked the demon in the boy and it left him, and from that moment the boy was well. [19]Afterwards the disciples asked Jesus privately, "Why couldn't we cast that demon out?" [20]"Because of your little faith," Jesus told them. "For if you had faith even as small as a tiny mustard seed you could say to this mountain, 'Move!' and it would go far away. Nothing would be impossible. [21]But this kind of demon won't leave unless you have prayed and gone without food." Mk 9:14–29.

Mt 28:17. There they met him and worshiped him—but some of them weren't sure it really was Jesus!

Mk 16:10, 11. She found the disciples wet-eyed with grief and exclaimed that she had seen Jesus, and he was alive! But they didn't believe her!

Lk 12:27. Look at the lilies! They don't toil and spin, and yet Solomon in all his glory was not robed as well as they are. [28]And if God provides clothing for the flowers that are here today and gone tomorrow, don't you suppose that he will provide clothing for you, you doubters?

Lk 24:35. Then the two from Emmaus told their story of how Jesus had appeared to them as they were walking along the road and how they had recognized him as he was breaking the bread. [36]And just as they were telling about it, Jesus himself was suddenly standing there among them, and greeted them. [37]But the whole group was terribly frightened, thinking they were seeing a ghost! [38]"Why are you frightened?" he asked. "Why do you doubt that it is really I? [39]Look at my hands! Look at my feet! You can see that it is I, myself! Touch me and make sure that I am not a ghost! For ghosts don't have bodies, as you see that I do!" [40]As he spoke, he held out his hands for them to see [the marks of the nails], and showed them [the wounds in] his feet. [41]Still they stood there undecided, filled with joy and doubt.

Jn 14:8. Philip said, "Sir, show us the Father and we will be satisfied." [9]Jesus replied, "Don't you even yet know who I am, Philip, even after all this time I have been with you? Anyone who has seen me has seen the Father! So why are you asking to see him? [10]Don't you believe that I am in the Father and the Father is in me? The words I say are not my own but are from my Father who lives in me. And he does his work through me. [11]Just believe it—that I am in the Father and the Father is in me. Or else believe it because of the mighty miracles you have seen me do.

Acts 9:13. "But Lord," exclaimed Ananias, "I have heard about the terrible things this man has done to the believers in Jerusalem! [14]And we hear that he has arrest warrants with him from the chief priests, authorizing him to arrest every believer in Damascus!"

See *Cowardice; Murmuring.*

DOUGH First of, offered to God, Num 15:19–21; Neh 10:37. Kneaded, Jer 7:18; Hos 7:4. Part of, for priest, Ezk 44:30.

See *Bread; Oven.*

DOVE, TURTLE DOVE Sent out from the ark by Noah, Gen 8:8–11. Mourning of, Isa 38:14; 59:11; Nah 2:7. Nests of, Isa 60:8; Jer 48:28. Harmlessness of, typical of Christ's gentleness, Mt 10:16. Sacrificial uses of, Gen 15:9. Prescribed for purification: Of women, Lev 12:6, 8; Lk 2:24; of Nazirites, Num 6:10; of lepers, Lev 14:22. Burnt offering of, Lev 1:14–17. Trespass offering of, for the poor, Lev 5:7–10; 12:8. Sin offering, for those who touched any dead body, Num 6:10. Market for, in the temple, Mt 21:12; Jn 2:14.

Symbolical. Of the Holy Spirit, Mt 3:16; Lk 3:22; Jn 1:32.

See *Pigeon.*

DOWRY Ex 22:16. If a man seduces a girl who is not engaged to anyone, and sleeps with her, he must pay the usual dowry and accept her as his wife. [17]But if her father utterly refuses to let her marry him, then he shall pay the money anyway.

Ruth 4:3. Boaz said to his relative, "You know Naomi, who came back to us from Moab. She is selling our brother Elimelech's property. [4]I felt that I should speak to you about it so that you can buy it if you wish, with these respected men as witnesses. If you want it, let me know right away, for if you don't take it, I will. You have the first right to purchase it and I am next." The man replied, "All right, I'll buy it." [5]Then Boaz told him, "Your purchase of the land from Naomi requires your marriage to Ruth so that she can have children to carry on her husband's name, and to inherit the land." [6]"Then I can't do it," the man replied. "For her son would become an heir to my property, too; you buy it." [7]In those days it was the custom in Israel for a man transferring a right of purchase to pull off his sandal and hand it to the other party; this publicly validated the transaction. [8]So, as the man said to Boaz, "You buy it for yourself," he drew off his sandal. [9]Then Boaz said to the witnesses and to the crowd standing around, "You have seen that today I have bought all the property of Elimelech, Chilion, and Mahlon, from Naomi.

See *Women.*

DOXOLOGY See *Praise.*

DRAGON Any terrible creature, a sea serpent, Isa 27:1.

A term applied to Pharaoh, Isa 30:7; 51:9; Ezk 29:3; to Satan, Rev 20:2.

Symbolical. Ezk 29:3; 32:2; Rev 12; 13; 16:13.

DRAPERIES See *Curtains.*

DRAMA See *Pantomime.*

DRAWING Of pictures on brick, Ezk 4:1.

DREAM Evanescent, Job 20:8. Vanity of, Eccl 5:1–3, 6, 7.

Revelations by, Num 12:6; Job 33:15–18; Jer 23:28; Joel 2:28; Acts 2:17. The dreams of the wine taster and baker, Gen 40:8–23; Pharaoh, Gen 41:1–36.

Interpreted by Joseph, Gen 40:12, 13, 18, 19; 41:25–32; Daniel, Dan 2:16–23, 28–30; 4. Delusive, Isa 29:7, 8.

False prophets pretended to receive revelations through, Deut 13:1–5; Jer 23:25–32; 27:9; 29:8; Zech 10:2.

See *Vision.*

INSTANCES OF. Of Abimelech, concerning Sarah, Gen 20:3. Of Jacob, concerning the ladder, Gen 28:12; the streaked goats, Gen 31:10–13; concerning his going down into Egypt, Gen 46:2. Of Laban, concerning Jacob, Gen 31:24. Of Joseph, concerning the sheaves, Gen 37:5–10. Of the Midianite, concerning the loaf of barley bread, Judg 7:12, 13. Of Solomon, concerning his choice of wisdom, 1 Kgs 3:3–15. Of Eliphaz, of a spirit speaking to him, Job 4:12–21. Of Daniel, concerning the four beasts, Dan 7. Of Joseph, concerning Mary's innocence, Mt 1:20, 21; concerning the escape into Egypt, Mt 2:13; concerning the return into Palestine, Mt 2:19–22. Of Pilate's wife, concerning Jesus, Mt 27:19. Cornelius' vision, concerning Peter, Acts 10:3–6. Peter's vision of the unclean animals, Acts 10:9–16. Paul's vision of the man in Macedonia, crying, "Come over here and help us," Acts 16:9; relating to his going to Rome, Acts 23:11; concerning the shipwreck, and the safety of all on board, Acts 27:23, 24.

DREGS Settlings of wine, Ps 75:8.

DRESS Of fig leaves, Gen 3:7. Of skins, Gen 3:21. Of other materials, see *Hair; Goat, Hair of; Leather; Linen; Sackcloth; Silk; Wool.* Mixed materials in, forbidden, Lev 19:19; Deut 22:11. Men forbidden to wear women's, and women forbidden to wear men's, Deut 22:5. Rules with respect to women's, 1 Tim 2:9, 10; 1 Pet 3:3. Not to be held overnight as a pledge for debt, Ex 22:26. Ceremonial purification of, Lev 11:25, 32; 13:47–59; Num 19:7; 31:20. Tearing of, see *Mourning.*

Of the head: Caps, or turbans, prescribed by Moses, for the priests, Ex 28:40; 29:9; 39:28, 29; by Ezekiel, Ezk 44:18. Scarves, worn by women, Isa 3:20. Headbands, Isa 3:20. Veils, Isa 3:19, 23; Ezk 13:18, 21. See *Veil.*

Various articles of: Scarf, 1 Kgs 19:13. Robe, Ex 28:4, 40; 1 Sam 18:4; 2 Sam 13:17, 18; 1 Chron 15:27; Job 1:20; Ezk 5:3. Purple, Jn 19:2, 5, 23. Cape, Isa 3:22. Coat, Ex 28:4; 1 Sam 2:19; Acts 9:39; 2 Tim 4:13. Shirts and coats, Mt 5:40; Lk 6:29. Purse, Isa 3:22.

Changes of clothing, the folly of excessive, Job 27:16. Uniform vestments kept in store for worshipers of Baal, 2 Kgs 10:22, 23; Zeph 1:8; for wedding feasts, Mt 22:11. Presents made of changes of clothing, Gen 45:22; 1 Sam 18:4; 2 Kgs 5:5; Esther 6:7, 8; Dan 5:7. Vestments of priests, see *Priest;* of mourning, see *Mourning.*

FIGURATIVE. Filthy, of unrighteousness, Isa 64:6. Of righteousness and of sin, see *Color, Symbolism of.*

Symbolical. Filthy, of sin, Zech 3:3, 4.

DRINK Intoxicating, see *Abstinence, Total; Drunkard; Drunkenness; Wine.*

DRINK OFFERING See *Offerings.*

DRIVING Rapid, by Jehu, 2 Kgs 9:20.

DROMEDARY Esther 8:9, 10; Isa 60:6.

DROPSY Lk 14:1, 2.

DROSS FIGURATIVE. Prov 25:4, 5; Jer 6:29; Ezk 22:18–20; Mal 3:3.

DROUGHT Gen 31:40; 1 Kgs chapters 17, 18; Jer 14:1–6. Sent by God as a judgment, Deut 28:23, 24; 1 Kgs 8:35, 36; 2 Chron 6:26; 7:13; Hos 13:15.

See *Famine; Meteorology; Rain.*

FIGURATIVE. Ps 32:4; Isa 44:3.

DRUMS Used in worship, Ps 81:2; 149:3.

DRUNKARD Deut 21:20. And declare, "This son of ours is stubborn and rebellious and won't obey; he is a worthless drunkard." [21]Then the men of the city shall stone him to death. In this way you shall put away this evil from among you, and all the young men of Israel will hear about what happened and will be afraid.

Ps 69:12. I am the talk of the town and the song of the drunkards.

Prov 23:19–21. Oh my son, be wise and stay in God's paths; don't carouse with drunkards and gluttons, for they are on their way to poverty. And remember that too much sleep clothes a man with rags.

Isa 28:1. Woe to the city of Samaria, surrounded by her rich valley—Samaria, the pride and delight of the drunkards of Israel! Woe to her fading beauty, the crowning glory of a nation of men lying drunk in the streets! [3]The proud city of Samaria—yes, the joy and delight of the drunkards of Israel—will be hurled to the ground and trampled beneath the enemies' feet.

Joel 1:5. Wake up and weep, you drunkards, for all the grapes are ruined and all your wine is gone!

1 Cor 5:11. What I meant was that you are not to keep company with anyone who claims to be a brother Christian but indulges in sexual sins, or is greedy, or is a swindler, or worships idols, or is a drunkard, or abusive. Don't even eat lunch with such a person.

1 Cor 6:9, 10. Don't you know that those doing such things have no share in the Kingdom of God? Don't fool yourselves. Those who live immoral lives, who are idol worshipers, adulterers or homosexuals—will have no share in his kingdom. Neither will thieves or greedy people, drunkards, slanderers, or robbers.

See *Drunkenness.*

DRUNKENNESS Deut 21:20. And declare, "This son of ours . . . is a worthless drunkard." [21]Then the men of the city shall stone him to death. In this way you shall put away this evil from among you, and all the young men of Israel will hear about what happened and will be afraid.

1 Sam 1:14. "Must you come here drunk?" he demanded. "Throw away your bottle."

Ps 69:12. I am the talk of the town and the song of the drunkards.

Prov 20:1. Wine gives false courage; hard liquor leads to brawls; what fools men are to let it master them, making them reel drunkenly down the street!

Prov 21:17. A man who loves pleasure becomes poor; wine and luxury are not the way to riches!

Prov 23:19–21. O my son, be wise and stay in God's paths; don't carouse with drunkards and gluttons, for they are on their way to poverty. [29, 30]Whose heart is filled with anguish and sorrow? Who is always fighting and quarreling? Who is the man with bloodshot eyes and many wounds? It is the one who spends long hours in the taverns, trying out new mixtures. [31]Don't let the sparkle and the smooth taste of strong wine deceive you. [32]For in the end it bites like a poisonous serpent; it stings like an adder. [33]You will see hallucinations and have delirium tremens, and you will say foolish, silly things that would embarrass you no end when sober. [34]You will stagger like a sailor tossed at sea, clinging to a swaying mast. [35]And afterwards you will say, "I didn't even know it when they beat me up. . . . Let's go and have another drink!"

Prov 31:4. And it is not for kings, O Lemuel, to drink wine and whiskey. [5]For if they drink they may forget their duties and be unable to give justice to those who are oppressed. [6, 7]Hard liquor is for sick men at the brink of death, and wine for those in deep depression. Let them drink to forget their poverty and misery.

Isa 5:11. Woe to you who get up early in the morning to go on long drinking bouts that last till late at night—woe to you drunken bums. [12]You furnish lovely music at your grand parties; the orchestras are superb! But for the Lord you have no thought or care. [22]Woe to those who are "heroes" when it comes to drinking, and boast about the liquor they can hold.

Isa 19:14. The Lord has sent a spirit of foolishness on them, so that all their suggestions are wrong; they make Egypt stagger like a sick drunkard.

Isa 24:9. No more are the joys of wine and song; strong drink turns bitter in the mouth. [11]Mobs form in the streets, crying for wine; joy has reached its lowest ebb; gladness has been banished from the land.

Isa 28:1. Woe to the city of Samaria, surrounded by her rich valley—Samaria, the pride and delight of the drunkards of Israel! Woe to her fading beauty, the crowning glory of a nation of men lying drunk in the streets! [3]The proud city of Samaria—yes, the joy and delight of the drunkards of Israel—will be hurled to the ground and trampled beneath the enemies' feet. [7]But Jerusalem is now led by drunks! Her priests and prophets reel and stagger, making stupid errors and mistakes. [8]Their tables are covered with vomit; filth is everywhere.

Isa 56:12. "Come," they say. "We'll get some wine and have a party; let's all get drunk. This is really living; let it go on and on, and tomorrow will be better yet!"

Jer 25:27. Tell them, "The Lord of Hosts, the God of Israel, says, Drink from this cup of my wrath until you are drunk and vomit and fall and rise no more, for I am sending terrible wars upon you."

Hos 4:11. Wine, women, and song have robbed my people of their brains.

Hos 7:5. On the king's birthday, the princes get him drunk; he makes a fool of himself and drinks with those who mock him.

Joel 1:5. Wake up and weep, you drunkards, for all the grapes are ruined and all your wine is gone!

Joel 3:3. They divided up my people as their slaves; they traded a young lad for a prostitute, and a little girl for wine enough to get drunk.

Amos 2:8. At their religious feasts they lounge in clothing stolen from their debtors, and in my own Temple they offer sacrifices of wine they purchased with stolen money. [12]But you caused the Nazarites to sin by urging them to drink your wine, and you silenced my prophets, telling them, "Shut up!"

Amos 6:1. Woe to those lounging in luxury at Jerusalem and Samaria. [6]You drink wine by the bucketful and perfume yourselves with sweet ointments, caring nothing at all that your brothers need your help.

Mic 2:11. "I'll preach to you the joys of wine and drink"—that is the kind of drunken, lying prophet that you like!

Hab 2:15. Woe to you for making your neighboring lands reel and stagger like drunkards beneath your blows, and then gloating over their nakedness and shame. [16]Soon your own glory will be replaced by shame. Drink down God's judgment on yourselves. Stagger and fall! *v.* 17.

Mt 24:49. And begin oppressing your fellow servants, partying and getting drunk. Lk 12:45.

Lk 21:34, 35. Watch out! Don't let my sudden coming catch you unawares; don't let me find you living in careless ease, carousing and drinking, and occupied with the problems of this life, like all the rest of the world.

Rom 13:13. Be decent and true in everything you do so that all can approve your behavior. Don't spend your time in wild parties and getting drunk or in adultery and lust, or fighting, or jealousy.

1 Cor 5:11. You are not to keep company with anyone who claims to be a brother Christian but indulges in sexual sins . . . or is a drunkard. . . . Don't even eat lunch with such a person.

Gal 5:19. But when you follow your own wrong inclinations your lives will produce these evil results: impure thoughts, eagerness for lustful pleasure, [20]idolatry, spiritism (that is, encouraging the activity of demons), hatred and fighting, jealousy and anger, constant effort to get the best for yourself, complaints and criticisms, the feeling that everyone else is wrong except those in your own little group—and there will be wrong doctrine, [21]envy, murder, drunkenness, wild parties, and all that sort of thing. Let me tell you again as I have before, that anyone living that sort of life will not inherit the kingdom of God.

Eph 5:18. Don't drink too much wine, for many evils lie along that path; be filled instead with the Holy Spirit, and controlled by him.

1 Thess 5:7. Night is the time for sleep and the time when people get drunk. [8]But let us who live in the light keep sober.

Tit 1:7. These pastors must be men of blameless lives because they are God's ministers. They must not be . . . drunkards.

FIGURATIVE. Isa 28:8; 51:17, 21–23; 63:6; Jer 25: 15, 16, 27, 28; 51:7–9; Lam 3:15; Ezk 23:31–34; Hab 2:15, 16.

See *Abstinence; Drunkard; Sobriety; Wine.*

INSTANCES OF. Noah, Gen 9:20, 21. Lot, Gen 19:33. Nabal, 1 Sam 25:36. Uriah, 2 Sam 11:13. Amnon, 2 Sam 13:28. Elah, 1 Kgs 16:9. Benhadad and his 32 confederate kings, 1 Kgs 20:16. Ahasuerus, Esther 1:10, 11. Belshazzar, Dan 5:1–6. Corinthians, 1 Cor 11:21.

FALSELY ACCUSED OF. Hannah, 1 Sam 1:12–16. Jesus, Mt 11:19. The apostles, Acts 2:13–15.

DRUSILLA Wife of Felix, Acts 24:24.

DULCIMER Dan 3:5, 10.

See *Music, Instruments of.*

DUMAH 1. Son of Ishmael, Gen 25:12–15; 1 Chron 1:28–31.

2. A city of Canaan assigned to Judah, Josh 15: 48–62.

3. Or Edom, Isa 21:11.

DUMB Stricken by God, Ex 4:11; Lk 1:20, 64; miraculous healing of, by Jesus, Mt 9:32, 33; 12:22; 15:30, 31; Mk 7:37; 9:17, 25, 26.

See *Deafness.*

DUNG See *Fertilizer; Manure.*

DUNGEON In prisons, Gen 41:14; Isa 24:22; 51:14; Jer 32:2; 37:15, 16; Acts 16:24.

See *Prison.*

DURA Plain of, Dan 3:1.

DUST Man made from, Gen 2:7; 18:27; Job 34: 15; Ps 103:14; Eccl 3:20; Ezk 2:1; 3:17; 1 Cor 15:47, 48. Tossing of, in anger, 2 Sam 16:13; Acts 22:23. Shaking from feet, Mt 10:14; Mk 6:11; Lk 9:5; 10:11; Acts 13:51; 18:6. Put on the head in mourning, Josh 7:6; 1 Sam 4:12; 2 Sam 1:2; Job 2:12; 42:6; Lam 2:10.

FIGURATIVE. Job 4:19.

See *Clay.*

DUTY Tribute levied on foreign commerce by Solomon, 1 Kgs 10:15.

DUTY OF MAN TO GOD. Deut 6:5. You must love him with *all* your heart, soul, and might.

Deut 10:12, 13. And now, Israel, what does the Lord your God require of you except to listen carefully to all he says to you, and to obey for your own good the commandments I am giving you today, and to love him, and to worship him with all your hearts and souls?

Deut 11:1. You must love the Lord your God and obey every one of his commands.

Deut 30:15. Look, today I have set before you life and death, depending on whether you obey or disobey. [16]I have commanded you today to love the Lord your God and to follow his paths and to keep his laws, so that you will live and become a great nation, and so that the Lord your God will bless you and the land you are about to possess. [17]But if your hearts turn away and you won't listen—if you are drawn away to worship other gods— [18]then I declare to you this day that you shall surely perish; you will not have a long, good life in the land you are going in to possess. [19]I call heaven and earth to witness against you that today I have set before you life or death, blessing or curse. Oh, that you would choose life, that you and your children might live! [20]Choose to love the Lord your God and to obey him and to cling to him, for he is your life and the length of your days. You will then be able to live safely in the land the Lord promised your ancestors, Abraham, Isaac, and Jacob.

Josh 22:5. Be sure to continue to obey all of the commandments Moses gave you. Love the Lord and follow his plan for your lives. Cling to him and serve him enthusiastically.

Josh 23:11. So be very careful to keep on loving him.

Ps 31:23. Oh, love the Lord, all of you who are his people; for the Lord protects those who are loyal to him, but harshly punishes all who haughtily reject him.

Prov 23:26. O my son, trust my advice—.

Mt 4:10. "Get out of here, Satan," Jesus told him. "The Scriptures say, 'Worship only the Lord God. Obey only him.' "

Mt 12:50. Then he added, "Anyone who obeys my Father in heaven is my brother, sister and mother!"

Mt 22:21. "Well, then," he said, "give it to Caesar if it is his, and give God everything that belongs to God."

36"Sir, which is the most important command in the laws of Moses? 37Jesus replied, " 'Love the Lord your God with all your heart, soul, and mind.' 38, 39This is the first and greatest commandment. The second most important is similar: 'Love your neighbor as much as you love yourself.' 40All the other commandments and all the demands of the prophets stem from these two laws and are fulfilled if you obey them."

Lk 17:10. Just so, if you merely obey me, you should not consider yourselves worthy of praise. For you have simply done your duty!

Lk 21:3. "Really," he remarked, "this poor widow has given more than all the rest of them combined. 4For they have given a little of what they didn't need, but she, poor as she is, has given everything she has."

Jn 4:34. Then Jesus explained: "My nourishment comes from doing the will of God who sent me, and from finishing his work."

Jn 6:38. For I have come here from heaven to do the will of God who sent me, not to have my own way.

Jn 14:15. If you love me, obey me. 21The one who obeys me is the one who loves me; and because he loves me, my Father will love him.

Jn 15:14. And you are my friends if you obey me.

Acts 4:19. But Peter and John replied, "You decide whether God wants us to obey you instead of him! 20We cannot stop telling about the wonderful things we saw Jesus do and heard him say."

Acts 5:29. But Peter and the apostles replied, "We must obey God rather than men."

Jude 1:21. Stay always within the boundaries where God's love can reach and bless you.

See *Commandments; Faithfulness; Obedience; Responsibility.*

OF MAN TO MAN. Lev 19:18. But love your neighbor as yourself, for I am Jehovah.

Isa 58:6. No, the kind of fast I want is that you stop oppressing those who work for you and treat them fairly and give them what they earn. 7I want you to share your food with the hungry and bring right into your own homes those who are helpless, poor and destitute. Clothe those who are cold and don't hide from relatives who need your help.

Mt 7:12. Do for others what you want them to do for you. This is the teaching of the laws of Moses in a nutshell.

Mt 25:34. Then I, the King, shall say to those at my right, "Come, blessed of my Father, into the Kingdom prepared for you from the founding of the world. 35For I was hungry and you fed me; I was thirsty and you gave me water; I was a stranger and you invited me into your homes; 36naked and you clothed me; sick and in prison, and you visited me." 37Then these righteous ones will reply, "Sir, when did we ever see you hungry and feed you? Or thirsty and give you anything to drink? 38Or a stranger, and help you? Or naked, and clothe you? 39When did we ever see you sick or in prison, and visit you?" 40And I, the King, will tell them, "When you did it to these my brothers you were doing it to me!" 41Then I will turn to those on my left and say, "Away with you, you cursed ones, into the eternal fire prepared for the devil and his demons. 42For I was hungry and you wouldn't feed me; thirsty, and you wouldn't give me anything to drink; 43a stranger, and you refused me hospitality; naked, and you wouldn't clothe me; sick, and in prison, and you didn't visit me." 44Then they will reply, "Lord, when did we ever see you hungry or thirsty or a stranger or naked or sick or in prison, and not help you?" 45And I will answer, "When you refused to help the least of these my brothers, you were refusing help to me." 46And they shall go away into eternal punishment; but the righteous into everlasting life.

Lk 10:25. One day an expert on Moses' laws came to test Jesus' orthodoxy by asking him this question: "Teacher, what does a man need to do to live forever in heaven?" 26Jesus replied, "What does Moses' law say about it?" 27"It says," he replied, "that you must love the Lord your God with all your heart, and with all your soul, and with all your strength, and with all your mind. And you must love your neighbor just as much as you love yourself." 28"Right!" Jesus told him. "*Do* this and *you* shall live!" 29The man wanted to justify (his lack of love for some kinds of people), so he asked, "Which neighbors?" 30Jesus replied with an illustration: "A Jew going on a trip from Jerusalem to Jericho was attacked by bandits. They stripped him of his clothes and money and beat him up and left him lying half dead beside the road. 31By chance a Jewish priest came along; and when he saw the man lying there, he passed to the other side of the road and passed him by. 32A Jewish Temple-assistant walked over and looked at him lying there, but then went on. 33But a despised Samaritan came along, and when he saw him, he felt deep pity. 34Kneeling beside him the Samaritan soothed his wounds with medicine and bandaged them. Then he put the man on his donkey and walked along beside him till they came to an inn, where he nursed him through the night. 35The next day he handed the innkeeper two twenty-dollar bills and told him to take care of the man, "If his bill runs higher than that,' he said, 'I'll pay the difference the next time I am here.' 36Now which of these three would you say was a neighbor to the bandits' victim?" [37]The man replied, "The one who showed him some pity." Then Jesus said, "Yes, now go and do the same."

See *Commandments; Children; Husband; Minister, Duties of; Parents; Responsibility; Wife.*

DWARFS Forbidden to be priests, Lev 21:20.

DYEING Ex 25:1–7; 26:14; 35:23; 36:19; 39:33–40; Ezk 27:7, 16.

DYING See *Death.*

DYSENTERY Acts 28:8.

DYSPEPSIA Of Timothy, 1 Tim 5:23.

E

EAGLE Forbidden as food, Lev 11:13–19; Deut 14:11–18. Swift flight of, Deut 28:49; Job 9:26; Prov 30:18, 19; Jer 4:13; Lam 4:19. Nest of, Deut 32:11; Job 39:27–30; Jer 49:16. Carries her young on her wings, Ex 19:4, Deut 32:11. Long life of, Ps 103:5.

FIGURATIVE. Ex 19:4; Deut 32:11.

Symbolical. Ezk 1:10; 10:14; 17:3, 4; Dan 7:4; Rev 4:7; 12:14.

EAR Blood put on, in consecration of priests, Ex 29:19, 20; Lev 8:23; in cleansing lepers, Lev 14:17, 25. Bored as a sign of servitude, Ex 21:5, 6.

FIGURATIVE. Anthropomorphic uses of:

Ps 17:6. Why am I praying like this? Because I know you will answer me, O God! Yes, listen as I pray.

Ps 39:12. Hear my prayer, O Lord; listen to my cry!

Ps 77:1. I cry to the Lord. . . . Oh, that he would listen.

Ps 80:1. O shepherd of Israel . . . bend down your ear and listen as I plead.

Ps 84:8. O Jehovah . . . hear my prayer!

For more extended anthropomorphic uses, consult concordances.

EARNEST See *Guarantee; Token.*

EARNESTNESS See *Zeal.*

EARRING Of gold, Judg 8:23, 24. Offering of, for the golden calf, Ex 32:2, 3; for the tabernacle, Ex 35:22. Worn for idolatrous purposes, Gen 35:4; Isa 3:20.

EARTH Primitive condition of, Gen 1:2, 6; Job 26:7; Ps 104:5–9; Jer 4:23. Design of, 1 Sam 2:8; Isa 45:18. Foundations and corners of, Job 9:6; Rev 7:1. Cursed by God, Gen 3:17, 18; Rom 8:19–22. Circle of, Isa 40:22. God's footstool, Isa 66:1; Lam 2:1. Given to man, Ps 115:16. Early divisions of, Gen 10; 11; Deut 32:8. Perpetuity of, Gen 49:26; Deut 33:15; Ps 78:69; 104:5; Eccl 1:3–7; Hab 3:6.

A new earth, Isa 65:17; 66:22; Rev 21:1.

CREATED BY GOD. Gen 1:1. When God began creating the heavens and the earth.

2 Kgs 19:15. You created the heavens and the earth.

2 Chron 2:12. Blessed be the Lord God of Israel who made the heavens and the earth.

Neh 9:6. Then Ezra prayed, "You alone are God. You have made the skies and the heavens, the earth and the seas, and everything in them. You preserve it all; and all the angels of heaven worship you."

Ps 90:2. Before the mountains were created, before the earth was formed, you are God without beginning or end.

Ps 102:25. In ages past you laid the foundations of the earth, and made the heavens with your hands!

Ps 115:15. Yes, Jehovah who made heaven and earth will personally bless you!

Ps 146:6. The God who made both earth and heaven, the seas and everything in them.

Prov 8:22. The Lord formed me in the beginning, before he created anything else. [23]From ages past, I am. I existed before the earth began. [24]I lived before the oceans were created, before the springs bubbled forth their waters onto the earth; [25]before the mountains and the hills were made. [26]Yes, I was born before God made the earth and fields, and high plateaus.

Isa 37:16. O Lord of Hosts, God of Israel enthroned above the cherubim, *you alone* are God of all the kingdoms of the earth. You alone made heaven and earth.

Isa 45:18. For Jehovah created the heavens and earth and put everything in place, and he made the world to be lived in, not to be an empty chaos. I am Jehovah, he says, and there is no other!

Jer 10:12. But our God formed the earth by his power and wisdom, and by his intelligence he hung the stars in space and stretched out the heavens.

Jer 27:5. By my great power I have made the earth and all mankind and every animal; and I give these things of mine to anyone I want to.

Jer 32:17. O Lord God! You have made the heavens and earth by your great power; nothing is too hard for you!

Jer 51:15. God made the earth by his power and wisdom. He stretched out the heavens by his understanding.

Jn 17:24. You gave me the glory because you loved me before the world began!

2 Pet 3:5, 6. They deliberately forget this fact: that God did destroy the world with a mighty flood, long after he had made the heavens by the word of his command, and had used the wa-

ters to form the earth and surround it.

Rev 10:6. And swore by him who lives forever and ever, who created heaven and everything in it and the earth and all that it contains and the sea and its inhabitants, that there should be no more delay.

Rev 14:7. "Fear God," he shouted, "and extol his greatness. For the time has come when he will sit as Judge. Worship him who made the heaven and the earth, the sea and all its sources."

By Christ. Jn 1:3. He created everything there is —nothing exists that he didn't make. [10]But although he made the world, the world didn't recognize him when he came.

Heb 1:10. God also called him "Lord" when he said, "Lord, in the beginning you made the earth, and the heavens are the work of your hands."

See *Creation; God, Creator.*

DESTRUCTION OF. Ps 102:25. In ages past you laid the foundations of the earth, and made the heavens with your hands! [26]They shall perish, but you go on forever. They will grow old, like worn-out clothing, and you will change them like a man putting on a new shirt and throwing away the old one! [27]But you yourself never grow old. You are forever, and your years never end. Heb 1:10–12.

Isa 24:19. The earth has broken down in utter collapse; everything is lost, abandoned and confused. [20]The world staggers like a drunkard; it shakes like a tent in a storm. It falls and will not rise again, for the sins of the earth are very great.

Isa 51:6. Look high in the skies and watch the earth beneath, for the skies shall disappear like smoke, the earth shall wear out like a garment, and the people of the earth shall die like flies. But my salvation lasts forever; my righteous rule will never die nor end.

Mt 24:3. "When will this happen?" the disciples asked him later, as he sat on the slopes of the Mount of Olives. "What events will signal your return, and the end of the world?" [14]"And the Good News about the Kingdom will be preached throughout the whole world, so that all nations will hear it, and then, finally, the end will come. [29]Immediately after the persecution of those days the sun will be darkened, and the moon will not give light, and the stars will seem to fall from the heavens, and the powers overshadowing the earth will be convulsed. [30]And then at last the signal of my coming will appear in the heavens and there will be deep mourning all around the earth. And the nations of the world will see me arrive in the clouds of heaven, with power and great glory. [31]And I shall send forth my angels with the sound of a mighty trumpet blast, and they shall gather my chosen ones from the farthest ends of the earth and heaven. [35]Heaven and earth will disappear, but my words remain forever. [36]But no one knows the date and hour when the end will be—not even the angels. No, nor even God's Son. Only the Father knows. [37, 38]The world will be at ease—banquets and parties and weddings—just as it was in Noah's time before the sudden coming of the flood; [39]people wouldn't believe what was going to happen until the flood actually arrived and took them all away. So shall my coming be." Mk 13:24–37; Lk 21:26–36.

2 Pet 3:10. The day of the Lord is surely coming, as unexpectedly as a thief, and then the heavens will pass away with a terrible noise and the heavenly bodies will disappear in fire, and the earth and everything on it will be burned up. [11]And so since everything around us is going to melt away, what holy, godly lives we should be living! [12]You should look forward to that day and hurry it along—the day when God will set the heavens on fire, and the heavenly bodies will melt and disappear in flames. [13]But we are looking forward to God's promise of new heavens and a new earth afterwards, where there will be only goodness.

Rev 20:11. And I saw a great white throne and the one who sat upon it, from whose face the earth and sky fled away, but they found no place to hide.

Rev 21:1. Then I saw a new earth (with no oceans!) and a new sky, for the present earth and sky had disappeared.

EARTHENWARE See *Pottery.*

EARTHQUAKES Job 9:6; Ps 18:7; 46:2, 3; 104:32; Jer 4:24. As judgments, Ps 18:15; 60:2; Isa 13:13; 24:19, 20; 29:6; Nah 1:5. Prophecies of, Ezk 38:19; Zech 14:4; Mt 24:7; Mk 13:8; Lk 21:11; Rev 11:19.

INSTANCES OF. At Sinai, Ex 19:18; Ps 68:8; 77:18; 114:4–7; Heb 12:26. When Korah, Dathan, and Abiram were swallowed up, Num 16:31, 32. When Jonathan and his bodyguard attacked the garrison at Gibe-ah, 1 Sam 14:15. When the Lord revealed himself to Elijah in the whisper, 1 Kgs 19:11. In Canaan, in the days of Uzziah, king of Judah, Amos 1:2; Zech 14:5. At the crucifixion of Jesus, Mt 27:51. At the resurrection of Jesus, Mt 28:2. When Paul and Silas were in prison at Philippi, Acts 16:26.

FIGURATIVE. Ps 60:2.

Symbolical. Rev 6:12–14; 11:13; 16:18, 20.

EAST WIND See *Wind.*

EASTER See *Passover.*

EATING The host acting as waiter, Gen 18:8. Favored guests served an extra portion, Gen 43:34. Table used in, Judg 1:7. Sitting at table, Ex 32:6. Reclining on couches, Amos 6:4; Jn 13:23–25. Ablutions before, Mt 15:2.

See *Feasts; Food; Gluttony.*

EBAL 1. Son of Joktan, 1 Chron 1:20–23.

2. A Horite, Gen 36:23; 1 Chron 1:40.

3. A mountain of Ephraim. Half of the tribes of Israel stand on, to respond Amen to the curses of the law, Deut 11:29; 27:12, 13; Josh 8:33. Altar built on, Josh 8:30.

See *Gerizim.*

EBED 1. Father of Gaal, Judg 9:26–35.

2. A captive returned from Babylon, Ezra 8:2–14.

EBED-MELECH An Ethiopian. Jeremiah rescued by, Jer 38:7–13. Prophecy concerning, Jer 39:16–18.

EBENEZER 1. Philistines defeat the Israelites at, 1 Sam 4. Philistines remove the ark from, 1 Sam 5:1.

2. Name of a memorial stone, 1 Sam 7:12. 5:1.

EBER Called also *Heber.* 1. Gen 10:21–25; 11:14–17; 1 Chron 1:19, 24–27; Lk 3:23–38. Prophecy concerning, Num 24:23, 24. See *Hebrew.*

2. A Gadite, 1 Chron 5:13.

3. A Benjaminite, 1 Chron 8:12.

4. A Benjaminite of Jerusalem, 1 Chron 8:22.

5. A priest, Neh 12:12–21.

EBEZ A city of Issachar, Josh 19:17–23.

EBIASAPH Called also *Asaph.* A son of Korah, 1 Chron 6:22–24; 9:19; 26:1.

EBONY A hard, black wood. Merchandise in, Ezk 27:15.

EBRON A city of Asher, Josh 19:28.

ECBATANA A Persian city, Ezra 6:2.

ECCLESIASTICISM The Jewish, rebuked by Jesus, Mt 9:10–13; 23:2–4, 8–10, 13–35; Mk 9:49, 50; to be overthrown, Mt 21:19, 20, 28–44. Traditional rules of the Jewish, Mt 15:1–20; Mk 7:2–23. See *Commandments, of Men.* Arrogance of, Mt 12:2–7; 23:4.

See *Minister; Church; Usurpation, in Ecclesiastical Affairs.*

ECLIPSE Of the sun and moon, Isa 13:10; Ezk 32:7, 8; Joel 2:10, 31; 3:15; Amos 8:9; Mic 3:6; Mt 24:29; Mk 13:24; Acts 2:20; Rev 6:12, 13; 8:12.

See *Sun; Moon.*

FIGURATIVE. Isa 60:19.

ECONOMY Political, see *Economics; Government.*

ECONOMICS

Political. Gen 41:33–57.

Household. Prov 24:27; 31:10–31; Eccl 11:4–6; Jn 6:12, 13.

See *Family; Frugality; Industry.*

EDEN 1. The garden of Eden, Gen 2:8–17; 3:23, 24; 4:16; Isa 51:3; Ezk 28:13; 31:9, 16, 18; 36:35; Joel 2:3.

2. A mart of costly merchandise, 2 Kgs 19:12; Isa 37:12; Ezk 27:23.

3. A Gershonite, 2 Chron 29:12–14.

4. A Levite, 2 Chron 31:14, 15.

EDER 1. A tower near Ephrath, Gen 35:21.

2. A city of Judah, Josh 15:21–32.

3. A grandson of Merari, 1 Chron 23:23; 24:30.

4. A Benjaminite, 1 Chron 8:15.

EDOM Signifies red. 1. A name of Esau, possibly on account of his being covered with red hair, Gen 25:25, 30; 36:1.

2. A name of the land occupied by the descendants of Esau. It extended from the Elanitic Gulf to the Red Sea, and was called also *Seir* and *Idumea,* Gen 32:3; 36:20, 21; Jer 40:11.

Noted for its wise men, Obd 1:8. Sins of, Obd 1:10–14. Prophecies concerning, Jer 25:21; 27:1–11; Dan 11:41.

See *Edomites.*

FIGURATIVE. Of the foes of Zion, Isa 63:1.

Wilderness of, 2 Kgs 3:8.

EDOMITES Called also *Edom.* Descendants of Esau, Gen 36. Kings of, Gen 36:31–39; Num 20:14; 1 Chron 1:43–54; Ezk 32:29; Amos 2:1. Clan leaders of, Gen 36:9–43; Ex 15:15. Land of, Gen 32:3; Deut 2:4, 5, 12.

Protected by divine command from desolation by the Israelites, Deut 2:4–6; from being despised by the Israelites, Deut 23:7. Refuse the Israelites passage through their country, Num 20:18–22. Saul makes war against, 1 Sam 14:47. David conquers, 1 Kgs 11:14–18; 1 Chron 18:11–13; garrisons, 2 Sam 8:14; writes battle songs concerning his conquest of, Ps 60:8–10; 108:9, 10. Become confederates of Jehoshaphat, 2 Kgs 3:9, 26. Ruled by a deputy king, 1 Kgs 22:47. The Lord delivers the army of, into the hands of Jehoshaphat, 2 Chron 20:20, 23. Revolt in the days of Jehoram, 2 Kgs 8:20–22; 2 Chron 21:8–10. Amaziah, king of Judah, invades the territory of, 2 Kgs 14:5–7, 10; 2 Chron 25:11, 12. Join Babylon in war against the Israelites, Ezk 35:4, 5; Amos 1:9–11; Obd 1:11–16. A Jewish prophet in Babylon denounces, Ps 137:7; Ezk 25:12–14; 35:3–10. Grandchildren may enter the congregation of Israel, Deut 23:8. Prophecies concerning, Gen 25:23; 27:27–29, 37–40; Num 24:15–19; Isa 11:14; 21:11, 12; 34; 63:1–4; Jer 9:25, 26; 27:1–11; 49:7–22; Lam 4:21, 22; Ezk 25:12–14; 32:29, 30; 35; 36:5; Joel 3:19; Amos 1:11, 12; 9:12; Obd 1:1–21; Mal 1:2–5.

EDRE-I 1. A town of Bashan. Allotted to Manasseh, Josh 13:31. Israel defeats Og at, Num 21:33–35; Deut 1:1–5; 3:1–3.

2. A town allotted to Naphtali, Josh 19:35–39.

EDUCATION See *Instruction; Teachers; Schools.*

EGLAH Wife of David, 2 Sam 3:5; 1 Chron 3:3.

EGLON 1. King of Moab. Assassinated by Ehud, Judg 3:12–30.

2. An ancient city of Cannan. Taken by Joshua, Josh 10:22, 23, 34, 35. Allotted to Judah, Josh 15:37–44.

EGOTISM See *Conceit.*

EGYPT 1. The country of. Called Rahab, Ps 89:10; Isa 30:7. Limits of, Ezk 29:10. Fertility of, Gen 13:10. Productions of, Num 11:4, 5; Ps 78:47; Prov 7:16, 17; Isa 19:5–9. Irrigation used in, Deut 11:10. Imports of, Gen 37:25, 36. Exports of, Prov 7:16, 17; Ezk 27:7; of horses, 1 Kgs 10:28, 29.

Famine in, Gen 41; Acts 7:11. Armies of, Ex 14:7; Isa 31:1. Army of destroyed in the Red Sea, Ex 14:5–31; Isa 43:17. Wise men and magicians of, Gen 41:8; Ex 7:11; 1 Kgs 4:30; Acts 7:22. Priests of, Gen 41:45; 47:22. Idols of, Ezk 20:7, 8.

Flooded by the Nile, Amos 8:8; 9:5. Plagues in, see *Plague.* Joseph's captivity in, and subsequent rule over, see *Joseph.* Civil war in, Isa 19:2. The king acquires title to land of, Gen 47:18–26. Abraham lives in, Gen 12:10–20; 13:1. Israelites in slavery in, see *Israelites.* Joseph takes Jesus to, Mt 2:13–20.

Prophecies against, Gen 15:13, 14; Isa 19; 20:2–6; 45:14; Jer 9:25, 26; 43:8–13; 44:30; 46; Ezk chapters 29–32; Hos 8:13; Joel 3:11; Zech 10:11.

See *Egyptians.*

Symbolical. Rev 11:8, 9.

2. River of. A wadi or small stream in the Sinai peninsula, now called Wadi el-Arish, Gen 15:18; Num 34:5; Josh 15:2–4, 47; 2 Kgs 24:7; 2 Chron 7:8; Ezk 47:19; 48:27, 28.

EGYPTIANS Descendants of Mizraim, Gen 10:6, 13, 14. Wisdom of, 1 Kgs 4:30. The art of embalming the dead practiced by, Gen 50:2, 3, 26. Hospitality of, to Abraham, Gen 12:10–20. Slaves bought by, Gen 37:36. Oppress the Israelites, Ex chapters 1, 2. Refuse to release the Israelites, Ex chapters 5–10. Visited by plagues, Ex chapters 7–12; Ps 78:43–51; firstborn of, killed, Ex 12:29; Ps 78:51; 105:36; 136:10. Send the Israelites away, Ex 12:29–36. Pursue Israelites, and the army of, destroyed, Ex 14:5–30; Ps 106:11; Heb 11:29.

Despised shepherds, Gen 46:34. Refused to eat with Hebrews, Gen 43:32. Alliances with, forbidden to the Israelites, Isa 30:2; 31:1; 36:6; Ezk 17:15; 29:6. Eligible to membership in Israelitish congregation in the third generation, Deut 23:7, 8.

Invade the land of Israel: Under Shishak, 1 Kgs 14:25, 26; 2 Chron 12:2–9; Pharoah-Neco, 2 Kgs 23:29–35; 2 Chron 35:20–23; 36:3, 4. Aid the Israelites against the Babylonians, Jer 37:5–11. Intermarry with the Jews, 1 Kgs 3:1.

An enthusiastic Egyptian instigated rebellion against Roman government, Acts 21:38.

Prophecies of dispersion and restoration of, Ezk 29:12–15; 30:23, 26. Conversion of, foretold, Isa 19:18.

See *Egypt.*

EHI See *Ehud.*

EHUD 1. A Benjaminite, the assassin of Eglon, Judg 3:15.

2. A descendant of Benjamin, 1 Chron 7:10; 8:6, 7. Called *Ehi,* Gen 46:19–22. Probably identical with *Ahiram,* mentioned in Num 26:38–41, and *Aharah,* 1 Chron 8:1, 2, and *Ahoah,* vs. 3–5 and *Ahijah,* vs. 6, 7, and *Aher,* 1 Chron 7:12.

EKER Son of Ram, 1 Chron 2:27.

EKRON One of the five chief cities of the Philistines, Josh 13:2–7. Conquered and allotted to Judah, Josh 15:10, 11, 45; Judg 1:18. Allotted to Dan, Josh 19:41–46. The Ark of God taken to, 1 Sam 5:10. Temple of Baal-zebub at, 2 Kgs 1:2.

Prophecies against, Jer 25:20; Amos 1:8; Zeph 2:4; Zech 9:5.

ELA Father of Shime-i, 1 Kgs 4:8–19.

ELAH 1. A valley where David slew Goliath, 1 Sam 17:2, 19; 21:9.

2. An Edomitish king and clan, Gen 36:40–43; 1 Chron 1:51–54.

3. Son of Caleb, 1 Chron 4:15.

4. Son and successor of Baasha, king of Israel, 1 Kgs 16:8–14.

5. Father of Hoshea, 2 Kgs 15:30; 17:1, 2.

6. A Benjaminite chief, 1 Chron 9:7, 8.

ELAM 1. A district southeast of Babylon, on the Persian Gulf, Gen 14:1, 9; Dan 8:2. Prophecies concerning, Isa 11:11; 21:2; 22:6, 7; Jer 25:25; 49:34–39; Ezk 32:24. Jews from, Acts 2:9.

See *Elamites.*

2. Son of Shem and ancestor of the Elamites, Gen 10:22. See *Elam, 1,* above and *Elamites.*

3. A Korahite Levite, 1 Chron 26:3.

4. A Benjaminite leader, 1 Chron 8:22–25.

5. A Jewish captive, whose descendants, to the number of 1,254, returned from Babylon, Exra 2:3–35; Neh 7:8–38.

6. Another Elam whose descendants returned from Babylon, Ezra 2:3–35; Neh 7:8–38.

7. Jeshaiah's ancestor, Ezra 8:2–14.

8. Ancestor of several Israelites who divorced their heathen wives, Ezra 10:26.

9. A Levite musician, Neh 12:42.

10. One of the Israelite leaders with Nehemiah, Neh 10:14–27.

ELAMITES Descendants of Elam, whose name was given to the district of Elam, Gen 10:22. Present at Pentecost, Acts 2:9.

ELASAH 1. Son of Shaphan, Jer 29:3.

2. Son of Pashhur, Ezra 10:22.

ELATH Called also *Eloth.* A city of Edom, Deut 2:8; 1 Kgs 9:26; 2 Chron 8:17, 18.

Conquest of, by Uzziah, 2 Chron 26:2; by the Syrians, 2 Kgs 16:6.

ELDAAH A descendant of Abraham, Gen 25:4; 1 Chron 1:33.

ELDAD Prophesies in the camp of the Israelites, Num 11:26–29.

ELDER IN THE MOSAIC SYSTEM. Equivalent to the title senator, in present use. Elders, with delegated powers, were authorized to act for their constituency, Deut 1:13, 15.

See *Government, Mosaic.*

IN THE CHURCH. Acts 11:29. So the believers decided to send relief to the Christians in Judea, each giving as much as he could. [30]This they did, consigning their gifts to Barnabas and Paul to take to the elders of the church in Jerusalem.

Acts 14:23. Paul and Barnabas also appointed elders in every church and prayed for them with fasting, turning them over to the care of the Lord in whom they trusted.

Acts 15:2. Paul and Barnabas argued and discussed this with them at length, and finally the believers sent them to Jerusalem, accompanied by some local men, to talk to the apostles and elders there about this question. [*v.* 4.] [5]But then some of the men who had been Pharisees before their conversion stood to their feet and declared that all Gentile converts must be circumcised and required to follow all the Jewish customs and ceremonies. [6]So the apostles and church elders set a further meeting to decide this question. [7]At the meeting, after long discussion, Peter stood and addressed them as follows: "Brothers, you all know that God chose me from among you long ago to preach the Good News to the Gentiles, so that they also could believe. [8]God, who knows men's hearts, confirmed the fact that he accepts Gentiles by giving them the Holy Spirit, just as he gave him to us. [9]He made no distinction between them and us, for he cleansed their lives through faith, just as he did ours. [10]And now are you going to correct God by burdening the

Gentiles with a yoke that neither we nor our fathers were able to bear? [11]Don't you believe that all are saved the same way, by the free gift of the Lord Jesus?" [12]There was no further discussion, and everyone now listened as Barnabas and Paul told about the miracles God had done through them among the Gentiles. [13]When they had finished, James took the floor. "Brothers," he said, "listen to me. [14]Peter has told you about the first time God first visited the Gentiles to take from them a people to bring honor to his name. [15]And this fact of Gentile conversion agrees with what the prophets predicted. For instance, listen to this passage from the prophet Amos; [16]'Afterwards' [says the Lord], 'I will return and renew the broken contract with David, [17]so that Gentiles, too, will find the Lord—all those marked with my name.' [18]That is what the Lord says, who reveals his plans made from the beginning. [19]And so my judgment is that we should not insist that the Gentiles who turn to God must obey our Jewish laws, [20]except that we should write to them to refrain from eating meat sacrificed to idols, from all fornication, and also from eating unbled meat of strangled animals. [21]For these things have been preached against in Jewish synagogues in every city on every Sabbath for many generations." [22]Then the apostles and elders and the whole congregation voted to send delegates to Antioch with Paul and Barnabas, to report on this decision. The men chosen were two of the church leaders—Judas (also called Barsabbas) and Silas. [23]This is the letter they took along with them: "*From:* The apostles, elders and brothers at Jerusalem. *To:* The Gentile brothers in Antioch, Syria and Cilicia. Greetings! [24]We understand that some believers from here have upset you and questioned your salvation, but they had no such instructions from us. [25]So it seemed wise to us, having unanimously agreed on our decision, to send to you these two official representatives, along with our beloved Barnabas and Paul. [26]These men—Judas and Silas, who have risked their lives for the sake of our Lord Jesus Christ—will confirm orally what we have decided concerning your question. [27, 28, 29]For it seemed good to the Holy Spirit and to us to lay no greater burden of Jewish laws on you than to abstain from eating food offered to idols and from unbled meat of strangled animals, and, of course, from fornication. If you do this, it is enough. Farewell." *vs.* 1–35.

Acts 16:4. Then they went from city to city, making known the decision concerning the Gentiles, as decided by the apostles and elders in Jerusalem. [5]So the church grew daily in faith and numbers.

Acts 20:17. But when we landed at Miletus, he sent a message to the elders of the church at Ephesus asking them to come down to the boat to meet him. [28]"And now beware! Be sure that you feed and shepherd God's flock—his church, purchased with his blood—for the Holy Spirit is holding you responsible as overseers. [29]I know full well that after I leave you, false teachers, like vicious wolves, will appear among you, not sparing the flock. [30]Some of you yourselves will distort the truth in order to draw a following. [31]Watch out! Remember the three years I was with you—my constant watchcare over you night and day and my many tears for you. [32]And now I entrust you to God and his care and to his wonderful words which are able to build your faith and give you all the inheritance of those who are set apart for himself."

Acts 21:18. The second day Paul took us with him to meet with James and the elders of the Jerusalem church.

1 Tim 4:14. Be sure to use the abilities God has given you through his prophets when the elders of the church laid their hands upon your head.

1 Tim 5:17. Pastors who do their work well should be paid well and should be highly appreciated, especially those who work hard at both preaching and teaching. [18]For the Scriptures say, "Never tie up the mouth of an ox when it is treading out the grain—let him eat as he goes along!" And in another place, "Those who work deserve their pay!" [19]Don't listen to complaints against the pastor unless there are two or three witnesses to accuse him.

Tit 1:5. I left you there on the island of Crete so that you could do whatever was needed to help strengthen each of its churches, and I asked you to appoint pastors in every city who would follow the instructions I gave you. [6]The men you choose must be well thought of for their good lives; they must have only one wife and their children must love the Lord and not have a reputation for being wild or disobedient to their parents. [7]These pastors must be men of blameless lives because they are God's ministers. They must not be proud or impatient; they must not be drunkards or fighters or greedy for money. [8]They must enjoy having guests in their homes and must love all that is good. They must be sensible men, and fair. They must be clean minded and level headed. [9]Their belief in the truth which they have been taught must be strong and steadfast, so that they will be able to teach it to others and show those who disagree with them where they are wrong.

Heb 11:2. Men of God in days of old were famous for their faith.

Jas 5:14. Is anyone sick? He should call for the elders of the church and they should pray over him and pour a little oil upon him, calling on the Lord to heal him. [15]And their prayer, if offered in faith, will heal him, for the Lord will make him well; and if his sickness was caused by some sin, the Lord will forgive him.

1 Pet 5:1. And now, a word to you elders of the church. I, too, am an elder; with my own eyes I saw Christ dying on the cross; and I, too, will share his glory and his honor when he returns. Fellow elders, this is my plea to you: [2]Feed the flock of God; care for it willingly, not grudgingly; not for what you will get out of it, but because you are eager to serve the Lord. [3]Don't be tyrants, but lead them by your good example, [4]and when the Head Shepherd

comes, your reward will be a never-ending share in his glory and honor. [5]You younger men, follow the leadership of those who are older.

2 Jn 1:1. From: John, the old Elder of the church. *To:* That dear woman Cyria, one of God's very own, and to her children whom I love so much, as does everyone else in the church. 3 Jn 1:1.

Apocalyptic Vision of. Rev 4:4, 10; 5:5, 6, 8, 11, 14; 7:11, 13; 11:16; 14:3; 19:4.

See *Deacon; Overseer; Pastor; Church, Visible.*

ELE-AD A descendant of Ephraim, 1 Chron 7:21.

ELEADAH Son of Ephraim, 1 Chron 7:20, 21.

ELEALEH A city of Moab. Taken by the Israelites, Num 32:3, 4, 37, 38. Repossessed by the Moabites, Isa 15:4; 16:9.

ELEASAH 1. A descendant of Judah and son of Helez, 1 Chron 2:39.

2. A Benjaminite, 1 Chron 8:37; 9:43.

ELEAZAR 1. Son of Aaron, Ex 6:23; 28:1. Married a daughter of Putiel, who bore him Phinehas, Ex 6:25. After the death of Nadab and Abihu is made chief of the tribe of Levi, Num 3:31–35. Duties of, Num 4:16.

Succeeds Aaron as high priest, Num 20:26, 28; Deut 10:6. Assists Moses in the census, Num 26:63. With Joshua, divides Palestine, Num 34:16–28. Death and burial of, Josh 24:33. Descendants of, 1 Chron 24:1–19.

2. An inhabitant of Kiriath-jearim who attended the ark, 1 Sam 7:1, 2.

3. A Merarite Levite, 1 Chron 23:21, 22; 24:28.

4. Son of Dodo, and one of David's distinguished heroes, 2 Sam 23:9, 10, 13; 1 Chron 11:12.

5. Son of Phinehas, Ezra 8:33.

6. A priest who played the trumpet at the dedication of the wall, Neh 12:42.

7. A returned exile, Ezra 10:25.

8. An ancestor of Joseph, Mt 1:15.

ELECTION OF RULERS. By lot, Neh 11:1.

OF GRACE. Jn 15:16. You didn't choose me! I chose you! I appointed you to go and produce lovely fruit always, so that no matter what you ask for from the Father, using my name, he will give it to you.

Jn 17:6. I have told these men all about you. They were in the world, but then you gave them to me. Actually, they were always yours, and you gave them to me; and they have obeyed you.

Eph 1:4. Long ago, even before he made the world, God chose us to be his very own, through what Christ would do for us; he decided then to make us holy in his eyes, without a single fault—we who stand before him covered with his love.

Eph 2:10. It is God himself who has made us what we are and given us new lives from Christ Jesus; and long ages ago he planned that we should spend these lives in helping others.

2 Thess 2:13. But we must forever give thanks to God for you, our brothers loved by the Lord, because God chose from the very first to give you salvation, cleansing you by the work of the Holy Spirit and by your trusting in the Truth.

Of Christ as Messiah, Isa 42:1; 1 Pet 2:6. Of Israel, Deut 7:6; Isa 45:4. Of ministers, Lk 6:13; Acts 9:15. Of churches, 1 Pet 5:13.

See *Chosen, or Elected; Predestination.*

ELECTIONEERING By Absalom, 2 Sam 15:1–6. Adonijah, 1 Kgs 1:7.

ELEGY David's, on Saul and Jonathan: 2 Sam 1:17. Then David composed a dirge for Saul and Jonathan and afterward commanded that it be sung throughout Israel. [19]O Israel, your pride and joy lies dead upon the hills; mighty heroes have fallen. [20]Don't tell the Philistines, lest they rejoice. Hide it from the cities of Gath and Ashkelon, lest the heathen nations laugh in triumph. [21]O Mount Gilboa, let there be no dew nor rain upon you, let no crops of grain grow on your slopes. For there the mighty Saul has died; he is God's appointed king no more. [22]Both Saul and Jonathan slew their strongest foes, and did not return from battle empty-handed. [23]How much they were loved, how wonderful they were—both Saul and Jonathan! They were together in life and in death. They were swifter than eagles, stronger than lions. [24]But now, O women of Israel, weep for Saul; he enriched you with fine clothing and golden ornaments. [25]These mighty heroes have fallen in the midst of the battle. Jonathan is slain upon the hills. [26]How I weep for you, my brother Jonathan; how much I loved you! And your love for me was deeper than the love of women! [27]The mighty ones have fallen, stripped of their weapons, and dead.

On Abner: 2 Sam 3:33, 34. "Should Abner have died like a fool?" the king lamented. "Your hands were not bound, your feet were not tied—you were murdered—the victim of a wicked plot." And all the people wept again for him.

See the book of Lamentations. See also *Poetry.*

EL-ELOHE-ISRAEL Name of Jacob's altar at Shechem, Gen 33:20.

ELHANAN 1. A distinguished warrior in the time of David, who killed Lahmi, the brother of Goliath, the Gittite, 2 Sam 21:19. Compare 1 Chron 20:5.

2. Son of Dodo, one of David's heroes, 2 Sam 23:24–39; 1 Chron 11:26–47.

ELI High priest, 1 Sam 1:25; 2:11; 1 Kgs 2:27. Judge of Israel, 1 Sam 4:18. Misjudges and rebukes Hannah, 1 Sam 1:14. His benediction on Hannah, 1 Sam 1:17, 18; 2:20. Officiates when Samuel is presented at the tabernacle, 1 Sam 1:24–28. Indulgent to his corrupt sons, 1 Sam 2:22–25, 29; 3:11–14. His solicitude for the ark, 1 Sam 4:11–18. Death of, 1 Sam 4:18.

Prophecies of judgments upon his house, 1 Sam 2:27–36; 3, with 1 Kgs 2:27.

ELIAB 1. A Reubenite, progenitor of Dathan and Abiram, Num 26:5–11; 16:1, 11, 12; Deut 11:6.

2. Son of Helon, Num 1:2–15; 2:3–31; 7:24–29; 10:16.

3. Ancestor of Samuel, 1 Chron 6:25–27. Called also *Elihu,* 1 Sam 1:1; and *Eliel,* 1 Chron 6:33–38.

4. Son of Jesse, and eldest brother of David,

1 Sam 16:6; 17:13, 28; 1 Chron 2:13. A leader of the tribe of Judah, 1 Chron 27:18.

5. A hero of the tribe of Gad, 1 Chron 12:8–13.

6. A Levite and musician, 1 Chron 15:18, 20; 16: 5.

ELIADA 1. Son of David, 2 Sam 5:14–16; 1 Chron 3:6–8. Called *Beeliada,* 1 Chron 14:4–7.

2. A Benjaminite, 2 Chron 17:17.

ELIAHBA One of David's heroes, 2 Sam 23: 24–39; 1 Chron 11:26–47.

ELIAKIM 1. Son of Hilkiah, deputy of Hezekiah, 2 Kgs 18:18; 19:2; Isa 36:3, 11, 22; 37:2.

2. Original name of Jehoiakim, king of Judah, 2 Kgs 23:34; 2 Chron 36:4.

3. A priest, Neh 12:40, 41.

4. Son of Abiud, Mt 1:13. Probably same as *Shechaniah,* 1 Chron 3:21, 22.

5. Son of Melea, Lk 3:23–38.

ELIAM 1. Father of Bath-sheba, 2 Sam 11:3. Called *Ammi-el,* 1 Chron 3:5.

2. One of David's valiant men, 2 Sam 23:34. Called *Ahijah,* 1 Chron 11:26–47.

ELIASAPH 1. A leader of the tribe of Gad, Num 1:2–15; 2:3–31; 7:42–47; 10:20.

2. Son of Lael, Num 3:16–24.

ELIASHIB 1. A priest, 1 Chron 24:7–18.

2. Name of three Israelites, mentioned in Ezra 10:24, 27, 34–42.

3. High priest, Neh 3:1; 12:10,11; 13:4–9, 28.

4. Son of Eli-o-enai, 1 Chron 3:24.

ELIATHAH A musician, 1 Chron 25:4, 5,9–31.

ELIDAD A leader of Benjamin, Num 34:16–28.

ELIE-HO-ENAI 1. A Levite, 1 Chron 26:2, 3.

2. Son of Zerahiah, Ezra 8:2–14.

ELIEL 1. A chief of Manasseh, 1 Chron 5:24.

2. Son of Toah, 1 Chron 6:33–38.

3. Two Benjaminite chiefs, 1 Chron 8:19–25.

4. Three of David's heroes, having the same name, 1 Chron 11:26–47; 12:8–13.

5. Two leaders of Levites, 1 Chron 15:4–10, 11.

6. A Levite, who had charge of the temple, 2 Chron 31:12, 13.

ELI-ENAI A Benjaminite citizen of Jerusalem, 1 Chron 8:19–21.

ELIEZER 1. Abraham's servant, Gen 15:2,3; 24.

2. Son of Becher, 1 Chron 7:8.

3. Son of Moses, Ex 18:4; 1 Chron 23:14, 15, 17.

4. A priest, 1 Chron 15:24.

5. Son of Zichri, 1 Chron 27:16–22.

6. A prophet, 2 Chron 20:37.

7. A Jewish exile, Ezra 8:16.

8. A priest after the exile, Ezra 10:16–19.

9. A Levite, Ezra 10:23.

10. An Israelite after the exile, Ezra 10:31, 32.

11. Son of Jorim, Lk 3:23–38.

ELIHOREPH Son of Shisha, 1 Kgs 4:1–6.

ELIHU 1. A Buzite and one of Job's friends, Job chapters 32–37.

2. Son of Tohu, 1 Sam 1:1. Probably identical with *Eliel,* 1 Chron 6:33–38, and *Eliab,* 1 Chron 6:25–27.

3. A Manassite warrior, who joined David at Ziklag, 1 Chron 12:20.

4. A temple guard, 1 Chron 26:6, 7.

5. A chief of the tribe of Judah, 1 Chron 27: 16–22. Possibly *Eliab,* oldest brother of David, 1 Sam 16:6.

ELIJAH 1. The Tishbite, a Gileadite and prophet. Persecuted by Ahab, 1 Kgs 17:2–7; 18:7–10. Escapes to the wilderness, where he is miraculously fed by ravens, 1 Kgs 17:1–7. By divine direction goes to Zarephath, where he is fed by a widow, whose flour and oil are miraculously increased, 1 Kgs 17:8–16. Returns, and sends a message to Ahab, 1 Kgs 18:1–16. Meets Ahab and directs him to assemble the prophets of Baal, 1 Kgs 18:17–20. Derisively challenges the priest of Baal to offer sacrifices, 1 Kgs 18:25–29. Kills the prophets of Baal, 1 Kgs 18:40. Escapes to the wilderness from the fierceness of Jezebel, 1 Kgs 19:1–18. Fasts 40 days, 1 Kgs 19:8. Despondency and murmuring of, 1 Kgs 19:10, 14. Consolation given to, 1 Kgs 19:11–18. Flees to the wilderness; directed to anoint Hazael king over Syria, Jehu king over Israel, and Elisha to be a prophet in his own place, 1 Kgs 19:9–21. Personal appearance of, 2 Kgs 1:8.

Piety of, 1 Kgs 19:10, 14; Lk 1:17; Rom 11:2, 3; Jas 5:17. His translation, 2 Kgs 2:11. Appears to Jesus at His transfiguration, Mt 17:3, 4; Mk 9:4; Lk 9:30. Antitype of John the Baptist, Mt 11:14; 16:14; 17: 10–12; Mk 9:12, 13; Lk 1:17; Jn 1:21–25.

MIRACLES OF. Increases the oil of the widow of Zarephath, 1 Kgs 17:14–16. Revives from the dead the son of the woman of Zarephath, 1 Kgs 17:17–24. Causes rain after a drought of three and a half years, 1 Kgs 18:41–45; Jas 5:17, 18. Causes fire to burn the sacrifice, 1 Kgs 18:24, 36–38. Calls lightning down upon the soldiers of Ahaziah, 2 Kgs 1: 10–12; Lk 9:54.

PROPHECIES OF. Foretells a drought, 1 Kgs 17: 1; the destruction of Ahab and his family, 1 Kgs 21: 17–29; 2 Kgs 9:25–37; the death of Ahaziah, 2 Kgs 1:2–17; the plague sent as a judgment upon the people in the time of Jehoram, king of Israel, 2 Chron 21:12–15.

2. A Benjaminite chief, 1 Chron 8:26, 27.

3. Two post-exilic Jews, Ezra 10:21, 26.

ELIKA One of David's officers, 2 Sam 23:25.

ELIM Second camp of the Israelites after crossing the Red Sea, Ex 15:27; Num 33:9.

ELIMELECH With Naomi, his wife, and two sons, emigrate to Moab, Ruth 1:1–3; 4:3, 9.

ELI-O-ENAI See also *Elie-ho-enai.*

1. Son of Becher, 1 Chron 7:8.

2. A chief of Simeon, 1 Chron 4:34–39.

3. A priest, Ezra 10:22. Possibly identical with one mentioned in Neh 12:41, which see.

4. An Israelite, Ezra 10:27.

5. Son of Neariah, 1 Chron 3:23, 24.

ELIPHAL A captain in David's army, 1 Chron 11:35.

ELIPHAZ 1. Son of Esau, Gen 36:4, 10–16; 1 Chron 1:35.

2. Friend of Job, Job 2:11; 4; 5; 22; 42:7–9.

ELIPHELEHU A Levite musician, 1 Chron 15:18, 21.

ELIPHELET 1. A distinguished warrior, 2 Sam 23:24–39.

2. A son of David, 1 Chron 3:6–8. Called *Elpelet,* 1 Chron 14:4–7.

3. A son of David, probably identical with 2, above, 2 Sam 5:14–16; 1 Chron 3:6–8; 14:4–7.

4. A descendant of Saul, 1 Chron 8:39.

5. A companion of Ezra, Ezra 8:2–14.

6. An Israelite, probably identical with no. 5, above, Ezra 10:33.

ELISHA Successor to the prophet Elijah. Elijah instructed to anoint, 1 Kgs 19:16. Called by Elijah, 1 Kgs 19:19. Ministers to Elijah, 1 Kgs 19:21. Witnesses Elijah's translation, receives a double portion of his power, 2 Kgs 2:1–15; 3:11. Mocked by the children of Bethel, 2 Kgs 2:23, 24. Causes the king to restore the property of the Shunemmite woman, 2 Kgs 8:1–6. Instructs that Jehu be anointed king of Israel, 2 Kgs 9:1–3. Life of, sought by Jehoram, 2 Kgs 6:31–33. Death of, 2 Kgs 13:14–20. Bones of, restore a dead man to life, 2 Kgs 13:20, 21.

MIRACLES OF. Divides the Jordan, 2 Kgs 2:13, 14. Purifies the waters of Jericho by throwing salt into the well, 2 Kgs 2:19–22. Increases the oil of the woman whose sons were to be sold for debt, 2 Kgs 4:1–7. Raises from the dead the son of the Shunemmite, 2 Kgs 4:18–37. Neutralizes the poison of the stew, 2 Kgs 4:38–41. Increases the bread to feed one hundred men, 2 Kgs 4:42–44. Heals Naaman the leper, 2 Kgs 5:1–19; Lk 4:27. Sends leprosy as a judgment upon Gehazi, 2 Kgs 5:26, 27. Recovers the axhead that had fallen into a river by causing it to float, 2 Kgs 6:6. Reveals the secrets of the king of Syria, 2 Kgs 6:12. Opens the eyes of his servant to see the army of the Lord, 2 Kgs 6:17. Brings blindness upon the army of Syria, 2 Kgs 6:18.

PROPHECIES OF. Foretells a son to the Shunemmite woman, 2 Kgs 4:15, 16; plenty to the starving in Samaria, 2 Kgs 7:1; seven years' famine in Israel, 2 Kgs 8:1–3; death of Ben-hadad, king of Syria, 2 Kgs 8:7–10; elevation of Hazael to the throne, 2 Kgs 8:11–15; the victory of Joash over Syria, 2 Kgs 13:14–19.

ELISHAH A descendant of Noah, Gen 10:4; 1 Chron 1:5–9.

ELISHAMA 1. Leader of Ephraim and grandfather of Joshua, Num 1:2–15; 2:3–31; 7:48–53; 10:22; 1 Chron 7:25–27.

2. A son of David, 2 Sam 5:14–16; 1 Chron 3:6–8; 14:4–7.

3. Another son of David, elsewhere called *Elishu-a,* which see. 1 Chron 3:6–8.

4. A descendant of Judah, 1 Chron 2:41.

5. Probably identical with no. 4, Jer 41:1.

6. A secretary to Jehoiakim, Jer 36:12, 20, 21.

7. A priest sent by Jehoshaphat to teach the law, 2 Chron 17:7–9.

ELISHAPHAT A Jewish officer, 2 Chron 23:1.

ELISHEBA Wife of Aaron, Ex 6:23.

ELISHU-A A son of David, 2 Sam 5:14–16; 1 Chron 14:4–7. Called *Elishama,* 1 Chron 3:6–8.

ELIUD An ancestor of Jesus, Mt 1:14, 15.

ELIZABETH Wife of Zacharias and mother of John the Baptist, Lk 1:5–60.

ELIZAPHAN 1. A Levite, Ex 6:22; Lev 10:4; Num 3:25–30; 1 Chron 15:4–10.

2. A leader of Zebulun, Num 34:16–28.

3. Probably identical with 1, above, 2 Chron 29:12–14.

ELIZUR Leader of Reuben, Num 1:2–15; 2:3–31; 7:30–35; 10:18.

ELKANAH 1. Grandson of Korah, Ex 6:24; 1 Chron 6:22–24.

2. Father of Samuel; a descendant of preceding, 1 Sam 1:1, 4, 8, 19, 21, 23; 2:11, 20; 1 Chron 6:25–27, 33–38.

3. A Levite and ancestor of Samuel, 1 Chron 6:25–27, 33–38.

4. Another Levite and ancestor of Samuel, 1 Chron 6:25–27, 33–38.

5. A Levite, 1 Chron 9:15, 16.

6. A warrior who joined David at Ziklag, 1 Chron 12:3–7.

7. A guard for the Ark, perhaps identical with 6, above, 1 Chron 15:23.

8. A officer of Ahaz, 2 Chron 28:7.

ELLASAR A city of Chaldea. Its king invades Canaan, Gen 14:1, 8, 9.

ELMADAM An ancestor of Jesus, Lk 3:23–38.

ELNA-AM Father of two distinguished warriors, 1 Chron 11:26–47.

ELNATHAN 1. Father of Nehushta, the mother of king Jehoiachin, 2 Kgs 24:8, 9; Jer 26:22; 36:12, 24, 25.

2. Name of three Levites in the time of Ezra, Ezra 8:16.

ELOI Mk 15:34.

ELON 1. Father-in-law of Esau, Gen 26:34; 36:2, 3.

2. A son of Zebulun, Gen 46:8–14; Num 26:26, 27.

3. A town of Dan, Josh 19:41–46.

4. A Hebrew judge, Judg 12:11, 12.

ELON-BETH-HANAN A town of Dan, 1 Kgs 4:8–19. Perhaps identical with *Elon* in Josh 19:41–46.

ELONITES Descendants of Elon, son of Zebulun, Num 26:26, 27.

ELOTH See *Elath.*

ELPAAL A Benjaminite, 1 Chron 8:11, 12, 17, 18.

EL-PARAN A place in the wilderness of Paran, Gen 14:5, 6.

ELPELET A son of David, 1 Chron 14:4–7. Called *Eliphelet* in 1 Chron 3:6–8.

ELTEKEH A city of Dan, Josh 19:41–46. Spelled *Elteke* in Josh 21:23, 24.

ELTEKON A city of Judah, Josh 15:48–62.

ELTOLAD A city of Judah, Josh 15:21–32; 19:2–7. Called *Tolad* in 1 Chron 4:29.

ELUL See *Calendar.*

ELUZAI A Benjaminite, 1 Chron 12:3–7.

ELYMAS A false prophet, punished with blindness, Acts 13:8–11.

ELZABAD 1. A Gadite, 1 Chron 12:8–13.

2. A Korhite, 1 Chron 26:6, 7.

ELZAPHAN See *Elizaphan, 1.*

EMANCIPATION Of all Jewish servants, Ex 21:2; Lev 25:8–16, 39–41; Deut 15:12.

Proclamation of: By Zedekiah, Jer 34:8–11; by Cyrus, 2 Chron 36:22, 23; Ezra 1:1–4.

See *Exodus; Jubilee.*

EMBALMING Of Jacob, Gen 50:2, 3; of Joseph, Gen 50:26; of Asa, 2 Chron 16:13, 14; of Jesus, Mk 15:46; 16:1; Jn 19:39, 40.

EMBEZZLEMENT Lk 16:1–7.

See *Dishonesty.*

EMBROIDERY In blue and purple and scarlet on the curtains of the tabernacle, Ex 26:1, 2, 36; 27:16; on the ephod and sash of the high priest, mixed with gold, Ex 28:33, 34, 39. On the garments of Sisera, Judg 5:30. On the garments of rulers, Ezk 26:16. On the garments of women, Ps 45:14; Ezk 16:9, 10, 13, 18. Bezalel and Oholiab divinely inspired for, in the work of the tabernacle, Ex 35:30–35; 38:22, 23.

See *Tapestry.*

EMEK-KEZIZ A city of Benjamin, Josh 18: 21–28.

EMERALD A precious stone. Color of the rainbow, Rev 4:3. Merchandise of, in Tyre, Ezk 27: 16; 28:13. Set in the chestpiece, Ex 28:17, 18.

Symbolical. In the foundation of the holy city, Rev 21:18–20.

EMERGENCY Ex 14:15. Then the Lord said to Moses, "Quit praying and get the people moving! Forward, march!"

Josh 7:10, 11. But the Lord said to Joshua, "Get up off your face! Israel has sinned and disobeyed my commandment and has taken loot when I said it was not to be taken; and they have not only taken it, they have lied about it and have hidden it among their belongings. 12That is why the people of Israel are being defeated. That is why your men are running from their enemies—for they are cursed. I will not stay with you any longer unless you completely rid yourselves of this sin. 13Get up! Tell the people, 'Each of you must undergo purification rites in preparation for tomorrow, for the Lord your God of Israel says that someone has stolen from him, and you cannot defeat your enemies until you deal with this sin."

See *Decision.*

EMIM A race of giants, Gen 14:5, 6; Deut 2: 10, 11.

EMMANUEL Mt 1:23.

See *Immanuel; Jesus.*

EMMAUS A village about seven miles (11.2 kilometers) from Jerusalem. Appearance of Jesus in, after his resurrection, Lk 24:13.

EMMER A small grain grown in Egypt, Ex 9:32.

EMPLOYEE Lev 19:13. You shall not rob nor oppress anyone, and you shall pay your hired workers promptly. If something is due them, don't even keep it overnight.

Lev 25:6. Any crops that do grow that year shall be free to all—for you, your servants, your slaves, and any foreigners living among you.

Deut 15:18. But when you free a slave you must not feel bad, for remember that for six years he has cost you less than half the price of a hired hand! And the Lord your God will prosper all you do because you have released him!

Deut 24:14, 15. Never oppress a poor hired man, whether a fellow Israelite or a foreigner living in your town. Pay him his wage each day before sunset, for since he is poor he needs it right away; otherwise he may cry out to the Lord against you and it would be counted as a sin against you.

Prov 25:13. A faithful employee is as refreshing as a cool day in the hot summertime.

Mt 10:10. Don't even carry a duffle bag with extra clothes or shoes, or even a walking stick; for those you help should feed and care for you.

Lk 10:7. And don't hesitate to accept hospitality, for the workman is worthy of his wages!

1 Tim 5:18. For the Scriptures say, "Never tie up the mouth of an ox when it is treading out the grain —let him eat as he goes along!" And in another place, "Those who work deserve their pay!"

CHARACTER OF UNRIGHTEOUS. Job 7:1. How mankind must struggle. A man's life is long and hard, like that of a slave. 2How he longs for the day to end. How he grinds on to the end of the week and his wages. 3And so to me also have been allotted months of frustration, these long and weary nights.

Job 14:1. How frail is man, how few his days, how full of trouble! 6So give him a little rest, won't you? Turn away your angry gaze and let him have a few moments of relief before he dies.

Prov 10:26. A lazy fellow is a pain to his employers—like smoke in their eyes or vinegar that sets the teeth on edge.

Mt 20:1. Here is another illustration of the Kingdom of Heaven. "The owner of an estate went out early one morning to hire workers for his harvest field. 2He agreed to pay them $20 a day and sent them out to work. 3A couple of hours later he was passing a hiring hall and saw some men standing around waiting for jobs, 4so he sent them also into his fields, telling them he would pay them whatever was right at the end of the day. 5At noon and again around three o'clock in the afternoon he did the same thing. 6At five o'clock that evening he was in town again and saw some more men standing around and asked them, 'Why haven't you been working today?' 7'Because no one hired us,' they replied. 'Then go on out and join the others in my fields,' he told them. 8That evening he told the paymaster to call the men in and pay them, beginning with the last men first. 9When the men hired at five o'clock were paid, each received $20. 10So when the men hired earlier came to get theirs, they assumed they would receive much more. But they, too, were paid $20. 11, 12They protested, 'Those fellows worked only one hour, and yet you've paid them just as much as those of us who worked all day in the scorching heat.' 13'Friend,' he answered one of them, 'I did you no wrong! Didn't you agree to work all day for $20? 14Take it and go. It is my desire to pay all the same; 15is it against the law to give away my money if I want to? Should you be angry because I am kind?' "

Mt 21:33. "Now listen to this story: A certain landowner planted a vineyard with a hedge around it, and built a platform for the watchman, then leased the vineyard to some farmers on a sharecrop basis, and went away to live in another country. 34At the time of the grape harvest he sent his agents to the farmers to collect his share. 35But the farmers attacked his men, beat one, killed one and stoned another. 36Then he sent a larger group of his men to collect for him, but the results were the same. 37Finally the owner sent his son, thinking they would surely respect him. 38But when these farmers saw the son coming they said among themselves, 'Here comes the heir to this estate; come on, let's kill him and get it for ourselves!' 39So they dragged him out of the vineyard and killed him. 40When the owner returns, what do you think he will do to those farmers?" 41The Jewish leaders replied, "He will put the wicked men to a horrible death, and lease the vineyard to others who will pay him promptly."

Jn 10:12. A hired man will run when he sees a wolf coming and will leave the sheep, for they aren't his and he isn't their shepherd. And so the wolf leaps on them and scatters the flock. 13The hired man runs because he is hired and has no real concern for the sheep.

KINDNESS TO. Ruth 2:4. Boaz arrived from the city. . . . After exchanging greetings with the reapers. . . .

Lk 15:17. When he finally came to his senses, he said to himself, "At home even the hired men have food enough and to spare, and here I am, dying of hunger! 18I will go home to my father and say, 'Father, I have sinned against both heaven and you, 19and am no longer worthy of being called your son. Please take me on as a hired man.' "

OPPRESSIONS OF. Prov 22:16. He who gains by oppressing the poor or by bribing the rich shall end in poverty.

Mal 3:5. "At that time my punishments will be quick and certain; I will move swiftly against . . . all those who cheat their hired hands, or oppress widows and orphans, or defraud strangers, and do not fear me," says the Lord of Hosts.

Lk 15:15. He persuaded a local farmer to hire him to feed his pigs. 16The boy became so hungry that even the pods he was feeding the swine looked good to him. And no one gave him anything.

Jas 5:4. For listen! Hear the cries of the field workers whom you have cheated of their pay. Their cries have reached the ears of the Lord of Hosts.

See *Servant; Employer; Master.*

EMPLOYER Lev 25:53. If he sells himself to a foreigner, the foreigner must treat him as a hired servant rather than as a slave or as property.

Deut 5:14. But the seventh day is the Sabbath of the Lord your God; no work shall be done that day by you or by any of your household—your sons, daughters, servants, oxen, donkeys, or cattle; even foreigners living among you must obey this law. Everybody must rest as you do.

Deut 24:14, 15. Never oppress a poor hired man, whether a fellow Israelite or a foreigner living in your town. Pay him his wage each day before sunset, for since he is poor he needs it right away; otherwise he might cry out to the Lord against you and it would be counted as a sin against you. Lev 19:13.

Job 31:13. If I have been unfair to my servants, 14how could I face God? What could I say when he questioned me about it? 15For God made me, and made my servant too. He created us both.

Prov 22:16. He who gains by oppressing the poor or by bribing the rich shall end in poverty.

Prov 29:21. Pamper a servant from childhood, and he will expect you to treat him as a son!

Jer 22:13. And woe to you, King Jehoiakim, for you are building your great palace with forced labor. By not paying wages you are building injustice into its walls and oppression into its doorframes and ceilings.

Mal 3:5. I will move swiftly against . . . all those who cheat their hired hands.

Mt 10:10. For those you help should feed and care for you.

Mt 20:1. Here is another illustration of the Kingdom of Heaven. "The owner of an estate went out early one morning to hire workers for his harvest field. 2He agreed to pay them $20 a day and sent them out to work. 3A couple of hours later he was passing a hiring hall and saw some men standing around waiting for jobs, 4so he sent them also into his field, telling them he would pay them whatever was right at the end of the day. 5At noon and again around three o'clock in the afternoon he did the same thing. 6At five o'clock that evening he was in town again and saw some more men standing around and asked them, 'Why haven't you been working today?' 7'Because no one hired us,' they replied. 'Then go on out and join the others in my fields,' he told them. 8That evening he told the paymaster to call the men in and pay them, beginning with the last men first. 9When the men hired at five o'clock were paid, each received $20. 10So when the men hired earlier came to get theirs, they assumed they would receive much more. But they, too, were paid $20. 11,12They protested, 'Those fellows worked only one hour, and yet you've paid them just as much as those of us who worked all day in the scorching heat.' 13'Friend,' he answered one of them, 'I did you no wrong! Didn't you agree to work all day for $20? 14Take it and go. It is my desire to pay all the same; 15is it against the law to give away my money if I want to? Should you be angry because I am kind?' "

Lk 10:7. For the workman is worthy of his wages!

Eph 6:9. And you slave owners must treat your slaves right, just as I have told them to treat you. Don't keep threatening them; remember, you yourselves are slaves to Christ; you have the same Master they do, and he has no favorites.

Col 4:1. You slave owners must be just and fair to all your slaves. Always remember that you, too, have a Master in heaven who is closely watching you.

1 Tim 5:18. For the Scriptures say, "Never tie up the mouth of an ox when it is treading out the grain—let him eat as he goes along!" And in another place, "Those who work deserve their pay!"

Philemon 1:15. Perhaps you could think of it this way: that he ran away from you for a little while so that now he can be yours forever, [16]no longer only a slave, but something much better—a beloved brother, especially to me. Now he will mean much more to you too, because he is not only a servant but also your brother in Christ.

Jas 5:4. For listen! Hear the cries of the field workers whom you have cheated of their pay. Their cries have reached the ears of the Lord of Hosts. [5]You have spent your years here on earth having fun, satisfying your every whim, and now your fat hearts are ready for the slaughter.

See *Master; Employee; Labor; Servant.*

EMULATION Rom 11:11. Does this mean that God has rejected his Jewish people forever? Of course not! His purpose was to make his salvation available to the Gentiles, and then the Jews would be jealous and begin to want God's salvation for themselves. [14]So that if possible I can make them want what you Gentiles have and in that way save some of them.

2 Cor 8:1. Now I want to tell you what God in his grace has done for the churches in Macedonia. [2]Though they have been going through much trouble and hard times, they have mixed their wonderful joy with their deep poverty, and the result has been an overflow of giving to others. [3]They gave not only what they could afford, but far more; and I can testify that they did it because they wanted to, and not because of nagging on my part. [4]They begged us to take the money so they could share in the joy of helping the Christians in Jerusalem. [5]Best of all, they went beyond our highest hopes, for their first action was to dedicate themselves to the Lord and to us, for whatever directions God might give to them through us. [6]They were so enthusiastic about it that we have urged Titus, who encouraged your giving in the first place, to visit you and encourage you to complete your share in this ministry of giving. [7]You people there are leaders in so many ways—you have so much faith, so many good preachers, so much learning, so much enthusiasm, so much love for us. Now I want you to be leaders also in the spirit of cheerful giving. [8]I am not giving you an order; I am not saying you must do it, but others are eager for it. This is one way to prove that your love is real, that it goes beyond mere words.

2 Cor 9:1. I realize that I really don't even need to mention this to you, about helping God's people. [2]For I know how eager you are to do it, and I have boasted to the friends in Macedonia that you were ready to send an offering a year ago. In fact, it was this enthusiasm of yours that stirred up many of them to begin helping. [3]But I am sending these men just to be sure that you really are ready, as I told them you would be, with your money all collected; I don't want it to turn out that this time I was wrong in my boasting about you. [4]I would be very much ashamed—and so would you—if some of these Macedonian people come with me, only to find that you still aren't ready after all I have told them! [5]So I have asked these other brothers to arrive ahead of me to see that the gift you promised is on hand and waiting. I want it to be a real gift and not look as if it were being given under pressure.

Heb 10:24. In response to all he has done for us, let us outdo each other in being helpful and kind to each other and in doing good.

ILLUSTRATED. In Esau's marriages, Gen 28:6–9. In Jacob's household, Gen 30:1–24.

ENAM A city of Judah, Josh 15:33–36.

ENAN A man of Naphtali, Num 1:2–15; 2:3–31; 7:78–83; 10:27.

ENCHANTMENT See *Magician; Sorcery.*

EN-DOR A city of Manasseh, Josh 17:11. The medium of, consulted by Saul, 1 Sam 28:7–25. Deborah triumphs at, over Sisera, Judg 4; Ps 83:10.

ENDURANCE Mt 10:22. Everyone shall hate you because you belong to me. But all of you who endure to the end shall be saved. Mk 13:13.

2 Cor 6:4. We patiently endure suffering and hardship and trouble of every kind. [5]We have been beaten, put in jail, faced angry mobs, worked to exhaustion, stayed awake through sleepless nights of watching, and gone without food. [6]We have proved ourselves to be what we claim by our wholesome lives and by our understanding of the Gospel and by our patience. We have been kind and truly loving and filled with the Holy Spirit.

Col 1:11. We are praying, too, that you will be filled with his mightly, glorious strength so that you can keep going no matter what happens—always full of the joy of the Lord.

Col 3:12. Since you have been chosen by God who has given you this new kind of life, and because of his deep love and concern for you, you should practice tenderhearted mercy and kindness to others. Don't worry about making a good impression on them but be ready to suffer quietly and patiently. [13]Be gentle and ready to forgive; never hold grudges. Remember, the Lord forgave you, so you must forgive others.

See *Perseverance.*

EN-EGLAIM A place near the Dead Sea, Ezk 47:10.

ENEMY Ex 23:5. If you see your enemy trying to get his donkey onto its feet beneath a heavy load, you must not go on by, but must help him.

Job 31:29. If I have rejoiced at harm to an enemy —[30](But actually I have never cursed anyone nor asked for revenge)—.

Ps 35:1. O Lord, fight those fighting me; declare war on them for their attacks on me. [2]Put on your armor, take your shield and protect me by standing in front. [3]Lift your spear in my defense, for my pursuers are getting very close. Let me hear you say that you will save me from them. [4]Dishonor those who are trying to kill me. Turn them back and confuse them. [5]Blow them away like chaff in the wind—wind sent by the Angel of the Lord. [6]Make their path dark and slippery before them, with the Angel of the Lord pursuing them. [7]For though I did them no wrong, yet they laid a trap for me and dug a pitfall in my path. *vs.* 8–28.

Prov 24:17. Do not rejoice when your enemy meets trouble. Let there be no gladness when he falls—[18]for the Lord may be displeased with you and stop punishing him!

Prov 25:21, 22. If your enemy is hungry, give him food! If he is thirsty, give him something to drink! This will make him feel ashamed of himself, and God will reward you.

Mt 5:43. There is a saying, 'Love your *friends* and hate your enemies.' [44]But I say: Love your *enemies!* Pray for those who *persecute* you! [45]In that way you will be acting as true sons of your Father in heaven. For he gives his sunlight to both the evil and the good, and sends rain on the just and on the unjust too. [46]If you love only those who love you, what good is that? Even scoundrels do that much. [47]If you are friendly only to your friends, how are you different from anyone else? Even the heathen do that. [48]But you are to be perfect, even as your Father in heaven is perfect. *v.* 25.

Lk 6:27. Listen, all of you. Love your *enemies.* Do *good* to those who *hate* you. [28]Pray for the happiness of those who *curse* you; implore God's blessing on those who *hurt* you. [29]If someone slaps you on one cheek, let him slap the other too! If someone demands your coat, give him your shirt besides. [30]Give what you have to anyone who asks you for it; and when things are taken away from you, don't worry about getting them back. [31]Treat others as you want them to treat you. [32]Do you think you deserve credit for merely loving those who love you? Even the godless do that! [33]And if you do good only to those who do you good—is that so wonderful? Even sinners do that much! [34]And if you lend money only to those who can repay you, what good is that? Even the most wicked will lend to their own kind for full return! [35]Love your *enemies!* Do good to *them!* Lend to *them!* And don't be concerned about the fact that they won't repay. Then your reward from heaven will be very great, and you will truly be acting as sons of God: for he is kind to the *unthankful* and to those who are *very wicked.* [36]Try to show as much compassion as your Father does.

Rom 12:14. If someone mistreats you because you are a Christian, don't curse him; pray that God will bless him. [20]Instead, feed your enemy if he is hungry. If he is thirsty give him something to drink and you will be "heaping coals of fire on his head."

The wickedness of David's, Ps 56:5; 57:4, 6; 62:3, 4; 69:4, 9; 71:10; 102:8; 109:2–5; 129:1–4. His imprecations against, see *Prayer, Imprecatory.*

Instances of forgiveness of: David, of Absalom, and co-conspirators, 2 Sam 19:6, 11–13. Jesus, of his persecutors, Lk 23:34. Stephen, of his murderers, Acts 7:60.

ENGAGEMENT Of Jacob, Gen 29:18–30. Laws concerning, Ex 21:9–11; 22:16, 17; Lev 19:20. Exempts from military duty, Deut 20:7. A quasi marriage, Mt 1:18; Lk 1:27.

FIGURATIVE. Isa 62:4; 2 Cor 11:2.

See *Betrothal; Marriage.*

EN-GANNIM 1. A city of Judah, Josh 15:33–36.

2. A city of Issachar, Josh 19:17–23; 21:28, 29.

EN-GEDI Called *Hazazon-tamar.* A spring and city allotted to Judah, Josh 15:48–62. Built by the Amorites, Gen 14:7; 2 Chron 20:2. Famous for its gardens, Song 1:14.

Wilderness of, in the vicinity of the Dead Sea. David uses as a stronghold, 1 Sam 23:29; 24. Cave of, 1 Sam 24:3.

ENGINE Of war, 2 Chron 26:15; Ezk 26:9.

See *Armies; Fort.*

ENGRAVING In making idols, Ex 32:4. On the stones set in the priest's ephod and chestpiece, Ex 28:9–11, 21; 39:6, 8–14; in the priest's turban, Ex 28:36; 39:30.

EN-HADDAH A city of Issachar, Josh 19:17–23.

EN-HAZOR A city of Naphtali, Josh 19:35–39.

EN-MISHPAT Ancient name of Kadesh, Gen 14:7.

See *Kadesh.*

ENOCH 1. Eldest son of Cain, Gen 4:17, 18.

2. A city built by Cain, Gen 4:17.

3. Father of Methuselah, 1 Chron 1:3; Lk 3:37; Jude 1:14. Translation of, Gen 5:18–24; Heb 11:5.

ENOSH Son of Seth, Gen 4:26; 5:6–11; 1 Chron 1:1–4. Called *Enos,* Lk 3:23–38.

EN-RIMMON A city of Judah, probably identical with *Ain* and *Rimmon,* Neh 11:25–30.

EN-ROGEL A spring near Jerusalem, Josh 15:7; 18:16; 2 Sam 17:17. A rebellious feast at, 1 Kgs 1:9.

EN-SHEMESH A spring between Judah and Benjamin, Josh 15:7; 18:17.

ENTHUSIASM INSTANCES OF. Gideon, Judg chapters 6, 7; Jehu, 2 Kgs 9:1–14; 10:1–28.

See *Zeal.*

ENUMERATION See *Census.*

ENVY Ps 37:1. Never envy the wicked! [7]Rest in the Lord; wait patiently for him to act. Don't be envious of evil men who prosper. Prov 24:19, 20.

Ps 49:16. So do not be dismayed when evil men grow rich and build their lovely homes. Deut 5:21.

Ps 73:3. For I was envious of the prosperity of the proud and wicked. *vs.* 17–20.

Ps 112:10. Evil-minded men will be infuriated

when they see all this; they will gnash their teeth in anger and slink away, their hopes thwarted.

Prov 3:31. Don't envy violent men. Don't copy their ways.

Prov 14:30. A relaxed attitude lengthens a man's life; jealousy rots it away.

Prov 23:17. Don't envy evil men but continue to reverence the Lord all the time.

Prov 24:1. Don't envy godless men; don't even enjoy their company. *vs.* 19, 20.

Prov 27:4. Jealousy is more dangerous and cruel than anger.

Eccl 4:4. Then I observed that the basic motive for success is the driving force of envy and jealousy!

Song 8:6. Seal me in your heart with permanent betrothal, for love is strong as death and jealousy is as cruel as Sheol. It flashes fire, the very flame of Jehovah.

Isa 26:11. Show them how much you love your people. Perhaps then they will be ashamed! Yes, let them be burned up by the fire reserved for your enemies. 1 Sam 2:32.

Ezk 35:11. Therefore as I live, the Lord God says, I will pay back your angry deeds with mine—I will punish you for all your acts of envy and of hate. And I will honor my name in Israel by what I do to you.

Rom 1:29. Their lives became full of every kind of wickedness and sin, of greed and hate, envy, murder, fighting, lying, bitterness, and gossip.

Rom 13:13. Be decent and true in everything you do so that all can approve your behavior. Don't spend your time in wild parties and getting drunk or in adultery and lust, or fighting, or jealousy.

1 Cor 3:3. When you are jealous of one another and divide up into quarreling groups, doesn't that prove you are still babies, wanting your own way? In fact, you are acting like people who don't belong to the Lord at all.

1 Cor 13:4. Love is very patient and kind, never jealous or envious, never boastful or proud.

2 Cor 12:20. For I am afraid that when I come to visit you I won't like what I find, and then you won't like the way I will have to act. I am afraid that I will find you quarreling, and envying each other, and being angry with each other, and acting big, and saying wicked things about each other and whispering behind each other's backs, filled with conceit and disunity.

Gal 5:19. But when you follow your own wrong inclinations your lives will produce these evil results: impure thoughts, eagerness for lustful pleasure, [20]idolatry, spiritism (that is, encouraging the activity of demons), hatred and fighting, jealousy and anger, constant effort to get the best for yourself, complaints and criticisms, the feeling that everyone else is wrong except those in your own little group—and there will be wrong doctrine, [21]envy, murder, drunkenness, wild parties, and all that sort of thing. Let me tell you again as I have before, that anyone living that sort of life will not inherit the kingdom of God. [26]Then we won't need to look for honors and popularity, which leads to jealousy and hard feelings. Mk 7:20–23.

1 Tim 6:4. He is quibbling over the meaning of Christ's words and stirring up arguments ending in jealousy and anger, which only lead to name-calling, accusations, and evil suspicions. [5]These arguers—their minds warped by sin—don't know how to tell the truth; to them the Good News is just a means of making money. Keep away from them.

Tit 3:3. Once we, too, were foolish and disobedient; we were misled by others and became slaves to many evil pleasures and wicked desires. Our lives were full of resentment and envy. We hated others and they hated us.

Jas 3:14. And by all means don't brag about being wise and good if you are bitter and jealous and selfish; that is the worst sort of lie. [16]For wherever there is jealousy or selfish ambition, there will be disorder and every other kind of evil.

Jas 5:9. Don't grumble about each other, brothers. Are you yourselves above criticism? For see! The great Judge is coming. He is almost here. [Let him do whatever criticizing must be done.]

1 Pet 2:1. So get rid of your feelings of hatred. Don't just pretend to be good! Be done with dishonesty and jealousy and talking about others behind their backs. *vs.* 2, 3.

INSTANCES OF. Cain, of Abel, Gen 4:4–8. Sarah, of Hagar, Gen 16:5, 6; 21:9, 10. Philistines, of Isaac, Gen 26:14. Rachel, of Leah, Gen 30:1. Leah, of Rachel, Gen 30:15. Laban's sons, of Jacob, Gen 31:1. Joseph's brothers of Joseph, Gen 37:4–11, 19, 20; Acts 7:9. Joshua, of Eldad and Medad, Num 11:28–30. Miriam and Aaron, of Moses, Num 12:1–10. Korah, Dathan, and Abiram, of Moses, Num 16:3; Ps 106:16–18. Saul, of David, 1 Sam 18:8, 9, 29; 20:31. Haman, of Mordecai, Esther 5:13. The rulers of Babylon, of Daniel, Dan 6:4. Priests, of Jesus, Mt 27:18; Mk 15:10; Jn 11:47. Jews, of Paul, Barnabas, and Silas, Acts 13:45; 17:5.

EPAENETUS A friend of Paul, Rom 16:5.

EPAPHRAS A fellow worker with Paul, Col 1:7; 4:12; Philemon 1:23.

EPAPHRODITUS A messenger of Paul, Phil 2:25; 4:18. Sick at Rome, Phil 2:26, 27, 30.

EPHAH 1. A son of Midian, Gen 25:4; 1 Chron 1:33; Isa 60:6.

2. Caleb's concubine, 1 Chron 2:46.

3. Son of Jahdai, 1 Chron 2:47.

4. A dry measure of about 1.5 bushels (22 liters), Ezk 45:11; 46:7. Equal to the liquid measure, *bath*.

EPHAI An Israelite, Jer 40:8.

EPHER 1. A son of Midian, Gen 25:4; 1 Chron 1:33.

2. Son of Ezrah, 1 Chron 4:17.

3. A chief of Manasseh, 1 Chron 5:24.

EPHES-DAMMIN A place in Judah, 1 Sam 17:1.

EPHESIANS Paul's letter to, see Epistle to the Ephesians. See also *Ephesus*.

EPHESUS Paul visits and preaches in, Acts 18:19–21; 19; 20:16–38. Apollos visits and preaches in, Acts 18:18–28. Sceva's sons attempt to expel a demon in, Acts 19:13–16. Timothy directed by Paul to remain at, 1 Tim 1:3, 4. Paul sends Tychicus to, 2 Tim 4:12. Onesiphorus lives at, 2 Tim 1:18. Church at, Rev 1:11. See the Epistle to the Ephesians. Apocalyptic message to, Rev 2:1–7.

EPHLAL A descendant of Judah, 1 Chron 2:37.

EPHOD 1. A sacred vestment worn by the high priest. Described, Ex 28:5–14, 32–35; 25:1–7. Making of, Ex 39:2–26. Chestpiece attached to, Ex 28:22–29. Worn by Aaron, Ex 28:12; 39:1.

Used as an oracle, 1 Sam 23:9, 12; 30:7, 8.

An inferior, was worn by the common priests, 1 Sam 22:18; by Samuel, 1 Sam 2:18; David, 2 Sam 6:14. It was called *Coat,* Lev 10:5 and *Robe,* Ex 28:40; 29:8; 39:27; 40:14; Lev 8:13.

Made by Gideon, became an idol to Israel, Judg 8:27; 17:5; 18:14.

2. A man of Manasseh, Num 34:16–28.

EPHRAIM 1. Second son of Joseph, Gen 41:52. Adopted by Jacob, Gen 48:5. Blessed before Manasseh; prophecies concerning, Gen 48:14–20. Descendants of, Num 26:28–37; 1 Chron 7:20–27. Mourns for his sons, 1 Chron 7:21, 22.

2. A tribe of Israel. Prophecy concerning, Gen 49:25, 26; Isa 7; 9:18–21; 11:13; 28:1; Jer 31; Hos 5:14; Zech 9:10; 10:7. Numbered at Sinai and in plains of Moab, Num 1:20–46; 26:28–37. Place in camp and march, Num 2:3–31; 10:22. Blessed by Moses, Deut 33:13–17.

Territory allotted to, after the conquest of Canaan, Josh 16:5–9; 17:9, 10, 15–18; 1 Chron 7:28. Fail to expel the Canaanites, Josh 16:10. Take Bethel in battle, Judg 1:22–25. Chide Gideon for not summoning them to join the war against the Midianites, Judg 8:1. Join Gideon against the Midianites, Judg 7:24, 25. Their jealousy of Jephthah, Judg 12:1. Defeated by him, Judg 12:4–6. Receive Ishbosheth as king, 2 Sam 2:9. Jeroboam places a golden calf in Bethel, 1 Kgs 12:29. Revolt from house of David, 1 Kgs 12:25; 2 Chron 10:16. Some of tribe join Judah under Asa, 2 Chron 15:9. Chastise Ahaz and Judah, 2 Chron 28:7. Join Hezekiah in reinstituting the passover, 2 Chron 30:17–19. Join in the destruction of idols in Jerusalem, 2 Chron 31:1. Submit to the rule of Josiah, 2 Chron 34:1–6. Envied by other tribes, Isa 11:13; Jer 7:15; Ezk 37:16–20; Hos 13:1. Worshiped Baal, Hos 13:1. Sin of, remembered by God, Hos 13:12. Reallotment of territory to, by Ezekiel, Ezk 48:5–7.

Name of, applied to the ten tribes, 2 Chron 17:2; Isa 7:8, 9; Jer 31:18, 20; Hos 6:4, 10; 8:11; 12:14. Tribe of, called *Joseph,* Rev 7:4–8.

3. Mount of. A range of low mountains, Josh 17:15–18. Joshua has his inheritance in, Judg 2:7–9. Residence of Micah, Judg 17:7, 8. A place of hiding for Israelites, 1 Sam 14:22. Sheba resides in, 2 Sam 20:21. Noted for rich pastures, Jer 50:19. Prophecy concerning its conversion, Jer 31:6.

4. A forest east of the Jordan. Absalom killed in, 2 Sam 18:6–17.

5. A gate of Jerusalem, 2 Kgs 14:13; 2 Chron 25:23; Neh 8:16; 12:39.

6. A city in the territory of Ephraim. Jesus escapes to, from the persecution of Caiaphas, Jn 11:54.

EPHRAIMITES See *Ephraim, 2.*

EPHRATAH 1. Called also *Ephrath.* The ancient name of Bethlehem, Gen 35:16, 19; 48:7; Ps 132:6; Mic 5:2.

2. Second wife of Caleb, mother of Hur, 1 Chron 2:19, 24, 50; 4:3,4.

EPHRATH See *Ephratah, 1.*

EPHRON 1. Son of Zohar, the Hethite. Sells to Abraham the field containing the cave Machpelah, Gen 23:8–18; 25:9, 10; 49:29, 30; 50:12, 13.

2. A mountain on the boundary line between Judah and Benjamin, Josh 15:9.

3. A city in Benjamin, 2 Chron 13:18, 19.

EPIC Heroic poetry. Miriam's song, Ex 15:1–19, 21. Deborah's song, Judg 5. David's war song, 2 Sam 22.

See *Poetry.*

EPICUREANS Reject John the Baptist, Mt 11:18; Lk 7:33. Doctrines propagated by, familiar to Solomon, Eccl 2:1–10; to Paul, 1 Cor 15:32. Dispute with Paul, Acts 17:18.

See *Sensuality.*

EPISTLES From the church at Jerusalem to the Gentiles, Acts 15:23–29. Of Luke to Theophilus, Lk 1:1–4; Acts 1:1,2. Of Paul, see the books of Romans, Corinthians, Galatians, Ephesians, Philippians, Colossians, Thessalonians, Timothy and Titus; of James, Peter and John, see books of the New Testament, bearing their names. Of Christ to the seven churches, Rev 2, 3.

See *Letters.*

EQUALITY Of men, see *Man, Equality of.*

EQUITY See *Justice.*

ER 1. Son of Judah, Gen 38:3–7; 46:8–14; Num 26:19–22; 1 Chron 2:3.

2. A son of Shelah, 1 Chron 4:21, 22.

3. An ancestor of Jesus, Lk 3:23–38.

ERAN A grandson of Ephraim, Num 26:28–37.

ERASTUS 1. A friend of Paul, Acts 19:22; 2 Tim 4:20.

2. Convert of Paul's, probably same as preceding, Rom 16:23.

ERECH A city of Shinar, Gen 10:10.

ERI A son of Gad, Gen 46:16, 17; Num 26:15–18.

ERRORS In teachers and doctrines, see *Teachers, False.*

ESAR-HADDON King of Assyria. Succeeds Sennacherib, 2 Kgs 19:37; Isa 37:38. Called *Osnapper,* Ezra 4:10.

ESAU Oldest of twin sons born to Isaac and Rebekah. Birth of, Gen 25:19–26; 1 Chron 1:34. Called *Edom,* Gen 36:1, 9. A hunter, Gen 25:27, 28. Beloved by Isaac, Gen 25:27, 28. Sells his birthright for stew, Gen 25:29–34; Mal 1:2, 3; Rom 9:10–13; Heb 12:16. Marries a Hethite, Gen 26:34. His marriage to, a grief to Isaac and Rebekah, Gen 26:35. Polygamy of, Gen 26:34; 28:9; 36:2, 3. Is defrauded of his father's blessing by Jacob, Gen 27; Heb 11:20. Meets Jacob on the return of the latter from Haran, Gen 33:1. With Jacob, buries his father, Gen 35:28, 29. Descendants of, Gen 36; 1 Chron 1:35–37. Enmity of descendants of, toward descendants of Jacob, Obd 1:10–14. Ancestor of Edomites, Jer 49:8. His name used to denote his descendants and their country, Deut 2:4; Jer 49:9, 10. Prophecies concerning, Obd 1:18.

ESCAPE NONE, FROM THE JUDGMENTS OF GOD. Gen 3:7. And as they ate it, suddenly they became aware of their nakedness, and were embarrassed. So they strung fig leaves together to cover themselves around the hips. [8]That evening they heard the sound of the Lord God walking in the garden; and they hid themselves among the trees. [9]The Lord God called to Adam, "Why are you hiding?" [10]And Adam replied, "I heard you coming and didn't want you to see me naked. So I hid." [11]"Who told you you were naked?" the Lord God asked. "Have you eaten fruit from the tree I warned you about?"

Gen 4:9. But afterwards the Lord asked Cain, "Where is your brother? Where is Abel?" "How should I know?" Cain retorted. "Am I supposed to keep track of him wherever he goes?" [10]But the Lord said, "Your brother's blood calls to me from the ground. What have you done? [11]You are hereby banished from this ground which you have defiled with your brother's blood."

Job 34:21. For God carefully watches the goings on of all mankind; he sees them all. [22]No darkness is thick enough to hide evil men from his eyes.

Isa 10:3. Oh, what will you do when I visit you in that day when I send desolation upon you from a distant land? To whom will you turn then for your help? Where will your treasures be safe?

Mt 23:33. Snakes! Sons of vipers! How shall you escape the judgment of hell?

Rom 2:3. Do you think that God will judge and condemn others for doing them and overlook you when you do them, too?

1 Thess 5:2. For you know perfectly well that no one knows. That day of the Lord will come unexpectedly like a thief in the night. [3]When people are saying, "All is well, everything is quiet and peaceful"—then, all of a sudden, disaster will fall upon them as suddenly as a woman's birth pains begin when her child is born. And these people will not be able to get away anywhere—there will be no place to hide.

Heb 2:2, 3. For since the messages from angels have always proved true and people have always been punished for disobeying them, [3]what makes us think that we can escape if we are indifferent to this great salvation announced by the Lord Jesus himself, and passed on to us by those who heard him speak?

Heb 12:25. So see to it that you obey him who is speaking to you. For if the people of Israel did not escape when they refused to listen to Moses, the earthly messenger, how terrible our danger if we refuse to listen to God who speaks to us from heaven! [26]When he spoke from Mount Sinai his voice shook the earth, but, "Next time," he says, "I will not only shake the earth, but the heavens too."

Rev 6:15. The kings of the earth, and world leaders and rich men, and high-ranking military officers, and all men great and small, slave and free, hid themselves in the caves and rocks of the mountains, [16]and cried to the mountains to crush them. "Fall on us," they pleaded, "and hide us from the face of the one sitting on the throne, and from the anger of the Lamb, [17]because the great day of their anger has come, and who can survive it?"

See *Sin, Fruits of, Punishment of; Judgments, No Escape from.*

ESCAPE, ROCK OF In the wilderness of Maon, 1 Sam 23:28.

ESCHATOLOGY The doctrine of last things, see *Prophecy.*

ESEK A well dug by the servants of Isaac, Gen 26:20.

ESHAN A city in Judah, Josh 15:48–62.

ESH-BAAL See *Ish-Bosheth.*

ESHBAN A son of Dishon, Gen 36:26; 1 Chron 1:41.

ESHCOL 1. An Amorite, and ally of Abraham, Gen 14:13, 24.

2. A valley or brook near Hebron, Num 13:23, 24; 32:9; Deut 1:24, 25.

ESHEK A Benjaminite, 1 Chron 8:39.

ESHTAOL A town of Judah, Josh 15:33–36. Allotted to Dan, Josh 19:41–46; Judg 18:2, 8, 11. Samson moved by the Spirit of the Lord near, Judg 13:25. Samson buried near, Judg 16:31.

ESHTEMOA 1. Called also *Eshtemoh.* A town of Canaan assigned to Judah, Josh 15:48–62. Allotted to the Aaronites, Josh 21:9–16; 1 Chron 6: 58, 59. David shared spoil with, 1 Sam 30:27–31.

2. A descendant of Ezrah, 1 Chron 4:17, 19.

ESHTON Son of Mahir, 1 Chron 4:11, 12.

ESLI An ancestor of Jesus, Lk 3:23–38.

ESTATE Vast landed, Isa 5:8.

See *Land.*

ESTHER Called also *Hadassah.* Cousin of Mordecai, Esther 2:7, 15. Chosen queen, Esther 2: 17. Tells the king of the plot to assassinate him, Esther 2:22. Fasts on account of the decree to destroy the Israelites; accuses Haman to the king; intercedes for her people, Esther chapters 4–9.

ETAM 1. A village of Simeon, 1 Chron 4:32, 33.

2. A city in Judah, 2 Chron 11:5–10.

3. A name in list of Judah's descendants, but probably referring to No. 2, 1 Chron 4:3, 4.

4. A rock where Samson was captured and delivered to the Philistines, Judg 15:8, 11–13.

ETERNAL LIFE See *Life, Eternal.*

ETERNAL PUNISHMENT See *Punishment, Eternal.*

ETERNITY God inhabits, Isa 57:15; Mic 5:2; rules, Jer 10:10.

See *God, Eternity of.*

UNCLASSIFIED SCRIPTURES RELATING TO. Ps 30:12. O Lord my God, I will keep on thanking you forever!

Ps 41:13. Bless the Lord, the God of Israel, who exists from everlasting ages past—and on into everlasting eternity ahead.

Ps 72:17. His name will be honored forever; it will continue as the sun; and all will be blessed in him; all nations will praise him.

Ps 90:2. Before the mountains were created, before the earth was formed, you are God without beginning or end.

Ps 110:4. Jehovah has taken oath, and will not rescind his vow, that you are a priest forever like Melchizedek.

Ps 119:142. Your justice is eternal for your laws are perfectly fair.

2 Cor 9:9. It is as the Scriptures say: "The godly man gives generously to the poor. His good deeds will be an honor to him forever."

Rev 20:10. Then the devil who had betrayed them will again be thrown into the Lake of Fire burning with sulfur where the Creature and False Prophet are, and they will be tormented day and night forever and ever.

See *Life, Eternal; Punishment, Eternal.*

ETHAM Second camping place of Israel, Ex 13:20; Num 33:5, 6.

ETHAN 1. A renowned sage, 1 Kgs 4:31.

2. Son of Zerah, 1 Chron 2:6, 8.

3. Two Levites, 1 Chron 6:39–43; and 6:44–47; 15:17, 19.

ETHANIM See *Calendar.*

ETHBAAL King of Sidon, 1 Kgs 16:31.

ETHER A city of Caanan. Assigned to Judah, Josh 15:37–44. Subsequently allotted to Simeon, Josh 19:2–7. Called *Tochen* in 1 Chron 4:32, 33.

ETHIOPIA A region in Africa, inhabited by the descendants of Ham. The inhabitants of, black, Jer 13:23. Within the Babylonian empire, Esther 1:1–3. Rivers of, Isa 18:1; Zeph 3:10. Bordered Egypt on the south, Ezk 29:10. Was called the land of Cush, mentioned in Gen 10:6; 1 Chron 1:5–9. Warriors of, Jer 46:9; 2 Chron 12:3; Ezk 38:5. Defeated by Asa, 2 Chron 14:9–15; 16:8. Invaded Syria, 2 Kgs 19:9. Merchandise of, Isa 45:14. Moses marries a woman of, Num 12:1. Ebel-melech, at the court of Babylon, native of; treats Jeremiah kindly, Jer 38:7–13; 39:15–18. Candace, queen of, Acts 8:27. A eunuch from, becomes a disciple under the preaching of Philip, Acts 3:27–39. Prophecies concerning the conversion of, Ps 68:31; 87:4; Isa 45:14; Dan 11:43. Desolation of, Isa 18:1–6; 20:2–6; 43:3; Ezk 30:4–9; Hab 3:7; Zeph 2:12.

ETHKAZIN A town on the boundary of Zebulun, Josh 19:13.

ETHNAN Son of Ashhur, 1 Chron 4:7.

ETHNI An ancestor of Asaph, 1 Chron 6:39–43.

ETIQUETTE See *Manners.*

EUBULUS A friend of Paul, 2 Tim 4:21.

EUCHARIST See *Lord's Supper.*

EUNICE Timothy's mother, 2 Tim 1:5. See Acts 16:1.

EUNUCH Mt 19:12. Prohibited from certain privileges of the congregation, Deut 23:1; Isa 56:3–5. Influential court officials, 2 Kgs 23:11; Esther 1:10, 11; 2:3–21; 4:4, 5; Jer 38:7–13; Dan 1:3, 4. Those who voluntarily became (continent, probably) for the kingdom of heaven's sake, Mt 19:12. Baptism of the Ethiopian, Acts 8:26–39.

EUODIAS A Christian woman of Philippi, Phil 4:2.

EUPHRATES A river in the garden of Eden, Gen 2:14. The eastern limit of the kingdom of Israel, Gen 15:18; Ex 23:31; Deut 1:7; 11:24; Josh 1:4; 2 Sam 8:3; 1 Kgs 4:21; 1 Chron 5:9; 18:3. Pharaoh Necho, king of Egypt, made conquest to, 2 Kgs 24:7; Jer 46: 2–10. On the banks of, Jeremiah symbolically buries his loincloth, Jer 13:1–7. Casts the scroll containing the prophecies against Babylon into, Jer 51:59–64.

Symbolical. The flooding of, of the extension of the empire of Assyria, Isa 8:6–8. In the symbolisms of the Apocalypse, Rev 9:14; 16:12.

EUTYCHUS A young man of Troas, restored to life by Paul, Acts 20:9–12.

EVANGELISM Mk 10:43–45.

Mt 28:19. Therefore go and make disciples in all the nations, baptizing them into the name of the Father and of the Son and of the Holy Spirit, [20]and then teach these new disciples to obey all the commands I have given you; and be sure of this—that I am with you always, even to the end of the world.

Jn 3:34. For this one—sent by God—speaks God's words, for God's Spirit is upon him without measure or limit.

Jn 4:35. Do you think the work of harvesting will not begin until the summer ends four months from now? Look around you! Vast fields of human souls are ripening all around us, and are ready now for reaping. [36]The reapers will be paid good wages and will be gathering eternal souls into the granaries of heaven! What joys await the sower and the reaper, both together! [37]For it is true that one sows and someone else reaps. [38]I sent you to reap where you didn't sow; others did the work, and you received the harvest.

Jn 15:27. And you also must tell everyone about me, because you have been with me from the beginning.

Jn 20:23. If you forgive anyone's sins, they are forgiven. If you refuse to forgive them, they are unforgiven.

Jn 21:15. After breakfast Jesus said to Simon Peter, "Simon, son of John, do you love me more than these others?" "Yes," Peter replied, "You know I am your friend." "Then feed my lambs," Jesus told him. [16]Jesus repeated the question: "Simon, son of John, do you *really* love me?" "Yes, Lord," Peter said, "you know I am your friend." "Than take care of my sheep," Jesus said. [17]Once more he asked him, "Simon, son of John, are you even my friend?" Peter was grieved at the way Jesus asked the question this third time. "Lord, you know my heart; you know I am," he said. Jesus said, "Then feed my little sheep."

Acts 1:21, 22. So now we must choose someone

else to take Judas' place and to join us as witnesses of Jesus' resurrection. Let us select someone who has been with us constantly from our first association with the Lord—from the time he was baptized by John until the day he was taken from us into heaven.

Acts 5:20. Go over to the Temple and preach about this Life!

Acts 6:2. So the Twelve called a meeting of all the believers. "We should spend our time preaching, not administering a feeding program," they said. [4]"Then we can spend our time in prayer, preaching, and teaching."

Acts 10:42. And he sent us to preach the Good News everywhere and to testify that Jesus is ordained of God to be the Judge of all—living and dead.

Acts 18:9. One night the Lord spoke to Paul in a vision and told him, "Don't be afraid! Speak out! Don't quit! [10]For I am with you and no one can harm you. Many people here in this city belong to me."

Acts 20:28. And now beware! Be sure that you feed and shepherd God's flock—his church, purchased with his blood—for the Holy Spirit is holding you responsible as overseers.

Acts 22:15. You are to take his message everywhere, telling what you have seen and heard.

Acts 26:16. Now stand up! For I have appeared to you to appoint you as my servant and my witness. You are to tell the world about this experience and about the many other occasions when I shall appear to you. [17]And I will protect you from both your own people and the Gentiles. Yes, I am going to send you to the Gentiles [18]to open their eyes to their true condition so that they may repent and live in the light of God instead of in Satan's darkness, so that they may receive forgiveness for their sins and God's inheritance along with all people everywhere whose sins are cleansed away, who are set apart by faith in me.

Rom 1:14. For I owe a great debt to you and to everyone else, both to civilized people and uncivilized alike; yes, to the educated and uneducated alike. [15]So, to the fullest extent of my ability, I am ready to come also to you in Rome to preach God's Good News.

Rom 12:6. God has given each of us the ability to do certain things well. So if God has given you the ability to prophesy, then prophesy whenever you can—as often as your faith is strong enough to receive a message from God. [7]If your gift is that of serving others, serve them well. If you are a teacher, do a good job of teaching. [8]If you are a preacher, see to it that your sermons are strong and helpful. If God has given you money, be generous in helping others with it. If God has given you administrative ability and put you in charge of the work of others, take the responsibility seriously. Those who offer comfort to the sorrowing should do so with Christian cheer. *vs.* 3–5.

1 Cor 4:1. So Apollos and I should be looked upon as Christ's servants who distribute God's blessings by explaining God's secrets. [2]Now the most important thing about a servant is that he does just what his master tells him to.

1 Cor 9:16. For just preaching the Gospel isn't any special credit to me—I couldn't keep from preaching it if I wanted to. I would be utterly miserable. Woe unto me if I don't. [17]If I were volunteering my services of my own free will, then the Lord would give me a special reward; but that is not the situation, for God has picked me out and given me this sacred trust and I have no choice.

2 Cor 1:24. When I come, although I can't do much to help your faith, for it is strong already, I want to be able to do something about your joy: I want to make you happy, not sad.

2 Cor 4:1. It is God himself, in his mercy, who has given us this wonderful work [of telling his Good News to others], and so we never give up. [2]We do not try to trick people into believing—we are not interested in fooling anyone. We never try to get anyone to believe that the Bible teaches what it doesn't. All such shameful methods we forego. We stand in the presence of God as we speak and so we tell the truth, as all who know us will agree. [5]We don't go around preaching about ourselves, but about Christ Jesus as Lord. All we say of ourselves is that we are your slaves because of what Jesus has done for us.

2 Cor 5:14. Whatever we do, it is certainly not for our own profit, but because Christ's love controls us now. Since we believe that Christ died for all of us, we should also believe that we have died to the old life we used to live. [18]All these new things are from God who brought us back to himself through what Christ Jesus did. And God has given us the privilege of urging everyone to come into his favor and be reconciled to him. [20]We are Christ's ambassadors. God is using us to speak to you: we beg you, as though Christ himself were here pleading with you, receive the love he offers you—be reconciled to God.

2 Cor 6:3. We try to live in such a way that no one will ever be offended or kept back from finding the Lord by the way we act, so that no one can find fault with us and blame it on the Lord. [4]In fact, in everything we do we try to show that we are true ministers of God. We patiently endure suffering and hardship and trouble of every kind. [5]We have been beaten, put in jail, faced angry mobs, worked to exhaustion, stayed awake through sleepless nights of watching, and gone without food. [6]We have proved ourselves to be what we claim by our wholesome lives and by our understanding of the Gospel and by our patience. We have been kind and truly loving and filled with the Holy Spirit. [7]We have been truthful, with God's power helping us in all we do. All of the godly man's arsenal—weapons of defense, and weapons of attack—have been ours. [8]We stand true to the Lord whether others honor us or despise us, whether they criticize us or commend us. We are honest, but they call us liars. [9]The world ignores us, but we are known to God; we live close to death, but here we

are, still very much alive. We have been injured but kept from death. [10]Our hearts ache, but at the same time we have the joy of the Lord. We are poor, but we give rich spiritual gifts to others. We own nothing, and yet we enjoy everything.

2 Cor 7:4. I have the highest confidence in you, and my pride in you is great. You have greatly encouraged me; you have made me so happy in spite of all my suffering. [5]When we arrived in Macedonia there was no rest for us; outside, trouble was on every hand and all around us; within us, our hearts were full of dread and fear. [6]Then God who cheers those who are discouraged refreshed us by the arrival of Titus. [7]Not only was his presence a joy, but also the news that he brought of the wonderful time he had with you. When he told me how much you were looking forward to my visit, and how sorry you were about what had happened, and about your loyalty and warm love for me, well, I overflowed with joy! [8]I am no longer sorry that I sent that letter to you, though I was very sorry for a time, realizing how painful it would be to you. But it hurt you only for a little while. [9]Now I am glad I sent it, not because it hurt you, but because the pain turned you to God. It was a good kind of sorrow you felt, the kind of sorrow God wants his people to have, so that I need not come to you with harshness. [12]I wrote as I did so the Lord could show how much you really do care for us. That was my purpose even more than to help the man who sinned, or his father to whom he did the wrong. [15]He [Titus] loves you more than ever when he remembers the way you listened to him so willingly and received him so anxiously and with such deep concern.

2 Cor 8:23. If anyone asks who Titus is, say that he is my partner, my helper in helping you, and you can also say that the other two brothers represent the assemblies here and are splendid examples of those who belong to the Lord.

2 Cor 10:8. I may seem to be boasting more than I should about my authority over you—authority to help you, not to hurt you—but I shall make good every claim.

2 Cor 12:15. I am glad to give you myself and all I have for your spiritual good, even though it seems that the more I love you, the less you love me. [19]I suppose you think I am saying all this to get back into your good graces. That isn't it at all. I tell you, with God listening as I say it, that I have said this to help *you,* dear friends—to build you up spiritually and not to help myself.

Gal 1:10. You can see that I am not trying to please you by sweet talk and flattery; no, I am trying to please God. If I were still trying to please men I could not be Christ's servant.

Eph 3:8. Just think! Though I did nothing to deserve it, and though I am the most useless Christian there is, yet I was the one chosen for this special joy of telling the Gentiles the Glad News of the endless treasures available to them in Christ; [9]and to explain to everyone that God is the Savior of the Gentiles too, just as he who made all things had secretly planned from the very beginning. [10]And his reason? To show to all the rulers in heaven how perfectly wise he is when all of his family—Jews and Gentiles alike—are seen to be joined together in his church.

Eph 4:11. Some of us have been given special ability as apostles; to others he has given the gift of being able to preach well; some have special ability in winning people to Christ, helping them to trust him as their Savior; still others have a gift for caring for God's people as a shepherd does his sheep, leading and teaching them in the ways of God. [12]Why is it that he gives us these special abilities to do certain things best? It is that God's people will be equipped to do better work for him, building up the church, the body of Christ, to a position of strength and maturity.

Eph 6:20. I am in chains now for preaching this message from God. But pray that I will keep on speaking out boldly for him even here in prison, as I should.

Col 4:17. And say to Archippus, "Be sure that you do all the Lord has told you to."

1 Thess 2:4. For we speak as messengers from God, trusted by him to tell the truth; we change his message not one bit to suit the taste of those who hear it; for we serve God alone, who examines our hearts' deepest thoughts. [5]Never once did we try to win you with flattery, as you very well know, and God knows we were not just pretending to be your friends so that you would give us money! [6]As for praise, we have never asked for it from you or anyone else, although as apostles of Christ we certainly had a right to some honor from you. [7]But we were as gentle among you as a mother feeding and caring for her own children. [8]We loved you dearly—so dearly that we gave you not only God's message, but our own lives too. [10]You yourselves are our witnesses—as is God—that we have been pure and honest and faultless toward every one of you. [11]We talked to you as a father to his own children—don't you remember?—pleading with you, encouraging you and even demanding [12]that your daily lives should not embarrass God, but bring joy to him who invited you into his kingdom to share his glory.

1 Thess 3:2. And send Timothy, our brother and fellow worker, God's minister, to visit you to strengthen your faith and encourage you.

1 Thess 5:12. Dear brothers, honor the officers of your church who work hard among you and warn you against all that is wrong.

2 Thess 3:4. And we trust the Lord that you are putting into practice the things we taught you, and that you always will.

1 Tim 1:3, 4. As I said when I left for Macedonia, please stay there in Ephesus and try to stop the men who are teaching such wrong doctrine. Put an end to their myths and fables, and their idea of being saved by finding favor with an endless chain of angels leading up to God—wild ideas that stir up questions and arguments instead of helping people accept God's plan of faith. [10,11]Yes, these laws were made to identify as sinners all who are im-

moral and impure: homosexuals, kidnappers, liars, and all others who do things that contradict the glorious Good News of our blessed God, whose messenger I am. [18]Now, Timothy, my son, here is my command to you: Fight well in the Lord's battles, just as the Lord told us through his prophets that you would. [19]Cling tightly to your faith in Christ and always keep your conscience clear, doing what you know is right. For some people have disobeyed their consciences and have deliberately done what they knew was wrong.

1 Tim 2:7. And I have been chosen—this is the absolute truth—as God's minister and missionary to teach this truth to the Gentiles, and to show them God's plan of salvation through faith.

1 Tim 4:6. If you explain this to the others you will be doing your duty as a worthy pastor who is fed by faith and by the true teaching you have followed. [7]Don't waste time arguing over foolish ideas and silly myths and legends. Spend your time and energy in the exercise of keeping spiritually fit. [12]Don't let anyone think little of you because you are young. Be their ideal; let them follow the way you teach and live; be a pattern for them in your love, your faith, and your clean thoughts. [13]Until I get there, read and explain the Scriptures to the church; preach the Word. [14]Be sure to use the abilities God has given you through his prophets when the elders of the church laid their hands upon your head. [15]Put these abilities to work; throw yourself into your tasks so that everyone may notice your improvement and progress. [16]Keep a close watch on all you do and think. Stay true to what is right and God will bless you and use you to help others.

1 Tim 6:3. Some may deny these things, but they are the sound, wholesome teachings of the Lord Jesus Christ and are the foundation for a godly life. [4]Anyone who says anything different is both proud and stupid. He is quibbling over the meaning of Christ's words and stirring up arguments ending in jealousy and anger, which only lead to name-calling, accusations, and evil suspicions. [10]For the love of money is the first step toward all kinds of sin. Some people have even turned away from God because of their love for it, and as a result have pierced themselves with many sorrows. [11]Oh, Timothy, you are God's man. Run from all these evil things and work instead at what is right and good, learning to trust him and love others, and be patient and gentle. [12]Fight on for God. Hold tightly to the eternal life which God has given you, and which you have confessed with such a ringing confession before many witnesses. [13]I command you before God who gives life to all, and before Christ Jesus who gave a fearless testimony before Pontius Pilate, [14]that you fulfill all he has told you to do, so that no one can find fault with you from now until our Lord Jesus Christ returns. [17]Tell those who are rich not to be proud and not to trust in their money, which will soon be gone, but their pride and trust should be in the living God who always richly gives us all we need for our enjoyment. [18]Tell them to use their money to do good. They should be rich in good works and should give happily to those in need, always being ready to share with others whatever God has given them. [19]By doing this they will be storing up real treasure for themselves in heaven—it is the only safe investment for eternity! And they will be living a fruitful Christian life down here as well. [20]Oh, Timothy, don't fail to do these things that God entrusted to you. Keep out of foolish arguments with those who boast of their "knowledge" and thus prove their lack of it. [21]Some of these people have missed the most important thing in life—they don't know God. May God's mercy be upon you.

2 Tim 1:6. This being so, I want to remind you to stir into flame the strength and boldness that is in you, that entered into you when I laid my hands upon your head and blessed you. [7]For the Holy Spirit, God's gift, does not want you to be afraid of people, but to be wise and strong, and to love them and enjoy being with them. [8]If you will stir up this inner power, you will never be afraid to tell others about our Lord, or to let them know that I am your friend even though I am here in jail for Christ's sake. You will be ready to suffer with me for the Lord, for he will give you strength in suffering.

2 Tim 2:2. For you must teach others those things you and many others have heard me speak about. Teach these great truths to trustworthy men who will, in turn, pass them on to others. [3]Take your share of suffering as a good soldier of Jesus Christ, just as I do, [4]and as Christ's soldier do not let yourself become tied up in worldly affairs, for then you cannot satisfy the one who has enlisted you in his army. [5]Follow the Lord's rules for doing his work, just as an athlete either follows the rules or is disqualified and wins no prize. [6]Work hard, like a farmer who gets paid well if he raises a large crop. [7]Think over these three illustrations, and may the Lord help you to understand how they apply to you. [14]Remind your people of these great facts, and command them in the name of the Lord not to argue over unimportant things. Such arguments are confusing and useless, and even harmful. [15]Work hard so God can say to you, "Well done." Be a good workman, one who does not need to be ashamed when God examines your work. Know what his Word says and means. [16]Steer clear of foolish discussions which lead people into the sin of anger with each other. [23]Again I say, don't get involved in foolish arguments which only upset people and make them angry. [24]God's people must not be quarrelsome; they must be gentle, patient teachers of those who are wrong. [25]Be humble when you are trying to teach those who are mixed up concerning the truth. For if you talk meekly and courteously to them they are more likely, with God's help, to turn away from their wrong ideas and believe what is true.

2 Tim 4:1. And so I solemnly urge you before God and before Christ Jesus—who will some day judge the living and the dead when he appears to set up his kingdom—[2]to preach the Word of God

urgently at all times, whenever you get the chance, in season and out, when it is convenient and when it is not. Correct and rebuke your people when they need it, encourage them to do right, and all the time be feeding them patiently with God's Word. [5]Stand steady, and don't be afraid of suffering for the Lord. Bring others to Christ. Leave nothing undone that you ought to do.

1 Pet 5:1. And now, a word to you elders of the church. I, too, am an elder. . . . [2]Feed the flock of God; care for it willingly, not grudgingly; not for what you will get out of it, but because you are eager to serve the Lord. [3]Don't be tyrants, but lead them by your good example, [4]and when the Head Shepherd comes, your reward will be a never-ending share in his glory and honor.

2 Pet 1:12. I plan to keep on reminding you of these things even though you already know them and are really getting along quite well! [13, 14]But the Lord Jesus Christ has showed me that my days here on earth are numbered, and I am soon to die. As long as I am still here I intend to keep sending these reminders to you, [15]hoping to impress them so clearly upon you that you will remember them long after I have gone. [16]For we have not been telling you fairy tales when we explained to you the power of our Lord Jesus Christ and his coming again. My own eyes have seen his splendor and his glory.

See *Missions; Zeal.*

EVAPORATION Ps 135:7; Jer 10:13; 51:16; Amos 5:8; 9:6.

EVE Creation of, Gen 1:26–28; 2:21–24; 1 Tim 2:13. Named by Adam, Gen 2:23; 3:20. Deceived by Satan, Gen 3; 2 Cor 11:3; 1 Tim 2:14. Clothed with fig leaves, Gen 3:7; with skins, Gen 3:21. Curse pronounced against, Gen 3:16. Messiah promised to, Gen 3:15. Children of, Gen 4:1, 2, 25; 5:3–5.

EVERLASTING FIRE See *Fire, Everlasting.*

EVERLASTING LIFE See *Life, Eternal.*

EVERLASTING PUNISHMENT See *Punishment, Eternal.*

EVI Prince of Midian, killed, Num 31:8; Josh 13:21.

EVICTION Of tenants, Mt 21:41; Mk 12:9.

EVIDENCE LAWS CONCERNING. Ex 20:16. You must not lie.

Ex 23:1. Do not pass along untrue reports. Do not cooperate with an evil man by affirming on the witness stand something you know is false. [7]Keep far away from falsely charging anyone with evil; never let an innocent person be put to death. I will not stand for this.

Lev 5:1. Anyone refusing to give testimony concerning what he knows about a crime is guilty.

Lev 24:14. Take him outside the camp and tell all who heard him to lay their hands upon his head; then all the people are to execute him by stoning.

Num 35:30. All murderers must be executed, but only if there is more than one witness; no man shall die with only one person testifying against him.

Deut 17:6. However, never put a man to death on the testimony of only one witness; there must be at least two or three. [7]The witnesses shall throw the first stones, and then all the people shall join in. In this way you will purge all evil from among you.

Deut 19:15. Never convict anyone on the testimony of one witness. There must be at least two, and three is even better. [16]If anyone gives false witness, claiming he has seen someone do wrong when he hasn't, [17]both men shall be brought before the priests and judges on duty before the Lord at the time. [18]They must be closely questioned, and if the witness is lying, [19]his penalty shall be the punishment he thought the other man would get. In this way you will purge out evil from among you. [20]Then those who hear about it will be afraid to tell lies on the witness stand. [21]You shall not show pity to a false witness. Life for life, eye for eye, tooth for tooth, hand for hand, foot for foot; this is your rule in such cases.

Prov 24:28. Don't testify spitefully against an innocent neighbor. Why lie about him?

Mt 18:16. But if not, then take one or two others with you and go back to him again, proving everything you say by these witnesses.

Mt 19:18. And Jesus replied . . . "don't lie."

Heb 10:28. A man who refused to obey the laws given by Moses was killed without mercy if there were two or three witnesses to his sin.

SELF-INCRIMINATING. Josh 7:19. Joshua said to Achan, "My son, give glory to the God of Israel and make your confession. Tell me what you have done." [20]Achan replied, "I have sinned against the Lord, the God of Israel. [21]For I saw a beautiful robe imported from Babylon, and some silver worth $200, and a bar of gold worth $500. I wanted them so much that I took them, and they are hidden in the ground beneath my tent, with the silver buried deeper than the rest."

See *Witness; False Witness; Accusation, False; Self-Incrimination.*

EVIL APPEARANCE OF, TO BE AVOIDED. Rom 14:1. Give a warm welcome to any brother who wants to join you, even though his faith is weak. Don't criticize him for having different ideas from yours about what is right and wrong. [2]For instance, don't argue with him about whether or not to eat meat that has been offered to idols. You may believe there is no harm in this, but the faith of others is weaker; they think it is wrong, and will go without any meat at all and eat vegetables rather than eat that kind of meat. [3]Those who think it is all right to eat such meat must not look down on those who won't. And if you are one of those who won't, don't find fault with those who do. For God has accepted them to be his children. [4]They are God's servants, not yours. They are responsible to him, not to you. Let him tell them whether they are right or wrong. And God is able to make them do as they should. [5]Some think that Christians should observe the Jewish holidays as special days to worship God, but others say it is wrong and foolish to go to all that trouble, for every day alike belongs to God. On questions of this kind everyone must decide for himself. [6]If you have special days for worshiping the Lord, you are trying to honor him; you are doing a good thing. So is the person who eats meat that has been offered to idols; he is thankful to the Lord for it; he is doing right. And the person who won't touch such meat, he, too, is anxious to please the Lord, and is thankful. [7]We are not our own bosses to live or die as we ourselves might choose. [8]Living or dying we follow the Lord. Either way we are his. [9]Christ died and rose again for this very purpose, so that he can be our Lord both while we live and when we die. [10]You have no right to criticize your brother or look down on him. Remember, each of us will stand personally before the Judgment Seat of God. [11]For it is written, "As I live," says the Lord, "every knee shall bow to me and every tongue confess to God." [12]Yes, each of us will give an account of himself to God. [13]So don't criticize each other any more. Try instead to live in such a way that you will never make your brother stumble by letting him see you doing something he thinks is wrong. [14]As for myself, I am perfectly sure on the authority of the Lord Jesus that there is nothing really wrong with eating meat that has been offered to idols. But if someone believes it is wrong, then he shouldn't do it because for him it is wrong. [15]And if your brother is bothered by what you eat, you are not acting in love if you go ahead and eat it. Don't let your eating ruin someone for whom Christ died. [16]Don't do anything that will cause criticism against yourself even though you know that what you do is right. [17]For, after all, the important thing for us as Christians is not what we eat or drink but stirring up goodness and peace and joy from the Holy Spirit. [18]If you let Christ be Lord in these affairs, God will be glad; and so will others. [19]In this way aim for harmony in the church and try to build each other up. [20]Don't undo the work of God for a chunk of meat. Remember, there is nothing wrong with the meat, but it is wrong to eat it if it makes another stumble. [21]The right thing to do is to quit eating meat or drinking wine or doing anything else that offends your brother or makes him sin. [22]You may know that there is nothing wrong with what you do, even from God's point of view, but keep it to yourself; don't flaunt your faith in front of others who might be hurt by it. In this situation, happy is the man who does not sin by doing what he knows is right. [23]But anyone who believes that something he wants to do is wrong shouldn't do it. He sins if he does, for he thinks it is wrong, and so for him it *is* wrong. Anything that is done apart from what he feels is right is sin.

1 Cor 8:7. However, some Christians don't realize this. All their lives they have been used to thinking of idols as alive, and have believed that food offered to the idols is really being offered to actual gods. So when they eat such food it bothers them and hurts their tender consciences. [8]Just remember that God doesn't care whether we eat it or not. We are no worse off if we don't eat it, and no better off if we do. [9]But be careful not to use your freedom to eat it, lest you cause some Christian brother to sin whose conscience is weaker than yours. [10]You see, this is what may happen: Someone who thinks it is wrong to eat this food will see you eating at a temple restaurant, for you know there is no harm in it. Then he will become bold enough to do it too, although all the time he still feels it is wrong. [11]So because you "know it is all right to do it," you will be responsible for causing great spiritual damage to a brother for whom Christ died. [12]And it is a sin against Christ to sin against your brother by encouraging him to do something he thinks is wrong. [13]So if eating meat offered to idols is going to make my brother sin, I'll not eat any of it as long as I live, because I don't want to do this to him.

1 Cor 10:28. But if someone warns you that this meat has been offered to idols, then don't eat it for the sake of the man who told you, and of his conscience. [29]In this case *his* feeling about it is the important thing, not yours. But why, you may ask, must I be guided and limited by what someone else thinks? [30]If I can thank God for the food and enjoy it, why let someone spoil everything just because he thinks I am wrong? [31]Well, I'll tell you why. It is because you must do everything for the glory of God, even your eating and drinking. [32]So don't be a stumbling block to anyone, whether they are Jews or Gentiles or Christians. [33]That is the plan I follow, too. I try to please everyone in everything I do, not doing what I like or what is best for me, but what is best for them, so that they may be saved.

1 Thess 4:11. This should be your ambition: to live a quiet life, minding your own business and doing your own work, just as we told you before. [12]As a result, people who are not Christians will trust and respect you, and you will not need to depend on others for enough money to pay your bills.

1 Thess 5:22. Keep away from every kind of evil.

INSTANCES OF. Paul, in refusing to eat that which had been offered to idols, 1 Cor 8:13. In supporting himself, 1 Cor 9:7–23.

EVIL FOR EVIL See *Retaliation.*

EVIL FOR GOOD Ps 7:3. It would be different, Lord, if I were doing evil things—[4]if I were paying back evil for good or unjustly attacking those I dislike. [5]Then it would be right for you to let my enemies destroy me, crush me to the ground, and trample my life in the dust.

Ps 35:12. I do them good, but they return me harm. I am sinking down to death.

Ps 109:5. They return evil for good, and hatred for love.

Prov 17:13. If you repay evil for good, a curse is upon your home.

INSTANCES OF. Joseph accuses his brothers of returning, Gen 44:4. Israelites, to Moses, Ex 5:21; 14:11; 15:24; 16:2, 3; 17:3, 4. Nabal returns, to David, 1 Sam 25:21. Saul returns, to David, 1 Sam 19:1, 4, 5, 9, 10. David, to Uriah, 2 Sam 11; to Joab, 1 Kgs 2:4, 5, 6.

See *Enemy; Good for Evil.*

EVIL-MERODACH Son and successor of Nebuchadnezzar. Released Jehoiachin from prison, 2 Kgs 25:27–30; Jer 52:31–34.

EVIL SPEAKING See *Speaking, Evil.*

EXALTATION OF CHRIST. See *Jesus, Exaltation of.*

OF SELF. See *Self-Exaltation.*

EXAMPLE BAD, WARNINGS AGAINST. Lev 18:1, 2. The Lord then told Moses to tell the people of Israel, "I am Jehovah your God, [3]so don't act like heathen—like the people of Egypt where you lived so long, or the people of Canaan where I am going to take you."

Lev 20:23. You must not follow the customs of the nations I cast out before you, for they do all these things I have warned you against; that is the reason I abhor them.

Deut 18:9. When you arrive in the Promised Land you must be very careful lest you be corrupted by the horrible customs of the nations now living there.

2 Chron 30:7. Do not be like your fathers and brothers who sinned against the Lord God of their fathers and were destroyed.

Prov 22:24, 25. Keep away from angry, short-tempered men, lest you learn to be like them and endanger your soul.

Isa 8:11. The Lord has said in strongest terms: Do not under any circumstances, go along with the plans of Judah to surrender to Syria and Israel.

Jer 16:12. *And you have been worse than your fathers were!* You follow evil to your hearts' content and refuse to listen to me.

Jer 17:1. My people sin as though commanded to, as though their evil were laws chiseled with an iron pen or diamond point upon their stony hearts or on the corners of their altars. [2]Their youths do not forget to sin, worshiping idols beneath each tree, high in the mountains or in the open country down below.

Ezk 20:18. Then I spoke to their children and said: Don't follow your fathers' footsteps. Don't defile yourselves with their idols.

Hos 4:9. And thus it is: "Like priests, like people"—because the priests are wicked, the people are too. Therefore, I will punish both priests and people for all their wicked deeds.

15. But though Israel is a prostitute, may Judah stay far from such a life. O Judah, do not join with those who insincerely worship me at Gilgal and at Bethel. Their worship is mere pretense.

Hos 5:5. The very arrogance of Israel testifies against her in my court. She will stumble under her load of guilt, and Judah, too, shall fall.

Zech 1:4. Don't be like your fathers were! The earlier prophets pled in vain with them to turn from all their evil ways. "Come, return to me," the Lord God said. But no, they wouldn't listen; they paid no attention at all.

Mt 23:1. Then Jesus said to the crowds, and to his disciples, [2]"You would think these Jewish leaders and these Pharisees were Moses, the way they keep making up so many laws! [3]And of course you should obey their every whim! It may be all right to do what they say, but above anything else, *don't follow their example.* For they don't do what they tell you to do.

1 Cor 8:9. But be careful not to use your freedom to eat it, lest you cause some Christian brother to sin whose conscience is weaker than yours. [10]You see, this is what may happen: Someone who thinks it is wrong to eat this food will see you eating at a temple restaurant, for you know there is no harm in it. Then he will become bold enough to do it too, although all the time he still feels it is wrong. [11]So because you "know it is all right to do it," you will be responsible for causing great spiritual damage to a brother with a tender conscience for whom Christ died. [12]And it is a sin against Christ to sin against your brother by encouraging him to do something he thinks is wrong. [13]So if eating meat offered to idols is going to make my brother sin, I'll not eat any of it as long as I live, because I don't want to do this to him.

1 Cor 10:6. From this lesson we are warned that we must not desire evil things as they did.

Eph 4:17. Let me say this, then, speaking for the Lord: Live no longer as the unsaved do, for they are blinded and confused.

3 Jn 1:11. Dear friend, don't let this bad example influence you. Follow only what is good. Remember that those who do what is right prove that they are God's children; and those who continue in evil prove that they are far from God.

See *Influence.*

GOOD. Neh 5:8. At the trial I shouted at them, "The rest of us are doing all we can to *help* our Jewish brothers who have returned from exile as slaves in distant lands, but you are forcing them right back into slavery again. How often must we redeem them?" And they had nothing to say in their own defense. [9]Then I pressed further. "What you are doing is very evil," I exclaimed. "Should you not walk in the fear of our God? Don't we have enough enemies among the nations around us who are trying to destroy us? [10]The rest of us are lending money and grain to our fellow-Jews without any interest. I beg you, gentlemen, stop this business of usury. [11]Restore their fields, vineyards, oliveyards, and homes to them this very day and drop your claims against them." [12]So they agreed to do it and said that they would assist their brothers without requiring them to mortgage their lands and sell them their children. Then I summoned the priests and made these men formally vow to carry out their promises. [13]And I invoked the curse of God upon any of them who refused. "May God destroy your homes and livelihood if you fail to keep this promise," I declared. And all the people shouted, "Amen," and praised the Lord. And the rich men did as they had promised. [14]I would like to mention that for the entire twelve years that I was governor of Judah—from the twentieth until the thirty-second year of the reign of King Ar-taxerxes—my aides and I accepted no salaries or other assistance from the people of Israel. [15]This was quite a contrast to the former governors who had demanded food and wine and $100 a day in cash, and had put the population at the mercy of their aides, who tyrannized them; but I obeyed God and did not act that way. [16]I stayed at work on the wall and refused to speculate in land; I also required my officials to spend time on the wall. [17]All this despite the fact that I regularly fed 150 Jewish officials at my table, besides visitors from other countries! [18]The provisions required for each day were one ox, six fat sheep, and a large number of domestic fowls; and we needed a huge supply of all kinds of wines every ten days. Yet I refused to make a special levy against the people, for they were already having a difficult time. [19]O my God, please keep in mind all that I've done for these people and bless me for it.

Ps 101:2. I will try to walk a blameless path, but how I need your help, especially in my own home, where I long to act as I should.

1 Thess 1:6. So you became our followers and the Lord's; for you received our message with joy from the Holy Spirit in spite of the trials and sorrows it brought you. [7]Then you yourselves became an example to all the other Christians in Greece. [8]And now the Word of the Lord has spread out from you to others everywhere, far beyond your boundaries, for wherever we go we find people telling us about your remarkable faith in God.

1 Tim 4:12. Don't let anyone think little of you because you are young. Be their ideal; let them follow the way you teach and live; be a pattern for them in your love, your faith, and your clean thoughts.

Tit 2:7. And here you yourself must be an example to them of good deeds of every kind. Let everything you do reflect your love of the truth and the fact that you are in dead earnest about it. [8]Your conversation should be so sensible and logical that anyone who wants to argue will be ashamed of himself because there won't be anything to criticize in anything you say!

Heb 13:7. Remember your leaders who have taught you the Word of God. Think of all the good that has come from their lives, and try to trust the Lord as they do.

Jas 5:10. For examples of patience in suffering, look at the Lord's prophets. [11]We know how happy they are now because they stayed true to him then, even though they suffered greatly for it. Job is an example of a man who continued to trust the Lord in sorrow; from his experiences we can see how the Lord's plan finally ended in food, for he is full of tenderness and mercy.

1 Pet 2:11. Dear brothers, you are only visitors here. Since your real home is in heaven I beg you to keep away from the evil pleasures of this world; they are not for you, for they fight against your very souls. [12]Be careful how you behave among your unsaved neighbors; for then, even if they are suspicious of you and talk against you, they will end up praising God for your good works when Christ returns. [13]For the Lord's sake, obey every law of your government: those of the king as head of the state, [14]and those of the king's officers, for he has sent them to punish all who do wrong, and to honor those who do right. [15]It is God's will that your good lives should silence those who foolishly condemn the Gospel without knowing what it can do for them, having never experienced its power. [16]You are free from the law, but that doesn't mean you are free to do wrong. Live as those who are free to do only God's will at all times. [17]Show respect for everyone. Love Christians everywhere. Fear God and honor the government. [18]Servants, you must respect your masters and do whatever they tell you—not only if they are kind and reasonable, but even if they are tough and cruel. [19]Praise the Lord if you are punished for doing right! [20]Of course, you get no credit for being patient if you are beaten for doing wrong; but if you do right and suffer for it, and are patient beneath the blows, God is well pleased. [21]This suffering is all part of the work God has given you. Christ, who suffered for you, is your example. Follow in his steps: [22]He never sinned, never told a lie, [23]never answered back when insulted; when he suffered he did not threaten to get even; he left his case in the hands of God who always judges fairly. [24]He personally carried the load of our sins in his own body when he died on the cross, so that we can be finished with sin and live a good life from now on. For his wounds have healed ours! [25]Like sheep you wandered away from God, but now you have returned to your Shepherd, the Guardian of your souls who keeps you safe from all attacks.

1 Pet 3:5. That kind of deep beauty was seen in the saintly women of old, who trusted God and fitted in with their husbands' plans. [6]Sarah, for instance, obeyed her husband Abraham, honoring him as head of the house. And if you do the same, you will be following in her steps like good daughters and doing what is right; then you will not need to fear [offending your husbands].

1 Pet 5:3. Don't be tyrants, but lead them by your good example.

See *Influence.*

GOD, OUR. Lev 11:44. I am the Lord your God. Keep yourselves pure concerning these things, and be holy, for I am holy; therefore do not defile yourselves by touching any of these things that crawl upon the earth.

Lev 19:1, 2. The Lord also told Moses to tell the people of Israel, "You must be holy because I, the Lord your God, am holy."

Mt 5:48. But you are to be perfect, even as your Father in heaven is perfect.

Lk 6:36. Try to show as much compassion as your Father does.

Eph 6:9. And you slave owners must treat your slaves right, just as I have told them to treat you. Don't keep threatening them; remember, you yourselves are slaves to Christ; you have the same Master they do, and he has no favorites.

CHRIST, OUR. Mk 10:43. But among you it is different. Whoever wants to be great among you must be your servant. [44]And whoever wants to be greatest of all must be the slave of all. [45]For even I, the Messiah, am not here to be served, but to help others, and to give my life as a ransom for many. Mt 20:28.

Lk 22:27. Out in the world the master sits at the table and is served by his servants. But not here! For I am your servant.

Jn 13:13. You call me 'Master' and 'Lord,' and you do well to say it, for it is true. [14]And since I, the Lord and Teacher, have washed your feet, you ought to wash each other's feet. [15]I have given you an example to follow: do as I have done to you. [16]How true it is that a servant is not greater than his master. Nor is the messenger more important than the one who sends him. [17]You know these things—now do them! That is the path of blessing. [34]And so I am giving a new commandment to you now—love each other just as much as I love you.

Rom 15:2. Let's please the other fellow, not ourselves, and do what is for his good and thus build him up in the Lord. [3]Christ didn't please himself. As the Psalmist said, "He came for the very purpose of suffering under the insults of those who were against the Lord." [4]These things that were written in the Scriptures so long ago are to teach us patience and to encourage us, so that we will look forward expectantly to the time when God will conquer sin and death. [5]May God who gives patience, steadiness, and encouragement help you to live in complete harmony with each other—each with the attitude of Christ toward the other. [6]And then all of us can praise the Lord together with one voice, giving glory to God, the Father of our Lord Jesus Christ. [7]So, warmly welcome each other into the church, just as Christ has warmly welcomed you; then God will be glorified.

2 Cor 8:9. You know how full of love and kindness our Lord Jesus was: though he was so very rich, yet to help you he became so very poor, so that by being poor he could make you rich. [With context.]

2 Cor 10:1. I plead with you—yes, I, Paul—and I plead gently, as Christ himself would do.

Eph 5:1. Follow God's example in everything you do just as a much loved child imitates his father. [2]Be full of love for others, following the example of Christ who loved you and gave himself to God as a sacrifice to take away your sins. And God was pleased, for Christ's love for you was like sweet perfume to him.

Phil 2:5. Your attitude should be the kind that was shown us by Jesus Christ, [6]who, though he was God, did not demand and cling to his rights as God, [7]but laid aside his mighty power and glory, taking the disguise of a slave and becoming like men. [8]And he humbled himself even further, going so far as actually to die a criminal's death on a cross.

Col 3:13. Be gentle and ready to forgive; never hold grudges. Remember, the Lord forgave you, so you must forgive others.

Heb 12:2. Keep your eyes on Jesus, our leader and instructor. He was willing to die a shameful death on the cross because of the joy he knew would be his afterwards; and now he sits in the place of honor by the throne of God. [3]If you want to keep from becoming fainthearted and weary, think about his patience as sinful men did such terrible things to him.

1 Pet 2:21. This suffering is all part of the work God has given you. Christ, who suffered for you, is your example. Follow in his steps.

1 Pet 3:17. Remember, if God wants you to suffer, it is better to suffer for doing good than for doing wrong! [18]Christ also suffered. He died once for the sins of all us guilty sinners, although he himself was innocent of any sin at any time, that he might bring us safely home to God. But though his body died, his spirit lived on.

1 Pet 4:1. Since Christ suffered and underwent pain, you must have the same attitude he did; you must be ready to suffer, too. For remember, when your body suffers, sin loses its power.

1 Jn 2:6. Anyone who says he is a Christian should live as Christ did.

1 Jn 3:16. We know what real love is from Christ's example in dying for us. And so we also ought to lay down our lives for our Christian brothers.

Rev 3:21. I will let everyone who conquers sit beside me on my throne, just as I took my place with my Father on his throne when I had conquered.

PAUL, OUR. Acts 20:35. And I was a constant example to you in helping the poor; for I remembered the words of the Lord Jesus, "It is more blessed to give than to receive."

1 Cor 4:16. So I beg you to follow my example, and do as I do.

1 Cor 7:7. I wish that everyone could get along without marrying, just as I do. But we are not all the same. God gives some the gift of a husband or wife, and others he gives the gift of being able to stay happily unmarried. [8]So I say to those who aren't married, and to widows—better to stay unmarried if you can, just as I am.

1 Cor 11:1. And you should follow my example, just as I follow Christ's.

Phil 3:17. Dear brothers, pattern your lives after mine and notice who else lives up to my example.

Phil 4:9. Keep putting into practice all you learned from me and saw me doing, and the God of peace will be with you.

2 Thess 3:7. For you well know that you ought to follow our example: you never saw us loafing; [8]we never accepted food from anyone without buying it; we worked hard day and night for the money we needed to live on, in order that we would not be a burden to any of you. [9]It wasn't that we didn't have the right to ask you to feed us, but we wanted to show you, firsthand, how you should work for your living. [10]Even while we were still there with you we gave you this rule: "He who does not work shall not eat."

1 Tim 1:16. But God had mercy on me so that Christ Jesus could use me as an example to show

everyone how patient he is with even the worst sinners, so that others will realize that they, too, can have everlasting life.

2 Tim 1:13. Hold tightly to the pattern of truth I taught you, especially concerning the faith and love Christ Jesus offers you.

See *Influence.*

EXCHANGERS See *Money Changers.*

EXCOMMUNICATION See *Church, Visible, Discipline of.*

EXCUSES Gen 3:12. "Yes," Adam admitted, "but it was the woman you gave me who brought me some, and I ate it." [13]Then the Lord God asked the woman, "How could you do such a thing?" "The serpent tricked me," she replied.

Ex 4:1. But Moses said, "They won't believe me! They won't do what *I* tell them to. They'll say, 'Jehovah never appeared to you!' " [10]But Moses pleaded, "O Lord, I'm just not a good speaker. I never have been, and I'm not now, even after you have spoken to me, for I have a speech impediment." [11]"Who makes mouths?" Jehovah asked him. "Isn't it I, the Lord? Who makes a man so that he can speak or not speak, see or not see, hear or not hear? [12]Now go ahead and do as I tell you, for I will help you to speak well, and I will tell you what to say." [13]But Moses said, "Lord, please! Send someone else." [14]Then the Lord became angry. "All right," he said, "your brother Aaron is a good speaker. And he is coming here to look for you, and will be very happy when he finds you."

Ex 32:22. "Don't get so upset," Aaron replied. "You know these people and what a wicked bunch they are. [23]They said to me, 'Make us a god to lead us, for something has happened to this fellow Moses who led us out of Egypt.' [24]Well, I told them, 'Bring me your gold earrings.' So they brought them to me and I threw them into the fire, and . . . well . . . this calf came out!"

Deut 30:11. Obeying these commandments is not something beyond your strength and reach; [12]for these laws are not in the far heavens, so distant that you can't hear and obey them, and with no one to bring them down to you; [13]nor are they beyond the ocean, so far that no one can bring you their message; [14]but they are very close at hand—in your hearts and on your lips—so that you can obey them.

Judg 6:12. The Angel of the Lord appeared to him and said, "Mighty soldier, the Lord is with you!" [13]"Stranger," Gideon replied, "if the Lord is with us, why has all this happened to us? And where are all the miracles our ancestors have told us about—such as when God brought them out of Egypt? Now the Lord has thrown us away and let the Midianites completely ruin us." [14]Then the Lord turned to him and said, "I will make you strong! Go and save Israel from the Midianites! I am sending you!" [15]But Gideon replied, "Sir, how can *I* save Israel? My family is the poorest in the whole tribe of Manasseh, and I am the least thought of in the entire family!" [16]Whereupon the Lord said to him, "But I, Jehovah, will be with you! And you shall quickly destroy the Midianite hordes!" [17]Gideon replied, "If it is really true that you are going to help me like that, then do some miracle to prove it! Prove that it is really Jehovah who is talking to me!"

1 Kgs 19:19. So Elijah went and found Elisha who was plowing a field with eleven other teams ahead of him; he was at the end of the line with the last team. Elijah went over to him and threw his coat across his shoulders and walked away again. [20]Elisha left the oxen standing there and ran after Elijah and said to him, "First let me go and say good-bye to my father and mother, and then I'll go with you!" Elijah replied, "Go on back! Why all the excitement?" [21]Elisha then returned to his oxen, killed them, and used wood from the plow to build a fire to roast their flesh. He passed around the meat to the other plowmen, and they all had a great feast. Then he went with Elijah, as his assistant.

2 Kgs 5:10. Elisha sent a messenger out to tell him to go and wash in the Jordan River seven times and he would be healed of every trace of his leprosy! [11]But Naaman was angry and stalked away. "Look," he said, "I thought at least he would come out and talk to me! I expected him to wave his hand over the leprosy and call upon the name of the Lord his God, and heal me! [12]Aren't the Abana River and Pharpar River of Damascus better than all the rivers of Israel put together? If it's rivers I need, I'll wash at home and get rid of my leprosy." So he went away in a rage. [13]But his officers tried to reason with him and said, "If the prophet had told you to do some great thing, wouldn't you have done it? So you should certainly obey him when he says simply to go and wash and be cured!" [14]So Naaman went down to the Jordan River and dipped himself seven times, as the prophet had told him to. And his flesh became as healthy as a little child's and he was healed!

Jer 1:1. These are God's messages to Jeremiah the priest (the son of Hilkiah) who lived in the town of Anathoth in the land of Benjamin. [4]The Lord said to me, [5]"I knew you before you were formed within your mother's womb; before you were born I sanctified you and appointed you as my spokesman to the world." [6]"O Lord God," I said, "I can't do that! I'm far too young! I'm only a youth!" [7]"Don't say that," he replied, "for you will go wherever I send you and speak whatever I tell you to. [8]And don't be afraid of the people, for I, the Lord, will be with you and see you through." [9]Then he touched my mouth and said, "See, I have put my words in your mouth! [10]Today your work begins, to warn the nations and the kingdoms of the world. In accord with my words spoken through your mouth I will tear down some and destroy them, and plant others and nurture them and make them strong and great."

Mt 8:21. Another of his disciples said, "Sir, when my father is dead, then I will follow you."

Lk 9:59. Another time, when he invited a man to come with him and to be his disciple, the man agreed—but wanted to wait until his father's death. [60]Jesus replied, "Let those without eternal life concern themselves with things like that. Your duty is to come and preach the coming of the Kingdom of God to all the world." [61]Another said, "Yes, Lord, I will come, but first let me ask permission of those at home." [62]But Jesus told him, "Anyone who lets himself be distracted from the work I plan for him is not fit for the Kingdom of God."

Lk 14:18. But they all began making excuses. One said he had just bought a field and wanted to inspect it, and asked to be excused. [19]Another said he had just bought five pair of oxen and wanted to try them out. [20]Another had just been married and for that reason couldn't come.

Jn 15:22. They would not be guilty if I had not come and spoken to them. But now they have no excuse for their sin.

Acts 24:25. And as he reasoned with them about righteousness and self-control and the judgment to come, Felix was terrified. "Go away for now," he replied, "and when I have a more convenient time, I'll call for you again."

Rom 1:20. Since earliest times men have seen the earth and sky and all God made, and have known of his existence and great eternal power. So they will have no excuse [when they stand before God at Judgment Day].

Rom 2:1. "Well," you may be saying, "what terrible people you have been talking about!" But wait a minute! You are just as bad. When you say they are wicked and should be punished, you are talking about yourselves, for you do these very same things.

EXECUTION See *Punishment.*

EXECUTIONER Gen 37:36; Prov 16:14; Dan 2:14; Acts 7:58.

Symbolical. Ezk 21:9–11; Zeph 1:7.

See *Punishment.*

EXILE Absalom, 2 Sam 14:13, 14, 24. Ittai, 2 Sam 15:19.

See *Banishment; Captivity.*

EXODUS Of early tribes, Gen 11:2. Of Israel from Egypt, see *Israel.*

EXORCISM Casting out demons by sorcery, see *Sorcery.*

EXPEDIENCY Rom 14:14. As for myself, I am perfectly sure on the authority of the Lord Jesus that there is nothing really wrong with eating meat that has been offered to idols. But if someone believes it is wrong, then he shouldn't do it because for him it is wrong. [15]And if your brother is bothered by what you eat, you are not acting in love if you go ahead and eat it. Don't let your eating ruin someone for whom Christ died. [16]Don't do anything that will cause criticism against yourself even though you know that what you do is right. [17]For, after all, the important thing for us as Christians is not what we eat or drink but stirring up goodness and peace and joy from the Holy Spirit. [18]If you let Christ be Lord in these affairs, God will be glad; and so will others. [19]In this way aim for harmony in the church and try to build each other up. [20]Don't undo the work of God for a chunk of meat. Remember, there is nothing wrong with the meat, but it is wrong to eat it if it makes another stumble. [21]The right thing to do is to quit eating meat or drinking wine or doing anything else that offends your brother or makes him sin. [22]You may know that there is nothing wrong with what you do, even from God's point of view, but keep it to yourself; don't flaunt your faith in front of others who might be hurt by it. In this situation, happy is the man who does not sin by doing what he knows is right.

1 Cor 6:12. I can do anything I want to if Christ has not said no, but some of these things aren't good for me. Even if I am allowed to do them, I'll refuse to if I think they might get such a grip on me that I can't easily stop when I want to.

1 Cor 8:8. Just remember that God doesn't care whether we eat it or not. We are no worse off if we don't eat it, and no better off if we do. [9]But be careful not to use your freedom to eat it, lest you cause some Christian brother to sin whose conscience is weaker than yours. [10]You see, this is what may happen: Someone who thinks it is wrong to eat this food will see you eating at a temple restaurant, for you know there is no harm in it. Then he will become bold enough to do it too, although all the time he still feels it is wrong. [11]So because you "know it is all right to do it," you will be responsible for causing great spiritual damage to a brother with a tender conscience for whom Christ died. [12]And it is a sin against Christ to sin against your brother by encouraging him to do something he thinks is wrong. [13]So if eating meat offered to idols is going to make my brother sin, I'll not eat any of it as long as I live, because I don't want to do this to him.

1 Cor 9:19. And this has a real advantage: I am not bound to obey anyone just because he pays my salary; yet I have freely and happily become a servant of any and all so that I can win them to Christ. [20]When I am with the Jews I seem as one of them so that they will listen to the Gospel and I can win them to Christ. When I am with Gentiles who follow Jewish customs and ceremonies I don't argue, even though I don't agree, because I want to help them. [21]When with the heathen I agree with them as much as I can, except of course that I must always do what is right as a Christian. And so, by agreeing, I can win their confidence and help them too. [22]When I am with those whose consciences bother them easily, I don't act as though I know it all and don't say they are foolish; the result is that they are willing to let me help them. Yes, whatever a person is like, I try to find common ground with him so that he will let me tell him about Christ and let Christ save him. [23]I do this to get the Gospel to them and also for the blessing I myself receive when I see them come to Christ.

1 Cor 10:23. You are certainly free to eat food offered to idols if you want to; it's not against God's laws to eat such meat, but that doesn't mean that you should go ahead and do it. It may be perfectly legal, but it may not be best and helpful.

[24]Don't think only of yourself. Try to think of the other fellow, too, and what is best for him. [25]Here's what you should do. Take any meat you want that is sold at the market. Don't ask whether or not it was offered to idols, lest the answer hurt your conscience. [26]For the earth and every good thing in it belongs to the Lord and is yours to enjoy. [27]If someone who isn't a Christian asks you out to dinner, go ahead; accept the invitation if you want to. Eat whatever is on the table and don't ask any questions about it. Then you won't know whether or not it has been used as a sacrifice to idols, and you won't risk having a bad conscience over eating it. [28]But if someone warns you that this meat has been offered to idols, then don't eat it for the sake of the man who told you, and of his conscience. [29]In this case *his* feeling about it is the important thing, not yours. But why, you may ask, must I be guided and limited by what someone else thinks? [30]If I can thank God for the food and enjoy it, why let someone spoil everything just because he thinks I am wrong? [31]Well, I'll tell you why. It is because you must do everything for the glory of God, even your eating and drinking. [32]So don't be a stumbling block to anyone, whether they are Jews or Gentiles or Christians. [33]That is the plan I follow, too. I try to please everyone in everything I do, not doing what I like or what is best for me, but what is best for them, so that they may be saved.

See *Evil, Appearance of, to be Avoided; Prudence.*

EXPERIENCE Solomon's, Eccl 1:2.

RELIGIOUS, RELATING OF. See *Testimony, Religious.*

EXPERIMENT In worldly pleasure, Solomon's, Eccl 1; 2.

EXPIATION See *Atonement.*

EXPORTS From Egypt: Of horses and chariots, 1 Kgs 10:28, 29; 2 Chron 1:16, 17; of grain, Gen 42; 43. From Gilead: of spices, Gen 37:25. From Ophir: of gold, 1 Kgs 10:11; 22:48; 1 Chron 29: 4, 5. From Tarshish: of gold, silver, ivory, apes, and peacocks, 1 Kgs 10:22; silver, iron, tin, lead, Ezk 27: 12. From Africa: slaves and bronze, Ezk 27:13. From Arabia: of sheep and goats, Ezk 27:21. Palestine: wheat, honey, oil and balm, Ezk 27:17.

See *Imports; Commerce.*

EXPOSTULATION See *Reproof.*

EXTERMINATION See *War of.*

EXTORTION Ps 109:11. May creditors seize his entire estate and strangers take all he has earned.

Isa 3:14. First to feel his wrath will be the elders and the princes, for they have defrauded the poor. They have filled their barns with grain extorted from the helpless peasants. Hab 2:6.

Ezk 22:12. Hired murderers, loan racketeers and extortioners are everywhere. You never even think of me and my commands, the Lord God says. *vs.* 25, 29.

Mic 3:2. Yet you are the very ones who hate good and love evil; you skin my people and strip them to the bone. [3]You devour them, flog them, break their bones, and chop them up like meat for the cooking pot. Mic 6:12.

Mt 23:25. Woe to you, Pharisees, and you religious leaders—hypocrites! You are so careful to polish the outside of the cup, but the inside is foul with extortion and greed.

Lk 18:11. The proud Pharisee "prayed" this prayer: "Thank God, I am not a sinner like everyone else, especially like that tax collector over there! For I never cheat, I don't commit adultery." Lk 3:12–14.

1 Cor 5:10. But when I said that I wasn't talking about unbelievers who live in sexual sin, or are greedy cheats and thieves and idol worshippers. For you can't live in this world without being with people like that. [11]What I meant was that you are not to keep company with anyone who claims to be a brother Christian but indulges in sexual sins, or is greedy, or is a swindler, or worships idols, or is a drunkard, or abusive. Don't even eat lunch with such a person.

1 Cor 6:10. Those who live immoral lives, who are idol worshippers, adulterers or homosexuals—will have no share in his kingdom. Neither will thieves or greedy people, drunkards, slanderers, or robbers. Ps 62:10, 11.

See *Usury.*

INSTANCES OF. Jacob in demanding Esau's birthright for some stew, Gen 25:31. Pharaoh in exacting of the Egyptians lands and persons, for grain, Gen 47:13–26. Menahem in exacting tax from the wealthy to pay off Pul, 2 Kgs 15:19, 20.

EXTRADITION 1 Kgs 18:7. Suddenly Obadiah saw Elijah coming toward him! Obadiah recognized him at once and fell to the ground before him. "Is it really you, my lord Elijah? [10]For I swear by God that the king has searched every nation and kingdom on earth from end to end to find you. And each time when he was told 'Elijah isn't here,' King Ahab forced the king of that nation to swear to the truth of his claim."

Jer 26:21. But when King Jehoiakim and the army officers and officials heard what he was saying, the king sent to kill him. Uriah heard about it and fled to Egypt. [22]Then King Jehoiakim sent Elnathan (son of Achbor) to Egypt along with several other men to capture Uriah. [23]They took him prisoner and brought him back to King Jehoiakim, who butchered him with a sword and had him buried in an unmarked grave.

Acts 9:2. He requested a letter addressed to synagogues in Damascus, requiring their cooperation in the persecution of any believers he found there, both men and women, so that he could bring them in chains to Jerusalem. [14]"And we hear that he has arrest warrants with him from the chief priests, authorizing him to arrest every believer in Damascus!"

Acts 22:5. The High Priest or any member of the Council can testify that this is so. For I asked them for letters to the Jewish leaders in Damascus, with instructions to let me bring any Christians I found to Jerusalem in chains to be punished.

EXTRAVAGANCE Prov 21:17. A man who

loves pleasure becomes poor; wine and luxury are not the way to riches! [20]The wise man saves for the future, but the foolish man spends whatever he gets.

Lk 16:19. "There was a certain rich man," Jesus said, "who was splendidly clothed and lived each day in mirth and luxury."

See *Gluttony.*

EYE ANTHROPOMORPHIC USES OF. Deut 32:10. God protected them in the howling wilderness as though they were the apple of his eye.

Ps 33:18, 19. But the eyes of the Lord are watching over those who fear him, who rely upon his steady love. He will keep them from death even in times of famine!

Ps 34:15. For the eyes of the Lord are intently watching all who live good lives. Amos 9:8; 1 Pet 3:12.

Ps 121:3, 4. He will never let me stumble, slip or fall. For he is always watching, never sleeping. [5]Jehovah himself is caring for you! He is your defender. *v.* 8.

Isa 1:15. From now on, when you pray with your hands stretched out to heaven, I won't look or listen.

Zech 2:8. The Lord of Glory has sent me against the nations that oppressed you, for he who harms you sticks his finger in Jehovah's eye!

2 Cor 2:17. Only those who, like ourselves, are men of integrity, sent by God, speaking with Christ's power, with God's eye upon us.

For additional anthropomorphic uses of, see *Anthropomorphisms.*

FIGURATIVE. Of evil desire, never satisfied, Prov 27:20; Eccl 1:8. The offending, Mt 5:29.

EYE FOR EYE See *Retaliation.*

EYELIDS Painted, 2 Kgs 9:30; Ezk 23:40.

EZBAI Father of Naarai, 1 Chron 11:26–47. Possibly identical with *Paarai* in 2 Sam 23:24–39.

EZBON 1. A son of Gad, Gen 46:16, 17. Called *Ozni* in Num 26:15–18.

2. Son of Bela, 1 Chron 7:7.

EZEKIEL A priest. Time of his prophecy, Ezk 1:1–3. Persecution of, Ezk 3:25.

Visions of: of God's glory, Ezk 1:8; 10; 11:22; of Jews' sins, Ezk 8:5, 6; of their punishment, Ezk 9: 10; of the valley of dry bones, Ezk 37:1–14; of a man with measuring instruments, Ezk chapters 40–48; of the river, Ezk 47:1–5.

Teaches by pantomime: Feigns dumbness, Ezk 3:26; 24:27; 33:22; symbolizes the seige of Jerusalem by drawings on a brick, Ezk 4; shaves himself, Ezk 5:1–4; removes his belongings to illustrate the approaching Jewish captivity, Ezk 12:3–7; sighs, Ezk 21:6, 7; employs a boiling pot to symbolize the destruction of Jerusalem, Ezk 24:1–14; refrains from mourning at the death of his wife, Ezk 24: 16–27; prophesies by parable of an eagle, Ezk 17: 2–10. Other parables, Ezk 15; 16; 19; 23.

Prophecies of, concerning various nations, Ezk 25–29. His popularity, Ezk 33:31, 32.

Prophecies of, concerning the invasion of Palestine in the latter days by a northern confederacy of nations, Ezk 38, 39.

EZEM A city assigned to Judah, then Simeon, Josh 15:29; 19:3; 1 Chron 4:29.

EZER 1. A Horite, Gen 36:21, 27; 1 Chron 1:38, 39, 42.

2. A son of Ephraim, 1 Chron 7:20, 21.

3. A priest, Neh 12:42.

4. A man of Judah, 1 Chron 4:3, 4. Perhaps identical with the *Ezrah* of 1 Chron 4:17.

5. A Gadite chief, 1 Chron 12:8–13.

6. A Levite, Neh 3:19.

EZION-GABER Last encampment of Israel before coming to the "wilderness of Zin," Num 33: 15–37; Deut 2:8. Solomon built a navy at, 1 Kgs 9: 26. Solomon visits, 2 Chron 8:17, 18. Jehoshaphat built a navy at, 2 Chron 20:36. Ships of Jehoshaphat wrecked at, 1 Kgs 22:48.

EZNITE See *Adino.*

EZRA A famous scribe and priest, son of Seriah, Ezra 7:1–5, 6, 10, 21; Neh 12:35, 36. Appoints a fast, Ezra 8:21. Commissioned by Ar-ta-xerxes, returns to Jerusalem with a large company of Jews, Ezra 7:7–9. His charge to the priests, Ezra 8:29. Exhorts people to divorce their heathen wives, Ezra 9; 10:1–17. Reads the law, Neh 8. Reforms corruptions, Ezra 10; Neh 13. Dedicates the wall of Jerusalem, Neh 12:27–43.

EZRAH A descendant of Judah, 1 Chron 4:17.

EZRAHITE See *Ethan, 1.*

EZRI An overseer king David's estates, 1 Chron 27:26.

F

FABLE 1 Tim 1:3, 4; 4:7; Tit 1:14; 2 Pet 1:16.

FACE Character revealed in, Gen 4:5; Ps 4:6; Prov 15:13; Isa 3:9; Ezk 27:35; Dan 5:6. Transfigured: of Moses, Ex 34:29–35; 2 Cor 3:7, 13; Jesus, Mt 17:2, Lk 9:29. Covering of, Isa 6:2. Disfiguring of, in fasting, Mt 6:16.

FAINTING Lam 2:11; Dan 8:27.

FAIR HAVENS A harbor in Crete, Paul stays at, on his way to Rome, Acts 27:8.

FAIRY, FOLK TALES See *Fable.*

FAITH 2 Sam 22:31. As for God, his way is perfect; the word of the Lord is true. He shields all who hide behind him.

Ps 5:11. But make everyone rejoice who puts his trust in you. Keep them shouting for joy because you are defending them. Fill all who love you with your happiness.

Ps 7:1. I am depending on you, O Lord my God, to save me from my persecutors.

Ps 9:9. All who are oppressed may come to him. He is a refuge for them in their times of trouble. [10]All those who know your mercy, Lord, will count on you for help. For you have never yet forsaken those who trust in you.

Ps 18:30. He is a shield for everyone who hides behind him.

Ps 32:10. Many sorrows come to the wicked, but abiding love surrounds those who trust in the Lord.

Ps 33:18, 19. But the eyes of the Lord are watching over those who fear him, who rely upon his steady love. He will keep them from death even in times of famine!

Ps 34:8. Oh, put God to the test and see how kind he is! See for yourself the way his mercies shower down on all who trust in him. [22]But as for those who serve the Lord, he will redeem them; everyone who takes refuge in him will be freely pardoned. *vs.* 1–8; Ps 2:12.

Ps 36:7. How precious is your constant love, O God! All humanity takes refuge in the shadow of your wings.

Ps 40:4. Many blessings are given to those who trust the Lord.

Ps 64:10. And the godly shall rejoice in the Lord, and trust and praise him.

Ps 78:7. In this way each generation has been able to obey his laws and to set its hope anew on God and not forget his glorious miracles. *vs.* 5–7.

Ps 84:5. Happy are those who are strong in the Lord, who want above all else to follow your steps. [12]O Lord of the armies of heaven, blessed are those who trust in you.

Ps 112:5. And all goes well for the generous man who conducts his business fairly. [7]He does not fear bad news, nor live in dread of what may happen. For he is settled in his mind that Jehovah will take care of him. [8]That is why he is not afraid, but can calmly face his foes.

Ps 118:8. It is better to trust the Lord than to put confidence in men. [9]It is better to take refuge in him than in the mightiest king!

Ps 125:1. Those who trust in the Lord are steady as Mount Zion, unmoved by any circumstance.

Ps 147:11. But his joy is in those who reverence him, those who expect him to be loving and kind.

Prov 3:5. Then trust the Lord completely; don't ever trust yourself.

Prov 14:26. Reverence for God gives a man deep strength; his children have a place of refuge and security.

Prov 22:17–19. Listen to this wise advice; follow it closely, for it will do you good, and you can pass it on to others: *Trust in the Lord.*

Prov 28:25. Trusting God leads to prosperity.

Prov 29:25. Fear of man is a dangerous trap, but to trust in God means safety.

Prov 30:5. Every word of God proves true. He defends all who come to him for protection.

Isa 10:20. Then at last, those left in Israel and in Judah will trust the Lord, the Holy One of Israel, instead of fearing the Assyrians.

Isa 14:32. Tell them that the Lord has founded Jerusalem and is determined that the poor of his people will find a refuge within her walls.

Isa 26:3. He will keep in perfect peace all those who trust in him, whose thoughts turn often to the Lord!

Isa 30:15. For the Lord God, the Holy One of Israel, says: Only in returning to me and waiting for me will you be saved; in quietness and confidence is your strength.

Isa 57:13. But he who trusts in me shall possess the land and inherit my Holy Mountain.

Jer 17:7. But blessed is the man who trusts in the Lord and has made the Lord his hope and confidence. [8]He is like a tree planted along a riverbank, with its roots reaching deep into the water—a tree not bothered by the heat nor worried by long months of drought. Its leaves stay green and it goes right on producing all its luscious fruit.

Jer 39:18. As a reward for trusting me, I will preserve your life and keep you safe.

Nah 1:7. The Lord is good. When trouble comes, he is the place to go! And he knows everyone who trusts in him!

Mt 9:22. Jesus turned around and spoke to her. "Daughter," he said, "all is well! Your faith has healed you." And the woman was well from that moment.

Mt 21:21. Then Jesus told them, "Truly, if you have faith, and don't doubt, you can do things like this and much more. You can even say to this Mount of Olives, 'Move over into the ocean,' and it will. [22]You can get anything—*anything* you ask for in prayer—if you believe."

Mk 9:23. "If I can?" Jesus asked. "Anything is possible if you have faith." [24]The father instantly replied, "I *do* have faith; oh, help me to have *more!*"

Mk 11: 22, 23. In reply Jesus said to the disciples, "If you only have faith in God—this is the absolute truth—you can say to this Mount of Olives, 'Rise up and fall into the Mediterranean,' and your command will be obeyed. All that's required is that you really believe and have no doubt! [24]Listen to me! You can pray for *anything,* and *if you believe, you have it;* it's yours!

Lk 7:50. And Jesus said to the woman, "Your faith has saved you; go in peace."

Lk 8:48. "Daughter," he said to her, "your faith has healed you. Go in peace." [49]While he was still speaking to her, a messenger arrived from the Jairus' home with the news that the little girl was dead. "She's gone," he told her father; "there's no use troubling the Teacher now." [50]But when Jesus heard what had happened, he said to the father, "Don't be afraid! Just trust me, and she'll be all right."

Lk 17:5. One day the apostles said to the Lord, "We need more faith; tell us how to get it."

Lk 18:8. When I, the Messiah, return, how many will I find who have faith [and are praying]?

Jn 11:25. Jesus told her, "I am the one who raises the dead and gives them life again. Anyone who believes in me, even though he dies like anyone else, shall live again. [26]He is given eternal life for believing in me and shall never perish. Do you believe this, Martha?" [27]"Yes, Master," she told him. "I believe you are the Messiah, the Son of God, the one we have so long awaited."

Acts 3:16. Jesus' name has healed this man—and you know how lame he was before. Faith in Jesus' name—faith given us from God—has caused this perfect healing.

Acts 13:48. When the Gentiles heard this, they were very glad and rejoiced in Paul's message; and as many as wanted eternal life, believed.

Acts 26:18. So that they may receive forgiveness for their sins and God's inheritance along with all people everywhere whose sins are cleansed away, who are set apart by faith in me.

Rom 1:16. For I am not ashamed of this Good News about Christ. It is God's powerful method of bringing all who believe it to heaven. This message was preached first to the Jews alone, but now everyone is invited to come to God in this same way. [17]This Good News tells us that God makes us ready for heaven—makes us right in God's sight—when we put our faith and trust in Christ to save us. This is accomplished from start to finish by faith. As the Scripture says it, "The man who finds life will find it through trusting God."

Rom 4:1, 2. Abraham was, humanly speaking, the founder of our Jewish nation. What were his experiences concerning this question of being saved by faith? Was it because of his good deeds that God accepted him? If so, then he would have something to boast about. But from God's point of view Abraham had no basis at all for pride. [3]For the Scriptures tell us Abraham *believed God,* and that is why God canceled his sins and declared him "not guilty." [4, 5]But didn't he earn his right to heaven by all the good things he did? No, for being saved is a gift; if a person could earn it by being good, then it wouldn't be free—but it is! It is *given* to those who do *not* work for it. For God declares sinners to be good in his sight if they have faith in Christ to save them from God's wrath. [6]King David spoke of this, describing the happiness of an undeserving sinner who is declared "not guilty" by God. [7]"Blessed, and to be envied," he said, "are those whose sins are forgiven and put out of sight. [8]Yes, what joy there is for anyone whose sins are no longer counted against him by the Lord." [9]Now then, the question: Is this blessing given only to those who have faith in Christ but also keep the Jewish laws, or is the blessing also given to those who do not keep the Jewish rules, but only trust in Christ? Well, what about Abraham? We say that he received these blessings through his faith. Was it by faith alone? Or because he also kept the Jewish rules? [10]For the answer to that question, answer this one: *When* did God give this blessing to Abraham? It was *before he became a Jew*—before he went through the Jewish initiation ceremony of circumcision. [11]It wasn't until later on, *after* God had promised to bless him *because of his faith,* that he was circumcised. The circumcision ceremony was a sign that Abraham already had faith and that God had already accepted him and declared him just and good in his sight—before the ceremony took place. So Abraham is the spiritual father of those who believe and are saved without obeying Jewish laws. We see, then, that those who do not keep these rules are justified by God through faith. [12]And Abraham is also the spiritual father of those Jews who have been circumcised. They can see from his example that it is not this ceremony that saves them, for Abraham found favor with God by faith alone, *before he was circumcised.* [13]It is clear, then, that God's promise to give the whole earth to Abraham and his descendants was not because Abraham obeyed God's laws but because he trusted God to keep his promise. [14]So if you still claim that God's blessings go to those who are "good enough," then you are saying that God's promises to those who have faith are meaningless, and faith is foolish. [15]But the fact of the matter is this: when we try to gain God's blessing and salvation by keeping his laws we always end up under his anger, for we always fail to keep them. The only way we can keep from breaking laws is not to have any to break! [16]So God's blessings are given to us by faith, as a free gift; we are certain to get them whether or not we follow Jewish customs if we have faith like Abraham's, for Abraham is the father of us all when it comes to these matters of faith. [17]That is what the Scriptures mean when they say that God made Abraham the father of many nations. God will accept all people in every nation who trust God as Abraham did. And this promise is from God himself, who makes the dead live again and speaks of future events with as much certainty as though they were already past. [18]So, when God told Abraham that he would give him a son who would have many descendants and become a great nation, Abraham believed God even though such a promise just couldn't come to pass! [19]And because his faith was strong, he didn't worry about the fact that he was too old to be a father, at the age of one hundred, and that Sarah his wife, at ninety, was also much too old to have a baby. [20]But Abraham never doubted. He believed God, for his faith and trust grew ever stronger, and he praised God for this blessing even before it happened. [21]He was completely sure that God was well able to do anything he promised. [22]And because of Abraham's faith God forgave his sins and declared him "not guilty." [23]Now this wonderful statement—that he was accepted and approved through his faith—wasn't just for Abraham's benefit. [24]It was for us, too, assuring us that God will accept us in the same way he accepted Abraham—when we believe the promises of God who brought back Jesus our Lord from the dead. [25]He died for ours sins and rose again to make us right with God, filling us with God's goodness.

Rom 5:1. So now, since we have been made right in God's sight by faith in his promises, we can have real peace with him because of what Jesus Christ our Lord has done for us.

Rom 9:31. But the Jews, who tried so hard to get right with God by keeping his laws, never succeeded. [32]Why not? Because they were trying to be saved by keeping the law and being good instead of by depending on faith. They have stumbled over the great stumbling stone. [33]God warned them of this in the Scriptures when he said, "I have put a Rock in the path of the Jews, and many will stumble over him (Jesus). Those who believe in him will never be disappointed."

Rom 10:6. But the salvation that comes through faith says, "You don't need to search the heavens to find Christ and bring him down to help you," and, [7]"You don't need to go among the dead to bring Christ back to life again." [8]For salvation that comes from trusting Christ—which is what we preach—is already within easy reach of each of us; in fact, it is as near as our own hearts and mouths. [9]For if you tell others with your own mouth that Jesus Christ is your Lord, and believe in your own heart that God has raised him from the dead, you will be saved. [10]For it is by believing in his heart that a man becomes right with God; and with his mouth he tells others of his faith, confirming his salvation.

Rom 11:20. Watch out! Remember that those branches, the Jews, were broken off because they didn't believe God, and you are there only because you do. [23]On the other hand, if the Jews leave their unbelief behind them and come back to God, God will graft them back into the tree again.

Rom 15:13. So I pray for you Gentiles that God who gives you hope will keep you happy and full of peace as you believe in him. I pray that God will help you overflow with hope in him through the Holy Spirit's power within you.

1 Cor 1:21. For God in his wisdom . . . stepped in and saved all those who believed his message, which the world calls foolish and silly.

1 Cor 2:5. I did this because I wanted your faith to stand firmly upon God, not on man's great ideas.

1 Cor 12:8. To one person the Spirit gives the ability to give wise advice; someone else may be especially good at studying and teaching, and this is his gift from the same Spirit. [9]He gives special faith to another, and to someone else the power to heal the sick.

2 Cor 1:24. When I come, although I can't do much to help your faith, for it is strong already, I want to be able to do something about your joy: I want to make you happy, not sad.

Gal 3:1. Oh, foolish Galatians! What magician has hypnotized you and cast an evil spell upon you? For you used to see the meaning of Jesus Christ's death as clearly as though I had waved a placard before you with a picture on it of Christ dying on the cross. [2]Let me ask you this one question: Did you receive the Holy Spirit by trying to keep the Jewish laws? Of course not, for the Holy Spirit came upon you only after you heard about Christ and trusted him to save you. [3]Then have you gone completely crazy? For if trying to obey the Jewish laws never gave you spiritual life in the first place, why do you think that trying to obey them now will make you stronger Christians? [4]You have suffered so much for the Gospel. Now are you going to just throw it all overboard? I can hardly believe it! [5]I ask you again, does God give you the power of the Holy Spirit and work miracles among you as a result of your trying to obey the Jewish laws? No, of course not. It is when you believe in Christ and fully trust him. [6]Abraham had the same experience—God declared him fit for heaven only because he believed God's promises. [7]You can see from this that the real children of Abraham are all the men of faith who truly trust in God. [8, 9]What's more, the Scriptures looked forward to this time when God would save the Gentiles also, through their faith. God told Abraham about this long ago when he said, "I will bless those in every nation who trust in me as you do." And so it is: all who trust in Christ share the same blessing Abraham received. [10]Yes, and those who depend on the Jewish laws to save them are under God's curse, for the Scriptures point out very clearly, "Cursed is everyone who at any time breaks a single one of these laws that are written in God's Book of the Law." [11]Consequently, it is clear that no one can ever win God's favor by trying to keep the Jewish laws, because God has said that the only way we can be right in his sight is by faith. As the prophet Habakkuk says it, "The man who finds life will find it through trusting God." [12]How different from this way of faith is the way of law which says that a man is saved by obeying every law of God, without one slip. [13]But Christ has bought us out from under the doom of that impossible system by taking the curse for our wrongdoing upon himself. For it is written in the Scripture, "Anyone who is hanged on a tree is cursed" [as Jesus was hung upon a wooden cross]. [14]Now God can bless the Gentiles, too, with this same blessing he promised to Abraham; and all of us as Christians can have the promised Holy Spirit through this faith. [15]Dear brothers, even in everyday life a promise made by one man to another, it it is written down and signed, cannot be changed. He cannot decide afterward to do something else instead. [16]Now, God gave some promises to Abraham and his Child. And notice that it doesn't say the promises were to his *children,* as it would if all his sons—all the Jews—were being spoken of, but to his *Child*—and that, of course, means Christ. [17]Here's what I am trying to say: God's promise to save through faith—and God wrote this promise down and signed it—could not be canceled or changed four hundred and thirty years later when God gave the Ten Commandments. [18]If *obeying those laws* could save us, then it is obvious that this would be a different way of gaining God's favor than Abraham's way, for he simply accepted God's promise. [19]Well then, why were the laws given? They were added after the promise was given, to show men how guilty they are of breaking God's laws. But this system of law was to last only until the coming of Christ, the Child to whom God's promise was made. (And there is this further difference. God gave his laws to angels to give to Moses, who then gave them to the people; [20]but when God gave his promise to Abraham, he did it by himself alone, without angels or Moses as go-betweens.) [21, 22]Well then, are God's laws and God's promises against each other? Of course not! If we could be saved by his laws, then God would not have had to give us a different way to get out of the grip of sin—for the Scriptures insist we are all its prisoners. The only way out is through faith in Jesus Christ; the way of escape is open to all who believe him. [23]Until Christ came we were guarded by the law, kept in protective custody, so to speak, until we could believe in the coming Savior. [24]Let me put it another way. The Jewish laws were our teacher and guide until Christ came to give us right standing with God through our faith. [25]But now that Christ has come, we don't need those laws any longer to guard us and lead us to him. [26]For now we are all children of God through faith in Jesus Christ, [27]and we who have been baptized into union with Christ are enveloped by him. [28]We are no longer Jews or Greeks or slaves or free men or even merely men or women, but we are all the same—we are Christians; we are one in Christ Jesus. [29]And now that we are Christ's we are the true descendants of Abraham, and all of God's promises to him belong to us.

Gal 5:22. But when the Holy Spirit controls our lives he will produce this kind of fruit in us: love, joy, peace, patience, kindness, goodness, faithfulness.

Eph 2:8. Because of his kindness you have been saved through trusting Christ. And even trusting is not of yourselves; it too is a gift from God.

Eph 6:16. In every battle you will need faith as your shield to stop the fiery arrows aimed at you by Satan.

Col 1:23. The only condition is that you fully believe the Truth, standing in it steadfast and firm, strong in the Lord, convinced of the Good News that Jesus died for you, and never shifting from trusting him to save you.

Col 2:12. For in baptism you see how your old, evil nature died with him and was buried with him; and then you came up out of death with him into a new life because you trusted the Word of the mighty God who raised Christ from the dead.

1 Thess 2:13. And we will never stop thanking God for this: that when we preached to you, you didn't think of the words we spoke as being just our own, but you accepted what we said as the very Word of God—which, of course, it was—and it changed your lives when you believed it.

1 Thess 5:8. But let us who live in the light keep sober, protected by the armor of faith and love.

2 Thess 2:13. God chose from the very first to give you salvation, cleansing you by the work of the Holy Spirit and by your trusting in the Truth.

1 Tim 1:5. What I am eager for is that all the Christians there will be filled with love that comes from pure hearts, and that their minds will be clean and their faith strong.

1 Tim 2:15. So God sent pain and suffering to women when their children are born, but he will save their souls if they trust in him, living quiet, good, and loving lives.

1 Tim 4:10. We work hard and suffer much in order that people will believe it, for our hope is in the living God who died for all, and particularly for those who have accepted his salvation.

1 Tim 6:11. Work instead at what is right and good, learning to trust him and love others, and to be patient and gentle. [12]Fight on for God. Hold tightly to the eternal life which God has given you, and which you have confessed with such a ringing confession before many witnesses. [17]Tell those who are rich not to be proud and not to trust in their money, which will soon be gone, but their pride and trust should be in the living God who always richly gives us all we need for our enjoyment.

2 Tim 4:7. I have fought long and hard for my Lord, and through it all I have kept true to him. . . . [8]In heaven a crown is waiting for me which the Lord, the righteous Judge, will give me on that great day of his return. And not just to me, but to all those whose lives show that they are eagerly looking forward to his coming back again.

Heb 4:1. Although God's promise still stands—his promise that all may enter his place of rest—we ought to tremble with fear because some of you may be on the verge of failing to get there after all. [2]For this wonderful news—the message that God wants to save us—has been given to us just as it was to those who lived in the time of Moses. But it didn't do them any good because they didn't believe it. They didn't mix it with faith. [3]For only we who believe God can enter into his place of rest. He has said, "I have sworn in my anger that those who don't believe me will never get in," even though he has been ready and waiting for them since the world began. [4]We know he is ready and waiting because it is written that God rested on the seventh day of creation, having finished all that he had planned to make. [5]Even so they didn't get in, for God finally said, "They shall never enter my rest." [6]Yet the promise remains and some get in—but not those who had the first chance, for they disobeyed God and failed to enter. [7]But he has set another time for coming in, and that time is now. He announced this through King David long years after man's first failure to enter, saying in the words already quoted, "Today when you hear him calling, do not harden your hearts against him." [8]This new place of rest he is talking about does not mean the land of Israel that Joshua led them into. If that were what God meant, he would not have spoken long afterwards about "today" being the time to get in. [9]So there is a full complete rest *still waiting* for the people of God. [10]Christ has already entered there. He is resting from his work, just as God did after the creation. [11]Let us do our best to go into that place of rest, too, being careful not to disobey God as the children of Israel did, thus failing to get in.

Heb 6:1. Let us stop going over the same old ground again and again, always teaching those first lessons about Christ. Let us go on instead to other things and become mature in our understanding, as strong Christians ought to be. Surely we don't need to speak further about the foolishness of trying to be saved by being good, or about the necessity of faith in God. [7]When a farmer's land has had many showers upon it and good crops come up, that land has experienced God's blessing upon it. [12]Then, knowing what lies ahead for you, you won't become bored with being a Christian, nor become spiritually dull and indifferent, but you will be anxious to follow the example of those who receive all that God has promised them because of their strong faith and patience. [18]He has given us both his promise and his oath, two things we can completely count on, for it is impossible for God to tell a lie. Now all those who flee to him to save them can take new courage when they hear such assurances from God; now they can know without doubt that he will give them the salvation he has promised them.

Heb 10:35. Do not let this happy trust in the Lord die away, no matter what happens. Remember your reward! [38]And those whose faith has made them good in God's sight must live by faith, trusting him in everything. Otherwise, if they shrink back, God will have no pleasure in them. [39]But we have never turned our backs on God and sealed our fate. No, our faith in him assures our souls' salvation.

Heb 11:1. What is faith? It is the confident assurance that something we want is going to happen. It is the certainty that what we hope for is waiting for us, even though we cannot see it up ahead. [2]Men of God in days of old were famous for their faith. [3]By faith—by believing God—we know that the world and the stars—in fact, all things—were made at God's command; and that they were all made from things that can't be seen. [6]You can never please God without faith, without depending on him. Anyone who wants to come to God must believe that there is a God and that he rewards those who sincerely look for him.

Heb 13:5. For God has said, "I will never, *never* fail you nor forsake you." [6]That is why we can say without any doubt or fear, "The Lord is my Helper and I am not afraid of anything that mere man can do to me."

Jas 1:6. But when you ask him, be sure that you really expect him to tell you.

Jas 2:1. Dear brothers, how can you claim that you belong to the Lord Jesus Christ, the Lord of glory, if you show favoritism to rich people and look down on poor people? [2]If a man comes into your church dressed in expensive clothes and with valuable gold rings on his fingers, and at the same moment another man comes in who is poor and dressed in threadbare clothes, [3]and you make a lot of fuss over the rich man and give him the best seat in the house and say to the poor man, "You can stand over there if you like, or else sit on the floor"—well, [4]judging a man by his wealth shows that you are guided by wrong motives. [5]Listen to me, dear brothers: God has chosen poor people to be rich in faith, and the Kingdom of Heaven is theirs, for that is the gift God has promised to all those who love him. [6]And yet, of the two strangers, you have despised the poor man. Don't you realize that it is usually the rich men who pick on you and drag you into court? [7]And all too often they are the ones who laugh at Jesus Christ, whose noble name you bear. 8Yes indeed, it is good when you truly obey our Lord's command, "You must love and help your neighbors just as much as you love and take care of yourself." 9But you are breaking this law of our Lord's when you favor the rich and fawn over them; it is sin. 10And the person who keeps every law of God, but makes one little slip, is just as guilty as the person who has broken every law there is. 11For the God who said you must not marry a woman who already has a husband, also said you must not murder, so even though you have not broken the marriage laws by committing adultery, but have murdered someone, you have entirely broken God's laws and stand utterly guilty before him. 12You will be judged on whether or not you are doing what Christ wants you to. So watch what you do and what you think; 13for there will be no mercy to those who have shown no mercy. But if you have been merciful, then God's mercy toward you will win out over his judgment against you. 14Dear brothers, what's the use of saying that you have faith and are Christians if you aren't proving it by helping others? Will *that* kind of faith save anyone? 15If you have a friend who is in need of food and clothing, 16and you say to him, "Well, good-bye and God bless you; stay warm and eat hearty," and then don't give him clothes or food, what good does that do? 17So you see, it isn't enough just to have faith. You must also do good to prove you have it. Faith that doesn't show itself by good works is no faith at all—it is dead and useless. 18But someone may well argue, "You say the way to God is by faith alone, plus nothing; well, I say that good works are important too, for without good works you can't prove whether you have faith or not; but anyone can see that I have faith by the way I act." 19Are there still some among you who hold that "only believing" is enough? Believing in one God? Well, remember that the demons believe this too—so strongly that they tremble in terror! 20Fool! When will you ever learn that "believing" is useless without *doing* what God wants you to? Faith that does not result in good deeds is not real faith. 21Don't you remember that even our father Abraham was declared good because of what he *did,* when he was willing to obey God, even if it meant offering his son Isaac to die on the altar? 22You see, he was trusting God so much that he was willing to do whatever God told him to; his faith was made complete by what he did, by his actions, his good deeds. 23And so it happened just as the Scriptures say, that Abraham trusted God, and the Lord declared him good in God's sight, and he was even called "the friend of God." 24So you see, a man is saved by what he does, as well as by what he believes. 25Rahab, the prostitute, is another example of this. She was saved because of what she did when she hid those messengers and sent them safely away by a different road. 26Just as the body is dead when there is no spirit in it, so faith is dead if it is not the kind that results in good deeds.

1 Pet 1:5. And God, in his mighty power, will make sure that you get there safely to receive it, because you are trusting him. It will be yours in that coming last day for all to see. 7These trials are only to test your faith, to see whether it is strong and pure. It is being tested as fire tests gold and purifies it—and your faith is far more precious to God than mere gold; so if your faith remains strong after being tried in the test tube of fiery trials, it will bring you much praise and glory and honor on the day of his return. 9And your further reward for trusting him will be the salvation of your souls. 21Because of this, your trust can be in God who raised Christ from the dead and gave him great glory. Now your faith and hope can rest in him alone.

1 Pet 3:5. That kind of deep beauty was seen in the saintly women of old, who trusted God and fitted in with their husbands' plans.

1 Jn 3:21. But, dearly loved friends, if our consciences are clear, we can come to the Lord with perfect assurance and trust.

1 Jn 5:4. For every child of God can obey him, defeating sin and evil pleasure by trusting Christ to help him.

Rev 22:7. Blessed are those who believe it and all else written in the scroll.

See *Faith, in Christ.*

COMMANDED. Ex 14:13. But Moses told the people, "Don't be afraid. Just stand where you are and watch, and you will see the wonderful way the Lord will rescue you today."

Deut 20:1. When you go to war and see before you vast numbers of horses and chariots, an army far greater than yours, don't be frightened! The Lord your God is with you—the same God who brought you safely out of Egypt! Num 21:34; Deut 1:19–31; 3:1, 2, 22; 7:17–21; 31:23; Josh 10:25; Judg 6:14–16; 2 Kgs 19:5–7; 2 Chron 20:15, 17.

Deut 31:8. Don't be afraid, for the Lord will go before you and will be with you; he will not fail nor forsake you. *vs.* 6–8.

Josh 1:9. Yes, be bold and strong! Banish fear and doubt! For remember, the Lord your God is with you wherever you go. *vs.* 5–9.

2 Chron 15:7. But you men of Judah, keep up the good work and don't get discouraged, for you will be rewarded.

2 Chron 16:9. For the eyes of the Lord search back and forth across the whole earth, looking for people whose hearts are perfect toward him, so that he can show his great power helping them.

2 Chron 20:20. Believe in the Lord your God, and you shall have success! Believe his prophets, and everything will be all right!

2 Chron 32:7. Be strong, be brave, and do not be afraid of the king of Assyria or his mighty army, for there is someone with us who is far greater than he is! 8He has a great army, but they are all mere men, while we have the Lord our God to fight our battles for us!

Neh 4:14. Don't be afraid! Remember the Lord who is great and glorious.

Job 35:14. And it is even more false to say that he doesn't see what is going on. He *does* bring about justice at last, if you will only wait.

Ps 4:5. Put your trust in the Lord, and offer him pleasing sacrifices.

Ps 27:14. Don't be impatient. Wait for the Lord, and he will come and save you! Be brave, stout-hearted and courageous. Yes, wait and he will help you.

Ps 31:19. Oh, how great is your goodness to those who publicly declare that you will rescue them. For you have stored up great blessings for those who trust and reverence you. [24]So cheer up! Take courage if you are depending on the Lord.

Ps 37:3. Trust in the Lord instead. Be kind and good to others; then you will live safely here in the land and prosper, feeding in safety. [5]Commit everything you do to the Lord. Trust him to help you do it and he will. [7]Rest in the Lord; wait patiently for him to act. [39]The Lord saves the godly! He is their salvation and their refuge when trouble comes. [40]Because they trust in him, he helps them and delivers them from the plots of evil men.

Ps 55:22. Give your burdens to the Lord. He will carry them. He will not permit the godly to slip or fall.

Ps 62:8. O my people, trust him all the time. Pour out your longings before him, for he can help!

Ps 115:9. O Israel, trust the Lord! He is your helper. He is your shield. [11]All of you, his people, trust in him. He is your helper; he is your shield.

Ps 130:7. O Israel, hope in the Lord; for he is loving and kind, and comes to us with armloads of salvation.

Prov 3:5. Then trust the Lord completely; don't ever trust yourself. [6]In everything you do, put God first, and he will direct you and crown your efforts with success. [24-26]With them on guard you can sleep without fear; you need not be afraid of disaster or the plots of wicked men, for the Lord is with you; he protects you.

Prov 16:3. Commit your work to the Lord, then it will succeed.

Isa 26:4. Trust in the Lord God always, for in the Lord Jehovah is your everlasting strength. [20]Go home, my people, and lock the doors! Hide for a little while until the Lord's wrath against your enemies has passed.

Isa 35:3. With this news bring cheer to all discouraged ones. [4]Encourage those who are afraid. Tell them, "Be strong, fear not, for your God is coming to destroy your enemies. He is coming to save you."

Isa 37:6. Then Isaiah replied, "Tell King Hezekiah that the Lord says, Don't be disturbed by this speech from the servant of the king of Assyria, and his blasphemy."

Isa 41:10. Fear not, for I am with you. Do not be dismayed. I am your God. I will strengthen you; I will help you; I will uphold you with my victorious right hand. [13]I am holding you by your right hand—I, the Lord your God—and I say to you, Don't be afraid; I am here to help you. [14]Despised though you are, fear not, O Israel; for I will help you. I am the Lord, your Redeemer; I am the Holy One of Israel.

Isa 43:1. But now the Lord who created you, O Israel, says, Don't be afraid, for I have ransomed you; I have called you by name; you are mine. [2]When you go through deep waters and great trouble, I will be with you. When you go through rivers of difficulty, you will not drown! When you walk through the fire of oppression, you will not be burned up—the flames will not consume you. [5]Don't be afraid, for I am with you. I will gather you from east and west. [10]You are my witnesses and my servants, chosen to know and to believe me and to understand that I alone am God.

Isa 44:2. The Lord who made you, who will help you, says, O servant of mine, don't be afraid. O Jerusalem, my chosen ones, don't be afraid. [8]Don't, don't be afraid. Haven't I proclaimed from ages past (that I would save you)? You are my witnesses—is there any other God? No! None that I know about! There is no other Rock!

Isa 50:10. Who among you fears the Lord and obeys his Servant? If such men walk in darkness, without one ray of light, let them trust the Lord, let them rely upon their God.

Jer 42:11. Don't fear the king of Babylon any more, for I am with you to save you and to deliver you from his hand.

Jer 49:11. But I will preserve your fatherless children who remain, and let your widows depend upon me.

Joel 2:21. Fear not, my people; be glad now and rejoice, for he has done amazing things for you.

Joel 3:16. But to his people Israel, the Lord will be very gentle. He is their Refuge and Strength.

Hab 2:3. Slowly, steadily, surely, the time approaches when the vision will be fulfilled. If it seems slow, do not despair, for these things will surely come to pass. Just be patient! They will not be overdue a single day! . . . [4]But the righteous man trusts in me, and lives!

Zeph 3:16. On that day the announcement to Jerusalem will be, "Cheer up, don't be afraid. [17]For the Lord your God has arrived to live among you. He is a mighty Savior. He will give you victory. He will rejoice over you in great gladness; he will love you and not accuse you."

Zech 8:9. The Lord of Hosts says, "Get on with the job and finish it! You have been listening long enough! For since you began laying the foundation of the Temple, the prophets have been telling you about the blessings that await you when it's finished."

Zech 9:12. Come to the place of safety, all you prisoners, for there is yet hope! I promise right now, I will repay you two mercies for each of your woes!

Mt 6:25. So my counsel is: Don't worry about *things*—food, drink, and clothes. For you already have life and a body—and they are far more important than what to eat and wear. [26]Look at the birds! They don't worry about what to eat—they don't need to sow or reap or store up food—for your heavenly Father feeds them. And you are far more valuable to him than they are. [27]Will all your worries add a single moment to your life? [28]And why worry about your clothes? Look at the field lilies! They don't worry about theirs. [29]Yet King Solomon in all his glory was not clothed as beautifully as they. [30]And if God cares so wonderfully for flowers that are here today and gone tomorrow, won't he more surely care for you, O men of little faith? [31, 32]So don't worry at all about having enough food and clothing. Why be like the heathen? For they take pride in all these things and are deeply concerned about them. But your heavenly Father already knows perfectly well that you need them, [33]and he will give them to you if you give him first place in your life and live as he wants you to. [34]So don't be anxious about tomorrow. God will take care of your tomorrow too. Live one day at a time. Lk 12:22–32.

Mt 17:18. Then Jesus rebuked the demon in the boy and it left him, and from that moment the boy was well. [19]Afterwards the disciples asked Jesus privately, "Why couldn't we cast that demon out?" [20]"Because of your little faith," Jesus told them. "For if you had faith even as small as a tiny mustard seed you could say to this mountain, 'Move!' and it would go far away. Nothing would be impossible." Mk 11:22–24.

Mk 1:15. Turn from your sins and act on this glorious news!

Mk 11:22. In reply Jesus said to the disciples, "If you only have faith in God—"

Lk 12:32. So don't be afraid, little flock. For it gives your Father great happiness to give you the Kingdom.

Lk 17:6. "If your faith were only the size of a mustard seed," Jesus answered, "it would be large enough to uproot that mulberry tree over there and send it hurtling into the sea! Your command would bring immediate results!"

1 Cor 16:13. Keep your eyes open for spiritual danger; stand true to the Lord; act like men; be strong.

1 Tim 1:19. Cling tightly to your faith in Christ and always keep your conscience clear, doing what you know is right. For some people have disobeyed their consciences and have deliberately done what they knew was wrong. It isn't surprising that soon they lost their faith in Christ after defying God like that.

1 Tim 4:12. Don't let anyone think little of you because you are young. Be their ideal; let them follow the way you teach and live; be a pattern for them in you love, your faith, and your clean thoughts.

Instances of. See after the following sub-topic.

EXEMPLIFIED. Gen 6:22. And Noah did everything as God commanded him.

Gen 16:13. Thereafter Hagar spoke of Jehovah—for it was he who appeared to her—as "the God who looked upon me," for she thought, "I saw God and lived to tell it."

Gen 24:7. For the Lord God of heaven told me to leave that land and my people, and promised to give me and my children this land. [40]For my Lord, in whose presence I have walked, will send his angel with you and make your mission successful.

Gen 48:21. Then Israel said to Joseph, "I am about to die, but God will be with you and will bring you again to Canaan, the land of your fathers."

Gen 50:20. "As far as I am concerned, God turned into good what you meant for evil, for he brought me to this high position I have today so that I could save the lives of many people. [24]Soon I will die," Joseph told his brothers, "but God will surely come and get you, and bring you out of this land of Egypt and take you back to the land he promised to the descendants of Abraham, Isaac and Jacob."

Ex 15:2. The Lord is my strength, my song, and my salvation. He is my God, and I will praise him. He is my father's God—I will exalt him. [16]Terror and dread have overcome them. O Lord, because of your great power they won't attack us! Your people whom you purchased will pass by them in safety. [17]You will bring them in and plant them on your mountain, your own homeland, Lord. *vs.* 1–19.

Ex 18:11. I know now that the Lord is greater than any other god because he delivered his people from the proud and cruel Egyptians.

Num 10:29. One day Moses said to his brother-in-law Hobab (son of Reuel, the Midianite), "At last we are on our way to the Promised Land. Come with us and we will do you good; for the Lord has given wonderful promises to Israel!"

Num 14:8. And the Lord loves us. He will bring us safely into the land and give it to us. . . . [9]Oh, do not rebel against the Lord, and do not fear the people of the land. For they are but bread for us to eat! The Lord is with us and he has removed his protection from them! Don't be afraid of them!

Josh 14:12. But if the Lord is with me I shall drive them out of the land.

1 Sam 14:6. "Yes, let's go across to those heathen," Jonathan had said to his bodyguard. "Perhaps the Lord will do a miracle for us. For it makes no difference to him how many enemy troops there are!"

1 Sam 17:36. I have done this to both lions and bears, and I'll do it to this heathen Philistine too, for he has defied the armies of the living God! [37]The Lord who saved me from the claws and teeth of the lion and the bear will save me from this Philistine!" Saul finally consented, "All right, go ahead," he said, "and may the Lord be with you!" [45]David shouted in reply, "You come to me with a sword and a spear, but I come to you in the name of the Lord of the armies of heaven and of Israel—the very God whom you have defied. [46]Today the Lord will conquer you and I will kill you and cut off your head; and then I will give the dead bodies of *your* men to the birds and wild animals, and the whole world will know that there is a God in Israel! [47]And

Israel will learn that the Lord does not depend on weapons to fulfill his plans—he works without regard to human means! He will give you to us!"

2 Sam 7:28. For you are indeed God, and your words are truth; and you have promised me these good things—.

2 Sam 23:5. Yes, God has made an everlasting covenant with me; his agreement is eternal, final, sealed. He will constantly look after my safety and success.

2 Kgs 18:5. He [Hezekiah] trusted very strongly in the Lord God of Israel.

1 Chron 28:20. Then he [David] continued, "Be strong and courageous and get to work. Don't be frightened by the size of the task, for the Lord my God is with you; he will not forsake you. He will see to it that everything is finished correctly."

2 Chron 13:10. But as for us, the Lord is our God and we have not forsaken him. Only the descendants of Aaron are our priests, and the Levites alone may help them in their work. [11]They burn sacrifices to the Lord every morning and evening—burnt offerings and sweet incense; and they place the Bread of the Presence upon the holy table. The golden lampstand is lighted every night, for we are careful to follow the instructions of the Lord our God; but you have forsaken him.

2 Chron 14:11. "O Lord," he [Asa] cried out to God, "no one else can help us! Here we are, powerless against this mighty army. Oh, help us, Lord our God! For we trust in you alone to rescue us, and in your name we attack this vast horde. Don't let mere men defeat you!"

2 Chron 20:12. O our God, won't you stop them? We have no way to protect ourselves against this mighty army. We don't know what to do, but we are looking to you.

2 Chron 32:7. "Be strong, be brave, and do not be afraid of the king of Assyria or his mighty army, for there is someone with us who is far greater than he is! [8]He has a great army, but they are all mere men, while we have the Lord our God to fight our battles for us!" This greatly encouraged them.

Ezra 8:22. After all, we had told the king that our God would protect all those who worshiped him.

Neh 1:10. We are your servants, the people you rescued by your great power. *vs.* 8–10.

Neh 2:20. But I replied, "The God of heaven will help us, and we, his servants, will rebuild this wall; but you may have no part in this affair."

Job 4:7, 8. Stop and think! Have you ever known a truly good and innocent person who was punished? Experience teaches that it is those who sow sin and trouble who harvest the same. [9]They die beneath the hand of God. [10]Though they are fierce as young lions, they shall all be broken and destroyed. [11]Like aged, helpless lions they shall starve, and all their children shall be scattered. [12]This truth was given me in secret, as though whispered in my ear. [13]It came in a nighttime vision as others slept. [14]Suddenly, fear gripped me; I trembled and shook with terror, [15]as a spirit passed before my face—my hair stood up on end. [16]I felt the spirit's presence, but couldn't see it standing there. Then out of the dreadful silence came this voice: [17]"Is mere man more just than God? More pure than his Creator?" [18, 19]If God cannot trust his own messengers (for even angels make mistakes), how much less men made of dust, who are crushed to death as easily as moths! [20]They are alive in the morning, but by evening they are dead, gone forever with hardly a thought from anyone. [21]Their candle of life is snuffed out. They die and no one cares.

Job 5:8. My advice to you is this: Go to God and confess your sins to him. [9]For he does wonderful miracles, marvels without number.

Job 10:12. You gave me life and were so kind and loving to me, and I was preserved by your care.

Job 13:15. God may kill me for saying this—in fact, I expect him to. Nevertheless I am going to argue my case with him. [16]This at least will be in my favor, that I am not godless, to be rejected instantly from his presence.

Job 14:15. You would call and I would come, and you would reward all I do.

Job 16:19. Yet even now the Witness to my innocence is there in heaven; my Advocate is there on high.

Job 19:25. But as for me, I know that my Redeemer lives, and that he will stand upon the earth at last. [26]And I know that after this body has decayed, this body shall see God! [27]Then he will be on *my* side! Yes, I shall see him, not as a stranger, but as a friend! What a glorious hope!

Job 23:6. Would he merely overpower me with his greatness? No, he would listen with sympathy.

Job 42:2. I know that you can do anything and that no one can stop you.

Ps 3:3. But Lord, you are my shield, my glory, and my only hope. You alone can lift my head, now bowed in shame. [5]Then I lay down and slept in peace and woke up safely, for the Lord was watching over me. [6]And now, although ten thousand enemies surround me on every side, I am not afraid.

Ps 4:3. Mark this well: The Lord has set apart the redeemed for himself. Therefore he will listen to me and answer when I call to him. [8]I will lie down in peace and sleep, for though I am alone, O Lord, you will keep me safe.

Ps 6:8. For the Lord has heard my weeping [9]and my pleading. He will answer all my prayers.

Ps 7:1. I am depending on you, O Lord my God, to save me from my persecutors. [10]God is my shield; he will defend me. He saves those whose hearts and lives are true and right.

Ps 9:3. My enemies will fall back and perish in your presence; [4]you have vindicated me; you have endorsed my work, declaring from your throne that it is good.

Ps 11:1. How dare you tell me, "Flee to the mountains for safety," when I am trusting in the Lord?

Ps 13:5. But I will always trust in you and in your mercy and shall rejoice in your salvation.

Ps 16:1. Save me, O God, because I have come to you for refuge. [2]I said to him, "You are my Lord, I have no other help but yours." [5]The Lord himself is my inheritance, my prize. He is my food and drink, my highest joy! He guards all that is mine. [8]I am always thinking of the Lord; and because he is so near, I never need to stumble or to fall. [11]You have let me experience the joys of life and the exquisite pleasures of your own eternal presence.

Ps 17:6. Why am I praying like this? Because I know you will answer me, O God! Yes, listen as I pray.

Ps 18:1. Lord, how I love you! For you have done such tremendous things for me. [2]The Lord is my fort where I can enter and be safe; no one can follow me in and slay me. He is a rugged mountain where I hide; he is my Savior, a rock where none can reach me, and a tower of safety. He is my shield. He is like the strong horn of a mighty fighting bull. [3]All I need to do is cry to him—oh, praise the Lord—and I am saved from all my enemies! [18]On the day when I was weakest, they attacked. But the Lord held me steady. [28]You have turned on my light! The Lord my God has made my darkness turn to light. [29]Now in your strength I can scale any wall, attack any troop. 2 Sam 22: 2–5.

Ps 20:5. May there be shouts of joy when we hear the news of your victory, flags flying with praise to God for all that he has done for you. May he answer all your prayers! [6]"God save the king"—I know he does! He hears me from highest heaven and sends great victories. [7]Some nations boast of armies and of weaponry, but our boast is in the Lord our God.

Ps 21:7. And because the king trusts in the Lord, he will never stumble, never fall.

Ps 22:4. The praises of our fathers surrounded your throne; they trusted you and you delivered them. [5]You heard their cries for help and saved them; they were never disappointed when they sought your aid.

Ps 23:1. Because the Lord is my Shepherd, I have everything I need! *vs.* 1–6.

Ps 25:1. To you, O Lord, I pray. [2]Don't fail me, Lord, for I am trusting you. [5]Lead me; teach me; for you are the God who gives me salvation. I have no hope except in you. [15]My eyes are ever looking to the Lord for help, for he alone can rescue me. [20]Save me from them! Deliver my life from their power! Oh, let it never be said that I trusted you in vain!

Ps 26:1. Dismiss all the charges against me, Lord, for I have tried to keep your laws and have trusted you without wavering. [12]I publicly praise the Lord for keeping me from slipping and falling.

Ps 27:1. The Lord is my light and my salvation; whom shall I fear? [5]There I'll be when troubles come. He will hide me. He will set me on a high rock [6]out of reach of all my enemies. Then I will bring him sacrifices and sing his praises with much joy. [10]For if my father and mother should abandon me, you would welcome and comfort me.

Ps 28:7. He is my strength, my shield from every danger. I trusted in him, and he helped me.

Ps 31:1. Lord, I trust in you alone. Don't let my enemies defeat me. [3]Yes, you are my Rock and my fortress; honor your name by leading me out of this peril. [4]Pull me from the trap my enemies have set for me. For you alone are strong enough. [5, 6]Into your hand I commit my spirit. You have rescued me, O God who keeps his promises. I worship only you; how you hate all those who worship idols, those imitation gods. [14, 15]But I was trusting you, O Lord. I said, "You alone are my God; my times are in your hands. Rescue me from those who hunt me down relentlessly."

Ps 32:7. You are my hiding place from every storm of life; you even keep me from getting into trouble! You surround me with songs of victory.

Ps 33:20. We depend upon the Lord alone to save us. Only he can help us; he protects us like a shield. [21]No wonder we are happy in the Lord! For we are trusting him. We trust his holy name. [22]Yes, Lord, let your constant love surround us, for our hopes are in you alone.

Ps 35:10. From the bottom of my heart praise rises to him. Where is his equal in all of heaven and earth? Who else protects the weak and helpless from the strong, and the poor and needy from those who would rob them?

Ps 38:9. Lord, you know how I long for my health once more. You hear my every sigh. [15]For I am waiting for you, O Lord my God. Come and protect me.

Ps 39:7. And so, Lord, my only hope is in you.

Ps 40:3. He has given me a new song to sing, of praises to our God. Now many will hear of the glorious things he did for me, and stand in awe before the Lord, and put their trust in him. [4]Many blessings are given to those who trust the Lord, and have no confidence in those who are proud, or who trust in idols. [17]I am poor and needy, yet the Lord is thinking about me right now! O my God, you are my helper. You are my Savior; come quickly, and save me. Please don't delay!

Ps 41:12. You have preserved me because I was honest; you have admitted me forever to your presence.

Ps 42:6. Yet I am standing here depressed and gloomy, but I will meditate upon your kindness. [8]Yet day by day the Lord also pours out his steadfast love upon me, and through the night I sing his songs and pray to God who gives me life.

Ps 43:5. O my soul, why be so gloomy and discouraged? Trust in God! I shall again praise him for his wondrous help; he will make me smile again, *for he is my God!* Ps 42:4, 5.

Ps 44:5. For it is only by your power and through your name that we tread down our enemies. [8]My constant boast is God. I can never thank you enough!

Ps 46:1. God is our refuge and strength, a tested help in times of trouble. [2]And so we need not fear even if the world blows up, and the mountains crumble into the sea. [3]Let the oceans roar and foam; let the mountains tremble! [5]God himself is living in that City; therefore it stands unmoved despite the turmoil everywhere. He will not delay his help. [7]The Commander of the armies of heaven is here among us. He, the God of Jacob, has come to rescue us.

Ps 47:3. He subdues the nations before us, [4]and will personally select his choicest blessings for his Jewish people—the very best for those he loves.

Ps 48:8. We have heard of the city's glory—the city of our God, the Commander of the armies of heaven. And now we see it for ourselves! God has established Jerusalem forever. [14]For this great God is our God forever and ever. He will be our guide until we die.

Ps 52:8. I trust in the mercy of God forever and ever.

Ps 54:4. But God is my helper. He is a friend of mine!

Ps 55:16. But I will call upon the Lord to save me —and he will. [17]I will pray morning, noon, and night, pleading aloud with God; and he will hear and answer.

Ps 56:3, 4. But when I am afraid, I will put my confidence in you. Yes, I will trust the promises of God. And since I am trusting him, what can mere man do to me? [8]You have seen me tossing and turning through the night. You have collected all my tears and preserved them in your bottle! You have recorded every one in your book. [9]The very day I call for help, the tide of battle turns. My enemies flee! This one thing I *know: God is for me! vs.* 10,11; Ps 55:23.

Ps 57:1. O God, have pity, for I am trusting you! I will hide beneath the shadow of your wings until this storm is past. [2]I will cry to the God of heaven who does such wonders for me. [3]He will send down help from heaven to save me, because of his love and his faithfulness. He will rescue me from these liars who are so intent upon destroying me.

Ps 59:9. O God my Strength! I will sing your praises, for you are my place of safety. [10]My God is changeless in his love for me and he will come and help me. He will let me see my wish come true upon my enemies. [17]O my Strength, to you I sing my praises; for you are my high tower of safety, my God of mercy.

Ps 60:9,10. Who will bring me in triumph into Edom's strong cities? God will! He who cast us off! He who abandoned us to our foes! [12]With God's help we shall do mighty things, for he will trample down our foes. Ps 108:10–13.

Ps 61:2. For wherever I am, though far away at the ends of the earth, I will cry to you for help. When my heart is faint and overwhelmed, lead me to the mighty, towering Rock of safety. [4]I shall live forever in your tabernacle; oh, to be safe beneath the shelter of your wings! [6]You will give me added years of life, as rich and full as those of many generations, all packed into one. [7]And I shall live before the Lord forever.

Ps 62:1. I stand silently before the Lord, waiting for him to rescue me. For salvation comes from him alone. [5]But I stand silently before the Lord, waiting for him to rescue me. For salvation comes from him alone. [6]Yes, he alone is my Rock, my rescuer, defense and fortress—why then should I be tense with fear when troubles come? [7]My protection and success come from God alone. He is my refuge, a Rock where no enemy can reach me.

Ps 63:6. I lie awake at night thinking of you— [7]of how much you have helped me—and how I rejoice through the night beneath the protecting shadow of your wings.

Ps 66:9. For he holds our lives in his hands. And he holds our feet to the path.

Ps 67:6. God, even our own God, will bless us.

Ps 69:19. You know how they talk about me, and how they so shamefully dishonor me. You see them all and know what each has said. [35]For God will save Jerusalem; he rebuilds the cities of Judah. His people shall live in them and not be dispossessed. [36]Their children shall inherit the land; all who love his name shall live there safely.

Ps 70:5. But I am in deep trouble. Rush to my aid, for only you can help and save me. O Lord, don't delay.

Ps 71:1. Lord, you are my refuge! Don't let me down! [3]Be to me a great protecting Rock, where I am always welcome, safe from all attacks. For you have issued the order to save me. [5]O Lord, you alone are my hope; I've trusted you from childhood. [6]Yes, you have been with me from birth and have helped me constantly—no wonder I am always praising you! [7]My success—at which so many stand amazed—is because you are my mighty protector. [14]I will keep on expecting you to help me. I praise you more and more. [16]I walk in the strength of the Lord God. I tell everyone that you alone are just and good. [20]You have let me sink down deep in desperate problems. But you will bring me back to life again, up from the depths of the earth. [21]You will give me greater honor than before, and turn again and comfort me.

Ps 73:23. But even so, you love me! You are holding my right hand! [24]You will keep on guiding me all my life with your wisdom and counsel; and afterwards receive me into the glories of heaven! [26]My health fails; my spirits droop, yet God remains! He is the strength of my heart; he is mine forever! [28]But as for me, I get as close to him as I can! I have chosen him and I will tell everyone about the wonderful ways he rescues me.

Ps 74:12. God is my King from ages past; you have been actively helping me everywhere throughout the land.

Ps 77:10. And I said: This is my fate, that the blessings of God have changed to hate. [11]I recall the many miracles he did for me so long ago. [12]Those wonderful deeds are constantly in my thoughts. I cannot stop thinking about them.

Ps 86:2. Protect me from death, for I try to follow all your laws. Save me, for I am serving you and trusting you. [7]I will call to you whenever trouble strikes, and you will help me.

Ps 89:18. Yes, our protection is from the Lord

himself and he, the Holy One of Israel, has given us our king. 26You are my Father, my God, and my Rock of Salvation.

Ps 90:1. Lord, through all the generations you have been our home!

Ps 91:1. We live within the shadow of the Almighty, sheltered by the God who is above all gods. 2This I declare, that he alone is my refuge, my place of safety; he is my God, and I am trusting him. 9For Jehovah is my refuge! I choose the God above all gods to shelter me. 10How then can evil overtake me or any plague come near?

Ps 92:10. But you have made me as strong as a wild bull. How refreshed I am by your blessings! 15He is my shelter. There is nothing but goodness in him!

Ps 94:14. The Lord will not forsake his people, for they are his prize. 15Judgment will again be just and all the upright will rejoice. 17I would have died unless the Lord had helped me. 18I screamed, "I'm slipping, Lord!" and he was kind and saved me. 22The Lord my God is my fortress—the mighty Rock where I can hide.

Ps 102:13. I know that you will come and have mercy on Jerusalem—and now is the time to pity her—the time you promised help.

Ps 115:12. Jehovah is constantly thinking about us and he will surely bless us. He will bless the people of Israel and the priests of Aaron, 13and all, both great and small, who reverence him. 14May the Lord richly bless both you and your children.

Ps 116:7. Now I can relax. For the Lord has done this wonderful miracle for me.

Ps 118:6. He is for me! How can I be afraid? What can mere man do to me? 7The Lord is on my side, he will help me. Let those who hate me beware. 10Though all the nations of the world attack me, I will march out behind his banner and destroy them. 14He is my strength and song in the heat of battle, and now he has given me the victory. 17I shall not die, but live to tell of all his deeds.

Ps 119:42. Then I will have an answer for those who taunt me, for I trust your promises. 43May I never forget your words; for they are my only hope. 57Jehovah is mine! And I promise to obey! 74All those who fear and trust in you will welcome me because I too am trusting in your Word. 81I faint for your salvation; but I expect your help, for you have promised it. 114You are my refuge and my shield, and your promises are my only source of hope. 151But you are near, O Lord; all your commandments are based on truth. 166I long for your salvation, Lord, and so I have obeyed your laws.

Ps 121:2. No! My help is from Jehovah who made the mountains! And the heavens too! Ps 124:8.

Ps 130:5. That is why I wait expectantly, trusting God to help, for he has promised. 6I long for him more than sentinels long for the dawn.

Ps 138:7. Though I am surrounded by troubles, you will bring me safely through them. You will clench your fist against my angry enemies! Your power will save me. 8The Lord will work out his plans for my life—for your lovingkindness, Lord, continues forever. Don't abandon me—for you made me.

Ps 140:6–8. O Jehovah, my Lord and Savior, my God and my shield—hear me as I pray! Don't let these wicked men succeed; don't let them prosper and be proud. 12But the Lord will surely help those they persecute; he will maintain the rights of the poor.

Ps 141:8. I look to you for help, O Lord God. You are my refuge. Don't let them slay me.

Ps 142:3. For I am overwhelmed and desperate, and you alone know which way I ought to turn to miss the traps my enemies have set for me. 5Then I prayed to Jehovah. "Lord," I pled, "you are my only place of refuge. Only you can keep me safe."

Ps 143:8. Let me see your kindness to me in the morning, for I am trusting you. Show me where to walk, for my prayer is sincere. 9Save me from my enemies, O Lord, I run to you to hide me.

Ps 144:2. He is always kind and loving to me; he is my fortress, my tower of strength and safety, my deliverer. He stands before me as a shield. He subdues my people under me. 10For you grant victory to kings! You are the one who will rescue your servant David from the fatal sword.

Isa 8:10. Call your councils of war, develop your strategies, prepare your plans of attacking us, and perish! For God is with us. 17I will wait for the Lord to help us, though he is hiding now. My only hope is in him.

Isa 12:2. See, God has come to save me! I will trust and not be afraid, for the Lord is my strength and song; he is my salvation.

Isa 25:9. In that day the people will proclaim, "This is our God, in whom we trust, for whom we waited. Now at last he is here." What a day of rejoicing!

Isa 26:1. Listen to them singing! In that day the whole land of Judah will sing this song: "Our city is strong! We are surrounded by the walls of his salvation!" 8O Lord, we love to do your will! Our hearts' desire is to glorify your name.

Isa 33:2. But to us, O Lord, be merciful, for we have waited for you. 22For the Lord is our Judge, our Lawgiver and our King; he will care for us and save us.

Isa 38:16. O Lord, your discipline is good and leads to life and health. Oh, heal me and make me live!

Isa 50:7. Because the Lord God helps me, I will not be dismayed; therefore, I have set my face like flint to do his will, and I know that I will triumph. 8He who gives me justice is near. Who will dare to fight against me now? Where are my enemies? Let them appear! 9See, the Lord God is for me! Who shall declare me guilty? All my enemies shall be destroyed like old clothes eaten up by moths!

Isa 63:16. Surely you are still our Father! Even if Abraham and Jacob would disown us, still you would be our Father, our Redeemer from ages past.

Isa 64:8. And yet, O Lord, you are our Father. We are the clay and you are the Potter. We are all formed by your hand.

Jer 10:23. O Lord, I know it is not within the power of man to map his life and plan his course.

Jer 14:9. O Lord, you are right here among us, and we carry your name; we are known as your people. O Lord, don't desert us now! [22]What heathen god can give us rain? Who but you alone, O Lord our God, can do such things as this? Therefore we will wait for you to help us.

Jer 16:19. O Lord, my Strength and Fortress, my Refuge in the day of trouble.

Jer 17:12. But our refuge is your throne, eternal, high and glorious. [17]Lord, don't desert me now! You alone are my hope.

Jer 20:11. But the Lord stands beside me like a great warrior, and before him, the Mighty, Terrible One, they shall stumble. They cannot defeat me; they shall be shamed and thoroughly humiliated, and they shall have a stigma upon them forever.

Lam 3:24. My soul claims the Lord as my inheritance; therefore I will hope in him. *vs.* 25–32.

Dan 3:16. Shadrach, Meshach, and Abednego replied, "O Nebuchadnezzar, we are not worried about what will happen to us. [17]If we are thrown into the flaming furnace, our God is able to deliver us; and he will deliver us out of your hand, Your Majesty."

Dan 6:16. The king said to him, "May your God, whom you worship continually, deliver you."

Jon 2:2. In my great trouble I cried to the Lord and he answered me; from the depths of death I called, and Lord, you heard me! *vs.* 3–9.

Mic 7:7. As for me, I look to the Lord for his help; I wait for God to save me; he will hear me. [8]Do not rejoice against me, O my enemy, for though I fall, I will rise again! When I sit in darkness, the Lord himself will be my Light. [9]I will be patient while the Lord punishes me, for I have sinned against him; then he will defend me from my enemies, and punish them for all the evil they have done to me. God will bring me out of my darkness into the light, and I will see his goodness. [20]You will bless us as you promised Jacob long ago. You will set your love upon us, as you promised our father Abraham!

Hab 1:12. O Lord my God, my Holy One, you who are eternal—is your plan in all of this to wipe us out? Surely not!

Hab 3:17. Even though the fig trees are all destroyed, and there is neither blossom left nor fruit, and though the olive crops all fail, and the fields lie barren; even if the flocks die in the fields and the cattle barns are empty, [18]yet I will rejoice in the Lord; I will be happy in the God of my salvation. [19]The Lord God is my Strength, and he will give me the speed of a deer and bring me safely over the mountains.

Zeph 3:12. Those who are left will be the poor and the humble and they will trust in the name of the Lord.

Lk 1:38. Mary said, "I am the Lord's servant, and I am willing to do whatever he wants. May everything you said come true."

Lk 7:50. And Jesus said to the woman, "Your faith has saved you; go in peace."

Jn 3:33. Those who believe him discover that God is a fountain of truth.

Acts 16:34. Then he brought them up into his house and set a meal before them. How he and his household rejoiced because all were now believers!

Acts 24:14. But one thing I do confess, that I believe in the way of salvation, which they refer to as a sect; I follow that system of serving the God of our ancestors; I firmly believe in the Jewish law and everything written in the books of prophecy; [15]and I believe, just as these men do, that there will be a resurrection of both the righteous and ungodly.

Acts 27:25. So take courage! For I believe God! It will be just as he said!

Rom 8:18. Yet what we suffer now is nothing compared to the glory he will give us later. [28]And we know that all that happens to us is working for our good if we love God and are fitting into his plans. [38]For I am convinced that nothing can ever separate us from his love. Death can't, and life can't. The angels won't, and all the powers of hell itself cannot keep God's love away. Our fears for today, our worries about tomorrow, [39]or where we are—high above the sky, or in the deepest ocean—nothing will ever be able to separate us from the love of God demonstrated by our Lord Jesus Christ when he died for us.

Rom 15:29. And I am sure that when I come the Lord will give me a great blessing for you.

1 Cor 9:26. So I run straight to the goal with purpose in every step. I fight to win. I'm not just shadow-boxing or playing around.

2 Cor 1:10. And he did help us, and saved us from a terrible death; yes, and we expect him to do it again and again.

2 Cor 4:8. We are pressed on every side by troubles, but not crushed and broken. We are perplexed because we don't know why things happen as they do, but we don't give up and quit. [9]We are hunted down, but God never abandons us. We get knocked down, but we get up again and keep going. [13]We boldly say what we believe [trusting God to care for us], just as the Psalm writer did when he said, "I believe and therefore I speak." [16]That is why we never give up. Though our bodies are dying, our inner strength in the Lord is growing every day. [17]These troubles and sufferings of ours are, after all, quite small and won't last very long. Yet this short time of distress will result in God's richest blessing upon us forever and ever! [18]So we do not look at what we can see right now, the troubles all around us, but we look forward to the joys in heaven which we have not yet seen.

2 Cor 5:7. We know these things are true by believing, not by seeing.

Gal 5:5. But we by the help of the Holy Spirit are counting on Christ's death to clear away our sins and make us right with God.

Phil 1:19. I am going to keep on being glad, for I know that as you pray for me, and as the Holy

Spirit helps me, this is all going to turn out for my good. [20]For I live in eager expectation and hope that I will never do anything that will cause me to be ashamed of myself but that I will always be ready to speak out boldly for Christ while I am going through all these trials here, just as I have in the past; and that I will always be an honor to Christ, whether I live or whether I must die. [21]For to me, living means opportunities for Christ, and dying—well, that's better yet!

1 Tim 4:9,10. This is the truth and everyone should accept it. We work hard and suffer much in order that people will believe it, for our hope is in the living God who died for all, and particularly for those who have accepted his salvation.

2 Tim 1:12. That is why I am suffering here in jail and I am certainly not ashamed of it, for I know the one in whom I trust, and I am sure that he is able to safely guard all that I have given him until the day of his return.

2 Tim 2:11. I am comforted by this truth, that when we suffer and die for Christ it only means that we will begin living with him in heaven. [12]And if we think that our present service for him is hard, just remember that some day we are going to sit with him and rule with him. But if we give up when we suffer, and turn against Christ, then he must turn against us. [13]Even when we are too weak to have any faith left, he remains faithful to us and will help us, for he cannot disown us who are part of himself, and he will always carry out his promises to us.

Heb 10:34. You suffered with those thrown into jail, and you were actually joyful when all you owned was taken from you, knowing that better things were awaiting you in heaven, things that would be yours forever.

Heb 11:4. It was by faith that Abel obeyed God and brought an offering that pleased God more than Cain's offering did. God accepted Abel and proved it by accepting his gift; and though Abel is long dead, we can still learn lessons from him about trusting God. [5]Enoch trusted God too, and that is why God took him away to heaven without dying; suddenly he was gone because God took him. Before this happened God had said how pleased he was with Enoch. [7]Noah was another who trusted God. When he heard God's warning about the future, Noah believed him even though there was then no sign of a flood, and wasting no time, he built the ark and saved his family. Noah's belief in God was in direct contrast to the sin and disbelief of the rest of the world—which refused to obey—and because of his faith he became one of those whom God has accepted. [8]Abraham trusted God, and when God told him to leave home and go far away to another land which he promised to give him, Abraham obeyed. Away he went, not even knowing where he was going. [9]And even when he reached God's promised land, he lived in tents like a mere visitor, as did Isaac and Jacob, to whom God gave the same promise. [10]Abraham did this because he was confidently waiting for God to bring him to that strong heavenly city whose designer and builder is God. [11]Sarah, too, had faith, and because of this she was able to become a mother in spite of her old age, for she realized that God, who gave her his promise, would certainly do what he said. [13]These men of faith I have mentioned died without ever receiving all that God had promised them; but they saw it all awaiting them on ahead and were glad, for they agreed that this earth was not their real home but that they were just strangers visiting down here. [14]And quite obviously when they talked like that, they were looking forward to their real home in heaven. [16]They were living for heaven. And now God is not ashamed to be called their God, for he has made a heavenly city for them. [17]While God was testing him, Abraham still trusted in God and his promises, and so he offered up his son Isaac, and was ready to slay him on the altar of sacrifice; [18]yes, to slay even Isaac, through whom God had promised Abraham a whole nation of descendants! He believed that if Isaac died God would bring him back to life again; and that is just about what happened, for as far as Abraham was concerned, Isaac was doomed to death, but he came back again alive! [20]It was by faith that Isaac knew God would give future blessings to his two sons, Jacob and Esau. [21]By faith Jacob, when he was old and dying, blessed each of Joseph's two sons as he stood and prayed, leaning on the top of his cane. [22]And it was by faith that Joseph, as he neared the end of his life, confidently spoke of God bringing the people of Israel out of Egypt; and he was so sure of it that he made them promise to carry his bones with them when they left! [23]Moses' parents had faith too. When they saw that God had given them an unusual child, they trusted that God would save him from the death the king commanded, and they hid him for three months, and were not afraid. [24, 25]It was by faith that Moses, when he grew up, refused to be treated as the grandson of the king, but chose to share ill-treatment with God's people instead of enjoying the fleeting pleasures of sin. [26]He thought that it was better to suffer for the promised Christ than to own all the treasures of Egypt, for he was looking forward to the great reward that God would give him. [27]And it was because he trusted God that he left the land of Egypt and wasn't afraid of the king's anger. Moses kept right on going; it seemed as though he could see God right there with him. [28]And it was because he believed God would save his people that he commanded them to kill a lamb as God had told them to and sprinkle the blood on the doorposts of their homes, so that God's terrible Angel of Death could not touch the oldest child in those homes, as he did among the Egyptians. [29]The people of Israel trusted God and went right through the Red Sea as though they were on dry ground. But when the Egyptians chasing them tried it, they all were drowned. [30]It was faith that brought the walls of Jericho tumbling down after the people of Israel had walked around them seven days, as God had commanded them. [31]By faith—because she believed in God and his power—Rahab the harlot did not die with all the others in her city when they refused to obey God, for she gave a friendly welcome to the spies. [32]Well, how much more do I need to say? It would take too long to recount the stories of the faith of Gideon and Barak and Samson and Jephthah and David and Samuel and all the other prophets. [33]These people all trusted God and as a result won battles, overthrew kingdoms, ruled their people well, and received what God had promised them; they were kept from harm in a den of lions, [34]and in a fiery furnace. Some, through their faith, escaped death by the sword. Some were made strong again after they had been weak or sick. Others were given real power in battle; they made whole armies turn and run away. [35]And some women, through faith, received their loved ones back again from death. But others trusted God and were beaten to death, preferring to die rather than turn from God and be free—trusting that they would rise to a better life afterwards. [36]Some were laughed at and their backs cut open with whips, and others were chained in dungeons. [37, 38]Some died by stoning and some by being sawed in two; others were promised freedom if they would renounce their faith, then were killed with the sword. Some went about in skins of sheep and goats, wandering over deserts and mountains, hiding in dens and caves. They were hungry and sick and ill-treated—too good for this world. [39]And these men of faith, though they trusted God and won his approval, none of them received all that God had promised them.

Heb 13:14. For this world is not our home; we are looking forward to our everlasting home in heaven.

2 Pet 3:13. But we are looking forward to God's promise of new heavens and a new earth afterwards, where there will be only goodness.

1 Jn 4:16. We know how much God loves us because we have felt his love and because we believe him when he tells us that he loves us dearly.

INSTANCES OF. Abel, Heb 11:4; Noah, in building the ark, Gen 6:14–22; Heb 11:7. Abraham, in leaving his homeland at the command of God, Gen 12:1–4; believing the promise of many descendants, Gen 12:7; 15:4–8; in the offering up of Isaac, Gen 22:1–10; Rom 4:18–21; Heb 11:8–19. Jacob, in blessing Joseph's sons, Heb 11:21. Joseph, concerning God's providence in his being sold into Egypt, and the final deliverance of Israel, Gen 50:20; Heb 11:22. Jochebed, in caring for Moses, Ex 2:2; 6:20; Heb 11:23. Egyptians, who obeyed the Lord, Ex 9:20. Moses, in espousing the cause of his people, Heb 11:24–28; at the death of Korah, Num 16:28, 29.

Israelites, when Aaron declared the mission of himself and Moses, Ex 4:31; in the battle with the Cannanites, 1 Chron 5:20, and other conquests, 2 Chron 13:8–19. See *Miracles, of Moses.* Caleb, in advising to take the land of promise, Num 13:30; 14:6–9. Rahab, in hospitality to the spies, Josh 2:9, 11; Heb 11:31. The spies, sent to reconnoiter Jericho, Josh 2:24. Conquest of Jericho, Josh 6. Manoah's wife, Judg 13:23. Hannah, 1 Sam 1. Jonathan, in killing the Philistines, 1 Sam 14:6. David, in killing Goliath, 1 Sam 17:37, 46, 47; in choosing to fall into the hands of the Lord as his punishment for numbering Israel, 2 Sam 24:14; in believing God's promise, that his kingdom would be a perpetual kingdom, Acts 2:30. Elijah, in his controversy with the priests of Baal, 1 Kgs 18:32–38. Widow of Zarephath in feeding Elijah, 1 Kgs 17:13–15. Amaziah, in dismissing the Ephraimites in obedience to the command of God, and going alone to battle against the Edomites, 2 Chron 25:7–10. Hezekiah, 2 Kgs 18:5; 19; 20:1–11. Daniel, in the lions' den, Dan 6. The three Hebrews, who refused to worship Nebuchadnezzar's statue, Dan 3:13–27. Ninevites, in obeying Jonah, Jon 3:5. Ezra, in making the journey from Babylon to Jersualem without a military escort, Ezra 8:22. Eliphaz, in the overruling providence of God, that trials are for the good of the righteous, Job 5:6–27. Mordecai, in the deliverance of the Jews, Esther 4:14. Joseph, in obeying the dream about Mary and to escape to Egypt, Mt 1:18–24; 2:13, 14. Simeon, when he saw Jesus in the temple, Lk 2:25–35. Conquests by, Heb 11:32–34.

See *Faith, Trial of,* below; *Faith, in Christ, Instances of,* below.

IN CHRIST. Mt 7:24. All who listen to my instructions and follow them are wise, like a man who builds his house on solid rock. [25]Though the rain comes in torrents, and the floods rise and the storm winds beat against his house, it won't collapse, for it is built on rock. Lk 6:46–49.

Mt 8:2. Look! A leper is approaching. He kneels before him, worshiping. "Sir," the leper pleads, "if you want to, you can heal me." [13]Then Jesus said to the Roman officer, "Go on home. What you have believed has happened!"

Mt 9:22. Jesus turned around and spoke to her. "Daughter," he said, "all is well! Your faith has healed you." [29]Then he touched their eyes and said, "Because of your faith it will happen."

Mt 11:6. Then give him this message, "Blessed are those who don't doubt me." [28]Come to me and I will give you rest—all of you who work so hard beneath a heavy yoke. [29, 30]Wear my yoke—for it fits perfectly—and let me teach you; for I am gentle and humble, and you shall find rest for your souls; for I give you only light burdens.

Mt 14:27. But Jesus immediately spoke to them, reassuring them. "Don't be afraid!" he said. Jn 6:20.

Mt 15:28. "Woman," Jesus told her, "your faith is large, and your request is granted."

Mt 17:7. Jesus came over and touched them. "Get up," he said, "don't be afraid."

Mk 9:23. "If I can?" Jesus asked. "*Anything* is possible if you have faith."

Mk 16:16. Those who believe and are baptized will be saved. But those who refuse to believe will be condemned.

Lk 7:9. Jesus was amazed. Turning to the crowd he said, "Never among all the Jews in Israel have I met a man with faith like this." [50]And Jesus said to the woman, "Your faith has saved you; go in peace."

Lk 8:50. But when Jesus heard what had happened, he said to the father, "Don't be afraid! Just trust me, and she'll be all right." Mk 5:36.

Lk 17:6. "If your faith were only the size of a mustard seed," Jesus answered, "it would be large enough to uproot that mulberry tree over there and send it hurtling into the sea! Your command would bring immediate results!"

Lk 18:42. And Jesus said, "All right, begin seeing! Your faith has healed you."

Jn 1:12. But to all who received him, he gave the right to become children of God. All they needed to do was to trust him to save them.

Jn 3:14. And as Moses in the wilderness lifted up the bronze image of a serpent on a pole, even so I must be lifted up upon a pole, [15]so that anyone who believes in me will have eternal life. [16]For God loved the world so much that he gave his only Son so that anyone who believes in him shall not perish but have eternal life. [Jn 6:40] [18]There is no eternal doom awaiting those who trust him to save them. But those who don't trust him have already been tried and condemned for not believing in the only Son of God. [36]And all who trust him—God's Son—to save them have eternal life; those who don't believe and obey him shall never see heaven, but the wrath of God remains upon them. Jn 6:47.

Jn 5:24. I say emphatically that anyone who listens to my message and believes in God who sent me has eternal life, and will never be damned for his sins, but has already passed out of death into life.

Jn 6:29. Jesus told them, "This is the will of God, that you believe in the one he has sent. [35]No one coming to me will ever be hungry again. Those believing in me will never thirst. [45]As it is written in the Scriptures, 'They shall all be taught of God.' Those the Father speaks to, who learn the truth from him, will be attracted to me."

Jn 7:38. For the Scriptures declare that rivers of living water shall flow from the inmost being of anyone who believes in me.

Jn 9:35. Jesus . . . found the man and said, "Do you believe in the Messiah?"

Jn 11:25. Jesus told her, "I am the one who raises the dead and gives them life again. Anyone who believes in me, even though he dies like anyone else, shall live again. [26]He is given eternal life for believing in me and shall never perish. Do you believe this, Martha? [40]But didn't I tell you that you will see a wonderful miracle from God if you believe?" Jesus asked her.

Jn 12:36. "Make use of the Light while there is still time; then you will become light bearers." [44]Jesus shouted to the crowds, "If you trust me, you are really trusting God. [46]I have come as a Light to shine in this dark world, so that all who put their trust in me will no longer wander in the darkness."

Jn 13:7. Jesus replied, "You don't understand now why I am doing it; some day you will. [20]Truly, anyone welcoming my messenger is welcoming me. And to welcome me is to welcome the Father who sent me."

Jn 14:1. Let not your heart be troubled. You are trusting God, now trust in me. [11]Just believe it—that I am in the Father and the Father is in me. Or else believe it because of the mighty miracles you have seen me do. [12]In solemn truth I tell you, anyone believing in me shall do the same miracles I have done, and even greater ones, because I am going to be with the Father.

Jn 16:27. For the Father himself loves you dearly because you love me and believe that I came from the Father. [33]I have told you all this so that you will have peace of heart and mind. Here on earth you will have many trials and sorrows; but cheer up, for I have overcome the world.

Jn 18:37. All who love the truth are my followers.

Jn 20:27. "Don't be faithless any longer. Believe!" [29]Then Jesus told him, "You believe because you have seen me. But blessed are those who haven't seen me and believe anyway." [31]But these are recorded so that you will believe that he is the Messiah, the Son of God, and that believing in him you will have life. 2 Tim 3:15.

Acts 3:16. Jesus' name has healed this man—and you know how lame he was before. Faith in Jesus' name—faith given us from God—has caused this perfect healing.

Acts 10:43. And all the prophets have written about him, saying that everyone who believes in him will have their sins forgiven through his name.

Acts 15:9. He made no distinction between them and us, for he cleansed their lives through faith, just as he did ours. [11]Don't you believe that all are saved the same way, by the free gift of the Lord Jesus?

Acts 16:31. They replied, "Believe on the Lord Jesus and you will be saved, and your entire household."

Acts 20:21. I have had one message for Jews and Gentiles alike—the necessity of turning from sin to God through faith in our Lord Jesus Christ.

Acts 26:18. So that they may receive forgiveness for their sins and God's inheritance along with all people everywhere whose sins are cleansed away, who are set apart by faith in me.

Rom 3:22. Now God says he will accept and acquit us—declare us "not guilty"—if we trust Jesus Christ to take away our sins. And we all can be saved in this same way, by coming to Christ, no matter who we are or what we have been like. [23]Yes, all have sinned; all fall short of God's glorious ideal; [24]yet now God declares us "not guilty" of offending him if we trust in Jesus Christ, who in his kindness freely takes away our sins. [25]For God sent Christ Jesus to take the punishment for our sins and to end all God's anger against us. He used Christ's blood and our faith as the means of saving us from his wrath. . . . [26]And now in these days also he can receive sinners in this same way, because Jesus took away their sins. But isn't this unfair for God to let criminals go free, and say that they are innocent? No, for he does it on the basis of their trust in Jesus who took away their sins. [27]Then what can we boast about doing, to earn our salvation? Nothing at all. Why? Because our acquittal is not based on our good deeds; it is based on what Christ has done and our faith in him. [28]So it is that we are saved by faith in Christ and not by the good things we do.

Rom 9:33. God warned them of this in the Scriptures when he said, "I have put a Rock in the path of the Jews, and many will stumble over him (Jesus). Those who believe in him will never be disappointed."

Rom 10:4. They don't understand that Christ gives to those who trust in him everything they are trying to get by keeping his laws. He ends all of that. [9]For if you tell others with your own mouth that Jesus Christ is your Lord, and believe in your own heart that God has raised him from the dead, you will be saved.

Gal. 2:16. And yet we Jewish Christians know very well that we cannot become right with God by obeying our Jewish laws, but only by faith in Jesus Christ to take away our sins. And so we, too, have trusted Jesus Christ, that we might be accepted by God because of faith—and not because we have obeyed the Jewish laws.

Gal 3:1. Oh, foolish Galatians! What magician has hypnotized you and cast an evil spell upon you? For you used to see the meaning of Jesus Christ's death as clearly as though I had waved a placard before you with a picture on it of Christ dying on the cross. [2]Let me ask you this one question: Did you receive the Holy Spirit by trying to keep the Jewish laws? Of course not, for the Holy Spirit came upon you only after you heard about Christ and trusted him to save you. [3]Then have you gone completely crazy? For if trying to obey the Jewish laws never gave you spiritual life in the first place, why do you think that trying to obey them now will make you stronger Christians? [4]You have suffered so much for the Gospel. Now are you going to just throw it all overboard? I can hardly believe it! [5]I ask you again, does God give you the power of the Holy Spirit and work miracles among you as a result of your trying to obey the Jewish laws? No, of course not. It is when you believe in Christ and fully trust him. [6]Abraham had the same experience—God declared him fit for heaven only because he believed God's promises. [7]You can see from this that the real children of Abraham are all the men of faith who truly trust in God. [8, 9]What's more, the Scriptures looked forward to this time when God would save the Gentiles also, through their faith. God told Abraham about this long ago when he said, "I will bless those in every nation who trust in me as you do." And so it is: all who trust in Christ share the same blessing Abraham received. [10]Yes, and those who depend on the Jewish laws to save them are under God's curse, for the Scriptures point out very clearly, "Cursed is everyone who at any time breaks a single one of these laws that are written in God's Book of the Law." [11]Consequently, it is clear that no one can ever win God's favor by trying to keep the Jewish laws, because God has said that the only way we can be right in his sight is by faith. As the prophet Habakkuk says it, "The man who finds life will find it through trusting God." [12]How different from this way of faith is the way of law which says that a man is saved by obeying every law of God, without one slip. [13]But Christ has bought us out from under the doom of that impossible system by taking the curse for our wrongdoing upon himself. For it is written in the Scripture, "Anyone who is hanged on a tree is cursed" [as Jesus was hung upon a wooden cross]. [14]Now God can bless the Gentiles, too, with this same blessing he promised to Abraham; and all of us as Christians can have the promised Holy Spirit through this faith. [15]Dear brothers, even in everyday life a promise made by one man to another, if it is written down and signed, cannot be changed. He cannot decide afterward to do something else instead. [16]Now, God gave some promises to Abraham and his Child. And notice that it doesn't say the promises were to his *children,* as it would if all his sons—all the Jews—were being spoken of, but to his *Child*—and that, of course, means Christ. [17]Here's what I am trying to say: God's promise to save through faith—and God wrote this promise down and signed it—could not be canceled or changed four hundred and thirty years later when God gave the Ten Commandments. [18]If *obeying those laws* could save us, then it is obvious that this would be a different way of gaining God's favor than Abraham's way, for he simply accepted God's promise. [19]Well then, why were the laws given? They were added after the promise was given to show men how guilty they are of breaking God's laws. But this system of law was to last only until the coming of Christ, the Child to whom God's promise was made. (And there is this further difference. God gave his laws to angels to give to Moses, who then gave them to the people; [20]but when God gave his promise to Abraham, he did it by himself alone, without angels or Moses as go-betweens.) [21, 22]Well then, are God's laws and God's promises against each other? Of course not! If we could be saved by his laws, then God would not have had to give us a different way to get out of the grip of sin—for the Scriptures insist we are all its prisoners. The only way out is through faith in Jesus Christ; the way of escape is open to all who believe him. [23]Until Christ came we were guarded by the law, kept in protective custody, so to speak, until we could believe in the coming Savior. [24]Let me put it another way. The Jewish laws were our teacher and guide until Christ came to give us right standing with God through our faith. [25]But now that Christ has come, we don't need those laws any longer to guard us and lead us to him. [26]For now we are all children of God through faith in Jesus Christ, [27]and we who have been baptized into union with Christ are enveloped by him. [28]We are no longer Jews or Greeks or slaves or free men or even merely men or women, but we are all the same—we are Christians; we are one in Christ Jesus. [29]And now that we are Christ's we are the true descendants of Abraham, and all of God's promises to him belong to us.

Gal 5:6. And we to whom Christ has given eternal life don't need to worry about whether we have been circumcised or not, or whether we are obeying the Jewish ceremonies or not; for all we need is faith working through love.

Eph 1:12. God's purpose in this was that we should praise God and give glory to him for doing these mighty things for us, who were the first to trust in Christ. [13]And because of what Christ did, all you others too, who heard the Good News about how to be saved, and trusted Christ, were marked as belonging to Christ by the Holy Spirit, who long ago had been promised to all of us Christians. [14]His presence within us is God's guarantee that he really will give us all that he promised; and the Spirit's seal upon us means that God has already purchased us and that he guarantees to bring us to himself. This is just one more reason for us to praise our glorious God.

Eph 3:12. Now we can come fearlessly right into God's presence, assured of his glad welcome when we come with Christ and trust in him. [17]And I pray that Christ will be more and more at home in your hearts, living within you as you trust in him.

Eph 4:13. Until finally we all believe alike about our salvation and about our Savior, God's Son, and all become full-grown in the Lord—yes, to the point of being filled full with Christ.

Phil 3:9. And become one with him, no longer counting on being saved by being good enough or by obeying God's laws, but by trusting Christ to save me; for God's way of making us right with himself depends on faith—counting on Christ alone.

Col 2:7. Let your roots grow down into him and draw up nourishment from him.

1 Tim 1:16. But God had mercy on me so that Christ Jesus could use me as an example to show everyone how patient he is with even the worst sinners, so that others will realize that they, too, can have everlasting life.

2 Tim 1:13. Hold tightly to the pattern of truth I taught you, especially concerning the faith and love Christ Jesus offers you.

2 Tim 2:1. Oh, Timothy, my son, be strong with the strength Jesus Christ gives you.

2 Tim 3:15. You know how, when you were a small child, you were taught the holy Scriptures; and it is these that make you wise to accept God's salvation by trusting in Christ Jesus.

Heb 4:16. So let us come boldly to the very throne of God and stay there to receive his mercy and to find grace to help us in our times of need.

Heb 6:19. This certain hope of being saved is a strong and trustworthy anchor for our souls, connecting us with God himself behind the sacred curtains of heaven.

Heb 10:22. Let us go right in, to God himself, with true hearts fully trusting him to receive us.

Heb 12:2. Keep your eyes on Jesus, our leader and instructor.

Heb 13:7. Remember your leaders who have taught you the Word of God. Think of all the good that has come from their lives, and try to trust the Lord as they do.

1 Pet 1:8. You love him even though you have never seen him; though not seeing him, you trust him; and even now you are happy with the inexpressible joy that comes from heaven itself.

1 Pet 2:6. As the Scriptures express it, "See, I am sending Christ to be the carefully chosen, precious Cornerstone of my church, and I will never disappoint those who trust in him." [7]Yes, he is very precious to you who believe. Isa 28:16.

2 Pet 1:1. From: Simon Peter, a servant and missionary of Jesus Christ. *To:* All of you who have our kind of faith. The faith I speak of is the kind that Jesus Christ our God and Savior gives to us.

1 Jn 3:23. And this is what God says we must do: Believe on the name of his Son Jesus Christ, and love one another.

1 Jn 5:4. For every child of God can obey him, defeating sin and evil pleasure by trusting Christ to help him. [5]But who could possibly fight and win this battle except by believing that Jesus is truly the Son of God? [10]All who believe this know in their hearts that it is true. [13]I have written this to you who believe in the Son of God so that you may know you have eternal life.

14. And we are sure of this, that he will listen to us whenever we ask him for anything in line with his will.

Jude 1:21. Stay always within the boundaries where God's love can reach and bless you. Wait patiently for the eternal life that our Lord Jesus Christ in his mercy is going to give you.

Rev 1:17. "Don't be afraid! Though I am the First and Last."

Rev 3:18. My advice to you is to buy pure gold from me, gold purified by fire—only then will you truly be rich. And to purchase from me white garments, clean and pure, so you won't be naked and ashamed. [20]Look! I have been standing at the door and I am constantly knocking. If anyone hears me calling him and opens the door, I will come in and fellowship with him and he with me.

IN CHRIST, EXEMPLIFIED. Mt 8:2. "Sir," the leper pleads, "if you want to, you can heal me."

Mt 9:18. "My little daughter has just died," he said, "but you can bring her back to life again if you will only come and touch her." [21]For she thought, "If I only touch him, I will be healed." [Mk 5:28; Lk 8:48.] [28]"Do you believe I can make you see?" "Yes, Lord," they told him, "we do."

Mt 14:33. The others sat there, awestruck. "You really are the Son of God!" they exclaimed.

Mt 15:27. "Yes, it is!" she replied, "for even the puppies beneath the table are permitted to eat the crumbs that fall." *vs.* 26, 28; Mk 7:27–30.

Mt 16:16. Simon Peter answered, "The Christ, the Messiah, the Son of the living God."

Mk 9:24. The father instantly replied, "I *do* have faith; oh, help me to have *more!*" Jn 9:38.

Lk 5:5. "Sir," Simon replied, "we worked hard all last night and didn't catch a thing. But if you say so, we'll try again."

Lk 7:3. When the captain heard about Jesus, he sent some respected Jewish elders to ask him to come and heal his slave. [4]So they began pleading earnestly with Jesus to come with them and help the man. They told him what a wonderful person the captain was. "If anyone deserves your help, it is he," they said, [5]"for he loves the Jews and even paid personally to build us a synagogue!" [6, 7, 8]Jesus went with them; but just before arriving at the house, the captain sent some friends to say, "Sir, don't inconvenience yourself by coming to my home, for I am not worthy of any such honor or even to come and meet you. Just speak a word from where you are, and my servant boy will be healed! I know, because I am under the authority of my superior officers, and I have authority over my men. I only need to say 'Go!' and they go; or 'Come!' and they come; and to my slave, 'Do this or that,' and he does it. So just say, 'Be healed!' and my servant will be well again!" [9]Jesus was amazed. Turning to the crowd he said, "Never among all the Jews in Israel have I met a man with faith like this." Mt 8:5–10.

Lk 23:42. Then he said, "Jesus, remember me when you come into your Kingdom."

Jn 4:29. "Come and meet a man who told me everything I ever did! Can this be the Messiah?" [42]Then they said to the woman, "Now we believe because we have heard him ourselves, not just because of what you told us. He is indeed the Savior of the world."

Jn 6:14. When the people realized what a great miracle had happened, they exclaimed, "Surely, he is the Prophet we have been expecting!" [68]Simon Peter replied, "Master, to whom shall we go? You alone have the words that give eternal life, [69]and we believe them and know you are the holy Son of God."

Jn 7:31. Many among the crowds at the Temple believed on him. "After all," they said, "what miracles do you expect the Messiah to do that this man hasn't done?"

Jn 10:41. And many followed him. "John didn't do miracles," they remarked to one another, "but all his predictions concerning this man have come true." [42]And many came to the decision that he was the Messiah.

Jn 11:21. Martha said to Jesus, "Sir, if you had been here, my brother wouldn't have died. [22]And even now it's not too late, for I know that God will bring my brother back to life again, if you will only ask him to. [27]I believe you are the Messiah, the Son of God, the one we have so long awaited." *v.* 32.

Jn 16:30. Now we understand that you know everything and don't need anyone to tell you anything. From this we believe that you came from God.

Jn 20:28. "My Lord and my God!" Thomas said.

Acts 8:37. And the eunuch replied, "I believe that Jesus Christ is the Son of God."

Acts 11:17. And since it was *God* who gave these Gentiles the same gift he gave us when we believed on the Lord Jesus Christ, who was I to argue?

Rom 7:24,25. Oh, what a terrible predicament I'm in! Who will free me from my slavery to this deadly lower nature? Thank God! It has been done by Jesus Christ our Lord. He has set me free.

Rom 8:35. Who then can ever keep Christ's love from us? When we have trouble or calamity, when we are hunted down or destroyed, is it because he doesn't love us anymore? And if we are hungry, or penniless, or in danger, or threatened with death, has God deserted us? [37]But despite all this, overwhelming victory is ours through Christ who loved us enough to die for us.

2 Cor 12:9. Now I am glad to boast about how weak I am; I am glad to be a living demonstration of Christ's power, instead of showing off my own power and abilities. [10]Since I know it is all for Christ's good, I am quite happy about "the thorn," and about insults and hardships, persecutions and difficulties.

Gal 2:20. I have been crucified with Christ: and I myself no longer live, but Christ lives in me. And the real life I now have within this body is a result of my trusting in the Son of God, who loved me and gave himself for me.

Phil 4:13. For I can do everything God asks me to with the help of Christ who gives me the strength and power.

1 Tim 1:14. Oh, how kind our Lord was, for he showed me how to trust him and become full of the love of Christ Jesus.

2 Tim 1:12. For I know the one in whom I trust, and I am sure that he is able to safely guard all that I have given him until the day of his return.

2 Tim 4:18. Yes, and the Lord will always deliver me from all evil and will bring me into his heavenly kingdom.

INSTANCES OF FAITH IN CHRIST. The astrologers of the east, Mt 2:1, 2, 11. Peter, Mt 4:18–22; Mk 1:16–20; Lk 5:4, 5; Jn 6:68, 69. Andrew, Mt 4: 18–22; Mk 1:16–20; Jn 1:41. James and John, Mt 4: 21, 22; Mk 1:19, 20. The woman with internal bleeding, Mt 9:21, 22. Jairus, for the healing of his daughter, Mt 9:18, 23–25. Two blind men, Mt 9:29, 30. Blind Bartimaeus and a fellow blind man, Mt 20:30–34; Mk 10:46–52; Lk 18:35–42. The Samaritan leper, Lk 17:11–19. The sick of Gennesaret, Mt 14:36; Mk 3:10; 6:54–56. Those who brought the paralytic to Jesus, Lk 5:18–20. The Canaanite woman, Mt 15:22–28; Mk 7:25–30. The woman who anointed Jesus' feet, Lk 7:36–50. Those who brought paralyzed boy, Mt 9:2. Philip, Jn 1:45, 46. Nathanael, Jn 1:49. The Samaritans, who believed through the preaching of Jesus, Jn 4:39–42; through the preaching of Philip, Acts 8:9–12. The official whose child was sick, Jn 4:46–53. Abraham, Jn 8:56. The blind man whom Jesus healed on the Sabbath, Jn 9:13–38. Mary, sister of Martha, Lk 10: 38–42; Jn 11:32. John the disciple, Jn 20:8. The disciples, through the miracle at Cana of Galilee, Jn 2:11. Jews at Jerusalem, Jn 2:23; 8:30, 31; 11:45; 12:11. Three thousand at Pentecost, Acts 2:41. Five thousand, Acts 4:4. Crowds, Acts 5:14. The cripple at Lystra, Acts 14:9. Stephen, Acts 6:8. Ethiopian eunuch, Acts 8:37. People of Lydda and Sharon, Acts 9:35; of Joppa, Acts 9:42; of Antioch, Acts 11: 21–24. Barnabas, Acts 11:24. Eunice, Lois, and Timothy, 2 Tim 1:5; Acts 16:1. Lydia, Acts 16:14. Philippian jailer, Acts 16:31–34. Crispus, Acts 18:8. The Corinthians, Acts 18:8; 1 Cor 15:11. Jews at Rome, Acts 28:24. Ephesians, Eph 1:13, 15. Colossians, Col 1:2, 4. Thessalonians, 1 Thess 1:6; 3:6–8; 2 Thess 1:3, 4. Philemon, Philemon 1:5. Church at Thyatria, Rev 2:19.

TRIAL OF. 1 Chron 29:17. I know, my God, that you test men to see if they are good; for you enjoy good men.

Ps 26:2. Cross-examine me, O Lord, and see that this is so; test my motives and affections too.

Ps 81:7. I tested your faith at Meribah, when you complained there was no water.

Mt 13:19. The hard path where some of the seeds fell represents the heart of a person who hears the Good News about the Kingdom and doesn't understand it; then Satan comes and snatches away the seeds from his heart. [20]The shallow, rocky soil represents the heart of a man who hears the message and receives it with real joy, [21]but he doesn't have much depth in his life, and the seeds don't root very deeply, and after a while when trouble comes, or persecution begins because of his beliefs, his enthusiasm fades, and he drops out. [22]The ground covered with thistles represents a man who hears the message, but the cares of this life and his longing for money choke out God's Word, and he does less and less for God. Lk 8:13,14.

Mt 24:21. For there will be persecution such as the world has never before seen in all its history, and will never see again. [22]In fact, unless those days are shortened, all mankind will perish. But they will be shortened for the sake of God's chosen people. [23]Then if anyone tells you, "The Messiah has arrived at such and such a place, or has appeared here or there," don't believe it. [24]For false Christs shall arise, and false prophets, and will do wonderful miracles, so that if it were possible, even God's chosen ones would be deceived. [25]See, I have warned you.

2 Thess 1:3. Dear brothers, giving thanks to God for you is not only the right thing to do, but it is our duty to God, because of the really wonderful way your faith has grown, and because of your growing love for each other. [4]We are happy to tell other churches about your patience and complete faith in God, in spite of all the crushing troubles and hardships you are going through. [5]This is only one example of the fair, just way God does things, for he is using your sufferings to make you ready for his kingdom.

Heb 6:13. For instance, there was God's promise to Abraham: God took an oath in his own name, since there was no one greater to swear by, [14]that he would bless Abraham again and again, and give him a son and make him the father of a great nation of people. [15]Then Abraham waited patiently until finally God gave him a son, Isaac, just as he had promised.

Jas 1:3. For when the way is rough, your patience has a chance to grow. [12]Happy is the man who doesn't give in and do wrong when he is tempted, for afterwards he will get as his reward the crown of life that God has promised those who love him.

1 Pet 1:7. These trials are only to test your faith, to see whether or not it is strong and pure. It is being tested as fire tests gold and purifies it—and your faith is far more precious to God than mere gold; so if your faith remains strong after being tried in the test tube of fiery trials, it will bring you much praise and glory and honor on the day of his return.

See *Temptation.*

INSTANCES OF TRIAL OF. Noah, Gen 6:14–22; Heb 11:7. Abraham, when commanded to leave his native land and go he knew not where, Gen 12:1–4; Heb 11:8; when commanded to offer Isaac, Gen 22: 1–19; Heb 11:17–19. Moses, when sent to Pharaoh, Ex 3:11, 12; 4:10–17; Heb 11:24–29; at the Red Sea, by the murmurings of the people, Ex 14; 15. Joshua and the children of Israel, in the method of taking Jericho, Josh 6; Heb 11:30. Gideon, when commanded to save Israel, Judg 6:36–40; 7; Heb 11:32. Job, by affliction and adversity, Job 1; 2. Ezra, in leaving Babylon without a military escort, Ezra 8: 22. Daniel, when forbidden to pray to God, Dan 6: 4–23; Heb 11:32, 33. The three Hebrews, when commanded to worship the statue, Dan 3:8–30; Heb 11: 32–34.

The Canaanite woman, Mt 15:21–28; Mk 7:24–30. The two blind men who appealed to Jesus for sight, Mt 9:28. The disciples, when Jesus came walking on the Sea of Galilee, Mt 14:25–33.

The disciples: by the question of Jesus, as to who he was, Mt 16:15–20; Lk 9:20, 21; by their inability to cast out the demon from the lunatic, Mt 17:14–21; Mk 9:14–29; Lk 9:37–42; in the storm on the lake, Mt 8:23–27; Mk 4:36–41; Lk 8:22–26. Of Philip, when questioned by Jesus as to how the multitude would be fed, Jn 6:1–6. Of Peter, when asked whether he loved Jesus, Jn 21:16, 17.

See *Afflictions, Design of.*

STRENGTHENED BY MIRACLES. See *Miracles, Design of.*

SUM TOTAL OF BELIEF AND LIFE. Rom 1:8; Jude 1:3.

WEAK. See *Doubting.*

FAITHFULNESS Ps 12:1. Lord! Help! Godly men are fast disappearing. Where in all the world can dependable men be found?

Ps 31:23. Oh, love the Lord, all of you who are his people; for the Lord protects those who are loyal to him.

Ps 103:17, 18. But the lovingkindness of the Lord is from everlasting to everlasting, to those who reverence him; his salvation is to children's children of those who are faithful to his covenant and remember to obey him!

Prov 20:6. Most people will tell you what loyal friends they are, but are they telling the truth?

Jer 23:28. Let these false prophets tell their dreams and let my true messengers faithfully proclaim my every word. There is a difference between chaff and wheat!

Mt 10:22. Everyone shall hate you because you belong to me. But all of you who endure to the end shall be saved.

Mt 24:45. Are you a wise and faithful servant of the Lord? Have I given you the task of managing my household, to feed my children day by day? [46]Blessings on you if I return and find you faithfully doing your work. [47]I will put such faithful ones in charge of everything I own! Lk 12:42–44.

Mt 25:14. Again, the Kingdom of Heaven can be illustrated by the story of a man going into another country, who called together his servants, and loaned them money to invest for him while he was gone. [15]He gave $5,000 to one, $2,000 to another, and $1,000 to the last—dividing it in proportion to their abilities—and then left on his trip. [16]The man who received the $5,000 began immediately to buy and sell with it and soon earned another $5,000. [17]The man with $2,000 went right to work, too, and earned another $2,000. [18]But the man who received the $1,000 dug a hole in the ground and hid the money for safekeeping. [19]After a long time their master returned from his trip and called them to him to account for his money. [20]The man to whom he had entrusted the $5,000 brought him $10,000. [21]His master praised him for good work. "You have been faithful in handling this small amount," he told him, "so now I will give you many more responsibilities. Begin the joyous tasks I have assigned to you." [22]Next came the man who had received the $2,000, with the report, "Sir, you gave me $2,000 to use, and I have doubled it." [23]"Good work," his master said. "You are a good and faithful servant. You have been faithful over this small amount, so now I will give you much more." Lk 19:12–27.

Lk 16:10. *No!* For unless you are honest in small matters, you won't be in large ones. If you cheat even a little, you won't be honest with greater responsibilities. [11]And if you are untrustworthy about worldly wealth, who will trust you with the true riches of heaven? [12]And if you are not faithful with other people's money, why should you be entrusted with money of your own?

1 Cor 4:2. Now the most important thing about a servant is that he does just what his master tells him to.

Col 3:22. You slaves must always obey your earthly masters, not only trying to please them when they are watching you but all the time; obey them willingly because of your love for the Lord and because you want to please him. Eph 6:5–9.

Rev 2:10. Remain faithful even when facing death and I will give you the crown of life—an unending, glorious future.

See *Obedience, Commanded; Perseverance; Minister, Faithful; Reproof, Faithfulness in.*

INSTANCES OF. Abraham, Gal 3:8,9. Moses, Heb 3:5. David, 2 Sam 22:22–35. Elijah, 1 Kgs 19:10,14. Abijah, 2 Chron 13:4–20. Jehoshaphat, 2 Chron 20:1–30. Job, Job 1:21,22; 2:9,10. Timothy, 1 Cor 4:17.

See *Hezekiah; Joash; Josiah; Daniel.*

OF GOD. See *God, Faithfulness of.*

FALCON A carnivorous bird, forbidden as food, Lev 11:13–19; Deut 14:11–18.

See *Vulture.*

FALL OF MAN Gen 3:1. The serpent was the craftiest of all the creatures the Lord God had made. So the serpent came to the woman. "Really?" he asked. "*None* of the fruit in the garden? God says you mustn't eat *any* of it?" [2, 3]"Of course we may eat it," the woman told him. "It's only the fruit from the tree at the *center* of the garden that we are not to eat. God says we mustn't eat it or even touch it, or we will die." [Gen 2:16,17.] [4]"That's a lie!" the serpent hissed. "You'll not die! [5]God knows very well that the instant you eat it you will become like him, for your eyes will be opened—you will be able to distinguish good from evil!" [6]The woman was convinced. How lovely and fresh looking it was! And it would make her so wise! So she ate some of the fruit and gave some to her husband, and he ate it too. [7]And as they ate it, suddenly they became aware of their nakedness, and were embarrassed. So they strung fig leaves together to cover themselves around the hips. [8]That evening they heard the sound of the Lord God walking in the garden; and they hid themselves among the trees. [9]The Lord God called to Adam, "Why are you hiding?" [10]And Adam replied, "I heard you coming and didn't want you to see me naked. So I hid." [11]"Who told you you were naked?" the Lord God asked. "Have you eaten fruit from the tree I warned you about?" [12]"Yes," Adam admitted, "but it was the woman you gave me who brought me some, and I ate it." [13]Then the Lord God asked the woman, "How could you do such a thing?" "The serpent tricked me," she replied. [14]So the Lord God said to the serpent, "This is your punishment: You are singled out from among all the domestic and wild animals of the whole earth—to be cursed. You shall grovel in the dust as long as you live, crawling along on your belly. [15]From now on you and the woman will be enemies, as will all of your offspring and hers. And I will put the fear of you into the woman, and between your offspring and hers. He shall strike you on your head, while you will strike at his heel." [16]Then God said to the woman, "You shall bear children in intense pain and suffering; yet even so, you shall welcome your husband's affections, and he shall be your master." [17]And to Adam, God said, "Because you listened to your wife and ate the fruit when I told you not to, I have placed a curse upon the soil. All your life you will struggle to extract a living from it. [18]It will grow thorns and thistles for you, and you shall eat its grasses. [19]All your life you will sweat to master it, until your dying day. Then you will return to the ground from which you came. For you were made from the ground, and to the ground you will return."

Job 31:33. Or if, like Adam, I have tried to hide my sins.

Eccl 7:29. And I found that though God has made men upright, each has turned away to follow his own downward road.

Isa 43:27. From the very first your ancestors sinned against me—all your forebears transgressed my law.

Hos 6:7. But like Adam, you broke my covenant; you refused my love.

Rom 5:12. When Adam sinned, sin entered the entire human race. His sin spread death throughout all the world, so everything began to grow old and die, for all sinned. [14]So when their bodies died it was not for their own sins since they themselves had never disobeyed God's special law against eating the forbidden fruit, as Adam had. What a contrast between Adam and Christ who was yet to come! [18]Yes, Adam's *sin* brought *punishment* to all, but Christ's *righteousness* makes men *right with God,* so that they can live. *vs.* 19,21.

1 Cor 15:21. Death came into the world because of what one man (Adam) did, and it is because of what this other man (Christ) has done that now there is the resurrection from the dead. [22]Everyone dies because all of us are related to Adam, being members of his sinful race, and wherever there is sin, death results. But all who are related to Christ will rise again.

2 Cor 11:3. But I am frightened, fearing that in some way you will be led away from your pure and simple devotion to our Lord, just as Eve was deceived by Satan in the Garden of Eden.

1 Tim 2:14. And it was not Adam who was fooled by Satan, but Eve, and sin was the result.

See *Depravity.*

FALSE ACCUSATION See *Accusation, False.*

FALSE CONFIDENCE In self, Deut 29:19; 1 Kgs 20:11; Prov 3:4,5; 23:4,5; 26:12; 28:26; Isa 5:21; Rom 12:16; 2 Cor 1:9. In outward resources, Ps 20:7; 33:16,17; 44:6; 49:6; Prov 11:28; Isa 22:9–11; 31:1–3; Jer 48:7; Zech 4:6; Mk 10:24. In man, Ps 33:16, 17; 62:9; 118:8; 146:3,4; Isa 2:22; Jer 17:5; Hos 5:13; 7:11.

INSTANCES OF. At Babel, Gen 11:3,4. Sennacherib, in the siege of Jerusalem, 2 Kgs 19:23. Asa, in relying on Syria rather than on God, 2 Chron. 16:7–9. Hezekiah, in the defenses of Jerusalem, Isa 22:9–11. Peter, in asserting his devotion to Jesus, Mt 26:35; Lk 22:33,34; Jn 13:37,38.

See *Confidence, False.*

FALSEHOOD See *Lying.*

FALSE TEACHERS See *Teachers, False.*

FALSE WITNESS Ex 20:16. You must not lie. Deut 5:20; Mt 19:18; Lk 18:20; Rom 13:9.

Ex 23:1. Do not pass along untrue reports. Do not cooperate with an evil man by affirming on the witness stand something you know is false.

Lev 6:2. If anyone sins against me . . . [3]by finding a lost article and lying about it, swearing that he doesn't have it.

Lev 19:11. You must not steal nor lie nor defraud.

12. You must not swear to a falsehood, thus bringing reproach upon the name of your God, for I am Jehovah.

16. Don't gossip. Don't falsely accuse your neighbor of some crime, for I am Jehovah. Ex 20:16.

Deut 19:16. If anyone gives false witness, claiming he has seen someone do wrong when he hasn't, [17]both men shall be brought before the priests and judges on duty before the Lord at the time. [18]They must be closely questioned, and if the witness is lying, [19]his penalty shall be the punishment he thought the other man would get. In this way you will purge out evil from among you. [20]Then those who hear about it will be afraid to tell lies on the witness stand.

Ps 27:12. Don't let them get me, Lord! Don't let me fall into their hands! For they accuse me of things I never did, and all the while are plotting cruelty.

Ps 35:11. These evil men swear to a lie. They accuse me of things I have never even heard about.

Prov 6:16. For there are six things the Lord hates —no, seven: Haughtiness, lying, murdering, plotting evil, eagerness to do wrong, a false witness, sowing discord among brothers.

Prov 12:17. A good man is known by his truthfulness; a false man by deceit and lies.

Prov 14:5. A truthful witness never lies; a false witness always lies. [8]The fool attempts to fool himself and won't face facts. [25]A witness who tells the truth saves good men from being sentenced to death, but a false witness is a traitor.

Prov 18:5. It is wrong for a judge to favor the wicked and condemn the innocent.

Prov 19:9. A false witness shall be punished and a liar shall be caught. [22]Kindness makes a man attractive. And it is better to be poor than dishonest. [28]A worthless witness cares nothing for truth—he enjoys his sinning too much.

Prov 21:28. A false witness must be punished; an honest witness is safe.

Prov 24:28. Don't testify spitefully against an innocent neighbor. Why lie about him?

Prov 25:18. Telling lies about someone is as harmful as hitting him with an axe, or wounding him with a sword, or shooting him with a sharp arrow.

Zech 5:3. "This scroll," he told me, "represents the words of God's curse going out over the entire land. It says that all who steal and lie have been judged and sentenced to death. [4]I am sending this curse into the home of every thief and everyone who swears falsely by my name," says the Lord of Hosts. "And my curse shall remain upon his home and completely destroy it."

Mt 15:19. For from the heart come evil thoughts . . . lying and slander.

Lk 3:14. "And us," asked some soldiers, "what

about us?" John replied, "Don't extort money by threats and violence; don't accuse anyone of what you know he didn't do; and be content with your pay!"

1 Tim 1:9. But they were not made for us, whom God has saved; they are for sinners who hate God, have rebellious hearts. . . . [10,11]Yes, these laws are made to identify as sinners all liars, and all others who do things that contradict the glorious Good News.

See *Perjury; Evidence, Laws concerning; Lying; Witness.*

INSTANCES OF. Witnesses against Naboth, 1 Kgs 21:13; against Jesus, Mt 26:59–61; Mk 14: 54–59; against Stephen, Acts 6:11, 13; against Paul, Acts 16:20, 21; 17:5–7; 24:5; 25:7, 8.

FAMILIAR SPIRITS See *Demons; Necromancy; Sorcery; Witchcraft.*

FAMILY OF BELIEVERS. Blessed, Ps 128:1, 3, 6. Should be taught God's word, Deut 4:9, 10. Worship God together, 1 Cor 16:19. Be duly regulated, Prov 31:27; 1 Tim 3:4, 5, 12. Live in unity, Gen 45:24; Ps 133:1. Live in mutual forbearance, Gen 50:16–21; Mt 18:21, 22. Rejoice together before God, Deut 14:26. Deceivers and liars should be removed from, Ps 101:7. Warned against turning away from God, Deut 29:18.

GOOD, EXEMPLIFIED. Abraham, Gen 18:19. Jacob, Gen 35:2. Joshua, Josh 24:15. David, 2 Sam 6:20; Job 1:5. Lazarus of Bethany, Jn 11:1–5. Cornelius, Acts 10:2, 33. Lydia, Acts 16:15. Jailer of Philippi, Acts 16:31–34. Crispus, Acts 18:8. Lois, 2 Tim 1:5.

See *Children; Husband; Wife; Orphan; Widow.*

INSTITUTED. Gen 2:23. "This is it!" Adam exclaimed. "She is part of my own bone and flesh! Her name is 'woman' because she was taken out of a man." [24]This explains why a man leaves his father and mother and is joined to his wife in such a way that the two become one person.

GOVERNMENT OF. Gen 3:16. Then God said to the woman . . . "You shall welcome your husband's affections, and he shall be your master."

Gen 18:19. And I have picked him out to have godly descendants and and godly household—men who are just and good—so that I can do for him all I have promised.

Esther 1:20. When this decree is published throughout your great kingdom, husbands everywhere, whatever their rank, will be respected by their wives! [22]Every man should rule his home, and should assert his authority.

1 Cor 7:10. Now, for those who are married I have a command, not just a suggestion. And it is not a command from me, for this is what the Lord himself has said: A wife must not leave her husband. [11]But if she is separated from him, let her remain single or else go back to him. And the husband must not divorce his wife.

1 Cor 11:3. A wife is responsible to her husband, her husband is responsible to Christ, and Christ is responsible to God. [7]God's glory is man made in his image, and man's glory is the woman. [8]The first man didn't come from woman, but the first woman came out of man. [9]And Adam, the first man, was not made for Eve's benefit, but Eve was made for Adam.

Eph 5:21. Honor Christ by submitting to each other. [22]You wives must submit to your husbands' leadership in the same way you submit to the Lord. [23]For a husband is in charge of his wife in the same way Christ is in charge of his body the church. (He gave his very life to take care of it and be its Savior!) [24]So you wives must willingly obey your husbands in everything, just as the church obeys Christ. [25]And you husbands, show the same kind of love to your wives as Christ showed to the church when he died for her.

Col 3:18. You wives, submit yourselves to your husbands, for that is what the Lord has planned for you. [19]And you husbands must be loving and kind to your wives and not bitter against them, nor harsh. *v.* 20.

1 Tim 3:2. For a pastor must be a good man whose life cannot be spoken against. He must have only one wife, and he must be hard working and thoughtful, orderly, and full of good deeds. He must enjoy having guests in his home, and must be a good Bible teacher. [4]He must have a well-behaved family, with children who obey quickly and quietly. [5]For if a man can't make his own little family behave, how can he help the whole church?

1 Pet 3:1. Wives, fit in with your husbands' plans. [6]Sarah, for instance, obeyed her husband Abraham, honoring him as head of the house. [7]You husbands must be careful of your wives, being thoughtful of their needs and honoring them as the weaker sex. Remember that you and your wife are partners in receiving God's blessing, and if you don't treat her as you should, your prayers will not get ready answers.

UNHAPPY. Prov 11:22. A beautiful woman lacking discretion and modesty is like a fine gold ring in a pig's snout.

Prov 12:4. A worthy wife is her husband's joy and crown; the other kind corrodes his strength and tears down everything he does.

Prov 14:1. A wise woman builds her house, while a foolish woman tears hers down by her own efforts.

Prov 15:17. It is better to eat soup with someone you love than steak with someone you hate.

Prov 18:19. It is harder to win back the friendship of an offended brother that to capture a fortified city. His anger shuts you out like iron bars.

Prov 19:13. A rebellious son is a calamity to his father, and a nagging wife annoys like constant dripping.

Prov 21:9. It is better to live in the corner of an attic than with a crabby woman in a lovely home. [Prov 25:24.] [19]Better to live in the desert than with a quarrelsome, complaining woman.

Prov 27:15. A constant dripping on a rainy day and a cranky woman are much alike! [16]You can no more stop her complaining than you can stop the wind or hold onto anything with oil-slick hands.

Prov 30:21–23. There are three things that make the earth tremble—no, four it cannot stand. A slave who becomes a king. A rebel who prospers. A bitter woman when she finally marries. A servant girl who marries her mistress' husband.

INSTANCES OF UNHAPPINESS IN. Of Abraham, on account of Hagar, Gen 16:5; 21:10, 11. Of Isaac, on account of disagreement between Jacob and Easu, Gen 27:2–46. Of Jacob, jealousy between Leah and Rachel, Gen 29:30–34; 30:1–25. Moses and Zipporah, Ex 4:25, 26. Of Elkanah, on account of Peninnah and Hannah, 1 Sam 1:4–7. David and Michal, 2 Sam 6:16, 20–23. Ahasuerus, on account of Vashti's refusing to appear before his drunken courtiers, Esther 1:10–22.

PERSIAN, DOMESTIC CUSTOMS. Esther 1:10–22.

See *Harem.*

RELATIONSHIP TO GOD. Gen 12:7. Then Jehovah appeared to Abram and said, "I am going to give this land to your descendants." And Abram built an altar there to commemorate Jehovah's visit. [8]Afterwards Abram left that place and traveled southward to the hilly country between Bethel on the west and Ai on the east. There he made camp, and made an altar to the Lord and prayed to him.

Gen 13:3,4. Then they continued northward toward Bethel where he had camped before, between Bethel and Ai—to the place where he had built the altar. And there he again worshiped the Lord.

Gen 17:12. Every male shall be circumcised on the eighth day after birth. This applies to every foreign-born slave as well as to everyone born in your household. . . . [13]All must be circumcised. Your bodies will thus be marked as participants in my everlasting covenant. [14]Anyone who refuses these terms shall be cut off from his people; for he has violated my contract.

Gen 18:19. And I have picked him out to have godly descendants and a godly household—men who are just and good—so that I can do for him all I have promised.

Deut 4:9. But watch out! Be very careful never to forget what you have seen God doing for you. May his miracles have a deep and permanent effect upon your lives! Tell your children and your grandchildren about the glorious miracles he did. [10]Tell them especially about the day you stood before the Lord at Mount Horeb, and he told me, "Summon the people before me and I will instruct them, so that they will learn always to reverence me, and so that they can teach my laws to their children."

Deut 11:19. Teach them to your children. Talk about them when you are sitting at home, when you are out walking, at bedtime, and before breakfast! [20]Write them upon the doors of your houses and upon your gates.

Deut 12:5. Rather, you must build a sanctuary for him at a place he himself will select as his home. [6]There you shall bring to the Lord your burnt offerings and other sacrifices—your tithes, your offerings presented by the gesture of waving before the altar, your offerings to fulfill your vows, your freewill offerings, and your offerings of the firstborn animals of your flocks and herds. [7]There you and your families shall feast before the Lord your God, and shall rejoice in all he has done for you. [11]Then you must bring all your burnt sacrifices and other offerings to his sanctuary, the place he will choose as his home. [12]You shall rejoice there before the Lord with your sons and daughters and servants; and remember to invite the Levites to feast with you, for they have no land of their own.

Jos 24:15. But as for me and my family, we will serve the Lord.

Ps 101:2. I will try to walk a blameless path, but how I need your help, especially in my own home, where I long to act as I should.

Jer 7:18. No wonder my anger is great! Watch how the children gather wood and the fathers build fires, and the women knead dough and make cakes to offer to "The Queen of Heaven" and to their other idol-gods!

Acts 10:1. In Caesarea there lived a Roman army officer, Cornelius, a captain of an Italian regiment. [2]He was a godly man, deeply reverent, as was his entire household. He gave generously to charity and was a man of prayer. [3]While wide awake one afternoon he had a vision—it was about three o'clock—and in this vision he saw an angel of God coming toward him. "Cornelius!" the angel said. [4]Cornelius stared at him in terror. "What do you want, sir?" he asked the angel. And the angel replied, "Your prayers and charities have not gone unnoticed by God! [5,6]Now send some men to Joppa to find a man named Simon Peter, who is staying with Simon, the tanner, down by the shore, and ask him to come and visit you." [33]"So I sent for you at once, and you have done well to come so soon. Now here we are, waiting before the Lord, anxious to hear what he has told you to tell us!"

44. Even as Peter was saying these things, the Holy Spirit fell upon all those listening! [47]Peter asked, "Can anyone object to my baptizing them, now that they have received the Holy Spirit just as we did?" [48]So he did, baptizing them in the name of Jesus, the Messiah.

Acts 16:25. Around midnight, as Paul and Silas were praying and singing hymns to the Lord—and the other prisoners were listening— [26]suddenly there was a great earthquake; the prison was shaken to its foundations, all the doors flew open —and the chains of every prisoner fell off! [27]The jailer wakened to see the prison doors wide open, and assuming the prisoners had escaped, he drew his sword to kill himself. [28]But Paul yelled at him, "Don't do it! We are all here!" [29]Trembling with fear, the jailer called for lights and ran to the dungeon and fell down before Paul and Silas. [30]He brought them out and begged them, "Sirs, what must I do to be saved?" [31]They replied, "Believe on the Lord Jesus and you will be saved, and your entire household." [32]Then they told him and all his household the Good News from the Lord. [33]That same hour he washed their stripes and he and all his family were baptized. [34]Then he brought them up into his house and set a meal before them. How he and his household rejoiced because all were now believers!

Acts 18:8. However, Crispus, the leader of the synagogue, and all his household believed in the Lord and were baptized—as were many others in Corinth.

1 Cor 1:16. Oh, yes, and I baptized the family of Stephanas.

FAMINE Pharaoh forewarned of, in dreams, Gen 41. Described, Deut 28:53–57; Isa 5:13; 9:18–21; 17:11; Jer 5:17; 14:1–6; 48:33; Lam 1:11, 19; 2:11–22; 4:3–10; Joel 1:17–20. Sent as a judgment, Lev 26:19–29; Deut 28:23, 24, 38–42; 1 Kgs 17:1; 2 Kgs 8:1; 1 Chron 21:12; Ps 105:16; 107:33, 34; Isa 3:1–8; 14:30; Jer 14:15–22; 19:9; 29:16,17; Lam 5:4, 5, 10; Ezk 4:16, 17; 5:16, 17; 14:13; Joel 1:15, 16; Amos 4:6–9; 5:16, 17; Hag 1:10, 11; Mt 24:7; Lk 21:11; Rev 6:5–8.

Cannibalism in, Deut 28:53; 2 Kgs 6:26–30. Righteous kept from, Job 5:20; Ps 33:18, 19; 37:19.

FIGURATIVE. Amos 8:11.

INSTANCES OF. In Canaan, Gen 12:10; 26:1; 2 Sam 21:1; 1 Kgs 17; 18:1; 2 Kgs 6:25–30; 7:4. In Jerusalem, from siege, 2 Kgs 25:3; Jer 52:6. In Egypt, Gen 41:53–57. Universal, Acts 11:28.

FARMING See *Agriculture; Vineyard.*

FASTING Observed on occasions of public calamities, 2 Sam 1:12; afflictions, Ps 35:13; Dan 6:18; private grief, 2 Sam 12:16; approaching danger, Esther 4:16; ordination of ministers, Acts 13:3; 14:23.

Accompanied by prayer, Dan 9:3; repentence, 1 Sam 7:6; Neh 9:1–3; humiliation, Deut 9:18; Neh 9:1; reading of the Scriptures, Jer 36:6.

Habitual: by John's disciples, Mt 9:14; by Anna, Lk 2:36, 37; by Pharisees, Mt 9:14; Mk 2:18; Lk 18:12; by Paul, 2 Cor 6:5; 11:27.

In times of bereavement: of the people of Jabesh-gilead, for Saul and his sons, 1 Sam 31:13; 1 Chron 10:12; of David, at the time of Saul's death, 2 Sam 1:12; of his child's sickness, 2 Sam 12:16, 21–23; of Abner's death, 2 Sam 3:35, 36.

Prolonged: for three weeks, by Daniel, Dan 10:2, 3; forty days, by Moses, Ex 24:18; 34:28; Deut 9:9, 18; Elijah, 1 Kgs 19:8; Jesus, Mt 4:2; Mk 1:12, 13; Lk 4:1, 2.

See *Humiliation; Humility.*

UNCLASSIFIED SCRIPTURES RELATING TO. Ezra 8:21. Then I declared a fast while we were at the Ahava River so that we would humble ourselves before our God; and we prayed that he would give us a good journey and protect us, our children, and our goods as we traveled. [22]For I was ashamed to ask the king for soldiers and cavalry to accompany us and protect us from the enemies along the way. After all, we had told the king that our God would protect all those who worshiped him, and that disaster could come only to those who had forsaken him! [23]So we fasted and begged God to take care of us. And he did.

Ps 35:13. When they were ill, I mourned before the Lord in sackcloth, asking him to make them well; I refused to eat; I prayed for them with utmost earnestness, but God did not listen.

Ps 69:10. How they scoff and mock me when I mourn and fast before the Lord!

Isa 58:3. "We have fasted before you," they say. "Why aren't you impressed? Why don't you see our sacrifices? Why don't you hear our prayers? We have done much penance, and you don't even notice it!" I'll tell you why! Because you are living in evil pleasure even while you are fasting, and you keep right on oppressing your workers. [4]Look, what good is fasting when you keep on fighting and quarreling? This kind of fasting will never get you anywhere with me. [5]Is this what I want—this doing of penance and bowing like reeds in the wind and putting on sackcloth and covering yourselves with ashes? Is this what you call fasting? [6]No, the kind of fast I want is that you stop oppressing those who work for you and treat them fairly and give them what they earn. [7]I want you to share your food with the hungry and bring right into your own homes those who are helpless, poor and destitute. Clothe those who are cold and don't hide from relatives who need your help.

Jer 14:12. When they fast, I will not pay any attention.

Dan 10:2. When this vision came to me (Daniel said later) I had been in mourning for three full weeks. [3]All that time I tasted neither wine nor meat, and of course I went without desserts. I neither washed nor shaved nor combed my hair.

Joel 1:14. Announce a fast; call a solemn meeting. Gather the elders and all the people into the Temple of the Lord your God, and weep before him there.

Joel 2:12. That is why the Lord says, "Turn to me now, while there is time. Give me all your hearts. Come with fasting, weeping, mourning. [13]Let your remorse tear at your hearts and not your garments." Return to the Lord your God, for he is gracious and merciful. He is not easily angered; he is full of kindness, and anxious not to punish you.

Zech 7:5. During those seventy years of exile when you fasted and mourned in August and October, were you really in earnest about leaving your sins behind, and coming back to me? No, not at all!

Zech 8:19. The traditional fasts and times of mourning you have kept in July, August, October, and January are ended. They will be changed to joyous festivals if you love truth and peace!

Mt 6:16. And now about fasting. When you fast, declining your food for a spiritual purpose, don't do it publicly, as the hypocrites do, who try to look wan and disheveled so people will feel sorry for them. Truly, that is the only reward they will ever get. [17]But when you fast, put on festive clothing, [18]so that no one will suspect you are hungry, except your Father who knows every secret. And he will reward you.

Mt 9:14. One day the disciples of John the Baptist came to Jesus and asked him, "Why don't your disciples fast as we do and as the Pharisees do?"

[15]"Should the bridegroom's friends mourn and go without food while he is with them?" Jesus asked. "But the time is coming when I will be taken from them. Time enough then for them to refuse to eat."

Mt 17:21. But this kind of demon won't leave unless you have prayed and gone without food.

Acts 27:33. As the darkness gave way to the early morning light, Paul begged everyone to eat. "You haven't touched food for two weeks," he said. [34]"Please eat something now for your own good! For not a hair of your heads shall perish!"

INSTANCES OF. Of the Israelites, in the conflict between the other tribes with the tribe of Benjamin, on account of the crime against a Levite's concubine, Judg 20:26; when they went to Mizpah for the ark, 1 Sam 7:6. Of David, at the death of Saul, 2 Sam 1:12; during the sickness of his child by Bath-sheba, 2 Sam 12:16–22; while interceding in prayer for his friends, Ps 35:13; in his zeal for Israel, Ps 69:10; in prayer for himself and his enemies, Ps 109:4, 24. Of Ahab, when Elijah prophesied the destruction of himself and his family, 1 Kgs 21:27; with verses 20–29. Of Jehoshaphat, at the time of the invasion of the confederated armies of the Canaanites and Syrians, 2 Chron 20:3. Of Ezra, on account of the heathen marriages of the Jews, Ezra 10:6. Of Nehemiah, on account of the desolation of Jerusalem and the temple, Neh 1:4. Of the Jews, when Jeremiah prophesied against Israel and Judah, Jer 36:9; in Babylon, with prayer for divine protection, Ezra 8:21, 23. Of Darius, when he put Daniel in the lions' den, Dan 6:18. Of Daniel, on account of the captivity of the people, with prayer for their deliverance, Dan 9:3; at the time of his vision, Dan 10:1–3. Ninevites, when Jonah preached to them, Jon 3:4–10. By Paul, at the time of his conversion, Acts 9:8, 9. Of the disciples, at the time of the dedication of Barnabas and Saul, Acts 13:2, 3. At the appointment of the elders, Acts 14:23.

FAT Offered in sacrifice, Ex 23:18; 29:13, 22; Lev 1:8; 3:3–5, 9–11, 14–16; 4:8–10; 7:3–5; 8:15, 16, 25; 10:15; 17:6; 1 Sam 2:15, 16; Isa 43:24. Belonged to the Lord, Lev 3:15, 16. Forbidden as food, Lev 3:17; 7: 23. Idolatrous sacrifices of, Deut 32:38.

FIGURATIVE. Gen 45:18.

FATHER Forbidden to be used as a title among the disciples, Mt 23:9.

See *Parents; God, Fatherhood of.*

FATHERHOOD OF GOD. See *God, Fatherhood of.*

FATHER-IN-LAW Hospitable to son-in-law, a man of Bethlehem, Judg 19:3–9. Unjust, Laban to Jacob, Gen 29:21–23; 31:7, 39–42.

FATHERLESS See *Orphan.*

FATTED CALF Lk 15:23.

FAULT FINDING See *Murmuring; Uncharitableness.*

FAVOR See *God, Grace of.*

FAVORITISM INSTANCES OF. Jacob, for Rachel, Gen 29:30, 34. Elkanah, for Hannah, 1 Sam 1:4, 5. Rebekah, for Jacob, Gen 27:6–17. Jacob, for Joseph, Gen 37:3, 4. Joseph, for Benjamin, Gen 43:34. Forbidden in parents, Deut 21: 15–17.

See *Partiality.*

FEAR See *Cowardice.* Also *Fear of God,* below.

FEAR OF GOD REVERENCE. Gen 35:5. Then they started on again. And the terror of God was upon all the cities they journeyed through, so that they were not attacked.

Ex 18:21. Find some capable, godly, honest men who hate bribes, and appoint them as judges, one judge for each 1000 people; he in turn will have ten judges under him, each in charge of a hundred; and under each of them will be two judges, each responsible for the affairs of fifty people; and each of these will have five judges beneath him, each counseling ten persons.

Ex 20:18. All the people saw the lightning and the smoke billowing from the mountain, and heard the thunder and the long, frightening trumpet blast; and they stood at a distance, shaking with fear. [19]They said to Moses, "You tell us what God says and we will obey, but don't let God speak directly to us, or it will kill us." [20]"Don't be afraid," Moses told them, "for God has come in this way to show you his awesome power, so that from now on you will be afraid to sin against him!"

Lev. 22:32. You must not treat me as common and ordinary. Revere me and hallow me, for I, the Lord, made you holy to myself.

Deut 4:10. Summon the people before me and I will instruct them, so that they will learn always to reverence me, and so that they can teach my laws to their children.

Deut 6:2. The purpose of these laws is to cause you, your sons, and your grandsons to reverence the Lord your God by obeying all of his instructions as long as you live.

Deut 10:20. You must fear the Lord your God and worship him and cling to him and take oaths by his name alone. [21]He is your praise and he is your God, the one who has done mighty miracles you yourselves have seen. Deut 6:13; 13:4; 14:23.

Deut 28:49. The Lord will bring a distant nation against you, swooping down upon you like an eagle; a nation whose language you don't understand. [58]If you refuse to obey all the laws written in this book, thus refusing reverence to the glorious and fearful name of Jehovah your God, then Jehovah will send perpetual plagues upon you and upon your children.

Josh 4:24. He did this so that all the nations of the earth will realize that Jehovah is the mighty God, and so that all of you will worship him forever.

Josh 24:14. So revere Jehovah and serve him in sincerity and truth.

1 Sam 2:30. I will honor only those who honor me, and I will despise those who despise me.

1 Sam 12:14. Now if you will fear and worship the Lord and listen to his commandments and not rebel against the Lord, and if both you and your king follow the Lord your God then all will be well.

[24]Trust the Lord and sincerely worship him; think of all the tremendous things he has done for you.

2 Sam 23:3. The Rock of Israel said to me: "One shall come who rules righteously, who rules in the fear of God."

1 Kgs 8:40. In this way they will always learn to reverence you as they continue to live in this land which you have given their fathers. *vs.* 41–43.

2 Kgs 17:36. They were to worship only the Lord who had brought them out of the land of Egypt with such tremendous miracles and power. [39]*You must worship only the Lord; he will save you from all your enemies. vs.* 27, 28.

1 Chron 16:30. Tremble before him, all the earth!

2 Chron 19:7. "Be very much afraid to give any other decision than what God tells you to. For there must be no injustice among God's judges, no partiality, no taking of bribes." [9]These were his instructions to them: "You are to act always in the fear of God, with honest hearts."

Ezra 10:3. For we agree before our God to divorce our heathen wives and to send them away with our children; we will follow your commands, and the commands of the others who fear our God. We will obey the laws of God. Ezra 9:4.

Neh 5:9. Then I pressed further. "What you are doing is very evil," I exclaimed. "Should you not walk in the fear of our God? Don't we have enough enemies among the nations around us who are trying to destroy us?"

Job 28:28. And this is what he says to all mankind: "Look, to fear the Lord is true wisdom; to forsake evil is real understanding."

Job 37:24. No wonder men everywhere fear him! For he is not impressed by the world's wisest men!

Ps 2:11. Serve the Lord with reverent fear; rejoice with trembling.

Ps 4:4. Stand before the Lord in awe, and do not sin against him. Lie quietly upon your bed in silent meditation.

Ps 22:23. "Praise the Lord, each one of you who fears him," I will say. "Each of you must fear and reverence his name. Let all Israel sing his praises." [25]Yes, I will stand and praise you before all the people. I will publicly fulfill my vows in the presence of all who reverence your name.

Ps 25:12. Where is the man who fears the Lord? God will teach him how to choose the best. [13]He shall live within God's circle of blessing, and his children shall inherit the earth. [14]Friendship with God is reserved for those who reverence him. With them alone he shares the secrets of his promises.

Ps 31:19. Oh, how great is your goodness to those who publicly declare that you will rescue them. For you have stored up great blessings for those who trust and reverence you.

Ps 33:8. Let everyone in all the world—men, women and children—fear the Lord and stand in awe of him. [18]But the eyes of the Lord are watching over those who fear him, who rely upon his steady love.

Ps 34:7. For the Angel of the Lord guards and rescues all who reverence him. [9]If you belong to the Lord, reverence him; for everyone who does this has everything he needs. [11]Sons and daughters, come and listen and let me teach you the importance of trusting and fearing the Lord.

Ps 46:10. Stand silent! Know that I am God! I will be honored by every nation in the world!

Ps 52:6. The followers of God will see it happen. They will watch in awe.

Ps 64:9. Then everyone shall stand in awe and confess the greatness of the miracles of God; at last they will realize what amazing things he does.

Ps 67:7. God, even our God, will bless us. And peoples from remotest lands will worship him.

Ps 72:5. May the poor and needy revere you constantly, as long as sun and moon continue in the skies! Yes, forever!

Ps 85:9. Surely his salvation is near to those who reverence him; our land will be filled with his glory.

Ps 86:11. Tell me where you want me to go and I will go there. May every fiber of my being unite in reverence to your name.

Ps 89:7. The highest of angelic powers stand in dread and awe of him. Who is as revered as he by those surrounding him?

Ps 90:11. Who can realize the terrors of your anger? Which of us can fear you as he should?

Ps 96:4. For the Lord is great beyond description, and greatly to be praised. Worship only him among the gods! [9]Let the earth tremble before him.

Ps 99:1. Jehovah is King! Let the nations tremble! He is enthroned upon the cherubim. Let the whole earth shake.

Ps 102:15. Now let the nations and their rulers tremble before the Lord, before his glory.

Ps 103:11. For his mercy toward those who fear and honor him is as great as the height of the heavens above the earth. [13]He is like a father to us, tender and sympathetic to those who reverence him. [17]But the lovingkindness of the Lord is from everlasting to everlasting, to those who reverence him.

Ps 111:5. He gives food to those who trust him. [10]How can men be wise? The only way to begin is by reverence for God. Prov 1:7–9; 9:10.

Ps 112:1. Praise the Lord! For all who fear God and trust in him are blessed beyond expression. Yes, happy is the man who delights in doing his commands.

Ps 115:11. All of you, his people, trust in him. [12]. . . He will bless . . . [13]all, both great and small, who reverence him.

Ps 119:63. Anyone is my brother who fears and trusts the Lord and obeys him. [74]All those who fear and trust in you will welcome me because I too am trusting in your Word. [79]Let all others join me, who trust and fear you, and we will discuss your laws. Ps 66:16.

Ps 128:1. Blessings on all who reverence and trust the Lord—on all who obey him! [4]This is God's reward to those who reverence and trust him.

Ps 135:20. Oh, bless his name, all of you who trust and reverence him.

Ps 145:19. He fulfills the desires of those who

reverence and trust him; he hears their cries for help and rescues them.

Ps 147:11. But his joy is in those who reverence him, those who expect him to be loving and kind.

Prov 1:7. How does a man become wise? The first step is to trust and reverence the Lord! Only fools refuse to be taught. Prov 9:10.

Prov 2:5. You will soon learn the importance of reverence for the Lord and of trusting him.

Prov 3:7. Don't be conceited, sure of your own wisdom. Instead, trust and reverence the Lord, and turn your back on evil.

Prov 8:13. If anyone respects and fears God, he will hate evil.

Prov 10:27. Reverence for God adds hours to each day.

Prov 13:13. Despise God's Word and find yourself in trouble. Obey it and succeed.

Prov 14:2. To do right honors God; to sin is to despise him. [26]Reverence for God gives a man deep strength .... [27]Reverence for the Lord is a fountain of life; its waters keep a man from death.

Prov 15:16. Better a little with reverence for God, than great treasure and trouble with it. [33]Humility and reverence for the Lord will make you both wise and honored.

Prov 16:6. Evil is avoided by reverence for God.

Prov 19:23. Reverence for God gives life, happiness, and protection from harm.

Prov 22:4. True humility and respect for the Lord lead a man to riches, honor and long life.

Prov 23:17. But continue to reverence the Lord all the time.

Prov 28:14. Blessed is the man who reveres God.

Prov 31:30. But a woman who fears and reverences God shall be greatly praised.

Eccl 3:14. And I know this, that whatever God does is final—nothing can be added or taken from it; God's purpose in this is that man should fear the all-powerful God.

Eccl 7:18. Tackle every task that comes along, and if you fear God you can expect his blessing.

Eccl 8:12. I know very well that those who fear God will be better off.

Eccl 12:13. Here is my final conclusion: fear God and obey his commandments, for this is the entire duty of man. Eccl 5:6,7; 1 Pet 2:17.

Isa 2:10. Crawl into the caves in the rocks and hide in terror from his glorious majesty. [19]When the Lord stands up from his throne to shake up the earth, his enemies will crawl with fear into the holes in the rocks and into the caves because of the glory of his majesty. [20]Then at last they will abandon their gold and silver idols to the moles and bats, [21]and crawl into the caverns to hide among the jagged rocks at the tops of the cliffs to try to get away from the terror of the Lord and the glory of his majesty when he rises to terrify the earth.

Isa 8:13. Don't fear anything except the Lord of the armies of heaven! If you fear him, you need fear nothing else.

Isa 25:3. Therefore strong nations will shake with fear before you; ruthless nations will obey and glorify your name.

Isa 29:23. Then they will fear and rejoice in my name, and praise the Holy One of Israel, and stand in awe of him.

Isa 33:6. An abundance of salvation is stored up for Judah in a safe place, along with wisdom and knowledge and reverence for God. [13]Listen to what I have done, O nations far away! And you that are near, acknowledge my might!

Isa 50:10. Who among you fears the Lord and obeys his Servant? . . . Let them trust the Lord, let them rely upon their God. Isa 51:13.

Isa 59:19. Then at last they will reverence and glorify the name of God from west to east.

Jer 5:22. Have you no respect at all for me? the Lord God asks. How can it be that you don't even tremble in my presence? I set the shorelines of the world by perpetual decrees, so that the oceans, though they toss and roar, can never pass those bounds. Isn't such a God to be feared and worshiped? *vs.* 23, 24.

Jer 10:7. Who would not fear you, O King of nations? (And that title belongs to you alone!) Among all the wise men of the earth and in all the kingdoms of the world there isn't anyone like you.

Jer 32:39. And I will give them one heart and mind to worship me forever, for their own good and for the good of all their descendants. [40]. . . I will put a desire into their hearts to worship me, and they shall never leave me.

Jer 33:9. The people of the world will see the good I do for my people and will tremble with awe!

Hos 3:5. Afterward they will return to the Lord their God, and to the Messiah, their King, and they shall come trembling, submissive to the Lord and to his blessings, in the end times.

Mic 7:16. "All the world will stand amazed at what I will do for you, and be embarrassed at their puny might. They will stand in silent awe, deaf to all around them." [17]They will see what snakes they are, lowly as worms crawling from their holes. They will come trembling out from their fortresses to meet the Lord our God. They will fear him; they will stand in awe.

Zeph 1:7. Stand in silence in the presence of the Lord.

Zeph 3:7. I thought, "Surely they will listen to me now—surely they will heed my warnings, so that I'll not need to strike again."

Zech 2:13. Be silent, all mankind, before the Lord, for he has come to earth from heaven, from his holy home.

Mal 1:6. A son honors his father, a servant honors his master. I am your Father and Master, yet you don't honor me, O priests, but you despise my name.

Mal 3:16. Then those who feared and loved the Lord spoke often of him to each other. And he had a Book of Remembrance drawn up in which he recorded the names of those who feared him and loved to think about him.

Mal 4:2. But for you who fear my name, the Sun

of Righteousness will rise with healing in his wings.

Mt 10:28. Don't be afraid of those who can kill only your bodies—but can't touch your souls! Fear only God who can destroy both soul and body in hell.

Lk 1:50. His mercy goes on from generation to generation, to all who reverence him.

Lk 12:5. But I'll tell you whom to fear—fear God who has the power to kill and then cast into hell.

Lk 23:40. But the other criminal protested. "Don't you even fear God when you are dying?"

Acts 10:35. In every nation he has those who worship him and do good deeds and are acceptable to him.

Acts 13:16. So Paul stood, waved a greeting to them and began. "Men of Israel," he said, "and all others here who reverence God, [let me begin my remarks with a bit of history]. [26]Brothers—you sons of Abraham, and also all of you Gentiles here who reverence God—this salvation is for all of us!" Acts 9:31.

2 Cor 7:1. Let us turn away from everything wrong, whether of body or spirit, and purify ourselves, living in the wholesome fear of God, giving ourselves to him alone.

Phil 2:12. Do the good things that result from being saved, obeying God with deep reverence, shrinking back from all that might displease him.

Col 3:22. You slaves must always obey your earthly masters, not only trying to please them when they are watching you but all the time; obey them willingly because of your love for the Lord and because you want to please him.

Heb 5:7. And God heard his prayers because of his strong desire to obey God at all times.

Heb 12:28. Since we have a kingdom nothing can destroy, let us please God by serving him with thankful hearts, and with holy fear and awe. [29]For our God is a consuming fire.

Jas 2:19. Believing in one God? Well, remember that the demons believe this too—so strongly that they tremble in terror!

1 Pet 1:17. He will judge you with perfect justice for everything you do; so act in reverent fear of him from now on until you get to heaven.

1 Jn 4:16. We know how much God loves us because we have felt his love and because we believe him when he tells us that he loves us dearly. God is love, and anyone who lives in love is living with God and God is living in him. [17]And as we live with Christ, our love grows more perfect and complete; so we will not be ashamed and embarrassed at the day of judgment, but can face him with confidence and joy, because he loves us and we love him too. [18]We need have no fear of someone who loves us perfectly; his perfect love for us eliminates all dread of what he might do to us. If we are afraid, it is for fear of what he might do to us, and shows that we are not fully convinced that he really loves us.

Rev 11:18. It is time to judge the dead, and reward your servants—prophets and people alike, all who fear your Name, both great and small.

Rev 14:7. "Fear God." he shouted, "and extol his greatness. For the time has come when he will sit as Judge."

Rev 19:5. Praise our God, all you his servants, small and great who fear him.

CONSPICUOUS INSTANCES OF THOSE WHO FEARED. Noah, in building the ark, Heb 11:7. Abraham, tested in the offering of his son Isaac, Gen 22:12. Jacob, in the dream of the ladder, and the covenant of God, Gen 28:16, 17; 42:18. The midwives of Egypt, in refusing to take the lives of the Hebrew children, Ex 1:17, 21. The Egyptians, at the time of the hailstorm, Ex 9:20. The nine and one-half tribes of Israel west of Jordan, Josh 22: 15–20. Phinehas, in turning away the anger of God at the time of the plague, Num 25:11, with verses 6–15. Obadiah, in hiding one hundred prophets from Jezebel, 1 Kgs 18:3, 4. Jehoshaphat, in proclaiming a fast, when the land was about to be invaded by the armies of the Ammonites and Moabites, 2 Chron 20:3, of his neighboring kingdoms, 2 Chron 17:10; 20:29. Nehemiah, in his reform of the public administration, Neh 5:15. Hanani, which qualified him to be ruler over Jerusalem, Neh 7:2. Job, according to the testimony of Satan, Job 1:1,8; 2:3. David, Ps 5:7; 119:38. Hezekiah, in his treatment of the prophet Micah, who prophesied punishment against Jerusalem, Jer 26:19. Jonah, in the storm, Jon 1:9, 10. The Jews, in obeying the message from the Lord, Hag 1:12. The women at the tomb, Mt 28:8. Cornelius, who, with all his household, feared God, Acts 10:2.

See *Conviction, of Sin; Faith.*

CULTIVATED. Ex 3:5. "Don't come any closer," God told him. "Take off your shoes, for you are standing on holy ground."

Ex 19:12. Set boundary lines the people may not pass, and tell them, "Beware! Do not go up into the mountain, or even touch its boundaries; whoever does shall die— [13]no hand shall touch him, but he shall be stoned or shot to death with arrows, whether man or animal." Stay away from the mountain entirely until you hear a ram's horn sounding one long blast; then gather at the foot of the mountain!

Heb 12:18. You have not had to stand face to face with terror, flaming fire, gloom, darkness and a terrible storm, as the Israelites did at Mount Sinai when God gave them his laws. [19]For there was an awesome trumpet blast, and a voice with a message so terrible that the people begged God to stop speaking. [20]They staggered back under God's command that if even an animal touched the mountain it must die. [21]Moses himself was so frightened at the sight that he shook with terrible fear. [22]But you have come right up into Mount Zion, to the city of the living God, the heavenly Jerusalem, and to the gathering of countless happy angels; [23]and to the church, composed of all those registered in heaven; and to God who is Judge of all; and to the spirits of the redeemed in heaven, already made perfect; [24]and to Jesus himself, who has brought us his wonderful new agreement; and to the sprinkled blood which graciously forgives instead of crying out for vengeance as the blood of Abel did.

GUILTY. Job 15:20. A wicked man is always in trouble throughout his life. [21]He is surrounded by terrors, and if there are good days they will soon be gone. [22]He dares not go out into the darkness, lest he be murdered. [23,24]He wanders around begging for food. He lives in fear, distress, and anguish. His enemies conquer him as a king defeats his foes. [25,26]Armed with his tin shield, he clenches his fist against God, defying the Almighty, stubbornly assaulting him.

Job 18:11. He has good cause for fear—his enemy is close behind him!

Prov 1:24. I have called you so often but still you won't come. I have pleaded, but all in vain. [25]For you have spurned my counsel and reproof. [26]Some day you'll be in trouble, and I'll laugh! Mock me, will you?—I'll mock you! [27]When a storm of terror surrounds you, and when you are engulfed by anguish and distress.

Prov 10:24. The wicked man's fears will all come true.

Dan 5:6. His face blanched with fear, and such terror gripped him that his knees knocked together and his legs gave way beneath him.

Jas 2:19. Well, remember that the demons believe this too—so strongly that they tremble in terror!

INSTANCES OF GUILTY FEAR. Adam and Eve, Gen 3:8–13. The guards at Jesus' tomb, Mt 28:4. Thief on the cross, Lk 23:40. Judas, Mt 27:3–5. Demons, Jas 2:19.

See *Conviction, of Sin.*

A MOTIVE OF OBEDIENCE. Lev 19:14. You must not curse the deaf nor trip up a blind man as he walks. Fear your God; I am Jehovah! [32]You shall give due honor and respect to the elderly, in the fear of God. I am Jehovah. Mal 3:5.

Lev 25:17. You must fear your God and not overcharge! For I am Jehovah. [36]Fear your God and let your brother live with you; and don't charge him interest on the money you lend him. [43]Fear your God.

Num 32:15. If you turn away from God like this, he will make the people stay even longer in the wilderness, and you will be responsible for destroying his people and bringing disaster to this entire nation!

Deut 6:13. When you are full, don't forget to be reverent to him and to serve him and to use *his* name alone to endorse your promises. [14]You must not worship the gods of the neighboring nations, [15]for Jehovah your God who lives among you is a jealous God, and his anger may rise quickly against you, and wipe you off the face of the earth.

Deut 7:4. That would surely result in your young people's beginning to worship their gods. Then the anger of the Lord would be hot against you and he would surely destroy you.

Deut 8:5. So you should realize that, as a man punishes his son, the Lord punishes you to help you. [6]Obey the laws of the Lord your God. Walk in his ways and fear him.

Deut 10:12,13. And now, Israel, what does the Lord your God require of you except to listen carefully to all he says to you, and to obey for your own good the commandments I am giving you today, and to love him, and to worship him with all your hearts and souls? [20]You must fear the Lord your God and worship him and cling to him and take oaths by his name alone.

Deut 13:4. You must *never* worship any God but Jehovah; obey only his commands and cling to him. [6, 7]If your nearest relative or closest friend, even a brother, son, daughter, or beloved wife whispers to you to come and worship these foreign gods, [8]do not consent nor listen, and have no pity: Do not spare that person from the penalty; don't conceal his horrible suggestion. [9]Execute him! Your own hand shall be the first upon him to put him to death, then the hands of all the people. [10]Stone him to death because he has tried to draw you away from the Lord your God who brought you from the land of Egypt, the place of slavery. [11]Then all Israel will hear about his evil deed, and will fear such wickedness as this among you.

Deut 14:23. Bring this tithe to eat before the Lord your God at the place he shall choose as his sanctuary; this applies to your tithes of grain, new wine, olive oil, and the firstborn of your flocks and herds. The purpose of tithing is to teach you always to put God first in your lives.

Deut 15:9. Beware! Don't refuse a loan because the year of debt cancellation is close at hand! If you refuse to make the loan and the needy man cries out to the Lord, it will be counted against you as a sin.

Deut 17:11. The sentence he imposes is to be fully executed. [12]If the defendant refuses to accept the decision of the priest or judge appointed by God for this purpose, the penalty is death. Such sinners must be purged from Israel. [13]Then everyone will hear about what happened to the man who refused God's verdict, and they will be afraid to defy the court's judgment a second time.

Deut 19:16. If anyone gives false witness, claiming he has seen someone do wrong when he hasn't, [17]both men shall be brought before the priests and judges on duty before the Lord at the time. [18]They must be closely questioned, and if the witness is lying, [19]his penalty shall be the punishment he thought the other man would get. In this way you will purge out evil from among you. [20]Then those who hear about it will be afraid to tell lies on the witness stand.

Deut 21:18. If a man has a stubborn, rebellious son who will not obey his father or mother, even though they punish him, [19]then his father and mother shall take him before the elders of the city [20]and declare, "This son of ours is stubborn and rebellious and won't obey; he is a worthless drunkard." [21]Then the men of the city shall stone him to death. In this way you shall put away this evil from among you, and all the young men of Israel will hear about what happened and will be afraid.

Deut 28:14. But each of these blessings depends on your not turning aside in any way from the laws

I have given you; and you must never worship
other gods. [15-19]If you won't listen to the Lord your
God and won't obey these laws I am giving you
today, then all of these curses shall come upon you:
curses in the city; curses in the fields; curses on
your fruit and bread; the curse of barren wombs;
curses upon your crops; curses upon the fertility of
your cattle and flocks; curses when you come in;
curses when you go out. [20]For the Lord himself will
send his personal curse upon you. You will be
confused and a failure in everything you do, until
at last you are destroyed because of the sin of
forsaking him. [21]He will send disease among you
until you are destroyed from the face of the land
which you are about to enter and possess. [22]He will
send tuberculosis, fever, infections, plague, and
war. He will blight your crops, covering them with
mildew. All these devastations shall pursue you
until you perish. [23]The heavens above you will be
as unyielding as bronze, and the earth beneath will
be as iron. [24]The land will become as dry as dust
for lack of rain, and dust storms shall destroy you.
[25]The Lord will cause you to be defeated by your
enemies. You will march out to battle gloriously,
but flee before your enemies in utter confusion; and
you will be tossed to and fro among all the nations
of the earth. [26]Your dead bodies will be food to the
birds and wild animals, and no one will be there to
chase them away. [27]He will send upon you Egyptian boils, tumors, scurvy, and itch, for none of
which will there be a remedy. [28]He will send madness, blindness, fear, and panic upon you. [29]You
shall grope in the bright sunlight just as the blind
man gropes in darkness. You shall not prosper in
anything you do; you will be oppressed and robbed
continually, and nothing will save you. [30]Someone
else will marry your fiancee; someone else will live
in the house you build; someone else will eat the
fruit of the vineyard you plant. [31]Your oxen shall
be butchered before your eyes, but you won't get
a single bit of the meat. Your donkeys will be
driven away as you watch, and will never return to
you again. Your sheep will be given to your enemies. And there will be no one to protect you.
[32]You will watch as your sons and daughters are
taken away as slaves. Your heart will break with
longing for them, but you will not be able to help
them. [33]A foreign nation you have not even heard
of will eat the crops you will have worked so hard
to grow. You will always be oppressed and
crushed. [34]You will go mad because of all the tragedy you see around you. [35]The Lord will cover you
with boils from head to foot. [36]He will exile you and
the king you will choose, to a nation to whom
neither you nor your ancestors gave a second
thought; and while in exile you shall worship gods
of wood and stone! [37]You will become an object of
horror, a proverb and a byword among all the
nations, for the Lord will thrust you away. [38]You
will sow much but reap little, for the locusts will
eat your crops. [39]You will plant vineyards and care
for them, but you won't eat the grapes or drink the
wine, for worms will destroy the vines. [40]Olive trees
will be growing everywhere, but there won't be
enough olive oil to anoint yourselves! For the trees
will drop their fruit before it is matured. [41]Your
sons and daughters will be snatched away from you
as slaves. [42]The locusts shall destroy your trees and
vines. [43]Foreigners living among you shall become
richer and richer while you become poorer and
poorer. [44]They shall lend to you, not you to them!
They shall be the head and you shall be the tail!
[45]All these curses shall pursue and overtake you
until you are destroyed—all because you refuse to
listen to the Lord your God. [46]These horrors shall
befall you and your descendants as a warning:
[47, 48]You will become slaves to your enemies because of your failure to praise God for all that he
has given you. The Lord will send your enemies
against you, and you will be hungry, thirsty, naked,
and in want of everything. A yoke of iron shall be
placed around your neck until you are destroyed!
[49]The Lord will bring a distant nation against you,
swooping down upon you like an eagle; a nation
whose language you don't understand—[50]a nation
of fierce and angry men who will have no mercy
upon young or old. [51]They will eat you out of house
and home until your cattle and crops are gone.
Your grain, new wine, olive oil, calves, and lambs
will all disappear. [52]That nation will lay siege to
your cities and knock down your highest walls—
the walls you will trust to protect you. [53]You will
even eat the flesh of your own sons and daughters
in the terrible days of siege that lie ahead. [54]The
most tenderhearted man among you will be utterly
callous toward his own brother and his beloved
wife and his children who are still alive. [55]He will
refuse to give them a share of the flesh he is devouring—the flesh of his own children—because he is
starving in the midst of the siege of your cities.
[56, 57]The most tender and delicate woman among
you—the one who would not so much as touch her
feet to the ground—will refuse to share with her
beloved husband, son, and daughter. She will hide
from them the afterbirth and the new baby she has
borne, so that she herself can eat them: so terrible
will be the hunger during the siege and the awful
distress caused by your enemies at your gates.
[58, 59]If you refuse to obey all the laws written in this
book, thus refusing reverence to the glorious and
fearful name of Jehovah your God, then Jehovah
will send perpetual plagues upon you and upon
your children. [60]He will bring upon you all the
diseases of Egypt which you feared so much, and
they shall plague the land. [61]And that is not all! The
Lord will bring upon you every sickness and
plague there is, even those not mentioned in this
book, until you are destroyed. [62]There will be few
of you left, though before you were as numerous as
stars. All this if you do not listen to the Lord your
God. [63]Just as the Lord has rejoiced over you and
has done such wonderful things for you and has
multiplied you, so the Lord at that time will rejoice
in destroying you; and you shall disappear from
the land. [64]For the Lord will scatter you among all
the nations from one end of the earth to the other.

There you will worship heathen gods that neither you nor your ancestors have known, gods made of wood and stone! [65]There among those nations you shall find no rest, but the Lord will give you trembling hearts, darkness, and bodies wasted from sorrow and fear. [66]Your lives will hang in doubt. You will live night and day in fear, and will have no reason to believe that you will see the morning light. [67]In the morning you will say, "Oh, that night were here!" And in the evening you will say, "Oh, that morning were here!" You will say this because of the awesome horrors surrounding you. [68]Then the Lord will send you back to Egypt in ships, a journey I promised you would never need to make again; and there you will offer to sell yourselves to your enemies as slaves—but no one will even want to buy you.

Deut 31:10, 11. The Lord commanded that these laws be read to all the people . . . when all Israel would assemble before the Lord at the sanctuary. [12]"Call them all together," the Lord instructed, " —men, women, children, and foreigners living among you—to hear the laws of God and to learn his will, so that you will reverence the Lord your God and obey his laws. [13]Do this so that your little children who have not known these laws will hear them and learn how to revere the Lord your God as long as you live in the Promised Land." Josh 23: 11–16.

1 Sam 12:24. Trust the Lord and sincerely worship him; think of all the tremendous things he has done for you. [25]But if you continue to sin, you and your king will be destroyed. *vs.* 14, 15.

Job 13:21. Don't abandon me. And don't terrify me with your awesome presence.

Job 31:1. I made a covenant with my eyes not to look with lust upon a girl. [2, 3]I know full well that Almighty God above sends calamity on those who do. [4]He sees everything I do, and every step I take. [13]If I have been unfair to my servants, [14]how could I face God? What could I say when he questioned me about it? [15]For God made me, and made my servant too. He created us both. [23]Rather that than face the judgment sent by God; that I dread more than anything else. For if the majesty of God opposes me, what hope is there?

Ps 36:1. Sin lurks deep in the hearts of the wicked, forever urging them on to evil deeds. They have no fear of God to hold them back.

Prov 16:6. Iniquity is atoned for by mercy and truth; evil is avoided by reverence for God.

Isa 1:20. But if you keep on turning your backs and refusing to listen to me, you will be killed by your enemies; I, the Lord, have spoken.

Jer 4:4. Cleanse your minds and hearts, not just your bodies, or else my anger will burn you to a crisp because of all your sins. And no one will be able to put the fire out.

Jer 22:5. But if you refuse to pay attention to this warning, I swear by my own name, says the Lord, that this palace shall become a shambles.

Mt 10:28. Don't be afraid of those who can kill only your bodies—but can't touch your souls! Fear only God who can destroy both soul and body in hell. Lk 12:4, 5.

2 Cor 5:10. For we must all stand before Christ to be judged and have our lives laid bare—before him. Each of us will receive whatever he deserves for the good or bad things he has done in his earthly body. [11]It is because of this solemn fear of the Lord, which is ever present in our minds, that we work so hard to win others.

2 Tim 4:1. And so I solemnly urge you before God and before Christ Jesus—who will some day judge the living and the dead when he appears to set up his kingdom—[2]to preach the Word of God urgently at all times, whenever you get the chance, in season and out, when it is convenient and when it is not. Correct and rebuke your people when they need it, encourage them to do right, and all the time be feeding them patiently with God's Word.

2 Pet 3:10. The day of the Lord is surely coming, as unexpectedly as a thief, and then the heavens will pass away with a terrible noise and the heavenly bodies will disappear in fire, and the earth and everything on it will be burned up. [11]And so since everything around us is going to melt away, what holy, godly lives we should be living! [12]You should look forward to that day and hurry it along—the day when God will set the heavens on fire, and the heavenly bodies will melt and disappear in flames.

Rev 14:9. Then a third angel followed them shouting, "Anyone worshiping the Creature from the sea and his statute and accepting his mark on the forehead or the hand, [10]must drink the wine of the anger of God; it is poured out undiluted into God's cup of wrath. And they will be tormented with fire and burning sulphur in the presence of the holy angels and the Lamb.

See *Punishment, Design of, to Secure Obedience; Reward, a Motive for Faithfulness.*

FEASTS Ancient customs at: Men alone present at, Gen 40:20; 43:32, 34; 1 Sam 9:22; Esther 1: 8; Mk 6:21; women alone, Esther 1:9. Men and women attend, Ex 32:6, with vs. 2, 3; Dan 5:1–4. Riddles propounded at, Judg 14:12. Marriage feasts provided by the bridegroom, Judg 14:10, 17. Guests arranged according to age, Gen 43:33; rank, 1 Sam 9:22; Lk 14:8–10. Reclined on couches, Amos 6:4, 7; Jn 13:23–25. Served in one dish, Mt 26:23. Were presided over by a master of ceremonies, Jn 2:7–9. Host served, Gen 18:8. Wine served at, Esther 5:6; 7:2. Music at, Isa 5:12; Amos 6:5; Lk 15: 25. Dancing at, Mt 14:6; Lk 15:25. Given by kings, 1 Sam 20:5; 25:36; 2 Sam 9:10, 11, 1 Kgs 2:7; 4:22; 18:19; Esther 1:1–8; Dan 5:1–4. Drunkenness at, 1 Sam 25:36; Esther 1:10; Dan 5:1–4.

Covenants ratified by, Gen 26:28–30. Celebrations by: Birthdays, Gen 40:20; Mk 6:21; coronations, 1 Kgs 1:25; 1 Chron 12:38–40; national deliverances, Esther 8:17; 9:17–19.

FIGURATIVE. Mt 22:1–14; Lk 14:16–24; Rev 19: 9, 17.

ANNUAL FESTIVALS. Instituted by Moses, Lev 23:4; Num 15:3; 29:39; 2 Chron 8:13; Ezra 3:5, Isa 1:14; Lam 2:6; Ezk 46:9. First and last days were

Sabbatic, Lev 23:39, 40; Num 28:18–25; 29:12, 35; Neh 8:1–18. Kept with rejoicing, Lev 23:40; Deut 16:11–14; 2 Chron 30:21–26; Ezra 6:21, 22; Neh 8: 9–12, 17; Ps 42:45; 122:4; Isa 30:29; Zech 8:19. Divine protection given during, Ex 34:24.

The three principal, were *Passover* (Unleavened Bread), *Pentecost* (Harvest), *Tabernacles* (In-gathering), Ex 23:14–17; Lev 23. All males were required to attend, Ex 23:17; 34:23; Deut 16:16; Ps 122: 4; Lk 2:41, 42; Jn 4:45; 7. Aliens permitted to attend, Jn 12:20; Acts 2:1–11. Attended by women, 1 Sam 1:3, 9; Lk 2:41, 42. Observed: by Jesus, Mt 26: 17–19; Lk 2:41, 42; 22:15; Jn 2:13, 23; 5:1; 7:10; 10:22, 23; by Paul, Acts 18:21; 19:21; 20:6, 16; 24:11, 17.

See for full treatment of annual feasts, *Passover; Pentecost; Purim; Tabernacles; Trumpets.*

FEBRUARY See *Calendar.*

FEET Bells worn on, Isa 3:16, 18. Washing of, as an example, by Jesus, Jn 13:4–14. Sitting at, Lk 10:39; Acts 22:3.

See *Ablution.*

FELIX Governor of Judea. Paul tried before, Acts 23:23–35; 24. Trembles under Paul's preaching, Acts 24:25. Leaves Paul in prison, Acts 24:26, 27; 25:14.

FELLOWSHIP INDEX OF SUB-TOPICS. *With God; With Christ; Of the Holy Spirit; Of the Righteous; With the Wicked; With the Wicked Forbidden; With the Wicked Exemplified; Instances of Those Who Avoided Fellowship with the Wicked.*

Eccl 4:9. Two can accomplish more than twice as much as one, for the results can be much better. [10]If one falls, the other pulls him up; but if a man falls when he is alone, he's in trouble. [11]Also, on a cold night, two under the same blanket gain warmth from each other, but how can one be warm alone? [12]And one standing alone can be attacked and defeated, but two can stand back-to-back and conquer; three is even better, for a triple-braided cord is not easily broken.

Amos 3:3. For how can we walk together with your sins between us?

See *Fraternity.*

WITH GOD. Gen 5:21–24. Enoch was sixty-five years old when his son Methuselah was born. Afterwards he lived another 300 years in fellowship with God, and produced sons and daughters; then, when he was 365, and in constant touch with God, he disappeared, for God took him!

Gen 6:8. But Noah was a pleasure to the Lord. Here is the story of Noah: [9]He was the only truly righteous man living on the earth at that time. He tried always to conduct his affairs according to God's will.

Ex 29:45. And I will live among the people of Israel and be their God.

Ex 33:14. And the Lord replied, "I myself will go with you and give you success." [15]For Moses had said, "If you aren't going with us, don't let us move a step from this place. [16]If you don't go with us, who will ever know that I and my people have found favor with you, and that we are different from any other people upon the face of the earth?" [17]And the Lord had replied to Moses, "Yes, I will do what you have asked, for you have certainly found favor with me, and you are my friend."

Lev 26:12. I will walk among you and be your God, and you shall be my people.

Isa 57:15. The high and lofty one who inhabits eternity, the Holy One, says this: I live in that high and holy place where those with contrite, humble spirits dwell; and I refresh the humble and give new courage to those with repentant hearts.

Zech 2:10. "Sing, Jerusalem, and rejoice! For I have come to live among you," says the Lord.

Mk 9:37. Anyone who welcomes a little child like this in my name is welcoming me, and anyone who welcomes me is welcoming my Father who sent me!

Jn 14:23. Jesus replied, "Because I will only reveal myself to those who love me and obey me. The Father will love them too, and we will come to them and live with them."

Jn 17:21. My prayer for all of them is that they will be of one heart and mind, just as you and I are, Father—that just as you are in me and I am in you, so they will be in us, [23]I in them and you in me, all being perfected into one—so that the world will know you sent me and will understand that you love them as much as you love me.

2 Cor 6:16. And what union can there be between God's temple and idols? For you are God's temple, the home of the living God, and God has said of you, "I will live in them and walk among them, and I will be their God and they shall be my people."

2 Cor 13:11. I close my letter with these last words: Be happy. Grow in Christ. Pay attention to what I have said. Live in harmony and peace. And may the God of love and peace be with you.

1 Jn 1:3. Again I say, we are telling you about what we ourselves have actually seen and heard, so that you may share the fellowship and the joys we have with the Father and with Jesus Christ his Son. [5]God is Light and in him is no darkness at all. [6]So if we say we are his friends, but go on living in spiritual darkness and sin, we are lying. [7]But if we are living in the light of God's presence, just as Christ does, then we have wonderful fellowship and joy with each other, and the blood of Jesus his Son cleanses us from every sin.

1 Jn 3:24. Those who do what God says—they are living with God and he with them. We know this is true because the Holy Spirit he has given us tells us so.

Rev 21:3. I heard a loud shout from the throne saying, "Look, the home of God is now among men, and he will live with them and they will be his people; yes, God himself will be among them. [4]He will wipe away all tears from their eyes, and there shall be no more death, now sorrow, nor crying, nor pain. All of that has gone forever."

See *Communion, with God.*

WITH CHRIST. Mt 12:48. He remarked, "Who is my mother? Who are my brothers?" [49]He pointed to his disciples. "Look!" he said, "these are my mother and brothers." [50]Then he added, "Anyone who obeys my Father in heaven is my brother, sister and mother!" Lk 8:21.

Mt 18:20. For where two or three gather together because they are mine, I will be right there among them.

Mk 9:37. Anyone who welcomes a little child like this in my name is welcoming me, and anyone who welcomes me is welcoming my Father who sent me!

Lk 24:32. They began telling each other how their hearts had felt strangely warm as he talked with them and explained the Scriptures during the walk down the road.

Jn 6:53. Unless you eat the flesh of the Messiah and drink his blood, you cannot have eternal life within you. [56]Everyone who eats my flesh and drinks my blood is in me, and I in him. *vs.* 47–58.

Jn 14:20. "When I come back to life again, you will know that I am in my Father, and you in me, and I in you. [21]The one who obeys me is the one who loves me; and because he loves me, my Father will love him; and I will too, and I will reveal myself to him." [22]Judas (not Judas Iscariot, but his other disciple with that name) said to him, "Sir, why are you going to reveal yourself only to us disciples and not to the world at large?" [23]Jesus replied, "Because I will only reveal myself to those who love me and obey me. The Father will love them too, and we will come to them and live with them."

Jn 15:4. Take care to live in me, and let me live in you. For a branch can't produce fruit when severed from the vine. Nor can you be fruitful apart from me. [5]Yes, I am the Vine; you are the branches. Whoever lives in me and I in him shall produce a large crop of fruit. For apart from me you can't do a thing. [7]But if you stay in me and obey my commands, you may ask any request you like, and it will be granted! *vs.* 1–8.

Jn 17:21. My prayer for all of them is that they will be of one heart and mind, just as you and I are, Father—that just as you are in me and I am in you, so they will be in us, and the world will believe you sent me. [22]I have given them the glory you gave me —the glorious unity of being one, as we are—[23]I in them and you in me, all being perfected into one —so that the world will know you sent me and will understand that you love them as much as you love me. [26]And I have revealed you to them, and will keep on revealing you so that the mighty love you have for me may be in them, and I in them.

Rom 7:4. Your "husband," your master, used to be the Jewish law; but you "died," as it were, with Christ on the cross; and since you are "dead," you are no longer "married to the law," and it has no more control over you. Then you came back to life again when Christ did, and are a new person. And now you are "married," so to speak, to the one who rose from the dead, so that you can produce good fruit, that is, good deeds for God. Ps 45:9–16; Song, chapters 1–8.

Rom 8:1. So there is now no condemnation awaiting those who belong to Christ Jesus. [10]Yet, even though Christ lives within you, your body will die because of sin; but your spirit will live, for Christ has pardoned it. [17]And since we are his children, we will share his treasures—for all God gives to his Son Jesus is now ours too. But if we are to share his glory, we must also share his suffering.

Rom 11:17. And you Gentiles who were branches from, we might say, a wild olive tree, were grafted in. So now you, too, receive the blessing God has promised Abraham and his children, sharing in God's rich nourishment of his own special olive tree.

Rom 12:4, 5. Just as there are many parts to our bodies, so it is with Christ's body. We are all parts of it, and it takes every one of us to make it complete, for we each have different work to do. So we each belong to each other, and each needs all the others.

1 Cor 1:9. God will surely do this for you, for he always does just what he says, and he is the one who invited you into this wonderful friendship with his Son, even Christ our Lord.

1 Cor 6:13. But sexual sin is never right: our bodies were not made for that, but for the Lord, and the Lord wants to fill our bodies with himself. [14]And God is going to raise our bodies from the dead by his power just as he raised up the Lord Jesus Christ. [15]Don't you realize that your bodies are actually parts and members of Christ? [17]But if you give yourself to the Lord, you and Christ are joined together as one person.

1 Cor 10:16. When we ask the Lord's blessing upon our drinking from the cup of wine at the Lord's Table, this means, doesn't it, that all who drink it are sharing together the blessing of Christ's blood? And when we break off pieces of the bread from the loaf to eat there together, this shows that we are sharing together in the benefits of his body.

1 Cor 12:12. Our bodies have many parts, but the many parts make up only one body when they are all put together. So it is with the "body" of Christ. [27]All of you together are the one body of Christ and each one of you is a separate and necessary part of it.

2 Cor 11:2. I am anxious for you with the deep concern of God himself—anxious that your love should be for Christ alone, just as a pure maiden saves her love for one man only, for the one who will be her husband.

2 Cor 13:5. Do you feel Christ's presence and power more and more within you? Or are you just pretending to be Christians when actually you aren't at all?

Eph 5:29, 30. No one hates his own body but lovingly cares for it, just as Christ cares for his body the church, of which we are parts. [32]I know this is hard to understand, but it is an illustration of the way we are parts of the body of Christ.

Col 1:26, 27. He has kept this secret for centuries and generations past, but now at last it has pleased him to tell it to those who love him and live for him, and the riches and glory of his plan are for you Gentiles too. And this is the secret: *that Christ in your hearts is your only hope of glory.*

Col 3:3. You should have as little desire for this world as a dead person does. Your real life is in heaven with Christ and God.

1 Thess 5:9. For God has not chosen to pour out his anger upon us, but to save us through our Lord Jesus Christ; [10]he died for us so that we can live with him forever, whether we are dead or alive at the time of his return.

Heb 2:11. We who have been made holy by Jesus, now have the same Father he has. That is why Jesus is not ashamed to call us his brothers.

1 Jn 2:6. Anyone who says he is a Christian should live as Christ did. [24]So keep on believing what you have been taught from the beginning. If you do, you will always be in close fellowship with both God the Father and his Son. [28]And now, my little children, stay in happy fellowship with the Lord so that when he comes you will be sure that all is well, and will not have to be ashamed and shrink back from meeting him.

1 Jn 3:6. So if we stay close to him, obedient to him, we won't be sinning either. [24]Those who do what God says—they are living with God and he with them. We know this is true because the Holy Spirit he has given us tells us so.

1 Jn 4:13. And he has put his own Holy Spirit into our hearts as a proof to us that we are living with him and he with us.

1 Jn 5:12. So whoever has God's Son has life; whoever does not have his Son, does not have life. [20]And we know that Christ, God's Son, has come to help us understand and find the true God. And now we are in God because we are in Jesus Christ his Son, who is the only true God; and he is eternal Life.

2 Jn 1:9. If you are loyal to Christ's teachings, you will have God too. Then you will have both the Father and the Son.

Rev 3:20. Look! I have been standing at the door and I am constantly knocking. If anyone hears me calling him and opens the door, I will come in and fellowship with him and he with me.

See *Communion.*

OF THE HOLY SPIRIT. Rom 8:9. But you are not like that. You are controlled by your new nature if you have the Spirit of God living in you. (And remember that if anyone doesn't have the Spirit of Christ living in him, he is not a Christian at all.)

1 Cor 3:16. Don't you realize that all of you together are the house of God, and that the Spirit of God lives among you in his house?

2 Cor 13:14. May the grace of our Lord Jesus Christ be with you all. May God's love and the Holy Spirit's friendship be yours.

See *Communion; Holy Spirit.*

OF THE RIGHTEOUS. Ps 55:14. What fellowship we had, what wonderful discussions as we walked together to the Temple of the Lord on holy days.

Ps 119:63. Anyone is my brother who fears and trusts the Lord and obeys him.

Amos 3:3. For how can we walk together with your sins between us?

Mal 3:16. Then those who feared and loved the Lord spoke often of him to each other. And he had a Book of Remembrance drawn up in which he recorded the names of those who feared him and loved to think about him.

Mt 17:4. Peter blurted out, "Sir, it's wonderful that we can be here! If you want me to, I'll make three shelters, one for you and one for Moses and one for Elijah."

Mt 20:25. But Jesus called them together and said, "Among the heathen, kings are tyrants and each minor official lords it over those beneath him. [26]But among you it is quite different. Anyone wanting to be a leader among you must be your servant. [27]And if you want to be right at the top, you must serve like a slave. [28]Your attitude must be like my own, for I, the Messiah, did not come to be served, but to serve, and to give my life as a ransom for many."

Mt 23:8. Don't ever let anyone call you that. For only God is your Rabbi and all of you are on the same level, as brothers.

Mk 10:42. So Jesus called them to him and said, "As you know, the kings and great men of the earth lord it over the people; [43]but among you it is different. Whoever wants to be great among you must be your servant. [44]And whoever wants to be greatest of all must be the slave of all. [45]For even I, the Messiah, am not here to be served, but to help others, and to give my life as a ransom for many."

Lk 22:32. So when you have repented and turned to me again, strengthen and build up the faith of your brothers.

Lk 24:13. That same day, Sunday, two of Jesus' followers were walking to the village of Emmaus, seven miles out of Jerusalem. [14]As they walked along they were talking of Jesus' death, [15]when suddenly Jesus himself came along and joined them and began walking beside them.

Jn 13:34. And so I am giving a new commandment to you now—love each other just as much as I love you.

Jn 15:12. I demand that you love each other as much as I love you.

Jn 17:11. Now I am leaving the world, and leaving them behind, and coming to you. Holy Father, keep them in your own care—all those you have given me—so that they will be united just as we are, with none missing. [21]My prayer for all of them is that they will be of one heart and mind, just as you and I are, Father—that just as you are in me and I am in you, so they will be in us, and the world will believe you sent me. [22]I have given them the glory you gave me—the glorious unity of being one, as we are—[23]I in them and you in me, all being perfected into one—so that the world will know you sent me and will understand that you love them as much as you love me.

Acts 1:14. Here is the list of those who were present at the meeting: Peter, John, James, Andrew, Philip, Thomas, Bartholomew, Matthew, James (son of Alphaeus), Simon (also called "The Zealot"), Judas (son of James), and the brothers of Jesus. Several women, including Jesus' mother, were also there. [15]This prayer meeting went on for several days.

Acts 2:1. The Day of Pentecost had now arrived. As the believers met together that day. [42]They joined with the other believers in regular attendance at the apostles' teaching sessions and at the Communion services and prayer meetings. [44]And all the believers met together constantly and shared everything with each other, [45]selling their possessions and dividing with those in need. [46]They worshiped together regularly at the Temple each day, met in small groups in homes for Communion, and shared their meals with great joy and thankfulness, [47]praising God. The whole city was favorable to them, and each day God added to them all who were being saved.

Acts 17:4. Some who listened were persuaded and became converts—including a large number of godly Greek men, and also many important women of the city.

Acts 20:35. And I was a constant example to you in helping the poor; for I remembered the words of the Lord Jesus, "It is more blessed to give than to receive."

Rom 1:12. Then, too, I need your help, for I want not only to share my faith with you but to be encouraged by yours: Each of us will be a blessing to the other.

Rom 14:1. Give a warm welcome to any brother who wants to join you, even though his faith is weak. Don't criticize him for having different ideas from yours about what is right and wrong. [2]For instance, don't argue with him about whether or not to eat meat that has been offered to idols. You may believe there is no harm in this, but the faith of others is weaker; they think it is wrong, and will go without any meat at all and eat vegetables rather than eat that kind of meat. [3]Those who think it is all right to eat such meat must not look down on those who won't. And if you are one of those who won't, don't find fault with those who do. For God has accepted them to be his children. [4]They are God's servants, not yours. They are responsible to him, not to you. Let him tell them whether they are right or wrong. And God is able to make them do as they should. [10]You have no right to criticize your brother or look down on him. Remember, each of us will stand personally before the Judgment Seat of God. [13]So don't criticize each other any more. Try instead to live in such a way that you will never make your brother stumble by letting him see you doing something he thinks is wrong. [14]As for myself, I am perfectly sure on the authority of the Lord Jesus that there is nothing really wrong with eating meat that has been offered to idols. But if someone believes it is wrong, then he shouldn't do it because for him it is wrong. [15]And if your brother is bothered by what you eat, you are not acting in love if you go ahead and eat it. Don't let your eating ruin someone for whom Christ died. [16]Don't do anything that will cause criticism against yourself even though you know that what you do is right. [18]If you let Christ be Lord in these affairs, God will be glad; and so will others. [19]In this way aim for harmony in the church and try to build each other up. [20]Don't undo the work of God for a chunk of meat. Remember, there is nothing wrong with the meat, but it is wrong to eat it if it makes another stumble. [21]The right thing to do is to quit eating meat or drinking wine or doing anything else that offends your brother or makes him sin.

Rom 15:1, 2. Even if we believe that it makes no difference to the Lord whether we do these things, still we cannot just go ahead and do them to please ourselves; for we must bear the "burden" of being considerate of the doubts and fears of others—of those who feel these things are wrong. Let's please the other fellow, not ourselves, and do what is for his good and thus build him up in the Lord. [3]Christ didn't please himself. As the Psalmist said, "He came for the very purpose of suffering under the insults of those who were against the Lord." [4]These things that were written in the Scriptures so long ago are to teach us patience and to encourage us, so that we will look forward expectantly to the time when God will conquer sin and death. [5]May God who gives patience, steadiness, and encouragement help you to live in complete harmony with each other—each with the attitude of Christ toward the other. [6]And then all of us can praise the Lord together with one voice, giving glory to God, the Father of our Lord Jesus Christ. [7]So, warmly welcome each other into the church, just as Christ has warmly welcomed you; then God will be glorified.

1 Cor 1:10. But, dear brothers, I beg you in the name of the Lord Jesus Christ to stop arguing among yourselves. Let there be real harmony so that there won't be splits in the church. I plead with you to be of one mind, united in thought and purpose.

1 Cor 10:16. When we ask the Lord's blessing upon our drinking from the cup of wine at the Lord's Table, this means, doesn't it, that all who drink it are sharing together the blessing of Christ's blood? And when we break off pieces of the bread from the loaf to eat there together, this shows that we are sharing together in the benefits of his body. [17]No matter how many of us there are, we all eat from the same loaf, showing that we are all parts of the one body of Christ.

1 Cor 12:13. Each of us is a part of the one body of Christ. Some of us are Jews, some are Gentiles, some are slaves and some are free. But the Holy Spirit has fitted us all together into one body. We have been baptized into Christ's body by the one Spirit, and have all been given that same Holy Spirit.

1 Cor 16:19. The churches here in Asia send you their loving greetings. Aquila and Priscilla send you their love and so do all the others who meet

in their home for their church service. [20]All the friends here have asked me to say "hello" to you for them. And give each other a loving handshake when you meet.

Gal 2:7, 8, 9. In fact, when Peter, James, and John, who were known as the pillars of the church, saw how greatly God had used me in winning the Gentiles, just as Peter had been blessed so greatly in his preaching to the Jews—for the same God gave us each our special gifts—they shook hands with Barnabas and me and encouraged us to keep right on with our preaching to the Gentiles while they continued their work with the Jews.

Gal 6:2. Share each other's troubles and problems, and so obey our Lord's command. [10]That's why whenever we can we should always be kind to everyone, and especially to our Christian brothers.

Eph 2:14. For Christ himself is our way of peace. He has made peace between us Jews and you Gentiles by making us all one family, breaking down the wall of contempt that used to separate us. [15]By his death he ended the angry resentment between us, caused by the Jewish laws which favored the Jews and excluded the Gentiles, for he died to annul that whole system of Jewish laws. Then he took the two groups that had been opposed to each other and made them parts of himself; thus he fused us together to become one new person, and at last there was peace. [16]As parts of the same body, our anger against each other has disappeared, for both of us have been reconciled to God. And so the feud ended at last at the cross. [17]And he has brought this Good News of peace to you Gentiles who were very far away from him, and to us Jews who were near. [18]Now all of us, whether Jews or Gentiles, may come to God the Father with the Holy Spirit's help because of what Christ has done for us. [19]Now you are no longer strangers to God and foreigners to heaven, but you are members of God's very own family, citizens of God's country, and you belong in God's household with every other Christian. [20]What a foundation you stand on now: the apostles and the prophets; and the cornerstone of the building is Jesus Christ himself! [21]We who believe are carefully joined together with Christ as parts of a beautiful, constantly growing temple for God. [22]And you also are joined with him and with each other by the Spirit, and are part of this dwelling place of God.

Eph 5:2. Be full of love for others, following the example of Christ who loved you and gave himself to God as a sacrifice to to take away your sins. And God was pleased, for Christ's love for you was like sweet perfume to him. [19]Talk with each other much about the Lord, quoting psalms and hymns and singing sacred songs, making music in your hearts to the Lord. [30]No one hates his own body but lovingly cares for it, just as Christ cares for his body the church, of which we are parts.

Phil 1:3. All my prayers for you are full of praise to God! [5]Because of all your wonderful help in making known the Good News about Christ from the time you first heard it until now. [27]But whatever happens to me, remember always to live as Christians should, so that, whether I ever see you again or not, I will keep on hearing good reports that you are standing side by side with one strong purpose —to tell the Good News.

Phil 2:1. Is there any such thing as Christians cheering each other up? Do you love me enough to want to help me? Does it mean anything to you that we are brothers in the Lord, sharing the same Spirit? Are your hearts tender and sympathetic at all? [2]Then make me truly happy by loving each other and agreeing wholeheartedly with each other, working together with one heart and mind and purpose.

Col 2:2. This is what I have asked of God for you: that you will be encouraged and knit together by strong ties of love, and that you will have the rich experience of knowing Christ with real certainty and clear understanding. *For God's secret plan, now at last made known, is Christ himself.*

Col 3:16. Remember what Christ taught and let his words enrich your lives and make you wise; teach them to each other and sing them out in psalms and hymns and spiritual songs, singing to the Lord with thankful hearts.

1 Thess 4:18. So comfort and encourage each other with this news.

1 Thess 5:11. So encourage each other to build each other up, just as you are already doing. [14]Dear brothers, warn those who are lazy; comfort those who are frightened; take tender care of those who are weak; and be patient with everyone.

Heb 3:13. Speak to each other about these things every day while there is still time, so that none of you will become hardened against God, being blinded by the glamor of sin.

Heb 10:24. Let us outdo each other in being helpful and kind to each other and in doing good. [25]Let us not neglect our church meetings, as some people do, but encourage and warn each other.

Heb 13:1. Continue to love each other with true brotherly love.

Jas 5:16. Admit your faults to one another and pray for each other so that you may be healed.

1 Pet 2:17. Love Christians everywhere.

1 Pet 3:8. And now this word to all of you: You should be like one big happy family, full of sympathy toward each other, loving one another with tender hearts and humble minds. [9]Don't repay evil for evil. Don't snap back at those who say unkind things about you. Instead, pray for God's help for them, for we are to be kind to others, and God will bless us for it.

1 Jn 1:3. Again I say, we are telling you about what we ourselves have actually seen and heard, so that you may share the fellowship and the joys we have with the Father and with Jesus Christ his Son. [7]But if we are living in the light of God's presence, just as Christ does, then we have wonderful fellowship and joy with each other.

1 Jn 3:14. If we love other Christians it proves that we have been delivered from hell and given eternal life. But a person who doesn't have love for

others is headed for eternal death.

1 Jn 4:7. Dear friends, let us practice loving each other, for love comes from God and those who are loving and kind show that they are the children of God, and that they are getting to know him better. [8]But if a person isn't loving and kind, it shows that he doesn't know God—for God is love. [11]Dear friends, since God loved us as much as that, we surely ought to love each other too. [12]For though we have never yet seen God, when we love each other God lives in us and his love within us grows ever stronger. [13]And he has put his own Holy Spirit into our hearts as a proof to us that we are living with him and he with us.

See *Communion, of Saints.*

WITH THE WICKED. Gen 49:6. O my soul, stay away from them. May I never be a party to their wicked plans. For in their anger they murdered a man, and maimed oxen just for fun.

Ex 33:15. For Moses had said, "If you aren't going with us, don't let us move a step from this place. [16]If you don't go with us, who will ever know that I and my people have found favor with you, and that we are different from any other people upon the face of the earth?"

Ex 34:13. Instead, you must break down their heathen altars, smash the obelisks they worship, and cut down their shameful idols. [14]For you must worship no other gods, but only Jehovah, for he is a God who claims absolute loyalty and exclusive devotion. [15]No, do not make a peace treaty of any kind with the people living in the land, for they are spiritual prostitutes, committing adultery against me by sacrificing to their gods. If you become friendly with them and one of them invites you to go with him and worship his idol, you are apt to do it. [Deut 31:16, 17.] [16]And you would accept their daughters, who worship other gods, as wives for your sons—and then your sons would commit adultery against me by worshiping their wives' gods.

Num 25:1. While Israel was camped at Acacia, some of the young men began going to wild parties with the local Moabite girls. [2]These girls also invited them to attend the sacrifices to their gods, and soon the men were not only attending the feasts, but also bowing down and worshiping the idols. [3]Before long all Israel was joining freely in the worship of Baal, the god of Moab; and the anger of the Lord was hot against his people. [4]He issued the following command to Moses: "Execute all the tribal leaders of Israel. Hang them up before the Lord in broad daylight, so that his fierce anger will turn away from the people." [5]So Moses ordered the judges to execute all who had worshiped Baal.

6. But one of the Israeli men insolently brought a Midianite girl into the camp, right before the eyes of Moses and all the people, as they were weeping at the door of the Tabernacle. [7]When Phinehas (son of Eleazar and grandson of Aaron the priest) saw this, he jumped up, grabbed a spear, [8]and rushed after the man into his tent, where he had taken the girl. He thrust the spear all the way through the man's body and into her stomach. So the plague was stopped.

Josh 23:12. If you don't, and if you begin to intermarry with the nations around you, [13]then know for a certainty that the Lord your God will no longer chase those nations from your land. Instead, they will be a snare and a trap to you, a pain in your side and a thorn in your eyes, and you will disappear from this good land which the Lord your God has given you.

Ezra 6:21, 22. And some of the heathen people who had been relocated in Judah turned from their immoral customs and joined the Israelis in worshiping the Lord God. They, with the entire nation, ate the Passover feast and celebrated the Feast of Unleavened Bread for seven days.

Ezra 9:14. We have broken your commandments again and intermarried with people who do these awful things. Surely your anger will destroy us now until not even this little remnant escapes.

Ps 6:8. Go, leave me now, you men of evil deeds, for the Lord has heard my weeping.

Ps 26:4. I do not have fellowship with tricky, two-faced men; they are false and hypocritical. [5]I hate the sinners' hangouts and refuse to enter them.

Ps 50:18. You see a thief and help him, and spend your time with evil and immoral men.

Ps 102:7. I lie awake, lonely as a solitary sparrow on the roof. *vs.* 6–8.

Prov 28:19. Hard work brings prosperity; playing around brings poverty. chapter 12:11.

Prov 29:24. A man who assists a thief must really hate himself! For he knows the consequence but does it anyway.

1 Cor 5:11. What I meant was that you are not to keep company with anyone who claims to be a brother Christian but indulges in sexual sins, or is greedy, or is a swindler, or worships idols, or is a drunkard, or abusive. Don't even eat lunch with such a person.

1 Cor 15:33. Don't be fooled by those who say such things. If you listen to them you will start acting like them.

2 Pet 2:18. They proudly boast about their sins and conquests, and, using lust as their bait, they lure back into sin those who have just escaped from such wicked living. [19]"You aren't saved by being good," they say, "so you might as well be bad. Do what you like, be free." But these very teachers who offer this "freedom" from law are themselves slaves to sin and destruction. For a man is a slave to whatever controls him.

2 Pet 3:17. I am warning you ahead of time, dear brothers, so that you can watch out and not be carried away by the mistakes of these wicked men, lest you yourselves become mixed up too.

See the following sub-topics:

Punishment of. Num 33:56; Josh 23:13; Judg 2:3; 3:5–8; Ezra 9:7, 14; Ps 106:41, 42; Rev 2:16, 22, 23.

See *Company, Evil; Influence.*

WITH THE WICKED FORBIDDEN. Ex 23:32.

You must make no covenant with them, nor have anything to do with their gods. [33]Don't let them live among you! For I know that they will infect you with their sin of worshiping false gods, and that would be an utter disaster to you.

Ex 34:12. Be very, very careful never to compromise with the people there in the land where you are going, for if you do, you will soon be following their evil ways. Judg 2:2.

Num 16:26. "Quick!" he told the people, "get away from the tents of these wicked men, and don't touch anything that belongs to them, lest you be included in their sins [and be destroyed with them]."

Deut 7:2. When the Lord your God delivers them over to you to be destroyed, do a complete job of it—don't make any treaties or show them mercy; utterly wipe them out. [3]Do not intermarry with them, nor let your sons and daughters marry their sons and daughters. [4]That would surely result in your young people's beginning to worship their gods. Then the anger of the Lord would be hot against you and he would surely destroy you. Deut 12:30; Ezra 9:1,2.

Deut 13:6, 7. If your nearest relative or closest friend, even a brother, son, daughter, or beloved wife whispers to you to come and worship these foreign gods, [8]do not consent nor listen, and have no pity: Do not spare that person from the penalty; don't conceal his horrible suggestion. [9]Execute him! Your own hand shall be the first upon him to put him to death, then the hands of all the people. [10]Stone him to death because he has tried to draw you away from the Lord your God who brought you from the land of Egypt, the place of slavery. [11]Then all Israel will hear about his evil deed, and will fear such wickedness as this among you.

Josh 23:6. But be very sure to follow all the instructions written in the book of the laws of Moses; do not deviate from them the least little bit. [7]Be sure that you do not mix with the heathen people still remaining in the land; do not even mention the names of their gods, much less swear by them or worship them.

13. Then know for a certainty that the Lord your God will no longer chase those nations from your land. Instead, they will be a snare and a trap to you, a pain in your side and a thorn in your eyes, and you will disappear from this good land which the Lord your God has given you.

Ezra 9:12. You told us not to let our daughters marry their sons, and not to let our sons marry their daughters, and not to help those nations in any way. You warned us that only if we followed this rule could we become a prosperous nation and forever leave that prosperity to our children as an inheritance.

Ezra 10:11. Confess your sin to the Lord God of your fathers and do what he demands: separate yourselves from the heathen people about you and from these women.

Ps 1:1. Oh, the joys of those who do not follow evil men's advice, who do not hang around with sinners, scoffing at the things of God.

Prov 1:10. If young toughs tell you, "Come and join us"—turn your back on them! [11]"We'll hide and rob and kill," they say. [12]"Good or bad, we'll treat them all alike. [13]And the loot we'll get! All kinds of stuff! [14]Come on, throw in your lot with us; we'll split with you in equal shares." [15]Don't do it, son! Stay far from men like that.

Prov 4:14. Don't do as the wicked do. [15]Avoid their haunts—turn away, go somewhere else.

Prov 9:6. Leave behind your foolishness and begin to live; learn how to be wise.

Prov 14:7. If you are looking for advice, stay away from fools.

Mt 18:17. If he still refuses to listen, then take your case to the church, and if the church's verdict favors you, but he won't accept it, then the church should excommunicate him.

Rom 16:17. And now there is one more thing to say before I end this letter. Stay away from those who cause divisions and are upsetting people's faith, teaching things about Christ that are contrary to what you have been taught.

1 Cor 5:9. When I wrote to you before I said not to mix with evil people. [10]But when I said that I wasn't talking about unbelievers who live in sexual sin, or are greedy cheats and thieves and idol worshipers. For you can't live in this world without being with people like that. [11]What I meant was that you are not to keep company with anyone who claims to be a brother Christian but indulges in sexual sins, or is greedy, or is a swindler, or worships idols, or is a drunkard, or abusive. Don't even eat lunch with such a person.

2 Cor 6:14. Don't be teamed with those who do not love the Lord, for what do the people of God have in common with the people of sin? How can light live with darkness? [15]And what harmony can there be between Christ and the devil? How can a Christian be a partner with one who doesn't believe? [16]And what union can there be between God's temple and idols? For you are God's temple, the home of the living God, and God has said of you, "I will live in them and walk among them, and I will be their God and they shall be my people." [17]That is why the Lord has said, "Leave them; separate yourselves from them; don't touch their filthy things, and I will welcome you."

Eph 5:11. Take no part in the worthless pleasures of evil and darkness, but instead, rebuke and expose them.

2 Thess 3:6. Now here is a command, dear brothers, given in the name of our Lord Jesus Christ by his authority: Stay away from any Christian who spends his days in laziness and does not follow the ideal of hard work we set up for you. [14]If anyone refuses to obey what we say in this letter, notice who he is and stay away from him, that he may be ashamed of himself. [15]Don't think of him as an enemy, but speak to him as you would to a brother who needs to be warned.

1 Tim 6:3. Some may deny these things, but they are the sound, wholesome teachings of the Lord

Jesus Christ and are the foundation for a godly life. [4]Anyone who says anything different is both proud and stupid. He is quibbling over the meaning of Christ's words and stirring up arguments ending in jealousy and anger, which only lead to name-calling, accusations, and evil suspicions. [5]These arguers—their minds warped by sin—don't know how to tell the truth; to them the Good News is just a means of making money. Keep away from them.

2 Tim 3:2. For people will love only themselves and their money; they will be proud and boastful, sneering at God, disobedient to their parents, ungrateful to them, and thoroughly bad. [3]They will be hardheaded and never give in to others; they will be constant liars and troublemakers and will think nothing of immorality. They will be rough and cruel, and sneer at those who try to be good. [4]They will betray their friends; they will be hotheaded, puffed up with pride, and prefer good times to worshiping God. [5]They will go to church, yes, but they won't really believe anything they hear. Don't be taken in by people like that. [6]They are the kind who craftily sneak into other people's homes and make friendships with silly, sin-burdened women and teach them their new doctrines. [7]Women of that kind are forever following new teachers, but they never understand the truth.

2 Pet 3:17. I am warning you ahead of time, dear brothers, so that you can watch out and not be carried away by the mistakes of these wicked men, lest you yourselves become mixed up too.

2 Jn 1:9. For if you wander beyond the teaching of Christ, you will leave God behind; while if you are loyal to Christ's teachings, you will have God too. Then you will have both the Father and the Son. [10]If anyone comes to teach you, and he doesn't believe what Christ taught, don't even invite him into your home. Don't encourage him in any way. [11]If you do you will be a partner with him in his wickedness.

Rev 18:1. After all this I saw another angel come down from heaven with great authority, and the earth grew bright with his splendor. [2]He gave a mighty shout, "Babylon the Great is fallen, is fallen; she has become a den of demons, a haunt of devils and every kind of evil spirit. [3]For all the nations have drunk the fatal wine of her intense immorality. The rulers of earth have enjoyed themselves with her, and businessmen throughout the world have grown rich from all her luxurious living." [4]Then I heard another voice calling from heaven, "Come away from her, my people; do not take part in her sins, or you will be punished with her."

The Evil of Fellowship with the Wicked Exemplified. By Solomon, 1 Kgs 11:1–8; Rehoboam, 1 Kgs 12:8, 9; Jehoshaphat, 2 Chron 18:2; 19:2; 20:35–37; Jehoram, 2 Chron 21:6; Ahaziah, 2 Chron 22:3–5; Israelites, Ezra 9:1, 2; Ezk 44:7; Judas Iscariot, Mt 26:14–16.

INSTANCES OF THOSE WHO AVOIDED FELLOWSHIP WITH THE WICKED. Prophet of God, 1 Kgs 13:7–10. Nehemiah, Neh 6:2–4; 10:29–31. David, Ps 101:4–7; 119:115. Jeremiah, Jer 15:17, 18. Joseph of Arimathea, Lk 23:50–52. Church of Ephesus, Rev 2:6.

See *Company, Evil; Influence, Evil.*

FENCE Song 4:12; Isa 5:5. Hedge, Nah 3:17; Mt 21:33; Hos 2:6. Of the Tabernacle, Num 3:25–30; 4:26, 32.

See *Walls.*

FERRYBOAT 2 Sam 19:18.

FERTILIZER Isa 25:10; Lk 13:8; 14:34, 35.

See *Manure.*

FESTIVALS See *Feasts.*

FESTUS Called also *Porcius Festus,* governor of Judea, and successor to Felix, Acts 24:27. Tries Paul, Acts 25.

FETTERS Ps 105:18.

See *Chains; Handcuffs; Shackles.*

FEVER Lev 26:16; Deut 28:22; Job 30:30; Mt 8:14; Mk 1:29, 30; Lk 4:38; Jn 4:52; Acts 28:8.

FICKLENESS See *Instability.*

FIG Common to Palestine, Num 13:23; Deut 8:8; to Egypt, Ps 105:33. Used as a remedy, 2 Kgs 20:7; Isa 38:21. Traffic in, Neh 13:15. Cakes of, 1 Sam 30:11, 12; 1 Kgs 14:3; sent by Abigail to David, 1 Sam 25:18–35. Aprons made of fig leaves, by Adam and Eve, Gen 3:7. Jeremiah's parable of, Jer 24:2, 3.

FIG TREE In an allegory, Judg 9:11. Barren, parable of, Lk 13:6–9; 21:29–31.

FIGURATIVE. Mt 24:32; Rev 6:13.

FIGHT OF FAITH 1 Tim 6:12; 2 Tim 4:7; Eph 6:12; Heb 10:32; 11:34. See 2 Chron 20:17.

FIGHTING See *Strife; War.*

FIGURE See *Figurative* under principal topics throughout the work. See also *Allegory; Pantomime; Parable; Symbols; Types.*

FINANCES Methods of raising money, see *Tribute; Temple; Money.*

FINE A penalty. Ex 22:1. If a man steals an ox or sheep and then kills or sells it, he shall pay a fine of five to one—five oxen shall be returned for each stolen ox. For sheep, the fine shall be four to one—four sheep returned for each sheep stolen. [4]If he is caught in the act of stealing a live ox or donkey or sheep or whatever it is, he shall pay double value as his fine. [7]If someone gives money or goods to anyone to keep for him, and it is stolen, the thief shall pay double if he is found. [8]But if no thief is found, then the man to whom the valuables were entrusted shall be brought before God to determine whether or not he himself has stolen his neighbor's property. [9]In every case in which an ox, donkey, sheep, clothing, or anything else is lost, and the owner believes he has found it in the possession of someone else who denies it, both parties to the dispute shall come before God for a decision, and the one whom God declares guilty shall pay double to the other.

Lev 5:15. If anyone sins by unintentionally defiling what is holy, then he shall bring a ram without defect, worth whatever fine you charge against him, as his guilt offering to the Lord. [16]And he shall make restitution for the holy thing he has spoiled, or the tithe omitted, by paying for the loss, plus a twenty percent penalty; he shall bring it to the priest, and the priest shall make atonement for him with the ram of the guilt offering, and he shall be forgiven. Num 5:5–8.

Lev 6:5. He shall restore what he took, adding a twenty percent fine, and give it to the one he has harmed; and on the same day he shall bring his guilt offering to the Tabernacle. [6]His guilt offering shall be a ram without defect, and must be worth whatever value you demand. He shall bring it to the priest.

Prov 6:30. Excuses might even be found for a thief, if he steals when he is starving! [31]But even so, he is fined seven times as much as he stole, though it may mean selling everything in his house to pay it back.

See *Damages.*

FINGER Six on one hand, 2 Sam 21:20, 21.

FIR TREE Ps 104:17; Song 1:17; Isa 41:19; 55:13. Wood of, used for building, 2 Chron 2:8. Ships made of, Ezk 27:5. Of Lebanon, Isa 14:8; 60:13.

See *Cypress.*

FIRE Used as a signal in war, Jer 6:1. Furnaces of, Dan 3:6. Children sacrificed in, 2 Kgs 16:3; 17:17.

Miracles connected with: Miraculously descends on, and burns, Abraham's sacrifice, Gen 15:17; David's, 1 Chron 21:26; Elijah's, 1 Kgs 18:38; Solomon's, at dedication of the Temple, 2 Chron 7:1. Display of, in the plagues of Egypt, Ex 9:23; at Elijah's translation, 2 Kgs 2:11. Destroys the conspirators with Korah, Dathan, and Abiram, Num 16:35; the captain and his soldiers, 2 Kgs 1:9–12.

Torture by, Lev 21:9; Jer 29:22; Ezk 23:25, 47; Dan 3.

Pillar of fire, Ex 13:21, 22; 14:19, 24; 40:38; Num 9:15–23.

See *Cloud, Pillar of.*

FIGURATIVE. Of cleansing, Isa 6:6, 7; spiritual power, Ps 104:4; Jer 20:9; Mt 3:11; Lk 3:16; judgments, Deut 4:24; 32:22; Isa 33:14; Jer 23:29; Amos 1:4, 7, 10, 12, 14; 2:2; Mal 3:2; Lk 12:49; Rev 20:9; of the destruction of the wicked, Mt 13:42, 50; 25:41; Mk 9:48; Rev 9:2; 21:8.

EVERLASTING FIRE. Isa 33:14; Mt 25:41; Mk 9:48.

A Symbol. Of God's presence, Gen 15:17; Ezk 1:4; in the burning bush, Ex 3:2; on Sinai, Ex 19:18; Deut 4:12. Tongues of, on the believers, Acts 2:3.

See *Arson.*

FIREBRAND FIGURATIVE. Prov 26:18, 19; Amos 4:11; Zech 3:2.

See *Torch.*

FIREPAN Ex 38:3; Num 4:14; 1 Kgs 7:50; 2 Kgs 25:14, 15; 2 Chron 4:22; Jer 52:19.

See *Censer.*

FIRMAMENT The expanse above the earth, Ps 150:1; Ezk 1:25.

FIRSTBORN Of man and beast, reserved for himself by God, Ex 13:2, 12–16; 22:29, 30; 34:19, 20; Lev 27:26; Num 3:13; 8:17, 18; Deut 15:19–23; Neh 10:36.

Redemption of, Ex 13:13; 34:20; Lev 27:27; Num 3:40–51; 18:14–17. Levites taken instead of firstborn of the families of Israel, Num 3:11, 12, 40–45; 8:16–18.

Of Egyptians killed, Ex 11:5; 12:12, 29; 13:15; Num 33:3, 4; Ps 78:51; 105:36; 136:10. Of idolaters, sacrificed, Ezk 20:26.

BIRTHRIGHT OF THE. Had precedence over other sons of the family, including a double portion of inheritance, Deut 21:15–17; royal succession, 2 Chron 21:3, 4. Honorable distinction of, Ex 4:22; Ps 89:27; Jer 31:9; Rom 8:29; Col 1:15; Heb 1:5, 6; Rev 1:5. Sold by Esau, Gen 25:29–34; 27:36; Rom 9:10–13; Heb 12:16. Forfeited by Reuben, Gen 49:3, 4; 1 Chron 5:1, 2. Set aside: that of Manasseh, Gen 48:15–20; Adonijah, 1 Kgs 2:15; Hosah's son, 1 Chron 26:10.

See *Birthright.*

FIRST FRUITS First ripe of fruits, grain, oil, wine, and first of fleece, required as an offering, Ex 22:29; Lev 2:12–16; Num 18:12; Deut 18:4; 2 Chron 31:5,6; Neh 10:35, 37, 39, 40; Prov 3:9, 10; Jer 2:3; Rom 11:16. Offerings of, must be the best quality, Num 18:12; presented at the tabernacle, Ex 23:19; 34:26; Deut 26:2–10; belonged to the priests, Lev 23:20; Num 18:12, 13; Deut 18:3–5. Freewill offerings of, given to the prophets, 2 Kgs 4:42.

Wave offering of, Lev 23:9–14, 17. To be offered as a thank offering after entering the Land of Promise, Deut 26:3–10.

FIGURATIVE. 1 Cor 15:20, 23.

FISH Creation of, Gen 1:20–22. Appointed for food, Gen 9:2, 3. Clean and unclean, Lev 11:9–12; Deut 14:9, 10. Caught with nets, Eccl 9:12; Hab 1:14–17; Mt 4:21; Lk 5:2–6; Jn 21:6–8; hooks, Isa 19:8; Amos 4:2; Mt 17:27; harpoons, Job 41:7.

Traffic in, Neh 13:16; Jn 21:13. Broiled, Jn 21:9–13; Lk 24:42. Miracles connected with: Jonah swallowed by, Jon 1:17; 2; Mt 12:39, 40; of the loaves and fish, Mt 14:19; 15:36; Lk 9:13–17; coin obtained from mouth of, Mt 17:27; great draft of, Lk 5:4–7; Jn 21:6; eaten by Jesus after his resurrection, Lk 24:42; Jn 21:9–13.

FIGURATIVE. Ezk 47:9, 10.

FISHERMEN Certain apostles, Mt 4:18–21; Mk 1:16, 19; Jn 21:2, 3.

FIGURATIVE. Jer 16:16; Mt 4:19; Mk 1:17; Lk 5:10.

FISH GATE 2 Chron 33:14; Neh 3:3; 12:39.

FISHHOOK Amos 4:2.

FLAG Of the Lord, Ex 17:15, 16. Used by each tribe of Israel in camp and march, Num 1:52, 2:2. Battle, Isa 18:3; 31:19.

FIGURATIVE. Ps 20:5; Isa 11:12; 13:2; 62:10.

See *Banner; Signal.*

FLAGON Ex 25:29; 37:15, 16.

FLAIL An implement for threshing grain, Isa 28:27.

FLASK Of perfume, Mk 14:3; Lk 7:37.

FLATTERY Job 32:21, 22. Don't insist that I be cautious lest I insult someone, and don't make me flatter anyone. Let me be frank, lest God should strike me dead.

Job 41:3. Will he beg you to desist or try to flatter you from your intentions?

Ps 5:8. Lord, lead me as you promised me you would; otherwise my enemies will conquer me. Tell me clearly what to do, which way to turn. [9]For they cannot speak one truthful word. Their hearts are filled to the brim with wickedness. Their suggestions are full of the stench of sin and death. Their tongues are filled with flatteries to gain their wicked ends.

Ps 12:2. Everyone deceives and flatters and lies. There is no sincerity left.

Ps 49:13. Such is the folly of these men, though after they die they will be quoted as having great wisdom. [18]Though a man calls himself happy all through his life—and the world loudly applauds success—. Prov 6:24.

Ps 78:36. But it was only with their words they followed him, not with their hearts. Rom 16:18.

Prov 5:3. For the lips of a prostitute are as sweet as honey, and smooth flattery is her stock in trade.

Prov 7:5. Let her hold you back from visiting a prostitute, from listening to her flattery. [21]So she seduced him with her pretty speech, her coaxing and her wheedling, until he yielded to her. He couldn't resist her flattery. Prov 2:16, 17.

Prov 14:20. Even his own neighbors despise the poor man, while the rich have many "friends."

Prov 19:4. A wealthy man has many "friends"; the poor man has none left. [6]Many beg favors from a man who is generous; everyone is his friend!

Prov 24:24. He who says to the wicked, "You are innocent," shall be cursed by many people of many nations.

Prov 25:26. If a godly man compromises with the wicked, it is like polluting a fountain or muddying a spring.

Prov 26:28. Flattery is a form of hatred and wounds cruelly.

Prov 27:21. The purity of silver and gold can be tested in a crucible, but a man is tested by his reaction to men's praise.

Prov 28:23. In the end, people appreciate frankness more than flattery.

Prov 29:5, 6. Flattery is a trap; evil men are caught in it, but good men stay away and sing for joy.

Dan 11:21. Next to come to power will be an evil man not directly in line for royal succession. But during a crisis he will take over the kingdom by flattery and intrigue. [34]Eventually these pressures will subside, and some ungodly men will come, pretending to offer a helping hand, only to take advantage of them. *v.* 32.

Lk 6:26. And what sadness is ahead for those praised by the crowds—for *false* prophets have *always* been praised.

Gal 1:10. You can see that I am not trying to please you by sweet talk and flattery; no, I am trying to please God. If I were still trying to please men I could not be Christ's servant.

1 Thess 2:4. For we speak as messengers from God, trusted by him to tell the truth; we change his message not one bit to suit the taste of those who hear it; for we serve God alone, who examines our hearts' deepest thoughts. [5]Never once did we try to win you with flattery, as you very well know, and God knows we were not just pretending to be your friends so that you would give us money! [6]As for praise, we have never asked for it from you or anyone else, although as apostles of Christ we certainly had a right to some honor from you.

Jude 1:16. They are loud-mouthed "show-offs," and when they show respect for others, it is only to get something from them in return.

INSTANCES OF. By Jacob, Gen 33:10. By Gideon, Judg 8:1–3. By Mephibosheth, 2 Sam 9:8. By woman of Tekoa, 2 Sam 14:17–20. By Absalom, 2 Sam 15:2–6. By Israel and Judah, 2 Sam 19:41–43. By Adonijah, 1 Kgs 1:42. By Ahab, 1 Kgs 20:4. By false prophets, 1 Kgs 22:13. By Darius's courtiers, Dan 6:7. By Herodians, Luke 20:21. By Tyrians, Acts 12:22. Tertullus flatters Felix, Acts 24:2–4. Paul flatters Felix, Acts 24:10; Agrippa, Acts 26:2, 3.

FLAX In Egypt, Ex 9:31. In Palestine, Josh 2: 6. Linen made from, Prov 31:13; Isa 19:9.

See *Linen.*

FLEA 1 Sam 24:14; Jer 43:12.

FLESH Gen 2:23. "This is it!" Adam exclaimed. "She is part of my own bone and flesh! Her name is 'woman' because she was taken out of a man."

Lev 17:11. For the life of the flesh is in the blood, and I have given you the blood to sprinkle upon the altar as an atonement for your souls; it is the blood that makes atonement, because it is the life.

Lev 20:9. Anyone who curses his father or mother shall surely be put to death—for he has cursed his own flesh and blood.

Deut 32:42. My arrows shall be drunk with blood! My sword devours the flesh and the blood of all the slain and captives.

Job 6:12. Am I unfeeling, like stone? Is my flesh made of brass?

Job 10:11. You gave me skin and flesh and knit together bones and sinews.

Job 16:9. God hates me and angrily tears at my flesh; he has gnashed upon me with his teeth, and watched to snuff out any sign of life.

1 Cor 15:50. I tell you this, my brothers: an earthly body made of flesh and blood cannot get into God's kingdom. These perishable bodies of ours are not the right kind to live forever.

Eph 6:12. For we are not fighting against people made of flesh and blood, but against persons without bodies—the evil rulers of the unseen world, those mighty satanic beings and great evil princes of darkness who rule this world; and against huge numbers of wicked spirits in the spirit world.

Heb 2:14. Since we, God's children, are human beings—made of flesh and blood—he became flesh and blood too by being born in human form; for only as a human being could he die and in dying break the power of the devil who had the power of death.

Symbolical. Body of Christ symbolized by the bread of the Lord's Supper, Jn 6:48–63.

See *Body; Heart, Known to God; Jesus, Humility of; Lust; Man.*

FLESHHOOK Or meat hook. Used in the Tabernacle, Ex 27:3; 38:3; Num 4:14; 1 Sam 2:13, 14. Made of gold, 1 Chron 28:17; of bronze, 2 Chron 4:12–16.

FLIES Eccl 10:1. Plague of, Ex 8:21–32; Ps 78:45; 105:31.

FIGURATIVE. Isa 7:18.

FLINT Gen 22:6, 7; Ex 4:25, 26; Deut 32:13; Josh 5:2, 3; Job 28:9; Ps 114:8; Isa 50:7; Zech 7:12.

FLOOD The deluge. Foretold, Gen 6:12, 13, 17. History of, Genesis chapters 6–8. References to, Job 22:15, 16; Ps 90:5, 6; Mt 24:37, 38; Lk 17:26, 27; Heb 11:7; 1 Pet 3:20; 2 Pet 2:5. The promise that it should not recur, Gen 8:20, 21; Isa 54:9.

See *Meteorology.*

FLOUR See *Barley; Bread; Offerings; Wheat.*

FLOWERS See *Botany.*

FLUTE Gen 4:21; 1 Sam 10:5; Dan 3:5, 7, 10; Isa 30:29; 1 Cor 14:7.

See *Music, Instruments of.*

FLY See *Flies.*

FOOD ARTICLES OF. Milk, Gen 49:12; Deut 32:14; Prov 27:25–27; butter, 2 Sam 17:28, 29; cheese, 1 Sam 17:18; Job 10:10; bread, 1 Sam 17:17; 2 Sam 6:19; roasted grain, Ruth 2:14; 1 Sam 17:17; meat, Deut 32:14; fish, Mt 7:10; Lk 24:42; vegetables, Rom 14:2; fruit, 2 Sam 16:2; raisin cakes, 1 Sam 25:18; 2 Sam 6:19; fig cakes, 1 Sam 25:18; 30:11, 12; grapes, Num 6:3; honey, Song 5:1; Isa 7:15; oil, Deut 12:17; wine, Num 6:3, 4; 2 Sam 6:19; Prov 21:17; Jn 2:3, 10. Manna from heaven, Ex 16:4; Num 11:6; Deut 8:3; Josh 5:11, 12.

Prepared by females, Gen 27:8–10; 1 Sam 8:13; Prov 31:15. Thanks given before, Mk 8:6; Acts 27:35. A hymn sung after, Mt 26:30. Men and women did not eat together, Gen 18:8, 9; Esther, 1:1–3, 9.

See *Bread; Eating; Oven.*

FROM GOD. Gen 1:29. And look! I have given you the seed-bearing plants throughout the earth, and all the fruit trees for your food. [30]And I've given all the grass and plants to the animals and birds for their food.

Gen 9:2, 3. "All wild animals and birds and fish will be afraid of you," God told him; "for I have placed them in your power, and they are yours to use for food, in addition to grain and vegetables."

Ps 23:5. You provide delicious food for me in the presence of my enemies. You have welcomed me as your guest; blessings overflow!

Ps 103:5. He fills my life with good things! My youth is renewed like the eagle's!

Ps 104:14. The tender grass grows up at his command to feed the cattle, and there are fruit trees, vegetables and grain for man to cultivate, [15]and wine to make him glad, and olive oil as lotion for his skin, and bread to give him strength.

Ps 111:5. He gives food to those who trust him; he never forgets his promises.

Ps 136:25. He gives food to every living thing, for his loving-kindness continues forever.

Ps 145:15. The eyes of all mankind look up to you for help; you give them their food as they need it.

Ps 147:9. He feeds the wild animals and the young ravens cry to him for food.

Prov 30:8. First, help me never to tell a lie. Second, give me neither poverty nor riches! Give me just enough to satisfy my needs!

Isa 3:1. The Lord of Hosts will cut off Jerusalem's and Judah's food and water supplies.

Mt 6:11. Give us our food again today, as usual.

Mk 7:18. "Don't you understand either?" he asked. "Can't you see that what you eat won't harm your soul? [19]For food doesn't come in contact with your heart, but only passes through the digestive system." (By saying this he showed that every kind of food is kosher.)

Rom 14:14. As for myself, I am perfectly sure on the authority of the Lord Jesus that there is nothing really wrong with eating meat that has been offered to idols. But if someone believes it is wrong, then he shouldn't do it because for him it is wrong. [21]The right thing to do is to quit eating meat or drinking wine or doing anything else that offends your brother or makes him sin.

1 Tim 4:3. They will say it is wrong to be married and wrong to eat meat, even though God gave these things to well-taught Christians to enjoy and be thankful for. [4]For everything God made is good, and we may eat it gladly if we are thankful for it, [5]and if we ask God to bless it, for it is made good by the Word of God and prayer.

THINGS PROHIBITED AS FOOD. Ex 22:31. And since you yourselves are holy—my special people—do not eat any animal that has been attacked and killed by a wild animal. Leave its carcass for the dogs to eat.

Lev 11:1. Then the Lord said to Moses and Aaron, [2, 3]"Tell the people of Israel that the animals which may be used for food include any animal with cloven hooves which chews its cud. [4-7]This means that the following may *not* be eaten: the camel (it chews the cud but does not have cloven hooves); the coney, or rock badger (because although it chews the cud, it does not have cloven hooves); the hare (because although it chews the cud, it does not have cloven hooves); the swine (because although it has cloven hooves, it does not chew the cud). [8]You may not eat their meat or even touch their dead bodies; they are forbidden foods for you. [9]As to fish, you may eat whatever has fins and scales, whether taken from rivers or from the sea; [10]but all other water creatures are strictly forbidden to you. [11]You mustn't eat their meat or even touch their dead bodies. [12]I'll repeat it again—any water creature that does not have fins or scales is forbidden to you. [13-19]Among the birds, these are the ones you may *not* eat: the eagle, the metire, the osprey, the falcon (all kinds), the kite, the raven (all kinds), the ostrich, the nighthawk, the seagull, the hawk (all kinds), the owl, the cormorant, the ibis, the marsh hen, the pelican, the vulture, the stork, the heron (all kinds), the hoopoe, the bat.

[20]Flying insects with four legs must not be eaten, [21, 22]with the exception of those that jump; locusts of all varieties—ordinary locusts, bald locusts, crickets, and grasshoppers—may be eaten. [23]All other things that fly and have four feet are forbidden to you. [24]Anyone touching their dead bodies shall be defiled until the evening, [25]and must wash his clothes immediately. He must also quarantine himself until nightfall, as being ceremonially defiled. [26]You are also defiled by touching any animal with only semi-parted hoofs, or any animal that does not chew the cud. [27]Any animal that walks on paws is forbidden to you as food. Anyone touching the dead body of such an animal shall be defiled until evening. [28]Anyone carrying away the carcass shall wash his clothes and be ceremonially defiled until evening; for it is forbidden to you. [29, 30]These are the forbidden small animals which scurry about your feet or crawl upon the ground: the mole, the rat, the great lizard, the gecko, the mouse, the lizard, the snail, the chameleon. [31]Anyone touching their dead bodies shall be defiled until evening, [32]and anything upon which the carcass falls shall be defiled—any article of wood, or of clothing, a rug, or a sack; anything it touches must be put into water, and is defiled until evening. After that it may be used again. [33]If it falls into a pottery bowl, anything in the bowl is defiled, and you shall smash the bowl. [34]If the water used to cleanse the defiled article touches any food, all of it is defiled. Any drink which is in the defiled bowl is also contaminated. [35]If the dead body of such an animal touches any clay oven, it is defiled and must be smashed. [36]If the body falls into a spring or cistern where there is water, that water is not defiled; yet anyone who pulls out the carcass is defiled. [37]And if the carcass touches grain to be sown in the field, it is not contaminated; [38]but if the seeds are wet and the carcass falls upon it, the seed is defiled. [39]If an animal which you are permitted to eat dies of disease, anyone touching the carcass shall be defiled until evening. [40]Also, anyone eating its meat or carrying away its carcass shall wash his clothes and be defiled until evening. [41, 42]Animals that crawl shall not be eaten. This includes all reptiles that slither along upon their bellies as well as those that have legs. No crawling thing with many feet may be eaten, for it is defiled. [43]Do not defile yourselves by touching it. [44]I am the Lord your God. Keep yourselves pure concerning these things, and be holy, for I am holy; therefore do not defile yourselves by touching any of these things that crawl upon the earth. [45]For I am the Lord who brought you out of the land of Egypt to be your God. You must therefore be holy, for I am holy." [46]These are the laws concerning animals, birds, and whatever swims in the water or crawls upon the ground. [47]These are the distinctions between what is ceremonially clean and may be eaten, and what is ceremonially defiled and may not be eaten, among all animal life upon the earth. Deut 14.

Lev 17:13. Anyone, whether an Israelite or a foreigner living among you, who goes hunting and kills an animal or bird of a kind permitted for food must pour out the blood and cover it with dust, [14]for the blood is the life. That is why I told the people of Israel never to eat it, for the life of every bird and animal is its blood. Therefore, anyone who eats blood must be excommunicated. [15]And anyone—native born or foreigner—who eats the dead body of an animal that dies of itself, or is torn by wild animals, must wash his clothes and bathe himself and be defiled until evening; after that he shall be declared cleansed.

FOOL Ps 14:1. That man is a fool who says to himself, "There is no God!" Ps 53:1.

Ps 107:17. Others, the fools, were ill because of their sinful ways.

Prov 1:7. How does a man become wise? The first step is to trust and reverence the Lord! Only fools refuse to be taught. [22]"You simpletons!" she cries. "How long will you go on being fools? How long will you scoff at wisdom and fight the facts?"

Prov 3:35. The wise are promoted to honor, but fools are promoted to shame!

Prov 9:6. Leave behind your foolishness and begin to live; learn how to be wise. [7, 8]If you rebuke a mocker, you will only get a smart retort; yes, he will snarl at you. So don't bother with him; he will only hate you for trying to help him. But a wise man, when rebuked, will love you all the more.

Prov 10:8. But a self-sufficient fool falls flat on his face. *v.* 10.

13. Men with common sense are admired as counselors; those without it are beaten as servants.

14. A wise man holds his tongue. Only a fool blurts out everything he knows; that only leads to sorrow and trouble.

18. To hate is to be a liar; to slander is to be a fool.

23. A fool's fun is being bad; a wise man's fun is being wise!

Prov 13:16. A wise man thinks ahead; a fool doesn't, and even brags about it.

Prov 14:1. A wise woman builds her house, while a foolish woman tears hers down by her own efforts.

7. If you are looking for advice, stay away from fools. [8]The wise man looks ahead. The fool attempts to fool himself and won't face facts.

15. Only a simpleton believes what he is told!

16. A wise man is cautious and avoids danger; a fool plunges ahead with great confidence.

Prov 15:5. Only a fool despises his father's advice.

21. If a man enjoys folly, something is wrong! The sensible stay on the pathways of right.

Prov 17:24. Wisdom is the main pursuit of sensible men, but a fool's goals are at the ends of the earth! Eccl 2:12–14.

Prov 18:6, 7. A fool gets into constant fights. His mouth is his undoing! His words endanger him.

Prov 20:3. It is an honor for a man to stay out of a fight. Only fools insist on quarreling.

Prov 21:20. The wise man saves for the future, but the foolish man spends whatever he gets.

Prov 26:4, 5. When arguing with a rebel, don't

use foolish arguments as he does, or you will become as foolish as he is! Prick his conceit with silly replies!

7. In the mouth of a fool a proverb becomes as useless as a paralyzed leg.

11. As a dog returns to his vomit, so a fool repeats his folly.

12. There is one thing worse than a fool, and that is a man who is conceited.

Prov 29:9. There's no use arguing with a fool. He only rages and scoffs, and tempers flare.

Eccl 4:5. The fool won't work and almost starves.

Eccl 7:9. Don't be quick-tempered—that is being a fool. Prov 14:17.

Eccl 10:2. A wise man's heart leads him to do right, and a fool's heart leads him to do evil.

12, 13. It is pleasant to listen to wise words, but a fool's speech brings him to ruin. Since he begins with a foolish premise, his conclusion is sheer madness.

14. A fool knows all about the future and tells everyone in detail! But who can really know what is going to happen?

15. A fool is so upset by a little work that he has no strength for the simplest matter.

Isa 44:25. I make wise men give opposite advice to what they should, and make them into fools.

Mt 7:26. But those who hear my instructions and ignore them are foolish, like a man who builds his house on sand. [27]For when the rains and floods come, and storm winds beat against his house, it will fall with a mighty crash.

Rom 1:22. Claiming themselves to be wise without God, they became utter fools instead.

Tit 3:3. Once we, too, were foolish and disobedient; we were misled by others and became slaves to many evil pleasures and wicked desires. Our lives were full of resentment and envy. We hated others and they hated us.

PARABLES OF. Of the foolish virgins, Mt 25:1–13; of the rich fool, Lk 12:16–20.

See *Rebel.*

FOOT Washing the feet of the disciples by Jesus, Jn 13:4–16.

See *Ablution; Purification.*

For footwear, see *Shoe.*

FIGURATIVE. Mt 18:8.

FOOTMAN A runner before kings and princes, 2 Sam 15:1; 1 Kgs 1:5.

FOOTSTOOL 2 Chron 9:18.

FIGURATIVE. Of the earth, Isa 66:1; Mt 5:35; Acts 7:48, 49; Temple, 1 Chron 28:2; Lam 2:1; Ezk 43:7; sanctuary, Ps 132:7; enemies of Jesus, Mk 12:36.

FOREIGNER FIGURATIVE. Eph 2:19.

See *Aliens; Gentiles; Strangers.*

FOREKNOWLEDGE OF GOD See *God, Foreknowledge of, Wisdom of.*

FOREMAN See *Master Workman.*

FOREORDINATION See *Predestination.*

FORGERY By Jezebel, 1 Kgs 21:8.

FORGETTING GOD A characteristic of the wicked, Prov 2:16, 17; Isa 65:11. Backsliders guilty of, Jer 2:32; 3:21.

Is forgetting his covenant, Deut 4:23; 2 Kgs 17:38; miracles, Ps 78:7, 11, 12; 106:13; benefits, Ps 103:2; 106:7; word, Heb 12:5; Jas 1:25; law, Ps 119:153, 176; Hos 4:6; church, Ps 137:5; past rescues, Judg 8:34; Ps 78:42; power to deliver, Isa 51:13–15.

Encouraged by false teachers, Jer 23:27. Prosperity leads to, Deut 8:12–14; Hos 13:6. Trials should not lead to, Ps 44:17–19. Resolve against, Deut 6:10–12; 8:11. Exhortation to those guilty of, Ps 50:22.

Punishment of, Job 8:11–13; Ps 9:17; Isa 17:10, 11; Ezk 23:35; Hos 8:14; threatened, Job 8:11–13; Ps 9:17; 50:22; Isa 17:10; Jer 2:32; Hos 8:14.

See *Backslider.*

FORGIVENESS OF ENEMIES. Ex 23:4. If you come upon an enemy's ox or donkey that has strayed away, you must take it back to its owner. [5]If you see your enemy trying to get his donkey onto its feet beneath a heavy load, you must not go on by, but must help him.

Prov 19:11. A wise man restrains his anger and overlooks insults. This is to his credit.

Prov 24:17. Do not rejoice when your enemy meets trouble. Let there be no gladness when he falls. [29]Don't say, "Now I can pay him back for all his meanness to me!"

Prov 25:21, 22. If your enemy is hungry, give him food! If he is thirsty, give him something to drink! This will make him feel ashamed of himself, and God will reward you. Rom 12:20.

Mt 5:7. Happy are the kind and merciful, for they shall be shown mercy. [39]But I say: Don't resist violence! If you are slapped on one cheek, turn the other too. [40]If you are ordered to court, and your shirt is taken from you, give your coat too. [41]If the military demand that you carry their gear for a mile, carry it two. [43]There is a saying, "Love your *friends* and hate your enemies." [44]But I say: Love your *enemies!* Pray for those who *persecute* you! [45]In that way you will be acting as true sons of your Father in heaven. For he gives his sunlight to both the evil and the good, and sends rain on the just and on the unjust too. [46]If you love only those who love you, what good is that? Even scoundrels do that much. *vs.* 47, 48; Lk 6:27–34.

Mt 6:12. And forgive us our sins, just as we have forgiven those who have sinned against us. [Lk 11:4.] [14, 15]Your heavenly Father will forgive you if you forgive those who sin against you; but if *you* refuse to forgive *them, he* will not forgive *you.*

Mt 18:21. Then Peter came to him and asked, "Sir, how often should I forgive a brother who sins against me? Seven times?" [22]"No!" Jesus replied, "seventy times seven! [23]The Kingdom of Heaven can be compared to a king who decided to bring his accounts up to date. [24]In the process, one of his debtors was brought in who owed him $10,000,000! [25]He couldn't pay, so the king ordered him sold for the debt, also his wife and children and everything he had. [26]But the man fell down before the king, his face in the dust, and said, 'Oh, sir, be patient with me and I will pay it all.' [27]Then the king was filled with pity for him and released him and forgave his debt. [28]But when the man left the king, he went to a man who owed him $2,000 and grabbed him by the throat and demanded instant payment. [29]The man fell down before him and begged him to give him a little time. 'Be patient and I will pay it,' he pled. [30]But his creditor wouldn't wait. He had the man arrested and jailed until the debt would be paid in full. [31]Then the man's friends went to the king and told him what had happened. [32]And the king called before him the man he had forgiven and said, 'You evil-hearted wretch! Here I forgave you all that tremendous debt, just because you asked me to—[33]shouldn't you have mercy on others, just as I had mercy on you?' [34]Then the angry king sent the man to the torture chamber until he had paid every last penny due. [35]So shall my heavenly Father do to you if you refuse to truly forgive your brothers."

Mk 11:25. But when you are praying, first forgive anyone you are holding a grudge against, so that your Father in heaven will forgive you your sins too.

Lk 6:35. Love your *enemies!* Do good to *them!* Lend to *them!* And don't be concerned about the fact that they won't repay. Then your reward from heaven will be very great, and you will truly be acting as sons of God: for he is kind to the *unthankful* and to those who are *very wicked.* [36]Try to show as much compassion as your Father does. [37]Never criticize or condemn—or it will all come back on you. Go easy on others; and they will do the same for you.

Lk 17:3. Rebuke your brother if he sins, and forgive him if he is sorry. [4]Even if he wrongs you seven times a day and each time turns again and asks forgiveness, forgive him. Mt 18:21, 22.

Rom 12:14. If someone mistreats you because you are a Christian, don't curse him; pray that God will bless him. [17]Never pay back evil for evil. Do things in such a way that everyone can see you are honest clear through. [19]Dear friends, never avenge yourselves. Leave that to God, for he has said that he will repay those who deserve it. [Don't take the law into your own hands.] [21]Don't let evil get the upper hand but conquer evil by doing good.

1 Cor 4:12. We have blessed those who cursed us. We have been patient with those who injured us. [13]We have replied quietly when evil things have been said about us.

Eph 4:32. Instead, be kind to each other, tenderhearted, forgiving one another, just as God has forgiven you because you belong to Christ.

Col 3:13. Be gentle and ready to forgive; never hold grudges. Remember, the Lord forgave you, so you must forgive others.

Philemon 1:10. My plea is that you show kindness to my child Onesimus. [18]If he has harmed you in any way or stolen anything from you, charge me for it.

1 Pet 3:9. Don't repay evil for evil. Don't snap back at those who say unkind things about you. Instead, pray for God's help for them, for we are to be kind to others, and God will bless us for it.

See *Enemy.*

Instances of. Esau forgives Jacob, Gen 33:4, 11. Joseph, his brothers, Gen 45:5–15; 50:19–21. Moses, the Israelites, Num 12:1–13. David forgives Saul, 1 Sam 24:9–12; 26:9, 23; 2 Sam 1:14–16; and Shime-i, 2 Sam 16:9–13; 19:23, with 1 Kgs 2:8, 9. Solomon forgives Adonijah, 1 Kgs 1:53. The prophet of Judah forgives Jeroboam, 1 Kgs 13:3–6. Jesus forgives his enemies, Lk 23:34.

OF SINS. See *Sin, Forgiveness of.*

FORK See *Fleshhook.*

FORM IN RELIGIOUS SERVICE. 1 Chron 15:13. "The Lord destroyed us before because we handled the matter improperly—you were not carrying it." [14]So the priests and the Levites underwent the ceremonies of sanctification in preparation for bringing home the Ark of Jehovah, the God of Israel.

2 Chron 29:34. But there were too few priests to prepare the burnt offerings, so their brothers the Levites helped them until the work was finished—and until more priests had reported to work—for the Levites were much more ready to sanctify themselves than the priests were.

IRREGULARITY IN. 2 Chron 30:2, 3. The king, his aides, and all the assembly of Jerusalem had voted to celebrate the Passover in May this time, rather than at the normal time in April, because not enough priests were sanctified at the earlier date, and there wasn't enough time to get notices out. [4]The king and his advisors were in complete agreement in this matter, [5]so they sent a Passover proclamation throughout Israel, from Dan to Beer-sheba, inviting everyone. They had not kept it in great numbers as prescribed. [17, 18, 19]Since many of the people arriving from Ephraim, Manasseh, Issachar, and Zebulun were ceremonially impure because they had not undergone the purification rites, the Levites killed their Passover lambs for them, to sanctify them. Then King Hezekiah prayed for them and they were permitted to eat the Passover anyway, even though this was contrary to God's rules. But Hezekiah said, "May the good Lord pardon everyone who determines to follow the Lord God of his fathers, even though he is not properly sanctified for the ceremony." [20]And the Lord listened to Hezekiah's prayer and did not destroy them.

Mt 12:3. But Jesus said to them, "Haven't you ever read what King David did when he and his friends were hungry? [4]He went into the Temple and they ate the special bread permitted to the priests alone. That was breaking the law too."

FORMALISM 1 Sam 15:22. Samuel replied, "Has the Lord as much pleasure in your burnt offerings and sacrifices as in your obedience? Obedience is far better than sacrifice. He is much more interested in your listening to him than in your offering the fat of rams to him."

Ps 50:8. I have no complaint about the sacrifices you bring to my altar, for you bring them regularly. [9]But it isn't sacrificial bullocks and goats that I really want from you. [10, 11]For all the animals of field and forest are mine! The cattle on a thousand hills! And all the birds upon the mountains! [12]If I were hungry, I would not mention it to you—for all the world is mine, and everything in it. [13]No, I don't need your sacrifices of flesh and blood. [14, 15]What I want from you is your true thanks; I want your promises fulfilled. *I want you to trust me in your times of trouble, so I can rescue you, and you can give me glory.*

Ps 51:16. You don't want penance; if you did, how gladly I would do it! You aren't interested in offerings burned before you on the altar. [17]It is a broken spirit you want—remorse and penitence. A broken and a contrite heart, O God, you will not ignore.

Ps 69:30. Then I will praise God with my singing! My thanks will be his praise—[31]that will please him more than sacrificing a bullock or an ox.

Isa 1:11. I am sick of your sacrifices. Don't bring me any more of them. I don't want your fat rams; I don't want to see the blood from your offerings. [12, 13]Who wants your sacrifices when you have no sorrow for your sins? The incense you bring me is a stench in my nostrils. Your holy celebrations of the new moon and the Sabbath, and your special days for fasting—even your most pious meetings—all are frauds! I want nothing more to do with them. [14]I hate them all; I can't stand the sight of them. [15]From now on, when you pray with your hands stretched out to heaven, I won't look or listen. Even though you make many prayers, I will not hear, for your hands are those of murders; they are covered with the blood of your innocent victims.

Isa 29:13. And so the Lord says, "Since these people say they are mine but they do not obey me, and since their worship amounts to mere words learned by rote, [14]therefore I will take awesome vengeance on these hypocrites, and make their wisest counselors as fools." [15]Woe to those who try to hide their plans from God, who try to keep him in the dark concerning what they do! "God can't see us," they say to themselves. "He doesn't know what is going on!" [16]How stupid can they be! Isn't he, the Potter, greater than the jars he makes? Will you say to him, "He didn't make us?" Does a machine call its inventor dumb?

Jer 6:20. There is no use now in burning sweet incense from Sheba before me! Keep your expensive perfumes! I cannot accept your offerings; they have no sweet fragrance for me.

Jer 14:12. When they fast, I will not pay any attention; when they present their offerings and sacrifices to me, I will not accept them. What I will give them in return is war and famine and disease.

Hos 6:6. I don't want your sacrifices—I want your love; I don't want your offerings—I want you to know me.

Amos 5:21. I hate your show and pretense—your hypocrisy of "honoring" me with your religious feasts and solemn assemblies. [22]I will not accept your burnt offerings and thank offerings. I will not look at your offerings of peace. [23]Away with your hymns of praise—they are mere noise to my ears. I will not listen to your music, no matter how lovely it is.

Mic 6:6. "How can we make up to you for what we've done?" you ask. "Shall we bow before the Lord with offerings of yearling calves?" Oh, no! [7]For if you offered him thousands of rams and ten thousands of rivers of olive oil—would that please him? Would he be satisfied? If you sacrificed your oldest child, would that make him glad? Then would he forgive your sins? Of course not!

Mal 1:6. "A son honors his father, a servant honors his master. I am your Father and Master, yet you don't honor me, O priests, but you despise my name." "Who? Us?" you say. "When did we ever despise your name?" [8]"You tell the people, 'Lame animals are all right to offer on the altar of the Lord—yes, even the sick and the blind ones.' And you claim this isn't evil? Try it on your governor sometime—give him gifts like that—and see how pleased he is! [10]Oh, to find one priest among you who would shut the doors and refuse this kind of sacrifice. I have no pleasure in you," says the Lord of Hosts, "and I will not accept your offerings. [13]You say, 'Oh, it's too difficult to serve the Lord and do what he asks.' And you turn up your noses at the rules he has given you to obey. Think of it! Stolen animals, lame and sick—as offerings to God! Should I accept such offerings as these?" asks the Lord. [14]"Cursed is that man who promises a fine ram from his flock, and substitutes a sick one to sacrifice to God. For I am a Great King," says the Lord of Hosts, "and my name is to be mightily revered among the Gentiles."

Mt 9:13. Then he added, "Now go away and learn the meaning of this verse of Scripture, 'It isn't your sacrifices and your gifts I want—I want you to be merciful.' For I have come to urge sinners, not the self-righteous, back to God."

Mt 12:7. But if you had known the meaning of this Scripture verse, 'I want you to be merciful more than I want your offerings,' you would not have condemned those who aren't guilty!

Mt 15:8. These people say they honor me, but their hearts are far away. [9]Their worship is worthless, for they teach their manmade laws instead of those from God.

Lk 13:24, 25. The door to heaven is narrow. Work hard to get in, for the truth is that many will try to enter but when the head of the house has locked the door, it will be too late. Then if you stand outside knocking, and pleading, "Lord, open the door for us," he will reply, "I do not know you." [26]"But we ate with you, and you taught in our streets," you will say. [27]And he will reply, "I tell you, I don't know you. You can't come in here, guilty as you are. Go away."

Rom 2:17. You Jews think all is well between yourselves and God because he gave his laws to you; you brag that you are his special friends. [18]Yes, you know what he wants; you know right from wrong and favor the right because you have been taught his laws from earliest youth. [19]You are so sure of the way to God that you could point it out to a blind man. You think of yourselves as beacon lights, directing men who are lost in darkness to God. [20]You think that you can guide the simple and teach even children the affairs of God, for you really know his laws, which are full of all knowledge and truth. [21]Yes, you teach others—then why don't you teach yourselves? You tell others not to steal—do *you* steal? [22]You say it is wrong to commit adultery—do *you* do it? You say, "Don't pray to idols," and then make money your god instead. [23]You are so proud of knowing God's laws, *but you dishonor him by breaking them.* [24]No wonder the Scriptures say that the world speaks evil of God because of you. [25]Being a Jew is worth something if you obey God's laws; but if you don't, then you are no better off than the heathen. [26]And if the heathen obey God's laws, won't God give them all the rights and honors he planned to give the Jews? [27]In fact, those heathen will be much better off than you Jews who know so much about God and have his promises but don't obey his laws. [28]For you are not real Jews just because you were born of Jewish parents or because you have gone through the Jewish initiation ceremony of circumcision. [29]No, a real Jew is anyone whose heart is right with God. For God is not looking for those who cut their bodies in actual body circumcision, but he is looking for those with changed hearts and minds. Whoever has that kind of change in his life will get his praise from God, even if not from you.

1 Cor 7:19. For it doesn't make any difference at all whether a Christian has gone through this ceremony or not. But it makes a lot of difference whether he is pleasing God and keeping God's commandments. That is the important thing.

Phil 3:4. Yet if anyone ever had reason to hope that he could save himself, it would be I. If others could be saved by what they are, certainly I could! [5]For I went through the Jewish initiation ceremony when I was eight days old, having been born into a pure-blooded Jewish home that was a branch of the old original Benjamin family. So I was a real Jew if there ever was one! What's more, I was a member of the Pharisees who demand the strictest obedience to every Jewish law and custom. [6]And sincere? Yes, so much so that I greatly persecuted the church; and I tried to obey every Jewish rule and regulation right down to the very last point. [7]But all these things that I once thought very worthwhile—now I've thrown them all away so that I can put my trust and hope in Christ alone.

2 Tim 3:1. You may as well know this too, Timothy, that in the last days it is going to be very difficult to be a Christian. [2]For people will love only themselves and their money; they will be proud and boastful, sneering at God, disobedient to their parents, ungrateful to them, and thoroughly bad. [3]They will be hardheaded and never give in to others; they will be constant liars and troublemakers and will think nothing of immorality. They will be rough and cruel, and sneer at those who try to be good. [4]They will betray their friends; they will be hotheaded, puffed up with pride, and prefer good times to worshiping God. [5]They will go to church, yes, but they won't really believe anything they hear. Don't be taken in by people like that.

See *Ordinance; Works.*

FORNICATION See *Adultery; Lasciviousness.*

FORT A military defense. Field fortifications, Deut 20:19, 20; Ezk 4:1, 2; 26:8. Defenses of cities, 2 Chron 26:15; Isa 25:12. See *Castle; Tower; Walls.* Erected in vineyards and herding grounds, Isa 5:2; Mk 12:1; in the desert, 2 Chron 26:10. Caves used for, Judg 6:2; 1 Sam 23:29; Isa 33:16.

FIGURATIVE. Of God's care, 2 Sam 22:2, 3, 47; Ps 18:2; 31:3; 62:2, 6; 94:21, 22; 144:2; Prov 18:10; Jer 16:19.

FORTITUDE See *Courage.*

FORTRESS 1 Chron 11:5–7; 2 Chron 17:12; 27:4.

See *Armory; Castle.*

FORTUNATUS A Christian of Corinth, 1 Cor 16:17.

FORTUNE Change of. See illustrated in lives of Joseph, from slave to prime minister; Pharaoh's wine taster and baker, Gen 40; David, from shepherd boy to king. See also *Jeroboam; Haman; Mordecai; Esther; Job; Daniel.*

FORTUNE TELLING See *Sorcery.*

FORTY Remarkable coincidences in the number.

DAYS. Of rain, at the time of the flood, Gen 7:17; of flood, before sending out the raven, Gen 8:6, 7. For embalming, Gen 50:3. Of fasting: By Moses, Ex 24:18; 34:28; Deut 9:9, 25; Elijah, 1 Kgs 19:8; Jesus, Mt 4:2. Spies in the land of Canaan, Num 13:25. Of probation, given to the Ninevites, Jon 3:4, 5. Christ's stay after the resurrection, Acts 1:3. Symbolical, Ezk 4:6.

YEARS. Wanderings of the Israelites in the wilderness, Ex 16:35; Num 14:34, 35. Peace in Israel, Judg 3:11; 5:31; 8:28. Egypt to be desolated, Ezk 29:11; to be restored after, Ezk 29:13.

STRIPES. Administered in punishing criminals, Deut 25:1–3.

FOUNDATION Of the Temple, 1 Kgs 5:17; Ezra 3:6, 10, 11; Isa 6:4; Hag 2:18, 19. Of the earth, Job 38:4; Ps 102:25; Isa 48:13; Zech 12:1. Spiritual, Eph 2:20; 1 Tim 6:3; 2 Tim 2:19; Heb 12:27; Jude 1:20. Christ as, Ps 118:22; Isa 28:16; Mt 21:42; Mk 12:10; Lk 20:17; Acts 4:11; 1 Cor 3:10, 11.

FIGURATIVE. 2 Sam 22:8; Job 9:6; Ps 82:5.

See *Founding.*

FOUNDING 1. See *Molding.*

2. Of Egypt, Ex 9:18.

Of the world. Kingdom prepared from the founding of the world, Mt 25:34. God's servants murdered since the founding of the world, Lk 11:50. Christ loved by God the Father from before the founding of the world, Jn 17:24; purpose determined before, 1 Pet 1:20. Believers chosen in Christ before the founding of the world, Eph 1:4; Rev 13:8; names written in the Book of Life before the founding of the world, Rev 17:8.

FOUNTAIN FIGURATIVE. Of divine grace, Ps 36:9; Jer 2:13; of the salvation of the gospel, Joel 3:18; Zech 13:1; Rev 7:17. The polluted, of the debasement of character, Prov 25:26.

FOX Dens of, Mt 8:20; Lk 9:58. Samson uses, to burn the fields of the Philistines, Judg 15:4. Plundering of, Song 2:15.

FIGURATIVE. Of false prophets, Ezk 13:4. Of craftiness, Lk 13:32. Of heretics, Song 2:15.

FRACTURES Treatment of, Ezk 30:21.

FRANKINCENSE An ingredient of the sacred incense, Ex 30:34. Used with showbread, Lev 24:5–8. Prohibited, in making an offering of suspicion, Num 5:15. A perfume, Song 3:6. Commerce in, Rev 18:11–13. Gift of, Mt 2:11.

FRATERNITY, BROTHERHOOD Gen 13:8. Then Abram talked it over with Lot. "This fighting between our men has got to stop," he said. "We can't afford to let a rift develop between our clans. Close relatives such as we are must present a united front!"

Deut 15:7. But if, when you arrive in the land the Lord will give you, there are any among you who are poor, you must not shut your heart or hand against them; [8]you must lend them as much as they need. [9]Beware! Don't refuse a loan because the year of debt cancellation is close at hand! If you refuse to make the loan and the needy man cries out to the Lord, it will be counted against you as a sin. [10]You must lend him what he needs, and don't moan about it either! For the Lord will prosper you in everything you do because of this. [11]There will always be some among you who are poor; that is why this commandment is necessary. You must lend to them liberally.

12. If you buy a Hebrew slave, whether a man or woman, you must free him at the end of the sixth year you have owned him, [13]and don't send him away empty-handed! [14]Give him a large farewell present from your flock, your olive press, and your wine press. Share with him in proportion as the Lord your God has blessed you. [15]Remember that you were slaves in the land of Egypt and the Lord your God rescued you! That is why I am giving you this command.

Ps 22:22. I will praise you to all my brothers.

Ps 133:1. How wonderful it is, how pleasant, when brothers live in harmony! [2]For harmony is as precious as the fragrant anointing oil that was poured over Aaron's head, and ran down onto his beard, and onto the border of his robe. [3]Harmony is as refreshing as the dew on Mount Hermon, on the mountains of Israel. And God has pronounced this eternal blessing on Jerusalem, even life forevermore.

Zech 11:14. Then I broke my other staff, "Union," to show that the bond of unity between Judah and Israel was broken.

Mal 2:10. We are children of the same father, Abraham, all created by the same God. And yet we are faithless to each other, violating the covenant of our fathers!

Mt 5:22. But I have added to that rule, and tell you that if you are only *angry,* even in your own home, you are in danger of judgment! If you call your friend an idiot, you are in danger of being brought before the court. And if you curse him, you are in danger of the fires of hell. [23]So if you are standing before the altar in the Temple, offering a sacrifice to God, and suddenly remember that a friend has something against you, [24]leave your sacrifice there beside the altar and go and apologize and be reconciled to him, and then come and offer your sacrifice to God.

Mt 18:15. If a brother sins against you, go to him privately and confront him with his fault. If he listens and confesses it, you have won back a brother. [16]But if not, then take one or two others with you and go back to him again, proving everything you say by these witnesses. [17]If he still refuses to listen, then take your case to the church, and if the church's verdict favors you, but he won't accept it, then the church should excommunicate him. [18]And I tell you this—whatever you bind on earth is bound in heaven, and whatever you free on earth will be freed in heaven.

21. Then Peter came to him and asked, "Sir, how often should I forgive a brother who sins against me? Seven times?" [22]"No!" Jesus replied, "seventy times seven!

35. So shall my heavenly Father do to you if you refuse to truly forgive your brothers.

Mt 23:8. Don't ever let anyone call you that. For only God is your Rabbi and all of you are on the same level, as brothers.

Mt 25:40. And I, the King, will tell them, "When you did it to these my brothers you were doing it to me!"

Jn 13:34. And so I am giving a new commandment to you now—love each other just as much as I love you. Jn 15:12.

Jn 20:17. "Don't touch me," he cautioned, "for I haven't yet ascended to the Father. But go find my brothers and tell them that I ascend to my Father and your Father, my God and your God."

Rom 12:10. Love each other with brotherly affection and take delight in honoring each other.

1 Cor 6:1. How is it that when you have something against another Christian, you "go to law" and ask a heathen court to decide the matter instead of taking it to other Christians to decide which of you is right? [2]Don't you know that some day we Christians are going to judge and govern the world? So why can't you decide even these little things among yourselves? [3]Don't you realize that we Christians will judge and reward the very angels in heaven? So you should be able to decide your problems down here on earth easily enough. [4]Why then go to outside judges who are not even Christians? [5]I am trying to make you ashamed. Isn't there anyone in all the church who is wise enough to decide these arguments? [6]But, instead, one Christian sues another and accuses his Chris-

tian brother in front of unbelievers. [7]To have such lawsuits at all is a real defeat for you as Christians. Why not just accept mistreatment and leave it at that? It would be far more honoring to the Lord to let yourselves be cheated. [8]But, instead, you yourselves are the ones who do wrong, cheating others, even your own brothers.

1 Cor 8:1. Next is your question about eating food that has been sacrificed to idols. On this question everyone feels that only his answer is the right one! But although being a "know-it-all" makes us feel important, what is really needed to build the church is love. [2]If anyone thinks he knows all the answers, he is just showing his ignorance. [3]But the person who truly loves God is the one who is open to God's knowledge. [4]So now, what about it? Should we eat meat that has been sacrificed to idols? Well, we all know that an idol is not really a god, and that there is only one God, and no other. [5]According to some people, there are a great many gods, both in heaven and on earth. [6]But we know that there is only one God, the Father, who created all things and made us to be his own; and one Lord Jesus Christ, who made everything and gives us life. [7]However, some Christians don't realize this. All their lives they have been used to thinking of idols as alive, and have believed that food offered to the idols is really being offered to actual gods. So when they eat such food it bothers them and hurts their tender consciences. [8]Just remember that God doesn't care whether we eat it or not. We are no worse off if we don't eat it, and no better off if we do. [9]But be careful not to use your freedom to eat it, lest you cause some Christian brother to sin whose conscience is weaker than yours. [10]You see, this is what may happen: Someone who thinks it is wrong to eat this food will see you eating at a temple restaurant, for you know there is no harm in it. Then he will become bold enough to do it too, although all the time he still feels it is wrong. [11]So because you "know it is all right to do it," you will be responsible for causing great spiritual damage to a brother with a tender conscience for whom Christ died. [12] And it is a sin against Christ to sin against your brother by encouraging him to do something he thinks is wrong. [13]So if eating meat offered to idols is going to make my brother sin, I'll not eat any of it as long as I live, because I don't want to do this to him.

Gal 6:1. Dear brothers, if a Christian is overcome by some sin, you who are godly should gently and humbly help him back onto the right path, remembering that next time it might be one of you who is in the wrong. [2]Share each other's troubles and problems, and so obey our Lord's command.

1 Thess 4:9. But concerning the pure brotherly love that there should be among God's people, I don't need to say very much, I'm sure! For God himself is teaching you to love one another.

2 Thess 3:14. If anyone refuses to obey what we say in this letter, notice who he is and stay away from him, that he may be ashamed of himself. [15]Don't think of him as an enemy, but speak to him as you would to a brother who needs to be warned.

Heb 13:1. Continue to love each other with true brotherly love.

1 Pet 1:22. Now you can have real love for everyone because your souls have been cleansed from selfishness and hatred when you trusted Christ to save you; so see to it that you really do love each other warmly, with all your hearts.

1 Pet 2:17. Love Christians everywhere.

1 Pet 3:8. And now this word to all of you: You should be like one big happy family, full of sympathy toward each other, loving one another with tender hearts and humble minds.

2 Pet 1:7. This will make possible the next step, which is for you to enjoy other people and to like them, and finally you will grow to love them deeply.

1 Jn 2:9. Anyone who says he is walking in the light of Christ but dislikes his fellow man, is still in darkness. [10]But whoever loves his fellow man is "walking in the light" and can see his way without stumbling around in darkness and sin. [11]For he who dislikes his brother is wandering in spiritual darkness and doesn't know where he is going, for the darkness had made him blind so that he cannot see the way.

1 Jn 3:17. But if someone who is supposed to be a Christian has money enough to live well, and sees a brother in need, and won't help him—how can God's love be within *him?*

See *Brother; Church, The True; Fellowship; Friendship.*

INSTANCES OF. The Nazirites, vows of, Num 6:1–21; Amos 2:11, 12; Acts 21:24–31. See *Nazirites.*

FRATRICIDE INSTANCES OF. Cain, Gen 4:8. Abimelech, Judg 9:5. Absalom, 2 Sam 13:28–30. Solomon, 1 Kgs 2:23–25. Jehoram, 2 Chron 21: 3, 4.

See *Homicide.*

FRAUD See *Dishonesty.*

FREEDMEN Cult of, Acts 6:9.

See *Emancipation.*

FREEDOM From servitude, see *Emancipation; Jubilee.*

FREE WILL See *Blessings, Divine, Contingent on Obedience.*

FREE-WILL OFFERINGS Lev 22:21, 23; Num 29:39; Deut 12:6, 17; 16:10; Ezra 3:5; 7:16; 8:28.

See *Benevolence; Giving; Liberality; Offerings.*

FRIENDS Jesus calls his disciples, Lk 12:4; Jn 15:14, 15.

FALSE FRIENDS. Instances of: Pharaoh's wine taster false to Joseph, Gen 40:23. Delilah to Samson, Judg 16:1–20. The Ephraimite's wife, Judg 19: 1–2. David to Joab, 1 Kgs 2:5, 6; to Uriah, 2 Sam 11. Ahithophel to David, 2 Sam 15:12. David's friends to David, Ps 35:11–16; 41:9; 55:12–14, 20, 21; 88:8, 18. Judas, Mt 26:48, 49. Disciples, Mt 26:56, 58.

See *Hypocrisy.*

FRIENDSHIP Deut 13:6, 7. If your nearest relative or closest friend, even a brother, son, daughter, or beloved wife whispers to you to come and worship these foreign gods, [8]do not consent nor listen, and have no pity: Do not spare that person from the penalty; don't conceal his horrible suggestion. [9]Execute him! Your own hand shall be the first upon him to put him to death, then the hands of all the people.

Job 6:14. One should be kind to a fainting friend, but you have accused me without the slightest fear of God. [15]My brother, you have proved as unreliable as a brook; it floods when there is ice and snow, but in hot weather, disappears.

Job 16:2. I have heard all this before. What miserable comforters all of you are. [20]My friends scoff at me, but I pour out my tears to God.

Job 19:13. He has sent away my brothers, and my friends. [14]My relatives have failed me; my friends have all forsaken me. [15]Those living in my home, even my servants, regard me as a stranger. I am like a foreigner to them. [16]I call my servant, but he doesn't come; I even beg him! [17]My own wife and brothers refuse to recognize me. [18]Even young children despise me. When I stand to speak, they mock. [19]My best friends abhor me. Those I loved have turned against me. [20]I am skin and bones and have escaped death by the skin of my teeth. [21]Oh, my friends, pity me, for the angry hand of God has touched me. [22]Why must you persecute me as God does? Why aren't you satisfied with my anguish?

Ps 35:13. When they were ill, I mourned before the Lord in sackcloth, asking him to make them well; I refused to eat; I prayed for them with utmost earnestness, but God did not listen. [14]I went about sadly as though it were my mother, friend or brother who was sick and nearing death.

Ps 41:9. Even my best friend has turned against me—a man I completely trusted; how often we ate together.

Ps 55:12. It was not an enemy who taunted me—then I could have borne it; I could have hidden and escaped. [13]But it was you, a man like myself, my companion and my friend. [14]What fellowship we had, what wonderful discussions as we walked together to the Temple of the Lord on holy days.

Ps 88:8. You have made my friends to loathe me, and they have gone away. I am in a trap with no way out. [18]Lover, friend, acquaintance—all are gone. There is only darkness everywhere.

Prov 11:13. A gossip goes around spreading rumors, while a trustworthy man tries to quiet them.

Prov 17:9. Love forgets mistakes; nagging about them parts the best of friends. [17]A true friend is always loyal, and a brother is born to help in time of need.

Prov 18:24. There are "friends" who pretend to be friends, but there is a friend who sticks closer than a brother.

Prov 22:24, 25. Keep away from angry, short-tempered men, lest you learn to be like them and endanger your soul. [26, 27]Unless you have the extra cash on hand, don't countersign a note. Why risk everything you own? They'll even take your bed!

Prov 25:17. Don't visit your neighbor too often, or you will outwear your welcome! [19]Putting confidence in an unreliable man is like chewing with a sore tooth, or trying to run on a broken foot.

Prov 27:6. Wounds from a friend are better than kisses from an enemy. [9]Friendly suggestions are as pleasant as perfume. [10]Never abandon a friend—either yours or your father's. Then you won't need to go to a distant relative for help in your time of need. [14]If you shout a pleasant greeting to a friend too early in the morning, he will count it as a curse! [17]A friendly discussion is as stimulating as the sparks that fly when iron strikes iron. [19]A mirror reflects a man's face, but what he is really like is shown by the kind of friends he chooses.

Eccl 4:9. Two can accomplish more than twice as much as one, for the results can be much better. [10]If one falls, the other pulls him up; but if a man falls when he is alone, he's in trouble. [11]Also, on a cold night, two under the same blanket gain warmth from each other, but how can one be warm alone? [12]And one standing alone can be attacked and defeated, but two can stand back-to-back and conquer; three is even better, for a triple-braided cord is not easily broken.

Amos 3:3. For how can we walk together with your sins between us?

2 Tim 4:16. The first time I was brought before the judge no one was here to help me. Everyone had run away. I hope that they will not be blamed for it.

Jas 4:4. Don't you realize that making friends with God's enemies—the evil pleasures of this world—makes you an enemy of God? I say it again, that if your aim is to enjoy the evil pleasure of the unsaved world, you cannot also be a friend of God. Rom 2:2; 1 Jn 2:15.

INSTANCES OF. Abraham and Lot, Gen 14:14–16. Ruth and Naomi, Ruth 1:16, 17. Samuel and Saul, 1 Sam 15:35; 16:1. David and Jonathan, 1 Sam 18:1–4; 20; 23:16–18; 2 Sam 1:17–27; 9:1–13. David and Abiathar, 1 Sam 22:23. David and Nahash, 2 Sam 10:2. David and Hiram, 1 Kgs 5:1. David and Mephibosheth, 2 Sam 9. David and Hushai, 2 Sam 15:32–37; 16; 17:1–22. David and Ittai, 2 Sam 15:19–21. Joram and Ahaziah, 2 Kgs 8:28, 29; 9:16. Jehu and Jehonadab, 2 Kgs 10:15–27. Job and his three friends, Job 2:11–13. Daniel and his three companions, Dan 2:49.

Mary, Martha, and Lazarus, and Jesus, Lk 10:38–42; Jn 11:1–46. The Marys, and Joseph of Arimathaea, for Jesus, Mt 27:55–61; 28:1–8; Lk 24:10; Jn 20:11–18; Luke and Theophilus, Acts 1:1. Paul and his nephew, Acts 23:16. Paul, Priscilla, and Aquila, Rom 16:3, 4. Paul, Timothy, and Epaphroditus, Phil 2:19, 20, 22, 25.

FRINGES Lengthened by the Pharisees, Mt 23:5.

See *Tassels.*

FROGS Plague of, Ex 8:2–14; Ps 78:45; 105:30. *Symbolical.* Rev 16:13.

FRUGALITY 1 Kgs 17:5. So he did as the Lord had told him to, and camped beside the brook. [6]The ravens brought him bread and meat each morning and evening, and he drank from the brook. [10]So he went to Zarephath. As he arrived at the gates of the city he saw a widow gathering sticks; and he asked her for a cup of water. [11]As she was going to get it, he called to her, "Bring me a bite of bread, too." [12]But she said, "I swear by the Lord your God that I haven't a single piece of bread in the house. And I have only a handful of flour left and a little cooking oil in the bottom of the jar. I was just gathering a few sticks to cook this last meal, and then my son and I must die of starvation." [13]But Elijah said to her, "Don't be afraid! Go ahead and cook that 'last meal,' but bake me a little loaf of bread first; and afterwards there will still be enough food for you and your son."

Prov 12:27. A lazy man won't even dress the game he gets while hunting, but the diligent man makes good use of everything he finds.

Prov 13:22. When a good man dies, he leaves an inheritance to his grandchildren; but when a sinner dies, his wealth is stored up for the godly.

Prov 21:17. A man who loves pleasure becomes poor; wine and luxury are not the way to riches! [20]The wise man saves for the future, but the foolish man spends whatever he gets.

Prov 22:3. A prudent man foresees the difficulties ahead and prepares for them; the simpleton goes blindly on and suffers the consequences.

Prov 23:20, 21. Don't carouse with drunkards and gluttons, for they are on their way to poverty. And remember that too much sleep clothes a man with rags.

Prov 31:27. She watches carefully all that goes on throughout her household, and is never lazy.

Mt 14:20. And everyone ate until full! And when the scraps were picked up afterwards, there were twelve basketfuls left over!

Mt 15:37, 38. And everyone ate until full—4,000 men besides the women and children! And afterwards, when the scraps were picked up, there were seven basketfuls left over!

Mk 7:28. She replied, "That's true, sir, but even the puppies under the table are given some scraps from the children's plates."

Mk 14:4, 5. Some of those at the table were indignant among themselves about this "waste," as they called it. "Why, she could have sold that perfume for a fortune and given the money to the poor!" they snarled.

Eph 4:28. If anyone is stealing he must stop it and begin using those hands of his for honest work so he can give to others in need.

See *Extravagance; Industry.*

INSTANCES OF. The provisions made by the Egyptians against famine, Gen 41:48–49, 53, 54. The gathering of manna, Ex 16:17, 18, 22–24.

FRUITS NATURAL. Gen 1:11, 12. And he said, "Let the earth burst forth with every sort of grass and seed-bearing plant, and fruit trees with seeds inside the fruit, so that these seeds will produce the kinds of plants and fruits they came from." And so it was, and God was pleased. [27]So God made man like his Maker. Like God did God make man; man and maid did he make them. [28]And God blessed them and told them, "Multiply and fill the earth and subdue it; you are masters of the fish and birds and all the animals. [29]And look! I have given you the seed-bearing plants throughout the earth, and all the fruit trees for your food." Ps 104:14.

See under the respective headings of various fruit-producing trees.

SPIRITUAL. See *Righteousness, Fruits of; Sin, Fruits of.*

FRUIT TREES Care for, Lev 19:23; Deut 20:19, 20.

FRYING PAN Lev 2:7; 7:9.

FUEL For Temple, how provided, Neh 10:34; 13:30, 31.

FUGITIVES From slavery, not to be returned, Deut 23:15, 16.

INSTANCES OF. From slavery, Shime-i's servants, 1 Kgs 2:39; Onesimus, Philemon 1:10, 11.

See *Exodus.*

From justice: Moses, Ex 2:15; Absalom, 2 Sam 13:34–39.

From the anger of the king: David, 1 Sam 21:10; Jeroboam, 1 Kgs 11:40; Joseph, to Egypt, Mt 2:13–15.

FULLER'S FIELD A spot near Jerusalem, where cloth was bleached, 2 Kgs 18:17; Isa 7:3; 36:2.

FUNERALS See *Burial; Elegy.*

FURNACE Uses of: For refining silver, Ezk 22:22; Mal 3:3; gold, Prov 17:3. For melting lead and tin, Ezk 22:20. For capital punishment, Shadrach, Meshach, and Abednego thrown into, by Nebuchadnezzar, Dan 3:6–26.

FIGURATIVE. Of affliction, 1 Kgs 8:51; Isa 48:10; Of intrigue, Hos 7:7. Of hell, Mal 4:1; Mt 13:42; Rev 9:2.

FUTURE PUNISHMENT See *Punishment, Eternal.*

G

GAAL Conspires against and is defeated by Abimelech, Judg 9:26–41.

GAASH A mountain. Joshua's estate included, Josh 24:30. Joshua buried on the north side of, Josh 24:30; Judg 2:7–9. Brooks of, 2 Sam 23:24–39.

GABA See *Geba.*

GABBAI A Benjaminite leader, Neh 11:8.

GABBATHA A place of judgment in Jerusalem, where Pilate passed sentence on Jesus, Jn 19:13.

GABRIEL A messenger of God. Appeared to Daniel, Dan 8:16; 9:21; to Zacharias, Lk 1:11–19; to Mary, Lk 1:26–29.

GAD 1. Jacob's seventh son, Gen 30:11; 35:26; Ex 1:4. Children of, Gen 46:16, 17; Num 26:15–18; 1 Chron 5:11. Prophecy concerning, Gen 49:19.

2. A tribe of Israel. Blessed by Moses, Deut 33:20. Census of, at Sinai, Num 1:2–15, 20–46; in the plains of Moab, Num 26:15–18; during the reign of Jotham, 1 Chron 5:11–17. Place of, in camp and march, Num 2:3–31. Wealth of, in livestock, and spoils, Josh 22:1, 7, 8; Num 32:1. Petition for their portion of land east of the Jordan, Num 32:1–5; Deut 3:12, 16, 17; 29:8. Boundaries of territory, Josh 13:24–28; 1 Chron 5:11. Aid in the conquest of the region west of the Jordan, Num 32:16–32; Josh 4:12, 13; 22:1–8. Erect a monument to signify the unity of the tribes east of the Jordan with the tribes west of the river, Josh 22:10–14, 34.

Opposed to Saul as king, and joined the faction under David in the wilderness of Hebron, 1 Chron 12:8–15, 38. Join the Reubenites in the war against the Hagrites, 1 Chron 5:10, 18–22. Conquered by Hazael, 2 Kgs 10:32, 33. Taken captive by the Assyrians, 1 Chron 5:26. Land of, occupied by the Ammonites, after the tribe is taken captive, Jer 49:1. Reallotment of territory to, by Ezekiel, Ezk 48:27–29.

3. A prophet of David, 2 Sam 24:11. Tells David to leave Adullam, 1 Sam 22:5. Gives God's message to David, offering a choice between three evils, for his presumption in taking a census of Israel, 2 Sam 24:11–14; 1 Chron 21:9–13. Tells David to build an altar on threshing floor of Araunah, 2 Sam 24:18, 19; 1 Chron 21:18, 19. Assists David in arranging temple service, 2 Chron 29:25, 26. Writings of, 1 Chron 29:29.

GADARENES Called also *Gerasene.* Jesus visits and works miracles in, but is rejected, Mt 8:28–34; Mk 5:1–19; Lk 8:26–37.

GADDI A leader of Manasseh. One of the twelve spies who explored Canaan, Num 13:3–15.

GADDIEL A leader of Zebulun. One of the twelve spies, Num 13:3–15.

GADI Father of Menahem, 2 Kgs 15:14.

GAHAM Son of Nahor, Gen 22:24.

GAHAR One of the returned exiles Ezra 2:43–54; Neh 7:46–56.

GAIUS 1. A Macedonian, and a companion of Paul. Seized at Ephesus, Acts 19:29.

2. A man of Derbe, accompanied Paul from Macedonia, Acts 20:4.

3. A Corinthian, whom Paul baptized, Rom 16:23; 1 Cor 1:14.

4. Man to whom John's third epistle was addressed. 3 Jn.

GALAL 1. A Levite, 1 Chron 9:15, 16.

2. Son of Jeduthun, 1 Chron 9:15, 16; Neh 11:15–17.

GALATIA A province of Asia Minor. Its churches visited by Paul, Acts 16:6; 18:23. Collection taken in, for Christians at Jerusalem, 1 Cor 16:1. Peter's address to, 1 Pet 1:1. Churches in, Gal 1:1, 2. See Paul's epistle to Galatians.

GALBANUM A fragrant gum used in the holy incense, Ex 30:34.

GALEED Called also *Jegar-sahadutha.* The monument of Jacob's and Laban's covenant, Gen 31:47, 48.

GALILEE 1. The northern district of Palestine. A city of refuge in, Josh 20:7; 21:32; 1 Chron 6:76. Cities in, given to Hiram, 1 Kgs 9:11, 12. Taken by king of Assyria, 2 Kgs 15:29. Prophecy concerning, Isa 9:1; Mt 4:15, 16. Herod, ruler of, Mk 6:21; Lk 3:1; 23:6, 7. Jesus lives in, Mt 17:22, 23; 19:1; Jn 7:1, 9. Teaching and miracles of Jesus in, Mt 4:23, 25; 15:29–31; Mk 1:14, 28, 39; 3:7, 8; Lk 4:14, 31: 5:17; 23:5; Jn 1:43; 4:3, 43–45; Acts 10:36, 37. People of, welcome Jesus, Jn 4:45, 53. Disciples were chiefly from, Acts 1:11; 2:7. Women from, ministered to Jesus, Mt 27:55, 56; Mk 15:41; Lk 23:49, 55. Jesus appeared to his disciples in, after his resurrection, Mt 26:32; 28:7, 10, 16, 17; Mk 14:28; 16:7; Jn 21.

Routes from, to Judea, Judg 21:19; Jn 4:3–5.

Called *Gennesaret,* Mt 14:34; Mk 6:53. Churches in, Acts 9:31.

2. Sea of. Called *Sea of Tiberias,* Jn 6:1; *Lake Gennesaret,* Lk 5:1; *Sea of Chinnereth,* Deut 3:17. Jesus calls disciples on the shore of, Mt 4:18–22; Lk 5:1–11. Jesus teaches from a boat on, Mt 13:1–3. Miracles of Jesus on, Mt 8:24–32; 14:22–33; 17:26, 27; Mk 4:37–39; Lk 5:1–9; 8:22–24; Jn 21:1–11.

GALL FIGURATIVE. Gall of bitterness, Acts 8:23.

GALL BLADDER Burnt with sacrifice, Ex 29:13, 22; Lev 3:3–5, 9–11, 15, 16; 4:9; 7:4; 8:25; 9:10, 19.

GALLIM A town, probably in Benjamin, 1 Sam 25:44; Isa 10:30.

GALLIO Governor (specifically, proconsul) of Achaia. Dismisses complaint of Jews against Paul, Acts 18:12–17.

GALLON See *Measure.*

GALLOWS Used for execution of criminals, Ezra 6:11; Esther 5:14; 6:4; 7:9, 10; 9:13, 24, 25.

See *Punishment.*

GAMAD Men of, were warriors or watchmen, Ezk 27:11.

GAMALIEL 1. A celebrated teacher. Speech of, before the Council (Sanhedrin), Acts 5:33–40. Paul's teacher, Acts 22:3.

2. A leader of Manasseh, Num 1:2–15; 2:3–31; 10:23. Offering of, at dedication of the Tabernacle, Num 7:54–59.

GAMES Foot races, 1 Cor 9:24, 26; Heb 12:1. Gladiatorial, 1 Cor 4:9; 9:26; 15:32; 2 Tim 4:7.

FIGURATIVE. Of the Christian life, 1 Cor 9:24, 26; Phil 3:14; Heb 12:1. Of spiritual conflict, 1 Cor 4:9; 9:26; 15:32; 2 Tim 4:7.

GAMUL A priest in the time of David, 1 Chron 24:7–18.

GARDEN Of Eden, see *Eden.* Of Gethsemane, see *Gethsemane.*

FIGURATIVE. Hos 14:7.

GAREB 1. One of David's mighty men, 2 Sam 23:24–39; 1 Chron 11:26–47.

2. A hill, Jer 31:38, 39.

GARLIC Num 11:4, 5.

GARMENT Of righteousness, Isa 61:10; Rev 3:18; 7:14; 16:15; 19:8.

See *Dress; Robe.*

GARRISON A military camp, 1 Sam 13:3, 4; 2 Sam 8:6, 14; 23:14.

GATAM Grandson of Esau, Gen 36:10–12, 15, 16; 1 Chron 1:36.

GATEKEEPERS Guards at the city gates, the doors of the king's palace, and doors of the Tabernacle, 1 Chron 9:17–32; 2 Chron 35:15. Lived near the Tabernacle in order to open the doors in the morning, 1 Chron 9:27. One-third guarded the Temple entrance, 2 Chron 23:4; one-third served in the palace, 2 Chron 23:5, 6; and one-third were stationed at the Lower Gate, 2 Chron 23:5, 6. They served, also, as collectors at the gates, Neh 12:25. They served in the 24 divisions, 1 Chron 26:13–19. Their posts were determined by coin-toss, 1 Chron 24:31; 26:13–19.

GATES Of cities, Deut 3:5; Josh 6:26; 2 Sam 18:24; 2 Chron 8:5. Made of iron, Acts 12:10; wood, Neh 1:3; brass, Ps 107:16; Isa 45:2. Double doors, Ezk 41:24.

The open square of, a place for idlers, Gen 19:1; 1 Sam 4:18; Jer 17:19, 20. Religious services held at, Acts 14:13. The law read at, Neh 8. Place for the transaction of public business, announcement of legal transactions, Gen 23:10, 16–18; conferences on public affairs, Gen 34:20; holding courts of justice, Ruth 4:1; 2 Sam 15:2. Place for public concourse, Prov 8:3. Thrones of kings at, 1 Kgs 22:10; 2 Chron 18:9; Jer 38:7, 8; 39:3. Punishment of criminals outside of, Deut 17:5; Jer 20:2; Acts 7:58; Heb 13:12. Closed at night, Josh 2:5, 7; on the Sabbath, Neh 13:19. Guards at, 2 Kgs 7:17; Neh 13:19, 22. Jails made in the towers of, Jer 20:2. Bodies of criminals exposed to view at, 2 Kgs 10:8.

FIGURATIVE. Of the gospel, Isa 60:11. Of the powers of death, Job 38:17, 18; of Sheol, Isa 38:10. Of righteousness, Ps 118:19. Of salvation, Ps 24:7; 118:19, 20; Isa 26:2; Mt 7:13. Of death, Isa 38:10.

Symbolical. Rev 21:12, 13, 21, 25.

GATH One of the five chief cities of the Philistines, Josh 13:2–7; 1 Sam 6:17; Amos 6:2; Mic 1:10. Anakim, a race of giants, inhabitants of, Josh 11:21, 22. Goliath lived in, 1 Sam 17:4; 1 Chron 20:5–8. Obed-edom from, 2 Sam 6:10. The ark taken to, 1 Sam 5:8. David takes refuge at, 1 Sam 21:10–15; 27:2–7. Band of Gittites, attached to David, 2 Sam 15:17–22. Taken by David, 1 Chron 18:1. Shime-i's servants escape to, 1 Kgs 2:39–41. Fortified by Rehoboam, 2 Chron 11:5–10. Taken, by Hazael, 2 Kgs 12:17. Recovered, by Joash, 2 Kgs 13:25. Captured, by Uzziah, 2 Chron 26:6.

GATH-HEPHER A city of Zebulun, Josh 19:13; 2 Kgs 14:25.

GATH-RIMMON 1. A Levitical city of Dan, Josh 19:41–46.

2. A city of Manasseh, Josh 21:25; 1 Chron 6:66–69. Called also *Bile-am,* 1 Chron 6:70.

GAZA A city of the Philistines, Josh 13:3; Jer 25:19, 20. One of the border cities of the Canaanites, Gen 10:15–19. A city of the Avvim and Anakim, Deut 2:23; Josh 11:22. Allotted to Judah, Josh 15:47; Judg 1:18. A temple of Dagon, situated at, Judg 16:23, 24. Samson dies at, Judg 16:21–31. On the western boundary of the kingdom of Israel in the time of Solomon, 1 Kgs 4:24. Captured by Pharaoh, Jer 47:1.

Prophecies relating to, Amos 1:6, 7; Zeph 2:4; Zech 9:5.

Desert of, Acts 8:26–39.

GAZEZ 1. A son of Caleb, 1 Chron 2:46.

2. A grandson of Caleb, 1 Chron 2:46.

GAZZAM One of the returned exiles, Ezra 2:43–54; Neh 7:46–56.

GEBA Called also *Gaba.* A city of Canaan, allotted to Benjamin, Josh 18:24; Ezra 2:3–35; Neh 7:8–38. A city of Benjamin, 1 Kgs 15:22; 2 Kgs 23:8; 1 Chron 8:6; 2 Chron 16:6; Neh 11:31; 12:29; Isa 10:29; Zech 14:10. Assigned to the Levites, Josh 21:17, 18; 1 Chron 6:60. Philistines defeated at, 1 Sam 13:3, 4; 2 Sam 5:25.

GEBAL 1. A city on the Mediterranean. Given to Israel, Josh 13:5. People of, work for Solomon, 1 Kgs 5:18. Shipbuilders in, Ezk 27:9.

2. A district near the Dead Sea, Ps 83:7.

GEBER Name of two men, called also *Bengeber,* officers of Solomon, 1 Kgs 4:8–19.

GEBIM A city of Benjamin, Isa 10:31.

GEDALIAH 1. Governor of Judah, appointed by Nebuchadnezzar after the defeat and exile of the Jews, 2 Kgs 25:22–24. Jeremiah committed to the care of, Jer 39:14; 40:5, 6. Warned by Johanan of the conspiracy of Ishmael, Jer 40:13–16. Killed by Ishmael, 2 Kgs 25:25, 26; Jer 41:1–10.

2. A musician, 1 Chron 25:3, 9–31.

3. A priest, who divorced his Gentile wife after the exile, Ezra 10:16–19.

4. Ancestor of Zephaniah, Zeph 1:1.

5. A prince who caused imprisonment of Jeremiah, Jer 38:1.

GEDER An ancient city of Canaan, Josh 12:8–24. Possibly identical with *Gedor, 2 or 3.*

GEDERAH A city in plain of Judah, Josh 15:33–36.

GEDEROTH A city in plain of Judah, Josh 15:37–44; 2 Chron 28:17, 18.

GEDEROTHAIM A city in plain of Judah, Josh 15:33–36.

GEDOR 1. A city in hill country of Judah, Josh 15:48–62.

2. The town of Jeroham, 1 Chron 12:3–7. Possibly identical with *Geder,* which see.

3. Valley of, taken by Simeonites, 1 Chron 4:34–39. See *Geder.*

4. An ancestor of Saul, 1 Chron 8:30–32; 9:35–37.

5. Either a place or a person, authorities disagree, 1 Chron 4:4, 18.

GEHAZI Servant of Elisha, 2 Kgs 4:12, 29, 31. Greed of, and the judgment of leprosy on, 2 Kgs 5:20–27. Mentions to King Jehoram the miracles of Elisha, his master, 2 Kgs 8:4, 5.

GEHENNA The Greek word rendered hell in Mt 5:22, 29, 30; 10:28; 18:9; 23:15, 33; Mk 9:43–47; Lk 12:5; Jas 3:6. Synonymous with the Lake of Fire, Rev 19:20; 20:10, 14, 15, it refers to the place to which evil men and angels are committed forever, separated from God.

The word is derived from the valley of Hinnom, Josh 15:8; 18:16, a deep ravine to the south of Jerusalem, now filled with the debris of the centuries. There Solomon erected a temple for Molech, 1 Kgs 11:7, an evil false god given special mention in Lev 18:21; 20:1–5. Manasseh sacrificed his children there in a pagan ceremony, as did others, 2 Chron 33:6, cf. 2 Kgs 23:10; Jer 19:1–6. Infants were offered in sacrifice in Topheth, in the southeastern part of Hinnom, 2 Kgs 23:10; Jer 7:31. King Josiah destroyed the altar of Topheth in the valley, 2 Kgs 23:10. Afterward the bodies of executed criminals were cast into it and it was called "the graveyard and ash dump," Jer 31:40. Worms fed on the carcasses, perpetual fires were kept burning to consume the refuse.

The name Gehenna became a symbol for "the unquenchable fires of hell," Mk 9:43, 44.

See *Hades; Pit; Sheol; Tartarus; Wicked, Punishment of.*

GELILOTH A place mentioned, Josh 18:17, as marking the boundary of Benjamin. In Josh 15:7, Gilgal is substituted.

GEMALLI Father of Ammiel, Num 13:3–15.

GEMARIAH 1. Son of Shaphan, Jer 36:10–12, 24, 25.

2. An ambassador of Zedekiah to Nebuchadnezzar, Jer 29:3.

GEMS See *Jewels; Precious Stones.*

GENEALOGY Num 1:17–19; 2 Chron 12:15; Ezra 2:59; Neh 7:5; Heb 7:3. Of no spiritual significance, Mt 3:9.

From Adam to Noah, Gen 4:16–22; 5; 1 Chron 1:1–4; to Abraham, Gen 11:10–32; 1 Chron 1:1–27; to Jesus, Mt 1:1–16; Lk 3:23–38. Of the descendants of Noah, Gen 10; of Nahor, Gen 22:20–24; of Abraham, by his wife Keturah, Gen 25:1–4; 1 Chron 1:32, 33; of Ishmael, Gen 25:12–16; 1 Chron 1:28–31; of Esau, Gen 36; 1 Chron 1:35–54; of Jacob, Gen 35:23–26; Ex 1:1–5; 6:14–27; Num 26; 1 Chron chapters 2–9; of Perez to David, Ruth 4:18–22. Of Ezra, Ezra 7:1–5. Of the Jews who returned from Babylon, Ezra 8:1–15; Neh 7. Of Joseph, Mt 1; Lk 3:23–38.

GENERAL Of an army, 1 Sam 14:50, 51; 17:25. Distinguished, see *Abraham; Joshua; Saul; David; Joab; Amasa; Gideon; Benaiah; Naaman; Jephthah; Benhadad; Sennacherib.* See *Captain; Officer; Armies.*

GENEROSITY See *Liberality.*

GENIUS Mechanical, a skill given by God, Ex 28:3; 31:1–11; 35:30–35; 36:1.

GENNESARET See *Galilee.*

GENTILES The Hebrew word *goy* is variously rendered in the Old Testament by the words Gentiles, heathen, and nations. In the New Testament the Greek word *ethnos* is rendered by the same three English words. More than 750 references appear, and refer to people not of Israel, whether believers or not.

See *Heathen; Nations.*

UNCLASSIFIED SCRIPTURES RELATING TO. Jer 10:2, 3. Don't act like the people who make horoscopes and try to read their fate and future in the stars! Don't be frightened by predictions such as theirs, for it is all a pack of lies. Their ways are futile and foolish. They cut down a tree and carve an idol.

Mt 6:7, 8. Don't recite the same prayer over and over as the heathen do, who think prayers are answered only by repeating them again and again. Remember, your Father knows exactly what you need even before you ask him! [31, 32]So don't worry at all about having enough food and clothing. Why be like the heathen? For they take pride in all these things and are deeply concerned about them. But your heavenly Father already knows perfectly well that you need them.

Acts 14:16. In bygone days he permitted

the nations to go their own ways.

Acts 17:4. Some who listened were persuaded and became converts—including a large number of godly Greek men, and also many important women of the city. [16]While Paul was waiting for them in Athens, he was deeply troubled by all the idols he saw everywhere throughout the city. [17]He went to the synagogue for discussions with the Jews and the devout Gentiles, and spoke daily in the public square to all who happened to be there. [22]So Paul, standing before them at the Mars Hill forum, addressed them as follows: "Men of Athens, I notice that you are very religious, [23]for as I was out walking I saw your many altars, and one of them had this inscription on it—'To the Unknown God.' You have been worshiping him without knowing who he is, and now I wish to tell you about him. [24]He made the world and everything in it, and since he is Lord of heaven and earth, he doesn't live in man-made temples; [25]and human hands can't minister to his needs—for he has no needs! He himself gives life and breath to everything, and satisfies every need there is. [26]He created all the people of the world from one man, Adam, and scattered the nations across the face of the earth. He decided beforehand which should rise and fall, and when. He determined their boundaries. [27]His purpose in all of this is that they should seek after God, and perhaps feel their way toward him and find him—though he is not far from any one of us."

Rom 1:18. But God shows his anger from heaven against all sinful, evil men who push away the truth from them. [19]For the truth about God is known to them instinctively; God has put this knowledge in their hearts. [20]Since earliest times men have seen the earth and sky and all God made, and have known of his existence and great eternal power. So they will have no excuse [when they stand before God at Judgment Day]. [21]Yes, they knew about him all right, but they wouldn't admit it or worship him or even thank him for all his daily care. And after awhile they began to think up silly ideas of what God was like and what he wanted them to do. The result was that their foolish minds became dark and confused. [22]Claiming themselves to be wise without God, they became utter fools instead. [23]And then, instead of worshiping the glorious, ever-living God, they took wood and stone and made idols for themselves, carving them to look like mere birds and animals and snakes and puny men. [24]So God let them go ahead into every sort of sex sin, and do whatever they wanted to—yes, vile and sinful things with each other's bodies. [25]Instead of believing what they knew was the truth about God, they deliberately chose to believe lies. So they prayed to the things God made, but wouldn't obey the blessed God who made these things. [26]That is why God let go of them and let them do all these evil things, so that even their women turned against God's natural plan for them and indulged in sex sin with each other. [27]And the men, instead of having a normal sex relationship with women, burned with lust for each other, men doing shameful things with other men and, as a result, getting paid within their own souls with the penalty they so richly deserved. [28]So it was that when they gave God up and would not even acknowledge him, God gave them up to doing everything their evil mind could think of. [29]Their lives became full of every kind of wickedness and sin, of greed and hate, envy, murder, fighting, lying, bitterness, and gossip. [30]They were backbiters, haters of God, insolent, proud braggarts, always thinking of new ways of sinning and continually being disobedient to their parents. [31]They tried to misunderstand, broke their promises, and were heartless—without pity. [32]They were fully aware of God's death penalty for these crimes, yet they went right ahead and did them anyway, and encouraged others to do them, too.

Rom 2:1. "Well," you may be saying, "what terrible people you have been talking about!" But wait a minute! You are just as bad. When you say they are wicked and should be punished, you are talking about yourselves, for you do these very same things. [2]And we know that God, in justice, will punish anyone who does such things as these. [3]Do you think that God will judge and condemn others for doing them and overlook you when you do them, too? [4]Don't you realize how patient he is being with you? Or don't you care? Can't you see that he has been waiting all this time without punishing you, to give you time to turn from your sin? His kindness is meant to lead you to repentance. [5]But no, you won't listen; and so you are saving up terrible punishment for yourselves because of your stubbornness in refusing to turn from your sin; for there is going to come a day of wrath when God will be the just Judge of all the world. [6]He will give each one whatever his deeds deserve. [7]He will give eternal life to those who patiently do the will of God, seeking for the unseen glory and honor and eternal life that he offers. [8]But he will terribly punish those who fight against the truth of God and walk in evil ways—God's anger will be poured out upon them. [9]There will be sorrow and suffering for Jews and Gentiles alike who keep on sinning. [10]But there will be glory and honor and peace from God for all who obey him, whether they are Jews or Gentiles. [11]For God treats everyone the same. [12-15]He will punish sin wherever it is found. He will punish the heathen when they sin, even though they never had God's written laws, for down in their hearts they know right from wrong. God's laws are written within them; their own conscience accuses them, or sometimes excuses them. And God will punish the Jews for sinning because they have his written laws but don't obey them. They know what is right but they don't do it. After all, salvation is not given to those who know what to do, unless they do it.

1 Cor 10:20. What I am saying is that those who offer food to these idols are united together in sacrificing to demons, certainly not to God.

1 Cor 12:2. You will remember that before you

became Christians you went around from one idol to another, not one of which could speak a single word.

Gal 2:15. You and I are Jews by birth, not mere Gentile sinners.

Eph 2:12. Remember that in those days you were living utterly apart from Christ; you were enemies of God's children and he had promised you no help. You were lost, without God, without hope.

Eph 4:17, 18. Let me say this, then, speaking for the Lord: Live no longer as the unsaved do, for they are blinded and confused. Their closed hearts are full of darkness; they are far away from the life of God because they have shut their minds against him, and they cannot understand his ways. [19]They don't care anymore about right and wrong and have given themselves over to impure ways. They stop at nothing, being driven by their evil minds and reckless lusts.

Eph 5:12. It would be shameful even to mention here those pleasures of darkness which the ungodly do.

1 Thess 4:5. Not in lustful passion as the heathen do, in their ignorance of God and his ways.

1 Pet 4:3. You have had enough in the past of the evil things the godless enjoy—sex sin, lust, getting drunk, wild parties, drinking bouts, and the worship of idols, and other terrible sins. [4]Of course, your former friends will be very surprised when you don't eagerly join them any more in the wicked things they do, and they will laugh at you in contempt and scorn.

See *Idolatry; Missions.*

PROPHECIES OF THE CONVERSION OF. Gen 12:3. And the entire world will be blessed because of you. *v.* 5.

Gen 22:18. And be a blessing to all the nations of the earth—all because you have obeyed me.

Gen 49:10. The scepter shall not depart from Judah until Shiloh comes, whom all people shall obey.

Deut 32:21. They have made me very jealous of their idols, which are not gods at all. Now I, in turn, will make them jealous by giving my affections to the foolish Gentile nations of the world.

Ps 2:8. Only ask, and I will give you all the nations of the world.

Ps 22:27. The whole earth shall see it and return to the Lord; the people of every nation shall worship him. [28]For the Lord is King and rules the nations. [29]Both proud and humble together, all who are mortal—born to die—shall worship him. [30]Our children too shall serve him, for they shall hear from us about the wonders of the Lord; [31]generations yet unborn shall hear of all the miracles he did for us.

Ps 46:4. There is a river of joy flowing through the City of our God—the sacred home of the God above all gods. [10]"Stand silent! Know that I am God! I will be honored by every nation in the world!"

Ps 65:2. And because you answer prayer, all mankind will come to you with their requests. [5]You are the only hope of all mankind throughout the world and far away upon the sea.

Ps 66:4. All the earth shall worship you and sing of your glories.

Ps 68:31. Egypt will send gifts of precious metals. Ethiopia will stretch out her hands to God in adoration. [32]Sing to the Lord, O kingdoms of the earth—sing praises to the Lord.

Ps 72:8. Let him reign from sea to sea, and from the Euphrates River to the ends of the earth. [9]The desert nomads shall bow before him; his enemies shall fall face downward in the dust. [10]Kings along the Mediterranean coast—the kings of Tarshish and the islands—and those from Sheba and from Seba—all will bring their gifts. [11]Yes, kings from everywhere! All will bow before him! All will serve him! [16]Bless us with abundant crops throughout the land, even on the highland plains; may there be fruit like that of Lebanon; may the cities be as full of people as the fields are of grass. [19]Blessed be his glorious name forever! Let the whole earth be filled with his glory. Amen, and amen! *vs.* 1–20.

Ps 86:9. All the nations—and you made each one—will come and bow before you, Lord, and praise your great and holy name.

Ps 102:15. Now let the nations and their rulers tremble before the Lord, before his glory. [18]I am recording this so that future generations will also praise the Lord for all that he has done. And a people that shall be created shall praise the Lord. [19]Tell them that God looked down from his temple in heaven, [20]and heard the groans of his people in slavery—they were children of death—and released them, [21, 22]so that multitudes would stream to the Temple in Jerusalem to praise him, and his praises were sung throughout the city; and many rulers throughout the earth came to worship him.

Ps 145:10. All living things shall thank you, Lord, and your people will bless you. [11]They will talk together about the glory of your kingdom and mention examples of your power.

Isa 2:2. In the last days Jerusalem and the Temple of the Lord will become the world's greatest attraction, and people from many lands will flow there to worship the Lord. [3]"Come," everyone will say, "let us go up the mountain of the Lord, to the Temple of the God of Israel; there he will teach us his laws, and we will obey them." For in those days the world will be ruled from Jerusalem. [4]The Lord will settle international disputes; all the nations will convert their weapons of war into implements of peace. Then at the last all wars will stop and all military training will end. *v.* 5.

Isa 9:2. The people who walk in darkness shall see a great Light—a Light that will shine on all those who live in the land of the shadow of death. [6]For unto us a Child is born; unto us a Son is given; and the government shall be upon his shoulder. These will be his royal titles: "Wonderful," "Counselor," "The Mighty God," "The Everlasting Father," "The Prince of Peace." [7]His ever-expanding, peaceful government will never end. He will rule with perfect fairness and justice from the throne of his father David. He will bring true justice and peace to all the nations of the world. This is going to happen because the Lord of heaven's armies has dedicated himself to do it! *vs.* 1–7.

Isa 11:6. In that day the wolf and the lamb will lie down together, and the leopard and goats will be at peace. Calves and fat cattle will be safe among lions, and a little child shall lead them all. [7]The cows will graze among bears; cubs and calves will lie down together, and lions will eat grass like the cows. [8]Babies will crawl safely among poisonous snakes, and a little child who puts his hand in a nest of deadly adders will pull it out unharmed. [9]Nothing will hurt or destroy in all my holy mountain, for as the waters fill the sea, so shall the earth be full of the knowledge of the Lord. [10]In that day he who created the royal dynasty of David will be a banner of salvation to all the world. The nations will rally to him, for the land where he lives will be a glorious place. *vs.* 1–10.

Isa 18:7. But the time will come when that strong and mighty nation, a terror to all both far and near, that conquering, destroying nation whose land the rivers divide, will bring gifts to the Lord of Hosts in Jerusalem, where he has placed his name.

Isa 24:16. Hear them singing to the Lord from the ends of the earth, singing glory to the Righteous One!

Isa 35:1. Even the wilderness and desert will rejoice in those days; the desert will blossom with flowers. [2]Yes, there will be an abundance of flowers and singing and joy! The deserts will become as green as the Lebanon mountains, as lovely as Mount Carmel's pastures and Sharon's meadows; for the Lord will display his glory there, the excellency of our God. [5]And when he comes, he will open the eyes of the blind, and unstop the ears of the deaf. [6]The lame man will leap up like a deer, and those who could not speak will shout and sing! Springs will burst forth in the wilderness, and streams in the desert. [7]The parched ground will become a pool, with springs of water in the thirsty land. Where desert jackals lived, there will be reeds and rushes! *vs.* 1–10.

Isa 40:5. The glory of the Lord will be seen by all mankind together. The Lord has spoken—it shall be. *vs.* 4–11.

Isa 42:1. See my Servant, whom I uphold; my Chosen One, in whom I delight. I have put my Spirit upon him; he will reveal justice to the nations of the world. [4]He won't be satisfied until truth and righteousness prevail throughout the earth, not until even distant lands beyond the seas have put their trust in him. *vs.* 1–12.

Isa 45:8. Open up, O heavens. Let the skies pour out their righteousness. Let salvation and righteousness sprout up together from the earth. I, Jehovah, created them. [22]Let all the world look to me for salvation! For I am God; there is no other. [23]I have sworn by myself and I will never go back on my word, for it is true—that every knee in all the world shall bow to me, and every tongue shall swear allegiance to my name. [24]"In Jehovah is all my righteousness and strength," the people shall declare. And all who were angry with him shall come to him and be ashamed. *v.* 6.

Isa 49:1. Listen to me, all of you in far-off lands: The Lord called me before my birth. From within the womb he called me by my name. [5]"And now," said the Lord—the Lord who formed me from my mother's womb to serve him who commissioned me to restore to him his people Israel, who has given me the strength to perform this task and honored me for doing it!—[6]"you shall do more than restore Israel to me. I will make you a Light to the nations of the world to bring my salvation to them too. [18]Look and see, for the Lord has vowed that all your enemies shall come and be your slaves. They will be as jewels to display, as bridal ornaments. [19]Even the most desolate parts of your abandoned land shall soon be crowded with your people, and your enemies who enslaved you shall be far away. [20]The generations born in exile shall return and say, 'We need more room! It's crowded here!' [21]Then you will think to yourself, 'Who has given me all these? For most of my children were killed and the rest were carried away into exile, leaving me here alone. Who bore these? Who raised them for me?' " [22]The Lord God says, "See, I will give a signal to the Gentiles and they shall carry your little sons back to you in their arms, and your daughters on their shoulders. [23]Kings and queens shall serve you; they shall care for all your needs. They shall bow to the earth before you, and lick the dust from off your feet; then you shall know I am the Lord. Those who wait for me shall never be ashamed."

Isa 54:1. Sing, O childless woman! Break out into loud and joyful song, Jerusalem, for she who was abandoned has more blessings now than she whose husband stayed! [2]Enlarge your house; build on additions; spread out your home! [3]For you will soon be bursting at the seams! And your descendants will possess the cities left behind during the exile, and rule the nations that took their lands.

Isa 55:5. You also will command the nations and they will come running to obey, not because of your own power or virtue but because I, the Lord your God, have glorified you.

Isa 56:3. And my blessings are for Gentiles, too, when they accept the Lord; don't let them think that I will make them second-class citizens. And this is for the eunuchs too. They can be as much mine as anyone. [6]As for the Gentiles, the outsiders who join the people of the Lord and serve him and love his name, and are his servants and don't desecrate the Sabbath, and have accepted his covenant and promises, [7]I will bring them also to my holy mountain of Jerusalem, and make them full of joy within my House of Prayer. I will accept their sacrifices and offerings, for my Temple shall be called "A House of Prayer for All People"! [8]For the Lord God who brings back the outcasts of Israel says, I will bring others too besides my people Israel.

Isa 60:1. Arise, my people! Let your light shine

for all the nations to see! For the glory of the Lord is streaming from you. [3]All nations will come to your light; mighty kings will come to see the glory of the Lord upon you. [4]Lift up your eyes and see! For your sons and daughters are coming home to you from distant lands. [5]Your eyes will shine with joy, your hearts will thrill, for merchants from around the world will flow to you, bringing you the wealth of many lands. [8]And who are these who fly like a cloud to Israel, like doves to their nests? [9]I have reserved the ships of many lands, the very best, to bring the sons of Israel home again from far away, bringing their wealth with them. For the Holy One of Israel, known around the world, has glorified you in the eyes of all. [10]Foreigners will come and build your cities. Presidents and kings will send you aid. For though I destroyed you in my anger, I will have mercy on you through my grace. [11]Your gates will stay wide open around the clock to receive the wealth of many lands. The kings of the world will cater to you. [12]For the nations refusing to be your allies will perish; they shall be destroyed. [13]The glory of Lebanon will be yours—the forests of firs and pines, and box trees —to beautify my sanctuary. My Temple will be glorious. [14]The sons of anti-Semites will come and bow before you! They will kiss your feet. They will call Jerusalem "The City of the Lord" and "The Glorious Mountain of the Holy One of Israel."

Isa 65:1. The Lord says, People who never before inquired about me are now seeking me out. Nations who never before searched for me are finding me.

Isa 66:12. Prosperity shall overflow Jerusalem like a river, says the Lord, for I will send it; the riches of the Gentiles will flow to her. Her children shall be nursed at her breasts, carried on her hips and dandled on her knees. [19]I will perform a mighty miracle against them, and I will send those who escape, as missionaries to the nations—to Tarshish, Put, Lud, Meshech, Rosh, Tubal, Javan, and to the lands beyond the sea that have not heard my fame nor seen my glory. There they shall declare my glory to the Gentiles. [23]All mankind shall come to worship me from week to week and month to month. *vs.* 7–23.

Jer 3:17. For the Lord himself will be among you, and the whole city of Jerusalem will be known as the throne of the Lord, and all nations will come to him there and no longer stubbornly follow their evil desires.

Jer 4:2. And if you will swear by me alone, the living God, and begin to live good, honest, clean lives, then you will be a testimony to the nations of the world and they will come to me and glorify my name.

Jer 16:19. O Lord, my Strength and Fortress, my Refuge in the day of trouble, nations from around the world will come to you saying, "Our fathers have been foolish, for they have worshiped worthless idols! [20]Can men make God? The gods they made are not real gods at all." [21]And when they come in that spirit, I will show them my power and might and make them understand at last that I alone am God.

Ezk 47:3. Measuring as he went, he took me 1,500 feet east along the stream and told me to go across. At that point the water was up to my ankles. [4]He measured off another 1,500 feet and told me to cross again. This time the water was up to my knees. [5]Fifteen hundred feet after that it was up to my waist. Another, 1,500 feet and it had become a river so deep I wouldn't be able to get across unless I were to swim. It was too deep to cross on foot.

Dan 2:35. But the Rock that knocked the statue down became a great mountain that covered the whole earth. [44]During the reigns of those kings, the God of heaven will set up a kingdom that will never be destroyed; no one will ever conquer it. It will shatter all these kingdoms into nothingness, but it shall stand forever, indestructible. *v.* 45.

Dan 7:13. Next I saw the arrival of a Man—or so he seemed to be—brought there on clouds from heaven; he approached the Ancient of Days and was presented to him. [14]He was given the ruling power and glory over all the nations of the world, so that all people of every language must obey him. His power is eternal—it will never end; his government shall never fall.

Hos 2:23. At that time I will sow a crop of Israelites and raise them for myself! I will pity those who are "not pitied," and I will say to those who are "not my people," "Now you are my people"; and they will reply, "You are our God!"

Joel 2:28. After I have poured out my rains again, I will pour out my Spirit upon all of you! Your sons and daughters will prophesy; your old men will dream dreams, and your young men see visions. [29]And I will pour out my Spirit even on your slaves, men and women alike, [30]and put strange symbols in the earth and sky—blood and fire and pillars of smoke. [31]The sun will be turned into darkness and the moon to blood before the great and terrible Day of the Lord shall come. [32]Everyone who calls upon the name of the Lord will be saved; even in Jerusalem some will escape, just as the Lord has promised, for he has chosen some to survive.

Amos 9:11. "Then, at that time, I will rebuild the City of David, which is now lying in ruins, and return it to its former glory, [12]and Israel will possess what is left of Edom, and of all the nations that belong to me." For so the Lord, who plans it all, has said.

Mic 4:3. He will arbitrate among the nations, and dictate to strong nations far away. They will beat their swords into plowshares and their spears into pruning-hooks; nations shall no longer fight each other, for all war will end. There will be universal peace, and all the military academies and training camps will be closed down. [4]Everyone will live quietly in his own home in peace and prosperity, for there will be nothing to fear. The Lord himself has promised this.

Hag 2:7. "I will shake all nations, and the Desire

of All Nations shall come to this Temple, and I will fill this place with my glory," says the Lord of Hosts.

Zech 2:10. "Sing, Jerusalem, and rejoice! For I have come to live among you," says the Lord. [11]"At that time many nations will be converted to the Lord, and they too shall be my people; I will live among them all. *Then you will know it was the Lord of Hosts who sent me to you.*"

Zech 6:15. These three who have come from so far away represent many others who will some day come from distant lands to rebuild the Temple of the Lord.

Zech 8:20, 21. People from around the world will come on pilgrimages and pour into Jerusalem from many foreign cities to attend these celebrations. People will write their friends in other cities and say, "Let's go to Jerusalem to ask the Lord to bless us, and be merciful to us. I'm going! Please come with me. Let's go *now!*" [22]Yes, many people, even strong nations, will come to the Lord of Hosts in Jerusalem to ask for his blessing and help. *vs.* 1–23.

23. In those days ten men from ten different nations will clutch at the coat sleeves of one Jew and say, "Please be my friend, for I know that God is with you."

Zech 9:1. This is the message concerning God's curse on the lands of Hadrach and Damascus, for the Lord is closely watching all mankind, as well as Israel. [10]"I will disarm all peoples of the earth, including my people in Israel, and he shall bring peace among the nations. His realm shall stretch from sea to sea, from the river to the ends of the earth." *vs.* 9–17.

Zech 14:8. Life-giving waters will flow out from Jerusalem, half toward the Dead Sea and half towards the Mediterranean, flowing continuously both in winter and in summer. [9]And the Lord shall be King over all the earth. In that day there shall be one Lord—his name alone will be worshiped. [16]In the end, those who survive the plague will go up to Jerusalem each year to worship the King, the Lord of Hosts, to celebrate a time of thanksgiving. *vs.* 8–21.

Mal 1:11. "But my name will be honored by the Gentiles from morning till night. All around the world they will offer sweet incense and pure offerings in honor of my name. For my name shall be great among the nations," says the Lord of Hosts.

Mt 3:9. Don't try to get by as you are, thinking, "We are safe for we are Jews—descendants of Abraham." That proves nothing. God can change these stones here into Jews!

Mt 8:11. And I tell you this, that many Gentiles [like this Roman officer], shall come from all over the world and sit down in the Kingdom of Heaven with Abraham, Isaac, and Jacob.

Mt 12:17. This fulfilled the prophecy of Isaiah concerning him: [18]"Look at my Servant. See my Chosen One. He is my Beloved, in whom my soul delights. I will put my Spirit upon him, and he will judge the nations. [19]He does not fight nor shout; He does not raise his voice! [20]He does not crush the weak, or quench the smallest hope; he will end all conflict with his final victory, [21]and his name shall be the hope of all the world."

Mt 19:30. But many who are first now will be last then; and some who are last now will be first then. Mk 10:31.

Lk 13:29. For people will come from all over the world to take their places there. [30]And note this: some who are despised now will be greatly honored then; and some who are highly thought of now will be least important then.

Lk 21:24. They will be brutally killed by enemy weapons, or sent away as exiles and captives to all the nations of the world; and Jerusalem shall be conquered and trampled down by the Gentiles until the period of Gentile triumph ends in God's good time.

Jn 10:16. I have other sheep, too, in another fold. I must bring them also, and they will heed my voice; and there will be one flock with one Shepherd.

Acts 9:15. But the Lord said, "Go and do what I say. For Paul is my chosen instrument to take my message to the nations and before kings, as well as to the people of Israel."

CONVERSION OF. Acts 10:45. The Jews who came with Peter were amazed that the gift of the Holy Spirit would be given to Gentiles too!

Acts 11:1. Soon the news reached the apostles and other brothers in Judea that Gentiles also were being converted! [2]But when Peter arrived back in Jerusalem, the Jewish believers argued with him. [3]"You fellowshiped with Gentiles and even ate with them," they accused. [4]Then Peter told them the whole story. [5]"One day in Joppa," he said, "while I was praying, I saw a vision—a huge sheet, let down by its four corners from the sky. [6]Inside the sheet were all sorts of animals, reptiles and birds [which are not to eat]. [7]And I heard a voice say, 'Kill and eat whatever you wish.' [8]"Never, Lord,' I replied. 'For I have never yet eaten anything forbidden by our Jewish laws!' [9]But the voice came again, 'Don't say it isn't right when God declares it is!' [10]This happened *three times* before the sheet and all it contained disappeared into heaven. [11]Just then three men who had come to take me with them to Caesarea arrived at the house where I was staying! [12]The Holy Spirit told me to go with them and not to worry about their being Gentiles! These six brothers here accompanied me, and we soon arrived at the home of the man who had sent the messengers. [13]He told us how an angel had appeared to him and told him to send messengers to Joppa to find Simon Peter! [14]"He will tell you how you and all your household can be saved!' the angel had told him. [15]Well, I began telling them the Good News, but just as I was getting started with my sermon, the Holy Spirit fell on them, just as he fell on us at the beginning! [16]Then I thought of the Lord's words when he said, 'Yes, John baptized with water, but you shall be baptized with the Holy Spirit.' [17]And since it was *God* who gave these Gentiles the same gift he gave us when we believed on the Lord Jesus Christ, who was I to argue?" [18]When the others heard this, all their objections were answered and they began praising God! "Yes," they said, "God has given to the Gentiles, too, the privilege of turning to him and receiving eternal life!"

Acts 13:2. One day as these men were worshiping and fasting the Holy Spirit said, "Dedicate Barnabas and Paul for a special job I have for them." [46]Then Paul and Barnabas spoke out boldly and declared, "It was necessary that this Good News from God should be given first to you Jews. But since you have rejected it, and shown yourselves unworthy of eternal life—well, we will offer it to Gentiles. [47]For this is as the Lord commanded when he said, 'I have made you a light to the Gentiles, to lead them from the farthest corners of the earth to my salvation.' " [48]When the Gentiles heard this, they were very glad and rejoiced in Paul's message; and as many as wanted eternal life, believed.

Acts 14:27. Upon arrival they called together the believers and reported on their trip, telling how God had opened the door of faith to the Gentiles too.

Acts 15:7. At the meeting, after long discussion, Peter stood and addressed them as follows: "Brothers, you all know that God chose me from among you long ago to preach the Good News to the Gentiles, so that they also could believe. [8]God, who knows men's hearts, confirmed the fact that he accepts Gentiles by giving them the Holy Spirit, just as he gave him to us. [9]He made no distinction between them and us, for he cleansed their lives through faith, just as he did ours." [12]There was no further discussion, and everyone now listened as Barnabas and Paul told about the miracles God had done through them among the Gentiles. [13]When they had finished, James took the floor. "Brothers," he said, "listen to me. [14]Peter has told you about the time God first visited the Gentiles to take from them a people to bring honor to his name. [15]And this fact of Gentile conversion agrees with what the prophets predicted. For instance, listen to this passage from the prophet Amos: [16]'Afterwards' [says the Lord], 'I will return and renew the broken contract with David, [17]So that Gentiles, too, will find the Lord—all those marked with my name.' [18]That is what the Lord says, who reveals his plans made from the beginning. [19]And so my judgment is that we should not insist that the Gentiles who turn to God must obey our Jewish laws, [20]except that we should write to them to refrain from eating meat sacrificed to idols, from all fornication, and also from eating unbled meat of strangled animals. [21]For these things have been preached against in Jewish synagogues in every city on every Sabbath for many generations." [22]Then the apostles and elders and the whole congregation voted to send delegates to Antioch with Paul and Barnabas, to report on this decision. The men chosen were two of the church leaders—Judas (also called Barsabbas) and Silas. [23]This is the letter they took along with them: "*From:* The apostles, elders and brothers at Jerusalem. *To:* The Gentile brothers in Antioch, Syria and Cilicia. Greetings! [24]We understand that some believers from here have upset you and questioned your salvation, but they had no such instructions from us. [25]So it seemed wise to us, having unanimously agreed on our decision, to send to you these two official representatives, along with our beloved Barnabas and Paul. [26]These men—Judas and Silas, who have risked their lives for the sake of our Lord Jesus Christ—will confirm orally what we have decided concerning your question. [27, 28, 29]For it seemed good to the Holy Spirit and to us to lay no greater burden of Jewish laws on you than to abstain from eating food offered to idols and from unbled meat of strangled animals, and, of course, from fornication. If you do this, it is enough. Farewell." [30]The four messengers went at once to Antioch, where they called a general meeting of the Christians and gave them the letter. [31]And there was great joy throughout the church that day as they read it.

Acts 18:4. Each Sabbath found Paul at the synagogue, trying to convince the Jews and Greeks alike. [5]And after the arrival of Silas and Timothy from Macedonia, Paul spent his full time preaching and testifying to the Jews that Jesus is the Messiah. [6]But when the Jews opposed him and blasphemed, hurling abuse at Jesus, Paul shook off the dust from his robe and said, "Your blood be upon your own heads—I am innocent—from now on I will preach to the Gentiles."

Acts 26:16. Now stand up! For I have appeared to you to appoint you as my servant and my witness. You are to tell the world about this experience and about the many other occasions when I shall appear to you. [17]And I will protect you from both your own people and the Gentiles. Yes, I am going to send you to the Gentiles [18]to open their eyes to their true condition so that they may repent and live in the light of God instead of in Satan's darkness, so that they may receive forgiveness for their sins and God's inheritance along with all people everywhere whose sins are cleansed away, who are set apart by faith in me.

Acts 28:28, 29. So I want you to realize that this salvation from God is available to the Gentiles too, and they will accept it.

Rom 1:5. And now, through Christ, all the kindness of God has been poured out upon us undeserving sinners; and now he is sending us out around the world to tell all people everywhere the great things God has done for them, so that they, too, will believe and obey him. [6, 7]And you, dear friends in Rome, are among those he dearly loves; you, too, are invited by Jesus Christ to be God's very own—yes, his holy people. May all God's mercies and peace be yours from God our Father and from Jesus Christ our Lord.

Rom 9:22. Does not God have a perfect right to show his fury and power against those who are fit only for destruction, those he has been patient with for all this time? [23, 24]And he has a right to take others such as ourselves, who have been made for pouring the riches of his glory into, whether we are Jews or Gentiles, and to be kind to us so that everyone can see how very great his glory is. [25]Remember what the prophecy of Hosea says? There God says that he will find other children for himself (who are not from his Jewish family) and will love them, though no one had ever loved them before. [26]And the heathen, of whom it once was said, "You are not my people," shall be called "sons of the Living God." [27]Isaiah the prophet cried out concerning the Jews that though there would be millions of them, only a small number would ever be saved. [28]"For the Lord will execute his sentence upon the earth, quickly ending his dealings, justly cutting them short." [29]And Isaiah says in another place that except for God's mercy all the Jews would be destroyed—all of them—just as everyone in the cities of Sodom and Gomorrah perished. [30]Well then, what shall we say about these things? Just this, that God has given the Gentiles the opportunity to be acquitted by faith, even though they had not been really seeking God.

Rom 10:19. And did they understand [that God would give his salvation to others if they refused to take it]? Yes, for even back in the time of Moses, God has said that he would make his people jealous and try to wake them up by giving his salvation to the foolish heathen nations. [20]And later on Isaiah said boldly that God would be found by people who weren't even looking for him.

Rom 11:11. Does this mean that God has rejected his Jewish people forever? Of course not! His purpose was to make his salvation available to the Gentiles, and then the Jews would be jealous and begin to want God's salvation for themselves. [12]Now if the whole world became rich as a result of God's offer of salvation, when the Jews stumbled over it and turned it down, think how much greater a blessing the world will share in later on when the Jews, too, come to Christ. [13]As you know, God has appointed me as a special messenger to you Gentiles. I lay great stress on this and remind the Jews about it as often as I can. [17]But some of these branches from Abraham's tree, some of the Jews, have been broken off. And you Gentiles who were branches from, we might say, a wild olive tree, were grafted in. So now you, too, receive the blessing God has promised Abraham and his children, sharing in God's rich nourishment of his own special olive tree. [18]But you must be careful not to brag about being put in to replace the branches that were broken off. Remember that you are important only because you are now a part of God's tree; you are just a branch not a root. [19]"Well," you may be saying, "those branches were broken off to make room for me so I must be pretty good." [20]Watch out! Remember that those branches, the Jews, were broken off because they didn't believe God, and you are there only because you do. Do not be proud; be humble and grateful—and careful. [21]For if God did not spare the branches he put there in the first place, he won't spare you either. [25]I want you to know about this truth from God, dear brothers, so that you will not feel proud and start bragging. Yes, it is true that some of the Jews have set themselves against the Gospel now, but this will last only until all of you Gentiles have come to Christ—those of you who will.

Rom 15:9. And remember that he came also that the Gentiles might be saved and give glory to God for his mercies to them. That is what the Psalmist meant when he wrote: "I will praise you among the Gentiles, and sing to your name." [10]And in another place, "Be glad, O you Gentiles, along with his people the Jews." [11]And yet again, "Praise the Lord, O you Gentiles, let everyone praise him." [12]And the prophet Isaiah said, "There shall be an Heir in the house of Jesse, and he will be King over the Gentiles; they will pin their hopes on him alone."

Gal 1:15. But then something happened! For even before I was born God had chosen me to be his, and called me—what kindness and grace—[16]to reveal his Son within me so that I could go to the Gentiles and show them the Good News about Jesus. When all this happened to me I didn't go at once and talk it over with anyone else.

Gal 2:2. I went there with definite orders from God to confer with the brothers there about the message I was preaching to the Gentiles. I talked privately to the leaders of the church so that they would all understand just what I had been teaching and, I hoped, agree that it was right.

Gal 3:14. Now God can bless the Gentiles, too, with this same blessing he promised to Abraham; and all of us as Christians can have the promised Holy Spirit through this faith.

Eph 3:1. I Paul, the servant of Christ, am here in jail because of you—for preaching that you Gentiles are a part of God's house. [2, 3]No doubt you already know that God has given me this special work of showing God's favor to you Gentiles, as I briefly mentioned before in one of my letters. God himself showed me this secret plan of his, that the Gentiles, too, are included in his kindness. [4]I say this to explain to you how I know about these things. [5]In olden times God did not share this plan with his people, but now he has revealed it by the Holy Spirit to his apostles and prophets. [6]And this is the secret: that the Gentiles will have their full share with the Jews in all the riches inherited by God's sons; both are invited to belong to his church, and all of God's blessings through Christ apply to them both when they accept the Good News about Christ and what he has done for them. [7]God has given me the wonderful privilege of telling everyone about this plan of his; and he has given me his power and special ability to do it well. [8]Just think! Though I did nothing to deserve it, and though I am the most useless Christian there is, yet I was the one chosen for this special joy of telling the Gentiles the Glad News of the endless treasures available to them in Christ.

Col 3:11. In this new life one's nationality or race or education or social position is unimportant;

such things mean nothing. Whether a person has Christ is what matters, and he is equally available to all.

1 Thess 2:16. Trying to keep us from preaching to the Gentiles for fear some might be saved; and so their sins continue to grow. But the anger of God has caught up with them at last.

1 Tim 3:16. It is quite true that the way to live a godly life is not an easy matter. But the answer lies in Christ, who came to earth as a man, was proved spotless and pure in his Spirit, was served by angels, was preached among the nations, was accepted by men everywhere and was received up again to his glory in heaven.

2 Tim 1:11. And God has chosen me to be his missionary, to preach to the Gentiles and teach them.

Rev 15:4. Who shall not fear, O Lord, and glorify your Name? For you alone are holy. All nations will come and worship before you, for your righteous deeds have been disclosed.

See *Missions.*

GENTLENESS OF CHRIST. Isa 40:11; Mt 11: 29, 30; 2 Cor 10:1.

See *Jesus, Compassion of, Humility of, Meekness of.*

OF GOD. 2 Sam 22:36; Ps 18:35; Isa 40:11.

See *God, Compassion of, Long-suffering of.*

Of Paul, 1 Thess 2:7.

EXHORTATIONS TO. Gal 5:22. But when the Holy Spirit controls our lives he will produce this kind of fruit in us: love, joy, peace, patience, kindness, goodness, faithfulness, [23]gentleness and self-control.

2 Tim 2:24. God's people must not be quarrelsome; they must be gentle, patient teachers of those who are wrong. [25]Be humble when you are trying to teach those who are mixed up concerning the truth. For if you talk meekly and courteously to them they are more likely, with God's help, to turn away from their wrong ideas and believe what is true. [26]Then they will come to their senses and escape from Satan's trap of slavery to sin which he uses to catch them whenever he likes, and then they can begin doing the will of God.

Tit 3:1. Remind your people. . . . [2]They must not speak evil of anyone, nor quarrel, but be gentle and truly courteous to all.

Jas 3:17. But the wisdom that comes from heaven is first of all pure and full of quiet gentleness. Then it is peace-loving and courteous. It allows discussion and is willing to yield to others; it is full of mercy and good deeds. It is wholehearted and straightforward and sincere.

See *Humility; Kindness; Meekness; Patience.*

GENUBATH Son of Hadad, 1 Kgs 11:20.

GEOLOGY Gen 1:9, 10. Then God said, "Let the water beneath the sky be gathered into oceans so that the dry land will emerge." And so it was. Then God named the dry land "earth," and the water "seas." And God was pleased.

1 Sam 2:8. For all the earth is the Lord's and he has set the world in order.

2 Sam 22:16. By the blast of his breath was the sea split in two. The bottom of the sea appeared.

Job 12:7, 8, 9. Who doesn't know that the Lord does things like that? Ask the dumbest beast—he knows that it is so; ask the birds—they will tell you; or let the earth teach you, or the fish of the sea.

Job 28:9. Men know how to tear apart flinty rocks and how to overturn the roots of mountains. [10]They drill tunnels in the rocks and lay bare precious stones. [11]They dam up streams of water and pan the gold.

Ps 18:15. Then at your command, O Lord, the sea receded from the shore. At the blast of your breath the depths were laid bare.

Ps 24:1. The earth belongs to God! Everything in all the world is his! [2]He is the one who pushed the oceans back to let dry land appear.

Ps 104:5. You bound the world together so that it would never fall apart. [6]You clothed the earth with floods of water covering up the mountains. [7, 8]You spoke, and at the sound of your shout the water collected into its vast ocean beds, and mountains rose and valleys sank to the levels you decreed. [9]And then you set a boundary for the seas, so that they would never again cover the earth. [10]He placed springs in the valleys, and streams that gush from the mountains. [11]They give water for all the animals to drink. There the wild donkeys quench their thirst, [12]and the birds nest beside the streams and sing among the branches of the trees. [13]He sends rain upon the mountains and fills the earth with fruit.

Ps 136:6. Praise him who planted the water within the earth, for his lovingkindness continues forever.

Prov 30:4. Who else but God goes back and forth to heaven? Who else holds the wind in his fists, and wraps up the oceans in his cloak? If there is any other, what is his name—and his son's name—if you know it?

Jer 31:37. Not until the heavens can be measured and the foundations of the earth explored, will I consider casting them away forever for their sins!

Hab 3:8. Was it in anger, Lord, you smote the rivers and parted the sea?

2 Pet 3:5, 6. They deliberately forget this fact: that God did destroy the world with a mighty flood, long after he had made the heavens by the word of his command, and had used the waters to form the earth and surround it. [7]And God has commanded that the earth and the heavens be stored away for a great bonfire at the judgment day, when all ungodly men will perish.

See *Creation; Earth; Meteorology; Astronomy.*

See also *Hot Springs.*

GERA Possibly the name of three men; more probably of one. The son of Bela, Gen 46:21; Judg 3:15; 2 Sam 16:5; 19:16; 1 Kgs 2:8; 1 Chron 8:3–7.

GERAH A unit of weight equal to 1/50 ounce (.6 gram) and used primarily as the smallest measure of money, the value of which varied according to the metal used, Ex 30:13; Lev 27:25; Num 3:47, 48.

See *Money.*

GERAR 1. A city of the Philistines, Gen 10:15–19. Abimelech, king of, Gen 20:1, 2; 26:1. Visited by Abraham, Gen 20:1; by Isaac, Gen 26:1. Ethiopians defeated at, 2 Chron 14:13, 14.

2. A valley, Gen 26:17–22.

GERASENE See *Gadarenes.*

GERIZIM Mount of blessing, Deut 11:29; 27:12; Josh 8:33. Jotham addresses the Shechemites from, against the conspiracy of Abimelech, Judg 9:7. Samaritans worship at, Jn 4:20.

GERSHOM 1. Son of Moses, Ex 2:22; 18:3; Judg 18:30; 1 Chron 23:14–16; 26:23, 24.

2. See *Gershon.*

3. A descendant of Phinehas, Ezra 8:2–14.

GERSHON Called also *Gershom.* Son of Levi, Gen 46:8–14; Ex 6:16, 17; Num 3:16–24; 4:21–28, 38–41; 7:7; 10:17; 26:57; Josh 21:6; 1 Chron 6:1, 16, 17, 19–21, 39–43, 62, 71; 15:7; 23:6.

GESHAN A descendant of Caleb, 1 Chron 2:47.

GESHEM An Arab. Opposed Nehemiah in building Jerusalem, Neh 2:19; 6:1–6.

GESHUR District east of the sources of the Jordan. The inhabitants of, not expelled by the Israelites, Deut 3:14; Josh 13:2–13; 1 Chron 2:23. Inhabitants of one of the villages of, exterminated, and the spoils taken by David, 1 Sam 27:8. David marries a princess of, 2 Sam 3:3; 1 Chron 3:2. Absalom takes refuge in, after the murder of Amnon, 2 Sam 13:37–39; 15:7, 8.

GETHSEMANE A garden near Jerusalem. Jesus betrayed in, Mt 26:36–50; Mk 14:32–46; Lk 22:39–49; Jn 18:1, 2.

GEZER Called also *Gob.* A Canaanitish royal city; king of, defeated by Joshua, Josh 10:33; 12:8–24. Canaanites not all expelled from, but served as slaves, Josh 16:10; Judg 1:29. Allotted to Ephraim, Josh 16:1–4, 10; 1 Chron 7:28. Assigned to Levites, Josh 21:20–22. Battle with Philistines at, 2 Sam 5:25; 21:18; 1 Chron 14:16; 20:4; Conquered by David, 1 Sam 27:8. Fortified by Solomon, 1 Kgs 9:15–18.

GHOST See *Spirit; Man, Spirit.*

GIAH A place on the way to the Gibeon desert, 2 Sam 2:24.

GIANTS There are numerous references to giants in the Bible, including passages which speak of individuals and others dealing with the race. The subject is introduced to the pages of Scripture in Gen 6:4, where giants are mentioned in connection with the wickedness which led to the flood. These *Nephilim,* or fallen ones (Heb.) first appeared on the earth when the sons of God took human women as wives, Gen 6:2–4. They appeared "also after that," under the same strange circumstances, prior to the invasion of Palestine by the Hebrews, Num 13:33. The *Nephilim* were destroyed on the first occasion by the flood, and on the second by the Israelites.

Num 13:33 also contains the word *gibbor,* or powerful ones. Other references to giants are translations of the Hebrew *Rephaim,* which see. Various tribes gave different names to the later descendants of the *Nephilim,* all of them believed to be branches of the same race of gigantic beings. These names are:

Anakims, Num 13:28, 33; Deut 1:28; 2:10, 11, 21; 9:1–3; Josh 14:12, 15. Descendents of Anak, Num 13:22; Deut 9:2; Josh 11:21, 22; 15:13, 14; Judg 1:20. Emims, Gen 14:5, 6; Deut 2:10, 11. Zamzummims, Deut 2:20. Zuzims, Gen 14:5, 6.

Individuals named in Scripture are Goliath, 1 Sam 17:4–7, 23; 21:9; 22:9, 10; 2 Sam 21:19; 1 Chron 20:5. Ishbi-benob, 2 Sam 21:16. Og, Num 21:33; 32:33; Deut 1:1–5; 3:1–10, 11, 13; 4:47; 29:7; 31:4; Josh 2:10; 9:10; 12:4; 13:12, 30, 31; 1 Kgs 4:8–19; Neh 9:22; Ps 135:11; 136:20.

References to the size of these beings are found in Num 13:32, 33; Deut 2:10, 11, 20, 21; 9:1–3; 1 Sam 17:4–7. The size of Og's iron bedstead is given in Deut 3:11; the curious fact is mentioned in 2 Sam 21:20, 21, that one of the giants had six fingers on each hand and six toes on each foot.

See *Anak; Anakim; Emim; Rephaim; Zamzummims.*

GIBBAR Ezra 2:3–35.

See *Gibeon.*

GIBBETHON A city of Dan, Josh 19:41–46. Allotted to the Levites, Josh 21:23, 24. Besieged by Israel, while in possession of Philistines, 1 Kgs 15:27; 16:15–17.

GIBE-A A descendant of Judah, 1 Chron 2:48, 49.

GIBEAH 1. Of Judah, Josh 15:48–62.

2. Of Saul. Called also *Gibeah of Benjamin,* Josh 18:28. The people's wickedness, Judg 19:12–30; Hos 9:9; 10:9. Destroyed by the Israelites, Judg 20. The city of Saul, 1 Sam 10:26; 15:34; 22:6. The ark of the covenant taken to, by the Philistines, 1 Sam 7:1; 2 Sam 6:3. Deserted, Isa 10:28, 29.

3. Of Ephraim, Josh 24:33.

GIBEON 1. A city of the Hivites, Josh 9:3–5, 17; 2 Sam 21:2. The people of, trick Joshua into a treaty, Josh 9. Made servants by the Israelites, when their trickery was discovered, Josh 9:27. The sun stands still over, during Joshua's battle with the five confederated kings, Josh 10:12–14. Assigned to Benjamin, Josh 18:21–28. Assigned to the Aaronites, Josh 21:17, 18. The tabernacle located at, 1 Kgs 3:4; 1 Chron 16:39; 21:29; 2 Chron 1:2, 3, 13. Philistines defeated at, by David, 1 Chron 14:16. Seven sons of Saul killed at, to avenge the inhabitants of, 2 Sam 21:1–9. Solomon worships at, and offers sacrifices, 1 Kgs 3:4; God appears to him in dreams, 1 Kgs 3:5; 9:2, 3. Abner kills Asahel at, 2 Sam 3:30. Ishmael, the son of Nethaniah, escapes Johanan at, Jer 41:11–16.

2. Pool of, 2 Sam 2:13; Jer 41:12.

GIDDALTI A son of Heman, 1 Chron 25:4, 5, 9–31.

GIDDEL 1. One of the Nethinim, Ezra 2:43–54; Neh 7:46–56.

2. One of Solomon's officials, Ezra 2:55–57; Neh 7:57–59.

GIDEON Call of, by an angel, Judg 6:11, 14.

His excuses, Judg 6:15. Promises of the Lord to, Judg 6:16. Angel proves the Lord's call to, by miracle, Judg 6:21–24. He destroys the altar of Baal, and builds one to the Lord, Judg 6:25–27. His prayer tests, Judg 6:36–40. Leads an army against, and defeats the Midianites, Judg 6:33–35; 7; 8:4–12. Ephraimites chide, for not inviting them to join in the campaign against the Midianites, Judg 8:1–3. Avenges himself upon the people of Succoth, Judg 8:14–17. Israel desires to make him king, he refuses, Judg 8:22–24. Makes an ephod which becomes an idol to the Israelites, Judg 8:23–27. Had seventy sons, Judg 8:30. Death of, Judg 8:32. Faith of, Heb 11:32.

GIDEONI Father of Abidan, Num 1:2–15; 2:3–31; 7:60–65; 10:24.

GIDOM Limit of pursuit after battle of Gibeah, Judg 20:45.

GIFTS See *Presents.*

GIFTS FROM GOD.

Spiritual. Christ, the Savior, Isa 42:6; Jn 3:16; 4:10; 6:32, 33. The Holy Spirit, the Comforter, see *Holy Spirit.* Strength, Jas 4:6. Wisdom, Prov 2:6; Jas 1:5. Repentance, Acts 11:18. Trust, Eph 2:8; Phil 1:29.

Temporal. Food and clothing, Mt 6:25, 33. Rain and harvests, Gen 8:22; 27:27–29; Lev 26:4, 5; Isa 30:23; Acts 14:17. Wisdom, 2 Chron 1:12. Peace, Lev 26:6; 1 Chron 22:9.

To be used and enjoyed, Eccl 3:13; 5:19, 20; 1 Tim 4:4, 5. Should cause us to remember God, Deut 8:18. All creatures share in, Ps 136:25; 145:15, 16. Prayer for, Zech 10:1; Mt 6:11.

UNCLASSIFIED SCRIPTURES RELATING TO BOTH TEMPORAL AND SPIRITUAL. Ps 4:7. Yes, the gladness you have given me is far greater than their joys at harvest time as they gaze at their bountiful crops.

Ps 21:2. For you have given him his heart's desire, everything he asks you for!

Ps 34:10. Even strong young lions sometimes go hungry, but those of us who reverence the Lord will never lack any good thing.

Ps 68:18. He ascends the heights, leading many captives in his train. He receives gifts for men, even those who once were rebels. God will live among us here. [35]What awe we feel, kneeling here before him in the sanctuary. The God of Israel gives strength and mighty power to his people. Blessed be God! Ps 29:11.

Ps 84:11. For Jehovah God is our Light and our Protector. He gives us grace and glory. No good thing will he withhold from those who walk along his paths.

Eccl 2:26. For God gives those who please him wisdom, knowledge, and joy; but if a sinner becomes wealthy, God takes the wealth away from him and gives it to those who please him. So here, too, we see an example of foolishly chasing the wind.

Isa 42:5. The Lord God who created the heavens and stretched them out and created the earth and everything in it, and gives life and breath and spirit to everyone in all the world, he is the one who says [to his Servant, the Messiah].

Ezk 11:19. I will give you one heart and a new spirit; I will take from you your hearts of stone and give you tender hearts of love for God.

Dan 2:21. World events are under his control. He removes kings and sets others on their thrones. He gives wise men their wisdom, and scholars their intelligence. [22]He reveals profound mysteries beyond man's understanding. He knows all hidden things, for he is light, and darkness is no obstacle to him. [23]I thank and praise you, O God of my fathers, for you have given me wisdom and glowing health, and now, even this vision of the king's dream, and the understanding of what it means.

Mt 11:28. Come to me and I will give you rest—all of you who work so hard beneath a heavy yoke.

Mt 25:14. Again, the Kingdom of Heaven can be illustrated by the story of a man going into another country, who called together his servants and loaned them money to invest for him while he was gone. [15]He gave $5,000 to one, $2,000 to another, and $1,000 to the last—dividing it in proportion to their abilities—and then left on his trip. *vs.* 14–30.

Jn 6:27. But you shouldn't be so concerned about perishable things like food. No, spend your energy seeking the eternal life that I, the Messiah, can give you. For God the Father has sent me for this very purpose.

Jn 16:23. At that time you won't need to ask me for anything, for you can go directly to the Father and ask him, and he will give you what you ask for because you use my name. [24]You haven't tried this before, [but begin now]. Ask, using my name, and you will receive, and your cup of joy will overflow.

Jn 17:22. I have given them the glory you gave me—the glorious unity of being one, as we are.

Rom 5:16. Adam's *one* sin brought the penalty of death to many, while Christ freely takes away *many* sins and gives glorious life instead. [17]The sin of this one man, Adam, caused *death to be king over all,* but all who will take God's gift of forgiveness and acquittal are *kings of life* because of this one man, Jesus Christ. [18]Yes, Adam's *sin* brought *punishment* to all, but Christ's *righteousness* makes men *right with God,* so that they can live.

Rom 6:23. For the wages of sin is death, but the free gift of God is eternal life through Jesus Christ our Lord.

Rom 8:32. Since he did not spare even his own Son for us all, won't he also surely give us everything else?

Rom 11:29. For God's gifts and his call can never be withdrawn; he will never go back on his promises.

Rom 12:6. God has given each of us the ability to do certain things well. So if God has given you the ability to prophesy, then prophesy whenever you can—as often as your faith is strong enough to receive a message from God. [7]If your gift is that of serving others, serve them well. If you are a teacher, do a good job of teaching. [8]If you are a preacher, see to it that your sermons are strong and helpful. If God has given you money, be generous in helping others with it. If God has given you administrative ability and put you in charge of the work of others, take the responsibility seriously. Those who offer comfort to the sorrowing should do so with Christian cheer.

1 Cor 1:5. He has enriched your whole life. He has helped you speak out for him and has given you a full understanding of the truth; [6]what I told you Christ could do for you has happened! [7]Now you have every grace and blessing; every spiritual gift and power for doing his will are yours during this time of waiting for the return of our Lord Jesus Christ.

1 Cor 7:7. But we are not all the same. God gives some the gift of a husband or wife, and others he gives the gift of being able to stay happily unmarried.

1 Cor 12:4. Now God gives us many kinds of special abilities, but it is the same Holy Spirit who is the source of them all. [5]There are different kinds of service to God, but it is the same Lord we are serving. [6]There are many ways in which God works in our lives, but it is the same God who does the work in and through all of us who are his. [7]The Holy Spirit displays God's power through each of us as a means of helping the entire church. [8]To one person the Spirit gives the ability to give wise advice; someone else may be especially good at studying and teaching, and this is his gift from the same Spirit. [9]He gives special faith to another, and to someone else the power to heal the sick. [10]He gives power for doing miracles to some, and to others power to prophesy and preach. He gives someone else the power to know whether evil spirits are speaking through those who claim to be giving God's messages—or whether it is really the Spirit of God who is speaking. Still another person is able to speak in languages he never learned; and others, who do not know the language either, are given power to understand what he is saying. [11]It is the same and only Holy Spirit who gives all these gifts and powers, deciding which each one of us should have.

1 Cor 13:2. If I had the gift of prophecy and knew all about what is going to happen in the future, knew everything about *everything,* but didn't love others, what good would it do? Even if I had the gift of faith so that I could speak to a mountain and make it move, I would still be worth nothing at all without love.

Eph 4:7. However, Christ has given each of us special abilities—whatever he wants us to have out of his rich storehouse of gifts. [8]The Psalmist tells about this, for he says that when Christ returned triumphantly to heaven after his resurrection and victory over Satan, he gave generous gifts to men.

1 Tim 6:17. Tell those who are rich not to be proud and not to trust in their money, which will soon be gone, but their pride and trust should be in the living God who always richly gives us all we need for our enjoyment.

Jas 1:17. But whatever is good and perfect comes to us from God, the Creator of all light, and he shines forever without change or shadow.

1 Pet 4:10. God has given each of you some special abilities; be sure to use them to help each other, passing on to others God's many kinds of blessings.

2 Pet 1:3. For as you know him better, he will give you, through his great power, everything you need for living a truly good life: he even shares his own glory and his own goodness with us!

See *Blessing, Temporal, From God.*

GIHON 1. A river, possibly in Egypt, of the Garden of Eden, Gen 2:13.

2. Spring and brook near Jerusalem, 1 Kgs 1:33, 38, 45. Hezekiah brings the waters of, by an aqueduct into the city of Jerusalem, 2 Chron 32:4, 30; 33:14; Neh 2:13–15; 3:13–16; Isa 7:3; 22:9–11; 36:2.

GILALAI A priest and musician, Neh 12:35, 36.

GILBOA A mountain south of Jezreel, where Saul was defeated by the Philistines, and died, 1 Sam 28:4; 31:1–8; 1 Chron 10:1–8.

GILEAD 1. A region east of the Jordan allotted to the tribes of Reuben and Gad and half-tribe of Manasseh, Num 32:1–30; Deut 3:13; 34:1; 2 Kgs 10:32, 33. Reubenites defeat Hagrites in, 1 Chron 5:9, 10, 18–22. Ammonites make war against; defeated by Jephthah, Judg 11; Amos 1:13. The prophet Elijah a native of, 1 Kgs 17:1. David retreats to, at the time of Absalom's rebellion, 2 Sam 17:16, 22, 24. Pursued into, by Absalom, 2 Sam 17:26. Absalom defeated and killed in the forest of, 2 Sam 18:9.

Hazael, king of Syria, conquers, 2 Kgs 10:32, 33; Amos 1:3. Invaded by Tiglath-pileser, king of Syria, 2 Kgs 15:29. A grazing country, Num 32:1; 1 Chron 5:9. Exported spices, gum, and medicine, Gen 37:25; Jer 8:22; 46:11.

FIGURATIVE. Of prosperity, Jer 22:6; 50:19.

2. A mountain, Song 4:1; 6:5. Laban overtakes Jacob at, Gen 31:21–25.

3. A city, Hos 6:8; 12:11.

4. Grandson of Manasseh, Num 26:28–37; 27:1; 36:1; Josh 17:1, 3; 1 Chron 2:21; 7:14, 17.

5. Father of Jephthah, Judg 11:1, 2.

6. A descendent of Gad, 1 Chron 5:14.

GILGAL 1. Place of the first encampment of the Israelites west of the Jordan, Josh 4:19; 9:6; 10:6, 43; 14:6. Monument erected in, to commemorate the crossing of the Jordan by the nation of Israel, Josh 4:19–24. Circumcision renewed at, Josh 5:2–9. Passover kept at, Josh 5:10. Manna ceased at, after the Passover, Josh 5:11, 12. Quarries at, Judg 3:17–19. Eglon, king of Moab, is killed at, Judg 3:14–26. A judgment seat, where Israel, in that district, came to be judged by Samuel, 1 Sam 7:16. Saul crowned king over all Israel at, 1 Sam 11:15. An altar built at, and sacrifice offered, 1 Sam 11:15; 13:3–15; 15:6–23. Agag, king of the Amalekites, killed at, by Samuel, 1 Sam 15:33. Tribe of Judah assembles at, to proceed to the east side of the Jordan to escort king David back after the defeat of Absalom, 2 Sam 19:14, 15, 40–43.

Prophecies concerning, Hos 4:15; 9:15; 12:11; Amos 4:4; 5:5.

2. A place near Mounts Ebal and Gerizim, Deut 11:30.

3. A place Elijah and Elisha visited, 2 Kgs 2:1, 2; 4:38.

4. A royal city in Canaan. Conquered by Joshua, Josh 12:8–24.

5. A place on the northern border of Judah, Josh 15:7.

GILOH A town in Judah, Josh 15:48–62; 2 Sam 15:12.

GIMZO A city of Judah, 2 Chron 28:18.

GINATH Father of Tibni, 1 Kgs 16:21.

GINNETHON Called also *Ginnethoi,* a companion of Nehemiah, Neh 10:1–8; 12:1–7, 12–21.

GIRGASHITES Land of, given to Abraham and his descendants, Gen 15:21; Deut 7:1; Josh 3:10; Neh 9:8. Delivered to the children of Israel, Josh 24:11.

GISHPA An overseer of the Nethinim, Neh 11:21.

GITTAIM A place of which little is known, 2 Sam 4:2, 3; Neh 11:33.

GITTITE See *Gath.*

GIVING RULES FOR. Mt 6:1. Take care! don't do your good deeds publicly, to be admired, for then you will lose the reward from your Father in heaven. [2]When you give a gift to a beggar, don't shout about it as the hypocrites do—blowing trumpets in the synagogues and streets to call attention to their acts of charity! I tell you in all earnestness, they have received all the reward they will ever get. [3]But when you do a kindness to someone, do it secretly—don't tell your left hand what your right hand is doing. [4]And your Father who knows all secrets will reward you.

1 Cor 16:2. On every Lord's Day each of you should put aside something from what you have earned during the week, and use it for this offering.

2 Cor 8:11. Having started the ball rolling so enthusiastically, you should carry this project through to completion just as gladly, giving whatever you can out of whatever you have. [12]If you are really eager to give, then it isn't important how much you have to give. God wants you to give what you have, not what you haven't. [13]Of course, I don't mean that those who receive your gifts should have an easy time of it at your expense, [14]but you should divide with them. Right now you have plenty and can help them; then at some other time they can share with you when you need it. In this way each will have as much as he needs.

2 Cor 9:6. But remember this—if you give little, you will get little. A farmer who plants just a few seeds will get only a small crop, but if he plants much, he will reap much. [7]Every one must make up his own mind as to how much he should give. Don't force anyone to give more than he really wants to, for cheerful givers are the ones God prizes.

See *Benevolence; Charity; Liberality.*

GIZONITE Town of Judah, 1 Chron 11:26–47.

GLADNESS See *Joy.*

GLASS Job 28:17. Symbolical: Rev 21:18–21. Ocean of, Rev 15:2.

See *Mirror.*

GLEANING Laws concerning, Lev 19:9, 10; 23:22; Deut 24:19–21.

See *Orphan; Strangers; Widow.*

FIGURATIVE. Judg 8:2, 3; Isa 17:6; Jer 49:9, 10; Mic 7:1.

INSTANCES OF. Ruth in the field of Boaz, Ruth 2:2, 3.

GLORIFYING GOD Commanded, 1 Chron 16:28; Ps 22:23; Isa 42:12. Due to him, 1 Chron 16:29; for his holiness, Ps 99:9; Rev 15:3, 4; mercy and truth, Ps 115:1; Rom 15:9; wonderful works, Isa 25:1; Mt 15:31; Acts 4:21; judgments, Isa 25:3; Ezk 28:22; Rev 14:7; rescues, Ps 50:15; grace to others, Acts 11:18; 2 Cor 9:13; Gal 1:24.

Accomplished by: Relying on his promises, Rom 4:20; praising him, Ps 50:23; doing all to glorify him, 1 Cor 10:31; dying for him, Jn 21:19; suffering for Christ, 1 Pet 4:14, 16; glorifying Christ, Acts 19:17; 2 Thess 1:12; producing spiritual fruits, Jn 15:8; Phil 1:11; patience in trouble, Isa 24:14–16; faithfulness, 1 Pet 4:11. Required in body and spirit, 1 Cor 6:20. Shall be universal, Ps 86:9; Rev 5:13.

Believers: Should resolve on, Ps 69:30; 118:27, 28; unite in, Ps 34:3; Rom 15:6; persevere in, Ps 86:12. All the blessings of God are designed to lead to, Isa 60:21; 61:3. The good deeds of believers may lead to, Mt 5:16; 1 Pet 2:12.

All, by nature, fail in, Rom 3:23. The wicked adverse to, Dan 5:23; Rom 1:21. Punishment for not, Dan 5:23, 30; Mal 2:1, 2; Acts 12:23; Rom 1:21. Heavenly creatures engaged in, Rev 4:11.

EXEMPLIFIED. By David, Ps 57:5; the crowds, Mt 9:8; 15:31; the virgin Mary, Lk 1:46; the angels, Lk 2:14; the shepherds, Lk 2:20; by Jesus, Jn 17:4; the paralyzed man, Lk 5:25; the handicapped woman, Lk 13:13; the leper, Lk 17:15; the blind man, Lk 18:43; the Roman captain, Lk 23:47; the church at Jerusalem, Acts 11:18; the Gentiles at Antioch, Acts 13:48; Abraham, Rom 4:20; Paul, Rom 11:36.

See *Praise.*

GLORY God is, to his people, Ps 3:3; Zech 2:5. Christ is, to his people, Isa 60:1; Lk 2:32. The gospel ordained to be, to believers, 1 Cor 2:7. Of the gospel exceeds that of the law, 2 Cor 3:9, 10.

SPIRITUAL. Is given by God, Ps 84:11; is given by Christ, Jn 17:22; is the work of the Holy Spirit, 2 Cor 3:18.

ETERNAL. Procured by the death of Christ, Heb 2:10; accompanies salvation of Christ, 2 Tim 2:10; inherited by believers, 1 Sam 2:8; Ps 73:24; Col 3:4; believers called to, 2 Thess 2:14; 1 Pet 5:10; believers prepared for, Rom 9:23; enhanced by distress, 2 Cor 4:17; present sufferings not to be compared with, Rom 8:18; the bodies of believers shall be revived in, 1 Cor 15:43; Phil 3:21; believers shall be, of their ministers, 1 Thess 2:19, 20; sufferings of ministers are, to believers, Eph 3:13.

TEMPORAL. Is given by God, Dan 2:37; passes away, 1 Pet 1:24. The devil tries to seduce by, Mt

4:8. Of hypocrites turned to disgrace, Hos 4:7. Ask not, from man, Mt 6:2; 1 Thess 2:6. Of the wicked is in their shame, Phil 3:19. Ends in destruction, Isa 5:14.

OF GOD. Exhibited in Christ, Mt 25:31; Lk 9:26; Jn 1:14; 2 Cor 4:6; Heb 1:3. Ascribed to God, Gal 1:5.

Exhibited in his name, Deut 28:58, 59; Neh 9:5; his majesty, Job 37:22; Ps 93:1; 104:1; 145:5; 12; Isa 2:10; his power, Ex 15:1, 6; Rom 6:4; his works, Ps 19:1; 111:3; his holiness, Ex 15:11.

First seen, Ex 16:7–10; cf. 13:21, 22. Departs from Jerusalem, Ezk 8:4; 9:3; 10:4, 18; 11:22, 23. Returns, Ezk 43:2, 4, 5.

Described as great, Ps 138:5; eternal, Ps 104:31; rich, Eph 3:16; highly exalted, Ps 8:1; 113:4.

Exhibited to Moses, Ex 34:5–7; with Ex 33:18–23; Stephen, Acts 7:55; Israel, Deut 5:24; Ps 102:16.

Illuminates Jerusalem, Rev 21:11, 23. Believers desire to see, Ps 63:2; 90:16. God is jealous of, Isa 42:8. The earth is full of, Isa 6:3. The knowledge of, shall fill the earth, Hab 2:14.

GLUTTONY Ex 16:20. But of course some of them wouldn't listen, and left it until morning; and when they looked, it was full of maggots and had a terrible odor; and Moses was very angry with them. [21]So they gathered the food morning by morning, each home according to its need; and when the sun became hot upon the ground, the food melted and disappeared. [27]But some of the people went out anyway to gather food, even though it was the Sabbath, but there wasn't any.

Num 11:32. So the people caught and killed quail all that day and through the night and all the next day too! The least anyone gathered was 100 bushels! Quail were spread out all around the camp. [33]But as everyone began eating the meat, the anger of the Lord rose against the people and he killed large numbers of them with a plague.

Prov 23:19–21. Only son, be wise and stay in God's paths; don't carouse with drunkards and gluttons, for they are on their way to poverty. And remember that too much sleep clothes a man with rags.

Eccl 10:17. Happy the land whose king is a nobleman, and whose leaders work hard before they feast and drink, and then only to strengthen themselves for the tasks ahead!

Isa 22:13. But instead, you sing and dance and play, and feast and drink. "Let us eat, drink, and be merry," you say: "What's the difference, for tomorrow we die."

Amos 6:4. You lie on ivory beds surrounded with luxury, eating the meat of the tenderest lambs and the choicest calves. [5]You sing idle songs to the sound of the harp, and fancy yourselves to be as great musicians as King David was. [6]You drink wine by the bucketful and perfume yourselves with sweet ointments, caring nothing at all that your brothers need your help. [7]Therefore you will be the first to be taken as slaves; suddenly your revelry will end.

Lk 12:19. And I'll sit back and say to myself, "Friend, you have enough stored away for years to come. Now take it easy! Wine, women, and song for you!" [20]But God said to him, "Fool! Tonight you die. Then who will get it all?"

Rom 13:13. Put on the armor of right living, as we who live in the daylight should! Be decent and true in everything you do so that all can approve your behavior. Don't spend your time in wild parties and getting drunk or in adultery and lust, or fighting, or jealousy. [14]But ask the Lord Jesus Christ to help you live as you should, and don't make plans to enjoy evil.

1 Cor 15:32. And what value was there in fighting wild beasts—those men of Ephesus—if it was only for what I gain in this life down here? If we will never live again after we die, then we might as well go and have ourselves a good time: let us eat, drink, and be merry. What's the difference? For tomorrow we die, and that ends everything!

Phil 3:19. Their future is eternal loss, for their god is their appetite: they are proud of what they should be ashamed of; and all they think about is this life here on earth.

1 Pet 4:3. You have had enough in the past of the evil things the godless enjoy—sex sin, lust, getting drunk, wild parties, drinking bouts, and the worship of idols, and other terrible sins.

Jude 1:12. When these men join you at the love feasts of the church, they are evil smears among you, laughing and carrying on, gorging and stuffing themselves without a thought for others.

INSTANCES OF. Esau, Gen 25:30–34, with Heb 12:16, 17. Israel, Num 11:4, 5, with Ps 78:18. Sons of Eli, 1 Sam 2:12–17. Belshazzar, Dan 5:1.

GNASHING OF TEETH Job 16:9; Ps 112:10; Lam 2:16; Mt 13:42; 22:13; 24:51; 25:30; Lk 13:28. See *Teeth*.

GNAT Mt 23:24.

GOAD An instrument used for prodding cattle, 1 Sam 13:21. Six hundred men killed with, by Shamgar, a judge of Israel, Judg 3:31.

FIGURATIVE. Of mental incentive, Eccl 12:11.

GOAH A place near Jerusalem, Jer 31:39.

GOAT Designated as one of the clean animals to be eaten, Deut 14:3–5, with Lev 11:1–8. Used for food, Gen 27:8–10; 1 Sam 16:20; for the Passover feast, Ex 12:5; 2 Chron 35:7; as a sacrifice by Abraham, Gen 15:9; by Gideon, Judg 6:19; Manoah, Judg 13:19. Milk of, used for food, Prov 27:25–27. Hair of, used for clothing, Num 31:20; pillows, 1 Sam 19:13; curtains of the Tabernacle, Ex 26:7, 8; 35:23; 36:14. Skins of, used for covering the Tabernacle, Ex 25:1–7; 26:14; 35:5–9, 23; 36:19; 39:33–40; Num 4:6, 8, 10, 11, 12, 14, 25; used for tents, see *Tabernacle*. Regulations of Mosaic law required that a kid should not be killed before it was eight days old, Lev 22:27; nor boiled in its mother's milk, Ex 23:19. Numerous, Deut 32:14; Song 4:1; 6:5; 1 Sam 25:2; 2 Chron 17:11. Wild, in Palestine, 1 Sam 24:2; Ps 104:18; Isa 51:20. Surefootedness, 2 Sam 22:34.

GOB Also called *Gezer*, which see.

GOBLET See *Cup*.

GOD INDEX OF SUB-TOPICS. *Miscellany; Unclassified Scriptures Relating to; Access to; Compassion of; Creator; Creator of Man; Eternity of; Faithfulness of; Fatherhood of; Favor of; Foreknowledge of; Glory of; Goodness of; Grace of; Guide; Holiness of; Human Forms and Appearance of; Impartial; Incomprehensible; Infinite; Invisible; Jealous; Judge, and his Justice; Knowledge of; Long-suffering; Long-suffering of, Abused; Love of; Love of, Exemplified; Mercy of; Omnipotent; Omnipresent; Omniscient; Perfection of; Personality of; Power of; Presence of; Preserver; Providence of; Providence of, Overruling Intervention Showing the; Providence of, Mysterious and Misinterpreted; Righteousness of; Savior; Self-existent; Sovereign; A Spirit; Truth; Ubiquitous; Unchangeable; Unity of; Unsearchable; Voice of; Wisdom of; Works of.*

Appearances of; To Adam, Gen 3:8–21; Abraham, Gen 18:2–33; Jacob, at Bethel, Gen 35:7, 9; Moses, in the burning bush, Ex 3:2; at Sinai, Ex 19:16–24; 24:10; Moses and Joshua, Deut 31:14, 15; Israel, Judg 2:1–5; Gideon, Judg 6:11–24; Solomon, 1 Kgs 3:5; 9:2, 3; 11:9, 10; 2 Chron 1:7–12; 7:12–22; Isaiah, Isa 6:1–5; Ezekiel, Ezk 1:26–28.

Name of: Proclaimed, Ex 34:5, 6, 14; see Ex 6:2, 3; 15:3; Ps 83:18; to be reverenced, Ex 20:7; Deut 5:11; 28:58, 59; Ps 111:9; 1 Tim 6:1; praised, Ps 34:3; 72:17; not to be profaned, Ex 20:7; Lev 18:21; 19:12; 20:3; 21:6; 22:1, 2, 32, 33; Deut 5:11; Ps 139:20; Prov 30:9; Isa 52:5; Rom 2:24; Rev 16:9; profaned, Ps 139:20; Mt 26:74. See *Blasphemy; Perjury.*

Repentance attributed to: Gen 6:6, 7; Ex 32:14; Judg 2:18; 1 Sam 15:35; 2 Sam 24:16; 1 Chron 21:15; Ps 106:45; Jer 26:19; Amos 7:3; Jon 3:10. For other anthropomorphic scriptures, see *Anthropomorphisms.*

Rejected: By Israel, 1 Sam 8:7, 8; Isa 65:12; 66:4; Saul, 1 Sam 15:26. See *Jesus, Rejected.*

Comforter, Job 35:10. See *Affliction, Consolation in; Holy Spirit.* Covenant keeping, see *Covenant.*

Anger of: See *Anger, of God.* Attributes of, see each in alphabetical order below. Condescension of, see *Condescension of God.*

UNCLASSIFIED SCRIPTURES RELATING TO. Job 5:8. My advice to you is this: Go to God and confess your sins to him. [9]For he does wonderful miracles, marvels without number. [10]He sends the rain upon the earth to water the fields, [11]and gives prosperity to the poor and humble, and takes sufferers to safety. [12]He frustrates the plans of crafty men. [13]They are caught in their own traps; he thwarts their schemes. [14]They grope like blind men in the daylight; they see no better in the daytime than at night. [15]God saves the fatherless and the poor from the grasp of these oppressors. [16]And so at last the poor have hope, and the fangs of the wicked are broken. [17]How enviable the man whom God corrects! Oh, do not despise the chastening of the Lord when you sin. [18]For though he wounds, he binds and heals again. [19]He will deliver you again and again, so that no evil can touch you. [20]He will keep you from death in famine, and from the power of the sword in time of war.

Job 9:2. Sure, I know all that. You're not telling me anything new. But how can a man be truly good in the eyes of God? [3]If God decides to argue with him, can a man answer even one question of a thousand he asks? [4]For God is so wise and so mighty. Who has ever opposed him successfully? [5]Suddenly he moves the mountains, overturning them in his anger. [6]He shakes the earth to its foundations. [7]The sun won't rise, the stars won't shine, if he commands it so! [8]Only he has stretched the heavens out and stalked along the seas. [9]He made the Bear, Orion and the Pleiades, and the constellations of the southern Zodiac. [10]He does incredible miracles, too many to count. [11]He passes by, invisible; he moves along, but I don't see him go. [12]When he sends death to snatch a man away, who can stop him? Who dares to ask him, "What are you doing?" [13]And God does not abate his anger. The pride of man collapses before him. [14]And who am I that I should try to argue with Almighty God, or even reason with him? [15]Even if I were sinless I wouldn't say a word. I would only plead for mercy. [16]And even if my prayers were answered I could scarce believe that he had heard my cry. [17]For he is the one who destroys, and multiplies my wounds without a cause. [18]He will not let me breathe, but fills me with bitter sorrows. He alone is strong and just. [20]But I? Am I righteous? My own mouth says no. Even if I were perfect, God would prove me wicked. [21]And even if I am utterly innocent, I dare not think of it. I despise what I am. [22]Innocent or evil, it is all the same to him, for he destroys both kinds. [23]He will laugh when calamity crushes the innocent. [24]The whole earth is in the hands of the wicked. God blinds the eyes of the judges and lets them be unfair. If not he, then who? [30]Even if I were to wash myself with purest water and cleanse my hands with lye to make them utterly clean, [31]even so you would plunge me into the ditch and mud; and even my clothing would be less filthy than you consider me to be! [32,33]And I cannot defend myself, for you are no mere man as I am. If you were, then we could discuss it fairly, but there is no umpire between us, no middle man, no mediator to bring us together. [34]Oh, let him stop beating me, so that I need no longer live in terror of his punishment. [35]Then I could speak without fear to him, and tell him boldly that I am not guilty.

Job 10:2. I will say to God, "Don't just condemn me—tell me *why* you are doing it. [3]Does it really seem right to you to oppress and despise me, a man you have made; and to send joy and prosperity to the wicked? [4-7]Are you unjust like men? Is your life so short that you must hound me for sins you know full well I've not committed? Is it because you know no one can save me from your hand? [8]You have made me, and yet you destroy me. [9]Oh, please remember that I'm made of dust—will you change me back again to dust so soon? [10]You have already poured me from bottle to bottle like milk, and curdled me like cheese. [11]You gave me skin and flesh and knit together bones and sinews. [12]You gave me life and were so kind and loving to me, and

I was preserved by your care. 13,14Yet all the time your real motive in making me was to destroy me if I sinned; and to refuse to forgive my iniquity. 15Just the slightest wickedness, and I am done for. And if I'm good, that doesn't count. I am filled with frustration. 16If I start to get up off the ground, you leap upon me like a lion and quickly finish me off. 17Again and again you witness against me and pour out an ever-increasing volume of wrath upon me and bring fresh armies against me. 18Why then did you ever let me be born? Why didn't you let me die at birth?"

Job 12:7–9. Who doesn't know that the Lord does things like that? Ask the dumbest beast—he knows that it is so; ask the birds—they will tell you; or let the earth teach you, or the fish of the sea. 10For the soul of every living thing is in the hand of God, and the breath of all mankind. 11Just as my mouth can taste good food, so my mind tastes truth when I hear it. 12And as you say, older men like me are wise. They understand. 13But true wisdom and power are God's. He alone knows what we should do; he understands. 14And how great is his might! What he destroys can't be rebuilt. When he closes in on a man, there is no escape. 15He withholds the rain, and the earth becomes a desert; he sends the storms, and floods the ground. 16Yes, with him is strength and wisdom. Deceivers and deceived are both his slaves. 17He makes fools of counselors and judges. 18He reduces kings to slaves and frees their servants. 19Priests are led away as slaves. He overthrows the mighty. 20He takes away the voice of orators, and the insight of the elders.

Job 26:7. God stretches out heaven over empty space, and hangs the earth upon nothing. 8He wraps the rain in his thick clouds and the clouds are not split by the weight. 9He shrouds his throne with his clouds. 10He sets a boundary for the ocean, yes, and a boundary for the day and for the night. 11The pillars of heaven tremble at his rebuke. 12And by his power the sea grows calm; he is skilled at crushing its pride! 13The heavens are made beautiful by his Spirit; he pierces the swiftly gliding serpent. 14These are some of the minor things he does, merely a whisper of his power. Who then can withstand his thunder?

Job 33:12. All right, here is my reply: In this very thing, you have sinned by speaking of God that way. For God is greater than man. 13Why should you fight against him just because he does not give account to you of what he does? 14For God speaks again and again, 15in dreams, in visions of the night when deep sleep falls on men as they lie on their beds. 16He opens their ears in times like that, and gives them wisdom and instruction, 17, 18causing them to change their minds, and keeping them from pride, and warning them of the penalties of sin, and keeping them from falling into some trap. 19Or, God sends sickness and pain, even though no bone is broken, 20so that a man loses all taste and appetite for food and doesn't care for even the daintiest dessert. 21He becomes thin, mere skin and bones, 22and draws near to death. 23, 24But if a messenger from heaven is there to intercede for him as a friend, to show him what is right, then God pities him and says, "Set him free. Do not make him die, for I have found a substitute." 25Then his body will become as healthy as a child's, firm and youthful again. 26And when he prays to God, God will hear and answer and receive him with joy, and return him to his duties. 27And he will declare to his friends, "I sinned, but God let me go. 28He did not let me die. I will go on living in the realm of light." 29Yes, God often does these things for man—30brings back his soul from the pit, so that he may live in the light of the living.

Job 34:10. Listen to me, you with understanding. Surely everyone knows that *God doesn't sin!* 11Rather, he punishes the sinners. 12There is no truer statement than this: *God is never wicked or unjust.* 13He alone has authority over the earth and dispenses justice for the world. 14If God were to withdraw his Spirit, 15all life would disappear and mankind would turn again to dust. 16Listen now and try to understand. 17Could God govern if he hated justice? Are you going to condemn the Almighty Judge? 18Are you going to condemn this God who says to kings and nobles, "You are wicked and unjust"? 19For he doesn't care how great a man may be, and doesn't pay any more attention to the rich than to the poor. He made them all. 20In a moment they die, and at midnight great and small shall suddenly pass away, removed by no human hand. 21For God carefully watches the goings on of all mankind; he sees them all. 22No darkness is thick enough to hide evil men from his eyes, 23So there is no need to wait for some great crime before a man is called before God in judgment. 24Without making a federal case of it, God simply shatters the greatest of men, and puts others in their place. 25He watches what they do and in a single night he overturns them, destroying them, 26or openly strikes them down as wicked men. 27For they turned aside from following him, 28causing the cry of the poor to come to the attention of God. Yes, he hears the cries of those being oppressed. 29, 30Yet when he chooses not to speak, who can criticize? Again, he may prevent a vile man from ruling, thus saving a nation from ruin, and he can depose an entire nation just as easily.

Job 37:1. "My heart trembles at this. 2Listen, listen to the thunder of his voice. 3It rolls across the heavens and his lightning flashes out in every direction. 4Afterwards comes the roaring of the thunder—the tremendous voice of his majesty. 5His voice is glorious in the thunder. We cannot comprehend the greatness of his power. 6For he directs the snow, the showers, and storm to fall upon the earth. 7Man's work stops at such a time, so that all men everywhere may recognize his power. 8The wild animals hide in the rocks or in their dens. 9From the south comes the rain; from the north, the cold. 10God blows upon the rivers, and even the widest torrents freeze. 11He loads the clouds with moisture and they send forth his lightning. 12The lightning bolts are directed by his hand, and do whatever he commands throughout the earth. [13]He sends the storms as punishment, or, in his loving-kindness, to encourage. [14]Listen, O Job, stop and consider the wonderful miracles of God. [15]Do you know how God controls all nature, and causes the lightning to flash forth from the clouds? [16, 17]Do you understand the balancing of the clouds with wonderful perfection and skill? Do you know why you become warm when the south wind is blowing and everything is still? [18]Can you spread out the gigantic mirror of the skies as he does? [19, 20]You who think you know so much, teach the rest of us how we should approach God. For we are too dull to know! With your wisdom, would we then dare to approach him? Well, does a man wish to be swallowed alive? [21]For as we cannot look at the sun for its brightness when the winds have cleared away the clouds, [22]neither can we gaze at the terrible majesty of God breaking forth upon us from heaven, clothed in dazzling splendor. [23]We cannot imagine the power of the Almighty, and yet he is so just and merciful that he does not destroy us. [24]No wonder men everywhere fear him! For he is not impressed by the world's wisest men!

Job 38:1. *Then the Lord answered Job from the whirlwind:* [2]"Why are you using your ignorance to deny my providence? [3]Now get ready to fight, for I am going to demand some answers from you, and you must reply. [4]Where were you when I laid the foundations of the earth? Tell me, if you know so much. [5]Do you know how its dimensions were determined, and who did the surveying? [6, 7]What supports its foundations, and who laid its cornerstone, as the morning stars sang together and all the angels shouted for joy? [8, 9]Who decreed the boundaries of the seas when they gushed from the depths? Who clothed them with clouds and thick darkness, [10]and barred them by limiting their shores, [11]and said, 'Thus far and no farther shall you come, and here shall your proud waves stop!'? [12]Have you ever once commanded the morning to appear, and caused the dawn to rise in the east? [13]Have you ever told the daylight to spread to the ends of the earth, to end the night's wickedness? [14]Have you ever robed the dawn in red, [15]and disturbed the haunts of wicked men and stopped the arm raised to strike? [16]Have you explored the springs from which the seas come, or walked in the sources of their depths? [17, 18]Has the location of the gates of Death been revealed to you? Do you realize the extent of the earth? Tell me about it if you know! [19]Where does the light come from, or how do you get there? Or tell me about the darkness. Where does it come from? [20]Can you find its boundaries, or go to its source? [21]But of course you know all this! For you were born before it was all created, and you are so very experienced! [22, 23]Have you visited the treasuries of the snow, or seen where hail is made and stored? For I have reserved it for the time when I will need it in war. [24]Where is the path to the distribution point of light? Where is the home of the east wind? [25-27]Who dug the valleys for the torrents of rain? Who laid out the path for the lightning, causing the rain to fall upon the barren deserts, so that the parched and barren ground is satisfied with water, and tender grass springs up? [28]Has the rain a father? Where does dew come from? [29]Who is the mother of the ice and frost? [30]For the water changes and turns to ice, as hard as rock. [31]Can you hold back the stars? Can you restrain Orion or Pleiades? [32]Can you ensure the proper sequence of the seasons, or guide the constellation of the Bear with her satellites across the heavens? [33]Do you know the laws of the universe and how the heavens influence the earth? [34]Can you shout to the clouds and make it rain? [35]Can you make lightning appear and cause it to strike as you direct it? [36]Who gives intuition and instinct? [37, 38]Who is wise enough to number all the clouds? Who can tilt the water jars of heaven, when everything is dust and clods? [39, 40]Can you stalk prey like a lioness, to satisfy the young lions' appetites as they lie in their dens, or lie in wait in the jungle? [41]Who provides for the ravens when their young cry out to God as they try to struggle up from their nest in hunger?"

Job 40:1. *The Lord went on:* [2]"Do you still want to argue with the Almighty? Or will you yield? Do you—God's critic—have the answers?" [3]*Then Job replied to God:* [4]"I am nothing—how could I ever find the answers? I lay my hand upon my mouth in silence. [5]I have said too much already." [6]*Then the Lord spoke to Job again from the whirlwind:* [7]"Stand up like a man and brace yourself for battle. Let me ask you a question, and give me the answer. [8]Are you going to discredit my justice and condemn me, so that you can say you are right? [9]Are you as strong as God, and can you shout as loudly as he? [10]All right then, put on your robes of state, your majesty and splendor. [11]Give vent to your anger. Let it overflow against the proud. [12]Humiliate the haughty with a glance; tread down the wicked where they stand. [13]Knock them into the dust, stone-faced in death. [14]If you can do that, then I'll agree with you that your own strength can save you."

Job 42:1. *Then Job replied to God:* [2]"I know that you can do anything and that no one can stop you. [3]You ask who it is who has so foolishly denied your providence. It is I. I was talking about things I knew nothing about and did not understand, things far too wonderful for me. [4][You said,] 'Listen and I will speak! Let me put the questions to you! See if you can answer them!' [5][But now I say,] 'I had heard about you before, but now I have seen you, [6]and I loathe myself and repent in dust and ashes.' "

Ps 8:3. When I look up into the night skies and see the work of your fingers—the moon and the stars you have made—[4]I cannot understand how you can bother with mere puny man, to pay any attention to him! [5]And yet you have made him only a little lower than the angels, and placed a crown of glory and honor upon his head. [6]You have put him in charge of everything you made;

everything is put under his authority.

Ps 97:6. The heavens declare his perfect righteousness; every nation sees his glory.

Ps 104:1. I bless the Lord: O Lord my God, how great you are! You are robed with honor and with majesty and light! You stretched out the starry curtain of the heavens, [3]and hollowed out the surface of the earth to form the seas. The clouds are his chariots. He rides upon the wings of the wind. [4]The angels are his messengers—his servants of fire! [5]You bound the world together so that it would never fall apart. [6]You clothed the earth with floods of waters covering up the mountains. [7, 8]You spoke, and at the sound of your shout the water collected into its vast ocean beds, and mountains rose and valleys sank to the levels you decreed. [9]And then you set a boundary for the seas, so that they would never again cover the earth. [10]He placed springs in the valleys, and streams that gush from the mountains. [11]They give water for all the animals to drink. There the wild donkeys quench their thirst, [12]and the birds nest beside the streams and sing among the branches of the trees. [13]He sends rain upon the mountains and fills the earth with fruit. [14]The tender grass grows up at his command to feed the cattle, and there are fruit trees, vegetables and grain for man to cultivate, [15]and wine to make him glad, and olive oil as lotion for his skin, and bread to give him strength. [16]The Lord planted the cedars of Lebanon. They are tall and flourishing. [17]There the birds make their nests, the storks in the firs. [18]High in the mountains are pastures for the wild goats, and rock-badgers burrow in among the rocks and find protection there. [19]He assigned the moon to mark the months, and the sun to mark the days. [20]He sends the night and darkness, when all the forest folk come out. [21]Then the young lions roar for their food, but they are dependent on the Lord. [22]At dawn they slink back into their dens to rest, [23]and men go off to work until the evening shadows fall again. [24]O Lord, what a variety you have made! And in wisdom you have made them all! The earth is full of your riches. [25]There before me lies the mighty ocean, teeming with life of every kind, both great and small. [26]And look! See the ships! And over there, the whale you made to play in the sea. [27]Every one of these depends on you to give them daily food. [28]You supply it, and they gather it. You open wide your hand to feed them and they are satisfied with all your bountiful provision. [29]But if you turn away from them, then all is lost. And when you gather up their breath, they die and turn again to dust. [30]Then you send your Spirit, and new life is born to replenish all the living of the earth. [31]Praise God forever! How he must rejoice in all his work! [32]The earth trembles at his glance; the mountains burst into flame at his touch.

Ps 107:23. And then there are the sailors sailing the seven seas, plying the trade routes of the world. [24]They, too, observe the power of God in action. [25]He calls to the storm winds; the waves rise high. [26]Their ships are tossed to the heavens and sink again to the depths; the sailors cringe in terror.

Ps 119:90, 91. Your faithfulness extends to every generation, like the earth you created; it endures by your decree, for everything serves your plans.

Ps 135:6. He does whatever pleases him throughout all of heaven and earth, and in the deepest seas. [7]He makes mists rise throughout the earth and sends the lightning to bring down the rain; and sends the winds from his treasuries.

Ps 147:15. He sends his orders to the world. How swiftly his word flies. [16]He sends the snow in all its lovely whiteness, and scatters the frost upon the ground, [17]and hurls the hail upon the earth. Who can stand before his freezing cold? [18]But then he calls for warmer weather, and the spring winds blow and all the river ice is broken.

Ps 148:3. Praise him, sun and moon, and all you twinkling stars. [4]Praise him, skies above. Praise him, vapors high above the clouds. [5]Let everything he has made give praise to him. For he issued his command, and they came into being; [6]he established them forever and forever. His orders will never be revoked.

Eccl 3:14. And I know this, that whatever God does is final—nothing can be added or taken from it; God's purpose in this is that man should fear the all-powerful God. [15]Whatever is, has been long ago; and whatever is going to be has been before; God brings to pass again what was in the distant past and disappeared.

Isa 2:19. When the Lord stands up from his throne to shake up the earth, his enemies will crawl with fear into the holes in the rocks and into the caves because of the glory of his majesty.

Isa 13:13. For I will shake the heavens in my wrath and fierce anger, and the earth will move from its place in the skies.

Isa 29:6. In an instant, I, the Lord of Hosts, will come upon them with thunder, earthquake, whirlwind and fire.

Isa 48:13. It was my hand that laid the foundations of the earth; the palm of my right hand spread out the heavens above; I spoke and they came into being.

Isa 50:2. Was I too weak to save you? Is that why the house is silent and empty when I come home? Have I no longer power to deliver? No, that is not the reason! For I can rebuke the sea and make it dry! I can turn the rivers into deserts, covered with dying fish. [3]I am the one who sends the darkness out across the skies.

Isa 64:3. So it was before when you came down, for you did awesome things beyond our highest expectations, and how the mountains quaked!

Jer 5:24. Though I am the one who gives them rain each year in spring and fall and sends the harvest times, yet they have no respect or fear for me.

Jer 10:2. Don't act like the people who make horoscopes and try to read their fate and future in the stars! Don't be frightened by predictions such as theirs, for it is all a pack of lies. [13]It is his voice that echoes in the thunder of the storm clouds. He causes mist to rise upon the earth; he sends the lightning and brings the rain, and from his treasuries he brings the wind.

Jer 31:35. The Lord who gives us sunlight in the daytime and the moon and stars to light the night, and who stirs the sea to make the roaring waves—his name is Lord of Hosts—says this: [36]I am as likely to reject my people Israel as I am to do away with these laws of nature! [37]Not until the heavens can be measured and the foundations of the earth explored, will I consider casting them away forever for their sins!

Jer 33:20, 21. If you can break my covenant with the day and with the night so that day and night don't come on their usual schedule, only then will my covenant with David, my servant, be broken so that he shall not have a son to reign upon his throne; and my covenant with the Levite priests, my ministers, is non-cancelable. [25, 26]But this is the Lord's reply: I would no more reject my people than I would change my laws of night and day, of earth and sky. I will never abandon the Jews, or David my servant, or change the plan that his Child will someday rule these descendants of Abraham, Isaac and Jacob. Instead I will restore their prosperity and have mercy on them.

Jer 51:16. When he speaks there is thunder in the heavens and he causes the vapors to rise around the world; he brings the lightning with the rain and the winds from his treasuries.

Dan 2:21. World events are under his control. He removes kings and sets others on their thrones. He gives wise men their wisdom, and scholars their intelligence.

Amos 5:8. Seek him who created the Seven Stars and the constellation Orion, who turns darkness into morning, and day into night, who calls forth the water from the ocean and pours it out as rain upon the land. The Lord, Jehovah, is his name.

Nah 1:3. He is slow in getting angry, but when aroused, his power is incredible, and he does not easily forgive. He shows his power in the terrors of the cyclone and the raging storms; clouds are billowing dust beneath his feet! [4]At his command the oceans and rivers become dry sand; the lush pastures of Bashan and Carmel fade away; the green forests of Lebanon wilt. [5]In his presence mountains quake and hills melt; the earth crumbles and its people are destroyed. [6]Who can stand before an angry God? His fury is like fire; the mountains tumble down before his anger.

Rom 1:19. For the truth about God is known to them instinctively; God has put this knowledge in their hearts. [20]Since earliest times men have seen the earth and sky and all God made, and have known of his existence and great eternal power. So they will have no excuse [when they stand before God at Judgment Day].

ACCESS TO. Deut 4:7. For what other nation, great or small, has God among them, as the Lord our God is here among us whenever we call upon him?

Ps 24:3. Who may climb the mountain of the Lord and enter where he lives? Who may stand before the Lord? [4]Only those with pure hands and hearts, who do not practice dishonesty and lying.

Ps 27:4. The one thing I want from God, the thing I seek most of all, is the privilege of meditating in his Temple, living in his presence every day of my life, delighting in his incomparable perfections and glory.

Ps 43:3. Oh, send out your light and your truth—let them lead me. Let them lead me to your Temple on your holy mountain, Zion.

Ps 65:4. How greatly to be envied are those you have chosen to come and live with you within the holy tabernacle courts! What joys await us among all the good things there.

Ps 145:18. He is close to all who call on him sincerely. [19]He fulfills the desires of those who reverence and trust him; he hears their cries for help and rescues them.

Isa 55:3. Come to me with your ears wide open. Listen, for the life of your soul is at stake. I am ready to make an everlasting covenant with you, to give you all the unfailing mercies and love that I had for King David.

Mt 6:6. But when you pray, go away by yourself, all alone, and shut the door behind you and pray to your Father secretly, and your Father, who knows your secrets, will reward you.

Jn 14:6. Jesus told him, "I am the Way—yes, and the Truth and the Life. No one can get to the Father except by means of me."

Acts 14:27. Upon arrival they called together the believers and reported on their trip, telling how God had opened the door of faith to the Gentiles too.

Rom 5:2. For because of our faith, he has brought us into this place of highest privilege where we now stand, and we confidently and joyfully look forward to actually becoming all that God has had in mind for us to be.

Eph 2:13. But now you belong to Jesus Christ, and though you once were far away from God, now you have been brought very near to him because of what Jesus Christ has done for you with his blood. [18]Now all of us, whether Jews or Gentiles, may come to God the Father with the Holy Spirit's help because of what Christ has done for us.

Eph 3:12. Now we can come fearlessly right into God's presence, assured of his glad welcome when we come with Christ and trust in him.

Col 1:21. This includes you who were once so far away from God. You were his enemies and hated him and were separated from him by your evil thoughts and actions, yet now he has brought you back as his friends. [22]He has done this through the death on the cross of his own human body, and now as a result Christ has brought you into the very presence of God, and you are standing there before him with nothing left against you—nothing left that he could even chide you for.

Heb 4:16. So let us come boldly to the very throne of God and stay there to receive his mercy and to find grace to help us in our times of need.

Heb 7:19. It [the law] never made anyone really right with God. But now we have a far better hope, for Christ makes us acceptable to God, and now we may draw near to him. [25]He is able to save completely all who come to God through him. Since he will live forever, he will always be there to remind God that he has paid for their sins with his blood.

Heb 10:19. And so, dear brothers, now we may walk right into the very Holy of Holies where God is, because of the blood of Jesus. [22]Let us go right in, to God himself, with true hearts fully trusting him to receive us, because we have been sprinkled with Christ's blood to make us clean, and because our bodies have been washed with pure water.

Heb 11:6. You can never please God without faith, without depending on him. Anyone who wants to come to God must believe that there is a God and that he rewards those who sincerely look for him.

Jas 4:8. And when you draw close to God, God will draw close to you. Wash your hands, you sinners, and let your hearts be filled with God alone to make them pure and true to him.

1 Pet 1:17. And remember that your heavenly Father to whom you pray has no favorites when he judges. He will judge you with perfect justice for everything you do; so act in reverent fear of him from now on until you get to heaven.

1 Pet 3:18. Christ also suffered. He died once for the sins of all us guilty sinners, although he himself was innocent of any sin at any time, that he might bring us safely home to God. But though his body died, his spirit lived on.

1 Jn 4:16. We know how much God loves us because we have felt his love and because we believe him when he tells us that he loves us dearly. God is love, and anyone who lives in love is living with God and God is living in him.

See *Penitent; Repentance; Seeker.*

COMPASSION OF. See *God, Long-suffering of, Mercy of,* below.

CREATOR. Gen 1:1. When God began creating the heavens and the earth, [2]the earth was at first a shapeless, chaotic mass, with the Spirit of God brooding over the dark vapors. [3]Then God said, "Let there be light." And light appeared. [4, 5]And God was pleased with it, and divided the light from the darkness. So he let it shine for awhile, and then there was darkness again. He called the light "daytime," and the darkness "nighttime." Together they formed the first day.

6. And God said, "Let the vapors separate to form the sky above and the oceans below." [7, 8]So God made the sky, dividing the vapor above from the water below. This all happened on the second day.

9, 10. Then God said, "Let the water beneath the sky be gathered into oceans so that the dry land will emerge." And so it was. Then God named the dry land "earth," and the water "seas." And God was pleased. [11, 12]And he said, "Let the earth burst forth with every sort of grass and seed-bearing plant, and fruit trees with seeds inside the fruit, so that these seeds will produce the kinds of plants and fruits they came from." And so it was, and God was pleased. [13]This all occurred on the third day.

14, 15. Then God said, "Let there be bright lights in the sky to give light to the earth and to identify the day and the night; they shall bring about the seasons on the earth, and mark the days and years." And so it was. [16]For God made two huge lights, the sun and moon, to shine down upon the earth—the larger one, the sun, to preside over the day and the smaller one, the moon, to preside through the night; he also made the stars. [17]And God set them in the sky to light the earth, [18]and to preside over the day and night, and to divide the light from the darkness. And God was pleased. [19]This all happened on the fourth day.

20. Then God said, "Let the waters teem with fish and other life, and let the skies be filled with birds of every kind." [21, 22]So God created great sea creatures, and every sort of fish and every kind of bird. And God looked at them with pleasure, and blessed them all. "Multiply and stock the oceans," he told them, and to the birds he said, "Let your numbers increase. Fill the earth!" [23]That ended the fifth day.

24. And God said, "Let the earth bring forth every kind of animal—cattle and reptiles and wildlife of every kind." And so it was. [25]God made all sorts of wild animals and cattle and reptiles. And God was pleased with what he had done.

26. Then God said, "Let us make a man—someone like ourselves, to be the master of all life upon the earth and in the skies and in the seas." [27]So God made man like his Maker. Like God did God make man; Man and maid did he make them. [28]And God blessed them and told them, "Multiply and fill the earth and subdue it; you are masters of the fish and birds and all the animals." [31]Then God looked over all that he had made, and it was excellent in every way. This ended the sixth day.

Gen 2:1. Now at last the heavens and earth were successfully completed, with all that they contained. [2]So on the seventh day, having finished his task, God ceased from this work he had been doing, [3]and God blessed the seventh day and declared it holy, because it was the day when he ceased this work of creation. [4]Here is a summary of the events in the creation of the heavens and earth which the Lord God made. [7]The time came when the Lord God formed a man's body from the dust of the ground and breathed into it the breath of life. And man became a living person. Gen 2: 1–25.

Gen 5:1. Here is a list of some of the descendants of Adam—the man who was like God from the day of his creation. [2]God created man and woman and blessed them, and called them Man from the start.

Gen 9:5, 6. And murder is forbidden. Man-killing animals must die, and any man who murders shall be killed; for to kill a man is to kill one made like God.

Ex 20:11. For in six days the Lord made the heaven, earth, and sea, and everything in them. Ps 146:6.

1 Sam 2:8. For all the earth is the Lord's and he has set the world in order.

2 Kgs 19:15. Then he prayed this prayer: "O Lord God of Israel, sitting on your throne high above the angels, you alone are the God of all the kingdoms of the earth. You created the heavens and the earth."

1 Chron 16:26. The other so-called gods are demons, but the Lord made the heavens.

Neh 9:6. Then Ezra prayed, "You alone are God. You have made the skies and the heavens, the earth and the seas, and everything in them. You preserve it all; and all the angels of heaven worship you."

Job 9:8. Only he has stretched the heavens out and stalked along the seas. [9]He made the Bear, Orion and the Pleiades, and the constellations of the southern Zodiac.

Job 10:3. Does it really seem right to you to oppress and despise me, a man you have made; and to send joy and prosperity to the wicked? [8]You have made me, and yet you destroy me.

Job 12:7–9. Who doesn't know that the Lord does things like that? Ask the dumbest beast—he knows that it is so; ask the birds—they will tell you; or let the earth teach you, or the fish of the sea.

Job 26:7. God stretches out heaven over empty space, and hangs the earth upon nothing. [13]The heavens are made beautiful by his Spirit; he pierces the swiftly gliding serpent. *vs.* 8–12.

Job 28:23, 24. And God surely knows where it is to be found, for he looks throughout the whole earth, under all the heavens. [25]He makes the winds blow and sets the boundaries of the oceans. [26]He makes the laws of the rain and a path for the lightning.

Job 37:16, 17. Do you understand the balancing of the clouds with wonderful perfection and skill? Do you know why you become warm when the south wind is blowing and everything is still? [18]Can you spread out the gigantic mirror of the skies as he does?

Job 38:4. Where were you when I laid the foundations of the earth? Tell me, if you know so much. [7]As the morning stars sang together and all the angels shouted for joy? [8, 9]Who decreed the boundaries of the seas when they gushed from the depths? Who clothed them with clouds and thick darkness, [10]and barred them by limiting their shores. *vs.* 4–38.

Ps 8:3. When I look up into the night skies and see the work of your fingers—the moon and the stars you have made.

Ps 19:1. The heavens are telling the glory of God; they are a marvelous display of his craftsmanship. [4]The sun lives in the heavens where God placed it.

Ps 24:1. The earth belongs to God! Everything in all the world is his! [2]He is the one who pushed the oceans back to let dry land appear.

Ps 33:6. He merely spoke, and the heavens were formed, and all the galaxies of stars. [7]He made the oceans, pouring them into his vast reservoirs. [9]For when he but spoke, the world began! It appeared at his command!

Ps 65:6. He formed the mountains by his mighty strength.

Ps 74:16. Day and night alike belong to you; you made the starlight and the sun. [17]All nature is within your hands; you make the summer and the winter too.

Ps 78:69. There he built his towering temple, solid and enduring as the heavens and the earth.

Ps 89:11. The heavens are yours, the world, everything—for you created them all. [12]You created north and south! [47]Oh, remember how short you have made man's lifespan. Is it an empty, futile life you give the sons of men?

Ps 90:2. Before the mountains were created, before the earth was formed, you are God without beginning or end.

Ps 95:4. He controls the formation of the depths of the earth and the mightiest mountains; all are his. [5]He made the sea and formed the land; they too are his.

Ps 102:25. In ages past you laid the foundations of the earth, and made the heavens with your hands! Ps 96:5.

Ps 104:2. You stretched out the starry curtain of the heavens, [3]and hollowed out the surface of the earth to form the seas. The clouds are his chariots. He rides upon the wings of the wind. [5]You bound the world together so that it would never fall apart. [6]You clothed the earth with floods of waters covering up the mountains. [24]O Lord, what a variety you have made! And in wisdom you have made them all! The earth is full of your riches. [30]Then you send your Spirit, and new life is born to replenish all the living of the earth. *v.* 31.

Ps 119:90, 91. Your faithfulness extends to every generation, like the earth you created; it endures by your decree, for everything serves your plans.

Ps 121:2. No! My help is from Jehovah who made the mountains! And the heavens too!

Ps 124:8. Our help is from the Lord who made heaven and earth.

Ps 136:5. Praise him who made the heavens . . . . [6]Praise him who planted the water within the earth. . . . [7]Praise him who made the heavenly lights . . . [8]the sun to rule the day . . . [9]and the moon and stars at night.

Ps 146:5. But happy is the man who has the God of Jacob as his helper, whose hope is in the Lord his God—[6]the God who made both earth and heaven, the seas and everything in them. He is the God who keeps every promise.

Ps 148:5. Let everything he has made give praise to him. For he issued his command, and they came into being; [6]he established them forever and forever. His orders will never be revoked.

Prov 3:19. The Lord's wisdom founded the earth; his understanding established all the universe and space.

Prov 8:26. Yes, I was born before God made the earth and fields, and high plateaus. [27-29]I was there when he established the heavens and formed the great springs in the depths of the oceans. I was there when he set the limits of the seas and gave them his instructions not to spread beyond their boundaries. I was there when he made the blueprint for the earth and oceans.

Prov 16:4. The Lord has made everything for his own purposes—even the wicked, for punishment.

Prov 22:2. The rich and the poor are alike before the Lord who made them all.

Prov 30:4. Who else but God goes back and forth to heaven? Who else holds the wind in his fists, and wraps up the oceans in his cloak? Who but God has created the world? If there is any other, what is his name—and his son's name—if you know it?

Eccl 3:11. Everything is appropriate in its own time. But though God has planted eternity in the hearts of men, even so, man cannot see the whole scope of God's work from beginning to end.

Eccl 7:29. And I found that though God has made men upright, each has turned away to follow his own downward road.

Eccl 11:5. God's ways are as mysterious as the pathway of the wind, and as the manner in which a human spirit is infused into the little body of a baby while it is yet in its mother's womb.

Isa 17:7. Then at last they will think of God their Creator and have respect for the Holy One of Israel.

Isa 37:16. O Lord of Hosts, God of Israel enthroned above the cherubim, *you alone* are God of all the kingdoms of the earth. You alone made heaven and earth.

Isa 40:12. Who else has held the oceans in his hands and measured off the heavens with his ruler? Who else knows the weight of all the earth and weighs the mountains and the hills? [26]Look up into the heavens! Who created all these stars? As a shepherd leads his sheep, calling each by its pet name, and counts them to see that none are lost or strayed, so God does with stars and planets! [28]Don't you yet understand? Don't you know by now that the everlasting God, the Creator of the farthest parts of the earth, never grows faint or weary? No one can fathom the depths of his understanding.

Isa 42:5. The Lord God who created the heavens and stretched them out and created the earth and everything in it, and gives life and breath and spirit to everyone in all the world.

Isa 44:24. The Lord, your Redeemer who made you, says, All things were made by me; I alone stretched out the heavens. By myself I made the earth and everything in it.

Isa 45:7. I form the light and make the dark. I send good times and bad. I, Jehovah, am he who does these things. [12]I have made the earth and created man upon it. With my hands I have stretched out the heavens and commanded all the vast myriads of stars. [18]For Jehovah created the heavens and earth and put everything in place, and he made the world to be lived in, not to be an empty chaos. I am Jehovah, he says, and there is no other!

Isa 48:13. It was my hand that laid the foundations of the earth; the palm of my right hand spread out the heavens above; I spoke and they came into being.

Isa 51:13. And yet you have no fear of God, your Maker—you have forgotten him, the one who spread the stars throughout the skies and made the earth. [16]And I have put my words in your mouth and hidden you safe within my hand. I planted the stars in place and molded all the earth. I am the one who says to Israel, "You are mine."

Isa 66:2. My hand has made both earth and skies, and they are mine. Yet I will look with pity on the man who has a humble and a contrite heart, who trembles at my word.

Jer 5:22. Have you no respect at all for me? the Lord God asks. How can it be that you don't even tremble in my presence? I set the shorelines of the world by perpetual decrees, so that the oceans, though they toss and roar, can never pass those bounds.

Jer 10:12. But our God formed the earth by his power and wisdom, and by his intelligence he hung the stars in space and stretched out the heavens. [16]But the God of Jacob is not like these foolish idols. He is the Creator of all, and Israel is his chosen nation. The Lord of Hosts is his name. Jer 51:19.

Jer 27:5. By my great power I have made the earth and all mankind and every animal; and I give these things of mine to anyone I want to.

Jer 31:35. The Lord who gives us sunlight in the daytime and the moon and stars to light the night, and who stirs the sea to make the roaring waves—his name is Lord of Hosts.

Jer 32:17. O Lord God! You have made the heavens and earth by your great power; nothing is too hard for you!

Jer 33:2. The Lord, the Maker of heaven and earth—Jehovah is his name.

Jer 51:15. God made the earth by his power and wisdom. He stretched out the heavens by his understanding. [16]When he speaks there is thunder in the heavens and he causes the vapors to rise around the world; he brings the lightning with the rain and the winds from his treasuries. Jer 10:13.

Amos 4:13. For you are dealing with the one who formed the mountains and made the winds, and knows your every thought; he turns the morning to darkness and crushes down the mountains underneath his feet: Jehovah, the Lord, the God of Hosts, is his name.

Amos 5:8. Seek him who created the Seven Stars and the constellation Orion, who turns darkness into morning, and day into night.

Amos 9:6. The upper stories of his home are in the heavens, the first floor on the earth. He calls for the vapor to rise from the ocean and pours it down as rain upon the ground. Jehovah, the Lord, is his name.

Jon 1:9. And he said, "I am a Jew; I worship Jehovah, the God of heaven, who made the earth and sea."

Zech 12:1. This is the fate of Israel, as pronounced by the Lord, who stretched out the heavens and laid the foundation of the earth, and formed the spirit of man within him.

Mk 10:6. For from the very first he made man and woman to be joined together permanently in marriage.

Mk 13:19. For those will be days of such horror as have never been since the beginning of God's creation, nor will ever be again.

Acts 4:24. Then all the believers united in this prayer: "O Lord, Creator of heaven and earth and of the sea and everything in them—."

Acts 7:50. Didn't I make both heaven and earth?

Acts 14:15. We have come to bring you the Good News that you are invited to turn from the worship of these foolish things and to pray instead to the living God who made heaven and earth and sea and everything in them.

Acts 17:24. He made the world and everything in it, and since he is Lord of heaven and earth, he doesn't live in man-made temples; [25]and human hands can't minister to his needs—for he has no needs! He himself gives life and breath to everything, and satisfies every need there is. [26]He created all the people of the world from one man, Adam, and scattered the nations across the face of the earth. He decided beforehand which should rise and fall, and when. He determined their boundaries.

Rom 1:20. Since earliest times men have seen the earth and sky and all God made, and have known of his existence and great eternal power.

Rom 11:36. For everything comes from God alone. Everything lives by his power, and everything is for his glory. To him be glory evermore.

1 Cor 8:6. But we know that there is only one God, the Father, who created all things and made us to be his own; and one Lord Jesus Christ, who made everything and gives us life.

2 Cor 4:6. For God, who said, "Let there be light in the darkness," has made us understand that it is the brightness of his glory that is seen in the face of Jesus Christ.

2 Cor 5:18. All these new things are from God. 1 Cor 11:12.

Eph 3:9. And to explain to everyone that God is the Savior of the Gentiles too, just as he who made all things had secretly planned from the very beginning.

1 Tim 6:13. I command you before God who gives life to all.

Heb 1:1. Long ago God spoke. . . . [2]But now in these days he has spoken to us through his Son to whom he has given everything, and through whom he made the world and everything there is.

Heb 2:10. And it was right and proper that God, who made everything for his own glory, should allow Jesus to suffer, for in doing this he was bringing vast multitudes of God's people to heaven; for his suffering made Jesus a perfect Leader, one fit to bring them into their salvation.

Heb 3:4. And many people can build houses, but only God made everything.

Heb 11:3. By faith—by believing God—we know that the world and the stars—in fact, all things—were made at God's command; and that they were all made from things that can't be seen. [10]Abraham did this because he was confidently waiting for God to bring him to that strong heavenly city whose designer and builder is God.

Rev 4:11. O Lord, you are worthy to receive the glory and the honor and the power, for you have created all things. They were created and called into being by your act of will.

Rev 10:6. And swore by him who lives forever and ever, who created heaven and everything in it and the earth and all that it contains and the sea and its inhabitants, that there should be no more delay.

Rev 14:7. "Fear God," he shouted, "and extol his greatness. . . . Worship him who made the heaven and the earth, the sea and all its sources."

CREATOR OF MAN. Gen 1:26. Then God said, "Let us make a man—someone like ourselves. . . ." [27]So God made man like his Maker. Like God did God make man; man and maid did he make them. Gen 2:7.

Gen 5:1. Adam—the man who was like God from the day of his creation. [2]God created man and woman and blessed them, and called them Man from the start.

Gen 9:6. For to kill a man is to kill one made like God.

Ex 4:11. "Who makes mouths?" Jehovah asked him. "Isn't it I, the Lord? Who makes a man so that he can speak or not speak, see or not see, hear or not hear?"

Num 16:22. But Moses and Aaron fell face downward to the ground before the Lord. "O God, the God of all mankind," they pleaded, "must you be angry with all the people when one man sins?" Num 27:16.

Deut 4:32. In all history, going back to the time when God created man upon the earth.

Deut 32:6. Is this the way you treat Jehovah? O foolish people, Is not God your Father? Has he not created you? Has he not established you and made you strong? [18]They spurned the Rock who had made them, forgetting it was God who had given them birth.

Job 10:8. You have made me. . . . [9]Oh, please remember that I'm made of dust—will you change me back again to dust so soon? [11]You gave me skin and flesh and knit together bones and sinews. [12]You gave me life and were so kind and loving to me, and I was preserved by your care. Ps 119:73.

Job 12:10. For the soul of every living thing is in the hand of God, and the breath of all mankind.

Job 27:3. That as long as I live, while I have breath from God.

Job 31:15. For God made me, and made my servant too. He created us both.

Job 33:4. For the Spirit of God has made me, and the breath of the Almighty gives me life.

Job 34:19. For he doesn't care how great a man may be, and doesn't pay any more attention to the rich than to the poor. He made them all.

Job 38:36. Who gives intuition and instinct?

Ps 33:13–15. The Lord gazes down upon mankind from heaven where he lives. He has made their hearts and closely watches everything they do.

Ps 86:9. All the nations—and you made each one —will come and bow before you, Lord, and praise your great and holy name.

Ps 94:9. Is God deaf and blind—he who makes ears and eyes?

Ps 95:6. Come, kneel before the Lord our Maker.

Ps 100:3. Try to realize what this means—the Lord is God! He made us—we are his people, the sheep of his pasture.

Ps 139:13. You made all the delicate, inner parts of my body, and knit them together in my mother's womb.

Ps 149:2. O Israel, rejoice in your Maker. O people of Jerusalem, exult in your King.

Prov 16:4. The Lord has made everything for his own purposes—even the wicked, for punishment.

Prov 20:12. If you have good eyesight and good hearing, thank God who gave them to you.

Prov 22:2. The rich and the poor are alike before the Lord who made them all.

Eccl 12:1. Don't let the excitement of being young cause you to forget about your Creator.

Isa 42:5. The Lord God . . . gives life and breath and spirit to everyone in all the world.

Isa 43:1. But now the Lord who created you, O Israel, says, [7]All who claim me as their God will come, for I have made them for my glory; I created them. [15]I am the Lord, your Holy One, Israel's Creator and King.

Isa 44:2. The Lord who made you, who will help you, says, O servant of mine, don't be afraid. *v.* 24.

Isa 45:12. I have made the earth and created man upon it. [18]For Jehovah created the heavens and earth and put everything in place, and he made the world to be lived in, not to be an empty chaos.

Isa 51:13. And yet you have no fear of God, your Maker—you have forgotten him.

Isa 64:8. And yet, O Lord, you are our Father. We are the clay and you are the Potter. We are all formed by your hand.

Jer 27:5. By my great power I have made the earth and all mankind and every animal; and I give these things of mine to anyone I want to.

Dan 5:23. But you have not praised the God who gives you the breath of life and controls your destiny!

Zech 12:1. The Lord, who stretched out the heavens . . . and formed the spirit of man within him.

Mal 2:10. We are children of the same father, Abraham, all created by the same God.

Acts 17:24. He made the world and everything in it . . . . [25]He himself gives life and breath to everything, and satisfies every need there is. [26]He created all the people of the world from one man, Adam, and scattered the nations across the face of the earth. He decided beforehand which should rise and fall, and when. He determined their boundaries. [28]For in him we live and move and are! As one of your own poets says it, "We are the sons of God." *v.* 29.

1 Cor 12:18. He has made many parts for our bodies and has put each part just where he wants it. [24]So God has put the body together in such a way that extra honor and care are given to those parts that mighty otherwise seem less important. [25]This makes for happiness among the parts, so that the parts have the same care for each other that they do for themselves.

1 Cor 15:38. Then God gives it a beautiful new body—just the kind he wants it to have; a different kind of plant grows from each kind of seed.

1 Pet 4:19. So if you are suffering according to God's will, keep on doing what is right and trust yourself to the God who made you, for he will never fail you.

See *Life, from God; Man.*

ETERNITY OF. Gen 21:33. And Abraham planted a tamarisk tree beside the well, and prayed there to the Lord, calling upon the Eternal God [to witness the covenant]. Rom 16:25–27.

Ex 3:15. Yes, tell them, "Jehovah, the God of your ancestors Abraham, Isaac, and Jacob, has sent me to you." (This is my eternal name, to be used throughout all generations.)

Deut 33:27. The eternal God is your Refuge, and underneath are the everlasting arms.

1 Chron 16:36. Blessed be Jehovah, God of Israel, forever and forevermore.

1 Chron 29:10. While still in the presence of the whole assembly, David expressed his praises to the Lord: "O Lord God of our father Israel, praise your name for ever and ever!"

Neh 9:5. Stand up and praise the Lord your God, for he lives from everlasting to everlasting.

Job 36:26. God is so great that we cannot begin to know him. No one can begin to understand eternity.

Ps 9:7. But the Lord lives on forever.

Ps 33:11. But his own plan stands forever. His intentions are the same for every generation.

Ps 41:13. Bless the Lord, the God of Israel, who exists from everlasting ages past—and on into everlasting eternity ahead.

Ps 55:19. God himself—God from everlasting ages past—will answer them! For they refuse to fear him or even honor his commands.

Ps 68:33. To him who rides upon the ancient heavens, whose mighty voice thunders from the sky.

Ps 90:1. Lord, through all the generations you have been our home! [2]Before the mountains were created, before the earth was formed, you are God without beginning or end. [4]A thousand years are but as yesterday to you! They are like a single hour!

Ps 92:8. But the Lord continues forever, exalted in the heavens.

Ps 93:2. O Lord, you have reigned from prehistoric times, from the everlasting past. Mic 5:2.

Ps 102:12. While you, Lord, are a famous King forever. Your fame will endure to every generation. [24]O God, you live forever and forever! . . . [25]In ages past you laid the foundations of the earth, and made the heavens with your hands! [26]They shall perish, but you go on forever. They will grow old, like worn-out clothing, and you will change them like a man putting on a new shirt and throwing away the old one! [27]But you yourself never grow old. You are forever, and your years never end.

Ps 104:31. Praise God forever! How he must rejoice in all his work!

Ps 111:3. For his miracles demonstrate his honor, majesty, and eternal goodness.

Ps 135:13. O Jehovah, your name endures forever; your fame is known to every generation.

Ps 145:13. For your kingdom never ends. You rule generation after generation.

Ps 146:10. The Lord will reign forever. O Jerusalem, your God is King in every generation! Ex 15:18.

Prov 8:23. From ages past, I am. I existed before the earth began. [24]I lived before the oceans were created, before the springs bubbled forth their waters onto the earth; [25]before the mountains and the hills were made.

Isa 26:4. Trust in the Lord God always, for in the Lord Jehovah is your everlasting strength.

Isa 40:28. Don't you know by now that the everlasting God, the Creator of the farthest parts of the earth, never grows faint or weary?

Isa 41:4. Who has done such mighty deeds, directing the affairs of generations of mankind as they march by? It is I, the Lord, the First and Last; I alone am he.

Isa 43:13. From eternity to eternity I am God.

Isa 44:6. I am the First and Last; there is no other God.

Isa 46:4. I will be your God through all your lifetime, yes, even when your hair is white with age. I made you and I will care for you. I will carry you along and be your Savior.

Isa 48:12. Listen to me, my people, my chosen ones! I alone am God. I am the First; I am the Last.

Isa 57:15. The high and lofty one who inhabits eternity, the Holy One, says this.

Isa 63:16. Still you would be our Father, our Redeemer from ages past.

Jer 10:10. But the Lord is the only true God, the living God, the everlasting King.

Jer 17:12. But our refuge is your throne, eternal, high and glorious.

Lam 5:19. O Lord, forever you remain the same! Your throne continues from generation to generation.

Dan 4:34. At the end of seven years I, Nebuchadnezzar, looked up to heaven, and my sanity returned, and I praised and worshiped the Most High God and honored him who lives forever, whose rule is everlasting, his kingdom evermore. *v.* 3.

Hab 1:12. O Lord my God, my Holy One, you who are eternal—.

Hab 3:6. He stops; he stands still for a moment, gazing at the earth. Then he shakes the nations, scattering the everlasting mountains and leveling the hills. His power is just the same as always!

Rom 1:20. Since earliest times men have seen the earth and sky and all God made, and have known of his existence and great eternal power.

Eph 3:21. May he be given glory forever and ever through endless ages because of his master plan of salvation for the church through Jesus Christ.

1 Tim 1:17. Glory and honor to God forever and ever. He is the King of the ages, the unseen one who never dies; he alone is God, and full of wisdom.

1 Tim 6:15. For in due season Christ will be revealed from heaven by the blessed and only Almighty God, the King of kings and Lord of lords, [16]who alone can never die, who lives in light so terrible that no human being can approach him. No mere man has ever seen him, nor ever will. Unto him be honor and everlasting power and dominion forever and ever.

Heb 1:8. But of his Son he says, "Your kingdom, O God, will last forever and ever; its commands are always just and right."

Heb 9:14. Just think how much more surely the blood of Christ will transform our lives and hearts. His sacrifice frees us from the worry of having to obey the old rules, and makes us want to serve the living God. For by the help of the eternal Holy Spirit, Christ willingly gave himself to God to die for our sins—he being perfect, without a single sin or fault.

2 Pet 3:8. But don't forget this, dear friends, that a day or a thousand years from now is like tomorrow to the Lord.

1 Jn 2:13. I am saying these things to you older men because you really know Christ, the one who has been alive from the beginning.

Rev 1:6. He has gathered us into his kingdom and made us priests of God his Father. Give to him everlasting glory! He rules forever!

Rev 4:8. Day after day and night after night they kept on saying, "Holy, holy, holy, Lord God Almighty—the one who was, and is, and is to come." [9]And when the Living Beings gave glory and honor and thanks to the one sitting on the throne, who lives forever and ever, *v.* 10; Rev 1:4; 5:13; 11:17; 15:7.

Rev 10:6. And swore by him who lives forever and ever, who created heaven and everything in it and the earth and all that it contains and the sea and its inhabitants, that there should be no more delay.

Rev 16:5. And I heard this angel of the waters declaring, "You are just in sending this judgment, O Holy One, who is and was."

See *God, Self-existent.*

FAITHFULNESS OF. Gen 9:16, 17. For I will see the rainbow in the cloud and remember my eternal promise to every living being on the earth. *v.* 15; Gen 6:18.

Gen 21:1, 2. Then God did as he had promised, and Sarah became pregnant and gave Abraham a baby son in his old age, at the time God had said.

Gen 24:27. "Thank you, Lord God of my master Abraham," he prayed; "thank you for being so kind and true to him."

Gen 28:15. What's more, I am with you, and will protect you wherever you go, and will bring you back safely to this land; I will be with you constantly until I have finished giving you all I am promising.

Gen 32:10. I am not worthy of the least of all your loving kindnesses shown me again and again just as you promised me.

Ex 6:4. And I entered into a solemn covenant with them; under its terms I promised to give them and their descendants the land of Canaan where they were living. [5]And now I have heard the groanings of the people of Israel, in slavery now to the Egyptians, and I remember my promise. Ex 2:24.

Ex 12:41. And it was on the last day of the 430th year that all of Jehovah's people left the land.

Ex 34:6. Then the Lord . . . passed in front of him and announced the meaning of his name. "I am Jehovah, the merciful and gracious God," he said, "slow to anger and rich in steadfast love and truth."

Lev 26:44. But despite all they have done, I will not utterly destroy them and my covenant with them, for I am Jehovah their God. [45]For their sakes I will remember my promises to their ancestors, to be their God.

Deut 4:31. For the Lord your God is merciful—he will not abandon you nor destroy you nor forget the promises he has made to your ancestors. Judg 2:1.

Deut 7:8. It was just because he loves you, and because he kept his promise to your ancestors. That is why he brought you out of slavery in Egypt with such amazing power and mighty miracles. [9]Understand, therefore, that the Lord your God is the faithful God who for a thousand generations keeps his promises and constantly loves those who love him and who obey his commands. Neh 1:5.

Deut 9:5. It is not at all because you are such fine, upright people that the Lord will drive them out from before you! I say it again, it is only because of the wickedness of the other nations, and because of his promises to your ancestors, Abraham, Isaac, and Jacob, that he will do it.

Deut 32:4. He is the Rock. His work is perfect. Everything he does is just and fair. He is faithful, without sin.

Josh 23:14. You know very well that God's promises to you have all come true. Josh 21:45.

1 Sam 12:22. The Lord will not abandon his chosen people, for that would dishonor his great name. He made you a special nation for himself—just because he wanted to!

2 Sam 7:28. For you are indeed God, and your words are truth; and you have promised me these good things—.

2 Sam 23:5. And it is my family he has chosen! Yes, God has made an everlasting covenant with me; his agreement is eternal, final, sealed. He will constantly look after my safety and success.

1 Kgs 8:23. You keep your promises to your people if they do their best to do your will. [24]Today you have fulfilled your promise to my father David, who was your servant. [56]Blessed be the Lord who has fulfilled his promise and given rest to his people Israel; not one word has failed of all the wonderful promises proclaimed by his servant Moses. *vs.* 15, 20; 2 Chron 6:4–15.

2 Kgs 8:19. Nevertheless, because God had promised his servant David that he would watch over and guide his descendants, he did not destroy Judah. 2 Chron 21:7.

2 Kgs 13:23. But the Lord was gracious to the people of Israel, and they were not totally destroyed. For God pitied them, and also he was honoring his contract with Abraham, Isaac, and Jacob. And this is still true.

1 Chron 17:27. May this blessing rest upon my children forever, for when you grant a blessing, Lord, it is an eternal blessing!

1 Chron 28:20. For the Lord my God is with you; he will not forsake you. He will see to it that everything is finished correctly. Deut 31:6.

Ezra 9:9. For we were slaves, but in your love and mercy you did not abandon us to slavery.

Neh 9:7. You are the Lord God who chose Abram. . . . [8]And now you have done what you promised, for you are always true to your word. *v.* 32.

Ps 9:10. All those who know your mercy, Lord, will count on you for help. For you have never yet forsaken those who trust in you.

Ps 18:30. What a God he is! How perfect in every way! All his promises prove true. He is a shield for everyone who hides behind him. 2 Sam 22:31.

Ps 25:10. And when we obey him, every path he guides us on is fragrant with his lovingkindness and his truth.

Ps 31:5. Into your hand I commit my spirit. You have rescued me, O God who keeps his promises.

Ps 33:4. For all God's words are right, and everything he does is worthy of our trust.

Ps 36:5. Your steadfast love, O Lord, is as great as all the heavens. Your faithfulness reaches beyond the clouds.

Ps 37:28. For the Lord loves justice and fairness; he will never abandon his people. They will be kept safe forever.

Ps 57:3. He will send down help from heaven to save me, because of his love and his faithfulness.

Ps 71:22. I will praise you with music, telling of your faithfulness to all your promises, O Holy One of Israel.

Ps 89:1. Forever and ever I will sing about the tender kindness of the Lord! . . . [2]Your love and kindness are forever; your truth is as enduring as the heavens. [5]All heaven shall praise your miracles, O Lord; myriads of angels will praise you for your faithfulness. [8]O Jehovah, Commander of the heavenly armies, where is there any other Mighty One like you? Faithfulness is your very character. [14]Mercy and Truth walk before you as your attendants. [24]I will protect and bless him constantly and surround him with my love. [28]I will love him forever, and be kind to him always; my covenant with him will never end. [33]But I will never completely take away my loving-kindness from them, nor let my promise fail. [34]No, I will not break my covenant; I will not take back one word of what I said. 2 Sam 7:14, 15.

Ps 92:1. It is good to say, "Thank you" to the Lord, to sing praises to the God who is above all gods. [2]Every morning tell him, "Thank you for your kindness," and every evening rejoice in all his faithfulness. [15]This honors the Lord, and exhibits his faithful care. He is my shelter. There is nothing but goodness in him! *v.* 14.

Ps 94:14. The Lord will not forsake his people, for they are his prize.

Ps 98:2, 3. He has announced this victory and revealed it to every nation by fulfilling his promise to be kind to Israel.

Ps 100:5. And his faithfulness goes on and on to each succeeding generation.

Ps 103:17. But the lovingkindness of the Lord is from everlasting to everlasting, to those who reverence him; his salvation is to children's children.

Ps 105:8. Though a thousand generations pass he never forgets his promise. [42]For he remembered his sacred promises to Abraham his servant.

Ps 108:4. For your lovingkindness is great beyond measure, high as the heavens. Your faithfulness reaches the skies.

Ps 111:5. He never forgets his promises. [7]All he does is just and good, and all his laws are right, [8]for they are formed from truth and goodness, and stand firm forever. [9]He has paid a full ransom for his people; now they are always free to come to Jehovah (what a holy, awe-inspiring name that is).

Ps 117:2. For he loves us very dearly, and his truth endures. Praise the Lord.

Ps 119:65. Lord, I am overflowing with your blessings, just as you promised. [89]Forever, O Lord, your Word stands firm in heaven. [90]Your faithfulness extends to every generation.

Ps 121:3, 4. He will never let me stumble, slip or fall. For he is always watching, never sleeping.

Ps 132:11. For you promised me that my son would sit on my throne and succeed me. And surely you will never go back on a promise!

Ps 138:2. I will face your Temple as I worship, giving thanks to you for all your lovingkindness and your faithfulness, for your promises are backed by all the honor of your name.

Ps 146:6. He is the God who keeps every promise.

Isa 25:1. You do such wonderful things! You planned them long ago, and now you have accomplished them, just as you said!

Isa 42:16. He will bring blind Israel along a path they have not seen before. He will make the darkness bright before them and smooth and straighten out the road ahead. He will not forsake them.

Isa 44:21. Pay attention, Israel, for you are my servant; I made you, and I will not forget to help you.

Isa 49:7. The Lord, the Redeemer and Holy One of Israel, says to the one who is despised, rejected by mankind, and kept beneath the heel of earthly rulers: "Kings shall stand at attention when you pass by; princes shall bow low because the Lord has chosen you; he, the faithful Lord, the Holy One of Israel, chooses you." [16]See, I have tattooed your name upon my palm and ever before me is a picture of Jerusalem's walls in ruins.

Isa 51:6. Look high in the skies and watch the earth beneath, for the skies shall disappear like smoke, the earth shall wear out like a garment, and the people of the earth shall die like flies. But my salvation lasts forever; my righteous rule will never die nor end. [8]For the moth shall destroy them like garments; the worm shall eat them like wool; but my justice and mercy shall last forever, and my salvation from generation to generation.

Isa 54:9. Just as in the time of Noah I swore that I would never again permit the waters of a flood to cover the earth and destroy its life, so now I swear that I will never again pour out my anger on you as I have during this exile. [10]For the mountains may depart and the hills disappear, but my kindness shall not leave you. My promise of peace for you will never be broken, says the Lord who has mercy upon you.

Isa 65:16. And yet, the days will come when all who invoke a blessing or take an oath shall swear by the God of Truth; for I will put aside my anger and forget the evil that you did.

Jer 29:10. The truth is this: You will be in Babylon for a lifetime. But then I will come and do for you all the good things I have promised, and bring you home again.

Jer 31:36. I am as likely to reject my people Israel as I am to do away with these laws of nature! [37]Not until the heavens can be measured and the foundations of the earth explored, will I consider casting them away forever for their sins!

Jer 32:40. And I will make an everlasting covenant with them, promising never again to desert them, but only to do them good.

Jer 33:14. Yes, the day will come, says the Lord, when I will do for Israel and Judah all the good I promised them. [20, 21]If you can break my covenant with the day and with the night so that day and night don't come on their usual schedule, only then will my covenant with David, my servant, be broken so that he shall not have a son to reign upon his throne; and my covenant with the Levite priests, my ministers, is noncancelable. *vs.* 25, 26.

Jer 51:5. For the Lord of Hosts has not forsaken Israel and Judah. He is still their God, but the land of the Chaldeans is filled with sin against the Holy One of Israel.

Lam 3:23. Great is his faithfulness; his lovingkindness begins afresh each day.

Ezk 16:60. Yet I will keep the pledge I made to you when you were young. I will establish an everlasting covenant with you forever.

Dan 9:4. "O Lord," I prayed, "you are a great and awesome God; you always fulfill your promises of mercy to those who love you and who keep your laws."

Hos 2:19. And I will bind you to me forever with chains of righteousness and justice and love and mercy. [20]I will betroth you to me in faithfulness and love, and you will really know me then as you never have before.

Mic 7:20. You will bless us as you promised Jacob long ago. You will set your love upon us, as you promised our father, Abraham!

Hag 2:5. For I promised when you left Egypt that my Spirit would remain among you; so don't be afraid.

Zech 9:11. I have delivered you from death in a waterless pit because of the covenant I made with you, sealed with blood.

Mt 24:34. Then at last this age will come to its close. [35]Heaven and earth will disappear, but my words remain forever.

Lk 1:54. And how he has helped his servant Israel! He has not forgotten his promise to be merciful. [55]For he promised our fathers—Abraham and his children—to be merciful to them forever. [68]Praise the Lord, the God of Israel, for he has come to visit his people and has redeemed them. [69]He is sending us a Mighty Savior from the royal line of his servant David, [70]just as he promised through his holy prophets long ago. [72, 73]He has been merciful to our ancestors, yes, to Abraham himself, by remembering his sacred promise to him.

Jn 8:26. For I say only what I am told to by the one who sent me; and he is Truth.

Acts 13:32, 33. God's promise to our ancestors has come true in our own time, in that God brought Jesus back to life again.

Rom 3:3. True, some of them were unfaithful, but just because they broke their promises to God, does that mean God will break his promises? [4]Of course not! Though everyone else in the world is a liar, God is not.

Rom 11:2. No, God has not discarded his own people whom he chose from the very beginning. [29]For God's gifts and his call can never be withdrawn; he will never go back on his promises. *v.* 1.

Rom 15:8. Remember that Jesus Christ came to show that God is true to his promises and to help the Jews.

1 Cor 1:9. God will surely do this for you, for he always does just what he says, and he is the one who invited you into this wonderful friendship with his Son, even Christ our Lord.

1 Cor 10:13. You can trust God to keep the temptation from becoming so strong that you can't stand up against it, for he has promised this and will do what he says.

2 Cor 1:20. He carries out and fulfills all of God's promises.

1 Thess 5:24. God, who called you to become his child, will do all this for you, just as he promised.

2 Tim 2:13. Even when we are too weak to have any faith left, he remains faithful to us and will help us, for he cannot disown us who are part of himself, and he will always carry out his promises to us. [19]God's truth. . . . is a foundation stone with these words written on it: "The Lord knows those who are really his."

Tit 1:2. So that they can have eternal life, which God promised them before the world began—and he cannot lie.

Heb 6:10. For God is not unfair. How can he forget your hard work for him, or forget the way you used to show your love for him—and still do —by helping his children? [13]For instance, there was God's promise to Abraham: God took an oath in his own name, since there was no one greater to swear by, [14]that he would bless Abraham again and again, and give him a son and make him the father of a great nation of people. [15]Then Abraham waited patiently until finally God gave him a son, Isaac, just as he had promised. [16]When a man takes an oath, he is calling upon someone greater than himself to force him to do what he has promised, or to punish him if he later refuses to do it; the oath ends all argument about it. [17]God also bound himself with an oath, so that those he promised to help would be perfectly sure and never need to wonder whether he might change his plans. [18]He has given us both his promise and his oath, two things we can completely count on, for it is impossible for God to lie. Now all those who flee to him to save them can take new courage when they hear such assurances from God; now they can know without doubt that he will give them the salvation he has promised them. [19]This certain hope of being saved is a strong and trustworthy anchor for our souls, connecting us with God himself behind the sacred curtains of heaven.

Heb 10:22. Let us go right in, to God himself, with true hearts fully trusting him to receive us, because we have been sprinkled with Christ's blood to make us clean, and because our bodies have been washed with pure water. [23]Now we can look forward to the salvation God has promised us. There is no longer any room for doubt, and we can tell others that salvation is ours, for there is no question that he will do what he says. [37]His coming will not be delayed much longer.

1 Pet 4:19. So if you are suffering according to God's will, keep on doing what is right and trust yourself to the God who made you, for he will never fail you.

2 Pet 3:9. He isn't really being slow about his promised return, even though it sometimes seems that way.

1 Jn 1:9. But if we confess our sins to him, he can be depended on to forgive us and to cleanse us from every wrong.

Rev 6:10. They called loudly to the Lord and said, "O Sovereign Lord, holy and true, how long will it be before you judge the people of the earth for what they've done to us? When will you avenge our blood against those living on the earth?"

Rev 15:3. And they were singing the song of Moses, the servant of God, and the song of the Lamb: "Great and marvelous are your doings, Lord God Almighty. Just and true are your ways, O King of Ages."

FATHERHOOD OF. Ex 4:22. Then you are to tell him, "Jehovah says, 'Israel is my eldest son.'"

Deut 14:1. Since you are the people of God, never cut yourselves [as the heathen do when they worship their idols] nor shave the front halves of your heads for funerals.

Deut 32:5. But Israel has become corrupt, smeared with sin. They are no longer his; they are a stubborn, twisted generation. [6]Is this the way you treat Jehovah? O foolish people, is not God your Father? Has he not created you? Has he not established you and made you strong?

2 Sam 7:14. I will be his father and he shall be my son. If he sins, I will use other nations to punish him.

1 Chron 28:6. He has told me, "Your son Solomon shall build my temple; for I have chosen him as my son and I will be his father."

1 Chron 29:10. While still in the presence of the whole assembly, David expressed his praises to the Lord: "O Lord God of our father Israel, praise your name for ever and ever!"

Ps 68:5. He is a father to the fatherless; he gives justice to the widows, for he is holy.

Ps 89:26. And he will cry to me, "You are my Father, my God, and my Rock of Salvation."

Isa 1:2. Listen, O heaven and earth, to what the Lord is saying: The children I raised and cared for so long and tenderly have turned against me.

Isa 9:6. For unto us a Child is born; unto us a Son is given; and the government shall be upon his shoulder. These will be his royal titles: "Wonderful," "Counselor," "The Mighty God," "The Everlasting Father," "The Prince of Peace."

Isa 63:16. Surely you are still our Father! Even if Abraham and Jacob would disown us, still you would be our Father, our Redeemer from ages past.

Isa 64:8. And yet, O Lord, you are our Father. We are the clay and you are the Potter. We are all formed by your hand.

Jer 3:19. And I thought how wonderful it would be for you to be here among my children. I planned to give you part of this beautiful land, the finest in the world. I looked forward to your calling me "Father," and thought that you would never turn away from me again.

Hos 1:10. You are my sons, children of the Living God.

Hos 11:1. When Israel was a child I loved him as a son and brought him out of Egypt.

Mt 3:17. And a voice from heaven said, "This is my beloved Son, and I am wonderfully pleased with him."

Mt 5:45. In that way you will be acting as true sons of your Father in heaven.

Mt 6:4. And your Father who knows all secrets will reward you. [*v.* 6.] [8]Remember, your Father knows exactly what you need even before you ask him! [9]Pray along these lines: "Our Father in heaven, we honor your holy name." Lk 11:2.

Mt 7:11. And if you hardhearted, sinful men know how to give good gifts to your children, won't your Father in heaven even more certainly give good gifts to those who ask him for them?

Mt 10:20. For it won't be you doing the talking—it will be the Spirit of your heavenly Father speaking through you! [29]Not one sparrow (What do they cost? Two for a penny?) can fall to the ground without your Father knowing it. [32]If anyone publicly acknowledges me as his friend, I will openly acknowledge him as my friend before my father in heaven. [33]But if anyone publicly denies me, I will openly deny him before my Father in heaven.

Mt 11:25. And Jesus prayed this prayer: "O Father, Lord of heaven and earth, thank you for hiding the truth from those who think themselves so wise, and for revealing it to little children. [26]Yes, Father, for it pleased you to do it this way! . . . [27]Everything has been entrusted to me by my Father. Only the Father knows the Son, and the Father is known only by the Son and by those to whom the Son reveals him."

Mt 12:50. Then he added, "Anyone who obeys my Father in heaven is my brother, sister and mother!"

Mt 13:43. Then the godly shall shine as the sun in their Father's Kingdom.

Mt 15:13. Jesus replied, "Every plant not planted by my Father shall be rooted up."

Mt 16:17. "God has blessed you, Simon, son of Jonah," Jesus said, "for my Father in heaven has personally revealed this to you—this is not from any human source. [27]For I, the Son of Mankind, shall come with my angels in the glory of my Father."

Mt 18:10. Beware that you don't look down upon a single one of these little children. For I tell you that in heaven their angels have constant access to my Father. [14]Just so, it is not my Father's will that even one of these little ones should perish. [19]I also tell you this—if two of you agree down here on earth concerning anything you ask for, my Father in heaven will do it for you.

Mt 20:23. But I have no right to say who will sit on the thrones next to mine. Those places are reserved for the persons my Father selects.

Mt 26:29. Mark my words—I will not drink this wine again until the day I drink it new with you in my Father's Kingdom. [39]My Father! If it is possible, let this cup be taken away from me. But I want your will, not mine. *v.* 42.

Mk 8:38. And anyone who is ashamed of me and my message in these days of unbelief and sin, I, the Messiah, will be ashamed of him when I return in the glory of my Father, with the holy angels.

Mk 11:25. But when you are praying, first forgive anyone you are holding a grudge against, so that your Father in heaven will forgive you your sins too.

Mk 13:32. However, no one, not even the angels in heaven, nor I myself, knows the day or hour when these things will happen; only the Father knows.

Lk 2:49. "But why did you need to search?" he asked. "Didn't you realize that I would be here at the Temple, in my Father's House?"

Lk 10:21. Then he was filled with the joy of the Holy Spirit and said, "I praise you, O Father, Lord of heaven and earth, for hiding these things from the intellectuals and worldly wise and for revealing them to those who are as trusting as little children. Yes, thank you, Father, for that is the way you wanted it. [22]I am the Agent of my Father in everything; and no one really knows the Son except the Father, and no one really knows the Father except the Son and those to whom the Son chooses to reveal him."

Lk 11:13. And if even sinful persons like yourselves give children what they need, don't you realize that your heavenly Father will do at least as much, and give the Holy Spirit to those who ask for him?

Lk 22:29. And because my Father has granted me a Kingdom, I, here and now, grant you the right [30]to eat and drink at my table in that Kingdom.

Lk 23:46. Then Jesus shouted, "Father, I commit my spirit to you," and with those words he died.

Lk 24:49. And now I will send the Holy Spirit upon you, just as my Father promised. Don't begin telling others yet—stay here in the city until the Holy Spirit comes and fills you with power from heaven.

Jn 1:14. And Christ became a human being and lived here on earth among us and was full of loving forgiveness and truth. And some of us have seen his glory—the glory of the only Son of the heavenly Father! [18]No one has ever actually seen God, but of course, his only Son has, for he is the companion of the Father and has told us all about him.

Jn 2:16. Then, going over to the men selling doves, he told them, "Get these things out of here. Don't turn my Father's House into a market!"

Jn 4:21–23. Jesus replied, "The time is coming, ma'am, when we will no longer be concerned about whether to worship the Father here or in Jerusalem. . . . is our worship spiritual and real? Do we have the Holy Spirit's help? For God is Spirit, and we must have his help to worship as we should. The Father wants this kind of worship from us."

Jn 5:17. But Jesus replied, "My Father constantly does good, and I'm following his example." [18]Then the Jewish leaders were all the more eager to kill him because in addition to disobeying their Sabbath laws, he had spoken of God as his Father, thereby making himself equal with God. [19]Jesus replied, "The Son can do nothing by himself. He does only what he sees the Father doing, and in the same way. [20]For the Father loves the Son, and tells him everything he is doing; and the Son will do far more awesome miracles than this man's healing. [21]He will even raise from the dead anyone he wants to, just as the Father does. [22]And the Father leaves all judgment of sin to his Son, [23]so that everyone will honor the Son, just as they honor the Father. But if you refuse to honor God's Son, whom he sent to you, then you are certainly not honoring the Father. [36]But I have a greater witness than John. I refer to the miracles I do; these have been assigned me by the Father, and they prove that the Father has sent me. [37]And the Father himself has also testified about me, though not appearing to you personally, or speaking to you directly. [43]I know, because I have come to you representing my Father and you refuse to welcome me, though you readily enough receive those who aren't sent from him, but represent only themselves!"

Jn 6:27. "But you shouldn't be so concerned about perishable things like food. No, spend your energy seeking the eternal life that I, the Messiah, can give you. For God the Father has sent me for this very purpose." [32]Jesus said, "Moses didn't give it to them. My Father did. And now he offers you true Bread from heaven. [44]For no one can come to me unless the Father who sent me draws him to me, and at the Last Day I will cause all such to rise again from the dead. [45]As it is written in the Scriptures, 'They shall all be taught of God.' Those the Father speaks to, who learn the truth from him, will be attracted to me. [46](Not that anyone actually sees the Father, for only I have seen him.)"

Jn 8:19. "Where is your father?" they asked. Jesus answered, "You don't know who I am, so you don't know who my Father is. If you knew me, then you would know him too." [27]But they still didn't understand that he was talking to them about God. [38]"I am telling you what I saw when I was with my Father. But you are following the advice of *your* father. [41]No, you are obeying your *real* father when you act that way." They replied, "We were not born out of wedlock—our true Father is God himself." [42]Jesus told them, "If that were so, then you would love me, for I have come to you from God. I am not here on my own, but he sent me." [49]Jesus said, "I have no demon in me. For I honor my Father—and you dishonor me."

Jn 10:15. Just as my Father knows me and I know the Father; and I lay down my life for the sheep. [29]For my Father has given them to me, and he is more powerful than anyone else, so no one can kidnap them from me. [30]I and the Father are one. [32]Jesus said, "At God's direction I have done many a miracle to help the people. For which one are you killing me?" [33]They replied, "Not for any good work, but for blasphemy; you, a mere man, have declared yourself to be God."

36. "Do you call it blasphemy when the one sanctified and sent into the world by the Father says, 'I am the Son of God'? [37]Don't believe me unless I do miracles of God. [38]But if I do, believe them even if you don't believe me. Then you will become convinced that the Father is in me, and I in the Father."

Jn 12:26. "If these Greeks want to be my disciples, tell them to come and follow me, for my servants must be where I am. And if they follow me, the Father will honor them. [27]Now my soul is deeply troubled. Shall I pray, 'Father, save me from what lies ahead'? But that is the very reason why I came! [28]Father, bring glory and honor to your name." Then a voice spoke from heaven saying, "I have already done this, and I will do it again."

49. For these are not my own ideas, but I have told you what the Father said to tell you. [50]And I know his instructions lead to eternal life; so whatever he tells me to say, I say!

Jn 13:3. Jesus knew that the Father had given him everything and that he had come from God and would return to God.

Jn 14:2. "There are many homes up there where my Father lives, and I am going to prepare them for your coming." [6]Jesus told him, "I am the Way—yes, and the Truth and the Life. No one can get to the Father except by means of me. [7]If you had known who I am, then you would have known who my Father is. From now on you know him—and have seen him!" [8]Philip said, "Sir, show us the Father and we will be satisfied." [9]Jesus replied, "Don't you even yet know who I am, Philip, even after all this time I have been with you? Anyone who has seen me has seen the Father! So why are you asking to see him? [10]Don't you believe that I am in the Father and the Father is in me? The words I say are not my own but are from my Father who lives in me. And he does his work through me. [11]Just believe it—that I am in the Father and the Father is in me. Or else believe it because of the mighty miracles you have seen me do. [12, 13]In solemn truth I tell you, anyone believing in me shall do the same miracles I have done, and even greater ones, because I am going to be with the Father. You can ask him for *anything,* using my name, and I will do it, for this will bring praise to the Father because of what I, the Son, will do for you. [16]And I will ask the Father and he will give you another Comforter, and he will never leave you. [20]When I come back to life again, you will know that I am in my Father, and you in me, and I in you. [21]The one who obeys me is the one who loves me; and because he loves me, my Father will love him; and I will too, and I will reveal myself to him." [23]Jesus replied, "Because I will only reveal myself to those who love me and obey me. The Father will love them too, and we will come to them and live with them. [24]Anyone who doesn't obey me doesn't love me. And remember, I am not making up this answer to your question! It is the answer given by the Father who sent me. [26]But when the Father sends the Comforter instead of me—and by the Comforter I mean the Holy Spirit—he will teach you much, as well as remind you of everything I myself have told you. [31]But I will freely do what the Father requires of me so that the world will know that I love the Father."

Jn 15:8. My true disciples produce bountiful harvests. This brings great glory to my Father. [9]I have loved you even as the Father has loved me. Live within my love. [10]When you obey me you are living in my love, just as I obey my Father and live in his love. [16]You didn't choose me! I chose you! I appointed you to go and produce lovely fruit always, so that no matter what you ask for from the Father, using my name, he will give it to you. [23]Anyone hating me is also hating my Father. [24]If I hadn't done such mighty miracles among them they would not be counted guilty. But as it is, they saw these miracles and yet they hated both of us—me and my Father. [26]But I will send you the Comforter—the Holy Spirit, the source of all truth. He will come to you from the Father and will tell you all about me.

Jn 16:3. This is because they have never known the Father or me. [10]There is righteousness available because I go to the Father and you shall see me no more. [15]All the Father's glory is mine. [23]At that time you won't need to ask me for anything, for you can go directly to the Father and ask him, and he will give you what you ask for because you use my name. [25]I have spoken of these matters very guardedly, but the time will come when this will not be necessary and I will tell you plainly all about the Father. [26]Then you will present your petitions over my signature! And I won't need to ask the Father to grant you these requests, [27]for the Father himself loves you dearly because you love me and believe that I came from the Father. [28]Yes, I came from the Father into the world and will leave the world and return to the Father.

Jn 17:1. When Jesus had finished saying all these things he looked up to heaven and said, "Father, the time has come. Reveal the glory of your Son so that he can give the glory back to you. [5]And now, Father, reveal my glory as I stand in your presence, the glory we shared before the world began. [11]Now I am leaving the world, and leaving them behind, and coming to you. Holy Father, keep them in your own care—all those you have given me—so that they will be united just as we are, with none missing. [21]My prayer for all of them is that they will be of one heart and mind, just as you and I are, Father—that just as you are in me and I am in you, so they will be in us, and the world will believe you sent me. [24]Father, I want them with me—these you've given me—so that they can see my glory. You gave me the glory because you loved me before the world began!"

Jn 20:17. "Don't touch me," he cautioned, "for I haven't yet ascended to the Father. But go find my brothers and tell them that I ascend to my Father and your Father, my God and your God." [21]He spoke to them again and said, "As the Father has sent me, even so I am sending you."

Acts 1:4. In one of these meeting he told them not to leave Jerusalem until the Holy Spirit came upon them in fulfillment of the Father's promise, a matter he had previously discussed with them.

Acts 2:33. And now he sits on the throne of highest honor in heaven, next to God. And just as promised, the Father gave him the authority to send the Holy Spirit—with the results you are seeing and hearing today.

Rom 1:3. It is the Good News about his Son, Jesus Christ our Lord, who came as a human baby, born into King David's royal family line; [4]and by being raised from the dead he was proved to be the mighty Son of God, with the holy nature of God himself. [6, 7]And you, dear friends in Rome, are among those he dearly loves; you, too, are invited by Jesus Christ to be God's very own—yes, his holy people. May all God's mercies and peace be yours from God our Father and from Jesus Christ our Lord. 1 Cor 1:3; Gal 1:3; Eph 1:2; 6:23; Phil 1:2; Col 1:2; 1 Thess 1:1; 2 Thess 1:2; Tit 1:4.

Rom 8:15. And so we should not be like cringing, fearful slaves, but we should behave like God's very own children, adopted into the bosom of his family, and calling to him, "Father, Father."

1 Cor 8:6. But we know that there is only one God, the Father, who created all things and made us to be his own.

1 Cor 15:24. After that the end will come when he will turn the kingdom over to God the Father, having put down all enemies of every kind.

2 Cor 1:3. What a wonderful God we have—he is the Father of our Lord Jesus Christ, the source of every mercy, and the one who so wonderfully comforts and strengthens us in our hardships and trials.

2 Cor 6:18. And be a Father to you, and you will be my sons and daughters.

Gal 1:1, 2. From: Paul the missionary. . . . I was not called to be a missionary by any group or agency. My call is from Jesus Christ himself, and from God the Father who raised him from the dead. [4]He died for our sins just as God our Father planned, and rescued us from this evil world in which we live.

Gal 4:4. But when the right time came, the time God decided on, he sent his Son, born of a woman, born as a Jew, [5]to buy freedom for us who were slaves to the law so that he could adopt us as his very own sons. [6]And because we are his sons God has sent the Spirit of his Son into our hearts, so now we can rightly speak of God as our dear Father. [7]Now we are no longer slaves, but God's own sons. And since we are his sons, everything he has belongs to us, for that is the way God planned.

Eph 1:3. How we praise God, the Father of our Lord Jesus Christ, who has blessed us with every blessing in heaven because we belong to Christ. [17]I pray for you constantly, asking God, the glorious Father of our Lord Jesus Christ, to give you wisdom to see clearly and really understand who Christ is and all that he has done for you.

Eph 2:18. Now all of us, whether Jews or Gentiles, may come to God the Father with the Holy Spirit's help because of what Christ has done for us.

Eph 3:14. When I think of the wisdom and scope of his plan I fall down on my knees and pray to the Father of all the great family of God.

Eph 4:6. And we all have the same God and Father who is over us all and in us all, and living through every part of us.

Eph 5:20. Always give thanks for everything to our God and Father in the name of our Lord Jesus Christ.

Col 1:3. Whenever we pray for you we always begin by giving thanks to God the Father of our Lord Jesus Christ. [12]And always thankful to the Father who has made us fit to share all the wonderful things that belong to those who live in the kingdom of light.

Col 3:17. And whatever you do or say, let it be as a representative of the Lord Jesus, and come with him into the presence of God the Father to give him your thanks.

1 Thess 1:1. From: Paul, Silas and Timothy. *To:* The Church at Thessalonica—to you who belong to God the Father and the Lord Jesus Christ: May blessing and peace of heart be your rich gifts from God our Father, and from Jesus Christ our Lord. [3]We never forget your loving deeds as we talk to our God and Father about you, and your strong faith and steady looking forward to the return of our Lord Jesus Christ.

1 Thess 3:11. May God our Father himself and our Lord Jesus send us back to you again. [13]This will result in your hearts being made strong, sinless and holy by God our Father, so that you may stand before him guiltless.

2 Thess 1:1. From: Paul, Silas and Timothy. *To:* The church of Thessalonica—kept safe in God our Father and in the Lord Jesus Christ. [2]May God the Father and the Lord Jesus Christ give you rich blessings and peace-filled hearts and minds.

2 Thess 2:16. May our Lord Jesus Christ himself and God our Father, who has loved us and given us everlasting comfort and hope which we don't deserve.

Heb 1:5, 6. For God never said to any angel, "You are my Son, and today I have given you the honor that goes with that name." But God said it about Jesus. Another time he said, "I am his Father and he is my Son." And still another time—when his firstborn Son came to earth—God said, "Let all the angels of God worship him."

Heb 12:9. Since we respect our fathers here on earth, though they punish us, should we not all the more cheerfully submit to God's training so that we can begin really to live?

Jas 1:27. The Christian who is pure and without fault, from God the Father's point of view, is the one who takes care of orphans and widows, and who remains true to the Lord—not soiled and dirtied by his contacts with the world.

Jas 3:9. Sometimes it [our tongue] praises our heavenly Father.

1 Pet 1:2. Dear friends, God the Father chose you long ago and knew you would become his children. . . . [3]All honor to God, the God and Father of our Lord Jesus Christ; for it is his boundless mercy that has given us the privilege of being born again, so that we are now members of God's own family. Now we live in the hope of eternal life because

Christ rose again from the dead. [17]And remember that your heavenly Father to whom you pray has no favorites when he judges. He will judge you with perfect justice for everything you do; so act in reverent fear of him from now on until you get to heaven.

1 Jn 1:2. This one who is Life from God has been shown to us and we guarantee that we have seen him; I am speaking of Christ, who is eternal Life. He was with the Father and then was shown to us.

1 Jn 2:1. But if you sin, there is someone to plead for you before the Father. His name is Jesus Christ, the one who is all that is good and who pleases God completely. [13]And I am writing to you younger boys and girls because you, too, have learned to know God our Father. [22]And who is the greatest liar? The one who says that Jesus is not Christ. Such a person is antichrist, for he does not believe in God the Father and in his Son. [23]For a person who doesn't believe in Christ, God's Son, can't have God the Father either. But he who has Christ, God's Son, has God the Father also. [24]So keep on believing what you have been taught from the beginning. If you do, you will always be in close fellowship with both God the Father and his Son.

1 Jn 3:1. See how very much our heavenly Father loves us, for he allows us to be called his children—think of it—and we really *are!*

1 Jn 4:14. And furthermore, we have seen with our own eyes and now tell all the world that God sent his Son to be their Savior.

2 Jn 1:3. God the Father and Jesus Christ his Son will bless us with great mercy and much peace, and with truth and love. [4]How happy I am to find some of your children here, and to see that they are living as they should, following the Truth, obeying God's command. [9]While if you are loyal to Christ's teachings, you will have God too. Then you will have have both the Father and the Son.

Rev 1:5. All praise to him who always loves us and who set us free from our sins by pouring out his lifeblood for us. [6]He has gathered us into his kingdom and made us priests of God his Father. Give to him everlasting glory! He rules forever! Amen!

Rev 3:5. Everyone who conquers will be clothed in white, and I will not erase his name from the Book of Life, but I will announce before my Father and his angels that he is mine.

Rev 14:1. Then I saw a Lamb standing on Mount Zion in Jerusalem, and with him were 144,000 who had his Name and his Father's Name written on their foreheads.

See *Adoption.*

FAVOR OF. See *God, Grace of,* below.

FOREKNOWLEDGE OF. 1 Sam 23:10. "O Lord God of Israel," David said, "I have heard that Saul is planning to come and destroy Keilah because I am here. [11]Will the men of Keilah surrender me to him? And will Saul actually come, as I have heard? O Lord God of Israel, please tell me." And the Lord said, "He will come." [12]"And will these men of Keilah betray me to Saul?" David persisted. And the Lord replied, "Yes, they will betray you."

Isa 42:9. Everything I prophesied came true, and now I will prophesy again. I will tell you the future before it happens.

Isa 44:7. Who else can tell you what is going to happen in the days ahead? Let them tell you if they can, and prove their power. Let them do as I have done since ancient times.

Isa 45:11. Jehovah, the Holy One of Israel, Israel's Creator, says: What right have you to question what I do? Who are you to command me concerning the work of my hands?

Isa 46:9. For I am God—I only—and there is no other like me. [10]Who can tell you what is going to happen? All I say will come to pass, for I do whatever I wish.

Isa 48:5. That is why I told you ahead of time what I was going to do, so that you could never say, "My idol did it; my carved image commanded it to happen!" [*v.* 3.] [6]You have heard my predictions and seen them fulfilled, but you refuse to agree it is so. Now I will tell you new things I haven't mentioned before, secrets you haven't heard.

Jer 1:5. I knew you before you were formed within your mother's womb; before you were born I sanctified you and appointed you as my spokesman to the world.

Dan 2:28. But there is a God in heaven who reveals secrets, and he has told you in your dream what will happen in the future. This was your dream: [29]You dreamed of coming events. He who reveals secrets was speaking to you.

Mt 6:8. Remember, your Father knows exactly what you need even before you ask him!

Mt 24:36. But no one knows the date and hour when the end will be—not even the angels. No, nor even God's Son. Only the Father knows.

Acts 15:18. That is what the Lord says, who reveals his plans made from the beginning.

Rom 8:29. For from the very beginning God decided that those who came to him—and all along he knew who would—should become like his Son.

Rom 11:2. No, God has not discarded his own people whom he chose from the very beginning.

1 Pet 1:2. Dear friends, God the Father chose you long ago and knew you would become his children.

See *God, Knowledge of, Wisdom of,* below; *Predestination.*

GLORY OF. Ex 3:2. Suddenly the Angel of Jehovah appeared to him as a flame of fire in a bush.

Ex 19:18. All Mt. Sinai was covered with smoke because Jehovah descended upon it in the form of fire; the smoke billowed into the sky as from a furnace, and the whole mountain shook with a violent earthquake. *vs.* 16, 19; Ex 20:18, 19; Deut 4:11, 12, 33, 36; 5:5, 24, 25.

Ex 24:10. And they saw the God of Israel; under his feet there seemed to be a pavement of brilliant sapphire stones, as clear as the heavens. [17]Those at the bottom of the mountain saw the awesome sight: the glory of the Lord on the mountain top looked like a raging fire.

Ex 33:20. But you may not see the glory of my face, for man may not see me and live. [22]And when my glory goes by, I will put you in the cleft of the rock and cover you with my hand until I have passed. *v.* 23.

Ex 34:5. Then the Lord descended in the form of a pillar of cloud and stood there with him, and passed in front of him and announced the meaning of his name. *vs.* 29–35; Ex 33:18, 19.

Ex 40:34. Then the cloud covered the Tabernacle and the glory of the Lord filled it. [35]Moses was not able to enter because the cloud was standing there, and the glory of the Lord filled the Tabernacle.

Deut 10:17. Jehovah your God is God of gods and Lord of lords. He is the great and mighty God, the God of terror who shows no partiality and takes no bribes. Deut 7:21.

Deut 28:58, 59. If you refuse to obey all the laws written in this book, thus refusing reverence to the glorious and fearful name of Jehovah your God, then Jehovah will send perpetual plagues upon you and upon your children.

Deut 33:2. He shone from Mount Paran, surrounded by ten thousands of holy angels. [26]There is none like the God of Jerusalem—he descends from the heavens in majestic splendor to help you.

1 Kgs 19:12. After the earthquake, there was a fire, but the Lord was not in the fire. And after the fire, there was the sound of a gentle whisper.

Job 9:32, 33. And I cannot defend myself, for you are no mere man as I am. If you were, then we could discuss it fairly, but there is no umpire between us, no middle man, no mediator to bring us together.

Job 13:11. Doesn't his majesty strike terror to your heart? How can you do this thing?

Job 22:12. God is so great—higher than the heavens, higher than the stars.

Job 25:3. Who is able to number his hosts of angels? And his light shines down on all the earth.

Job 35:5. Look up there into the sky, high above you. [6]If you sin, does that shake the heavens and knock God from his throne? Even if you sin again and again, what effect will that have upon him? [7]Or if you are good, is this some great gift to him?

Job 37:5. His voice is glorious in the thunder. We cannot comprehend the greatness of his power. [22]Neither can we gaze at the terrible majesty of God. *v.* 4.

Ps 8:9. O Jehovah, our Lord, the majesty and glory of your name fills the earth.

Ps 18:9. He bent the heavens down and came to my defense; thick darkness was beneath his feet. [10]Mounted on the cherubim, he sped swiftly to my aid with wings of wind. [11]He enshrouded himself with darkness, veiling his approach with dense clouds dark as murky waters. *vs.* 7–15; 2 Sam 22.

Ps 19:1. The heavens are telling the glory of God; they are a marvelous display of his craftsmanship. *vs.* 2–4.

Ps 24:8. Who is this King of Glory? The Lord, strong and mighty, invincible in battle. [9]Yes, open wide the gates and let the King of Glory in. *v.* 10.

Ps 29:2. Praise him for his majestic glory, the glory of his name. Come before him clothed in sacred garments. *vs.* 3, 4.

Ps 46:10. Stand silent! Know that I am God! I will be honored by every nation in the world!

Ps 57:5. Lord, be exalted above the highest heavens! Show your glory high above the earth. *v.* 11.

Ps 68:24. The procession of God my King moves onward to the sanctuary—.

Ps 72:18. Blessed be Jehovah God, the God of Israel, who only does wonderful things! [19]Blessed be his glorious name forever! Let the whole earth be filled with his glory. Amen, and amen!

Ps 76:4. The everlasting mountains cannot compare with you in glory!

Ps 96:3. Publish his glorious acts throughout the earth. Tell everyone about the amazing things he does. [4]For the Lord is great beyond description, and greatly to be praised. Worship only him among the gods! [6]Honor and majesty surround him; strength and beauty are in his Temple. [7]O nations of the world, confess that God alone is glorious and strong. 1 Chron 16:24, 25.

Ps 97:2. Clouds and darkness surround him. Righteousness and justice are the foundation of his throne. [6]The heavens declare his perfect righteousness; every nation sees his glory. [9]You reign in majesty over the entire earth and are far greater than these other gods. *vs.* 3–5.

Ps 102:16. For Jehovah will rebuild Jerusalem! He will appear in his glory! [21, 22]So that multitudes would stream to the Temple in Jerusalem to praise him, and his praises were sung throughout the city; and many rulers throughout the earth came to worship him.

Ps 104:31. Praise God forever! How he must rejoice in all his work!

Ps 106:8. Even so you saved them—to defend the honor of your name and demonstrate your power to all the world.

Ps 113:4. For he is high above the nations; his glory is far greater than the heavens.

Ps 145:5. I will meditate about your glory, splendor, majesty and miracles. [11]They will talk together about the glory of your kingdom and mention examples of your power. [12]They will tell about your miracles and about the majesty and glory of your reign.

Isa 1:24. Therefore the Lord of Hosts, the Mighty One of Israel, says.

Isa 2:10. Crawl into the caves in the rocks and hide in terror from his glorious majesty.

Isa 6:1. The year King Uzziah died I saw the Lord! He was sitting on a lofty throne and the Temple was filled with his glory. [3]In a great antiphonal chorus they sang, "Holy, holy, holy is the Lord of Hosts; the whole earth is filled with his glory." *vs.* 1–5.

Isa 12:6. Let all the people of Jerusalem shout his praise with joy. For great and mighty is the Holy One of Israel, who lives among you.

Isa 24:23. Then the Lord of heaven's armies will mount his throne in Zion and rule gloriously in

Jerusalem, in the sight of all the elders of his people.

Isa 26:15. O praise the Lord! He has made our nation very great. He has widened the boundaries of our land!

Isa 28:5. Then at last the Lord of Hosts himself will be their crowning glory, the diadem of beauty to his people who are left.

Isa 29:23. For when they see the surging birth rate and the expanding economy, then they will fear and rejoice in my name, and praise the Holy One of Israel, and stand in awe of him.

Isa 30:30. And the Lord shall cause his majestic voice to be heard and shall crush down his mighty arm upon his enemies with angry indignation and with devouring flames and tornados and terrible storms and huge hailstones.

Isa 33:5. The Lord is very great, and lives in heaven. He will make Jerusalem the home of justice and goodness and righteousness. [10]But the Lord says, I will stand up and show my power and might.

Isa 35:2. For the Lord will display his glory there, the excellency of our God.

Isa 40:5. The glory of the Lord will be seen by all mankind together.

Isa 43:7. All who claim me as their God will come, for I have made them for my glory; I created them. [21]I have made Israel for myself, and these my people will some day honor me before the world.

Isa 44:23. For the Lord redeemed Jacob and is glorified in Israel!

Isa 48:11. Yet for my own sake—yes, *for my own sake*—I will save you from my anger and not destroy you lest the heathen say their gods have conquered me. I will not let them have my glory. *v.* 9.

Isa 49:3. He said to me: "You are my Servant, a Prince of Power with God, and you shall bring me glory. [26]All the world shall know that I, the Lord, am your Savior and Redeemer, the Mighty One of Israel."

Isa 52:10. The Lord has bared his holy arm before the eyes of all the nations; the ends of the earth shall see the salvation of our God.

Isa 55:9. For just as the heavens are higher than the earth, so are my ways higher than yours, and my thoughts than yours.

Isa 57:15. The high and lofty one who inhabits eternity, the Holy One, says this.

Isa 60:1. Arise, my people! Let your light shine for all the nations to see! For the glory of the Lord is streaming from you. [2]Darkness as black as night shall cover all the peoples of the earth, but the glory of the Lord will shine from you. [6]Vast droves of camels will converge upon you . . . bringing gold and incense to add to the praise of God. [19]For the Lord your God will be your everlasting light, and he will be your glory. [20]Your sun shall never set; the moon shall not go down—for the Lord will be your everlasting light; your days of mourning all will end. [21]All your people will be good. They will possess their land forever, for I will plant them there with my own hands; this will bring me glory.

Isa 61:3. To all who mourn in Israel he will give: beauty for ashes; joy instead of mourning; praise instead of heaviness. For God has planted them like strong and graceful oaks for his own glory.

Isa 62:3. He will hold you aloft in his hands for all to see—a splendid crown for the King of kings.

Isa 63:12. Where is he whose mighty power divided the sea before them when Moses lifted up his hand, and established his reputation forever? *v.* 14.

Isa 66:1. Heaven is my throne and the earth is my footstool: What Temple can you build for me as good as that? [2]My hand has made both earth and skies, and they are mine. [18]So I will gather together all nations and people against Jerusalem, where they shall see my glory.

Jer 13:11. Even as a loincloth clings to a man's loins, so I made Judah and Israel to cling to me, says the Lord. They were my people, an honor to my name.

Jer 17:12. But our refuge is your throne, eternal, high and glorious.

Jer 33:9. Then this city will be an honor to me, and it will give me joy and be a source of praise and glory to me before all the nations of the earth! The people of the world will see the good I do for my people and will tremble with awe!

Ezk 1:26. For high in the sky above them was what looked like a throne made of beautiful blue sapphire stones, and upon it sat someone who appeared to be a Man. [27, 28]From his waist up, he seemed to be all glowing bronze, dazzling like fire; and from his waist down he seemed to be entirely flame, and there was a glowing halo like a rainbow all around him. That was the way the glory of the Lord appeared to me. And when I saw it I fell face downward on the ground, and heard the voice of someone speaking to me.

Ezk 3:12. Then the Spirit lifted me up and the glory of the Lord began to move away, accompanied by the sound of a great earthquake. [23]I arose and went, and oh, I saw the glory of the Lord there, just as in my first vision! And I fell to the ground on my face.

Ezk 8:4. Suddenly the glory of the God of Israel was there, just as I had seen it before in the valley.

Ezk 20:14. But again I refrained in order to protect the honor of my name, lest the nations who saw me bring them out of Egypt would say that it was because I couldn't care for them that I destroyed them. [44]And when I have honored my name by blessing you despite your wickedness, then, O Israel, you will know I am the Lord.

Ezk 36:22. Therefore say to the people of Israel: The Lord God says, I am bringing you back again, but not because you deserve it; I am doing it to protect my holy name which you tarnished among the nations. [23]I will honor my great name that you defiled, and the people of the world shall know I am the Lord. I will be honored before their eyes by delivering you from exile among them.

Ezk 43:4. And the glory of the Lord came into the Temple through the eastern passageway. [5]Then the Spirit took me up and brought me into the inner court; and the glory of the Lord filled the Temple.

Hab 3:3. His glory fills the heavens, and the earth is full of his praise! . . . [4]From his hands flash rays of brilliant light. He rejoices in his awesome power. [5]Pestilence marches before him; plague follows close behind. *v.* 6.

Mt 6:9. Our Father in heaven, we honor your holy name.

Lk 2:14. "Glory to God in the highest heaven," they sang, "and peace on earth for all those pleasing him."

Jn 8:50. And though I have no wish to make myself great, God wants this for me and judges [those who reject me].

Jn 12:28. "Father, bring glory and honor to your name." Then a voice spoke from heaven saying, "I have already done this, and I will do it again."

Jn 13:31. The glory of God will soon surround me —and God shall receive great praise because of all that happens to me. [32]And God shall give me his own glory, and this so very soon.

Jn 14:13. You can ask him for *anything,* using my name, and I will do it, for this will bring praise to the Father because of what I, the Son, will do for you.

Jn 17:1. Reveal the glory of your Son so that he can give the glory back to you. [10]And all of them, since they are mine, belong to you; and you have given them back to me with everything else of yours, and so *they are my glory!*

Acts 7:55. But Stephen, full of the Holy Spirit, gazed steadily upward into heaven and saw the glory of God and Jesus standing at God's right hand.

Rom 1:23. And then, instead of worshiping the glorious, ever-living God, they took wood and stone and made idols for themselves, carving them to look like mere birds and animals and snakes and puny men.

Rom 11:36. For everything comes from God alone. Everything lives by his power, and everything is for his glory. To him be glory evermore.

2 Cor 1:20. He carries out and fulfills all of God's promises, no matter how many of them there are; and we have told everyone how faithful he is, giving glory to his name.

2 Cor 4:15. These sufferings of ours are for your benefit. And the more of you who are won to Christ, the more there are to thank him for his great kindness, and the more the Lord is glorified.

Eph 1:6. Now all praise to God for his wonderful kindness to us and his favor that he has poured out upon us, because we belong to his dearly loved Son. [12]God's purpose in this was that we should praise God and give glory to him for doing these mighty things for us, who were the first to trust in Christ. [14]And the Spirit's seal upon us means that God has already purchased us and that he guarantees to bring us to himself. This is just one more reason for us to praise our glorious God.

Eph 2:7. And now God can always point to us as examples of how very, very rich his kindness is, as shown in all he has done for us through Jesus Christ.

Eph 3:21. May he be given glory forever and ever through endless ages because of his master plan of salvation for the church through Jesus Christ.

Phil 1:11. May you always be doing those good, kind things which show that you are a child of God, for this will bring much praise and glory to the Lord.

Phil 2:11. And every tongue shall confess that Jesus Christ is Lord, to the glory of God the Father.

Phil 4:19. And it is he who will supply all your needs from his riches in glory, because of what Christ Jesus has done for us.

1 Tim 6:15. For in due season Christ will be revealed from heaven by the blessed and only Almighty God, the King of Kings and Lord of lords, [16]who alone can never die, who lives in light so terrible that no human being can approach him. No mere man has ever seen him, nor ever will. Unto him be honor and everlasting power and dominion forever and ever.

Heb 12:18. You have not had to stand face to face with terror, flaming fire, gloom, darkness and a terrible storm, as the Israelites did at Mount Sinai when God gave them his laws. [19]For there was an awesome trumpet blast, and a voice with a message so terrible that the people begged God to stop speaking. [20]They staggered back under God's command that if even an animal touched the mountain it must die. [21]Moses himself was so frightened at the sight that he shook with terrible fear.

Jude 1:24. And now—all glory to him who alone is God, who saves us through Jesus Christ our Lord; yes, splendor and majesty, all power and authority are his from the beginning; his they are and his they evermore shall be.

Rev 4:11. O Lord, you are worthy to receive the glory and the honor and the power, for you have created all things. They were created and called into being by your act of will.

Rev 15:8. The temple was filled with smoke from his glory and power.

Rev 21:10. In a vision he took me to a towering mountain peak and from there I watched that wondrous city, the holy Jerusalem, descending out of the skies from God. [11]It was filled with the glory of God. [23]And the city has no need of sun or moon to light it, for the glory of God and of the Lamb illuminate it.

See *Glory; Praise.*

GOODNESS OF. Ex 33:19. The Lord replied, "I will make my goodness pass before you."

Ex 34:6. "I am Jehovah, the merciful and gracious God," he said, "slow to anger and rich in steadfast love and truth."

Deut 30:9. The Lord your God will prosper everything you do and give you many children and much cattle and wonderful crops; for the Lord will again rejoice over you as he did over your fathers.

2 Chron 5:13, 14. The band and chorus united as one to praise and thank the Lord; their selections

were interspersed with trumpet obbligatos, the clashing of cymbals, and the loud playing of other musical instruments—all praising and thanking the Lord. Their theme was "He is so good! His lovingkindness lasts forever!" And at that moment the glory of the Lord, coming as a bright cloud, filled the Temple so that the priests could not continue their work. chapter 7:3.

1 Kgs 8:66. Afterwards Solomon sent the people home, happy for all the goodness that the Lord had shown to his servant David and to his people Israel. And they blessed the king.

Ps 8:4. I cannot understand how you can bother with mere puny man, to pay any attention to him! *vs.* 1–9; Ps 144:3.

Ps 11:7. For God is good, and he loves goodness; the godly shall see his face.

Ps 17:7. Show me your strong love in wonderful ways, O Savior of all those seeking your help against their foes.

Ps 23:6. Your goodness and unfailing kindness shall be with me all of my life.

Ps 25:8. The Lord is good and glad to teach the proper path to all who go astray. *vs.* 9, 10.

Ps 31:19. Oh, how great is your goodness to those who publicly declare that you will rescue them. For you have stored up great blessings for those who trust and reverence you.

Ps 33:5. He loves whatever is just and good.

Ps 68:19. What a glorious Lord! He who daily bears our burdens also gives us our salvation.

Ps 69:16. For your lovingkindness is wonderful; your mercy is so plentiful, so tender and so kind.

Ps 73:1. How good God is to Israel—to those whose hearts are pure.

Ps 86:5. O Lord, you are so good and kind, so ready to forgive; so full of mercy for all who ask your aid.

Ps 100:5. For the Lord is always good. He is always loving and kind, and his faithfulness goes on and on to each succeeding generation.

Ps 106:1. Hallelujah! Thank you, Lord! How good you are! Your love for us continues on forever.

Ps 107:8. Oh, that these men would praise the Lord for his lovingkindness, and for all of his wonderful deeds! [9]For he satisfies the thirsty soul and fills the hungry soul with good. [43]Listen, if you are wise, to what I am saying. Think about the lovingkindness of the Lord!

Ps 118:29. Oh, give thanks to the Lord, for he is so good! For his lovingkindness is forever. 1 Chron 16:34; Ps 135:3; 136:1.

Ps 119:64. O Lord, the earth is full of your lovingkindness! [68]You are good and do only good.

Ps 139:17, 18. How precious it is, Lord, to realize that you are thinking about me constantly! I can't even count how many times a day your thoughts turn towards me. And when I waken in the morning, you are still thinking of me!

Ps 143:10. Lead me in good paths, for your Spirit is good.

Ps 145:7. Everyone will tell about how good you are, and sing about your righteousness. [9]He is good to everyone, and his compassion is intertwined with everything he does.

Isa 63:7. I will tell of the lovingkindnesses of God. I will praise him for all he has done; I will rejoice in his great goodness to Israel, which he has granted in accordance with his mercy and love.

Jer 9:24. . . . I am the Lord of justice and of righteousness whose love is steadfast; and that I love to be this way.

Lam 3:25. The Lord is wonderfully good to those who wait for him, to those who seek for him.

Mic 7:9. God will bring me out of my darkness into the light, and I will see his goodness.

Nah 1:7. The Lord is good. When trouble comes, he is the place to go! And he knows everyone who trusts in him!

Mt 7:11. And if you hardhearted, sinful men know how to give good gifts to your children, won't your Father in heaven even more certainly give good gifts to those who ask him for them?

Mt 19:17. "When you call me good you are calling me God," Jesus replied, "for God alone is truly good." Mk 10:18; Lk 18:19.

Lk 6:35. For he is kind to the *unthankful* and to those who are *very wicked.*

Rom 2:4. Don't you realize how patient he is being with you? Or don't you care? Can't you see that he has been waiting all this time without punishing you, to give you time to turn from your sin? His kindness is meant to lead you to repentance.

Rom 11:22. Notice how God is both kind and severe. He is very hard on those who disobey, but very good to you if you continue to love and trust him. But if you don't, you too will be cut off.

2 Thess 1:11. And so we keep on praying for you that our God will make you the kind of children he wants to have—will make you as good as you wish you could be!—rewarding your faith with his power.

Tit 3:4. But when the time came for the kindness and love of God our Savior to appear.

Jas 1:5. If you want to know what God wants you to do, ask him, and he will gladly tell you, for he is always ready to give a bountiful supply of wisdom to all who ask him; he will not resent it. [17]But whatever is good and perfect comes to us from God, the Creator of all light.

1 Jn 4:8. For God is love.

See *God, Grace of, Long-suffering of, Love of, Mercy of,* below.

GRACE OF. Gen 18:26. And God replied, "If I find fifty godly people there, I will spare the entire city for their sake."

Gen 32:28. It [your name] is Israel—one who has power with God. Because you have been strong with God, you shall prevail with men.

Gen 46:4. And I will go down with you into Egypt and I will bring your descendants back again.

Ex 3:12. Then God told him, "I will certainly be with you, and this is the proof that I am the one who is sending you: When you have led the people out of Egypt, you shall worship God here upon this mountain!"

Ex 20:24. Build altars only where I tell you to, and I will come and bless you there.

Ex 24:2. Moses alone shall come near to the Lord. Ex 20:21.

Ex 33:11. Inside the tent the Lord spoke to Moses face to face, as a man speaks to his friend. [17]"For you have certainly found favor with me, and you are my friend. [22]And when my glory goes by, I will put you in the cleft of the rock and cover you with my hand until I have passed. [23]Then I will remove my hand and you shall see my back, but not my face." *v.* 12.

Lev 26:11. And I will live among you, and not despise you. [12]I will walk among you and be your God, and you shall be my people.

Num 6:27. This is how Aaron and his sons shall call down my blessings upon the people of Israel; and I myself will personally bless them.

Num 14:14. They have told this to the inhabitants of this land, who are well aware that you are with Israel and that you talk with her face to face. They see the pillar of cloud and fire standing above us, and they know that you lead and protect us day and night.

Num 23:20, 21. Look! I have received a command to bless them, for God has blessed them, and I cannot reverse it! He has not seen sin in Jacob. He will not trouble Israel! Jehovah their God is with them. He is their king! Num 22:12; 24:1.

Deut 4:7. For what other nation, great or small, has God among them, as the Lord our God is here among us whenever we call upon him?

Deut 33:23. O Naphtali, you are satisfied with all the blessings of the Lord.

Josh 1:5. For I will be with you just as I was with Moses; I will not abandon you or fail to help you. [9]For remember, the Lord your God is with you wherever you go. Deut 31:6, 8.

1 Kgs 6:13. I will live among the people of Israel and never forsake them.

2 Chron 15:2. The Lord will stay with you as long as you stay with him! Whenever you look for him, you will find him. But if you forsake him, he will forsake you.

Job 10:12. You gave me life and were so kind and loving to me, and I was preserved by your care.

Job 22:27. You will pray to him, and he will hear you.

Job 29:3. When he lighted the way before me and I walked safely through the darkness; [4]yes, in my early years, when the friendship of God was felt in my home; [5]when the Almighty was still with me.

Ps 3:8. What joys he gives to all his people.

Ps 5:12. For you bless the godly man, O Lord; you protect him with your shield of love.

Ps 11:7. For God is good, and he loves goodness; the godly shall see his face.

Ps 18:19. He led me to a place of safety, for he delights in me. [25]Lord, how merciful you are to those who are merciful. And you do not punish those who run from evil. *v.* 26; 2 Sam 22:20.

Ps 24:4. Only those with pure hands and hearts. . . . [5]They will receive God's own goodness as their blessing from him.

Ps 25:14. Friendship with God is reserved for those who reverence him. With them alone he shares the secrets of his promises.

Ps 30:7. The Lord has shown me his favor. He has made me steady as a mountain.

Ps 36:9. For you are the Fountain of life; our light is from your Light.

Ps 37:18. Day by day the Lord observes the good deeds done by godly men. [23]The steps of good men are directed by the Lord. He delights in each step they take.

Ps 41:11. I know you are pleased with me because you haven't let my enemies triumph over me. [12]You have preserved me because I was honest; you have admitted me forever to your presence.

Ps 44:3. They did not conquer by their own strength and skill, but by your mighty power and because you smiled upon them and favored them.

Ps 46:7. The Commander of the armies of heaven is here among us. He, the God of Jacob, has come to rescue us.

Ps 58:11. Then at last everyone will know that good is rewarded.

Ps 68:16. Well may you look with envy at Mount Zion, the mount where God has chosen to live forever. [18]He receives gifts for men, even those who once were rebels. God will live among us here.

Ps 84:11. He gives us grace and glory.

Ps 89:17. You are their strength. What glory! Our power is based on your favor!

Ps 92:10. But you have made me as strong as a wild bull. How refreshed I am by your blessings! Ps 75:10; 112:9.

Ps 94:19. Lord, when doubts fill my mind, when my heart is in turmoil, quiet me and give me renewed hope and cheer.

Ps 102:13. I know that you will come and have mercy on Jerusalem—and now is the time to pity her—the time you promised help.

Ps 115:12. Jehovah is constantly thinking about us and he will surely bless us. He will bless the people of Israel and the priests of Aaron, [13]and all, both great and small, who reverence him. *v.* 15.

Ps 132:13. O Lord, you have chosen Jerusalem as your home: [14]"This is my permanent home where I shall live," you said, "for I have always wanted it this way."

Ps 147:11. But his joy is in those who reverence him, those who expect him to be loving and kind.

Ps 149:4. For Jehovah enjoys his people; he will save the humble.

Prov 3:4. If you want favor with both God and man, and a reputation for good judgment and common sense, then trust the Lord completely. [32]But he gives his friendship to the godly. [35]The wise are promoted to honor. *v.* 23.

Prov 8:35. For whoever finds me finds life and wins approval from the Lord.

Prov 10:6. The good man is covered with blessings from head to foot. [22]The Lord's blessing is our greatest wealth. All our work adds nothing to it! [24]The wicked man's fears will all come true, and so will the good man's hopes.

Prov 11:20. The Lord hates the stubborn but delights in those who are good. [27]If you search for good you will find God's favor.

Prov 12:2. The Lord blesses good men and condemns the wicked.

Prov 14:9. The common bond of godly people is good will.

Prov 16:7. When a man is trying to please God, God makes even his worst enemies to be at peace with him.

Isa 28:5. Then at last the Lord of Hosts himself will be their crowning glory, the diadem of beauty to his people who are left.

Isa 30:26. The moon will be as bright as the sun, and the sunlight brighter than seven days! So it will be when the Lord begins to heal his people and to cure the wounds he gave them.

Isa 33:17. Your eyes will see the King in his beauty, and the highlands of heaven far away. [21]The glorious Lord will be to us as a wide river of protection. *v.* 22.

Isa 41:10. Fear not, for I am with you. Do not be dismayed. I am your God. Isa 43:5.

Isa 43:21. I have made Israel for myself, and these my people will some day honor me before the world.

Isa 54:8. But with everlasting love I will have pity on you, says the Lord, your Redeemer.

Isa 60:10. I will have mercy on you through my grace.

Jer 15:20. For I am with you to protect and deliver you, says the Lord.

Lam 3:24. My soul claims the Lord as my inheritance; therefore I will hope in him.

Ezk 37:27. And I will make my home among them.

Ezk 39:29. And I will never hide my face from them again, for I will pour out my Spirit upon them, says the Lord God.

Ezk 48:35. And the name of the city will be "The City of God."

Hos 14:4. And my love will know no bounds, for my anger will be forever gone!

Joel 2:27. And you will know that I am here among my people Israel, and that I alone am the Lord, your God. And my people shall never again be dealt a blow like this. *v.* 26.

Joel 3:16. But to his people Israel, the Lord will be very gentle. He is their Refuge and Strength. [17]Then you shall know at last that I am the Lord your God in Zion, my holy mountain. *vs.* 20, 21.

Amos 3:2. Of all the peoples of the earth, I have chosen you alone.

Zeph 3:15. And the Lord himself, the King of Israel, will live among you! At last your troubles will be over—you need fear no more. *v.* 17, 18.

Hag 1:13. Then the Lord told them . . . "I am with you; I will bless you."

Zech 2:5. For the Lord himself will be a wall of fire protecting them and all Jerusalem; he will be the glory of the city.

Zech 8:3. Now I am going to return to my land and I, myself, will live within Jerusalem.

Zech 9:16. The Lord their God will save his people in that day, as a Shepherd caring for his sheep. They shall shine in his land as glittering jewels in a crown.

Lk 1:28. Gabriel appeared to her and said, "Congratulations, favored lady! The Lord is with you! [30]Don't be frightened, Mary," the angel told her, "for God has decided to wonderfully bless you!" [66]For the hand of the Lord is surely upon him [John] in some special way.

Lk 2:52. So Jesus grew both tall and wise, and was loved by God and man. 1 Sam 2:26.

Jn 14:16. And I will ask the Father and he will give you another Comforter, and he will never leave you. [17]He is the Holy Spirit, the Spirit who leads into all truth. The world . . . doesn't recognize him. But you do, for he lives with you now and some day shall be in you. [18]No, I will not abandon you or leave you as orphans in the storm—I will come to you. [19]In just a little while I will be gone from the world, but I will still be present with you. For I will live again—and you will too. [20]When I come back to life again, you will know that I am in my Father, and you in me, and I in you. [21]. . . The one who loves me . . . my Father will love him; and I will too, and I will reveal myself to him. [23]Because I only reveal myself to those who love me and obey me. The Father will love them too, and we will come to them and live with them.

Jn 15:15. I no longer call you slaves, for a master doesn't confide in his slaves; now you are my friends, proved by the fact that I have told you everything the Father told me.

Acts 10:35. In every nation he has those who worship him and do good deeds and are acceptable to him.

Rom 2:29. No, a real Jew is anyone whose heart is right with God. For God is not looking for those who cut their bodies in actual body circumcision, but he is looking for those with changed hearts and minds. Whoever has that kind of change in his life will get his praise from God, even if not from you.

1 Cor 1:9. God will surely do this for you, for he always does just what he says, and he is the one who invited you into this wonderful friendship with his Son, even Christ our Lord.

1 Cor 3:21. For God has already given you everything you need. [22]He has given you Paul and Apollos and Peter as your helpers. He has given you the whole world to use, and life and even death are your servants. He has given you all of the present and all of the future. All are yours, [23]and you belong to Christ, and Christ is God's.

2 Cor 4:15. These sufferings of ours are for your benefit. And the more of you who are won to Christ, the more there are to thank him for his great kindness, and the more the Lord is glorified.

2 Cor 10:18. When someone boasts about himself and how well he has done, it doesn't count for

much. But when the Lord commends him, that's different!

Gal 4:6. And because we are his sons God has sent the Spirit of his Son into our hearts, so now we can rightly speak of God as our dear Father.

Eph 1:6. Now all praise to God for his wonderful kindness to us and his favor that he has poured out upon us, because we belong to his dearly loved Son.

Eph 2:13. But now you belong to Christ Jesus, and though you once were far away from God, now you have been brought very near to him because of what Jesus Christ has done for you with his blood. [14]For Christ himself is our way of peace. [18]Now all of us, whether Jews or Gentiles, may come to God the Father with the Holy Spirit's help because of what Christ has done for us. [22]And you also are joined with him and with each other by the Spirit, and are part of this dwelling place of God. *v.* 19; Eph 2:16.

Eph 3:12. Now we can come fearlessly right into God's presence, assured of his glad welcome when we come with Christ and trust in him. Rom 5:2.

Heb 4:16. So let us come boldly to the very throne of God and stay there to receive his mercy and to find grace to help us in our times of need.

Heb 10:19. And so, dear brothers, now we may walk right into the very Holy of Holies where God is, because of the blood of Jesus. [22]Let us go right in, to God himself, with true hearts fully trusting him to receive us.

Heb 11:5. Suddenly he was gone because God took him. Before this happened God had said how pleased he was with Enoch.

1 Pet 2:9. . . . for you have been chosen by God himself—you are priests of the King, you are holy and pure, you are God's very own—.

1 Jn 1:3. So that you may share the fellowship and the joys we have with the Father and with Jesus Christ his Son.

1 Jn 3:19. Then we will know for sure, by our actions, that we are on God's side, and our consciences will be clear, even when we stand before the Lord.

1 Jn 4:17. And as we live with Christ, our love grows more perfect and complete; so we will not be ashamed and embarrassed at the day of judgment, but can face him with confidence and joy, because he loves us and we love him too. [18]We need have no fear of someone who loves us perfectly; his perfect love for us eliminates all dread of what he might do to us. If we are afraid, it is for fear of what he might do to us, and shows that we are not fully convinced that he really loves us.

Rev 1:5. All praise to him who always loves us and who set us free from our sins by pouring out his lifeblood for us. [6]He has gathered us into his kingdom and made us priests of God his Father. Give to him everlasting glory! He rules forever! Amen!

Rev 3:20. Look! I have been standing at the door and I am constantly knocking. If anyone hears me calling him and opens the door, I will come in and fellowship with him and he with me. Rev 19:9.

Rev 21:3. I heard a loud shout from the throne saying, "Look, the home of God is now among men, and he will live with them and they will be his people; yes, God himself will be among them."

See *Grace of God.*

Instances of Special Grace. To Enoch, Gen 5: 21–24. To Noah, Gen 6:8. To Abraham, Gen 12:2. To Jacob, Gen 32:28; 46:3, 4. To Moses, Ex 3:12; 33:12, 14. To Solomon, 1 Chron 22:18.

GUIDE. Gen 12:1. After the death of Abram's father, God told him, "Leave your own country behind you, and your own people, and go to the land I will guide you to."

Ex 13:21. The Lord guided them by a pillar of cloud during the daytime, and by a pillar of fire at night. So they could travel either by day or night.

Ex 15:13. You have led the people you redeemed. But in your lovingkindness you have guided them wonderfully to your holy land.

Ex 33:13. "Please, if this is really so, guide me clearly along the way you want me to travel so that I will understand you and walk acceptably before you. For don't forget that this nation is your people." [14]And the Lord replied, "I myself will go with you and give you success." [15]For Moses had said, "If you aren't going with us, don't let us move a step from this place."

Num 10:33. They traveled for three days after leaving Mount Sinai, with the Ark at the front of the column to choose a place for them to stop.

Deut 32:10. God protected them in the howling wilderness as though they were the apple of his eye. [12]When the Lord alone was leading them, and they lived without foreign gods.

2 Sam 22:20. O Lord, you are my light! You make my darkness bright.

2 Chron 32:22. That is how the Lord saved Hezekiah and the people of Jerusalem. And now there was peace at last throughout his realm.

Neh 9:19. But in your great mercy you didn't abandon them to die in the wilderness! The pillar of cloud led them forward day by day, and the pillar of fire showed them the way through the night. [20]You sent your good Spirit to instruct them, and you did not stop giving them bread from heaven or water for their thirst.

Ps 5:8. Lord, lead me as you promised me you would; otherwise my enemies will conquer me. Tell me clearly what to do, which way to turn.

Ps 23:2, 3. He lets me rest in the meadow grass and leads me beside the quiet streams. He restores my failing health. He helps me do what honors him the most.

Ps 25:5. Lead me; teach me; for you are the God who gives me salvation. I have no hope except in you. [9]He will teach the ways that are right and best to those who humbly turn to him.

Ps 27:11. Tell me what to do, O Lord, and make it plain because I am surrounded by waiting enemies.

Ps 31:3. Yes, you are my Rock and my fortress; honor your name by leading me out of this peril.

Ps 32:8. I will instruct you (says the Lord) and guide you along the best pathway for your life; I will advise you and watch your progress.

Ps 48:14. For this great God is our God forever and ever. He will be our guide until we die.

Ps 61:2. For wherever I am, though far away at the ends of the earth, I will cry to you for help. When my heart is faint and overwhelmed, lead me to the mighty, towering Rock of safety.

Ps 73:24. You will keep on guiding me all my life with your wisdom and counsel; and afterwards receive me into the glories of heaven!

Ps 78:52. But he led forth his own people like a flock, guiding them safely through the wilderness.

Ps 80:1. O Shepherd of Israel who leads Israel like a flock; O God enthroned above the cherubim, bend down your ear and listen as I plead. Display your power and radiant glory.

Ps 107:7. He led them straight to safety and a place to live.

Ps 139:9. If I ride the morning winds to the farthest oceans, [10]even there your hand will guide me, your strength will support me. [24]Point out anything you find in me that makes you sad, and lead me along the path of everlasting life.

Prov 8:20. My paths are those of justice and right.

Isa 40:11. He will feed his flock like a shepherd; he will carry the lambs in his arms and gently lead the ewes with young.

Isa 42:16. He will bring blind Israel along a path they have not seen before. He will make the darkness bright before them and smooth and straighten out the road ahead. He will not forsake them.

Isa 48:17. The Lord, your Redeemer, the Holy One of Israel, says, I am the Lord your God, who punishes you for your own good and leads you along the paths that you should follow.

Isa 57:18. I have seen what they do, but I will heal them anyway! I will lead them and comfort them, helping them to mourn and to confess their sins.

Isa 58:11. And the Lord will guide you continually, and satisfy you with all good things, and keep you healthy too; and you will be like a well-watered garden, like an ever-flowing spring.

Lk 1:79. To give light to those who sit in darkness and death's shadow, and to guide us to the path of peace.

Jn 10:3. The gatekeeper opens the gate for him, and the sheep hear his voice and come to him; and he calls his own sheep by name and leads them out. [4]He walks ahead of them; and they follow him, for they recognize his voice.

Jn 16:13. When the Holy Spirit, who is truth, comes, he shall guide you into all truth, for he will not be presenting his own ideas, but will be passing on to you what he has heard. He will tell you about the future.

See *God, Providence of.*

HOLINESS OF. Ex 3:5. "Don't come any closer," God told him. "Take off your shoes, for you are standing on holy ground." Josh 5:15.

Ex 15:11. Who else is like the Lord among the gods? Who is glorious in holiness like him? Who is so awesome in splendor, a wonder-working God?

Lev 19:2. You must be holy because I, the Lord your God, am holy. Lev 11:44; 20:26; 21:8.

Deut 32:4. He is the Rock. His work is perfect. Everything he does is just and fair. He is faithful, without sin.

Josh 24:19. But Joshua replied to the people, "You can't worship the Lord God, for he is holy and jealous; he will not forgive your rebellion and sins."

1 Sam 2:2. No one is as holy as the Lord! There is no other God, nor any Rock like our God.

1 Sam 6:20. "Who is able to stand before Jehovah, this holy God?" they cried out. "Where can we send the Ark from here?"

1 Chron 16:10. Glory in his holy name. Ps 105:3.

Job 4:17. Is mere man more just than God? More pure than his Creator? *vs.* 18, 19.

Job 6:10. This, at least, gives me comfort despite all the pain—that I have not denied the words of the holy God.

Job 15:15. Why, God doesn't even trust the angels! Even the heavens can't be absolutely pure compared with him!

Job 25:5. God is so glorious that even the moon and stars are less than nothing as compared to him.

Job 34:10. Listen to me, you with understanding. Surely everyone knows that *God doesn't sin!*

Job 36:23. Who can say that what he does is absurd or evil?

Ps 11:7. For God is good, and he loves goodness; the godly shall see his face.

Ps 18:30. What a God he is! How perfect in every way!

Ps 22:3. For *you are holy.*

Ps 30:4. Oh, sing to him you saints of his; give thanks to his holy name.

Ps 33:4. For all God's words are right, and everything he does is worthy of our trust. [5]He loves whatever is just and good; the earth is filled with his tender love.

Ps 47:8. He reigns above the nations, sitting on his holy throne.

Ps 48:1. How great is the Lord! How much we should praise him. He lives upon Mount Zion in Jerusalem.

Ps 60:6. God has promised to help us. He has vowed it by his holiness! Ps 108:7.

Ps 89:35. For I have sworn to David (and a holy God can never lie).

Ps 92:15. This honors the Lord, and exhibits his faithful care. He is my shelter. There is nothing but goodness in him!

Ps 99:3. Let them reverence your great and holy name. [5]Exalt the Lord our holy God! Bow low before his feet. *v.* 9.

Ps 111:9. He has paid a full ransom for his people; now they are always free to come to Jehovah (what a holy, awe-inspiring name that is).

Ps 119:142. Your justice is eternal for your laws are perfectly fair.

Ps 145:17. The Lord is fair in everything he does, and full of kindness.

Isa 5:16. For he alone is holy, just and good.

Isa 6:3. Holy, holy, holy is the Lord of Hosts; the whole earth is filled with his glory.

Isa 12:6. Let all the people of Jerusalem shout his praise with joy. For great and mighty is the Holy One of Israel, who lives among you.

Isa 29:19. The meek will be filled with fresh joy from the Lord, and the poor shall exult in the Holy One of Israel. [23]Then they will fear and rejoice in my name, and praise the Holy One of Israel, and stand in awe of him. Isa 41:14.

Isa 43:14. The Lord, your Redeemer, the Holy One of Israel, says: For your sakes I will send an invading army against Babylon, that will walk in almost unscathed. The boasts of the Babylonians will turn to cries of fear. [15]I am the Lord, your Holy One, Israel's Creator and King.

Isa 45:19. No, for I, Jehovah, speak only truth and righteousness.

Isa 47:4. The Lord of Hosts is his name, the Holy One of Israel.

Isa 49:7. The Lord, the Redeemer and Holy One of Israel, says to the one who is despised, rejected by mankind, and kept beneath the heel of earthly rulers: "Kings shall stand at attention when you pass by; princes shall bow low because the Lord has chosen you; he, the faithful Lord, the Holy One of Israel, chooses you."

Isa 52:10. The Lord has bared his holy arm before the eyes of all the nations. Ps 98:1.

Isa 57:15. The high and lofty one who inhabits eternity, the Holy One.

Jer 2:4, 5. O Israel, says the Lord, why did your fathers desert me? What sin did they find in me that turned them away and changed them into fools who worship idols?

Ezk 39:7. Thus I will make known my holy name among my people Israel; I will not let it be mocked at anymore. And the nations too shall know I am the Lord, the Holy One of Israel. *v* 25; Ezk 36:21, 22.

Dan 4:8. At last Daniel came in—the man I named Belteshazzar after my god—the man in whom is the spirit of the holy gods, and I told him the dream.

Hos 11:9. For I am God and not man; I am the Holy One living among you, and I did not come to destroy.

Hab 1:12. O Lord my God, my Holy One, you who are eternal. . . . [13]We are wicked, but they far more! Will you, who cannot allow sin in any form, stand idly by while they swallow us up? Should you be silent while the wicked destroy those who are better than they?

Mt 5:48. But you are to be perfect, even as your Father in heaven is perfect.

Mt 19:17. For God alone is truly good. Mk 10:18; Lk 18:19.

Lk 1:49. For he, the mighty Holy One, has done great things to me.

Jn 7:28. So Jesus, in a sermon in the Temple, called out, "Yes, you know me and where I was born and raised, but I am the representative of one you don't know, and he is Truth."

Jn 17:11. Holy Father, keep them in your own care—all those you have given me.

Rom 1:23. And then, instead of worshiping the glorious, ever-living God, they took wood and stone and made idols for themselves, carving them to look like mere birds and animals and snakes and puny men.

Heb 1:8. But of his son he says, "Your kingdom, O God, will last forever and ever, its commands are always just and right."

Jas 1:13. And remember, when someone wants to do wrong it is never God who is tempting him, for God never wants to do wrong and never tempts anyone else to do it.

1 Pet 1:15. But be holy now in everything you do, just as the Lord is holy, who invited you to be his child. [16]He himself has said, "You must be holy, for I am holy."

1 Jn 1:5. God is Light and in him is no darkness at all.

Rev 4:8. Holy, holy, holy, Lord God Almighty —the one who was, and is, and is to come.

Rev 6:10. They called loudly to the Lord and said, "O Sovereign Lord, holy and true, how long will it be before you judge the people of the earth for what they've done to us? When will you avenge our blood against those living on the earth?"

Rev 15:4. Who shall not fear, O Lord, and glorify your Name? For you alone are holy.

See *Sin, Separates from God; God, Perfection of, Righteousness of.*

HUMAN FORMS AND APPEARANCE OF. See *Anthropomorphisms.*

IMPARTIAL. Deut 10:17. Jehovah your God is God of gods and Lord of lords. He is the great and mighty God, the God of terror who shows no partiality and takes no bribes.

Job 36:5. God is almighty and yet does not despise anyone! And he is perfect in his understanding.

Job 37:24. No wonder men everywhere fear him! For he is not impressed by the world's wisest men!

Acts 10:34. Then Peter replied, "I see very clearly that the Jews are not God's only favorites! [35]In every nation he has those who worship him and do good deeds and are acceptable to him."

Rom 2:6. He will give each one whatever his deeds deserve. [11]For God treats everyone the same.

Gal 2:6. And the great leaders of the church who were there had nothing to add to what I was preaching. (By the way, their being great leaders made no difference to me, for all are the same to God.)

Eph 6:8. Remember, the Lord will pay you for each good thing you do, whether you are slave or free.

Col 3:25. And if you don't do your best for him, he will pay you in a way that you won't like—for he has no special favorites who can get away with shirking.

1 Pet 1:17. And remember that your heavenly Father to whom you pray has no favorites when he judges. He will judge you with perfect justice for everything you do; so act in reverent fear of him from now on until you get to heaven.

INCOMPREHENSIBLE. Ex 20:21. As the people stood in the distance, Moses entered into the deep darkness where God was.

Deut 4:11. You stood at the foot of the mountain, and the mountain burned with fire; flames shot far into the sky, surrounded by black clouds and deep darkness.

Deut 5:22. The Lord has given these laws to each one of you from the heart of the fire, surrounded by clouds and thick darkness that engulfed Mount Sinai. Those were the only commandments he gave you at that time.

1 Kgs 8:12. Now King Solomon prayed this invocation: "The Lord has said that he would live in the thick darkness."

Job 11:7. Do you know the mind and purposes of God? Will long searching make them known to you? Are you qualified to judge the Almighty? [8]He is as faultless as heaven is high—but who are you? His mind is fathomless—what can you know in comparison? [9]His Spirit is broader than the earth and wider than the sea.

Job 15:8. Have you heard the secret counsel of God?

Job 37:1. My heart trembles at this. [2]Listen, listen to the thunder of his voice. [3]It rolls across the heavens and his lightning flashes out in every direction. [4]Afterwards comes the roaring of the thunder —the tremendous voice of his majesty. [5]His voice is glorious in the thunder. We cannot comprehend the greatness of his power. [6]For he directs the snow, the showers, and storm to fall upon the earth. [7]Man's work stops at such a time, so that all men everywhere may recognize his power. [8]The wild animals hide in the rocks or in their dens. [9]From the south comes the rain; from the north, the cold. [10]God blows upon the rivers, and even the widest torrents freeze. [11]He loads the clouds with moisture and they send forth his lightning. [12]The lightning bolts are directed by his hand, and do whatever he commands throughout the earth. [13]He sends the storms as punishment, or, in his loving-kindness, to encourage. [14]Listen, O Job, stop and consider the wonderful miracles of God. [15]Do you know how God controls all nature, and causes the lightning to flash forth from the clouds? [16, 17]Do you understand the balancing of the clouds with wonderful perfection and skill? Do you know why you become warm when the south wind is blowing and everything is still? [18]Can you spread out the gigantic mirror of the skies as he does? [19, 20]You who think you know so much, teach the rest of us how we should approach God. For we are too dull to know! With your wisdom, would we then dare to approach him? Well, does a man wish to be swallowed alive? [21]For as we cannot look at the sun for its brightness when the winds have cleared away the clouds, [22]neither can we gaze at the terrible majesty of God breaking forth upon us from heaven, clothed in dazzling splendor. [23]We cannot imagine the power of the Almighty, and yet he is so just and merciful that he does not destroy us. [24]No wonder men everywhere fear him! For he is not impressed by the world's wisest men!"

Ps 18:11. He enshrouded himself with darkness, veiling his approach with dense clouds dark as murky waters.

Ps 97:2. Clouds and darkness surround him. Righteousness and justice are the foundation of his throne.

Eccl 3:11. Man cannot see the whole scope of God's work from beginning to end.

Isa 40:12. Who else has held the oceans in his hands and measured off the heavens with his ruler? Who else knows the weight of all the earth and weighs the mountains and the hills? [13]Who can advise the Spirit of the Lord or be his teacher or give him counsel? [14]Has he ever needed anyone's advice? Did he need instruction as to what is right and best? [15]No, for all the peoples of the world are nothing in comparison with him—they are but a drop in the bucket, dust on the scales. He picks up the islands as though they had no weight at all. [16]All of Lebanon's forests do not contain sufficient fuel to consume a sacrifice large enough to honor him, nor are all its animals enough to offer to our God. [17]All the nations are as nothing to him; in his eyes they are less than nothing—mere emptiness and froth. [18]How can we describe God? With what can we compare him? [19]With an idol? An idol, made from a mold, overlaid with gold, and with silver chains around its neck? [20]The man too poor to buy expensive gods like that will find a tree free from rot and hire a man to carve a face on it, and that's his god—a god that cannot even move! [21]Are you so ignorant? Are you so deaf to the words of God—the words he gave before the worlds began? Have you never heard nor understood? [22]It is God who sits above the circle of the earth. (The people below must seem to him like grasshoppers!) He is the one who stretches out the heavens like a curtain and makes his tent from them. [23]He dooms the great men of the world and brings them all to naught. [24]They hardly get started, barely take root, when he blows on them and their work withers and the wind carries them off like straw. [25]"With whom will you compare me? Who is my equal?" asks the Holy One. [26]Look up into the heavens! Who created all these stars? As a shepherd leads his sheep, calling each by its pet name, and counts them to see that none are lost or strayed, so God does with stars and planets! [27]O Jacob, O Israel, how can you say that the Lord doesn't see your troubles and isn't being fair? [28]Don't you yet understand? Don't you know by now that the everlasting God the Creator of the farthest parts of the earth, never grows faint or weary? No one can fathom the depths of his understanding. [29]He gives power to the tired and worn out, and strength to the weak. [30]Even the youths shall be exhausted, and the young men will all give up. [31]But they that wait upon the Lord shall renew their strength. They shall mount up with wings like eagles; they shall run and not be weary; they shall walk and not faint.

Isa 55:8. This plan of mine is not what you would work out, neither are my thoughts the same as yours! [9]For just as the heavens are higher than the earth, so are my ways higher than yours, and my thoughts than yours.

1 Cor 2:16. For certainly he has never been one to know the Lord's thoughts, or to discuss them with him, or to move the hands of God by prayer.

Symbolized. By a pillar of fire, Ex 14:19, 20. By the darkness of the Most Holy Place in the Temple, 1 Kgs 8:12, 13; by the general structure of the Most Holy Place, see Lev 16:2.

See *God, Unsearchable,* below.

INFINITE. 1 Kgs 8:27. But is it possible that God would really live on earth? Why, even the skies and the highest heavens cannot contain you, much less this Temple I have built! 2 Chron 2:6; 6:1, 2, 18.

Ps 147:5. How great he is! His power is absolute! His understanding is unlimited.

Jer 23:24. Am I not everywhere in all of heaven and earth?

See *God, Incomprehensible,* above; *Ubiquitous, Unsearchable,* below.

INVISIBLE. Ex 20:21. As the people stood in the distance, Moses entered into the deep darkness where God was.

Ex 33:20. But you may not see the glory of my face, for man may not see me and live.

Deut 4:11. You stood at the foot of the mountain, and the mountain burned with fire; flames shot far into the sky, surrounded by black clouds and deep darkness. [15]You didn't see the form of God that day as he spoke to you from the fire at Mount Horeb.

Deut 5:22. The Lord has given these laws to each one of you from the heart of the fire, surrounded by the clouds and thick darkness that engulfed Mount Sinai. Those were the only commandments he gave you at that time.

1 Kgs 8:12. Now King Solomon prayed this invocation: "The Lord has said that he would live in the thick darkness."

Job 9:11. He passes by, invisible; he moves along, but I don't see him go.

Job 23:8. But I search in vain. I seek him here, I seek him there, and cannot find him. [9]I seek him in his workshop in the North, but cannot find him there; nor can I find him in the South; there, too, he hides himself.

Ps 18:11. He enshrouded himself with darkness, veiling his approach with dense clouds dark as murky waters.

Ps 97:2. Clouds and darkness surround him. Righteousness and justice are the foundation of his throne.

Jn 1:18. No one has ever actually seen God, but, of course, his only Son has, for he is the companion of the Father and has told us all about him.

Jn 5:37. And the Father himself has also testified about me, though not appearing to you personally, or speaking to you directly.

Jn 6:46. Not that anyone actually sees the Father, for only I have seen him.

Col 1:13. For he has rescued us out of the darkness and gloom of Satan's kingdom and brought us into the kingdom of his dear Son, [14]who bought our freedom with his blood and forgave us all our sins. [15]Christ is the exact likeness of the unseen God. He existed before God made anything at all.

1 Tim 1:17. Glory and honor to God forever and ever. He is the King of the ages, the unseen one who never dies; he alone is God, and full of wisdom. Amen.

1 Tim 6:16. Who alone can never die, who lives in light so terrible that no human being can approach. No mere man has ever seen him, nor ever will.

1 Jn 4:12. For though we have never yet seen God, when we love each other God lives in us and his love within us grows ever stronger.

See *God, Incomprehensible, Infinite,* above; *Unsearchable,* below.

JEALOUS. Ex 20:5. For I, the Lord your God, am very possessive. [7]You shall not use the name of Jehovah your God irreverently, nor use it to swear to a falsehood. You will not escape punishment if you do. Deut 5:9–11.

Ex 34:14. For you must worship no other gods, but only Jehovah, for he is a God who claims absolute loyalty and exclusive devotion. Deut 6:15.

Deut 4:24. He is a devouring fire, a jealous God.

Deut 29:20. For the Lord will not pardon! His anger and jealousy will be hot against that man.

Deut 32:16. Israel began to follow foreign gods, and Jehovah was very angry; he was jealous of his people. [21]They have made me very jealous of their idols, which are not gods at all.

Josh 24:19. You can't worship the Lord God, for he is holy and jealous; he will not forgive your rebellion and sins.

2 Chron 16:7. About that time the prophet Hanai came to King Asa and told him, "Because you have put your trust in the king of Syria instead of in the Lord your God, the army of the king of Syria has escaped from you. [8]Don't you remember what happened to the Ethiopians and Libyans and their vast army, with all of their chariots and cavalrymen? But you relied then on the Lord, and he delivered them all into your hand. [9]For the eyes of the Lord search back and forth across the whole earth, looking for people whose hearts are perfect toward him, so that he can show his great power in helping them. What a fool you have been! From now on you shall have wars." [10]Asa was so angry with the prophet for saying this that he threw him into jail. And Asa oppressed all the people at that time.

Isa 30:1. Woe to my rebellious children, says the Lord; you ask advice from everyone but me, and decide to do what I don't want you to do. You yoke yourselves with unbelievers, thus piling up your sins. [2]For without consulting me you have gone down to Egypt to find aid and have put your trust in Pharaoh for his protection.

Isa 31:1. Woe to those who run to Egypt for help, trusting their mighty cavalry and chariots instead of looking to the Holy One of Israel and consulting him. [3]For these Egyptians are mere men, not God! Their horses are puny flesh, not mighty spirits! When the Lord clenches his fist against them, they will stumble and fall among those they are trying to help. All will fail together.

Ezk 23:25. And I will send my jealousy against you.

Ezk 36:5. My anger is afire against these nations, especially Edom, for grabbing my land with relish, in utter contempt for me, to take it for themselves.

Joel 2:18. Then the Lord will pity his people and be indignant for the honor of his land!

Nah 1:2. God is jealous over those he loves; that is why he takes vengeance on those who hurt them. He furiously destroys their enemies.

Zech 1:14. Shout out this message from the Lord of Hosts: Don't you think I care about what has happened to Judah and Jerusalem? I am as jealous as a husband for his captive wife.

JUDGE, AND HIS JUSTICE. Gen 16:5. Then Sarai said to Abram, "It's all your fault. . . . May the Lord judge you for doing this to me!"

Gen 18:21. "I am going down to see whether these reports are true or not. Then I will know." [25]"That wouldn't be right! Surely you wouldn't do such a thing, to kill the godly with the wicked! Why, you would be treating godly and wicked exactly the same! Surely you wouldn't do that! Should not the Judge of all the earth be fair?"

Num 16:22. But Moses and Aaron fell face downward to the ground before the Lord. "O God, the God of all mankind," they pleaded, "must you be angry with all the people when one man sins?"

Deut 10:17. Jehovah your God is God of gods and Lord of lords. He is the great and mighty God, the God of terror who shows no partiality and takes no bribes. 2 Sam 14:14; Rom 2:11.

Deut 32:4. He is the Rock. His work is perfect. Everything he does is just and fair. He is faithful, without sin. [35]Vengeance is mine.

Josh 24:19. You can't worship the Lord God, for he is holy and jealous; he will not forgive your rebellion and sins. Ex 20:5; 34:7.

Judg 11:27. But Jehovah the Judge will soon show which of us is right—Israel or Ammon.

1 Sam 2:3. The Lord knows what you have done, and he will judge your deeds. [10]Those who fight against the Lord shall be broken; he thunders against them from heaven. He judges throughout the earth.

1 Sam 24:12. The Lord will decide between us. Perhaps he will kill you for what you are trying to do to me, but I will never harm you. [15]May the Lord judge as to which of us is right and punish whichever one of us is guilty. He is my lawyer and defender, and he will rescue me from your power!

2 Sam 22:25. That is why the Lord has done so much for me, for he sees that I am clean. [26]You are merciful to the merciful; you show your perfections to the blameless. [27]To those who are pure, you show yourself pure; but you destroy those who are evil. Ps 18:25, 26.

1 Kgs 8:32. Hear him in heaven and do what is right; judge whether or not he did it. Judg 9:56, 57; 2 Chron 6:22, 23.

1 Chron 16:33. Let the trees in the woods sing for joy before the Lord, for he comes to judge the earth.

2 Chron 19:7. For there must be no injustice among God's judges, no partiality, no taking of bribes.

Neh 9:33. Every time you punished us you were being perfectly fair; we have sinned so greatly that you gave us only what we deserved.

Job 4:17. Is mere man more just than God? More pure than his Creator?

Job 8:3. Does God twist justice?

Job 9:15. Even if I were sinless I wouldn't say a word. I would only plead for mercy. [28]For I know that you will not hold me innocent, O God.

Job 21:22. But who can rebuke God, the supreme Judge?

Job 31:13. If I have been unfair to my servants, [14]how could I face God? What could I say when he questioned me about it? [15]For God made me, and made my servant too. He created us both.

Job 34:10. Listen to me, you with understanding. Surely everyone knows that God doesn't sin! [11]Rather, he punishes the sinners. [12]There is no truer statement than this: *God is never wicked or unjust.* [17]Could God govern if he hated justice? Are you going to condemn the Almighty Judge? [19]For he doesn't care how great a man may be, and doesn't pay any more attention to the rich than to the poor. He made them all. [23]So there is no need to wait for some great crime before a man is called before God in judgment.

Job 35:14, 15. And it is even more false to say that he doesn't see what is going on. He *does* bring about justice at last, if you will only wait.

Job 36:3. I will give you many illustrations of the righteousness of my Maker.

Job 37:23. We cannot imagine the power of the Almighty, and yet he is so just and merciful that he does not destroy us.

Ps 7:9. For you, the righteous God, look deep within the hearts of men and examine all their motives and their thoughts. [11]God is a judge who is perfectly fair, and he is angry with the wicked every day.

Ps 9:4. You have vindicated me; you have endorsed my work, declaring from your throne that it is good. [7, 8]But the Lord lives on forever; he sits upon his throne to judge justly the nations of the world.

Ps 11:4. He closely watches everything that happens here on earth. [5]He puts the righteous and the wicked to the test; he hates those loving violence. [7]For God is good, and he loves goodness; the godly shall see his face.

Ps 19:9. God's laws are pure, eternal, just.

Ps 26:1. Dismiss all the charges against me, Lord, for I have tried to keep your laws and have trusted you without wavering. [2]Cross-examine me, O Lord, and see that this is so; test my motives and my affections too.

Ps 33:5. He loves whatever is just and good; the earth is filled with his tender love.

Ps 35:24. Declare me "not guilty," for you are just.

Ps 43:1. O God, defend me from the charges of these merciless, deceitful men.

Ps 50:4. He has come to judge his people. [6]God will judge them with complete fairness, for all heaven declares he is just.

Ps 51:4. It is against you and you alone I sinned, and did this terrible thing. You saw it all, and your sentence against me is just.

Ps 58:11. Then at last everyone will know that good is rewarded, and that there is a God who judges justly here on earth.

Ps 62:12. He is loving and kind and rewards each one of us according to the work we do for Him.

Ps 67:4. How glad the nations will be, singing for joy because you are their King and will give true justice to their people!

Ps 71:19. Your power and goodness, Lord, reach to the highest heavens. You have done such wonderful things. Where is there another God like you?

Ps 76:8. You pronounce sentence on them from heaven; the earth trembles and stands silently before you. [9]You stand up to punish the evil-doers and to defend the meek of the earth.

Ps 85:10. Mercy and truth have met together. Grim justice and peace have kissed!

Ps 89:14. Your throne is founded on two strong pillars—the one is Justice and the other Righteousness. Mercy and Truth walk before you as your attendants.

Ps 90:8. You spread out our sins before you—our secret sins—and see them all. [11]Who can realize the terrors of your anger? Which of us can fear you as he should?

Ps 92:15. This honors the Lord, and exhibits his faithful care. He is my shelter. There is nothing but goodness in him!

Ps 94:1, 2. Lord God, to whom vengeance belongs, let your glory shine out. Arise and judge the earth; sentence the proud to the penalties they deserve. [10]He punishes the nations—won't he also punish you? Ps 82:8.

Ps 96:13. For the Lord is coming to judge the earth; he will judge the nations fairly and with truth! *v.* 10.

Ps 97:2. Clouds and darkness surround him. Righteousness and justice are the foundation of his throne.

Ps 98:2. He has announced this victory and revealed it to every nation by fulfilling his promise to be kind to Israel. The whole earth has seen God's salvation of his people. *vs.* 8, 9.

Ps 99:4. This mighty King is determined to give justice. Fairness is the touchstone of everything he does. He gives justice throughout Israel. [8]O Jehovah our God! You answered them and forgave their sins, yet punished them when they went wrong.

Ps 103:6. He gives justice to all who are treated unfairly.

Ps 111:7. All he does is just and good, and all his laws are right.

Ps 119:137. O Lord, you are just and your punishments are fair.

Ps 135:14. For Jehovah will vindicate his people, and have compassion on his servants.

Ps 143:2. Don't bring me to trial! For as compared with you, no one is perfect.

Ps 145:17. The Lord is fair in everything he does, and full of kindness.

Prov 11:31. Even the godly shall be rewarded here on earth; how much more the wicked!

Prov 16:2. We can always "prove" that we are right, but is the Lord convinced?

Prov 21:2. We can justify our every deed but God looks at our motives. [3]God is more pleased when we are just and fair than when we give him gifts.

Prov 24:11, 12. Rescue those who are unjustly sentenced to death; don't stand back and let them die. Don't try to disclaim responsibility by saying you didn't know about it. For God, who knows all hearts, knows yours, and he knows you knew! And he will reward everyone according to his deeds.

Prov 29:13. Rich and poor are alike in this: each depends on God for light. [26]Do you want justice? Don't fawn on the judge, but ask the Lord for it!

Eccl 3:15. Whatever is, has been long ago; and whatever is going to be has been before; God brings to pass again what was in the distant past and disappeared. [17]I said to myself, "In due season God will judge everything man does, both good and bad."

Eccl 11:9. Young man, it's wonderful to be young! Enjoy every minute of it! Do all you want to; take in everything, but realize that you must account to God for everything you do.

Eccl 12:14. For God will judge us for everything we do, including every hidden thing, good or bad.

Isa 1:27. Those who return to the Lord, who are just and good, shall be redeemed.

Isa 3:13. The Lord stands up! He is the great Prosecuting Attorney presenting his case against his people! [14]First to feel his wrath will be the elders and the princes, for they have defrauded the poor. They have filled their barns with grain extorted from the helpless peasants.

Isa 10:17. God, the Light and Holy One of Israel, will be the fire and flame that will destroy them. In a single night he will burn those thorns and briars, the Assyrians who destroyed the land of Israel. [18]Assyria's vast army is like a glorious forest, yet it will be destroyed. The Lord will destroy them, soul and body, as when a sick man wastes away.

Isa 26:7. But for good men the path is not uphill and rough! God does not give them a rough and treacherous path, but smooths the road before them.

Isa 28:17. I will take the line and plummet of justice to check the foundation wall you built; it looks so fine, but it is so weak a storm of hail will knock it down! The enemy will come like a flood and sweep it away, and you will be drowned. [21]The Lord will come suddenly and in anger, as at Mount Perazim and Gibeon, to do a strange, unusual thing—to destroy his own people!

Isa 30:18. Yet the Lord still waits for you to come to him, so he can show you his love; he will conquer you to bless you, just as he said. For the Lord is faithful to his promises. Blessed are all those who wait for him to help them. [27]See, the Lord comes from afar, aflame with wrath, surrounded by thick rising smoke. His lips are filled with fury; his words consume like fire. [30]And the Lord shall cause his majestic voice to be heard and shall crush down his mighty arm upon his enemies with angry indignation and with devouring flames and tornados and terrible storms and huge hailstones.

Isa 31:2. In his wisdom, he will send great evil on his people and will not change his mind. He will rise against them for the evil they have done, and crush their allies too.

Isa 33:22. For the Lord is our Judge, our Lawgiver and our King; he will care for us and save us.

Isa 45:21. Consult together, argue your case and state your proofs that idol-worship pays! Who but God has said that these things concerning Cyrus would come true? What idol ever told you they would happen? For there is no other God but me —a just God and a Savior—no, not one!

Isa 61:8. For I, the Lord, love justice; I hate robbery and wrong. I will faithfully reward my people for their suffering and make an everlasting covenant with them.

Jer 9:24. Let them boast in this alone: That they truly know me, and understand that I am the Lord of justice and of righteousness whose love is steadfast; and that I love to be this way.

Jer 10:10. But the Lord is the only true God, the living God, the everlasting King. The whole earth shall tremble at his anger; the world shall hide before his displeasure.

Jer 11:20. O Lord of Hosts, you are just. See the hearts and motives of these men. Repay them for all that they have planned! I look to you for justice. Jer 20:12.

Jer 12:1. O Lord, you always give me justice when I bring a case before you to decide. Now let me bring you this complaint: Why are the wicked so prosperous? Why are evil men so happy?

Jer 32:19. You have all wisdom and do great and mighty miracles; for your eyes are open to all the ways of men, and you reward everyone according to his life and deeds.

Jer 50:7. All who found them devoured them and said, "We are permitted to attack them freely, for they have sinned against the Lord, the God of justice, the hope of their fathers."

Jer 51:10. The Lord has vindicated us. Come, let us declare in Jerusalem all the Lord our God has done.

Lam 1:18. And the Lord is right, for we rebelled. And yet, O people everywhere, behold and see my anguish and despair, for my sons and daughters are taken far away as slaves to distant lands.

Ezk 14:21. And the Lord says: Four great punishments await Jerusalem to destroy all life: war, famine, ferocious beasts, plague. [23]You will agree, when you meet them, that it is not without cause that all these things are being done to Israel.

Ezk 18:25. Yet you say: "The Lord isn't being fair!" Listen to me, O people of Israel. Am I the one who is unfair, or is it you? [*v.* 29.] [30]I will judge each of you, O Israel, and punish or reward each according to your own actions. Oh, turn from your sins while there is yet time.

Ezk 33:7. So with you, son of dust. I have appointed you as a watchman for the people of Israel; therefore listen to what I say and warn them for me. [8]When I say to the wicked, "O wicked man, you will die!" and you don't tell him what I say, so that he does not repent—that wicked person will die in his sins, but I will hold you responsible for his death. [9]But if you warn him to repent and he doesn't, he will die in his sin, and you will not be responsible. [10]O people of Israel, you are saying: "Our sins are heavy upon us; we pine away with guilt. How can we live?" [11]Tell them: As I live, says the Lord God, I have no pleasure in the death of the wicked; *I desire that the wicked turn from his evil ways and live.* Turn, turn from your wickedness, for why will you die, O Israel? [12]For the good works of a righteous man will not save him if he turns to sin; and the sins of an evil man will not destroy him if he repents and turns from his sins. [13]I have said the good man will live. But if he sins, expecting his past goodness to save him, then none of his good deeds will be remembered. I will destroy him for his sins. [14]And when I tell the wicked he will die and then he turns from his sins and does what is fair and right—[15]if he gives back the borrower's pledge and returns what he has stolen and walks along the paths of right, not doing evil—he shall surely live. He shall not die. [16]None of his past sins shall be brought up against him, for he has turned to the good and shall surely live. [17]And yet your people are saying the Lord isn't fair. The trouble is *they* aren't fair. [18]For again I say, when the good man turns to evil, he shall die. [19]But if the wicked turns from his wickedness and does what's fair and just, he shall live.

Dan 4:37. Now, I, Nebuchadnezzar, praise and glorify and honor the King of Heaven, the Judge of all, whose every act is right and good; for he is able to take those who walk proudly and push them into the dust!

Dan 7:9. I watched as thrones were put in place and the Ancient of Days—the Almighty God—sat down to judge. His clothing was as white as snow, his hair like whitest wool. He sat upon a fiery throne brought in on flaming wheels, and [10]a river of fire flowed from before him. Millions of angels ministered to him and hundreds of millions of people stood before him, waiting to be judged. Then the court began its session and The Books were opened.

Dan 9:7. O Lord, you are righteous; but as for us, we are always shamefaced with sin, just as you see us now; yes, all of us—the men of Judah, the people of Jerusalem, and all Israel, scattered near and far wherever you have driven us because of our disloyalty to you. [14]And so the Lord deliberately crushed us with the calamity he prepared; he is fair in everything he does, but we would not obey.

Hos 10:10. I will come against you for your disobedience; I will gather the armies of the nations against you to punish you for your heaped-up sins.

Amos 8:7. The Lord, the Pride of Israel, has sworn: "I won't forget your deeds!"

Nah 1:3. He is slow in getting angry, but when aroused, his power is incredible, and he does not easily forgive. He shows his power in the terrors of the cyclone and the raging storms; clouds are billowing dust beneath his feet! [6]Who can stand before an angry God? His fury is like fire; the mountains tumble down before his anger.

Zeph 3:5. But the Lord is there within the city, and he does no wrong. Day by day his justice is more evident, but no one heeds—the wicked know no shame.

Mal 3:5. "At that time my punishments will be quick and certain; I will move swiftly against wicked men who trick the innocent, against adulterers, and liars, against all those who cheat their hired hands, or oppress widows and orphans, or defraud strangers, and do not fear me," says the Lord of Hosts. [18]"Then you will see the difference between God's treatment of good men and bad, between those who serve him and those who don't."

Acts 17:31. For he has set a day for justly judging the world by the man he has appointed, and has pointed him out by bringing him back to life again.

Rom 1:32. They were fully aware of God's death penalty for these crimes, yet they went right ahead and did them anyway, and encouraged others to do them, too.

Rom 2:2. And we know that God, in justice, will punish anyone who does such things as these. [5]But no, you won't listen; and so you are saving up terrible punishment for yourselves because of your stubbornness in refusing to turn from your sin; for there is going to come a day of wrath when God will be the just Judge of all the world. [6]He will give each one whatever his deeds deserve. [7]He will give eternal life to those who patiently do the will of God, seeking for the unseen glory and honor and eternal life that he offers. [8]But he will terribly punish those who fight against the truth of God and walk in evil ways—God's anger will be poured out upon them. [9]There will be sorrow and suffering for Jews and Gentiles alike who keep on sinning. [10]But there will be glory and honor and peace from God for all who obey him, whether they are Jews or Gentiles. [11]For God treats everyone the same. [12-15]He will punish sin wherever it is found. He will punish the heathen when they sin, even though they never had God's written laws, for down in their hearts they know right from wrong. God's laws are written within them; their own conscience accuses them, or sometimes excuses them. And God will punish the Jews for sinning because they have his written laws but don't obey them. They know what is right but don't do it. After all, salvation is not given to those who know what to do, unless they do it. [16]The day will surely come when at God's command Jesus Christ will judge the secret lives of everyone, their inmost thoughts and motives; this is all part of God's great plan which I proclaim.

Rom 3:4. Of course not! Though everyone else in the world is a liar, God is not. Do you remember what the book of Psalms says about this? That God's words will always prove true and right, no matter who questions them. [5]"But," some say, "our breaking faith with God is good, our sins serve a good purpose, for people will notice how good God is when they see how bad we are. Is it fair, then, for him to punish us when our sins are helping him?" (That is the way some people talk.) [6]God forbid! Then what kind of God would he be, to overlook sin? How could he ever condemn anyone? [26]And now in these days also he can receive sinners in this same way, because Jesus took away their sins. But isn't this unfair for God to let criminals go free, and say that they are innocent? No, for he does it on the basis of their trust in Jesus who took away their sins.

Rom 9:14. Was God being unfair? Of course not.

Rom 11:22. Notice how God is both kind and severe. He is very hard on those who disobey, but very good to you if you continue to love and trust him. But if you don't, you too will be cut off.

Eph 6:8. Remember, the Lord will pay you for each good thing you do, whether you are slave or free. [9]And you slave owners must treat your slaves right, just as I have told them to treat you. Don't keep threatening them; remember, you yourselves are slaves to Christ; you have the same Master they do, and he has no favorites. Col 3:25; Acts 10:34.

2 Thess 1:4. We are happy to tell other churches about your patience and complete faith in God, in spite of all the crushing troubles and hardships you are going through. [5]This is only one example of the fair, just way God does things, for he is using your sufferings to make you ready for his kingdom, [6]while at the same time he is preparing judgment and punishment for those who are hurting you.

Heb 6:10. For God is not unfair. How can he forget your hard work for him or forget the way you used to show your love for him—and still do—by helping his children?

Heb 10:30. For we know him who said, "Justice belongs to me; I will repay them"; who also said, "The Lord himself will handle these cases." [31]It is a fearful thing to fall into the hands of the living God.

Heb 12:22. But you have come right up into Mount Zion, to the city of the living God, the heavenly Jerusalem, and to the gathering of countless happy angels; [23]and to the church, composed of all those registered in heaven; and to God who is Judge of all; and to the spirits of the redeemed in heaven, already made perfect. [29]For our God is a consuming fire. Deut 4:24.

1 Pet 1:17. And remember that your heavenly Father to whom you pray has no favorites when he judges. He will judge you with perfect justice for everything you do; so act in reverent fear of him from now on until you get to heaven.

2 Pet 2:9. So also the Lord can rescue you and me from the temptations that surround us, and continue to punish the ungodly until the day of final judgment comes.

1 Jn 1:9. But if we confess our sins to him, he can be depended on to forgive us and to cleanse us from every wrong. [And it is perfectly proper for God to do this for us because Christ died to wash away our sins.]

Jude 1:6. And I remind you of those angels who were once pure and holy, but turned to a life of sin. Now God has them chained up in prisons of darkness, waiting for the judgment day.

Rev 6:16. And cried to the mountains to crush them. "Fall on us," they pleaded, "and hide us from the face of the one sitting on the throne, and from the anger of the Lamb, [17]because the great day of their anger has come, and who can survive it?"

Rev 11:18. The nations were angry with you, but now it is your turn to be angry with them. It is time to judge the dead, and reward your servants—prophets and people alike, all who fear your Name, both great and small—and to destroy those who have caused destruction upon the earth.

Rev 15:3. And they were singing the song of Moses, the servant of God, and the song of the Lamb: "Great and marvelous are your doings, Lord God Almighty. Just and true are your ways, O King of Ages."

Rev 16:5. And I heard this angel of the waters declaring, "You are just in sending this judgment, O Holy One, who is and was, [6]for your saints and prophets have been martyred and their blood poured out upon the earth; and now, in turn, you have poured out the blood of those who murdered them; it is their just reward." [7]And I heard the angel of the altar say, "Yes, Lord God Almighty, your punishments are just and true."

Rev 18:8. Therefore the sorrows of death and mourning and famine shall overtake her in a single day, and she shall be utterly consumed by fire; for mighty is the Lord who judges her.

Rev 19:2. For his judgments are just and true. He has punished the Great Prostitute who corrupted the earth with her sin; and he has avenged the murder of his servants.

See *Jesus, Judge; Government, God in; God, Holiness of,* above; and *Righteousness of,* below; also *Judgments; Sin, Punishment of.*

KING. See *God, Sovereign,* below.

KNOWLEDGE OF. Gen 16:13. Thereafter Hagar spoke of Jehovah—for it was he who appeared to her—as "the God who looked upon me," for she thought, "I saw God and lived to tell it."

Ex 3:7. Then the Lord told him, "I have seen the deep sorrows of my people in Egypt, and have heard their pleas for freedom from their harsh taskmasters." *vs.* 3, 4, 9, 19, 20; Ex 6:1; 11:1; 14:3, 4.

Num 14:26, 27. Then the Lord added to Moses and to Aaron, "How long will these wicked people complain about me? For I have heard all that they have been saying."

Deut 2:7. The Lord your God has watched over you and blessed you every step of the way for all these forty years as you have wandered around in this great wilderness; and you have lacked nothing in all that time.

Deut 31:21. And great disasters come upon them, then this song will remind them of the reason for their woes. (For this song will live from generation to generation.) I know now, even before they enter the land, what these people are like.

1 Sam 2:3. Quit acting so proud and arrogant! The Lord knows what you have done, and he will judge your deeds. Gen 20:6.

1 Sam 16:7. But the Lord said to Samuel, "Don't judge by a man's face or height for this is not the one. I don't make decisions the way you do! Men judge by outward appearance, but I look at a man's thoughts and intentions."

2 Sam 7:20. What can I say? For you know what I am like!

1 Kgs 8:39. Hear them from heaven and forgive and answer all who have made an honest confession; for you know each heart. 2 Chron 6:30.

2 Kgs 19:27. I know everything about you. I know all your plans and where you are going next; and I also know the evil things you have said about me.

1 Chron 28:9. Solomon, my son, get to know the God of your fathers. Worship and serve him with a clean heart and a willing mind, for the Lord sees every heart and understands and knows every thought. If you seek him, you will find him; but if you forsake him, he will permanently throw you aside.

1 Chron 29:17. I know, my God, that you test men to see if they are good; for you enjoy good men. I have done all this with good motives, and I have watched your people offer their gifts willingly and joyously.

2 Chron 16:9. For the eyes of the Lord search back and forth across the whole earth, looking for people whose hearts are perfect toward him, so that he can show his great power in helping them. What a fool you have been! From now on you shall have wars. Zech 4:10.

Neh 9:10. You displayed great miracles against Pharaoh and his people, for you knew how brutally the Egyptians were treating them; you have a glorious reputation because of those never-to-be-forgotten deeds.

Job 11:11. For he knows perfectly all the faults and sins of mankind; he sees all sin without searching.

Job 12:13. But true wisdom and power are God's. He alone knows what we should do; he understands. [22]He floods the darkness with light, even the dark shadow of death. *v.* 16.

Job 22:13. But you reply, "That is why he can't see what I am doing! How can he judge through the thick darkness? [14]For thick clouds swirl about him so that he cannot see us. He is way up there, walking on the vault of heaven."

Job 23:10. But he knows every detail of what is happening to me; and when he has examined me, he will pronounce me completely innocent—as pure as solid gold!

Job 26:5, 6. The dead stand naked, trembling before God in the place where they go.

Job 28:12. But though men can do all these things, they don't know where to find wisdom and understanding. [23, 24]And God surely knows where it is to be found, for he looks throughout the whole earth, under all the heavens.

Job 31:4. He sees everything I do, and every step I take.

Job 34:21. For God carefully watches the goings on of all mankind; he sees them all. [22]No darkness is thick enough to hide evil men from his eyes. [25]He watches what they do and in a single night he overturns them, destroying them.

Job 36:4. I am telling the honest truth, for I am a man of well-rounded knowledge. [5]God is almighty and yet does not despise anyone! And he is perfect in his understanding.

Job 42:2. I know that you can do anything and that no one can stop you.

Ps 1:6. For the Lord watches over all the plans and paths of godly men, but the paths of the godless lead to doom.

Ps 7:9. End all wickedness, O Lord, and bless all who truly worship God; for you, the righteous God, look deep within the hearts of men and examine all their motives and their thoughts.

Ps 10:11. "God isn't watching," they say to themselves; "he'll never know!" Ps 94:6, 7.

Ps 11:4. But the Lord is still in his holy temple; he still rules from heaven. He closely watches everything that happens here on earth.

Ps 33:13–15. The Lord gazes down upon mankind from heaven where he lives. He has made their hearts and closely watches everything they do.

Ps 37:18. Day by day the Lord observes the good deeds done by godly men, and gives them eternal rewards.

Ps 38:9. Lord, you know how I long for my health once more. You hear my every sigh.

Ps 44:21. Would God not know it? Yes, he knows the secrets of every heart.

Ps 66:7. Because of his great power he rules forever. He watches every movement of the nations. O rebel lands, he will deflate your pride.

Ps 69:19. You know how they talk about me, and how they so shamefully dishonor me. You see them all and know what each has said.

Ps 73:11. "Does God realize what is going on?" they ask.

Ps 92:5. O Lord, what miracles you do! And how deep are your thoughts!

Ps 94:9. Is God deaf and blind—he who makes ears and eyes? [10]He punishes the nations—won't he also punish you? He knows everything—doesn't he also know what you are doing? [11]The Lord is fully aware of how limited and futile the thoughts of mankind are. 1 Cor 3:20.

Ps 103:14. For he knows we are but dust.

Ps 104:24. O Lord, what a variety you have made! And in wisdom you have made them all! The earth is full of your riches.

Ps 119:168. Yes, I have searched for them. You know this because everything I do is known to you.

Ps 121:3, 4. He will never let me stumble, slip or fall. For he is always watching, never sleeping.

Ps 139:1. O Lord, you have examined my heart and know everything about me. [2]You know when I sit or stand. When far away you know my every thought. [3]You chart the path ahead of me, and tell me where to stop and rest. Every moment, you know where I am. [4]You know what I am going to say before I even say it. [12]For even darkness cannot hide from God; to you the night shines as bright as day. Darkness and light are both alike to you. [14]Thank you for making me so wonderfully complex! It is amazing to think about. Your workmanship is marvelous—and how well I know it. [15]You were there while I was being formed in utter seclusion! [16]You saw me before I was born and scheduled each day of my life before I began to breathe. Every day was recorded in your Book! *vs.* 1–24.

Ps 142:3. For I am overwhelmed and desperate, and you alone know which way I ought to turn to miss the traps my enemies have set for me.

Ps 147:4. He counts the stars and calls them all by name. [5]How great he is! His power is absolute! His understanding is unlimited. Isa 40:26.

Prov 3:19. The Lord's wisdom founded the earth; his understanding established all the universe and space. [20]The deep fountains of the earth were broken open by his knowledge, and the skies poured down rain.

Prov 5:21. *For God is closely watching you,* and he weighs carefully everything you do.

Prov 15:3. The Lord is watching everywhere and keeps his eye on both the evil and the good. [11]The depths of hell are open to God's knowledge. How much more the hearts of all mankind!

Prov 16:2. We can always "prove" that we are right, but is the Lord convinced?

Prov 24:12. Don't try to disclaim responsibility by saying you didn't know about it. For God, who knows all hearts, knows yours, and he knows you knew! And he will reward everyone according to his deeds. Prov 21:2.

Isa 28:29. The Lord of Hosts is a wonderful teacher and gives the farmer wisdom.

Isa 29:15. Woe to those who try to hide their plans from God, who try to keep him in the dark concerning what they do! "God can't see us," they say to themselves. "He doesn't know what is going on!" [16]How stupid can they be! Isn't he, the Potter, greater than you, the jars he makes? Will you say to him, "He didn't make us"? Does a machine call its inventor dumb?

Isa 37:28. But I know you well—your comings and goings and all you do—and the way you have raged against me.

Isa 40:13. Who can advise the Spirit of the Lord or be his teacher or give him counsel? [14]Has he ever needed anyone's advice? Did he need instruction as to what is right and best? [27]O Jacob, O Israel, how can you say that the Lord doesn't see your troubles and isn't being fair? [28]Don't you yet understand? Don't you know by now that the everlasting God, the Creator of the farthest parts of the earth, never grows faint or weary? No one can fathom the depths of his understanding.

Isa 41:4. Who has done such mighty deeds, directing the affairs of generations of mankind as they march by? It is I, the Lord, the First and Last; I alone am he.

Isa 42:9. Everything I prophesied came true, and now I will prophesy again. I will tell you the future before it happens.

Isa 44:7. Who else can tell you what is going to happen in the days ahead? Let them tell you if they can, and prove their power. Let them do as I have done since ancient times.

Isa 45:4. And why have I named you for this work? For the sake of Jacob, my servant—Israel, my chosen. I called you by name when you didn't know me. *v.* 21.

Isa 46:10. Who can tell you what is going to happen. All I say will come to pass, for I do whatever I wish.

Isa 48:5. This is why I told you ahead of time what I was going to do, so that you could never say, "My idol did it; my carved image commanded it to happen!" [6]You have heard my predictions and seen them fulfilled, but you refuse to agree it is so. Now I will tell you new things I haven't mentioned before, secrets you haven't heard. *v.* 3.

Isa 66:18. I see full well what they are doing; I know what they are thinking, so I will gather together all nations and people against Jerusalem, where they shall see my glory.

Jer 5:3. O Lord, you will take naught but truth. You have tried to get them to be honest, for you have punished them, but they won't change! You have destroyed them but they refuse to turn from their sins. They are determined, with faces hard as rock, not to repent.

Jer 10:7. Who would not fear you, O King of nations? (And that title belongs to you alone!) Among all the wise men of the earth and in all the kingdoms of the world there isn't anyone like you.

Jer 11:20. O Lord of Hosts, you are just. See the hearts and motives of these men. Repay them for all that they have planned! I look to you for justice. Jer 20:12.

Jer 17:10. Only the Lord knows! He searches all hearts and examines deepest motives so he can give to each person his right reward, according to his deeds—how he has lived.

Jer 23:24. Can anyone hide from me? Am I not everywhere in all of heaven and earth?

Jer 32:19. You have all wisdom and do great and mighty miracles; for your eyes are open to all the ways of men, and you reward everyone according to his life and deeds.

Jer 51:15. God made the earth by his power and wisdom. He stretched out the heavens by his understanding. Jer 10:12.

Ezk 9:9. But he said to me, "The sins of the people of Israel and Judah are very great and all the land is full of murder and injustice, for they say, 'The Lord doesn't see it! He has gone away!' "

Ezk 11:5. Then the Spirit of the Lord came upon me and told me to say: "The Lord says to the people of Israel: Is that what you are saying? Yes, I know it is, for I know everything you think—every thought that comes into your minds."

Dan 2:20. Saying, "Blessed be the name of God forever and ever, for he alone has all wisdom and all power. [22]He reveals profound mysteries beyond man's understanding. He knows all hidden things, for he is light, and darkness is no obstacle to him. [28]But there is a God in heaven who reveals secrets, and he has told you in your dream what will happen in the future."

Amos 4:13. For you are dealing with the one who formed the mountains and made the winds, and knows your every thought; he turns the morning to darkness and crushes down the mountains underneath his feet: Jehovah, the Lord, the God of Hosts, is his name.

Amos 9:2. Though they dig down to Sheol, I will reach down and pull them up; though they climb into the heavens, I will bring them down. [3]Though they hide among the rocks at the top of Carmel, I will search them out and capture them. Though they hide at the bottom of the ocean, I will send the sea-serpent after them to bite and destroy them. [4]Though they volunteer for exile, I will command the sword to kill them there. I will see to it that they receive evil and not good.

Mt 6:4. And your Father who knows all secrets will reward you. [8]Remember, your Father knows exactly what you need even before you ask him! [18]So that no one will suspect you are hungry, except your Father who knows every secret. And he will reward you. [32]But your heavenly Father already knows perfectly well that you need them.

Mt 10:29. Not one sparrow (What do they cost? Two for a penny?) can fall to the ground without your Father knowing it. [30]And the very hairs of your head are all numbered.

Mt 24:36. But no one knows the date and hour when the end will be—not even the angels. No, nor even God's Son. Only the Father knows. Mk 13:32.

Lk 16:15. Then he said to them, "You wear a noble, pious expression in public, but God knows your evil hearts. Your pretense brings you honor from the people, but it is an abomination in the sight of God."

Acts 1:24, 25. Then they all prayed for the right man to be chosen. "O Lord," they said, "you know every heart; show us which of these men you have chosen as an apostle to replace Judas the traitor, who has gone on to his proper place."

Acts 2:23. But God, following his prearranged plan, let you use the Roman government to nail him to the cross and murder him.

Acts 15:8. God, who knows men's hearts, confirmed the fact that he accepts Gentiles by giving them the Holy Spirit, just as he gave him to us.
[18]This is what the Lord says, who reveals his plans made from the beginning.

Rom 8:27. And the Father who knows all hearts knows, of course, what the Spirit is saying as he pleads for us in harmony with God's own will.
[29]For from the very beginning God decided that those who came to him—and all along he knew who would—should become like his Son, so that his Son would be the First, with many brothers.

Rom 11:33. Oh, what a wonderful God we have! How great are his wisdom and knowledge and riches! How impossible it is for us to understand his decisions and his methods! [34]For who among us can know the mind of the Lord? Who knows enough to be his counselor and guide?

1 Cor 1:25. This so-called "foolish" plan of God is far wiser than the wisest plan of the wisest man, and God in his weakness—Christ dying on the cross—is far stronger than any man.

1 Cor 2:7. Our words are wise because they are from God, telling of God's wise plan to bring us into the glories of heaven. This plan was hidden in former times, though it was made for our benefit before the world began.

1 Cor 3:20. And again, in the book of Psalms, we are told that the Lord knows full well how the human mind reasons, and how foolish and futile it is.

1 Cor 8:3. But the person who truly loves God is the one who is open to God's knowledge.

Gal 4:9. And now that you have found God (or I should say, now that God has found you) how can it be that you want to go back again and become slaves once more to another poor, weak, useless religion of trying to get to heaven by obeying God's laws?

Eph 1:8. And he has showered down upon us the richness of his grace—for how well he understands us and knows what is best for us at all times.

Eph 3:10. And his reason? To show to all the rulers in heaven how perfectly wise he is when all of his family—Jews and Gentiles alike—are seen to be joined together in his church.

1 Thess 2:4. For we speak as messengers from God, trusted by him to tell the truth; we change his message not one bit to suit the taste of those who hear it; for we serve God alone, who examines our hearts' deepest thoughts.

1 Tim 1:17. Glory and honor to God forever and ever. He is the King of the ages, the unseen one who never dies; he alone is God, and full of wisdom. Amen. Rom 16:25–27; Jude 1:24, 25.

2 Tim 2:19. But God's truth stands firm like a great rock, and nothing can shake it. It is a foundation stone with these words written on it: "The Lord knows those who are really his," and "A person who calls himself a Christian should not be doing things that are wrong."

Heb 4:13. He knows about everyone, everywhere. Everything about us is bare and wide open to the all-seeing eyes of our living God; nothing can be hidden from him to whom we must explain all that we have done.

1 Pet 1:2. Dear friends, God the Father chose you long ago and knew you would become his children. And the Holy Spirit has been at work in your hearts, cleansing you with the blood of Jesus Christ and making you to please him. May God bless you richly and grant you increasing freedom from all anxiety and fear.

1 Jn 1:5. This is the message God has given us to pass on to you: that God is Light and in him is no darkness at all.

1 Jn 3:20. But if we have bad consciences and feel that we have done wrong, the Lord will surely feel it even more, for he knows everything we do.

See *God, Foreknowledge of,* above; *Wisdom of,* below.

LONG-SUFFERING OF. Gen 6:3. Then Jehovah said, "My Spirit must not forever be disgraced in man, wholly evil as he is. I will give him 120 years to mend his ways."

Gen 15:16. After four generations they will return here to this land; for the wickedness of the Amorite nations living here now will not be ready for punishment until then.

Ex 34:6. "I am Jehovah, the merciful and gracious God," he said, "slow to anger and rich in steadfast love and truth."

Num 14:17, 18. Oh, please, show the great power (of your patience) by forgiving our sins and showing us your steadfast love. Forgive us, even though you have said that you don't let sin go unpunished, and that you punish the father's fault in the children to the third and fourth generation.

Ps 86:15. But you are merciful and gentle, Lord, slow in getting angry, full of constant lovingkindness and of truth.

Ps 103:8. He is merciful and tender toward those who don't deserve it; he is slow to get angry and full of kindness and love. [9]He never bears a grudge, nor remains angry forever. [10]He has not punished us as we deserve for all our sins.

Isa 5:1. Now I will sing a song about his vineyard to the one I love. *My Beloved has a vineyard on a very fertile hill.* [2]*He plowed it and took out all the rocks and planted his vineyard with the choicest vines. He built a watchtower and cut a winepress in the rocks. Then he waited for the harvest, but the grapes that grew were wild and sour and not at all the sweet ones he expected.* [3]Now, men of Jerusalem and Judah, you have heard the case! You be the judges! [4]What more could I have done? Why did my vineyard give me wild grapes instead of sweet?

Isa 30:18. Yet the Lord still waits for you to come

to him, so he can show you his love; he will conquer you to bless you, just as he said. For the Lord is faithful to his promises. Blessed are all those who wait for him to help them.

Isa 48:9. Yet for my own sake and for the honor of my name I will hold back my anger and not wipe you out. [11]Yet for my own sake—yes, *for my own sake*—I will save you from my anger and not destroy you lest the heathen say their gods have conquered me. I will not let them have my glory.

Jer 7:13. And now, says the Lord, I will do the same thing here because of all this evil you have done. Again and again I spoke to you about it, rising up early and calling, but you refused to hear or answer. [23]But what I told them was: *Obey* me and I will be your God and you shall be my people; only do as I say and all shall be well! [24]But they wouldn't listen; they kept on doing whatever they wanted to, following their own stubborn, evil thoughts. They went backward instead of forward. [25]Ever since the day your fathers left Egypt until now, I have kept on sending them my prophets, day after day. Isa 42:14; Jer 11:7.

Jer 15:15. Then Jeremiah replied, "Lord, you know it is for your sake that I am suffering. They are persecuting me because I have proclaimed your word to them. Don't let them kill me! Rescue me from their clutches, and give them what they deserve!"

Ezk 20:17. Nevertheless, I spared them. I didn't finish them off in the wilderness.

Joel 2:13. Let your remorse tear at your hearts and not your garments. Return to the Lord your God, for he is gracious and merciful. He is not easily angered; he is full of kindness, and anxious not to punish you.

Hab 1:2. O Lord, how long must I call for help before you will listen? I shout to you in vain; there is no answer. "Help! Murder!" I cry, but no one comes to save. [3]Must I forever see this sin and sadness all around me? Wherever I look there is oppression and bribery and men who love to argue and to fight. [4]The law is not enforced and there is no justice given in the courts, for the wicked far outnumber the righteous, and bribes and trickery prevail.

Mt 21:33. "Now listen to this story: A certain landowner planted a vineyard with a hedge around it, and built a platform for the watchman, then leased the vineyard to some farmers on a sharecrop basis, and went away to live in another country. [34]At the time of the grape harvest he sent his agents to the farmers to collect his share. [35]But the farmers attacked his men, beat one, killed one and stoned another. [36]Then he sent a larger group of his men to collect for him, but the results were the same. [37]Finally the owner sent his son, thinking they would surely respect him. [38]But when these farmers saw the son coming they said among themselves, 'Here comes the heir to this estate; come on, let's kill him and get it for ourselves!' [39]So they dragged him out of the vineyard and killed him. [40]When the owner returns, what do you think he will do to those farmers?" [41]The Jewish leaders replied, "He will put the wicked men to a horrible death, and lease the vineyard to others who will pay him promptly." Mk 12:1–9; Lk 20:9–16.

Mt 23:37. O Jerusalem, Jerusalem, the city that kills the prophets, and stones all those God sends to her! How often I have wanted to gather your children together as a hen gathers her chicks beneath her wings, but you wouldn't let me. Lk 13:34.

Lk 13:6. Then he used this illustration: "A man planted a fig tree in his garden and came again and again to see if he could find any fruit on it, but he was always disappointed. [7]Finally he told his gardener to cut it down. 'I've waited three years and there hasn't been a single fig!' he said. 'Why bother with it any longer? It's taking up space we can use for something else.' [8]'Give it one more chance,' the gardener answered. 'Leave it another year, and I'll give it special attention and plenty of fertilizer. [9]If we get figs next year, fine; if not, I'll cut it down.' "

Acts 14:16. In bygone days he permitted the nations to go their own ways.

Acts 17:30. God tolerated man's past ignorance about these things, but now he commands everyone to put away idols and worship only him.

Rom 2:4. Don't you realize how patient he is being with you? Or don't you care? Can't you see that he has been waiting all this time without punishing you, to give you time to turn from your sin? His kindness is meant to lead you to repentance.

Rom 3:25. For God sent Christ Jesus to take the punishment for our sins and to end all God's anger against us. He used Christ's blood and our faith as the means of saving us from his wrath. In this way he was being entirely fair, even though he did not punish those who sinned in former times. For he was looking forward to the time when Christ would come and take away those sins.

Rom 9:22. Does not God have a perfect right to show his fury and power against those who are fit only for destruction, those he has been patient with for all this time? [23, 24]And he has a right to take others such as ourselves, who have been made for pouring the riches of his glory into, whether we are Jews or Gentiles, and to be kind to us so that everyone can see how very great his glory is.

Rom 15:5. May God who gives patience, steadiness, and encouragement help you to live in complete harmony with each other—each with the attitude of Christ toward the other.

1 Pet 3:20. Spirits of those who, long before in the days of Noah, had refused to listen to God, though he waited patiently for them while Noah was building the ark.

2 Pet 3:9. He isn't really being slow about his promised return, even though it sometimes seems that way. But he is waiting, for the good reason that he is not willing that any should perish, and he is giving more time for sinners to repent. [15]And remember why he is waiting. He is giving us time to get his message of salvation out to others.

Rev 2:21. I gave her time to change her mind and

attitude, but she refused. [22]Pay attention now to what I am saying: I will lay her upon a sickbed of intense affliction, along with all her immoral followers, unless they turn again to me, repenting of their sin with her.

See *God, Love of, Mercy of,* below.

LONG-SUFFERING OF, ABUSED. Neh 9:28. But when all was going well, your people turned to sin again, and once more you let their enemies conquer them. Yet whenever your people returned to you and cried to you for help, once more you listened from heaven, and in your wonderful mercy delivered them! [29]You punished them in order to turn them toward your laws; but even though they should have obeyed them, they were proud and wouldn't listen, and continued to sin. [30]You were patient with them for many years. You sent your prophets to warn them about their sins, but still they wouldn't listen. So once again you allowed the heathen nations to conquer them. [31]But in your great mercy you did not destroy them completely or abandon them forever. What a gracious and merciful God you are!

Prov 1:24. I have called you so often but still you won't come. I have pleaded, but all in vain. [25]For you have spurned my counsel and reproof. [26]Some day you'll be in trouble, and I'll laugh! Mock me, will you?—I'll mock you!

Prov 29:1. The man who is often reproved but refuses to accept criticism will suddenly be broken and never have another chance.

Eccl 8:11. Because God does not punish sinners instantly, people feel it is safe to do wrong.

Mt 24:48. But if you are evil and say to yourself, "My Lord won't be coming for a while," [49]and begin oppressing your fellow servants, partying and getting drunk, [50]your Lord will arrive unannounced and unexpected, [51]and severely whip you and send you off to the judgment of the hypocrites; there will be weeping and gnashing of teeth.

Lk 13:6. Then he used this illustration: "A man planted a fig tree in his garden and came again and again to see if he could find any fruit on it, but he was always disappointed. [7]Finally he told his gardener to cut it down. 'I've waited three years and there hasn't been a single fig!' he said. 'Why bother with it any longer? It's taking up space we can use for something else.' [8]'Give it one more chance,' the gardener answered. 'Leave it another year, and I'll give it special attention and plenty of fertilizer. [9]If we get figs next year, fine; if not, I'll cut it down.' "

LOVE OF. Deut 4:37. It was because he loved your ancestors and chose to bless their descendants that he personally brought you out from Egypt with a great display of power. Deut 9:29; 1 Kgs 8:51–53.

Deut 7:7. He didn't choose you and pour out his love upon you because you were a larger nation than any other, for you were the smallest of all! [8]It was just because he loves you, and because he kept his promise to your ancestors. That is why he brought you out of slavery in Egypt with such amazing power and mighty miracles. [13]And he will love you and bless you and make you into a great nation. He will make you fertile and give fertility to your ground and to your animals, so that you will have large crops of grain, grapes, and olives, and great flocks of cattle, sheep, and goats when you arrive in the land he promised your fathers to give you.

Deut 10:15. And yet he rejoiced in your fathers and loved them so much that he chose you, their children, to be above every other nation, as is evident today. [18]He gives justice to the fatherless and widows. He loves foreigners and gives them food and clothing.

Deut 23:5. But the Lord wouldn't listen to Balaam; instead, he turned the intended curse into a blessing for you, because the Lord loves you.

Deut 33:3. "How he loves his people—his holy ones are in his hands. They followed in your steps, O Lord. They have received their directions from you." [12]Concerning the tribe of Benjamin, Moses said: "He is beloved of God and lives in safety beside him. God surrounds him with his loving care, and preserves him from every harm."

2 Sam 12:24. Then David comforted Bath-sheba; and when he slept with her, she conceived and gave birth to a son and named him Solomon. And the Lord loved the baby. Neh 13:26.

Ps 42:8. Yet day by day the Lord also pours out his steadfast love upon me, and through the night I sing his songs and pray to God who gives me life.

Ps 47:4. And will personally select his choicest blessings for his Jewish people—the very best for those he loves.

Ps 63:3. For your love and kindness are better to me than life itself. How I praise you!

Ps 78:68. And chose the tribe of Judah—and Mount Zion which he [the Lord] loved. *vs.* 61, 62.

Ps 89:33. But I will never completely take away my loving-kindness from them, nor let my promise fail.

Ps 103:13. He is like a father to us, tender and sympathetic to those who reverence him.

Ps 146:8. And opens the eyes of the blind; he lifts the burdens from those bent down beneath their loads. For the Lord loves good men.

Prov 15:9. The Lord despises the deeds of the wicked, but loves those who try to be good.

Isa 38:17. Yes, now I see it all—it was good for me to undergo this bitterness, for you have lovingly delivered me from death; you have forgiven all my sins.

Isa 43:4. Others died that you might live; I traded their lives for yours because you are precious to me and honored, and I love you.

Jer 31:3. For long ago the Lord had said to Israel: I have loved you, O my people, with an everlasting love; with loving-kindness I have drawn you to me.

Hos 11:1. When Israel was a child I loved him as a son and brought him out of Egypt.

Mal 1:2. "I have loved you very deeply," says the Lord.

Jn 3:16. For God loved the world so much that he gave his only Son so that anyone who believes in him shall not perish but have eternal life.

Jn 5:20. For the Father loves the Son, and tells him everything he is doing; and the Son will do far more awesome miracles than this man's healing.

Jn 14:21. "The one who obeys me is the one who loves me; and because he loves me, my Father will love him; and I will too, and I will reveal myself to him." [23]Jesus replied, "Because I will only reveal myself to those who love me and obey me. The Father will love them too, and we will come to them and live with them."

Jn 16:27. For the Father himself loves you dearly because you love me and believe that I came from the Father.

Jn 17:10. And all of them, since they are mine, belong to you; and you have given them back to me with everything else of yours, and so *they are my glory!* [23]I in them and you in me, all being perfected into one—so that the world will know you sent me and will understand that you love them as much as you love me. [26]And I have revealed you to them, and will keep on revealing you so that the mighty love you have for me may be in them, and I in them.

Jn 20:17. "Don't touch me," he cautioned, "for I haven't yet ascended to the Father. But go find my brothers and tell them that I ascend to my Father and your Father, my God and your God."

Rom 1:6, 7. And you, dear friends in Rome, are among those he dearly loves; you, too, are invited by Jesus Christ to be God's very own—yes, his holy people. May all God's mercies and peace be yours from God our Father and from Jesus Christ our Lord.

Rom 5:8. But God showed his great love for us by sending Christ to die for us while we were still sinners.

Rom 11:28. Now many of the Jews are enemies of the Gospel. They hate it. But this has been a benefit to you, for it has resulted in God's giving his gifts to you Gentiles. Yet the Jews are still beloved of God because of his promises to Abraham, Issac, and Jacob.

2 Cor 13:11. I close my letter with these last words: Be happy. Grow in Christ. Pay attention to what I have said. Live in harmony and peace. And may the God of love and peace be with you.

Eph 2:4. But God is so rich in mercy; he loved us so much [5]that even though we were spiritually dead and doomed by our sins, he gave us back our lives again when he raised Christ from the dead—only by his undeserved favor have we ever been saved.

2 Thess 2:16. May our Lord Jesus Christ himself and God our Father, who has loved us and given us everlasting comfort and hope which we don't deserve.

Tit 3:4. But when the time came for the kindness and love of God our Savior to appear, [5]then he saved us—not because we were good enough to be saved, but because of his kindness and pity—by washing away our sins and giving us the new joy of the indwelling Holy Spirit.

Heb 12:6. For when he punishes you, it proves that he loves you. When he whips you it proves you are really his child.

1 Jn 3:1. See how very much our heavenly Father loves us, for he allows us to be called his children —think of it—and we really *are!* But since most people don't know God, naturally they don't understand that we are his children.

1 Jn 4:8. But if a person isn't loving and kind, it shows that he doesn't know God—for God is love. [9]God showed how much he loved us by sending his only Son into this wicked world to bring to us eternal life through his death. [10]In this act we see what real love is: it is not our love for God, but his love for us when he sent his Son to satisfy God's anger against our sins. [12]For though we have never yet seen God, when we love each other God lives in us and his love within us grows ever stronger. [13]And he has put his own Holy Spirit into our hearts as a proof to us that we are living with him and he with us. [15]Anyone who believes and says that Jesus is the Son of God has God living in him, and he is living with God. [16]We know how much God loves us because we have felt his love and because we believe him when he tells us that he loves us dearly. God is love, and anyone who lives in love is living with God and God is living in him. [19]So you see, our love for him comes as a result of his loving us first.

Jude 1:21. Stay always within the boundaries where God's love can reach and bless you. Wait patiently for the eternal life that our Lord Jesus Christ in his mercy is going to give you.

Rev 3:12. As for the one who conquers, I will make him a pillar in the temple of my God; he will be secure, and will go out no more; and I will write my God's Name on him, and he will be a citizen in the city of my God—the New Jerusalem, coming down from heaven from my God; and he will have my new Name inscribed upon him.

Rev 14:1. Then I saw a Lamb standing on Mount Zion in Jerusalem, and with him were 144,000 who had his Name and his Father's Name written on their foreheads.

LOVE OF, EXEMPLIFIED. Gen 17:7. And I will continue this agreement between us generation after generation, forever, for it shall be between me and your children as well. It is a contract that I shall be your God and the God of your posterity.

Ex 3:6. I am the God of your fathers—the God of Abraham, Isaac, and Jacob. Gen 46:3, 4.

Ex 6:7. And I will accept them as my people and be their God. And they shall know that I am Jehovah their God who has rescued them from the Egyptians. Ex 29:45, 46.

Ex 19:4. You have seen what I did to the Egyptians, and how I brought you to myself as though on eagle's wings. [5]Now if you will obey me and keep your part of my contract with you, you shall be my own little flock from among all the nations of the earth; for all the earth is mine. [6]And you shall be a kingdom of priests to God, a holy nation.

Lev 20:26. You shall be holy to me, for I the Lord am holy, and I have set you apart from all other peoples, to be mine. *v.* 24.

Lev 22:32, 33. You must not treat me as common and ordinary. Revere me and hallow me, for I, the Lord, made you holy to myself and rescued you from Egypt to be my own people! Lev 11:44, 45; 25:38; Num 15:41.

Lev 25:23. And remember, the land is mine, so that you may not sell it permanently. You are merely my tenants and sharecroppers! [42]For I brought you from the land of Egypt, and you are my servants; so you may not be sold as ordinary slaves. *v.* 55.

Lev 26:12. I will walk among you and be your God, and you shall be my people.

Deut 4:20. The Lord has rescued you from prison—Egypt—to be his special people, his own inheritance; this is what you are today. [34]Where else will you ever find another example of God's removing a nation from its slavery by sending terrible plagues, mighty miracles, war, and terror? Yet that is what the Lord your God did for you in Egypt, right before your very eyes. [37]It was because he loved your ancestors and chose to bless their descendants that he personally brought you out from Egypt with a great display of power. Ex 15: 13; Deut 9:29; 1 Kgs 8:51–53.

Deut 7:7. He didn't choose you and pour out his love upon you because you were a larger nation than any other, for you were the smallest of all! [8]It was just because he loves you, and because he kept his promise to your ancestors. That is why he brought you out of slavery in Egypt with such amazing power and mighty miracles. [13]And he will love you and bless you and make you into a great nation. He will make you fertile and give fertility to your ground and to your animals, so that you will have large crops of grain, grapes, and olives, and great flocks of cattle, sheep, and goats when you arrive in the land he promised your fathers to give you.

Deut 10:15. And yet he rejoiced in your fathers and loved them so much that he chose you, their children, to be above every other nation, as is evident today.

Deut 14:2. You belong exclusively to the Lord your God, and he has chosen you to be his own possession, more so than any other nation on the face of the earth. Deut 7:6.

Deut 23:5. But the Lord wouldn't listen to Balaam; instead, he turned the intended curse into a blessing for you, because the Lord loves you.

Deut 26:18. And the Lord has declared today that you are his very own people, just as he promised, and that you must obey all of his laws. [19]If you do, he will make you greater than any other nation, allowing you to receive praise, honor, and renown; but to attain this honor and renown you must be a holy people to the Lord your God, as he requires.

Deut 27:9. Then Moses and the Levite-priests addressed all Israel as follows: "O Israel, listen! Today you have become the people of the Lord your God."

Deut 28:9. He will change you into a holy people dedicated to himself; this he has promised to do if you will only obey him and walk in his ways. [10]All the nations in the world shall see that you belong to the Lord, and they will stand in awe. Deut 29:13.

Deut 32:9. But he appointed none for Israel; for Israel was God's own personal possession! [10]God protected them in the howling wilderness as though they were the apple of his eye. [11]He spreads his wings over them, even as an eagle overspreads her young. She carries them upon her wings—as does the Lord his people! [12]When the Lord alone was leading them, and they lived without foreign gods.

Deut 33:3. How he loves his people—his holy ones are in his hands. They followed in your steps, O Lord. They have received their directions from you. [12]Concerning the tribe of Benjamin, Moses said: "He is beloved of God and lives in safety beside him. God surrounds him with his loving care, and preserves him from every harm."

2 Sam 7:23. What other nation in all the earth has received such blessings as Israel, your people? For you have rescued your chosen nation in order to bring glory to your name. You have done great miracles to destroy Egypt and its gods. [24]You chose Israel to be your people forever, and you became our God.

2 Sam 12:24. Then David comforted Bath-sheba; and when he slept with her, she conceived and gave birth to a son and named him Solomon. And the Lord loved the baby. Neh 13:26.

Ps 4:3. Mark this well: The Lord has set apart the redeemed for himself. Therefore he will listen to me and answer when I call to him.

Ps 31:19. Oh, how great is your goodness to those who publicly declare that you will rescue them. For you have stored up great blessings for those who trust and reverence you. [21]Blessed is the Lord, for he has shown me that his never-failing love protects me like the walls of a fort!

Ps 42:8. Yet day by day the Lord also pours out his steadfast love upon me, and through the night I sing his songs and pray to God who gives me life.

Ps 47:4. And will personally select his choicest blessings for his Jewish people—the very best for those he loves.

Ps 48:9. Lord, here in your Temple we meditate upon your kindness and your love. [14]For this great God is our God forever and ever. He will be our guide until we die.

Ps 50:5. Gather together my own people who by their sacrifice upon my altar have promised to obey me. [7]O my people, listen! For I am your God. Listen! Here are my charges against you.

Ps 63:3. For your love and kindness are better to me than life itself. How I praise you!

Ps 73:1. How good God is to Israel—to those whose hearts are pure.

Ps 74:2. Remember that we are your people—

the ones you chose in ancient times from slavery and made the choicest of your possessions. You chose Jerusalem as your home on earth!

Ps 78:68. And [the Lord] chose the tribe of Judah—and Mount Zion which he loved. *vs.* 61, 62.

Ps 81:13. But oh, that my people would listen to me! Oh, that Israel would follow me, walking in my paths!

Ps 89:33. But I will never completely take away my lovingkindness from them, nor let my promise fail.

Ps 90:1. Lord, through all the generations you have been our home!

Ps 100:3. Try to realize what this means—the Lord is God! He made us—we are his people, the sheep of his pasture. Ps 79:13; 95:7.

Ps 103:4. He ransoms me from hell. He surrounds me with lovingkindness and tender mercies.

Ps 105:5, 6. Think of the mighty deeds he did for us, his chosen ones—descendants of God's servant Abraham, and of Jacob. Remember how he destroyed our enemies.

Ps 114:2. Then the lands of Judah and of Israel became God's new home and kingdom.

Ps 135:4. For the Lord has chosen Israel as his personal possession.

Ps 148:14. He has made his people strong, honoring his godly ones—the people of Israel, the people closest to him.

Prov 11:20. The Lord hates the stubborn but delights in those who are good.

Prov 15:9. The Lord despises the deeds of the wicked, but loves those who try to be good.

Isa 5:7. I have given you the story of God's people. They are the vineyard that I spoke about, Israel and Judah are his pleasant acreage!

Isa 41:8. But as for you, O Israel, you are mine, my chosen ones; for you are Abraham's family, and he was my friend. [9]I have called you back from the ends of the earth and said that you must serve but me alone, for I have chosen you and will not throw you away. [10]Fear not, for I am with you. Do not be dismayed. I am your God. I will strengthen you; I will help you; I will uphold you with my victorious right hand.

Isa 43:1. But now the Lord who created you, O Israel, says, Don't be afraid, for I have ransomed you; I have called you by name; you are mine. [2]When you go through deep waters and great trouble, I will be with you. When you go through rivers of difficulty, you will not drown! When you walk through the fire of oppression, you will not be burned up—the flames will not consume you. [3]For I am the Lord your God, your Savior, the Holy One of Israel. I gave Egypt and Ethiopia and Seba (to Cyrus) in exchange for your freedom, as your ransom. [4]Others died that you might live; I traded their lives for yours because you are precious to me and honored, and I love you. [7]All who claim me as their God will come, for I have made them for my glory; I created them.

Isa 44:1. Listen to me, O my servant Israel, O my chosen ones: [2]The Lord who made you, who will help you, says, O servant of mine, don't be afraid. O Jerusalem, my chosen ones, don't be afraid. [21]Pay attention, Israel, for you are my servant; I made you, and I will not forget to help you. [22]I've blotted out your sins; they are gone like morning mist at noon! Oh, return to me, for I have paid the price to set you free.

Isa 48:12. Listen to me, my people, my chosen ones! I alone am God. I am the First; I am the Last.

Isa 49:13. Sing for joy, O heavens; shout, O earth. Break forth with song, O mountains, for the Lord has comforted his people, and will have compassion upon them in their sorrow. [14]Yet they say, "My Lord deserted us; he has forgotten us." [15]Never! Can a mother forget her little child and not have love for her own son? Yet even if that should be, I will not forget you. [16]See, I have tattooed your name upon my palm and ever before me is a picture of Jerusalem's walls in ruins. [17]Soon your rebuilders shall come and chase away all those destroying you.

Isa 51:16. And I have put my words in your mouth and hidden you safe within my hand. I planted the stars in place and molded all the earth. I am the one who says to Israel, "You are mine."

Isa 54:5. For your Creator will be your "husband." The Lord of Hosts is his name; he is your Redeemer, the Holy One of Israel, the God of all the earth. [6]For the Lord has called you back from your grief—a young wife abandoned by her husband. [10]For the mountains may depart and the hills disappear, but my kindness shall not leave you. My promise of peace for you will never be broken, says the Lord who has mercy upon you.

Isa 62:4. Never again shall you be called "The God-forsaken Land" or the "Land that God Forgot." Your new name will be "The Land of God's Delight" and "The Bride," for the Lord delights in you and will claim you as his own. [5]Your children will care for you, O Jerusalem, with joy like that of a young man who marries a virgin; and God will rejoice over you as a bridegroom with his bride.

Isa 63:7. I will tell of the lovingkindnesses of God. I will praise him for all he has done; I will rejoice in his great goodness to Israel, which he has granted in accordance with his mercy and love. [8]He said, "They are my very own; surely they will not be false again." And he became their Savior. [9]In all their affliction he was afflicted, and he personally saved them. In his love and pity he redeemed them and lifted them up and carried them through all the years.

Isa 65:19. And I will rejoice in Jerusalem, and in my people; and the voice of weeping and crying shall not be heard there any more.

Isa 66:13. I will comfort you there as a little one is comforted by its mother.

Jer 3:14. O sinful children, come home, for I am your Master and I will bring you again to the land of Israel—one from here and two from there, wherever you are scattered. [15]And I will give you leaders after my own heart, who will guide you with wisdom and understanding.

Jer 10:16. But the God of Jacob is not like these foolish idols. He is the Creator of all, and Israel is his chosen nation. The Lord of Hosts is his name. Jer 51:19.

Jer 12:7. Then the Lord said: I have abandoned my people, my inheritance; I have surrendered my dearest ones to their enemies.

Jer 13:11. Even as a loincloth clings to a man's loins, so I made Judah and Israel to cling to me, says the Lord. They were my people, an honor to my name. But then they turned away.

Jer 15:16. Your words are what sustain me; they are food to my hungry soul. They bring joy to my sorrowing heart and delight me. How proud I am to bear your name, O Lord.

Jer 31:3. For long ago the Lord had said to Israel: I have loved you, O my people, with an everlasting love; with lovingkindness I have drawn you to me. [14]I will feast the priests with the abundance of offerings brought to them at the Temple; I will satisfy my people with my bounty, says the Lord.

Jer 32:41. I will rejoice to do them good and will replant them in this land, with great joy.

Ezk 16:8. Later, when I passed by and saw you again, you were old enough for marriage; and I wrapped my cloak around you to legally declare my marriage vow. I signed a covenant with you, and you became mine. *vs.* 1–14.

Ezk 34:31. You are my flock, the sheep of my pasture. You are my men and I am your God, so says the Lord.

Ezk 37:27. And I will make my home among them. Yes, I will be their God and they shall be my people.

Hos 2:19. And I will bind you to me forever with chains of righteousness and justice and love and mercy. [20]I will betroth you to me in faithfulness and love, and you will really know me then as you never have before. [23]At that time I will sow a crop of Israelites and raise them for myself! I will pity those who are "not pitied," and I will say to those who are "not my people," "Now you are my people"; and they will reply, "You are our God!" 1 Pet 2:10.

Hos 9:10. O Israel, how well I remember those first delightful days when I led you through the wilderness! How refreshing was your love! How satisfying, like the early figs of summer in their first season!

Hos 11:1. When Israel was a child I loved him as a son and brought him out of Egypt. [3]I trained him from infancy, I taught him to walk, I held him in my arms. But he doesn't know or even care that it was I who raised him. [4]As a man would lead his favorite ox, so I led Israel with my ropes of love. I loosened his muzzle so he could eat. I myself have stooped and fed him.

Zeph 3:17. "For the Lord your God has arrived to live among you. He is a mighty Savior. He will give you victory. He will rejoice over you in great gladness; he will love you and not accuse you." Is that a joyous choir I hear? No, it is the Lord himself exulting over you in happy song.

Hag 2:23. "But when that happens, I will take you, O Zerubbabel my servant, and honor you like a signet ring upon my finger; for I have specially chosen you," says the Lord of Hosts.

Zech 1:14. Then the angel said, "Shout out this message from the Lord of Hosts: Don't you think I care about what has happened to Judah and Jerusalem? I am as jealous as a husband for his captive wife."

Zech 2:8. The Lord of Glory has sent me against the nations that oppressed you, for he who harms you sticks his finger in Jehovah's eye!

Zech 8:8. I will bring them home again to live safely in Jerusalem, and they will be my people, and I will be their God, just and true and yet forgiving them their sins! Jer 30:22.

Zech 13:9. I will bring the third that remain through the fire and make them pure, as gold and silver are refined and purified by fire. They will call upon my name and I will hear them; I will say, "These are my people," and they will say, "The Lord is our God."

Mal 1:2, 3. "I have loved you very deeply," says the Lord. But you retort, "Really? When was this?" And the Lord replies, "I showed my love for you by loving your father, Jacob. I didn't need to. I even rejected his very own brother, Esau, and destroyed Esau's mountains and inheritance, to give it to the jackals of the desert."

Mal 3:16. Then those who feared and loved the Lord spoke often of him to each other. And he had a Book of Remembrance drawn up in which he recorded the names of those who feared him and loved to think about him. [17]"They shall be mine," says the Lord of Hosts, "in that day when I make up my jewels. And I will spare them as a man spares an obedient and dutiful son."

Mt 18:11. And I, the Messiah, came to save the lost. [12]If a man has a hundred sheep, and one wanders away and is lost, what will he do? Won't he leave the ninety-nine others and go out into the hills to search for the lost one? [13]And if he finds it, he will rejoice over it more than over the ninety-nine others safe at home! [14]Just so, it is not my Father's will that even one of these little ones should perish.

Lk 15:4. If you had a hundred sheep and one of them strayed away and was lost in the wilderness, wouldn't you leave the ninety-nine others to go and search for the lost one until you found it? [5]And then you would joyfully carry it home on your shoulders. [6]When you arrived you would call together your friends and neighbors to rejoice with you because your lost sheep was found. [7]Well, in the same way heaven will be happier over one lost sinner who returns to God than over ninety-nine others who haven't strayed away!

11. A man had two sons. [12]When the younger told his father, "I want my share of your estate now, instead of waiting until you die!" his father agreed to divide his wealth between his sons. [13]A few days later this younger son packed all his belongings

and took a trip to a distant land, and there wasted all his money on parties and prostitutes. [14]About the time his money was gone a great famine swept over the land, and he began to starve. [15]He persuaded a local farmer to hire him to feed his pigs. [16]The boy became so hungry that even the pods he was feeding the swine looked good to him. And no one gave him anything. [17]When he finally came to his senses, he said to himself, "At home even the hired men have food enough and to spare, and here I am, dying of hunger! [18]I will go home to my father and say, 'Father, I have sinned against both heaven and you, [19]and am no longer worthy of being called your son. Please take me on as a hired man.' " [20]So he returned home to his father. And while he was still a long distance away, his father saw him coming, and was filled with loving pity and ran and embraced him and kissed him. [21]His son said to him, "Father, I have sinned against heaven and you, and am not worthy of being called your son—" [22]But his father said to the slaves, "Quick! Bring the finest robe in the house and put it on him. And a jeweled ring for his finger; and shoes! [23]And kill the calf we have in the fattening pen. We must celebrate with a feast, [24]for this son of mine was dead and has returned to life. He was lost and is found." So the party began. [25]Meanwhile, the older son was in the fields working; when he returned home, he heard dance music coming from the house, [26]and he asked one of the servants what was going on. [27]"Your brother is back," he was told, "and your father has killed the calf we were fattening and has prepared a great feast to celebrate his coming home again unharmed."

Jn 14:21. "The one who obeys me is the one who loves me; and because he loves me, my Father will love him; and I will too, and I will reveal myself to him." [23]Jesus replied, "Because I will only reveal myself to those who love me and obey me. The Father will love them too, and we will come to them and live with them."

Jn 16:27. For the Father himself loves you dearly because you love me and believe that I came from the Father.

Jn 17:10. And all of them, since they are mine, belong to you; and you have given them back to me with everything else of yours, and so *they are my glory!* [23]I in them and you in me, all being perfected into one—so that the world will know you sent me and will understand that you love them as much as you love me. [26]And I have revealed you to them, and will keep on revealing you so that the mighty love you have for me may be in them, and I in them.

Rom 1:6, 7. And you, dear friends in Rome, are among those he dearly loves; you, too, are invited by Jesus Christ to be God's very own—yes, his holy people. May all God's mercies and peace be yours from God our Father and from Jesus Christ our Lord.

Rom 5:8. But God showed his great love for us by sending Christ to die for us while we were still sinners.

Rom 8:31. What can we ever say to such wonderful things as these? If God is on our side, who can ever be against us? [32]Since he did not spare even his own Son for us but gave him up for us all, won't he also surely give us everything else? [39]Or where we are—high above the sky, or in the deepest ocean —nothing will ever be able to separate us from the love of God demonstrated by our Lord Jesus Christ when he died for us.

Rom 11:28. Now many of the Jews are enemies of the Gospel. They hate it. But this has been a benefit to you, for it has resulted in God's giving his gifts to you Gentiles. Yet the Jews are still beloved of God because of his promises to Abraham, Isaac, and Jacob.

1 Cor 2:9. That is what is meant by the Scriptures which say that no mere man has ever seen, heard or even imagined what wonderful things God has ready for those who love the Lord. Isa 64:4.

1 Cor 3:9. We are only God's co-workers. You are *God's* garden, not ours; you are *God's* building, not ours.

1 Cor 6:19. Haven't you yet learned that your body is the home of the Holy Spirit God gave you, and that he lives within you? Your own body does not belong to you. [20]For God has bought you with a great price. So use every part of your body to give glory back to God, because he owns it. 1 Cor 7:23.

2 Cor 5:18. All these new things are from God who brought us back to himself through what Christ Jesus did. And God has given us the privilege of urging everyone to come into his favor and be reconciled to him. [19]For God was in Christ, restoring the world to himself, no longer counting men's sins against them but blotting them out. This is the wonderful message he has given us to tell others. [20]We are Christ's ambassadors. God is using us to speak to you: we beg you, as though Christ himself were here pleading with you, receive the love he offers you—be reconciled to God. [21]For God took the sinless Christ and poured into him our sins. Then, in exchange, he poured God's goodness into us!

2 Cor 6:16. And what union can there be between God's temple and idols? For you are God's temple, the home of the living God, and God has said of you, "I will live in them and walk among them, and I will be their God, and they shall be my people."

2 Cor 13:14. May the grace of our Lord Jesus Christ be with you all. May God's love and the Holy Spirit's friendship be yours.

Eph 1:3. How we praise God, the Father of our Lord Jesus Christ, who has blessed us with every blessing in heaven because we belong to Christ. [4]Long ago, even before he made the world, God chose us to be his very own, through what Christ would do for us; he decided then to make us holy in his eyes, without a single fault—we who stand before him covered with his love. [5]His unchanging plan has always been to adopt us into his own family by sending Jesus Christ to die for us. And he did this because he wanted to! [6]Now all praise to God for his wonderful kindness to us and his favor that he has poured out upon us, because we belong to his dearly loved Son.

Col 3:12. Since you have been chosen by God who has given you this new kind of life, and because of his deep love and concern for you, you should practice tenderhearted mercy and kindness to others. Don't worry about making a good impression on them but be ready to suffer quietly and patiently.

Heb 11:16. But they didn't want to. They were living for heaven. And now God is not ashamed to be called their God, for he has made a heavenly city for them.

Jas 1:18. And it was a happy day for him when he gave us our new lives, through the truth of his Word, and we became, as it were, the first children in his new family.

MERCY OF. Gen 8:21. And Jehovah was pleased with the sacrifice and said to himself, "I will never do it again—I will never again curse the earth, destroying all living things, even though men's bent is always toward evil from his earliest youth, and even though he does such wicked things."

Gen 18:26. And God replied, "If I find fifty godly people there, I will spare the entire city for their sake." *vs.* 27–32.

Gen 19:16. When Lot still hesitated, the angels seized his hand and the hands of his wife and two daughters and rushed them to safety, outside the city, for the Lord was merciful.

Ex 22:27. For it is probably his only warmth; how can he sleep without it? If you don't return it, and he cries to me for help, I will hear and be very gracious to him (at your expense), for I am very compassionate.

Ex 25:17. And make a lid of pure gold, 3 3/4 feet long and 2 1/4 feet wide. This is the place of mercy for your sins. Ps 80:1; Heb 4:16.

Ex 32:14. So the Lord changed his mind and spared them.

Ex 33:19. The Lord replied, "I will make my goodness pass before you, and I will announce to you the meaning of my name Jehovah, the Lord. I show kindness and mercy to anyone I want to."

Ex 34:6. "I am Jehovah, the merciful and gracious God," he said, "slow to anger and rich in
steadfast love and truth. [7]I, Jehovah, show this
steadfast love to many thousands by forgiving their sins; or else I refuse to clear the guilty, and require that a father's sins be punished in the sons and grandsons, and even later generations."

Lev 26:44. But despite all they have done, I will not utterly destroy them and my covenant with
them, for I am Jehovah their God. [45]For their sakes
I will remember my promises to their ancestors, to be their God. For I brought their forefathers out of Egypt as all the nations watched in wonder. I am Jehovah. *vs.* 40–43.

Num 14:17, 18. "Oh, please, show the great power (of your patience) by forgiving our sins and showing us your steadfast love. Forgive us, even though you have said that you don't let sin go unpunished, and that you punish the father's fault in the children to the third and fourth generation. [19]Oh, I
plead with you, pardon the sins of this people because of your magnificent, steadfast love, just as you have forgiven them all the time from when we
left Egypt until now." [20]Then the Lord said, "All
right, I will pardon them as you have requested."

Num 16:48. And he stood between the living and the dead, and the plague was stopped.

Num 21:8. Then the Lord told him, "Make a bronze replica of one of these snakes and attach it to the top of a pole; anyone who is bitten shall live if he simply looks at it!"

Deut 4:31. For the Lord your God is merciful—he will not abandon you nor destroy you nor forget the promises he has made to your ancestors.

Deut 5:10. But I will show kindness to a thousand generations of those who love me and keep
my commandments. [29]Oh, that they would always
have such a heart for me, wanting to obey my commandments. Then all would go well with them in the future, and with their children throughout all generations!

Deut 7:9. Understand, therefore, that the Lord your God is the faithful God who for a thousand generations keeps his promises and constantly loves those who love him and who obey his commands.

Deut 32:29. Oh, that they were wise! Oh, that they could understand! Oh, that they would know
what they are getting into! [36]The Lord will see his
people righted, and will have compassion on them when they slip. He will watch their power ebb away, both slave and free. Deut 30:1–3.

Judg 2:18. Each judge rescued the people of Israel from their enemies throughout his lifetime, for the Lord was moved to pity by the groaning of his people under their crushing oppressions; so he helped them as long as that judge lived. Ex 2:24, 25; Judg 3:9, 15.

Judg 10:16. Then they destroyed their foreign gods and worshiped only the Lord; and he was grieved by their misery.

2 Sam 12:13. "I have sinned against the Lord," David confessed to Nathan. Then Nathan replied, "Yes, but the Lord has forgiven you, and you won't die for this sin."

2 Sam 14:14. All of us must die eventually; our lives are like water that is poured out on the ground—it can't be gathered up again. But God will bless you with a longer life if you will find a way to bring your son back from his exile.

2 Sam 24:14. "This is a hard decision," David replied, "but it is better to fall into the hand of the Lord (for his mercy is great) than into the hands
of men." [16]But as the death angel was preparing to
destroy Jerusalem, the Lord was sorry for what was happening and told him to stop. He was by the threshing floor of Araunah the Jebusite at the time.

1 Kgs 8:23. O Lord God of Israel, there is no god like you in heaven or earth, for you are loving and kind and you keep your promises to your people if they do their best to do your will.

1 Kgs 11:39. But because of Solomon's sin I will punish the descendants of David—though not forever.

2 Kgs 13:23. But the Lord was gracious to the people of Israel, and they were not totally destroyed. For God pitied them, and also he was honoring his contract with Abraham, Isaac, and Jacob. And this is still true.

2 Kgs 14:26. For the Lord saw the bitter plight of Israel—she had no one to help her. [27]And he had not said that he would blot out the name of Israel, so he used King Jeroboam II to save her.

1 Chron 16:34. Oh, give thanks to the Lord, for he is good; his love and his kindness go on forever.

2 Chron 5:13, 14. The band and chorus united as one to praise and thank the Lord; their selections were interspersed with trumpet obbligatos, the clashing of cymbals, and the loud playing of other musical instruments—all praising and thanking the Lord. Their theme was "He is so good! His lovingkindness lasts forever!" And at that moment the glory of the Lord, coming as a bright cloud, filled the Temple so that the priests could not continue their work.

2 Chron 7:3. All the people had been watching and now they fell flat on the pavement, and worshiped and thanked the Lord. "How good he is!" they exclaimed. "He is always so loving and kind." [6]The priests were standing at their posts of duty, and the Levites were playing their thanksgiving song, "His Lovingkindness Is Forever," using the musical instruments that King David himself had made and had used to praise the Lord. Then, when the priests blew the trumpets, all the people stood again. [14]Then if my people will humble themselves and pray, and search for me, and turn from their wicked ways, I will hear them from heaven and forgive their sins and heal their land.

2 Chron 30:9. For if you turn to the Lord again, your brothers and your children will be treated mercifully by their captors, and they will be able to return to this land. For the Lord your God is full of kindness and mercy and will not continue to turn away his face from you if you return to him.

2 Chron 36:15. Jehovah the God of their fathers sent his prophets again and again to warn them, for he had compassion on his people and on his Temple. Jer 7:25.

Ezra 9:9. For we were slaves, but in your love and mercy you did not abandon us to slavery; instead you caused the kings of Persia to be favorable to us. They have even given us their assistance in rebuilding the Temple of our God and in giving us Jerusalem as a walled city in Judah. [13]And now, even after our punishment in exile because of our wickedness (and we have been punished far less than we deserved), and even though you have let some of us return. *vs.* 7–14; Job 11:6.

Neh 1:10. We are your servants, the people you rescued by your great power.

Neh 9:17. They refused to obey and didn't pay any attention to the miracles you did for them; instead, they rebelled and appointed a leader to take them back into slavery in Egypt! But you are a God of forgiveness, always ready to pardon, gracious and merciful, slow to become angry, and full of love and mercy; you didn't abandon them. [27]So you gave them to their enemies. But in their time of trouble they cried to you and you heard them from heaven, and in great mercy you sent them saviors who delivered them from their enemies. [28]But when all was going well, your people turned to sin again, and once more you let their enemies conquer them. Yet whenever your people returned to you and cried to you for help, once more you listened from heaven, and in your wonderful mercy delivered them! [29]You punished them in order to turn them toward your laws; but even though they should have obeyed them, they were proud and wouldn't listen, and continued to sin. [30]You were patient with them for many years. You sent your prophets to warn them about their sins, but still they wouldn't listen. So once again you allowed the heathen nations to conquer them. [31]But in your great mercy you did not destroy them completely or abandon them forever. What a gracious and merciful God you are! *vs.* 17–20; 2 Chron 24:19.

Job 23:2. My complaint today is still a bitter one, and my punishment far more severe than my fault deserves. [3]Oh, that I knew where to find God—that I could go to his throne and talk with him there. [4, 5]I would tell him all about my side of this argument, and listen to his reply, and understand what he wants. [6]Would he merely overpower me with his greatness? No, he would listen with sympathy.

Job 33:14. For God speaks again and again, [15]in dreams, in visions of the night when deep sleep falls on men as the lie on their beds. [16]He opens their ears in times like that, and gives them wisdom and instruction, [17, 18]causing them to change their minds, and keeping them from pride, and warning them of the penalties of sin, and keeping them from falling into some trap. [19]Or, God sends sickness and pain, even though no bone is broken, [20]so that a man loses all taste and appetite for food and doesn't care for even the daintiest dessert. [21]He becomes thin, mere skin and bones, [22]and draws near to death. [23, 24]But if a messenger from heaven is there to intercede for him as a friend, to show him what is right, then God pities him and says, "Set him free. Do not make him die, for I have found a substitute." [25]Then his body will become as healthy as a child's, firm and youthful again. [26]And when he prays to God, God will hear and answer and receive him with joy, and return him to his duties. [27]And he will declare to his friends, "I sinned, but God let me go. [28]He did not let me die. I will go on living in the realm of light." [29]Yes, God often does these things for man—[30]brings back his soul from the pit, so that he may live in the light of the living.

Ps 18:50. Many times you have miraculously rescued me, the king you appointed. You have been loving and kind to me and will be to my descendants.

Ps 25:6, 7. Overlook my youthful sins, O Lord!

Look at me instead through eyes of mercy and forgiveness, through eyes of everlasting love and kindness. [8]The Lord is good and glad to teach the proper path to all who go astray.

Ps 30:5. His anger lasts a moment; his favor lasts for life! Weeping may go on all night, but in the morning there is joy.

Ps 31:7. I am radiant with joy because of your mercy, for you have listened to my troubles and have seen the crisis in my soul.

Ps 32:1, 2. What happiness for those whose guilt has been forgiven! What joys when sins are covered over! What relief for those who have confessed their sins and God has cleared their record. [5]I said to myself, "I will confess them to the Lord." And you forgave me! All my guilt is gone.

Ps 50:21. I remained silent—you thought I didn't care—but now your time of punishment has come, and I list all the above charges against you.

Ps 57:10. Your kindness and love are as vast as the heavens. Your faithfulness is higher than the skies.

Ps 62:12. He is loving and kind and rewards each one of us according to the work we do for him.

Ps 65:3. Though sins fill our hearts, you forgive them all.

Ps 69:16. O Jehovah, answer my prayers, for your lovingkindness is wonderful; your mercy is so plentiful, so tender and so kind.

Ps 78:38. Yet he was merciful and forgave their sins and didn't destroy them all. Many and many a time he held back his anger. [39]For he remembered that they were merely mortal men, gone in a moment like a breath of wind. *vs.* 4–72; Ps 106:43–46.

Ps 85:2. And forgiven the sins of your people—yes, covered over each one, [3]so that all your wrath, your blazing anger, is now ended. [10]Mercy and truth have met together. Grim justice and peace have kissed!

Ps 86:5. O Lord, you are so good and kind, so ready to forgive; so full of mercy for all who ask your aid. [13]For you love me so much! You are constantly so kind! You have rescued me from deepest hell. [15]But you are merciful and gentle, Lord, slow in getting angry, full of constant lovingkindness and of truth.

Ps 89:2. Your love and kindness are forever; your truth is as enduring as the heavens. [14]Mercy and Truth walk before you as your attendants. [28]I will love him forever, and be kind to him always; my covenant with him will never end.

Ps 99:8. O Jehovah our God! You answered them and forgave their sins, yet punished them when they went wrong.

Ps 100:5. For the Lord is always good. He is always loving and kind, and his faithfulness goes on and on to each succeeding generation.

Ps 103:3. He forgives all my sins. He heals me. [8]He is merciful and tender toward those who don't deserve it; he is slow to get angry and full of kindness and love. [9]He never bears a grudge, nor remains angry forever. [10]He has not punished us as we deserve for all our sins, [11]for his mercy toward those who fear and honor him is as great as the height of the heavens above the earth. [12]He has removed our sins as far away from us as the east is from the west. [13]He is like a father to us, tender and sympathetic to those who reverence him. [14]For he knows we are but dust. [17, 18]But the lovingkindness of the Lord is from everlasting to everlasting, to those who reverence him; his salvation is to children's children of those who are faithful to his covenant and remember to obey him!

Ps 107:1. Say "Thank you" to the Lord for being so good, for always being so loving and kind.

Ps 108:4. For your lovingkindness is great beyond measure, high as the heavens. Your faithfulness reaches the skies.

Ps 111:4. Who can forget the wonders he performs—deeds of mercy and of grace?

Ps 116:5. How kind he is! How good he is! So merciful, this God of ours!

Ps 119:64. O Lord, the earth is full of your lovingkindness! Teach me your good paths. [156]Lord, how great is your mercy; oh, give me back my life again.

Ps 130:3, 4. Lord, if you keep in mind our sins then who can ever get an answer to his prayers? But you forgive! What an awesome thing this is! [7]O Israel, hope in the Lord; for he is loving and kind, and comes to us with armloads of salvation. [8]He himself shall ransom Israel from her slavery to sin.

Ps 135:14. For Jehovah will vindicate his people, and have compassion on his servants.

Ps 138:2. I face your Temple as I worship, giving thanks to you for all your lovingkindness and your faithfulness, for your promises are backed by all the honor of your name.

Ps 145:8. Jehovah is kind and merciful, slow to get angry, full of love. [9]He is good to everyone, and his compassion is intertwined with everything he does.

Ps 146:7. And gives justice to the poor and oppressed, and food to the hungry. He frees the prisoners, [8]and opens the eyes of the blind; he lifts the burdens from those bent down beneath their loads. For the Lord loves good men.

Prov 16:6. Iniquity is atoned for by mercy and truth; evil is avoided by reverence for God.

Prov 28:13. A man who refuses to admit his mistakes can never be successful. But if he confesses and forsakes them, he gets another chance.

Isa 1:5. Oh, my people, haven't you had enough of punishment? Why will you force me to whip you again and again? Must you forever rebel? [18]Come, let's talk this over! says the Lord; no matter how deep the stain of your sins, I can take it out and make you as clean as freshly fallen snow. Even if you are stained as red as crimson, I can make you white as wool!

Isa 6:7. He touched my lips with it and said, "Now you are pronounced 'Not guilty' because this coal has touched your lips. Your sins are all forgiven."

Isa 12:1. On that day you will say, "Praise the Lord! He was angry with me, but now he comforts me."

Isa 17:6. Oh, a very few of her people will be left, just as a few stray olives are left on the trees when the harvest is ended, two or three in the highest branches, four or five out on the tips of the limbs. That is how it will be in Damascus and Israel—stripped bare of people except for a few of the poor who remain. Isa 24:13.

Isa 54:9. Just as in the time of Noah I swore that I would never again permit the waters of a flood to cover the earth and destroy its life, so now I swear that I will never again pour out my anger on you as I have during this exile.

Isa 55:7. Let men cast off their wicked deeds; let them banish from their minds the very thought of doing wrong! Let them turn to the Lord that he may have mercy upon them, and to our God, for he will abundantly pardon! [8]This plan of mine is not what you would work out, neither are my thoughts the same as yours! [9]For just as the heavens are higher than the earth, so are my ways higher than yours, and my thoughts than yours.

Isa 57:11. Why were you more afraid of them than of me? How is it that you gave not even a second thought to me? Is it because I've been too gentle, that you have no fear of me? [15]The high and lofty one who inhabits eternity, the Holy One, says this: I live in that high and holy place where those with contrite, humble spirits dwell; and I refresh the humble and give new courage to those with repentant hearts. [16]For I will not fight against you forever, nor always show my wrath; if I did, all mankind would perish—the very souls that I have made. [18]I have seen what they do, but I will heal them anyway! I will lead them and comfort them, helping them to mourn and to confess their sins. [19]Peace, peace to them, both near and far, for I will heal them all.

Isa 60:10. Foreigners will come and build your cities. Presidents and kings will send you aid. For though I destroyed you in my anger, I will have mercy on you through my grace.

Isa 65:2. But my own people—though I have been spreading out my arms to welcome them all day long—have rebelled; they follow their own evil paths and thoughts. [8]But I will not destroy them all, says the Lord; for just as good grapes are found among a cluster of bad ones (and someone will say, "Don't throw them all away—there are some good grapes there!") so I will not destroy all Israel, for I have true servants there.

Jer 2:9. But I will not give you up—I will plead for you to return to me, and will keep on pleading; yes, even with your children's children in the years to come!

Jer 3:12. Therefore go and say to Israel, O Israel, my sinful people, come home to me again, for I am merciful; I will not be forever angry with you. [22]O my rebellious children, come back to me again and I will heal you from your sins. And they reply, Yes, we will come, for you are the Lord our God. *vs.* 1–22.

Jer 4:27. The Lord's decree of desolation covers all the land. "Yet," he says, "there will be a little remnant of my people left."

Jer 5:10. Go down the rows of the vineyards and destroy them! But leave a scattered few to live. Strip the branches from each vine, for they are not the Lord's.

Jer 9:24. Let them boast in this alone: That they truly know me, and understand that I am the Lord of justice and of righteousness whose love is steadfast; and that I love to be this way.

Jer 29:11. For I know the plans I have for you, says the Lord. They are plans for good and not for evil, to give you a future and a hope.

Jer 30:11. For I am with you and I will save you, says the Lord. Even if I utterly destroy the nations where I scatter you, I will not exterminate you; I will punish you, yes—you will not go unpunished. Jer 46:28.

Jer 31:20. And the Lord replies: Ephraim is still my son, my darling child. I had to punish him, but I still love him. I long for him and surely will have mercy on him. [34]At that time it will no longer be necessary to admonish one another to know the Lord. For everyone, both great and small, shall really know me then, says the Lord, and I will forgive and forget their sins. [37]Not until the heavens can be measured and the foundations of the earth explored, will I consider casting them away forever for their sins!

Jer 32:18. You are loving and kind to thousands, yet children suffer for their fathers' sins; you are the great and mighty God, the Lord of Hosts.

Jer 33:8. And I will cleanse away all their sins against me, and pardon them. [11]The people will sing: "Praise the Lord! For he is good and his mercy endures forever!" For I will make this land happier and more prosperous than it has ever been before.

Jer 36:3. Perhaps when the people of Judah see in writing all the terrible things I will do to them, they will repent. And then I can forgive them. *vs.* 6, 7.

Jer 50:20. In those days, says the Lord, no sin shall be found in Israel or in Judah, for I will pardon the remnant I preserve.

Jer 51:5. For the Lord of Hosts has not forsaken Israel and Judah. He is still their God, but the land of the Chaldeans is filled with sin against the Holy One of Israel.

Lam 3:22. *His compassion never ends.* It is only the Lord's mercies that have kept us from complete destruction. [23]Great is his faithfulness; his lovingkindness begins afresh each day. [31]For the Lord will not abandon him forever. [32]Although God gives him grief, yet he will show compassion too, according to the greatness of his lovingkindness. [33]For he does not enjoy afflicting men and causing sorrow.

Ezk 14:22. If there are survivors and they come here to join you as exiles in Babylon, you will see with your own eyes how wicked they are, and you will know it was right for me to destroy Jerusalem.

Ezk 16:6. But I came by and saw you there,

covered with your own blood, and I said, "Live! Thrive like a plant in the field!" [42]Then at last my fury against you will die away; my jealousy against you will end, and I will be quiet and not be angry with you anymore. [63]Despite all you have done, I will be kind to you again; you will cover your mouth in silence and in shame when I forgive you all that you have done, says the Lord God.

Ezk 18:23. Do you think I like to see the wicked die? asks the Lord. O course not! I only want him to turn from his wicked ways and live. [31]Put them behind you and receive a new heart and a new spirit. For why will you die, O Israel? [32]I do not enjoy seeing you die, the Lord God says. Turn, turn and live!

Ezk 20:17. Nevertheless, I spared them. I didn't finish them off in the wilderness. [42]Then, when I have brought you home to the land I promised your fathers, you will know I am the Lord. *vs.* 11–44.

Ezk 33:11. Tell them: As I live, says the Lord God, I have no pleasure in the death of the wicked; *I desire that the wicked turn from his evil ways and live.* Turn, turn from your wickedness, for why will you die, O Israel?

Ezk 36:25. Then it will be as though I had sprinkled clean water on you, for you will be clean—your filthiness will be washed away, your idol worship gone.

Dan 4:22. That tree, Your Majesty, is you. For you have grown strong and great; your greatness reaches up to heaven, and your rule to the ends of the earth. [23]Then you saw God's angel coming down from heaven and saying, "Cut down the tree and destroy it, but leave the stump and the roots in the earth surrounded by tender grass, banded with a chain of iron and brass. Let him be wet with the dew of heaven. For seven years let him eat grass with the animals of the field." [24]Your Majesty, the Most High God has decreed—and it will surely happen—[25]that your people will chase you from your palace, and you will live in the fields like an animal, eating grass like a cow, your back wet with dew from heaven. For seven years this will be your life, until you learn that the Most High God dominates the kingdoms of men, and gives power to anyone he chooses. [26]But the stump and the roots were left in the ground! This means that you will get your kingdom back again, when you have learned that heaven rules. [27]O King Nebuchadnezzar, listen to me—stop sinning; do what you know is right; be merciful to the poor. Perhaps even yet God will spare you.

Dan 9:4. "O Lord," I prayed, "you are a great and awesome God; you always fulfill your promises of mercy to those who love you and who keep your laws. [9]But the Lord our God is merciful, and pardons even those who have rebelled against him."

Hos 2:14. But I will court her again, and bring her into the wilderness, and speak to her tenderly there. [23]At that time I will sow a crop of Israelites and raise them for myself! I will pity those who are "not pitied," and I will say to those who are "not my people," "Now you are my people"; and they will reply, "You are our God!" *vs.* 14–23; Rom 9:15, 18; 1 Pet 2:10.

Hos 11:8. Oh, how can I give you up, my Ephraim? How can I let you go? How can I forsake you like Admah and Zeboiim? My heart cries out within me; how I long to help you! [9]No, I will not punish you as much as my fierce anger tells me to. This is the last time I will destroy Ephraim. For I am God and not man; I am the Holy One living among you, and I did not come to destroy.

Hos 14:4. Then I will cure you of idolatry and faithlessness, and my love will know no bounds, for my anger will be forever gone! *vs.* 1–8.

Joel 2:13. Let your remorse tear at your hearts and not your garments. Return to the Lord your God, for he is gracious and merciful. He is not easily angered; he is full of kindness, and anxious not to punish you. [18]Then the Lord will pity his people and be indignant for the honor of his land!

Amos 7:3. So the Lord relented, and did not fulfill the vision. "I won't do it," he told me.

Jon 4:2. He complained to the Lord about it: "This is exactly what I thought you'd do, Lord, when I was there in my own country and you first told me to come here. That's why I ran away to Tarshish. For I knew you were a gracious God, merciful, slow to get angry, and full of kindness; I knew how easily you could cancel your plans for destroying these people." [10]Then the Lord said, "You feel sorry for yourself when your shelter is destroyed, though you did no work to put it there, and it is, at best, short-lived. [11]And why shouldn't I feel sorry for a great city like Nineveh with its 120,000 people in utter spiritual darkness, and all its cattle?"

Mic 7:18. Where is another God like you, who pardons the sins of the survivors among his people? You cannot stay angry with your people, for you love to be merciful. [19]Once again you will have compassion on us. You will tread our sins beneath your feet; you will throw them into the depths of the ocean!

Zeph 2:7. There the little remnant of the tribe of Judah will be pastured. They will lie down to rest in the abandoned houses in Ashkelon. For the Lord God will visit his people in kindness and restore their prosperity again.

Zech 1:16. Therefore the Lord declares: I have returned to Jerusalem filled with mercy; my Temple will be rebuilt, says the Lord of Hosts, and so will all Jerusalem. [17]Say it again: The Lord of Hosts declares that the cities of Israel will again overflow with prosperity, and the Lord will again comfort Jerusalem and bless her and live in her.

Zech 3:9. He will be the Foundation Stone of the Temple that Joshua is standing beside, and I will engrave this inscription on it seven times: *I will remove the sins of this land in a single day.*

Zech 10:6. I will strengthen Judah, yes, and Israel too; I will reestablish them because I love them. It will be as though I had never cast them all away, for I, the Lord their God, will hear their cries.

Mal 3:6. For I am the Lord—I do not change. That is why you are not already utterly destroyed (for my mercy endures forever).

Mt 6:14. Your heavenly Father will forgive you if you forgive those who sin against you.

Mt 18:11. And I, the Messiah, came to save the lost. [12]If a man has a hundred sheep, and one wanders away and is lost, what will he do? Won't he leave the ninety-nine others and go out into the hills to search for the lost one? [13]And if he finds it, he will rejoice over it more than over the ninety-nine others safe at home! [14]Just so, it is not my Father's will that even one of these little ones should perish.

23. The Kingdom of Heaven can be compared to a king who decided to bring his accounts up to date. [24]In the process, one of his debtors was brought in who owed him $10,000,000! [25]He couldn't pay, so the king ordered him sold for the debt, also his wife and children and everything he had. [26]But the man fell down before the king, his face in the dust, and said, "Oh, sir, be patient with me and I will pay it all." [27]Then the king was filled with pity for him and released him and forgave his debt. Lk 15:3–7.

Lk 1:50. His mercy goes on from generation to generation, to all who reverence him. [77]You will tell his people how to find salvation through forgiveness of their sins. [78]All this will be because the mercy of our God is very tender, and heaven's dawn is about to break upon us.

Lk 6:36. Try to show as much compassion as your Father does.

Acts 3:19. Now change your mind and attitude to God and turn to him so he can cleanse away your sins and send you wonderful times of refreshment from the presence of the Lord.

Acts 17:30. God tolerated man's past ignorance about these things, but now he commands everyone to put away idols and worship only him.

Acts 26:18. To open their eyes to their true condition so that they may repent and live in the light of God instead of in Satan's darkness, so that they may receive forgiveness for their sins and God's inheritance along with all people everywhere whose sins are cleansed away, who are set apart by faith in me.

Rom 10:12. Jew and Gentile are the same in this respect: they all have the same Lord who generously gives his riches to all those who ask him for them. [13]Anyone who calls upon the name of the Lord will be saved.

Rom 11:32. For God has given them all up to sin so that he could have mercy upon all alike.

Rom 15:9. And remember that he came also that the Gentiles might be saved and give glory to God for his mercies to them. That is what the Psalmist meant when he wrote: "I will praise you among the Gentiles, and sing to your name."

1 Cor 15:10. But whatever I am now it is all because God poured out such kindness and grace upon me—and not without results: for I have worked harder than all the other apostles, yet actually I wasn't doing it, but God working in me, to bless me.

2 Cor 1:3. What a wonderful God we have—he is the Father of our Lord Jesus Christ, the source of every mercy, and the one who so wonderfully comforts and strengthens us in our hardships and trials.

2 Cor 4:15. These sufferings of ours are for your benefit. And the more of you who are won to Christ, the more there are to thank him for his great kindness, and the more the Lord is glorified.

2 Cor 12:9. Each time he said, "No. But I am with you; that is all you need. My power shows up best in weak people." Now I am glad to boast about how weak I am; I am glad to be a living demonstration of Christ's power, instead of showing off my own power and abilities.

Eph 1:6. Now all praise to God for his wonderful kindness to us and his favor that he has poured out upon us, because we belong to his dearly loved Son. [7]So overflowing is his kindness towards us that he took away all our sins through the blood of his Son, by whom we are saved; [8]and he has showered down upon us the richness of his grace—for how well he understands us and knows what is best for us at all times.

Eph 2:4. But God is so rich in mercy; he loved us so much [5]that even though we were spiritually dead and doomed by our sins, he gave us back our lives again when he raised Christ from the dead—only by his undeserved favor have we ever been saved—[6]and lifted us up from the grave into glory along with Christ, where we sit with him in the heavenly realms—all because of what Christ Jesus did. [7]And now God can always point to us as examples of how very, very rich his kindness is, as shown in all he has done for us through Jesus Christ.

1 Tim 1:13. Even though I used to scoff at the name of Christ. I hunted down his people, harming them in every way I could. But God had mercy on me because I didn't know what I was doing, for I didn't know Christ at that time.

Tit 3:5. Then he saved us—not because we were good enough to be saved, but because of his kindness and pity—by washing away our sins and giving us the new joy of the indwelling Holy Spirit.

Heb 4:16. So let us come boldly to the very throne of God and stay there to receive his mercy and to find grace to help us in our times of need.

Heb 8:12. But I will be merciful to them in their wrongdoings, and I will remember their sins no more.

Jas 2:13. For there will be no mercy to those who have shown no mercy. But if you have been merciful, then God's mercy toward you will win out over his judgment against you.

Jas 4:8. And when you draw close to God, God will draw close to you. Wash your hands, you sinners, and let your hearts be filled with God alone to make them pure and true to him.

Jas 5:11. We know how happy they are now because they stayed true to him then, even though they suffered greatly for it. Job is an example of a man who continued to trust the Lord in sorrow; from his experiences we can see how the Lord's plan finally ended in good, for he is full of tenderness and mercy. [15]And their prayer, if offered in faith, will heal him, for the Lord will make him well; and if his sickness was caused by some sin, the Lord will forgive him.

1 Pet 1:3. All honor to God, the God and Father of our Lord Jesus Christ; for it is his boundless mercy that has given us the privilege of being born again, so that we are now members of God's own family. Now we live in the hope of eternal life because Christ rose again from the dead.

1 Pet 5:10. After you have suffered a little while, our God, who is full of kindness through Christ, will give you his eternal glory. He personally will come and pick you up, and set you firmly in place, and make you stronger than ever.

2 Pet 3:9. He isn't really being slow about his promised return, even though it sometimes seems that way. But he is waiting, for the good reason that he is not willing that any should perish, and he is giving more time for sinners to repent. [15]And remember why he is waiting. He is giving us time to get his message of salvation out to others.

1 Jn 1:9. But if we confess our sins to him, he can be depended on to forgive us and to cleanse us from every wrong. (And it is perfectly proper for God to do this for us because Christ died to wash away our sins.)

Rev 2:21. I gave her time to change her mind and attitude, but she refused.

See *God, Long-suffering of, Love of,* above.

OMNIPOTENT. Gen 17:1. When Abram was ninety-nine years old, God appeared to him and told him, "I am the Almighty; obey me and live as you should."

Gen 18:14. Is anything too hard for God? Next year, just as I told you, I will certainly see to it that Sarah has a son.

Job 42:2. I know that you can do anything and that no one can stop you.

Isa 26:4. Trust in the Lord God always, for in the Lord Jehovah is your everlasting strength.

Mt 19:26. Jesus looked at them intently and said, "Humanly speaking, no one. But with God, everything is possible."

Lk 1:37. For every promise from God shall surely come true.

Acts 26:8. But is it a crime to believe in the resurrection of the dead? Does it seem incredible to you that God can bring men back to life again?

Rev 19:6. Then I heard again what sounded like the shouting of a huge crowd, or like the waves of a hundred oceans crashing on the shore, or like the mighty rolling of great thunder, "Praise the Lord. For the Lord our God, the Almighty, reigns."

Rev 21:22. No temple could be seen in the city, for the Lord God Almighty and the Lamb are worshiped in it everywhere.

For uses of the term Almighty consult Concordances.

See *God, Creator,* above; *Power of, Preserver,* below.

OMNIPRESENT. Gen 28:16. Then Jacob woke up. "God lives here!" he exclaimed in terror.

1 Kgs 8:27. But is it possible that God would really live on earth? Why, even the skies and the highest heavens cannot contain you, much less this Temple I have built! 2 Chron 2:6, Acts 7:48, 49.

Ps 139:3. You chart the path ahead of me, and tell where to stop and rest. Every moment, you know where I am. [5]You both precede and follow me, and place your hand of blessing on my head. [7]I can *never* be lost to your Spirit! I can *never* get away from my God! [8]If I go up to heaven, you are there; if I go down to the place of the dead, you are there. [9]If I ride the morning winds to the farthest oceans, [10]even there your hand will guide me, your strength will support me.

Jer 23:23. Am I a God who is only in one place and cannot see what they are doing? [24]Can anyone hide from me? Am I not everywhere in all of heaven and earth?

Acts 17:24. He made the world and everything in it, and since he is the Lord of heaven and earth, he doesn't live in man-made temples. [27]His purpose in all of this is that they should seek after God, and perhaps feel their way toward him and find him—though he is not far from any one of us. [28]For in him we live and move and are! As one of your own poets says it, "We are the sons of God."

See *God, Presence of, Ubiquitous,* below.

OMNISCIENT. See *God, Knowledge of,* above; *Wisdom of,* below.

PERFECTION OF. Deut 32:4. He is the Rock. His work is perfect. Everything he does is just and fair. He is faithful, without sin.

2 Sam 22:31. As for God, his way is perfect; the word of the Lord is true. He shields all who hide behind him.

Ps 18:30. What a God he is! How perfect in every way!

Mt 5:48. But you are to be perfect, even as your Father in heaven is perfect.

Jas 1:17. But whatever is good and perfect comes to us from God, the Creator of all light, and he shines forever without change or shadow.

See *God, Holiness of; Judge, and his Justice; Knowledge of,* above; *Wisdom of,* below.

PERSONALITY OF. Ex 8:10. "Do it tomorrow," Pharaoh said. "All right," Moses replied, "it shall be as you have said; then you will know that there is no one like the Lord our God." Ex 3:14.

Ex 15:11. Who else is like the Lord among the gods? Who is glorious in holiness like him? Who is so awesome in splendor, a wonder-working God?

Ex 20:3. You may worship no other god than me. Deut 5:7.

Ex 34:14. For you must worship no other gods, but only Jehovah, for he is a God who claims absolute loyalty and exclusive devotion.

Deut 4:35. He did these things so you would

realize that Jehovah is God, and that there is no one else like him. [39]This is your wonderful thought for the day: Jehovah is God both in heaven and down here upon the earth; and there is no God other than him!

Deut 6:4. O Israel, listen: Jehovah is our God, Jehovah alone.

Deut 10:17. Jehovah your God is God of gods and Lord of lords. He is the great and mighty God, the God of terror who shows no partiality and takes no bribes.

Deut 32:12. When the Lord alone was leading them, and they lived without foreign gods. [39]Don't you see that I alone am God? I kill and make live. I wound and heal—no one delivers from my power.

Josh 22:22. We swear by Jehovah, the God of gods, that we have not built the altar in rebellion against the Lord.

1 Sam 2:2. No one is as holy as the Lord! There is no other God, nor any Rock like our God.

1 Sam 7:3. At that time Samuel said to them, "If you are really serious about wanting to return to the Lord, get rid of your foreign gods and your Ashtaroth idols. Determine to obey only the Lord; then he will rescue you from the Philistines."

2 Sam 7:22. How great you are, Lord God! We have never heard of any other god like you. And there is no other god.

2 Sam 22:32. Our Lord alone is God; we have no other Savior. Ps 18:31.

1 Kgs 8:23. O Lord God of Israel, there is no god like you in heaven or earth, for you are loving and kind and you keep your promises to your people if they do their best to do your will. [60]May people all over the earth know that the Lord is God, and that there is no other god at all. 2 Chron 6:14.

2 Kgs 17:36. They were to worship only the Lord who had brought them out of the land of Egypt with such tremendous miracles and power.

2 Kgs 19:15. Then he prayed this prayer: "O Lord God of Israel, sitting on your throne high above the angels, you alone are the God of all the kingdoms of the earth. You created the heavens and the earth." Isa 37:16, 17; Ps 86:10.

Ezra 1:3. All Jews throughout the kingdom may now return to Jerusalem to rebuild this Temple of Jehovah, who is the God of Israel and of Jerusalem. May his blessings rest upon you.

Neh 9:6. Then Ezra prayed, "You alone are God. You have made the skies and the heavens, the earth and the seas, and everything in them. You preserve it all; and all the angels of heaven worship you."

Ps 96:5. For the gods of other nations are merely idols, but our God made the heavens!

Isa 40:25. "With whom will you compare me? Who is my equal?" asks the Holy One.

Isa 42:8. I am the Lord! That is my name, and I will not give my glory to anyone else; I will not share my praise with carved idols.

Isa 43:10. But I have witnesses, O Israel, says the Lord! You are my witnesses and my servants, chosen to know and to believe me and to understand that I alone am God. There is no other God; there never was and never will be. [11]I am the Lord, and there is no other Savior.

Isa 44:6. The Lord, the King of Israel, says—yes, it is Israel's Redeemer, the Lord of Hosts, who says it—I am the First and Last; there is no other God. [8]Don't, don't be afraid. Haven't I proclaimed from ages past (that I would save you)? You are my witnesses—is there any other God? No! None that I know about! There is no other Rock!

Isa 45:5. I am Jehovah; there is no other God. I will strengthen you and send you out to victory even though you don't know me, [6]and all the world from east to west will know there is no other God. I am Jehovah and there is no one else. I alone am God. [21]Consult together, argue your case and state your proofs that idol-worship pays! Who but God has said that these things concerning Cyrus would come true? What idol ever told you they would happen? For there is no other God but me—a just God and a Savior—no, not one! *v.* 18.

Isa 46:5. With what in all of heaven and earth do I compare? Whom can you find who equals me? [9]And don't forget the many times I clearly told you what was going to happen in the future. For I am God—I only—and there is no other like me. Isa 45: 22.

Jer 10:6. O Lord, there is no other god like you. For you are great and your name is full of power. [7]Who would not fear you, O King of nations? (And that title belongs to you alone!) Among all the wise men of the earth and in all the kingdoms of the world there isn't anyone like you. [10]But the Lord is the only true God, the living God, the everlasting King. The whole earth shall tremble at his anger; the world shall hide before his displeasure.

Jer 14:22. What heathen god can give us rain? Who but you alone, O Lord our God, can do such things as this? Therefore we will wait for you to help us.

Jer 32:27. I am the Lord, the God of all mankind; is there anything too hard for me?

Hos 13:4. I alone am God, your Lord, and have been ever since I brought you out from Egypt. You have no God but me, for there is no other Savior.

Mal 2:10. We are children of the same father, Abraham, all created by the same God.

Mt 4:10. "Get out of here, Satan," Jesus told him. "The Scriptures say, 'Worship only the Lord God. Obey only him.'"

Mt 23:9. And don't address anyone here on earth as "Father," for only God in heaven should be addressed like that.

Mk 12:32. The teacher of religion replied, "Sir, you have spoken a true word in saying that there is only one God and no other."

Jn 14:9. Jesus replied, "Don't you even yet know who I am, Philip, even after all this time I have been with you? Anyone who has seen me has seen the Father! So why are you asking to see him?"

Jn 17:3. And this is the way to have eternal life—by knowing you, the only true God, and Jesus

Christ, the one you sent to earth!

Rom 1:25. Instead of believing what they knew was the truth about God, they deliberately chose to believe lies. So they prayed to the things God made, but wouldn't obey the blessed God who made these things.

1 Cor 8:4. So now, what about it? Should we eat meat that has been sacrificed to idols? Well, we all know that an idol is not really a god, and that there is only one God, and no other. [5]According to some people, there are a great many gods, both in heaven and on earth. [6]But we know that there is only one God, the Father, who created all things and made us to be his own; and one Lord Jesus Christ, who made everything and gives us life.

2 Cor 4:4. Satan, who is the god of this evil world, has made him blind, unable to see the glorious light of the Gospel that is shining upon him, or to understand the amazing message we preach about the glory of Christ, who is God.

Gal 3:20. But when God gave his promise to Abraham, he did it by himself alone, without angels or Moses as go betweens.

Eph 4:6. And we all have the same God and Father who is over us all and in us all, and living through every part of us.

Col 1:15. Christ is the exact likeness of the unseen God. He existed before God made anything at all.

1 Thess 1:9. For *they* keep telling *us* about the wonderful welcome you gave us, and how you turned away from your idols to God so that now the living and true God only is your Master.

1 Tim 2:5. *That God is on one side and all the people on the other side, and Christ Jesus, himself man, is between them to bring them together.*

Heb 1:3. God's Son shines out with God's glory, and all that God's Son is and does marks him as God. He regulates the universe by the mighty power of his command. He is the one who died to cleanse us and clear our record of all sin, and then sat down in highest honor beside the great God of heaven.

See *God, Unity of,* below.

POWER OF. Ex 15:3. The Lord is a warrior—yes, Jehovah is his name. [6]Your right hand, O Lord, is glorious in power; it dashes the enemy to pieces. [7]In greatness of your majesty you overthrew all those who rose against you. You sent forth your anger, and it consumed them as fire consumes straw. [11]Who else is like the Lord among the gods? Who is glorious in holiness like him? Who is so awesome in splendor, a wonder-working God? [12]You reached out your hand and the earth swallowed them. *vs.* 8, 10.

Num 11:23. Then the Lord said to Moses, "When did I become weak? Now you shall see whether my word comes true or not!" Deut 11:2.

Num 23:20. Look! I have received a command to bless them, for God has blessed them, and I cannot reverse it!

Deut 3:23–25. At that time I made this plea to God: "O Lord God, please let me cross over into the Promised Land—the good land beyond the Jordan River with its rolling hills—and Lebanon. I want to see the result of all the greatness and power you have been showing us; for what God in all of heaven or earth can do what you have done for us?"

Deut 7:21. No, do not be afraid of those nations, for the Lord your God is among you, and he is a great and awesome God.

Deut 32:39. Don't you see that I alone am God? I kill and make live. I wound and heal—no one delivers from my power. Job 10:4–7.

Deut 33:26. There is none like the God of Jerusalem—he descends from the heavens in majestic splendor to help you. [27]The eternal God is your Refuge, and underneath are the everlasting arms. He thrusts out your enemies before you; it is he who cries, "Destroy them!"

Josh 4:24. He did this so that all the nations of the earth will realize that Jehovah is the mighty God, and so that all of you will worship him forever.

1 Sam 2:6. The Lord kills, the Lord gives life. [7]Some he causes to be poor and others to be rich. He cuts one down and lifts another up. [10]Those who fight against the Lord shall be broken; he thunders against them from heaven. He judges throughout the earth. And gives mighty strength to his King, and gives great glory to his anointed one. *v.* 8.

1 Sam 14:6. "Yes, let's go across to those heathen," Jonathan had said to his bodyguard. "Perhaps the Lord will do a miracle for us. For it makes no difference to him how many enemy troops there are!"

2 Sam 22:13. The earth was radiant with his brightness. [16]By the blast of his breath was the sea split in two. The bottom of the sea appeared. Ps 18.

1 Chron 29:11. Yours is the mighty power and glory and victory and majesty. Everything in the heavens and earth is yours, O Lord, and this is your kingdom. We adore you as being in control of everything. [12]Riches and honor come from you alone, and you are the Ruler of all mankind; your hand controls power and might, and it is at your discretion that men are made great and given strength.

2 Chron 14:11. "O Lord," he cried out to God, "no one else can help us! Here we are, powerless against this mighty army. Oh, help us, Lord our God! For we trust in you alone to rescue us, and in your name we attack this vast horde. Don't let mere men defeat you!"

2 Chron 16:9. For the eyes of the Lord search back and forth across the whole earth, looking for people whose hearts are perfect toward him, so that he can show his great power in helping them. What a fool you have been! From now on you shall have wars.

2 Chron 20:6. O Lord God of our fathers—the only God in all the heavens, the Ruler of all the kingdoms of the earth—you are so powerful, so mighty. Who can stand against you?

2 Chron 25:8. "If you let them go with your

troops to battle, you will be defeated no matter how well you fight; for God has power to help or to frustrate." [9]"But the money!" Amaziah whined. "What shall I do about that?" And the prophet replied, "The Lord is able to give you much more than this!"

Ezra 8:22. For I was ashamed to ask the king for soldiers and cavalry to accompany us and protect us from the enemies along the way. After all, we had told the king that our God would protect all those who worshiped him, and that disaster could come only to those who had forsaken him!

Neh 1:10. We are your servants, the people you rescued by your great power.

Job 9:4. For God is so wise and so mighty. Who has ever opposed him successfully? [5]Suddenly he moves the mountains, overturning them in his anger. [6]He shakes the earth to its foundations. [7]The sun won't rise, the stars won't shine, if he commands it so! [10]He does incredible miracles, too many to count. [12]When he sends death to snatch a man away, who can stop him? Who dares to ask him, "What are you doing?" [13]And God does not abate his anger. The pride of man collapses before him. [19]He alone is strong and just. Job 5:9.

Job 11:10. If he rushes in and makes an arrest, and calls the court to order, who is going to stop him?

Job 12:14. And how great is his might! What he destroys can't be rebuilt. When he closes in on a man, there is no escape. [16]Yes, with him is strength and wisdom. Deceivers and deceived are both his slaves. *v.* 15.

Job 14:20. Always you are against him, and then he passes off the scene. You make him old and wrinkled, then send him away.

Job 23:13. Nevertheless, his mind concerning me remains unchanged, and who can turn him from his purposes? Whatever he wants to do, he does. [14]So he will do to me all he has planned, and there is more ahead.

Job 26:11. The pillars of heaven tremble at his rebuke. [14]These are some of the minor things he does, merely a whisper of his power. Who then can withstand his thunder? *v.* 12.

Job 34:14. If God were to withdraw his Spirit, [15]all life would disappear and mankind would turn again to dust.

Job 36:5. God is almighty and yet does not despise anyone! And he is perfect in his understanding. [22]Look, God is all-powerful. Who is a teacher like him? *vs.* 27–33.

Job 37:23. We cannot imagine the power of the Almighty, and yet he is so just and merciful that he does not destroy us. *vs.* 1–22.

Job 38:8. Who decreed the boundaries of the seas when they gushed from the depths? [11]And said, "Thus far and no farther shall you come, and here shall your proud waves stop!"? *v.* 37, 38.

Job 40:9. Are you as strong as God, and can you shout as loudly as he?

Job 41:10. No one dares to stir *him* up, let alone try to conquer him. And if no one can stand before *him,* who can stand before *me?* [11]I owe no one anything. Everything under the heaven is mine.

Job 42:2. I know that you can do anything and that no one can stop you.

Ps 21:13. Accept our praise, O Lord, for all your glorious power. We will write songs to celebrate your mighty acts!

Ps 29:3. The voice of the Lord echoes from the clouds. The God of glory thunders through the skies. [4]So powerful is his voice; so full of majesty. *vs.* 5–9.

Ps 33:9. For when he but spoke, the world began! It appeared at his command!

Ps 46:6. The nations rant and rave in anger—but when God speaks, the earth melts in submission and kingdoms totter into ruin.

Ps 65:6. He formed the mountains by his mighty strength. [7]He quiets the raging oceans and all the world's clamor.

Ps 66:3. How awe-inspiring are your deeds, O God! How great your power! No wonder your enemies surrender! [7]Because of his great power he rules forever. He watches every movement of the nations. O rebel lands, he will deflate your pride.

Ps 68:33. To him who rides upon the ancient heavens, whose mighty voice thunders from the sky. *vs.* 34, 35.

Ps 74:13. You divided the Red Sea with your strength; you crushed the sea-god's heads! [15]At your command the springs burst forth to give your people water; and then you dried a path for them across the ever-flowing Jordan.

Ps 76:6. When you rebuked them, God of Jacob, steeds and riders fell. [7]No wonder you are greatly feared! Who can stand before an angry God?

Ps 77:14. You are the God of miracles and wonders! You still demonstrate your awesome power. [16]When the Red Sea saw you, how it feared! It trembled to its depths! [18]There was thunder in the whirlwind; the lightning lighted up the world! The earth trembled and shook.

Ps 78:26. And he led forth the east wind and guided the south wind by his mighty power. *vs.* 11–16, 43–51.

Ps 79:11. Listen to the sighing of the prisoners and those condemned to die. Demonstrate the greatness of your power by saving them.

Ps 89:8. O Jehovah, Commander of the heavenly armies, where is there any other Mighty One like you? Faithfulness is your very character. [9]You rule the oceans when their waves arise in fearful storms; you speak, and they lie still. [13]Strong is your arm! Strong is your hand! Your right hand is lifted high in glorious strength.

Ps 90:3. You speak, and man turns back to dust.

Ps 93:1. Jehovah is King! He is robed in majesty and strength. The world is his throne. [4]You are mightier than all the breakers pounding on the seashores of the world!

Ps 97:3. Fire goes forth before him and burns up all his foes. [4]His lightning flashes out across the world. The earth sees and trembles. [5]The mountains melt like wax before the Lord of all the earth.

Ps 104:7. You spoke, and at the sound of your

shout the water collected into its vast ocean beds. [9]And then you set a boundary for the seas, so that they would never again cover the earth. [29]But if you turn away from them, then all is lost. And when you gather up their breath, they die and turn again to dust. [30]Then you send your Spirit, and new life is born to replenish all the living of the earth. [32]The earth trembles at his glance; the mountains burst into flame at his touch. Ps 105; 114:3–8; 135:8–12; 136:10–22.

Ps 106:8. Even so you saved them—to defend the honor of your name and demonstrate your power to all the world.

Ps 107:25. He calls to the storm winds; the waves rise high. [29]He calms the storm and stills the waves.

Ps 111:6. He has shown his great power to his people by giving them the land of Israel, though it was the home of many nations living there.

Ps 114:7. Tremble, O earth, at the presence of the Lord, the God of Jacob. [8]For he caused gushing streams to burst from flinty rock.

Ps 115:3. For he is in the heavens, and does as he wishes.

Ps 118:16. The strong arm of the Lord has done glorious things!

Ps 135:6. He does whatever pleases him throughout all of heaven and earth, and in the deepest seas.

Ps 144:5. Bend down the heavens, Lord, and come. The mountains smoke beneath your touch.

Ps 145:6. Your awe-inspiring deeds shall be on every tongue; I will proclaim your greatness. [16]You constantly satisfy the hunger and thirst of every living thing.

Ps 147:5. How great he is! His power is absolute! His understanding is unlimited. [16]He sends the snow in all its lovely whiteness, and scatters the frost upon the ground. [18]But then he calls for warmer weather, and the spring winds blow and all the river ice is broken.

Ps 148:5. Let everything he has made give praise to him. For he issued his command, and they came into being. [8]Let fire and hail, snow, rain, wind and weather, all obey.

Prov 21:30. No one, regardless of how shrewd or well-advised he is, can stand against the Lord.

Prov 30:4. Who else but God goes back and forth to heaven? Who else holds the wind in his fists, and wraps up the oceans in his cloak? Who but God has created the world? If there is any other, what is his name—and his son's name—if you know it?

Isa 14:24. He has taken an oath to do it! For this is his purpose and plan. [27]The Lord, the God of battle, has spoken—who can change his plans? When his hand moves, who can stop him?

Isa 17:13. But though they roar like breakers rolling upon a beach, God will silence them. They will flee, scattered like chaff by the wind, like whirling dust before a storm. Ps 2:4, 5.

Isa 19:1. This is God's message concerning Egypt: Look, the Lord is coming against Egypt, riding on a swift cloud; the idols of Egypt tremble; the hearts of the Egyptians melt with fear.

Isa 23:11. The Lord holds out his hand over the seas; he shakes the kingdoms of the earth; he has spoken out against this great merchant city, to destroy its strength.

Isa 26:4. Trust in the Lord God always, for in the Lord Jehovah is your everlasting strength.

Isa 27:4. My anger against Israel is gone. If I find thorns and briars bothering her, I will burn them up.

Isa 31:3. For these Egyptians are mere men, not God! Their horses are puny flesh, not mighty spirits! When the Lord clenches his fist against them, they will stumble and fall among those they are trying to help. All will fail together.

Isa 33:3. The enemy runs at the sound of your voice. When you stand up, the nations flee. [13]Listen to what I have done, O nations far away! And you that are near, acknowledge my might!

Isa 40:12. Who else has held the oceans in his hands and measured off the heavens with his ruler? Who else knows the weight of all the earth and weighs the mountains and the hills? [22]It is God who sits above the circle of the earth. (The people below must seem to him like grasshoppers!) He is the one who stretches out the heavens like a curtain and makes his tent from them. [24]They hardly get started, barely take root, when he blows on them and their work withers and the wind carries them off like straw. [26]Look up into the heavens! Who created all these stars? As a shepherd leads his sheep, calling each by its pet name, and counts them to see that none are lost or strayed, so God does with stars and planets! [28]Don't you yet understand? Don't you know by now that the everlasting God, the Creator of the farthest parts of the earth, never grows faint or weary? No one can fathom the depths of his understanding.

Isa 43:13. From eternity to eternity I am God. No one can oppose what I do. [16]I am the Lord, who opens a way through the waters, making a path right through the sea. [17]I called forth the mighty army of Egypt with all its chariots and horses, to lie beneath the waves, dead, their lives snuffed out like candlewicks.

Isa 44:27. When I speak to the rivers and say, "Be dry!" they shall be dry.

Isa 46:10. Who can tell you what is going to happen. All I say will come to pass, for I do whatever I wish. [11]I will call that swift bird of prey from the east—that man Cyrus from far away. And he will come and do my bidding. I have said I would do it and I will.

Isa 48:13. It was my hand that laid the foundations of the earth; the palm of my right hand spread out the heavens above; I spoke and they came into being.

Isa 50:2. Was I too weak to save you? Is that why the house is silent and empty when I come home? Have I no longer power to deliver? No, that is not the reason! For I can rebuke the sea and make it dry! I can turn the rivers into deserts, covered with dying fish. [3]I am the one who sends the darkness out across the skies.

Isa 51:10. Are you not the same today, the mighty

God who dried up the sea, making a path right through it for your ransomed ones? *v.* 15.

Isa 52:10. The Lord has bared his holy arm before the eyes of all the nations; the ends of the earth shall see the salvation of our God.

Isa 59:1. Listen now! the Lord isn't too weak to save you. And he isn't getting deaf! He can hear you when you call!

Isa 60:16. Powerful kings and mighty nations shall provide you with the choicest of their goods to satisfy your every need, and you will know at last and really understand that I, the Lord, am your Savior and Redeemer, the Mighty One of Israel.

Isa 63:12. Where is he whose mighty power divided the sea before them when Moses lifted up his hand, and established his reputation forever?

Jer 5:22. Have you no respect at all for me? the Lord God asks. How can it be that you don't even tremble in my presence? I set the shorelines of the world by perpetual decrees, so that the oceans, though they toss and roar, can never pass those bounds. Isn't such a God to be feared and worshiped?

Jer 10:6. O Lord, there is no other god like you. For you are great and your name is full of power. [12]But our God formed the earth by his power and wisdom, and by his intelligence he hung the stars in space and stretched out the heavens. (chapter 51: 15) [13]It is his voice that echoes in the thunder of the storm clouds. He causes mist to rise upon the earth; he sends the lightning and brings the rain, and from his treasuries he brings the wind.

Jer 20:11. But the Lord stands beside me like a great warrior, and before him, the Mighty, Terrible One, they shall stumble. They cannot defeat me; they shall be shamed and thoroughly humiliated, and they shall have a stigma upon them forever.

Jer 27:5. By my great power I have made the earth and all mankind and every animal; and I give these things of mine to anyone I want to.

Jer 32:17. O Lord God! You have made the heavens and earth by your great power; nothing is too hard for you! [27]I am the Lord, the God of all mankind; is there anything too hard for me?

Jer 50:44. I will send against them an invader who will come upon them suddenly, like a lion from the jungles of Jordan that leaps upon the grazing sheep. I will put her defenders to flight and appoint over them whomsoever I please. For who is like me? What ruler can oppose my will? Who can call me to account?

Dan 2:20. Saying, "Blessed be the name of God forever and ever, for he alone has all wisdom and all power."

Dan 3:17. If we are thrown into the flaming furnace, our God is able to deliver us; and he will deliver us out of your hand, Your Majesty.

Dan 4:35. All the people of the earth are nothing when compared to him; he does whatever he thinks best among the hosts of heaven, as well as here among the inhabitants of earth. No one can stop him or challenge him, saying "What do you mean by doing these things?"

Dan 6:27. He delivers his people, preserving them from harm; he does great miracles in heaven and earth; it is he who delivered Daniel from the power of the lions.

Joel 2:11. The Lord leads them with a shout. This is his mighty army and they follow his orders. The day of the judgment of the Lord is an awesome, terrible thing. Who can endure it?

Joel 3:16. The Lord shouts from his Temple in Jerusalem and the earth and sky begin to shake. But to his people Israel, the Lord will be very gentle. He is their Refuge and Strength. Amos 1:2.

Amos 4:13. For you are dealing with the one who formed the mountains and made the winds, and knows your every thought; he turns the morning to darkness and crushes down the mountains underneath his feet: Jehovah, the Lord, the God of Hosts, is his name.

Amos 9:5. The Lord God of Hosts touches the land and it melts, and all its people mourn. It rises like the river Nile in Egypt, and then sinks again. [6]The upper stories of his home are in the heavens, the first floor on the earth. He calls for the vapor to rise from the ocean and pours it down as rain upon the ground. Jehovah, the Lord, is his name.

Mic 1:3. Look! He is coming! He leaves his throne in heaven and comes to earth, walking on the mountaintops. [4]They melt beneath his feet, and flow into the valleys like wax in fire, like water pouring down a hill.

Nah 1:3. He is slow in getting angry, but when aroused, his power is incredible, and he does not easily forgive. He shows his power in the terrors of the cyclone and the raging storms; clouds are billowing dust beneath his feet! [4]At his command the oceans and rivers become dry sand; the lush pastures of Bashan and Carmel fade away; the green forests of Lebanon wilt. [5]In his presence mountains quake and hills melt; the earth crumbles and its people are destroyed. [6]Who can stand before an angry God? His fury is like fire; the mountains tumble down before his anger.

Hab 3:6. He stops; he stands still for a moment, gazing at the earth. Then he shakes the nations, scattering the everlasting mountains and leveling the hills. His power is just the same as always! [9]All saw your power! Then springs burst forth upon the earth at your command! [10]The mountains watched and trembled. Onward swept the raging water. The mighty deep cried out, announcing its surrender to the Lord. [11]The lofty sun and moon began to fade, obscured by brilliance from your arrows and the flashing of your glittering spear. [15]Your horsemen marched across the sea; the mighty waters piled high.

Zech 9:14. The Lord shall lead his people as they fight! His arrows shall fly like lightning; the Lord God shall sound the trumpet call and go out against his enemies like a whirlwind off the desert from the south.

Mt 3:9. Don't try to get by as you are, thinking, "We are safe for we are Jews—descendants of

Abraham." That proves nothing. God can change these stones here into Jews!

Mt 10:28. Don't be afraid of those who can kill only your bodies—but can't touch your souls! Fear only God who can destroy both soul and body in hell.

Mt 19:26. Jesus looked at them intently and said, "Humanly speaking, no one. But with God, everything is possible." Mk 10:27; Lk 18:27.

Mt 22:29. But Jesus said, Your error is caused by your ignorance of the Scriptures and of God's power!

Mk 14:36. "Father, Father," he said, "everything is possible for you. Take away this cup from me. Yet I want your will, not mine."

Lk 1:37. For every promise from God shall surely come true. [49]For he, the mighty Holy One, has done great things to me. [51]How powerful is his mighty arm! How he scatters the proud and haughty ones!

Lk 11:20. But if I am casting out demons because of power from God, it proves that the Kingdom of God has arrived.

Rom 1:20. Since earliest times men have seen the earth and sky and all God made, and have known of his existence and great eternal power. So they will have no excuse (when they stand before God at Judgment Day).

Rom 4:21. He was completely sure that God was well able to do anything he promised.

1 Cor 6:14. And God is going to raise our bodies from the dead by his power just as he raised up the Lord Jesus Christ.

2 Cor 13:4. His weak, human body died on the cross, but now he lives by the mighty power of God. We, too, are weak in our bodies, as he was, but now we live and are strong, as he is, and have all of God's power to use in dealing with you.

Eph 1:19. I pray that you will begin to understand how incredibly great his power is to help those who believe him. It is that same mighty power [20]that raised Christ from the dead and seated him in the place of honor at God's right hand in heaven.

Eph 3:20. Now glory be to God who by his mighty power at work within us is able to do far more than we would ever dare to ask or even dream of—infinitely beyond our highest prayers, desires, thoughts, or hopes. [21]May he be given glory forever and ever through endless ages because of his master plan of salvation for the church through Jesus Christ.

Heb 1:3. God's Son shines out with God's glory, and all that God's Son is and does marks him as God. He regulates the universe by the mighty power of his command. He is the one who died to cleanse us and clear our record of all sin, and then sat down in highest honor beside the great God of heaven.

Heb 12:26. When he spoke from Mount Sinai his voice shook the earth, but, "Next time," he says, "I will not only shake the earth, but the heavens too." [29]For our God is a consuming fire.

Jas 4:12. Only he who made the law can rightly judge among us. He alone decides to save us or destroy. So what right do you have to judge or criticize others?

1 Pet 1:5. And God, in his mighty power, will make sure that you get there safely to receive it, because you are trusting him. It will be yours in that coming last day for all to see.

Rev 4:11. O Lord, you are worthy to receive the glory and the honor and the power, for you have created all things. They were created and called into being by your act of will. Rev 5:13.

Rev 11:17. We give thanks, Lord God Almighty, who is and was, for now you have assumed your great power and have begun to reign.

Rev 19:1. After this I heard the shouting of a vast crowd in heaven, "Halleluah! Praise the Lord! Salvation is from our God. Honor and authority belong to him alone." [6]Then I heard again what sounded like the shouting of a huge crowd, or like the waves of a hundred oceans crashing on the shore, or like the mighty rolling of great thunder, "Praise the Lord. For the Lord our God, the Almighty, reigns."

See *God, Omnipotent,* above.

PRESENCE OF. Gen 16:13. Thereafter Hagar spoke of Jehovah—for it was he who appeared to her—as "the God who looked upon me," for she thought, "I saw God and lived to tell it."

Gen 28:16. Then Jacob woke up. "God lives here!" he exclaimed in terror.

Ex 20:24. The altars you make for me must be simple altars of earth. Offer upon them your sacrifices to me—your burnt offerings and peace offerings of sheep and oxen. Build altars only where I tell you to, and I will come and bless you there.

Deut 4:34. Where else will you ever find another example of God's removing a nation from its slavery by sending terrible plagues, mighty miracles, war, and terror? Yet that is what the Lord your God did for you in Egypt, right before your very eyes. [35]He did these things so you would realize that Jehovah is God, and that there is no one else like him. [36]He let you hear his voice instructing you from heaven, and he let you see his great pillar of fire upon the earth; you even heard his words from the center of the fire. [39]This is your wonderful thought for the day: Jehovah is God both in heaven and down here upon the earth; and there is no God other than him! Josh 2:11.

1 Kgs 8:27. But is it possible that God would really live on earth? Why, even the skies and the highest heavens cannot contain you, much less this Temple I have built! 2 Chron 2:6; Acts 7:48, 49.

Ps 139:3. You chart the path ahead of me, and tell me where to stop and rest. Every moment, you know where I am. [5]You both precede and follow me, and place your hand of blessing on my head. [7]I can *never* be lost to your Spirit! I can *never* get away from my God! [8]If I go up to heaven, you are there; if I go down to the place of the dead, you are there. [9]If I ride the morning winds to the farthest oceans, [10]Even there your hand will guide me, your strength will support me.

Isa 57:15. The high and lofty one who inhabits eternity, the Holy One, says this: I live in that high and holy place where those with contrite, humble spirits dwell; and I refresh the humble and give new courage to those with repentant hearts.

Isa 66:1. Heaven is my throne and the earth is my footstool: What Temple can you build for me as good as that?

Jer 23:23. Am I a God who is only in one place and cannot see what they are doing? [24]Can anyone hide from me? Am I not everywhere in all of heaven and earth?

Jer 32:18. You are loving and kind to thousands, yet children suffer for their fathers' sins; you are the great and mighty God, the Lord of Hosts. [19]You have all wisdom and do great and mighty miracles; for your eyes are open to all the ways of men, and you reward everyone according to his life and deeds.

Jon 1:3. But Jonah was afraid to go and ran away from the Lord. He went down to the seacoast, to the port of Joppa, where he found a ship leaving for Tarshish. He bought a ticket, went on board, and climbed down into the dark hold of the ship to hide there from the Lord. [4]But as the ship was sailing along, suddenly the Lord flung a terrific wind over the sea, causing a great storm that threatened to send them to the bottom.

Acts 17:24. He made the world and everything in it, and since he is Lord of heaven and earth, he doesn't live in man-made temples. [27]His purpose in all of this is that they should seek after God, and perhaps feel their way toward him and find him—though he is not far from any one of us. [28]For in him we live and move and are!

1 Cor 12:6. There are many ways in which God works in our lives, but it is the same God who does the work in and through all of us who are his.

Eph 1:23. Which is his body, filled with himself, the Author and Giver of everything everywhere.

See *God, Omnipresent,* above; *Preserver,* below.

PRESERVER. Gen 14:19, 20. Then Melchizedek blessed Abram with this blessing: "The blessing of the supreme God, Creator of heaven and earth, be upon you, Abram; and blessed be God, who has delivered your enemies over to you."

Gen 28:15. What's more, I am with you, and will protect you wherever you go, and will bring you back safely to this land; I will be with you constantly until I have finished giving you all I am promising. Gen 31:3, 13.

Gen 48:15. Then he blessed Joseph with this blessing: "May God, the God of my fathers Abraham and Isaac, the God who has shepherded me all my life, wonderfully bless these boys. [16]He is the Angel who has kept me from all harm. May these boys be an honor to my name and to the names of my fathers Abraham and Isaac; and may they become a mighty nation."

Gen 49:24. But their weapons were shattered by the Mighty One of Jacob, the Shepherd, the Rock of Israel. [25]May the God of your fathers, the Almighty, bless you with blessings of heaven above and of the earth beneath—blessings of the breasts and of the womb.

Ex 6:6. Therefore tell the descendants of Israel that I will use my mighty power and perform great miracles to deliver them from slavery, and make them free. [7]And I will accept them as my people and be their God. And they shall know that I am Jehovah their God who has rescued them from the Egyptians. Ex 3:17.

Ex 8:22. But it will be very different in the land of Goshen where the Israelis live. No flies will be there; thus you will know that I am the Lord God of all the earth. *v.* 23; Ex 11:7.

Ex 9:26. The only spot in all Egypt without hail that day was the land of Goshen where the people of Israel lived.

Ex 11:7. But not a dog shall move his tongue against any of the people of Israel, nor shall any of their animals die. Then you will know that Jehovah makes a distinction between Egyptians and Israelis.

Ex 12:13. The blood you have placed on the doorposts will be proof that you obey me, and when I see the blood I will pass over you and I will not destroy your firstborn children when I smite the land of Egypt. [17]The annual "Celebration with Unleavened Bread" will cause you always to remember today as the day when I brought you out of the land of Egypt; so it is a law that you must celebrate this day annually, generation after generation. [23]For Jehovah will pass through the land and kill the Egyptians; but when he sees the blood upon the panel at the top of the door and on the two side pieces, he will pass over that home and not permit the Destroyer to enter and kill your firstborn.

Ex 13:21. The Lord guided them by a pillar of cloud during the daytime, and by a pillar of fire at night. So they could travel either by day or night. [22]The cloud and fire were never out of sight.

Ex 14:29. The people of Israel had walked through on dry land, and the waters had been walled up on either side of them. [30]Thus Jehovah saved Israel that day from the Egyptians; and the people of Israel saw the Egyptians dead, washed up on the seashore.

Ex 15:2. The Lord is my strength, my song, and my salvation. He is my God, and I will praise him. He is my father's God—I will exalt him. [13]You have led the people you redeemed. But in your lovingkindness you have guided them wonderfully to your holy land. [16]Terror and dread have overcome them. O Lord, because of your great power they won't attack us! Your people whom you purchased will pass by them in safety. [17]You will bring them in and plant them on your mountain, your own homeland, Lord—the sanctuary you made for them to live in.

Ex 16:15. When the people of Israel saw it they asked each other, "What is it?" And Moses told them, It is the food Jehovah has given you to eat."

Ex 19:4. You have seen what I did to the Egyptians, and how I brought you to myself as though on eagle's wings.

Ex 23:20. See, I am sending an Angel before you to lead you safely to the land I have prepared for you. *vs.* 21–31.

Ex 34:24. No one will attack and conquer your land when you go up to appear before the Lord your God those three times each year. For I will drive out the nations from before you and enlarge your boundaries.

Num 10:33. They traveled for three days after leaving Mount Sinai, with the Ark at the front of the column to choose a place for them to stop.

Num 23:23. No curse can be placed on Jacob, and no magic shall be done against him. For now it shall be said of Israel, "What wonders God has done for them!"

Deut 1:30. The Lord God is your leader, and he will fight for you with his mighty miracles, just as you saw him do in Egypt. [31]And you know how he has cared for you again and again here in the wilderness, just as a father cares for his child!

Deut 7:21. No, do not be afraid of those nations, for the Lord your God is among you, and he is a great and awesome God. [22]He will cast them out a little at a time; he will not do it all at once, for if he did, the wild animals would multiply too quickly and become dangerous.

Deut 9:3. But the Lord your God will go before you as a devouring fire to destroy them, so that you will quickly conquer them and drive them out.

Deut 11:25. No one will be able to stand against you, for the Lord your God will send fear and dread ahead of you wherever you go, just as he has promised.

Deut 23:14. The camp must be holy, for the Lord walks among you to protect you and to cause your enemies to fall before you; and the Lord does not want to see anything indecent lest he turn away from you.

Deut 30:4. Though you are at the ends of the earth, he will go and find you and bring you back again. [20]Choose to love the Lord your God and to obey him and to cling to him, for he is your life and the length of your days. You will then be able to live safely in the land the Lord promised your ancestors, Abraham, Isaac, and Jacob.

Deut 31:3. But the Lord himself will lead you, and will destroy the nations living there, and you shall overcome them. Joshua is your new commander, as the Lord has instructed.

Deut 32:10. God protected them in the howling wilderness as though they were the apple of his eye.

Deut 33:12. He is beloved of God and lives in safety beside him. God surrounds him with his loving care, and preserves him from every harm. [25]May you be protected with strong bolts of iron and bronze, and may your strength match the length of your days! [26]There is none like the God of Jerusalem—he descends from the heavens in majestic splendor to help you. [27]The eternal God is your Refuge, and underneath are the everlasting arms. He thrusts out your enemies before you; it is he who cries, "Destroy them!" [28]So Israel dwells safely, prospering in a land of corn and wine, while the gentle rains descend from heaven. *v.* 29.

Josh 23:10. Each one of you has put to flight a thousand of the enemy, for the Lord your God fights for you, just as he has promised.

1 Sam 2:6. The Lord kills, the Lord gives life. [9]He will protect his godly ones, but the wicked shall be silenced in darkness. No one shall succeed by strength alone.

1 Sam 9:16. About this time tomorrow I will send you a man from the land of Benjamin. You are to anoint him as the leader of my people. He will save them from the Philistines, for I have looked down on them in mercy and have heard their cry.

2 Sam 22:28. You will save those in trouble, but you bring down the haughty; for you watch their every move.

2 Kgs 20:6. I will add fifteen years to his life and save him and this city from the king of Assyria. And it will be done for the glory of my own name and for the sake of my servant David.

2 Chron 16:9. For the eyes of the Lord search back and forth across the whole earth, looking for people whose hearts are perfect toward him, so that he can show his great power in helping them. What a fool you have been! From now on you shall have wars.

2 Chron 20:15. "Listen to me, all you people of Judah and Jerusalem, and you, O king Jehoshaphat!" he exclaimed, "The Lord says, 'Don't be afraid! Don't be paralyzed by this mighty army! For the battle is not yours, but God's! [17]But you will not need to fight! Take your places; stand quietly and see the incredible rescue operation God will perform for you, O people of Judah and Jerusalem! Don't be afraid or discouraged! Go out there tomorrow, for the Lord is with you!' "

Ezra 8:22. For I was ashamed to ask the king for soldiers and cavalry to accompany us and protect us from the enemies along the way. After all, we had told the king that our God would protect all those who worshiped him, and that disaster could come only to those who had forsaken him! [23]So we fasted and begged God to take care of us. And he did.

Neh 9:6. Then Ezra prayed, "You alone are God. You have made the skies and the heavens, the earth and the seas, and everything in them. You preserve it all; and all the angels of heaven worship you."

Job 1:10. You have always protected him and his home and his property from all harm. You have prospered everything he does—look how rich he is! No wonder he "worships" you!

Job 4:7. Stop and think! Have you ever known a truly good and innocent person who was punished?

Job 5:11. And gives prosperity to the poor and humble, and takes sufferers to safety. [18]For though he wounds, he binds and heals again. [19]He will deliver you again and again, so that no evil can touch you. [20]He will keep you from death in famine, and from the power of the sword in time of war. [21]You will be safe from slander; no need to fear the future. *vs.* 22–24.

Job 10:12. You gave me life and were so kind and loving to me, and I was preserved by your care.

Job 11:18. You will have courage because you will have hope. You will take your time, and rest in safety. [19]You will lie down unafraid and many will look to you for help.

Job 27:3. That as long as I live, while I have breath from God, [4]my lips shall speak no evil, my tongue shall speak no lies.

Job 33:17, 18. Causing them to change their minds, and keeping them from pride, and warning them of the penalties of sin, and keeping them from falling into some trap.

Job 36:7. He does not ignore the good men but honors them by placing them upon eternal, kingly thrones. [16]How he wanted to lure you away from danger into a wide and pleasant valley and to prosper you there.

Ps 1:6. For the Lord watches over all the plans and paths of godly men, but the paths of godless lead to doom.

Ps 3:3. But Lord, you are my shield, my glory, and my only hope. You alone can lift my head, now bowed in shame.

Ps 9:9. All who are oppressed may come to him. He is a refuge for them in their times of trouble.

Ps 10:17. Lord, you know the hopes of humble people. Surely you will hear their cries and comfort their hearts by helping them. [18]You will be with the orphans and all who are oppressed, so that mere earthly man will terrify them no longer.

Ps 12:7. O Lord, we know that you will forever preserve your own from the reach of evil men.

Ps 14:5. Terror shall grip them, for God is with those who love him. [6]He is the refuge of the poor and humble when evildoers are oppressing them.

Ps 17:7. Show me your strong love in wonderful ways, O Savior of all those seeking your help against their foes.

Ps 18:17. He delivered me from my strong enemy, from those who hated me—I who was helpless in their hands. [27]You deliver the humble but condemn the proud and haughty ones.

Ps 19:14. May my spoken words and unspoken thoughts be pleasing even to you, O Lord my Rock and my Redeemer.

Ps 25:8. The Lord is good and glad to teach the proper path to all who go astray; [9]he will teach the ways that are right and best to those who humbly turn to him. [12]Where is the man who fears the Lord? God will teach him how to choose the best.

Ps 31:20. Hide your loved ones in the shelter of your presence, safe beneath your hand, safe from all conspiring men. [23]Oh, love the Lord, all of you who are his people; for the Lord protects those who are loyal to him, but harshly punishes all who haughtily reject him.

Ps 32:6. Now I say that each believer should confess his sins to God when he is aware of them, while there is time to be forgiven. Judgment will not touch him if he does. [8]I will instruct you (says the Lord) and guide you along the best pathway for your life; I will advise you and watch your progress.

Ps 34:15. For the eyes of the Lord are intently watching all who live good lives, and he gives attention when they cry to him. [17]Yes, the Lord hears the good man when he calls to him for help, and saves him out of all his troubles. [19]The good man does not escape all troubles—he has them too. But the Lord helps him in each and every one. [20]God even protects him from accidents. *vs.* 21, 22.

Ps 37:17. For the strength of evil men shall be broken, but the Lord takes care of those he has forgiven. [23]The steps of good men are directed by the Lord. He delights in each step they take. [24]If they fall it isn't fatal, for the Lord holds them with his hand. [28]For the Lord loves justice and fairness; he will never abandon his people. They will be kept safe forever; but all who love wickedness shall perish. [32]Evil men spy on the godly, waiting for an excuse to accuse them and then demanding their death. [33]But the Lord will not let these evil men succeed, nor let the godly be condemned when they are brought before the judge.

Ps 41:1. God blesses those who are kind to the poor. He helps them out of their troubles. [2]He protects them and keeps them alive; he publicly honors them and destroys the power of their enemies. [3]He nurses them when they are sick, and soothes their pains and worries.

Ps 46:1. God is our refuge and strength, a tested help in times of trouble. [5]God himself is living in that City; therefore it stands unmoved despite the turmoil everywhere. He will not delay his help. [7]The Commander of the armies of heaven is here among us. He, the God of Jacob, has come to rescue us.

Ps 48:3. God himself is the defender of Jerusalem.

Ps 50:15. I want you to trust me in your times of trouble, so I can rescue you, and you can give me glory.

Ps 61:3. For you are my refuge, a high tower where my enemies can never reach me. [6]You will give me added years of life, as rich and full as those of many generations, all packed into one.

Ps 68:6. He gives families to the lonely, and releases prisoners from jail, singing with joy! But for rebels there is famine and distress. [22]The Lord says, "Come," to all his people's enemies; they are hiding on Mount Hermon's highest slopes and deep within the sea!

Ps 72:14. He will save them from oppression and from violence, for their lives are precious to him.

Ps 73:23. But even so, you love me! You are holding my right hand!

Ps 80:1. O shepherd of Israel who leads Israel like a flock; O God enthroned above the cherubim, bend down your ear and listen as I plead. Display your power and radiant glory.

Ps 84:11. For Jehovah God is our Light and our Protector. He gives us grace and glory. No good thing will he withhold from those who walk along his paths.

Ps 87:5. But someday the highest honor will be to be a native of Jerusalem! For the God above all gods will personally bless this city.

Ps 91:1. We live within the shadow of the Almighty, sheltered by the God who is above all gods. [3]For he rescues you from every trap, and protects you from the fatal plague. [4]He will shield you with his wings! They will shelter you. His faithful promises are your armor. [7]Though a thousand fall at my side, though ten thousand are dying around me, the evil will not touch me. [9]For Jehovah is my refuge! I choose the God above all gods to shelter me. [10]How then can evil overtake me or any plague come near? [14]For the Lord says, "Because he loves me, I will rescue him; I will make him great because he trusts in my name. [15]When he calls on me I will answer; I will be with him in trouble, and rescue him and honor him. *vs.* 1–16.

Ps 97:10. The Lord loves those who hate evil; he protects the lives of his people, and rescues them from the wicked.

Ps 102:19. Tell them that God looked down from his temple in heaven, [20]and heard the groans of his people in slavery—they were children of death—and released them.

Ps 103:2. Yes, I will bless the Lord and not forget the glorious things he does for me. [3]He forgives all my sins. He heals me. [4]He ransoms me from hell. He surrounds me with lovingkindness and tender mercies. [5]He fills my life with good things! My youth is renewed like the eagle's!

Ps 107:9. For he satisfies the thirsty soul and fills the hungry soul with good. [10]Who are these who sit in darkness, in the shadow of death, crushed by misery and slavery?

Ps 112:4. When darkness overtakes him, light will come bursting in. He is kind and merciful.

Ps 115:10. O priests of Aaron, trust the Lord! He is your helper; he is your shield.

Ps 116:6. The Lord protects the simple and the childlike; I was facing death and then he saved me.

Ps 118:13. You did your best to kill me, O my enemy, but the Lord helped me.

Ps 121:3, 4. He will never let me stumble, slip or fall. For he is always watching, never sleeping. [7]He keeps you from all evil, and preserves your life. [8]He keeps his eye upon you as you come and go, and always guards you. *vs.* 5, 6.

Ps 124:1. If the Lord had not been on our side (let all Israel admit it), if the Lord had not been on our side, [2, 3]we would have been swallowed alive by our enemies, destroyed by their anger. [4, 5]We would have drowned beneath the flood of these men's fury and pride. [6]Blessed be Jehovah who has not let them devour us. [7]We have escaped with our lives as a bird from a hunter's snare. The snare is broken and we are free! [8]Our help is from the Lord who made heaven and earth.

Ps 125:1. Those who trust in the Lord are steady as Mount Zion, unmoved by any circumstance. [2]Just as the mountains surround and protect Jerusalem, so the Lord surrounds and protects his people. [3]For the wicked shall not rule the godly, lest the godly be forced to do wrong.

Ps 127:1. Unless the Lord builds a house, the builders' work is useless. Unless the Lord protects a city, sentries do no good.

Ps 145:14. The Lord lifts the fallen and those bent beneath their loads. [19]He fulfills the desires of those who reverence and trust him; he hears their cries for help and rescues them. [20]He protects all those who love him, but destroys the wicked. Prov 22:12.

Ps 146:7. And gives justice to the poor and oppressed, and food to the hungry. He frees the prisoners, [8]and opens the eyes of the blind; he lifts the burdens from those bent down beneath their loads. For the Lord loves good men.

Ps 147:2. He is rebuilding Jerusalem and bringing back the exiles. [3]He heals the brokenhearted, binding up their wounds.

Prov 2:7, 8. He grants good sense to the godly—his saints. He is their shield, protecting them and guarding their pathway.

Prov 3:6. In everything you do, put God first, and he will direct you and crown your efforts with success.

Prov 10:3. The Lord will not let a good man starve to death, nor will he let the wicked man's riches continue forever. [30]The good shall never lose God's blessings, but the wicked shall lose everything.

Prov 11:8. God rescues good men from danger while letting the wicked fall into it.

Prov 12:3. Wickedness never brings real success; only the godly have that. [21]No real harm befalls the good, but there is constant trouble for the wicked. *v.* 13.

Prov 14:26. Reverence for God gives a man deep strength; his children have a place of refuge and security.

Prov 15:19. A lazy fellow has trouble all through life; the good man's path is easy!

Prov 16:9. We should make plans—counting on God to direct us. [33]We toss the coin, but it is the Lord who controls its decision.

Prov 19:23. Reverence for God gives life, happiness, and protection from harm.

Prov 20:22. Don't repay evil for evil. Wait for the Lord to handle the matter. [24]Since the Lord is directing our steps, why try to understand everything that happens along the way?

Prov 21:31. Go ahead and prepare for the conflict, but victory comes from God.

Prov 24:16. Don't you know that this good man, though you trip him up seven times, will each time rise again? But one calamity is enough to lay you low.

Isa 4:5. Then the Lord will provide shade on all Jerusalem—over every home and all its public grounds—a canopy of smoke and cloud throughout the day, and clouds of fire at night, covering the Glorious Land, [6]protecting it from daytime heat and from rains and storms.

Isa 10:27. On that day God will end the bondage of his people. He will break the slave-yoke off their necks, and destroy it as decreed.

Isa 14:3. In that wonderful day when the Lord gives his people rest from sorrow and fear, from slavery and chains.

Isa 26:7. But for good men the path is not uphill and rough! God does not give them a rough and treacherous path, but smooths the road before them.

Isa 27:3. Israel is my vineyard; I, the Lord, will tend the fruitful vines; every day I'll water them, and day and night I'll watch to keep all enemies away.

Isa 30:21. And if you leave God's paths and go astray, you will hear a Voice behind you say, "No, this is the way; walk here." [26]The moon will be as bright as the sun, and the sunlight brighter than seven days! So it will be when the Lord begins to heal his people and to cure the wounds he gave them.

Isa 31:4, 5. But the Lord has told me this: When a lion, even a young one, kills a sheep, he pays no attention to the shepherd's shouts and noise. He goes right on and eats. In such a manner the Lord will come and fight upon Mount Zion. He will not be frightened away! He, the Lord of Hosts, will hover over Jerusalem as birds hover round their nests, and he will defend the city and deliver it. [9]Even their generals will quake with terror and flee when they see the battle flags of Israel, says the Lord. For the flame of God burns brightly in Jerusalem.

Isa 32:2. He will shelter Israel from the storm and wind. He will refresh her as a river in the desert and as the cooling shadow of a mighty rock within a hot and weary land. [18]My people will live in safety, quietly at home,

Isa 33:16. Such as these shall dwell on high. The rocks of the mountains will be their fortress of safety; food will be supplied to them and they will have all the water they need. [20]Instead you will see Jerusalem at peace, a place where God is worshiped, a city quiet and unmoved.

Isa 35:9. No lion will lurk along its course, nor will there be any other dangers; only the redeemed will travel there.

Isa 37:32. For a remnant shall go out from Jerusalem to repopulate the land; the power of the Lord of Hosts will cause all this to come to pass. [35]For my own honor I will defend it, and in memory of my servant David.

Isa 40:11. He will feed his flock like a shepherd; he will carry the lambs in his arms and gently lead the ewes with young. [29]He gives power to the tired and worn out, and strength to the weak. [31]But they that wait upon the Lord shall renew their strength. They shall mount up with wings like eagles; they shall run and not be weary; they shall walk and not faint.

Isa 42:13. The Lord will be a mighty warrior, full of fury toward his foes. He will give a great shout and prevail. [16]He will bring blind Israel along a path they have not seen before. He will make the darkness bright before them and smooth and straighten out the road ahead. He will not forsake them.

Isa 43:2. When you go through deep waters and great trouble, I will be with you. When you go through rivers of difficulty, you will not drown! When you walk through the fire of oppression, you will not be burned up—the flames will not consume you.

Isa 45:2. I will go before you, Cyrus, and level the mountains and smash down the city gates of brass and iron bars. *v.* 4.

Isa 46:4. I will be your God through all your lifetime, yes, even when your hair is white with age. I made you and I will care for you. I will carry you along and be your Savior. *v.* 3.

Isa 48:17. The Lord, your Redeemer, the Holy One of Israel, says, I am the Lord your God, who punishes you for your own good and leads you along the paths that you should follow.

Isa 49:9. They will be my sheep, grazing in green pastures and on the grassy hills. [10]They shall neither hunger nor thirst; the searing sun and scorching desert winds will not reach them any more. For the Lord in his mercy will lead them beside the cool waters. [17]Soon your rebuilders shall come and chase away all those destroying you. [25]But the Lord says, "Even the captives of the most mighty and most terrible shall all be freed; for I will fight those who fight you, and I will save your children."

Isa 51:9. Awake, O Lord! Rise up and robe yourself with strength. Rouse yourself as in the days of old when you slew Egypt, the dragon of the Nile. [10]Are you not the same today, the mighty God who dried up the sea, making a path right through it for your ransomed ones? [22]This is what the Lord says, the Lord your God who cares for his people: "See, I take from your hands the terrible cup; you shall drink no more of my fury; it is gone at last."

Isa 52:12. You shall not leave in haste, running for your lives; for the Lord will go ahead of you, and he, the God of Israel, will protect you from behind.

Isa 54:14. You will live under a government that is just and fair. Your enemies will stay far away; you will live in peace. Terror shall not come near. [15]If any nation comes to fight you, it will not be sent by me to punish you. Therefore it will be routed, for I am on your side. [17]But in that coming day, no weapon turned against you shall succeed, and you will have justice against every courtroom lie. This is the heritage of the servants of the Lord. This is the blessing I have given you, says the Lord.

Isa 57:14. I will say, Rebuild the road! Clear away the rocks and stones. Prepare a glorious highway for my people's return from captivity.

Isa 58:11. And the Lord will guide you continually, and satisfy you with all good things, and keep you healthy too; and you will be like a well-watered garden, like an ever-flowing spring.

Isa 59:19. Then at last they will reverence and glorify the name of God from west to east. For he will come like a floodtide driven by Jehovah's breath.

Isa 63:9. In all their affliction he was afflicted, and he personally saved them. In his love and pity he redeemed them and lifted them up and carried them through all the years.

Jer 2:3. In those days Israel was a holy people, the first of my children. All who harmed them were counted deeply guilty, and great evil fell on anyone who touched them. [6]They ignore the fact that it was I, the Lord, who brought them safely out of Egypt and led them through the barren wilderness, a land of deserts and rocks, of drought and death, where no one lives or even travels.

Jer 3:4. And yet you say to me, "O Father, you have always been my Friend; surely you won't be angry about such a little thing! Surely you will just forget it?"

Jer 11:4. For I told them at the time I brought them out of slavery in Egypt that if they would obey me and do whatever I commanded them, then they and all their children would be mine and I would be their God.

Jer 30:7. Alas, in all history when has there ever been a time of terror such as in that coming day? It is a time of trouble for my people—for Jacob—such as they have never known before. Yet God will rescue them! [8]For on that day, says the Lord of Hosts, I will break the yoke from their necks and snap their chains, and foreigners shall no longer be their masters! [11]For I am with you and I will save you, says the Lord. Even if I utterly destroy the nations where I scatter you, I will not exterminate you; I will punish you, yes—you will not go unpunished. *v.* 17.

Jer 31:9. Tears of joy shall stream down their faces, and I will lead them home with great care. They shall walk beside the quiet streams and not stumble. For I am a Father to Israel, and Ephraim is my oldest child. [10]Listen to this message from the Lord, you nations of the world, and publish it abroad: The Lord who scattered his people will gather them back together again and watch over them as a shepherd does his flock. [28]In the past I painstakingly destroyed the nation but now I will carefully build it up.

Ezk 9:4. And said to him, "Walk through the streets of Jerusalem and put a mark on the foreheads of the men who weep and sigh because of all the sins they see around them. [6]Kill them all—old and young, girls, women and little children; but don't touch anyone with the mark. And begin right here at the Temple." And so they began by killing the seventy elders.

Ezk 11:16. But tell the exiles that the Lord God says: Although I have scattered you in the countries of the world, yet I will be a sanctuary to you for the time that you are there.

Ezk 34:11. For the Lord God says: I will search and find my sheep. [12]I will be like a shepherd looking for his flock. I will find my sheep and rescue them from all the places they were scattered in that dark and cloudy day. [15, 16]I myself will be the Shepherd of my sheep, and cause them to lie down in peace, the Lord God says. I will seek my lost ones, those who strayed away, and bring them safely home again. I will put splints and bandages upon their broken limbs and heal the sick. [22]So I myself will save my flock; no more will they be picked on and destroyed. And I will notice which is plump and which is thin, and why! [31]You are my flock, the sheep of my pasture. You are my men and I am your God, so says the Lord. *vs.* 13, 14.

Dan 3:27. Then the princes, governors, captains, and counselors crowded around them and saw that the fire hadn't touched them—not a hair of their heads was singed; their coats were unscorched, and they didn't even smell of smoke! [28]Then Nebuchadnezzar said, "Blessed be the God of Shadrach, Meshach, and Abednego, for he sent his angel to deliver his trusting servants when they defied the king's commandment, and were willing to die rather than serve or worship any god except their own."

Dan 12:1. At that time Michael, the mighty angelic prince who stands guard over your nation, will stand up (and fight for you in heaven against satanic forces), and there will be a time of anguish for the Jews greater than any previous suffering in Jewish history. And yet every one of your people whose names are written in the Book will endure it.

Hos 2:18. At that time I will make a treaty between you and the wild animals, birds, and snakes, not to fear each other any more; and I will destroy all weapons, and all wars will end. Then you will lie down in peace and safety, unafraid.

Hos 13:10. Where is your king? Why don't you call on him for help? Where are all the leaders of the land? You asked for them, now let them save you!

Joel 2:18. Then the Lord will pity his people and be indignant for the honor of his land!

Amos 5:8. Seek him who created the Seven Stars and the constellation Orion, who turns darkness into morning, and day into night, who calls forth the water from the ocean and pours it out as rain upon the land. The Lord, Jehovah, is his name. [9]With blinding speed and violence he brings destruction on the strong, breaking all defenses.

Amos 9:9. For I have commanded that Israel be sifted by the other nations as grain is sifted in a sieve, yet not one true kernel will be lost.

Mic 2:13. The Messiah will lead you out of exile and bring you through the gates of your cities of captivity, back to your own land. Your King will go before you—the Lord leads on.

Nah 1:12. But the Lord is not afraid of him! "Though he build his army millions strong," the Lord declares, "it will vanish."

Zeph 3:13. They will not be sinners, full of lies and deceit. They will live quietly, in peace, and lie down in safety, and no one will make them afraid. [15]For the Lord will remove his hand of judgment, and disperse the armies of your enemy. And the Lord himself, the King of Israel, will live among you! At last your troubles will be over—you need fear no more. [17]For the Lord your God has arrived to live among you. He is a mighty Savior. He will give you victory. He will rejoice over you in great gladness; he will love you and not accuse you. Is that a joyous choir I hear? No, it is the Lord himself exulting over you in happy song. [19]"And I will deal severely with all who have oppressed you. I will save the weak and helpless ones, and bring together those who were chased away. I will give glory to my former exiles, mocked and shamed." *v.* 20.

Zech 2:5. For the Lord himself will be a wall of fire protecting them and all Jerusalem; he will be the glory of the city. [8]The Lord of Glory has sent me against the nations that oppressed you, for he who harms you sticks his finger in Jehovah's eye.

Zech 4:6. Then he said, "This is God's message to Zerubbabel: 'Not by might, nor by power, but by my Spirit, says the Lord of Hosts—you will succeed because of my Spirit, though you are few and weak.' [7]Therefore no mountain, however high, can stand before Zerubbabel! For it will flatten out before him! And Zerubbabel will finish building this Temple with mighty shouts of thanksgiving for God's mercy, declaring that all was done by grace alone. [10]Do not despise this small beginning, for the eyes of the Lord rejoice to see the work begin, to see the plumbline in the hand of Zerubbabel. For these seven lamps represent the eyes of the Lord that see everywhere around the world."

Zech 9:8. "And I will surround my Temple like a guard to keep invading armies from entering Israel. I am closely watching their movements and I will keep them away; no foreign oppressors will again overrun my people's land." [14]The Lord shall lead his people as they fight! His arrows shall fly like lightning; the Lord God shall sound the trumpet call and go out against his enemies like a whirlwind off the desert from the south. [15]He will defend his people and they will subdue their enemies, treading them beneath their feet. They will taste victory and shout with triumph. They will slaughter their foes, leaving horrible carnage everywhere. [16]The Lord their God will save his people in that day, as a Shepherd caring for his sheep. They shall shine in his land as glittering jewels in a crown. How wonderful and beautiful all shall be!

Zech 12:8. The Lord will defend the people of Jerusalem; the weakest among them will be mighty as King David! And the royal line will be as God, like the Angel of the Lord who goes before them!

Mt 4:6. "Jump off," he said, "and prove you are the Son of God; for the Scriptures declare, 'God will send his angels to keep you from harm,' . . . they will prevent you from smashing on the rocks below."

Mt 10:29. Not one sparrow (What do they cost? Two for a penny?) can fall to the ground without your Father knowing it. [30]And the very hairs of your head are all numbered. [31]So don't worry! You are more valuable to him than many sparrows. Lk 12:6, 7.

Mt 24:22. In fact, unless those days are shortened, all mankind will perish. But they will be shortened for the sake of God's chosen people. [31]And I shall send forth my angels with the sound of a mighty trumpet blast, and they shall gather my chosen ones from the farthest ends of the earth and heaven. Mk 13:20.

Lk 18:7. Don't you think that God will surely give justice to his people who plead with him day and night? [8]Yes! He will answer them quickly! But the question is: When I, the Messiah, return, how many will I find who have faith (and are praying)?

Lk 21:18. But not a hair of your head will perish!

Acts 17:28. For in him we live and move and are!

Rom 8:28. And we know that all that happens to us is working for our good if we love God and are fitting into his plans.

1 Cor 10:13. But remember this—the wrong desires that come into your life aren't anything new and different. Many others have faced exactly the same problems before you. And no temptation is irresistible. You can trust God to keep the temptation from becoming so strong that you can't stand up against it, for he has promised this and will do what he says. He will show you how to escape temption's power so that you can bear up patiently against it.

2 Thess 3:3. But the Lord is faithful; he will make you strong and guard you from satanic attacks of every kind.

Heb 1:14. No, for the angels are only spirit-messengers sent out to help and care for those who are to receive his salvation.

Jas 4:15. What you ought to say is, "If the Lord wants us to, we shall live and do this or that."

1 Pet 3:12. For the Lord is watching his children, listening to their prayers; but the Lord's face is hard against those who do evil. [13]Usually no one will hurt you for wanting to do good.

2 Pet 2:9. So also the Lord can rescue you and me from the temptations that surround us, and continue to punish the ungodly until the day of final judgment comes.

Rev 3:10. Because you have patiently obeyed me despite the persecution, therefore I will protect you from the time of Great Tribulation and temptation, which will come upon the world to test everyone alive.

Rev 7:3. Wait! Don't do anything yet—hurt neither earth nor sea nor trees—until we have placed the Seal of God upon the foreheads of his servants.

Rev 12:6. The woman fled into the wilderness, where God had prepared a place for her, to take care of her for 1,260 days.

His Preserving Care Exemplified. To Noah and his family, at the time of the flood, Gen 6:8, 12–21; 7; 8:1, 15, 16. To Abraham and Sarah, in Egypt, Gen 12:17; in Gerar, Gen 20:3. To Lot, when Sodom was destroyed, Gen 19. To Hagar, when Abraham sent her away, Gen 21:17, 19. To Jacob, when he fled from Laban, his father-in-law, Gen 31:24, 29; when he met Esau, Gen 33:3–10; as he journeyed in the land of Canaan, Gen 35:5. To Joseph, in Egypt, Gen 39:2, 21. To Moses, in his infancy, Ex 2:1–10. To the Israelites, in bringing about their rescue from slavery, Ex 1:9–12; 2:23–25; 3:7–9; in exempting the land of Goshen from the plague of flies, Ex 8:22; in preserving their cattle from the plague, Ex 9:4–7; in exempting the land of Goshen from the plague of darkness, Ex 10:21–23; in saving the firstborn, when the plague of death destroyed the firstborn of Egypt, Ex 12:13, 23; deliverance from Egypt, Ex 13:3, 17–22; 14; 19:4; Lev 26:13; in the wilderness, Ex 40:36–38; Num 9:17–23; 10:33; 22:12; 23:7–10; Deut 1:31; 23:5. Victories over the Canaanites under Joshua, Josh chapters 6–11; 24:11–13; under Othni-el, Judg 3:9–11; under Ehud, Judg 3:15–30; under Shamgar, Judg 3:31; under Deborah, Judg 4:5; under Gideon, Judg 7; 8:1–24; under Jephthah, Judg 11:29–40; on account of Samuel's intercession, 1 Sam 7:7–10; under David, 1 Sam 17:45–49; Ahab, 1 Kgs 20. Delivering the kingdom of Israel from Syria, 2 Sam 8; delivering Israel by Jeroboam II, 2 Kgs 14:26, 27; by Abijah, 2 Chron 13:4–19; in delivering from the oppression of the king of Syria, 2 Kgs 13:2–5.

To the kingdom of Judah: In delivering from the Egyptians, 2 Chron 12:2–12; the Ethiopian army, 2 Chron 14:11–14; in giving peace with other nations, 2 Chron 17; delivering them from the the Assyrian army, 2 Kgs 19.

To David, 2 Sam 7; 1 Chron 11:13, 14; Hezekiah, 2 Kgs 19; Job, Job 1:9–12; 2:6; Jeremiah and Baruch, Jer 36:26; Daniel and the three Hebrew captives, Dan 2:18–23; 3:27; 6. Jonah, Jon 1:17; the astrologers of the east, Mt 2:12; Jesus and his parents, Mt 2:13, 19–22; Peter, Acts 12:3–17; Paul and Silas, Acts 16:26–39; Paul, Acts 27:24; 28:5, 6, with Mk 16:18.

See *Affliction, Comfort in; Faith; God, Grace of; Savior; Poor, God's Care of.*

See instances under the sub-topic *God, Providence of.*

PROVIDENCE OF. Gen 1:29. And look! I have given you the seed-bearing plants throughout the earth, and all the fruit trees for your food. [30]And I've given all the grass and plants to the animals and birds for their food.

Gen 2:16. But the Lord God gave the man this warning: "You may eat any fruit in the garden except fruit from the Tree of Conscience."

Gen 8:22. As long as the earth remains, there will be springtime and harvest, cold and heat, winter and summer, day and night.

Gen 9:1. God blessed Noah and his sons and told them to have many children and to repopulate the earth. [2, 3]"All wild animals and birds and fish will be afraid of you," God told him; "for I have placed them in your power, and they are yours to use for food, in addition to grain and vegetables."

Gen 22:14. Abraham named the place "Jehovah provides"—and it still goes by that name to this day. [17]"I will bless you with incredible blessings and multiply your descendants into countless thousands and millions, like the stars above you in the sky, and like the sands along the seashore. These descendants of yours will conquer their enemies." Gen 26:4, 5.

Gen 28:20. And Jacob vowed this vow to God: "If God will help and protect me on this journey and give me food and clothes, [21]and will bring me back safely to my father, then I will choose Jehovah as my God!"

Gen 49:24. But their weapons were shattered by the Mighty One of Jacob, the Shepherd, the Rock of Israel. [25]May the God of your fathers, the Almighty, bless you with blessings of heaven above and of the earth beneath—blessings of the breasts and of the womb. *vs.* 11, 12, 20.

Ex 23:22. But if you are careful to obey him, following all my instructions, then I will be an enemy to your enemies.

Ex 34:24. No one will attack and conquer your land when you go up to appear before the Lord your God those three times each year. For I will drive out the nations from before you and enlarge your boundaries.

Lev 25:20. But you will ask, "What shall we eat the seventh year, since we are not allowed to plant or harvest crops that year?" [21, 22]The answer is, "I will bless you with bumper crops the sixth year that will last you until the crops of the eighth year are harvested!"

Lev 26:4, 5. I will give you regular rains, and the land will yield bumper crops, and the trees will be loaded with fruit long after the normal time! And grapes will still be ripening when sowing time comes again. You shall eat your fill, and live safely in the land. [6]for I will give you peace, and you will go to sleep without fear. I will chase away the dangerous animals. [10]You will have such a surplus of crops that you won't know what to do with them when the new harvest is ready!

Deut 1:10. For the Lord has multiplied you like stars!

Deut 2:7. The Lord your God has watched over you and blessed you every step of the way for all these forty years as you have wandered around in this great wilderness; and you have lacked nothing in all that time.

Deut 4:4. But all of you who were faithful to the Lord your God are still alive today. *v.* 40; Num 10:29; Deut 6:2–25; 5:33; 12:28.

Deut 5:29. Oh, that they would always have such a heart for me, wanting to obey my commandments. Then all would go well with them in the future, and with their children throughout all generations! Deut 29:9.

Deut 7:13. And he will love you and bless you and make you into a great nation. He will make you fertile and give fertility to your ground and to your animals, so that you will have large crops of grain, grapes, and olives, and great flocks of cattle, sheep, and goats when you arrive in the land he promised your fathers to give you. [14]You will be blessed above all the nations of the earth; not one of you, whether male or female, shall be barren, not even your cattle. [15]And the Lord will take away all your sickness and will not let you suffer any of the diseases of Egypt you remember so well; he will give them all to your enemies! *vs.* 16–24; Ex 15:26;

23:25, 26; Lev 25:17–19; Deut 6:2, 3; 11:7, 8; 13:17, 18; 30:15–20.

Deut 8:3. Yes, he humbled you by letting you go hungry and then feeding you with manna, a food previously unknown to both you and your ancestors. He did it to help you realize that food isn't everything, and that real life comes by obeying every command of God. [18]Always remember that it is the Lord your God who gives you power to become rich, and he does it to fulfill his promise to your ancestors.

Deut 10:18. He gives justice to the fatherless and widows. He loves foreigners and gives them food and clothing.

Deut 11:12. A land that the Lord your God personally cares for! His eyes are always upon it, day after day throughout the year! *vs.* 13–15.

Deut 12:7. There you and your families shall feast before the Lord your God, and shall rejoice in all he has done for you.

Deut 15:4, 5. No one will become poor because of this, for the Lord will greatly bless you in the land he is giving you if you obey this command. The only prerequisite for his blessing is that you carefully heed all the commands of the Lord your God that I am giving you today. [6]He will bless you as he has promised. You shall lend money to many nations but will never need to borrow! You shall rule many nations, but they shall not rule over you! Deut 26:19; 28:2–13.

Deut 29:5. For forty years God has led you through the wilderness, yet your clothes haven't become old, and your shoes haven't worn out! Deut 8:4.

Deut 32:11. He spreads his wings over them, even as an eagle overspreads her young. She carries them upon her wings—as does the Lord his people! [12]When the Lord alone was leading them, and they lived without foreign gods, [13]God gave them fertile hilltops, rolling, fertile fields, honey from the rock, and olive oil from stony ground! [14]He gave them milk and meat—choice Bashan rams, and goats—and the finest of the wheat; they drank the sparkling wine. [47]These laws are not mere words—they are your life! Through obeying them you will live long, plentiful lives in the land you are going to possess across the Jordon River.

Josh 1:8. Constantly remind the people about these laws, and you yourself must think about them every day and every night so that you will be sure to obey all of them. For only then will you succeed.

Ruth 1:6. She decided to return to Israel with her daughters-in-law, for she had heard that the Lord had blessed his people by giving them good crops again.

1 Sam 2:7. Some he causes to be poor and others to be rich. He cuts one down and lifts another up. [8]He lifts the poor from the dust—yes, from a pile of ashes—and treats them as princes sitting in the seats of honor. For all the earth is the Lord's and he has set the world in order.

1 Sam 14:6. "Yes, let's go across to those heathen," Jonathan had said to his bodyguard. "Perhaps the Lord will do a miracle for us. For it makes no difference to him how many enemy troops there are!"

2 Sam 7:8. Now go and give this message to David from the Lord of heaven: "I chose you to be the leader of my people Israel when you were a mere shepherd, tending your sheep in the pastureland. [9]I have been with you wherever you have gone and have destroyed your enemies. And I will make your name greater yet, so that you will be one of the most famous men in the world!" 1 Chron 17: 7, 8.

1 Kgs 2:3. Obey the laws of God and follow all his ways; keep each of his commands written in the law of Moses so that you will prosper in everything you do, wherever you turn. [4]If you do this, then the Lord will fulfill the promise he gave me, that if my children and their descendants watch their step and are faithful to God, one of them shall always be the king of Israel—my dynasty will never end. 1 Kgs 9:4, 5; 1 Chron 22:9, 13; 2 Chron 7:17, 18; Ps 132:14, 15.

1 Chron 28:8. Then David turned to Solomon and said: "Here before the leaders of Israel, the people of God, and in the sight of our God, I am instructing you to search out every commandment of the Lord so that you may continue to rule this good land and leave it to your children to rule forever."

1 Chron 29:12. Riches and honor come from you alone, and you are the Ruler of all mankind; your hand controls power and might, and it is at your discretion that men are made great and given strength. [14]But who am I and who are my people that we should be permitted to give anything to you? Everything we have has come from you, and we only give you what is yours already! [16]O Lord our God, all of this material that we have gathered to build a temple for your holy name comes from you! It all belongs to you!

2 Chron 1:12. Yes, I am giving you the wisdom and knowledge you asked for! And I am also giving you such riches, wealth and honor as no other king has ever had before you! And there will never again be so great a king in all the world!

2 Chron 20:17. But you will not need to fight! Take your places; stand quietly and see the incredible rescue operation God will perform for you, O people of Judah and Jerusalem! Don't be afraid or discouraged! Go out there tomorrow, for the Lord is with you! *vs.* 3–30.

2 Chron 30:9. For if you turn to the Lord again, your brothers and your children will be treated mercifully by their captors, and they will be able to return to this land. For the Lord your God is full of kindness and mercy and will not continue to turn away his face from you if you return to him.

2 Chron 31:10. And Azariah the High Priest from the clan of Zadok replied, "These are tithes! We have been eating from these stores of food for many weeks, but all this is left over, for the Lord has blessed his people."

Ezra 8:22. For I was ashamed to ask the king for soldiers and cavalry to accompany us and protect us from the enemies along the way. After all, we had told the king that our God would protect all those who worshiped him, and that disaster could come only to those who forsaken him!

Neh 9:25. Your people captured fortified cities and fertile land; they took over houses full of good things, with cisterns and vineyards and oliveyards and many, many fruit trees; so they ate and were full and enjoyed themselves in all your blessings.

Job 5:6. Misery comes upon them to punish them for sowing seeds of sin. [7]Mankind heads for sin and misery as predictably as flames shoot upwards from a fire. [8]My advice to you is this: Go to God and confess your sins to him. [9]For he does wonderful miracles, marvels without number. [10]He sends the rain upon the earth to water the fields, [11]and gives prosperity to the poor and humble, and takes sufferers to safety.

Job 5:24. You need not worry about your home while you are gone; nothing shall be stolen from your barns. [25]Your sons shall become important men; your descendants shall be as numerous as grass! [26]You shall live a long, good life; like standing grain, you'll not be harvested until it's time!

Job 8:7. And though you started with little, you would end with much. [20]But look! God will not cast away a good man, nor prosper evildoers. [21]He will yet fill your mouth with laughter and your lips with shouts of joy. *v.* 6

Job 11:17. And your life will be cloudless; any darkness will be as bright as morning! [18]You will have courage because you will have hope. You will take your time, and rest in safety. [19]You will lie down unafraid and many will look to you for help.

Job 12:23. He raises up a nation and then destroys it. He makes it great, and then reduces it to nothing.

Job 22:18. Yet they forgot that he had filled their homes with good things. [24]If you give up your lust for money, and throw your gold away, [25]then the Almighty himself shall be your treasure; he will be your precious silver! [26]Whatever you wish will happen! And the light of heaven will shine upon the road ahead of you.

Job 29:5. When the Almighty was still with me and my children were around me. [19]For everything I did prospered; the dew lay all night upon my fields and watered them. [20]Fresh honors were constantly given me, and my abilities were constantly refreshed and renewed.

Job 33:14. For God speaks again and again, [15]in dreams, in visions of the night when deep sleep falls on men as they lie on their beds. [16]He opens their ears in times like that, and gives them wisdom and instruction, [17,18]causing them to change their minds, and keeping them from pride, and warning them of the penalties of sin, and keeping them from falling into some trap. [19]Or, God sends sickness and pain, even though no bone is broken, [20]so that a man loses all taste and appetite for food and doesn't care for even the daintiest dessert. [21]He becomes thin, mere skin and bones, [22]and draws near to death. [23, 24]But if a messenger from heaven is there to intercede for him as a friend, to show him what is right, then God pities him and says, "Set him free. Do not make him die, for I have found a substitute." [25]Then his body will become as healthy as a child's, firm and youthful again. [26]And when he prays to God, God will hear and answer and receive him with joy, and return him to his duties. [27]And he will declare to his friends, "I sinned, but God let me go. [28]He did not let me die. I will go on living in the realm of light." [29]Yes, God often does these things for man—[30]brings back his soul from the pit, so that he may live in the light of the living.

Job 36:11. If they listen and obey him, then they will be blessed with prosperity throughout their lives.

Job 37:6. For he directs the snow, the showers, and storm to fall upon the earth. [7]Man's work stops at such a time, so that all men everywhere may recognize his power. [8]The wild animals hide in the rocks or in their dens. [9]From the south comes the rain; from the north, the cold. [10]God blows upon the rivers, and even the widest torrents freeze. [11]He loads the clouds with moisture and they send forth his lightning. [12]The lightning bolts are directed by his hand, and do whatever he commands throughout the earth. [13]He sends the storms as punishment, or, in his lovingkindness, to encourage. [14]Listen, O Job, stop and consider the wonderful miracles of God. [15]Do you know how God controls all nature, and causes the lightning to flash forth from the clouds? [16, 17]Do you understand the balancing of the clouds with wonderful perfection and skill? Do you know why you become warm when the south wind is blowing and everything is still? [18]Can you spread out the gigantic mirror of the skies as he does? [19, 20]You who think you know so much, teach the rest of us how we should approach God. For we are too dull to know! With your wisdom, would we then dare to approach him? Well, does a man wish to be swallowed alive? [21]For as we cannot look at the sun for its brightness when the winds have cleared away the clouds, [22]neither can we gaze at the terrible majesty of God breaking forth upon us from heaven, clothed in dazzling splendor. [23]We cannot imagine the power of the Almighty, and yet he is so just and merciful that he does not destroy us. [24]No wonder men everywhere fear him! For he is not impressed by the world's wisest men!

Job 38:25–27. Who dug the valleys for the torrents of rain? Who laid out the path for the lightning, causing the rain to fall upon the barren deserts, so that the parched and barren ground is satisfied with water, and tender grass springs up? [41]Who provides for the ravens when their young cry out to God as they try to struggle up from their nest in hunger?

Job 39:5. Who makes the wild donkeys wild? [6]I have placed them in the wilderness and given them salt plains to live in.

Ps 21:3. You welcomed him to the throne with

success and prosperity. You set a kingly crown of purest gold upon his head. [4]He asked for a long, good life, and you have granted his request; the days of his life stretch on and on forever. [5]You have given him fame and honor. You have clothed him with splendor and majesty.

Ps 23:1. Because the Lord is my Shepherd, I have everything I need! [2, 3]He lets me rest in the meadow grass and leads me beside the quiet streams. He restores my failing health. He helps me do what honors him the most. [4]Even when walking through the dark valley of death I will not be afraid, for you are close beside me, guarding, guiding all the way. [5]You provide delicious food for me in the presence of my enemies. You have welcomed me as your guest; blessings overflow! [6]Your goodness and unfailing kindness shall be with me all of my life, and afterwards I will live with you forever in your home.

Ps 33:12. Blessed is the nation whose God is the Lord, whose people he has chosen as his own. [15]He has made their hearts and closely watches everything they do.

Ps 34:7. For the Angel of the Lord guards and rescues all who reverence him. [9]If you belong to the Lord, reverence him; for everyone who does this has everything he needs. [10]Even strong young lions sometimes go hungry, but those of us who reverence the Lord will never lack any good thing.

Ps 36:6. Your justice is as solid as God's mountains. Your decisions are as full of wisdom as the oceans are with water. You are concerned for men and animals alike. [7]How precious is your constant love, O God! All humanity takes refuge in the shadow of your wings.

Ps 37:3. Trust in the Lord instead. Be kind and good to others; then you will live safely here in the land and prosper, feeding in safety. [19]He cares for them when times are hard; even in famine, they will have enough. [22]Those blessed by the Lord shall inherit the earth, but those cursed by him shall die. [25]I have been young and now I am old. And in all my years I have never seen the Lord forsake a man who loves him; nor have I seen the children of the godly go hungry. [34]Don't be impatient for the Lord to act! Keep traveling steadily along his pathway and in due season he will honor you with every blessing, and you will see the wicked destroyed.

Ps 40:5. O Lord my God, many and many a time you have done great miracles for us, and we are ever in your thoughts. Who else can do such glorious things? No one else can be compared with you. There isn't time to tell of all your wonderful deeds.

Ps 44:1, 2. O God, we have heard of the glorious miracles you did in the days of long ago. Our forefathers have told us how you drove the heathen nations from this land and gave it all to us, spreading Israel from one end of the country to the other. [3]They did not conquer by their own strength and skill, but by your mighty power and because you smiled upon them and favored them.

Ps 65:9. He waters the earth to make it fertile. The rivers of God will not run dry! He prepares the earth for his people and sends them rich harvests of grain. [10]He waters the furrows with abundant rain. Showers soften the earth, melting the clods and causing seeds to sprout across the land. [11, 12]Then he crowns it all with green, lush pastures in the wilderness; hillsides blossom with joy. [13]The pastures are filled with flocks of sheep, and the valleys are carpeted with grain. All the world shouts with joy, and sings.

Ps 67:6. For the earth has yielded abundant harvests. God, even our own God, will bless us.

Ps 68:6. He gives families to the lonely, and releases prisoners from jail, singing with joy! But for rebels there is famine and distress. [9, 10]You sent abundant rain upon your land, O God, to refresh it in its weariness! There your people lived, for you gave them this home when they were destitute.

Ps 69:35. For God will save Jerusalem; he rebuilds the cities of Judah. His people shall live in them and not be dispossessed. [36]Their children shall inherit the land; all who love his name shall live there safely.

Ps 71:6. Yes, you have been with me from birth and have helped me constantly—no wonder I am always praising you! [7]My success—at which so many stand amazed—is because you are my mighty protector. [15]I cannot count the times when you have faithfully rescued me from danger. I will tell everyone how good you are, and of your constant, daily care.

Ps 72:16. Bless us with abundant crops throughout the land, even on the highland plains; may there be fruit like that of Lebanon; may the cities be as full of people as the fields are of grass.

Ps 78:52. But he led forth his own people like a flock, guiding them safely through the wilderness. [53]He kept them safe, so they were not afraid. But the Sea closed in upon their enemies and overwhelmed them. [54]He brought them to the border of his land of blessing, to this land of hills he made for them. [55]He drove out the nations occupying the land, and gave each tribe of Israel its apportioned place as its home.

Ps 81:16. But he would feed you with the choicest foods. He would satisfy you with honey for the taking. *vs.* 13–15.

Ps 85:12. Yes, the Lord pours down his blessings on the land and it yields its bountiful crops.

Ps 87:5. But someday the highest honor will be to a native of Jerusalem! For the God above all gods will personally bless this city.

Ps 100:3. Try to realize what this means—the Lord is God! He made us—we are his people, the sheep of his pasture.

Ps 103:3. He forgives all my sins. He heals me. [4]He ransoms me from hell. He surrounds me with lovingkindness and tender mercies. [5]He fills my life with good things! My youth is renewed like the eagle's!

Ps 104:10. He placed springs in the valleys, and streams that gush from the mountains. [11]They give water for all the animals to drink. There the wild donkeys quench their thirst, [12]and the birds nest beside the streams and sing among the branches of the trees. 13He sends rain upon the mountains and fills the earth with fruit. 14The tender grass grows up at his command to feed the cattle, and there are fruit trees, vegetables and grain for man to cultivate, 15and wine to make him glad, and olive oil as lotion for his skin, and bread to give him strength. 16The Lord planted the cedars of Lebanon. They are tall and flourishing. 17There the birds make their nests, the storks in the firs. 18High in the mountains are pastures for the wild goats, and rock-badgers burrow in among the rocks and find protection there. 19He assigned the moon to mark the months, and the sun to mark the days. 24O Lord, what a variety you have made! And in wisdom you have made them all! The earth is full of your riches. 25There before me lies the mighty ocean, teeming with life of every kind, both great and small. 26And look! See the ships! And over there the whale you made to play in the sea. 27Every one of these depends on you to give them daily food. 28You supply it, and they gather it. You open wide your hand to feed them and they are satisfied with all your bountiful provision. 29But if you turn away from them, then all is lost. And when you gather up their breath, they die and turn again to dust. 30Then you send your Spirit, and new life is born to replenish all the living of the earth.

Ps 105:14. But through it all he would not let one thing be done to them apart from his decision. He destroyed many a king who tried! 15"Touch not these chosen ones of mine," he warned, "and do not hurt my prophets." 16He called for a famine on the land of Canaan, cutting off its food supply. 17Then he sent Joseph as a slave to Egypt to save his people from starvation. 18There in prison they hurt his feet with fetters, and placed his neck in an iron collar, 19until God's time finally came—how God tested his patience! 20Then the king sent for him and set him free. 21He was put in charge of all the king's possessions. 22At his pleasure he could imprison the king's aides and teach the king's advisors. 23Then Jacob (Israel) arrived in Egypt and lived there with his sons. 24In the years that followed, the people of Israel multiplied explosively, until they were a greater nation than their rulers. 25At that point God turned the Egyptians against the Israelis; they hated and enslaved them. 26But God sent Moses as his representative, and Aaron with him, 27to call down miracles of terror upon the land of Egypt. 28They followed his instructions and he sent thick darkness through the land, 29and turned the nation's water into blood, poisoning the fish. 30Then frogs invaded in enormous numbers; they were found even in the king's private rooms. 31When Moses spoke, the flies and other insects swarmed in vast clouds from one end of Egypt to the other. 32Instead of rain he sent down murderous hail, and lightning flashes overwhelmed the nation. 33Their grape vines and fig trees were ruined; all the trees lay broken on the ground. 34He spoke, and hordes of locusts came, 35and ate up everything green, destroying all the crops. 36Then he killed the oldest child in each Egyptian home, their pride and joy—37and brought his people safely out from Egypt, loaded with silver and gold; there were no sick and feeble folk among them then. 38Egypt was glad when they were gone, for the dread of them was great. 39He spread out a cloud above them to shield them from the burning sun, and gave them a pillar of flame at night to give light. 40They asked for meat and he sent them quail, and gave them manna—bread from heaven. 41He opened up a rock, and water gushed out to form a river through the dry and barren land; 42for he remembered his sacred promises to Abraham his servant. 43So he brought his chosen ones singing into the Promised Land. 44He gave them the lands of the Gentiles, complete with their growing crops; they ate what others planted. 45This was done to make them faithful and obedient to his laws. Hallelujah! Acts 7:34–36.

Ps 107:1. Say "Thank you" to the Lord for being so good, for always being so loving and kind. 2Has the Lord redeemed you? Then speak out! Tell others he has saved you from your enemies. 3He brought the exiles back from the farthest corners of the earth. 4They were wandering homeless in the desert, 5hungry and thirsty and faint. 6"Lord, help!" they cried, and he did! 7He led them straight to safety and a place to live. 8Oh, that these men would praise the Lord for his lovingkindness, and for all of his wonderful deeds! 9For he satisfies the thirsty soul and fills the hungry soul with good. 10Who are these who sit in darkness, in the shadow of death, crushed by misery and slavery? 11They rebelled against the Lord, scorning him who is the God above all gods. 12That is why he broke them with hard labor; they fell and none could help them rise again. 13Then they cried to the Lord in their troubles, and he rescued them! 14He led them from the darkness and shadow of death and snapped their chains. 15Oh, that these men would praise the Lord for his lovingkindness and for all of his wonderful deeds! 16For he broke down their prison gates of brass and cut apart their iron bars. 17Others, the fools, were ill because of their sinful ways. 18Their appetites were gone and death was near. 19Then they cried to the Lord in their troubles, and he helped them and delivered them. 20He spoke, and they were healed—snatched from the door of death. 21Oh, that these men would praise the Lord for his lovingkindness and for all of his wonderful deeds! 22Let them tell him "Thank you" as their sacrifice, and sing about his glorious deeds. 23And then there are the sailors sailing the seven seas, plying the trade routes of the world. 24They, too, observe the power of God in action. 25He calls to the storm winds; the waves rise high. 26Their ships are tossed to the heavens and sink again to the depths; the sailors cringe in terror. 27They reel and stagger like drunkards and are at their wit's end. 28Then they cry to the Lord in their trouble, and he saves them. 29He calms the storm and stills the waves. 30What a blessing is that stillness, as he brings them safely into harbor! 31Oh, that these men would praise the Lord for his lovingkindness and for all of his wonderful deeds! 32Let them praise him publicly before the congregation, and before the leaders of the nation. 33He dries up rivers, 34and turns the good land of the wicked into deserts of salt. 35Again, he turns deserts into fertile, watered valleys. 36He brings the hungry to settle there and build their cities, 37to sow their fields and plant their vineyards, and reap their bumper crops! 38How he blesses them! They raise big families there, and many cattle. 39But others become poor through oppression, trouble and sorrow. 40For God pours contempt upon the haughty and causes princes to wander among ruins; 41but he rescues the poor who are godly and gives them many children and much prosperity. 42Good men everywhere will see it and be glad, while evil men are stricken silent. 43Listen, if you are wise, to what I am saying. Think about the lovingkindness of the Lord!

Ps 111:5. He gives food to those who trust him; he never forgets his promises.

Ps 113:6. Far below him are the heavens and the earth; he stoops to look, 7and lifts the poor from the dirt, and the hungry from the garbage dump, 8and sets them among princes! 9He gives children to the childless wife, so that she becomes a happy mother. Hallelujah! Praise the Lord.

Ps 115:16. The heavens belong to the Lord, but he has given the earth to all mankind.

Ps 116:1. I love the Lord because he hears my prayers and answers them. 2Because he bends down and listens, I will pray as long as I breathe! 3Death stared me in the face—I was frightened and sad. 4Then I cried, "Lord, save me!" 5How kind he is! How good he is! So merciful, this God of ours! 6The Lord protects the simple and the childlike; I was facing death and then he saved me. 7Now I can relax. For the Lord has done this wonderful miracle for me. 8He has saved me from death, my eyes from tears, my feet from stumbling. 9I shall live! Yes, in his presence—here on earth! 10, 11In my discouragement I thought, "They are lying when they say I will recover." 12But now what can I offer Jehovah for all he has done for me? 13I will bring him an offering of wine and praise his name for saving me. 14I will publicly bring him the sacrifice I vowed I would. 15His loved ones are very precious to him and he does not lightly let them die.

Ps 118:5. In my distress I prayed to the Lord and he answered me and rescued me. 6He is for me! How can I be afraid? What can mere man do to me? 13You did your best to kill me, O my enemy, but the Lord helped me. 14He is my strength and song in the heat of battle, and now he has given me the victory.

Ps 127:1. Unless the Lord builds a house, the builders' work is useless. Unless the Lord protects a city, sentries do no good. *vs.* 2–5.

Ps 128:2. Their reward shall be prosperity and happiness. 3Your wife shall be contented in your home. And look at all those children! There they sit around the dinner table as vigorous and healthy as young olive trees. 4That is God's reward to those who reverence and trust him. 5May the Lord continually bless you with heaven's blessings as well as with human joys. 6May you live to enjoy your grandchildren! And may God bless Israel!

Ps 135:7. He makes mists rise throughout the earth and sends the lightning to bring down the rain; and sends the winds from his treasuries. *vs.* 6–12.

Ps 136:25. He gives food to every living thing, for his lovingkindness continues forever. *vs.* 5–25.

Ps 144:12–15. Here is my description of a truly happy land where Jehovah is God: Sons vigorous and tall as growing plants. Daughters of graceful beauty like the pillars of a palace wall. Barns full to the brim with crops of every kind. Sheep by the thousands out in our fields. Oxen loaded down with produce. No enemy attacking the walls, but peace everywhere. No crime in our streets. Yes, happy are those whose God is Jehovah.

Ps 145:15. The eyes of all mankind look up to you for help; you give them their food as they need it. 16You constantly satisfy the hunger and thirst of every living thing.

Ps 146:7. And gives justice to the poor and oppressed, and food to the hungry. He frees the prisoners, 8and opens the eyes of the blind; he lifts the burdens from those bent down beneath their loads. For the Lord loves good men. 9He protects the immigrants, and cares for the orphans and widows. But he turns topsy-turvy the plans of the wicked.

Ps 147:8. He covers the heavens with clouds, sends down the showers and makes the green grass grow in mountain pastures. 9He feeds the wild animals and the young ravens cry to him for food. 13For he has fortified your gates against all enemies, and blessed your children. 14He sends peace across your nation, and fills your barns with plenty of the finest wheat.

Prov 2:21. For only good men enjoy life to the full.

Prov 3:1, 2. My son, never forget the things I've taught you. If you want a long and satisfying life, closely follow my instructions.

Prov 10:22. The Lord's blessing is our greatest wealth. All our work adds nothing to it! 27Reverence for God adds hours to each day; so how can the wicked expect a long, good life?

Prov 11:10. The whole city celebrates a good man's success—and also the godless man's death. 11The good influence of godly citizens causes a city to prosper, but the moral decay of the wicked drives it downhill. 31Even the godly shall be rewarded here on earth; how much more the wicked!

Prov 13:25. The good man eats to live, while the evil man lives to eat.

Prov 14:11. The work of the wicked shall perish; the work of the godly will flourish. 19Evil men shall bow before the godly. 34Godliness exalts a nation, but sin is a reproach to any people. Eccl 2:24–26.

Prov 15:6. There is treasure in being good, but trouble dogs the wicked.

Prov 16:7. When a man is trying to please God, God makes even his worst enemies to be at peace with him. [9]We should make plans—counting on God to direct us.

Prov 28:10. A curse on those who lead astray the godly. But men who encourage the upright to do good shall be given a worthwhile reward.

Eccl 2:24. So I decided that there was nothing better for a man to do than to enjoy his food and drink, and his job. Then I realized that even this pleasure is from the hand of God. Eccl 3:13.

Eccl 5:19. And, of course, it is very good if a man has received wealth from the Lord, and the good health to enjoy it. To enjoy your work and to accept your lot in life—that is indeed a gift from God.

Isa 1:19. If you will only let me help you, if you will only obey, then I will make you rich!

Isa 25:4. But to the poor, O Lord, you are a refuge from the storm, a shadow from the heat, a shelter from merciless men who are like a driving rain that melts down an earthen wall.

Isa 30:23. Then God will bless you with rain at planting time and with wonderful harvests and with ample pastures for your cows. [26]The moon will be as bright as the sun, and the sunlight brighter than seven days! So it will be when the Lord begins to heal his people and to cure the wounds he gave them. *vs.* 24, 25.

Isa 33:16. Such as these shall dwell on high. The rocks of the mountains will be their fortress of safety; food will be supplied to them and they will have all the water they need.

Isa 43:20. The wild animals in the fields will thank me, the jackals and ostriches too, for giving them water in the wilderness, yes, springs in the desert, so that my people, my chosen ones, can be refreshed.

Isa 46:3. Listen to me, all Israel who are left; I have created you and cared for you since you were born. [4]I will be your God through all your lifetime, yes, even when your hair is white with age. I made you and I will care for you. I will carry you along and be your Savior.

Isa 48:17. The Lord, your Redeemer, the Holy One of Israel, says, I am the Lord your God, who punishes you for your own good and leads you along the paths that you should follow. [21]They were not thirsty when he led them through the deserts; he divided the rock, and water gushed out for them to drink.

Isa 51:2. Yes, think about your ancestors Abraham and Sarah, from whom you came. You worry at being so small and few, but Abraham was only *one* when I called him. But when I blessed him, he became a great nation.

Isa 55:10. As the rain and snow come down from heaven and stay upon the ground to water the earth, and cause the grain to grow and to produce seed for the farmer and bread for the hungry.

Isa 61:9. Their descendants shall be known and honored among the nations; all shall realize that they are a people God has blessed.

Isa 62:9. You raised it; you shall keep it, praising God. Within the Temple courts you yourselves shall drink the wine you pressed.

Isa 65:13. Therefore the Lord God says, You shall starve, but my servants shall eat; you shall be thirsty while they drink; you shall be sad and ashamed, but they shall rejoice. [23]Their harvests will not be eaten by their enemies; their children will not be born to be cannon fodder. For they are the children of those the Lord has blessed; and their children, too, shall be blessed.

Jer 5:24. Though I am the one who gives them rain each year in spring and fall and sends the harvest times, yet they have no respect or fear for me.

Jer 10:13. It is his voice that echoes in the thunder of the storm clouds. He causes mist to rise upon the earth; he sends the lightning and brings the rain, and from his treasuries he brings the wind. Jer 51:16.

Jer 14:22. What heathen god can gives us rain? Who but you alone, O Lord our God, can do such things as this? Therefore we will wait for you to help us.

Jer 22:15. But a beautiful palace does not make a great king! Why did your father Josiah reign so long? Because he was just and fair in all his dealings. That is why God blessed him. [16]He saw to it that justice and help were given the poor and the needy and all went well for him. This is how a man lives close to God.

Jer 27:6. So now I have given all your countries to King Nebuchadnezzar of Babylon, who is my deputy. And I have handed over to him all your cattle for his use.

Jer 30:19. The cities will be filled with joy and great thanksgiving, and I will multiply my people and make of them a great and honored nation.

Jer 31:35. The Lord who gives us sunlight in the daytime and the moon and stars to light the night, and who stirs the sea to make the roaring waves—his name is Lord of Hosts—says this.

Jer 33:10, 11. The Lord declares that the happy voice of bridegrooms and of brides, and the joyous song of those bringing thanksgiving offerings to the Lord will be heard again in this doomed land. The people will sing: "Praise the Lord! For he is good and his mercy endures forever!" For I will make this land happier and even more prosperous than it has ever been before.

Ezk 36:9. See, I am for you, and I will come and help you as you prepare the ground and sow your crops. [10]I will greatly increase your population throughout all Israel, and the ruined cities will be rebuilt and filled with people. [11]Not only the people, but your flocks and herds will also greatly multiply. O mountains of Israel, again you will be filled with homes. I will do even more for you than I did before. Then you shall know I am the Lord. [30]I will give you huge harvests from your fruit trees and fields, and never again will the surrounding nations be able to scoff at your land for its famines. [36]Then the nations all around—all those still left—will know that I, the Lord, rebuilt the ruins and planted lush crops in the wilderness. For I, the Lord, have promised it, and I will do it. [38]Let them but ask and I will multiply them like the flocks that fill Jerusalem's streets at time of sacrifice. The ruined cities will be crowded once more, and everyone will know I am the Lord. *vs.* 28–38.

Dan 5:18. Your Majesty, the Most High God gave Nebuchadnezzar, who long ago preceded you, a kingdom and majesty and glory and honor.

Dan 6:20. And called out in anguish, "O Daniel, servant of the Living God, was your God, whom you worship continually, able to deliver you from the lions?" [21]Then he heard a voice! "Your Majesty, live forever!" It was Daniel! [22]"My God has sent his angel," he said, "to shut the lions' mouths so that they can't touch me; for I am innocent before God, nor, sir, have I wronged you."

Hos 2:8. She doesn't realize that all she has, has come from me. It was I who gave her all the gold and silver that she used in worshiping Baal, her god!

21, 22. In that day, says the Lord, I will answer the pleading of the sky for clouds, to pour down water on the earth in answer to its cry for rain. Then the earth can answer the parched cry of the grain, the grapes, and the olive trees for moisture and for dew—and the whole grand chorus shall sing together that "God sows!" He has given all!

Hos 11:3. I trained him from infancy, I taught him to walk, I held him in my arms. But he doesn't know or even care that it was I who raised him.

Joel 2:21. Fear not, my people; be glad now and rejoice, for he has done amazing things for you. [23]Rejoice, O people of Jerusalem, rejoice in the Lord your God! For the rains he sends are tokens of forgiveness. Once more the autumn rains will come, as well as those of spring. [26]Once again you will have all the food you want. Praise the Lord, who does these miracles for you. Never again will my people experience disaster such as this. *vs.* 18–26.

Amos 4:7. "I ruined your crops by holding back the rain three months before the harvest. I sent rain on one city, but not another. While rain fell on one field, another was dry and withered. [8]People from two or three cities would make their weary journey for a drink of water to a city that had rain, but there wasn't ever enough. Yet you wouldn't return to me," says the Lord. [9]"I sent blight and mildew on your farms and your vineyards; the locusts ate your figs and olive trees. And still you wouldn't return to me," says the Lord. [10]"I sent you plagues like those of Egypt long ago. I killed your lads in war and drove away your horses. The stench of death was terrible to smell. And yet you refused to come. [11]I destroyed some of your cities, as I did Sodom and Gomorrah; those left are like half-burned firebrands snatched away from fire. And still you won't return to me," says the Lord. [12]Therefore I will bring upon you all these further evils I have spoken of. Prepare to meet your God in judgment, Israel."

Amos 9:13. The time will come when there will be such abundance of crops, that the harvest time will scarcely end before the farmer starts again to sow another crop, and the terraces of grapes upon the hills of Israel will drip sweet wine!

Jon 4:6. And when the leaves of the shelter withered in the heat, the Lord arranged for a vine to grow up quickly and spread its broad leaves over Jonah's head to shade him. This made him comfortable and very grateful.

Hag 2:19. Notice, I am giving you this promise now before you have even begun to rebuild the Temple structure, and before you have harvested your grain, and before the grapes and figs and pomegranates and olives have produced their next crops: *From this day I will bless you.*

Zech 3:7. The Lord of Hosts declares: "If you will follow the paths I set for you and do all I tell you to, then I will put you in charge of my Temple, to keep it holy; and I will let you walk in and out of my presence with these angels."

Zech 8:12. For I am sowing peace and prosperity among you. Your crops will prosper; the grapevines will be weighted down with fruit; the ground will be fertile, with plenty of rain; all these blessings will be given to the people left in the land.

Zech 9:17. How wonderful and beautiful all shall be! The abundance of grain and wine will make the young men and girls flourish; they will be radiant with health and happiness.

Zech 10:1. Ask the Lord for rain in the springtime, and he will answer with lightning and showers. Every field will become a lush pasture.

Mal 3:10. Bring all the tithes into the storehouse so that there will be food enough in my Temple; if you do, I will open up the windows of heaven for you and pour out a blessing so great you won't have room enough to take it in! Try it! Let me prove it to you! [12]And all nations will call you blessed, for you will be a land sparkling with happiness. These are the promises of the Lord of Hosts. *v.* 11.

Mt 5:5. The meek and lowly are fortunate! for the whole wide world belongs to them. [45]In that way you will be acting as true sons of your Father in heaven. For he gives his sunlight to both the evil and the good, and sends rain on the just and on the unjust too.

Mt 6:26. Look at the birds! They don't worry about what to eat—they don't need to sow or reap or store up food—for your heavenly Father feeds them. And you are far more valuable to him than they are. [30]And if God cares so wonderfully for flowers that are here today and gone tomorrow, won't he more surely care for you, O men of little faith? [31, 32]So don't worry at all about having enough food and clothing. Why be like the heathen? For they take pride in all these things and are deeply concerned about them. But your heavenly Father already knows perfectly well that you need them, [33]and he will give them to you if you give him first place in your life and live as he wants you to.

Mt 10:29. Not one sparrow (What do they cost? Two for a penny?) can fall to the ground without your Father knowing it. [30]And the very hairs of your head are all numbered. (Lk 12:6, 7, 24–28.)

[31]So don't worry! You are more valuable to him than many sparrows.

Lk 22:35. Then Jesus asked them, "When I sent you out to preach the Good News and you were without money, duffle bag, or extra clothing, how did you get along?" "Fine," they replied.

Jn 6:31. Give us free bread every day, like our fathers had while they journeyed through the wilderness! As the Scriptures say, "Moses gave them bread from heaven."

Acts 14:17. But he never left himself without a witness; there were always his reminders—the kind things he did such as sending you rain and good crops and giving you food and gladness.

1 Cor. 2:9. That is what is meant by the Scriptures which say that no mere man has ever seen, heard or even imagined what wonderful things God has ready for those who love the Lord.

1 Cor 16:2. On every Lord's Day each of you should put aside something from what you have earned during the week, and use it for this offering. The amount depends on how much the Lord has helped you earn. Don't wait until I get there and then try to collect it all at once.

2 Cor 9:8. God is able to make it up to you by giving you everything you need and more, so that there will not only be enough for your own needs, but plenty left over to give joyfully to others. [9]It is as the Scriptures say: "The godly man gives generously to the poor. His good deeds will be an honor to him forever." [10]For God, who gives seed to the farmer to plant, and later on, good crops to harvest and eat, will give you more and more seed to plant and will make it grow so that you can give away more and more fruit from your harvest.

Instances of. Saving Noah, Gen 7:1. The call of Abraham, Gen 12:1. Protecting Abraham, Sarah, and Abimelech, Gen 20:3–6. Deliverance of Lot, Gen 19. Care of Isaac, Gen 26:2, 3. The mission of Joseph, Gen 39:2, 3, 23; 45:7, 8; 50:20; Ps 105:17–22. Warning Pharaoh of famine, Gen 41. Delivering the Israelites, Ex 3:8; 11:3; 13:17, 18; Acts 7:34–36. The pillar of cloud, Ex 13:21; 14:19, 20. Dividing the Red Sea, Ex 14:21. Delaying and destroying Pharaoh, Ex 14:25–30. Purifying the waters of Marah, Ex 15:25. Supplying manna and quail, Ex 16:13–15; Num 11:31, 32; water at Meribah, Num 20:7–13; Neh 9:10–25. Protection of homes while at feasts, Ex 34:24. In the conquest of Canaan, Ps 44:1–3. Saving David's army, 2 Sam 5:23–25. The revolt of the ten tribes, 1 Kgs 12:15, 23, 24; 2 Chron 10:15. Fighting the battles of Israel, 2 Chron 13:12, 18, 19; 14:9–14; 16:7–9; 20:15, 17, 22, 23; 32:21, 22. Restoring Manasseh after his conversion, 2 Chron 33:12, 13. Feeding Elijah and the widow, 1 Kgs 17; 19:1–8. In prospering Hezekiah, 2 Kgs 18:6, 7; 2 Chron 32:28, 29; and Asa, 2 Chron 14:6, 7; and Jehoshaphat, 2 Chron 17:3, 5; 20:30; and Uzziah, 2 Chron 26: 5–15; and Jotham, 2 Chron 27:6; and Job, Job 1:10; 42:10, 12; and Daniel, Dan 1:9. In causing the king of Assyria to favor the Jews, Ezra 6:21, 22. In rescuing Jeremiah, Lam 3:52–58, with Jer 38:6–13. Restoration of the Jews, 2 Chron 36:22, 23; Ezra 1:1. Rescuing the Jews from Haman's plot, the book of Esther. Rebuilding the walls of Jerusalem, Neh 6:16. Warning Joseph in dreams, Mt 1:20; 2:13, 19, 20; and the astrologers of the east, Mt 2:12, 13. Restoring Epaphroditus, Phil 2:27. In the banishment of John to Patmos, Rev 1:9.

See *God, Goodness of; Preserver,* above; and *Overruling Intervention Showing the,* below.

PROVIDENCE OF, OVERRULING INTERVENTION SHOWING THE. Gen 50:20. As far as I am concerned, God turned into good what you meant for evil, for he brought me to this high position I have today so that I could save the lives of many people. Gen 45:5–7; Ps 105:17; Acts 7:9, 10.

Ex 14:4. And once again I will harden Pharaoh's heart and he will chase after you. I have planned this to gain great honor and glory over Pharaoh and all his armies, and the Egyptians shall know that I am the Lord.

Num 23:7, 8. This was Balaam's message: "King Balak, king of Moab, has brought me from the land of Aram, from the eastern mountains. 'Come,' he told me, 'curse Jacob for me! Let your anger rise on Israel.' But how can I curse what God has not cursed? How can I denounce a people God has not denounced?" [23]"No curse can be placed on Jacob, and no magic shall be done against him. For now it shall be said of Israel, 'What wonders God has done for them!' " *vs.* 1–30; Num 22:12–18; 24:10–13.

Deut 2:30. But King Sihon refused because Jehovah your God made him obstinate, so that he could destroy Sihon by the hands of Israel, as has now been done. Josh 11:20.

Deut 23:4. The reason for this law is that these nations did not welcome you with food and water when you came out of Egypt; they even tried to hire Balaam, the son of Beor from Pethor, Mesopotamia, to curse you. [5]But the Lord wouldn't listen to Balaam; instead, he turned the intended curse into a blessing for you, because the Lord loves you.

Judg 9:22, 23. Three years later God stirred up trouble between King Abimelech and the citizens of Shechem, and they revolted. [24]In the events that followed, both Abimelech and the citizens of Shechem who aided him in butchering Gideon's seventy sons were given their just punishment for these murders.

1 Sam 2:6. The Lord kills, the Lord gives life. [7]Some he causes to be poor and others to be rich. He cuts one down and lifts another up. [8]He lifts the poor from the dust—yes, from a pile of ashes—and treats them as princes sitting in the seats of honor. For all the earth is the Lord's and he has set the world in order. [9]He will protect his godly ones, but the wicked shall be silenced in darkness. No one shall succeed by strength alone.

2 Sam 17:14. Then Absalom and all the men of Israel said, "Hushai's advice is better than Ahithophel's." For the Lord had arranged to defeat the counsel of Ahithophel, which really was the better plan, so that he could bring disaster upon Absalom!

1 Kgs 12:15. So the king refused the people's de-

mands. (But the Lord's hand was in it—he caused the new king to do this in order to fulfill his promise to Jeroboam, made through Ahijah, the prophet from Shiloh.) 1 Kgs 11:14–40; 2 Chron 10:15.

1 Chron 5:26. So God caused King Pul of Assyria (also known as Tilgath-pilneser III) to invade the land and deport the men of Reuben, Gad, and the half-tribe of Manasseh. They took them to Halah, Habor, Hara, and the Gozan River, where they remain to this day.

2 Chron 36:22, 23. But in the first year of King Cyrus of Persia, the Lord stirred up the spirit of Cyrus to make this proclamation throughout his kingdom, putting it into writing: "All the kingdoms of the earth have been given to me by the Lord God of heaven, and he has instructed me to build him a Temple in Jerusalem, in the land of Judah. All among you who are the Lord's people, return to Israel for this task, and the Lord be with you." This also fulfilled the prediction of Jeremiah the prophet. Ezra 1:1.

Ezra 5:5. But because the Lord was overseeing the entire situation, our enemies did not force us to stop building, but let us continue while King Darius looked into the matter and returned his decision.

Ezra 6:22. There was great joy throughout the land because the Lord had caused the king of Assyria to be generous to Israel and to assist in the construction of the Temple.

Neh 6:16. When our enemies and the surrounding nations heard about it, they were frightened and humiliated, and they realized that the work had been done with the help of our God.

Esther 7:9, 10. Then Harbona, one of the king's aides, said "Sir, Haman has just ordered a 75-foot gallows constructed, to hang Mordecai, the man who saved the king from assassination! It stands in Haman's courtyard." "Hang Haman on it," the king ordered. So they did, and the king's wrath was pacified. Esther 6:1–12; 9:24, 25.

Esther 9:1. So on the 28th day of February, the day the two decrees of the king were to be put into effect—the day the Jews' enemies had hoped to vanquish them, though it turned out quite to the contrary—the Jews gathered in their cities throughout all the king's provinces to defend themselves against any who might try to harm them; but no one tried, for they were greatly feared.

Job 5:12. He frustrates the plans of crafty men. [13]They are caught in their own traps; he thwarts their schemes. Isa 8:9, 10.

Ps 17:13, 14. Lord, arise and stand against them. Push them back! Come and save me from these men of the world whose only concern is earthly gain—these men whom you have filled with your treasures so that their children and grandchildren are rich and prosperous.

Ps 33:10. And with a breath he can scatter the plans of all the nations who oppose him.

Ps 75:6, 7. For promotion and power come from nowhere on earth, but only from God. He promotes one and deposes another.

Ps 76:10. Man's futile wrath will bring you glory. You will use it as an ornament!

Ps 127:1. Unless the Lord builds a house, the builders' work is useless. Unless the Lord protects a city, sentries do no good. [2]It is senseless for you to work so hard from early morning until late at night, fearing you will starve to death; for God wants his loved ones to get their proper rest.

Prov 13:22. When a good man dies, he leaves an inheritance to his grandchildren; but when a sinner dies, his wealth is stored up for the godly.

Prov 14:19. Evil men shall bow before the godly.

Prov 16:7. When a man is trying to please God, God makes even his worst enemies to be at peace with him. [33]We toss the coin, but it is the Lord who controls its decision.

Prov 19:21. Man proposes, but God disposes.

Prov 21:1. Just as water is turned into irrigation ditches, so the Lord directs the king's thoughts. He turns them wherever he wants to. [18]The wicked will finally lose; the righteous will finally win.

Prov 28:8. Income from exploiting the poor will end up in the hands of someone who pities them.

Eccl 2:26. But if a sinner becomes wealthy, God takes the wealth away from him and gives it to those who please him.

Eccl 3:1. There is a right time for everything: [10]I have thought about this in connection with all the various kinds of work God has given to mankind.

Isa 10:5, 6. Assyria is the whip of my anger; his military strength is my weapon upon this godless nation, doomed and damned; he will enslave them and plunder them and trample them like dirt beneath his feet. [7]But the king of Assyria will not know that it is I who sent him. He will merely think he is attacking my people as part of his plan to conquer the world.

Isa 13:3. I, the Lord, have set apart these armies for this task; I have called those rejoicing in their strength to do this work, to satisfy my anger. [4]Hear the tumult on the mountains! Listen as the armies march! It is the tumult and the shout of many nations. The Lord of Hosts has brought them here, [5]from countries far away. They are his weapons against you, O Babylon. They carry his anger with them and will destroy your whole land.

Isa 41:2. Who has stirred up this one from the east, whom victory meets at every step? Who, indeed, but the Lord? God has given him victory over many nations and permitted him to trample kings underfoot and to put entire armies to the sword. [4]Who has done such mighty deeds, directing the affairs of generations of mankind as they march by? It is I, the Lord, the First and Last; I alone am he.

Isa 43:14. The Lord, your Redeemer, the Holy One of Israel, says: For your sakes I will send an invading army against Babylon, that will walk in almost unscathed. The boasts of the Babylonians will turn to cries of fear.

Isa 44:28. When I say of Cyrus, "He is my shepherd," he will certainly do as I say; and Jerusalem will be rebuilt and the Temple restored, for I have spoken it.

Isa 45:5. I am Jehovah; there is no other God. I will strengthen you and send you out to victory even though you don't know me, [6]and all the world from east to west will know there is no other God. I am Jehovah and there is no one else. I alone am God. [13]I have raised up Cyrus to fulfill my righteous purpose, and I will direct all his paths. He shall restore my city and free my captive people—and not for a reward! *vs.* 1–5.

Isa 48:14. Come, all of you, and listen. Among all your idols, which one has ever told you this: "The Lord loves Cyrus. He will use him to put an end to the empire of Babylonia. He will utterly rout the armies of the Chaldeans"? [15]But I am saying it. I have called Cyrus; I have sent him on this errand and I will prosper him.

Isa 54:16. I have created the smith who blows the coals beneath the forge and makes the weapons of destruction. And I have created the armies that destroy. [17]But in that coming day, no weapon turned against you shall succeed, and you will have justice against every courtroom lie. This is the heritage of the servants of the Lord. This is the blessing I have given you, says the Lord.

Jer 51:20. Cyrus is God's battleaxe and sword. I will use you, says the Lord, to break nations in pieces and to destroy many kingdoms. [21]With you I will crush armies, destroying the horse and his rider, the chariot and the charioteer.

Jer 52:3. Things became so bad at last that the Lord, in his anger, saw to it that Zedekiah rebelled against the king of Babylon until he and the people of Israel were ejected from the Lord's presence in Jerusalem and Judah, and were taken away as captives to Babylon.

Ezk 21:26. Take off your jeweled crown, the Lord God says. The old order changes. Now the poor are exalted, and the rich brought very low. [27]I will overturn, overturn, overturn the kingdom, so that even the new order that emerges will not succeed until the Man appears who has a right to it. And I will give it all to him.

Ezk 29:19. Therefore, the Lord God says, I will give the land of Egypt to Nebuchadnezzar, king of Babylon, and he will carry off her wealth, plundering everything she has, for his army. [20]Yes, I have given him the land of Egypt for his salary, because he was working for me during those thirteen years at Tyre, says the Lord.

Dan 11:27. Both these kings will be plotting against each other at the conference table, attempting to deceive each other. But it will make no difference, for neither can succeed until God's appointed time has come.

Acts 3:17. Dear brothers, I realize that what you did to Jesus was done in ignorance; and the same can be said of your leaders. [18]But God was fulfilling the prophecies that the Messiah must suffer all these things.

Acts 5:38. And so my advice is, leave these men alone. If what they teach and do is merely on their own, it will soon be overthrown. [39]But if it is of God, you will not be able to stop them, lest you find yourselves fighting even against God.

Rom 1:10. And one of the things I keep on praying for is the opportunity, God willing, to come at last to see you and, if possible, that I will have a safe trip.

Rom 8:28. And we know that all that happens to us is working for our good if we love God and are fitting into his plans.

1 Cor 4:19. But I will come, and soon, if the Lord will let me, and then I'll find out whether these proud men are just big talkers or whether they really have God's power.

1 Cor 16:7. This time I don't want to make just a passing visit and then go right on; I want to come and stay awhile, if the Lord will let me.

Phil 1:12. And I want you to know this, dear brothers: Everything that has happened to me here has been a great boost in getting out the Good News concerning Christ. [19]I am going to keep on being glad, for I know that as you pray for me, and as the Holy Spirit helps me, this is all going to turn out for my good.

Philemon 1:15. Perhaps you could think of it this way: that he ran away from you for a little while so that now he can be yours forever.

Jas 4:15. What you ought to say is, "If the Lord wants us to, we shall live and do this or that."

Rev 17:17. For God will put a plan into their minds, a plan that will carry out his purposes: They will mutually agree to give their authority to the scarlet animal, so that the words of God will be fulfilled.

See *God, Goodness of, Preserver,* above.

PROVIDENCE OF, MYSTERIOUS AND MISINTERPRETED: Job 10:15. Just the slightest wickedness, and I am done for. And if I'm good, that doesn't count. I am filled with frustration.

Job 12:6. For robbers prosper. Go ahead and provoke God—it makes no difference! He will supply your every need anyway!

Job 21:7. The truth is that the wicked live on to a good old age, and become great and powerful.

Job 24:1. Why doesn't God open the court and listen to my case? Why must the godly wait for him in vain? *vs.* 1–12.

Job 33:13. Why should you fight against him just because he does not give account to you of what he does?

Ps 10:5. Yet there is success in everything they do, and their enemies fall before them. They do not see your punishment awaiting them.

Ps 73:2. But as for me, I came *so* close to the edge of the cliff! My feet were slipping and I was almost gone. [3]For I was envious of the prosperity of the proud and wicked. [13]Have I been wasting my time? Why take the trouble to be pure? [14]All I get out of it is trouble and woe—every day and all day long! [15]If I had really said that, I would have been a traitor to your people. [16]Yet it is so hard to explain it—this prosperity of those who hate the Lord. [17]Then one day I went into God's sanctuary to meditate, and thought about the future of these evil men. *vs.* 4, 5, 12.

Ps 89:47. Oh, remember how short you have made man's lifespan. Is it an empty, futile life you give the sons of men?

Prov 28:5. Evil men don't understand the importance of justice, but those who follow the Lord are much concerned about it.

Eccl 7:15. In this silly life I have seen everything, including the fact that some of the good die young and some of the wicked live on and on.

Eccl 8:14. There is a strange thing happening here upon the earth: Providence seems to treat some good men as though they were wicked, and some wicked men as though they were good. This is all very vexing and troublesome! *vs.* 12–17.

Eccl 9:2. The same providence confronts everyone, whether good or bad, religious or irreligious, profane or godly. It seems so unfair, that one fate comes to all. [11]Again I looked throughout the earth and saw that the swiftest person does not always win the race, nor the strongest man the battle, and that wise men are often poor, and skillful men are not necessarily famous; but it is all by chance, by happening to be at the right place at the right time.

Jer 12:1. O Lord, you always give me justice when I bring a case before you to decide. Now let me bring you this complaint: Why are the wicked so prosperous? Why are evil men so happy? [2]You plant them. They take root and their business grows. Their profits multiply, and they are rich. They say, "Thank God!" But in their hearts they give no credit to you.

Jer 50:7. All who found them devoured them and said, "We are permitted to attack them freely, for they have sinned against the Lord, the God of justice, the hope of their fathers."

Dan 12:10. Many shall be purified by great trials and persecutions. But the wicked shall continue in their wickedness, and none of them will understand. Only those who are willing to learn will know what it means.

Mic 4:12. But they do not know my thoughts nor understand my plan, for the time will come when the Lord will gather together the enemies of his people like sheaves upon the threshing floor.

Hab 1:2. O Lord, how long must I call for help before you will listen? I shout to you in vain; there is no answer. "Help! Murder!" I cry, but no one comes to save. [3]Must I forever see this sin and sadness all around me? [11]They sweep past like wind and are gone, but their guilt is deep, for they claim their power is from their gods. [13]We are wicked, but they far more! Will you, who cannot allow sin in any form, stand idly by while they swallow us up? Should you be silent while the wicked destroy those who are better than they? [14]Are we but fish, to be caught and killed? Are we but creeping things that have no leader to defend them from their foes?

Mal 3:14, 15. "Listen; you have said, 'It is foolish to worship God and obey him. What good does it do to obey his laws, and to sorrow and mourn for our sins? From now on, as far as we're concerned, "Blessed are the arrogant." For those who do evil shall prosper, and those who dare God to punish them shall get off scot-free.' "

See *Blindness, Spiritual.*

Instances of. Elijah's trials, 1 Kgs 19. Job's, Job 3:19–23, with chapters 1; 2. Israelites, Ex 5:20–23.

RIGHTEOUSNESS OF. Judg 5:11. The village musicians gather at the village well to sing of the triumphs of the Lord. Again and again they sing the ballad of how the Lord saved Israel with an army of peasants! The people of the Lord marched through the gates!

Job 36:3. I will give you many illustrations of the righteousness of my Maker.

Ps 7:9. End all wickedness, O Lord, and bless all who truly worship God; for you, the righteous God, look deep within the hearts of men and examine all their motives and their thoughts.

Ps 71:15. I cannot count the times when you have faithfully rescued me from danger. I will tell everyone how good you are, and of your constant, daily care. [19]Your power and goodness, Lord, reach to the highest heavens. You have done such wonderful things. Where is there another God like you?

Ps 85:11. Truth rises from the earth and righteousness smiles down from heaven.

Ps 89:14, 15. Your throne is founded on two strong pillars—the one is Justice and the other Righteousness. Mercy and Truth walk before you as your attendants. Blessed are those who hear the joyful blast of the trumpet, for they shall walk in the light of your presence. [16]They rejoice all day long in your wonderful reputation and in your perfect righteousness.

Ps 97:2. Clouds and darkness surround him. Righteousness and justice are the foundation of his throne. [6]The heavens declare his perfect righteousness; every nation sees his glory.

Ps 111:3. For his miracles demonstrate his honor, majesty, and eternal goodness.

Ps 112:4. When darkness overtakes him, light will come bursting in. He is kind and merciful.

Ps 116:5. How kind he is! How good he is! So merciful, this God of ours!

Ps 143:1. Hear my prayer, O Lord; answer my plea, because you are faithful to your promises.

Ps 145:7. Everyone will tell about how good you are, and sing about your righteousness. [17]The Lord is fair in everything he does, and full of kindness.

Isa 24:15, 16. And those in the east will respond with praise. Hear them singing to the Lord from the ends of the earth, singing glory to the Righteous One!

Isa 32:1. Look, a righteous King is coming, with honest princes!

Isa 41:10. Fear not, for I am with you. Do not be dismayed. I am your God. I will strengthen you; I will help you; I will uphold you with my victorious right hand.

Isa 42:6. I the Lord have called you to demonstrate my righteousness. I will guard and support you, for I have given you to my people as the personal confirmation of my covenant with them.

[21]The Lord has magnified his law and made it truly glorious. Through it he had planned to show the world that he is righteous.

Isa 45:19. No, for I, Jehovah, speak only truth and righteousness.

Isa 56:1. Be just and fair to all, the Lord God says. Do what's right and good, for I am coming soon to rescue you.

Isa 59:12. For your sins keep piling up before the righteous God, and testify against you.

Isa 61:11. The Lord will show the nations of the world his justice; all will praise him. His righteousness shall be like a budding tree, or like a garden in early spring, full of young plants springing up everywhere.

Isa 62:1. Because I love Zion, because my heart yearns for Jerusalem, I will not cease to pray for her or to cry out to God on her behalf until she shines forth in his righteousness and is glorious in his salvation.

Jer 4:2. And if you will swear by me alone, the living God, and begin to live good, honest, clean lives, then you will be a testimony to the nations of the world and they will come to me and glorify my name.

Jer 9:24. Let them boast in this alone: That they truly know me, and understand that I am the Lord of justice and of righteousness whose love is steadfast; and that I love to be this way.

Jer 33:16. In that day the people of Judah and Jerusalem shall live in safety and their motto will be, "The Lord is our righteousness!"

Dan 9:7. O Lord, you are righteous; but as for us, we are always shamefaced with sin, just as you see us now; yes, all of us—the men of Judah, the people of Jerusalem, and all Israel, scattered near and far wherever you have driven us because of our disloyalty to you. [14]And so the Lord deliberately crushed us with the calamity he prepared; he is fair in everything he does, but we would not obey.

Hos 14:9. Whoever is wise, let him understand these things. Whoever is intelligent, let him listen. For the paths of the Lord are true and right, and good men walk along them. But sinners trying it will fail.

Mic 7:9. I will be patient while the Lord punishes me, for I have sinned against him; then he will defend me from my enemies, and punish them for all the evil they have done to me. God will bring me out of my darkness into the light, and I will see his goodness.

Mal 4:2. But for you who fear my name, the Sun of Righteousness will rise with healing in his wings. And you will go free, leaping with joy like calves let out to pasture.

Mt 6:33. And he will give them to you if you give him first place in your life and live as he wants you to.

Jn 17:25. O righteous Father, the world doesn't know you, but I do; and these disciples know you sent me.

Rom 1:17. This Good News tells us that God makes us ready for heaven—makes us right in God's sight—when we put our faith and trust in Christ to save us. This is accomplished from start to finish by faith. As the Scripture says it, "The man who finds life will find it through trusting God."

Rom 3:4. O course not! Though everyone else in the world is a liar, God is not. Do you remember what the book of Psalms says about this? That God's words will always prove true and right, no matter who questions them. [5]"But," some say, "our breaking faith with God is good, our sins serve a good purpose, for people will notice how good God is when they see how bad we are. Is it fair, then, for him to punish us when our sins are helping him?" (That is the way some people talk.) [6]God forbid! Then what kind of God would he be, to overlook sin? How could he ever condemn anyone? [21, 22]But now God has shown us a different way to heaven—not by "being good enough" and trying to keep his laws, but by a new way (though not new, really, for the Scriptures told about it long ago). Now God says he will accept and acquit us —declare us "not guilty"—if we trust Jesus Christ to take away our sins. And we all can be saved in this same way, by coming to Christ, no matter who we are or what we have been like.

Rom 10:3. For they don't understand that Christ has died to make them right with God. Instead they are trying to make themselves good enough to gain God's favor by keeping the Jewish laws and customs, but that is not God's way of salvation. [4]They don't understand that Christ gives to those who trust in him everything they are trying to get by keeping his laws. He ends all of that.

2 Tim 4:8. In heaven a crown is waiting for me which the Lord, the righteous Judge, will give me on that great day of his return. And not just to me, but to all those whose lives show that they are eagerly looking forward to his coming back again.

2 Pet 1:1. From: Simon Peter, a servant and missionary of Jesus Christ. *To:* All of you who have our kind of faith. The faith I speak of is the kind that Jesus Christ our God and Savior gives to us. How precious it is, and how just and good he is to give this same faith to each of us.

1 Jn 2:1. My little children, I am telling you this so that you will stay away from sin. But if you sin, there is someone to plead for you before the Father. His name is Jesus Christ, the one who is all that is good and who pleases God completely.

Rev 16:5. And I heard this angel of the waters declaring, "You are just in sending this judgment, O Holy One, who is and was."

See *God, Holiness of; Judge, and his Justice,* above.

SAVIOR. Gen 48:16. He is the Angel who has kept me from all harm. May these boys be an honor to my name and to the names of my fathers Abraham and Isaac; and may they become a mighty nation.

Ex 15:2. The Lord is my strength, my song, and my salvation. He is my God, and I will praise him. He is my father's God—I will exalt him.

Deut 32:15. But Israel was soon overfed; yes, fat

and bloated; then, in plenty, they forsook their God. They shrugged away the Rock of their salvation. [31]But the rock of other nations is not like our Rock; prayers to their gods are valueless. [39]Don't you see that I alone am God? I kill and make live. I wound and heal—no one delivers from my power.

Deut 33:29. What blessings are yours, O Israel! Who else has been saved by the Lord? He is your shield and your helper! He is your excellent sword! Your enemies shall bow low before you, and you shall trample on their backs! *vs.* 25–29.

Job 33:23, 24. But if a messenger from heaven is there to intercede for him as a friend, to show him what is right, then God pities him and says, "Set him free. Do not make him die, for I have found a substitute." [27]And he will declare to his friends, "I sinned, but God let me go. [28]He did not let me die. I will go on living in the realm of light." [29]Yes, God often does these things for man— [30]brings back his soul from the pit, so that he may live in the light of the living.

Ps 3:8. For salvation comes from God. What joys he gives to all his people.

Ps 18:30. What a God he is! How perfect in every way! All his promises prove true. He is a shield for everyone who hides behind him. [31]For who is God except our Lord? Who but he is as a rock? 1 Sam 2:2.

Ps 19:14. May my spoken words and unspoken thoughts be pleasing even to you, O Lord my Rock and my Redeemer.

Ps 25:5. Lead me; teach me; for you are the God who gives me salvation. I have no hope except in you.

Ps 27:1. The Lord is my light and my salvation; whom shall I fear?

Ps 28:8. The Lord protects his people and gives victory to his anointed king.

Ps 31:5. Into your hand I commit my spirit. You have rescued me, O God who keeps his promises.

Ps 33:18, 19. But the eyes of the Lord are watching over those who fear him, who rely upon his steady love. He will keep them from death even in times of famine!

Ps 34:22. But as for those who serve the Lord, he will redeem them; everyone who takes refuge in him will be freely pardoned.

Ps 36:9. For you are the Fountain of life; our light is from your Light.

Ps 37:39. The Lord saves the godly! He is their salvation and their refuge when trouble comes. [40]Because they trust in him, he helps them and delivers them from the plots of evil men.

Ps 50:23. But true praise is a worthy sacrifice; this really honors me. Those who walk my paths will receive salvation from the Lord.

Ps 62:1. I stand silently before the Lord, waiting for him to rescue me. For salvation comes from him alone. [6]Yes, he alone is my Rock, my rescuer, defense and fortress—why then should I be tense with fear when troubles come? [7]My protection and success come from God alone. He is my refuge, a Rock where no enemy can reach me. *v.* 2.

Ps 65:5. With dread deeds and awesome power you will defend us from our enemies, O God who saves us. You are the only hope of all mankind throughout the world and far away upon the sea.

Ps 68:19. What a glorious Lord! He who daily bears our burdens also gives us our salvation. [20]He frees us! He rescues us from death.

Ps 71:16. I walk in the strength of the Lord God. I tell everyone that you alone are just and good.

Ps 74:12. God is my King from ages past; you have been actively helping me everywhere throughout the land.

Ps 76:8. You pronounce sentence on them from heaven; the earth trembles and stands silently before you. [9]You stand up to punish the evil-doers and to defend the meek of the earth.

Ps 85:9. Surely his salvation is near to those who reverence him; our land will be filled with his glory.

Ps 88:1. O Jehovah, God of my salvation, I have wept before you day and night.

Ps 96:2. Sing out his praises! Bless his name. Each day tell someone that he saves.

Ps 98:2, 3. He has announced this victory and revealed it to every nation by fulfilling his promise to be king to Israel. The whole earth has seen God's salvation of his people.

Ps 111:9. He has paid a full ransom for his people; now they are always free to come to Jehovah (what a holy, awe-inspiring name that is).

Ps 118:14. He is my strength and song in the heat of battle, and now he has given me the victory. [21]O Lord, thank you so much for answering my prayer and saving me. [27]Jehovah God is our light.

Ps 121:7. He keeps you from all evil, and preserves your life.

Ps 133:3. Harmony is as refreshing as the dew on Mount Hermon, on the mountains of Israel. And God has pronounced this eternal blessing on Jerusalem, even life forevermore. Ps 145:9.

Ps 149:4. For Jehovah enjoys his people; he will save the humble.

Isa 12:2. See, God has come to save me! I will trust and not be afraid, for the Lord is my strength and song; he is my salvation.

Isa 25:4. But to the poor, O Lord, you are a refuge from the storm, a shadow from the heat, a shelter from merciless men who are like a driving rain that melts down an earthen wall. [9]In that day the people will proclaim, "This is our God, in whom we trust, for whom we waited. Now at last he is here." What a day of rejoicing!

Isa 26:1. Listen to them singing! In that day the whole land of Judah will sing this song: "Our city is strong! We are surrounded by the walls of his salvation!"

Isa 33:22. For the Lord is our Judge, our Lawgiver and our King; he will care for us and save us.

Isa 35:4. Encourage those who are afraid. Tell them, "Be strong, fear not, for your God is coming to destroy your enemies. He is coming to save you."

Isa 41:14. Despised though you are, fear not, O

Israel; for I will help you. I am the Lord, your Redeemer; I am the Holy One of Israel. Isa 48:17.

Isa 43:3. For I am the Lord your God, your Savior, the Holy One of Israel. I gave Egypt and Ethiopia and Seba (to Cyrus) in exchange for your freedom, as your ransom. [11]I am the Lord, and there is no other Savior. [12]Whenever you have thrown away your idols, I have shown you my power. With one word I have saved you. You have seen me do it; you are my witnesses that it is true. *v.* 14.

Isa 44:22. I've blotted out your sins; they are gone like morning mist at noon! Oh, return to me, for I have paid the price to set you free. [23]Sing, O heavens, for the Lord has done this wondrous thing. Shout, O earth; break forth into song, O mountains and forests, yes, and every tree; for the Lord redeemed Jacob and is glorified in Israel! [24]The Lord, your Redeemer who made you, says, All things were made by me; I alone stretched out the heavens. By myself I made the earth and everything in it. *v.* 6.

Isa 45:15. Truly, O God of Israel, Savior, you work in strange, mysterious ways. [17]But Israel shall be saved by Jehovah with eternal salvation; they shall never be disappointed in their God through all eternity. [21]Consult together, argue your case and state your proofs that idol-worship pays! Who but God has said that these things concerning Cyrus would come true? What idol ever told you they would happen? For there is no other God but me—a just God and a Savior—no, not one! [22]Let all the world look to me for salvation! For I am God; there is no other.

Isa 46:12. Listen to me, you stubborn, evil men! [13]For I am offering you my deliverance; not in the distant future, but right now! I am ready to save you, and I will restore Jerusalem, and Israel, who is my glory.

Isa 47:4. So speaks our Redeemer, who will save Israel from Babylon's mighty power; the Lord of Hosts is his name, the Holy One of Israel.

Isa 49:25. But the Lord says, "Even the captives of the most mighty and most terrible shall all be freed; for I will fight those who fight you, and I will save your children."

Isa 50:2. Was I too weak to save you? Is that why the house is silent and empty when I come home? Have I no longer power to deliver? No, that is not the reason! For I can rebuke the sea and make it dry! I can turn the rivers into deserts, covered with dying fish.

Isa 52:3. For the Lord says, When I sold you into exile I asked no fee from your oppressors; now I can take you back again and owe them not a cent! [9]Let the ruins of Jerusalem break into joyous song, for the Lord has comforted his people; he has redeemed Jerusalem. [10]The Lord has bared his holy arm before the eyes of all the nations; the ends of the earth shall see the salvation of our God.

Isa 59:1. Listen now! The Lord isn't too weak to save you. And he isn't getting deaf! He can hear you when you call!

Isa 60:16. Powerful kings and mighty nations shall provide you with the choicest of their goods to satisfy your every need, and you will know at last and really understand that I, the Lord, am your Savior and Redeemer, the Mighty One of Israel.

Isa 63:8. He said, "They are my very own; surely they will not be false again." And he became their Savior. [16]Surely you are still our Father! Even if Abraham and Jacob would disown us, still you would be our Father, our Redeemer from ages past.

Jer 3:23. We are weary of worshiping idols on the hills and of having orgies on the mountains. It is all a farce. Only in the Lord our God can Israel ever find her help and her salvation.

Jer 8:22. Is there no medicine in Gilead? Is there no physician there? Why doesn't God do something? Why doesn't he help?

Jer 14:8. O Hope of Israel, our Savior in times of trouble, why are you as a stranger to us, as one passing through the land who is merely stopping for the night?

Jer 30:17. I will give you back your health again and heal your wounds. Now you are called "The Outcast" and "Jerusalem, the Place Nobody Wants."

Jer 33:6. Nevertheless the time will come when I will heal Jerusalem's damage and give her prosperity and peace.

Jer 50:34. But their Redeemer is strong. His name is the Lord of Hosts. He will plead for them and see that they are freed to live again in quietness in Israel.

Ezk 37:23. They shall stop polluting themselves with idols and their other sins, for I will save them from all this foulness. Then they shall truly be my people and I their God.

Hos 1:7. But I *will* have mercy on the tribe of Judah. I will personally free her from her enemies without any help from her armies or her weapons.

Hos 13:4. I alone am God, your Lord, and have been ever since I brought you out from Egypt. You have no God but me, for there is no other Savior. [9]O Israel, if I destroy you, who can save you?

Joel 3:16. The Lord shouts from his Temple in Jerusalem and the earth and sky begin to shake. But to his people Israel, the Lord will be very gentle. He is their Refuge and Strength.

Jon 2:9. I will never worship anyone but you! For how can I thank you enough for all you have done? I will surely fulfill my promises. For my deliverance comes from the Lord alone.

Zech 9:11. I have delivered you from death in a waterless pit because of the covenant I made with you, sealed with blood. [12]Come to the place of safety, all you prisoners, for there is yet hope! I promise right now, I will repay you two mercies for each of your woes! [16]The Lord their God will save his people in that day, as a Shepherd caring for his sheep. They shall shine in his land as glittering jewels in a crown. How wonderful and beautiful all shall be!

Lk 1:68. Praise the Lord, the God of Israel, for he has come to visit his people and has redeemed them.

Jn 3:16. For God loved the world so much that he gave his only Son so that anyone who believes in him shall not perish but have eternal life. [17]God did not send his Son into the world to condemn it, but to save it.

Jn 6:39. And this is the will of God, that I should not lose even one of all those he has given me, but that I should raise them to eternal life at the Last Day.

Rom 1:16. For I am not ashamed of this Good News about Christ. It is God's powerful method of bringing all who believe it to heaven. This message was preached first to the Jews alone, but now everyone is invited to come to God in this same way.

Rom 6:23. For the wages of sin is death, but the free gift of God is eternal life through Jesus Christ our Lord.

Rom 8:30. And having chosen us, he called us to come to him; and when we came, he declared us "not guilty," filled us with Christ's goodness, gave us right standing with himself, and promised us his glory. [31]What can we ever say to such wonderful things as these? If God is on our side, who can ever be against us? [32]Since he did not spare even his own Son for us but gave him up for us all, won't he also surely give us everything else?

1 Cor 1:18. I know very well how foolish it sounds to those who are lost, when they hear that Jesus died to save them. But we who are saved recognize this message as the very power of God.

2 Cor 5:18. All these new things are from God who brought us back to himself through what Christ Jesus did. And God has given us the privilege of urging everyone to come into his favor and be reconciled to him.

Eph 1:3. How we praise God, the Father of our Lord Jesus Christ, who has blessed us with every blessing in heaven because we belong to Christ. [5]His unchanging plan has always been to adopt us into his own family by sending Jesus Christ to die for us. And he did this because he wanted to!

1 Thess 5:9. For God has not chosen to pour out his anger upon us, but to save us through our Lord Jesus Christ.

2 Thess 2:16. May our Lord Jesus Christ himself and God our Father, who has loved us and given us everlasting comfort and hope which we don't deserve, [17]comfort your hearts with all comfort, and help you in every good thing you say and do.

1 Tim 2:3. This is good and pleases God our Savior, [4]for he longs for all to be saved and to understand this truth.

1 Tim 4:10. We work hard and suffer much in order that people will believe it, for our hope is in the living God who died for all, and particularly for those who have accepted his salvation.

2 Tim 1:9. It is he who saved us and chose us for his holy work, not because we deserved it but because that was his plan long before the world began—to show his love and kindness to us through Christ.

Tit 1:2. So that they can have eternal life, which God promised them before the world began—and he cannot lie. [3]And now in his own good time he has revealed this Good News and permits me to tell it to everyone. By command of God our Savior I have been trusted to do this work for him.

Tit 2:10. Nor steal, but must show themselves to be entirely trustworthy. In this way they will make people want to believe in our Savior and God. [11]For the free gift of eternal salvation is now being offered to everyone.

Tit 3:4. But when the time came for the kindness and love of God our Savior to appear, [5]then he saved us—not because we were good enough to be saved, but because of his kindness and pity—by washing away our sins and giving us the new joy of the indwelling Holy Spirit.

1 Pet 1:5. And God, in his mighty power, will make sure that you get there safely to receive it, because you are trusting him. It will be yours in that coming last day for all to see.

1 Jn 4:9. God showed how much he loved us by sending his only Son into this wicked world to bring to us eternal life through his death. [10]In this act we see what real love is: it is not our love for God, but his love for us when he sent his Son to satisfy God's anger against our sins.

1 Jn 5:11. And what is it that God has said? That he has given us eternal life, and that this life is in his Son.

Rev 7:10. And they were shouting with a mighty shout, "Salvation comes from our God upon the throne, and from the Lamb."

Rev 19:1. After this I heard the shouting of a vast crowd in heaven, "Hallelujah! Praise the Lord! Salvation is from our God. Honor and authority belong to him alone."

See *God, Preserver,* above.

SELF-EXISTENT. Ex 3:14. " 'The Sovereign God,' " was the reply. "Just say, 'I Am has sent me!' "

Deut 32:40. I raise my hand to heaven and vow by my existence.

Job 35:6. If you sin, does that shake the heavens and knock God from his throne? Even if you sin again and again, what effect will it have upon him? [7]Or if you are good, is this some great gift to him? [8]Your sins may hurt another man, or your good deeds may profit him.

Isa 44:6. The Lord, the King of Israel, says—yes, it is Israel's Redeemer, the Lord of Hosts, who says it—I am the First and Last; there is no other God.

Jer 10:10. But the Lord is the only true God, the living God, the everlasting King. The whole earth shall tremble at his anger; the world shall hide before his displeasure.

Jn 5:26. The Father has life in himself, and has granted his Son to have life in himself.

Acts 17:24. He made the world and everything in it, and since he is Lord of heaven and earth, he doesn't live in man-made temples; [25]and human hands can't minister to his needs—for he has no needs! He himself gives life and breath to everything, and satisfies every need there is.

See *God, Eternity of,* above.

SOVEREIGN: Gen 14:18. And Melchizedek, the king of Salem (Jerusalem), who was a priest of the God of Highest Heaven, brought him bread and wine. [*v.* 22] [19, 20]Then Melchizedek blessed Abram with this blessing: "The blessing of the supreme God, Creator of heaven and earth, be upon you, Abram; and blessed be God, who has delivered your enemies over to you." Then Abram gave Melchizedek a tenth of all the spoils.

Gen 24:3. Swear by Jehovah, the God of Heaven and earth, that you will not let my son marry one of these local girls, these Canaanites.

Ex 8:22. But it will be very different in the land of Goshen where the Israelis live. No flies will be there; thus you will know that I am the Lord God of all the earth.

Ex 9:29. All right, Moses replied, as soon as I have left the city I will spread out my hands to the Lord, and the thunder and hail will stop. This will prove to you that the earth is controlled by Jehovah. Josh 3:11.

Ex 15:18. Jehovah shall reign forever and forever.

Ex 18:11. I know now that the Lord is greater than any other god because he delivered his people from the proud and cruel Egyptians.

Num 27:16. O Jehovah, the God of the spirits of all mankind, (before I am taken away) please appoint a new leader for the people.

Deut 2:18. Today Israel shall cross the borders of Moab at Ar, [19]into the land of the Ammonites. But do not attack them, for I will not give you any of their land. I have given it to the descendants of Lot.

Deut 4:39. This is your wonderful thought for the day: Jehovah is God both in heaven and down here upon the earth; and there is no God other than him!

Deut 10:14. Earth and highest heaven belong to the Lord your God. [17]Jehovah your God is God of gods and Lord of lords. He is the great and mighty God, the God of terror who shows no partiality and takes no bribes. Ex 19:5.

Deut 32:8. When God divided up the world among the nations, he gave each of them a supervising angel! [39]"Don't you see that I alone am God? I kill and make live. I wound and heal—no one delivers from my power. [40-43]I raise my hand to heaven and vow by my existence, that I will whet the lightning of my sword! And hurl my punishments upon my enemies! My arrows shall be drunk with blood! My sword devours the flesh and blood of all the slain and captives. The heads of the enemy are gory with blood." Praise his people, O Gentile nations, for he will avenge his people, taking vengeance on his enemies, purifying his land and his people.

Josh 2:11. No wonder we are afraid of you! No one has any fight left in him after hearing things like that, for your God is the supreme God of heaven, not just an ordinary god.

Josh 3:11. Think of it! The Ark of God, who is Lord of the whole earth, will lead you across the river!

1 Sam 2:6. The Lord kills, the Lord gives life. [7]Some he causes to be poor and others to be rich. He cuts one down and lifts another up. [8]He lifts the poor from the dust—yes, from a pile of ashes—and treats them as princes sitting in the seats of honor. For all the earth is the Lord's and he has set the world in order.

2 Kgs 19:15. Then he prayed this prayer: "O Lord God of Israel, sitting on your throne high above the angels, you alone are the God of all the kingdoms of the earth. You created the heavens and the earth."

1 Chron 29:11. Yours is the mighty power and glory and victory and majesty. Everything in the heavens and earth is yours, O Lord, and this is your kingdom. We adore you as being in control of everything. [12]Riches and honor come from you alone, and you are the Ruler of all mankind; your hand controls power and might, and it is at your discretion that men are made great and given strength.

2 Chron 20:6. O Lord God of our fathers—the only God in all the heavens, the Ruler of all the kingdoms of the earth—you are so powerful, so mighty. Who can stand against you?

Neh 9:6. Then Ezra prayed, "You alone are God. You have made the skies and the heavens, the earth and the seas, and everything in them. You preserve it all; and all the angels of heaven worship you."

Job 9:12. When he sends death to snatch a man away, who can stop him? Who dares to ask him, "What are you doing?"

Job 12:10. For the soul of every living thing is in the hand of God, and the breath of all mankind. [16]Yes, with him is strength and wisdom. Deceivers and deceived are both his slaves. [17]He makes fools of counselors and judges.

Job 25:2. God is powerful and dreadful. He enforces peace in heaven.

Job 33:13. Why should you fight against him just because he does not give account to you of what he does?

Job 34:13. He alone has authority over the earth and dispenses justice for the world. [24]Without making a federal case of it, God simply shatters the greatest of men, and puts others in their place. [33]Must God tailor his justice to your demands? Must he change the order of the universe to suit your whims? The answer must be obvious even to you!

Job 36:23. Who can say that what he does is absurd or evil? *vs.* 1–33.

Job 41:11. I owe no one anything. Everything under the heaven is mine.

Ps 10:16. The Lord is King forever and forever. Those who follow other gods shall be swept from his land.

Ps 22:28. For the Lord is King and rules the nations. [29]Both proud and humble together, all who are mortal—born to die—shall worship him.

Ps 24:1. The earth belongs to God! Everything in all the world is his! [10]Who is this King of Glory? The Commander of all of heaven's armies! 1 Cor 10: 26.

Ps 29:10. At the Flood, the Lord showed his control of all creation. Now he continues to unveil his power.

Ps 44:4. You are my King and my God. Decree victories for your people.

Ps 47:2. For the Lord, the God above all gods, is awesome beyond words; he is the great King of all the earth. [3]He subdues the nations before us. [6, 7]Sing out your praises to our God, our King. Yes, sing your highest praises to our King, the King of all the earth. Sing thoughtful praises! [8]He reigns above the nations, sitting on his holy throne.

Ps 50:10, 11. For all the animals of field and forest are mine! The cattle on a thousand hills! And all the birds upon the mountains! [12]If I were hungry, I would not mention it to you—for all the world is mine, and everything in it.

Ps 59:13. And let the nations find out too that God rules in Israel and will reign throughout the world.

Ps 65:5. With dread deeds and awesome power you will defend us from our enemies, O God who saves us. You are the only hope of all mankind throughout the world and far away upon the sea.

Ps 66:7. Because of his great power he rules forever. He watches every movement of the nations. O rebel lands, he will deflate your pride.

Ps 67:4. How glad the nations will be, singing for joy because you are their King and will give true justice to their people!

Ps 74:12. God is my King from ages past; you have been actively helping me everywhere throughout the land.

Ps 75:6, 7. For promotion and power come from nowhere on earth, but only from God. He promotes one and deposes another.

Ps 76:11. Fulfill all your vows that you have made to Jehovah your God. Let everyone bring him presents. He should be reverenced and feared, [12]for he cuts down princes and does awesome things to the kings of the earth.

Ps 82:1. God stands up to open heaven's court. He pronounces judgment on the judges. [8]Stand up, O God, and judge the earth. For all of it belongs to you. All nations are in your hands.

Ps 83:18. Until they learn that you alone, Jehovah, are the God above all gods in supreme charge of all the earth.

Ps 89:11. The heavens are yours, the world, everything—for you created them all. [18]Yes, our protection is from the Lord himself and he, the Holy One of Israel, has given us our king.

Ps 93:1, 2. Jehovah is King! He is robed in majesty and strength. The world is his throne. [2]O Lord, you have reigned from prehistoric times, from the everlasting past.

Ps 95:3. For the Lord is a great God, the great King of all gods. [4]He controls the formation of the depths of the earth and the mightiest mountains; all are his. [5]He made the sea and formed the land; they too are his.

Ps 96:10. Tell the nations that Jehovah reigns! He rules the world. His power can never be overthrown. He will judge all nations fairly.

Ps 97:1. Jehovah is King! Let all the earth rejoice! Tell the farthest islands to be glad. [2]Clouds and darkness surround him. Righteousness and justice are the foundation of his throne. [*v.* 5.] [8, 9]Jerusalem and all the cities of Judah have heard your justice, Lord, and are glad that you reign in majesty over the entire earth and are far greater than these other gods.

Ps 98:6. Let the cornets and trumpets shout! Make a joyful symphony before the Lord, the King!

Ps 99:1. Jehovah is King! Let the nations tremble! He is enthroned upon the cherubim. Let the whole earth shake.

Ps 103:19. The Lord has made the heavens his throne; from there he rules over everything there is.

Ps 105:7. He is the Lord our God. His goodness is seen everywhere throughout the land.

Ps 113:4. For he is high above the nations; his glory is far greater than the heavens.

Ps 115:3. For he is in the heavens, and does as he wishes. [16]The heavens belong to the Lord, but he has given the earth to all mankind.

Ps 135:5. I know the greatness of the Lord—that he is greater far than any other god. [6]He does whatever pleases him throughout all of heaven and earth, and in the deepest seas.

Ps 136:2. Give thanks to the God of gods, for his lovingkindness continues forever. [3]Give thanks to the Lord of lords, for his lovingkindness continues forever.

Ps 145:11. They will talk together about the glory of your kingdom and mention examples of your power. [12]They will tell about your miracles and about the majesty and glory of your reign. [13]For your kingdom never ends. You rule generation after generation.

Ps 146:10. The Lord will reign forever. O Jerusalem, your God is King in every generation! Hallelujah! Praise the Lord! Isa 52:7.

Eccl 9:1. This, too, I carefully explored—that godly and wise men are in God's will; no one knows whether he will favor them or not. All is chance!

Isa 24:23. Then the Lord of heaven's armies will mount his throne in Zion and rule gloriously in Jerusalem, in the sight of all the elders of his people. Such glory there will be that all the brightness of the sun and moon will seem to fade away.

Isa 33:22. For the Lord is our Judge, our Lawgiver and our King; he will care for us and save us.

Isa 37:16. O Lord of Hosts, God of Israel enthroned above the cherubim, *you alone* are God of all the kingdoms of the earth. You alone made heaven and earth.

Isa 40:22. It is God who sits above the circle of

the earth. (The people below must seem to him like grasshoppers!) He is the one who stretches out the heavens like a curtain and makes his tent from them. [23]He dooms the great men of the world and brings them all to naught.

Isa 43:15. I am the Lord, your Holy One, Israel's Creator and King.

Isa 44:6. The Lord, the King of Israel, says—yes, it is Israel's Redeemer, the Lord of Hosts, who says it—I am the First and Last; there is no other God.

Isa 45:7. I form the light and make the dark. I send good times and bad. I, Jehovah, am he who does these things. [23]I have sworn by myself and I will never go back on my word, for it is true—that every knee in all the world shall bow to me, and every tongue shall swear allegiance to my name.

Isa 54:5. For your Creator will be your "husband." The Lord of Hosts is his name; he is your Redeemer, the Holy One of Israel, the God of all the earth.

Jer 10:10. For the Lord is the only true God, the living God, the everlasting King. The whole earth shall tremble at his anger; the world shall hide before his displeasure.

Jer 18:6. O Israel, can't I do to you as this potter has done to his clay? As the clay is in the potter's hand, so are you in my hand. *vs.* 1–23.

Jer 27:5. By my great power I have made the earth and all mankind and every animal; and I give these things of mine to anyone I want to. [6]So now I have given all your countries to King Nebuchadnezzar of Babylon, who is my deputy. And I have handed over to him all your cattle for his use. *v.* 7; Jer 32:27, 28.

Lam 3:37. For who can act against you without the Lord's permission? [38]It is the Lord who helps one and harms another.

Lam 5:19. O Lord, forever you remain the same! Your throne continues from generation to generation.

Ezk 16:50. She insolently worshiped many idols as I watched. Therefore I crushed her.

Ezk 17:24. And everyone shall know that it is I, the Lord, who cuts down the high trees and exalts the low, that I make the green tree wither and the dry tree grow. I, the Lord, have said that I would do it, and I will.

Ezk 18:4. For all souls are mine to judge—fathers and sons alike—and my rule is this: It is for a man's own sins that he will die.

Dan 2:20. Saying, "Blessed be the name of God forever and ever, for he alone has all wisdom and all power. [21]World events are under his control. He removes kings and sets others on their thrones. He gives wise men their wisdom, and scholars their intelligence." [47]"Truly, O Daniel," the king said, "your God is the God of gods, Ruler of kings, the Revealer of mysteries, because he has told you this secret."

Dan 4:3. It was incredible—a mighty miracle! And now I know for sure that his kingdom is everlasting; he reigns forever and ever. [17]For this has been decreed by the Watchers, demanded by the Holy Ones. The purpose of this decree is that all the world may understand that the Most High dominates the kingdoms of the world, and gives them to anyone he wants to, even the lowliest of men! [25]That your people will chase you from your palace, and you will live in the fields like an animal, eating grass like a cow, your back wet with dew from heaven. For seven years this will be your life, until you learn that the Most High God dominates the kingdoms of men, and gives power to anyone he chooses. [35]All the people of the earth are nothing when compared to him; he does whatever he thinks best among the hosts of heaven, as well as here among the inhabitants of earth. No one can stop him or challenge him, saying, "What do you mean by doing these things?" [37]Now, I, Nebuchadnezzar, praise and glorify and honor the King of Heaven, the Judge of all, whose every act is right and good; for he is able to take those who walk proudly and push them into the dust! *v.* 34.

Dan 5:18. Your Majesty, the Most High God gave Nebuchadnezzar, who long ago preceded you, a kingdom and majesty and glory and honor. [26]This is what it means: *Mene* means "numbered" —God has numbered the days of your reign, and they are ended. [27]*Tekel* means "weighed"—you have been weighed in God's balances and have failed the test. [28]*Parsin* means "divided"—your kingdom will be divided and given to the Medes and Persians.

Dan 6:26. For his God is the living, unchanging God whose kingdom shall never be destroyed and whose power shall never end.

Mic 4:7. And make them strong again in their own land, a mighty nation, and the Lord himself shall be their King from Mount Zion forever. [13]Rise, thresh, O daughter of Zion; I will give you horns of iron and hoofs of brass and you will trample to pieces many people, and you will give their wealth as offerings to the Lord, the Lord of all the earth.

Hag 2:8. "For I have plenty of silver and gold to do it! And here I will give peace," says the Lord.

Mal 1:14. "Cursed is that man who promises a fine ram from his flock, and substitutes a sick one to sacrifice to God. For I am a Great King," says the Lord of Hosts, "and my name is to be mightily revered among the Gentiles."

Mt 6:10. We ask that your kingdom will come now. May your will be done here on earth, just as it is in heaven.

Mt 11:25. And Jesus prayed this prayer: "O Father, Lord of heaven and earth, thank you for hiding the truth from those who think themselves so wise, and for revealing it to little children." Lk 10:21.

Mt 20:15. Is it against the law to give away my money if I want to? Should you be angry because I am kind?

Lk 1:53. He has satisfied the hungry hearts and sent the rich away with empty hands.

Jn 10:29. For my Father has given them to me, and he is more powerful than anyone else, so no one can kidnap them from me.

Jn 19:11. Then Jesus said, "You would have no power at all over me unless it were given to you from above. So those who brought me to you have the greater sin."

Acts 17:24. He made the world and everything in it, and since he is Lord of heaven and earth, he doesn't live in man-made temples; [25]and human hands can't minister to his needs—for he has no needs! He himself gives life and breath to everything, and satisfies every need there is. [26]He created all the people of the world from one man, Adam, and scattered the nations across the face of the earth. He decided beforehand which should rise and fall, and when. He determined their boundaries.

Rom 9:19. Well then, why does God blame them for not listening? Haven't they done what he made them do?

Rom 14:11. For it is written, "As I live," says the Lord, "every knee shall bow to me and every tongue confess to God."

Eph 4:6. And we all have the same God and Father who is over us all and in us all, and living through every part of us.

1 Tim 6:15. For in due season Christ will be revealed from heaven by the blessed and only Almighty God, the King of kings and Lord of lords, [16]who alone can never die, who lives in light so terrible that no human being can approach him. No mere man has ever seen him, nor ever will. Unto him be honor and everlasting power and dominion forever and ever. Amen.

Heb 1:3. God's Son shines out with God's glory, and all that God's Son is and does marks him as God. He regulates the universe by the mighty power of his command. He is the one who died to cleanse us and clear our record of all sin, and then sat down in highest honor beside the great God of heaven.

Jas 4:12. Only he who made the law can rightly judge among us. He alone decides to save us or destroy. So what right do you have to judge or criticize others?

Rev 1:6. He has gathered us into his kingdom and made us priests of God his Father. Give to him everlasting glory! He rules forever! Amen!

Rev 4:11. O Lord, you are worthy to receive the glory and the honor and the power, for you have created all things. They were created and called into being by your act of will.

Rev 11:4. These two prophets are the two olive trees, and two candlesticks standing before the God of all the earth. [13]The same hour there will be a terrible earthquake that levels a tenth of the city, leaving 7,000 dead. Then everyone left will, in their terror, give glory to the God of heaven. [17]"We give thanks, Lord God Almighty, who is and was, for now you have assumed your great power and have begun to reign."

Rev 19:6. Then I heard again what sounded like the shouting of a huge crowd, or like the waves of a hundred oceans crashing on the shore, or like the mighty rolling of great thunder, "Praise the Lord. For the Lord our God, the Almighty, reigns."

See *God, Power of.*

A SPIRIT. Num 27:16. O Jehovah, the God of the spirits of all mankind, [before I am taken away] please appoint a new leader for the people.

Jn 4:24. For God is Spirit, and we must have his help to worship as we should. The Father wants this kind of worship from us. 2 Cor 3:17.

See *Holy Spirit; Life, Spiritual.*

TRUTH. Num 23:19. God is not a man, that he should lie; he doesn't change his mind like humans do. Has he ever promised, without doing what he said?

1 Sam 15:29. And he who is the glory of Israel is not lying, nor will he change his mind, for he is not a man!

2 Sam 7:28. For you are indeed God, and your words are truth; and you have promised me these good things.

Ps 25:10. And when we obey him, every path he guides us on is fragrant with his lovingkindness and his truth.

Ps 31:5. Into your hand I commit my spirit. You have rescued me, O God who keeps his promises.

Ps 33:4. For all God's words are right, and everything he does is worthy of our trust.

Ps 40:10. I have not kept this Good News hidden in my heart, but have proclaimed your lovingkindness and truth to all the congregation.

Ps 43:3. Oh, send out your light and your truth —let them lead me. Let them lead me to your Temple on your holy mountain, Zion.

Ps 61:7. And I shall live before the Lord forever. Oh, send your lovingkindness and truth to guard and watch over me.

Ps 86:15. But you are merciful and gentle, Lord, slow in getting angry, full of constant lovingkindness and truth.

Ps 89:14. Mercy and Truth walk before you as your attendants.

Ps 115:1. Glorify your name, not ours, O Lord! Cause everyone to praise your lovingkindness and your truth.

Ps 117:2. For he loves us very dearly, and his truth endures. Praise the Lord.

Ps 132:11. For you promised me that my son would sit on my throne and succeed me. And surely you will never go back on a promise!

Ps 138:2. I face your Temple as I worship, giving thanks to you for all your lovingkindness and your faithfulness, for your promises are backed by all the honor of your name.

Ps 146:6. The God who made both earth and heaven, the seas and everything in them. He is the God who keeps every promise.

Isa 25:1. O Lord, I will honor and praise your name, for you are my God; you do such wonderful things! You planned them long ago, and now you have accomplished them, just as you said!

Isa 65:16. And yet, the days will come when all who invoke a blessing or take an oath shall swear by the God of Truth; for I will put aside my anger and forget the evil that you did.

Jer 10:10. But the Lord is the only true God, the living God, the everlasting King. The whole earth shall tremble at his anger; the world shall hide before his displeasure.

Dan 9:13. Every curse against us written in the law of Moses has come true; all the evils he predicted—all have come. But even so we still refuse to satisfy the Lord our God by turning from our sins and doing right.

Jn 3:33, 34. Those who believe him discover that God is a fountain of truth. For this one—sent by God—speaks God's words, for God's Spirit is upon him without measure or limit.

Jn 7:28. Yes, you know me and where I was born and raised, but I am representative of one you don't know, and he is Truth.

Jn 8:26. I could condemn you for much and teach you much, but I won't, for I say only what I am told to by the one who sent me; and he is Truth.

Jn 17:17. Make them pure and holy through teaching them your words of truth. [19]And I consecrate myself to meet their need for growth in truth and holiness.

Rom 3:4. Of course not! Though everyone else in the world is a liar, God is not. Do you remember what the book of Psalms says about this? That God's words will always prove true and right, no matter who questions them. [7]For he could not judge and condemn me as a sinner if my dishonesty brought him glory by pointing up his honesty in contrast to my lies.

2 Tim 2:19. But God's truth stands firm like a great rock, and nothing can shake it.

Tit 1:2. So that they can have eternal life, which God promised them before the world began—and he cannot lie.

Rev 6:10. They called loudly to the Lord and said, "O Sovereign Lord, holy and true, how long will it be before you judge the people of the earth for what they've done to us? When will you avenge our blood against those living on the earth?"

Rev 15:3. And they were singing the song of Moses, the servant of God, and the song of the Lamb: "Great and marvelous are your doings, Lord God Almighty. Just and true are your ways, O King of Ages."

See *God, Faithfulness of, Judge, and his Justice, Righteousness of,* above. See also *Truth.*

UBIQUITOUS. See above, *Eternity of, Infinite, Omnipresent, Power of, Presence of, Providence of.*

UNCHANGEABLE. Num 23:19, 20. God is not a man, that he should lie; he doesn't change his mind like humans do. Has he ever promised, without doing what he said? Look! I have received a command to bless them, for God has blessed them, and I cannot reverse it!

1 Sam 15:29. And he who is the glory of Israel is not lying, nor will he change his mind, for he is not a man!

Job 23:13. Nevertheless, his mind concerning me remains unchanged, and who can turn him from his purposes? Whatever he wants to do, he does.

Ps 33:11. But his own plan stands forever. His intentions are the same for every generation.

Ps 119:89. Forever, O Lord, your Word stands firm in heaven. [90, 91]Your faithfulness extends to every generation, like the earth you created; it endures by your decree, for everything serves your plans.

Prov 19:21. Man proposes, but God disposes.

Eccl 3:14. And I know this, that whatever God does is final—nothing can be added or taken from it.

Eccl 7:13. See the way God does things and fall into line. Don't fight the facts of nature.

Isa 31:2. In his wisdom, he will send great evil on his people and will not change his mind.

Isa 40:28. Don't you yet understand? Don't you know by now that the everlasting God, the Creator of the farthest parts of the earth, never grows faint or weary?

Isa 59:1. Listen now! the Lord isn't too weak to save you. And he isn't getting deaf! He can hear you when you call!

Hos 13:14. Shall I ransom him from hell? Shall I redeem him from Death? O Death, bring forth your terrors for his tasting! O Grave, demonstrate your plagues! For I will not relent!

Mal 3:6. For I am the Lord—I do not change. That is why you are not already utterly destroyed (for my mercy endures forever).

Rom 11:29. For God's gifts and his call can never be withdrawn; he will never go back on his promises.

Heb 6:17. God also bound himself with an oath, so that those he promised to help would be perfectly sure and never need to wonder whether he might change his plans. [18]He has given us both his promise and his oath, two things we can completely count on, for it is impossible for God to tell a lie.

Jas 1:17. But whatever is good and perfect comes to us from God, the Creator of all light, and he shines forever without change or shadow.

UNITY OF. Deut 6:4. O Israel, listen: Jehovah is our God, Jehovah alone. Mk 12:29.

1 Kgs 8:60. May people all over the earth know that the Lord is God, and that there is no other god at all.

1 Kgs 20:28. Then a prophet went to the king of Israel with this message from the Lord: "Because the Syrians have declared, 'The Lord is a God of the hills and not of the plains,' I will help you defeat this vast army, and you shall know that I am indeed the Lord."

Isa 42:8. I am the Lord! That is my name, and I will not give my glory to anyone else; I will not share my praise with carved idols.

Mk 12:29. Jesus replied, "The one that says, 'Hear, O Israel! The Lord our God is the one and only God.' " [32]The teacher of religion replied, "Sir, you have spoken a true word in saying that there is only one God and no other."

Jn 17:3. And this is the way to have eternal life

—by knowing you, the only true God, and Jesus Christ, the one you sent to earth!

1 Cor 8:4. So now, what about it? Should we eat meat that has been sacrificed to idols? Well, we all know that an idol is not really a god, and that there is only one God, and no other. [6]But we know that there is only one God, the Father, who created all things and made us to be his own; and one Lord Jesus Christ, who made everything and gives us life.

Gal 3:20. But when God gave his promise to Abraham, he did it by himself alone, without angels or Moses as go-betweens.

1 Tim 2:5. That God is on one side and all the people on the other side, and Christ Jesus, himself man, is between them to bring them together.

Jas 2:19. Are there still some among you who hold that "only believing" is enough? Believing in one God? Well, remember that the demons believe this too—so strongly that they tremble in terror!

UNSEARCHABLE. Deut 29:29. There are secrets the Lord your God has not revealed to us, but these words which he has revealed are for us and our children to obey forever.

Judg 13:18. "Don't even ask my name," the Angel replied, "for it is a secret." Gen 32:29.

1 Kgs 8:12. Now King Solomon prayed this invocation: "The Lord has said that he would live in the thick darkness. [27]But is it possible that God would really live on earth? Why, even the skies and the highest heavens cannot contain you, much less this Temple I have built!" 2 Chron 2:6; 6:1, 2, 18.

Job 5:8. My advice to you is this: Go to God and confess your sins to him. [9]For he does wonderful miracles, marvels without number. Job 9:10.

Job 11:7. Do you know the mind and purposes of God? Will long searching make them known to you? Are you qualified to judge the Almighty? [8]He is as faultless as heaven is high—but who are you? His mind is fathomless—what can you know in comparison? [9]His Spirit is broader than the earth and wider than the sea.

Job 26:9. He shrouds his throne with his clouds. [14]These are some of the minor things he does, merely a whisper of his power. Who then can withstand his thunder?

Job 36:26. God is so great that we cannot begin to know him. No one can begin to understand eternity.

Job 37:5. His voice is glorious in the thunder. We cannot comprehend the greatness of his power. [23]We cannot imagine the power of the Almighty, and yet he is so just and merciful that he does not destroy us.

Ps 77:19. Your road led by a pathway through the sea—a pathway no one knew was there!

Ps 92:5. O Lord, what miracles you do! And how deep are your thoughts!

Ps 97:2. Clouds and darkness surround him. Righteousness and justice are the foundation of his throne.

Ps 139:6. This is too glorious, too wonderful to believe!

Ps 145:3. Great is Jehovah! Greatly praise him! His greatness is beyond discovery!

Prov 25:2. It is God's privilege to conceal things.

Prov 30:4. Who else but God goes back and forth to heaven? Who else holds the wind in his fists, and wraps up the oceans in his cloak? Who but God has created the world? If there is any other, what is his name—and his son's name—if you know it?

Eccl 3:11. Everything is appropriate in its own time. But though God has planted eternity in the hearts of men, even so, man cannot see the whole scope of God's work from beginning to end.

Eccl 7:24. Wisdom is far away, and very difficult to find.

Eccl 11:5. God's ways are as mysterious as the pathway of the wind, and as the manner in which a human spirit is infused into the little body of a baby while it is yet in its mother's womb.

Isa 40:28. Don't you yet understand? Don't you know by now that the everlasting God, the Creator of the farthest parts of the earth, never grows faint or weary? No one can fathom the depths of his understanding.

Isa 45:15. Truly, O God of Israel, Savior, you work in strange, mysterious ways.

Isa 55:8. This plan of mine is not what you would work out, neither are my thoughts the same as yours! [9]For just as the heavens are higher than the earth, so are my ways higher than yours, and my thoughts than yours.

Jer 23:24. Can anyone hide from me? Am I not everywhere in all of heaven and earth?

Nah 1:3. He is slow in getting angry, but when aroused, his power is incredible, and he does not easily forgive. He shows his power in the terrors of the cyclone and the raging storms; clouds are billowing dust beneath his feet!

Mt 11:27. Everything has been entrusted to me by my Father. Only the Father knows the Son, and the Father is known only by the Son and by those to whom the Son reveals him.

Rom 11:33. Oh, what a wonderful God we have! How great are his wisdom and knowledge and riches! How impossible it is for us to understand his decisions and his methods! [34]For who among us can know the mind of the Lord? Who knows enough to be his counselor and guide?

1 Cor 2:10. But we know about these things because God has sent his Spirit to tell us, and his Spirit searches out and shows us all of God's deepest secrets. [11]No one can really know what anyone else is thinking, or what he is really like, except that person himself. And no one can know God's thoughts except God's own Spirit.

1 Cor 2:16. How could he? For certainly he has never been one to know the Lord's thoughts, or to discuss them with him, or to move the hands of God by prayer. But, strange as it seems, we Christians actually do have within us a portion of the very thoughts and mind of Christ.

Eph 3:8. Just think! Though I did nothing to deserve it, and though I am the most useless Christian there is, yet I was the one chosen for this special joy of telling the Gentiles the Glad News of the endless treasures available to them in Christ.

See *Mysteries and Secrets.*

VOICE OF. See *Anthropomorphism.*

WISDOM OF. Ezra 7:25. And you, Ezra, are to use the wisdom God has given you to select and appoint judges and other officials to govern all the people west of the Euphrates River; if they are not familiar with the laws of your God, you are to teach them.

Job 9:4. For God is so wise and so mighty. Who has ever opposed him successfully?

Job 12:13. But true wisdom and power are God's. He alone knows what we should do; he understands. [16]Yes, with him is strength and wisdom. Deceivers and deceived are both his slaves.

Ps 104:24. O Lord, what a variety you have made! And in wisdom you have made them all! The earth is full of your riches.

Ps 147:5. How great he is! His power is absolute! His understanding is unlimited.

Prov 3:19. The Lord's wisdom founded the earth; his understanding established all the universe and space. [20]The deep fountains of the earth were broken open by his knowledge, and the skies poured down rain.

Prov 8:12. Wisdom and good judgment live together, for wisdom knows where to discover knowledge and understanding. [22]The Lord formed me in the beginning, before he created anything else. [27-29]I was there when he established the heavens and formed the great springs in the depths of the oceans. I was there when he set the limits of the seas and gave them his instructions not to spread beyond their boundaries. I was there when he made the blueprint for the earth and oceans. [30]I was always at his side like a little child. I was his constant delight, laughing and playing in his presence. [31]And how happy I was with what he created—his wide world and all his family of mankind!

Isa 31:2. In his wisdom, he will send great evil on his people and will not change his mind. He will rise against them for the evil they have done, and crush their allies too.

Jer 10:7. Who would not fear you, O King of nations? (And that title belongs to you alone!) Among all the wise men of the earth and in all the kingdoms of the world there isn't anyone like you. [12]But our God formed the earth by his power and wisdom, and by his intelligence he hung the stars in space and stretched out the heavens. Jer 51:15.

Dan 2:20. Saying, "Blessed be the name of God forever and ever, for he alone has all wisdom and all power. [21]World events are under his control. He removes kings and set others on their thrones. He gives wise men their wisdom, and scholars their intelligence. [22]He reveals profound mysteries beyond man's understanding. He knows all hidden things, for he is light, and darkness is no obstacle to him. [28]But there is a God in heaven who reveals secrets, and he has told you in your dream what will happen in the future."

Rom 16:27. To God, who alone is wise, be the glory forever through Jesus Christ our Lord. Amen.

1 Cor 1:24. But God has opened the eyes of those called to salvation, both Jews and Gentiles, to see that Christ is the mighty power of God to save them; Christ himself is the center of God's wise plan for their salvation. [25]This so-called "foolish" plan of God is far wiser than the wisest plan of the wisest man, and God in his weakness—Christ dying on the cross—is far stronger than any man.

Eph 1:8. And he has showered down upon us the richness of his grace—for how well he understands us and knows what is best for us at all times.

Eph 3:10. And his reason? To show to all the rulers in heaven how perfectly wise he is when all of his family—Jews and Gentiles alike—are seen to be joined together in his church.

1 Tim 1:17. Glory and honor to God forever and ever. He is the King of the ages, the unseen one who never dies; he alone is God, and full of wisdom. Amen.

Rev 7:12. "Amen!" they said. "Blessing, and glory, and wisdom, and thanksgiving, and honor, and power, and might, be to our God forever and forever. Amen!"

See *God, Knowledge of, Omniscient, above.*

WORKS OF. Gen 1:10. And God was pleased. *vs.* 18, 21, 22, 25.

Deut 32:4. He is the Rock. His work is perfect. Everything he does is just and fair. He is faithful, without sin.

Ps 26:7. Singing a song of thanksgiving and telling about your miracles.

Ps 33:4. For all God's words are right, and everything he does is worthy of our trust.

Ps 40:5. O Lord my God, many and many a time you have done great miracles of us, and we are ever in your thoughts. Who else can do such glorious things? No one else can be compared with you. There isn't time to tell of all your wonderful deeds.

Ps 66:3. How awe-inspiring are your deeds, O God! How great your power! No wonder your enemies surrender!

Ps 75:1. How we thank you, Lord! Your mighty miracles give proof that you care.

Ps 86:8. Where among the heathen gods is there a god like you? Where are their miracles?

Ps 92:4. You have done so much for me, O Lord. No wonder I am glad! I sing for joy. [5]O Lord, what miracles you do! And how deep are your thoughts!

Ps 111:1, 2. I want to express publicly before his people my heartfelt thanks to God for his mighty miracles. All who are thankful should ponder them with me. [4]Who can forget the wonders he performs —deeds of mercy and of grace? [6]He has shown his great power to his people by giving them the land of Israel, though it was the home of many nations living there.

Ps 118:17. I shall not die, but live to tell of all his deeds.

Ps 136:4. Praise him who alone does mighty miracles, for his lovingkindness continues forever. [5]Praise him who made the heavens, for his lovingkindness continues forever. [6]Praise him who planted the water within the earth, for his lovingkindness continues forever. [7]Praise him who made the heavenly lights, for his lovingkindness continues forever: [8]the sun to rule the day, for his lovingkindness continues forever; [9]and the moon and stars at night, for his lovingkindness continues forever. *vs.* 1–26.

Ps 139:14. Thank you for making me so wonderfully complex! It is amazing to think about. Your workmanship is marvelous—and how well I know it.

Eccl 3:11. Everything is appropriate in its own time. But though God has planted eternity in the hearts of men, even so, man cannot see the whole scope of God's work from beginning to end. [14]And I know this, that whatever God does is final—nothing can be added or taken from it; God's purpose in this is that man should fear the all-powerful God.

See Job 9; and chapters 37–41; Psalms 8; 19; 89; 104; 111; 145; 147; 148; Jer 10:12.

See *Creation; God, Creator,* above.

GODLESSNESS Deut 7:10. But those who hate him shall be punished publicly and destroyed. He will deal with them personally.

Deut 32:15. But Israel was soon overfed; yes, fat and bloated; then, in plenty, they forsook their God. They shrugged away the Rock of their salvation.

1 Sam 2:30. Therefore, I, the Lord God of Israel, declare that although I promised that your branch of the tribe of Levi could always be my priests, it is ridiculous to think that what you are doing can continue. I will honor only those who honor me, and I will despise those who despise me.

Job 8:11–13. Those who forget God have no hope. They are like rushes without any mire to grow in; or grass without water to keep it alive. Suddenly it begins to wither, even before it is cut.

Job 35:10. Yet none of them cry to God, asking, "Where is God my Maker who gives songs in the night."

Ps 2:2. For a summit conference of the nations has been called to plot against the Lord and his Messiah, Christ the King. [4]But God in heaven merely laughs! He is amused by all their puny plans.

Ps 9:17. The wicked shall be sent away to hell; this is the fate of all the nations forgetting the Lord.

Ps 10:4. These wicked men, so proud and haughty, seem to think that God is dead. They wouldn't think of looking for him!

Ps 14:2. The Lord looks down from heaven on all mankind to see if there are any who are wise, who want to please God. [3]But no, all have strayed away; all are rotten with sin. Not one is good, not one! Ps 53:2, 3; Rom 3:11, 18.

Ps 28:5. They care nothing for God or what he has done or what he has made; therefore God will dismantle them like old buildings, never to be rebuilt again. Isa 5:12.

Ps 36:1. Sin lurks deep in the hearts of the wicked, forever urging them on to evil deeds. They have no fear of God to hold them back.

Ps 50:22. This is the last chance for all of you who have forgotten God, before I tear you apart—and no one can help you then.

Ps 52:7. See what happens to those who despise God and trust in their wealth, and become ever more bold in their wickedness.

Ps 53:4. How can this be? Can't they understand anything? For they devour my people like bread and refuse to come to God.

Ps 54:3. For violent men have risen against me—ruthless men who care nothing for God are seeking my life.

Ps 55:19. God himself—God from everlasting ages past—will answer them! For they refuse to fear him or even honor his commands.

Ps 86:14. O God, proud and insolent men defy me; violent, godless men are trying to kill me.

Prov 14:2. To do right honors God; to sin is to despise him.

Isa 1:3. Even the animals—the donkey and the ox—know their owner and appreciate his care for them, but not my people Israel. No matter what I do for them, they still don't care.

Isa 17:10. Why? Because you have turned from the God who can save you—the Rock who can hide you; therefore, even though you plant a wonderful, rare crop of greatest value.

Isa 22:11. But all your feverish plans will not avail, for you never ask for help from God, who lets this come upon you. He is the one who planned it long ago.

Isa 30:1. Woe to my rebellious children, says the Lord; you ask advice from everyone but me, and decide to do what I don't want you to do. You yoke yourselves with unbelievers, thus piling up your sins. [*v.* 2.] [9]For if you don't write it, they will claim I never warned them. "Oh, no," they'll say, "you never told us that!" For they are stubborn rebels. [10, 11]They tell my prophets, "Shut up-we don't want any more of your reports!" Or they say, "Don't tell us the truth; tell us nice things; tell us lies. Forget all this gloom; we've heard more than enough about your 'Holy One of Israel' and all he says." [12]This is the reply of the Holy One of Israel: Because you despise what I tell you and trust instead in frauds and lies and won't repent, [13]therefore calamity will come upon you suddenly, as upon a bulging wall that bursts and falls; in one moment it comes crashing down.

Isa 31:1. Woe to those who run to Egypt for help, trusting their mighty cavalry and chariots instead of looking to the Holy One of Israel and consulting him.

Jer 2:32. How can you disown your God like that? Can a girl forget her jewels? What bride will seek to hide her wedding dress? Yet for years on end my people have forgotten me—the most precious of their treasures.

Dan 5:23. For you have defied the Lord of Heaven, and brought here these cups from his Temple; and you and your officers and wives and concubines have been drinking wine from them while praising gods of silver, gold, brass, iron, wood, and stone—gods that neither see nor hear, nor know anything at all. But you have not praised the God who gives you the breath of life and controls your destiny!

Hos 7:2. Her people never seem to recognize that I am watching them. Their sinful deeds give them away on every side; I see them all. [3]The king is glad about their wickedness; the princes laugh about their lies. [4]They are all adulterers; as a baker's oven is constantly aflame—except while he kneads the dough and waits for it to rise—so are these people constantly aflame with lust.

Mal 2:17. You have wearied the Lord with your words. "Wearied him?" you ask in fake surprise. "How have we wearied him?" By saying that evil is good, that it pleases the Lord! Or by saying that God won't punish us—he doesn't care.

Mal 3:8. Will a man rob God? Surely not! And yet you have robbed me. "What do you mean? When did we ever rob you?" You have robbed me of the tithes and offerings due to me.

Jn 5:42. For as I know so well, you don't have God's love within you. [44]No wonder you can't believe! For you gladly honor each other, but you don't care about the honor that comes from the only God!

Jn 15:23. Anyone hating me is also hating my Father. [24]If I hadn't done such mighty miracles among them they would not be counted guilty. But as it is, they saw these miracles and yet they hated both of us—me and my Father. [25]This had fulfilled what the prophets said concerning the Messiah, "They hated me without reason."

Rom 1:21. Yes, they knew about him all right, but they wouldn't admit it or worship him or even thank him for all his daily care. And after awhile they began to think up silly ideas of what God was like and what he wanted them to do. The result was that their foolish minds became dark and confused. [22]Claiming themselves to be wise without God, they became utter fools instead. [28]So it was that when they gave God up and would not even acknowledge him, God gave them up to doing everything their evil minds could think of.

Rom 8:6. Following after the Holy Spirit leads to life and peace, but following after the old nature leads to death, [7]because the old sinful nature within us is against God. It never did obey God's laws and it never will. [8]That's why those who are still under the control of their old sinful selves, bent on following their old evil desires, can never please God.

Eph 4:18. Their closed hearts are full of darkness; they are far away from the life of God because they have shut their minds against him, and they cannot understand his ways.

Col 1:21. This includes you who were once so far away from God. You were his enemies and hated him and were separated from him by your evil thoughts and actions, yet now he has brought you back as his friends.

Heb 10:26. If anyone sins deliberately by rejecting the Savior after knowing the truth of forgiveness, this sin is not covered by Christ's death; there is no way to get rid of it. [27]There will be nothing to look forward to but the terrible punishment of God's awful anger which will consume all his enemies.

Jas 4:4. You are like an unfaithful wife who loves her husband's enemies. Don't you realize that making friends with God's enemies—the evil pleasures of this world—makes you an enemy of God? I say it again, that if your aim is to enjoy the evil pleasure of the unsaved world, you cannot also be a friend of God.

See *Impenitence; Obduracy; Prayerlessness; Reprobate; Unbelief; Wicked.*

GODLINESS See *Holiness; Righteousness.*

GODLY See *Righteous.*

GODS See *Idol; Idolatry; Image.*

GOG 1. A Reubenite, 1 Chron 5:4.

2. King of Meshech and Tubal. Prophecy against, Ezk 38; 39; Rev 20:8. Valley of, burial place of the armies of Gog, Ezk 39:15, 16.

GOLAN A town in Bashan. Given to Manasseh as a city of refuge, Deut 4:43; Josh 20:8. A Levitical city, Josh 21:27; 1 Chron 6:71.

GOLD Exported from Havilah, Gen 2:11, 12. From Ophir, 1 Kgs 9:27, 28; 10:11; 1 Chron 29:4; 2 Chron 8:17, 18; Job 28:16; Isa 13:12; Tarshish, 2 Chron 9:21; Parvaim, 2 Chron 3:6; Sheba, 1 Kgs 10:10; 2 Chron 9:9; Ps 72:15; Uphaz, Jer 10:9.

Refined, Job 28:19; Prov 8:19; 17:3; 27:21; Zech 13:9; Mal 3:3. Used in the arts: Beaten work, 2 Chron 9:15; made into wire threads and woven into embroidered tapestry, Ex 39:3; clothing, Ps 45:13; in decorating the priests' garments; Ex 39; modeled into forms of fruits, Prov 25:11; into ornaments, Gen 24:22; Ex 3:22; 11:2; 28:11; Num 31:50; Ps 45:9; Song 5:14; Ezk 16:17; crowns made of, Ex 39:30; Esther 8:15; Ps 21:3; Zech 6:10, 11; lampstands made of, for the tabernacle, Ex 25:31–38; 37:17–24; shields of, 1 Kgs 10:16, 17; overlaying with, Ex 25:11, 13, 14, 24, 28, with 1–40; 26:26, 27, 29; 30:5; 36:34, 36, 38; 37:2, 4, 11; 26; 1 Kgs 6:20–28, 30, 32, 35; benches made of, Esther 1:6. Bar of, Josh 7:21.

Used as money, Gen 44:8, with verse 1; 1 Chron 21:25; Ezra 8:25–28; Isa 13:17; Ezk 28:4; Mt 2:11; 1 Pet 1:18. Solomon rich in, 1 Kgs 10:2, 14, 21.

Dishes and utensils made of, for the tabernacle, Ex 25:29, 38, 39; 37:16; for the temple, 1 Chron 18:11; 22:14, 16; 29:2–7. Altar, lamps, and other articles made of, 1 Kgs 7:48–51; 2 Kgs 25:14, 15; Ezra 8:26, 27; Jer 52:19; Dan 5:2–4; see *Overlaying with,* above.

Belongs to God, Ezk 16:17.

FIGURATIVE. Eccl 12:6; Jer 51:7; Lam 4:1; 1 Cor 3:12. Also Job 23:10; Prov 17:3; Mal 3:3; 1 Pet 1:7; Rev 3:18.

Symbolical. Dan 2:32–45; Rev 21:18–21.

See *Goldsmith.*

GOLDEN ALTAR See *Altar.*

GOLDEN CALF See *Calf.*

GOLDEN CANDLESTICK See *Candlestick.*

GOLDEN RULE Lev 19:18. Don't seek vengeance. Don't bear a grudge; but love your neighbor as yourself, for I am Jehovah. Rom 13:9; Gal 5:14.

Mt 7:12. Do for others what you want them to do for you. This is the teaching of the laws of Moses in a nutshell.

Lk 6:31. Treat others as you want them to treat you.

GOLDSMITH 2 Chron 2:7, 14; Neh 3:8, 31, 32; Isa 41:7; 46:6, Jer 10:9.

See *Gold.*

GOLGOTHA Hebrew name of the place where Jesus was crucified, Mt 27:33; Mk 15:22; Lk 23:33; Jn 19:17.

GOLIATH A giant champion of Gath. Defied armies of Israel and is killed by David, 1 Sam 17; 21:9; 22:9, 10. His brother, 2 Sam 21:15–22; 1 Chron 20:4–8.

GOMER 1. Son of Japheth, Gen 10:2, 3; 1 Chron 1:5–9.

2. A people descended from Gomer, Ezk 38:6.

3. Wife, or concubine, of Hosea, Hos 1:3.

GOMORRAH One of the "cities of the plain," Gen 10:19; 13:10. Its king defeated by Chedor-laomer, Gen 14:2, 8–11. Wickedness of, Gen 18:20. Destroyed, Gen 19:24–28; Deut 29:23; 32:32; Isa 1:9, 10; 13:19; Jer 23:14; 49:18; 50:40; Amos 4:11; Zeph 2:9; Mt 10:15; Rom 9:29; 2 Pet 2:6; Jude 1:7.

GOOD AND EVIL Choice between, by Adam and Eve, Gen 3. Exhortation to choose between, Josh 24:15. Conflict between, Rev 16:13–21. Subjective conflict between, Rom 7:9–25.

GONORRHEA Lev 15.

See *Disease.*

GOOD FOR EVIL Mt 5:44. But I say: Love your *enemies!* Pray for those who *persecute* you! [45]In that way you will be acting as true sons of your Father in heaven. For he gives his sunlight to both the evil and the good, and sends rain on the just and on the unjust too. [46]If you love only those who love you, what good is that? Even scoundrels do that much. [47]If you are friendly only to your friends, how are you different from anyone else? Even the heathen do that. [48]But you are to be perfect, even as your Father in heaven is perfect.

Lk 6:27. Listen, all of you. Love your *enemies.* Do *good* to those who *hate* you. [28]Pray for the happiness of those who *curse* you; implore God's blessing on those who *hurt* you. [29]If someone slaps you on one cheek, let him slap the other too! If someone demands your coat, give him your shirt besides. [30]Give what you have to anyone who asks you for it; and when things are taken away from you, don't worry about getting them back. [31]Treat others as you want them to treat you. [32]Do you think you deserve credit for merely loving those who love you? Even the godless do that! [33]And if you do good only to those who do you good—is that so wonderful? Even sinners do that much! [34]And if you lend money only to those who can repay you, what good is that? Even the most wicked will lend to their own kind for full return! [35]Love your *enemies!* Do good to *them!* Lend to *them!* And don't be concerned about the fact that they won't repay. Then your reward from heaven will be very great, and you will truly be acting as sons of God: for he is kind to the *unthankful* and to those who are *very wicked.* [36]Try to show as much compassion as your Father does.

RETURNING.

Instances of. Abraham, to Abimelech, Gen 20:14–18. David, to Saul, 1 Sam 24:17; 26. Elisha, to the Syrians, 2 Kgs 6:22, 23. David, to his enemies, Ps 35:12–14. Jesus, to his crucifiers, Lk 23:34. Stephen, Acts 7:60.

See *Golden Rule; Evil for Good.*

GOOD NEWS Prov 15:30; 25:25.

GOSHEN 1. A district in Egypt especially adapted to herds and flocks. Israelites lived in, Gen 45:10; 46:28; 47. Exempted from plagues, Ex 8:22; 9:26.

2. A town and district of Judah, Josh 10:41; 11:16; 15:48–62.

GOSPEL The New Testament word means "good news." Occurrences of this and related expressions: *Gospel,* Rom 11:28; 15:15, 16, 27; 16:25–27; 1 Cor 1:17; 4:15; 9:14, 16, 20, 23; 13:3; 15:1, 11; 2 Cor 2:14; 6:6; Gal 1:9; 2:14; Col 1:5; 1 Pet 2:15; 3 Jn 1:3; *Gospel of Christ,* Rom 15:9; *Gospel of peace with God,* Rom 10:15; *Glorious light of the Gospel,* 2 Cor 4:4; *Good News,* 1 Cor 9:18; 13:1; Phil 1:27; Col 1:6; *God's Good News,* Rom 1:1; *Good News of our beloved God,* 1 Tim 1:1; *Good News about Christ,* Rom 1:16; *Good News about the Kingdom,* Mt 4:23; 24:14; Lk 16:16; *Good News about God's mighty kindness and love,* Acts 20:24; *Good News about how to be saved,* Eph 1:13; *Good News of peace with God,* Eph 6:15; *Story of Jesus the Messiah,* Mk 1:1; *Truth concerning Christ,* Gal 1:7; *God's message,* 1 Thess 2:8; *Wonderful message,* 2 Cor 5:19; *Word of God,* 1 Thess 2:13; *Word of life,* Phil 2:16; *Foundation for a godly life,* 1 Tim 6:3; *Pattern of truth,* 2 Tim 1:13.

Likened to a feast, Lk 14:16–24.

UNCLASSIFIED SCRIPTURES RELATING TO:

Mt 4:23. Jesus traveled all through Galilee teaching in the Jewish synagogues, everywhere preaching the Good News about the Kingdom of Heaven. And he healed every kind of sickness and disease.

Mt 11:4. Jesus told them, "Go back to John and tell him about the miracles you've seen me do— [5]the blind people I've healed, and the lame people now walking without help, and the cured lepers, and the deaf who hear, and the dead raised to life; and tell him about my preaching the Good News to the poor. [6]Then give him this message, 'Blessed are those who don't doubt me.' " Lk 7:20–22.

Mt 13:17. Many a prophet and godly man has longed to see what you have seen, and hear what you have heard, but couldn't.

Mt 24:14. And the Good News about the Kingdom will be preached throughout the whole world, so that all nations will hear it, and then, finally, the end will come.

Mt 28:18. He told his disciples, "I have been given all authority in heaven and earth. [19]Therefore go and make disciples in all the nations, baptizing them into the name of the Father and of the Son and of the Holy Spirit, [20]and then teach these new disciples to obey all the commands I have given you; and be sure of this—that I am with you always, even to the end of the world."

Mk 1:14. Later on, after John was arrested by King Herod, Jesus went to Galilee to preach God's Good News. [15]"At last the time has come!" he announced. "God's Kingdom is near! Turn from your sins and act on this glorious news!"

Mk 13:10. And the Good News must first be made known in every nation before the end-time finally comes. Mk 16:15.

Lk 1:67. Then his father Zacharias was filled with the Holy Spirit and gave this prophecy: [68]"Praise the Lord, the God of Israel, for he has come to visit his people and has redeemed them. [69]He is sending us a Mighty Savior from the royal line of his servant David, [70]just as he promised through his holy prophets long ago—[71]someone to save us from our enemies, from all who hate us. [72, 73]He has been merciful to our ancestors, yes, to Abraham himself, by remembering his sacred promise to him, [74]and by granting us the privilege of serving God fearlessly, freed from our enemies, [75]and by making us holy and acceptable, ready to stand in his presence forever. [76]And you, my little son, shall be called the prophet of the glorious God, for you will prepare the way for the Messiah. [77]You will tell his people how to find salvation through forgiveness of their sins. [78]All this will be because the mercy of our God is very tender, and heaven's dawn is about to break upon us, [79]to give light to those who sit in darkness and death's shadow, and to guide us to the path of peace."

Lk 2:10. But the angel reassured them. "Don't be afraid!" he said. "I bring you the most joyful news ever announced, and it is for everyone! [11]The Savior—yes, the Messiah, the Lord—has been born tonight in Bethlehem! [12]How will you recognize him? You will find a baby wrapped in a blanket, lying in a manger!" [13]Suddenly the angel was joined by a vast host of others—the armies of heaven—praising God: [14]"Glory to God in the highest heaven," they sang, "and peace on earth for all those pleasing him." [34]Simeon blessed them but then said to Mary, "A sword shall pierce your soul, for this child shall be rejected by many in Israel, and this to their undoing. But he will be the greatest joy of many others. And the deepest thoughts of many hearts shall be revealed."

Lk 4:18, 19. The Spirit of the Lord is upon me; he has appointed me to preach Good News to the poor; he has sent me to heal the brokenhearted and to announce that captives shall be released and the blind shall see, that the downtrodden shall be freed from their oppressors, and that God is ready to give blessings to all who come to him.

Lk 10:23. Then, turning to the twelve disciples, he said quietly, "How privileged you are to see what you have seen. [24]Many a prophet and king of old has longed for these days, to see and hear what you have seen and heard!"

Lk 16:16. Until John the Baptist began to preach, the laws of Moses and the messages of the prophets were your guides. But John introduced the Good News that the Kingdom of God would come soon. And now eager multitudes are pressing in. Acts 12:24; 19:20.

Lk 17:20. One day the Pharisees asked Jesus, "When will the Kingdom of God begin?" Jesus replied, "The Kingdom of God isn't ushered in with visible signs. [21]You won't be able to say, 'It has begun here in this place or there in that part of the country.' For the Kingdom of God is within you."

Jn 1:16. We have all benefited from the rich blessings he brought to us—blessing upon blessing heaped upon us! [17]For Moses gave us only the Law with its rigid demands and merciless justice, while Jesus Christ brought us loving forgiveness as well.

Jn 4:14. "But the water I give them," he said, "becomes a perpetual spring within them, watering them forever with eternal life."

Jn 8:32. And you will know the truth, and the truth will set you free.

Jn 12:35. Jesus replied, "My light will shine out for you just a little while longer. Walk in it while you can, and go where you want to go before the darkness falls, for then it will be too late for you to find your way. [50]And I know his instructions lead to eternal life; so whatever he tells me to say, I say!"

Jn 17:7. Now they know that everything I have is a gift from you, [8]for I have passed on to them the commands you gave me; and they accepted them and know of a certainty that I came down to earth from you, and they believe you sent me. Jn 13:20.

Jn 18:36. Then Jesus answered, "I am not an earthly king. If I were, my followers would have fought when I was arrested by the Jewish leaders. But my Kingdom is not of the world."

Acts 2:11. And we all hear these men telling in our own languages about the mighty miracles of God!

Acts 5:20. Go over to the Temple and preach about this Life!

Acts 10:36, 37. I'm sure you have heard about the Good News for the people of Israel—that there is peace with God through Jesus, the Messiah, who is Lord of all creation. This message has spread all through Judea, beginning with John the Baptist in Galilee.

Acts 13:32, 33. And now Barnabas and I are here to bring you this Good News—that God's promise to our ancestors has come true in our own time, in that God brought Jesus back to life again. This is what the second Psalm is talking about when it says concerning Jesus, "Today I have honored you as my son."

Acts 14:3. Nevertheless, they stayed there a long time, preaching boldly, and the Lord proved their message was from him by giving them power to do great miracles.

Acts 16:17. She followed along behind us shouting, "These men are servants of God and they have come to tell you how to have your sins forgiven."

Acts 20:24. But life is worth nothing unless I use it for doing the work assigned me by the Lord Jesus—the work of telling others the Good News about God's mighty kindness and love. [32]And now I entrust you to God and his care and to his wonderful words which are able to build your faith and give you all the inheritance of those who are set apart for himself. Acts 14:3.

Rom 1:16. For I am not ashamed of this Good News about Christ. It is God's powerful method of bringing all who believe it to heaven. This message was preached first to the Jews alone, but now everyone is invited to come to God in this same way. [17]This Good News tells us that God makes us ready for heaven—makes us right in God's sight—when we put our faith and trust in Christ to save us. This is accomplished from start to finish by faith. As the Scriptures says it, "The man who finds life will find it through trusting God."

Rom 10:15. And how will anyone go and tell them unless someone sends him? That is what the Scriptures are talking about when they say "How beautiful are the feet of those who preach the Gospel of peace with God and bring glad tidings of good things." In other words, how welcome are those who come preaching God's Good News! [16]But not everyone who hears the Good News has welcomed it, for Isaiah the prophet said, "Lord, who has believed me when I told them?" [17]Yet faith comes from listening to this Good News—the Good News about Christ. [18]But what about the Jews? Have they heard God's Word? Yes, for it has gone wherever they are; the Good News has been told to the ends of the earth.

Rom 16:25, 26. I commit you to God, who is able to make you strong and steady in the Lord, just as the Gospel says, and just as I have told you. This is God's plan of salvation for you Gentiles, kept secret from the beginning of time. But now as the prophets foretold and as God commands, this message is being preached everywhere, so that people all around the world will have faith in Christ and obey him.

1 Cor 1:18. I know very well how foolish it sounds to those who are lost, when they hear that Jesus died to save them. But we who are saved recognize this message as the very power of God. [21]For God in his wisdom saw to it that the world would never find God through human brilliance, and then he stepped in and saved all those who believed his message, which the world calls foolish and silly. [24]But God has opened the eyes of those called to salvation, both Jews and Gentiles, to see that Christ is the mighty power of God to save them; Christ himself is the center of God's wise plan for their salvation. [25]This so-called "foolish" plan of God is far wiser than the wisest plan of the wisest man, and God in his weakness—Christ dying on the cross—is far stronger than any man.

1 Cor 2:4. And my preaching was very plain, not with a lot of oratory and human wisdom, but the Holy Spirit's power was in my words, proving to those who heard them that the message was from God. [5]I did this because I wanted your faith to stand firmly upon God, not on man's great ideas. [6]Yet when I am among mature Christians I do speak with words of great wisdom, but not the kind that comes from here on earth, and not the kind that appeals to the great men of this world, who are doomed to fall. [7]Our words are wise because they are from God, telling of God's wise plan to bring us into the glories of heaven. This plan was hidden in former times, though it was made for our benefit before the world began. [9]That is what is meant by the Scriptures which say that no mere man has ever seen, heard or even imagined what wonderful things God has ready for those who love the Lord.

1 Cor 4:20. The Kingdom of God is not just talking; it is living by God's power.

1 Cor 9:16. For just preaching the Gospel isn't any special credit to me—I couldn't keep from preaching it if I wanted to. I would be utterly miserable. Woe unto me if I don't. [17]If I were volunteering my services of my own free will, then the Lord would give me a special reward; but that is not the situation, for God has picked me out and given me this sacred trust and I have no choice. [18]Under this circumstance, what is my pay? It is the special joy I get from preaching the Good News without expense to anyone, never demanding my rights.

1 Cor 15:1. Now let me remind you, brothers, of what the Gospel really is, for it has not changed—it is the same Good News I preached to you before. You welcomed it then and still do now, for your faith is squarely built upon this wonderful message; [2]and it is this Good News that saves you if you still firmly believe it, unless of course you never really believed it in the first place.

2 Cor 3:6. He is the one who has helped us tell others about his new agreement to save them. We do not tell them that they must obey every law of God or die; but we tell them there is life for them from the Holy Spirit. The old way, trying to be saved by keeping the Ten Commandments, ends in death; in the new way, the Holy Spirit gives them life. [7]Yet that old system of law that led to death began with such glory that people could not bear to look at Moses' face. For as he gave them God's law to obey, his face shone out with the very glory of God—though the brightness was already fading away. [8]Shall we not expect far greater glory in these days when the Holy Spirit is giving life? [9]If the plan that leads to doom was glorious, much more glorious is the plan that makes men right with God. [10]In fact, that first glory as it shone from Moses' face is worth nothing at all in comparison with the overwhelming glory of the new agreement. [11]So if the old system that faded into nothing was full of heavenly glory, the glory of God's new plan for our salvation is certainly far greater, for it is eternal.

[18]But we Christians have no veil over our faces; we can be mirrors that brightly reflect the glory of the Lord. And as the Spirit of the Lord works within us, we become more and more like him.

2 Cor 4:3. If the Good News we preach is hidden to anyone, it is hidden from the one who is on the road to eternal death. [4]Satan, who is the god of this evil world, has made him blind, unable to see the glorious light of the Gospel that is shining upon him, or to understand the amazing message we preach about the glory of Christ, who is God. [6]For God, who said, "Let there be light in the darkness," has made us understand that it is the brightness of his glory that is seen in the face of Jesus Christ.

2 Cor 9:15. Thank God for his Son—his Gift too wonderful for words.

2 Cor 10:4. I use God's mighty weapons, not those made by men, to knock down the devil's strongholds. [5]These weapons can break down every proud argument against God and every wall that can be built to keep men from finding him. With these weapons I can capture rebels and bring them back to God, and change them into men whose hearts' desire is obedience to Christ.

Gal 2:2. I went there with definite orders from God to confer with the brothers there about the message I was preaching to the Gentiles. I talked privately to the leaders of the church so that they would all understand just what I had been teaching and, I hoped, agree that it was right.

Gal 3:8, 9. What's more, the Scriptures looked forward to this time when God would save the Gentiles also, through their faith. God told Abraham about this long ago when he said, "I will bless those in every nation who trust in me as you do." And so it is: all who trust in Christ share the same blessing Abraham received.

Eph 1:13. And because of what Christ did, all you others too, who heard the Good News about how to be saved, and trusted Christ, were marked as belonging to Christ by the Holy Spirit, who long ago had been promised to all of us Christians. [14]His presence within us is God's guarantee that he really will give us all that he promised; and the Spirit's seal upon us means that God has already purchased us and that he guarantees to bring us to himself. This is just one more reason for us to praise our glorious God.

Eph 3:8. Just think! Though I did nothing to deserve it, and though I am the most useless Christian there is, yet I was the one chosen for this special joy of telling the Gentiles the Glad News of the endless treasures available to them in Christ; [9]and to explain to everyone that God is the Savior of the Gentiles too, just as he who made all things had secretly planned from the very beginning. [10]And his reason? To show to all the rulers in heaven how perfectly wise he is when all of his family—Jews and Gentiles alike—are seen to be joined together in his church, [11]in just the way he had always planned it through Jesus Christ our Lord.

Eph 6:15. Wear shoes that are able to speed you on as you preach the Good News of peace with God. [17]And you will need the helmet of salvation and the sword of the Spirit—which is the Word of God. [19]Pray for me, too, and ask God to give me the right words as I boldly tell others about the Lord, and as I explain to them that his salvation is for the Gentiles too. [20]I am in chains now for preaching this message from God. But pray that I will keep on speaking out boldly for him even here in prison, as I should.

Col 1:5. And you are looking forward to the joys of heaven, and have been ever since the Gospel first was preached to you. [6]The same Good News that came to you is going out all over the world and changing lives everywhere, just as it changed yours that very first day you heard it and understood about God's great kindness to sinners. [23]The only condition is that you fully believe the Truth, standing in it steadfast and firm, strong in the Lord, convinced of the Good News that Jesus died for you, and never shifting from trusting him to save you. This is the wonderful news that came to each of you and is now spreading all over the world. And I, Paul, have the joy of telling it to others. [26, 27]He has kept this secret for centuries and generations past, but now at last it has pleased him to tell it to those who love him and live for him, and the riches and glory of his plan are for you Gentiles too. And this is the secret: *that Christ in your hearts is your only hope of glory.* [28]So everywhere we go we talk about Christ to all who will listen, warning them and teaching them as well as we know how. We want to be able to present each one to God, perfect because of what Christ has done for each of them. [29]This is my work, and I can do it only because Christ's mighty energy is at work within me.

1 Thess 1:5. For when we brought you the Good News, it was not just meaningless chatter to you; no, you listened with great interest. What we told you produced a powerful effect upon you, for the Holy Spirit gave you great and full assurance that what we said was true. And you know how our very lives were further proof to you of the truth of our message.

1 Thess 2:13. And we will never stop thanking God for this: that when we preached to you, you didn't think of the words we spoke as being just our own, but you accepted what we said as the very Word of God—which, of course, it was—and it changed your lives when you believed it.

2 Thess 1:10. When he comes to receive praise and admiration because of all he has done for his people, his saints. And you will be among those praising him, because you have believed what we told you about him.

2 Thess 2:10. He will completely fool those who are on their way to hell because they have said "no" to the Truth; they have refused to believe it and love it, and let it save them. [14]Through us he told you the Good News. Through us he called you to share in the glory of our Lord Jesus Christ.

1 Tim 1:10, 11. Yes, these laws are made to identify as sinners all who are immoral and impure: homosexuals, kidnappers, liars, and all others who do things that contradict the glorious Good News of our blessed God, whose messenger I am.

1 Tim 2:4. For he longs for all to be saved and to understand this truth.

1 Tim 3:16. It is quite true that the way to live a godly life is not an easy matter. But the answer lies in Christ, who came to earth as a man, was proved spotless and pure in his Spirit, was served by angels, was preached among the nations, was accepted by men everywhere and was received up again to his glory in heaven.

1 Tim 4:6. If you explain this to the others you will be doing your duty as a worthy pastor who is fed by faith and by the true teaching you have followed.

2 Tim 1:10. And now he has made all of this plain to us by the coming of our Savior Jesus Christ, who broke the power of death and showed us the way of everlasting life through trusting him.

2 Tim 2:3. Take your share of suffering as a good soldier of Jesus Christ, just as I do.

Heb 4:2. For this wonderful news—the message that God wants to save us—has been given to us just as it was to those who lived in the time of Moses. But it didn't do them any good because they didn't believe it. They didn't mix it with faith.

Heb 5:13. And when a person is still living on milk it shows he isn't very far along in the Christian life, and doesn't know much about the difference between right and wrong. He is still a baby-Christian!

Heb 6:1. Let us stop going over the same old ground again and again, always teaching those first lessons about Christ. Let us go on instead to other things and become mature in our understanding, as strong Christians ought to be. Surely we don't need to speak further about the foolishness of trying to be saved by being good, or about the necessity of faith in God.

Heb 7:18. Yes, the old system of priesthood based on family lines was canceled because it didn't work. It was weak and useless for saving people. [19]It never made anyone really right with God. But now we have a far better hope, for Christ makes us acceptable to God, and now we may draw near to him.

Jas 1:18. And it was a happy day for him when he gave us our new lives, through the truth of his Word, and we became, as it were, the first children in his new family. [21]So get rid of all that is wrong in your life, both inside and outside, and humbly be glad for the wonderful message we have received, for it is able to save our souls as it takes hold of our hearts. [25]But if anyone keeps looking steadily into God's law for free men, he will not only remember it but he will do what it says, and God will greatly bless in everything he does.

1 Pet 1:23. For you have a new life. It was not passed on to you from your parents, for the life they gave you will fade away. This new one will last forever, for it comes from Christ, God's ever-living Message to men. [25]But the Word of the Lord will last forever. And his message is the Good News that was preached to you. Isa 40:8.

1 Pet 4:6. That is why the Good News was preached even to those who were dead—killed by the flood—so that although their bodies were punished with death, they could still live in their spirits as God lives.

1 Pet 5:12. I am sending this note to you through the courtesy of Silvanus who is, in my opinion, a very faithful brother. I hope I have encouraged you by this letter for I have given you a true statement of the way God blesses. What I have told you here should help you to stand firmly in his love.

2 Pet 1:16. For we have not been telling you fairy tales when we explained to you the power of our Lord Jesus Christ and his coming again. My own eyes have seen his splendor and his glory. [19]So we have seen and proved that what the prophets said came true. You will do well to pay close attention to everything they have written, for, like lights shining into dark corners, their words help us to understand many things that otherwise would be dark and difficult. But when you consider the wonderful truth of the prophets' words, then the light will dawn in your souls and Christ the Morning Star will shine in your hearts.

2 Pet 2:2. Many will follow their evil teaching that there is nothing wrong with sexual sin. And because of them Christ and his way will be scoffed at. [21]It would be better if he had never known about Christ at all than to learn of him and then afterwards turn his back on the holy commandments that were given to him.

1 Jn 2:8. Yet it is always new, and works for you just as it did for Christ; and as we obey this commandment, *to love one another,* the darkness in our lives disappears and the new light of life in Christ shines in.

Jude 1:3. Dearly loved friends, I had been planning to write you some thoughts about the salvation God has given us, but now I find I must write of something else instead, urging you to stoutly defend the truth which God gave, once for all, to his people to keep without change through the years.

Rev 14:6. And I saw another angel flying through the heavens, carrying the everlasting Good News to preach to those on earth—to every nation, tribe, language and people. [7]"Fear God," he shouted, "and extol his greatness. For the time has come when he will sit as Judge. Worship him who made the heaven and the earth, the sea and all its sources."

GOOD NEWS OF THE NEW COVENANT. Jer 31:31. The day will come, says the Lord, when I will make a new contract with the people of Israel and Judah. [32]It won't be like the one I made with their fathers when I took them by the hand to bring them out of the land of Egypt—a contract they broke, forcing me to reject them, says the Lord. [33]But this is the new contract I will make with them: I will inscribe my laws upon their hearts, so that they shall want to honor me; then they shall truly be my people and I will be their God. [34]At that time it will no longer be necessary to admonish one another to know the Lord. For everyone, both great and small, shall really know me then, says the Lord, and I will forgive and forget their sins.

Heb 7:22. Because of God's oath, Christ can guarantee forever the success of this new and better arrangement.

Heb 8:6. But Christ, as a Minister in heaven, has been rewarded with a far more important work than those who serve under the old laws, because the new agreement which he passes on to us from God contains far more wonderful promises. [7]The old agreement didn't even work. If it had, there would have been no need for another to replace it. [8]But God himself found fault with the old one, for he said, "The day will come when I will make a new agreement with the people of Israel and the people of Judah. [9]This new agreement will not be like the old one I gave to their fathers on the day when I took them by the hand to lead them out of the land of Egypt; they did not keep their part in that agreement, so I had to cancel it. [10]But this is the new agreement I will make with the people of Israel, says the Lord: I will write my laws in their minds so that they will know what I want them to do without my even telling them, and these laws will be in their hearts so that they will want to obey them, and I will be their God and they shall be my people. [11]And no one then will need to speak to his friend or neighbor or brother, saying, 'You, too, should know the Lord,' because everyone, great and small, will know me already. [12]And I will be merciful to them in their wrongdoings, and I will remember their sins no more." [13]God speaks of these new promises, of this new agreement, as taking the place of the old one; for the old one is out of date now and has been put aside forever.

Heb 9:8. And the Holy Spirit uses all this to point out to us that under the old system the common people could not go into the Holy of Holies as long as the outer room and the entire system it represents were still in use. [9]This has an important lesson for us today. For under the old system, gifts and sacrifices were offered, but these failed to cleanse the hearts of the people who brought them. [10]For the old system dealt only with certain rituals —what foods to eat and drink, rules for washing themselves, and rules about this and that. The people had to keep these rules to tide them over until Christ came with God's new and better way. [11]He came as High Priest of this better system which we now have. He went into that greater, perfect tabernacle in heaven, not made by men nor part of this world, [12]and once for all took blood into that inner room, the Holy of Holies, and sprinkled it on the mercy seat; but it was not the blood of goats and calves. No, he took his own blood, and with it he, by himself, made sure of our eternal salvation. [13]And if under the old system the blood of bulls and goats and the ashes of young cows could cleanse men's bodies from sin, [14]just think how much more surely the blood of Christ will transform our lives and hearts. His sacrifice frees us from the worry of having to obey the old rules, and makes us want to serve the living God. For by the help of the eternal Holy Spirit, Christ willingly gave himself to God to die for our sins—he being perfect, without a single sin or fault. [15]Christ came with this new agreement so that all who are invited may come and have forever all the wonders God has promised them. For Christ died to rescue them from the penalty of the sins they had committed while still under that old system.

Heb 10:9. He then added, "Here I am. I have come to give my life." He cancels the first system in favor of a far better one.

Heb 12:22. But you have come right up into Mount Zion, to the city of the living God, the heavenly Jerusalem, and to the gathering of countless happy angels; [23]and to the church, composed of all those registered in heaven; and to God who is Judge of all; and to the spirits of the redeemed in heaven, already made perfect; [24]and to Jesus himself, who has brought us his wonderful new agreement; and to the sprinkled blood which graciously forgives instead of crying out for vengeance as the blood of Abel did.

GOOD NEWS REGARDING ISRAEL'S FUTURE. Ps 46:4. There is a river of joy flowing through the City of our God—the sacred home of the God above all gods.

Isa 2:3. "Come," everyone will say, "let us go up the mountain of the Lord, to the Temple of the God of Israel; there he will teach us his laws, and we will obey them." For in those days the world will be ruled from Jerusalem. [4]The Lord will settle international disputes; all the nations will convert their weapons of war into implements of peace. Then at the last all wars will stop and all military training will end. [5]O Israel, come, let us walk in the light of the Lord, and be obedient to his laws!

Isa 4:2, 3, 4, Those whose names are written down to escape the destruction of Jerusalem will be washed and rinsed of all their moral filth by the horrors and the fire. They will be God's holy people. And the land will produce for them its lushest bounty and its richest fruit. [5]Then the Lord will provide shade on all Jerusalem—over every home and all its public grounds—a canopy of smoke and cloud throughout the day, and clouds of fire at night, covering the Glorious Land, [6]protecting it from daytime heat and from rains and storms.

Isa 9:2. The people who walk in darkness shall see a great Light—a Light that will shine on all those who live in the land of the shadow of death. [6]For unto us a Child is born; unto us a Son is given; and the government shall be upon his shoulder. These will be his royal titles: "Wonderful," "Counselor," "The Mighty God," "The Everlasting Father," "The Prince of Peace." [7]His ever-expanding, peaceful government will never end. He will rule with perfect fairness and justice from the throne of his father David. He will bring true justice and peace to all the nations of the world. This is going to happen because the Lord of heaven's armies has dedicated himself to do it!

Isa 25:7. At that time he will remove the cloud of gloom, the pall of death that hangs over the earth.

Isa 29:18. In that day the deaf will hear the words of a book, and out of their gloom and darkness the blind will see my plans. [24]Those in error will believe the truth, and complainers will be willing to be taught!

Isa 32:3. Then at last the eyes of Israel will open wide to God; his people will listen to his voice.

Isa 35:5. And when he comes, he will open the eyes of the blind, and unstop the ears of the deaf.

Isa 40:9. O Crier of Good News, shout to Jerusalem from the mountain tops! Shout louder—don't be afraid—tell the cities of Judah, "Your God is coming!"

Isa 41:27. I was the first to tell Jerusalem, "Look! Look! Help is on the way!"

Isa 42:6. I the Lord have called you to demonstrate my righteousness. I will guard and support you, for I have given you to my people as the personal confirmation of my covenant with them. You shall also be a light to guide the nations unto me. [7]You will open the eyes of the blind, and release those who sit in prison darkness and despair.

Isa 43:18. But forget all that—it is nothing compared to what I'm going to do! [19]For I'm going to do a brand new thing. See, I have already begun! Don't you see it? I will make a road through the wilderness of the world for my people to go home, and create rivers for them in the desert! [20]The wild animals in the fields will thank me, the jackals and ostriches too, for giving them water in the wilderness, yes, springs in the desert, so that my people, my chosen ones, can be refreshed. [21]I have made Israel for myself, and these my people will some day honor me before the world.

Isa 46:13. For I am offering you my deliverance; not in the distant future, but right now! I am ready to save you, and I will restore Jerusalem, and Israel, who is my glory.

Isa 49:13. Sing for joy, O heavens; shout, O earth. Break forth with song, O mountains, for the Lord has comforted his people, and will have compassion upon them in their sorrow.

Isa 51:4. Listen to me, my people; listen, O Israel, for I will see that right prevails. [5]My mercy and justice are coming soon; your salvation is on the way. I will rule nations; they shall wait for me and long for me to come. [6]Look high in the skies and watch the earth beneath, for the skies shall disappear like smoke, the earth shall wear out like a garment, and the people of the earth shall die like flies. But my salvation lasts forever; my righteous rule will never die nor end.

Isa 52:7. How beautiful upon the mountains are the feet of those who bring the happy news of peace and salvation, the news that the God of Israel reigns.

Isa 55:1. Say there! Is anyone thirsty? Come and drink—even if you have no money! Come, take your choice of wine and milk—it's all free! [2]Why spend your money on foodstuffs that don't give you strength? Why pay for groceries that don't do you any good? Listen and I'll tell you where to get good food that fattens up the soul! [3]Come to me with your ears wide open. Listen, for the life of your soul is at stake. I am ready to make an everlasting covenant with you, to give you all the unfailing mercies and love that I had for King David. [4]He proved my power by conquering foreign nations. [5]You also will command the nations and they will come running to obey, not because of your own power or virtue but because I, the Lord your God, have glorified you.

Isa 60:1. Arise, my people! Let your light shine for all the nations to see! For the glory of the Lord is streaming from you. [2]Darkness as black as night shall cover all the peoples of the earth, but the glory of the Lord will shine from you. [3]All nations will come to your light; mighty kings will come to see the glory of the Lord upon you. [4]Lift up your eyes and see! For your sons and daughters are coming home to you from distant lands. [5]Your eyes will shine with joy, your hearts will thrill, for merchants from around the world will flow to you, bringing you the wealth of many lands. [6]Vast droves of camels will converge upon you, dromedaries from Midian and Sheba and Ephah, too, bringing gold and incense to add to the praise of God. [7]The flocks of Kedar shall be given you, and the rams of Nabaioth for my altars, and I will glorify my glorious Temple in that day. [8]And who are these who fly like a cloud to Israel, like doves to their nests? [9]I have reserved the ships of many lands, the very best, to bring the sons of Israel home again from far away, bringing their wealth with them. For the Holy One of Israel, known around the world, has glorified you in the eyes of all. [10]Foreigners will come and build your cities. Presidents and kings will send you aid. For though I destroyed you in my anger, I will have mercy on you through my grace. [11]Your gates will stay wide open around the clock to receive the wealth of many lands. The kings of the world will cater to you. [12]For the nations refusing to be your allies will perish; they shall be destroyed. [13]The glory of Lebanon will be yours—the forests of firs and pines, and box trees—to beautify my sanctuary. My Temple will be glorious. [14]The sons of anti-Semites will come and bow before you! They will kiss your feet! They will call Jerusalem "The City of the Lord" and "The Glorious Mountain of the Holy One of Israel." [15]Though once despised and hated and rebuffed by all, you will be beautiful forever, a joy for all the generations of the world, for I will make you so. [16]Powerful kings and mighty nations shall provide you with the choicest of their goods to satisfy your every need, and you will know at last and really understand that I, the Lord, am your Savior and Redeemer, the Mighty One of Israel. [17]I will exchange your brass for gold, your iron for silver, your wood for brass, your stones for iron. Peace and righteousness shall be your taskmasters! [18]Violence will disappear out of your land —all war will end. Your walls will be "Salvation" and your gates "Praise." [19]No longer will you need the sun or moon to give you light, for the Lord your God will be your everlasting light, and he will be your glory. [20]Your sun shall never set; the moon shall not go down—for the Lord will be your everlasting light; your days of mourning all will end. [21]All your people will be good. They will possess their land forever, for I will plant them there with my own hands; this will bring me glory. [22]The smallest family shall multiply into a clan; the tiny group shall be a mighty nation. I, the Lord, will bring it all to pass when it is time.

Isa 61:1. The Spirit of the Lord God is upon me, because the Lord has anointed me to bring good news to the suffering and afflicted. He has sent me to comfort the broken-hearted, to announce liberty to captives and to open the eyes of the blind. [2]He has sent me to tell those who mourn that the time of God's favor to them has come, and the day of his wrath to their enemies. [3]To all who mourn in Israel he will give: Beauty for ashes; joy instead of mourning; praise instead of heaviness. For God has planted them like strong and graceful oaks for his own glory.

Ezk 34:23. And I will set one Shepherd over all my people, even my Servant, David. He shall feed them and be a Shepherd to them. [24]And I, the Lord, will be their God, and my Servant David shall be a Prince among my people. I, the Lord, have spoken it. [25]I will make a peace pact with them, and drive away the dangerous animals from the land so that my people can safely camp in the wildest places and sleep safely in the woods. [26]I will make my people and their homes around my hill a blessing. And there shall be showers, showers of blessing, for I will not shut off the rains but send them in their seasons. [27]Their fruit trees and fields will yield bumper crops, and everyone will live in safety. When I have broken off their chains of slavery and delivered them from those who profiteered at their expense, they shall know I am the Lord. [28]No more will other nations conquer them nor wild animals attack. They shall live in safety and no one shall make them afraid. [29]And I will raise up a notable Vine [the Messiah], in Israel so that my people will never again go hungry nor be shamed by heathen conquest. [30]In this way they will know that I, the Lord their God, am with them, and that they, the people of Israel, are my people, says the Lord God. [31]You are my flock, the sheep of my pasture. You are my men and I am your God, so says the Lord.

Ezk 47:8. He told me: This river flows east through the desert and the Jordan Valley to the Dead Sea, where it will heal the salty waters and make them fresh and pure. [12]All kinds of fruit trees will grow along the river banks. The leaves will never turn brown and fall, and there will always be fruit. There will be a new crop every month—without fail! For they are watered by the river flowing from the Temple. The fruit will be for food and the leaves for medicine. *vs.* 1–12.

Joel 2:28. After I have poured out my rains again, I will pour out my Spirit upon all of you! Your sons and daughters will prophesy; your old men will dream dreams, and your young men see visions. [29]And I will pour out my Spirit even on your slaves, men and women alike, [30]and put strange symbols in the earth and sky—blood and fire and pillars of smoke. [31]The sun will be turned into darkness and the moon to blood before the great and terrible Day of the Lord shall come. [32]Everyone who calls upon the name of the Lord will be saved; even in Jerusalem some will escape, just as the Lord has promised, for he has chosen some to survive.

Mic 4:1. But in the last days Mount Zion will be the most renowned of all the mountains of the world, praised by all nations; people from all over the world will make pilgrimages there. [2]"Come," they will say to one another, "let us visit the mountain of the Lord, and see the Temple of the God of Israel; he will tell us what to do, and we will do it." For in those days the whole world will be ruled by the Lord from Jerusalem! He will issue his laws and announce his decrees from there. [3]He will arbitrate among the nations, and dictate to strong nations far away. They will beat their swords into plowshares and their spears into pruninghooks; nations shall no longer fight each other, for all war will end. There will be universal peace, and all the military academies and training camps will be closed down. [4]Everyone will live quietly in his own home in peace and prosperity, for there will be nothing to fear. The Lord himself has promised this. [5](Therefore we will follow the Lord our God forever and ever, even though all the nations around us worship idols!) [6]In that coming day, the Lord says that he will bring back his punished people—sick and lame and dispossessed—[7]and make them strong again in their own land, a mighty nation, and the Lord himself shall be their King from Mount Zion forever.

See *Church, The True; Israel.*

GOSSIP Ps 15:1. Lord, who may go and find refuge and shelter in your tabernacle up on your holy hill? [2]Anyone who leads a blameless life and is truly sincere. [3]Anyone who refuses to slander others, does not listen to gossip, never harms his neighbor.

Prov 11:13. A gossip goes around spreading rumors, while a trustworthy man tries to quiet them.

Prov 16:28. An evil man sows strife; gossip separates the best of friends.

Prov 17:9. Love forgets mistakes, nagging about them parts the best of friends.

Prov 18:8. What dainty morsels rumors are. They are eaten with great relish!

Prov 26:20. Fire goes out for lack of fuel, and tensions disappear when gossip stops. [21]A quarrelsome man starts fights as easily as a match sets fire to paper. [22]Gossip is a dainty morsel eaten with great relish.

1 Tim 5:11. The younger widows should not become members of this special group because after awhile they are likely to disregard their vow to Christ and marry again. [13]Besides, they are likely to be lazy and spend their time gossiping around from house to house, getting into other people's business.

FORBIDDEN. Lev 19:16. Don't gossip. Don't falsely accuse your neighbor of some crime, for I am Jehovah.

Ps 50:20. You slander your own brother.

Prov 11:13. A gossip goes around spreading rumors, while a trustworthy man tries to quiet them.

Prov 20:19. Don't tell your secrets to a gossip unless you want them broadcast to the world.

Ezk 22:9. Prisoners are falsely accused and sent to their death. Every mountain top is filled with idols; lewdness is everywhere.

See *Busybody; Slander; Speaking, Evil.*

GOURD The wild gourd mentioned 2 Kgs 4:39 is supposed to be a plant in appearance like the cucumber.

GOUT 2 Chron 16:12.

GOVERNMENT Paternal functions of, Gen 41:25–57. Civil service school provided by, Dan 1:3–20. Maintains a system of public instruction, 2 Chron 17:7–9.

Executive departments in. See *Cabinet; King; Ruler.*

Judicial department in. See *Court; Judge; Justice; Levite; Priest.*

MOSIAC.

Administrative and Judicial System. Ex 18:13. The next day Moses sat as usual to hear the people's complaints against each other, from morning to evening. [14]When Moses' father-in-law saw how much time this was taking, he said, "Why are you trying to do all this alone, with people standing here all day long to get your help?" [15, 16]"Well, because the people come to me with their disputes, to ask for God's decisions," Moses told him. "I am their judge, deciding who is right and who is wrong, and instructing them in God's ways. I apply the laws of God to their particular disputes." [17]"It's not right!" his father-in-law exclaimed. [18]"You're going to wear yourself out—and if you do, what will happen to the people? Moses, this job is too heavy a burden for you to try to handle all by yourself. [19, 20]Now listen, and let me give you a word of advice, and God will bless you: Be these people's lawyer—their representative before God—bringing him their questions to decide; you will tell them his decisions, teaching them God's laws, and showing them the principles of godly living. [21]Find some capable, godly, honest men who hate bribes, and appoint them as judges, one judge for each 1000 people; he in turn will have ten judges under him, each in charge of a hundred; and under each of them will be two judges, each responsible for the affairs of fifty people; and each of these will have five judges beneath him, each counseling ten persons. [22]Let these men be responsible to serve the people with justice at all times. Anything that is too important or complicated can be brought to you. But the smaller matters they can take care of themselves. That way it will be easier for you because you will share the burden with them. [23]If you follow this advice, and if the Lord agrees, you will be able to endure the pressures, and there will be peace and harmony in the camp." [24]Moses listened to his father-in-law's advice, and followed this suggestion. [25]He chose able men from all over Israel and made them judges over the people—thousands, hundreds, fifties, and tens. [26]They were constantly available to administer justice. They brought the hard cases to Moses but judged the smaller matters themselves.

Num 11:16. Then the Lord said to Moses, "Summon before me seventy of the leaders of Israel; bring them to the Tabernacle, to stand there with you. [17]I will come down and talk with you there and I will take of the Spirit which is on you and will put it upon them also; they shall bear the burden of the people along with you, so that you will not have the task alone." [24]So Moses left the Tabernacle and reported Jehovah's words to the people; and he gathered the seventy elders and placed them around the Tabernacle. [25]And the Lord came down in the Cloud and talked with Moses, and the Lord took of the Spirit that was upon Moses and put it upon the seventy elders; and when the Spirit rested upon them, they prophesied for some time.

Deut 1:9. At that time I told the people, "I need help! You are a great burden for me to carry all by myself, [10]for the Lord has multiplied you like stars! [11]And may he multiply you a thousand times more, and bless you as he promised, [12]but what can one man do to settle all your quarrels and problems? [13]So choose some men from each tribe who are wise, experienced, and understanding, and I will appoint them as your leaders." [14]They agreed to do this; [15]I took the men they selected, some from every tribe, and appointed them as administrative assistants in charge of thousands, hundreds, fifties, and tens to decide their quarrels and assist them in every way. [16]I instructed them to be perfectly fair at all times, even to foreigners! [17]"When giving your decisions," I told them, "never favor a man because he is rich; be fair to great and small alike. Don't fear their displeasure, for you are judging in the place of God. Bring me any cases too difficult for you, and I will handle them."

Popular, by a National Assembly, or its Representatives. Accepted, and agreed to, the law given by Moses, Ex 19:7, 8; 24:3, 7; Deut 29:10–15. Refused to make conquest of Canaan, Num 14:1–11. Chose, or ratified, the chief ruler, Num 27:18–23; 1 Sam 10:24, with 1 Sam 8:4–22; 11:14, 15; 2 Sam 3:17–21; 5:1–3; 1 Chron 29:22; 2 Chron 23:2, 3. Possessed veto power over the king's purposes, 1 Sam 14:44, 45. The court in certain capital cases, Num 35:12, 24, 25.

The Delegated, Senatorial Council. Closely associated Moses and subsequent leaders, Ex 3:16. "Call together all the elders of Israel," God instructed him, "and tell them about Jehovah appearing to you here in this burning bush and that he said to you, 'I have visited my people, and have seen what is happening to them there in Egypt.' [18]The elders of the people of Israel will accept your message. They must go with you to the king of Egypt and tell him, 'Jehovah, the God of the Hebrews, has met with us and instructed us to go three days' journey into the desert to sacrifice to him. Give us your permission.' "

Ex 4:29. So Moses and Aaron returned to Egypt and summoned the elders of the people of Israel to a council meeting. [Ex 12:21; 17:5, 6; 18:12; Lev 9:1; Num 16:25; Deut 5:23.] [30]Aaron told them what Jehovah had said to Moses, and Moses performed the miracles as they watched. [31]Then the elders believed that God had sent them, and when they heard that Jehovah had visited them and had seen their sorrows, and had decided to rescue them, they all rejoiced and bowed their heads and worshiped.

Ex 19:7. Moses returned from the mountain and called together the leaders of the people and told them what the Lord had said. [8]They all responded in unison, "We will certainly do everything he asks of us." Moses reported the words of the people to the Lord.

Ex 24:1. The Lord now instructed Moses, "Come up here with Aaron, Nadab, Abihu, and seventy of the elders of Israel. All of you except Moses are to worship at a distance." [14]He told the elders, "Stay here and wait for us until we come back; if there are any problems while I am gone, consult with Aaron and Hur."

Lev 4:15. Where the leaders of the nation shall lay their hands upon the animal's head and kill it before the Lord.

Num 11:16. Then the Lord said to Moses, "Summon before me seventy of the leaders of Israel; bring them to the Tabernacle, to stand there with you. [17]I will come down and talk with you there and I will take of the Spirit which is on you and will put it upon them also; they shall bear the burden of the people along with you, so that you will not have the task alone. [18]And tell the people to purify themselves, for tomorrow they shall have meat to eat. Tell them, 'The Lord has heard your tearful complaints about all you left behind in Egypt, and he is going to give you meat. You shall eat it.' " [30]Then Moses returned to the camp with the elders of Israel.

Deut 1:13. "So choose some men from each tribe who are wise, experienced, and understanding, and I will appoint them as your leaders." [14]They agreed to this; [15]I took the men they selected, some from every tribe, and appointed them as administrative assistants in charge of thousands, hundreds, fifties, and tens to decide their quarrels and assist them in every way.

Deut 27:1. Then Moses and the elders of Israel gave the people these further instructions to obey.

Deut 29:10. All of you—your leaders, the people, your judges, and your administrative officers—are standing today before the Lord your God, [11]along with your little ones and your wives and the foreigners that are among you—those who chop your wood and carry your water. [12]You are standing here to enter into a contract with Jehovah your God, a contract he is making with you today. [13]He wants to confirm you today as his people, and to confirm that he is your God, just as he promised your ancestors, Abraham, Isaac, and Jacob. [14, 15]This contract is not with you alone as you stand before him today, but with all future generations of Israel as well.

Deut 31:9. Then Moses wrote out the laws he had already delivered to the people and gave them to the priests, the sons of Levi, who carried the Ark containing the Ten Commandments of the Lord. Moses also gave copies of the laws to the elders of Israel. [28]Now summon all the elders and officers of your tribes so that I can speak to them, and call heaven and earth to witness against them.

Josh 7:6. Joshua and the elders of Israel tore their clothing and lay prostrate before the Ark of the Lord until evening, with dust on their heads.

Josh 8:10. Early the next morning Joshua roused his men and started toward Ai, accompanied by the elders of Israel. [32]And as the people of Israel watched, Joshua carved upon the stones of the altar each of the Ten Commandments. [33]Then all the people of Israel—including the elders, officers, judges, and the foreigners living among them—divided into two groups, half of them standing at the foot of Mount Gerizim and half at the foot of Mount Ebal. Between them stood the priests with the Ark, ready to pronounce their blessing. (This was all done in accordance with the instructions given long before by Moses.)

Josh 23:2. He called for the leaders of Israel—the elders, judges, and officers—and said to them, "I am an old man now, [3]and you have seen all that the Lord your God has done for you during my lifetime. He has fought for you against your enemies and has given you their land. [6]But be very sure to follow all the instructions written in the book of the laws of Moses; do not deviate from them the least little bit."

Josh 24:1. Then Joshua summoned all the people of Israel to him at Shechem, along with their leaders—the elders, officers, and judges. So they came and presented themselves before God. [24]The people replied to Joshua, "Yes, we will worship and obey the Lord alone." [25]So Joshua made a covenant with them that day at Shechem, committing them to a permanent and binding contract between themselves and God.

Judg 21:16. "What shall we do for wives for the others, since all the women of the tribe of Benjamin are dead?" the leaders of Israel asked. [17]"There must be some way to get wives for them, so that an entire tribe of Israel will not be lost forever." *vs.* 18–25.

Acts 5:17. The High Priest and his relatives and friends among the Sadducees reacted with violent jealousy [18]and arrested the apostles, and put them in the public jail. [21]They arrived at the Temple about daybreak, and immediately began preaching! Later that morning the High Priest and his courtiers arrived at the Temple, and convening the Jewish Council and the entire Senate, they sent for the apostles to be brought for trial. *vs.* 22–41.

Miscellany of Facts Relating to the Council. Demand a king, 1 Sam 8:4–10, 19–22. Saul pleads to be honored before, 1 Sam 15:30. Chooses David as king, 2 Sam 3:17–21; 5:3, 1 Chron 11:3. Closely associated with David, 2 Sam 12:17; 1 Chron 15:25; 21:16. Joins Absalom in his usurpation, 2 Sam 17:4. David chides, 2 Sam 19:11, 12. Assists Solomon at the dedication of the temple, 1 Kgs 8:1, 2; 2 Chron 5:2, 3. Counsels King Rehoboam, 1 Kgs 12:6–8, 13, 14. Counsels King Ahab, 1 Kgs 20:7, 8. Josiah assembles to hear the law of the Lord, 2 Kgs 23:1, 2; 2 Chron 34:29, 31.

Legislates with Ezra in reforming certain marriages with the heathen, Ezra 9:1; 10:7–14. Legislates in later times, Mt 15:2, 7–9; Mk 7:1–13. Sits as a court, Jer 26:10–24. Constitutes, with priests and other leaders, a court for the trial of both civil and ecclesiastical causes, Mt 21:23; 26:3–5, 57–68; 27:1, 2; Mk 8:31; 14:43–65; 15:1; Lk 22:52–71; Acts 4:1–21; 6:9–15; 7:1–59. Unfaithful to the city, Lam 1:19. Seeks counsel from prophets, Ezk 8:1; 14:1; 20:1, 3; Joel 1:14; 2:16. Corrupt, 1 Kgs 21:8–14; Ezk 8:11, 12; Mt 26:14, 15; with chapter 27:3, 4.

A similar council existed among the Egyptians, Gen 50:7, with Gen 41:37, 38; Ex 10:1, 7; 12:30; 14:5; and among the Midianites and Moabites, Num 22:4, 7, and Gibeonites, Josh 9:11.

Executive Officers of Tribes and Cities, Called Chiefs, Mayors or Princes. Num 7:2, 18–86; 10:4; 17:1–3, 6; Neh 3:9, 12, 16, 18, 19.

The Mosaic Judicial System. See *Court; Judge; Priest; Levite; Ruler; Sanhedrin; Synagogue.*

Forms and facts of government after the death of Moses and the leaders who survived Moses. See *Israel, History of,* under the sub-topics *Judges; Kings.*

See *Constitution.*

See *Church, Visible.*

IMPERIAL. Gen 14:1; Josh 11:10; Esther 1:1; Dan 4:1; 6:1–3; Lk 2:1.

MONARCHICAL. Tyranny in, Instances of. By Saul, 1 Sam 22:6, 11–19. By David, 2 Sam 1:13–16; 4:9–12; 11:14–17. By Solomon, 1 Kgs 2:23–25, 28–34, 36–46. By Rehoboam, 1 Kgs 12:1–15. By Ahab, 1 Kgs 21:7–16; 2 Kgs 10. By Ahasuerus, Esther chapters 2; 3. By Nebuchadnezzar, Dan 1:10; 2:5–13; 5:19. By Herod, Mk 6:27, 28. See *Israel, History of,* under the sub-topic *Kings.* Also see *Assyria; Babylon; Chaldea; Syria.*

Limited. See *Constitution.*

MUNICIPAL. Conducted by a local council, elders and judges, Deut 19:12; 21:2–8, 18–21; 22:13–21; 25:7–9; Josh 20:4; Judg 8:14–16; 11:5–11; Ruth 4:2–11; 1 Sam 11:3; 16:4; 30:26; 1 Kgs 21:8–14; 2 Kgs 10:1–7; Ezra 10:7, 8, 14; Neh 3:9, 12, 16, 18, 19; Lam 5:14.

PATRIARCHAL. Gen 27:27–29, 37.

PROVINCIAL. Ezra 4:8, 9; 5:3, 6; 6:6; 8:36; Neh 2:7, 9; 5:14; Dan 6:1–3; Mt 27:2; 28:14; Lk 3:1, 2; Acts 23:25, 26. See *Herod; Pilate.*

REPRESENTATIVE. Deut 1:13–15; Josh 9:11. See *Delegated, Senatorial Council,* above. Also see *Elder.*

THEOCRATIC. Ex 19:3. Moses climbed the rugged mountain to meet with God, and from somewhere in the mountain God called to him and said, "Give these instructions to the people of Israel. Tell them, [4]"You have seen what I did to the Egyptians, and how I brought you to myself as though on eagle's wings. [5]Now if you will obey me and keep your part of my contract with you, you shall be my own little flock from among all the nations of the earth; for all the earth is mine. [6]And you shall be a kingdom of priests to God, a holy nation.' " [7]Moses returned from the mountain and called together the leaders of the people and told them what the Lord had said. [8]They all responded in unison, "We will certainly do everything he asks of us." Moses reported the words of the people to the Lord. Deut 26:16–19.

Deut 29:1. It was on the plains of Moab that Moses restated the covenant which the Lord had made with the people of Israel at Mount Horeb. [2, 3]He summoned all Israel before him and told them, "You have seen with your own eyes the great plagues and mighty miracles that the Lord brought upon Pharaoh and his people in the land of Egypt. [4]But even yet the Lord hasn't given you hearts that understand or eyes that see or ears that hear! [5]For forty years God has led you through the wilderness, yet your clothes haven't become old, and your shoes haven't worn out! [6]The reason he hasn't let you settle down to grow grain for bread or grapes for wine and strong drink, is so that you would realize that it is the Lord your God who has been caring for you. [7]When we came here, King of Sihon of Heshbon and King Og of Bashan came out against us in battle, but we destroyed them, [8]and took their land and gave it to the tribes of Reuben and Gad and to the half-tribe of Manasseh as their inheritance. [9]Therefore, obey the terms of this covenant so that you will prosper in everything you do. [10]All of you—your leaders, the people, your judges, and your administrative officers—are standing today before the Lord your God, [11]along with your little ones and your wives and the foreigners that are among you—those who chop your wood and carry your water. [12]You are standing here to enter into a contract with Jehovah your God, a contract he is making with you today. [13]He wants to confirm you today as his people, and to confirm that he is your God, just as he promised your ancestors, Abraham, Isaac, and Jacob."

1 Sam 8:6. Samuel was terribly upset and went to the Lord for advice. [7]"Do as they say," the Lord replied, "for I am the one they are rejecting, not you—they don't want me to be their king any longer."

See *Government, God in,* below. Also see *Ruler; Judge; Elder.*

CORRUPTION IN. 1 Kgs 21:5. "What in the world is the matter?" his wife, Jezebel, asked him.

"Why aren't you eating? What has made you so upset and angry?" [6]"I asked Naboth to sell his vineyard, or to trade it, and he refused!" Ahab told her. [7]"Are you the king of Israel or not?" Jezebel demanded. "Get up and eat and don't worry about it. I'll get you Naboth's vineyard!" [8]So she wrote letters in Ahab's name, sealed them with his seal, and addressed them to the civic leaders of Jezreel, where Naboth lived. [9]In her letter she commanded: "Call the citizens together for fasting and prayer. Then summon Naboth, [10]and find two scoundrels who will accuse him of cursing God and the king. Then take him out and execute him." [11]The city fathers followed the queen's instructions. [12]They called the meeting and put Naboth on trial. [13]Then two men who had no conscience accused him of cursing God and the king; and he was dragged outside the city and stoned to death.

Prov 25:5. When you remove corrupt men from the king's court, his reign will be just and fair.

Mic 3:1. Listen, you leaders of Israel—you are supposed to know right from wrong, [2]yet you are the very ones who hate good and love evil; you skin my people and strip them to the bone. [3]You devour them, flog them, break their bones, and chop them up like meat for the cooking pot—[4]and then you plead with the Lord for his help in times of trouble! Do you really expect him to listen? He will look the other way! [9]Listen to me, you leaders of Israel who hate justice and love unfairness, [10]and fill Jerusalem with murder and sin of every kind—[11]you leaders who take bribes; you priests and prophets who won't preach and prophesy until you're paid. (And yet you fawn upon the Lord and say, "All is well—the Lord is here among us. No harm can come to us.")

See *Court, Corrupt.*

Instances of. Pilate, in delivering Jesus to death to please the crowd, Jn 19:12–16; Mt 27:24. Felix, who expected a bribe from Paul, Acts 24:26. See *Ruler, Wicked, Instances of.*

DUTY OF CITIZENS TO. Mt 22:17. "Now tell us, is it right to pay taxes to the Roman government or not?" [18]But Jesus saw what they were after. "You hypocrites!" he exclaimed. "Who are you trying to fool with your trick questions? [19]Here, show me a coin." And they handed him a penny. [20]"Whose picture is stamped on it?" he asked them. "And whose name is this beneath the picture?" [21]"Caesar's," they replied. "Well, then," he said, "give it to Caesar if it is his, and give God everything that belongs to God." Lk 20:25.

Rom 13:1. Obey the government, for God is the one who has put it there. There is no government anywhere that God has not placed in power. [2]So those who refuse to obey the laws of the land are refusing to obey God, and punishment will follow. [3]For the policeman does not frighten people who are doing right; but those doing evil will always fear him. So if you don't want to be afraid, keep the laws and you will get along well. [4]The policeman is sent by God to help you. But if you are doing something wrong, of course you should be afraid, for he will have you punished. He is sent by God for that very purpose. [5]Obey the laws, then, for two reasons: first, to keep from being punished, and second, just because you know you should. [6]Pay your taxes too, for these same two reasons. For government workers need to be paid so that they can keep on doing God's work, serving you. [7]Pay everyone whatever he ought to have: pay your taxes and import duties gladly, obey those over you, and give honor and respect to all those to whom it is due.

Tit 3:1. Remind your people to obey the government and its officers, and always to be obedient and ready for any honest work.

1 Pet 2:13. For the Lord's sake, obey every law of your government: those of the king as head of the state, [14]and those of the king's officers, for he has sent them to punish all who do wrong, and to honor those who do right. [15]It is God's will that your good lives should silence those who foolishly condemn the Gospel without knowing what it can do for them, having never experienced its power. [16]You are free from the law, but that doesn't mean you are free to do wrong. Live as those who are free to do only God's will at all times. [17]Show respect for everyone. Love Christians everywhere. Fear God and honor the government.

See *Citizen.*

GOD IN. In appointment of Saul as king, 1 Sam 9:15–17; 10:1. In Saul's rejection, 1 Sam 15:26–28; Acts 13:22. In appointment of David, 1 Sam 16:1, 7, 13; 2 Sam 7:13–16; Ps 89:19–37; Acts 13:22. In counseling Solomon, 1 Kgs 9:2–9. In prospering him, 1 Chron 29:25. In denouncing Solomon's wickedness, 1 Kgs 11:9–13. In raising enemies against Solomon, 1 Kgs 11:14, 23. In dividing the Jewish nation in two, 1 Kgs 11:12, 13; 12:1–24; 2 Chron 10:15; 11:4; 22:7. In destroying the dynasty of Jeroboam, 1 Kgs 14:7–16; 15:27–30. In appointment of kings, 1 Kgs 14:14; 16:1–14; 1 Chron 28:4, 5; 29:25; Ps 22:28; Prov 8:14–16; Dan 2:20, 21, 37; 5:20–23. In destruction of nations, Amos 9:8. See *Government, Theocratic,* above. Also see *God, Sovereign.*

Unclassified Scriptures Relating to God in. Ps 22:28. For the Lord is King and rules the nations.

Prov 8:15. Because of my strength, kings reign in power. I show the judges who is right and who is wrong. [16]Rulers rule well with my help.

Isa 9:6. For unto us a Child is born; unto us a Son is given; and the government shall be upon his shoulder. These will be his royal titles: "Wonderful," "Counselor," "The Mighty God," "The Everlasting Father," "The Prince of Peace." [7]His ever-expanding, peaceful government will never end. He will rule with perfect fairness and justice from the throne of his father David. He will bring true justice and peace to all the nations of the world. This is going to happen because the Lord of heaven's armies has dedicated himself to do it!

Jer 1:9. Then he touched my mouth and said, "See, I have put my words in your mouth! [10]Today your work begins, to warn the nations and the kingdoms of the world. In accord with my words spoken through your mouth I will tear down some and destroy them, and plant others and nurture them and make them strong and great."

Jer 18:6. O Israel, can't I do to you as this potter has done to his clay? As the clay is in the potter's hand, so are you in my hand. [7]Whenever I announce that a certain nation or kingdom is to be taken up and destroyed, [8]then if that nation renounces its evil ways, I will not destroy it as I had planned. [9]And if I announce that I will make a certain nation strong and great, [10]but then that nation changes its mind and turns to evil and refuses to obey me, then I too will change my mind and not bless that nation as I had said I would.

Jer 25:12. Then, after these years of slavery are ended, I will punish the king of Babylon and his people for their sins; I will make the land of Chaldea an everlasting waste. [13]I will bring upon them all the terror I have promised in this book—all the penalties announced by Jeremiah against the nations. [14]For many nations and great kings shall enslave the Chaldeans, just as they enslaved my people; I will punish them in proportion to their treatment of my people. [15]For the Lord God said to me: "Take from my hand this wine cup filled to the brim with my fury, and make all the nations to whom I send you drink from it. [16]They shall drink from it and reel, crazed by the death blows I rain upon them." [17]So I took the cup of fury from the Lord and made all the nations drink from it—every nation God had sent me to. *vs.* 18–33.

Ezk 21:25. O King Zedekiah, evil prince of Israel, your final day of reckoning is here. [26]Take off your jeweled crown, the Lord God says. The old order changes. Now the poor are exalted, and the rich brought very low. [27]I will overturn, overturn, overturn the kingdom, so that even the new order that emerges will not succeed until the Man appears who has a right to it. And I will give it all to him.

Ezk 29:19. Therefore, the Lord God says, I will give the land of Egypt to Nebuchadnezzar, king of Babylon, and he will carry off her wealth, plundering everything she has, for his army. [20]Yes, I have given him the land of Egypt for his salary, because he was working for me during those thirteen years at Tyre, says the Lord.

Dan 2:20. Saying, "Blessed be the name of God forever and ever, for he alone has all wisdom and all power. [21]World events are under his control. He removes kings and sets others on their thrones. He gives wise men their wisdom, and scholars their intelligence. [37]Your Majesty, you are a king over many kings, for the God of heaven has given you your kingdom, power, strength and glory."

Dan 4:17. For this has been decreed by the Watchers, demanded by the Holy Ones. The purpose of this decree is that all the world may understand that the Most High dominates the kingdoms of the world, and gives them to anyone he wants to, even the lowliest of men!

Dan 5:18. Your Majesty, the Most High God gave Nebuchadnezzar, who long ago preceded you, a kingdom and majesty and glory and honor. [19]He gave him such majesty that all the nations of the world trembled before him in fear. He killed any who offended him, and spared any he liked. At his whim they rose or fell. [20]But when his heart and mind were hardened in pride, God removed him from his royal throne and took away his glory, [21]and he was chased out of his palace into the fields. His thoughts and feelings became those of an animal, and he lived among the wild donkeys; he ate grass like the cows and his body was wet with the dew of heaven, until at last he knew that the Most High overrules the kingdoms of men, and that he appoints anyone he desires to reign over them. [22]And you, his successor, O Belshazzar—you knew all this, yet you have not been humble. [23]For you have defied the Lord of Heaven, and brought here these cups from his Temple; and you and your officers and wives and concubines have been drinking wine from them while praising gods of silver, gold, brass, iron, wood and stone—gods that neither see nor hear, nor know anything at all. But you have not praised the God who gives you the breath of life and controls your destiny! [24, 25]And so God sent those fingers to write this message: *"Mene," "Mene," "Tekel," "Parsin."* [26]This is what it means: *Mene* means "numbered"—God has numbered the days of your reign, and they are ended. [27]*Tekel* means "weighed"—you have been weighed in God's balances and have failed the test. [28]*Parsin* means "divided"—your kingdom will be divided and given to the Medes and Persians.

Dan 10:13. But for twenty-one days the mighty Evil Spirit who overrules the kingdom of Persia blocked my way. Then Michael, one of the top officers of the heavenly army, came to help me, so that I was able to break through these spirit rulers of Persia.

Hos 8:4. She has appointed kings and princes, but not with my consent. They have cut themselves off from my help by worshiping the idols that they made from their silver and gold.

Amos 9:8. The eyes of the Lord God are watching Israel, that sinful nation, and I will root her up and scatter her across the world. *Yet I have promised that this rooting out will not be permanent.*

Hag 2:21. Tell Zerubbabel, the governor of Judah, "I am about to shake the heavens and the earth, [22]and to overthrow thrones and destroy the strength of the kingdoms of the nations. I will overthrow their armed might, and brothers and companions will kill each other."

Jn 19:10. "You won't talk to me?" Pilate demanded. "Don't you realize that I have the power to release you or to crucify you?" [11]Then Jesus said, "You would have no power at all over me unless it were given to you from above. So those who brought me to you have the greater sin."

See *God, Sovereign.*

GOVERNOR Gen 42:6; 2 Kgs 25:22; 2 Chron 18:25; 34:8; Ezra 4:8, 9, 17; 5:3, 14; 6:6; Neh 5:14; 7:70; 8:9; 10:1–8; Dan 6:1; Hag 1:1; Mt 27:2; Lk

2:2; 3:19, 20; Acts 13:6–8; 18:12; 23:23, 24; 28:7. A title of Jesus, Mt 2:6.

See *Cabinet.*

GOZAN A district in Assyria. Israelites deported to, after the conquest of Samaria, 1 Chron 5:26; 2 Kgs 17:6; 18:11; 19:12.

GRACE OF GOD Gen 15:6. And Abram believed God; then God considered him righteous on account of his faith.

Gen 20:6. "Yes, I know," the Lord replied. "That is why I held you back from sinning against me; that is why I didn't let you touch her."

Deut 7:6. For you are a holy people, dedicated to the Lord your God. He has chosen you from all the people on the face of the whole earth to be his own chosen ones. [7]He didn't choose you and pour out his love upon you because you were a larger nation than any other, for you were the smallest of all! [8]It was just because he loves you, and because he kept his promise to your ancestors. That is why he brought you out of slavery in Egypt with such amazing power and mighty miracles. [9]Understand, therefore, that the Lord your God is the faithful God who for a thousand generations keeps his promises and constantly loves those who love him and who obey his commands.

Deut 9:4. Then, when the Lord has done this for you, don't say to yourselves, "The Lord has helped us because we are so good!" No, it is because of the wickedness of the other nations that he is doing it. [5]It is not at all because you are such fine, upright people that the Lord will drive them out from before you! I say it again, it is only because of the wickedness of the other nations, and because of his promises to your ancestors, Abraham, Isaac, and Jacob, that he will do it. [6]I say it yet again: *Jehovah your God is not giving you this good land because you are good, for you are not*—you are a wicked, stubborn people.

Job 10:12. You gave me life and were so kind and loving to me, and I was preserved by your care.

Job 22:2. Is mere man of any worth to God? Even the wisest is of value only to himself! [3]Is it any pleasure to the Almighty if you are righteous? Would it be any gain to him if you were perfect?

Ps 94:17. I would have died unless the Lord had helped me. [18]I screamed, "I'm slipping, Lord!" and he was kind and saved me. [19]Lord, when doubts fill my mind, when my heart is in turmoil, quiet me and give me renewed hope and cheer.

Ps 138:3. When I pray, you answer me, and encourage me by giving me the strength I need.

Ps 143:11. Lord, saving me will bring glory to your name. Bring me out of all this trouble because you are true to your promises.

Dan 9:18. O my God, bend down your ear and listen to my plea. Open your eyes and see our wretchedness, how your city lies in ruins—for everyone knows that it is yours. We don't ask because we merit help, but because you are so merciful despite our grievous sins.

Dan 10:18. Then the one who seemed to be man touched me again, and I felt my strength returning. [19]"God loves you very much," he said; "don't be afraid! Calm yourself; be strong—yes, strong!" Suddenly, as he spoke these words, I felt stronger and said to him, "Now you can go ahead and speak, sir, for you have strengthened me."

Jn 6:44. For no one can come to me unless the Father who sent me draws him to me, and at the Last Day I will cause all such to rise again from the dead. [45]As it is written in the Scriptures, "They shall all be taught of God." Those the Father speaks to, who learn the truth from him, will be attracted to me.

Jn 17:11. Now I am leaving the world, and leaving them behind, and coming to you. Holy Father, keep them in your own care—all those you have given me—so that they will be united just as we are, with none missing. [12]During my time here I have kept safe within your family all of these you gave me. I guarded them so that not one perished, except the son of hell, as the Scriptures foretold. [15]I'm not asking you to take them out of the world, but to keep them safe from Satan's power.

Acts 4:29. And now, O Lord, hear their threats, and grant to your servants great boldness in their preaching, [30]and send your healing power, and may miracles and wonders be done by the name of your holy servant Jesus.

Acts 26:22. But God protected me so that I am still alive today to tell these facts to everyone, both great and small.

Rom 3:22. Now God says he will accept and acquit us—declare us "not guilty"—if we trust Jesus Christ to take away our sins. And we all can be saved in this same way, by coming to Christ, no matter who we are or what we have been like. [23]Yes, all have sinned; all fall short of God's glorious ideal; [24]yet now God declares us "not guilty" of offending him if we trust in Jesus Christ, who in his kindness freely takes away our sins. Acts 15:11.

Rom 4:4, 5. But didn't he earn his right to heaven by all the good things he did? No, for being saved is a gift; if a person could earn it by being good, then it wouldn't be free—but it is! It is *given* to those who do *not* work for it. For God declares sinners to be good in his sight if they have faith in Christ to save them from God's wrath. [16]So God's blessings are given to us by faith, as a free gift; we are certain to get them whether or not we follow Jewish customs if we have faith like Abraham's, for Abraham is the father of us all when it comes to these matters of faith.

Rom 5:2. For because of our faith, he has brought us into this place of highest privilege where we now stand, and we confidently and joyfully look forward to actually becoming all that God has had in mind for us to be. [6]When we were utterly helpless with no way of escape, Christ came at just the right time and died for us sinners who had no use for him. [7]Even if we were good, we really wouldn't expect anyone to die for us, though, of course, that might be barely possible. [8]But God showed his great love for us by sending Christ to die for us while we were still sinners.

15And what a difference between man's sin and God's forgiveness! For this one man, Adam, brought death to many through his *sin.* But this one man, Jesus Christ, brought forgiveness to many through God's *mercy.* 16Adam's *one* sin brought the penalty of death to many, while Christ freely takes away *many* sins and gives glorious life instead. 17The sin of this one man, Adam, caused *death to be king over all,* but all who will take God's gift of forgiveness and acquittal are *kings of life* because of this one man, Jesus Christ. 18Yes, Adam's *sin* brought *punishment* to all, but Christ's *righteousness* makes men *right with God,* so that they can live. 19Adam caused many to be sinners because he *disobeyed* God, and Christ caused many to be made acceptable to God because he *obeyed.* 20The Ten Commandments were given so that all could see the extent of their failure to obey God's laws. But the more we see our sinfulness, the more we see God's abounding grace forgiving us. 21Before, sin ruled over all men and brought them to death, but now God's kindness rules instead, giving us right standing with God and resulting in eternal life through Jesus Christ our Lord.

Rom 9:10–13. And years later, when this son, Isaac, was grown up and married, and Rebecca his wife was about to bear him twin children, God told her that Esau, the child born first, would be a servant to Jacob, his twin brother. In the words of the Scripture, "I chose to bless Jacob, but not Esau." And God said this before the children were even born, before they had done anything either good or bad. This proves that God was doing what he had decided from the beginning; it was not because of what the children did but because of what God wanted and chose. 14Was God being unfair? Of course not. 15For God had said to Moses, "If I want to be kind to someone, I will. And I will take pity on anyone I want to." 16And so God's blessings are not given just because someone decides to have them or works hard to get them. They are given because God takes pity on those he wants to.

Rom 11:5. It is the same today. Not all the Jews have turned away from God; there are a few being saved as a result of God's kindness in choosing them. 6And if it is by God's kindness, then it is not by their being good enough. For in that case the free gift would no longer be free—it isn't free when it is earned.

1 Cor 1:4. I can never stop thanking God for all the wonderful gifts he has given you, now that you are Christ's: 5he has enriched your whole life. He has helped you speak out for him and has given you a full understanding of the truth; 6what I told you Christ could do for you has happened! 7Now you have every grace and blessing; every spiritual gift and power for doing his will are yours during this time of waiting for the return of our Lord Jesus Christ. 8And he guarantees right up to the end that you will be counted free from all sin and guilt on that day when he returns.

1 Cor 10:13. But remember this—the wrong desires that come into your life aren't anything new and different. Many others have faced exactly the same problems before you. And no temptation is irresistible. You can trust God to keep the temptation from becoming so strong that you can't stand up against it, for he has promised this and will do what he says. He will show you how to escape temptation's power so that you can bear up patiently against it.

1 Cor 15:10. But whatever I am now it is all because God poured out such kindness and grace upon me—and not without results: for I have worked harder than all the other apostles, yet actually I wasn't doing it, but God working in me, to bless me.

2 Cor 1:12. We are so glad that we can say with utter honesty that in all our dealings we have been pure and sincere, quietly depending upon the Lord for his help, and not on our own skills. And that is even more true, if possible, about the way we have acted toward you.

Gal 1:15. But then something happened! For even before I was born God had chosen me to be his, and called me—what kindness and grace—16to reveal his Son within me so that I could go to the Gentiles and show them the Good News about Jesus.

Eph 1:5. His unchanging plan has always been to adopt us into his own family by sending Jesus Christ to die for us. And he did this because he wanted to! 6Now all praise to God for his wonderful kindness to us and his favor that he has poured out upon us, because we belong to his dearly loved Son. 7So overflowing is his kindness towards us that he took away all our sins through the blood of his Son, by whom we are saved; 8and he has showered down upon us the richness of his grace—for how well he understands us and knows what is best for us at all times. 9God has told us his secret reason for sending Christ, a plan he decided on in mercy long ago. 11Moreover, because of what Christ has done we have become gifts to God that he delights in, for as part of God's sovereign plan we were chosen from the beginning to be his, and all things happen just as he decided long ago. 12God's purpose in this was that we should praise God and give glory to him for doing these mighty things for us, who were the first to trust in Christ.

Eph 2:8. Because of his kindness you have been saved through trusting Christ. And even trusting is not of yourselves; it too is a gift from God. 9Salvation is not a reward for the good we have done, so none of us can take any credit for it.

Eph 3:16. That out of his glorious, unlimited resources he will give you the mighty inner strengthening of his Holy Spirit.

Eph 4:7. However, Christ has given each of us special abilities—whatever he wants us to have out of his rich storehouse of gifts.

Eph 6:10. Last of all I want to remind you that your strength must come from the Lord's mighty power within you.

Phil 1:19. I am going to keep on being glad, for I know that as you pray for me, and as the Holy

Spirit helps me, this is all going to turn out for my good.

Phil 2:13. For God is at work within you, helping you want to obey him, and then helping you do what he wants.

1 Thess 1:1. May blessing and peace of heart be your rich gifts from God our Father, and from Jesus Christ our Lord. 1 Thess 5:28; 2 Pet 1:2.

1 Tim 1:14. Oh, how kind our Lord was, for he showed me how to trust him and become full of the love of Christ Jesus.

2 Tim 1:1. From: Paul, Jesus Christ's missionary, sent out by God to tell men and women everywhere about the eternal life he has promised them through faith in Jesus Christ. [9]It is he who saved us and chose us for his holy work not because we deserved it but because that was his plan long before the world began—to show his love and kindness to us through Christ.

Tit 3:7. So that he could declare us good in God's eyes—all because of his great kindness; and now we can share in the wealth of the eternal life he gives us, and we are eagerly looking forward to receiving it.

1 Pet 1:5. And God, in his mighty power, will make sure that you get there safely to receive it, because you are trusting him. It will be yours in that coming last day for all to see.

1 Pet 4:10. God has given each of you some special abilities; be sure to use them to help each other, passing on to others God's many kinds of blessings.

1 Pet 5:10. After you have suffered a little while, our God, who is full of kindness through Christ, will give you his eternal glory. He personally will come and pick you up, and set you firmly in place, and make you stronger than ever.

Jude 1:1. From: Jude, a servant of Jesus Christ, and a brother of James. *To:* Christians everywhere—beloved of God and chosen by him. [21]Stay always within the boundaries where God's love can reach and bless you. Wait patiently for the eternal life that our Lord Jesus Christ in his mercy is going to give you. [24, 25]And now—all glory to him who alone is God, who saves us through Jesus Christ our Lord; yes, splendor and majesty, all power and authority are his from the beginning; his they are and his they evermore shall be. And he is able to keep you from slipping and falling away, and to bring you, sinless and perfect, into his glorious presence with mighty shouts of everlasting joy.

Rev 3:10. Because you have patiently obeyed me despite the persecution, therefore I will protect you from the time of Great Tribulation and temptation, which will come upon the world to test everyone alive.

See *God, Grace of.*

GROWTH IN. Ps 84:7. They will grow constantly in strength and each of them is invited to meet with the Lord in Zion.

Prov 4:18. But the good man walks along in the everbrightening light of God's favor; the dawn gives way to morning splendor,

Phil 1:6. And I am sure that God who began the good work within you will keep right on helping you grow in his grace until his task within you is finally finished on that day when Jesus Christ returns. [9]My prayer for you is that you will overflow more and more with love for others, and at the same time keep on growing in spiritual knowledge and insight, [10]for I want you always to see clearly the difference between right and wrong, and to be inwardly clean, no one being able to criticize you from now until our Lord returns. [11]May you always be doing those good, kind things which show that you are a child of God, for this will bring much praise and glory to the Lord.

Phil 3:12. I don't mean to say I am perfect. I haven't learned all I should even yet, but I keep working toward that day when I will finally be all that Christ saved me for and wants me to be. [13]No, dear brothers, I am still not all I should be but I am bringing all my energies to bear on this one thing: Forgetting the past and looking forward to what lies ahead, [14]I strain to reach the end of the race and receive the prize for which God is calling us up to heaven because of what Christ Jesus did for us. [15]I hope all of you who are mature Christians will see eye-to-eye with me on these things, and if you disagree on some point, I believe that God will make it plain to you.

Col 1:10. And asking that the way you live will always please the Lord and honor him, so that you will always be doing good, kind things for others, while all the time you are learning to know God better and better. [11]We are praying, too, that you will be filled with his mighty, glorious strength so that you can keep going no matter what happens—always full of the joy of the Lord.

Col 2:19. But they are not connected to Christ, the Head to which all of us who are his body are joined; for we are joined together by his strong sinews and we grow only as we get our nourishment and strength from God.

1 Thess 3:10. For night and day we pray on and on for you, asking God to let us see you again, to fill up any little cracks there may yet be in your faith. [12]And may the Lord make your love to grow and overflow to each other and to everyone else, just as our love does toward you. [13]This will result in your hearts being made strong, sinless and holy by God our Father, so that you may stand before him guiltless on that day when our Lord Jesus Christ returns with all those who belong to him.

2 Thess 1:3. Dear brothers, giving thanks to God for you is not only the right thing to do, but it is our duty to God, because of the really wonderful way your faith has grown, and because of your growing love for each other.

Heb 6:1. Let us stop going over the same old ground again and again, always teaching those first lessons about Christ. Let us go on instead to other things and become mature in our understanding, as strong Christians ought to be. Surely we don't need to speak further about the foolishness of trying to be saved by being good, or about the necessity of faith in God; [2]you don't need further instruction about baptism and spiritual gifts and the resurrection of the dead and eternal judgment. [3]The Lord willing, we will go on now to other things.

1 Pet 2:1. So get rid of your feelings of hatred. Don't just pretend to be good! Be done with dishonesty and jealousy and talking about others behind their backs. [2,3]Now that you realize how kind the Lord has been to you, put away all evil, deception, envy, and fraud. Long to grow up into the fullness of your salvation; cry for this as a baby cries for his milk.

2 Pet 3:18. But grow in spiritual strength and become better acquainted with our Lord and Savior Jesus Christ. To him be all glory and splendid honor, both now and forevermore.

GRACES Christian. Mt 5:3. "Humble men are very fortunate!" he told them, "for the Kingdom of Heaven is given to them. [4]Those who mourn are fortunate! for they shall be comforted. [5]The meek and lowly are fortunate! for the whole wide world belongs to them. [6]Happy are those who long to be just and good, for they shall be completely satisfied. [7]Happy are the kind and merciful, for they shall be shown mercy. [8]Happy are those whose hearts are pure, for they shall see God. [9]Happy are those who strive for peace—they shall be called the sons of God. [10]Happy are those who are persecuted because they are good, for the Kingdom of Heaven is theirs. [11]When you are reviled and persecuted and lied about because you are my followers—wonderful!"

Rom 5:3. We can rejoice, too, when we run into problems and trials for we know that they are good for us—they help us learn to be patient. [4]And patience develops strength of character in us and helps us trust God more each time we use it until finally our hope and faith are strong and steady. [5]Then, when that happens, we are able to hold our heads high no matter what happens and know that all is well, for we know how dearly God loves us, and we feel this warm love everywhere within us because God has given us the Holy Spirit to fill our hearts with his love.

1 Cor 13:1. If I had the gift of being able to speak in other languages without learning them, and could speak in every language there is in all of heaven and earth, but didn't love others, I would only be making noise. [2]If I had the gift of prophecy and knew all about what is going to happen in the future, knew everything about *everything,* but didn't love others, what good would it do? Even if I had the gift of of faith so that I could speak to a mountain and make it move, I would still be worth nothing at all without love. [3]If I gave everything I have to poor people, and if I were burned alive for preaching the Gospel but didn't love others, it would be of no value whatever. [4]Love is very patient and kind, never jealous or envious, never boastful or proud, [5]never haughty or selfish or rude. Love does not demand its own way. It is not irritable or touchy. It does not hold grudges and will hardly even notice when others do it wrong. [6]It is never glad about injustice, but rejoices whenever truth wins out. [7]If you love someone you will be loyal to him no matter what the cost. You will always believe in him, always expect the best of him, and always stand your ground in defending him. [8]All the special gifts and powers from God will someday come to an end, but love goes on forever. Someday prophecy, and speaking in unknown languages, and special knowledge—these gifts will disappear. [13]There are three things that remain—faith, hope, and love—and the greatest of these is love.

Gal 5:22. But when the Holy Spirit controls our lives he will produce this kind of fruit in us: love, joy, peace, patience, kindness, goodness, faithfulness, [23]gentleness and self-control; and here there is no conflict with Jewish laws.

2 Pet 1:5. But to obtain these gifts, you need more than faith; you must also work hard to be good, and even that is not enough. For then you must learn to know God better and discover what he wants you to do. [6]Next, learn to put aside our own desires so that you will become patient and godly, gladly letting God have his way with you. [7]This will make possible the next step, which is for you to enjoy other people and to like them, and finally you will grow to love them deeply. [8]The more you go on in this way, the more you will grow strong spiritually and become fruitful and useful to our Lord Jesus Christ. [9]But anyone who fails to go after these additions to faith is blind indeed, or at least very shortsighted, and has forgotten that God delivered him from the old life of sin so that now he can live a strong, good life for the Lord.

See *Character; Charitableness; Courage; Endurance; Gentleness; Hope; Kindness; Knowledge; Love; Meekness; Mercy; Patience; Peace; Perseverance; Purity; Righteousness, Fruits of; Stability; Temperance; Wisdom.*

GRAFTING Rom 11:17–24.

GRAIN A product of Egypt, Gen 41:47–49. Mosaic laws concerning, Ex 22:6; Lev 2:1; 11:37; 19:9; Num 15:19–21; Deut 23:25; 25:4. Eaten by the Israelites, Josh 5:11, 12. Shocks of, burned, Judg 15:5. Parched, Ruth 2:14; 1 Sam 17:17; 25:18; 2 Sam 17:28. Ground, 2 Sam 17:19. Cultivated in Canaan, Isa 28:25; in valleys, Ps 65:13; Mk 4:28. Heads of, broken by Christ's disciples, Mt 12:1.

Symbolical. Gen 41:5.

See *Corn; Wheat.*

GRAPE Cultivated in vineyards, by Noah, Gen 9:20, 21; the Canaanites, Num 13:24; Deut 6:10–12; Josh 24:13; Edomites, Num 20:17; Amorites, Num 21:22; Moabites, Isa 16:8, 9. Grown, at Ammon, Judg 11:33; Baal-hamon, Song 8:11; Carmel, 2 Chron 26:10; Jezreel, 1 Kgs 21:1; Lebanon, Hos 14:7; Samaria, Jer 31:5; Shechem, Judg 9:27; Shiloh, Judg 21:20, 21; Timnath, Judg 14:5.

Culture of, Lev 25:3, 11; Deut 28:39; 2 Chron 26:10; Song 2:15; 6:11; Isa 5:1; Jer 31:5.

Wine made of, Jer 25:30. Wine of, forbidden to Nazirites, Num 6:3, 4. See *Nazirites.*

See *Vine; Vineyard; Wine.*

FIGURATIVE. Deut 32:32; Ezk 15; Hos 10:1; Rev 14:18–20.

FABLE OF. Judg 9:12, 13.

PARABLES OF THE VINE. Ps 80:8–14; Ezk 17:6–10; 19:10–14; Jn 15:1–5.

PROVERB OF. Ezk 18:2.

See *Vine; Vineyard; Wine.*

GRASS Created on the third creative day, Gen 1:11, 12; Watered, Ps 72:6.

FIGURATIVE. Ps 90:5, 6; 129:6; Isa 40:6; 47:14; Lk 7:24; 1 Pet 1:24.

See *Chaff; Straw.*

GRASSHOPPER Lev 11:21, 22; Num 13:33; Ps 109:22, 23; Isa 40:22; Nah 3:15, 17.

See *Locust.*

GRATING Ex 27:4, 5; 38:4, 5.

GRATITUDE See *Thankfulness.*

GRAVE Prepared by Jacob, Gen 50:5. Defilement from touching, Num 19:16, 18. Weeping at, 2 Sam 3:32, Jn 11:31; 20:11. Of parents, honored, 2 Sam 19:37. Welcomed, Job 3:20–22. Resurrection from: Of Lazarus, Jn 11:43, 44; 12:17; of Jesus, Mt 28:5, 6; 1 Cor 15:12–20; of saints after Jesus' resurrection, Mt 27:52, 53; of all the dead, foretold, Jn 5:28; 1 Cor 15:22–54.

FIGURATIVE. Prov 23:26–28.

See *Burial; Hell.*

GRAVEL FIGURATIVE. Prov 20:17; Lam 3:16.

GREAT SEA See *Mediterranean Sea.*

GREECE Inhabitants of, called Gentiles, Mk 7:26; Jn 7:35; Rom 2:10; 3:9; 1 Cor 10:32; 12:13; desire to see Jesus, Jn 12:20–22; marry among the Jews, Acts 16:1; accept the Messiah, Acts 17:2–4, 12, 34; persecute the early Christians, Acts 6:9–14; 18:17. Gentiles called Greeks, Gal 3:28.

Schools of philosophy in Athens, Acts 17:16–18. Philosophy of, 1 Cor 1:22, 23. Poets of, Acts 17:28.

See *Athens; Epicureans; Stoicism.*

GREED See *Covetousness.*

GREEK Philosophy of, 1 Cor 1:22, 23.

See *Greece.*

GREETINGS By kissing, 2 Sam 20:8–10; Mt 26:49; by bowing, Gen 23:7; 27:27–29; 33:3; 37:10; 41:43; 43:26, 28; 49:8; 1 Sam 25:23; 2 Sam 18:28; 1 Kgs 1:16; Esther 8:3; Mt 2:11; Mk 5:22. Addresses in: "Sirs," Gen 19:2; "God be gracious to you," Gen 43:29; "May God prosper you," 1 Sam 25:6; "I'm glad to see you, my brother," 2 Sam 20:9; "Hello, Master," Mt 26:49; "Good morning," Mt 28:9. By letter, 1 Cor 16:21; 2 Cor 13:13; Phil 4:21; Col 4:18; 2 Thess 3:17; 2 Jn 1:13; 3 Jn 1:14, 15. To rulers, see *King.*

See *Manners.*

GRIEF Attributed to the Holy Spirit, Eph 4:30.

See *Afflictions; Mourning; Sorrow.*

GRINDING See *Mill.*

GRINDING OF TEETH See *Gnashing of Teeth.*

GROUND Man made from, Gen 2:7; 3:19, 23; Job 4:18, 19. Animals from, Gen 2:19, 20. Vegetables from, Gen 2:9.

Cursed, Gen 3:17; 5:28–31.

GROVE Location of idol worship. Forbidden to be established, Isa 1:29; 17:8; Mic 5:14. Worshiped in by Israelites, 1 Kgs 14:23; 2 Kgs 16:4; 17:10; 21:3–7; Jer 17:2, 3. Destroyed by Hezekiah, 2 Kgs 18:4; Josiah, 2 Kgs 23:14; Asa, 2 Chron 14:3; Jehoshaphat, 2 Chron 17:6.

See *Ashtoreth; Idolatry.*

GUARANTEE Ps 86:17; 2 Cor 1:22; 5:5; Eph 1:14.

GUARD See *Gatekeepers; Watchman.*

GUARDIAN 1. A title of Jesus, 1 Pet 2:25.

2. See *Tutor.*

GUDGODAH A stopping-place of the Israelites in the wilderness, Deut 10:7; probably identical with *Hor-haggidgad* in Num 33:15–37.

GUEST Greetings to, Gen 18:2. Abraham's hospitality to, see *Hospitality.* Rules for the conduct of, Prov 23:1–3, 6–8; 25:6, 7, 17; Lk 10:5–7; 14:7–11; 1 Cor 10:27.

See *Hospitality.*

GUIDANCE See *Counsel; God, Guide.*

GUILE See *Conspiracy; Deceit; Dishonesty; Hypocrisy.*

GUILT See *Conviction, of Sin; Conscience.*

GUILT OFFERINGS See *Offerings, Guilt.*

GUM Sap of the balm tree, Gen 37:25.

GUNI 1. Son of Naphtali, Gen 46:23–25; Num 26:48–50; 1 Chron 7:13.

2. Father of Abdi-el, 1 Chron 5:15.

GUR Place where Jehu killed Ahaziah, 2 Kgs 9:27.

GURBALL A town between Canaan and Arabia, 2 Chron 26:7.

HAAHASHTARI Son of Ashhur, 1 Chron 4:6.

HABAIAH A priest, whose descendants returned from captivity, Ezra 2:61; Neh 7:63.

HABAKKUK A prophet and poet, who prophesied after the destruction of Nineveh, probably, Hab 1:1; 3:1. His hymn of praise of the majesty of God, Hab 3.

HABAZZINIAH Head of the family of Rechabites, Jer 35:3.

HABOR A river of Assyria, 2 Kgs 17:6; 18:11; 1 Chron 5:26.

HACHILAH A hill in Judah where David and his followers hid from Saul, 1 Sam 23:19; 26:1.

HACHMONI 1. Family of Jashobeam, 1 Chron 11:11.

2. Father of Jehiel, 1 Chron 27:32.

HADAD 1. A successor of Husham as king of Edom. Defeated the Midianites in the fields of Moab, Gen 36:31–39; 1 Chron 1:46.

2. A son of Ishmael, Gen 25:15; 1 Chron 1:28–31.

3. Successor of Baal-hanan, king of Edom, Gen 36:31–39; 1 Chron 1:50.

4. A prince of Edom. Enemy of Solomon, 1 Kgs 11:14–22, 25.

HADADEZER King of Zobah, defeated by David, 2 Sam 8:3–13; 10:15–19; 1 Kgs 11:23; 1 Chron 18:3–10; 19:6–19.

HADAD-RIMMON A place in the valley of Megiddon, Zech 12:11.

HADASHAH A town in Judah, Josh 15:37–44.

HADASSAH Jewish name of Esther, Esther 2:7.

See *Esther.*

HADATTAH Probably an adjective qualifying Hazor, making it equivalent to *New Hazor,* Josh 15:21–32.

HADES The unseen world; the place of the dead; the exact equivalent of the Old Testament Hebrew word *Sheol,* Lk 16:23.

See *Hell; Pit; Sheol; Tartarus.*

HADID A city of Benjamin. Captives of, returned from Babylon, Ezra 2:3–35; Neh 7:8–38; 11:31–35.

HADLAI An Ephraimite, 2 Chron 28:12.

HADORAM 1. Descendant of Shem, Gen 10:26–30; 1 Chron 1:20–23.

2. Son of Tou, 1 Chron 18:10. Called *Joram,* 2 Sam 8:10.

3. Official in charge of forced labor under Rehoboam, 2 Chron 10:18. Probably identical with *Adoniram* of 1 Kgs 4:1–6; 5:14; and *Adoram* of 2 Sam 20:24.

HADRACH A district of Syria, Zech 9:1.

HA-ELEPH A town allotted to Benjamin, Josh 18:28.

HAGAB One of the Nethinim, Ezra 2:43–54.

HAGABA Called also *Hagabah.* One of the Nethinim, Ezra 2:43–54; Neh 7:48.

HAGAR A servant of Abraham and maid of Sarah. Given by Sarah to Abraham to be his wife, Gen 16. Descendants of, Gen 25:12–15; 1 Chron 5:10, 19–22; Ps 83:6.

FIGURATIVE. Gal 4:24, 25.

HAGGAI One of the minor prophets. Urges the Jews to rebuild the Temple, Ezra 5:1; 6:14. See the book of Haggai.

HAGGI Son of Gad, Gen 46:16, 17; Num 26:15–18.

HAGGIAH A Levite, 1 Chron 6:29, 30.

HAGGITH Wife of David. Mother of Adonijah, 2 Sam 3:4; 1 Kgs 1:5, 11; 2:13; 1 Chron 3:2.

HAGRI Father of Mibhar, 1 Chron 11:26–47.

HAIL Job 38:22; Hag 2:16, 17. Plague of, in Egypt, Ex 9:18–29; Ps 78:48; 105:32. Destroys army of the Amorites, Josh 10:11.

FIGURATIVE. Isa 28:2; Rev 16:21.

HAIR Numbered, Mt 10:30; Lk 12:7. Worn long by women, Isa 3:24; Lk 7:38; 1 Cor 11:5, 6, 14, 15; 1 Pet 3:3; Rev 9:8; by Absalom, 2 Sam 14:26. Worn short by men, 1 Cor 11:14, 15. Symbolical dividing of, Ezk 5:1, 2.

See *Baldness; Leprosy; Mourning; Nazirite.*

HAKKATAN Father of Johanan, Ezra 8:2–14.

HAKKOZ A priest, 1 Chron 24:7–18. Descendants of, excluded from the priesthood because of defective genealogies, Ezra 2:61; Neh 7:63; repair walls of Jerusalem, Neh 3:4, 21.

HAKUPHA One of the Nethinim, Ezra 2:43–54; Neh 7:46–56.

HALAH A place to which Israelite captives

were transported, 2 Kgs 17:6; 18:11; 1 Chron 5:26.

HALAK A mountain, the southern limit of Joshua's conquest, Josh 11:17; 12:7.

HALHUL A city in Judah, Josh 15:48–62.

HALI A border town of Asher, Josh 19:24–26.

HALLELUJAH An exclamatory expression of praise or adoration, Ps 104:35; 105:45; 106:1, 48; 111:1; 113:1, 9; 115:18; 135:1, 21; 146:10; 147:1, 20; 148:14; 149:1, 9; 150:1, 6; Rev 19:1, 4.

See *Praise.*

HALLOHESH Father of Shallum, Neh 3:12. Signed the covenant with Nehemiah, Neh 10:14–27.

HAM 1. Son of Noah, Gen 5:32; 9:18, 24, 25; 1 Chron 1:5–9. Provokes his father's wrath and the curse on Canaan, Gen 9:18–27. His children, Gen 10:6–20; 1 Chron 1:5–16; 4:40.

2. Place where Ched-or-laomer defeated the Zuzim, Gen 14:5, 6.

HAMAN Prime minister of Ahasuerus, Esther 3:1. Plotted against Esther and the Jews; thwarted by Esther and Mordecai; hanged, Esther chapters 3–9.

HAMATH A city of upper Syria, Num 13:21; 34:7–9; Josh 13:2–7; Ezk 47:16. Inhabited by Canaanites, Gen 10:15–19. Prosperity of, Amos 6:2. David receives gifts of gold and silver from Toi (Tou), king of, 2 Sam 8:9, 10; 1 Chron 18:3, 9, 10. Conquest of, by Jeroboam, 2 Kgs 14:25, 28. Israelites taken captive to, Isa 11:11. Prophecy concerning, Jer 49:23. Solomon builds supply centers in, 2 Chron 8:4.

HAMATH-ZOBAH A town on the border of Palestine. Conquered by Solomon, 2 Chron 8:3.

HAMMATH 1. A fortified city of Naphtali, Josh 19:35–39.

See *Hammon, 2; Hammoth-Dor.*

2. Ancestor of the family of Rechab, 1 Chron 2:55.

HAMMEDATHA Father of Haman, Esther 3:1, 10; 9:7–10, 24, 25.

HAMMER Judg 4:21; 5:26; 1 Kgs 6:7; Jer 10:4.

FIGURATIVE. Jer 23:29; 50:23.

HAMMOLECHETH Daughter of Machir, and sister of Gilead, 1 Chron 7:17, 18.

HAMMON 1. A city of Asher, Josh 19:28.

2. A Levitical city of Naphtali, 1 Chron 6:76. Possibly identical with *Hammath* and *Hammoth-dor,* which see.

HAMMOTH-DOR A city of refuge of Naphtali, Josh 21:32. Possibly identical with *Hammath,* Josh 19:35–39. Called *Hammon,* 1 Chron 6:76.

HAMMU-EL A Simeonite, 1 Chron 4:26.

HAMOR Father of Shechem. Jacob buys ground from, Gen 33:19; Josh 24:32. Murdered by the sons of Jacob, Gen 34:26; 49:6.

HAMRAN Son of Dishon, 1 Chron 1:41.

HAMUL Son of Perez, Gen 46:8–14; Num 26:19–22; 1 Chron 2:5.

HAMUTAL Mother of Jehoahaz and Zedekiah, 2 Kgs 23:31, 32; 24:18, 19; Jer 52:1.

HANAMEL Cousin of Jeremiah, to whom he sold a farm in Anathoth, Jer 32:7–12.

HANAN 1. Son of Shashak, 1 Chron 8:22–25.

2. Son of Azel, 1 Chron 8:38; 9:44.

3. One of David's mighty men, 1 Chron 11:26–47.

4. One of the Nethinim, Ezra 2:43–54; Neh 7:46–56.

5. A Levite, Neh 8:7, 8; 10:9–13. Probably identical with the one mentioned in Neh 13:13.

6. Two leaders who signed the covenant with Nehemiah, Neh 10:14–27.

7. Son of Igdaliah, Jer 35:4.

HANANEL Name of a tower forming part of the wall of Jerusalem, Neh 3:1; 12:39; Jer 31:38, 39; Zech 14:10.

HANANI 1. Son of Heman, 1 Chron 25:4, 5, 9–31.

2. A prophet who rebuked Asa, king of Judah, 2 Chron 16:7.

3. Father of Jehu the prophet, 2 Chron 19:2; 20:34. Possibly identical with 2, above.

4. A priest, Ezra 10:20.

5. A brother of Nehemiah and governor of Jerusalem, Neh 1:2; 7:2.

6. A priest and musician, Neh 12:35, 36.

HANANIAH 1. Son of Heman, 1 Chron 25:4, 5, 9–31.

2. A commander of Uzziah's army, 2 Chron 26:11.

3. Father of Zedekiah, Jer 36:12.

4. A prophet of Gibeon who prophesied falsely in the temple during the reign of Zedekiah, Jer 28.

5. Grandfather of Irijah, Jer 37:13.

6. Son of Shashak, 1 Chron 8:22–25.

7. Hebrew name of *Shadrach,* which see.

8. Son of Zerubbabel, 1 Chron 3:19–22.

9. Son of Bebai, Ezra 10:28.

10. A perfumer, Neh 3:8.

11. Son of Shelemiah, Neh 3:30.

12. A governor of Jerusalem, Neh 7:2.

13. One who signed the covenant, Neh 10:14–27.

14. A priest in the time of Jehoiakim, Neh 12:12–21, 40, 41.

HAND Laying on of hands, Acts 6:6; 13:3; 1 Tim 4:14; Heb 6:2; in consecration, Gen 48:14; Ex 29:10, 15, 16, 19, 20; Lev 1:4; 3:2, 7, 8, 13; 4:15, 24, 33; 16:21; in ordaining the Levites, Num 8:10, 11; Joshua, Num 27:18–23; Deut 34:9; Timothy, 1 Tim 4:14; 2 Tim 1:6; in healing, Mk 6:5; 7:32; 16:18; Lk 4:40; Acts 28:8; in blessing children, Mt 19:13; Mk 10:16; in solemnizing testimony, Lev 24:13, 14. Lifted up in blessing and prayer, Lev 9:22; Lk 24:50; and see also *Worship, Attitudes in.*

Ceremonial washing of, Mt 15:2; Mk 7:2–5. See *Ablution.*

Washing of, a symbol of innocency, Deut 21:6; Isa 23:11; 41:10; Mt 27:24. Shaking of, in friendship, 2 Kgs 10:15; Rom 16:16; 1 Cor 16:20; 1 Thess 5:26. Right hand, a symbol of power, Isa 23:11; 41:10; place of honor, Ps 80:17.

FIGURATIVE. Mt 5:30; 18:8; Mk 9:43, 44. Anthropomorphic use of, Deut 2:14, 15; Job 2:10; 1 Pet 5:6. For extended anthropomorphisms consult concordances under the word *hand.*

See *Anthropomorphisms.*

HANDCUFFS Used for securing prisoners, Mk 5:3, 4.

See *Chains; Fetters; Shackles.*

HANDKERCHIEF Acts 19:12.

HANDS A place in Egypt, Isa 30:4.

HANGING Capital punishment by, Josh 8:29; 2 Sam 4:12; Esther 7:10. The curse of death by, Deut 21:22, 23; Gal 3:13.

See *Punishment.*

HANGINGS See *Curtains.*

HANNAH Mother of Samuel. Her trials and prayer, and promise, 1 Sam 1:1–18. Samuel born to, dedicates him to God, leaves him at the Tabernacle, 1 Sam 1:19–28. Her hymn of praise, 1 Sam 2:1–10. Visits Samuel from year to year, 1 Sam 2:18, 19. Children of, 1 Sam 2:20, 21.

HANNATHON A city of Zebulun, Josh 19:14.

HANNIEL 1. A son of Ephod, appointed by Moses to divide the land among the tribes, Num 34:16–28.

2. A son of Ulla, 1 Chron 7:39.

HANOCH 1. Son of Midian, Gen 25:4; 1 Chron 1:33.

2. Eldest son of Reuben, Gen 46:8–14; Ex 6:14; Num 26:5–11; 1 Chron 5:3.

HANUN 1. Successor of Nahash as king of Ammon, humiliates David's ambassadors, 2 Sam 10; 1 Chron 19.

2. One, or two, who assisted in rebuilding the Valley Gate and wall of Jerusalem, Neh 3:13, 30.

HAPHARAIM A city of Issachar, Josh 19:17–23.

HAPPINESS OF THE WICKED. Limited to this life, Ps 17:13, 14; Lk 16:25; short, Job 20:5; uncertain, Lk 12:20; vain, Eccl 2:1; 7:6.

Is derived from their wealth, Job 21:12, 13; Ps 52:7; their power, Job 21:7; Ps 37:35; their worldly prosperity, Ps 17:13, 14; 73:3, 4, 7; Hab 1:16; gluttony, Isa 22:13; drunkenness, Isa 5:11; 56:12; pleasure, Job 21:12, 13; Isa 5:12; successful oppression, Hab 1:15. Marred by jealousy, Esther 5:13; often interrupted by judgments, Num 11:33; Job 15:21; Ps 73:18–20; Jer 25:10, 11. Leads to sorrow, Prov 14:13. Leads to recklessness, Isa 22:13. Sometimes a stumbling block to believers, Ps 73:3, 16; Jer 12:1; Hab 1:13. Believers often permitted to see the end of, Ps 73:17–20; not to be envied, Ps 37:1. Woe to, Amos 6:1; Lk 6:25. Illustrated, Ps 37:35, 36; Lk 12:16–20; 16:19–25.

Exemplified: Israel, Num 11:33. Haman, Esther 5:9–11. Belshazzar, Dan 5:1. Herod, Acts 12:21–23.

OF THE RIGHTEOUS. Job 5:17. How enviable the man whom God corrects! Oh, do not despise the chastening of the Lord when you sin. [18]For though he wounds, he binds and heals again. [19]He will deliver you again and again, so that no evil can touch you. [20]He will keep you from death in famine, and from the power of the sword in time of war. [21]You will be safe from slander; no need to fear the future. [22]You shall laugh at war and famine; wild animals will leave you alone. [23]Dangerous animals will be at peace with you. [24]You need not worry about your home while you are gone; nothing shall be stolen from your barns. [25]Your sons shall become important men; your descendants shall be as numerous as grass! [26]You shall live a long, good life; like standing grain, you'll not be harvested until it's time! [27]I have found from experience that all of this is true. For your own good, listen to my counsel.

Ps 1:1. Oh, the joys of those who do not follow evil men's advice, who do not hang around with sinners, scoffing at the things of God: [2]But they delight in doing everything God wants them to, and day and night are always meditating on his laws and thinking about ways to follow him more closely.

Ps 36:8. You feed them with blessings from your own table and let them drink from your rivers of delight.

Ps 40:8. And I delight to do your will, my God, for your law is written upon my heart!

Ps 63:5. At last I shall be fully satisfied; I will praise you with great joy.

Ps 106:3. Happiness comes to those who are fair to others and are always just and good.

Ps 119:1. Happy are all who perfectly follow the laws of God. [2]Happy are all who search for God, and always do his will.

Ps 128:1. Blessings on all who reverence and trust the Lord—on all who obey him! [2]Their reward shall be prosperity and happiness.

Ps 133:1. How wonderful it is, how pleasant, when brothers live in harmony!

Ps 144:15. Yes, happy are those whose God is Jehovah.

Ps 146:5. But happy is the man who has the God of Jacob as his helper, whose hope is in the Lord his God.

Prov 3:13–15. The man who knows right from wrong and has good judgment and common sense is happier than the man who is immensely rich! For such wisdom is far more valuable than precious jewels. Nothing else compares with it. [16, 17]Wisdom gives: A long, good life, riches, honor, pleasure, peace. [18]Wisdom is a tree of life to those who eat her fruit; happy is the man who keeps on eating it.

Prov 8:32. And so, young men, listen to me, for how happy are all who follow my instructions.

Prov 16:20. God blesses those who obey him; happy the man who puts his trust in the Lord.

Eccl 2:24–26. So I decided that there was nothing better for a man to do than to enjoy his food and drink, and his job. Then I realized that even this pleasure is from the hand of God. For who can eat or enjoy apart from him? For God gives those who please him wisdom, knowledge, and joy; but if a sinner becomes wealthy, God takes the wealth away from him and gives it to those who please him. So here, too, we see an example of foolishly chasing the wind.

Eccl 3:12. So I conclude that, first, there is nothing better for a man than to be happy and to enjoy himself as long as he can; [13]and second, that he should eat and drink and enjoy the fruits of his labors, for these are gifts from God. [22]So I saw that there is nothing better for men than that they should be happy in their work, for that is what they are here for, and no one can bring them back to life to enjoy what will be in the future, so let them enjoy it now.

Isa 12:2. See, God has come to save me! I will trust and not be afraid, for the Lord is my strength and song; he is my salvation. [3]Oh, the joy of drinking deeply from the Fountain of Salvation!

Mt 5:3. "Humble men are very fortunate!" he told them, for the Kingdom of Heaven is given to them. [4]Those who mourn are fortunate! for they shall be comforted. [5]The meek and lowly are fortunate! for the whole wide world belongs to them. [6]Happy are those who long to be just and good, for they shall be completely satisfied. [7]Happy are the kind and merciful, for they shall be shown mercy. [8]Happy are those whose hearts are pure, for they shall see God. [9]Happy are those who strive for peace—they shall be called the sons of God. [10]Happy are those who are persecuted because they are good, for the Kingdom of Heaven is theirs. [11]When you are reviled and persecuted and lied about because you are my followers—wonderful! [12]Be *happy* about it! Be *very glad!* for a *tremendous reward* awaits you up in heaven. And remember, the ancient prophets were persecuted too.

Rom 5:2. For because of our faith, he has brought us into this place of highest privilege where we now stand, and we confidently and joyfully look forward to actually becoming all that God has had in mind for us to be.

2 Cor 12:10. Since I know it is all for Christ's good, I am quite happy about "the thorn," and about insults and hardships, persecutions and difficulties; for when I am weak, then I am strong—the less I have, the more I depend on him.

Phil 4:7. If you do this you will experience God's peace, which is far more wonderful than the human mind can understand. His peace will keep your thoughts and your hearts quiet and at rest as you trust in Christ Jesus.

1 Pet 4:12. Dear friends, don't be bewildered or surprised when you go through the fiery trials ahead, for this is no strange, unusual thing that is going to happen to you. [13]Instead, be really glad—because these trials will make you partners with Christ in his suffering, and afterwards you will have the wonderful joy of sharing his glory in that coming day when it will be displayed.

See *Joy; Peace; Praise.*

HAPPIZZEZ A leader of the Temple, 1 Chron 24:7–18.

HARA A place in Assyria. Israelitish captives carried to, 1 Chron 5:26.

HARADAH One of the camps of Israel, Num 33:15–37.

HARAN 1. Father of Lot and brother of Abraham, Gen 11:26–31.

2. Son of Caleb, 1 Chron 2:46.

3. A Levite, 1 Chron 23:8, 9.

4. Called also *Charran.* A place in Mesopotamia to which Terah and Abraham migrated, Gen 11:31; 12:4, 5; Acts 7:4. Death of Terah at, Gen 11:32. Abraham leaves, by divine command, Gen 12:1–5. Jacob flees to, Gen 27:43; 28:10; 29; returns from, with Rachel and Leah, Gen 31:17–21. Destruction of, by king of Assyria, 2 Kgs 19:12. Merchants of, Ezk 27:23. Idolatry in, Josh 24:2, 14; Isa 37:12.

HAR-BAANA See *Baanah, 3.*

HARBONA An aide of Ahasuerus, Esther 1:10; 7:9.

HARE Forbidden as food, Lev 11:4–7; Deut 14:7.

HAREM Persian household, Esther 2:3, 12–14.

HAREPH Son of Hur, 1 Chron 2:51.

HARHAIAH Father of Uzziel, Neh 3:8.

HARHAS Grandfather of the husband of Huldah, the prophetess, 2 Kgs 22:14. Called *Hasrah,* 2 Chron 34:22.

HARHUR One of the Nethinim, Ezra 2:43–54; Neh 7:46–56.

HARIM 1. A priest, 1 Chron 24:8. Possibly the same as 3, below.

2. An Israelite whose descendants returned from Babylon, Ezra 2:3–35; 10:31, 32; Neh 10:1–8. Possibly the same as 4, below.

3. Ancestor of priests who returned from exile with Zerubbabel, Ezra 2:36–39; Neh 7:39–42.

4. Son of Malchijah, Neh 3:11.

5. Ancestor of a family of priests, Neh 12:12–21.

HARIPH One of the exiles, Neh 7:8–38. Signed the covenant, Neh 10:14–27. Probably the same as *Jorah,* Ezra 2:18.

HARLOT See *Prostitute.*

HARLOTRY See *Prostitution.*

HAROD A spring by which Gideon and his army camped, Judg 7:1.

HAROEH Called also *Re-aiah.* Son of Shobal, 1 Chron 2:52; 4:2.

HAROSHETH-HA-GOIIM A town of Galilee. The home of Sisera, Judg 4:2, 3, 13, 16.

HARP A stringed musical instrument, Hab 3:19. With ten strings, Ps 144:9. Originated with Jubal, Gen 4:21. Made of algum wood, 1 Kgs 10:12. David a skillful harpist, 1 Sam 16:15, 16, 23. Used in worship, 1 Sam 10:5; 2 Sam 6:5; 1 Chron 16:5; 25:1–7; 2 Chron 5:11, 12; 29:25, 26; Ps 33:2; 43:4; 49:4; 57:8; 81:2; 92:3; 98:5; 108:2; 144:9; 147:7; 150:3; Rev 5:8. Used, in national celebrations, after the triumph over the armies of Ammon and Moab, 2 Chron 20:28, with verses 20–29; when the new walls of Jerusalem were dedicated, Neh 12:27, 36. Used in festivities, Gen 31:27; Isa 24:8; Ezk 26:13; Rev 18:22. Discordant, 1 Cor 14:7. Hung on the willows by the captive Jews, Ps 137:2. Heard in heaven, in John's apocalyptic vision, Rev 5:8; 14:2; 15:2.

See *Music, Instruments of.*

HARPOON Job 41:7.

HARROW An agricultural implement, Job 39:10; Isa 28:23, 24; Hos 10:11. Used as an instrument of torture, 2 Sam 12:31.

HARSHA One of the Nethinim, Ezra 2:43–54; Neh 7:46–56.

HARUM A descendant of Judah, 1 Chron 4: 8.

HARUMAPH Father of Jedaiah, Neh 3:10.

HARUZ Father-in-law of King Manasseh, 2 Kgs 21:19.

HARVEST Sabbath to be observed in, Ex 34: 21. Sabbath desecrated in, Neh 13:15–22.

Of wheat at Pentecost, in Palestine, Ex 34:22; Lev 23:15–17; and before vintage, Lev 26:4, 5. Of barley, before wheat, Ex 9:31, 32.

Celebrated with joy, Judg 9:27; Isa 9:3; 16:10; Jer 48:33. Promises of plentiful, Gen 8:22; Jer 5:23, 24; Joel 2:23, 24.

FIGURATIVE. Job 24:6; Prov 10:5; Jer 8:20; Joel 3:13; Mt 9:37; 13:39; Lk 10:2; Rev 14:15.

See *Pentecost, Feast of; Tabernacles, Feast of; First Fruits; Reaping; Gleaning.*

HASADIAH Son of Zerubbabel, 1 Chron 3: 19, 20.

HASHABIAH 1. Son of Amaziah, a Levite, 1 Chron 6:44–47.

2. Son of Jeduthun, a Levite, 1 Chron 25:3, 9–31.

3. A Levite of Hebron, 1 Chron 26:30.

4. Son of Kemuel, 1 Chron 27:16–22.

5. A chief Levite, 2 Chron 35:9.

6. Son of Bunni, 1 Chron 9:14; Neh 11:15–17.

7. Son of Mattaniah, a Levite, Neh 11:22, 23.

8. A chief priest who had charge of the bullion and other valuables of the Temple, at Jerusalem, Ezra 8:24. Probably identical with the one mentioned in Neh 12:12–21.

9. Merarite Levite, Ezra 8:19.

10. An Israelite who divorced his heathen wife, Ezra 10:25.

11. Three Levites, Neh 3:17; 10:9–13; 12:24.

HASHABNAH One who signed the covenant, Neh 10:14–27.

HASHABNEIAH 1. Father of Hattush, Neh 3:10.

2. A Levite, Neh 9:5.

HASH-BADDENAH A companion of Ezra, Neh 8:1–5.

HASHEM Father of several members of David's guard, 1 Chron 11:26–47.

HASHMONAH A camp of the Israelites, Num 33:15–37.

HASHUBAH A descendant of King Jehoiakim, 1 Chron 3:19, 20.

HASHUM 1. Ancestor of certain Jews who returned from exile, Ezra 2:3–35; 10:33; Neh 7: 8–38.

2. A priest, Neh 8:4.

3. One who signed the covenant with Nehemiah, Neh 10:14–27.

HASRAH See *Harhas.*

HASSENUAH A Benjaminite, 1 Chron 9:7, 8; Neh 11:7–9.

HASSHUB 1. Son of Pahath-moab, Neh 3:11.

2. One who assisted in repairing the wall of Jerusalem, Neh 3:23.

3. A leader who signed the covenant with Nehemiah, Neh 10:14–27.

4. A Levite, 1 Chron 9:14; Neh 11:15–17.

HASSOPHERETH See *Sophereth.*

HASTE Gen 19:22; Ex 10:16; 12:11; Deut 16:3; 1 Sam 21:8; 2 Kgs 7:15; 2 Chron 35:21; Prov 28:20. In judgment, by Moses and the Israelites, Num 32: 1–19; Josh 22:10–34.

See *Rashness.*

HASUPHA A Nethinim family, Ezra 2:43–54; Neh 7:46–56.

HAT See *Dress.*

HATHACH A eunuch in the court of Ahasuerus, Esther 4:5, 6, 9, 10, 12.

HATHATH A son of Othni-el, 1 Chron 4:13.

HATIPHA One of the Nethinim, Ezra 2:43–54; Neh 7:46–56.

HATITA A gatekeeper of the Temple, Ezra 2: 40–42.

HATRED Of evil, justified, Ps 97:10; 101:3; 119: 104, 128, 163; 139:21, 22. Of God, Ps 5:5; 45:7; Mal 2:16.

SCRIPTURES RELATING TO. Lev 19:17. Don't hate your brother. Rebuke anyone who sins; don't let him get away with it, or you will be equally guilty.

Ps 25:19. See how many enemies I have and how viciously they hate me!

Ps 35:19. Don't give victory to those who fight me without any reason! Don't let them rejoice at my fall—let them die.

Prov 10:12. Hatred stirs old quarrels, but love overlooks insults.

18. To hate is to be a liar; to slander is to be a fool.

Prov 15:17. It is better to eat soup with someone you love than steak with someone you hate.

Prov 26:24–26. A man with hate in his heart may sound pleasant enough, but don't believe him; for he is cursing you in his heart. Though he pretends to be so kind, his hatred will finally come to light for all to see.

Mt 5:43. There is a saying, "Love your *friends* and hate your enemies." [44]But I say: Love your *enemies!* Pray for those who *persecute* you!

Mt 6:14, 15. Your heavenly Father will forgive you if you forgive those who sin against you; but if *you* refuse to forgive *them, he* will not forgive *you.*

Mt 10:22. Everyone shall hate you because you belong to me. But all of you who endure to the end shall be saved.

Jn 15:18. For you get enough hate from the world! But then, it hated me before it hated you. [19]The world would love you if you belonged to it; but you don't—for I chose you to come out of the world, and so it hates you. [23]Anyone hating me is also hating my Father. [24]If I hadn't done such mighty miracles among them they would not be counted guilty. But as it is, they saw these miracles and yet they hated both of us—me and my Father. [25]This has fulfilled what the prophets said concerning the Messiah, "They hated me without reason."

Jn 17:14. I have given them your commands. And the world hates them because they don't fit in with it, just as I don't.

Gal 5:19. But when you follow your own wrong inclinations your lives will produce these evil results [20]. . . hatred and fighting, jealousy and anger.

Eph 4:31. Stop being mean, bad-tempered and angry. Quarreling, harsh words, and dislike of others should have no place in your lives.

Col 3:8. But now is the time to cast off and throw away all these rotten garments of anger, hatred, cursing, and dirty language.

1 Jn 2:9. Anyone who says he is walking in the light of Christ but dislikes his fellow man, is still in darkness. [11]For he who dislikes his brother is wandering in spiritual darkness and doesn't know where he is going, for the darkness had made him blind so that he cannot see the way.

1 Jn 3:10. So now we can tell who is a child of God and who belongs to Satan. Whoever is living a life of sin and doesn't love his brother shows that he is not in God's family. [13]So don't be surprised, dear friends, if the world hates you. [14]If we love other Christians it proves that we have been delivered from hell and given eternal life. But a person who doesn't have love for others is headed for eternal death. [15]Anyone who hates his Christian brother is really a murderer at heart; and you know that no one wanting to murder has eternal life within.

1 Jn 4:20. If anyone says "I love God," but keeps on hating his brother, he is a liar; for if he doesn't love his brother who is right there in front of him, how can he love God whom he has never seen?

See *Envy; Jealousy; Malice; Revenge.*

HATTIL A returned exile, Ezra 2:55–57; Neh 7:57–59.

HATTUSH 1. A descendant of David, 1 Chron 3:21, 22; Ezra 8:2–14.

2. One who helped to repair the wall of Jerusalem, Neh 3:10.

3. One who signed the covenant with Nehemiah, Neh 10:4; 12:2.

HAUGHTINESS See *Pride.*

HAUNT For birds, unclean, Rev 18:2.

HAURAN A district probably south of Damascus and east of the Jordan, Ezk 47:16, 18.

HAVILAH 1. Son of Cush, Gen 10:7; 1 Chron 1:5–9.

2. A son of Joktan, Gen 10:26–30; 1 Chron 1:20–23.

3. An unknown region, Gen 2:11, 12.

4. A district east of Amalek, Gen 25:18; 1 Sam 15:7.

HAVVOTH-JAIR Certain villages east of the Jordan, Num 32:41; Deut 3:14; Judg 10:4.

HAWK A carnivorous and unclean bird, Lev 11:13–19; Deut 14:11–18; Job 39:26; Isa 34:11.

HAY Prov 27:25–27; 1 Cor 3:12.

HAZAEL King of Syria. Anointed king by Elijah, 1 Kgs 19:15. Conquests by, 2 Kgs 8:28, 29; 9:14; 10:32, 33; 12:17, 18; 13:3, 22; 2 Chron 22:5, 6. Conspires against, murders and succeeds to the throne of Ben-hadad, 2 Kgs 8:8–15. Death of, 2 Kgs 13:24.

HAZAIAH A man of Judah, Neh 11:4–6.

HAZARADDAR A place on the southern boundary of Canaan, Num 34:4.

HAZAR-ENAN The northeast boundary point of the promised land, Num 34:7–11; also called *Hazar-enon,* Ezk 47:17; 48:1.

HAZAR-GADDAH A town in the southern district of Judah, Josh 15:21–32.

HAZARMAVETH Son of Joktan, Gen 10:26–30; 1 Chron 1:20–23.

HAZAR-SHUAL A town on the south of Judah, Josh 15:21–32; 19:2–7; 1 Chron 4:28; Neh 11:25–30.

HAZAR-SUSAH Called also *Hazar-susim,* a city of Judah, Josh 19:5; 1 Chron 4:31.

HAZAZON-TAMAR Ancient name of En-gedi, Gen 14:7; 2 Chron 20:2.

HAZER-HATTICON A place on the boundary of Hauran, probably east of Damascus, Ezk 47:16.

HAZEROTH A station in the journeyings of the Israelites, Num 11:35; 12:16; 33:15–37; Deut 1:1.

HAZIEL A Levite, 1 Chron 23:8, 9.

HAZO A son of Nahor, Gen 22:20–23.

HAZOR 1. A fortified city of Naphtali, Josh 11:1–3, 10, 11, 13; 12:8–24; 19:35–39; Judg 4:2, 3, 17; 1 Sam 12:9; 1 Kgs 9:15; 2 Kgs 15:29.

2. A city in the south of Judah, Josh 15:21–32.

3. A place north of Jerusalem, Neh 11:33.

4. An area of Arabia, prophesied against by Jeremiah, Jer 49:28–33.

HAZOR-HADATTAH A city of Judah, Josh 15:21–32.

HAZZELELPONI Daughter of Etam, 1 Chron 4:3, 4.

HEAD Shaving of, Lev 13:33; 14:8; Num 6:9, 18; Deut 21:12; Acts 21:24. Diseases of, Isa 3:17. Anointed, Lev 14:18, 29.

HEADBANDS Isa 3:20.

HEADSHIP Christ is the head of the corner, Acts 4:11; 1 Pet 2:7; head over every man, 1 Cor 11:3; head over the church which is his body, Eph 4:15, 16; Col 1:18; 2:19; head over the bride, Eph 5:23–33; head over every other power, Col 2:10. The head of Christ is God, 1 Cor 11:3. The head of the woman is the man, 1 Cor 11:3; Eph 5:23.

HEALING, DIVINE God heals by medicine, 2 Kgs 20:7; 1 Tim 5:23; through physicians, Col 4:14; directly through Christ's word, Mt 12:10–13; by his disciples, in the name of Christ, Acts 3:6–8; in answer to the faith of friends, Mk 2:5; in answer to the prayers of elders, Jas 5:15; in answer to the prayers of fellow believers, Jas 5:16; God did not heal Daniel, Dan 8:27; Elisha, 2 Kgs 13:14; Timothy, 1 Tim 5:23; Trophimus, 2 Tim 4:20; Paul, 2 Cor 12:7–10.

See *Afflictions; Disease.*

HEARERS Ezk 33:30. Son of dust, your people are whispering behind your back. They talk about you in their houses and whisper about you at the doors, saying, "Come on, let's have some fun! Let's go hear him tell us what the Lord is saying!" [31]So they come as though they are sincere and sit before you listening. But they have no intention of doing what I tell them to; they talk very sweetly about loving the Lord, but with their hearts they are loving their money. [32]You are very entertaining to them, like someone who sings lovely songs with a beautiful voice or plays well on an instrument. They hear what you say but don't pay any attention to it!

Mt 7:24. All who listen to my instructions and follow them are wise, like a man who builds his house on solid rock. [25]Though the rain comes in torrents, and the floods rise and the storm winds beat against his house, it won't collapse, for it is built on rock. [26]But those who hear my instructions and ignore them are foolish, like a man who builds his house on sand. [27]For when the rains and floods come, and storm winds beat against his house, it will fall with a mighty crash. Lk 6:49.

Mt 13:14. This fulfills the prophecy of Isaiah: "They hear, but don't understand; they look, but don't see! [15]For their hearts are fat and heavy, and their ears are dull, and they have closed their eyes in sleep." [19]The hard path where some of the seeds fell represents the heart of a person who hears the Good News about the Kingdom and doesn't understand it; then Satan comes and snatches away the seeds from his heart. [20]The shallow, rocky soil represents the heart of a man who hears the message and receives it with real joy, [21]but he doesn't have much depth in his life, and the seeds don't root very deeply, and after a while when trouble comes, or persecution begins because of his beliefs, his enthusiasm fades, and he drops out. [22]The ground covered with thistles represents a man who hears the message, but the cares of this life and his longing for money choke out God's Word, and he does less and less for God. [23]The good ground represents the heart of a man who listens to the message and understands it and goes out and brings thirty, sixty, or even a hundred others into the Kingdom. Lk 8:11–15.

Jas 1:19. Dear brothers, don't ever forget that it is best to listen much, speak little, and not become angry. [22]And remember, it is a message to obey, not just to listen to. So don't fool yourselves. [23]For if a person just listens and doesn't obey, he is like a man looking at his face in a mirror; [24]as soon as he walks away, he can't see himself anymore or remember what he looks like. [25]But if anyone keeps looking steadily into God's law for free men, he will not only remember it but he will do what it says, and God will greatly bless him in everything he does.

HEART Seat of the affections.

RENEWED. Deut 30:6; Ps 51:10; Ezk 11:19; 18:31; 36:26; Rom 2:29; Eph 4:23; Col 3:10. Regenerated, Jn 3:3, 7. Affected by God, 1 Sam 10:26; 1 Chron 29:18; Ezra 6:21, 22; 7:27; Prov 16:1; 21:1; Jer 20:9; Acts 16:14. Strengthened, Ps 27:14; 112:8; 1 Thess 3:13. Enlightened, 2 Cor 4:6. Examined and tested, 1 Chron 29:17; Ps 7:9; 26:2; Prov 17:3; Jer 11:20; 12:3; 20:12, 30; 1 Thess 2:4; Heb 11:17; Rev 2:2, 10.

It should give to God obedience, Deut 10:12, 13; 11:13; 26:16; Ps 119:1, 12; Rom 6:17; Eph 6:6, 7; faith, 1 Kgs 2:4; Ps 27:3; 112:7; Acts 8:37; Rom 10:10; trust, Prov 3:4, 5; love, Mt 22:37; reverence, Ps 119:161; Jer 32:40; fidelity, Neh 9:8; zeal, 2 Chron 17:16; Jer 20:9.

It should seek God, 2 Chron 19:3; 30:17–19; Ezra 7:10; Ps 10:17; 84:2; be joyful, 1 Sam 2:1; Ps 4:7; 97:11; Isa 65:14; Zech 10:7; perfect, 1 Kgs 8:61; Ps 101:2; upright, Ps 97:11; 125:4; clean, Ps 51:10; 73:1; pure, Ps 24:4; Mt 5:8; 1 Tim 1:5; 2 Tim 2:22; Jas 4:8; 1 Pet 1:22; sincere, Lk 8:15; Acts 2:46; Eph 6:5; Col 3:22; Heb 10:22; repentant, Deut 30:2; Ps 34:18; 51:17; devout, 1 Sam 1:12, 13; Ps 4:4; 9:1; 27:8; 77:6; 119:10, 69, 145; wise, 1 Kgs 3:9, 12; 4:29; Prov 8:10; 10:8; 11:29; 14:33; 23:15; tender, 1 Sam 24:5; 2 Kgs 22:18, 19; Job 23:16, 17; Ps 22:14; Eph 4:32; holy, Ps 66:18; 1 Pet 3:15; compassionate, Song 5:4; Jer 4:19; Lam 3:51; Phil 2:1; humble, Mt 11:29.

THE UNREGENERATE. Is full of evil, Gen 6:5; 8:21; Prov 6:14, 16–19; 11:20; Eccl 8:11; 9:2, 3; Jer 4:14, 18; 17:9; Rom 1:21. Loves evil, Deut 29:18; Ps 95:10; Jer 17:5. Produces evil, Job 15:35; Mt 12:34, 35; Mk 7:21. See *Depravity.* Is wayward, 2 Chron 12:14; Prov 6:14; 11:20; 12:8; 17:20; Jer 5:23, 24; Heb 3:10; blind, Rom 1:21; Eph 4:17, 18. See *Blindness, Spiritual.* Is false, Ps 12:2; Hos 10:2; Jas 1:6–8; Isa 10:12; Zech 7:12. See *Instability.* Is hard, Ezk 2:4; 3:7; 11:19; 36:26; Mk 6:52; 10:5; 16:14; Jn 12:40; Rom 2:5. See *Impenitence; Obduracy.* Is deceitful, Jer 17:9. Is proud, 2 Kgs 14:10; 2 Chron 25:19; Ps 101:5; Prov 18:12; 28:25; Jer 48:29; 49:16. See *Pride.* Is sensual, Ezk 6:9; Hos 13:6; Rom 8:7. See *Lasciviousness.* Is worldly, 2 Chron 26:16; Dan 5:20; Acts 8:21, 22. Is judicially hardened, Ex 9:12; 14:17; Isa 6:10; Acts 28:26, 27. Is malicious, Ps 28:3; 140:2; Prov 24:2; Eccl 7:26; Ezk 25:15. See *Malice.* Is impenitent, Rom 2:5. See *Impenitence.* Is diabolical, Jn 13:1–3; Acts 5:3. Is covetous, Jer 22:17; 2 Pet 2:14. See *Covetousness.* Is foolish, Prov 12:23; 22:15; Eccl 9:2, 3.

UNCLASSIFIED SCRIPTURES DESCRIPTIVE OF THE SEAT OF THE AFFECTIONS. Deut 5:29. Oh, that they would always have such a heart for me, wanting to obey my commandments. Then all would go well with them in the future, and with their children throughout all generations!

Deut 6:5. You must love him with *all* your heart, soul, and might. [6]And you must think constantly about these commandments I am giving you today.

1 Kgs 8:39. Hear them from heaven and forgive and answer all who have made an honest confession; for you know each heart.

1 Chron 28:9. Solomon, my son, get to know the God of your fathers. Worship and serve him with a clean heart and a willing mind, for the Lord sees every heart and understands and knows every thought. If you seek him, you will find him; but if you forsake him, he will permanently throw you aside.

Ps 22:26. The poor shall eat and be satisfied; all who seek the Lord shall find him and shall praise his name. Their hearts shall rejoice with everlasting joy.

Ps 34:18. The Lord is close to those whose hearts are breaking; he rescues those who are humbly sorry for their sins.

Ps 51:10. Create in me a new, clean heart, O God, filled with clean thoughts and right desires. [17]It is a broken spirit you want—remorse and penitence. A broken and a contrite heart, O God, you will not ignore.

Ps 57:7. O God, my heart is quiet and confident. No wonder I can sing your praises!

Prov 4:23. *Above all else, guard your affections.* For they influence everything else in your life. Lk 6:45.

Prov 12:25. Anxious hearts are very heavy but a word of encouragement does wonders!

Prov 15:13. A happy face means a glad heart; a sad face means a breaking heart.

Prov 17:22. A cheerful heart does good like medicine, but a broken spirit makes one sick.

Prov 20:9. Who can ever say, "I have cleansed my heart; I am sinless"?

Jer 17:1. My people sin as though commanded to, as though their evil were laws chiseled with an iron pen or diamond point upon their stony hearts or on the corners of their altars. [9]The heart is the most deceitful thing there is, and desperately wicked. No one can really know how bad it is! [10]Only the Lord knows! He searches all hearts and examines deepest motives so he can give to each person his right reward according to his deeds—how he has lived.

Mt 5:8. Happy are those whose hearts are pure, for they shall see God.

Mt 12:33. A tree is identified by its fruit. A tree from a select variety produces good fruit; poor varieties don't. [34]You brood of snakes! How could evil men like you speak what is good and right? For a man's heart determines his speech.

Mt 15:18. But evil words come from an evil heart, and defile the man who says them. [19]For from the heart come evil thoughts, murder, adultery, fornication, theft, lying and slander. [20]These are what defile; but there is no spiritual defilement from eating without first going through the ritual of ceremonial handwashing! Mk 7:21.

Mt 23:26. Blind Parisees! First cleanse the inside of the cup, and then the whole cup will be clean.

Lk 16:15. Then he said to them, "You wear a noble, pious expression in public, but God knows your evil hearts. Your pretense brings you honor from the people, but it is an abomination in the sight of God."

1 Cor 4:5. So be careful not to jump to conclusions before the Lord returns as to whether someone is a good servant or not. When the Lord comes, he will turn on the light so that everyone can see exactly what each one of us is really like, deep down in our hearts. Then everyone will know why we have been doing the Lord's work. At that time God will give to each one whatever praise is coming to him.

Heb 3:7, 8. And since Christ is so much superior, the Holy Spirit warns us to listen to him, to be careful to hear his voice today and not let our hearts become set against him, as the people of Israel did. They steeled themselves against his love and complained against him in the desert while he was testing them. *v.* 15.

INSTANCES OF HARDENED HEARTS. Pharaoh, Ex 4:21; 7:3, 13, 22; 8:15, 31, 32; 9:12, 34, 35; 10: 1, 20, 27; 11:9, 10; 14:4, 8, 17. Sihon, Deut 2:30. King of Canaan, Josh 11:20. Others, 1 Sam 6:6.

KNOWN TO GOD. Deut 31:21. And great disasters come upon them, then this song will remind them of the reason for their woes. (For this song will live from generation to generation.) I know now, even before they enter the land, what these people are like.

1 Sam 16:7. But the Lord said to Samuel, "Don't judge by a man's face or height, for this is not the one. I don't make decisions the way you do! Men judge by outward appearances, but I look at a man's thoughts and intentions."

2 Sam 7:20. What can I say? For you know what I am like!

1 Kgs 8:39. Hear them from heaven and forgive and answer all who have made an honest confession; for you know each heart.

1 Chron 28:9. Solomon, my son, get to know the God of your fathers. Worship and serve him with a clean heart and a willing mind, for the Lord sees every heart and understands and knows every thought. If you seek him, you will find him; but if you forsake him, he will permanently throw you aside.

Job 11:11. For he knows perfectly all the faults and sins of mankind; he sees all sin without searching.

Job 16:19. Yet even now the Witness to my innocence is there in heaven; my Advocate is there on high.

Job 31:4. He sees everything I do, and every step I take.

Ps 1:6. For the Lord watches over all the plans and paths of godly men, but the paths of the godless lead to doom.

Ps 44:21. Would God not know it? Yes, he knows the secrets of every heart.

Ps 51:10. Create in me a new, clean heart, O God, filled with clean thoughts and right desires.

Ps 94:11. The Lord is fully aware of how limited and futile the thoughts of mankind are.

Ps 139:1. O Lord, you have examined my heart and know everything about me. [2]You know when I sit or stand. When far away you know my every thought. [3]You chart the path ahead of me, and tell me where to stop and rest. Every moment, you know where I am. [4]You know what I am going to say before I even say it. [5]You both precede and follow me, and place your hand of blessing on my head. [6]This is too glorious, too wonderful to believe! [7]I can *never* be lost to your spirit! I can *never* get away from my God! [8]If I go up to heaven, you are there; if I go down to the place of the dead, you are there. [9]If I ride the morning winds to the farthest oceans, [10]even there your hand will guide me, your strength will support me. [11]If I try to hide in the darkness, the night becomes light around me. [12]For even darkness cannot hide from God; to you the night shines as bright as day. Darkness and light are both alike to you.

Prov 5:21. *For God is closely watching you,* and he weighs carefully everything you do.

Prov 16:2. We can always "prove" that we are right, but is the Lord convinced?

Prov 24:12. For God, who knows all hearts, knows yours, and he knows you knew! And he will reward everyone according to his deeds.

Isa 66:18. I see full well what they are doing; I know what they are thinking, so I will gather together all nations and people against Jerusalem, where they shall see my glory.

Jer 12:3. But as for me—Lord, you know my heart—you know how much it longs for you. (And I am poor, O Lord!) Lord, drag them off like helpless sheep to the slaughter. Judge them, O God!

Jer 17:10. Only the Lord knows! He searches all hearts and examines deepest motives so he can give to each person his right reward, according to his deeds—how he has lived.

Ezk 11:5. Then the Spirit of the Lord came upon me and told me to say: "The Lord says to the people of Israel: Is that what you are saying? Yes, I know it is, for I know everything you think—every thought that comes into your minds. [19]I will give you one heart and a new spirit; I will take from you your hearts of stone and give you tender hearts of love for God, [20]so that you can obey my laws and be my people, and I will be your God. [21]But as for those now in Jerusalem, who long for idols, I will repay them fully for their sins," the Lord God says. Ezk 36:25, 26.

Lk 16:15. Then he said to them, "You wear a noble, pious expression in public, but God knows your evil hearts. Your pretense brings you honor from the people, but it is an abomination in the sight of God."

Acts 1:24. Then they all prayed for the right man to be chosen. "O Lord," they said, "you know every heart; show us which of these men you have chosen."

Acts 15:8. God, who knows men's hearts, confirmed the fact that he accepts Gentiles by giving them the Holy Spirit, just as he gave him to us.

Rom 8:27. And the Father who knows all hearts knows, of course, what the Spirit is saying as he pleads for us in harmony with God's own will.

1 Cor 3:20. And again, in the book of Psalms, we are told that the Lord knows full well how the human mind reasons, and how foolish and futile it is.

Heb 4:12. For whatever God says to us is full of living power: it is sharper than the sharpest dagger, cutting swift and deep into our innermost thoughts and desires with all their parts, exposing us for what we really are.

Rev 2:23. And I will strike her children dead. And all the churches shall know that I am he who searches deep within men's hearts, and minds; I will give to each of you whatever you deserve.

CHANGE OF.

Instances of. Saul, 1 Sam 10:9. Solomon, 1 Kgs 3: 11, 12. Saul (Paul) of Tarsus, Acts 9:1–18.

See *Regeneration; Sanctification.*

HEARTH Lev 6:9; Isa 30:14; Jer 36:22, 23. See *Brazier.*

HEAT Jonah overcome with, Jon 4:8. See *Sunstroke.*

HEATHEN Hebrew *goy,* variously rendered as Gentiles, heathen, nations. It refers to all men who are neither Jews or Christians, 1 Cor 10:32. The equivalent Greek word in the N.T. is *ethnos,* also rendered as Gentiles, heathen, nations; occurs some 150 times. Thrown out of Canaan, Lev 18:24, 25; Ps 44:2; and their land given to Israel, Ps 78: 55; 105:44; 135:12; 136:21, 22; Isa 54:1–3. Excluded from the temple, Lam 1:10.

Wicked practices of, see *Idolatry.*

Divine revelations given to: Abimelech, Gen 20: 3–7; Pharaoh, Gen 41:1–28; Balaam, Num 22; Nebuchadnezzar, Dan 4:1–18; Belshazzar, Dan 5:5, 24–29; Cyrus, 2 Chron 36:22, 23; Ezra 1:1–4; the Magi, Mt 2:1–11; the Roman captain, Mt 8:5–13; Lk 7:2–9; Cornelius, Acts 10:1–7.

Pious people among, Isa 65:5; Acts 10:35.

INSTANCES OF. Melchizedek, Gen 14:18–20. Abimelech, Gen 20. Balaam, Num 22. Jethro, Ex 18. Cyrus, Ezra 1:1–3. Eliphaz, Job 4. Bildad, Job 8. Zophar, Job 11. Elihu, Job 32. Nebuchadnezzar, after his restoration, Dan 4. The Ninevites, Jon 3: 4–10. The Magi, Mt 2:1–12. The Roman captain of Capernaum, Mt 8:5–13; Lk 7:2–9. Cornelius, Acts 10.

See *Gentiles; Nations.*

HEAVE OFFERING See *Offerings.*

HEAVEN GOD'S HOME. Deut 26:15. Look down from your holy home in heaven and bless your people and the land you have given us, as you promised our ancestors; make it a land "flowing with milk and honey"! Isa 63:15; Zech 2:13.

1 Kgs 8:30. Listen to every plea of the people of Israel whenever they face this place to pray; yes, hear in heaven where you live, and when you hear, forgive. *vs.* 39, 43, 49; 2 Chron 6:18, 20, 21, 27, 30, 33, 35, 39; Jer 23:24.

1 Chron 16:31. Let the heavens be glad, the earth rejoice; let all the nations say, "It is the Lord who reigns."

1 Chron 21:26. And built an altar to the Lord there, and sacrificed burnt offerings and peace offerings upon it; and he called out to the Lord, who answered by sending down fire from heaven to burn up the offering on the altar. 2 Chron 7:14; Neh 9:27.

2 Chron 2:6. But who can ever build him a worthy home? Not even the highest heaven would be beautiful enough! And who am I to be allowed to build a temple for God? But it will be a place to worship him.

2 Chron 30:27. Then the priests and Levites stood and blessed the people, and the Lord heard their prayers from his holy temple in heaven.

Job 22:12. God is so great—higher than the

heavens, higher than the stars. [14]For thick clouds swirl about him so that he cannot see us. He is way up there, walking on the vault of heaven.

Ps 2:4. But God in heaven merely laughs! He is amused by all their puny plans.

Ps 11:4. But the Lord is still in his holy temple; he still rules from heaven. He closely watches everything that happens here on earth.

Ps 20:6. "God save the king"—I know he does! He hears me from highest heaven and sends great victories.

Ps 33:13–15. The Lord gazes down upon mankind from heaven where he lives. He has made their hearts and closely watches everything they do.

Ps 102:19. Tell them that God looked down from his temple in heaven.

Ps 103:19. The Lord has made the heavens his throne; from there he rules over everything there is. Ps 135:6; Dan 4:35.

Ps 113:5. Who can be compared with God enthroned on high?

Ps 123:1. O God enthroned in heaven, I lift my eyes to you.

Isa 57:15. The high and lofty one who inhabits eternity, the Holy One, says this: I live in that high and holy place where those with contrite, humble spirits dwell; and I refresh the humble and give new courage to those with repentant hearts.

Isa 63:15. O Lord, look down from heaven and see us from your holy, glorious home; where is the love for us you used to show—your power, your mercy and your compassion? Where are they now?

Isa 66:1. Heaven is my throne and the earth is my footstool: What Temple can you build for me as good as that?

Lam 3:41. Let us lift our hearts and hands to him in heaven. [50]Oh, that the Lord might look down from heaven and respond to my cry!

Dan 5:23. For you have defied the Lord of Heaven, and brought here these cups from his Temple; and you and your officers and wives and concubines have been drinking wine from them while praising gods of silver, gold, brass, iron, wood, and stone—gods that neither see nor hear, nor know anything at all. But you have not praised the God who gives you the breath of life and controls your destiny!

Mt 5:34. But I say: Don't make any vows! And even to say, "By heavens!" is a sacred vow to God, for the heavens are God's throne. [45]In that way you will be acting as true sons of your Father in heaven. For he gives his sunlight to both the evil and the good, and sends rain on the just and on the unjust too.

Mt 6:9. Pray along these lines: "Our Father in heaven, we honor your holy name." Mt 18:10; Mk 11:25.

Mt 10:32. If anyone publicly acknowledges me as his friend, I will openly acknowledge him as my friend before my Father in heaven. [33]But if anyone publicly denies me, I will openly deny him before my Father in heaven.

Mt 11:25. And Jesus prayed this prayer: "O Father, Lord of heaven and earth, thank you for hiding the truth from those who think themselves so wise, and for revealing it to little children."

Mt 12:50. Then he added, "Anyone who obeys my Father in heaven is my brother, sister and mother!"

Mt 16:17. "God has blessed you, Simon, son of Jonah," Jesus said, "for my Father in heaven has personally revealed this to you—this is not from any human source."

Mk 16:19. When the Lord Jesus had finished talking with them, he was taken up into heaven and sat down on God's right hand.

Acts 7:49. "The heaven is my throne," says the Lord.

Rom 1:18. But God shows his anger from heaven against all sinful, evil men who push away the truth from them.

Heb 8:1. What we are saying is this: Christ, whose priesthood we have just described, is our High Priest, and is in heaven at the place of greatest honor next to God himself.

Rev 8:1. When the Lamb had broken the seventh seal, there was silence throughout all heaven for what seemed like half an hour.

Rev 12:7. Then there was war in heaven; Michael and the angels under his command fought the Dragon and his hosts of fallen angels. [8]And the Dragon lost the battle and was forced from heaven. [9]This great Dragon—the ancient serpent called the devil, or Satan, the one deceiving the whole world—was thrown down onto the earth with all his army.

Rev 21:22. No temple could be seen in the city, for the Lord God Almighty and the Lamb are worshiped in it everywhere. [23]And the city has no need of sun or moon to light it, for the glory of God and of the Lamb illuminate it. [24]Its light will light the nations of the earth, and the rulers of the world will come and bring their glory to it. [25]Its gates never close; they stay open all day long—and there is no night! [26]And the glory and honor of all the nations shall be brought into it. [27]Nothing evil will be permitted in it—no one immoral or dishonest—but only those whose names are written in the Lamb's Book of Life.

Rev 22:1. And he pointed out to me a river of pure Water of Life, clear as crystal, flowing from the throne of God and the Lamb, [2]coursing down the center of the main street. On each side of the river grew Trees of Life, bearing twelve crops of fruit, with a fresh crop each month; the leaves were used for medicine to heal the nations. [3]There shall be nothing in the city which is evil; for the throne of God and of the Lamb will be there, and his servants will worship him. [4]And they shall see his face; and his name shall be written on their foreheads. [5]And there will be no night there—no need for lamps or sun—for the Lord God will be their light; and they shall reign forever and ever.

THE FUTURE HOME OF THE RIGHTEOUS. The wicked excluded from, Mt 25:41; 1 Cor 6:9, 10; Gal 5:21; Eph 5:5; Rev 21:8; 22:15.

Unclassified Scriptures Relating to. 2 Kgs 2:11.

As they were walking along, talking, suddenly a chariot of fire, drawn by horses of fire, appeared and drove between them, separating them, and Elijah was carried by a whirlwind into heaven.

Job 3:17. For there in death the wicked cease from troubling, and there the weary are at rest.

Ps 16:11. You have let me experience the joys of life and the exquisite pleasures of your own eternal presence.

Ps 17:15. But as for me, my contentment is not in wealth but in seeing you and knowing all is well between us. And when I awake in heaven, I will be fully satisfied, for I will see you face to face.

Ps 23:6. Your goodness and unfailing kindness shall be with me all of my life, and afterwards I will live with you forever in your home.

Ps 24:3. Who may climb the mountain of the Lord and enter where he lives? Who may stand before the Lord? [7]Open up, O ancient gates, and let the King of Glory in.

Ps 73:24. You will keep on guiding me all my life with your wisdom and counsel; and afterwards receive me into the glories of heaven!

Isa 33:17. Your eyes will see the King in his beauty, and the highlands of heaven far away.

Dan 12:3. And those who are wise—the people of God—shall shine as brightly as the sun's brilliance, and those who turn many to righteousness will glitter like stars forever.

Mal 3:17. "They shall be mine," says the Lord of Hosts, "in that day when I make up my jewels. And I will spare them as a man spares an obedient and dutiful son."

Mt 5:3. "Humble men are very fortunate!" he told them, "for the Kingdom of Heaven is given to them. [8]Happy are those whose hearts are pure, for they shall see God. [12]Be *happy* about it! Be *very glad!* for a *tremendous reward* awaits you up in heaven. And remember, the ancient prophets were persecuted too. [20]But I warn you—unless your goodness is greater than that of the Pharisees and other Jewish leaders, you can't get into the Kingdom of Heaven at all!"

Mt 6:20. Store them in heaven where they will never lose their value, and are safe from thieves. Lk 12:33.

Mt 8:11. And I tell you this, that many Gentiles (like this Roman officer), shall come from all over the world and sit down in the Kingdom of Heaven with Abraham, Issac, and Jacob.

Mt 13:30. Let both grow together until the harvest, and I will tell the reapers to sort out the thistles and burn them, and put the wheat in the barn. [43]Then the godly shall shine as the sun in their Father's Kingdom. Let those with ears, listen! [49]That is the way it will be at the end of the world —the angels will come and separate the wicked people from the godly. Mt 3:12.

Mt 18:10. Beware that you don't look down upon a single one of these little children. For I tell you that in heaven their angels have constant access to my Father.

Mt 19:21. Jesus told him, "If you want to be perfect, go and sell everything you have and give the money to the poor, and you will have treasure in heaven; and come, follow me."

Mt 25:34. Then I, the King, shall say to those at my right, "Come, blessed of my Father, into the Kingdom prepared for you from the founding of the world." [46]And they shall go away into eternal punishment; but the righteous into everlasting life.

Lk 10:20. However, the important thing is not that demons obey you, but that your names are registered as citizens of heaven.

Lk 12:32. So don't be afraid, little flock. For it gives your Father great happiness to give you the Kingdom.

Lk 15:6. When you arrived you would call together your friends and neighbors to rejoice with you because your lost sheep was found. [7]Well, in the same way heaven will be happier over one lost sinner who returns to God than over ninety-nine others who haven't strayed away! [*v.* 10] [32]But it is right to celebrate. For he is your brother; and he was dead and has come back to life! He was lost and is found!

Lk 16:22. Finally the beggar died and was carried by the angels to be with Abraham in the place of the righteous dead.

Lk 20:34, 35. Jesus replied, "Marriage is for people here on earth, but when those who are counted worthy of being raised from the dead get to heaven, they do not marry. [Mt 22:30.] [36]And they never die again; in these respects they are like angels, and are sons of God, for they are raised up in new life from the dead."

Lk 22:29. And because my Father has granted me a Kingdom, I, here and now, grant you the right [30]to eat and drink at my table in that Kingdom; and you will sit on thrones judging the twelve tribes of Israel.

Lk 23:43. And Jesus replied, "Today you will be with me in Paradise. This is a solemn promise."

Jn 5:28. Don't be so surprised! Indeed the time is coming when all the dead in their graves shall hear the voice of God's Son, [29]and shall rise again —those who have done good, to eternal life; and those who have continued in evil, to judgment.

Jn 10:28. I give them eternal life and they shall never perish. No one shall snatch them away from me.

Jn 12:26. If these Greeks want to be my disciples, tell them to come and follow me, for my servants must be where I am. And if they follow me, the Father will honor them.

Jn 13:36. Simon Peter said, "Master, where are you going?" And Jesus replied, "You can't go with me now; but you will follow me later."

Jn 14:2, 3. There are many homes up there where my Father lives, and I am going to prepare them for your coming. When everything is ready, then I will come and get you, so that you can always be with me where I am. If this weren't so, I would tell you plainly.

Jn 17:22. I have given them the glory you gave me—the glorious unity of being one, as we are—.

[24]Father, I want them with me—these you've given me—so that they can see my glory. You gave me the glory because you loved me before the world began!

Acts 7:55. But Stephen, full of the Holy Spirit, gazed steadily upward into heaven and saw the glory of God and Jesus standing at God's right hand. *v.* 56.

Rom 5:17. The sin of this one man, Adam, caused *death to be king over all,* but all who will take God's gift of forgiveness and acquittal are *kings of life* because of this one man, Jesus Christ.

2 Cor 5:1. For we know that when this tent we live in now is taken down—when we die and leave these bodies—we will have wonderful new bodies in heaven, homes that will be ours forevermore, made for us by God himself, and not by human hands.

2 Cor 12:2, 3. Fourteen years ago I was taken up to heaven for a visit. Don't ask me whether my body was there or just my spirit, for I don't know; only God can answer that. But anyway, there I was in paradise, [4]and heard things so astounding that they are beyond a man's power to describe or put in words (and anyway I am not allowed to tell them to others).

Eph 1:18. I pray that your hearts will be flooded with light so that you can see something of the future he has called you to share. I want you to realize that God has been made rich because we who are Christ's have been given to him!

Col 1:5. And you are looking forward to the joys of heaven, and have been ever since the Gospel first was preached to you. [6]The same Good News that came to you is going out all over the world and changing lives everywhere, just as it changed yours that very first day you heard it and understood about God's great kindness to sinners. [12]And always thankful to the Father who has made us fit to share all the wonderful things that belong to those who live in the kingdom of light.

Col 3:4. And when Christ who is our real life comes back again, you will shine with him and share in all his glories.

1 Thess 2:12. That your daily lives should not embarrass God, but bring joy to him who invited you into his kingdom to share his glory.

1 Thess 4:17. Then we who are still alive and remain on the earth will be caught up with them in the clouds to meet the Lord in the air and remain with him forever.

2 Thess 1:7. And so I would say to you who are suffering, God will give you rest along with us when the Lord Jesus appears suddenly from heaven in flaming fire with his mighty angels.

2 Thess 2:14. Through us he told you the Good News. Through us he called you to share in the glory of our Lord Jesus Christ.

Heb 10:34. You suffered with those thrown into jail, and you were actually joyful when all you owned was taken from you, knowing that better things were awaiting you in heaven, things that would be yours forever.

Heb 11:10. Abraham did this because he was confidently waiting for God to bring him to that strong heavenly city whose designer and builder is God. [16]But they didn't want to. They were living for heaven. And now God is not ashamed to be called their God, for he has made a heavenly city for them.

Heb 12:22. But you have come right up into Mount Zion, to the city of the living God, the heavenly Jerusalem, and to the gathering of countless happy angels; [23]and to the church, composed of all those registered in heaven; and to God who is Judge of all; and to the spirits of the redeemed in heaven, already made perfect; [24]and to Jesus himself, who has brought us his wonderful new agreement; and to the sprinkled blood which graciously forgives instead of crying out for vengeance as the blood of Abel did. [28]Since we have a kingdom nothing can destroy, let us please God by serving him with thankful hearts, and with holy fear and awe.

Heb 13:14. For this world is not our home; we are looking forward to our everlasting home in heaven.

1 Pet 1:4. And God has reserved for his children the priceless gift of eternal life; it is kept in heaven for you, pure and undefiled, beyond the reach of change and decay.

2 Pet 1:11. And God will open wide the gates of heaven for you to enter into the eternal kingdom of our Lord and Savior Jesus Christ.

2 Pet 3:13. But we are looking forward to God's promise of new heavens and a new earth afterwards, where there will be only goodness.

Rev 2:7. Let this message sink into the ears of anyone who listens to what the Spirit is saying to the churches: To everyone who is victorious, I will give fruit from the Tree of Life in the Paradise of God.

Rev 3:21. I will let every one who conquers sit beside me on my throne, just as I took my place with my Father on his throne when I had conquered. Lk 12:8.

Rev 4:4. Twenty-four smaller thrones surrounded his, with twenty-four Elders sitting on them; all were clothed in white, with golden crowns upon their heads.

Rev 5:9. They were singing him a new song with these words: "You are worthy to take the scroll and break its seals and open it; for you were slain, and your blood has bought people from every nation as gifts for God."

Rev 7:9. After this I saw a vast crowd, too great to count, from all nations and provinces and languages, standing in front of the throne and before the Lamb, clothed in white, with palm branches in their hands. [13]Then one of the twenty-four Elders asked me, "Do you know who these are, who are clothed in white, and where they come from?" [14]"No, sir," I replied. "Please tell me." "These are the ones coming out of the Great Tribulation," he said; "they washed their robes and whitened them by the blood of the Lamb. [15]That is why they are here before the throne of God, serving him day and night in his temple. The one sitting on the throne will shelter them; [16]they will never be hungry again, nor thirsty, and they will be fully protected from the scorching noontime heat. [17]For the Lamb standing in front of the throne will feed them and be their Shepherd and lead them to the springs of the Water of Life. And God will wipe their tears away." Isa 49:8–10.

Rev 14:1. Then I saw a Lamb standing on Mount Zion in Jerusalem, and with him were 144,000 who had his Name and his Father's Name written on their foreheads. [2]And I heard a sound from heaven like the roaring of a great waterfall or the rolling of mighty thunder. It was the singing of a choir accompanied by harps. [3]This tremendous choir—144,000 strong—sang a wonderful new song in front of the throne of God and before the four Living Beings and the twenty-four Elders; and no one could sing this song except those 144,000 who had been redeemed from the earth.

Rev 15:2. Spread out before me was what seemed to be an ocean of fire and glass, and on it stood all those who had been victorious over the Evil Creature and his statue and his mark and number. All were holding harps of God.

Rev 21:1. Then I saw a new earth (with no oceans!) and a new sky, for the present earth and sky had disappeared. [2]And I, John, saw the Holy City, the new Jerusalem, coming down from God out of heaven. It was a glorious sight, beautiful as a bride at her wedding. [3]I heard a loud shout from the throne saying, "Look, the home of God is now among men, and he will live with them and they will be his people; yes, God himself will be among them. [4]He will wipe away all tears from their eyes, and there shall be no more death, nor sorrow, nor crying, nor pain. All of that has gone forever." [5]And the one sitting on the throne said, "See, I am making all things new!" [9]Then one of the seven angels, who had emptied the flasks containing the seven last plagues, came and said to me, "Come with me and I will show you the bride, the Lamb's wife." [10]In a vision he took me to a towering mountain peak and from there I watched that wondrous city, the holy Jerusalem, descending out of the skies from God.

11. It was filled with the glory of God, and flashed and glowed like a precious gem, crystal clear like jasper. [18, 19]The city itself was pure, transparent gold like glass! The wall was made of jasper, and was built on twelve layers of foundation stones inlaid with gems. [21]The twelve gates were made of pearls—each gate from a single pearl! And the main street was pure, transparent gold, like glass.

22. No temple could be seen in the city, for the Lord God Almighty and the Lamb are worshiped in it everywhere. [23]And the city has no need of sun or moon to light it, for the glory of God and of the Lamb illuminate it. [24]Its light will light the nations of the earth, and the rulers of the world will come and bring their glory to it.

25. Its gates never close; they stay open all day long—and there is no night! [27]Nothing evil will be permitted in it—no one immoral or dishonest—but only those whose names are written in the Lamb's Book of Life.

Rev 22:1. And he pointed out to me a river of pure Water of Life, clear as crystal, flowing from the throne of God and the Lamb, [2]coursing down the center of the main street. On each side of the river grew Trees of Life, bearing twelve crops of fruit, with a fresh crop each month; the leaves were used for medicine to heal the nations. [3]There shall be nothing in the city which is evil; for the throne of God and of the Lamb will be there, and his servants will worship him.

4. And they shall see his face; and his name shall be written on their foreheads. [5]And there will be no night there—no need for lamps or sun—for the Lord God will be their light; and they shall reign forever and ever.

See *Righteous, Promises to.*

THE PHYSICAL HEAVENS. Gen 1:1. When God began creating the heavens and the earth. Job 37:18; Ps 33:6; 136:5; Jer 10:12.

Ps 19:1. The heavens are telling the glory of God; they are a marvelous display of his craftsmanship.

Ps 50:6 God will judge them with complete fairness, for all heaven declares that he is just.

Ps 68:33. To him who rides upon the ancient heavens, whose mighty voice thunders from the sky.

Ps 89:29. He will always have an heir; his throne will be as endless as the days of heaven.

Ps 97:6. The heavens declare his perfect righteousness; every nation sees his glory.

Ps 103:11. For his mercy toward those who fear and honor him is as great as the height of the heavens above the earth.

Ps 113:4. For he is high above the nations; his glory is far greater than the heavens.

Ps 115:16. The heavens belong to the Lord, but he has given the earth to all mankind.

Jer 31:37. Not until the heavens can be measured and the foundations of the earth explored, will I consider casting them away forever for their sins!

Ezk 1:1–3. Ezekiel was a priest (the son of Buzi) who lived with the Jewish exiles beside the Chebar Canal in Babylon. One day late in June, when I was thirty years old, the heavens were suddenly opened to me and I saw visions from God.

Mt 24:29. Immediately after the persecution of those days the sun will be darkened, and the moon will not give light, and the stars will seem to fall from the heavens, and the powers overshadowing the earth will be convulsed. [30]And then at last the signal of my coming will appear in the heavens and there will be deep mourning all around the earth. And the nations of the world will see me arrive in the clouds of heaven, with power and great glory.

Acts 2:19. And I will cause strange demonstrations in the heavens and on the earth—blood and fire and clouds of smoke; [20]the sun shall turn black and the moon blood-red before that awesome Day of the Lord arrives.

See sub-topics, below.

Physical Heavens, Creation of. Gen 1:1. When God began creating the heavens and the earth.

Gen 2:1. Now at last the heavens and earth were successfully completed, with all that they contained.

1 Chron 16:26. The other so-called gods are demons, but the Lord made the heavens.

2 Chron 2:12. Blessed be the Lord God of Israel who made the heavens and the earth and who has given to David such a wise, intelligent, and understanding son to build God's Temple, and a royal palace for himself.

Neh 9:6. Then Ezra prayed, "You alone are God. You have made the skies and the heavens, the earth and the seas, and everything in them. You preserve it all; and all the angels of heaven worship you."

Job 9:8. Only he has stretched the heavens out and stalked along the seas.

Ps 8:3. When I look up into the night skies and see the work of your fingers—the moon and the stars you have made.

Ps 19:1. The heavens are telling the glory of God; they are a marvelous display of his craftsmanship.

Ps 33:6. He merely spoke, and the heavens were formed, and all the galaxies of stars. [9]For when he but spoke, the world began! It appeared at his command!

Ps 148:4. Praise him, skies above. Praise him, vapors high above the clouds. [5]Let everything he has made give praise to him. For he issued his command, and they came into being; [6]he established them forever and forever. His orders will never be revoked.

Prov 8:27. I was there when he established the heavens and formed the great springs in the depths of the oceans.

Isa 37:16. O Lord of Hosts, God of Israel enthroned above the cherubim, *you alone* are God of all the kingdoms of the earth. You alone made heaven and earth.

Isa 40:22. It is God who sits above the circle of the earth. (The people below must seem to him like grasshoppers!) He is the one who stretches out the heavens like a curtain and makes his tent from them.

Isa 42:5. The Lord God who created the heavens and stretched them out and created the earth and everything in it. Isa 45:18.

Isa 45:12. I have made the earth and created man upon it. With my hands I have stretched out the heavens and commanded all the vast myriads of stars.

Jer 10:12. But our God formed the earth by his power and wisdom, and by his intelligence he hung the stars in space and stretched out the heavens.

Jer 32:17. O Lord God! You have made the heavens and earth by your great power; nothing is too hard for you!

Jer 51:15. God made the earth by his power and wisdom. He stretched out the heavens by his understanding.

Acts 4:24. Then all the believers united in this prayer: "O Lord, Creator of heaven and earth and of the sea and everything in them—." Acts 14:15.

Heb 1:10. God also called him "Lord" when he said, "Lord, in the beginning you made the earth, and the heavens are the work of your hands."

Rev 10:6. And swore by him who lives forever and ever, who created heaven and everything in it and the earth and all that it contains and the sea and its inhabitants, that there should be no more delay.

Rev 14:7. "Fear God," he shouted, "and extol his greatness. For the time has come when he will sit as Judge. Worship him who made the heaven and the earth, the sea and all its sources."

See *Creation; God, Creator; Heavens, New,* below.

Physical Heavens, Destruction of. Job 14:12. So a man lies down for the last time, and does not rise again until the heavens are no more; he shall not awaken, nor be roused from his sleep.

Ps 102:25. In ages past you laid the foundations of the earth, and made the heavens with your hands! [26]They shall perish but you go on forever. They will grow old, like worn-out clothing, and you will change them like a man putting on a new shirt, and throwing away the old one!

Isa 34:4. At that time the heavens above will melt away and disappear just like a rolled-up scroll, and the stars will fall as leaves, as ripe fruit from the trees.

Isa 51:6. Look high in the skies and watch the earth beneath, for the skies shall disappear like smoke, the earth shall wear out like a garment, and the people of the earth shall die like flies. But my salvation lasts forever; my righteous rule will never die nor end.

Mt 24:35. Heaven and earth will disappear, but my words remain forever.

Heb 1:10. God also called him "Lord" when he said, "Lord, in the beginning you made the earth, and the heavens are the work of your hands. [11]They will disappear into nothingness, but you will remain forever. They will become worn out like old clothes, [12]and some day you will fold them up and replace them. But you yourself will never change, and your years will never end."

2 Pet 3:10. The day of the Lord is surely coming, as unexpectedly as a thief, and then the heavens will pass away with a terrible noise and the heavenly bodies will disappear in fire, and the earth and everything on it will be burned up. [12]You should look forward to that day and hurry it along—the day when God will set the heavens on fire, and the heavenly bodies will melt and disappear in flames.

Rev 6:12. I watched as he broke the sixth seal, and there was a vast earthquake; and the sun became dark like black cloth, and the moon was blood-red. [13]Then the stars of heaven appeared to be falling to earth—like green fruit from fig trees buffeted by mighty winds. [14]And the starry heavens disappeared as though rolled up like a scroll and taken away; and every mountain and island shook and shifted.

Rev 20:11. And I saw a great white throne and the one who sat upon it, from whose face the earth and sky fled away, but they found no place to hide.

Rev 21:1. Then I saw a new earth (with no oceans!) and a new sky, for the present earth and sky had disappeared. [4]He will wipe away all tears from their eyes, and there shall be no more death, nor sorrow, nor crying, nor pain. All of that has gone forever.

NEW HEAVENS. Isa 65:17. For see, I am creating new heavens and a new earth—so wonderful that no one will even think about the old ones anymore.

Isa 66:22. As surely as my new heavens and earth shall remain, so surely shall you always be my people, with a name that shall never disappear.

2 Pet 3:13. But we are looking forward to God's promise of new heavens and a new earth afterwards, where there will be only goodness.

Rev 21:1. Then I saw a new earth (with no oceans!) and a new sky, for the present earth and sky had disappeared. [2]And I, John, saw the Holy City, the new Jerusalem, coming down from God out of heaven. It was a glorious sight, beautiful as a bride at her wedding. [3]I heard a loud shout from the throne saying, "Look, the home of God is now among men, and he will live with them and they will be his people; yes, God himself will be among them. [4]He will wipe away all tears from their eyes, and there shall be no more death, nor sorrow, nor crying, nor pain. All of that has gone forever."

HEBER 1. A son of Beriah, Gen 46:16, 17; Num 26:44–47; 1 Chron 7:31, 32.

2. Husband of Jael, Judg 4:11, 17, 21; 5:24.

3. A Judahite, 1 Chron 4:18.

4. A Benjaminite, 1 Chron 8:17, 18.

HEBREW The name may be derived from Eber, an ancestor of Abraham, Gen 10:21–25, or it may come from a root meaning "the traveller," or "the one who crossed the river," the Euphrates, Josh 24:2, 3. See *Genealogy.* Applied to Abraham, Gen 14:13; and his descendants, Gen 39:14, 15; 40:15; 43:32; Ex 2:6; Deut 15:12; 1 Sam 14:21; Jon 1:9, 10; Acts 6:1; 2 Cor 11:22. Used to denote the language of the Jews, Jn 19:20; Acts 21:40; 22:2; 26:14; Rev 9:11; 16:16.

See *Israelites; Jews.*

HEBRON 1. A city of Judah, south of Jerusalem. When built, Num 13:22. Fortified, 2 Chron 11:10. Called *Kiriaath-arba,* Gen 35:7; *Arba,* Josh 15:13. Abraham lives and Sarah dies in, Gen 23:2. Hohom, king of, confederated with other kings of the Canaanites against Joshua, Josh 10:3–39. Descendants of Anak live in, Num 13:22; Josh 11:21. Conquest of, by Caleb, Josh 14:6–15; Judg 1:10, 20. A city of refuge, Josh 20:7; 21:9–16. David crowned king of Judah at, 2 Sam 2:1–11; 3; of Israel, 2 Sam 5:1–5. The burial place of Sarah, Gen 23:2; Abner, 2 Sam 3:32; Ish-bosheth, 2 Sam 4:12. The conspirators against Ish-bosheth hanged at, 2 Sam 4:12. Absalom made king at, 2 Sam 15:9, 10. Jews of the Babylonian captivity live in, Neh 11:25.

Pool of, 2 Sam 4:12.

2. Son of Kohath, Ex 6:18; Num 3:25–30; 1 Chron 6:2, 18; 23:12, 19.

3. The son of Mareshah, 1 Chron 2:42, 43; 15:4–10.

HECALIAH Father of Nehemiah, Neh 1:1.

HEDGE A fence, Jer 49:3; Nah 3:17; Mt 21:33; of thorns, Mic 7:4. People sheltered in, Lk 14:23. See *Fence.*

HEDGEHOG Zeph 2:14.

HEGAI Eunuch in the court of Ahasuerus, Esther 2:3, 9, 15.

HEIFER When used as sacrifice, must be without defect and never been yoked, Num 19:2; Deut 21:3. An atonement for murder, Deut 21:1–9. The red heifer used for the water of purification, Num 19; Heb 9:13.

Used for plowing, Judg 14:18. Stubborn, Hos 4:16.

See *Cattle; Offerings.*

FIGURATIVE. Of backsliders, Hos 4:16.

HEIR Gal 4:1, 2.

Gen 15:2, 3. But Abram replied, "O Lord Jehovah, what good are all your blessings when I have no son? For without a son, some other member of my household will inherit all my wealth." [4]Then Jehovah told him, "No, no one else will be your heir, for you will have a son to inherit everything you own."

Gen 21:10. She turned upon Abraham and demanded, "Get rid of that slave girl and her son. He is not going to share your property with my son. I won't have it." Gal 4:30.

Gen 25:5. Abraham deeded everything he owned to Isaac; [6]however, he gave gifts to the sons of his concubines and sent them off into the east, away from Isaac.

Lev 25:45. And you may purchase the children of the foreigners living among you, even though they have been born in your land. [46]They will be permanent slaves for you to pass on to your children after you; but your brothers, the people of Israel, shall not be treated so.

Num 27:8. Moreover, this is a general law among you, that if a man dies and has no sons, then his inheritance shall be passed on to his daughters. [9]And if he has no daughter, it shall belong to his brothers. [10]And if he has no brother, then it shall go to his uncles. [11]But if he has no uncles, then it shall go to the nearest relative.

Num 36:1, 2. Then the heads of the sub-clan of Gilead (of the clan of Machir, of the tribe of Manasseh, one of the sons of Joseph) came to Moses and the leaders of Israel with a petition: "The Lord instructed you to divide the land by lot among the people of Israel," they reminded Moses, "and to give the inheritance of our brother Zelophehad to his daughters. [3]But if they marry into another tribe, their land will go with them to the tribe into which they marry. In this way the total area of our tribe will be reduced, [4]and will not be returned at the Year of Jubilee." [5]Then Moses replied publicly, giving them these instructions from the Lord: "The men of the tribe of Joseph have a proper complaint. [6]This is what the Lord has further commanded concerning the daughters of Zelophehad: 'Let them be married to anyone they like, so long as it is within their own tribe. [7]In this way none of the land of the tribe shall shift to any other tribe, for the inheritance of every tribe is to remain permanently as it was first allotted. [8]The girls throughout the tribes of Israel who are heiresses must marry within their own tribe, so that their land won't leave the tribe.' " Josh 17:3–6.

Deut 21:15. If a man has two wives but loves one and not the other, and both have borne him children, and the mother of his oldest son is the wife he doesn't love, [16]he may not give a larger inheritance to his younger son, the son of the wife he loves. [17]He must give the customary double portion to his oldest son, who is the beginning of his strength and who owns the rights of a firstborn son, even though he is the son of the wife his father doesn't love.

Ruth 4:1. So Boaz went down to the market place and found the relative he had mentioned. "Say, come over here," he called to him. "I want to talk to you a minute." So they sat down together. [2]Then Boaz called for ten of the chief men of the village, and asked them to sit as witnesses. [3]Boaz said to his relative, "You know Naomi, who came back to us from Moab. She is selling our brother Elimelech's property. [4]I felt that I should speak to you about it so that you can buy it if you wish, with these respected men as witnesses. If you want it, let me know right away, for if you don't take it, I will. You have the first right to purchase it and I am next." The man replied, "All right, I'll buy it." [5]Then Boaz told him, "Your purchase of the land from Naomi requires your marriage to Ruth so that she can have children to carry on her husband's name, and to inherit the land." [6]"Then I can't do it," the man replied. "For her son would become an heir to my property, too; you buy it." [7]In those days it was the custom in Israel for a man transferring a right of purchase to pull off his sandal and hand it to the other party; this publicly validated the transaction. [8]So, as the man said to Boaz, "You buy it for yourself," he drew off his sandal. [9]Then Boaz said to the witnesses and to the crowd standing around, "You have seen that today I have bought all the property of Elimelech, Chilion, and Mahlon, from Naomi, [10]and that with it I have purchased Ruth the Moabitess, the widow of Mahlon, to be my wife, so that she can have a son to carry on the family name of her dead husband." [11]And all the people standing there, and the witnesses replied, "We are witnesses. May the Lord make this woman, who has now come into your home, as fertile as Rachel and Leah, from whom all the nation of Israel descended! May you be a great and successful man in Bethlehem, [12]and may the descendants the Lord will give you from this young woman be as numerous and honorable as those of our ancestor Perez, the son of Tamar and Judah."

Eccl 2:18. And I am disgusted about this, that I must leave the fruits of all my hard work to others. [19]And who can tell whether my son will be a wise man or a fool? And yet all I have will be given to him—how discouraging!

See *Birthright; Firstborn; Inheritance; Orphan; Will, a Testament.*

FIGURATIVE. Rom 8:14. For all who are led by the Spirit of God are sons of God. [15]And so we should not be like cringing, fearful slaves, but we should behave like God's very own children, adopted into the bosom of his family, and calling to him, "Father, Father." [16]For his Holy Spirit speaks to us deep in our hearts, and tells us that we really are God's children. [17]And since we are his children, we will share his treasures—for all God gives to his Son Jesus is now ours too. But if we are to share his glory, we must also share his suffering.

Gal 3:29. And now that we are Christ's we are the true descendants of Abraham, and all of God's promises to him belong to us.

Gal 4:6. And because we are his sons God has sent the Spirit of his Son into our hearts, so now we can rightly speak of God as our dear Father. [7]Now we are no longer slaves, but God's own sons. And since we are his sons, everything he has belongs to us, for that is the way God planned.

Tit 3:7. So that he could declare us good in God's eyes—all because of his great kindness; and now we can share in the wealth of the eternal life he gives us, and we are eagerly looking forward to receiving it.

Jas 2:5. Listen to me, dear brothers: God has chosen poor people to be rich in faith, and the Kingdom of Heaven is theirs, for that is the gift God has promised to all those who love him.

See *Adoption; Inheritance.*

HELAH A wife of Ashhur, 1 Chron 4:5, 7.

HELAM A place east of the Jordan, 2 Sam 10:15–17.

HELBAH A town of Asher, Judg 1:31, 32.

HELBON A village near Damascus, noted for fine wines, Ezk 27:18.

HELDAI 1. A Netophathite. One of David's heroes, 1 Chron 27:15. Called *Heled,* 1 Chron 11:26–47; and *Heleb,* 2 Sam 23:24–39.

2. An Israelite, Zech 6:10, 11.

HELEB See *Heldai, 2.*

HELEK Son of Gilead, Num 26:28–37; Josh 17:2.

HELEM A descendant of Asher, called *Hotham,* 1 Chron 7:32, 35.

HELEPH Town of Naphtali, Josh 19:34.

HELEZ 1. One of David's mighty men, 2 Sam 23:24–39; 1 Chron 11:26–47; 27:10.

2. A man of Judah, 1 Chron 2:39.

HELI Father of Joseph, Lk 3:23–38.

HELIOPOLIS A city in Egypt, Gen 41:45; 46:19–22; Isa 19:18; Jer 43:13; Ezk 30:17.

HELKAI A priest, Neh 12:12–21.

HELKATH Called also *Hukok.* A Levitical town, 1 Chron 6:75; Josh 19:25; 21:30, 31.

HELL The word is used in the *Living Bible* version of the Old Testament to translate the Hebrew word *sheol,* signifying the unseen world, in 2 Sam 22:6; Ps 9:17; 86:13; Prov 5:5; 7:27; 9:18; 15:11, 24; 23:13, 14; Isa 5:14; 14:9, 15; 57:9; Ezk 31:16; Hab 2:5.

A translation of the Greek word *hades* in the New Testament *Living Bible,* the unseen world, Mt 11:23; 16:18; Lk 10:15; 16:23; Acts 2:27, 31; Rev 1:17, 18; 6:8; 20:14; of the Greek word *gehenna,* signifying the place of torment, Mt 5:22, 29, 30; 10:28; 18:9; 23:15, 33; Mk 9:43–47; Lk 12:5; Jas 3:6; of the Greek word *tartarus,* signifying an infernal region, 2 Pet 2:4.

In all of the following passages Sheol is rendered hell:

2 Sam 22:6. I was trapped, and bound by hell and death.

Ps 9:17. The wicked shall be sent away to hell; this is the fate of all the nations forgetting the Lord.

Ps 86:13. For you love me so much! You are constantly so kind! You have rescued me from deepest hell.

Prov 5:5. She leads me down to death and hell.

Prov 7:27. If you want to find the road to hell, look for her house.

Prov 9:18. But they don't realize that her former guests are now citizens of hell.

Prov 15:11. The depths of hell are open to God's knowledge. How much more the hearts of all mankind!

Prov 15:24. The road of the godly leads upward, leaving hell behind.

Prov 23:14. They won't die if you use a stick on them! Punishment will keep them out of hell.

Isa 5:14. Hell is licking its chops in anticipation of this delicious morsel, Jerusalem. Her great and small shall be swallowed up, and all her drunken throngs.

Isa 14:9. The denizens of hell crowd to meet you as you enter their domain. World leaders and earth's mightiest kings, long dead, are there to see you. [15]But instead, you will be brought down to the pit of hell, down to its lowest depths.

Isa 57:9. You have taken pleasant incense and perfume to Molech as your gift. You have traveled far, even to hell itself, to find new gods to love.

Ezk 31:16. I made the nations shake with fear at the sound of her fall, for I threw her down to hell with all the others like her. And all the other proud trees of Eden, the choicest and the best of Lebanon, the ones whose roots went deep into the water, are comforted to find her there with them in hell. [17]Her allies too are all destroyed and perish with her. They went down with her to the nether world—those nations that had lived beneath her shade.

Hab 2:5. What's more, these arrogant Chaldeans are betrayed by all their wine, for it is treacherous. In their greed they have collected many nations, but like death and hell, they are never satisfied.

See *Gehenna; Hades; Pit; Sheol; Tartarus; Wicked, Punishment of.*

HEMAN 1. A man noted for wisdom, to whom Solomon is compared, 1 Kgs 4:31; 1 Chron 2:6.

2. "The Cantor," a chief Levite, and musician, 1 Chron 6:33–38; 15:17, 19; 16:41. The king's chaplain, 1 Chron 25:5. His sons and daughters temple musicians, 1 Chron 25:1–7.

HEMDAN Son of Dishon, Gen 36:26.

HEMORRHAGE A woman suffers twelve years, Mt 9:20; Mk 5:25–29; Lk 8:43.

See *Disease.*

HEN FIGURATIVE. Mt 23:37; Lk 13:34.

HENA A city on the Euphrates, 2 Kgs 18:34; 19:13; Isa 37:13.

HENADAD A Levite, Ezra 3:9; Neh 3:18, 24; 10:9–13.

HEPHER 1. Son of Gilead, and father of Zelophehad, Num 26:28–37; 27:1; Josh 17:2, 3.

2. Son of Asshur, 1 Chron 4:6.

3. One of David's heroes, 1 Chron 11:26–47.

4. A city west of the Jordan, Josh 12:8–24; 1 Kgs 4:8–19.

HEPHZIBAH Wife of Hezekiah, 2 Kgs 21:1, 2.

HERALD Dan 3:4. Signified by the word missionary, 1 Tim 2:7; 2 Tim 1:11.

HERBS Gen 37:25; bitter, Ex 12:8; Num 9:11; Mk 15:23.

See *Vegetation.*

HEREDITY Gen 5:3. *Adam:* Adam was 130 years old when his son Seth was born, the very image of his father in every way.

Ex 20:5. You must never bow to an image or worship it in any way; for I, the Lord your God, am very possessive. I will not share your affection with any other God! And when I punish people for their sins, the punishment continues upon the children, grandchildren, and greatgrandchildren of those who hate me; [Ex 34:7; Num 14:17, 18.] [6]but I lavish my love upon thousands of those who love me and obey my commandments.

Job 14:4. How can you demand purity in one born impure?

Job 21:19. "Well," you say, "at least God will punish their children!" But I say that God should punish the man who sins, not his children! Let him feel the penalty himself.

Ps 51:5. But I was born a sinner, yes, from the moment my mother conceived me.

Ps 58:3. These men are born sinners, lying from their earliest words!

Isa 14:20. No monument will be given you, for you have destroyed your nation and slain your people. Your son will not succeed you as the king. [21]Slay the children of this sinner. Do not let them rise and conquer the land nor rebuild the cities of the world.

Isa 48:8. Yes, I'll tell you things entirely new, for I know so well what traitors you are, rebels from earliest childhood, rotten through and through.

Isa 65:6. See, here is my decree all written out before me: *I will not stand silent; I will repay. Yes, I will repay them*—[7]not only for their own sins but for those of their fathers too, says the Lord, for they also burned incense on the mountains and insulted me upon the hills. I will pay them back in full.

Jer 31:29. The people shall no longer quote this proverb—"Children pay for their fathers' sins." [30]For everyone shall die for his own sins—the person eating sour grapes is the one whose teeth are set on edge.

Jer 32:18. You are loving and kind to thousands, yet children suffer for their fathers' sins; you are the great and mighty God, the Lord of Hosts.

Ezk 18:2. Why do people use this proverb about the land of Israel: The children are punished for their fathers' sins?

Ezk 18:19. "What?" you ask. "Doesn't the son pay for his father's sins?" No! For if the son does what is right and keeps my laws, he shall surely live. [20]The one who sins is the one who dies. The son shall not be punished for his father's sins, nor the father for his son's. The righteous person will be rewarded for his own goodness and the wicked person for his wickedness.

Mt 3:9. Don't try to get by as you are, thinking, "We are safe for we are Jews—descendants of Abraham." That proves nothing. God can change these stones here into Jews!

Jn 3:6. Men can only reproduce human life, but the Holy Spirit gives new life from heaven; [7]so don't be surprised at my statement that you must be born again!

Jn 9:2. "Master," his disciples asked him, "why was this man born blind? Was it a result of his own sins or those of his parents?"

Rom 5:12. When Adam sinned, sin entered the entire human race. His sin spread death throughout all the world, so everything began to grow old and die, for all sinned.

1 Cor 15:22. Everyone dies because all of us are related to Adam, being members of his sinful race, and wherever there is sin, death results. But all who are related to Christ will rise again.

Eph 2:3. All of us used to be just as they are, our lives expressing the evil within us, doing every wicked thing that our passions or our evil thoughts might lead us into. We started out bad, being born with evil natures, and were under God's anger just like everyone else.

HERES 1. A mountain, Judg 1:35.

2. A place east of the Jordan, Judg 8:13.

HERESH A Levite, 1 Chron 9:15, 16.

HERESY Propagandism of, forbidden under severe penalties, Deut 13; Tit 3:10, 11; 2 Jn 1:10, 11. Teachers of, among early Christians, Acts 15:24; 2 Cor 11:4; Gal 1:7; 2:4; 2 Pet 2; Jude 1:3–16; Rev 2:2. Paul and Silas accused of, Acts 16:20, 21, 23. Paul accused of, Acts 18:13. Disavowed by Paul, Acts 24:13–16.

See *Teachers, False.*

HERETH A forest in which David hid from Saul, 1 Sam 22:5.

HERMAS A Christian at Rome, Rom 16:14.

HERMES A Greek Christian, Rom 16:14.

HERMOGENES A Christian, who deserted Paul, 2 Tim 1:15.

HERMON A mountain in the north of Palestine, Josh 11:1, 17; 12:1, 5; 13:2–7, 11; Ps 42:6; 68:22; 89:12; 133:3; Jer 18:14. Called *Sirion,* Deut 3:9; Ps 29:6; Deut 4:48; *Senir,* Deut 3:9; 1 Chron 5:23.

HEROD 1. The Great, King of Judea, Mt 2.

2. Antipas, Tetrarch (governor) of Galilee, Lk 3:1; 23:7. Incest of, Mt 14:3, 4; Mk 6:17–19. Beheads John the Baptist, Mt 14:3–11; Mk 6:16–28. Desires to see Jesus, Lk 9:7, 9; 23:8. Tyranny of, Lk 13:31, 32. Jesus tried by, Lk 23:6–12, 15; Acts 4:27.

3. Agrippa I, son of Aristobulus, Acts 12:1–23.

HERODIANS A Jewish faction. Seek to trap Jesus, Mt 22:16; Mk 12:13. Conspire to kill Jesus, Mk 3:6.

HERODIAS Daughter of Aristobulus and wife of Herod's brother Philip, Mt 14:3, 6; Mk 6:17–19; Lk 3:19, 20.

HERODION A Roman Christian, Rom 16:11.

HERON Lev 11:13–19; Deut 14:11–18.

HESHBON A city of the Amorites, Num 21:25–35; Deut 1:1–5. Built by Reuben, Num 32:37, 38. Allotted to Gad, Josh 21:38, 39. Pools at, Song 7:4. Prophecy concerning, Isa 16:8; Jer 48:2–4, 34; 49:1–3.

HESHMON A town in the south of Judah, Josh 15:21–32.

HETH Son of Canaan, and ancestor of the Hittites, Gen 10:15–19; 23:3, 5, 7, 10, 16, 18; 49:32; 1 Chron 1:13–16.

See *Hittites.*

HETHLON A place on the northern frontier of Palestine, Ezk 47:15; 48:1.

HEZEKIAH 1. King of Judah, 2 Kgs 16:20; 18:1–3; 1 Chron 3:10–14; 2 Chron 29:1; Mt 1:9. Religious zeal of, 2 Chron 29; 30; 31. Purges the nation of idolatry, 2 Kgs 18:4; 2 Chron 31:1; 33:3. Restores the true forms of worship, 2 Chron 31:2–21. His piety, 2 Kgs 18:5, 6; 2 Chron 29:2; 31:20, 21; 32:32; Jer 26:19. Military operations of, 2 Kgs 18:19; 1 Chron 4:40–43; 2 Chron 32; Isa 36, 37. Sickness and restoration of, 2 Kgs 20:1–11; 2 Chron 32:24; Isa 38:1–8. His psalm of thanksgiving, Isa 38:9–22. His lack of wisdom in showing his resources to ambassadors from Babylon, 2 Kgs 20:12–19; 2 Chron 32:25, 26, 31; Isa 39. Prospered by God, 2 Kgs 18:7; 2 Chron 32:27–30. Conducts the brook Gihon into Jerusalem, 2 Kgs 18:17; 20:20; 2 Chron 32:4, 30; 33:14; Neh 2:13–15; Isa 7:3; 22:9–11; 36:2. Scribes of, Prov 25:1. Death and burial of, 2 Kgs 20:21; 2 Chron 32:33. Prophecies concerning, 2 Kgs 19:20–34; 20:5, 6, 16–18; Isa 38:5–8; 39:5–7; Jer 26:18, 19.

2. One of the exiles, Ezra 2:3–35; Neh 7:8–38; 10:17.

HEZIR 1. A Levite, 1 Chron 24:7–18.

2. A leader of Judah, Neh 10:14–27.

HEZRO A Carmelite, 2 Sam 23:24–39; 1 Chron 11:26–47.

HEZRON 1. Son of Perez, Gen 46:8–14, and ancestor of Jesus, Mt 1:3; Lk 3:23–38. Ancestor of the Hezronites, Num 26:5–11, 19–22; 1 Chron 2:5, 9, 18, 21, 24.

2. A son of Reuben, Gen 46:8–14; Ex 6:14; 1 Chron 5:3. Descendants of, called Hezronites, Num 26:5–11.

3. A town of Judah, Josh 15:2–4.

HIDDAI One of David's heroes, 2 Sam 23: 24–39. Called *Hurai,* 1 Chron 11:26–47.

HIEL Rebuilder of Jericho, 1 Kgs 16:34. In him was fulfilled the curse pronounced by Joshua, Josh 6:26.

HIERAPOLIS A city of Asia. Christians in, Col 4:13.

HIGH PLACES A term used to describe places of idol worship, 2 Kgs 17:9.

See *Grove; Idolatry.*

HIGH PRIEST See *Priest.*

HIGHWAYS FIGURATIVE. Isa 11:16. He will make a highway from Assyria for the remnant there, just as he did for all of Israel long ago when they returned from Egypt.

Isa 35:8. And a main road will go through that once-deserted land; it will be named "The Holy Highway." No evilhearted men may walk upon it. God will walk there with you; even the most stupid cannot miss the way. [9]No lion will lurk along its course, nor will there be any other dangers; only the redeemed will travel there. [10]These, the ransomed of the Lord, will go home along that road to Zion, singing the songs of everlasting joy. For them all sorrow and all sighing will be gone forever; only joy and gladness will be there.

Isa 40:3. Listen! I hear the voice of someone shouting, "Make a road for the Lord through the wilderness; make him a straight, smooth road through the desert. [4]Fill the valleys; level the hills; straighten out the crooked paths and smooth off the rough spots in the road." Mt 3:3.

Mt 7:13. Heaven can be entered only through the narrow gate! The highway to hell is broad, and its gate is wide enough for all the multitudes who choose its easy way. [14]But the Gateway to Life is small, and the road is narrow, and only a few ever find it.

See *Roads; Way.*

HILEN A city of Judah. Assigned to the priests, 1 Chron 6:58, 59. Called *Holon,* Josh 15: 48–62; 21:9–16.

HILKIAH 1. Father of Hezekiah's prime minister, 2 Kgs 18:37; Isa 22:20; 36:3, 22.

2. High priest, 2 Kgs 22:3, 4, 8–10, 12–14; 23:4, 24; 1 Chron 6:4–15; 9:10, 11; 2 Chron 34:9, 14, 15, 16, 18, 20; Ezra 7:1–5.

3. Name of two Levites, 1 Chron 6:44–47; 26:11.

4. Two priests, Neh 8:1–5; 12:1–7, 12–21.

5. Father of Gemariah, Jer 29:3.

6. Father of Jeremiah, Jer 1:1.

HILLEL Father of Abdon, Judg 12:13.

HILLS Perpetual, Gen 49:26; Hab 3:6.

HIND See *Deer.*

HINNOM A valley south of Jerusalem, Josh 15:8; 18:16; Neh 11:30. Containing Topheth, where children were burned in sacrifice to pagan gods, Jer 7:31; destroyed by Josiah, 2 Kgs 23:10. The name Hinnom appears in the New Testament in the word derived from it, Gehenna, rendered hell in the *Living Bible.*

See *Gehenna; Topheth.*

HIRAH An Adullamite, Gen 38:1, 12.

HIRAM 1. King of Tyre. Builds a house for David, 2 Sam 5:11; 1 Chron 14:1; 2 Chron 2:3. Aids Solomon in building the temple, 1 Kgs 5; 2 Chron 2:3–16. Dissatisfied with cities given by Solomon, 1 Kgs 9:11–13. Makes presents of gold and sailors to Solomon, 1 Kgs 9:14, 26–28; 10:11.

2. Called also *Huramabi.* An artificer sent by King Hiram to execute the artistic work of the interior of the temple, 1 Kgs 7:13–46; 2 Chron 2:13; 4:11–16.

HISTORY Job 8:8–10.

See *Books;* books of Genesis, Exodus, Numbers, Deuteronomy, Joshua, Judges, Ruth, Samuel, Kings, Chronicles, Ezra, Nehemiah, Esther; *Israel, History of; Jesus, Life of.*

HIRE Law concerning hired property, Ex 22: 14, 15.

See *Wages; Employer; Master; Servant.*

HITTITES Or *Hethites,* a tribe of Canaanites. Children of Heth, Gen 10:15–19; 23:3. Sell a burying-ground to Abraham, Gen 23. Esau intermarries with, Gen 26:34; 36:2, 3. Home of, Gen 23: 17–20; Num 13:29; Josh 1:4; Judg 1:26. Their land given to the Israelites, Ex 3:8; Deut 7:1; Josh 1:4. Conquered by Joshua, Josh 9:1, 2; chapters 10–12; 24:11. Intermarry with Israelites, Judg 3:5–7; Ezra 9:1. Solomon intermarries with, 1 Kgs 11:1; Neh 13: 26. Slaves under Solomon, 1 Kgs 9:20, 21. Retain their own kings, 1 Kgs 10:29; 2 Chron 1:17. Officers from, in David's army, 1 Sam 26:5–7; 2 Sam 11:6; 23:24–39.

HIVITES A tribe of Canaanites, Gen 10:15–19; 1 Chron 1:15. Shechemites and Gibeonites were families of, Gen 34:2; Josh 9:7. Esau intermarries with, Gen 36:2, 3. Home of, Josh 11:1–3; Judg 3:1–3; 2 Sam 24:7. Their land given to the Israelites, Ex 23:23, 28; Deut 20:17; Judg 3:5. Conquered by Joshua, Josh 9:1; 12:8–24; 24:11. Slaves under Solomon, 1 Kgs 9:20, 21; 2 Chron 8:7, 8.

HIZKI A Benjaminite, 1 Chron 8:17, 18.

HIZKIAH Son of Neariah, 1 Chron 3:23.

HOBAB Son of Reuel, Num 10:29; Judg 4:11.

HOBAH A place north of Damascus, Gen 14: 15.

HOD A son of Zophah, 1 Chron 7:36, 37.

HODAVIAH 1. Son of Eli-o-enai, 1 Chron 3: 24.

2. A chief of the half-tribe of Manasseh, whose inheritance was east of the Jordan, 1 Chron 5:24.

3. A Benjaminite, 1 Chron 9:7, 8.

4. A Levite, Ezra 2:40–42.

HODESH Wife of Shaharaim, 1 Chron 8:8–10.

HODEVAH A Levite, Neh 7:43–45.

HODIAH 1. A Judahite, 1 Chron 4:19.

2. A Levite, Neh 8:7, 8; 9:5.

3. Two Levites who signed the covenant, Neh 10: 9–13.

4. An Israelitish leader, Neh 10:14–27.

HOGLAH A daughter of Zelophehad, Num 26:28–37; 27:1, 2; 36:11, 12; Josh 17:3.

HOGS See *Swine.*

HOHAM King of Hebron, Josh 10:3.

HOLIDAY Contracted from Holy Day (Old English). For rest, see *Sabbath.* One year in seven, Lev 25:1–7.

See *Jubilee.*

HOLINESS Gen 17:1. When Abram was ninety-nine years old, God appeared to him and told him, "I am the Almighty; obey me and live as you should."

Gen 35:2. So Jacob instructed all those in his household to destroy the idols they had brought with them, and to wash themselves and to put on fresh clothing.

Ex 19:6. And you shall be a kingdom of priests to God, a holy nation.

Ex 22:31. And since you yourselves are holy—my special people—do not eat any animal that has been attacked and killed by a wild animal. Leave its carcass for the dogs to eat.

Lev 10:8, 9. Now the Lord instructed Aaron, "Never drink wine or strong drink when you go into the Tabernacle, lest you die; and this rule applies to your sons and to all your descendants from generation to generation. [10]Your duties will be to arbitrate for the people, to teach them the difference between what is holy and what is ordinary, what is pure and what is impure."

Lev 11:44. "I am the Lord your God. Keep yourselves pure concerning these things, and be holy, for I am holy; therefore do not defile yourselves by touching any of these things that crawl upon the earth. [45]For I am the Lord who brought you out of the land of Egypt to be your God. You must therefore be holy, for I am holy." (Lev 19:1, 2; 20:7.) [47]These are the distinctions between what is ceremonially clean and may be eaten, and what is ceremonially defiled and may not be eaten, among all animal life upon the earth.

Lev 20:26. You shall be holy to me, for I the Lord am holy, and I have set you apart from all other peoples, to be mine.

Deut 13:17. Keep none of the booty! Then the Lord will turn from his fierce anger and be merciful to you, and have compassion upon you, and make you a great nation just as he promised your ancestors.

Deut 14:2. You belong exclusively to the Lord your God, and he has chosen you to be his own possession, more so than any other nation on the face of the earth. Deut 26:19.

Deut 18:13. You must walk blamelessly before the Lord your God.

Deut 28:9. He will change you into a holy people dedicated to himself; this he has promised to do if you will only obey him and walk in his ways.

Deut 30:2. If at that time you want to return to the Lord your God, and you and your children have begun wholeheartedly to obey all of the commandments I have given you today. [10]He will rejoice if you but obey the commandments written in this book of the law, and if you turn to the Lord your God with all your hearts and souls.

Josh 7:12. That is why the people of Israel are being defeated. That is why your men are running from their enemies—for they are cursed. I will not stay with you any longer unless you completely rid yourselves of this sin. [13]Get up! Tell the people, "Each of you must undergo purification rites in preparation for tomorrow, for the Lord your God of Israel says that someone has stolen from him, and you cannot defeat your enemies until you deal with this sin."

Job 28:28. And this is what he says to all mankind: "Look, to fear the Lord is true wisdom; to forsake evil is real understanding."

Job 36:21. Turn back from evil, for it was to prevent you from getting into a life of evil that God sent this suffering.

Ps 4:4. Stand before the Lord in awe, and do not sin against him. Lie quietly upon your bed in silent meditation.

Ps 24:3. Who may climb the mountain of the Lord and enter where he lives? Who may stand before the Lord? [4]Only those with pure hands and hearts, who do not practice dishonesty and lying. [5]They will receive God's own goodness as their blessing from him, planted in their lives by God himself, their Savior. Ps 15:1–5.

Ps 32:2. What relief for those who have confessed their sins and God has cleared their record.

Ps 37:27. So if you want an eternal home, leave your evil, lowdown ways and live good lives.

Ps 73:1. How good God is to Israel—to those whose hearts are pure.

Ps 94:15. Judgment will again be just and all the upright will rejoice.

Ps 97:10. The Lord loves those who hate evil; he protects the lives of his people, and rescues them from the wicked.

Ps 119:1. Happy are all who perfectly follow the laws of God. [2]Happy are all who search for God, and always do his will, [3]rejecting compromise with evil, and walking only in his paths.

Prov 11:23. The good man can look forward to happiness, while the wicked can expect only wrath.

Prov 12:5. A good man's mind is filled with honest thoughts; an evil man's mind is crammed with lies.

Prov 16:17. The path of the godly leads away from evil; he who follows that path is safe.

Prov 21:8. A man is known by his actions. An evil man lives an evil life; a good man lives a godly life. [15]A good man loves justice, but it is a calamity to evil-doers. [29]An evil man is stubborn, but a godly man will reconsider.

Prov 22:1. If you must choose, take a good name rather than great riches; for to be held in loving esteem is better than silver and gold. Eccl 7:1.

Isa 4:2, 3. Those whose names are written down to escape the destruction of Jerusalem will be washed and rinsed of all their moral filth by the horrors and the fire. They will be God's holy people.

Isa 26:2. Open the gates to everyone, for all may enter in who love the Lord. [8]O Lord, we love to do your will! Our hearts' desire is to glorify your name. [9]All night long I search for you; earnestly I seek for God; for only when you come in judgment on the earth to punish it will people turn away from wickedness and do what is right.

Isa 35:8. And a main road will go through that once-deserted land; it will be named "The Holy Highway." No evilhearted men may walk upon it. God will walk there with you; even the most stupid cannot miss the way.

Isa 51:7. Listen to me, you who know the right from wrong and cherish my laws in your hearts: don't be afraid of people's scorn or their slanderous talk.

Isa 52:1. Wake up, wake up, Jerusalem, and clothe yourselves with strength (from God). Put on your beautiful clothes, O Zion, Holy City; for sinners—those who turn from God—will no longer enter your gates. [11]Go now, leave your bonds and slavery. Put Babylon and all it represents far behind you—it is unclean to you. You are the holy people of the Lord; purify yourselves, all you who carry home the vessels of the Lord.

Isa 57:2. For the godly who die shall rest in peace.

Isa 60:1. Arise, my people! Let your light shine for all the nations to see! For the glory of the Lord is streaming from you. [21]All your people will be good. They will possess their land forever, for I will plant them there with my own hands; this will bring me glory.

Isa 61:3. To all who mourn in Israel he will give: beauty for ashes; joy instead of mourning; praise instead of heaviness. For God has planted them like strong and graceful oaks for his own glory. [9]Their descendants shall be known and honored among the nations; all shall realize that they are a people God has blessed. [10]Let me tell you how happy God has made me! For he has clothed me with garments of salvation and draped about me the robe of righteousness. I am like a bridegroom in his wedding suit or a bride with her jewels. [11]The Lord will show the nations of the world his justice; all will praise him. His righteousness shall be like a budding tree, or like a garden in early spring, full of young plants springing up everywhere.

Mic 6:8. No, he has told you what he wants, and this is all it is: *to be fair and just and merciful, and to walk humbly with your God.*

Zeph 2:3. Beg him to save you, all who are humble—all who have tried to obey. Walk humbly and do what is right; perhaps even yet the Lord will protect you from his wrath in that day of doom.

Zech 8:3. Now I am going to return to my land and I, myself, will live within Jerusalem, and Jerusalem shall be called "The Faithful City," and "The Holy Mountain," and "The Mountain of the Lord of Hosts."

Zech 14:20. In that day the bells on the horses will have written on them, "These Are Holy Property"; and the trash cans in the Temple of the Lord will be as sacred as the bowls beside the altar. [21]In fact, every container in Jerusalem and Judah shall be sacred to the Lord of Hosts; all who come to worship may use any of them free of charge to boil their sacrifices in; there will be no more grasping traders in the Temple of the Lord of Hosts!

Mt 5:6. Happy are those who long to be just and good, for they shall be completely satisfied. [8]Happy are those whose hearts are pure, for they shall see God. [29]So if your eye—even if it is your best eye!—causes you to lust, gouge it out and throw it away. Better for part of you to be destroyed than for all of you to be cast into hell. [30]And if your hand—even your right hand—causes you to sin, cut it off and throw it away. Better that than find yourself in hell. [48]But you are to be perfect, even as your Father in heaven is perfect.

Mt 12:33. A tree is identified by its fruit. A tree from a select variety produces good fruit; poor varieties don't.

Mk 9:50. Good salt is worthless if it loses its saltiness; it can't season anything. So don't lose your flavor! Live in peace with each other.

Lk 1:74. And by granting us the privilege of serving God fearlessly, freed from our enemies, [75]and by making us holy and acceptable, ready to stand in his presence forever.

Lk 6:45. A good man produces good deeds from a good heart. And an evil man produces evil deeds from his hidden wickedness. Whatever is in the heart overflows into speech.

Jn 1:47. As they approached, Jesus said, "Here comes an honest man—a true son of Israel."

Jn 4:14. "But the water I give them," he said, "becomes a perpetual spring within them, watering them forever with eternal life."

Jn 5:14. But afterwards Jesus found him in the Temple and told him, "Now you are well; don't sin as you did before, or something even worse may happen to you."

Jn 6:35. Jesus replied, "I am the Bread of Life. No one coming to me will ever be hungry again. Those believing in me will never thirst."

Jn 15:19. The world would love you if you belonged to it; but you don't—for I chose you to come out of the world, and so it hates you.

Jn 17:23. I in them and you in me, all being perfected into one—so that the world will know you sent me and will understand that you love them as much as you love me.

Acts 24:16. Because of this I try with all my strength to always maintain a clear conscience before God and man.

Rom 2:28. For you are not real Jews just because you were born of Jewish parents or because you have gone through the Jewish initiation ceremony of circumcision. [29]No, a real Jew is anyone whose heart is right with God. For God is not looking for those who cut their bodies in actual body circumcision, but he is looking for those with changed hearts and minds. Whoever has that kind of change in his life will get his praise from God, even if not from you.

Rom 6:1. Well then, shall we keep on sinning so that God can keep on showing us more and more kindness and forgiveness? [2, 3]Of course not! Should we keep on sinning when we don't have to? For sin's power over us was broken when we became Christians and were baptized to become a part of Jesus Christ; through his death the power of your sinful nature was shattered. [4]Your old sin-loving nature was buried with him by baptism when he died, and when God the Father, with glorious power, brought him back to life again, you were given his wonderful new life to enjoy. [5]For you have become a part of him, and so you died with him, so to speak, when he died; and now you share his new life, and shall rise as he did. [6]Your old evil desires were nailed to the cross with him; that part of you that loves to sin was crushed and fatally wounded, so that your sin-loving body is no longer under sin's control, no longer needs to be a slave to sin; [7]for when you are deadened to sin you are freed from all its allure and its power over you. [8]And since your old sin-loving nature "died" with Christ, we know that you will share his new life. [9]Christ rose from the dead and will never die again. Death no longer has any power over him. [10]He died once for all to end sin's power, but now he lives forever in unbroken fellowship with God. [11]So look upon your old sin nature as dead and unresponsive to sin, and instead be alive to God, alert to him, through Jesus Christ our Lord. [12]Do not let sin control your puny body any longer; do not give in to its sinful desires. [13]Do not let any part of your bodies become tools of wickedness, to be used for sinning; but give yourselves completely to God—every part of you—for you are back from death and you want to be tools in the hands of God, to be used for his good purposes. [14]Sin need never again be your master, for now you are no longer tied to the law where sin enslaves you, but you are free under God's favor and mercy. [15]Does this mean that now we can go ahead and sin and not worry about it? (For our salvation does not depend on keeping the law, but on receiving God's grace!) Of course not! [16]Don't you realize that you can choose your own master? You can choose sin (with death) or else obedience (with acquittal). The one to whom you offer yourself—he will take you and be your master and you will be his slave. [17]Thank God that though you once chose to be slaves of sin, now you have obeyed with all your heart the teaching to which God has committed you. [18]And now you are free from your old master, sin; and you have become slaves to your new master, righteousness. [19]I speak this way, using the illustration of slaves and masters, because it is easy to understand: just as you used to be slaves to all kinds of sin, so now you must let yourselves be slaves to all that is right and holy. [20]In those days when you were slaves of sin you didn't bother much with goodness. [21]And what was the result? Evidently not good, since you are ashamed now even to think about those things you used to do, for all of them end in eternal doom. [22]And now you are free from the power of sin and are slaves of God, and his benefits to you include holiness and everlasting life. [23]For the wages of sin is death, but the free gift of God is eternal life through Jesus Christ our Lord.

Rom 7:4. Your "husband," your master, used to be the Jewish law; but you "died," as it were, with Christ on the cross; and since you are "dead," you are no longer "married to the law," and it has no more control over you. Then you came back to life again when Christ did, and are a new person. And now you are "married," so to speak, to the one who rose from the dead, so that you can produce good fruit, that is, good deeds for God. [6]But now you need no longer worry about the Jewish laws and customs because you "died" while in their captivity, and now you can really serve God; not in the old way, mechanically obeying a set of rules, but in the new way, (with all of your hearts and minds).

Rom 8:1. So there is now no condemnation awaiting those who belong to Christ Jesus. [4]So now we can obey God's laws if we follow after the Holy Spirit and no longer obey the old evil nature within us. [12]So, dear brothers, you have no obligations whatever to your old sinful nature to do what it begs you to do.

Rom 11:16. And since Abraham and the prophets are God's people, their children will be too. For if the roots of the tree are holy, the branches will be too.

Rom 12:1. And so, dear brothers, I plead with you to give your bodies to God. Let them be a living sacrifice, holy—the kind he can accept. When you think of what he has done for you, is this too much to ask? [2]Don't copy the behavior and customs of this world, but be a new and different person with a fresh newness in all you do and think. Then you will learn from your own experience how his ways will really satisfy you. [9]Don't just pretend that you love others: really love them. Hate what is wrong. Stand on the side of the good.

Rom 13:12, 13. The night is far gone, the day of his return will soon be here. So quit the evil deeds of darkness and put on the armor of right living, as we who live in the daylight should! Be decent and true in everything you do so that all can approve your behavior. Don't spend your time in wild parties and getting drunk or in adultery and lust, or fighting, or jealousy. [14]But ask the Lord Jesus Christ to help you live as you should, and don't make plans to enjoy evil.

Rom 14:17. For, after all, the important thing for us as Christians is not what we eat or drink but stirring up goodness and peace and joy from the Holy Spirit.

Rom 16:19. But everyone knows that you stand loyal and true. This makes me very happy. I want you always to remain very clear about what is right, and to stay innocent of any wrong.

1 Cor 3:16. Don't you realize that all of you together are the house of God, and that the Spirit of God lives among you in his house? [17]If anyone defiles and spoils God's home, God will destroy

him. For God's home is holy and clean, and you are that home.

1 Cor 5:7. Remove this evil cancer—this wicked person—from among you, so that you can stay pure. Christ, God's Lamb, has been slain for us.

1 Cor 6:12. I can do anything I want to if Christ has not said no, but some of these things aren't good for me. Even if I am allowed to do them, I'll refuse to if I think they might get such a grip on me that I can't easily stop when I want to. [13]For instance, take the matter of eating. God has given us an appetite for food and stomachs to digest it. But that doesn't mean we should eat more than we need. Don't think of eating as important, because some day God will do away with both stomachs and food. But sexual sin is never right: our bodies were not made for that, but for the Lord, and the Lord wants to fill our bodies with himself. [19]Haven't you yet learned that your body is the home of the Holy Spirit God gave you, and that he lives within you? Your own body does not belong to you. [20]For God has bought you with a great price. So use every part of your body to give glory back to God, because he owns it.

1 Cor 7:23. You have been bought and paid for by Christ, so you belong to him—be free now from all these earthly prides and fears.

1 Cor 8:12. And it is a sin against Christ to sin against your brother by encouraging him to do something he thinks is wrong.

1 Cor 10:21. You cannot drink from the cup at the Lord's Table and at Satan's table, too. You cannot eat bread both at the Lord's Table and at Satan's table. [31]Well, I'll tell you why. It is because you must do everything for the glory of God, even your eating and drinking. [32]So don't be a stumbling block to anyone, whether they are Jews or Gentiles or Christians.

1 Cor 12:31. No, but try your best to have the more important of these gifts.

1 Cor 15:34. Get some sense and quit your sinning. For to your shame I say it, some of you are not even Christians at all and have never really known God.

2 Cor 6:14. Don't be teamed with those who do not love the Lord, for what do the people of God have in common with the people of sin? How can light live with darkness? [15]And what harmony can there be between Christ and the devil? How can a Christian be a partner with one who doesn't believe? [16]And what union can there be between God's temple and idols? For you are God's temple, the home of the living God, and God has said of you, "I will live in them and walk among them, and I will be their God and they shall be my people." [17]That is why the Lord has said, "Leave them; separate yourselves from them; don't touch their filthy things, and I will welcome you."

2 Cor 7:1. Having such great promises as these, dear friends, let us turn away from everything wrong, whether of body or spirit, and purify ourselves, living in the wholesome fear of God, giving ourselves to him alone.

2 Cor 10:3. It is true that I am an ordinary, weak human being, but I don't use human plans and methods to win my battles. [5]These weapons can break down every proud argument against God and every wall that can be built to keep men from finding him. With these weapons I can capture rebels and bring them back to God, and change them into men whose hearts' desire is obedience to Christ.

2 Cor 11:2. I am anxious for you with the deep concern of God himself—anxious that your love should be for Christ alone, just as a pure maiden saves her love for one man only, for the one who will be her husband.

2 Cor 13:7. I pray that you will live good lives, not because that will be a feather in our caps, proving that what we teach is right; no, for we want you to do right even if we ourselves are despised. [8]Our responsibility is to encourage the right at all times, not to hope for evil.

Gal 2:17. But what if we trust Christ to save us and then find that we are wrong, and that we cannot be saved without being circumcised and obeying all the other Jewish laws? Wouldn't we need to say that faith in Christ had ruined us? God forbid that anyone should dare to think such things about our Lord.

Gal 5:22. But when the Holy Spirit controls our lives he will produce this kind of fruit in us: love, joy, peace, patience, kindness, goodness, faithfulness, [23]gentleness and self-control; and here there is no conflict with Jewish laws. [24]Those who belong to Christ have nailed their natural evil desires to his cross and crucified them there. [25]If we are living now by the Holy Spirit's power, let us follow the Holy Spirit's leading in every part of our lives.

Gal 6:15. It doesn't make any difference now whether we have been circumcised or not; what counts is whether we really have been changed into new and different people.

Eph 1:4. Long ago, even before he made the world, God chose us to be his very own, through what Christ would do for us; he decided then to make us holy in his eyes, without a single fault—we who stand before him covered with his love. [13]And because of what Christ did, all you others too, who heard the Good News about how to be saved, and trusted Christ, were marked as belonging to Christ by the Holy Spirit, who long ago had been promised to all of us Christians. [14]His presence within us is God's guarantee that he really will give us all that he promised; and the Spirit's seal upon us means that God has already purchased us and that he guarantees to bring us to himself. This is just one more reason for us to praise our glorious God.

Eph 2:21. We who believe are carefully joined together with Christ as parts of a beautiful, constantly growing temple for God. [22]And you also are joined with him and with each other by the Spirit, and are part of this dwelling place of God.

Eph 4:20. But that isn't the way Christ taught you! [21]If you have really heard his voice and learned from him the truths concerning himself, [22]then throw off your old evil nature—the old you that was a partner in your evil ways—rotten through and through, full of lust and sham. [23]Now your attitudes and thoughts must all be constantly changing for the better. [24]Yes, you must be a new and different person, holy and good. Clothe yourself with this new nature.

Eph 5:1. Follow God's example in everything you do just as a much loved child imitates his father. [3]Let there be no sex sin, impurity or greed among you. Let no one be able to accuse you of any such things. [8]For though once your heart was full of darkness, now it is full of light from the Lord, and your behavior should show it! [9]Because of this light within you, you should do only what is good and right and true. [10]Learn as you go along what pleases the Lord. [11]Take no part in the worthless pleasures of evil and darkness, but instead, rebuke and expose them.

Phil 1:10. For I want you always to see clearly the difference between right and wrong, and to be inwardly clean, no one being able to criticize you from now until our Lord returns. [11]May you always be doing those good, kind things which show that you are a child of God, for this will bring much praise and glory to the Lord.

Phil 2:15. So that no one can speak a word of blame against you. You are to live clean, innocent lives as children of God in a dark world full of people who are crooked and stubborn. Shine out among them like beacon lights.

Phil 4:8. And now, brothers, as I close this letter let me say this one more thing: Fix your thoughts on what is true and good and right. Think about things that are pure and lovely, and dwell on the fine, good things in others. Think about all you can praise God for and be glad about.

Col 1:22. He has done this through the death on the cross of his own human body, and now as a result Christ has brought you into the very presence of God, and you are standing there before him with nothing left against you—nothing left that he could even chide you for.

Col 3:5. Away then with sinful, earthly things; deaden the evil desires lurking within you; having nothing to do with sexual sin, impurity, lust and shameful desires; don't worship the good things of life, for that is idolatry. [6]God's terrible anger is upon those who do such things. [7]You used to do them when your life was still part of this world; [8]but now is the time to cast off and throw away all these rotten garments of anger, hatred, cursing, and dirty language. [9]Don't tell lies to each other; it was your old life with all its wickedness that did that sort of thing; now it is dead and gone. [10]You are living a brand new kind of life that is continually learning more and more of what is right, and trying constantly to be more and more like Christ who created this new life within you. [12]Since you have been chosen by God who has given you this new kind of life, and because of his deep love and concern for you, you should practice tenderhearted mercy and kindness to others. Don't worry about making a good impression on them but be ready to suffer quietly and patiently. [13]Be gentle and ready to forgive; never hold grudges. Remember, the Lord forgave you, so you must forgive others. [14]Most of all, let love guide your life, for then the whole church will stay together in perfect harmony. [15]Let the peace of heart which comes from Christ be always present in your hearts and lives, for this is your responsibility and privilege as members of his body. And always be thankful.

1 Thess 2:12. That your daily lives should not embarrass God, but bring joy to him who invited you into his kingdom to share his glory.

1 Thess 3:13. This will result in your hearts being made strong, sinless and holy by God our Father, so that you may stand before him guiltless on the day when our Lord Jesus Christ returns with all those who belong to him.

1 Thess 4:3, 4. For God wants you to be holy and pure, and to keep clear of all sexual sin so that each of you will marry in holiness and honor. [7]For God has not called us to be dirty-minded and full of lust, but to be holy and clean.

1 Thess 5:5. For you are all children of the light and of the day, and do not belong to darkness and night. [22]Keep away from every kind of evil. [23]May the God of peace himself make you entirely pure and devoted to God; and may your spirit and soul and body be kept strong and blameless until that day when our Lord Jesus Christ comes back again.

2 Thess 2:13. But we must forever give thanks to God for you, our brothers loved by the Lord, because God chose from the very first to give you salvation, cleansing you by the work of the Holy Spirit and by your trusting in the Truth.

1 Tim 1:5. What I am eager for is that all the Christians there will be filled with love that comes from pure hearts, and that their minds will be clean and their faith strong.

1 Tim 4:8. Bodily exercise is all right, but spiritual exercise is much more important and is a tonic for all you do. So exercise yourself spiritually and practice being a better Christian, because that will help you not only now in this life, but in the next life too. [12]Don't let anyone think little of you because you are young. Be their ideal; let them follow the way you teach and live; be a pattern for them in your love, your faith, and your clean thoughts.

1 Tim 5:22. Never be in a hurry about choosing a pastor; you may overlook his sins and it will look as if you approve of them. Be sure that you yourself stay away from all sin.

1 Tim 6:6. Do you want to be truly rich? You already are if you are happy and good. [11]Oh, Timothy, you are God's man. Run from all these evil things and work instead at what is right and good, learning to trust him and love others, and to be patient and gentle. [12]Fight on for God. Hold tightly to the eternal life which God has given you, and which you have confessed with such a ringing confession before many witnesses.

2 Tim 2:19. But God's truth stands firm like a great rock, and nothing can shake it. It is a foundation stone with these words written on it: "the Lord knows those who are really his," and "A person who calls himself a Christian should not be doing things that are wrong." [21]If you stay away from sin you will be like one of these dishes made of purest gold—the very best in the house—so that Christ himself can use you for his highest purposes. [22]Run from anything that gives you the evil thoughts that young men often have, but stay close to anything that makes you want to do right. Have faith and love, and enjoy the companionship of those who love the Lord and have pure hearts. *vs.* 16, 17.

2 Tim 3:17. It is God's way of making us well prepared at every point, fully equipped to do good to everyone.

Tit 1:15. A person who is pure of heart sees goodness and purity in everything.

Tit 2:9. Urge slaves to [10]. . . show themselves to be entirely trustworthy. In this way they will make people want to believe in our Savior and God. [12]And along with this gift comes the realization that God wants us to turn from godless living and sinful pleasures and to live good, God-fearing lives day after day.

Heb 4:3. For only we who believe God can enter into his place of rest. He has said, "I have sworn in my anger that those who don't believe me will never get in," even though he has been ready and waiting for them since the world began. [9]So there is a full complete rest *still waiting* for the people of God.

Heb 10:22. Let us go right in, to God himself, with true hearts fully trusting him to receive us, because we have been sprinkled with Christ's blood to make us clean, and because our bodies have been washed with pure water.

Heb 12:1. Since we have such a huge crowd of men of faith watching us from the grandstands, let us strip off anything that slows us down or holds us back, and especially those sins that wrap themselves so tightly around our feet and trip us up; and let us run with patience the particular race that God has set before us. [14]Try to stay out of all quarrels and seek to live a clean and holy life, for one who is not holy will not see the Lord. [15]Look after each other so that not one of you will fail to find God's best blessings. Watch out that no bitterness takes root among you, for as it springs up it causes deep trouble, hurting many in their spiritual lives. *v.* 10.

Heb 13:9. So do not be attracted by strange, new ideas. Your spiritual strength comes as a gift from God, not from ceremonial rules about eating certain foods—a method which, by the way, hasn't helped those who have tried it!

Jas 1:21. So get rid of all that is wrong in your life, both inside and outside, and humbly be glad for the wonderful message we have received, for it is able to save our souls as it takes hold of our hearts. [27]The Christian who is pure and without fault, from God the Father's point of view, is the one who takes care of orphans and widows, and who remains true to the Lord—not soiled and dirtied by his contacts with the world.

Jas 3:17. But the wisdom that comes from heaven is first of all pure and full of quiet gentleness. Then it is peace-loving and courteous. It allows discussion and is willing to yield to others; it is full of mercy and good deeds. It is wholehearted and straightforward and sincere.

Jas 4:4. You are like an unfaithful wife who loves her husband's enemies. Don't you realize that making friends with God's enemies—the evil pleasures of this world—makes you an enemy of God? I say it again, that if your aim is to enjoy the evil pleasure of the unsaved world, you cannot also be a friend of God.

1 Pet 1:14. Obey God because you are his children; don't slip back into your old ways—doing evil because you knew no better. [15]But be holy now in everything you do, just as the Lord is holy, who invited you to be his child. [16]He himself has said, "You must be holy, for I am holy."

1 Pet 2:1. So get rid of your feelings of hatred. Don't just pretend to be good! Be done with dishonesty and jealousy and talking about others behind their backs. [5]And now you have become living building-stones for God's use in building his house. What's more, you are his holy priests; so come to him—(you who are acceptable to him because of Jesus Christ)—and offer to God those things that please him. [9]But you are not like that, for you have been chosen by God himself—you are priests of the King, you are holy and pure, you are God's very own—all this so that you may show to others how God called you out of the darkness into his wonderful light. [11]Dear brothers, you are only visitors here. Since your real home is in heaven I beg you to keep away from the evil pleasures of this world; they are not for you, for they fight against your very souls. [12]Be careful how you behave among your unsaved neighbors; for then, even if they are suspicious of you and talk against you, they will end up praising God for your good works when Christ returns. [24]He personally carried the load of our sins in his own body when he died on the cross, so that we can be finished with sin and live a good life from now on. For his wounds have healed ours!

1 Pet 3:11. Turn away from evil and do good. Try to live in peace even if you must run after it to catch and hold it! Ps 34:14.

1 Pet 4:1. Since Christ suffered and underwent pain, you must have the same attitude he did; you must be ready to suffer, too. For remember, when your body suffers, sin loses its power, [2]and you won't be spending the rest of your life chasing after evil desires, but will be anxious to do the will of God. [6]That is why the Good News was preached even to those who were dead—killed by the flood —so that although their bodies were punished with death, they could still live in their spirits as God lives. [7]The end of the world is coming soon. Therefore be earnest, thoughtful men of prayer.

2 Pet 1:5. But to obtain these gifts, you need more than faith: you must also work hard to be good, and even that is not enough. For then you must learn to know God better and discover what he wants you to do. 6Next, learn to put aside your own desires so that you will become patient and godly, gladly letting God have his way with you. 7This will make possible the next step, which is for you to enjoy other people and to like them, and finally you grow to love them deeply. 8The more you go on in this way, the more you will grow strong spiritually and become fruitful and useful to our Lord Jesus Christ. *vs.* 2–4.

2 Pet 3:11. And so since everything around us is going to melt away, what holy, godly lives we should be living! 12You should look forward to that day and hurry it along—the day when God will set the heavens on fire, and the heavenly bodies will melt and disappear in flames. 14Dear friends, while you are waiting for these things to happen and for him to come, try hard to live without sinning; and be at peace with everyone so that he will be pleased with you when he returns.

1 Jn 1:6. So if we say we are his friends, but go on living in spiritual darkness and sin, we are lying. 7But if we are living in the light of God's presence, just as Christ does, then we have wonderful fellowship and joy with each other, and the blood of Jesus his Son cleanses us from every sin.

1 Jn 2:1. My little children, I am telling you this so that you will stay away from sin. But if you sin, there is someone to plead for you before the Father. His name is Jesus Christ, the one who is all that is good and who pleases God completely. 5But those who do what Christ tells them to will learn to love God more and more. That is the way to know whether or not you are a Christian. 29Since we know that God is always good and does only right, we may rightly assume that all those who do right are his children.

1 Jn 3:3. And everyone who really believes this will try to stay pure because Christ is pure. 6So if we stay close to him, obedient to him, we won't be sinning either; but as for those who keep on sinning, they should realize this: They sin because they have never really known him or become his. 9The person who has been born into God's family does not make a practice of sinning, because now God's life is in him; so he can't keep on sinning, for this new life has been born into him and controls him—he has been *born again.* 10So now we can tell who is a child of God and who belongs to Satan. Whoever is living a life of sin and doesn't love his brother shows that he is not in God's family. *vs.* 7, 8.

1 Jn 5:4. For every child of God can obey him, defeating sin and evil pleasure by trusting Christ to help him. 5But who could possibly fight and win this battle except by believing that Jesus is truly the Son of God? 18No one who has become part of God's family makes a practice of sinning, for Christ, God's Son, holds him securely and the devil cannot get his hands on him. 21Dear children, keep away from anything that might take God's place in your hearts.

2 Jn 1:4. How happy I am to find some of your children here, and to see that they are living as they should, following the Truth, obeying God's command.

3 Jn 1:11. Dear friend, don't let this bad example influence you. Follow only what is good. Remember that those who do what is right prove that they are God's children; and those who continue in evil prove that they are far from God.

Rev 14:4. For they are spiritually undefiled, pure as virgins, following the Lamb wherever he goes. They have been purchased from among the men on the earth as a consecrated offering to God and the Lamb. 5No falsehood can be charged against them; they are blameless.

Rev 18:4. Then I heard another voice calling from heaven, "Come away from her, my people; do not take part in her sins, or you will be punished with her."

Rev 19:8. She is permitted to wear the cleanest and whitest and finest of linens. (Fine linen represents the good deeds done by the people of God.)

Rev 22:11. And when that time comes, all doing wrong will do it more and more; the vile will become more vile; good men will be better; those who are holy will continue on to greater holiness.

See *Desire, Spiritual; God, Holiness of; Righteousness; Sanctification; Sinlessness.*

HOLY BREAD See *Bread of the Presence.*

HOLY DAY See *Holiday.*

HOLY PLACE In the Tabernacle, Ex 28:29; in the Temple, 2 Chron 4:22; in the city of Jerusalem in prophecy, Mt 24:15; in the millenial temple, Ezk 42:14. See *Tabernacle; Temple.*

HOLY SPIRIT Gen 1:2. The earth was at first a shapeless, chaotic mass, with the Spirit of God brooding over the dark vapors.

Gen 6:3. Then Jehovah said, "My Spirit must not forever be disgraced in man, wholly evil as he is. I will give him 120 years to mend his ways."

Gen 41:38. As they discussed who should be appointed for the job, Pharaoh said, "Who could do it better than Joseph? For he is a man who is obviously filled with the Spirit of God."

Ex 31:3. And have filled him with the Spirit of God, giving him great wisdom, ability, and skill in constructing the Tabernacle and everything it contains.

Num 27:18. The Lord replied, "Go and get Joshua (son of Nun), who has the Spirit in him."

Neh 9:20. You sent your good Spirit to instruct them, and you did not stop giving them bread from heaven or water for their thirst.

Job 16:19. Yet even now the Witness to my innocence is there in heaven; my Advocate is there on high.

Job 32:8, 9. But it is not mere age that makes men wise. Rather, it is the spirit in a man, the breath of the Almighty which makes him intelligent.

Job 33:4. For the Spirit of God has made me, and the breath of the Almighty gives me life.

Ps 51:11. Don't toss me aside, banished forever from your presence. Don't take your Holy Spirit from me. [12]Restore to me again the joy of your salvation, and make me willing to obey you.

Ps 139:7. I can *never* be lost to your Spirit! I can *never* get away from my God!

Isa 11:2. And the Spirit of the Lord shall rest upon him, the Spirit of wisdom, understanding, counsel and might; the Spirit of knowledge and of the fear of the Lord.

Isa 30:21. And if you leave God's paths and go astray, you will hear a voice behind you say, "No, this is the way; walk here."

Isa 32:15. Until at last the Spirit is poured down on us from heaven. Then once again enormous crops will come.

Isa 40:13. Who can advise the Spirit of the Lord or be his teacher or give him counsel?

Isa 42:1. See my Servant, whom I uphold; my Chosen One, in whom I delight. I have put my Spirit upon him; he will reveal justice to the nations of the world.

Isa 44:3. For I will give you abundant water for your thirst and for your parched fields. And I will pour out my Spirit and my blessings on your children. [4]They shall thrive like watered grass, like willows on a river bank.

Isa 48:16. Come closer and listen. I have always told you plainly what would happen, so that you could clearly understand. And now the Lord God and his Spirit have sent me (with this message).

Isa 51:12. I, even I, am he who comforts you and gives you all this joy. So what right have you to fear mere mortal men, who wither like the grass and disappear?

Isa 59:19. Then at last they will reverence and glorify the name of God from west to east. For he will come like a flood-tide driven by Jehovah's breath. [21]"As for me, this is my promise to them," says the Lord: "My Holy Spirit shall not leave them, and they shall want the good and hate the wrong—they and their children and their children's children forever."

Isa 61:1. The Spirit of the Lord God is upon me, because the Lord has anointed me to bring good news to the suffering and afflicted. He has sent me to comfort the broken-hearted, to announce liberty to captives and to open the eyes of the blind. Lk 4: 18, 19.

Isa 63:10. But they rebelled against him and grieved his Holy Spirit. That is why he became their enemy and personally fought against them. [11]Then they remembered those days of old when Moses, God's servant, led his people out of Egypt and they cried out, "Where is the one who brought Israel through the sea, with Moses as their shepherd? Where is the God who sent his Holy Spirit to be among his people? [14]Like cattle grazing in the valleys, so the Spirit of the Lord gave them rest. Thus he gave himself a magnificent reputation."

Ezk 36:27. And I will put my Spirit within you so that you will obey my laws and do whatever I command.

Ezk 37:9. Then he told me to call to the wind and say: "The Lord God says: Come from the four winds, O Spirit, and breathe upon these slain bodies, that they may live again. [14]I will put my Spirit into you, and you shall live and return home again to your own land. Then you will know that I, the Lord, have done just what I promised you."

Ezk 39:29. And I will never hide my face from them again, for I will pour out my Spirit upon them, says the Lord God.

Joel 2:28. After I have poured out my rains again, I will pour out my Spirit upon all of you! Your sons and daughters will prophesy; your old men will dream dreams, and your young men see visions. [29]And I will pour out my Spirit even on your slaves, men and women alike. Prov 1:23.

Mic 2:7. Is that the right reply for you to make, O House of Jacob? Do you think the Spirit of the Lord likes to talk to you so roughly? No! His threats are for your good, to get you on the path again.

Mic 3:8. But as for me, I am filled with power, with the Spirit of the Lord, fearlessly announcing God's punishment on Israel for her sins.

Hag 2:5. For I promised when you left Egypt that my Spirit would remain among you; so don't be afraid.

Zech 4:6. Then he said, "This is God's message to Zerubbabel: 'Not by might, nor by power, but by my Spirit, says the Lord of Hosts—you will succeed because of my Spirit, though you are few and weak.' " *vs.* 1–7.

Zech 12:10. Then I will pour out the spirit of grace and prayer on all the people of Jerusalem, and they will look on him they pierced, and mourn for him as for an only son, and grieve bitterly for him as for an oldest child who died.

Mt 1:18. These are the facts concerning the birth of Jesus Christ: His mother, Mary, was engaged to be married to Joseph. But while she was still a virgin she became pregnant by the Holy Spirit. *v.* 20.

Mt 3:11. "With water I baptize those who repent of their sins; but someone else is coming, far greater than I am, so great that I am not worthy to carry his shoes! He shall baptize you with the Holy Spirit and with fire." [Jn 1:33; Acts 11:16.] [16]After his baptism, as soon as Jesus came up out of the water, the heavens were opened to him and he saw the Spirit of God coming down in the form of a dove. [17]And a voice from heaven said, "This is my beloved Son, and I am wonderfully pleased with him." Mk 1:10; Lk 3:22; Jn 1:32.

Mt 4:1. Then Jesus was led out into the wilderness by the Holy Spirit, to be tempted there by Satan.

Mt 10:20. For it won't be you doing the talking —it will be the Spirit of your heavenly Father speaking through you! Mk 13:11.

Mt 12:28. But if I am casting out demons by the Spirit of God, then the Kingdom of God has arrived among you.

Mt 28:19. Therefore go and make disciples in all

the nations, baptizing them into the name of the Father and of the Son and of the Holy Spirit.

Mk 12:36. For David himself said—and the Holy Spirit was speaking through him when he said it—"God said to my Lord, sit at my right hand until I make your enemies your footstool."

Mk 13:11. But when you are arrested and stand trial, don't worry about what to say in your defense. Just say what God tells you to. Then you will not be speaking, but the Holy Spirit will.

Lk 1:15. "For he will be one of the Lord's great men. He must never touch wine or hard liquor—and he will be filled with the Holy Spirit, even from before his birth!" [35]The angel replied, "The Holy Spirit shall come upon you, and the power of God shall overshadow you; so the baby born to you will be utterly holy—the Son of God." [67]Then his father Zacharias was filled with the Holy Spirit and gave this prophecy.

Lk 2:25. That day a man named Simeon, a Jerusalem resident, was in the Temple. He was a good man, very devout, filled with the Holy Spirit and constantly expecting the Messiah to come soon. [26]For the Holy Spirit had revealed to him that he would not die until he had seen him—God's anointed King. [27]The Holy Spirit had impelled him to go to the Temple that day; and so, when Mary and Joseph arrived to present the baby Jesus to the Lord in obedience to the law, [28]Simeon was there and took the child in his arms, praising God.

Lk 11:13. And if even sinful persons like yourselves give children what they need, don't you realize that your heavenly Father will do at least as much, and give the Holy Spirit to those who ask for him?

Lk 12:12. For the Holy Spirit will give you the right words even as you are standing there.

Lk 24:49. And now I send the Holy Spirit upon you, just as my Father promised, Don't begin telling others yet—stay here in the city until the Holy Spirit comes and fills you with power from heaven.

Jn 3:5. Jesus replied, "What I am telling you so earnestly is this: Unless one is born of water and the Spirit, he cannot enter the Kingdom of God. [6]Men can only reproduce human life, but the Holy Spirit gives new life from heaven." [34]"For this one —sent by God—speaks God's words, for God's Spirit is upon him without measure or limit."

Jn 4:14. "But the water I give them," he said, "becomes a perpetual spring within them, watering them forever with eternal life."

Jn 6:63. Only the Holy Spirit gives eternal life. Those born only once, with physical birth, will never receive this gift. But now I have told you how to get this true spiritual life.

Jn 7:38. "For the Scriptures declare that rivers of living water shall flow from the inmost being of anyone who believes in me." [39](He was speaking of the Holy Spirit, who would be given to everyone believing in him; but the Spirit had not yet been given, because Jesus had not yet returned to his glory in heaven.)

Jn 14:15, 16. If you love me, obey me; and I will ask the Father and he will give you another Comforter, and he will never leave you. [17]He is the Holy Spirit, the Spirit who leads into all truth. The world at large cannot receive him, for it isn't looking for him and doesn't recognize him. But you do, for he lives with you now and some day shall be in you. [26]But when the Father sends the Comforter instead of me—and by the Comforter I mean the Holy Spirit—he will teach you much, as well as remind you of everything I myself have told you.

Jn 15:26. But I will send you the Comforter—the Holy Spirit, the source of all truth. He will come to you from the Father and will tell you all about me.

Jn 16:7. But the fact of the matter is that it is best for you that I go away, for if I don't, the Comforter won't come. If I do, he will—for I will send him to you. [8]And when he has come he will convince the world of its sin, and of the availability of God's goodness, and of deliverance from judgment. [9]The world's sin is unbelief in me; [10]there is righteousness available because I go to the Father and you shall see me no more; [11]there is deliverance from judgment because the prince of this world has already been judged. [12]Oh, there is so much more I want to tell you, but you can't understand it now. [13]When the Holy Spirit, who is truth, comes, he shall guide you into all truth, for he will not be presenting his own ideas, but will be passing on to you what he has heard. He will tell you about the future. [14]He shall praise me and bring me great honor by showing you my glory.

Jn 20:22. Then he breathed on them and told them, "Receive the Holy Spirit."

Acts 1:2. And how he returned to heaven after giving his chosen apostles further instructions from the Holy Spirit. [5]"John baptized you with water," he reminded them, "but you shall be baptized with the Holy Spirit in just a few days. [8]But when the Holy Spirit has come upon you, you will receive power to testify about me with great effect, to the people in Jerusalem, throughout Judea, in Samaria, and to the ends of the earth, about my death and resurrection." [16]"Brothers, it was necessary for the Scriptures to come true concerning Judas, who betrayed Jesus by guiding the mob to him, for this was predicted long ago by the Holy Spirit, speaking through King David."

Acts 2:2. Suddenly there was a sound like the roaring of a mighty windstorm in the skies above them and it filled the house where they were meeting. [3]Then, what looked like flames or tongues of fire appeared and settled on their heads. [4]And everyone present was filled with the Holy Spirit and began speaking in languages they didn't know, for the Holy Spirit gave them this ability. [33]"And now he sits on the throne of highest honor in heaven, next to God. And just as promised, the Father gave him the authority to send the Holy Spirit—with the results you are seeing and hearing today." [38]And Peter replied, "Each one of you must turn from sin, return to God, and be baptized in the name of Jesus Christ for the forgiveness of your sins; then you also shall receive this gift, the Holy Spirit."

Acts 4:8. Then Peter, filled with the Holy Spirit, said to them, "Honorable leaders and elders of our nation." [31]After this prayer, the building where they were meeting shook and they were all filled with the Holy Spirit and boldly preached God's message.

Acts 5:3. But Peter said, "Ananias, Satan has filled your heart. When you claimed this was the full price, you were lying to the Holy Spirit. [4]The property was yours to sell or not, as you wished. And after selling it, it was yours to decide how much to give. How could you do a thing like this? You weren't lying to us, but to God." [9]And Peter said, "How could you and your husband even think of doing a thing like this—conspiring together to test the Spirit of God's ability to know what is going on? Just outside the door are the young men who buried your husband, and they will carry you out too."

32. And we are witnesses of these things, and so is the Holy Spirit, who is given by God to all who obey him.

Acts 6:5. This sounded reasonable to the whole assembly, and they elected the following: Stephen (a man unusually full of faith and the Holy Spirit).

Acts 7:51. You stiff-necked heathen! Must you forever resist the Holy Spirit? But your fathers did, and so do you!

Acts 8:15. As soon as they arrived, they began praying for these new Christians to receive the Holy Spirit, [16]For as yet he had not come upon any of them. For they had only been baptized in the name of the Lord Jesus. [17]Then Peter and John laid their hands upon these believers, and they received the Holy Spirit. [18]When Simon saw this—that the Holy Spirit was given when the Apostles placed their hands upon people's heads—he offered money to buy this power. [19]"Let me have this power too," he exclaimed, "so that when I lay my hands on people, they will receive the Holy Spirit!"

Acts 9:31. Meanwhile, the church had peace throughout Judea, Galilee and Samaria, and grew in strength and numbers. The believers learned how to walk in the fear of the Lord and in the comfort of the Holy Spirit.

Acts 10:19. Meanwhile, as Peter was puzzling over the vision, the Holy Spirit said to him, "Three men have come to see you. [20]Go down and meet them and go with them. All is well, I have sent them." [44]Even as Peter was saying these things, the Holy Spirit fell upon all those listening! [45]The Jews who came with Peter were amazed that the gift of the Holy Spirit would be given to Gentiles too! [46, 47]But there could be no doubt about it, for they heard them speaking in tongues and praising God. Peter asked, "Can anyone object to my baptizing them, now that they have received the Holy Spirit just as we did?" Acts 11:17.

Acts 11:15. Well, I began telling them the Good News, but just as I was getting started with my sermon, the Holy Spirit fell on them, just as he fell on us at the beginning! [16]Then I thought of the Lord's words when he said, "Yes, John baptized with water, but you shall be baptized with the Holy Spirit."

24. Barnabas was a kindly person, full of the Holy Spirit and strong in faith. As a result large numbers of people were added to the Lord.

Acts 13:2. One day as these men were worshiping and fasting the Holy Spirit said, "Dedicate Barnabas and Paul for a special job I have for them." [4]Directed by the Holy Spirit they went to Seleucia and then sailed for Cyprus.

9. Then Paul, filled with the Holy Spirit, glared angrily at the sorcerer.

52. And their converts were filled with joy and with the Holy Spirit.

Acts 15:8. God, who knows men's hearts, confirmed the fact that he accepts Gentiles by giving them the Holy Spirit, just as he gave him to us. [28]For it seemed good to the Holy Spirit and to us to lay no greater burden of Jewish laws on you.

Acts 16:6. Next they traveled through Phrygia and Galatia, because the Holy Spirit had told them not to go into the Turkish province of Ausia at that time. [7]Then going along the borders of Mysia they headed north for the province of Bithynia, but again the Spirit of Jesus said no.

Acts 19:2. "Did you receive the Holy Spirit when you believed?" he asked them. "No," they replied, "we don't know what you mean. What is the Holy Spirit?" [3]"Then what beliefs did you acknowledge at your baptism?" he asked. And they replied, "What John the Baptist taught." [4]Then Paul pointed out to them that John's baptism was to demonstrate a desire to turn from sin to God and that those receiving his baptism must then go on to believe in Jesus, the one John said would come later. [5]As soon as they heard this, they were baptized in the name of the Lord Jesus. [6]Then, when Paul laid his hands upon their heads, the Holy Spirit came on them, and they spoke in other languages and prophesied.

Acts 20:28. And now beware! Be sure that you feed and shepherd God's flock—his church, purchased with his blood—for the Holy Spirit is holding you responsible as overseers.

Rom 5:5. Then, when that happens, we are able to hold our heads high no matter what happens and know that all is well, for we know how dearly God loves us, and we feel this warm love everywhere within us because God has given us the Holy Spirit to fill our hearts with his love. *vs.* 3–5.

Rom 8:1. So there is now no condemnation awaiting those who belong to Christ Jesus. [2]For the power of the life-giving Spirit—and this power is mine through Christ Jesus—has freed me from the vicious circle of sin and death. [4]So now we can obey God's laws if we follow after the Holy Spirit and no longer obey the old evil nature within us. [9]But you are not like that. You are controlled by your new nature if you have the Spirit of God living in you. (And remember that if anyone doesn't have the Spirit of Christ living in him, he is not a Christian at all.) [11]And if the Spirit of God, who raised up Jesus from the dead, lives in you, he will make your dying bodies live again after you die, by means of this same Holy Spirit living within you. [13]For if you keep on following it you are lost and will perish, but if through the power of the Holy Spirit you crush it and its evil deeds, you shall live. [14]For all who are led by the Spirit of God are sons of God. [15]And so we should not be like cringing, fearful slaves, but we should behave like God's very own children, adopted into the bosom of his family, and calling to him, "Father, Father." [16]For his Holy Spirit speaks to us deep in our hearts, and tells us that we really are God's children. [23]And even we Christians, although we have the Holy Spirit within us as a foretaste of future glory, also groan to be released from pain and suffering. We, too, wait anxiously for that day when God will give us our full rights as his children, including the new bodies he has promised us—bodies that will never be sick again and will never die. [26]And in the same way—by our faith—the Holy Spirit helps us with our daily problems and in our praying. For we don't even know what we should pray for, nor how to pray as we should; but the Holy Spirit prays for us with such feeling that it cannot be expressed in words. [27]And the Father who knows all hearts knows, of course, what the Spirit is saying as he pleads for us in harmony with God's own will. *vs.* 1–27.

Rom 9:1. Oh, Israel, my people! Oh, my Jewish brothers! How I long for you to come to Christ. My heart is heavy within me and I grieve bitterly day and night because of you. Christ knows and the Holy Spirit knows that it is no mere pretense when I say that I would be willing to be forever damned if that would save you.

Rom 14:17. For, after all, the important thing for us as Christians is not what we eat or drink but stirring up goodness and peace and joy from the Holy Spirit.

Rom 15:13. So I pray for you Gentiles that God who gives hope will keep you happy and full of peace as you believe in him. I pray that God will help you overflow with hope in him through the Holy Spirit's power within you. [16]For I am, by God's grace, a special messenger from Jesus Christ to you Gentiles, bringing you the Gospel and offering you up as a fragrant sacrifice to God; for you have been made pure and pleasing to him by the Holy Spirit. [18]I dare not judge how effectively he has used others, but I know this: he has used me to win the Gentiles to God. [19]I have won them by my message and by the good way I have lived before them, and by the miracles done through me as signs from God—all by the Holy Spirit's power. In this way I have preached the full Gospel of Christ all the way from Jerusalem clear over into Illyricum. [30]Will you be my prayer partners? For the Lord Jesus Christ's sake, and because of your love for me—given to you by the Holy Spirit—pray much with me for my work.

1 Cor 2:4. And my preaching was very plain, not with a lot of oratory and human wisdom, but the Holy Spirit's power was in my words, proving to those who heard them that the message was from God. [10]But we know about these things because God has sent his Spirit to tell us, and his Spirit searches out and shows us all of God's deepest secrets. [Rom 11:33, 34.] [11]No one can really know what anyone else is thinking, or what he is really like, except that person himself. And no one can know God's thoughts except God's own Spirit. [12]And God has actually given us his Spirit (not the world's spirit) to tell us about the wonderful free gifts of grace and blessing that God has given us. [13]In telling you about these gifts we have even used the very words given to us by the Holy Spirit, not words that we as men might choose. So we use the Holy Spirit's words to explain the Holy Spirit's facts. [14]But the man who isn't a Christian can't understand and can't accept these thoughts from God, which the Holy Spirit teaches us. They sound foolish to him, because only those who have the Holy Spirit within them can understand what the Holy Spirit means. Others just can't take it in.

1 Cor 3:16. Don't you realize that all of you together are the house of God, and that the Spirit of God lives among you in his house? 1 Cor 6:19.

1 Cor 6:11. There was a time when some of you were just like that but now your sins are washed away, and you are set apart for God, and he has accepted you because of what the Lord Jesus Christ and the Spirit of our God have done for you. [19]Haven't you yet learned that your body is the home of the Holy Spirit God gave you, and that he lives within you? Your own body does not belong to you.

1 Cor 12:3. But now you are meeting people who claim to speak messages from the Spirit of God. How can you know whether they are really inspired by God or whether they are fakes? Here is the test: no one speaking by the power of the Spirit of God can curse Jesus, and no one can say, "Jesus is Lord," and really mean it, unless the Holy Spirit is helping him. [4]Now God gives us many kinds of special abilities, but it is the same Holy Spirit who is the source of them all. [5]There are different kinds of service to God, but it is the same Lord we are serving. [6]There are many ways in which God works in our lives, but it is the same God who does the work in and through all of us who are his. [7]The Holy Spirit displays God's power through each of us as a means of helping the entire church. [8]To one person the Spirit gives the ability to give wise advice; someone else may be especially good at studying and teaching, and this is his gift from the same Spirit. [9]He gives special faith to another, and to someone else the power to heal the sick. [10]He gives power for doing miracles to some, and others power to prophesy and preach. He gives someone else the power to know whether evil spirits are speaking through those who claim to be giving God's messages—or whether it is really the Spirit of God who is speaking. Still another person is able to speak in languages he never learned; and others,

who do not know the language either, are given power to understand what he is saying. [11]It is the same and only Holy Spirit who gives all these gifts and powers, deciding which each one of us should have.

2 Cor 1:22. He has put his brand upon us—his mark of ownership—and given us his Holy Spirit in our hearts as guarantee that we belong to him, and as the first installment of all that he is going to give us. 2 Cor 5:5.

2 Cor 3:3. They can see that you are a letter from Christ, written by us. It is not a letter written with pen and ink, but by the Spirit of the living God; not one carved on stone, but in human hearts. [6]He is the one who has helped us tell others about his new agreement to save them. We do not tell them that they must obey every law of God or die; but we tell them there is life for them from the Holy Spirit. The old way, trying to be saved by keeping the Ten Commandments, ends in death; in the new way, the Holy Spirit gives them life. [8]Shall we not expect far greater glory in these days when the Holy Spirit is giving life? [17]The Lord is the Spirit who gives them life, and where he is there is freedom (from trying to be saved by keeping the laws of God). [18]But we Christians have no veil over our faces; we can be mirrors that brightly reflect the glory of the Lord. And as the Spirit of the Lord works within us, we become more and more like him.

2 Cor 5:5. This is what God has prepared for us and, as a guarantee, he has given us his Holy Spirit.

2 Cor 6:4. In fact, in everything we do we try to show that we are true ministers of God. [6]We have proved ourselves to be what we claim by our wholesome lives and by our understanding of the Gospel and by our patience. We have been kind and truly loving and filled with the Holy Spirit.

2 Cor 13:14. May the grace of our Lord Jesus Christ be with you all. May God's love and the Holy Spirit's friendship be yours.

Gal 3:2. Let me ask you this one question: Did you receive the Holy Spirit by trying to keep the Jewish laws? Of course not, for the Holy Spirit came upon you only after you heard about Christ and trusted him to save you. [3]Then have you gone completely crazy? For if trying to obey the Jewish laws never gave you spiritual life in the first place, why do you think that trying to obey them now will make you stronger Christians? [14]Now God can bless the Gentiles, too, with this same blessing he promised to Abraham; and all of us as Christians can have the promised Holy Spirit through this faith.

Gal 4:6. And because we are his sons God has sent the Spirit of his Son into our hearts, so now we can rightly speak of God as our dear Father.

Gal 5:5. But we by the help of the Holy Spirit are counting on Christ's death to clear away our sins and make us right with God. [16]I advise you to obey only the Holy Spirit's instructions. He will tell you where to go and what to do, and then you won't always be doing the wrong things your evil nature wants you to. [17]For we naturally love to do evil things that are just the opposite from the things that the Holy Spirit tells us to do; and the good things we want to do when the Spirit has his way with us are just the opposite of our natural desires. These two forces within us are constantly fighting each other to win control over us, and our wishes are never free from their pressures. [18]When you are guided by the Holy Spirit you need no longer force yourself to obey Jewish laws. [22]But when the Holy Spirit controls our lives he will produce this kind of fruit in us: love, joy, peace, patience, kindness, goodness, faithfulness, [23]gentleness and self-control; and here there is no conflict with Jewish laws. [25]If we are living now by the Holy Spirit's power, let us follow the Holy Spirit's leading in every part of our lives.

Gal 6:8. If he sows to please his own wrong desires, he will be planting seeds of evil and he will surely reap a harvest of spiritual decay and death; but if he plants the good things of the Spirit, he will reap the everlasting life which the Holy Spirit gives him.

Eph 1:12. God's purpose in this was that we should praise God and give glory to him for doing these mighty things for us, who were the first to trust in Christ. [13]And because of what Christ did, all you others too, who heard the Good News about how to be saved, and trusted Christ, were marked as belonging to Christ by the Holy Spirit, who long ago had been promised to all of us Christians. [14]His presence within us is God's guarantee that he really will give us all that he promised; and the Spirit's seal upon us means that God has already purchased us and that he guarantees to bring us to himself. This is just one more reason for us to praise our glorious God.

Eph 2:18. Now all of us, whether Jews or Gentiles, may come to God the Father with the Holy Spirit's help because of what Christ has done for us. [22]And you also are joined with him and with each other by the Spirit, and are part of this dwelling place of God.

Eph 3:5. In olden times God did not share this plan with his people, but now he has revealed it by the Holy Spirit to his apostles and prophets. [16]That out of his glorious, unlimited resources he will give you the mighty inner strengthening of his Holy Spirit.

Eph 4:3. Try always to be led along together by the Holy Spirit, and so be at peace with one another. [4]We are all parts of one body, we have the same Spirit, and we have all been called to the same glorious future. [30]Don't cause the Holy Spirit sorrow by the way you live. Remember, he is the one who marks you to be present on that day when salvation from sin will be complete.

Eph 5:9. Because of this light within you, you should do only what is good and right and true. [18]Don't drink too much wine, for many evils lie along that path; be filled instead with the Holy Spirit, and controlled by him.

Eph 6:17. And you will need the helmet of salvation and the sword of the Spirit—which is the

Word of God. [18]Pray all the time. Ask God for anything in line with the Holy Spirit's wishes. Plead with him, reminding him of your needs, and keep praying earnestly for all Christians everywhere.

Phil 1:19. I am going to keep on being glad, for I know that as you pray for me, and as the Holy Spirit helps me, this is all going to turn out for my good.

Phil 2:1. Is there any such thing as Christians cheering each other up? Do you love me enough to want to help me? Does it mean anything to you that we are brothers in the Lord, sharing the same Spirit? Are your hearts tender and sympathetic at all?

Col 1:8. And he is the one who has told us about the great love for others which the Holy Spirit has given you.

1 Thess 1:5. For when we brought you the Good News, it was not just meaningless chatter to you; no, you listened with great interest. What we told you produced a powerful effect upon you, for the Holy Spirit gave you great and full assurance that what we said was true. And you know how our very lives were further proof to you of the truth of our message. [6]So you became our followers and the Lord's; for you received our message with joy from the Holy Spirit in spite of the trials and sorrows it brought you.

1 Thess 4:8. If anyone refuses to live by these rules he is not disobeying the rules of men but of God who gives his *Holy* Spirit to you. [9]But concerning the pure brotherly love that there should be among God's people, I don't need to say very much, I'm sure! For God himself is teaching you to love one another.

1 Thess 5:19. Do not smother the Holy Spirit.

2 Thess 2:13. But we must forever give thanks to God for you, our brothers loved by the Lord, because God chose from the very first to give you salvation, cleansing you by the work of the Holy Spirit and by your trusting in the Truth.

1 Tim 4:1. But the Holy Spirit tells us clearly that in the last times some in the church will turn away from Christ and become eager followers of teachers with devil-inspired ideas.

2 Tim 1:7. For the Holy Spirit, God's gift, does not want you to be afraid of people, but to be wise and strong, and to love them and enjoy being with them. [14]Guard well the splendid, God-given ability you received as a gift from the Holy Spirit who lives within you.

Tit 3:5. Then he saved us—not because we were good enough to be saved, but because of his kindness and pity—by washing away our sins and giving us the new joy of the indwelling Holy Spirit [6]whom he poured out upon us with wonderful fullness—and all because of what Jesus Christ our Savior did.

Heb 2:4. God always has shown us that these messages are true by signs and wonders and various miracles and by giving certain special abilities from the Holy Spirit to those who believe; yes, God has assigned such gifts to each of us.

Heb 3:7. And since Christ is so much superior, the Holy Spirit warns us to listen to him.

Heb 6:4. There is no use trying to bring you back to the Lord again if you have once understood the Good News and tasted for yourself the good things of heaven and shared in the Holy Spirit.

Heb 9:14. Just think how much more surely the blood of Christ will transform our lives and hearts. His sacrifice frees us from the worry of having to obey the old rules, and makes us want to serve the living God. For by the help of the eternal Holy Spirit, Christ willingly gave himself to God to die for our sins—he being perfect, without a single sin or fault.

Heb 10:15. And the Holy Spirit testifies that this is so. [29]Think how much more terrible the punishment will be for those who have trampled underfoot the Son of God and treated his cleansing blood as though it were common and unhallowed, and insulted and outraged the Holy Spirit who brings God's mercy to his people.

1 Pet 1:2. Dear friends, God the Father chose you long ago and knew you would become his children. And the Holy Spirit has been at work in your hearts, cleansing you with the blood of Jesus Christ and making you to please him. May God bless you richly and grant you increasing freedom from all anxiety and fear. [11]They wondered what the Spirit of Christ within them was talking about, for he told them to write down the events which, since then, have happened to Christ: his suffering, and his great glory afterwards. And they wondered when and to whom all this would happen. [12]They were finally told that these things would not occur during their lifetime, but long years later, during yours. And now at last this Good News has been plainly announced to all of us. It was preached to us in the power of the same heaven-sent Holy Spirit who spoke to them; and it is all so strange and wonderful that even the angels in heaven would give a great deal to know more about it.

1 Pet 3:18. Christ also suffered. He died once for the sins of all us guilty sinners, although he himself was innocent of any sin at any time, that he might bring us safely home to God. But though his body died, his spirit lived on.

1 Pet 4:14. Be happy if you are cursed and insulted for being a Christian, for when that happens the Spirit of God will come upon you with great glory.

2 Pet 1:20, 21. For no prophecy recorded in Scripture was ever thought up by the prophet himself. It was the Holy Spirit within these godly men who gave them true messages from God. 2 Tim 3:16.

1 Jn 2:20. But you are not like that, for the Holy Spirit has come upon you, and you know the truth.

1 Jn 3:24. Those who do what God says—they are living with God and he with them. We know this is true because the Holy Spirit he has given us tells us so.

1 Jn 4:2. And the way to find out if their message is from the Holy Spirit is to ask: Does it really agree that Jesus Christ, God's Son, actually became man with a human body? If so, then the message is from God. [13]And he has put his own Holy Spirit into our hearts as a proof to us that we are living with him and he with us.

1 Jn 5:6, 7, 8. And we know he is, because God said so with a voice from heaven when Jesus was baptized, and again as he was facing death—yes, not only at his baptism but also as he faced death. And the Holy Spirit, forever truthful, says it too. So we have these three witnesses: the voice of the Holy Spirit in our hearts, the voice from heaven at Christ's baptism, and the voice before he died. And they all say the same thing: that Jesus Christ is the Son of God.

Jude 1:19. They stir up arguments; they love the evil things of the world; they do not have the Holy Spirit living in them. [20]But you, dear friends, must build up your lives ever more strongly upon the foundation of our holy faith, learning to pray in the power and strength of the Holy Spirit.

Rev 1:4. May you have grace and peace from God who is, and was, and is to come! and from the seven-fold Spirit before his throne. Rev 4:5; 5:6.

Rev 2:7. Let this message sink into the ears of anyone who listens to what the Spirit is saying to the churches: To everyone who is victorious, I will give fruit from the Tree of Life in the Paradise of God. *vs.* 11, 29.

Rev 11:11. But after three and a half days, the spirit of life from God will enter them and they will stand up! And great fear will fall on everyone.

Rev 14:13. And I heard a voice in the heavens above me saying, "Write this down: At last the time has come for his martyrs to enter into their full reward. Yes, says the Spirit, they are blest indeed, for now they shall rest from all their toils and trials; for their good deeds follow them to heaven!"

Rev 22:17. The Spirit and the bride say, "Come." Let each one who hears them say the same, "Come." Let the thirsty one come—anyone who wants to; let him come and drink the Water of Life without charge.

See *God, a Spirit; Word of God, Inspiration of.*

INSPIRATION OF.

Instances of. Joseph, Gen 41:38. Bezalel, Ex 31:3. The seventy elders, Num 11:17. Balaam, Num 24:2. Joshua, Num 27:18.

The judges: Othni-el, Judg 3:10; Gideon, Judg 6:34; Jephthah, Judg 11:29; Samson, Judg 13:25; 14:6, 19.

King David, 1 Chron 28:11, 12.

The prophets: Azariah, 2 Chron 15:1; Zechariah, 2 Chron 24:20; Zech 1:1; Ezekiel, Ezk 8:3; 11:1, 5, 24; Daniel, Dan 4:8; Zacharias, Lk 1:67; Elizabeth, Lk 1:41; Simeon, Lk 2:25, 26.

The disciples, Acts 6:3; 7:55; 8:29; 9:17; 10:45.

See *Inspiration.*

SIN AGAINST. Isa 63:10. But they rebelled against him and grieved his Holy Spirit. That is why he became their enemy and personally fought against them.

Mt 12:31, 32. Even blasphemy against me or any other sin, can be forgiven—all except one: speaking against the Holy Spirit shall never be forgiven, either in this world or in the world to come. Lk 12:10.

Mk 3:29. But blasphemy against the Holy Spirit can never be forgiven. It is an eternal sin. Lk 2:10; 1 Jn 5:16; Acts 5:9.

Acts 5:3. But Peter said, "Ananias, Satan has filled your heart. When you claimed this was the full price, you were lying to the Holy Spirit." [9]And Peter said, "How could you and your husband even think of doing a thing like this—conspiring together to test the Spirit of God's ability to know what is going on? Just outside that door are the young men who buried your husband, and they will carry you out too."

Acts 7:51. You stiff-necked heathen! Must you forever resist the Holy Spirit? But your fathers did, and so do you!

Acts 8:18. When Simon saw this—that the Holy Spirit was given when the apostles placed their hands upon people's heads—he offered money to buy this power. [19]"Let me have this power too," he exclaimed, "so that when I lay my hands on people, they will receive the Holy Spirit!" [20]But Peter replied, "Your money perish with you for thinking God's gift can be bought! [21]You can have no part in this, for your heart is not right before God. [22]Turn from this great wickedness and pray. Perhaps God will yet forgive your evil thoughts.

Eph 4:30. Don't cause the Holy Spirit sorrow by the way you live. Remember, he is the one who marks you to be present on that day when salvation from sin will be complete.

Heb 10:29. Think how much more terrible the punishment will be for those who have trampled underfoot the Son of God and treated his cleansing blood as though it were common and unhallowed, and insulted and outraged the Holy Spirit who brings God's mercy to his people.

WITHDRAWN. Gen 6:3. Then Jehovah said, "My Spirit must not forever be disgraced in man, wholly evil as he is. I will give him 120 years to mend his ways."

Deut 32:30. How could one single enemy chase a thousand of them, and two put ten thousand to flight, unless their Rock had abandoned them, unless the Lord had destroyed them?

Ps 51:11. Don't toss me aside, banished forever from your presence. Don't take your Holy Spirit from me.

Prov 1:24. I have called you so often but still you won't come. I have pleaded, but all in vain. [25]For you have spurned my counsel and reproof. [26]Some day you'll be in trouble, and I'll laugh! Mock me, will you?—I'll mock you! [27]When a storm of terror surrounds you, and when you are engulfed by anguish and distress, [28]then I will not answer your cry for help. It will be too late though you search for me ever so anxiously.

Jer 7:29. O Jerusalem, shave your head in shame and weep alone upon the mountains; for the Lord has rejected and forsaken this people of his wrath.

Hos 5:6. Then at last, they will come with their flocks and herds to sacrifice to God, but it will be too late—they will not find him. He has withdrawn from them and they are left alone.

Hos 9:12. And if your children grow, I will take them from you; all are doomed. Yes, it will be a sad day when I turn away and leave you alone.

Mt 15:14. They are blind guides leading the blind, and both will fall into a ditch.

Lk 13:7. Finally he told his gardener to cut it down. "I've waited three years and there hasn't been a single fig!" he said. "Why bother with it any longer? It's taking up space we can use for something else."

Rom 1:24. So God let them go ahead into every sort of sex sin, and do whatever they wanted to—yes, vile and sinful things with each other's bodies. 26That is why God let go of them and let them do all these evil things, so that even their women turned against God's natural plan for them and indulged in sex sin with each other. 28So it was that when they gave God up and would not acknowledge him, God gave them up to doing everything their evil minds could think of.

2 Thess 2:6. And you know what is keeping him from being here already; for he can come only when his time is ready. 7As for the work this man of rebellion and hell will do when he comes, it is already going on, but he himself will not come until the one who is holding him back steps out of the way. 8Then this wicked one will appear, whom the Lord Jesus will burn up with the breath of his mouth and destroy by his presence when he returns.

See *Reprobate.*

Instances of. Antediluvians, Gen 6:3–7. People of Sodom, Gen 19:13, 24, 25. Israelites, Num 14:26–45; Deut 1:42; 28:15–68; 31:17, 18. Samson, Judg 16:20. Saul, 1 Sam 16:14; 18:10–12; 19:9–11; 20:30–33; 22:7–19; 28:15, 16; 2 Sam 7:15.

HOMAGE Refused by Peter, Acts 10:26; by Paul and Barnabas, Acts 14:11–18; by the angel seen by John in his vision, Rev 19:10; 22:8, 9. See *Worship.* Rendered to kings, 1 Kgs 1:16, 22, 23, 31; officials, Esther 3:2.

HOMAM Called also *Heman.* An Edomite, Gen 36:22; 1 Chron 1:38, 39.

HOME See *Family.*

HOMER A dry measure, about 6 bushels (220 liters), Ezk 45:11. Equal to 10 ephahs.

HOMESTEAD Mortgaged, Neh 5:2–4. When salable, and when not salable, Lev 25:25–34. See *Lands.*

HOMICIDE ACCIDENTAL. Ex 21:13. But if it is accidental—an act of God—and not intentional, then I will appoint a place where he can run and get protection. 28If an ox gores a man or woman to death, the ox shall be stoned and its flesh not eaten, but the owner shall not be held—29unless the ox was known to gore people in the past, and the owner had been notified and still the ox was not kept under control; in that case, if it kills someone, the ox shall be stoned and the owner also shall be killed. 30But the dead man's relatives may accept a fine instead, if they wish. The judges will determine the amount. 31The same law holds if the ox gores a boy or a girl. 32But if the ox gores a slave, whether male or female, the slave's master shall be given thirty pieces of silver, and the ox shall be stoned.

Num 35:11. Cities of Refuge shall be designated for anyone to flee into if he has killed someone accidentally. 12These Cities will be places of protection from the dead man's relatives who want to avenge his death; for the slayer must not be killed unless a fair trial establishes his guilt. 13, 14Three of these six Cities of Refuge are to be located in the land of Canaan, and three on the east side of the Jordan River. 15These are not only for the protection of Israelites, but also for foreigners and travelers. 22, 23But if it is an accident—a case in which something is thrown unintentionally, or in which a stone is thrown without anger, without realizing it will hit anyone, and without wanting to harm an enemy—yet the man dies, 24then the people shall judge whether or not it was an accident, and whether or not to hand the killer over to the avenger of the dead man. 25If it is decided that it was accidental, then the people shall save the killer from the avenger; the killer shall be permitted to stay in the City of Refuge; and he must live there until the death of the High Priest. 26If the slayer leaves the City, 27and the avenger finds him outside and kills him, it is not murder, 28for the man should have stayed inside the City until the death of the High Priest. But after the death of the High Priest, the man may return to his own land and home. 32Nor may a payment be accepted from a refugee in a City of Refuge, permitting him to return to his home before the death of the High Priest. Deut 4:41–43; 19:1–10.

Josh 20:1. The Lord said to Joshua, 2"Tell the people of Israel to designate now the Cities of Refuge, as I instructed Moses. 3If a man is guilty of killing someone unintentionally, he can run to one of these cities and be protected from the relatives of the dead man, who may try to kill him in revenge. 4When the innocent killer reaches any of these cities, he will meet with the city council and explain what happened, and they must let him come in and must give him a place to live among them. 5If a relative of the dead man comes to kill him in revenge, the innocent slayer must not be released to them, for the death was accidental. 6The man who caused the accidental death must stay in that city until he has been tried by the judges, and must live there until the death of the High Priest who was in the office at the time of the accident. But then he is free to return to his own city and home." 7The cities chosen as Cities of Refuge were Kedesh of Galilee in the hill country of Naphtali; Shechem, in the hill country of Ephraim; and Kiriath-arba (also known as Hebron) in the hill country of Judah. 8The Lord also instructed that three cities be set aside for this purpose on the east side of the Jordan River, across from Jericho. They were Bezer, in the wilderness of the land of the tribe of Reuben; Ramoth of Gilead, in the territory of the tribe of Gad; and Golan of Bashan, in the land of the tribe of Manasseh. [9]These Cities of Refuge were for foreigners living in Israel as well as for the Israelis themselves, so that anyone who accidentally killed another man could run to that place for a trial, and not be killed in revenge.

FELONIOUS, OR MURDER. Gen 4:9. But afterwards the Lord asked Cain, "Where is your brother? Where is Abel?" "How should I know?" Cain retorted. "Am I supposed to keep track of him wherever he goes?" [10]But the Lord said, "Your brother's blood calls to me from the ground. What have you done? [11]You are hereby banished from this ground which you have defiled with your brother's blood." *v.* 12.

Gen 9:5, 6. And murder is forbidden. Man-killing animals must die, and any man who murders shall be killed; for to kill a man is to kill one made like God.

Gen 49:7. Cursed be their anger, for it is fierce and cruel. Therefore, I will scatter their descendants throughout Israel.

Ex 20:13. You must not murder. Deut 5:17; Rom 13:9.

Ex 21:29. Unless the ox was known to gore people in the past, and the owner had been notified and still the ox was not kept under control; in that case, if it kills someone, the ox shall be stoned and the owner also shall be killed. [30]But the dead man's relatives may accept a fine instead, if they wish. The judges will determine the amount. [31]The same law holds if the ox gores a boy or a girl. [32]But if the ox gores a slave, whether male or female, the slave's master shall be given thirty pieces of silver, and the ox shall be stoned.

Num 35:16. But if someone is struck and killed by a piece of iron, it must be presumed to be murder, and the murderer must be executed. [17]Or if the slain man was struck down with a large stone, it is murder, and the murderer shall die. [18]The same is true if he is killed with a wooden weapon. [19]The avenger of his death shall personally kill the murderer when he meets him. [20]So, if anyone kills another out of hatred by throwing something at him, or ambushing him, [21]or angrily striking him with his fist so that he dies, he is a murderer; and the murderer shall be executed by the avenger. [30]All murderers must be executed, but only if there is more than one witness; no man shall die with only one person testifying against him. [31]Whenever anyone is judged guilty of murder, he must die—no ransom may be accepted for him.

Deut 17:6. However, never put a man to death on the testimony of only one witness; there must be at least two or three.

Deut 21:1. If, when you arrive in the Promised Land, a murder victim is found lying in a field and no one has seen the murder, [2]the elders and judges shall measure from the body to the nearest city. [3]Then the elders of that city shall take a heifer that has never been yoked, [4]and lead it to a valley where there is running water—a valley neither plowed nor sowed—and there break its neck. [5]Then the priests shall come (for the Lord your God has chosen them to minister before him and to pronounce his blessings and decide lawsuits and punishments), [6]and shall wash their hands over the heifer, [7]and say, "Our hands have not shed this blood, neither have our eyes seen it. [8]O Lord, forgive your people Israel whom you have redeemed, and do not charge them with murdering an innocent man. Forgive us the guilt of this man's blood." [9]In this way you will put away the guilt from among you by following the Lord's directions.

Deut 22:8. Every new house must have a guardrail around the edge of the flat rooftop to prevent anyone from falling off and bringing guilt to both the house and its owner.

Deut 27:24. "Cursed is he who secretly slays another." And all the people shall reply, "Amen." [25]"Cursed is he who accepts a bribe to kill an innocent person." And all the people shall reply, "Amen."

1 Kgs 21:19. Give him this message from me: "Isn't killing Naboth bad enough? Must you rob him, too? Because you have done this, dogs shall lick your blood outside the city just as they licked the blood of Naboth!"

2 Chron 24:22. That was how King Joash repaid Jehoiada for his love and loyalty—by killing his son. Zechariah's last words as he died were "Lord, see what they are doing and pay them back."

Job 24:14. They are murderers who rise in the early dawn to kill the poor and needy; at night they are thieves and adulterers. *vs.* 1–25.

Ps 5:6. You will destroy them for their lies; how you abhor all murder and deception.

Ps 9:12. He who avenges murder has an open ear to those who cry to him for justice. He does not ignore the prayers of men in trouble when they call to him for help.

Ps 10:2. Come and deal with all these proud and wicked men who viciously persecute the poor. Pour upon these men the evil they planned for others! [8]They lurk in dark alleys of the city and murder passersby.

Ps 26:9, 10. Don't treat me as a common sinner or murderer who plots against the innocent and demands bribes.

Ps 37:32. Evil men spy on the godly, waiting for an excuse to accuse them and then demanding their death.

Ps 38:12. Meanwhile my enemies are trying to kill me. They plot my ruin and spend all their waking hours planning treachery.

Ps 55:23. He will send my enemies to the pit of destruction. Murderers and liars will not live out half their days. But I am trusting you to save me.

Ps 94:3. Lord, how long shall the wicked be allowed to triumph and exult? [6]They murder widows, immigrants, and orphans.

Prov 1:11. "We'll hide and rob and kill," they say. [12]"Good or bad, we'll treat them all alike." [15]Don't do it, son! Stay far from men like that, [16]for crime is their way of life, and murder is their specialty. Isa 59:7.

Prov 6:16, 17. For there are six things the Lord hates—no, seven: Haughtiness, lying, murdering.

Prov 28:17. A murderer's conscience will drive him into hell. Don't stop him!

Isa 26:21. Look! The Lord is coming from the heavens to punish the people of the earth for their sins. The earth will no longer hide the murderers. The guilty will be found.

Isa 59:3. For your hands are those of murderers and your fingers are filthy with sin. You lie and grumble and oppose the good.

Jer 2:34. Your clothing is stained with the blood of the innocent and the poor. Brazenly you murder without a cause. Jer 19:4.

Jer 7:9. Do you really think that you can steal, murder, commit adultery, lie, and worship Baal and all of those new gods of yours, [10]and then come here and stand before me in my Temple and chant, "We are saved!"—only to go right back to all these evil things again?

Jer 22:3. The Lord says: Be fairminded. Do what is right! Help those in need of justice! Quit your evil deeds! Protect the rights of aliens and immigrants, orphans and widows; stop murdering the innocent!

Ezk 22:9. Prisoners are falsely accused and sent to their death. Every mountain top is filled with idols; lewdness is everywhere.

Ezk 35:6. As I live, the Lord God says, since you enjoy blood so much, I will give you a blood bath —your turn has come!

Hos 1:4, 5. And the Lord said, "Name the child Jezreel, for in the Valley of Jezreel I am about to punish King Jehu's dynasty to avenge the murders he committed; in fact, I will put an end to Israel as an independent kingdom, breaking the power of the nation in the Valley of Jezreel."

Hos 4:1. Hear the word of the Lord, O people of Israel. The Lord has filed a lawsuit against you listing the following charges: There is no faithfulness, no kindness, no knowledge of God in your land. [2]You swear and lie and kill and steal and commit adultery. There is violence everywhere, with one murder after another. [3]That is why your land is not producing; it is filled with sadness, and all living things grow sick and die; the animals, the birds, and even the fish begin to disappear.

Hab 2:10. By the murders you commit, you have shamed your name and forfeited your lives. [12]Woe to you who build cities with money gained from murdering and robbery!

Mt 5:21. Under the laws of Moses the rule was, "If you kill, you must die." [22]But I have added to that rule, and tell you that if you are only *angry,* even in your own home, you are in danger of judgment! If you call your friend an idiot, you are in danger of being brought before the court. And if you curse him, you are in danger of the fires of hell.

Mt 15:19. For from the heart come evil thoughts, murder, adultery, fornication, theft, lying and slander. Mk 7:21.

Mt 19:18. "Which ones?" the man asked. And Jesus replied, "Don't kill, don't commit adultery, don't steal, don't lie. Mk 10:19; Lk 18:20.

Gal 5:19. But when you follow your own wrong inclinations your lives will produce these evil results: impure thoughts, eagerness for lustful pleasure, [20]idolatry, spiritism (that is, encouraging the activity of demons), hatred and fighting, jealousy and anger, constant effort to get the best for yourself, complaints and criticisms, the feeling that everyone else is wrong except those in your own little group—and there will be wrong doctrine, [21]envy, murder, drunkenness, wild parties, and all that sort of thing. Let me tell you again as I have before, that anyone living that sort of life will not inherit the kingdom of God.

1 Tim 1:9. But they were not made for us, whom God has saved; they are for sinners who hate God, have rebellious hearts, curse and swear, attack their fathers and mothers, and murder.

Jas 2:11. For the God who said you must not marry a woman who already has a husband, also said you must not murder, so even though you have not broken the marriage laws by committing adultery, but have murdered someone, you have entirely broken God's laws and stand utterly guilty before him.

1 Pet 4:15. Don't let me hear of your suffering for murdering or stealing or making trouble or being a busybody and prying into other people's affairs.

1 Jn 3:15. Anyone who hates his Christian brother is really a murderer at heart; and you know that no one wanting to murder has eternal life within. *v.* 12.

Rev 9:21. Neither did they change their mind and attitude about all their murders and witchcraft, their immorality and theft.

Rev 21:8. But cowards who turn back from following me, and those who are unfaithful to me, and the corrupt, and murderers, and the immoral, and those conversing with demons, and idol worshipers and all liars—their doom is in the Lake that burns with fire and sulphur. This is the Second Death.

Rev 22:15. Outside the city are those who have strayed away from God, and the sorcerers and the immoral and murderers and idolaters, and all who love to lie, and do so.

See *Conspiracy; Fratricide; Parricide; Patricide; Regicide; Suicide.*

David's Repentance for, and Confession of, the Murder of Uriah. Ps 51:1. O loving and kind God, have mercy. Have pity upon me and take away the awful stain of my transgressions. [2]Oh, wash me, cleanse me from this guilt. Let me be pure again. [3]For I admit my shameful deed—it haunts me day and night. [4]It is against you and you alone I sinned, and did this terrible thing. You saw it all, and your sentence against me is just. [5]But I was born a sinner, yes, from the moment my mother conceived me. [6]You deserve honesty from the heart; yes, utter sincerity and truthfulness. Oh, give me this wisdom. [7]Sprinkle me with the cleansing blood and I shall be clean again. Wash me and I shall be whiter than snow. [8]And after you have punished me, give me back my joy again. [9]Don't keep looking at my sins—erase them from your sight. [10]Create in me a new, clean heart, O God, filled with clean thoughts and right desires. [11]Don't toss me aside, banished forever from your presence. Don't take your Holy Spirit from me. [12]Restore to me again the joy of your salvation, and make me willing to obey you. [13]Then I will teach your ways to other sinners, and they—guilty like me—will repent and return to you. [14, 15]Don't sentence me to death. O my God, you alone can rescue me. Then I will sing of your forgiveness, for my lips will be unsealed—oh, how I will praise you. [16]You don't want penance; if you did, how gladly I would do it! You aren't interested in offerings burned before you on the altar. [17]It is a broken spirit you want—remorse and penitence. A broken and a contrite heart, O God, you will not ignore.

Instances of Felonious. By Cain, Gen 4:8. Lamech, Gen 4:23, 24. Simeon and Levi, Gen 34: 25–31. Pharaoh, Ex 1:15, 16, 22. Moses, Ex 2:12. Ehud, Judg 3:16–23. Jael, Judg 4:21. Abimelech, Judg 9:5, 18, 56, 57. An Amalekite, 2 Sam 1:16. Abner, 2 Sam 2:18–24. Joab, 2 Sam 3:24–27; 2 Sam 20:8–10; 1 Kgs 2:5. Solomon, 1 Kgs 2:23–46. Rechab and Baanah, 2 Sam 4:5–8. David, 2 Sam 11: 14–17; 12:9; Ps 51:14, 15. Of Amon, 2 Kgs 21:23. Absalom, 2 Sam 13:21–30. Baasha, 1 Kgs 15:27–29. Zimri, 1 Kgs 16:9–11. Ahab and Jezebel, 1 Kgs 21: 10–24; 2 Kgs 6:32. Hazael, 2 Kgs 8:15. Jehu, 2 Kgs 9:24–37; 2 Kgs 10:1–25. Athaliah, 2 Kgs 11: 1. Of Joash by his aides, 2 Kgs 12:20, 21. Menahem, 2 Kgs 15:16. Of Sennacherib, 2 Kgs 19:37; Isa 37:38. Manasseh, 2 Kgs 21:16; 24:3, 4. Jehoram, 2 Chron 21:3, 4. Joash, 2 Chron 24:21. Amaziah's soldiers, 2 Chron 25:12. Nebuchadnezzar, Jer 39:6. Ishmael, Jer 41:1–7. Ammonites, Amos 1:13–15. Herod I., Mt 2:16. Herod II., Mt 14:10; Mk 6:27. Barabbas, Mk 15:7; Acts 3:14. Sanhedrin and Pilate, Mt 26; 27. Sanhedrin, Acts 7:54–60. Herod, Acts 12:2, 19. By raping, Judg 19:25–28.

PUNISHMENT OF. Gen 4:13. Cain replied to the Lord, "My punishment is greater than I can bear. [14]For you have banished me from my farm and from you, and made me a fugitive and a tramp; and everyone who sees me will try to kill me." [15]The Lord replied, "They won't kill you, for I will give seven times your punishment to anyone who does." Then the Lord put an identifying mark on Cain as a warning not to kill him.

Gen 9:5, 6. And murder is forbidden. Man-killing animals must die, and any man who murders shall be killed; for to kill a man is to kill one made like God.

Gen 27:43. "This is what to do," she said. "Flee to your Uncle Laban in Haran. [44]Stay there with him awhile until your brother's fury is spent, [45]and he forgets what you have done. Then I will send for you. For why should I be bereaved of both of you in one day?"

Ex 21:12. Anyone who hits a man so hard that he dies shall surely be put to death. [14]However, if a man deliberately attacks another, intending to kill him, drag him even from my altar, and kill him.

Lev 24:17. Also, all murderers must be executed.

Num 35:16. But if someone is struck and killed by a piece of iron, it must be presumed to be murder, and the murderer must be executed. [17]Or if the slain man was struck down with a large stone, it is murder, and the murderer shall die. [18]The same is true if he is killed with a wooden weapon. [19]The avenger of his death shall personally kill the murderer when he meets him. [20]So, if anyone kills another out of hatred by throwing something at him, or ambushing him, [21]or angrily striking him with his fist so that he dies, he is a murderer; and the murderer shall be executed by the avenger. [30]All murderers must be executed, but only if there is more than one witness; no man shall die with only one person testifying against him. [31]Whenever anyone is judged guilty of murder, he must die—no ransom may be accepted for him. [32]Nor may a payment be accepted from a refugee in a City of Refuge, permitting him to return to his home before the death of the High Priest. [33]In this way the land will not be polluted, for murder pollutes the land, and no atonement can be made for murder except by the execution of the murderer.

Deut 19:11. But if anyone hates his neighbor and springs out of hiding and kills him, and then flees into one of the Cities of Refuge, [12]the elders of his home town shall send for him and shall bring him home and deliver him over to the dead man's avenger, to kill him. [13]Don't pity him! Purge all murderers from Israel! Only then will all go well with you.

2 Sam 12:9. Why, then, have you despised the laws of God and done this horrible deed? For you have murdered Uriah and stolen his wife. [10]Therefore murder shall be a constant threat in your family from this time on, because you have insulted me by taking Uriah's wife. [11]I vow that because of what you have done I will cause your own household to rebel against you. I will give your wives to another man, and he will go to bed with them in public view. [12]You did it secretly, but I will do this to you openly, in the sight of all Israel.

Instances of the Punishment of Murderers. Cain, Gen 4:11–15. David, 2 Sam 12:9, 10. Joab, 1 Kgs 2: 31–34. Haman, Esther 7:10.

The murderer of Saul, 2 Sam 1:15, 16; of Ishbosheth, 2 Sam 4:11, 12. The murderers of Joash, 2 Kgs 14:5.

HOMOSEXUALITY Gen 19:5–8; Judg 19: 22; 1 Kgs 14:24; 15:12; 22:46; 2 Kgs 23:7; Rom 1:24, 26, 27. Forbidden, Lev 18:22; 1 Tim 1:9–11. Punishment of, Lev 20:13; 1 Cor 6:9, 10. Offerings of a homosexual detestable to God, Deut 23:17, 18.

See *Adultery; Sodomites.*

HONESTY Lev 19:35, 36. You must be impartial in judgment. Use accurate measurements—lengths, weights, and volumes—and give full measure, for I am Jehovah your God who brought you from the land of Egypt.

Deut 16:20. Justice must prevail. That is the only

way you will be successful in the land which the Lord your God is giving you.

Deut 25:13–15. In all your transactions you must use accurate scales and honest measurements, so that you will have a long, good life in the land the Lord your God is giving you. [16]All who cheat with unjust weights and measurements are detestable to the Lord your God.

Job 27:6. I am *not* a sinner—I repeat it again and again. My conscience is clear for as long as I live.

Ps 7:3. It would be different Lord, if I were doing evil things—[4]if I were paying back evil for good or unjustly attacking those I dislike.

Ps 15:5. Does not crush his debtors with high interest rates, and refuses to testify against the innocent despite the bribes offered him—such a man shall stand firm forever.

Ps 24:4. Only those with pure hands and hearts, who do not practice dishonesty and lying.

Prov 4:25. Look straight ahead; don't even turn your head to look.

Prov 11:1. The Lord hates cheating and delights in honesty.

Prov 12:22. God delights in those who keep their promises, and abhors those who don't.

Prov 16:11. The Lord demands fairness in every business deal. He established this principle.

Prov 20:10. The Lord despises every kind of cheating. *v.* 23.

Isa 33:15. I will tell you who can live here: All who are honest and fair, who reject making profit by fraud, who hold back their hands from taking bribes, who refuse to listen to those who plot murder, who shut their eyes to all enticement to do wrong. [16]Such as these shall dwell on high. The rocks of the mountains will be their fortress of safety; food will be supplied to them and they will have all the water they need.

Ezk 45:10. You must use honest scales, honest bushels, honest gallons.

Mk 10:19. You know the commandments: don't kill, don't commit adultery, don't steal, don't lie, don't cheat.

Lk 3:12. Even tax collectors—notorious for their corruption—came to be baptized and asked, "How shall we prove to you that we have abandoned our sins?" [13]"By your honesty," he replied. "Make sure you collect no more taxes than the Roman government requires you to to."

Lk 6:31. Treat others as you want them to treat you. Mt 7:12.

Acts 24:16. Because of this I try with all my strength to always maintain a clear conscience before God and man.

2 Cor 4:1. It is God himself, in his mercy, who has given us this wonderful work (of telling his Good News to others), and so we never give up. [2]We do not try to trick people into believing—we are not interested in fooling anyone. We never try to get anyone to believe that the Bible teaches what it doesn't. All such shameful methods we forego. We stand in the presence of God as we speak and so we tell the truth, as all who know us will agree.

2 Cor 7:2. Please open your hearts to us again, for not one of you has suffered any wrong from us. Not one of you was led astray. We have cheated no one nor taken advantage of anyone.

2 Cor 8:21. God knows we are honest, but I want everyone else to know it too.

Phil 4:8. Fix your thoughts on what is true and good and right.

Col 3:22. Not only trying to please them when they are watching you but all the time; obey them willingly because of your love for the Lord and because you want to please him.

1 Thess 4:11. This should be your ambition: to live a quiet life, minding your own business and doing your own work, just as we told you before. [12]As a result, people who are not Christians will trust and respect you, and you will not need to depend on others for enough money to pay your bills.

Heb 13:18. Pray for us, for our conscience is clear and we want to keep it that way.

1 Pet 2:12. Be careful how you behave among your unsaved neighbors; for then, even if they are suspicious of you and talk against you, they will end up praising God for your good works when Christ returns.

INSTANCES OF. Jacob, returning money placed in the sacks, Gen 43:12. The superintendents of the Temple repairs, 2 Kgs 12:15; 22:4–7. Treasurers of the Temple, Neh 13:13.

See *Integrity; Righteousness; Dishonesty.*

HONEY Ex 16:31; 2 Sam 17:28, 29; Prov 25:27; Song 4:11; Isa 7:15, 16; Mt 3:4. Not to be offered with sacrifices, Lev 2:11. Found in rocks, Deut 32:13; Ps 81:16; on the ground, 1 Sam 14:24, 25. Samson's riddle concerning, Judg 14:14. Sent as a present by Jacob to Egypt, Gen 43:11. Plentiful in Palestine, Ex 3:8; Lev 20:24; Deut 8:8; Ezk 20:5, 6; in Assyria, 2 Kgs 18:31, 32. An article of merchandise from Palestine, Ezk 27:17.

FIGURATIVE. Ps 19:10; 119:102, 103; Prov 5:3; 16:24; Ezk 3:3.

HOOF Cloven, one of the physical marks used for distinguishing clean and unclean animals, Lev 11:2–8; Deut 14:3–8.

HOOKS For Tabernacle, made of gold, Ex 26:32, 37; 36:36; silver, Ex 27:9, 10; 38:10–12, 17, 19. In the Temple, seen in Ezekiel's vision, Ezk 40:43. Used for catching fish, Ezk 29:4. For pruning, Isa 2:4; Joel 3:10.

See *Fleshhook.*

FIGURATIVE. Ezk 38:4.

HOOPOE A bird forbidden as food, Lev 11:13–19; Deut 14:11–18.

HOPE Ps 9:18. For the needs of the needy shall not be ignored forever; the hopes of the poor shall not always be crushed.

Ps 25:5. Lead me; teach me; for you are the God who gives me salvation. I have no hope except in you.

Ps 31:24. So cheer up! Take courage if you are depending on the Lord.

Ps 33:22. Yes, Lord, let you constant love surround us, for our hopes are in your alone.

Ps 39:7. And so, Lord, my only hope is in you.

Ps 40:11. O Lord, don't hold back your tender mercies from me! My only hope is in your love and faithfulness.

Ps 43:5. O my soul, why be so gloomy and discouraged? Trust in God! I shall again praise him for his wondrous help; he will make me smile again, *for he is my God!*

Ps 65:5. With dread deeds and awesome power you will defend us from our enemies, O God who saves us. You are the only hope of all mankind throughout the world and far away upon the sea.

Ps 71:5. O Lord, you alone are my hope; I've trusted you from childhood. Ps 22:9–11.

Ps 78:5. For he gave his laws to Israel, and commanded our fathers to teach them to their children,
[6]so that they in turn could teach their children too.
Thus his laws pass down from generation to generation. [7]In this way each generation has been able to
obey his laws and to set its hope anew on God and not forget his glorious miracles.

Ps 86:3. Be merciful, O Lord, for I am looking up to you in constant hope.

Ps 119:43. May I never forget your words; for
they are my only hope. [114]You are my refuge and
my shield, and your promises are my only source of hope.

Ps 130:7. O Israel, hope in the Lord; for he is loving and kind.

Ps 146:5. But happy is the man who has the God of Jacob as his helper, whose hope is in the Lord his God.

Prov 10:28. The hope of good men is eternal happiness.

Prov 13:12. Hope deferred makes the heart sick; but when dreams come true at last, there is life and joy.

Prov 23:18. For surely you have a wonderful future ahead of you. There is hope for you yet!

Prov 24:14. When you enjoy becoming wise, there is hope for you! A bright future lies ahead!

Isa 38:18. For dead men cannot praise you. They cannot be filled with hope and joy.

Jer 17:7. But blessed is the man who trusts in the Lord and has made the Lord his hope and confidence.

Lam 3:21. *Yet there is one ray of hope.* [24]My soul
claims the Lord as my inheritance; therefore I will
hope in him. [26]It is good both to hope and wait
quietly for the salvation of the Lord.

Hos 2:15. There I will . . . transform her Valley of Troubles into a Door of Hope.

Joel 3:16. But to his people Israel, the Lord will be very gentle. He is their Refuge and Strength.

Zech 9:12. Come to the place of safety, all you prisoners, for there is yet hope!

Acts 23:6. And I am being tried here today because I believe in the resurrection of the dead!

Acts 24:14. But one thing I do confess, that I believe in the way of salvation, which they refer to as a sect; I follow that system of serving the God of our ancestors; I firmly believe in the Jewish law
and everything written in the books of prophecy;
[15]and I believe, just as these men do, that there will
be a resurrection of both the righteous and ungodly.

Acts 26:6. But the real reason behind their accusations is something else—it is because I am looking forward to the fulfillment of God's promise
made to our ancestors. [7]The twelve tribes of Israel
strive night and day to attain this same hope I have! Yet, O King, for me it is a crime, they say!

Rom 4:18. So, when God told Abraham that he would give him a son who would have many descendants and become a great nation, Abraham believed God even though such a promise just couldn't come to pass!

Rom 5:2. For because of our faith, he has brought us into this place of highest privilege where we now stand, and we confidently and joyfully look forward to actually becoming all that
God has had in mind for us to be. [3]We can rejoice,
too, when we run into problems and trials for we know that they are good for us—they help us learn
to be patient. [4]And patience develops strength of
character in us and helps us trust God more each time we use it until finally our hope and faith are
strong and steady. [5]Then, when that happens, we
are able to hold our heads high no matter what happens and know that all is well, for we know how dearly God loves us, and we feel this warm love everywhere within us because God has given us the Holy Spirit to fill our hearts with his love.

Rom 8:24. We are saved by trusting. And trusting means looking forward to getting something we don't yet have—for a man who already has something doesn't need to hope and trust that he will get
it. [25]But if we must keep trusting God for something that hasn't happened yet, it teaches us to wait patiently and confidently.

Rom 12:12. Be glad for all God is planning for you.

Rom 15:4. These things that were written in the Scriptures so long ago are to teach us patience and to encourage us, so that we will look forward expectantly to the time when God will conquer sin
and death. [13]So I pray for you Gentiles that God
who gives you hope will keep you happy and full of peace as you believe in him. I pray that God will help you overflow with hope in him through the Holy Spirit's power within you.

1 Cor 13:13. There are three things that remain—faith, hope, and love.

Gal 5:5. But we by the help of the Holy Spirit are counting on Christ's death to clear away our sins and make us right with God.

Eph 1:18. I pray that your hearts will be flooded with light so that you can see something of the future he has called you to share.

Phil 1:20. For I live in eager expectation and hope that I will never do anything that will cause me to be ashamed of myself but that I will always be ready to speak out boldly for Christ while I am going through all these trials here, just as I have in the past; and that I will always be an honor to Christ, whether I live or whether I must die.

Phil 3:7. But all these things that I once thought very worthwhile—now I've thrown them all away so that I can put my trust and hope in Christ alone.

Col 1:5. And you are looking forward to the joys of heaven, and have been ever since the Gospel first was preached to you. [23]The only condition is that you fully believe the Truth, standing in it steadfast and firm, strong in the Lord, convinced of the Good News that Jesus died for you, and never shifting from trusting him to save you. [27]And the riches and glory of his plan are for you Gentiles too. And this is the secret: *that Christ in your hearts is your only hope of glory.*

1 Thess 1:3. We never forget your loving deeds as we talk to our God and Father about you, and your strong faith and steady looking forward to the return of our Lord Jesus Christ.

1 Thess 5:8. But let us who live in the light keep sober, protected by the armor of faith and love, and wearing as our helmet the happy hope of salvation.

2 Thess 2:16. May our Lord Jesus Christ himself and God our Father, who has loved us and given us everlasting comfort and hope which we don't deserve.

1 Tim 1:1. From: Paul, a missionary of Jesus Christ, sent out by the direct command of God our Savior and by Jesus Christ our Lord—our only hope.

Tit 1:2. So that they can have eternal life, which God promised them before the world began—and he cannot lie.

Tit 2:13. Looking forward to that wonderful time we've been expecting, when his glory shall be seen —the glory of our great God and Savior Jesus Christ.

Tit 3:7. So that he could declare us good in God's eyes—all because of his great kindness; and now we can share in the wealth of the eternal life he gives us, and we are eagerly looking forward to receiving it.

Heb 3:6. But Christ, God's faithful Son, is in complete charge of God's house. And we Christians are God's house—he lives in us!—if we keep up our courage firm to the end, and our joy and our trust in the Lord.

Heb 6:11. And we are anxious that you keep on loving others as long as life lasts, [18]He has given us both his promise and his oath, two things we can completely count on, for it is impossible for God to tell a lie. Now all those who flee to him to save them can take new courage when they hear such assurances from God; now they can know without doubt that he will give them the salvation he has promised them. [19]This certain hope of being saved is a strong and trustworthy anchor for our souls, connecting us with God himself behind the sacred curtains of heaven.

Heb 11:1. What is faith? . . . It is the certainty that what we hope for is waiting for us, even though we cannot see it up ahead.

1 Pet 1:3. All honor to God, the God and Father of our Lord Jesus Christ; for it is his boundless mercy that has given us the privilege of being born again, so that we are now members of God's own family. Now we live in the hope of eternal life because Christ rose again from the dead. [13]So now you can look forward soberly and intelligently to more of God's kindness to you when Jesus Christ returns. [21]Now your faith and hope can rest in him alone.

See *Faith.*

OF THE WICKED. Job 8:11. Those who forget God have no hope.

Job 11:20. But the wicked shall find no way to escape; their only hope is death.

Job 27:8. But what hope has the godless when God cuts him off and takes away his life?

Job 31:23. For if the majesty of God opposes me, what hope is there? [24]If I have put my trust in money, [25]if my happiness depends on wealth. [28]It should mean that I denied the God of heaven.

Prov 6:15. But he will be destroyed suddenly, broken beyond hope of healing.

Prov 10:28. The hope of good men is eternal happiness; the hopes of evil men are all in vain.

Zech 9:5. Ashkelon will see it happen and be filled with fear; Gaza will huddle in desperation and Ekron will shake with terror, for their hope that Tyre would stop the enemies' advance will all be dashed.

Eph 2:12. Remember that in those days you were living utterly apart from Christ; you were enemies of God's children and he had promised you no help. You were lost, without God, without hope.

HOPHNI Son of Eli, 1 Sam 1:3. Sin of, 1 Sam 2:12–36; 3:11–14. Death of, 1 Sam 4:4, 11, 17.

HOPHRA See *Pharaoh.*

HOR Mountain on which Aaron died, Num 20:21–29; 21:4; 33:38, 39; Deut 32:50.

2. A mountain in northern Palestine, Num 34: 7–9.

HORAM King of Gezer, Josh 10:33.

HOREB A mountain, same as Mount Sinai, Ex 3:1; 4:27; 17:5, 6; Deut 1:1–6, 19–21; 4:10, 15; 5:2, 3; 9:8; 18:16; 29:1; 1 Kgs 8:9; 19:8; 2 Chron 5:10; Mal 4:4.

See *Sinai.*

HOREM A fortified city in Naphtali, Josh 19: 38.

HOR-HAGIDGAD One of the stations of the Israelites in the wilderness, Num 33:15–37.

HORI 1. Son of Lotan, Gen 36:22; 1 Chron 1: 38, 39.

2. A Simeonite, Num 13:3–15.

HORMAH A city southwest of the Dead Sea, Num 14:45; 21:1–3; Deut 1:44. Taken by Judah and Simeon, Judg 1:17; Josh 12:8–24. Allotted to Simeon, Josh 19:2–7; 1 Chron 4:30. Within the territory allotted to Judah, Josh 15:21–32; 1 Sam 30: 27–31.

HORN Used for a trumpet, see *Trumpet.*

FIGURATIVE. Of power, 1 Kgs 22:11.

Symbolical. Dan 7:7–24; 8:3–9, 20; Mic 4:13; Zech 1:18–21; Rev 5:6; 12:3; 13:1, 11; 17:3–16.

Horns of the altar, see *Altar.*

HORNED OWL Forbidden as food, Deut 14:11–18.

HORNET Or wasp, Ex 23:28; Deut 7:20; Josh 24:12.

HORONAIM A town of Moab, Isa 15:5; Jer 48:2–4, 34.

HORONITE Sanballat, the, Neh 2:10; 13:28.

HORSE Description of: Great strength, Job 39:19–25; Isa 5:28; swifter than eagles, Jer 4:13; snorting and neighing of, Jer 8:16; a vain thing for safety, Ps 33:16, 17; Prov 21:31. Used by the Egyptians in war, Ex 14:9; 15:19; the Israelites, 1 Kgs 22:4. Used for cavalry, 2 Kgs 18:23; Jer 47:3; 51:21. Egypt famous for, Isa 31:1. Forbidden to kings of Israel, Deut 17:16. Hamstrung by Joshua, Josh 11:6, 9; David, 2 Sam 8:4. Israel reproved for keeping, Isa 2:7; 31:1; Ezk 17:15. Exported from Egypt, 1 Kgs 10:28, 29; 2 Chron 9:25, 28; from Babylon, Ezra 2:66, 67; Neh 7:68, 69. Bits for, Jas 3:3; bells for, Zech 14:20; harness for, Jer 46:4. Color of, Zech 1:8. Commerce in, Rev 18:13; see *Exported,* above. Dedicated to idols, 2 Kgs 23:11.

Symbolical. Zech 1:8; Rev 6:2–8; 9:17, 18; 19:11–21.

HORTICULTURE Encouraged, Lev 19:23–25; Deut 20:19, 20.

See *Agriculture; Pruning.*

HOSAH 1. A city of Asher, Josh 19:29.

2. A Levite, 1 Chron 16:38; 26:10, 11.

HOSEA One of the minor prophets, Rom 9:25. See the book of Hosea.

HOSHAIAH 1. One of the returned exiles, Neh 12:31–33.

2. Father of Azariah, Jer 43:2, 3.

HOSHAMA Son of Jeconiah, 1 Chron 3:17, 18.

HOSHEA 1. The original name of Joshua, Num 13:3–15, 16. See *Joshua, 1.*

2. A leader of Ephraim, 1 Chron 27:16–22.

3. King of Israel. Assassinates Pekah and usurps the throne, 2 Kgs 15:30. Evil reign of, 2 Kgs 17:1, 2. Becomes subject to Assyria, 2 Kgs 17:3. Conspires against Assyria and is imprisoned, 2 Kgs 17:4. Last king of Israel, 2 Kgs 17:6; 18:9–12; Hos 10:3, 7.

4. A Jewish leader who signed the covenant with Nehemiah, Neh 10:23.

HOSPITALITY Ex 22:21. You must not oppress a stranger in any way; remember, you yourselves were foreigners in the land of Egypt.

Ex 23:9. Do not oppress foreigners; you know what it's like to be a foreigner; remember your own experience in the land of Egypt.

Lev 19:10. It is the same with your grape crop—don't strip every last piece of fruit from the vines, and don't pick up the grapes that fall to the ground. Leave them for the poor and for those traveling through, for I am Jehovah your God. [33]Do not take advantage of foreigners in your land; do not wrong them. [34]They must be treated like any other citizen; love them as yourself, for remember that you too were foreigners in the land of Egypt. I am Jehovah your God.

Lev 24:22. You shall have the same law for the foreigner as for the home-born citizen, for I am Jehovah your God.

Deut 10:18. He gives justice to the fatherless and widows. He loves foreigners and gives them food and clothing. [19](You too must love foreigners, for you yourselves were foreigners in the land of Egypt.)

Deut 26:12. Every third year is a year of special tithing. That year you are to give all your tithes to the Levites, migrants, orphans, and widows, so that they will be well fed. [13]Then you shall declare before the Lord your God, "I have given all of my tithes to the Levites, the migrants, the orphans, and the widows, just as you commanded me; I have not violated or forgotten any of your rules."

Deut 27:19. "Cursed is he who is unjust to the foreigner, the orphan, and the widow." And all the people shall reply, "Amen."

Prov 9:1. Wisdom has built a palace supported on seven pillars, [2]and has prepared a great banquet, and mixed the wines, [3]And sent out her maidens inviting all to come. She calls from the busiest intersections in the city, [4]"Come, you simple ones without good judgment; [5]come to wisdom's banquet and drink the wines that I have mixed."

Prov 23:6, 7, 8. Don't associate with evil men; don't long for their favors and gifts. Their kindness is a trick; they want to use you as their pawn. The delicious food they serve will turn sour in your stomach and you will vomit it, and have to take back your words of appreciation for their "kindness."

Isa 58:6. No, the kind of fast I want is that you stop oppressing those who work for you and treat them fairly and give them what they earn. [7]I want you to share your food with the hungry and bring right into your own homes those who are helpless, poor and destitute. Clothe those who are cold and don't hide from relatives who need your help.

Mt 22:1, 2. Jesus told several other stories to show what the Kingdom of Heaven is like. "For instance," he said, "it can be illustrated by the story of a king who prepared a great wedding dinner for his son. [3]Many guests were invited, and when the banquet was ready he sent messengers to notify everyone that it was time to come. But all refused! [4]So he sent other servants to tell them, 'Everything is ready and the roast is in the oven. Hurry!' [5]But the guests he had invited merely laughed and went on about their business, one to his farm, another to his store; [6]others beat up his messengers and treated them shamefully, even killing some of them. [7]Then the angry king sent out his army and destroyed the murderers and burned their city. [8]And he said to his servants, 'The wedding feast is ready, and the guests I invited aren't worthy of the honor. [9]Now go out to the street corners and invite everyone you see.' [10]So the servants did, and brought in all they could find, good and bad alike; and the banquet hall was filled with guests."

Mt 25:34. "Then I, the King, shall say to those at my right, 'Come, blessed of my Father, into the

Kingdom prepared for you from the founding of the world. [35]For I was hungry and you fed me; I was thirsty and you gave me water; I was a stranger and you invited me into your homes; [36]naked and you clothed me; sick and in prison, and you visited me.' [37]Then these righteous ones will reply, 'Sir, when did we ever see you hungry and feed you? Or thirsty and give you anything to drink? [38]Or a stranger, and help you? Or naked, and clothe you? [39]When did we ever see you sick or in prison, and visit you?' [40]And I, the King, will tell them, 'When you did it to these my brothers you were doing it to me!' [41]Then I will turn to those on my left and say, 'Away with you, you cursed ones, into the eternal fire prepared for the devil and his demons. [42]For I was hungry and you wouldn't feed me; thirsty, and you wouldn't give me anything to drink; [43]a stranger, and you refused me hospitality; naked, and you wouldn't clothe me; sick, and in prison, and you didn't visit me.' [44]Then they will reply, 'Lord, when did we ever see you hungry or thirsty or a stranger or naked or sick or in prison, and not help you?' [45]And I will answer, 'When you refused to help the least of these my brothers, you were refusing help to me.' [46]And they shall go away into eternal punishment; but the righteous into everlasting life."

Lk 14:12. Then he turned to his host. "When you put on a dinner," he said, "don't invite friends, brothers, relatives, and rich neighbors! For they will return the invitation. [13]Instead, invite the poor, the crippled, the lame, and the blind. [14]Then at the resurrection of the godly, God will reward you for inviting those who can't repay you."

Rom 12:13. When God's children are in need, you be the one to help them out. And get into the habit of inviting guests home for dinner or, if they need lodging, for the night.

Rom 16:1, 2. Phoebe, a dear Christian woman from the town of Cenchreae, will be coming to see you soon. She has worked hard in the church there. Receive her as your sister in the Lord, giving her a warm Christian welcome. Help her in every way you can, for she has helped many in their needs, including me.

1 Tim 3:2. For a pastor must be a good man whose life cannot be spoken against. He must have only one wife, and he must be hard working and thoughtful, orderly, and full of good deeds. He must enjoy having guests in his home, and must be a good Bible teacher.

1 Tim 5:10. She must be well thought of by everyone because of the good she has done. Has she brought up her children well? Has she been kind to strangers as well as to other Christians? Has she helped those who are sick and hurt? Is she always ready to show kindness?

Tit 1:7. These pastors must be men of blameless lives because they are God's ministers. They must not be proud or impatient; they must not be drunkards or fighters or greedy for money. [8]They must enjoy having guests in their homes and must love all that is good. They must be sensible men, and fair. They must be clean minded and level headed.

Heb 13:2. Don't forget to be kind to strangers, for some who have done this have entertained angels without realizing it!

1 Pet 4:9. Cheerfully share your home with those who need a meal or a place to stay for the night. [10]God has given each of you some special abilities; be sure to use them to help each other, passing on to others God's many kinds of blessings. [11]Are you called to preach? Then preach as though God himself were speaking through you. Are you called to help others? Do it with all the strength and energy that God supplies, so that God will be glorified through Jesus Christ—to him be glory and power forever and ever. Amen.

3 Jn 1:5. Dear friend, you are doing a good work for God in taking care of the traveling teachers and missionaries who are passing through. [6]They have told the church here of your friendship and your loving deeds. I am glad when you send them on their way with a generous gift. [7]For they are traveling for the Lord, and take neither food, clothing, shelter, nor money from those who are not Christians, even though they have preached to them. [8]So we ourselves should take care of them in order that we may become partners with them in the Lord's work.

See *Guest; Strangers.*

INSTANCES OF. Pharaoh to Abraham, Gen 12:16. Melchizedek to Abraham, Gen 14:18. Abraham to the angels, Gen 18:1–8. Lot to the angel, Gen 19:1–11. Abimelech to Abraham, Gen 20:14, 15. Men of Heth to Abraham, Gen 23:5, 6, 11. Laban to Abraham's servant, Gen 24:31; to Jacob, Gen 29:12–14. Isaac to Abimelech, Gen 26:30. Joseph to his brothers, Gen 43:31–34. Pharaoh to Jacob, Gen 45:16–20; 47:7–12. Reuel to Moses, Ex 2:20. Rahab to the spies, Josh 2:1–16. Man of Gibe-ah to the Levite, Judg 19:16–21. Samuel to Saul, 1 Sam 9:22. David to Mephibosheth, 2 Sam 9:7–13. Pharaoh to Hadad, 1 Kgs 11:16–18, 22. The widow of Zarephath to Elijah, 1 Kgs 17:10–24. The Shunemmite to Elisha, 2 Kgs 4:8. Elisha to the Syrian spies, 2 Kgs 6:22. Job to strangers, Job 31:32.

Matthew to Jesus, Mt 9:9, 10; Mk 2:13–15; Lk 5:27–29. Martha to Jesus, Lk 10:38; Jn 12:1, 2. Pharisees to Jesus, Lk 11:37, 38. Zacchaeus to Jesus, Lk 19:1–10. The tanner to Peter, Acts 10:5, 6, 23. Lydia to Paul and Silas, Acts 16:15. Publius to Paul, Acts 28:7; Phoebe to Paul, Rom 16:1, 2. Onesiphorus to Paul, 2 Tim 1:16. Gaius, 3 Jn 1:5–8.

REWARDED.

Instances of. Rahab's, Josh 6:17, 22–25. Widow of Zarephath's, 1 Kgs 17:10–24.

See *Feasts; Strangers.*

HOSTAGE 2 Kgs 14:14; 2 Chron 25:24.

HOTHAM Son of Heber, 1 Chron 7:32.

2. An Aroerite, 1 Chron 11:26–47.

HOTHIR Son of Heman, 1 Chron 25:4, 5, 9–31.

HOT SPRINGS Gen 36:24.

HOURS A division of time. Twelve, in the day, Jn 11:9; in the night, Acts 23:23, 24. The third, sixth, and ninth hours of the day, mentioned in the New Testament were the more marked divisions of the twelve.

Symbolical. Rev 8:1; 9:15.

HOUSE Built of stone, Lev 14:40–45; Amos 5:11; brick, Gen 11:3, 4; Ex 1:11–14; wood, Isa 9:8–10. Built into city walls, Josh 2:15.

Used for worship, Acts 1:13, 14; 12:12; Rom 16:5; 1 Cor 16:19; Col 4:15; Philemon 1:1, 2.

Is private, Deut 24:10, 11.

ARCHITECTURE OF. Foundations of stone, 1 Kgs 5:17; 1 Kgs 7:9; Ezra 6:3; Jer 51:26. Figurative: Ps 87:1; Isa 28:16; 48:13; 1 Cor 3:11; Eph 2:20; Rev 21:14. Corner stone, Job 38:6, 7. Figurative: Ps 118: 22; Isa 28:16; Eph 2:20; 1 Pet 2:6.

Porches, Judg 3:22, 23; 1 Kgs 7:6, 7; 2 Kgs 1:2; Mt 24:17; courtyards, Neh 8:16; Esther 1:5; summer apartment, Judg 3:20, with Amos 3:15; 1 Kgs 17:19; inner room, 1 Kgs 22:25; bedrooms, Gen 43:30; 2 Sam 18:33; 2 Kgs 4:10; upstairs rooms, Mk 14:14; Acts 1:13; 9:37; 20:8; pillars, Prov 9:1; windows, Judg 5:28; Prov 7:6; plastered, Dan 5:5; hinges, Prov 26:14.

Roofs, flat, Josh 2:6; Judg 16:27; 1 Sam 9:25; 2 Sam 11:2; 16:22; Isa 22:1; Mt 24:17; Lk 12:3; guardrails required in Mosaic law, Deut 22:8. Prayer on, Acts 10:9, 10. Altars on, 2 Kgs 23:12; Jer 19:13; 32:29; Zeph 1:5. Huts on, Neh 8:16. Used as place to sleep, Josh 2:8.

Painted, Jer 22:14; Ezk 8:10. Texts of scripture on doorposts of, Deut 6:9. Laws regarding sale of, Lev 25:29–33; Neh 5:2–4. Dedicated, Deut 20:5.

FIGURATIVE. Ps 23:6; 36:8; Jn 14:2, 3; 2 Cor 5: 1; Heb 3:2.

HOUSE OF GOD A place of prayer, Mt 21: 13; Mk 11:17; Lk 19:46. Holy, Ezk 43:12; 1 Cor 3:17.

Proper behavior in, 1 Tim 3:15. "We Christians are God's house," Heb 3:6. Christ a high priest over, Heb 10:21. Judgment begins at, 1 Pet 4:17. See Mt 12:4; Mk 2:25, 26; Lk 6:4; cf. Jn 2:16, 17; 14:2, 3.

See *Synagogue; Tabernacle; Temple.*

HUKKOK A place on the boundary line of Naphtali, Josh 19:34.

HUKOK See *Helkath.*

HUL Son of Aram, Gen 10:23; 1 Chron 1:17.

HULDAH A prophetess. Foretells the destruction of Jerusalem, 2 Kgs 22:14–20; 2 Chron 34: 22–28.

HUMAN SACRIFICE See *Offerings, Human.*

HUMBLE Deut 8:2, 16; 2 Chron 7:14; 34:27; Ps 18:27; 37:11; 69:32; Prov 6:3; 16:19; 29:23; Isa 57: 15; Mt 18:4; 23:12; Jas 4:6, 10; 1 Pet 5:5, 6.

HUMILIATION AND SELF-EXAMINATION COMMANDED. Lev 16:29, 30. This is a permanent law: You must do no work on the twenty-fifth day of September, but must spend the day in self-examination and humility. This applies whether you are born in the land or are a foreigner living among the people of Israel; for this is the day commemorating the atonement, cleansing you in the Lord's eyes from all of your sins. [31]It is a Sabbath of solemn rest for you, and you shall spend the day in quiet humility; this is a permanent law.

Lev 23:26, 27. *The Day of Atonement* follows nine days later: All the people are to come together before the Lord, saddened by their sin; and they shall offer sacrifices by fire to the Lord. [28]Don't do any work that day, for it is a special day for making atonement before the Lord your God. [29]Anyone who does not spend the day in repentance and sorrow for sin shall be excommunicated from his people. [30, 31]And I will put to death anyone who does any kind of work that day. This is a law of Israel from generation to generation. [32]For this is a Sabbath of solemn rest, and in it you shall humble your souls and be filled with remorse; this time for atonement begins on the previous evening and goes on until the next evening.

2 Chron 7:14. Then if my people will humble themselves and pray and search for me, and turn from their wicked ways, I will hear them from heaven and forgive their sins and heal their land.

Ezra 8:21. Then I declared a fast while we were at the Ahava River so that we would humble ourselves before our God; and we prayed that he would give us a good journey and protect us, our children, and our goods as we traveled. [22]For I was ashamed to ask the king for soldiers and cavalry to accompany us and protect us from the enemies along the way. After all, we had told the king that our God would protect all those who worshiped him, and that disaster could come only to those who had forsaken him! [23]So we fasted and begged God to take care of us. And he did.

See *Fasting; Humility.*

HUMILITY Deut 9:7. Don't you remember (oh, never forget it!) how continually angry you made the Lord your God out in the wilderness. *vs.* 4–29.

Deut 15:15. Remember that you were slaves in the land of Egypt and the Lord your God rescued you!

Job 5:11. And gives prosperity to the poor and humble, and takes sufferers to safety.

Job 22:29. If you are attacked and knocked down, you will know that there is someone who will lift you up again. Yes, he will save the humble.

Job 25:5. God is so glorious that even the moon and stars are less than nothing as compared to him. [6]How much less is man, who is but a worm in his sight?

Ps 9:12. He who avenges murder has an open ear to those who cry to him for justice. He does not ignore the prayers of men in trouble when they call to him for help.

Ps 10:17. Lord, you know the hopes of humble people. Surely you will hear their cries and comfort their hearts by helping them.

Ps 22:6. But I am a worm, not a man, scorned and despised by my own people and by all mankind.

Ps 25:9. He will teach the ways that are right and best to those who humbly turn to him.

Ps 37:11. But all who humble themselves before

the Lord shall be given every blessing, and shall have wonderful peace.

Ps 69:32. The humble shall see their God at work for them. No wonder they will be so glad! All who seek for God shall live in joy.

Ps 86:1. Bend down and hear my prayer, O Lord, and answer me, for I am deep in trouble.

Ps 131:1. Lord, I am not proud and haughty. I don't think myself better than others. I don't pretend to "know it all." [2]I am quiet now before the Lord, just as a child who is weaned from the breast. Yes, my begging has been stilled.

Ps 138:6. Yet though he is so great, he respects the humble.

Ps 147:6. The Lord supports the humble.

Ps 149:4. For Jehovah enjoys his people; he will save the humble.

Prov 3:34. The Lord mocks at mockers, but helps the humble.

Prov 10:8. The wise man is glad to be instructed, but a self-sufficient fool falls flat on his face.

Prov 11:2. Proud men end in shame, but the meek become wise.

Prov 12:15. A fool thinks he needs no advice, but a wise man listens to others.

Prov 15:33. Humility and reverence for the Lord will make you both wise and honored. Prov 18:12.

Prov 16:19. Better poor and humble than proud and rich.

Prov 22:4. True humility and respect for the Lord lead a man to riches, honor and long life.

Prov 25:6, 7. Don't demand an audience with the king as though you were some powerful prince. It is better to wait for an invitation rather than to be sent back to the end of the line, publicly disgraced!

Prov 27:2. Don't praise yourself; let others do it!

Prov 29:23. Pride ends in a fall, while humility brings honor.

Prov 30:32. If you have been a fool by being proud or plotting evil, don't brag about it—cover your mouth with your hand in shame.

Eccl 5:2. Don't be a fool who doesn't even realize it is sinful to make rash promises to God, for he is in heaven and you are only here on earth, so let your words be few.

Isa 29:19. The meek will be filled with fresh joy from the Lord, and the poor shall exult in the Holy One of Israel.

Isa 51:1. Listen to me, all who hope for deliverance, who seek the Lord! Consider the quarry from which you were mined, the rock from which you were cut! Deut 32:7.

Isa 57:15. I live in that high and holy place where those with contrite, humble spirits dwell; and I refresh the humble and give new courage to those with repentant hearts.

Isa 66:2. Yet I will look with pity on the man who has a humble and a contrite heart, who trembles at my word.

Jer 45:5. Are you seeking great things for yourself? Don't do it!

Ezk 16:63. Despite all you have done, I will be kind to you again; you will cover your mouth in silence and in shame when I forgive you all that you have done, says the Lord God.

Mic 6:8. No, he has told you what he wants, and this is all it is: . . . *to walk humbly with your God.*

Zeph 2:3. Beg him to save you, all who are humble—all who have tried to obey. Walk humbly and do what is right; perhaps even yet the Lord will protect you from his wrath in that day of doom.

Zeph 3:11. I will remove all your proud and arrogant men from among you; there will be no pride or haughtiness on my holy mountain. [12]Those who are left will be the poor and the humble, and they will trust in the name of the Lord.

Mt 5:3. "Humble men are very fortunate!" he told them, "for the Kingdom of Heaven is given to them." Lk 6:20.

Mt 11:29, 30. Wear my yoke—for it fits perfectly—and let me teach you; for I am gentle and humble, and you shall find rest for your souls; for I give you only light burdens.

Mt 18:2. Jesus called a small child over to him and set the little fellow down among them, [3]and said, "Unless you turn to God from your sins and become as little children, you will never get into the Kingdom of Heaven. [4]Therefore anyone who humbles himself as this little child, is the greatest in the Kingdom of Heaven." Mk 9:33–37; Lk 9:46–48.

Mt 20:26. Anyone wanting to be a leader among you must be your servant. [27]And if you want to be right at the top, you must serve like a slave. Mk 10:43, 44; Lk 22:26.

Mt 23:12. But those who think themselves great shall be disappointed and humbled; and those who humble themselves shall be exalted. Lk 14:11.

Lk 1:52. He has torn princes from their thrones and exalted the lowly.

Lk 10:21. I praise you, O Father, Lord of heaven and earth, for hiding these things from the intellectuals and worldly wise and for revealing them to those who are as trusting as little children.

Lk 14:10. Do this instead—start at the foot; and when your host sees you he will come and say, "Friend, we have a better place than this for you!" *v.* 11; Prov 25:6, 7.

Lk 17:10. Just so, if you merely obey me, you should not consider yourselves worthy of praise. For you have simply done your duty!

Lk 18:13. But the corrupt tax collector stood at a distance and dared not even lift his eyes to heaven as he prayed, but beat upon his chest in sorrow, exclaiming, "God, be merciful to me, a sinner." [14]I tell you, this sinner, not the Pharisee, returned home forgiven! For the proud shall be humbled, but the humble shall be honored. Mt 23:12.

Lk 22:24. And they began to argue among themselves as to who would have the highest rank [in the coming Kingdom]. [25]Jesus told them, "In this world the kings and great men order their slaves around, and the slaves have no choice but to like it! [26]But among you, the one who serves you best will be your leader. [27]Out in the world the master sits at the table and is served by his servants. But not here! For I am your servant.

Jn 13:14. And since I, the Lord and Teacher, have washed your feet, you ought to wash each other's feet. [15]I have given you an example to follow: do as I have done to you. [16]How true it is that a servant is not greater than his master. Nor is the messenger more important than the one who sends him.

Rom 11:18. But you must be careful not to brag about being put in to replace the branches that were broken off. Remember that you are important only because you are now a part of God's tree; you are just a branch, not a root. [20]Do not be proud; be humble and grateful—and careful. [25]I want you to know about this truth from God, dear brothers, so that you will not feel proud and start bragging. Yes, it is true that some of the Jews have set themselves against the Gospel now, but this will last only until all of you Gentiles have come to Christ —those of you who will.

Rom 12:3. As God's messenger I give each of you God's warning: Be honest in your estimate of yourselves, measuring your value by how much faith God has given you. [10]Take delight in honoring each other. [16]Don't try to get into the good graces of important people, but enjoy the company of ordinary folks. And don't think you know it all!

1 Cor 1:28. He has chosen a plan despised by the world, counted as nothing at all, and used it to bring down to nothing those the world considers great, [29]so that no one anywhere can ever brag in the presence of God.

1 Cor 2:1. Dear brothers, even when I first came to you I didn't use lofty words and brilliant ideas to tell you God's message. [2]For I decided that I would speak only of Jesus Christ and his death on the cross. [3]I came to you in weakness—timid and trembling.

1 Cor 3:18. Stop fooling yourselves. If you count yourself above average in intelligence, as judged by this world's standards, you had better put this all aside and be a fool rather than let it hold you back from the true wisdom from above.

1 Cor 10:12. So be careful. If you are thinking, "Oh, I would never behave like that"—let this be a warning to you. For you too may fall into sin.

1 Cor 13:4. Love is very patient and kind, never jealous or envious, never boastful or proud.

2 Cor 11:30. But if I must brag, I would rather brag about the things that show how weak I am.

2 Cor 12:5. That experience is something worth bragging about, but I am not going to do it. I am going to boast only about how weak I am and how great God is to use such weakness for his glory. [6]I have plenty to boast about and would be no fool in doing it, but I don't want anyone to think more highly of me than he should from what he can actually see in my life and my message. [7]I will say this: because these experiences I had were so tremendous, God was afraid I might be puffed up by them; so I was given a physical condition which has been a thorn in my flesh, a messenger from Satan to hurt and bother me, and prick my pride. [8]Three different times I begged God to make me well again. [9]Each time he said, "No. But I am with you; that is all you need. My power shows up best in weak people." Now I am glad to boast about how weak I am; I am glad to be a living demonstration of Christ's power, instead of showing off my own power and abilities. [10]Since I know it is all for Christ's good, I am quite happy about "the thorn," and about insults and hardships, persecutions and difficulties; for when I am weak, then I am strong —the less I have, the more I depend on him. [11]You have made me act like a fool—boasting like this— for you people ought to be writing about me and not making me write about myself. There isn't a single thing these other marvelous fellows have that I don't have too, even though I am really worth nothing at all. [12]When I was there I certainly gave you every proof that I was truly an apostle, sent to you by God himself: for I patiently did many wonders and signs and mighty works among you.

Gal 5:26. Then we won't need to look for honors and popularity.

Gal 6:14. As for me, God forbid that I should boast about anything except the cross of our Lord Jesus Christ. Because of that cross my interest in all the attractive things of the world was killed long ago, and the world's interest in me is also long dead.

Eph 4:2. Be humble and gentle. Be patient with each other, making allowance for each other's faults because of your love.

Eph 5:21. Honor Christ by submitting to each other.

Phil 2:3. Don't be selfish; don't live to make a good impression on others. Be humble, thinking of others as better than yourself. [4]Don't just think about your own affairs, but be interested in others, too, and in what they are doing. [5]Your attitude should be the kind that was shown us by Jesus Christ, [6]who, though he was God, did not demand and cling to his rights as God, [7]but laid aside his mighty power and glory, taking the disguise of a slave and becoming like men. [8]And he humbled himself even further, going so far as actually to die a criminal's death on a cross. [9]Yet it was because of this that God raised him up to the heights of heaven and gave him a name which is above every other name, [10]that at the name of Jesus every knee shall bow in heaven and on earth and under the earth, [11]and every tongue shall confess that Jesus Christ is Lord, to the glory of God the Father.

Col 3:12. Since you have been chosen by God . . . and because of his deep love and concern for you, you should practice tenderhearted mercy and kindness to others. Don't worry about making an impression on them but be ready to suffer quietly and patiently.

Jas 1:9. A Christian who doesn't amount to much in this world should be glad, for he is great in the Lord's sight. [10]But a rich man should be glad that his riches mean nothing to the Lord, for he will soon be gone, like a flower that has lost its beauty and fades away. [19]Dear brothers, don't ever forget that it is best to listen much, speak little, and not become angry.

Jas 3:1. Dear brothers, don't be too eager to tell others their faults, for we all make many mistakes; and when we teachers of religion, who should know better, do wrong, our punishment will be greater than it would be for others.

Jas 4:6. God gives strength to the humble, but sets himself against the proud and haughty. [10]Then when you realize your worthlessness before the Lord, he will lift you up, encourage and help you.

1 Pet 5:3. Don't be tyrants, but lead them by your good example. [5]You younger men, follow the leadership of those who are older. And all of you serve each other with humble spirits, for God gives special blessings to those who are humble, but sets himself against those who are proud. [6]If you will humble yourselves under the mighty hand of God, in his good time he will lift you up.

EXEMPLIFIED. Gen 18:27. Since I have begun, let me go on and speak further to the Lord, though I am but dust and ashes. *v.* 32.

Gen 32:10. I am not worthy of the least of all your loving kindnesses shown me again and again just as you promised me.

Ex 3:11. "But I'm not the person for a job like that!" Moses exclaimed.

Ex 4:10. But Moses pleaded, "O Lord, I'm just not a good speaker. I never have been, and I'm not now, even after you have spoken to me, for I have a speech impediment."

2 Sam 7:18. Then David went into the Tabernacle and sat before the Lord and prayed, "O Lord God, why have you showered your blessings on such an insignificant person as I am? [19]And now, in addition to everything else, you speak of giving me an eternal dynasty! Such generosity is far beyond any human standard!" 1 Chron 17:17.

1 Kgs 3:7. O Lord my God, now you have made me the king instead of my father David, but I am as a little child who doesn't know his way around. 2 Chron 1:10.

1 Chron 29:14. But who am I and who are my people that we should be permitted to give anything to you? Everything we have has come from you, and we only give you what is yours already!

2 Chron 2:6. And who am I to be allowed to build a temple for God? But it will be a place to worship him.

Ezra 9:13. And now, even after our punishment in exile because of our wickedness (and we have been punished far less than we deserved).

Job 9:14. And who am I that I should try to argue with Almighty God, or even reason with him? [15]Even if I were sinless I wouldn't say a word. I would only plead for mercy. Job 10:15.

Job 33:7. I, too, am made of common clay.

Job 40:4. I am nothing—how could I ever find the answers? I lay my hand upon my mouth in silence. [5]I have said too much already.

Job 42:4. [You said,] "Listen and I will speak! . . . [5][But now I say,] "I had heard about you before, but now I have seen you, [6]and I loathe myself and repent in dust and ashes."

Ps 8:3. When I look up into the night skies . . . [4]I cannot understand how you can bother with mere puny man, to pay any attention to him! Job 7:17, 18; Ps 144:3, 4.

Ps 73:22. I saw myself so stupid and so ignorant; I must seem like an animal to you, O God.

Ps 131:1. Lord, I am not proud and haughty. I don't think myself better than others. I don't pretend to "know it all." [2]I am quiet now before the Lord, just as a child who is weaned from the breast. Yes, my begging has been stilled.

Ps 141:5. Let the godly smite me! It will be a kindness! If they reprove me, it is medicine! Don't let me refuse it.

Prov 30:2. I am tired out, O God, and ready to die. I am too stupid even to call myself a human being! [3]I cannot understand man, let alone God.

Isa 6:5. Then I said, "My doom is sealed, for I am a foul-mouthed sinner, a member of a sinful, foul-mouthed race; and I have looked upon the King, the Lord of heaven's armies."

Jer 1:6. "O Lord God," I said, "I can't do that! I'm far too young! I'm only a youth!"

Jer 10:23. O Lord, I know it is not within the power of man to map his life and plan his course —[24]so you correct me, Lord; but please be gentle. Don't do it in your anger, for I would die.

Dan 2:30. But remember, it's not because I am wiser than any living person that I know this secret of your dream. Gen 41:16; Acts 3:12.

Mt 3:14. John didn't want to do it. "This isn't proper," he said. "I am the one who needs to be baptized by you."

Mt 15:27. "Yes, it is!" she replied, "for even the puppies beneath the table are permitted to eat the crumbs that fall."

Mt 25:37. Then these righteous ones will reply, "Sir, when did we ever see you hungry and feed you? Or thirsty and give you anything to drink? [38]Or a stranger, and help you? Or naked, and clothe you? [39]When did we ever see you sick or in prison, and visit you?" [40]And I, the King, will tell them, "When you did it to these my brothers you were doing it to me!"

Lk 7:6, 7. Sir, don't inconvenience yourself by coming to my home, for I am not worthy of any such honor or even to come and meet you. Just speak a word from where you are, and my servant boy will be healed! Mt 8:8, 9.

Jn 1:27. Who will soon begin his ministry among you, and I am not even fit to be his slave.

Jn 3:29. The bride will go where the bridegroom is! A bridegroom's friends rejoice with him. I am the Bridegroom's friend, and I am filled with joy at his success. [30]He must become greater and greater, and I must become less and less.

Rom 7:18. I know I am rotten through and through so far as my old sinful nature is concerned.

1 Cor 15:10. But whatever I am now it is all because God poured out such kindness and grace upon me—and not without results: for I have worked harder than all the other apostles, yet actu-

ally I wasn't doing it, but God working in me, to bless me.

2 Cor 3:5. And not because we think we can do anything of lasting value by ourselves. Our only power and success comes from God.

2 Cor 12:7. Because these experiences I had were so tremendous, God was afraid I might be puffed up by them; so I was given a physical condition which has been a thorn in my flesh, a messenger from Satan to hurt and bother me, and prick my pride.

Eph 3:8. Though I am the most useless Christian there is, yet I was the one chosen for this special joy.

Phil 3:12. I don't mean to say I am perfect. I haven't learned all I should even yet, but I keep working toward that day when I will finally be all that Christ saved me for and wants me to be. [13]No, dear brothers, I am still not all I should be.

Phil 4:12. I know how to live on almost nothing or with everything.

1 Tim 1:15. How true it is, and how I long that everyone should know it, that Christ Jesus came into the world to save sinners—and I was the greatest of them all. 1 Cor 15:9.

Rev 4:10. The twenty-four Elders fell down before him and worshiped him, the Eternal Living One, and cast their crowns before the throne.

INSTANCES OF. Joseph, Gen 41:16. David, 1 Sam 18:18–23; 24:14; 26:20; 2 Sam 7:18–29; 1 Chron 17:16–27. Mephibosheth, 2 Sam 9:8. Ahab, 1 Kgs 21:29. Josiah, 2 Chron 34:27; Elihu, Job 32: 4–7. Isaiah, Isa 6:5. Elisabeth, Lk 1:43. John the Baptist, Mk 1:7; Lk 3:16. Cornelius, Acts 10:33. Paul, Rom 1:11, 12; 16:7. Peter, Lk 5:8; 1 Pet 5:1. John, Rev 1:9.

See *Modesty.*

HUMTAH A city of Judah, Josh 15:48–62.

HUNDRED, TOWER OF THE Neh 3:1; 12:39.

HUNGER Of Jesus, Mt 4:2–4; 21:18; Mk 11:12; Lk 4:1–4; Jn 4:8. A stimulus to work, Prov 16:26. No hunger in heaven, Rev 7:16, 17.

See *Famine.*

SPIRITUAL. Prov 2:3, 4, 5. Yes, if you want better insight and discernment, and are searching for them as you would for lost money or hidden treasure, then wisdom will be given you, and knowledge of God himself; you will soon learn the importance of reverence for the Lord and of trusting him.

Isa 55:1. Say there! is anyone thirsty? Come and drink—even if you have no money! Come, take your choice of wine and milk—it's all free! [2]Why spend your money on foodstuffs that don't give you strength? Why pay for groceries that don't do you any good? Listen and I'll tell you where to get good food that fattens up the soul!

Amos 8:11. "The time is surely coming," says the Lord God, "when I will send a famine on the land —not a famine of bread or water, but of hearing the words of the Lord. [12]Men will wander everywhere from sea to sea, seeking the Word of the Lord, searching, running here and going there, but will not find it. [13]Beautiful girls and young men alike will grow faint and weary, thirsting for the Word of God."

Mt 5:6. Happy are those who long to be just and good, for they shall be completely satisfied.

Lk 6:21. What happiness there is for you who are now hungry, for you are going to be satisfied! What happiness there is for you who weep, for the time will come when you shall laugh with joy!

1 Pet 2:2, 3. Now that you realize how kind the Lord has been to you, put away all evil, deception, envy, and fraud. Long to grow up into the fullness of your salvation; cry for this as a baby cries for his milk.

See *Desire, Spiritual; Thirst.*

HUNTING Authorized in the Mosaic law, Lev 17:13. By Nimrod, Gen 10:9. By Esau, Gen 27: 2–4, 30, 33. By Ishmael, Gen 21:20. Of lion, Job 10: 16. Fowling, 1 Sam 26:20; Ps 140:5; 141:9, 10; Prov 1:17; Eccl 9:12; Lam 3:52; Amos 3:5.

FIGURATIVE. Jer 16:16.

HUPHAM A Benjaminite, Num 26:38–41. Probably identical with *Huppim,* which see.

HUPPAH A priest, 1 Chron 24:7–18.

HUPPIM A Benjaminite, Gen 46:19–22; 1 Chron 7:12, 15.

HUR 1. An Israelite who assisted in supporting Moses's hands during battle, Ex 17:10, 12; 24:14.

2. A son of Caleb, Ex 31:1, 2; 35:30, 31; 38:22; 1 Chron 2:19, 20; 2 Chron 1:5, 6.

3. A king of Midian, Num 31:8; Josh 13:21.

4. Called Ben-hur, an officer of Solomon's commissary, 1 Kgs 4:8–19.

5. Son of Ephratah, 1 Chron 2:50; 4:3, 4.

6. A son of Judah, 1 Chron 4:1.

7. Father of Rephaiah, Neh 3:9.

HURAI One of David's warriors, 1 Chron 11: 26–47.

HURAM Son of Bela, 1 Chron 8:3–5.

HURAMABI See *Hiram, 2.*

HURI Father of Abihail, 1 Chron 5:14.

HUSBAND Gen 2:23. "This is it!" Adam exclaimed. "She is part of my own bone and flesh! Her name is 'woman' because she was taken out of a man." [24]This explains why a man leaves his father and mother and is joined to his wife in such a way that the two become one person. Mt 19:5, 6; Mk 10: 6, 7.

Num 5:11, 12. And the Lord said to Moses, "Tell the people of Israel that if a man's wife commits adultery, [13]but there is no proof, there being no witness, [14]and he is jealous and suspicious, [15]the man shall bring his wife to the priest with an offering for her of a tenth of a bushel of barley meal without oil or frankincense mingled with it—for it is a suspicion offering—to bring out the truth as to whether or not she is guilty. [16]The priest shall bring her before the Lord, [17]and take holy water in a clay jar and mix into it dust from the floor of the Tabernacle. [18]He shall unbind her hair and place the suspicion offering in her hands to determine whether or not her husband's suspicions are justified. The priest shall stand before her holding the jar of bitter water that brings a curse. [19]He shall require her to swear that she is innocent, and then he shall say to her, 'If no man has slept with you except your husband, be free from the effects of this bitter water that causes the curse. [20]But if you have committed adultery, [21, 22]then Jehovah shall make you a curse among your people, for he will make your thigh rot away and your body swell.' And the woman shall be required to say, 'Yes, let it be so.' [23]Then the priest shall write these curses in a book and wash them off into the bitter water. [24](When he requires the woman to drink the water it becomes bitter within her [if she is guilty].) [25]Then the priest shall take the suspicion offering from the woman's hand and wave it before Jehovah, and carry it to the altar. [26]He shall take a handful, representing all of it, and burn the handful upon the altar, and then require the woman to drink the water. [27]If she has been defiled, having committed adultery against her husband, the water will become bitter within her, and her body will swell and her thigh will rot, and she shall be a curse among her people. [28]But if she is pure and has not committed adultery, she shall be unharmed and will soon become pregnant. [29]This, then, is the law concerning a wayward wife—or a husband's suspicions against his wife—[30]to determine whether or not she has been unfaithful to him. He shall bring her before the Lord and the priest shall handle the situation as outlined above. [31]Her husband shall not be brought to trial for causing her horrible disease, for she is responsible."

Deut 22:13, 14. If a man marries a girl, then after sleeping with her accuses her of having had premarital intercourse with another man, saying, "She was not a virgin when I married her," [15]then the girl's father and mother shall bring the proof of her virginity to the city judges. [16]Her father shall tell them, "I gave my daughter to this man to be his wife, and now he despises her, [17, 18]and has accused her of shameful things, claiming that she was not a virgin when she married; yet here is the proof." And they shall spread the garment before the judges. The judges shall sentence the man to be whipped, [19]and fine him one hundred dollars to be given to the girl's father, for he has falsely accused a virgin of Israel. She shall remain his wife and he may never divorce her. [20]But if the man's accusations are true, and she was not a virgin, [21]the judges shall take the girl to the door of her father's home where the men of the city shall stone her to death. She has defiled Israel by flagrant crime, being a prostitute while living at home with her parents; and such evil must be cleansed from among you.

Deut 24:5. A newly married man is not to be drafted into the army nor given any other special responsibilities; for a year he shall be free to be at home, happy with his wife.

Prov 5:15. Drink from your own well, my son—be faithful and true to your wife. [16]Why should you beget children with women of the street? [17]Why share your children with those outside your home? [18]Let your manhood be a blessing; rejoice in the wife of your youth. [19]Let her charms and tender embrace satisfy you. Let her love alone fill you with delight.

Eccl 9:9. Live happily with the woman you love through the fleeting days of life, for the wife God gives you is your best reward down here for all your earthly toil.

Mal 2:14. "Why has God abandoned us?" you cry. I'll tell you why; it is because the Lord has seen your treachery in divorcing your wives who have been faithful to you through the years, the companions you promised to care for and keep. [15]You were united to your wife by the Lord. In God's wise plan, when you married, the two of you became one person in his sight. And what does he want? Godly children from your union. Therefore guard your passions! Keep faith with the wife of your youth. [16]For the Lord, the God of Israel, says he hates divorce and cruel men. Therefore control your passions—let there be no divorcing of your wives.

1 Cor 7:3. The man should give his wife all that is her right as a married woman, and the wife should do the same for her husband. [5]So do not refuse these rights to each other. The only exception to this rule would be the agreement of both husband and wife to refrain from the rights of marriage for a limited time, so that they can give themselves more completely to prayer. Afterwards, they should come together again so that Satan won't be able to tempt them because of their lack of self-control.

1 Cor 7:14. For perhaps the husband who isn't a Christian may become a Christian with the help of his Christian wife. And the wife who isn't a Christian may become a Christian with the help of her Christian husband. Otherwise, if the family separates, the children might never come to know the Lord; whereas a united family may, in God's plan, result in the children's salvation. [16]For, after all, there is no assurance to you wives that your husbands will be converted if they stay; and the same may be said to you husbands concerning your wives. [33]But a married man can't do that so well; he has to think about his earthly responsibilities and how to please his wife.

1 Cor 11:3. But there is one matter I want to remind you about: that a wife is responsible to her husband, her husband is responsible to Christ, and Christ is responsible to God.

Eph 5:22. You wives must submit to your husbands' leadership in the same way you submit to the Lord. [23]For a husband is in charge of his wife in the same way Christ is in charge of his body the church. (He gave his very life to take care of it and be its Savior!) [24]So you wives must willingly obey your husbands in everything, just as the church obeys Christ. [25]And you husbands, show the same kind of love to your wives as Christ showed to the church when he died for her, [26]to make her holy and clean, washed by baptism and God's Word; [27]so that he could give her to himself as a glorious church without a single spot or wrinkle or any other blemish, being holy and without a single fault. [28]That is how husbands should treat their wives, loving them as parts of themselves. For since a man and his wife are now one, a man is really doing himself a favor and loving himself when he loves his wife! [29, 30]No one hates his own body but lovingly cares for it, just as Christ cares for his body the church, of which we are parts. [31](That the husband and wife are one body is proved by the Scripture which says, "A man must leave his father and mother when he marries, so that he can be perfectly joined to his wife, and the two shall be one.") [32]I know this is hard to understand, but it is an illustration of the way we are parts of the body of Christ. [33]So again I say, a man must love his wife as a part of himself; and the wife must see to it that she deeply respects her husband —obeying, praising and honoring him.

Col 3:18. You wives, submit yourselves to your husbands, for that is what the Lord has planned for you. [19]And you husbands must be loving and kind to your wives and not bitter against them, nor harsh.

1 Tim 5:8. But anyone who won't care for his own relatives when they need help, especially those living in his own family, has no right to say he is a Christian. Such a person is worse than the heathen.

1 Pet 3:7. You husbands must be careful of your wives, being thoughtful of their needs and honoring them as the weaker sex. Remember that you and your wife are partners in receiving God's blessings, and if you don't treat her as you should, your prayers will not get ready answers.

FAITHFUL. *Instances of:* Isaac, Gen 24:67; Joseph, Mt 1:19.

UNREASONABLE AND OPPRESSIVE. Ahasuerus, Esther 1:10–22.

FIGURATIVE. Isa 54:5, 6; Hos 2:19, 20.

See *Family; Marriage; Wife.*

HUSBANDMAN An agriculturist, Mt 21:33–46; Mk 12:1–9; Jn 15:1; 1 Cor 3:9.

See *Agriculture.*

HUSBANDRY See *Husbandman; Agriculture; Animals.*

HUSHAH Son of Ezer, 1 Chron 4:3, 4. Probably called *Shuhah,* 1 Chron 4:11, 12.

HUSHAI David's friend, 2 Sam 15:32–37; 16:16–19; 17; 1 Chron 27:33.

HUSHAM A Temanite, Gen 36:31–39; 1 Chron 1:45, 46.

HUSHIM 1. Son of Dan, Gen 46:23–25. Called *Shuham,* Num 26:42, 43.

2. A Benjaminite, 1 Chron 7:12.

3. Wife of Shaharaim, 1 Chron 8:8–11.

HUT See *Booth.*

HYBRIDIZING Forbidden, Lev 19:19.

HYGIENE 1 Cor 6:18; 9:25.

See *Sanitation.*

HYMENAEUS A false teacher, 1 Tim 1:20; 2 Tim 2:17.

HYMN See *Psalms; Song.*

HYPOCRISY Job 8:14. A man without God is trusting in a spider's web. Everything he counts on will collapse. [15]If he counts on his home for security, it won't last.

Job 15:31. Let him no longer trust in foolish riches; let him no longer deceive himself, for the money he trusts in will be his only reward. [32]Before he dies, all this futility will become evident to him. For all he counted on will disappear, [33]and fall to the ground like a withered grape. How little will come of his hopes! [34]For the godless are barren: they can produce nothing truly good. God's fire consumes them with all their possessions.

Job 27:8. But what hope has the godless when God cuts him off and takes away his life? [9]Will God listen to his cry when trouble comes upon him? [10]For he does not delight himself in the Almighty or pay any attention to God except in times of crisis. *vs.* 13–18.

Job 31:33. Or if, like Adam, I have tried to hide my sins, [34]fearing the crowd and its contempt, so that I refused to acknowledge my sin and do not go out of my way to help others.

Ps 5:9. For they cannot speak one truthful word. Their hearts are filled to the brim with wickedness. Their suggestions are full of the stench of sin and death. Their tongues are filled with flatteries to gain their wicked ends.

Ps 50:16. But God says to evil men: Recite my laws no longer, and stop claiming my promises, [17]for you have refused my discipline, disregarding my laws.

Ps 52:4. You love to slander—you love to say anything that will do harm, O man with the lying tongue.

Ps 55:12. It was not an enemy who taunted me —then I could have borne it; I could have hidden and escaped. [13]But it was you, a man like myself, my companion and my friend. [14]What fellowship we had, what wonderful discussions as we walked together to the Temple of the Lord on holy days. [20]This friend of mine betrayed me—I who was at peace with him. He broke his promises. [21]His words were oily smooth, but in his heart was war. His words were sweet, but underneath were daggers. [23]He will send my enemies to the pit of destruction. Murderers and liars will not live out half their days.

Ps 78:34. Then at last, when he had ruined them, they walked awhile behind him; how earnestly they turned around and followed him! [35]Then they remembered that God was their Rock—that their Savior was the God above all gods. [36]But it was only with their words they followed him, not with their hearts; [37]their hearts were far away. They did not keep their promises.

Ps 101:7. But I will not allow those who deceive and lie to stay in my house.

Prov 7:10. She approached him, saucy and pert, and dressed seductively. [11, 12]She was the brash, coarse type, seen often in the streets and markets, soliciting at every corner for men to be her lovers. [13]She put her arms around him and kissed him, and with a saucy look she said, [14]"I've decided to forget our quarrel! [15]I was just coming to look for you and here you are! [16, 17]My bed is spread with lovely, colored sheets of finest linen imported from Egypt, perfumed with myrrh, aloes and cinnamon. [18]Come on, let's take our fill of love until morning, [19]for my husband is away on a long trip. [20]He has taken a wallet full of money with him, and won't return for several days. [21]So she seduced him with her pretty speech, her coaxing and her wheedling, until he yielded to her. He couldn't resist her flattery.

Prov 14:8. The wise man looks ahead. The fool attempts to fool himself and won't face facts.

Prov 15:8. The Lord hates the gifts of the wicked.

Prov 20:14. "Utterly worthless!' says the buyer as he haggles over the price. But afterwards he brags about his bargain!

Prov 21:27. God loathes the gifts of evil men, especially if they are trying to bribe him!

Prov 23:6–8. Don't associate with evil men; don't long for their favors and gifts. Their kindness is a trick; they want to use you as their pawn. The delicious food they serve will turn sour in your stomach and you will vomit it, and have to take back your words of appreciation for their "kindness."

Prov 25:19. Putting confidence in an unreliable man is like chewing with a sore tooth, or trying to run on a broken foot.

Prov 26:18, 19. A man who is caught lying to his neighbor and says, "I was just fooling," is like a madman throwing around firebrands, arrows and death! [23]Pretty words may hide a wicked heart, just as a pretty glaze covers a common clay pot. [24-26]A man with hate in his heart may sound pleasant enough, but don't believe him for he is cursing you in his heart. Though he pretends to be so kind, his hatred will finally come to light for all to see.

Isa 1:12, 13. Who wants your sacrifices when you have no sorrow for your sins? The incense you bring me is a stench in my nostrils. Your holy celebrations of the new moon and the Sabbath, and your special days for fasting—even your most pious meetings—all are frauds! I want nothing more to do with them. [15]From now on, when you pray with your hands stretched out to heaven, I won't look or listen. Even though you make many prayers, I will not hear, for your hands are those of murderers; they are covered with the blood of your innocent victims. *vs.* 11–14. Isa 66:3–5.

Isa 9:17. That is why the Lord has no joy in their young men, and no mercy upon even the widows and orphans, for they are all filthy-mouthed, wicked liars.

Isa 29:13. And so the Lord says, "Since these people say they are mine but they do not obey me, and since their worship amounts to mere words learned by rote, [Mt 15:8] [14]therefore I will take awesome vengeance on these hypocrites, and make their wisest counselors as fools." [15]Woe to those who try to hide their plans from God, who try to keep him in the dark concerning what they do! "God can't see us," they say to themselves. "He doesn't know what is going on!" [16]How stupid can they be! Isn't he, the Potter, greater than you, the jars he makes?

Isa 32:5. In those days the ungodly, the atheists, will not be heroes! Wealthy cheaters will not be spoken of as generous, outstanding men! [6]Everyone will recognize an evil man when he sees him, and hypocrites will fool no one at all. Their lies about God and their cheating of the hungry will be plain for all to see.

Isa 48:1, 2. Hear me, my people: you swear allegiance to the Lord without meaning a word of it, when you boast of living in the Holy City and brag about depending on the God of Israel.

Isa 58:2. Yet they act so pious! They come to the Temple every day and are so delighted to hear the reading of my laws—just as though they would obey them—just as though they don't despise the commandments of their God! How anxious they are to worship correctly; oh, how they love the Temple services! [3]"We have fasted before you," they say. "Why aren't you impressed? Why don't you see our sacrifices? Why don't you hear our prayers? We have done much penance, and you don't even notice it!" I'll tell you why! Because you are living in evil pleasure even while you are fasting, and you keep right on oppressing your workers. [4]Look, what good is fasting when you keep on fighting and quarreling? This kind of fasting will never get you anywhere with me. [5]Is this what I want—this doing of penance and bowing like reeds in the wind and putting on sackcloth and covering yourselves with ashes? Is this what you call fasting?

Isa 65:5. Yet they say to one another, "Don't come too close, you'll defile me! For I am holier than you!" They stifle me. Day in and day out they infuriate me.

Jer 3:10. Then, afterwards, this faithless one "returned" to me, but her "sorrow" was only faked, the Lord God says. *v.* 11.

Jer 5:2. Even under oath, they lie.

Jer 6:20. There is no use now in burning sweet incense from Sheba before me! Keep your expensive perfumes! I cannot accept your offerings; they have no sweet fragrance for me.

Jer 7:4. But don't be fooled by those who lie to you and say that since the Temple of the Lord is here, God will never let Jerusalem be destroyed. [8]Do you think that because the Temple is here, you will never suffer? Don't fool yourselves! [9]Do you really think that you can steal, murder, commit adultery, lie, and worship Baal and all of those new gods of yours, [10]and then come here and stand before me in my Temple and chant, "We are saved!"—only to go right back to all these evil things again?

Jer 9:4. Beware of your neighbor! Beware of your brother! All take advantage of one another and spread their slanderous lies. [8]For their tongues aim lies like poisoned spears. They speak cleverly to their neighbors while planning to kill them.

Jer 12:2. You plant them. They take root and their business grows. Their profits multiply, and they are rich. They say, "Thank God!" But in their hearts they give no credit to you.

Jer 17:9. The heart is the most deceitful thing there is, and desperately wicked. No one can really know how bad it is!

Jer 42:20. For you were deceitful when you sent me to pray for you and said, "Just tell us what God says and we will do it!" *vs.* 21, 22.

Lam 1:2. She sobs through the night; tears run down her cheeks. Among all her lovers, there is none to help her. All her friends are now her enemies.

Ezk 14:7. I the Lord will personally punish everyone . . . who rejects me for idols, and then comes to a prophet to ask for my help and advice. [8]I will turn upon him and make a terrible example of him, destroying him; and you shall know I am the Lord. *v.* 4.

Ezk 20:39. O Israel, the Lord God says: If you insist on worshiping your idols, go right ahead, but then don't bring your gifts to me as well! Such desecration of my holy name must stop! Ezk 5:11; Hos 8:13; 9:4.

Ezk 33:30. Son of dust, your people are whispering behind your back. They talk about you in their houses and whisper about you at the doors, saying, "Come on, let's have some fun! Let's go hear him tell us what the Lord is saying!" [31]So they come as though they are sincere and sit before you listening. But they have no intention of doing what I tell them to; they talk very sweetly about loving the Lord, but with their hearts they are loving their money. [32]You are very entertaining to them, like someone who sings lovely songs with a beautiful voice or plays well on an instrument. They hear what you say but don't pay any attention to it!

Hos 6:4. O Ephraim and Judah, what shall I do with you? For your love vanishes like morning clouds, and disappears like dew.

Hos 7:14. They lie there sleepless with anxiety, but won't ask my help. [16]They look everywhere except to heaven, to the Most High God. They are like a crooked bow that always misses targets.

Hos 8:2. Now Israel pleads with me and says, "Help us, for you are our God!" [3]But it is too late! Israel has thrown away her chance with contempt, and now her enemies will chase her.

Hos 10:1. How prosperous Israel is—a luxuriant vine all filled with fruit! But the more wealth I give her, the more she pours it on the altars of her heathen gods. [4]They make promises they don't intend to keep.

Hos 11:12. Israel surrounds me with lies and deceit.

Amos 5:21. I hate your show and pretense—your hypocrisy of "honoring" me with your religious feasts and solemn assemblies. [22]I will not accept your burnt offerings and thank offerings. I will not look at your offerings of peace. [23]Away with your hymns of praise—they are mere noise to my ears. I will not listen to your music, no matter how lovely it is. [24]I want to see a mighty flood of justice —a torrent of doing good. *vs.* 25–27.

Obd 1:7. All your allies will turn against you and help to push you out of your land. They will promise peace while plotting your destruction. Your trusted friends will set traps for you and all your counterstrategy will fail.

Mic 3:11. You leaders who take bribes; you priests and prophets who won't preach and prophesy until you're paid. (And yet you fawn upon the Lord and say, "All is well—the Lord is here among us. No harm can come to us.")

Mic 7:5. Don't trust anyone, not your best friend —not even your wife!

Zech 7:5. During those seventy years of exile when you fasted and mourned in August and October, were you really in earnest about leaving your sins behind, and coming back to me? No, not at all! [6]And even now in your holy feasts to God, you don't think of me, but only of the food and fellowship and fun.

Zech 13:6. And if someone asks, "Then what are these scars on your chest and your back?" he will say, "I got into a brawl at the home of a friend!"

Mal 1:6. "A son honors his father, a servant honors his master. I am your Father and Master, yet you don't honor me, O priests, but you despise my name." "Who? Us?" you say. "When did we ever despise your name?" [7]"When you offer polluted sacrifices on my altar." "Polluted sacrifices? When have we ever done a thing like that?" "Every time you say, 'Don't bother bringing anything very valuable to offer to God!' [8]You tell the people, 'Lame animals are all right to offer on the alter of the Lord—yes, even the sick and the blind ones.' And you claim this isn't evil? Try it on your governor sometime—give him gifts like that—and see how pleased he is! [13]You say, 'Oh, it's too difficult to serve the Lord and do what he asks.' And you turn up your noses at the rules he has given you to obey. Think of it! Stolen animals, lame and sick—as offerings to God! Should I accept such offerings as these?" asks the Lord. [14]"Cursed is that man who promises a fine ram from his flock, and substitutes a sick one to sacrifice to God. For I am a Great King," says the Lord of Hosts." *vs.* 9–12.

Mal 2:13. Yet you cover the altar with your tears because the Lord doesn't pay attention to your offerings anymore, and you receive no blessing from him.

Mal 3:14. Listen; you have said, "It is foolish to worship God and obey him. What good does it do to obey his laws, and to sorrow and mourn for our sins?"

Mt 3:7. "You sons of snakes!" he warned. "Who said that you could escape the coming wrath of God? [8]Before being baptized, prove that you have turned from sin by doing worthy deeds."

Mt 6:1. Take care! don't do your good deeds publicly, to be admired, for then you will lose the reward from your Father in heaven. [2]When you give a gift to a beggar, don't shout about it as the hypocrites do—blowing trumpets in the synagogues and streets to call attention to their acts of charity! I tell you in all earnestness, they have received all the reward they will ever get. 5And now about prayer. When you pray, don't be like the hypocrites who pretend piety by praying publicly on street corners and in the synagogues where everyone can see them. Truly, that is all the reward they will ever get. 16And now about fasting. When you fast, declining your food for a spiritual purpose, don't do it publicly, as the hypocrites do, who try to look wan and disheveled so people will feel sorry for them. Truly, that is the only reward they will ever get.

24. You cannot serve two masters: God and money. For you will hate one and love the other, or else the other way around.

Mt 7:5. Hypocrite! First get rid of the board. Then you can see to help your brother. 15Beware of false teachers who come disguised as harmless sheep, but are wolves and will tear you apart. 21Not all who sound religious are really godly people. They may refer to me as "Lord," but still won't get to heaven. For the decisive question is whether they obey my Father in heaven. 22At the Judgment many will tell me, "Lord, Lord, we told others about you and used your name to cast out demons and to do many other great miracles." 23But I will reply, "You have never been mine. Go away, for your deeds are evil." Lk 13:26, 27.

Mt 9:13. Now go away and learn the meaning of this verse of Scripture, "It isn't your sacrifices and your gifts I want—I want you to be merciful." For I have come to urge sinners, not the self-righteous back to God.

Mt 15:7. You hypocrites! Well did Isaiah prophesy of you, 8"These people say they honor me, but their hearts are far away. [Mk 7:6, 7.] 9Their worship is worthless, for they teach their man-made laws instead of those from God."

Mt 21:28. "But what do you think about this? A man with two sons told the older boy, 'Son, go out and work on the farm today.' 29'I won't,' he answered, but later he changed his mind and went. 30Then the father told the youngest, 'You go!' and he said, 'Yes, sir, I will.' But he didn't. 31Which of the two was obeying his father?" They replied, "The first, of course." Then Jesus explained his meaning: "Surely evil men and prostitutes will get into the Kingdom before you do. 32For John the Baptist told you to repent and turn to God, and you wouldn't, while very evil men and prostitutes did. And even when you saw this happening, you refused to repent, and so you couldn't believe."

Mt 22:12. " 'Friend,' he asked, 'how does it happen that you are here without a wedding robe?' And the man had no reply. 13Then the king said to his aides, 'Bind him hand and foot and throw him out into the outer darkness where there is weeping and gnashing of teeth.' " 18But Jesus saw what they were after. "You hypocrites!" he exclaimed. "Who are you trying to fool with your trick questions?"

Mt 23:2. You would think these Jewish leaders and these Pharisees were Moses, the way they keep making up so many laws! 3And of course you should obey their every whim! It may be all right to do what they say, but above anything else *don't follow their example.* For they don't do what they tell you to do. 4They load you with impossible demands that they themselves don't even try to keep. 5Everything they do is done for show. They act holy by wearing on their arms little prayer boxes with Scripture verses inside, and by lengthening the memorial fringes of their robes. 6And how they love to sit at the head table at banquets, and in the reserved pews in the synagogue! 7How they enjoy the deference paid them on the streets, and to be called "Rabbi" and "Master"! 8Don't ever let anyone call you that. For only God is your Rabbi and all of you are on the same level, as brothers. 9And don't address anyone here on earth as "Father," for only God in heaven should be addressed like that. 10And don't be called "Master," for only one is your master, even the Messiah. 11The more lowly your service to others, the greater you are. To be the greatest, be a servant. 12But those who think themselves great shall be disappointed and humbled; and those who humble themselves shall be exalted. 13, 14Woe to you, Pharisees, and you other religious leaders. Hypocrites! For you won't let others enter the Kingdom of Heaven, and won't go in yourselves. And you pretend to be holy, with all your long, public prayers in the streets, while you are evicting widows from their homes. Hypocrites! 15Yes, woe upon you hypocrites. For you go to all lengths to make one convert, and then turn him into twice the son of hell you are yourselves. 16Blind guides! Woe upon you! For your rule is that to swear "By God's Temple" means nothing—you can break that oath, but to swear "By the gold in the Temple" is binding! 17Blind fools! Which is greater, the gold, or the Temple that sanctifies the gold? 18And you say that to take an oath "By the altar" can be broken, but to swear "By the gifts on the altar" is binding! 19Blind! For which is greater, the gift on the altar, or the altar itself that sanctifies the gift? 20When you swear "By the altar" you are swearing by it and everything on it, 21and when you swear "By the Temple" you are swearing by it, and by God who lives in it. 22And when you swear "By heavens" you are swearing by the Throne of God and by God himself. 23Yes, woe upon you, Pharisees, and you other religious leaders—hypocrites! For you tithe down to the last mint leaf in your garden, but ignore the important things—justice and mercy and faith. Yes, you should tithe, but you shouldn't leave the more important things undone. 24Blind guides! You strain out a gnat and swallow a camel. 25Woe to you, Pharisees, and you religious leaders—hypocrites! You are so careful to polish the outside of the cup, but the inside is foul with extortion and greed. 26Blind Pharisees! First cleanse the inside of the cup and then the whole cup will be clean. 27Woe to you, Pharisees, and you religious leaders! You are like beautiful mausoleums—full of dead men's bones, and of foulness and corruption. [28]You try to look like saintly men, but underneath those pious robes of yours are hearts besmirched with every sort of hypocrisy and sin. [29, 30]Yes, woe to you Pharisees, and you religious leaders—hypocrites! For you build monuments to the prophets killed by your fathers and lay flowers on the graves of the godly men they destroyed, and say, 'We certainly would never have acted as our fathers did.' [31]In saying that, you are accusing yourselves of being the sons of wicked men. [32]And you are following in their steps, filling up the full measure of their evil. [33]Snakes! Sons of vipers! How shall you escape the judgment of hell?

Mt 24:50. Your Lord will arrive unannounced and unexpected, [51]and severely whip you and send you off to the judgment of the hypocrites; there will be weeping and gnashing of teeth.

Mt 25:41. Then I will turn to those on my left and say, "Away with you, you cursed ones, into the eternal fire prepared for the devil and his demons. [42]For I was hungry and you wouldn't feed me; thirsty, and you wouldn't give me anything to drink; [43]a stranger, and you refused me hospitality; naked, and you wouldn't clothe me; sick, and in prison, and you didn't visit me." [44]Then they will reply, "Lord, when did we ever see you hungry or thirsty or a stranger or naked or sick or in prison, and not help you?" [45]And I will answer, "When you refused to help the least of these my brothers, you were refusing help to me."

Mk 7:6, 7. Jesus replied, "You bunch of hypocrites! Isaiah the prophet described you very well when he said, 'These people speak very prettily about the Lord but they have no love for him at all. Their worship is a farce, for they claim that God commands the people to obey their petty rules.' How right Isaiah was! [8]For you ignore God's specific orders and substitute your own traditions." Mt 15:7–9.

Mk 12:38. Here are some of the other things he taught them at this time: "Beware of the teachers of religion! For they love to wear the robes of the rich and scholarly, and to have everyone bow to them as they walk through the markets. [39]They love to sit in the best seats in the synagogues, and at the places of honor at banquets—[40]but they shamelessly cheat widows out of their homes and then, to cover up the kind of men they really are, they pretend to be pious by praying long prayers in public. Because of this, their punishment will be the greater."

Lk 6:46. So why do you call me "Lord" when you won't obey me?

Lk 8:18. And whoever does not have, even what he thinks he has shall be taken away from him.

Lk 11:39. Then Jesus said to him, "You Pharisees wash the outside, but inside you are still dirty—full of greed and wickedness! [42]But woe to you Pharisees! For though you are careful to tithe even the smallest part of your income, you completely forget about justice and the love of God. You should tithe, yes, but you should not leave these other things undone. [44]Yes, awesome judgment is awaiting you. For you are like hidden graves in a field. Men go by you with no knowledge of the corruption they are passing. [52]Woe to you experts in religion! For you hide the truth from the people. You won't accept it for yourselves, and you prevent others from having a chance to believe it." *vs.* 39–52.

Lk 12:1. More than anything else, beware of these Pharisees and the way they pretend to be good when they aren't. But such hypocrisy cannot be hidden forever. [2]It will become as evident as yeast in dough. Mt 16:6, 12; Mk 8:15.

Lk 12:56. Hypocrites! You interpret the sky well enough, but you refuse to notice the warnings all around you about the crisis ahead.

Lk 13:13. He touched her, and instantly she could stand straight. How she praised and thanked God! [14]But the local Jewish leader in charge of the synagogue was very angry about it because Jesus had healed her on the Sabbath day. "There are six days of the week to work," he shouted to the crowd. "Those are the days to come for healing, not on the Sabbath!" [15]But the Lord replied, "You hypocrite! You work on the Sabbath! Don't you untie your cattle from their stalls on the Sabbath and lead them out for water? [16]And is it wrong for me just because it is the Sabbath day, to free this Jewish woman from the bondage in which Satan has held her for eighteen years?" [17]This shamed his enemies. And all the people rejoiced at the wonderful things he did.

Lk 14:34. What good is salt that has lost its saltiness? *v.* 35; Mk 9:50.

Lk 16:13. For neither you nor anyone else can serve two masters. You will hate one and show loyalty to the other, or else the other way around —you will be enthusiastic about one and despise the other. You cannot serve both God and money. [15]You wear a noble, pious expression in public, but God knows your evil hearts. Your pretense brings you honor from the people, but it is an abomination in the sight of God.

Lk 18:11. The proud Pharisee "prayed" this prayer: "Thank God, I am not a sinner like everyone else, especially like that tax collector over there! For I never cheat, I don't commit adultery, [12]I go without food twice a week, and I give to God a tenth of everything I earn."

Lk 20:46. Beware of these experts in religion, for they love to parade in dignified robes and to be bowed to by the people as they walk along the street. And how they love the seats of honor in the synagogues and at religious festivals! [47]But even while they are praying long prayers with great outward piety, they are planning schemes to cheat widows out of their property. Therefore God's heaviest sentence awaits these men. Mt 23:13, 14; Mk 12:38–40.

Lk 21:16. Even those closest to you—your parents, brothers, relatives, and friends will betray you and have you arrested; and some of you will be killed.

Jn 6:26. "The truth of the matter is that you

want to be with me because I fed you, not because you believe in me." [70]Then Jesus said, "I chose the twelve of you, and one is a devil."

Jn 7:19. None of *you* obeys the laws of Moses! So why pick on *me* for breaking them? Why kill *me* for this?

Jn 15:2. He lops off every branch that doesn't produce. [6]If anyone separates from me, he is thrown away like a useless branch, withers, and is gathered into a pile with all the others and burned.

Rom 1:18. But God shows his anger from heaven against all sinful, evil men who push away the truth from them.

Rom 2:1. You are just as bad. When you say they are wicked and should be punished, you are talking about yourselves, for you do these very same things. [3]Do you think that God will judge and condemn others for doing them and overlook you when you do them, too? [17]You Jews think all is well between yourselves and God because he gave his laws to you; you brag that you are his special friends. [18]Yes, you know what he wants; you know right from wrong and favor the right because you have been taught his laws from earliest youth. [19]You are so sure of the way to God that you could point it out to a blind man. You think of yourselves as beacon lights, directing men who are lost in darkness to God. [20]You think that you can guide the simple and teach even children the affairs of God, for you really know his laws, which are full of all knowledge and truth. [21]Yes, you teach others —then why don't you teach yourselves? You tell others not to steal—do *you* steal? [22]You say it is wrong to commit adultery—do *you* do it? You say, "Don't pray to idols," and then make money your god instead. [23]You are so proud of knowing God's laws, *but you dishonor him by breaking them.* [24]No wonder the Scriptures say that the world speaks evil of God because of you. [25]Being a Jew is worth something if you obey God's laws; but if you don't, then you are no better off than the heathen. [26]And if the heathen obey God's laws, won't God give them all the rights and honors he planned to give the Jews? [27]In fact, those heathen will be much better off than you Jews who know so much about God and have his promises but don't obey his laws. [28]For you are not real Jews just because you were born of Jewish parents or because you have gone through the Jewish initiation ceremony of circumcision. [29]No, a real Jew is anyone whose heart is right with God. For God is not looking for those who cut their bodies in actual circumcision, but he is looking for those with changed hearts and minds. Whoever has that kind of change in his life will get his praise from God, even if not from you.

Rom 9:6. And not everyone born into a Jewish family is truly a Jew! [7]Just the fact that they come from Abraham doesn't make them truly Abraham's children.

Rom 16:18. Such teachers are not working for our Lord Jesus, but only want gain for themselves. They are good speakers, and simple-minded people are often fooled by them.

1 Cor 13:1. If I had the gift of being able to speak in other languages without learning them, and could speak in every language there is in all of heaven and earth, but didn't love others, I would only be making noise.

2 Cor 4:2. We do not try to trick people into believing—we are not interested in fooling anyone. We never try to get anyone to believe that the Bible teaches what it doesn't. All such shameful methods we forego. We stand in the presence of God as we speak and so we tell the truth, as all who know us will agree.

2 Cor 5:12. Are we trying to pat ourselves on the back again? No, I am giving you some good ammunition! You can use this on those preachers of yours who brag about how well they look and preach, but don't have true and honest hearts. You can boast about us that we, at least, are well intentioned and honest.

Gal 6:3. If anyone thinks he is too great to stoop to this, he is fooling himself. He is really a nobody.

Phil 3:2. Watch out for those wicked men—dangerous dogs, I call them—who say you must be circumcised. [18]For I have told you often before, and I say it again now with tears in my eyes, there are many who walk along the Christian road who are really enemies of the cross of Christ. [19]Their future is eternal loss.

1 Tim 4:2. These teachers will tell lies with straight faces and do it so often that their consciences won't even bother them.

2 Tim 3:5. They will go to church, yes, but they won't really believe anything they hear. [13]In fact, evil men and false teachers will become worse and worse, deceiving many, they themselves having been deceived by Satan.

Tit 1:16. Such persons claim they know God, but from seeing the way they act, one knows they don't. They are rotten and disobedient, worthless so far as doing anything good is concerned.

Jas 1:22. And remember, it is a message to obey, not just to listen to. So don't fool yourselves. [23]For if a person just listens and doesn't obey, he is like a man looking at his face in a mirror; [24]as soon as he walks away, he can't see himself anymore or remember what he looks like. [26]Anyone who says he is a Christian but doesn't control his sharp tongue is just fooling himself, and his religion isn't worth much.

Jas 2:14. Dear brothers, what's the use of saying that you have faith and are Christians if you aren't proving it by helping others? Will *that* kind of faith save anyone? [15]If you have a friend who is in need of food and clothing, [16]and you say to him, "Well, goodbye and God bless you; stay warm and eat hearty," and then don't give him clothes or food, what good does that do? [17]So you see, it isn't enough just to have faith. You must also do good to prove that you have it. Faith that doesn't show itself by good works is no faith at all—it is dead and useless. [18]But someone may well argue, "You say the way to God is by faith alone, plus nothing; well, I say that good works are important too, for without good works you can't prove whether you have faith or not; but anyone can see that I have faith by the way I act." [19]Are there still some among you who hold that "only believing" is enough? Believing in one God? Well, remember that the demons believe this too—so strongly that they tremble in terror! [20]Fool! When will you ever learn that "believing" is useless without *doing* what God wants you to? Faith that does not result in good deeds is not real faith. [21]Don't you remember that even our father Abraham was declared good because of what he *did,* when he was willing to obey God, even if it meant offering his son Isaac to die on the altar? [22]You see, he was trusting God so much that he was willing to do whatever God told him to; his faith was made complete by what he did, by his actions, his good deeds. [23]And so it happened just as the Scriptures say, that Abraham trusted God, and the Lord declared him good in God's sight, and he was even called "the friend of God." [24]So you see, a man is saved by what he does, as well as by what he believes. [25]Rahab, the prostitute, is another example of this. She was saved because of what she did when she hid those messengers and sent them safely away by a different road. [26]Just as the body is dead when there is no spirit in it, so faith is dead if it is not the kind that results in good deeds.

1 Pet 2:1. Don't just pretend to be good! Be done with dishonesty and jealousy and talking about others behind their backs. [16]You are free from the law, but that doesn't mean you are free to do wrong. Live as those who are free to do only God's will at all times.

2 Pet 2:1. Just as there will be false teachers among you. [2]Many will follow their evil teaching that there is nothing wrong with sexual sin. And because of them Christ and his way will be scoffed at. [3]These teachers in their greed will tell you anything to get hold of your money. But God condemned them long ago and their destruction is on the way. [17]These men are as useless as dried-up springs of water, promising much and delivering nothing; they are as unstable as clouds driven by the storm winds. They are doomed to the eternal pits of darkness. [19]"You aren't saved by being good," they say, "so you might as well be bad. Do what you like, be free." But these very teachers who offer this "freedom" from law are themselves slaves to sin and destruction. For a man is a slave to whatever controls him.

1 Jn 1:6. So if we say we are his friends, but go on living in spiritual darkness and sin, we are lying. [10]If we claim we have not sinned, we are lying and calling God a liar, *for he says we have sinned.*

1 Jn 2:4. Someone may say, "I am a Christian; I am on my way to heaven; I belong to Christ." But if he doesn't do what Christ tells him to, he is a liar. [9]Anyone who says he is walking in the light of Christ but dislikes his fellow man, is still in darkness. [19]These "against-Christ" people used to be members of our churches, but they never really belonged with us or else they would have stayed. When they left us it proved that they were not of us at all.

1 Jn 4:20. If anyone says "I love God," but keeps on hating his brother, he is a liar; for if he doesn't love his brother who is right there in front of him, how can he love God whom he has never seen?

Jude 1:12. When these men join you at the love feasts of the church, they are evil smears among you, laughing and carrying on, gorging and stuffing themselves without a thought for others. They are like clouds blowing over dry land without giving rain, promising much, but producing nothing. They are like fruit trees without any fruit at picking time. They are not only dead, but doubly dead, for they have been pulled out, roots and all, to be burned. [13]All they leave behind them is shame and disgrace like the dirty foam left along the beach by the wild waves. They wander around looking as bright as stars, but ahead of them is the everlasting gloom and darkness that God has prepared for them.

Rev 2:9. I know the slander of those opposing you, who say that they are Jews—the children of God—but they aren't, for they support the cause of Satan. Rev 3:9.

Rev 3:1. I know your reputation as a live and active church, but you are dead.

See *Deceit; Deception.*

INSTANCES OF. Jacob, in impersonating Esau and deceiving his father, Gen 27. Jacob's sons, in deception of their father concerning Joseph, Gen 37:29–35. Joseph's deception of his brothers, Gen chapters 42–44. Pharaoh, Ex 8:15, 28, 29, 31, 32; 9:27–35; 10:8–29. Balaam, Jude 1:11, with Num chapters 22–24. Delilah, the wife of Samson, Judg 16. Jael, Judg 4:8–21. Ehud, Judg 3:15–25. Rabshakeh, 2 Kgs 18:17–37. Ahaz, Isa 7:12, with *vs.* 17–25. Johanan, Jer 42:1–12, 20, 22. Ishmael, Jer 41:6, 7. The false prophets, Ezk 13:1–23. Herod, Mt 2:8. Judas, Mt 26:25, 48; Jn 12:5, 6. Pilate, Mt 27:24. Pharisees, Mt 15:1–9; 22:11; Mk 12:13, 14; Jn 8:4–9; 9:24; 19:15. The ruler, Lk 13:14–17. Spies sent to trap Jesus, Lk 20:21. Priests and Levites, Lk 10:31, 32. Chief priests, Jn 18:28. Ananias and Sapphira, Acts 5:1–10. Simon Magus, Acts 8:18–23. Peter and other Christians at Antioch, Gal 2:11–14. Judaizing Christians in Galatia, Gal 6:13. False teachers at Ephesus, Rev 2:2.

See *Conspiracy; Treachery.*

HYSSOP A plant indigenous to western Asia and northern Africa, 1 Kgs 4:33. The Israelites used, in sprinkling the blood of the paschal lamb upon the lintels of their doors, Ex 12:22; in sprinkling blood in purifications, Lev 14:4, 6, 51, 52; Heb 9:19. Used in the sacrifices of separation, Num 19:6. Used in giving Jesus wine on the cross, Jn 19:29.

FIGURATIVE. Of spiritual cleansing, Ps 51:7.

I

I AM A name of God, Ex 3:14; Rev 1:4, 11, 17, 18.

IBEX A type of wild goat, Deut 14:3–5.

IBHAR Son of David, 2 Sam 5:14–16; 1 Chron 3:6–8; 14:4–7.

IBLEAM A city of Manasseh, Josh 17:11; Judg 1:27; 2 Kgs 9:27.

IBNEIAH A Benjaminite, 1 Chron 9:7, 8.

IBNIJAH A Benjaminite, 1 Chron 9:7, 8.

IBRI A Levite, 1 Chron 24:26, 27.

IBSAM Son of Tola, 1 Chron 7:2.

IBZAN A Bethlehemite, and judge of Israel, Judg 12:8–10.

ICE Job 6:15–18; 38:29; Ps 147:17, 18.

ICHABOD Son of Phinehas, and grandson of Eli, 1 Sam 4:21, 22; 14:3.

ICONIUM A city of Asia Minor. Paul preaches in, Acts 13:51; 14:21, 22; 16:2; is persecuted by the people of, Acts 14:1–6; 2 Tim 3:11.

ICONOCLASM Idols to be destroyed, Ex 23:24; 34:13; Num 33:52; Deut 7:5, 25, 26; 12:1–5; Judg 2:2; Jer 50:2. Destroyed by Jacob, Gen 35: 2–4; Moses, Ex 32:19, 20; Gideon, Judg 6:28–32; David, 2 Sam 5:21; 1 Chron 14:12; Jehu, 2 Kgs 10: 26–28; Jehoiada, 2 Kgs 11:18; Hezekiah, 2 Kgs 18: 1–6; Josiah, 2 Kgs 23:4–20; Asa, 2 Chron 14:3–5; 15: 8–16; Jehoshaphat, 2 Chron 17:6; 19:3; Jews, 2 Chron 30:14; Manasseh, 2 Chron 33:15.

See *Idolatry.*

IDALAH A town of Zebulun, Josh 19:15, 16.

IDBASH A descendant of Judah, 1 Chron 4: 3, 4.

IDDO 1. Father of Ahinadab, 1 Kgs 4:8–19.

2. A descendant of Gershom, 1 Chron 6:19–21.

3. A son of Zechariah, 1 Chron 27:16–22.

4. A prophet, 2 Chron 9:29; 12:15; 13:22.

5. Ancestor of Zechariah, Ezra 5:1; 6:14; Zech 1: 1, 7.

6. A priest, Neh 12:1–7, 12–21.

7. The leader of the Jews established at Casiphia, Ezra 8:17.

IDLENESS Prov 6:6. Take a lesson from the ants, you lazy fellow. Learn from their ways and be wise! [9]But you—all you do is sleep. When will you wake up? [10]"Let me sleep a little longer!" Sure, just a little more! [11]And as you sleep, poverty creeps upon you like a robber and destroys you; want attacks you in full armor. Prov 24:32, 33.

Prov 10:4. Lazy men are soon poor. . . . [5]but what a shame to see a lad who sleeps away his hour of opportunity. [26]A lazy fellow is a pain to his employers—like smoke in their eyes or vinegar that sets the teeth on edge.

Prov 12:9. It is better to get your hands dirty—and eat, than to be too proud to work—and starve. [24]Work hard and become a leader; be lazy and never succeed. [27]A lazy man won't even dress the game he gets while hunting.

Prov 13:4. Lazy people want much but get little.

Prov 14:23. Work brings profit; talk brings poverty!

Prov 15:19. A lazy fellow has trouble all through life.

Prov 18:9. A lazy man is brother to the saboteur.

Prov 19:15. A lazy man sleeps soundly—and goes hungry! [24]Some men are so lazy they won't even feed themselves!

Prov 20:4. If you won't plow in the cold, you won't eat at the harvest. [13]If you love sleep, you will end in poverty.

Prov 21:25, 26. The lazy man longs for many things but his hands refuse to work. He is greedy to get.

Prov 23:21. And remember that too much sleep clothes a man with rags.

Prov 24:30, 31. I walked by the field of a certain lazy fellow and saw that it was overgrown with thorns, and covered with weeds; and its walls were broken down. [32, 33]Then, as I looked, I learned this lesson: "A little extra sleep, a little more slumber, a little folding of the hands to rest" [34]means that poverty will break in upon you suddenly like a robber, and violently like a bandit.

Prov 26:13. The lazy man won't go out and work. "There might be a lion outside!" he says. [Prov 22: 13.] [14]He sticks to his bed like a door to its hinges! [15]He is too tired even to lift his food from his dish to his mouth! [16]Yet in his own opinion he is smarter than seven wise men.

Eccl 4:5. The fool won't work and almost starves.

Eccl 10:18. Laziness lets the roof leak, and soon the rafters begin to rot.

Isa 56:10. For the leaders of my people—the

Lord's watchmen, his shepherds—are all blind to every danger. They are featherbrained and give no warning when danger comes. They love to lie there, love to sleep, to dream.

Ezk 16:49. Your sister Sodom's sins were pride and laziness and too much food. Lk 19:20–25.

Mt 20:6. At five o'clock that evening he was in town again and saw some more men standing around and asked them, "Why haven't you been working today?" [7]"Because no one hired us," they replied.

Acts 17:21. I should explain that all the Athenians as well as the foreigners in Athens seemed to spend all their time discussing the latest new ideas!

2 Thess 3:10. Even while we were still there with you we gave you this rule: "He who does not work shall not eat." [11]Yet we hear that some of you are living in laziness, refusing to work, and wasting your time in gossiping.

1 Tim 5:13. Besides, they are likely to be lazy and spend their time gossiping around from house to house, getting into other people's business.

See *Laziness; Industry.*

IDOL Manufacture of, Ex 20:4; 32:4, 20; Deut 4:23; Isa 40:19, 20; 44:9–12, 17; Hab 2:18; Acts 19:24, 25. Manufacture of, forbidden, Ex 20:4; 34:17. Made of gold, Ex 32:2–4; Ps 115:4–7; 135:15–17; Isa 2:20; 30:22; 31:7; Hos 8:4; silver, Isa 2:20; 30:22; 31:7; Hos 8:4; wood and stone, Lev 26:1; Deut 4:28; 2 Kgs 19:18; Isa 37:19; 40:20; 44:13–19; Ezk 20:32.

Coverings of, Ezk 16:18. Prayer to, unanswered, 1 Kgs 18:25–29; Isa 16:12. Things offered to, not to be eaten, 1 Cor 8:4, 7. Demons are associated with, 1 Cor 10:19, 20. Called an abomination, evil, and horrible, 1 Kgs 11:5, 7; 2 Kgs 23:13; Dan 9:27; 11:31; 12:11; Mt 24:15; Mk 13:14.

See *Iconoclasm.*

IDOLATRY WICKED PRACTICES OF. Human sacrifices, Lev 18:21; 20:1–5; Deut 12:31; 18:10; 2 Kgs 3:26, 27; 16:3; 17:17, 18; 21:6; 23:10; 2 Chron 28:3; 33:6; Ps 106:37, 38; Isa 57:5; Jer 7:31; 19:4–7; 32:35; Ezk 16:20, 21; 20:26, 31; 23:37, 39; Mic 6:7; practices of, relating to the dead, Deut 14:1; licentiousness of, Ex 32:6, 25; Num 25:1–3; 1 Kgs 14:24; 15:12; 2 Kgs 17:30; 23:7; Ezk 16:17; 23:1–44; Hos 4:12–14; Mic 1:7; Rom 1:24, 26, 27; 1 Cor 10:7, 8; 1 Pet 4:3, 4; Rev 2:14, 20–22; 9:20, 21; 14:8; 17:1–6.

OTHER CUSTOMS OF. Offered burnt offerings, Ex 32:6; 1 Kgs 18:26; Acts 14:13; libations, Jer 19:13; 32:29; 44:19; Ezk 20:27, 28; of wine, Deut 32:38; of blood, Zech 9:7; food offerings, Jer 7:18; Ezk 16:19; peace offerings, Ex 32:6.

Incense burned on altars, 1 Kgs 12:32, 33; 2 Chron 30:14; Isa 65:3; Jer 11:12, 17; 48:35; Ezk 16:18; 23:41; Hos 11:2. Prayers to idols, Judg 10:14; Isa 44:17; 45:20; 46:7; Jon 1:5. Praise, Judg 16:23, 24; Dan 5:4.

Singing and dancing, Ex 32:18, 19. Music, Dan 3:5–7. Cutting the flesh, Deut 14:1; 1 Kgs 18:28; Jer 41:5. Kissing, 1 Kgs 19:18; Job 31:27; Hos 13:2. Bowing, 1 Kgs 19:18; 2 Kgs 5:18. Tithes and gifts, 2 Kgs 23:11; Dan 11:38; Amos 4:4, 5.

ANNUAL FEASTS. 1 Kgs 12:32, 33; Ezk 18:6, 11, 12, 15; 22:9; Dan 3:2, 3.

OBJECTS OF. Sun, moon, and stars, Deut 4:19; 2 Kgs 17:16; 21:3–5; 2 Chron 33:3–5; Job 31:26–28; Jer 7:17–20; 8:2; Ezk 8:15, 16; Zeph 1:4, 5; Acts 7:42. Angels, Col 2:18. Images of animals, Rom 1:23. Gods of Egypt, Ex 12:12. Golden calf, Ex 32:4; 1 Kgs 12:28. Bronze serpent, 2 Kgs 18:4. Nets, Hab 1:16. Pictures on walls, Ezk 8:10. Earrings, Gen 35:4.

See *Shrine.*

DENUNCIATIONS AGAINST. Gen 35:2. So Jacob instructed all those in his household to destroy the idols they had brought with them, and to wash themselves and to put on fresh clothing.

Ex 20:3. You may worship no other god than me. [4]You shall not make yourselves any idols: any images resembling animals, birds, or fish. [5]You must never bow to an image or worship it in any way; for I, the Lord your God, am very possessive. I will not share your affection with any other god! And when I punish people for their sins, the punishment continues upon the children, grandchildren, and greatgrandchildren of those who hate me; [6]but I lavish my love upon thousands of those who love me and obey my commandments. [23]Remember, you must not make or worship idols made of silver or gold or of anything else! Deut 5:7–10.

Ex 23:13. And remember—never mention the name of any other god. 1 Cor 10:7.

Lev 19:3, 4. Do not make or worship idols, for I am Jehovah your God.

Lev 26:1. You must have no idols; you must never worship carved images, obelisks, or shaped stones, for I am the Lord your God. [30]And I will destroy the altars on the hills where you worship your idols, and I will cut down your incense altars, leaving your dead bodies to rot among your idols; and I will abhor you. Deut 16:21, 22.

Deut 4:15. But beware! You didn't see the form of God that day as he spoke to you from the fire at Mount Horeb, [16, 17]so do not defile yourselves by trying to make a statue of God—an idol in any form, whether of a man, woman. [19]And do not look up into the sky to worship the sun, moon, or stars. The Lord may permit other nations to get away with this, but not you. *vs.* 15–23, 25–28; Deut 11:16, 17, 28; 28:15–68; 30:17, 18; 31:16–21, 29; 32:15–26; 1 Kgs 9:6–9.

Deut 12:31. You must not insult the Lord your God like that! These nations have done horrible things that he hates, all in the name of their religion. They have even roasted their sons and daughters before their gods.

Deut 27:15. The curse of God be upon anyone who makes and worships an idol, even in secret, whether carved of wood or made from molten metal—for these handmade gods are hated by the Lord. Ex 34:17.

1 Sam 15:23. For rebellion is as bad as the sin of witchcraft, and stubbornness is as bad as worshiping idols. And now because you have rejected the

word of Jehovah, he has rejected you from being king.

Job 31:26. Or if I have looked at the sun shining in the skies, or the moon walking down her silver pathway, [27]and my heart has been secretly enticed, and I have worshiped them by kissing my hand to them, [28]this, too, must be punished by the judges. For if I had done such things, it would mean that I denied the God of heaven.

Ps 16:4. Those choosing other gods shall all be filled with sorrow; I will not offer the sacrifices they do or even speak the names of their gods.

Ps 44:20. If we had turned away from worshiping our God, and were worshiping idols, [21]would God not know it? Yes, he knows the secrets of every heart.

Ps 59:8. Lord, laugh at them! (And scoff at these surrounding nations too.)

Ps 79:6. Pour out your wrath upon the godless nations, not on us! And on kingdoms that refuse to pray, that will not call upon your name!

Ps 81:9. *You must never worship any other god,* nor ever have an idol in your home.

Ps 97:7. Let those who worship idols be disgraced—all who brag about their worthless gods—for every god must bow to him!

Isa 42:17. But those who trust in idols and call them gods will be greatly disappointed; they will be turned away. Isa 45:16.

Joel 3:12. Collect the nations; bring them to the Valley of Jehoshaphat, for there I will sit to pronounce judgment on them all.

Jon 2:8. Those who worship false gods have turned their backs on all the mercies waiting for them from the Lord!

Mic 5:15. And I will pour out my vengeance upon the nations who refuse to obey me.

Hab 1:16. Then they will worship their nets and burn incense before them!

Acts 15:29. Than to abstain from eating food offered to idols. *v.* 20; 1 Cor 8:1–13.

Acts 17:16. While Paul was waiting for them in Athens, he was deeply troubled by all the idols he saw everywhere throughout the city.

Rom 1:25. Instead of believing what they knew was the truth about God, they deliberately chose to believe lies. So they prayed to the things God made, but wouldn't obey the blessed God who made these things.

1 Cor 6:9, 10. Don't fool yourselves. Those who live immoral lives, who are idol worshipers . . . will have no share in his kingdom. Eph 5:5, 6.

1 Cor 10:14. So, dear friends, carefully avoid idol-worship of every kind. [20]What I am saying is that those who offer food to these idols are united together in sacrificing to demons, certainly not to God. And I don't want any of you to be partners with demons. *vs.* 21, 22.

1 Jn 5:21. Dear children, keep away from anything that might take God's place in your hearts.

Rev 21:8. And idol worshipers . . . their doom is in the Lake that burns with fire and sulphur. This is the Second Death. Rev 22:15.

See *Iconoclasm.*

WARNINGS AGAINST, AND PUNISHMENTS OF. Deut 16:21; 17:2–5; 1 Kgs 14:15; 2 Chron 28:23; Neh 9:27–37; Ps 78:58–64; 106:34–42; Isa 1:29–31; 2:6–22; 30:22; 57:3–13; 65:3–7; Jer 1:15, 16; 3:1–11; 5:1–17; 7; 8:1, 2, 19; 13:8–27; 16; 17:1–6; 18:13–15; 19; 22:9; 32:35; 44; 48:8; Ezk 6; 7:19; 8:5–18; 9; 14:1–14; 16; 20; 22:4; 23; 44:10–12; Hos 1:2; 2:2–5; 4:12–19; 5:1–3; 8:5–14; 9:10; 10; 11:2; 12:11–14; 13:1–4; 14:8; Amos 3:14; 4:4, 5; 5:5; Mic 1:1–9; 5:12–14; 6:16; Zeph 1; Mal 2:11–13.

PROPHECIES RELATING TO. Ex 12:12. For I will pass through the land of Egypt tonight and kill all the oldest sons and firstborn male animals in all the land of Egypt, and execute judgment upon all the gods of Egypt—for I am Jehovah. Num 33:3, 4.

Isa 2:18. And all idols will be utterly abolished and destroyed. [20]Then at last they will abandon their gold and silver idols to the moles and bats. Isa 31:7.

Isa 17:7. Then at last they will think of God their Creator and have respect for the Holy One of Israel. [8]They will no longer ask their idols for help in that day, neither will they worship what their hands have made! They will no longer have respect for the images of Ashtaroth and the sun idols.

Isa 19:1. Look, the Lord is coming against Egypt, riding on a swift cloud; the idols of Egypt tremble; the hearts of the Egyptians melt with fear.

Isa 27:9. It was to purge away her sins, to rid her of all her idol altars and her idols. They will never be worshiped again.

Jer 10:11. Your so-called gods, who have not made the heavens and earth, shall vanish from the earth. [15]All are worthless, silly; they will be crushed when their makers perish.

Jer 51:44. And I will punish Bel, the god of Babylon, and pull from his mouth what he has taken. The nations shall no longer come and worship him. [47]I will punish this great city and all her idols. *v.* 52; Isa 21:8, 9.

Ezk 43:7. And the Lord said to me: "Son of dust, this is the place of my throne, and my footstool, where I shall remain, living among the people of Israel forever. They and their kings will not defile my holy name any longer through the adulterous worship of other gods or by worshiping the totem poles erected by their kings. [8]They built their idol temples beside mine, with only a wall between, and worshiped their idols. Because they sullied my holy name by such wickedness, I consumed them in my anger. [9]Now let them put away their idols and the totem poles erected by their kings, and I will live among them forever.

Hos 10:2. The hearts of her people are false toward God. They are guilty and must be punished. God will break down their heathen altars and smash their idols.

Mic 5:13. And destroy all your idols. Never again will you worship what you have made.

Zeph 2:11. The Lord will do terrible things to

them. He will starve out all those gods of foreign powers.

Zech 13:2. In that day I will get rid of every vestige of idol worship throughout the land, so that even the names of the idols will be forgotten. All false prophets and fortune-tellers will be wiped out.

Mt 24:15. So, when you see the horrible thing (told about by Daniel the prophet) standing in a holy place (Note to the reader: You know what is meant!), [16]then those in Judea must flee into the Judean hills. Mk 13:14.

Rev 13:14. And he ordered the people of the world to make a great statue of the first Creature, who was fatally wounded and then came back to life. [15]He was permitted to give breath to this statue and even make it speak! Then the statue ordered that anyone refusing to worship it must die!

Rev 14:9. Anyone worshiping the Creature from the sea and his statue and accepting his mark on the forehead or the hand, [10]must drink the wine of the anger of God.

Rev 15:2. Spread out before me was what seemed to be an ocean of fire and glass, and on it stood all those who had been victorious over the Evil Creature and his statue and his mark and number. All were holding harps of God.

Rev 16:2. And horrible, malignant sores broke out on everyone who had the mark of the Creature and was worshiping his statue.

Rev 19:20. And the Evil Creature was captured, and with him the False Prophet, who could do mighty miracles when the Evil Creature was present—miracles that deceived all who had accepted the Evil Creature's mark, and who worshiped his statue. Both of them—the Evil Creature and his False Prophet—were thrown alive into the Lake of Fire that burns with sulphur.

Rev 20:4. Then I saw thrones, and sitting on them were those who had been given the right to judge. And I saw the souls of those who had been beheaded for their testimony about Jesus, for proclaiming the Word of God, and who had not worshiped the Creature or his statue, nor accepted his mark on their foreheads or their hands. They had come to life again and now they reigned with Christ for a thousand years.

FOLLY OF. Deut 4:28. There, far away, you will worship idols made from wood and stone, idols that neither see nor hear nor eat nor smell.

1 Kgs 18:27. About noontime, Elijah began mocking them. "You'll have to shout louder than that," he scoffed, "to catch the attention of your god! Perhaps he is talking to someone, or is out sitting on the toilet, or maybe he is away on a trip, or is asleep and needs to be wakened!" Judg 6:31; 1 Sam 5:3, 4.

2 Chron 25:15. This made the Lord very angry and he sent a prophet to demand, "Why have you worshiped gods who couldn't even save their own people from you?" 1 Sam 12:21; 2 Kgs 3:13; Isa 16:12; 36:18.

2 Chron 28:22. In this time of deep trial, King Ahaz collapsed spiritually. [23]He sacrificed to the gods of the people of Damascus who had defeated him, for he felt that since these gods had helped the kings of Syria, they would help him too if he sacrificed to them. But instead, they were his ruin, and that of all his people.

Ps 115:4. Their gods are merely man-made things of silver and of gold. [5]They can't talk or see, despite their eyes and mouths! [8]And those who make and worship them are just as foolish as their idols are. Ps 96:5; 135:15–18; Isa 2:8.

Isa 40:12. Who else had held the oceans in his hands and measured off the heavens with his ruler? Who else knows the weight of all the earth and weighs the mountains and the hills? [13]Who can advise the Spirit of the Lord or be his teacher or give him counsel? [14]Has he ever needed anyone's advice? Did he need instruction as to what is right and best? [15]No, for all the peoples of the world are nothing in comparison with him—they are but a drop in the bucket, dust on the scales. He picks up the islands as though they had no weight at all. [16]All of Lebanon's forests do not contain sufficient fuel to consume a sacrifice large enough to honor him, nor are all its animals enough to offer to our God. [17]All the nations are as nothing to him; in his eyes they are less than nothing—mere emptiness and froth. [18]How can we describe God? With what can we compare him? [19]With an idol? An idol, made from a mold, overlaid with gold, and with silver chains around its neck? [20]The man too poor to buy expensive gods like that will find a tree free from rot and hire a man to carve a face on it, and that's his god—a god that cannot even move! [21]Are you so ignorant? Are you so deaf to the words of God—the words he gave before the worlds began? Have you never heard nor understood? [22]It is God who sits above the circle of the earth. (The people below must seem to him like grasshoppers!) He is the one who stretches out the heavens like a curtain and makes his tent from them. [23]He dooms the great men of the world and brings them all to naught. [24]They hardly get started, barely take root, when he blows on them and their work withers and the wind carries them off like straw. [25]"With whom will you compare me? Who is my equal?" asks the Holy One. [26]Look up into the heavens! Who created all these stars? As a shepherd leads his sheep, calling each by its pet name, and counts them to see that none are lost or strayed, so God does with stars and planets!

Isa 41:23. Yes, that's it! If you are gods, tell what will happen in the days ahead! Or do some mighty miracle that makes us stare, amazed. [24]But no! You are less than nothing, and can do nothing at all. Anyone who chooses you needs to have his head examined! *vs.* 26–29.

Isa 44:19. The man never stops to think or figure out, "Why, it's just a block of wood! I've burned it for heat and used it to bake my bread and roast my meat. How can the rest of it be a god? Should I fall down before a chunk of wood?" *vs.* 9–20.

Isa 45:20. What fools they are who carry around the wooden idols and pray to gods that cannot save!

Isa 46:1, 2. The idols of Babylon, Bel and Nebo, are being hauled away on ox carts! But look! The beasts are stumbling! The cart is turning over! The gods are falling out onto the ground! Is that the best that they can do? If they cannot even save themselves from such a fall, how can they save their worshipers from Cyrus? [6]Will you compare me with an idol made lavishly with silver and with gold? They hire a goldsmith to take your wealth and make a god from it! Then they fall down and worship it! [7]They carry it around on their shoulders, and when they set it down it stays there, for it cannot move! And when someone prays to it there is no answer, for it cannot get him out of his trouble.

Isa 47:13. You have advisors by the ton—your astrologers and stargazers, who try to tell you what the future holds. [14]But they are as useless as dried grass burning in the fire. They cannot even deliver themselves! You'll get no help from them at all. Theirs is no fire to sit beside to make you warm! *vs.* 12–15; 2 Kgs 19:18; Isa 37:19; Zech 10:2.

Isa 57:13. Let's see if the whole collection of your idols can help you when you cry to them to save you! They are so weak that the wind can carry them off! A breath can puff them away.

Jer 2:28. Why don't you call on these gods you have made? When danger comes, let *them* go out and save you if they can! For you have as many gods as there are cities in Judah. Deut 32:37, 38; Judg 10:14.

Jer 10:5. And there stands their god like a helpless scarecrow in a garden! It cannot speak, and it must be carried, for it cannot walk. Don't be afraid of such a god for it can neither harm nor help, nor do you any good. *vs.* 2–16; Jer 48:13; 51:17; Hab 2: 18, 19.

Jer 11:12. Then they will pray to their idols and burn incense before them, but that cannot save them from their time of anguish and despair.

Jer 14:22. What heathen god can give us rain?

Jer 16:19. O Lord, my Strength and Fortress, my Refuge in the day of trouble, nations from around the world will come to you saying, "Our fathers have been foolish, for they have worshiped worthless idols! [20]Can men make God? The gods they made are not real gods at all."

Hos 8:5. O Samaria, I reject this calf—this idol you have made. My fury burns against you. How long will it be before one honest man is found among you? [6]When will you admit this calf you worship was made by human hands! It is not God! Therefore, it must be smashed to bits. Ex 32:20; Ps 106:19, 20.

Acts 14:15. We are merely human beings like yourselves! We have come to bring you the Good News that you are invited to turn from the worship of these foolish things and to pray instead to the living God.

Acts 17:22. So Paul, standing before them at the Mars Hill forum, addressed them as follows: "Men of Athens, I notice that you are very religious, [23]for as I was out walking I saw your many altars, and one of them had this inscription on it—'To the Unknown God.' [29]We shouldn't think of God as an idol made by men from gold or silver or chipped from stone."

Rom 1:22. Claiming themselves to be wise without God, they became utter fools instead. [23]And then, instead of worshiping the glorious, everliving God, they took wood and stone and made idols for themselves, carving them to look like mere birds and animals and snakes and puny men.

1 Cor 8:4. Well, we all know that an idol is not really a god, and that there is only one God, and no other. *with* 8:5; 10:19.

1 Cor 12:2. You will remember that before you became Christians you went around from one idol to another, not one of which could speak a single word.

Gal 4:8. Before you Gentiles knew God you were slaves to so-called gods that did not even exist.

Rev 9:20. But the men left alive after these plagues *still refused to worship God!* They would not renounce their demon-worship, nor their idols made of gold and silver, brass, stone, and wood—which neither see nor hear nor walk! Deut 4:28; Dan 5:23.

IDUMEA See *Edom.*

IFS, OF THE BIBLE See *Blessing, Divine, Contingent on Obedience.*

IGAL 1. One of the spies sent to Canaan, Num 13:3–15.

2. Called also *Joel.* One of David's guards, 2 Sam 23:24–39; 1 Chron 11:26–47.

3. Son of Shemaiah, 1 Chron 3:22.

IGDALIAH Father of Hanan, Jer 35:4.

IGNORANCE Job 8:9. For we were born but yesterday and know so little; our days here on earth are as transient as shadows.

Job 11:7. Do you know the mind and purposes of God? Will long searching make them known to you? Are you qualified to judge the Almighty? [8]He is as faultless as heaven is high—but who are you? His mind is fathomless—what can you know in comparison? [12]Mere man is as likely to be wise as a wild donkey's colt is likely to be born a man!

Job 28:12. But though men can do all these things, they don't know where to find wisdom and understanding. [13]They not only don't know how to get it, but, in fact, it is not to be found among the living. [20]Then where can we get it? Where can it be found? [21]For it is hid from the eyes of all mankind.

Job 36:26. God is so great that we cannot begin to know him. No one can begin to understand eternity. [29]Can anyone really understand the spreading of the clouds, and the thunders within?

Job 37:5. His voice is glorious in the thunder. We cannot comprehend the greatness of his power. [15]Do you know how God controls all nature, and causes the lightning to flash forth from the clouds? [16]Do you understand the balancing of the clouds with wonderful perfection and skill? [19]You who think you know so much, teach the rest of us how we should approach God. For we are too dull to know! [23]We cannot imagine the power of the Almighty, chapters 38; 39.

Prov 7:6. I was looking out the window of my house one day, [7]and saw a simple-minded lad, a young man lacking common sense, [8, 9]walking at twilight down the street to the house of this wayward girl, a prostitute. [10]She approached him, saucy and pert, and dressed seductively. [11, 12]She was the brash, coarse type, seen often in the streets and markets, soliciting at every corner for men to be her lovers. [13]She put her arms around him and kissed him, and with a saucy look she said, [14]"I've decided to forget our quarrel! [15]I was just coming to look for you and here you are! [16, 17]My bed is spread with lovely, colored sheets of finest linen imported from Egypt, perfumed with myrrh, aloes and cinnamon. [18]Come on, let's take our fill of love until morning, [19]for my husband is away on a long trip. [20]He has taken a wallet full of money with him, and won't return for several days." [21]So she seduced him with her pretty speech, her coaxing and her wheedling, until he yielded to her. He couldn't resist her flattery. [22]He followed her as an ox going to the butcher, or as a stag that is trapped, [23]waiting to be killed with an arrow through its heart. He was as a bird flying into a snare, not knowing the fate awaiting it there.

Prov 8:5. Let me give you understanding. O foolish ones, let me show you common sense!

Prov 9:14. She sits at the door of her house or stands at the street corners of the city, [15]whispering to men going by, and to those minding their own business. [16]"Come home with me," she urges simpletons. [17]"Stolen melons are the sweetest; stolen apples taste the best!" [18]But they don't realize that her former guests are now citizens of hell.

Prov 19:2. It is dangerous and sinful to rush into the unknown.

Prov 20:24. Since the Lord is directing our steps, why try to understand everything that happens along the way?

Prov 22:3. A prudent man foresees the difficulties ahead and prepares for them; the simpleton goes blindly on and suffers the consequences. Prov 27:12.

Prov 27:1. Don't brag about your plans for tomorrow—wait and see what happens.

Prov 30:4. Who else but God goes back and forth to heaven? Who else holds the wind in his fists, and wraps up the oceans in his cloak? Who but God has created the world? If there is any other, what is his name—and his son's name—if you know it?

Eccl 3:11. Everything is appropriate in its own time. But though God has planted eternity in the hearts of men, even so, man cannot see the whole scope of God's work from beginning to end.

Eccl 6:11. The more words you speak, the less they mean, so why bother to speak at all? [12]In these few days of our empty lifetimes, who can say how one's days can best be spent? Who can know what will prove best for the future after he is gone? For who knows the future?

Eccl 7:23. I have tried my best to be wise. I declared, "I *will* be wise," but it didn't work. [24]Wisdom is far away, and very difficult to find.

Eccl 8:6, 7. Yes, there is a time and a way for everything, though man's trouble lies heavy upon him; for how can he avoid what he doesn't know is going to happen? [16, 17]In my search for wisdom I observed all that was going on everywhere across the earth—ceaseless activity, day and night. (Of course, only God can see everything, and even the wisest man who says he knows everything, doesn't!)

Eccl 9:12. A man never knows when he is going to run into bad luck. He is like a fish caught in a net, or a bird caught in a snare.

Eccl 11:5. God's ways are as mysterious as the pathway of the wind, and as the manner in which a human spirit is infused into the little body of a baby while it is yet in its mother's womb.

Jer 10:23. O Lord, I know it is not within the power of man to map his life and plan his course.

Jn 13:7. Jesus replied, "You don't understand now why I am doing it; some day you will."

Acts 1:7. "The Father sets those dates," he replied, "and they are not for you to know."

Acts 17:23. For as I was out walking I saw your many altars, and one of them had this inscription on it—"To the Unknown God." You have been worshiping him without knowing who he is, and now I wish to tell you about him. [30]God tolerated man's past ignorance about these things, but now he commands everyone to put away idols and worship only him.

Rom 8:24. We are saved by trusting. And trusting means looking forward to getting something we don't yet have—for a man who already has something doesn't need to hope and trust that he will get it. [25]But if we must keep trusting God for something that hasn't happened yet, it teaches us to wait patiently and confidently. [26]And in the same way—by our faith—the Holy Spirit helps us with our daily problems and in our praying. For we don't even know what we should pray for, nor how to pray as we should; but the Holy Spirit prays for us with such feeling that it cannot be expressed in words.

1 Cor 2:7. Our words are wise because they are from God, telling of God's wise plan to bring us into the glories of heaven. [8]But the great men of the world have not understood it; if they had, they never would have crucified the Lord of Glory. [9]That is what is meant by the Scriptures which say that no mere man has ever seen, heard or even imagined what wonderful things God has ready for those who love the Lord. [10]But we know about these things because God has sent his Spirit to tell us, and his Spirit searches out and shows us all of God's deepest secrets.

1 Cor 3:19. For the wisdom of this world is foolishness to God. As it says in the book of Job, God uses man's own brilliance to trap him.

1 Cor 13:9. Now we know so little, even with our special gifts, and the preaching of those most gifted is still so poor. [12]We can see and understand only a little about God now, as if we were peering at his reflection in a poor mirror; but someday we are

going to see him in his completeness, face to face. Now all that I know is hazy and blurred.

Jas 1:5. If you want to know what God wants you to do, ask him, and he will gladly tell you, for he is always ready to give a bountiful supply of wisdom to all who ask him; he will not resent it. [6]But when you ask him, be sure that you really expect him to tell you, for a doubtful mind will be as unsettled as a wave of the sea that is driven and tossed by the wind.

See *Knowledge; Wisdom.*

SINS OF. Gen 20:1. Now Abraham moved south to the Negeb, and settled between Kadesh and Shur. One day, when visiting the city of Gerar, [2]he remarked that Sarah was his sister! Then King Abimelech sent for her, and had her brought to him at his palace. [3]But that night God came to him in a dream and told him, "You are a dead man, for that woman you took is married." [4]But Abimelech hadn't slept with her yet, so he said, "Lord, will you slay an innocent man? [5]He told me, 'She is my sister,' and she herself said, 'Yes, he is my brother.' I hadn't the slightest intention of doing anything wrong." [6]"Yes, I know," the Lord replied. "That is why I held you back from sinning against me; that is why I didn't let you touch her. [7]Now restore her to her husband, and he will pray for you (for he is a prophet) and you shall live. But if you don't return her to him, you are doomed to death along with all your household."

Lev 4:1. Then the Lord gave these further instructions to Moses: [2]"Tell the people of Israel that these are the laws concerning anyone who unintentionally breaks any of my commandments. [3]If a priest sins unintentionally, and so brings guilt upon the people, he must offer a young bull without defect as a sin offering to the Lord. [4]He shall bring it to the door of the Tabernacle, and shall lay his hand upon its head and kill it there before Jehovah. [5]Then the priest shall take the animal's blood into the Tabernacle, [6]and shall dip his finger in the blood and sprinkle it seven times before the Lord in front of the veil that bars the way to the Holy of Holies. [7]Then the priest shall put some of the blood upon the horns of the incense altar before the Lord in the Tabernacle; the remainder of the blood shall be poured out at the base of the altar for burnt offerings, at the entrance to the Tabernacle. [8]Then he shall take all the fat on the entrails, [9]the two kidneys and the loin-fat on them, and the gall bladder, [10]and shall burn them on the altar of burnt offering, just as in the case of a bull or cow sacrificed as a thank-offering. [11, 12]But the remainder of the young bull—the skin, meat, head, legs, internal organs, and intestines—shall be carried to a ceremonially clean place outside the camp—a place where the ashes are brought from the altar—and burned there on a wood fire. [13]If the entire nation of Israel sins without realizing it, and does something that Jehovah has said not to do, all the people are guilty. [14]When they realize it, they shall offer a young bull for a sin offering, bringing it to the Tabernacle [15]where the leaders of the nation shall lay their hands upon the animal's head and kill it before the Lord. [16]Then the priest shall bring its blood into the Tabernacle, [17]and shall dip his finger in the blood and sprinkle it seven times before the Lord, in front of the veil. [18]Then he shall put blood upon the horns of the altar there in the Tabernacle before the Lord, and all the remainder of the blood shall be poured out at the base of the burnt offering altar, at the entrance to the Tabernacle. [19]All the fat shall be removed and burned upon the altar. [20]He shall follow the same procedure as for a sin offering; in this way the priest shall make atonement for the nation, and everyone will be forgiven. [21]The priest shall then cart the young bull outside the camp and burn it there, just as though it were a sin offering for an individual, only this time it is a sin offering for the entire nation. [22]If one of the leaders sins without realizing it and is guilty of disobeying one of God's laws, [23]as soon as it is called to his attention he must bring as his sacrifice a billy goat without any physical defect. [24]He shall lay his hand upon its head and kill it at the place where the burnt offerings are killed, and present it to the Lord. This is his sin offering. [25]Then the priest shall take some of the blood of this offering and place it with his finger upon the horns of the altar of burnt offerings, and the rest of the blood shall be poured out at the base of the altar. [26]All the fat shall be burned upon the altar, just as if it were the fat of the sacrifice of a thank-offering; thus the priest shall make atonement for the leader concerning his sin, and he shall be forgiven. [27]If any one of the common people sins and doesn't realize it, he is guilty. [28]But as soon as he does realize it, he is to bring as his sacrifice a nanny goat without defect to atone for his sin. [29]He shall bring it to the place where the animals for burnt offerings are killed, and there lay his hand upon the head of the sin offering and kill it. [30]And the priest shall take some of the blood with his finger and smear it upon the horns of the burnt offering altar. Then the priest shall pour out the remainder of the blood at the base of the altar. [31]All the fat shall be taken off, just as in the procedure for the thank-offering sacrifice, and the priest shall burn it upon the altar; and the Lord will appreciate it. Thus the priest shall make atonement for that man, and he shall be forgiven. [32]However, if he chooses to bring a lamb as his sin offering, it must be a female without physical defect. [33]He shall bring it to the place where the burnt offerings are killed, and lay his hand upon its head and kill it there as a sin offering. [34]The priest shall take some of the blood with his finger and smear it upon the horns of the burnt offering altar, and all the rest of the blood shall be poured out at the base of the altar. [35]The fat shall be used just as in the case of a thank-offering lamb—the priest shall burn the fat on the altar as in any other sacrifice made to Jehovah by fire; and the priest shall make atonement for the man, and his sin shall be forgiven."

Lev 5:4. "If anyone makes a rash vow, whether the vow is good or bad, when he realizes what a foolish vow he has taken, he is guilty. [5]In any of these cases, he shall confess his sin [6]and bring his guilt offering to the Lord, a female lamb or goat, and the priest shall make atonement for him, and he shall be freed from his sin, and need not fulfill the vow. [7]If he is too poor to bring a lamb to the Lord, then he shall bring two turtledoves or two young pigeons as his guilt offering; one of the birds shall be his sin offering and the other his burnt offering. [8]The priest shall offer as the sin sacrifice whichever bird is handed to him first, wringing its neck, but not severing its head from its body. [9]Then he shall sprinkle some of the blood at the side of the altar and the rest shall be drained out at the base of the altar; this is the sin offering. [10]He shall offer the second bird as a burnt offering, following the customary procedures that have been set forth; so the priest shall make atonement for him concerning his sin and he shall be forgiven. [11]If he is too poor to bring turtledoves or young pigeons as his sin offering, then he shall bring a tenth of a bushel of fine flour. He must not mix it with olive oil or put any incense on it, because it is a sin offering. [12]He shall bring it to the priest and the priest shall take out a handful as a representative portion, and burn it on the altar just as any other offering to Jehovah made by fire; this shall be his sin offering. [13]In this way the priest shall make atonement for him for any sin of this kind, and he shall be forgiven. The rest of the flour shall belong to the priest, just as was the case with the grain offering." [14]And the Lord said to Moses, [15]"If anyone sins by unintentionally defiling what is holy, then he shall bring a ram without defect, worth whatever fine you charge against him, as his guilt offering to the Lord. [16]And he shall make restitution for the holy thing he has spoiled, or the tithe omitted, by paying for the loss, plus a twenty percent penalty; he shall bring it to the priest, and the priest shall make atonement for him with the ram of the guilt offering, and he shall be forgiven. [17, 18]Anyone who disobeys some law of God without realizing it is guilty anyway, and must bring his sacrifice of a value determined by Moses. This sacrifice shall be a ram without blemish taken to the priest as a guilt offering; with it the priest shall make atonement for him, so that he will be forgiven for whatever it is he has done without realizing it. [19]It must be offered as a guilt offering, for he is certainly guilty before the Lord."

Lev 22:14. If someone should eat of the holy sacrifices without realizing it, he shall return to the priest the amount he has used, with twenty per cent added.

Num 15:22. If by mistake you or future generations fail to carry out all of these regulations which the Lord has given you over the years through Moses, [23, 24]then when the people realize their error, they must offer one young bull for a burnt offering. It will be a pleasant odor before the Lord, and must be offered along with the usual grain offering and drink offering, and one male goat for a sin offering. [25]And the priest shall make atonement for all of the people of Israel and they shall be forgiven; for it was an error, and they have corrected it with their sacrifice made by fire before the Lord, and by their sin offering. [26]All the people shall be forgiven, including the foreigners living among them, for the entire population is involved in such error and forgiveness. [27]If the error is made by a single individual, then he shall sacrifice a one-year old female goat for a sin offering, [28]and the priest shall make atonement for him before the Lord, and he shall be forgiven. [29]This same law applies to individual foreigners who are living among you.

Ezk 33:6. But if the watchman sees the enemy coming and doesn't sound the alarm and warn the people, he is responsible for their deaths. They will die in their sins, but I will charge the watchman with their deaths. [Ezk 3:18.] [8]When I say to the wicked, "O wicked man, you will die!" and you don't tell him what I say, so that he does not repent —that wicked person will die in his sins, but I will hold you responsible for his death.

Ezk 45:20. Do this also on the seventh day of that month for anyone who has sinned through error or ignorance, and so the Temple will be cleansed.

Hos 4:6. My people are destroyed because they don't know me, and it is all your fault, you priests, for you yourselves refuse to know me; therefore I refuse to recognize you as my priests. Since you have forgotten my laws, I will "forget" to bless your children.

Lk 12:48. But anyone who is not aware that he is doing wrong will be punished only lightly. Much is required from those to whom much is given, for their responsibility is greater.

Lk 23:34. "Father, forgive these people," Jesus said, "for they don't know what they are doing."

Jn 16:2. For you will be excommunicated from the synagogues, and indeed the time is coming when those who kill you will think they are doing God a service.

Acts 3:14. You didn't want him freed—this holy, righteous one. Instead you demanded the release of a murderer. [15]And you killed the Author of Life; but God brought him back to life again. And John and I are witnesses of this fact. [17]Dear brothers, I realize that what you did to Jesus was done in ignorance; and the same can be said of your leaders.

1 Cor 2:8. But the great men of the world have not understood it; if they had, they never would have crucified the Lord of Glory.

Gal 1:13. You know what I was like when I followed the Jewish religion—how I went after the Christians mercilessly, hunting them down and doing my best to get rid of them all. [14]I was one of the most religious Jews of my own age in the whole country, and tried as hard as I possibly could to follow all the old, traditional rules of my religion. [15]But then something happened! For even before I was born God had chosen me to be his, and called me—what kindness and grace—[16]to reveal his Son within me so that I could go to the Gentiles and show them the Good News about Jesus. When all this happened to me I didn't go at once and talk it over with anyone else.

Eph 4:18. Their closed hearts are full of darkness; they are far away from the life of God because they have shut their minds against him, and they cannot understand his ways. [19]They don't care anymore about right and wrong and have given themselves over to impure ways. They stop at nothing, being driven by their evil minds and reckless lusts.

1 Tim 1:12. How thankful I am to Christ Jesus our Lord for choosing me as one of his messengers, and giving me the strength to be faithful to him, [13]even though I used to scoff at the name of Christ. I hunted down his people, harming them in every way I could. But God had mercy on me because I didn't know what I was doing, for I didn't know Christ at that time.

INSTANCES OF PUNISHMENT OF SINS OF. Pharaoh, Gen 12:11–17; Abimelech, Gen 20:1–18.

IIM A town in the extreme south of Judah, Josh 15:21–32.

IJON A town of Naphtali, 1 Kgs 15:20; 2 Kgs 15:29; 2 Chron 16:4.

IKKESH Father of Ira, 2 Sam 23:24–39; 1 Chron 11:26–47; 27:9.

ILAI An Ahohite, 1 Chron 11:26–47.

ILLYRICUM A province north of Greece, called also *Dalmatia.* Visited by Paul, Rom 15:19; by Titus, 2 Tim 4:10.

IMAGE See *Idol.*

FIGURATIVE. Man created in, of God, Gen 1:26, 27; 5:1; 9:5, 6; 1 Cor 11:7; Jas 3:9. Regenerated into, Rom 8:29; 2 Cor 3:18; Eph 4:24; Col 3:10; 1 Jn 3:1–3. Christ, of God, Col 1:15; Heb 1:3. Of jealousy, Ezk 8:3, 5.

See *Idol; Idolatry.*

IMAGINATION Gen 8:21. And Jehovah was pleased with the sacrifice and said to himself, "I will never do it again—I will never again curse the earth, destroying all living things, even though man's bent is always toward evil from his earliest youth, and even though he does such wicked things."

Deut 29:19. Let no one blithely think, when he hears the warnings of this curse, "I shall prosper even though I walk in my own stubborn way!" [20]For the Lord will not pardon! His anger and jealousy will be hot against that man. And all the curses written in this book shall lie heavily upon him, and the Lord will blot out his name from under heaven.

1 Chron 28:9. Solomon, my son, get to know the God of your fathers. Worship and serve him with a clean heart and a willing mind, for the Lord sees every heart and understands and knows every thought. If you seek him, you will find him; but if you forsake him, he will permanently throw you aside.

Prov 6:16–18. For there are six things the Lord hates—no seven: Haughtiness, lying, murdering, plotting evil, eagerness to do wrong.

Mt 5:28. But I say: Anyone who even looks at a woman with lust in his eye has already committed adultery with her in his heart.

Rom 1:21. Yes, they knew about him all right, but they wouldn't admit it or worship him or even thank him for all his daily care. And after awhile they began to think up silly ideas of what God was like and what he wanted them to do. The result was that their foolish minds became dark and confused.

2 Cor 10:3. It is true that I am an ordinary, weak human being, but I don't use human plans and methods to win my battles. [5]These weapons can break down every proud argument against God and every wall that can be built to keep men from finding him. With these weapons I can capture rebels and bring them back to God, and change them into men whose hearts' desire is obedience to Christ.

IMLAH Father of Micaiah the prophet, 1 Kgs 22:8; 2 Chron 18:6–8.

IMMANUEL A name of Jesus, Isa 7:14. Called *Emmanuel,* Mt 1:23.

See *Jesus, Names of.*

IMMER 1. A family of priests, 1 Chron 9:12; Ezra 2:36–39; 10:20; Neh 7:40; 11:10–14.

2. A priest at the time of David, head of a division of priests, 1 Chron 24:14.

3. Father of Zadok, Neh 3:29.

4. Father of Pashhur, Jer 20:1, 2.

5. A Persian town named for inhabitants, Ezra 2:59; Neh 7:61.

IMMORALITY See *Adultery; Lewdness; Lust.*

IMMORTALITY Deathlessness, or exemption from the physical death of the body.

Rom 2:6. He will give each one whatever his deeds deserve. [7]He will give eternal life to those who patiently do the will of God, seeking for the unseen glory and honor and eternal life that he offers.

1 Cor 15:51. But I am telling you this strange and wonderful secret; we shall not all die, but we shall all be given new bodies! [52]It will all happen in a moment, in the twinkling of an eye, when the last trumpet is blown. For there will be a trumpet blast from the sky and all the Christians who have died will suddenly become alive, with new bodies that will never, never die; and then we who are still alive shall suddenly have new bodies too. [53]For our earthly bodies, the ones we have now that can die, must be transformed into heavenly bodies that cannot perish but will live forever. [54]When this happens, then at last this Scripture will come true—"Death is swallowed up in victory."

1 Tim 1:17. Glory and honor to God forever and ever. He is the King of the ages, the unseen one who never dies; he alone is God, and full of wisdom. Amen.

1 Tim 6:14. That you fulfill all he has told you to do, so that no one can find fault with you from now until our Lord Jesus Christ returns. [15]For in due season Christ will be revealed from heaven by the blessed and only Almighty God, the King of kings and Lord of lords, [16]who alone can never die, who

lives in light so terrible that no human being can approach him. No mere man has ever seen him, nor ever will. Unto him be honor and everlasting power and dominion forever and ever. Amen.

2 Tim 1:10. And now he has made all of this plain to us by the coming of our Savior Jesus Christ, who broke the power of death and showed us the way of everlasting life through trusting him.

See *Incorruption; Life, Eternal; Resurrection.*

IMNA Son of Helem, 1 Chron 7:35.

IMNAH 1. Firstborn of Asher, Gen 46:16, 17; Num 26:44–47; 1 Chron 7:30.

2. A Levite, 2 Chron 31:14, 15.

IMPENITENCE Lev 23:26, 27. *The Day of Atonement* follows nine days later: All the people are to come together before the Lord, saddened by their sin; and they shall offer sacrifices by fire to the Lord. [28]Don't do any work that day, for it is a special day for making atonement before the Lord your God. [29]Anyone who does not spend the day in repentance and sorrow for sin shall be excommunicated from his people.

Lev 26:21. And if even then you will not obey me and listen to me, I will send you seven times more plagues because of your sins. *vs.* 22–24.

Deut 29:19. Let no one blithely think, when he hears the warnings of this curse, "I shall prosper even though I walk in my own stubborn way!" [20]For the Lord will not pardon! His anger and jealousy will be hot against that man. And all the curses written in this book shall lie heavily upon him, and the Lord will blot out his name from under heaven. [21]The Lord will separate that man from all the tribes of Israel, to pour out upon him all the curses (which are recorded in this book) that befall those who break this contract.

1 Sam 15:23. For rebellion is as bad as the sin of witchcraft, and stubbornness is as bad as worshiping idols. And now because you have rejected the word of Jehovah, he has rejected you from being king.

Job 9:2. But how can a man be truly good in the eyes of God? [4]Who has ever opposed him successfully?

Job 24:13. The wicked rebel against the light and are not acquainted with the right and the good.

Ps 7:11. God is a judge who is perfectly fair, and he is angry with the wicked every day. [12]Unless they repent, he will sharpen his sword and slay them. *v.* 13.

Ps 10:3. For these men brag of all their evil lusts; they revile God and congratulate those the Lord abhors, whose only goal in life is money.

Ps 32:9. Don't be like a senseless horse or mule that has to have a bit in its mouth to keep it in line!

Ps 50:17. For you have refused my discipline, disregarding my laws. [21]I remained silent—you thought I didn't care—but now your time of punishment has come, and I list all the above charges against you.

Ps 52:1. You call yourself a *hero,* do you? You *boast* about this evil deed of yours against God's people. [7]See what happens to those who despise God and trust in their wealth, and become ever more bold in their wickedness.

Ps 58:3. These men are born sinners, lying from their earliest words! [4, 5]They are poisonous as deadly snakes, cobras that close their ears to the most expert of charmers.

Ps 68:21. But he will crush his enemies, for they refuse to leave their guilty, stubborn ways.

Ps 78:8. Thus they did not need to be as their fathers were—stubborn, rebellious, unfaithful, refusing to give their hearts to God.

Ps 81:11. But no, my people won't listen. Israel doesn't want me around. [12]So I am letting them go their blind and stubborn way, living according to their own desires.

Ps 82:5. But you are so foolish and so ignorant! Because you are in darkness, all the foundations of society are shaken to the core.

Ps 95:8. Don't harden your hearts as Israel did in the wilderness at Meribah and Massah. Heb 3: 7, 8.

Ps 106:24. They refused to enter the Promised Land, for they wouldn't believe his solemn oath to care for them. [25]Instead, they pouted in their tents and mourned and despised his command.

Ps 107:11. They rebelled against the Lord, scorning him who is the God above all gods. [12]That is why he broke them with hard labor; they fell and none could help them rise again.

Prov 1:24. I have called you so often but still you won't come. I have pleaded, but all in vain. [25]For you have spurned my counsel and reproof. [26]Some day you'll be in trouble, and I'll laugh! Mock me, will you?—I'll mock you! [27]When a storm of terror surrounds you, and when you are engulfed by anguish and distress, [28]then I will not answer your cry for help. It will be too late though you search for me ever so anxiously. [29]For you closed your eyes to the facts and did not choose to reverence and trust the Lord, [30]and you turned your back on me, spurning my advice. [31]That is why you must eat the bitter fruit of having your own way and experience the full terrors of the pathway you have chosen.

Prov 11:3. A good man is guided by his honesty; the evil man is destroyed by his dishonesty.

Prov 15:9, 10. The Lord despises the deeds of the wicked, but loves those who try to be good. If they stop trying, the Lord will punish them; if they rebel against that punishment, they will die. [32]But to reject criticism is to harm yourself and your own best interests.

Prov 19:16. Keep the commandments and keep your life; despising them means death.

Prov 21:29. An evil man is stubborn, but a godly man will reconsider.

Prov 26:11. As a dog returns to his vomit, so a fool repeats his folly.

Prov 28:13. A man who refuses to admit his mistakes can never be successful. . . . [14]Blessed is the man who reveres God, but the man who doesn't care is headed for serious trouble.

Prov 29:1. The man who is often reproved but refuses to accept criticism will suddenly be broken and never have another chance.

Eccl 8:11. Because God does not punish sinners instantly, people feel it is safe to do wrong. [13]Their days shall pass away as quickly as shadows because they don't fear God.

Isa 26:10. Your kindness to the wicked doesn't make them good; they keep on doing wrong and take no notice of your majesty.

Isa 28:12. They could have rest in their own land if they would obey him, if they were kind and good. He told them that, but they wouldn't listen to him.

Isa 32:9. Listen, you women who loll around in lazy ease; listen to me and I will tell you your reward: [10]In a short time—in just a little more than a year—suddenly you'll care, O careless ones. For the crops of fruit will fail; the harvest will not take place. [11]Tremble, O women of ease; throw off your unconcern. Strip off your pretty clothes—wear sackcloth for your grief.

Isa 42:22. But what a sight his people are—these who were to demonstrate to all the world the glory of his law; for they are robbed, enslaved, imprisoned, trapped, fair game for all, with no one to protect them. [23]Won't even one of you apply these lessons from the past and see the ruin that awaits you up ahead? [24]Who let Israel be robbed and hurt? Did not the Lord? It is the Lord they sinned against, for they would not go where he sent them nor listen to his laws. [25]That is why God poured out such fury and wrath on his people and destroyed them in battle. Yet, though set on fire and burned, they will not understand the reason why—that it is God, wanting them to repent.

Isa 46:12. Listen to me, you stubborn, evil men! [13]For I am offering you my deliverance; not in the distant future, but right now!

Isa 48:4. I knew how hard and obstinate you are. Your necks are as unbending as iron; you are as hardheaded as brass. [8]Yes, I'll tell you things entirely new, for I know so well what traitors you are, rebels from earliest childhood, rotten through and through.

Isa 57:11. Why were you more afraid of them than of me? How is it that you gave not even a second thought to me? Is it because I've been too gentle, that you have no fear of me?

Isa 65:12. Therefore I will "destine" you to the sword, and your "fate" shall be a dark one; for when I called, you didn't answer; when I spoke, you wouldn't listen. You deliberately sinned before my very eyes, choosing to do what you know I despise. [15]Your name shall be a curse word among my people, for the Lord God will slay you and call his true servants by another name. Isa 66:4.

Jer 3:10. Then, afterwards, this faithless one "returned" to me, but her "sorrow" was only faked, the Lord God says. *vs.* 7–9.

Jer 5:21. Listen, O foolish, senseless people—you with the eyes that do not see and the ears that do not listen—[22]have you no respect at all for me? the Lord God asks. How can it be that you don't even tremble in my presence? . . . [23]But my people have rebellious hearts; they have turned against me and gone off into idolatry. [24]Though I am the one who gives them rain each year in spring and fall and sends the harvest times, yet they have no respect or fear for me.

Jer 6:10. But who will listen when I warn them? Their ears are closed and they refuse to hear. The word of God has angered them; they don't want it at all. [16]Yet the Lord pleads with you still: Ask where the good road is, the godly paths you used to walk in, in the days of long ago. Travel there, and you will find rest for your souls. But you reply, "No, that is not the road we want!" [17]I set watchmen over you who warned you: "Listen for the sound of the trumpet! It will let you know when trouble comes." But you said, "No! We won't pay any attention!" [19]I will bring evil upon this people; it will be the fruit of their own sin, because they will not listen to me. They reject my law.

Jer 7:13. And now, says the Lord, I will do the same thing here because of all this evil you have done. Again and again I spoke to you about it, rising up early and calling, but you refused to hear or answer. [14]Yes, I will destroy this Temple, as I did in Shiloh—this Temple called by my name, which you trust for help, and this place I gave to you and to your fathers. [24]But they wouldn't listen; they kept on doing whatever they wanted to, following their own stubborn, evil thoughts. They went backward instead of forward. [28]Say to them: This is the nation that refuses to obey the Lord its God, and refuses to be taught. She continues to live a lie. *vs.* 13–34; Jer 11:8; 25:4; 26:4–6; 32:33; 35:14–17; Zech 1:4.

Jer 8:5. But these people keep on along their evil path, even though I warn them. [6]I listen to their conversation and what do I hear? Is anyone sorry for sin? Does anyone say, "What a terrible thing I have done?" No, all are rushing pell-mell down the path of sin as swiftly as a horse rushing to the battle! [7]The stork knows the time of her migration, as does the turtledove, and the crane, and the swallow. They all return at God's appointed time each year; but not my people! They don't accept the laws of God. [20]The harvest is finished; the summer is over and we are not saved. *vs.* 4–22.

Jer 12:11. The whole land is desolate and no one cares.

Jer 13:17. Do you still refuse to listen? Then in loneliness my breaking heart shall mourn because of your pride. My eyes will overflow with tears because the Lord's flock shall be carried away as slaves. [27]I am keenly aware of your apostasy, your faithlessness to me, and your abominable idol worship in the fields and on the hills. Woe upon you, O Jerusalem! How long before you will be pure? *v.* 15; Jer 19:15.

Jer 14:10. But the Lord replies: You have loved to wander far from me and have not tried to follow in my paths. Now I will no longer accept you as my people; now I will remember all the evil you have done, and punish your sins. *vs.* 1–16.

Jer 15:6. You have forsaken me and turned your backs upon me. Therefore I will clench my fists against you to destroy you. I am tired of always giving you another chance. [7]I will sift you at the gates of your cities and take from you all that you hold dear, and I will destroy my own people because they refuse to turn back to me from all their evil ways.

Jer 16:12. *And you have been worse than your fathers were!* You follow evil to your hearts' content and refuse to listen to me.

Jer 17:23. But they didn't listen or obey. They stubbornly refused to pay attention and be taught.

Jer 18:12. But they replied, "Don't waste your breath. We have no intention whatever of doing what God says. We will continue to live as we want to, free from any restraint, full of stubborness and wickedness!" Jer 2:25.

Jer 22:21. When you were prosperous I warned you, but you replied, "Don't bother me." Since childhood you have been that way—you just won't listen.

Jer 29:19. For they refuse to listen to me though I spoke to them again and again through my prophets.

Jer 44:10. And even until this very hour there has been no apology; no one has wanted to return to me, or follow the laws I gave you and your fathers before you. [16]"We will not listen to your false 'Messages from God'! [17]We will do whatever we want to. We will burn incense to the 'Queen of Heaven' and sacrifice to her just as much as we like—just as we and our fathers before us, . . . for in those days we had plenty to eat and we were well off and happy!"

Ezk 2:5. And whether they listen or not (for remember, they are rebels), they will at least know they have had a prophet among them.

Ezk 3:5. I am not sending you to some far-off foreign land where you can't understand the language—[6]no, not to tribes with strange, difficult tongues. (If I did, they would listen!) [7]I am sending you to the people of Israel, and they won't listen to me! For the whole lot of them are hard, impudent and stubborn. [19]But if you warn them and they keep on sinning, and refuse to repent, they will die in their sins, but you are blameless—you have done all you could. [26]And I will make your tongue stick to the roof of your mouth so that you can't reprove them; for they are rebels. *vs.* 1–11; Ezk 2:4; 33:9.

Ezk 12:2. "Son of dust," he said, "you live among rebels who could know the truth if they wanted to, but they don't want to; they could hear me if they would listen, but they won't,

Ezk 20:8. But they rebelled against me and would not listen. They didn't get rid of their idols, nor forsake the gods of Egypt. Then I thought, I will pour out my fury upon them and fulfill my anger against them while they are still in Egypt. [13]But Israel rebelled against me. There in the wilderness they refused my laws. They would not obey my rules even though obeying them means life. And they misused my Sabbaths. Then I thought, I will pour out my fury upon them and utterly consume them in the desert. [21]But their children too rebelled against me. They refused my laws—the laws that, if a person keeps them, he shall live. And they defiled my Sabbaths. So then I said: Now at last I will pour out my fury upon you in the wilderness.

Ezk 33:4. Then anyone who hears the alarm and refuses to heed it—well, if he dies the fault is his own. [5]For he heard the warning and wouldn't listen; the fault is his. If he had heeded the warning, he would have saved his life.

Dan 9:13. Every curse against us written in the law of Moses has come true; all the evils he predicted—all have come. But even so we still refuse to satisfy the Lord our God by turning from our sins and doing right.

Hos 4:17. Stay away from her [Israel], for she is wedded to idolatry.

Hos 5:4. Your deeds won't let you come to God again, for the spirit of adultery is deep within you, and you cannot know the Lord.

Hos 7:13. Woe to my people for deserting me; let them perish, for they have sinned against me. I wanted to redeem them but their hard hearts would not accept the truth. [15]I have helped them, and made them strong, yet now they turn against me.

Hos 11:2. But the more I called to him, the more he rebelled, sacrificing to Baal and burning incense to idols. [7]For my people are determined to desert me. And so I have sentenced them to slavery, and no one shall set them free.

Zech 7:11. Your fathers would not listen to this message. They turned stubbornly away and put their fingers in their ears to keep from hearing me. [12]They hardened their hearts like flint, afraid to hear the words that God, the Lord of Hosts, commanded them—the laws he had revealed to them by his Spirit through the early prophets. That is why such great wrath came down on them from God. [13]I called but they refused to listen, so when they cried to me, I turned away. *vs.* 4–14.

Mal 2:2. If you don't change your ways and give glory to my name, then I will send terrible punishment upon you, and instead of giving you blessings as I would like to, I will turn on you with curses. Indeed, I have cursed you already because you haven't taken seriously the things that are most important to me. [17]You have wearied the Lord with your words. "Wearied him?" you ask in fake surprise. "How have we wearied him?" By saying that evil is good, that it pleases the Lord! Or by saying that God won't punish us—he doesn't care.

Mt 11:16. "What shall I say about this nation? These people are like children playing, who say to their little friends, [17]'We played wedding and you weren't happy, so we played funeral but you weren't sad.' [18]For John the Baptist doesn't even drink wine and often goes without food, and you say, 'He's crazy.' [19]And I, the Messiah, feast and drink, and you complain that I am 'a glutton and a drinking man, and hang around with the worst sort of sinners!' But brilliant men like you can justify your every inconsistency!" [Lk 7:35.] [20]Then he began to pour out his denunciations against the cities where he had done most of his miracles, because they hadn't turned to God. [21]"Woe to you, Chorazin, and woe to you, Bethsaida! For if the miracles I did in your streets had been done in wicked Tyre and Sidon their people would have repented long ago in shame and humility." *vs.* 20–24; Mt 12:41, 42; Lk 10:13.

Mt 13:15. For their hearts are fat and heavy, and their ears are dull, and they have closed their eyes in sleep, [16]so they won't see and hear and understand and turn to God again, and let me heal them.

Mt 23:37. O Jerusalem, Jerusalem, the city that kills the prophets, and stones all those God sends to her! How often I have wanted to gather your children together as a hen gathers her chicks beneath her wings, but you wouldn't let me. [38]And now your house is left to you, desolate. Lk 13:34.

Mt 24:38. The world will be at ease—banquets and parties and weddings—just as it was in Noah's time before the sudden coming of the flood; [39]people wouldn't believe what was going to happen until the flood actually arrived and took them all away. So shall my coming be. [48]But if you are evil and say to yourself, "My Lord won't be coming for a while," [49]and begin oppressing your fellow servants, partying and getting drunk, [50]your Lord will arrive unannounced and unexpected, [51]and severely whip you and send you off to the judgment of the hypocrites; there will be weeping and gnashing of teeth.

Mt 27:4. "I have sinned," he declared, "for I have betrayed an innocent man." "That's your problem," they retorted. [25]And the mob yelled back, "His blood be on us and on our children!"

Mk 3:5. Looking around at them angrily, for he was deeply disturbed by their indifference to human need.

Lk 13:1. About this time he was informed that Pilate had butchered some Jews from Galilee as they were sacrificing at the Temple in Jerusalem. [2]"Do you think they were worse sinners than other men from Galilee?" he asked. "Is that why they suffered? [3]Not at all! And don't you realize that you also will perish unless you leave your evil ways and turn to God?" *v.* 5.

Lk 16:31. But Abraham said, "If they won't listen to Moses and the prophets, they won't listen even though someone rises from the dead."

Acts 7:51. You stiff-necked heathen! Must you forever resist the Holy Spirit? But your fathers did, and so do you!

Rom 2:4. Don't you realize how patient he is being with you? Or don't you care? Can't you see that he has been waiting all this time without punishing you, to give you time to turn from your sin? His kindness is meant to lead you to repentance. [5]But no, you won't listen; and so you are saving up terrible punishment for yourselves because of your stubbornness in refusing to turn from your sin; for there is going to come a day of wrath when God will be the just Judge of all the world.

2 Cor 12:21. Yes, I am afraid that when I come God will humble me before you and I will be sad and mourn because many of you who have sinned became sinners and don't even care about the wicked, impure things you have done: your lust and immorality, and the taking of other men's wives.

Heb 12:17. And afterwards, when he wanted those rights back again, it was too late, even though he wept bitter tears of repentance. So remember, and be careful.

Rev 2:5. Think about those times of your first love (how different now!) and turn back to me again and work as you did before; or else I will come and remove your candlestick from its place among the churches. [16]Change your mind and attitude, or else I will come to you suddenly and fight against them with the sword of my mouth. [21]I gave her time to change her mind and attitude, but she refused. [22]Pay attention now to what I am saying: I will lay her upon a sickbed of intense affliction, along with all her immoral followers, unless they turn again to me, repenting of their sin with her.

Rev 3:3. Go back to what you heard and believed at first; hold to it firmly and turn to me again. Unless you do, I will come suddenly upon you, unexpected as a thief, and punish you.

Rev 9:20. But the men left alive after these plagues *still refused to worship God!* They would not renounce their demon-worship, nor their idols made of gold and silver, brass, stone, and wood—which neither see nor hear nor walk! [21]Neither did they change their mind and attitude about all their murders and witchcraft, their immorality and theft.

Rev 16:9. Everyone was burned by this blast of heat, and they cursed the name of God who sent the plagues—they did not change their mind and attitude to give him glory. [21]And there was an incredible hailstorm from heaven; hailstones weighing a hundred pounds fell from the sky onto the people below, and they cursed God because of the terrible hail.

See *Affliction, Impenitence in; Backslider; Blindness, Spiritual; Infidelity; Obduracy; Unbelief.*

INSTANCES OF. Pharaoh, Ex 9:30, 34; 10:27; 14: 5–9. Israelites, Num 14:22, 23; 2 Kgs 17:14; 2 Chron 24:19; 36:16, 17; Neh 9:16, 17, 29, 30; Jer 36: 31. Eli's sons, 1 Sam 2:23–25. Amaziah, 2 Chron 25: 16. Manasseh, 2 Chron 33:10. Amon, 2 Chron 33: 23. Zedekiah, 2 Chron 36:12, 13; Jer 37:2. Jehoiakim and his servants, Jer 36:22–25. Belshazzar, Dan 5: 22, 23. The rich young man, Mt 19:22.

IMPORTS Of Jerusalem: horses and chariots, 1 Kgs 10:28, 29; 2 Chron 1:16; gold, ivory, apes, peacocks, 2 Chron 9:21. Of Egypt: gum, spices, and herbs, Gen 37:25. Of Tyre, Ezk 27:12–25.

See *Commerce; Exports; Tribute.*

IMPORTUNITY See *Prayer.*

IMPRECATION INSTANCES OF. Ruth, Ruth 1:17. Samuel, 1 Sam 3:16, 17. David, 2 Sam 1: 21; 3:28, 29. Shimei, 2 Sam 16:5, 13.

See *Prayer, Imprecatory.*

IMPRISONMENT Of Joseph, Gen 39:20.

Jeremiah, Jer 38:6. John the Baptist, Mt 11:2; 14:3. Apostles, Acts 5:18. Paul and Silas, Acts 16:24. Peter, Acts 12:4.

Of debtors, Mt 5:26; 18:30.

See *Prison; Prisoners; Punishment.*

IMPUTATION Reckoning over, or ascribing, to one's account. Of Adam's sin to the human race, Rom 5:12–21. Of the sin of the race to Christ, Isa 53:5, 6; 1 Pet 2:24; 2 Cor 5:21. Of the righteousness of God to the believer, Rom 3:21, 22; 10:3; Phil 3:9.

IMRAH A chief of the tribe of Asher, 1 Chron 7:36, 37.

IMRI 1. A man of Judah, 1 Chron 9:4.

2. Father of Zaccur, Neh 3:2.

INCARNATION See *Jesus, Incarnation of.*

INCENDIARISM See *Arson.*

INCENSE Formula for compounding, Ex 30:34, 35. Uses of, Ex 30:36–38; Lev 2:1, 2, 15, 16; 6:15; 16:12; Num 16:17, 40, 46; Deut 33:10. Compounded by Bezalel, Ex 37:29; by priests, 1 Chron 9:30. Offered morning and evening, Ex 30:7, 8; 2 Chron 13:11; on the golden altar, Ex 30:1–7; 40:5, 27; 2 Chron 2:4; 32:12; in making atonement, Lev 16:12, 13; Num 16:46, 47; Lk 1:10. Prohibited, in sin offerings, Lev 5:11. Unlawfully offered by Nadab and Abihu, Lev 10:1, 2; by Korah, Dathan, and Abiram, Num 16:16–35; by Uzziah, 2 Chron 26:16–21. Offered in idolatrous worship, 1 Kgs 12:32, 33; Jer 41:5; Ezk 8:11. Presented by the wise men to Jesus, Mt 2:11.

See *Altar, of Incense.*

FIGURATIVE. Mal 1:11. Of prayer, Ps 141:2. Of an acceptable sacrifice, Eph 5:2.

Symbolical. Of the prayers of saints, Rev 5:8; 8:3, 4.

INCEST DEFINED AND FORBIDDEN. Lev 18:6. None of you shall marry a near relative, for I am the Lord. [7]A girl may not marry her father; nor a son his mother, [8]nor any other of his father's wives, [9]nor his sister or half-sister, whether the daughter of his father or his mother, whether born in the same house or elsewhere. [10]You shall not marry your granddaughter—the daughter of either your son or your daughter—for she is a close relative. [11]You may not marry a half-sister—your father's wife's daughter; [12]nor your aunt—your father's sister—because she is so closely related to your father; [13]nor your aunt—your mother's sister—because she is a close relative of your mother; [14]nor your aunt—the wife of your father's brother. [15]You may not marry your daughter-in-law—your son's wife; [16]nor your brother's wife, for she is your brother's. [17]You may not marry both a woman and her daughter or granddaughter, for they are near relatives, and to do so is horrible wickedness. [18]You shall not marry two sisters, for they will be rivals. However, if your wife dies, then it is all right to marry her sister.

Lev 20:11. If a man sleeps with his father's wife, he has defiled what is his father's; both the man and the woman must die, for it is their own fault. [12]And if a man has sexual intercourse with his daughter-in-law, both shall be executed: they have brought it upon themselves by defiling each other. [17]If a man has sexual intercourse with his sister, whether the daughter of his father or of his mother, it is a shameful thing, and they shall publicly be cut off from the people of Israel. He shall bear his guilt. [19]Sexual intercourse is outlawed between a man and his maiden aunt—whether the sister of his mother or of his father—for they are near of kin; they shall bear their guilt. [20]If a man has intercourse with his uncle's widow, he has taken what belongs to his uncle; their punishment is that they shall bear their sin and die childless. [21]If a man marries his brother's widow, this is impurity; for he has taken what belongs to his brother, and they shall be childless.

Deut 22:30. A man shall not sleep with his father's widow since she belonged to his father.

Deut 27:20. "Cursed is he who commits adultery with one of his father's wives, for she belongs to his father." And all the people shall reply, "Amen." [22]"Cursed is he who has sexual intercourse with his sister, whether she be a full sister or a half-sister." And all the people shall reply, "Amen." [23]"Cursed is he who has sexual intercourse with his widowed mother-in-law." And all the people shall reply, "Amen."

Ezk 22:11. Adultery with a neighbor's wife, a daughter-in-law, a half-sister—this is common.

1 Cor 5:1. Everyone is talking about the terrible thing that has happened there among you, something so evil that even the heathen don't do it: you have a man in your church who is living in sin with his father's wife.

INSTANCES OF. Lot with his daughters, Gen 19:31–36. Abraham, Gen 20:11–13. Nahor, Gen 11:29. Reuben, Gen 35:22; 49:4. Amram, Ex 6:20. Judah, Gen 38:16–18; 1 Chron 2:4. Amnon, 2 Sam 13:14. Absalom, 2 Sam 16:21, 22. Herod, Mt 14:3, 4; Mk 6:17, 18; Lk 3:19, 20. Israel, Amos 2:7.

Instances of marriage of near relatives; Isaac with Rebekah, Gen 24:15, 16, 67. Jacob with Leah and Rachel, Gen 29:23, 30. Rehoboam, 2 Chron 11:18.

INCINERATION See *Cremation.*

INCONSISTENCY Mt 7:3. And why worry about a speck in the eye of a brother when you have a board in your own? [4]Should you say, "Friend, let me help you get that speck out of your eye," when you can't even see because of the board in your own? [5]Hypocrite! First get rid of the board. Then you can see to help your brother.

Mt 23:3. And of course you should obey their every whim! It may be all right to do what they say, but above anything else, *don't follow their example.* [4]For they don't do what they tell you to do. They load you with impossible demands that they themselves don't even try to keep.

Rom 2:1. "Well," you may be saying, "what terrible people you have been talking about!" But wait a minute! You are just as bad. When you say they are wicked and should be punished, you are talking about yourselves, for you do these very same things. [21]Yes, you teach others—then why don't you teach yourselves? You tell others not to steal —do *you* steal? [22]You say it is wrong to commit adultery—do *you* do it? You say, "Don't pray to idols," and then make money your god instead. [23]You are so proud of knowing God's laws, *but you dishonor him by breaking them.*

See *Deceit; Deception; Hypocrisy.*

INSTANCES OF. Jehu, 2 Kgs 10:16–31. The Jews, in oppressing the poor, Neh 5:9; in accusing Jesus of violating the Sabbath, Jn 7:21–23.

INCORRUPTION Not subject to decay, used of the body after resurrection, as immortality is used of the body after it has become exempt from physical death.

1 Cor 15:42. In the same way, our earthly bodies which die and decay are different from the bodies we shall have when we come back to life again, for they will never die. [43]The bodies we now have embarrass us for they become sick and die; but they will be full of glory when we come back to life again. Yes, they are weak, dying bodies now, but when we live again they will be full of strength. [50]I tell you this, my brothers: an earthly body made of flesh and blood cannot get into God's kingdom. These perishable bodies of ours are not the right kind to live forever. [51]But I am telling you this strange and wonderful secret: we shall not all die, but we shall all be given new bodies! [52]It will all happen in a moment, in the twinkling of an eye, when the last trumpet is blown. For there will be a trumpet blast from the sky and all the Christians who have died will suddenly become alive, with new bodies that will never, never die; and then we who are still alive shall suddenly have new bodies too. [53]For our earthly bodies, the ones we have now that can die, must be transformed into heavenly bodies that cannot perish but will live forever. [54]When this happens, then at last this Scripture will come true—"Death is swallowed up in victory."

Incorruptible reward, 1 Cor 9:25. The dead raised incorruptible, 1 Cor 15:52. Incorruptible gift, 1 Pet 1:4. Incorruptible life, 1 Pet 1:23.

See *Immortality; Death; Resurrection.*

INDECISION 1 Kgs 18:21. Then Elijah talked to them. "How long are you going to waver between two opinions?" he asked the people. "If the Lord is God, *follow* him! But if Baal is God, then follow *him!*"

Hos 10:2. The hearts of her people are false toward God. They are guilty and must be punished.

Mt 6:24. You cannot serve two masters: God and money. For you will hate one and love the other, or else the other way around.

Mt 26:41. Keep alert and pray. Otherwise temptation will overpower you. For the spirit indeed is willing, but how weak the body is!

Jas 1:8. If you don't ask with faith, don't expect the Lord to give you any solid answer.

Jas 4:17. Remember, too, that knowing what is right to do and then not doing it is sin.

See *Decision; Instability; Lukewarmness.*

INSTANCES OF. Moses at the Red Sea, Ex 14:15. Joshua at Ai, Josh 7:8–11. Esther, Esther 5:7, 8. Rulers, who believed in Jesus, Jn 12:42. Felix, Acts 24:25.

INDIA Probably the eastern limit of the kingdom of Ahasuerus, Esther 1:1; 8:9.

INDICTMENT INSTANCES OF. Naboth on false charge of blasphemy, 1 Kgs 21:13, with *vs.* 1–16. Jeremiah of treasonable prophecy, but of which he was acquitted, Jer 26:1–24; a second indictment, Jer 37:13–16. Three Jewish captives on the charge of contempt, Dan 3:12, with *vs.* 1–28. Daniel, of contempt, Dan 6:13 with *vs.* 1–24. Jesus, under two charges, first, of blasphemy, Mt 26:60, 61; Mk 14:58; Mt 26:63–66; Mk 14:61–64; Lk 22:67–71; Jn 19:7; the second, of treason, Mt 27:11, 37; Mk 15:2, 26; Lk 23:2, 3, 38; Jn 18:30, 33; 19:12, 19–22.

Stephen for blasphemy, Acts 6:11, 13. Paul, Acts 17:7; 18:13; 24:5; 25:18, 19, 26, 27. Paul and Silas, Acts 16:20, 21.

Indictment quashed, Acts 18:14–16.

INDUSTRY Gen 2:15. The Lord God placed the man in the Garden of Eden as its gardener, to tend and care for it.

Ex 23:12. Work six days only, and rest the seventh. Deut 5:13.

Ex 35:2. Work six days only; the seventh day is a day of solemn rest, a holy day to be used to worship Jehovah.

Prov 10:4. Lazy men are soon poor; hard workers get rich. [5]A wise youth makes hay while the sun shines.

Prov 12:11. Hard work means prosperity; only a fool idles away his time. [24]Work hard and become a leader; be lazy and never succeed. [27]A lazy man won't even dress the game he gets while hunting, but the diligent man makes good use of everything he finds.

Prov 13:4. Lazy people want much but get little, while the diligent are prospering. [11]Wealth from hard work grows.

Prov 14:4. An empty stable stays clean—but there is no income from an empty stable. [23]Work brings profit.

Prov 16:26. Hunger is good—if it makes you work to satisfy it!

Prov 20:13. If you love sleep, you will end in poverty. Stay awake, work hard, and there will be plenty to eat!

Prov 21:5. Steady plodding brings prosperity; hasty speculation brings poverty.

Prov 22:29. Do you know a hard-working man? He shall be successful and stand before kings!

Prov 28:19. Hard work brings prosperity.

Prov 30:25. Ants: they aren't strong, but store up food for the winter.

Prov 31:27. She watches carefully all that goes on throughout her household, and is never lazy. *vs.* 13–27.

Eccl 1:3. For what does a man get for all his hard work?

Eccl 2:10. Anything I wanted, I took and did not restrain myself from any joy. I even found great pleasure in hard work. This pleasure was, indeed, my only reward for all my labors. [11]But as I looked at everything I had tried, it was all so useless, a chasing of the wind, and there was nothing really worthwhile anywhere. [17]So now I hate life because it is all so irrational; all is foolishness, chasing the wind. [18]And I am disgusted about this, that I must leave the fruits of all my hard work to others. [19]And who can tell whether my son will be a wise man or a fool? And yet all I have will be given to him—how discouraging! [20]So I turned in despair from hard work as the answer to my search for satisfaction. [21]For though I spend my life searching for wisdom, knowledge, and skill, I must leave all of it to someone who hasn't done a day's work in his life; he inherits all my efforts, free of charge. [22]This is not only foolish, but unfair. So what does a man get for all his hard work?

Eccl 9:10. Whatever you do, do well, for in death, where you are going, there is no working or planning, or knowing, or understanding.

Eccl 11:4. If you wait for perfect conditions, you will never get anything done. Keep on sowing your seed, for you never know which will grow—perhaps it all will.

Rom 12:11. Never be lazy in your work but serve the Lord enthusiastically.

Eph 4:28. If anyone is stealing he must stop it and begin using those hands of his for honest work so he can give to others in need.

1 Thess 4:11. This should be your ambition: to live a quiet life, minding your own business and doing your own work, just as we told you before. [12]As a result, people who are not Christians will trust and respect you, and you will not need to depend on others for enough money to pay your bills.

2 Thess 3:10. Even while we were still there with you we gave you this rule: "He who does not work shall not eat." [11]Yet we hear that some of you are living in laziness, refusing to work, and wasting your time in gossiping. [12]In the name of the Lord Jesus Christ we appeal to such people—we command them—to quiet down, get to work, and earn their own living.

1 Tim 5:8. But anyone who won't care for his own relatives when they need help, especially those living in his own family, has no right to say he is a Christian. Such a person is worse than the heathen.

See *Frugality, Labor.* Also see *Idleness; Laziness.*

INSTANCES OF. Jeroboam, 1 Kgs 11:27, 28. Paul, Acts 18:2, 3; 20:33, 34; 2 Thess 3:8.

INFANTICIDE Ex 1:15, 16; Mt 2:16–18; Acts 7:19.

INFANTS See *Children.*

INFECTION Deut 28:22.

See *Disease.*

INFIDELITY OR DISLOYALTY TO GOD Gen 3:1. "Really?" he asked. "*None* of the fruit in the garden? God says you mustn't eat *any* of it?" *v.* 4.

Ex 5:2. "Is that so?" retorted Pharaoh. "And who is Jehovah, that I should listen to him and let Israel go? I don't know Jehovah and I will not let Israel go."

Ex 14:11. And they turned against Moses, whining, "Have you brought us out here to die in the desert because there were not enough graves for us in Egypt? Why did you make us leave Egypt?" *v.* 12. Ex 16:3, 7; Num 14:26–35; 16:41; 21:5.

Ex 17:7. Moses named the place Massah (meaning "tempting Jehovah to slay us"), and sometimes they referred to it as Meribah (meaning "argument" and "strife!")—for it was there that the people of Israel argued against God and tempted him to slay them by saying, "Is Jehovah going to take care of us or not?"

Num 15:30. But anyone who deliberately makes the "mistake," whether he is a native Israeli or a foreigner, is blaspheming Jehovah, and shall be cut off from among his people. *v.* 31.

Deut 29:19. Let no one blithely think, when he hears the warnings of this curse, "I shall prosper even though I walk in my own stubborn way!" [20]For the Lord will not pardon! His anger and jealousy will be hot against that man. And all the curses written in this book shall lie heavily upon him, and the Lord will blot out his name from under heaven. *v.* 21.

Deut 32:15. But Israel was soon overfed; Yes, fat and bloated; Then, in plenty, they forsook their God. They shrugged away the Rock of their salvation.

1 Kgs 20:28. Because the Syrians have declared, "The Lord is a God of the hills and not of the plains," I will help you defeat this vast army, and you shall know that I am indeed the Lord.

1 Kgs 22:24. Then Zedekiah (son of Chenaanah) walked over and slapped Micaiah on the face. "When did the Spirit of the Lord leave me and speak to you?" he demanded.

2 Kgs 2:23. Some young boys from the city began mocking and making fun of him because of his bald head. *v.* 24.

2 Chron 30:6. "Come back to the Lord God of Abraham, Isaac, and Israel," the king's letter said, "so that he will return to us who have escaped from the power of the kings of Assyria." [10]So the messengers went from city to city throughout Ephraim and Manasseh and as far as Zebulun. But for the most part they were received with laughter and scorn!

2 Chron 32:15. Don't let Hezekiah fool you! Don't believe him. I say it again—no god of any nation has ever yet been able to rescue his people from me or my ancestors; how much less your God! *vs.* 16–19.

2 Chron 36:16. But the people mocked these messengers of God and despised their words, scoffing at the prophets until the anger of the Lord could no longer be restrained, and there was no longer any remedy.

Job 15:25, 26. Armed with his tin shield, he clenches his fist against God, defying the Almighty, stubbornly assaulting him.

Job 21:14. All this despite the fact that they ordered God away and wanted no part of him and his ways. [15]"Who is Almighty God?" they scoff. "Why should we obey him? What good will it do us?"

Job 22:13. But you reply, "That is why he can't see what I am doing! How can he judge through the thick darkness? [14]For thick clouds swirl about him so that he cannot see us. He is way up there, walking on the vault of heaven." [17]For they said to God, "Go away, God! What can you do for us?"

Job 34:7. Who else is as arrogant as Job? [9]He must have spent much time with evil men, for he said, "Why waste time trying to please God?" [17]Are you going to condemn the Almighty Judge? [18]Are you going to condemn the God who says to kings and nobles, "You are wicked and unjust"? [19]For he doesn't care how great a man may be, and doesn't pay any more attention to the rich than to the poor. He made them all. [33]Must God tailor his justice to your demands? Must he change the order of the universe to suit your whims? The answer must be obvious even to you!

Job 35:2, 3. Do you think it is right for you to claim, "I haven't sinned, but I'm no better off before God than if I had"?

Job 36:23. Who can say that what he [God] does is absurd or evil?

Ps 1:1. Oh, the joys of those who do not follow evil men's advice, who do not hang around with sinners, scoffing at the things of God.

Ps 3:2. So many say that God will never help me.

Ps 4:6. Many say that God will never help us. Prove them wrong, O Lord, by letting the light of your face shine down upon us.

Ps 10:11. "God isn't watching," they say to themselves; "he'll never know!" [13]Why do you let the wicked get away with this contempt for God? For they think that God will never call them to account.

Ps 12:3, 4. But the Lord will not deal gently with people who act like that; he will destroy those proud liars who say, "We will lie to our hearts' content. Our lips are our own; who can stop us?"

Ps 14:1. That man is a fool who says to himself, "There is no God!" [6]He is the refuge of the poor and humble when evil-doers are oppressing them. Ps 53:1.

Ps 42:3. Day and night I weep for his help, and all the while my enemies taunt me. "Where is this God of yours?" they scoff.

Ps 50:21. I remained silent—you thought I didn't care—but now your time of punishment has come, and I list all the above charges against you.

Ps 59:7. I hear them shouting insults and cursing God, for "No one will hear us," they think.

Ps 64:5. They encourage each other to do evil. They meet in secret to set their traps. "He will never notice them here," they say.

Ps 73:11. "Does God realize what is going on?" they ask.

Ps 78:19,20. They even spoke against God himself. "Why can't he give us decent food as well as water?" they grumbled. *vs.* 20–22. Ps 107:11, 12.

Ps 94:7. "The Lord isn't looking," they say, "and besides, he doesn't care." [8]Fools! [9]Is God deaf and blind—he who makes ears and eyes?

Ps 106:24. They refused to enter the Promised Land, for they wouldn't believe his solemn oath to care for them. [25]Instead, they pouted in their tents and mourned and despised his command.

Prov 1:22. "You simpletons!" she cries. "How long will you go on being fools? How long will you scoff at wisdom and fight the facts?"

Prov 3:34. The Lord mocks at mockers.

Prov 9:12. Wisdom is its own reward, and if you scorn her, you hurt only yourself.

Prov 14:6. A mocker never finds the wisdom he claims he is looking for. [9]The common bond of rebels is their guilt.

Prov 19:29. Mockers and rebels shall be severely punished.

Prov 24:9. The rebel's schemes are sinful, and the mocker is the scourge of all mankind.

Isa 3:8. Israel's civil government will be in utter ruin because the Jews have spoken out against their Lord and will not worship him; they offend his glory.

Isa 5:18. Woe to those who drag their sins behind them like a bullock on a rope. [19]They even mock the Holy One of Israel and dare the Lord to punish them. "Hurry up and punish us, O Lord," they say. "We want to see what you can do!" [24]Therefore God will deal with them and burn them. They will disappear like straw on fire. Their roots will rot and their flowers wither, for they have thrown away the laws of God and despised the Word of the Holy One of Israel. [25]That is why the anger of the Lord is hot against his people.

Isa 10:15. But the Lord says, "Shall the axe boast greater power then the man who uses it? Is the saw greater than the man who saws? Can a rod strike unless a hand is moving it? Can a cane walk by itself?"

Isa 28:9. "Who does Isaiah think he is," the people say, "to speak to us like this! Are we little children, barely old enough to talk? [10]He tells us everything over and over again, a line at a time and in such simple words!" [14]Therefore hear the word of the Lord, you scoffing rulers in Jerusalem: [15]You have struck a bargain with Death, you say, and sold yourselves to the devil in exchange for his protection against the Assyrians. "They can never touch us," you say, "for we are under the care of one who will deceive and fool them." [17]I will take the line and plummet of justice to check the foundation wall you built; it looks so fine, but it is so weak a storm of hail will knock it down! The enemy will come like a flood and sweep it away, and you will be drowned. [18]I will cancel your agreement of compromise with Death and the devil, so when the terrible enemy floods in, you will be trampled into the ground. [19]Again and again that flood will come and carry you off, until at last the unmixed horror of the truth of my warnings will finally dawn on you. [20]The bed you have made is far too short to lie on; the blankets are too narrow to cover you. [21]The Lord will come suddenly and in anger, as at Mount Perazim and Gibeon, to do a strange, unusual thing—to destroy his own people! [22]So scoff no more, lest your punishment be made even greater, for the Lord God of Hosts has plainly told me that he is determined to crush you.

Isa 29:15. Woe to those who try to hide their plans from God, who try to keep him in the dark concerning what they do! "God can't see us," they say to themselves. "He doesn't know what is going on!" [16]How stupid can they be! Isn't he, the Potter, greater than you, the jars he makes? Will you say to him, "He didn't make us"? Does a machine call its inventor dumb? [20]Bullies will vanish and scoffers will cease, and all those plotting evil will be killed.

Isa 45:9. Woe to the man who fights with his Creator. Does the pot argue with its maker? Does the clay dispute with him who forms it, saying, "Stop, you're doing it wrong!" or the pot exclaim, "How clumsy can you be!"? [10]Woe to the baby just being born who squalls to his father and mother, "Why have you produced me? Can't you do anything right at all?"

Isa 47:10. You felt secure in all your wickedness. "No one sees me," you said. Your "wisdom" and "knowledge" have caused you to turn away from me and claim that you yourself are Jehovah. [11]That is why disaster shall overtake you suddenly—so suddenly that you won't know where it comes from. And there will be no atonement then to cleanse away your sins.

Isa 57:4. Who is it you mock, making faces and sticking out your tongues? You children of sinners and liars! [11]Why were you more afraid of them than of me? How is it that you gave not even a second thought to me? Is it because I've been too gentle, that you have no fear of me? *vs.* 5–10.

Jer 2:31. O my people, listen to the words of God: Have I been unjust to Israel? Have I been to them a land of darkness and of evil? Why then do my people say, "At last we are free from God; we won't have anything to do with him again!"

Jer 5:12. They have lied and said, "He won't bother us! No evil will come upon us! There will be neither famine nor war!" [14]Therefore this is what the Lord God of Hosts says to his prophets: Because of talk like this I'll take your words and prophecies and turn them into raging fire and burn up these people like kindling wood.

Jer 17:15. Men scoff at me and say, "What is this word of the Lord you keep talking about? If these threats of yours are really from God, why don't they come true?" Jer 43:2, 3.

Jer 48:42. Moab shall no longer be a nation, for she has boasted against the Lord. *v.* 26.

Jer 50:24. O Babylon, I have set a trap for you and you are caught, for you have fought against the Lord. [29]Send out a call for archers to come to Babylon; surround the city so that none can escape. Do to her as she has done to others, for she has haughtily defied the Lord, the Holy One of Israel.

Lam 1:7. And now in the midst of all Jerusalem's sadness she remembers happy bygone days. She thinks of all the precious joys she had before her mocking enemy struck her down—and there was no one to give her aid.

Ezk 9:9. But he said to me, "The sins of the people of Israel and Judah are very great and all the land is full of murder and injustice, for they say, 'The Lord doesn't see it! He has gone away!' [10]And so I will not spare them nor have any pity on them, and I will fully repay them for all that they have done." Ezk 8:12.

Ezk 12:22. Son of dust, what is that proverb they quote in Israel—"The days as they pass make liars out of every prophet." Ezk 11:3.

Ezk 18:2. Why do people use this proverb about the land of Israel: The children are punished for their fathers' sins? [29]And yet the people of Israel keep saying: "The Lord is unfair!" O people of Israel, it is you who are unfair, not I. Ezk 33:17.

Ezk 20:49. Then I said, "O Lord God, they say of me, 'He only talks in riddles!' "

Ezk 33:20. Yet you are saying the Lord isn't fair. But I will judge each of you in accordance with his deeds. [30]Son of dust, your people are whispering behind your back. They talk about you in their houses and whisper about you at the doors, saying, "Come on, let's have some fun! Let's go hear him tell us what the Lord is saying!"

Ezk 36:2. Your enemies have sneered at you and claimed your ancient heights as theirs.

Dan 3:15. And what god can deliver you out of my hands then?

Dan 8:25. He will be a master of deception. . . . So great will he fancy himself to be that he will even take on the Prince of Princes in battle; but in so doing he will deal his own doom, for he shall be broken by the hand of God, though no human means could overpower him. *v.* 10. Dan 7:25; 11:36, 37.

Hos 7:5. On the king's birthday, the princes get him drunk; he makes a fool of himself and drinks with those who mock him. [13]Woe to my people for deserting me; let them perish, for they have sinned against me. I wanted to redeem them but their hard hearts would not accept the truth. [15]I have helped them, and made them strong, yet now they turn against me.

Amos 5:18. You say, "If only the Day of the Lord were here, for then God would deliver us from all our foes." But you have no idea what you ask. For that day will *not* be light and prosperity, but darkness and doom! How terrible the darkness will be for you; not a ray of joy or hope will shine.

Amos 7:16. Now therefore listen to this message to you from the Lord. You say, "Don't prophesy against Israel." [17]The Lord's reply is this: . . . "You yourself will die in a heathen land."

Mic 7:10. Then my enemy will see that God is for me, and be ashamed for taunting me, "Where is that God of yours?" Now with my own eyes I see them trampled down like mud in the street.

Zeph 1:12. I will search with lanterns in Jerusalem's darkest corners to find and punish those who sit contented in their sins, indifferent to God, thinking he will let them alone.

Mal 1:7. "When you offer polluted sacrifices on my altar." "Polluted sacrifices? When have we ever done a thing like that?" "Every time you say, "Don't bother bringing anything very valuable to offer to God!' "

Mal 3:13. "Your attitude toward me has been proud and arrogant," says the Lord. "But you say, 'What do you mean? What have we said that we shouldn't?' [14]Listen; you have said, 'It is foolish to worship God and obey him. What good does it do to obey his laws, and to sorrow and mourn for our sins?' "

Mt 12:24. But when the Pharisees heard about the miracle they said, "He can cast out demons because he is Satan, king of devils." Mk 3:22; Lk 11:15; 16:14.

Mt 25:24, 25. Then the man with the $1,000 came and said, "Sir, I knew you were a hard man, and I was afraid you would rob me of what I earned, so I hid your money in the earth and here it is!" [26]But his master replied, "Wicked man! Lazy slave! Since you knew I would demand your profit, [27]you should at least have put my money into the bank so I could have some interest."

Mt 27:39. And the people passing by hurled abuse, shaking their heads at him and saying, [40]"So! You can destroy the Temple and build it again in three days, can you? Well, then come on down from the cross if you are the Son of God!" [41-43]And the chief priests and Jewish leaders also mocked him. "He saved others," they scoffed, "but he can't save himself! So you are the King of Israel, are you? Come down from the cross and we'll believe you! He trusted God—let God show his approval by delivering him! Didn't he say, 'I am God's Son'?" [44]And the robbers also threw the same in his teeth.

Lk 4:23. Then he said, "Probably you will quote me that proverb, 'Physician, heal yourself'—meaning, 'Why don't you do miracles here in your home town like those you did in Capernaum?' "

Lk 19:14. But some of his people hated him and sent him their declaration of independence, stating that they had rebelled and would not acknowledge him as their king. [27]"And now about these enemies of mine who revolted—bring them in and execute them before me."

Acts 2:13. But others in the crowd were mocking. "They're drunk, that's all!" they said.

Acts 13:45. But when the Jewish leaders saw the crowds, they were jealous, and cursed and argued against whatever Paul said.

Acts 17:18. He also had an encounter with some of the Epicurean and Stoic philosophers. Their reaction, when he told them about Jesus and his resurrection, was, "He's a dreamer," or, "He's pushing some foreign religion." [32]When they heard Paul speak of the resurrection of a person who had been dead, some laughed.

Acts 23:8. For the Sadducees say there is no resurrection or angels or even eternal spirit within us. Mt 22:23.

Rom 9:20. No, don't say that. Who are you to criticize God? Should the thing made say to the one who made it, "Why have you made me like this?" [21]When a man makes a jar out of clay, doesn't he have a right to use the same lump of clay to make one jar beautiful, to be used for holding flowers, and another to throw garbage into? Rom 3:5.

Heb 10:29. Think how much more terrible the punishment will be for those who have trampled underfoot the Son of God and treated his cleansing blood as though it were common and unhallowed, and insulted and outraged the Holy Spirit who brings God's mercy to his people.

2 Pet 2:1. But there were false prophets, too, in those days, just as there will be false teachers among you. They will cleverly tell their lies about God, turning against even their Master who bought them; but theirs will be a swift and terrible end.

2 Pet 3:3. First, I want to remind you that in the last days there will come scoffers who will do every wrong they can think of, and laugh at the truth. [4]This will be their line of argument: "So Jesus promised to come back, did he? Then where is he? He'll never come! Why, as far back as anyone can remember everything has remained exactly as it was since the first day of creation." *vs.* 5, 6.

Jude 1:4. I say this because some godless teachers have wormed their way in among you, saying that after we become Christians we can do just as we like without fear of God's punishment. The fate of such people was written long ago, for they have turned against our only Master and Lord, Jesus Christ. [15]He will bring the people of the world before him in judgment, to receive just punishment, and to prove the terrible things they have done in rebellion against God, revealing all they have said against him. [18]That in the last times there would come these scoffers whose whole purpose in life is to enjoy themselves in every evil way imaginable. *v.* 19.

See *Presumption; Skepticism; Unbelief.*

INFIRMITY See *Ailment; Disease.*

INFLUENCE EVIL. 1 Kgs 11:3. He had seven hundred wives and three hundred concubines; and sure enough, they turned his heart away from the Lord, [4]especially in his old age. They encouraged him to worship their gods instead of trusting completely in the Lord as his father David had done.

1 Kgs 15:25. Meanwhile, over in Israel, Nadab the son of Jeroboam had become king. He reigned two years, beginning in the second year of the reign of King Asa of Judah. [26]But he was not a good king; like his father, he worshiped many idols and led all of Israel into sin.

1 Kgs 21:25. No one else was so completely sold out to the devil as Ahab, for his wife Jezebel encouraged him to do every sort of evil.

1 Kgs 22:51. It was during the seventeenth year of the reign of King Jehoshaphat of Judah that Ahaziah, Ahab's son, began to reign over Israel in Samaria; and he reigned two years. [52, 53]But he

was not a good king, for he followed in the footsteps of his father and mother and of Jeroboam, who had led Israel into the sin of worshiping idols. So Ahaziah made the Lord God of Israel very angry.

2 Kgs 8:16. King Jehoram, the son of King Jehoshaphat of Judah, began his reign during the fifth year of the reign of King Joram of Israel, the son of Ahab. [17]Jehoram was thirty-two years old when he became king, and he reigned in Jerusalem for eight years. [18]But he was as wicked as Ahab and the other kings of Israel; he even married one of Ahab's daughters. [25]Then his son Ahaziah became the new king during the twelfth year of the reign of King Joram of Israel, the son of Ahab. [26]Ahaziah was twenty-two years old when he began to reign but he reigned only one year, in Jerusalem. His mother was Athaliah, the granddaughter of King Omri of Israel. [27]He was an evil king, just as all of King Ahab's descendants were—for he was related to Ahab by marriage.

2 Kgs 17:21. For Israel split off from the kingdom of David and chose Jeroboam I (the son of Nebat) as its king. Then Jeroboam drew Israel away from following the Lord. He made them sin a great sin, [22]and the people of Israel never quit doing the evil things that Jeroboam led them into.

2 Kgs 21:9. But the people did not listen to the Lord, and Manasseh enticed them to do even more evil than the surrounding nations had done, even though Jehovah had destroyed those nations for their evil ways when the people of Israel entered the land.

2 Chron 21:5. He was thirty-two years old when he began to reign, and he reigned eight years, in Jerusalem. [6]But he was as wicked as the kings who were over in Israel. Yes, as wicked as Ahab, for Jehoram had married one of the daughters of Ahab, and his whole life was one constant binge of doing evil.

2 Chron 22:3. He, too, walked in the evil ways of Ahab, for his mother encouraged him in doing wrong. [4]Yes, he was as evil as Ahab, for Ahab's family became his advisors after his father's death, and they led him on to ruin. [5]Following their evil advice, Ahaziah made an alliance with King Jehoram of Israel (the son of Ahab), who was at war with King Hazael of Syria at Ramoth-gilead. Ahaziah led his army there to join the battle.

2 Chron 33:9. But Manasseh encouraged the people of Judah and Jerusalem to do even more evil than the nations the Lord destroyed when Israel entered the land.

Prov 22:24. Keep away from angry, short-tempered men, [25]lest you learn to be like them and endanger your soul.

Prov 29:12. A wicked ruler will have wicked aides on his staff.

Jer 17:1. My people sin as though commanded to, as though their evil were laws chiseled with an iron pen or diamond point upon their stony hearts or on the corners of their altars. [2]Their youths do not forget to sin, worshiping idols beneath each tree, high in the mountains or in the open country down below.

Hos 4:9. And thus it is: "Like priests, like people"—because the priests are wicked, the people are too. Therefore, I will punish both priests and people for all their wicked deeds.

Mt 13:24. Here is another illustration Jesus used: "The Kingdom of Heaven is like a farmer sowing good seed in his field; [25]but one night as he slept, his enemy came and sowed thistles among the wheat."

Lk 12:1. More than anything else, beware of these Pharisees and the way they pretend to be good when they aren't.

1 Cor 5:6. What a terrible thing it is that you are boasting about your purity, and yet you let this sort of thing go on. Don't you realize that if even one person is allowed to go on sinning, soon all will be affected? [7]Remove this evil cancer—this wicked person—from among you, so that you can stay pure. Christ, God's Lamb, has been slain for us. [8]So let us feast upon him and grow strong in the Christian life, leaving entirely behind us the cancerous old life with all its hatreds and wickedness. Let us feast instead upon the pure bread of honor and sincerity and truth.

Gal 3:1. Oh, foolish Galatians! What magician has hypnotized you and cast an evil spell upon you? For you used to see the meaning of Jesus Christ's death as clearly as though I had waved a placard before you with a picture on it of Christ dying on the cross.

Gal 5:7. You were getting along so well. Who has interfered with you to hold you back from following the truth? [8]It certainly isn't God who has done it, for he is the one who has called you to freedom in Christ. [9]But it takes only one wrong person among you to infect all the others.

2 Tim 2:14. Remind your people of these great facts, and command them in the name of the Lord not to argue over unimportant things. Such arguments are confusing and useless, and even harmful. [17]Things will be said that will burn and hurt for a long time to come. Hymenaeus and Philetus, in their love of argument, are men like that. [18]They have left the path of truth, preaching the lie that the resurrection of the dead has already occurred; and they have weakened the faith of some who believe them.

Heb 12:15. Look after each other so that not one of you will fail to find God's best blessings. Watch out that no bitterness takes root among you, for as it springs up it causes deep trouble, hurting many in their spiritual lives.

See *Example.*

Instances of. Satan over Adam and Eve, Gen 3:1–5. Eve over Adam, Gen 3:6.

GOOD. 1 Sam 19:1. Saul now urged his aides and his son Jonathan to assassinate David. But Jonathan, because of his close friendship with David, [2]told him what his father was planning. "Tomorrow morning," he warned him, "you must find a hiding place out in the fields. [3]I'll ask my father to go out there with me, and I'll talk to him about you; then I'll tell you everything I can find out." 4The next morning as Jonathan and his father were talking together, he spoke well of David and begged him not to be against David. "He's never done anything to harm you," Jonathan pleaded. "He has always helped you in any way he could. 5Have you forgotten about the time he risked his life to kill Goliath, and how the Lord brought a great victory to Israel as a result? You were certainly happy about it then. Why should you now murder an innocent man by killing him? There is no reason for it at all!" 6Finally Saul agreed, and vowed, "As the Lord lives, he shall not be killed."

1 Sam 20:4. "Tell me what I can do," Jonathan begged. 5And David replied, "Tomorrow is the beginning of the celebration of the new moon. Always before, I've been with your father for this occasion, but tomorrow I'll hide in the field and stay there until the evening of the third day. 6If your father asks where I am, tell him that I asked permission to go home to Bethlehem for an annual family reunion. 7If he says, 'Fine!' then I'll know that all is well. But if he is angry, then I'll know that he is planning to kill me. 8Do this for me as my sworn brother. Or else kill me yourself if I have sinned against your father, but don't betray me to him!" 9"Of course not!" Jonathan exclaimed. "Look, wouldn't I say so if I knew that my father was planning to kill you?"

1 Kgs 22:42. Jehoshaphat was thirty-five years old when he ascended to the throne, and he reigned in Jerusalem for twenty-five years. His mother was Azubah, the daughter of Shilhi. 43He did as his father Asa had done, obeying the Lord in all but one thing: he did not destroy the shrines on the hills, so the people sacrificed and burned incense there.

2 Kgs 15:1. New king of Judah: Azariah; name of his father: Amaziah, the former king; name of his mother: Jecoliah of Jerusalem; length of his reign: 52 years, in Jerusalem; 2his age at the beginning of his reign: 16 years old; reigning in Israel at this time: King Jeroboam, who had been the king there for 27 years. 3Azariah was a good king, and he pleased the Lord just as his father Amaziah had.

32. New king of Judah: Jotham; father's name: King Uzziah; 33his age when he became king: 25 years old; duration of his reign: 16 years, in Jerusalem; mother's name: Jerusha (daughter of Zadok); reigning in Israel at this time: Pekah (son of Remaliah), who had been the king there for 2 years. 34Generally speaking, Jotham was a good king. Like his father Uzziah, he followed the Lord.

Mt 5:13. You are the world's seasoning, to make it tolerable. If you lose your flavor, what will happen to the world? And you yourselves will be thrown out and trampled underfoot as worthless. 14You are the world's light—a city on a hill, glowing in the night for all to see. 15, 16Don't hide your light! Let it shine for all; let your good deeds glow for all to see, so that they will praise your heavenly Father.

Mk 4:21. Then he asked them, "When someone lights a lamp, does he put a box over it to shut out the light? Of course not! The light couldn't be seen or used. A lamp is placed on a stand to shine and be useful. 22All that is now hidden will someday come to light."

Lk 11:33. No one lights a lamp and hides it! Instead, he puts it on a lampstand to give light to all who enter the room. 34Your eyes light up your inward being. A pure eye lets sunshine into your soul. A lustful eye shuts out the light and plunges you into darkness. 35So watch out that the sunshine isn't blotted out. 36If you are filled with light within, with no dark corners, then your face will be radiant too, as though a floodlight is beamed upon you.

Jn 7:38. For the Scriptures declare that rivers of living water shall flow from the inmost being of anyone who believes in me.

1 Cor 7:16. For, after all, there is no assurance to you wives that your husbands will be converted if they stay; and the same may be said to you husbands concerning your wives.

Phil 2:15. So that no one can speak a word of blame against you. You are to live clean, innocent lives as children of God in a dark world full of people who are crooked and stubborn. Shine out among them like beacon lights.

1 Thess 1:7. Then you yourselves became an example to all the other Christians in Greece. 8And now the Word of the Lord has spread out from you to others everywhere, far beyond your boundaries, for wherever we go we find people telling us about your remarkable faith in God.

1 Tim 6:1. Christian slaves should work hard for their owners and respect them; never let it be said that Christ's people are poor workers. Don't let the name of God or his teaching be laughed at because of this.

Heb 11:4. It was by faith that Abel obeyed God and brought an offering that pleased God more than Cain's offering did. God accepted Abel and proved it by accepting his gift; and though Abel is long dead, we can still learn lessons from him about trusting God.

1 Pet 2:11. Dear brothers, you are only visitors here. Since your real home is in heaven I beg you to keep away from the evil pleasures of this world; they are not for you, for they fight against your very souls. 12Be careful how you behave among your unsaved neighbors; for then, even if they are suspicious of you and talk against you, they will end up praising God for your good works when Christ returns.

1 Pet 3:1, 2. Wives, fit in with your husbands' plans; for then if they refuse to listen when you talk to them about the Lord, they will be won by your respectful, pure behavior. Your godly lives will speak to them better than any words. 15Quietly trust yourself to Christ your Lord and if anybody asks why you believe as you do, be ready to tell him, and do it in a gentle and respectful way. 16Do what is right; then if men speak against you, calling

you evil names, they will become ashamed of themselves for falsely accusing you when you have only done what is good.

See *Example.*

Instances of. Ezra, Ezra 10:1, with chapter 9. Nehemiah, Neh chapters 4; 5. Hezekiah, 2 Chron chapters 29–31. Josiah, 2 Kgs chapters 22; 23; 2 Chron chapters 34; 35. Manasseh, 2 Chron 33: 12–19.

POLITICAL. 1 Kgs 2:13. One day Adonijah the son Haggith came to see Solomon's mother, Bath-sheba. "Have you come to make trouble?" she asked him. "No," he replied, "I come in peace.
[14]As a matter of fact, I have a favor to ask of you."
"What is it?" she asked. [15]"Everything was going well for me," he said, "and the kingdom was mine: everyone expected me to be the next king. But the tables are turned, and everything went to my brother instead; for that is the way the Lord
wanted it. [16]But now I have just a small favor to ask of you; please don't turn me down." "What is it?"
she asked. [17]He replied, "Speak to King Solomon on my behalf (for I know he will do anything you request) and ask him to give me Abishag, the Shunammite, as my wife." [18]"All right," Bath-sheba replied, "I'll ask him."

2 Kgs 4:11, 12. Once when he was resting in the room he said to his servant Gehazi, "Tell the woman I want to speak to her." When she came,
[13]he said to Gehazi, "Tell her that we appreciate her kindness to us. Now ask her what we can do for her. Does she want me to put in a good word for her to the king or to the general of the army?" "No," she replied, "I am perfectly content."

Neh 6:17. During those fifty-two days many letters went back and forth between Tobiah and the wealthy politicians of Judah. [18]For many in Judah had sworn allegiance to him because his father-in-law was Shecaniah (son of Arah) and because his son Jehohanan was married to the daughter of Meshullam (son of Berechiah). [19]They all told me what a wonderful man Tobiah was, and then they told him everything I had said; and Tobiah sent many threatening letters to frighten me.

Prov 19:6. Many beg favors from a man who is generous; everyone is his friend!

Prov 29:26. Do you want justice? Don't fawn on the judge, but ask the Lord for it!

Dan 5:10. But when the queen-mother heard what was happening, she rushed to the banquet hall and said to Belshazzar, "Calm yourself, Your Majesty, don't be so pale and frightened over this.
[11]For there is a man in your kingdom who has within him the spirit of the holy gods. In the days of your father this man was found to be as full of wisdom and understanding as though he were himself a god. And in the reign of King Nebuchadnezzar, he was made chief of all the magicians, astrologers, Chaldeans and soothsayers of Babylon. [12]Call for this man, Daniel—or Belteshazzar, as the king called him—for his mind is filled with divine knowledge and understanding. He can interpret dreams, explain riddles, and solve knotty problems. He will tell you what the writing means."

Mt 20:20. Then the mother of James and John, the sons of Zebedee, brought them to Jesus and respectfully asked a favor. [21]"What is your request?" he asked. She replied, "In your Kingdom, will you let my two sons sit on two thrones next to yours?" [22]But Jesus told her, "You don't know what you are asking!" Then he turned to James and John and asked them, "Are you able to drink from the terrible cup I am about to drink from?" "Yes," they replied, "we are able!" [23]"You shall indeed drink from it," he told them. "But I have no right to say who will sit on the thrones next to mine. Those places are reserved for the persons my Father selects." [24]The other ten disciples were indignant when they heard what James and John had asked for.

Acts 12:20. While he was in Caesarea, a delegation from Tyre and Sidon arrived to see him. He was highly displeased with the people of those two cities, but the delegates made friends with Blastus, the royal secretary, and asked for peace, for their cities were economically dependent upon trade with Herod's country.

See *Politics.*

INGATHERING, FEAST OF See *Tabernacles, Feast of.*

INGRATITUDE OF MAN TO GOD. Num 16:9. Then Moses spoke again to Korah: "Does it seem a small thing to you that the God of Israel has chosen you from among all the people of Israel to be near to himself as you work in the Tabernacle of Jehovah, and to stand before the people to minister to them? [10]Is it nothing to you that he has given this task to only you Levites? And now are you demanding the priesthood also?

Deut 8:12. For when you have become full and prosperous and have built fine homes to live in,
[13]and when your flocks and herds have become very large, and your silver and gold have multiplied, [14]that is the time to watch out that you don't become proud, and forget the Lord your God who brought you out of your slavery in the land of Egypt. Deut 6:10–12.

Deut 28:47, 48. You will become slaves to your enemies because of your failure to praise God for all that he has given you. The Lord will send your enemies against you, and you will be hungry, thirsty, naked, and in want of everything. A yoke of iron shall be placed around your neck until you are destroyed!

Deut 31:16. And said to Moses, "You shall die and join your ancestors. After you are gone, these people will begin worshiping foreign gods in the Promised Land. They will forget about me and break the contract I have made with them.

Deut 32:6. Is this the way you treat Jehovah? O foolish people, is not God your Father? Has he not created you? Has he not established you and made you strong? [15]But Israel was soon overfed; yes, fat and bloated; then, in plenty, they forsook their God. They shrugged away the Rock of their salvation. [18]They spurned the Rock who had made them, forgetting it was God who had given them birth. *v.* 13.

Judg 2:10. But finally all that generation died; and the next generation did not worship Jehovah as their God, and did not care about the mighty miracles he had done for Israel. [11]They did many things which the Lord had expressly forbidden. . . . [12]They abandoned Jehovah, the God loved and worshiped by their ancestors—the God who had brought them out of Egypt. Instead, they were worshiping and bowing low before the idols of the neighboring nations. So the anger of the Lord flared out against all Israel. Neh 9:26, 27.

Judg 8:34. They no longer considered the Lord as their God, though he had rescued them from all their enemies on every side. [35]Nor did they show any kindness to the family of Gideon despite all he had done for them.

Judg 10:11, 13, 14. But the Lord replied, "Didn't I save you from the Egyptians, the Amorites, the Ammonites, the Philistines. [13]Yet you continue to abandon me and to worship other gods. So go away; I won't save you any more. [14]Go and cry to the new gods you have chosen! Let them save you in your hour of distress!" Neh 9:25, 35; Ps 106:7, 21, 22; Jer 2:6, 7.

1 Sam 8:7. "Do as they say," the Lord replied, "for I am the one they are rejecting, not you—they don't want me to be their king any longer. [8]Ever since I brought them from Egypt they have continually forsaken me and followed other gods. And now they are giving you the same treatment."

1 Sam 10:18, 19. I brought you from Egypt and rescued you from the Egyptians and from all of the nations that were torturing you. But although I have done so much for you, you have rejected me and have said, "We want a king instead!"

1 Sam 15:17. And Samuel told him, "When you didn't think much of yourself, God made you king of Israel. [19]Then why didn't you obey the Lord? Why did you rush for the loot and do exactly what God said not to?"

2 Sam 12:7. I made you king of Israel and saved you from the power of Saul. [8]I gave you his palace and his wives and the kingdoms of Israel and Judah; and if that had not been enough, I would have given you much, much more. [9]Why, then, have you despised the laws of God and done this terrible deed? For you have murdered Uriah and stolen his wife. 2 Chron 12:1.

1 Kgs 16:1. A message of condemnation from the Lord was delivered to King Baasha at this time by the prophet Jehu: [2]"I lifted you out of the dust," the message said, "to make you king of my people Israel; but you have walked in the evil paths of Jeroboam. You have made my people sin, and I am angry! So now I will destroy you and your family, just as I did the descendants of Jeroboam."

2 Chron 26:15. So he became very famous, for the Lord helped him wonderfully until he was very powerful. [16]But at that point he became proud—and corrupt. He sinned against the Lord his God by entering the forbidden sanctuary of the Temple and personally burning incense upon the altar.

2 Chron 32:25. However, Hezekiah didn't respond with true thanksgiving and praise, for he had become proud, and so the anger of God was upon him and upon Judah and Jerusalem.

Ps 78:16. Streams poured from the rock, flowing like a river! [17]Yet they kept on with their rebellion, sinning against the God who is above all gods. [27]He rained down birds as thick as dust, clouds of them like sands along the shore! [28]He caused the birds to fall to the ground among the tents. [29]The people ate their fill. He gave them what they asked for. [30]But they had hardly finished eating, and the meat was yet in their mouths, [31]when the anger of the Lord rose against them and killed the finest of Israel's young men. [32]Yet even so the people kept on sinning and refused to believe in miracles.

Ps 106:7. They weren't impressed by the wonder of your miracles in Egypt, and soon forgot your many acts of kindness to them.

Isa 1:2. The children I raised and cared for so long and tenderly have turned against me.

Jer 2:17. And you have brought this on yourselves by rebelling against the Lord your God when he wanted to lead you and show you the way! [31]Have I been unjust to Israel? Have I been to them a land of darkness and of evil? Why then do my people say, "At last we are free from God; we won't have anything to do with him again!"

Jer 5:7. How can I pardon you? For even your children have turned away, and worship gods that are not gods at all. I fed my people until they were fully satisfied, and their thanks was to commit adultery wholesale and to gang up at the city's brothels. [9]Shall I not punish them for this? Shall I not send my vengeance on such a nation as this? [24]Though I am the one who gives them rain each year in spring and fall and sends the harvest times, yet they have no respect or fear for me.

Ezk 16:17. You took the very jewels and gold and silver ornaments I gave to you and made statues of men and worshiped them, which is adultery against me. *vs.* 17–22.

Dan 5:18. Your Majesty, the Most High God gave Nebuchadnezzar, who long ago preceded you, a kingdom and majesty and glory and honor. [20]But when his heart and mind were hardened in pride, God removed him from his royal throne and took away his glory, [21]and he was chased out of his palace into the fields. . . . until at last he knew that the Most High overrules the kingdoms of men, and that he appoints anyone he desires to reign over them.

Hos 2:8. She doesn't realize that all she has, has come from me. It was I who gave her all the gold and silver that she used in worshiping Baal, her god! [9]But now I will take back the wine and ripened corn I constantly supplied, and the clothes I gave her to cover her nakedness—I will no longer give her rich harvests of grain in its season, or wine at the time of the grape harvest.

Hos 4:7. The more my people multiplied, the

more they sinned against me. They exchanged the glory of God for the disgrace of idols.

Hos 7:13. Woe to my people for deserting me; let them perish, for they have sinned against me. I wanted to redeem them but their hard hearts would not accept the truth. [15]I have helped them, and made them strong, yet now they turn against me.

Hos 11:1. When Israel was a child I loved him as a son. [3]I trained him from infancy, I taught him to walk, I held him in my arms. But he doesn't know or even care that it was I who raised him.

Hos 13:6. But when you had eaten and were satisfied, then you became proud and forgot me.

Amos 3:1. Listen! This your doom! It is spoken by the Lord against both Israel and Judah—against the entire family I brought from Egypt: [2]"Of all the peoples of the earth, I have chosen you alone. That is why I must punish you the more for all your sins."

Mic 6:3. O my people, what have I done that makes you turn away from me? Tell me why your patience is exhausted! Answer me! [4]For I brought you out of Egypt, and cut your chains of slavery.

Lk 17:17. Jesus asked, "Didn't I heal ten men? Where are the nine? [18]Does only this foreigner return to give glory to God?"

Jn 1:11. Even in his own land and among his own people, the Jews, he was not accepted.

Rom 1:21. Yes, they knew about him all right, but they wouldn't admit it or worship him or even thank him for all his daily care. And after awhile they began to think up silly ideas of what God was like and what he wanted them to do. The result was that their foolish minds became dark and confused.

2 Tim 3:2. For people will love only themselves . . . sneering at God.

OF MAN TO MAN. Prov 17:13; 2 Tim 3:2.

Instances of: Laban to Jacob, Gen 31. Pharaoh's wine taster to Joseph, Gen 40:23. Israelites to Moses, Ex 16:3; 17:2–4; Num 16:12–14; to Gideon, Judg 8:35. Shechemites, Judg 9:17, 18. Men of Keilah to David, 1 Sam 23:5–12. Saul to David, 1 Sam 24. Nabal, 1 Sam 25:21. David to Joab, 1 Kgs 2:5, 6; with the history of Joab's services to David, see *Joab.* David to Uriah, 2 Sam 11:6–17. David's companions to David, Ps 35:11–16; 38:20; 41:9; 109:4, 5. Citizens, Eccl 9:14–16. Joash, 2 Chron 24:22. Jeremiah's enemies, Jer 18:20.

INHERITANCE Provisions for inheritance under Levirate marriages, Gen 38:7–11; Num 36:6–9; Deut 25:5–10; Ruth 3:1–8; 4:7–17.

UNCLASSIFIED SCRIPTURES RELATING TO. Gen 15:2, 3. But Abraham replied, "O Lord Jehovah, what good are all your blessings when I have no son? For without a son, some other member of my household will inherit all my wealth."

Gen 21:9. But when Sarah noticed Ishmael—the son of Abraham and the Egyptian girl Hagar—teasing Isaac, [10]she turned upon Abraham and demanded, "Get rid of the slave girl and her son. He is not going to share your property with my son. I won't have it." [11]This upset Abraham very much, for after all, Ishmael too was his son.

Gen 24:36. Now when Sarah, my master's wife, was very old, she gave birth to my master's son, and my master has given him everything he owns.

Gen 25:5. Abraham deeded everything he owned to Isaac; [6]however, he gave gifts to the sons of his concubines and sent them off into the east, away from Isaac.

Gen 48:21. Then Israel said to Joseph, "I am about to die, but God will be with you and will bring you again to Canaan, the land of your fathers. [22]And I have given the choice land of Shekem to you instead of to your brothers, as your portion of that land which I took from the Amorites with my sword and with my bow."

Num 27:6. And the Lord replied to Moses, [7]"The daughters of Zelophehad are correct. Give them land along with their uncles; give them the property that would have been given to their father if he had lived. [8]Moreover, this is a general law among you, that if a man dies and has no sons, then his inheritance shall be passed on to his daughters. [9]And if he has no daughter, it shall belong to his brothers. [10]And if he has no brother, then it shall go to his uncles. [11]But if he has no uncles then it shall go to the nearest relative."

Deut 21:15. If a man has two wives but loves one and not the other, and both have borne him children, and the mother of his oldest son is the wife he doesn't love, [16]he may not give a larger inheritance to his younger son, the son of the wife he loves. [17]He must give the customary double portion to his oldest son, who is the beginning of his strength and who owns the rights of a first-born son, even though he is the son of the wife his father doesn't love.

1 Kgs 21:3. But Naboth replied, "Not on your life! That land has been in my family for generations."

2 Chron 21:3. Their father had given each of them valuable gifts of money and jewels, also the ownership of some of the fortified cities of Judah. However, he gave the kingship to Jehoram because he was the oldest.

Job 42:15. And in all the land there were no other girls as lovely as the daughters of Job; and their father put them into his will along with their brothers.

Prov 17:2. A wise slave will rule his master's wicked sons and share their estate.

Prov 20:21. A fortune can be made from cheating, but there is a curse that goes with it.

Eccl 2:18. And I am disgusted about this, that I must leave the fruits of all my hard work to others. [19]And who can tell whether my son will be a wise man or a fool?

Jer 32:6, 7. Then this message from the Lord came to Jeremiah: Your cousin Hanamel (son of Shallum) will soon arrive to ask you to buy the farm he owns in Anathoth, for by law you have a chance to buy before it is offered to anyone else. [8]So Hanamel came, as the Lord had said he would, and visited me in the prison. "Buy my field in Anathoth, in the land of Benjamin," he said, "for the law gives you the first right to purchase it." Then I knew for sure that the message I had heard was really from the Lord.

Ezk 46:16. The Lord God says: If the prince gives a gift of land to one of his sons, it will belong to him forever. [17]But if he gives a gift of land to one of his servants, the servant may keep it only until the Year of Release (every seventh year) when he is set free; then the land returns to the prince. Only gifts to his sons are permanent. [18]And the prince may never take anyone's property by force. If he gives property to his sons, it must be from his own land, for I don't want my people losing their property and having to move away.

Lk 15:12. When the younger told his father, "I want my share of your estate now, instead of waiting until you die!" his father agreed to divide his wealth between his sons. [25]Meanwhile, the older son was in the fields working; when he returned home he heard dance music coming from the house, [26]and he asked one of the servants what was going on. [27]"Your brother is back," he was told, "and your father has killed the calf we were fattening and has prepared a great feast to celebrate his coming home again unharmed." [28]The older brother was angry and wouldn't go in. His father came out and begged him, [29]but he replied, "All these years I've worked hard for you and never once refused to do a single thing you told me to; and in all that time you never gave me even one young goat for a feast with my friends. [30]Yet when this son of yours comes back after spending your money on prostitutes, you celebrate by killing the finest calf we have on the place." [31]"Look, dear son," his father said to him, "you and I are very close, and everything I have is yours."

Gal 3:15. Dear brothers, even in everyday life a promise made by one man to another, if it is written down and signed, cannot be changed. He cannot decide afterward to do something else instead.

Heb 9:16. Now, if someone dies and leaves a will —a list of things to be given away to certain people when he dies—no one gets anything until it is proved that the person who wrote the will is dead. [17]The will goes into effect only after the death of the person who wrote it. While he is still alive no one can use it to get any of those things he has promised them.

See *Will; Heir.*

OF THE SAINTS. Ps 37:29. The godly shall be firmly planted in the land, and live there forever.

Acts 20:32. And now I entrust you to God and his care and to his wonderful words which are able to build your faith and give you all the inheritance of those who are set apart for himself.

Acts 26:18. To open their eyes to their true condition so that they may repent and live in the light of God instead of in Satan's darkness, so that they may receive forgiveness for their sins and God's inheritance along with all people everywhere whose sins are cleansed away, who are set apart by faith in me.

Rom 8:16. For his Holy Spirit speaks to us deep in our hearts, and tells us that we really are God's children. [17]And since we are his children, we will share his treasures—for all God gives to his Son Jesus is now ours too. But if we are to share his glory, we must also share his suffering.

Eph 1:11. Moreover, because of what Christ has done we have become gifts to God that he delights in, for as part of God's sovereign plan we were chosen from the beginning to be his, and all things happen just as he decided long ago. [12]God's purpose in this was that we should praise God and give glory to him for doing these mighty things for us, who were the first to trust in Christ. [13]And because of what Christ did, all you others too, who heard the Good News about how to be saved, and trusted Christ, were marked as belonging to Christ by the Holy Spirit, who long ago had been promised to all of us Christians. [14]His presence within us is God's guarantee that he really will give us all that he promised;

Tit 3:7. So that he could declare us good in God's eyes—all because of his great kindness; and now we can share in the wealth of the eternal life he gives us, and we are eagerly looking forward to receiving it.

Heb 1:14. No, for the angels are only spirit-messengers sent out to help and care for those who are to receive his salvation.

Heb 9:15. Christ came with this new agreement so that all who are invited may come and have forever all the wonders God has promised them. For Christ died to rescue them from the penalty of the sins they had committed while still under that old system.

1 Pet 1:3. All honor to God, the God and Father of our Lord Jesus Christ; for it is his boundless mercy that has given us the privilege of being born again, so that we are now members of God's own family. Now we live in the hope of eternal life because Christ rose again from the dead. [4]And God has reserved for his children the priceless gift of eternal life; it is kept in heaven for you, pure and undefiled, beyond the reach of change and decay.

See *Firstborn; Heir; Will.*

INHOSPITABLENESS INSTANCES OF. Toward the Israelites: Edom, Num 20:18–22; Sihon, Num 21:22, 23; Ammonites and Moabites, Deut 23:3–6. Men of Gibe-ah toward a Levite, Judg 19:15. Nabal toward David, 1 Sam 25:10–17. Samaritans toward Jesus, Lk 9:53.

See *Hospitality.*

INJUSTICE Ex 22:21. You must not oppress a stranger in any way; [22]you must not exploit widows or orphans.

Ex 23:1. Do not pass along untrue reports. Do not cooperate with an evil man by affirming on the witness stand something you know is false.

2. Don't join mobs intent on evil. When on the witness stand, don't be swayed in your testimony by the mood of the majority present, [3]and do not slant your testimony in favor of a man just because he is poor.

6. A man's poverty is no excuse for twisting justice against him. [7]Keep far away from falsely charging anyone with evil; never let an innocent person be put to death. I will not stand for this.

Lev 19:15. Judges must always be just in their sentences, not noticing whether a person is poor or rich; they must always be perfectly fair.

35, 36. You must be impartial in judgment. Use accurate measurements—lengths, weights, and volumes—and give full measure, for I am Jehovah your God who brought you from the land of Egypt.

Deut 16:19. Never twist justice to benefit a rich man, and never accept bribes. For bribes blind the eyes of the wisest and corrupt their decisions. [20]Justice must prevail. That is the only way you will be successful in the land which the Lord your God is giving you.

Deut 24:17. Justice must be given to migrants and orphans and you must never accept a widow's garment in pledge of her debt. [Deut 27:19.] [18]Always remember that you were slaves in Egypt, and that the Lord your God rescued you; that is why I have given you this command.

Job 16:16. My eyes are red with weeping and on my eyelids is the shadow of death. [17]Yet I am innocent, and my prayer is pure.

Job 31:13. If I have been unfair to my servants, [14]how could I face God? What could I say when he questioned me about it? [15]For God made me, and made my servant too. He created us both.

Ps 12:5. The Lord replies, "I will arise and defend the oppressed, the poor, the needy. I will rescue them as they have longed for me to do."

Ps 43:1. O God, defend me from the charges of these merciless, deceitful men.

Ps 82:2. How long will you judges refuse to listen to the evidence? How long will you shower special favors on the wicked?

Prov 11:7. When an evil man dies, his hopes all perish, for they are based upon this earthly life.

Prov 17:15. The Lord despises those who say that bad is good, and good is bad.

Prov 28:8. Income from exploiting the poor will end up in the hands of someone who pities them.

Prov 29:27. The good hate the badness of the wicked. The wicked hate the goodness of the good.

Prov 31:4. And it is not for kings, O Lemuel, to drink wine and whiskey. [5]For if they drink they may forget their duties and be unable to give justice to those who are oppressed.

Eccl 3:16. Moreover, I noticed that throughout the earth justice is giving way to crime and even the police courts are corrupt.

Eccl 5:8. If you see some poor man being oppressed by the rich, with miscarriage of justice anywhere throughout the land, don't be surprised! For every official is under orders from higher up, and the higher officials look up to their superiors. And so the matter is lost in red tape and bureaucracy.

Isa 26:10. Your kindness to the wicked doesn't make them good; they keep on doing wrong and take no notice of your majesty.

Jer 22:3. The Lord says: Be fairminded. Do what is right! Help those in need of justice! Quit your evil deeds! Protect the rights of aliens and immigrants, orphans and widows; stop murdering the innocent! [4]If you put an end to all these terrible deeds you are doing, then I will deliver this nation and once more give kings to sit on David's throne, and there shall be prosperity for all. [5]But if you refuse to pay attention to this warning, I swear by my own name, says the Lord, that this palace shall become a shambles.

Lam 3:34. But you have trampled and crushed beneath your feet the lowly of the world, [35]and deprived men of their God-given rights, and refused them justice. [36]No wonder the Lord has had to deal with you!

Amos 5:11. You trample the poor and steal their smallest crumb by all your taxes, fines, and usury; therefore you will never live in the beautiful stone houses you are building, nor drink the wine from the lush vineyards you are planting. [12]For many and great are your sins. I know them all so well. You are the enemies of everything good; you take bribes; you refuse justice to the poor.

Zeph 3:5. The wicked know no shame.

Lk 3:14. "And us," asked some soldiers, "what about us?" John replied, "Don't extort money by threats and violence; don't accuse anyone of what you know he didn't do; and be content with your pay!"

Lk 16:10. For unless you are honest in small matters, you won't be in large ones. If you cheat even a little, you won't be honest with greater responsibilities.

1 Thess 4:6. And this also is God's will: that you never cheat in this matter by taking another man's wife, because the Lord will punish you terribly for this, as we have solemnly told you before.

Rev 22:11. And when that time comes, all doing wrong will do it more and more; the vile will become more vile.

See *Court; Dishonesty; Justice.*

INK Jer 36:18; 2 Cor 3:3.

INN Josh 2:1; 2 Kgs 10:12; Lk 2:7; 10:34.

INNOCENCY Signified by washing the hands, Deut 21:6; Ps 26:6; Mt 27:24. Found in Daniel, Dan 6:22; Jeremiah, Jer 2:35. Professed by Pilate, Mt 27:24.

Contrasted with guilt, compare Gen 2:25; 3:7–11.

INNUENDO Ps 35:19; Prov 6:13; 10:10.

See *Accusation, False.*

INQUEST Deut 21:1–9.

INQUIRING OF GOD See *Afflictions, Prayer in; Prayer.*

INSANITY Prov 26:18. Feigned by David, 1 Sam 21:13–15. Sent as a judgment from God, Deut 28:28; Zech 12:4. Nebuchadnezzar's, Dan 4:32–34. Jesus accused of, Mk 3:21; Jn 10:20. Paul, Acts 26:24, 25. Cured by Jesus, Mt 4:24; 17:15. Demoniacal: Saul, 1 Sam 16:14; 18:10.

See *Demons, Possession by.*

INSCRIPTION "Consecrated to Jehovah," worn on the high priest's turban, Ex 28:36; 39:30.

Precepts written on door posts and gates, and worn on the hand and forehead, Deut 6:6–9; 11:18–20; "Holy to the Lord," engraved on bells of horses, Zech 14:20. "This is Jesus, the King of the Jews," over Jesus at the crucifixion, Mt 27:37; see also Mk 15:26; Lk 23:38; Jn 19:19.

INSECTS Clean and unclean, Lev 11:21–25; Deut 14:19, 20.

See *Ant; Bee; Caterpillar; Cricket; Flea; Flies; Gnat; Grasshopper; Hornet; Leech; Lice; Locust; Moth; Scorpion; Snail; Spider; Worm.*

INSINCERITY See *Hypocrisy.*

INSINUATION See *Innuendo.*

INSOMNIA INSTANCES OF. Ahasuerus, Esther 6:1. Nebuchadnezzar, Dan 6:18.

INSPIRATION See *Prophecy; Prophets; Word of God, Inspiration of.*

INSTABILITY Gen 49:3. Reuben, you are my oldest son, the child of my vigorous youth. You are the head of the list in rank and in honor. [4]But you are unruly as the wild waves of the sea, and you shall be first no longer. I am demoting you, for you slept with one of my wives and thus dishonored me.

Ex 8:15. But when Pharaoh saw that the frogs were gone, he hardened his heart and refused to let the people go, just as the Lord had predicted. *v.* 32.

Ex 9:34. When Pharaoh saw this, he and his officials sinned yet more by their stubborn refusal to do what they had promised; Ex 10:16–20; 14:5.

Ex 32:8. "And have quickly abandoned all my laws. They have molded themselves a calf, and worshiped it, and sacrificed to it, and said, 'This is your god, O Israel, that brought you out of Egypt.' " [9]Then the Lord said, "I have seen what a stubborn, rebellious lot these people are. [10]Now let me alone and my anger shall blaze out against them and destroy them all; and I will make you, Moses, into a great nation instead of them." with Ex 19:8; 24:3, 7.

Judg 2:17. Yet even then Israel would not listen to the judges, but broke faith with Jehovah by worshiping other gods instead. How quickly they turned away from the true faith of their ancestors, for they refused to obey God's commands.

1 Kgs 18:21. Then Elijah talked to them. "How long are you going to waver between two opinions?" he asked the people. "If the Lord is God, *follow* him! But if Baal is God, then follow *him!*"

Ps 106:12. Then at last his people believed him. Then they finally sang his praise. [13]Yet how quickly they forgot again! They wouldn't wait for him to act.

Prov 24:21. My son, watch your step before the Lord and the king, and don't associate with radicals. [22]For you will go down with them to sudden disaster, and who knows where it all will end?

Prov 27:8. A man who strays from home is like a bird that wanders from its nest.

Jer 2:36. First here, then there, you flit about, going from one ally to another for their help; but it's all no good—your new friends in Egypt will forsake you as Assyria did before.

Hos 6:4. O Ephraim and Judah, what shall I do with you? For your love vanishes like morning clouds, and disappears like dew. [5]I sent my prophets to warn you of your doom; I have slain you with the words of my mouth, threatening you with death. Suddenly, without warning, my judgment will strike you as surely as day follows night.

Mt 6:24. You cannot serve two masters: God and money. For you will hate one and love the other, or else the other way around.

Mt 12:25. Jesus knew their thoughts and replied, "A divided kingdom ends in ruin. A city or home divided against itself cannot stand."

Mk 4:14. The farmer I talked about is anyone who brings God's message to others, trying to plant good seed within their lives. [15]The hard pathway, where some of the seed fell, represents the hard hearts of some of those who hear God's message; Satan comes at once to try to make them forget it. [16]The rocky soil represents the hearts of those who hear the message with joy, [17]but, like young plants in such soil, their roots don't go very deep, and though at first they get along fine, as soon as persecution begins, they wilt. [18]The thorny ground represents the hearts of people who listen to the Good News and receive it, [19]but all too quickly the attractions of this world and the delights of wealth, and the search for success and lure of nice things come in and crowd out God's message from their hearts, so that no crop is produced. Mt 13:20, 21; Lk 8:13, 14.

Luke 9:57. As they were walking along someone said to Jesus, "I will always follow you no matter where you go." [58]But Jesus replied, "Remember, I don't even own a place to lay my head. Foxes have dens to live in, and birds have nests, but I, the Messiah, have no earthly home at all." [59]Another time, when he invited a man to come with him and to be his disciple, the man agreed—but wanted to wait until his father's death. [60]Jesus replied, "Let those without eternal life concern themselves with things like that. Your duty is to come and preach the coming of the Kingdom of God to all the world." [61]Another said, "Yes, Lord, I will come, but first let me ask permission of those at home." [62]But Jesus told him, "Anyone who lets himself be distracted from the work I plan for him is not fit for the Kingdom of God." Mt 8:19, 20.

Lk 17:32. Remember what happened to Lot's wife!

Jn 5:35. John shone brightly for a while, and you benefited and rejoiced.

Gal 1:6. I am amazed that you are turning away so soon from God who, in his love and mercy, invited you to share the eternal life he gives through Christ; you are already following a different "way to heaven," which really doesn't go to heaven at all.

Gal 4:9. And now that you have found God (or I should say, now that God has found you) how can it be that you want to go back again and become slaves once more to another poor, weak, useless religion of trying to get to heaven by obeying

God's laws? [10]You are trying to find favor with God by what you do or don't do on certain days or months or seasons or years. [11]I fear for you. I am afraid that all my hard work for you was worth nothing.

Eph 4:14. Then we will no longer be like children, forever changing our minds about what we believe because someone has told us something different, or has cleverly lied to us and made the lie sound like the truth.

Heb 13:9. So, do not be attracted by strange, new ideas. Your spiritual strength comes as a gift from God.

Jas 1:6. But when you ask him, be sure that you really expect him to tell you, for a doubtful mind will be as unsettled as a wave of the sea that is driven and tossed by the wind; [7, 8]and every decision you then make will be uncertain, as you turn first this way, and then that. If you don't ask with faith, don't expect the Lord to give you any solid answer.

Jas 4:8. And when you draw close to God, God will draw close to you. Wash your hands, you sinners, and let your hearts be filled with God alone to make them pure and true to him.

2 Pet 2:14. No woman can escape their sinful stare, and of adultery they never have enough. They make a game of luring unstable women. They train themselves to be greedy; and are doomed and cursed.

Rev 2:4. Yet, there is one thing wrong; you don't love me as at first!

Rev 3:2. Now wake up! Strengthen what little remains—for even what is left is at the point of death. Your deeds are far from right in the sight of God. [15]I know you well—you are neither hot nor cold; I wish you were one or the other! [16]But since you are merely lukewarm, I will spit you out of my mouth!

See *Backslider; Hypocrisy; Indecision.*

INSTANCES OF. Reuben, Gen 49:4. Saul, in his feelings toward David, 1 Sam 18:19. David, in his yielding to lust, 2 Sam 11:2–9. Solomon, in yielding to his idolatrous wives, 1 Kgs 11:1–8. Ephraim and Judah, Hos 6:4. Lot's wife, Lk 17:32. Disciples of Jesus, Jn 6:66; John Mark, Acts 15:38.

INSTINCT Of animals, Prov 1:17; Isa 1:3. Of birds, Jer 8:7.

See *Animals; Birds.*

INSTRUCTION From nature, Prov 24:30–34; Eccl 1:12–18; 3; 4:1; Mt 6:25–30. See *Parable.* From the study of human nature, Eccl chapters 3–12.

By object lessons: The container of manna, Ex 16:32. The pillar of twelve stones at the fords of the Jordan, Josh 4:19–24. Tassels on the hems of clothing, Num 15:37–39. Symbolically going naked and barefoot, Isa 20:2, 3. The linen loincloth, Jer 13:1–11. Clay jar, Jer 19:1–12. Basket of figs, Jer 24. Yoke, Jer 27:2–11; 28. Illustrations on a brick, Ezk 4:1–3. Lying on one side in public view for a long period, Ezk 4:4–8. Eating bread baked over a fire of dung, Ezk 4:12. Shaving the head, Ezk 5. Moving household goods, Ezk 12:3–16. Eating and drinking sparingly, Ezk 12:18–20. Sighing, Ezk 21:6, 7. The boiling pot, Ezk 24:1–14. Widowhood, Ezk 24:16–27. Two sticks joined together, Ezk 37:16–22. By symbols and parables, see *Symbols; Parable.*

See *Animals, Clean and Unclean; Firstborn; Passover; Pillar; Purification.* See also Prov 24:30–34.

UNCLASSIFIED SCRIPTURES RELATING TO. 2 Chron 15:3. For a long time now, over in Israel, the people haven't worshiped the true God, and have not had a true priest to teach them. They have lived without God's laws.

2 Chron 17:7. In the third year of his reign he began a nationwide religious education program. He sent out top government officials as teachers in all the cities of Judah. [8]These men included Ben-hail, Obadiah, Zechariah, Nethanel, and Micaiah. He also used the Levites for this purpose, including Shemaiah, Nethaniah, Zebadiah, Asahel, Shemiramoth, Jehonathan, Adonijah, Tobijah, and Tobadonijah; also the priests, Elishama and Jehoram. [9]They took copies of *The Book of the Law of the Lord* to all the cities of Judah, to teach the Scriptures to the people.

Ezra 7:10. This was because Ezra had determined to study and obey the laws of the Lord and to become a Bible teacher, teaching those laws to the people of Israel.

Ps 50:17. For you have refused my discipline, disregarding my laws.

Ps 78:2. For I will show you lessons from our history, [3]stories handed down to us from former generations. [4]I will reveal these truths to you so that you can describe these glorious deeds of Jehovah to your children, and tell them about the mighty miracles he did. [5]For he gave his laws to Israel, and commanded our fathers to teach them to their children, [6]so that they in turn could teach their children too. Thus his laws pass down from generation to generation. [7]In this way each generation has been able to obey his laws and to set its hope anew on God and not forget his glorious miracles. [8]Thus they did not need to be as their fathers were—stubborn, rebellious, unfaithful, refusing to give their hearts to God.

Ps 119:12. Blessed Lord, teach me your rules. *vs.* 3–125.

Ps 143:8. Let me see your kindness to me in the morning, for I am trusting you. Show me where to walk, for my prayer is sincere. [10]Help me to do your will, for you are my God. Lead me in good paths, for your Spirit is good.

Prov 1:1. These are the proverbs of King Solomon of Israel, David's son: [2]He wrote them to teach his people how to live—how to act in every circumstance, [3]for he wanted them to be understanding, just and fair in everything they did. [4]"I want to make the simple-minded wise!" he said. "I want to warn young men about some problems they will face. [5,6]I want those already wise to become the wiser and become leaders by exploring the depths of meaning in these nuggets of truth."

[Prov 9:9.] [20]Wisdom shouts in the streets for a hearing. [21]She calls out to the crowds along Main Street, and to the judges in their courts, and to everyone in all the land: [22]"You simpletons!" she cries. "How long will you go on being fools? How long will you scoff at wisdom and fight the facts? [23]Come here and listen to me! I'll pour out the spirit of wisdom upon you, and make you wise. [24]I have called you so often but still you won't come, I have pleaded, but all in vain. [25]For you have spurned my counsel and reproof. [26]Some day you'll be in trouble, and I'll laugh! Mock me, will you?—I'll mock you! [27]When a storm of terror surrounds you, and when you are engulfed by anguish and distress, [28]then I will not answer your cry for help. It will be too late though you search for me ever so anxiously. [29]For you closed your eyes to the facts and did not choose to reverence and trust the Lord, [30]and you turned your back on me, spurning my advice."

Prov 22:17–19. Listen to this wise advice; follow it closely, for it will do you good, and you can pass it on to others: *Trust in the Lord.* [20,21]In the past, haven't I been right? Then believe what I am telling you now, and share it with others.

Prov 23:12. Don't refuse to accept criticism; get all the help you can. [23]Get the facts at any price, and hold on tightly to all the good sense you can get.

Prov 24:30. I walked by the field of a certain lazy fellow [31]and saw that it was overgrown with thorns, and covered with weeds; and its walls were broken down. [32, 33]Then, as I looked, I learned this lesson: "A little extra sleep, a little more slumber, a little folding of the hands to rest" [34]means that poverty will break in upon you suddenly like a robber, and violently like a bandit.

Jer 32:33. They have turned their backs upon me and refused to return; day after day, year after year, I taught them right from wrong, but they would not listen or obey.

Dan 1:3. Then he ordered Ashpenaz, who was in charge of his palace personnel, to select some of the Jewish youths brought back as captives—young men of the royal family and nobility of Judah [4]—and to teach them the Chaldean language and literature. "Pick strong, healthy, good-looking lads," he said; "those who have read widely in many fields, are well informed, alert and sensible, and have enough poise to look good around the palace." [5]The king assigned them the best of food and wine from his own kitchen during their three-year training period, planning to make them his counselors when they graduated. [17]God gave these four youths great ability to learn and they soon mastered all the literature and science of the time, and God gave to Daniel special ability in understanding the meanings of dreams and visions. [18]When the three-year training period was completed, the superintendent brought all the young men to the king for oral exams, as he had been ordered to do. [19]King Nebuchadnezzar had long talks with each of them, and none of them impressed him as much as Daniel, Hananiah, Misha-el, and Azariah. So they were put on his regular staff of advisors. [20]And in all matters requiring information and balanced judgment, the king found these young men's advice ten times better than that of all the skilled magicians and wise astrologers in his realm.

Lk 20:1. On one of those days when he was teaching and preaching the Good News in the Temple, he was confronted by the chief priests and other religious leaders and councilmen. [2]They demanded to know by what authority he had driven out the merchants from the Temple.

Lk 21:37, 38. Every day Jesus went to the Temple to teach, and the crowds began gathering early in the morning to hear him. And each evening he returned to spend the night on the Mount of Olives.

Rom 2:18. Yes, you know what he wants; you know right from wrong and favor the right because you have been taught his laws from earliest youth.

1 Cor 12:28. Here is a list of some of the parts he has placed in his church, which is his body: apostles, prophets—those who preach God's Word, teachers, those who do miracles, those who have the gift of healing, those who can help others, those who can get others to work together, those who speak in languages they have never learned. [29]Is everyone an apostle? Of course not. Is everyone a preacher? No. Are all teachers? Does everyone have the power to do miracles?

Gal 3:24. Let me put it another way. The Jewish laws were our teacher and guide until Christ came to give us right standing with God through our faith. [25]But now that Christ has come, we don't need those laws any longer to guard us and lead us to him.

Gal 4:1. But remember this, that if a father dies and leaves great wealth for his little son, that child is not much better off than a slave until he grows up, even though he actually owns everything his father had. [2]He has to do what his guardians and managers tell him to, until he reaches whatever age his father set.

Eph 4:11. Some of us have been given special ability as apostles; to others he has given the gift of being able to preach well; some have special ability in winning people to Christ, helping them to trust him as their Savior; still others have a gift for caring for God's people as a shepherd does his sheep, leading and teaching them in the ways of God. [12]Why is it that he gives us these special abilities to do certain things best? It is that God's people will be equipped to do better work for him, building up the chruch, the body of Christ, to a position of strength and maturity.

OF CHILDREN. Ex 10:2. What stories you can tell your children and grandchildren about the incredible things I am doing in Egypt! Tell them what fools I made of the Egyptians, and how I proved to you that I am Jehovah.

Ex 12:26. And your children ask, "What does all this mean? What is this ceremony about?" [27]You will reply, "It is the celebration of Jehovah's passing over us, for he passed over the homes of the people of Israel, though he killed the Egyptians; he passed over our houses and did not come in to destroy us." And all the people bowed their heads and worshiped. Ex 13:14–16.

Ex 13:8. During those celebration days each year you must explain to your children why you are celebrating—it is a celebration of what the Lord did for you when you left Egypt. [9]This annual memorial week will brand you as his own unique people, just as though he had branded his mark of ownership upon your hands or your forehead. [10]So celebrate the event annually in late March.

Deut 4:9. But watch out! Be very careful never to forget what you have seen God doing for you. May his miracles have a deep and permanent effect upon your lives! Tell your children and your grandchildren about the glorious miracles he did. [10]Tell them especially about the day you stood before the Lord at Mount Horeb, and he told me, "Summon the people before me and I will instruct them, so that they will learn always to reverence me, and so that they can teach my laws to their children."

Deut 6:6. And you must think constantly about these commandments I am giving you today. [7]You must teach them to your children and talk about them when you are at home or out for a walk; at bedtime and the first thing in the morning. [8]Tie them on your finger, wear them on your forehead, [9]and write them on the doorposts of your house!

Deut 11:18. So keep these commandments carefully in mind. Tie them to your hand to remind you to obey them, and tie them to your forehead between your eyes! [19]Teach them to your children. Talk about them when you are sitting at home, when you are out walking, at bedtime, and before breakfast! [20]Write them upon the doors of your houses and upon your gates, [21]so that as long as there is sky above the earth, you and your children will enjoy the good life awaiting you in the land the Lord has promised you.

Deut 31:9. Then Moses wrote out the laws he had already delivered to the people and gave them to the priests, the sons of Levi, who carried Ark containing the Ten Commandments of the Lord. Moses also gave copies of the laws to the elders of Israel. [10]The Lord commanded that these laws be read to all the people at the end of every seventh year—the Year of Release—at the Festival of Tabernacles, [11]when all Israel would assemble before the Lord at the sanctuary. [12]"Call them all together," the Lord instructed,"—men, women, children, and foreigners living among you—to hear the laws of God and to learn his will, so that you will reverence the Lord your God and obey his laws. [13]Do this so that your little children who have not known these laws will hear them and learn how to revere the Lord your God as long as you live in the Promised Land." Josh 8:35.

Ps 34:11. Sons and daughters, come and listen and let me teach you the importance of trusting and fearing the Lord.

Ps 78:5. For he gave his laws to Israel, and commanded our fathers to teach them to their children, [6]so that they in turn could teach their children too. Thus his laws pass down from generation to generation. [7]In this way each generation has been able to obey his laws and to set its hope anew on God and not forget his glorious miracles. [8]Thus they did not need to be as their fathers were—stubborn, rebellious, unfaithful, refusing to give their hearts to God.

Prov 20:7. It is a wonderful heritage to have an honest father.

Prov 22:6. Teach a child to choose the right path, and when he is older he will remain upon it.

Isa 38:19. One generation makes known your faithfulness to the next.

Acts 22:3. "I am a Jew," he said, "born in Tarsus, a city in Cilicia, but educated here in Jerusalem under Gamaliel, at whose feet I learned to follow our Jewish laws and customs very carefully. I became very anxious to honor God in everything I did, just as you have tried to do today."

Eph 6:4. And now a word to you parents. Don't keep on scolding and nagging your children, making them angry and resentful. Rather, bring them up with the loving discipline the Lord himself approves, with suggestions and godly advice.

2 Tim 3:15. You know how, when you were a small child, you were taught the holy Scriptures; and it is these that make you wise to accept God's salvation by trusting in Christ Jesus.

See *Children.*

IN RELIGION. Ex 13:11. And remember, when the Lord brings you into the land he promised to your ancestors long ago, where the Canaanites are now living, [12]all firstborn sons and firstborn male animals belong to the Lord, and you shall give them to him. [13]A firstborn donkey may be purchased back from the Lord in exchange for a lamb or baby goat; but if you decide not to trade, the donkey shall be killed. However, you *must* buy back your firstborn sons. [14]And in the future, when your children ask you, "What is this all about?" you shall tell them, "With mighty miracles Jehovah brought us out of Egypt from our slavery. [15]Pharaoh wouldn't let us go, so Jehovah killed all the firstborn males throughout the land of Egypt, both of men and animals; that is why we now give all the firstborn males to the Lord—except that all the eldest sons are always bought back." [16]Again I say, this celebration shall identify you as God's people, just as much as if his brand of ownership were placed upon your foreheads. It is a reminder that the Lord brought us out of Egypt with great power.

Lev 11:44. "I am the Lord your God. Keep yourselves pure concerning these things, and be holy, for I am holy; therefore do not defile yourselves by touching any of these things that crawl upon the earth. [45]For I am the Lord who brought you out of the land of Egypt to be your God. You must therefore be holy, for I am holy." [46]These are the laws concerning animals, birds, and whatever swims in the water or crawls upon the ground. [47]These are the distinctions between what is ceremonially clean and may be eaten, and what is ceremonially defiled and may not be eaten, among all animal life upon the earth.

Num 15:37, 38. The Lord said to Moses, "Tell the people of Israel to make tassels for the hems of their clothes (this is a permanent regulation from generation to generation) and to attach the tassels to their clothes with a blue cord. [39]The purpose of this regulation is to remind you, whenever you notice the tassels, of the commandments of the Lord, and that you are to obey his laws instead of following your own desires and going your own ways, as you used to do in serving other gods."

Deut 27:1. Then Moses and the elders of Israel gave the people these further instructions to obey: [2, 3, 4]"When you cross the Jordan River and go into the Promised Land—a land 'flowing with milk and honey'—take out boulders from the river bottom and immediately pile them into a monument on the other side, at Mount Ebal. Face the stones with a coating of lime and then write the laws of God in the lime. [5, 6]And build an altar there to the Lord your God. Use uncut boulders, and on the altar offer burnt offerings to the Lord your God. [7]Sacrifice peace offerings upon it also, and feast there with great joy before the Lord your God. [8]Write all of these laws plainly [upon the monument]." [9]Then Moses and the Levite-priests addressed all Israel as follows: "O Israel, listen! Today you have become the people of the Lord your God, [10]so today you must begin to obey all of these commandments I have given you." [11]That same day Moses gave this charge to the people: [12]"When you cross into the Promised Land, the tribes of Simeon, Levi, Judah, Issachar, Joseph, and Benjamin shall stand upon Mount Gerizim to proclaim a blessing, [13]and the tribes of Reuben, Gad, Asher, Zebulun, Dan, and Naphtali shall stand upon Mount Ebal to proclaim a curse. [14]Then the Levites standing between them shall shout to all Israel, [15]'The curse of God be upon anyone who makes and worships an idol, even in secret, whether carved of wood or made from molten metal—for these handmade gods are hated by the Lord.' And all the people shall reply, 'Amen.' [16]'Cursed is anyone who despises his father or mother.' And all the people shall reply, 'Amen.' [17]'Cursed is he who moves the boundary marker between his land and his neighbor's.' And all the people shall reply, 'Amen.' [18]'Cursed is he who takes advantage of a blind man.' And all the people shall reply, 'Amen.' [19]'Cursed is he who is unjust to the foreigner, the orphan, and the widow,' And all the people shall reply, 'Amen.' [20]'Cursed is he who commits adultery with one of his father's wives, for she belongs to his father.' And all the people shall reply, 'Amen.' [21]'Cursed is he who has sexual intercourse with an animal.' And all the people shall reply, 'Amen.' [22]'Cursed is he who has sexual intercourse with his sister, whether she be a full sister or a half-sister.' And all the people shall reply, 'Amen.' [23]'Cursed is he who has sexual intercourse with his widowed mother-in-law.' And all the people shall reply, 'Amen.' [24]'Cursed is he who secretly slays another.' And all the people shall reply, 'Amen.' [25]'Cursed is he who accepts a bribe to kill an innocent person.' And all the people shall reply, 'Amen.' [26]'Cursed is anyone who does not obey these laws.' And all the people shall reply, 'Amen.' "

Deut 31:19. Now write down the words of this song, and teach it to the people of Israel as my warning to them.

Deut 32:1. "Listen, O heavens and earth! Listen to what I say! [2]My words shall fall upon you like the gentle rain and dew, like rain upon the tender grass, like showers on the hillside. [3]I will proclaim the greatness of the Lord. How glorious he is! [4]He is the Rock. His work is perfect. Everything he does is just and fair. He is faithful, without sin. [5]But Israel had become corrupt, smeared with sin. They are no longer his; they are a stubborn, twisted generation. [6]Is this the way you treat Jehovah? O foolish people, is not God your Father? Has he not created you? Has he not established you and made you strong? [7]Remember the days of long ago! (Ask your father and the aged men; they will tell you all about it.) [8]When God divided up the world among the nations, he gave each of them a supervising angel! [9]But he appointed none for Israel; for Israel was God's own personal possession! [10]God protected them in the howling wilderness as though they were the apple of his eye. [11]He spreads his wings over them, even as an eagle overspreads her young. She carries them upon her wings—as does the Lord his people! [12]When the Lord alone was leading them, and they lived without foreign gods, [13]God gave them fertile hilltops, rolling, fertile fields, honey from the rock, and olive oil from stony ground! [14]He gave them milk and meat—choice Bashan rams, and goats—and the finest of the wheat; they drank the sparkling wine. [15]But Israel was soon overfed; yes, fat and bloated; then, in plenty, they forsook their God. They shrugged away the Rock of their salvation. [16]Israel began to follow foreign gods, and Jehovah was very angry; he was jealous of his people. [17]They sacrificed to heathen gods, to new gods never before worshiped. [18]They spurned the Rock who had made them, forgetting it was God who had given them birth. [19]God saw what they were doing, and detested them! His sons and daughters were insulting him. [20]He said, 'I will abandon them; see what happens to them then! For they are a stubborn, faithless generation. [21]They have made me very jealous of their idols, which are not gods at all. Now I, in turn, will make them jealous by giving my affections to the foolish Gentile nations of the world. [22]For my anger has kindled a fire that burns to the depths of the underworld, consuming the earth and all of its crops, and setting its mountains on fire. [23]I will heap evils upon them and shoot them down with my arrows. [24]I will waste them with hunger, burning fever, and fatal disease. I will devour them! I will set wild beasts upon them, to rip them apart with their teeth; and deadly serpents crawling in the dust. [25]Outside, the enemies' sword—inside, the plague—shall terrorize young men and girls alike; the baby nursing at the breast, and aged men. [26]I had decided to scatter them to distant lands, so that even the memory of them would disappear.' [27]But then I thought, 'My enemies will boast, "Israel is destroyed by our own might; it was not the Lord who did it!" ' [28]Israel is a stupid nation; foolish, without understanding. [29]Oh, that they were wise! Oh, that they could understand! Oh, that they would know what they are getting into! [30]How could one single enemy chase a thousand of them, and two put ten thousand to flight, unless their Rock had abandoned them, unless the Lord had destroyed them? [31]But the rock of other nations is not like our Rock; prayers to their gods are valueless. [32]They act like men of Sodom and Gomorrah: their deeds are bitter with poison; [33]they drink the wine of serpent venom. [34]But Israel is my special people, sealed as jewels within my treasury. [35]Vengeance is mine, and I decree the punishment of all her enemies: their doom is sealed. [36]The Lord will see his people righted, and will have compassion on them when they slip. He will watch their power ebb away, both slave and free. [37]Then God will ask, 'Where are their gods—the rocks they claimed to be their refuge? [38]Where are these gods now, to whom they sacrificed their fat and wine? Let those gods arise, and help them! [39]Don't you see that I alone am God? I kill and make live. I wound and heal—no one delivers from my power. [40]I raise my hand to heaven and vow by my existence, [41]that I will whet the lightning of my sword! And hurl my punishments upon my enemies! [42]My arrows shall be drunk with blood! My sword devours the flesh and blood of all the slain and captives. The heads of the enemy are gory with blood.' [43]Praise his people, O Gentile nations, for he will avenge his people, taking vengeance on his enemies, purifying his land and his people." [44, 45]When Moses and Joshua had recited all the words of this song to the people, [46]Moses made these comments: "Meditate upon all the laws I have given you today, and pass them on to your children. [47]These laws are not mere words—they are your life! Through obeying them you will live long, plentiful lives in the land you are going to possess across the Jordan River."

2 Chron 17:7. In the third year of his reign he began a nationwide religious education program. He sent out top government officials as teachers in all the cities of Judah. [8]These men included Benhail, Obadiah, Zechariah, Nethanel, and Micaiah. He also used the Levites for this purpose, including Shemaiah, Nethaniah, Zebadiah, Asahel, Shemiramoth, Jehonathan, Adonijah, Tobijah, and Tobadonijah; also the priests, Elishama and Jehoram. [9]They took copies of *The Book of the Law of the Lord* to all the cities of Judah, to teach the Scriptures to the people.

Neh 8:7, 8. As Ezra read from the scroll, Jeshua, Bani, Sherebiah, Jamin, Akkub, Shabbethai, Hodiah, Ma-aseiah, Kelita, Azariah, Joazbad, Hanan, Pelaiah, and the Levites went among the people and explained the meaning of the passage that was being read.

Isa 28:9. "Who does Isaiah think he is," the people say, "to speak to us like this! Are we little children, barely old enough to talk? [10]He tells us everything over and over again, a line at a time and in such simple words!"

Mt 5:12. One day as the crowds were gathering, he went up the hillside with his disciples and sat down and taught them there. *vs.* 3–48; chapters 6; 7.

Lk 4:16. When he came to the village of Nazareth, his boyhood home, he went as usual to the synagogue on Saturday, and stood up to read the Scriptures. [17]The book of Isaiah the prophet was handed to him, and he opened it to the place where it says: [18, 19]"The Spirit of the Lord is upon me; he has appointed me to preach Good News to the poor; he has sent me to heal the brokenhearted and to announce that captives shall be released and the blind shall see, that the downtrodden shall be freed from their oppressors, and that God is ready to give blessings to all who come to him." [20]He closed the book and handed it back to the attendant and sat down, while everyone in the synagogue gazed at him intently. [21]Then he added, "These Scriptures came true today!"

Lk 24:27. Then Jesus quoted them passage after passage from the writings of the Prophets, beginning with the book of Genesis and going right on through the Scriptures, explaining what the passages meant and what they said about himself.

Jn 7:14. Then, midway through the festival, Jesus went up to the Temple and preached openly. Mk 12:35; Lk 19:47; 20:1–18; Jn 8:2. See *Jesus, History of.*

Rom 2:19. You are so sure of the way to God that you could point it out to a blind man. You think of yourselves as beacon lights, directing men who are lost in darkness to God. [20]You think that you can guide the simple and teach even children the affairs of God, for you really know his laws, which are full of all knowledge and truth.

Gal 6:6. Those who are taught the Word of God should help their teachers by paying them.

2 Tim 2:2. For you must teach others those things you and many others have heard me speak about. Teach these great truths to trustworthy men who will, in turn, pass them on to others.

See *Children, Instruction of; Doctrine; Minister, Duties of; School; Teachers.*

IN MUSIC. See *Music.*

INSTRUMENTALITY See *Agency.*

INSTRUMENTS, MUSICAL See *Music.*

INSURGENTS Army of, David's, 1 Sam 22: 1, 2.

INSURRECTION Ps 64:2. Described by David in Psalm 55. Led by Sheba, 2 Sam 20; Absalom, see *Absalom;* Barabbas, Mk 15:7.

INTEGRITY Gen 18:19. And I have picked him out to have godly descendants and a godly household—men who are just and good—so that I can do for him all I have promised.

Ex 18:21. Find some capable, godly, honest men who hate bribes, and appoint them as judges.

Deut 16:19. Never twist justice to benefit a rich man, and never accept bribes. For bribes blind the eyes of the wisest and corrupt their decisions. [20]Justice must prevail. That is the only way you will be successful in the land which the Lord your God is giving you.

Job 10:4–7. Are you unjust like men? Is your life so short that you must hound me for sins you know full well I've not committed? Is it because you know no one can save me from your hand?

Job 13:15. God may kill me for saying this—in fact, I expect him to. Nevertheless I am going to argue my case with him. [18]This is my case: *I know that I am righteous.*

Job 16:17. Yet I am innocent, and my prayer is pure.

Job 27:4. My lips shall speak no evil, my tongue shall speak no lies. [5]I will never, never, agree that you are right; until I die I will vow my innocence. [6]I am *not* a sinner—I repeat it again and again. My conscience is clear for as long as I live.

Job 29:14. All I did was just and honest, for righteousness was my clothing!

Job 31:1. "I made a covenant with my eyes not to look with lust upon a girl. [2, 3]I know full well that Almighty God above sends calamity on those who do. [4]He sees everything I do, and every step I take. [5]If I have lied and deceived—[6]but God knows that I am innocent—[7, 8]or if I have stepped off God's pathway, or if my heart has lusted for what my eyes have seen, or if I am guilty of any other sin, then let someone else reap the crops I have sown and let all that I have planted be rooted out. [9]Or if I have longed for another man's wife, [10]then may I die, and may my wife be in another man's home, and someone else become her husband. [11]For lust is a shameful sin, a crime that should be punished. [12]It is a devastating fire that destroys to hell, and would root out all I have planted. [13]If I have been unfair to my servants, [14]how could I face God? What could I say when he questioned me about it? [15]For God made me, and made my servant too. He created us both. [16]If I have hurt the poor or caused widows to weep, [17]or refused food to hungry orphans—[18](But we have always cared for orphans in our home, treating them as our own children)—[19, 20]or if I have seen anyone freezing and not given him clothing, or fleece from my sheep to keep him warm, [21]or if I have taken advantage of an orphan because I thought I could get away with it—[22]if I have done any of these things, then let my arm be torn from its socket! Let my shoulder be wrenched out of place! [23]Rather that than face the judgment sent by God; that I dread more than anything else. For if the majesty of God opposes me, what hope is there? [24]If I have put my trust in money, [25]if my happiness depends on wealth, [26]or if I have looked at the sun shining in the skies, or the moon walking down her silver pathway, [27]and my heart has been secretly enticed, and I have worshiped them by kissing my hand to them, [28]this, too, must be punished by the judges. For if I had done such things, it would mean that I denied the God of heaven. [29]If I have rejoiced at harm to an enemy—[30](but actually I have never cursed anyone nor asked for revenge)—[31]or if any of my servants have ever gone hungry—[32](actually I have never turned away even a stranger but have opened my doors to all)—[33]or if, like Adam, I have tried to hide my sins, [34]fearing the crowd and its contempt, so that I refused to acknowledge my sin and do not go out of my way to help others—[35](oh, that there were someone who would listen to me and try to see my side of this argument. Look, I will sign my signature to my defense; now let the Almighty show me that I am wrong; let *him* approve the indictments made against me by my enemies. [36]I would treasure it like a crown. [37]Then I would tell him exactly what I have done and why, presenting my defense as one he listens to.) [38, 39]Or if my land accuses me because I stole the fruit it bears, or if I have murdered its owners to get their land for myself, [40]then let thistles grow on that land instead of wheat, and weeds instead of barley." *Job's words are ended.*

Ps 7:3. It would be different, Lord, if I were doing evil things—[4]if I were paying back evil for good or unjustly attacking those I dislike. [5]Then it would be right for you to let my enemies destroy me. [8]But justify me publicly; establish my honor and truth before them all.

Ps 15:1. Lord, who may go and find refuge and shelter in your tabernacle up on your holy hill? [2]Anyone who leads a blameless life and is truly sincere. [3]Anyone who refuses to slander others, does not listen to gossip, never harms his neighbor, [4]speaks out against sin, criticizes those committing it, commends the faithful followers of the Lord, keeps a promise even if it ruins him, [5]does not crush his debtors with high interest rates, and refuses to testify against the innocent despite the bribes offered him—such a man shall stand firm forever.

Ps 17:3. You have tested me and seen that I am good. You have come even in the night and found nothing amiss and know that I have told the truth.

Ps 18:20. The Lord rewarded me for doing right and being pure. 2 Sam 22:21.

Ps 24:3. Who may climb the mountain of the Lord and enter where he lives? Who may stand before the Lord? [4]Only those with pure hands and hearts, who do not practice dishonesty and lying. [5]They will receive God's own goodness as their blessing from him, planted in their lives by God himself, their Savior.

Ps 25:21. Assign me Godliness and Integrity as my bodyguards, for I expect you to protect me [22]and to ransom Israel from all her troubles.

Ps 26:1. Dismiss all the charges against me, Lord, for I have tried to keep your laws and have trusted you without wavering. [2]Cross-examine me, O Lord, and see that this is so; test my motives and affections too. [3]For I have taken your lovingkindness and your truth as my ideals.

Ps 73:15. If I had really said that, I would have

been a traitor to your people. With *vs.* 2–22.

Ps 119:121. For I have done what is right; I've been perfectly fair.

Prov 2:1, 2. Every young man who listens to me and obeys my instructions will be given wisdom and good sense. [5]You will soon learn the importance of reverence for the Lord and of trusting him. [9]He shows how to distinguish right from wrong, how to find the right decision every time. Prov 1:3.

Prov 3:3. Never forget to be truthful and kind. Hold these virtues tightly. Write them deep within your heart.

Prov 4:25. Look straight ahead; don't even turn your head to look. [26]Watch your step. Stick to the path and be safe. [27]Don't sidetrack; pull back your foot from danger.

Prov 10:9. A good man has firm footing.

Prov 11:3. A good man is guided by his honesty. [5]The upright are directed by their honesty.

Prov 12:22. God delights in those who keep their promises, and abhors those who don't.

Prov 15:21. The sensible stay on the pathways of right.

Prov 16:11. The Lord demands fairness in every business deal. He established this principle.

Prov 19:1. Better be poor and honest than rich and dishonest. Prov 28:6.

Prov 20:7. It is a wonderful heritage to have an honest father.

Prov 21:3. God is more pleased when we are just and fair than when we give him gifts. [15]A good man loves justice.

Prov 22:11. He who values grace and truth is the king's friend.

Prov 28:20. The man who wants to do right will get a rich reward.

Isa 26:7. But for good men the path is not uphill and rough! God does not give them a rough and treacherous path, but smooths the road before them.

Isa 33:15. I will tell you who can live here: All who are honest and fair, who reject making profit by fraud, who hold back their hands from taking bribes, who refuse to listen to those who plot murder, who shut their eyes to all enticement to do wrong. [16]Such as these shall dwell on high. The rocks of the mountains will be their fortress of safety; food will be supplied to them and they will have all the water they need.

Isa 56:1. Be just and fair to all, the Lord God says. Do what's right and good.

Jer 7:5. You may remain under these conditions only: If you stop your wicked thoughts and deeds, and are fair to others. [7]Then, and only then, will I let you stay in this land that I gave to your fathers to keep forever.

Ezk 18:5. But if a man is just and does what is lawful and right. [7]And is a merciful creditor, not holding on to the items given to him in pledge by poor debtors, and is no robber, but gives food to the hungry and clothes to those in need, [8]and grants loans without interest, and stays away from sin, and is honest and fair when judging others, [9]and obeys my laws—that man is just, says the Lord, and he shall surely live.

Mic 6:8. No, he has told you what he wants, and this is all it is: *to be fair and just and merciful, and to walk humbly with your God.*

Zech 7:8, 9. Then this message from the Lord came to Zechariah. "Tell them to be honest and fair—and not to take bribes—and to be merciful and kind to everyone."

Mal 2:6. He passed on to the people all the truth he got from me. He did not lie or cheat; he walked with me, living a good and righteous life, and turned many from their lives of sin.

Lk 3:13. "By your honesty," he replied. "Make sure you collect no more taxes than the Roman government requires you to." [14]"And us," asked some soldiers, "what about us?" John replied, "Don't extort money by threats and violence; don't accuse anyone of what you know he didn't do; and be content with your pay!"

Lk 6:31. Treat others as you want them to treat you.

Lk 11:42. But woe to you Pharisees! For though you are careful to tithe even the smallest part of your income, you completely forget about justice and the love of God. You should tithe, yes, but you should not leave these other things undone.

Lk 16:10. *No!* For unless you are honest in small matters, you won't be in large ones. If you cheat even a little, you won't be honest with greater responsibilities.

Acts 24:16. Because of this I try with all my strength to always maintain a clear conscience before God and man. Acts 23:1.

Rom 9:1–3. Oh, Israel, my people! Oh, my Jewish brothers! How I long for you to come to Christ. My heart is heavy within me and I grieve bitterly day and night because of you. Christ knows and the Holy Spirit knows that it is no mere pretense when I say that I would be willing to be forever damned if that would save you.

Rom 13:5. Obey the laws, then, for two reasons: first, to keep from being punished, and second, just because you know you should.

Rom 14:5. Some think that Christians should observe the Jewish holidays as special days to worship God, but others say it is wrong and foolish to go to all that trouble, for every day alike belongs to God. On questions of this kind everyone must decide for himself. [14]As for myself, I am perfectly sure on the authority of the Lord Jesus that there is nothing really wrong with eating meat that has been offered to idols. But if someone believes it is wrong, then he shouldn't do it because for him it is wrong. [22]You may know that there is nothing wrong with what you do, even from God's point of view, but keep it to yourself; don't flaunt your faith in front of others who might be hurt by it. In this situation, happy is the man who does not sin by doing what he knows is right.

2 Cor 4:2. We do not try to trick people into believing—we are not interested in fooling anyone.

We never try to get anyone to believe that the Bible teaches what it doesn't. All such shameful methods we forego. We stand in the presence of God as we speak and so we tell the truth, as all who know us will agree. 2 Cor 5:11.

2 Cor 7:2. Please open your hearts to us again, for not one of you has suffered any wrong from us. Not one of you was led astray. We have cheated no one nor taken advantage of anyone.

2 Cor 8:21. God knows we are honest, but I want everyone else to know it too. That is why we have made this arrangement.

Phil 4:8. And now, brothers, as I close this letter let me say this one more thing: Fix your thoughts on what is true and good and right. Think about things that are pure and lovely, and dwell on the fine, good things in others. Think about all you can praise God for and be glad about.

Col 3:22. You slaves must always obey your earthly masters, not only trying to please them when they are watching you but all the time; obey them willingly because of your love for the Lord and because you want to please him. [23]Work hard and cheerfully at all you do, just as though you were working for the Lord and not merely for your masters. Eph 6:6, 7.

1 Thess 2:4. For we speak as messengers from God, trusted by him to tell the truth; we change his message not one bit to suit the taste of those who hear it; for we serve God alone, who examines our hearts' deepest thoughts.

1 Tim 1:5. What I am eager for is that all the Christians there will be filled with love that comes from pure hearts, and that their minds will be clean and their faith strong.

1 Tim 3:9. They must be earnest, wholehearted followers of Christ who is the hidden Source of their faith.

Tit 1:7. These pastors must be men of blameless lives because they are God's ministers. . . . [8]They must enjoy having guests in their homes and must love all that is good. They must be sensible men, and fair. They must be clean minded and level headed.

Heb 13:18. Pray for us, for our conscience is clear and we want to keep it that way.

1 Pet 2:12. Be careful how you behave among your unsaved neighbors; for then, even if they are suspicious of you and talk against you, they will end up praising God for your good works when Christ returns.

1 Pet 3:16. Do what is right; then if men speak against you, calling you evil names, they will become ashamed of themselves for falsely accusing you when you have only done what is good.

See *Character; Dishonesty; Honesty; Justice; Righteousness.*

INSTANCES OF. Pharaoh, when he learned that Sarah was Abraham's wife, Gen 12:18. Abimelech, when warned by God that the woman he had taken into his household was Abraham's wife, Gen 26: 9–11. Jacob, in the care of Laban's property, Gen 31: 39. Joseph, in resisting Potiphar's wife, Gen 39: 8–12; innocent of the charge on which he was thrown into prison, Gen 40:15. Jacob's sons, when accused by Joseph of robbery, Gen 43:15–22; 44: 7–16. The Egyptian midwives, when commanded to destroy the newborn Hebrew babies, Ex 1:17–21. Moses, in taking nothing from the Israelites in consideration of his services, Num 16:15. Samuel, in exacting nothing from the people for his services, 1 Sam 12:4. David, in self-reproach for the cutting Saul's robe, 1 Sam 24:5; in preventing foraging by his men, 1 Sam 25:15; in his conduct while in refuge with the Philistines, 1 Sam 29:6, 9, with *vs.* 1–11. Workmen, who repaired the temple, 2 Kgs 12:15; 22:7. Joab, when ordered by David to number the military forces of Israel, 1 Chron 21:6. Priests, who received the offerings of gold and other gifts for the renewing of the temple under Ezra, Ezra 8:24–30. Nehemiah, reforming the civil service, and receiving no compensation for his own services, Neh 5: 14–19. The Rechabites, in keeping the Nazarite vows, Jer 35:12–17. Daniel, in his temperance, Dan 1:8–20; in maintaining uprightness of character and consistent devoutness, Dan 6:4. Joseph, the husband of Mary, in not jealously accusing her of immorality, Mt 1:19. Zacchaeus, in the administration of his wealth, Lk 19:8. Nathanael, an honest man, Jn 1:47. Joseph, a counselor, Lk 23:50–52. Peter, when offered money by Simon, Acts 8:18–23. Paul and Barnabas, when the people of Lystra desired to deify them, Acts 14:12–15.

INTEMPERANCE See *Drunkard; Drunkenness; Wine; Abstinence; Temperance.*

INTERCESSION OF MAN WITH MAN. 1 Sam 2:25. It is an awful thing to make the Lord's people sin. Ordinary sin receives heavy punishment, but how much more this sin of yours which has been committed against the Lord?

Instances of. Reuben for Joseph, Gen 37:21, 22. Judah for Joseph, Gen 37:26, 27. Pharaoh's wine taster for Joseph, Gen 41:9–13, with Gen 40:14. Jonathan for David, 1 Sam 19:1–7. Abigail for Nabal, 1 Sam 25:23–35. Joab for Absalom, 2 Sam 14:1–24. Bath-sheba for Solomon, 1 Kgs 1:15–31; for Adonijah, 1 Kgs 2:13–25. Ebed-melech for Jeremiah, Jer 38:7–13. Elisha offers to see the king for the Shunammite, 2 Kgs 4:13. The king of Syria for Naaman, 2 Kgs 5:6–8. Paul for Onesimus, Philemon 1:10–21.

OF MAN WITH GOD. Gen 20:7. Now restore her to her husband, and he will pray for you (for he is a prophet) and you shall live. But if you don't return her to him, you are doomed to death along with all your household.

Ex 28:12. Fasten the two stones upon the shoulders of the ephod, as memorial stones for the people of Israel: Aaron will carry their names before the Lord as a constant reminder. [29]In this way Aaron shall carry the names of the tribes of Israel on the chestpiece over his heart (it is God's oracle) when he goes in to the Holy Place; thus Jehovah will be reminded of them continually. [30, 31]Insert into the pocket of the chestpiece the Urim and Thummim, to be carried over Aaron's heart when he goes in before Jehovah. Thus Aaron shall always be carrying the oracle over his heart when he goes in before the Lord. [36]Next, make a plate of pure gold and engrave on it, just as you would upon a seal, "Consecrated to Jehovah." [37, 38]This plate is to be attached by means of a blue ribbon to the front of Aaron's turban. In this way Aaron will be wearing it upon his forehead, and thus bear the guilt connected with any errors regarding the offerings of the people of Israel. It shall always be worn when he goes into the presence of the Lord, so that the people will be accepted and forgiven.

Ex 32:9. Then the Lord said, "I have seen what a stubborn, rebellious lot these people are. [10]Now let me alone and my anger shall blaze out against them and destroy them all; and I will make you, Moses, into a great nation instead of them." [11]But Moses begged God not to do it. "Lord," he pleaded, "why is your anger so hot against your own people whom you brought from the land of Egypt with such great power and mighty miracles? [12]Do you want the Egyptians to say, 'God tricked them into coming to the mountains so that he could slay them, destroying them from off the face of the earth'? Turn back from your fierce wrath. Turn away from this terrible evil you are planning against your people! [13]Remember your promise to your servants—to Abraham, Isaac, and Israel. For you swore by your own self, 'I will multiply your posterity as the stars of heaven, and I will give them all of this land I have promised to your descendants, and they shall inherit it forever.' " [14]So the Lord changed his mind and spared them.

Num 6:23. Now the Lord said to Moses, "Tell Aaron and his sons that they are to give this special blessing to the people of Israel: [24]'May the Lord bless and protect you; [25]may the Lord's face radiate with joy because of you; [26]may he be gracious to you, show you his favor, and give you his peace.' "

Num 14:11. And the Lord said to Moses, "How long will these people despise me? Will they *never* believe me, even after all the miracles I have done among them? [12]I will disinherit them and destroy them with a plague, and I will make you into a nation far greater and mightier than they are!" [13]"But what will the Egyptians think when they hear about it?" Moses pleaded with the Lord. "They know full well the power you displayed in rescuing your people. [14]They have told this to the inhabitants of this land, who are well aware that you are with Israel and that you talk with her face to face. They see the pillar of cloud and fire standing above us, and they know that you lead and protect us day and night. [15]Now if you kill all your people, the nations that have heard your fame will say, [16]'The Lord had to kill them because he wasn't able to take care of them in the wilderness. He wasn't strong enough to bring them into the land he swore he would give them.' [17]Oh, please show the great power (of your patience) by forgiving our sins and showing us your steadfast love. [18]Forgive us, even though you have said that you don't let sin go unpunished, and that you punish the father's fault in the children to the third and fourth generation. [19]Oh, I plead with you, pardon the sins of this people because of your magnificent, steadfast love, just as you have forgiven them all the time from when we left Egypt until now." [20]Then the Lord said, "All right, I will pardon them as you have requested."

Num 16:46. And Moses said to Aaron, "Quick, take a censer and place fire in it from the altar; lay incense on it, and carry it quickly among the people and make atonement for them; for God's anger has gone out among them—the plague has already begun." [47]Aaron did as Moses had told him to, and ran among the people, for the plague had indeed already begun; and he put on the incense and made atonement for them. [48]And he stood between the living and the dead, and the plague was stopped, [49]but not before 14,700 people had died (in addition to those who had died the previous day with Korah.) [50]Then Aaron returned to Moses at the entrance of the Tabernacle; and so the plague was stopped.

Deut 5:5. I stood as an intermediary between you and Jehovah, for you were afraid of the fire and did not go up to him on the mountain.

Deut 7:9. Understand, therefore, that the Lord your God is the faithful God who for a thousand generations keeps his promises and constantly loves those who love him and who obey his commands.

Deut 9:18. Then, for another forty days and nights I lay before the Lord, neither eating bread nor drinking water, for you had done what the Lord hated most, thus provoking him to great anger. [20]Aaron was in great danger because the Lord was so angry with him; but I prayed, and the Lord spared him. [25]That is why I fell down before him for forty days and nights when the Lord was ready to destroy you. [26]I prayed to him, "O Lord God, don't destroy your own people. They are your inheritance saved from Egypt by your mighty power and glorious strength. [27]Don't notice the rebellion and stubbornness of these people, but remember instead your promises to your servants Abraham, Isaac, and Jacob. Oh, please overlook the awful wickedness and sin of these people. [28]For if you destroy them the Egyptians will say, 'It is because the Lord wasn't able to bring them to the land he promised them,' or 'He destroyed them because he hated them: he brought them into the wilderness to slay them.' [29]They are your people and your inheritance which you brought from Egypt by your great power and your mighty arm."

1 Sam 7:5. Then Samuel told them, "Come to Mizpah, all of you, and I will pray to the Lord for you." [6]So they gathered there and, in a great ceremony, drew water from the well and poured it out before the Lord. They also went without food all day as a sign of sorrow for their sins. So it was at Mizpah that Samuel became Israel's judge. [7]When the Philistine leaders heard about the great crowds at Mizpah, they mobilized their army and advanced. The Israelis were badly frightened when

they learned that the Philistines were approaching. [8]"Plead with God to save us!" they begged Samuel. 1 Chron 20:3, 4.

1 Sam 12:23. As for me, far be it from me, that I should sin against the Lord by ending my prayers for you; and I will continue to teach you those things which are good and right.

1 Sam 15:24. "I have sinned," Saul finally admitted. "Yes, I have disobeyed your instructions and the command of the Lord, for I was afraid of the people and did what they demanded. [25]Oh, please pardon my sin now and go with me to worship the Lord." [26]But Samuel replied, "It's no use! Since you have rejected the commandment of the Lord, he has rejected you from being the king of Israel." [30]Then Saul pleaded again, "I have sinned; but oh, at least honor me before the leaders and before my people by going with me to worship the Lord your God."

Job 1:5. When these birthday parties ended—and sometimes they lasted several days—Job would summon his children to him and sanctify them, getting up early in the morning and offering a burnt offering for each of them. For Job said, "Perhaps my sons have sinned and turned away from God in their hearts." This was Job's regular practice.

Job 9:32, 33. And I cannot defend myself, for you are no mere man as I am. If you were, then we could discuss it fairly, but there is no umpire between us, no middle man, no mediator to bring us together.

Job 16:20. My friends scoff at me, but I pour out my tears to God, [21]pleading that he will listen as a man would listen to his neighbor.

Job 42:8. "Now take seven young bulls and seven rams and go to my servant Job and offer a burnt offering for yourselves; and my servant Job will pray for you, and I will accept his prayer on your behalf, and won't destroy you as I should because of your sin, your failure to speak rightly concerning my servant Job." [9]So Eliphaz the Temanite, and Bildad the Shuhite, and Zophar the Naamathite did as the Lord commanded them, and the Lord accepted Job's prayer on their behalf. [10]Then, when Job prayed for his friends, the Lord restored his wealth and happiness! In fact, the Lord gave him twice as much as before!

Ps 122:6. Pray for the peace of Jerusalem. May all who love this city prosper.

Isa 62:6, 7. O Jerusalem, I have set intercessors on your walls who shall cry to God all day and all night for the fulfillment of his promises. Take no rest, all you who pray, and give God no rest until he establishes Jerusalem and makes her respected and admired throughout the earth.

Isa 65:8. But I will not destroy them all, says the Lord; for just as good grapes are found among a cluster of bad ones (and someone will say, "Don't throw them all away—there are some good grapes there!") so I will not destroy all Israel, for I have true servants there.

Jer 5:1. Run up and down through every street in all Jerusalem; search high and low and see if you can find one fair and honest man! Search every square, and if you find just one, I'll not destroy the city!

Jer 7:16. Pray no more for these people, Jeremiah. Neither weep for them nor pray nor beg that I should help them, for I will not listen.

Jer 11:14. Therefore, Jeremiah, pray no longer for this people, neither weep nor plead for them; for I will not listen to them when they are finally desperate enough to beg me for help. Jer 14:11.

Jer 15:1. Then the Lord said to me, Even if Moses and Samuel stood before me pleading for these people, even then I wouldn't help them—away with them! Get them out of my sight!

Jer 29:7. And work for the peace and prosperity of Babylon. Pray for her, for if Babylon has peace, so will you.

Ezk 22:30. I looked in vain for anyone who would build again the wall of righteousness that guards the land, who could stand in the gap and defend you from my just attacks, but I found not one.

Mt 8:5, 6. When Jesus arrived in Capernaum, a Roman army captain came and pled with him to come to his home and heal his servant boy who was in bed paralyzed and racked with pain. [7]"Yes," Jesus said, "I will come and heal him." [8, 9]Then the officer said, "Sir, I am not worthy to have you in my home; (and it isn't necessary for you to come). If you will only stand here and say, 'Be healed,' my servant will get well! I know, because I am under the authority of my superior officers and I have authority over my soldiers, and I say to one, 'Go,' and he goes, and to another, 'Come,' and he comes, and to my slave boy, 'Do this or that,' and he does it. And I know you have authority to tell his sickness to go—and it will go!" [10]Jesus stood there amazed! Turning to the crowd he said, "I haven't seen faith like this in all the land of Israel! [11]And I tell you this, that many Gentiles (like this Roman officer), shall come from all over the world and sit down in the Kingdom of Heaven with Abraham, Isaac, and Jacob. [12]And many an Israelite—those for whom the Kingdom was prepared—shall be cast into outer darkness, into the place of weeping and torment." [13]Then Jesus said to the Roman officer, "Go on home. What you have believed has happened!" And the boy was healed that same hour!

Mk 6:55. And ran throughout the whole area to spread the news of his arrival, and began carrying sick folks to him on mats and stretchers. [56]Wherever he went—in villages and cities, and out on the farms—they laid the sick in the market plazas and streets, and begged him to let them at least touch the fringes of his clothes; and as many as touched him were healed.

Eph 6:18. Pray all the time. Ask God for anything in line with the Holy Spirit's wishes. Plead with him, reminding him of your needs, and keep praying earnestly for all Christians everywhere.

1 Tim 2:1. Here are my directions: Pray much for

others; plead for God's mercy upon them; give thanks for all he is going to do for them. [2]Pray in this way for kings and all others who are in authority over us.

Heb 13:18. Pray for us.

Jas 5:14. Is anyone sick? He should call for the elders of the church and they should pray over him and pour a little oil upon him, calling on the Lord to heal him. [15]And their prayer, if offered in faith, will heal him, for the Lord will make him well; and if his sickness was caused by some sin, the Lord will forgive him. [16]Admit your faults to one another and pray for each other so that you may be healed. The earnest prayer of a righteous man has great power and wonderful results. [17]Elijah was as completely human as we are, and yet when he prayed earnestly that no rain would fall, none fell for the next three and one half years! [18]Then he prayed again, this time that it *would* rain, and down it poured and the grass turned green and the gardens began to grow again. [19]Dear brothers, if anyone has slipped away from God and no longer trusts the Lord, and someone helps him understand the Truth again, [20]that person who brings him back to God will have saved a wandering soul from death, bringing about the forgiveness of his many sins.

1 Pet 2:5 And now you have become living building-stones for God's use in building his house. What's more, you are his holy priests; so come to him (you who are acceptable to him because of Jesus Christ)—and offer to God those things that please him. *v.* 9.

1 Jn 5:16. If you see a Christian sinning in a way that does not end in death, you should ask God to forgive him and God will give him life, unless he has sinned that one fatal sin. But there is that one sin which ends in death and if he has done that, there is no use praying for him.

EXEMPLIFIED. Gen 48:16. He is the Angel who has kept me from all harm. May these boys be an honor to my name and to the names of my fathers Abraham and Isaac; and may they become a mighty nation. *vs.* 15–20.

Ex 32:31. So Moses returned to the Lord and said, "Oh, these people have sinned a great sin, and have made themselves gods of gold. [32]Yet now if you will only forgive their sin—and if not, then blot *me* out of the book you have written."

Ex 34:9. And he said, "If it is true that I have found favor in your sight, O Lord, then please go with us to the Promised Land; yes, it is an unruly, stubborn people, but pardon our iniquity and our sins, and accept us as your own."

Num 10:35. As the Ark was carried forward, Moses cried out, "Arise, O Lord, and scatter your enemies; let them flee before you." [36]And when the Ark was set down he said, "Return, O Lord, to the millions of Israel."

Num 27:16. O Jehovah, the God of the spirits of all mankind, (before I am taken away) please appoint a new leader for the people, [17]a man who will lead them into battle and care for them, so that the people of the Lord will not be as sheep without a shepherd.

Josh 7:8. O Lord, what am I to do now that Israel has fled from her enemies! [9]For when the Canaanites and the other nearby nations hear about it, they will surround us and attack us and wipe us out. And then what will happen to the honor of your great name? *vs.* 7–26.

Judg 5:31. O Lord, may all your enemies perish as Sisera did, but may those who love the Lord shine as the sun!

Ruth 2:12. May the Lord God of Israel, under whose wings you have come to take refuge, bless you for it.

1 Sam 1:17. "In that case," Eli said, "cheer up! May the Lord of Israel grant you your petition, whatever it is!"

1 Sam 12:23. As for me, far be it from me that I should sin against the Lord by ending my prayers for you.

2 Sam 24:17. When David saw the angel, he said to the Lord, "Look, I am the one who has sinned! What have these sheep done? Let your anger be only against me and my family."

1 Kgs 8:29. Please watch over this Temple night and day—this place you have promised to live in—and as I face toward the Temple and pray, whether by night or by day, please listen to me and answer my requests. [38]Then when the people realize their sin and pray toward this Temple, [39]hear them from heaven and forgive and answer all who have made an honest confession; for you know each heart. [44]When you send your people out to battle against their enemies and they pray to you, looking toward your chosen city of Jerusalem and toward this temple which I have built for your name, [45]hear their prayer and help them.

1 Chron 29:18. O Lord God of our fathers: Abraham, Isaac, and Israel! Make your people always want to obey you, and see to it that their love for you never changes. [19]Give my son Solomon a good heart toward God, so that he will want to obey you in the smallest detail, and will look forward eagerly to finishing the building of your temple, for which I have made all of these preparations.

2 Chron 6:40. Yes, O my God, be wide awake and attentive to all the prayers made to you in this place. [41]And now, O Lord God, arise and enter this resting place of yours where the Ark of your strength has been placed. Let your priests, O Lord God, be clothed with salvation, and let your saints rejoice in your kind deeds.

2 Chron 30:18. May the good Lord pardon everyone [19]who determines to follow the Lord God of his fathers, even though he is not properly sanctified for the ceremony.

Ps 7:9. End all wickedness, O Lord, and bless all who truly worship God.

Ps 12:1. Lord! Help! Godly men are fast disappearing. Where in all the world can dependable men be found?

Ps 20:1. In your day of trouble, may the Lord be

with you! May the God of Jacob keep you from all harm. [2]May he send you aid from his sanctuary in Zion. [3]May he remember with pleasure the gifts you have given him, your sacrifices and burnt offerings. [4]May he grant you your heart's desire and fulfill all your plans.

Ps 25:22. And to ransom Israel from all her troubles.

Ps 28:9. Defend your people, Lord; defend and bless your chosen ones. Lead them like a shepherd and carry them forever in your arms.

Ps 36:10. Pour out your unfailing love on those who know you! Never stop giving your salvation to those who long to do your will.

Ps 51:18. And Lord, don't punish Israel for my sins—help your people and protect Jerusalem.

Ps 80:1. O shepherd of Israel who leads Israel like a flock; O God enthroned above the cherubim, bend down your ear and listen as I plead. Display your power and radiant glory. [2]Let Ephraim, Benjamin and Manasseh see you rouse yourself and use your mighty power to rescue us. [14]Come back, we beg of you, O God of the armies of heaven, and bless us. Look down from heaven and see our plight and care for this your vine! [15]Protect what you yourself have planted, this son you have raised for yourself. [17]Strengthen the man you love, the son of your choice. [19]Turn us again to yourself, O God of the armies of heaven. Look down on us, your face aglow with joy and love—only then shall we be saved.

Ps 122:7. O Jerusalem, may there be peace within your walls and prosperity in your palaces. [8]This I ask for the sake of all my brothers and my friends who live here; [9]and may there be peace as a protection to the Temple of the Lord.

Ps 125:4. O Lord, do good to those who are good, whose hearts are right with the Lord.

Ps 132:9. We will clothe the priests in white, the symbol of all purity. May our nation shout for joy. [10]Do not reject your servant David—the king you chose for your people. *v.* 8.

Ps 134:3. The Lord bless you from Zion—the Lord who made heaven and earth.

Ps 141:5. Let the godly smite me! It will be a kindness! If they reprove me, it is medicine! Don't let me refuse it. But I am in constant prayer against the wicked and their deeds.

Isa 62:1. Because I love Zion, because my heart yearns for Jerusalem, I will not cease to pray for her or to cry out to God on her behalf until she shines forth in his righteousness and is glorious in his salvation.

Isa 63:17. O Lord, why have you hardened our hearts and made us sin and turn against you? Return and help us, for we who belong to you need you so. [18]How briefly we possessed Jerusalem! And now our enemies have destroyed her. [19]O God, why do you treat us as though we weren't your people, as though we were a heathen nation that never called you "Lord"?

Isa 64:8. And yet, O Lord, you are our Father. We are the clay and you are the Potter. We are all formed by your hand. [9]Oh, be not so angry with us, Lord, nor forever remember our sins. Oh, look and see that we are all your people. [10]Your holy cities are destroyed; Jerusalem is a desolate wilderness. [11]Our holy, beautiful Temple where our fathers praised you is burned down, and all the things of beauty are destroyed. [12]After all of this, must you still refuse to help us, Lord? Will you stand silent and still punish us?

Jer 18:20. Should they repay evil for good? They have set a trap to kill me, yet I spoke well of them to you and tried to defend them from your anger.

Ezk 9:8. While they were fulfilling their orders, I was alone. I fell to the ground on my face and cried out: "O Lord God! Will your fury against Jerusalem wipe out everyone left in Israel?" Ezk 11:13.

Dan 9:3. So I earnestly pleaded with the Lord God (to end our captivity and send us back to our own land). As I prayed, I fasted, and wore rough sackcloth, and sprinkled myself with ashes, [4]and confessed my sins and those of my people. "O Lord," I prayed, "you are a great and awesome God; you always fulfill your promises of mercy to those who love you and who keep your laws. [5]But we have sinned so much; we have rebelled against you and scorned your commands. [6]We have refused to listen to your servants the prophets, whom you sent again and again down through the years, with your messages to our kings and princes and to all the people. [7]O Lord, you are righteous; but as for us, we are always shamefaced with sin, just as you see us now; yes, all of us—the men of Judah, the people of Jerusalem, and all Israel, scattered near and far wherever you have driven us because of our disloyalty to you. [8]O Lord, we and our kings and princes and fathers are weighted down with shame because of all our sins. [9]But the Lord our God is merciful, and pardons even those who have rebelled against him. [10]O Lord our God, we have disobeyed you; we have flouted all the laws you gave us through your servants, the prophets. [11]All Israel has disobeyed; we have turned away from you and haven't listened to your voice. And so the awesome curse of God has crushed us—the curse written in the law of Moses your servant. [12]And you have done exactly as you warned us you would do, for never in all history has there been a disaster like what happened at Jerusalem to us and our rulers. [13]Every curse against us written in the law of Moses has come true; all the evils he predicted—all have come. But even so we still refuse to satisfy the Lord our God by turning from our sins and doing right. [14]And so the Lord deliberately crushed us with the calamity he prepared; he is fair in everything he does, but we would not obey. [15]O Lord our God, you brought lasting honor to your name by removing your people from Egypt in a great display of power. Lord, do it again! Though we have sinned so much and are full of wickedness, [16]yet because of all your faithful mercies, Lord, please turn away your furious anger from Jerusalem, your own city, your holy mountain. For the heathen mock at you because your city lies in ruins for our sins. [17]O our God, hear your servant's prayer! Listen as I plead! Let your face shine again with peace and joy upon your desolate sanctuary —for your own glory, Lord. [18]O my God, bend down your ear and listen to my plea. Open your eyes and see our wretchedness, how your city lies in ruins—for everyone knows that it is yours. We don't ask because we merit help, but because you are so merciful despite our grievous sins. [19]O Lord, hear; O Lord, forgive. O Lord, listen to me and act! Don't delay—for your own sake, O my God, because your people and your city bear your name."

Joel 2:17. The priests, the ministers of God, will stand between the people and the altar, weeping; and they will pray, "Spare your people, O our God; don't let the heathen rule them, for they belong to you."

Mic 7:14 O Lord, come and rule your people; lead your flock; make them live in peace and prosperity; let them enjoy the fertile pastures of Bashan and Gilead as they did long ago.

Mt 5:44. Love your *enemies!* Pray for those who *persecute* you!

Mt 6:10. We ask that your kingdom will come now. May your will be done here on earth, just as it is in heaven.

Acts 7:60. Lord, don't charge them with this sin!

Acts 8:15. As soon as they arrived, they began praying for these new Christians to receive the Holy Spirit,

Rom 1:9. Day and night I bring you and your needs in prayer to the one I serve.

Rom 10:1. Dear brothers, the longing of my heart and my prayer is that the Jewish people might be saved.

1 Cor 1:3. May God our Father and the Lord Jesus Christ give you all of his blessings, and great peace of heart and mind. Gal 1:3.

2 Cor 9:10. For God, who gives seed to the farmer to plant, and later on, good crops to harvest and eat, will give you more and more seed to plant and will make it grow so that you can give away more and more fruit from your harvest. [14]And they will pray for you with deep fervor and feeling because of the wonderful grace of God shown through you.

2 Cor 13:7. I pray that you will live good lives, not because that will be a feather in our caps, proving that what we teach is right; no, for we want you to do right even if we ourselves are despised.

Gal 6:16. May God's mercy and peace be upon all of you who live by this principle and upon those everywhere who are really God's own.

Eph 1:15. That is why . . . [16]I have never stopped thanking God for you. I pray for you constantly, [17]asking God, the glorious Father of our Lord Jesus Christ, to give you wisdom to see clearly and really understand who Christ is and all that he has done for you. [18]I pray that your hearts will be flooded with light so that you can see something of the future he has called you to share. I want you to realize that God has been made rich because we who are Christ's have been given to him! [19]I pray that you will begin to understand how incredibly great his power is to help those who believe him. 1 Thess 1:2.

Eph 3:14, 15. When I think of the wisdom and scope of his plan I fall down on my knees and pray to the Father of all the great family of God—some of them already in heaven and some down here on earth—[16]that out of his glorious, unlimited resources he will give you the mighty inner strengthening of his Holy Spirit. [17]And I pray that Christ will be more and more at home in your hearts, living within you as you trust in him. May your roots go down deep into the soil of God's marvelous love; [18, 19]and may you be able to feel and understand, as all God's children should, how long, how wide, how deep, and how high his love really is; and to experience this love for yourselves, though it is so great that you will never see the end of it or fully know or understand it. And so at last you will be filled up with God himself.

Phil 1:3. All my prayers for you are full of praise to God! [4]When I pray for you, my heart is full of joy, [5]because of all your wonderful help in making known the Good News about Christ from the time you first heard it until now. [9]My prayer for you is that you will overflow more and more with love for others, and at the same time keep on growing in spiritual knowledge and insight. *v.* 10.

Col 1:3. Whenever we pray for you we always begin by giving thanks to God the Father of our Lord Jesus Christ, [4]for we have heard how much you trust the Lord. [9]So ever since we first heard about you we have kept on praying and asking God to help you understand what he wants you to do; asking him to make you wise about spiritual things.

Col 2:1. I wish you could know how much I have struggled in prayer for you and for the church at Laodicea, and for my many other friends who have never known me personally. [2]This is what I have asked of God for you: that you will be encouraged and knit together by strong ties of love, and that you will have the rich experience of knowing Christ with real certainty and clear understanding. *For God's secret plan, now at last made known, is Christ himself.* Col 4:12.

1 Thess 3:10. For night and day we pray on and on for you, asking God to let us see you again, to fill up any little cracks there may yet be in your faith. [12]And may the Lord make your love to grow and overflow to each other and to everyone else, just as our love does toward you. [13]This will result in your hearts being made strong, sinless and holy by God our Father, so that you may stand before him guiltless on that day when our Lord Jesus Christ returns with all those who belong to him. 2 Tim 1:3.

1 Thess 5:23. May the God of peace himself make you entirely pure and devoted to God; and may your spirit and soul and body be kept strong and blameless until that day when our Lord Jesus Christ comes back again.

2 Thess 1:11. And so we keep on praying for you

that our God will make you the kind of children he wants to have—will make you as good as you wish you could be!—rewarding your faith with his power.

2 Thess 2:16. May our Lord Jesus Christ himself and God our Father, who has loved us and given us everlasting comfort and hope which we don't deserve, 17comfort your hearts with all comfort, and help you in every good thing you say and do.

2 Thess 3:5. May the Lord bring you into an ever deeper understanding of the love of God and of the patience that comes from Christ. 16May the Lord of peace himself give you his peace no matter what happens. The Lord be with you all.

2 Tim 1:18. May the Lord give him a special blessing at the day of Christ's return.

2 Tim 2:7. And may the Lord help you to understand.

2 Tim 4:16. The first time I was brought before that judge no one was here to help me. Everyone had run away. I hope that they will not be blamed for it.

Philem 1:4. I always thank God when I am praying for you. 6And I pray that as you share your faith with others it will grip their lives too, as they see the wealth of good things in you that come from Christ Jesus.

Heb 13:20, 21. And now may the God of peace, . . . produce in you through the power of Christ all that is pleasing to him.

1 Pet 5:10. After you have suffered a little while, our God, who is full of kindness through Christ, will give you his eternal glory. He personally will come and pick you up, and set you firmly in place, and make you stronger than ever.

See *Prayer, Intercessory.*

ADDITIONAL INSTANCES OF. Abraham, in behalf of Sodom, Gen 18:23–32; in behalf of Abimelech, Gen 20:17, 18. Abraham's servant, in behalf of his master, Gen 24:12. Jacob, in behalf of his children, Gen 49. Moses, in behalf of Pharaoh, Ex 8: 12, 13, 30, 31; 9:33; 10:18, 19. Moses, for Israel, Num 16:20–22; 21:7; Deut 33:6–17; Ps 106:23; for Miriam, Num 12:13–15. David, for Israel, 2 Sam 24:17. Solomon, for Israel, 1 Kgs 8:29–53. Ezra, for Israel, Ezra 9:5–15. Nehemiah, in behalf of Judah and Jerusalem, Neh 1:4–9. Asaph, for the church, Ps 80:83. Korah, for the chruch, Ps 85:1–7. Jeremiah, for Israel, Jer 14:7–22. Amos, for Israel, Amos 7: 2–6. Canaanite woman, for her daughter, Mt 15:22. Disciples, in behalf of Simon's mother-in-law, Lk 4:38, 39. Parents, for deranged son, Mt 17:15; Mk 9:17–27. Others, who sought Jesus in behalf of the disabled, Mt 12:22; 15:22, 30; 17:14–18; Mk 1:32, 33; 2:3; Lk 5:18–20; Jn 4:47, 49. Paul, for the church, Acts 20:32; Onesiphorus, 2 Tim 1:16, 18. For Paul, by the churches, Acts 14:26; 15:40, 41.

SOLICITED.

Instances of. By Pharaoh, of Moses, Ex 8:8, 28; 9:28; 10:17; 12:32; and by the Israelites, Num 21:7. By Israel, of Samuel, 1 Sam 12:19. By Jeroboam, of a prophet, 1 Kgs 13:6. By Hezekiah, of Isaiah, 2 Kgs 19:1–4. By Zedekiah, of Jeremiah, Jer 37:3; and by Johanan, Jer 42:1–6. By Daniel, of Hananiah, Misha-el, and Azariah, Dan 2:17, 18. By Darius, of the Jews, Ezra 6:10. By Simon, of Peter, Acts 8:24. By Paul, of the churches, Rom 15:30–32; 2 Cor 1:11; Eph 6:19, 20; 1 Thess 5:25; 2 Thess 3:1; Heb 13:18.

ANSWERED.

Instances of. Of Moses, in behalf of Pharaoh, for the plague of frogs to be stopped, Ex 8:12, 15; the plague of flies, Ex 8:30–32; the plague of rain, thunder, and hail, Ex 9:27–35; plague of locusts, Ex 10: 16–20; plague of darkness, Ex 10:21–23. Of Moses, for the Israelites, during the battle with the Amalekites, Ex 17:11–14; after the Israelites had made the golden calf, Ex 32:11–14, 31–34; Deut 9:18–29; 10:10; Ps 106:23; after the complaining of the people, Ex 33:15–17; when the fire of the Lord destroyed the people, Num 11:1, 2; when the people complained on account of the report of the spies, Num 14:11–20; that the poisonous serpents might be stopped, Num 21:4–9; that Miriam's leprosy might be healed, Num 12:13; in behalf of Aaron, on account of his sin in making the golden calf, Deut 9:20. Of Samuel, for deliverance from the oppressions of the Philistines, 1 Sam 7:5–14. The prophet of Judah, for the restoration of Jeroboam's paralyzed hand, 1 Kgs 13:1–6. Of Elijah, for the reviving from the dead the son of the hospitable widow, 1 Kgs 17: 20–23. Of Elisha, for the reviving from the dead the son of the Shunemmite woman, 2 Kgs 4:33–36. Of Isaiah, in behalf of Hezekiah and the people, to be delivered from Sennacherib, 2 Kgs 19.

INTERCESSIONAL INFLUENCE OF THE RIGHTEOUS. Gen 18:26. And God replied, "If I find fifty godly people there, I will spare the entire city for their sake." *vs.* 29, 30, 32.

Gen 19:22. But hurry! For I can do nothing until you are there.

Gen 26:4. "And I will cause your descendants to become as numerous as the stars! And I will give them all of these lands; and they shall be a blessing to all the nations of the earth. 5I will do this because Abraham obeyed my commandments and laws." 24Jehovah appeared to him on the night of his arrival. "I am the God of Abraham your father," he said. "Fear not, for I am with you and will bless you, and will give you so many descendants that they will become a great nation—because of my promise to Abraham, who obeyed me."

1 Kgs 11:12. However, for the sake of your father David, I won't do this while you are still alive. I will take the kingdom away from your son. 13And even so I will let him be king of one tribe, for David's sake and for the sake of Jerusalem, my chosen city. 34I will not take the kingdom from him now, however; for the sake of my servant David, my chosen one who obeyed my commandments, I will let Solomon reign for the rest of his life.

1 Kgs 15:4. But despite Abijam's sin, the Lord remembered David's love and did not end the line of David's royal descendants.

2 Kgs 8:19. Nevertheless, because God had promised his servant David that he would watch over

and guide his descendants, he did not destroy Judah. 2 Chron 21:7.

Ps 103:17, 18. But the lovingkindness of the Lord is from everlasting to everlasting, to those who reverence him; his salvation is to children's children of those who are faithful to his covenant and remember to obey him!

Isa 37:35. For my own honor I will defend it, and in memory of my servant David.

Jer 5:1. Run up and down through every street in all Jerusalem; search high and low and see if you can find one fair and honest man! Search every square, and if you find just one, I'll not destroy the city!

Ezk 14:14. If Noah, Daniel and Job were here today, they alone would be saved by their righteousness, and I would destroy the remainder of Israel, says the Lord God. [16]Even if these three men were here, the Lord God swears that it would do no good—it would not save the people from their doom. These three only would be saved, but the land would be devastated. *vs.* 18, 20.

Rev 5:8. And as he took the scroll, the twenty-four Elders fell down before the Lamb, each with a harp and golden vials filled with incense—the prayers of God's people!

Rev 8:3. Then another angel with a golden censer came and stood at the altar; and a great quantity of incense was given to him to mix with the prayers of God's people, to offer upon the golden altar before the throne. [4]And the perfume of the incense mixed with prayers ascended up to God from the altar where the angel had poured them out.

See *Children, of the Righteous, Blessed by God; Jesus, Meditation of.*

INTEREST Income from loaning money, sometimes called usury in the scriptures, but not generally signifying unlawful or unjust rates.

Ex 22:25. If you lend money to a needy fellow-Hebrew, you are not to handle the transaction in an ordinary way, with interest.

Lev 25:36. Fear your God and let your brother live with you; and don't charge him interest on the money you lend him. [37]Remember—no interest; and give him what he needs, at your cost: don't try to make a profit!

Deut 23:19. Don't demand interest on loans you make to a brother Israelite, whether it is in the form of money, food, or anything else. [20]You may take interest from a foreigner, but not from an Israeli. For if you take interest from a brother, an Israeli, the Lord your God won't bless you when you arrive in the Promised Land.

Neh 5:1. About this time there was a great outcry of protest from parents against some of the rich Jews who were profiteering on them. [2-4]What was happening was that families who ran out of money for food had to sell their children or mortgage their fields, vineyards, and homes to these rich men; and some couldn't even do that, for they already had borrowed to the limit to pay their taxes. [5]"We are their brothers, and our children are just like theirs," the people protested. "Yet we must sell our children into slavery to get enough money to live. We have already sold some of our daughters, and we are helpless to redeem them, for our fields, too, are mortgaged to these men." [6]I was very angry when I heard this; [7]so after thinking about it I spoke out against these rich government officials. "What is this you are doing?" I demanded. "How dare you demand a mortgage as a condition for helping another Israelite?" Then I called a public trial to deal with them. [8]At the trial I shouted at them, "The rest of us are doing all we can to *help* our Jewish brothers who have returned from exile as slaves in distant lands, but you are forcing them right back into slavery again. How often must we redeem them?" And they had nothing to say in their own defense. [9]Then I pressed further. "What you are doing is very evil," I exclaimed. "Should you not walk in the fear of our God? Don't we have enough enemies among the nations around us who are trying to destroy us? [10]The rest of us are lending money and grain to our fellow-Jews without any interest. I beg you, gentlemen, stop this business of usury. [11]Restore their fields, vineyards, oliveyards, and homes to them this very day and drop your claims against them." [12]So they agreed to do it and said that they would assist their brothers without requiring them to mortgage their lands and sell them their children. Then I summoned the priests and made these men formally vow to carry out their promises. [13]And I invoked the curse of God upon any of them who refused. "May God destroy your homes and livelihood if you fail to keep this promise," I declared. And all the people shouted, "Amen," and praised the Lord. And the rich men did as they had promised.

Ps 15:5. Does not crush his debtors with high interest rates, and refuses to testify against the innocent despite the bribes offered him—such a man shall stand firm forever.

Prov 28:8. Income from exploiting the poor will end up in the hands of someone who pities them.

Isa 24:2. Priests and people, servants and masters, slave girls and mistresses, buyers and sellers, lenders and borrowers, bankers and debtors—none will be spared.

Ezk 18:8. And grants loans without interest, and stays away from sin, and is honest and fair when judging others, [9]and obeys my laws—that man is just, says the Lord, and he shall surely live. [13]And loans out his money at interest—shall that man live? No! He shall surely die, and it is his own fault. [17]And helps the poor and does not loan money at interest, and obeys my laws—he shall not die because of his father's sins; he shall surely live.

Ezk 22:12. Hired murderers, loan racketeers and extortioners are everywhere. You never even think of me and my commands, the Lord God says.

See *Borrowing; Debt; Debtor; Lending; Money; Usury.*

INTERMEDIATE STATE A theological term referring to the condition of mankind between death and the resurrection of the body. Torment for the unsaved, Lk 16:23; Jude 1:7. Paradise for the saved, Lk 23:43; cf. 2 Cor 12:1–10; Rev 6:9–11. Compare, for the present experience of believers, Acts 7:59; 2 Cor 5:6; 1 Thess 4:13; Ps 16:11; Phil 1:21.

See *Hades; Paradise.*

INTERPRETATION Of dreams, see *Dream.* Of foreign tongues, 1 Cor 14:9–19, see *Tongues.*

INTERPRETER Of dreams, Gen 40:8; 41:16; Dan 2:18–30. Of languages, Gen 42:23; Neh 8:7, 8. In Christian churches, 1 Cor 12:10, 30; 14:5, 13, 26–28.

INTESTINES Diseased, 2 Chron 21:15, 19.

See *Bowels.*

INTOLERANCE Religious. Exemplified by Cain, Gen 4:8; Joshua, Num 11:24–28; James and John, Mk 9:38, 39; Lk 9:49; the Jews, in persecuting Jesus, see *Jesus, History of;* and in persecuting the disciples, Acts 4:1–3, 15–21; 17:13; and Stephen, Acts 6:9–15; 7:57–59; 8:1–3; and Paul, Acts 13:50; 17:5; 18:13; 21:28–31; 22:22, 23; 23:2.

Of idolatrous religions, taught by Moses, Ex 22:20; Deut 13; 17:1–7. Exemplified by Elijah, 1 Kgs 18:40; Jehu, 2 Kgs 10:18–32; by the Jews, at the time of the religious revival under the leadership of Azariah, 2 Chron 15:12, 13.

See *Persecution.*

INTOXICANTS See *Wine.*

INTOXICATION See *Drunkenness; Abstinence.*

INTRIGUE See *Conspiracy.*

INVECTIVE See *Satire.*

INVENTION Of musical instruments: By Jubal, Gen 4:21; by David, 1 Chron 23:5; 2 Chron 7:6; 29:26; Amos 6:5. The use of metals, Gen 4:22. Engines of war, 2 Chron 26:15.

INVESTIGATION Eccl 1:12–18; 2:1–12; 12:9–14.

IOB See *Jashub. 1.*

IPHDEIAH A Benjaminite, 1 Chron 8:22–25.

IPHTAH A city of Judah, Josh 15:37–44.

IPHTAHEL A valley in Zebulun, Josh 19:14, 27.

IR A Benjaminite, 1 Chron 7:12.

IRA 1. A priest, 2 Sam 20:26.

2. The Ithrite, one of David's heroes, 2 Sam 23:38; 1 Chron 11:40.

3. A Tekoite, one of David's heroes, 2 Sam 23:26; 1 Chron 11:28; 27:9.

IRAD Son of Enoch, Gen 4:18.

IRAM A king of Edom, Gen 36:43; 1 Chron 1:54.

IRAQ See *Mesopotamia.*

IRI A son of Bela, 1 Chron 7:7.

IRIJAH The guard who arrested the prophet Jeremiah, Jer 37:13, 14.

IR-NAHASH Son of Tehinnah, 1 Chron 4:12.

IRON First recorded use of, Gen 4:22. Ore of, Deut 8:9; Job 28:2. Melted, Ezk 22:18–20. Used in the temple, 1 Chron 22:3; 29:2, 6, 7. Strength of, Jer 15:12, 13. Articles made of: Ax, 2 Kgs 6:6; Eccl 10:10; Isa 10:34; bedstead, Deut 3:11; breastplate, Rev 9:9; chariot, Josh 17:16–18; Judg 1:19; 4:3; fetters, Ps 105:18; 107:16; 149:8; furnace, 1 Kgs 8:51; gate, Acts 12:10; harrow, 2 Sam 12:31; horn, 1 Kgs 22:11; 2 Chron 18:10; Mic 4:13; idols, Dan 2:33; 5:4, 23; pans, Ezk 4:3; 27:19; pen, Job 19:23, 24; Jer 17:1; pillars, Jer 1:18; rods for scourging, Ps 2:9; Rev 2:27; threshing instruments, Amos 1:3; tools, 1 Kgs 6:7; utensils, Josh 6:24; weapons, Num 35:16; 1 Sam 17:7; Job 41:7; yokes, Deut 28:48; Jer 28:13, 14.

Stones of, Deut 8:9; Job 28:2; Isa 60:17.

FIGURATIVE. Jer 15:12, 13.

IRONY INSTANCES OF. Michal to David, 2 Sam 6:20. Elijah to the priests of Baal, 1 Kgs 18:27. Job to his accusers, Job 12:2. Ezekiel to the prince of Tyre, Ezk 28:2–5. Micaiah, 1 Kgs 22:15. Amos to the Samaritans, Amos 4:4. Jesus to Pharisees, Mk 2:17. Pharisees and Herodians to Jesus, Mt 22:16. Roman soldiers to Jesus, Mt 27:29; Mk 15:16–19; Lk 23:11; Jn 19:2, 3. Pilate, calling Jesus king, Mk 15:19; Jn 19:15. Superscription of Pilate over Jesus, Mt 27:37; Mk 15:26; Lk 23:38; Jn 19:19. Agrippa to Paul, Acts 26:28.

See *Sarcasm; Satire.*

IRPEEL A city of Benjamin, Josh 18:27.

IRRIGATION Deut 11:10; Prov 21:1; Eccl 2:4–6; Isa 58:11.

FIGURATIVE. 1 Cor 3:6–8.

IR-SHEMESH A city of Dan, Josh 19:41.

IRU Eldest son of Caleb, 1 Chron 4:15.

ISAAC Miraculous son of Abraham, Gen 17:15–19; 18:1–15; 21:1–8; Josh 24:3; 1 Chron 1:28; Gal 4:28; Heb 11:11. Ancestor of, Jesus, Mt 1:2. Offered in sacrifice by his father, Gen 22:1–19; Heb 11:17; Jas 2:21. Is provided a wife from among his relatives, Gen 24; 25:20. Abrahamic covenant confirmed in, Gen 26:2–5; 1 Chron 16:15–19. Lives in the south country at Beer-lahai-roi, Gen 24:62; 25:11. With Ishmael, buries his father in the cave of Machpelah, Gen 25:9, 10. Esau and Jacob born to, Gen 25:19–26; 1 Chron 1:34; Josh 24:4. Lives in Gerar, Gen 26:7–11. Prospers, Gen 26:12–14. Possesses large flocks and herds, Gen 26:14. Digs wells, and is defrauded of them by the shepherds of Abimelech, Gen 26:15, 21. Moves to the valley of Gerar, afterward called Beer-sheba, Gen 26:22–33. His old age, last blessing on his sons, Gen 27:18–40. Death and burial of, Gen 35:27–29; 49:31. His filial obedience, Gen 22:9. His peaceableness, Gen 26:14–22. Was a prophet, Gen 27:27–29, 38–40; Heb 11:20. His devoutness, Gen 24:63; 25:21; 26:25; Mt 8:11; Lk 13:28. Prophecies concerning, Gen 17:16–21; 18:10–14; 21:12; 26:2–5, 24; Ex 32:13; 1 Chron 16:16; Rom 9:7.

ISAIAH Son of Amoz, Isa 1:1. Prophesies in the days of Uzziah, Jotham, Ahaz, and Hezekiah, kings of Judah, Isa 1:1; 6:1; 7:1, 3; 14:28; 20:1; 36:1; 38:1; 39:1; at the time when Sargon, of Assyria, sends his army, Isa 20:1. Symbolically walks naked and barefoot, as a sign to Israel, Isa 20:2, 3. Comforts and encourages Hezekiah and the people in the siege of Jerusalem, 2 Kgs 18; 19; Isa 37:6, 7.

Comforts Hezekiah in his illness, 2 Kgs 20:1–11; Isa 38. Performs the miracle of the returning shadow to confirm Hezekiah's faith, 2 Kgs 20:8–11. Reproves Hezekiah's folly in exhibiting his resources to the ambassadors from Babylon, 2 Kgs 20:12–19; Isa 39. Is chronicler of the times of Uzziah and Hezekiah, 2 Chron 26:22; 32:32.

PROPHECIES, REPROOFS, AND EXHORTATIONS OF. Foretells punishment of the Jews for idolatry, and reproves self-confidence and distrust of God, Isa 2:6–20. Foretells the destruction of the Jews, Isa 3. Promises to the remnant restoration of divine favor, Isa 4:2–6; 6. Delineates in the parable of the vineyard the ingratitude of the Jews, and reproves it, Isa 5:1–10. Denounces existing corruptions, Isa 5:8–30. Foretells the ill success of the plot of the Israelites and Syrians against Judah, Isa 7:1–16. Denounces calamities against Israel and Judah, Isa 7:16–25; 9:2–6. Foretells prosperity under Hezekiah, and the manifestation of the Messiah, Isa 9:1–7. Denounces vengeance upon the enemies of Israel, Isa 9:8–12. Denounces the wickedness of Israel, and foretells the judgments of God, Isa 9:13–21. Denounces the unjust, Isa 10:1–4. Foretells the destruction of the Assyrian army, Isa 10:5–34; the restoration of Israel and the triumph of the Messiah's kingdom, Isa 11. The burden of Babylon, Isa 13; 14:1–28. Denunciation against the Philistines, Isa 14:9–32. Burden of Moab, Isa 15; 16. Burden of Damascus, Isa 17. Obscure prophecy, supposed by some authorities to be directed against the Assyrians, by others against the Egyptians, and by others against the Ethiopians, Isa 18. The burden of Egypt, Isa 19; 20. Denunciations against Babylon, Isa 21:1–10. Prophecy concerning Edom, Isa 21:11, 12; Arabia, Isa 21:13–17; concerning the conquest of Jerusalem, the captivity of Shebna, and the promotion of Eliakim, Isa 22:1–22; the overthrow of Tyre, Isa 23; the judgments upon the land, but that a remnant of the Jews would be saved, Isa 25; 26; 27. Foretells the destruction of Samaria, Isa 28:1–5. Declares the glory of God upon the remnant who are saved, Isa 28:5, 6. Exposes the corruptions in Jerusalem and exhorts to repentance, Isa 28:7–29. Foretells the seige of Jerusalem, the distress of the Jews, and the destruction of their enemies, Isa 29:1–8. Denounces the hypocrisy of the Jews, Isa 29:9–17. Promises a reformation, Isa 29:18–24. Reproves the people for their confidence in Egypt, and their contempt of God, Isa 30:1–17; 31:1–6. Declares the goodness and longsuffering of God toward them, Isa 30:18–26; chapters 32–35. Reproves the Jews for their spiritual blindness and infidelity, Isa 42:18–25. Promises ultimate restoration of the Jews, Isa 43:1–13. Foretells the ultimate destruction of Babylon, Isa 43:14–17; 47. Exhorts the people to repent, Isa 43:22–28. Comforts Israel with promises, exposes the folly of idolatry, and prophesies Israel's deliverance from captivity by Cyrus, Isa 44; 45:1–5; 48:20. Foretells the conversion of the Gentiles, Isa 45:5–25. Denounces the evils of idolatry, Isa 46. Reproves the Jews for their idolatries and other wickedness, Isa 48. Exhorts to sanctification, Isa 56:1–8. Foretells calamities to Judah, Isa 59:9–12, with chapters 57–59.

Foreshadows the person and the kingdom of the Messiah, Isa chapters 32–35; 42; 45; 49–56; 59:15–21, and chapters 60–66.

ISCAH Son of Haran and brother of Lot and Milcah, Gen 11:29.

ISCARIOT See *Judas, 1.*

ISHBAH Ancestor of Eshtemoa, 1 Chron 4:17.

ISHBAK Son of Abraham and Keturah, Gen 25:2; 1 Chron 1:32.

ISHBI-BENOB A giant slain by Abishai, 2 Sam 21:16.

ISH-BOSHETH Son of Saul. Called *Eshbaal* in 1 Chron 8:33; 9:39. Made king by Abner, 2 Sam 2:8, 9. Deserted by Abner, 2 Sam 3:6–12. Restores Michal, David's wife, to David, 2 Sam 3:14–16. Assassinated, 2 Sam 4:5–8. Avenged by David, 2 Sam 4:9–12.

ISHHOD One of the tribe of Manasseh, 1 Chron 7:18.

ISHI 1. A son of Appaim, 1 Chron 2:31.

2. A descendant of Judah, 1 Chron 4:20.

3. A Simeonite, 1 Chron 4:42.

4. One of the heads of Manasseh, 1 Chron 5:24.

ISHMA A descendant of Judah, 1 Chron 4:3.

ISHMAEL 1. Son of Abraham, Gen 16:9–12, 15, 16; 1 Chron 1:28. Prayer of Abraham for, Gen 17:18, 20. Circumcised, Gen 17:23–27. Promised to be the father of a nation, Gen 16:9–12; 17:20; 21:12, 13, 18. Sent away by Abraham, Gen 21:6–21. With Isaac buries his father, Gen 25:9, 10. Children of, Gen 25:12–18; 1 Chron 1:28–31. Daughter of, marries Esau, Gen 28:9; 36:2, 3. Death of, Gen 25:17, 18.

2. Father of Zebadiah, 2 Chron 19:11.

3. A son of Azel, 1 Chron 8:38; 9:44.

4. An army officer, 2 Chron 23:1.

5. A priest of the exile, Ezra 10:22.

6. A son of Nethaniah. Assassinated Gedaliah, governor of Judah under king of Babylon, and takes captive many Jews, Jer 40:8–16; 41:1–10; 2 Kgs 25:23–25. Defeated by Johanan, and escapes, Jer 41:11–15.

ISHMAELITES Region occupied by, Gen 25:18. Traders of, buy Joseph, Gen 37:25–36; 39:1. Called *Midianites,* Gen 37:28, 36; Judg 8:23, 24. Enemies to Israel, Ps 83:6.

See *Ishmael.*

ISHMAIAH 1. A Gibeonite who joined David at Ziklag, 1 Chron 12:3–7.

2. An officer of Zebulun, 1 Chron 27:19.

ISHMERAI A chief Benjaminite, 1 Chron 8:18.

ISHPAH A chief Benjaminite, 1 Chron 8:15, 16.

ISHPAN A chief Benjaminite, 1 Chron 8:22–25.

ISHTAR See *Ashtoreth.*

ISHVAH Son of Asher, Gen 46:17; 1 Chron 7:30.

ISHVI 1. Son of Asher, Gen 46:17; Num 26: 44–47; 1 Chron 7:30.

2. Son of Saul, 1 Sam 14:49.

ISLANDS, OR COASTS Prophecies concerning. Ps 72:10; 97:1; Isa 11:11; Ezk 39:6; Rev 6:14; 16:20.

ISMACHIAH A Levite, 2 Chron 31:12, 13.

ISRAEL 1. A name given to Jacob, Gen 32: 22–32; 2 Kgs 17:34; Hos 12:3, 4.

2. A name of the Christ in prophecy, Isa 49:3.

3. A name given to the descendants of Jacob, a nation. Called also *Israelis, Israelites, and Hebrews,* Gen 43:32; Ex 1:15, 16; 9:7; 10:3; 21:2; Lev 23:42; Josh 13:6, etc.; 1 Sam 4:6; 13:3, 4, 19; 14:11, 21.

Tribes of Israel were named after the sons of Jacob. In lists usually the names Levi and Joseph, two sons of Jacob, do not appear. The descendants of Levi were consecrated to religious service, and the two sons of Joseph, Ephraim and Manasseh, were adopted by Jacob in Joseph's place, Gen 48: 5; Josh 14:4, and their names appear in the lists of tribes instead of those of Levi and Joseph, as follows: Asher, Benjamin, Dan, Ephraim, Gad, Issachar, Judah, Manasseh, Naphtali, Reuben, Simeon, Zebulun.

Names of, seen in John's vision, on the gates of the New Jerusalem, Rev 21:12.

Prophecies concerning, Gen 15:5, 13; 25:23; 26:4; 27:27–29, 39, 40. 48:19; 49; Deut 33; of the great number of, Gen 13:16; 15:5; 22:17; 26:4; 28:14; of their captivity in Egypt, Gen 15:13, 14; Acts 7:6, 7.

Divided into families, each of which had a chief, Num 25:14; 26; 36:1; Josh 7:14; 1 Chron chapters 4–8.

Number of, who went into Egypt, Gen 46:8–27; Ex 1:5; Deut 10:22; Acts 7:14. Number of, at the time of the exodus, Ex 12:37, 38, with Gen 47:27; Ex 1:7–20; Ps 105:24; Acts 7:17, 18. Number of, fit for military service when they left Egypt, Ex 12:37; at Sinai, by tribes, Num 1:1–50; after the plague, Num 26; when David numbered, 2 Sam 24:1–9; 1 Chron 21:5, 6; 27:23, 24; after the captivity, Ezra 2:64, 65; Neh 7:66, 67; in John's apocalyptic vision, Rev 7:1–8.

Lived in Goshen, Gen 46:28–34; 47:4–10, 27, 28. Lived in Egypt 430 years, Ex 12:40, 41, with Gen 15: 13; Acts 7:6; Gal 3:17. Were enslaved and oppressed by the Egyptians, Ex 1; 2; 5; Acts 7:17–36. Their groaning heard by God, Ex 2:23–25. Moses commissioned as deliverer, Ex 3:2–22; 4:1–17. The land of Egypt plagued on their account, see *Egypt.* Exempt from the plagues, Ex 8:22, 23; 9:4–6, 26; 10: 23; 11:7; 12:13. Children were spared when the firstborn of the Egyptians were killed, Ex 12:13, 23. Instituted the passover, Ex 12:1–28. Borrowed jewels from the Egyptians, Ex 11:2, 3; 12:35, 36; Ps 105: 37. Urged by the Egyptians to depart, Ex 12:31–39. Travel from Rameses to Succoth, Ex 12:37–39. Made the trip by night, Ex 12:42. The day of their deliverance to be a memorial, Ex 12:42; 13:3–16. Led of God, Ex 13:17, 18, 21, 22. Providentially cared for, Deut 8:3, 4; 29:5, 6; 34:7; Neh 9:21; Ps 105:37. See *Manna; Cloud, Pillar of.*

Travel from Succoth to Etham, Ex 13:20; to Piha-hiroth, Ex 14:2; Num 33:5–7. Pursued by the Egyptians, Ex 14:5–31. Pass through the Red Sea, Ex 14:19–22; Deut 11:4; Ps 78; 105; 106; 107; 136. Order of march, Num 2. Travel to Marah, Ex 15: 23; Num 33:8. Murmur on account of the bitter water, Ex 15:23–25; water of, sweetened, Ex 15:25. Travel to Elim, Ex 15:27; Num 33:9. For the itinerary, see Num 33.

Murmured for food, Ex 16:2, 3. Provided with manna and quails, Ex 16:4–36. Murmured for lack of water at Rephidim, Ex 17:2–7; water miraculously supplied from the rock at Meribah, Ex 17: 5–7. Defeat the Amalekites, Ex 17:13; Deut 25:17, 18. Arrive at Sinai, Ex 19:1; Num 33:15. At the suggestion of Jethro, Moses's father-in-law, they organize a system of government, Ex 18:25; Deut 1: 9–18. The message of God to them, requiring that they will obey his instructions and as a reward they would be to him a holy nation, and their reply, Ex 19:3–8. Sanctify themselves for receiving the law, Ex 19:10–15. The law delivered to, Ex 20; 21; 22; 23; 24:1–4; 25; 26; 27; 28; 29; 30; 31; Lev chapters 1–25; 27; Deut 5; 15; 16. The people receive it and covenant obedience to it, Ex 24:3, 7. Idolatry of, Ex 32; Deut 9:17–21. The anger of the Lord in consequence, Ex 32:9–14. Moses' indignation; breaks the stone tablets; enters the camp; commands the Levites; 3,000 killed, Ex 32:19–35. Visited by a plague, Ex 32:35. Stubbornness of, Ex 33:3; 34:9; Deut 9: 12–29. God withdraws his presence, Ex 33:1–3. The mourning of, when God refused to lead them, Ex 33:4–10. Tablets renewed, Ex 34. Plans for the tabernacle and the furnishings, and forms of worship to be observed, Ex chapters 25–31. Gifts consecrated for the creation of the tabernacle, Ex 35; 36: 1–7; Num 7. The erection of the tabernacle; the manufacture of the furnishings, including the garments of the priests; and their sanctification, Ex 36: 8–38; chapters 37–40. First sacrifice offered by, under the law, Lev 8:14–36; 9:8–24. Second passover observed, Num 9:1–5.

March out of the wilderness, Num 10:11–36. For itinerary, see Num 33. Order of camp and march, Num 2. Arrive at the border of Canaan, Num 12: 16. Send twelve spies to survey the land, Num 13; 32:8; Deut 1:22, 25; Josh 14:7. Return with a majority and minority report, Num 13:26–33; 14:6–11. Murmuring over the report, Num 14:1–5. The judgment of God upon them because of their unbelief and murmuring, Num 14:13–39. Reaction, and their decision to enter the land; are defeated by the Amalekites, Num 14:40–45; Deut 1:41–45. Stay at Kadesh, Deut 1:46. Return to the wilderness, where they remain 38 years, and all die except Joshua and Caleb, Num 14:20–39. Rebellion of Korah, Dathan, and Abiram, Num 16:1–40; Deut 11:6. Murmur against Moses and Aaron; are plagued; 14,700 die; plague stopped, Num 16:41–50. Murmur for lack of water in Meribah; the rock is struck, Num 20:1–13. Are refused passage through the country of Edom, Num 20:14–21. The death of Aaron, Num 20:24, 28, 29; 33:38, 39; Deut 10:6.

Defeat the Canaanites, Num 21:1–3. Are punished with snakes, Num 21:4–9. Defeat the Amorites, Num 21:21–32; Deut 2:24–36, and the king of Bashan, Num 21:33–35; Deut 3:1–17. Arrive in the plains of Moab, at the Jordan River, Num 22:1; 33: 48, 49. Commit idolatry with the people of Moab, Num 25:1–5. Punished by a plague as a result; 24, 000 die, Num 25:6–15; 26:1. The people numbered for the allotment of the land, Num 26. The daughters of Zelophehad sue for an inheritance, Num 27: 1–11; Josh 17:3–6. Conquest of the Midianites, Num 31. Nations dread, Deut 2:25. Renew the covenant, Deut 29. Moses dies, and people mourn, Deut 34. Joshua appointed leader, Num 27:18–23, Deut 31: 23. See *Joshua.*

All who were numbered at Sinai perished in the wilderness except Caleb and Joshua, Num 26:63–65; Deut 2:14, 15. Faithfulness of those who entered Canaan, Josh 23:8; Judg 2:7–9; Jer 2:2, 3. Men chosen to divide the lands of Canaan among the tribes and families, Num 34:16–29. Move from Acacia to Jordan, Josh 3:1. Cross Jordan, Josh 4. Circumcision observed and passover celebrated, Josh 5. Jericho taken, Josh 6. Ai taken, Josh 7 and 8. Make a treaty with the Gibeonites, Josh 9. Defeat the five Amorite kings, Josh 10. Conquest of the land, Josh 21:43–45, with Judg 1. The land allotted, Josh chapters 15–21.

Troops of the two and one-half tribes on the west side of the Jordan erect a monument to signify the unity of the tribes; the monument misunderstood; the controversy which followed; its amicable settlement, Josh 22. Joshua's exhortation immediately before his death, Josh 23. Covenant renewed, death of Joshua, Josh 24; Judg 2:7–9. Religious fidelity during the life of Joshua, Josh 24:31; Judg 2:7–9.

UNDER THE JUDGES. Public affairs administered 450 years by the judges, Judg 2:16–19; Acts 13: 20. The original inhabitants not fully expelled, Judg 1:27–36; 3:1–7. Reproved by an angel for not expelling the original inhabitants, Judg 2:1–5. People turn to idolatry, Judg 2:10–23. Delivered for their idolatry to the king of eastern Syria during eight years; their repentance and deliverance, Judg 3:8–11. Renew their idolatry, and are put under tribute to the king of Moab during 18 years; repent and are delivered by Ehud; 80 years of peace follow, Judg 3:12–30. Shamgar resists a foray of the Philistines and saves Israel, Judg 3:31. People again sin and are conquered for 20 years to the king of Hazor, Judg 4:1–3. Delivered by Deborah, a prophetess, and judged, Judg 4; 5. Seven years of bondage to the Midianites; delivered by Gideon, Judg 6; 7; 8:1–28; see *Gideon.* Return to idolatry, Judg 8:33, 34. Abimelech foments an inter-tribal war, Judg 9. Judged by Tola 23 years, Judg 10:1, 2; by Jair 22 years, Judg 10:3, 4. People backslide, and are given over to the Philistines for chastisement 18 years; repent and turn to the Lord; delivered by Jephthah, Judg 10:6–18; 11. Ephraimites go to war against other tribes; defeated by Jephthah, Judg 12: 1–7. Judged by Ibzan seven years, Judg 12:8–10; by Elon ten years, Judg 12:11, 12; by Abdon eight years, Judg 12:13–15. Backslide again and are subject to the Philistines 40 years, Judg 13:1. Judged by Samson 20 years, Judg 15:20, with chapters 13–16. Scandal of the Levite's concubine, and the consequent war between the Benjaminites and other tribes, Judg chapters 19–21. Judged by Eli 40 years, 1 Sam 4:18, with chapters 1–4. Defeated by the Philistines at Ebenezer, 1 Sam 4:1, 2, 10, 11. Demand a king, 1 Sam 8:5–20; Hos 13:10.

UNDER THE KINGS BEFORE THE SEPARATION INTO TWO KINGDOMS. Saul anointed king, 1 Sam 10; 11:12–15; 12:13. Ammonites invade Israel, are defeated, 1 Sam 11. Philistines defeated, 1 Sam 14. Amalekites defeated, 1 Sam 15. David anointed king, 1 Sam 16:10–13. Goliath killed, 1 Sam 17. Israel defeated by the Philistines, and Saul and his sons killed, 1 Sam 31. See *Saul.*

David defeats the Amalekites, 1 Sam 30; 2 Sam 1:1; made king, 2 Sam 2:4, 10, 11. Ishbosheth made king, 2 Sam 2:8–11.

The conflict between the two political factions, 2 Sam 2:12–32; 3:1.

David made king over all Israel, 2 Sam 5:1–5. Conquests of David, 2 Sam 8; Absalom's rebellion, 2 Sam chapters 15–18. See *David.*

Solomon anointed king, 1 Kgs 1:32–40. Temple built, 1 Kgs 6. Solomon's palace built, 1 Kgs 7. Solomon's death, 1 Kgs 11:41–43. See *Solomon.*

THE REVOLT OF THE TEN TRIBES. Foreshadowing circumstances indicating the separation: Disagreement after Saul's death, 2 Sam 2; 1 Chron 12:23–40; 13. Lukewarmness of the ten tribes, and zeal of Judah for David in Absalom's rebellion, 2 Sam 19:41–43. The rebellion of Sheba, 2 Sam 20. The two factions are distinguished as Israel and Judah during David's reign, 2 Sam 21: 2. Providential, Zech 11:14.

Revolt consummated under Rehoboam, son and successor of Solomon, 1 Kgs 12.

4. The name of the ten tribes that revolted from the house of David. Called also *Jacob,* Hos 12:2.

List of the kings of Israel, and the period of time in which they reigned. For the facts of their reigns see under each name:

1. Jeroboam, 22 years.
2. Nadab, about two years.
3. Baasha, 24 years.
4. Elah, two years.
5. Zimri, seven days.
6. Omri, 12 years.
7. Ahab, 22 years.
8. Ahaziah, two years.
9. Jehoram, 12 years.
10. Jehu, 28 years.
11. Jehoahaz, 17 years.
12. Joash, 16 years.
13. Jeroboam II, 41 years.
14. Zechariah, six months.
15. Shallum, one month.
16. Menahem, ten years.
17. Pekahiah, two years.
18. Pekah, 20 years.
19. Hoshea, nine years.

The ten tribes carried captive to Assyria.

History of. War continued between the two kingdoms all the days of Rehoboam and Jeroboam, 1 Kgs 14:30; and between Jeroboam and Abijam, 1 Kgs 15:6, and between Baasha and Asa, 1 Kgs 15:16, 32, 33. Famine prevails in the reign of Ahab, 1 Kgs 18:1–6. Israel, called also *Samaria,* invaded by, but defeats, Ben-hadad, king of Syria, 1 Kgs 20. Moab, rebels, 2 Kgs 1:1; 3. Army of Syria invades Israel, but peacefully withdraws through the tact of the prophet Elisha, 2 Kgs 6:8–23. Samaria besieged, 2 Kgs 6:24–33; 7; city of, taken, and the people carried to Assyria, 2 Kgs 17. The land recolonized, 2 Kgs 17:24.

The remnant that remained after the ablebodied were carried into captivity affiliated with the kingdom of Judah, 2 Chron 30:17–26; 34:6; 35:18.

Prophecies concerning. Of captivity, famine, and judgments, 1 Kgs 14:15, 16; 17:1; 20:13–28; 2 Kgs 7:1, 2, 17; 8:1; Isa 7:8; 8:4–8; 9:8–21; 17:3–11; 28:1–8; Hos 1:1–9; 2:1–13; chapters 4; 8; 9; 10; 11:5, 6; 12:7–14; 13; Amos 2:6–16; chapters 3–9.

Of restoration, Hos 2:14–23; 11:9–11; 13:13, 14; 14:8.

Of the reunion of the ten tribes and Judah, Jer 3:18; Ezk 37:16–22.

See the following:

5. Judah. The nation composed of the tribes of Judah and Benjamin, called *Judah,* Isa 11:12, 13; Jer 4:3, and *Jews,* (see *Jews,*) ruled by the descendants of David.

In the historical books of the Kings and the Chronicles the nation is called *Judah,* but in the prophecies it is frequently referred to as *Israel,* as in Isa 49:7.

List of rulers and the periods of time over which they reigned:

1. Rehoboam, 17 years.
2. Abijah, or Abijam, three years.
3. Asa, 41 years.
4. Jehoshaphat, 25 years.
5. Jehoram, eight years.
6. Ahaziah, one year.

Athaliah's usurpation, six years.

7. Joash, or Jehoash, 40 years.
8. Amaziah, 29 years.
9. Uzziah, or Azariah, 52 years.
10. Jotham, 16 years.
11. Ahaz, 16 years.
12. Hezekiah, 29 years.
13. Manasseh, 55 years.
14. Amon, two years.
15. Josiah, 31 years.
16. Jehoahaz, Josiah's son, three months.
17. Jehoiakim, Josiah's son, 11 years.
18. Jehoiachin, or Jeconiah, Jehoiakim's son, three months.
19. Zedekiah, or Mattaniah, Josiah's son, 11 years.

For the history of the above kings see under each name.

Rehoboam succeeds Solomon. As a result of his arbitrary policy ten tribes rebel, 1 Kgs 12. Other circumstances of his reign, 1 Kgs 14:21–31; 2 Chron 10; 11; 12. Death of Rehoboam, 1 Kgs 14:31. Abijam's wicked reign, 1 Kgs 15:1–8; 2 Chron 13. Asa's good reign, 1 Kgs 15:9–24; 2 Chron 14; 15; 16. Asa makes an alliance with Ben-hadad, king of Syria, to make war against Israel, 1 Kgs 15:16–24. Jehoshaphat succeeds Asa, 1 Kgs 15:24; 2 Chron 17; 18; 19; 20; 21:1; joins Ahab against the king of Syria, 1 Kgs 22. See *Jehoshaphat, 3.* Jehoram, called also *Joram,* reigns in the stead of his father, Jehoshaphat, 2 Kgs 8:16–24; 2 Chron 21. Edom revolts, 2 Kgs 8:20–22. Ahaziah, called also *Jehoahaz,* 2 Chron 21:17; succeeds Jehoram, 2 Kgs 8:24–29; 2 Chron 22; killed by Jehu, 2 Kgs 9:27–29; 2 Chron 22:8, 9. Athaliah, his mother, succeeds him, 2 Kgs 11:1–16; 2 Chron 22:10–12; 23:1–14. Joash succeeds Athaliah, 2 Kgs 11:21; 12:1–21; 2 Chron 24. The temple repaired, 2 Kgs 12. Amaziah reigns, and Judah is invaded by the king of Israel; Jerusalem is taken and the sacred things of the temple carried away, 2 Kgs 14:1–20; 2 Chron 25. Azariah, called also *Uzziah,* succeeds him, 2 Kgs 14:21, 22; 15:1–7; 2 Chron 26. Jotham succeeds Uzziah, 2 Kgs 15:7, 32–38; 2 Chron 27. Rezin, king of Syria, invades Judah, 2 Kgs 15:37. Jotham is succeeded by Ahaz, 2 Kgs 16:1; 2 Chron 28. Judah is invaded by kings of Israel and Syria; Ahaz hires the king of Assyria to make war on Israel and Syria, 2 Kgs 16:5–9. Ahaz changes the design of the altar in the temple, 2 Kgs 16:10–18. Hezekiah succeeds Ahaz, 2 Kgs 16:19, 20; 2 Chron chapters 29–32. His good reign, 2 Kgs 18:1–8. He revolts from the sovereignty of the king of Assyria, 2 Kgs 18:7. King of Assyria invades Judah, and blasphemes the God of Judah; his army overthrown, 2 Kgs 18:9–37; 19. Hezekiah's sickness and miraculous recovery, 2 Kgs 20. Succeeded by Manasseh, 2 Kgs 20:21; 2 Chron 33:1–19. Manasseh's wicked reign, 2 Kgs 21:1–18. Amon succeeds Manasseh on the throne, 2 Kgs 21:18–26; 2 Chron 33:20–25. Josiah, succeeds Amon; the temple is repaired; the scroll containing the law recovered; religious revival follows; and the king dies, 2 Kgs 22; 23:1–30; 2 Chron 34; 35. Josiah is succeeded by Jehoahaz, who reigned three months, is deposed by the king of Egypt, and the land put under taxation, 2 Kgs 23:30–35; 2 Chron 36:1–3. Jehoiakim is elevated to the throne; becomes tributary to Nebuchadnezzar for three years; rebels; is conquered and carried to Babylon, 2 Kgs 24:1–6; 2 Chron 36:4–8. Jehoiachin is made king; suffers invasion and is carried to Babylon, 2 Kgs 24:8–16; 2 Chron 36:9, 10. Zedekiah is made king by Nebuchadnezzar; rebels; Nebuchadnezzar invades Judah, takes Jerusalem, and carries the people to Babylon, destroys the temple, 2 Kgs 24:17–20; 25; 2 Chron 36:11–21. The poorest of the people were left to occupy the country, and were joined by fragments of the army of Judah, the dispersed Israelites in other lands, and the king's daughters, 2 Kgs 25:12, 22, 23; Jer 39:10; 40:7–12; 41:10; 52:16. Gedaliah appointed governor over, 2 Kgs 25:22. His administration favorable to the people, 2 Kgs 25:23, 24; Jer 40:7–12. Conspired against and killed by Ishmael, 2 Kgs 25:25; Jer 40:13–16; 41:1–3. Ishmael attempts to betray the people to the Ammonites, Jer 41:1–18. The people, in fear, take refuge in Egypt, 2 Kgs 25:26; Jer 41:13–18; 42:13–18.

Captivity of. Great wickedness the cause of their troubles, Ezk 5; 6; 7; 16; 23:22–44. Live in Babylon, Dan 5:13; 6:13; Jer 52:28–30; by the Chebar Canal, Ezk 1:1; 10:15. Patriotism of, Ps 137. Plotted against by Haman, Esther 3. Are saved by Esther, Esther chapters 4–9. Cyrus decrees their restoration, 2 Chron 36:22, 23; Ezra 1:1–4. Cyrus directs the rebuilding of the temple, and the restoration of the vessels which had been taken to Babylon, 2 Chron 36:22, 23; Ezra 1:3–11. Proclamation renewed by Darius and Ar-ta-xerxes, Ezra 6:1–14. Temple rebuilt and dedicated, Ezra chapters 3–6. Ar-ta-xerxes issues proclamation to restore the temple service, Ezra 7. Priests and Levites authorized to return, Ezra 8. Corruptions among the returned captives; their reform, Ezra 9; 10.

Nehemiah is commissioned to lead the remainder of the captivity, 49,942, back to Canaan, Neh 2; 7:5–67; Ps 85; 87; 107; 126. Wall of Jerusalem rebuilt and dedicated, Neh chapters 2–6; 12. The law read and expounded, Neh 8. Solemn feast is kept; priests are purified; and the covenant sealed, Neh chapters 8–10. One-tenth of the people, to be determined by lot, volunteer to live in Jerusalem, and the remaining nine parts live in other cities, Neh 11. List of the priests and Levites who accompanied Zerubbabel, Neh 12. Nehemiah reforms various abuses, Neh 13. Expect a Messiah, Lk 3:15. Many accept Jesus as the Christ, Jn 2:23; 10:42; 11:45; 12:11; Acts 21:20. Reject Jesus, see *Jesus, Rejected.*

Prophecies Concerning. Of their rejection of the Messiah, Isa 8:14, 15; 49:5, 7; 52:14, 15; 53:1–3; Zech 11; 13; Mt 21:33; 22:1.

Of war and other judgments: Deut 28:49–57; 2 Kgs 20:17, 18; 21:12–15; 22:15–17; 23:26, 27; Isa 1:1–24; 3; 4:1; 5; 6:9–13; 7:17–25; 8:14–22; 9; 10:12; 22:1–14; 28:14–22; 29:1–10; 30:1–17; 31:1–3; 32:9–14; Jer 1:11–16; 4:5–31; 6; 7:8–34; 8; 9:9–26; 10:17–22; 11:9–23; 13:8–27; 14:14–18; 15:1–14; 16; 17:1–4; 18:15–17; 19; 20:5; 21:3–7; 22:24–30; 25:8–38; chapters 28; 34; 37; 38:1–3; 42:13–22; chapters 43; 44; 45; Lam 5:6; Ezk 4; 5; 11:7–12; chapters 12; 15; 16; 17; 19; 22:13–22; 23:22–35; 24; 33:21–29; Dan 9:26–27; Joel 2:1–17; Amos 2:4; 5; Mic 2:10; 3; 4:8–10; Hab 1:6–11; Zeph 1; Zech 11; 14:1–3; Mal 4:1; Mt 21:33, 34; 23:35–38; 24:2, 14–42; Mk 13:1–13; Lk 13:34, 35; 19:43, 44; 21:5–25; 23:28–31; Rev 1:7.

Dispersion of: Isa 24:1; Jer 9:16; Ezk 4:13; 5:10, 12; 20:23, 24; 36:19; Dan 9:7; Hos 9:17; Joel 3:6; Amos 9:9; Jn 7:35; Acts 2:5.

Of blessing and restoration: Isa 1:25–27; 2:1–5; 4:2–6; 11:11–13; 25; 26:1, 2, 12–19; 27:13; 29:18–24; 30:18–26; 32:15–20; 33:13–24; 35; 37:31, 32; 40:2, 9; 41:27; 44; 49:13–23; 51; 52:1–12; 60; 61:4–9; 62; 66:5–22; Jer 3:14–18; 4:3–18; 12:14–16; 23:3; 24:1–7; 29:1–14; 30:3–22; 32:36–44; 33; 44:28; Ezk 14:22, 23; 16:59–63; 20:40, 41; 36; 37:12, 21; Dan 11:30–45; 12:1; Joel 3; Amos 9:9–15; Obd 1:17–21; Mic 2:12, 13; 5:3; Zeph 2:7; Zech 1:14–21; 2; 8; 10:5–12; 12; 13; 14:3–21; Mal 3:4; Rom 11; 2 Cor 3:16; Rev 7:4–8.

See *Jews.*

ISRAELITES See *Israel.*

ISSACHAR 1. Son of Jacob, Gen 30:18; Ex 1:1–4; 1 Chron 2:1, 2. Jacob's prophetic benedictions on, Gen 49:14, 15. In the time of David, 1 Chron 7:1, 5. See *Tribe of,* below.

2. Tribe of. Military forces of, taken at Sinai, Num 1:20–46; 2:3–31; on the plains of Moab, Num 26:23–25. Moses' blessing on, Deut 33:18, 19. Place in march and camp, Num 2:3–31; 10:14, 15. Parts of Canaan allotted to, Josh 19:17–23, with Josh 17:10, 11.

Join Deborah and Barak in war against Sisera, Judg 5:15. Insurgents from, joined David, 1 Chron 12:24–37, 40. Join with the kingdom of Judah after the conquest of the land by, 2 Chron 30:17–19. For things common to all the tribes, see *Israel, Tribes of.*

ISSHIAH 1. A descendant of Issachar, 1 Chron 7:3.

2. A disaffected Israelite who joined David at Ziklag, 1 Chron 12:3–7.

3. A Levite and descendant of Uzziel, 1 Chron 23:20; 24:24, 25.

4. A Levite, son of Rehabiah, 1 Chron 24:21.

ISSHIJAH One of the sons of Harim, Ezra 10:31.

ITALY Acts 27:6; Heb 13:24, 25. Aquila and Priscilla expelled from, Acts 18:2, 3.

ITCH Lev 22:22; Deut 28:27.

ITHAI Called also *Ittai.* One of David's valiant men, 2 Sam 23:24–39; 1 Chron 11:26–47.

ITHAMAR Son of Aaron, Ex 6:23; 28:1; 1 Chron 6:3. Charged with duties of the Tabernacle, Ex 38:21; Num 4:28; 7:8. Forbidden to mourn the death of his brothers, Nadab and Abihu, Lev 10:6, 7. Descendants of, 1 Chron 24:1–19.

ITHIEL 1. A Benjaminite, Neh 11:7–9.

2. An unidentified person mentioned in Prov 30:1.

ITHLAH A city of Dan, Josh 19:41–46.

ITHMAH A Moabite, 1 Chron 11:26–47.

ITHNAN A town in the extreme south of Judah, Josh 15:21–32.

ITHRA Called also *Jether.* Father of Amasa, 2 Sam 17:25; 1 Chron 2:17.

ITHRAN 1. Son of Dishon, Gen 36:26; 1 Chron 1:41.

2. Son of Zophah, 1 Chron 7:36, 37.

ITHREAM Son of David, 2 Sam 3:5; 1 Chron 3:3.

ITHRITES Patronymic of the family of Jether, 2 Sam 23:24–39; 1 Chron 2:53.

ITINERARY Of the Israelites, Num 33; Deut 10:6, 7.

See *Israel.*

ITTAI 1. One of David's commanders, 2 Sam 18:2. Supports David against Absalom, 2 Sam 15:19–22; 18:2, 5.

2. One of David's warriors, called *Ithai,* 2 Sam 23:24–39; 1 Chron 11:31.

ITUREA Small province in the northwest of Palestine, Lk 3:1. See also 1 Chron 1:31; 5:19.

IVORY Song 5:14; 7:4; Ezk 27:15. Exported from Tarshish, 1 Kgs 10:22; 2 Chron 9:21. Ahab's palace made of, 1 Kgs 22:39. Other houses made of, Ps 45:8; Amos 3:15. Other articles made of: Rev 18:12; thrones, 1 Kgs 10:18; 2 Chron 9:17; beds, Amos 6:4.

IVVAH A city in Samaria conquered by the Assyrians, 2 Kgs 18:34; 19:13; Isa 37:13.

IYEABARIM A camping place of the Israelites, Num 21:11; 33:44.

IZHAR 1. Son of Kohath, Ex 6:18, 21; 1 Chron 6:2, 18, 33–38; 23:12, 18.

2. Son of Asshur, 1 Chron 4:7.

IZLIAH A Benjaminite, 1 Chron 8:17, 18.

IZRAHIAH Grandson of Tola, 1 Chron 7:3.

IZRI Perhaps the same as *Zeri.* Leader of the fourth division of Levitical singers, 1 Chron 25:9–31.

J

JAAKAN Called also *Akan.* Son of Ezer, Gen 36:27; 1 Chron 1:42.
See *Bene-jaakan.*

JA-AKOBAH Descendant of Simeon, 1 Chron 4:34–39.

JAALA Called also *Jaalah.* A descendant of one of Solomon's officials, returned from exile, Ezra 2:56; Neh 7:58.

JAARESHIAH Son of Jeroham, 1 Chron 8:26, 27.

JA-ASIEL 1. One of David's warriors, 1 Chron 11:26–47.
2. Son of Abner, 1 Chron 27:16–22.

JAASU Of the family of Bani, Ezra 10:34–42.

JA-AZANIAH 1. Called also *Jezaniah.* A captain who joined Gedaliah at Mizpah, 2 Kgs 25:23; Jer 40:8.
2. A Rechabite, Jer 35:3.
3. An idolatrous zealot, Ezk 8:11.
4. A wicked officer of Judah, Ezk 11:1–13.

JA-AZIAH A descendant of Merari, 1 Chron 24:26, 27.

JA-AZIEL A Levite musician, 1 Chron 15:18.

JABAL Son of Lamech and a shepherd, Gen 4:20.

JABBOK A river on the east of Jordan, the northern boundary of the Ammonites, Num 21:24; Judg 11:13; of the Reubenites and the Gadites, Josh 12:2; Deut 3:16. The northern boundary of the Amorites, Judg 11:21, 22. Jacob wrestles at, Gen 32:22–24.

JABESH 1. Father of Shallum, 2 Kgs 15:10, 13.
2. See *Jabesh-gilead.*

JABESH-GILEAD A city east of the Jordan, Judg 21:8–15. Besieged by the Ammonites, 1 Sam 11:1–11. Saul and his sons buried at, 1 Sam 31:11–13; 1 Chron 10:11, 12; 2 Sam 2:4. Bones of Saul and his sons removed, by David, and buried at Zelah, 2 Sam 21:12–14.

JABEZ 1. A city of Judah, 1 Chron 2:55.
2. The head of a family, 1 Chron 4:9, 10.

JABIN Names of two kings of Hazor, Josh 11:1–14; Judg 4:2, 3, 7, 17, 23, 24; Ps 83:9.

JABNEEL 1. A city in Judah, Josh 15:10, 11.
2. A city of Naphtali, Josh 19:33.

JABNEH A Philistine city, 2 Chron 26:6; probably identical to *Jabneel, 1.*

JACAN A Gadite, 1 Chron 5:13.

JACHIN 1. Son of Simeon, Gen 46:8–14; Ex 6:15; Num 26:12–14. Called *Jarib,* 1 Chron 4:24.
2. Name of a pillar, 1 Kgs 7:16–22; 2 Chron 3:17. See *Boaz, 2.*
3. A priest, who returned from exile to Jerusalem, 1 Chron 9:10; 10; Neh 11:10–14.
4. A priest, head of one of priestly groups, 1 Chron 24:7–18.

JACINTH A precious stone, Ex 39:12; Rev 21:18–20.

JACKAL A carnivorous animal, Mal 1:2, 3; plundering, Ps 63:10.

JACKAL'S WELL A well at Jerusalem, Neh 2:13.

JACOB Son of Isaac, and twin brother of Esau, Gen 25:24–26; Josh 24:4; 1 Chron 1:34; Acts 7:8. Ancestor of Jesus, Mt 1:2. Given in answer to prayer, Gen 25:21. Obtains Esau's birthright for a portion of stew, Gen 25:29–34; Heb 12:16. Fraudulently obtains his father's blessing, Gen 27:1–29; Heb 11:20. Esau seeks to kill, escapes to Paddan-aram, Gen 27:41–46; 28:1–5; Hos 12:12. His vision of the ladder, Gen 28:10–22. God confirms the covenant of Abraham to, Gen 28:13–22; 35:9–15; 1 Chron 16:12–18.

Lives in Haran with his uncle, Laban, Gen 29; 30; Hos 12:12. Serves 14 years for Leah and Rachel, Gen 29:15–20; Hos 12:12. Sharp practice of, with the flocks and herds of Laban, Gen 30:31–43. Dissatisfied with Laban's treatment and returns to the land of Canaan, Gen 31. Meets angels of God on the trip, and calls the place "God's territory," Gen 32:1, 2. Dreads to meet Esau; sends him presents; wrestles with an angel, Gen 32. Name of, changed to Israel, Gen 32:28; 35:10. Reconciliation of, with Esau, Gen 33:4. Travels to Succoth, Gen 33:17; to Shechem, where he purchases a parcel of ground from Hamor, and erects an altar, Gen 33:18–20. His daughter, Dinah, raped, Gen 34. Returns to Bethel, where he builds an altar, Gen 35:1–7. Deborah, Rebekah's nurse, dies, and is buried at Bethel, Gen 35:8. Travels to Ephrath; Benjamin is born to; Rachel dies, and is "buried near the road to Ephrath, (also called Bethlehem)," Gen 35:16–19;

48:7. Erects a monument at Rachel's grave, Gen 35:20. The incest of his son, Reuben, and his concubine, Bilhah, Gen 35:22. List of the names of his twelve sons, Gen 35:23–26. Returns to Kiriatharba, the city of his father, Gen 35:27. Settles in the land of Canaan, Gen 37:1. His partiality for his son, Joseph, and the consequent jealousy of his other sons, Gen 37:3, 4. Joseph's prophetic dream concerning, Gen 37:9–11. His grief over the loss of Joseph, Gen 37:34, 35. Sends into Egypt to buy grain, Gen 42:1, 2; 43:1–14. His grief over the detention of Simeon, and the demand for Benjamin to be taken into Egypt, Gen 42:36. His love for Benjamin, Gen 43:14; 44:29. Hears that Joseph still lives, Gen 45:26–28.

Moves to Egypt, Gen 46:1–7; 1 Sam 12:8; Ps 105: 23; Acts 7:14, 15. List of his children and grandchildren who went into Egypt, Gen 46:8–27. Meets Joseph, Gen 46:28–34. Pharaoh receives him, and is blessed by Jacob, Gen 47:1–10. The land of Goshen assigned to, Gen 47:11, 12, 27. Lives in Egypt 17 years, Gen 47:28. Exacts a promise from Joseph to bury him with his fathers, Gen 47:29–31. His benediction upon Joseph and his two sons, Gen 48:15–22. Gives the land of the Amorites to Joseph, Gen 48:22; Jn 4:5, 6. His final prophetic benedictions on his sons: On Reuben, Gen 49:3, 4; Simeon and Levi, Gen 49:5–7; Judah, Gen 49:8–12; Zebulun, Gen 49:13; Issachar, Gen 49:14, 15; Dan, Gen 49:16–18; Gad, Gen 49:19; Asher, Gen 49:20; Naphtali, Gen 49:21; Joseph, Gen 49:22–26; Benjamin, Gen 49:27. Charges his sons to bury him in the field of Mach-pelah, Gen 49:29, 30. Death of, Gen 49: 33. Body of, embalmed, Gen 50:2. Forty days mourning for, Gen 50:3. Burial of, Gen 50:4–13. Descendants of, Gen 29:31–35; 30:1–24; 35:18, 22–26; 46:8–27; Ex 1:1–5; 1 Chron chapters 2–9.

Prophecies concerning himself and descendants, Gen 25:33; 27:27–29; 28:10–15; Gen 31:3; 35:9–12; 46:3, 4; Deut 1:8; Ps 105:10, 11. His wealth, Gen 36: 6–8. Well of, Jn 4:5–30.

JADDAI One who divorced his heathen wife, Ezra 10:43.

JAEL Wife of Heber, and killer of Sisera, Judg 4:17–22; 5:6, 24.

JAGUR A town of Judah, Josh 15:21–32.

JAHATH Name of five Levites, 1 Chron 4:2; 6:19–21, 39–43; 23:10, 11; 24:22; 2 Chron 34:12.

JAHAZ Called also *Jahzah*. A Levitical city in Reuben, taken from the Moabites, Josh 13:18; 21: 36, 37; 1 Chron 6:78, 79; Isa 15:4; Jer 48:21. Sihon defeated at, Num 21:23; Deut 2:32; Judg 11:20.

JAHAZIEL 1. A disaffected Israelite who joined David at Ziklag, 1 Chron 12:3–7.

2. A priest, 1 Chron 16:6.

3. Son of Hebron, 1 Chron 23:19; 24:23.

4. A Levite, and prophet, 2 Chron 20:14.

5. Father of a leader among the exiles who returned from Babylon, Ezra 8:2–14.

JAHDAI A descendant of Caleb, 1 Chron 2: 47.

JAHDI-EL Heard of a clan of Manasseh, 1 Chron 5:24.

JAHDO Descendent of Buz, 1 Chron 5:14.

JAHLEEL Son of Zebulun, Gen 46:8–14; Num 26:26, 27.

JAHMAI Son of Tola, 1 Chron 7:2.

JAHZAH See *Jahaz*.

JAHZEEL Called also *Jahzi-el*. A son of Naphtali, Gen 46:23–25; Num 26:48–50; 1 Chron 7: 13.

JAHZEIAH A returned exile, Ezra 10:15.

JAHZERAH A priest, 1 Chron 9:12.

JAHZIEL See *Jahzeel*.

JAILER Of Philippi, converted, Acts 16:27–34.

JAIR 1. Son of Manasseh. Founder of a number of cities in Gilead, Num 32:41; Deut 3:14; Josh 13:30; 1 Kgs 4:8–19; 1 Chron 2:22, 23.

2. A judge of Israel, Judg 10:3–5.

3. A Benjaminite, Esther 2:5.

4. Father of Elhanan, 1 Chron 20:5.

JAIRUS A rabbi of the synagogue in Capernaum, Mt 9:18. Daughter of, restored to life, Mt 9: 18, 23–26; Mk 5:22–43; Lk 8:41–56.

JAKEH Father of Agur, Prov 30:1.

JAKIM 1. A Benjaminite, 1 Chron 8:19–21.

2. Head of a priestly group in the tabernacle service, 1 Chron 24:7–18.

JALAM Son of Esau, Gen 36:5, 18; 1 Chron 1: 35.

JALON Son of Ezrah, 1 Chron 4:17.

JAMBRES An Egyptian magician, Ex 7:11; 2 Tim 3:8, 9.

JAMES 1. An apostle. Son of Zebedee and Salome, Mt 4:21; 27:56. See *Salome*. Brother of John, and a fisherman, Lk 5:10. Called to be an apostle, Mt 4:21, 22; 10:2–4; Mk 1:19, 20; Lk 6:14–16; Acts 1:14. Called "Son of thunder" by Jesus, Mk 3: 17. An intimate companion of Jesus, and present with him: At the great draught of fishes, Lk 5:10; the healing of Peter's mother-in-law, Mk 1:29, 30; the raising of Jairus' daughter, Mk 5:37; Lk 8:51; the transfiguration of Jesus, Mt 17:1; Mk 9:2; Lk 9: 28; in Gethsemane, Mt 26:37; Mk 14:33. Asks Jesus concerning his second coming, Mk 13:3, 4. Bigotry of, Lk 9:54. Civil ambitions of, Mt 20:20–23; Mk 10:35–41. Present at the sea of Galilee when Jesus revealed himself to the disciples after his resurrection, Jn 21:2. Martyred, Acts 12:2.

2. James the Younger, Mk 15:40; son of Alphaeus, Mt 10:2–4; Mk 3:16–19; Lk 6:14–16; Acts 1:14; and son of Mary, sister of the mother of Jesus, Mt 27:56; Mk 15:40; Lk 24:10. He was one of the 12 apostles. He had a brother, Joseph, or Joses, Mt 27: 56; Mk 15:40.

3. Brother of Jesus, Mt 13:55; Mk 6:2, 3. He was not one of the twelve, did not at first believe, Jn 7: 5; but did afterward, Acts 1:13, 14. Saw the risen Lord, 1 Cor 15:7; was called an apostle, Gal 1:19; was prominent in the Jerusalem church, Gal 1:18, 19; 2:12; and presided at the first council there, Acts 15:13; 21:18. He was the author of the epistle of James, Jas 1:1. Some students, especially those who do not accept Matthew 13:55 literally, identify James the Younger and James the brother of Jesus.

See Bible dictionaries and encyclopedias.

4. Father of Judas, Lk 6:14–16; Acts 1:14.

JAMIN 1. Son of Simeon, Gen 46:8–14; Ex 6:15; Num 26:12–14; 1 Chron 4:24.

2. Descendant of Hezron, 1 Chron 2:27.

3. A priest who explained the law to the exiles who returned to Jerusalem, Neh 8:7, 8.

JAMLECH Descendant of Simeon, 1 Chron 4:34–39.

JANAI A Gadite leader, 1 Chron 5:12.

JANIM A city of Judah, Josh 15:48–62.

JANNAI Ancestor of Joseph, Lk 3:23–38.

JANNES An Egyptian magician, Ex 7:11; 2 Tim 3:8, 9.

JANOAH 1. A city on the border of Ephraim, Josh 16:5–7.

2. A city of Naphtali, 2 Kgs 15:29.

JANUARY See *Calendar.*

JAPHETH Son of Noah, Gen 5:32; 6:9, 10; 9:18; 10:21. His life preserved at the time of the flood, Gen 7:13; 9:18. Prudence of, on the occasion of Noah's drunkenness, Gen 9:23, 26, 27. Descendants of, Gen 10:2–5; 1 Chron 1:5–7.

JAPHIA 1. King of Lachish, Josh 10:3.

2. A town of Zebulun, Josh 19:12.

3. A son of David, 2 Sam 5:14–16; 1 Chron 3:6–8; 14:4–7.

JAPHLET Grandson of Beriah, 1 Chron 7:32.

JAPHLETITES A tribe living in the territory allotted to the tribes of Joseph, Josh 16:1–4.

JAR Made of clay, Jer 19:1, 10; 48:12. Used by Gideon in his battle with the Midianites, Judg 7:10–20.

See *Bottle.*

JARAH Son of Ahaz, 1 Chron 9:42.

JARED A descendant of Seth, Gen 5:15–20; 1 Chron 1:1–4. An ancestor of Jesus, Lk 3:23–38.

JARHA An Egyptian, 1 Chron 2:34, 35.

JARIB 1. Son of Simeon, 1 Chron 4:24.

2. A Levite leader during the captivity, Ezra 8:16.

3. A priest who married a heathen wife, Ezra 10:16–19.

JARMUTH 1. A city in Judah, Josh 10:3, 5, 22, 23; 12:8–24; 15:33–36; Neh 11:25–30.

2. A Levitical city in Issachar, Josh 21:28, 29.

JAROAH A descendant of Gad, 1 Chron 5:14.

JASHEN Father of one or more of David's heroes, 2 Sam 23:24–39.

JASHOBEAM 1. Also called *Adino* and *Josheb-basshebeth.* David's leading warrior, 2 Sam 23:8; 1 Chron 11:11; 27:2, 3.

2. A Korahite Levite, 1 Chron 12:3–7.

JASHUB 1. Son of Issachar, Num 26:23–25; 1 Chron 7:1. Called *Iob* in Gen 46:8–14.

2. Of the family of Bani, Ezra 10:29.

JASON A Christian at Thessalonica, Acts 17:5–9; and probably Paul's relative, mentioned in Romans 16:21.

JASPER A precious stone, Ezk 28:13; set in the high priest's chestpiece, Ex 28:20; 39:13. Walls of new Jerusalem made of, Rev 21:11, 18–20.

JATHNI-EL Son of Meshelemiah, 1 Chron 26:2, 3.

JATTIR A Levitical city in Judah, Josh 15:48–62; 21:9–16; 1 Sam 30:27–31; 1 Chron 6:58, 59.

JAVAN 1. Son of Japheth, Gen 10:2, 4; 1 Chron 1:5–7.

2. A city in Asia Minor, Isa 66:19; Ezk 27:13.

3. A city, possibly in Arabia, Ezk 27:19.

JAVELIN A heavy lance, Job 39:21–23; 41:29; Ezk 39:9; used by Goliath, 1 Sam 17:4–7.

JAWS FIGURATIVE. Of death, Jon 2:6.

JAZER A city of refuge east of the Jordan, Josh 21:38, 39. Taken from the Amorites, Num 21:31, 32; 32:1, 3, 4, 34–36; Josh 13:25. Controlled by Moabites, Isa 16:8, 9; Jer 48:32.

JAZIZ A shepherd, 1 Chron 27:31.

JEALOUSY Prov 6:34; 27:4; Eccl 4:4; Song 8:6. Law concerning, when husband is jealous of his wife, Num 5:11–31. Forbidden, Rom 13:12, 13.

Attributed to God, Ex 20:5; 34:13, 14; Deut 4:24; 5:9, 10; 29:20; 32:16, 21; Ps 79:5; Isa 30:1, 2; 31:1, 3; Ezk 16:42; 23:25; 38:19; Zeph 1:18; 3:8; Zech 1:14.

See *Anthropomorphisms.*

A spirit of emulation, Rom 10:19; 11:11.

See *Emulation; Envy.*

INSTANCES OF. Cain, of Abel, Gen 4:5, 6, 8. Sarah, of Hagar, Gen 16:5. Joseph's brothers, of Joseph, Gen 37:4–11, 18–28. Saul, of David, 1 Sam 18:8–30; 19:8–24; 20:24–34. Joab, of Abner, 2 Sam 3:24–27. Nathan, of Adonijah, 1 Kgs 1:24–26. Ephraimites, of Gideon, Judg 8:1; of Jephthah, Judg 12:1. The brother of the prodigal son, Lk 15:25–32. Sectional, between Israel, and the tribe of Judah, 2 Sam 19:41–43.

JEATHERAI Descendant of Gershom, 1 Chron 6:19–21.

JEBERECHIAH Father of Zechariah, Isa 8:2.

JEBUS See *Jerusalem.*

JEBUSITES One of the tribes of Canaan, Deut 7:1. Land of, given to Abraham and his descendants, Gen 15:19–21; Ex 3:8, 17; 23:23, 24; 33:2; 34:10, 11; Deut 20:17. Conquered by Joshua, Joshua chapters 10–12; and 24:11; by David, 2 Sam 5:6–9. Jerusalem within the territory of, Josh 18:21–28. Not exterminated, but intermarry with the Israelites, Judg 3:5, 6; Ezra 9:1, 2; 10:16–44. Slaves under Solomon, 1 Kgs 9:20, 21.

JECOLIAH Mother of Azariah, 2 Kgs 15:1, 2; 2 Chron 26:3.

JECONIAH See *Jehoiachin.*

JEDAIAH 1. Descendant of Simeon, 1 Chron 4:34–39.

2. A returned exile, Neh 3:10.

3. Leader of a priestly division, 1 Chron 24:7–18.

4. Ancestor of returned exiles, Ezra 2:36–39; Neh 7:39–42. Possibly the same as 3, above.

5. A priest who returned from exile, 1 Chron 9:10, 11; Neh 11:10–14; 12:1–7, 12–21.

6. Another priest, who returned from Babylon with Nehemiah, Neh 12:1–7, 12–21.

7. Returned exile bearing gifts, Zech 6:10, 11, 14. Possibly identical with 5 or 6, above.

8. An exile bearing gifts of gold and silver, Zech 6:10–14.

JEDIA-EL 1. Son of Benjamin, 1 Chron 7:6, 10, 11.

2. Son of Shimri, 1 Chron 11:26–47.

3. A Manassite officer, who joined David at Ziklag, 1 Chron 12:20.

4. Son of Meshelemiah, 1 Chron 26:2.

JEDIDAH Wife of Amon, 2 Kgs 22:1, 2.

JEDIDIAH A name given to Solomon, 2 Sam 12:25.

JEDUTHUN A temple musician, 1 Chron 16:41; 25:1. Called *Ethan,* 1 Chron 6:44–47; 15:17.

JEGAR-SAHADUTHA Called also *Galeed.* A heap of stones on Mount Gilead, Gen 31:47, 48.

JEHALLELEL 1. Descendant of Judah, 1 Chron 4:16.

2. Descendant of Merari, 2 Chron 29:12–14.

JEHDEIAH 1. Son of Shubael, 1 Chron 24:20.

2. One of David's overseers, 1 Chron 27:30.

JEHEZKEL A priest, and head of the twentieth group in the tabernacle service, 1 Chron 24:16.

JEHIAH A Levite, and guard for the ark, 1 Chron 15:24.

JEHIEL 1. A Levite doorkeeper, 1 Chron 15:18; 16:5.

2. A Gershonite Levite, 1 Chron 23:8, 9; 29:8.

3. A tutor of David's sons, 1 Chron 27:32.

4. Son of Jehoshaphat, 2 Chron 21:2.

5. A Levite overseer in the temple, 2 Chron 31:12, 13.

6. A priest who gave extraordinary offerings for the passover, 2 Chron 35:8.

7. Father of Obadiah, Ezra 8:2–14.

8. Father of Shechaniah, Ezra 10:2.

9. A priest who married a heathen wife, Ezra 10:21.

10. Citizen who married a heathen wife, Ezra 10:26.

JEHIELI Son of Ladan, 1 Chron 26:20–22. Possibly identical to *Jehiel, 2.*

JEHIZKIAH Son of Shallum, 2 Chron 28:12.

JEHOADDAH Son of Ahaz, 1 Chron 8:36.

JEHO-ADDAN Or *Jeho-addin,* mother of Amaziah, 2 Kgs 14:2; 2 Chron 25:1.

JEHOAHAZ 1. Son of Jehu, and king of Israel, 2 Kgs 10:35; 13:1–8.

2. Son of Jehoram, king of Judah, 2 Chron 22:1. See *Ahaziah, 1.*

3. Called also *Shallum.* King of Judah, and successor of Josiah, 2 Kgs 23:30–32; 1 Chron 3:15; 2 Chron 36:1; Jer 22:11. Wicked reign of, 2 Kgs 23:31, 32. Pharaoh-Neco, king of Egypt, invades the kingdom of, defeats him, and takes him captive to Egypt, 2 Kgs 23:33–35; 2 Chron 36:3, 4. Prophecies concerning, Jer 22:10, 11, 12.

JEHOHANAN 1. A Temple guard, 1 Chron 26:2, 3.

2. A military commander under Jehoshaphat, whose army consisted of 280,000 men, 2 Chron 17:14, 15.

3. Father of Ishmael, 2 Chron 23:1.

4. A priest, Ezra 10:6. See *Johanan, 8.*

5. Son of Bebai, Ezra 10:28.

6. Son of Tobiah, Neh 6:18.

7. A priest among the exiles who returned from Babylon, Neh 12:12–21.

8. A singer in the Temple, Neh 12:42.

JEHOIACHIN King of Judah and successor to Jehoiakim, 2 Kgs 24:6–9; 2 Chron 36:8, 9. Called *Jeconiah,* 1 Chron 3:16; Jer 24:1. Called *Coniah,* Jer 22:24, 25; 37:1. Wicked reign of, 2 Chron 36:9. Nebuchadnezzar invades his kingdom, takes him captive to Babylon, 2 Kgs 24:10–16; 2 Chron 36:10; Esther 2:6; Jer 27:19–21; 29:1, 2. Confined in prison 37 years, 2 Kgs 25:27. Released from prison by Evil-merodach, and promoted above other kings, and honored until death, 2 Kgs 25:27–30; Jer 52:31–34. Prophecies concerning, Jer 22:24–30; 28:4. Sons of, 1 Chron 3:17, 18. Ancestor of Jesus, Mt 1:12.

JEHOIADA 1. Father of Benaiah, one of David's officers, 2 Sam 8:18; 23:20.

2. A high priest. Overthrows Athaliah, the usurping queen of Judah, and establishes Joash upon the throne, 2 Kgs 11; 2 Chron 23. Beneficial influence of, over Joash, 2 Kgs 12:2; 2 Chron 24:2, 22. Directs the repairs of the temple, 2 Kgs 12:4–16; 2 Chron 24:4–14. Death of, 2 Chron 24:15, 16.

3. A priest who led 3700 priests armed for war, 1 Chron 12:24–37.

4. Son of Benaiah, 1 Chron 27:34.

5. A priest mentioned in Jeremiah's letter to the captive Jews, Jer 29:26.

6. See *Joida, 2.*

JEHOIAKIM Called also *Eliakim.* King of Judah, 1 Chron 3:15. Ancestor of Jesus, Mt 1:11. Wicked reign and final overthrow of, 2 Kgs 23:34–37; 24:1–6; 2 Chron 36:4–8; Jer 22:13–19; 26:22, 23; 36; Dan 1:1, 2. Dies, and is succeeded by his son, Jehoiachin, 2 Kgs 24:6.

JEHOIARIB Or *Joiarib,* two priests bearing the same name, 1 Chron 9:10, 11; Neh 11:10–14; 1 Chron 24:7–18.

JEHONADAB See *Jonadab, 2.*

JEHONATHAN 1. A Levite sent to instruct the people in the law, 2 Chron 17:7–9.

2. An obscure priest, Neh 12:12–21.

JEHORAM Or *Joram.* 1. King of Judah, 1 Kgs 22:50; 2 Kgs 8:16; 1 Chron 3:10–14; 2 Chron 21:5. Ancestor of Jesus, Mt 1:8. Marries Athaliah, who influences his reign for evil, 2 Kgs 8:18, 19; 2 Chron 21:6–13.

Kills his brothers to strengthen himself in his sovereignty, 2 Chron 21:3, 4, 13. Edom revolts from, 2 Kgs 8:20–22; 2 Chron 21:8–10. Philistines and Arabs invade his territory, 2 Chron 21:16, 17. Death of, 2 Chron 21:18–20; 2 Kgs 8:24, 25. Prophecy concerning, 2 Chron 21:12–15.

2. A son of Ahab. See *Joram, 2.*

3. A priest commissioned to go through Israel and instruct the people in the law, 2 Chron 17:7–9.

JEHOSHABEATH See *Jehosheba.*

JEHOSHAPHAT 1. David's historian,

2 Sam 8:16; 20:24; 1 Kgs 4:3; 1 Chron 18:15.

2. One of Solomon's officials, 1 Kgs 4:8–19.

3. King of Judah. Succeeds Asa, 1 Kgs 15:24; 22:41; 1 Chron 3:10–14; 2 Chron 17:1; Mt 1:8. Strengthens himself against Israel, 2 Chron 17:2. Inaugurates a system of public instruction in the law, 2 Chron 17:7–9. His wise reign, 1 Kgs 22:43; 2 Chron 17:7–9; 19:3–11. His system of tribute, 2 Chron 17:11. His military forces and armament, 2 Chron 17:12–19. Joins Ahab in an invasion of Ramoth-gilead, 1 Kgs 22; 2 Chron 18. Rebuked by the prophet Jehu, 2 Chron 19:2. The allied forces of the Amorites, Moabites, and other tribes invade his territory, and are defeated by, 2 Chron 20. Builds ships for commerce with Tarshish, ships are destroyed, 1 Kgs 22:48, 49; 2 Chron 20:35–37. Joins Jehoram, king of Israel, in an invasion of the land of Moab, defeats the Moabites, 2 Kgs 3. Makes valuable gifts to the temple, 2 Kgs 12:18. Death of, 1 Kgs 22:50; 2 Chron 21:1. Religious zeal of, 1 Kgs 22:43, 46; 2 Chron 17:1–9; 19; 20:1–32; 22:9. Prosperity of, 1 Kgs 22:45, 48; 2 Chron chapters 17–20. Bequests of, to his children, 2 Chron 21:2–4.

4. Father of Jehu, 2 Kgs 9:2, 14.

5. A valley. Called *Valley Where Jehovah Judges,* Joel 3:2, 12, 14. Possibly the wide valley of Zech 14:4.

JEHOSHEBA Called also *Jehoshabeath.* Daughter of Jehoram, 2 Kgs 11:2, 3; 2 Chron 22:11.

JEHOVAH The name of God most frequently used in the Old Testament. Where the word *Yahweh* appears in the Hebrew text, the *Living Bible* renders it as *Jehovah* or *Lord.* It means "the self-existent One"; the key to this meaning is found in Ex 3:14.

JEHOVAH-NISSI "Jehovah is my flag." An altar, Ex 17:15, 16.

JEHOVAH-SHAMMAH "The Lord is there," the figurative name of Jerusalem in the millennium, Ezk 48:35.

JEHOZABAD 1. Son of Shomer, and one of the assassins of King Joash, 2 Kgs 12:21; 2 Chron 24:26.

2. Son of Obed-edom, 1 Chron 26:4, 5.

3. A Benjaminite officer who commanded 180,000 men, 2 Chron 17:18.

JEHOZADAK Called also *Josedech* and *Jozadak.* A priest of the exile, 1 Chron 6:4–15; Ezra 3:1, 2, 8; 5:1, 2; Neh 12:26; Hag 1:1, 12; Zech 6:11.

JEHU 1. The prophet who announced the wrath of Jehovah against Baasha, king of Israel, 1 Kgs 16:1, 12; 2 Chron 19:2; 20:34.

2. Son of Jehoshaphat, king of Israel, 1 Kgs 19:16; 2 Kgs 9:1–14. Religious zeal of, in killing idolaters, 2 Kgs 9:14–37; 10:1–28; 2 Chron 22:8, 9. His territory invaded by Hazael, king of Syria, 2 Kgs 10:32, 33. Prophecies concerning, 1 Kgs 19:17; 2 Kgs 10:30; 15:12; Hos 1:4, 5. Death of, 2 Kgs 10:35.

3. Son of Obed, 1 Chron 2:38.

4. A Simeonite, 1 Chron 4:34–39.

5. A Benjaminite, 1 Chron 12:3–7.

JEHUBBAH An Asherite, 1 Chron 7:34.

JEHUCAL Called also *Jucal.* Son of Shelemiah, Jer 37:3; 38:1.

JEHUD A city of Dan, Josh 19:41–46.

JEHUDI A representative of King Jehoiakim, Jer 36:14, 15, 21, 23.

JEHUEL Son of Heman, 2 Chron 29:12–14.

JEIEL 1. A Reubenite, 1 Chron 5:7, 8.

2. A Benjaminite, 1 Chron 8:29; 9:35–37.

3. One of David's heroes, 1 Chron 11:26–47.

4. A Levite, and musician in the Tabernacle service, 1 Chron 15:18, 21; 16:5.

5. A Levite, ancestor of Jahaziel, who encouraged Judah against their enemies, 2 Chron 20:14.

6. A secretary during the reign of Uzziah, 2 Chron 26:11.

7. A Levite leader who gave, with other leaders, 5,500 sheep, goats and oxen for sacrifice, 2 Chron 35:9.

8. A priest who was defiled by marriage to a heathen woman, Ezra 10:43.

JEKABZEEL A city in the south of Judah, Neh 11:25–30.

JEKAMEAM Son of Hebron, 1 Chron 23:19; 24:23.

JEKAMIAH A Judahite, son of Shallum, 1 Chron 2:41.

2. Son of Jeconiah, 1 Chron 3:17, 18.

JEKUTHIEL Son of Mered, 1 Chron 4:18.

JEMIMA Job's daughter, Job 42:13, 14.

JEMUEL Son of Simeon, Gen 46:8–14; Ex 6:15.

JEPHTHAH A judge of Israel. Illegitimate, and therefore not entitled to inherit his father's property, Judg 11:1, 2. Escapes the violence of his half-brothers, lives in the land of Tob, Judg 11:3. Recalled from the land of Tob by the leaders of Gilead, Judg 11:5. Made commander-in-chief, Judg 11:5–11; and made king of the land of Gilead, Judg 11:7–11. His message to the king of the Ammonites, Judg 11:12–28. Leads the army of Israel against the Ammonites, Judg 11:29–33. His rash vow concerning his daughter, Judg 11:30–40. Falsely accused by the Ephraimites, Judg 12:1. Leads the army of Gilead against the Ephraimites, Judg 12:4. Judges Israel six years, dies, and is buried in Gilead, Judg 12:7. Faith of, Heb 11:32.

JEPHUNNEH 1. Father of Caleb, Num 13:3–15.

2. An Asherite, 1 Chron 7:38.

JERAH Son of Joktan, Gen 10:26–30; 1 Chron 1:20–23.

JERAHMEEL 1. Son of Hezron, 1 Chron 2:9.

2. Son of Kish, 1 Chron 24:29.

3. An officer of Jehoiakim, king of Judah, Jer 36:26.

JERED A Judahite, 1 Chron 4:18.

JEREMAI Of the family of Hashum, Ezra 10:33.

JEREMIAH 1. Of Libnah, grandfather of Jehoahaz, 2 Kgs 23:31, 32; 24:18, 19; Jer 52:1.

2. A chief of Manasseh, 1 Chron 5:24.

3. An Israelite who joined David at Ziklag, 1 Chron 12:3–7.

4. Two Gadites who joined David at Ziklag, 1 Chron 12:8–13.

5. The prophet, Jer 1:1. A Rechabite, Jer 35:3. A priest, Jer 1:1. Call of, Jer 1:4–19. Time of his prophecies, Jer 3:6; 21:1, 2; 24:1; 25:1–3; 26:1; 28:1; 32:1; 34:1; 45:1; 49:34. Letter to the captives in Babylon, Jer 29. Sorrow of, under persecution, Jer 15:10, 15; 17:15–18. Conspiracy against, Jer 11:21–23; 18:18–23. Foretells the desolation of Jerusalem, Jer 19. Pashhur, the head priest of the temple, whips and imprisons him, Jer 20:1–3. Denounces Pashhur, Jer 20:3–6. His melancholy and murmuring against God, because of persecution, Jer 20:7–18. Imprisoned by Zedekiah, Jer 32; 33:1; 37:15–21; 38:6–13; 39:15–18; Lam 3: 53–55. Nebuchadnezzar directs the release of, Jer 39:11–14; 40:1–4. Has a friend in Ahikam, Jer 26:24. Ebedmelech, the Ethiopian, intercedes with the king for him, and secures his release, Jer 38:7–13.

Prophecies of, written down by Baruch, Jer 36: 1–7, 32; 45:1. Prophecies of, destroyed by Jehoiakim, Jer 36:8–32. Scroll containing prophecies of, delivered to Seraiah, with a charge from Jeremiah, Jer 51:59–64. Zedekiah seeks help from God by, Jer 21:1, 2; 37:3; 38:14. His intercession asked: By Johanan and all the people, Jer 42:1–6; by Zedekiah, Jer 37:3. Johanan forces Jeremiah into Egypt, Jer 43: 1–7. Foretells the conquest of Egypt by Babylon, Jer 43:8–13. Prophecies of, studied by Daniel, Dan 9:2. Celibacy of, Jer 16:2. Purchases a field, Jer 32: 6–10. Lamentations of: Over Josiah, 2 Chron 35:24, 25; over the prosperity of the wicked, Jer 12:1–6; over the desolation of God's inheritance, Jer 12: 7–13; over Jerusalem, Jer 4:14–18; 8; 9:1; 10:19–22; 18: 11. See the book of Lamentations. Lives at Mizpah, Jer 40:6. Prayers of, Jer 14:7–9; 32:17–25. Zeal of, Jer 15:16.

6. A priest who signed the covenant with Nehemiah, Neh 10:1–8.

7. A priest who accompanied Zerubbabel, Neh 12:1–7, 12–21.

8. A Judean leader at the dedication of the wall, Neh 12:34.

9. Father of Jaazaniah, Jer 35:3.

JEREMOTH 1. Two Benjaminites, 1 Chron 7:8; 8:14.

2. One of the sons of Elam, Ezra 10:26.

3. One of the family of Zattu, Ezra 10:27.

4. One of the family of Bani, Ezra 10:29.

5. A ruler of the tribe of Naphtali, 1 Chron 27: 16–22.

6. See *Jerimoth, 3.*

7. See *Jerimoth, 4.*

JERIAH Called also *Jerijah.* A descendant of Hebron, 1 Chron 23:19; 24:23; 26:31.

JERIBAI A valiant man of David's guard, 1 Chron 11:26–47.

JERICHO 1. A city east of Jerusalem and near the Jordan, Num 22:1; 26:3, 4; Deut 34:1. Called the *City of Palm Trees,* Deut 34:3. Situation of, beautiful, 2 Kgs 2:19. Rahab the prostitute lived in, Josh 2; Heb 11:31. Joshua sees the "Commander-in-Cheif of the Lord's army" near, Josh 5:13–15. Besieged by Joshua seven days; fall and destruction of, Josh 6; 24:11. Situated within the territory allotted to Benjamin, Josh 18:12, 21–28. The Kenites lived at, Judg 1:16. King of Moab conquers, and establishes his capital at, Judg 3:13. Rebuilt by Hiel, 1 Kgs 16:34. Young prophets live at, 2 Kgs 2: 4, 5, 15, 18. Captives of Judah, taken by the king of Israel, released at, because of Oded's warning, 2 Chron 28:7–15. Inhabitants of, taken captive to Babylon, return to, with Ezra and Nehemiah, Ezra 2:3–35; Neh 7:8–38; assist in repairing the walls of Jerusalem, Neh 3:2. Blind men healed at, by Jesus, Mt 20:29–34; Mk 10:46; Lk 18:35. Zacchaeus lived at, Lk 19:1–10.

2. Plain of, 2 Kgs 25:4, 5; Jer 52:8.

3. Waters of, purified by Elisha, 2 Kgs 2:18–22.

JERI-EL Son of Tola, 1 Chron 7:2.

JERIMOTH 1. Son of Bela, 1 Chron 7:7.

2. A disaffected Israelite, who denounced Saul and joined David at Ziklag, 1 Chron 12:3–7.

3. Son of Mushi, 1 Chron 23:23; called *Jeremoth,* 1 Chron 24:30.

4. Son of Heman, 1 Chron 25:4, 5; called *Jeremoth,* 1 Chron 25:9–31.

5. A son of David, 2 Chron 11:18.

6. A Levite who assisted Conaniah in the Temple storerooms, 2 Chron 31:12, 13.

JERIOTH Wife of Caleb, 1 Chron 2:18. Possibly another name for *Azubah,* in same verse.

JEROBOAM 1. First king of Israel after the revolt. Promoted by Solomon, 1 Kgs 11:27, 28. Ahijah's prophecy concerning, 1 Kgs 11:29–39; 14:5–16. Flees to Egypt to escape from Solomon, 1 Kgs 11: 26–40. Recalled from Egypt by the ten tribes on account of disaffection toward Rehoboam, and made king, 1 Kgs 12:1–20; 2 Chron 10:12–19. Subverts the religion of Moses, 1 Kgs 12:25–33; 13:33, 34; 14:9, 16; 16:2, 26; 2 Chron 11:13, 14; 13:8, 9. Hand of, paralyzed, 1 Kgs 13:1–10. His wife sent to consult the prophet Ahijah concerning her child, 1 Kgs 14: 1–18. His wars with Rehoboam, 1 Kgs 14:30; 15:6; 2 Chron 11:1–4. His war with Abijah, 1 Kgs 15:7; 2 Chron 13. Death of, 1 Kgs 14:20; 2 Chron 13:20.

2. King of Israel. Successor to Joash, 2 Kgs 14: 16, 23. Recovers Hamath and Damascus, 2 Kgs 14: 25–28. Wicked reign of, 2 Kgs 14:24. Prophecies concerning, Amos 7:7–13. Death of, 2 Kgs 14:29. Genealogy written during his reign, 1 Chron 5:17.

JEROHAM 1. A Levite, probably living in Ephraim, and grandfather of Samuel, 1 Sam 1:1; 1 Chron 6:25–27, 33–38.

2. A chief of the tribe of Benjamin, 1 Chron 8:26, 27.

3. A descendant of Benjamin, 1 Chron 9:7, 8.

4. A priest, and father of Adaiah, who lived in Jerusalem after the exile, 1 Chron 9:12; Neh 11: 10–14.

5. Father of two Israelites who joined David at Ziklag, 1 Chron 12:3–7.

6. The father of Azarel, 1 Chron 27:16–22.

7. Father of Azariah, 2 Chron 23:1.

JERUBBAAL See *Gideon.*

JERUEL A wilderness in the south of Judah, 2 Chron 20:16.

JERUSALEM Called *Jebus,* Josh 18:21–28; Judg 19:10; *Zion,* 1 Kgs 8:1; 2 Chron 5:2; *City of David;* 2 Sam 5:7; 1 Chron 11:5, 6; *Salem,* Gen 14:18; Heb 7:1, 2; *Ariel,* Isa 29:1, 2; *City of our God,* Ps 46:4; *Most Beautiful in all the World, Joy of all the Earth,* Lam 2:15; *The Throne of the Lord,* Jer 3:17; *Holy Mountain,* Dan 9:16, 20; *Holy City,* Neh 11:1; Isa 52:1; *The Faithful City, The Holy Mountain, The Mountain of the Lord of Hosts,* Zech 8:3; to be called *The Lord is our Righteousness,* Jer 33:16; *Jehovah-Shammah,* Ezk 48:35; *New Jerusalem,* Rev 21:2, 10–27.

Situation and appearance of, Ps 122:2, 3; 125:2; Song 6:4; Mic 4:8. Walls of, Jer 39:4.

Gates of: Old gate, fish gate, sheep gate, prison gate, Neh 3:1, 3, 32; 12:39. Gate of Ephraim, 2 Chron 25:23; Neh 12:39. Gate of Benjamin, Jer 37:13; Zech 14:10. Old gate, Neh 3:6; 12:39; Zech 14:10. Corner gate, Zech 14:10. Valley gate, Neh 2:13; 3:13. Dung gate, Neh 2:13; 3:13; 12:31, 32. Fountain gate, Neh 2:14, 15; 3:15; 12:37. Water gate, Neh 3:26; 8:1; 12:37. Horse gate, Neh 3:28. Royal gate, 1 Chron 9:18. Shallecheth, 1 Chron 26:16. Upper gate, 2 Chron 23:20. East gate, Neh 3:29. Muster gate, Neh 3:31. Middle gate, Jer 39:3.

Buildings: High Priest's palace, Jn 18:15. Castle, Acts 21:34. Stairs, Neh 3:15.

Plazas: Around the Temple, 2 Chron 29:4; Ezra 10:9; near Water and Ephraim gates, Neh 8:16.

Towers of, see *Hananel; Millo; Ophel; Siloam; Tower of the Hundred.*

Places in and around: Moriah, 2 Chron 3:1. The tomb of Jesus, Jn 19:41. See *Gethsemane; Golgotha; Olives, Mount of; Jehoshaphat, Valley of; Topheth.*

Measurement of, in Ezekiel's vision, Ezk 45:6. Names of the gates of, in Ezekiel's vision, Ezk 48:30–34.

The capital of David's kingdom by divine appointment, 1 Kgs 15:4; 2 Kgs 19:34; 2 Chron 6:6; 12:13. To be called God's throne, Jer 3:17. The cantors live in, 1 Chron 9:33, 34. The high priest lived at, Jn 18:15. Annual feasts kept at, Ezk 36:37, 38, with Deut 16:16, and Ps 122:2–5; Lk 2:41, 42; Jn 4:20; 5:1; 7:1–14; 12:20; Acts 18:21. Prayers of the Israelites made toward, 1 Kgs 8:38; Dan 6:10. Beloved, Ps 122:6; 137:1–6; Isa 62:1–7. See *Country, Love of; Patriotism.*

Oaths taken in the name of, Mt 5:35.

Melchizedek ancient king and priest of, Gen 14:18. King of, confederated with the four other kings of the Amorites, against Joshua and the people of Israel, Josh 10:1–5. Confederated kings defeated, and the king of Jerusalem killed by Joshua, Josh 10:15–26. Falls to Benjamin in the allotment of the land of Canaan, Josh 18:21–28. Conquest of, made by David, 2 Sam 5:7. The inhabitants of, not expelled, Josh 15:63; Judg 1:21. Conquest of the fortress of Zion in, made by David, 1 Chron 11:4–6. The fortress of Mount Zion, occupied by David, and called the *City of David,* 2 Sam 5:4–9; 1 Chron 11:7. Ark brought to, by David, 2 Sam 6:12–19. The threshing floor of Araunah within the fortress of, 2 Sam 24:16. David purchases and erects and altar upon it, 2 Sam 24:16–25. The city built around the citadel, 1 Chron 11:8.

Fortified by Solomon, 1 Kgs 3:1; 9:15. The temple built within the fortress, see *Temple.*

Captured and pillaged by: Shishak, king of Egypt, 1 Kgs 14:25, 26; 2 Chron 12:9; by Joash, king of Israel, 2 Kgs 14:13, 14; 2 Chron 25:23, 24; Nebuchadnezzar, king of Babylon, 2 Kgs 24:10–16; 25:1–17; 2 Chron 36:17–21; Jer 1:3; 32:2; 39; 52:4–7, 12–25; Lam 1:5–8. Walls of, restored and fortified: By Uzziah, 2 Chron 26:9, 10; by Jotham, 2 Chron 27:3; Manasseh, 2 Chron 33:14. Water supply brought in from the Gihon by Hezekiah, 2 Kgs 18:17; 20:20; 2 Chron 32:3, 4, 30; Neh 2:13–15; Isa 7:3; 22:9–11; 36:2. Besieged: By Pekah, 2 Kgs 16:5; by the Philistines, 2 Chron 21:16, 17; by Sennacherib, 2 Kgs 18:13–37; 19:20–37; 2 Chron 32. Rebuilding of, ordered by proclamation of Cyrus, 2 Chron 36:22, 23; Ezra 1:1–4. Rebuilt by Nehemiah under the direction of Ar-ta-xerxes, Neh chapters 2–6. Wall of, dedicated, Neh 12:27–43. Temple restored, see *Temple.*

Roman rulers resided at: Herod I, Mt 2:3; Pontius Pilate, Mt 27:2; Mk 15:1; Lk 23:1–7; Jn 18:28, 29; Herod III, Acts 12:1–23.

Life and miracles of Jesus connected with, see *Jesus, History of.*

Gospel first preached at, Mic 4:2; Lk 24:47; Acts 1:4; 2:14. Pentecostal revival occurs at, Acts 2. Stephen martyred at, Acts 6:8–15; 7. Believers persecuted and dispersed from, Acts 8:1–4; 11:19–21.

For personal incidents occurring in, see biographies of individuals; see also *Israel.*

Wickedness of, Luke 13:33, 34. List of sins in, Ezk 22:3–12, 25–30; 23; 33:25, 26. Led Judah to sin, Mic 1:5.

Prophecies against, Isa 3:1–8; Jer 9:11; 19:6, 15; 21:10; 26:9, 11; Dan 9:2, 27; Mic 1:1; 3:12; of disease, famine, and war in, Jer 34:2; Ezk 5:12; Joel 3:2, 3; Amos 2:5; of the destruction of, Jer 7:32–34; 26:18; 32:29, 31, 32; Dan 9:24–27. Destruction of, foretold by Jesus, Mt 23:37, 38; Mk 13:14–23; Lk 13:35; 17:26–37; 19:41–44; 21:20–24; Rev 11:1–12.

Prophecies of the rebuilding of, Isa 44:28; Jer 31:38–40; Ezk 48:15–22; Dan 9:25; Zech 14:8–11. Of final restoration of, Joel 3:20, 21; Obd 1:17, 21; Zech 2:2–5; 8.

Historical Notices of. Melchizedek was ancient king of, Gen 14:18.

JERUSHA Daughter of Zadok, 2 Kgs 15:32, 33; called *Jerushah* in 2 Chron 27:1.

JESHAIAH 1. Grandson of Zerubbabel, 1 Chron 3:21, 22.

2. Son of Jeduthun, 1 Chron 25:3, 9–31.

3. Grandson of Eliezer, 1 Chron 26:25.

4. A Jew of the family of Elam, who returned from exile, Ezra 8:2–14.

5. A Levite who joined Ezra to return to Jerusalem, Ezra 8:19.

6. A Benjaminite ancestor of one selected by lot to live in Jerusalem after the exile, Neh 11:7–9.

JESHANAH A city in the north of Benjamin, 1 Sam 7:12; 2 Chron 13:18, 19.

JESHARELAH A Levite musician, 1 Chron 25:9–31.

JESHEBEAB A priest, and head of the 14th priestly group, 1 Chron 24:7–18.

JESHER Son of Caleb, 1 Chron 2:18.

JESHISHAI A Gadite, 1 Chron 5:14.

JESHOHAIAH A descendant of Simeon, 1 Chron 4:34–39.

JESHUA 1. A priest, head of the ninth priestly group, 1 Chron 24:7–18. Nine hundred and seventy-three of his descendants returned from Babylon, Ezra 2:36–39; Neh 7:39–42.

2. A Levite who assisted in distributing the tithes, 2 Chron 31:14, 15.

3. A priest who accompanied Zerubbabel from Babylon, Ezra 2:2; Neh 7:7; 12:1. Descendants of, Neh 12:10, 11. He rebuilt the altar, Ezra 3:2. Rebuilt the temple, Ezra 3:8–13. Contends with those who tried to defeat the rebuilding, Ezra 4:1–3; 5:1, 2.

4. Ancestor of Levites who returned with Zerubbabel, Ezra 2:40–42; Neh 7:43–45.

5. Father of Jozabad, Ezra 8:33.

6. Son of Pahath-moab, Ezra 2:3–35; Neh 7:8–38.

7. Father of Ezer, Neh 3:19.

8. A Levite who explained the law to the people when Ezra read it, Neh 8:7, 8.

9. A Levite who signed Nehemiah's covenant, Neh 10:9–13.

10. A city of Judah, Neh 11:25–30.

JESHURUN A name used poetically for Israel, Deut 32:15.

JESIMI-EL A descendant of Simeon, 1 Chron 4:34–39.

JESSE Father of David, Ruth 4:16, 17; 1 Sam 17:12. Ancestor of Jesus, Mt 1:5, 6. Samuel visits, under divine command, to select from his sons a successor to Saul, 1 Sam 16:1–13. Saul asks, to send David to become his bodyguard, 1 Sam 16:19–23. Sons in Saul's army, 1 Sam 17:13–28. Lives in Moab, 1 Sam 22:3, 4. Descendants of, 1 Chron 2:13–17.

JESTING Foolish, forbidden, Eph 5:4. See Mt 12:36.

JESUS CHRIST INDEX OF SUBTOPICS. *History of; Miscellaneous Facts Concerning; Unclassified Scriptures Relating to; Ascension of; Atonement by; Attributes of; Birth of; Compassion of; Confessing; Creator; Death of; Design of his Death; Death of, Voluntary; Deity of; Denial of; Eternity of; Exaltation of; Example, an; Faith in; Foreknowledge of; Genealogy of; Healing by; Holiness of; Humanity of; Humility of; Impeccability of; Incarnation of; Intercession of; Judge; Justice of; King; Kingdom of; Love of; Mediation of; Meekness of; Messiah; Miracles of; Mission of; Names and Titles of; Obedience of; Omnipotence of; Omnipresence of; Omniscience of; Parables of; Passion of; Perfections of; Persecutions of; Power of, to Forgive Sins; Prayers of; Preexistence of; Priesthood of; Promises of; Prophecies Concerning; Prophet; Received; Redeemer; Rejected; Relation of, to the Father; Resurrection of; Revelations of; Righteousness of; Salvation by; Savior; Second Coming of; Shepherd; Son of God; Son of Man; Sovereignty of; Sufferings of; Sympathy of; Teacher; Temptation of; Types of; Unchangeable; Union of, with the Righteous; Wisdom of; Worship of; Zeal of.*

HISTORY OF. Genealogy of, Mt 1:1–17; Lk 3:23–38.

Facts before the birth of: The angel Gabriel appears to Mary (Nazareth), Lk 1:26–38. Mary visits Elizabeth (Hebron?), Lk 1:39–56. Mary's *magnificat* (Hebron?), Lk 1:46–55. An angel appears to Joseph concerning Mary, Mt 1:18–25.

Birth of (Bethlehem), Lk 2:1–7.

Angels appear to the shepherds, Lk 2:8–20.

Magi visit (Bethlehem), Mt 2:1–12.

Circumcision of (Bethlehem), Lk 2:21. Is presented in the temple (Jerusalem), Lk 2:22–38.

Flight into, and return from, Egypt, Mt 2:13–23.

Debates with the teachers in the temple (Jerusalem), Lk 2:41–52.

Is baptized by John (Jordan), Mt 3:13–17; Mk 1:9–11; Lk 3:21, 22.

Temptation of (Desert of Judea), Mt 4:1–11; Mk 1:12, 13; Lk 4:1–13.

John's testimony concerning him, Jn 1:1–18.

Testimony of John the Baptist concerning (Bethany), Jn 1:19–34.

Disciples adhere to, Jn 1:35–51.

Miracle at Cana of Galilee, Jn 2:1–12.

Drives the money changers from the temple (Jerusalem), Jn 2:13–25. Nicodemus comes to (Jerusalem), Jn 3:1–21.

Baptizes (Aenon), Jn 3:22, with chapter 4:1, 2.

Returns to Galilee, Mt 4:12, 13; Mk 1:14; Lk 4:14; Jn 4:1–3.

Visits Sychar, and teaches the Samaritan woman, Jn 4:4–42.

Teaches in Galilee, Mt 4:17; Mk 1:14, 15; Lk 4:14, 15; Jn 4:43–45.

Heals a Capernaum official's son (Cana of Galilee), Jn 4:46–54.

Is rejected by the people of Nazareth, moves to Capernaum, Mt 4:13–16; Lk 4:16–31.

Chooses Peter, Andrew, James, and John as disciples, miracle of the draught of fish (Capernaum), Mt 4:18–22; Mk 1:16–20; Lk 5:1–11.

Preaches throughout Galilee, Mt 4:23–25; Mk 1:35–39; Lk 4:42–44.

Heals a demoniac (Capernaum), Mk 1:21–28; Lk 4:31–37.

Heals Peter's mother-in-law (Capernaum), Mt 8:14–17; Mk 1:29–34; Lk 4:38–41.

Heals a leper in Galilee, Mt 8:2–4; Mk 1:40–45; Lk 5:12–16.

Heals a paralytic (Capernaum), Mt 9:2–8; Mk 2:1–12; Lk 5:17–26.

Calls Matthew (Capernaum), Mt 9:9; Mk 2:13, 14; Lk 5:27, 28.

Heals an impotent man at the pool of Bethesda on the Sabbath day, is persecuted, and makes his defense, John 5.

Defines the law of the Sabbath on the occasion of his disciples breaking the heads of wheat, (Capernaum), Mt 12:1–8; Mk 2:23–28; Lk 6:1–5.

Heals a man with a deformed hand (Capernaum), Mt 12:9–13; Mk 3:1–6; Lk 6:6–11.

Withdraws from Capernaum to the Sea of Galilee where he heals many, Mt 12:15–21; Mk 3:7–12.

Goes up into the hills, and calls and ordains twelve disciples (Galilee), Mt 10:2–4; Mk 3:13–19; Lk 6:12–16.

Delivers the "Sermon on the Mount" (Galilee), Mt 5; 6; 7; Lk 6:20–49.

Heals the servant of the Roman army officer (near Capernaum), Mt 8:5–13; Lk 7:1–10.

Revives the son of the widow of Nain, Lk 7:11–17.

Receives the message from John the Baptist (Galilee), Mt 11:2–19; Lk 7:18–35.

Chides the unbelieving cities near Capernaum, Mt 11:20–30.

Anointed by a prostitute (Capernaum), Lk 7:36–50.

Preaches in the cities of Galilee, Lk 8:1–3.

Heals a demoniac, and denounces the Pharisees (Galilee), Mt 12:22–37; Mk 3:19–30; Lk 11:14–26.

Replies to the Jewish leaders and Pharisees who ask for a miracle (Galilee), Mt 12:38–45; Lk 11:16–36.

Denounces the Pharisees and other hypocrites (Galilee), Lk 11:37–54.

Discourses to his disciples (Galilee), Lk 12:1–59.

Parable of the fig tree (Galilee), Lk 13:6–9.

Parable of the sower (Sea of Galilee), Mt 13:1–23; Mk 4:1–25; Lk 8:4–18.

Parable of the thistles, and other teachings (Galilee), Mt 13:24–54; Mk 4:26–34.

Crosses the Sea of Galilee, and quiets the storm, Mt 8:18–27; Mk 4:35–41; Lk 8:22–25.

Miracle of the swine (Gadara), Mt 8:28–34; Mk 5:1–21; Lk 8:26–40.

Returns to Capernaum, Mt 9:1; Mk 5:21; Lk 8:40.

Eats with tax collectors and sinners, and discourses on fasting (Capernaum), Mt 9:10–17; Mk 2:15–22; Lk 5:29–39.

Brings to life the daughter of Jairus, and heals the woman who has the hemorrhage (Capernaum), Mt 9:18–26; Mk 5:22–43; Lk 8:41–56.

Heals two blind men, and casts out a dumb spirit (Capernaum), Mt 9:27–34.

Returns to Nazareth, Mt 13:53–58; Mk 6:1–6.

Teaches in various cities in Galilee, Mt 9:35–38.

Instructs his disciples, and empowers them to heal diseases and cast out demons, Mt 10; Mk 6:6–13; Lk 9:1–6.

Herod falsely supposes him to be John, whom he had beheaded, Mt 14:1, 2, 6–12; Mk 6:14–16, 21–29; Lk 9:7–9.

The twelve return; he goes to the desert; crowds follow him; he feeds 5,000 (Sea of Galilee), Mt 14:13–21; Mk 6:30–44; Lk 9:10–17; Jn 6:1–14.

Walks on the water (Galilee), Mt 14:22–36; Mk 6:45–56; Jn 6:15–21.

Teaches in the synagogue in Capernaum, Jn 6:22–65.

Many disciples desert him (Capernaum), Jn 6:66–71.

He justifies his disciples in eating without ceremonial washing (Capernaum), Mt 15:1–20; Mk 7:1–23.

Heals the daughter of the Syro-phoenician woman (Tyre and Sidon), Mt 15:21–28; Mk 7:24–30.

Heals a speech-impaired deaf man (Decapolis), Mt 15:29–31; Mk 7:31–37.

Feeds 4,000, Mt 15:32–39; Mk 8:1–9.

Refuses to give a sign to the Pharisees (region of Magdala), Mt 16:1–4; Mk 8:10–12.

Cautions his disciples against the "yeast" of hypocrisy (Sea of Galilee), Mt 16:4–12; Mk 8:13–21.

Heals a blind man (Bethsaida), Mk 8:22–26.

Foretells his death and resurrection (near Caesarea Philippi), Mt 16:21–28; Mk 8:31–38; 9:1; Lk 9:21–27.

Is transfigured, Mt 17:1–13; Mk 9:2–13; Lk 9:28–36.

Heals a demoniac (Caesarea Philippi), Mt 17:14–21; Mk 9:14–29; Lk 9:37–43.

Foretells his death and resurrection (Galilee), Mt 17:22, 23; Mk 9:30–32; Lk 9:43–45.

Miracle of tax money in the fish's mouth, Mt 17:24–27.

Reproves the ambition of his disciples (Capernaum), Mt 18:1–35; Mk 9:33–50; Lk 9:46–50.

Reproves the intolerance of his disciples, Mk 9:38, 39; Lk 9:49, 50.

Travels to Jerusalem to attend the Feast of Tabernacles, passing through Samaria, Lk 9:51–62; Jn 7:2–11.

Commissions the seventy (Samaria), Lk 10:1–16.

Heals ten lepers, Lk 17:11–19.

Teaches in Jerusalem at the Feast of Tabernacles, Jn 7:14–53; 8.

Answers a lawyer, who tests his wisdom with the question, "What does a man need to do to live forever in heaven?" by the parable of the good Samaritan (Jerusalem), Lk 10:25–37.

Hears the report of the seventy (Jerusalem), Lk 10:17–24.

Teaches in the house of Mary, Martha, and Lazarus, in Bethany, Lk 10:38–42.

Teaches his disciples to pray, Lk 11:1–13.

Heals a blind man, who, because of his faith in Jesus, was excommunicated, Jn 9.

Teaches in Jerusalem, Jn 9:39–41; 10:1–21.

Teaches in the temple at Jerusalem, at the Dedication Celebration, Jn 10:22–39.

Escapes the violence from the Jewish leaders, Jn 10:40–42; 11:3–16.

Returns to Bethany, and raises Lazarus from the dead, Jn 11:1–46.

Escapes to the city of Ephraim from the conspiracy led by Caiaphus, the high priest (Judea), Jn 11:47–54.

Travels toward Jerusalem to attend the passover; heals many who are diseased, and teaches the people (Perea), Mt 19:1, 2; Mk 10:1; Lk 13:10–35.

Dines with a Pharisee on the Sabbath (Perea), Lk 14:1–24.

Teaches the crowds the conditions of discipleship (Perea), Lk 14:25–35.

Relates the parables of the lost sheep, the lost silver coin, prodigal son, unjust accountant (Perea), Lk 15:1–32; 16:1–13.

Reproves the hypocrisy of the Pharisees (Perea), Lk 16.

Relates the parable of the rich man and Lazarus (Perea), Lk 16:19–31.

Teaches his disciples concerning offenses, meekness, and humility (Perea), Lk 17:1–10.

Teaches the Pharisees concerning the coming of his Kingdom (Perea), Lk 17:20–37.

Relates the parables of the unjust judge, and the Pharisee and tax collector praying in the temple (Perea), Lk 18:1–14.

Interprets the law concerning marriage and divorce (Perea), Mt 19:3–12; Mk 10:2–12.

Blesses little children (Perea), Mt 19:13–15; Mk 10:13–16; Lk 18:15–17.

Receives the rich young leader, who asks what he shall do to get to heaven (Perea), Mt 19:16–22; Mk 10:17–22; Lk 18:18–24.

Enunciates the parable of the vineyard (Perea), Mt 20:1–16.

Foretells his death and resurrection (Perea), Mt 20:17–19; Mk 10:32–34; Lk 18:31–34.

Listens to the mother of James and John in behalf of her sons (Perea), Mt 20:20–28.

Heals two blind men at Jericho, Mt 20:29–34; Mk 10:46–50; Lk 18:35–43.

Visits Zacchaeus, Lk 19:1–10.

Relates the parable of the money (pounds) (Jericho), Lk 19:11–28.

Goes to Bethany six days before the passover, Jn 12:1–9.

Triumphal entry into Jerusalem, while the people throw palm branches in the way, Mt 21:1–11; Mk 11:1–11; Lk 19:29–44; Jn 12:12–19.

Enters the temple, Mt 21:12; Mk 11:11; Lk 19:45.

Drives the money changers out of the temple, Mt 21:12, 13; Lk 19:45, 46.

Heals the disabled in the temple, Mt 21:14.

Teaches daily in the temple, Lk 19:47, 48.

Performs the miracle of causing the barren fig tree to wither, Mt 21:17–22; Mk 11:12–14, 20, 21.

Relates the parable of the two sons, Mt 21:28–31; the parable of the wicked husbandmen, Mt 21:33–46; Mk 12:1–12; Lk 20:9–19; of the marriage, Mt 22:1–14; Lk 14:16–24.

Tested by the Pharisees and Herodians, and explains the duty of the citizen to his government, Mt 22:15–22; Mk 12:13–17; Lk 20:20–26.

Tried by the Sadducees concerning the resurrection of the dead, Mt 22:23–33; Mk 12:18–27; Lk 20:27–40; and by a lawyer, Mt 22:34–40; Mk 12:28–34.

Exposes the hypocrisies of the Jewish leaders and Pharisees, Mt 23; Mk 12:38–40; Lk 20:45–47.

Extols the widow who threw two pennies into the treasury, Mk 12:41–44; Lk 21:1–4.

Verifies the prophecy of Isaiah concerning the unbelieving Jews, Jn 12:37–50.

Foretells the destruction of the temple, and of Jerusalem, Mt 24; Mk 13; Lk 21:5–36.

Laments over Jerusalem, Mt 23:37; Lk 19:41–44.

Relates the parables of the ten virgins and of the investments, Mt 25:1–30.

Foretells scenes of judgment, Mt 25:31–46.

Anointed with perfume (Bethany), Mt 26:6–13; Mk 14:3–9; Jn 12:1–8.

Last passover, and institution of the sacrament of holy communion, Mt 26:17–30; Mk 14:12–25; Lk 22:7–20.

Washes the disciples' feet, Jn 13:1–17.

Foretells his betrayal, Mt 26:23; Mk 14:18–21; Lk 22:21; Jn 13:18.

Accuses Judas of his betrayal, Mt 26:20–25; Mk 14:18–21; Lk 22:21–23; Jn 13:21–30.

Teaches his disciples, and comforts them with promises, and promises the gift of the Holy Spirit, Jn 14; 15; 16.

Last prayer (Jerusalem), Jn 17.

Repairs to Gethsemane (Mount of Olives), Mt 26:30, 36–46; Mk 14:26, 32–42; Lk 22:39–46; Jn 18:1.

Is betrayed and apprehended (Gethsemane), Mt 26:47–56; Mk 14:43–54, 66–72; Lk 22:47–53; Jn 18:2–12.

Trail of, before Caiaphas (Jerusalem), Mt 26:57, 58, 69–75; Mk 14:53, 54, 66–72; Lk 22:54–62; Jn 18:13–18, 25–27.

Tried by the council, Mt 26:59–68; Mk 14:55–65; Lk 22:63–71; Jn 18:19–21.

Led by the council to Pilate, Mt 27:1, 2, 11–14; Mk 15:1–5; Lk 23:1–5; Jn 18:28–38.

Arraigned before Herod, Lk 23:6–12.

Tried before Pilate, Mt 27:15–26; Mk 15:6–15; Lk 23:13–25; Jn 18:39, 40; 19:1–16.

Mocked by the soldiers, Mt 27:27–31; Mk 15:16–20.

Is led away to be crucified, Mt 27:31–34; Mk 15:20–23; Lk 23:26–33; Jn 19:16, 17.

Crucified, Mt 27:35–56; Mk 15:24–41; Lk 23:32–49; Jn 19:18–30.

Taken from the cross and buried, Mt 27:57–66; Mk 15:42–47; Lk 23:50–56; Jn 19:31–42.

Comes back to life, Mt 28:2–15; Mk 16:1–11; Lk 24:1–12; Jn 20:1–18.

Is seen by Mary Magdalene, Mt 28:1–10; Mk 16:9; Jn 20:11–17; by Peter, Lk 24:33, 34; 1 Cor 15:5.

Appears to two disciples walking to Emmaus, Mk 16:12, 13; Lk 24:13–35.

Appears to the disciples, when Thomas is absent (Jerusalem), Mk 16:14–18; Lk 24:36–49; Jn 20:19–23; when Thomas was present (Jerusalem), Jn 20:26–29; at the Sea of Galilee, Mt 28:16; Jn 21:1–14; to the apostles and more than 500 Christian brothers on a mountain in Galilee, Mt 28:16–20; with Acts 10:40–42. See also Acts 13:31; 1 Cor 15:6, 7.

Appears to James, and also to all the apostles (Jerusalem), Acts 1:3–8; 1 Cor 15:7.

Ascends to heaven (Bethany), Mk 16:19, 20; Lk 24:50–53; Acts 1:9–12.

Appears to Paul, Acts 9:3–17; 18:9; 22:14, 17, 18; 23:11; 26:16; 1 Cor 9:1; 15:8.

Stephen's vision of, Acts 7:55, 56.

Appears to John on Patmos, Rev 1:10–18.

MISCELLANEOUS FACTS CONCERNING.

Brethren of, Mt 13:55; Mk 6:2, 3; 1 Cor 9:5; Gal 1:19. Sisters of, Mt 13:56; Mk 6:2, 3.

Was with the Israelites in the wilderness, 1 Cor 10:3, 4, 9.

UNCLASSIFIED SCRIPTURES RELATING TO. Jn 6:35. Jesus replied, "I am the Bread of Life. No one coming to me will ever be hungry again. Those believing in me will never thirst." [41]Then the Jews began to murmur against him because he claimed to be the Bread from heaven. [48-51]"Yes, I am the Bread of Life! When your fathers in the wilderness ate bread from the skies, they all died. But the Bread from heaven gives eternal life to everyone who eats it. I am that Living Bread that came down out of heaven. Anyone eating this Bread shall live forever; this Bread is my flesh given to redeem humanity." [53]So Jesus said it again, "With all the earnestness I possess I tell you this: Unless you eat the flesh of the Messiah and drink his blood, you cannot have eternal life within you. [54]But anyone who does eat my flesh and drink my blood has eternal life, and I will raise him at the Last Day. [55]For my flesh is the true food, and my blood is the true drink. [56]Everyone who eats my flesh and drinks my blood is in me, and I in him. [57]I live by the power of the living Father who sent me, and in the same way those who partake of me shall live because of me! [58]I am the true Bread from heaven; and anyone who eats this Bread shall live forever."

Jn 8:12. Later, in one of his talks, Jesus said to the people, "I am the Light of the world. So if you follow me, you won't be stumbling through the darkness, for living light will flood your path."

Jn 10:9. Yes, I am the Gate. Those who come in by way of the Gate will be saved and will go in and out and find green pastures. [10]The thief's purpose is to steal, kill and destroy. My purpose is to give life in all its fullness. [11]I am the Good Shepherd. The Good Shepherd lays down his life for the sheep. *v.* 14

Jn 11:25. Jesus told her, "I am the one who raises the dead and gives them life again. Anyone who believes in me, even though he dies like anyone else, shall live again."

Jn 14:6. Jesus told him, "I am the Way—yes, and the Truth and the Life. No one can get to the Father except by means of me."

Jn 15:1. I am the true Vine, and my Father is the Gardener. [5]Yes, I am the Vine; you are the branches. Whoever lives in me and I in him shall produce a large crop of fruit. For apart from me you can't do a thing. [6]If anyone separates from me, he is thrown away like a useless branch, withers, and is gathered into a pile with all the others and burned. [7]But if you stay in me and obey my commands, you may ask any request you like, and it will be granted!

Col 3:4. And when Christ who is our real life comes back again, you will shine with him and share in all his glories.

2 Tim 1:10. And now he has made all of this plain to us by the coming of our Savior Jesus Christ, who broke the power of death and showed us the way of everlasting life through trusting him.

Rev 1:18. Don't be afraid! Though I am the First and Last, the Living One who died, who is now alive forevermore, who has the keys of hell and death—don't be afraid!

Rev 22:13. I am the A and the Z, the Beginning and the End, the First and Last. Chapters 1–17.

ASCENSION OF. Ps 68:18. He ascends the heights, leading many captives in his train. Eph 4:8.

Mk 16:19. When the Lord Jesus had finished talking with them, he was taken up into heaven and sat down at God's right hand.

Lk 24:26. "Wasn't it clearly predicted by the prophets that the Messiah would have to suffer all these things before entering his time of glory?" [50]Then Jesus led them out along the road to Bethany, and lifting his hands to heaven, he blessed them, [51]and then began rising into the sky, and went on to heaven.

Jn 1:51. You will even see heaven open and the angels of God coming back and forth to me, the Messiah.

Jn 6:62. Then what will you think if you see me, the Messiah, return to heaven again?

Jn 7:33. But Jesus told them, "[Not yet!] I am to be here a little longer. Then I shall return to the one who sent me. [34]You will search for me but not find me. And you won't be able to come where I am!" [39](He was speaking of the Holy Spirit, who would be given to everyone believing in him; but the Spirit had not yet been given, because Jesus had not yet returned to his glory in heaven.)

Jn 14:2, 3. There are many homes up there where my Father lives, and I am going to prepare them for your coming. When everything is ready, then I will come and get you, so that you can always be with me where I am. If this weren't so, I would tell you plainly. [4]And you know where I am going and how to get there.

12. I am going to be with the Father. [28]Remember what I told you—I am going away, but I will come back to you again. If you really love me, you will be very happy for me, for now I can go to the Father, who is greater than I am.

Jn 16:5. But now I am going away to the one who sent me. [7]But the fact of the matter is that it is best for you that I go away, for if I don't, the Comforter won't come. If I do, he will—for I will send him to you. [10]I go to the Father and you shall see me no more. [16]In just a little while I will be gone, and you will see me no more; but just a little while after that, and you will see me again! [25]I have spoken of these matters very guardedly, but the time will come when this will not be necessary and I will tell you plainly all about the Father. [28]Yes, I came from the Father into the world and will leave the world and return to the Father.

Jn 17:5. And now, Father, reveal my glory as I stand in your presence, the glory we shared before the world began. [13]And now I am coming to you. I have told them many things while I was with them so that they would be filled with my joy.

Jn 20:17. "Don't touch me," he cautioned, "for I haven't yet ascended to the Father."

Acts 1:9. It was not long afterwards that he rose into the sky and disappeared into a cloud, leaving them staring after him.

Acts 3:21. For he must remain in heaven until the final recovery of all things from sin.

Eph 1:20. That raised Christ from the dead and seated him in the place of honor at God's right hand in heaven.

Eph 4:8. The Psalmist tells about this, for he says that when Christ returned triumphantly to heaven after his resurrection and victory over Satan, he gave generous gifts to men. [9]Notice that it says he returned to heaven. This means that he had first come down from the heights of heaven, far down to the lowest parts of the earth. [10]The same one who came down is the one who went back up, that he might fill all things everywhere with himself, from the very lowest to the very highest.

1 Tim 3:16. It is quite true that the way to live a godly life is not an easy matter. But the answer lies in Christ, who came to earth as a man, was proved spotless and pure in his spirit, was served by angels, was preached among the nations, was accepted by men everywhere and was received up again to his glory in heaven.

Heb 1:3. He is the one who died to cleanse us and clear our record of all sin, and then sat down in highest honor beside the great God of heaven.

Heb 4:14. But Jesus the Son of God is our great High Priest who has gone to heaven itself to help us.

Heb 9:24. For Christ has entered into heaven itself, to appear now before God as our Friend.

See *Jesus, Exaltation of.*

ATONEMENT BY. See *Atonement.*

ATTRIBUTES OF. See each one in its alphabetical order, below.

BIRTH OF. See *Incarnation of.*

COMPASSION OF. Isa 40:11. He will feed his flock like a shepherd; he will carry the lambs in his arms and gently lead the ewes with young.

Isa 42:3. He will not break the bruised reed, nor quench the dimly burning flame.

Isa 63:9. In all their affliction he was afflicted, and he personally saved them. In his love and pity he redeemed them and lifted them up and carried them through all the years. *vs.* 7, 8.

Mt 8:3. Jesus touches the man. "I want to," he says. "Be healed." And instantly the leprosy disappears. [16]That evening several demon-possessed people were brought to Jesus; and when he spoke a single word, all the demons fled; and all the sick were healed. [17]This fulfilled the prophecy of Isaiah, "He took our sicknesses and bore our diseases." Isa 53:4.

Mt 9:36. And what pity he felt for the crowds that came, because their problems were so great and they didn't know what to do or where to go for help. They were like sheep without a shepherd.

Mt 14:14. So when Jesus came out of the wilderness, a vast crowd was waiting for him and he pitied them and healed their sick.

Mt 15:32. I pity these people—they've been here with me for three days now, and have nothing left to eat; I don't want to send them away hungry or they will faint along the road.

Mt 18:11. And I, the Messiah, came to save the lost. [12]If a man has a hundred sheep, and one wanders away and is lost, what will he do? Won't he leave the ninety-nine others and go out into the hills to search for the lost one? [13]And if he finds it, he will rejoice over it more than over the ninety-nine others safe at home!

Mt 20:34. Jesus was moved with pity for them and touched their eyes. And instantly they could see, and followed him.

Mt 23:37. O Jerusalem, Jerusalem, the city that kills the prophets, and stones all those God sends to her! How often I have wanted to gather your children together as a hen gathers her chicks beneath her wings, but you wouldn't let me.

Mk 6:34. So the usual vast crowd was there as he stepped from the boat; and he had pity on them because they were like sheep without a shepherd, and he taught them many things they needed to know.

Mk 8:2. "I pity these people," he said, "for they have been here three days, and have nothing left to eat. [3]And if I send them home without feeding them, they will faint along the road! For some of them have come a long distance."

Lk 7:13. When the Lord saw her, his heart overflowed with sympathy. "Don't cry!" he said.

Lk 19:41. But as they came closer to Jerusalem and he saw the city ahead, he began to cry. [42]"Eternal peace was within your reach and you turned it down," he wept, "and now it is too late."

Jn 11:34. "Where is he buried?" he asked them. They told him, "Come and see." [35]Tears came to Jesus' eyes. [36]"They were close friends," the Jewish leaders said. "See how much he loved him." [37, 38]But some said, "This fellow healed a blind man —why couldn't he keep Lazarus from dying?" And again Jesus was moved with deep anger. Then they came to the tomb. It was a cave with a heavy stone rolled across its door.

Jn 18:8. "I told you I am he," Jesus said; "and since I am the one you are after, let these others go." [9]He did this to carry out the prophecy he had just made, "I have not lost a single one of those you gave me. . . ."

2 Cor 8:9. You know how full of love and kindness our Lord Jesus was: though he was so very rich, yet to help you he became so very poor, so that by being poor he could make you rich.

Heb 4:15. This High Priest of ours understands our weaknesses, since he had the same temptations we do, though he never once gave way to them and sinned.

See *Jesus, Love of,* below.

CONFESSING. See *Confession, of Christ; Testimony, Religious.*

CREATOR. Jn 1:3. He created everything there is—nothing exists that he didn't make. [10]But although he made the world, the world didn't recognize him when he came.

Eph 3:9. And to explain to everyone that God is the Savior of the Gentiles too, just as he who made all things had secretly planned from the very beginning.

Col 1:16. Christ himself is the Creator who made everything in heaven and earth, the things we can see and the things we can't; the spirit world with its kings and kingdoms, its rulers and authorities; all were made by Christ for his own use and glory. [17]He was before all else began and it is his power that holds everything together.

Heb 1:2. But now in these days he has spoken to us through his Son to whom he has given everything, and through whom he made the world and everything there is. [10]God also called him "Lord" when he said, "Lord, in the beginning you made the earth, and the heavens are the work of your hands."

Rev 3:14. *Write this letter to the leader of the church in Laodicea:* This message is from the one who stands firm, the faithful and true Witness (of all that is or was or evermore shall be), the primeval source of God's creation.

See *Jesus, Preexistence of,* below.

DEATH OF. Gen 3:15. From now on you and the woman will be enemies, as will all of your offspring and hers. And I will put the fear of you into the woman, and between your offspring and hers. He shall strike you on your head, while you will strike at his heel. Heb 2:14.

Ps 22:1. My God, my God, why have you forsaken me? Why do you refuse to help me or even to listen to my groans? [Mt 27:46.] [13]They come at me with open jaws, like roaring lions attacking their prey. [16]They have pierced my hands and feet. [18]They divide my clothes among themselves by a toss of the dice. Lk 23:34; Jn 19:23, 24.

Ps 69:21. For food they gave me poison; for my awful thirst they offered me vinegar. [Mt 27:34; Mk 15:23; Jn 19:28–30.] [26]For they persecute the one you have smitten, and scoff at the pain of the one you have pierced.

Ps 109:25. I am a symbol of failure to all mankind; when they see me they shake their heads. Mt 27:39.

Isa 52:14, 15. Yet many shall be amazed when they see him. . . . For they shall see and understand what they had not been told before. They shall see my Servant beaten and bloodied, so disfigured one would scarcely know it was a person standing there.

Isa 53:7. He was oppressed and he was afflicted, yet he never said a word. He was brought as a lamb to the slaughter; and as a sheep before her shearers is dumb, so he stood silent before the ones condemning him. [8]From prison and trial they led him away to his death. But who among the people of that day realized it was their sins that he was dying for—that he was suffering their punishment? [9]He was buried like a criminal in a rich man's grave; but he had done no wrong, and had never spoken an evil word. [10]Yet it was the Lord's good plan to bruise him and fill him with grief. But when his soul has been made an offering for sin, then he shall have a multitude of children, many heirs. He shall live again and God's program shall prosper in his hands. [11]And when he sees all that is accomplished by the anguish of his soul, he shall be satisfied; and because of what he has experienced, my righteous Servant shall make many to be counted righteous before God, for he shall bear all their sins. [12]Therefore I will give him the honors of one who is mighty and great, because he has poured out his soul unto death. He was counted as a sinner, and he bore the sins of many, and he pled with God for sinners.

Dan 9:26. After this period of 434 years, the Anointed One will be killed, his kingdom still unrealized . . . and a king will arise whose armies will destroy the city and the Temple. They will be overwhelmed as with a flood, and war and its miseries are decreed from that time to the very end.

Zech 12:9. For my plan is to destroy all the nations that come against Jerusalem. [10]Then I will pour out the spirit of grace and prayer on all the people of Jerusalem, and they will look on him they pierced, and mourn for him as for an only son, and grieve bitterly for him as for an oldest child who died.

Zech 13:6. "And if someone asks, 'Then what are these scars on your chest and your back?' he will say, 'I got into a brawl at the home of a friend!' [7]Awake, O sword, against my Shepherd, the man who is my associate and equal," says the Lord of Hosts. "Strike down the Shepherd and the sheep will scatter, but I will come back and comfort and care for the lambs."

Mt 12:40. For as Jonah was in the great fish for three days and three nights, so I, the Messiah, shall be in the heart of the earth three days and three nights. Lk 11:29, 30.

Mt 16:4. "This evil, unbelieving nation is asking for some strange sign in the heavens, but no further proof will be given except the miracle that happened to Jonah." Then Jesus walked out on them. [21]From then on Jesus began to speak plainly to his disciples about going to Jerusalem, and what would happen to him there—that he would suffer at the hands of the Jewish leaders, that he would be killed, and that three days later he would be raised to life again. Lk 9:22.

Mt 17:12. "And, in fact, he has already come, but he wasn't recognized, and was badly mistreated by many. And I, the Messiah, shall also suffer at their hands." [13]Then the disciples realized he was speaking of John the Baptist. [22, 23]One day while they were still in Galilee, Jesus told them, "I am going to be betrayed into the power of those who will kill me, and on the third day afterwards I will be brought back to life again." And the disciples' hearts were filled with sorrow and dread.

Mt 20:17. As Jesus was on the way to Jerusalem, he took the twelve disciples aside, [18]and talked to them about what would happen to him when they arrived. "I will be betrayed to the chief priests and other Jewish leaders, and they will condemn me to die. [19]And they will hand me over to the Roman government, and I will be mocked and crucified, and the third day I will rise to life again." Mk 10: 32, 34.

Mt 21:33. Now listen to this story: A certain landowner planted a vineyard with a hedge around it, and built a platform for the watchman, then leased the vineyard to some farmers on a sharecrop basis, and went away to live in another country. [34]At the time of the grape harvest he sent his agents to the farmers to collect his share. [35]But the farmers attacked his men, beat one, killed one and stoned another. [36]Then he sent a larger group of his men to collect for him, but the results were the same. [37]Finally the owner sent his son, thinking they would surely respect him. [38]But when these farmers saw the son coming they said among themselves, "Here comes the heir to this estate; come on, let's kill him and get it for ourselves!" [39]So they dragged him out of the vineyard and killed him.

Mt 26:2. As you know, the Passover celebration begins in two days, and I shall be betrayed and crucified.

18. He replied, "Go into the city and see Mr. So-and-So, and tell him, 'Our Master says, my time has come, and I will eat the Passover meal with my disciples at your house.' "

Mk 8:31. Then he began to tell them about the terrible things he would suffer, and that he would be rejected by the elders and the Chief Priests and the other Jewish leaders—and be killed, and that he would rise again three days afterwards.

Mk 9:31. He would say to them, "I, the Messiah, am going to be betrayed and killed and three days later I will return to life again."

Mk 10:33. "When we get there," he told them, "I, the Messiah, will be arrested and taken before the chief priests and the Jewish leaders, who will sentence me to die and hand me over to the Romans to be killed. [34]They will mock me and spit on me and flog me with their whips and kill me; but after three days I will come back to life again." Mt 20:18, 19; Lk 18:31–33.

Lk 2:34, 35. Simeon blessed them but then said to Mary, "A sword shall pierce your soul, for this child shall be rejected by many in Israel, and this to their undoing. But he will be the greatest joy of many others. And the deepest thoughts of many hearts shall be revealed."

Lk 9:22. "For I, the Messiah, must suffer much," he said, "and be rejected by the Jewish leaders—the elders, chief priests, and teachers of the Law—and be killed; and three days later I will come back to life again! [44]Listen to me and remember what I say. I, the Messiah, am going to be betrayed."

Lk 12:50. There is a terrible baptism ahead of me, and how I am pent up until it is accomplished!

Lk 17:25. But first I must suffer terribly and be rejected by this whole nation.

Lk 22:15. And he said, "I have looked forward to this hour with deep longing, anxious to eat this Passover meal with you before my suffering begins. [37]For the time has come for this prophecy about me to come true: 'He will be condemned as a criminal!' Yes, everything written about me by the prophets will come true."

Jn 10:11. I am the Good Shepherd. The Good Shepherd lays down his life for the sheep. [15]And I lay down my life for the sheep. [17]The Father loves me because I lay down my life that I may have it back again. [18]No one can kill me without my consent—I lay down my life voluntarily. For I have the right and power to lay it down when I want to and also the right and power to take it again. For the Father has given me this right.

Jn 12:7. Jesus replied, "Let her alone. She did it in preparation for my burial. [32]And when I am lifted up (on the cross), I will draw everyone to me." [33]He said this to indicate how he was going to die. Mt 26:12; Mk 14:9.

34. "Die?" asked the crowd. "We understood that the Messiah would live forever and never die. Why are you saying he will die? What Messiah are you talking about?"

Jn 13:18. "The Scripture declares, 'One who eats supper with me will betray me,' and this will soon come true. [19]I tell you this now so that when it happens, you will believe on me." [21]Now Jesus was in great anguish of spirit and exclaimed, "Yes, it is true—one of you will betray me." Mt 26:20, 21; Mk 14:18; Lk 22:21.

Jn 14:19. In just a little while I will be gone from the world, but I will still be present with you. For I will live again—and you will too.

Jn 15:13. And here is how to measure it—the greatest love is shown when a person lays down his life for his friends.

Jn 16:20. The world will greatly rejoice over what is going to happen to me, and you will weep. But your weeping shall suddenly be turned to wonderful joy (when you see me again).

Jn 18:11. Shall I not drink from the cup the Father has given me?

Acts 26:22. But God protected me so that I am still alive today to tell these facts to everyone, both great and small. I teach nothing except what the prophets and Moses said—[23]that the Messiah would suffer, and be the First to rise from the dead, to bring light to Jews and Gentiles alike.

1 Cor 1:17. For Christ didn't send me to baptize, but to preach the Gospel; and even my preaching sounds poor, for I do not fill my sermons with profound words and high sounding ideas, for fear of diluting the mighty power there is in the simple message of the cross of Christ. [18]I know very well how foolish it sounds to those who are lost, when they hear that Jesus died to save them. But we who are saved recognize this message as the very power of God. [23]So when we preach about Christ dying to save them, the Jews are offended and the Gentiles say it's all nonsense. [24]But God has opened the eyes of those called to salvation, both Jews and Gentiles, to see that Christ is the mighty power of God to save them; Christ himself is the center of God's wise plan for their salvation.

1 Cor 2:2. For I decided that I would speak only of Jesus Christ and his death on the cross.

1 Cor 15:3. I passed on to you right from the first what had been told to me, that Christ died for our sins just as the Scriptures said he would, [4]and that he was buried, and that three days afterwards he arose from the grave just as the prophets foretold.

2 Cor 4:10. These bodies of ours are constantly facing death just as Jesus did; so it is clear to all that it is only the living Christ within (who keeps us safe). [11]Yes, we live under constant danger to our lives because we serve the Lord, but this gives us constant opportunitites to show forth the power of Jesus Christ within our dying bodies.

1 Thess 4:14. For since we believe that Jesus died and then came back to life again, we can also believe that when Jesus returns, God will bring back with him all the Christians who have died.

Rev 5:12. "The Lamb is worthy" (loudly they sang it!)"—the Lamb who was slain. He is worthy to receive the power, and the riches, and the wisdom, and the strength, and the honor, and the glory, and the blessing."

Rev 13:8. And all mankind—whose names were not written down before the founding of the world in the slain Lamb's Book of Life—worshiped the evil Creature.

For circumstances of the death of, see *Jesus, History of,* above.

DESIGN OF HIS DEATH. Gen 3:15. From now on you and the woman will be enemies, as will all of your offspring and hers. And I will put the fear of you into the woman, and between your offspring and hers. He shall strike you on your head, while you will strike at his heel.

Isa 53:4. Yet it was *our* grief he bore, *our* sorrows that weighed him down. And we thought his troubles were a punishment from God, for his *own* sins! [5]But he was wounded and bruised for *our* sins. He was chastised that we might have peace; he was lashed—and we were healed! [6]*We* are the ones who strayed away like sheep! *We,* who left God's paths to follow our own. Yet God laid on *him* the guilt and sins of every one of us! [8]From prison and trial they led him away to his death. But who among the people of that day realized it was their sins that he was dying for—that he was suffering their punishment? [10]Yet it was the Lord's good plan to bruise him and fill him with grief. But when his soul has been made an offering for sin, then he shall have a multitude of children, many heirs. He shall live again and God's program shall prosper in his hands. [11]And when he sees all that is accomplished by the anguish of his soul, he shall be satisfied; and because of what he has experienced, my righteous Servant shall make many to be counted righteous before God, for he shall bear all their sins. [12]Therefore I will give him the honors of one who is mighty and great, because he has poured out his soul unto death. He was counted as a sinner, and he bore the sins of many, and he pled with God for sinners. *vs.* 1–12.

Dan 9:24. The Lord has commanded 490 years of further punishment upon Jerusalem and your people. Then at last they will learn to stay away from sin, and their guilt will be cleansed; then the kingdom of everlasting righteousness will begin, and the Most Holy Place (in the Temple) will be rededicated, as the prophets have declared. [26]After this period of 434 years, the Anointed One will be killed, his kingdom still unrealized . . . and a king will arise whose armies will destroy the city and the Temple. They will be overwhelmed as with a flood, and war and its miseries are decreed from that time to the very end.

Zech 9:11. I have delivered you from death in a waterless pit because of the covenant I made with you, sealed with blood.

Zech 13:1. At that time a Fountain will be opened to the people of Israel and Jerusalem, a Fountain to cleanse them from all their sins and uncleanness.

Mt 20:28. Your attitude must be like my own, for I, the Messiah, did not come to be served, but to serve, and to give my life as a ransom for many. Mk 10:45.

Mt 26:28. For this is my blood, sealing the New Covenant. It is poured out to forgive the sins of multitudes. Mk 14:24.

Lk 22:19. Then he took a loaf of bread; and when he had thanked God for it, he broke it apart and gave it to them, saying, "This is my body, given for you. Eat it in remembrance of me." [20]After supper he gave them another glass of wine, saying, "This wine is the token of God's new agreement to save you—an agreement sealed with the blood I shall pour out to purchase back your souls."

Lk 24:26. Wasn't it clearly predicted by the prophets that the Messiah would have to suffer all these things before entering his time of glory?

Jn 1:29. The next day John saw Jesus coming toward him and said, "Look! There is the Lamb of God who takes away the world's sin!"

Jn 3:14. And as Moses in the wilderness lifted up the bronze image of a serpent on a pole, even so I must be lifted up upon a pole, [15]so that anyone who believes in me will have eternal life. [16]For God loved the world so much that he gave his only Son so that anyone who believes in him shall not perish but have eternal life. [17]God did not send his Son into the world to condemn it, but to save it.

Jn 6:51. I am that Living Bread that came down out of heaven. Anyone eating this Bread shall live forever; this Bread is my flesh given to redeem humanity.

Jn 10:11. I am the Good Shepherd. The Good Shepherd lays down his life for the sheep. [15]Just as my Father knows me and I know the Father; and I lay down my life for the sheep. [17]The Father loves me because I lay down my life that I may have it back again.

Jn 11:49. And one of them, Caiaphas, who was High Priest that year, said, "You stupid idiots—[50]let this one man die for the people—why should the whole nation perish?" [51]This prophecy that Jesus should die for the entire nation came from Caiaphas in his position as High Priest—he didn't think of it by himself, but was inspired to say it. [52]It was a prediction that Jesus' death would not be for Israel only, but for all the children of God scattered around the world.

Jn 12:24. "Unless I die I will be alone—a single seed. But my death will produce many new wheat kernels—a plentiful harvest of new lives. [31]The time of judgment for the world has come—and the time when Satan, the prince of this world, shall be cast out. [32]And when I am lifted up [on the cross], I will draw everyone to me." [33]He said this to indicate how he was going to die.

Jn 14:19. In just a little while I will be gone from the world, but I will still be present with you. For I will live again—and you will too.

Jn 15:13. And here is how to measure it—the greatest love is shown when a person lays down his life for his friends.

Acts 5:30. The God of our ancestors brought Jesus back to life again after you had killed him by hanging him on a cross. [31]Then, with mighty power, God exalted him to be a Prince and Savior, so that the people of Israel would have an opportunity for repentance, and for their sins to be forgiven.

Acts 20:28. And now beware! Be sure that you feed and shepherd God's flock—his church, purchased with his blood—for the Holy Spirit is holding you responsible as overseers.

Acts 26:23. That the Messiah would suffer, and be the First to rise from the dead, to bring light to Jews and Gentiles alike.

Rom 3:24. Yet now God declares us "not guilty" of offending him if we trust in Jesus Christ, who in his kindness freely takes away our sins. [25]For God sent Christ Jesus to take the punishment for our sins and to end all God's anger against us. He used Christ's blood and our faith as the means of saving us from his wrath. In this way he was being entirely fair, even though he did not punish those who sinned in former times. For he was looking forward to the time when Christ would come and take away those sins.

Rom 4:25. He died for our sins and rose again to make us right with God, filling us with God's goodness.

Rom 5:6. When we were utterly helpless with no way of escape, Christ came at just the right time and died for us sinners who had no use for him. [7]Even if we were good, we really wouldn't expect anyone to die for us, though, of course, that might be barely possible. [8]But God showed his great love for us by sending Christ to die for us while we were still sinners. [9]And since by his blood he did all this for us as sinners, how much more will he do for us now that he has declared us not guilty? Now he will save us from all of God's wrath to come. [10]And since, when we were his enemies, we were brought back to God by the death of his Son, what blessings he must have for us now that we are his friends, and he is living within us! [11]Now we rejoice in our wonderful new relationship with God—all because of what our Lord Jesus Christ has done in dying for our sins—making us friends of God.

Rom 6:3. For sin's power over us was broken when we became Christians and were baptized to become a part of Jesus Christ; through his death the power of your sinful nature was shattered. [4]Your old sin-loving nature was buried with him by baptism when he died, and when God the Father, with glorious power, brought him back to life again, you were given his wonderful new life to enjoy. [5]For you have become a part of him, and so you died with him, so to speak, when he died; and now you share his new life, and shall rise as he did. [9]Christ rose from the dead and will never die again. Death no longer has any power over him. [10]He died once for all to end sin's power, but now he lives forever in unbroken fellowship with God.

Rom 8:3. We aren't saved from sin's grasp by knowing the commandments of God, because we can't and don't keep them, but God put into effect a different plan to save us. He sent his own Son in a human body like ours—except that ours are sinful—and destroyed sin's control over us by giving himself as a sacrifice for our sins. [32]Since he did not spare even his own Son for us but gave him up for us all, won't he also surely give us everything else? [34]Who then will condemn us? Will Christ? *No!* For he is the one who died for us and came back to life again for us and is sitting at the place of highest honor next to God, pleading for us there in heaven. [39]Or where we are—high above the sky, or in the deepest ocean—nothing will ever be able to separate us from the love of God demonstrated by our Lord Jesus Christ when he died for us.

Rom 14:9. Christ died and rose again for this very purpose, so that he can be our Lord both while we live and when we die. [15]And if your brother is bothered by what you eat, you are not acting in love if you go ahead and eat it. Don't let your eating ruin someone for whom Christ died.

1 Cor 5:7. Christ, God's Lamb has been slain for us.

1 Cor 6:20. For God has bought you with a great price. So use every part of your body to give glory back to God, because he owns it.

1 Cor 8:11. So because you "know it is all right to do it," you will be responsible for causing great spiritual damage to a brother with a tender conscience for whom Christ died.

1 Cor 15:3. I passed on to you right from the first what had been told to me, that Christ died for our sins just as the Scriptures said he would.

2 Cor 5:14. Whatever we do, it is certainly not for our own profit, but because Christ's love controls us now. Since we believe that Christ died for all of us, we should also believe that we have died to the old life we used to live. [15]He died for all so that all who live—having received eternal life from him—might live no longer for themselves, to please themselves, but to spend their lives pleasing Christ who died and rose again for them. [19]For God was in Christ, restoring the world to himself, no longer counting men's sins against them but blotting them out. This is the wonderful message he has given us to tell others. [21]For God took the sinless Christ and

poured into him our sins. Then, in exchange, he poured God's goodness into us!

2 Cor 8:9. You know how full of love and kindness our Lord Jesus was: though he was so very rich, yet to help you he became so very poor, so that by being poor he could make you rich.

Gal 1:4. He died for our sins just as God our Father planned, and rescued us from this evil world in which we live.

Gal 2:20. I have been crucified with Christ: and I myself no longer live, but Christ lives in me. And the real life I now have within this body is a result of my trusting in the Son of God, who loved me and gave himself for me.

Gal 3:13. But Christ has bought us out from under the doom of that impossible system by taking the curse for our wrongdoing upon himself. For it is written in the Scripture, "Anyone who is hanged on a tree is cursed" (as Jesus was hung upon a wooden cross).

Gal 4:4. But when the right time came, the time God decided on, he sent his Son, born of a woman, born as a Jew, [5]to buy freedom for us who were slaves to the law so that he could adopt us as his very own sons.

Eph 1:6. Now all praise to God for his wonderful kindness to us and his favor that he has poured out upon us, because we belong to his dearly loved Son. [7]So overflowing is his kindness towards us that he took away all our sins through the blood of his Son, by whom we are saved.

Eph 2:13. But now you belong to Christ Jesus, and though you once were far away from God, now you have been brought very near to him because of what Jesus Christ has done for you with his blood. [14]For Christ himself is our way of peace. He has made peace between us Jews and you Gentiles by making us all one family, breaking down the wall of contempt that used to separate us. [15]By his death he ended the angry resentment between us, caused by the Jewish laws which favored the Jews and excluded the Gentiles, for he died to annul that whole system of Jewish laws. Then he took the two groups that had been opposed to each other and made them parts of himself; thus he fused us together to become one new person, and at last there was peace. [16]As parts of the same body, our anger against each other has disappeared, for both of us have been reconciled to God. And so the feud ended at last at the cross.

Eph 5:2. Be full of love for others, following the example of Christ who loved you and gave himself to God as a sacrifice to take away your sins. And God was pleased, for Christ's love for you was like sweet perfume to him. [25]And you husbands, show the same kind of love to your wives as Christ showed to the church when he died for her, [26]to make her holy and clean, washed by baptism and God's Word; [27]so that he could give her to himself as a glorious church without a single spot or wrinkle or any other blemish, being holy and without a single fault.

Col 1:14. Who bought our freedom with his blood and forgave us all our sins. [20]It was through what his Son did that God cleared a path for everything to come to him—all things in heaven and on earth —for Christ's death on the cross has made peace with God for all by his blood. [21]This includes you who were once so far away from God. You were his enemies and hated him and were separated from him by your evil thoughts and actions, yet now he has brought you back as his friends. [22]He has done this through the death on the cross of his own human body, and now as a result Christ has brought you into the very presence of God, and you are standing there before him with nothing left against you—nothing left that he could even chide you for.

Col 2:14. And blotted out the charges proved against you, the list of his commandments which you had not obeyed. He took this list of sins and destroyed it by nailing it to Christ's cross. [15]In this way God took away Satan's power to accuse you of sin, and God openly displayed to the whole world Christ's triumph at the cross where your sins were all taken away.

1 Thess 1:10. Jesus, whom God brought back to life—and he is our only Savior from God's terrible anger against sin.

1 Thess 5:9. For God has not chosen to pour out his anger upon us, but to save us through our Lord Jesus Christ; [10]he died for us so that we can live with him forever, whether we are dead or alive at the time of his return.

1 Tim 2:6. By giving his life for all mankind.

Tit 2:14. He died under God's judgment against our sins, so that he could rescue us from constant falling into sin and make us his very own people, with cleansed hearts and real enthusiasm for doing kind things for others.

Heb 1:3. God's Son shines out with God's glory, and all that God's Son is and does marks him as God. He regulates the universe by the mighty power of his command. He is the one who died to cleanse us and clear our record of all sin, and then sat down in highest honor beside the great God of heaven.

Heb 2:9. But we do see Jesus—who for awhile was a little lower than the angels—crowned now by God with glory and honor because he suffered death for us. Yes, because of God's great kindness, Jesus tasted death for everyone in all the world. [10]And it was right and proper that God, who made everything for his own glory, should allow Jesus to suffer, for in doing this he was bringing in vast multitudes of God's people to heaven; for his suffering made Jesus a perfect Leader, one fit to bring them into their salvation. [14]Since we, God's children, are human beings—made of flesh and blood —he became flesh and blood too by being born in human form; for only as a human being could he die and in dying break the power of the devil who had the power of death. [15]Only in that way could he deliver those who through fear of death have been living all their lives as slaves to constant dread. [18]For since he himself has now been through suffering and temptation, he knows what it is like when we suffer and are tempted, and he is wonderfully able to help us.

Heb 7:27. He never needs the daily blood of animal sacrifices, as other priests did, to cover over first their own sins and then the sins of the people; for he finished all sacrifices, once and for all, when he sacrificed himself on the cross.

Heb 9:12. And once for all took blood into that inner room, the Holy of Holies, and sprinkled it on the mercy seat; but it was not the blood of goats and calves. No, he took his own blood, and with it he, by himself, made sure of our eternal salvation.
[13]And if under the old system the blood of bulls and goats and the ashes of young cows could cleanse men's bodies from sin, [14]just think how much more surely the blood of Christ will transform our lives and hearts. His sacrifice frees us from the worry of having to obey the old rules, and makes us want to serve the living God. For by the help of the eternal Holy Spirit, Christ willingly gave himself to God to die for our sins—he being perfect, without a single sin or fault. [15]Christ came with this new agreement so that all who are invited may come and have forever all the wonders God has promised them. For Christ died to rescue them from the penalty of the sins they had committed while still under that old system. [16]Now, if someone dies and leaves a will—a list of things to be given away to certain people when he dies—no one gets anything until it is proved that the person who wrote the will is dead. [17]The will goes into effect only after the death of the person who wrote it. While he is still alive no one can use it to get any of those things he has promised them. [25]Nor has he offered himself again and again, as the high priest down here on earth offers animal blood in the Holy of Holies each year. [26]If that had been necessary, then he would have had to die again and again, ever since the world began. But no! He came once for all, at the end of the age, to put away the power of sin forever by dying for us. [28]So also Christ died only once as an offering for the sins of many people; and he will come again, but not to deal again with our sins. This time he will come bringing salvation to all those who are eagerly and patiently waiting for him.

Heb 10:10. Under this new plan we have been forgiven and made clean by Christ's dying for us once and for all. [12]But Christ gave himself to God for our sins as one sacrifice for all time, and then sat down in the place of highest honor at God's right hand. [14]For by that one offering he made forever perfect in the sight of God all those whom he is making holy. [17]And then he adds, "I will never again remember their sins and lawless deeds." [18]Now, when sins have once been forever forgiven and forgotten, there is no need to offer more sacrifices to get rid of them. [19]And so, dear brothers, now we may walk right into the very Holy of Holies where God is, because of the blood of Jesus. [20]This is the fresh, new, life-giving way which Christ has opened up for us by tearing the curtain—his human body—to let us into the holy presence of God.

Heb 12:2. Keep your eyes on Jesus, our leader and instructor. He was willing to die a shameful death on the cross because of the joy he knew would be his afterwards; and now he sits in the place of honor by the throne of God. [24]And to Jesus himself, who has brought us his wonderful new agreement; and to the sprinkled blood which graciously forgives instead of crying out for vengeance as the blood of Abel did.

Heb 13:11. Under the system of Jewish laws the high priest brought the blood of the slain animals into the sanctuary as a sacrifice for sin, and then the bodies of the animals were burned outside the city. [12]That is why Jesus suffered and died outside the city, where his blood washed our sins away.

1 Pet 1:2. Dear friends, God the Father chose you long ago and knew you would become his children. And the Holy Spirit has been at work in your hearts, cleansing you with the blood of Jesus Christ and making you to please him. May God bless you richly and grant you increasing freedom from all anxiety and fear. [18]God paid a ransom to save you from the impossible road to heaven which your fathers tried to take, and the ransom he paid was not mere gold or silver, as you very well know. [19]But he paid for you with the precious lifeblood of Christ, the sinless, spotless Lamb of God. [20]God chose him for this purpose long before the world began, but only recently was he brought into public view, in these last days, as a blessing to you. [21]Because of this, your trust can be in God who raised Christ from the dead and gave him great glory. Now your faith and hope can rest in him alone.

1 Pet 2:21. This suffering is all part of the work God has given you. Christ, who suffered for you, is your example. Follow in his steps. [24]He personally carried the load of our sins in his own body when he died on the cross, so that we can be finished with sin and live a good life from now on. For his wounds have healed ours!

1 Pet 3:18. Christ also suffered. He died once for the sins of all of us guilty sinners, although he himself was innocent of any sin at any time, that he might bring us safely home to God. But though his body died, his spirit lived on.

1 Pet 4:1. Since Christ suffered and underwent pain, you must have the same attitude he did; you must be ready to suffer, too. For remember, when your body suffers, sin loses its power.

1 Jn 1:7. But if we are living in the light of God's presence, just as Christ does, then we have wonderful fellowship and joy with each other, and the blood of Jesus his Son cleanses us from every sin.

1 Jn 2:2. He is the one who took God's wrath against our sins upon himself, and brought us into fellowship with God; and he is the forgiveness for our sins, and not only ours but all the world's.

1 Jn 3:16. We know what real love is from Christ's example in dying for us. And so we also ought to lay down our lives for our Christian brothers.

1 Jn 4:10. In this act we see what real love is: it

is not our love for God, but his love for us when he sent his Son to satisfy God's anger against our sins.

Rev 1:5. All praise to him who always loves us and who set us free from our sins by pouring out his lifeblood for us. [6]He has gathered us into his kingdom and made us priests of God his Father.

Rev 5:9. They were singing him a new song with these words: "You are worthy to take the scroll and break its seals and open it; for you were slain, and your blood has bought people from every nation as gifts for God. [10]And you have gathered them into a kingdom and made them priests of our God; they shall reign upon the earth."

Rev 7:14. "These are the ones coming out of the Great Tribulation," he said; "they washed their robes and whitened them by the blood of the Lamb. [15]That is why they are here before the throne of God, serving him day and night in his temple. The one sitting on the throne will shelter them."

Rev 13:8. And all mankind—whose names were not written down before the founding of the world in the slain Lamb's Book of Life—worshiped the evil Creature.

See *Atonement; Reconciliation; Satan, Kingdom of, to be Destroyed.*

DEATH OF, VOLUNTARY. Isa 50:6. I give my back to the whip, and my cheeks to those who pull out the beard. I do not hide from shame—they spit in my face.

Isa 53:12. He has poured out his soul unto death. He was counted as a sinner, and he bore the sins of many, and he pled with God for sinners.

Mt 26:24. For I must die just as was prophesied, but woe to the man by whom I am betrayed. Far better for that one if he had never been born. [39]My Father! If it is possible, let this cup be taken away from me. But I want your will, not mine. [42]My Father! If this cup cannot go away until I drink it all, your will be done. [Mk 14:36, 39.] [53]Don't you realize that I could ask my Father for thousands of angels to protect us, and he would send them instantly? [54]But if I did, how would the Scriptures be fulfilled that describe what is happening now?

Lk 9:51. As the time drew near for his return to heaven, he moved steadily onward towards Jerusalem with an iron will.

Lk 12:50. There is a terrible baptism ahead of me, and how I am pent up until it is accomplished! Lk 22:15.

Lk 22:42. Father, if you are willing, please take away this cup of horror from me. But I want your will, not mine.

Jn 10:17. The Father loves me because I lay down my life that I may have it back again. [18]No one can kill me without my consent—I lay down my life voluntarily. For I have the right and power to lay it down when I want to and also the right and power to take it again.

Jn 18:5. He asked, "Whom are you looking for?" "Jesus of Nazareth," they replied. "I am he," Jesus said. [8]"I told you I am he," Jesus said; "and since I am the one you are after, let these others go." [11]But Jesus said to Peter, "Put your sword away. Shall I not drink from the cup the Father has given me?"

Jn 19:11. Then Jesus said, "You would have no power at all over me unless it were given to you from above. So those who brought me to you have the greater sin."

Phil 2:8. And he humbled himself even further, going so far as actually to die a criminal's death on a cross.

Heb 7:27. He never needs the daily blood of animal sacrifices, as other priests did, to cover over first their own sins and then the sins of the people; for he finished all sacrifices, once and for all, when he sacrificed himself on the cross.

Heb 9:26. If that had been necessary, then he would have had to die again and again, ever since the world began. But no! He came once for all, at the end of the age, to put away the power of sin forever by dying for us.

DEITY OF. As Jehovah, Isa 40:3, with Mt 3:3; Jehovah of glory, Ps 24:7, 10, with 1 Cor 2:8; Jas 2:1; Jehovah our righteousness, Jer 23:5, 6, with 1 Cor 1:30; Jehovah above all, Ps 97:8, 9, with Jn 3:31; Jehovah the first and the last, Isa 44:6, with Rev 1:17, 18; Isa 48:12–16, with Rev 22:13; Jehovah's associate and equal, Zech 13:7; Phil 2:6; Jehovah of hosts, Isa 6:1–3, with Jn 12:41; Isa 8:13–15, with 1 Pet 2:8; Jehovah, Ps 110:1, with Mt 22:42–45; Jehovah the shepherd, Isa 40:10, 11; Heb 13:20, 21; Jehovah, for whose glory all things were created, Prov 16:4, with Col 1:16; Jehovah the messenger of the covenant, Mal 3:1, with Lk 7:27. Invoked as Jehovah, Joel 2:32, with 1 Cor 1:2; as the eternal God and Creator, Ps 102:24–27, with Heb 1:8, 10–12; the mighty God, Isa 9:6; the great God and Savior, Tit 2:13; God over all, Rom 9:5; God the Judge, Eccl 12:14, with 1 Cor 4:5; 2 Cor 5:10; 2 Tim 4:1; Immanuel, Isa 7:14, with Mt 1:23; King of kings and Lord of lords, Dan 10:17, with Rev 1:5; 17:14; the Holy One, 1 Sam 2:2, with Acts 3:14; the Lord from heaven, 1 Cor 15:47; Lord of the sabbath, Gen 2:3, with Mt 12:8; Lord of all, Acts 10:36, 37; Rom 10:11–13; Son of God, Mt 26:63–67; the only Son of the Father, Jn 1:14, 18; 3:16, 18; 1 Jn 4:9. One with the Father, Jn 10:30, 38; 12:45; 14:1–10; 17:10. As sending the Spirit equally with the Father, Jn 14:15, 16, with Jn 15:26. As unsearchable equally with the Father, Prov 30:4; Mt 11:27. As Creator of all things, Isa 40:28; Jn 1:3; Col 1:16; supporter and preserver of all things, Neh 9:6, with Col 1:17; Heb 1:3. Acknowledged by Old Testament saints, Gen 17:1, with Gen 48:15, 16; 32:22–30, with Hos 12:3–5; Judg 6:22–24; 13:21, 22; Job 19:25–27.

Unclassified Scriptures Relating to the Deity of. Ex 23:20. See I am sending an Angel before you to lead you safely to the land I have prepared for you. [21]Reverence him and obey all of his instructions; do not rebel against him, for he will not pardon your transgression; he is my representative—he bears my name.

Ps 24:10. Who is this King of Glory? The Commander of all of heaven's armies! 1 Cor 2:8.

Ps 45:6. Your throne, O God, endures forever. Justice is your royal scepter. [7]You love what is good and hate what is wrong. Therefore God, your God, has given you more gladness than anyone else. Heb 1:8.

Isa 6:1. The year King Uzziah died I saw the Lord! He was sitting on a lofty throne, and the Temple was filled with his glory. Jn 12:41.

Isa 8:13. Don't fear anything except the Lord of the armies of heaven! If you fear him, you need fear nothing else. [14]He will be your safety; but Israel and Judah have refused his care and thereby stumbled against the Rock of their salvation and lie fallen and crushed beneath it. 1 Pet 2:8.

Isa 9:6. These will be his royal titles: "Wonderful," "Counselor," "The Mighty God," "The Everlasting Father," "The Prince of Peace." Tit 2:13.

Isa 40:3. Listen! I hear the voice of someone shouting, "Make a road for the Lord through the wilderness; make him a straight, smooth road through the desert. [9]Tell the cities of Judah, "Your God is coming!" [10]Yes, the Lord God is coming with mighty power; he will rule with awesome strength. Mt 3:3.

Mal 3:1. "Listen: I will send my messenger before me to prepare the way. And then the one you are looking for will come suddenly to his Temple —the Messenger of God's promises, to bring you great joy. Yes, he is surely coming," says the Lord of Hosts. Mt 11:10.

Mt 1:23. *Listen! The virgin shall conceive a child!* She shall give birth to a Son, and he shall be called "Emmanuel" (meaning "God is with us"). Isa 7:14.

Mt 8:29. They began screaming at him, "What do you want with us, O Son of God? You have no right to torment us yet." Lk 8:28.

Mt 9:5, 6. "I, the Messiah, have the authority on earth to forgive sins. But talk is cheap—anybody could say that. So I'll prove it to you by healing this man." Then, turning to the paralyzed man, he commanded, "Pick up your stretcher and go on home, for you are healed."

Mt 22:43. "Then why does David, speaking under the inspiration of the Holy Spirit, call him 'Lord'?" Jesus asked. "For David said, [44]'God said to my Lord, Sit at my right hand until I put your enemies beneath your feet.' [45]Since David called him 'Lord,' how can he be merely his son?" Ps 110:1.

Mt 28:17. There they met him and worshiped him—but some of them weren't sure it really was Jesus! [18]He told his disciples, "I have been given all authority in heaven and earth."

Mk 5:6. When Jesus was still far out on the water, the man had seen him and had run to meet him, and fell down before him. [7, 8]Then Jesus spoke to the demon within the man and said, "Come out, you evil spirit." It gave a terrible scream, shrieking, "What are you going to do to me, Jesus, Son of the Most High God? For God's sake, don't torture me!"

Lk 4:12. Jesus replied, "The Scriptures also say, 'Do not put the Lord your God to a foolish test.' "

33. Once as he was teaching in the synagogue, a man possessed by a demon began shouting at Jesus, [34]"Go away! We want nothing to do with you, Jesus from Nazareth. You have come to destroy us. I know who you are—the Holy Son of God."

Lk 9:43. Awe gripped the people as they saw this display of the power of God. Meanwhile, as they were exclaiming over all the wonderful things he was doing, Jesus said to his disciples, [44]"Listen to me and remember what I say. I, the Messiah, am going to be betrayed."

Jn 1:1, 2. Before anything else existed, there was Christ, with God. He has always been alive and is himself God.

Jn 5:17. But Jesus replied, "My Father constantly does good, and I'm following his example." [18]Then the Jewish leaders were all the more eager to kill him because in addition to disobeying their Sabbath laws, he had spoken of God as his Father, thereby making himself equal with God. [21]"He will even raise from the dead anyone he wants to, just as the Father does. [22]And the Father leaves all judgment of sin to his Son, [23]so that everyone will honor the Son, just as they honor the Father. But if you refuse to honor God's Son, whom he sent to you, then you are certainly not honoring the Father."

Jn 10:30. "I and the Father are one." [31]Then again the Jewish leaders picked up stones to kill him. [32]Jesus said, "At God's direction I have done many a miracle to help the people. For which one are you killing me?" [33]They replied, "Not for any good work, but for blasphemy; you, a mere man, have declared yourself to be God."

Jn 12:45. For when you see me, you are seeing the one who sent me.

Jn 20:28. "My Lord and my God!" Thomas said.

Acts 7:37. Moses himself told the people of Israel, "God will raise up a Prophet much like me from among your brothers." [38]How true this proved to be, for in the wilderness, Moses was the go-between—the mediator between the people of Israel and the Angel who gave them the Law of God—the Living Word—on Mount Sinai. [39]But our fathers rejected Moses and wanted to return to Egypt.

Acts 20:28. Be sure that you feed and shepherd God's flock—his church, purchased with his blood.

Rom 1:7. May all God's mercies and peace be yours from God our Father and from Jesus Christ our Lord. 1 Cor 1:3; 2 Cor 1:2; Phil 1:2; 1 Thess 1:1; 2 Thess 1:1, 2; 2 Tim 1:2.

Rom 9:5. Great men of God were your fathers, and Christ himself was one of you, a Jew so far as his human nature is concerned, he who now rules over all things. Praise God forever!

1 Cor 8:6. But we know that there is only one God, the Father, who created all things and made us to be his own; and one Lord Jesus Christ, who made everything and gives us life.

1 Cor 10:9. And don't try the Lord's patience—they did, and died from snake bites. Num 21:6.

1 Cor 15:47. Adam was made from the dust of the earth, but Christ came from heaven above.

Gal 1:1, 2. I was not called to be a missionary by any group or agency. My call is from Jesus Christ himself, and from God the Father who raised him from the dead. [3]May peace and blessing be yours from God the Father and from the Lord Jesus Christ.

Eph 1:2. May his blessings and peace be yours, sent to you from God our Father and Jesus Christ our Lord.

Eph 6:23. May God give peace to you, my Christian brothers, and love, with faith from God the Father and the Lord Jesus Christ.

Phil 2:6. Who, though he was God, did not demand and cling to his rights as God. *vs.* 5–11.

1 Thess 3:11. May God our Father himself and our Lord Jesus send us back to you again.

2 Thess 2:16. May our Lord Jesus Christ himself and God our Father, who has loved us and given us everlasting comfort and hope which we don't deserve, [17]comfort your hearts with all comfort, and help you in every good thing you say and do.

1 Tim 3:16. It is quite true that the way to live a godly life is not an easy matter. But the answer lies in Christ, who came to earth as a man, was proved spotless and pure in his Spirit, was served by angels, was preached among the nations, was accepted by men everywhere and was received up again to his glory in heaven.

Tit 2:13. Looking forward to that wonderful time we've been expecting, when his glory shall be seen—the glory of our great God and Savior Jesus Christ.

Heb 1:8. But of his Son he says, "Your kingdom, O God, will last forever and ever; its commands are always just and right." [10]God also called him "Lord" when he said, "Lord, in the beginning you made the earth, and the heavens are the work of your hands." Ps 102:24–27; *vs.* 1–14, with Gen 1:1.

1 Jn 5:20. And we know that Christ, God's Son, has come to help us understand and find the true God. And now we are in God because we are in Jesus Christ his Son, who is the only true God; and he is eternal Life.

See *Jesus, Creator, Judge, Son of God, Son of Man; Trinity.*

DENIAL OF. See *Jesus, Rejected.*

ETERNITY OF. Prov 8:22. The Lord formed me in the beginning, before he created anything else. [23]From ages past, I am. I existed before the earth began. [24]I lived before the oceans were created, before the springs bubbled forth their waters onto the earth; [25]before the mountains and the hills were made.

Isa 9:6. For unto us a Child is born; unto us a Son is given; and the government shall be upon his shoulder. These will be his royal titles: "Wonderful," "Counselor," "The Mighty God," "The Everlasting Father," "The Prince of Peace."

Mic 5:2. O Bethlehem Ephrathah, you are but a small Judean village, yet you will be the birthplace of my King who is alive from everlasting ages past!

Mk 12:36. For David himself said—and the Holy Spirit was speaking through him when he said it—"God said to my Lord, sit at my right hand until I make your enemies your footstool." [37]Since David called him his Lord, how can he be his *son?* (This sort of reasoning delighted the crowd and they listened to him with great interest.)

Jn 1:1, 2. Before anything else existed, there was Christ, with God. He has always been alive and is himself God. [4]Eternal life is in him, and this life gives light to all mankind. [15]Someone is coming who is greater by far than I am—for he existed long before I did.

Jn 6:62. Then what will you think if you see me, the Messiah, return to heaven again?

Jn 8:23. Then he said to them, "You are from below; I am from above. You are of this world; I am not." [58]*Jesus:* "The absolute truth is that I was in existence before Abraham was ever born!"

Jn 12:41. Isaiah was referring to Jesus when he made this prediction, for he had seen a vision of the Messiah's glory.

Jn 17:5. And now, Father, reveal my glory as I stand in your presence, the glory we shared before the world began.

24. Father, I want them with me—these you've given me—so that they can see my glory. You gave me the glory because you loved me before the world began!

25. O righteous Father, the world doesn't know you, but I do; and these disciples know you sent me.

Eph 3:21. May he be given glory forever and ever through endless ages because of his master plan of salvation for the church through Jesus Christ.

Eph 4:10. The same one who came down is the one who went back up, that he might fill all things everywhere with himself, from the very lowest to the very highest.

Col 1:17. He was before all else began and it is his power that holds everything together.

2 Tim 1:9. It is he who saved us and chose us for his holy work, not because we deserved it but because that was his plan long before the world began—to show his love and kindness to us through Christ.

Heb 1:10. God also called him "Lord" when he said, "Lord, in the beginning you made the earth, and the heavens are the work of your hands. [11]They will disappear into nothingness, but you will remain forever. They will become worn out like old clothes. [12]And some day you will fold them up and replace them. But you yourself will never change, and your years will never end." Ps 102:24–27.

Heb 7:16. Did not become a priest by meeting the old requirement of belonging to the tribe of Levi, but on the basis of power flowing from a life that cannot end. [24]But Jesus lives forever and continues to be a Priest so that no one else is needed. [25]He is able to save completely all who come to God through him. Since he will live forever, he will always be there to remind God that he has paid for their sins with his blood. Heb 6:20.

Heb 13:8. Jesus Christ is the same yesterday, today, and forever.

1 Pet 1:20. God chose him for this purpose long before the world began, but only recently was he brought into public view, in these last days, as a blessing to you.

1 Jn 1:1. Christ was alive when the world began, yet I myself have seen him with my own eyes and listened to him speak. I have touched him with my own hands. He is God's message of Life. [2]This one who is Life from God has been shown to us and we guarantee that we have seen him; I am speaking of Christ, who is eternal Life. He was with the Father and then was shown to us.

1 Jn 2:13. I am saying these things to you older men because you really know Christ, the one who has been alive from the beginning. And you young men, I am talking to you because you have won your battle with Satan. And I am writing to you younger boys and girls because you, too, have learned to know God our Father. [14]And so I say to you fathers who know the eternal God, and to you young men who are strong, with God's Word in your hearts, and have won your struggle against Satan.

Rev 1:8. "I am the A and the Z, the Beginning and the Ending of all things," says God, who is the Lord, the All Powerful One who is, and was, and is coming again! [11]Saying, "I am A and Z, the First and Last! [17, 18]I am the First and Last, the Living One who died, who is now alive forevermore."

Rev 5:13. And then I heard everyone in heaven and earth, and from the dead beneath the earth and in the sea, exclaiming, "The blessing and the honor and the glory and the power belong to the one sitting on the throne, and to the Lamb forever and ever." [14]And the four Living Beings kept saying, "Amen!" And the twenty-four Elders fell down and worshiped him.

See *Jesus, Preexistence of,* below.

EXALTATION OF. Ps 2:8. Only ask, and I will give you all the nations of the world. [9]Rule them with an iron rod; smash them like clay pots!

Ps 24:7. Open up, O ancient gates, and let the King of Glory in. *vs.* 8–10.

Ps 68:18. He ascends the heights, leading many captives in his train. He receives gifts for men, even those who once were rebels. God will live among us here. Eph 4:8.

Mk 16:19. When the Lord Jesus had finished talking with them, he was taken up into heaven and sat down at God's right hand.

Lk 22:69. But the time is soon coming when I, the Messiah, shall be enthroned beside Almighty God.

Lk 24:26. Wasn't it clearly predicted by the prophets that the Messiah would have to suffer all these things before entering his time of glory?

Jn 7:39. He was speaking of the Holy Spirit, who would be given to everyone believing in him; but the Spirit had not yet been given, because Jesus had not yet returned to his glory in heaven.

Jn 13:31. As soon as Judas left the room, Jesus said, "My time has come; the glory of God will soon surround me—and God shall receive great praise because of all that happens to me. [32]And God shall give me his own glory, and this so very soon."

Jn 17:5. And now, Father, reveal my glory as I stand in your presence, the glory we shared before the world began.

Acts 2:33. And now he sits on the throne of highest honor in heaven, next to God. And just as promised, the Father gave him the authority to send the Holy Spirit—with the results you are seeing and hearing today. [34](No, David was not speaking of himself in these words of his I have quoted), for he never ascended into the skies. Moreover, he further stated, "God spoke to my Lord, the Messiah, and said to him, Sit here in honor beside me."

Acts 3:20. And send Jesus your Messiah back to you again. [21]For he must remain in heaven until the final recovery of all things from sin.

Acts 5:31. Then, with mighty power, God exalted him to be a Prince and Savior, so that the people of Israel would have an opportunity for repentance, and for their sins to be forgiven.

Acts 7:55. But Stephen, full of the Holy Spirit, gazed steadily upward into heaven and saw the glory of God and Jesus standing at God's right hand. [56]And he told them, "Look, I see the heavens opened and Jesus the Messiah standing beside God, at his right hand!"

Rom 8:17. And since we are his children, we will share his treasures—for all God gives to his Son Jesus is now ours too. But if we are to share his glory, we must also share his suffering. [34]Who then will condemn us? Will Christ? *No!* For he is the one who died for us and came back to life again for us and is sitting at the place of highest honor next to God, pleading for us there in heaven.

Eph 1:20. That raised Christ from the dead and seated him in the place of honor at God's right hand in heaven.

Eph 4:10. The same one who came down is the one who went back up, that he might fill all things everywhere with himself, from the very lowest to the very highest.

Phil 2:9. Yet it was because of this that God raised him up to the heights of heaven and gave him a name which is above every other name, [10]that at the name of Jesus every knee shall bow in heaven and earth and under the earth, [11]and every tongue shall confess that Jesus Christ is Lord, to the glory of God the Father.

Col 2:15. In this way God took away Satan's power to accuse you of sin, and God openly displayed to the whole world Christ's triumph at the cross where your sins were all taken away.

Col 3:1. Since you became alive again, so to speak, when Christ arose from the dead, now set your sights on the rich treasures and joys of heaven where he sits beside God in the place of honor and power.

1 Tim 3:16. The answer lies in Christ, who came to earth as a man. . . . and was received up again to his glory in heaven.

Heb 1:3. God's Son shines out with God's glory, and all that God's Son is and does marks him as God. He regulates the universe by the mighty power of his command. He is the one who died to cleanse us and clear our record of all sin, and then sat down in highest honor beside the great God of heaven.

Heb 2:9. But we do see Jesus—who for awhile was a little lower than the angels—crowned now by God with glory and honor because he suffered death for us. Yes, because of God's great kindness, Jesus tasted death for everyone in all the world.

Heb 4:10. Christ has already entered there. He is resting from his work, just as God did after the creation. [14]But Jesus the Son of God is our great High Priest who has gone to heaven itself to help us; therefore let us never stop trusting him.

Heb 6:20. Where Christ has gone ahead to plead for us from his position as our High Priest, with the honor and rank of Melchizedek.

Heb 7:26. He is, therefore, exactly the kind of High Priest we need; for he is holy and blameless, unstained by sin, undefiled by sinners, and to him has been given the place of honor in heaven.

Heb 8:1. What we are saying is this: Christ, whose priesthood we have just described, is our High Priest, and is in heaven at the place of greatest honor next to God himself.

Heb 9:12. And once for all took blood into that inner room, the Holy of Holies, and sprinkled it on the mercy seat; but it was not the blood of goats and calves. No, he took his own blood, and with it he, by himself, made sure of our eternal salvation. [24]For Christ has entered into heaven itself, to appear now before God as our Friend. It was not in the earthly place of worship that he did this, for that was merely a copy of the real temple in heaven.

Heb 10:12. For Christ gave himself to God for our sins as one sacrifice for all time, and then sat down in the place of highest honor at God's right hand, [13]waiting for his enemies to be laid under his feet.

Heb 12:2. Keep your eyes on Jesus, our leader and instructor. He was willing to die a shameful death on the cross because of the joy he knew would be his afterwards; and now he sits in the place of honor by the throne of God.

1 Pet 3:22. And now Christ is in heaven, sitting in the place of honor next to God the Father, with all the angels and powers of heaven bowing before him and obeying him.

EXAMPLE, AN. Mt 11:29. Wear my yoke—for it fits perfectly—and let me teach you; for I am gentle and humble, and you shall find rest for your souls.

Mt 20:28. Your attitude must be like my own, for I, the Messiah, did not come to be served, but to serve, and to give my life as a ransom for many.

Mk 10:43. But among you it is different. Whoever wants to be great among you must be your servant. [44]And whoever wants to be greatest of all must be the slave of all. [45]For even I, the Messiah, am not here to be served, but to help others, and to give my life as a ransom for many.

Lk 22:26. But among you, the one who serves you best will be your leader. [27]Out in the world the master sits at the table and is served by his servants. But not here! For I am your servant.

Jn 10:4. He walks ahead of them; and they follow him, for they recognize his voice.

Jn 13:13. You call me "Master" and "Lord," and you do well to say it, for it is true. [14]And since I, the Lord and Teacher, have washed your feet, you ought to wash each other's feet. [15]I have given you an example to follow: do as I have done to you. [34]And so I am giving a new commandment to you now—love each other just as much as I love you.

Jn 17:14. I have given them your commands. And the world hates them because they don't fit in with it, just as I don't. [18]As you sent me into the world, I am sending them into the world. [21]My prayer for all of them is that they will be of one heart and mind, just as you and I are, Father—that just as you are in me and I am in you, so they will be in us, and the world will believe you sent me. [22]I have given them the glory you gave me—the glorious unity of being one, as we are.

Rom 8:29. For from the very beginning God decided that those who came to him—and all along he knew who would—should become like his Son, so that his Son would be the First, with many brothers.

Rom 13:14. But ask the Lord Jesus Christ to help you live as you should, and don't make plans to enjoy evil.

Rom 15:2. Let's please the other fellow, not ourselves, and do what is for his good and thus build him up in the Lord. [3]Christ didn't please himself. As the Psalmist said, "He came for the very purpose of suffering under the insults of those who were against the Lord." [5]May God who gives patience, steadiness, and encouragement help you to live in complete harmony with each other—each with the attitude of Christ toward the other. [7]So, warmly welcome each other into the church, just as Christ has warmly welcomed you; then God will be glorified.

2 Cor 4:10. These bodies of ours are constantly facing death just as Jesus did; so it is clear to all that it is only the living Christ within (who keeps us safe).

2 Cor 8:9. You know how full of love and kindness our Lord Jesus was: though he was so very rich, yet to help you he became so very poor, so that by being poor he could make you rich.

2 Cor 10:1. I plead with you—yes, I, Paul—and I plead gently, as Christ himself would do. Yet some of you are saying, "Paul's letters are bold enough when he is far away, but when he gets here he will be afraid to raise his voice!"

Gal 3:27. And we who have been baptized into union with Christ are enveloped by him.

Gal 6:2. Share each other's troubles and problems, and so obey our Lord's command.

Eph 4:13. Until finally we all believe alike about our salvation and about our Savior, God's Son, and all become full-grown in the Lord—yes, to the point of being filled full with Christ. [15]Instead, we will lovingly follow the truth at all times—speaking truly, dealing truly, living truly—and so become more and more in every way like Christ who is the Head of his body, the church. [24]Yes, you must be a new and different person, holy and good. Clothe yourself with this new nature. *v.* 32.

Eph 5:2. Be full of love for others, following the example of Christ who loved you and gave himself to God as a sacrifice to take away your sins. And God was pleased, for Christ's love for you was like sweet perfume to him.

Eph 6:9. And you slave owners must treat your slaves right, just as I have told them to treat you. Don't keep threatening them; remember, you yourselves are slaves to Christ; you have the same Master they do, and he has no favorites.

Phil 2:5. Your attitude should be the kind that was shown us by Jesus Christ, [6]who, though he was God, did not demand and cling to his rights as God, [7]but laid aside his mighty power and glory, taking the disguise of a slave and becoming like men. [8]And he humbled himself even further, going so far as actually to die a criminal's death on a cross.

Col 3:10. You are living a brand new kind of life that is continually learning more and more of what is right, and trying constantly to be more and more like Christ who created this new life within you. [11]. . . Whether a person has Christ is what matters, and he is equally available to all. [13]Be gentle and ready to forgive; never hold grudges. Remember, the Lord forgave you, so you must forgive others.

1 Thess 1:6. So you became our followers and the Lord's; for you received our message with joy from the Holy Spirit in spite of the trials and sorrows it brought you.

Heb 3:1. Therefore, dear brothers whom God has set apart for himself—you who are chosen for heaven—I want you to think now about this Jesus who is God's Messenger and the High Priest of our faith.

Heb 12:2. Keep your eyes on Jesus, our leader and instructor. He was willing to die a shameful death on the cross because of the joy he knew would be his afterwards; and now he sits in the place of honor by the throne of God. [3]If you want to keep from becoming fainthearted and weary, think about his patience as sinful men did such terrible things to him. [4]After all, you have never yet struggled against sin and temptation until you sweat great drops of blood.

1 Pet 1:15. But be holy now in everything you do, just as the Lord is holy, who invited you to be his child. *v.* 16.

1 Pet 2:21. This suffering is all part of the work God has given you. Christ, who suffered for you, is your example. Follow in his steps: [22]He never sinned, never told a lie, [23]never answered back when insulted; when he suffered he did not threaten to get even; he left his case in the hands of God who always judges fairly. [24]He personally carried the load of our sins in his own body when he died on the cross, so that we can be finished with sin and live a good life from now on. For his wounds have healed ours!

1 Pet 3:17. Remember, if God wants you to suffer, it is better to suffer for doing good than for doing wrong! [18]Christ also suffered. He died once for the sins of all us guilty sinners, although he himself was innocent of any sin at any time, that he might bring us safely home to God. But though his body died, his spirit lived on.

1 Jn 2:6. Anyone who says he is a Christian should live as Christ did.

1 Jn 3:1. See how very much our heavenly Father loves us, for he allows us to be called his children —think of it—and we really *are!* But since most people don't know God, naturally they don't understand that we are his children. [2]Yes, dear friends, we are already God's children, right now, and we can't even imagine what it is going to be like later on. But we do know this, that when he comes we will be like him, as a result of seeing him as he really is. [3]And everyone who really believes this will try to stay pure because Christ is pure. [16]We know what real love is from Christ's example in dying for us. And so we also ought to lay down our lives for our Christian brothers.

1 Jn 4:17. And as we live with Christ, our love grows more perfect and complete; so we will not be ashamed and embarrassed at the day of judgment, but can face him with confidence and joy, because he loves us and we love him too.

Rev 3:21. I will let every one who conquers sit beside me on my throne, just as I took my place with my Father on his throne when I had conquered.

Rev 14:4. For they are spiritually undefiled, pure as virgins, following the Lamb wherever he goes.

FAITH IN. See *Faith; Salvation, Conditions of.*

FOREKNOWLEDGE OF. See *Jesus, Omniscience of.*

GENEALOGY OF. See *Jesus, History of,* at beginning of the topic.

HEALING BY. See *Miracles.*

HOLINESS OF. Ps 45:7. You love what is good and hate what is wrong. Therefore God, your God, has given you more gladness than anyone else. Heb 1:9.

Isa 11:4. But will defend the poor and the exploited. He will rule against the wicked who oppress them. [5]For he will be clothed with fairness and with truth.

Isa 32:1. Look, a righteous King is coming, with honest princes!

Isa 42:21. The Lord has magnified his law and made it truly glorious. Through it he had planned to show the world that he is righteous.

Isa 49:7. The Lord, the Redeemer and Holy One of Israel, says to the one who is despised, rejected by mankind, and kept beneath the heel of earthly rulers: "Kings shall stand at attention when you pass by; princes shall bow low because the Lord has chosen you; he, the faithful Lord, the Holy One of Israel, chooses you."

Isa 50:5. The Lord God has spoken to me and I have listened; I do not rebel nor turn away.

Isa 53:9. But he had done no wrong, and had never spoken an evil word.

Isa 59:17. He put on righteousness as armor, and the helmet of salvation on his head. He clothed himself with robes of vengeance and of godly fury.

Jer 23:5. For the time is coming, says the Lord, when I will place a righteous Branch upon King David's throne.

Zech 9:9. Rejoice greatly, O my people! Shout with joy! For look—your King is coming! He is the Righteous One, the Victor! Yet he is lowly, riding on a donkey's colt!

Mk 1:24. "Why are you bothering us, Jesus of Nazareth—have you come to destroy us demons? I know who you are—the holy Son of God!"

Lk 1:35. So the baby born to you will be utterly holy—the Son of God.

Lk 4:34. I know who you are—the Holy Son of God.

Lk 23:40, 41. But the other criminal protested. "Don't you even fear God when you are dying? We deserve to die for our evil deeds, but this man hasn't done one thing wrong." [47]When the captain of the Roman military unit handling the executions saw what had happened, he was stricken with awe before God and said, "Surely this man was innocent."

Jn 5:30. But I pass no judgment without consulting the Father. I judge as I am told. And my judgment is absolutely fair and just, for it is according to the will of God who sent me and is not merely my own.

Jn 8:46. Which of you can truthfully accuse me of one single sin? (No one!)

Jn 14:30. For the evil prince of this world approaches. He has no power over me.

Acts 3:14. You didn't want him freed—this holy, righteous one. Instead you demanded the release of a murderer.

Acts 4:27. For Herod the king, and Pontius Pilate the governor, and all the Romans—as well as the people of Israel—are united against Jesus, your anointed Son, your holy servant.

30. And send your healing power, and may miracles and wonders be done by the name of your holy servant Jesus.

Acts 13:28. They found no just cause to execute him, but asked Pilate to have him killed anyway. [35]In another Psalm he explained more fully, saying, "God will not let his Holy One decay."

2 Cor 4:4. Satan, who is the god of this evil world, has made him blind, unable to see the glorious light of the Gospel that is shining upon him, or to understand the amazing message we preach about the glory of Christ, who is God.

2 Cor 5:21. For God took the sinless Christ and poured into him our sins. Then, in exchange, he poured God's goodness into us!

Heb 1:9. You love right and hate wrong; so God, even your God, has poured out more gladness upon you than on anyone else.

Heb 4:15. This High Priest of ours understands our weaknesses, since he had the same temptations we do, though he never once gave way to them and sinned.

Heb 7:26. He is, therefore, exactly the kind of High Priest we need; for he is holy and blameless, unstained by sin, undefiled by sinners, and to him has been given the place of honor in heaven. [27]He never needs the daily blood of animal sacrifices, as other priests did, to cover over first their own sins and then the sins of the people; for he finished all sacrifices, once and for all, when he sacrificed himself on the cross. [28]Under the old system, even the high priests were weak and sinful men who could not keep from doing wrong, but later God appointed by his oath his Son who is perfect forever.

Heb 9:14. For by the help of the eternal Holy Spirit, Christ willingly gave himself to God to die for our sins—he being perfect, without a single sin or fault.

1 Pet 1:19. But he paid for you with the precious lifeblood of Christ, the sinless, spotless Lamb of God.

1 Pet 2:22. He never sinned, never told a lie.

1 Jn 2:29. Since we know that God is always good and does only right, we may rightly assume that all those who do right are his children.

1 Jn 3:5. There is no sin in him.

Rev 3:7. *Write this letter to the leader of the church in Philadelphia.* This message is sent to you by the one who is holy and true, and has the key of David to open what no one can shut and to shut what no one can open.

HUMANITY OF. Gen 3:15. From now on you and the woman will be enemies, as will all of your offspring and hers. And I will put the fear of you into the woman, and between your offspring and hers. He shall strike you on your head, while you will strike at his heel.

Deut 18:15. Instead, he will raise up for you a Prophet like me, an Israeli, a man to whom you must listen and whom you must obey. [16]For this is what you yourselves begged of God at Mount Horeb. There at the foot of the mountain you begged that you might not have to listen to the terrifying voice of God again, or see the awesome fire on the mountain, lest you die. [17]"All right," the Lord said to me, "I will do as they have requested. [18]I will raise up from among them a Prophet, an Israeli like you. I will tell him what to say, and he shall be my spokesman to the people. [19]I will personally deal with anyone who will not listen to him and heed his messages from me."

Ps 22:22. I will praise you to all my brothers; I will stand up before the congregation and testify of the wonderful things you have done.

Isa 8:18. I and the children God has given me have symbolic names that reveal the plans of the Lord of heaven's armies for his people.

Isa 9:6. For unto us a Child is born; unto us a Son is given; and the government shall be upon his shoulder. These will be his royal titles: "Wonderful," "Counselor," "The Mighty God," "The Everlasting Father," "The Prince of Peace."

Dan 7:13. Next I saw the arrival of a Man—or so he seemed to be—brought there on clouds from heaven; he approached the Ancient of Days and was presented to him.

Mt 16:27. For I, the Son of Mankind, shall come with my angels in the glory of my Father and judge each person according to his deeds. [28]And some of you standing right here now will certainly live to see me coming in my Kingdom.

Mt 20:28. Your attitude must be like my own, for I, the Messiah, did not come to be served, but to serve, and to give my life as a ransom for many. [30]Two blind men were sitting beside the road and when they heard that Jesus was coming that way, they began shouting, "Sir, King David's Son, have mercy on us!" [31]The crowd told them to be quiet, but they only yelled the louder.

Mt 21:9. Then the crowds surged on ahead and pressed along behind, shouting, "God bless King David's Son!" . . . "God's Man is here!" . . . "Bless him, Lord!" . . . "Praise God in highest heaven!"

Mt 26:26. As they were eating, Jesus took a small loaf of bread and blessed it and broke it apart and gave it to the disciples and said, "Take it and eat it, for this is my body." [27]And he took a cup of wine and gave thanks for it and gave it to them and said, "Each one drink from it, [28]for this is my blood, sealing the New Covenant. It is poured out to forgive the sins of multitudes." [36]Then Jesus brought them to a garden grove, Gethsemane, and told them to sit down and wait while he went on ahead to pray. [37]He took Peter with him and Zebedee's two sons James and John, and began to be filled with anguish and despair. [38]Then he told them, "My soul is crushed with horror and sadness to the point of death . . . stay here . . . stay awake with me." [39]He went forward a little, and fell face downward on the ground, and prayed, "My Father! If it is possible, let this cup be taken away from me. But I want your will, not mine." [40]Then he returned to the three disciples and found them asleep. "Peter," he called, "couldn't you even stay awake with me one hour? [41]Keep alert and pray. Otherwise temptation will overpower you. For the spirit indeed is willing, but how weak the body is!" [42]Again he left them and prayed, "My Father! If this cup cannot go away until I drink it all, your will be done." [43]He returned to them again and found them sleeping, for their eyes were heavy, [44]so he went back to prayer the third time, saying the same things again. [45]Then he came to the disciples and said, "Sleep on now and take your rest . . . but no! The time has come! I am betrayed into the hands of evil men!" Mk 14:34, 42.

Lk 2:11. The Savior—yes, the Messiah, the Lord—has been born tonight in Bethlehem! [12]How will you recognize him? You will find a baby wrapped in a blanket, lying in a manger! [13]Suddenly, the angel was joined by a vast host of others—the armies of heaven—praising God: [14]"Glory to God in the highest heaven," they sang, "and peace on earth for all those pleasing him."

Jn 1:14. And Christ became a human being and lived here on earth among us and was full of loving forgiveness and truth. And some of us have seen his glory—the glory of the only Son of the heavenly Father!

Jn 5:27. And to judge the sins of all mankind because he is the Son of Man.

Acts 17:31. For he has set a day for justly judging the world by the man he has appointed, and has pointed him out by bringing him back to life again.

Rom 8:3. We aren't saved from sin's grasp by knowing the commandments of God, because we can't and don't keep them, but God put into effect a different plan to save us. He sent his own Son in a human body like ours—except that ours are sinful—and destroyed sin's control over us by giving himself as a sacrifice for our sins.

Gal 4:4. But when the right time came, the time God decided on, he sent his Son, born of a woman, born as a Jew.

Phil 2:7. But laid aside his mighty power and glory, taking the disguise of a slave and becoming like men. [8]And he humbled himself even further, going so far as actually to die a criminal's death on a cross.

1 Tim 2:5. That God is on one side and all the people on the other side, and Jesus Christ, himself man, is between them to bring them together.

Heb 2:9. But we do see Jesus—who for awhile was a little lower than the angels—crowned now by God with glory and honor because he suffered death for us. Yes, because of God's great kindness, Jesus tasted death for everyone in all the world. [10]And it was right and proper that God, who made everything for his own glory, would allow Jesus to suffer, for in doing this he was bringing vast multitudes of God's people to heaven; for his suffering made Jesus a perfect Leader, one fit to bring them into their salvation. [14]Since we, God's children, are human beings—made of flesh and blood—he became flesh and blood too by being born in human form; for only as a human being could he die and in dying break the power of death. [15]Only in that way could he deliver those who through fear of death have been living all their lives as slaves to constant dread. [16]We all know he did not come as an angel but as a human being—yes, a Jew. [17]And it was necessary for Jesus to be like us, his brothers, so that he could be our merciful and faithful High Priest before God, a Priest who would be both merciful to us and faithful to God in dealing with the sins of the people. [18]For since he himself has now been through suffering and temptation, he knows what it is like when we suffer and are tempted, and he is wonderfully able to help us.

1 Jn 4:2. And the way to find out if their message is from the Holy Spirit is to ask: Does it really agree that Jesus Christ, God's Son, actually became man with a human body? If so, then the

message is from God. [3]If not, the message is not from God but from one who is against Christ, like the "Antichrist" you have heard about who is going to come, and his attitude of enmity against Christ is already abroad in the world.

2 Jn 1:7. Watch out for the false leaders—and there are many of them around—who don't believe that Jesus Christ came to earth as a human being with a body like ours. Such people are against the truth and against Christ.

Rev 1:13. And standing among them was one who looked like Jesus who called himself the Son of Man, wearing a long robe circled with a golden band across his chest.

Rev 14:14. Then the scene changed and I saw a white cloud, and someone sitting on it who looked like Jesus, who was called "The Son of Man," with a crown of solid gold upon his head and a sharp sickle in his hand.

See *Jesus, Incarnation of, History of, Relation of, to the Father, Prophecies Concerning the Coming of.*

HUMILITY OF. Zech 9:9. Yet he is lowly, riding on a donkey's colt! Mt 21:5.

Mt 9:10. Later, as Jesus and his disciples were eating dinner [at Matthew's house], there were many notorious swindlers there as guests! Mk 2:14; Lk 5:27, 28.

Lk 22:27. Out in the world the master sits at the table and is served by his servants. But not here! For I am your servant.

Jn 13:5. Poured water into a basin, and began to wash the disciples' feet and to wipe them with the towel he had around him. [14]"And since I, the Lord and Teacher, have washed your feet, you ought to wash each other's feet."

Acts 8:32. The passage of Scripture he had been reading from was this: "He was led as a sheep to the slaughter, and as a lamb is silent before the shearers, so he opened not his mouth; [33]in his humiliation, justice was denied him; and who can express the wickedness of the people of his generation? For his life is taken from the earth."

2 Cor 8:9. You know how full of love and kindness our Lord Jesus was: though he was so very rich, yet to help you he became so very poor, so that by being poor he could make you rich.

2 Cor 10:1. I plead with you—yes, I, Paul—and I plead gently, as Christ himself would do.

Phil 2:7. But laid aside his mighty power and glory, taking the disguise of a slave and becoming like men. [8]And he humbled himself even further, going so far as actually to die a criminal's death on a cross.

See *Jesus, Meekness of, below; Meekness.*

IMPECCABILITY OF. See *Holiness of,* above; *Temptation of,* below.

INCARNATION OF. Gen 3:15. From now on you and the woman will be enemies, as will all of your offspring and hers. And I will put the fear of you into the woman, and between your offspring and hers. He shall strike you on your head, while you will strike at his heel.

Deut 18:15. Instead, he will raise up for you a Prophet like me, an Israeli, a man to whom you must listen and whom you must obey. [16]For this is what you yourselves begged of God at Mount Horeb. There at the foot of the mountain you begged that you might not have to listen to the terrifying voice of God again, or see the awesome fire on the mountain, lest you die. [17]"All right," the Lord said to me, "I will do as they have requested. [18]I will raise up from among them a Prophet, an Israeli like you. I will tell him what to say, and he shall be my spokesman to the people."

1 Chron 5:2. Although Joseph received the birthright, yet Judah was a powerful and influential tribe in Israel, and from Judah came a Prince.

Ps 2:7. His chosen one replies, "I will reveal the everlasting purposes of God, for the Lord has said to me, 'You are my Son. This is your Coronation Day.' " Acts 13:32, 33.

Ps 40:7. Then I said, "See, I have come, just as all the prophets foretold. [8]And I delight to do your will, my God, for your law is written upon my heart!"

Ps 80:17. Strengthen the man you love, the son of your choice.

Ps 89:19. In a vision you spoke to your prophet and said, "I have chosen a splendid young man from the common people to be the king.

Isa 7:14. All right then, the Lord himself will choose the sign—a child shall be born to a virgin! And she shall call him Immanuel (meaning, "God is with us"). [15, 16]By the time this child is weaned and knows right from wrong, the two kings you fear so much—the kings of Israel and Syria—will both be dead.

Isa 9:6. For unto us a Child is born; unto us a Son is given; and the government shall be upon his shoulder. These will be his royal titles: "Wonderful," "Counselor," "The Mighty God," "The Everlasting Father," "The Prince of Peace."

Isa 11:1. The royal line of David will be cut off, chopped down like a tree; but from the stump will grow a Shoot—yes, a new Branch from the old root.

Isa 32:2. He will shelter Israel from the storm and wind. He will refresh her as a river in the desert and as the cooling shadow of a mighty rock within a hot and weary land.

Isa 49:1. Listen to me, all of you in far-off lands: The Lord called me before my birth. From within the womb he called me by my name. [5]"And now," said the Lord—the Lord who formed me from my mother's womb to serve him who commissioned me to restore to him his people Israel, who has given me the strength to perform this task and honored me for doing it!

Jer 23:5. For the time is coming, says the Lord, when I will place a righteous Branch upon King David's throne. He shall be a King who shall rule with wisdom and justice and cause righteousness to prevail everywhere throughout the earth.

Mic 5:2. O Bethlehem Ephrathah, you are but a small Judean village, yet you will be the birthplace of my King who is alive from everlasting ages past! [3]God will abandon his people to their enemies until the time of Israel's spiritual rebirth; then at last the exile remnants of Israel will rejoin their brethren in their own land. Mt 2:5, 6.

Mt 1:1. These are the ancestors of Jesus Christ, a descendant of King David and of Abraham. [16]Jacob was the father of Joseph (who was the husband of Mary, the mother of Jesus Christ the Messiah). [17]These are fourteen of the generations from Abraham to King David; and fourteen from King David's time to the exile; and fourteen from the exile to Christ. [Lk 3:23–38.] [18]These are the facts concerning the birth of Jesus Christ: His mother, Mary, was engaged to be married to Joseph. But while she was still a virgin she became pregnant by the Holy Spirit. [23]*"Listen! The virgin shall conceive a child!* She shall give birth to a Son, and he shall be called 'Emmanuel' (meaning 'God is with us')."

Mt 8:20. But Jesus said, "Foxes have dens and birds have nests, but I, the Messiah, have no home of my own—no place to lay my head."

Mt 13:55. "How is this possible?" the people exclaimed. "He's just a carpenter's son, and we know Mary his mother and his brothers—James, Joseph, Simon, and Judas. [56]And his sisters—they all live here. How can be be so great?"

Mt 22:45. Since David called him "Lord," how can he be merely his son?

Lk 1:26. The following month God sent the angel Gabriel to Nazareth, a village in Galilee, [27]to a virgin, Mary, engaged to be married to a man named Joseph, a descendant of King David. [28]Gabriel appeared to her and said, "Congratulations, favored lady! The Lord is with you!" [29]Confused and disturbed, Mary tried to think what the angel could mean. [30]"Don't be frightened, Mary," the angel told her, "for God has decided to wonderfully bless you! [31]Very soon now, you will become pregnant and have a baby boy, and you are to name him 'Jesus.' [32]He shall be very great and shall be called the Son of God. And the Lord God shall give him the throne of his ancestor David. [33]And he shall reign over Israel forever; his Kingdom shall never end!" [34]Mary asked the angel, "But how can I have a baby? I am a virgin." [35]The angel replied, "The Holy Spirit shall come upon you, and the power of God shall overshadow you; so the baby born to you will be utterly holy—the Son of God." [38]Mary said, "I am the Lord's servant, and I am willing to do whatever he wants. May everything you said come true." And then the angel disappeared. [39, 40]A few days later Mary hurried to the highlands of Judea to the town where Zacharias lived, to visit Elizabeth. [41]At the sound of Mary's greeting, Elizabeth's child leaped within her and she was filled with the Holy Spirit. [42]She gave a glad cry and exclaimed to Mary, "You are favored by God above all other women, and your child is destined for God's mightiest praise. [43]What an honor this is, that the mother of my Lord should visit me! [44]When you came in and greeted me, the instant I heard your voice, my baby moved in me for joy! [45]You believed that God would do what he said; that is why he has given you this wonderful blessing." [46]Mary responded, "Oh, how I praise the Lord. [47]How I rejoice in God my Savior! [48]For he took notice of his lowly servant girl, and now generation after generation forever shall call me blest of God. [49]For he, the mighty Holy One, has done great things to me. [50]His mercy goes on from generation to generation, to all who reverence him. [51]How powerful is his mighty arm! How he scatters the proud and haughty ones! [52]He has torn princes from their thrones and exalted the lowly. [53]He has satisfied the hungry hearts and sent the rich away with empty hands. [54]And how he has helped his servant Israel! He has not forgotten his promise to be merciful. [55]For he promised our fathers—Abraham and his children—to be merciful to them forever." [56]Mary stayed with Elizabeth about three months and then went back to her own home.

Lk 2:1. About this time Caesar Augustus, the Roman Emperor, decreed that a census should be taken throughout the nation. [2](This census was taken when Quirinius was governor of Syria.) [3]Everyone was required to return to his ancestral home for this registration. [4]And because Joseph was a member of the royal line, he had to go to Bethlehem in Judea, King David's ancient home—journeying there from the Galilean village of Nazareth. [5]He took with him Mary, his fiancee, who was obviously pregnant by this time. [6]And while they were there, the time came for her baby to be born; [7]and she gave birth to her first child, a son. She wrapped him in a blanket and laid him in a manger, because there was no room for them in the village inn. [8]That night some shepherds were in the fields outside of the village, guarding their flocks of sheep. [9]Suddenly an angel appeared among them, and the landscape shone bright with the glory of the Lord. They were badly frightened, [10]but the angel reassured them. "Don't be afraid!" he said. "I bring you the most joyful news ever announced, and it is for everyone! [11]The Savior—yes, the Messiah, the Lord—has been born tonight in Bethlehem! [12]How will you recognize him? You will find a baby wrapped in a blanket, lying in a manger!" [13]Suddenly, the angel was joined by a vast host of others—the armies of heaven—praising God: [14]"Glory to God in the highest heaven," they sang, "and peace on earth for all those pleasing him." [15]When this great army of angels had returned again to heaven, the shepherds said to each other, "Come on! Let's go to Bethlehem! Let's see this wonderful thing that has happened, which the Lord has told us about." [16]They ran to the village and found their way to Mary and Joseph. And there was the baby, lying in the manger. [17]The shepherds told everyone what had happened and what the angel had said to them about this child. [18]All who heard the shepherds' story expressed astonishment, [19]but Mary quietly treasured these things in her heart and often thought about them. [20]Then the shepherds went back again to their fields and flocks, praising God for the visit of the angels, and because they had seen the child, just as the angel had told them. [21]Eight days later, at the baby's circumcision ceremony, he was named Jesus, the name given him by the angel before he was even conceived.

Lk 24:39. Look at my hands! Look at my feet! You can see that it is I, myself! Touch me and make sure that I am not a ghost! For ghosts don't have bodies, as you see that I do!

Jn 1:14. And Christ became a human being and lived here on earth among us and was full of loving forgiveness and truth. And some of us have seen his glory—the glory of the only Son of the heavenly Father!

Jn 7:42. For the Scriptures clearly state that the Messiah will be born of the royal line of David, in *Bethlehem,* the village where David was born.

Jn 20:27. Then he said to Thomas, "Put your finger into my hands. Put your hand into my side. Don't be faithless any longer. Believe!"

Acts 2:30. But he was a prophet and knew God had promised with an unbreakable oath that one of David's own descendants would (be the Messiah and) sit on David's throne. 2 Sam 7:12; Ps 89:35, 36.

Acts 3:22. Moses, for instance, said long ago, "The Lord God will raise up a Prophet among you, who will resemble me! Listen carefully to everything he tells you." Deut 18:15–19.

Acts 13:23. And it is one of King David's descendants, Jesus, who is God's promised Savior of Israel!

Rom 1:3. It is the Good News about his Son, Jesus Christ our Lord, who came as a human baby, born into King David's royal family line.

Rom 8:3. We aren't saved from sin's grasp by knowing the commandments of God, because we can't and don't keep them, but God put into effect a different plan to save us. He sent his own Son in a human body like ours—except that ours are sinful—and destroyed sin's control over us by giving himself as a sacrifice for our sins.

Rom 9:5. Christ himself was one of you, a Jew so far as his human nature is concerned, he who now rules over all things. Praise God forever!

1 Cor 15:47. Adam was made from the dust of the earth, but Christ came from heaven above.

2 Cor 5:16. So stop evaluating Christians by what the world thinks about them or by what they seem to be like on the outside. Once I mistakenly thought of Christ that way, merely as a human being like myself. How differently I feel now!

Gal 3:16. Now, God gave some promises to Abraham and his Child. And notice that it doesn't say the promises were to his *children,* as it would if all his sons—all the Jews—were being spoken of, but to his *Child*—and that, of course, means Christ. Gen 12:3; 17:7, 8; 22:18.

Gal 4:4. But when the right time came, the time God decided on, he sent his Son, born of a woman, born as a Jew.

Phil 2:7. But laid aside his mighty power and glory, taking the disguise of a slave and becoming like men. [8]And he humbled himself even further, going so far as actually to die a criminal's death on a cross.

Col 1:15. Christ is the exact likeness of the unseen God. He existed before God made anything at all.

1 Tim 3:16. It is quite true that the way to live a godly life is not an easy matter. But the answer lies in Christ, who came to earth as a man . . . .

Heb 1:3. God's Son shines out with God's glory, and all that God's Son is and does marks him as God. [6]And still another time—when his firstborn Son came to earth—God said, "Let all the angels of God worship him."

Heb 2:9. But we do see Jesus—who for awhile was a little lower than the angels—crowned now by God with glory and honor because he suffered death for us. [14]Since we, God's children, are human beings—made of flesh and blood—he became flesh and blood too by being born in human form. [16]We all know he did not come as an angel but as a human being—yes, a Jew. [17]And it was necessary for Jesus to be like us, his brothers, so that he could be our merciful and faithful High Priest before God, a Priest who would be both merciful to us and faithful to God in dealing with the sins of the people. [18]For since he himself has now been through suffering and temptation, he knows what it is like when we suffer and are tempted, and he is wonderfully able to help us. *vs.* 9–17.

Heb 7:14. As we all know, Christ did not belong to the priest-tribe of Levi, but came from the tribe of Judah.

Heb 10:5. That is why Christ said, as he came into the world, "O God, the blood of bulls and goats cannot satisfy you, so you have made ready this body of mine for me to lay as a sacrifice upon your altar."

1 Jn 1:1. Christ was alive when the world began, yet I myself have seen him with my own eyes and listened to him speak. I have touched him with my own hands. He is God's message of Life. [2]This one who is Life from God has been shown to us and we guarantee that we have seen him; I am speaking of Christ, who is eternal Life. He was with the Father and then was shown to us. [3]Again I say, we are telling you about what we ourselves have actually seen and heard, so that you may share the fellowship and the joys we have with the Father and with Jesus Christ his Son.

1 Jn 4:2. And the way to find out if their message is from the Holy Spirit is to ask: Does it really agree that Jesus Christ, God's Son, actually became man with a human body? If so, then the message is from God. [3]If not, the message is not from God but from one who is against Christ, like the "Antichrist" you have heard about who is going to come, and his attitude of enmity against Christ is already abroad in the world.

2 Jn 1:7. Watch out for the false leaders—and there are many of them around—who don't believe that Jesus Christ came to earth as a human being with a body like ours. Such people are against the truth and against Christ.

Rev 22:16. I am both David's Root and his Descendant. I am the bright Morning Star.

See *Jesus, Humanity of; Relation of, to the Father.*

INTERCESSION OF. See *Jesus, Mediator.*

JUDGE. Ps 72:2. Help him to give justice to your people, even to the poor. [4]Help him to defend the poor and needy and to crush their oppressors.

Ps 75:2. "Yes," the Lord replies, "and when I am ready, I will punish the wicked!"

Ps 96:13. For the Lord is coming to judge the earth; he will judge the nations fairly and with truth!

Ps 110:6. He will punish the nations, and fill them with their dead. He will crush many heads.

Isa 2:4. The Lord will settle international disputes. Mic 4:3.

Isa 11:3. His delight will be obedience to the Lord. He will not judge by appearance, false evidence, or hearsay, [4]but will defend the poor and the exploited. He will rule against the wicked who oppress them.

Mic 5:1. Mobilize! The enemy lays siege to Jerusalem! With a rod they shall strike the Judge of Israel on the face.

Mal 3:2. But who can live when he appears? Who can endure his coming? For he is like a blazing fire refining precious metal and he can bleach the dirtiest garments! [3]Like a refiner of silver he will sit and closely watch as the dross is burned away. He will purify the Levites, the ministers of God, refining them like gold or silver, so that they will do their work for God with pure hearts.

Mt 19:28. And Jesus replied, "When I, the Messiah, shall sit upon my glorious throne in the Kingdom, you my disciples shall certainly sit on twelve thrones judging the twelve tribes of Israel."

Mt 25:31. But when I, the Messiah, shall come in my glory, and all the angels with me, then I shall sit upon my throne of glory. [32]And all the nations shall be gathered before me. And I will separate the people as a shepherd separates the sheep from the goats, [33]and place the sheep at my right hand, and the goats at my left. [34]Then I, the King, shall say to those at my right, "Come, blessed of my Father, into the Kingdom prepared for you from the founding of the world."

Lk 3:17. He will separate chaff from grain, and burn up the chaff with eternal fire and store away the grain. Mt 3:12; Jn 5:22; 12:48.

Acts 10:42. And he sent us to preach the Good News everywhere and to testify that Jesus is ordained of God to be the Judge of all—living and dead.

Acts 17:31. For he has set a day for justly judging the world by the man he has appointed, and has pointed him out by bringing him back to life again.

Rom 2:16. The day will surely come when at God's command Jesus Christ will judge the secret lives of everyone, their inmost thoughts and motives; this is all part of God's great plan which I proclaim.

Rom 14:10. You have no right to criticize your brother or look down on him. Remember, each of us will stand personally before the Judgment Seat of God.

1 Cor 4:4. My conscience is clear, but even that isn't final proof. It is the Lord himself who must examine me and decide. [5]So be careful not to jump to conclusions before the Lord returns as to whether someone is a good servant or not. When the Lord comes, he will turn on the light so that everyone can see exactly what each one of us is really like, deep down in our hearts. Then everyone will know why we have been doing the Lord's work. At that time God will give to each one whatever praise is coming to him.

2 Cor 5:10. For we must all stand before Christ to be judged and have our lives laid bare—before him. Each of us will receive whatever he deserves for the good or bad things he has done in his earthly body.

2 Tim 4:1. And so I solemnly urge you before God and before Christ Jesus—who will some day judge the living and the dead when he appears to set up his kingdom. [8]In heaven a crown is waiting for me which the Lord, the righteous Judge, will give me on that great day of his return. And not just to me, but to all those whose lives show that they are eagerly looking forward to his coming back again.

Jas 5:9. Don't grumble about each other, brothers. Are you yourselves above criticism? For see! The great Judge is coming. He is almost here. (Let him do whatever criticizing must be done.)

Rev 2:23. And I will strike her children dead. And all the churches shall know that I am he who searches deep within men's hearts, and minds; I will give to each of you whatever you deserve.

See *God, Judge.*

JUSTICE OF. 2 Sam 23:3. The Rock of Israel said to me: "One shall come who rules righteously, who rules in the fear of God."

Zech 9:9. Rejoice greatly, O my people! Shout with joy! For look—your King is coming! He is the Righteous One, the Victor! Yet he is lowly, riding on a donkey's colt!

Mt 27:19. Just then, as he was presiding over the court, Pilate's wife sent him this message: "Leave that good man alone; for I had a terrible nightmare concerning him last night."

Jn 5:30. But I pass no judgment without consulting the Father. I judge as I am told. And my judgment is absolutely fair and just, for it is according to the will of God who sent me and is not merely my own.

Acts 3:14. You didn't want him freed—this holy, righteous one.

See *Jesus, Holiness of, Judge.*

KING. Gen 49:10. The scepter shall not depart from Judah until Shiloh comes, whom all people shall obey.

Num 24:17. I see in the future of Israel, far down the distant trail, that there shall come a star from Jacob! This ruler of Israel shall smite the people of Moab.

1 Sam 2:10. Those who fight against the Lord shall be broken; he thunders against them from heaven. He judges throughout the earth. He gives mighty strength to his King, and gives great glory to his anointed one.

Ps 2:6. For the Lord declares, "This is the King of my choice, and I have enthroned him in Jerusalem, my holy city."

Ps 18:43, 44. You gave me victory in every battle. The nations came and served me. Even those I didn't know before come now and bow before me. Foreigners who have never seen me submit instantly.

Ps 24:8. Who is this King of Glory? The Lord, strong and mighty, invincible in battle. *vs.* 7–10.

Ps 45:3. Arm yourself, O Mighty One, so glorious, so majestic! [4]And in your majesty go on to victory, defending truth, humility, and justice. Go forth to awe-inspiring deeds! [5]Your arrows are sharp in your enemies' hearts; they fall before you. [6]Your throne, O God, endures forever. Justice is your royal scepter. [7]You love what is good and hate what is wrong. Therefore God, your God, has given you more gladness than anyone else. Song 1: 4, 12.

Ps 72:5. May the poor and needy revere you constantly, as long as sun and moon continue in the skies! Yes, forever! [8]Let him reign from sea to sea, and from the Euphrates River to the ends of the earth. [11]Yes, kings from everywhere! All will bow before him! All will serve him!

Ps 89:3, 4. The Lord God says, "I have made a solemn agreement with my chosen servant David. I have taken an oath to establish his descendants as kings forever on his throne, from now until eternity!" [19]In a vision you spoke to your prophet and said, "I have chosen a splendid young man from the common people to be the king—[20]he is my servant David! I have anointed him with my holy oil. [21]I will steady him and make him strong. [23]I will beat down his adversaries before him, and destroy those who hate him. [27]I will treat him as my firstborn son, and make him the mightiest king in all the earth. [29]He will always have an heir; his throne will be as endless as the days of heaven. [36]His dynasty will go on forever, and his throne will continue to the end of time. [37]It shall be eternal as the moon, my faithful witness in the sky!"

Ps 110:1. Jehovah said to my Lord the Messiah, "Rule as my regent—I will subdue your enemies and make them bow low before you." [2]Jehovah has established your throne in Jerusalem to rule over your enemies.

Ps 132:11. For you promised me that my son would sit on my throne and succeed me. And surely you will never go back on a promise! [17]David's power shall grow, for I have decreed for him a mighty Son. [18]I'll clothe his enemies with shame, but he shall be a glorious King.

Isa 6:1. The year King Uzziah died I saw the Lord! He was sitting on a lofty throne and the Temple was filled with his glory. *vs.* 2, 3; Jn 12:41.

Isa 9:6. For unto us a Child is born; unto us a Son is given; and the government shall be upon his shoulder. These will be his royal titles: "Wonderful," "Counselor," "The Mighty God," "The Everlasting Father," "The Prince of Peace." [7]His ever-expanding, peaceful government will never end. He will rule with perfect fairness and justice from the throne of his father David. He will bring true justice and peace to all the nations of the world. This is going to happen because the Lord of heaven's armies has dedicated himself to do it!

Isa 11:10. In that day he who created the royal dynasty of David will be a banner of salvation to all the world. The nations will rally to him, for the land where he lives will be a glorious place.

Isa 32:1. Look, a righteous King is coming, with honest princes!

Isa 33:17. Your eyes will see the King in his beauty, and the highlands of heaven far away.

Isa 40:10. Yes, the Lord God is coming with mighty power; he will rule with awesome strength. See, his reward is with him, to each as he has done.

Isa 52:7. How beautiful upon the mountains are the feet of those who bring the happy news of peace and salvation, the news that the God of Israel reigns. [13]See, my Servant shall prosper; he shall be highly exalted.

Jer 23:5, 6. For the time is coming, says the Lord, when I will place a righteous Branch upon King David's throne. He shall be a King who shall rule with wisdom and justice and cause righteousness to prevail everywhere throughout the earth. And this is his name: *The Lord Our Righteousness.* At that time Judah will be saved and Israel will live in peace.

Jer 30:9. For they shall serve the Lord their God, and David their King, whom I will raise up for them, says the Lord.

Jer 33:17. For the Lord declares that from then on, David shall forever have an heir sitting on the throne of Israel.

Ezk 37:24. And David, my Servant—the Messiah—shall be their King, their only Shepherd; and they shall obey my laws and all my wishes. [25]They shall live in the land of Israel where their fathers lived, the land I gave my servant Jacob. They and their children after them shall live there, and their grandchildren, for all generations. And my Servant David, their Messiah, shall be their Prince forever.

Dan 2:35. But the Rock that knocked the statue down became a mountain that covered the whole earth. [44]During the reigns of those kings, the God of heaven will set up a kingdom that will never be destroyed; no one will ever conquer it. It will shatter all these kingdoms into nothingness, but it shall stand forever, indestructible.

Dan 7:13. Next I saw the arrival of a Man—or so he seemed to be—brought there on clouds from heaven; he approached the Ancient of Days and was presented to him. [14]He was given the ruling power and glory over all the nations of the world, so that all people of every language must obey him. His power is eternal—it will never end; his government shall never fall.

Dan 8:23. Toward the end of their kingdoms, when they have become morally rotten, an angry king shall rise to power with great shrewdness and intelligence. [25]He will be a master of deception, defeating many by catching them off guard as they bask in false security. Without warning he will destroy them. So great will he fancy himself to be that he will even take on the Prince of Princes in battle; but in so doing he will seal his own doom, for he shall be broken by the hand of God, though no human means could overpower him.

Dan 9:25. Now listen! It will be forty-nine years plus 434 years from the time the command is given to rebuild Jerusalem, until the Anointed One comes! Jerusalem's streets and walls will be rebuilt despite the perilous times.

Hos 3:5. Afterward they will return to the Lord their God, and to the Messiah, their King, and they shall come trembling, submissive to the Lord and to his blessings, in the end times.

Mic 5:2. O Bethlehem Ephrathah, you are but a small Judean village, yet you will be the birthplace of my King who is alive from everlasting ages past! [4]And he shall stand and feed his flock in the strength of the Lord, in the majesty of the name of the Lord his God, and his people shall remain there undisturbed, for he will be greatly honored all around the world.

Zech 6:13. To him belongs the royal title. He will rule both as King and as Priest, with perfect harmony between the two!

Zech 9:9. Rejoice greatly, O my people! Shout with joy! For look—your King is coming! He is the Righteous One, the Victor! Yet he is lowly, riding on a donkey's colt! [10]I will disarm all peoples of the earth, including my people in Israel, and he shall bring peace among the nations. His realm shall stretch from sea to sea, from the river to the ends of the earth.

Mt 2:2. Where is the newborn King of the Jews? for we have seen his star in far-off eastern lands, and have come to worship him. [6]O little town of Bethlehem, you are not just an unimportant Judean village, for a Governor shall rise from you to rule my people Israel.

Mt 3:12. He will separate the chaff from the grain, burning the chaff with never-ending fire, and storing away the grain. Lk 3:17.

Mt 12:6. And truly, one is here who is greater than the Temple!

Mt 13:41. I will send my angels and they will separate out of the Kingdom every temptation and all who are evil.

Mt 19:28. And Jesus replied, "When I, the Messiah, shall sit upon my glorious throne in the Kingdom, you my disciples shall certainly sit on twelve thrones judging the twelve tribes of Israel."

Mt 21:5. Tell Jerusalem her King is coming to her, riding humbly on a donkey's colt!

Mt 25:31. But when I, the Messiah, shall come in my glory, and all the angels with me, then I shall sit upon my throne of glory. [32]And all the nations shall be gathered before me. And I will separate the people as a shepherd separates the sheep from the goats, [33]and place the sheep at my right hand, and the goats at my left. [34]Then I, the King, shall say to those at my right, "Come, blessed of my Father, into the Kingdom prepared for you from the founding of the world."

Mt 26:64. "Yes," Jesus said, "I am. And in the future you will see me, the Messiah, sitting at the right hand of God and returning on the clouds of heaven." Mk 14:62; Lk 22:69.

Mt 27:11. Now Jesus was standing before Pilate, the Roman governor. "Are you the Jews' Messiah?" the governor asked him. "Yes," Jesus replied.

Mt 28:18. He told his disciples, "I have been given all authority in heaven and earth."

Lk 1:32. He shall be very great and shall be called the Son of God. And the Lord God shall give him the throne of his ancestor David. [33]And he shall reign over Israel forever; his Kingdom shall never end!

Lk 2:11. The Savior—yes, the Messiah, the Lord—has been born tonight in Bethlehem!

Lk 10:22. I am the Agent of my Father in everything; and no one really knows the Son except the Father, and no one really knows the Father except the Son and those to whom the Son chooses to reveal him. Mt 11:27.

Lk 19:27. "And now about these enemies of mine who revolted—bring them in and execute them before me." [38]"God has given us a King!" they exulted. "Long live the King! Let all heaven rejoice! Glory to God in the highest heavens!"

Lk 22:29. And because my Father has granted me a Kingdom, I, here and now, grant you the right [30]to eat and drink at my table in that Kingdom; and you will sit on thrones judging the twelve tribes of Israel.

Lk 23:42. Then he said, "Jesus, remember me when you come into your Kingdom."

Jn 1:49. Nathanael replied, "Sir, you are the Son of God—the King of Israel!"

Jn 3:31. He has come from heaven and is greater than anyone else. I am of the earth, and my understanding is limited to the things of earth.

Jn 12:13. Took palm branches and went down the road to meet him, shouting, "The Savior! God bless the King of Israel! Hail to God's Ambassador!" [15]"Don't be afraid of your King, people of Israel, for he will come to you meekly, sitting on a donkey's colt!" Mt 21:5.

Jn 13:3. Jesus knew that the Father had given him everything and that he had come from God and would return to God. And how he loved his disciples!

Jn 18:36. Then Jesus answered, "I am not an earthly king. If I were, my followers would have fought when I was arrested by the Jewish leaders. But my Kingdom is not of the world." [37]Pilate replied, "But you are a king then?" "Yes," Jesus said. "I was born for that purpose. And I came to bring truth to the world. All who love the truth are my followers."

Jn 19:19. And Pilate posted a sign over him reading, "Jesus of Nazareth, the King of the Jews."

Acts 2:30. But he was a prophet, and knew God had promised with an unbreakable oath that one of David's own descendants would (be the Messiah and) sit on David's throne.

Acts 3:15. And you killed the Author of Life; but God brought him back to life again. And John and I are witnesses of this fact, for after you killed him we saw him alive!

Acts 5:31. Then, with mighty power, God exalted him to be a Prince and Savior.

Acts 10:36. I'm sure you have heard about the Good News for the people of Israel—that there is peace with God through Jesus, the Messiah, who is Lord of all creation.

Rom 9:5. Great men of God were your fathers, and Christ himself was one of you, a Jew so far as his human nature is concerned, he who now rules over all things. Praise God forever!

Rom 14:9. Christ died and rose again for this very purpose, so that he can be our Lord both while we live and when we die.

1 Cor 15:23. Each, however, in his own turn: Christ rose first; then when Christ comes back, all his people will become alive again. [24]After that the end will come when he will turn the kingdom over to God the Father, having put down all enemies of every kind. [25]For Christ will be King until he has defeated all his enemies, [26]including the last enemy —death. This too must be defeated and ended. [27]For the rule and authority over all things has been given to Christ by his Father; except, of course, Christ does not rule over the Father himself, who gave him this power to rule. [28]When Christ has finally won the battle against all his enemies, then he, the Son of God, will put himself also under his Father's orders, so that God who has given him the victory over everything else will be utterly supreme.

Eph 1:20. That raised Christ from the dead and seated him in the place of honor at God's right hand in heaven, [21]far, far above any other king or ruler or dictator or leader. Yes, his honor is far more glorious than that of anyone else either in this world or in the world to come. [22]And God has put all things under his feet and made him the supreme Head of the church.

Phil 2:9. Yet it was because of this that God raised him up to the heights of heaven and gave him a name which is above every other name, [10]that at the name of Jesus every knee shall bow in heaven and on earth and under the earth, [11]and every tongue shall confess that Jesus Christ is Lord, to the glory of God the Father.

1 Tim 6:15. For in due season Christ will be revealed from heaven by the blessed and only Almighty God, the King of kings and Lord of lords, [16]who alone can never die, who lives in light so terrible that no human being can approach him. No mere man has ever seen him, nor ever will. Unto him be honor and everlasting power and dominion forever and ever. Amen.

2 Tim 4:8. In heaven a crown is waiting for me which the Lord, the righteous Judge, will give me on that great day of his return. And not just to me, but to all those whose lives show that they are eagerly looking forward to his coming back again.

Heb 2:7. For though you made him lower than the angels for a little while, now you have crowned him with glory and honor. [8]And you have put him in complete charge of everything there is. Nothing is left out.

Heb 10:12. But Christ gave himself to God for our sins as one sacrifice for all time, and then sat down in the place of highest honor at God's right hand, [13]waiting for his enemies to be laid under his feet.

1 Pet 3:22. And now Christ is in heaven, sitting in the place of honor next to God the Father, with all the angels and powers of heaven bowing before him and obeying him.

Rev 1:5. And from Jesus Christ who faithfully reveals all truth to us. He was the first to rise from death, to die no more. He is far greater than any king in all the earth. All praise to him who always loves us and who set us free from our sins by pouring out his lifeblood for us. [6]He has gathered us into his kingdom and made us priests of God his Father. Give to him everlasting glory! He rules forever! Amen! [7]See! He is arriving, surrounded by clouds; and every eye shall see him—yes, and those who pierced him. And the nations will weep in sorrow and in terror when he comes. Yes! Amen! Let it be so! [18]"Though I am the First and Last, the Living One who died, who is now alive forevermore, who has the keys of hell and death—don't be afraid!"

Rev 3:7. *Write this letter to the leader of the church in Philadelphia.* "This message is sent to you by the one who is holy and true, and has the key of David to open what no one can shut and to shut what no one can open." [14]*Write this letter to the leader of the church in Laodicea:* "This message is from one who stands firm, the faithful and true Witness (of all that is or was or evermore shall be), the primeval source of God's creation. [21]I will let every one who conquers sit beside me on my throne, just as I took my place with my Father on his throne when I had conquered." Isa 22:22.

Rev 5:5. But one of the twenty-four Elders said to me, "Stop crying, for look! The Lion of the tribe of Judah, the Root of David, has conquered, and proved himself worthy to open the scroll and to break its seven seals." [12]"The Lamb is worthy" (loudly they sang it!) "—the Lamb who was slain. He is worthy to receive the power, and the riches, and the wisdom, and the strength, and the honor, and the glory, and the blessing."

Rev 6:2. I looked, and there in front of me was a white horse. Its rider carried a bow, and a crown was placed upon his head; he rode out to conquer in many battles and win the war. [15]The kings of the earth, and world leaders and rich men, and high-ranking military officers, and all men great and small, slave and free, hid themselves in the caves and rocks of the mountains, [16]and cried to the mountains to crush them. "Fall on us," they pleaded, "and hide us from the face of the one sitting on the throne, and from the anger of the Lamb, [17]because the great day of their anger has come, and who can survive it?"

Rev 11:15. For just then the seventh angel blew his trumpet, and there were loud voices shouting down from heaven, "The kingdom of this world now belongs to our Lord, and to his Christ; and he shall reign forever and ever."

Rev 12:10. Then I heard a loud voice shouting across the heavens, "It has happened at last! God's salvation and the power and the rule, and the authority of his Christ are finally here; for the Accuser of our brothers has been thrown down from heaven onto earth—he accused them day and night before our God."

Rev 14:14. Then the scene changed and I saw a white cloud, and someone sitting on it who looked like Jesus, who was called "The Son of Man," with a crown of solid gold upon his head and a sharp sickle in his hand.

Rev 17:14. Together they will wage war against the Lamb, and the Lamb will conquer them; for he is Lord over all lords, and King of kings, and his people are the called and chosen and faithful ones.

Rev 19:11. Then I saw heaven opened and a white horse standing there; and the one sitting on the horse was named "Faithful and True"—the one who justly punishes and makes war. [12]His eyes were like flames, and on his head were many crowns. A name was written on his forehead, and only he knew its meaning. [15]In his mouth he held a sharp sword to strike down the nations; he ruled them with an iron grip; and he trod the winepress of the fierceness of the wrath of Almighty God. [16]On his robe and thigh was written this title: "King of Kings and Lord of Lords."

Rev 20:4. Then I saw thrones, and sitting on them were those who had been given the right to judge. And I saw the souls of those who had been beheaded for their testimony about Jesus, for proclaiming the Word of God, and who had not worshiped the Creature or his statue, nor accepted his mark on their foreheads or their hands. They had come to life again and now they reigned with Christ for a thousand years. [6]Blessed and holy are those who share in the First Resurrection. For them the Second Death holds no terrors, for they will be priests of God and of Christ, and shall reign with him a thousand years.

KINGDOM OF. See *Kingdom.*

LOVE OF. Ps 72:14. He will save them from oppression and from violence, for their lives are precious to him.

Prov 8:17. I love all who love me. Those who search for me shall surely find me.

Isa 40:11. He will feed his flock like a shepherd; he will carry the lambs in his arms and gently lead the ewes with young.

Isa 42:3. He will not break the bruised reed, nor quench the dimly burning flame. He will encourage the fainthearted, those tempted to despair. He will see full justice given to all who have been wronged.

Isa 63:9. In all their affliction he was afflicted, and he personally saved them. In his love and pity he redeemed them and lifted them up and carried them through all the years. *vs.* 7, 8.

Mic 5:4. And he shall stand and feed his flock in the strength of the Lord, in the majesty of the name of the Lord his God, and his people shall remain there undisturbed, for he will be greatly honored all around the world.

Mt 8:17. This fulfilled the prophecy of Isaiah, "He took our sicknesses and bore our diseases." Isa 53:4.

Mt 9:36. And what pity he felt for the crowds that came, because their problems were so great and they didn't know what to do or where to go for help. They were like sheep without a shepherd.

Mt 12:49. He pointed to his disciples. "Look!" he said, "these are my mother and brothers." [50]Then he added, "Anyone who obeys my Father in heaven is my brother, sister and mother!" Mk 3:31–35; Lk 8:19–21.

Mt 14:14. So when Jesus came out of the wilderness, a vast crowd was waiting for him and he pitied them and healed their sick.

Mt 15:32. Then Jesus called his disciples to him and said, "I pity these people—they've been here with me for three days now, and have nothing left to eat; I don't want to send them away hungry or they will faint along the road."

Mt 18:6. But if any of you causes one of these little ones who trusts in me to lose his faith, it would be better for you to have a rock tied to your neck and be thrown into the sea. [10]Beware that you don't look down upon a single one of these little children. For I tell you that in heaven their angels have constant access to my Father. Mk 9:37, 42; Lk 9:48.

Mt 18:11. And I, the Messiah, came to save the lost. [12]If a man has a hundred sheep, and one wanders away and is lost, what will he do? Won't he leave the ninety-nine others and go out into the hills to search for the lost one? [13]And if he finds it, he will rejoice over it more than over the ninety-nine others safe at home!

Mt 23:37. O Jerusalem, Jerusalem, the city that kills the prophets, and stones all those God sends to her! How often I have wanted to gather your children together as a hen gathers her chicks beneath her wings, but you wouldn't let me.

Mt 28:10. Then Jesus said to them, "Don't be frightened! Go tell my brothers to leave at once for Galilee, to meet me there."

Mk 8:12. He sighed deeply when he heard this and he said, "Certainly not. How many more miracles do you people need?"

Mk 9:36. Then he placed a little child among them; and taking the child in his arms he said to them, [37]"Anyone who welcomes a little child like this in my name is welcoming me, and anyone who welcomes me is welcoming my Father who sent me!" Mt 18:2–5; Lk 9:48.

Mk 10:13. Once when some mothers were bringing their children to Jesus to bless them, the disciples shooed them away, telling them not to bother him. [14]But when Jesus saw what was happening he was very much displeased with his disciples and said to them, "Let the children come to me, for the Kingdom of God belongs to such as they. Don't send them away!" [16]Then he took the children into his arms and placed his hands on their heads and he blessed them. [21]Jesus felt genuine love for this man [the rich young man] as he looked at him. Mt 19:13–15; Lk 18:15–17.

Lk 7:13. When the Lord saw her, his heart overflowed with sympathy. "Don't cry!" he said.

Lk 22:31. Simon, Simon, Satan has asked to have you, to sift you like wheat, [32]but I have pleaded in prayer for you that your faith should not completely fail. So when you have repented and turned to me again, strengthen and build up the faith of your brothers.

Lk 23:28. But Jesus turned and said to them, "Daughters of Jerusalem, don't weep for me, but for yourselves and for your children."

Lk 24:38. "Why are you frightened?" he asked. "Why do you doubt that it is really I? [39]Look at my hands! Look at my feet! You can see that it is I, myself! Touch me and make sure that I am not a ghost! For ghosts don't have bodies, as you see that I do!" [40]As he spoke, he held out his hands for them to see (the marks of the nails), and showed them (the wounds in) his feet.

Jn 10:3. The gatekeeper opens the gate for him, and the sheep hear his voice and come to him; and he calls his own sheep by name and leads them out. [4]He walks ahead of them; and they follow him, for they recognize his voice. [11]I am the Good Shepherd. The Good Shepherd lays down his life for the sheep. [14]I am the Good Shepherd and know my own sheep, and they know me, [15]just as my Father knows me and I know the Father; and I lay down my life for the sheep. [16]I have other sheep, too, in another fold. I must bring them also, and they will heed my voice; and there will be one flock with one Shepherd.

Jn 11:5. Although Jesus was very fond of Martha, Mary and Lazarus. [33]When Jesus saw her weeping and the Jewish leaders wailing with her, he was moved with indignation and deeply troubled. [34]"Where is he buried?" he asked them. They told him, "Come and see." [35]Tears came to Jesus' eyes. [36]"They were close friends," the Jewish leaders said. "See how much he loved him."

Jn 13:1. And how he loved his disciples! [23]I was sitting next to Jesus at the table, being his closest friend. [34]"And so I am giving a new commandment to you now—love each other just as much as I love you."

Jn 14:1. Let not your heart be troubled. You are trusting God, now trust in me. [2, 3]There are many homes up there where my Father lives, and I am going to prepare them for your coming. When everything is ready, then I will come and get you, so that you can always be with me where I am. If this weren't so, I would tell you plainly. [18]No, I will not abandon you or leave you as orphans in the storm —I will come to you. [21]The one who obeys me is the one who loves me; and because he loves me, my Father will love him; and I will too, and I will reveal myself to him. [27]I am leaving you with a gift —peace of mind and heart! And the peace I give isn't fragile like the peace the world gives. So don't be troubled or afraid.

Jn 15:9. I have loved you even as the Father has loved me. Live within my love. [10]When you obey me you are living in my love, just as I obey my Father and live in his love. [11]I have told you this so that you will be filled with my joy. Yes, your cup of joy will overflow! [12]I demand that you love each other as much as I love you. [13]And here is how to measure it—the greatest love is shown when a person lays down his life for his friends. [15]I no longer call you slaves, for a master doesn't confide in his slaves; now you are my friends, proved by the fact that I have told you everything the Father told me.

Jn 17:12. During my time here I have kept safe within your family all of these you gave me. I guarded them so that not one perished, except the son of hell, as the Scriptures foretold. [15]I'm not asking you to take them out of the world, but to keep them safe from Satan's power. [19]And I consecrate myself to meet their need for growth in truth and holiness.

Jn 18:8. "I told you I am he," Jesus said; "and since I am the one you are after, let these others go." [9]He did this to carry out the prophecy he had just made, "I have not lost a single one of those you gave me. . . ."

Jn 19:26. When Jesus saw his mother standing there beside me, his close friend, he said to her, "He is your son." [27]And to me he said, "She is your mother!"

Jn 20:17. "Don't touch me," he cautioned, "for I haven't yet ascended to the Father. But go find my brothers and tell them that I ascend to my Father and your Father, my God and your God." [27]Then he said to Thomas, "Put your finger into my hands. Put your hand into my side. Don't be faithless any longer. Believe!"

Jn 21:15. After breakfast Jesus said to Simon Peter, "Simon, son of John, do you love me more than these others?" "Yes," Peter replied, "You know I am your friend." [16]Jesus repeated the question: "Simon, son of John, do you *really* love me?" . . . [17]Once more he asked him, "Simon, son of John, are you even my friend?" Peter was grieved at the way Jesus asked the question this third time. "Lord, you know my heart; you know I am," he said. Jesus said, "Then feed my little sheep."

Acts 9:4. He fell to the ground and heard a voice saying to him, "Paul! Paul! Why are you persecuting me?" [5]"Who is speaking, sir?" Paul asked. And the voice replied, "I am Jesus, the one you are persecuting!"

Acts 10:38. And you no doubt know that Jesus of Nazareth was anointed by God with the Holy Spirit and with power, and he went around doing good and healing all who were possessed by demons, for God was with him.

Rom 8:35. Who then can ever keep Christ's love from us? When we have trouble or calamity, when we are hunted down or destroyed, is it because he doesn't love us anymore? And if we are hungry, or penniless, or in danger, or threatened with death, has God deserted us?

37. But despite all this, overwhelming victory is ours through Christ who loved us enough to die for us. [38]For I am convinced that nothing can ever separate us from his love. Death can't, and life can't. The angels won't, and all the powers of hell itself cannot keep God's love away. Our fears for today, our worries about tomorrow, [39]or where we are—high above the sky, or in the deepest ocean—nothing will ever be able to separate us from the love of God demonstrated by our Lord Jesus Christ when he died for us.

Rom 15:3. Christ didn't please himself. As the Psalmist said, "He came for the very purpose of suffering under the insults of those who were against the Lord."

2 Cor 5:13, 14. Are we insane (to say such things about ourselves)? If so, it is to bring glory to God. And if we are in our right minds, it is for your benefit. Whatever we do, it is certainly not for our own profit, but because Christ's love controls us now. Since we believe that Christ died for all of us, we should also believe that we have died to the old life we used to live.

2 Cor 8:9. You know how full of love and kindness our Lord Jesus was: though he was so very rich, yet to help you he became so very poor, so that by being poor he could make you rich.

Gal 2:20. And the real life I now have within this body is a result of my trusting in the Son of God, who loved me and gave himself for me.

Eph 3:17. And I pray that Christ will be more and more at home in your hearts, living within you as you trust in him. May your roots go down deep into the soil of God's marvelous love; [18, 19]and may you be able to feel and understand, as all God's children should, how long, how wide, how deep, and how high his love really is; and to experience this love for yourselves, though it is so great that you will never see the end of it or fully know or understand it. And so at last you will be filled up with God himself.

Eph 5:2. Be full of love for others, following the example of Christ who loved you and gave himself to God as a sacrifice to take away your sins. And God was pleased, for Christ's love for you was like sweet perfume to him. [25]And you husbands, show the same kind of love to your wives as Christ showed to the church when he died for her. [29, 30]No one hates his own body but lovingly cares for it, just as Christ cares for his body the church, of which we are parts.

2 Thess 2:13. But we must forever give thanks to God for you, our brothers loved by the Lord, because God chose from the very first to give you salvation, cleansing you by the work of the Holy Spirit and by your trusting in the Truth.

Heb 2:11. We who have been made holy by Jesus, now have the same Father he has. That is why Jesus is not ashamed to call us his brothers. [18]For since he himself has now been through suffering and temptation, he knows what it is like when we suffer and are tempted, and he is wonderfully able to help us.

Heb 4:15. This High Priest of ours understands our weaknesses, since he had the same temptations we do, though he never once gave way to them and sinned.

1 Jn 3:16. We know what real love is from Christ's example in dying for us. And so we also ought to lay down our lives for our Christian brothers.

Rev 1:5. All praise to him who always loves us and who set us free from our sins by pouring out his lifeblood for us.

Rev 3:9. Note this: I will force those supporting the causes of Satan while claiming to be mine (but they aren't—they are lying) to fall at your feet and acknowledge that you are the ones I love. [19]I continually discipline and punish everyone I love.

See *Jesus, Compassion of, above.*

MEDIATION OF. Deut 18:18. I will raise up from among them a Prophet, an Israeli like you. I will tell him what to say, and he shall be my spokesman to the people.

Ps 110:4. Jehovah has taken oath, and will not rescind his vow, that you are a priest forever like Melchizedek.

Isa 53:10. Yet it was the Lord's good plan to bruise him and fill him with grief. But when his soul has been made an offering for sin, then he shall have a multitude of children, many heirs. He shall live again and God's program shall prosper in his hands. [11]And when he sees all that is accomplished by the anguish of his soul, he shall be satisfied; and because of what he has experienced, my righteous Servant shall make many to be counted righteous before God, for he shall bear all their sins. [12]Therefore I will give him the honors of one who is mighty and great, because he has poured out his soul unto death. He was counted as a sinner, and he bore the sins of many, and he pled with God for sinners.

Zech 1:12. Upon hearing this, the Angel of the Lord prayed this prayer: "O Lord of Hosts, for seventy years your anger has raged against Jerusalem and the cities of Judah. How long will it be until you again show mercy to them?" [13]And the Lord answered the angel who stood beside me, speaking words of comfort and assurance.

Zech 6:13. To him belongs the royal title. He will rule both as King and as Priest, with perfect harmony between the two!

Mt 18:20. For where two or three gather together because they are mine, I will be right there among them.

Lk 22:31. Simon, Simon, Satan has asked to have you, to sift you like wheat, [32]but I have pleaded in prayer for you that your faith should not completely fail. So when you have repented and turned to me again, strengthen and build up the faith of your brothers.

Lk 23:32, 33. Two others, criminals, were led out to be executed with him at a place called "The Skull." There all three were crucified—Jesus on the center cross, and the two criminals on either side. [34]"Father, forgive these people," Jesus said, "for they don't know what they are doing."

Jn 14:6. Jesus told him, "I am the Way—yes, and the Truth and the Life. No one can get to the Father except by means of me. [13]You can ask him for *anything,* using my name, and I will do it, for this will bring praise to the Father because of what I, the Son, will do for you. [14]Yes, ask *anything,* using my name, and I will do it! [16]I will ask the Father and he will give you another Comforter, and he will never leave you."

Jn 16:23. At that time you won't need to ask me for anything, for you can go directly to the Father and ask him, and he will give you what you ask for because you use my name. [24]You haven't tried this before, (but begin now). Ask, using my name, and you will receive, and your cup of joy will overflow. [26]Then you will present your petitions over my signature! And I won't need to ask the Father to grant you these requests.

Jn 17:9. My plea is not for the world but for those you have given me because they belong to you. [11]Holy Father, keep them in your own care—all those you have given me—so that they will be united just as we are, with none missing. [15]I'm not asking you to take them out of the world, but to keep them safe from Satan's power. [16]They are not part of this world any more than I am. [17]Make them pure and holy through teaching them your words of truth. [20]I am not praying for these alone but also for the future believers who will come to me because of the testimony of these. [21]My prayer for all of them is that they will be of one heart and mind, just as you and I are, Father—that just as you are in me and I am in you, so they will be in us, and the world will believe you sent me. [22]I have given them the glory you gave me—the glorious unity of being one, as we are. *vs.* 1–26.

Jn 20:31. But these are recorded so that you will believe that he is the Messiah, the Son of God, and that believing in him you will have life.

Rom 1:8. How I thank God through Jesus Christ for this good report, and for each one of you.

Rom 5:1. So now, since we have been made right in God's sight by faith in his promises, we can have real peace with him because of what Jesus Christ our Lord has done for us. [2]For because of our faith, he has brought us into this place of highest privilege where we now stand, and we confidently and joyfully look forward to actually becoming all that God has had in mind for us to be.

Rom 6:23. For the wages of sin is death, but the free gift of God is eternal life through Jesus Christ our Lord.

Rom 8:34. Who then will condemn us? Will Christ? *No!* For he is the one who died for us and came back to life again for us and is sitting at the place of highest honor next to God, pleading for us there in heaven.

Rom 16:27. To God, who alone is wise, be the glory forever through Jesus Christ our Lord. Amen.

1 Cor 6:11. There was a time when some of you were just like that but now your sins are washed away, and you are set apart for God, and he has accepted you because of what the Lord Jesus Christ and the Spirit of our God have done for you.

1 Cor 15:57. How we thank God for all of this! It is he who makes us victorious through Jesus Christ our Lord!

2 Cor 1:20. He carries out and fulfills all of God's promises, no matter how many of them there are; and we have told everyone how faithful he is, giving glory to his name.

Gal 4:7. Now we are no longer slaves, but God's own sons. And since we are his sons, everything he has belongs to us, for that is the way God planned.

Eph 2:13. But now you belong to Christ Jesus, and though you once were far away from God, now you have been brought very near to him because of what Jesus Christ has done for you with his blood. [14]For Christ himself is our way of peace. He has made peace between us Jews and you Gentiles by making us all one family, breaking down the wall of contempt that used to separate us. [15]By his death he ended the angry resentment between us, caused by the Jewish laws which favored the Jews and excluded the Gentiles, for he died to annul that whole system of Jewish laws. Then he took the two groups that had been opposed to each other and made them parts of himself; thus he fused us together to become one new person, and at last there was peace. [16]As parts of the same body, our anger against each other has disappeared, for both of us have been reconciled to God. And so the feud ended at last at the cross. [17]And he has brought this Good News of peace to you Gentiles who were very far away from him, and to us Jews who were near. [18]Now all of us, whether Jews or Gentiles, may come to God the Father with the Holy Spirit's help because of what Christ has done for us.

Eph 3:12. Now we can come fearlessly right into God's presence, assured of his glad welcome when we come with Christ and trust in him.

Eph 4:32. Instead, be kind to each other, tenderhearted, forgiving one another, just as God has forgiven you because you belong to Christ.

Eph 5:20. Always give thanks for everything to our God and Father in the name of our Lord Jesus Christ.

Col 3:17. And whatever you do or say, let it be as a representative of the Lord Jesus, and come with him into the presence of God the Father to give him your thanks.

1 Tim 2:1. Here are my directions: Pray much for others; plead for God's mercy upon them; give thanks for all he is going to do for them. [3]This is good and pleases God our Savior. [5]*That God is on one side and all the people on the other side, and*

Christ Jesus, himself man, is between them to bring them together.

Heb 2:17. And it was necessary for Jesus to be like us, his brothers, so that he could be our merciful and faithful High Priest before God, a Priest who would be both merciful to us and faithful to God in dealing with the sins of the people.

Heb 3:1. Therefore, dear brothers whom God has set apart for himself—you who are chosen for heaven—I want you to think now about this Jesus who is God's Messenger and the High Priest of our faith. [2]For Jesus was faithful to God who appointed him High Priest, just as Moses also faithfully served in God's house.

Heb 4:14. But Jesus the Son of God is our great High Priest who has gone to heaven itself to help us; therefore let us never stop trusting him. [15]This High Priest of ours understands our weaknesses, since he had the same temptations we do, though he never once gave way to them and sinned.

Heb 5:5. That is why Christ did not elect himself to the honor of being High Priest; no, he was chosen by God. God said to him, "My Son, today I have honored you." [6]And another time God said to him, "You have been chosen to be a priest forever, with the same rank as Melchizedek." [10]For remember that God has chosen him to be a High Priest with the same rank as Melchizedek.

Heb 6:19. This certain hope of being saved is a strong and trustworthy anchor for our souls, connecting us with God himself behind the sacred curtains of heaven, [20]where Christ has gone ahead to plead for us from his position as our High Priest, with the honor and rank of Melchizedek. Heb 7:21.

Heb 7:1. This Melchizedek was king of the city of Salem, and also a priest of the Most High God. [3]Melchizedek had no father or mother and there is no record of any of his ancestors. He was never born and he never died but his life is like that of the Son of God—a priest forever. [19]It never made anyone really right with God. But now we have a far better hope, for Christ makes us acceptable to God, and now we may draw near to him. [24]But Jesus lives forever and continues to be a Priest so that no one else is needed. [25]He is able to save completely all who come to God through him. Since he will live forever, he will always be there to remind God that he has paid for their sins with his blood. [26]He is, therefore, exactly the kind of High Priest we need; for he is holy and blameless, unstained by sin, undefiled by sinners, and to him has been given the place of honor in heaven. [27]He never needs the daily blood of animal sacrifices, as other priests did, to cover over first their own sins and then the sins of the people; for he finished all sacrifices, once and for all, when he sacrificed himself on the cross. [28]Under the old system, even the high priests were weak and sinful men who could not keep from doing wrong, but later God appointed by his oath his Son who is perfect forever.

Heb 8:1. What we are saying is this: Christ, whose priesthood we have just described, is our High Priest, and is in heaven at the place of greatest honor next to God himself. [2]He ministers in the temple in heaven, the true place of worship built by the Lord and not by human hands. [6]But Christ, as a Minister in heaven, has been rewarded with a far more important work than those who serve under the old laws, because the new agreement which he passes on to us from God contains far more wonderful promises.

Heb 9:11. He came as High Priest of this better system which we now have. He went into that greater, perfect tabernacle in heaven, not made by men nor part of this world, [12]and once for all took blood into that inner room, the Holy of Holies, and sprinkled it on the mercy seat; but it was not the blood of goats and calves. No, he took his own blood, and with it he, by himself, made sure of our eternal salvation. [15]Christ came with this new agreement so that all who are invited may come and have forever all the wonders God has promised them. For Christ died to rescue them from the penalty of the sins they had committed while still under that old system.

24. For Christ has entered into heaven itself, to appear now before God as our Friend. It was not in the earthly place of worship that he did this, for that was merely a copy of the real temple in heaven. *vs.* 11–28. See Rev 8:3, 4.

Heb 10:11. Under the old agreement the priests stood before the altar day after day offering sacrifices that could never take away our sins. [12]But Christ gave himself to God for our sins as one sacrifice for all time, and then sat down in the place of highest honor at God's right hand. [19]And so, dear brothers, now we may walk right into the very Holy of Holies where God is, because of the blood of Jesus. [20]This is the fresh, new, life-giving way which Christ has opened up for us by tearing the curtain—his human body—to let us into the holy presence of God. [21]And since this great High Priest of ours rules over God's household. *vs.* 1–21.

Heb 12:24. And to Jesus himself, who has brought us his wonderful new agreement; and to the sprinkled blood which graciously forgives instead of crying out for vengeance as the blood of Abel did.

Heb 13:15. With Jesus' help we will continually offer our sacrifice of praise to God by telling others of the glory of his name.

1 Pet 2:5. And now you have become living building-stones for God's use in building his house. What's more, you are his holy priests; so come to him—(you who are acceptable to him because of Jesus Christ)—and offer to God those things that please him.

1 Jn 2:1. But if you sin, there is someone to plead for you before the Father. His name is Jesus Christ, the one who is all that is good and who pleases God completely. [2]He is the one who took God's wrath against our sins upon himself, and brought us into fellowship with God; and he is the forgiveness for our sins, and not only ours but all the world's. [12]I am writing these things to all of you, my little children, because your sins have been

forgiven in the name of Jesus our Savior.

Typified: Moses, Deut 5:5; Gal 3:19. Aaron, Num 16:48.

See *Jesus, Intercession of.*

MEEKNESS OF. Ps 45:4. And in your majesty go on to victory, defending truth, humility, and justice.

Isa 42:2. He will be gentle—he will not shout nor quarrel in the streets.

Isa 50:5. The Lord God has spoken to me and I have listened; I do not rebel nor turn away. [6]I give my back to the whip, and my cheeks to those who pull out the beard. I do not hide from shame—they spit in my face.

Isa 52:13. See, my Servant shall prosper; he shall be highly exalted.

Isa 53:7. He was oppressed and he was afflicted, yet he never said a word. He was brought as a lamb to the slaughter; and as a sheep before her shearers is dumb, so he stood silent before the ones condemning him. Acts 8:32.

Mt 11:29. And let me teach you; for I am gentle and humble.

Mt 12:19. He does not fight nor shout; he does not raise his voice! [20]He does not crush the weak, or quench the smallest hope; he will end all conflict with his final victory.

Mt 21:5. Tell Jerusalem her King is coming to her, riding humbly on a donkey's colt!

Mt 26:49. So now Judas came straight to Jesus and said, "Hello, Master!" and embraced him in friendly fashion. [50]Jesus said, "My friend, go ahead and do what you have come for." Then the others grabbed him. [51]One of the men with Jesus pulled out a sword and slashed off the ear of the High Priest's servant. [52]"Put away your sword," Jesus told him. "Those using swords will get killed. [53]Don't you realize that I could ask my Father for thousands of angels to protect us, and he would send them instantly?"

54. "But if I did, how would the Scriptures be fulfilled that describe what is happening now?" [55]Then Jesus spoke to the crowd. "Am I some dangerous criminal," he asked "that you had to arm yourselves with swords and clubs before you could arrest me? I was with you teaching daily in the Temple and you didn't stop me then. [56]But this is all happening to fulfill the words of the prophets as recorded in the Scriptures." At that point, all the disciples deserted him and fled. [57]Then the mob led him to the home of Caiaphas the High Priest, where all the Jewish leaders were gathering. [58]Meanwhile, Peter was following far to the rear, and came to the courtyard of the High Priest's house and went in and sat with the soldiers, and waited to see what was going to be done to Jesus. [59]The chief priests and, in fact, the entire Jewish Supreme Court assembled there and looked for witnesses who would lie about Jesus, in order to build a case against him that would result in a death sentence. [60, 61]But even though they found many who agreed to be false witnesses, these always contradicted each other. Finally two men were found who declared, "This man said, 'I am able to destroy the Temple of God and rebuild it in three days.' " [62]Then the High Priest stood up and said to Jesus, "Well, what about it? Did you say that, or didn't you?" [63]But Jesus remained silent.

Mt 27:12. But when the chief priests and other Jewish leaders made their many accusations against him, Jesus remained silent. [13]"Don't you hear what they are saying?" Pilate demanded. [14]But Jesus said nothing, much to the governor's surprise.

Mk 2:6. But some of the Jewish religious leaders said to themselves as they sat there, [7]"What? This is blasphemy! Does he think he is God? For only God can forgive sins." [8]Jesus could read their minds and said to them at once, "Why does this bother you? [9, 10, 11]I, the Messiah, have the authority on earth to forgive sins. But talk is cheap—anybody could say that. So I'll prove it to you by healing this man." Then, turning to the paralyzed man, he commanded, "Pick up your stretcher and go on home, for you are healed!"

Lk 22:27. For I am your servant.

Lk 23:34. "Father, forgive these people," Jesus said, "for they don't know what they are doing."

Jn 8:48. "You Samaritan! Foreigner! Devil!" the Jewish leaders snarled. "Didn't we say all along you were possessed by a demon?" [49]"No," Jesus said, "I have no demon in me. For I honor my Father—and you dishonor me. [50]And though I have no wish to make myself great, God wants this for me and judges (those who reject me)."

Jn 13:5. Poured water into a basin, and began to wash the disciples' feet and to wipe them with the towel he had around him. [14]"And since I, the Lord and Teacher, have washed your feet, you ought to wash each other's feet."

2 Cor 10:1. I plead with you—yes, I, Paul—and I plead gently, as Christ himself would do.

Phil 2:7. But laid aside his mighty power and glory, taking the disguise of a slave and becoming like men. [8]And he humbled himself even further, going so far as actually to die a criminal's death on a cross.

Heb 12:2. Keep your eyes on Jesus, our leader and instructor. He was willing to die a shameful death on the cross because of the joy he knew would be his afterwards; and now he sits in the place of honor by the throne of God. [3]If you want to keep from becoming fainthearted and weary, think about his patience as sinful men did such terrible things to him.

1 Pet 2:23. Never answered back when insulted; when he suffered he did not threaten to get even; he left his case in the hands of God who always judges fairly.

MESSIAH.

Messianic Psalms. Ps 2:1. What fools the nations are to rage against the Lord! How strange that men should try to outwit God! [2]For a summit conference of the nations has been called to plot against the Lord and his Messiah, Christ the King. [3]"Come, let us break his chains," they say, "and free ourselves from all this slavery to God." [4]But God in heaven merely laughs! He is amused by all their puny plans. [5]And then in fierce fury he rebukes them and fills them with fear. [6]For the Lord declares, "This is the King of my choice, and I have enthroned him in Jerusalem, my holy city." [7]His chosen one replies, "I will reveal the everlasting purposes of God, for the Lord has said to me, 'You are my Son. This is your Coronation Day. Today I am giving you your glory.' " [8]"Only ask, and I will give you all the nations of the world. [9]Rule them with an iron rod; smash them like clay pots!" [10]O kings and rulers of the earth, listen while there is time. [11]Serve the Lord with reverent fear; rejoice with trembling. [12]Fall down before his Son and kiss his feet before his anger is roused and you perish. I am warning you—his wrath will soon begin. But oh, the joys of those who put their trust in him!

Ps 16:7. I will bless the Lord who counsels me; he gives me wisdom in the night. He tells me what to do. [8]I am always thinking of the Lord; and because he is so near, I never need to stumble or to fall. [9]Heart, body, and soul are filled with joy. [10]For you will not leave me among the dead; you will not allow your beloved one to rot in the grave. [11]You have let me experience the joys of life and the exquisite pleasures of your own eternal presence.

Ps 67:1. O God, in mercy bless us; let your face beam with joy as you look down at us. [2]Send us around the world with the news of your saving power and your eternal plan for all mankind. [3]How everyone throughout the earth will praise the Lord! [4]How glad the nations will be, singing for joy because you are their King and will give true justice to their people! [5]Praise God, O world! May all the peoples of the earth give thanks to you. [6, 7]For the earth has yielded abundant harvests. God, even our own God, will bless us. And peoples from remotest lands will worship him.

Ps 68:28. Summon your might; display your strength, O God, for you have done such mighty things for us. [29]The kings of the earth are bringing their gifts to your temple in Jerusalem. [30]Rebuke our enemies, O Lord. Bring them—submissive, tax in hand. Scatter all who delight in war. [31]Egypt will send gifts of precious metals. Ethiopia will stretch out her hands to God in adoration. [32]Sing to the Lord, O kingdoms of the earth—sing praises to the Lord, [33]to him who rides upon the ancient heavens, whose mighty voice thunders from the sky. [34]Power belongs to God! His majesty shines down on Israel; his strength is mighty in the heavens. [35]What awe we feel, kneeling here before him in the sanctuary. The God of Israel gives strength and mighty power to his people. Blessed be God!

Ps 69:1, 2. Save me, O my God. The floods have risen. Deeper and deeper I sink in the mire; the waters rise around me. [3]I have wept until I am exhausted; my throat is dry and hoarse; my eyes are swollen with weeping, waiting for my God to act. [4]I cannot even count all those who hate me without cause. They are influential men, these who plot to kill me though I am innocent. They demand that I be punished for what I didn't do. [5]O God, you know so well how stupid I am, and you know all my sins. [6]O Lord God of the armies of heaven, don't let me be a stumbling block to those who trust in you. O God of Israel, don't let me cause them to be confused, [7]though I am mocked and cursed and shamed for your sake. [8]Even my own brothers pretend they don't know me! [9]My zeal for God and his work burns hot within me. And because I advocate your cause, your enemies insult me even as they insult you. [10]How they scoff and mock me when I mourn and fast before the Lord! [11]How they talk about me when I wear sackcloth to show my humiliation and sorrow for my sins! [12]I am the talk of the town and the song of the drunkards. [13]But I keep right on praying to you, Lord. For now is the time—you are bending down to hear! You are ready with a plentiful supply of love and kindness. Now answer my prayer and rescue me as you promised. [14]Pull me out of this mire. Don't let me sink in. Rescue me from those who hate me, and from these deep waters I am in. [15]Don't let the floods overwhelm me, or the ocean swallow me; save me from the pit that threatens me. [16]O Jehovah, answer my prayers, for your lovingkindness is wonderful; your mercy is so plentiful, so tender and so kind. [17]Don't hide from me, for I am in deep trouble. Quick! Come and save me. [18]Come, Lord, and rescue me. Ransom me from all my enemies. [19]You know how they talk about me, and how they so shamefully dishonor me. You see them all and know what each has said. [20]Their contempt has broken my heart; my spirit is heavy within me. If even one would show some pity, if even one would comfort me! [21]For food they gave me poison; for my awful thirst they offered me vinegar. [22]Let their joys turn to ashes and their peace disappear; [23]let darkness, blindness and great feebleness be theirs. [24]Pour out your fury upon them; consume them with the fierceness of your anger. [25]Let their homes be desolate and abandoned. [26]For they persecute the one you have smitten, and scoff at the pain of the one you have pierced. [27]Pile their sins high and do not overlook them. [28]Let these men be blotted from the list of the living; do not give them the joys of life with the righteous. [29]But rescue me, O God, from my poverty and pain. [30]Then I will praise God with my singing! My thanks will be his praise—[31]that will please him more than sacrificing a bullock or an ox. [32]The humble shall see their God at work for them. No wonder they will be so glad! All who seek for God shall live in joy. [33]For Jehovah hears the cries of his needy ones, and does not look the other way. [34]Praise him, all heaven and earth! Praise him, all the seas and everything in them! [35]For God will save Jerusalem; he rebuilds the cities of Judah. His people shall live in them and not be dispossessed. [36]Their children shall inherit the land; all who love his name shall live there safely.

Ps 72:1. O God, help the king to judge as you would, and help his son to walk in godliness. [2]Help him to give justice to your people, even to the poor. [3]May the mountains and hills flourish in prosperity because of his good reign. [4]Help him to defend the poor and needy and to crush their oppressors. [5]May the poor and needy revere you constantly, as long as sun and moon continue in the skies! Yes, forever! [6]May the reign of this son of mine be as gentle and fruitful as the springtime rains upon the grass—like showers that water the earth! [7]May all good men flourish in his reign, with abundance of peace to the end of time. [8]Let him reign from sea to sea, and from the Euphrates River to the ends of the earth. [9]The desert nomads shall bow before him; his enemies shall fall face downward in the dust. [10]Kings along the Mediterranean coast—the kings of Tarshish and the islands—and those from Sheba and from Seba—all will bring their gifts. [11]Yes, kings from everywhere! All will bow before him! All will serve him! [12]He will take care of the helpless and poor when they cry to him; for they have no one else to defend them. [13]He feels pity for the weak and needy, and will rescue them. [14]He will save them from oppression and from violence, for their lives are precious to him. [15]And he shall live; and to him will be given the gold of Sheba, and there will be constant praise for him. His people will bless him all day long. [16]Bless us with abundant crops throughout the land, even on the highland plains; may there be fruit like that of Lebanon; may the cities be as full of people as the fields are of grass. [17]His name will be honored forever; it will continue as the sun; and all will be blessed in him; all nations will praise him. [18]Blessed be Jehovah God, the God of Israel, who only does wonderful things! [19]Blessed be his glorious name forever! Let the whole earth be filled with his glory. Amen, and amen!

Ps 93:1, 2. Jehovah is King! He is robed in majesty and strength. The world is his throne. O Lord, you have reigned from prehistoric times, from the everlasting past. [3]The mighty oceans thunder your praise. [4]You are mightier than all the breakers pounding on the seashores of the world! [5]Your royal decrees cannot be changed. Holiness is forever the keynote of your reign.

Ps 96:1. Sing a new song to the Lord! Sing it everywhere around the world! [2]Sing out his praises! Bless his name. Each day tell someone that he saves. [3]Publish his glorious acts throughout the earth. Tell everyone about the amazing things he does. [4]For the Lord is great beyond description, and greatly to be praised. Worship only him among the gods! [5]For the gods of other nations are merely idols, but our God made the heavens! [6]Honor and majesty surround him; strength and beauty are in his Temple. [7]O nations of the world, confess that God alone is glorious and strong. [8]Give him the glory he deserves! Bring your offering and come to worship him. [9]Worship the Lord with the beauty of holy lives. Let the earth tremble before him. [10]Tell the nations that Jehovah reigns! He rules the world. His power can never be overthrown. He will judge all nations fairly. [11]Let the heavens be glad, the earth rejoice; let the vastness of the roaring seas demonstrate his glory. [12]Praise him for the growing fields, for they display his greatness. Let the trees of the forest rustle with praise. [13]For the Lord is coming to judge the earth; he will judge the nations fairly and with truth!

Ps 97:1. Jehovah is King! Let all the earth rejoice! Tell the farthest islands to be glad. [2]Clouds and darkness surround him. Righteousness and justice are the foundation of his throne. [3]Fire goes forth before him and burns up all his foes. [4]His lightning flashes out across the world. The earth sees and trembles. [5]The mountains melt like wax before the Lord of all the earth. [6]The heavens declare his perfect righteousness; every nation sees his glory. [7]Let those who worship idols be disgraced—all who brag about their worthless gods—for every god must bow to him! [8, 9]Jerusalem and all the cities of Judah have heard of your justice, Lord, and are glad that you reign in majesty over the entire earth and are far greater than these other gods. [10]The Lord loves those who hate evil; he protects the lives of his people, and rescues them from the wicked. [11]Light is sown for the godly and joy for the good. [12]May all who are godly be happy in the Lord and crown him, our holy God.

Ps 98:1. Sing a new song to the Lord telling about his mighty deeds! For he has won a mighty victory by his power and holiness. [2, 3]He has announced this victory and revealed it to every nation by fulfilling his promise to be kind to Israel. The whole earth has seen God's salvation of his people. [4]That is why the earth breaks out in praise to God, and sings for utter joy! [5]Sing your praise accompanied by music from the harp. [6]Let the cornets and trumpets shout! Make a joyful symphony before the Lord, the King! [7]Let the sea in all its vastness roar with praise! Let the earth and all those living on it shout, "Glory to the Lord." [8, 9]Let the waves clap their hands in glee and the hills sing out their songs of joy before the Lord, for he is coming to judge the world with perfect justice.

Ps 99:1. Jehovah is King! Let the nations tremble! He is enthroned upon the cherubim. Let the whole earth shake. [2]Jehovah sits in majesty in Zion, supreme above all rulers of the earth. [3]Let them reverence your great and holy name. [4]This mighty King is determined to give justice. Fairness is the touchstone of everything he does. He gives justice throughout Israel. [5]Exalt the Lord our holy God! Bow low before his feet. [6]When Moses and Aaron and Samuel, his prophet, cried to him for help, he answered them. [7]He spoke to them from the pillar of cloud and they followed his instructions. [8]O Jehovah our God! You answered them and forgave their sins, yet punished them when they went wrong. [9]Exalt the Lord our God, and worship at his holy mountain in Jerusalem, for he is holy.

Ps 110:1. Jehovah said to my Lord the Messiah, "Rule as my regent—I will subdue your enemies and make them bow low before you." [2]Jehovah has established your throne in Jerusalem to rule over your enemies. [3]In that day of your power your people shall come to you willingly, dressed in holy altar robes. And your strength shall be renewed day by day like morning dew. [4]Jehovah has taken oath, and will not rescind his vow, that you are a priest forever like Melchizedek. [5]God stands beside you to protect you. He will strike down many kings in the day of his anger. [6]He will punish the nations, and fill them with their dead. He will crush many heads. [7]But he himself shall be refreshed from springs along the way.

Ps 118:19. Open the gates of the Temple—I will go in and give him my thanks. [20]Those gates are the way into the presence of the Lord, and the godly enter there. [21]O Lord, thank you so much for answering my prayer and saving me. [22]The stone rejected by the builders has now become the capstone of the arch! [23]This is the Lord's doing, and it is marvelous to see! [24]This is the day the Lord has made. We will rejoice and be glad in it. [25]O Lord, please help us. Save us. Give us success. [26]Blessed is the one who is coming, the one sent by the Lord. We bless you from the Temple. [27, 28]Jehovah God is our light. I present to him my sacrifice upon the altar, for you are my God, and I shall give you this thanks and this praise. [29]Oh, give thanks to the Lord, for he is so good! For his lovingkindness is forever.

Other Scriptures Relating to his Messiahship. Dan 9:25. Now listen! It will be forty-nine years plus 434 years from the time the command is given to rebuild Jerusalem, until the Anointed One comes! Jerusalem's streets and walls will be rebuilt despite the perilous times. [26]After this period of 434 years, the Anointed One will be killed, his kingdom still unrealized.

Mt 11:3. "Are you really the one we are waiting for, or shall we keep on looking?" [4]Jesus told them, "Go back to John and tell him about the miracles you've seen me do—[5]the blind people I've healed, and the lame people now walking without help, and the cured lepers, and the deaf who hear, and the dead raised to life; and tell him about my preaching the Good News to the poor. [6]Then give him this message, 'Blessed are those who don't doubt me.' "

Mt 16:15. Then he asked them, "Who do *you* think I am?" [16]Simon Peter answered, "The Christ, the Messiah, the Son of the living God."

Mt 26:63. But Jesus remained silent. Then the High Priest said to him, "I demand in the name of the living God that you tell us whether you claim to be the Messiah, the Son of God." [64]"Yes," Jesus said, "I am. And in the future you will see me, the Messiah, sitting at the right hand of God and returning on the clouds of heaven."

Lk 2:28. Simeon was there and took the child in his arms, praising God. [29-31]"Lord," he said, "now I can die content! For I have seen him as you promised me I would. I have seen the Savior you have given to the world. [32]He is the Light that will shine upon the nations, and he will be the glory of your people Israel!" [38]She [Anna] came along just as Simeon was talking with Mary and Joseph, and she also began thanking God and telling everyone in Jerusalem who had been awaiting the coming of the Savior that the Messiah had finally arrived.

Lk 20:41. Then he presented *them* with a question. "Why is it," he asked, "that Christ, the Messiah, is said to be a descendant of King David? [42, 43]For David himself wrote in the book of Psalms: 'God said to my Lord, the Messiah, "Sit at my right hand until I place your enemies beneath your feet." ' [44]How can the Messiah be both David's son and David's God at the same time?" Mt 22:42–45; Mk 12:35–37.

Lk 24:25. Then Jesus said to them, "You are such foolish, foolish people! You find it so hard to believe all that the prophets wrote in the Scriptures! [26]Wasn't it clearly predicted by the prophets that the Messiah would have to suffer all these things before entering his time of glory?" [27]Then Jesus quoted them passage after passage from the writings of the prophets, beginning with the book of Genesis and going right on through the Scriptures, explaining what the passages meant and what they said about himself.

Jn 1:41. Andrew then went to find his brother Peter and told him, "We have found the Messiah!" [45]"We have found the Messiah!—the very person Moses and the prophets told about! His name is Jesus, the son of Joseph from Nazareth!"

Jn 4:25. The woman said, "Well, at least I know that the Messiah will come—the one they call Christ—and when he does, he will explain everything to us." [26]Then Jesus told her, "I am the Messiah!" [29]"Come and meet a man who told me everything I ever did! Can this be the Messiah?" [42]Then they said to the woman, "Now we believe because we have heard him ourselves, not just because of what you told us. He is indeed the Savior of the world."

Jn 5:33. You have gone out to listen to his preaching, and I can assure you that all he says about me is true! [36]But I have a greater witness than John. I refer to the miracles I do; these have been assigned me by the Father, and they prove that the Father has sent me. [37]And the Father himself has also testified about me, though not appearing to you personally, or speaking to you directly. [39]You search the Scriptures, for you believe they give you eternal life. And the Scriptures point to me! [46]For you have refused to believe Moses. He wrote about me, but you refuse to believe him, so you refuse to believe in me.

Jn 6:27. But you shouldn't be so concerned about perishable things like food. No, spend your energy seeking the eternal life that I, the Messiah, can give you. For God the Father has sent me for this very purpose.

Jn 8:14. Jesus told them, "These claims are true even though I make them concerning myself. For I know where I came from and where I am going, but you don't know this about me. [17]Your laws say that if two men agree on something that has happened, their witness is accepted as fact. [18]Well, I am one witness, and my Father who sent me is the other." [25]"Tell us who you are," they demanded. He replied, "I am the one I have always claimed to be." [28]So Jesus said, "When you have killed the Messiah, then you will realize that I am he and that I have not been telling you my own ideas, but have spoken what the Father taught me. [56]Your father Abraham rejoiced to see my day. He knew I was coming and was glad."

Jn 13:19. I tell you this now so that when it happens, you will believe on me.

Acts 3:18. But God was fulfilling the prophecies that the Messiah must suffer all these things. [20]And send Jesus your Messiah back to you again. [24]Samuel and every prophet since have all spoken about what is going on today.

Acts 4:26. The kings of the earth unite to fight against him, and against the anointed Son of God! [27]. . . For Herod the king, and Pontius Pilate the governor, and all the Romans—as well as the people of Israel—are united against Jesus, your anointed Son, your holy servant. Ps 2:2.

Acts 9:22. Paul became more and more fervent in his preaching, and the Damascus Jews couldn't withstand his proofs that Jesus was indeed the Christ.

Acts 13:27. The Jews in Jerusalem and their leaders fulfilled prophecy by killing Jesus; for they didn't recognize him, or realize that he is the one the prophets had written about, though they heard the prophets' words read every Sabbath.

Acts 17:2. As was Paul's custom, he went there to preach, and for three Sabbaths in a row he opened the Scriptures to the people, [3]explaining the prophecies about the sufferings of the Messiah and his coming back to life, and proving that Jesus is the Messiah.

Acts 26:6. But the real reason behind their accusations is something else—it is because I am looking forward to the fulfillment of God's promise made to our ancestors. [7]The twelve tribes of Israel strive night and day to attain this same hope I have! Yet, O King, for me it is a crime, they say! [22]But God protected me so that I am still alive today to tell these facts to everyone, both great and small. I teach nothing except what the prophets and Moses said—[23]that the Messiah would suffer, and be the First to rise from the dead, to bring light to Jews and Gentiles alike.

Acts 28:23. He told them about the Kingdom of God and taught them about Jesus from the Scriptures—from the five books of Moses and the books of prophecy.

Rom 1:1. This letter is from Paul, Jesus Christ's slave, chosen to be a missionary, and sent out to preach God's Good News. [2]This Good News was promised long ago by God's prophets in the Old Testament. [3]It is the Good News about his Son, Jesus Christ our Lord, who came as a human baby, born into King David's royal family line.

1 Cor 15:3. I passed on to you right from the first what had been told to me, that Christ died for our sins just as the Scriptures said he would.

1 Pet 1:10. This salvation was something the prophets did not fully understand. Though they wrote about it, they had many questions as to what it all could mean. [11]They wondered what the Spirit of Christ within them was talking about, for he told them to write down the events which, since then, have happened to Christ: his suffering, and his great glory afterwards.

2 Pet 1:16. For we have not been telling you fairy tales when we explained to you the power of our Lord Jesus Christ and his coming again. My own eyes have seen his splendor and his glory: [17, 18]I was there on the holy mountain when he shone out with honor given him by God his Father; I heard that glorious, majestic voice calling down from heaven, saying, "This is my much-loved Son; I am well pleased with him."

1 Jn 5:6, 7, 8. And we know he is, because God said so with a voice from heaven when Jesus was baptized, and again as he was facing death—yes, not only at his baptism but also as he faced death. And the Holy Spirit, forever truthful, says it too. So we have these three witnesses: the voice of the Holy Spirit in our hearts, the voice from heaven at Christ's baptism, and the voice before he died. And they all say the same thing: that Jesus Christ is the Son of God. [9]We believe men who witness in our courts, and so surely we can believe whatever God declares. And God declares that Jesus is his Son.

See *Jesus, Deity of, King,* above.

MIRACLES OF. Water made wine, Jn 2:1–11.

Heals the government official's son, Jn 4:46–54.

First miraculous draught of fishes, Lk 5:1–11.

Demoniac in the synagogue healed, Mk 1:23–26; Lk 4:33–36.

Heals Simon's wife's mother, Mt 8:14, 15; Mk 1: 29–31; Lk 4:38, 39.

Heals diseases in Galilee, Mt 4:23, 24; Mk 1:34.

Miracles at Jerusalem, Jn 2:23.

Heals the leper, Mt 8:1–4; Mk 1:40–45; Lk 5: 12–16.

Heals the paralytic, Mt 9:1–8; Mk 2:1–12; Lk 5: 17–26.

Heals the disabled man, Jn 5:1–16.

Restores the deformed hand, Mt 12:9–13; Mk 3: 1–5; Lk 6:6–11.

Heals multitudes from Judea, Jerusalem, and coasts of Tyre and Sidon, Lk 6:17–19.

Heals the Roman army officer's servant, Mt 8: 5–13; Lk 7:1–10.

Heals demoniacs, Mt 8:16, 17; Lk 4:40, 41.

Raises the widow's son, Lk 7:11–16.

Heals in Galilee, Lk 7:20–22.

Heals a demoniac, Mt 12:22–37; Mk 3:11, 20–30; Lk 11:14, 15, 17–23.

Stills the storm, Mt 8:23–27; 14:32; Mk 4:35–41; Lk 8:22–25.

Healing of the sick in the land of Gennesaret, Mt 14:34–36.

The demoniacs in Gadara healed, Mt 8:28–34; Mk 5:1–20; Lk 8:26–29.

Raises Jairus's daughter, Mt 9:18, 19, 23–26; Mk 5:22–24, 35–43; Lk 8:41, 42, 49–56.

Heals the woman with the hemorrhage, Mt

9:20–22; Mk 5:25–34; Lk 8:43–48.

Opens the eyes of two blind men in the house, Mt 9:27–31.

A demon cast out and a dumb man cured, Mt 9:32, 33.

Five thousand fed, Mt 14:15–21; Mk 6:35–44; Lk 9:12–17; Jn 6:1–14.

Heals sick in Galilee, Mt 14:14.

Walking on the sea, Mt 14:22–33; Mk 6:45–52; Jn 6:14–21.

The daughter of the Syrophoenician healed, Mt 15:21–28; Mk 7:24–30.

Healing the lame, blind, dumb, and maimed, near the Sea of Galilee, Mt 15:30.

Four thousand fed, Mt 15:32–39; Mk 8:1–9.

One deaf man with a speech impediment cured, Mk 7:31–37.

One blind man cured, Mk 8:22–36.

Child possessed by a demon healed, Mt 17:14–21; Mk 9:14–29; Lk 9:37–43.

Piece of money in the fish's mouth, Mt 17:24–27.

The ten lepers cured, Lk 17:11–19.

Opening the eyes of one born blind, Jn 9.

Raising of Lazarus, Jn 11:1–54.

Handicapped woman cured, Lk 13:10–17.

The dropsy cured, Lk 14:1–6.

Two blind men cured near Jericho, Mt 20:29–34; Mk 10:46–52; Lk 18:35–43.

The fig tree blighted, Mt 21:17–22; Mk 11:12–14, 20–24.

Healing of Malchus's ear, Lk 22:49–51.

Second draught of fishes, Jn 21:6.

Not particularly described, Mt 4:23, 24; 14:14; 15:30; Mk 1:34; Lk 6:17–19; 7:20–22; Jn 2:23; 3:1, 2. Resurrection, Mt 28:6; Mk 16:6; Lk 24:6, 7; Jn 20:1–18. Holds the vision of his disciples, that they should not recognize him, Lk 24:16, 31, 35. His appearances and disappearances, Lk 24:15, 31, 36–45; Jn 20:19, 26. Opening the understanding of his disciples, Lk 24:45. His ascension, Lk 24:51; Acts 1:9.

See *Miracles.*

MISSION OF. In addition to passages dealing with the reasons why Christ came, and will come again, not directly related to his death on the cross, a number of passages reveal various purposes accomplished in his death. These include:

1. To take the place of sinners as their substitute, Mt 20:28.

2. To provide redemption from sin, Rom 3:24.

3. To provide reconciliation toward man, Col 1:21.

4. To provide propitiation toward God, Rom 3:25; 1 Jn 2:2; 4:10.

5. To fulfill the law and bring in grace, Rom 10:4; Gal 3:19–25.

6. To judge the sin nature, Rom 6:10.

7. To provide the basis for the forgiveness of believers, 1 Jn 2:1, 2.

8. To provide the basis for the deferring of predicted divine judgments, 2 Pet 3:9–14.

9. To provide the basis for the forgiveness of pre-cross sins, Rom 3:25.

10. To provide the basis for the national salvation of Israel, Rom 9–11.

11. To provide the basis for the future blessing of the Gentiles, Isa 42:1–7.

12. To provide the basis for making peace, Eph 2:14, 15.

13. To spoil Satan's power, Col 2:14, 15.

14. To provide the basis for the purification of things in heaven, Heb 9:23, 24.

2 Sam 23:3. The Rock of Israel said to me: "One shall come who rules righteously, who rules in the fear of God. [4]He shall be as the light of the morning; a cloudless sunrise when the tender grass springs forth upon the earth; as sunshine after rain."

Isa 42:6. I the Lord have called you to demonstrate my righteousness. I will guard and support you, for I have given you to my people as the personal confirmation of my covenant with them. You shall also be a light to guide the nations unto me. [7]You will open the eyes of the blind, and release those who sit in prison darkness and despair.

Isa 61:1. The Spirit of the Lord God is upon me, because the Lord has anointed me to bring good news to the suffering and afflicted. He has sent me to comfort the broken-hearted, to announce liberty to captives and to open the eyes of the blind. [2]He has sent me to tell those who mourn that the time of God's favor to them has come, and the day of his wrath to their enemies. [3]To all who mourn in Israel he will give: beauty for ashes; joy instead of mourning; praise instead of heaviness. For God has planted them like strong and graceful oaks for his own glory.

Dan 9:24. The Lord has commanded 490 years of further punishment upon Jerusalem and your people. Then at last they will learn to stay away from sin, and their guilt will be cleansed; then the kingdom of everlasting righteousness will begin, and the Most Holy Place (in the Temple) will be rededicated, as the prophets have declared. [27]This king will make a seven-year treaty with the people, but after half that time, he will break his pledge and stop the Jews from all their sacrifices and their offerings; then, as a climax to all his terrible deeds, the Enemy shall utterly defile the sanctuary of God. But in God's time and plan, his judgment will be poured out upon this Evil One.

Mic 5:2. O Bethlehem Ephrathah, you are but a small Judean village, yet you will be the birthplace of my King who is alive from everlasting ages past!

Zech 13:1. At that time a Fountain will be opened to the people of Israel and Jerusalem, a Fountain to cleanse them from all their sins and uncleanness.

Mal 3:2. But who can live when he appears? Who can endure his coming? For he is like a blazing fire refining precious metal and he can bleach the dirtiest garments! [3]Like a refiner of silver he will sit and closely watch as the dross is burned away. He will purify the Levites, the ministers of God, refining them like gold or silver, so that they will do their work for God with pure hearts.

Mt 1:21. For he will save his people from their sins.

Mt 3:11. With water I baptize those who repent of their sins; but someone else is coming, far greater than I am, so great that I am not worthy to carry his shoes! He shall baptize you with the Holy Spirit and with fire. [12]He will separate the chaff from the grain, burning the chaff with never-ending fire, and storing away the grain.

Mt 4:23. Jesus traveled all through Galilee teaching in the Jewish synagogues, everywhere preaching the Good News about the Kingdom of Heaven. And he healed every kind of sickness and disease.

Mt 5:17. Don't misunderstand why I have come—it isn't to cancel the laws of Moses and the warnings of the prophets. No, I came to fulfill them, and to make them all come true.

Mt 9:13. For I have come to urge sinners, not the self-righteous, back to God. Lk 5:30–32.

Mt 10:34. Don't imagine that I came to bring peace to the earth! No, rather, a sword. [35]I have come to set a man against his father, and a daughter against her mother, and a daughter-in-law against her mother-in-law—[36]a man's worst enemies will be right in his own home! Lk 12:49–53; Mic 7:6.

Mt 15:24. Then he said to the woman, "I was sent to help the Jews—the lost sheep of Israel—not the Gentiles."

Mt 18:11. And I, the Messiah, came to save the lost. [Lk 19:9, 10.] [12]If a man has a hundred sheep, and one wanders away and is lost, what will he do? Won't he leave the ninety-nine others and go out into the hills to search for the lost one? [13]And if he finds it, he will rejoice over it more than over the ninety-nine others safe at home! [14]Just so, it is not my Father's will that even one of these little ones should perish. Lk 15:3–7.

Mt 20:28. Your attitude must be like my own, for I, the Messiah, did not come to be served, but to serve, and to give my life as a ransom for many. Mk 10:45.

Mk 1:38. But he replied, "We must go on to other towns as well, and give my message to them too, for that is why I came." Lk 4:43.

Mk 2:15. That night Levi invited his fellow tax collectors and many other notorious sinners to be his dinner guests so that they could meet Jesus and his disciples. (There were many men of this type among the crowds that followed him.) [16]But when some of the Jewish religious leaders saw him eating with these men of ill repute, they said to his disciples, "How can he stand it, to eat with such scum?" [17]When Jesus heard what they were saying, he told them, "Sick people need the doctor, not healthy ones! I haven't come to tell good people to repent, but the bad ones." [18]John's disciples and the Jewish leaders sometimes fasted, that is, went without food as part of their religion. One day some people came to Jesus and asked why his disciples didn't do this too. [19]Jesus replied, "Do friends of the bridegroom refuse to eat at the wedding feast? Should they be sad while he is with them? [20]But some day he will be taken away from them, and then they will mourn. [21](Besides, going without food is part of the old way of doing things.) It is like patching an old garment with unshrunk cloth! What happens? The patch pulls away and leaves the hole worse than before. [22]You know better than to put new wine into old wineskins. They would burst. The wine would be spilled out and the wineskins ruined. New wine needs fresh wineskins."

Lk 1:78. All this will be because the mercy of our God is very tender, and heaven's dawn is about to break upon us, [79]to give light to those who sit in darkness and death's shadow, and to guide us to the path of peace.

Lk 2:30, 31. "For I have seen him as you promised me I would. I have seen the Savior you have given to the world. [32]He is the Light that will shine upon the nations, and he will be the glory of your people Israel!" [34, 35]Simeon blessed them but then said to Mary, "A sword shall pierce your soul, for this child shall be rejected by many in Israel, and this to their undoing. But he will be the greatest joy of many others. And the deepest thoughts of many hearts shall be revealed." [38]She [Anna] came along just as Simeon was talking with Mary and Joseph, and she also began thanking God and telling everyone in Jerusalem who had been awaiting the coming of the Savior that the Messiah had finally arrived.

Lk 4:18, 19. "The Spirit of the Lord is upon me; he has appointed me to preach Good News to the poor; he has sent me to heal the brokenhearted and to announce that captives shall be released and the blind shall see, that the downtrodden shall be freed from their oppressors, and that God is ready to give blessings to all who come to him." [43]But he replied, "I must preach the Good News of the Kingdom of God in other places too, for that is why I was sent."

Lk 8:1. Not long afterwards he began a tour of the cities and villages of Galilee to announce the coming of the Kingdom of God, and took his twelve disciples with him.

Lk 12:49. I have come to bring fire to the earth, and, oh, that my task were completed! [50]There is a terrible baptism ahead of me, and how I am pent up until it is accomplished! [51]Do you think I have come to give peace to the earth? *No!* Rather, strife and division! [52]From now on families will be split apart, three in favor of me, and two against—or perhaps the other way around. [53]A father will decide one way about me; his son, the other; mother and daughter will disagree; and the decision of an honored mother-in-law will be spurned by her daughter-in-law.

Lk 24:26. "Wasn't it clearly predicted by the prophets that the Messiah would have to suffer all these things before entering his time of glory?" [46]And he said, "Yes, it was written long ago that the Messiah must suffer and die and rise again from the dead on the third day; [47]and that this message of salvation should be taken from Jerusalem to all the nations: *There is forgiveness of sins for all who turn to me.*"

Jn 3:13. For only I, the Messiah, have come to earth and will return to heaven again. [14]And as Moses in the wilderness lifted up the bronze image of a serpent on a pole, even so I must be lifted up upon a pole, [15]so that anyone who believes in me will have eternal life. [16]For God loved the world so much that he gave his only Son so that anyone who believes in him shall not perish but have eternal life. [17]God did not send his Son into the world to condemn it, but to save it.

Jn 4:34. Then Jesus explained: "My nourishment comes from doing the will of God who sent me, and from finishing his work."

Jn 6:51. I am that Living Bread that came down out of heaven. Anyone eating this Bread shall live forever; this Bread is my flesh given to redeem humanity.

Jn 8:12. Later, in one of his talks, Jesus said to the people, "I am the Light of the world. So if you follow me, you won't be stumbling through the darkness, for living light will flood your path."

Jn 9:39. Then Jesus told him, "I have come into the world to give sight to those who are spiritually blind and to show those who think they see that they are blind."

Jn 10:10. My purpose is to give life in all its fullness.

Jn 11:50. "Let this one man die for the people—why should the whole nation perish?" [51]This prophecy that Jesus should die for the entire nation came from Caiaphas in his position as High Priest—he didn't think of it by himself, but was inspired to say it. [52]It was a prediction that Jesus' death would not be for Israel only, but for all the children of God scattered around the world.

Jn 12:27. Now my soul is deeply troubled. Shall I pray, "Father, save me from what lies ahead"? But that is the very reason why I came! [46]I have come as a Light to shine in this dark world, so that all who put their trust in me will no longer wander in the darkness. [47]If anyone hears me and doesn't obey me, I am not his judge—for I have come to save the world and not to judge it.

Jn 18:37. I was born for that purpose. And I came to bring truth to the world.

Acts 5:31. Then, with mighty power, God exalted him to be a Prince and Savior, so that the people of Israel would have an opportunity for repentance, and for their sins to be forgiven.

Acts 10:43. And all the prophets have written about him, saying that everyone who believes in him will have their sins forgiven through his name.

Acts 26:23. That the Messiah would suffer, and be the First to rise from the dead, to bring light to Jews and Gentiles alike.

Rom 4:25. He died for our sins and rose again to make us right with God, filling us with God's goodness.

Rom 5:6. When we were utterly helpless with no way of escape, Christ came at just the right time and died for us sinners who had no use for him. [7]Even if we were good, we really wouldn't expect anyone to die for us, though, of course, that might be barely possible. [8]But God showed his great love for us by sending Christ to die for us while we were still sinners.

Rom 8:3. We aren't saved from sin's grasp by knowing the commandments of God, because we can't and don't keep them, but God put into effect a different plan to save us. He sent his own Son in a human body like ours—except that ours are sinful—and destroyed sin's control over us by giving himself as a sacrifice for our sins. [4]So now we can obey God's laws if we follow after the Holy Spirit and no longer obey the old evil nature within us.

Rom 10:4. They don't understand that Christ gives to those who trust in him everything they are trying to get by keeping his laws. He ends all of that.

Rom 14:9. Christ died and rose again for this very purpose, so that he can be our Lord both while we live and when we die. [15]And if your brother is bothered by what you eat, you are not acting in love if you go ahead and eat it. Don't let your eating ruin someone for whom Christ died.

Rom 15:8. Remember that Jesus Christ came to show that God is true to his promises and to help the Jews. [9]And remember that he came also that the Gentiles might be saved and give glory to God for his mercies to them. That is what the Psalmist meant when he wrote: "I will praise you among the Gentiles, and sing to your name."

2 Cor 5:14. Christ's love controls us now. Since we believe that Christ died for all of us, we should also believe that we have died to the old life we used to live. [15]He died for all so that all who live—having received eternal life from him—might live no longer for themselves, to please themselves, but to spend their lives pleasing Christ who died and rose again for them.

Gal 1:3. May peace and blessing be yours from God the Father and from the Lord Jesus Christ. [4]He died for our sins just as God our Father planned, and rescued us from this evil world in which we live.

Gal 4:4. But when the right time came, the time God decided on, he sent his Son, born of a woman, born as a Jew, [5]to buy freedom for us who were slaves to the law so that he could adopt us as his very own sons.

Eph 4:10. The same one who came down is the one who went back up, that he might fill all things everywhere with himself, from the very lowest to the very highest.

1 Tim 1:15. How true it is, and how I long that everyone should know it, that Christ Jesus came into the world to save sinners—and I was the greatest of them all.

Heb 2:9. But we do see Jesus—who for awhile was a little lower than the angels—crowned now by God with glory and honor because he suffered death for us. Yes, because of God's great kindness, Jesus tasted death for everyone in all the world. [14]Since we, God's children, are human beings—

made of flesh and blood—he became flesh and blood too by being born in human form; for only as a human being could he die and in dying break the power of the devil who had the power of death. [15]Only in that way could he deliver those who through fear of death have been living all their lives as slaves to constant dread. [18]For since he himself has now been through suffering and temptation, he knows what it is like when we suffer and are tempted, and he is wonderfully able to help us.

Heb 9:26. If that had been necessary, then he would have had to die again and again, ever since the world began. But no! He came once for all, at the end of the age, to put away the power of sin forever by dying for us.

1 Jn 3:5. And you know that he became a man so that he could take away our sins, and that there is no sin in him, no missing of God's will at any time in any way. [8]But if you keep on sinning, it shows that you belong to Satan, who since he first began to sin has kept steadily at it. But the Son of God came to destroy these works of the devil.

1 Jn 4:10. In this act we see what real love is: it is not our love for God, but his love for us when he sent his Son to satisfy God's anger against our sins.

NAMES AND TITLES OF. A and Z, Rev 1:8. Adam, 1 Cor 15:45. Advocate, Job 16:19. All Powerful One, Rev 1:8. Alpha and Omega, Rev 1:8. Amen, Rev 3:14. Angel, Gen 48:16; Ex 23:20, 21. Angel of his Presence, Isa 63:9. Anointed, Ps 2:2. Author of Life, Acts 3:15.

Beginning and the End, Rev 22:13. Beloved one, Ps 16:10. Branch, Jer 23:5, 6; Zech 3:8; 6:12. Bread of Life, Jn 6:48–51. Bridegroom, Mt 9:15. Bright Morning Star, Rev 22:16.

Carpenter, Mk 6:2, 3. Carpenter's son, Mt 13:55. Child, Isa 9:6. Chosen One, Isa 42:1. Christ, Eph 5:23; 1 Pet 5:10, 14. Christ Jesus, Rom 8:1; 1 Cor 1: 2, 30. Christ Jesus our Lord, 1 Tim 1:12. Christ Jesus our Savior, Tit 1:4. Christ of God, Lk 9:20. Christ the Morning Star, 2 Pet 1:19. Christ the power of God, 1 Cor 1:24. Commander-in-Chief of the Lord's army, Josh 5:14. Consolation of Israel, Lk 2:25. Cornerstone, Eph 2:20; 1 Pet 2:6. Counsellor, Isa 9:6. Covenant with the people, Isa 42:6.

David, Jer 30:9. David's Root and Descendant, Rev 22:16. Deliverer, Rom 11:26. Desire of all nations, Hag 2:7.

Eternal life, 1 Jn 5:20. Everlasting Father, Isa 9: 6. Everlasting light, Isa 60:20.

Faithful and True, Rev 19:11. Faithful and true witness, Rev 3:14. First and last, Rev 1:17, 18; 2:8; 22:13. Firstborn of the dead, Rev 1:5. Firstborn Son, Ps 89:27; Heb 1:6. Foundation, Isa 28:16. Foundation of Rock, 1 Pet 2:4. Fountain, Zech 13:1.

Gate, Jn 10:7. Gift, 2 Cor 9:15. Glory of Israel, Lk 2:32. God, Jn 1:1. God is with us, Mt 1:23. God of all the earth, Isa 54:5. God of Israel, the Savior, Isa 45:15. God our savior, 1 Tim 2:3. God's Anointed King, Lk 2:27. God's Chosen One, Lk 23:35. God's dear Son, Col 1:13. God's Lamb, 1 Cor 5:7. God's Messenger, Heb 3:1. Good Master, Mt 19:16. Governor, Mt 2:6. Great shepherd of the sheep, Heb 13:20, 21. Guardian, 1 Pet 2:25.

Head of the church, Col 1:18. Head of the corner, Mt 21:42. Head Shepherd, 1 Pet 5:4. High Priest, Heb 3:1; 4:14. Holy servant Jesus, Acts 4:30. Holy one, Acts 3:14. Holy One of Israel, Isa 41:14; 54:5. Holy, righteous one, Acts 3:14. Holy son of God, Mk 1:24. Hope (our), 1 Tim 1:1.

Immanuel, Isa 7:14. Israel, Isa 49:3.

Jesus, Mt 1:21. Jesus Christ, Mt 1:1; Jn 1:17; 17:3; Acts 2:38; 9:34; 16:18; Rom 1:1, 3, 6, 7; 2:16; 5:15, 17; 6:3; 1 Cor 1:1; 1 Cor 2:2; 2 Cor 1:19; 4:6; Gal 2:16; Phil 1:8; 2:11; Heb 13:8. Jesus Christ our Lord, Rom 1:3; 6:11, 23. Jesus Christ the Messiah, Mt 1:16. Jesus Christ our Savior, Tit 3:6. Jesus of Nazareth, Mk 1:24; Lk 24:19. Jesus of Nazareth, King of the Jews, Jn 19:19. Jesus, the King of the Jews, Mt 27:37. Jesus, the Son of God, Acts 9:20; Heb 4:14. Jesus, the son of Joseph, Jn 6:42. Judge, Acts 10:42.

King, Mt 21:5. King of Israel, Jn 1:49. King of the Jews, Mt 2:2. King of Ages, Rev 15:3. King of Glory, Ps 24:7–10. King of kings, 1 Tim 6:15; Rev 17:14. King over all the earth, Zech 14:9.

Lamb, Rev 5:6, 8; 6:16; 7:9, 10, 17; 12:11; 13:8, 11; 14:1, 4; 15:3, 4; 17:14; 19:7, 9; 21:9, 14, 22, 23, 27. Lamb of God, Jn 1:29, 36. Lawgiver, Isa 33:22. Leader, Heb 2:10. Leader and instructor, Heb 12:2. Life, Jn 14:6. Light, Jn 8:12. Light of the world, Jn 8:12. Light to guide the nations, Isa 42:6. Lion of the tribe of Judah, Rev 5:5. Living Bread, Jn 6:48–51. Living Foundation of Rock, 1 Pet 2:4. Lord, Isa 40: 3; Rom 1:3. Lord and Savior Jesus Christ, 2 Pet 1: 11; 2:20; 3:18. Lord Christ, Col 3:24. Lord God Almighty, Rev 15:3, 4. Lord Jesus, Acts 7:49; Col 3:17; 1 Thess 4:1, 2. Lord Jesus Christ, Acts 11:17; 16: 31; 20:21; Rom 5:11; 8:39; 13:14; Jas 1:1. Lord of all creation, Acts 10:36, 37. Lord of glory, 1 Cor 2:8; Jas 2:1. Lord of Hosts, Isa 44:6. Lord of lords, Rev 17:14; 19:16. Lord our righteousness, Jer 23:5, 6. Lord, strong and mighty, Ps 24:8. Lord, your Holy One, Isa 43:15. Lord, your Redeemer, Isa 43:14.

Man, 2 Tim 2:8. Man of sorrows, Isa 53:3. Master, Mt 26:49. Mediator, 1 Sam 20:23. Message of Life, 1 Jn 1:1. Messenger of God's promises, Mal 3: 1. Messiah, Lk 2:11; Jn 1:41. Messiah, a King, Lk 23: 1, 2. Messiah, the Son of God, Mk 14:61. Mighty God, Isa 9:6. Mighty One, Ps 45:3. Mighty one of Israel, Isa 49:26. Mighty Savior, Lk 1:69. Mighty to save, Isa 63:1. Minister of the temple in heaven, Heb 8:2. Morning star, 2 Pet 1:19; Rev 22:16.

Nazarene, Mt 2:23.

Only son of the heavenly Father, Jn 1:14.

Power of God, 1 Cor 1:24. Precious cornerstone, Isa 28:16. Priest, Heb 7:17. Prince, Acts 5:31. Prince of peace, Isa 9:6. Prince of Princes, Dan 9:25. Prophet, Deut 18:15, 18; Mt 21:11; Lk 24:19.

Rabbi, Mt 26:25. Redeemer, Isa 59:20. Resurrection and life, Jn 11:25. Righteous branch, Jer 23: 5, 6. Righteous judge, 2 Tim 4:8. Righteous One, Acts 7:52; 22:14. Righteous Servant, Isa 53:11. Rock, 1 Cor 10:3, 4. Root of David, Rev 5:5. Root of Jesse, Isa 11:10. Rose of Sharon, Song 2:1. Ruler of Israel, Num 24:15–19.

Safety, Isa 8:14. Savior, Lk 2:11; Jn 4:42. Savior,

Jesus Christ, 2 Tim 1:10; Tit 2:13. Savior of the body, Eph 5:23. Savior of the world, 1 Jn 4:14. Servant, Isa 42:1. Shepherd, Mk 14:27. Shepherd and Guardian of souls, 1 Pet 2:25. Shepherd, Head, 1 Pet 5:4. Shepherd, Good, Jn 10:11. Shepherd, great, Heb 13:20, 21. Shepherd of Israel, Ps 80:1. Shiloh, Gen 49:10. Son of God, see *Jesus, Son of God.* Son of Man, see *Jesus, Son of Man.* Son of King David, Mt 9:27. Star, Num 24:15–19. Sun of righteousness, Mal 4:2. Stone, Mt 21:42. Stone of stumbling, 1 Pet 2:8.

True God, 1 Jn 5:20. True Light, Jn 1:9. True vine, Jn 15:1. Truth, Jn 14:6.

Vine, Jer 33:15; Ezk 34:29; Jn 15:1.

Way, Jn 14:6. Who is, was, and is to come, Rev 1:4. Wonderful, Isa 9:6. Word, Jn 1:1. Word of God, Rev 19:13.

Those who use his name must not do wrong, 2 Tim 2:19.

In His Name. 1 Cor 6:11; Phil 2:9, 10; Col 3:17; Rev 19:16. Prayer, Jn 14:13; 16:23, 24, 26; Eph 5:20; Col 3:17; Heb 13:15. Miracles performed, Acts 3:6; 4:10; 19:13; baptism, Mt 28:19; Acts 2:38. Preaching, Lk 24:47. Faith, Mt 12:21; Jn 1:11, 12; 2:23. Forgiveness of sins, Lk 24:47; Acts 10:43; 1 Jn 2:12. Salvation, Acts 4:12; 10:43.

See *Jesus, Intercession of,* above; and *Priesthood of,* below.

OBEDIENCE OF. Ps 40:8. And I delight to do your will, my God, for your law is written upon my heart!

Isa 42:21. The Lord has magnified his law and made it truly glorious. Through it he had planned to show the world that he is righteous.

Isa 50:5. The Lord God has spoken to me and I have listened; I do not rebel nor turn away. [6]I give my back to the whip, and my cheeks to those who pull out the beard. I do not hide from shame—they spit in my face.

Mt 3:15. But Jesus said, "Please do it, for I must do all that is right." So then John baptized him.

Mt 26:39. He went forward a little, and fell face downward on the ground, and prayed, "My Father! If it is possible, let this cup be taken away from me. But I want your will, not mine." [42]Again he left them and prayed, "My Father! If this cup cannot go away until I drink it all, your will be done." Mk 14:36; Lk 22:41, 42.

Lk 2:49. "But why did you need to search?" he asked. "Didn't you realize that I would be here at the Temple, in my Father's House?"

Jn 4:34. Then Jesus explained: "My nourishment comes from doing the will of God who sent me, and from finishing his work."

Jn 5:30. But I pass no judgment without consulting the Father. I judge as I am told. And my judgment is absolutely fair and just, for it is according to the will of God who sent me and is not merely my own. [36]But I have a greater witness than John. I refer to the miracles I do; these have been assigned me by the Father, and they prove that the Father has sent me.

Jn 6:38. For I have come here from heaven to do the will of God who sent me, not to have my own way.

Jn 7:18. Anyone presenting his own ideas is looking for praise for himself, but anyone seeking to honor the one who sent him is a good and true person.

Jn 8:39. And he who sent me is with me—he has not deserted me—for I always do those things that are pleasing to him. [46]Which of you can truthfully accuse me of one single sin? [55]But it is true—I know him and fully obey him.

Jn 9:4. All of us must quickly carry out the tasks assigned us by the one who sent me, for there is little time left before the night falls and all work comes to an end.

Jn 14:31. But I will freely do what the Father requires of me so that the world will know that I love the Father.

Jn 15:10. When you obey me you are living in my love, just as I obey my Father and live in his love.

Jn 17:4. I brought glory to you here on earth by doing everything you told me to.

Jn 19:30. When Jesus had tasted it, he said, "It is finished," and bowed his head and dismissed his spirit.

Phil 2:8. And he humbled himself even further, going so far as actually to die a criminal's death on a cross.

Heb 5:8. And even though Jesus was God's Son, he had to learn from experience what it was like to obey, when obeying meant suffering.

Heb 10:7. "Then I said, 'See, I have come to do your will, to lay down my life, just as the Scriptures said that I would.' " [8]After Christ said this, about not being satisfied with the various sacrifices and offerings required under the old system, [9]he then added, "Here I am. I have come to give my life."

OMNIPOTENCE OF. Ps 45:3. Arm yourself, O Mighty One, so glorious, so majestic! [4]And in your majesty go on to victory, defending truth, humility, and justice. Go forth to awe-inspiring deeds! [5]Your arrows are sharp in your enemies' hearts; they fall before you.

Ps 110:3. In that day of your power your people shall come to you willingly.

Isa 9:6. The government shall be upon his shoulder. These will be his royal titles: "Wonderful," "Counselor," "The Mighty God," "The Everlasting Father," "The Prince of Peace."

Isa 40:10. Yes, the Lord God is coming with mighty power; he will rule with awesome strength. See, his reward is with him, to each as he has done.

Isa 50:2. Was I too weak to save you? Is that why the house is silent and empty when I come home? Have I no longer power to deliver? No, that is not the reason! For I can rebuke the sea and make it dry! I can turn the rivers into deserts, covered with dying fish. [3]I am the one who sends the darkness out across the skies. *v.* 4.

Isa 63:1. Who is this who comes from Edom, from the city of Bozrah, with his magnificent garments of crimson? Who is this in kingly robes, marching in the greatness of his strength? "It is I, the Lord, announcing your salvation; I, the Lord, the one who is mighty to save!"

Mt 8:3. *Jesus touches the man. "I want to," he says. "Be healed." And instantly the leprosy disappears.* [16]And when he spoke a single word, all the demons fled; and all the sick were healed. [27]The disciples just sat there, awed! "Who is this," they asked themselves, "that even the winds and the sea obey him?"

Mt 10:1. Jesus called his twelve disciples to him, and gave them authority to cast out evil spirits and to heal every kind of sickness and disease. Mk 6:7; Lk 9:1.

Mt 12:13. Then he said to the man, "Stretch out your arm." And as he did, his hand became normal, just like the other one! [28]"But if I am casting out demons by the Spirit of God, then the Kingdom of God has arrived among you. [29]One cannot rob Satan's kingdom without first binding Satan. Only then can his demons be cast out!" Mk 3:27; Lk 11:20–22.

Mt 28:18. He told his disciples, "I have been given all authority in heaven and earth."

Lk 5:17. And the Lord's healing power was upon him.

Jn 2:19. "All right," Jesus replied, "this is the miracle I will do for you: Destroy this sanctuary and in three days I will raise it up!"

Jn 5:21. He will even raise from the dead anyone he wants to, just as the Father does. [28]Don't be so surprised! Indeed the time is coming when all the dead in their graves shall hear the voice of God's Son, [29]and shall rise again.

Jn 10:17. The Father loves me because I lay down my life that I may have it back again. [18]No one can kill me without my consent—I lay down my life voluntarily. For I have the right and power to lay it down when I want to and also the right and power to take it again. For the Father has given me this right. [28]I give them eternal life and they shall never perish. No one shall snatch them away from me.

Jn 17:1. When Jesus had finished saying all these things he looked up to heaven and said, "Father, the time has come. Reveal the glory of your Son so that he can give the glory back to you. [2]For you have given him authority over every man and woman in all the earth. He gives eternal life to each one you have given him."

Phil 3:20. But our homeland is in heaven, where our Savior the Lord Jesus Christ is; and we are looking forward to his return from there. [21]When he comes back he will take these dying bodies of ours and change them into glorious bodies like his own, using the same mighty power that he will use to conquer all else everywhere.

Col 1:17. He was before all else began and it is his power that holds everything together.

2 Thess 1:9. They will be punished in everlasting hell, forever separated from the Lord, never to see the glory of his power.

1 Tim 6:16. . . . . Unto him be honor and everlasting power and dominion forever and ever. Amen.

Heb 1:3. God's Son shines out with God's glory, and all that God's Son is and does marks him as God. He regulates the universe by the mighty power of his command. He is the one who died to cleanse us and clear our record of all sin, and then sat down in highest honor beside the great God of heaven.

Heb 7:25. He is able to save completely all who come to God through him.

2 Pet 1:16. For we have not been telling you fairy tales when we explained to you the power of our Lord Jesus Christ and his coming again.

Rev 1:8. "I am the A and the Z, the Beginning and the Ending of all things," says God, who is the Lord, the All Powerful One who is, and was, and is coming again!

Rev 3:7. This message is sent to you by the one who is holy and true, and has the key of David to open what no one can shut and to shut what no one can open.

Rev 5:12. "The Lamb is worthy" (loudly they sang it!) "—the Lamb who was slain. He is worthy to receive the power, and the riches, and the wisdom, and the strength, and the honor, and the glory, and the blessing."

See *Jesus, Miracles of.*

OMNIPRESENCE OF. Mt 18:20. For where two or three gather together because they are mine, I will be right there among them.

Mt 28:20. I am with you always, even to the end of the world.

Jn 3:13. For only I, the Messiah, have come to earth and will return to heaven again.

Eph 1:23. Which is his body, filled with himself, the Author and Giver of everything everywhere.

OMNISCIENCE OF. Prov 8:14, 15. I, Wisdom, give good advice and common sense. Because of my strength, kings reign in power. I show the judges who is right and who is wrong. [16]Rulers rule well with my help.

Isa 11:2. And the Spirit of the Lord shall rest upon him, the Spirit of wisdom, understanding, counsel and might; the Spirit of knowledge and of the fear of the Lord. [3]His delight will be obedience to the Lord. He will not judge by appearance, false evidence, or hearsay.

Isa 50:4. The Lord God has given me his words of wisdom so that I may know what I should say to all these weary ones. Morning by morning he wakens me and opens my understanding to his will.

Mt 9:4. Jesus knew what they were thinking and asked them, "Why are you thinking such evil thoughts?"

Mt 11:27. Everything has been entrusted to me by my Father. Only the Father knows the Son, and the Father is known only by the Son and by those to whom the Son reveals him.

Mt 12:25. Jesus knew their thoughts and replied, "A divided kingdom ends in ruin. A city or home divided against itself cannot stand."

Mt 13:54. He returned to his home town, Nazareth in Galilee, and taught there in the synagogue and astonished everyone with his wisdom and his miracles.

Mt 22:18. But Jesus saw what they were after. "You hypocrites!" he exclaimed. "Who are you trying to fool with your trick questions?

Mt 24:25. See, I have warned you.

Mt 26:46. Look! Here comes the man who is betraying me! Mk 14:42.

Mk 2:8. Jesus could read their minds and said to them at once, "Why does this bother you?"

Mk 5:30. Jesus realized at once that healing power had gone out from him, so he turned around in the crowd and asked, "Who touched my clothes?"

Lk 2:40. There the child became a strong, robust lad, and was known for wisdom beyond his years; and God poured out his blessings on him. [47]He was in the Temple, discussing deep questions with them and amazing everyone with his understanding and answers. [52]So Jesus grew both tall and wise, and was loved by God and man.

Lk 5:22. Jesus knew what they were thinking, and he replied, "Why is it blasphemy?

Lk 6:8. How well he knew their thoughts!

Lk 9:46. Now came an argument among them as to which of them would be greatest [in the coming Kingdom]! [47]But Jesus knew their thoughts, so he stood a little child beside him [48]and said to them, "Anyone who takes care of a little child like this is caring for me! And whoever cares for me is caring for God who sent me. Your care for others is the measure of your greatness."

Lk 22:10. And he replied, "As soon as you enter Jerusalem, you will see a man walking along carrying a pitcher of water. Follow him into the house he enters, [11]and say to the man who lives there, 'Our Teacher says for you to show us the guest room where he can eat the Passover meal with his disciples.' [12]He will take you upstairs to a large room all ready for us. That is the place. Go ahead and prepare the meal there." [13]They went off to the city and found everything just as Jesus had said, and prepared the Passover supper. Mk 14:13–15.

Jn 1:48. "How do you know what I am like?" Nathanael demanded. And Jesus replied, "I could see you under the fig tree before Philip found you."

Jn 2:24, 25. But Jesus didn't trust them, for he knew mankind to the core. No one needed to tell him how changeable human nature is!

Jn 3:32. He tells what he has seen and heard, but how few believe what he tells them!

Jn 4:16. "Go and get your husband," Jesus told her. [17, 18]"But I'm not married," the woman replied. "All too true!" Jesus said. "For you have had five husbands, and you aren't even married to the man you're living with now." [19]"Sir," the woman said, "you must be a prophet." [28, 29]Then the woman left her waterpot beside the well and went back to the village and told everyone, "Come and meet a man who told me everything I ever did! Can this be the Messiah?"

Jn 5:30. But I pass no judgment without consulting the Father. I judge as I am told. And my judgment is absolutely fair and just, for it is according to the will of God who sent me and is not merely my own. [42]For as I know so well, you don't have God's love within you.

Jn 6:64. "But some of you don't believe me." (For Jesus knew from the beginning who didn't believe and knew the one who would betray him.)

Jn 8:16. But if I were, it would be an absolutely correct judgment in every respect, for I have with me the Father who sent me.

Jn 13:1, 3. Jesus knew on the evening of Passover Day that it would be his last night on earth before returning to his Father. . . . Jesus knew that the Father had given him everything and that he had come from God and would return to God. [10]Jesus replied. . . ."Now you are clean—but that isn't true of everyone here." [11]For Jesus knew who would betray him. That is what he meant when he said, "Not all of you are clean."

Jn 16:30. "Now we understand that you know everything and don't need anyone to tell you anything." [32]"But the time is coming—in fact, it is here—when you will be scattered, each one returning to his own home, leaving me alone."

Jn 17:1. When Jesus had finished saying all these things he looked up to heaven and said, "Father, the time has come. Reveal the glory of your Son so that he can give the glory back to you."

Jn 18:4. Jesus fully realized all that was going to happen to him. Stepping forward to meet them he asked, "Whom are you looking for?"

Jn 21:17. Peter was grieved. . . . "Lord, you know my heart; you know I am [your friend]."

Acts 1:24. Then they all prayed for the right man to be chosen. "O Lord," they said, "you know every heart; show us which of these men you have chosen."

Col 2:3. In him lie hidden all the mighty, untapped treasures of wisdom and knowledge.

Rev 2:18. This is a message from the Son of God, whose eyes penetrate like flames of fire, whose feet are like glowing brass. [23]And all the churches shall know that I am he who searches deep within men's hearts, and minds; I will give to each of you whatever you deserve.

Rev 5:5. "Stop crying, for look! The Lion of the tribe of Judah, the Root of David, has conquered, and proved himself worthy to open the scroll and to break its seven seals." [12]"The Lamb is worthy" (loudly they sang it) "—the Lamb who was slain. He is worthy to receive the power, and the riches, and the wisdom."

PARABLES OF. The wise and foolish builders, Mt 7:24–27; Lk 6:47–49.

Two debtors, Lk 7:41–43.

The rich fool, Lk 12:16–21.

The servants waiting for their Lord, Lk 12:35–40.

Barren fig tree, Lk 13:6–9.

The sower, Mt 13:2–9, 18–23; Mk 4:1–9, 14–20; Lk 8:5–8, 11–15.

The thistles, Mt 13:24–30, 36–43.

Seed growing unattended, Mk 4:26–29.

Mustard seed, Mt 13:31, 32; Mk 4:30–32; Lk 13:18, 19.

Yeast, Mt 13:33; Lk 13:20, 21.
Hidden treasure, Mt 13:44.
Pearl of great value, Mt 13:45, 46.
Fishnet, Mt 13:47–50.
Unmerciful creditor, Mt 18:23–35.
Good Samaritan, Lk 10:30–37.
Friend at midnight, Lk 11:5–8.
Good shepherd, Jn 10:1–16.
Great feast, Lk 14:15–24.
Lost sheep, Lk 15:3–7; Mt 18:12–14.
Lost piece of money, Lk 15:8–10.
The prodigal son and his brother, Lk 15:11–32.
The dishonest steward, Lk 16:1–9.
Rich man and Lazarus, Lk 16:19–31.
Persistent widow, Lk 18:1–8.
Pharisee and tax collector, Lk 18:9–14.
Workers in the field, Mt 20:1–16.
The nobleman and $20,000, Lk 19:11–27.
The two sons, Mt 21:28–32.
Wicked husbandmen, Mt 21:33–44; Mk 12:1–12; Lk 20:9–18.
Marriage of the king's son, Mt 22:1–14.
Fig tree leafing, Mt 24:32; Mk 13:28, 29.
Man taking a trip, Mk 13:34–37.
Ten virgins, Mt 25:1–13.
Investments, Mt 25:14–30.
The vine, Jn 15:1–5.

PASSION OF. See *Sufferings of.*

PERFECTIONS OF. Not classified under preceding topics: Ps 45:2. You are the fairest of all; Your words are filled with grace.

Isa 11:5. For he will be clothed with fairness and with truth.

Isa 49:2. God will make my words of judgment sharp as swords. He has hidden me in the shadow of his hand; I am like a sharp arrow in his quiver.

Isa 53:9. But he had done no wrong, and had never spoken an evil word.

Ezk 34:29. And I will raise up a notable Vine (the Messiah), in Israel so that my people will never again go hungry nor be shamed by heathen conquest.

Mic 5:4. And he shall stand and feed his flock in the strength of the Lord, in the majesty of the name of the Lord his God.

Hag 2:7. I will shake all nations, and the Desire of All Nations shall come to this Temple.

Mt 12:41. . . . And now a greater than Jonah is here. . . . [42]And now a greater than Solomon is here.

Mt 27:3. About that time Judas, who betrayed him, when he saw that Jesus had been condemned to die, changed his mind and deeply regretted what he had done, and brought back the money to the chief priests and other Jewish leaders. [4]"I have sinned," he declared, "for I have betrayed an innocent man."

Lk 3:16. But someone is coming soon who has far higher authority than mine; in fact, I am not even worthy of being his slave. Mt 3:11; Mk 1:7, 8.

Lk 23:41. But this man hasn't done one thing wrong.

Jn 1:14. And some of us have seen his glory—the glory of the only Son of the heavenly Father! [18]No one has ever actually seen God, but, of course, his only Son has, for he is the companion of the Father and has told us all about him.

Jn 5:30. And my judgment is absolutely fair and just, for it is according to the will of God who sent me and is not merely my own. [34]But the truest witness I have is not from a man. [41]Your approval or disapproval means nothing to me.

Jn 7:18. Anyone presenting his own ideas is looking for praise for himself, but anyone seeking to honor the one who sent him is a good and true person.

Acts 13:28. They found no just cause to execute him.

1 Cor 1:24. Christ is the mighty power of God to save them; Christ himself is the center of God's wise plan for their salvation.

1 Cor 15:45. But Christ is more than that, for he was life-giving Spirit. [47]Christ came from heaven above.

2 Cor 1:19. He isn't one to say "yes" when he means "no." He always does exactly what he says.

2 Cor 4:4. The amazing message we preach about the glory of Christ, who is God.

2 Cor 5:21. For God took the sinless Christ and poured into him our sins. Then, in exchange, he poured God's goodness into us!

Eph 3:8. I was the one chosen for this special joy of telling the Gentiles the Glad News of the endless treasures available to them in Christ.

Col 1:19. For God wanted all of himself to be in his Son.

2 Thess 3:3. But the Lord is faithful; he will make you strong and guard you from satanic attacks of every kind.

2 Tim 2:13. He remains faithful to us and will help us, for he cannot disown us who are part of himself.

Heb 1:3. God's Son shines out with God's glory, and all that God's Son is and does marks him as God.

Heb 2:10. And it was right and proper that God, who made everything for his own glory, should allow Jesus to suffer, for in doing this he was bringing vast multitudes of God's people to heaven; for his suffering made Jesus a perfect Leader, one fit to bring them into their salvation.

Heb 3:2. For Jesus was faithful to God who appointed him High Priest.

PERSECUTIONS OF. See *Persecution, of Jesus.*

POWER OF, TO FORGIVE SINS. Mt 9:2. When Jesus saw their faith, he said to the sick boy, "Cheer up, son! For I have forgiven your sins! [5, 6]I, the Messiah, have the authority on earth to forgive sins. But talk is cheap—anybody could say that. So I'll prove it to you by healing this man." Then, turning to the paralyzed man, he commanded, "Pick up your stretcher and go on home, for you are healed." Mk 2:5, 9–11; Lk 5:20, 23, 24.

Lk 7:47. "Therefore her sins—and they are many—are forgiven, for she loved me much . . ." [48]And he said to her, "Your sins are forgiven." [49]Then the men at the table said to themselves,

"Who does this man think he is, going around forgiving sins?" 50And Jesus said to the woman, "Your faith has saved you; go in peace."

Acts 5:31. Then, with mighty power, God exalted him to be a Prince and Savior, so that the people of Israel would have an opportunity for repentance, and for their sins to be forgiven.

Col 3:13. Remember, the Lord forgave you, so you must forgive others.

See *Jesus, Deity of.*

PRAYERS OF. Mt 11:25. O Father, Lord of heaven and earth, thank you for hiding the truth from those who think themselves so wise, and for revealing it to little children. 26Yes, Father, for it pleased you to do it this way!

Mt 14:23. Then afterwards he went up into the hills to pray. Mk 6:46.

Mt 15:36. And he took the seven loaves and the fish, and gave thanks to God for them, and divided them into pieces.

Mt 19:13. Little children were brought for Jesus to lay his hands on them and pray.

Mt 26:26. As they were eating, Jesus took a small loaf of bread and blessed it and broke it apart and gave it to the disciples and said, "Take it and eat it, for this is my body." 27And he took a cup of wine and gave thanks for it. [1 Cor 11:24.] 36Then Jesus brought them to a garden grove, Gethsemane, and told them to sit down and wait while he went on ahead to pray. 39He went forward a little, and fell face downward on the ground, and prayed, "My Father! If it is possible, let this cup be taken away from me. But I want your will, not mine." 42Again he left them and prayed, "My Father! If this cup cannot go away until I drink it all, your will be done." 44So he went back to prayer the third time, saying the same things again. Mk 14:32–39.

Mt 27:46. Jesus shouted, "Eli, Eli, lama sabachthani," which means, "My God, my God, why have you forsaken me?"

Mk 1:35. The next morning he was up long before daybreak and went out alone into the wilderness to pray.

Mk 6:41. He took the five loaves and two fish and looking up to heaven, gave thanks for the food.

Lk 3:21. Then one day, after the crowds had been baptized, Jesus himself was baptized; and as he was praying, the heavens opened.

Lk 5:16. But he often withdrew to the wilderness for prayer.

Lk 6:12. One day soon afterwards he went out into the mountains to pray, and prayed all night.

Lk 9:18. One day as he was alone, praying, with his disciples nearby. 28Eight days later he took Peter, James, and John with him into the hills to pray. 29And as he was praying, his face began to shine, and his clothes became dazzling white and blazed with light.

Lk 11:1. Once when Jesus had been out praying, one of his disciples came to him as he finished and said, "Lord, teach us a prayer to recite just as John taught one to his disciples."

Lk 22:32. But I have pleaded in prayer for you that your faith should not completely fail. 41, 42He walked away, perhaps a stone's throw, and knelt down and prayed this prayer: "Father, if you are willing, please take away this cup of horror from me. But I want your will, not mine." 43Then an angel from heaven appeared and strengthened him, 44for he was in such agony of spirit that he broke into a sweat of blood, with great drops falling to the ground as he prayed more and more earnestly.

Lk 23:34. "Father, forgive these people," Jesus said, "for they don't know what they are doing." 46Then Jesus shouted, "Father, I commit my spirit to you," and with those words he died.

Jn 11:41. Then Jesus looked up to heaven and said, "Father, thank you for hearing me. 42(You always hear me, of course, but I said it because of all these people standing here, so that they will believe you sent me.)"

Jn 12:27. "Now my soul is deeply troubled. Shall I pray, 'Father, save me from what lies ahead'? But that is the very reason why I came! 28Father, bring glory and honor to your name." Then a voice spoke from heaven saying, "I have already done this, and I will do it again."

Jn 17:1. When Jesus had finished saying all these things he looked up to heaven and said, "Father, the time has come. Reveal the glory of your Son so that he can give the glory back to you. 2For you have given him authority over every man and woman in all the earth. He gives eternal life to each one you have given him. 3And this is the way to have eternal life—by knowing you, the only true God, and Jesus Christ, the one you sent to earth! 4I brought glory to you here on earth by doing everything you told me to. 5And now, Father, reveal my glory as I stand in your presence, the glory we shared before the world began. 6I have told these men all about you. They were in the world, but then you gave them to me. Actually, they were always yours, and you gave them to me; and they have obeyed you. 7Now they know that everything I have is a gift from you, 8for I have passed on to them the commands you gave me; and they accepted them and know of a certainty that I came down to earth from you, and they believe you sent me. 9My plea is not for the world but for those you have given me because they belong to you. 10And all of them, since they are mine, belong to you; and you have given them back to me with everything else of yours, and so *they are my glory!* 11Now I am leaving the world, and leaving them behind, and coming to you. Holy Father, keep them in your own care—all those you have given me—so that they will be united just as we are, with none missing. 12During my time here I have kept safe within your family all of these you gave me. I guarded them so that no one perished, except the son of hell, as the Scriptures foretold. 13And now I am coming to you. I have told them many things while I was with them so that they would be filled with my joy. 14I have given them your commands. And the world hates them because they don't fit in with it, just as I don't. 15I'm not asking you to take them out of the world, but to keep them safe from Satan's power. [16]They are not part of this world any more than I am. [17]Make them pure and holy through teaching them your words of truth. [18]As you sent me into the world, I am sending them into the world, [19]and I consecrate myself to meet their need for growth in truth and holiness. [20]I am not praying for these alone but also for the future believers who will come to me because of the testimony of these. [21]My prayer for all of them is that they will be of one heart and mind, just as you and I are, Father—that just as you are in me and I am in you, so they will be in us, and the world will believe you sent me. [22]I have given them the glory you gave me—the glorious unity of being one, as we are—[23]I in them and you in me, all being perfected into one—so that the world will know you sent me and will understand that you love them as much as you love me. [24]Father, I want them with me—these you've given me—so that they can see my glory. You gave me the glory because you loved me before the world began! [25]O righteous Father, the world doesn't know you, but I do; and these disciples know you sent me. [26]And I have revealed you to them, and will keep on revealing you so that the mighty love you have for me may be in them, and I in them."

Heb 5:7. Yet while Christ was here on earth he pleaded with God, praying with tears and agony of soul to the only one who would save him from [premature] death. And God heard his prayers because of his strong desire to obey God at all times.

See *Jesus, Mediation of, Priesthood of.*

PREEXISTENCE OF. Gen 1:26. Then God said, "Let us make a man—someone like ourselves, to be the master of all life upon the earth and in the skies and in the seas."

Ps 102:25. In ages past you laid the foundations of the earth, and made the heavens with your hands! [26]They shall perish, but you go on forever. They will grow old, like worn-out clothing, and you will change them like a man putting on a new shirt and throwing away the old one! [27]But you yourself never grow old. You are forever, and your years never end. with Heb 1:8–12.

Prov 8:22. The Lord formed me in the beginning, before he created anything else. [23]From ages past, I am. I existed before the earth began. [24]I lived before the oceans were created, before the springs bubbled forth their waters onto the earth; [25]before the mountains and the hills were made. [26]Yes, I was born before God made the earth and fields, and high plateaus. [27-29]I was there when he established the heavens and formed the great springs in the depths of the oceans. I was there when he set the limits of the seas and gave them his instructions not to spread beyond their boundaries. I was there when he made the blueprint for the earth and oceans. [30]I was always at his side like a little child. I was his constant delight, laughing and playing in his presence. [31]And how happy I was with what he created—his wide world and all his family of mankind! [32]And so, young men, listen to me, for how happy are all who follow my instructions. [33]Listen to my counsel—oh, don't refuse it—and be wise. [34]Happy is the man who is so anxious to be with me that he watches for me daily at my gates, or waits for me outside my home! [35]For whoever finds me finds life and wins approval from the Lord. [36]But the one who misses me has injured himself irreparably. Those who refuse me show that they love death.

Jn 1:1, 2. Before anything else existed, there was Christ, with God. He has always been alive and is himself God. [3]He created everything there is—nothing exists that he didn't make.

Jn 3:13. For only I, the Messiah, have come to earth and will return to heaven again.

Jn 6:62. Then what will you think if you see me, the Messiah, return to heaven again?

Jn 8:56. "Your father Abraham rejoiced to see my day. He knew I was coming and was glad." [57]*The Jewish Leaders:* "You aren't even fifty years old—sure, you've seen Abraham!" [58]*Jesus:* "The absolute truth is that I was in existence before Abraham was ever born!"

Jn 17:5. And now, Father, reveal my glory as I stand in your presence, the glory we shared before the world began.

Rom 11:36. For everything comes from God alone. Everything lives by his power, and everything is for his glory. To him be glory evermore.

1 Cor 8:6. But we know that there is only one God, the Father, who created all things and made us to be his own; and one Lord Jesus Christ, who made everything and gives us life.

Phil 2:5. Your attitude should be the kind that was shown us by Jesus Christ, [6]who, though he was God, did not demand and cling to his rights as God, [7]but laid aside his mighty power and glory, taking the disguise of a slave and becoming like men.

Col 1:15. Christ is the exact likeness of the unseen God. He existed before God made anything at all, and, in fact, [16]Christ himself is the Creator who made everything in heaven and earth, the things we can see and the things we can't; the spirit world with its kings and kingdoms, its rulers and authorities; all were made by Christ for his own use and glory. [17]He was before all else began and it is his power that holds everything together.

Heb 1:1. Long ago God spoke in many different ways to our fathers through the prophets (in visions, dreams, and even face to face), telling them little by little about his plans. [2]But now in these days he has spoken to us through his Son to whom he has given everything, and through whom he made the world and everything there is.

Heb 2:9. But we do see Jesus—who for awhile was a little lower than the angels—crowned now by God with glory and honor because he suffered death for us. Yes, because of God's great kindness, Jesus tasted death for everyone in all the world. [14]Since we, God's children, are human beings—made of flesh and blood—he became flesh and blood too by being born in human form; for only as a human being could he die and in dying break the power of the devil who had the power of death. [15]Only in that way could he deliver those who through fear of death have been living all their lives as slaves to constant dread. [16]We all know he did not come as an angel but as a human being—yes, a Jew.

Rev 4:11. O Lord, you are worthy to receive the glory and the honor and the power, for you have created all things. They were created and called into being by your act of will.

See above, *Jesus, Creator, Eternity of, Incarnation of, Omnipotence of, Omnipresence of, Omniscience of.*

PRIESTHOOD OF. Appointed and called by God, Heb 3:1, 2; 5:4, 5; after the manner of Melchizedek, Ps 110:4, with Heb 5:6; 6:20; 7:15, 17; superior to Aaron and the Levitical priests, Heb 7:11, 16, 22; 8:1, 2, 6. Consecrated with an oath, Heb 7:20, 21. Has unchangeable priesthood, Heb 7:23, 28. Is of unblemished purity, Heb 7:26, 28; faithful, Heb 3:2. Needed no sacrifice for himself, Heb 7:27.

Offered himself a sacrifice, Heb 9:14, 26. His sacrifice superior to all others, Heb 9:13, 14, 23. Offered sacrifice but once, Heb 7:27. Made reconciliation, Heb 2:17. Obtained redemption for us, Heb 9:12. Entered into heaven, Heb 4:14; 10:12. Sympathizes with us, Heb 2:18; 4:15. Intercedes, Heb 7:25; 9:24. Blesses, Num 6:23–26, with Acts 3:26. On his throne, Zech 6:13. Appointment of, an encouragement to steadfastness, Heb 4:14.

Typified: Melchizedek, Gen 14:18–20. Aaron and his sons, Ex 40:12–15.

PROMISES OF.

Prophetic. Mt 19:28. And Jesus replied, "When I, the Messiah, shall sit upon my glorious throne in the Kingdom, you my disciples shall certainly sit on twelve thrones judging the twelve tribes of Israel. [29]And anyone who gives up his home, brothers, sisters, father, mother, wife, children, or property, to follow me, shall receive a hundred times as much in return, and shall have eternal life." Lk 18:29, 30.

Mk 10:29. And Jesus replied, "Let me assure you that no one has ever given up anything—home, brothers, sisters, mother, father, children, or property—for love of me and to tell others the Good News, [30]who won't be given back, a hundred times over, homes, brothers, sisters, mothers, children, and land—with persecutions!" Lk 18:29, 30.

Lk 22:29. And because my Father has granted me a Kingdom, I, here and now, grant you the right [30]to eat and drink at my table in that Kingdom; and you will sit on thrones judging the twelve tribes of Israel.

Lk 23:43. And Jesus replied, "Today you will be with me in Paradise. This is a solemn promise."

Lk 24:49. And now I will send the Holy Spirit upon you, just as my Father promised. Don't begin telling others yet—stay here in the city until the Holy Spirit comes and fills you with power from heaven.

Jn 5:25. And I solemnly declare that the time is coming, in fact, it is here, when the dead shall hear my voice—the voice of the Son of God—and those who listen shall live. [26]The Father has life in himself, and has granted his Son to have life in himself, [27]and to judge the sins of all mankind because he is the Son of Man. [28]Don't be so surprised! Indeed the time is coming when all the dead in their graves shall hear the voice of God's Son, [29]and shall rise again—those who have done good, to eternal life; and those who have continued in evil, to judgment.

Jn 6:54. But anyone who does eat my flesh and drink my blood has eternal life, and I will raise him at the Last Day. [57]I live by the power of the living Father who sent me, and in the same way those who partake of me shall live because of me! [58]I am the true Bread from heaven; and anyone who eats this Bread shall live forever, and not die as your fathers did—though they ate bread from heaven.

Jn 7:39. He was speaking of the Holy Spirit, who would be given to everyone believing in him; but the Spirit had not yet been given, because Jesus had not yet returned to his glory in heaven.

Jn 12:25. If you love your life down here—you will lose it. If you despise your life down here—you will exchange it for eternal glory. [26]If these Greeks want to be my disciples, tell them to come and follow me, for my servants must be where I am. And if they follow me, the Father will honor them.

Jn 14:16. And I will ask the Father and he will give you another Comforter, and he will never leave you. [26]But when the Father sends the Comforter instead of me—and by the Comforter I mean the Holy Spirit—he will teach you much, as well as remind you of everything I myself have told you.

Jn 15:26. But I will send you the Comforter—the Holy Spirit, the source of all truth. He will come to you from the Father and will tell you all about me. [27]And you also must tell everyone about me, because you have been with me from the beginning.

Jn 16:7. But the fact of the matter is that it is best for you that I go away, for if I don't, the Comforter won't come. If I do, he will—for I will send him to you. [8]And when he has come he will convince the world of its sin, and of the availability of God's goodness, and of deliverance from judgment. [9]The world's sin is unbelief in me; [10]there is righteousness available because I go to the Father and you shall see me no more; [11]there is deliverance from judgment because the prince of this world has already been judged. [12]Oh, there is so much more I want to tell you, but you can't understand it now. [13]When the Holy Spirit, who is truth, comes, he shall guide you into all truth, for he will not be presenting his own ideas, but will be passing on to you what he has heard. He will tell you about the future. [14]He shall praise me and bring me great honor by showing you my glory. [15]All the Father's glory is mine; this is what I mean when I say that he will show you my glory. [16]In just a little while I will be gone, and you will see me no more; but just a little while after that, and you will see me again! [20]The world will greatly rejoice over what is going to happen to me, and you will weep. But your weeping shall suddenly be turned to wonderful joy (when you see me again). [21]It will be the same joy as that of a woman in labor when her child is born—her anguish gives place to rapturous joy and the pain is forgotten. [22]You have sorrow now, but I will see you again and then you will rejoice; and no one can rob you of that joy. [23]At that time you won't need to ask me for anything, for you can go directly to the Father and ask him, and he will give you what you ask for because you use my name. [24]You haven't tried this before, (but begin now). Ask, using my name, and you will receive, and your cup of joy will overflow. [25]I have spoken of these matters very guardedly, but the time will come when this will not be necessary and I will tell you plainly all about the Father. [26]Then you will present your petitions over my signature! And I won't need to ask the Father to grant you these requests. [33]I have told you all this so that you will have peace of heart and mind. Here on earth you will have many trials and sorrows; but cheer up, for I have overcome the world.

Acts 1:4. In one of these meetings he told them not to leave Jerusalem until the Holy Spirit came upon them in fulfillment of the Father's promise, a matter he had previously discussed with them. [5]"John baptized you with water," he reminded them, but you shall be baptized with the Holy Spirit in just a few days." [6]And another time when he appeared to them, they asked him, "Lord, are you going to free Israel (from Rome) now and restore us as an independent nation?" [7]"The Father sets those dates," he replied, "and they are not for you to know. [8]But when the Holy Spirit has come upon you, you will receive power to testify about me with great effect, to the people in Jerusalem, throughout Judea, in Samaria, and to the ends of the earth, about my death and resurrection."

PROPHECIES CONCERNING.

Coming of. Gen 3:15. From now on you and the woman will be enemies, as will all of your offspring and hers. And I will put the fear of you into the woman, and between your offspring and hers. He shall strike you on your head, while you will strike at his heel.

Gen 12:3. I will bless those who bless you and curse those who curse you; and the entire world will be blessed because of you.

Gen 49:10. The scepter shall not depart from Judah until Shiloh comes, whom all people shall obey.

Deut 32:18. They spurned the Rock who had made them, forgetting it was God who had given them birth.

1 Sam 2:10. Those who fight against the Lord shall be broken; he thunders against them from heaven. He judges throughout the earth. He gives mighty strength to his King, and gives great glory to his anointed one.

Job 19:25. But as for me, I know that my Redeemer lives, and that he will stand upon the earth at last.

Ps 21:5. You have given him fame and honor. You have clothed him with splendor and majesty. [6]You have endowed him with eternal happiness. You have given him the unquenchable joy of your presence. [7]And because the king trusts in the Lord, he will never stumble, never fall; for he depends upon the steadfast love of the God who is above all gods.

Ps 40:6. It isn't sacrifices and offerings which you really want from your people. Burnt animals bring no special joy to your heart. But you have accepted the offer of my lifelong service. [7]Then I said, "See, I have come, just as all the prophets foretold. [8]And I delight to do your will, my God, for your law is written upon my heart!" [9]I have told everyone the Good News that you forgive men's sins. I have not been timid about it, as you well know, O Lord. [10]I have not kept this Good News hidden in my heart, but have proclaimed your lovingkindness and truth to all the congregation.

Ps 68:18. He ascends the heights, leading many captives in his train. He receives gifts for men, even those who once were rebels. God will live among us here.

Ps 118:22. The stone rejected by the builders has now become the capstone of the arch! [23]This is the Lord's doing, and it is marvelous to see! [24]This is the day the Lord has made. We will rejoice and be glad in it. [26]Blessed is the one who is coming, the one sent by the Lord. We bless you from the Temple.

Isa 11:1. The royal line of David will be cut off, chopped down like a tree; but from the stump will grow a Shoot—yes, a new Branch from the old root. [Rom 15:12.] [2]And the Spirit of the Lord shall rest upon him, the Spirit of wisdom, understanding, counsel and might; the Spirit of knowledge and of the fear of the Lord. [3]His delight will be obedience to the Lord. He will not judge by appearance, false evidence, or hearsay, [4]but will defend the poor and the exploited. He will rule against the wicked who oppress them. [5]For he will be clothed with fairness and with truth. [6]In that day the wolf and the lamb will lie down together, and the leopard and goats will be at peace. Calves and fat cattle will be safe among lions, and a little child shall lead them all. [7]The cows will graze among bears; cubs and calves will lie down together, and lions will eat grass like the cows. [8]Babies will crawl safely among poisonous snakes, and a little child who puts his hand in a nest of deadly adders will pull it out unharmed. [9]Nothing will hurt or destroy in all my holy mountain, for as the waters fill the sea, so shall the earth be full of the knowledge of the Lord. [10]In that day he who created the royal dynasty of David will be a banner of salvation to all the world. The nations will rally to him, for the land where he lives will be a glorious place. *vs.* 11–16.

Isa 28:16. But the Lord God says, See, I am placing a Foundation Stone in Zion—a firm, tested, precious Cornerstone that is safe to build on. He who believes need never run away again.

Isa 40:3. Listen! I hear the voice of someone

shouting, "Make a road for the Lord through the wilderness; make him a straight, smooth road through the desert. [Lk 3:4.] [11]He will feed his flock like a shepherd; he will carry the lambs in his arms and gently lead the ewes with young.

Isa 42:1. See my Servant, whom I uphold; my Chosen One, in whom I delight. I have put my Spirit upon him; he will reveal justice to the nations of the world. [2]He will be gentle—he will not shout nor quarrel in the streets. [3]He will not break the bruised reed, nor quench the dimly burning flame. He will encourage the fainthearted, those tempted to despair. He will see full justice given to all who have been wronged. [4]He won't be satisfied until truth and righteousness prevail throughout the earth, nor until even distant lands beyond the seas have put their trust in him.

Isa 49:1. Listen to me, all of you in far-off lands: The Lord called me before my birth. From within the womb he called me by my name. [2]God will make my words of judgment sharp as swords. He has hidden me in the shadow of his hand; I am like a sharp arrow in his quiver. [3]He said to me: "You are my Servant, a Prince of Power with God, and you shall bring me glory." [4]I replied, "But my work for them seems all in vain; I have spent my strength for them without response. Yet I leave it all with God for my reward." [5]"And now," said the Lord—the Lord who formed me from my mother's womb to serve him who commissioned me to restore to him his people Israel, who has given me the strength to perform this task and honored me for doing it!—[6]"you shall do more than restore Israel to me. I will make you a Light to the nations of the world to bring my salvation to them too." [7]The Lord, the Redeemer and Holy One of Israel, say to the one who is despised, rejected by mankind, and kept beneath the heel of earthly rulers: "Kings shall stand at attention when you pass by; princes shall bow low because the Lord has chosen you; he, the faithful Lord, the Holy One of Israel, chooses you." [8, 9]The Lord says, "Your request has come at a favorable time. I will keep you from premature harm and give you as a token and pledge to Israel, proof that I will reestablish the land of Israel and reassign it to its own people again. Through you I am saying to the prisoners of darkness, 'Come out! I am giving you your freedom!' [10]They shall neither hunger nor thirst; the searing sun and scorching desert winds will not reach them any more. For the Lord in his mercy will lead them beside the cool waters. [11]And I will make my mountains into level paths for them; the highways shall be raised above the valleys. [12]See, my people shall return from far away, from north and west and south." *vs.* 13–26; Isa 53.

Isa 55:3. Come to me with your ears wide open. Listen, for the life of your soul is at stake. I am ready to make an everlasting covenant with you, to give you all the unfailing mercies and love that I had for King David. [4]He proved my power by conquering foreign nations. [5]You also will command the nations and they will come running to obey, not because of your own power or virtue but because I, the Lord your God, have glorified you.

Isa 56:1. Be just and fair to all, the Lord God says. Do what's right and good, for I am coming soon to rescue you.

Isa 59:16. He saw no one was helping you, and wondered that no one intervened. Therefore he himself stepped in to save you through his mighty power and justice. [17]He put on righteousness as armor, and the helmet of salvation on his head. He clothed himself with robes of vengeance and of godly fury. [18]He will repay his enemies for their evil deeds—fury for his foes in distant lands. [20]He will come as a Redeemer to those in Zion who have turned away from sin.

Isa 62:10. "Go out! Go out! Prepare the roadway for my people to return! Build the roads, pull out the boulders, raise the flag of Israel." [11]See, the Lord has sent his messengers to every land and said, "Tell my people, I, the Lord your God, am coming to save you and will bring you many gifts."

Jer 23:5, 6. For the time is coming, says the Lord, when I will place a righteous Branch upon King David's throne. He shall be a King who shall rule with wisdom and justice and cause righteousness to prevail everywhere throughout the earth. And this is his name: *The Lord Our Righteousness.* At that time Judah will be saved and Israel will live in peace.

Jer 33:15. At that time I will bring to the throne the true Son of David, and he shall rule justly. [16]In that day the people of Judah and Jerusalem shall live in safety and their motto will be, "The Lord is our righteousness!" [17]For the Lord declares that from then on, David shall forever have an heir sitting on the throne of Israel. [18]And there shall always be Levites to offer burnt offerings and meal offerings and sacrifices to the Lord.

Dan 7:13. Next I saw the arrival of a Man—or so he seemed to be—brought there on clouds from heaven; he approached the Ancient of Days and was presented to him. [14]He was given the ruling power and glory over all the nations of the world, so that all people of every language must obey him. His power is eternal—it will never end; his government shall never fall.

Dan 9:24. The Lord has commanded 490 years of further punishment upon Jerusalem and your people. Then at last they will learn to stay away from sin, and their guilt will be cleansed; then the kingdom of everlasting righteousness will begin, and the Most Holy Place (in the Temple) will be rededicated, as the prophets have declared. [25]Now listen! It will be forty-nine years plus 434 years from the time the command is given to rebuild Jerusalem, until the Anointed One comes! Jerusalem's streets and walls will be rebuilt despite the perilous times. [26]After this period of 434 years, the Anointed One will be killed, his kingdom still unrealized . . . and a king will arise whose armies will destroy the city and the Temple. They will be overwhelmed as with a flood, and war and its miseries are decreed from that time to the very end. [27]This king will make a seven-year treaty with the people, but after half that time, he will break his pledge and stop the Jews from all their sacrifices and their offerings; then, as a climax to all his terrible deeds, the Enemy shall utterly defile the sanctuary of God. But in God's time and plan, his judgment will be poured out upon this Evil One.

Hag 2:7. "I will shake all nations, and the Desire of All Nations shall come to this Temple, and I will fill this place with my glory," says the Lord of Hosts.

Zech 3:8. Listen to me, O Joshua the High Priest, and all you other priests, you are illustrations of the good things to come. Don't you see?—Joshua represents my servant the Branch whom I will send.

Zech 9:9. Rejoice greatly, O my people! Shout with joy! For look—your King is coming! He is the Righteous One, the Victor! Yet he is lowly, riding on a donkey's colt!

Zech 13:1. At that time a Fountain will be opened to the people of Israel and Jerusalem, a Fountain to cleanse them from all their sins and uncleanness.

Mal 3:1. "Listen: I will send my messenger before me to prepare the way. And then the one you are looking for will come suddenly to his Temple—the Messenger of God's promises, to bring you great joy. Yes, he is surely coming," says the Lord of Hosts. [2]"But who can live when he appears? Who can endure his coming? For he is like a blazing fire refining precious metal and he can bleach the dirtiest garments! [3]Like a refiner of silver he will sit and closely watch as the dross is burned away. He will purify the Levites, the ministers of God, refining them like gold or silver, so that they will do their work for God with pure hearts."

Mal 4:2. But for you who fear my name, the Sun of Righteousness will rise with healing in his wings. And you will go free, leaping with joy like calves let out to pasture.

Mt 1:20. As he lay awake considering this, he fell into a dream, and saw an angel standing beside him. "Joseph, son of David," the angel said, "don't hesitate to take Mary as your wife! For the child within her has been conceived by the Holy Spirit. [21]And she will have a Son and you shall name him Jesus (meaning 'Savior'), for he will save his people from their sins. [22]This will fulfill God's message through his prophets—[23]'*Listen! The virgin shall conceive a child!* She shall give birth to a Son, and he shall be called "Emmanuel" (meaning "God is with us").'"

Lk 1:26. The following month God sent the angel Gabriel to Nazareth, a village in Galilee, [27]to a virgin, Mary, engaged to be married to a man named Joseph, a descendant of King David. [28]Gabriel appeared to her and said, "Congratulations, favored lady! The Lord is with you!" [29]Confused and disturbed, Mary tried to think what the angel could mean. [30]"Don't be frightened, Mary," the angel told her, "for God has decided to wonderfully bless you! [31]Very soon now, you will become pregnant and have a baby boy, and you are to name him 'Jesus.' [32]He shall be very great and shall be called the Son of God. And the Lord God shall give him the throne of his ancestor David. [33]And he shall reign over Israel forever; his Kingdom shall never end!" [34]Mary asked the angel, "But how can I have a baby? I am a virgin." [35]The angel replied, "The Holy Spirit shall come upon you, and the power of God shall overshadow you; so the baby born to you will be utterly holy—the Son of God. [36]Furthermore, six months ago your Aunt Elizabeth—'the barren one,' they called her—became pregnant in her old age! [37]For every promise from God shall surely come true." [41]At the sound of Mary's greeting, Elizabeth's child leaped within her and she was filled with the Holy Spirit. [42]She gave a glad cry and exclaimed to Mary, "You are favored by God above all other women, and your child is destined for God's mightiest praise. [43]What an honor this is, that the mother of my Lord should visit me! [44]When you came in and greeted me, the instant I heard your voice, my baby moved in me for joy! [45]You believed that God would do what he said; that is why he has given you this wonderful blessing."

Lk 2:26. For the Holy Spirit had revealed to him that he would not die until he had seen him—God's anointed King. [31]"I have seen the Savior you have given to the world. [32]He is the Light that will shine upon the nations, and he will be the glory of your people Israel!" [34, 35]Simeon blessed them but then said to Mary, "A sword shall pierce your soul, for this child shall be rejected by many in Israel, and this to their undoing. But he will be the greatest joy of many others. And the deepest thoughts of many hearts shall be revealed." [38]She [Anna] came along just as Simeon was talking with Mary and Joseph, and she also began thanking God and telling everyone in Jerusalem who had been awaiting the coming of the Savior that the Messiah had finally arrived.

Jn 8:56. Your father Abraham rejoiced to see my day. He knew I was coming and was glad.

Acts 3:22. Moses, for instance, said long ago, "The Lord God will raise up a Prophet among you, who will resemble me! Listen carefully to everything he tells you. [23]Anyone who will not listen to him shall be utterly destroyed." [24]Samuel and every prophet since have all spoken about what is going on today.

Rom 1:2. This Good News was promised long ago by God's prophets in the Old Testament. [3]It is the Good News about his Son, Jesus Christ our Lord, who came as a human baby, born into King David's royal family line.

Heb 7:16. Did not become a priest by meeting the old requirement of belonging to the tribe of Levi, but on the basis of power flowing from a life that cannot end.

Heb 10:9. He then added, "Here I am. I have come to give my life." He cancels the first system in favor of a far better one.

The Future Glory and Power of. Mk 14:62. Jesus said, "I am, and you will see me sitting at the right hand of God, and returning to earth in the clouds of heaven."

1 Pet 3:22. And now Christ is in heaven, sitting in the place of honor next to God the Father, with all the angels and powers of heaven bowing before him and obeying him.

Jude 1:14. Enoch, who lived seven generations after Adam, knew about these men and said this about them: "See, the Lord is coming with millions of his holy ones. [15]He will bring the people of the world before him in judgment, to receive just punishment, and to prove the terrible things they have done in rebellion against God, revealing all they have said against him."

Rev 1:5. And from Jesus Christ who faithfully reveals all truth to us. He was the first to rise from death, to die no more. He is far greater than any king in all the earth. All praise to him who always loves us and who set us free from our sins by pouring out his lifeblood for us. [6]He has gathered us into his kingdom and made us priests of God his Father. Give to him everlasting glory! He rules forever! Amen! [7]See! He is arriving, surrounded by clouds; and every eye shall see him—yes, and those who pierced him. And the nations will weep in sorrow and in terror when he comes. Yes! Amen! Let it be so! [18]"Though I am the First and Last, the Living One who died, who is now alive forevermore, who has the keys of hell and death—don't be afraid!"

Rev 2:23. And I will strike her children dead. And all the churches shall know that I am he who searches deep within men's hearts, and minds; I will give to each of you whatever you deserve.

Rev 3:7. This message is sent to you by the one who is holy and true, and has the key of David to open what no one can shut and to shut what no one can open. [14]This message is from the one who stands firm, the faithful and true Witness (of all that is or was or evermore shall be), the primeval source of God's creation. [21]I will let every one who conquers sit beside me on my throne, just as I took my place with my Father on his throne when I had conquered. Isa 22:22.

Rev 5:5. But one of the twenty-four Elders said to me, "Stop crying, for look! The Lion of the tribe of Judah, the Root of David, has conquered, and proved himself worthy to open the scroll and to break its seven seals." [12]"The Lamb is worthy" (loudly they sang it!) "—the Lamb who was slain. He is worthy to receive the power, and the riches, and the wisdom, and the strength, and the honor, and the glory, and the blessing."

Rev 6:16. And cried to the mountains to crush them. "Fall on us," they pleaded, "and hide us from the face of the one sitting on the throne, and from the anger of the Lamb, [17]because the great day of their anger has come, and who can survive it?"

Rev 7:9. After this I saw a vast crowd, too great to count, from all nations and provinces and languages, standing in front of the throne and before the Lamb, clothed in white, with palm branches in their hands. [10]And they were shouting with a mighty shout, "Salvation comes from our God upon the throne, and from the Lamb." [11]And now all the angels were crowding around the throne and around the Elders and the four Living Beings, and falling face down before the throne and worshiping God. [12]"Amen!" they said. "Blessing, and glory, and wisdom, and thanksgiving, and honor, and power, and might, be to our God forever and forever. Amen!" [13]Then one of the twenty-four Elders asked me, "Do you know who these are, who are clothed in white, and where they come from?" [14]"No, sir," I replied. "Please tell me." "These are the ones coming out of the Great Tribulation," he said; "they washed their robes and whitened them by the blood of the Lamb. [15]That is why they are here before the throne of God, serving him day and night in his temple. The one sitting on the throne will shelter them; [16]they will never be angry again, nor thirsty, and they will be fully protected from the scorching noontime heat. [17]For the Lamb standing in front of the throne will feed them and be their Shepherd and lead them to the springs of the Water of Life. And God will wipe their tears away."

Rev 11:15. The kingdom of this world now belongs to our Lord, and to his Christ; and he shall reign forever and ever.

Rev 12:10. It has happened at last! God's salvation and the power and the rule, and the authority of his Christ are finally here; for the Accuser of our brothers has been thrown down from heaven onto earth.

Rev 14:14. Then the scene changed and I saw a white cloud, and someone sitting on it who looked like Jesus, who was called "The Son of Man," with a crown of solid gold upon his head and a sharp sickle in his hand.

Rev 17:14. Together they will wage war against the Lamb, and the Lamb will conquer them; for he is Lord over all lords, and King of kings, and his people are the called and chosen and faithful ones.

Rev 19:11. Then I saw heaven opened and a white horse standing there; and the one sitting on the horse was named "Faithful and True"—the one who justly punishes and makes war. [12]His eyes were like flames, and on his head were many crowns. A name was written on his forehead, and only he knew its meaning. [15]In his mouth he held a sharp sword to strike down the nations; he ruled them with an iron grip; and he trod the winepress of the fierceness of the wrath of Almighty God. [16]On his robe and thigh was written this title: "King of Kings and Lord of Lords."

Rev 20:4. Then I saw thrones, and sitting on them were those who had been given the right to judge. And I saw the souls of those who had been beheaded for their testimony about Jesus, for proclaiming the Word of God, and who had not worshiped the Creature or his statue, nor accepted his mark on their foreheads or their hands. They had come to life again and now they reigned with Christ for a thousand years. [6]Blessed and holy are those who share in the First Resurrection. For them the Second Death holds no terrors, for they will be priests of God and of Christ, and shall reign with him a thousand years.

See above, *Jesus, Exaltation of, Kingdom of.*

PROPHET. Foretold, Isa 52:7; Nah 1:15. Anointed with the Holy Spirit Isa 42:1; 61:1, with Lk 4:18, 19; Jn 3:33, 34. Reveals God, Mt 11:27; Jn 3:1, 2, 13, 33, 34; 17:6, 14, 26; Heb 1:1, 2. Declared his doctrine to be that of the Father, Jn 8:26, 28; 12:49, 50; 14:10, 24; 15:15; 17:8, 26. Foretold things to come, Mt 24:3–35; Lk 19:41–44. Faithful, Lk 4: 43; Jn 17:8; Heb 3:2; Rev 1:5; 3:14. Abounded in wisdom, Lk 2:40, 46, 47, 52; Col 2:3. Mighty in deed and word, Mt 13:53, 54; Mk 1:27; Lk 4:32; Jn 7:46. Unostentatious in his teaching, Isa 42:2; Mt 12:17–20. God commands us to hear, Deut 18:15; Acts 3:21, 22. God will punish neglect of, Deut 18: 19; Acts 3:23; Heb 2:3.

Deut 18:15. Instead, he will raise up for you a Prophet like me, an Israeli, a man to whom you must listen and whom you must obey. [18]I will raise up from among them a Prophet, an Israeli like you. I will tell him what to say, and he shall be my spokesman to the people. Acts 3:21–23; 7:37.

Mt 21:11. And the crowds replied, "It's Jesus, the prophet from Nazareth up in Galilee." [46]They wanted to get rid of him, but were afraid to try because of the crowds, for they accepted Jesus as a prophet.

Lk 7:16. A great fear swept the crowd, and they exclaimed with praises to God, "A mighty prophet has risen among us," and, "We have seen the hand of God at work today." [39]When Jesus' host, a Pharisee, saw what was happening and who the woman was, he said to himself, "This proves that Jesus is no prophet, for if God had really sent him, he would know what kind of woman this one is!"

Lk 13:33. Yes, today, tomorrow, and the next day! For it wouldn't do for a prophet of God to be killed except in Jerusalem!

Lk 24:19. "What things?" Jesus asked. "The things that happened to Jesus, the Man from Nazareth," they said. "He was a Prophet who did incredible miracles and was a mighty Teacher, highly regarded by both God and man."

Jn 3:2. "Sir," he said, "we all know that God has sent you to teach us. Your miracles are proof enough of this."

Jn 4:19. "Sir," the woman said, "you must be a prophet."

John 6:14. When the people realized what a great miracle had happened, they exclaimed, "Surely, he is the Prophet we have been expecting!"

Jn 9:17. Then the Pharisees turned on the man who had been blind and demanded, "This man who opened your eyes—who do you say he is?" "I think he must be a prophet sent from God," the man replied.

RECEIVED. Mt 4:24. The report of his miracles spread far beyond the borders of Galilee so that sick folk were soon coming to be healed from as far away as Syria. And whatever their illness and pain, or if they were possessed by demons, or were insane, or paralyzed—he healed them all. [25]Enormous crowds followed him wherever he went—people from Galilee, and the Ten Cities, and Jerusalem, and from all over Judea, and even from across the Jordan River. Mt 8:1; 19:1, 2; Mk 3:7, 8; 5:21; 10:1.

Mt 7:28. The crowds were amazed at Jesus' sermons, [29]for he taught as one who had great authority, and not as their Jewish leaders. Mk 1:22; Lk 4: 32.

Mt 9:8. A chill of fear swept through the crowd as they saw this happen right before their eyes. How they praised God for giving such authority to a man! [27]As Jesus was leaving her home, two blind men followed along behind, shouting, "O Son of King David, have mercy on us." [33]How the crowds marveled! "Never in all our lives have we seen anything like this," they exclaimed.

Mt 12:23. The crowd was amazed. "Maybe Jesus is the Messiah!" they exclaimed.

Mt 13:2. Where an immense crowd soon gathered. He got into a boat and taught from it while the people listened on the beach. [54]He returned to his home town, Nazareth in Galilee, and taught there in the synagogue and astonished everyone with his wisdom and his miracles. Mk 4:1.

Mt 14:33. The others sat there, awestruck. "You really are the Son of God!" they exclaimed. Mk 6: 51, 52.

Mt 16:1. One day the Pharisees and Sadducees came to test Jesus' claim of being the Messiah by asking him to show them some great demonstrations in the skies. [13]When Jesus came to Caesarea Philippi, he asked his disciples, "Who are the people saying I am?" [14]"Well," they replied, "some say John the Baptist; some, Elijah; some, Jeremiah or one of the other prophets." Mt 12:38; Mk 8:11, 28; Lk 9:19; 11:16.

Mt 21:8. And some in the crowd threw down their coats along the road ahead of him, and others cut branches from the trees and spread them out before him. [9]Then the crowds surged on ahead and pressed along behind, shouting, "God bless King David's Son!" . . . "God's Man is here! . . . Bless him, Lord!" . . . "Praise God in highest heaven!" [10]The entire city of Jerusalem was stirred as he entered. "Who is this?" they asked. [Mk 11:8–10; Lk 19:36–38; Jn 12:12, 13.] [11]And the crowds replied, "It's Jesus, the prophet from Nazareth up in Galilee." [15]But when the chief priests and other Jewish leaders saw these wonderful miracles, and heard even the little children in the Temple shouting, "God bless the Son of David," they were disturbed and indignant.

Mt 27:54. The soldiers at the crucifixion and their sergeant were terribly frightened by the earthquake and all that happened. They exclaimed, "Surely this was God's Son." Mk 15:39; Lk 23:47.

Mk 1:36, 37. Later, Simon and the others went out to find him, and told him, "Everyone is asking for you."

45. But as the man went on his way he began to

shout the good news that he was healed; as a result, such throngs soon surrounded Jesus that he couldn't publicly enter a city anywhere, but had to stay out in the barren wastelands. And people from everywhere came to him there.

Mk 2:2. Soon the house where he was staying was so packed with visitors that there wasn't room for a single person more, not even outside the door. And he preached the Word to them. [12]Then how they praised God. "We've never seen anything like this before!" they all exclaimed. [15]That night Levi invited his fellow tax collectors and many other notorious sinners to be his dinner guests so that they could meet Jesus and his disciples. (There were many men of this type among the crowds that followed him.) Mk 1:32, 33.

Mk 3:20. The crowds began to gather again, and soon it was so full of visitors that he couldn't even find time to eat. [21]When his friends heard what was happening they came to try to take him home with them. "He's out of his mind," they said.

Mk 5:42. Her parents just couldn't get over it. Lk 8:56.

Mk 6:33. But many people saw them leaving and ran on ahead along the shore and met them as they landed. [55]And ran throughout the whole area to spread the news of his arrival, and began carrying sick folks to him on mats and stretchers. [56]Wherever he went—in villages and cities, and out on the farm—they laid the sick in the market plazas and streets, and begged him to let them at least touch the fringes of his clothes; and as many as touched him were healed. Mt 14:13, 35; Lk 9:11; Jn 6:2–5.

Mk 7:37. For they were overcome with utter amazement. Again and again they said, "Everything he does is wonderful; he even corrects deafness and stammering!" Mt 15:31.

Mk 12:37. This sort of reasoning delighted the crowd and they listened to him with great interest.

Lk 4:14. . . . Soon he became well known throughout all that region [15]for his sermons in the synagogues; everyone praised him. [22]All who were there spoke well of him and were amazed by the beautiful words that fell from his lips. "How can this be?" they asked. "Isn't this Joseph's son?" [36]Amazed, the people asked, "What is in this man's words that even demons obey him?" [37]The story of what he had done spread like wildfire throughout the whole region. [42]The crowds searched everywhere for him and when they finally found him they begged him not to leave them, but to stay at Capernaum. Mk 1:27.

Lk 5:1. Great crowds pressed in on him to listen to the Word of God. [17]One day while he was teaching, some Jewish religious leaders and teachers of the Law were sitting nearby. (It seemed that these men showed up from every village in all Gallilee and Judea, as well as from Jerusalem.) [18, 19]Then—look! Some men came carrying a paralyzed man on a sleeping mat. They tried to push through the crowd to Jesus but couldn't reach him. So they went up on the roof above him, took off some tiles and lowered the sick man down into the crowd, still on his sleeping mat, right in front of Jesus. [26]Everyone present was gripped with awe and fear. And they praised God, remarking over and over again, "We have seen strange things today."

Lk 6:17, 18. When they came down the slopes of the mountain, they stood with Jesus on a large, level area, surrounded by many of his followers who, in turn, were surrounded by the crowds. For people from all over Judea and from Jerusalem and from as far north as the seacoasts of Tyre and Sidon had come to hear him or to be healed. And he cast out many demons. [19]Everyone was trying to touch him, for when they did healing power went out from him and they were cured.

Lk 7:16. A great fear swept the crowd, and they exclaimed with praises to God, "A mighty prophet has risen among us," and, "We have seen the hand of God at work today." [17]The report of what he did that day raced from end to end of Judea and even out across the borders. [18]The disciples of John the Baptist soon heard of all that Jesus was doing. [29]And all who heard John preach—even the most wicked of them—agreed that God's requirements were right, and they were baptized by him.

Lk 12:1. Meanwhile the crowds grew until thousands upon thousands were milling about and crushing each other.

Lk 13:17. And all the people rejoiced at the wonderful things he did.

Lk 18:43. And instantly the man could see, and followed Jesus, praising God. And all who saw it happen praised God too.

Lk 19:37. And as they reached the place where the road started down from the Mount of Olives, the whole procession began to shout and sing as they walked along, praising God for all the wonderful miracles Jesus had done. [47]But the chief priests and other religious leaders and the business community were trying to find some way to get rid of him. [48]But they could think of nothing, for he was a hero to the people—they hung on every word he said. Mk 11:18.

Lk 21:38. Every day Jesus went to the Temple to teach, and the crowds began gathering early in the morning to hear him. Jn 8:2.

Lk 23:27. Great crowds trailed along behind, and many grief-stricken women.

Jn 2:11. This miracle at Cana in Galilee was Jesus' first public demonstration of his heaven-sent power. And his disciples believed that he really was the Messiah. [23]Because of the miracles he did in Jerusalem at the Passover celebration, many people were convinced that he was indeed the Messiah.

Jn 7:31. Many among the crowds at the Temple believed on him. "After all," they said, "what miracles do you expect the Messiah to do that this man hasn't done?" [40]When the crowds heard him say this, some of them declared, "This man surely is the prophet who will come just before the Messiah." [41, 42]Others said, "He *is* the Messiah." Still others, "But he *can't* be! Will the Messiah come from *Galilee?* For the Scriptures clearly state that the Messiah will be born of the royal line of David, in *Bethlehem,* the village where David was born." [43]So the crowd was divided about him. [44]And some wanted him arrested, but no one touched him. [46]"He says such wonderful things!" they mumbled. "We've never heard anything like it."

Jn 8:30. Then many of the Jewish leaders who heard him say these things began believing him to be the Messiah.

Jn 9:17. Then the Pharisees turned on the man who had been blind and demanded, "This man who opened your eyes—who do you say he is?" "I think he must be a prophet sent from God," the man replied. [24]"Give the glory to God, not to Jesus, for we know Jesus is an evil person." [25]"I don't know whether he is good or bad," the man replied, "but I know this: *I was blind, and now I see!*" [29]"We know God has spoken to Moses, but as for this fellow, we don't know anything about him." [30]"Why, that's very strange!" the man replied. "He can heal blind men, and yet you don't know anything about him! [33]If this man were not from God, he couldn't do it."

Jn 10:41. And many followed him. "John didn't do miracles," they remarked to one another, "but all his predictions concerning this man have come true." [42]And many came to the decision that he was the Messiah.

Jn 11:37. But some said, "This fellow healed a blind man—why couldn't he keep Lazarus from dying?" [45]And so at last many of the Jewish leaders who were with Mary and saw it happen, finally believed on him. [46]But some went away to the Pharisees and reported it to them. [47]Then the chief priests and Pharisees convened a council to discuss the situation. "What are we going to do?" they asked each other. "For this man certainly does miracles. [48]If we let him alone the whole nation will follow him."

Jn 12:9. When the ordinary people of Jerusalem heard of his arrival, they flocked to see him and also to see Lazarus—the man who had come back to life again. [11]For it was because of him that many of the Jewish leaders had deserted and believed in Jesus as their Messiah. [18]That was the main reason why so many went out to meet him—because they had heard about this mighty miracle. [19]Then the Pharisees said to each other, "We've lost. Look—the whole world has gone after him!" [20]Some Greeks who had come to Jerusalem to attend the Passover [21]paid a visit to Philip, who was from Bethsaida, and said, "Sir, we want to meet Jesus." [34]"Die?" asked the crowd. "We understood that the Messiah would live forever and never die. Why are you saying he will die? What Messiah are you talking about?" [42]However, even many of the Jewish leaders believed him to be the Messiah but wouldn't admit it to anyone because of their fear that the Pharisees would excommunicate them from the synagogue.

Instances of. By Matthew, Mt 9:9, 10. Simon Peter and other disciples, Mk 1:16–20; Lk 5:3–11. Zacchaeus, Lk 19:1–10. Philip, Jn 1:43, 45. Nathanael, Jn 1:45–51. Three thousand at Pentecost, Acts 2:41; 4:4. The eunuch, Acts 8:27–39.

See *Faith, in Christ, Instances of.*

REDEEMER. See *Jesus, Savior; Redemption.*

REJECTED. Ps 2:1. What fools the nations are to rage against the Lord! How strange that men should try to outwit God! [2]For a summit conference of the nations has been called to plot against the Lord and his Messiah, Christ the King. [3]"Come, let us break his chans," they say, "and free ourselves from all this slavery to God."

Ps 118:22. The stone rejected by the builders has now become the capstone of the arch! Lk 20:17, 18.

Isa 8:14. He will be your safety; but Israel and Judah have refused his care and thereby stumbled against the Rock of their salvation and lie fallen and crushed beneath it.

Isa 49:4. I replied, "But my work for them seems all in vain; I have spent my strength for them without response. Yet I leave it all with God for my reward."

Isa 50:1. The Lord asks, Did I sell you to my creditors? Is that why you aren't here? Is your mother gone because I divorced her and sent her away? No, you sold yourselves for your sins. And your mother was taken in payment for your debts. [2]Was I too weak to save you? Is that why the house is silent and empty when I come home? Have I no longer power to deliver? No, that is not the reason! For I can rebuke the sea and make it dry! I can turn the rivers into deserts, covered with dying fish. [3]I am the one who sends the darkness out across the skies. [4]The Lord God has given me his words of wisdom so that I may know what I should say to all these weary ones. Morning by morning he wakens me and opens my understanding to his will. [5]The Lord God has spoken to me and I have listened; I do not rebel nor turn away. [6]I give my back to the whip, and my cheeks to those who pull out the beard. I do not hide from shame—they spit in my face. [7]Because the Lord God helps me, I will not be dismayed; therefore, I have set my face like flint to do his will, and I know that I will triumph. [8]He who gives me justice is near. Who will dare to fight against me now? Where are my enemies? Let them appear! [9]See, the Lord God is for me! Who shall declare me guilty? All my enemies shall be destroyed like old clothes eaten up by moths! [10]Who among you fears the Lord and obeys his Servant? If such men walk in darkness, without one ray of light, let them trust the Lord, let them rely upon their God. [11]But see here, you who live in your own light, and warm yourselves from your own fires and not from God's; you will live among sorrows.

Isa 53:1. But, oh, how few believe it! Who will listen? To whom will God reveal his saving power? [2]In God's eyes he was like a tender green shoot, sprouting from a root in dry and sterile ground. But in our eyes there was no attractiveness at all, nothing to make us want him. [3]We despised him and rejected him—a man of sorrows, acquainted with bitterest grief. We turned our backs on him and looked the other way when he went by. He was despised and we didn't care. [4]Yet it was *our* grief he bore, *our* sorrows that weighed him down. And we thought his troubles were a punishment from God, for his *own* sins!

Mt 7:26. But those who hear my instructions and ignore them are foolish, like a man who builds his house on sand. [27]For when the rains and floods come, and storm winds beat against his house, it will fall with a mighty crash. Lk 6:46–49.

Mt 8:12. "And many an Israelite—those for whom the Kingdom was prepared—shall be cast into outer darkness, into the place of weeping and torment." [34]And the entire population came rushing out to see Jesus, and begged him to go away and leave them alone. Mk 5:17; Lk 8:37.

Mt 10:14. Any city or home that doesn't welcome you—shake off the dust of that place from your feet as you leave. [15]Truly, the wicked cities of Sodom and Gomorrah will be better off at Judgment Day than they. [33]But if anyone publicly denies me, I will openly deny him before my Father in heaven.

Mt 11:16. What shall I say about this nation? These people are like children playing, who say to their little friends, [17]"We played wedding and you weren't happy, so we played funeral but you weren't sad." [18]For John the Baptist doesn't even drink wine and often goes without food, and you say, "He's crazy." [19]And I, the Messiah, feast and drink, and you complain that I am "a glutton and a drinking man, and hang around with the worst sort of sinners!" But brilliant men like you can justify your every inconsistency! Lk 7:31–35.

Mt 12:38. One day some of the Jewish leaders, including some Pharisees, came to Jesus asking him to show them a miracle. [39, 40]But Jesus replied, "Only an evil, faithless nation would ask for further proof; and none will be given except what happened to Jonah the prophet! For as Jonah was in the great fish for three days and three nights, so I, the Messiah, shall be in the heart of the earth three days and three nights. [41]The men of Nineveh shall arise against this nation at the judgment and condemn you. For when Jonah preached to them, they repented and turned to God from all their evil ways. And now a greater than Jonah is here—and you refuse to believe him. [42]The Queen of Sheba shall rise against this nation in the judgment, and condemn it; for she came from a distant land to hear the wisdom of Solomon; and now a greater than Solomon is here—and you refuse to believe him. [43-45]This evil nation is like a man possessed by a demon. For if the demon leaves, it goes into the deserts for a while, seeking rest but finding none. Then it says, 'I will return to the man I came from.' So it returns and finds the man's heart clean but empty! Then the demon finds seven other spirits more evil than itself, and all enter the man and live in him. And so he is worse off than before."

Mt 13:13. "That is why I use these illustrations, so people will hear and see but not understand." [58]And so he did only a few great miracles there, because of their unbelief. *vs.* 1–14; Isa 6:9, 10.

Mt 17:17. Jesus replied, "Oh, you stubborn, faithless people! How long shall I bear with you?"

Mt 21:32. For John the Baptist told you to repent and turn to God, and you wouldn't, while very evil men and prostitutes did. And even when you saw this happening, you refused to repent, and so you couldn't believe.

38. "But when these farmers saw the son coming they said among themselves, 'Here comes the heir to this estate; come on, let's kill him and get it for ourselves!' [39]So they dragged him out of the vineyard and killed him. [40]When the owner returns, what do you think he will do to those farmers?" [41]The Jewish leaders replied, "He will put the wicked men to a horrible death, and lease the vineyard to others who will pay him promptly." [42]Then Jesus asked them, "Didn't you ever read in the Scriptures: 'The stone rejected by the builders has been made the honored cornerstone; how remarkable! what an amazing thing the Lord has done'? [43]What I mean is that the Kingdom of God shall be taken away from you, and given to a nation that will give God his share of the crop. [44]All who stumble on this rock of truth shall be broken, but those it falls on will be scattered as dust." [45]When the chief priests and other Jewish leaders realized that Jesus was talking about them—that they were the farmers in his story—[46]they wanted to get rid of him, but were afraid to try because of the crowds, for they accepted Jesus as a prophet. Mk 12:1–12; Lk 20:9–18.

Mt 26:31. Then Jesus said to them, "Tonight you will all desert me. For it is written in the Scriptures that God will smite the Shepherd, and the sheep of the flock will be scattered. [32]But after I have been brought back to life again I will go to Galilee, and meet you there." [33]Peter declared, "If everyone else deserts you, I won't." [34]Jesus told him, "The truth is that this very night, before the cock crows at dawn, you will deny me three times!" [35]"I would die first!" Peter insisted. And all the other disciples said the same thing. [69]Meanwhile, as Peter was sitting in the courtyard a girl came over and said to him, "You were with Jesus, for both of you are from Galilee." [70]But Peter denied it loudly. "I don't even know what you are talking about," he angrily declared. [71]Later, out by the gate, another girl noticed him and said to those standing around, "This man was with Jesus—from Nazareth." [72]Again Peter denied it, this time with an oath. "I don't even know the man," he said. [73]But after a while the men who had been standing there came over to him and said, "We know you are one of his disciples, for we can tell by your Galilean accent." [74]Peter began to curse and swear. "I don't even know the man," he said. And immediately the cock crowed. [75]Then Peter remembered what Jesus had said, "Before the cock crows, you will deny me three times." And he went away, crying bitterly. Mk 14:27–31, 66–72; Lk 22:31–34, 54–62; Jn 18:15–27.

Mk 6:3. "He's no better than we are," they said.

"He's just a carpenter, Mary's boy, and a brother of James and Joseph, Judas and Simon. And his sisters live right here among us." And they were offended! [4]Then Jesus told them, "A prophet is honored everywhere except in his home town and among his relatives and by his own family." [5]And because of their unbelief he couldn't do any mighty miracles among them except to place his hands on a few sick people and heal them. [6]And he could hardly accept the fact that they wouldn't believe in him. Then he went out among the villages, teaching.

Mk 16:16. But those who refuse to believe will be condemned.

Lk 7:30. All, that is, except the Pharisees and teachers of Moses' Law. They rejected God's plan for them and refused John's baptism. [34]"'But I eat my food and drink my wine, and you say, 'What a glutton Jesus is! And he drinks! And has the lowest sort of friends!' "

Lk 10:16. Then he said to the disciples, "Those who welcome you are welcoming me. And those who reject you are rejecting me. And those who reject me are rejecting God who sent me."

Lk 11:23. Anyone who is not for me is against me; if he isn't helping me, he is hurting my cause. [24]When a demon is cast out of a man, it goes to the deserts, searching there for rest; but finding none, it returns to the person it left, [25]and finds that its former home is all swept and clean. [26]Then it goes and gets seven other demons more evil than itself, and they all enter the man. And so the poor fellow is seven times worse off than he was before.

Lk 13:34. O Jerusalem, Jerusalem! The city that murders the prophets. The city that stones those sent to help her. How often I have wanted to gather your children together even as a hen protects her brood under her wings, but you wouldn't let me.

Lk 14:16. Jesus replied with this illustration: "A man prepared a great feast and sent out many invitations. [17]When all was ready, he sent his servant around to notify the guests that it was time for them to arrive. [18]But they all began making excuses. One said he had just bought a field and wanted to inspect it, and asked to be excused. [19]Another said he had just bought five pair of oxen and wanted to try them out. [20]Another had just been married and for that reason couldn't come. [21]The servant returned and reported to his master what they had said. His master was angry and told him to go quickly into the streets and alleys of the city and invite the beggars, crippled, lame, and blind. [22]But even then, there was still room. [23]'Well, then,' said his master, 'go out into the country lanes and out behind the hedges and urge anyone you find to come, so that the house will be full. [24]For none of those I invited first will get even the smallest taste of what I had prepared for them.' " Mt 22:1–13.

Lk 17:25. But first I must suffer terribly and be rejected by this whole nation.

Lk 19:42. "Eternal peace was within your reach and you turned it down," he wept, "and now it is too late."

Lk 22:67, 68. And instructed to state whether or not he claimed to be the Messiah. But he replied, "If I tell you, you won't believe me or let me present my case."

Lk 24:25. Then Jesus said to them, "You are such foolish, foolish people! You find it so hard to believe all that the prophets wrote in the Scriptures!" *vs.* 11, 15–25, 37–39.

Jn 1:11. Even in his own land and among his own people, the Jews, he was not accepted.

Jn 3:11. "I am telling you what I know and have seen—and yet you won't believe me. [12]But if you don't even believe me when I tell you about such things as these that happen here among men, how can you possibly believe if I tell you what is going on in heaven? [18]There is no eternal doom awaiting those who trust him to save them. But those who don't trust him have already been tried and condemned for not believing in the only Son of God. [19]Their sentence is based on this fact: that the Light from heaven came into the world, but they loved the darkness more than the Light, for their deeds were evil." [32]He tells what he has seen and heard, but how few believe what he tells them!

Jn 5:38. But you are not listening to him, for you refuse to believe me—the one sent to you with God's message. [40]Yet you won't come to me so that I can give you this life eternal! [43]I know, because I have come to you representing my Father and you refuse to welcome me, though you readily enough receive those who aren't sent from him, but represent only themselves!

Jn 6:36. "But the trouble is, as I have told you before, you haven't believed even though you have seen me." [60]Even his disciples said, "This is very hard to understand. Who can tell what he means?" [61]Jesus knew within himself that his disciples were complaining and said to them, "Does *this* offend you? [62]Then what will you think if you see me, the Messiah, return to heaven again? [63]Only the Holy Spirit gives eternal life. Those born only once, with physical birth, will never receive this gift. But now I have told you how to get this true spiritual life. [64]But some of you don't believe me." (For Jesus knew from the beginning who didn't believe and knew the one who would betray him.) [65]And he remarked, "That is what I meant when I said that no one can come to me unless the Father attracts him to me." [66]At this point many of his disciples turned away and deserted him. [67]Then Jesus turned to the Twelve and asked, "Are you going too?" [68]Simon Peter replied, "Master, to whom shall we go? You alone have the words that give eternal life."

Jn 7:3. And Jesus' brothers urged him to go to Judea for the celebration. "Go where more people can see your miracles!" they scoffed. [4]"You can't be famous when you hide like this! If you're so great, prove it to the world!" [5]For even his brothers didn't believe in him. [12]There was a lot of discussion about him among the crowds. Some said, "He's a wonderful man," while others said, "No, he's duping the public." [13]But no one had the courage to speak out for him in public for fear of reprisals from the Jewish leaders. [15]The Jewish leaders were surprised when they heard him. "How can he know so much when he's never been to our schools?" they asked. [25]Some of the people who lived there in Jerusalem said among themselves, "Isn't this the man they are trying to kill? [26]But here he is preaching in public, and they say nothing to him. Can it be that our leaders have learned, after all, that he really is the Messiah? [27]But how could he be? For we know where this man was born; when Christ comes, he will just appear and no one will know where he comes from."

Jn 8:13. The Pharisees replied, "You are boasting —and lying!" [21]Later he said to them again, "I am going away; and you will search for me, and die in your sins. And you cannot come where I am going." [22]The Jews asked, "Is he planning suicide? What does he mean, 'You cannot come where I am going'?" [24]"That is why I said that you will die in your sins; for unless you believe that I am the Messiah, the Son of God, you will die in your sins." [30]Then many of the Jewish leaders who heard him say these things began believing him to be the Messiah. [with *vs.* 25–29.] [45]"And so when I tell the truth, you just naturally don't believe it! [46]Which of you can truthfully accuse me of one single sin? (No one!) And since I am telling you the truth, why don't you believe me? [47]Anyone whose Father is God listens gladly to the words of God. Since you don't, it proves you aren't his children." [53]"So you are greater than our father Abraham, who died? And greater than the prophets, who died? Who do you think you are?"

Jn 9:16. Some of them said, "Then this fellow Jesus is not from God, because he is working on the Sabbath." Others said, "But how could an ordinary sinner do such miracles?" So there was a deep division of opinion among them. [17]Then the Pharisees turned on the man who had been blind and demanded, "This man who opened your eyes— who do you say he is?" "I think he must be a prophet sent from God," the man replied. [24]They called in the man who had been blind and told him, "Give the glory to God, not to Jesus, for we know Jesus is an evil person."

Jn 10:20. Some of them said, "He has a demon or else is crazy. Why listen to a man like that?" [21]Others said, "This doesn't sound to us like a man possessed by a demon! Can a demon open the eyes of blind men?" [24]The Jewish leaders surrounded him and asked, "How long are you going to keep us in suspense? If you are the Messiah, tell us plainly." [33]They replied, "Nor for any good work, but for blasphemy; you, a mere man, have declared yourself to be God."

Jn 11:46. But some went away to the Pharisees and reported it to them. [47]Then the chief priests and Pharisees convened a council to discuss the situation. "What are we going to do?" they asked each other. "For this man certainly does miracles. [48]If we let him alone the whole nation will follow him."

Jn 12:37. But despite all the miracles he had done, most of the people would not believe he was the Messiah. [48]"But all who reject me and my message will be judged at the Day of Judgment by the truths I have spoken."

Jn 15:18. For you get enough hate from the world! But then, it hated me before it hated you. [20]Do you remember what I told you? "A slave isn't greater than his master!" So since they persecuted me, naturally they will persecute you. And if they had listened to me, they would listen to you! [24]If I hadn't done such mighty miracles among them they would not be counted guilty. But as it is, they saw these miracles and yet they hated both of us— me and my Father.

Acts 13:46. Then Paul and Barnabas spoke out boldly and declared, "It was necessary that this Good News from God should be given first to you Jews. But since you have rejected it, and shown yourselves unworthy of eternal life—well, we will offer it to Gentiles."

Acts 18:5. And after the arrival of Silas and Timothy from Macedonia, Paul spent his full time preaching and testifying to the Jews that Jesus is the Messiah. [6]But when the Jews opposed him and blasphemed, hurling abuse at Jesus, Paul shook off the dust from his robe and said, "Your blood be upon your own heads—I am innocent—from now on I will preach to the Gentiles."

Acts 22:18. Leave Jerusalem, for the people here won't believe you when you give them my message.

Acts 28:24. Some believed, and some didn't. [25]But after they had argued back and forth among themselves, they left with this final word from Paul ringing in their ears: "The Holy Spirit was right when he said through Isaiah the prophet. [27]'For your hearts are too fat and your ears don't listen and you have closed your eyes against understanding, for you don't want to see and hear and understand and turn to me to heal you.' "

Rom 3:3. True, some of them were unfaithful, but just because they broke their promises to God, does that mean God will break his promises?

Rom 9:31. But the Jews, who tried so hard to get right with God by keeping his laws, never succeeded. [32]Why not? Because they were trying to be saved by keeping the law and being good instead of by depending on faith. They have stumbled over the great stumbling stone.

Rom 10:16. But not everyone who hears the Good News has welcomed it, for Isaiah the prophet said, "Lord, who has believed me when I told them?" [21]In the meantime, he keeps on reaching out his hands to the Jews, but they keep arguing and refusing to come.

1 Cor 1:18. I know very well how foolish it sounds to those who are lost, when they hear that Jesus died to save them. But we who are saved recognize this message as the very power of God. [23]So when we preach about Christ dying to save them, the Jews are offended and the Gentiles say it's all nonsense.

2 Tim 2:12. And if we think that our present

service for him is hard, just remember that some day we are going to sit with him and rule with him. But if we give up when we suffer, and turn against Christ, then he must turn against us.

Heb 6:6. And then have turned against God. You cannot bring yourself to repent again if you have nailed the Son of God to the cross again by rejecting him, holding him up to mocking and to public shame.

Heb 10:29. Think how much more terrible the punishment will be for those who have trampled underfoot the Son of God and treated his cleansing blood as though it were common and unhallowed, and insulted and outraged the Holy Spirit who brings God's mercy to his people.

1 Pet 2:4. Come to Christ, who is the living Foundation of Rock upon which God builds; though men have spurned him, he is very precious to God who has chosen him above all others. [7]"The same Stone that was rejected by the builders has become the Cornerstone, the most honored and important part of the building." [8]. . ."He is the Stone that some will stumble over, and the Rock that will make them fall." They will stumble because they will not listen to God's Word, nor obey it.

2 Pet 2:1. But there were false prophets, too, in those days, just as there will be false teachers among you. They will cleverly tell their lies about God, turning against even their Master who bought them; but theirs will be a swift and terrible end.

1 Jn 2:22. And who is the greatest liar? The one who says that Jesus is not Christ. Such a person is antichrist, for he does not believe in God the Father and in his Son. [23]For a person who doesn't believe in Christ, God's Son, can't have God the Father either.

2 Jn 1:7. Watch out for the false leaders—and there are many of them around—who don't believe that Jesus Christ came to earth as a human being with a body like ours. Such people are against the truth and against Christ.

Jude 1:4. I say this because some godless teachers have wormed their way in among you, saying that after we become Christians we can do just as we like without fear of God's punishment. The fate of such people was written long ago, for they have turned against our only Master and Lord, Jesus Christ.

RELATION OF, TO THE FATHER. Ps 110:1. Jehovah said to my Lord the Messiah, "Rule as my regent—I will subdue your enemies and make them bow low before you."

Isa 42:1. See my Servant, whom I uphold; my Chosen One, in whom I delight. I have put my Spirit upon him.

Isa 49:5. "And now," said the Lord—the Lord who formed me from my mother's womb to serve him who commissioned me to restore to him his people Israel, who has given me the strength to perform this task and honored me for doing it!— [6]"you shall do more than restore Israel to me. I will make you a Light to the nations of the world to bring my salvation to them too."

Isa 61:1. The Spirit of the Lord God is upon me, because the Lord has anointed me to bring good news to the suffering and afflicted. He has sent me to comfort the broken-hearted, to announce liberty to captives and to open the eyes of the blind.

Mic 5:4. And he shall stand and feed his flock in the strength of the Lord, in the majesty of the name of the Lord his God, and his people shall remain there undisturbed, for he will be greatly honored all around the world.

Mt 20:23. "You shall indeed drink from it," he told them. "But I have no right to say who will sit on the thrones next to mine. Those places are reserved for the persons my Father selects."

Mt 26:39. He went forward a little, and fell face downward on the ground, and prayed, "My Father! If it is possible, let this cup be taken away from me. But I want your will, not mine."

Mk 10:40. But I do not have the right to place you on thrones next to mine. Those appointments have already been made.

Mk 13:32. However, no one, not even the angels in heaven, nor I myself, knows the day or hour when these things will happen; only the Father knows.

Jn 1:1, 2. Before anything else existed, there was Christ, with God. He has always been alive and is himself God. [14]And Christ became a human being and lived here on earth among us and was full of loving forgiveness and truth. And some of us have seen his glory—the glory of the only Son of the heavenly Father!

Jn 3:34. For this one—sent by God—speaks God's words, for God's Spirit is upon him without measure or limit. [35]The Father loves this man because he is his Son, and God has given him everything there is.

Jn 4:34. Then Jesus explained: "My nourishment comes from doing the will of God who sent me, and from finishing his work."

Jn 5:19. Jesus replied, "The Son can do nothing by himself. He does only what he sees the Father doing, and in the same way. [20]For the Father loves the Son, and tells him everything he is doing; and the Son will do far more awesome miracles than this man's healing. [21]He will even raise from the dead anyone he wants to, just as the Father does. [22]And the Father leaves all judgment of sin to his Son, [23]so that everyone will honor the Son, just as they honor the Father. But if you refuse to honor God's Son, whom he sent to you, then you are certainly not honoring the Father. [24]I say emphatically that anyone who listens to my message and believes in God who sent me has eternal life, and will never be damned for his sins, but has already passed out of death into life. [25]And I solemnly declare that the time is coming, in fact, it is here, when the dead shall hear my voice—the voice of the Son of God—and those who listen shall live. [26]The Father has life in himself, and has granted his Son to have life in himself, [27]and to judge the sins of all mankind because he is the Son of Man.

[28]Don't be surprised! Indeed the time is coming when all the dead in their graves shall hear the voice of God's Son, [29]and shall rise again—those who have done good, to eternal life; and those who have continued in evil, to judgment. [30]But I pass no judgment without consulting the Father. I judge as I am told. And my judgment is absolutely fair and just, for it is according to the will of God who sent me and is not merely my own. [31]When I make claims about myself they aren't believed. [37]And the Father himself has also testified about me, though not appearing to you personally, or speaking to you directly. [45]Yet it is not I who will accuse you of this to the Father—Moses will! Moses, on whose laws you set your hopes of heaven."

Jn 6:32. Jesus said, "Moses didn't give it to them. My Father did. And now he offers you true Bread from heaven. [33]The true Bread is a Person—the one sent by God from heaven, and he gives life to the world. [38]For I have come here from heaven to do the will of God who sent me, not to have my own way. [39]And this is the will of God, that I should not lose even one of all those he has given me, but that I should raise them to eternal life at the Last Day. [40]For it is my Father's will that everyone who sees his Son and believes on him should have eternal life —that I should raise him at the Last Day. [44]For no one can come to me unless the Father who sent me draws him to me, and at the Last Day I will cause all such to rise again from the dead. [45]As it is written in the Scriptures, 'They shall all be taught of God.' Those the Father speaks to, who learn the truth from him, will be attracted to me. [46](Not that anyone actually sees the Father, for only I have seen him.)"

Jn 7:16. So Jesus told them, "I'm not teaching you my own thoughts, but those of God who sent me." [28]So Jesus, in a sermon in the Temple, called out, "Yes, you know me and where I was born and raised, but I am the representative of one you don't know, and he is Truth. [29]I know him because I was with him, and he sent me to you." [33]But Jesus told them, "(Not yet!) I am to be here a little longer. Then I shall return to the one who sent me."

Jn 8:15. You pass judgment on me without knowing the facts. I am not judging you now, [16]but if I were, it would be an absolutely correct judgment in every respect, for I have with me the Father who sent me." [19]"Where is your father?" they asked. Jesus answered, "You don't know who I am, so you don't know who my Father is. If you knew me, then you would know him too." [28]So Jesus said, "When you have killed the Messiah, then you will realize that I am he and that I have not been telling you my own ideas, but have spoken what the Father taught me. [29]And he who sent me is with me—he has not deserted me—for I always do those things that are pleasing to him. [38]I am telling you what I saw when I was with my Father. But you are following the advice of *your* father. [40]But instead you are trying to kill me—and all because I told you the truth I heard from God. Abraham wouldn't do a thing like that!" [42]Jesus told them, "If that were so, then you would love me, for I have come to you from God. I am not here on my own, but he sent me." [49]"No," Jesus said, "I have no demon in me. For I honor my Father—and you dishonor me." [54]Then Jesus told them this: "If I am merely boasting about myself, it doesn't count. But it is my Father—and you claim him as your God—who is saying these glorious things about me. [55]But you do not even know him. I do. If I said otherwise, I would be as great a liar as you! But it is true—I know him and fully obey him."

Jn 9:4. All of us must quickly carry out the tasks assigned us by the one who sent me, for there is little time left before the night falls and all work comes to an end.

Jn 10:15. "Just as my Father knows me and I know the Father; and I lay down my life for the sheep. [18]No one can kill me without my consent— I lay down my life voluntarily. For I have the right and power to lay it down when I want to and also the right and power to take it again. For the Father has given me this right. [25]I have already told you, and you don't believe me," Jesus replied. "The proof is in the miracles I do in the name of my Father. [29]For my Father has given them to me, and he is more powerful than anyone else, so no one can kidnap them from me. [30]I and the Father are one." [32]Jesus said, "At God's direction I have done many a miracle to help the people. For which one are you killing me?" [33]They replied, "Not for any good work, but for blasphemy; you, a mere man, have declared yourself to be God." [36]"Do you call it blasphemy when the one sanctified and sent into the world by the Father says, 'I am the Son of God'? [37]Don't believe me unless I do miracles of God. [38]But if I do, believe them even if you don't believe me. Then you will become convinced that the Father is in me, and I in the Father."

Jn 11:41. So they rolled the stone aside. Then Jesus looked up to heaven and said, "Father, thank you for hearing me. [42](You always hear me, of course, but I said it because of all these people standing here, so that they will believe you sent me.)"

Jn 12:44. Jesus shouted to the crowds, "If you trust me, you are really trusting God. [49]For these are not my own ideas, but I have told you what the Father said to tell you. [50]And I know his instructions lead to eternal life; so whatever he tells me to say, I say!"

Jn 14:7. "If you had known who I am, then you would have known who my Father is. From now on you know him—and have seen him!" [9]Jesus replied, "Don't you even yet know who I am, Philip, even after all this time I have been with you? Anyone who has seen me has seen the Father! So why are you asking to see him? [10]Don't you believe that I am in the Father and the Father is in me? The words I say are not my own but are from my Father who lives in me. And he does his work through me. [11]Just believe it—that I am in the Father and the Father is in me. Or else believe it because of the mighty miracles you have seen me do. [12, 13]In solemn truth I tell you, anyone believing in me shall do the same miracles I have done, and even greater ones, because I am going to be with the Father. You can ask him for *anything,* using my name, and I will do it, for this will bring praise to the Father because of what I, the Son, will do for you. [14]Yes, ask *anything,* using my name, and I will do it! [20]When I come back to life again, you will know that I am in my Father, and you in me, and I in you. [24]Anyone who doesn't obey me doesn't love me. And remember, I am not making up this answer to your question! It is the answer given by the Father who sent me. [28]Remember what I told you—I am going away, but I will come back to you again. If you really love me, you will be very happy for me, for now I can go to the Father, who is greater than I am. [31]But I will freely do what the Father requires of me so that the world will know that I love the Father. Come, let's be going."

Jn 15:9. I have loved you even as the Father has loved me. Live within my love. [10]When you obey me you are living in my love, just as I obey my Father and live in his love. [15]I no longer call you slaves, for a master doesn't confide in his slaves; now you are my friends, proved by the fact that I have told you everything the Father told me. [23]Anyone hating me is also hating my Father. [24]If I hadn't done such mighty miracles among them they would not be counted guilty. But as it is, they saw these miracles and yet they hated both of us—me and my Father. [25]This has fulfilled what the prophets said concerning the Messiah, "They hated me without reason." [26]But I will send you the Comforter—the Holy Spirit, the source of all truth. He will come to you from the Father and will tell you all about me.

Jn 16:5. But now I am going away to the one who sent me; and none of you seems interested in the purpose of my going; none wonders why. [10]There is righteousness available because I go to the Father and you shall see me no more. [15]All the Father's glory is mine; this is what I mean when I say that he will show you my glory. [23]At that time you won't need to ask me for anything, for you can go directly to the Father and ask him, and he will give you what you ask for because you use my name. [25]I have spoken of these matters very guardedly, but the time will come when this will not be necessary and I will tell you plainly all about the Father. [27]For the Father himself loves you dearly because you love me and believe that I came from the Father. [28]Yes, I came from the Father into the world and will leave the world and return to the Father. [32]But the time is coming—in fact, it is here—when you will be scattered, each one returning to his own home, leaving me alone. Yet I will not be alone, for the Father is with me.

Jn 17:1. When Jesus had finished saying all these things he looked up to heaven and said, "Father, the time has come. Reveal the glory of your Son so that he can give the glory back to you. [2]For you have given him authority over every man and woman in all the earth. He gives eternal life to each one you have given him. [3]And this is the way to have eternal life—by knowing you, the only true God, and Jesus Christ, the one you sent to earth! [4]I brought glory to you here on earth by doing everything you told me to. [5]And now, Father, reveal my glory as I stand in your presence, the glory we shared before the world began. [6]I have told these men all about you. They were in the world, but then you gave them to me. Actually, they were always yours, and you gave them to me; and they have obeyed you. [7]Now they know that everything I have is a gift from you, [8]for I have passed on to them the commands you gave me; and they accepted them and know of a certainty that I came down to earth from you, and they believe you sent me. [9]My plea is not for the world but for those you have given me because they belong to you. [10]And all of them, since they are mine, belong to you; and you have given them back to me with everything else of yours, and so *they are my glory!* [11]Now I am leaving the world, and leaving them behind, and coming to you. Holy Father, keep them in your care—all those you have given me—so that they will be united just as we are, with none missing. [12]During my time here I have kept safe within your family all of these you gave me. I guarded them so that not one perished, except the son of hell, as the Scriptures foretold. [13]And now I am coming to you. I have told them many things while I was with them so that they would be filled with my joy. [14]I have given them your commands. And the world hates them because they don't fit in with it, just as I don't. [15]I'm not asking you to take them out of the world, but to keep them safe from Satan's power. [16]They are not part of this world any more than I am. [17]Make them pure and holy through teaching them your words of truth. [18]As you sent me into the world, I am sending them into the world, [19]and I consecrate myself to meet their need for growth in truth and holiness. [20]I am not praying for these alone but also for the future believers who will come to me because of the testimony of these. [21]My prayer for all of them is that they will be of one heart and mind, just as you and I are, Father—that just as you are in me and I am in you, so they will be in us, and the world will believe you sent me. [22]I have given them the glory you gave me—the glorious unity of being one, as we are— [23]I in them and you in me, all being perfected into one—so that the world will know you sent me and will understand that you love them as much as you love me. [24]Father, I want them with me—these you've given me—so that they can see my glory. You gave me the glory because you loved me before the world began! [25]O righteous Father, the world doesn't know you, but I do; and these disciples know you sent me. [26]And I have revealed you to them, and will keep on revealing you so that the mighty love you have for me may be in them, and I in them."

Acts 2:33. And now he sits on the throne of

highest honor in heaven, next to God. And just as promised, the Father gave him the authority to send the Holy Spirit—with the results you are seeing and hearing today. [36]Therefore I clearly state to everyone in Israel that God has made this Jesus you crucified to be the Lord, the Messiah!

Acts 10:38. And you no doubt know that Jesus of Nazareth was anointed by God with the Holy Spirit and with power, and he went around doing good and healing all who were possessed by demons, for God was with him.

Acts 13:37. (No, it was a reference to another)—someone God brought back to life, whose body was not touched at all by the ravages of death.

Rom 1:4. And by being raised from the dead he was proved to be the mighty Son of God, with the holy nature of God himself.

Rom 8:32. Since he did not spare even his own Son for us but gave him up for us all.

1 Cor 1:30. For it is from God alone that you have your life through Christ Jesus. He showed us God's plan of salvation; he was the one who made us acceptable to God; he made us pure and holy and gave himself to purchase our salvation.

1 Cor 3:23. And you belong to Christ, and Christ is God's.

1 Cor 11:3. But there is one matter I want to remind you about: that a wife is responsible to her husband, her husband is responsible to Christ, and Christ is responsible to God.

1 Cor 15:24. After that the end will come when he will turn the kingdom over to God the Father, having put down all enemies of every kind. [27]For the rule and authority over all things has been given to Christ by his Father; except, of course, Christ does not rule over the Father himself, who gave him this power to rule. [28]When Christ has finally won the battle against all his enemies, then he, the Son of God, will put himself also under his Father's orders, so that God who has given him the victory over everything else will be utterly supreme.

2 Cor 4:4. Satan, who is the god of this evil world, has made him blind, unable to see the glorious light of the Gospel that is shining upon him, or to understand the amazing message we preach about the glory of Christ, who is God. [6]For God, who said, "Let there be light in the darkness," has made us understand that it is the brightness of his glory that is seen in the face of Jesus Christ.

Eph 1:17. I pray for you constantly, asking God, the glorious Father of our Lord Jesus Christ, to give you wisdom to see clearly and really understand who Christ is and all that he has done for you. [20]That raised Christ from the dead and seated him in the place of honor at God's right hand in heaven, [21]far, far above any other king or ruler or dictator or leader. Yes, his honor is far more glorious than that of anyone else either in this world or in the world to come. [22]And God has put all things under his feet and made him the supreme Head of the church.

Phil 2:6. Who, though he was God, did not demand and cling to his rights as God. [11]And every tongue shall confess that Jesus Christ is Lord, to the glory of God the Father.

Col 1:15. Christ is the exact likeness of the unseen God. He existed before God made anything at all. [19]For God wanted all of himself to be in his Son.

1 Thess 5:18. No matter what happens, always be thankful, for this is God's will for you who belong to Christ Jesus.

Heb 1:2. But now in these days he has spoken to us through his Son to whom he has given everything, and through whom he made the world and everything there is. [3]God's Son shines out with God's glory, and all that God's Son is and does marks him as God. He regulates the universe by the mighty power of his command. He is the one who died to cleanse us and clear our record of all sin, and then sat down in highest honor beside the great God of heaven.

Heb 2:9. But we do see Jesus—who for awhile was a little lower than the angels—crowned now by God with glory and honor because he suffered death for us. Yes, because of God's great kindness, Jesus tasted death for everyone in all the world.

Heb 3:2. For Jesus was faithful to God who appointed him High Priest, just as Moses also faithfully served in God's house.

Heb 5:5. That is why Christ did not elect himself to the honor of being High Priest; no, he was chosen by God. God said to him, "My Son, today I have honored you." [6]And another time God said to him, "You have been chosen to be a priest forever, with the same rank as Melchizedek." [7]Yet while Christ was here on earth he pleaded with God, praying with tears and agony of soul to the only one who would save him from (premature) death. And God heard his prayers because of his strong desire to obey God at all times. [8]And even though Jesus was God's Son, he had to learn from experience what it was like to obey, when obeying meant suffering. [9]It was after he had proved himself perfect in this experience that Jesus became the Giver of eternal salvation to all those who obey him. [10]For remember that God has chosen him to be a High Priest with the same rank as Melchizedek.

1 Pet 1:21. Because of this, your trust can be in God who raised Christ from the dead and gave him great glory. Now your faith and hope can rest in him alone.

1 Pet 2:4. Come to Christ, who is the living Foundation of Rock upon which God builds; though men have spurned him, he is very precious to God who has chosen him above all others. [23]Never answered back when insulted; when he suffered he did not threaten to get even; he left his case in the hands of God who always judges fairly.

2 Pet 1:17, 18. I was there on the holy mountain when he shone out with honor given him by God his Father; I heard that glorious, majestic voice calling down from heaven, saying, "This is my much-loved Son; I am well pleased with him."

1 Jn 4:9. God showed how much he loved us by sending his only Son into this wicked world to bring

to us eternal life through his death. [10]In this act we see what real love is: it is not our love for God, but his love for us when he sent his Son to satisfy God's anger against our sins. [14]And furthermore, we have seen with our own eyes and now tell all the world that God sent his Son to be their Savior.

Rev 2:27. You will rule them with a rod of iron just as my Father gave me the authority to rule them; they will be shattered like a pot of clay that is broken into tiny pieces.

Rev 3:12. As for the one who conquers, I will make him a pillar in the temple of my God; he will be secure, and will go out no more; and I will write my God's Name on him, and he will be a citizen in the city of my God—the New Jerusalem, coming down from heaven from my God; and he will have my new Name inscribed upon him. [21]I will let every one who conquers sit beside me on my throne, just as I took my place with my Father on his throne when I had conquered.

See *Jesus, Deity of, Humanity of, Son of God.*

RESURRECTION OF. Ps 2:7. For the Lord has said to me, "You are my Son. This is your Coronation Day." Acts 13:32, 33.

Ps 16:9. Heart, body, and soul are filled with joy. [10]For you will not leave me among the dead; you will not allow your beloved one to rot in the grave.

Mt 12:40. For as Jonah was in the great fish for three days and three nights, so I, the Messiah, shall be in the heart of the earth three days and three nights.

Mt 16:4. "This evil, unbelieving nation is asking for some strange sign in the heavens, but no further proof will be given except the miracle that happened to Jonah." [21]From then on Jesus began to speak plainly to his disciples about going to Jerusalem, . . . that he would be killed, and that three days later he would be raised to life again. Mt 17:22, 23; Lk 9:22, 31; 24:6, 7.

Mt 20:19. And they will hand me over to the Roman government, and I will be mocked and crucified, and the third day I will rise to life again. Mk 10:34.

Mt 26:32. But after I have been brought back to life again I will go to Galilee, and meet you there. Mk 14:28.

Mt 27:52. And tombs opened, and many godly men and women who had died came back to life again. [53]After Jesus' resurrection, they left the cemetery and went into Jerusalem, and appeared to many people there. [63]And told him, "Sir, that liar once said, 'After three days I will come back to life again.'" Mk 8:31.

Mt 28:6. But he isn't here! For he has come back to life again, just as he said he would. Come in and see where his body was lying. . . . [7]And now, go quickly and tell his disciples that he has risen from the dead, and that he is going to Galilee to meet them there. That is my message to them. Mk 16:6, 7; Lk 24:5–7; Jn 20:1–18.

Mk 9:9. As they descended the mountainside he told them never to mention what they had seen until after he had risen from the dead. [10]So they kept it to themselves, but often talked about it, and wondered what he meant by "rising from the dead."

Lk 18:33. And lashed and killed. And the third day I will rise again.

Lk 24:46. And he said, "Yes, it was written long ago that the Messiah must suffer and die and rise again from the dead on the third day."

Jn 2:19. "All right," Jesus replied, "this is the miracle I will do for you: Destroy this sanctuary and in three days I will raise it up!" [21]But by "this sanctuary" he meant his body. *v.* 22; Mk 14:58.

Jn 12:23. Jesus replied that the time had come for him to return to his glory in heaven.

Jn 16:16. In just a little while I will be gone, and you will see me no more; but just a little while after that, and you will see me again! [22]You have sorrow now, but I will see you again and then you will rejoice; and no one can rob you of that joy.

Acts 1:3. During the forty days after his crucifixion he appeared to the apostles from time to time, actually alive, and proved to them in many ways that it was really he himself they were seeing. And on these occasions he talked to them about the Kingdom of God. [22]Let us select someone who has been with us constantly from our first association with the Lord—from the time he was baptized by John until the day he was taken from us into heaven.

Acts 2:24. Then God released him from the horrors of death and brought him back to life again, for death could not keep this man within its grip. [31]David was looking far into the future and predicting the Messiah's resurrection, and saying that the Messiah's soul would not be left in hell and his body would not decay. [32]He was speaking of Jesus, and we all are witnesses that Jesus rose from the dead. Ps 16:9, 10.

Acts 3:15. And you killed the Author of Life; but God brought him back to life again. And John and I are witnesses of this fact, for after you killed him we saw him alive!

Acts 4:10. "Let me clearly state to you and to all the people of Israel that it was done in the name and power of Jesus from Nazareth, the Messiah, the man you crucified—but God raised back to life again. It is by his authority that this man stands here healed!" [33]And the apostles preached powerful sermons about the resurrection of the Lord Jesus, and there was warm fellowship among all the believers.

Acts 5:30. The God of our ancestors brought Jesus back to life again after you had killed him by hanging him on a cross. [31]Then, with mighty power, God exalted him to be a Prince and Savior, so that the people of Israel would have an opportunity for repentance, and for their sins to be forgiven. [32]And we are witnesses of these things, and so is the Holy Spirit, who is given by God to all who obey him.

Acts 10:40, 41. But God brought him back to life again three days later and showed him to certain witnesses God had selected beforehand—not to the general public, but to us who ate and drank with him after he rose from the dead.

Acts 13:30. But God brought him back to life again! [31]And he was seen many times during the next few days by the men who had accompanied him to Jerusalem from Galilee—these men have constantly testified to this in public witness. [32, 33]And now Barnabas and I are here to bring you this Good News—that God's promise to our ancestors has come true in our own time, in that God brought Jesus back to life again. This is what the second Psalm is talking about when it says concerning Jesus, "Today I have honored you as my son." [34]For God had promised to bring him back to life again, no more to die. This is stated in the Scripture that says, "I will do for you the wonderful thing I promised David." Ps 2:7.

Acts 17:2. As was Paul's custom, he went there to preach, and for three Sabbaths in a row he opened the Scriptures to the people, [3]explaining the prophecies about the sufferings of the Messiah and his coming back to life, and proving that Jesus is the Messiah.

31. For he has set a day for justly judging the world by the man he has appointed, and has pointed him out by bringing him back to life again.

Acts 26:23. That the Messiah would suffer, and be the First to rise from the dead, to bring light to Jews and Gentiles alike. *v.* 26.

Rom 1:4. And by being raised from the dead he was proved to be the mighty Son of God, with the holy nature of God himself.

Rom 4:24. It was for us, too, assuring us that God will accept us in the same way he accepted Abraham—when we believe the promises of God who brought back Jesus our Lord from the dead. [25]He died for our sins and rose again to make us right with God, filling us with God's goodness.

Rom 5:10. And since, when we were his enemies, we were brought back to God by the death of his Son, what blessings he must have for us now that we are his friends, and he is living within us!

Rom 6:4. And when God the Father, with glorious power, brought him back to life again. . . . [5]For you have become a part of him, and so you died with him, so to speak, when he died; and now you share his new life, and shall rise as he did. [9]Christ rose from the dead and will never die again. Death no longer has any power over him. [10]He died once for all to end sin's power, but now he lives forever in unbroken fellowship with God.

Rom 8:11. And if the Spirit of God, who raised up Jesus from the dead, lives in you, he will make your dying bodies live again after you die, by means of this same Holy Spirit living within you. [34]Who then will condemn us? Will Christ? *No!* For he is the one who died for us and came back to life again for us and is sitting at the place of highest honor next to God, pleading for us there in heaven.

Rom 10:9. For if you tell others with your own mouth that Jesus Christ is your Lord, and believe in your own heart that God has raised him from the dead, you will be saved.

1 Cor 6:14. And God is going to raise our bodies from the dead by his power just as he raised up the Lord Jesus Christ.

1 Cor 15:3. I passed on to you right from the first what had been told to me, that Christ died for our sins just as the Scriptures said he would, [4]and that he was buried, and that three days afterwards he arose from the grave just as the prophets foretold. [20]But the fact is that Christ did actually rise from the dead, and has become the first of millions who will come back to life again some day. [21]Death came into the world because of what one man (Adam) did, and it is because of what this other man (Christ) has done that now there is the resurrection from the dead. [22]Everyone dies because all of us are related to Adam, being members of his sinful race, and wherever there is sin, death results. But all who are related to Christ will rise again. [23]Each, however, in his own turn: Christ rose first; then when Christ comes back, all his people will become alive again. *vs.* 5–8, 12–20.

2 Cor 4:10. These bodies of ours are constantly facing death just as Jesus did; so it is clear to all that it is only the living Christ within (who keeps us safe). [11]Yes, we live under constant danger to our lives because we serve the Lord, but this gives us constant opportunities to show forth the power of Jesus Christ within our dying bodies. [14]We know that the same God who brought the Lord Jesus back from death will also bring us back to life again with Jesus, and present us to him along with you.

2 Cor 5:15. He died for all so that all who live—having received eternal life from him—might live no longer for themselves, to please themselves, but to spend their lives pleasing Christ who died and rose again for them.

2 Cor 13:4. His weak, human body died on the cross, but now he lives by the mighty power of God. We, too, are weak in our bodies, as he was, but now we live and are strong, as he is, and have all of God's power to use in dealing with you.

Gal 1:1, 2. I was not called to be a missionary by any group or agency. My call is from Jesus Christ himself, and from God the Father who raised him from the dead.

Eph 1:20. That raised Christ from the dead and seated him in the place of honor at God's right hand in heaven.

Phil 3:10. Now I have given up everything else —I have found it to be the only way to really know Christ and to experience the mighty power that brought him back to life again, and to find out what it means to suffer and to die with him.

Col 1:18. He is the Head of the body made up of his people—that is, his church—which he began; and he is the Leader of all those who arise from the dead, so that he is first in everything.

Col 2:12. For in baptism you see how your old, evil nature died with him and was buried with him; and then you came up out of death with him into a new life because you trusted the Word of the mighty God who raised Christ from the dead.

1 Thess 1:10. And they speak of how you are

looking forward to the return of God's Son from heaven—Jesus, whom God brought back to life—and he is our only Savior from God's terrible anger against sin.

1 Thess 4:14. For since we believe that Jesus died and then came back to life again, we can also believe that when Jesus returns, God will bring back with him all the Christians who have died.

2 Tim 2:8. Don't ever forget the wonderful fact that Jesus Christ was a Man, born into King David's family; and that he was God, as shown by the fact that he rose again from the dead.

Heb 13:20. And now may the God of peace, who brought again from the dead our Lord Jesus, equip you with all you need for doing his will.

1 Pet 1:3. All honor to God, the God and Father of our Lord Jesus Christ; for it is his boundless mercy that has given us the privilege of being born again, so that we are now members of God's own family. Now we live in the hope of eternal life because Christ rose again from the dead. [21]Because of this, your trust can be in God who raised Christ from the dead and gave him great glory. Now your faith and hope can rest in him alone.

1 Pet 3:18. Christ also suffered. He died once for the sins of all us guilty sinners, although he himself was innocent of any sin at any time, that he might bring us safely home to God. But though his body died, his Spirit lived on. [21]That, by the way, is what baptism pictures for us: In baptism we show that we have been saved from death and doom by the resurrection of Christ.

Rev 1:5. And from Jesus Christ who faithfully reveals all truth to us. He was the first to rise from death, to die no more. [18]"Don't be afraid! Though I am the First and Last, the Living One who died, who is now alive forevermore, who has the keys of hell and death—don't be afraid!"

See *Resurrection.*

REVELATIONS OF. Concerning his kingdom: Mt 8:11, 12; Lk 13:28, 29; Mt 10:23, 34; 13:24–50; 16:18, 28; 25; Mk 9:1; Lk 9:27; Mt 21:43, 44; 24:14; Mk 16:17, 18; Lk 12:40–53; 13:24–35; 17:20–37; Jn 4:21–24; 5:25–29; 6:39, 54; 12:35; 13:19; 14:29; 16:4; his rejection by the Jews, Mt 21:33–44; Lk 17:25; his betrayal, Mt 26:20–25; crucifixion, Jn 3:14; 8:28; 12:32; judgments upon the Jews, Mt 23:37–39; Mk 11:12–14; Lk 23:28–31; the destruction of the temple, and Jerusalem, Mt 24; Mk 13; Lk 19:41–48; the destruction of Capernaum, Mt 11:23; Lk 10:15.

Concerning persecutions, Mt 23:34–36; his being forsaken by his disciples, Jn 16:32. Concerning Lazarus, Jn 11:4, 11, 23, 40. Concerning Peter, Jn 21:18–23; fame of the woman who anointed his head, Mt 26:13; Mk 14:8, 9. Antichrist, Mt 24:4, 5, 23–26; Mk 13:5, 6, 21–23; Lk 17:23, 24; 21:8.

Concerning his death and resurrection, Mt 12:39, 40; 16:21; 17:22, 23; 20:18, 19; 26:2, 20, 21, 23, 24, 45, 46; Mk 8:31; 9:30, 31; 10:32–34; Lk 9:22–24; 18:31–33; Jn 2:19; 12:7, 23, 24; 13:18–27, 36–38; 16:32; ascension, Jn 7:33, 34; 8:21; 12:8; 13:33; 17:10, 16.

RIGHTEOUSNESS OF. See *Holiness of,* above.

SALVATION BY. See *Savior,* below.

SAVIOR. Gen 12:3. I will bless those who bless you and curse those who curse you; and the entire world will be blessed because of you.

Gen 49:18. I trust in your salvation, Lord.

2 Sam 23:6. But the godless are as thorns to be thrown away, for they tear the hand that touches them. [7]One must be armed to chop them down; they shall be burned.

Job 33:23, 24. But if a messenger from heaven is there to intercede for him as a friend, to show him what is right, then God pities him and says, "Set him free. Do not make him die, for I have found a substitute."

Ps 14:7. Oh, that the time of their rescue were already here, that God would come from Zion now to save his people. What gladness when the Lord has rescued Israel!

Ps 72:4. Help him to defend the poor and needy and to crush their oppressors. [12]He will take care of the helpless and poor when they cry to him; for they have no one else to defend them. [13]He feels pity for the weak and needy, and will rescue them. [14]He will save them from oppression and from violence, for their lives are precious to him. [17]His name will be honored forever; it will continue as the sun; and all will be blessed in him; all nations will praise him.

Ps 80:17. Strengthen the man you love, the son of your choice.

Ps 89:19. In a vision you spoke to your prophet and said, "I have chosen a splendid young man from the common people to be the king."

Isa 8:14. He will be your safety.

Isa 28:16. But the Lord God says, See, I am placing a Foundation Stone in Zion—a firm, tested, precious Cornerstone that is safe to build on. He who believes need never run away again.

Isa 32:2. He will shelter Israel from the storm and wind. He will refresh her as a river in the desert and as the cooling shadow of a mighty rock within a hot and weary land.

Isa 40:10. Yes, the Lord God is coming with mighty power; he will rule with awesome strength. See, his reward is with him, to each as he has done. [11]He will feed his flock like a shepherd; he will carry the lambs in his arms and gently lead the ewes with young.

Isa 42:6. I the Lord have called you to demonstrate my righteousness. I will guard and support you, for I have given you to my people as the personal confirmation of my covenant with them. You shall also be a light to guide the nations unto me. [7]You will open the eyes of the blind, and release those who sit in prison darkness and despair.

Isa 49:6. "You shall do more than restore Israel to me. I will make you a Light to the nations of the world to bring my salvation to them too." [8, 9]The Lord says, "Your request has come at a favorable time. I will keep you from premature harm and give you as a token and pledge to Israel, proof that I will reestablish the land of Israel and reassign it to its own people again. Through you I am saying to the prisoners of darkness, 'Come out! I am giving you your freedom!' They will be my sheep, grazing in green pastures and on the grassy hills." Acts 13:47.

Isa 50:2. Was I too weak to save you? Is that why the house is silent and empty when I come home? Have I no longer power to deliver? [8]He who gives me justice is near. Who will dare to fight against me now? Where are my enemies? Let them appear! [9]See, the Lord God is for me! Who shall declare me guilty?

Isa 53:10. Yet it was the Lord's good plan to bruise him and fill him with grief. But when his soul has been made an offering for sin, then he shall have a multitude of children, many heirs. He shall live again and God's program shall prosper in his hands. [11]And when he sees all that is accomplished by the anguish of his soul, he shall be satisfied; and because of what he has experienced, my righteous Servant shall make many to be counted righteous before God, for he shall bear all their sins.

Isa 59:16. He saw no one was helping you, and wondered that no one intervened. Therefore he himself stepped in to save you through his mighty power and justice. [17]He put on righteousness as armor, and the helmet of salvation on his head. He clothed himself with robes of vengeance and of godly fury. [20]He will come as a Redeemer to those in Zion who have turned away from sin.

Isa 61:1. The Spirit of the Lord God is upon me, because the Lord has anointed me to bring good news to the suffering and afflicted. He has sent me to comfort the broken-hearted, to announce liberty to captives and to open the eyes of the blind. [2]He has sent me to tell those who mourn that the time of God's favor to them has come, and the day of his wrath to their enemies. [3]To all who mourn in Israel he will give: beauty for ashes; joy instead of mourning; praise instead of heaviness. For God has planted them like strong and graceful oaks for his own glory.

Isa 62:11. See, the Lord has sent his messengers to every land and said, "Tell my people, I, the Lord your God, am coming to save you and will bring you many gifts."

Isa 63:1. Who is this who comes from Edom, from the city of Bozrah, with his magnificent garments of crimson? Who is this in kingly robes, marching in the greatness of his strength? "It is I, the Lord, the one who is mighty to save!" [5]I looked but no one came to help them; I was amazed and appalled. So I executed vengeance alone; unaided, I meted out judgment. [8]He said, "They are my very own; surely they will not be false again." And he became their Savior. [9]In all their affliction he was afflicted, and he personally saved them. In his love and pity he redeemed them and lifted them up and carried them through all the years.

Jer 23:5, 6. For the time is coming, says the Lord, when I will place a righteous Branch upon King David's throne. He shall be a King who shall rule with wisdom and justice and cause righteousness to prevail everywhere throughout the earth. And this is his name: *The Lord Our Righteousness.* At that time Judah will be saved and Israel will live in peace. Jer 33:15, 16.

Ezk 34:23. And I will set one Shepherd over all my people, even my Servant, David. He shall feed them and be a Shepherd to them.

Hag 2:7. And the Desire of All Nations shall come to this Temple.

Zech 4:7. And Zerubbabel will finish building this Temple with mighty shouts of thanksgiving for God's mercy, declaring that all was done by grace alone.

Zech 9:9. Rejoice greatly, O my people! Shout with joy! For look—your King is coming! He is the Righteous One, the Victor! Yet he is lowly, riding on a donkey's colt!

Mal 4:2. But for you who fear my name, the Sun of Righteousness will rise with healing in his wings. And you will go free, leaping with joy like calves let out to pasture.

Mt 1:21. And you shall name him Jesus (meaning "Savior"), for he will save his people from their sins.

Mt 15:24. Then he said to the woman, "I was sent to help the Jews—the lost sheep of Israel—not the Gentiles."

Mt 18:11. And I, the Messiah, came to save the lost. [12]If a man has a hundred sheep, and one wanders away and is lost, what will he do? Won't he leave the ninety-nine others and go out into the hills to search for the lost one? [13]And if he finds it, he will rejoice over it more than over the ninety-nine others safe at home! Lk 15:1–6.

Lk 1:68. Praise the Lord, the God of Israel, for he has come to visit his people and has redeemed them. [69]He is sending us a Mighty Savior from the royal line of his servant David, [70]just as he promised through his holy prophets long ago—[71]someone to save us from our enemies, from all who hate us. [72, 73]He has been merciful to our ancestors, yes, to Abraham himself, by remembering his sacred promise to him, [74]and by granting us the privilege of serving God fearlessly, freed from our enemies, [75]and by making us holy and acceptable, ready to stand in his presence forever. [76]And you, my little son, shall be called the prophet of the glorious God, for you will prepare the way for the Messiah. [77]You will tell his people how to find salvation through forgiveness of their sins.

Lk 2:11. "The Savior—yes, the Messiah, the Lord—has been born tonight in Bethlehem." [30, 31]"For I have seen him as you promised me I would. I have seen the Savior you have given to the world. [32]He is the Light that will shine upon the nations, and he will be the glory of your people Israel!" [34]Simeon blessed them but then said to Mary, "A sword shall pierce your soul, for this child shall be rejected by many in Israel, and this to their undoing."

Lk 5:31. Jesus answered them, "It is the sick who need a doctor, not those in good health. [32]My purpose is to invite sinners to turn from their sins, not to spend my time with those who think themselves already good enough." Mt 9:12, 13.

Lk 19:10. This man was one of the lost sons of Abraham, and I, the Messiah, have come to search for and to save such souls as his. Lk 15:3–10.

Jn 1:9. Later on, the one who is the true Light arrived to shine on everyone coming into the world. [29]The next day John saw Jesus coming toward him and said, "Look! There is the Lamb of God who takes away the world's sin!"

Jn 3:16. For God loved the world so much that he gave his only Son so that anyone who believes in him shall not perish but have eternal life. [17]God did not send his Son into the world to condemn it, but to save it.

Jn 4:14. "But the water I give them," he said, "becomes a perpetual spring within them, watering them forever with eternal life." [42]Then they said to the woman, "Now we believe because we have heard him ourselves, not just because of what you told us. He is indeed the Savior of the world."

Jn 5:26. The Father has life in himself, and has granted his Son to have life in himself. [33]You have gone out to listen to his preaching, and I can assure you that all he says about me is true! [34]But the truest witness I have is not from a man, though I have reminded you about John's witness so that you will believe in me and be saved. [40]Yet you won't come to me so that I can give you this life eternal!

Jn 6:27. "But you shouldn't be so concerned about perishable things like food. No, spend your energy seeking the eternal life that I, the Messiah, can give you. For God the Father has sent me for this very purpose." [32]Jesus said, "Moses didn't give it to them. My Father did. And now he offers you true Bread from heaven. [33]The true Bread is a Person—the one sent by God from heaven, and he gives life to the world." [35]Jesus replied, "I am the Bread of Life. No one coming to me will ever be hungry again. Those believing in me will never thirst. [37]But some will come to me—those the Father has given me—and I will never, never reject them. [39]And this is the will of God, that I should not lose even one of all those he has given me, but that I should raise them to eternal life at the Last Day. [51]I am that Living Bread that came down out of heaven. Anyone eating this Bread shall live forever; this Bread is my flesh given to redeem humanity." [53]So Jesus said it again, "With all the earnestness I possess I tell you this: Unless you eat the flesh of the Messiah and drink his blood, you cannot have eternal life within you. [54]But anyone who does eat my flesh and drink my blood has eternal life, and I will raise him at the Last Day. [55]For my flesh is the true food, and my blood is the true drink. [56]Everyone who eats my flesh and drinks my blood is in me, and I in him. [57]I live by the power of the living Father who sent me, and in the same way those who partake of me shall live because of me! [58]I am the true Bread from heaven; and anyone who eats this Bread shall live forever, and not die as your fathers did—though they ate bread from heaven." [68]Simon Peter replied, "Master, to whom shall we go? You alone have the words that give eternal life."

Jn 7:37. On the last day, the climax of the holidays, Jesus shouted to the crowds, "If anyone is thirsty, let him come to me and drink. [38]For the Scriptures declare that rivers of living water shall flow from the inmost being of anyone who believes in me." [39](He was speaking of the Holy Spirit, who would be given to everyone believing in him; but the Spirit had not yet been given, because Jesus had not yet returned to his glory in heaven.)

Jn 8:12. Later, in one of his talks, Jesus said to the people, "I am the Light of the world. So if you follow me, you won't be stumbling through the darkness, for living light will flood your path."

Jn 9:5. "But while I am still here in the world, I give it my light." [39]Then Jesus told him, "I have come into the world to give sight to those who are spiritually blind and to show those who think they see that they are blind."

Jn 10:7. So he explained it to them. "I am the Gate for the sheep," he said. [9]"Yes, I am the Gate. Those who come in by way of the Gate will be saved and will go in and out and find green pastures. [10]The thief's purpose is to steal, kill and destroy. My purpose is to give life in all its fullness. [11]I am the Good Shepherd. The Good Shepherd lays down his life for the sheep. [14]I am the Good Shepherd and know my own sheep, and they know me, [15]just as my Father knows me and I know the Father; and I lay down my life for the sheep. [16]I have other sheep, too, in another fold. I must bring them also, and they will heed my voice; and there will be one flock with one Shepherd. [27]My sheep recognize my voice, and I know them, and they follow me. [28]I give them eternal life and they shall never perish. No one shall snatch them away from me."

Jn 11:25. Jesus told her, "I am the one who raises the dead and gives them life again. Anyone who believes in me, even though he dies like anyone else, shall live again. [26]He is given eternal life for believing in me and shall never perish. Do you believe this, Martha?" [27]"Yes, Master," she told him. "I believe you are the Messiah, the Son of God, the one we have so long awaited."

Jn 12:47. If anyone hears me and doesn't obey me, I am not his judge—for I have come to save the world and not to judge it.

Jn 14:6. Jesus told him, "I am the Way—yes, and the Truth and the Life. No one can get to the Father except by means of me. [19]For I will live again—and you will too."

Jn 16:33. But cheer up, for I have overcome the world.

Jn 17:2. For you have given him authority over every man and woman in all the earth. He gives eternal life to each one you have given him. [3]And this is the way to have eternal life—by knowing you, the only true God, and Jesus Christ, the one you sent to earth!

Acts 3:26. As soon as God had brought his servant to life again, he sent him first of all to you men of Israel, to bless you by turning you back from your sins.

Acts 4:12. There is salvation in no one else! Under all heaven there is no other name for men to call upon to save them.

Acts 5:31. Then, with mighty power, God exalted him to be a Prince and Savior, so that the people of Israel would have an opportunity for repentance, and for their sins to be forgiven.

Acts 13:23. And it is one of King David's descendants, Jesus, who is God's promised Savior of Israel! [38]Brothers! Listen! In this man Jesus, there is forgiveness for your sins! [39]Everyone who trusts in him is freed from all guilt and declared righteous —something the Jewish law could never do.

Acts 15:11. Don't you believe that all are saved the same way, by the free gift of the Lord Jesus?

Acts 16:31. They replied, "Believe on the Lord Jesus and you will be saved, and your entire household."

Rom 3:24. Yet now God declares us "not guilty" of offending him if we trust in Jesus Christ, who in his kindness freely takes away our sins. [25]For God sent Christ Jesus to take the punishment for our sins and to end all God's anger against us. He used Christ's blood and our faith as the means of saving us from his wrath. In this way he was being entirely fair, even though he did not punish those who sinned in former times. For he was looking forward to the time when Christ would come and take away those sins. [26]And now in these days also he can receive sinners in this same way, because Jesus took away their sins. But isn't this unfair for God to let criminals go free, and say that they are innocent? No, for he does it on the basis of their trust in Jesus who took away their sins.

Rom 4:25. He died for our sins and rose again to make us right with God, filling us with God's goodness.

Rom 5:1. So now, since we have been made right in God's sight by faith in his promises, we can have real peace with him because of what Jesus Christ our Lord has done for us. [6]When we were utterly helpless with no way of escape, Christ came at just the right time and died for us sinners who had no use for him. [8]But God showed his great love for us by sending Christ to die for us while we were still sinners. [9]And since by his blood he did all this for us as sinners, how much more will he do for us now that he has declared us not guilty? Now he will save us from all of God's wrath to come. [10]And since, when we were his enemies, we were brought back to God by the death of his Son, what blessings he must have for us now that we are his friends, and he is living within us! [11]Now we rejoice in our wonderful new relationship with God—all because of what our Lord Jesus Christ has done in dying for our sins—making us friends of God.

15. And what a difference between man's sin and God's forgiveness! For this one man, Adam, brought death to many through his *sin.* But this one man, Jesus Christ, brought forgiveness to many through God's *mercy.* [17]The sin of this one man, Adam, caused *death to be king over all,* but all who will take God's gift of forgiveness and acquittal are *kings of life* because of this one man, Jesus Christ. [18]Yes, Adam's *sin* brought *punishment* to all, but Christ's *righteousness* makes men *right with God,* so that they can live. [19]Adam caused many to be sinners because he *disobeyed* God, and Christ caused many to be acceptable to God because he *obeyed.* [21]Before, sin ruled over all men and brought them to death, but now God's kindness rules instead, giving us right standing with God and resulting in eternal life through Jesus Christ our Lord.

Rom 6:23. But the free gift of God is eternal life through Jesus Christ our Lord.

Rom 8:2. For the power of the life-giving Spirit —and this power is mine through Christ Jesus— has freed me from the vicious circle of sin and death.

Rom 10:9. For if you tell others with your own mouth that Jesus Christ is your Lord, and believe in your own heart that God has raised him from the dead, you will be saved. [11]For the Scriptures tell us that no one who believes in Christ will ever be disappointed.

Rom 15:7. So, warmly welcome each other into the church, just as Christ has warmly welcomed you; then God will be glorified. [8]Remember that Jesus Christ came to show that God is true to his promises and to help the Jews. [9]And remember that he came also that the Gentiles might be saved and give glory to God for his mercies to them. That is what the Psalmist meant when he wrote: "I will praise you among the Gentiles, and sing to your name."

1 Cor 1:30. For it is from God alone that you have your life through Christ Jesus. He showed us God's plan of salvation; he was the one who made us acceptable to God; he made us pure and holy and gave himself to purchase our salvation.

1 Cor 3:11. And no one can ever lay any other real foundation than that one we already have—Jesus Christ.

1 Cor 6:11. But now your sins are washed away, and you are set apart for God, and he has accepted you because of what the Lord Jesus Christ and the Spirit of our God have done for you.

1 Cor 10:3, 4. And by a miracle God sent them food to eat and water to drink there in the desert; they drank the water that Christ gave them. He was there with them as a mighty Rock of spiritual refreshment.

1 Cor 15:17. And you are very foolish to keep on trusting God to save you, and you are still under condemnation for your sins. [57]How we thank God for all of this! It is he who makes us victorious through Jesus Christ our Lord!

2 Cor 5:18. All these new things are from God who brought us back to himself through what Christ Jesus did. And God has given us the privilege of urging everyone to come into his favor and be reconciled to him. [19]For God was in Christ, restoring the world to himself, no longer counting

men's sins against them but blotting them out. This is the wonderful message he has given us to tell others. [21]For God took the sinless Christ and poured into him our sins. Then, in exchange, he poured God's goodness into us!

Gal 1:3. May peace and blessing be yours from God the Father and from the Lord Jesus Christ. [4]He died for our sins just as God our Father planned, and rescued us from this evil world in which we live.

Gal 2:20. I have been crucified with Christ: and I myself no longer live, but Christ lives in me. And the real life I now have within this body is a result of my trusting in the Son of God, who loved me and gave himself for me.

Gal 4:7. Now we are no longer slaves, but God's own sons. And since we are his sons, everything he has belongs to us, for that is the way God planned.

Eph 1:10. And this was his purpose: that when the time is ripe he will gather us all together from wherever we are—in heaven or on earth—to be with him in Christ, forever. [11]Moreover, because of what Christ has done we have become gifts to God that he delights in.

Eph 2:7. And now God can always point to us as examples of how very, very rich his kindness is, as shown in all he has done for us through Jesus Christ. [13]But now you belong to Christ Jesus, and though you once were far away from God, now you have been brought very near to him because of what Jesus Christ has done for you with his blood. [14]For Christ himself is our way of peace. He has made peace between us Jews and you Gentiles by making us all one family, breaking down the wall of contempt that used to separate us. [15]By his death he ended the angry resentment between us, caused by the Jewish laws which favored the Jews and excluded the Gentiles, for he died to annul that whole system of Jewish laws. Then he took the two groups that had been opposed to each other and made them parts of himself; thus he fused us together to become one new person, and at last there was peace. [16]As parts of the same body, our anger against each other has disappeared, for both of us have been reconciled to God. And so the feud ended at last at the cross. [17]And he has brought this Good News of peace to you Gentiles who were very far away from him, and to us Jews who were near. [18]Now all of us, whether Jews or Gentiles, may come to God the Father with the Holy Spirit's help because of what Christ has done for us. [20]What a foundation you stand on now: the apostles and the prophets; and the cornerstone of the building is Jesus Christ himself!

Eph 4:8. The Psalmist tells about this, for he says that when Christ returned triumphantly to heaven after his resurrection and victory over Satan, he gave generous gifts to men.

Eph 5:2. Be full of love for others, following the example of Christ who loved you and gave himself to God as a sacrifice to take away your sins. And God was pleased, for Christ's love for you was like sweet perfume to him. [14]That is why God says in the Scriptures, "Awake, O sleeper, and rise up from the dead; and Christ shall give you light." [23]Christ is in charge of his body the church. (He gave his very life to take care of it and be its Savior!)

25. And you husbands, show the same kind of love to your wives as Christ showed to the church when he died for her, [26]to make her holy and clean, washed by baptism and God's Word.

Phil 3:20. But our homeland is in heaven, where our Savior the Lord Jesus Christ is.

Col 1:12. And always thankful to the Father . . . [13]For he has rescued us out of the darkness and gloom of Satan's kingdom and brought us into the kingdom of his dear Son, [14]who bought our freedom with his blood and forgave us all our sins. [27]And this is the secret: *that Christ in your hearts is your only hope of glory.* [28]So everywhere we go we talk about Christ to all who will listen, warning them and teaching them as well as we know how. We want to be able to present each one to God, perfect because of what Christ has done for each of them.

Col 2:8. Don't let others spoil your faith and joy with their philosophies, their wrong and shallow answers built on men's thoughts and ideas, instead of on what Christ has said. [10]*So you have everything when you have Christ.* . . . He is the highest Ruler, with authority over every other power.

Col 3:3. You should have as little desire for this world as a dead person does. Your real life is in heaven with Christ and God. [4]And when Christ who is our real life comes back again, you will shine with him and share in all his glories. [11]Whether a person has Christ is what matters, and he is equally available to all.

1 Thess 1:10. And they speak of how you are looking forward to the return of God's Son from heaven—Jesus, whom God brought back to life—and he is our only Savior from God's terrible anger against sin.

1 Thess 5:9. For God has not chosen to pour out his anger upon us, but to save us through our Lord Jesus Christ; [10]he died for us so that we can live with him forever, whether we are dead or alive at the time of his return.

2 Thess 1:12. Then everyone will be praising the name of the Lord Jesus Christ because of the results they see in you; and your greatest glory will be that you belong to him. The tender mercy of our God and of the Lord Jesus Christ has made all this possible for you.

1 Tim 1:1. From: Paul, a missionary of Jesus Christ, sent out by the direct command of God our Savior and by Jesus Christ our Lord—our only hope. [15]How true it is, and how I long that everyone should know it, that Christ Jesus came into the world to save sinners—and I was the greatest of them all.

2 Tim 1:1. From: Paul, Jesus Christ's missionary, sent out by God to tell men and women everywhere about the eternal life he has promised them through faith in Jesus Christ. [9]It is he who saved

us and chose us for his holy work, not because we deserved it but because that was his plan long before the world began—to show his love and kindness to us through Christ. [10]And now he has made all of this plain to us by the coming of our Savior Jesus Christ, who broke the power of death and showed us the way of everlasting life through trusting him. [12]For I know the one in whom I trust, and I am sure that he is able to safely guard all that I have given him until the day of his return.

2 Tim 2:10. I am more than willing to suffer if that will bring salvation and eternal glory in Christ Jesus to those God has chosen.

2 Tim 3:15. You know how, when you were a small child, you were taught the holy Scriptures; and it is these that make you wise to accept God's salvation by trusting in Christ Jesus.

Tit 1:4. To Titus, who is truly my son in the affairs of the Lord. May God the Father and Christ Jesus our Savior give you his blessings and his peace.

Tit 2:13. Looking forward to that wonderful time we've been expecting, when his glory shall be seen —the glory of our great God and Savior Jesus Christ. [14]He died under God's judgment against our sins, so that he could rescue us from constant falling into sin and make us his very own people, with cleansed hearts and real enthusiasm for doing kind things for others.

Heb 2:3. What makes us think that we can escape if we are indifferent to this great salvation announced by the Lord Jesus himself, and passed on to us by those who heard him speak? [17]And it was necessary for Jesus to be like us, his brothers, so that he could be our merciful and faithful High Priest before God, a Priest who would be both merciful to us and faithful to God in dealing with the sins of the people.

Heb 5:9. It was after he had proved himself perfect in this experience that Jesus became the Giver of eternal salvation to all those who obey him.

Heb 7:22. Because of God's oath, Christ can guarantee forever the success of this new and better arrangement. [25]He is able to save completely all who come to God through him. Since he will live forever, he will always be there to remind God that he has paid for their sins with his blood.

Heb 13:10. We have an altar—the cross where Christ was sacrificed—where those who continue to seek salvation by obeying Jewish laws can never be helped. [20]And now may the God of peace, who brought again from the dead our Lord Jesus, equip you with all you need for doing his will. May he who became the great Shepherd of the sheep by an everlasting agreement between God and you, signed with his blood.

1 Pet 1:3. All honor to God, the God and Father of our Lord Jesus Christ; for it is his boundless mercy that has given us the privilege of being born again, so that we are now members of God's own family. Now we live in the hope of eternal life because Christ rose again from the dead. [18]God paid a ransom to save you from the impossible road to heaven which your fathers tried to take, and the ransom he paid was not mere gold or silver, as you very well know. [19]But he paid for you with the precious lifeblood of Christ, the sinless, spotless Lamb of God.

1 Pet 2:4. Come to Christ, who is the living Foundation of Rock upon which God builds; though men have spurned him, he is very precious to God who has chosen him above all others. [5]And now you have become living building-stones for God's use in building his house. What's more, you are his holy priests; so come to him—(you who are acceptable to him because of Jesus Christ)—and offer to God those things that please him. [6]As the Scriptures express it, "See, I am sending Christ to be the carefully chosen, precious Cornerstone of my church, and I will never disappoint those who trust in him." [7]Yes, he is very precious to you who believe . . . "The same Stone that was rejected by the builders has become the Cornerstone." [25]Like sheep you wandered away from God, but now you have returned to your Shepherd, the Guardian of your souls who keeps you safe from all attacks.

1 Pet 3:18. Christ also suffered. He died once for the sins of all us guilty sinners, although he himself was innocent of any sin at any time, that he might bring us safely home to God. But though his body died, his Spirit lived on. [21]That, by the way, is what baptism pictures for us: In baptism we show that we have been saved from death and doom by the resurrection of Christ; not because our bodies are washed clean by the water, but because in being baptized we are turning to God and asking him to cleanse our *hearts* from sin.

1 Pet 5:10. After you have suffered a little while, our God, who is full of kindness through Christ, will give you his eternal glory. He personally will come and pick you up, and set you firmly in place, and make you stronger than ever.

2 Pet 1:3. For as you know him better, he will give you, through his great power, everything you need for living a truly good life: he even shares his own glory and his own goodness with us! [11]And God will open wide the gates of heaven for you to enter into the eternal kingdom of our Lord and Savior Jesus Christ.

2 Pet 2:20. And when a person has escaped from the wicked ways of the world by learning about our Lord and Savior Jesus Christ, and then gets tangled up with sin and becomes its slave again, he is worse off than he was before.

1 Jn 3:5. And you know that he became a man so that he could take away our sins, and that there is no sin in him, no missing of God's will at any time in any way. [8]But the Son of God came to destroy these works of the devil.

1 Jn 4:9. God showed how much he loved us by sending his only Son into this wicked world to bring to us eternal life through his death. [10]In this act we see what real love is: it is not our love for God, but his love for us when he sent his Son to satisfy God's anger against our sins. [14]And furthermore, we have seen with our own eyes and now tell

all the world that God sent his Son to be their Savior.

1 Jn 5:11. And what is it that God has said? That he has given us eternal life, and that this life is in his Son. [12]So whoever has God's Son has life; whoever does not have his Son, does not have life. [13]I have written this to you who believe in the Son of God so that you may know you have eternal life. [20]And we know that Christ, God's Son, has come to help us understand and find the true God. And now we are in God because we are in Jesus Christ his Son, who is the only true God; and he is eternal Life.

Rev 2:7. To everyone who is victorious, I will give fruit from the Tree of Life in the Paradise of God.

Rev 3:18. My advice to you is to buy pure gold from me, gold purified by fire—only then will you truly be rich. And to purchase from me white garments, clean and pure, so you won't be naked and ashamed; and to get medicine from me to heal your eyes and give you back your sight.

Rev 5:5. But one of the twenty-four Elders said to me, "Stop crying, for look! The Lion of the tribe of Judah, the Root of David, has conquered, and proved himself worthy to open the scroll and to break its seven seals." [6]I looked and saw a Lamb standing there before the twenty-four Elders, in front of the throne and the Living Beings, and on the Lamb were wounds that once had caused his death. He had seven horns and seven eyes, which represent the seven-fold Spirit of God, sent out into every part of the world. [7]He stepped forward and took the scroll from the right hand of the one sitting upon the throne. [8]And as he took the scroll, the twenty-four Elders fell down before the Lamb, each with a harp and golden vials filled with incense—the prayers of God's people! [9]They were singing him a new song with these words: "You are worthy to take the scroll and break its seals and open it; for you were slain, and your blood has bought people from every nation as gifts for God. [10]And you have gathered them into a kingdom and made them priests of our God; they shall reign upon the earth." [11]Then in my vision I heard the singing of millions of angels surrounding the throne and the Living Beings and the Elders: [12]"The Lamb is worthy" (loudly they sang it!) "—the Lamb who was slain. He is worthy to receive the power, and the riches, and the wisdom, and the strength, and the honor, and the glory, and the blessing." [13]And then I heard everyone in heaven and earth, and from the dead beneath the earth and in the sea, exclaiming, "The blessing and the honor and the glory and the power belong to the one sitting on the throne, and to the Lamb forever and ever." [14]And the four Living Beings kept saying, "Amen!" And the twenty-four Elders fell down and worshiped him.

Rev 7:10. Salvation comes from our God upon the throne, and from the Lamb.

Rev 14:4. For they are spiritually undefiled, pure as virgins, following the Lamb wherever he goes. They have been purchased from among the men on the earth as a consecrated offering to God and the Lamb.

Rev 21:27. Nothing evil will be permitted in it . . . but only those whose names are written in the Lamb's Book of Life.

Rev 22:1. And he pointed out to me a river of pure Water of Life, clear as crystal, flowing from the throne of God and the Lamb, [2]coursing down the center of the main street. On each side of the river grew Trees of Life, bearing twelve crops of fruit, with a fresh crop each month; the leaves were used for medicine to heal the nations.

See *Jesus, Design of his Death, Faith in.*

See also *Jesus, Ascension of.*

SECOND COMING OF. Job 19:25. But as for me, I know that my Redeemer lives, and that he will stand upon the earth at last. [26]And I know that after this body has decayed, this body shall see God!

Mt 16:27. For I, the Son of Mankind, shall come with my angels in the glory of my Father and judge each person according to his deeds. [28]And some of you standing right here now will certainly live to see me coming in my Kingdom. Mk 9:1; Lk 9:27.

Mt 23:39. For I tell you this, you will never see me again until you are ready to welcome the one sent to you from God.

Mt 24:3. "When will this happen?" the disciples asked him later, as he sat on the slopes of the Mount of Olives. "What events will signal your return, and the end of the world?" "[27]For as the lightning flashes across the sky from east to west, so shall my coming be, when I, the Messiah, return. [30]And then at last the signal of my coming will appear in the heavens and there will be deep mourning all around the earth. And the nations of the world will see me arrive in the clouds of heaven, with power and great glory. [31]And I shall send forth my angels with the sound of a mighty trumpet blast, and they shall gather my chosen ones from the farthest ends of the earth and heaven.

37, 38. The world will be at ease—banquets and parties and weddings—just as it was in Noah's time before the sudden coming of the flood; [39]people wouldn't believe what was going to happen until the flood actually arrived and took them all away. So shall my coming be.

42. So be prepared, for you don't know what day your Lord is coming. [43]Just as a man can prevent trouble from thieves by keeping watch for them, [44]so you can avoid trouble by always being ready for my unannounced return. *vs.* 1–51; Mk 13:1–37; Lk 21:5–35; 17:22–37; 12:40.

Mt 25:5, 6. So, when the bridegroom was delayed, they lay down to rest until midnight, when they were roused by the shout, "The bridegroom is coming! Come out and welcome him!" [10]But while they were gone, the bridegroom came, and those who were ready went in with him to the marriage feast, and the door was locked. [13]So stay awake and be prepared, for you do not know the date or moment of my return. [19]After a long time their master returned from his trip and called them to him to account for his money. [31]But when I, the Messiah, shall come in my glory, and all the angels with me, then I shall sit upon my throne of glory. *vs.* 1–13, 31–46.

Mt 26:64. "Yes," Jesus said, "I am. And in the future you will see me, the Messiah, sitting at the right hand of God and returning on the clouds of heaven."

Mk 13:27. And I will send out the angels to gather together my chosen ones from all over the world—from the farthest bounds of earth and heaven. [32]However, no one, not even the angels in heaven, nor I myself, knows the day or the hour when these things will happen; only the Father knows. [35, 36]Keep a sharp lookout! For you do not know when I will come, at evening, at midnight, early dawn or late daybreak. Don't let me find you sleeping. Mt 24:36.

Mk 14:62. Jesus said, "I am, and you will see me sitting at the right hand of God, and returning to earth in the clouds of heaven."

Lk 9:26. When I, the Messiah, come in my glory and in the glory of the Father and the holy angels, I will be ashamed then of all who are ashamed of me and of my words now. Mk 8:38.

Lk 12:37. There will be great joy for those who are ready and waiting for his return. He himself will seat them and put on a waiter's uniform and serve them as they sit and eat! [38]He may come at nine o'clock at night—or even at midnight. But whenever he comes there will be joy for his servants who are ready! [39]Everyone would be ready for him if they knew the exact hour of his return —just as they would be ready for a thief if they knew when he was coming. [40]So be ready all the time. For I, the Messiah, will come when least expected.

Lk 17:30. Yes, it will be "business as usual" right up to the hour of my return.

Lk 18:8. When I, the Messiah, return, how many will I find who have faith (and are praying)?

Lk 19:12. A nobleman living in a certain province was called away to the distant capital of the empire to be crowned king of his province. [13]Before he left he called together ten assistants and gave them each $2,000 to invest while he was gone. [15]Upon his return he called in the men to whom he had given the money, to find out what they had done with it, and what their profits were.

Lk 21:27. "Then the peoples of the earth shall see me, the Messiah, coming in a cloud with power and great glory. [28]So when all these things begin to happen, stand straight and look up! For your salvation is near." [29]Then he gave them this illustration: "Notice the fig tree, or any other tree. [30]When the leaves come out, you know without being told that summer is near. [31]In the same way, when you see the events taking place that I've described you can be just as sure that the Kingdom of God is near. [32]I solemnly declare to you that when these things happen, the end of this age has come. [33]And though all heaven and earth shall pass away, yet my words remain forever true. [34, 35]Watch out! Don't let my sudden coming catch you unawares; don't let me find you living in careless ease, carousing and drinking, and occupied with the problems of this life, like all the rest of the world. [36]Keep a constant watch. And pray that if possible you may arrive in my presence without having to experience these horrors."

Jn 14:3. When everything is ready, then I will come and get you, so that you can always be with me where I am. If this weren't so, I would tell you plainly. [18]No, I will not abandon you or leave you as orphans in the storm—I will come to you.

28. Remember what I told you—I am going away, but I will come back to you again. If you really love me, you will be very happy for me, for now I can go to the Father, who is greater than I am. [29]I have told you these things before they happen so that when they do, you will believe (in me).

Acts 1:11. Jesus has gone away to heaven, and some day, just as he went, he will return!

Acts 3:20. And send Jesus your Messiah back to you again. [21]For he must remain in heaven until the final recovery of all things from sin, as prophesied from ancient times.

1 Cor 1:7. Every spiritual gift and power for doing his will are yours during this time of waiting for the return of our Lord Jesus Christ. [8]And he guarantees right up to the end that you will be counted free from all sin and guilt on that day when he returns.

1 Cor 4:5. So be careful not to jump to conclusions before the Lord returns as to whether someone is a good servant or not. When the Lord comes, he will turn on the light so that everyone can see exactly what each one of us is really like, deep down in our hearts.

1 Cor 11:26. For every time you eat this bread and drink this cup you are re-telling the message of the Lord's death, that he has died for you. Do this until he comes again.

1 Cor 15:23. Each, however, in his own turn: Christ rose first; then when Christ comes back, all his people will become alive again.

Phil 3:20. But our homeland is in heaven, where our Savior the Lord Jesus Christ is; and we are looking forward to his return from there. [21]When he comes back he will take these dying bodies of ours and change them into glorious bodies like his own, using the same mighty power that he will use to conquer all else everywhere.

Phil 4:5. Let everyone see that you are unselfish and considerate in all you do. Remember that the Lord is coming soon.

Col 3:4. And when Christ who is our real life comes back again, you will shine with him and share in all his glories.

1 Thess 1:10. And they speak of how you are looking forward to the return of God's Son from heaven—Jesus, whom God brought back to life—and he is our only Savior from God's terrible anger against sin.

1 Thess 2:19. For what is it we live for, that gives us hope and joy and is our proud reward and crown? It is you! Yes, you will bring us much joy as we stand together before our Lord Jesus Christ when he comes back again.

1 Thess 3:13. This will result in your hearts being made strong, sinless and holy by God our Father, so that you may stand before him guiltless on that day when our Lord Jesus Christ returns with all those who belong to him.

1 Thess 4:15. I can tell you this directly from the Lord: that we who are still living when the Lord returns will not rise to meet him ahead of those who are in their graves. [16]For the Lord himself will come down from heaven with a mighty shout and with the soul-stirring cry of the archangel and the great trumpet-call of God. And the believers who are dead will be the first to rise to meet the Lord. [17]Then we who are still alive and remain on the earth will be caught up with them in the clouds to meet the Lord in the air and remain with him forever.

1 Thess 5:2. For you know perfectly well that no one knows. That day of the Lord will come unexpectedly like a thief in the night. [3]When people are saying, "All is well, everything is quiet and peaceful"—then, all of a sudden, disaster will fall upon them as suddenly as a woman's birth pains begin when her child is born. And these people will not be able to get away anywhere—there will be no place to hide. [23]May the God of peace himself make you entirely pure and devoted to God; and may your spirit and soul and body be kept strong and blameless until that day when our Lord Jesus Christ comes back again.

2 Thess 1:7. And so I would say to you who are suffering, God will give you rest along with us when the Lord Jesus appears suddenly from heaven in flaming fire with his mighty angels, [8]bringing judgment on those who do not wish to know God, and who refuse to accept his plan to save them through our Lord Jesus Christ. [9]They will be punished in everlasting hell, forever separated from the Lord, never to see the glory of his power, [10]when he comes to receive praise and admiration because of all he has done for his people, his saints. And you will be among those praising him, because you have believed what we told you about him.

2 Thess 2:1. And now, what about the coming again of our Lord Jesus Christ, and our being gathered together to meet him? [2]Please don't be upset and excited, dear brothers, by the rumor that this day of the Lord has already begun. If you hear of people having visions and special messages from God about this, or letters that are supposed to have come from me, don't believe them. [3]Don't be carried away and deceived regardless of what they say. For that day will not come until two things happen: first, there will be a time of great rebellion against God, and then the man of rebellion will come—the son of hell. [5]Don't you remember that I told you this when I was with you? [8]Then this wicked one will appear, whom the Lord Jesus will burn up with the breath of his mouth and destroy by his presence when he returns.

1 Tim 6:14. That you fulfill all he has told you to do, so that no one can find fault with you from now until our Lord Jesus Christ returns. [15]For in due season Christ will be revealed from heaven by the blessed and only Almighty God, the King of kings and Lord of lords.

2 Tim 4:1. And so I solemnly urge you before God and before Christ Jesus—who will some day judge the living and the dead when he appears to set up his kingdom. [8]In heaven a crown is waiting for me which the Lord, the righteous Judge, will give me on that great day of his return. And not just to me, but to all those whose lives show that they are eagerly looking forward to his coming back again.

Tit 2:13. Looking forward to that wonderful time we've been expecting, when his glory shall be seen —the glory of our great God and Savior Jesus Christ.

Heb 9:28. So also Christ died only once as an offering for the sins of many people; and he will come again, but not to deal again with our sins. This time he will come bringing salvation to all those who are eagerly and patiently waiting for him.

Jas 5:7. Now as for you, dear brothers who are waiting for the Lord's return, be patient, like a farmer who waits until the autumn for his precious harvest to ripen. [8]Yes, be patient. And take courage, for the coming of the Lord is near. [9] . . . For see! The great Judge is coming. He is almost here.

1 Pet 1:7. These trials are only to test your faith. . . . so if your faith remains strong after being tried in the test tube of fiery trials, it will bring you much praise and glory and honor on the day of his return. [13]So now you can look forward soberly and intelligently to more of God's kindness to you when Jesus Christ returns.

1 Pet 4:13. Instead, be really glad—because these trials will make you partners with Christ in his suffering, and afterwards you will have the wonderful joy of sharing his glory in that coming day when it will be displayed.

1 Pet 5:4. And when the Head Shepherd comes, your reward will be a never-ending share in his glory and honor.

2 Pet 1:16. For we have not been telling you fairy tales when we explained to you the power of our Lord Jesus Christ and his coming again.

2 Pet 3:3. First, I want to remind you that in the last days there will come scoffers who will do every wrong they can think of, and laugh at the truth. [4]This will be their line of argument: "So Jesus promised to come back, did he? Then where is he? He'll never come! Why, as far back as anyone can remember everything has remained exactly as it was since the first day of creation." [10]The day of the Lord is surely coming, as unexpectedly as a thief, and then the heavens will pass away with a terrible noise and the heavenly bodies will disappear in fire,

and the earth and everything on it will be burned up. [11]And so since everything around us is going to melt away, what holy, godly lives we should be living! [12]You should look forward to that day and hurry it along—the day when God will set the heavens on fire, and the heavenly bodies will melt and disappear in flames. *vs.* 8–14.

1 Jn 2:28. And now, my little children, stay in happy fellowship with the Lord so that when he comes you will be sure that all is well, and will not have to be ashamed and shrink back from meeting him.

1 Jn 3:2. But we do know this, that when he comes we will be like him, as a result of seeing him as he really is.

Jude 1:14. Enoch, who lived seven generations after Adam, knew about these men and said this about them: "See, the Lord is coming with millions of his holy ones. [15]He will bring the people of the world before him in judgment."

Rev 1:7. See! He is arriving, surrounded by clouds; and every eye shall see him—yes, and those who pierced him. And the nations will weep in sorrow and in terror when he comes.

Rev 3:11. Look, I am coming soon! Hold tightly to the little strength you have—so that no one will take away your crown.

Rev 16:15. Take note: I will come as unexpectedly as a thief!

Rev 22:12. "See, I am coming soon, and my reward is with me, to repay everyone according to the deeds he has done. [20]He who has said all these things declares: Yes, I am coming soon!" Amen! Come, Lord Jesus!

See *Millennium.*

SHEPHERD.

Jesus the True. Foretold, Gen 49:24; Isa 40:11; Ezk 34:23; 37:24. The chief, 1 Pet 5:4. The good, Jn 10:11, 14. The great, Mic 5:4; Heb 13:20, 21.

His sheep he knows, Jn 10:14, 27. He calls, Jn 10: 3. He gathers, Isa 40:11; Jn 10:16. He guides, Ps 23: 2, 3; Jn 10:3, 4. He feeds, Ps 23:1–3; Jn 10:9. He cherishes tenderly, Isa 40:11. He protects and preserves, Jer 31:10; Ezk 34:9, 10; Zech 9:16, 17; Jn 10: 28. He laid down his life for, Zech 13:7; Mt 26:31; Jn 10:11, 15; Acts 20:28. He gives eternal life to, Jn 10:28.

Typified: David, 1 Sam 16:10, 11.

SON OF GOD. Ps 2:7. His chosen one replies, "I will reveal the everlasting purposes of God, for the Lord has said to me, 'You are my Son. This is your Coronation Day.' "

Ps 89:26. And he will cry to me, "You are my Father, my God, and my Rock of Salvation." [27]I will treat him as my firstborn son, and make him the mightiest king in all the earth.

Mt 3:17. And a voice from heaven said, "This is my beloved Son, and I am wonderfully pleased with him." Mk 1:11; Lk 3:22.

Mt 4:3. Then Satan tempted him to get food by changing stones into loaves of bread. "It will prove you are the Son of God," he said. [6]"Jump off," he said, "and prove you are the Son of God; for the Scriptures declare; 'God will send his angels to keep you from harm,' . . . they will prevent you from smashing on the rocks below."

Mt 10:40. Those who welcome you are welcoming me. And when they welcome me they are welcoming God who sent me.

Mt 11:27. Everything has been entrusted to me by my Father. Only the Father knows the Son, and the Father is known only by the Son and by those to whom the Son reveals him. Lk 10:22.

Mt 14:33. The others sat there, awestruck. "You really are the Son of God!" they exclaimed.

Mt 15:13. Jesus replied, "Every plant not planted by my Father shall be rooted up."

Mt 16:15. Then he asked them, "Who do *you* think I am?" [16]Simon Peter answered, "The Christ, the Messiah, the Son of the living God." [17]"God has blessed you, Simon, son of Jonah," Jesus said, "for my Father in heaven has personally revealed this to you—this is not from any human source."

Mt 17:5. But even as he said it, a bright cloud came over them, and a voice from the cloud said, "*This* is my beloved Son, and I am wonderfully pleased with him. Obey *him.*" Mk 9:7; Lk 9:35; 2 Pet 1:17, 18.

Mt 18:10. Beware that you don't look down upon a single one of these little children. For I tell you that in heaven their angels have constant access to my Father. [19]I also tell you this—if two of you agree down here on earth concerning anything you ask for, my Father in heaven will do it for you.

Mt 20:23. But I have no right to say who will sit on the thrones next to mine. Those places are reserved for the persons my Father selects.

Mt 21:37. Finally the owner sent his son, thinking they would surely respect him. Lk 20:13.

Mt 26:53. "Don't you realize that I could ask my Father for thousands of angels to protect us, and he would send them instantly?" [63]Then the High Priest said to him, "I demand in the name of the living God that you tell us whether you claim to be the Messiah, the Son of God." [64]"Yes," Jesus said, "I am. And in the future you will see me, the Messiah, sitting at the right hand of God and returning on the clouds of heaven."

Mt 27:43. "He trusted God—let God show his approval by delivering him! Didn't he say, 'I am God's Son'?" [54]The soldiers at the crucifixion and their sergeant were terribly frightened by the earthquake and all that happened. They exclaimed, "Surely this was God's Son."

Mk 1:1. Here begins the wonderful story of Jesus the Messiah, the Son of God.

Mk 3:11. And whenever those possessed by demons caught sight of him they would fall down before him shrieking, "You are the Son of God!"

Mk 5:7, 8. It gave a terrible scream, shrieking, "What are you going to do to me, Jesus, Son of the Most High God? For God's sake, don't torture me!" Lk 8:28.

Mk 14:61. Then the High Priest asked him. "Are you the Messiah, the Son of God?" [62]Jesus said, "I am, and you will see me sitting at the right hand of God, and returning to earth in the clouds of heaven."

Mk 15:39. When the Roman officer standing beside his cross saw how he dismissed his spirit, he exclaimed, "Truly, this was the Son of God!"

Lk 1:32. "He shall be very great and shall be called the Son of God. And the Lord God shall give him the throne of his ancestor David." [35]The angel replied, "The Holy Spirit shall come upon you, and the power of God shall overshadow you; so the baby born to you will be utterly holy—the Son of God."

Lk 4:3. Satan said, "If you are God's Son, tell this stone to become a loaf of bread." [9]Then Satan took him to Jerusalem to a high roof of the Temple and said, "If you are the Son of God, jump off!"

41. Some were possessed by demons; and the demons came out at his command, shouting, "You are the Son of God." But because they knew he was the Christ, he stopped them and told them to be silent.

Lk 9:35. And a voice from the cloud said, *"This* is my Son, my Chosen One; listen to *him."*

Lk 10:22. I am the Agent of my Father in everything; and no one really knows the Son except the Father, and no one really knows the Father except the Son and those to whom the Son chooses to reveal him.

Lk 22:29. And because my Father has granted me a Kingdom, I, here and now, grant you the right [30]to eat and drink at my table in that Kingdom. [70]They all shouted, "Then you claim you are the Son of God?" And he replied, "Yes, I am." Mk 14:61.

Jn 1:1, 2. Before anything else existed, there was Christ, with God. He has always been alive and is himself God. [14]And Christ became a human being and lived here on earth among us and was full of loving forgiveness and truth. And some of us have seen his glory—the glory of the only Son of the heavenly Father! [18]No one has ever actually seen God, but, of course, his only Son has, for he is the companion of the Father and has told us all about him. [34]I saw it happen to this man, and I therefore testify that he is the Son of God. [49]Nathanael replied, "Sir, you are the Son of God—the King of Israel!" [50]Jesus asked him, "Do you believe all this just because I told you I had seen you under the fig tree? You will see greater proofs than this."

Jn 3:16. For God loved the world so much that he gave his only Son so that anyone who believes in him shall not perish but have eternal life. [17]God did not send his Son into the world to condemn it, but to save it. [18]There is no eternal doom awaiting those who trust him to save them. But those who don't trust him have already been tried and condemned for not believing in the only Son of God. [34]For this one—sent by God—speaks God's words, for God's Spirit is upon him without measure or limit. [35]The Father loves this man because he is his Son, and God has given him everything there is. [36]And all who trust him—God's Son—to save them have eternal life; those who don't believe and obey him shall never see heaven, but the wrath of God remains upon them.

Jn 5:19. Jesus replied, "The Son can do nothing by himself. He does only what he sees the Father doing, and in the same way. [20]For the Father loves the Son, and tells him everything he is doing; and the Son will do far more awesome miracles than this man's healing. [21]He will even raise from the dead anyone he wants to, just as the Father does. [23]So that everyone will honor the Son, just as they honor the Father. But if you refuse to honor God's Son, whom he sent to you, then you are certainly not honoring the Father. [26]The Father has life in himself, and has granted his Son to have life in himself, [27]and to judge the sins of all mankind because he is the Son of Man. [30]But I pass no judgment without consulting the Father. I judge as I am told. And my judgment is absolutely fair and just, for it is according to the will of God who sent me and is not merely my own. [32,33]But someone else, yes, John the Baptist, is making these claims for me too. . . . and I can assure you that all he says about me is true! [36]But I have a greater witness than John. I refer to the miracles I do; these have been assigned me by the Father, and they prove that the Father has sent me. [37]And the Father himself has also testified about me, though not appearing to you personally, or speaking to you directly."

Jn 6:27. "For God the Father has sent me for this very purpose. [38]For I have come here from heaven to do the will of God who sent me, not to have my own way. [40]For it is my Father's will that everyone who sees his Son and believes on him should have eternal life—that I should raise him at the Last Day. [46]Not that anyone actually sees the Father, for only I have seen him. [57]I live by the power of the living Father who sent me." [68]Simon Peter replied, "Master, to whom shall we go? You alone have the words that give eternal life, [69]and we believe them and know you are the holy Son of God."

Jn 7:16. So Jesus told them, "I'm not teaching you my own thoughts, but those of God who sent me. [28]But I am the representative of one you don't know, and he is Truth. [29]I know him because I was with him, and he sent me to you."

Jn 8:16. "For I have with me the Father who sent me." [19]"Where is your father?" they asked. Jesus answered, "You don't know who I am, so you don't know who my Father is. If you knew me, then you would know him too. [26]I could condemn you for much and teach you much, but I won't, for I say only what I am told to by the one who sent me; and he is Truth." [27]But they still didn't understand that he was talking to them about God. [28]So Jesus said, "When you have killed the Messiah, then you will realize that I am he and that I have not been telling you my own ideas, but have spoken what the Father taught me. [29]And he who sent me is with me—he has not deserted me—for I always do those things that are pleasing to him. [38]I am telling you what I saw when I was with my Father. But you are following the advice of *your* father.

[40]But instead you are trying to kill me—and all because I told you the truth I heard from God." [42]Jesus told them, "If that were so, then you would love me, for I have come to you from God. I am not here on my own, but he sent me. [49]For I honor my Father—and you dishonor me." [54]Then Jesus told them this: "If I am merely boasting about myself, it doesn't count. But it is my Father—and you claim him as your God—who is saying these glorious things about me."

Jn 10:15. Just as my Father knows me and I know the Father. [17]The Father loves me because I lay down my life that I may have it back again. [18]. . . For the Father has given me this right. [29]For my Father has given them to me, and he is more powerful than anyone else, so no one can kidnap them from me. [30]I and the Father are one. [36]Do you call it blasphemy when the one sanctified and sent into the world by the Father says, "I am the Son of God"? [37]Don't believe me unless I do miracles of God. [38]But if I do, believe them even if you don't believe me. Then you will become convinced that the Father is in me, and I in the Father.

Jn 11:4. But when Jesus heard about it he said, "The purpose of his illness is not death, but for the glory of God. I, the Son of God, will receive glory from this situation." [27]"Yes, Master," she told him "I believe you are the Messiah, the Son of God, the one we have so long awaited." [41]Then Jesus . . . said, "Father, thank you for hearing me."

Jn 12:49. For these are not my own ideas, but I have told you what the Father said to tell you. [50]And I know his instructions lead to eternal life; so whatever he tells me to say, I say!

Jn 13:3. Jesus knew that the Father had given him everything and that he had come from God and would return to God. And how he loved his disciples!

Jn 14:7. "If you had known who I am, then you would have known who my Father is. From now on you know him—and have seen him!" [9]Jesus replied, "Don't you even yet know who I am, Philip, even after all this time I have been with you? Anyone who has seen me has seen the Father! So why are you asking to see him? [10]Don't you believe that I am in the Father and the Father is in me? The words I say are not my own but are from my Father who lives in me. And he does his work through me. [11]Just believe it—that I am in the Father and the Father is in me. Or else believe it because of the mighty miracles you have seen me do. [13]You can ask him for *anything,* using my name, and I will do it, for this will bring praise to the Father because of what I, the Son, will do for you. [16]I will ask the Father and he will give you another Comforter, and he will never leave you. [20]When I come back to life again, you will know that I am in my Father, and you in me, and I in you. [24]And remember, I am not making up this answer to your question! It is the answer given by the Father who sent me. [28]If you really love me, you will be very happy for me, for now I can go to the Father, who is greater than I am. [31]But I will freely do what the Father requires of me so that the world will know that I love the Father."

Jn 15:1. I am the true Vine, and my Father is the Gardener. [8]My true disciples produce bountiful harvests. This brings great glory to my Father. [9]I have loved you even as the Father has loved me. Live within my love. [10]When you obey me you are living in my love, just as I obey my Father and live in his love. [23]Anyone hating me is also hating my Father. [24] . . . But as it is, they saw these miracles and yet they hated both of us—me and my Father.

Jn 16:5. But now I am going away to the one who sent me. [15]All the Father's glory is mine. [27]For the Father himself loves you dearly because you love me and believe that I came from the Father. [28]Yes, I came from the Father into the world and will leave the world and return to the Father. [32]Yet I will not be alone, for the Father is with me.

Jn 17:1. Father, the time has come. Reveal the glory of your Son so that he can give the glory back to you. *vs.* 1–26.

Jn 19:7. They replied, "By our laws he ought to die because he called himself the Son of God."

Jn 20:17. "For I haven't yet ascended to the Father. But go find my brothers and tell them that I ascend to my Father and your Father, my God and your God. [21]As the Father has sent me, even so I am sending you." [31]But these are recorded so that you will believe that he is the Messiah, the Son of God, and that believing in him you will have life.

Acts 13:33. God's promise to our ancestors has come true in our own time, in that God brought Jesus back to life again. This is what the second Psalm is talking about when it says concerning Jesus, "Today I have honored you as my son."

Rom 1:3. It is the Good News about his Son, Jesus Christ our Lord, who came as a human baby, born into King David's royal family line; [4]and by being raised from the dead he was proved to be the mighty Son of God, with the holy nature of God himself. [9]God knows how often I pray for you. Day and night I bring you and your needs in prayer to the one I serve with all my might, telling others the Good News about his Son.

Rom 8:3. We aren't saved from sin's grasp by knowing the commandments of God, because we can't and don't keep them, but God put into effect a different plan to save us. He sent his own Son in a human body like ours—except that ours are sinful—and destroyed sin's control over us by giving himself as a sacrifice for our sins. [29]From the very beginning God decided that those who came to him—and all along he knew who would—should become like his Son, so that his Son would be the First, with many brothers. [32]Since he did not spare even his own Son for us but gave him up for us all.

1 Cor 1:9. God will surely do this for you, for he always does just what he says, and he is the one who invited you into this wonderful friendship with his Son, even Christ our Lord.

1 Cor 15:24. After that the end will come when he will turn the kingdom over to God the Father. [27]For the rule and authority over all things has

been given to Christ by his Father; except, of course, Christ does not rule over the Father himself, who gave him this power to rule. [28]When Christ has finally won the battle against all his enemies, then he, the Son of God, will put himself also under his Father's orders, so that God who has given him the victory over everything else will be utterly supreme.

2 Cor 1:3. What a wonderful God we have—he is the Father of our Lord Jesus Christ. [19]Timothy and Silvanus and I have been telling you about Jesus Christ the Son of God. He isn't one to say "yes" when he means "no." He always does exactly what he says.

Gal 1:16. To reveal his Son within me so that I could go to the Gentiles and show them the Good News about Jesus.

Gal 4:4. But when the right time came, the time God decided on, he sent his Son, born of a woman, born as a Jew.

Eph 1:3. How we praise God, the Father of our Lord Jesus Christ.

Eph 3:14. When I think of the wisdom and scope of his plan I fall down on my knees and pray to the Father of all the great family of God.

Col 1:3. Whenever we pray for you we always begin by giving thanks to God the Father of our Lord Jesus Christ. [15]Christ is the exact likeness of the unseen God. He existed before God made anything at all. [19]For God wanted all of himself to be in his Son.

Col 3:17. And whatever you do or say, let it be as a representative of the Lord Jesus, and come with him into the presence of God the Father to give him your thanks.

1 Thess 1:10. And they speak of how you are looking forward to the return of God's Son from heaven—Jesus, whom God brought back to life—and he is our only Savior from God's terrible anger against sin.

Heb 1:2. But now in these days he [God] has spoken to us through his Son to whom he has given everything, and through whom he made the world and everything there is. [3]God's Son shines out with God's glory, and all that God's Son is and does marks him as God. He regulates the universe by the mighty power of his command. He is the one who died to cleanse us and clear our record of all sin, and then sat down in highest honor beside the great God of heaven. [5]For God never said to any angel, "You are my Son, and today I have given you the honor that goes with that name." But God said it about Jesus. Another time he said, "I am his Father and he is my Son."

Heb 4:14. But Jesus the Son of God is our great High Priest who has gone to heaven itself to help us; therefore let us never stop trusting him.

Heb 5:5. That is why Christ did not elect himself to the honor of being High Priest; no, he was chosen by God. God said to him, "My Son, today I have honored you." [8]And even though Jesus was God's Son, he had to learn from experience what it was like to obey, when obeying meant suffering. [10]For remember that God has chosen him to be a High Priest with the same rank as Melchizedek.

Heb 6:6. You cannot bring yourself to repent again if you have nailed the Son of God to the cross again by rejecting him, holding him up to mocking and to public shame.

Heb 7:3. Melchizedek had no father or mother and there is no record of any of his ancestors. He was never born and he never died but his life is like that of the Son of God—a priest forever.

Heb 10:29. Think how much more terrible the punishment will be for those who have trampled underfoot the Son of God and treated his cleansing blood as though it were common and unhallowed, and insulted and outraged the Holy Spirit who brings God's mercy to his people.

1 Jn 1:7. But if we are living in the light of God's presence, just as Christ does, then we have wonderful fellowship and joy with each other, and the blood of Jesus his Son cleanses us from every sin.

1 Jn 2:22. And who is the greatest liar? The one who says that Jesus is not Christ. Such a person is antichrist, for he does not believe in God the Father and in his Son. [23]For a person who doesn't believe in Christ, God's Son, can't have God the Father either. But he who has Christ, God's Son, has God the Father also. [24]So keep on believing what you have been taught from the beginning. If you do, you will always be in close fellowship with both God the Father and his Son.

1 Jn 3:8. But the Son of God came to destroy these works of the devil. [23]And this is what God says we must do: Believe on the name of his Son Jesus Christ, and love one another.

1 Jn 4:9. God showed how much he loved us by sending his only Son into this wicked world to bring to us eternal life through his death. [10]In this act we see what real love is: it is not our love for God, but his love for us when he sent his Son to satisfy God's anger against our sins. [14]And furthermore, we have seen with our own eyes and now tell all the world that God sent his Son to be their Savior.

1 Jn 5:5. But who could possibly fight and win this battle except by believing that Jesus is truly the Son of God? [9]We believe men who witness in our courts, and so surely we can believe whatever God declares. And God declares that Jesus is his Son. [10]All who believe this know in their hearts that it is true. If anyone doesn't believe this, he is actually calling God a liar, because he doesn't believe what God has said about his Son. [13]I have written this to you who believe in the Son of God so that you may know you have eternal life. [20]And we know that Christ, God's Son, has come to help us understand and find the true God. And now we are in God because we are in Jesus Christ his Son, who is the only true God; and he is eternal Life.

2 Jn 1:3. God the Father and Jesus Christ his Son will bless us with great mercy and much peace, and with truth and love.

Rev 2:18. *Write this letter to the leader of the church in Thyatira:* This is a message from the Son of God, whose eyes penetrate like flames of fire, whose feet are like glowing brass.

See *Jesus, Deity of, Relation of, to the Father,* above.

SON OF MAN. See *Humanity of,* above.

SOVEREIGNTY OF. See *Jesus, King, Sufferings of.*

SUFFERINGS OF. Mt 26:38. Then he told them, "My soul is crushed with horror and sadness to the point of death . . . stay here . . . stay awake with me." [39]He went forward a little, and fell face downward on the ground, and prayed, "My Father! If it is possible, let this cup be taken away from me. But I want your will, not mine." [40]Then he returned to the three disciples and found them asleep. "Peter," he called, "couldn't you even stay awake with me one hour? [41]Keep alert and pray. Otherwise temptation will overpower you. For the spirit indeed is willing, but how weak the body is!" [42]Again he left them and prayed, "My Father! If this cup cannot go away until I drink it all, your will be done." [43]He returned to them again and found them sleeping, for their eyes were heavy, [44]so he went back to prayer the third time, saying the same things again. [45]Then he came to the disciples and said, "Sleep on now and take your rest . . . but no! The time has come! I am betrayed into the hands of evil men!"

Mt 27:24. When Pilate saw that he wasn't getting anywhere, and that a riot was developing, he sent for a bowl of water and washed his hands before the crowd, saying, "I am innocent of the blood of this good man. The responsibility is yours!" [25]And the mob yelled back, "His blood be on us and on our children!" [26]Then Pilate released Barabbas to them. And after he had whipped Jesus, he gave him to the Roman soldiers to take away and crucify. [27]But first they took him into the armory and called out the entire contingent. [28]They stripped him and put a scarlet robe on him, [29]and made a crown from long thorns and put it on his head, and placed a stick in his right hand as a scepter and knelt before him in mockery. "Hail, King of the Jews," they yelled. [30]And they spat on him and grabbed the stick and beat him on the head with it. [31]After the mockery, they took off the robe and put his own garment on him again, and took him out to crucify him. [32]As they were on the way to the execution grounds they came across a man from Cyrene, in Africa—Simon was his name —and forced him to carry Jesus' cross. [33]Then they went out to an area known as Golgotha, that is, "Skull Hill," [34]where the soldiers gave him drugged wine to drink; but when he had tasted it, he refused. [35]After the crucifixion, the soldiers threw dice to divide up his clothes among themselves. [36]Then they sat around and watched him as he hung there. [37]And they put a sign above his head, "This is Jesus, the King of the Jews." [38]Two robbers were also crucified there that morning, one on either side of him. [39]And the people passing by hurled abuse, shaking their heads at him and saying, [40]"So! You can destroy the Temple and build it again in three days, can you? Well, then, come on down from the cross if you are the Son of God!" [41-43]And the chief priests and Jewish leaders also mocked him. "He saved others," they scoffed, "but he can't save himself! So you are the King of Israel, are you? Come down from the cross and we'll believe you! He trusted God—let God show his approval by delivering him! Didn't he say, 'I am God's Son'?" [44]And the robbers also threw the same in his teeth. [45]That afternoon, the whole earth was covered with darkness for three hours, from noon until three o'clock. [46]About three o'clock, Jesus shouted, "Eli, Eli, lama sabachthani," which means, "My God, my God, why have you forsaken me?" [47]Some of the bystanders misunderstood and thought he was calling for Elijah. [48]One of them ran and filled a sponge with sour wine and put it on a stick and held it up to him to drink. [49]But the rest said, "Leave him alone. Let's see whether Elijah will come and save him." [50]Then Jesus shouted out again, dismissed his spirit, and died. Mark 14;-15; Luke 22; 23; John 18; 19.

Mk 15:34. Then Jesus called out with a loud voice, "Eli, Eli, lama sabachthani?" ("My God, my God, why have you deserted me?")

Lk 2:34. A sword shall pierce your soul, for this child shall be rejected by many in Israel, and this to their undoing.

Lk 4:28. These remarks stung them to fury; [29]and jumping up, they mobbed him and took him to the edge of the hill on which the city was built, to push him over the cliff.

Lk 22:44. For he was in such agony of spirit that he broke into a sweat of blood, with great drops falling to the ground as he prayed more and more earnestly.

Lk 24:46. And he said, "Yes, it was written long ago that the Messiah must suffer and die and rise again from the dead on the third day."

Jn 4:6. Jesus was tired from the long walk in the hot sun and sat wearily beside the well.

Jn 11:33. When Jesus saw her weeping and the Jewish leaders wailing with her, he was moved with indignation and deeply troubled. [35]Tears came to Jesus' eyes.

Jn 12:27. Now my soul is deeply troubled. Shall I pray, "Father, save me from what lies ahead"? But that is the very reason why I came!

Jn 18:11. Shall I not drink from the cup the Father has given me?

Jn 19:28. Jesus knew that everything was now finished, and to fulfill the Scriptures said, "I'm thirsty."

Acts 3:18. But God was fulfilling the prophecies that the Messiah must suffer all these things.

Acts 17:3. Explaining the prophecies about the sufferings of the Messiah and his coming back to life, and proving that Jesus is the Messiah.

2 Cor 1:5. You can be sure that the more we undergo sufferings for Christ, the more he will shower us with his comfort and encouragement.

Phil 2:7. But laid aside his mighty power and glory, taking the disguise of a slave and becoming like men. [8]And he humbled himself even further, going so far as actually to die a criminal's death on a cross.

Phil 3:10. Now I have given up everything else —I have found it to be the only way to really know Christ and to experience the mighty power that brought him back to life again, and to find out what it means to suffer and to die with him.

Heb 2:9. But we do see Jesus—who for awhile was a little lower than the angels—crowned now by God with glory and honor because he suffered death for us.

Heb 4:15. This High Priest of ours understands our weaknesses, since he had the same temptations we do, though he never once gave way to them and sinned.

Heb 5:7. Yet while Christ was here on earth he pleaded with God, praying with tears and agony of soul to the only one who would save him from (premature) death. And God heard his prayers because of his strong desire to obey God at all times. [8]And even though Jesus was God's Son, he had to learn from experience what it was like to obey, when obeying meant suffering.

Heb 12:2. Keep your eyes on Jesus, our leader and instructor. He was willing to die a shameful death on the cross because of the joy he knew would be his afterwards; and now he sits in the place of honor by the throne of God. [3]If you want to keep from becoming fainthearted and weary, think about his patience as sinful men did such terrible things to him.

1 Pet 1:11. They wondered what the Spirit of Christ within them was talking about, for he told them to write down the events which, since then, have happened to Christ: his suffering, and his great glory afterwards. And they wondered when and to whom all this would happen.

1 Pet 2:21. This suffering is all part of the work God has given you. Christ, who suffered for you, is your example. Follow in his steps: [22]He never sinned, never told a lie, [23]never answered back when insulted; when he suffered he did not threaten to get even; he left his case in the hands of God who always judges fairly.

1 Pet 4:1. Since Christ suffered and underwent pain, you must have the same attitude he did; you must be ready to suffer too. For remember, when your body suffers, sin loses its power.

Rev 5:6. I looked and saw a Lamb standing there before the twenty-four Elders, in front of the throne and the Living Beings, and on the Lamb were wounds that once had caused his death.

Rev 19:13. He was clothed with garments dipped in blood, and his title was "The Word of God."

See *Jesus, Death of,* above; *Persecution, of Jesus.*

Prophecies Concerning. Ps 22:6. But I am a worm, not a man, scorned and despised by my own people and by all mankind. [7]Everyone who sees me mocks and sneers and shrugs. [8]"Is this the one who rolled his burden on the Lord?" they laugh. "Is this the one who claims the Lord delights in him? We'll believe it when we see God rescue him!" [11]Don't leave me now, for trouble is near and no one else can possibly help. [12]I am surrounded by fearsome enemies, strong as the giant bulls from Bashan. [13]They come at me with open jaws, like roaring lions attacking their prey. [17]I can count every bone in my body. See these men of evil gloat and stare; [18]they divide my clothes among themselves by a toss of the dice. [Mt 27:35; Mk 15:24; Lk 23:34; Jn 19:23, 24.] [19]O Lord, don't stay away. O God my Strength, hurry to my aid. [20]Rescue me from death; spare my precious life from all these evil men. [21]Save me from these lions' jaws and from the horns of these wild oxen. Yes, God will answer me and rescue me.

Ps 69:7. Though I am mocked and cursed and shamed for your sake. [8]Even my own brothers pretend they don't know me! [9]My zeal for God and his work burns hot within me. And because I advocate your cause, your enemies insult me even as they insult you. [20]Their contempt has broken my heart; my spirit is heavy within me. If even one would show some pity, if even one would comfort me!

Ps 109:25. I am a symbol of failure to all mankind; when they see me they shake their heads.

Isa 50:6. I give my back to the whip, and my cheeks to those who pull out the beard. I do not hide from shame—they spit in my face.

Isa 52:13. See, my Servant shall prosper; he shall be highly exalted. [14, 15]Yet many shall be amazed when they see him—yes, even far-off foreign nations and their kings; they shall stand dumbfounded, speechless in his presence. For they shall see and understand what they had not been told before. They shall see my Servant beaten and bloodied, so disfigured one would scarcely know it was a person standing there.

Isa 53:1. But, oh, how few believe it! Who will listen? To whom will God reveal his saving power? [Jn 12:38.] [2]In God's eyes he was like a tender green shoot, sprouting from a root in dry and sterile ground. But in our eyes there was no attractiveness at all, nothing to make us want him. [3]We despised him and rejected him—a man of sorrows, acquainted with bitterest grief. We turned our back on him and looked the other way when he went by. He was despised and we didn't care. [4]Yet it was *our* grief he bore, *our* sorrows that weighed him down. And we thought his troubles were a punishment from God, for his *own* sins! [5]But he was wounded and bruised for *our* sins. He was chastised that we might have peace; he was lashed—and we were healed! [6]*We* are the ones who strayed away like sheep! *We,* who left God's paths to follow our own. Yet God laid on *him* the guilt and sins of every one of us! [7]He was oppressed and he was afflicted, yet he never said a word. He was brought as a lamb to the slaughter; and as a sheep before her shearers is dumb, so he stood silent before the ones condemning him. [8]From prison and trial they led him away to his death. But who among the people of that day realized it was their sins that he was dying for—that he was suffering their punishment? [9]He was buried like a criminal in a rich man's grave; but he had done no wrong, and had never spoken an evil word. [10]Yet it was the Lord's good plan to bruise him and fill him with grief. But when his soul has been made an offering for sin, then he shall have a multitude of children, many heirs. He shall live again and God's program shall prosper in his hands. [11]And when he sees all that is accomplished by the anguish of his soul, he shall be satisfied; and because of what he has experienced, my righteous Servant shall make many to be counted righteous before God, for he shall bear all their sins. [12]Therefore I will give him the honors of one who is mighty and great, because he has poured out his soul unto death. He was counted as a sinner, and he bore the sins of many, and he pled with God for sinners. Lk 22:37.

Mic 5:1. Mobilize! The enemy lays siege to Jerusalem! With a rod they shall strike the Judge of Israel on the face.

Zech 11:12. And I said to their leaders, "If you like, give me my pay, whatever I am worth; but only if you want to." So they counted out thirty little silver coins as my wages. [13]And the Lord told me, "Toss it into the Temple treasury—this magnificent sum they value you at!" So I took the thirty coins and threw them in.

Zech 13:6. "And if someone asks, 'Then what are these scars on your chest and your back?' he will say, 'I got into a brawl at the home of a friend!' [7]Awake, O sword, against my Shepherd, the man who is my associate and equal," says the Lord of Hosts. "Strike down the Shepherd and the sheep will scatter, but I will come back and comfort and care for the lambs."

Mt 16:21. From then on Jesus began to speak plainly to his disciples about going to Jerusalem, and what would happen to him there—that he would suffer at the hands of the Jewish leaders, that he would be killed, and that three days later he would be raised to life again.

Mt 17:12. "And, in fact, he has already come, but he wasn't recognized, and was badly mistreated by many. And I, the Messiah, shall also suffer at their hands." [22,23]One day while they were still in Galilee, Jesus told them, "I am going to be betrayed into the power of those who will kill me, and on the third day afterwards I will be brought back to life again." And the disciples' hearts were filled with sorrow and dread.

Mt 20:17. As Jesus was on the way to Jerusalem, he took the twelve disciples aside, [18]and talked to them about what would happen to him when they arrived. "I will be betrayed to the chief priests and other Jewish leaders, and they will condemn me to die. [19]And they will hand me over to the Roman government, and I will be mocked and crucified, and the third day I will rise to life again." Mk 10: 32–34; Lk 18:31–33.

Mk 8:31. Then he began to tell them about the terrible things he would suffer, and that he would be rejected by the elders and the Chief Priests and the other Jewish leaders—and be killed, and that he would rise again three days afterwards.

Lk 2:34, 35. Simeon blessed them but then said to Mary, "A sword shall pierce your soul, for this child shall be rejected by many in Israel, and this to their undoing. But he will be the greatest joy of many others. And the deepest thoughts of many hearts shall be revealed."

Lk 9:22. "For I, the Messiah, must suffer much," he said, "and be rejected by the Jewish leaders—the elders, chief priests, and teachers of the Law—and be killed; and three days later I will come back to life again!"

1 Pet 1:11. They wondered what the Spirit of Christ within them was talking about, for he told them to write down the events which, since then, have happened to Christ; his suffering, and his great glory afterwards.

SYMPATHY OF. See *Compassion of; Love of.*

TEACHER. Mt 4:23. Jesus traveled all through Galilee teaching in the Jewish synagogues, everywhere preaching the Good News about the Kingdom of Heaven.

Mt 7:29. For he taught as one who had great authority, and not as their Jewish leaders.

Mt 11:1. When Jesus had finished giving these instructions to his twelve disciples, he went off preaching in the cities where they were scheduled to go.

Mt 21:23. When he had returned to the Temple and was teaching, the chief priests and other Jewish leaders came up to him and demanded to know by whose authority he had thrown out the merchants the day before.

Mt 22:16. They decided to send some of their men along with the Herodians to ask him this question: "Sir, we know you are very honest and teach the truth regardless of the consequences, without fear or favor." Mk 12:14; Lk 20:21.

Mt 23:8. Don't ever let anyone call you that. For only God is your Rabbi and all of you are on the same level, as brothers.

Mt 26:55. Then Jesus spoke to the crowd. "Am I some dangerous criminal," he asked, "that you had to arm yourselves with swords and clubs before you could arrest me? I was with you teaching daily in the Temple and you didn't stop me then."

Mk 4:1. Once again an immense crowd gathered around him on the beach as he was teaching, so he got into a boat and sat down and talked from there. Mt 5:1.

Lk 4:14. Soon he became well known throughout all that region [15]for his sermons in the synagogues; everyone praised him.

Lk 6:6. On another Sabbath he was in the synagogue teaching, and a man was present whose right hand was deformed.

Jn 3:2. "Sir," he said, "we all know that God has sent you to teach us. Your miracles are proof enough of this."

Acts 1:1. Dear friend who loves God: In my first letter I told you about Jesus' life and teachings.

TEMPTATION OF. Isa 7:15, 16. By the time this child is weaned and knows right from wrong, the two kings you fear so much—the kings of Israel and Syria—will both be dead.

Mt 4:1. Then Jesus was led out into the wilderness by the Holy Spirit, to be tempted there by Satan. [2]For forty days and forty nights he ate nothing and became very hungry. [3]Then Satan tempted him to get food by changing stones into loaves of bread. "It will prove you are the Son of God," he said. [4]But Jesus told him, "No! For the Scriptures tell us that bread won't feed men's souls: obedience to every word of God is what we need." [5]Then Satan took him to Jerusalem to the roof of the Temple. [6]"Jump off," he said, "and prove you are the Son of God; for the Scriptures declare, 'God will send his angels to keep you from harm,'. . . they will prevent you from smashing on the rocks below." [7]Jesus retorted, "It also says not to put the Lord your God to a foolish test!" [8]Next Satan took him to the peak of a very high mountain and showed him the nations of the world and all their glory. [9]"I'll give it all to you," he said, "if you will only kneel and worship me." [10]"Get out of here, Satan," Jesus told him. "The Scriptures say, 'Worship only the Lord God. Obey only him.' " [11]Then Satan went away, and angels came and cared for Jesus. Mk 1:12, 13; Lk 4:1–13.

Lk 22:28. Nevertheless, because you have stood true to me in these terrible days.

Jn 14:30. For the evil prince of this world approaches. He has no power over me.

Heb 2:18. For since he himself has now been through suffering and temptation, he knows what it is like when we suffer and are tempted, and he is wonderfully able to help us.

Heb 4:15. This High Priest of ours understands our weaknesses, since he had the same temptations we do, though he never once gave way to them and sinned.

TYPES OF. See *Types.*

UNCHANGEABLE. Heb 13:8. Jesus Christ is the same yesterday, today, and forever.

UNION OF, WITH THE RIGHTEOUS. See *Righteous, Unity of, with Christ.*

WISDOM OF. See *Omniscience of,* above.

WORSHIP OF. Mt 2:2. "Where is the newborn King of the Jews? for we have seen his star in far-off eastern lands, and have come to worship him." [11]Entering the house where the baby and Mary his mother were, they threw themselves down before him, worshiping.

Mt 9:18. As he was saying this, the rabbi of the local synagogue came and worshiped him. "My little daughter has just died," he said, "but you can bring her back to life again if you will only come and touch her."

Mt 14:33. The others sat there, awestruck. "You really are the Son of God!" they exclaimed.

Mt 15:25. But she came and worshiped him and pled again, "Sir, help me!"

Mt 28:9. "Good morning!" he said. And they fell to the ground before him, holding his feet and worshiping him. [16]Then the eleven disciples left for Galilee, going to the mountain where Jesus had said they would find him. [17]There they met him and worshiped him—but some of them weren't sure it really was Jesus!

Mk 3:11. And whenever those possessed by demons caught sight of him they would fall down before him shrieking, "You are the Son of God!"

Mk 5:6. When Jesus was still far out on the water, the man had seen him and had run to meet him, and fell down before him. [7, 8] . . . It gave a terrible scream, shrieking, "What are you going to do to me, Jesus, Son of the Most High God? For God's sake, don't torture me!"

Mk 11:9. He was in the center of the procession with crowds ahead and behind, and all of them shouting, "Hail to the King!" "Praise God for him who comes in the name of the Lord!" . . . [10]"Praise God for the return of our father David's kingdom . . ." "Hail to the King of the universe!" Mt 21:9; Jn 12:13.

Lk 4:41. Some were possessed by demons; and the demons came out at his command, shouting, "You are the Son of God." But because they knew he was the Christ, he stopped them and told them to be silent.

Lk 5:8. When Simon Peter realized what had happened, he fell to his knees before Jesus and said, "Oh, sir, please leave us—I'm too much of a sinner for you to have around."

Lk 23:42. Then he said, "Jesus, remember me when you come into your Kingdom."

Lk 24:52. And they worshiped him, and returned to Jerusalem filled with mighty joy.

Jn 5:23. So that everyone will honor the Son, just as they honor the Father. But if you refuse to honor God's Son, whom he sent to you, then you are certainly not honoring the Father.

Jn 9:38. "Yes, Lord," the man said, "I believe!" And he worshiped Jesus.

Acts 7:59. And as the murderous stones came hurtling at him, Stephen prayed, "Lord Jesus, receive my spirit." [60]And he fell to his knees, shouting, "Lord, don't charge them with this sin!" and with that, he died. Acts 1:24, 25.

1 Cor 1:2. *And to:* All Christians everywhere—whoever calls upon the name of Jesus Christ, our Lord and theirs.

2 Cor 12:8. Three different times I begged God to make me well again. [9]Each time he said, "No. But I am with you; that is all you need. My power shows up best in weak people."

Phil 2:10. That at the name of Jesus every knee shall bow in heaven and on earth and under the earth, [11]and every tongue shall confess that Jesus Christ is Lord, to the glory of God the Father.

1 Tim 1:12. How thankful I am to Christ Jesus our Lord for choosing me as one of his messengers, and giving me the strength to be faithful to him.

Heb 1:6. And still another time—when his firstborn Son came to earth—God said, "Let all the angels of God worship him."

2 Pet 3:18. But grow in spiritual strength and become better acquainted with our Lord and Savior Jesus Christ. To him be all glory and splendid

honor, both now and forevermore.

Rev 5:8. And as he took the scroll, the twenty-four Elders fell down before the Lamb, each with a harp and golden vials filled with incense—the prayers of God's people! [9]They were singing him a new song with these words: "You are worthy to take the scroll and break its seals and open it; for you were slain, and your blood has bought people from every nation as gifts for God. [12]"The Lamb is worthy" (loudly they sang it!) "—the Lamb who was slain. He is worthy to receive the power, and the riches, and the wisdom, and the strength, and the honor, and the glory, and the blessing." [13]And then I heard everyone in heaven and earth, and from the dead beneath the earth and in the sea, exclaiming, "The blessing and the honor and the glory and the power belong to the one sitting on the throne, and to the Lamb forever and ever." [14]And the four Living Beings kept saying, "Amen!" And the twenty-four Elders fell down and worshiped him.

Rev 7:10. And they were shouting with a mighty shout, "Salvation comes from our God upon the throne, and from the Lamb."

ZEAL OF.

Isa 59:17. He put on righteousness as armor, and the helmet of salvation on his head. He clothed himself with robes of vengeance and of godly fury.

Mt 4:23. Jesus traveled all through Galilee teaching in the Jewish synagogues, everywhere preaching the Good News about the Kingdom of Heaven. And he healed every kind of sickness and disease. Mt 9:35; Mk 6:6.

Mk 3:20. The crowds began to gather again, and soon it was so full of visitors that he couldn't even find time to eat. [21]When his friends heard what was happening they came to try to take him home with them. "He's out of his mind," they said.

Lk 2:49. "But why did you need to search?" he asked. "Didn't you realize that I would be here at the Temple, in my Father's House?"

Lk 4:43. But he replied, "I must preach the Good News of the Kingdom of God in other places too, for that is why I was sent." Mk 1:38.

Lk 8:1. Not long afterwards he began a tour of the cities and villages of Galilee to announce the coming of the Kingdom of God.

Lk 9:51. As the time drew near for his return to heaven, he moved steadily onward towards Jerusalem with an iron will.

Lk 12:50. There is a terrible baptism ahead of me, and how I am pent up until it is accomplished!

Lk 13:32. Jesus replied, "Go tell that fox that I will keep on casting out demons and doing miracles of healing today and tomorrow; and the third day I will reach my destination. [33]Yes, today, tomorrow, and the next day! For it wouldn't do for a prophet of God to be killed except in Jerusalem!"

Jn 2:17. Then his disciples remembered this prophecy from the Scriptures: "Concern for God's House will be my undoing."

Jn 4:32. "No," he said, "I have some food you don't know about." [34]Then Jesus explained: "My nourishment comes from doing the will of God who sent me, and from finishing his work."

Jn 9:4. All of us must quickly carry out the tasks assigned us by the one who sent me, for there is little time left before the night falls and all work comes to an end.

Acts 10:38. He went around doing good and healing all who were possessed by demons, for God was with him.

Rom 15:3. Christ didn't please himself. As the Psalmist said, "He came for the very purpose of suffering under the insults of those who were against the Lord."

1 Tim 6:13. I command you before God . . . and before Christ Jesus who gave a fearless testimony before Pontius Pilate.

JESUS JUSTUS A Christian in Rome, Col 4:11.

JETHER 1. Son of Gideon. Feared to kill the Midianite kings, Judg 8:20.

2. An Ismaelite who married David's sister, 1 Chron 2:17. Called *Ithra,* 2 Sam 17:25.

3. A son of Jada, 1 Chron 2:32.

4. A son of Ezra, 1 Chron 4:17.

5. A chief of the line of Asher, 1 Chron 7:38.

JETHETH A king of Edom, Gen 36:40–43; 1 Chron 1:51–54.

JETHRO Called *Reuel.* A priest of Midian. Moses spent 40 years of exile with, and married his daughter, Ex 21:15–22; 3:1; 4:18; Num 10:29.

JETUR Son of Ishmael, Gen 25:15; 1 Chron 1:28–31.

JEUEL 1. A descendant of Zerah, 1 Chron 9:6.

2. A Levite who cleansed the Temple, 2 Chron 29:13.

3. A son of Adonikam, an exile who returned to Jerusalem with Ezra, Ezra 8:2–14.

JEUSH 1. Son of Esau, Gen 36:5, 18; 1 Chron 1:35.

2. A Benjaminite, 1 Chron 7:10.

3. Son of Eshek, 1 Chron 8:39.

4. A Gershonite Levite, 1 Chron 23:10, 11.

5. Son of Rehoboam, 2 Chron 11:19.

JEUZ Head of a Benjaminite family, 1 Chron 8:8–10.

JEWELER Cuts precious stones, Ex 31:5; 35:33.

JEWELS Engagement presents of, Gen 24:53. Borrowed from Egyptians by Israelites, Ex 3:22; 11:2; 12:35. Dedicated to the Tabernacle, Ex 35:22; Num 31:50–52. Regarded by Jacob as a hindrance to holiness, Gen 35:4; Ex 33:4–6; Isa 3:18–21. Tokens of love, Ezk 16:11–13. Worn by men, Ezk 23:42. Exported from Sheba, 1 Kgs 10:2, 10; 2 Chron 9:9, 10; Ezk 27:22; Ophir, 1 Kgs 10:11.

FIGURATIVE. Prov 20:15; Isa 54:11, 12; Mal 3:17; Rev 17:4. Believers' works as, 1 Cor 3:12.

See *Bracelet; Chains; Earring; Pearl; Ring; Seal; Stones, Precious.*

JEWS The word is derived from Judah, and was originally applied to the people of the southern kingdom, Judah and Benjamin, 2 Kgs 16:6; 2 Chron 32:18. Later the term was used of all

Israelites. "Jewess" appears in Acts 16:1; 24:24; "Jewish folktales" are mentioned in Tit 1:14; "the Jewish religion" in Gal 1:13, 14. The Jews are distinguished from Gentiles and Christians, 1 Cor 10:32.

See *Israel.*

JEZANIAH See *Ja-azaniah, 1.*

JEZEBEL Daughter of Ethbaal, a Sidonian, and wife of Ahab, 1 Kgs 16:31. Was an idolatress and persecuted the prophets of God, 1 Kgs 18:3, 4, 13, 19; 2 Kgs 3:2, 13; 9:7, 22. Vowed to kill Elijah, 1 Kgs 19:1–3. Wickedly accomplishes the death of Naboth, 1 Kgs 21:5–16. Death of, foretold, 1 Kgs 21:23; 2 Kgs 9:10. Death of, at the hand of Jehu, 2 Kgs 9:30–37.

FIGURATIVE. Rev 2:20.

JEZER Son of Naphtali, Gen 46:23–25; Num 26:48–50; 1 Chron 7:13.

JEZI-EL A disaffected Israelite who joined David at Ziklag, 1 Chron 12:3–7.

JEZRAHIAH A choirmaster, Neh 12:42.

JEZREEL 1. A city in the south of Judah, Josh 15:48–62; 1 Sam 25:43; 27:2, 3.

2. A city of Issachar, Josh 19:17–23; 2 Sam 2:9. Ahab's residence in, 1 Kgs 18:45, 46; 21:1. Naboth's vineyard in, 1 Kgs 21:1. Joram's residence in, 2 Kgs 8:29. Israelites camp at, 1 Sam 29:1, 11. Jehu kills Joram, Jezebel, and the family and friends of Ahab at, 2 Kgs 9:15–37; 10:11. Prophecies concerning, Hos 1:4, 5, 11.

3. A valley, Josh 17:16–18. Place of Gideon's battle with the Midianites, Judg 6:33. Place of the defeat of the Israelites under Saul and Jonathan, 1 Sam 29:1, 11; 31:1–6; 2 Sam 4:4.

4. A descendant of Etam, 1 Chron 4:3, 4.

5. Figurative of Israel, Hos 1:4, 5, 11; 2:22.

JIDLAPH Son of Nahor, Gen 22:20–23.

JOAB 1. Son of David's sister, 1 Chron 2:16. Commander of David's army, 2 Sam 8:16; 20:23; 1 Chron 11:5, 6; 18:15; 27:34. Dedicated spoils of his battles, 1 Chron 26:28. Defeated the Jebusites, 1 Chron 11:5, 6. Defeats and kills Abner, 2 Sam 2:13–32; 3:27; 1 Kgs 2:5. Destroys all the males in Edom, 1 Kgs 11:15. (See Ps 60, title.) Defeats the Ammonites, 2 Sam 10:7–14; 1 Chron 19:6–15. Captures Rabbah, 2 Sam 11:1, 15–25; 12:26–28; 1 Chron 20:1, 2.

Procures the return of Absalom to Jerusalem, 2 Sam 14:1–24. Barley field of, burned by Absalom, 2 Sam 14:29–33. Pursues and kills Absalom, 2 Sam 18. Censures David for mourning the death of Absalom, 2 Sam 19:1–7. Replaced by Amasa as commander of David's army, 2 Sam 17:25; 19:13. Kills Amasa, 2 Sam 20:8–13; 1 Kgs 2:5. Causes Sheba to be put to death, 2 Sam 20:16–22. Opposes the census, 2 Sam 24:3; 1 Chron 21:3. Counts the people, 2 Sam 24:4–9; 1 Chron 21:4, 5; 27:23, 24. Supports Adonijah as successor to David, 1 Kgs 1:7; 2:28. Killed by Benaiah, under Solomon's order, 1 Kgs 2:29–34.

2. Son of Seraiah, 1 Chron 4:14.

3. An Israelite (or the name of two Israelites) whose descendants returned from Babylon to Jerusalem, Ezra 2:3–35; 8:2–14; Neh 7:8–38.

JOAH 1. Son of Asaph, 2 Kgs 18:18, 26; Isa 36:3, 11, 22.

2. A descendant of Gershom, 1 Chron 6:19–21; 2 Chron 29:12–14.

3. A son of Obed-edom, 1 Chron 26:4, 5.

4. Son of Joahaz, and one who repaired the temple, 2 Chron 34:8.

JOAHAZ Father of Joah, 2 Chron 34:8.

JOANAN An ancestor of Jesus, Lk 3:23–38.

JOANNA Wife of Chuza, Herod's steward, and a disciple of Jesus, Lk 8:3; 24:10.

JOASH 1. Son of Becher, 1 Chron 7:8.

2. Keeper of the olive oil supplies, 1 Chron 27:28.

3. Father of Gideon, Judg 6:11, 29, 31; 7:14; 8:32.

4. Son of Ahab, king of Israel, 1 Kgs 22:26; 2 Chron 18:25.

5. Son of Ahaziah and king of Judah. Saved from his grandmother by Jehosheba, his aunt, and hidden for six years, 2 Kgs 11:1–3; 2 Chron 22:11, 12. Anointed king by the priest, Jehoiada, 2 Kgs 11:12–21; 2 Chron 23. Righteousness of, under influence of Jehoiada, 2 Kgs 12:2; 2 Chron 24:2. Repaired the temple, 2 Kgs 12:4–16; 2 Chron 24:4–14, 27. Wickedness of, after Jehoiada's death, 2 Chron 24:17–22. Procured peace from Hazael, king of Syria, by gift of sacred objects from the temple, 2 Kgs 12:17, 18; 2 Chron 24:23, 24. Prophecy against, 2 Chron 24:19, 20. Put Jehoiada's son to death, 2 Chron 24:20–22; Mt 23:35. Conspired against and killed, 2 Kgs 12:20, 21; 2 Chron 24:25, 26.

6. A king of Israel and successor of Jehoahaz, 2 Kgs 13:9–25. Defeats Amaziah, 2 Kgs 13:12; 14:8–15; 2 Chron 25:17–24. Death of, 2 Kgs 13:13; 14:16.

7. A descendant of Shelah, 1 Chron 4:21, 22.

8. One of David's officers, 1 Chron 12:3–7.

JOB A man who lived in Uz, Job 1:1. Righteousness of, Job 1:1, 5, 8; 2:3; Ezk 14:14, 20. Wealth of, Job 1:2, 3. Trial of, by affliction of Satan, Job 1:12–19; 2:7–10. Fortitude of, Job 1:20–22; 2:10; Jas 5:11. Visited by Eliphaz, Bildad, and Zophar as comforters, Job 2:11–13. Complaints of, and replies by his three friends to, Job chapters 3–31. Job and Elihu, chapters 32–37. Replied to by God, Job chapters 38–41. Submission of, to God, Job 40:3–5; 42:1–6. Later blessings and riches of, Job 42:10–16. Death of, Job 42:16, 17.

JOBAB 1. Son of Joktan, Gen 10:26–30; 1 Chron 1:20–23.

2. A king of Edom, Gen 36:31–39; 1 Chron 1:44, 45.

3. A king of Madon, Josh 11:1–3.

4. Name of two Benjaminites of whom little is known, 1 Chron 8:8–10, 17, 18.

JOCHEBED Mother of Miriam, Aaron, and Moses, Ex 6:20; Num 26:58, 59. Nurses Moses when he is adopted by Pharaoh's daughter, Ex 2:1–9.

JOED A Benjaminite, Neh 11:7–9.

JOEL 1. Son of Samuel, 1 Sam 8:2; 1 Chron 6:28, 33–38; 15:17.

2. A Simeonite, 1 Chron 4:34–39.

3. A Reubenite, 1 Chron 5:4, 7, 8.

4. A Gadite, 1 Chron 5:12.
5. A Kohathite Levite, 1 Chron 6:33–38.
6. A descendant of Issachar, 1 Chron 7:3.
7. One of David's valiant men, 1 Chron 11:26–47. Called "Igal, son of Nathan," 2 Sam 23:24–39.
8. Name of two Gershonites, 1 Chron 15:4–10, 11; 23:8, 9; and 1 Chron 26:22.
9. Leader of Manasseh, 1 Chron 27:16–22.
10. A Kohathite who assisted in the cleansing of the temple, 2 Chron 29:12–14.
11. One of Nebo's family, Ezra 10:43.
12. Son of Zichri, Neh 11:7–9.
13. One of the twelve minor prophets, probably lived in the days of Uzziah, Joel 1:1; Acts 2:16. Declares the terribleness of God's judgments, Joel 1; 2:1–11. Exhorts to repentance, Joel 1:12–32. Pronounces judgments against the enemies of God, Joel 3:1–17. Sets forth the blessings of Israel, Joel 3:16–21.

JO-ELAH Son of Jeroham, 1 Chron 12:3–7.

JO-EZER A Korahite, who joined David at Ziklag, 1 Chron 12:3–7.

JOGBEHAH A city in Gad, Num 32:34–36; Judg 8:11.

JOGLI A leader of Dan, Num 34:16–28.

JOHA 1. A Benjaminite, 1 Chron 8:15, 16.
2. One of David's valiant men, 1 Chron 11:26–47.

JOHANAN 1. A Jewish captain, 2 Kgs 25:22–24. Warns Gedaliah against Ishmael, Jer 40:13–16. Ishmael defeated by, Jer 41:11–15. Sought prayers of Jeremiah, Jer 42:1–3. Disobeyed Jeremiah and forced him to go to Egypt, Jer 43:1–7.
2. Son of Josiah, 1 Chron 3:15.
3. A son of Eli-o-enai, 1 Chron 3:24.
4. A Levite, 1 Chron 6:4–15.
5. Two Israelites who joined David at Ziklag, 1 Chron 12:3–7, 8–13.
6. An Ephraimite, 2 Chron 28:12.
7. A returned exile, Ezra 8:2–14.
8. A priest, Neh 12:22, 23. Called also *Jehoharan,* Ezra 10:26.

JOHN 1. The Baptist: Prophecies concerning, Isa 40:3; Mal 4:5, 6; Lk 1:11–17. Miraculous birth of, Lk 1:11–20, 57–65. Lives in the desert, Mt 3:1; Mk 1:4; Lk 1:80; 3:1–3. Mission of, Mt 17:11; Mk 1:2–8; Lk 1:15–17, 76–79; 3:4–6; Jn 1:6–8, 15, 22–28, 31–34; 5:32–35; Acts 13:24, 25; 19:4. Ministry of, Mt 3:1–3; Mk 1:4; Lk 3:3; Jn 1:6–8. His influence upon the public mind, Mt 3:5, 6; 14:5; 21:32; Mk 1:5; 11:32; Lk 3:7, 15; 20:6; Jn 1:35–40. Testifies to the messiahship of Jesus, Mt 3:11, 12; Mk 1:7, 8; Lk 3:16, 17; Jn 1:15, 26–36; 3:23–36; 5:32, 33; 10:41; Acts 13:25. Teaches his disciples to pray, Lk 11:1; to fast, Lk 5:33. The baptism which he taught, see *Baptism.* Baptizes Jesus, Mt 3:13–16; Mk 1:9–11; Lk 3:21, 22; Jn 1:32. The testimony of Jesus concerning, Mt 17:12, 13; 21:32; Mk 9:12, 13; Jn 5:32–35; see below. Jesus' discourses upon. His ministry not attested by miracles, Jn 10:41. Reproves Herod because of his immorality; Herod imprisons him; beheads him, Mt 4:12, 13; 14:1–12; Mk 6:16–29; 9:12, 13; Lk 3:18–20. Sends two disciples to Jesus, Mt 11:2–6; Lk 7:18–23. Herod falsely supposes Jesus to be, Mt 14:1, 2; 16:14; Mk 6:14, 16; Lk 9:19. Character of, Mk 6:20; Jn 5:35. Jesus talks about, Mt 11:7–19; Lk 7:24–33. Simplicity of his life in the deserts, Mt 11:18; Mk 1:6; Lk 1:80. A Nazirite, Mt 11:18; Lk 1:15; 7:33.
2. The Apostle: Intimately associated with Jesus, Jn 13:23–26; 21:20; is present when Jesus performs the following miracles: Healing of Peter's mother-in-law, Mt 8:14, 15; Mk 1:29–31; raising of the daughter of Jairus, Mk 5:37; Lk 8:51; the two draughts of fishes, Lk 5:10; Jn 21:1–7; transfiguration, Mt 17:1; Mk 9:2; Lk 9:28. Is present with Jesus in the garden, Mt 26:37; Mk 14:33; Lk 22:39. Intolerance of, Mk 9:38; Lk 9:49, 50, 54–56. Civil ambitions of, Mt 20:20–24; Mk 10:35–41. Prepares the passover, Mt 26:18, 19; Mk 14:13–16; Lk 22:8–13. Present at the trial of Jesus before the high priest, Jn 18:15, 16; at the crucifixion, Jn 19:26, 27; at the tomb, Jn 20:2–8; when Jesus appeared himself at the Sea of Galilee, Jn 21; with Peter in the Temple, Acts 3:1–11. Lives in Jerusalem, Acts 1:13. Is entrusted with the care of Mary, mother of Jesus, Jn 19:26. Imprisoned by the rulers of the Jews, Acts 4:1–19. Sent by the church with the commission to Samaria, Acts 8:14–17. A pillar of the church, Gal 2:7–9. Writes to the churches, see the epistles of John. Writes his apocalyptic vision from Patmos, Rev 1:9. Prophecy concerning, Rev 10:11.
3. A relative of Annas the high priest, Acts 4:6.
4. Whose surname was Mark. See *Mark.*
5. Father of Peter, Jn 1:42; 21:15–17. Called *Jonah,* Mt 16:17.

JOIADA 1. A returned exile, Neh 3:6.
2. Son and successor of Eliashib in the high priesthood, Neh 12:10, 11, 22; called *Jehoiada* in Neh 13:28.

JOIAKIM A high priest, Neh 12:10, 11, 26.

JOIARIB 1. A returned exile, Ezra 8:16.
2. A descendant of Judah, Neh 11:4–6.
3. A priest who returned from Babylon, Neh 12:1–7, 12–21.
4. See *Jehoiarib.*

JOKDE-AM A city of Judah, Josh 15:48–62.

JOKIM A descendant of Shelah, 1 Chron 4:21, 22.

JOKME-AM 1. A Levitical city of Ephraim, 1 Chron 6:66–69.
2. See *Jokne-am.*

JOKNE-AM A Levitical city of Zebulun, Josh 12:8–24; 21:34, 35. Called *Jeokne-am* in Josh 19:11; and *Jokme-am* in 1 Kgs 4:8–19.

JOKSHAN Son of Abraham, by Keturah, Gen 25:1–3, 6; 1 Chron 1:32.

JOKTAN Son of Eber, Gen 10:25, 29; 1 Chron 1:19, 20–23.

JOKTHE-EL 1. A city of Judah, Josh 15:37–44.
2. A name given by Amaziah to Sela, a stronghold of Edom, 2 Kgs 14:7.

JONADAB 1. Nephew of David. His complicity with Amnon in his rape of Tamar, 2 Sam 13:3–5. Comforts David on death of Amnon, 2 Sam 13:32–35.
2. Called also *Jehonadab.* A Rechabite and com-

panion of Jehu, 2 Kgs 10:15–23. His sons refuse to drink wine in obedience to his command, Jer 35: 5–10, 16–19.

See *Rechabites.*

JONAH 1. A prophet of Israel, 2 Kgs 14:25. Sent by God to warn Nineveh, Jon 1:1, 2. Disobedience and punishment of, Jon 1:3–17. Repentance and deliverance of, Jon 2; Mt 12:39, 40. Brought Ninevites to repentance, Jon 3; Mt 12:41. Displeased with God's mercy to Nineveh; reproved, Jon 4. Is a sign, Mt 16:4; Lk 11:29, 30.

2. See *John, 5.*

JONAM An ancestor of Christ, Lk 3:23–38.

JONATHAN 1. A Levite of Bethlehem, who becomes a priest for Micah; accepts idolatry; joins the Danites, Judg 17:7–13; 18:1–30.

2. Son of Saul, 1 Sam 14:49. Victory of, over the Philistine garrison of Geba, 1 Sam 13:3, 4, 16; over Philistines at Michmash, 1 Sam 14:1–18. Under Saul's curse pronounced against any who might take food before he had revenge on his enemies, 1 Sam 14:24–30, 43. Rescued by the people, 1 Sam 14:43–45. Love of, for David, 1 Sam 18:1–4; 19:1–7; 20; 23:16–18. Killed in battle with Philistines, 1 Sam 31:2, 6; 1 Chron 10:2; 2 Sam 21:12–14. Buried by inhabitants of Jabesh-gilead, 1 Sam 31:11–13. Mourned by David, 2 Sam 1:12, 17–27. Son of, cared for by David, 2 Sam 4:4; 9; 1 Chron 8:34.

3. Son of Abiathar, 2 Sam 15:27. Acts as spy for David, 2 Sam 15:27, 28; 17:17–22. Informs Adonijah of Solomon's succession to David, 1 Kgs 1:42–48.

4. Nephew of David, kills a giant, and becomes one of David's chief warriors, 2 Sam 21:20, 21; 1 Chron 20:6, 7.

5. One of David's heroes, 2 Sam 23:24–39; 1 Chron 11:26–47.

6. A son of Jada, 1 Chron 2:32, 33.

7. Son of Uzziah, 1 Chron 27:25.

8. David's uncle and counselor, 1 Chron 27:32.

9. Father of Ebed, Ezra 8:2–14.

10. Son of Asahel, Ezra 10:15.

11. Called also *Johanan.* A descendant of Jeshua, Neh 12:10, 11, 22.

12. Name of two priests, Neh 12:12–21, 35.

13. A scribe, Jer 37:15, 16; 38:26.

14. Son of Kareah, Jer 40:8.

JOPPA A seaport, Josh 19:46; 2 Chron 2:16; Ezra 3:7. Passenger traffic from, Jon 1:3. Peter performs a miracle at, Acts 9:36–43; has a vision of a sheet let down from heaven at, Acts 10:9–18.

JORAH Head of a family of returned exiles, Ezra 2:3–35.

JORAI A Gadite, 1 Chron 5:13.

JORAM 1. A son of Toi, 2 Sam 8:9, 10. Called *Hadoram,* 1 Chron 18:10.

2. Called also *Jehoram.* King of Israel, 2 Kgs 1: 17; 3:1. King of Syria sends Naaman to, that he may be healed of his leprosy, 2 Kgs 5:1–27. Has war with the king of Syria, 2 Kgs 6:8–23; 7; 8:28, 29; 2 Chron 22:5, 6. Inquires for the particulars concerning Elisha's miracles, 2 Kgs 8:4, 5. Killed by Jehu, 2 Kgs 9:14–26.

3. A Levite, 1 Chron 26:25.

JORDAN A river in Palestine. Empties into the Dead Sea, Josh 15:5. Fords of, Gen 32:10; Josh 2:7; Judg 3:28; 7:24; 8:4; 10:9; 12:5; 2 Sam 2:29; 17: 22, 24; 19:15, 31, 32; 1 Chron 19:17, 18. Seasonal flooding of, 1 Chron 12:15. Miraculously divides for the passage of the Israelites, Josh 3; 4; 5:1; Ps 114: 3; of Elijah, 2 Kgs 2:6–8; of Elisha, 2 Kgs 2:14. Crossed by a ferryboat, 2 Sam 19:18. Naaman washes in, for the healing of his leprosy, 2 Kgs 5: 10–14. John the Baptist baptizes in, Mt 3:6; Mk 1: 5; baptizes Jesus in, Mt 3:13; Mk 1:9.

PLAIN OF. Gen 13:10–12. Israelites camped in, Num 22:1; 26:3, 4, 63. Solomon's foundry in, 1 Kgs 7:41–46; 2 Chron 4:17, 18.

JORIM An ancestor of Jesus, Lk 3:23–38.

JORKE-AM Descendant of Caleb, 1 Chron 2:44.

JOSECH An ancestor of Jesus, Lk 3:23–38.

JOSEDECH See *Jehozadak.*

JOSEPH 1. Son of Jacob, Gen 30:23, 24. Personal appearance of, Gen 39:6. His father's favorite child, Gen 33:2; 37:3; 4, 35; 48:22; 1 Chron 5:2; Jn 4:5, 6. His father's partiality for, excites the jealousy of his brothers, Gen 37:4, 11, 18–28; Ps 105:17; Acts 7:9. His prophetic dreams of his fortunes in Egypt, Gen 37:5–11. Sold to traders, Gen 37:26–28. Is falsely reported to his father as killed by wild animals, Gen 37:29–35. Is bought by Potiphar, an officer of Pharaoh, Gen 37:36. Is prospered of God, Gen 39:2–5, 21, 23. Is falsely accused, and thrown into prison; is befriended by the chief jailer, Gen 39:40; Ps 105:18. Is an interpreter of dreams: of the two prisoners, Gen 40:5–23; of Pharaoh, Gen 41: 1–37. Given a name by Pharaoh, Gen 41:45. Is promoted to authority next to Pharaoh at thirty years of age, Gen 41:37–46; Ps 105:19–22. Takes as his wife the daughter of the priest of Heliopolis, Gen 41:45. Provides against the years of famine, Gen 41: 46–57. Exports the produce of Egypt to other countries, Gen 41:56, 57. Sells the stores of food to the people of Egypt, exacting of them all their money, flocks and herds, lands and lives, Gen 47: 13–26. Exempts the priests from taxes, Gen 47:22, 26.

His father sends down into Egypt to buy grain, Gen 42; 43; 44. Reveals himself to his brothers; sends for his father; provides the land of Goshen for his people; and sustains them during the famine, Gen chapters 45; 46; 47:1–12. His two sons, Gen 41:50–52. See *Ephraim; Manasseh.* Mourns the death of his father, Gen 50:1–14. Exacts a promise from his brothers to take his remains to Canaan, Gen 50:24, 25; Heb 11:22, with Ex 13:19; Josh 24:32; Acts 7:16. Death of, Gen 50:22–26.

Kindness of heart, Gen 40:7, 8. His integrity, Gen 39:7–12; humility, Gen 41:16; 45:7–9; wisdom, Gen 41:33–57; piety, Gen 41:51, 52; faith, Gen 45: 5–8. Was a prophet, Gen 41:38, 39; 50:25; Ex 13:19. God's providence with, Gen 39:2–5; Ps 105:17–22. His sons conjointly called *Joseph,* Deut 33:13–17. Descendants of, Gen 46:19–22; Num 26:28–37.

2. Father of Igal the spy, Num 13:3–15.

3. Of the sons of Asaph, 1 Chron 25:2, 9–31.

4. A returned exile, Ezra 10:34–42.

5. A priest, Neh 12:12–21.

6. Husband of Mary, Mt 13:55; Mk 6:2, 3; Mt 1:18–25; Lk 1:27. His genealogy, Mt 1:1–16; Lk 3: 23–38. An angel appears and testifies to the innocency of Mary, Mt 1:19–24. Lives in Nazareth, Lk 2:4. Belongs to the city of Bethlehem, Lk 2:4. Goes to Bethlehem for the census, Lk 2:1–4. Jesus born to, Mt 1:25; Lk 2:7. Presents Jesus in the temple, Lk 2:22–39. Returns to Nazareth, Lk 2:39. Warned in a dream to escape to Egypt in order to save the child's life, Mt 2:13–15. Warned in a dream to return to Nazareth, Mt 2:19–23. Attends the annual feast at Jerusalem with his family, Lk 2:41–51.

7. Of Arimathea. Begs the body of Jesus for burial in his own tomb, Mt 27:57–60; Mk 15:42–47; Lk 23:50–56; Jn 19:38–42.

8. Two ancestors of Joseph, Lk 3:23–38.

9. Called also *Barsabbas,* surnamed *Justus.* One of the two persons nominated in place of Judas, Acts 1:21–23.

10. See *Joses.*

11. A Levite, surnamed *Barnabas* by the apostles, Acts 4:36.

JOSES Or *Joseph,* one of Jesus' brothers, Mt 13:55; 27:56; Mk 6:2, 3; 15:40, 47.

JOSHAH A descendant of Simeon, 1 Chron 4:34–39.

JOSHAPHAT 1. One of David's valiant men, 1 Chron 11:43.

2. A priest who assisted in bringing the ark from Obed-edom, 1 Chron 15:24.

JOSHAVIAH One of David's bodyguard, 1 Chron 11:26–47.

JOSHBEKASHAH Son of Heman, 1 Chron 25:4, 5, 9–31.

JOSHEB-BASSHEBETH See *Jashobeam, 1.*

JOSHUA 1. Called also *Hoshea.* Son of Nun, Num 13:3–15; 1 Chron 7:25–27. Closely associated with Moses, Ex 24:13; 32:17; 33:11. His zeal, Num 11: 28. Sent with others to see the promised land, Num 13:3–15. Makes favorable report, Num 14:6–9. Rewarded for his courage and fidelity, Num 14:30, 36–38; 32:12. Commissioned, ordained, and charged with the responsibilities of Moses' office, Num 27:18–23; Deut 1:38; 3:28; 31:3, 7, 23; 34:9. Divinely inspired, Num 27:18; Deut 34:9; Josh 1:5, 9; 3:7; 8:8. His life miraculously preserved when he made a favorable report of the land, Num 14:10, 11. Promises to, Josh 1:5–9. Leads the people into the land of Canaan, Joshua chapters 1–4; Acts 7:45; Heb 4:8. Renews the circumcision rite for the male population of Israel; reestablishes the passover; has a vision of the angel of God, Josh 5. Besieges and takes Jericho, Josh 6. Takes Ai, Josh 8:1–28. Makes a treaty with the Gibeonites, Josh 9:3–27. The kings of six surrounding nations unite against him, Josh 9:1, 2; make war on Gibeonites; are defeated and killed, Josh 10. Defeats seven other kings, Josh 10:28–43. Makes conquest of Hazor, Josh 11. Completes the conquest of the whole land, Josh 11:23. List of the kings destroyed by Joshua, Josh 12. Allots the land, Josh chapters 13–19. Sets up the tabernacle in Shiloh, Josh 18:1. Sets apart cities of refuge, Josh 20; 48 cities for the Levites, Josh 21. Exhortation of, before his death, Josh 23; 24. Survives the Israelites who refused to enter Canaan, Num 26:63–65. His portion of the land, Josh 19:49, 50. Death and burial of, Josh 24:29, 30. Esteem in which he was held, Josh 1:16–18. Faith of, Josh 6:16. Military genius of, as exhibited at the defeat of the Amalekites, Ex 17:13; at Ai, Josh 8; in Gibeon, Josh 10; at Hazor, Josh 11. Age of, at death, Judg 2:7–9.

2. An Israelite, 1 Sam 6:14, 18.

3. A mayor of Jerusalem, 2 Kgs 23:8.

4. Called also *Jeshua.* The high priest of the captivity, Ezra 2:2. Assists Zerubbabel in restoring the temple, Ezra 3; 4:1–6; 5; Hag 1:1, 12–14; 2:2.

Symbolical. Of the restoration of Israel, Zech 3; 6:9–15.

5. An ancestor of Jesus, Lk 3:23–38.

JOSIAH 1. King of Judah, 2 Kgs 21:24–26; 22:1, 2; 1 Chron 3:10–14; 2 Chron 33:25. Ancestor of Jesus, Mt 1:10, 11. Killed in battle with Pharaoh-neco, 2 Kgs 23:29, 30; 2 Chron 35:20–25. Lamentations for, 2 Chron 35:24, 25. Piety of: exemplified in his repairing the temple, 2 Kgs 22:3–7; 2 Chron 34:1–4. Solicitude when the copy of the law was discovered and read to him, 2 Kgs 22: 8–20; 2 Chron 34:14–33; in keeping a solemn passover, 2 Kgs 23:21–23; 2 Chron 35:1–19. Prophecies concerning, 1 Kgs 13:1–3. Destroys the altar places of idolatry, and all forms of idol worship, 2 Kgs 23: 3–20, 24, 25.

2. Son of Zephaniah, Zech 6:10, 11.

JOSIPHIAH Father of Shelomith, Ezra 8: 2–14.

JOTBAH A place in Judah, 2 Kgs 21:19, 20.

JOTBATHAH A camping place of the Israelites, Num 33:15–37; Deut 10:7.

JOTHAM 1. Son of Gideon, Judg 9:5, 56, 57. Rebukes the Shechemites in the parable of the trees, Judg 9:7–21.

2. Son of Azariah, king of Judah, 2 Kgs 15:5–7, 32–38; 1 Chron 3:10–14; 2 Chron 26:21–23; 27. Piety of, 2 Chron 27. The moral condition of Israel during his reign, Hos 4. Ancestor of Jesus, Mt 1:9.

3. Son of Jahdai, 1 Chron 2:47.

JOY Attributed to God, Deut 28:63; 30:9; Jer 32:41 In heaven, Lk 15:7, 10–32.

UNCLASSIFIED SCRIPTURES RELATING TO. Deut 12:18. Rejoice before the Lord your God in everything you do.

1 Sam 2:1. How I rejoice in the Lord! How he has blessed me! Now I have an answer for my enemies, for the Lord has solved my problem. How I rejoice!

1 Chron 16:27. Majesty and honor march before him, strength and gladness walk beside him.

2 Chron 7:10. Then, on October 7, he sent the people home, joyful and happy because the Lord had been so good to David and Solomon and to his people Israel.

Ezra 6:22. They, with the entire nation, ate the Passover feast and celebrated the Feast of Unleavened Bread for seven days. There was great joy throughout the land because the Lord had caused the king of Assyria to be generous to Israel and to assist in the construction of the Temple.

Neh 8:10. "It is a time to celebrate with a hearty meal, and to send presents to those in need, for the joy of the Lord is your strength. You must not be dejected and sad!" [12]So the people went away to eat a festive meal and to send presents; it was a time of great and joyful celebration because they could hear and understand God's words.

Neh 12:43. Many sacrifices were offered on that joyous day, for God had given us cause for great joy. The women and children rejoiced too, and the joy of the people of Jerusalem was heard far away!

Job 8:21. He will yet fill your mouth with laughter and your lips with shouts of joy.

Job 22:21. Quit quarreling with God! Agree with him and you will have peace at last! His favor will surround you if you will only admit that you were wrong. [26]Then you will delight yourself in the Lord, and look up to God.

Job 33:26. And when he prays to God, God will hear and answer and receive him with joy, and return him to his duties.

Ps 2:11. Serve the Lord with reverent fear; rejoice with trembling.

Ps 4:7. Yes, the gladness you have given me is far greater than their joys at harvest time as they gaze at their bountiful crops.

Ps 5:11. But make everyone rejoice who puts his trust in you. Keep them shouting for joy because you are defending them. Fill all who love you with happiness.

Ps 9:2. I will be glad, yes, filled with joy because of you. I will sing your praises, O Lord God above all gods.

Ps 13:5. But I will always trust in you and in your mercy and shall rejoice in your salvation. Ps 9:14.

Ps 16:5. The Lord himself is my inheritance, my prize. He is my food and drink, my highest joy! He guards all that is mine. [6]He sees that I am given pleasant brooks and meadows as my share! What a wonderful inheritance! [8]I am always thinking of the Lord; and because he is so near, I never need to stumble or to fall. [9]Heart, body, and soul are filled with joy. [11]You have let me experience the joys of life and the exquisite pleasures of your own eternal presence.

Ps 17:15. But as for me, my contentment is not in wealth but in seeing you and knowing all is well between us. And when I awake in heaven, I will be fully satisfied, for I will see you face to face.

Ps 19:7, 8. God's laws are perfect. They protect us, make us wise, and give us joy and light.

Ps 20:5. May there be shouts of joy when we hear the news of your victory, flags flying with praise to God for all that he has done for you. May he answer all your prayers!

Ps 21:1. How the king rejoices in your strength, O Lord! How he exults in your salvation. [6]You have endowed him with eternal happiness. You have given him the unquenchable joy of your presence.

Ps 28:7. He is my strength, my shield from every danger. I trusted in him, and he helped me. Joy rises in my heart until I burst out in songs of praise to him.

Ps 30:5. Weeping may go on all night, but in the morning there is joy. [11]Then he turned my sorrow into joy! He took away my clothes of mourning and gave me gay and festive garments to rejoice in. *v.* 12.

Ps 32:11. So rejoice in him, all those who are his, and shout for joy, all those who try to obey him. *vs.* 1, 2.

Ps 33:21. No wonder we are happy in the Lord! For we are trusting him. We trust his holy name.

Ps 35:9. But I will rejoice in the Lord. He shall rescue me!

Ps 36:8. You feed them with blessings from your own table and let them drink from your rivers of delight.

Ps 40:16. But may the joy of the Lord be given to everyone who loves him and his salvation. May they constantly exclaim, "How great God is!" Ps 70:4.

Ps 42:4. Take courage, my soul! Do you remember those times . . . when you led a great procession to the Temple on festival days, singing with joy, praising the Lord?

Ps 43:4. There I will go to the altar of God my exceeding joy, and praise him with my harp. O God—my God!

Ps 45:15. What a joyful, glad procession as they enter in the palace gates!

Ps 46:4. There is a river of joy flowing through the City of our God—the sacred home of the God above all gods.

Ps 51:8. And after you have punished me, give me back my joy again. [12]Restore to me again the joy of your salvation.

Ps 53:6. Only when the Lord himself restores them can they ever be really happy again. Ps 14:7.

Ps 63:5. At last I shall be fully satisfied; I will praise you with great joy. [6]I lie awake at night thinking of you—[7]of how much you have helped me—and how I rejoice through the night beneath the protecting shadow of your wings. [11]But I will rejoice in God. All who trust in him exult.

Ps 64:10. And the godly shall rejoice in the Lord, and trust and praise him.

Ps 68:3. But may the godly man exult. May he rejoice and be merry.

Ps 69:32. The humble shall see their God at work for them. No wonder they will be so glad! All who seek for God shall live in joy.

Ps 71:23. I will shout and sing your praises for redeeming me.

Ps 85:6. Oh, revive us! Then your people can rejoice in you again.

Ps 89:15. Blessed are those who hear the joyful blast of the trumpet, for they shall walk in the light of your presence. [16]They rejoice all day long in your wonderful reputation and in your perfect righteousness.

Ps 97:11. Light is sown for the godly and joy for

the good. [12]May all who are godly be happy in the Lord.

Ps 100:1. Shout with joy before the Lord, O earth! [2]Obey him gladly; come before him, singing with joy.

Ps 104:34. May he be pleased by all these thoughts about him, for he is the source of all my joy.

Ps 105:3. Glory in the Lord; O worshipers of God, rejoice. [43]So he brought his chosen ones singing into the Promised Land.

Ps 119:1. Happy are all who perfectly follow the laws of God. [2]Happy are all who search for God, and always do his will. [13]I have recited your laws, [14]and rejoiced in them more than in riches. [16]I will delight in them and not forget them. [55]I obey them even at night and keep my thoughts, O Lord, on you. [111]Your laws are my joyous treasure forever. [162]I rejoice in your laws like one who finds a great treasure. [165]Those who love your laws have great peace of heart and mind and do not stumble.

Ps 126:5. Those who sow tears shall reap joy. [6]Yes, they go out weeping carrying seed for sowing, and return singing, carrying their sheaves.

Ps 132:16. I will clothe her priests with salvation; her saints shall shout for joy.

Ps 138:5. Yes, they shall sing about Jehovah's glorious ways, for his glory is very great.

Ps 149:2. O Israel, rejoice in your Maker. O people of Jerusalem, exult in your King. [5]Let his people rejoice in this honor. Let them sing for joy as they lie upon their beds.

Prov 10:28. The hope of good men is eternal happiness.

Prov 13:9. The good man's life is full of light.

Prov 19:23. Reverence for God gives life, happiness, and protection from harm.

Prov 29:5, 6. Flattery is a trap; evil men are caught in it, but good men stay away and sing for joy. Prov 28:12.

Eccl 2:26. For God gives those who please him wisdom, knowledge, and joy; but if a sinner becomes wealthy, God takes the wealth away from him and gives it to those who please him.

Isa 9:3. For Israel will again be great, filled with joy like that of reapers when the harvest time has come, and like that of men dividing up the plunder they have won.

Isa 12:1. On that day you will say, "Praise the Lord! He was angry with me, but now he comforts me. [2]See, God has come to save me! I will trust and not be afraid, for the Lord is my strength and song; he is my salvation. [3]Oh, the joy of drinking deeply from the Fountain of Salvation!" [4]In that wonderful day you will say, "Thank the Lord! Praise his name! Tell the world about his wondrous love. How mighty he is!" [5]Sing to the Lord, for he has done wonderful things. Make known his praise around the world. [6]Let all the people of Jerusalem shout his praise with joy. For great and mighty is the Holy One of Israel, who lives among you.

Isa 25:9. In that day the people will proclaim, "This is our God, in whom we trust, for whom we waited. Now at last he is here." What a day of rejoicing!

Isa 29:19. The meek will be filled with fresh joy from the Lord, and the poor shall exult in the Holy One of Israel.

Isa 30:29. But the people of God will sing a song of solemn joy, like songs in the night when holy feasts are held; his people will have gladness of heart, as when a flutist leads a pilgrim band to Jerusalem to the Mountain of the Lord, the Rock of Israel.

Isa 35:1. Even the wilderness and desert will rejoice in those days; the desert will blossom with flowers. [2]Yes, there will be an abundance of flowers and singing and joy! [10]These, the ransomed of the Lord, will go home along that road to Zion, singing the songs of everlasting joy. For them all sorrow and all sighing will be gone forever; only joy and gladness will be there.

Isa 41:16. And the joy of the Lord shall fill you full; you shall glory in the God of Israel.

Isa 44:23. Sing, O heavens, for the Lord has done this wondrous thing. Shout, O earth; break forth into song, O mountains and forests, yes, and every tree; for the Lord redeemed Jacob and is glorified in Israel! Isa 49:13; 52:9.

Isa 51:11. The time will come when God's redeemed will all come home again. They shall come with singing to Jerusalem, filled with joy and everlasting gladness; sorrow and mourning will all disappear. Isa 56:7.

Isa 55:12. You will live in joy and peace. The mountains and hills, the trees of the field—all the world around you—will rejoice.

Isa 61:3. To all who mourn in Israel he will give: Beauty for ashes; joy instead of mourning; praise instead of heaviness. [7]Instead of shame and dishonor, you shall have a double portion of prosperity and everlasting joy. [10]Let me tell you how happy God has made me! For he has clothed me with garments of salvation and draped about me the robe of righteousness. I am like a bridegroom in his wedding suit or a bride with her jewels.

Isa 65:14. While they [my servants] sing for joy. [18]Be glad; rejoice forever in my creation. Look! I will recreate Jerusalem as a place of happiness, and her people shall be a joy! [19]And I will rejoice in Jerusalem, and in my people; and the voice of weeping and crying shall not be heard there any more.

Isa 66:10. Rejoice with Jerusalem; be glad with her, all you who love her, you who mourned for her. [11]Delight in Jerusalem; drink deep of her glory even as an infant at a mother's generous breasts. [12]Prosperity shall overflow Jerusalem like a river, says the Lord, for I will send it; the riches of the Gentiles will flow to her. [14]When you see Jerusalem, your heart will rejoice; vigorous health will be yours. All the world will see the good hand of God upon his people.

Jer 15:16. Your words are what sustain me; they are food to my hungry soul. They bring joy to my sorrowing heart and delight me. How proud I am to bear your name, O Lord.

Jer 31:12. They shall come home and sing songs of joy upon the hills of Zion, and shall be radiant over the goodness of the Lord—the good crops, the wheat and the wine and the oil, and the healthy flocks and herds. Their life shall be like a watered garden, and all their sorrows shall be gone. [13]The young girls will dance for joy, and men folk—old and young—will take their part in all the fun; for I will turn their mourning into joy and I will comfort them and make them rejoice, for their captivity with all its sorrows will be behind them. [14]I will feast the priests with the abundance of offerings brought to them at the Temple; I will satisfy my people with my bounty, says the Lord. [25]For I have given rest to the weary and joy to all the sorrowing. [26](Then Jeremiah wakened. "Such sleep is very sweet!" he said.)

Jer 33:6. Nevertheless the time will come when I will heal Jerusalem's damage and give her prosperity and peace. [10, 11]The Lord declares that the happy voices of bridegrooms and brides, and the joyous song of those bringing thanksgiving offerings to the Lord will be heard again in this doomed land. The people will sing: "Praise the Lord! For he is good and his mercy endures forever!" For I will make this land happier and more prosperous than it has ever been before.

Joel 2:23. Rejoice, O people of Jerusalem, rejoice in the Lord your God!

Nah 1:15. See, the messengers come running down the mountains with glad news.

Hab 3:18. Yet I will rejoice in the Lord; I will be happy in the God of my salvation.

Zeph 3:14. Sing, O daughter of Zion; shout, O Israel; be glad and rejoice with all your heart, O daughter of Jerusalem.

Hag 2:9. "And here I will give peace," says the Lord.

Zech 2:10. "Sing, Jerusalem, and rejoice! For I have come to live among you," says the Lord.

Zech 9:9. Rejoice greatly, O my people! Shout with joy! For look—your King is coming!

Zech 10:7. They shall be like mighty warriors. They shall be happy as with wine. Their children, too, shall see the mercies of the Lord and be glad. Their hearts shall rejoice in the Lord.

Mt 25:21. His master praised him for good work. "You have been faithful in handling this small amount," he told him, "so now I will give you many more responsibilities. Begin the joyous tasks I have assigned to you."

Lk 1:47. How I rejoice in God my Savior!

Lk 2:10. But the angel reassured them. "Don't be afraid!" he said. "I bring you the most joyful news ever announced, and it is for everyone!"

Lk 6:22. What happiness it is when others hate you and exclude you and insult you and smear your name because you are mine! [23]When that happens, rejoice! Yes, leap for joy! For you will have a great reward awaiting you in heaven. And you will be in good company—the ancient prophets were treated that way too!

Lk 15:6. When you arrived you would call together your friends and neighbors to rejoice with you because your lost sheep was found. [7]Well, in the same way heaven will be happier over one lost sinner who returns to God than over ninety-nine others who haven't strayed away! [8]Or take another illustration: A woman has ten valuable silver coins and loses one. Won't she light a lamp and look in every corner of the house and sweep every nook and cranny until she finds it? [10]In the same way there is joy in the presence of the angels of God when one sinner repents. Mt 18:13.

22. But his father said to the slaves, "Quick! Bring the finest robe in the house and put it on him. And a jeweled ring for his finger; and shoes! [23]And kill the calf we have in the fattening pen. We must celebrate with a feast, [24]for this son of mine was dead and has returned to life. He was lost and is found." So the party began. [25]Meanwhile, the older son was in the fields working; when he returned home, he heard dance music coming from the house, [26]and he asked one of the servants what was going on. [27]"Your brother is back," he was told, "and your father has killed the calf we were fattening and has prepared a great feast to celebrate his coming home again unharmed." [28]The older brother was angry and wouldn't go in. His father came out and begged him, [29]but he replied, "All these years I've worked hard for you and never once refused to do a single thing you told me to; and in all that time you never gave me even one young goat for a feast with my friends. [30]Yet when this son of yours comes back after spending your money on prostitutes, you celebrate by killing the finest calf we have on the place." [31]"Look, dear son," his father said to him, "you and I are very close, and everything I have is yours. [32]But it is right to celebrate. For he is your brother; and he was dead and has come back to life! He was lost and is found!"

Lk 24:52. And they worshiped him, and returned to Jerusalem filled with mighty joy, [53]and were continually in the Temple, praising God.

Jn 15:11. I have told you this so that you will be filled with my joy. Yes, your cup of joy will overflow!

Jn 16:20. The world will greatly rejoice over what is going to happen to me, and you will weep. But your weeping shall suddenly be turned to wonderful joy (when you see me again). [22]You have sorrow now, but I will see you again and then you will rejoice; and no one can rob you of that joy. [24]You haven't tried this before, (but begin now). Ask, using my name, and you will receive, and your cup of joy will overflow. [33]I have told you all this so that you will have peace of heart and mind. Here on earth you will have many trials and sorrows; but cheer up, for I have overcome the world.

Jn 17:13. I have told them many things while I was with them so that they would be filled with my joy.

Acts 2:28. You will give me back my life, and give me wonderful joy in your presence.

Acts 8:8. So there was much joy in that city! [39]And when they came up out of the water, the Spirit of the Lord caught away Philip, and the eunuch never saw him again, but went on his way rejoicing.

Acts 13:52. And their converts were filled with joy and with the Holy Spirit.

Acts 16:25. Around midnight, as Paul and Silas were praying and singing hymns to the Lord. [34]Then he brought them up into his house and set a meal before them. How he and his household rejoiced because all were now believers!

Rom 5:2. For because of our faith, he has brought us into this place of highest privilege where we now stand, and we confidently and joyfully look forward to actually becoming all that God has had in mind for us to be. [11]Now we rejoice in our wonderful relationship with God—all because of what our Lord Jesus Christ has done in dying for our sins—making us friends of God.

Rom 12:12. Be glad for all God is planning for you.

Rom 14:17. For, after all, the important thing for us as Christians is not what we eat or drink but stirring up goodness and peace and joy from the Holy Spirit.

Rom 15:13. So I pray for you Gentiles that God who gives you hope will keep you happy and full of peace as you believe in him. I pray that God will help you overflow with hope in him through the Holy Spirit's power within you.

2 Cor 1:12. We are so glad that we can say with utter honesty that in all our dealings we have been pure and sincere. [24]When I come, although I can't do much to help your faith, for it is strong already, I want to be able to do something about your joy.

2 Cor 6:10. Our hearts ache, but at the same time we have the joy of the Lord. We are poor, but we give rich spiritual gifts to others. We own nothing, and yet we enjoy everything.

2 Cor 7:4. I have the highest confidence in you, and my pride in you is great. You have greatly encouraged me; you have made me so happy in spite of all my suffering.

2 Cor 8:2. Though they have been going through much trouble and hard times, they have mixed their wonderful joy with their deep poverty, and the result has been an overflow of giving to others.

2 Cor 12:10. Since I know it is all for Christ's good, I am quite happy about "the thorn," and about insults and hardships, persecutions and difficulties; for when I am weak, then I am strong—the less I have, the more I depend on him.

Gal 5:22. But when the Holy Spirit controls our lives he will produce this kind of fruit in us: love, joy, peace.

Eph 5:18. Don't drink too much wine, for many evils lie along that path; be filled instead with the Holy Spirit, and controlled by him. [19]Talk with each other much about the Lord, quoting psalms and hymns and singing sacred songs, making music in your hearts to the Lord.

Phil 3:3. For it isn't the *cutting of our bodies* that makes us children of God; it is *worshiping him with our spirits.* That is the only true "circumcision." We Christians glory in what Christ Jesus has done for us and realize that we are helpless to save ourselves.

Phil 4:4. Always be full of joy in the Lord; I say it again, rejoice!

Col 1:11. We are praying, too, that you will be filled with his mighty, glorious strength so that you can keep going no matter what happens—always full of the joy of the Lord.

1 Thess 1:6. So you became our followers, and the Lord's; for you received our message with joy from the Holy Spirit in spite of the trials and sorrows it brought you.

1 Thess 5:16. Always be joyful.

Heb 10:34. You suffered with those thrown into jail, and you were actually joyful when all you owned was taken from you, knowing that better things were awaiting you in heaven, things that would be yours forever.

Heb 12:2. Keep your eyes on Jesus, our leader and instructor. He was willing to die a shameful death on the cross because of the joy he knew would be his afterwards; and now he sits in the place of honor by the throne of God.

Jas 1:2. Dear brothers, is your life full of difficulties and temptations? Then be happy.

Jas 5:13. And those who have reason to be thankful should continually be singing praises to the Lord.

1 Pet 1:8. You love him even though you have never seen him; though not seeing him, you trust him, and even now you are happy with the inexpressible joy that comes from heaven itself.

1 Pet 4:13. Instead, be really glad—because these trials will make you partners with Christ in his suffering, and afterwards you will have the wonderful joy of sharing his glory in that coming day when it will be displayed.

1 Jn 1:4. And if you do as I say in this letter, then you, too, will be full of joy, and so will we.

Jude 1:25. And he is able to keep you from slipping and falling away, and to bring you, sinless and perfect, into his glorious presence with mighty shouts of everlasting joy.

INSTANCES OF. Of Moses and the Israelites, when Pharaoh and his army were destroyed, Ex 15:1–22. Of Deborah and the Israelites, when Sisera was overthrown, Judg 5. Of Jephthah's daughter, when he returned from his victory over the Ammonites, Judg 11:34. Of Hannah, when Samuel was born, 1 Sam 2:1–11. Of Naomi, when Boaz showed kindness to Ruth, Ruth 2:20; 4:14. Of the Israelites: When Saul was presented as their king, 1 Sam 10:24; when David killed Goliath, 1 Sam 18:6, 7; when they went to Hebron to make David king, 1 Chron 12:40; when they took the ark from Kiriath-jearim, 1 Chron 13:8; when they brought the ark from the house of Obed-edom to Jerusalem, 1 Chron 15:16, 25, 28; when they made gifts to the Temple, 1 Chron 29:9; when they kept the dedication of the temple, and the Feast of Unleavened

Bread under Ezra, Ezra 6:16, 21, 22. Of the Jews, after hearing, anew, the word of God, Neh 8:9–18; when they turned away from idolatry, 2 Chron 15:14, 15; 23:18, 21; 29:30, 36; 30:21, 23, 26; when the wall of Jerusalem was dedicated, Neh 12:43; when the foundation of the second temple was laid, Ezra 3:11–13.

Of David, over the offerings of the leaders and people for the house of God, 1 Chron 29:10–19. Jews, over the hanging of Haman, Esther 8:15, 16, with 7:10.

Of Elizabeth, when Mary visited her, Lk 1:5–44. Of Mary, when she visited Elizabeth, Lk 1:46–56. Of Zecharias, when John was born, Lk 1:67–79. Of angels, when Jesus was born, Lk 2:13, 14. Of the shepherds, when they saw the infant Jesus, Lk 2:20. Of the Magi, Mt 2:10. Of Simeon, when Jesus was presented in the temple, Lk 2:28–32. Of the disciples, because the demons obeyed them, Lk 10:17. Of the father, when his prodigal son returns, Lk 15:20–32. Of angels, when sinners repent, Lk 15:7, 10. Of the disciples, when Jesus triumphantly entered Jerusalem, Mt 21:8, 9: Mk 11:8–10. Of the women who returned from the Lord's tomb, Mt 28:8. Of the disciples, after the resurrection of Jesus, Lk 24:41. Of the disciples in the temple after the ascension of Jesus, Lk 24:53. Of the disciples in the temple because they had received the gift of the Holy Spirit, Acts 2:46, 47. Of the lame man, healed by Peter, Acts 3:7, 8. Of Paul, when he went up to Jerusalem, Acts 20:22–24. Of Paul and Silas, in the jail at Philippi, Acts 16:25. Of Rhoda, when she heard Peter at the gate, Acts 12:14. Of the disciples at Jerusalem, when Peter told them about the conversion of Cornelius and other Gentiles, Acts 11:18. Of Barnabas, when he saw the success of the gospel at Antioch, Acts 11:22, 23. Of Paul and the Corinthians, because the excommunicated member repented, 2 Cor 1:24; 2:3. Of Paul and Titus, because of the hospitality of the Corinthians, 2 Cor 7:13, with 8:6; Rom 15:32; 1 Cor 16:18. Of the Macedonians, when they made a contribution for the Christians at Jerusalem, 2 Cor 8:2. Of Paul when he prayed for the Philippians, Phil 1:4. Of Thessalonians, when they believed Paul's message, 1 Thess 1:6. Of Paul, rejoicing over his converts, 1 Thess 2:19, 20; 3:9; Philemon 1:7. Of early Christians, when they believed in Jesus, 1 Pet 1:8, 9.

OF THE WICKED. Job 20:5. The triumph of the wicked has been short-lived, and the joy of the godless but for a moment?

Prov 15:21. If a man enjoys folly, something is wrong! The sensible stay on the pathways of right.

Eccl 2:10. Anything I wanted, I took, and did not restrain myself from any joy. I even found great pleasure in hard work. This pleasure was, indeed, my only reward for all my labors.

Eccl 11:8. If a person lives to be very old, let him rejoice in every day of life, but let him also remember that eternity is far longer, and that everything down here is futile in comparison. [9]Young man, it's wonderful to be young! Enjoy every minute of it! Do all you want to; take in everything, but realize that you must account to God for everything you do.

Isa 16:10. Gone now is the gladness, gone the joy of harvest. The happy singing in the vineyards will be heard no more; the treading out of the grapes in the wine presses has ceased forever. I have ended all their harvest joys.

Jas 4:9. Let there be tears for the wrong things you have done. Let there be sorrow and sincere grief. Let there be sadness instead of laughter, and gloom instead of joy.

See *Happiness; Praise; Thanksgiving.*

JOZABAD 1. A famous archer who joined David at Ziklag, 1 Chron 12:3–7.

2. Two men of Manasseh, 1 Chron 12:20.

3. Two Levites, 2 Chron 31:12, 13; 35:9.

4. Son of Jeshua, Ezra 8:33.

5. A priest, Ezra 10:22.

6. Three Levites, Ezra 10:23; Neh 8:7, 8; 11:15–17.

JOZACHAR One of the two servants of Joash, king of Judah, who assassinated him in Millo, 2 Kgs 12:21. Called *Zabad,* 2 Chron 24:26.

JOZADAK See *Jehozadak.*

JUBAL Inventor of musical instruments, Gen 4:21.

JUBILEE Called *The Year of Release,* Ezk 46:17.

LAWS CONCERNING. Lev 25:8. Every fiftieth year, [9]on the Day of Atonement, let the trumpets blow loud and long throughout the land. [10]For the fiftieth year shall be holy, a time to proclaim liberty throughout the land to all enslaved debtors, and a time for the canceling of all public and private debts. It shall be a year when all the family estates sold to others shall be returned to the original owners or their heirs. [11]What a happy year it will be! In it you shall not sow, nor gather crops nor grapes; [12]for it is a holy Year of Jubilee for you. That year your food shall be the volunteer crops that grow wild in the fields. [13]Yes, during the Year of Jubilee everyone shall return home to his original family possession; if he has sold it, it shall be his again! [14-16]Because of this, if the land is sold or bought during the preceding forty-nine years, a fair price shall be arrived at by counting the number of years until the Jubilee. If the Jubilee is many years away, the price will be high; if few years, the price will be low; for what you are really doing is selling the number of crops the new owner will get from the land before it is returned to you. [17, 18]You must fear your God and not overcharge! For I am Jehovah. Obey my laws if you want to live safely in the land. [19]When you obey, the land will yield bumper crops and you can eat your fill in safety. [20]But you will ask, "What shall we eat the seventh year, since we are not allowed to plant or harvest crops that year?" [21, 22]The answer is, "I will bless you with bumper crops the sixth year that will last you until the crops of the eighth year are harvested!" [23]And remember, the land is mine, so you may not sell it permanently. You are merely my tenants and share-croppers! [24]In every contract of sale there must be a stipulation that the land can be redeemed at any time by the seller. [25]If anyone becomes poor and sells some of his land, then his nearest relatives may redeem it. [26]If there is no one else to redeem it, and he himself gets together enough money, [27]then he may always buy it back at a price proportionate to the number of harvests until the Jubilee, and the owner must accept the money and return the land to him. [28]But if the original owner is not able to redeem it, then it shall belong to the new owner until the Year of Jubilee; but at the Jubilee year it must be returned again. [29]If a man sells a house in the city, he has up to one year to redeem it, with full right of redemption during that time. [30]But if it is not redeemed within the year, then it will belong permanently to the new owner—it does not return to the original owner in the Year of Jubilee. [31]But village houses—a village is a settlement without fortifying walls around it—are like farmland, redeemable at any time, and are always returned to the original owner in the Year of Jubilee. [32]There is one exception: The homes of the Levites, even though in walled cities, may be redeemed at any time, [33]and must be returned to the original owners in the Year of Jubilee; for the Levites will not be given farmland like the other tribes, but will receive only houses in their cities, and the surrounding fields. [34]The Levites are not permitted to sell the fields of common land surrounding their cities, for these are their permanent possession, and they must belong to no one else. [35]If your brother becomes poor, you are responsible to help him; invite him to live with you as a guest in your home. [36]Fear your God and let your brother live with you; and don't charge him interest on the money you lend him. [37]Remember—no interest; and give him what he needs, at your cost; don't try to make a profit! [38]For I, the Lord your God, brought you out of the land of Egypt to *give* you the land of Canaan, and to be your God. [39]If a fellow Israelite becomes poor and sells himself to you, you must not treat him as an ordinary slave, [40]but rather as a hired servant or as a guest; and he shall serve you only until the Year of Jubilee. [41]At that time he can leave with his children, and return to his own family and possessions. [42]For I brought you from the land of Egypt, and you are my servants; so you may not be sold as ordinary slaves, [43]or treated harshly; fear your God. [44]However, you may purchase slaves from the foreign nations living around you, [45]and you may purchase the children of the foreigners living among you, even though they have been born in your land. [46]They will be permanent slaves for you to pass on to your children after you; but your brothers, the people of Israel, shall not be treated so. [47]If a foreigner living among you becomes rich, and an Israelite becomes poor and sells himself to the foreigner or to the foreigner's family, [48]he may be redeemed by one of his brothers, [49]his uncle, nephew, or anyone else who is a near relative. He may also redeem himself if he can find the money. [50]The price of his freedom shall be in proportion to the number of years left before the Year of Jubilee—whatever it would cost to hire a servant for that number of years. [51]If there are still many years until the Jubilee, he shall pay almost the amount he received when he sold himself; [52]if the years have passed and only a few remain until the Jubilee, then he will repay only a small part of the amount he received when he sold himself. [53]If he sells himself to a foreigner, the foreigner must treat him as a hired servant rather than as a slave or as property. [54]If he has not been redeemed by the time the Year of Jubilee arrives, then he and his children shall be freed at that time. [55]For the people of Israel are *my* servants; I brought them from the land of Egypt; I am the Lord your God.

Lev 27:17. If a man dedicates his field in the Year of Jubilee, then the whole estimate shall stand; [18]but if it is after the Year of Jubilee, then the value shall be in proportion to the number of years remaining until the next Year of Jubilee. [19]If the man decides to redeem the field, he shall pay twenty percent in addition to the priest's valuation, and the field will be his again. [20]But if he decides not to redeem the field, or if he has sold the field to someone else (and has given to the Lord his rights to it at the Year of Jubilee), it shall not be returned to him again. [21]When it is freed in the Year of Jubilee, it shall belong to the Lord as a field devoted to him, and it shall be given to the priests. [22]If a man dedicates to the Lord a field he has bought, but which is not part of his family possession, [23]the priest shall estimate the value until the Year of Jubilee, and he shall immediately give that estimated value to the Lord, [24]and in the Year of Jubilee the field shall return to the original owner from whom it was bought.

Num 36:3. But if they marry into another tribe, their land will go with them to the tribe into which they marry. In this way the total area of our tribe will be reduced, [4]and will not be returned at the Year of Jubilee.

See *Sabbatical Year.*

JUDAH 1. Son of Jacob, Gen 35:23. Intercedes for Joseph's life when his brothers were about to kill him, and proposes that they sell him to the Ishmaelites, Gen 37:26, 27. Takes a wife, Gen 38:1–6. Lives at Chezib, Gen 38:3–5. His incest with his daughter-in-law, Gen 38:12–26. Goes down into Egypt for grain, Gen 43:1–10; 44:14–34; 46:28. Prophetic benediction of his father on, Gen 49:8–12. The ancestor of Jesus, Mt 1:2, 3; Rev 5:5.

2. Tribe of: Prophecies concerning, Gen 49:10. Census of, at Sinai, Num 1:20–46; 2:3–31; at Bezek, 1 Sam 11:8; 2 Sam 24:9; in the plains of Moab, Num 26:19–22. Place of, in camp and march, Num 2:3–31; 10:14. By whom commanded, Num 2:3–31. Moses' blessing on, Deut 33:7. Commissioned by God to lead in the conquest of the promised land, Judg 1:1–3, with verses 4–21. Make David king, 2 Sam 2:1–11; 5:4, 5. Chided by David for lukewarmness toward him after Absalom's defeat, 2 Sam 19:11–15. Accused by the other tribes of stealing the heart of David, 2 Sam 19:41–43. Loyal to David at the time of the insurrection led by Sheba,

2 Sam 20:1, 2. Is accorded the leadership forfeited by Reuben, 1 Chron 5:1, 2; 28:4; Ps 60:6, 7. Loyal to the family of David at the time of the revolt of the ten tribes, 1 Kgs 12:20. Inheritance of, Josh 15; 19:1, 9.

3. Name of two exiled priests, Ezra 10:23; Neh 12:8.

4. A Benjaminite, Neh 11:7–9.

5. A leader who assisted in the dedication of the wall of Jerusalem, Neh 12:34.

6. A priest who played the trumpet at the dedication of the wall, Neh 12:35, 36.

7. Son of Joseph and ancestor of Jesus, Lk 3: 23–38.

JUDAISM 1. The religion of the Jews, Acts 26:5; Gal 1:13, 14.

2. A corrupt form of Christianity, Acts 15:1; 21: 20–25; Galatians chapters 3–6.

See *Teachers, False.*

JUDAS 1. Surnamed *Iscariot.* Chosen as an apostle, Mt 10:4; Mk 3:19; Lk 6:16; Acts 1:17. Treasurer of the disciples, Jn 12:6; 13:29. His greed exemplified by his protest against the use of the jar of perfume, Jn 12:4–6; buy his bargain to betray Jesus for a sum of money, Mt 26:14–16; Mk 14:10, 11; Lk 22:3–6; Jn 13:1–3. His apostasy, Jn 17:12. Betrays the Lord, Mt 26:47–50; Mk 14:43–45; Lk 22: 47–49; Jn 18:2–5; Acts 1:16–25. Returns the money to the rulers of the Jews, Mt 27:3–10. Suicide of, Mt 27:5; Acts 1:18. Prophecies concerning, Mt 26:20–25; Mk 14:18–21; Lk 22:21–23; Jn 13:18–26; 17:12; Acts 1:16, 20, with Ps 41:9; Zech 11:12, 13.

2. One of the brothers of Jesus, Mt 13:55; Mk 6: 2, 3.

3. An apostle, son or brother of James, and writer of the epistle of Jude, Lk 6:14–16; Jn 14:22; Acts 1:14; Jude 1:1. Called also *Thaddaeus,* Mt 10: 2–4.

4. Of Galilee, who stirred up a rebellion among the Jews soon after the birth of Jesus, Acts 5:37.

5. A disciple who entertained Paul, Acts 9:11.

6. Surnamed *Barsabbas.* A Christian sent to Antioch with Paul and Barnabas, Acts 15:22–32.

JUDEA 1. Called also *Judah.* The southern division of Palestine. It extended from the Jordan and Dead Sea to the Mediterranean, and from Shiloh on the north to the wilderness on the south, Mt 4:25; Lk 5:17; Jn 4:46, 47, 54. In Luke 1:5 the term applies to all Palestine. In Matthew 19:1, Mark 10: 1, and Luke 23:5 it applies to the territory east of Jordan.

2. Wilderness of. Called *Beth-arabah,* Josh 15:6, 48–62. Assigned to Benjamin, Josh 18:21–28. John the Baptist preaches in, Mt 3:1; Lk 3:3.

JUDGE Appointed by Persians, Ezra 7:25. Kings and other rulers as, 2 Sam 8:15; 15:2; 1 Kgs 3:16–28; 10:9; 2 Kgs 8:1–6; Ps 72:1–4; Mt 27:11–26; Acts 23:34, 35; 24; 25:10–12. Priests and Levites as, Deut 17:9; 2 Chron 19:8; Ezk 44:23, 24; Mt 26: 57–62. Women as: Deborah, Judg 4:4, 5.

Held circuit courts, 1 Sam 7:16. Paul and Silas before, Acts 16:19, 22, 35, 38.

See *Court; Justice; Witness.*

CHARACTER OF, AND PRECEPTS RELATING TO. Ex 18:21. Find some capable, godly, honest men who hate bribes, and appoint them as judges, one judge for each 1000 people; he in turn will have ten judges under him, each in charge of a hundred; and under each of them will be two judges, each responsible for the affairs of fifty people; and each of these will have five judges beneath him, each counseling ten persons. [22]Let these men be responsible to serve the people with justice at all times. Anything that is too important or complicated can be brought to you. But the smaller matters they can take care of themselves. That way it will be easier for you because you will share the burden with them.

Ex 22:28. You shall not blaspheme God, nor curse government officials—your judges and your rulers.

Lev 19:15. Judges must always be just in their sentences, not noticing whether a person is poor or rich; they must always be perfectly fair.

Deut 1:12. But what can one man do to settle all your quarrels and problems? [13]So choose some men from each tribe who are wise, experienced, and understanding, and I will appoint them as your leaders. [14]They agreed to this; [15]I took the men they selected, some from every tribe, and appointed them as administrative assistants in charge of thousands, hundreds, fifties, and tens to decide their quarrels and assist them in every way. [16]I instructed them to be perfectly fair at all times, even to foreigners! [17]"When giving your decisions," I told them, "never favor a man because he is rich; be fair to great and small alike. Don't fear their displeasure, for you are judging in the place of God. Bring me any cases too difficult for you, and I will handle them."

Deut 16:18. Appoint judges and administrative officials for all the cities the Lord your God is giving you. They will administer justice in every part of the land. [19]Never twist justice to benefit a rich man, and never accept bribes. For bribes blind the eyes of the wisest and corrupt their decisions. [20]Justice must prevail. That is the only way you will be successful in the land which the Lord your God is giving you.

Deut 17:8. If a case arises that is too hard for you to decide—for instance, whether someone is guilty of murder when there is insufficient evidence, or whether someone's rights have been violated—you shall take the case to the sanctuary of the Lord your God, [9]to the priests and Levites, and the chief judge on duty at the time will make the decision. [10]His decision is without appeal and is to be followed to the letter. [11]The sentence he imposes is to be fully executed.

Deut 19:16. If anyone gives false witness, claiming he has seen someone do wrong when he hasn't, [17]both men shall be brought before the priests and judges on duty before the Lord at the time. [18]They must be closely questioned, and if the witness is lying, [19]his penalty shall be the punishment he thought the other man would get. In this way you will purge out evil from among you.

Deut 25:1–3. If a man is guilty of a crime, and the penalty is a beating, the judge shall command him to lie down and be beaten in his presence with up to forty stripes in proportion to the seriousness of the crime; but no more than forty stripes may be given lest the punishment seem too severe, and your brother be degraded in your eyes.

1 Sam 2:25. "Ordinary sin receives heavy punishment, but how much more this sin of yours which has been committed against the Lord?" But they wouldn't listen to their father, for the Lord was already planning to kill them.

1 Sam 8:3. But they were not like their father, for they were greedy for money. They accepted bribes and were very corrupt in the administration of justice.

1 Kgs 3:9. Give me an understanding mind so that I can govern your people well and know the difference between what is right and what is wrong. For who by himself is able to carry such a heavy responsibility?

2 Chron 19:5. He appointed judges throughout the nation in all the larger cities, [6]and instructed them: "Watch your step—I have not appointed you—God has; and he will stand beside you and help you give justice in each case that comes before you. [7]Be very much afraid to give any other decision than what God tells you to. For there must be no injustice among God's judges, no partiality, no taking of bribes." [8]Jehoshaphat set up courts in Jerusalem, too, with the Levites and priests and clan leaders and judges. [9]These were his instructions to them: "You are to act always in the fear of God, with honest hearts. [10]Whenever a case is referred to you by the judges out in the provinces, whether murder cases or other violations of the laws and ordinances of God, you are to clarify the evidence for them and help them to decide justly, lest the wrath of God come down upon you and them; if you do this, you will discharge your responsibility."

Ps 58:1, 2. Justice? You high and mighty politicians don't even know the meaning of the word! Fairness? Which of you has any left? Not one! All your dealings are crooked; you give "justice" in exchange for bribes.

Ps 72:1. O God, help the king to judge as you would, and help his son to walk in godliness. [2]Help him to give justice to your people, even to the poor. [4]Help him to defend the poor and needy and to crush their oppressors. *vs.* 12–14.

Ps 82:2. How long will you judges refuse to listen to the evidence? How long will you shower special favors on the wicked? [3]Give fair judgment to the poor man, the afflicted, the fatherless, the destitute. [4]Rescue the poor and needy from the grasp of evil men.

Prov 24:23. It is wrong to sentence the poor, and let the rich go free. Prov 18:5.

Isa 5:22. Woe to those who are "heroes" when it comes to drinking, and boast about the liquor they can hold. [23]They take bribes to pervert justice, letting the wicked go free and putting innocent men in jail.

Isa 28:5. Then at last the Lord of Hosts himself will be their crowning glory, the diadem of beauty to his people who are left. [6]He will give a longing for justice to your judges and great courage to your soldiers who are battling to the last before your gates.

Ezk 44:24. They will serve as judges to resolve any disagreements among my people. Their decisions must be based upon my laws. And the priests themselves shall obey my rules and regulations at all the sacred festivals, and they shall see to it that the Sabbath is kept a sacred day.

Dan 9:12. And you have done exactly as you warned us you would do, for never in all history has there been a disaster like what happened at Jerusalem to us and our rulers.

Mic 7:3. They go at their evil deeds with both hands, and how skilled they are in using them! The governor and judge alike demand bribes. The rich man pays them off and tells them whom to ruin. Justice is twisted between them.

Zeph 3:3. Her leaders are like roaring lions hunting for their victims—out for everything that they can get. Her judges are like ravenous wolves at evening time, who by dawn have left no trace of their prey.

See *Justice; Court.*

CORRUPT.

Instances of. Eli's sons, 1 Sam 2:12–17, 22–25. Samuel's sons, 1 Sam 8:1–5. The judges of Jezreel, 1 Kgs 21:8–13. Pilate, Mt 27:24; Mk 15:15, with 19–24. Felix, Acts 24:26, 27.

GOD AS. See *God, Judge.*

JUDGES OF ISRAEL. During the time when the land was ruled by judges, Judg 2:16–19; Acts 13:19, 20.

1. Othni-el, Judg 3:9–11.
2. Ehud, Judg 3:15–30.
3. Shamgar, Judg 3:31.
4. Deborah, Judg 4:5.
5. Gideon, Judg 6:11–40; 7; 8.
6. Abimelech, Judg 9:1–54.
7. Tola, Judg 10:1, 2.
8. Jair, Judg 10:3–5.
9. Jephthah, Judg 11; 12:1–7.
10. Ibzan, Judg 12:8–10.
11. Elon, Judg 12:11, 12.
12. Abdon, Judg 12:13, 14.
13. Samson, Judg chapters 13–16.

Eli judged Israel, 1 Sam 4:18. Samuel as judge, 1 Sam 7:6, 15–17. The sons of Samuel, 1 Sam 8:1–5.

Judges in prophecy, Isa 1:26; Mt 19:28; Lk 22:30.

JUDGING See *Uncharitableness.*

JUDGMENT OF GOD UNCLASSIFIED SCRIPTURES RELATING TO. 1 Chron 16:33. Let the trees in the woods sing for joy before the Lord, for he comes to judge the earth.

Job 14:17. You bundle them all together as evidence against me.

Job 21:30. That the evil man is usually spared in the day of calamity, and allowed to escape.

Job 31:13. If I have been unfair to my servants, [14]how could I face God? What could I say when he questioned me about it? [15]For God made me, and made my servant too. He created us both.

Ps 9:7, 8. But the Lord lives on forever; he sits upon his throne to judge justly the nations of the world.

Ps 50:3. He comes with the noise of thunder, surrounded by devastating fire; a great storm rages round about him. [4]He has come to judge his people. To heaven and earth he shouts, [5]"Gather together my own people who by their sacrifice upon my altar have promised to obey me." [6]God will judge them with complete fairness, for all heaven declares that he is just.

Ps 96:13. For the Lord is coming to judge the earth; he will judge the nations fairly and with truth! Ps 98:8, 9.

Eccl 3:17. I said to myself, "In due season God will judge everything man does, both good and bad."

Eccl 11:9. Young man, it's wonderful to be young! Enjoy every minute of it! Do all you want to; take in everything, but realize that you must account to God for everything you do.

Eccl 12:14. For God will judge us for everything we do, including every hidden thing, good or bad.

Ezk 18:20. The one who sins is the one who dies. The son shall not be punished for his father's sins, nor the father for his son's. The righteous person will be rewarded for his own goodness and the wicked person for his wickedness. [21]But if a wicked person turns away from all his sins and begins to obey my laws and do what is just and right, he shall surely live and not die. [22]All his past sins will be forgotten, and he shall live because of his goodness. [23]Do you think I like to see the wicked die? asks the Lord. Of course not! I only want him to turn from his wicked ways and live. [24]However, if a righteous person turns to sinning and acts like any other sinner, should he be allowed to live? No, of course not. All his previous goodness will be forgotten and he shall die for his sins. [25]Yet you say: "The Lord isn't being fair!" Listen to me, O people of Israel. Am I the one who is unfair, or is it you? [26]When a good man turns away from being good and begins sinning and dies in his sins, he dies for the evil he has done. [27]And if a wicked person turns away from his wickedness and obeys the law, and does right, he shall save his soul, [28]for he has thought it over and decided to turn from his sins and live a good life. He shall surely live—he shall not die.

Dan 7:9. I watched as thrones were put in place and the Ancient of Days—the Almighty God—sat down to judge. His clothing was as white as snow, his hair like whitest wool. He sat upon a fiery throne brought in on flaming wheels, and [10]a river of fire flowed from before him. Millions of angels ministered to him and hundreds of millions of people stood before him, waiting to be judged. Then the court began its session and The Books were opened.

Amos 4:12. Therefore I will bring upon you all these further evils I have spoken of. Prepare to meet your God in Judgment, Israel.

Mt 3:12. He will separate the chaff from the grain, burning the chaff with never-ending fire, and storing away the grain. Lk 3:17.

Mt 7:22. At the Judgment many will tell me, "Lord, Lord, we told others about you and used your name to cast out demons and to do many other great miracles." [23]But I will reply, "You have never been mine. Go away, for your deeds are evil."

Mt 8:29. They began screaming at him, "What do you want with us, O Son of God? You have no right to torment us yet." With 2 Pet 2:4; Jude 1:6.

Mt 11:22. Truly, Tyre and Sidon will be better off on the Judgment Day than you! Mt 10:15.

Mt 12:36. And I tell you this, that you must give account on Judgment Day for every idle word you speak. [37]Your words now reflect your fate then: either you will be justified by them or you will be condemned. [41]The men of Nineveh shall arise against this nation at the judgment and condemn you. For when Jonah preached to them, they repented and turned to God from all their evil ways. And now a greater than Jonah is here—and you refuse to believe him. [42]The Queen of Sheba shall rise against this nation in the judgment, and condemn it; for she came from a distant land to hear the wisdom of Solomon; and now a greater than Solomon is here—and you refuse to believe him. Lk 11:31, 32.

Mt 13:30. Let both grow together until the harvest, and I will tell the reapers to sort out the thistles and burn them, and put the wheat in the barn. [40]Just as in this story the thistles are separated and burned, so shall it be at the end of the world: [41]I will send my angels and they will separate out of the Kingdom every temptation and all who are evil, [42]and throw them into the furnace and burn them. There shall be weeping and gnashing of teeth. [43]Then the godly shall shine as the sun in their Father's Kingdom. Let those with ears, listen! [49]That is the way it will be at the end of the world—the angels will come and separate the wicked people from the godly, [50]casting the wicked into the fire; there shall be weeping and gnashing of teeth.

Mt 16:27. For I, the Son of Mankind, shall come with my angels in the glory of my Father and judge each person according to his deeds. Mk 8:38.

Mt 22:13. Then the king said to his aides, "Bind him hand and foot and throw him out into the outer darkness where there is weeping and gnashing of teeth." *vs.* 11–13.

Mt 23:13, 14. Woe to you, Pharisees, and you other religious leaders. Hypocrites! . . . You pretend to be holy, with all your long, public prayers in the streets, while you are evicting widows from their homes. Hypocrites!

Mt 25:1. The Kingdom of Heaven can be illustrated by the story of ten bridesmaids who took their lamps and went to meet the bridegroom. [2,3,4]But only five of them were wise enough to fill their lamps with oil, while the other five were foolish and forgot. 5,6So, when the bridegroom was delayed, they lay down to rest until midnight, when they were roused by the shout, "The bridegroom is coming! Come out and welcome him!" 7,8All the girls jumped up and trimmed their lamps. Then the five who hadn't any oil begged the others to share with them, for their lamps were going out. 9But the others replied, "We haven't enough. Go instead to the shops and buy some for yourselves." 10But while they were gone, the bridegroom came, and those who were ready went in with him to the marriage feast, and the door was locked. 11Later, when the other five returned, they stood outside, calling, "Sir, open the door for us!" 12But he called back, "Go away! It is too late!" 13So stay awake and be prepared, for you do not know the date or moment of my return. 14Again, the Kingdom of Heaven can be illustrated by the story of a man going into another country, who called together his servants and loaned them money to invest for him while he was gone. [Lk 19:12–26.] 15He gave $5,000 to one, $2,000 to another, and $1,000 to the last—dividing it in proportion to their abilities—and then left on his trip. 16The man who received the $5,000 began immediately to buy and sell with it and soon earned another $5,000. 17The man with $2,000 went right to work, too, and earned another $2,000. 18But the man who received the $1,000 dug a hole in the ground and hid the money for safekeeping. 19After a long time their master returned from his trip and called them to him to account for his money. 20The man to whom he had entrusted the $5,000 brought him $10,000. 21His master praised him for good work. "You have been faithful in handling this small amount," he told him, "so now I will give you many more responsibilities. Begin the joyous tasks I have assigned to you." 22Next came the man who had received the $2,000, with the report, "Sir, you gave me $2,000 to use, and I have doubled it." 23"Good work," his master said. "You are a good and faithful servant. You have been faithful over this small amount, so now I will give you much more." 24, 25Then the man with the $1,000 came and said, "Sir, I knew you were a hard man, and I was afraid you would rob me of what I earned, so I hid your money in the earth and here it is!" 26But his master replied, "Wicked man! Lazy slave! Since you knew I would demand your profit, 27you should at least have put my money into the bank so I could have some interest. 28Take the money from this man and give it to the man with the $10,000. 29For the man who uses well what he is given shall be given more, and he shall have abundance. But from the man who is unfaithful, even what little responsibility he has shall be taken from him. 30And throw the useless servant out into outer darkness; there shall be weeping and gnashing of teeth." 31But when I, the Messiah, shall come in my glory, and all the angels with me, then I shall sit upon my throne of glory. 32And all the nations shall be gathered before me. And I will separate the people as a shepherd separates the sheep from the goats, 33and place the sheep at my right hand, and the goats at my left, 34Then I, the King, shall say to those at my right, "Come, blessed of my Father, into the Kingdom prepared for you from the founding of the world. 35For I was hungry and you fed me; I was thirsty and you gave me water; I was a stranger and you invited me into your homes; 36naked and you clothed me; sick and in prison, and you visited me." 37Then these righteous ones will reply, "Sir, when did we ever see you hungry and feed you? Or thirsty and give you anything to drink? 38Or a stranger, and help you? Or naked, and clothe you? 39When did we ever see you sick or in prison, and visit you?" 40And I, the King will tell them, "When you did it to these my brothers you were doing it to me!" 41Then I will turn to those on my left and say, "Away with you, you cursed ones, into the eternal fire prepared for the devil and his demons. 42For I was hungry and you wouldn't feed me; thirsty, and you wouldn't give me anything to drink; 43a stranger, and you refused me hospitality; naked, and you wouldn't clothe me; sick, and in prison, and you didn't visit me." 44Then they will reply, "Lord, when did we ever see you hungry or thirsty or a stranger or naked or sick or in prison, and not help you?" 45And I will answer, "When you refused to help the least of these my brothers, you were refusing help to me." 46And they shall go away into eternal punishment; but the righteous into everlasting life."

Mk 4:22. All that is now hidden will someday come to light.

Mk 13:32. However, no one, not even the angels in heaven, nor I myself, knows the day or hour when these things will happen; only the Father knows.

Lk 10:10. But if a town refuses you, go out into its streets and say, 11"We wipe the dust of your town from our feet as a public announcement of your doom. Never forget how close you were to the Kingdom of God!" 12Even wicked Sodom will be better off than such a city on the Judgment Day. 13What horrors await you, you cities of Chorazin and Bethsaida! For if the miracles I did for you had been done in the cities of Tyre and Sidon, their people would have sat in deep repentance long ago, clothed in sackcloth and throwing ashes on their heads to show their remorse. 14Yes, Tyre and Sidon will receive less punishment on the Judgment Day than you.

Lk 12:2. It will become as evident as yeast in dough. 3Whatever they have said in the dark shall be heard in the light, and what you have whispered in the inner rooms shall be broadcast from the housetops for all to hear! 4Dear friends, don't be afraid of these who want to murder you. They can only kill the body; they have no power over your soul. 5But I'll tell you whom to fear—fear God who has the power to kill and then cast into hell.

Lk 13:24, 25. The door to heaven is narrow. Work hard to get in, for the truth is that many will try to enter but when the head of the house has locked the door, it will be too late. Then if you stand outside knocking, and pleading, "Lord, open the door for us," he will reply, "I do not know you." [26]"But we ate with you, and you taught in our streets," you will say. [27]And he will reply, "I tell you, I don't know you. You can't come in here, guilty as you are. Go away." [28]And there will be great weeping and gnashing of teeth as you stand outside and see Abraham, Isaac, Jacob, and all the prophets within the Kingdom of God— [29]for people will come from all over the world to take their places there.

Lk 20:45. Then, with the crowds listening, he turned to his disciples and said, [46]"Beware of these experts in religion, for they love to parade in dignified robes and to be bowed to by the people as they walk along the street. And how they love the seats of honor in the synagogues and at religious festivals! [47]But even while they are praying long prayers with great outward piety, they are planning schemes to cheat widows out of their property. Therefore God's heaviest sentence awaits these men."

Jn 5:22. And the Father leaves all judgment of sin to his Son.

Jn 12:48. But all who reject me and my message will be judged at the Day of Judgment by the truths I have spoken.

Acts 2:19. And I will cause strange demonstrations in the heavens and on the earth—blood and fire and clouds of smoke; [20]the sun shall turn black and the moon blood-red before that awesome Day of the Lord arrives. [21]But anyone who asks for mercy from the Lord shall have it and shall be saved.

Acts 10:42. And he sent us to preach the Good News everywhere and to testify that Jesus is ordained of God to be the Judge of all—living and dead.

Acts 17:31. For he has set a day for justly judging the world by the man he has appointed, and has pointed him out by bringing him back to life again.

Acts 24:25. And as he reasoned with them about righteousness and self-control and the judgment to come, Felix was terrified.

Rom 2:5. But no, you won't listen; and so you are saving up terrible punishment for yourselves because of your stubbornness in refusing to turn from your sin; for there is going to come a day of wrath when God will be the just Judge of all the world. [6]He will give each one whatever his deeds deserve. [7]He will give eternal life to those who patiently do the will of God, seeking for the unseen glory and honor and eternal life that he offers. [8]But he will terribly punish those who fight against the truth of God and walk in evil ways—God's anger will be poured out upon them. [9]There will be sorrow and suffering for Jews and Gentiles alike who keep on sinning. [10]But there will be glory and honor and peace from God for all who obey him, whether they are Jews or Gentiles. [12-15]He will punish sin wherever it is found. He will punish the heathen when they sin, even though they never had God's written laws, for down in their hearts they know right from wrong. God's laws are written within them; their own conscience accuses them, or sometimes excuses them. And God will punish the Jews for sinning because they have his written laws but don't obey them. They know what is right but don't do it. After all, salvation is not given to those who know what to do, unless they do it. [16]The day will surely come when at God's command Jesus Christ will judge the secret lives of everyone, their inmost thoughts and motives; this is all part of God's great plan which I proclaim.

Rom 14:10. You have no right to criticize your brother or look down on him. Remember, each of us will stand personally before the Judgment Seat of God. [11]For it is written, "As I live," says the Lord, "every knee shall bow to me and every tongue confess to God." [12]Yes, each of us will give an account of himself to God.

1 Cor 3:13. There is going to come a time of testing at Christ's Judgment Day to see what kind of material each builder has used. Everyone's work will be put through the fire so that all can see whether or not it keeps its value, and what was really accomplished.

1 Cor 4:5. So be careful not to jump to conclusions before the Lord returns as to whether someone is a good servant or not. When the Lord comes, he will turn on the light so that everyone can see exactly what each one of us is really like, deep down in our hearts. Then everyone will know why we have been doing the Lord's work. At that time God will give to each one whatever praise is coming to him.

1 Cor 6:2. Don't you know that some day we Christians are going to judge and govern the world? So why can't you decide even these little things among yourselves?

2 Cor 5:10. For we must all stand before Christ to be judged and have our lives laid bare—before him. Each of us will receive whatever he deserves for the good or bad things he has done in his earthly body.

2 Thess 1:7. And so I would say to you who are suffering, God will give you rest along with us when the Lord Jesus appears suddenly from heaven in flaming fire with his mighty angels, [8]bringing judgment on those who do not wish to know God, and who refuse to accept his plan to save them through our Lord Jesus Christ.

2 Tim 4:1. And so I solemnly urge you before God and before Christ Jesus—who will some day judge the living and the dead when he appears to set up his kingdom. [8]In heaven a crown is waiting for me which the Lord, the righteous Judge, will give me on that great day of his return. And not just to me, but to all those whose lives show that they are eagerly looking forward to his coming back again.

Heb 6:2. You don't need further instruction about baptism and spiritual gifts and the resurrection of the dead and eternal judgment.

Heb 9:27. And just as it is destined that men die only once, and after that comes judgment.

Heb 10:27. There will be nothing to look forward

to but the terrible punishment of God's awful anger which will consume all his enemies.

1 Pet 4:5. But just remember that they must face the Judge of all, living and dead; they will be punished for the way they have lived. [7]The end of the world is coming soon. Therefore be earnest thoughtful men of prayer.

2 Pet 2:4. For God did not spare even the angels who sinned, but threw them into hell, chained in gloomy caves and darkness until the judgment day. [9]So also the Lord can rescue you and me from the temptations that surround us, and continue to punish the ungodly until the day of final judgment comes.

2 Pet 3:7. And God has commanded that the earth and the heavens be stored away for a great bonfire at the judgment day, when all ungodly men will perish. [10]The day of the Lord is surely coming, as unexpectedly as a thief, and then the heavens will pass away with a terrible noise and the heavenly bodies will disappear in fire, and the earth and everything on it will be burned up. [11]And so since everything around us is going to melt away, what holy godly lives we should be living! [12]You should look forward to that day and hurry it along—the day when God will set the heavens on fire, and the heavenly bodies will melt and disappear in flames.

1 Jn 4:17. And as we live with Christ, our love grows more perfect and complete; so we will not be ashamed and embarrassed at the day of judgment, but can face him with confidence and joy, because he loves us and we love him too.

Jude 1:6. And I remind you of those angels who were once pure and holy, but turned to a life of sin. Now God has them chained up in prisons of darkness, waiting for the judgment day. [14]Enoch, who lived seven generations after Adam, knew about these men and said this about them: "See, the Lord is coming with millions of his holy ones. [15]He will bring the people of the world before him in judgment, to receive just punishment, and to prove the terrible things they have done in rebellion against God, revealing all they have said against him." [24,25]And now—all glory to him who alone is God. . . . he is able to . . . bring you, sinless and perfect, into his glorious presence with mighty shouts of everlasting joy.

Rev 1:7. See! He is arriving, surrounded by clouds; and every eye shall see him—yes, and those who pierced him. And the nations will weep in sorrow and in terror when he comes. Yes! Amen! Let it be so!

Rev 6:15. The kings of the earth, and world leaders and rich men, and high-ranking military officers, and all men great and small, slave and free, hid themselves in the caves and rocks of the mountains, [16]and cried to the mountains to crush them. "Fall on us," they pleaded, "and hide us from the face of the one sitting on the throne, and from the anger of the Lamb, [17]because the great day of their anger has come, and who can survive it?"

Rev 11:18. The nations were angry with you, but now it is your turn to be angry with them. It is time to judge the dead, and reward your servants—prophets and people alike, all who fear your Name, both great and small—and to destroy those who have caused destruction upon the earth.

Rev 20:11. And I saw a great white throne and the one who sat upon it, from whose face the earth and sky fled away, but they found no place to hide. [12]I saw the dead, great and small, standing before God; and The Books were opened, including the Book of Life. And the dead were judged according to the things written in The Books, each according to the deeds he had done. [13]The oceans surrendered the bodies buried in them; and the earth and the underworld gave up the dead in them. Each was judged according to his deeds. [14]And Death and Hell were thrown into the Lake of Fire. This is the Second Death—the Lake of Fire. [15]And if anyone's name was not found recorded in the Book of Life, he was thrown into the Lake of Fire.

Rev 22:12. See, I am coming soon, and my reward is with me, to repay everyone according to the deeds he has done.

ACCORDING TO OPPORTUNITY AND WORKS. Gen 4:7. It can be bright with joy if you will do what you should! But if you refuse to obey, watch out. Sin is waiting to attack you, longing to destroy you. But you can conquer it!

Job 34:11. Rather, he punishes the sinners.

Prov 11:31. Even the godly shall be rewarded here on earth; how much more the wicked!

Prov 12:14. Telling the truth gives a man great satisfaction, and hard work returns many blessings to him.

Prov 24:11, 12. Rescue those who are unjustly sentenced to death; don't stand back and let them die. Don't try to disclaim responsibility by saying you didn't know about it. For God, who knows all hearts, knows yours, and he knows you knew! And he will reward everyone according to his deeds. Ps 62:12; 2 Tim 4:14.

Isa 3:10. But all is well for the godly man. Tell him, "What a reward you are going to get!" [11]But say to the wicked, "Your doom is sure. You too shall get your just deserts. Your well-earned punishment is on the way."

Isa 5:15. In that day the haughty shall be brought down to the dust; the proud shall be humbled; [16]but the Lord of Hosts is exalted above all, for he alone is holy, just and good.

Isa 24:2. Priests and people, servants and masters, slave girls and mistresses, buyers and sellers, lenders and borrowers, bankers and debtors—none will be spared.

Isa 59:18. He will repay his enemies for their evil deeds—fury for his foes in distant lands.

Jer 17:10. Only the Lord knows! He searches all hearts and examines deepest motives so he can give to each person his right reward, according to his deeds—how he has lived. [11]Like a bird that fills her nest with young she has not hatched and which will soon desert her and fly away, so is the man who gets his wealth by unjust means. Sooner or later he will lose his riches and at the end of his life become a poor old fool.

Jer 32:19. You have all wisdom and do great and mighty miracles; for your eyes are open to all the ways of men, and you reward everyone according to his life and deeds.

Ezk 7:3. No hope remains, for I will loose my anger on you for your worshiping of idols. [4]I will turn my eyes away and show no pity; I will repay you in full, and you shall know I am the Lord. [27]The people will tremble with fear, for I will do to them the evil they have done, and give them all their just deserts. They shall learn that I am the Lord.

Ezk 9:4. And said to him, "Walk through the streets of Jerusalem and put a mark on the foreheads of the men who weep and sigh because of all the sins they see around them." [5]Then I heard the Lord tell the other men: "Follow him through the city and kill everyone whose forehead isn't marked. Spare not nor pity them—[6]kill them all—old and young, girls, women and little children; but don't touch anyone with the mark. And begin right here at the Temple." And so they began by killing the seventy elders.

Ezk 16:59, 60. For the Lord God says: I will repay you for your broken promises. You lightly broke your solemn vows to me, yet I will keep the pledge I made to you when you were young. I will establish an everlasting covenant with you forever.

Ezk 18:4. For all souls are mine to judge—fathers and sons alike—and my rule is this: It is for a man's own sins that he will die. [*vs.* 5–9]. [19]"What?" you ask. "Doesn't the son pay for his father's sins?" No! For if the son does what is right and keeps my laws, he shall surely live. [20]The one who sins is the one who dies. The son shall not be punished for his father's sins, nor the father for his son's. The righteous person will be rewarded for his own goodness and the wicked person for his wickedness. [21]But if a wicked person turns away from all his sins and begins to obey my laws and do what is just and right, he shall surely live and not die. [22]All his past sins will be forgotten, and he shall live because of his goodness. [23]Do you think I like to see the wicked die? asks the Lord. Of course not! I only want him to turn from his wicked ways and live. [24]However, if a righteous person turns to sinning and acts like any other sinner, should he be allowed to live? No, of course not. All his previous goodness will be forgotten and he shall die for his sins. [25]Yet you say: "The Lord isn't being fair!" Listen to me, O people of Israel. Am I the one who is unfair, or is it you? [26]When a good man turns away from being good and begins sinning and dies in his sins, he dies for the evil he has done. [27]And if a wicked person turns away from his wickedness and obeys the law, and does right, he shall save his soul, [28]for he has thought it over and decided to turn from his sins and live a good life. He shall surely live—he shall not die. [29]And yet the people of Israel keep saying: "The Lord is unfair!" O people of Israel, it is you who are unfair, not I. [30]I will judge each of you, O Israel, and punish or reward each according to your own actions. Oh, turn from your sins while there is yet time. [31]Put them behind you and receive a new heart and a new spirit. For why will you die, O Israel? [32]I do not enjoy seeing you die, the Lord God says. Turn, turn and live!

Ezk 33:18. For again I say, when the good man turns to evil, he shall die. [19]But if the wicked turns from his wickedness and does what's fair and just, he shall live. [20]Yet you are saying the Lord isn't fair. But I will judge each of you in accordance with his deeds.

Ezk 39:24. I turned my face away and punished them in proportion to the vileness of their sins.

Hos 4:9. And thus it is: "Like priests, like people"—because the priests are wicked, the people are too. Therefore, I will punish both priests and people for all their wicked deeds. Hos 12:2.

Amos 3:2. Of all the peoples of the earth, I have chosen you alone. That is why I must punish you the more for all your sins.

Zech 1:5, 6. Your fathers and their prophets are now long dead, but remember the lesson they learned, that *God's Word endures!* It caught up with them and punished them. Then at last they repented.

Mt 10:14. Any city or home that doesn't welcome you—shake off the dust of that place from your feet as you leave. [15]Truly, the wicked cities of Sodom and Gomorrah will be better off at Judgment Day than they. Mt 11:24; Mk 6:11; Lk 9:5; 10: 12–15.

Mt 12:37. Your words now reflect your fate then: either you will be justified by them or you will be condemned.

Mt 23:13, 14. Woe to you, Pharisees, and you other religious leaders. Hypocrites! . . . . And you pretend to be holy, with all your long, public prayers in the streets, while you are evicting widows from their homes. Hypocrites! Lk 20:47.

Mk 14:21. I must die, as the prophets declared long ago; but, oh, the misery ahead for the man by whom I am betrayed. Oh, that he had never been born!

Lk 11:49. This is what God says about you: "I will send prophets and apostles to you, and you will kill some of them and chase away the others." [50]And you of this generation will be held responsible for the murder of God's servants from the founding of the world. *v.* 51.

Lk 12:47. He will be severely punished, for though he knew his duty he refused to do it. [48]But anyone who is not aware that he is doing wrong will be punished only lightly. Much is required from those to whom much is given, for their responsibility is greater. [See parable of the vineyard, Isa 5:1–6. Of the farmer, Isa 28:23–28. Of the wicked husbandmen, Mt 21:33–36. Of the investments, Mt 25:14–30.]

Lk 13:6. Then he used this illustration: "A man planted a fig tree in his garden and came again and again to see if he could find any fruit on it, but he was always disappointed. [7]Finally he told his gardener to cut it down. 'I've waited three years and there hasn't been a single fig!' he said. 'Why bother with it any longer? it's taking up space we can use for something else.' [8]"Give it one more chance,' the gardener answered. 'Leave it another year, and I'll give it special attention and plenty of fertilizer. [9]If we get figs next year, fine; if not, I'll cut it down.' "

Lk 19:12. A nobleman living in a certain province was called away to the distant capital of the empire to be crowned king of his province. [13]Before he left he called together ten assistants and gave them each $2,000 to invest while he was gone. [14]But some of his people hated him and sent him their declaration of independence, stating that they had rebelled and would not acknowledge him as their king. [15]Upon his return he called in the men to whom he had given the money, to find out what they had done with it, and what their profits were. [16]The first man reported a tremendous gain—ten times the original amount! [17]"Fine!" the king exclaimed. "You are a good man. You have been faithful with the little I entrusted to you, and as your reward, you shall be governor of ten cities." [18]The next man also reported a splendid gain—five times the original amount. [19]"All right!" his master said. "You can be governor over five cities." [20]But the third man brought back only the money he had started with. "I've kept it safe," he said, [21]"because I was afraid (you would demand my profits), for you are a hard man to deal with, taking what isn't yours and even confiscating the crops that others plant." [22]"You vile and wicked slave," the king roared. "Hard, am I? That's exactly how I'll be toward you! If you knew so much about me and how tough I am, [23]then why didn't you deposit the money in the bank so that I could at least get some interest on it?" [24]Then turning to the others standing by he ordered, "Take the money away from him and give it to the man who earned the most." [25]"But, sir," they said, "he has enough already!" [26]"Yes," the king replied, "but it is always true that those who have, get more, and those who have little, soon lose even that. [27]And now about those enemies of mine who revolted—bring them in and execute them before me."

Lk 21:1. As he stood in the Temple, he was watching the rich tossing their gifts into the collection box. [2]Then a poor widow came by and dropped in two small copper coins. [3]"Really," he remarked, "this poor widow has given more than all the rest of them combined. [4]For they have given a little of what they didn't need, but she, poor as she is, has given everything she has."

Jn 3:19. Their sentence is based on this fact: that the Light from heaven came into the world, but they loved the darkness more than the Light, for their deeds were evil. [20]They hated the heavenly Light because they wanted to sin in the darkness. They stayed away from that Light for fear their sins would be exposed and they would be punished.

Jn 5:45. Yet it is not I who will accuse you of this to the Father—Moses will! Moses, on whose laws you set your hopes of heaven.

Jn 9:41. "If you were blind, you wouldn't be guilty," Jesus replied. "But your guilt remains because you claim to know what you are doing."

Jn 12:48. But all who reject me and my message will be judged at the Day of Judgment by the truths I have spoken.

Jn 15:22. They would not be guilty if I had not come and spoken to them. But now they have no excuse for their sin. [24]If I hadn't done such mighty miracles among them they would not be counted guilty. But as it is, they saw these miracles and yet they hated both of us—me and my Father.

Rom 2:5. But no, you won't listen; and so you are saving up terrible punishment for yourselves because of your stubbornness in refusing to turn from your sin; for there is going to come a day of wrath when God will be the just Judge of all the world. [6]He will give each one whatever his deeds deserve. [7]He will give eternal life to those who patiently do the will of God, seeking for the unseen glory and honor and eternal life that he offers. [8]But he will terribly punish those who fight against the truth of God and walk in evil ways—God's anger will be poured out upon them. [9]There will be sorrow and suffering for Jews and Gentiles alike who keep on sinning. [10]But there will be glory and honor and peace from God for all who obey him, whether they are Jews or Gentiles. [11]For God treats everyone the same. [12]He will punish sin wherever it is found. He will punish the heathen when they sin, even though they never had God's written laws, for down in their hearts they know right from wrong. [27]In fact, those heathen will be much better off than you Jews who know so much about God and have have his promises but don't obey his laws.

1 Cor 3:8. Apollos and I are working as a team, with the same aim, though each of us will be rewarded for his own hard work. [13]There is going to come a time of testing at Christ's Judgment Day to see what kind of material each builder has used. Everyone's work will be put through the fire so that all can see whether or not it keeps its value, and what was really accomplished. [14]Then every workman who has built on the foundation with the right materials, and whose work still stands, will get his pay. [15]But if the house he has built burns up, he will have a great loss. He himself will be saved, but like a man escaping through a wall of flames. *v.* 12.

1 Cor 4:5. So be careful not to jump to conclusions before the Lord returns as to whether someone is a good servant or not. When the Lord comes, he will turn on the light so that everyone can see exactly what each one of us is really like, deep down in our hearts. Then everyone will know why we have been doing the Lord's work. At that time God will give to each one whatever praise is coming to him.

2 Cor 2:15. As far as God is concerned there is a sweet, wholesome fragrance in our lives. It is the fragrance of Christ within us, an aroma to both the saved and the unsaved all around us. [16]To those who are not being saved, we seem a fearful smell

of death and doom, while to those who know Christ we are a life-giving perfume. But who is adequate for such a task as this?

2 Cor 11:14. Satan can change himself into an angel of light, [15]so is it no wonder his servants can do it too, and seem like godly ministers. In the end they will get every bit of punishment their wicked deeds deserve.

Gal 6:5. Each of us must bear some faults and burdens of his own. For none of us is perfect! [6]Those who are taught the Word of God should help their teachers by paying them. [7]Don't be misled; remember that you can't ignore God and get away with it: a man will always reap just the kind of crop he sows! [8]If he sows to please his own wrong desires, he will be planting seeds of evil and he will surely reap a harvest of spiritual decay and death; but if he plants the good things of the Spirit, he will reap the everlasting life which the Holy Spirit gives him. [9]And let us not get tired of doing what is right, for after a while we will reap a harvest of blessing if we don't get discouraged and give up. [10]That's why whenever we can we should always be kind to everyone, and especially to our Christian brothers.

Eph 6:6, 7. Don't work hard only when your master is watching and then shirk when he isn't looking; work hard and with gladness all the time, as though working for Christ, doing the will of God with all your hearts. [8]Remember, the Lord will pay you for each good thing you do, whether you are slave or free.

Col 3:25. And if you don't do your best for him, he will pay you in a way that you won't like—for he has no special favorites who can get away with shirking.

1 Tim 1:13. Even though I used to scoff at the name of Christ, I hunted down his people, harming them in every way I could. But God had mercy on me because I didn't know what I was doing, for I didn't know Christ at that time.

Heb 2:2. For since the messages from angels have always proved true and people have always been punished for disobeying them, [3]what makes us think that we can escape if we are indifferent to this great salvation announced by the Lord Jesus himself, and passed on to us by those who heard him speak?

Heb 10:26. If anyone sins deliberately by rejecting the Savior after knowing the truth of forgiveness, this sin is not covered by Christ's death; there is no way to get rid of it. [27]There will be nothing to look forward to but the terrible punishment of God's awful anger which will consume all his enemies. [28]A man who refused to obey the laws given by Moses was killed without mercy if there were two or three witnesses to his sin. [29]Think how much more terrible the punishment will be for those who have trampled underfoot the Son of God and treated his cleansing blood as though it were common and unhallowed, and insulted and outraged the Holy Spirit who brings God's mercy to his people. [30]For we know him who said, "Justice belongs to me; I will repay them"; who also said, "The Lord himself will handle these cases."

Heb 12:25. So see to it that you obey him who is speaking to you. For if the people of Israel did not escape when they refused to listen to Moses, the earthly messenger, how terrible our danger if we refuse to listen to God who speaks to us from heaven!

Jas 2:12. You will be judged on whether or not you are doing what Christ wants you to. So watch what you do and what you think; [13]for there will be no mercy to those who have shown no mercy. But if you have been merciful, then God's mercy toward you will win out over his judgment against you.

1 Pet 1:17. And remember that your heavenly Father to whom you pray has no favorites when he judges. He will judge you with perfect justice for everything you do; so act in reverent fear of him from now on until you get to heaven.

2 Pet 2:20. And when a person has escaped from the wicked ways of the world by learning about our Lord and Savior Jesus Christ, and then gets tangled up with sin and becomes its slave again, he is worse off than he was before. [21]It would be better if he had never known about Christ at all than to learn of him and then afterwards turn his back on the holy commandments that were given to him.

Rev 2:23. And I will strike her children dead. And all the churches shall know that I am he who searches deep within men's hearts, and minds; I will give to each of you whatever you deserve.

Rev 20:12. I saw the dead, great and small, standing before God; and The Books were opened, including the Book of Life. And the dead were judged according to the things written in The Books, each according to the deeds he had done. [13]The oceans surrendered the bodies buried in them; and the earth and the underworld gave up the dead in them. Each was judged according to his deeds.

VARIOUS DIVINE JUDGMENTS.

1. Of sin at the cross, Jn 5:24; Rom 8:1–3; Gal 3:13; Heb 9:26–28; 1 Pet 2:24.

2. Of believers by correction, Jn 15:1–6; 1 Cor 11:29–32; Heb 12:3–15.

3. Of the believer's works, Rom 14:10; 1 Cor 3:11–15; 9:27; 2 Cor 5:10; Eph 6:8; 2 Tim 4:8; Rev 22:12.

4. Of Israel, Ezk 20:33–44; Mal 3:2–6; Mt 24:37–51; 25:1–30.

5. Of the nations, Joel 3:1, 2, 11–14; Mt 25:31–46.

6. Of angels, 1 Cor 6:3; 2 Pet 2:4; Jude 1:6.

7. Of the wicked dead, Rev 20:11–15.

See *God, Judge; Jesus, Judge; Punishment, According to Deeds.*

JUDGMENT SEAT of God, Rom 14:10.

JUDGMENT, VALLEY OF Joel 3:14.

JUDGMENTS, NOTABLE On the serpent, Gen 3:14, 15. Eve, Gen 3:16; Adam, Gen 3:17–19. Cain, Gen 4:11–15; the Antediluvians, Gen chapters 6, 7; Sodomites, Gen 19:23–25; Egyptians, the plagues and overthrow, Ex chapters 7–14;

Nadab and Abihu, Lev 10:1–3; Miriam, Num 12:1–15.

On the Israelites: For worshiping Aaron's calf, Ex 32:35; for complaining, Num 11:1, 33, 34; 14:22, 23, 32, 34–38; 21:6; 25:4, 5, 9. The 40 year's wandering a judgment, Num 14:26–39; 26:63–65; Deut 2:14–17; exiled to Assyria, 2 Kgs 17:6–41; Babylon, 2 Chron 36:14–21.

On the Canaanites, Lev 18:25; Deut 7; 12:29–32, with the conquest of, by Joshua. See *Canaanites.*

On Abimelech, Judg 9:52–57; Uzzah, 2 Sam 6:7; Hananiah, the false prophet, Jer 28:15–17; Eli's descendents, 1 Sam 2:27–36, with chapter 4:10–22; the prophet of Judah, for disobedience, 1 Kgs 13:1–25; Zimri, 1 Kgs 16:18, 19; Gehazi, 2 Kgs 5:27; Sennacherib, 2 Kgs 19:35–37.

Pronounced against Solomon, 1 Kgs 11:9–14, 23; Jeroboam, 1 Kgs 14:7–15; Ahab and Jezebel, 1 Kgs 21:19–24; Ahaziah, 2 Chron 22:7–9; Manasseh, 2 Chron 33:11.

Pronounced against disobedience, Lev 26:14–39; Deut 28:15–68; 29; 32:19–43.

Misunderstood, Jer 16:10; Joel 2:17. No escape from, Ex 20:7; 34:7; Isa 2:10, 12–19, 21; Ezk 14:13, 14; Amos 5:16–20; 9:1–4; Mt 23:33; Heb 2:1–3; 10:28, 29; 12:25; Rev 6:16, 17. See *Escape.* Executed by human instrumentality, Jer 51:2. Delayed, Ps 10:6; 50:21; 55:19. See *Punishment, Delayed.*

See *Chastisement; Punishment; Sin, Punishment of.*

DESIGN OF. Ex 14:17. "I will harden the hearts of the Egyptians and they will go in after you and you will see the honor I will get in defeating Pharaoh and all his armies, chariots, and horsemen. [18]And all Egypt shall know that I am Jehovah." [31]When the people of Israel saw the mighty miracle the Lord had done for them against the Egyptians, they were afraid and revered the Lord, and believed in him and in his servant Moses.

Lev 10:3. Then Moses said to Aaron, "This is what the Lord meant when he said, 'I will show myself holy among those who approach me, and I will be glorified before all the people.' " And Aaron was speechless.

Deut 29:22. Then your children and the generations to come and the foreigners that pass by from distant lands shall see the devastation of the land and the diseases the Lord will have sent upon it. [23]They will see that the whole land is alkali and salt, a burned over wasteland, unsown, without crops, without a shred of vegetation—just like Sodom and Gomorrah and Admah and Zeboiim, destroyed by the Lord in his anger. [24]"Why has the Lord done this to his land?" the nations will ask. "Why was he so angry?" [25]And they will be told, "Because the people of the land broke the contract made with them by Jehovah, the God of their ancestors, when he brought them out of the land of Egypt. [26]For they worshiped other gods, violating his express command. [27]That is why the anger of the Lord was hot against this land, so that all his curses (which are recorded in this book) broke forth upon them. [28]In great anger the Lord rooted them out of their land and threw them away into another land, where they still live today!"

Ps 9:16. The Lord is famous for the way he punishes the wicked in their own snares! [20]Make them tremble in fear; put the nations in their place until at last they know they are but puny men.

Ps 59:13. Angrily destroy them. Wipe them out. (And let the nations find out too that God rules in Israel and will reign throughout the world.)

Ps 83:16. Utterly disgrace them until they recognize your power and name, O Lord. [17]Make them failures in everything they do; let them be ashamed and terrified [18]until they learn that you alone, Jehovah, are the God above all gods in supreme charge of all the earth.

Isa 26:9. All night long I search for you; earnestly I seek for God; for only when you come in judgment on the earth to punish it will people turn away from wickedness and do what is right.

Isa 64:1. Oh, that you would burst forth from the skies and come down! How the mountains would quake in your presence! [2]The consuming fire of your glory would burn down the forests and boil the oceans dry. The nations would tremble before you; then your enemies would learn the reason for your fame!

Ezk 11:10. You will be slaughtered all the way to the borders of Israel, and you will know I am the Lord. [11]No, this city will not be an iron shield for you, and you safe within. I will chase you even to the borders of Israel, [12]and you will know I am the Lord—you who have not obeyed me, but rather have copied the nations all around you.

Ezk 12:16. But I will spare a few of them from death by war and famine and disease. I will save them to confess to the nations how wicked they have been, and they shall know I am the Lord.

Ezk 14:7. I the Lord will personally punish everyone, whether people of Israel or the foreigners living among you, who rejects me for idols, and then comes to a prophet to ask for my help and advice. [8]I will turn upon him and make a terrible example of him, destroying him; and you shall know I am the Lord.

Ezk 21:3. For the Lord says: I am against you, Israel. I will unsheath my sword and destroy your people, good and bad alike—[4]I will not spare even the righteous. I will make a clean sweep throughout the land from the Negeb to your northern borders. [5]All the world shall know that it is I, the Lord. His sword is in his hand, and it will not return to its sheath again until its work is finished.

Ezk 25:5. And I will turn the city of Rabbah into a pasture for camels and all the country of the Ammonites into a waste land where flocks of sheep can graze. Then you will know I am the Lord. [7]Therefore I will lay my hand heavily upon you, delivering you to many nations for devastation. I will cut you off from being a nation any more. I will destroy you; then you shall know I am the Lord. [11]Thus I will bring down my judgment upon the Moabites, and they shall know I am the Lord.

Ezk 26:6. And her mainland city shall perish by

the sword. Then they shall know I am the Lord.

Ezk 29:9. The land of Egypt shall become a desolate wasteland, and the Egyptians will know that I, the Lord, have done it. [16]Israel will no longer expect any help from Egypt. Whenever she thinks of asking for it, then she will remember her sin in seeking it before. Then Israel will know that I alone am God.

Ezk 30:8. And they will know I am the Lord when I have set Egypt on fire and destroyed her allies. [25]I will strengthen the hands of the king of Babylon, while the arms of Pharaoh fall useless to his sides. Yes, when I place my sword into the hand of the king of Babylon, and he swings it over the land of Egypt, Egypt shall know I am the Lord. [26]I will scatter the Egyptians among the nations; then they shall know I am the Lord.

Ezk 33:29. When I have ruined the land because of their sins, then they shall know I am the Lord.

Ezk 38:22. I will fight you with sword, disease, torrential floods, great hailstones, fire and brimstone! [23]Thus will I show my greatness and bring honor upon my name, and all the nations of the world will hear what I have done, and know that I am God! [23]Thus will I show my greatness and bring honor upon my name, and all the nations of the world will hear what I have done, and know that I am God!

Dan 4:17. "For this has been decreed by the Watchers, demanded by the Holy Ones. The purpose of this decree is that all the world may understand that the Most High dominates the kingdoms of the world, and gives them to anyone he wants to, even the lowliest of men! [24]Your Majesty, the Most High God has decreed—and it will surely happen—[25]that your people will chase you from your palace, and you will live in the fields like an animal, eating grass like a cow, your back wet with dew from heaven. For seven years this will be your life, until you learn that the Most High God dominates the kingdoms of men, and gives power to anyone he chooses. [26]But the stump and the roots were left in the ground! This means that you will get your kingdom back again, when you have learned that heaven rules." [34]"At the end of seven years, I, Nebuchadnezzar, looked up to heaven, and my sanity returned, and I praised and worshiped the Most High God and honored him who lives forever, whose rule is everlasting, his kingdom evermore."

Rom 9:17. Pharaoh, king of Egypt, was an example of this fact. For God told him he had given him the kingdom of Egypt for the very purpose of displaying the awesome power of God against him: so that all the world would hear about God's glorious name. [22]Does not God have a perfect right to show his fury and power against those who are fit only for destruction, those he has been patient with for all this time?

1 Cor 10:6. From this lesson we are warned that we must not desire evil things as they did. [11]All these things happened to them as examples—as object lessons to us—to warn us against doing the same things; they were written down so that we could read about them and learn from them in these last days as the world nears its end.

Rev 2:23. And I will strike her children dead. And all the churches shall know that I am he who searches deep within men's hearts, and minds; I will give to each of you whatever you deserve.

For judgments on various nations, cities, etc., see under each name.

See *Afflictions, Design of.*

See also *Chastisement; Punishment; Sin, Punishment of.*

JUDITH A wife of Esau, Gen 26:34. Called *Oholibamah,* Gen 36:2, 3.

JULIA A Christian woman in Rome, Rom 16:15.

JULIUS A Roman officer, Acts 27:1, 3, 43.

JULY See *Calendar.*

JUNE See *Calendar.*

JUNIAS A relative of Paul, Rom 16:7.

JUPITER A Greek and Roman deity, Acts 14:12, 13.

JURY Of ten men, Ruth 4:2. Of seventy men, elders (senators), Num 11:16, 17, 24, 25.

JUSHAB-HESED Son of Zerubbabel, 1 Chron 3:20.

JUSTICE Ex 23:1. Do not pass along untrue reports. Do not cooperate with an evil man by affirming on the witness stand, something you know is false. [2, 3]Don't join mobs intent on evil. When on the witness stand, don't be swayed in your testimony by the mood of the majority present, and do not slant your testimony in favor of a man just because he is poor. [6]A man's poverty is no excuse for twisting justice against him. [7]Keep far away from falsely charging anyone with evil; never let an innocent person be put to death. I will not stand for this. [8]Take no bribes, for a bribe makes you unaware of what you clearly see! A bribe hurts the cause of the person who is right.

Lev 19:13. You shall not rob nor oppress anyone, and you shall pay your hired workers promptly. If something is due them, don't even keep it overnight. [Col 4:1] [14]You must not curse the deaf nor trip up a blind man as he walks. Fear your God; I am Jehovah! [15]Judges must always be just in their sentences, not noticing whether a person is poor or rich; they must always be perfectly fair.

Deut 16:18. Appoint judges and administrative officials for all the cities the Lord your God is giving you. They will administer justice in every part of the land. [19]Never twist justice to benefit a rich man, and never accept bribes. For bribes blind the eyes of the wisest and corrupt their decisions. [20]Justice must prevail. That is the only way you will be successful in the land which the Lord your God is giving you.

Deut 25:1–3. If a man is guilty of a crime, and the penalty is a beating, the judge shall command him to lie down and be beaten in his presence with up to forty stripes in proportion to the seriousness of the crime; but no more than forty stripes may be given lest the punishment seem too severe, and your brother be degraded in your eyes. [4]Don't muzzle an ox as it treads out the grain.

Ezra 7:26. Anyone refusing to obey the law of your God and the law of the king shall be punished immediately by death, banishment, confiscation of goods, or imprisonment.

Ps 72:1. O God, help the king to judge as you would, and help his son to walk in godliness. [2]Help him to give justice to your people, even to the poor.

Ps 82:2. How long will you judges refuse to listen to the evidence? How long will you shower special favors on the wicked? [3]Give fair judgment to the poor man, the afflicted, the fatherless, the destitute. [4]Rescue the poor and needy from the grasp of evil men.

Prov 17:15. The Lord despises those who say that bad is good, and good is bad.

26. How short-sighted to fine the godly for being good! And to punish nobles for being honest!

Prov 18:5. It is wrong for a judge to favor the wicked and condemn the innocent.

17. Any story sounds true until someone tells the other side and sets the record straight.

Prov 20:8. A king sitting as judge weighs all the evidence carefully, distinguishing the true from false.

Prov 22:27. Why risk everything you own? They'll even take your bed!

Prov 24:23. It is wrong to sentence the poor, and let the rich go free.

Prov 28:21. Giving preferred treatment to rich people is a clear case of selling one's soul for a piece of bread.

Prov 29:26. Do you want justice? Don't fawn on the judge, but ask the Lord for it!

Eccl 3:16. Moreover, I notice that throughout the earth justice is giving way to crime and even the police courts are corrupt. [17]I said to myself, "In due season God will judge everything man does, both good and bad."

Eccl 5:8. If you see some poor man being oppressed by the rich, with miscarriage of justice anywhere, throughout the land, don't be surprised! For every official is under orders from higher up, and the higher officials look up to their superiors. And so the matter is lost in red tape and bureaucracy.

Eccl 7:7. The wise man is turned into a fool by a bribe; it destroys his understanding.

Isa 1:17. Learn to do good, to be fair and to help the poor, the fatherless, and widows.

Isa 56:1. Be just and fair to all, the Lord God says. Do what's right and good, for I am coming soon to rescue you. Mic 6:8.

Isa 59:14. Our courts oppose the righteous man; fairness is unknown. Truth falls dead in the streets, and justice is outlawed. [15]Yes, truth is gone, and anyone who tries a better life is soon attacked. The Lord saw all the evil and was displeased to find no steps taken against sin.

Jer 22:1. Then the Lord said to me: Go over and speak directly to the king of Judah and say, [2]Listen to this message from God, O king of Judah, sitting on David's throne; and let your servants and your people listen too. [3]The Lord says: Be fairminded. Do what is right! Help those in need of justice! Quit your evil deeds! Protect the rights of aliens and immigrants, orphans and widows; stop murdering the innocent! [4]If you put an end to all these terrible deeds you are doing, then I will deliver this nation and once more give kings to sit on David's throne, and there shall be prosperity for all.

Lam 3:34–36. But you have trampled and crushed beneath your feet the lowly of the world, and deprived men of their God-given rights, and refused them justice. No wonder the Lord has had to deal with you!

Amos 5:7. O evil men, you make "justice" a bitter pill for the poor and oppressed. "Righteousness" and "fair play" are meaningless fictions to you! [11]You trample the poor and steal their smallest crumb by all your taxes, fines, and usury; therefore you will never live in the beautiful stone houses you are building, nor drink the wine from the lush vineyards you are planting. [12]For many and great are your sins. I know them all so well. You are the enemies of everything good; you take bribes; you refuse justice to the poor.

Mic 7:3. They go at their evil deeds with both hands, and how skilled they are in using them! The governor and judge alike demand bribes. The rich man pays them off and tells them whom to ruin. Justice is twisted between them.

Hab 1:4. The law is not enforced and there is no justice given in the courts, for the wicked far outnumber the righteous, and bribes and trickery prevail.

Zech 8:16. Here is your part: Tell the truth. Be fair. Live at peace with everyone.

Mt 5:23. So if you are standing before the altar in the Temple, offering a sacrifice to God, and suddenly remember that a friend has something against you, [24]leave your sacrifice there beside the altar and go and apologize and be reconciled to him, and then come and offer your sacrifice to God.

Mt 12:7. But if you had known the meaning of this Scripture verse, "I want you to be merciful more than I want your offerings," you would not have condemned those who aren't guilty!

Jn 7:51. "Is it legal to convict a man before he is even tried?" he asked.

1 Cor 13:6. It is never glad about injustice, but rejoices whenever truth wins out.

See *Court; Judge; Witness; Lawyer.*

JUSTIFICATION Gen 15:6. And Abram believed God; then God considered him righteous on account of his faith. Rom 4:3.

Ps 32:2. What relief for those who have confessed their sins and God has cleared their record. Rom 4:6.

Ps 71:16. I walk in the strength of the Lord God. I tell everyone that you alone are just and good.

Ps 89:16. They rejoice all day long in your wonderful reputation and in your perfect righteousness.

Isa 42:21. The Lord has magnified his law and made it truly glorious. Through it he had planned to show the world that he is righteous.

Isa 45:24. "In Jehovah is all my righteousness and strength," the people shall declare. And all who were angry with him shall come to him and be ashamed. [25]In Jehovah all the generations of Israel shall be justified, triumphant.

Isa 46:12. Listen to me, you stubborn, evil men! [13]For I am offering you my deliverance; not in the distant future, but right now! I am ready to save you, and I will restore Jerusalem, and Israel, who is my glory.

Isa 50:8. He who gives me justice is near. Who will dare to fight against me now? Where are my enemies? Let them appear!

Isa 51:5. My mercy and justice are coming soon; your salvation is on the way. I will rule the nations; they shall wait for me and long for me to come. [6]Look high in the skies and watch the earth disappear like smoke, the earth shall wear out like a garment, and the people of the earth shall die like flies. But my salvation lasts forever; my righteous rule will never die nor end.

Isa 53:11. And when he sees all that is accomplished by the anguish of his soul, he shall be satisfied; and because of what he has experienced, my righteous Servant shall make many to be counted righteous before God, for he shall bear all their sins.

Isa 54:17. But in that coming day, no weapon turned against you shall succeed, and you will have justice against every courtroom lie. This is the heritage of the servants of the Lord. This is the blessing I have given you, says the Lord.

Isa 56:1. Be just and fair to all, the Lord God says. Do what's right and good, for I am coming soon to rescue you.

Isa 61:10. Let me tell you how happy God has made me! For he has clothed me with garments of salvation and draped about me the robe of righteousness. I am like a bridegroom in his wedding suit or a bride with her jewels.

Jer 23:6. And this is his name: *The Lord Our Righteousness.* At that time Judah will be saved and Israel will live in peace.

Zech 3:4. Then the Angel said to the others standing there, "Remove his filthy clothing." And turning to Joshua he said, "See, I have taken away your sins, and now I am giving you these fine new clothes."

Jn 5:24. I say emphatically that anyone who listens to my message and believes in God who sent me has eternal life, and will never be damned for his sins, but has already passed out of death into life.

Acts 13:29. When they had fulfilled all the prophecies concerning his death, he was taken from the cross and placed in a tomb.

Rom 1:16. For I am not ashamed of this Good News about Christ. It is God's powerful method of bringing all who believe it to heaven. This message was preached first to the Jews alone, but now everyone is invited to come to God in this same way. [17]This Good News tells us that God makes us ready for heaven—makes us right in God's sight—when we put our faith and trust in Christ to save us. This is accomplished from start to finish by faith. As the Scripture says it, "The man who finds life will find it through trusting God." Hab 2:4; Gal 3:11.

Rom 2:12–15. . . . After all, salvation is not given to those who know what to do, unless they do it.

Rom 3:21, 22. But now God has shown us a different way to heaven—not by "being good enough" and trying to keep his laws, but by a new way (though not new, really, for the Scriptures told about it long ago). Now God says he will accept and acquit us—declare us "not guilty"—if we trust Jesus Christ to take away our sins. And we all can be saved in this same way, by coming to Christ, no matter who we are or what we have been like. [24]Yet now God declares us "not guilty" of offending him if we trust in Jesus Christ, who in his kindness freely takes away our sins. [25]For God sent Christ Jesus to take the punishment for our sins and to end all God's anger against us. He used Christ's blood and our faith as the means of saving us from his wrath. In this way he was being entirely fair, even though he did not punish those who sinned in former times. For he was looking forward to the time when Christ would come and take away those sins. [26]And now in these days also he can receive sinners in this same way, because Jesus took away their sins. But isn't this unfair for God to let criminals go free, and say that they are innocent? No, for he does it on the basis of their trust in Jesus who took away their sins. [28]So it is that we are saved by faith in Christ and not by the good things we do. [30]God treats us all the same; all, whether Jews or Gentiles, are acquitted if they have faith.

Rom 4:5. It is *given* to those who do *not* work for it. For God declares sinners to be good in his sight if they have faith in Christ to save them from God's wrath. [6]King David spoke of this, describing the happiness of an undeserving sinner who is declared "not guilty" by God. [7]"Blessed, and to be envied," he said, "are those whose sins are forgiven and put out of sight. [8]Yes, what joy there is for anyone whose sins are no longer counted against him by the Lord. [9]Now then, the question: Is this blessing given only to those who have faith in Christ but also keep the Jewish laws, or is the blessing also given to those who do not keep the Jewish rules, but only trust in Christ? Well, what about Abraham? We say that he received these blessings through his faith. Was it by faith alone? Or because he also kept the Jewish rules? [10]For the answer to that question, answer this one: *When* did God give this blessing to Abraham? It was *before he became a Jew*—before he went through the Jewish initiation ceremony of circumcision. [11]It wasn't until later on, *after* God had promised to bless him *because of his faith,* that he was circumcised. The circumcision ceremony was a sign that Abraham already had faith and that God had already accepted him and declared him just and good in his sight—before the ceremony took place. So Abraham is the spiritual father of those who believe and are saved without obeying Jewish laws. We see, then, that those who do not keep these rules are justified by God through faith. [12]And Abraham is also the spiritual father of those Jews who have been circumcised. They can see from his example that it is not this ceremony that saves them, for Abraham found favor with God by faith alone, *before he was circumcised.* [13]It is clear, then, that God's promise to give the whole earth to Abraham and his descendants was not because Abraham obeyed God's laws but because he trusted God to keep his promise. [14]So if you still claim that God's blessings go to those who are "good enough," then you are saying that God's promises to those who have faith are meaningless, and faith is foolish. [15]But the fact of the matter is this: when we try to gain God's blessing and salvation by keeping his laws we always end up under his anger, for we always fail to keep them. The only way we can keep from breaking laws is not to have any to break! [16]So God's blessings are given to us by faith, as a free gift; we are certain to get them whether or not we follow Jewish customs if we have faith like Abraham's, for Abraham is the father of us all when it comes to these matters of faith. [17]That is what the Scriptures mean when they say that God made Abraham the father of many nations. God will accept all people in every nation who trust God as Abraham did. And this promise is from God himself, who makes the dead live again and speaks of future events with as much certainty as though they were already past. [18]So, when God told Abraham that he would give him a son who would have many descendants and become a great nation, Abraham believed God even though such a promise just couldn't come to pass! [19]And because his faith was strong, he didn't worry about the fact that he was too old to be a father, at the age of one hundred, and that Sarah his wife, at ninety, was also much too old to have a baby. [20]But Abraham never doubted. He believed God, for his faith and trust grew ever stronger, and he praised God for this blessing even before it happened. [21]He was completely sure that God was well able to do anything he promised. [22]And because of Abraham's faith God forgave his sins and declared him "not guilty." [23]Now this wonderful statement —that he was accepted and approved through his faith—wasn't just for Abraham's benefit. [24]It was for us, too, assuring us that God will accept us in the same way he accepted Abraham—when we believe the promises of God who brought back Jesus our Lord from the dead. [25]He died for our sins and rose again to make us right with God, filling us with God's goodness.

Rom 5:1. So now, since we have been made right in God's sight by faith in his promises, we can have real peace with him because of what Jesus Christ our Lord has done for us. [9]And since by his blood he did all this for us as sinners, how much more will he do for us now that he has declared us not guilty? Now he will save us from all of God's wrath to come. [11]Now we rejoice in our wonderful new relationship with God—all because of what our Lord Jesus Christ has done in dying for our sins—making us friends of God. [16]Adam's *one* sin brought the penalty of death to many, while Christ freely takes away *many* sins and gives glorious life instead. [17]The sin of this one man, Adam, caused *death to be king over all,* but all who will take God's gift of forgiveness and acquittal are *kings of life* because of this one man, Jesus Christ. [18]Yes, Adam's *sin* brought *punishment* to all, but Christ's *righteousness* makes men *right with God,* so that they can live. [21]Before, sin ruled over all men and brought them to death, but now God's kindness rules instead, giving us right standing with God and resulting in eternal life through Jesus Christ our Lord. *vs.* 12–21.

Rom 6:22. But now you are free from the power of sin and are slaves of God, and his benefits to you include holiness and everlasting life.

Rom 7:4. Your "husband," your master, used to be the Jewish law; but you "died," as it were, with Christ on the cross; and since you are "dead," you are no longer "married to the law," and it has no more control over you. Then you came back to life again when Christ did, and are a new person. And now you are "married," so to speak, to the one who rose from the dead, so that you can produce good fruit, that is, good deeds for God. *vs.* 1–25.

Rom 8:1. So there is now no condemnation awaiting those who belong to Christ Jesus. [30]And having chosen us, he called us to come to him; and when we came, he declared us "not guilty," filled us with Christ's goodness, gave us right standing with himself, and promised us his glory. [31]What can we ever say to such wonderful things as these? If God is on our side, who can ever be against us? [33]Who dares accuse us whom God has chosen for his own? Will God? No! He is the one who has forgiven us and given us right standing with himself. [34]Who then will condemn us? Will Christ? *No!* For he is the one who died for us and came back to life again for us and is sitting at the place of highest honor next to God, pleading for us there in heaven.

Rom 9:30. Well then, what shall we say about these things? Just this, that God has given the Gentiles the opportunity to be acquitted by faith, even though they had not been really seeking God. [31]But the Jews, who tried so hard to get right with God by keeping his laws, never succeeded. [32]Why not? Because they were trying to be saved by keeping the law and being good instead of by depending on faith. They have stumbled over the great stumbling stone.

Rom 10:4. They don't understand that Christ gives to those who trust in him everything they are trying to get by keeping his laws. He ends all of that. [5]For Moses wrote that if a person could be perfectly good and hold out against temptation all his life and never sin once, only then could he be pardoned and saved. [6]But the salvation that comes through faith says, "You don't need to search the heavens to find Christ and bring him down to help you." [8]For salvation that comes from trusting Christ—which is what we preach—is already within easy reach of each of us; in fact, it is as near as our own hearts and mouths. [9]For if you tell others with your own mouth that Jesus Christ is your Lord, and believe in your own heart that God has raised him from the dead, you will be saved. [10]For it is by believing in his heart that a man becomes right with God; and with his mouth he tells others of his faith, confirming his salvation. [11]For the Scriptures tell us that no one who believes in Christ will ever be disappointed. *vs.* 1–21.

1 Cor 1:30. For it is from God alone that you have your life through Christ Jesus. He showed us God's plan of salvation; he was the one who made us acceptable to God; he made us pure and holy and gave himself to purchase our salvation.

1 Cor 6:11. There was a time when some of you were just like that but now your sins are washed away, and you are set apart for God, and he has accepted you because of what the Lord Jesus Christ and the Spirit of our God have done for you.

2 Cor 5:19. For God was in Christ, restoring the world to himself, no longer counting men's sins against them but blotting them out. This is the wonderful message he has given us to tell others.

Gal 2:16. And yet we Jewish Christians know very well that we cannot become right with God by obeying our Jewish laws, but only by faith in Jesus Christ to take away our sins. And so we, too, have trusted Jesus Christ, that we might be accepted by God because of faith—and not because we have obeyed the Jewish laws. For no one will ever be saved by obeying them. *vs.* 14–21.

Gal 3:8, 9. What's more, the Scriptures looked forward to this time when God would save the Gentiles also, through their faith. God told Abraham about this long ago when he said, "I will bless those in every nation who trust in me as you do." And so it is: all who trust in Christ share the same blessing Abraham received. (*v.* 6.) [21, 22]Well then, are God's laws and God's promises against each other? Of course not! If we could be saved by his laws, then God would not have had to give us a different way to get out of the grip of sin—for the Scriptures insist we are all its prisoners. The only way out is through faith in Jesus Christ; the way of escape is open to all who believe him. [24]Let me put it another way. The Jewish laws were our teacher and guide until Christ came to give us right standing with God through our faith. Gal 4:21–31.

Gal 5:4. Christ is useless to you if you are counting on clearing your debt to God by keeping those laws; you are lost from God's grace. [5]But we by the help of the Holy Spirit are counting on Christ's death to clear away our sins and make us right with God. [6]And we to whom Christ has given eternal life don't need to worry about whether we have been circumcised or not, or whether we are obeying the Jewish ceremonies or not; for all we need is faith working through love.

Eph 6:14. But to do this, you will need the strong belt of truth and the breastplate of God's approval.

Phil 3:8. In order that I can have Christ, [9]and become one with him, no longer counting on being saved by being good enough or by obeying God's laws, but by trusting Christ to save me; for God's way of making us right with himself depends on faith—counting on Christ alone.

Col 2:13. You were dead in sins, and your sinful desires were not yet cut away. Then he gave you a share in the very life of Christ, for he forgave all your sins, [14]and blotted out the charges proved against you, the list of his commandments which you had not obeyed. He took this list of sins and destroyed it by nailing it to Christ's cross.

Tit 3:7. So that he could declare us good in God's eyes—all because of his great kindness; and now we can share in the wealth of the eternal life he gives us, and we are eagerly looking forward to receiving it.

Heb 11:4. It was by faith that Abel obeyed God and brought an offering that pleased God more than Cain's offering did. God accepted his gift; and though Abel is long dead, we can still learn lessons from him about trusting God. [7]Noah was another who trusted God. When he heard God's warning about the future, Noah believed him even though there was then no sign of a flood, and wasting no time, he built the ark and saved his family. Noah's belief in God was in direct contrast to the sin and disbelief of the rest of the world—which refused to obey—and because of his faith he became one of those whom God has accepted.

Jas 2:20. Fool! When will you ever learn that "believing" is useless without *doing* what God wants you to? Faith that does not result in good deeds is not real faith. [21]Don't you remember that even our father Abraham was declared good because of what he *did,* when he was willing to obey God, even if it meant offering his son Isaac to die on the altar? [22]You see, he was trusting God so much that he was willing to do whatever God told him to; his faith was made complete by what he did, by his actions, his good deeds. [23]And so it happened just as the Scriptures say, that Abraham trusted God, and the Lord declared him good in God's sight, and he was even called "the friend of God." [26]Just as the body is dead when there is no spirit in it, so faith is dead if it is not the kind that results in good deeds.

See *Adoption; Forgiveness; Regeneration; Sanctification; Sin; Confession of, Forgiveness of.*

JUSTUS 1. A disciple nominated with Matthias to succeed Judas Iscariot, Acts 1:23.

2. A believer in Corinth, Acts 18:7.

3. Called also *Jesus.* A disciple in Rome, Col 4:11.

JUTTAH A Levitical city in Judah, Josh 15:48–62; 21:9–16.

K

KABUL 1. A city of Asher, Josh 19:27.

2. Names given by Hiram to certain cities in Galilee, called in 1 Kgs 9:13, "the wasteland."

KABZEEL A city of Judah, Josh 15:21–32; 2 Sam 23:20; 1 Chron 11:22.

KADESH Called also *Kadesh-barnea.* A city on the southern boundary of Palestine, Josh 15:2–4. Conquered by Ched-or-laomer, Gen 14:7. Abraham lives by the wells near, Gen 20:1 with 14:7; 16:14. Israel camps at, Num 13:26; 20:1; 33:15–37. Canaanites defeated at, Josh 10:41.

KADMI-EL 1. A Levite, Ezra 2:40–42; 3:9; Neh 7:43–45; 12:8, 24.

2. A Levite who assisted in leading the worship of the people, Neh 9:4, 5; 10:9–13. Probably identical to 1, above.

KAIN A city of Judah, Josh 15:57.

KAIWAN Called also *Kaiway,* a god of the Phoenicians, Amos 5:26; Acts 7:43.

KALLAI A priest, Neh 12:12–21.

KAMON Place where Jair was buried, Judg 10:5.

KANAH 1. A brook dividing Ephraim from Manasseh, Josh 16:8; 17:9.

2. A town in Asher, Josh 19:28.

KAREAH Father of Johanan and Jonathan, 2 Kgs 25:23; Jer 40:8, 13, 14; 41:11.

KARKOR A city in Gad, Judg 8:10.

KARTAH A city of Zebulun, Josh 21:34, 35.

KARTAN A Levitical city of Naphtali, Josh 21:32.

KATTATH A city in Zebulun, Josh 19:15, 16.

KEDAR 1. Son of Ishmael, Gen 25:12–15; 1 Chron 1:28–31.

2. A nomadic clan of the Ishmaelites, Ps 120:5, 6; Song 1:5; Isa 21:16; 42:11; 60:7; Jer 49:28. Flocks of, Isa 60:7; Jer 49:28, 29. Princes and commerce of, Ezk 27:21.

KEDEMAH Son of Ishmael, Gen 25:12–15; 1 Chron 1:28–31.

KEDEMOTH A city of Moab, allotted to Reuben and the Merarite Levites, Josh 13:18; 21:36, 37; 1 Chron 6:78, 79. Circled by a wilderness of the same name, Deut 2:26.

KEDESH 1. A city of Judah, Josh 15:21–32. Possibly identical with *Kadesh-barnea.*

2. Called also *Kishion.* A Canaanite city taken by Joshua, allotted to Issachar and the Levites, Josh 12:8–24; 19:17–23; 21:28, 29; 1 Chron 6:72.

3. Called also *Kedesh of Galilee, in Naphtali.* A city of refuge, Josh 20:7; 21:32. Home of Barak and Heber, Judg 4:6, 9, 11. Captured by Tiglath-pileser, 2 Kgs 15:29.

KEHELATHAH A camping place of Israel, Num 33:15–37.

KEILAH 1. One of a group of nine cities in the southern part of Palestine allotted to Judah, Josh 15:37–44. Philistines raid, after harvest, 1 Sam 23:1. David rescues, 1 Sam 23:2–13. Rulers of, aid in rebuilding the wall of Jerusalem after the captivity, Neh 3:17, 18.

2. A descendant of Caleb, 1 Chron 4:19.

KELAIAH Called also *Kelita.* A Levite who divorced his Gentile wife after the captivity, and assisted Ezra in explaining the law, Ezra 10:23; Neh 8:7, 8; 10:9–13.

KELITA See *Kelaiah.*

KEMUEL 1. Son of Nahor, Gen 22:20–23.

2. A leader of Ephraim, Num 34:16–28.

3. A Levite, 1 Chron 27:16–22.

KENAN See *Cainan, 1.*

KENATH called also *Nobah.* A city of Gilead, Num 32:42; 1 Chron 2:23.

KENAZ 1. Grandson of Esau, Gen 36:10–16; 1 Chron 1:36.

2. A king of Edom, Gen 36:40–43; 1 Chron 1:51–54.

3. Brother of Caleb, Josh 15:17; Judg 1:13; 3:9; 1 Chron 4:13.

4. Grandson of Caleb, 1 Chron 4:15.

KENITES 1. A Canaanite nation whose country was given to Abraham, Gen 15:19–21; Num 24:21, 22.

2. The descendants of Jethro, a Midianite, father-in-law of Moses. Join the Israelites in the wilderness, Judg 1:16; 4:11; 1 Chron 2:55. Jael, one of the, betrays and kills Sisera, Judg 4:17–21.

KENIZZITES An Edomite nation whose land was promised to Abraham, Gen 15:19–21.

KERCHIEF See *Handkerchief.*

KEREN-HAPPUCH Youngest daughter of Job, Job 42:13, 14.

KERIOTH A city of Moab, Jer 48:24; Amos 2:2.

KERI-OTH-HEZRON A city of Judah, Josh 15:21–32.

KETURAH Wife or concubine of Abraham, Gen 25:1–4; 1 Chron 1:32.

KEY Judg 3:25. A symbol of authority, Mt 16:19; Rev 1:17, 18; 3:7; 9:1; 20:1.

KEZIA A daughter of Job, Job 42:13, 14.

KIBROTH-HATTAAVAH A place where the Israelites were miraculously fed with quail, Num 11:31–35; 33:15–37; Deut 9:22.

KIBZA-IM A Levitical city in Ephraim, Josh 21:20–22.

KIDNAPPING Forbidden, Ex 21:16; Deut 24:7.

INSTANCE OF. Judg 21:20–23.

KIDNEY Burnt offering of the, Ex 29:13, 22; Lev 3; 4:9, 10; 7:4, 5; 8:15, 16; 9:10.

KIDRON A valley and brook between Jerusalem and the Mount of Olives, 1 Kgs 2:36, 37; Neh 2:14, 15; Jer 31:40. David escapes from Absalom across, 2 Sam 15:23. Destruction of idols at, by Asa, Josiah, and the Levites, 1 Kgs 15:13; 2 Kgs 23:6, 12; 2 Chron 29:16. Source of, closed by Hezekiah, 2 Chron 32:4. Jesus crossed, on the night of his arrest, Jn 18:1.

KILLING See *Homicide.*

KINAH A city of Judah, Josh 15:21–32.

KINDNESS Lev 19:34. They must be treated like any other citizen; love them as yourself, for remember that you too were foreigners in the land of Egypt. I am Jehovah your God.

Deut 22:1. If you see someone's ox or sheep wandering away, don't pretend you didn't see it; take it back to its owner.

Ps 112:5. And all goes well for the generous man who conducts his business fairly.

Prov 14:21. To despise the poor is to sin. Blessed are those who pity them.

Prov 19:22. Kindness makes a man attractive. And it is better to be poor than dishonest.

Prov 31:26. When she speaks, her words are wise, and kindness is the rule for everything she says.

Isa 11:13. Then, at last, the jealousy between Israel and Judah will end; they will not fight each other any more.

Zech 7:8, 9. Then this message from the Lord came to Zechariah. "Tell them to be honest and fair—and not to take bribes—and to be merciful and kind to everyone. [10]Tell them to stop oppressing widows and orphans, foreigners and poor people, and to stop plotting evil against each other."

Mt 5:7. Happy are the kind and merciful, for they shall be shown mercy. [42]Give to those who ask, and don't turn away from those who want to borrow. Lk 6:30.

Mt 25:34. Then I, the King, shall say to those at my right, "Come, blessed of my Father, into the Kingdom prepared for you from the founding of the world. [35]For I was hungry and you fed me; I was thirsty and you gave me water; I was a stranger and you invited me into your homes; [36]naked and you clothed me; sick and in prison, and you visited me."

Lk 6:34. And if you lend money only to those who can repay you, what good is that? Even the most wicked will lend to their own kind for full return! [35]Love your *enemies!* Do good to *them!* Lend to *them!* And don't be concerned about the fact that they won't repay. Then your reward from heaven will be very great, and you will truly be acting as sons of God: for he is kind to the *unthankful* and to those who are *very wicked.*

Acts 20:35. And I was a constant example to you in helping the poor; for I remembered the words of the Lord Jesus, "It is more blessed to give than to receive."

Rom 12:15. When others are happy, be happy with them. If they are sad, share their sorrow.

Rom 15:1, 2. Even if we believe that it makes no difference to the Lord whether we do these things, still we cannot just go ahead and do them to please ourselves; for we must bear the "burden" of being considerate of the doubts and fears of others—of those who feel these things are wrong. Let's please the other fellow, not ourselves, and do what is for his good and thus build him up in the Lord. [5]May God who gives patience, steadiness, and encouragement help you to live in complete harmony with each other—each with the attitude of Christ toward the other.

1 Cor 13:4. Love is very patient and kind, never jealous or envious, never boastful or proud, [5]never haughty or selfish or rude. Love does not demand its own way. It is not irritable or touchy. It does not hold grudges and will hardly even notice when others do it wrong. [6]It is never glad about injustice, but rejoices whenever truth wins out. [7]If you love someone you will be loyal to him no matter what the cost. You will always believe in him, always expect the best of him, and always stand your ground in defending him.

Gal 6:1. Dear brothers, if a Christian is overcome by some sin, you who are godly should gently and humbly help him back onto the right path, remembering that next time it might be one of you who is in the wrong. [2]Share each other's troubles and problems, and so obey our Lord's command. [10]That's why whenever we can we should always be kind to everyone, and especially to our Christian brothers.

Eph 4:32. Instead, be kind to each other, tenderhearted, forgiving one another, just as God has forgiven you because you belong to Christ.

Col 3:12. Since you have been chosen by God who has given you this new kind of life, and because of his deep love and concern for you, you should practice tenderhearted mercy and kindness to others. Don't worry about making a good impression on them but be ready to suffer quietly and patiently. [14]Most of all, let love guide your life, for then the whole church will stay together in perfect harmony.

1 Tim 5:9. A widow who wants to become one of the special church workers should be at least sixty

years old and have been married only once. [10]She must be well thought of by everyone because of the good she has done. Has she brought up her children well? Has she been kind to strangers as well as to other Christians? Has she helped those who are sick and hurt? Is she always ready to show kindness?

Heb 5:2, 3. And because he is a man he can deal gently with other men, though they are foolish and ignorant, for he, too, is surrounded with the same temptations and understands their problems very well.

1 Pet 3:8. And now this word to all of you: You should be like one big happy family, full of sympathy toward each other, loving one another with tender hearts and humble minds. *v.* 9.

1 Pet 4:8. Most important of all, continue to show deep love for each other, for love makes up for many of your faults.

2 Pet 1:7. This will make possible the next step, which is for you to enjoy other people and to like them, and finally you will grow to love deeply.

1 Jn 3:17. But if someone who is supposed to be a Christian has money enough to live well, and sees a brother in need, and won't help him—how can God's love be within *him?* [18]Little children, let us stop just *saying* we love people; let us *really* love them, and *show it* by our *actions.*

INSTANCES OF. Pharaoh to Jacob, Gen 45:16–20; 47:5, 6. Pharaoh's daughter to Moses, Ex 2:6–10. Rahab to the spies, Josh 2:6–16. David to Mephibosheth, 2 Sam 9:1–13. Joab to Absalom, 2 Sam 14:1–24. Ahab to Ben-hadad, 1 Kgs 20:32–34. Elisha to the woman whose son he restored to life, 2 Kgs 8:1. Evil-merodach to Jehoiachin, 2 Kgs 25:28–30. Jehoshabeath to Joash, 2 Chron 22:11. Wealthy Jews to the people, Neh 5:8–19. Mordecai to Esther, Esther 2:7. Nebuchadnezzar to Jeremiah, Jer 39:11, 12.

Joseph to Mary, Mt 1:19. Roman officer to his servant, Lk 7:2–8. Jews to Mary and Martha, Jn 11:19, 33. John to Mary, Jn 19:27. Felix to Paul, Acts 24:23. Julius to Paul, Acts 27:3, 43. Onesiphorus to Paul, 2 Tim 1:16–18.

See *Mercy.*

KING The word is used of the rulers of towns or cities, Gen 14:1, 2; Josh 12:8–24; Judg 1:7; of powerful rulers like Nebuchadnezzar, Dan 2:31; and of the Roman emperor, 1 Pet 2:13. Divinely authorized, Deut 17:15; 1 Sam 9:16, 17; 16:12; 1 Chron 22:10; 2 Chron 2:11, 12; Prov 8:14, 15; Dan 2:21, 27; 4:17; 5:20; Hos 8:4; 13:11.

How chosen: By divine appointment, Saul, 1 Sam 10:1; David and the Davidic dynasty, 1 Sam 16:1–13. Hereditary succession, 2 Sam 7:12–16; 1 Kgs 1:28–30; 2 Chron 21:3, 4; Ps 89:35–37. See *Israel, Kings of Judah.* Not hereditary, 1 Chron 1:43–50. See *Israel, Kings of Israel,* after the revolt. By lot, 1 Sam 10:20, 21. Modes of induction into office: By anointing, see *Anointing.* By proclamation, 2 Sam 15:10; 1 Kgs 1:33, 34; 2 Kgs 9:13; 11:12; by an oath, 2 Kgs 11:4. Ceremonial recognition of: Prostration, 2 Sam 9:8; obeisance, 2 Sam 9:5, 6; 1 Kgs 1:16, 22, 23, 31; kneeling before, Mt 27:29; salutation to: "Your majesty, live forever," Dan 6:6, 21.

Acts as judge, 2 Sam 8:15; 15:2; 1 Kgs 10:9; 2 Kgs 8:1–6; Ps 72:1–4; 122:5; Acts 25:10, 11, 12, 20. Precepts concerning, Deut 17:14–19; Prov 31:4, 5; Ezk 46:16–18. Obedience to, commanded, Eccl 8:2–5; Rom 13:1. Rights and duties of, Prov 25:2–7, 15; 29:4, 12, 14; Jer 21:12. Exercises executive clemency, 1 Sam 11:13. Constitutional restrictions of, Deut 17:18–20; 1 Sam 10:24, 25; 2 Sam 5:3; 2 Kgs 11:12, 17; 2 Chron 23:11; Jer 34:8–11; Dan 6:12–15. Influenced by popular opinion: Saul, 1 Sam 14:45; 15:24; David, 2 Chron 20:21; Hezekiah, 2 Chron 30:2, 3; Zedekiah, Jer 38:19, 24–27; Herod, Mt 14:5; Acts 12:2, 3; Pilate, Jn 19:6–13.

Religious duties of, Ezk 45:9–25; 46:2, 4–8. Deification of, Ezk 28:2, 3, 9. Loyalty to, commanded, Prov 16:14, 15; Eccl 10:20. Influence of queens over: Bath-sheba, 1 Kgs 1:28–34; Jezebel, 1 Kgs 18:3, 4, 13; 19:1–3; 21:5–16; Esther, Esther 5:1–8. Respect due to, Isa 8:21; Mt 22:21; Mk 12:17.

Compensation of: Confiscations of property, 2 Sam 16:4; 1 Kgs 21:1–16. Spoils, 2 Sam 12:29, 30; 1 Chron 26:27; 2 Chron 24:23. Tariff on imports, and internal revenue on merchandise, 1 Kgs 10:15–29. Forced labor, 2 Sam 20:24; 1 Kgs 12:18. Tribute, 2 Sam 8:2; 2 Chron 9:24; 17:11. Poll tax, Mt 17:24–27. Presents, 1 Sam 10:27; 16:20; 1 Kgs 10:2, 10, 25; Ps 72:10. Commissary of, 1 Kgs 4:7–19, 27, 28; 1 Chron 27:25–31; 2 Chron 26:10; 32:28, 29.

Stables of, Judg 12:14; 1 Kgs 1:33; 4:26; 10:25; 2 Chron 9:24, 25; Esther 6:7, 8.

Chief officers of: general of the army, 2 Sam 8:16; 1 Kgs 4:1–6; secretary of state, 2 Sam 8:16; 1 Kgs 4:1–6; secretary, 2 Sam 8:17; 20:25; 1 Kgs 4:1–6; priests, 2 Sam 8:17; 20:25; 1 Kgs 4:1–6; captain of the bodyguard, 2 Sam 8:18; 20:23; 1 Chron 11:25; superintendent of public works, 2 Sam 20:24; 1 Kgs 4:1–6; historian, 2 Sam 20:24; chaplain, 2 Sam 20:26; 1 Kgs 4:1–6; prime minister, Esther 3:1, 2; 8:1, 2, 15; 10:3; counselor, 1 Kgs 4:1–6; provincial governors, Dan 6:1–3.

Subordinate officers of: Manager of palace affairs, 1 Kgs 4:1–6; 2 Chron 28:7; tailor, 2 Kgs 22:14; 2 Chron 34:22.

Drunkenness of, forbidden, Prov 31:4, 5. Drunken, instances of, Hos 7:5; Elah, 1 Kgs 16:9; Ben-hadad, 1 Kgs 20:16; Belshazzar, Dan 5:1–4, 23; Ahasuerus, Esther 1:7, 10; 5:6; 7:2.

Prayer for, Ezra 6:10. Prayer for, commanded, 1 Tim 2:1, 2.

Decrees of, irrevocable, Esther 8:8; Dan 6:8, 9, 12–15.

History of, recorded; 1 Kgs 11:41; 14:19; 2 Kgs 21:25; 1 Chron 9:1; 27:24; 29:29; 2 Chron 9:29; 12:15; 20:34; 26:22; 32:32; Ezra 5:17; Esther 6:1, 2.

See *Government; Ruler; King of Kings.*

For the kings of Israel, before and after the revolt of the ten tribes, see *Israel.*

KING OF KINGS A term used of Jesus Christ as universal sovereign, 1 Tim 6:15; Rev 17:14; 19:16, cf. Rev 1:5. The same term, not capitalized, is used of great human kings in the Old Testament, Ezra 7:12; Ezk 26:7; Dan 2:37.

KINGDOM More space in the prophetic Scriptures is devoted to a future rule of God on earth than to any other theme. A number of expressions are used in the New Testament with reference to various aspects of God's sovereign rule, a vast and complex revelation, encompassing his government on earth and in heaven. These include: kingdom of God, Jn 3:3; kingdom of heaven, Mt 3:2; their Father's kingdom, Mt 13:43; 6:10; my kingdom, Mt 16:28; Jn 18:36; the kingdom of his dear Son, Col 1:13; a kingdom nothing can destroy, Heb 12:28; the Kingdom of Heaven, Jas 2:5; the kingdom of Christ and of God, Eph 5:5; his kingdom, 1 Thess 2:12; Rev 1:9; his heavenly kingdom, 2 Tim 4:18; the kingdom of our Lord, and of his Christ, Rev 11:15. Old Testament references include: 2 Sam 7:12–16; 1 Chron 17:11–14; Ps 22:28; 45:6; 103:19; 145:13; Isa 9:7; Dan 2:44; 4:3, 17, 25, 32; 5:21; Obd 1:21.

Representative facts about the coming kingdom: The Lord Jesus Christ is to occupy the throne of his ancestor David, Lk 1:32, 33; He will rule from Zion, in Jerusalem, Ps 2:6, 8; Jer 3:17; Zeph 3:15; called Jehovah Shammah, Ezk 48:35, or "The Lord is there." When the government is placed on his shoulder, Isa 9:6, 7, he will reign in righteousness, Isa 32:1, with an iron rod, Ps 2:9.

The saints of all ages will have a part in the kingdom, Dan 7:13–18; Rev 3:21; 5:9, 10; 20:4, 6, including the church, 2 Tim 2:12. The disciples will be judges in Israel, Isa 1:26; Mt 19:28.

As the kingdom begins, Satan and his demons are imprisoned, Rev 20:1–3; Isa 24:21, 22. All evil men are removed from the earth, Mt 13:41–43; 25:31–46. The Holy Spirit is poured out on all, Joel 2:28; Isa 32:15; Ezk 39:29. The awareness of the glory of the Lord fills the earth, Hab 2:14. Wars will end, Isa 2:4; Ps 46:9, the earth becomes a place of singing, Isa 14:7. Cities are filled with people, Ezk 36:37, 38.

With the curse lifted, thorns and briars will be gone, Isa 32:13, 15. Animal nature will be changed, Isa 11:6, 9. Rainfall and sunlight will be plentiful, Isa 30:26; 35:6, 7. Abundant crops will be produced, Amos 9:13; Ps 72:16; the wilderness will blossom with flowers, Isa 35:1. There will be unprecedented prosperity, Mic 4:4. Longevity will be tremendously increased as sickness and handicaps end, Isa 35:5, 6; 65:21, 22.

This golden age of man on the earth will come to an end when Satan is released, after 1,000 years, Rev 20:1–7. He gathers together all men who have yielded only feigned obedience to Christ, they are destroyed by fire from heaven, Rev 20:7–9.

At last the earth is burned up, 2 Pet 3:10, the wicked dead are judged at the great white throne, Rev 20:11–15, God creates a new heaven and a new earth, Isa 65:17; Rev 21:1–8, and eternity dawns.

The constitution of the coming kingdom (commonly called the millennium) is given in the Sermon on the Mount, Mt 5, 6, 7. All aspects of the kingdom are comprehended under Ps 103:19, "The Lord has made the heavens his throne; from there he rules over everything there is." After the Messianic kingdom of Christ has run its course, all things will be subject to the Father, "that God . . . will be utterly supreme," (1 Cor 15:27, 28).

KINGDOM OF GOD, KINGDOM OF HEAVEN. Bible students differ in all good conscience before God as to the precise meanings of these terms. The kingdom of God is mentioned in Mark, Luke, John, and throughout the New Testament, but the expression *kingdom of heaven* appears mainly in Matthew. It is derived from Dan 2:44; 4:25, 32, and refers to the rule of the heavens over the earth.

Those who regard the two terms as identical point to the similarities between the two, including: both are to be established on the earth, Mt 3:2; Mk 1:15; both were preached, Mt 4:23; Mk 1:14, 15; there are mysteries or previously unrevealed sacred secrets associated with both, Mt 13:11; Lk 8:10; the rich have difficulty entering both, Mt 19:23; Mk 10:23; the parable of the yeast was spoken about both, Mt 13:33; Lk 13:18–21.

Students who think the two terms must be distinguished point to the differences between them, including: the kingdom of God is entered only by the new birth, Jn 3:3, 5, while exhibiting righteousness is mentioned instead as the basis for entering the kingdom of heaven, Mt 5:20; 7:21. Those within the kingdom of God are secure, Jn 3:18; 5:24; 10:28, 29; 2 Tim 4:18; Jas 2:5, but those within the kingdom of heaven may be cast out, Mt 8:12; 13:41, 42, 47–50; 24:50, 51; 25:30. The kingdom of God is eternal, Dan 4:2, 3; Heb 1:8, while the kingdom of heaven comes to an end, 1 Cor 15:24; Rev 20:6. Only saved persons are found in the kingdom of God, Jn 3:3, 5; 1 Thess 2:12, 13, but unsaved persons are found within the kingdom of heaven, Mt 13:37–43, 47–50.

PROPHECIES CONCERNING THE EXTENT OF THE KINGDOM. Gen 12:3. And the entire world will be blessed because of you.

Gen 49:10. The scepter shall not depart from Judah until Shiloh comes, whom all people shall obey.

Ps 2:8. Only ask, and I will give you all the nations of the world.

Ps 22:27. The whole earth shall see it and return to the Lord; the people of every nation shall worship him. [28]For the Lord is King and rules the nations. [29]Both proud and humble together, all who are mortal—born to die—shall worship him. [30]Our children too shall serve him, for they shall hear from us about the wonders of the Lord; [31]generations yet unborn shall hear of all the miracles he did for us.

Ps 47:8. He reigns above the nations, sitting on his holy throne.

Ps 65:2. And because you answer prayer, all mankind will come to you with their requests.

Ps 66:4. All the earth shall worship you and sing of your glories.

Ps 68:31. Egypt will send gifts of precious metals. Ethiopia will stretch out her hands to God in adoration. [32]Sing to the Lord, O kingdoms of the earth —sing praises to the Lord.

Ps 72:5. May the poor and needy revere you constantly, as long as sun and moon continue in the skies! Yes, forever! [8]Let him reign from sea to sea, and from the Euphrates River to the ends of the earth. [9]The desert nomads shall bow before him; his enemies shall fall face downward in the dust. [10]Kings along the Mediterranean coast—the kings of Tarshish and the islands—and those from Sheba and from Seba—all will bring their gifts. [11]Yes, kings from everywhere! All will bow before him! All will serve him! [16]Bless us with abundant crops throughout the land, even on the highland plains; may there be fruit like that of Lebanon; may the cities be as full of people as the fields are of grass. [17]His name will be honored forever; it will continue as the sun; and all will be blessed in him; all nations will praise him. [19]Blessed be his glorious name forever! Let the whole earth be filled with his glory. Amen, and amen!

Ps 85:10. Mercy and truth have met together. Grim justice and peace have kissed! [11]Truth rises from the earth and righteousness smiles down from heaven. [12]Yes, the Lord pours down his blessings on the land and it yields its bountiful crops.

Ps 86:9. All the nations—and you made each one —will come and bow before you, Lord, and praise your great and holy name.

Ps 87:1, 2. High on his holy mountain stands Jerusalem, the city of God, the city he loves more than any other! [3]O city of God, what wondrous tales are told of you! [4]Nowadays when I mention among my friends the names of Egypt and Babylonia, Philistia and Tyre, or even distant Ethiopia, someone boasts that he was born in one or another of those countries. [5]But someday the highest honor will be to be a native of Jerusalem! For the God above all gods will personally bless this city.

Ps 89:25. He will hold sway from the Euphrates River to the Mediterranean Sea. [29]He will always have an heir; his throne will be as endless as the days of heaven. [36]His dynasty will go on forever, and his throne will continue to the end of time. [37]It shall be eternal as the moon, my faithful witness in the sky! *vs.* 1–37.

Ps 96:11. Let the heavens be glad, the earth rejoice; let the vastness of the roaring seas demonstrate his glory. [12]Praise him for the growing fields, for they display his greatness. Let the trees of the forest rustle with praise. [13]For the Lord is coming to judge the earth; he will judge the nations fairly and with truth! *vs.* 1–13.

Ps 102:13. I know that you will come and have mercy on Jerusalem—and now is the time to pity her—the time you promised help. [14]For your people love every stone in her walls and feel sympathy for every grain of dust in her streets. [15]Now let the nations and their rulers tremble before the Lord, before his glory. [16]For Jehovah will rebuild Jerusalem! He will appear in his glory!

Ps 110:1. Jehovah said to my Lord the Messiah, "Rule as my regent—I will subdue your enemies and make them bow low before you." [2]Jehovah has established your throne in Jerusalem to rule over your enemies. [3]In that day of your power your people shall come to you willingly, dressed in holy altar robes. And your strength shall be renewed day by day like morning dew. [4]Jehovah has taken oath, and will not rescind his vow, that you are a priest forever like Melchizedek. [5]God stands beside you to protect you. He will strike down many kings in the day of his anger. [6]He will punish the nations, and fill them with their dead. He will crush many heads.

Ps 113:3. Praise him from sunrise to sunset!

Ps 138:4. Every king in all the earth shall give you thanks, O Lord, for all of them shall hear your voice. [5]Yes, they shall sing about Jehovah's glorious ways, for his glory is very great.

Ps 145:10. All living things shall thank you, Lord, and your people will bless you. [11]They will talk together about the glory of your kingdom and mention examples of your power.

Isa 2:2. In the last days Jerusalem and the Temple of the Lord will become the world's greatest attraction, and people from many lands will flow there to worship the Lord. [3]"Come," everyone will say, "let us go up the mountain of the Lord, to the Temple of the God of Israel; there he will teach us his laws, and we will obey them." For in those days the world will be ruled from Jerusalem. [4]The Lord will settle international disputes; all the nations will convert their weapons of war into implements of peace. Then at the last all wars will stop and all military training will end. *v.* 5.

Isa 4:2, 3, 4. Those whose names are written down to escape the destruction of Jerusalem will be washed and rinsed of all their moral filth by the horrors and the fire. They will be God's holy people. And the land will produce for them its lushest bounty and its richest fruit.

Isa 9:7. His ever-expanding, peaceful government will never end. He will rule with perfect fairness and justice from the throne of his father David. He will bring true justice and peace to all the nations of the world. This is going to happen because the Lord of heaven's armies has dedicated himself to do it! *vs.* 1–7.

Isa 11:6. In that day the wolf and the lamb will lie down together, and the leopard and goats will be at peace. Calves and fat cattle will be safe among lions, and a little child shall lead them all. [7]The cows will graze among bears; cubs and calves will lie down together, and lions will eat grass like the cows. [8]Babies will crawl safely among poisonous snakes, and a little child who puts his hand in a nest of deadly adders will pull it out unharmed. [9]Nothing will hurt or destroy in all my holy mountain, for as the waters fill the sea, so shall the earth be full of the knowledge of the Lord. [10]In that day he who created the royal dynasty of David will be a banner of salvation to all the world. The nations will rally to him, for the land where he lives will be a glorious place. *vs.* 1–10.

Isa 24:16. Hear them singing to the Lord from

the ends of the earth, singing glory to the Righteous One!

Isa 25:6. Here on Mount Zion in Jerusalem, the Lord of Hosts will spread a wondrous feast for everyone around the world—a delicious feast of good food, with clear, well-aged wine and choice beef. [7]At that time he will remove the cloud of gloom, the pall of death that hangs over the earth; [8]he will swallow up death forever. The Lord God will wipe away all tears and take away forever all insults and mockery against his land and people. The Lord has spoken—he will surely do it!

Isa 29:18. In that day the deaf will hear the words of a book, and out of their gloom and darkness the blind will see my plans. [19]The meek will be filled with fresh joy from the Lord, and the poor shall exult in the Holy One of Israel.

Isa 32:15. Until at last the Spirit is poured down on us from heaven. Then once again enormous crops will come. [16]Then justice will rule through all the land, [17]and out of justice, peace. Quietness and confidence will reign forever more.

Isa 35:1. Even the wilderness and desert will rejoice in those days; the desert will blossom with flowers. [2]Yes, there will be an abundance of flowers and singing and joy! The deserts will become as green as the Lebanon mountains, as lovely as Mount Carmel's pastures and Sharon's meadows; for the Lord will display his glory there, the excellency of our God.

Isa 40:5. "The glory of the Lord will be seen by all mankind together." The Lord has spoken—it shall be. *vs.* 4–11.

Isa 42:3. He will see full justice given to all who have been wronged. [4]He won't be satisfied until truth and righteousness prevail throughout the earth, nor until even distant lands beyond the seas have put their trust in him.

Isa 45:8. Open up, O heavens. Let the skies pour out their righteousness. Let salvation and righteousness sprout up together from the earth. I, Jehovah, created them. [23]I have sworn by myself and I will never go back on my word, for it is true —that every knee in all the world shall bow to me, and every tongue shall swear allegiance to my name. [24]"In Jehovah is all my righteousness and strength," the people shall declare. And all who were angry with him shall come to him and be ashamed.

Isa 49:12. See, my people shall return from far away, from north and west and south. [18]Look and see, for the Lord has vowed that all your enemies shall come and be your slaves. They will be as jewels to display, as bridal ornaments. *vs.* 1–26.

Isa 53:10. Yet it was the Lord's good plan to bruise him and fill him with grief. But when his soul has been made an offering for sin, then he shall have a multitude of children, many heirs. He shall live again and God's program shall prosper in his hands. [11]And when he sees all that is accomplished by the anguish of his soul, he shall be satisfied; and because of what he has experienced, my righteous Servant shall make many to be counted righteous before God, for he shall bear all their sins. [12]Therefore I will give him the honors of one who is mighty and great, because he has poured out his soul unto death. He was counted as a sinner, and he bore the sins of many, and he pled with God for sinners.

Isa 54:1. Sing, O childless woman! Break out into loud and joyful song, Jerusalem, for she who was abandoned has more blessings now than she whose husband stayed! [2]Enlarge your house; build on additions; spread out your home! [3]For you will soon be bursting at the seams! And your descendants will possess the cities left behind during the exile, and rule the nations that took their lands.

Isa 55:5. You also will command the nations and they will come running to obey, not because of your own power or virtue but because I, the Lord your God, have glorified you. [10]As the rain and snow come down from heaven and stay upon the ground to water the earth, and cause the grain to grow and to produce seed for the farmer and bread for the hungry, [11]so also is my Word. I send it out and it always produces fruit. It shall accomplish all I want it to, and prosper everywhere I send it. [12]You will live in joy and peace. The mountains and hills, the trees of the field—all the world around you—will rejoice. [13]Where once were thorns, fir trees will grow; where briars grew, the myrtle trees will sprout up. This miracle will make the Lord's name very great and be an everlasting sign (of God's power and love).

Isa 56:7. I will bring them also to my holy mountain of Jerusalem, and make them full of joy within my House of Prayer. I will accept their sacrifices and offerings, for my Temple shall be called "A House of Prayer for All People"! [8]For the Lord God who brings back the outcasts of Israel says, I will bring others too besides my people Israel. *vs.* 3–8.

Isa 59:19. Then at last they will reverence and glorify the name of God from west to east. For he will come like a floodtide driven by Jehovah's breath. *vs.* 19–21.

Isa 60:1. Arise, my people! Let your light shine for all the nations to see! For the glory of the Lord is streaming from you. [2]Darkness as black as night shall cover all the peoples of the earth, but the glory of the Lord will shine from you. [3]All nations will come to your light; mighty kings will come to see the glory of the Lord upon you. [4]Lift up your eyes and see! For your sons and daughters are coming home to you from distant lands. [5]Your eyes will shine with joy, your hearts will thrill, for merchants from around the world will flow to you, bringing you the wealth of many lands. [7]The flocks of Kedar shall be given you, and the rams of Nabaioth for my altars, and I will glorify my glorious Temple in that day. [8]And who are these who fly like a cloud to Israel, like doves to their nests? [9]I have reserved the ships of many lands, the very best, to bring the sons of Israel home again from far away, bringing their wealth with them. For the Holy One of Israel, known around the world, has glorified you in the eyes of all.

Isa 66:12. Prosperity shall overflow Jerusalem like a river, says the Lord, for I will send it; the riches of the Gentiles will flow to her. Her children shall be nursed at her breasts, carried on her hips and dandled on her knees. [19]I will perform a mighty miracle against them, and I will send those who escape, as missionaries to the nations—to Tarshish, Put, Lud, Meshech, Rosh, Tubal, Javan, and to the lands beyond the sea that have not heard my fame nor seen my glory. There they shall declare my glory to the Gentiles. [23]All mankind shall come to worship me from week to week and month to month. *vs.* 7–23.

Jer 3:17. For the Lord himself will be among you, and the whole city of Jerusalem will be known as the throne of the Lord, and all nations will come to him there and no longer stubbornly follow their evil desires.

Jer 4:2. And if you will swear by me alone, the living God, and begin to live good, honest, clean lives, then you will be a testimony to the nations of the world and they will come to me and glorify my name.

Jer 16:19. O Lord, my Strength and Fortress, my Refuge in the day of trouble, nations from around the world will come to you saying, "Our fathers have been foolish, for they have worshiped worthless idols! [20]Can men make God? The gods they made are not real gods at all." [21]And when they come in that spirit, I will show them my power and might and make them understand at last that I alone am God.

Jer 31:34. At that time it will no longer be necessary to admonish one another to know the Lord. For everyone, both great and small, shall really know me then, says the Lord, and I will forgive and forget their sins.

Ezk 17:22, 23. The Lord God says: I, myself, will take the finest and most tender twig from the top of the highest cedar, and I, myself, will plant it on the top of Israel's highest mountain. It shall become a noble cedar, bringing forth branches and bearing fruit. Animals of every sort will gather under it; its branches will shelter every kind of bird.

Dan 2:35. But the Rock that knocked the statue down became a great mountain that covered the whole earth. [44]During the reigns of those kings, the God of heaven will set up a kingdom that will never be destroyed; no one will ever conquer it. It will shatter all these kingdoms into nothingness, but it shall stand forever, indestructible.

Dan 7:13. Next I saw the arrival of a Man—or so he seemed to be—brought there on clouds from heaven; he approached the Ancient of Days and was presented to him. [14]He was given the ruling power and glory over all the nations of the world, so that all people of every language must obey him. His power is eternal—it will never end; his government shall never fall. [18]"But in the end the people of the Most High God shall rule the governments of the world forever and forever." [22]Until the Ancient of Days came and opened his court and vindicated his people, giving them worldwide powers of government. [27]"Then every nation under heaven, and all their power, shall be given to the people of God; they shall rule all things forever, and all rulers shall serve and obey them."

Joel 2:28. After I have poured out my rains again, I will pour out my Spirit upon all of you! Your sons and daughters will prophesy; your old men will dream dreams, and your young men see visions. [29]And I will pour out my Spirit even on your slaves, men and women alike.

Mic 4:1. But in the last days Mount Zion will be the most renowned of all the mountains of the world, praised by all nations; people from all over the world will make pilgrimages there. [2]"Come," they will say to one another, "let us visit the mountain of the Lord, and see the Temple of the God of Israel; he will tell us what to do, and we will do it." For in those days the whole world will be ruled by the Lord from Jerusalem! He will issue his laws and announce his decrees from there. [3]He will arbitrate among the nations, and dictate to strong nations far away. They will beat their swords into plowshares and their spears into pruning-hooks; nations shall no longer fight each other, for all war will end. There will be universal peace, and all the military academies and training camps will be closed down. [4]Everyone will live quietly in his own home in peace and prosperity, for there will be nothing to fear. The Lord himself has promised this.

Hab 2:14. The time will come when all the earth is filled, as the waters fill the sea, with an awareness of the glory of the Lord.

Zeph 2:11. The Lord will do terrible things to them. He will starve out all those gods of foreign powers, and everyone shall worship him, each in his own land throughout the world.

Zeph 3:9. At that time I will change the speech of my returning people to pure Hebrew so that all can worship the Lord together.

Hag 2:7. "I will shake all nations, and the Desire of All Nations shall come to this Temple, and I will fill this place with my glory," says the Lord of Hosts. [8, 9]"The future splendor of this Temple will be greater than the splendor of the first one! For I have plenty of silver and gold to do it! And here I will give peace," says the Lord.

Zech 2:10. "Sing, Jerusalem, and rejoice! For I have come to live among you," says the Lord. [11]"At that time many nations will be converted to the Lord, and they too shall be my people; I will live among them all. *Then you will know it was the Lord of Hosts who sent me to you.*"

Zech 4:10. Do not despise this small beginning, for the eyes of the Lord rejoice to see the work begin, to see the plumbline in the hand of Zerubbabel. For these seven lamps represent the eyes of the Lord that see everywhere around the world.

Zech 6:15. These three who have come from so far away represent many others who will some day come from distant lands to rebuild the Temple of the Lord.

Zech 8:20, 21. People from around the world will come on pilgrimages and pour into Jerusalem from many foreign cities to attend these celebrations. People will write their friends in other cities and say, "Let's go to Jerusalem to ask the Lord to bless us, and be merciful to us. I'm going! Please come with me. Let's go *now!*" [22]Yes, many people, even strong nations, will come to the Lord of Hosts in Jerusalem to ask for his blessing and help. [23]In those days ten men from ten different nations will clutch at the coat sleeves of one Jew and say, "Please be my friend, for I know that God is with you."

Zech 9:1. For the Lord is closely watching all mankind, as well as Israel. [10]I will disarm all peoples of the earth, including my people in Israel, and he shall bring peace among the nations. His realm shall stretch from sea to sea, from the river to the ends of the earth.

Zech 14:8. Life-giving waters will flow out from Jerusalem, half toward the Dead Sea and half toward the Mediterranean, flowing continuously both in winter and in summer. [9]And the Lord shall be King over all the earth. In that day there shall be one Lord—his name alone will be worshiped. [16]In the end, those who survive the plague will go up to Jerusalem each year to worship the King, the Lord of Hosts, to celebrate a time of thanksgiving. [20]In that day the bells on the horses will have written on them, "These Are Holy Property"; and the trash cans in the Temple of the Lord will be as sacred as the bowls beside the altar. [21]In fact, every container in Jerusalem and Judah shall be sacred to the Lord of Hosts; all who come to worship may use any of them free of charge to boil their sacrifices in; there will be no more grasping traders in the Temple of the Lord of Hosts!

Mal 1:11. "But my name will be honored by the Gentiles from morning till night. All around the world they will offer sweet incense and pure offerings in honor of my name. For my name shall be great among the nations," says the Lord of Hosts.

Mt 8:11. And I tell you this, that many Gentiles (like this Roman officer), shall come from all over the world and sit down in the Kingdom of Heaven with Abraham, Isaac, and Jacob.

Lk 1:33. And he shall reign over Israel forever; his Kingdom shall never end!

Lk 2:10. But the angel reassured them. "Don't be afraid!" he said. "I bring you the most joyful news ever announced, and it is for everyone!"

Jn 10:16. I have other sheep, too, in another fold. I must bring them also, and they will heed my voice; and there will be one flock with one Shepherd.

Acts 2:34. (No, David was not speaking of himself in these words of his I have quoted), for he never ascended into the skies. Moreover, he further stated, "God spoke to my Lord, the Messiah, and said to him, Sit here in honor beside me [35]Until I bring your enemies into complete subjection."

1 Cor 15:24. After that the end will come when he will turn the kingdom over to God the Father, having put down all enemies of every kind. [25]For Christ will be King until he has defeated all his enemies, [26]including the last enemy—death. This too must be defeated and ended. [27]For the rule and authority over all things has been given to Christ by his Father; except, of course, Christ does not rule over the Father himself, who gave him this power to rule. [28]When Christ has finally won the battle against all his enemies, then he, the Son of God, will put himself also under his Father's orders, so that God who has given him the victory over everything else will be utterly supreme.

Eph 1:10. And this was his purpose: that when the time is ripe he will gather us all together from wherever we are—in heaven or on earth—to be with him in Christ, forever.

Phil 2:10. That at the name of Jesus every knee shall bow in heaven and on earth and under the earth, [11]and every tongue shall confess that Jesus Christ is Lord, to the glory of God the Father.

Heb 8:11. And no one then will need to speak to his friend or neighbor or brother, saying, "You, too, should know the Lord," because everyone, great and small, will know me already.

Heb 10:13. Waiting for his enemies to be laid under his feet.

Heb 12:23. And to the church, composed of all those registered in heaven; and to God who is Judge of all; and to the spirits of the redeemed in heaven, already made perfect; [24]and to Jesus himself, who has brought us his wonderful new agreement; and to the sprinkled blood which graciously forgives instead of crying out for vengeance as the blood of Abel did. [27]By this he means that he will sift out everything without solid foundations, so that only unshakable things will be left. [28]Since we have a kingdom nothing can destroy, let us please God by serving him with thankful hearts, and with holy fear and awe.

Rev 5:9. They were singing him a new song with these words: "You are worthy to take the scroll and break its seals and open it; for you were slain, and your blood has bought people from every nation as gifts for God. [10]And you have gathered them into a kingdom and made them priests of our God; they shall reign upon the earth." [13]And then I heard everyone in heaven and earth, and from the dead beneath the earth and in the sea, exclaiming, "The blessing and the honor and the glory and the power belong to the one sitting on the throne, and to the Lamb forever and ever." [14]And the four Living Beings kept saying, "Amen!" And the twenty-four Elders fell down and worshiped him.

Rev 11:15. For just then the seventh angel blew his trumpet, and there were loud voices shouting down from heaven, "The kingdom of this world now belongs to our Lord, and to his Christ; and he shall reign forever and ever."

Rev 12:10. Then I heard a loud voice shouting across the heavens, "It has happened at last! God's salvation and the power and the rule, and the authority of his Christ are finally here; for the Accuser of our brothers has been thrown down from heaven onto earth—he accused them day and night before our God."

Rev 14:6. And I saw another angel flying through the heavens, carrying the everlasting Good News to preach to those on earth—to every nation, tribe, language and people.

Rev 15:4. Who shall not fear, O Lord, and glorify your Name? For you alone are holy. All nations will come and worship before you, for your righteous deeds have been disclosed.

Rev 17:14. Together they will wage war against the Lamb, and the Lamb will conquer them; for he is Lord over all lords, and King of kings, and his people are the called and chosen and faithful ones.

Rev 19:6. Then I heard again what sounded like the shouting of a huge crowd, or like the waves of a hundred oceans crashing on the shore, or like the mighty rolling of great thunder, "Praise the Lord. For the Lord our God, the Almighty reigns." 11Then I saw heaven opened and a white horse standing there; and the one sitting on the horse was named "Faithful and True"—the one who justly punishes and makes war. 12His eyes were like flames, and on his head were many crowns. A name was written on his forehead, and only he knew its meaning. 13He was clothed with garments dipped in blood, and his title was "The Word of God." 14The armies of heaven, dressed in finest linen, white and clean, followed him on white horses. 15In his mouth he held a sharp sword to strike down the nations; he ruled them with an iron grip; and he trod the winepress of the fierceness of the wrath of Almighty God. 16On his robe and thigh was written this title: "King of Kings and Lord of Lords." 17Then I saw an angel standing in the sunshine, shouting loudly to the birds, "Come! Gather together for the supper of the Great God! 18Come and eat the flesh of kings, and captains, and great generals; of horses and riders; and of all humanity, both great and small, slave and free." 19Then I saw the Evil Creature gathering the governments of the earth and their armies to fight against the one sitting on the horse and his army. 20And the Evil Creature was captured, and with him the False Prophet, who could do mighty miracles when the Evil Creature was present—miracles that deceived all who had accepted the Evil Creature's mark, and who worshiped his statue. Both of them—the Evil Creature and his False Prophet—were thrown alive into the Lake of Fire that burns with sulphur. 21And their entire army was killed with the sharp sword in the mouth of the one riding the white horse, and all the birds of heaven were gorged with their flesh.

Rev 20:1. Then I saw an angel come down from heaven with the key to the bottomless pit and a heavy chain in his hand. 2He seized the Dragon—that old Serpent, the devil, Satan—and bound him in chains for 1,000 years, 3and threw him into the bottomless pit, which he then shut and locked, so that he could not fool the nations any more until the thousand years were finished. Afterwards he would be released again for a little while.

UNCLASSIFIED PROPHECIES CONCERNING THE KINGDOM. Gen 22:18. And be a blessing to all the nations of the earth—all because you have obeyed me.

Gen 49:10. The scepter shall not depart from Judah until Shiloh comes, whom all people shall obey.

Ps 2:9. Rule them with an iron rod; smash them like clay pots!

Ps 46:9. And causes wars to end throughout the earth, breaking and burning every weapon.

Ps 67:1. O God, in mercy bless us; let your face beam with joy as you look down at us. 2Send us around the world with the news of your saving power and your eternal plan for all mankind. 3How everyone throughout the earth will praise the Lord! 4How glad the nations will be, singing for joy because you are their King and will give true justice to their people! 5Praise God, O world! May all the peoples of the earth give thanks to you. 6, 7For the earth has yielded abundant harvests. God, even our own God, will bless us. And peoples from remotest lands will worship him.

Ps 72:12. He will take care of the helpless and poor when they cry to him; for they have no one else to defend them.

Isa 2:2. In the last days Jerusalem and the Temple of the Lord will become the world's greatest attraction, and people from many lands will flow there to worship the Lord. 3"Come," everyone will say, "let us go up the mountain of the Lord, to the Temple of the God of Israel; there he will teach us his laws, and we will obey them." For in those days the world will be ruled from Jerusalem. 4The Lord will settle international disputes; all the nations will convert their weapons of war into implements of peace. Then at the last all wars will stop and all military training will end.

Isa 9:5. In that glorious day of peace there will no longer be the issuing of battle gear; no more the blood-stained uniforms of war; all such will be burned.

Isa 11:1. The royal line of David will be cut off, chopped down like a tree; but from the stump will grow a Shoot—yes, a new Branch from the old root. 2And the Spirit of the Lord shall rest upon him, the Spirit of wisdom, understanding, counsel and might; the Spirit of knowledge and of the fear of the Lord. 3His delight will be obedience to the Lord. He will not judge by appearance, false evidence, or hearsay, 4but will defend the poor and the exploited. He will rule against the wicked who oppress them. 5For he will be clothed with fairness and with truth. 6In that day the wolf and the lamb will lie down together, and the leopard and goats will be at peace. Calves and fat cattle will be safe among lions, and a little child shall lead them all. 7The cows will graze among bears; cubs and calves will lie down together, and lions will eat grass like the cows. 8Babies will crawl safely among poisonous snakes, and a little child who puts his hand in a nest of deadly adders will pull it out unharmed. 9Nothing will hurt or destroy in all my holy mountain, for as the waters fill the sea, so shall the earth be full of the knowledge of the Lord. 10In that day he who created the royal dynasty of David will be a banner of salvation to all the world. The nations will rally to him, for the land where he lives will be a glorious place. 11At that time the Lord will bring back a remnant of his people for the second time, returning them to the land of Israel from Assyria, Upper and Lower Egypt, Ethiopia, Elam, Babylonia, Hamath and all the distant coastal lands. 12He will raise a flag among the nations for them to rally to; he will gather the scattered Israelites from the ends of the earth. 13Then, at last, the jealousy between Israel and Judah will end; they will not fight each other any more.

Isa 25:6. Here on Mount Zion in Jerusalem, the Lord of Hosts will spread a wondrous feast for everyone around the world—a delicious feast of good food, with clear, well-aged wine and choice beef.

Isa 35:1. Even the wilderness and desert will rejoice in those days; the desert will blossom with flowers. 2Yes, there will be an abundance of flowers and singing and joy! The deserts will become as green as the Lebanon mountains, as lovely as Mount Carmel's pastures and Sharon's meadows; for the Lord will display his glory there, the excellency of our God. 3With this news bring cheer to all discouraged ones. 4Encourage those who are afraid. Tell them, "Be strong, fear not, for your God is coming to destroy your enemies, He is coming to save you." 5And when he comes, he will open the eyes of the blind, and unstop the ears of the deaf. [Mt 11:5.] 6The lame man will leap up like a deer, and those who could not speak will shout and sing! Springs will burst forth in the wilderness, and streams in the desert. 7The parched ground will become a pool, with springs of water in the thirsty land. Where desert jackals lived, there will be reeds and rushes! 8And a main road will go through that once-deserted land; it will be named "The Holy Highway." No evil-hearted men may walk upon it. God will walk there with you; even the most stupid cannot miss the way. 9No lion will lurk along its course, nor will there be any other dangers; only the redeemed will travel there. 10These, the ransomed of the Lord, will go home along that road to Zion, singing the songs of everlasting joy. For them all sorrow and all sighing will be gone forever; only joy and gladness will be there.

Isa 42:1. See my Servant, whom I uphold; my Chosen One, in whom I delight. I have put my Spirit upon him; he will reveal justice to the nations of the world. 2He will be gentle—he will not shout nor quarrel in the streets. [Mt 12:18–21.] 3He will not break the bruised reed, nor quench the dimly burning flame. He will encourage the fainthearted, those tempted to despair. He will see full justice given to all who have been wronged. 4He won't be satisfied until truth and righteousness prevail throughout the earth, nor until even distant lands beyond the seas have put their trust in him. 5The Lord God who created the heavens and stretched them out and created the earth and everything in it, and gives life and breath and spirit to everyone in all the world, he is the one who says (to his Servant, the Messiah), 6"I the Lord have called you to demonstrate my righteousness. I will guard and support you, for I have given you to my people as the personal confirmation of my covenant with them. You shall also be a light to guide the nations unto me. 7You will open the eyes of the blind, and release those who sit in prison darkness and despair." 18Oh, how blind and deaf you are towards God! Why won't you listen? Why won't you see? 19Who in all the world is as blind as my own people, who are designed to be my messengers of truth? Who is so blind as my "dedicated one," the "Servant of the Lord"? 20You see and understand what is right but won't heed nor do it; you hear but you won't listen. 21The Lord has magnified his law and made it truly glorious. Through it he had planned to show the world that he is righteous.

Isa 45:14. Jehovah says: The Egyptians, Ethiopians and Sabeans shall be subject to you. They shall come to you with all their merchandise and it shall all be yours. They shall follow you as prisoners in chains, and fall down on their knees before you and say, "The only God there is, is your God!"

Isa 49:5. "And now," said the Lord—the Lord who formed me from my mother's womb to serve him who commissioned me to restore to him his people Israel, who has given me the strength to perform this task and honored me for doing it! 18Look and see, for the Lord has vowed that all your enemies shall come and be your slaves. They will be as jewels to display, as bridal ornaments. 19Even the most desolate parts of your abandoned land shall soon be crowded with your people, and your enemies who enslaved you shall be far away. 20The generations born in exile shall return and say, 'We need more room! It's crowded here!' 21Then you will think to yourself, 'Who has given me all these? For most of my children were killed and the rest were carried away into exile, leaving me here alone. Who bore these? Who raised them for me?' " 22The Lord God says, "See, I will give a signal to the Gentiles and they shall carry your little sons back to you in their arms, and your daughters on their shoulders. 23Kings and queens shall serve you; they shall care for all your needs. They shall bow to the earth before you, and lick the dust from off your feet; then you shall know I am the Lord. Those who wait for me shall never be ashamed."

Isa 55:1. Say there! Is anyone thirsty? Come and drink—even if you have no money! Come, take your choice of wine and milk—it's all free! 2Why spend your money on foodstuffs that don't give you strength? Why pay for groceries that don't do you any good? Listen and I'll tell you where to get good food that fattens up the soul! 3Come to me with your ears wide open. Listen, for the life of your soul is at stake. I am ready to make an everlasting covenant with you, to give you all the unfailing mercies and love that I had for King David. 4He proved my power by conquering foreign nations. [5]You also will command the nations and they will come running to obey, not because of your own power or virtue but because I, the Lord your God, have glorified you. [6]Seek the Lord while you can find him. Call upon him now while he is near. [7]Let men cast off their wicked deeds; let them banish from their minds the very thought of doing wrong! Let them turn to the Lord that he may have mercy upon them, and to our God, for he will abundantly pardon! [8]This plan of mine is not what you would work out, neither are my thoughts the same as yours! [9]For just as the heavens are higher than the earth, so are my ways higher than yours, and my thoughts than yours. [10]As the rain and snow come down from heaven and stay upon the ground to water the earth, and cause the grain to grow and to produce seed for the farmer and bread for the hungry, [11]so also is my Word. I send it out and it always produces fruit. It shall accomplish all I want it to, and prosper everywhere I send it. [12]You will live in joy and peace. The mountains and hills, the trees of the field—all the world around you—will rejoice. [13]Where once were thorns, fir trees will grow; where briars grew, the myrtle trees will sprout up. This miracle will make the Lord's name very great and be an everlasting sign (of God's power and love).

Isa 62:11. See, the Lord has sent his messengers to every land and said, "Tell my people, I, the Lord your God, am coming to save you and will bring you many gifts."

Isa 65:17. For see, I am creating new heavens and a new earth—so wonderful that no one will even think about the old ones anymore. [18]Be glad; rejoice forever in my creation. Look! I will recreate Jerusalem as a place of happiness, and her people shall be a joy! [19]And I will rejoice in Jerusalem, and in my people; and the voice of weeping and crying shall not be heard there any more. [20]No longer will babies die when only a few days old; no longer will men be considered old at 100! Only sinners will die that young! [21, 22]In those days when a man builds a house, he will keep on living in it—it will not be destroyed by invading armies as in the past. My people will plant vineyards and eat the fruit themselves—their enemies will not confiscate it. For my people will live as long as trees and will long enjoy their hard-won gains. [23]Their harvests will not be eaten by their enemies; their children will not be born to be cannon fodder. For they are the children of those the Lord has blessed; and their children, too, shall be blessed. [24]I will answer them before they even call to me. While they are still talking to me about their needs, I will go ahead and answer their prayers! [25]The wolf and lamb shall feed together, the lion shall eat straw as the ox does, and poisonous snakes shall strike no more! In those days nothing and no one shall be hurt or destroyed in all my Holy Mountain, says the Lord.

Isa 66:19. I will perform a mighty miracle against them, and I will send those who escape, as missionaries to the nations—to Tarshish, Put, Lud, Meshech, Rosh, Tubal, Javan, and to the lands beyond the sea that have not heard my fame nor seen my glory. There they shall declare my glory to the Gentiles.

Jer 3:14. O sinful children, come home, for I am your Master and I will bring you again to the land of Israel—one from here and two from there, wherever you are scattered. [15]And I will give you leaders after my own heart, who will guide you with wisdom and understanding. [16]Then, when your land is once more filled with people, says the Lord, you will no longer wish for "the good old days of long ago" when you possessed the Ark of God's covenant. Those days will not be missed or even thought about, and the Ark will not be reconstructed, [17]for the Lord himself will be among you, and the whole city of Jerusalem will be known as the throne of the Lord, and all nations will come to him there and no longer stubbornly follow their evil desires. [18]At that time the people of Judah and of Israel will return together from their exile in the north, to the land I gave their fathers as an inheritance forever. [19]And I thought how wonderful it would be for you to be here among my children. I planned to give you part of this beautiful land, the finest in the world. I looked forward to your calling me "Father," and thought that you would never turn away from me again.

Dan 2:44. During the reigns of those kings, the God of heaven will set up a kingdom that will never be destroyed; no one will ever conquer it. It will shatter all these kingdoms into nothingness, but it shall stand forever, indestructible.

Dan 7:9. I watched as thrones were put in place and the Ancient of Days—the Almighty God—sat down to judge. His clothing was as white as snow, his hair like whitest wool. He sat upon a fiery throne brought in on flaming wheels, and, [10]a river of fire flowed from before him. Millions of angels ministered to him and hundreds of millions of people stood before him, waiting to be judged. Then the court began its session and The Books were opened. [11]As I watched, the brutal fourth animal was killed and its body handed over to be burned because of its arrogance against Almighty God, and the boasting of its little horn. [12]As for the other three animals, their kingdoms were taken from them, but they were allowed to live a short time longer. [13]Next I saw the arrival of a Man—or so he seemed to be—brought there on clouds from heaven; he approached the Ancient of Days and was presented to him. [14]He was given the ruling power and glory over all the nations of the world, so that all people of every language must obey him. His power is eternal—it will never end; his government shall never fall. [27]Then every nation under heaven, and all their power, shall be given to the people of God; they shall rule all things forever, and all rulers shall serve and obey them.

Hos 2:18. At that time I will make a treaty between you and the wild animals, birds, and snakes, not to fear each other any more; and I will destroy all weapons, and all wars will end. [23]And I will say to those who are "not my people," "Now you are my people"; and they will reply, "You are our God!"

Amos 9:11. "Then, at that time, I will rebuild the City of David, which is now lying in ruins, and return it to its former glory, [12]and Israel will possess what is left of Edom, and of all the nations that belong to me." For so the Lord, who plans it all, has said.

Mic 4:1. But in the last days Mount Zion will be the most renowned of all the mountains of the world, praised by all nations; people from all over the world will make pilgrimages there. [2]"Come," they will say to one another, "let us visit the mountain of the Lord, and see the Temple of the God of Israel; he will tell us what to do, and we will do it." For in those days the whole world will be ruled by the Lord from Jerusalem! He will issue his laws and announce his decrees from there. [3]He will arbitrate among the nations, and dictate to strong nations far away. They will beat their swords into plowshares and their spears into pruning-hooks; nations shall no longer fight each other, for all war will end. There will be universal peace, and all the military academies and training camps will be closed down. [4]Everyone will live quietly in his own home in peace and prosperity, for there will be nothing to fear. The Lord himself has promised this. [5](Therefore we will follow the Lord our God forever and ever, even though all the nations around us worship idols!) [6]In that coming day, the Lord says that he will bring back his punished people—sick and lame and dispossessed— [7]and make them strong again in their own land, a mighty nation, and the Lord himself shall be their King from Mount Zion forever.

Zech 8:20, 21. People from around the world will come on pilgrimages and pour into Jerusalem from many foreign cities to attend these celebrations. People will write their friends in other cities and say, "Let's go to Jerusalem to ask the Lord to bless us, and be merciful to us. I'm going! Please come with me. Let's go *now!*" [22]Yes, many people, even strong nations, will come to the Lord of Hosts in Jerusalem to ask for his blessing and help. [23]In those days ten men from ten different nations will clutch at the coat sleeves of one Jew and say, "Please be my friend, for I know that God is with you."

Lk 1:32. He shall be very great and shall be called the Son of God. And the Lord God shall give him the throne of his ancestor David. [33]And he shall reign over Israel forever; his Kingdom shall never end!

Lk 22:29. And because my Father has granted me a Kingdom, I, here and now, grant you the right [30]to eat and drink at my table in that Kingdom; and you will sit on thrones judging the twelve tribes of Israel.

Heb 1:8. But of his Son he says, "Your kingdom, O God, will last forever and ever; its commands are always just and right."

2 Pet 1:11. And God will open wide the gates of heaven for you to enter into the eternal kingdom of our Lord and Savior Jesus Christ.

KINGDOM OF SATAN Mt 12:26; Mk 3:23, 24; Lk 11:18. Satan or Beelzebub, the king of the demons, Mt 9:34; 12:24; Mk 3:22; Lk 11:15, 18. The prince of this world, Jn 12:31; 14:30; 16:11. The god of this world, 2 Cor 4:4. The prince of the power of the air, Eph 2:2. Leader of the powers of darkness, Eph 6:11, 12. Leader of the evil angels, Mt 25:41; Rev 12:7–9.

See *Satan; Demons.*

KING'S VALLEY Gen 14:17; 2 Sam 18:18.

KINSMAN REDEEMER See *Redeemer.*

KIR The inhabitants of Damascus taken into captivity to, by the king of Assyria, 2 Kgs 16:9. Prophecies concerning, Isa 22:6, 7; Amos 1:5; 9:7.

KIR-HARASETH Called also *Kir-haresh, Kir-hareseth,* and *Kir-heres.* A city of Moab, 2 Kgs 3:25; Isa 16:7, 11; Jer 48:31, 36. Called *Kir of Moab,* Isa 15:1.

KIRIATHAIM 1. A city of Reuben, Num 32:37, 38; Josh 13:19. Plain of, originally populated by the Emim, Gen 14:5, 6. Prophecies concerning, Jer 48:1, 23; Ezk 25:9, 10.

2. A Levitical city in Naphtali, 1 Chron 6:76.

KIRIATH-ARBA An early name of *Hebron,* Gen 35:27; Josh 14:15; Judg 1:10.

KIRIATH-BAAL See *Kiriath-jearim.*

KIRIATH-HUZOTH A residence of Balak, Num 22:39.

KIRIATH-JEARIM Called also *Baalah* and *Kiriath-baal,* one of the four cities of the Gibeonites. Inhabitants of, not destroyed, because of the treaty made by the Israelites with the Gibeonites, but put under servitude, Josh 9:17; with verses 3–27.

In the territory allotted to Judah, Josh 15:9, 48–62; 18:14. The Philistines bring the Ark to, 1 Sam 6:21, with verses 1–21; Ark remains 20 years at, 1 Sam 7:1, 2; 1 Chron 13:5, 6. David brings the Ark from, 2 Chron 1:4. Inhabitants of, who were taken into captivity to Babylon, returned, Ezra 2:3–35; Neh 7:8–38. Uriah, the prophet, an inhabitant of, Jer 26:20.

KIRIATH-SANNAH A city of Judah, Josh 15:48–62.

See *Debir, 1.*

KIRIATH-SEPHER Josh 15:15, 16.

See *Debir, 1.*

KISH 1. Father of Saul, 1 Sam 9:1–3; 10:21; 2 Sam 21:12–14; Acts 13:21.

2. A Benjaminite, 1 Chron 8:30–32; 9:35–37.

3. A Levite, 1 Chron 23:21, 22; 24:29.

4. A Levite, 2 Chron 29:12–14.

5. Great-grandfather of Mordecai, Esther 2:5.

KISHI Called also *Kushaiah.* Father of Ethan, a chief assistant in the Temple music, 1 Chron 6:44–47; 15:17.

KISHION See *Kedesh, 2.*

KISHON A noted river of Palestine emptying into the Mediterranean near the northern base of Mount Carmel; Sisera defeated at, and his army destroyed in, Judg 4:7, 13; 5:21; Ps 83:9. Prophets of Baal killed by Elijah at, 1 Kgs 18:40.

KISLEV See *Calendar.*

KISS Of affection, Gen 27:26; 31:55; 33:4; 48:10; 50:1; Ruth 1:14; 2 Sam 14:33; 19:39; Lk 15:20; Acts 20:37. The feet of Jesus kissed by the penitent woman, Lk 7:38. Deceitful, Prov 27:6; of Joab, when he killed Amasa, 2 Sam 20:8–10; of Judas, when he betrayed Jesus, Mt 26:48; Lk 22:48. Idolatrous, 1 Kgs 19:18; Job 31:27; Hos 13:2.

KITE Isa 34:15, 16. A bird forbidden as food, Lev 11:13–19.

See *Vulture.*

KITRON A city of Zebulun, Judg 1:30.

KITTIM Son of Javan, Gen 10:4.

KNEADING TROUGH Ex 8:3; 12:34.

KNIFE An edged tool, Josh 5:2, 3; carried by Abraham, Gen 22:6. Used in the Temple, Ezk 40:42. Used for cutting, Jer 36:23; Ezk 5:2. Self-injury with, in idolatrous worship, 1 Kgs 18:28.

FIGURATIVE. Prov 30:13, 14.

KNOWLEDGE Of good and bad, Gen 2:9, 16, 17; 3:22. Is power, Prov 3:20. Desire for, 1 Kgs 3:9; Ps 119:66; Prov 2; 3; 12:1; 15:14; 18:15. Rejected, Hos 4:6. Those who reject are destroyed, Hos 4:6. Fools hate, Prov 1:22, 29. A spiritual gift, 1 Cor 12:8. Is pleasant, Prov 2:10. Shall be increased, Dan 12:4.

The earth shall be full of, Isa 11:9. Reverence of the Lord is the first step toward, Prov 1:7–9. Of more value than gold, Prov 8:10. The priest's lips should flow with, Mal 2:7.

Of salvation, Lk 1:77. Now we know so little, 1 Cor 13:9–12. Of God more than offerings, Hos 6:6. Of Christ, Phil 3:8.

See *Wisdom.*

KOA Enemy of Jerusalem, Ezk 23:23.

KOHATH Son of Levi, Gen 46:8–14; Ex 6:16. Grandfather of Moses, Aaron, and Miriam, Num 26:58, 59. Father of the Kohathites, one of the divisions of the Levites, Ex 6:18; Num 3:25–30.

See *Levites.*

KOLAIAH 1. A Benjaminite and ancestor of Sallu, Neh 11:7–9.

2. Father of the false prophet Ahab, Jer 29:21.

KORAH 1. A son of Esau, Gen 36:5, 18, 19.

2. Son of Eliphaz, Gen 36:15, 16.

3. A Korahite Levite, Ex 6:18, 21, 24; jealous of Moses, leads 250 leaders in a rebellion, and is swallowed up in the earth, Num 16; 26:5–11; Deut 11:6; Ps 106:17; Jude 1:11.

4. Son of Hebron, 1 Chron 2:43.

5. Son of Kohath, and head of the family of sacred musicians among the Levites, 1 Chron 6:22–24.

KORAHITES A division of the Levites. See *Levites.*

KORE 1. A Korahite, 1 Chron 9:19; 26:1.

2. A Levite, keeper of the East Gate, 2 Chron 31:14, 15.

KOSHER LAWS See *Food.*

KOZ Father of Anub, 1 Chron 4:8.

KUSHAIAH See *Kishi.*

L

LAADAH Son of Shelah, 1 Chron 4:21, 22.

LABAN 1. Son of Bethuel, Gen 28:5. Brother of Rebekah, Gen 22:20–23; 24:15, 16, 29, 30. Welcomes the servant of Abraham, Gen 24:29–33. Receives Jacob, and gives him his daughters in marriage, Gen 29:12–30. Jacob becomes his servant, Gen 29:15–20, 27; 30:27–43. Outwitted by Jacob, Gen 30:37–43; 31:1–21. Pursues Jacob, overtakes him at Mount Gilead, and makes peace with him, Gen 31:22–55.

2. A city, possibly located in the plains of Moab, Deut 1:1–5.

LABOR Gen 3:19. All your life you will sweat to master it, until your dying day. Then you will return to the ground from which you came. For you were made from the ground, and to the ground you will return.

Ex 20:9. Six days a week are for your daily duties and your regular work, [10]but the seventh day is a day of Sabbath rest before the Lord your God. On that day you are to do no work of any kind, nor shall your son, daughter, or slaves—whether men or women— or your cattle or your house guests. [11]For in six days the Lord made the heaven, earth, and sea, and everything in them, and rested the seventh day; so he blessed the Sabbath day and set it aside for rest.

Ex 23:12. Work six days only and rest the seventh; this is to give your oxen and donkeys a rest, as well as the people of your household—your slaves and visitors.

Ex 34:21. Even during plowing and harvest times, work only six days, and rest on the seventh. Lev 23:3.

Lev 19:13. You shall not rob nor oppress anyone, and you shall pay your hired workers promptly. If something is due them, don't even keep it overnight.

Deut 24:14, 15. Never oppress a poor hired man, whether a fellow Israelite or a foreigner living in your town. Pay him his wage each day before sunset, for since he is poor he needs it right away; otherwise he may cry out to the Lord against you and it would be counted as a sin against you.

Deut 25:4. Don't muzzle an ox as it treads out the grain. 1 Cor 9:9; 1 Tim 5:18.

Eccl 5:12. The man who works hard sleeps well whether he eats little or much, but the rich must worry and suffer insomnia.

Jer 22:13. And woe to you, King Jehoiakim, for you are building your great palace with forced labor. By not paying wages you are building injustice into its walls and oppression into its doorframes and ceilings.

Mal 3:5. "At that time my punishments will be quick and certain; I will move swiftly against wicked men who trick the innocent, against adulterers, and liars, against all those who cheat their hired hands, or oppress widows and orphans, or defraud strangers, and do not fear me," says the Lord of Hosts.

Mt 20:1. Here is another illustration of the Kingdom of Heaven. "The owner of an estate went out early one morning to hire workers for his harvest field. [2]He agreed to pay them $20 a day and sent them out to work. [3]A couple of hours later he was passing a hiring hall and saw some men standing around waiting for jobs, [4]so he sent them also into his fields, telling them he would pay them whatever was right at the end of the day. [5]At noon and again around three o'clock in the afternoon he did the same thing. [6]At five o'clock that evening he was in town again and saw some more men standing around and asked them, 'Why haven't you been working today?' [7]'Because no one hired us,' they replied. 'Then go on out and join the others in my fields,' he told them. [8]That evening he told the paymaster to call the men in and pay them, beginning with the last men first. [9]When the men hired at five o'clock were paid, each received $20. [10]So when the men hired earlier came to get theirs, they assumed they would receive much more. But they, too, were paid $20. [11, 12]They protested, 'Those fellows worked only one hour, and yet you've paid them just as much as those of us who worked all day in the scorching heat.' [13]'Friend,' he answered one of them, 'I did you no wrong! Didn't you agree to work all day for $20? [14]Take it and go. It is my desire to pay all the same; [15]is it against the law to give away my money if I want to? Should you be angry because I am kind?' "

Lk 10:7. The workman is worthy of his wages!

Eph 4:28. If anyone is stealing he must stop it and begin using those hands of his for honest work so he can give to others in need.

1 Thess 4:11. This should be your ambition: to live a quiet life, minding your own business and doing your own work, just as we told you before. [12]As a result, people who are not Christians will trust and respect you, and you will not need to depend on others for enough money to pay your bills.

2 Thess 3:7. For you well know that you ought to follow our example: you never saw us loafing; [8]we never accepted food from anyone without buying it; we worked hard day and night for the money we needed to live on, in order that we would not be a burden to any of you. [9]It wasn't that we didn't have the right to ask you to feed us, but we wanted to show you, firsthand, how you should work for your living. [10]Even while we were still there with you we gave you this rule: "He who does not work shall not eat." [11]Yet we hear that some of you are living in laziness, refusing to work, and wasting your time in gossiping. [12]In the name of the Lord Jesus Christ we appeal to such people—to quiet down, get to work, and earn their own living. [13]And to the rest of you I say, dear brothers, never be tired of doing right.

Jas 5:4. For listen! Hear the cries of the field workers whom you have cheated of their pay. Their cries have reached the ears of the Lord of Hosts.

See *Employee; Employer; Idleness; Industry; Master; Servant.*

LACHISH A city. King of, besieges Gibeon, Josh 10:3–5. Captured by Joshua, Josh 10:31, 32. Allotted to Judah, Josh 15:37–44. Fortified by Rehoboam, 2 Chron 11:5–10. Assassination of Amaziah at, 2 Kgs 14:19. Besieged by Sennacherib, 2 Kgs 18:13–17; 19:8; 2 Chron 32:9; by Nebuchadnezzar, Jer 34:7. Prophecy concerning, Mic 1:13.

LADAN 1. A descendant of Ephraim, 1 Chron 7:25–27.

2. A Levite, called also *Libni,* 1 Chron 6:17; 23:7–9; 26:20–22.

LADDER In Jacob's dream, Gen 28:12.

LAHAD A descendant of Judah, 1 Chron 4:2.

LAHMAM A city of Judah, Josh 15:37–44.

LAHMI Brother of Goliath. Killed by Elhanan, 2 Sam 21:19; 1 Chron 20:5.

LAISH 1. Called also *Leshem.* See *Dan, 3.*

2. A native of Gallim, 1 Sam 25:44.

3. A town near Jerusalem, Isa 10:30.

LAKE 1. Of fire, Rev 19:20; 20:10, 14, 15; 21:8.

2. See *Galilee, Sea of.*

LAKUM A city in Naphtali, Josh 19:33.

LAMA SABACHTHANI The dying cry of Jesus, Mt 27:46; Mk 15:34. See Ps 22:1.

LAMB Offering of, Ex 29:38–41; Lev 3:7, 8; 4:32; 5:6; 22:23; 23:19; Num 6:12; 7:15; 28:3–8.

LAMB OF GOD A name of Jesus, Jn 1:29, 36; 1 Cor 5:7; 1 Pet 1:19; Rev 6:16; 7:9, 10, 14, 17; 12:11; 13:8; 14:1, 4; 15:3, 4; 17:14; 19:7; 21:9, 14, 22, 23, 27; 22:1, 3.

LAMECH 1. Father of Jabal, Jubal, and Tubal-cain, Gen 4:18–24.

2. Son of Methuselah, and father of Noah, lived 777 years, Gen 5:25–31; 1 Chron 1:1–4. Ancestor of Jesus, Lk 3:23–38.

LAMENESS Disqualified priests from exercising priestly duties, Lev 21:18. Disqualified animals for sacrificial uses, Deut 15:21. Hated by David, 2 Sam 5:8. Healed by Jesus, Mt 11:5; 15:31; 21:14; Lk 7:20–22; by Peter, Acts 3:2–11. Non-existent during the kingdom, Isa 35:5, 6.

FIGURATIVE. Heb 12:13.

LAMENTATIONS Of David, Ps 60:1–3. Of Jeremiah, see the book of Lamentations. Of Ezekiel, Ezk 19; 28:12–19.

See *Elegy; Mourning; Sorrow.*

LAMING Of horses, Josh 11:6, 9; 2 Sam 8:4; 1 Chron 18:4.

LAMP For the Tabernacle, Ex 25:31–40; 37:17–24. Kept burning continually in the Tabernacle and cared for by priests, Ex 27:20, 21; Lev 24:1–4. Trimmed every morning, Ex 30:7.

See *Torch.*

Symbolical. Zech 4:2–10; Rev 4:5.

See *Candlestick; Lampstand.*

LAMPSTAND Called also *Candlestick.*

OF THE TABERNACLE. Made after divine pattern, Ex 25:31–40; 37:17–24; Num 8:4. Place of, Ex 26:35; 40:24; Heb 9:1, 2. Accessories of, Ex 25:38; 37:23, 24; Num 4:9, 10. Carried by Kohathites, Num 4:4, 15.

OF THE TEMPLE. Ten branches of, 1 Kgs 7:49, 50. Of gold, 1 Chron 28:15; 2 Chron 4:20. Taken with other spoils to Babylon, Jer 52:19.

Symbolical. Zech 4:2, 11; Rev 1:12, 20; 2:5; 11:4.

LAND Appeared on third creative day, Gen 1:9, 10. Original title to, from God, Gen 13:14–17; 15:7; Ex 23:31; Lev 25:23. Bought and sold, Gen 23:3–18; 33:19; Acts 4:34, 35; 5:1–8.

Sale and redemption of, laws concerning, Lev 25:14–16, 23–33; 27:17–24; Num 36:4; Jer 32:6–16, 25, 44; Ezk 46:18. Conveyance of, by written deeds and other forms, Gen 23:3–20; Ruth 4:3–8, 11; Jer 32:9–14; witnessed, Gen 23:10, 11; Ruth 4:9–11; Jer 32:9–14.

Sold for debt, Neh 5:2–5. Rights in, alienated, 2 Kgs 8:1–6. Leased, Lk 20:9–16; Mt 21:33–41.

Priest's part in, Gen 47:22; Ezk 48:10, 11. King's part in, Ezk 48:21, 22. Widow's dower in, Ruth 4:3–9. Unmarried woman's rights in, Num 27:1–11; 36:1–12.

To rest every seventh year for the benefit of the poor, Ex 23:11. Monopoly of, Gen 47:20–26; Isa 5:8; Mic 2:1, 2. See *Mortgage.*

Rules for apportioning Canaan among the tribes, see *Canaan;* also Ezk 47:22.

LANDMARKS Protected from fraudulent removal, Deut 19:14; Job 24:2; Prov 22:28.

See *Boundary.*

LANGUAGE Unity of, Gen 11:1, 6. Confusion of, Gen 10:5, 20, 31; 11:1–9. Dialects of the Jews, Judg 12:6; Mt 26:73. Many spoken at Jerusalem, Jn 19:20; Acts 2:8–11. Speaking in unknown, in church, forbidden, 1 Cor 14:2–28.

Gift of, Mk 16:17; Acts 2:7, 8; 10:46, 47; 19:6; 1 Cor 12:10; 14.

Mention in scripture: Of Ashdod, Neh 13:24; Chaldean, Dan 1:3, 4; Egyptian, Acts 2:10; Ps 114: 1; Greek, Jn 19:20; Acts 21:37, 38; Latin, Jn 19:20; Lycaonian, Acts 14:11; Parthian and others, Acts 2: 9–11; Aramaic, 2 Kgs 18:26; Ezra 4:7; Dan 2:4.

LANTERN Zeph 1:12; Jn 18:3.

LAODICEA A Phrygian city. Paul's concern for, Col 2:1. Epaphras's zeal for, Col 4:13. Letter to the Colossians to be read in, Col 4:15, 16. Message to, through John, Rev 1:11; 3:14–22.

LAPIS LAZULI A semiprecious stone. Exported from Havilah, Gen 2:11, 12.

LAPPIDOTH Husband of Deborah, Judg 4: 4.

LARCENY See *Theft.*

LASCIVIOUSNESS Ex 32:6. So they were up early the next morning and began offering burnt offerings and peace offerings to the calf-idol; afterwards they sat down to feast and drink at a wild party, followed by sexual immorality.

Prov 2:16, 17. Only wisdom from the Lord can save a man from the flattery of prostitutes; these girls have abandoned their husbands and flouted the laws of God. [18]Their houses lie along the road to death and hell.

Prov 5:3. For the lips of a prostitute are as sweet as honey, and smooth flattery is her stock in trade. [4]But afterwards only a bitter conscience is left to you, sharp as a double-edged sword. [5]She leads you down to death and hell. [8]*Run from her! Don't go near her house,* [9]lest you fall to her temptation and lose your honor, and give the remainder of your life to the cruel and merciless; [10]lest strangers obtain your wealth, and you become a slave of foreigners. [11]Lest afterwards you groan in anguish and in shame, when syphilis consumes your body, [12]and you say, "Oh, if only I had listened! If only I had not demanded my own way! [13]Oh, why wouldn't I take advice? Why was I so stupid?"

Prov 7:6. I was looking out the window of my house one day, [7]and saw a simple-minded lad, a young man lacking common sense, [8, 9]walking at twilight down the street to the house of this wayward girl, a prostitute. [10]She approached him, saucy and pert, and dressed seductively. [11, 12]She was the brash, coarse type, seen often in the streets and markets, soliciting at every corner for men to be her lovers. [13]She put her arms around him and kissed him, and with a saucy look she said, [14]"I've decided to forget our quarrel! [15]I was just coming to look for you and here you are! [16, 17]My bed is spread with lovely, colored sheets of finest linen imported from Egypt, perfumed with myrrh, aloes and cinnamon. [18]Come on, let's take our fill of love until morning, [19]for my husband is away on a long trip. [20]He has taken a wallet full of money with him and won't return for several days." [21]So she seduced him with her pretty speech, her coaxing and her wheedling, until he yielded to her. He couldn't resist her flattery. [22]He followed her as an ox going to the butcher, or as a stag that is trapped, [23]waiting to be killed with an arrow through its heart. He was as a bird flying into a snare, not knowing the fate awaiting it there. [24]Listen to me, young men, and not only listen but obey; [25]don't let your desires get out of hand; don't let yourself think about her. Don't go near her; stay away from where she walks, lest she tempt you and seduce you. [26]For she has been the ruin of multitudes—a vast host of men have been her victims. [27]If you want to find the road to hell, look for her house.

Prov 9:13. A prostitute is loud and brash, and never has enough of lust and shame. [14]She sits at the door of her house or stands at the street corners of the city, [15]whispering to men going by, and to those minding their own business. [16]"Come home with me," she urges simpletons. [17]"Stolen melons are the sweetest; stolen applies taste the best!" [18]But they don't realize that her former guests are now citizens of hell.

Prov 30:18, 19. There are three things too wonderful for me to understand—no four! How an eagle glides through the sky. How a serpent crawls upon a rock. How a ship finds its way across the heaving ocean. The growth of love between a man and a girl. [20]There is another thing too: how a prostitute can sin and then say, "What's wrong with that?"

Joel 3:3. They divided up my people as their slaves; they traded a young lad for a prostitute, and a little girl for wine enough to get drunk.

Mk 7:21. For from within, out of men's hearts, come evil thoughts of lust, theft, murder, adultery, [22]wanting what belongs to others, wickedness, deceit, lewdness, envy, slander, pride, and all other folly. [23]All these vile things come from within; they are what pollute you and make you unfit for God.

Rom 1:22. Claiming themselves to be wise without God, they became utter fools instead. [23]And then, instead of worshiping the glorious, everliving God, they took wood and stone and made idols for themselves, carving them to look like mere birds and animals and snakes and puny men. [24]So God let them go ahead into every sort of sex sin, and do whatever they wanted to—yes, vile and sinful things with each other's bodies. [25]Instead of believing what they knew was the truth about God, they deliberately chose to believe lies. So they prayed to the things God made, but wouldn't obey the blessed God who made these things. [26]That is why God let go of them and let them do all these evil things, so that even their women turned against God's natural plan for them and indulged in sex sin with each other. [27]And the men, instead of having a normal sex relationship with women, burned with lust for each other, men doing shameful things with other men and, as a result, getting paid within their own souls with the penalty they so richly deserved. [28]So it was that when they gave God up and would not even acknowledge him, God gave them up to doing everything their evil minds could think of. [29]Their lives became full of every kind of wickedness and sin, of greed and hate, envy, murder, fighting, lying, bitterness, and gossip.

Rom 7:8. But sin used this law against evil desires by reminding me that such desires are wrong and arousing all kinds of forbidden desires within me!

Rom 13:13. Be decent and true in everything you do so that all can approve your behavior. Don't spend your time in wild parties and getting drunk or in adultery and lust, or fighting, or jealousy.

1 Cor 6:9, 10. Don't you know that those doing such things have no share in the Kingdom of God? Don't fool yourselves. Those who live immoral lives, who are idol worshipers, adulterers or homosexuals—will have no share in his kingdom. Neither will thieves or greedy people, drunkards, slanderers, or robbers. [13]For instance, take the matter of eating. God has given us an appetite for food and stomachs to digest it. But that doesn't mean we should eat more than we need. Don't think of eating as important, because some day God will do away with both stomachs and food. But sexual sin is never right: our bodies were not made for that, but for the Lord, and the Lord wants to fill our bodies with himself. [15]Don't you realize that your bodies are actually parts and members of Christ? So should I take part of Christ and join him to a prostitute? Never! [16]And don't you know that if a man joins himself to a prostitute she becomes a part of him and he becomes a part of her? For God tells us in the Scripture that in his sight the two become one person. [17]But if you give yourself to the Lord, you and Christ are joined together as one person. [18]That is why I say to run from sex sin. No other sin affects the body as this one does. When you sin this sin it is against your own body.

1 Cor 9:27. Like an athlete I punish my body, treating it roughly, training it to do what it should, not what it wants to. Otherwise I fear that after enlisting others for the race, I myself might be declared unfit and ordered to stand aside.

2 Cor 12:21. Yes, I am afraid that when I come God will humble me before you and I will be sad and mourn because many of you who have sinned became sinners and don't even care about the wicked, impure things you have done: your lust and immorality, and the taking of other men's wives.

Gal 5:19. But when you follow your own wrong inclinations your lives will produce these evil results: impure thoughts, eagerness for lustful pleasure, [20]idolatry, spiritism (that is, encouraging the activity of demons), hatred and fighting, jealousy and anger, constant effort to get the best for yourself, complaints and criticisms, the feeling that everyone else is wrong except those in your own little group—and there will be wrong doctrine, [21]envy, murder, drunkenness, wild parties, and all that sort of thing. Let me tell you again as I have before, that anyone living that sort of life will not inherit the kingdom of God.

Eph 4:17, 18. Let me say this, then, speaking for the Lord: Live no longer as the unsaved do, for they are blinded and confused. Their closed hearts are full of darkness; they are far away from the life of God because they have shut their minds against him, and they cannot understand his ways. [19]They don't care anymore about right and wrong and have given themselves over to impure ways. They stop at nothing, being driven by their evil minds and reckless lusts.

Eph 5:5. You can be sure of this: The kingdom of Christ and of God will never belong to anyone who is impure or greedy, for a greedy person is really an idol worshiper—he loves and worships the good things of this life more than God.

Col 3:5. Away then with sinful, earthly things; deaden the evil desires lurking within you; have nothing to do with sexual sin, impurity, lust and shameful desires; don't worship the good things of life, for that is idolatry.

1 Thess 4:5. Not in lustful passion as the heathen do, in their ignorance of God and his ways.

2 Tim 3:6. They are the kind who craftily sneak into other people's homes and make friendships with silly, sin-burdened women and teach them their new doctrines.

1 Pet 4:2. And you won't be spending the rest of your life chasing after evil desires, but will be anxious to do the will of God. [3]You have had enough in the past of the evil things the godless enjoy—sex sin, lust, getting drunk, wild parties, drinking bouts, and the worship of idols, and other terrible sins.

Jude 1:4. I say this because some godless teachers have wormed their way in among you, saying that after we become Christians we can do just as we like without fear of God's punishment. The fate of such people was written long ago, for they have turned against our only Master and Lord, Jesus Christ. [7]And don't forget the cities of Sodom and Gomorrah and their neighboring towns, all full of lust of every kind including lust of men for other men. Those cities were destroyed by fire and continue to be a warning to us that there is a hell in which sinners are punished.

See *Adultery; Bestiality; Homosexuality; Idolatry, Licentiousness; Incest; Lust; Prostitute; Prostitution; Rape; Sensuality.*

FIGURATIVE. Ezk 16:15–59. See *Prostitution.*

INSTANCES OF. Sodomites, Gen 19:5. Lot's daughters, Gen 19:30–38. Judah, Gen 38:15, 16. The Gibeahites, Judg 19:22–25. Eli's sons, 1 Sam 2:22. David, 2 Sam 5:13; 11:2–27. Amnon, 2 Sam 13:1–14. Solomon, 1 Kgs 11:1–3. Rehoboam, 2 Chron 11:21–23. Persian kings, Esther 2:3, 12–14, 19.

LASEA A city of Crete, Acts 27:7, 8.

LASHA A place at the southern extremity of Canaan, Gen 10:15–19.

LASHARON King of, killed by Joshua, Josh 12:8–24.

LATIN Jn 19:20.

LATTICE 1 Kgs 7:16–22.

LAUGHTER A time for, Eccl 3:4. Attributed to God, Ps 37:12, 13; 59:8; Prov 1:26.

In prophecy, Ps 2:4; Prov 1:26; Lk 6:21. At the cross, Ps 22:7. See also Ps 126:2; Prov 14:13; Eccl 2:1, 2; 7:3; 10:19; Jas 4:9.

See *Happiness; Joy.*

LAVER Or basin. Directions for making, Ex 30:17–20; 31:9. Position of, Ex 40:7. Sanctified, Ex 30:28; 40:11; Lev 8:11. Used for washing, Ex 40:30–32.

Bronze, made by Solomon for the temple, 1 Kgs 7:23–26, 38, 39; 2 Chron 4:2–16. Altered by Ahaz, 2 Kgs 16:17. Broken and carried to Babylon, 2 Kgs 25:13, 16; Jer 52:17, 20.

LAW Ps 19:7, 8. God's laws are perfect. They protect us, make us wise, and give us joy and light. [9]God's laws are pure, eternal, just.

Ps 119:1. Happy are all who perfectly follow the laws of God. [2]Happy are all who search for God, and always do his will, [3]rejecting compromise with evil, and walking only in his paths. [4]You have given us your laws to obey—[5]oh, how I want to follow them consistently. [6]Then I will not be disgraced, for I will have a clean record. [7]After you have corrected me I will thank you by living as I should! [8]I *will* obey! Oh, don't forsake me and let me slip back into sin again.

Prov 28:4. To complain about the law is to praise wickedness. To obey the law is to fight evil. [5]Evil men don't understand the importance of justice, but those who follow the Lord are much concerned about it.

Mt 22:21. "Caesar's," they replied. "Well then," he said, "give it to Caesar if it is his, and give God everything that belongs to God." Luke 20:22–25.

Lk 16:17. But that doesn't mean that the Law has lost its force in even the smallest point. It is as strong and unshakable as heaven and earth.

Rom 2:12–15. He will punish sin wherever it is found. He will punish the heathen when they sin, even though they never had God's written laws, for down in their hearts they know right from wrong. God's laws are written within them; their own conscience accuses them, or sometimes excuses them. And God will punish the Jews for sinning because they have his written laws but don't obey them. They know what is right but don't do it. After all, salvation is not given to those who know what to do, unless they do it.

Rom 7:7. No, the law is not sinful but it was the law that showed me my sin. I would never have known the sin in my heart—the evil desires that are hidden there—if the law had not said "You must not have evil desires in your heart." [12]But still, you see, the law itself was wholly right and good. [14]The law is good, then, and the trouble is not there but with *me,* because I am sold into slavery with Sin as my owner.

Rom 13:10. Love does no wrong to anyone. That's why it fully satisfies all of God's requirements. It is the only law you need.

1 Tim 1:5. What I am eager for is that all the Christians there will be filled with love that comes from pure hearts, and that their minds will be clean and their faith strong. [8]Those laws are good when used as God intended. [9]But they were not made for us, whom God has saved; they are for sinners who hate God, have rebellious hearts, curse and swear, attack their fathers and mothers, and murder. [10, 11]Yes, these laws are made to identify as sinners all who are immoral and impure: homosexuals, kidnappers, liars, and all others who do things that contradict the glorious Good News of our blessed God, whose messenger I am.

Jas 1:25. But if anyone keeps looking steadily into God's law for free men, he will not only remember it but he will do what it says, and God will greatly bless him in everything he does.

1 Jn 3:4. But those who keep on sinning are against God, for every sin is done against the will of God.

1 Jn 5:3. Loving God means doing what he tells us to do, and really, that isn't hard at all.

See *Litigation; Commandments; Duty, of Man to God.*

OF MOSES. Contained in the books, Exodus, Leviticus, Numbers, and Deuteronomy. Given at Sinai, Ex 19; Deut 1:1–5; 4:10–13, 44–46; 33:2; Hab 3:3. Received through angels, Deut 33:2; Ps 68:17; Acts 7:53; Gal 3:19; Heb 2:2. Was given because of sins until the Messiah came, Gal 3:19. Engraved on stone, Ex 20:3–17, with 24:12; 31:18; 32:16; 34:29; 40:20; Deut 4:13; 5:4–22; 9:10. See *Tablet; Commandments.* Preserved in the Ark of the Covenant, Ex 25:16; Deut 31:9, 26. Found by Hilkiah in the Temple, 2 Kgs 22:8. Written on monuments, Deut 27:2–8; Josh 8:30–35. To be written on doorposts, Deut 6:9; 11:20; on the forehead, and tied on the hand, Ex 13:9, 16; Deut 6:4–9; 11:18–21. Children instructed in, see *Children; Instruction.* Taught by the priests and Levites, Lev 10:11; Deut 33:10; 2 Chron 35:3; Ezra 7:10; Neh 8:1–18; from city to city, 2 Chron 17:7–10; in synagogues, Lk 4:16, 31; Acts 13:14–52; 15:21, with 9:20; 14:1; 17:1–3; 18:4, 25, 26. Read to all the people at the feast of tabernacles in the sabbatic year, Deut 31:10–13. Renewed by Moses, Deut 4:44–46.

Curses of, responsively read by Levites and people at Ebal and Gerizim, Deut 27:12–26; Josh 8:33–35. Formed a constitution on which the civil government of the Israelites was founded, and according to which kings were required to rule, Deut 17:18–20; 2 Kgs 11:12; 2 Chron 23:11. See *Constitution.* Divine authority for, Ex 19:16–24; 20:1–17; 24:12–18; 31:18; 32:15, 16; 34:1–4, 27, 28; Lev 26:46; Deut 4:10–13, 36; 5:1–22; 9:10, 11; 10:1–5; 33:2–4; 1 Kgs 8:9; Ezra 7:6; Neh 1:6, 7; 8:1; 9:14; Ps 78:5; 103:7; Isa 33:22; Mal 4:4; Acts 7:38, 53; Gal 3:19; Heb 9:18–21.

Prophecies in, of the Messiah, Lk 24:44; Jn 1:45; 5:46; 12:34; Acts 26:22, 23; 28:23; Rom 3:21, 22. See *Jesus, Prophecies Concerning.* Epitomized by Jesus, Mt 22:40; Mk 12:29–33; Lk 10:27.

Scroll containing, found by Hilkiah in the Temple, 2 Kgs 22:8; 2 Chron 34:14.

TEMPORARY. Jer 3:16. Then, when your land is once more filled with people, says the Lord, you will no longer wish for "the good old days of long ago" when you possessed the Ark of God's covenant. Those days will not be missed or even thought about, and the Ark will not be reconstructed.

Dan 9:27. This king will make a seven-year

treaty with the people, but after half that time, he will break his pledge and stop the Jews from all their sacrifices and their offerings; then, as a climax to all his terrible deeds, the Enemy shall utterly defile the sanctuary of God. But in God's time and plan, his judgment will be poured out upon this Evil One.

Mt 5:17. Don't misunderstand why I have come—it isn't to cancel the laws of Moses and the warnings of the prophets. No, I came to fulfill them, and to make them all come true. 18With all the earnestness I have I say: Every law in the Book will continue until its purpose is achieved. 19And so if anyone breaks the least commandment, and teaches others to, he shall be the least in the Kingdom of Heaven. But those who teach God's laws *and obey them* shall be great in the Kingdom of Heaven. 20But I warn you—unless your goodness is greater than that of the Pharisees and other Jewish leaders, you can't get into the Kingdom of Heaven at all! 21Under the laws of Moses the rule was, "If you kill, you must die." 22But I have added to that rule, and tell you that if you are only *angry,* even in your own home, you are in danger of judgment! If you call your friend an idiot, you are in danger of being brought before the court. And if you curse him, you are in danger of the fires of hell. 23So if you are standing before the altar in the Temple, offering a sacrifice to God, and suddenly remember that a friend has something against you, 24leave your sacrifice there beside the altar and go and apologize and be reconciled to him, and then come and offer your sacrifice to God. 25Come to terms quickly with your enemy before it is too late and he drags you into court and you are thrown into a debtor's cell, 26for you will stay there until you have paid the last penny. 27The laws of Moses said, "You shall not commit adultery." 28But I say: Anyone who even looks at a woman with lust in his eye has already committed adultery with her in his heart. 29So if your eye—even if it is your best eye!—causes you to lust, gouge it out and throw it away. Better for part of you to be destroyed than for all of you to be cast into hell. 30And if your hand—even your right hand—causes you to sin, cut it off and throw it away. Better that than find yourself in hell. 31The law of Moses says, "If anyone wants to be rid of his wife, he can divorce her merely by giving her a letter of dismissal." 32But I say that a man who divorces his wife, except for fornication, causes her to commit adultery if she marries again. And he who marries her commits adultery. 33Again, the law of Moses says, "You shall not break your vows to God, but must fulfill them all." 34But I say: Don't make any vows! And even to say, "By heavens!" is a sacred vow to God, for the heavens are God's throne. 35And if you say "By the earth!" it is a sacred vow, for the earth is his footstool. And don't swear "By Jerusalem!" for Jerusalem is the capital of the great King. 36Don't even swear "By my head!" for you can't turn one hair white or black. 37Say just a simple "Yes, I will" or "No, I won't." Your word is enough. To strengthen your promise with a vow shows that something is wrong. 38The law of Moses says, "If a man gouges out another's eye, he must pay with his own eye. If a tooth gets knocked out, knock out the tooth of the one who did it." 39But I say: Don't resist violence! If you are slapped on one cheek, turn the other too. 40If you are ordered to court, and your shirt is taken from you, give your coat too. 41If the military demand that you carry their gear for a mile, carry it two. 42Give to those who ask, and don't turn away from those who want to borrow. 43There is a saying, "Love your *friends* and hate your enemies." 44But I say: Love your *enemies!* Pray for those who *persecute* you! 45In that way you will be acting as true sons of your Father in heaven. For he gives his sunlight to both the evil and the good, and sends rain on the just and on the unjust too.

Lk 16:16. Until John the Baptist began to preach, the laws of Moses and the messages of the prophets were your guides. But John introduced the Good News that the Kingdom of God would come soon. And now eager multitudes are pressing in. 17But that doesn't mean that the Law has lost its force in even the smallest point. It is as strong and unshakable as heaven and earth.

Jn 1:17. For Moses gave us only the Law with its rigid demands and merciless justice, while Jesus Christ brought us loving forgiveness as well.

Jn 4:20. "But say, tell me, why is it that you Jews insist that Jerusalem is the only place of worship, while we Samaritans claim it is here (at Mount Gerazim), where our ancestors worshiped?" 21-24Jesus replied, "The time is coming, ma'am, when we will no longer be concerned about whether to worship the Father here or in Jerusalem. For it's not *where* we worship that counts, but *how* we worship—is our worship spiritual and real? Do we have the Holy Spirit's help? For God is Spirit, and we must have his help to worship as we should. The Father wants this kind of worship from us. But you Samaritans know so little about him, worshiping blindly, while we Jews know all about him, for salvation comes to the world through the Jews."

Jn 8:35 And slaves don't have rights, but the Son has every right there is! See Gal 4:30, 31, below.

Acts 6:14. They declared, "We have heard him say that this fellow Jesus of Nazareth will destroy the Temple, and throw out all of Moses' laws."

Acts 10:28. Peter told them, "You know it is against the Jewish laws for me to come into a Gentile home like this. But God has shown me in a vision that I should never think of anyone as inferior."

Acts 13:39. Everyone who trusts in him is freed from all guilt and declared righteous—something the Jewish law could never do.

Acts 15:1. While Paul and Barnabas were at Antioch, some men from Judea arrived and began to teach the believers that unless they adhered to the ancient Jewish custom of circumcision, they could not be saved. 2Paul and Barnabas argued and discussed this with them at length, and finally the believers sent them to Jerusalem, accompanied by some local men, to talk to the apostles and elders there about this question. [3]After the entire congregation had escorted them out of the city the delegates went on to Jerusalem, stopping along the way in the cities of Phoenicia and Samaria to visit the believers, telling them—much to everyone's joy—that the Gentiles, too, were being converted. [4]Arriving in Jerusalem, they met with the church leaders—all the apostles and elders were present—and Paul and Barnabas reported on what God had been doing through their ministry. [5]But then some of the men who had been Pharisees before their conversion stood to their feet and declared that all Gentile converts must be circumcised and required to follow all the Jewish customs and ceremonies. [6]So the apostles and church elders set a further meeting to decide this question. [7]At the meeting, after long discussion, Peter stood and addressed them as follows: "Brothers, you all know that God chose me from among you long ago to preach the Good News to the Gentiles, so that they also could believe. [8]God, who knows men's hearts, confirmed the fact that he accepts Gentiles by giving them the Holy Spirit, just as he gave him to us. [9]He made no distinction between them and us, for he cleansed their lives through faith, just as he did ours. [10]And now are you going to correct God by burdening the Gentiles with a yoke that neither we nor our fathers were able to bear? [11]Don't you believe that all are saved the same way, by the free gift of the Lord Jesus?" [12]There was no further discussion, and everyone now listened as Barnabas and Paul told about the miracles God had done through them among the Gentiles. [13]When they had finished, James took the floor. "Brothers," he said, "listen to me. [14]Peter has told you about the time God first visited the Gentiles to take from them a people to bring honor to his name. [15]And this fact of Gentile conversion agrees with what the prophets predicted. For instance, listen to this passage from the prophet Amos: [16]'Afterwards' (says the Lord), 'I will return and renew the broken contract with David, [17]so that Gentiles, too, will find the Lord—all those marked with my name.' [18]That is what the Lord says, who reveals his plans made from the beginning. [19]And so my judgment is that we should not insist that the Gentiles who turn to God must obey our Jewish laws, [20]except that we should write to them to refrain from eating meat sacrificed to idols, from all fornication, and also from eating unbled meat of strangled animals. [21]For these things have been preached against in Jewish synagogues in every city on every Sabbath for many generations." [22]Then the apostles and elders and the whole congregation voted to send delegates to Antioch with Paul and Barnabas, to report on this decision. The men chosen were two of the church leaders—Judas (also called Barsabbas) and Silas. [23]This is the letter they took along with them: "*From:* The Apostles, elders and brothers at Jerusalem. *To:* The Gentile brothers in Antioch, Syria and Cilicia. Greetings! [24]We understand that some believers from here have upset you and questioned your salvation, but they had no such instructions from us. [25]So it seemed wise to us, having unanimously agreed on our decision, to send to you these two official representatives, along with our beloved Barnabas and Paul. [26]These men—Judas and Silas, who have risked their lives for the sake of our Lord Jesus Christ—will confirm orally what we have decided concerning your question. [27-29]For it seemed good to the Holy Spirit and to us to lay no greater burden of Jewish laws on you than to abstain from eating food offered to idols and from unbled meat of strangled animals, and, of course, from fornication. If you do this, it is enough. Farewell."

Acts 21:20. They praised God but then said, "You know, dear brother, how many thousands of Jews have also believed, and they are all very insistent that Jewish believers must continue to follow the Jewish traditions and customs. [21]Our Jewish Christians here at Jerusalem have been told that you are against the laws of Moses, against our Jewish customs, and that you forbid the circumcision of their children. [22]Now what can be done? For they will certainly hear that you have come. [23]We suggest this: We have four men here who are preparing to shave their heads and take some vows. [24]Go with them to the Temple and have your head shaved too—and pay for theirs to be shaved. Then everyone will know that you approve of this custom for the Hebrew Christians and that you yourself obey the Jewish laws and are in line with our thinking in these matters. [25]As for the Gentile Christians, we aren't asking them to follow these Jewish customs at all—except for the ones we wrote to them about: not to eat food offered to idols, not to eat unbled meat from strangled animals, and not to commit fornication."

Rom 3:1. Then what's the use of being a Jew? Are there any special benefits for them from God? Is there any value in the Jewish circumcision ceremony? [2]Yes, being a Jew has many advantages. First of all, God trusted them with his laws (so that they could know and do his will).

Rom 7:1. Don't you understand yet, dear Jewish brothers in Christ, that when a person dies the law no longer holds him in its power? [2]Let me illustrate: when a woman marries, the law binds her to her husband as long as he is alive. But if he dies, she is no longer bound to him; the laws of marriage no longer apply to her. [3]Then she can marry someone else if she wants to. That would be wrong while he was alive, but it is perfectly all right after he dies. [4]Your "husband," your master, used to be the Jewish law; but you "died," as it were, with Christ on the cross; and since you are "dead," you are no longer "married to the law," and it has no more control over you. Then you came back to life again when Christ did, and are a new person. And now you are "married," so to speak, to the one who rose from the dead, so that you can produce good fruit, that is, good deeds for God. [5]When your old nature was still active, sinful desires were at work within you, making you want to do whatever God said not to, and producing sinful deeds, the rotting fruit of death. [6]But now you need no longer worry about the Jewish laws and customs because you "died" while in their captivity, and now you can really serve God; not in the old way, mechanically obeying a set of rules, but in the new way, (with all of your hearts and minds).

Rom 8:3. We aren't saved from sin's grasp by knowing the commandments of God, because we can't and don't keep them, but God put into effect a different plan to save us. He sent his own Son in a human body like ours—except that ours are sinful—and destroyed sin's control over us by giving himself as a sacrifice for our sins.

Rom 10:4. They don't understand that Christ gives to those who trust in him everything they are trying to get by keeping his laws. He ends all of that.

2 Cor 3:7. Yet that old system of law that led to death began with such glory that people could not bear to look at Moses' face. For as he gave them God's law to obey, his face shone out with the very glory of God—though the brightness was already fading away. [8]Shall we not expect far greater glory in these days when the Holy Spirit is giving life? [9]If the plan that leads to doom was glorious, much more glorious is the plan that makes men right with God. [10]In fact, that first glory as it shone from Moses' face is worth nothing at all in comparison with the overwhelming glory of the new agreement. [11]So if the old system that faded into nothing was full of heavenly glory, the glory of God's new plan for our salvation is certainly far greater, for it is eternal. [12]Since we know that this new glory will never go away, we can preach with great boldness, [13]and not as Moses did, who put a veil over his face so that the Israelis could not see the glory fade away. [14]Not only Moses' face was veiled, but his people's minds and understanding were veiled and blinded too. Even now when the Scripture is read it seems as though Jewish hearts and minds are covered by a thick veil, because they cannot see and understand the real meaning to the Scriptures. For this veil of misunderstanding can be removed only by believing in Christ.

Gal 2:3. And they did agree; they did not even demand that Titus, my companion, should be circumcised, though he was a Gentile. [4]Even that question wouldn't have come up except for some so-called "Christians" there—false ones, really—who came to spy on us and see what freedom we enjoyed in Christ Jesus, as to whether we obeyed the Jewish laws or not. They tried to get us all tied up in their rules, like slaves in chains. [5]But we did not listen to them for a single moment, for we did not want to confuse you into thinking that salvation can be earned by being circumcised and by obeying Jewish laws. [6]And the great leaders of the church who were there had nothing to add to what I was preaching. (By the way, their being great leaders made no difference to me, for all are the same to God.) [7-9]In fact, when Peter, James, and John, who were known as the pillars of the church, saw how greatly God had used me in winning the Gentiles, just as Peter had been blessed so greatly in his preaching to the Jews—for the same God gave us each our special gifts—they shook hands with Barnabas and me and encouraged us to keep right on with our preaching to the Gentiles while they continued their work with the Jews.

Gal 4:30. But the Scriptures say that God told Abraham to send away the slave-wife and her son, for the slave-wife's son could not inherit Abraham's home and lands along with the free woman's son. [31]Dear brothers, we are not slave children, obligated to the Jewish laws, but children of the free woman, acceptable to God because of our faith.

Eph 2:15. By his death he ended the angry resentment between us, caused by the Jewish laws which favored the Jews and excluded the Gentiles, for he died to annul that whole system of Jewish laws. Then he took the two groups that had been opposed to each other and made them parts of himself; thus he fused us together to become one new person, and at last there was peace.

Col 2:14. And blotted out the charges proved against you, the list of his commandments which you had not obeyed. He took this list of sins and destroyed it by nailing it to Christ's cross. [15]In this way God took away Satan's power to accuse you of sin, and God openly displayed to the whole world Christ's triumph at the cross where your sins were all taken away. [16]So don't let anyone criticize you for what you eat or drink, or for not celebrating Jewish holidays and feasts or new moon ceremonies or Sabbaths. [17]For these were only temporary rules that ended when Christ came. They were only shadows of the real thing—of Christ himself. [18]Don't let anyone declare you lost when you refuse to worship angels, as they say you must. They have seen a vision, they say, and know you should. These proud men (though they claim to be so humble) have a very clever imagination. [19]But they are not connected to Christ, the Head to which all of us who are his body are joined; for we are joined together by his strong sinews and we grow only as we get our nourishment and strength from God. [20]Since you died, as it were, with Christ and this has set you free from following the world's ideas of how to be saved—by doing good and obeying various rules—why do you keep right on following them anyway, still bound by such rules as [21]not eating, tasting, or even touching certain foods? [22]Such rules are mere human teachings, for food was made to be eaten and used up. [23]These rules may seem good, for rules of this kind require strong devotion and are humiliating and hard on the body, but they have no effect when it comes to conquering a person's evil thoughts and desires. They only make him proud.

Heb 8:4. The sacrifice he offers is far better than those offered by the earthly priests. (But even so, if he were here on earth he wouldn't even be permitted to be a priest, because down here the priests still follow the old Jewish system of sacrifices.) [5]Their work is connected with a mere earthly model of the real tabernacle in heaven; for when Moses was getting ready to build the tabernacle, God warned him to follow exactly the pattern of the heavenly tabernacle as shown to him on Mount Sinai. [6]But Christ, as a Minister in heaven, has been rewarded with a far more important work than those who serve under the old laws, because the new agreement which he passes on to us from God contains far more wonderful promises. [7]The old agreement didn't even work. If it had, there would have been no need for another to replace it. [8]But God himself found fault with the old one, for he said, "The day will come when I will make a new agreement with the people of Israel and the people of Judah. [9]This new agreement will not be like the old one I gave to their fathers on the day when I took them by the hand to lead them out of the land of Egypt; they did not keep their part in that agreement, so I had to cancel it. [10]But this is the new agreement I will make with the people of Israel, says the Lord: I will write my laws in their minds so that they will know what I want them to do without my even telling them, and these laws will be in their hearts so that they will want to obey them, and I will be their God and they shall be my people. [11]And no one then will need to speak to his friend or neighbor or brother, saying, 'You, too, should know the Lord,' because everyone, great and small, will know me already. [12]And I will be merciful to them in their wrongdoings, and I will remember their sins no more." [13]God speaks of these new promises, of this new agreement, as taking the place of the old one; for the old one is out of date now and has been put aside forever.

Heb 9:8. And the Holy Spirit uses all this to point out to us that under the old system the common people could not go into the Holy of Holies as long as the outer room and the entire system it represents were still in use. [9]This has an important lesson for us today. For under the old system, gifts and sacrifices were offered, but these failed to cleanse the hearts of the people who brought them. [10]For the old system dealt only with certain rituals —what foods to eat and drink, rules for washing themselves, and rules about this and that. The people had to keep these rules to tide them over until Christ came with God's new and better way. [11]He came as High Priest of this better system which we now have. He went into that greater, perfect tabernacle in heaven, not made by men nor part of this world, [12]and once for all took blood into that inner room, the Holy of Holies, and sprinkled it on the mercy seat; but it was not the blood of goats and calves. No, he took his own blood, and with it he, by himself, made sure of our eternal salvation. [13]And if under the old system the blood of bulls and goats and the ashes of young cows could cleanse men's bodies from sin, [14]just think how much more surely the blood of Christ will transform our lives and hearts. His sacrifice frees us from the worry of having to obey the old rules, and makes us want to serve the living God. For by the help of the eternal Holy Spirit, Christ willingly gave himself to God to die for our sins—he being perfect, without a single sin or fault. [15]Christ came with this new agreement so that all who are invited may come and have forever all the wonders God has promised them. For Christ died to rescue them from the penalty of the sins they had committed while still under that old system. [16]Now, if someone dies and leaves a will—a list of things to be given away to certain people when he dies—no one gets anything until it is proved that the person who wrote the will is dead. [17]The will goes into effect only after the death of the person who wrote it. While he is still alive no one can use it to get any of those things he has promised them. [18]That is why blood was sprinkled (as proof of Christ's death) before even the first agreement could go into effect. [19]For after Moses had given the people all of God's laws, he took the blood of calves and goats, along with water, and sprinkled the blood over the book of God's laws and over all the people, using branches of hyssop bushes and scarlet wool to sprinkle with. [20]Then he said, "This is the blood that marks the beginning of the agreement between you and God, the agreement God commanded me to make with you." [21]And in the same way he sprinkled blood on the sacred tent and on whatever instruments were used for worship. [22]In fact we can say that under the old agreement almost everything was cleansed by sprinkling it with blood, and without the shedding of blood there is no forgiveness of sins. [23]That is why the sacred tent down here on earth, and everything in it—all copied from things in heaven —all had to be made pure by Moses in this way, by being sprinkled with the blood of animals. But the real things in heaven, of which these down here are copies, were made pure with far more precious offerings. [24]For Christ has entered into heaven itself, to appear now before God as our Friend. It was not in the earthly place of worship that he did this, for that was merely a copy of the real temple in heaven.

Heb 10:1. The old system of Jewish laws gave only a dim foretaste of the good things Christ would do for us. The sacrifices under the old system were repeated again and again, year after year, but even so they could never save those who lived under their rules. [2]If they could have, one offering would have been enough; the worshipers would have been cleansed once for all, and their feeling of guilt would be gone. [3]But just the opposite happened: those yearly sacrifices reminded them of their disobedience and guilt instead of relieving their minds. [4]For it is not possible for the blood of bulls and goats really to take away sins. [5]That is why Christ said, as he came into the world, "O God, the blood of bulls and goats cannot satisfy you, so you have made ready this body of mine for me to lay as a sacrifice upon your altar. [6]You were not satisfied with the animal sacrifices, slain and burnt before you as offerings for sin. [7]Then I said,

'See, I have come to do your will, to lay down my life, just as the Scriptures said that I would.' " [8]After Christ said this, about not being satisfied with the various sacrifices and offerings required under the old system, [9]he then added, "Here I am. I have come to give my life." He cancels the first system in favor of a far better one. [10]Under this new plan we have been forgiven and made clean by Christ's dying for us once and for all. [11]Under the old agreement the priests stood before the altar day after day offering sacrifices that could never take away our sins. [12]But Christ gave himself to God for our sins as one sacrifice for all time, and then sat down in the place of highest honor at God's right hand, [13]waiting for his enemies to be laid under his feet. [14]For by that one offering he made forever perfect in the sight of God all those whom he is making holy. [15]And the Holy Spirit testifies that this is so, for he has said, [16]"This is the agreement I will make with the people of Israel, though they broke their first agreement: I will write my laws into their minds so that they will always know my will, and I will put my laws in their hearts so that they will want to obey them." [17]And then he adds, "I will never again remember their sins and lawless deeds." [18]Now, when sins have once been forever forgiven and forgotten, there is no need to offer more sacrifices to get rid of them.

Heb 11:40. For God wanted them to wait and share the even better rewards that were prepared for us.

Heb 12:18. You have not had to stand face to face with terror, flaming fire, gloom, darkness and a terrible storm, as the Israelites did at Mount Sinai when God gave them his laws. [19]For there was an awesome trumpet blast, and a voice with a message so terrible that the people begged God to stop speaking. [27]By this he means that he will sift out everything without solid foundations, so that only unshakeable things will be left.

LAWSUITS Deut 21:5; 2 Sam 15:4; Isa 59:4. To be avoided, Prov 25:8–10; Mt 5:25, 26; 1 Cor 6: 1–8.

FIGURATIVE. Hos 4:1; 12:2.

See *Actions at Law; Adjudication; Arbitration; Compromise; Court; Justice.*

LAWYER One versed in the Mosaic law. Test Jesus with questions, Mt 22:34, 35; Lk 10: 25–37. Jesus' satire against, Lk 11:45–52. Tertullus, a, Acts 24:1. Zenas, a, Tit 3:13.

FIGURATIVE. God called, 1 Sam 24:15; Jer 51: 36; Lam 3:58.

See *Litigation.*

LAYING ON OF HANDS See *Hand, Laying on of.*

LAZARUS 1. Brother of Mary and Martha. Sickness and death of, Jn 11:1–14. Resurrection of, Jn 11:37–44; 12:17, 18. Dined with Jesus, Jn 12:1, 2, 9. Plotted against by the chief priests, Jn 12:10, 11.

2. The beggar in Jesus' parable, Lk 16:19.

LAZINESS Job 3:26. I was not fat and lazy, yet trouble struck me down.

Prov 6:6. Take a lesson from the ants, you lazy fellow. Learn from their ways and be wise! [7]For though they have no king to make them work, [8]yet they labor hard all summer, gathering food for the winter. [9]But you—all you do is sleep. When will you wake up? [10]"Let me sleep a little longer!" Sure, just a little more! [11]And as you sleep, poverty creeps upon you like a robber and destroys you; want attacks you in full armor.

Prov 10:4. Lazy men are soon poor; hard workers get rich. [5]A wise youth makes hay while the sun shines, but what a shame to see a lad who sleeps away his hour of opportunity. [26]A lazy fellow is a pain to his employers—like smoke in their eyes or vinegar that sets the teeth on edge.

Prov 12:24. Work hard and become a leader; be lazy and never succeed. [27]A lazy man won't even dress the game he gets while hunting, but the diligent man makes good use of everything he finds.

Prov 13:4. Lazy people want much but get little, while the diligent are prospering.

Prov 15:19. A lazy fellow has trouble all through life; the good man's path is easy!

Prov 18:9. A lazy man is brother to the saboteur.

Prov 19:15. A lazy man sleeps soundly—and goes hungry! [24]Some men are so lazy they won't even feed themselves!

Prov 20:4. If you won't plow in the cold, you won't eat at the harvest.

Prov 21:25. The lazy man longs for many things but his hands refuse to work.

Prov 23:21. And remember that too much sleep clothes a man with rags.

Prov 24:30, 31. I walked by the field of a certain lazy fellow and saw that it was overgrown with thorns, and covered with weeds; and its walls were broken down. [32, 33]Then, as I looked, I learned this lesson: "A little extra sleep, a little more slumber, a little folding of the hands to rest" [34]means that poverty will break in upon you suddenly like a robber, and violently like a bandit.

Prov 26:13. The lazy man won't go out and work. "There might be a lion outside!" he says. [chapter 22:13.] [14]He sticks to his bed like a door to its hinges! [15]He is too tired even to lift his food from his dish to his mouth! [16]Yet in his own opinion he is smarter than seven wise men.

Prov 31:27. She watches carefully all that goes on throughout her household, and is never lazy.

Eccl 10:18. Laziness lets the roof leak, and soon the rafters begin to rot.

Isa 56:10. For the leaders of my people—the Lord's watchmen, his shepherds—are all blind to every danger. They are featherbrained and give no warning when danger comes. They love to lie there, love to sleep, to dream.

Mt 25:26. But his master replied, "Wicked man! Lazy slave! Since you knew I would demand your profit, [27]you should at least have put my money into the bank so I could have some interest."

Rom 12:11. Never be lazy in your work but serve the Lord enthusiastically.

2 Thess 3:6. Now here is a command, dear broth-

ers, given in the name of our Lord Jesus Christ by his authority: Stay away from any Christian who spends his days in laziness and does not follow the ideal of hard work we set up for you. [10]Even while we were still there with you we gave you this rule: "He who does not work shall not eat." [11]Yet we hear that some of you are living in laziness, refusing to work, and wasting your time gossiping. [12]In the name of the Lord Jesus Christ we appeal to such people—we command them—to quiet down, get to work, and earn their own living. 1 Thess 5:14; 1 Tim 5:13.

Heb 6:12. Then knowing what lies ahead for you, you won't become bored with being a Christian, nor become spiritually dull and indifferent, but you will be anxious to follow the example of those who receive all that God has promised them because of their strong faith and patience.

See *Idleness; Industry.*

LEAD A mineral, Ex 15:10. Purified by fire, Num 31:22; Ezk 22:18–20. Trade in, Ezk 27:12. Used for weighing, Zech 5:7, 8.

LEADER Of the tribes, Num 2. Of God's people, 1 Sam 9:16; 2 Kgs 20:5. Of 400 men, 1 Sam 22:2.

God called, 2 Chron 13:12. Christ called, Heb 2:10.

See *Armies; Captain; Officers.*

LEADERSHIP INSTANCES OF. Abraham, Moses, Joshua, Gideon, Deborah, see each respectively.

LEAGUE See *Alliances; Treaty.*

LEAH Daughter of Laban, Gen 29:16. Married to Jacob, Gen 29:31–35; 30:9–13, 17–21. Children of, Gen 29:31–35; 30:9–13, 17–21. Escapes with Jacob, Gen 31:4, 14, 17–20; 33:2–7. Ancestor of the nation of Israel, Ruth 4:11.

LEARNING See *Instruction; Knowledge.*

LEASE Of real estate, Mt 21:33–41; Mk 12:1–9; Lk 20:9–16.

See *Land.*

LEATHER Belts of, 2 Kgs 1:8; Mt 3:4; Mk 1:6. Tanning of, Acts 9:43; 10:5, 6. Called skin, Gen 3:21; hide, Lev 8:17.

LEAVEN See *Yeast.*

LEBANAH Called also *Lebana.* One of the Nethinim, Ezra 2:43–54; Neh 7:46–56.

LEBANON A mountain range. Northern boundary of the land of Canaan, Deut 1:7; 3:23–25; 11:24; Josh 1:4; 9:1. Early inhabitants of, Judg 3:1–3. Snow of, Jer 18:14. Streams of, Song 4:15. Cedars of, Judg 9:15; 2 Kgs 19:23; 2 Chron 2:8; Ps 29:5; 37:35; 104:16; Isa 2:13; 14:8; Ezk 27:5. Other trees of, 2 Kgs 19:23; 2 Chron 2:8. Animals of, Isa 40:16. Fertility and productiveness of, Hos 14:5–7; Nah 1:4. "Hall of the Forest of," 1 Kgs 7:2–5. Valley of, Josh 11:17; 12:7. Tower of, Song 7:4. Solomon had storage cities in, 1 Kgs 9:19.

FIGURATIVE. Isa 29:17; Jer 22:6.

LEBAOTH A city of Simeon, Josh 15:21–32. See *Beth-lebaoth.*

LEBONAH A city on the highway from Bethel to Shechem, Judg 21:19.

LECAH A descendant of Shelah, 1 Chron 4:21, 22.

LEECH Prov 30:15, 16.

LEEK Num 11:4, 5.

LEFT-HANDED Judg 3:15; 20:16.

LEGEND See *Fable; Inscription.*

LEGGINGS Bronze, 1 Sam 17:4–7.

LEGION Demons, Mk 5:9; Lk 8:30.

LEGISLATION Class, forbidden, Ex 12:49; Lev 24:22; Num 9:14; 15:15, 16, 29; Gal 3:28.

Supplemental, concerning Sabbath-breaking, Num 15:32–35; inheritance, Num 27:1–11.

See *Government; Law.*

LEGS Of the crucified, broken, Jn 19:31, 32.

LEHABIM A people whose ancestor was Mizraim, Gen 10:13, 14; 1 Chron 1:11, 12.

LEHEM Possibly a place in Judah, 1 Chron 4:21, 22.

LEHI A district of Judah, where Samson killed 1,000 Philistines with the donkey's jawbone, Judg 15:9–19.

LEMUEL A king. Possibly refers to Solomon, Prov 31:1, 4.

LENDING Ex 22:25. If you lend money to a needy fellow-Hebrew, you are not to handle the transaction in an ordinary way, with interest. [26]If you take his clothing as a pledge of his repayment, you must let him have it back at night. [27]For it is probably his only warmth; how can he sleep without it? If you don't return it, and he cries to me for help, I will hear and be very gracious to him (at your expense), for I am very compassionate.

Lev 25:35. If your brother becomes poor, you are responsible to help him; invite him to live with you as a guest in your home. [36]Fear your God and let your brother live with you; and don't charge him interest on the money you lend him. [37]Remember—no interest and give him what he needs at your cost: don't try to make a profit!

Deut 15:1. At the end of every seventh year there is to be a canceling of all debts! [2]Every creditor shall write "Paid in full" on any promissory note he holds against a fellow Israelite, for the Lord has released everyone from his obligation. [3](This release does not apply to foreigners.) [4,5]No one will become poor because of this, for the Lord will greatly bless you in the land he is giving you if you obey this command. The only prerequisite for his blessing is that you carefully heed all the commands of the Lord your God that I am giving you today. [6]He will bless you as he has promised. You shall lend money to many nations but will never need to borrow! You shall rule many nations, but they shall not rule over you! [7]But if, when you arrive in the land the Lord will give you, there are any among you who are poor, you must not shut your heart or hand against them; [8]you must lend them as much as they need. [9]Beware! Don't refuse a loan because the year of debt cancellation is close at hand! If you refuse to make the loan and the needy man cries out to the Lord, it will be counted against you as a sin. [10]You must lend him what he needs, and don't moan about it either! For the Lord will prosper you in everything you do because of this! [11]There will always be some among you who are poor; that is why this commandment is necessary. You must lend to them liberally.

Deut 23:19. Don't demand interest on loans you make to a brother Israelite, whether it is in the form of money, food, or anything else. [20]You may take interest from a foreigner, but not from an Israeli. For if you take interest from a brother, an Israeli, the Lord your God won't bless you when you arrive in the Promised Land.

Deut 24:6. It is illegal to take a millstone as a pledge, for it is a tool by which its owner gains his livelihood. [10]If you lend anything to another man, you must not enter his house to get his security. [11]Stand outside! The owner will bring it out to you. [12, 13]If the man is poor and gives you his cloak as security, you are not to sleep in it. Take it back to him at sundown so that he can use it through the night and bless you; and the Lord your God will count it as righteousness for you. [17]Justice must be given to migrants and orphans and you must never accept a widow's garment in pledge of her debt.

Neh 5:1. About this time there was a great outcry of protest from parents against some of the rich Jews who were profiteering on them. [2-4]What was happening was that families who ran out of money for food had to sell their children or mortgage their fields, vineyards, and homes to these rich men; and some couldn't even do that, for they already had borrowed to the limit to pay their taxes. [5]"We are their brothers, and our children are just like theirs," the people protested. "Yet we must sell our children into slavery to get enough money to live. We have already sold some of our daughters, and we are helpless to redeem them, for our fields, too, are mortgaged to these men." [6]I was very angry when I heard this; [7]so after thinking about it I spoke out against these rich government officials. "What is this you are doing?" I demanded. "How dare you demand a mortgage as a condition for helping another Israelite?" Then I called a public trial to deal with them. [8]At the trial I shouted at them, "The rest of us are doing all we can to *help* our Jewish brothers who have returned from exile as slaves in distant lands, but you are forcing them right back into slavery again. How often must we redeem them?" And they had nothing to say in their own defense. [9]Then I pressed further. "What you are doing is very evil," I exclaimed. "Should you not walk in the fear of our God? Don't we have enough enemies among the nations around us who are trying to destroy us? [10]The rest of us are lending money and grain to our fellow-Jews without any interest. I beg you, gentlemen, stop this business of usury. [11]Restore their fields, vineyards, olive-yards, and homes to them this very day and drop your claims against them." [12]So they agreed to do it and said that they would assist their brothers without requiring them to mortgage their lands and sell them their children. Then I summoned the priests and made these men formally vow to carry out their promises. [13]And I invoked the curse of God upon any of them who refused. "May God destroy your homes and livelihood if you fail to keep this promise," I declared. And all the people shouted, "Amen," and praised the Lord. And the rich men did as they had promised.

Ps 37:25. I have been young and now I am old. And in all my years I have never seen the Lord forsake a man who loves him; nor have I seen the children of the godly go hungry. [26]Instead, the godly are able to be generous with their gifts and loans to others, and their children are a blessing.

Ps 112:5. And all goes well for the generous man who conducts his business fairly.

Prov 19:17. When you help the poor you are lending to the Lord—and he pays wonderful interest on your loan!

Prov 22:7. Just as the rich rule the poor, so the borrower is servant to the lender.

Prov 28:8. Income from exploiting the poor will end up in the hands of someone who pities them.

Isa 24:1. Look! The Lord is overturning the land of Judah and making it a vast wasteland of destruction. See how he is emptying out all its people and scattering them over the face of the earth. [2]Priests and people, servants and masters, slave girls and mistresses, buyers and sellers, lenders and borrowers, bankers and debtors—none will be spared.

Ezk 18:13. And loans out his money at interest—shall that man live? No! He shall surely die, and it is his own fault.

Mt 5:42. Give to those who ask, and don't turn away from those who want to borrow.

Lk 6:34. And if you lend money only to those who can repay you, what good is that? Even the most wicked will lend to their own kind for full return! [35]Love your *enemies!* Do good to *them!* Lend to *them!* And don't be concerned about the fact that they won't repay. Then your reward from heaven will be very great, and you will truly be acting as sons of God: for he is kind to the *unthankful* and to those who are *very wicked.*

See *Borrowing; Interest; Money.*

LENTIL 2 Sam 17:28, 29; 23:11, 12; Ezk 4:9. See *Peas.*

LEOPARD Fierceness of, Jer 5:6; 13:23; Hos 13:7; Hab 1:8.

FIGURATIVE. Dan 7:6; Rev 13:2. Taming of, during the Kingdom age, Isa 11:6.

LEPROSY Laws concerning, Lev 13; 14; 22:4; Num 5:1–3; 12:14; Deut 24:8; Mt 8:4; Lk 5:14; 17:14. Sent as a judgment: On Miriam, Num 12:1–10; Gehazi, 2 Kgs 5:27; Uzziah, 2 Chron 26:20, 21. Entailed, 2 Kgs 5:27. Isolation of lepers, Lev 13:46; Num 5:1, 2; 12:14; 2 Kgs 15:5; 2 Chron 26:21. Separate burial of, 2 Chron 26:23.

Instances of leprosy not mentioned above: Four lepers outside Samaria, 2 Kgs 7:3; Azariah, 2 Kgs 15:5; Simon, Mk 14:3.

HEALED. Miriam, Num 12:13, 14; Naaman, 2 Kgs 5:8–14; by Jesus, Mt 8:3; Mk 1:40–42; Lk 5:13; 17:12–14.

Disciples empowered to heal, Mt 10:8.

LESHEM Called also *Laish.* See *Dan, 3.*

LETTERS Written by David to Joab, 2 Sam 11:14; king of Syria to king of Israel, 2 Kgs 5:5, 6; Rabshakeh to Hezekiah, Isa 37:9–14; King of Babylon to Hezekiah, Isa 39:1; Sennacherib to Hezekiah, 2 Kgs 19:14. Of Ar-ta-xerxes to Nehemiah, Neh 2:7–9. Open letter from Sanballat to Nehemiah, Neh 6:5, 6. Luke to Theophilus, the books of Luke and Acts, Acts 1:1, 2. Claudius Lysias to Felix, Acts 23:25–30. Letters of intercession by Paul to Philemon on behalf of Onesimus, Philemon 1:1, 2; of recommendation, 2 Cor 3:1.

See *Epistles.*

LETUSHIM A son of Dedan, Gen 25:3.

LEUMMIM A son of Dedan, Gen 25:3.

LEVI Son of Jacob, Gen 29:34; 35:23; 1 Chron 2:1. Avenges the rape of Dinah, Gen 34: 49: 5–7. Jacob's prophecy regarding, Gen 49:5–7. His age at death, Ex 6:16. Descendants of, made ministers of religion, see *Levites.*

LEVIATHAN Possibly a crocodile, Job 41. The serpent, Isa 27:1.

LEVITES The descendants of Levi. Set apart as ministers of religion, Num 1:47–54; 3:6–15; 16:8, 9; 26:57–62; Deut 10:8; 1 Chron 15:2. Substituted in the place of the firstborn, Num 3:11, 12, 41–45; 8:14, 16–18; 18:6. Religious zeal of, Ex 32:26–28; Deut 33: 9, 10; Mal 2:4, 5. Consecration of, Num 8:5–21. Rebellion of, led by Korah, Dathan, Abiram, and On, because of jealousy toward Moses and Aaron, Num 16 with 4:17–20.

Three divisions of, each having the name of one of its progenitors, Gershon, Kohath, and Merari, Ex 6:16. Gershonites and their duties, Num 3:16–30; 4:24–26; 10:17. Ruling chief over the Gershonites was the second son of the ruling high priest, Num 4:28. Kohathites, consisting of the families of the Amramites, Izharites, Hebronites, Uzzielites, Num 3:25–30; 4:17–20. Of the Amramites, Aaron and his family were set apart as priests, Ex 28:1; 29: 9; Num 3:31–35; 8:1–14; 17; 18:1; the remaining families appointed to take charge of the Ark, table, lampstand, altars, and utensils of the sanctuary, the hangings, and all the service, Num 3:25–37; 4: 2–15. The leader of the Kohathites was the oldest son of the ruling high priest, Num 3:31–35; 1 Chron 9:20. Merarites, Num 3:31–37; 4:30–33; 7: 8; 10:17; 1 Chron 6:19–21, 29, 30; 23:21–23. The leader of the Merarites was the second son of the ruling high priest, Num 4:33.

Place of, in camp and march, Num 1:50–53; 2: 3–31; 3:16–35. Cities assigned to, in the land of Canaan, Josh 21. Lodged near and in the temple, 1 Chron 9:27, 33, 34; Ezk 40:44–46. Resided also in villages outside of Jerusalem, Neh 12:29.

Age of, when inducted into office, Num 4:3, 29, 46–48; 8:23, 24; 1 Chron 23:3, 24; Ezra 3:8; when retired from office, Num 4:3, 46–48; 8:23, 24.

Functions of: Had charge of the Tabernacle in camp and on the march, Num 1:50–53; 3:6–9, 25–37; 4:1–15, 17–49; 8:19, 22; 18:2–6; and of the temple, 1 Chron 9:27–29; 23:2–32; Ezra 8:24–34.

Carried the Ark of the Covenant, Deut 10:8; 1 Chron 15:2, 26, 27. Ministered before the Ark, 1 Chron 16:4. Custodians and administrators of the tithes and other offerings, 1 Chron 9:26–29; 26:28; 29:8; 2 Chron 24:5, 11; 31:11–19; 34:9; Ezra 8:29, 30, 33; Neh 12:44. Prepared the Bread of the Presence, 1 Chron 23:29. Assisted the priests in preparing the sacrifice, 2 Chron 29:12–36; 35:1–18. Prepared the passover for the returned captives, Ezra 6:20, 21. Teachers of the law, Deut 33:10; 2 Chron 17:7–9; 35: 3; Neh 8:7–13; Mal 2:6, 7. Were judges, Deut 17:9; 1 Chron 23:4, 5; 26:29; 2 Chron 19:8–11. See *Judges.*

Were scribes of the sacred books, see *Scribes.* Pronounced the blessings of the law in the responsive service at Mount Gerizim, Deut 27:12; Josh 8: 33. Were gatekeepers, see *Gatekeepers.* Were overseers in building and the repairs of the temple, 1 Chron 23:2–5; Ezra 3:8, 9. Were musicians of the temple service, see *Music.* Supervised weights and measures, 1 Chron 23:29.

List of those who returned from captivity, Ezra 2:40–63; 7:7–9; 8:16–20; Neh 7:43–73; 12. Signed the covenant with Nehemiah, Neh 10:9–28.

Compensations of: In lieu of landed inheritance, 48 cities with suburbs were assigned to them, Num 35:2–8, with 18:24 and 26:62; Deut 10:9; 12:12, 18, 19; 14:27–29; 18:1–8; Josh 13:14; 14:3, 4; 18:7; 1 Chron 6: 54–81; 13:2; 2 Chron 23:2, 3; Ezk 34:1–5. Assigned to, by families, Josh 21:4–40. Suburbs of their cities were not to be sold for debt, Lev 25:32–34. Tithes and other offerings, Num 18:24, 25–32; Deut 18:1–8; 26:11–13; Josh 13:14; Neh 10:38–40; 12:44, 47. Spoils of war, including captives, Num 31:30, 42–47. See *Tithes.* Tithes withheld from, Neh 13:10–13; Mal 3: 10. Pensioned, 2 Chron 31:16–18. Owned lands, Deut 18:8, with 1 Kgs 2:26. Land allotted to, by Ezekiel, Ezk 48:13, 14.

Census of, at Sinai, Num 1:47–49; 2:32, 33; 3: 14–39; 4:1–3; 26:57–62; 1 Chron 23:3–5. Degraded from the Levitical office by Jeroboam, 2 Chron 11: 13–17; 13:9–11. Loyal to the king, 2 Kgs 11:6–11; 2 Chron 23:7.

Intermarry with Canaanites, Ezra 9:1, 2; 10:23, 24. Exempt from enrollment for military duty, Num 1:47–54, with 1 Chron 12:24–37. Subordinate to the sons of Aaron, Num 3:7–9; 8:19; 18:6.

Prophecies concerning, Jer 33:18; Ezk 44:10–14; Mal 3:3; of their repentance of the crucifixion of the Messiah, Zech 12:10–14. John's vision concerning, Rev 7:4–8.

LIARS All men liars, Ps 116:10, 11. Satan, a, Jn 8:44, 55. Destiny of, Rev 21:8.

See *Deceit; Deception; Hypocrisy; Lying.*

LIBERALITY Generosity. Ex 22:29. You must be prompt in giving me the tithe of your crops and your wine, and the redemption payment for your oldest son. [30]As to the firstborn of the oxen and the sheep, give it to me on the eighth day, after leaving it with its mother for seven days. Ex 13:1, 2, 12.

Ex 23:15. The first is the Pilgrimage of Unleavened Bread, when for seven days you are not to eat bread with yeast, just as I commanded you before. This celebration is to be an annual event at the regular time in March, the month you left Egypt;

everyone must bring me a sacrifice at that time. Ex 34:20.

Ex 25:1–7. Jehovah said to Moses, "Tell the people of Israel that everyone who wants to may bring me an offering from this list: Gold, silver, bronze, blue cloth, purple cloth, scarlet cloth, fine-twined linen, goat's hair, red-dyed ram's skins, goat-skins, acacia wood, olive oil for the lamps, spices for the anointing oil and for the fragrant incense, onyx stones, stones to be set in the ephod and in the breastplate. [8]For I want the people of Israel to make me a sacred Temple where I can live among them."

Ex 35:4. Then Moses said to all the people, "This is what the Lord has commanded: [5-9]All of you who wish to, all those with generous hearts, may bring these offerings to Jehovah: Gold, silver, and bronze; blue, purple, and scarlet cloth, made of fine-twined linen or of goat's hair; tanned rams' skins and specially treated goatskins; acacia wood; olive oil for the lamps; spices for the anointing oil and for the incense; onyx stones and stones to be used for the ephod and chestpiece. [10-19]Come, all of you who are skilled craftsmen having special talents, and construct what God has commanded us: The Tabernacle tent, and its coverings, clasps, frames, bars, pillars, and bases; the Ark and its poles; the place of mercy; the veil to enclose the Holy Place; the table, its carrying poles, and all of its utensils; the Bread of the Presence; lamp holders, with lamps and oil; the incense altar and its carrying poles; the anointing oil and sweet incense; the curtain for the door of the Tabernacle; the altar for the burnt offerings; the bronze grating of the altar, and its carrying poles and utensils; the basin with its pedestal; the drapes for the walls of the court; the pillars and their bases; drapes for the entrance to the court; the posts of the Tabernacle court, and their cords; the beautiful clothing for the priests, to be used when ministering in the Holy Place; the holy garments for Aaron the priest, and for his sons." [20]So all the people went to their tents to prepare their gifts. [21]Those whose hearts were stirred by God's Spirit returned with their offerings of materials for the Tabernacle, its equipment, and for the holy garments. [22]Both men and women came, all who were willing-hearted. They brought to the Lord their offerings of gold, jewelry—earrings, rings from their fingers, necklaces—and gold objects of every kind. [23]Others brought blue, purple, and scarlet cloth made from the fine-twined linen or goats' hair; and ram skins dyed red, and specially treated goatskins. [24]Others brought silver and bronze as their offering to the Lord; and some brought the acacia wood needed in the construction. [25]The women skilled in sewing and spinning prepared blue, purple, and scarlet thread and cloth, and fine-twined linen, and brought them in. [26]Some other women gladly used their special skill to spin the goats' hair into cloth. [27]The leaders brought onyx stones to be used for the ephod and the chestpiece; [28]and spices, and oil—for the light, and for compounding the anointing oil and the sweet incense. [29]So the people of Israel—every man and woman who wanted to assist in the work given to them by the Lord's command to Moses—brought their freewill offerings to him.

Ex 36:3. Moses gave them the materials donated by the people and additional gifts were received each morning. [4-7]But finally the workmen all left their task to meet with Moses and told him, "We have more than enough materials on hand now to complete the job!" So Moses sent a message throughout the camp announcing that no more donations were needed. Then at last the people were restrained from bringing more!

Ex 38:8. The bronze washbasin and its bronze pedestal were cast from the solid bronze mirrors donated by the women who assembled at the entrance to the Tabernacle.

Lev 19:5. When you sacrifice a peace offering to the Lord, offer it correctly so that it will be accepted. Lev 22:29, 30; Num 35:8.

Deut 12:11. Then you must bring all your burnt sacrifices and other offerings to his sanctuary, the place he will choose as his home. [12]You shall rejoice there before the Lord with your sons and daughters and servants; and remember to invite the Levites to feast with you, for they have no land of their own. [17]But none of the offerings may be eaten at home. Neither the tithe of your grain and new wine and olive oil, nor the firstborn of your flocks and herds, nor anything you have vowed to give the Lord, nor your freewill offerings, nor the offerings to be presented to the Lord by waving them before his altar. [18]All these must be brought to the central altar where you, your children, and the Levites shall eat them before the Lord your God. He will tell you where this altar must be located. Rejoice before the Lord your God in everything you do. [19](By the way, be very careful not to forget about the Levites. Share with them.)

Deut 14:27. Don't forget to share your income with the Levites in your community, for they have no property or crops as you do. [28]Every third year you are to use your entire tithe for local welfare programs: [29]Give it to the Levites who have no inheritance among you, or to foreigners, or to widows and orphans within your city, so that they can eat and be satisfied; and then Jehovah your God will bless you and your work.

Deut 15:7. But if, when you arrive in the land the Lord will give you, there are any among you who are poor, you must not shut your heart or hand against them; [8]you must lend them as much as they need. [9]Beware! Don't refuse a loan because the year of debt cancellation is close at hand! If you refuse to make the loan and the needy man cries out to the Lord, it will be counted against you as a sin. [10]You must lend him what he needs, and don't moan about it either! For the Lord will prosper you in everything you do because of this! [11]There will always be some among you who are poor; that is why this commandment is necessary. You must lend to them liberally. [12]If you buy a Hebrew slave, whether a man or woman, you must free him at the end of the sixth year you have owned him, [13]and don't send him away empty-handed! [14]Give him a large farewell present from your flock, your olive press, and your wine press. Share with him in proportion as the Lord your God has blessed you. [15]Remember that you were slaves in the land of Egypt and the Lord your God rescued you! That is why I am giving you this command. [16]But if your Hebrew slave doesn't want to leave—if he says he loves you and enjoys your pleasant home and gets along well with you—[17]then take an awl and pierce his ear into the door, and after that he shall be your slave forever. Do the same with your women slaves. [18]But when you free a slave you must not feel bad, for remember that for six years he has cost you less than half the price of a hired hand! And the Lord your God will prosper all you do because you have released him!

Deut 16:10. There shall be another festival before the Lord your God called the Festival of Weeks. At that time bring to him a free-will offering proportionate in size to his blessing upon you as judged by the amount of your harvest. [17]Give as you are able, according as the Lord has blessed you.

Deut 18:1. Remember that the priests and all the other members of the Levite tribe will not be given property like the other tribes. So the priests and Levites are to be supported by the sacrifices brought to the altar of the Lord and by the other offerings the people bring to him. [2]They don't need to own property, for the Lord is their property! That is what he promised them! [3]The shoulder, the cheeks, and the stomach of every ox or sheep brought for sacrifice must be given to the priests. [4]In addition, the priests shall receive the harvest samples brought in thanksgiving to the Lord—the first of the grain, the new wine, the olive oil, and of the fleece at shearing time. [5]For the Lord your God has chosen the tribe of Levi, of all the tribes, to minister to the Lord from generation to generation. [6, 7]Any Levite, no matter where he lives in the land of Israel, has the right to come to the sanctuary at any time and minister in the name of the Lord, just like his brother Levites who work there regularly. [8]He shall be given his share of the sacrifices and offerings as his right, not just if he is in need.

Deut 24:19. If, when reaping your harvest, you forget to bring in a sheaf from the field, don't go back after it. Leave it for the migrants, orphans, and widows; then the Lord your God will bless and prosper all you do. [20]When you beat the olives from your olive trees, don't go over the boughs twice; leave anything remaining for the migrants, orphans, and widows. [21]It is the same for the grapes in your vineyard; don't glean the vines after they are picked, but leave what's left for those in need. [22]Remember that you were slaves in the land of Egypt—that is why I am giving you this command.

2 Sam 24:24. But the king said to Araunah, "No, I will not have it as a gift. I will buy it, for I don't want to offer to the Lord my God burnt offerings that have cost me nothing." So David paid him for the threshing floor and the oxen.

1 Chron 22:19. Now try with every fiber of your being to obey the Lord your God, and you will soon be bringing the Ark and the other holy articles of worship into the Temple of the Lord!

1 Chron 28:10. "So be very careful, for the Lord has chosen you to build his holy temple. Be strong and do as he commands." [20]Then he continued, "Be strong and courageous and get to work. Don't be frightened by the size of the task, for the Lord my God is with you; he will not forsake you. He will see to it that everything is finished correctly."

1 Chron 29:5. Now then, who will follow my example? Who will give himself and all that he has to the Lord?"

2 Chron 15:7. "But you men of Judah, keep up the good work and don't get discouraged, for you will be rewarded." [18]He brought back into the Temple the silver and gold bowls which he and his father had dedicated to the Lord.

Ezra 1:2. Cyrus, King of Persia, hereby announces that Jehovah, the God of heaven who gave me my vast empire, has now given me the responsibility of building him a Temple in Jerusalem, in the land of Judah. [3]All Jews throughout the kingdom may now return to Jerusalem to rebuild this Temple of Jehovah, who is the God of Israel and of Jerusalem. May his blessings rest upon you. [4]Those Jews who do not go should contribute toward the expenses of those who do, and also supply them with clothing, transportation, supplies for the journey, and a freewill offering for the Temple.

Ps 41:1. God blesses those who are kind to the poor. He helps them out of their troubles. [2]He protects them and keeps them alive; he publicly honors them and destroys the power of their enemies. [3]He nurses them when they are sick, and soothes their pains and worries.

Ps 76:11. Fulfill all your vows that you have made to Jehovah your God. Let everyone bring him presents. He should be reverenced and feared.

Ps 112:5. And all goes well for the generous man who conducts his business fairly. [9]He gives generously to those in need. His deeds will never be forgotten. He shall have influence and honor.

Ps 132:1. Lord, do you remember that time when my heart was so filled with turmoil? [2-5]I couldn't rest, I couldn't sleep, thinking how I ought to build a permanent home for the Ark of the Lord, a Temple for the mighty one of Israel. Then I vowed that I would do it; I made a solemn promise to the Lord.

Prov 3:9, 10. Honor the Lord by giving him the first part of all your income, and he will fill your barns with wheat and barley and overflow your wine vats with the finest wines.

Prov 11:24, 25. It is possible to give away and become richer! . . . Yes, the liberal man shall be rich! By watering others, he waters himself.

Prov 13:7. Some rich people are poor, and some poor people have great wealth!

Prov 14:21. To despise the poor is to sin. Blessed are those who pity them.

Prov 19:6. Many beg favors from a man who is generous; everyone is his friend! [17]When you help the poor you are lending to the Lord—and he pays wonderful interest on your loan!

Prov 21:26. He is greedy to get, while the godly love to give!

Prov 22:9. Happy is the generous man, the one who feeds the poor.

Prov 28:27. If you give to the poor, your needs will be supplied.

Prov 31:19, 20. She sews for the poor, and generously gives to the needy.

Eccl 11:1. Give generously, for your gifts will return to you later. [2]Divide your gifts among many, for in the days ahead you yourself may need much help.

Isa 32:8. But good men will be generous to others and will be blessed of God for all they do.

Isa 60:7. The flocks of Kedar shall be given you, and the rams of Nabaioth for my altars, and I will glorify my glorious Temple in that day. [9]I have reserved the ships of many lands, the very best, to bring the sons of Israel home again from far away, bringing their wealth with them. For the Holy One of Israel, known around the world, has glorified you in the eyes of all. [17]I will exchange your brass for gold, your iron for silver, your wood for brass, your stones for iron. Peace and righteousness shall be your taskmasters!

Hag 1:8. "Then go up into the mountains and bring down timber, and rebuild my Temple, and I will be pleased with it and appear there in my glory," says the Lord.

Hag 2:18, 19. But now note this: From today, this 24th day of the month, as the foundation of the Lord's Temple is finished, and from this day onward, I will bless you. Notice, I am giving you this promise now before you have even begun to rebuild the Temple structure, and before you have harvested your grain, and before the grapes and figs and pomegranates and olives have produced their next crops: *From this day I will bless you.*

Mal 3:10. "Bring all the tithes into the storehouse so that there will be food enough in my Temple; if you do, I will open up the windows of heaven for you and pour out a blessing so great you won't have room enough to take it in! Try it! Let me prove it to you! [11]Your crops will be large, for I will guard them from insects and plagues. Your grapes won't shrivel away before they ripen," says the Lord of Hosts. [12]"And all nations will call you blessed, for you will be a land sparkling with happiness. These are the promises of the Lord of Hosts."

Mt 6:1. Take care! don't do your good deeds publicly, to be admired, for then you will lose the reward from your Father in heaven. [2]When you give a gift to a beggar, don't shout about it as the hypocrites do—blowing trumpets in the synagogues and streets to call attention to their acts of charity! I tell you in all earnestness, they have received all the reward they will ever get. [3]But when you do a kindness to someone, do it secretly —don't tell your left hand what your right hand is doing. [4]And your Father who knows all secrets will reward you.

Mt 19:21. Jesus told him, "If you want to be perfect, go and sell everything you have and give the money to the poor, and you will have treasure in heaven; and come, follow me." [22]But when the young man heard this, he went away sadly, for he was very rich.

Mt 25:34. Then I, the King, shall say to those at my right, "Come, blessed of my Father, into the Kingdom prepared for you from the founding of the world. [35]For I was hungry and you fed me; I was thirsty and you gave me water; I was a stranger and you invited me into your homes; [36]naked and you clothed me; sick and in prison, and you visited me." [37]Then these righteous ones will reply, "Sir, when did we ever see you hungry and feed you? Or thirsty and give you anything to drink? [38]Or a stranger, and help you? Or naked, and clothe you? [39]When did we ever see you sick or in prison, and visit you?" [40]And I, the King, will tell them, "When you did it to these my brothers you were doing it to me!"

Lk 3:10. The crowd replied, "What do you want us to do?" [11]"If you have two coats," he replied, "give one to the poor. If you have extra food, give it away to those who are hungry."

Lk 6:38. For if you give, you will get! Your gift will return to you in full and overflowing measure, pressed down, shaken together to make room for more, and running over. Whatever measure you use to give—large or small—will be used to measure what is given back to you. Mt 5:42.

Lk 11:41. Purity is best demonstrated by generosity.

Lk 12:33. Sell what you have and give to those in need. This will fatten your purses in heaven! And the purses of heaven have no rips or holes in them. Your treasures there will never disappear; no thief can steal them; no moth can destroy them. [34]Wherever your treasure is, there your heart and thoughts will also be.

Lk 16:9. But shall I tell *you* to act that way, to buy friendship through cheating? Will this ensure your entry into an everlasting home in heaven?

Acts 10:4. Cornelius stared at him in terror. "What do you want, sir?" he asked the angel. And the angel replied, "Your prayers and charities have not gone unnoticed by God!"

Acts 20:35. And I was a constant example to you in helping the poor; for I remembered the words of the Lord Jesus, "It is more blessed to give than to receive."

Rom 12:8. If God has given you money, be generous in helping others with it. [13]When God's children are in need, you be the one to help them out. And get into the habit of inviting guests home for dinner or, if they need lodging, for the night.

Rom 15:27. They were very glad to do this, for they feel that they owe a real debt to the Jerusalem Christians. Why? Because the news about Christ came to these Gentiles from the church in Jerusalem. And since they received this wonderful spiritual gift of the Gospel from there, they feel that the least they can do in return is to give some material aid.

1 Cor 13:3. If I gave everything I have to poor people, and if I were burned alive for preaching the Gospel but didn't love others, it would be of no value whatever.

1 Cor 16:1. Now here are the directions about the money you are collecting to send to the Christians in Jerusalem; (and, by the way, these are the same directions I gave to the churches in Galatia). [2]On every Lord's Day each of you should put aside something from what you have earned during the week, and use it for this offering. The amount depends on how much the Lord has helped you earn. Don't wait until I get there and then try to collect it all at once. [3]When I come I will send your loving gift with a letter to Jerusalem, to be taken there by trustworthy messengers you yourselves will choose.

2 Cor 8:7. You people there are leaders in so many ways—you have so much faith, so many good preachers, so much learning, so much enthusiasm, so much love for us. Now I want you to be leaders also in the spirit of cheerful giving. [9]You know how full of love and kindness our Lord Jesus was: though he was so very rich, yet to help you he became so very poor, so that by being poor he could make you rich. [11]Having started the ball rolling so enthusiastically, you should carry this project through to completion just as gladly, giving whatever you can out of whatever you have. Let your enthusiastic idea at the start be equalled by your realistic action now. [12]If you are really eager to give, then it isn't important how much you have to give. God wants you to give what you have, not what you haven't. [13]Of course, I don't mean that those who receive your gifts should have an easy time of it at your expense, [14]but you should divide with them. Right now you have plenty and can help them; then at some other time they can share with you when you need it. In this way each will have as much as he needs. [24]Please show your love for me to these men and do for them all that I have publicly boasted you would. *vs.* 8, 15.

2 Cor 9:6. A farmer who plants just a few seeds will get only a small crop, but if he plants much, he will reap much. [7]Every one must make up his own mind as to how much he should give. Don't force anyone to give more than he really wants to, for cheerful givers are the ones God prizes. [8]God is able to make it up to you by giving you everything you need and more, so that there will not only be enough for your own needs, but plenty left over to give joyfully to others. [*v.* 9] [10]For God, who gives seed to the farmer to plant, and later on, good crops to harvest and eat, will give you more and more seed to plant and will make it grow so that you can give away more and more fruit from your harvest. [11]Yes, God will give you much so that you can give away much, and when we take your gifts to those who need them they will break out into thanksgiving and praise to God for your help. [12]So, two good things happen as a result of your gifts—those in need are helped, and they overflow with thanks to God. *v.* 13.

Eph 4:28. If anyone is stealing he must stop it and begin using those hands of his for honest work so he can give to others in need.

1 Tim 5:16. Let me remind you again that a widow's relatives must take care of her, and not leave this to the church to do. Then the church can spend its money for the care of widows who are all alone and have nowhere else to turn.

1 Tim 6:17. Tell those who are rich not to be proud and not to trust in their money, which will soon be gone, but their pride and trust should be in the living God who always richly gives us all we need for our enjoyment. [18]Tell them to use their money to do good. They should be rich in good works and should give happily to those in need, always being ready to share with others whatever God has given them. [19]By doing this they will be storing up real treasure for themselves in heaven—it is the only safe investment for eternity! And they will be living a fruitful Christian life down here as well.

Philemon 1:14. But I didn't want to do it without your consent. I didn't want you to be kind because you had to but because you wanted to.

Heb 6:10. For God is not unfair. How can he forget your hard work for him, or forget the way you used to show your love for him—and still do—by helping his children?

Heb 13:16. Don't forget to do good and to share what you have with those in need, for such sacrifices are very pleasing to him.

1 Jn 3:17. But if someone who is supposed to be a Christian has money enough to live well, and sees a brother in need, and won't help him—how can God's love be within *him?* [18]Little children, let us stop just *saying* we love people; let us *really* love them, and *show* it by our *actions.*

See *Benevolence; Charitableness; Charity; Giving; Poor, Duty to; Rich; Riches; Tithes.*

INSTANCES OF. King of Sodom to Abraham, Gen 14:21. Jacob, Gen 28:22. Pharaoh to Joseph's people, Gen 45:18–20. Israelites at the erection of the tabernacle, Ex 35:21–29; 36:3–7; 38:8; Num 7: 2–86; Josh 18:1. Reubenites, Josh 22:24–29. David, 2 Sam 7:2; 1 Chron 17:1; 2 Sam 8:11, 12; 1 Kgs 7:51; 8:17, 18; 1 Chron 21:22, 24; 26:26; 28:2; 29:2–5, 17, 18; Ps 132:1–5. Barzillai and others to David, 2 Sam 17:27–29; 19:31, 32. Araunah for sacrifice, 2 Sam 24:22, 23. Joab to David, 2 Sam 12:26–28.

Israelites' offerings for the Temple, 1 Chron 29: 6–9, 16, 17. Samuel, 1 Chron 26:27, 28. Solomon, 1 Kgs 4:29; 5:4, 5; 2 Chron 2:1–6; 1 Kgs 6; 7:51; 8: 12, 13. Queen of Sheba to Solomon, 1 Kgs 10:10. Asa and Abijam, 1 Kgs 15:15. Elisha toward Elijah, 1 Kgs 19:21. Jehoshaphat, 2 Kgs 12:18. Joash and his people, 2 Kgs 12:4–14; 2 Chron 24:4–14. David, 1 Chron 16:3. Hezekiah, 2 Chron 29; 30:1–12; 31: 1–10, 21. Manasseh, 2 Chron 33:16. Josiah, 2 Kgs 22: 3–6; 2 Chron 34:8–13; 35:1–19.

Jews after the captivity, Ezra 1:5, 6; 2:68, 69; 3:1–9; 5:1–6; 6:14–22; 8:25–35; Neh 3; 4:6; 6:3; 7:70–72; 10:32–40; 13:12, 31; Hag 1:12–15; 2:18, 19. Cyrus, Ezra 1:2–4, 7–11; 3:7; 5:13–15; 6:3. Darius, Ezra 6:7–12. Ar-ta-xerxes, Ezra 7:13–27; 8:24–36. The Magi, Mt 2:11. Roman army captain, Lk 7:4, 5. Mary Magdalene, Lk 8:2, 3. The good Samaritan, Lk 10:33–35. Poor widow, Lk 21:2–4. Christians in Jerusalem, Acts 2:44, 45; 4:32–37; in Antioch, Acts 11:29; at Philippi, Phil 4:18; Corinth, 2 Cor 8:19; 9:1–13; Macedonia, 2 Cor 8:14. People of Malta to Paul, Acts 28:10.

LIBERTY Proclaimed in the year of jubilee, Lev 25:10; Jer 34:8, 15–17. Political, Judg 17:6; 21:25; Acts 22:28.

See *Jubilee.*

FIGURATIVE. Isa 61:1; 63:4; Lk 4:18; Jn 8:32, 33, 36; Gal 3:28; Eph 6:8.

LIBNAH 1. A camping place of the Israelites in the desert, Num 33:15–37.

2. A city of Judah, captured by Joshua, Josh 10:29–32, 39; 12:8–24. Allotted to the priests, Josh 21:9–16. Sennacherib besieged; his army defeated near, 2 Kgs 19:8, 35; Isa 37:8–36.

LIBNI 1. Son of Gershon, Ex 6:17; Num 3:16–24; 1 Chron 6:17, 19–21. Descendants called *Libnites,* Num 26:58, 59.

2. Grandson of Merari, 1 Chron 6:29, 30.

LIBYA Region of north Africa, Ezk 30:5; Nah 3:9; Acts 2:10. Called also *Put,* which see.

LIBYANS The inhabitants of Libya, 2 Chron 12:3; 16:8; Dan 11:43.

LICE Plague of, Ex 8:16–19.

LICENTIOUSNESS See *Adultery; Lasciviousness.*

LIEUTENANT Of the police, Jn 18:12.

See *Armies; Captain; Officer.*

LIFE INDEX OF SUB-TOPICS. *Miscellany of Minor Sub-Topics; Brevity and Uncertainty of; Eternal or Everlasting; From God; Long; Spiritual.*

MISCELLANY OF MINOR SUB-TOPICS. Breath of, Gen 2:7. Called *breath from God,* Job 27:3. Tree of, Gen 2:9; 3:22, 24; Prov 3:18; 13:12; Rev 2:7. Sacredness of, an inference from what is taught in the law concerning murder, see *Homicide.*

Long life promised to obedient children, Ex 20:12; Deut 5:16; to those who keep the commandments, Deut 4:40; 32:47; 1 Kgs 3:14.

Futility of, Eccl chapters 1–7. Hated, Eccl 2:17. To be hated for Christ's sake, Lk 14:26. What shall a man give in exchange for, Mt 16:26; Mk 8:37. He that loses it will save it, Mt 10:39; 16:25, 26; Lk 9:24; Jn 12:25.

Weary of: Job, Job 3; 7:1–3; 10:18, 19. Jeremiah, Jer 20:14–18. Elijah, 1 Kgs 19:1–8. Jonah, Jon 4:8, 9. See *Suicide.*

Life of Christ, a ransom, Mt 20:28; Mk 10:45; 1 Tim 2:6. See *Spiritual,* below.

BREVITY AND UNCERTAINTY OF. Gen 47:9. Jacob replied, "I have lived 130 long, hard years, and I am not nearly as old as many of my ancestors."

1 Sam 20:3. But the truth is that I am only a step away from death! I swear it by the Lord and by your own soul!

2 Sam 14:14. All of us must die eventually; our lives are like water that is poured out on the ground—it can't be gathered up again.

1 Chron 29:15. For we are here for but a moment, strangers in the land as our fathers were before us; our days on earth are like a shadow, gone so soon, without a trace.

Job 4:19. How much less men made of dust, who are crushed to death as easily as moths! [20]They are alive in the morning, but by evening they are dead, gone forever with hardly a thought from anyone. [21]Their candle of life is snuffed out. They die and no one cares.

Job 7:6. My life flies by—day after hopeless day. [7]My life is but a breath, and nothing good is left. [8]You see me now, but not for long. Soon you'll look upon me dead. [9]As a cloud disperses and vanishes, so those who die shall go away forever—[10]gone forever from their family and their home—never to be seen again. *v.* 17.

Job 8:9. For we were born but yesterday and know so little; our days here on earth are as transient as shadows.

Job 9:25. My life passes swiftly away, filled with tragedy. [26]My years disappear like swift ships, like the eagle that swoops upon its prey.

Job 10:9. Oh, please remember that I'm made of dust—will you change me back again to dust so soon? [20, 21]Can't you see how little time I have left? Oh, let me alone that I may have a little moment of comfort before I leave for the land of darkness and the shadow of death, never to return.

Job 13:12. These tremendous statements you have made have about as much value as ashes. Your defense of God is as fragile as a clay vase! [25]Would you blame a leaf that is blown about by the wind? Will you chase dry, useless straws? [28]I am like a fallen, rotten tree, like a moth-eaten coat. Gen 18:27.

Job 14:1. How frail is man, how few his days, how full of trouble! [2]He blossoms for a moment like a flower—and withers; as the shadow of a passing cloud, he quickly disappears.

Job 17:1. I am sick and near to death; the grave is ready to receive me.

Ps 22:29. Both proud and humble together, all who are mortal—born to die—shall worship him.

Ps 39:4. Lord, help me to realize how brief my time on earth will be. Help me to know that I am here for but a moment more. [5, 6]My life is no longer than my hand! My whole lifetime is but a moment to you. Proud man! Frail as breath! A shadow! And all his busy rushing ends in nothing. He heaps up riches for someone else to spend. [11]When you punish a man for his sins, he is destroyed, for he is as fragile as a moth-infested cloth; yes, man is frail as breath.

Ps 78:39. For he remembered that they were merely mortal men, gone in a moment like a breath of wind.

Ps 89:47. Oh, remember how short you have

made man's lifespan. Is it an empty, futile life you give the sons of men? [48]No man can live forever. All will die. Who can rescue his life from the power of the grave?

Ps 90:3. You speak, and man turns back to dust. [5, 6]We glide along the tides of time as swiftly as a racing river, and vanish as quickly as a dream. We are like grass that is green in the morning but mowed down and withered before the evening shadows fall. [9]No wonder the years are long and heavy here beneath your wrath. All our days are filled with sighing. [10]Seventy years are given us! And some may even live to eighty. But even the best of these years are often emptiness and pain; soon they disappear, and we are gone.

Ps 102:11. My life is passing swiftly as the evening shadows. I am withering like grass.

Ps 103:14. For he knows we are but dust, [15]and that our days are few and brief, like grass, like flowers, [16]blown by the wind and gone forever.

Ps 144:4. For man is but a breath; his days are like a passing shadow. *v.* 3.

Ps 146:4. For every man must die. His breathing stops, life ends, and in a moment all he planned for himself is ended.

Prov 27:1. Don't brag about your plans for tomorrow—wait and see what happens.

Eccl 1:4. Generations come and go but it makes no difference.

Eccl 6:12. In these few days of our empty lifetimes, who can say how one's days can best be spent? Who can know what will prove best for the future after he is gone? For who knows the future?

Isa 2:22. Puny man! Frail as his breath! Don't ever put your trust in him!

Isa 38:12. My life is blown away like a shepherd's tent; it is cut short as when a weaver stops his working at the loom. In one short day my life hangs by a thread.

Isa 40:6. "Shout that man is like the grass that dies away, and all his beauty fades like dying flowers. [7]The grass withers, the flower fades beneath the breath of God. And so it is with fragile man." [24]They hardly get started, barely take root, when he blows on them and their work withers and the wind carries them off like straw. 1 Pet 1:24.

Isa 51:8. For the moth shall destroy them like garments; the worm shall eat them like wool. [12]So what right have you to fear mere mortal men, who wither like the grass and disappear?

Isa 64:6. Like autumn leaves we fade, wither and fall.

Lk 12:20. But God said to him, "Fool! Tonight you die. Then who will get it all?"

Jas 1:10, 11. But a rich man should be glad that his riches mean nothing to the Lord, for he will soon be gone, like a flower that has lost its beauty and fades away, withered—killed by the scorching summer sun. So it is with rich men. They will soon die and leave behind all their busy activities.

Jas 4:14. How do you know what is going to happen tomorrow? For the length of your lives is as uncertain as the morning fog—now you see it; soon it is gone. *v.* 15.

See *Death.*

ETERNAL OR EVERLASTING. Gen 5:24. And in constant touch with God, he [Enoch] disappeared, for God took him!

2 Sam 12:23. But why should I fast when he is dead? Can I bring him back again? I shall go to him, but he shall not return to me.

2 Kgs 2:11. As they were walking along, talking, suddenly a chariot of fire, drawn by horses of fire, appeared and drove between them, separating them, and Elijah was carried by a whirlwind into heaven.

Neh 9:5. Stand up and praise the Lord your God, for he lives from everlasting to everlasting. Praise his glorious name! It is far greater than we can think or say.

Job 4:17. "Is mere man more just than God? More pure than his Creator?" [18, 19]If God cannot trust his own messengers (for even angels make mistakes), how much less men made of dust, who are crushed to death as easily as moths! [20]They are alive in the morning, but by evening they are dead, gone forever with hardly a thought from anyone. [21]Their candle of life is snuffed out. They die and no one cares.

Job 14:13. Oh, that you would hide me with the dead, and forget me there until your anger ends; but mark your calendar to think of me again!

Ps 16:10. For you will not leave me among the dead; you will not allow your beloved one to rot in the grave. [11]You have let me experience the joys of life and the exquisite pleasures of your own eternal presence.

Ps 21:4. He asked for a long, good life, and you have granted his request; the days of his life stretch on and on forever.

Ps 22:26. The poor shall eat and be satisfied; all who seek the Lord shall find him and shall praise his name. Their hearts shall rejoice with everlasting joy.

Ps 23:6. Your goodness and unfailing kindness shall be with me all of my life, and afterwards I will live with you forever in your home.

Ps 31:5. Into your hand I commit my spirit. You have rescued me, O God who keeps his promises.

Ps 36:9. For you are the Fountain of life; our light is from your Light.

Ps 37:18. Day by day the Lord observes the good deeds done by godly men, and gives them eternal rewards. [27]So if you want an eternal home, leave your evil, lowdown ways and live good lives.

Ps 49:7. Yet not one of them, though rich as kings, can ransom his own brother from the penalty of sin! For God's forgiveness does not come that way. [8, 9]For a soul is far too precious to be ransomed by mere earthly wealth. There is not enough of it in all the earth to buy eternal life for just one soul, to keep it out of hell.

14. Death is the shepherd of all mankind. And "in the morning" those who are evil will be the slaves of those who are good. For the power of

their wealth is gone when they die; they cannot take it with them. [15]But as for me, God will redeem my soul from the power of death, for he will receive me.

Ps 73:26. My health fails; my spirits droop, yet God remains! He is the strength of my heart; he is mine forever!

Ps 86:12. With all my heart I will praise you. I will give glory to your name forever.

Ps 102:24. But I cried to him, "O God, you live forever and forever! Don't let me die half through my years! [25]In ages past you laid the foundations of the earth, and made the heavens with your hands! [26]They shall perish, but you go on forever. They will grow old, like worn-out clothing, and you will change them like a man putting on a new shirt and throwing away the old one! [27]But you yourself never grow old. You are forever, and your years never end. [28]But our families will continue; generation after generation will be preserved by your protection."

Ps 121:8. He keeps his eye upon you as you come and go, and always guards you.

Ps 133:3. Harmony is as refreshing as the dew on Mount Hermon, on the mountains of Israel. And God has pronounced this eternal blessing on Jerusalem, even life forevermore.

Ps 145:1, 2. I will praise you, my God and King, and bless your name each day and forever.

Prov 14:32. The godly have a refuge when they die, but the wicked are crushed by their sins.

Eccl 3:21. For who can prove that the spirit of man goes upward and the spirit of animals goes downward into dust?

Eccl 12:7. And the dust returns to the earth as it was, and the spirit returns to God who gave it.

Isa 14:9. The denizens of hell crowd to meet you as you enter their domain. World leaders and earth's mightiest kings, long dead, are there to see you.

Isa 25:8. He will swallow up death forever.

Isa 26:19. Yet we have this assurance: Those who belong to God shall live again. Their bodies shall rise again! Those who dwell in the dust shall awake and sing for joy! For God's light of life will fall like dew upon them!

Isa 38:18. For dead men cannot praise you. They cannot be filled with hope and joy. [19]The living, only the living, can praise you as I do today. One generation makes known your faithfulness to the next.

Ezk 32:31. When Pharaoh arrives, he will be comforted to find that he is not alone in having all his army slain, says the Lord God.

Dan 12:2. And many of those whose bodies lie dead and buried will rise up, some to everlasting life and some to shame and everlasting contempt. [3]And those who are wise—the people of God—shall shine as brightly as the sun's brilliance, and those who turn many to righteousness will glitter like stars forever.

Mt 10:28. Don't be afraid of those who can kill only your bodies—but can't touch your souls! Fear only God who can destroy both soul and body in hell.

Mt 16:26. What profit is there if you gain the whole world—and lose eternal life? What can be compared with the value of eternal life?

Mt 19:16. Someone came to Jesus with this question: "Good master, what must I do to have eternal life?" [17]"When you call me good you are calling me God," Jesus replied, "for God alone is truly good. But to answer your question, you can get to heaven if you keep the commandments. [29]And anyone who gives up his home, brothers, sisters, father, mother, wife, children, or property, to follow me, shall receive a hundred times as much in return, and shall have eternal life." Mk 10:30; Lk 10:25–28.

Mt 25:46. And they shall go away into eternal punishment; but the righteous into everlasting life.

Mk 10:30. Who won't be given back, a hundred times over, homes, brothers, sisters, mothers, children, and land—with persecutions! All these will be his here on earth, and in the world to come he shall have eternal life.

Mk 12:26. But now as to whether there will be a resurrection—have you never read in the book of Exodus about Moses and the burning bush? God said to Moses, "I *am* the God of Abraham, and I *am* the God of Isaac, and I *am* the God of Jacob." [27]God was telling Moses that these men, though dead for hundreds of years, were still very much alive, for he would not have said, "I *am* the God" of those who don't exist! You have made a serious error.

Lk 9:25. And what profit is there in gaining the whole world when it means forfeiting one's self?

Lk 18:30. Will be repaid many times over now, as well as receiving eternal life in the world to come.

Lk 20:36. And they never die again; in these respects they are like angels, and are sons of God, for they are raised up in new life from the dead. [37, 38]But as to your real question—whether or not there is a resurrection—why, even the writings of Moses himself prove this. For when he describes how God appeared to him in the burning bush, he speaks of God as "the God of Abraham, the God of Isaac, and God of Jacob." To say that the Lord *is* some person's God means that person is *alive,* not dead! So from God's point of view, all men are living.

Jn 3:14. And as Moses in the wilderness lifted up the bronze image of a serpent on a pole, even so I must be lifted up upon a pole, [15]so that anyone who believes in me will have eternal life. [16]For God loved the world so much that he gave hs only Son so that anyone who believes in him shall not perish but have eternal life. [36]And all who trust him—God's Son—to save them have eternal life; those who don't believe and obey him shall never see heaven, but the wrath of God remains upon them.

Jn 4:14. "But the water I give them," he said, "becomes a perpetual spring within them, watering them forever with eternal life."

Jn 5:24. I say emphatically that anyone who

listens to my message and believes in God who sent me has eternal life, and will never be damned for his sins, but has already passed out of death into life. [25]And I solemnly declare that the time is coming, in fact, it is here, when the dead shall hear my voice—the voice of the Son of God—and those who listen shall live. [29]And shall rise again—those who have done good, to eternal life; and those who have continued in evil, to judgment.

39. You search the Scriptures, for you believe they give you eternal life. And the Scriptures point to me! [40]Yet you won't come to me so that I can give you this life eternal!

Jn 6:27. But you shouldn't be so concerned about perishable things like food. No, spend your energy seeking the eternal life that I, the Messiah, can give you. For God the Father has sent me for this very purpose.

Jn 6:39. "And this is the will of God, that I should not lose even one of all those he has given me, but that I should raise them to eternal life at the Last Day. [40]For it is my Father's will that everyone who sees his Son and believes on him should have eternal life—that I should raise him at the Last Day. [44]For no one can come to me unless the Father who sent me draws him to me, and at the Last Day I will cause all such to rise again from the dead. [47]How earnestly I tell you this—anyone who believes in me already has eternal life! [50, 51]But the Bread from heaven gives eternal life to everyone who eats it. I am that Living Bread that came down out of heaven. Anyone eating this Bread shall live forever; this Bread is my flesh given to redeem humanity." [53]So Jesus said it again, "With all the earnestness I possess I tell you this: Unless you eat the flesh of the Messiah and drink his blood, you cannot have eternal life within you. [54]But anyone who does eat my flesh and drink my blood has eternal life, and I will raise him at the Last Day. [58]I am the true Bread from heaven; and anyone who eats this Bread shall live forever, and not die as your fathers did—though they ate bread from heaven." [68]Simon Peter replied, "Master, to whom shall we go? You alone have the words that give eternal life."

Jn 10:10. My purpose is to give life in all its fullness. [27]My sheep recognize my voice, and I know them, and they follow me. [28]I give them eternal life and they shall never perish. No one shall snatch them away from me.

Jn 11:25. Jesus told her, "I am the one who raises the dead and gives them life again. Anyone who believes in me, even though he dies like anyone else, shall live again. [26]He is given eternal life for believing in me and shall never perish. Do you believe this, Martha?"

Jn 12:25. If you love your life down here—you will lose it. If you despise your life down here—you will exchange it for eternal glory. [50]And I know his instructions lead to eternal life.

Jn 14:19. In just a little while I will be gone from the world, but I will still be present with you. For I will live again—and you will too.

Jn 17:2. For you have given him authority over every man and woman in all the earth. He gives eternal life to each one you have given him. [3]And this is the way to have eternal life—by knowing you, the only true God, and Jesus Christ, the one you sent to earth!

Acts 13:46. Then Paul and Barnabas spoke out boldly and declared, "It was necessary that this Good News from God should be given first to you Jews. But since you have rejected it, and shown yourselves unworthy of eternal life—well, we will offer it to Gentiles." [48]When the Gentiles heard this, they were very glad and rejoiced in Paul's message; and as many as wanted eternal life, believed.

Acts 20:32. And now I entrust you to God and his care and to his wonderful words which are able to build your faith and give you all the inheritance of those who are set apart for himself.

Acts 23:8. For the Sadducees say there is no resurrection or angels or even eternal spirit within us, but the Pharisees believe in all of these. [9]So a great clamor arose. Some of the Jewish leaders jumped up to argue that Paul was all right. "We see nothing wrong with him," they shouted. "Perhaps a spirit or angel spoke to him (there on the Damascus road)."

Acts 26:7. The twelve tribes of Israel strive night and day to attain this same hope I have! Yet, O King, for me it is a crime they say! [8]But is it a crime to believe in the resurrection of the dead? Does it seem incredible to you that God can bring men back to life again? [18]"To open their eyes to their true condition so that they may repent and live in the light of God instead of in Satan's darkness, so that they may receive forgiveness for their sins and God's inheritance along with all people everywhere whose sins are cleansed away, who are set apart by faith in me."

Rom 2:7. He will give eternal life to those who patiently do the will of God, seeking for the unseen glory and honor and eternal life that he offers.

Rom 5:21. Before, sin ruled over all men and brought them to death, but now God's kindness rules instead, giving us right standing with God and resulting in eternal life through Jesus Christ our Lord.

Rom 6:22. But now you are free from the power of sin and are slaves of God, and his benefits to you include holiness and everlasting life. [23]For the wages of sin is death, but the free gift of God is eternal life through Jesus Christ our Lord.

1 Cor 15:12. But tell me this! Since you believe what we preach, that *Christ* rose from the dead, why are some of you saying that dead people will never come back to life again? [13]For if there is no resurrection of the dead, then Christ must still be dead. [14]And if he is still dead, then all our preaching is useless and your trust in God is empty, worthless, hopeless; [15]and we apostles are all liars because we have said that God raised Christ from the grave, and of course that isn't true if the dead do not come back to life again. [16]If they don't, then

Christ is still dead, [17]and you are very foolish to keep on trusting God to save you, and you are still under condemnation for your sins; [18]in that case all Christians who have died are lost! [19]And if being a Christian is of value to us only now in this life, we are the most miserable of creatures. [20]But the fact is that Christ did actually rise from the dead, and has become the first of millions who will come back to life again some day. [21]Death came into the world because of what one man (Adam) did, and it is because of what this other man (Christ) has done that now there is the resurrection from the dead. [22]Everyone dies because all of us are related to Adam, being members of his sinful race, and wherever there is sin, death results. But all who are related to Christ will rise again. [23]Each, however, in his own turn: Christ rose first; then when Christ comes back, all his people will become alive again. [24]After that the end will come when he will turn the kingdom over to God the Father, having put down all enemies of every kind. [25]For Christ will be King until he has defeated all his enemies, [26]including the last enemy—death. This too must be defeated and ended. [27]For the rule and authority over all things has been given to Christ by his Father; except, of course, Christ does not rule over the Father himself, who gave him this power to rule. [28]When Christ has finally won the battle against all his enemies, then he, the Son of God, will put himself also under his Father's orders, so that God who has given him the victory over everything else will be utterly supreme. [29]If the dead will not come back to life again, then what point is there in people being baptized for those who are gone? Why do it unless you believe that the dead will some day rise again? [30]And why should we ourselves be continually risking our lives, facing death hour by hour. [31]For it is a fact that I face death daily; that is as true as my pride in your growth in the Lord. [32]And what value was there in fighting wild beasts—those men of Ephesus—if it was only for what I gain in this life down here? If we will never live again after we die, then we might as well go and have ourselves a good time: let us eat, drink, and be merry. What's the difference? For tomorrow we die, and that ends everything! [33]Don't be fooled by those who say such things. If you listen to them you will start acting like them. [34]Get some sense and quit your sinning. For to your shame I say it, some of you are not even Christians at all and have never really known God. [35]But someone may ask, "How will the dead be brought back to life again? What kind of bodies will they have?" [36]What a foolish question! You will find the answer in your own garden! When you put a seed into the ground it doesn't grow into a plant unless it "dies" first. [37]And when the green shoot comes up out of the seed, it is very different from the seed you first planted. For all you put into the ground is a dry little seed of wheat, or whatever it is you are planting, [38]then God gives it a beautiful new body—just the kind he wants it to have; a different kind of plant grows from each kind of seed. [39]And just as there are different kinds of seeds and plants, so also there are different kinds of flesh. Humans, animals, fish, and birds are all different. [40]The angels in heaven have bodies far different from ours, and the beauty and the glory of their bodies is different from the beauty and the glory of ours. [41]The sun has one kind of glory while the moon and stars have another kind. And the stars differ from each other in their beauty and brightness. [42]In the same way, our earthly bodies which die and decay are different from the bodies we shall have when we come back to life again, for they will never die. [43]The bodies we have now embarrass us for they become sick and die; but they will be full of glory when we come back to life again. Yes, they are weak, dying bodies now, but when we live again they will be full of strength. [44]They are just human bodies at death, but when they come back to life they will be superhuman bodies. For just as there are natural, human bodies, there are also supernatural, spiritual bodies. [45]The Scriptures tell us that the first man, Adam, was given a natural, human body but Christ is more than that, for he was life-giving Spirit. [46]First, then, we have these human bodies and later on God gives us spiritual, heavenly bodies. [47]Adam was made from the dust of the earth, but Christ came from heaven above. [48]Every human being has a body just like Adam's, made of dust, but all who become Christ's will have the same kind of body as his—a body from heaven. [49]Just as each of us now has a body like Adam's, so we shall some day have a body like Christ's. [50]I tell you this, my brothers: an earthly body made of flesh and blood cannot get into God's kingdom. These perishable bodies of ours are not the right kind to live forever. [51]But I am telling you this strange and wonderful secret: we shall not all die, but we shall all be given new bodies! [52]It will all happen in a moment, in the twinkling of an eye, when the last trumpet is blown. For there will be a trumpet blast from the sky and all the Christians who have died will suddenly become alive, with new bodies that will never, never die; and then we who are still alive shall suddenly have new bodies too. [53]For our earthly bodies, the ones we have now that can die, must be transformed into heavenly bodies that cannot perish but will live forever. [54]When this happens, then at last this Scripture will come true—"Death is swallowed up in victory." [55]O death, where then your victory? Where then your sting?

2 Cor 5:1. For we know that when this tent we live in now is taken down—when we die and leave these bodies—we will have wonderful new bodies in heaven, homes that will be ours forevermore, made for us by God himself, and not by human hands.

Gal 6:8. If he sows to please his own wrong desires, he will be planting seeds of evil and he will surely reap a harvest of spiritual decay and death; but if he plants the good things of the Spirit, he will reap the everlasting life which the Holy Spirit gives him.

Col 1:5. And you are looking forward to the joys

of heaven, and have been ever since the Gospel first was preached to you. 6The same Good News that came to you is going out all over the world and changing lives everywhere, just as it changed yours that very first day you heard it and understood about God's great kindness to sinners.

1 Thess 4:13. And now, dear brothers, I want you to know what happens to a Christian when he dies so that when it happens, you will not be full of sorrow, as those are who have no hope. 14For since we believe that Jesus died and then came back to life again, we can also believe that when Jesus returns, God will bring back with him all the Christians who have died. 15I can tell you this directly from the Lord: that we who are still living when the Lord returns will not rise to meet him ahead of those who are in their graves. 16For the Lord himself will come down from heaven with a mighty shout and with the soul-stirring cry of the archangel and the great trumpet-call of God. And the believers who are dead will be the first to rise to meet the Lord. 17Then we who are still alive and remain on the earth will be caught up with them in the clouds to meet the Lord in the air and remain with him forever. 18So comfort and encourage each other with this news.

1 Thess 5:10. He died for us so that we can live with him forever, whether we are dead or alive at the time of his return.

2 Thess 1:7. And so I would say to you who are suffering, God will give you rest along with us when the Lord Jesus appears suddenly from heaven in flaming fire with his mighty angels, 8bringing judgment on those who do not wish to know God, and who refuse to accept his plan to save them through our Lord Jesus Christ. 9They will be punished in everlasting hell forever separated from the Lord, never to see the glory of his power.

2 Thess 2:16. May our Lord Jesus Christ himself and God our Father, who has loved us and given us everlasting comfort and hope which we don't deserve.

1 Tim 1:16. But God had mercy on me so that Christ Jesus could use me as an example to show everyone how patient he is with even the worst sinners, so that others will realize that they, too, can have everlasting life.

1 Tim 4:8. Bodily exercise is all right, but spiritual exercise is much more important and is a tonic for all you do. So exercise yourself spiritually and practice being a better Christian, because that will help you not only now in this life, but in the next life too.

1 Tim 6:12. Fight on for God. Hold tightly to the eternal life which God has given you. 19By doing this they will be storing up real treasure for themselves in heaven—it is the only safe investment for eternity! And they will be living a fruitful Christian life down here as well.

2 Tim 1:9. It is he who saved us and chose us for his holy work, not because we deserved it but because that was his plan long before the world began—to show his love and kindness to us through Christ. 10And now he has made all of this plain to us by the coming of our Savior Jesus Christ, who broke the power of death and showed us the way of everlasting life through trusting him.

Tit 1:2. I have been sent to bring faith to those God has chosen and to teach them to know God's truth—the kind of truth that changes lives—so that they can have eternal life, which God promised them before the world began—and he cannot lie.

Tit 3:7. So that he could declare us good in God's eyes—all because of his great kindness; and now we can share in the wealth of the eternal life he gives us, and we are eagerly looking forward to receiving it.

Heb 9:15. Christ came with this new agreement so that all who are invited may come and have forever all the wonders God has promised them. For Christ died to rescue *them from the penalty* of the sins they had committed while still under that old system.

Heb 10:34. You suffered with those thrown into jail, and you were actually joyful when all you owned was taken from you, knowing that better things were awaiting you in heaven, things that would be yours forever.

Heb 11:5. Enoch trusted God too, and that is why God took him away to heaven without dying; suddenly he was gone because God took him. 10Abraham did this because he was confidently waiting for God to bring him to that strong heavenly city whose designer and builder is God. 13These men of faith I have mentioned died without ever receiving all that God had promised them; but they saw it all awaiting them on ahead and were glad, for they agreed that this earth was not their real home but that they were just strangers visiting down here. 14And quite obviously when they talked like that, they were looking forward to their real home in heaven. 15If they had wanted to, they could have gone back to the good things of this world. 16But they didn't want to. They were living for heaven. And now God is not ashamed to be called their God, for he has made a heavenly city for them.

1 Pet 1:3. All honor to God, the God and Father of our Lord Jesus Christ; for it is his boundless mercy that has given us the privilege of being born again, so that we are now members of God's own family. Now we live in the hope of eternal life because Christ rose again from the dead. 4And God has reserved for his children the priceless gift of eternal life; it is kept in heaven for you, pure and undefiled, beyond the reach of change and decay. 5And God, in his mighty power, will make sure that you get there safely to receive it, because you are trusting him. It will be yours in that coming last day for all to see.

1 Jn 2:17. And this world is fading away, and these evil, forbidden things will go with it, but whoever keeps doing the will of God will live forever. 25And he himself has promised us this: *eternal life.*

1 Jn 3:15. And you know that no one wanting to murder has eternal life within.

1 Jn 5:11. And what is it that God has said? That he has given us eternal life, and that this life is in his Son. [12]So whoever has God's Son has life; whoever does not have his Son, does not have life.

13. I have written this to you who believe in the Son of God so that you may know you have eternal life.

20. And we know that Christ, God's Son, has come to help us understand and find the true God. And now we are in God because we are in Jesus Christ his Son, who is the only true God; and he is eternal Life.

Jude 1:21. Stay always within the boundaries where God's love can reach and bless you. Wait patiently for the eternal life that our Lord Jesus Christ in his mercy is going to give you.

Rev 1:7. See! He is arriving, surrounded by clouds; and every eye shall see him—yes, and those who pierced him. And the nations will weep in sorrow and in terror when he comes. Yes! Amen! Let it be so!

18. I am the First and Last, the Living One who died, who is now alive forevermore, who has the keys of hell and death.

Rev 3:4. Yet even there in Sardis some haven't soiled their garments with the world's filth; they shall walk with me in white, for they are worthy.

Rev 22:5. And there will be no night there—no need for lamps or sun—for the Lord God will be their light; and they shall reign forever and ever.

See *Immortality; Resurrection; Righteous, Promises to; Wicked, Punishment of.*

FROM GOD. Gen 2:7. The time came when the Lord God formed a man's body from the dust of the ground and breathed into it the breath of life. And man became a living person.

Deut 8:3. He did it to help you realize that food isn't everything, and that real life comes by obeying every command of God.

Deut 30:20. Choose to love the Lord your God and to obey him and to cling to him, for he is your life and the length of your days. You will then be able to live safely in the land the Lord promised your ancestors, Abraham, Isaac, and Jacob.

Deut 32:39. Don't you see that I alone am God? I kill and make live. I wound and heal—no one delivers from my power.

1 Sam 2:6. The Lord kills, the Lord gives life.

Job 27:3. That as long as I live, while I have breath from God. Chapter 12:10.

Job 34:14. If God were to withdraw his Spirit, [15]all life would disappear and mankind would turn again to dust.

Ps 30:3. You brought me back from the brink of the grave, from death itself, and here I am alive! Ps 66:9.

Ps 68:20. He frees us! He rescues us from death.

Ps 104:30. Then you send your Spirit, and new life is born to replenish all the living of the earth.

Eccl 12:7. And the dust returns to the earth as it was, and the spirit returns to God who gave it.

Isa 38:16. O Lord, your discipline is good and leads to life and health. Oh, heal me and make me live! [17]Yes, now I see it all—it was good for me to undergo this bitterness, for you have lovingly delivered me from death; you have forgiven all my sins. [18]For dead men cannot praise you. They cannot be filled with hope and joy. [19]The living, only the living, can praise you as I do today. One generation makes known your faithfulness to the next. [20]Think of it! The Lord healed me! Every day of my life from now on I will sing my songs of praise in the Temple, accompanied by the orchestra.

Acts 17:25. He himself gives life and breath to everything, and satisfies every need there is. [26]He created all the people of the world from one man, Adam, and scattered the nations across the face of the earth. He decided beforehand which should rise and fall, and when. He determined their boundaries. [28]For in him we live and move and are! As one of your own poets says it, "We are the sons of God."

Rom 4:17. And this promise is from God himself, who makes the dead live again and speaks of future events with as much certainty as though they were already past.

1 Tim 6:13. I command you before God who gives life to all.

Jas 4:15. What you ought to say is, "If the Lord wants us to, we shall live and do this or that."

LONG. See *Longevity.*

SPIRITUAL. Jn 3:3. Jesus replied, "With all the earnestness I possess I tell you this: Unless you are born again, you can never get into the Kingdom of God." [4]"Born again!" exclaimed Nicodemus. "What do you mean? How can an old man go back into his mother's womb and be born again?" [5]Jesus replied, "What I am telling you so earnestly is this: Unless one is born of water and the Spirit, he cannot enter the Kingdom of God. [6]Men can only reproduce human life, but the Holy Spirit gives new life from heaven; [7]so don't be surprised at my statement that you must be born again! [8]Just as you can hear the wind but can't tell where it comes from or where it will go next, so it is with the Spirit. We do not know on whom he will next bestow this life from heaven." [9]"What do you mean?" Nicodemus asked. [10, 11]Jesus replied, "You, a respected Jewish teacher, and yet you don't understand these things? I am telling you what I know and have seen —and yet you won't believe me. [12]But if you don't even believe me when I tell you about such things as these that happen here among men, how can you possibly believe if I tell you what is going on in heaven? [13]For only I, the Messiah, have come to earth and will return to heaven again. [14]And as Moses in the wilderness lifted up the bronze image of a serpent on a pole, even so I must be lifted up upon a pole, [15]so that anyone who believes in me will have eternal life. [16]For God loved the world so much that he gave his only Son so that anyone who believes in him shall not perish but have eternal life."

Jn 5:24. I say emphatically that anyone who

listens to my message and believes in God who sent me has eternal life, and will never be damned for his sins, but has already passed out of death into life. [25]And I solemnly declare that the time is coming, in fact, it is here, when the dead shall hear my voice—the voice of the Son of God—and those who listen shall live. [26]The Father has life in himself, and has granted his Son to have life in himself. [40]Yet you won't come to me so that I can give you this life eternal!

Jn 6:27. "But you shouldn't be so concerned about perishable things like food. No, spend your energy seeking the eternal life that I, the Messiah, can give you. For God the Father has sent me for this very purpose. [33]The true Bread is a Person—the one sent by God from heaven, and he gives life to the world." [35]Jesus replied, "I am the Bread of Life. No one coming to me will ever be hungry again. Those believing in me will never thirst. [40]For it is my Father's will that everyone who sees his Son and believes on him should have eternal life—that I should raise him at the Last Day. [47]How earnestly I tell you this—anyone who believes in me already has eternal life!"

Jn 10:10. The thief's purpose is to steal, kill and destroy. My purpose is to give life in all its fullness.

Jn 11:25. Jesus told her, "I am the one who raises the dead and gives them life again. Anyone who believes in me, even though he dies like anyone else, shall live again. [26]He is given eternal life for believing in me and shall never perish."

Jn 14:6. Jesus told him, "I am the Way—yes, and the Truth and the Life. No one can get to the Father except by means of me."

Jn 17:2. For you have given him authority over every man and woman in all the earth. He gives eternal life to each one you have given him. [3]And this is the way to have eternal life—by knowing you, the only true God, and Jesus Christ, the one you sent to earth!

Jn 20:31. But these are recorded so that you will believe that he is the Messiah, the Son of God, and that believing in him you will have life.

Rom 6:4. Your old sin-loving nature was buried with him by baptism when he died, and when God the Father, with glorious power, brought him back to life again, you were given his wonderful new life to enjoy. [Eph 2:5] [5]For you have become a part of him, and so you died with him, so to speak, when he died, and now you share his new life, and shall rise as he did. [8]And since your old sin-loving nature "died" with Christ, we know that you will share his new life. [11]So look upon your old sin nature as dead and unresponsive to sin, and instead be alive to God, alert to him, through Jesus Christ our Lord. [Gal 2:20] [13]Do not let any part of your bodies become tools of wickedness, to be used for sinning; but give yourselves completely to God—every part of you—for you are back from death and you want to be tools in the hands of God, to be used for his good purposes. [22]But now you are free from the power of sin and are slaves of God, and his benefits to you include holiness and everlasting life. [23]For the wages of sin is death, but the free gift of God is eternal life through Jesus Christ our Lord.

Rom 8:10. Yet, even though Christ lives within you, your body will die because of sin; but your spirit will live, for Christ has pardoned it.

Col 3:3. You should have as little desire for this world as a dead person does. Your real life is in heaven with Christ and God.

1 Jn 1:1. Christ was alive when the world began, yet I myself have seen him with my own eyes and listened to him speak. I have touched him with my own hands. He is God's message of Life. [2]This one who is Life from God has been shown to us and we guarantee that we have seen him; I am speaking of Christ, who is eternal Life. He was with the Father and then was shown to us.

See *Life, Eternal.*

LIGHT Created, Gen 1:3–5; Ps 74:16; Isa 45:7; 2 Cor 4:6. Miraculous, Mt 17:2; Acts 9:3.

FIGURATIVE AND SYMBOLICAL. Ps 27:1. The Lord is my light and my salvation; whom shall I fear?

Ps 84:11. For Jehovah God is our Light and Protector.

Ps 119:105. Your words are a flashlight to light the path ahead of me, and keep me from stumbling.

Prov 6:23. For their advice is a beam of light directed into the dark corners of your mind to warn you of danger and to give you a good life.

Prov 13:9. The good man's life is full of light. The sinner's road is dark and gloomy.

Prov 20:20. God puts out the light of the man who curses his father or mother.

Eccl 2:13. That wisdom is of more value than foolishness, just as light is better than darkness.

Isa 8:20. "Check these witches' words against the Word of God!" he says. "If their messages are different than mine, it is because I have not sent them; for they have no light or truth in them."

Isa 49:6. You shall do more than restore Israel to me. I will make you a Light to the nations of the world to bring my salvation to them too.

Isa 58:8. If you do these things, God will shed his own glorious light upon you. He will heal you; your godliness will lead you forward, and goodness will be a shield before you, and the glory of the Lord will protect you from behind.

Isa 60:19. No longer will you need the sun or moon to give you light, for the Lord your God will be your everlasting light, and he will be your glory. [20]Your sun shall never set; the moon shall not go down—for the Lord will be your everlasting light; your days of mourning all will end.

Mt 4:16. There the people who sat in darkness have seen a great Light; they sat in the land of death, and the Light broke through upon them.

Mt 5:14. You are the world's light—a city on a hill, glowing in the night for all to see.

Lk 2:32. He is the Light that will shine upon the nations, and he will be the glory of your people Israel!

Lk 11:34. Your eyes light up your inward being.

A pure eye lets sunshine into your soul. A lustful eye shuts out the light and plunges you into darkness.

Jn 1:4. Eternal life is in him, and this life gives light to all mankind. [5]His life is the light that shines through the darkness—and the darkness can never extinguish it. [6, 7]God sent John the Baptist as a witness to the fact that Jesus Christ is the true Light. [8]John himself was not the Light; he was only a witness to identify it. [9]Later on, the one who is the true Light arrived to shine on everyone coming into the world.

Jn 3:19. Their sentence is based on this fact: that the Light from heaven came into the world, but they loved the darkness more than the Light, for their deeds were evil. [20]They hated the heavenly light because they wanted to sin in the darkness. They stayed away from that Light for fear their sins would be exposed and they would be punished. [21]But those doing right come gladly to the Light to let everyone see that they are doing what God wants them to.

Jn 5:35. John shone brightly for a while, and you benefited and rejoiced.

Jn 8:12. Later, in one of his talks, Jesus said to the people, "I am the Light of the world. So if you follow me, you won't be stumbling through the darkness, for living light will flood your path."

Jn 9:5. But while I am still here in the world, I give it my light.

Jn 12:35. Jesus replied, "My light will shine out for you just a little while longer. Walk in it while you can, and go where you want to go before the darkness falls, for then it will be too late for you to find your way. [36]Make use of the Light while there is still time; then you will become light bearers." After saying these things, Jesus went away and was hidden from them. Lk 16:8.

Acts 26:18. To open their eyes to their true condition so that they may repent and live in the light of God instead of in Satan's darkness, so that they may receive forgiveness for their sins and God's inheritance along with all people everywhere whose sins are cleansed away, who are set apart by faith in me.

Eph 5:8. For though once your heart was full of darkness, now it is full of light from the Lord, and your behavior should show it! [14]"'Awake, O sleeper, and rise up from the dead; and Christ shall give you light."

Phil 2:15. So that no one can speak a word of blame against you. You are to live clean, innocent lives as children of God in a dark world full of people who are crooked and stubborn. Shine out among them like beacon lights.

1 Thess 5:5. For you are all children of the light and of the day, and do not belong to darkness and night.

1 Tim 6:16. Who alone can never die, who lives in light so terrible that no human being can approach him.

Jas 1:17. But whatever is good and perfect comes to us from God, the Creator of all light, and he shines forever without change or shadow.

1 Pet 2:9. But you are not like that, for you have been chosen by God himself—you are priests of the King, you are holy and pure, you are God's very own—all this so that you may show to others how God called you out of the darkness into his wonderful light.

2 Pet 1:19. So we have seen and proved that what the prophets said came true. You will do well to pay close attention to everything they have written, for, like lights shining into dark corners, their words help us to understand many things that otherwise would be dark and difficult. But when you consider the wonderful truth of the prophets' words, then the light will dawn in your souls and Christ the Morning Star will shine in your hearts.

1 Jn 1:5. This is the message God has given us to pass on to you: that God is Light and in him is no darkness at all. [7]But if we are living in the light of God's presence, just as Christ does, then we have wonderful fellowship and joy with each other, and the blood of Jesus his Son cleanses us from every sin.

Rev 21:23. And the city has no need of sun or moon to light it, for the glory of God and of the Lamb illuminate it.

LIGHTNING Job 28:26; 37:3; 38:25–27, 35; Ps 18:14; 77:18; 78:48; 97:4; 135:7; 144:6; Jer 10:13; 51:16; Ezk 1:13, 14; Dan 10:5, 6; Nah 2:4; Zech 9:14; 10:1; Mt 24:27; 28:3; Lk 10:18; Rev 4:5; 8:5; 11:19; 16:18.

LILY Song 6:2, 3. The principal pillars of the Temple ornamented with carvings of, 1 Kgs 7:16–22. Bronze laver in the Temple shaped like, 2 Chron 4:5. Lessons of trust gathered from, Mt 6:28–30; Lk 12:27.

FIGURATIVE. Song 2:1, 2, 16; 4:5; 5:13; 7:2; Hos 14:5.

LIME Deut 27:2–4; Isa 33:12.

LINEN Exported from Egypt, Ezk 27:7; from Edom, Ezk 27:16. Curtains of the tabernacle made of, Ex 26:1, 2; 27:9, 10. Clothing of priests made of, Ex 28:5–8, 15, 39–42; 39:28; Lev 6:10; 16:4; Ezk 44:18. Royal garments made of, Esther 8:15. Garments for men made of, Ezk 9:2; for women, Prov 31:22; Isa 3:23; Ezk 16:9–13. Bedding made of, Prov 7:16, 17. Mosaic law forbade its being woven with wool, Lev 19:19; Deut 22:11. The body of Jesus wrapped in, Mk 15:46; Jn 20:5.

FIGURATIVE. Pure and white, of righteousness, Rev 15:6; 19:8, 14.

LINUS A Christian at Rome, 2 Tim 4:21.

LION King of beasts, Mic 5:8. Fierceness of, Job 4:10; 28:8; Ps 7:2; Prov 22:13; Jer 2:15; 49:19; 50:44; Hos 13:8. The roaring of, Ps 22:13; Prov 20:2. Strength of, Prov 30:29–31; Isa 38:13; Joel 1:6. Instincts of, in taking prey, Ps 10:9; 17:12; Lam 3:10; Amos 3:4; Nah 2:12. Lair of, Jer 4:7; 25:38. The stands in the temple decorated with, 1 Kgs 7:27–30, 36. Twelve statues of, on the stairs leading to Solomon's throne, 1 Kgs 10:19, 20. Samson's riddle concerning, Judg 14:14, 18. Proverb of, Eccl 9:4. Parable of, Ezk 19:1–9. Kept in captivity, Dan 6. Sent as judgment on the Samaritans, 2 Kgs 17:25,

26. Killed by Samson, Judg 14:5–9; David, 1 Sam 17:34–36; Benaiah, 2 Sam 23:20. Disobedient prophet killed by, 1 Kgs 13:24–28; an unnamed person slain by, 1 Kgs 20:36. Used for the torture of criminals, Dan 6:16–24. 2 Tim 4:17.

FIGURATIVE. Of a king's anger, Prov 19:12; Jer 5:6; 50:17; Hos 5:14; of Satan, 1 Pet 5:8; of divine judgments, Isa 15:9.

Symbolical. Gen 49:9; Ezk 1:10; 10:14; Dan 7:4; Rev 4:7; 5:5; 9:8, 17, 18; 13:2.

LIST Genealogies kept in, Gen 5:1. Of the living, Ps 69:28.

See *Book.*

LITIGATION To be avoided, Mt 5:25; Lk 12:58; 1 Cor 6:1–8.

See *Actions at Law; Adjudication; Arbitration; Compromise.*

LITTER An Oriental contrivance for carrying persons, Isa 66:20. Made of wood, Song 3:7–9.

LIVER Superstitious rites with, Ezk 21:21.

LIVING WORD Scriptures called, Acts 7:38.

LIZARD Lev 11:29, 30; Prov 30:24–28; Ezk 8:10.

LO-AMMI A symbolical name given to a son of Hosea, Hos 1:9.

LOAVES Miracle of the five, Mt 14:15–21; 16:9; Lk 9:12–17; of the seven, Mt 15:34–38; 16:9, 10.

See *Bread.*

LOBBYING Ezra 4:4, 5.

See *Diplomacy; Influence, Political.*

LOCK Judg 3:22–25; Neh 3:13, 14; Song 5:5.

LOCUST Authorized as food, Lev 11:21, 22; used as, Mt 3:4; Mk 1:6. Plague of, Ex 10:1–19; Ps 105:34, 35. Devastation by, Deut 28:38; 1 Kgs 8:37; 2 Chron 7:13; Isa 33:4; Joel 1:4–7; 2:25; Amos 4:9; Rev 9:7–10. Sent as judgment, Joel 1:4; 2:25; Nah 3:15, 16. Instincts of, Prov 30:24–28.

See *Grasshopper.*

FIGURATIVE. Job 39:20.

Symbolical. Rev 9:3–10.

LOD A city in Benjamin, 1 Chron 8:12; Ezra 2:3–35; Neh 7:8–38; 11:31–35. Called *Lydda,* Acts 9:38.

LO-DEBAR Home of Mephibosheth, the lame son of Jonathan, 2 Sam 9:3–5.

LOINCLOTH *Symbolical.* Jer 13:1–11.

See *Belt; Sash.*

LOIS Grandmother of Timothy, commended by Paul for her faith, 2 Tim 1:5.

LONGEVITY Gen 6:3. Then Jehovah said, "My Spirit must not forever be disgraced in man, wholly evil as he is. I will give him 120 years to mend his ways."

Ex 20:12. Honor your father and mother, that you may have a long, good life in the land the Lord your God will give you.

1 Kgs 3:11. So he replied, "Because you have asked for wisdom in governing my people, and haven't asked for a long life or riches for yourself, or the defeat of your enemies— [12]yes, I'll give you what you asked for! I will give you a wiser mind than anyone else has ever had or ever will have! [13]And I will also give you what you didn't ask for —riches and honor! And no one in all the world will be as rich and famous as you for the rest of your life! [14]And I will give you a long life if you follow me and obey my laws as your father David did."

Job 5:26. You shall live a long, good life; like standing grain, you'll not be harvested until it's time!

Ps 21:4. He asked for a long, good life, and you have granted his request; the days of his life stretch on and on forever.

Ps 34:11. Sons and daughters, come and listen and let me teach you the importance of trusting and fearing the Lord. [12]Do you want a long, good life? [13]Then watch your tongue! Keep your lips from lying.

Ps 90:10. Seventy years are given us! And some may even live to eighty. But even the best of these years are often emptiness and pain; soon they disappear, and we are gone.

Ps 91:16. I will satisfy him with a full life and give him my salvation.

Prov 3:1, 2. My son, never forget the things I've taught you. If you want a long and satisfying life, closely follow my instructions. [16]Wisdom gives: A long, good life, riches, honor.

Prov 9:11. I, Wisdom, will make the hours of your day more profitable and the years of your life more fruitful.

Prov 10:27. Reverence for God adds hours to each day; so how can the wicked expect a long, good life?

Isa 65:20. No longer will babies die when only a few days old; no longer will men be considered old at 100! Only sinners will die that young! [21, 22]In those days, when a man builds a house, he will keep on living in it—it will not be destroyed by invading armies as in the past. My people will plant vineyards and eat the fruit themselves—their enemies will not confiscate it. For my people will live as long as trees and will long enjoy their hard-won gains.

1 Pet 3:10. If you want a happy, good life, keep control of your tongue, and guard your lips from telling lies. [11]Turn away from evil and do good. Try to live in peace even if you must run after it to catch and hold it!

See *Old Age.*

INSTANCES OF. Adam, 930 years, Gen 5:3–5. Seth, 912 years, Gen 5:6–8. Enosh, 905 years, Gen 5:9–11. Kenan, 910 years, Gen 5:12–14. Mahalalel, 895 years, Gen 5:15–17. Jared, 962 years, Gen 5:18–20. Enoch, 365 years, Gen 5:21–24. Methuselah, 969 years, Gen 5:25–27. Lamech, 777 years, Gen 5:28–31. Noah, 950 years, Gen 9:29. Shem, 600 years, Gen 11:10, 11. Arpachshad, 438 years, Gen 11:12, 13. Shelah, 433 years, Gen 11:14, 15. Eber, 464 years, Gen 11:16, 17. Peleg, 239 years, Gen 11:18, 19. Reu, 239 years, Gen 11:20, 21. Serug, 230 years, Gen 11:22, 23. Nahor, 148 years, Gen 11:24, 25. Terah, 205 years, Gen 11:32. Sarah, 127 years, Gen 23:1. Abraham, 175 years, Gen 25:7, 8. Isaac, 180 years,

Gen 35:28, 29. Jacob, 147 years, Gen 47:28. Joseph, 110 years, Gen 50:26. Amram, 137 years, Ex 6:20. Aaron, 123 years, Num 33:38, 39. Moses, 120 years, Deut 31:2; 34:7. Joshua, 110 years, Josh 24:29. Eli, 98 years, 1 Sam 4:15. Barzillai, 80 years, 2 Sam 19:31, 32. Job, 140 years, Job 42:16. Jehoiada, 130 years, 2 Chron 24:15. Anna, Lk 2:36, 37. Paul, Philemon 1:8, 9.

LONGSUFFERING See *Charitableness; Endurance; God, Longsuffering of; Patience.*

LOOKING-GLASS See *Mirror.*

LORD See *God; Jehovah; Jesus.*

LORD'S DAY The first day of the week, Sunday, which followed the regular Sabbath of the Jews, the day on which Christ was raised from the dead. By common consent Christians observe the first day as the Lord's day for worship and Christian activity, in honor of his resurrection. (The term *Christian Sabbath* is rejected by many believers as inappropriate.) Lev 23:9–11; Ps 118:22–24; Col 2:16, 17.

Mk 16:9. It was early on Sunday morning when Jesus came back to life, and the first person who saw him was Mary Magdalene. Mt 28:1, 5, 6, 9.

Jn 20:19. That evening the disciples were meeting behind locked doors, in fear of the Jewish leaders, when suddenly Jesus was standing there among them! [*vs* 1, 11–16.] [26]Eight days later the disciples were together again, and this time Thomas was with them. The doors were locked; but suddenly, as before, Jesus was standing among them and greeting them.

Acts 20:7. On Sunday, we gathered for a communion service, with Paul preaching. And since he was leaving the next day, he talked until midnight!

1 Cor 16:2. On every Lord's Day each of you should put aside something from what you have earned during the week, and use it for this offering. The amount depends on how much the Lord has helped you earn. Don't wait until I get there and then try to collect it all at once.

Rev 1:10. It was the Lord's Day and I was worshiping, when suddenly I heard a loud voice behind me, a voice that sounded like a trumpet blast.

See *Sabbath.*

LORD'S PRAYER Mt 6:9–13; Lk 11:2–4. More properly, Jn 17.

LORD'S SUPPER Mt 26:17. On the first day of the Passover ceremonies, when bread made with yeast was purged from every Jewish home, the disciples came to Jesus and asked, "Where shall we plan to eat the Passover?" [18]He replied, "Go into the city and see Mr. So-and-So, and tell him, 'Our Master says, my time has come, and I will eat the Passover meal with my disciples at your house.' " [19]So the disciples did as he told them, and prepared the supper there. [20, 21]That evening as he sat eating with the Twelve, he said, "One of you will betray me." [22]Sorrow chilled their hearts, and each one asked, "Am I the one?" [23]He replied, "It is the one I served first. [24]For I must die just as was prophesied, but woe to the man by whom I am betrayed. Far better for that one if he had never been born." [25]Judas, too, had asked him, "Rabbi, am I the one?" And Jesus had told him, "Yes." [26]As they were eating, Jesus took a small loaf of bread and blessed it and broke it apart and gave it to the disciples and said, "Take it and eat it, for this is my body." [27]And he took a cup of wine and gave thanks for it and gave it to them and said, "Each one drink from it, [28]for this is my blood, sealing the New Covenant. It is poured out to forgive the sins of multitudes. [29]Mark my words—I will not drink this wine again until the day I drink it new with you in my Father's Kingdom." [30]And when they had sung a hymn, they went out to the Mount of Olives. Mk 14:22–24; Lk 22:19, 20; Jn 13:1–4.

Lk 13:26. "But we ate with you, and you taught in our streets," you will say.

Acts 2:42. They joined with the other believers in regular attendance at the apostles' teaching sessions and at the Communion services and prayer meetings. [46]They worshiped together regularly at the Temple each day, met in small groups in homes for Communion, and shared their meals with great joy and thankfulness, [47]praising God. The whole city was favorable to them, and each day God added to them all who were being saved.

Acts 20:7. On Sunday, we gathered for a communion service, with Paul preaching. And since he was leaving the next day, he talked until midnight! *vs.* 10–12.

1 Cor 10:16. When we ask the Lord's blessing upon our drinking from the cup of wine at the Lord's Table, this means, doesn't it, that all who drink it are sharing together the blessing of Christ's blood? And when we break off pieces of the bread from the loaf to eat there together, this shows that we are sharing together in the benefits of his body. [17]No matter how many of us there are, we all eat from the same loaf, showing that we are all parts of the one body of Christ. [21]You cannot drink from the cup at the Lord's Table and at Satan's table, too. You cannot eat bread both at the Lord's Table and at Satan's table. [22]What? Are you tempting the Lord to be angry with you? Are you stronger than he is?

1 Cor 11:20. When you come together to eat, it isn't the Lord's Supper you are eating, [21]but your own. For I am told that everyone hastily gobbles all the food he can without waiting to share with the others, so that one doesn't get enough and goes hungry while another has too much to drink and gets drunk. [22]What? Is this really true? Can't you do your eating and drinking at home, to avoid disgracing the church and shaming those who are poor and can bring no food? What am I supposed to say about these things? Do you want me to praise you? Well, I certainly do not! [23]For this is what the Lord himself has said about his Table, and I have passed it on to you before: That on the night when Judas betrayed him, the Lord Jesus took bread, [24]and when he had given thanks to God for it, he broke it and gave it to his disciples and said, "Take this and eat it. This is my body, which

is given for you. Do this to remember me." [25]In the same way, he took the cup of wine after supper, saying, "This cup is the new agreement between God and you that has been established and set in motion by my blood. Do this in remembrance of me whenever you drink it." [26]For every time you eat this bread and drink this cup you are re-telling the message of the Lord's death, that he has died for you. Do this until he comes again. [27]So if anyone eats this bread and drinks from this cup of the Lord in an unworthy manner, he is guilty of sin against the body and the blood of the Lord. [28]That is why a man should examine himself carefully before eating the bread and drinking from the cup. [29]For if he eats the bread and drinks from the cup unworthily, not thinking about the body of Christ and what it means, he is eating and drinking God's judgment upon himself; for he is trifling with the death of Christ. [30]That is why many of you are weak and sick, and some have even died. [31]But if you carefully examine yourselves before eating you will not need to be judged and punished. [32]Yet, when we are judged and punished by the Lord, it is so that we will not be condemned with the rest of the world. [33]So, dear brothers, when you gather for the Lord's Supper—the communion service—wait for each other; [34]if anyone is really hungry he should eat at home so that he won't bring punishment upon himself when you meet together. I'll talk to you about the other matters after I arrive.

LO-RUHAMAH Hosea's daughter, Hos 1: 6–8.

LOST SHEEP Parable of, Mt 18:12, 13; Lk 15:3–7.

LOST, THE See *Wicked, Punishment of.*

LOT The son of Haran. Accompanies Terah from Ur of the Chaldeans to Haran, Gen 11:31. Migrates with Abraham to the land of Canaan, Gen 12:4. Accompanies Abraham to Egypt; returns with him to Bethel, Gen 12:10; 13:1–4. Wealthy with sheep, cattle and servants; separates from Abraham, and settles near Sodom, Gen 13: 5–14. Taken captive by Ched-or-laomer; rescues by Abraham, Gen 14:1–16. Providentially saved from destruction in Sodom, Gen 19; Lk 17:28, 29. Righteous, 2 Pet 2:7, 8. Disobediently protests against going to the mountains, and chooses Zoar, Gen 19: 17–22. His wife disobediently longs after Sodom, and becomes a pillar of salt, Gen 19:26; Lk 17:32. Commits incest with his daughters, Gen 19:30–38. Descendants of, see *Ammonites; Moabites.*

LOTS, LOTTERY Prov 18:18. The scapegoat chosen by, Lev 16:8–10.

The land of Canaan divided among the tribes by, Num 26:55, 56; Josh 15; 18:10; 19:51; 21; 1 Chron 6: 61, 64, 65. Saul chosen king by, 1 Sam 10:20, 21. Priests and Levites designated by, for Temple service, 1 Chron 24:5–31; Neh 10:34; Lk 1:8, 9. Used after the captivity, Neh 11:1. An apostle chosen by, Acts 1:26. Jonathan's guilt ascertained by, 1 Sam 14: 41, 42,

Used to fix the time for the execution of condemned persons, Esther 3:7; 9:24, 25. The garments of Jesus divided by, Ps 22:18; Mt 27:35; Mk 15:24; Jn 19:23, 24.

LOTS, FEAST OF See *Purim.*

LOVE OF CHILDREN FOR PARENTS. See *Children.*

OF GOD. See *God, Love of.*

OF MAN FOR GOD. Ex 20:6. But I lavish my love upon thousands of those who love me and obey my commandments. Deut 5:9, 10; Neh 1:5.

Deut 6:5. You must love him with *all* your heart, soul, and might.

Deut 7:9. Understand, therefore, that the Lord your God is the faithful God who for a thousand generations keeps his promises and constantly loves those who love him and who obey his commands.

Deut 10:12, 13. What does the Lord your God require of you except to listen carefully to all he says to you, and to obey for your own good the commandments I am giving you today, and to love him, and to worship him with all your hearts and souls?

Deut 11:1. You must love the Lord your God and obey every one of his commands.

Deut 13:3. For the Lord is testing you to find out whether or not you really love him with all your heart and soul.

Deut 30:6. He will cleanse your hearts and the hearts of your children and of your children's children so that you will love the Lord your God with all your hearts and souls, and Israel shall come alive again! *vs.* 16, 20.

Josh 22:5. Love the Lord and follow his plan for your lives. Cling to him and serve him enthusiastically. Deut 11:1, 13, 22.

Josh 23:11. So be very careful to keep on loving him.

Ps 18:1. Lord, how I love you! For you have done such tremendous things for me.

Ps 31:23. Oh, love the Lord, all of you who are his people.

Ps 37:4. Be delighted with the Lord. Then he will give you all your heart's desires.

Ps 45:10, 11. I advise you, O daughter, not to fret about your parents in your homeland far away. Your royal husband delights in your beauty. Reverence him, for he is your lord. See Song of Solomon.

Ps 63:5. At last I shall be fully satisfied; I will praise you with great joy. [6]I lie awake at night thinking of you.

Ps 69:35. For God will save Jerusalem; he rebuilds the cities of Judah. His people shall live in them and not be dispossessed. [36]Their children shall inherit the land; all who love his name shall live there safely.

Ps 73:25. Whom have I in heaven but you? And I desire no one on earth as much as you! [26]My health fails; my spirits droop, yet God remains! He is the strength of my heart; he is mine forever!

Ps 91:14. For the Lord says, "Because he loves me, I will rescue him; I will make him great because he trusts in my name."

Ps 116:1. I love the Lord because he hears my prayers and answers them.

Ps 145:20. He protects all those who love him, but destroys the wicked.

Prov 8:17. I love all who love me. Those who search for me shall surely find me.

Isa 56:6. As for the Gentiles, the outsiders who join the people of the Lord and serve him and love his name, and are his servants and don't desecrate the Sabbath, and have accepted his covenant and promises, [7]I will bring them also to my holy mountain of Jerusalem, and make them full of joy within my House of Prayer. I will accept their sacrifices and offerings.

Jer 2:2. Go and shout this in Jerusalem's streets: The Lord says, I remember how eager you were to please me as a young bride long ago and how you loved me and followed me even through the barren deserts. [3]In those days Israel was a holy people, the first of my children.

Mk 12:29. Jesus replied, "The one that says, 'Hear, O Israel! The Lord our God is the one and only God. [30]And you must love him with all your heart and soul and mind and strength.'" [32]The teacher of religion replied, "Sir, you have spoken a true word in saying that there is only one God and no other. [33]And I know it is far more important to love him with all my heart and understanding and strength, and to love others as myself, than to offer all kinds of sacrifices on the altar of the Temple." Mt 22:37.

Lk 11:42. For though you are careful to tithe even the smallest part of your income, you completely forget about justice and the love of God. You should tithe, yes, but you should not leave these other things undone.

Jn 5:42. For as I know so well, you don't have God's love within you.

Rom 5:5. Then, when that happens, we are able to hold our heads high no matter what happens and know that all is well, for we know how dearly God loves us, and we feel this warm love everywhere within us because God has given us the Holy Spirit to fill our hearts with his love.

Rom 8:28. And we know that all that happens to us is working for our good if we love God and are fitting into his plans.

1 Cor 8:3. But the person who truly loves God is the one who is open to God's knowledge.

Phil 1:9. My prayer for you is that you will overflow more and more with love for others, and at the same time keep on growing in spiritual knowledge and insight.

2 Thess 3:5. May the Lord bring you into an ever deeper understanding of the love of God and of the patience that comes from Christ.

1 Jn 2:5. But those who do what Christ tells them to will learn to love God more and more. That is the way to know whether or not you are a Christian. [15]Stop loving this evil world and all that it offers you, for when you love these things you show that you do not really love God.

1 Jn 3:17. But if someone who is supposed to be a Christian has money enough to live well, and sees a brother in need, and won't help him—how can God's love be within *him?* [18]Little children, let us stop just *saying* we love people; let us *really* love them, and *show it* by our *actions.*

1 Jn 4:12. For though we have never yet seen God, when we love each other God lives in us and his love within us grows ever stronger. [16]We know how much God loves us because we have felt his love and because we believe him when he tells us that he loves us dearly. God is love, and anyone who lives in love is living with God and God is living in him. [17]And as we live with Christ, our love grows more perfect and complete; so we will not be ashamed and embarrassed at the day of judgment, but can face him with confidence and joy, because he loves us and we love him too. [18]We need have no fear of someone who loves us perfectly; his perfect love for us eliminates all dread of what he might do to us. If we are afraid, it is for fear of what he might do to us, and shows that we are not fully convinced that he really loves us. [19]So you see, our love for him comes as a result of his loving us first. [20]If anyone says "I love God," but keeps on hating his brother, he is a liar; for if he doesn't love his brother who is right there in front of him, how can he love God whom he has never seen? [21]And God himself has said that one must love not only God, but his brother too.

1 Jn 5:1. If you believe that Jesus is the Christ—that he is God's Son and your Savior—then you are a child of God. And all who love the Father love his children too. [2]So you can find out how much you love God's children—your brothers and sisters in the Lord—by how much you love and obey God. [3]Loving God means doing what he tells us to do, and really, that isn't hard at all.

2 Jn 1:6. If we love God, we will do whatever he tells us to. And he has told us from the very first to love each other.

OF MAN FOR JESUS. Mt 10:37. If you love your father and mother more than you love me, you are not worthy of being mine; or if you love your son or daughter more than me, you are not worthy of being mine. *v.* 38.

Mt 25:34. Then I, the King, shall say to those at my right, "Come, blessed of my Father, into the Kingdom prepared for you from the founding of the world. [35]For I was hungry and you fed me; I was thirsty and you gave me water; I was a stranger and you invited me into your homes; [36]naked and you clothed me; sick and in prison, and you visited me." [37]Then these righteous ones will reply, "Sir, when did we ever see you hungry and feed you? Or thirsty and give you anything to drink? [38]Or a stranger, and help you? Or naked, and clothe you? [39]When did we ever see you sick or in prison, and visit you?" [40]And I, the King, will tell them, "When you did it to these my brothers you were doing it to me!"

Mt 27:55. And many women who had come down from Galilee with Jesus to care for him were watching from a distance. [56]Among them were

Mary Magdalene and Mary the mother of James and Joseph, and the mother of James and John (the sons of Zebedee). [57]When evening came, a rich man from Arimathea named Joseph, one of Jesus' followers, [58]went to Pilate and asked for Jesus' body. And Pilate issued an order to release it to him. [59]Joseph took the body and wrapped it in a clean linen cloth, [60]and placed it in his own new rock-hewn tomb, and rolled a great stone across the entrance as he left. [61]Both Mary Magdalene and the other Mary were sitting nearby watching.

Mk 9:41. If anyone so much as gives you a cup of water because you are Christ's—I say this solemnly—he won't lose his reward.

Lk 2:29, 30. "Lord," he said, "now I can die content! For I have seen him as you promised me I would."

Lk 7:47. Therefore her sins—and they are many —are forgiven, for she loved me much; but one who is forgiven little, shows little love.

Jn 8:42. Jesus told them, "If that were so, then you would love me, for I have come to you from God. I am not here on my own, but he sent me."

Jn 14:15. "If you love me, obey me. [21]The one who obeys me is the one who loves me; and because he loves me, my Father will love him; and I will too, and I will reveal myself to him." [23]Jesus replied, "Because I will only reveal myself to those who love me and obey me. The Father will love them too, and we will come to them and live with them. [28]If you really love me, you will be very happy for me, for now I can go to the Father, who is greater than I am."

Jn 15:9. I have loved you even as the Father has loved me. Live within my love.

Jn 16:27. For the Father himself loves you dearly because you love me and believe that I came from the Father.

Jn 17:26. And I have revealed you to them, and will keep on revealing you so that the mighty love you have for me may be in them, and I in them.

Jn 21:17. "Lord, you know my heart; you know I am [your friend]," he said.

Acts 21:13. For I am ready not only to be jailed at Jerusalem, but also to die for the sake of the Lord Jesus.

1 Cor 16:22. If anyone does not love the Lord, that person is cursed.

2 Cor 5:8. And we are not afraid, but are quite content to die, for then we will be at home with the Lord. [*v.* 6.] [14]Christ's love controls us now. Since we believe that Christ died for all of us, we should also believe that we have died to the old life we used to live. [15]He died for all so that all who live —having received eternal life from him—might live no longer for themselves, to please themselves, but to spend their lives pleasing Christ who died and rose again for them.

Gal 5:6. And we to whom Christ has given eternal life don't need to worry about whether we have been circumcised or not, or whether we are obeying the Jewish ceremonies or not; for all we need is faith working through love. [22]But when the Holy Spirit controls our lives he will produce this kind of fruit in us: love.

Gal 6:14. As for me, God forbid that I should boast about anything except the cross of our Lord Jesus Christ. Because of that cross my interest in all the attractive things of the world was killed long ago, and the world's interest in me is also long dead.

Eph 3:17. And I pray that Christ will be more and more at home in your hearts, living within you as you trust in him. May your roots go down deep into the soil of God's marvelous love; [18, 19]and may you be able to feel and understand, as all God's children should, how long, how wide, how deep, and how high his love really is, and to experience this love for yourselves, though it is so great that you will never see the end of it or fully know or understand it. And so at last you will be filled up with God himself.

Eph 4:15. Instead, we will lovingly follow the truth at all times—speaking truly, dealing truly, living truly—and so become more and more in every way like Christ who is the Head of his body, the church.

Eph 6:24. May God's grace and blessing be upon all who sincerely love our Lord Jesus Christ.

Phil 1:9. My prayer for you is that you will overflow more and more with love for others, and at the same time keep on growing in spiritual knowledge and insight.

Phil 1:23. Sometimes I want to live and at other times I don't, for I long to go and be with Christ. How much happier for *me* than being here! *vs.* 20, 21.

Phil 3:7. But all these things that I once thought very worthwhile—now I've thrown them all away so that I can put my trust and hope in Christ alone. [8]Yes, everything else is worthless when compared with the priceless gain of knowing Christ Jesus my Lord. I have put aside all else, counting it worth less than nothing, in order that I can have Christ.

Col 1:8. And he is the one who has told us about the great love for others which the Holy Spirit has given you.

2 Thess 3:5. May the Lord bring you into an ever deeper understanding of the love of God and of the patience that comes from Christ.

2 Tim 1:13. Hold tightly to the pattern of truth I taught you, especially concerning the faith and love Christ Jesus offers you.

2 Tim 4:8. In heaven a crown is waiting for me which the Lord, the righteous Judge, will give me on that great day of his return. And not just to me, but to all those whose lives show that they are eagerly looking forward to his coming back again.

Philemon 1:5. Because I keep hearing of your love and trust in the Lord Jesus and in his people.

Heb 6:10. For God is not unfair. How can he forget your hard work for him, or forget the way you used to show your love for him—and still do —by helping his children?

Jas 1:12. Happy is the man who doesn't give in and do wrong when he is tempted, for afterwards he will get as his reward the crown of life that God has promised those who love him.

Jas 2:5. Listen to me, dear brothers: God has chosen poor people to be rich in faith, and the Kingdom of Heaven is theirs, for that is the gift God has promised to all those who love him.

1 Pet 1:8. You love him even though you have never seen him; though not seeing him, you trust him; and even now you are happy with the inexpressible joy that comes from heaven itself.

1 Pet 2:7. Yes, he is very precious to you who believe.

Rev 2:4. Yet there is one thing wrong; you don't love me as at first!

Instances of Love for Jesus. Mary, Mt 26:6–13; Jn 12:3–8; Lk 10:39. Peter, Mt 17:4; Jn 13:37; 18:10; 20: 3–6; 21:7. Thomas, Jn 11:16. The disciples, Mk 16:10, 11; Lk 24:17–41; Jn 20:20. Mary Magdalene and other disciples, Mt 27:55, 56, 61; 28:1–9; Lk 8:2, 3; 23:27, 55, 56; 24:1–10; Jn 20:1, 2, 11–18. A man of Gadara out of whom Jesus cast a demon, Mk 5:18. Joseph of Aramathea, Mt 27:57–60. Nicodemus, Jn 19:39, 40. Women of Jerusalem, Lk 23:27.

OF MAN FOR MAN. Lev 19:18. But love your neighbor as yourself, for I am Jehovah. [34]They must be treated like any other citizen; love them as yourself, for remember that you too were foreigners in the land of Egypt.

Deut 10:19. You too must love foreigners, for you yourselves were foreigners in the land of Egypt.

Ps 133:1. How wonderful it is, how pleasant, when brothers live in harmony! [2]For harmony is as precious as the fragrant anointing oil that was poured over Aaron's head, and ran down onto his beard, and onto the border of his robe. [3]Harmony is as refreshing as the dew on Mount Hermon, on the mountains of Israel. And God has pronounced this eternal blessing on Jerusalem, even life forevermore.

Prov 10:12. Hatred stirs old quarrels, but love overlooks insults.

Prov 15:17. It is better to eat soup with someone you love than steak with someone you hate.

Prov 17:9. Love forgets mistakes; nagging about them parts the best of friends. [17]A true friend is always loyal, and a brother is born to help in time of need.

Song 8:6. For love is strong as death and jealousy is as cruel as Sheol. It flashes fire, the very flame of Jehovah. [7]Many waters cannot quench the flame of love, neither can the floods drown it. If a man tried to buy it with everything he owned, he couldn't do it.

Mt 5:41. If the military demand that you carry their gear for a mile, carry it two. [42]Give to those who ask and don't turn away from those who want to borrow. *vs.* 41–47.

Mt 10:41. If you welcome a prophet because he is a man of God, you will be given the same reward a prophet gets. And if you welcome good and godly men because of their godliness, you will be given a reward like theirs. [42]And if, as my representatives, you give even a cup of cold water to a little child, you will surely be rewarded.

Mt 19:19. And love your neighbor as yourself! Gal 5:14.

Mt 25:34. Then I, the King, shall say to those at my right, "Come, blessed of my Father into the Kingdom prepared for you from the founding of the world. [35]For I was hungry and you fed me; I was thirsty and you gave me water; I was a stranger and you invited me into your homes; [36]naked and you clothed me; sick and in prison, and you visited me." [37]Then these righteous ones will reply, "Sir, when did we ever see you hungry and feed you? Or thirsty and give you anything to drink? [38]Or a stranger, and help you? Or naked, and clothe you? [39]When did we ever see you sick or in prison, and visit you?" [40]And I, the King, will tell them, "When you did it to these my brothers you were doing it to me!"

Mk 9:41. If anyone so much as gives you a cup of water because you are Christ's—I say this solemnly—he won't lose his reward.

Mk 12:30. " 'And you must love him with all your heart and soul and mind and strength.' [31]The second is: 'You must love others as much as yourself.' No other commandments are greater than these." [32]The teacher of religion replied, "Sir, you have spoken a true word in saying that there is only one God and no other. [33]And I know it is far more important to love him with all my heart and understanding and strength, and to love others as myself, than to offer all kinds of sacrifices on the altar of the Temple."

Lk 6:31. Treat others as you want them to treat you. [32]Do you think you deserve credit for merely loving those who love you? Even the godless do that! [33]And if you do good only to those who do you good—is that so wonderful? Even sinners do that much! [34]And if you lend money only to those who can repay you, what good is that? Even the most wicked will lend to their own kind for full return! [35]Love your *enemies!* Do good to *them!* Lend to *them!* And don't be concerned about the fact that they won't repay. Then your reward from heaven will be very great, and you will truly be acting as sons of God: for he is kind to the *unthankful* and to those who are *very wicked.* Mt 7:12.

Lk 10:36. "Now which of these three would you say was a neighbor to the bandits' victim?" [37]The man replied, "The one who showed him some pity." Then Jesus said, "Yes, now go and do the same." *vs.* 30–37.

Jn 13:14. And since I, the Lord and Teacher, have washed your feet, you ought to wash each other's feet. [15]I have given you an example to follow: do as I have done to you. [34]And so I am giving a new commandment to you now—love each other just as much as I love you. [35]Your strong love for each other will prove to the world that you are my disciples.

Jn 15:12. I demand that you love each other as much as I love you. [13]And here is how to measure it—the greatest love is shown when a person lays down his life for his friends. *v.* 17.

Rom 12:9. Don't just pretend that you love others: really love them. Hate what is wrong. Stand on the side of the good. [10]Love each other with brotherly affection and take delight in honoring each other.

Rom 13:8. Pay all your debts except the debt of love for others—never finish paying that! For if you love them, you will be obeying all of God's laws, fulfilling all his requirements. [9]If you love your neighbor as much as you love yourself you will not want to harm or cheat him, or kill him or steal from him. And you won't sin with his wife or want what is his, or do anything else the Ten Commandments say is wrong. All ten are wrapped up in this one, to love your neighbor as you love yourself. [10]Love does no wrong to anyone. That's why it fully satisfies all of God's requirements. It is the only law you need.

1 Cor 8:1. But although being a "know-it-all" makes us feel important, what is really needed to build the church is love.

1 Cor 13:1. If I had the gift of being able to speak in other languages without learning them, and could speak in every language there is in all of heaven and earth, but didn't love others, I would only be making noise. [2]If I had the gift of prophecy and knew all about what is going to happen in the future, knew everything about *everything,* but didn't love others, what good would it do? Even if I had the gift of faith so that I could speak to a mountain and make it move, I would still be worth nothing at all without love. [3]If I gave everything I have to poor people, and if I were burned alive for preaching the Gospel but didn't love others, it would be of no value whatever. [4]Love is very patient and kind, never jealous or envious, never boastful or proud, [5]never haughty or selfish or rude. Love does not demand its own way. It is not irritable or touchy. It does not hold grudges and will hardly even notice when others do it wrong. [6]It is never glad about injustice, but rejoices whenever truth wins out. [7]If you love someone you will be loyal to him no matter what the cost. You will always believe in him, always expect the best of him, and always stand your ground in defending him. [8]All the special gifts and powers from God will someday come to an end, but love goes on forever. Someday prophecy, and speaking in unknown languages, and special knowledge—these gifts will disappear. [9]Now we know so little, even with our special gifts, and the preaching of these most gifted is still so poor. [10]But when we have been made perfect and complete, then the need for these inadequate special gifts will come to an end, and they will disappear. [11]It's like this: when I was a child I spoke and thought and reasoned as a child does. But when I became a man my thoughts grew far beyond those of my childhood, and now I have put away the childish things. [12]In the same way, we can see and understand only a little about God now, as if we were peering at his reflection in a poor mirror; but someday we are going to see him in his completeness, face to face. Now all that I know is hazy and blurred, but then I will see everything clearly, just as clearly as God sees into my heart right now. [13]There are three things that remain—faith, hope, and love—and the greatest of these is love.

1 Cor 14:1. Let love be your greatest aim.

1 Cor 16:14. And whatever you do, do it with kindness and love.

2 Cor 8:7. You people there are leaders in so many ways—you have so much faith, so many good preachers, so much learning, so much enthusiasm, so much love for us. Now I want you to be leaders also in the spirit of cheerful giving. [8]I am not giving you an order; I am not saying you must do it, but others are eager for it. This is one way to prove that your love is real, that it goes beyond mere words.

Gal 5:13. For, dear brothers, you have been given freedom: not freedom to do wrong, but freedom to love and serve each other. [22]But when the Holy Spirit controls our lives he will produce this kind of fruit in us: love, joy, peace, patience, kindness, goodness, faithfulness. [26]Then we won't need to look for honors and popularity, which lead to jealousy and hard feelings.

Eph 5:2. Be full of love for others, following the example of Christ who loved you and gave himself to God as a sacrifice to take away your sins. And God was pleased, for Christ's love for you was like sweet perfume to him.

Phil 1:9. My prayer for you is that you will overflow more and more with love for others, and at the same time keep on growing in spiritual knowledge and insight.

Phil 2:2. Then make me truly happy by loving each other and agreeing wholeheartedly with each other, working together with one heart and mind and purpose.

Col 2:2. This is what I have asked of God for you: that you will be encouraged and knit together by strong ties of love.

Col 3:12. Since you have been chosen by God who has given you this new kind of life, and because of his deep love and concern for you, you should practice tenderhearted mercy and kindness to others. Don't worry about making a good impression on them but be ready to suffer quietly and patiently. [13]Be gentle and ready to forgive; never hold grudges. Remember, the Lord forgave you, so you must forgive others. [14]Most of all, let love guide your life, for then the whole church will stay together in perfect harmony.

1 Thess 1:3. We never forget your loving deeds as we talk to our God and Father about you.

1 Thess 3:12. And may the Lord make your love to grow and overflow to each other and to everyone else, just as our love does toward you.

1 Thess 4:9. But concerning the pure brotherly love that there should be among God's people, I don't need to say very much, I'm sure! For God himself is teaching you to love one another.

1 Tim 1:5. What I am eager for is that all the Christians there will be filled with love that comes

from pure hearts, and that their minds will be clean and their faith strong. [14]Oh, how kind our Lord was, for he showed me how to trust him and become full of the love of Christ Jesus.

1 Tim 2:15. But he will save their souls if they trust in him, living quiet, good, and loving lives.

1 Tim 4:12. Don't let anyone think little of you because you are young. Be their ideal; let them follow the way you teach and live; be a pattern for them in your love, your faith, and your clean thoughts.

1 Tim 6:2. If their owner is a Christian, that is no excuse for slowing down; rather they should work all the harder because a brother in the faith is being helped by their efforts. [11]Work instead at what is right and good, learning to trust him and love others, and to be patient and gentle.

2 Tim 2:22. Run from anything that gives you the evil thoughts that young men often have, but stay close to anything that makes you want to do right. Have faith and love.

Tit 3:15. Please say "hello" to all of the Christian friends there.

Philemon 1:12. I am sending him back to you, and with him comes my own heart. [16]No longer only a slave, but something much better—a beloved brother, especially to me. Now he will mean much more to you too, because he is not only a servant but also your brother in Christ.

Heb 10:24. Let us outdo each other in being helpful and kind to each other and in doing good.

Jas 2:8. Yes indeed, it is good when you truly obey our Lord's command, "You must love and help your neighbors just as much as you love and take care of yourself."

1 Pet 1:22. Now you can have real love for everyone because your souls have been cleansed from selfishness and hatred when you trusted Christ to save you; so see to it that you really do love each other warmly, with all your hearts.

1 Pet 2:17. Show respect for everyone. Love Christians everywhere.

1 Pet 3:8. And now this word to all of you: You should be like one big happy family, full of sympathy toward each other, loving one another with tender hearts and humble minds. *v.* 9.

1 Pet 4:8. Most important of all, continue to show deep love for each other, for love makes up for many of your faults.

2 Pet 1:7. This will make possible the next step, which is for you to enjoy other people and to like them, and finally you will grow to love them deeply.

1 Jn 2:10. But whoever loves his fellow man is "walking in the light" and can see his way without stumbling around in darkness and sin. *vs.* 9, 11.

1 Jn 3:11. For the message to us from the beginning has been that we should love one another. [14]If we love other Christians it proves that we have been delivered from hell and given eternal life. But a person who doesn't have love for others is headed for eternal death. [16]We know what real love is from Christ's example in dying for us. And so we also ought to lay down our lives for our Christian brothers. [17]But if someone who is supposed to be a Christian has money enough to live well, and sees a brother in need, and won't help him—how can God's love be within *him?* [18]Little children, let us stop just *saying* we love people; let us *really* love them, and *show it* by our *actions.* [23]And this is what God says we must do . . . love one another. *v.* 19.

1 Jn 4:7. Dear friends, let us practice loving each other, for love comes from God and those who are loving and kind show that they are the children of God, and that they are getting to know him better. [11]Dear friends, since God loved us as much as that, we surely ought to love each other too. [12]For though we have never yet seen God, when we love each other God lives in us and his love within us grows ever stronger. [20]If anyone says "I love God," but keeps on hating his brother who is right in front of him, how can he love God whom he has never seen? [21]And God himself has said that one must love not only God, but his brother too.

1 Jn 5:1. If you believe that Jesus is the Christ—that he is God's Son and your Savior—then you are a child of God. And all who love the Father love his children too. [2]So you can find out how much you love God's children—your brothers and sisters in the Lord—by how much you love and obey God.

2 Jn 1:5. And now I want to urgently remind you, dear friends, of the old rule God gave us right from the beginning, that Christians should love one another.

Exemplification of the Love of Man for Man. Ex 32:31. So Moses returned to the Lord and said, "Oh, these people have sinned a great sin, and have made themselves gods of gold. [32]Yet now if you will only forgive their sin—and if not, then blot *me* out of the book you have written."

Ps 133:1. How wonderful it is, how pleasant, when brothers live in harmony! *vs.* 2, 3.

Prov 24:17. Do not rejoice when your enemy meets trouble. Let there be no gladness when he falls—[18]for the Lord may be displeased with you and stop punishing him!

Mt 5:41. If the military demand that you carry their gear for a mile, carry it two. [42]Give to those who ask and don't turn away from those who want to borrow.

Mt 10:41. If you welcome a prophet because he is a man of God, you will be given the same reward a prophet gets. And if you welcome good and godly men because of their godliness, you will be given a reward like theirs. [42]And if, as my representatives, you give even a cup of cold water to a little child, you will surely be rewarded.

Mt 25:34. Then I, the King, shall say to those at my right, "Come, blessed of my Father, into the Kingdom prepared for you from the founding of the world. [35]For I was hungry and you fed me; I was thirsty and you gave me water; I was a stranger and you invited me into your homes; [36]naked and you clothed me; sick and in prison, and you visited me." [37]Then these righteous ones will reply, "Sir, when did we ever see you hungry and feed you? Or thirsty and give you anything to drink? [38]Or a stranger, and help you? Or naked, and clothe you? [39]When did we ever see you sick or in prison, and visit you?" [40]And I, the King, will tell them, "When you did it to these my brothers you were doing it to me!"

Mk 9:41. If anyone so much as gives you a cup of water because you are Christ's—I say this solemnly—he won't lose his reward.

Lk 10:25. One day an expert on Moses' laws came to test Jesus' orthodoxy by asking him this question: "Teacher, what does a man need to do to live forever in heaven?" [26]Jesus replied, "What does Moses' law say about it?" [27]"It says," he replied, "that you must love the Lord your God with all your heart, and with all your soul, and with all your strength, and with all your mind. And you must love your neighbor just as much as you love yourself." [28]"Right!" Jesus told him. "*Do* this and *you* shall live!" [29]The man wanted to justify (his lack of love for some kinds of people), so he asked, "Which neighbors?" [30]Jesus replied with an illustration: "A Jew going on a trip from Jerusalem to Jericho was attacked by bandits. They stripped him of his clothes and money and beat him up and left him lying half dead beside the road. [31]By chance a Jewish priest came along; and when he saw the man lying there, he crossed to the other side of the road and passed him by. [32]A Jewish Temple-assistant walked over and looked at him lying there, but then went on. [33]But a despised Samaritan came along, and when he saw him, he felt deep pity. [34]Kneeling beside him the Samaritan soothed his wounds with medicine and bandaged them. Then he put the man on his donkey and walked along beside him till they came to an inn, where he nursed him through the night. [35]The next day he handed the innkeeper two twenty-dollar bills and told him to take care of the man. 'If his bill runs higher than that,' he said, 'I'll pay the difference the next time I am here.' [36]Now which of these three would you say was a neighbor to the bandits' victim?" [37]The man replied, "The one who showed him some pity." Then Jesus said, "Yes, now go and do the same."

Acts 20:26. Let me say plainly that no man's blood can be laid at my door, [27]for I didn't shrink from declaring all God's message to you. [31]Watch out! Remember the three years I was with you—my constant watchcare over you night and day and my many tears for you.

Acts 26:29. And Paul replied, "Would to God that whether my arguments are trivial or strong, both you and everyone here in this audience might become the same as I am, except for these chains."

Rom 1:12. For I want not only to share my faith with you but to be encouraged by yours: Each of us will be a blessing to the other.

Rom 5:7. Even if we were good, we really wouldn't expect anyone to die for us, though, of course, that might be barely possible.

Rom 9:3. Christ knows and the Holy Spirit knows that it is no mere pretense when I say that I would be willing to be forever damned if that would save you. *vs.* 1, 2.

Rom 12:15. When others are happy, be happy with them. If they are sad, share their sorrow. [16]Work happily together. Don't try to act big. Don't try to get into the good graces of important people, but enjoy the company of ordinary folks. And don't think you know it all!

Rom 14:19. In this way aim for harmony in the church and try to build each other up. [21]The right thing to do is to quit eating meat or drinking wine or doing anything else that offends your brother or makes him sin.

Rom 15:1, 2. Even if we believe that it makes no difference to the Lord whether we do these things, still we cannot just go ahead and do them to please ourselves; for we must bear the "burden" of being considerate of the doubts and fears of others—of those who feel these things are wrong. Let's please the other fellow, not ourselves, and do what is for his good and thus build him up in the Lord. [5]May God who gives patience, steadiness, and encouragement help you to live in complete harmony with each other—each with the attitude of Christ toward the other. [7]So, warmly welcome each other into the church, just as Christ has warmly welcomed you; then God will be glorified. [14]I know that you are wise and good, my brothers, and that you know these things so well that you are able to teach others all about them. [15]But even so I have been bold enough to emphasize some of these points, knowing that all you need is this reminder from me; for I am, by God's grace, a special messenger from Jesus Christ to you Gentiles. [24]For I am planning to take a trip to Spain, and when I do, I will stop off there in Rome, and after we have had a good time together for a little while, you can send me on my way again. [32]Then I will be able to come to you with a happy heart by the will of God, and we can refresh each other.

Rom 16:1, 2. Phoebe, a dear Christian woman from the town of Cenchreae, will be coming to see you soon. She has worked hard in the church there. Receive her as your sister in the Lord, giving her a warm Christian welcome. Help her in every way you can, for she has helped many in their needs, including me. [8]Say "hello" to Ampliatus, whom I love as one of God's own children. [19]But everyone knows that you stand loyal and true. This makes me very happy. I want you always to remain very clear about what is right, and to stay innocent of any wrong. *vs.* 1–16; Col 4:7.

1 Cor 1:4. I can never stop thanking God for all the wonderful gifts he has given you, now that you are Christ's.

1 Cor 4:14. I am not writing about these things to make you ashamed, but to warn and counsel you as beloved children. [15]For although you may have ten thousand others to teach you about Christ, remember that you have only me as your father. For I was the one who brought you to Christ when

I preached the Gospel to you. [16]So I beg you to follow my example, and do as I do.

1 Cor 8:13. So if eating meat offered to idols is going to make my brother sin, I'll not eat any of it as long as I live, because I don't want to do this to him.

1 Cor 10:24. Don't think only of yourself. Try to think of the other fellow, too, and what is best for him.

2 Cor 1:3, 4. What a wonderful God we have . . . who so wonderfully comforts and strengthens us in our hardships and trials. And why does he do this? So that when others are troubled, needing our sympathy and encouragement, we can pass on to them this same help and comfort God has given us. [5]You can be sure that the more we undergo sufferings for Christ, the more he will shower us with his comfort and encouragement. [6]We are in deep trouble for bringing you God's comfort and salvation. But in our trouble God has comforted us—and this, too, to help you; to show you from our personal experience how God will tenderly comfort you. [14]And even though you don't know me very well (I hope someday you will), I want you to try to accept me and be proud of me, as you already are to some extent; just as I shall be of you on that day when our Lord Jesus comes back again. *vs.* 23, 24.

2 Cor 2:4. Oh, how I hated to write that letter! It almost broke my heart and I tell you honestly that I cried over it. I didn't want to hurt you, but I had to show you how very much I loved you and cared about what was happening to you. *vs.* 1–17.

2 Cor 3:2. The only letter I need is you yourselves! By looking at the good change in your hearts, everyone can see that we have done a good work among you.

2 Cor 4:5. We don't go around preaching about ourselves, but about Christ Jesus as Lord. All we say of ourselves is that we are your slaves because of what Jesus has done for us.

2 Cor 6:4. In fact, in everything we do we try to show that we are true ministers of God. We patiently endure suffering and hardship and trouble of every kind. [5]We have been beaten, put in jail, faced angry mobs, worked to exhaustion, stayed awake through sleepless nights of watching, and gone without food. [6]We have proved ourselves to be what we claim by our wholesome lives and by our understanding of the Gospel and by our patience. We have been kind and truly loving and filled with the Holy Spirit. [11]Oh, my dear Corinthian friends! I have told you all my feelings; I love you with all my heart. [12]Any coldness still between us is not because of any lack of love on my part, but because your love is too small and does not reach out to me and draw me in. [13]I am talking to you now as if you truly were my very own children. Open your hearts to us! Return our love!

2 Cor 7:1. Having such great promises as these, dear friends, let us turn away from everything wrong, whether of body or spirit, and purify ourselves, living in the wholesome fear of God, giving ourselves to him alone. [2]Please open your hearts to us again, for not one of you has suffered any wrong from us. Not one of you was led astray. We have cheated no one nor taken advantage of anyone. [3]I'm not saying this to scold or blame you, for, as I have said before, you are in my heart forever and I live and die with you. [4]I have the highest confidence in you, and my pride in you is great. You have greatly encouraged me; you have made me so happy in spite of all my suffering. [7]Not only was his presence a joy, but also the news that he brought of the wonderful time he had with you. When he told me how much you were looking forward to my visit, and how sorry you were about what had happened, and about your loyalty and warm love for me, well, I overflowed with joy! [12]I wrote as I did so the Lord could show how much you really do care for us. That was my purpose even more than to help the man who sinned, or his father to whom he did the wrong.

2 Cor 11:2. I am anxious for you with the deep concern of God himself—anxious that your love should be for Christ alone, just as a pure maiden saves her love for one man only, for the one who will be her husband.

2 Cor 12:14. Now I am coming to you again, the third time; and it is still not going to cost you anything, for I don't want your money, I want *you!* And anyway, you are my children, and little children don't pay for their father's and mother's food—it's the other way around; parents supply food for their children. [15]I am glad to give you myself and all I have for your spiritual good, even though it seems that the more I love you, the less you love me. [16]Some of you are saying, "It's true that his visits didn't seem to cost us anything, but he is a sneaky fellow, that Paul, and he fooled us. As sure as anything he must have made money from us some way." [19]I suppose you think I am saying all this to get back into your good graces. That isn't it at all. I tell you, with God listening as I say it, that I have said this to help *you,* dear friends—to build you up spiritually and not to help myself. [20]For I am afraid that when I come to visit you I won't like what I find, and then you won't like the way I will have to act. I am afraid that I will find you quarreling, and envying each other, and being angry with each other, and acting big, and saying wicked things about each other and whispering behind each other's backs, filled with conceit and disunity. [21]Yes, I am afraid that when I come God will humble me before you and I will be sad and mourn because many of you who have sinned became sinners and don't even care about the wicked, impure things you have done: your lust and immorality, and the taking of other men's wives.

2 Cor 13:9. We are glad to be weak and despised if you are really strong. Our greatest wish and prayer is that you will become mature Christians.

Gal 4:11. I fear for you. I am afraid that all my hard work for you was worth nothing. [12]Dear brothers, please feel as I do about these things, for I am as free from these chains as you used to be.

You did not despise me then when I first preached to you, [13]even though I was sick when I first brought you the Good News of Christ. [14]But even though my sickness was revolting to you, you didn't reject me and turn me away. No, you took me in and cared for me as though I were an angel from God, or even Jesus Christ himself. [15]Where is that happy spirit that we felt together then? For in those days I know you would gladly have taken out your own eyes and given them to replace mine if that would have helped me. [16]And now have I become your enemy because I tell you the truth? [19]Oh, my children, how you are hurting me! I am once again suffering for you the pains of a mother waiting for her child to be born—longing for the time when you will finally be filled with Christ. [20]How I wish I could be there with you right now and not have to reason with you like this, for at this distance I frankly don't know what to do. *vs.* 11–20.

Gal 6:1. Dear brothers, if a Christian is overcome by some sin, you who are godly should gently and humbly help him back onto the right path, remembering that next time it might be one of you who is in the wrong. [2]Share each other's troubles and problems, and so obey our Lord's command. [10]That's why whenever we can we should always be kind to everyone, and especially to our Christian brothers.

Eph 3:13. So please don't lose heart at what they are doing to me here. It is for you I am suffering and you should feel honored and encouraged.

Eph 4:2. Be humble and gentle. Be patient with each other, making allowance for each other's faults because of your love. [32]Instead, be kind to each other, tenderhearted, forgiving one another, just as God has forgiven you because you belong to Christ.

Eph 6:22. I am sending him to you for just this purpose, to let you know how we are and be encouraged by his report. *v.* 24.

Phil 1:3. All my prayers for you are full of praise to God! [4]When I pray for you, my heart is full of joy, [5]because of all your wonderful help in making known the Good News about Christ from the time you first heard it until now. [7]How natural it is that I should feel as I do about you, for you have a very special place in my heart. We have shared together the blessings of God, both when I was in prison and when I was out, defending the truth and telling others about Christ. [8]Only God knows how deep is my love and longing for you—with the tenderness of Jesus Christ. [23]Sometimes I want to live and at other times I don't, for I long to go and be with Christ. How much happier for *me* than being here! [24]But the fact is that I can be of more help to *you* by staying! [25]Yes, I am still needed down here and so I feel certain I will be staying on earth a little longer, to help you grow and become happy in your faith; [26]my staying will make you glad and give you reason to glorify Christ Jesus for keeping me safe, when I return to visit you again.

Phil 2:19. If the Lord is willing, I will send Timothy to see you soon. Then when he comes back he can cheer me up by telling me all about you and how you are getting along.

Phil 3:18. For I have told you often before, and I say it again now with tears in my eyes, there are many who walk along the Christian road who are really enemies of the cross of Christ.

Phil 4:1. Dear brother Christians, I love you and long to see you, for you are my joy and my reward for my work. My beloved friends, stay true to the Lord.

Col 1:3. Whenever we pray for you we always begin by giving thanks to God the Father of our Lord Jesus Christ, [4]for we have heard how much you trust the Lord, and how much you love his people. [24]But part of my work is to suffer for you; and I am glad, for I am helping to finish up the remainder of Christ's sufferings for his body, the church. [28]So everywhere we go we talk about Christ to all who will listen, warning them and teaching them as well as we know how. We want to be able to present each one to God, perfect because of what Christ has done for each of them. [29]This is my work, and I can do it only because Christ's mighty energy is at work within me.

Col 2:1. I wish you could know how much I have struggled in prayer for you and for the church at Laodicea, and for my many other friends who have never known me personally. [5]For though I am far away from you my heart is with you, happy because you are getting along so well, happy because of your strong faith in Christ.

1 Thess 1:3. We never forget your loving deeds as we talk to our God and Father about you, and your strong faith and steady looking forward to the return of our Lord Jesus Christ. [4]We know that God has chosen you, dear brothers, much beloved of God.

1 Thess 2:7. But we were as gentle among you as a mother feeding and caring for her own children. [8]We loved you dearly—so dearly that we gave you not only God's message, but our own lives too. [11]We talked to you as a father to his own children—don't you remember?—pleading with you, encouraging you and even demanding [12]that your daily lives should not embarrass God, but bring joy to him who invited you into his kingdom to share his glory. [17]Dear brothers, after we left you and had been away from you but a very little while (though our hearts never left you), we tried hard to come back to see you once more. [18]We wanted very much to come and I, Paul, tried again and again, but Satan stopped us. [19]For what is it we live for, that gives us hope and joy and is our proud reward and crown? It is you! Yes, you will bring us much joy as we stand together before our Lord Jesus Christ when he comes back again. [20]For you are our trophy and joy.

1 Thess 3:5. As I was saying, when I could bear the suspense no longer I sent Timothy to find out whether your faith was still strong. I was afraid that perhaps Satan had gotten the best of you and that all our work had been useless. [7]So we are greatly comforted, dear brothers, in all of our own

crushing troubles and suffering here, now that we know you are standing true to the Lord. [8]We can bear anything as long as we know that you remain strong in him. [9]How can we thank God enough for you and for the joy and delight you have given us in our praying for you? [10]For night and day we pray on and on for you, asking God to let us see you again, to fill up any little cracks there may yet be in your faith. [12]And may the Lord make your love to grow and overflow to each other and to everyone else, just as our love does toward you.

1 Thess 5:8. But let us who live in the light keep sober, protected by the armor of faith and love, and wearing as our helmet the happy hope of salvation. [11]So encourage each other to build each other up, just as you are already doing. [14]Dear brothers, warn those who are lazy; comfort those who are frightened; take tender care of those who are weak; and be patient with everyone.

2 Thess 1:4. We are happy to tell other churches about your patience and complete faith in God, in spite of all the crushing troubles and hardships you are going through.

1 Tim 1:5. What I am eager for is that all the Christians there will be filled with love that comes from pure hearts, and that their minds will be clean and their faith strong.

1 Tim 5:9. A widow who wants to become one of the special church workers should be at least sixty years old and have been married only once. [10]She must be well thought of by everyone because of the good she has done. . . . Has she been kind to strangers as well as to other Christians? Has she helped those who are sick and hurt? Is she always ready to show kindness?

1 Tim 6:2. If their owner is a Christian, that is no excuse for slowing down; rather they should work all the harder because a brother in the faith is being helped by their efforts. [11]Work instead at what is right and good, learning to trust him and love others, and to be patient and gentle.

2 Tim 1:3. How I thank God for you, Timothy. I pray for you every day, and many times during the long nights I beg my God to bless you richly. He is my fathers' God, and mine, and my only purpose in life is to please him. [4]How I long to see you again. How happy I would be, for I remember your tears as we left each other. [8]If you will stir up this inner power, you will never be afraid to tell others about our Lord, or to let them know that I am your friend even though I am here in jail for Christ's sake.

2 Tim 2:10. I am more than willing to suffer if that will bring salvation and eternal glory in Christ Jesus to those God has chosen.

Philemon 1:8, 9. Now I want to ask a favor of you. I could demand it of you in the name of Christ because it is the right thing for you to do, but I love you and prefer just to ask you—I, Paul, an old man now, here in jail for the sake of Jesus Christ. [12]I am sending him [Onesimus] back to you, and with him comes my own heart. [16]No longer only a slave, but something much better—a beloved brother, especially to me. Now he will mean much more to you too, because he is not only a servant but also your brother in Christ. [17]If I am really your friend, give him the same welcome you would give to me if I were the one who was coming. [18]If he has harmed you in any way or stolen anything from you, charge me for it. [19]I will pay it back (I, Paul, personally guarantee this by writing it here with my own hand) but I won't mention how much you owe me! The fact is, you even owe me your very soul! [20]Yes, dear brother, give me joy with this loving act and my weary heart will praise the Lord. [21]I've written you this letter because I am positive that you will do what I ask and even more!

Heb 5:2, 3. And because he is a man he can deal gently with other men, though they are foolish and ignorant, for he, too, is surrounded with the same temptations and understands their problems very well.

Heb 6:9. Dear friends, even though I am talking like this I really don't believe that what I am saying applies to you. I am confident you are producing the good fruit that comes along with your salvation. [10]For God is not unfair. How can he forget your hard work for him, or forget the way you used to show your love for him—and still do—by helping his children?

Heb 13:1. Continue to love each other with true brotherly love. [2]Don't forget to be kind to strangers, for some who have done this have entertained angels without realizing it! [3]Don't forget about those in jail. Suffer with them as though you were there yourself. Share the sorrow of those being mistreated, for you know what they are going through. [22]Brethren, please listen patiently to what I have said in this letter, for it is a short one.

Jas 1:27. The Christian who is pure and without fault, from God the Father's point of view, is the one who takes care of orphans and widows, and who remains true to the Lord—not soiled and dirtied by his contacts with the world.

See *Fraternity.*

Instances of. Abraham for Lot, Gen 14:14–16. Joseph for Benjamin, Gen 43:30. Naomi, Ruth, and Boaz, Ruth 1–3. David and Jonathan, 1 Sam 20. David's subjects, 2 Sam 15:30; 17:27–29. Obadiah for the prophets, 1 Kgs 18:3, 4. Jehoshabeath for Joash, 2 Chron 22:11. Nehemiah for Israelites, Neh 5:10–15. Mordecai for Esther, Esther 2:7. Job's friends, Job 42:11. Roman officer for his slave, Lk 7:2–6. Roman Christians for Paul, Acts 28:15. Paul for the people of Israel, Rom 9:1–4.

OF MONEY. The first step toward sin, 1 Tim 6:10. See *Riches.*

OF PARENTS FOR CHILDREN. See *Parents.*

See also *Brother; Fraternity; Friendship.*

LOVEFEASTS Assemblies of Christian fellowship, 2 Pet 2:13; Jude 1:12.

See *Communion; Lord's Supper.*

LOVERS INSTANCES OF. Isaac and Rebekah, Gen 24:67. Jacob and Rachel, Gen 29:20, 30. Shechem and Dinah, Gen 34:3, 12. Boaz and Ruth, Ruth 2–5.

LOVINGKINDNESS The goodness, grace, and mercy of God toward men. Ps 26:3; 40:10; 69:16; 88:11; 89:33; 103:4; 107; 118; 119:149; 136; 138:2; Isa 63:7; Jer 16:5; 31:3; 32:18.

See *Mercy; God, Goodness of; Grace of God.*

LOYALTY Commanded, Ex 22:28; Num 27:20; Ezra 6:10; 7:26; Job 34:18; Prov 24:21, 22; Eccl 8:2, 3; 10:4; Rom 13:1; Tit 3:1. Enforced, Ezra 10:7, 8; Prov 17:11. Disloyalty, 2 Pet 2:10.

See *Patriotism.*

INSTANCES OF. Israelites, Josh 1:16–18; 2 Sam 3:35–37; 15:23, 30; 18:3; 21:17; 1 Chron 12:38. David, 1 Sam 24:6–10; 26:5–16; 2 Sam 1:14. Uriah, 2 Sam 11:9. Ittai, 2 Sam 15:21. Hushai, 2 Sam 17:15, 16. David's soldiers, 2 Sam 18:12, 13; 23:15, 16. Joab, 2 Sam 19:5, 6. Barzillai, 2 Sam 19:31, 32. Jehoiada, 2 Kgs 11:4–12. Mordecai, Esther 2:21–23.

LUCIFER A name for Satan, Isa 14:12.

LUCIUS 1. A Christian at Antioch, Acts 13:1.

2. A relative of Paul, Rom 16:21.

LUD, LUDIM 1. A son of Shem, Gen 10:22; 1 Chron 1:17.

2. Son of Mizraim, Gen 10:13, 14. Descendants of, 1 Chron 1:11, 12; were warriors, Isa 66:19; Jer 46:9; Ezk 27:10; 30:5.

LUHITH A city of Moab, Isa 15:5; Jer 48:5.

LUKE A disciple. A physician, Col 4:14. Wrote to Theophilus, Lk 1:1–4; Acts 1:1, 2. Accompanies Paul in his tour of Asia and Macedonia, Acts 16:10–13; 20:5, 6; to Jerusalem, Acts 21:1–18; to Rome, Acts 27; 28; 2 Tim 4:11; Philemon 1:24.

LUKEWARMNESS FIGURATIVE. Jer 9:3. "They bend their tongues like bows to shoot their arrows of untruth. They care nothing for right and go from bad to worse; they care nothing for me," says the Lord.

Ezk 13:5. O evil prophets, what have you ever done to strengthen the walls of Israel against her enemies—by strengthening Israel in the Lord?

Hos 6:4. O Ephraim and Judah, what shall I do with you? For your love vanishes like morning clouds, and disappears like dew.

Hos 10:2. The hearts of her people are false toward God. They are guilty and must be punished. God will break down their heathen altars and smash their idols.

Hag 1:2. "Why is everyone saying it is not the right time for rebuilding my Temple?" asks the Lord. *vs.* 4–11; Hag 2:15–17.

Mt 26:41. For the spirit indeed is willing, but how weak the body is!

Rev 2:4. Yet there is one thing wrong; you don't love me as at first!

Rev 3:2. Now wake up! Strengthen what little remains—for even what is left is at the point of death. Your deeds are far from right in the sight of God. [15]I know you well—you are neither hot nor cold; I wish you were one or the other! [16]But since you are merely lukewarm, I will spit you out of my mouth!

See *Backslider; Blindness, Spiritual.*

INSTANCES OF. The Reubenites, when Deborah called on them to assist Sisera, Judg 5:16. The Jews under Nehemiah, Neh 3:5; 13:11. The church at Pergamos, Rev 2:14–16; Thyatira, Rev 2:20–24; Sardis, Rev 3:1–3; Laodicea, Rev 3:14–16.

LUNACY See *Insanity; Demons.*

LUST Evil desire. Gen 3:6. The woman was convinced. How lovely and fresh looking it was! And it would make her so wise! So she ate some of the fruit and gave some to her husband, and he ate it too.

Ex 20:17. You must not be envious of your neighbor's house, or want to sleep with his wife, or want to own his slaves, oxen, donkeys, or anything else he has.

Job 22:24. If you give up your lust for money, and throw your gold away, [25]then the Almighty himself shall be your treasure, he will be your precious silver.

Job 31:9. Or if I have longed for another man's wife, [10]then may I die, and my wife be in another man's home, and someone else become her husband. [11]For lust is a shameful sin, a crime that should be punished. [12]It is a devastating fire that destroys to hell, and would root out all I have planted. Prov 21:4; 2 Cor 12:21.

Ps 81:12. So I am letting them go their blind and stubborn way, living according to their own desires. Rom 1:24–27; Jude 1:7.

Ps 141:4. Take away my lust for evil things; don't let me want to be with sinners, doing what they do, sharing their dainties.

Prov 6:24. Their counsel will keep you far away from prostitutes with all their flatteries. [25]Don't lust for their beauty. Don't let their coyness seduce you. Prov 9:13.

Hos 7:4. They are all adulterers; as a baker's oven is constantly aflame—except while he kneads the dough and waits for it to rise—so are these people constantly aflame with lust.

Mt 5:28. But I say: Anyone who even looks at a woman with lust in his eye has already committed adultery with her in his heart. Job 31:1.

Mk 4:19. But all too quickly the attractions of this world and the delights of wealth, and the search for success and lure of nice things come in and crowd out God's message from their hearts, so that no crop is produced. Ezk 28:18.

Jn 8:44. For you are the children of your father the devil and you love to do the evil things he does.

1 Cor 7:9. It is better to marry than to burn with lust.

1 Cor 9:27. Like an athlete I punish my body, treating it roughly, training it to do what it should, not what it wants to. Otherwise I fear that after enlisting others for the race, I myself might be declared unfit and ordered to stand aside.

1 Cor 10:6. From this lesson we are warned that we must not desire evil things as they did, [7]nor worship idols as they did. (The Scriptures tell us, "The people sat down to eat and drink and then got up to dance" in worship of the golden calf.) Num 11:34.

Eph 4:22. Then throw off your old evil nature—

the old you that was a partner in your evil ways—rotten through and through, full of lust and sham. 1 Thess 4:7; 2 Pet 1:4.

1 Tim 6:9. But people who long to be rich soon begin to do all kinds of wrong things to get money, things that hurt them and make them evil-minded and finally send them to hell itself.

2 Tim 2:22. Run from anything that gives you the evil thoughts that young men often have. Mk 7:20, 21; Col 3:5.

Tit 2:12. And along with this gift comes the realization that God wants us to turn from godless living and sinful pleasures and to live good, God-fearing lives day after day.

Jas 1:14. Temptation is the pull of man's own evil thoughts and wishes. [15]These evil thoughts lead to evil actions and afterwards to the death penalty from God.

Jas 4:1. What is causing the quarrels and fights among you? Isn't it because there is a whole army of evil desires within you? [2]You want what you don't have, so you kill to get it. You long for what others have, and can't afford it, so you start a fight to take it away from them. And yet the reason you don't have what you want is that you don't ask God for it. [3]And even when you do ask you don't get it because your whole aim is wrong—you want only what will give *you* pleasure.

1 Pet 2:11. Dear brothers, you are only visitors here. Since your real home is in heaven I beg you to keep away from the evil pleasures of this world; they are not for you, for they fight against your very souls.

1 Pet 4:3. You have had enough in the past of the evil things the godless enjoy—sex sin, lust, getting drunk, wild parties, drinking bouts, and the worship of idols, and other terrible sins.

2 Pet 2:18. They proudly boast about their sins and conquests, and, using lust as their bait, they lure back into sin those who have just escaped from such wicked living.

2 Pet 3:3. First, I want to remind you that in the last days there will come scoffers who will do every wrong they can think of, and laugh at the truth.

1 Jn 2:16. For all these worldly things, these evil desires—the craze for sex, the ambition to buy everything that appeals to you, and the pride that comes from wealth and importance—these are not from God. They are from this evil world itself. [17]And this world is fading away, and these evil, forbidden things will go with it, but whoever keeps doing the will of God will live forever. Rom 13: 12–14.

Jude 1:16. These men are constant gripers, never satisfied, doing whatever evil they feel like; they are loud-mouthed "show-offs," and when they show respect for others, it is only to get something from them in return. [18]That in the last times there would come these scoffers whose whole purpose in life is to enjoy themselves in every evil way imaginable.

See *Adultery; Bestiality; Covetousness; Homosexuality; Incest; Lasciviousness; Sensuality; Sodomites.*

LUTE 2 Kgs 3:15. Used in worship, Ps 92:3; 150:3.

LYCAONIA A province of Asia Minor. Paul visits towns of, Acts 14:5–21.

LYCIA A province of Asia Minor. Paul visits, Acts 27:5.

LYDDA Called also *Lod.* Peter heals Aeneas in, Acts 9:32–35.

LYDIA A woman of Thyatira, who with her household was converted through the preaching of Paul, Acts 16:14, 15. Entertains Paul and Silas, Acts 16:15, 40.

LYE Job 9:30; Jer 2:22.

LYING Lying spirit from God, 1 Kgs 22:21–23; 2 Chron 18:19–22. cf. Ex 20:16; Prov 6:16–19; 10: 18; Jer 7:4; 29:23; Dan 2:8, 9; 2 Thess 2:9; Rev 22: 15.

UNCLASSIFIED SCRIPTURES RELATING TO. Ex 23:1. Do not pass along untrue reports. Do not cooperate with an evil man by affirming on the witness stand something you know is false.

Lev 6:2. If anyone sins against me by refusing to return a deposit or something borrowed or rented, or by refusing to return something entrusted to him, or by robbery, or by oppressing his neighbor, [3]or by finding a lost article and lying about it, swearing that he doesn't have it—[4, 5]On the day he is found guilty of any such sin, he shall restore what he took, adding a twenty percent fine, and give it to the one he has harmed; and on the same day he shall bring his guilt offering to the Tabernacle. [6]His guilt offering shall be a ram without defect, and must be worth whatever value you demand. He shall bring it to the priest, [7]and the priest shall make atonement for him before the Lord, and he shall be forgiven.

Lev 19:11. You must not steal nor lie nor defraud. [12]You must not swear to a falsehood, thus bringing reproach upon the name of your God, for I am Jehovah. [16]Don't gossip. Don't falsely accuse your neighbor of some crime, for I am Jehovah. Ex 20: 16.

Job 27:4. My lips shall speak no evil, my tongue shall speak no lies.

Job 31:5. If I have lied and deceived—[6]but God knows that I am innocent. [33]Or if, like Adam, I have tried to hide my sins.

Job 36:4. I am telling you the honest truth, for I am a man of well-rounded knowledge.

Ps 5:6. You will destroy them for their lies; how you abhor all murder and deception. [9]For they cannot speak one truthful word. Their hearts are filled to the brim with wickedness. Their suggestions are full of the stench of sin and death. Their tongues are filled with flatteries to gain their wicked ends.

Ps 10:7. Their mouths are full of profanity and lies and fraud. They are always boasting of their evil plans.

Ps 12:2. Everyone deceives and flatters and lies. There is no sincerity left. [3, 4]But the Lord will not deal gently with people who act like that; he will destroy those proud liars who say, "We will lie to our hearts' content. Our lips are our own; who can stop us?"

Ps 28:3. Don't punish me with all the wicked ones who speak so sweetly to their neighbors while planning to murder them.

Ps 31:18. Their lying lips quieted at last—the lips of these arrogant men who are accusing honest men of evil deeds.

Ps 34:13. Then watch your tongue! Keep your lips from lying. 1 Pet 3:10.

Ps 36:3. Everything they say is crooked and deceitful; they are no longer wise and good.

Ps 50:19. You curse and lie, and vile language streams from your mouths. [20]You slander your own brother.

Ps 52:2. You are sharp as a tack in plotting your evil tricks. [3]How you love wickedness—far more than good! And lying more than truth! [4]You love to slander—you love to say anything that will do harm, O man with the lying tongue. [5]But God will strike you down and pull you from your home, and drag you away from the land of the living.

Ps 55:21. His words were oily smooth, but in his heart was war. His words were sweet, but underneath were daggers. [23]He will send my enemies to the pit of destruction. Murderers and liars will not live but half their days.

Ps 58:3. These men are born sinners, lying from their earliest words!

Ps 59:12. They are proud, cursing liars. Angrily destroy them. Wipe them out.

Ps 62:3, 4. But what is this? They pick on me at a time when my throne is tottering; they plot my death and use lies and deceit to try to force me from the throne. They are so friendly to my face while cursing in their hearts!

Ps 63:11. But I will rejoice in God. All who trust in him exult, while liars shall be silenced.

Ps 101:5. I will not tolerate anyone who secretly slanders his neighbors; I will not permit conceit and pride. [7]But I will not allow those who deceive and lie to stay in my house.

Ps 109:2. While the wicked slander me and tell their lies.

Ps 116:10, 11. In my discouragement I thought, "They are lying when they say I will recover."

Ps 119:69. Proud men have made up lies about me, but the truth is that I obey your laws with all my heart. [163]How I hate all falsehood but how I love your laws.

Ps 120:2. Deliver me, O Lord, from liars. [3]O lying tongue, what shall be your fate? [4]You shall be pierced with sharp arrows and burned with glowing coals.

Ps 144:8. Their mouths are filled with lies; they swear to the truth of what is false. [11]Save me! Deliver me from these enemies, these liars, these treacherous men.

Prov 3:3. Never forget to be truthful and kind. Hold these virtues tightly. Write them deep within your heart.

Prov 6:12, 13. Let me describe for you a worthless and a wicked man; first, he is a constant liar; he signals his true intentions to his friends with eyes and feet and fingers. [16-19]For there are six things the Lord hates—no seven: haughtiness, lying, murdering, plotting evil, eagerness to do wrong, a false witness, sowing discord among brothers.

Prov 10:9. A good man has firm footing, but a crook will slip and fall. [10]Winking at sin leads to sorrow; bold reproof leads to peace. [18]To hate is to be a liar; to slander is to be a fool. [31]The good man gives wise advice, but the liar's counsel is shunned.

Prov 11:9. Evil words destroy. Godly skill rebuilds.

Prov 12:17. A good man is known by his truthfulness; a false man by deceit and lies. [19]Truth stands the test of time; lies are soon exposed. [20]Deceit fills hearts that are plotting for evil; joy fills hearts that are planning for good! [22]God delights in those who keep their promises, and abhors those who don't.

Prov 13:5. A good man hates lies; wicked men lie constantly and come to shame.

Prov 14:5. A truthful witness never lies; a false witness always lies. [8]The wise man looks ahead. The fool attempts to fool himself and won't face facts. [25]A witness who tells the truth saves good men from being sentenced to death, but a false witness is a traitor.

Prov 17:4. The wicked enjoy fellowship with others who are wicked; liars enjoy liars. [7]Truth from a rebel or lies from a king are both unexpected.

Prov 19:5. Punish false witnesses. Track down liars. [*v.* 9.] [22]Kindness makes a man attractive. And it is better to be poor than dishonest. [28]A worthless witness cares nothing for truth—he enjoys his sinning too much.

Prov 20:17. Some men enjoy cheating, but the cake they buy with such ill-gotten gain will turn to gravel in their mouths.

Prov 21:6. Dishonest gain will never last, so why take the risk?

Prov 26:18, 19. A man who is caught lying to his neighbor and says, "I was just fooling," is like a madman throwing around firebrands, arrows and death! [24, 25, 26]A man with hate in his heart may sound pleasant enough, but don't believe him; for he is cursing you in his heart. Though he pretends to be so kind, his hatred will finally come to light for all to see. [28]Flattery is a form of hatred and wounds cruelly.

Prov 27:14. If you shout a pleasant greeting to a friend too early in the morning, he will count it as a curse!

Eccl 5:6. In that case, your mouth is making you sin. Don't try to defend yourself by telling the messenger from God that it was all a mistake [to make the vow]. That would make God very angry; and he might destroy your prosperity.

Isa 28:15. You have struck a bargain with Death, you say, and sold yourselves to the devil in exchange for his protection against the Assyrians. "They can never touch us," you say, "for we are under the care of one who will deceive and fool them."

Isa 32:7. The smooth tricks of evil men will be

exposed, as will all the lies they use to oppress the poor in the courts.

Isa 59:3. You lie and grumble and oppose the good. [4]No one cares about being fair and true. Your lawsuits are based on lies; you spend your time plotting evil deeds and doing them. [12]For your sins keep piling up before the righteous God, and testify against you. Yes, we know what sinners we are. [13]We know our disobedience; we have denied the Lord our God. We know what rebels we are and how unfair we are, for we carefully plan our lies.

Isa 63:8. He said, "They are my very own; surely they will not be false again." And he became their Savior.

Jer 7:28. Say to them: This is the nation that refuses to obey the Lord its God, and refuses to be taught. She continues to live a lie.

Jer 9:3. "They bend their tongues like bows to shoot their arrows of untruth. They care nothing for right and go from bad to worse; they care nothing for me," says the Lord. [5]With practiced tongues they fool and defraud each other; they wear themselves out with all their sinning. [6]"They pile evil upon evil, lie upon lie, and utterly refuse to come to me," says the Lord. [8]"For their tongues aim lies like poisoned spears. They speak cleverly to their neighbors while planning to kill them."

Jer 12:6. Even your own brothers, your own family, have turned against you. They have plotted to call for a mob to lynch you. Don't trust them, no matter how pleasantly they speak. Don't believe them.

Ezk 22:9. Prisoners are falsely accused and sent to their death. Every mountain top is filled with idols; lewdness is everywhere.

Hos 4:1. The Lord has filed a lawsuit against you . . . There is no faithfulness . . . in your land. [2]You swear and lie and kill and steal and commit adultery. There is violence everywhere, with one murder after another.

Obd 1:7. They will promise peace while plotting your destruction.

Mic 6:12. Your rich men are wealthy through extortion and violence; your citizens are so used to lying that their tongues can't tell the truth!

Nah 3:1. Woe to Nineveh, City of Blood, full of lies, crammed with plunder.

Zeph 3:13. They will not be sinners, full of lies and deceit. They will live quietly, in peace, and lie down in safety, and no one will make them afraid.

Mt 25:44. Then they will reply, "Lord, when did we ever see you hungry or thirsty or a stranger or naked or sick or in prison, and not help you?" [45]And I will answer, "When you refused to help the least of these my brothers, you were refusing help to me." [46]And they shall go away into eternal punishment; but the righteous into everlasting life.

Jn 8:44. For you are the children of your father the devil and you love to do the evil things he does. He was a murderer from the beginning and a hater of truth—there is not an iota of truth in him. When he lies, it is perfectly normal; for he is the father of liars. [45]And so when I tell the truth, you just naturally don't believe it!

Eph 4:25. Stop lying to each other; tell the truth, for we are parts of each other and when we lie to each other we are hurting ourselves. [29]Don't use bad language. Say only what is good and helpful to those you are talking to, and what will give them a blessing.

Col 3:9. Don't tell lies to each other; it was your old life with all its wickedness that did that sort of thing.

1 Tim 1:10. Yes, these laws are made to identify as sinners . . . liars, and all others who do things that contradict the glorious Good News.

1 Tim 4:2. These teachers will tell lies with straight faces and do it so often that their consciences won't even bother them.

1 Pet 3:16. Do what is right; then if men speak against you, calling you evil names, they will become ashamed of themselves for falsely accusing you when you have only done what is good.

Rev 21:8. And all liars—their doom is in the Lake that burns with fire and sulphur. [27]Nothing evil will be permitted in it [the Holy City]—no one immoral or dishonest.

Rev 22:15. Outside the city are those who have strayed away from God, . . . all who love to lie, and do so.

INSTANCES OF. Satan, in deceiving Eve, Gen 3: 4, 5; in impugning Job's motives for being righteous, Job 1:9, 10; 2:4, 5; in his false pretensions to Jesus, Mt 4:8, 9; Lk 4:6, 7. Adam and Eve, in attempting to evade responsibility, Gen 3:12, 13. Cain, in denying knowledge of his brother, Gen 4: 9. Abraham, in denying that Sarah was his wife, Gen 12:11–19; 20:2. Sarah, to the angels, denying her laugh in unbelief, Gen 18:15; in denying to the king of Gerar, that she was Abraham's wife, Gen 20:5, 16. Isaac, denying that Rebekah was his wife, Gen 26:7–10. Rebekah and Jacob, in the conspiracy against Esau, Gen 27:6–24, 46. Jacob's sons, in the scheme to destroy the Shechemites by first having them circumcised, Gen 34.

Joseph's brethren, in deceiving their father into a belief that Joseph was killed by wild animals, Gen 37:29–35. Potiphar's wife, in falsely accusing Joseph, Gen 39:14–17. Joseph, in the deception he carried on with his brothers, Gen 42–44. Pharaoh, in dealing deceitfully with the Israelites, Ex 7–12.

Aaron, in attempting to shift responsibility for the making of the golden calf, Ex 32:1–24. Rahab, in denying that the spies were in her house, Josh 2:4–6. The Gibeonites, ambassadors, in the deception they perpetrated upon Joshua and the elders of Israel in leading them to believe that they came from a distant land, when in fact they lived in the immediate vicinity, Josh 9. Ehud, in pretending to deliver secret messages to Eglon, king of Moab, while his object was to assassinate him, Judg 3: 16–23. Sisera, who instructed Jael to mislead his pursuers, Judg 4:20. Saul, in professing to Samuel to have obeyed the commandment to destroy all spoils of the Amalekites, when in fact he had not obeyed, 1 Sam 15:1–26; in accusing Ahimelech of conspiring with David against himself, 1 Sam 22:11–16. David lied to Ahimelech, professing to be on a mission for the king, in order that he might obtain provisions and armor, 1 Sam 21; in feigning insanity, 1 Sam 21:13–15; and other deceits with the Philistines, 1 Sam 27:8–12; the falsehood he put into Hushai's mouth, of loyalty to Absalom, 2 Sam 15:34–37.

Michal, in the false statement that David was sick, in order to save him from Saul's violence, 1 Sam 19:12–17. The Amalekite who claimed to have killed Saul, 2 Sam 1:10–12. Hushai, in false professions to Absalom, 2 Sam 16:16–19; in his deceitful counsel to Absalom, 2 Sam 17:7–14.

The wife of the Bahurimite who saved the lives of Hushai's messengers, sent to apprise David of the movements of Absalom's army, 2 Sam 17:15–22. The murder, under false pretense: Of Adonijah, 1 Kgs 2:23, 24; of Shime-i, 1 Kgs 2:42, 43; of Jeroboam's wife, 1 Kgs 14:2. The old prophet of Bethel who misguided the prophet of Judah, 1 Kgs 13:11–22; Jeroboam's wife, pretending to be another woman, 1 Kgs 14:5–7.

The conspirators against Naboth, 1 Kgs 21:7–13. Gehazi, when he ran after Naaman, and misrepresented that Elisha wanted silver and clothing, 2 Kgs 5:20–24. Hazael, servant of the king of Syria, lied to the king in misstating Elisha's message in regard to the king's recovery, 2 Kgs 8:7–15. Jehu lied to the worshipers of Baal in order to gain advantage over them, and destroy them, 2 Kgs 10:18–28. Zedekiah, in violating his oath of loyalty to Nebuchadnezzar, 2 Chron 36:13; Ezk 16:59, 60; 17:15–20. Samaritans, in their efforts to hinder the rebuilding of the temple at Jerusalem, Ezra 4. Sanballat, in trying to obstruct the rebuilding of Jerusalem, Neh 6. Haman, in his conspiracy against the Jews, Esther 3:8. Jeremiah's adversaries, in accusing him of joining the Babylonians, Jer 37:13–16. Princes of Israel, when they went to Jeremiah for a vision from the Lord, Jer 42:20.

Herod, to the astrologers, in professing to desire to worship Jesus, Mt 2:8.

Jews, in falsely accusing Jesus of being a glutton and a drinker, Mt 11:19; in refusing to speak truthfully concerning John the Baptist, Mt 21:24–27; falsely accusing Jesus of blasphemy, when he forgave sin, Mt 9:2–6; Mk 2:7; Lk 5:21; and announced that he was the Son of God, Mt 26:64–66; Mk 14:63, 64; Jn 10:33–38.

Peter, in denying Jesus, Mt 26:69–75; Mk 14:68–71; Lk 22:56–62; Jn 18:25–27. The Roman soldiers, who said the disciples stole the body of Jesus, Mt 28:13, 15.

The disobedient son, who promised to work on the farm, but did not, Mt 21:30. Ananias and Sapphira falsely state that they had sold their land for a given sum, Acts 5:1–10.

Stephen's accusers, who falsely accused him of blaspheming Moses and God, Acts 6:11–14. Paul's traducers, falsely accusing him of treason against Caesar, Acts 16:20, 21; 17:5–7; 24:5; 25:7, 8. The Cretans *are* always liars, lazy animals, Tit 1:12.

See *Accusation, False; Conspiracy; Deceit; Deception; False Witness; Flattery; Hypocrisy; Perjury; Teachers, False.*

LYRE Ps 137:2. Made of sandalwood, 2 Chron 9:11. Used in worship, 2 Sam 6:5; 2 Chron 5:11, 12; 20:28; Ps 33:2; 57:8; 81:2; 92:3; 108:2; 149:3.

LYSANIAS A tetrarch, or governor, Lk 3:1, 2.

LYSIAS Commander of Roman troops in Jerusalem, Acts 24:7, 22.

See *Claudius Lysias.*

LYSTRA One of two cities of Lycaonia, to which Paul and Barnabas fled from persecutions in Iconium, Acts 14:5–23; 2 Tim 3:11. Church of, elders ordained for, by Paul and Barnabas, Acts 14:23. Timothy a resident of, Acts 16:1–4.

M

MAACAH, MAACHAH 1. Son of Nahor, Gen 22:24.

2. Mother of Absalom, 2 Sam 3:3; 1 Chron 3:2.

3. Called also *Micaiah.* Mother of Abijam and grandmother of Asa, 1 Kgs 15:1, 2, 10–13; 2 Chron 13:2.

4. Concubine of Caleb, 1 Chron 2:48, 49.

5. Sister of Machir, 1 Chron 7:15.

6. Wife of Machir, 1 Chron 7:16.

7. Wife of Jeiel, 1 Chron 8:29; 9:35–37.

8. Father of Hanan, 1 Chron 11:26–47.

9. Father of Shephatiah, 1 Chron 27:16–22.

10. A small kingdom east of Bashan, Deut 3:14; Josh 12:5; 2 Sam 10:6–8. Called also *Aram-maacah,* 1 Chron 19:6, 7.

MA-ADAI A returned exile, Ezra 10:34–42.

MA-ADIAH A priest, Neh 12:1–8.

MAAI A priest, Neh 12:35, 36.

MAARATH A city of Judah, Josh 15:48–62.

MAASAI A priest, 1 Chron 9:12.

MA-ASEIAH 1. A Levite musician, 1 Chron 15:18, 20.

2. An officer, son of Adaiah, 2 Chron 23:1.

3. An officer of Uzziah, 2 Chron 26:11.

4. Son of Ahaz. Killed by Zichri, 2 Chron 28:7.

5. Governor of Jerusalem, 2 Chron 28:7.

6. The name of eight priests of the exile, Ezra 10:16–19, 21, 22; Neh 8:1–5, 7, 8; 12:41, 42; Jer 21:1; 29:25; 37:3.

7. A returned exile, Ezra 10:30.

8. Father of Azariah, Neh 3:23.

9. One who signed the covenant, Neh 10:14–27.

10. A descendant of Perez, Neh 11:4–6.

11. A Benjaminite, Neh 11:7–9.

12. Father of a false prophet, Jer 29:21.

13. A temple doorman, Jer 35:4.

MAATHAT An ancestor of Jesus, Lk 3:23–38.

MAAZ A son of Ram, 1 Chron 2:27.

MAAZIAH 1. A priest, 1 Chron 24:7–18.

2. A priest who signed the covenant with Nehemiah, Neh 10:1–8.

MACEDONIA A country in southeastern Europe. Paul has a dream concerning, Acts 16:9; preaches in, at Philippi, Acts 16:12; revisits, Acts 20:1–6; 2 Cor 2:13; 7:5. Church at, sends contributions to the poor in Jerusalem, Rom 15:26; 2 Cor 8:1–5. Timothy visits, Acts 19:22.

MACHBANNAI A Gadite warrior, 1 Chron 12:8–13.

MACHI A Gadite, Num 13:3–15.

MACHIR 1. One of the sons of Manasseh, Gen 50:23. Father of the Machirites, Num 26:28–37; 36:1. The land of Gilead allotted to, Num 32:39, 40; Deut 3:15; Josh 13:31. Certain cities of Bashan given to, Josh 13:31; 17:1.

2. A man of Lo-debar who took care of Jonathan's lame son, Mephibosheth, 2 Sam 9:4; 17:27.

MACHNADEBAI A descendant of Bani, Ezra 10:34–42.

MACH-PELAH The burying place of Sarah, Abraham, Isaac, Rebekah, Leah, and Jacob, Gen 23:9, 17–20; 25:9, 10; 49:30, 31; 50:12, 13; Acts 7:16.

MADAI Son of Jepheth, Gen 10:2; 1 Chron 1:5–9.

MADMANNAH A city of Judah, Josh 15:21–32.

MADMENAH A city of Benjamin, Isa 10:31.

MADNESS See *Insanity.*

MADON A Canaanite city, Josh 11:1–3; 12:8–24.

MAGADAN A city of Galilee. Christ visits, Mt 15:39.

MAGDALENE See *Mary, 2.*

MAGGOT See *Worm.*

MAGI The wise men who visited Jesus, Mt 2:1–12.

MAGIC See *Astrology; Magician; Necromancy; Sorcery; Witchcraft.*

MAGICIAN A person who works wonders which are beyond man's ordinary powers, Dan 1:20. Failed to interpret Pharaoh's dreams, Gen 41:8, 24; Nebuchadnezzar's, Dan 2:1–13; 4:7. Performed apparent miracles, Ex 7:11, 12, 22; 8:7. Balaam, Josh 13:22.

FIGURATIVE. Gal 3:1.

MAGISTRATE An officer of civil law, Dan 2:49.

See *Government; Ruler.*

MAGNANIMITY INSTANCES OF. Joshua and the leaders of Israel to the Gibeonites who had deceived the Israelites, Josh 9:3–27. Of Moses, see

Moses. David to Saul, 1 Sam 24:3–11. Ahab to Benhadad, 1 Kgs 20:32–34.

See *Charitableness.*

MAGNIFICAT Of Mary, Lk 1:46–55.

MAGOG Son of Japheth, Gen 10:2; 1 Chron 1:5–9. Prophecy concerning, Ezk 38:2, 3; 39:6.

Symbolic of the enemies of God, Rev 20:8.

MAGPIASH A leader who signed the covenant with Nehemiah, Neh 10:14–27.

MAHALALEL Son of Kenan, Gen 5:12–17; 1 Chron 1:1–4; Lk 3:23–38.

MAHALATH 1. Called also *Basemath.* Daughter of Ishmael, Gen 28:9; 36:2, 3.

2. A granddaughter of David, 2 Chron 11:18.

MAHALELEL A man of Judah, Neh 11:4–6.

MAHANAIM The town of, allotted to Gad, Josh 13:26, 30. One of the Levitical cities, Josh 21:38, 39. Ish-bosheth establishes himself at, when made king over Israel, 2 Sam 2:8–12. David stays at, at the time of Absalom's rebellion, 2 Sam 17:27–29; 1 Kgs 2:8.

MAHARAI One of David's warriors, 2 Sam 23:24–39; 1 Chron 11:26–47; 27:13.

MAHATH Name of two descendants of Kohath, 1 Chron 6:33–38; 2 Chron 29:12–14; 31:12, 13.

MAHAZI-OTH Son of Heman, 1 Chron 25:4, 5, 9–31.

MAHER-SHALAL-HASH-BAZ A symbolical name, Isa 8:1–4, 18.

MAHIR Son of Chelub, 1 Chron 4:11, 12.

MAHLAH 1. One of the daughters of Zelophehad. Special legislation in regard to the inheritance of, Num 26:28–37; 27:1–7; 36:1–12; Josh 17:3, 4.

2. Grandson of Manasseh, 1 Chron 7:18.

MAHLI 1. Son of Merari, Ex 6:19; 1 Chron 6:19–21; Ezra 8:18.

2. Son of Mushi, 1 Chron 6:44–47; 23:23; 24:30.

MAHLON Son of Naomi, and first husband of Ruth, Ruth 1:1–5; 4:9, 10.

MAHOL Father of Heman, Calcol, and Darda, 1 Kgs 4:31.

MAHSEIAH Grandfather of Baruch, Jer 32:12; 51:59.

MAIDEN See *Virgin; Servant.*

MAIL 1. Information, public or private. Carried by post, Esther 3:13; 8:9, 10.

2. Armor, 1 Sam 17:4–7; Jer 51:3. See *Armor.*

MAJORITY AND MINORITY REPORTS Of the spies, Num 13:26–33; 14:6–11.

MAKAZ A place in Judah, 1 Kgs 4:8–19.

MAKHELOTH A camping place of Israel, Num 33:15–37.

MAKKEDAH A city in Canaan, conquered by Joshua, Josh 10:28; 12:8–24. Five Amorite kings hide in a cave of, and are killed by Joshua, Josh 10:5, 16–27.

MALACHI Last of the minor prophets, Mal 1:1. Reproves Israel for its impiety, Mal 1; 2; 3:7–15. Foretells the coming of the Messiah, Mal 3:1–6; the judgments on the wicked and consolations of the righteous, Mal 4:1–3; the coming of the forerunner of the Messiah, Mal 4:4–6.

MALCAM A Benjaminite, 1 Chron 8:8–10.

MALCHIAH 1. See *Malchijah, 2.*

2. Owner of a cistern, Jer 38:6.

MALCHIEL Son of Beriah, Gen 46:17; Num 26:44–47; 1 Chron 7:31.

MALCHIJAH 1. A Gershonite, 1 Chron 6:39–43.

2. An Aaronite, 1 Chron 9:12; Neh 11:10–14. Called also *Malchiah,* Jer 21:1, 2; 38:1.

3. Head of a division of priests, 1 Chron 24:7–18.

4. Name of two exiles, Ezra 10:25, 31, 32. See also Neh 3:11.

5. A son of Rechab who repaired the Dung Gate of Jerusalem, Neh 3:14.

6. A Jew who helped repair the walls of Jerusalem, Neh 3:31.

7. A Jew who stood by Ezra when he read the law to the people, Neh 8:1–5.

8. A priest who signed the covenant with Nehemiah, Neh 10:1–8.

9. A priest appointed to assist in dedicating the walls of Jerusalem, Neh 12:42.

MALCHIRAM Son of Jeconiah, 1 Chron 3:17, 18.

MALCHISHUA Son of Saul, 1 Sam 14:49; 31:2; 1 Chron 8:33; 9:39; 10:2.

MALCHUS Servant of the high priest; Peter assaults in Gethsemane; healed by Jesus, Jn 18:10.

MALFEASANCE IN OFFICE INSTANCES OF. The lessees of the vineyard, in one of the parables of Jesus, Mk 12:1–8; Lk 20:9–15. The accountant mentioned in one of the parables of Jesus, Lk 16:1–7.

MALICE AND WICKEDNESS Gen 3:15. I will put the fear of you into the woman, and between your offspring and hers. He shall strike you on on your head, while you will strike at his heel.

Lev 19:14. You must not curse the deaf nor trip up a blind man as he walks. Fear your God; I am Jehovah! [17]Don't hate your brother. Rebuke anyone who sins; don't let him get away with it, or you will be equally guilty. [18]Don't seek vengeance. Don't bear a grudge; but love your neighbor as yourself, for I am Jehovah.

Deut 27:17. Cursed is he who moves the boundary marker between his land and his neighbor's. . . . [18]Cursed is he who takes advantage of a blind man.

Deut 32:32. They act like men of Sodom and Gomorrah: their deeds are bitter with poison; [33]they drink the wine of serpent venom.

2 Kgs 6:21. When the king of Israel saw them, he shouted to Elisha, "Oh, sir, shall I kill them? Shall I kill them?" [22]"Of course not!" Elisha told him. "Do we kill prisoners of war? Give them food and drink and send them home again."

Job 31:29. If I have rejoiced at harm to an enemy — [30](but actually I have never cursed anyone nor asked for revenge)—.

Ps 4:2. Sons of men, will you forever turn my glory into shame?

Ps 7:14. The wicked man conceives an evil plot, labors with its dark details, and brings to birth his treachery and lies; [15]let him fall into his own trap. [16]May the violence he plans for others boomerang upon himself; let him die. Job 15:35.

Ps 10:7. Their mouths are full of profanity and lies and fraud. They are always boasting of their evil plans. [8]They lurk in dark alleys of the city and murder passersby. [9]Like lions they crouch silently, waiting to pounce upon the poor. Like hunters they catch their victims in their traps. [10]The unfortunate are overwhelmed by their superior strength and fall beneath their blows. [14]Lord, you see what they are doing. You have noted each evil act. You know what trouble and grief they have caused. Now punish them.

Ps 21:11. For these men plot against you, Lord, but they cannot possibly succeed.

Ps 22:7. Everyone who sees me mocks and sneers and shrugs. [8]"Is this the one who rolled his burden on the Lord?" they laugh. "Is this the one who claims the Lord delights in him? We'll believe it when we see God rescue him!"

Ps 35:15. But now that I am in trouble they are glad; they come together in meetings filled with slander against me—I didn't even know some of those who were there. [16]For they gather with the worthless fellows of the town and spend their time cursing me. [19]Don't give victory to those who fight me without any reason! Don't let them rejoice at my fall—let them die. [20]They don't talk of peace and doing good, but of plots against innocent men who are minding their own business. [21]They shout that they have seen *me* doing wrong! "Aha!" they say. "With our own eyes we saw him do it."

Ps 38:16. Put an end to their arrogance, these who gloat when I am cast down! [19]But my enemies persecute with vigor, and continue to hate me—though I have done nothing against them to deserve it.

Ps 41:5. But my enemies say, "May he soon die and be forgotten!" [6]They act so friendly when they come to visit me while I am sick; but all the time they hate me and are glad that I am lying there upon my bed of pain. And when they leave, they laugh and mock. [7]They whisper together about what they will do when I am dead. [8]"It's fatal, whatever it is," they say. "He'll never get out of that bed!"

Ps 55:3. They surround me with terror and plot to kill me. Their fury and hatred rise to engulf me. [10]Though they patrol their walls night and day against invaders, their real problem is internal—wickedness and dishonesty are entrenched in the heart of the city. [11]There is murder and robbery there, and cheating in the markets and wherever you look.

Ps 56:5. They are always twisting what I say. All their thoughts are how to harm me. [6]They meet together to perfect their plans; they hide beside the trail, listening for my steps, waiting to kill me.

Ps 57:4. I am surrounded by fierce lions—hotheads whose teeth are sharp as spears and arrows. Their tongues are like swords. [6]My enemies have set a trap for me. Frantic fear grips me. They have dug a pitfall in my path. But look! They themselves have fallen into it!

Ps 59:3. They lurk in ambush for my life. Strong men are out there waiting. And not, O Lord, because I've done them wrong. [4]Yet they prepare to kill me. Lord, waken! See what is happening! Help me! [6]At evening they come to spy, slinking around like dogs that prowl the city. [7]I hear them shouting insults and cursing God, for "No one will hear us," they think.

Ps 62:3, 4. But what is this? They pick on me at a time when my throne is tottering; they plot my death and use lies and deceit to try to force me from the throne. They are so friendly to my face while cursing in their hearts!

Ps 64:2. Oh, preserve my life from the conspiracy of these wicked men, these gangs of criminals. [3]They cut me down with sharpened tongues; they aim their bitter words like arrows straight at my heart. [4]They shoot from ambush at the innocent. Suddenly the deed is done, yet they are not afraid. [5]They encourage each other to do evil. They meet in secret to set their traps. "He will never notice them here," they say. [6]They keep a sharp lookout for opportunities of crime. They spend long hours with all their endless evil thoughts and plans.

Ps 69:4. I cannot even count all those who hate me without cause. They are influential men, these who plot to kill me though I am innocent. They demand that I be punished for what I didn't do. [10]How they scoff and mock me when I mourn and fast before the Lord! [11]How they talk about me when I wear sackcloth to show my humiliation and sorrow for my sins! [12]I am the talk of the town and the song of the drunkards. [26]For they persecute the one you have smitten, and scoff at the pain of the one you have pierced.

Ps 70:2, 3. They are after my life, and delight in hurting me. Confuse them! Shame them! Stop them! Don't let them keep on mocking me!

Ps 71:10. My enemies are whispering, [11]"God has forsaken him! Now we can get him. There is no one to help him now!" *vs.* 13, 24.

Ps 74:20. Remember your promise! For the land is full of darkness and cruel men.

Ps 86:14. O God, proud and insolent men defy me; violent, godless men are trying to kill me.

Ps 102:8. My enemies taunt me day after day and curse at me.

Ps 109:2. While the wicked slander me and tell their lies. [3]They have no reason to hate and fight me, yet they do! [4]I love them, but even while I am praying for them, they are trying to destroy me. [5]They return evil for good, and hatred for love. [16]For he refused all kindness to others, and persecuted those in need, and hounded brokenhearted ones to death. [17]He loved to curse others; now you curse him. He never blessed others; now don't you bless him. [18]Cursing is as much a part of him as his clothing, or as the water he drinks, or as the rich food he eats.

Ps 119:150. Here come these lawless men to attack me. *v.* 78.

Ps 140:1. O Lord, deliver me from evil men. Preserve me from the violent, [2]who plot and stir up trouble all day long. [3]Their words sting like poisonous snakes. [4]Keep me out of their power. Preserve me from their violence, for they are plotting against me.

Prov 4:16. For evil men don't sleep until they've done their evil deed for the day. They can't rest unless they cause someone to stumble and fall. [17]They eat and drink wickedness and violence!

Prov 6:14. Next, his heart is full of rebellion. And he spends his time thinking of all the evil he can do, and stirring up discontent. [15]But he will be destroyed suddenly, broken beyond hope of healing. *vs.* 16–19.

Prov 10:6. But an evil man inwardly curses his luck. [12]Hatred stirs old quarrels.

Prov 11:17. Your own soul . . . is destroyed when you are cruel.

Prov 12:10. But even the kindness of godless men is cruel.

Prov 14:17. A short-tempered man is a fool. He hates the man who is patient. [22]Those who plot evil shall wander away and be lost.

Prov 15:17. It is better to eat soup with someone you love than steak with someone you hate.

Prov 16:30. The wicked man stares into space with pursed lips, deep in thought, planning his evil deeds.

Prov 17:5. Mocking the poor is mocking the God who made them. He will punish those who rejoice at others' misfortunes.

Prov 20:22. Don't repay evil for evil. Wait for the Lord to handle the matter.

Prov 21:10. An evil man loves to harm others; being a good neighbor is out of his line.

Prov 24:8. To plan evil is as wrong as doing it. [17]Do not rejoice when your enemy meets trouble. Let there be no gladness when he falls— [18]for the Lord may be displeased with you and stop punishing him! [29]Don't say, "Now I can pay him back for all his meanness to me!"

Prov 26:2. An undeserved curse has no effect. Its intended victim will be no more harmed by it than by a sparrow or swallow flitting through the sky. [27]The man who sets a trap for others will get caught in it himself. Roll a boulder down on someone, and it will roll back and crush you.

Prov 28:10. A curse on those who lead astray the godly.

Prov 30:14. They devour the poor with teeth as sharp as knives!

Isa 29:20. Bullies will vanish and scoffers will cease, and all those plotting evil will be killed— [21]the violent man who fights at the drop of a hat, the man who waits in hiding to beat up the judge who sentenced him, and the men who use any excuse to be unfair.

Isa 32:6. Everyone will recognize an evil man when he sees him, and hypocrites will fool no one at all. Their lies about God and their cheating of the hungry will be plain for all to see.

Isa 59:4. No one cares about being fair and true. Your lawsuits are based on lies; you spend your time plotting evil deeds and doing them. [5]You spend your time and energy in spinning evil plans which end up in deadly actions. [6]You cheat and short-change everyone. Everything you do is filled with sin; violence is your trademark. *v.* 7.

Jer 20:10. Yet on every side I hear their whispered threats, and am afraid. "We will report you," they say. Even those who were my friends are watching me, waiting for a fatal slip. "He will trap himself," they say, "and then we will get our revenge on him."

Lam 4:3, 4. Even the jackals feed their young, but not my people, Israel. They are like cruel desert ostriches, heedless of their babies' cries. The children's tongues stick to the roofs of their mouths for thirst, for there is not a drop of water left. Babies cry for bread but no one can give them any.

Ezk 18:18. But his father shall die for his own sins because he is cruel and robs and does wrong.

Ezk 25:3. Tell them: Listen to what the Lord God says. Because you scoffed when my Temple was destroyed, and mocked Israel in her anguish, and laughed at Judah when she was marched away captive. [6]For the Lord God says: Because you clapped and stamped and cheered with glee at the destruction of my people, [7]therefore I will lay my hand heavily upon you, delivering you to many nations for devastation. I will cut you off from being a nation any more. I will destroy you; then you shall know I am the Lord. [12]And the Lord God says: Because the people of Edom have sinned so greatly by avenging themselves upon the people of Judah. [15]And the Lord God says: Because the Philistines have acted against Judah out of revenge and long-standing hatred. [17]I will execute terrible vengeance upon them to rebuke them for what they have done. And when all this happens, then they shall know I am the Lord.

Ezk 26:2. Son of dust, Tyre has rejoiced over the fall of Jerusalem, saying "Ha! She who controlled the lucrative north-south trade routes along the coast and along the course of the Jordan River has been broken, and I have fallen heir! Because she has been laid waste, I shall become wealthy!" [3]Therefore the Lord God says: I will stand against you, Tyre, and I will bring nations against you like ocean waves.

Amos 1:11. The Lord says, "Edom has sinned again and again, and I will not forget it. I will not leave him unpunished any more. For he chased his brother, Israel, with the sword; he was pitiless in unrelenting anger."

Mic 2:1. Woe to you who lie awake at night, plotting wickedness; you rise at dawn to carry out your schemes; because you can, you do.

Zech 8:17. "Don't plot harm to others; don't swear that something is true when it isn't! How I hate all that sort of thing!" says the Lord. Zech 7:10.

Mt 5:38. The law of Moses says, "If a man

gouges out another's eye, he must pay with his own eye. If a tooth gets knocked out, knock out the tooth of the one who did it." [39]But I say: Don't resist violence! If you are slapped on one cheek, turn the other too. [40]If you are ordered to court, and your shirt is taken from you, give your coat too. [41]If the military demand that you carry their gear for a mile, carry it two. Lk 6:29.

Mt 6:15. But if *you* refuse to forgive *them, he* will not forgive *you.*

Mt 18:28. But when the man left the king, he went to a man who owed him $2,000 and grabbed him by the throat and demanded instant payment. [29]The man fell down before him and begged him to give him a little time. "Be patient and I will pay it," he pled. [30]But his creditor wouldn't wait. He had the man arrested and jailed until the debt would be paid in full. [31]Then the man's friends went to the king and told him what had happened. [32]And the king called before him the man he had forgiven and said, "You evil-hearted wretch! Here I forgave you all that tremendous debt, just because you asked me to— [33]shouldn't you have mercy on others, just as I had mercy on you?" [34]Then the angry king sent the man to the torture chamber until he had paid every last penny due. [35]So shall my heavenly Father do to you if you refuse to truly forgive your brothers.

Mt 26:52. "Put away your sword," Jesus told him. "Those using swords will get killed."

Mk 15:10. For he realized by now that this was a frameup, backed by the chief priests because they envied Jesus' popularity.

Jn 8:44. For you are the children of your father the devil and you love to do the evil things he does. He was a murderer from the beginning and a hater of truth—there is not an iota of truth in him. When he lies, it is perfectly normal; for he is the father of liars.

Jn 18:22. One of the soldiers standing there struck Jesus with his fist. "Is that the way to answer the High Priest?" he demanded. [23]"If I lied, prove it," Jesus replied. "Should you hit a man for telling the truth?"

Acts 23:12, 13. The next morning some forty or more of the Jews got together and bound themselves by a curse neither to eat nor drink until they had killed Paul! [14]Then they went to the chief priests and elders and told them what they had done.

Acts 28:19. But when the Jews protested the decision, I felt it necessary, with no malice against them, to appeal to Caesar.

Rom 1:29. Their lives became full of every kind of wickedness and sin, of greed and hate, envy, murder, fighting, lying, bitterness and gossip. [30]They were backbiters, haters of God, insolent, proud braggarts, always thinking of new ways of sinning and continually being disobedient to their parents. [31]They tried to misunderstand, broke their promises, and were heartless—without pity. [32]They were fully aware of God's death penalty for these crimes, yet they went right ahead and did them anyway, and encouraged others to do them, too.

Rom 12:19. Dear friends, never avenge yourselves. Leave that to God, for he has said that he will repay those who deserve it.

1 Cor 5:8. So let us feast upon him and grow strong in the Christian life, leaving entirely behind us the cancerous old life with all its hatreds and wickedness. Let us feast instead upon the pure bread of honor and sincerity and truth.

1 Cor 14:20. Dear brothers, don't be childish in your understanding of these things. Be innocent babies when it comes to planning evil, but be men of intelligence in understanding matters of this kind.

Gal 5:19. But when you follow your own wrong inclinations your lives will produce these evil results: impure thoughts, eagerness for lustful pleasure, [20]idolatry, spiritism (that is, encouraging the activity of demons), hatred and fighting, jealousy and anger, constant effort to get the best for yourself, complaints and criticisms, the feeling that everyone else is wrong except those in your own little group—and there will be wrong doctrine, [21]envy, murder, drunkenness, wild parties, and all that sort of thing. Let me tell you again as I have before, that anyone living that sort of life will not inherit the kingdom of God.

Eph 4:31. Stop being mean, bad-tempered and angry. Quarreling, harsh words, and dislike of others should have no place in your lives.

Phil 1:15. Some, of course, are preaching the Good News because they are jealous of the way God has used me. They want reputations as fearless preachers! But others have purer motives, [16, 17]preaching because they love me, for they know that the Lord has brought me here to defend the Truth. And some preach to make me jealous, thinking that their success will add to my sorrows here in jail!

Col 3:8. But now is the time to cast off and throw away all these rotten garments of anger, hatred, cursing, and dirty language.

1 Thess 5:15. See that no one pays back evil for evil.

Tit 3:3. Once we, too . . . were full of resentment and envy. We hated others and they hated us.

Jas 1:21. So get rid of all that is wrong in your life, both inside and outside, and humbly be glad for the wonderful message we have received, for it is able to save our souls as it takes hold of our hearts.

Jas 2:13. For there will be no mercy to those who have shown no mercy.

1 Pet 2:1. So get rid of your feelings of hatred. Don't just pretend to be good! Be done with dishonesty and jealousy and talking about others behind their backs.

1 Pet 3:9. Don't repay evil for evil. Don't snap back at those who say unkind things about you.

1 Jn 2:9. Anyone who says he is walking in the light of Christ but dislikes his fellow man, is still in darkness. [11]For he who dislikes his brother is wandering in spiritual darkness and doesn't know

where he is going, for the darkness had made him blind so that he cannot see the way.

1 Jn 3:10. So now we can tell who is a child of God and who belongs to Satan. Whoever is living a life of sin and doesn't love his brother shows that he is not in God's family. [13]So don't be surprised, dear friends, if the world hates you. [14]. . . But a person who doesn't have love for others is headed for eternal death. [15]Anyone who hates his Christian brother is really a murderer at heart; and you know that no one wanting to murder has eternal life within.

1 Jn 4:20. If anyone says "I love God," but keeps on hating his brother, he is a liar; for if he doesn't love his brother who is right there in front of him, how can he love God whom he has never seen?

3 Jn 1:10. When I come I will tell you some of the things he is doing and what wicked things he is saying about me and what insulting language he is using. He not only refuses to welcome the missionary travelers himself, but tells others not to, and when they do he tries to put them out of the church.

See *Conspiracy; Hatred; Homicide; Jealousy; Revenge; Wicked.*

INSTANCES OF. Cain toward Abel, Gen 4:8. Ishmael toward Sarah, Gen 21:9. Sarah toward Hagar, Gen 21:10. Philistines toward Isaac, Gen 26. Esau toward Jacob, Gen 27:41. Joseph's brothers toward Joseph, Gen 37; 42:21. Potiphar's wife toward Joseph, Gen 39:14–20. Ammonites toward the Israelites, Deut 23:3, 4. Saul toward David, 1 Sam 18:8–29; 19; 20:30–33; 22:6–18; 23:7–23; 26:17, 18. David toward Michal, 2 Sam 6:21–23; toward Joab, 1 Kgs 2:5, 6; Shime-i, 1 Kgs 2:8, 9. Shime-i toward David, 2 Sam 16:5–8. Ahithophel toward David, 2 Sam 17:1–3. Jezebel toward Elijah, 1 Kgs 19:1, 2. Ahaziah toward Elijah, 2 Kgs 1. Jehoram toward Elisha, 2 Kgs 6:31. Samaritans toward the Jews, Ezra 4; Neh 2:10; 4; 6. Haman toward Mordecai, Esther 3:5–15; 5:9–14. Jeremiah's enemies, Jer 26:7–11; 38. Nebuchadnezzar toward Zedekiah, Jer 52:10, 11. Daniel's enemies, Dan 6: 4–9. Herodias toward John, Mt 14:3–10; Mk 6:24–28. Herod toward Jesus, Lk 23:11. The Jews toward Jesus, Mt 27:18; Mk 12:12; 15:10; Lk 11:53, 54. James and John toward the Samaritans, Lk 9:54. Jews toward Paul, Acts 17:5; 23:12, 13; 25:3. Masters of the fortune-teller toward Paul, Acts 16:19–24.

MALINGERING INSTANCE OF. David feigning madness, 1 Sam 21:13–15.

MALLOTHI Son of Heman, a singer, 1 Chron 25:4, 5, 9–31.

MALLUCH 1. A Merarite Levite, 1 Chron 6: 44–47.

2. Son of Bani, who divorced his Gentile wife after the captivity, Ezra 10:29.

3. One of the family of Harim, who also divorced his Gentile wife after the captivity, Ezra 10:31, 32.

4. A priest who signed the covenant with Nehemiah, Neh 10:1–8.

5. A leader of the people who signed the covenant with Nehemiah, Neh 10:14–27.

6. A priest who accompanied Zerubbabel, Neh 12:1–7.

MALLUCHI A priest, Neh 12:12–21.

MALTA An island on the Mediterranean. Paul shipwrecked on the coast of, Acts 28:1–10.

MAMMON Wealth, Lk 16:9–13.

See *Money; Rich; Riches.*

MAMRE 1. A plain near Hebron. Abraham lives in, Gen 13:18; 14:13. Entertains three angels, and is promised a son, Gen 18:1–15. Isaac lives in, Gen 35:27.

2. An Amorite and ally of Abraham, Gen 14:13, 24.

MAN INDEX OF SUB-TOPICS. *Created; Created in the Image of God; Design of the Creation of; Dominion of; Duty of; Equality of; Ignorance of; Immortal; Insignificance of; Little Lower than the Angels; Mortal; Spirit; State of, after the Fall; State of, before the Fall; Young Men.*

CREATED. Gen 1:26. Then God said, "Let us make a man—someone like ourselves, to be the master of all life upon the earth and in the skies and in the seas." [27]So God made man like his Maker. Like God did God make man; man and maid did he make them.

Gen 2:7. The time came when the Lord God formed a man's body from the dust of the ground and breathed into it the breath of life. And man became a living person.

Gen 5:1. Here is a list of some of the descendants of Adam—the man who was like God from the day of his creation. [2]God created man and woman and blessed them, and called them Man from the start.

Deut 4:32. In all history, going back to the time when God created man upon the earth, search from one end of the heavens to the other to see if you can find anything like this.

Job 4:17. Is mere man more just than God? More pure than his Creator?

Job 10:2. I will say to God, "Don't just condemn me—tell me *why* you are doing it. [3]Does it really seem right to you to oppress and despise me, a man you have made; and to send joy and prosperity to the wicked? [8]You have made me, and yet you destroy me. [9]Oh, please remember that I'm made of dust—will you change me back again to dust so soon?"

Job 31:15. For God made me, and made my servant too. He created us both.

Job 33:4. For the Spirit of God has made me, and the breath of the Almighty gives me life.

Job 34:19. For he doesn't care how great a man may be, and doesn't pay any more attention to the rich than to the poor. He made them all.

Job 35:10. Yet none of them cry to God, asking, "Where is God my Maker who gives songs in the night."

Ps 8:5. And yet you have made him only a little lower than the angels, and placed a crown of glory and honor upon his head.

Ps 100:3. Try to realize what this means—the Lord is God! He made us—we are his people, the sheep of his pasture.

Ps 119:73. You made my body, Lord; now give me sense to heed your laws.

Ps 138:8. The Lord will work out his plans for my life—for your lovingkindness, Lord, continues forever. Don't abandon me—for you made me.

Ps 139:14. Thank you for making me so wonderfully complex! It is amazing to think about. Your workmanship is marvelous—and how well I know it.

Eccl 7:29. And I found that though God has made men upright, each has turned away to follow his own downward road.

Isa 17:7. Then at last they will think of God their Creator and have respect for the Holy One of Israel.

Isa 42:5. The Lord God who created the heavens and stretched them out and created the earth and everything in it, and gives life and breath and spirit to everyone in all the world.

Isa 43:7. All who claim me as their God will come, for I have made them for my glory; I created them.

Isa 45:12. I have made the earth and created man upon it. With my hands I have stretched out the heavens and commanded all the vast myriads of stars.

Isa 64:8. And yet, O Lord, you are our Father. We are the clay and you are the Potter. We are all formed by your hand.

Jer 27:5. By my great power I have made the earth and all mankind and every animal; and I give these things of mine to anyone I want to.

Zech 12:1. This is the fate of Israel as pronounced by the Lord, who stretched out the heavens and laid the foundation of the earth, and formed the spirit of man within him.

Mal 2:10. We are children of the same father, Abraham, all created by the same God.

Mk 10:6. For from the very first he made man and woman.

Heb 2:7. For though you made him lower than the angels for a little while, now you have crowned him with glory and honor. [8]And you have put him in complete charge of everything there is. Nothing is left out.

See *Man, Created in the Image of God,* below.

CREATED IN THE IMAGE OF GOD. Gen 1:26. Then God said, "Let us make a man—someone like ourselves, to be the master of all life upon the earth and in the skies and in the seas." [27]So God made man like his Maker. Like God did God make man; man and maid did he make them.

Gen 9:6. And any man who murders shall be killed; for to kill a man is to kill one made like God.

Eccl 7:29. And I found that though God has made men upright, each has turned away to follow his own downward road.

1 Cor 11:7. But a man should not wear anything on his head (when worshiping, for his hat is a sign of subjection to men). God's glory is man made in his image, and man's glory is the woman.

1 Cor 15:48. Every human being has a body just like Adam's, made of dust, but all who become Christ's will have the same kind of body as his—a body from heaven. [49]Just as each of us now has a body like Adam's, so we shall some day have a body like Christ's.

Jas 3:9. Sometimes it praises our heavenly Father, and sometimes it breaks out into curses against men who are made like God.

DESIGN OF THE CREATION OF. Ps 8:6. You have put him in charge of everything you made; everything is put under his authority; [7]all sheep and oxen, and wild animals too, [8]the birds and fish, and all the life in the sea.

Prov 16:4. The Lord has made everything for his own purposes—even the wicked, for punishment.

Isa 43:7. All who claim me as their God will come, for I have made them for my glory; I created them.

DOMINION OF. Gen 1:26. Then God said, "Let us make a man—someone like ourselves, to be the master of all life upon the earth and in the skies and in the seas." [28]And God blessed them and told them, "Multiply and fill the earth and subdue it; you are masters of the fish and birds and all the animals."

Gen 2:19, 20. So the Lord God formed from the soil every kind of animal and bird, and brought them to the man to see what he would call them; and whatever he called them, that was their name. But still there was no proper helper for the man.

Gen 9:2, 3. "All wild animals and birds and fish will be afraid of you," God told him; "for I have placed them in your power, and they are yours to use for food, in addition to grain and vegetables."

Jer 27:6. So now I have given all your countries to King Nebuchadnezzar of Babylon, who is my deputy. And I have handed over to him all your cattle for his use. Jer 28:14.

Dan 2:38. You rule the farthest provinces, and even animals and birds are under your control, as God decreed.

Heb 2:7. For though you made him lower than the angels for a little while, now you have crowned him with glory and honor. [8]And you have put him in complete charge of everything there is. Nothing is left out.

DUTY OF. See *Duty; Neighbor.*

EQUALITY OF. Job 31:13. If I have been unfair to my servants, [14]how could I face God? What could I say when he questioned me about it? [15]For God made me, and made my servant too. He created us both.

Ps 33:13–15. The Lord gazes down upon mankind from heaven where he lives. He has made their hearts and closely watches everything they do.

Prov 22:2. The rich and the poor are alike before the Lord who made them all.

Mt 20:25. But Jesus called them together and said, "Among the heathen, kings are tyrants and each minor official lords it over those beneath him. [26]But among you it is quite different. Anyone wanting to be a leader among you must be your servant. [27]And if you want to be right at the top, you must serve like a slave. [28]Your attitude must be like my own, for I, the Messiah, did not come to be served, but to serve, and to give my life as a ransom for many."

Mt 23:8. Don't ever let anyone call you that. For only God is your Rabbi and all of you are on the same level, as brothers. [11]The more lowly your service to others, the greater you are. To be the greatest, be a servant.

Mk 10:42. So Jesus called them to him and said, "As you know, the kings and great men of the earth lord it over the people; [43]but among you it is different. Whoever wants to be great among you must be your servant. [44]And whoever wants to be the greatest of all must be the slave of all.

Acts 10:28. Peter told them, "You know it is against the Jewish laws for me to come into a Gentile home like this. But God has shown me in a vision that I should never think of anyone as inferior."

Acts 17:26. He created all the people of the world from one man, Adam, and scattered the nations across the face of the earth. He decided beforehand which should rise and fall, and when. He determined their boundaries.

Gal 3:28. We are no longer Jews or Greeks or slaves or free men or even merely men or women, but we are all the same—we are Christians; we are one in Christ Jesus.

See *Race, Unity of.*

IGNORANCE OF. See *Ignorance.*

IMMORTAL. See *Immortality.*

INSIGNIFICANCE OF. Job 4:18, 19. If God cannot trust his own messengers (for even angels make mistakes), how much less men made of dust, who are crushed to death as easily as moths!

Job 15:14. What man in all the earth can be as pure and righteous as you claim to be?

Job 22:2. Is mere man of any worth to God? Even the wisest is of value only to himself! [3]Is it any pleasure to the Almighty if you are righteous? Would it be any gain to him if you were perfect? [4]Is it because you are good that he is punishing you? [5]Not at all! It is because of your wickedness! Your sins are endless!

Job 25:4. How can mere man stand before God and claim to be righteous? Who in all the earth can boast that he is clean? [5]God is so glorious that even the moon and stars are less than nothing as compared to him. [6]How much less is man, who is but a worm in his sight?

Job 35:2, 3. Do you think it is right for you to claim, "I haven't sinned, but I'm no better off before God than if I had"? [4]I will answer you, and all your friends too. [5]Look up there into the sky, high above you. [6]If you sin, does that shake the heavens and knock God from his throne? Even if you sin again and again, what effect will it have upon him? [7]Or if you are good, is this some great gift to him? [8]Your sins may hurt another man, or your good deeds may profit him.

Job 38:4. Where were you when I laid the foundations of the earth? Tell me, if you know so much. [12]Have you ever once commanded the morning to appear, and caused the dawn to rise in the east? [13]Have you ever told the daylight to spread to the ends of the earth, to end the night's wickedness?

Ps 8:3. When I look up into the night skies and see the work of your fingers—the moon and the stars you have made— [4]I cannot understand how you can bother with mere puny man, to pay any attention to him!

Ps 144:3. O Lord, what is man that you even notice him? Why bother at all with the human race? [4]For man is but a breath; his days are like a passing shadow.

LITTLE LOWER THAN THE ANGELS. Job 4:18, 19. If God cannot trust his own messengers (for even angels make mistakes), how much less men made of dust, who are crushed to death as easily as moths! [20]They are alive in the morning, but by evening they are dead, gone forever with hardly a thought from anyone. [21]Their candle of life is snuffed out. They die and no one cares.

Ps 8:5. And yet you have made him only a little lower than the angels, and placed a crown of glory and honor upon his head.

Heb 2:7. "For though you made him lower than the angels for a little while, now you have crowned him with glory and honor. [8]And you have put him in complete charge of everything there is. Nothing is left out." We have not yet seen all of this take place.

MORTAL. Job 4:17. Is mere man more just than God? More pure than his Creator?

Eccl 2:14. For the wise man sees, while the fool is blind. And yet I noticed that there was one thing that happened to wise and foolish alike— [15]Just as the fool will die, so will I. So of what value is all my wisdom? Then I realized that even wisdom is futile.

Eccl 3:20. All go to one place—the dust from which they came and to which they must return.

Isa 40:6. Shout that man is like the grass that dies away, and all his beauty fades like drying flowers.

Jer 17:5. The Lord says: Cursed is the man who puts his trust in mortal man and turns his heart away from God.

1 Cor 15:21. Death came into the world because of what one man (Adam) did, and it is because of what this other man (Christ) has done that now there is the resurrection from the dead. Rom 5:12.

Heb 9:27. And just as it is destined that men die only once, and after that comes judgment.

1 Pet 1:24. Yes, our natural lives will fade as grass does when it becomes all brown and dry.

See *Death.*

SPIRIT. Job 4:19. How much less men made of dust, who are crushed to death as easily as moths!

Job 32:8, 9. It is the spirit in a man, the breath of the Almighty which makes him intelligent.

Ps 31:5. Into your hand I commit my spirit. You have rescued me, O God who keeps his promises.

Prov 20:27. A man's conscience is the Lord's searchlight exposing his hidden motives.

Eccl 1:8. No matter how much we see, we are never satisfied; no matter how much we hear, we are not content.

Eccl 3:21. For who can prove that the spirit of man goes upward and the spirit of animals goes downward into dust?

Eccl 12:7. And the dust returns to the earth as it was, and the spirit returns to God who gave it.

Zech 12:1. This is the fate of Israel, as pronounced by the Lord, who stretched out the heavens and laid the foundation of the earth, and formed the spirit of man within him.

Mt 4:4. But Jesus told him, "No! For the Scriptures tell us that bread won't feed men's souls: obedience to every word of God is what we need."

Mt 10:28. Don't be afraid of those who can kill only your bodies—but can't touch your souls! Fear only God who can destroy both soul and body in hell.

Mt 26:41. For the spirit indeed is willing, but how weak the body is! Mk 14:38; Lk 22:40.

Lk 23:46. Then Jesus shouted, "Father, I commit my spirit to you," and with those words he died.

Lk 24:39. For ghosts don't have bodies, as you see that I do!

Jn 3:3. Jesus replied, "With all the earnestness I possess I tell you this: Unless you are born again, you can never get into the Kingdom of God." [4]"Born again!" exclaimed Nicodemus. "What do you mean? How can an old man go back into his mother's womb and be born again?" [5]Jesus replied, "What I am telling you so earnestly is this: Unless one is born of water and the Spirit, he cannot enter the Kingdom of God. [6]Men can only reproduce human life, but the Holy Spirit gives new life from heaven; [7]so don't be surprised at my statement that you must be born again! [8]Just as you can hear the wind but can't tell where it comes from or where it will go next, so it is with the Spirit. We do not know on whom he will next bestow this life from heaven."

Jn 4:24. Is our worship spiritual and real? Do we have the Holy Spirit's help? For God is Spirit, and we must have his help to worship as we should.

Acts 7:59. And as the murderous stones came hurtling at him, Stephen prayed, "Lord Jesus, receive my spirit."

Rom 2:29. No, a real Jew is anyone whose heart is right with God. For God is not looking for those who cut their bodies in actual body circumcision, but he is looking for those with changed hearts and minds. Whoever has that kind of change in his life will get his praise from God, even if not from you.

Rom 7:14. The law is good, then, and the trouble is not there but with *me,* because I am sold into slavery with Sin as my owner. [15]I don't understand myself at all, for I really want to do what is right, but I can't. I do what I don't want to—what I hate. [16]I know perfectly well that what I am doing is wrong, and my bad conscience proves that I agree with these laws I am breaking. [17]But I can't help myself, because I'm no longer doing it. It is sin inside me that is stronger than I am that makes me do these evil things. [18]I know I am rotten through and through so far as my old sinful nature is concerned. No matter which way I turn I can't make myself do right. I want to but I can't. [19]When I want to do good, I don't; and when I try not to do wrong, I do it anyway. [20]Now if I am doing what I don't want to, it is plain where the trouble is: sin still has me in its evil grasp. [21]It seems to be a fact of life that when I want to do what is right, I inevitably do what is wrong. [22]I love to do God's will so far as my new nature is concerned; [23-25]but there is something else deep within me, in my lower nature, that is at war with my mind and wins the fight and makes me a slave to the sin that is still within me. In my mind I want to be God's willing servant but instead I find myself still enslaved to sin. So you see how it is: my new life tells me to do right, but the old nature that is still inside me loves to sin. Oh, what a terrible predicament I'm in! Who will free me from my slavery to this deadly lower nature? Thank God! It has been done by Jesus Christ our Lord. He has set me free.

1 Cor 2:11. No one can really know what anyone else is thinking, or what he is really like, except that person himself. And no one can know God's thoughts except God's own Spirit.

1 Cor 6:20. For God has bought you with a great price. So use every part of your body to give glory back to God, because he owns it.

1 Cor 14:14. For if I pray in a language I don't understand, my spirit is praying but I don't know what I am saying.

2 Cor 4:6. For God, who said, "Let there be light in the darkness," has made us understand that it is the brightness of his glory that is seen in the face of Jesus Christ. [7]But this precious treasure—this light and power that now shine within us—is held in a perishable container, that is, our weak bodies. [16]That is why we never give up. Though our bodies are dying, our inner strength in the Lord is growing every day.

2 Cor 5:1. For we know that when this tent we live in now is taken down—when we die and leave these bodies—we will have wonderful new bodies in heaven, homes that will be ours forevermore, made for us by God himself, and not by human hands. [2]How weary we grow of our present bodies. That is why we look forward eagerly to the day when we shall have heavenly bodies which we shall put on like new clothes. [3]For we shall not be merely spirits without bodies. [4]These earthly bodies make us groan and sigh, but we wouldn't like to think of dying and having no bodies at all. We want to slip into our new bodies so that these dying bodies will, as it were, be swallowed up by everlasting life. [5]This is what God has prepared for us and, as a guarantee, he has given us his Holy Spirit. [6]Now we look forward with confidence to our heavenly bodies, realizing that every moment we spend in these earthly bodies is time spent away from our eternal home in heaven with Jesus. [7]We know these things are true by believing, not by seeing. [8]And we

are not afraid, but are quite content to die, for then we will be at home with the Lord. 9So our aim is to please him always in everything we do, whether we are here in this body or away from this body and with him in heaven.

Eph 3:16. That out of his glorious, unlimited resources he will give you the mighty inner strengthening of his Holy Spirit.

Eph 4:4. We are all parts of one body, we have the same Spirit, and we have all been called to the same glorious future.

1 Thess 5:23. May the God of peace himself make you entirely pure and devoted to God; and may your spirit and soul and body be kept strong and blameless until that day when our Lord Jesus Christ comes back again.

Heb 4:12. For whatever God says to us is full of living power; it is sharper than the sharpest dagger, cutting swift and deep into our innermost thoughts and desires with all their parts, exposing us for what we really are.

Jas 2:26. Just as the body is dead when there is no spirit in it, so faith is dead if it is not the kind that results in good deeds.

STATE OF, AFTER THE FALL. See *Depravity.*

STATE OF, BEFORE THE FALL. See above, *Created in the Image of God.*

YOUNG MEN. See *Young Men.*

MAN OF REBELLION The son of hell who is to be revealed after the One who now restrains evil is taken out of the way, 2 Thess 2:3–8. He is usually identified with the wicked king of Dan 7:24, 25; the angry king of Dan 8:23–25; the Antichrist of 1 Jn 2:18; the first beast of Rev 13:1–10. cf. Jn 5:43. See *Antichrist.*

MAN WHO LIVES IN TERROR, THE A symbolical name given by Jeremiah to Pashhur, Jer 20:3–6.

MANAEN Herod's foster brother and a Christian teacher, Acts 13:1.

MANAHATH 1. Son of Shobal, Gen 36:23; 1 Chron 1:40.

2. A city in Benjamin, 1 Chron 8:6, 7.

MANASSEH 1. Son of Joseph and Asenath, Gen 41:50, 51; 46:19–22; adopted by Jacob on his deathbed, Gen 48:1, 5–20.

2. Tribe of. Descendants of Joseph. The two sons of Joseph, Ephraim and Manasseh, were counted among the primogenitors of the twelve tribes, taking the places of Joseph and Levi.

Adopted by Jacob, Gen 48:5. Prophecy concerning, Gen 49:25, 26. Census of, Num 1:20–46; 26:28–37. Place of, in camp and march, Num 2:3–31; 10:22, 23. Blessing of Moses on, Deut 33:13–17. Inheritance of one-half of tribe east of Jordan, Num 32:33, 39–42. One-half of tribe west of Jordan, Josh 16:9; 17:5–11. The eastern half assist in the conquest of the country west of the Jordan, Deut 3:18–20; Josh 1:12–15; 4:12, 13. Join the other eastern tribes in erecting a monument to testify to the unity of all Israel; misunderstood; make satisfactory explanation, Josh 22. Join Gideon in war with the Midianites, Judg 6; 7. Malcontents of, join David, 1 Chron 12:19, 24–37. Conquered by Hazael, 2 Kgs 10:32, 33. Return from captivity, 1 Chron 9:3. Reallotment of territory to, by Ezekiel, Ezk 48:4. Affiliate with the Jews in the reign of Hezekiah, 2 Chron 30. Incorporated into kingdom of Judah, 2 Chron 15:9; 34:6, 7.

See *Israel, Tribes of.*

3. King of Judah. History of, 2 Kgs 21:1–18; 2 Chron 33:1–21.

4. Two Jews who divorced their Gentile wives after the captivity, Ezra 10:30, 33.

MANDRAKE Gen 30:14–16; Song 7:13.

MANEH A weight, Ezk 45:12.

See *Weights.*

MANGER Lk 2:7, 12, 16. Rendered stall, Lk 13:15.

MANNA Ex 16:4–35; Num 11:6–10; Deut 8:3, 16; Josh 5:11, 12; Neh 9:20; Ps 78:24; Jn 6:30, 31, 48–51, 58. Preserved in the Ark, Ex 16:33; Heb 9:4.

FIGURATIVE. Jn 6:48–51; Rev 2:17.

MANNERS Social customs. Courtesy to strangers, Gen 18:2; 19:1. Standing while guests eat, Gen 18:8; in presence of superiors, Gen 31:35; Job 29:8. Courteousness enjoined, Lev 19:32; 1 Pet 3:8. Rules for guests, Prov 23:1–3; 1 Cor 10:27.

See *Greetings.*

MANOAH A Danite of Zorah and father of Samson, Judg 13:2–24.

MANSIONS Isa 32:14; Amos 3:15.

MANSLAUGHTER See *Fratricide; Homicide; Regicide.*

MANURE 1 Kgs 14:10; 2 Kgs 9:36; Jer 9:22. Used as fuel, Ezk 4:12–15. In famine, 2 Kgs 6:25; 18:27. In prophecy, Mal 2:3. Dung gate, Neh 2:13; 3:13, 14; 12:31, 32.

See *Fertilizer.*

MAON A city allotted to Judah, Josh 15:48–62. Home of Nabal, 1 Sam 25:2. David with his insurgents camps near, 1 Sam 23:24, 25. Uzziah engages in war against the people of, called *Meunites,* 2 Chron 26:7.

MARAH The first stop of the Israelites, where Moses made the bitter waters sweet, Ex 15:22–25; Num 33:8, 9.

MARBLE In the Temple, 1 Chron 29:2. Pillars of, Esther 1:6; Song 5:15. Merchandise of, Rev 18:12. Mosaics of, Esther 1:6.

MARCH See *Calendar.*

MARDUK A Babylonian god, Jer 50:2.

MAREAL A place on the boundary of Zebulun, Josh 19:11.

MARESHAH 1. A city of Judah, Josh 15:37–44; 2 Chron 11:5–10; 14:9, 10. Birthplace of Eliezer the prophet, 2 Chron 20:37. Prophecy concerning, Mic 1:15.

2. Father of Hebron, 1 Chron 2:42.

3. A son of, or possibly a city founded by, Laadah, 1 Chron 4:21, 22.

MARK Or *John Mark.* A relative of Barnabas, Col 4:10. A disciple of Jesus, Acts 12:12, 25; 13:5. Paul and Barnabas contend concerning, Acts 15:36–39. A convert of Peter, 1 Pet 5:13. Fellow-worker with Paul at Rome, Col 4:10, 11; 2 Tim 4: 11; Philemon 1:24.

MARKET A place for general merchandise. Held at gates, see *Gates.* Judgment seat at, Acts 16: 19. Traffic of, in Tyre, consisted of slaves, horses, mules, bronze dishes, ivory, and ebony, emeralds, dyes, embroidery, linen, coral, agate, honey, balm, wine, wool, oil, yarn, wrought iron, cassia, calamus, saddlecloths, lambs, rams, goats, precious stones, and gold, spices, fabrics and carpets, Ezk 27:13–25.

See *Gates.*

MAROTH A city of Judah, Mic 1:12.

MARRIAGE Consanguineous, Abraham and Sarah, Gen 11:29; 12:11–13; 20:3, 9–16. Isaac and Rebekah, Gen 24:3, 4, 67; 28:2. Jacob and his wives, Gen 29:15–30; see below, in the elaborated text. Levirate (the brother required to marry a brother's widow), Gen 38:8, 11; Deut 25:5–10; Ruth 4:5; Mt 22:24; Mk 12:19–23; Lk 20:28.

Parents contract for their children: Hagar selects a wife for Ishmael, Gen 21:20, 21; Abraham for Isaac, Gen 24; Laban arranges for his daughters' marriage, Gen 29; Samson asks his parents to procure him a wife, Judg 14:2, 3. Parents' consent required in the Mosaic law, Ex 22:17. Presents given to parents to secure their favor, Gen 24:53; 34:12; Deut 22:28, 29; 1 Sam 18:25; Hos 3:2. Nuptial parties, Gen 29:22; Judg 14:10, 11; Esther 2:18; Mt 22:11, 12. Jesus present at, Jn 2:1–5. Ceremony attested by witnesses, Ruth 4:1–11; Isa 8:1–3. Bridegroom exempt one year from military duty, Deut 24:5. Bridal ornaments, Isa 49:18; 61:10; Jer 2:32. Bridal presents, Gen 24:53; Ps 45:12. Herald preceded the bridegroom, Mt 25:6.

Wives obtained by purchase, Gen 29:20; Ruth 4: 10; Hos 3:2; 12:12; by kidnapping, Judg 21:21–23. Given by kings, 1 Sam 17:25; 18:17, 21. Daughters given in, as rewards of valor, Judg 1:12; 1 Sam 17: 25; 18:27.

Wives taken by edict, Esther 2:2–4; 8–14. David gave 100 Philistine lives for a wife, 2 Sam 3:14.

Wives among the Israelites must be Israelites, Ex 34:16; Deut 7:3, 4; 1 Chron 23:22; Ezra 9:1, 2, 12; Neh 10:30; 13:26, 27; Mal 2:11; 1 Cor 7:39. Engagement a quasi-marriage, Mt 1:18; Lk 1:27. Engagement made with the spirit, Ezk 16:8. Celibacy deplored, Judg 11:38; Isa 4:1; Jer 16:9; advised, 1 Cor 7:7, 8, 24–40.

Obligations under, secondary to duty to God, Deut 13:6–10; Mt 19:29; Lk 14:26.

Not binding after death, Mt 22:29, 30; Mk 12:24, 25; Rom 7:2.

See *Bride; Bridegroom.*

UNCLASSIFIED SCRIPTURES RELATING TO. Gen 2:23. "This is it!" Adam exclaimed. "She is part of my own bone and flesh! Her name is 'woman' because she was taken out of a man." [24]This explains why a man leaves his father and mother and is joined to his wife in such a way that the two become one person. 1 Cor 6:16; Eph 5:31.

Ex 22:16. If a man seduces a girl who is not engaged to anyone, and sleeps with her, he must pay the usual dowry and accept her as his wife. [17]But if her father utterly refuses to let her marry him, then he shall pay the money anyway.

Lev 18:6. None of you shall marry a near relative, for I am the Lord. [7]A girl may not marry her father; nor a son his mother, [8]nor any other of his father's wives, [Deut 22:20] [9]nor his sister or half-sister, whether the daughter of his father or his mother, whether born in the same house or elsewhere. [10]You shall not marry your granddaughter—the daughter of either your son or your daughter—for she is a close relative. [11]You may not marry a half-sister—your father's wife's daughter; [12]nor your aunt—your father's sister—because she is so closely related to your father; [13]nor your aunt—your mother's sister—because she is a close relative of your mother; [14]nor your aunt—the wife of your father's brother. [15]You may not marry your daughter-in-law—your son's wife; [16]nor your brother's wife, for she is your brother's. [17]You may not marry both a woman and her daughter or granddaughter, for they are near relatives, and to do so is horrible wickedness. [18]You shall not marry two sisters, for they will be rivals. However, if your wife dies, then it is all right to marry her sister.

Lev 20:14. If a man has sexual intercourse with a woman and with her mother, it is a great evil. All three shall be burned alive to wipe out wickedness from among you. [17]If a man has sexual intercourse with his sister, whether the daughter of his father or of his mother, it is a shameful thing, and they shall publicly be cut off from the people of Israel. He shall bear his guilt. [19]Sexual intercourse is outlawed between a man and his maiden aunt—whether the sister of his mother or of his father—for they are near of kin; they shall bear their guilt. [20]If a man has intercourse with his uncle's widow, he has taken what belongs to his uncle; their punishment is that they shall bear their sin and die childless. [21]If a man marries his brother's widow, this is impurity; for he has taken what belongs to his brother, and they shall be childless.

Lev 21:7. A priest shall not marry a prostitute, nor a woman of another tribe, and he shall not marry a divorced woman, for he is a holy man of God. [13]He must marry a virgin. [14, 15]He may not marry a widow, nor a woman who is divorced, nor a prostitute. She must be a virgin from his own tribe, for he must not be the father of children of mixed blood—half priestly and half ordinary.

Num 36:8. The girls throughout the tribes of Israel who are heiresses must marry within their own tribe, so that their land won't leave the tribe.

Deut 21:10. When you go to war and the Lord your God delivers your enemies to you, [11]and you see among the captives a beautiful girl you want as your wife, [12]take her home with you. She must shave her head and pare her nails [13]and change her clothing, laying aside that which she was wearing when she was captured, then remain in your home in mourning for her father and mother for a full month. After that you may marry her. [14]However, if after marrying her you decide you don't like her, you must let her go free—you may not sell her or treat her as a slave, for you have humiliated her.

Deut 24:1. If a man doesn't like something about his wife, he may write a letter stating that he has divorced her, give her the letter, and send her away. [2]If she then remarries, [3]and the second husband also divorces her, or dies, [4]the former husband may not marry her again, for she has been defiled; this would bring guilt upon the land the Lord your God is giving you. [5]A newly married man is not to be drafted into the army nor given any other special responsibilities; for a year he shall be free to be at home, happy with his wife.

Prov 18:22. The man who finds a wife finds a good thing; she is a blessing to him from the Lord.

Prov 21:9. It is better to live in the corner of an attic than with a crabby woman in a lovely home. [19]Better to live in the desert than with a quarrelsome, complaining woman.

Jer 29:6. Marry and have children, and then find mates for them and have many grandchildren. Multiply! Don't dwindle away!

Hos 2:19. And I will bind you to me forever with chains of righteousness and justice and love and mercy. [20]I will betroth you to me in faithfulness and love, and you will really know me then as you never have before.

Mal 2:13. Yet you cover the altar with your tears because the Lord doesn't pay attention to your offerings anymore, and you receive no blessing from him. [14]"Why has God abandoned us?" you cry. I'll tell you why; it is because the Lord has seen your treachery in divorcing your wives who have been faithful to you through the years, the companions you promised to care for and keep. [15]You were united to your wife by the Lord. In God's wise plan, when you married, the two of you became one person in his sight. And what does he want? Godly children from your union. Therefore guard your passions! Keep faith with the wife of your youth. [16]For the Lord, the God of Israel, says he hates divorce and cruel men. Therefore control your passions—let there be no divorcing of your wives.

Mt 5:31. The law of Moses says, "If anyone wants to be rid of his wife, he can divorce her merely by giving her a letter of dismissal." [32]But I say that a man who divorces his wife, except for fornication, causes her to commit adultery if she marries again. And he who marries her commits adultery.

Mk 6:17, 18. For Herod had sent soldiers to arrest and imprison John because he kept saying it was wrong for the king to marry Herodias, his brother Philip's wife.

Mk 10:2. Some Pharisees came and asked him, "Do you permit divorce?" Of course they were trying to trap him. [3]"What did Moses say about divorce?" Jesus asked them. [4]"He said it was all right," they replied. "He said that all a man has to do is write his wife a letter of dismissal." [5]"And why did he say that?" Jesus asked. "I'll tell you why—it was a concession to your hardhearted wickedness. [6, 7]But it certainly isn't God's way. For from the very first he made man and woman to be joined together permanently in marriage; therefore a man is to leave his father and mother, [8]and he and his wife are united so that they are no longer two, but one. [9]And no man may separate what God has joined together." [10]Later, when he was alone with his disciples in the house, they brought up the subject again. [11]He told them, "When a man divorces his wife to marry someone else, he commits adultery against her. [12]And if a wife divorces her husband and remarries, she, too, commits adultery." Mt 19:2–9.

Lk 16:18. So anyone who divorces his wife and marries someone else commits adultery, and anyone who marries a divorced woman commits adultery.

Rom 7:1. Don't you understand yet, dear Jewish brothers in Christ, that when a person dies the law no longer holds him in its power? [2]Let me illustrate: when a woman marries, the law binds her to her husband as long as he is alive. But if he dies, she is no longer bound to him; the laws of marriage no longer apply to her. [3]Then she can marry someone else if she wants to. That would be wrong while he was alive, but it is perfectly all right after he dies.

1 Cor 7:1. Now about those questions you asked in your last letter: my answer is that if you do not marry, it is good. [2]But usually it is best to be married, each man having his own wife, and each woman having her own husband, because otherwise you might fall back into sin. [3]The man should give his wife all that is her right as a married woman, and the wife should do the same for her husband: [4]for a girl who marries no longer has full right to her own body, for her husband then has his rights to it, too; and in the same way the husband no longer has full right to his own body, for it belongs also to his wife. [5]So do not refuse these rights to each other. The only exception to this rule would be the agreement of both husband and wife to refrain from the rights of marriage for a limited time, so that they can give themselves more completely to prayer. Afterwards, they should come together again so that Satan won't be able to tempt them because of their lack of self-control. [6]I'm not saying you *must* marry; but you certainly *may* if you wish. [7]I wish everyone could get along without marrying, just as I do. But we are not all the same. God gives some the gift of a husband or wife, and others he gives the gift of being able to stay happily unmarried. [8]So I say to those who aren't married, and to widows—better to stay unmarried if you can, just as I am. [9]But if you can't control yourselves, go ahead and marry. It is better to marry than to burn with lust. [10]Now, for those who are married I have a command, not just a suggestion. And it is not a command from me, for this is what the Lord himself has said: A wife must not leave her husband. [11]But if she is separated from him, let her remain single or else go back to him. And the husband must not divorce his wife. [12]Here I want

to add some suggestions of my own. These are not direct commands from the Lord, but they seem right to me: If a Christian has a wife who is not a Christian, but she wants to stay with him anyway, he must not leave her or divorce her. [13]And if a Christian woman has a husband who isn't a Christian, and he wants her to stay with him, she must not leave him. [14]For perhaps the husband who isn't a Christian may become a Christian with the help of his Christian wife. And the wife who isn't a Christian may become a Christian with the help of her Christian husband. Otherwise, if the family separates, the children might never come to know the Lord; whereas a united family may, in God's plan, result in the children's salvation. [15]But if the husband or wife who isn't a Christian is eager to leave, it is permitted. In such cases the Christian husband or wife should not insist that the other stay, for God wants his children to live in peace and harmony. [16]For, after all, there is no assurance to you wives that your husbands will be converted if they stay; and the same may be said to you husbands concerning your wives. [17]But be sure in deciding these matters that you are living as God intended, marrying in accordance with God's direction and help, and accepting whatever situation God has put you into. This is my rule for all the churches. [18]For instance, a man who already has gone through the Jewish ceremony of circumcision before he became a Christian shouldn't worry about it; and if he hasn't been circumcised, he shouldn't do it now. [19]For it doesn't make any difference at all whether a Christian has gone through this ceremony or not. But it makes a lot of difference whether he is pleasing God and keeping God's commandments. That is the important thing. [20]Usually a person should keep on with the work he was doing when God called him. [21]Are you a slave? Don't let that worry you—but of course, if you get a chance to be free, take it. [22]If the Lord calls you, and you are a slave, remember that Christ has set you free from the awful power of sin; and if he has called you and you are free, remember that you are now a slave of Christ. [23]You have been bought and paid for by Christ, so you belong to him—be free now from all these earthly prides and fears. [24]So, dear brothers, whatever situation a person is in when he becomes a Christian, let him stay there, for now the Lord is there to help him. [25]Now I will try to answer your other question. What about girls who are not yet married? Should they be permitted to do so? In answer to this question, I have no special command for them from the Lord. But the Lord in his kindness has given me wisdom that can be trusted, and I will be glad to tell you what I think. [26]Here is the problem: We Christians are facing great dangers to our lives at present. In times like these I think it is best for a person to remain unmarried. [27]Of course, if you already are married, don't separate because of this. But if you aren't, don't rush into it at this time. [28]But if you men decide to go ahead anyway and get married now, it is all right; and if a girl gets married in times like these, it is no sin. However, marriage will bring extra problems that I wish you didn't have to face right now. [29]The important thing to remember is that our remaining time is very short, (and so are our opportunities for doing the Lord's work). For that reason those who have wives should stay as free as possible for the Lord; [30]happiness or sadness or wealth should not keep anyone from doing God's work. [31]Those in frequent contact with the exciting things the world offers should make good use of their opportunities without stopping to enjoy them; for the world in its present form will soon be gone. [32]In all you do, I want you to be free from worry. An unmarried man can spend his time doing the Lord's work and thinking how to please him. [33]But a married man can't do that so well; he has to think about his earthly responsibilities and how to please his wife. [34]His interests are divided. It is the same with a girl who marries. She faces the same problem. A girl who is not married is anxious to please the Lord in all she is and does. But a married woman must consider other things such as housekeeping and the likes and dislikes of her husband. [35]I am saying this to help you, not to try to keep you from marrying. I want you to do whatever will help you serve the Lord best, with as few other things as possible to distract your attention from him. [36]But if anyone feels he ought to marry because he has trouble controlling his passions, it is all right, it is not a sin; let him marry. [37]But if a man has the willpower not to marry and decides that he doesn't need to and won't, he has made a wise decision. [38]So the person who marries does well, and the person who doesn't marry does even better. [39]The wife is part of her husband as long as he lives; if her husband dies, then she may marry again, but only if she marries a Christian. [40]But in my opinion she will be happier if she doesn't marry again; and I think I am giving you counsel from God's Spirit when I say this.

1 Cor 9:5. If I had a wife, and if she were a believer, couldn't I bring her along on these trips just as the other disciples do, and as the Lord's brothers do, and as Peter does?

1 Cor 11:11. For remember that in God's plan men and women need each other. [12]For although the first woman came out of man, all men have been born from women ever since, and both men and women come from God their Creator.

1 Tim 3:2. For a pastor must be a good man whose life cannot be spoken against. He must have only one wife. [12]Deacons should have only one wife and they should have happy, obedient families.

1 Tim 4:1. But the Holy Spirit tells us clearly that in the last times some in the church will turn away from Christ and become eager followers of teachers with devil-inspired ideas. [3]They will say it is wrong to be married.

1 Tim 5:14. So I think it is better for these young widows to marry again and have children, and take care of their own homes; then no one will be able to say anything against them.

Heb 13:4. Honor your marriage and its vows, and

be pure; for God will surely punish all those who are immoral or commit adultery.

FIGURATIVE. Isa 54:5; 62:4, 5; Jer 31:32; Hos 1:2; 2:19, 20; Eph 5:29–32; Rev 19:7–9. Parables from, Mt 22:1, 2; 25:1–10.

See *Divorce; Husband; Wife.*

MARS HILL A hill in Athens, Acts 17:19–34.

MARSH HEN Forbidden as food, Lev 11:13–19.

MARTHA Sister of Mary and Lazarus, Jn 11:1, 2. Ministers to Jesus, Lk 10:38–42; Jn 12:2. Beloved by Jesus, Jn 11:5.

See *Lazarus; Mary, 4.*

MARTYRDOM Ps 44:22. But that is not our case. For we are facing death threats constantly because of serving you! We are like sheep awaiting slaughter. Rom 8:36.

Mt 10:21. Brother shall betray brother to death, and fathers shall betray their own children. And children shall rise against their parents and cause their deaths. [22]Everyone shall hate you because you belong to me. But all of you who endure to the end shall be saved. [Mk 13:12; Lk 21:16, 17.] [39]If you cling to your life, you will lose it; but if you give it up for me, you will save it. Mt 16:25; Jn 12:25.

Mt 23:34. I will send you prophets, and wise men, and inspired writers, and you will kill some by crucifixion, and rip open the backs of others with whips in your synagogues, and hound them from city to city, [Lk 11:50] [35]so that you will become guilty of all the blood of murdered godly men from righteous Abel to Zechariah (son of Barachiah), slain by you in the Temple between the altar and the sanctuary.

Mt 24:9. Then you will be tortured and killed and hated all over the world because you are mine.

Lk 9:24. Whoever loses his life for my sake will save it, but whoever insists on keeping his life will lose it. Jn 12:25.

1 Cor 13:3. If I gave everything I have to poor people, and if I were burned alive for preaching the Gospel but didn't love others, it would be of no value whatever.

Rev 6:9. And when he broke open the fifth seal, I saw an altar, and underneath it all the souls of those who had been martyred for preaching the Word of God and for being faithful in their witnessing. [10]They called loudly to the Lord and said, "O Sovereign Lord, holy and true, how long will it be before you judge the people of the earth for what they've done to us? When will you avenge our blood against those living on the earth?" [11]White robes were given to each of them, and they were told to rest a little longer until their other brothers, fellow servants of Jesus, had been martyred on the earth and joined them.

Rev 11:7. When they complete the three and a half years of their solemn testimony, the tyrant who comes out of the bottomless pit will declare war against them and conquer and kill them; [8, 9]and for three and a half days their bodies will be exposed in the streets of Jerusalem (the city fittingly described as "Sodom" or "Egypt")—the very place where their Lord was crucified. No one will be allowed to bury them, and people from many nations will crowd around to gaze at them. [10]And there will be a worldwide holiday—people everywhere will rejoice and give presents to each other and throw parties to celebrate the death of the two prophets who had tormented them so much! [11]But after three and a half days, the spirit of life from God will enter them and they will stand up! And great fear will fall on everyone. [12]Then a loud voice will shout from heaven, "Come up!" And they will rise to heaven in a cloud as their enemies watch.

Rev 12:11. They defeated him by the blood of the Lamb, and by their testimony; for they did not love their lives but laid them down for him.

Rev 16:6. For your saints and prophets have been martyred and their blood poured out upon the earth; and now, in turn, you have poured out the blood of those who murdered them; it is their just reward.

Rev 17:6. I could see that she was drunk—drunk with the blood of the martyrs of Jesus she had killed. I stared at her in horror. Rev 18:24.

See *Persecution.*

INSTANCES OF. Abel, Gen 4:3–8. Prophets killed by Jezebel, 1 Kgs 18:3, 4, 13. Zechariah, 2 Chron 24:21, 22. John the Baptist, Mk 6:17–28. Jesus, see *Jesus.* Stephen, Acts 7:58–60. James, the apostle, Acts 12:2. The prophets, Mt 22:6; 23:35; Rom 11:2, 3; 1 Thess 2:15; Heb 11:32–38. Antipas, Rev 2:13.

MARY 1. The mother of Jesus, Mt 1:16; Lk 1:26–38; 2:5–19. Visits her cousin Elizabeth, Lk 1:39–56. Attends the feast at Jerusalem with her husband and her son, starts on the return, misses Jesus, looks and finds him in the temple, Lk 2:41–51. Is present with Jesus at a marriage in Cana of Galilee, Jn 2:1–10. Looks for Jesus when he is teaching in a house, Mt 12:46, 47; Mk 3:31, 32; Lk 8:19. Present at the cross, Jn 19:25–27. Is committed to the care of John, Jn 19:27. Lives with the disciples in Jerusalem, Acts 1:14. Prophecies concerning, Isa 7:14; Lk 2:34, 35.

2. Magdalene. Possessed by demons, delivered by Jesus, Mk 16:9; Lk 8:2. Present at the crucifixion, Mt 27:56; Mk 15:40; Jn 19:25; at the tomb, Mt 27:61; 28:1–7; Mk 15:47; 16:1–7; Lk 23:55, 56; 24:1–7; Jn 20:1, 11–13. Recognizes Jesus after the resurrection, Mt 28:8–10; Mk 16:9; Jn 20:14–18.

3. Mary the wife of Cleophas, Jn 19:25, thought by some to be the sister of Mary, the mother of Jesus. Mother of James and Joses, Mt 27:56; Mk 15:40. At the tomb, Mt 27:61; 28:1; Mk 15:47. Assists in preparing the body of Jesus for burial, Mk 16:1. A witness of the resurrection, Lk 24:10.

4. Sister of Lazarus. Sits at Jesus' feet for instruction, Lk 10:38–42. Beloved of Jesus, Jn 11:5. Anoints Jesus, Mt 26:7–13; Mk 14:3–9; Jn 11:1, 2; 12:3.

5. Mother of Mark and related to Barnabas, Acts 12:12; Col 4:10.

6. A Christian woman in Rome, Rom 16:6.

MASH Son of Aram, Gen 10:23.

MASHAL Called also *Mishal.* A Levitical city in Asher, Josh 19:24–26; 21:30, 31; 1 Chron 6: 74.

MASHING By Tamar, Gen 38:14.

MASON A trade in the time of David, 2 Sam 5:11; of later times, 2 Kgs 12:11, 12; 22:5, 6; 1 Chron 14:1; Ezra 3:7.

MASREKAH A city in Edom, Gen 36:31–39; 1 Chron 1:47.

MASSA Son of Ishmael, Gen 25:12–15; 1 Chron 1:28–31.

MASSACRE Authorized by Moses, Deut 20:13, 16. Decree to destroy the Jews, Esther 3.

INSTANCES OF. Inhabitants of Heshbon, Deut 2:34; of Bashan, Deut 3:6; of Ai, Josh 8:24–26; of Hazor, Josh 11:11, 12; of the cities of the seven kings, Josh 10:28–40; of Jerusalem, Judg 1:7; of Zephath, Judg 1:17; of Luz, Judg 1:25. Midianites, Num 31:7, 8. Prophets of Baal, 1 Kgs 18:40. Worshipers of Baal, 2 Kgs 10:18–28. Sons of Ahab, 2 Kgs 10:1–8. Descendants of Athaliah, 2 Kgs 11:1. Edomites, 2 Kgs 14:7. Inhabitants of Tappuah, 2 Kgs 15:16.

See *Captive.*

MASSAH A camping place of the Israelites, Ex 17:7.

See *Meribah, 1.*

MASTER Jesus called, Mt 10:25; 23:7, 10; 26: 18, 49; Mk 14:45; Lk 8:24; Jn 9:2; 11:8; 13:13; 20:16. Jesus prohibited the appellation, Mt 23:7, 8. John called, Jn 3:26.

SCRIPTURES RELATING TO MASTERS OF SERVANTS. Ex 21:20. If a man beats his slave to death—whether the slave is male or female—that man shall surely be punished. [21]However, if the slave does not die for a couple of days, then the man shall not be punished—for the slave is his property. [26]If a man hits his slave in the eye, whether man or woman, and the eye is blinded, then the slave shall go free because of his eye. [27]And if a master knocks out his slave's tooth, he shall let him go free to pay for the tooth.

Lev 19:13. You shall not rob nor oppress anyone, and you shall pay your hired workers promptly. If something is due them, don't even keep it overnight.

Lev 25:42. So you may not be sold as ordinary slaves, [43]or treated harshly; fear your God.

Deut 5:14. But the seventh day is the Sabbath of the Lord your God; no work shall be done that day by you or by any of your household—your sons, daughters, servants, oxen, donkeys, or cattle; even foreigners living among you must obey this law. Everybody must rest as you do.

Deut 24:14, 15. Never oppress a poor hired man, whether a fellow Israelite or a foreigner living in your town. Pay him his wage each day before sunset, for since he is poor he needs it right away; otherwise he may cry out to the Lord against you and it would be counted as a sin against you. Lev 19:13.

Job 31:13. If I have been unfair to my servants, [14]how could I face God? What could I say when he questioned me about it? [15]For God made me, and made my servant too. He created us both.

Prov 22:16. He who gains by oppressing the poor or by bribing the rich shall end in poverty.

Prov 29:12. A wicked ruler will have wicked aides on his staff. [21]Pamper a servant from childhood, and he will expect you to treat him as a son!

Jer 22:13. And woe to you, King Jehoiakim, for you are building your great palace with forced labor. By not paying wages you are building injustice into its walls and oppression into its doorframes and ceilings.

Mal 3:5. At that time my punishments will be quick and certain; I will move swiftly against . . . all those who cheat their hired hands.

Rom 4:4. But didn't he earn his right to heaven by all the good things he did? No, for being saved is a gift.

Eph 6:9. And you slave owners must treat your slaves right, just as I have told them to treat you. Don't keep threatening them; remember, you yourselves are slaves to Christ; you have the same Master they do, and he has no favorites.

Col 4:1. You slave owners must be just and fair to all your slaves. Always remember that you, too, have a Master in heaven who is closely watching you.

1 Tim 5:18. For the Scriptures say, "Never tie up the mouth of an ox when it is treading out the grain —let him eat as he goes along!" And in another place, "Those who work deserve their pay!"

Philemon 1:10. My plea is that you show kindness to my child Onesimus, whom I won to the Lord while here in my chains. [11]Onesimus (whose name means "Useful") hasn't been of much use to you in the past, but now he is going to be of real use to both of us. [12]I am sending him back to you, and with him comes my own heart. [13]I really wanted to keep him here with me while I am in these chains for preaching the Good News, and you would have been helping me through him, [14]but I didn't want to do it without your consent. I didn't want you to be kind because you had to but because you wanted to. [15]Perhaps you could think of it this way: that he ran away from you for a little while so that now he can be yours forever, [16]no longer only a slave, but something much better—a beloved brother, especially to me. Now he will mean much more to you too, because he is not only a servant but also your brother in Christ.

Jas 5:4. For listen! Hear the cries of the field workers whom you have cheated of their pay. Their cries have reached the ears of the Lord of Hosts.

See *Servant.*

GOOD.

Instances of. Abraham, Gen 18:19; Job 31:13–15; the Roman captain, Lk 7:2.

UNJUST.

Instances of. Sarah to Hagar, Gen 16:6. Laban to Jacob, Gen 31:7; Potiphar's wife to Joseph, Gen 39: 7–20.

See *Employer.*

MASTER WORKMAN Prov 8:30.

INSTANCES OF. Tubal-cain, Gen 4:22; Bezalel, Ex 31:2–11; 35:30–35; Hiram, or Huramabi, 1 Kgs 7:13–50; 2 Chron 2:13, 14; 4:11–18.

See *Art.*

MATATTAH One of the family of Hashum, Ezra 10:33.

MATRED Mother of Mehetabel, Gen 36:31–39; 1 Chron 1:50.

MATRI A Benjaminite, 1 Sam 10:21.

MATTAN 1. A priest of Baal killed in the idol temple at Jerusalem, 2 Kgs 11:18; 2 Chron 23:15–17.

2. Father of Shephatiah, Jer 38:1.

MATTANAH A camping place of Israel, Num 21:17, 18.

MATTANIAH 1. Original name of Zedekiah, king of Judah, 2 Kgs 24:17.

See *Zedekiah.*

2. A Levite, descendant of Asaph, 1 Chron 9:15, 16; Neh 11:15–17, 22, 23; 12:8, 35, 36.

3. A Levite of the sons of Asaph, 2 Chron 20:14.

4. Son of Heman, who had charge of the ninth division of musicians, 1 Chron 25:4, 9–31.

5. Descendant of Asaph, who assisted in purifying the Temple, 2 Chron 29:12–14.

6. Four Israelites who put away their Gentile wives after the captivity, Ezra 10:26, 27, 30, 34–42.

7. A gatekeeper, Neh 12:25.

8. A Levite, father of Zaccur, Neh 13:13.

MATTATHA An ancestor of Jesus, Lk 3:23–38.

MATTATHIAS Two ancestors of Jesus, Lk 3:23–38.

MATTENAI 1. Two Israelites who divorced their Gentile wives after the captivity, Ezra 10:33, 34–42.

2. A priest in the time of Joiakim, Neh 12:12–21.

MATTHAN An ancestor of Jesus, Mt 1:15.

MATTHAT 1. Father of Heli, and ancestor of Joseph, Lk 3:23–38.

2. Father of Jorim, and ancestor of Joseph, Lk 3:23–38.

MATTHEW Called also *Levi.* A tax collector. Becomes a disciple of Jesus, Mt 9:9, 10; 10:2–4; Mk 2:14, 15; 3:16–19; Lk 5:27–29; 6:14–16; Acts 1:14.

MATTHIAS Chosen as an apostle in the place of Judas, Acts 1:15–26.

MATTITHIAH 1. A Levite who had charge of the baked offerings, 1 Chron 9:31.

2. A Levite musician, 1 Chron 15:18, 21; 16:5.

3. A chief of the fourteenth division of Temple musicians, 1 Chron 25:3, 21.

4. An Israelite who divorced his Gentile wife after the captivity, Ezra 10:43.

5. One who stood by Ezra when he read the law to the people, Neh 8:1–5.

MAY See *Calendar.*

MAYOR Acts 19:35.

MEAL See *Eating; Food.*

MEASURE DRY. See *Bushel; Ephah; Homer; Omer.*

LIQUID. See *Bath.*

LINEAR. See *Cubit.*

See *Weights.*

MUST BE JUST. Lev 19:35, 36. You must be impartial in judgment. Use accurate measurements—lengths, weights, and volumes—and give full measure, for I am Jehovah your God who brought you from the land of Egypt.

Deut 25:13–15. In all your transactions you must use accurate scales and honest measurements, so that you will have a long, good life in the land the Lord your God is giving you. [16]All who cheat with unjust weights and measurements are detestable to the Lord your God.

Prov 11:1. The Lord hates cheating and delights in honesty.

Prov 16:11. The Lord demands fairness in every business deal. He established this principle.

Prov 20:10. The Lord despises every kind of cheating. [23]The Lord loathes all cheating and dishonesty.

Hos 12:7. But no, my people are like crafty merchants selling from dishonest scales—they love to cheat. [8]Ephraim boasts, "I am so rich! I have gotten it all by myself!" But riches can't make up for sin. [9]I am the same Lord, the same God, who delivered you from slavery in Egypt, and I am the one who will consign you to living in tents again, as you do each year at the Tabernacle Feast.

Mic 6:10. For your sins are very great—is there to be no end of getting rich by cheating? The homes of the wicked are full of ungodly treasures and lying scales. [11]Shall I say "Good!" to all your merchants with their bags of false, deceitful weights? How could God be just while saying that? [12]Your rich men are wealthy through extortion and violence; your citizens are so used to lying that their tongues can't tell the truth!

Dishonest measures used, Amos 3:5.

See *Dishonesty; Integrity.*

MEAT OFFERING See *Offerings, Meat.*

MEBUNNAI One of David's guards, 2 Sam 23:24–39.

MECONAH A city of Judah, Neh 11:25–30.

MEDAD One of the seventy elders who did not go to the tabernacle with Moses, but prophesied in the camp, Num 11:26–29.

MEDAN Son of Abraham and Keturah, Gen 25:1, 2; 1 Chron 1:32.

MEDDLING See *Busybody; Gossip.*

MEDEBA A city of Moab, Num 21:27–30; Isa 15:2. Allotted to Reuben, Josh 13:9, 16. David defeats army and the Ammonites at, 1 Chron 19:7–15.

MEDES Inhabitants of Media. Israelites distributed among, when taken captive to Assyria, 2 Kgs 17:6; 18:11. Palace in the Babylonian province of, Ezra 6:2. An essential part of the Medo-Persian empire, Esther 1:1–19. Supremacy of, in the Chaldean empire, Dan 5:28, 31; 9:1; 11:1.

MEDIA See *Medes.*

MEDIA-PERSIA See *Persia.*

MEDIATION See *Intercession; Jesus, Mediation of.*

MEDIATOR One who reconciles persons at variance with one another, 1 Sam 20:23; Job 9:32,

33; Acts 7:38; Gal 3:19, 20; 1 Tim 2:5.

MEDICINE Prov 17:22. A cheerful heart does good like medicine, but a broken spirit makes one sick.

Isa 1:6. From head to foot you are sick and weak and faint, covered with bruises and welts and infected wounds, unanointed and unbound.

Isa 38:21. For Isaiah had told Hezekiah's servants, "Make an ointment of figs and spread it over the boil, and he will get well again."

Jer 8:22. Is there no medicine in Gilead? Is there no physician there? Why doesn't God do something? Why doesn't he help?

Jer 30:13. There is no one to help you or to bind up your wound and no medicine does any good.

Jer 46:11. Go up to Gilead for medicine, O virgin daughter of Egypt! Yet there is no cure for your wounds. Though you have used many medicines, there is no healing for you.

Jer 51:8. But now, suddenly Babylon too has fallen. Weep for her; give her medicine; perhaps she can yet be healed. [9]We would help her if we could, but nothing can save her now. Let her go. Abandon her and return to your own land, for God is judging her from heaven.

Ezk 47:12. All kinds of fruit trees will grow along the river banks. The leaves will never turn brown and fall, and there will always be fruit. There will be a new crop every month—without fail! For they are watered by the river flowing from the Temple. The fruit will be for food and the leaves for medicine.

Lk 10:34. Kneeling beside him the Samaritan soothed his wounds with medicine and bandaged them. Then he put the man on his donkey and walked along beside him till they came to an inn, where he nursed him through the night.

Rev 22:2. On each side of the river grew Trees of Life, bearing twelve crops of fruit, with a fresh crop each month; the leaves were used for medicine to heal the nations.

See *Disease; Physician.*

MEDITATION Josh 1:8. Constantly remind the people about these laws, and you yourself must think about them every day and every night so that you will be sure to obey all of them. For only then will you succeed. Deut 32:46.

Ps 1:2. But they delight in doing everything God wants them to, and day and night are always meditating on his laws and thinking about ways to follow him more closely.

Ps 4:4. Stand before the Lord in awe, and do not sin against him. Lie quietly upon your bed in silent meditation.

Ps 19:14. May my spoken words and unspoken thoughts be pleasing even to you, O Lord my Rock and my Redeemer.

Ps 39:2, 3. But as I stood there silently the turmoil within me grew to the bursting point. The more I mused, the hotter the fires inside. Then at last I spoke, and pled with God.

Ps 42:6. But I will meditate upon your kindness to this lovely land where the Jordan River flows and where Mount Hermon and Mount Mizar stand.

Ps 48:9. Lord, here in your Temple we meditate upon your kindness and your love. Ps 27:4.

Ps 63:5. At last I shall be fully satisfied; I will praise you with great joy. [6]I lie awake at night thinking of you.

Ps 73:12. "Look at these men of arrogance; they never have to lift a finger—theirs is a life of ease; and all the time their riches multiply." [13]Have I been wasting my time? Why take the trouble to be pure? [14]All I get out of it is trouble and woe—every day and all day long! [15]If I had really said that, I would have been a traitor to your people. [16]Yet it is so hard to explain it—this prosperity of those who hate the Lord. [17]Then one day I went into God's sanctuary to meditate, and thought about the future of these evil men. [18]What a slippery path they are on—suddenly God will send them sliding over the edge of the cliff and down to their destruction: [19]an instant end to all their happiness, an eternity of terror. [20]Their present life is only a dream! They will awaken to the truth as one awakens from a dream of things that never really were! [21]When I saw this, what turmoil filled my heart! [22]I saw myself so stupid and so ignorant; I must seem like an animal to you, O God.

Ps 77:10. And I said: This is my fate, that the blessings of God have changed to hate. [11]I recall the many miracles he did for me so long ago. [12]Those wonderful deeds are constantly in my thoughts. I cannot stop thinking about them.

Ps 104:34. May he be pleased by all these thoughts about him, for he is the source of all my joy.

Ps 119:11. I have thought much about your words, and stored them in my heart so that they would hold me back from sin. [15]I will meditate upon them and give them my full respect. [16]I will delight in them and not forget them. [23]For even princes sit and talk against me, but I will continue in your plans. [48]"Come, come to me," I call to them, for I love them and will let them fill my life. [55]I obey them even at night and keep my thoughts, O Lord, on you. [59, 60]I thought about the wrong direction in which I was headed, and turned around and came running back to you. [78]Let the proud be disgraced, for they have cut me down with all their lies. But I will concentrate my thoughts upon your laws. [97]Oh, how I love them. I think about them all day long. [98]They make me wiser than my enemies, because they are my constant guide. [99]Yes, wiser than my teachers, for I am ever thinking of your rules. [148]I stay awake through the night to think about your promises.

Ps 139:17, 18. How precious it is, Lord, to realize that you are thinking about me constantly! I can't even count how many times a day your thoughts turn towards me. And when I waken in the morning, you are still thinking of me!

Ps 145:5. I will meditate about your glory, splendor, majesty, and miracles.

INSTANCE OF. Isaac, Gen 24:63.

MEDITERRANEAN SEA Num 13:29; 34:5–9; Ps 89:25; Ezk 47:10–20; Mk 11:22, 23. As a border of the lands of Israel, Num 34:6, 7, 8, 9; Deut 1:7; 11:24; 34:2; Josh 1:3, 4. Prophecy concerning boundary to be re-established for Israel, Joel 2:20; Zech 14:8.

MEDIUM See *Sorcery; Witchcraft.*

MEEKNESS Ps 25:9. He will teach the ways that are right and best to those who humbly turn to him.

Ps 37:11. But all who humble themselves before the Lord shall be given every blessing, and shall have wonderful peace.

Ps 76:8. You pronounce sentence on them from heaven; the earth trembles and stands silently before you. [9]You stand up to punish the evil-doers and to defend the meek of the earth.

Ps 147:6. The Lord supports the humble, but brings the wicked into the dust.

Ps 149:4. For Jehovah enjoys his people; he will save the humble.

Prov 11:2. Proud men end in shame, but the meek become wise.

Prov 15:1. A soft answer turns away wrath, but harsh words cause quarrels. [18]A quick-tempered man starts fights; a cool-tempered man tries to stop them.

Prov 16:32. It is better to be slow-tempered than famous; it is better to have self-control than to control an army.

Prov 17:1. A dry crust eaten in peace is better than steak every day along with argument and strife.

Prov 20:3. It is an honor for a man to stay out of a fight. Only fools insist on quarreling.

Prov 25:15. Be patient and you will finally win, for a soft tongue can break hard bones.

Prov 29:8. Wise men try to keep peace.

Eccl 7:8. Finishing is better than starting! Patience is better than pride!

Eccl 10:4. If the boss is angry with you, don't quit! A quiet spirit will quiet his bad temper.

Isa 29:19. The meek will be filled with fresh joy from the Lord, and the poor shall exult in the Holy One of Israel.

Lam 3:28. For it causes him to sit apart in silence beneath the Lord's demands, [29]to lie face downward in the dust; then at last there is hope for him. [30]Let him turn the other cheek to those who strike him, and accept their awful insults.

Amos 2:7. They trample the poor in the dust and kick aside the meek.

Zeph 2:3. Beg him to save you, all who are humble—all who have tried to obey. Walk humbly and do what is right; perhaps even yet the Lord will protect you from his wrath in that day of doom.

Mt 5:5. The meek and lowly are fortunate! for the whole wide world belongs to them. [9]Happy are those who strive for peace—they shall be called the sons of God. [38]The law of Moses says, 'If a man gouges out another's eye, he must pay with his own eye. If a tooth gets knocked out, knock out the tooth of the one who did it.' [39]But I say: Don't resist violence! If you are slapped on one cheek, turn the other too. [40]If you are ordered to court, and your shirt is taken from you, give your coat too. [Lk 6:29.] [41]If the military demand that you carry their gear for a mile, carry it two. [42]Give to those who ask, and don't turn away from those who want to borrow.

Mt 11:29. Wear my yoke—for it fits perfectly—and let me teach you; for I am gentle and humble, and you shall find rest for your souls.

Mt 27:13. "Don't you hear what they are saying?" Pilate demanded. [14]But Jesus said nothing, much to the governor's surprise.

Mk 9:50. Good salt is worthless if it loses its saltiness; it can't season anything. So don't lose your flavor! Live in peace with each other.

Rom 12:14. If someone mistreats you because you are a Christian, don't curse him; pray that God will bless him. [18]Don't quarrel with anyone. Be at peace with everyone, just as much as possible.

Rom 14:19. In this way aim for harmony in the church and try to build each other up.

1 Cor 6:7. To have such lawsuits at all is a real defeat for you as Christians. Why not just accept mistreatment and leave it at that? It would be far more honoring to the Lord to let yourselves be cheated.

1 Cor 7:15. But if the husband or wife who isn't a Christian is eager to leave, it is permitted. In such cases the Christian husband or wife should not insist that the other stay, for God wants his children to live in peace and harmony.

1 Cor 10:32. So don't be a stumbling block to anyone, whether they are Jews or Gentiles or Christians.

1 Cor 13:4. Love is very patient and kind, never jealous or envious, never boastful or proud, [5]never haughty or selfish or rude. Love does not demand its own way. It is not irritable or touchy. It does not hold grudges and will hardly even notice when others do it wrong. [7]If you love someone you will be loyal to him no matter what the cost. You will always believe in him, always expect the best of him, and always stand your ground in defending him.

2 Cor 10:1. I plead with you—yes, I, Paul—and I plead gently, as Christ himself would do. Yet some of you are saying, "Paul's letters are bold enough when he is far away, but when he gets here he will be afraid to raise his voice!"

2 Cor 13:11. Be happy. Grow in Christ. Pay attention to what I have said. Live in harmony and peace. And may the God of love and peace be with you.

Gal 5:22. But when the Holy Spirit controls our lives he will produce this kind of fruit in us: love, joy, peace, patience, kindness, goodness, faithfulness, [23]gentleness and self-control; and here there is no conflict with Jewish laws. [26]Then we won't need to look for honors and popularity, which lead to jealousy and hard feelings.

Gal 6:1. Dear brothers, if a Christian is overcome by some sin, you who are godly should gently and humbly help him back onto the right path, remembering that next time it might be one of you who is in the wrong.

Eph 4:1. I beg you—I, a prisoner here in jail for serving the Lord—to live and act in a way worthy of those who have been chosen for such wonderful blessings as these. [2]Be humble and gentle. Be patient with each other, making allowance for each other's faults because of your love.

Phil 2:14. In everything you do, stay away from complaining and arguing, [15]so that no one can speak a word of blame against you. You are to live clean, innocent lives as children of God in a dark world full of people who are crooked and stubborn. Shine out among them like beacon lights.

Col 3:12. Since you have been chosen by God who has given you this new kind of life, and because of his deep love and concern for you, you should practice tenderhearted mercy and kindness to others. Don't worry about making a good impression on them but be ready to suffer quietly and patiently. [13]Be gentle and ready to forgive; never hold grudges. Remember, the Lord forgave you, so you must forgive others.

1 Thess 5:14. Dear brothers . . . be patient with everyone. [15]See that no one pays back evil for evil, but always try to do good to each other and to everyone else.

2 Thess 3:5. May the Lord bring you into an ever deeper understanding of the love of God and of the patience that comes from Christ.

1 Tim 3:2. For a pastor must be a good man whose life cannot be spoken against. He must have only one wife, and he must be hard working and thoughtful, orderly, and full of good deeds. He must enjoy having guests in his home, and must be a good Bible teacher. [3]He must not be a drinker or quarrelsome, but he must be gentle and kind, and not be one who loves money.

1 Tim 6:11. Oh, Timothy, you are God's man. Run from all these evil things and work instead at what is right and good, learning to trust him and love others, and to be patient and gentle. [12]Fight on for God. Hold tightly to the eternal life which God has given you, and which you have confessed with such a ringing confession before many witnesses.

2 Tim 2:24. God's people must not be quarrelsome; they must be gentle, patient teachers of those who are wrong. [25]Be humble when you are trying to teach those who are mixed up concerning the truth. For if you talk meekly and courteously to them they are more likely, with God's help, to turn away from their wrong ideas and believe what is true.

Tit 2:2. Teach the older men to be serious and unruffled; they must be sensible, knowing and believing the truth and doing everything with love and patience. [9]Urge slaves to obey their masters and to try their best to satisfy them. They must not talk back.

Tit 3:2. They must not speak evil of anyone, nor quarrel, but be gentle and truly courteous to all.

Heb 10:36. You need to keep on patiently doing God's will if you want him to do for you all that he has promised.

Heb 12:14. Try to stay out of all quarrels and seek to live a clean and holy life.

Jas 1:4. For when your patience is finally in full bloom, then you will be ready for anything, strong in character, full and complete. [19]Dear brothers, don't ever forget that it is best to listen much, speak little, and not become angry. [21]So get rid of all that is wrong in your life, both inside and outside, and humbly be glad for the wonderful message we have received, for it is able to save our souls as it takes hold of our hearts.

Jas 3:13. If you are wise, live a life of steady goodness, so that only good deeds will pour forth. And if you don't brag about them, then you will be truly wise! [17]But the wisdom that comes from heaven is first of all pure and full of quiet gentleness. Then it is peace-loving and courteous. It allows discussion and is willing to yield to others; it is full of mercy and good deeds. It is wholehearted and straightforward and sincere. [18]And those who are peacemakers will plant seeds of peace and reap a harvest of goodness.

1 Pet 2:18. Servants, you must respect your masters and do whatever they tell you—not only if they are kind and reasonable, but even if they are tough and cruel. [19]Praise the Lord if you are punished for doing right! [20]Of course, you get no credit for being patient if you are beaten for doing wrong; but if you do right and suffer for it, and are patient beneath the blows, God is well pleased. [21]This suffering is all part of the work God has given you. Christ, who suffered for you, is your example. Follow in his steps: [22]He never sinned, never told a lie, [23]never answered back when insulted; when he suffered he did not threaten to get even; he left his case in the hands of God who always judges fairly.

1 Pet 3:4. Be beautiful inside, in your hearts, with the lasting charm of a gentle and quiet spirit which is so precious to God. [11]Turn away from evil and do good. Try to live in peace even if you must run after it to catch and hold it! [15]Quietly trust yourself to Christ your Lord and if anybody asks why you believe as you do, be ready to tell him, and do it in a gentle and respectful way. Ps 34:14.

2 Pet 1:5. But to obtain these gifts, you need more than faith; you must also work hard to be good, and even that is not enough. For then you must learn to know God better and discover what he wants you to do. [6]Next, learn to put aside your own desires so that you will become patient and godly, gladly letting God have his way with you. [7]This will make possible the next step, which is for you to enjoy other people and to like them, and finally you will grow to love them deeply.

Jude 1:9. Yet Michael, one of the mightiest of the angels, when he was arguing with Satan about Moses' body, did not dare to accuse even Satan, or jeer at him, but simply said, "The Lord rebuke you."

INSTANCES OF. Abraham, Gen 13:8. Isaac, Gen 26:20–22. Moses, Ex 2:13; 14:13, 14; 15:24; 16:

7–9; Num 12:3, 4; 16:4–12. Gideon, Judg 8:2, 3. Hannah, 1 Sam 1:12–16. Saul, 1 Sam 10:27. David, 1 Sam 17:29; 2 Sam 16:9–14; Ps 38:13, 14; 120:5–7. Paul, Acts 21:20–26; 1 Thess 2:7; 2 Tim 4:16. The Thessalonians, 2 Thess 1:4. Job, Jas 5:11. Michael, Jude 1:9. For the meekness of Jesus, see below.

See *Humility; Kindness; Patience.*

OF JESUS. Isa 42:1. See my Servant, whom I uphold; my Chosen One, in whom I delight. I have put my Spirit upon him; he will reveal justice to the nations of the world. [2]He will be gentle—he will not shout nor quarrel in the streets. [3]He will not break the bruised reed, nor quench the dimly burning flame. He will encourage the fainthearted, those tempted to despair. He will see full justice given to all who have been wronged. [4]He won't be satisfied until truth and righteousness prevail throughout the earth, nor until even distant lands beyond the seas have put their trust in him. Mt 12: 19, 20.

Isa 53:7. He was oppressed and he was afflicted, yet he never said a word. He was brought as a lamb to the slaughter; and as a sheep before her shearers is dumb, so he stood silent before the ones condemning him.

Mt 26:47. At that very moment while he was still speaking, Judas, one of the Twelve, arrived with a great crowd armed with swords and clubs, sent by the Jewish leaders. [48]Judas had told them to arrest the man he greeted, for that would be the one they were after. [49]So now Judas came straight to Jesus and said "Hello, Master!" and embraced him in friendly fashion. [50]Jesus said, "My friend, go ahead and do what you have come for." Then the others grabbed him. [51]One of the men with Jesus pulled out a sword and slashed off the ear of the High Priest's servant. [52]"Put away your sword," Jesus told him. "Those using swords will get killed. [53]Don't you realize that I could ask my Father for thousands of angels to protect us, and he would send them instantly? [54]But if I did, how would the Scriptures be fulfilled that describe what is happening now?"

Jn 12:15. Don't be afraid of your King, people of Israel, for he will come to you meekly, sitting on a donkey's colt! Zech 9:9.

See *Jesus, Humility of.*

MEGIDDO Called also *Megiddon,* and probably *Armageddon.* A city of Manasseh in Issachar, situated on the southern edge of the plain of Esdraelon, Josh 17:11; 1 Chron 7:29. Conquest of, by Joshua, Josh 12:8–24. Walled by Solomon, 1 Kgs 9:15; included in one of Solomon's commissary districts, 1 Kgs 4:8–19. Ahaziah dies at, 2 Kgs 9:27. Valley of, Deborah defeats Sisera in, Judg 5:19. Josiah killed at, by King Neco, 2 Kgs 23:29, 30; 2 Chron 35:22, 23. Prophecy concerning, Zech 12:11.

MEHETABEL 1. Wife of Hadad, Gen 36: 31–39; 1 Chron 1:50.

2. A person whose grandson tried to intimidate Nehemiah, Neh 6:10.

MEHIDA A person whose descendants returned from Babylon, Ezra 2:43–54; Neh 7:46–56.

MEHOLATH Home of Adriel, 1 Sam 18:19.

MEHUJAEL Son of Irad, Gen 4:18.

MEHUMAN A eunuch of Ahasuerus, Esther 1:10.

ME-JARKON A city in Dan, Josh 19:41–46.

MELATIAH A Gibeonite who assisted in repairing the wall of Jerusalem, Neh 3:7.

MELCHI 1. Ancestor of Jesus, Lk 3:23–38.

2. Remote ancestor of Jesus, Lk 3:23–38.

MELCHIZEDEK King of Salem, Gen 14: 18–20; Heb 7:1. A priest and type of Christ, Ps 110: 4; Heb 5:6, 10; 6:20; 7:1–21.

MELECH Son of Micah, 1 Chron 8:35; 9:41.

MELONS Num 11:4, 5; Prov 9:17.

MEMORIAL Passover, Ex 12:14. See *Passover.* Firstborn set apart as a, Ex 13:12–16. Pot of manna, Ex 16:32–34. Festival of tabernacles, Lev 23:43. Shoulder stones of the ephod, Ex 28:12.

Lord's supper, Lk 22:19; 1 Cor 11:24–26.

See *Pillar.*

MEMPHIS A celebrated city of Egypt, Hos 9:6. Prophecies concerning, Isa 19:13; Jer 2:16; 46: 14, 19; Ezk 30:16; against Jews in, Jer 44.

MEMUCAN One of the seven officers of Ahasuerus who counsels the king to divorce Queen Vashti, Esther 1:14–21.

MENAHEM King of Israel, 2 Kgs 15:13–22.

MENE Dan 5:24–26.

MENNA An ancestor of Jesus, Lk 3:23–38.

MENSES See *Menstruation.*

MENSTRUATION Law relating to, Lev 15: 19–30; 20:18; Ezk 18:6. Cessation of, in old age, Gen 18:11. Immunities of women during, Gen 31:35.

FIGURATIVE. Ezk 36:17.

MEONENIM A place in Ephraim, Judg 9: 37.

MEONOTHAI Father of Ophrah, 1 Chron 4:14.

MEPHA-ATH A Levitical city in Reuben, Josh 13:18; 21:36, 37; 1 Chron 6:78, 79; Jer 48:21.

MEPHIBOSHETH 1. Son of Saul by Rizpah, whom David surrendered to the Gibeonites to be killed, 2 Sam 21:8, 9.

2. Son of Jonathan, 2 Sam 4:4. Called *Merib-baal,* 1 Chron 8:34; 9:40. Was lame, 2 Sam 4:4. David cares for, 2 Sam 9:1–7; 21:7. Property restored to, 2 Sam 9:9–11. His ingratitude to David at the time of Absalom's usurpation, 2 Sam 16:1–3; 19: 24–30. Property of, confiscated, 2 Sam 16:4; 19:29, 30.

MERAB Daughter of King Saul, 1 Sam 14:49. Promised to David by Saul, 1 Sam 18:17, 18; but given to Adriel to be his wife, 1 Sam 18:19.

MERAIAH A priest, Neh 12:12–21.

MERAIOTH 1. A high priest of the line of Eleazar, 1 Chron 6:4–15, 50–53; Ezra 7:1–5. Probably identical with the priest of same name in 1 Chron 9:10, 11; Neh 11:10–14.

2. A priestly clan in the time of Joiakim, Neh 12: 15.

MERARI Son of Levi, Gen 46:8–14. Head of the Merarite Levites, Num 3:31–35.

See *Levites.*

MERATHAIM Probably a poetical name for Babylon, Jer 50:21.

MERCENARIES See *Soldiers.*

MERCHANDISE See *Commerce.*

MERCHANT Gen 37:28; 1 Kgs 10:28; 2 Kgs 12:11, 12; 2 Chron 9:13, 14; Neh 3:32; 13:20; Job 41:6; Prov 31:24; Song 3:6; Isa 23:2, 3; Ezk 17:3, 4; 27:13, 17, 21–36; 38:13; Hos 12:7; Amos 8:4; Nah 3:16; Mt 13:45; 21:12; Lk 20:2; Jn 2:14; Rev 18:3, 11, 23.

See *Commerce.*

MERCURIUS Mercury. Paul taken for, in Lystra, Acts 14:11, 12.

MERCY 2 Sam 22:26. You are merciful to the merciful; you show your perfections to the blameless.

Ps 18:25. Lord, how merciful you are to those who are merciful.

Ps 37:25. I have been young and now I am old. And in all my years I have never seen the Lord forsake a man who loves him; nor have I seen the children of the godly go hungry. [26]Instead, the godly are able to be generous with their gifts and loans to others, and their children are a blessing.

Ps 85:10. Mercy and truth have met together. Grim justice and peace have kissed!

Prov 3:3. Never forget to be truthful and kind. Hold these virtues tightly. Write them deep within your heart.

Prov 11:17. Your own soul is nourished when you are kind; it is destroyed when you are cruel.

Prov 12:10. A good man is concerned for the welfare of his animals, but even the kindness of godless men is cruel.

Prov 14:21. To despise the poor is to sin. Blessed are those who pity them. [22]Those who plot evil shall wander away and be lost, but those who plan good shall be granted mercy and quietness. [31]Anyone who oppresses the poor is insulting God who made them. To help the poor is to honor God.

Prov 16:6. Iniquity is atoned for by mercy and truth; evil is avoided by reverence for God.

Prov 20:28. If a king is kind, honest and fair, his kingdom stands secure.

Prov 21:21. The man who tries to be good, loving and kind finds life, righteousness and honor.

Hos 4:1. Hear the word of the Lord, O people of Israel. The Lord has filed a lawsuit against you listing the following charges: There is no faithfulness, no kindness, no knowledge of God in your land.

Hos 12:6. Oh, come back to God. Live by the principles of love and justice, and always be expecting much from him, your God.

Mic 6:8. No, he has told you what he wants, and this is all it is: *to be fair and just and merciful, and to walk humbly with your God.*

Mt 5:7. Happy are the kind and merciful, for they shall be shown mercy.

Mt 23:23. Yes, woe upon you, Pharisees, and you other religious leaders—hypocrites! For you tithe down to the last mint leaf in your garden, but ignore the important things—justice and mercy and faith. Yes, you should tithe, but you shouldn't leave the more important things undone. Mt 9:13; 12:7.

Lk 6:36. Try to show as much compassion as your Father does.

Rom 12:8. Those who offer comfort to the sorrowing should do so with Christian cheer.

Col 3:12. Since you have been chosen by God who has given you this new kind of life, and because of his deep love and concern for you, you should practice tenderhearted mercy and kindness to others. Don't worry about making a good impression on them but be ready to suffer quietly and patiently. [13]Be gentle and ready to forgive; never hold grudges. Remember, the Lord forgave you, so you must forgive others.

Jas 2:13. For there will be no mercy to those who have shown no mercy. But if you have been merciful, then God's mercy toward you will win out over his judgment against you. Mt 18:32–35.

Jude 1:22. Try to help those who argue against you. Be merciful to those who doubt. *v.* 23.

See *God, Mercy of; Kindness.*

INSTANCES OF. The jailor, to Joseph, Gen 39:21–23. Joshua to Rahab, Josh 6:25. The Israelites to the man of Bethel, Judg 1:23–26. David to Saul, 1 Sam 24:9–13, 17.

MERCY PLACE See *Mercy Seat.*

MERCY SEAT Description of, Ex 25:17–22. Placed on the ark of the testimony, Ex 26:34; 30:6; 31:7; 40:20; Heb 9:5. Materials of, to be a freewill offering, Ex 35:4–12. Made by Bezalel, Ex 37:1, 6–9.

Sprinkled with blood, Lev 16:14, 15. The presence of God on, Ex 25:22; 30:6; Lev 16: 1, 2; Num 7:89; 1 Sam 4:4; 2 Sam 6:1, 2; 2 Kgs 19:15; 1 Chron 13:6; Ps 80:1; Ps 99:1; Isa 37:16, 17; Heb 4:16.

In Solomon's temple, 1 Chron 28:11.

See *Tabernacle.*

MERED Son of Ezrah, 1 Chron 4:17, 18.

MEREMOTH 1. A priest who was appointed to weigh and register gold and silver brought to Jerusalem, Ezra 8:33; Neh 3:4, 21.

2. A Jew who divorced his Gentile wife after the captivity, Ezra 10:34–42.

3. A priest who signed the covenant with Nehemiah, Neh 10:1–8; 12:1–7.

MERES One of the officials of Persia, Esther 1:13–15.

MERIBAH 1. A place in Rephidim, where Moses struck a rock and produced water, Ex 17:1–7.

2. A place at Kadesh, in the desert of Zin, where Moses again struck a rock for water, Num 20:13, 24.

MERIB-BAAL See *Mephibosheth.*

MERIT Personal, see *Graces.*

MERODACH-BALADAN King of Persia. Sends congratulatory letters and a present to Hezekiah, 2 Kgs 20:12; Isa 30:1.

MEROM The district near the springs of Jordan. Joshua conquered the confederacy of kings under Jabin, king of Hazor, near, Josh 11:5–7.

MEROZ A place north of Mount Tabor. Deborah and Barak curse the inhabitants of, in their song of triumph, Judg 5:23.

MESHA 1. King of Moab. Tributary to Ahab, 2 Kgs 3:4, 5.

2. Son of Caleb, 1 Chron 2:42.

3. A place in possession of the Joktanites, Gen 10:26–30.

4. A Benjaminite, 1 Chron 8:8–10.

MESHACH A name given by the superintendent to Misha-el, one of the three Hebrew children, Dan 1:7; 2:49; 3:12–30.

MESHECH 1. Son of Japheth, Gen 10:2; 1 Chron 1:5–9.

2. Son of Shem, 1 Chron 1:17.

3. A tribe, Ps 120:5, 6.

4. A Japhetic people associated with Tyre, Tubal, and Javan, Ezk 27:13; 32:26; 38:2, 3.

MESHELEMIAH A temple guard, 1 Chron 9:21; 26:1, 9.

MESHEZABEL 1. Ancestor of Meshullam, Neh 3:4.

2. A person who signed the covenant, Neh 10:14–27.

3. Father of Pethahiah, Neh 11:24.

MESHILLEMITH A priest, 1 Chron 9:12.

MESHILLEMOTH 1. Father of an Ephraimite who protested against the attempt of the Israelites to enslave the captive Judeans, 2 Chron 28:12, 13.

2. A priest, Neh 11:10–14.

MESHOBAB A Simeonite, 1 Chron 4:34–39.

MESHULLAM 1. Grandfather of Shaphan, 2 Kgs 22:3, 4.

2. A son of Zerubbabel, 1 Chron 3:19, 20.

3. A Gadite of Bashan, 1 Chron 5:13.

4. Three Benjaminites, 1 Chron 8:17,18; 1 Chron 9:7; Neh 11:7–9; 1 Chron 9:8.

5. An Aaronite, 1 Chron 9: 10, 11; Neh 11:10–14.

6. A priest, 1 Chron 9:12.

7. A Kohathite and superintendent of the temple repairs, 2 Chron 34:12.

8. A Levite leader who returned with Ezra, Ezra 8:16.

9. A returned exile, Ezra 10:5.

10. Son of Bani who divorced his Gentile wife, Ezra 10:29.

11. Two persons who rebuilt portions of the wall, Neh 3:4, 6, 30.

12. A leader who stood by Ezra when he read the law to the people, Neh 8:4.

13. Two priests who signed the covenant, Neh 10:1–8, 14–27.

14. Three priests who returned with Zerubbabel from Babylon, Neh 12:12–21, 33.

15. A Levite, Neh 12:25.

MESHULLEMETH Wife of Manasseh and mother of Amon, 2 Kgs 21:19, 20.

MESOPOTAMIA The country around and between the Tigris and the Euphrates, now Iraq and parts of Syria and Turkey. Abraham a native of, Acts 7:2. Nahor lived in, Gen 24:10. People who lived in, called Arameans, Gen 25:20. Balaam from, Deut 23:4. The children of Israel subjected to, eight years under the judgments of God, Judg 3:8; rescued by Othni-el, Judg 3:9, 10. Chariots hired from, by the Ammonites, 1 Chron 19:6, 7. People of, present at Pentecost, Acts 2:9.

See *Babylon; Chaldea; Syria.*

MESSENGER Of Hezekiah, 2 Chron 30:10; Ahasuerus, Esther 3:13, 15; 8:9, 10, 14.

FIGURATIVE. Hag 1:13; Mal 2:7; 3:1; Mt 11:10; Mk 1:2; Lk 7:27. Of Satan, 2 Cor 12:7.

A name of Jesus, Heb 3:1.

MESSIAH See *Jesus.*

METAL See *Brass; Bronze; Copper; Gold; Iron; Lead; Silver; Tin.*

METAPHOR Jesus spoke in, Mk 4:11, 12. See *Parable.*

METEOROLOGY AND CELESTIAL PHENOMENA Gen 2:5. There were no plants or grain sprouting up across the earth at first, for the Lord God hadn't sent any rain; nor was there anyone to farm the soil. [6](However, water welled up from the ground at certain places and flowed across the land.)

Job 9:7. The sun won't rise, the stars won't shine, if he commands it so!

Job 26:7. God stretches out heaven over empty space, and hangs the earth upon nothing. [8]He wraps the rain in his thick clouds and the clouds are not split by the weight. [11]The pillars of heaven tremble at his rebuke.

Job 27:20. Terror overwhelms him, and he is blown away in the storms of the night. [21]The east wind carries him away, and he is gone. It sweeps him into eternity.

Job 28:24. For he looks throughout the whole earth, under all the heavens. [25]He makes the winds blow and sets the boundaries of the oceans. [26]He makes the laws of the rain and a path for the lightning. [27]He knows where wisdom is and declares it to all who will listen. He established it and examined it thoroughly.

Job 29:19. The dew lay all night upon my fields and watered them.

Job 36:27. He draws up the water vapor and then distills it into rain, [28]which the skies pour down. [29]Can anyone really understand the spreading of the clouds, and the thunders within? [30]See how he spreads the lightning around him, and blankets the tops of the mountains. [31]By his fantastic powers in nature he punishes or blesses the people, giving them food in abundance. [32]He fills his hands with lightning bolts. He hurls each at its target. [33]We feel his presence in the thunder. May all sinners be warned.

Job 37:6. For he directs the snow, the showers, and storm to fall upon the earth. [7]Man's work stops at such a time, so that all men everywhere may recognize his power. [8]The wild animals hide in the rocks or in their dens. [9]From the south comes the rain; from the north, the cold. [10]God blows upon the rivers, and even the widest torrents freeze. [11]He loads the clouds with moisture and they send forth his lightning. [12]The lightning bolts are directed by his hand, and do whatever he commands throughout the earth. [13]He sends the storms as punishment, or, in his lovingkindness, to encourage. [14]Listen, O

Job, stop and consider the wonderful miracles of God. [15]Do you know how God controls all nature, and causes the lightning to flash forth from the clouds? [16, 17]Do you understand the balancing of the clouds with wonderful perfection and skill? Do you know why you become warm when the south wind is blowing and everything is still? [18]Can you spread out the gigantic mirror of the skies as he does? [19, 20]You who think you know so much, teach the rest of us how we should approach God. For we are too dull to know! With your wisdom, would we then dare to approach him? Well, does a man wish to be swallowed alive? [21]For as we cannot look at the sun for its brightness when the winds have cleared away the clouds, [22]neither can we gaze at the terrible majesty of God breaking forth upon us from heaven, clothed in dazzling splendor.

Job 38:9. Who clothed them with clouds and thick darkness? [with *vs.* 8–11.] [22]Have you visited the treasuries of the snow, or seen where hail is made and stored? [24]Where is the path to the distribution point of light? Where is the home of the east wind? [25-27]Who dug the valleys for the torrents of rain? Who laid out the path for the lightning, causing the rain to fall upon the barren deserts, so that the parched and barren ground is satisfied with water, and tender grass springs up? [28]Has the rain a father? Where does dew come from? [29]Who is the mother of the ice and frost? [31]Can you hold back the stars? Can you restrain Orion or Pleiades? [32]Can you ensure the proper sequence of the seasons, or guide the constellation of the Bear with her satellites across the heavens? [33]Do you know the laws of the universe and how the heavens influence the earth? [34]Can you shout to the clouds and make it rain? [35]Can you make lightning appear and cause it to strike as you direct it? [37]Who is wise enough to number all the clouds? Who can tilt the water jars of heaven, when everything is dust and clods?

Ps 18:8. Fierce flames leaped from his mouth, setting fire to the earth; smoke blew from his nostrils. [9]He bent the heavens down and came to my defense; thick darkness was beneath his feet. [10]Mounted on the cherubim, he sped swiftly to my aid with wings of wind. [11]He enshrouded himself with darkness, veiling his approach with dense clouds dark as murky waters. [12]Suddenly the brilliance of his presence broke through the clouds with lightning and a mighty storm of hail. [13]The Lord thundered in the heavens; the God above all gods has spoken—oh, the hailstones; oh, the fire! [14]He flashed his fearful arrows of lightning and routed all my enemies. See how they run! [15]Then at your command, O Lord, the sea receded from the shore. At the blast of your breath the depths were laid bare.

Ps 19:2. Day and night they keep on telling about God.

3, 4. Without a sound or word, silent in the skies, their message reaches out to all the world. The sun lives in the heavens where God placed it [5]and moves out across the skies as radiant as a bridegroom going to his wedding, or as joyous as an athlete looking forward to a race! [6]The sun crosses the heavens from end to end, and nothing can hide from its heat.

Ps 29:3. The voice of the Lord echoes from the clouds. The God of glory thunders through the skies. [4]So powerful is his voice; so full of majesty. [5, 6]It breaks down the cedars. It splits the giant trees of Lebanon. It shakes Mount Lebanon and Mount Sirion. They leap and skip before him like young calves! [7]The voice of the Lord thunders through the lightning. [8]It resounds through the deserts and shakes the wilderness of Kadesh. [9]The voice of the Lord spins and topples the mighty oaks. It strips the forests bare. They whirl and sway beneath the blast. But in his temple all are praising, "Glory, glory to the Lord." [10]At the Flood, the Lord showed his control of all creation. Now he continues to unveil his power.

Ps 65:8. In the farthest corners of the earth the glorious acts of God shall startle everyone. The dawn and sunset shout for joy! [9]He waters the earth to make it fertile. The rivers of God will not run dry! He prepares the earth for his people and sends them rich harvests of grain. [10]He waters the furrows with abundant rain. Showers soften the earth, melting the clods and causing seeds to sprout across the land. [11, 12]Then he crowns it all with green, lush pastures in the wilderness; hillsides blossom with joy.

Ps 104:2. You are robed with honor and with majesty and light! You stretched out the starry curtain of the heavens, [3]and hollowed out the surface of the earth to form the seas. The clouds are his chariots. He rides upon the wings of the wind. [7]You spoke, and at the sound of your shout the water collected into its vast ocean beds. [13]He sends rain upon the mountains and fills the earth with fruit. [19]He assigned the moon to mark the months, and the sun to mark the days. [20]He sends the night and darkness.

Ps 147:7. Sing out your thanks to him; sing praises to our God, accompanied by harps. [8]He covers the heavens with clouds, sends down the showers and makes the green grass grow in mountain pastures.

Ps 148:7. And praise him down here on earth, you creatures of the ocean depths. [8]Let fire and hail, snow, rain, wind and weather, all obey.

Prov 25:23. As surely as a wind from the north brings cold.

Prov 26:1. Honor doesn't go with fools any more than snow with summertime or rain with harvest time!

Prov 30:4. Who else but God goes back and forth to heaven? Who else holds the wind in his fists, and wraps up the oceans in his cloak? Who but God has created the world? If there is any other, what is his name—and his son's name—if you know it?

Eccl 1:6, 7. The wind blows south and north, here and there, twisting back and forth, getting nowhere. The rivers run into the sea but the sea is never full, and the water returns again to the rivers, and flows again to the sea.

Eccl 11:3. When the clouds are heavy, the rains come down.

Isa 5:5. I will tear down the fence and let my vineyard go to pasture to be trampled by cattle and sheep. [6]I won't prune it or hoe it, but let it be overgrown with briars and thorns. I will command the clouds not to rain on it any more.

Isa 13:13. For I will shake the heavens in my wrath and fierce anger, and the earth will move from its place in the skies.

Isa 24:18. For destruction falls from the heavens upon you; the world is shaken beneath you.

Isa 50:3. I am the one who sends the darkness out across the skies.

Jer 4:11, 12. At that time he will send a burning wind from the desert upon them—not in little gusts but in a roaring blast—and he will pronounce their doom.

Jer 10:13. It is his voice that echoes in the thunder of the storm clouds. He causes mist to rise upon the earth; he sends the lightning and brings the rain, and from his treasuries he brings the wind.

Jer 51:16. When he speaks there is thunder in the heavens and he causes the vapors to rise around the world; he brings the lightning with the rain and the winds from his treasuries.

Hos 6:4. O Ephraim and Judah, what shall I do with you? For your love vanishes like morning clouds, and disappears like dew.

Hos 8:7. They have sown the wind and they will reap the whirlwind.

Hos 13:15. He was called the most fruitful of all his brothers, but the east wind—a wind of the Lord from the desert—will blow hard upon him and dry up his land. All his flowing springs and green oases will dry away, and he will die of thirst.

Joel 2:30. And put strange symbols in the earth and sky—blood and fire and pillars of smoke. [31]The sun will be turned into darkness and the moon to blood before the great and terrible Day of the Lord shall come.

Amos 9:6. The upper stories of his home are in the heavens, the first floor on the earth. He calls for the vapor to rise from the ocean and pours it down as rain upon the ground. Jehovah, the Lord, is his name.

Nah 1:3. He shows his power in the terrors of the cyclone and the raging storm; clouds are billowing dust beneath his feet!

Mt 8:24. Suddenly a terrible storm came up, with waves higher than the boat. But Jesus was asleep. [25]The disciples went to him and wakened him, shouting, "Lord, save us! We're sinking!" [26]But Jesus answered, "O you men of little faith! Why are you so frightened?" Then he stood up and rebuked the wind and waves, and the storm subsided and all was calm. [27]The disciples just sat there, awed! "Who is this," they asked themselves, "that even the winds and the sea obey him?" Lk 8: 24, 25.

Mt 16:2, 3. He replied, "You are good at reading the weather signs of the skies—red sky tonight means fair weather tomorrow; red sky in the morning means foul weather all day—but you can't read the obvious signs of the times!"

Mt 24:27. For as the lightning flashes across the sky from east to west, so shall my coming be, when I, the Messiah, return. [29]Immediately after the persecution of those days the sun will be darkened, and the moon will not give light, and the stars will seem to fall from the heavens, and the powers overshadowing the earth will be convulsed.

Mt 27:45. That afternoon, the whole earth was covered with darkness for three hours, from noon until three o'clock. Lk 23:44, 45.

Lk 12:54. Then he turned to the crowd and said, "When you see clouds beginning to form in the west, you say, 'Here comes a shower.' And you are right. [55]When the south wind blows you say, 'Today will be a scorcher.' And it is. [56]Hypocrites! You interpret the sky well enough, but you refuse to notice the warnings all around you about the crisis ahead."

Lk 21:25. Then there will be strange events in the skies—warnings, evil omens and portents in the sun, moon and stars.

Jn 3:8. Just as you can hear the wind but can't tell where it comes from or where it will go next, so it is with the Spirit.

Acts 2:19. And I will cause strange demonstrations in the heavens and on the earth—blood and fire and clouds of smoke; [20]the sun shall turn black and the moon blood-red before that awesome Day of the Lord arrives.

Jas 5:17. Elijah was as completely human as we are, and yet when he prayed earnestly that no rain would fall, none fell for the next three and one half years! [18]Then he prayed again, this time that it *would* rain, and down it poured and the grass turned green and the gardens began to grow again.

2 Pet 2:17. These men are as useless as dried-up springs of water, promising much and delivering nothing; they are as unstable as clouds driven by the storm winds. They are doomed to the eternal pits of darkness.

Jude 1:12. When these men join you at the love feasts of the church, they are evil smears among you, laughing and carrying on, gorging and stuffing themselves without a thought for others. They are like clouds blowing over dry land without giving rain.

Rev 6:12. I watched as he broke the sixth seal, and there was a vast earthquake; and the sun became dark like black cloth, and the moon was blood-red. [13]Then the stars of heaven appeared to be falling to earth—like green fruit from fig trees buffeted by mighty winds. [14]And the starry heavens disappeared as though rolled up like a scroll and taken away; and every mountain and island shook and shifted.

Rev 7:1. Then I saw four angels standing at the four corners of the earth, holding back the four winds from blowing, so that not a leaf rustled in the trees, and the ocean became as smooth as glass.

Rev 8:5. Then the angel filled the censer with fire from the altar and threw it down upon the earth;

and thunder crashed and rumbled, lightning flashed, and there was a terrible earthquake. [7]The first angel blew his trumpet, and hail and fire mixed with blood were thrown down upon the earth. One-third of the earth was set on fire so that one-third of the trees were burned, and all the green grass. [10]The third angel blew, and a great flaming star fell from heaven upon a third of the rivers and springs. [12]The fourth angel blew his trumpet and immediately a third of the sun was blighted and darkened, and a third of the moon and the stars, so that the daylight was dimmed by a third, and the nighttime darkness deepened.

Rev 9:1. Then the fifth angel blew his trumpet and I saw one who was fallen to earth from heaven, and to him was given the key to the bottomless pit. [2]When he opened it, smoke poured out as though from some huge furnace, and the sun and air were darkened by the smoke.

Rev 11:6. They have power to shut the skies so that no rain will fall during the three and a half years they prophesy, and to turn rivers and oceans to blood, and to send every kind of plague upon the earth as often as they wish.

Rev 16:21. And there was an incredible hailstorm from heaven; hailstones weighing a hundred pounds fell from the sky onto the people below, and they cursed God because of the terrible hail.

PHENOMENA OF. The flood, Gen 7; 8. Fire from heaven on the cities of the plain, Gen 19:24, 25. Plagues of hail, thunder, and lightning in Egypt, Ex 9:22–29; Ps 78:17–23; of darkness, Ex 10:22, 23. East wind that divided the Red Sea, Ex 14:21; that brought the quails, Num 11:31, 32; Ps 78:26–28. Pillar of cloud and fire, see *Pillar.* Sun stood still, Josh 10:12, 13. Dew on Gideon's fleece, Judg 6:36–40. Stars of heaven fought against Sisera, Judg 5:20. Hailstorm, Josh 10:11. Fire from heaven at Elijah's command, 2 Kgs 1:10–14. The whirlwind which carried Elijah to heaven, 2 Kgs 2:1, 11.

Wind under God's control, Ps 48:7; 107:25. Rain, formation of, Ps 135:6, 7. Dew, Ps 133:3. Rain in answer to Samuel's prayer, 1 Sam 12:16–18; Elijah's prayer, 1 Kgs 18:41–45. Thunder routs the Philistine army, 1 Sam 7:10. Wind destroyed Job's children, Job 1:18, 19. Darkness at the crucifixion, Mt 27:45; Lk 23:44, 45. The autumn weather on the Mediterranean, Acts 27:9–14, 20.

In prophecy, Deut 28:23, 24; Ezk 38:22; 47:1–11; Joel 2:30, 31; Amos 8:9; Zech 14:4, 8, 10; Mt 24:29; Lk 21:25, 26. See under *Symbolical.*

See *Astronomy; Dew; Hail; Rain.*

Symbolical. Used in the Revelation, Rev 6:12–14; 7:1; 8:3–12; 9:1, 2, 17–19; 10:1–6; 11:6; 12:1–4, 7–9; 14; 15:1–4; 16:8, 17–21; 19:11–18; 20:11; 21:1.

METHUSAEL Father of Lamech, Gen 4:18.

METHUSELAH Son of Enoch and grandfather of Noah, Gen 5:21–27; 1 Chron 1:1–4.

ME-UNIM A person whose descendants returned from exile, Ezra 2:43–54; Neh 7:46–56.

MEZAHAB Grandfather of Mehetabel, Gen 36:31–39; 1 Chron 1:50.

MIBHAR One of David's valiant men, 1 Chron 11:26–47.

MIBSAM 1. Son of Ishmael, Gen 25:12–15; 1 Chron 1:28–31.

2. Son of Shallum, 1 Chron 4:25.

MIBZAR King of Edom, Gen 36:40–43; 1 Chron 1:51–54.

MICA 1. See *Micah, 3.*

2. A Levite who signed the covenant with Nehemiah, Neh 10:9–13.

3. Son of Zichri, 1 Chron 9:15, 16; Neh 11:15–17, 22, 23. Called *Micaiah* in Neh 12:35, 36.

MICAH 1. An Ephraimite. His robbery and idolatry, Judg 17; 18.

2. Head of a family of Reuben, 1 Chron 5:5.

3. Called also *Mica.* Son of Mephibosheth, 2 Sam 9:12; 1 Chron 8:34, 35; 9:40, 41.

4. A Kohathite, 1 Chron 23:20; 24:24, 25.

5. Father of Abdon, 2 Chron 34:20. Called *Michaiah* in 2 Kgs 22:12, 13.

6. One of the minor prophets, Jer 26:18, 19; Mic 1:1, 14, 15. Denounces the idolatry of his times, Mic 1; the oppressions of the covetous, Mic 2:1–11. Foretells the restoration of Israel, Mic 2:12, 13; the injustice of judges and falsehoods of false prophets, Mic 3. Prophesies the coming of the Messiah, Mic 4; 5. Denounces the oppressions, frauds, and other sins, Mic 6. Laments the condition of Israel, and foretells the triumphs, righteousness, and the mercies of God, Mic 7.

MICAIAH 1. A prophet who reproved King Ahab, 1 Kgs 22:8–28; 2 Chron 18:3–27.

2. An official sent by Jehoshaphat to teach the law in the cities of Judah, 2 Chron 17:7–9.

3. A priest of the family of Asaph, Neh 12:35, 36. See *Mica, 3.*

4. A priest who played the trumpet, Neh 12:40, 41.

5. Son of Gemariah. Who expounds to the officials the prophecies of Jeremiah read by Baruch to the people, Jer 36:11–15.

6. See *Maacah, 3.*

MICE See *Mouse.*

MICHAEL 1. An Asherite, Num 13:3–15.

2. Two Gadites, 1 Chron 5:13, 14.

3. A Gershonite Levite, 1 Chron 6:39–43.

4. A descendant of Issachar, 1 Chron 7:3.

5. A Benjaminite, 1 Chron 8:15, 16.

6. An officer of Manasseh who joined David at Ziklag, 1 Chron 12:20.

7. Father of Omri, 1 Chron 27:16–22.

8. Son of Jehoshaphat. Killed by his brother, Jehoram, 2 Chron 21:2–4.

9. Father of Zebadiah, Ezra 8:2–14.

10. The Archangel. His message to Daniel, Dan 10:13, 20, 21; 12:1. Contention with the devil, Jude 1:9. Fights with the dragon, Rev 12:7.

MICHAIAH Father of Achbor, 2 Kgs 22:12, 13.

See *Micah, 5.*

MICHAL Daughter of Saul. Given to David as a reward for killing 200 Philistines, 1 Sam 18:22–28. Rescues David from death, 1 Sam 19:9–17.

Saul forcibly separates them and she is given in marriage to Palti, 1 Sam 25:44. David recovers, to himself, 2 Sam 3:13–16. Ridicules David because of his religious zeal, 2 Sam 6:16, 20–23.

MICHMAS See *Michmash.*

MICHMASH A city of Benjamin, 1 Sam 13: 5. People of the captivity return to, and live in, Ezra 2:3–35; Neh 11:31–35. Prophecy concerning the armies of Assyria storing equipment at, Isa 10: 28. Is garrisoned by Saul, 1 Sam 13:2. Philistines killed at, by Jonathan, 1 Sam 14:31.

MICHMETHATH A city between Ephraim and Manasseh, Josh 16:5, 6; 17:7.

MICHRI A Benjaminite, 1 Chron 9:7, 8.

MIDDIN A city of Judah, Josh 15:48–62.

MIDIAN Son of Abraham by Keturah, Gen 25:1, 2, 4; 1 Chron 1:32, 33.

MIDIANITES Descendants of Midian, son of Abraham by Keturah, Gen 25: 1, 2, 4; 1 Chron 1:32, 33. Called *Ishmaelites,* Gen 37:25; Judg 8:23, 24. Were traders, Gen 37:28. Buy Joseph and sell him to Potiphar, Gen 37:28, 36. Defeated by the Israelites under Phinehas; five of their kings killed; the women taken captives; cities burned; and rich spoils taken, Num 31. Defeated by Gideon, Judg chapters 6–8. Owned vast droves of camels, and dromedaries, and large quantities of gold, Isa 60:6. A snare to the Israelites, Num 25: 16–18. Prophecies concerning, Isa 60:6; Hab 3:7.

MIDWIFERY Gen 35:17; Ex 1:15–21; Ezk 16: 4.

MIGDAL-EL A city of Naphtali, Josh 19: 35–39.

MIGDAL-GAD A city of Judah, Josh 15:37–44.

MIGDOL 1. A place near the Red Sea where the Israelites camped, Ex 14:2; Num 33:7, 8.

2. A city of the northeastern border of lower Egypt, Jer 44:1; 46:14.

MIGRON A city in Benjamin. Saul camps near, under a pomegranate tree, 1 Sam 14:2. Prophecy concerning, Isa 10:28, 29.

MIJAMIN 1. A priest in the time of David, 1 Chron 24:7–18.

2. A Jew who divorced his Gentile wife after the captivity, Ezra 10:25.

3. A priest who signed the covenant with Nehemiah, Neh 10:1–8.

4. A priest who returned with Zerubbabel from Babylon, Neh 12:1–7.

MIKLOTH 1. A Benjaminite of Jerusalem, 1 Chron 8:30–32; 9:35–38.

2. An officer in the reign of David, 1 Chron 27:4.

MIKNEIAH A door keeper of the Temple, and musician, 1 Chron 15:18, 21.

MILALAI A priest who took part in the dedication of the walls of Jerusalem, Neh 12:35, 36.

MILCAH 1. Wife of Nahor and mother of Bethuel, Gen 11:29; 22:20–23; 24:15, 16, 24, 47.

2. Daughter of Zelophehad. Special legislation in regard to the inheritance of, Num 26:33; 27:1–7; 36: 1–12; Josh 17:3, 4.

MILCOM See *Molech.*

MILDEW Deut 28:22; Amos 4:9; Hag 2:16, 17.

MILETUS A seaport in Asia Minor. Paul visits, Acts 20:15; and sends to Ephesus for the elders of the church, and addresses them at, Acts 20:17–38. Trophimus left sick at, 2 Tim 4:20.

MILITARY INSTRUCTION See *Armies.*

MILK Used for food, Gen 18:8; Judg 4:19; Song 5:1; Ezk 25:4; 1 Cor 9:7. Of goats, Prov 27: 25–27; sheep, Deut 32:14; Isa 7:21, 22; camels, Gen 32:13–15; cows, 1 Sam 6:7, 10. Churned, Prov 30:33. Kid not to be boiled in its mother's, Ex 23:19; Deut 14:21.

FIGURATIVE. Ex 3:8, 17; 13:4, 5; 33:3; Num 13: 27; Deut 26:9, 15; Isa 55:1; Jer 11:5; 32:22; Ezk 20: 5, 6; Joel 3:18; 1 Cor 3:2; Heb 5:12, 13; 1 Pet 2:2, 3.

MILL Stones of, Deut 24:6; Job 41:24; Isa 47: 2. Operated by captives, Judg 16:21; Lam 5:13. Manna ground in, Num 11:8. Sound of, to cease, Rev 18:22.

See *Millstone.*

MILLENNIUM A period of time during which Christ is to rule the world, described as 1,000 years.

Rev 20:1. Then I saw an angel come down from heaven with the key to the bottomless pit and a heavy chain in his hand. [2]He seized the Dragon—that old Serpent, the devil, Satan—and bound him in chains for 1,000 years, [3]and threw him into the bottomless pit, which he then shut and locked, so that he could not fool the nations any more until the thousand years were finished. Afterwards he would be released again for a little while. [4]Then I saw thrones, and sitting on them were those who had been given the right to judge. And I saw the souls of those who had been beheaded for their testimony about Jesus, for proclaiming the Word of God, and who had not worshiped the Creature or his statue, nor accepted his mark on their foreheads or their hands. They had come to life again and now they reigned with Christ for a thousand years. [5]This is the First Resurrection. (The rest of the dead did not come back to life until the thousand years had ended.) [6]Blessed and holy are those who share in the First Resurrection. For them the Second Death holds no terrors, for they will be priests of God and of Christ, and shall reign with him a thousand years. *vs.* 7–15.

The word *millennium* is associated with three views of this kingdom reign of Christ: the *postmillennial,* which holds that the gospel being proclaimed in the present age will bring about the kingdom of Christ on earth, after which Christ will return to reign; the *amillennial,* which holds that all Bible prophecies describing an earthly kingdom are figurative, and refer either to the present age or to the eternal state; and the *premillennial,* which holds that after his second coming, Christ will reign over a literal earthly kingdom for one thousand years before the eternal state begins.

For a selection of representative texts dealing with this subject, see *Kingdom.*

MILLO A name given to part of the citadel of Jerusalem, 2 Sam 5:9; 1 Chron 11:8. King Solomon raises a levy to repair, 1 Kgs 9:15, 24; 11:27, 28. Repaired by King Hezekiah, 2 Chron 32:5. King Joash murdered at, 2 Kgs 12:20.

MILLSTONE Not to be taken in pledge, Deut 24:6. Probably used in executions by drowning, Mt 18:6; Mk 9:42; Lk 17:2, 3. Abimelech killed by one being hurled on him, Judg 9:53. Figurative of the hard heart, Job 41:24.

MINCING Isa 3:16.

MINERALS See *Agate; Alkali; Amethyst; Asphalt; Beryl; Bitumen; Brimstone; Chalcedony; Chrysolyte; Chrysoprase; Copper; Coral; Diamond; Flint; Gold; Iron; Jacinth; Jasper; Lead; Lime; Lye; Marble; Pitch; Ruby; Salt; Sapphire; Sardius; Sardonyx; Silver; Slime; Soda; Stones; Tar; Tin; Topaz.* See *Stones, Precious.*

MINIAMIN 1. A Levite who assisted in the distribution of the offerings in the time of Hezekiah, 2 Chron 31:14, 15.

2. A priest who came from Babylon with Zerubbabel, Neh 12:12–21, 40, 41.

MINISTER, OLD TESTAMENT The Hebrew root means to serve, or servant. It usually occurs as a verb to describe the service of the priests of Israel, never of the prophets, and never of civil authority. See Ex 28:41; 29:44; Ezra 7:24; 8:17; Ps 103:21; 104:4; Isa 61:6; Jer 33:20, 21; Ezk 43:19; 44:11; 45:4, 5; 46:24; Joel 1:9, 13; 2:17. The following selection of passages includes references to prophets and other servants of God, as well as priests.

CALL OF. Ex 28:1. Consecrate Aaron your brother, and his sons Nadab, Abihu, Eleazer, and Ithamar, to be priests, to minister to me. Heb 5:4.

Num 3:5. Then the Lord said to Moses, [6]"Summon the tribe of Levi and present them to Aaron as his assistants. [7-9]They will follow his instructions and perform the sacred duties at the Tabernacle on behalf of all the people of Israel. For they are assigned to him as representatives of all the people of Israel. They are in charge of all the furnishings and maintenance of the Tabernacle. [10]However, only Aaron and his sons may carry out the duties of the priesthood; anyone else who presumes to assume this office shall be executed." [11, 12]And the Lord said to Moses, "I have accepted the Levites in substitution for all the oldest sons of the people of Israel. The Levites are mine [13]in exchange for all the oldest sons. From the day I killed all the oldest sons of the Egyptians, I took for myself all the firstborn in Israel of both men and animals! They are mine; I am Jehovah."

1 Sam 3:4,5. The Lord called out, "Samuel! Samuel!" "Yes?" Samuel replied. "What is it?" He jumped up and ran to Eli. "Here I am. What do you want?" he asked. "I didn't call you," Eli said. "Go on back to bed." So he did. [6]Then the Lord called again, "Samuel!" And again Samuel jumped up and ran to Eli. "Yes?" he asked. "What do you need?" "No, I didn't call you, my son," Eli said. "Go on back to bed." [7](Samuel had never had a message from Jehovah before.) [8]So now the Lord called the third time, and once more Samuel jumped up and ran to Eli. "Yes?" he asked. "What do you need?" Then Eli realized it was the Lord who had spoken to the child. [9]So he said to Samuel, "Go and lie down again, and if he calls again, say, 'Yes, Lord, I'm listening.'" So Samuel went back to bed. [10]And the Lord came and called as before, "Samuel! Samuel!" and Samuel replied, "Yes, I'm listening."

1 Kgs 19:16. "Then anoint Jehu (son of Himshi) to be king of Israel, and anoint Elisha (the son of Shaphat of Abel-meholah) to replace you as my prophet." [19]So Elijah went and found Elisha who was plowing a field with eleven other teams ahead of him; he was at the end of the line with the last team. Elijah went over to him and threw his coat across his shoulders and walked away again.

1 Chron 23:13. Amram was the ancestor of Aaron and Moses. Aaron and his sons were set apart for the holy service of sacrificing the people's offerings to the Lord. He served the Lord constantly and pronounced blessings in his name at all times.

Isa 6:8. Then I heard the Lord asking, "Whom shall I send as a messenger to my people? Who will go?" And I said, "Lord, I'll go! Send *me*." [9]And he said, "Yes, go. But tell my people this: 'Though you hear my words repeatedly, you won't understand them. Though you watch and watch as I perform my miracles, still you won't know what they mean.' [10]Dull their understanding, close their ears and shut their eyes. I don't want them to see or to hear or to understand, or to turn to me to heal them."

Jer 1:5. I knew you before you were formed within your mother's womb; before you were born I sanctified you and appointed you as my spokesman to the world.

Amos 2:11. "And I chose your sons to be Nazirites and prophets—can you deny this, Israel?" asks the Lord.

Jon 1:1. The Lord sent this message to Jonah, the son of Amittai: [2]"Go to the great city of Nineveh, and give them this announcement from the Lord: 'I am going to destroy you, for your wickedness rises before me; it smells to highest heaven.'" Jon 3:1, 2.

CHARACTER AND QUALIFICATIONS OF. Lev 10:3. Then Moses said to Aaron, "This is what the Lord meant when he said, 'I will show myself holy among those who approach me, and I will be glorified before all the people.'" And Aaron was speechless. [4]Then Moses called for Mishael and Elzaphon, Aaron's cousins, the sons of Uzziel, and told them, "Go and get the charred bodies from before the Tabernacle, and carry them outside the camp." [5]So they went over and got them, and carried them out in their coats as Moses had told them to. [6]Then Moses said to Aaron and his sons Eleazar and Ithamar, "Do not mourn—do not let your hair hang loose as a sign of your mourning, and do not tear your clothes. If you do, God will strike you dead too, and his wrath will come upon all the people of Israel. But the rest of the people of Israel may lament the death of Nadab and Abihu, and mourn because of the terrible fire the Lord has sent. [7]But you are not to leave the Tabernacle under penalty of death, for the anointing oil of Jehovah is upon you." And they did as Moses commanded. [8, 9]Now the Lord instructed Aaron, "Never drink wine or strong drink when you go into the Tabernacle, lest you die; and this rule applies to your sons and to all your descendants from generation to generation. [10]Your duties will be to arbitrate for the people, to teach them the difference between what is holy and what is ordinary, what is pure and what is impure; [11]and to teach them all the laws Jehovah has given through Moses."

Lev 21:6. They shall be holy unto their God, and shall not dishonor and profane his name; otherwise they will be unfit to make food offerings by fire to the Lord their God. 2 Chron 29:11.

Num 16:9. Does it seem a small thing to you that the God of Israel has chosen you from among all the people of Israel to be near to himself as you work in the Tabernacle of Jehovah, and to stand before the people to minister to them? [10]Is it nothing to you that he has given this task to only you Levites? And now are you demanding the priesthood also?

Deut 32:1. Listen, O heavens and earth! Listen to what I say! [2]My words shall fall upon you like the gentle rain and dew, like rain upon the tender grass, like showers on the hillside. [3]I will proclaim the greatness of the Lord. How glorious he is!

1 Sam 2:35. Then I will raise up a faithful priest who will serve me and do whatever I tell him to do. I will bless his descendants, and his family shall be priests to my kings forever.

1 Sam 12:7. Now stand here quietly before the Lord as I remind you of all the good things he has done for you and for your ancestors.

2 Chron 6:41. And now, O Lord God, arise and enter this resting place of yours where the Ark of your strength has been placed. Let your priests, O Lord God, be clothed with salvation, and let your saints rejoice in your kind deeds.

Ezra 7:10. This was because Ezra had determined to study and obey the laws of the Lord and to become a Bible teacher, teaching those laws to the people of Israel.

Prov 11:30. Godly men are growing a tree that bears life-giving fruit, and all who win souls are wise.

Isa 6:5. Then I said, "My doom is sealed, for I am a foul-mouthed sinner, a member of a sinful, foul-mouthed race; and I have looked upon the King, the Lord of heaven's armies." [6]Then one of the seraphs flew over to the altar and with a pair of tongs picked out a burning coal. [7]He touched my lips with it and said, "Now you are pronounced 'Not guilty' because this coal has touched your lips. Your sins are all forgiven." [8]Then I heard the Lord asking, "Whom shall I send as a messenger to my people? Who will go?" And I said, "Lord, I'll go! Send *me.*"

Isa 32:20. And God will greatly bless his people. Wherever they plant, bountiful crops will spring up, and their flocks and herds will graze in green pastures.

Isa 52:11. Purify yourselves, all you who carry home the vessels of the Lord.

Jer 1:7. "Don't say that," he replied, "for you will go wherever I send you and speak whatever I tell you to. [8]And don't be afraid of the people, for I, the Lord, will be with you and see you through."

Jer 3:15. And I will give you leaders after my own heart, who will guide you with wisdom and understanding.

Jer 20:9. Then his word in my heart is like fire that burns in my bones, and I can't hold it in any longer.

Ezk 34:2. The Lord God says to you: Woe to the shepherds who feed themselves instead of their flocks. Shouldn't shepherds feed the sheep? *vs.* 1–31.

Mal 2:6. He passed on to the people all the truth he got from me. He did not lie or cheat; he walked with me, living a good and righteous life, and turned many from their lives of sin. [7]Priests' lips should flow with the knowledge of God so the people will learn God's laws. The priests are the messengers of the Lord of Hosts, and men should come to them for guidance.

CHARGE DELIVERED TO. Num 18:1. The Lord now spoke to Aaron: "You and your sons and your family are responsible for any desecration of the sanctuary," he said, "and will be held liable for any impropriety in your priestly work. [2, 3]Your kinsmen, the tribe of Levi, are your assistants; but only you and your sons may perform the sacred duties in the Tabernacle itself. The Levites must be careful not to touch any of the sacred articles or the altar, lest I destroy both them and you. [4]No one who is not a member of the tribe of Levi shall assist you in any way. [5]Remember, only the priests are to perform the sacred duties within the sanctuary and at the altar. If you follow these instructions the wrath of God will never again fall upon any of the people of Israel for violating this law. [6]I say it again —your kinsmen the Levites are your assistants for the work of the Tabernacle. They are a gift to you from the Lord. [7]But you and your sons the priests, shall personally handle all the sacred service, including the altar and all that is within the veil, for the priesthood is your special gift of service. Anyone else who attempts to perform these duties shall die."

Num 27:18. The Lord replied, "Go and get Joshua (son of Nun), who has the Spirit in him, [19]and take him to Eleazar the priest, and as all the people watch, charge him with the responsibility of leading the people. [20]Publicly give him your authority so that all the people of Israel will obey him. [21]He shall be the one to consult with Eleazar the priest in order to get directions from the Lord. The Lord will speak to Eleazar through the use of the Urim, and Eleazar will pass on these instructions to Joshua and the people. In this way the Lord will continue to give them guidance." [22]So Moses did as Jehovah commanded, and took Joshua to Eleazar the priest. As the people watched, [23]Moses laid his hands upon him and dedicated him to his responsibilities, as the Lord had commanded.

Deut 31:7. Then Moses called for Joshua and said to him, as all Israel watched, "Be strong! Be courageous! For you shall lead these people into the land promised by the Lord to their ancestors; see to it that they conquer it. [8]Don't be afraid, for the Lord will go before you and will be with you; he will not fail nor forsake you." Deut 31:14–23.

Josh 1:1. After the death of Moses, the Lord's disciple, God spoke to Moses' assistant, whose name was Joshua (the son of Nun), and said to him, [2]"Now that my disciple is dead, (you are the new leader of Israel). Lead my people across the Jordan River into the Promised Land. [3]I say to you what I said to Moses: 'Wherever you go will be part of the land of Israel—[4]all the way from Negeb desert in the south to the Lebanon mountains in the north, and from the Mediterranean Sea in the west to the Euphrates River in the east, including all the land of the Hittites.' [5]No one will be able to oppose you as long as you live, for I will be with you just as I was with Moses; I will not abandon you or fail to help you. [6]Be strong and brave, for you will be a successful leader of my people; and they shall conquer all the land I promised to their ancestors. [7]You need only to be strong and courageous and to obey to the letter every law Moses gave you, for if you are careful to obey every one of them you will be successful in everything you do. [8]Constantly remind the people about these laws, and you yourself must think about them every day and every night so that you will be sure to obey all of them. For only then will you succeed. [9]Yes, be bold and strong! Banish fear and doubt! For remember, the Lord your God is with you wherever you go."

Ezk 3:4. Then he said: "Son of dust, I am sending you to the people of Israel with my messages."

DUTIES OF. Ex 4:12. Now go ahead and do as I tell you, for I will help you to speak well, and I will tell you what to say.

Lev 10:11. And to teach them all the laws Jehovah has given through Moses. *vs.* 8–11.

Josh 1:8. Constantly remind the people about these laws, and you yourself must think about them every day and every night so that you will be sure to obey all of them.

2 Kgs 17:27, 28. The king of Assyria then decreed that one of the exiled priests from Samaria should return to Israel and teach the new residents the laws of the god of the land. So one of them returned to Bethel and taught the colonists from Babylon how to worship the Lord.

2 Chron 29:11. My children, don't neglect your duties any longer, for the Lord has chosen you to minister to him and to burn incense.

Isa 40:1. Comfort, oh, comfort my people, says your God. [2]Speak tenderly to Jerusalem and tell her that her sad days are gone. Her sins are pardoned, and the Lord will give her twice as many blessings as he gave her punishment before. [3]Listen! I hear the voice of someone shouting, "Make a road for the Lord through the wilderness; make him a straight, smooth road through the desert." [9]O Crier of Good News, shout to Jerusalem from the mountain tops! Shout louder—don't be afraid—tell the cities of Judah, "Your God is coming!" [Nah 1:15.] [11]He will feed his flock like a shepherd; he will carry the lambs in his arms and gently lead the ewes with young.

Isa 52:11. Go now, leave your bonds and slavery. Put Babylon and all it represents far behind you—it is unclean to you. You are the holy people of the Lord; purify yourselves, all you who carry home the vessels of the Lord.

Isa 57:14. I will say, Rebuild the road! Clear away the rocks and stones. Prepare a glorious highway for my people's return from captivity.

Isa 58:1. Shout with the voice of a trumpet blast; tell my people of their sins!

Isa 62:6, 7. O Jerusalem, I have set intercessors on your walls who shall cry to God all day and all night for the fulfillment of his promises. Take no rest, all you who pray, and give God no rest until he establishes Jerusalem and makes her respected and admired throughout the earth.

Jer 1:7. "Don't say that," he replied, "for you will go wherever I send you and speak whatever I tell you to. [8]And don't be afraid of the people, for I, the Lord, will be with you and see you through. [17]Get up and dress and go out and tell them whatever I tell you to say. Don't be afraid of them, or else I will make a fool of you in front of them. [18]For see, today I have made you impervious to their attacks. They cannot harm you. You are strong like a fortified city that cannot be captured, like an iron pillar and heavy gates of brass. All the kings of Judah and its officers and priests and people will not be able to prevail against you. [19]They will try, but they will fail. For I am with you," says the Lord. "I will deliver you." Jer 15:20, 21.

Jer 6:27. Jeremiah, I have made you an assayer of metals, that you may test this my people and determine their value. Listen to what they are saying and watch what they are doing.

Jer 15:19. The Lord replied: "Stop this foolishness and talk some sense! Only if you return to trusting me will I let you continue as my spokesman. You are to influence *them,* not let them influence *you!*

Jer 23:4. And I will appoint responsible shepherds to care for them, and they shall not need to be afraid again; all of them shall be accounted for continually. [22]If they were mine, they would try to turn my people from their evil ways. [28]Let these false prophets tell their dreams and let my true messengers faithfully proclaim my every word. There is a difference between chaff and wheat!

Jer 26:2. Stand out in front of the Temple of the

Lord and make an announcement to all the people who have come there to worship from many parts of Judah. Give them the entire message; don't leave out one word of all I have for them to hear.

Ezk 2:6. Son of dust, don't be afraid of them; don't be frightened even though their threats are sharp and barbed and sting like scorpions. Don't be dismayed by their dark scowls. For remember, they are rebels! [7]You must give them my messages whether they listen or not (but they won't, for they are utter rebels). [8]Listen, son of dust, to what I say to you. Don't you be a rebel too! Open your mouth and eat what I give you.

Ezk 3:8. "But see, I have made you hard and stubborn too—as tough as they are. [9]I have made your forehead as hard as rock. So don't be afraid of them, or fear their sullen, angry looks, even though they are such rebels." [10]Then he added: "Son of dust, let all my words sink deep into your own heart first; listen to them carefully for yourself. [17]Son of dust, I have appointed you as a watchman for Israel; whenever I send my people a warning, pass it on to them at once. [18]If you refuse to warn the wicked when I want you to tell them, you are under the penalty of death, therefore repent and save your life—they will die in their sins, but I will punish you. I will demand your blood for theirs. [19]But if you warn them and they keep on sinning, and refuse to repent, they will die in their sins, but you are blameless—you have done all you could. [20]And if a good man becomes bad, and you refuse to warn him of the consequences, and the Lord destroys him, his previous good deeds won't help him—he shall die in his sin. But I will hold you responsible for his death, and punish you. [21]But if you warn him and he repents, he shall live and you have saved your own life too. [27]But whenever I give you a message, then I will loosen your tongue and let you speak, and you shall say to them: The Lord God says, Let anyone listen who wants to, and let anyone refuse who wants to, for they are rebels."

Ezk 6:11. The Lord God says: Raise your hands in horror and shake your head with deep remorse and say, Alas for all the evil we have done! For you are going to perish from war and famine and disease.

Ezk 33:1. Once again a message came to me from the Lord. He said: [2]"Son of dust, tell your people: When I bring an army against a country, and the people of that land choose a watchman, [3]and when he sees the army coming, and blows the alarm to warn them, [4]then anyone who hears the alarm and refuses to heed it—well, if he dies the fault is his own. [5]For he heard the warning and wouldn't listen; the fault is his. If he had heeded the warning, he would have saved his life. [6]But if the watchman sees the enemy coming and doesn't sound the alarm and warn the people, he is responsible for their deaths. They will die in their sins, but I will charge the watchman with their deaths. [7]So with you, son of dust. I have appointed you as a watchman for the people of Israel; therefore listen to what I say and warn them for me. [8]When I say to the wicked, 'O wicked man, you will die!' and you don't tell him what I say, so that he does not repent —that wicked person will die in his sins, but I will hold you responsible for his death. [9]But if you warn him to repent and he doesn't, he will die in his sin, and you will not be responsible."

Ezk 34:2. Son of dust, prophesy against the shepherds, the leaders of Israel, and say to them: The Lord God says to you: Woe to the shepherds who feed themselves instead of their flocks. Shouldn't shepherds feed the sheep? [3]You eat the best food and wear the finest clothes, but you let your flocks starve. [4]You haven't taken care of the weak nor tended the sick nor bound up the broken bones nor gone looking for those who have wandered away and are lost. Instead you have ruled them with force and cruelty. [5]So they were scattered without a shepherd. They have become a prey to every animal that comes along. [6]My sheep wandered through the mountains and hills and over the face of the earth, and there was no one to search for them or care about them. [7]Therefore, O shepherds, hear the word of the Lord: [8]As I live, says the Lord God, you abandoned my flock, leaving them to be attacked and destroyed, and you were no real shepherds at all, for you didn't search for them. You fed yourselves and let them starve; [9, 10]therefore I am against the shepherds, and I will hold them responsible for what has happened to my flock. I will take away their right to feed the flock—and take away their right to eat. I will save my flock from being taken for their food. [11]For the Lord God says: I will search and find my sheep. [12]I will be like a shepherd looking for his flock. I will find my sheep and rescue them from all the places they were scattered in that dark and cloudy day. [13]And I will bring them back from among the people and nations where they were, back home to their own land of Israel, and I will feed them upon the mountains of Israel and by the rivers where the land is fertile and good. [14]Yes, I will give them good pasture on the high hills of Israel. There they will lie down in peace and feed in luscious mountain pastures. [15, 16]I myself will be the Shepherd of my sheep, and cause them to lie down in peace, the Lord God says. I will seek my lost ones, those who strayed away, and bring them safely home again. I will put splints and bandages upon their broken limbs and heal the sick. And I will destroy the powerful, fat shepherds; I will feed them, yes—feed them punishment! [17]And as for you, O my flock—my people—the Lord God says, I will distinguish lambs from kids and rams from billy goats! [18]Is it a small thing to you, O evil shepherds, that you not only keep the best of the pastures for yourselves, but trample down the rest? That you take the best water for yourselves, and muddy the rest with your feet? [19]All that's left for my flock is what you've trampled down; all they have to drink is water that you've fouled. [20]Therefore the Lord God says: I will surely judge between these fat shepherds and their scrawny sheep. [21]For these shepherds push and butt and crowd my sick and hungry flock until they're scattered far away. [22]So I myself will save my flock; no more will they be picked on and destroyed. And I will notice which is plump and which is thin, and why! [23]And I will set one Shepherd over all my people, even my Servant, David. He shall feed them and be a Shepherd to them. [24]And I, the Lord, will be their God, and my Servant David shall be a Prince among my people. I, the Lord, have spoken it. [25]I will make a peace pact with them, and drive away the dangerous animals from the land so that my people can safely camp in the wildest places and sleep safely in the woods. [26]I will make my people and their homes around my hill a blessing. And there shall be showers, showers of blessing, for I will not shut off the rains but send them in their seasons. [27]Their fruit trees and fields will yield bumper crops, and everyone will live in safety. When I have broken off their chains of slavery and delivered them from those who profiteered at their expense, they shall know I am the Lord. [28]No more will other nations conquer them nor wild animals attack. They shall live in safety and no one shall make them afraid. [29]And I will raise up a notable Vine (the Messiah), in Israel so that my people will never again go hungry nor be shamed by heathen conquest. [30]In this way they will know that I, the Lord their God, am with them, and that they, the people of Israel, are my people, says the Lord God. [31]You are my flock, the sheep of my pasture. You are my men and I am your God, so says the Lord.

Ezk 44:23. He shall teach my people the difference between what is holy and what is secular, what is right and what is wrong.

Joel 1:13. O priests, robe yourselves in sackcloth. O ministers of my God, lie all night before the altar, weeping. For there are no more offerings of grain and wine for you. [14]Announce a fast; call a solemn meeting. Gather the elders and all the people into the Temple of the Lord your God, and weep before him there. [15]Alas, this terrible day of punishment is on the way. Destruction from the Almighty is almost here!

Joel 2:17. The priests, the ministers of God will stand between the people and the altar, weeping; and they will pray, "Spare your people, O our God; don't let the heathen rule them, for they belong to you. Don't let them be disgraced by the taunts of the heathen who say, 'Where is this God of theirs? How weak and helpless he must be!"

Jon 1:2. "Go to the great city of Nineveh, and give them this announcement from the Lord: 'I am going to destroy you, for your wickedness rises before me; it smells to highest heaven.' "

Hab 2:2. And the Lord said to me, "Write my answer on a billboard, large and clear, so that anyone can read it at a glance and rush to tell the others."

Mal 2:7. Priests' lips should flow with the knowledge of God so the people will learn God's laws. The priests are the messengers of the Lord of Hosts.

FALSE AND CORRUPT. Deut 13:1. If there is a prophet among you, or one who claims to foretell the future by dreams, [2]and if his predictions come true but he says, "Come, let us worship the gods of the other nations," [3]don't listen to him. For the Lord is testing you to find out whether or not you really love him with all your heart and soul. [4]You must *never* worship any God but Jehovah; obey only his commands and cling to him. [5]The prophet who tries to lead you astray must be executed, for he has attempted to foment rebellion against the Lord your God who brought you out of slavery in the land of Egypt. By executing him you will clear out the evil from among you.

Deut 18:20. But any prophet who falsely claims that his message is from me, shall die. And any prophet who claims to give a message from other gods must die. [21]If you wonder, "How shall we know whether the prophecy is from the Lord or not?" [22]this is the way to know: If the thing he prophesies doesn't happen, it is not the Lord who has given him the message; he has made it up himself. You have nothing to fear from him. Deut 13:3, 5.

1 Kgs 12:31. He also made shrines on the hills and ordained priests from the rank and file of the people—even those who were not from the priest-tribe of Levi.

2 Chron 29:34. But there were too few priests to prepare the burnt offerings, so their brothers the Levites helped them until the work was finished—and until more priests had reported to work—for the Levites were much more ready to sanctify themselves than the priests were.

2 Chron 30:15. On the first day of May the people killed their Passover lambs. Then the priests and Levites became ashamed of themselves for not taking a more active part, so they sanctified themselves and brought burnt offerings into the Temple.

Neh 13:29. Remember them, O my God, for they have defiled the priesthood and the promises and vows of the priests and Levites.

Prov 19:27. Stop listening to teaching that contradicts what you know is right.

Isa 3:12. O my people! Can't you see what fools your rulers are? . . . True leaders? No, misleaders! Leading you down the garden path to destruction.

Isa 5:20. They say that what is right is wrong, and what is wrong is right; that black is white and white is black; bitter is sweet and sweet is bitter.

Isa 8:19. So why are you trying to find out the future by consulting witches and mediums? Don't listen to their whisperings and mutterings. Can the living find out the future from the dead? Why not ask your God? [20]"Check these witches' words against the Word of God!" he says. "If their messages are different than mine, it is because I have not sent them; for they have no light or truth in them."

Isa 9:14, 15. Therefore the Lord, in one day, will destroy the leaders of Israel and the lying prophets. [16]For the leaders of his people have led them down the paths of ruin.

Isa 28:7. But Jerusalem is now led by drunks! Her priests and prophets reel and stagger, making stupid errors and mistakes.

Isa 29:10. For the Lord has poured out upon you a spirit of deep sleep. He has closed the eyes of your prophets and seers, [11]so all of these future events are a sealed book to them. When you give it to one who can read, he says, "I can't, for it's sealed."

Isa 30:10. They tell my prophets, "Shut up—we don't want any more of your reports!" Or they say, "Don't tell us the truth; tell us nice things; tell us lies."

Isa 43:27. From the very first your ancestors sinned against me—all your forebears transgressed my law. [28]That is why I have deposed your priests and destroyed Israel, leaving her to shame.

Isa 44:20. The poor, deluded fool feeds on ashes; he is trusting what can never give him any help at all. Yet he cannot bring himself to ask, "Is this thing, this idol that I'm holding in my hand, a lie?"

Isa 56:10. For the leaders of my people—the Lord's watchmen, his shepherds—are all blind to every danger. They are featherbrained and give no warning when danger comes. They love to lie there, love to sleep, to dream. [11]And they are as greedy as dogs, never satisfied; they are stupid shepherds who only look after their own interest, each trying to get as much as he can for himself from every possible source. [12]"Come," they say. "We'll get some wine and have a party; let's all get drunk."

Jer 2:8. Even their priests cared nothing for the Lord, and their judges ignored me; their rulers turned against me, and their prophets worshiped Baal and wasted their time on nonsense.

Jer 5:30. A horrible thing has happened in this land—[31]the priests are ruled by false prophets, and my people like it so! But your doom is certain. *vs.* 13, 14.

Jer 6:13. They are swindlers and liars, from the least of them right to the top! Yes, even my prophets and priests! [14]You can't heal a wound by saying it's not there! Yet the priests and prophets give assurances of peace when all is war. Jer 8:10, 11.

Jer 10:21. The shepherds of my people have lost their senses; they no longer follow God nor ask his will. Therefore they perish and their flocks are scattered.

Jer 12:10. Many foreign rulers have ravaged my vineyard, trampling down the vines, and turning all its beauty into barren wilderness.

Jer 13:20. See the armies marching from the north! Where is your flock, Jerusalem, your beautiful flock I gave you to take care of?

Jer 14:13. Then I said, O Lord God, their prophets are telling them that all is well—that no war or famine will come. They tell the people you will surely send them peace, that you will bless them. [14]Then the Lord said: The prophets are telling lies in my name. I didn't send them or tell them to speak or give them any message. They prophesy of visions and revelations they have never seen nor heard; they speak foolishness concocted out of their own lying hearts. [15]Therefore, the Lord says, I will punish these lying prophets who have spoken in my name though I did not send them, who say no war shall come nor famine. By war and famine they themselves shall die! [16]And the people to whom they prophesy—their bodies shall be thrown out into the streets of Jerusalem, victims of famine and war; there shall be no one to bury them. Husbands, wives, sons and daughters—all will be gone. For I will pour out terrible punishment upon them for their sins.

Jer 23:1. The Lord declares: I will send disaster upon the leaders of my people—the shepherds of my sheep—for they have destroyed and scattered the very ones they were to care for. [2]Instead of leading my flock to safety, you have deserted them and driven them to destruction. And now I will pour out judgment upon you for the evil you have done to them. [11]And the priests are like the prophets, all ungodly, wicked men. I have seen their despicable acts right here in my own Temple, says the Lord. [14]But the prophets of Jerusalem are even worse! The things they do are horrible; they commit adultery and love dishonesty. They encourage and compliment those who are doing evil, instead of turning them back from their sins. These prophets are as thoroughly depraved as the men of Sodom and Gomorrah were. [15]Therefore the Lord of Hosts says: I will feed them with bitterness and give them poison to drink. For it is because of them that wickedness fills this land. [16]This is my warning to my people, says the Lord of Hosts. Don't listen to these false prophets when they prophesy to you, filling you with futile hopes. They are making up everything they say. They do not speak for me! [21]I have not sent these prophets, yet they claim to speak for me; I gave them no message, yet they say their words are mine. [30, 31]So I stand against these "prophets" who get their messages from each other—these smooth-tongued prophets who say, "This message is from God!" [32]Their made-up dreams are flippant lies that lead my people into sin. I did not send them and they have no message at all for my people, says the Lord. [36]But stop using this term, "God's sad news." For what is sad is you and your lying. You are twisting my words and inventing "messages from God" that I didn't speak. *vs.* 25–39; Jer 27:9–18.

Jer 48:10. Cursed be those . . . refusing to do the work that God has given them!

Jer 50:6. My people have been lost sheep. Their shepherds led them astray and then turned them loose in the mountains. They lost their way and didn't remember how to get back to the fold.

Lam 2:14. Your "prophets" have said so many foolish things, false to the core. They have not tried to hold you back from slavery by pointing out your sins. They lied and said that all was well.

Lam 4:13. Yet God permitted it because of the sins of her prophets and priests, who defiled the city by shedding innocent blood. [14]Now these same men are blindly staggering through the streets, covered with blood, defiling everything they touch.

Ezk 13:2, 3. Son of dust, prophesy against the false prophets of Israel who are inventing their own visions and claiming to have messages from me when I have never told them anything at all. Woe upon them! [4]O Israel, these "prophets" of yours are as useless as foxes for rebuilding your walls! [5]O evil prophets, what have you ever done to strengthen the walls of Israel against her enemies—by strengthening Israel in the Lord? [10]For these evil men deceive my people by saying, "God will send peace," when that is not my plan at all! My people build a flimsy wall and these prophets praise them for it—and cover it with whitewash! [11]Tell these evil builders that their wall will fall. A heavy rainstorm will undermine it; great hailstones and mighty winds will knock it down. [16]For they were lying prophets, claiming Jerusalem will have peace when there is no peace, says the Lord God. [17]Son of dust, speak out against the women prophets too who pretend the Lord has given them his messages. [18]Tell them the Lord God says: Woe to these women who are damning the souls of my people, of both young and old alike, by tying magic charms on their wrists and furnishing them with magic veils and selling them indulgences. They refuse to even offer help unless they get a profit from it. [19]For the sake of a few paltry handfuls of barley or a piece of bread will you turn away my people from me? You have led those to death who should not die! And you have promised life to those who should not live, by lying to my people—and how they love it! [22]Your lies have discouraged the righteous, when I didn't want it so. And you have encouraged the wicked by promising life, though they continue in their sins. *vs.* 1–23.

Ezk 14:9. And if one of the false prophets gives him a message anyway, it is a lie. His prophecy will not come true, and I will stand against that "prophet" and destroy him from among my people Israel. [10]False prophets and hypocrites—evil people who say they want my words—all will be punished for their sins.

Ezk 22:25. Your "prophets" have plotted against you like lions stalking prey. They devour many lives; they seize treasures and extort wealth; they multiply the widows in the land. [26]Your priests have violated my laws and defiled my Temple and my holiness. To them the things of God are no more important than any daily task. They have not taught my people the difference between right and wrong, and they disregard my Sabbaths, so my holy name is greatly defiled among them. [28]Your "prophets" describe false visions and speak false messages they claim are from God, when he hasn't spoken one word to them at all. Thus they repair the walls with whitewash!

Ezk 34:2. Son of dust, prophesy against the shepherds, the leaders of Israel, and say to them: The Lord God says to you: Woe to the shepherds who feed themselves instead of their flocks. Shouldn't shepherds feed the sheep? [3]You eat the best food and wear the finest clothes, but you let your flocks starve. [4]You haven't taken care of the weak nor tended the sick nor bound up the broken bones nor gone looking for those who have wandered away and are lost. Instead you have ruled them with force and cruelty. [6]My sheep wandered through the mountains and hills and over the face of the earth, and there was no one to search for them or care about them. [9, 10]Therefore I am against the shepherds, and I will hold them responsible for what has happened to my flock. I will take away their right to feed the flock—and take away their right to eat. I will save my flock from being taken for their food. *vs.* 1–31.

Ezk 44:8. You have not kept the laws I gave you concerning these holy affairs, for you have hired foreigners to take charge of my sanctuary. [10]And the men of the tribe of Levi who abandoned me when Israel strayed away from God to idols must be punished for their unfaithfulness.

Hos 4:6. My people are destroyed because they don't know me, and it is all your fault, you priests, for you yourselves refuse to know me; therefore I refuse to recognize you as my priests. Since you have forgotten my laws, I will "forget" to bless your children. [8]The priests rejoice in the sins of the people; they lap it up and lick their lips for more! [9]And thus it is: "Like priests, like people"—because the priests are wicked, the people are too. Therefore, I will punish both priests and people for all their wicked deeds. *vs.* 10–13.

Hos 5:1. Listen to this, you priests and all of Israel's leaders; listen, all you men of the royal family: You are doomed! For you have deluded the people with idols at Mizpah and Tabor.

Hos 6:9. Her citizens are gangs of robbers, lying in ambush for their victims; packs of priests murder along the road to Shechem and practice every kind of sin.

Hos 9:8. I appointed the prophets to guard my people, but the people have blocked them at every turn and publicly declared their hatred, even in the Temple of the Lord. *v.* 7.

Amos 2:11. And I chose your sons to be Nazirites and prophets—can you deny this, Israel? asks the Lord. [12]But you caused the Nazirites to sin by urging them to drink your wine, and you silenced my prophets, telling them, "Shut up!"

Mic 2:11. "I'll preach to you the joys of wine and drink"—that is the kind of drunken, lying prophet that you like!

Mic 3:5. You false prophets! You who lead his people astray! You who cry "Peace" to those who give you food, and threaten those who will not pay! This is God's message to you: [6]The night will close about you and cut off all your visions; darkness will cover you, with never a word from God. The sun will go down upon you, and your day will end. [7]Then at last you will cover your faces in shame, and admit that your messages were not from God. [11]You leaders who take bribes; you priests and prophets who won't preach and prophesy until you're paid. (And yet you fawn upon the Lord and say, "All is well—the Lord is here among us. No harm can come to us.")

Zeph 3:4. Her "prophets" are liars seeking their own gain; her priests defile the Temple by their disobedience to God's laws.

Zech 10:3. My anger burns against your "shepherds"—your leaders—and I will punish them—these goats. For the Lord of Hosts has arrived to help his flock of Judah. I will make them strong and glorious like a proud steed in battle.

Zech 11:4. Then said the Lord my God to me, "Go and take a job as shepherd of a flock being fattened for the butcher. 5This will illustrate the way my people have been bought and slain by wicked leaders, who go unpunished. 'Thank God, now I am rich!' say those who have betrayed them—their own shepherds have sold them without mercy." 16And he said to me, "This illustrates how I will give this nation a shepherd who will not care for the dying ones, nor look after the young, nor heal the broken bones, nor feed the healthy ones, nor carry the lame that cannot walk; instead, he will eat the fat ones, even tearing off the feet. 17Woe to this worthless shepherd who doesn't care for the flock. God's sword will cut his arm and pierce through his right eye; his arm will become useless and his right eye blinded."

Zech 13:2. And the Lord of Hosts declares. . . . "All false prophets and fortune-tellers will be wiped out, 3and if anyone begins false prophecy again, his own father and mother will slay him! 'You must die,' they will tell him, 'for you are prophesying lies in the name of the Lord.' 4No one will be boasting then of his prophetic gift! No one will wear prophet's clothes to try to fool the people then. 5 'No,' he will say. 'I am not a prophet; I am a farmer. The soil has been my livelihood from my earliest youth.' "

Mal 1:6. "A son honors his father, a servant honors his master. I am your Father and Master, yet you don't honor me, O priests, but you despise my name." "Who? Us?" you say. "When did we ever despise your name?" *vs.* 7–10.

Mal 2:8. "For you have left God's paths. Your 'guidance' has caused many to stumble in sin. You have distorted the covenant of Levi, and made it into a grotesque parody," says the Lord of Hosts. 9"Therefore I have made you contemptible in the eyes of all the people; for you have not obeyed me, but you let your favorites break the law without rebuke." *vs.* 1–3.

PROMISES TO, AND JOYS OF. Ps 126:5. Those who sow tears shall reap joy. 6Yes, they go out weeping, carrying seed for sowing, and return singing, carrying their sheaves.

Jer 1:7. "Don't say that," he replied, "for you will go wherever I send you and speak whatever I tell you to. 8And don't be afraid of the people, for I, the Lord, will be with you and see you through." 9Then he touched my mouth and said, "See, I have put my words in your mouth! 10Today your work begins, to warn the nations and the kingdoms of the world. In accord with my words spoken through your mouth I will tear down some and destroy them, and plant others and nurture them and make them strong and great. 17Get up and dress and go out and tell them whatever I tell you to say. Don't be afraid of them, or else I will make a fool of you in front of them. 18For see, today I have made you impervious to their attacks. They cannot harm you. You are strong like a fortified city that cannot be captured, like an iron pillar and heavy gates of brass. All the kings of Judah and its officers and priests and people will not be able to prevail against you. 19They will try, but they will fail. For I am with you," says the Lord. "I will deliver you."

Jer 20:11. But the Lord stands beside me like a great warrior, and before him, the Mighty, Terrible One, they shall stumble. They cannot defeat me; they shall be shamed and thoroughly humiliated, and they shall have a stigma upon them forever.

Dan 12:3. And those who are wise—the people of God—shall shine as brightly as the sun's brilliance, and those who turn many to righteousness will glitter like stars forever.

TRIALS AND PERSECUTIONS OF. 1 Kgs 19:1. When Ahab told Queen Jezebel what Elijah had done, and that he had slaughtered the prophets of Baal, 2she sent this message to Elijah: "You killed my prophets, and now I swear by the gods that I am going to kill you by this time tomorrow night." 3So Elijah fled for his life; he went to Beer-sheba, a city of Judah, and left his servant there. 4Then he went on alone into the wilderness, traveling all day, and sat down under a broom bush and prayed that he might die. "I've had enough," he told the Lord. "Take away my life. I've got to die sometime, and it might as well be now." 5Then he lay down and slept beneath the broom bush. But as he was sleeping, an angel touched him and told him to get up and eat! 6He looked around and saw some bread baking on hot stones, and a jar of water! So he ate and drank and lay down again. 7Then the angel of the Lord came again and touched him and said, "Get up and eat some more, for there is a long journey ahead of you." 8So he got up and ate and drank, and the food gave him enough strength to travel forty days and forty nights to Mount Horeb, the mountain of God, 9where he lived in a cave. But the Lord said to him, "What are you doing here, Elijah?" 10He replied, "I have worked very hard for the Lord God of the heavens; but the people of Israel have broken their covenant with you and torn down your altars and killed your prophets, and only I am left; and now they are trying to kill me, too."

Isa 20:2. The Lord told Isaiah, the son of Amoz, to take off his clothing, including his shoes, and to walk around naked and barefoot. And Isaiah did as he was told. 3Then the Lord said, My servant Isaiah, who has been walking naked and barefoot for the last three years, is a symbol of the terrible troubles I will bring upon Egypt and Ethiopia.

Ezk 24:15. Again a message came to me from the Lord, saying: 16"Son of dust, I am going to take away your lovely wife. Suddenly, she will die. Yet you must show no sorrow. Do not weep; let there be no tears. [17]You may sigh, but only quietly. Let there be no wailing at her grave; don't bare your head nor feet, and don't accept the food brought to you by consoling friends." [18]I proclaimed this to the people in the morning, and in the evening my wife died. The next morning I did all the Lord had told me to.

Hos 1:2. Here is the first message: The Lord said to Hosea, "Go and marry a girl who is a prostitute, so that some of her children will be born to you from other men. This will illustrate the way my people have been untrue to me, committing open adultery against me by worshiping other gods."

Amos 5:10. How you hate honest judges! How you despise people who tell the truth!

Amos 7:10. But when Amaziah, the priest of Bethel, heard what Amos was saying, he rushed a message to Jeroboam, the king: "Amos is a traitor to our nation and is plotting your death. This is intolerable. It will lead to rebellion all across the land. [11]He says you will be killed, and Israel will be sent far away into exile and slavery." [12]Then Amaziah sent orders to Amos, "Get out of here, you prophet, you! Flee to the land of Judah and do your prophesying there. [13]Don't bother us here with your visions, not here in the capital, where the king's chapel is!" [14]But Amos replied, "I am not really one of the prophets. I do not come from a family of prophets. I am just a herdsman and fruit picker. [15]But the Lord took me from caring for the flocks and told me, 'Go and prophesy to my people Israel.' [16]Now therefore listen to this message to you from the Lord. You say, 'Don't prophesy against Israel.' [17]The Lord's reply is this: 'Because of your interference, your wife will become a prostitute in this city, and your sons and daughters will be killed and your land divided up. You yourself will die in a heathen land, and the people of Israel will certainly become slaves in exile, far from their land.' "

MINISTER, NEW TESTAMENT The Greek root, like the Old Testament Hebrew equivalent, means simply a servant, or to serve. The following serve as ministers: Christ, Mt 20:28; Mk 10:45; Rom 15:8; Heb 8:2, 6; Paul, Acts 26:16; Rom 15:15, 16; Eph 3:7; Col 1:23, 25; 1 Tim 2:7; Tychicus, Eph 6:21; Col 4:7; Epaphras, Col 1:7; Timothy, 1 Thess 3:2, 3; 1 Tim 4:6; Apollos, 1 Cor 3:5; angels, Heb 1:7, 14; civil authority, Rom 13:4, 6; the servants of Satan, 2 Cor 11:15. The following selection of passages includes references to various kinds of servants of God, as well as false teachers and others.

Called: *Angels of the church,* Rev 1:20; 2:1; *Apostles,* Lk 6:13; Rev 18:20.

Christ's ambassadors, 2 Cor 5:20; *Christ's servants,* 1 Cor 4:1.

Defenders of the truth, Phil 1:7.

Elders, 1 Pet 5:1; *Evangelists,* Acts 21:8.

Fishers of men, Mt 4:19; Mk 1:17.

God's partners, 2 Cor 6:1.

Laborers, Lk 10:2; *Lights,* Jn 5:35.

Men of God, 1 Tim 6:11; *Ministers of God,* 2 Cor 6:4; *of Christ,* Rom 15:15, 16; Tit 1:1, 2; *Missionaries,* Lk 6:13; 1 Tim 2:7.

Overseers, Acts 20:28.

Pastors, 1 Tim 3:1; 5:17; *Preachers,* Acts 4:36.

Servants of God, Jas 1:1; *of Jesus Christ,* Jude 1:1; *Slave of God,* Tit 1:1, 2; *of Jesus Christ,* Phil 1:1; *Soldiers of Christ,* 2 Tim 2:3, 4; *Stars,* Rev 1:20.

Teachers, Eph 4:11; 2 Tim 2:24.

Witnesses, Acts 5:32; 26:16; *Workers,* Mt 9:38, with Philemon 1:1, 2; 1 Thess 3:2, 3;

Likened to sowers, Mt 13:2–8; Mk 4:3–20; Lk 8:5–8.

Tact of, 1 Cor 9:20–23; 10:23, 28–33; 2 Cor 12:16. Recreations for, Mk 6:31, 32, 45. Take leave of congregations, Acts 20:17–38. Personal bearing of, Tit 2:7, 8. Preach without ecclesiastical authority, Gal 1:15–24; 2:1–9. Patience of, Jas 5:10. Work of, will be tried, 1 Cor 3:12–15. Responsibility of, Mt 10:14–40; Acts 18:6; 20:26, 27. Speaking evil of, forbidden, Jude 1:8–10.

Marriage of, Mt 8:14; 1 Cor 9:5; 1 Tim 3:2, 12; Tit 1:5–7. Incorruptible; 2 Pet 2:15, 16; Peter, Acts 8:18–23.

Love of, for the church, exemplified by Paul, Phil 1:7; 1 Thess 1:2–4; 2:8, 11. Examples to the flock, Phil 3:17; 2 Thess 3:9; 1 Tim 4:12; 1 Pet 5:3. Intolerance of, Mt 15:23; 19:13; Mk 10:13; Lk 18:15. Inconsistent, Mt 27:3–7. God's care of, Mt 10:29–31; Lk 12:6, 7. Their calling glorious, 2 Cor 3:7–11. Discouragements of, Mt 13:57; Mk 6:2–4; Lk 4:24; Jn 4:43, 44.

Beloved, Acts 20:37, 38; 21:5, 6.

Sent out two by two: Disciples, Mk 6:7. The seventy, Lk 10:1–20. Paul and Barnabas, Acts 13:2, 3. Judas and Silas, Acts 15:26. Barnabas and Mark, Acts 15:37, 39. Paul and Silas, Acts 15:40. Paul and Timothy, Acts 16:1–4. Paul and Titus, 2 Cor 8:19, 23. Timothy and Erastus, Acts 19:22. Titus and a companion, 2 Cor 12:18.

CALL OF. Mt 4:18. One day as he was walking along the beach beside the Lake of Galilee, he saw two brothers—Simon, also called Peter, and Andrew—out in a boat fishing with a net, for they were commercial fishermen. [19]Jesus called out, "Come along with me and I will show you how to fish for the souls of men!" [20]And they left their nets at once and went with him. [21]A little farther up the beach he saw two other brothers, James and John, sitting in a boat with their father Zebedee, mending their nets; and he called to them to come too. [22]At once they stopped their work and, leaving their father behind, went with him. Mk 1:17–20.

Mt 9:9. As Jesus was going on down the road, he saw a tax collector, Matthew, sitting at a tax collection booth. "Come and be my disciple," Jesus said to him, and Matthew jumped up and went along with him. Mt 10:1–6; Mk 2:14.

Lk 10:1. The Lord now chose seventy other disciples and sent them on ahead in pairs to all the towns and villages he planned to visit later. [2]These were his instructions to them: "Plead with the Lord of the harvest to send out more laborers to help you, for the harvest is so plentiful and the workers so few."

Jn 1:43. The next day Jesus decided to go to Galilee. He found Philip and told him, "Come with me."

Acts 13:2. One day as these men were worshiping and fasting the Holy Spirit said, "Dedicate Barnabas and Paul for a special job I have for them." [3]So after more fasting and prayer, the men laid their hands on them—and sent them on their way.

Acts 20:24. But life is worth nothing unless I use it for doing the work assigned me by the Lord Jesus—the work of telling others the Good News about God's mighty kindness and love.

Acts 22:12. There a man named Ananias, as godly a man as you could find for obeying the law, and well thought of by all the Jews of Damascus, [13]came to me, and standing beside me said, "Brother Saul, receive your sight!" And that very hour I could see him! [14]Then he told me, "The God of our fathers has chosen you to know his will and to see the Messiah and hear him speak. [15]You are to take his message everywhere, telling what you have seen and heard."

Acts 26:14. We all fell down, and I heard a voice speaking to me in Hebrew, "Saul, Saul, why are you persecuting me? You are only hurting yourself." [15]"Who are you, sir?" I asked. And the Lord replied, "I am Jesus, the one you are persecuting. [16]Now stand up! For I have appeared to you to appoint you as my servant and my witness. You are to tell the world about this experience and about the many other occasions when I shall appear to you. [17]And I will protect you from both your own people and the Gentiles. Yes, I am going to send you to the Gentiles [18]to open their eyes to their true condition so that they may repent and live in the light of God instead of in Satan's darkness, so that they may receive forgiveness for their sins and God's inheritance along with all people everywhere whose sins are cleansed away, who are set apart by faith in me."

Rom 1:1. Dear friends in Rome: This letter is from Paul, Jesus Christ's slave, chosen to be a missionary, and sent out to preach God's Good News.

Rom 10:14. But how shall they ask him to save them unless they believe in him? And how can they believe in him if they have never heard about him? And how can they hear about him unless someone tells them? [15]And how will anyone go and tell them unless someone sends him? That is what the Scriptures are talking about when they say, "How beautiful are the feet of those who preach the Gospel of peace with God and bring glad tidings of good things." In other words, how welcome are those who come preaching God's Good News!

1 Cor 1:1. From: Paul, chosen by God to be Jesus Christ's missionary, and from brother Sosthenes. [2 Cor 1:1; Col 1:1.] [27]Instead, God has deliberately chosen to use ideas the world considers foolish and of little worth in order to shame those people considered by the world as wise and great. [28]He has chosen a plan despised by the world, counted as nothing at all, and used it to bring down to nothing those the world considers great.

1 Cor 9:16. For just preaching the Gospel isn't any special credit to me—I couldn't keep from preaching it if I wanted to. I would be utterly miserable. Woe unto me if I don't. [17]If I were volunteering my services of my own free will, then the Lord would give me a special reward; but that is not the situation, for God has picked me out and given me this sacred trust and I have no choice. [18]Under this circumstance, what is my pay? It is the special joy I get from preaching the Good News without expense to anyone, never demanding my rights. [19]And this has a real advantage: I am not bound to obey anyone just because he pays my salary; yet I have freely and happily become a servant of any and all so that I can win them to Christ.

2 Cor 5:18. All these new things are from God who brought us back to himself through what Christ Jesus did. And God has given us the privilege of urging everyone to come into his favor and be reconciled to him. [19]For God was in Christ, restoring the world to himself, no longer counting men's sins against them but blotting them out. This is the wonderful message he has given us to tell others. [20]We are Christ's ambassadors. God is using us to speak to you: we beg you, as though Christ himself were here pleading with you, receive the love he offers you—be reconciled to God.

Gal 1:15. But then something happened! For even before I was born God had chosen me to be his, and called me—what kindness and grace—[16]to reveal his Son within me so that I could go to the Gentiles and show them the Good News about Jesus.

Eph 3:7. God has given me the wonderful privilege of telling everyone about this plan of his; and he has given me his power and special ability to do it well. [8]Just think! Though I did nothing to deserve it, and though I am the most useless Christian there is, yet I was the one chosen for this special joy of telling the Gentiles the Glad News of the endless treasures available to them in Christ.

Eph 4:11. Some of us have been given special ability as apostles; to others he has given the gift of being able to preach well; some have special ability in winning people to Christ, helping them to trust him as their Savior; still others have a gift for caring for God's people as a shepherd does his sheep, leading and teaching them in the ways of God. [12]Why is it that he gives us these special abilities to do certain things best? It is that God's people will be equipped to do better work for him, building up the church, the body of Christ, to a position of strength and maturity.

Col 1:25. God has sent me to help his church and to tell his secret plan to you Gentiles. [26, 27]He has kept this secret for centuries and generations past, but now at last it has pleased him to tell it to those who love him and live for him, and the riches and glory of his plan are for you Gentiles too. And this is the secret: *that Christ in your hearts is your only hope of glory.* [28]So everywhere we go we talk about Christ to all who will listen, warning them and teaching them as well as we know how. We want to be able to present each one to God, perfect because of what Christ has done for each of them. [29]This is my work, and I can do it only because Christ's mighty energy is at work within me.

Col 4:17. And say to Archippus, "Be sure that you do all the Lord has told you to."

1 Tim 1:12. How thankful I am to Christ Jesus our Lord for choosing me as one of his messengers, and giving me the strength to be faithful to him, [13]even though I used to scoff at the name of Christ. I hunted down his people, harming them in every way I could. But God had mercy on me because I didn't know what I was doing, for I didn't know Christ at that time. [14]Oh, how kind our Lord was, for he showed me how to trust him and become full of the love of Christ Jesus.

1 Tim 2:7. And I have been chosen—this is the absolute truth—as God's minister and missionary to teach this truth to the Gentiles, and to show them God's plan of salvation through faith. 2 Tim 1:11.

Tit 1:3. And now in his own good time he has revealed this Good News and permits me to tell it to everyone. By command of God our Savior I have been trusted to do this work for him.

CHARACTER AND QUALIFICATIONS OF. Mt 10:16. I am sending you out as sheep among wolves. Be as wary as serpents and harmless as doves. [17]But beware! For you will be arrested and tried, and whipped in the synagogues. [18]Yes, and you must stand trial before governors and kings for my sake. This will give you the opportunity to tell them about me, yes, to witness to the world. [19]When you are arrested, don't worry about what to say at your trial, for you will be given the right words at the right time. [20]For it won't be you doing the talking —it will be the Spirit of your heavenly Father speaking through you! [22]Everyone shall hate you because you belong to me. But all of you who endure to the end shall be saved. [23]When you are persecuted in one city, flee to the next! I will return before you have reached them all! [24]A student is not greater than his teacher. A servant is not above his master.

Mt 11:25. And Jesus prayed this prayer: "O Father, Lord of heaven and earth, thank you for hiding the truth from those who think themselves so wise, and for revealing it to little children. [Lk 10: 21.] [26]Yes, Father, for it pleased you to do it this way! . . ."

Mt 13:51. "Do you understand?" "Yes," they said, "we do." [52]Then he added, "Those experts in Jewish law who are now my disciples have double treasures—from the Old Testament as well as from the New!"

Mt 20:25. But Jesus called them together and said, "Among the heathen, kings are tyrants and each minor official lords it over those beneath him. [26]But among you it is quite different. Anyone wanting to be a leader among you must be your servant. [27]And if you want to be right at the top, you must serve like a slave. [28]Your attitude must be like my own, for I, the Messiah, did not come to be served, but to serve, and to give my life as a ransom for many." Lk 22:27; Jn 13:14, 15.

Mt 23:8. Don't ever let anyone call you that. For only God is your Rabbi and all of you are on the same level, as brothers. [9]And don't address anyone here on earth as "Father," for only God in heaven should be addressed like that. [10]And don't be called "Master," for only one is your master, even the Messiah. [11]The more lowly your service to others, the greater you are. To be the greatest, be a servant.

Lk 6:39. Here are some of the story-illustrations Jesus used in his sermons: "What good is it for one blind man to lead another? He will fall into a ditch and pull the other down with him."

Lk 12:42–44. And the Lord replied, "I'm talking to any faithful, sensible man whose master gives him the responsibility of feeding the other servants. If his master returns and finds that he has done a good job, there will be a reward—his master will put him in charge of all he owns." Mt 24:45.

Lk 24:49. And now I will send the Holy Spirit upon you, just as my Father promised. Don't begin telling others yet—stay here in the city until the Holy Spirit comes and fills you with power from heaven.

Jn 3:27. John replied, "God in heaven appoints each man's work. [34]For this one—sent by God—speaks God's words, for God's Spirit is upon him without measure or limit."

Jn 4:36. The reapers will be paid good wages and will be gathering eternal souls into the granaries of heaven! What joys await the sower and the reaper, both together! [37]For it is true that one sows and someone else reaps. [38]I sent you to reap where you didn't sow; others did the work, and you received the harvest.

Jn 10:2. For a shepherd comes through the gate. [3]The gatekeeper opens the gate for him, and the sheep hear his voice and come to him; and he calls his own sheep by name and leads them out. [4]He walks ahead of them; and they follow him, for they recognize his voice. [5]They won't follow a stranger but will run from him, for they don't recognize his voice. [11]I am the Good Shepherd. The Good Shepherd lays down his life for the sheep. [12]A hired man will run when he sees a wolf coming and will leave the sheep, for they aren't his and he isn't their shepherd. And so the wolf leaps on them and scatters the flock. [13]The hired man runs because he is hired and has no real concern for the sheep. [14]I am the Good Shepherd and know my own sheep, and they know me, [15]just as my Father knows me and I know the Father; and I lay down my life for the sheep.

Jn 13:13. You call me "Master" and "Lord," and you do well to say it, for it is true. [14]And since I, the Lord and Teacher, have washed your feet, you ought to wash each other's feet. [15]I have given you an example to follow: do as I have done to you. [16]How true it is that a servant is not greater than his master. Nor is the messenger more important than the one who sends him. [17]You know these things—now do them! That is the path of blessing.

Jn 15:20. Do you remember what I told you? "A slave isn't greater than his master!" So since they persecuted me, naturally they will persecute you. And if they had listened to me, they would listen to you! [21]The people of the world will persecute you because you belong to me, for they don't know God who sent me.

Jn 17:16. They are not part of this world any more than I am. [17]Make them pure and holy through teaching them your words of truth. [18]As you sent me into the world, I am sending them into the world. [20]I am not praying for these alone but also for the future believers who will come to me because of the testimony of these.

Acts 1:8. But when the Holy Spirit has come upon you, you will receive power to testify about me with great effect, to the people in Jerusalem, throughout Judea, in Samaria, and to the ends of the earth, about my death and resurrection.

Acts 4:8. Then Peter, filled with the Holy Spirit, said to them, "Honorable leaders and elders of our nation." [31]After this prayer, the building where they were meeting shook and they were all filled with the Holy Spirit and boldly preached God's message.

Acts 6:3. Now look around among yourselves, dear brothers, and select seven men, wise and full of the Holy Spirit, who are well thought of by everyone; and we will put them in charge of this business. [4]Then we can spend our time in prayer, preaching and teaching.

Acts 20:22. And now I am going to Jerusalem, drawn there irresistibly by the Holy Spirit, not knowing what awaits me, [23]except that the Holy Spirit has told me in city after city that jail and suffering lie ahead. [24]But life is worth nothing unless I use it for doing the work assigned me by the Lord Jesus—the work of telling others the Good News about God's mighty kindness and love.

Rom 2:21. Yes, you teach others—then why don't you teach yourselves? You tell others not to steal—do *you* steal? [22]You say it is wrong to commit adultery—do *you* do it? You say, "Don't pray to idols," and then make money your god instead. [23]You are so proud of knowing God's laws, *but you dishonor him by breaking them.*

1 Cor 1:23. So when we preach about Christ dying to save them, the Jews are offended and the Gentiles say it's all nonsense. [27]Instead, God has deliberately chosen to use ideas the world considers foolish and of little worth in order to shame those people considered by the world as wise and great. [28]He has chosen a plan despised by the world, counted as nothing at all, and used it to bring down to nothing those the world considers great, [29]so that no one anywhere can ever brag in the presence of God. [30]For it is from God alone that you have your life through Christ Jesus. He showed us God's plan of salvation; he was the one who made us acceptable to God; he made us pure and holy and gave himself to purchase our salvation.

1 Cor 2:2. For I decided that I would speak only of Jesus Christ and his death on the cross.

1 Cor 3:7. The person who does the planting or watering isn't very important, but God is important because he is the one who makes things grow. [8]Apollos and I are working as a team, with the same aim, though each of us will be rewarded for his own hard work. [9]We are only God's co-workers. You are *God's* garden, not ours; you are *God's* building, not ours. [10]God, in his kindness, has taught me how to be an expert builder. I have laid the foundation and Apollos has built on it. But he who builds on the foundation must be very careful.

1 Cor 4:10. Religion has made us foolish, you say, but of course you are all such wise and sensible Christians! We are weak, but not you! You are well thought of, while we are laughed at. [11]To this very hour we have gone hungry and thirsty, without even enough clothes to keep us warm. We have been kicked around without homes of our own. [12]We have worked wearily with our hands to earn our living. We have blessed those who cursed us. We have been patient with those who injured us. [13]We have replied quietly when evil things have been said about us. Yet right up to the present moment we are like dirt under foot, like garbage.

1 Cor 9:16. For just preaching the Gospel isn't any special credit to me—I couldn't keep from preaching it if I wanted to. I would be utterly miserable. Woe unto me if I don't. [17]If I were volunteering my services of my own free will, then the Lord would give me a special reward; but that is not the situation, for God has picked me out and given me this sacred trust and I have no choice. [18]Under this circumstance, what is my pay? It is the special joy I get from preaching the Good News without expense to anyone, never demanding my rights. [19]And this has a real advantage: I am not bound to obey anyone just because he pays my salary; yet I have freely and happily become a servant of any and all so that I can win them to Christ. [20]When I am with the Jews I seem as one of them so that they will listen to the Gospel and I can win them to Christ. When I am with Gentiles who follow Jewish customs and ceremonies I don't argue, even though I don't agree, because I want to help them. [21]When with the heathen I agree with them as much as I can, except of course that I must always do what is right as a Christian. And so, by agreeing, I can win their confidence and help them too. [22]When I am with those whose consciences bother them easily, I don't act as though I know it all and don't say they are foolish; the result is that they are willing to let me help them. Yes, whatever a person is like, I try to find a common ground with him so that he will let me tell him about Christ and let Christ save him. [23]I do this to get the Gospel to them and also for the blessing I myself receive when I see them come to Christ. [27]Like an athlete I punish my body, treating it roughly, training it to do what it should, not what

it wants to. Otherwise I fear that after enlisting others for the race, I myself might be declared unfit and ordered to stand aside.

1 Cor 15:10. But whatever I am now it is all because God poured out such kindness and grace upon me—and not without results: for I have worked harder than all the other apostles, yet actually I wasn't doing it, but God working in me, to bless me.

2 Cor 2:15. As far as God is concerned there is a sweet, wholesome fragrance in our lives. It is the fragrance of Christ within us, an aroma to both the saved and the unsaved all around us.
16To those who are not being saved, we seem a fearful smell of death and doom, while to those who know Christ we are a life-giving perfume. But who is adequate for such a task as this?
17Only those who, like ourselves, are men of integrity, sent by God, speaking with Christ's power, with God's eye upon us. We are not like those hucksters—and there are many of them—whose idea in getting out the Gospel is to make a good living out of it.

2 Cor 3:6. He is the one who has helped us tell others about his new agreement to save them. We do not tell them that they must obey every law of God or die; but we tell them there is life for them from the Holy Spirit. The old way, trying to be saved by keeping the Ten Commandments, ends in death; in the new way, the Holy Spirit gives the
them life.
7Yet that old system of law that led to death began with such glory that people could not bear to look at Moses' face. For as he gave them God's law to obey, his face shone out with the very glory of God—though the brightness was already
fading away.
8Shall we not expect far greater glory
in these days when the Holy Spirit is giving life?
9If the plan that leads to doom was glorious, much more glorious is the plan that makes men right
with God.
10In fact, that first glory as it shone from Moses' face is worth nothing at all in comparison with the overwhelming glory of the new agreement.

2 Cor 4:1. It is God himself, in his mercy, who has given us this wonderful work (of telling his Good News to others), and so we never give up.
2We do not try to trick people into believing—we are not interested in fooling anyone. We never try to get anyone to believe that the Bible teaches what it doesn't. All such shameful methods we forego. We stand in the presence of God as we speak and so we tell the truth, as all who know us will agree.
3If the Good News we preach is hidden to anyone, it is hidden from the one who is on the road to
eternal death.
4Satan, who is the god of this evil world, has made him blind, unable to see the glorious light of the Gospel that is shining upon him, or to understand the amazing message we preach
about the glory of Christ, who is God.
5We don't go around preaching about ourselves, but about Christ Jesus as Lord. All we say of ourselves is that we are your slaves because of what Jesus has done
for us.
6For God, who said, "Let there be light in the darkness," has made us understand that it is the brightness of his glory that is seen in the face
of Jesus Christ.
7But this precious treasure—this light and power that now shine within us—is held in a perishable container, that is, in our weak bodies. Everyone can see that the glorious power
within must be from God and is not our own.
8We are pressed on every side by troubles, but not crushed and broken. We are perplexed because we don't know why things happen as they do, but we
don't give up and quit.
9We are hunted down, but God never abandons us. We get knocked down,
but we get up again and keep going.
10These bodies of ours are constantly facing death just as Jesus did; so it is clear to all that it is only the living Christ within (who keeps us safe).

2 Cor 5:11. It is because of this solemn fear of the Lord, which is ever present in our minds, that we work so hard to win others. God knows our hearts, that they are pure in this matter, and I hope that,
deep within, you really know it too.
18All these new things are from God who brought us back to himself through what Jesus Christ did. And God has given us the privilege of urging everyone to come
into his favor and be reconciled to him.
19For God was in Christ, restoring the world to himself, no longer counting men's sins against them but blotting them out. This is the wonderful message he
has given us to tell others.
20We are Christ's ambassadors. God is using us to speak to you: we beg you, as though Christ himself were here pleading with you, receive the love he offers you—be reconciled to God.

2 Cor 6:3. We try to live in such a way that no one will ever be offended or kept back from finding the Lord by the way we act, so that no one can find
fault with us and blame it on the Lord.
4In fact, in everything we do we try to show that we are true ministers of God. We patiently endure suffering
and hardship and trouble of every kind.
5We have been beaten, put in jail, faced angry mobs, worked to exhaustion, stayed awake through sleepless
nights of watching, and gone without food.
6We have proved ourselves to be what we claim by our wholesome lives and by our understanding of the Gospel and by our patience. We have been kind and truly loving and filled with the Holy Spirit.
7We have been truthful, with God's power helping us in all we do. All of the godly man's arsenal—weapons of defense, and weapons of attack—have been ours.

2 Cor 10:1. I plead with you—yes, I, Paul—and I plead gently, as Christ himself would do. Yet some of you are saying, "Paul's letters are bold enough when he is far away, but when he gets here
he will be afraid to raise his voice!"
2I hope I won't need to show you when I come how harsh and rough I can be. I don't want to carry out my present plans against some of you who seem to think my deeds and words are merely those of an ordinary man.
8I may seem to be boasting more than I should about my authority over you—authority to help you, not to hurt you—but I shall make good every claim.

2 Cor 13:10. I am writing this to you now in the hope that I won't need to scold and punish when I come; for I want to use the Lord's authority which he has given me, not to punish you but to make you strong.

Gal 2:8. When Peter, James, and John . . . saw how greatly God had used me in winning the Gentiles, just as Peter had been blessed so greatly in his preaching to the Jews.

Gal 6:17. From now on please don't argue with me about these things, for I carry on my body the scars of the whippings and wounds from Jesus' enemies that mark me as his slave.

Phil 3:17. Dear brothers, pattern your lives after mine and notice who else lives up to my example.

1 Thess 2:3. So you can see that we were not preaching with any false motives or evil purposes in mind; we were perfectly straightforward and sincere. [4]For we speak as messengers from God, trusted by him to tell the truth; we change his message not one bit to suit the taste of those who hear it; for we serve God alone, who examines our hearts' deepest thoughts. [5]Never once did we try to win you with flattery, as you very well know, and God knows we were not just pretending to be your friends so that you would give us money! [6]As for praise, we have never asked for it from you or anyone else, although as apostles of Christ we certainly had a right to some honor from you. [7]But we were as gentle among you as a mother feeding and caring for her own children. [8]We loved you dearly—so dearly that we gave you not only God's message, but our own lives too. [9]Don't you remember, dear brothers, how hard we worked among you? Night and day we toiled and sweated to earn enough to live on so that our expenses would not be a burden to anyone there, as we preached God's Good News among you. [10]You yourselves are our witnesses—as is God—that we have been pure and honest and faultless toward every one of you. [11]We talked to you as a father to his own children—don't you remember?—pleading with you, encouraging you and even demanding [12]that your daily lives should not embarrass God, but bring joy to him who invited you into his kingdom to share his glory.

1 Tim 3:1. It is a true saying that if a man wants to be a pastor he has a good ambition. [2]For a pastor must be a good man whose life cannot be spoken against. He must have only one wife, and he must be hard working and thoughtful, orderly, and full of good deeds. He must enjoy having guests in his home, and must be a good Bible teacher. [3]He must not be a drinker or quarrelsome, but he must be gentle and kind, and not be one who loves money. [4]He must have a well-behaved family, with children who obey quickly and quietly. [5]For if a man can't make his own little family behave, how can he help the whole church? [6]The pastor must not be a new Christian, because he might be proud of being chosen so soon, and pride comes before a fall. (Satan's downfall is an example.) [7]Also, he must be well spoken of by people outside the church—those who aren't Christians—so that Satan can't trap him with many accusations, and leave him without freedom to lead his flock. [8]The deacons must be the same sort of good, steady men as the pastors. They must not be heavy drinkers and must not be greedy for money. [9]They must be earnest, wholehearted followers of Christ who is the hidden Source of their faith. [10]Before they are asked to be deacons they should be given other jobs in the church as a test of their character and ability, and if they do well, then they may be chosen as deacons. [11]Their wives must be thoughtful, not heavy drinkers, not gossipers, but faithful in everything they do. [12]Deacons should have only one wife and they should have happy, obedient families. [13]Those who do well as deacons will be well rewarded both by respect from others and also by developing their own confidence and bold trust in the Lord. [15]So that if I don't come for awhile you will know what kind of men you should choose as officers for the church of the living God.

1 Tim 5:17. Pastors who do their work well should be paid well and should be highly appreciated, especially those who work hard at both preaching and teaching. [21]I solemnly command you in the presence of God and the Lord Jesus Christ and of the holy angels to do this whether the pastor is a special friend of yours or not. All must be treated exactly the same.

1 Tim 6:11. Oh, Timothy, you are God's man. Run from all these evil things and work instead at what is right and good, learning to trust him and love others, and to be patient and gentle. [13]I command you before God who gives life to all, and before Christ Jesus who gave a fearless testimony before Pontius Pilate, [14]that you fulfill all he has told you to do, so that no one can find fault with you from now until our Lord Jesus Christ returns. [20]Oh, Timothy, don't fail to do these things that God entrusted to you. Keep out of foolish arguments with those who boast of their "knowledge" and thus prove their lack of it. [21]Some of these people have missed the most important thing in life—they don't know God. May God's mercy be upon you.

2 Tim 1:6. This being so, I want to remind you to stir into flame the strength and boldness that is in you, that entered into you when I laid my hands upon your head and blessed you. [7]For the Holy Spirit, God's gift, does not want you to be afraid of people, but to be wise and strong, and to love them and enjoy being with them. [8]If you will stir up this inner power, you will never be afraid to tell others about our Lord, or to let them know that I am your friend even though I am here in jail for Christ's sake. You will be ready to suffer with me for the Lord, for he will give you strength in suffering. [13]Hold tightly to the pattern of truth I taught you, especially concerning the faith and love Christ Jesus offers you. [14]Guard well the splendid God-given ability you received as a gift from the Holy Spirit who lives within you.

2 Tim 2:1. Oh, Timothy, my son, be strong with

the strength Christ Jesus gives you. [2]For you must teach others those things you and many others have heard me speak about. Teach these great truths to trustworthy men who will, in turn, pass them on to others. [3]Take your share of suffering as a good soldier of Jesus Christ, just as I do, [4]and as Christ's soldier do not let yourself become tied up in worldly affairs, for then you cannot satisfy the one who has enlisted you in his army. [5]Follow the Lord's rules for doing his work, just as an athlete either follows the rules or is disqualified and wins no prize. [6]Work hard, like a farmer who gets paid well if he raises a large crop. [7]Think over these three illustrations, and may the Lord help you to understand how they apply to you. [14]Remind your people of these great facts, and command them in the name of the Lord not to argue over unimportant things. Such arguments are confusing and useless, and even harmful. [15]Work hard so God can say to you, "Well done." Be a good workman, one who does not need to be ashamed when God examines your work. Know what his Word says and means. [16]Steer clear of foolish discussions which lead people into the sin of anger with each other. [20]In a wealthy home there are dishes made of gold and silver as well as some made from wood and clay. The expensive dishes are used for guests, and the cheap ones are used in the kitchen or to put garbage in. [21]If you stay away from sin you will be like one of these dishes made of purest gold—the very best in the house—so that Christ himself can use you for his highest purposes. [22]Run from anything that gives you the evil thoughts that young men often have, but stay close to anything that makes you want to do right. Have faith and love, and enjoy the companionship of those who love the Lord and have pure hearts. [23]Again I say, don't get involved in foolish arguments which only upset people and make them angry. [24]God's people must not be quarrelsome; they must be gentle, patient teachers of those who are wrong. [25]Be humble when you are trying to teach those who are mixed up concerning the truth. For if you talk meekly and courteously to them they are more likely, with God's help, to turn away from their wrong ideas and believe what is true. [26]Then they will come to their senses and escape from Satan's trap of slavery to sin which he uses to catch them whenever he likes, and then they can begin doing the will of God.

2 Tim 3:14. But you must keep on believing the things you have been taught. You know they are true for you know that you can trust those of us who have taught you. [16]The whole Bible was given to us by inspiration from God and is useful to teach us what is true and to make us realize what is wrong in our lives; it straightens us out and helps us do what is right. [17]It is God's way of making us well prepared at every point, fully equipped to do good to everyone.

Tit 1:5. I left you there on the island of Crete so that you could do whatever was needed to help strengthen each of its churches, and I asked you to appoint pastors in every city who would follow the instructions I gave you. [6]The men you choose must be well thought of for their good lives; they must have only one wife and their children must love the Lord and not have a reputation for being wild or disobedient to their parents. [7]These pastors must be men of blameless lives because they are God's ministers. They must not be proud or impatient; they must not be drunkards or fighters or greedy for money. [8]They must enjoy having guests in their homes and must love all that is good. They must be sensible men, and fair. They must be clean minded and level headed. [9]Their belief in the truth which they have been taught must be strong and steadfast, so that they will be able to teach it to others and show those who disagree with them where they are wrong. [13]So speak to the Christians there as sternly as necessary to make them strong in the faith, [14]and to stop them from listening to Jewish folk tales and the demands of men who have turned their backs on the truth.

Tit 2:1. But as for you, speak up for the right living that goes along with true Christianity. [7]And here you yourself must be an example to them of good deeds of every kind. Let everything you do reflect your love of the truth and the fact that you are in dead earnest about it. [8]Your conversation should be so sensible and logical that anyone who wants to argue will be ashamed of himself because there won't be anything to criticize in anything you say! [15]You must teach these things and encourage your people to do them, correcting them when necessary as one who has every right to do so. Don't let anyone think that what you say is not important.

Tit 3:1. Remind your people to obey the government and its officers, and always to be obedient and ready for any honest work. [2]They must not speak evil of anyone, nor quarrel, but be gentle and truly courteous to all. [8]These things I have told you are all true. Insist on them so that Christians will be careful to do good deeds all the time, for this is not only right, but it brings results. [9]Don't get involved in arguing over unanswerable questions and controversial theological ideas; keep out of arguments and quarrels about obedience to Jewish laws, for this kind of thing isn't worthwhile; it only does harm. [See Epistles to Timothy, and Titus, in full.]

Heb 5:1–3. The Jewish high priest is merely a man like anyone else, but he is chosen to speak for all other men in their dealings with God. He presents their gifts to God and offers to him the blood of animals that are sacrificed to cover the sins of the people and his own sins too. And because he is a man he can deal gently with other men, though they are foolish and ignorant, for he, too, is surrounded with the same temptations and understands their problems very well. [12, 13]You have been Christians a long time now, and you ought to be teaching others, but instead you have dropped back to the place where you need someone to teach you all over again the very first principles in God's Word. You are like babies who can drink only milk, not old enough for solid food. And when a person is still living on milk it shows he isn't very far along in the Christian life, and doesn't know much about the difference between right and wrong. He is still a baby-Christian! [14]You will never be able to eat solid spiritual food and understand the deeper things of God's Word until you become better Christians and learn right from wrong by practicing doing right.

Heb 13:6. That is why we can say without any doubt or fear, "The Lord is my Helper and I am not afraid of anything that mere man can do to me." [7]Remember your leaders who have taught you the Word of God. Think of all the good that has come from their lives, and try to trust the Lord as they do. [9]So do not be attracted by strange, new ideas. Your spiritual strength comes as a gift from God, not from ceremonial rules about eating certain foods—a method which, by the way, hasn't helped those who have tried it! [17]Obey your spiritual leaders and be willing to do what they say. For their work is to watch over your souls, and God will judge them on how well they do this. Give them reason to report joyfully about you to the Lord and not with sorrow, for then you will suffer for it too.

Jas 3:1. Dear brothers, don't be too eager to tell others their faults, for we all make many mistakes; and when we teachers of religion, who should know better, do wrong, our punishment will be greater than it would be for others. [13]If you are wise, live a life of steady goodness, so that only good deeds will pour forth. And if you don't brag about them, then you will be truly wise! [16]For wherever there is jealousy or selfish ambition, there will be disorder and every other kind of evil. [17]But the wisdom that comes from heaven is first of all pure and full of quiet gentleness. Then it is peace-loving and courteous. It allows discussion and is willing to yield to others; it is full of mercy and good deeds. It is wholehearted and straightforward and sincere. [18]And those who are peacemakers will plant seeds of peace and reap a harvest of goodness.

1 Pet 4:10. God has given each of you some special abilities; be sure to use them to help each other, passing on to others God's many kinds of blessings. [11]Are you called to preach? Then preach as though God himself were speaking through you. Are you called to help others? Do it with all the strength and energy that God supplies, so that God will be glorified through Jesus Christ—to him be glory and power forever and ever. Amen.

CHARGE DELIVERED TO. Mt 10:5. Jesus sent them out with these instructions: "Don't go to the Gentiles or the Samaritans, [6]but only to the people of Israel—God's lost sheep. [7]Go and announce to them that the Kingdom of Heaven is near. [8]Heal the sick, raise the dead, cure the lepers, and cast out demons. Give as freely as you have received! [9]Don't take any money with you; [10]don't even carry a duffle bag with extra clothes and shoes, or even a walking stick; for those you help should feed and care for you. [11]Whenever you enter a city or village, search for a godly man and stay in his home until you leave for the next town. [12]When you ask permission to stay, be friendly, [13]and if it turns out to be a godly home, give it your blessing; if not, keep the blessing. [14]Any city or home that doesn't welcome you—shake off the dust of that place from your feet as you leave. [15]Truly, the wicked cities of Sodom and Gomorrah will be better off at Judgment Day than they. [Mk 6:11.] [16]I am sending you out as sheep among wolves. Be as wary as serpents and harmless as doves. [17]But beware! For you will be arrested and tried, and whipped in the synagogues. [18]Yes, and you must stand trial before governors and kings for my sake. This will give you the opportunity to tell them about me, yes, to witness to the world. [19]When you are arrested, don't worry about what to say at your trial, for you will be given the right words at the right time. [20]For it won't be you doing the talking—it will be the Spirit of your heavenly Father speaking through you! [21]Brother shall betray brother to death, and fathers shall betray their own children. And children shall rise against their parents and cause their deaths. [22]Everyone shall hate you because you belong to me. But all of you who endure to the end shall be saved. [23]When you are persecuted in one city, flee to the next! I will return before you have reached them all! [24]A student is not greater than his teacher. A servant is not above his master. [25]The student shares his teacher's fate. The servant shares his master's! And since I, the master of the household, have been called 'Satan,' how much more will you! [26]But don't be afraid of those who threaten you. For the time is coming when the truth will be revealed: their secret plots will become public information. [27]What I tell you now in the gloom, shout abroad when daybreak comes. What I whisper in your ears, proclaim from the housetops! [28]Don't be afraid of those who can kill only your bodies—but can't touch your souls! Fear only God who can destroy both soul and body in hell. [29]Not one sparrow (What do they cost? Two for a penny?) can fall to the ground without your Father knowing it. [30]And the very hairs of your head are all numbered. [31]So don't worry! You are more valuable to him than many sparrows. [32]If anyone publicly acknowledges me as his friend, I will openly acknowledge him as my friend before my father in heaven. [33]But if anyone publicly denies me, I will openly deny him before my Father in heaven. [34]Don't imagine that I came to bring peace to the earth! No, rather, a sword. [35]I have come to set a man against his father, and a daughter against her mother, and a daughter-in-law against her mother-in-law—[36]a man's worst enemies will be right in his own home! [37]If you love your father and mother more than you love me, you are not worthy of being mine; or if you love your son or daughter more than me, you are not worthy of being mine. [38]If you refuse to take up your cross and follow me, you are not worthy of being mine. [39]If you cling to your life, you will lose it; but if you give it up for me, you will save it. [40]Those who welcome you are welcoming me. And when they welcome me they are welcoming God who sent me. [41]If you welcome a prophet because he is a man of God, you will be given the same reward a prophet gets. And if you welcome good and godly men because of their godliness, you will be given a reward like theirs. [42]And if, as my representatives, you give even a cup of cold water to a little child, you will surely be rewarded."

Lk 10:1. The Lord now chose seventy other disciples and sent them on ahead in pairs to all the towns and villages he planned to visit later. [2]These were his instructions to them: "Plead with the Lord of the harvest to send out more laborers to help you, for the harvest is so plentiful and the workers so few. [3]Go now, and remember that I am sending you out as lambs among wolves. [4]Don't take any money with you, or a beggar's bag, or even an extra pair of shoes. And don't waste time along the way. [5]Whenever you enter a home, give it your blessing. [6]If it is worthy of the blessing, the blessing will stand; if not, the blessing will return to you. [7]When you enter a village, don't shift around from home to home, but stay in one place, eating and drinking without question whatever is set before you. And don't hesitate to accept hospitality, for the workman is worthy of his wages! [8, 9]If a town welcomes you, follow these two rules: (1) Eat whatever is set before you. (2) Heal the sick; and as you heal them, say, 'The Kingdom of God is very near you now.' [10]But if a town refuses you, go out into its streets and say, [11]'We wipe the dust of your town from our feet as a public announcement of your doom. Never forget how close you were to the Kingdom of God!' [12]Even wicked Sodom will be better off than such a city on the Judgment Day. [13]What horrors await you, you cities of Chorazin and Bethsaida! For if the miracles I did for you had been done in the cities of Tyre and Sidon, their people would have sat in deep repentance long ago, clothed in sackcloth and throwing ashes on their heads to show their remorse. [14]Yes, Tyre and Sidon will receive less punishment on the Judgment Day than you. [15]And you people of Capernaum, what shall I say about you? Will you be exalted to heaven? No, you shall be brought down to hell." [16]Then he said to the disciples, "Those who welcome you are welcoming me. And those who reject you are rejecting me. And those who reject me are rejecting God who sent me."

1 Tim 1:18. Now, Timothy, my son, here is my command to you: Fight well in the Lord's battles, just as the Lord told us through his prophets that you would. [19]Cling tightly to your faith in Christ and always keep your conscience clear, doing what you know is right. For some people have disobeyed their consciences and have deliberately done what they knew was wrong. It isn't surprising that soon they lost their faith in Christ after defying God like that. [20]Hymenaeus and Alexander are two examples of this. I had to give them over to Satan to punish them until they could learn not to bring shame to the name of Christ.

1 Tim 2:1. Here are my directions: Pray much for others; plead for God's mercy upon them; give thanks for all he is going to do for them. [2]Pray in this way for kings and all others who are in authority over us, or are in places of high responsibility, so that we can live in peace and quietness, spending our time in godly living and thinking much about the Lord. [3]This is good and pleases God our Savior, [4]for he longs for all to be saved and to understand this truth: [5]*That God is on one side and all the people on the other side, and Christ Jesus, himself man, is between them to bring them together,* [6]*by giving his life for all mankind.* This is the message which at the proper time God gave to the world. [7]And I have been chosen—this is the absolute truth—as God's minister and missionary to teach this truth to the Gentiles, and to show them God's plan of salvation through faith. [8]So I want men everywhere to pray with holy hands lifted up to God, free from sin and anger and resentment. [9, 10]And the women should be the same way, quiet and sensible in manner and clothing. Christian women should be noticed for being kind and good, not for the way they fix their hair or because of their jewels or fancy clothes. [11]Women should listen and learn quietly and humbly. [12]I never let women teach men or lord it over them. Let them be silent in your church meetings. [13]Why? Because God made Adam first, and afterwards he made Eve. [14]And it was not Adam who was fooled by Satan, but Eve, and sin was the result. [15]So God sent pain and suffering to women when their children are born, but he will save their souls if they trust in him, living quiet, good, and loving lives.

1 Tim 3:1. It is a true saying that if a man wants to be a pastor he has a good ambition. [2]For a pastor must be a good man whose life cannot be spoken against. He must have only one wife, and he must be hard working and thoughtful, orderly, and full of good deeds. He must enjoy having guests in his home, and must be a good Bible teacher. [3]He must not be a drinker or quarrelsome, but he must be gentle and kind, and not be one who loves money. [4]He must have a well-behaved family, with children who obey quickly and quietly. [5]For if a man can't make his own little family behave, how can he help the whole church? [6]The pastor must not be a new Christian, because he might be proud of being chosen so soon, and pride comes before a fall. (Satan's downfall is an example.) [7]Also, he must be well spoken of by people outside the church—those who aren't Christians—so that Satan can't trap him with many accusations, and leave him without freedom to lead his flock. [8]The deacons must be the same sort of good, steady men as the pastors. They must not be heavy drinkers and must not be greedy for money. [9]They must be earnest, wholehearted followers of Christ who is the hidden Source of their faith. [10]Before they are asked to be deacons they should be given other jobs in the church as a test of their character and ability, and if they do well, then they may be chosen as dea-

cons. 11Their wives must be thoughtful, not heavy drinkers, not gossipers, but faithful in everything they do. 12Deacons should have only one wife and they should have happy, obedient families. 13Those who do well as deacons will be well rewarded both by respect from others and also by developing their own confidence and bold trust in the Lord. 14I am writing these things to you now, even though I hope to be with you soon, 15so that if I don't come for awhile you will know what kind of men you should choose as officers for the church of the living God, which contains and holds high the truth of God. 16It is quite true that the way to live a godly life is not an easy matter. But the answer lies in Christ, who came to earth as a man, was proved spotless and pure in his Spirit, was served by angels, was preached among the nations, was accepted by men everywhere and was received up again to his glory in heaven.

I Tim 4:1. But the Holy Spirit tells us clearly that in the last times some in the church will turn away from Christ and become eager followers of teachers with devil-inspired ideas. 2These teachers will tell lies with straight faces and do it so often that their consciences won't even bother them. 3They will say it is wrong to be married and wrong to eat meat, even though God gave these things to well-taught Christians to enjoy and be thankful for. 4For everything God made is good, and we may eat it gladly if we are thankful for it, 5and if we ask God to bless it, for it is made good by the Word of God and prayer. 6If you explain this to the others you will be doing your duty as a worthy pastor who is fed by faith and by the true teaching you have followed. 7Don't waste time arguing over foolish ideas and silly myths and legends. Spend your time and energy in the exercise of keeping spiritually fit. 8Bodily exercise is all right, but spiritual exercise is much more important and is a tonic for all you do. So exercise yourself spiritually and practice being a better Christian, because that will help you not only now in this life, but in the next life too. 9, 10This is the truth and everyone should accept it. We work hard and suffer much in order that people will believe it, for our hope is in the living God who died for all, and particularly for those who have accepted his salvation. 11Teach these things and make sure everyone learns them well. 12Don't let anyone think little of you because you are young. Be their ideal; let them follow the way you teach and live; be a pattern for them in your love, your faith, and your clean thoughts. 13Until I get there, read and explain the Scriptures to the church; preach God's Word. 14Be sure to use the abilities God has given you through his prophets when the elders of the church laid their hands upon your head. 15Put these abilities to work; throw yourself into your tasks so that everyone may notice your improvement and progress. 16Keep a close watch on all you do and think. Stay true to what is right and God will bless you and use you to help others.

I Tim 5:1. Never speak sharply to an older man, but plead with him respectfully just as though he were your own father. Talk to the younger men as you would to much loved brothers. 2Treat the older women as mothers, and the girls as your sisters, thinking only pure thoughts about them. 3The church should take loving care of women whose husbands have died, if they don't have anyone else to help them. 4But if they have children or grandchildren, these are the ones who should take the responsibility, for kindness should begin at home, supporting needy parents. This is something that pleases God very much. 5The church should care for widows who are poor and alone in the world, if they are looking to God for his help and spending much time in prayer; 6but not if they are spending their time running around gossiping, seeking only pleasure and thus ruining their souls. 7This should be your church rule so that the Christians will know and do what is right. 8But anyone who won't care for his own relatives when they need help, especially those living in his own family, has no right to say he is a Christian. Such a person is worse than the heathen. 9A widow who wants to become one of the special church workers should be at least sixty years old and have been married only once. 10She must be well thought of by everyone because of the good she has done. Has she brought up her children well? Has she been kind to strangers as well as to other Christians? Has she helped those who are sick and hurt? Is she always ready to show kindness? 11The younger widows should not become members of this special group because after awhile they are likely to disregard their vow to Christ and marry again. 12And so they will stand condemned because they broke their first promise. 13Besides, they are likely to be lazy and spend their time gossiping around from house to house, getting into other people's business. 14So I think it is better for these younger widows to marry again and have children, and take care of their own homes; then no one will be able to say anything against them. 15For I am afraid that some of them have already turned away from the church and been led astray by Satan. 16Let me remind you again that a widow's relatives must take care of her, and not leave this to the church to do. Then the church can spend its money for the care of widows who are all alone and have nowhere else to turn. 17Pastors who do their work well should be paid well and should be highly appreciated, especially those who work hard at both preaching and teaching. 18For the Scriptures say, "Never tie up the mouth of an ox when it is treading out the grain—let him eat as he goes along!" And in another place, "Those who work deserve their pay!" 19Don't listen to complaints against the pastor unless there are two or three witnesses to accuse him. 20If he has really sinned, then he should be rebuked in front of the whole church so that no one else will follow his example. 21I solemnly command you in the presence of God and the Lord Jesus Christ and of the holy angels to do this whether the pastor is a special friend of yours or not. All must be treated exactly the same. 22Never be in a hurry about choosing a pastor; you may overlook his sins and it will look as if you approve of them. Be sure that you yourself stay away from all sin.

1 Tim 6:1. Christian slaves should work hard for their owners and respect them; never let it be said that Christ's people are poor workers. Don't let the name of God or his teaching be laughed at because of this. [2]If their owner is a Christian, there is no excuse for slowing down; rather they should work all the harder because a brother in the faith is being helped by their efforts. Teach these truths, Timothy, and encourage all to obey them. [3]Some may deny these things, but they are the sound, wholesome teachings of the Lord Jesus Christ and are the foundation for a godly life. [4]Anyone who says anything different is both proud and stupid. He is quibbling over the meaning of Christ's words and stirring up arguments ending in jealousy and anger, which only lead to name-calling, accusations, and evil suspicions. [5]These arguers—their minds warped by sin—don't know how to tell the truth; to them the Good News is just a means of making money. Keep away from them. [6]Do you want to be truly rich? You already are if you are happy and good. [7]After all, we didn't bring any money with us when we came into the world, and we can't carry away a single penny when we die. [8]So we should be well satisfied without money if we have enough food and clothing. [9]But people who long to be rich soon begin to do all kinds of wrong things to get money, things that hurt them and make them evil-minded and finally send them to hell itself. [10]For the love of money is the first step toward all kinds of sin. Some people have even turned away from God because of their love for it, and as a result have pierced themselves with many sorrows. [11]Oh, Timothy, you are God's man. Run from all these evil things and work instead at what is right and good, learning to trust him and love others, and to be patient and gentle. [12]Fight on for God. Hold tightly to the eternal life which God has given you, and which you have confessed with such a ringing confession before many witnesses. [13]I command you before God who gives life to all, and before Christ Jesus who gave a fearless testimony before Pontius Pilate, [14]that you fulfill all he has told you to do, so that no one can find fault with you from now until our Lord Jesus Christ returns. [15]For in due season Christ will be revealed from heaven by the blessed and only Almighty God, the King of kings and Lord of lords, [16]who alone can never die, who lives in light so terrible that no human being can approach him. No mere man has ever seen him, nor ever will. Unto him be honor and everlasting power and dominion forever and ever. Amen. [17]Tell those who are rich not to be proud and not to trust in their money, which will soon be gone, but their pride and trust should be in the living God who always richly gives us all we need for our enjoyment. [18]Tell them to use their money to do good. They should be rich in good works and should give happily to those in need, always being ready to share with others whatever God has given them. [19]By doing this they will be storing up real treasure for themselves in heaven—it is the only safe investment for eternity! And they will be living a fruitful Christian life down here as well. [20]Oh, Timothy, don't fail to do these things that God entrusted to you. Keep out of foolish arguments with those who boast of their "knowledge" and thus prove their lack of it. [21]Some of these people have missed the most important thing in life—they don't know God. May God's mercy be upon you.

2 Tim 1:6. This being so, I want to remind you to stir into flame the strength and boldness that is in you, that entered into you when I laid my hands upon your head and blessed you. [7]For the Holy Spirit, God's gift, does not want you to be afraid of people, but to be wise and strong, and to love them and enjoy being with them. [8]If you will stir up this inner power, you will never be afraid to tell others about our Lord, or to let them know that I am your friend even though I am here in jail for Christ's sake. You will be ready to suffer with me for the Lord, for he will give you strength in suffering. [9]It is he who saved us and chose us for his holy work, not because we deserved it but because that was his plan long before the world began—to show his love and kindness to us through Christ. [10]And now he has made all of this plain to us by the coming of our Savior Jesus Christ, who broke the power of death and showed us the way of everlasting life through trusting him. [11]And God has chosen me to be his missionary, to preach to the Gentiles and teach them. [12]That is why I am suffering here in jail and I am certainly not ashamed of it, for I know the one in whom I trust, and I am sure that he is able to safely guard all that I have given him until the day of his return. [13]Hold tightly to the pattern of truth I taught you, especially concerning the faith and love Christ Jesus offers you.

2 Tim 2:1. Oh, Timothy, my son, be strong with the strength Christ Jesus gives you. [2]For you must teach others those things you and many others have heard me speak about. Teach these great truths to trustworthy men who will, in turn, pass them on to others. [3]Take your share of suffering as a good soldier of Jesus Christ, just as I do, [4]and as Christ's soldier do not let yourself become tied up in worldly affairs, for then you cannot satisfy the one who has enlisted you in his army. [5]Follow the Lord's rules for doing his work, just as an athlete either follows the rules or is disqualified and wins no prize. [6]Work hard, like a farmer who gets paid well if he raises a large crop. [7]Think over these three illustrations, and may the Lord help you to understand how they apply to you. [8]Don't ever forget the wonderful fact that Jesus Christ was a Man, born into King David's family; and that he was God, as shown by the fact that he rose again from the dead. [9]It is because I have preached these great truths that I am in trouble here and have been put in jail like a criminal. But the Word of God is not chained, even though I am. [10]I am more than

willing to suffer if that will bring salvation and eternal glory in Christ Jesus to those God has chosen. [11]I am comforted by this truth, that when we suffer and die for Christ it only means that we will begin living with him in heaven. [12]And if we think that our present service for him is hard, just remember that some day we are going to sit with him and rule with him. But if we give up when we suffer, and turn against Christ, then he must turn against us. [13]Even when we are too weak to have any faith left, he remains faithful to us and will help us, for he cannot disown us who are part of himself, and he will always carry out his promises to us. [14]Remind your people of these great facts, and command them in the name of the Lord not to argue over unimportant things. Such arguments are confusing and useless, and even harmful. [15]Work hard so God can say to you, "Well done," Be a good workman, one who does not need to be ashamed when God examines your work. Know what his Word says and means. [16]Steer clear of foolish discussions which lead people into the sin of anger with each other. [17]Things will be said that will burn and hurt for a long time to come. Hymenaeus and Philetus, in their love of argument, are men like that. [18]They have left the path of truth, preaching the lie that the resurrection of the dead has already occurred; and they have weakened the faith of some who believe them. [19]But God's truth stands firm like a great rock, and nothing can shake it. It is a foundation stone with these words written on it: "The Lord knows those who are really his," and "A person who calls himself a Christian should not be doing things that are wrong." [20]In a wealthy home there are dishes made of gold and silver as well as some made from wood and clay. The expensive dishes are used for guests, and the cheap ones are used in the kitchen or to put garbage in. [21]If you stay away from sin you will be like one of these dishes made of purest gold—the very best in the house—so that Christ himself can use you for his highest purposes. [22]Run from anything that gives you the evil thoughts that young men often have, but stay close to anything that makes you want to do right. Have faith and love, and enjoy the companionship of those who love the Lord and have pure hearts. [23]Again I say, don't get involved in foolish arguments which only upset people and make them angry. [24]God's people must not be quarrelsome; they must be gentle, patient teachers of those who are wrong. [25]Be humble when you are trying to teach those who are mixed up concerning the truth. For if you talk meekly and courteously to them they are more likely, with God's help, to turn away from their wrong ideas and believe what is true. [26]Then they will come to their senses and escape from Satan's trap of slavery to sin which he uses to catch them whenever he likes, and then they can begin doing the will of God.

2 Tim 3:1. You may as well know this too, Timothy, that in the last days it is going to be very difficult to be a Christian. [2]For people will love only themselves and their money; they will be proud and boastful, sneering at God, disobedient to their parents, ungrateful to them, and thoroughly bad. [3]They will be hardheaded and never give in to others; they will be constant liars and troublemakers and will think nothing of immorality. They will be rough and cruel, and sneer at those who try to be good. [4]They will betray their friends; they will be hot-headed, puffed up with pride, and prefer good times to worshiping God. [5]They will go to church, yes, but they won't believe anything they hear. Don't be taken in by people like that. [6]They are the kind who craftily sneak into other people's homes and make friendships with silly, sin-burdened women and teach them their new doctrines. [7]Women of that kind are forever following new teachers, but they never understand the truth. [8]And these teachers fight truth just as Jannes and Jambres fought against Moses. They have dirty minds, warped and twisted, and have turned against the Christian faith. [9]But they won't get away with all this forever. Some day their deceit will be well known to everyone, as was the sin of Jannes and Jambres. [10]But you know from watching me that I am not that kind of person. You know what I believe and the way I live and what I want. You know my faith in Christ and how I have suffered. You know my love for you, and my patience. [11]You know how many troubles I have had as a result of my preaching the Good News. You know about all that was done to me while I was visiting in Antioch, Iconium and Lystra, but the Lord delivered me. [12]Yes, and those who decide to please Christ Jesus by living godly lives will suffer at the hands of those who hate him. [13]In fact, evil men and false teachers will become worse and worse, deceiving many, they themselves having been deceived by Satan. [14]But you must keep on believing the things you have been taught. You know they are true for you know that you can trust those of us who have taught you. [15]You know how, when you were a small child, you were taught the holy Scriptures; and it is these that make you wise to accept God's salvation by trusting in Christ Jesus. [16]The whole Bible was given to us by inspiration from God and is useful to teach us what is true and to make us realize what is wrong in our lives; it straightens us out and helps us do what is right. [17]It is God's way of making us well prepared at every point, fully equipped to do good to everyone.

2 Tim 4:1. And so I solemnly urge you before God and before Christ Jesus—who will some day judge the living and the dead when he appears to set up his kingdom—[2]to preach the Word of God urgently at all times, whenever you get the chance, in season and out, when it is convenient and when it is not. Correct and rebuke your people when they need it, encourage them to do right, and all the time be feeding them patiently with God's Word. [3]For there is going to come a time when people won't listen to the truth, but will go around looking for teachers who will tell them just what they want to hear. [4]They won't listen to what the Bible says

but will blithely follow their own misguided ideas. [5]Stand steady, and don't be afraid of suffering for the Lord. Bring others to Christ. Leave nothing undone that you ought to do. [6]I say this because I won't be around to help you very much longer. My time has almost run out. Very soon now I will be on my way to heaven. [7]I have fought long and hard for my Lord, and through it all I have kept true to him. And now the time has come for me to stop fighting and rest. [8]In heaven a crown is waiting for me which the Lord, the righteous Judge, will give to me on that great day of his return. And not just to me, but to all those whose lives show that they are eagerly looking forward to his coming back again.

DUTIES OF THE CHURCH TO. 1 Cor 11:1. And you should follow my example, just as I follow Christ's. [2]I am so glad, dear brothers, that you have been remembering and doing everything I taught you.

1 Cor 16:15. Do you remember Stephanas and his family? They were the first to become Christians in Greece and they are spending their lives helping and serving Christians everywhere. [16]Please follow their instructions and do everything you can to help them as well as all others like them who work hard at your side with such real devotion.

Phil 3:17. Dear brothers, pattern your lives after mine and notice who else lives up to my example.

1 Thess 5:12. Dear brothers, honor the officers of your church who work hard among you and warn you against all that is wrong. [13]Think highly of them and give them your wholehearted love because they are straining to help you. And remember, no quarreling among yourselves.

Heb 13:7. Remember your leaders who have taught you the Word of God. Think of all the good that has come from their lives, and try to trust the Lord as they do. [17]Obey your spiritual leaders and be willing to do what they say. For their work is to watch over your souls, and God will judge them on how well they do this. Give them reason to report joyfully about you to the Lord and not with sorrow, for then you will suffer for it too. [18]Pray for us, for our conscience is clear and we want to keep it that way.

FALSE AND CORRUPT. Mt 5:19. And if anyone breaks the least commandment, and teaches others to, he shall be the least in the Kingdom of Heaven.

Mt 7:15. Beware of false teachers who come disguised as harmless sheep, but are wolves and will tear you apart. [22]At the Judgment many will tell me, "Lord, Lord, we told others about you and used your name to cast our demons and to do many other great miracles." [23]But I will reply, "You have never been mine. Go away, for your deeds are evil."

Mt 15:9. "Their worship is worthless, for they teach their manmade laws instead of those from God." [13, 14]Jesus replied, "Every plant not planted by my Father shall be rooted up, so ignore them. They are blind guides leading the blind, and both will fall into a ditch." Lk 6:39.

Mt 20:20. Then the mother of James and John, the sons of Zebedee, brought them to Jesus and respectfully asked a favor. [21]"What is your request?" he asked. She replied, "In your Kingdom, will you let my two sons sit on two thrones next to yours?" [22]But Jesus told her, "You don't know what you are asking!" Then he turned to James and John and asked them, "Are you able to drink from the terrible cup I am about to drink from?" "Yes," they replied, "we are able!" [23]"You shall indeed drink from it," he told them. "But I have no right to say who will sit on the thrones next to mine. Those places are reserved for the persons my Father selects." [24]The other ten disciples were indignant when they heard what James and John had asked for. [25]But Jesus called them together and said, "Among the heathen, kings are tyrants and each minor official lords it over those beneath him. [26]But among you it is quite different. Anyone wanting to be a leader among you must be your servant. [27]And if you want to be right at the top, you must serve like a slave." Mk 10:35–37; Lk 22:24.

Mt 23:3. And of course you should obey their every whim! It may be all right to do what they say, but above anything else, *don't follow their example.* For they don't do what they tell you to do. [4]They load you with impossible demands that they themselves don't even try to keep. [13]Woe to you, Pharisees, and you other religious leaders. Hypocrites! For you won't let others enter the Kingdom of Heaven, and won't go in yourselves.

Mt 24:4. Jesus told them, "Don't let anyone fool you. [5]For many will come claiming to be the Messiah, and will lead many astray. [24]For false Christs shall arise, and false prophets, and will do wonderful miracles, so that if it were possible, even God's chosen ones would be deceived." *vs.* 11, 26, 48–51; Lk 21:8.

Mk 9:33. And so they arrived at Capernaum. When they were settled in the house where they were to stay he asked them, "What were you discussing out on the road?" [34]But they were ashamed to answer, for they had been arguing about which of them was the greatest! [35]He sat down and called them around him and said, "Anyone wanting to be the greatest must be the least—the servant of all!" Lk 9:46.

Mk 13:21. And then if anyone tells you, "This is the Messiah," or, "That one is," don't pay any attention. [22]For there will be many false Messiahs and false prophets who will do wonderful miracles that would deceive, if possible, even God's own children.

Lk 11:35. So watch out that the sunshine isn't blotted out. [52]Woe to you experts in religion! For you hide the truth from the people. You won't accept it for yourselves, and you prevent others from having a chance to believe it. *vs.* 46–51.

Lk 12:45. But if the man begins to think, "My Lord won't be back for a long time," and begins to whip the men and women he is supposed to protect, and to spend his time at drinking parties and in drunkenness—[46]well, his master will return without notice and remove him from his position of trust and assign him to the place of the unfaithful.

Jn 3:10. Jesus replied, "You, a respected Jewish teacher, and yet you don't understand these things?"

Jn 5:43. I know, because I have come to you representing my Father and you refuse to welcome me, though you readily enough receive those who aren't sent from him, but represent only themselves!

Jn 10:1. Anyone refusing to walk through the gate into a sheepfold, who sneaks over the wall, must surely be a thief! [5]They won't follow a stranger but will run from him, for they don't recognize his voice. [8]All others who came before me were thieves and robbers. But the true sheep did not listen to them. [10]The thief's purpose is to steal, kill and destroy. My purpose is to give life in all its fullness. [12]A hired man will run when he sees a wolf coming and will leave the sheep, for they aren't his and he isn't their shepherd. And so the wolf leaps on them and scatters the flock. [13]The hired man runs because he is hired and has no real concern for the sheep.

Acts 20:29. I know full well that after I leave you, false teachers, like vicious wolves, will appear among you, not sparing the flock. [30]Some of you yourselves will distort the truth in order to draw a following.

Rom 2:19. You are so sure of the way to God that you could point it out to a blind man. You think of yourselves as beacon lights, directing men who are lost in darkness to God. [20]You think that you can guide the simple and teach even children the affairs of God, for you really know his laws, which are full of all knowledge and truth. [21]Yes, you teach others—then why don't you teach yourselves? You tell others not to steal—do *you* steal? [22]You say it is wrong to commit adultery—do *you* do it? You say, "Don't pray to idols," and then make money your god instead. [23]You are so proud of knowing God's laws, *but you dishonor him by breaking them.* [24]No wonder the Scriptures say that the world speaks evil of God because of you. [25]Being a Jew is worth something if you obey God's laws; but if you don't, then you are no better off than the heathen.

Rom 16:17. And now there is one more thing to say before I end this letter. Stay away from those who cause divisions and are upsetting people's faith, teaching things about Christ that are contrary to what you have been taught. [18]Such teachers are not working for our Lord Jesus, but only want gain for themselves. They are good speakers, and simple-minded people are often fooled by them.

1 Cor 3:10. God, in his kindness, has taught me how to be an expert builder. I have laid the foundation and Apollos has built on it. But he who builds on the foundation must be very careful. [11]And no one can ever lay any other real foundation than that one we already have—Jesus Christ. [12]But there are various kinds of materials that can be used to build on that foundation. Some use gold and silver and jewels; and some build with sticks, and hay, or even straw! [13]There is going to come a time of testing at Christ's Judgment Day to see what kind of material each builder has used. Everyone's work will be put through the fire so that all can see whether or not it keeps its value, and what was really accomplished. [14]Then every workman who has built on the foundation with the right materials, and whose work still stands will get his pay. [15]But if the house he has built burns up, he will have a great loss. He himself will be saved, but like a man escaping through a wall of flames. [16]Don't you realize that all of you together are the house of God, and that the Spirit of God lives among you in his house? [21]So don't be proud of following the wise men of this world. For God has already given you everything you need. *vs.* 1–4.

1 Cor 11:18. Everyone keeps telling me about the arguing that goes on in these meetings, and the divisions developing among you, and I can just about believe it. [19]But I suppose you feel this is necessary so that you who are always right will become known and recognized!

2 Cor 2:17. Only those who, like ourselves, are men of integrity, sent by God, speaking with Christ's power, with God's eye upon us. We are not like those hucksters—and there are many of them—whose idea in getting out the Gospel is to make a good living out of it.

2 Cor 11:3. But I am frightened, fearing that in some way you will be led away from your pure and simple devotion to our Lord, just as Eve was deceived by Satan in the Garden of Eden. [4]You seem so gullible: you believe whatever anyone tells you even if he is preaching about another Jesus than the one we preach, or a different spirit than the Holy Spirit you received, or shows you a different way to be saved. You swallow it all. [13]God never sent those men at all; they are "phonies" who have fooled you into thinking they are Christ's apostles. [14]Yet I am not surprised! Satan can change himself into an angel of light, [15]so it is no wonder his servants can do it too, and seem like godly ministers. In the end they will get every bit of punishment their wicked deeds deserve. *vs.* 1–33.

Gal 1:6. I am amazed that you are turning away so soon from God who, in his love and mercy, invited you to share the eternal life he gives through Christ; you are already following a different "way to heaven," which really doesn't go to heaven at all. [7]For there is no other way than the one we showed you; you are being fooled by those who twist and change the truth concerning Christ. [8]Let God's curses fall on anyone, including myself, who preaches any other way to be saved than the one we told you about; yes, if an angel comes from heaven and preaches any other message, let him be forever cursed.

Gal 5:10. I am trusting the Lord to bring you back to believing as I do about these things. God will deal with that person, whoever he is, who has been troubling and confusing you.

Eph 4:14. Then we will no longer be like children, forever changing our minds about what we believe because someone has told us something different, or has cleverly lied to us and made the lie sound like the truth.

Phil 1:15. Some, of course, are preaching the Good News because they are jealous of the way God has used me. They want reputations as fearless preachers! [17]And some preach to make me jealous, thinking that their success will add to my sorrows here in jail!

Phil 3:2. Watch out for those wicked men—dangerous dogs, I call them—who say you must be circumcised to be saved.

Col 2:4. I am saying this because I am afraid that someone may fool you with smooth talk. [8]Don't let others spoil your faith and joy with their philosophies, their wrong and shallow answers built on men's thoughts and ideas, instead of on what Christ has said. [18]Don't let anyone declare you lost when you refuse to worship angels, as they say you must. They have seen a vision, they say, and know you should. These proud men (though they claim to be so humble) have a very clever imagination. [19]But they are not connected to Christ, the Head to which all of us who are his body are joined; for we are joined together by his strong sinews and we grow only as we get our nourishment and strength from God.

1 Tim 1:3, 4. As I said when I left for Macedonia, please stay there in Ephesus and try to stop the men who are teaching such wrong doctrine. Put an end to their myths and fables, and their idea of being saved by finding favor with an endless chain of angels leading up to God—wild ideas that stir up questions and arguments instead of helping people accept God's plan of faith. [5]What I am eager for is that all the Christians there will be filled with love that comes from pure hearts, and that their minds will be clean and their faith strong. [6]But these teachers have missed this whole idea and spend their time arguing and talking foolishness. [7]They want to become famous as teachers of the laws of Moses when they haven't the slightest idea what those laws really show us. [19]Cling tightly to your faith in Christ and always keep your conscience clear, doing what you know is right. For some people have disobeyed their consciences and have deliberately done what they knew was wrong. It isn't surprising that soon they lost their faith in Christ after defying God like that.

1 Tim 4:1. But the Holy Spirit tells us clearly that in the last times some in the church will turn away from Christ and become eager followers of teachers with devil-inspired ideas. [2]These teachers will tell lies with straight faces and do it so often that their consciences won't even bother them. [3]They will say it is wrong to be married and wrong to eat meat, even though God gave these things to well-taught Christians to enjoy and be thankful for. [7]Don't waste time arguing over foolish ideas and silly myths and legends. Spend your time and energy in the exercise of keeping spiritually fit.

1 Tim 6:3. Some may deny these things, but they are the sound, wholesome teachings of the Lord Jesus Christ and are the foundation for a godly life. [4]Anyone who says anything different is both proud and stupid. He is quibbling over the meaning of Christ's words and stirring up arguments ending in jealousy and anger, which only lead to name-calling, accusations, and evil suspicions. [5]These arguers—their minds warped by sin—don't know how to tell the truth; to them the Good News is just a means of making money. Keep away from them. [20]Oh, Timothy, don't fail to do these things that God entrusted to you. Keep out of foolish arguments with those who boast of their "knowledge" and thus prove their lack of it. [21]Some of these people have missed the most important thing in life—they don't know God. May God's mercy be upon you.

2 Tim 2:14. Remind your people of these great facts, and command them in the name of the Lord not to argue over unimportant things. Such arguments are confusing and useless, and even harmful. [15]Work hard so God can say to you, "Well done." Be a good workman, one who does not need to be ashamed when God examines your work. Know what his Word says and means. [16]Steer clear of foolish discussions which lead people into the sin of anger with each other. [17]Things will be said that will burn and hurt for a long time to come. Hymenaeus and Philetus, in their love of argument, are men like that. [18]They have left the path of truth, preaching the lie that the resurrection of the dead has already occurred; and they have weakened the faith of some who believe them.

2 Tim 3:6. They are the kind who craftily sneak into other people's homes and make friendships with silly, sin-burdened women and teach them their new doctrines. [7]Women of that kind are forever following new teachers, but they never understand the truth. [8]And these teachers fight truth just as Jannes and Jambres fought against Moses. They have dirty minds, warped and twisted, and have turned against the Christian faith. [9]But they won't get away with all this forever. Some day their deceit will be well known to everyone, as was the sin of Jannes and Jambres. [13]In fact, evil men and false teachers will become worse and worse, deceiving many, they themselves having been deceived by Satan. 2 Tim 4:3.

Tit 1:10. For there are many who refuse to obey; this is especially true among those who say that all Christians must obey the Jewish laws. But this is foolish talk; it blinds people to the truth, [11]and it must be stopped. Already whole families have been turned away from the grace of God. Such teachers are only after your money. [12]One of their own men, a prophet from Crete, has said about them, "These men of Crete are all liars; they are like lazy animals, living only to satisfy their stomachs." [13]And this is true. So speak to the Christians there as sternly as necessary to make them strong in the faith, [14]and to stop them from listening to Jewish folk tales and the demands of men who have turned their backs on the truth.

Tit 3:10. If anyone is causing divisions among you, he should be given a first and second warning. After that have nothing more to do with him, [11]for such a person has a wrong sense of values. He is sinning, and he knows it.

Heb 13:9. So do not be attracted by strange, new ideas.

2 Pet 2:1. But there were false prophets, too, in those days, just as there will be false teachers among you. They will cleverly tell their lies about God, turning against even their Master who bought them; but theirs will be a swift and terrible end. [2]Many will follow their evil teaching that there is nothing wrong with sexual sin. And because of them Christ and his way will be scoffed at. [3]These teachers in their greed will tell you anything to get hold of your money. But God condemned them long ago and their destruction is on the way. [13]That is the pay these teachers will have for their sin. For they live in evil pleasures day after day. They are a disgrace and a stain among you, deceiving you by living in foul sin on the side while they join your love feasts as though they were honest men. [14]No woman can escape their sinful stare, and of adultery they never have enough. They make a game of luring unstable women. They train themselves to be greedy; and are doomed and cursed. [15]They have gone off the road and become lost like Balaam, the son of Beor, who fell in love with the money he could make by doing wrong; [16]but Balaam was stopped from his mad course when his donkey spoke to him with a human voice, scolding and rebuking him. [17]These men are as useless as dried-up springs of water, promising much and delivering nothing; they are as unstable as clouds driven by the storm winds. They are doomed to the eternal pits of darkness. [18]They proudly boast about their sins and conquests, and, using lust as their bait, they lure back into sin those who have just escaped from such wicked living. [19]"You aren't saved by being good," they say, "so you might as well be bad. Do what you like, be free." But these very teachers who offer this "freedom" from law are themselves slaves to sin and destruction. For a man is a slave to whatever controls him. *vs.* 1–22.

2 Pet 3:16. Some of his comments are not easy to understand, and there are people who are deliberately stupid, and always demand some unusual interpretation—they have twisted his letters around to mean something quite different from what he meant, just as they do the other parts of the Scripture—and the result is disaster for them.

1 Jn 2:18. Dear children, this world's last hour has come. You have heard about the Antichrist who is coming—the one who is against Christ—and already many such persons have appeared. This makes us all the more certain that the end of the world is near. [26]These remarks of mine about the Antichrist are pointed at those who would dearly love to blindfold you and lead you astray.

1 Jn 4:1. Dearly loved friends, don't always believe everything you hear just because someone says it is a message from God: test it first to see if it really is. For there are many false teachers around, [2]and the way to find out if their message is from the Holy Spirit is to ask: Does it really agree that Jesus Christ, God's Son, actually became man with a human body? If so, then the message is from God. [3]If not, the message is not from God but from one who is against Christ, like the "Antichrist" you have heard about who is going to come, and his attitude of enmity against Christ is already abroad in the world. [5]These men belong to this world, so, quite naturally, they are concerned about worldly affairs and the world pays attention to them.

2 Jn 1:7. Watch out for the false leaders—and there are many of them around—who don't believe that Jesus Christ came to earth as a human being with a body like ours. Such people are against the truth and against Christ. [10]If anyone comes to teach you, and he doesn't believe what Christ taught, don't even invite him into your home. Don't encourage him in any way. [11]If you do you will be a partner with him in his wickedness.

3 Jn 1:10. When I come I will tell you some of the things he is doing and what wicked things he is saying about me and what insulting language he is using. He not only refuses to welcome the missionary travelers himself, but tells others not to, and when they do he tries to put them out of the church.

Jude 1:4. I say this because some godless teachers have wormed their way in among you, saying that after we become Christians we can do just as we like without fear of God's punishment. The fate of such people was written long ago, for they have turned against our only Master and Lord, Jesus Christ. [11]Woe upon them! For they follow the example of Cain who killed his brother; and, like Balaam, they will do anything for money; and like Korah, they have disobeyed God and will die under his curse.

Rev 2:1. *Write a letter to the leader of the church at Ephesus and tell him this:* I write to inform you of a message from him who walks among the churches and holds their leaders in his right hand. He says to you: [2]I know how many good things you are doing. I have watched your hard work and your patience; I know you don't tolerate sin among your members, and you have carefully examined the claims of those who say they are apostles but aren't. You have found out how they lie. [12]*Write this letter to the leader of the church in Pergamos:* This message is from him who wields the sharp and double-bladed sword. [14]And yet I have a few things against you. You tolerate some among you who do as Balaam did when he taught Balak how to ruin the people of Israel by involving them in sexual sin and encouraging them to go to idol feasts. [15]Yes, you have some of these very same followers of Balaam among you! [18]*Write this letter to the leader of the church in Thyatira:* [20]Yet I have this against you: You are permitting that woman Jezebel, who calls herself a prophetess, to teach my servants that sex sin is not a serious matter; she urges them to practice immorality and to eat meat that has been sacrificed to idols. [21]I gave her time to change her mind and attitude, but she refused. [22]Pay attention now to what I am saying: I will lay her upon a sickbed of intense affliction, along with all her immoral followers, unless they turn again to me, repenting of their sin with her. [23]And I will strike her children dead.

HOSPITALITY TO. The islanders to Paul, Acts 28:1–10. Simon the tanner to Peter, Acts 9:43. The Philippian jailer, Acts 16:33, 34. Aquila and Priscilla to Paul, Acts 18:2, 3; to Apollos, Acts 18:25, 26. Titus Justus to Paul, Acts 18:7. Philip the Evangelist to Paul, Acts 21:8–10.

ORDINATION OF. Of Matthias, Acts 1:26; of seven deacons, Acts 6:5, 6; of Paul and Barnabas, Acts 13:3; Timothy, 1 Tim 4:14.

PRAYER FOR, COMMANDED. Mt 9:37. "The harvest is so great, and the workers are so few," he told his disciples. [38]"So pray to the one in charge of the harvesting, and ask him to recruit more workers for his harvest fields." Lk 10:2.

Rom 15:30. Will you be my prayer partners? For the Lord Jesus Christ's sake, and because of your love for me—given to you by the Holy Spirit—pray much with me for my work. [31]Pray that I will be protected in Jerusalem from those who are not Christians. Pray also that the Christians there will be willing to accept the money I am bringing them. [32]Then I will be able to come to you with a happy heart by the will of God, and we can refresh each other.

2 Cor 1:11. But you must help us too, by praying for us. For much thanks and praise will go to God from you who see his wonderful answers to your prayers for our safety!

Eph 6:18. Pray all the time. Ask God for anything in line with the Holy Spirit's wishes. Plead with him, reminding him of your needs, and keep praying earnestly for all Christians everywhere. [19]Pray for me, too, and ask God to give me the right words as I boldly tell others about the Lord, and as I explain to them that his salvation is for the Gentiles too. [20]I am in chains now for preaching this message from God. But pray that I will keep on speaking out boldly for him even here in prison, as I should.

Phil 1:19. I am going to keep on being glad, for I know that as you pray for me, and as the Holy Spirit helps me, this is all going to turn out for my good.

Col 4:2. Don't be weary in prayer; keep at it; watch for God's answers and remember to be thankful when they come. [3]Don't forget to pray for us too, that God will give us many chances to preach the Good News of Christ for which I am here in jail. [4]Pray that I will be bold enough to tell it freely and fully, and make it plain, as, of course, I should.

1 Thess 5:25. Dear brothers, pray for us.

2 Thess 3:1. Finally, dear brothers, as I come to the end of this letter I ask you to pray for us. Pray first that the Lord's message will spread rapidly and triumph wherever it goes, winning converts everywhere as it did when it came to you. [2]Pray too that we will be saved out of the clutches of evil men, for not everyone loves the Lord.

Philemon 1:22. Please keep a guest room ready for me, for I am hoping that God will answer your prayers and let me come to you soon.

Heb 13:18. Pray for us, for our conscience is clear and we want to keep it that way. [19]I especially need your prayers right now so that I can come back to you sooner.

PRAYER FOR, EXEMPLIFIED. Acts 1:24, 25. Then they all prayed for the right man to be chosen. "O Lord," they said, "you know every heart; show us which of these men you have chosen as an apostle to replace Judas the traitor, who has gone on to his proper place."

Acts 4:29. And now, O Lord, hear their threats, and grant to your servants great boldness in their preaching.

Acts 6:6. These seven were presented to the apostles, who prayed for them and laid their hands on them in blessing.

Acts 12:5. But earnest prayer was going up to God from the church for his safety all the time he was in prison.

Acts 14:23. Paul and Barnabas also appointed elders in every church and prayed for them with fasting, turning them over to the care of the Lord in whom they trusted.

PROMISES TO, AND JOYS OF. Mt 10:28. Don't be afraid of those who can kill only your bodies—but can't touch your souls! Fear only God who can destroy both soul and body in hell. [29]Not one sparrow (what do they cost? Two for a penny?) can fall to the ground without your Father knowing it. [30]And the very hairs of your head are all numbered. [31]So don't worry! You are more valuable to him than many sparrows.

Mt 28:20. And be sure of this—that I am with you always, even to the end of the world.

Lk 12:11. And when you are brought to trial before these Jewish rulers and authorities in the synagogues, don't be concerned about what to say in your defense, [12]for the Holy Spirit will give you the right words even as you are standing there.

Lk 24:49. And now I will send the Holy Spirit upon you, just as my Father promised. Don't begin telling others yet—stay here in the city until the Holy Spirit comes and fills you with power from heaven.

Jn 4:36. The reapers will be paid good wages and will be gathering eternal souls into the granaries of heaven! What joys await the sower and the reaper, both together! [37]For it is true that one sows and someone else reaps. [38]I sent you to reap where you didn't sow; others did the work, and you received the harvest.

Acts 1:4. In one of these meetings he told them not to leave Jerusalem until the Holy Spirit came upon them in fulfillment of the Father's promise, a matter he had previously discussed with them. [5]"John baptized you with water," he reminded them, "but you shall be baptized with the Holy Spirit in just a few days. [8]But when the Holy Spirit has come upon you, you will receive power to testify about me with great effect, to the people in Jerusalem, throughout Judea, in Samaria, and to the ends of the earth, about my death and resurrection."

1 Cor 9:9. For in the law God gave to Moses he said that you must not put a muzzle on an ox to keep it from eating when it is treading out the wheat. Do you suppose God was thinking only about oxen when he said this? [10]Wasn't he also thinking about us? Of course he was. He said this to show us that Christian workers should be paid by those they help. Those who do the plowing and threshing should expect some share of the harvest.

2 Cor 2:14. But thanks be to God! For through what Christ has done, he has triumphed over us so that now wherever we go he uses us to tell others about the Lord and to spread the Gospel like a sweet perfume. [15]As far as God is concerned there is a sweet, wholesome fragrance in our lives. It is the fragrance of Christ within us, an aroma to both the saved and the unsaved all around us. [16]To those who are not being saved, we seem a fearful smell of death and doom, while to those who know Christ we are a life-giving perfume. But who is adequate for such a task as this?

2 Cor 7:6. Then God who cheers those who are discouraged refreshed us by the arrival of Titus. [7]Not only was his presence a joy, but also the news that he brought of the wonderful time he had with you. When he told me how much you were looking forward to my visit, and how sorry you were about what had happened, and about your loyalty and warm love for me, well, I overflowed with joy!

Phil 2:16. Holding out to them the Word of Life. Then when Christ returns how glad I will be that my work among you was so worthwhile.

1 Thess 2:13. And we will never stop thanking God for this: that when we preached to you, you didn't think of the words we spoke as being just our own, but you accepted what we said as the very Word of God—which, of course, it was—and it changed your lives when you believed it. [19]For what is it we live for, that gives us hope and joy and is our proud reward and crown? It is you! Yes, you will bring us much joy as we stand together before our Lord Jesus Christ when he comes back again. [20]For you are our trophy and joy.

1 Thess 3:8. We can bear anything as long as we know that you remain strong in him. [9]How can we thank God enough for you and for the joy and delight you have given us in our praying for you?

3 Jn 1:4. I could have no greater joy than to hear such things about my children.

See *Righteous, Promises to.*

SUCCESS ATTENDING. Apostles, Acts 2:1–4, 41. Philip, Acts 8:6, 8, 12. Peter, Acts 9:32–35. Paul, Acts 13:16–43; 1 Cor 4:15; 9:2; 15:11; 2 Cor 3:2, 3; 12:12; 13:4; Phil 2:16; 1 Thess 1:5. Apollos, Acts 18:24–28.

See *Revival.*

TRIALS AND PERSECUTIONS OF. Mt 10:16. I am sending you out as sheep among wolves. Be as wary as serpents and harmless as doves. [17]But beware! For you will be arrested and tried, and whipped in the synagogues. [18]Yes, and you must stand trial before governors and kings for my sake. This will give you the opportunity to tell them about me, yes, to witness to the world. [19]When you are arrested, don't worry about what to say at your trial, for you will be given the right words at the right time. [20]For it won't be you doing the talking —it will be the Spirit of your heavenly Father speaking through you! [21]Brother shall betray brother to death, and fathers shall betray their own children. And children shall rise against their parents and cause their deaths. [22]Everyone shall hate you because you belong to me. But all of you who endure to the end shall be saved. [23]When you are persecuted in one city, flee to the next! I will return before you have reached them all! [24]A student is not greater than his teacher. A servant is not above his master. [25]The student shares his teacher's fate. The servant shares his master's! And since I, the master of the household, have been called "Satan," how much more will you! [Jn 13:16.] [26]But don't be afraid of those who threaten you. For the time is coming when the truth will be revealed: their secret plots will become public information. [27]What I tell you now in the gloom, shout abroad when daybreak comes. What I whisper in your ears, proclaim from the housetops!

Mt 23:34. I will send you prophets, and wise men, and inspired writers, and you will kill some by crucifixion, and rip open the backs of others with whips in your synagogues, and hound them from city to city.

1 Cor 2:1. Dear brothers, even when I first came to you I didn't use lofty words and brilliant ideas to tell you God's message. [2]For I decided that I would speak only of Jesus Christ and his death on the cross. [3]I came to you in weakness—timid and trembling. [4]And my preaching was very plain, not with a lot of oratory and human wisdom, but the Holy Spirit's power was in my words, proving to those who heard them that the message was from God.

1 Cor 4:9. Sometimes I think God has put us apostles at the very end of the line, like prisoners soon to be killed, put on display at the end of a victor's parade, to be stared at by men and angels alike. [10]Religion has made us foolish, you say, but of course you are all such wise and sensible Christians! We are weak, but not you! You are well thought of, while we are laughed at. [11]To this very hour we have gone hungry and thirsty, without even enough clothes to keep us warm. We have been kicked around without homes of our own. [12]We have worked wearily with our hands to earn our living. We have blessed those who cursed us. We have been patient with those who injured us.

[13]We have replied quietly when evil things have been said about us. Yet right up to the present moment we are like dirt under foot, like garbage.

2 Cor 6:4. In fact, in everything we do we try to show that we are true ministers of God. We patiently endure suffering and hardship and trouble of every kind. [5]We have been beaten, put in jail, faced angry mobs, worked to exhaustion, stayed awake through sleepless nights of watching, and gone without food. [6]We have proved ourselves to be what we claim by our wholesome lives and by our understanding of the Gospel and by our patience. We have been kind and truly loving and filled with the Holy Spirit. [7]We have been truthful, with God's power helping us in all we do. All of the godly man's arsenal—weapons of defense, and weapons of attack—have been ours. [8]We stand true to the Lord whether others honor us or despise us, whether they criticize us or commend us. We are honest, but they call us liars. [9]The world ignores us, but we are known to God; we live close to death, but here we are, still very much alive. We have been injured but kept from death. [10]Our hearts ache, but at the same time we have the joy of the Lord. We are poor, but we give rich spiritual gifts to others. We own nothing, and yet we enjoy everything.

2 Cor 7:5. When we arrived in Macedonia there was no rest for us; outside, trouble was on every hand and all around us; within us, our hearts were full of dread and fear.

2 Cor 11:23. They say they serve Christ? But I have served him far more! (Have I gone mad to boast like this?) I have worked harder, been put in jail oftener, been whipped times without number, and faced death again and again and again. [24]Five different times the Jews gave me their terrible thirty-nine lashes. [25]Three times I was beaten with rods. Once I was stoned. Three times I was shipwrecked. Once I was in the open sea all night and the whole next day. [26]I have traveled many weary miles and have been often in great danger from flooded rivers, and from robbers, and from my own people, the Jews, as well as from the hands of the Gentiles. I have faced grave dangers from mobs in the cities and from death in the deserts and in the stormy seas and from men who claim to be brothers in Christ but are not. [27]I have lived with weariness and pain and sleepless nights. Often I have been hungry and thirsty and have gone without food; often I have shivered with cold, without enough clothing to keep me warm. [28]Then, besides all this, I have the constant worry of how the churches are getting along: [29]Who makes a mistake and I do not feel his sadness? Who falls without my longing to help him? Who is spiritually hurt without my fury rising against the one who hurt him? [30]But if I must brag, I would rather brag about the things that show how weak I am. [31]God, the Father of our Lord Jesus Christ, who is to be praised forever and ever, knows I tell the truth. [32]For instance, in Damascus the governor under King Aretus kept guards at the city gates to catch me; [33]but I was let down by rope and basket from a hole in the city wall, and so I got away! (What popularity!)

2 Cor 12:7. I will say this: because these experiences I had were so tremendous, God was afraid I might be puffed up by them; so I was given a physical condition which has been a thorn in my flesh, a messenger from Satan to hurt and bother me, and prick my pride. [8]Three different times I begged God to make me well again. [9]Each time he said, "No. But I am with you; that is all you need. My power shows up best in weak people." Now I am glad to boast about how weak I am; I am glad to be a living demonstration of Christ's power, instead of showing off my own power and abilities. [10]Since I know it is all for Christ's good, I am quite happy about "the thorn," and about insults and hardships, persecutions and difficulties; for when I am weak, then I am strong—the less I have, the more I depend on him. [11]You have made me act like a fool—boasting like this—for you people ought to be writing about me and not making me write about myself. There isn't a single thing these other marvelous fellows have that I don't have too, even though I am really worth nothing at all. [12]When I was there I certainly gave you every proof that I was truly an apostle, sent to you by God himself: for I patiently did many wonders and signs and mighty works among you.

Gal 4:13. I was sick when I first brought you the Good News of Christ. [14]But even though my sickness was revolting to you, you didn't reject me and turn me away. No, you took me in and cared for me as though I were an angel from God, or even Jesus Christ himself.

Eph 3:1. I Paul, the servant of Christ, am here in jail because of you—for preaching that you Gentiles are a part of God's house. [13]So please don't lose heart at what they are doing to me here. It is for you I am suffering and you should feel honored and encouraged.

Instances of Persecution. The apostles, Acts 5: 17–42. Peter, Acts 12:3–19. Paul, Acts 9:23–25, 29, 30; 14:5–20; 16:11–40; 17:1–13; 20:3; 21:26–40; 22:17, 18, 21, 24–30; 23:11–35; 24; 25; 26; 2 Cor 11:31–33; Gal 1:21–24; 2 Tim 1:8, 16; 2:9; 4:16, 17.

ZEALOUS. Titus, 2 Cor 8:16, 17. Epaphroditus, Phil 2:25–30. Epaphras, Col 4:12, 13. Tychicus, Col 4:7. John, in his vision, Rev 5:4, 5.

See *Zeal.*

MINNI A district of Armenia, Jer 51:27.

MINNITH A place east of the Jordan, Judg 11:33; Ezk 27:17.

MINORS Legal status of, Gal 4:1, 2.

See *Orphan; Young Men.*

MINORITY REPORT See *Reports.*

MINT Mt 23:23.

MIRACLES INDEX OF SUB-TOPICS. *Catalog of, and Supernatural Events; Of Jesus, in Chronological Order; Of the Disciples of Jesus; Convincing Effect of; Design of; Miraculous Gifts of the Holy Spirit; Miscellany of Minor Sub-Topics.*

CATALOG OF, AND SUPERNATURAL

EVENTS. Creation, Gen 1. Flood, Gen 7; 8. Confusion of languages, Gen 11:1–9. Fire on Abraham's sacrifice, Gen 15:17. Conception of Isaac, Gen 17:17; 18:12; 21:1, 2. Destruction of Sodom, Gen 19. Lot's wife turned to salt, Gen 19:26. Barrenness of Abimelech's household, Gen 20:17, 18. Opening of Hagar's eyes, Gen 21:19. Conception of Jacob and Esau, Gen 25:21. Conception of Joseph, Gen 30:22. Flaming bush, Ex 3:2. Transformation of Moses's rod into a serpent, Ex 4:3, 4, 30; 7:10, 12; Moses's leprosy, Ex 4:6, 7, 30. Plagues in Egypt, see *Plague.* Pillar of cloud and fire, Ex 13:21, 22; 14:19, 20. Passage through the Red Sea, Ex 14:22. Destruction of Pharaoh and his army, Ex 14:23–30. Sweetening the waters of Marah, Ex 15:25. Manna, Ex 16: 4–31. Quails, Ex 16:13. Defeat of Amalek, Ex 17: 9–13. Transfiguration of the face of Moses, Ex 34: 29–35. Water from the rock, Ex 17:5–7. Thundering and lightning on Sinai, Ex 19:16–20; 24:10, 15–17; Deut 4:33. Miriam's leprosy, Num 12:10–15. Judgment by fire, Num 11:1–3. Destruction of Korah, Dathan, and Abiram, Num 16:31–35; Deut 11:6, 7. Plague, Num 16:46–50. Aaron's rod buds, Num 17:1–9. Water from the rock in Kadesh, Num 20:8–11. Judgment of serpents, Num 21:6–9. Destruction of Nadab and Abihu, Lev 10:1, 2. Balaam's donkey speaks, Num 22:22–30. Preservation of Moses, Deut 34:7. Jordan divided, Josh 3: 13–17; 4:15–18. Fall of Jericho, Josh 6:20. Midianites destroyed, Judg 7:16–22. Hail falls on the confederated kings, Josh 10:11. Sun and moon stand still, Josh 10:12–14. Dew on Gideon's fleece, Judg 6:37–40. Samson's strength, Judg 14:6; 16:3, 29, 30. Samson supplied with water, Judg 15:19. Fall of Dagon, 1 Sam 5:1–4. Cows return the ark, 1 Sam 6:7–14. Plagues, 1 Sam 5:9–12; 6:1–18. Destruction of 70 men of Beth-shemesh, 1 Sam 6:19, 20. Thunder, 1 Sam 12:16–18. Destruction of Uzzah, 2 Sam 6:1–8. Plague in Israel, 1 Chron 21:14–26. Fire on the sacrifices of Aaron, Lev 9:24; of Gideon, Judg 6:21; of Manoah, Judg 13:19, 20; of Solomon, 2 Chron 7:1; of Elijah, 1 Kgs 18:38. Jeroboam's hand paralyzed, 1 Kgs 13:3–6. Appearance of blood, 2 Kgs 3:20–23. Panic of the Syrians, 2 Kgs 7:6, 7. Elijah is fed by ravens, 1 Kgs 17:6; by an angel, 1 Kgs 19:1–8; increases the widow's flour and oil, 1 Kgs 17:8–16; Lk 4:25, 26; raises the widow's son, 1 Kgs 17:17–24. Rain in answer to Elijah's prayer, 1 Kgs 18:41–45. Elijah brings fire on Ahaziah's army, 2 Kgs 1:10–12; divides Jordan, 2 Kgs 2:8. Elijah's translation, 2 Kgs 2:11.

Elisha divides Jordan, 2 Kgs 2:13, 14; purifies the water of Jericho, 2 Kgs 2:19–22; increases a widow's oil, 2 Kgs 4:1–7; raises the Shunemmite's child, 2 Kgs 4:18–37; renders harmless the poisoned stew, 2 Kgs 4:38–41; feeds 100 men, 2 Kgs 4:42–44; cures Naaman, 2 Kgs 5:1–19; afflicts Gehazi with leprosy, 2 Kgs 5:26, 27; causes the axehead to float, 2 Kgs 6:6; reveals the secrets of the king of Syria, 2 Kgs 6:12; causes the eyes of his servant to be opened, 2 Kgs 6:17; blinds the army of the king of Syria, 2 Kgs 6:18; the dead man restored to life, 2 Kgs 13:20, 21.

Destruction of Sennacherib's army, 2 Kgs 19:35; Isa 37:36; return of the shadow on the sun dial, 2 Kgs 20:9–11; Hezekiah's cure, Isa 38:21; deliverance of Shadrach, Meshach, and Abednego, Dan 3: 23–27; of Daniel, Dan 6:22; the sea calmed on Jonah being thrown into it, Jon 1:15; Jonah in the fish's belly, Jon 1:17; 2:10; his vine, Jon 4:6, 7.

Conception by Elizabeth, Lk 1:18, 24, 25. The incarnation of Jesus, Mt 1:18–25; Lk 1:26–80. The appearance of the star of Bethlehem, Mt 2:1–9. The deliverance of Jesus, Mt 2:13–23.

Of Jesus, in Chronological Order. Water made wine, Jn 2:1–11.

Heals the government official's son, Jn 4:46–54.

Draught of fishes, Lk 5:1–11.

Heals the demoniac, Mk 1:23–26; Lk 4:33–36.

Heals Peter's mother-in-law, Mt 8:14, 15; Mk 1: 29–31; Lk 4:38, 39.

Heals the leper, Mt 8:1–4; Mk 1:40–45; Lk 5: 12–16.

Heals the paralytic, Mt 9:1–8; Mk 2:1–12; Lk 5: 17–26.

Healing of the disabled man, Jn 5:1–16.

Restoring the deformed hand, Mt 12:9–13; Mk 3: 1–5; Lk 6:6–11.

Restores the Roman army officer's servant, Mt 8:5–13; Lk 7:1–10.

Raises the widow's son to life, Lk 7:11–16.

Heals a demoniac, Mt 12:22–37; Mk 3:11, 20–30; Lk 11:14, 15.

Stills the storm, Mt 8:23–27; 14:32; Mk 4:35–41; Lk 8:22–25.

Heals two demoniacs in Gadara, Mt 8:28–34; Mk 5:1–20; Lk 8:26–39.

Raises Jairus's daughter, Mt 9:18, 19, 23–26; Mk 5:22–24, 35–43; Lk 8:41, 42, 49–56.

Cures the woman with the hemorrhage, Mt 9: 20–22; Mk 5:25–34; Lk 8:43–48.

Restores the sight of two blind men, Mt 9:27–31.

Heals a demoniac, Mt 9:32, 33.

Feeds 5,000 people, Mt 14:15–21; Mk 6:35–44; Lk 9:12–17; Jn 6:1–14.

Walks on the sea, Mt 14:22–33; Mk 6:45–52; Jn 6:16–21.

Heals the daughter of the Syrophoenician woman, Mt 15:21–28; Mk 7:24–30.

Feeds 4,000 people, Mt 15:32–39; Mk 8:1–9.

Restores one deaf man with a speech impediment, Mk 7:31–37.

Heals a blind man, Mk 8:22–26.

Restores a demoniac child, Mt 17:14–21; Mk 9: 14–29; Lk 9:37–43.

Tax money obtained from a fish's mouth, Mt 17: 24–27.

Cures 10 lepers, Lk 17:11–19.

Opens the eyes of a man born blind, Jn 9.

Raises Lazarus from the dead, Jn 11:1–54.

Heals the handicapped woman, Lk 13:10–17.

Cures a man with dropsy, Lk 14:1–6.

Heals two blind men near Jericho, Mt 20:29–34; Mk 10:46–52; Lk 18:35–43.

Curses a fig tree, Mt 21:17–22; Mk 11:12–14, 20–24.

Heals the ear of Malchus, Lk 22:49–51.
Second draught of fishes, Jn 21:6.

Of the Disciples of Jesus. By the seventy, Lk 10:17–20; by other disciples, Mk 9:39; Jn 14:12, 13; by the apostles, Acts 3:6, 12, 13, 16; 4:10, 30; 9:34, 35; 16:18. Peter cures the sick, Acts 5:15, 16; Aeneas, Acts 9:34; raises Dorcas, Acts 9:40; causes the death of Ananias and Sapphira, Acts 5:5, 10. Peter and John cure a lame man, Acts 3:2–11. Peter and other apostles delivered from prison, Acts 5:19–23; 12:6–11; 16:26. Philip carried away by the Spirit, Acts 8:39. Paul strikes Elymas with blindness, Acts 13:11; heals a cripple, Acts 14:10; casts out demons, and cures sick, Acts 16:18; 19:11, 12; 28:8, 9; raises Eutychus to life, Acts 20:9–12; shakes a snake off his hand, Acts 28:5. Paul cured of blindness, Acts 9:3–6, 17, 18.

CONVINCING EFFECT OF. Ex 4:28. Moses told Aaron what God had said they must do, and what they were to say, and told him about the miracles they must do before Pharaoh. [29]So Moses and Aaron returned to Egypt and summoned the elders of the people of Israel to a council meeting. [30]Aaron told them what Jehovah had said to Moses, and Moses performed the miracles as they watched. [31]Then the elders believed that God had sent them, and when they heard that Jehovah had visited them and had seen their sorrows, and had decided to rescue them, they all rejoiced and bowed their heads and worshiped.

Ex 10:7. The court officials now came to Pharaoh and asked him, "Are you going to destroy us completely? Don't you know even yet that all Egypt lies in ruins? Let the *men* go and serve Jehovah their God!" [16]Then Pharaoh sent an urgent call for Moses and Aaron and said to them, "I confess my sin against Jehovah your God and against you. [17]Forgive my sin only this once, and beg Jehovah your God to take away this death. I promise not to refuse afterwards to let you go."

Ex 12:31. And Pharaoh summoned Moses and Aaron during the night and said, "Leave us; please go away, all of you; go and serve Jehovah as you said. [32]Take your flocks and herds and be gone; and oh, give me a blessing as you go." [33]And the Egyptians were urgent upon the people of Israel, to get them out of the land as quickly as possible. For they said, "We are as good as dead."

Ex 14:25. Their chariot wheels began coming off, so that their chariots scraped along the dry ground. "Let's get out of here," the Egyptians yelled. "Jehovah is fighting for them and against us." [31]When the people of Israel saw the mighty miracle the Lord had done for them against the Egyptians, they were afraid and revered the Lord, and believed in him and in his servant Moses.

Judg 6:17. Gideon replied, "If it is really true that you are going to help me like that, then do some miracle to prove it! Prove that it is really Jehovah who is talking to me! [18]But stay here until I go and get a present for you." "All right," the Angel agreed. "I'll stay here until you return." [19]Gideon hurried home and roasted a young goat, and baked some unleavened bread from a bushel of flour. Then, carrying the meat in a basket and broth in a pot, he took it out to the Angel, who was beneath the oak tree, and presented it to him. [20]The Angel said to him, "Place the meat and the bread upon that rock over there, and pour the broth over it." When Gideon had followed these instructions, [21]the Angel touched the meat and bread with his staff, and fire flamed up from the rock and consumed them! And suddenly the Angel was gone! [22]When Gideon realized that it had indeed been the Angel of the Lord, he cried out, "Alas, O Lord God, for I have seen the Angel of the Lord face to face!" [36]Then Gideon said to God, "If you are really going to use me to save Israel as you promised, [37]prove it to me in this way: I'll put some wool on the threshing floor tonight, and if, in the morning, the fleece is wet and the ground is dry, I will know you are going to help me!" [38]And it happened just that way! When he got up the next morning he pressed the fleece together and wrung out a whole bowlful of water! [39]Then Gideon said to the Lord, "Please don't be angry with me, but let me make one more test: this time let the fleece remain dry while the ground around it is wet!" [40]So the Lord did as he asked; that night the fleece stayed dry, but the ground was covered with dew!

Judg 7:1. Jerubbaal (that is, Gideon—his other name) and his army got an early start and went as far as the spring of Harod. The armies of Midian were camped north of them, down in the valley beside the hill of Moreh.

Dan 3:28. Then Nebuchadnezzar said, "Blessed be the God of Shadrach, Meshach, and Abednego, for he sent his angel to deliver his trusting servants when they defied the king's commandment, and were willing to die rather than serve or worship any god except their own. [29]Therefore, I make the decree, that any person of any nation, language, or religion who speaks a word against the God of Shadrach, Meshach, and Abednego shall be torn limb from limb and his house knocked into a heap of rubble. For no other God can do what this one does."

Dan 4:2. I want you all to know about the strange thing that the Most High God did to me. [3]It was incredible—a mighty miracle! And now I know for sure that his kingdom is everlasting; he reigns forever and ever.

Lk 5:4. When he had finished speaking, he said to Simon, "Now go out where it is deeper and let down your nets and you will catch a lot of fish!" [5]"Sir," Simon replied, "we worked hard all last night and didn't catch a thing. But if you say so, we'll try again." [6]And this time their nets were so full that they began to tear! [7]A shout for help brought their partners in the other boat and soon both boats were filled with fish and on the verge of sinking. [8]When Simon Peter realized what had happened, he fell to his knees before Jesus and said, "Oh, sir, please leave us—I'm too much of a sinner for you to have around." [9]For he was awestruck by the size of their catch, as were the others with him,

[10]and his partners too—James and John, the sons of Zebedee. Jesus replied, "Don't be afraid! From now on you'll be fishing for the souls of men!" [11]And as soon as they landed, they left everything and went with him.

Jn 2:11. This miracle at Cana in Galilee was Jesus' first public demonstration of his heaven-sent power. And his disciples believed that he really was the Messiah. [22]After he came back to life again, the disciples remembered his saying this and realized that what he had quoted from the Scriptures really did refer to him, and had all come true! [23]Because of the miracles he did in Jerusalem at the Passover celebration, many people were convinced that he was indeed the Messiah.

Jn 4:48. Jesus asked, "Won't any of you believe in me unless I do more and more miracles?" [49]The official pled, "Sir, please come now before my child dies." [50]Then Jesus told him, "Go back home. Your son is healed!" And the man believed Jesus and started home. [51]While he was on his way, some of his servants met him with the news that all was well—his son had recovered. [52]He asked them when the lad had begun to feel better, and they replied, "Yesterday afternoon at about one o'clock his fever suddenly disappeared!" [53]Then the father realized it was the same moment that Jesus had told him, "Your son is healed." And the officer and his entire household believed that Jesus was the Messiah.

Jn 7:31. Many among the crowds at the Temple believed on him. "After all," they said, "what miracles do you expect the Messiah to do that this man hasn't done?"

Jn 11:43. Then he shouted, "Lazarus, come out!" [44]And Lazarus came—bound up in the gravecloth, his face muffled in a head swath. Jesus told them, "Unwrap him and let him go!" [45]And so at last many of the Jewish leaders who were with Mary and saw it happen, finally believed on him.

Jn 12:10. Then the chief priests decided to kill Lazarus too, [11]for it was because of him that many of the Jewish leaders had deserted and believed in Jesus as their Messiah.

Jn 20:30, 31. Jesus' disciples saw him do many other miracles besides the ones told about in this book, but these are recorded so that you will believe that he is the Messiah, the Son of God, and that believing in him you will have life.

Acts 8:6. Crowds listened intently to what he had to say because of the miracles he did.

Acts 9:32. Peter traveled from place to place to visit them, and in his travels came to the believers in the town of Lydda. [33]There he met a man named Aeneas, paralyzed and bedridden for eight years. [34]Peter said to him "Aeneas! Jesus Christ has healed you! Get up and make your bed." And he was healed instantly. [35]Then the whole population of Lydda and Sharon turned to the Lord when they saw Aeneas walking around. [36]In the city of Joppa there was a woman named Dorcas ("Gazelle"), a believer who was always doing kind things for others, especially for the poor. [37]About this time she became ill and died. Her friends prepared her for burial and laid her in an upstairs room. [38]But when they learned that Peter was nearby at Lydda, they sent two men to beg him to return with them to Joppa. [39]This he did; as soon as he arrived, they took him upstairs where Dorcas lay. The room was filled with weeping widows who were showing one another the coats and other garments Dorcas had made for them. [40]But Peter asked them all to leave the room; then he knelt and prayed. Turning to the body he said, "Get up, Dorcas," and she opened her eyes! And when she saw Peter, she sat up! [41]He gave her his hand and helped her up and called in the believers and widows, presenting her to them. [42]The news raced through the town, and many believed in the Lord.

Acts 13:8. But the sorcerer, Elymas (his name in Greek), interfered and urged the governor to pay no attention to what Paul and Barnabas said, trying to keep him from trusting the Lord. [9]Then Paul, filled with the Holy Spirit, glared angrily at the sorcerer and said, [10]"You son of the devil, full of every sort of trickery and villainy, enemy of all that is good, will you never end your opposition to the Lord? [11]And now God has laid his hand of punishment upon you, and you will be stricken awhile with blindness." Instantly mist and darkness fell upon him, and he began wandering around begging for someone to take his hand and lead him. [12]When the governor saw what happened he believed and was astonished at the power of God's message.

Acts 19:13. A team of itinerant Jews who were traveling from town to town casting out demons planned to experiment by using the name of the Lord Jesus. The incantation they decided on was this: "I adjure you by Jesus, whom Paul preaches, to come out!" [14]Seven sons of Sceva, a Jewish priest, were doing this. [15]But when they tried it on a man possessed by a demon, the demon replied, "I know Jesus and I know Paul, but who are you?" [16]And he leaped on two of them and beat them up, so that they fled out of his house naked and badly injured. [17]The story of what happened spread quickly all through Ephesus, to Jews and Greeks alike; and a solemn fear descended on the city, and the name of the Lord Jesus was greatly honored. [18]Many of the believers who had been practicing black magic confessed their deeds.

Rom 15:18. I dare not judge how effectively he has used others, but I know this: he has used me to win the Gentiles to God. [19]I have won them by my message and by the good way I have lived before them, and by the miracles done through me as signs from God—all by the Holy Spirit's power. In this way I have preached the full Gospel of Christ all the way from Jerusalem clear over into Illyricum.

See below, *Miracles, Design of.*

DESIGN OF. Ex 3:19. But I know that the king of Egypt will not let you go except under heavy pressure. [20]So I will give him all the pressure he needs! I will destroy Egypt with my miracles, and then at last he will let you go.

Ex 4:2. "What do you have there in your hand?" the Lord asked him. And he replied, "A shepherd's rod." [3]"Throw it down on the ground," the Lord told him. So he threw it down—and it became a serpent, and Moses ran from it! [4]Then the Lord told him, "Grab it by the tail!" He did, and it became a rod in his hand again! [5]"Do that and they will believe you!" the Lord told him. "Then they will realize that Jehovah, the God of their ancestors Abraham, Isaac, and Jacob, has really appeared to you. [6]Now reach your hand inside your robe, next to your chest." And when he did, and took it out again, it was white with leprosy! [7]"Now put it in again," Jehovah said. And when he did, and took it out again, it was normal, just as before! [8]"If they don't believe the first miracle, they will the second," the Lord said, [9]"and if they don't accept you after these two signs, then take water from the Nile River and pour it upon the dry land, and it will turn to blood."

Ex 7:5. "The Egyptians will find out that I am indeed God when I show them my power and force them to let my people go." [17]And now the Lord says this: "You are going to find out that I am God. For I have instructed Moses to hit the water of the Nile with his rod, and the river will turn to blood!"

Ex 8:8. Then Pharaoh summoned Moses and Aaron and begged, "Plead with God to take the frogs away, and I will let the people go and sacrifice to him." [9]"Be so kind as to tell me when you want them to go," Moses said, "and I will pray that the frogs will die at the time you specify, everywhere except in the river." [10]"Do it tomorrow," Pharaoh said. "All right," Moses replied, "it shall be as you have said; then you will know that there is no one like the Lord our God." [22]"But it will be very different in the land of Goshen where the Israelis live. No flies will be there; thus you will know that I am the Lord God of all the earth."

Ex 9:14. "This time I am going to send a plague that will really speak to you and to your servants and to all the Egyptian people, and prove to you there is no other God in all the earth. [15]I could have killed you all by now, [16]but I didn't, for I wanted to demonstrate my power to you and to all the earth." [29]"All right," Moses replied, "as soon as I have left the city I will spread out my hands to the Lord, and the thunder and hail will stop. This will prove to you that the earth is controlled by Jehovah."

Ex 10:1. Then the Lord said to Moses, "Go back again and make your demand upon Pharaoh; but I have hardened him and his officials, so that I can do more miracles demonstrating my power. [2]What stories you can tell your children and grandchildren about the incredible things I am doing in Egypt! Tell them what fools I made of the Egyptians, and how I proved to you that I am Jehovah." [16]Then Pharaoh sent an urgent call for Moses and Aaron and said to them, "I confess my sin against Jehovah your God and against you. [17]Forgive my sin only this once, and beg Jehovah your God to take away this death. I promise not to refuse afterwards to let you go."

Ex 11:1. Then the Lord said to Moses, "I will send just one more disaster on Pharaoh and his land, and after that he will let you go; in fact, he will be so anxious to get rid of you that he will practically throw you out of the country." [7]" 'But not a dog shall move his tongue against any of the people of Israel, nor shall any of their animals die. Then you will know that Jehovah makes a distinction between Egyptians and Israelis.' [8]All these officials of yours will come running to me bowing low and begging, 'Please leave at once, and take all your people with you.' Only then will I go!" Then, red-faced with anger, Moses stomped from the palace. [9]The Lord had told Moses, "Pharaoh won't listen, and this will give me the opportunity of doing mighty miracles to demonstrate my power."

Ex 12:29. And that night, at midnight, Jehovah killed all the first-born sons in the land of Egypt, from Pharaoh's oldest son to the oldest son of the captive in the dungeon; also all the firstborn of the cattle. [30]Then Pharaoh and his officials and all the people of Egypt got up in the night; and there was bitter crying throughout all the land of Egypt, for there was not a house where there was not one dead. [31]And Pharaoh summoned Moses and Aaron during the night and said, "Leave us; please go away, all of you; go and serve Jehovah as you said. [32]Take your flocks and herds and be gone; and oh, give me a blessing as you go." [33]And the Egyptians were urgent upon the people of Israel, to get them out of the land as quickly as possible. For they said, "We are as good as dead."

Ex 14:4. "And once again I will harden Pharaoh's heart and he will chase after you. I have planned this to gain great honor and glory over Pharaoh and all his armies, and the Egyptians shall know that I am the Lord." So they camped where they were told. [18]"And all Egypt shall know that I am Jehovah." [24]But in the early morning Jehovah looked down from the cloud of fire upon the array of the Egyptians, and began to harass them. [25]Their chariot wheels began coming off, so that their chariots scraped along the dry ground. "Let's get out of here," the Egyptians yelled. "Jehovah is fighting for them and against us." [31]When the people of Israel saw the mighty miracle the Lord had done for them against the Egyptians, they were afraid and revered the Lord, and believed in him and in his servant Moses.

Ex 16:4. Then the Lord said to Moses, "Look, I'm going to rain down food from heaven for them. Everyone can go out each day and gather as much food as he needs. And I will test them in this, to see whether they will follow my instructions or not. [5]Tell them to gather twice as much as usual on the sixth day of each week." [6]Then Moses and Aaron called a meeting of all the people of Israel and told them, "This evening you will realize that it was the Lord who brought you out of the land of Egypt."

Ex 19:4. "You have seen what I did to the Egyptians, and how I brought you to myself as though on eagle's wings. [5]Now if you will obey me and keep your part of my contract with you, you shall be my own little flock from among all the nations of the earth; for all the earth is mine." [9]Then he said to Moses, "I am going to come to you in the form of a dark cloud, so that the people themselves can hear me when I talk with you, and then they will always believe you."

Num 14:11. The Lord said to Moses, "How long will these people despise me? Will they *never* believe me, even after all the miracles I have done among them?"

Num 16:28. And Moses said, "By this you shall know that Jehovah has sent me to do all these things that I have done—for I have not done them on my own. [29]If these men die a natural death or from some ordinary accident or disease, then Jehovah has not sent me. [30]But if the Lord does a miracle and the ground opens up and swallows them and everything that belongs to them, and they go down alive into Sheol, then you will know that these men have despised the Lord." [31]He had hardly finished speaking the words when the ground suddenly split open beneath them, [32]and a great fissure swallowed them up, along with their tents and families and the friends who were standing with them, and everything they owned. [33]So they went down alive into Sheol and the earth closed upon them, and they perished. [34]All of the people of Israel fled at their screams, fearing that the earth would swallow them too. [35]Then fire came forth from Jehovah and burned up the 250 men who were offering incense.

Num 17:1. Then the Lord said to Moses, "Tell the people of Israel that each of their tribal chiefs is to bring you a wooden rod with his name inscribed upon it. Aaron's name is to be on the rod of the tribe of Levi. [4]Put these rods in the inner room of the Tabernacle where I meet with you, in front of the Ark. [5]I will use these rods to identify the man I have chosen: for buds will grow on his rod! Then at last this murmuring and complaining against you will stop!" [6]So Moses gave the instructions to the people, and each of the twelve chiefs (including Aaron) brought him a rod. [7]He put them before the Lord in the inner room of the Tabernacle, [8]and when he went in the next day, he found that Aaron's rod, representing the tribe of Levi, had budded and was blossoming, and had ripe almonds hanging from it! [9]When Moses brought them out to show the others, they stared in disbelief! Then each man except Aaron claimed his rod. [10]The Lord told Moses to place Aaron's rod permanently beside the Ark as a reminder of this rebellion. He was to (bring it out and show it to the people again) if there were any further complaints about Aaron's authority; this would ward off further catastrophe to the people. [11]So Moses did as the Lord commanded him. [12, 13]But the people of Israel only grumbled the more. "We are as good as dead," they whined. "Everyone who even comes close to the Tabernacle dies. Must we all perish?"

Deut 4:33. An entire nation heard the voice of God speaking to it from fire, as you did, and lived! [34]Where else will you ever find another example of God's removing a nation from its slavery by sending terrible plagues, mighty miracles, war, and terror? Yet that is what the Lord your God did for you in Egypt, right before your very eyes. [35]He did these things so you would realize that Jehovah is God, and that there is no one else like him.

Deut 11:1. You must love the Lord your God and obey every one of his commands. [2]Listen! I am not talking now to your children who have never experienced the Lord's punishments or seen his greatness and his awesome power. [3]They weren't there to see the miracles he did in Egypt against Pharaoh and all his land. [chapter 29:1–9.] [4]They didn't see what God did to the armies of Egypt and to their horses and chariots—how he drowned them in the Red Sea as they were chasing you, and how the Lord has kept them powerless against you until this very day! [5]They didn't see how the Lord cared for you time and again through all the years you were wandering in the wilderness, until your arrival here. [6]They weren't there when Dathan and Abiram (the sons of Eliab, descendants of Reuben) sinned, and the earth opened up and swallowed them, with their households and tents and all their belongings, as all Israel watched! [7]But *you* have seen these mighty miracles! [8]How carefully, then, you should obey these commandments I am going to give you today, so that you may have the strength to go in and possess the land you are about to enter.

Deut 29:5. For forty years God has led you through the wilderness, yet your clothes haven't become old, and your shoes haven't worn out! [6]The reason he hasn't let you settle down to grow grain for bread or grapes for wine and strong drink, is so that you would realize that it is the Lord your God who has been caring for you.

Josh 2:9. "I know perfectly well that your God is going to give my country to you," she told them. "We are all afraid of you; everyone is terrified if the word *Israel* is even mentioned. [10]For we have heard how the Lord made a path through the Red Sea for you when you left Egypt! And we know what you did to Sihon and Og, the two Amorite kings east of the Jordan, and how you ruined their land and completely destroyed their people. [11]No wonder we are afraid of you! No one has any fight left in him after hearing things like that, for your God is the supreme God of heaven, not just an ordinary god."

Josh 3:10. Today you are going to know for sure that the living God is among you and that he will, without fail, drive out the Canaanites, Hittites, Hivites, Perizzites, Girgashites, Amorites, and Jebusites—all the people who now live in the land you will soon occupy. [11]Think of it! The Ark of God, who is Lord of the whole earth, will lead you across the river!

Josh 4:23. Tell them how the Lord our God dried up the river right before our eyes, and then kept it dry until we were all across! It is the same thing the Lord did forty years ago at the Red Sea! [24]He did this so that all the nations of the earth will realize that Jehovah is the mighty God, and so that all of you will worship him forever.

Josh 5:1. When the nations west of the Jordan River—the Amorites and Canaanites who lived along the Mediterranean coast—heard that the Lord had dried up the Jordan River so the people of Israel could cross, their courage melted away completely and they were paralyzed with fear.

Judg 2:9. The people had remained true to the Lord throughout Joshua's lifetime, and as long afterward as the old men of his generation were still living—those who had seen the mighty miracles the Lord had done for Israel.

1 Sam 6:6. Don't be stubborn and rebellious as Pharaoh and the Egyptians were. They wouldn't let Israel go until God had destroyed them with dreadful plagues. [7]Now build a new cart and hitch to it two cows that have just had calves—cows that never before have been yoked—and shut their calves away from them in the barn. [8]Place the Ark of God on the cart beside a chest containing the gold models of the rats and tumors, and let the cows go wherever they want to. [9]If they cross the border of our land and go into Beth-shemesh, then you will know that it was God who brought this great evil upon us; if they don't, (but return to their calves,) then we will know that the plague was simply a coincidence and was not sent by God at all. *vs.* 10–18.

1 Sam 12:17. "You know that it does not rain at this time of the year, during the wheat harvest; I will pray for the Lord to send thunder and rain today, so that you will realize the extent of your wickedness in asking for a king!" [18]So Samuel called to the Lord, and the Lord sent thunder and rain; and all the people were very much afraid of the Lord and of Samuel.

1 Kgs 18:24. "Then pray to your god, and I will pray to the Lord; and the god who answers by sending fire to light the wood is the true God!" And all the people agreed to this test. [37]"O Lord, answer me! Answer me so these people will know that you are God and that you have brought them back to yourself." [38]Then, suddenly, fire flashed down from heaven and burned up the young bull, the wood, the stones, the dust, and even evaporated all the water in the ditch!

2 Kgs 5:14. So Naaman went down to the Jordan River and dipped himself seven times, as the prophet had told him to. And his flesh became as healthy as a little child's, and he was healed! [15]Then he and his entire party went back to find the prophet; and they stood humbly before him and Naaman said, "I know at last that there is no God in all the world except in Israel; now please accept my gifts."

2 Chron 7:1, 2. As Solomon finished praying, fire flashed down from heaven and burned up the sacrifices! And the glory of the Lord filled the Temple, so that the priests couldn't enter! [3]All the people had been watching and now they fell flat on the pavement, and worshiped and thanked the Lord. "How good he is!" they exclaimed. "He is always so loving and kind."

Ps 78:10. Because they didn't obey his laws. They refused to follow his ways. [11, 12]And they forgot about the wonderful miracles God had done for them, and for their fathers in Egypt. [13]For he divided the sea before them and led them through! The water stood banked up along both sides of them! [14]In the daytime he led them by a cloud, and at night by a pillar of fire. [15]He split open the rocks in the wilderness to give them plenty of water, as though gushing from a spring. [16]Streams poured from the rock, flowing like a river! [17]Yet they kept on with their rebellion, sinning against the God who is above all gods. [18]They murmured and complained, demanding other food than God was giving them. [19, 20]They even spoke against God himself. "Why can't he give us decent food as well as water?" they grumbled. [21]Jehovah heard them and was angry; the fire of his wrath burned against Israel, [22]because they didn't believe in God or trust in him to care for them, [23]even though he commanded the skies to open—he opened the windows of heaven—[24]and rained down manna for their food. He gave them bread from heaven! [25]They ate angel's food! He gave them all they could hold. [26]And he led forth the east wind and guided the south wind by his mighty power. [27]He rained down birds as thick as dust, clouds of them like sands along the shore! [28]He caused the birds to fall to the ground among the tents. [29]The people ate their fill. He gave them what they asked for. [30]But they had hardly finished eating, and the meat was yet in their mouths, [31]when the anger of the Lord rose against them and killed the finest of Israel's young men. [32]Yet even so the people kept on sinning and refused to believe in miracles.

Ps 106:9. You commanded the Red Sea to divide, forming a dry road across its bottom. Yes, as dry as any desert! [10]Thus you rescued them from their enemies. [11]Then the water returned and covered the road and drowned their foes; not one survived. [12]Then at last his people believed him. Then they finally sang his praise.

Jer 32:20. You have done incredible things in the land of Egypt—things still remembered to this day. And you have continued to do great miracles in Israel and all around the world. You have made your name very great, as it is today.

Dan 2:47. "Truly, O Daniel," the king said, "your God is the God of gods, Ruler of kings, the Revealer of mysteries, because he has told you this secret."

Dan 3:28. Then Nebuchadnezzar said, "Blessed be the God of Shadrach, Meshach, and Abednego, for he sent his angel to deliver his trusting servants when they defied the king's commandment, and were willing to die rather than serve or worship any god except their own. [29]Therefore, I make this decree, that any person of any nation, language, or religion who speaks a word against the God of Shadrach, Meshach, and Abednego shall be torn limb from limb and his house knocked into a heap of rubble. For no other God can do what this one does."

Dan 6:20. And called out in anguish, "O Daniel, servant of the Living God, was your God, whom you worship continually, able to deliver you from the lions?" [21]Then he heard a voice! "Your Majesty, live forever!" It was Daniel! [22]"My God has sent his angel," he said, "to shut the lions' mouths so that they can't touch me; for I am innocent before God, nor, sir, have I wronged you." [23]The king was beside himself with joy and ordered that Daniel be lifted from the den. And not a scratch was found on him, because he believed his God. [24]Then the king issued a command to bring the men who had accused Daniel, and throw them into the den along with their children and wives, and the lions leaped upon them and tore them apart before they even hit the bottom of the den. [25, 26]Afterward King Darius wrote this message addressed to everyone in his empire: "Greetings! I decree that everyone shall tremble and fear before the God of Daniel in every part of my kingdom. For his God is the living, unchanging God whose kingdom shall never be destroyed and whose power shall never end. [27]He delivers his people, preserving them from harm; he does great miracles in heaven and earth; it is he who delivered Daniel from the power of the lions."

Jon 1:14. Then they shouted out a prayer to Jehovah, Jonah's God. "O Jehovah," they pleaded, "don't make us die for this man's sin, and don't hold us responsible for his death, for it is not our fault—you have sent this storm upon him for your own good reasons." [15]Then they picked up Jonah and threw him overboard into the raging sea—and the storm stopped! [16]The men stood there in awe before Jehovah, and sacrificed to him and vowed to serve him.

Zech 2:9. I will smash them with my fist and their slaves will be their rulers! *Then you will know it was the Lord of Hosts who sent me.*

Mt 4:3. Then Satan tempted him to get food by changing stones into loaves of bread. "It will prove you are the Son of God," he said. Lk 4:3, 6, 7.

Mt 11:3. "Are you really the one we are waiting for, or shall we keep on looking?" [4]Jesus told them, "Go back to John and tell him about the miracles you've seen me do—[5]the blind people I've healed, and the lame people now walking without help, and the cured lepers, and the deaf who hear, and the dead raised to life; and tell him about my preaching the Good News to the poor."

Mk 2:9, 10, 11. "I, the Messiah, have the authority on earth to forgive sins. But talk is cheap—anybody could say that. So I'll prove it to you by healing this man." Then, turning to the paralyzed man, he commanded, "Pick up your stretcher and go on home, for you are healed!" [12]The man jumped up, took the stretcher, and pushed his way through the stunned onlookers! Then how they praised God. "We've never seen anything like this before!" they all exclaimed. Lk 5:26.

Lk 18:42. And Jesus said, "All right, begin seeing! Your faith has healed you." [43]And instantly the man could see, and followed Jesus, praising God. And all who saw it happen praised God too.

Jn 2:11. This miracle at Cana in Galilee was Jesus' first public demonstration of his heaven-sent power. And his disciples believed that he really was the Messiah.

Jn 4:48. Jesus asked, "Won't any of you believe in me unless I do more and more miracles?"

Jn 5:36. But I have a greater witness than John. I refer to the miracles I do; these have been assigned me by the Father, and they prove that the Father has sent me.

Jn 9:2. "Master," his disciples asked him, "why was this man born blind? Was it a result of his own sins or those of his parents?" [3]"Neither," Jesus answered. "But to demonstrate the power of God."

Jn 11:4. But when Jesus heard about it he said, "The purpose of his illness is not death, but for the glory of God. I, the Son of God, will receive glory from this situation." [40]"But didn't I tell you that you will see a wonderful miracle from God if you believe?" Jesus asked her. [41]So they rolled the stone aside. Then Jesus looked up to heaven and said, "Father, thank you for hearing me. [42](You always hear me, of course, but I said it because of all these people standing here, so that they will believe you sent me.)"

Acts 2:22. O men of Israel, listen! God publicly endorsed Jesus of Nazareth by doing tremendous miracles through him, as you well know.

Acts 3:1. Peter and John went to the Temple one afternoon to take part in the three o'clock prayer meeting. [2]As they approached the Temple, they saw a man lame from birth carried along the street and laid beside the Temple gate—the one called The Beautiful Gate—as was his custom every day. [3]As Peter and John were passing by, he asked them for some money. [4]They looked at him intently, and then Peter said, "Look here!" [5]The lame man looked at them eagerly, expecting a gift. [6]But Peter said, "We don't have any money for you! But I'll give you something else! I command you in the name of Jesus Christ of Nazareth, *walk!*" [7, 8]Then Peter took the lame man by the hand and pulled him to his feet. And as he did, the man's feet and ankle-bones were healed and strengthened so that he came up with a leap, stood there a moment and began walking! Then, walking, leaping, and praising God, he went into the Temple with them. [9]When the people inside saw him walking and heard him praising God, [10]and realized he was the lame beggar they had seen so often at The Beautiful Gate, they were inexpressibly surprised!

Acts 4:21. The Council then threatened them further, and finally let them go because they didn't know how to punish them without starting a riot. For everyone was praising God for this wonderful miracle—[22]the healing of a man who had been lame for forty years.

1 Cor 1:22. It seems foolish to the Jews because they want a sign from heaven as proof that what

is preached is true; and it is foolish to the Gentiles because they believe only what agrees with their philosophy and seems wise to them.

MIRACULOUS GIFTS OF THE HOLY SPIRIT. Foretold, Isa 35:4–6; Joel 2:28, 29. Of different kinds, 1 Cor 12:4–6. Enumerated, 1 Cor 12:8–10, 28. Christ was endowed with, Mt 12:28. Poured out on Pentecost, Acts 2:1–4. Given while preaching the gospel, Acts 10:44–47; by laying on of the apostles' hands, Acts 8:17, 18; 19:6; for the confirmation of the gospel, Mk 16:20; Acts 14:3; Rom 15:19; Heb 2:4; for the edification of the church, 1 Cor 12:7; 14:12, 13. To be sought after, 1 Cor 12:31; 14:1. Temporary nature of, 1 Cor 13:8. Not to be neglected, 1 Tim 4:14; 2 Tim 1:6; or despised, 1 Thess 5:20; or purchased, Acts 8:20.

MISCELLANY OF MINOR SUB-TOPICS. Called *Mighty Deeds,* Ps 105:5; *Mighty Miracles,* Jer 32:21; *Mighty Works,* 2 Cor 12:12.

Performed through the power of God, Jn 3:1, 2; Acts 14:3; 15:12; 19:11; of the Holy Spirit, Mt 12:28; Rom 15:19; 1 Cor 12:9, 10, 28, 30; in the name of Christ, Mk 16:17; Acts 3:16; 4:30. Faith required in those who perform, Mt 17:20; 21:21; Jn 14:12, 13; Acts 3:16; 6:8. Faith required in those for whom they were performed, Mt 9:28; Mk 9:22–24; Acts 14:9. Power to perform, given the disciples, Mk 3:14, 15; 16:17, 18, 20. Demanded by unbelievers, Mt 12:38–40; 16:1; Lk 11:16, 29, 30; 23:8. Alleged miracles performed by magicians, Ex 7:10–12, 22; 8:7; by other impostors, Mt 7:22. Performed through the powers of evil, 2 Thess 2:9; Rev 16:14. Performed in support of false religions, Deut 13:1, 2; by false christs, Mt 24:24; by false prophets, Mt 24:24; Rev 19:20; by the witch of Endor, 1 Sam 28:7–14; Simon the sorcerer, Acts 8:9–11. Not to be regarded, Deut 13:3. Deceive the ungodly, 2 Thess 2:10–12; Rev 13:14; 19:20. A mark of apostasy, 2 Thess 2:3, 9; Rev 13:13.

MIRE Isa 57:20; Jer 38:6.

FIGURATIVE. Job 8:11–13; Ps 40:2; 69:1, 2, 14.

See *Clay.*

MIRIAM Sister of Moses. Watches over Moses when he is hidden among the reeds, Ex 2:4–8. Song of, after the destruction of Pharaoh and his army, Ex 15:20, 21; Mic 6:4. Jealous of Moses, stricken with leprosy, healed because of the intercession of Moses, Num 12; Deut 24:9. Dies and is buried at Kadesh, Num 20:1.

MIRMAH A Benjaminite, 1 Chron 8:8–10.

MIRROR Job 37:18; Prov 27:19; Isa 3:23. Of bronze, donated by the Israelite women, Ex 38:8.

FIGURATIVE. 1 Cor 13:12; 2 Cor 3:18; Jas 1:23, 24.

MISCEGENATION See *Mixed Marriage.*

MISCHIEF See *Malice.*

MISER Eccl 4:7, 8.

MISHA-EL 1. A son of Uzziel, helps carry the bodies of Nadab and Abihu out of the camp, Ex 6:22; Lev 10:4.

2. A Jew who stood by Ezra when he read the law to the people, Neh 8:1–5.

3. Called also *Meshach.* One of three Hebrew children trained with Daniel at the court of Babylon, Dan 1:6, 7, 11–20. Assists Daniel in interpreting Nebuchadnezzar's dream, Dan 2:17–23. Thrown into the fiery furnace, Dan 3:13–30.

MISHAL See *Mashal.*

MISHAM A Benjaminite, 1 Chron 8:12.

MISHMA 1. Son of Ishmael, Gen 25:12–15; 1 Chron 1:28–31.

2. Of the tribe of Simeon, 1 Chron 4:25, 26.

MISHMANNAH A Gadite who joined David at Ziklag, 1 Chron 12:8–13.

MISHNEH A district of Jerusalem, 2 Kgs 22:14.

MISJUDGMENT INSTANCES OF. Of the Reubenites and Gadites, Num 32:1–33; Josh 22:11–31; of Hannah, 1 Sam 1:14–17.

See *Accusation, False; Uncharitableness.*

MISPAR See *Mispereth.*

MISPERETH Called also *Mispar.* A Jew who returned with Zerubbabel from Babylon, Ezra 2:2; Neh 7:7.

MISREPHOTH-MAIM A city of east Sidon, Josh 13:2–7.

MISSIONS BIBLE FACTS ABOUT MISSIONS. God is seeking men, Lk 15:3–10; Jn 4:21–24; 2 Pet 3:9.

The divine call, Mt 28:19, 20; Mk 16:15; Lk 24:46–48; Acts 26:16–18.

Divine appointment, Lk 10:1; 2 Tim 1:11.

Divine ordination, Jn 15:16; Acts 13:2, 3.

Divine preparation, Mt 4:19; Mk 1:17; Acts 26:16.

Divine guidance, Acts 16:6–10.

Divine protection, Lk 10:19; Acts 26:17.

Divine preparation of the lost, Jn 16:8–11.

Divine plan, Lk 10:1–20; Acts 1:8.

The believer's obligation, Rom 1:14–16; 12:1, 2.

Ambassadors of Christ, 2 Cor 5:20.

Entrusted with the gospel, 1 Thess 2:4; 1 Tim 1:10, 11; 6:20.

Sent out, Lk 10:1; Jn 17:18; Acts 26:17; Rom 10:15; 1 Cor 1:17.

Christ our example, Lk 4:18, 19; Jn 17:18; 6:38; 7:16, 17; 1 Pet 2:21.

Paul our example, 1 Cor 11:1; Phil 4:9.

Forsaking home, Mt 19:27–29; Acts 11:22; 13:4; 16:3.

Going to far places, Acts 22:21; 8:4; 13:47; Rom 10:18 (Prov 25:25); 2 Cor 10:16; where Christ is not named, Rom 15:20.

Among the Gentiles, Gal 1:16; all nations, Mt 28:19; Rom 1:5; 16:25–27.

Facing danger, Acts 15:26.

Open doors, 1 Cor 16:9; 2 Cor 2:12; Col 4:3; Rev 3:8, 20.

Bearing witness, Lk 24:48; Jn 15:27; Acts 22:15; 26:16; 1 Jn 1:2.

Preaching the gospel, Acts 10:42; 17:3; Rom 1:15, 16; Eph 3:8; Col 1:28, 29.

Using other languages, Acts 2:4, 11; 10:46, 47.

Roads and hedges, Mt 22:9; Lk 14:23.

Divine compulsion, 1 Cor 9:16.

Message defined, 1 Cor 15:1–4.

Establishing Bible schools, 2 Tim 2:2.

Using every means, 1 Cor 9:22; 2 Cor 9:8.

Having results, Jn 15:1–16; Rom 1:13; Gal 5:22, 23; Phil 4:17; Col 1:5, 6.

A plentiful harvest, Mt 9:37, 38; Lk 10:2; Jn 4:35–37.

Recounting successes, Acts 15:26; Lk 10:17.

Care of the churches, Acts 15:36; 2 Cor 11:28.

Urgency of the task, Mt 13:30–39; Jn 4:35; 9:4; Rev 14:15.

Sowing and reaping, Jn 4:37, 38; 2 Cor 9:6; Gal 6:7–9.

Helped by prayer, 2 Cor 1:11; 9:14; Phil 4:6; Col 4:12.

Church support, Lk 16:9; 1 Cor 16:2; 2 Cor 8:11–24; Heb 13:16, 17.

The presence of Christ, Mt 28:20; Heb 13:6.

See *Evangelism; Gentiles; Church.*

OUTSTANDING MISSIONARY TEXTS. (See also section above.) Gen 24:27. Thank you for being so kind and true to him, and for leading me.

Ex 3:10. Now I am going to send you to Pharaoh, to demand that he let you lead my people out of Egypt.

Ex 4:5. Then they will realize that Jehovah, the God of their ancestors Abraham, Isaac, and Jacob, has really appeared to you. Num 16:28.

Deut 32:3. I will proclaim the greatness of the Lord.

Josh 1:8. Constantly remind the people about these laws, and you yourself must think about them every day and every night so that you will be sure to obey all of them. For only then will you succeed. [9]Yes, be bold and strong! Banish fear and doubt! For remember, the Lord your God is with you wherever you go.

Josh 2:18. We cannot be responsible for what happens . . . unless all your relatives—your father, mother, brothers, and anyone else—are here inside the house. [19]If they go out into the street we assume no responsibility whatsoever; but we swear that no one inside this house will be killed or injured.

Josh 24:15. But if you are unwilling to obey the Lord, then decide today whom you will obey.

Ruth 1:16. I want to go wherever you go, and to live wherever you live; your people shall be my people, and your God shall be my God.

1 Sam 1:11. O Lord of heaven, if you will look down upon my sorrow and answer my prayer and give me a son, then I will give him back to you, and he'll be yours for his entire lifetime.

2 Kgs 4:9. She said to her husband, "I'm sure this man who stops in from time to time is a holy prophet. [10]Let's make a little room for him on the roof; we can put in a bed, a table, a chair, and a lamp, and he will have a place to stay whenever he comes by."

2 Kgs 7:9. This isn't right. This is wonderful news, and we aren't sharing it with anyone! Even if we wait until morning, some terrible calamity will certainly fall upon us; come on, let's go back and tell the people at the palace.

2 Kgs 17:28. So one of them returned to Bethel and taught the colonists from Babylon how to worship the Lord.

1 Chron 16:23. Sing to the Lord, O earth, declare each day that he is the one who saves! [24]Show his glory to the nations! Tell everyone about his miracles.

Job 33:24. Then God pities him and says, "Set him free. Do not make him die, for I have found a substitute."

Ps 2:8. Only ask, and I will give you all the nations of the world.

Ps 43:3. Oh, send out your light and your truth—let them lead me.

Ps 68:11. The Lord speaks. The enemy flees. The women at home cry out the happy news.

Ps 96:3. Publish his glorious acts throughout the earth. Tell everyone about the amazing things he does. Ps 98:2, 3.

Ps 119:53. I am very angry with those who spurn your commands. [136]I weep because your laws are disobeyed.

Ps 147:15. He sends his orders to the world. How swiftly his word flies.

Prov 3:5. Trust the Lord completely; don't ever trust yourself. [6]In everything you do, put God first, and he will direct you and crown your efforts with success.

Prov 22:20, 21. In the past, haven't I been right? Then believe what I am telling you now, and share it with others.

Isa 6:8. Then I heard the Lord asking, "Whom shall I send as a messenger to my people? Who will go?" And I said, "Lord, I'll go! Send *me.*"

Isa 54:2. Enlarge your house; build on additions; spread out your home!

Isa 55:11. So also is my Word. I send it out and it always produces fruit. It shall accomplish all I want it to, and prosper everywhere I send it.

Isa 61:1. The Spirit of the Lord God is upon me, because the Lord has anointed me to bring good news to the suffering and afflicted. He has sent me to comfort the broken-hearted, to announce liberty to captives and to open the eyes of the blind. [2]He has sent me to tell those who mourn that the time of God's favor to them has come, and the day of his wrath to their enemies.

Jer 1:7. You will go wherever I send you and speak whatever I tell you to.

Jer 27:13. Why do you insist on dying—you and your people?

Lam 1:12. Is it nothing to you, all you who pass by?

Ezk 3:4. Then he said: "Son of dust, I am sending you to the people of Israel with my messages. [5]I am not sending you to some far-off foreign land where you can't understand the language."

Jon 3:2. "Go to that great city, Nineveh," he said, "and warn them of their doom, as I told you to before!"

Mt 4:16. There the people who sat in darkness have seen a great Light; they sat in the land of death, and the Light broke through upon them.

Mt 5:14. You are the world's light.

Mt 9:36. And what pity he felt for the crowds that came. . . . [37]"The harvest is so great, and the workers are so few. . . . [38]So pray to the one in charge of the harvesting, and ask him to recruit more workers for his harvest fields." Lk 10:2.

Mt 10:16. I am sending you out as sheep among wolves. Be as wary as serpents and harmless as doves. [38]If you refuse to take up your cross and follow me, you are not worthy of being mine. [39]If you cling to your life, you will lose it; but if you give it up for me, you will save it.

Mt 21:3. Just say, "The Master needs them." Lk 19:31.

Mt 22:9. Now go out to the street corners and invite everyone you see.

Mt 28:18. He told his disciples, "I have been given all authority in heaven and earth. [19]Therefore go and make disciples in all the nations, baptizing them into the name of the Father and of the Son and of the Holy Spirit, [20]and then teach these new disciples to obey all the commands I have given you and be sure of this—that I am with you always, even to the end of the world."

Mk 1:17. Jesus called out to them, "Come, follow me! And I will make you fishermen for the souls of men!"

Mk 5:19. "Go home to your friends," he told him, "and tell them what wonderful things God has done for you; and how merciful he has been." [20]So the man started off to visit the Ten Towns of that region and began to tell everyone about the great things Jesus had done for him; and they were awestruck by his story.

Mk 10:29. And Jesus replied, "Let me assure you that no one has ever given up anything—home, brothers, sisters, mother, father, children, or property—for love of me and to tell others the Good News, [30]who won't be given back, a hundred times over, homes, brothers, sisters, mothers, children, and land—with persecutions! All these will be his here on earth, and in the world to come he shall have eternal life."

Mk 16:15. You are to go into all the world and preach the Good News to everyone, everywhere.

Lk 2:10. But the angel reassured them. "Don't be afraid!" he said. "I bring you the most joyful news ever announced, and it is for everyone!" [32]"He is the Light that will shine upon the nations, and he will be the glory of your people Israel!"

Lk 4:17. The book of Isaiah the prophet was handed to him, and he opened it to the place where it says: [18, 19]"The Spirit of the Lord is upon me; he has appointed me to preach Good News to the poor; he has sent me to heal the brokenhearted and to announce that captives shall be released and the blind shall see, that the downtrodden shall be freed from their oppressors, and that God is ready to give blessings to all who come to him."

Lk 9:60. Jesus replied, "Let those without eternal life concern themselves with things like that. Your duty is to come and preach the coming of the Kingdom of God to all the world."

Lk 10:1. The Lord now chose seventy other disciples and sent them on ahead in pairs to all the towns and villages he planned to visit later. [2]These were his instructions to them: "Plead with the Lord of the harvest to send out more laborers to help you, for the harvest is so plentiful and the workers so few. [16]Those who welcome you are welcoming me. And those who reject you are rejecting me. And those who reject me are rejecting God who sent me."

Lk 14:23. "Well, then," said his master, "go out into the country lanes and out behind the hedges and urge anyone you find to come, so that the house will be full."

Lk 24:46. And he said, "Yes, it was written long ago that the Messiah must suffer and die and rise again from the dead on the third day; [47]and that this message of salvation should be taken from Jerusalem to all the nations: *There is forgiveness of sins for all who turn to me.* [48]You have seen these prophecies come true."

Jn 4:23. For it's not *where* we worship that counts, but *how* we worship—is our worship spiritual and real? . . . The Father wants this kind of worship from us. [35]Do you think the work of harvesting will not begin until the summer ends four months from now? Look around you! Vast fields of human souls are ripening all around us, and are ready now for reaping.

Jn 8:12. I am the Light of the world.

Jn 10:16. I have other sheep, too, in another fold. I must bring them also, and they will heed my voice; and there will be one flock with one Shepherd.

Jn 13:20. Truly, anyone welcoming my messenger is welcoming me. And to welcome me is to welcome the Father who sent me.

Jn 15:8. My true disciples produce bountiful harvests. This brings great glory to my Father. [16]You didn't choose me! I chose you. I appointed you to go and produce lovely fruit always, so that no matter what you ask for from the Father, using my name, he will give it to you.

Jn 16:7. But the fact of the matter is that it is best for you that I go away, for if I don't, the Comforter won't come. If I do, he will—for I will send him to you. [8]And when he has come he will convince the world of its sin, and of the availability of God's goodness, and of deliverance from judgment.

Jn 17:18. As you sent me into the world, I am sending them into the world. [20]I am not praying for these alone but also for the future believers who will come to me because of the testimony of these.

Jn 20:21. He spoke to them again and said, "As the Father has sent me, even so I am sending you."

Acts 1:8. But when the Holy Spirit has come upon you, you will receive power to testify about me with great effect, to the people in Jerusalem, throughout Judea, in Samaria, and to the ends of the earth, about my death and resurrection.

Acts 2:11. And we all hear these men telling in our own languages about the mighty miracles of God! [39]For Christ promised him to each one of you who has been called by the Lord our God, and to your children and even to those in distant lands!

Acts 4:20. We cannot stop telling about the wonderful things we saw Jesus do and heard him say.

Acts 8:4. But the believers who had fled Jerusalem went everywhere preaching the Good News about Jesus! [5]Philip, for instance, went to the city of Samaria and told the people there about Christ. [8]So there was much joy in that city!

Acts 9:15. For Paul is my chosen instrument to take my message to the nations and before kings, as well as to the people of Israel. [16]And I will show him how much he must suffer for me.

Acts 10:42. And he sent us to preach the Good News everywhere and to testify that Jesus is ordained of God to be the Judge of all—living and dead. [43]And all the prophets have written about him, saying that everyone who believes in him will have their sins forgiven through his name. [44]Even as Peter was saying these things, the Holy Spirit fell upon all those listening!

Acts 13:2. One day as these men were worshiping and fasting the Holy Spirit said, "Dedicate Barnabas and Paul for a special job I have for them." [3]So after more fasting and prayer, the men laid their hands on them—and sent them on their way.

Acts 13:47. For this is as the Lord commanded when he said, "I have made you a light to the Gentiles, to lead them from the farthest corners of the earth to my salvation."

Acts 14:27. Upon arrival they called together the believers and reported on their trip, telling how God had opened the door of faith to the Gentiles too.

Acts 15:26. These men—Judas and Silas, who have risked their lives for the sake of our Lord Jesus Christ. [36]Several days later Paul suggested to Barnabas that they return again to Turkey, and visit each city where they had preached before, to see how the new converts were getting along.

Acts 16:6. Next they traveled through Phrygia and Galatia, because the Holy Spirit had told them not to go into the Turkish province of Ausia at that time. [7]Then going along the borders of Mysia they headed north for the province of Bithynia, but again the Spirit of Jesus said no. [8]So instead they went on through Mysia province to the city of Troas. [9]That night Paul had a vision. In his dream he saw a man over in Macedonia, Greece, pleading with him, "Come over here and help us." [10]Well, that settled it. We would go to Macedonia, for we could only conclude that God was sending us to preach the Good News there.

13. On the Sabbath, we went a little way outside the city to a river bank where we understood some people met for prayer; and we taught the Scriptures to some women who came. [14]One of them was Lydia, a saleswoman from Thyatira, a merchant of purple cloth. She was already a worshiper of God and, as she listened to us, the Lord opened her heart and she accepted all that Paul was saying. [30]He brought them out and begged them, "Sirs, what must I do to be saved?" [31]They replied, "Believe on the Lord Jesus and you will be saved, and your entire household." [32]Then they told him and all his household the Good News from the Lord. [33]That same hour he washed their stripes and he and all his family were baptized.

Acts 17:32. When they heard Paul speak of the resurrection of a person who had been dead, some laughed, but others said, "We want to hear more about this later." [34]But a few joined him and became believers.

Acts 18:23. He left for Turkey again, going through Galatia and Phrygia visiting all the believers, encouraging them and helping them grow in the Lord.

Acts 22:14. Then he told me, "The God of our fathers has chosen you to know his will and to see the Messiah and hear him speak. [15]You are to take his message everywhere, telling what you have seen and heard." [18]"Hurry! Leave Jerusalem, for the people here won't believe you when you give them my message." [21]But God said to me, "Leave Jerusalem, for I will send you far away to the *Gentiles!*"

Acts 26:16. "Now stand up! For I have appeared to you to appoint you as my servant and my witness. You are to tell the world about this experience and about the many other occasions when I shall appear to you. [17]And I will protect you from both your own people and the Gentiles. Yes, I am going to send you to the Gentiles [18]to open their eyes to their true condition so that they may repent and live in the light of God instead of in Satan's darkness, so that they may receive forgiveness for their sins and God's inheritance along with all people everywhere whose sins are cleansed away, who are set apart by faith in me." [19]And so, O King Agrippa, I was not disobedient to that vision from heaven! [20]I preached first to those in Damascus, then in Jerusalem and through Judea, and also to the Gentiles that all must forsake their sins and turn to God—and prove their repentance by doing good deeds. [22]But God protected me so that I am still alive today to tell these facts to everyone, both great and small. I teach nothing except what the prophets and Moses said—[23]that the Messiah would suffer, and be the First to rise from the dead, to bring light to Jews and Gentiles alike.

Acts 28:28, 29. So I want you to realize that this salvation from God is available to the Gentiles too, and they will accept it.

Rom 1:5. And now, through Christ, all the kindness of God has been poured out upon us undeserving sinners; and now he is sending us out around the world to tell all people everywhere the great things God has done for them, so that they, too, will believe and obey him. [13]I want you to know, dear brothers, that I planned to come many times before (but was prevented) so that I could work among you and see good results, just as I have among the other Gentile churches. [14]For I owe a great debt to you and to everyone else, both to civilized people and uncivilized alike; yes, to the educated and uneducated alike. [15]So, to the fullest extent of my ability, I am ready to come also to you in Rome to preach God's Good News.

Rom 9:25. Remember what the prophecy of Hosea says? There God says that he will find other children for himself (who are not from his Jewish family) and will love them, though no one had ever loved them before. [26]And the heathen, of whom it once was said, "You are not my people," shall be called "sons of the Living God."

Rom 10:14. But how shall they ask him to save them unless they believe in him? And how can they believe in him if they have never heard about him? And how can they hear about him unless someone tells them? [15]And how will anyone go and tell them unless someone sends him? That is what the Scriptures are talking about when they say, "How beautiful are the feet of those who preach the Gospel of peace with God and bring glad tidings of good things."

Rom 12:1. And so, dear brothers, I plead with you to give your bodies to God. Let them be a living sacrifice, holy—the kind he can accept. When you think of what he has done for you, is this too much to ask?

Rom 15:16. For I am, by God's grace, a special messenger from Jesus Christ to you Gentiles, bringing you the Gospel and offering you up as a fragrant sacrifice to God; for you have been made pure and pleasing to him by the Holy Spirit. [20]But all the while my ambition has been to go still farther, preaching where the name of Christ has never yet been heard, rather than where a church has already been started by someone else. [29]And I am sure that when I come the Lord will give me a great blessing for you.

1 Cor 1:17. For Christ didn't send me to baptize, but to preach the Gospel; and even my preaching sounds poor, for I do not fill my sermons with profound words and high sounding ideas, for fear of diluting the mighty power there is in the simple message of the cross of Christ.

1 Cor 9:14. In the same way the Lord has given orders that those who preach the Gospel should be supported by those who accept it. [16]For just preaching the Gospel isn't any special credit to me —I couldn't keep from preaching it if I wanted to. I would be utterly miserable. Woe unto me if I don't.

1 Cor 10:32. So don't be a stumbling block to anyone, whether they are Jews or Gentiles or Christians. [33]That is the plan I follow, too. I try to please everyone in everything I do, not doing what I like or what is best for me, but what is best for them, so that they may be saved.

1 Cor 11:1. And you should follow my example, just as I follow Christ's.

1 Cor 15:58. So, my dear brothers, since future victory is sure, be strong and steady, always abounding in the Lord's work, for you know that nothing you do for the Lord is ever wasted as it would be if there were no resurrection.

1 Cor 16:9. For there is a wide open door for me to preach and teach here. So much is happening, but there are many enemies.

2 Cor 1:11. But you must help us too, by praying for us.

2 Cor 2:12. The Lord gave me tremendous opportunities to preach the Gospel. [14]But thanks be to God! For through what Christ has done, he has triumphed over us so that now wherever we go he uses us to tell others about the Lord and to spread the Gospel like a sweet perfume. [15]As far as God is concerned there is a sweet, wholesome fragrance in our lives. It is the fragrance of Christ within us, an aroma to both the saved and the unsaved all around us. [16]To those who are not being saved, we seem a fearful smell of death and doom, while to those who know Christ we are a life-giving perfume. But who is adequate for such a task as this?

2 Cor 5:11. It is because of this solemn fear of the Lord, which is ever present in our minds, that we work so hard to win others. God knows our hearts, that they are pure in this matter. [14]Nor for our own profit, but because Christ's love controls us now. [18]All these new things are from God who brought us back to himself through what Christ Jesus did. And God has given us the privilege of urging everyone to come into his favor and be reconciled to him. [19]For God was in Christ, restoring the world to himself, no longer counting men's sins against them but blotting them out. This is the wonderful message he has given us to tell others. [20]We are Christ's ambassadors. God is using us to speak to you: we beg you, as though Christ himself were here pleading with you, receive the love he offers you—be reconciled to God.

2 Cor 10:16. After that, we will be able to preach the Good News to other cities that are far beyond you, where no one else is working; then there will be no question about being in someone else's field.

Gal 1:15. But then something happened! For even before I was born God had chosen me to be his, and called me—what kindness and grace—[16]to reveal his Son within me so that I could go to the Gentiles and show them the Good News about Jesus. When all this happened to me I didn't go at once and talk it over with anyone else.

Gal 2:7–9. In fact, when Peter, James, and John . . . saw how greatly God had used me in winning the Gentiles, just as Peter had been blessed so greatly in his preaching to the Jews—for the same God gave us each our special gifts—they shook hands with Barnabas and me and encouraged us to keep right on with our preaching to the Gentiles while they continued their work with the Jews.

Gal 6:6. Those who are taught the Word of God should help their teachers by paying them.

Eph 3:8. Just think! Though I did nothing to deserve it, and though I am the most useless Christian there is, yet I was the one chosen for this special joy of telling the Gentiles the Glad News of the endless treasures available to them in Christ.

Eph 6:15. Wear shoes that are able to speed you on as you preach the Good News of peace with God. [19]Pray for me, too, and ask God to give me the right words as I boldly tell others about the Lord, and as I explain to them that his salvation is for the Gentiles too. [20]I am in chains now for preaching this message from God. But pray that I will keep on speaking out boldly for him even here in prison, as I should.

Phil 1:12. And I want you to know this, dear brothers. Everything that has happened to me here has been a great boost in getting out the Good News concerning Christ.

Phil 2:15. Shine out among them like beacon lights, [16]holding out to them the Word of Life. Then when Christ returns how glad I will be that my work among you was so worthwhile.

Col 1:5. Ever since the Gospel first was preached to you. [6]The same Good News that came to you is going out all over the world and changing lives everywhere, just as it changed yours that very first day you heard it and understood about God's great kindness to sinners. [23]This is the wonderful news that came to each of you and is now spreading all over the world. And I, Paul, have the joy of telling it to others.

Col 4:2. Don't be weary in prayer; keep at it; watch for God's answers and remember to be thankful when they come. [3]Don't forget to pray for us too, that God will give us many chances to preach the Good News of Christ for which I am here in jail. [4]Pray that I will be bold enough to tell it freely and fully, and make it plain, as, of course, I should. [17]Be sure that you do all the Lord has told you to.

1 Thess 1:5. For when we brought you the Good News, it was not just meaningless chatter to you; no, you listened with great interest. What we told you produced a powerful effect upon you, for the Holy Spirit gave you great and full assurance that what we said was true. And you know how our very lives were further proof to you of the truth of our message. [6]So you became our followers and the Lord's; for you received our message with joy from the Holy Spirit in spite of the trials and sorrows it brought you. [7]Then you yourselves became an example to all the other Christians in Greece. [8]And now the Word of the Lord has spread out from you.

1 Thess 2:4. For we speak as messengers from God, trusted by him to tell the truth; we change his message not one bit to suit the taste of those who hear it; for we serve God alone, who examines our hearts' deepest thoughts.

1 Thess 5:12. Dear brothers, honor the officers of your church who work hard among you and warn you against all that is wrong. [13]Think highly of them and give them your whole-hearted love because they are straining to help you.

2 Thess 3:8. We never accepted food from anyone without buying it; we worked hard day and night for the money we needed to live on, in order that we would not be a burden to any of you. [9]It wasn't that we didn't have the right to ask you to feed us, but we wanted to show you, firsthand, how you should work for your living.

1 Tim 2:7. And I have been chosen—this is the absolute truth—as God's minister and missionary to teach this truth to the Gentiles, and to show them God's plan of salvation through faith.

1 Tim 5:18. Those who work deserve their pay!

1 Tim 6:20. Oh, Timothy, don't fail to do these things that God entrusted to you.

2 Tim 1:8. If you will stir up this inner power, you will never be afraid to tell others about our Lord, or to let them know that I am your friend even though I am here in jail for Christ's sake. You will be ready to suffer with me for the Lord, for he will give you strength in suffering.

2 Tim 2:2. For you must teach others those things you and many others have heard me speak about. Teach these great truths to trustworthy men who will, in turn, pass them on to others.

2 Tim 4:2. Preach the Word of God urgently at all times, whenever you get the chance, in season and out, when it is convenient and when it is not. Correct and rebuke your people when they need it, encourage them to do right, and all the time be feeding them patiently with God's Word. [5]Stand steady, and don't be afraid of suffering for the Lord. Bring others to Christ. Leave nothing undone that you ought to do. [17]But the Lord stood with me and gave me the opportunity to boldly preach a whole sermon for all the world to hear.

Heb 6:10. For God is not unfair. How can he forget your hard work for him, or forget the way you used to show your love for him—and still do—by helping his children?

1 Pet 4:11. Are you called to preach? Then preach as though God himself were speaking through you. Are you called to help others? Do it with all the strength and energy that God supplies.

2 Pet 3:9. He isn't really being slow about his promised return, even though it sometimes seems that way. But he is waiting, for the good reason that he is not willing that any should perish, and he is giving more time for sinners to repent.

3 Jn 1:7. For they are traveling for the Lord, and take neither food, clothing, shelter, nor money from those who are not Christians, even though they have preached to them. [8]So we ourselves should take care of them in order that we may become partners with them in the Lord's work.

Rev 3:8. Therefore I have opened a door to you that no one can shut.

Rev 5:9. They were singing him a new song with these words: "You are worthy to take the scroll and break its seals and open it; for you were slain, and your blood has bought people from every nation as gifts for God."

Rev 12:11. They defeated him by the blood of the Lamb, and by their testimony; for they did not love their lives but laid them down for him.

(See following section also.)

MISSIONS IN THE OLD TESTAMENT. God always had a witness, Acts 14:17; Prov 14:25.

All the prophets were witnesses, Acts 10:43.

God's messengers to his people, 2 Chron 36:15, 16.

The message preached, Isa 55:6–11.

Why will you die? Jer 27:13.

Isaiah's call, Isa 6:8.
Jeremiah's call, Jer 1:7–10.
Ezekiel's call, Ezk 3:5–9.
The words of truth made known, Prov 22:17–21.
The witness of creation, Ps 19:1–6.
Divine activity in ancient times, Job 33:14–30.
Examples of providential missionary witness: Lot in Sodom, 2 Pet 2:7, 8; Gideon to Israel, Judg 6:14; Moses in Egypt, Ex 3:10; Acts 7:34; Joseph in Egypt, Gen 45:7, 8; the two spies in Jericho, Josh 2:17–19; 6:17, 25; the maid and Naaman, 2 Kgs 5: 2–4; Jonah in Nineveh, Jon 1:2; 3:1, 2; 4:11; Daniel in Babylon, Dan 5:17–23.

MISSIONS IN THE TRIBULATION. World wide dispersion of Jews a factor, Deut 28:64.
The awakening in Israel, Zech 12:10–14.
The Jewish evangelists, Mt 24:14; 25:40; Rev 7: 1–8.
The two witnesses, Rev 11:3–12.
The message preached, Joel 2:32; Mt 3:2; 4:23; 24:14; Rev 12:11.
The results, Rev 7:9–14; Mt 24:34.

MISSIONS IN THE KINGDOM. The Jews are the Lord's witnesses, Isa 43:12, the ministers of God, Isa 61:6.
A great company publishes the Word, Ps 68:11.
Thirst for God satisfied, Isa 44:3.
The Holy Spirit is poured out, Joel 2:28.
God is active in making the Word known, Prov 1:23.
Gentiles seek out the Jews, Zech 8:23; Isa 55:4, 5.
The message is God's Word, Mic 4:2; Ps 68: 11–13; Prov 1:23.
World-wide knowledge of God, Ps 67:2; Hab 2: 14.
Missionary psalm, Ps 96.

MIST Ps 137:5; Isa 44:22; Jer 10:13; Hos 13:3; Acts 13:11.

MITHKAH A camping place of the Israelites, Num 33:15–37.

MITHREDATH 1. Treasurer of Cyrus, Ezra 1:8.
2. A Persian officer who joined in writing a letter hostile to the Jews, Ezra 4:7.

MITYLENE Capital of Lesbos. Paul visits, Acts 20:14.

MIXED MARRIAGE The covenant people of Israel were forbidden by God to marry individuals from the surrounding idol-worshiping nations. Intermarriage was a constant temptation to the Israelites and often resulted in the adoption of idolatrous practices. Abraham forbade Isaac to marry a Canaanite, Gen 28:1, ordered his servant not to take a wife from among the heathen Canaanites for Isaac, Gen 24:3, 37. The heathen Hethite wives of Esau a grief to his parents, Gen 26:35; 27: 46. Intermarriage with neighboring nations forbidden under Mosaic law, Ex 34:16; Deut 7:3; Josh 23: 12. Solomon's many marriages to foreign women, 1 Kgs 11:1, 2, called a sinful deed, Neh 13:23–27; cf. Neh 10:30. These marriages called a sin against God, Ezra 10:2, 10, brought the fierce wrath of God upon the Jews, Ezra 10:14, resulted in broken families, Ezra 10:2, 16–19, 44. Both mixed marriage and divorce denounced by Malachi, Mal 2:10–16.

The principle of avoiding spiritual intermarriage is suggested by Paul in 2 Cor 6:14–18. Christians are not voluntarily to be married to non-Christians, although Paul also advises converts to remain with nonbelieving marriage partners unless the non-Christian mate objects, 1 Cor 7:10–15.

See *Marriage.*

MIZAR A mountain, Ps 42:6.

MIZPAH Also *Mizpeh.* 1. A city allotted to Benjamin, Josh 18:21–28. The Israelites assemble at, Judg 20:1–3; and decree the penalty on the Benjaminites for their maltreatment of the Levite's concubine, Judg 20:10. Assembled by Samuel that he might reprove them for their idolatry, 1 Sam 7: 5. Crown Saul king of Israel at, 1 Sam 10:17–25. A judgment seat of Samuel, 1 Sam 7:16. Built by Asa, 1 Kgs 15:22; 2 Chron 16:6. Temporarily the capital of the country after the Israelites had been taken captive, 2 Kgs 25:23, 25; Jer 40:6–15; 41:1–14. Captives returned to, Neh 3:7, 15, 19.
2. The land of Mizpah, near Hermon, Josh 11: 1–3, 8.
3. A city in Moab. David gives his parents to the care of the king of, 1 Sam 22:3, 4.
4. A city in the lowland of Judah, Josh 15:37–44.
5. A place east of Jordan where Jephthah lived, Judg 10:17; 11:11, 34. Probably the same as *Ramath-mizpeh* of Gad, Josh 13:26.
6. The heap of stones raised by Jacob as witness to his covenant with Laban, Gen 31:44–49, origin of the so-called Mizpah benediction, *v.* 49.

MIZRAIM Or *Misream,* son of Ham, Gen 10:6, 13, 14; 1 Chron 1:5–9, 11, 12.

MIZZAH Son of Reuel, Gen 36:13, 14, 17; 1 Chron 1:37.

MNASON A native and Christian of Cyprus who entertained Paul, Acts 21:16.

MOAB 1. Son of Lot by his eldest daughter after the destruction of Sodom; progenitor of the Moabites, Gen 19:37.
2. Land of. Moses viewed the promised land from Mt. Nebo in, Deut 32:49; 34:1–4. Moses died and was buried in, Deut 34:5, 6. The place where Elimelech and Naomi lived, Ruth 1:1, 2.
3. Plains of. People of Israel camp in, Num 22: 1. Formerly a land of giants, Deut 2:18–23. Census of military forces in, Num 26:3, 4, 63. Moses reviews the law in, Num 35, 36; Deut 29–33. Israelites renewed their covenant in, Deut 29:1. Divided and distributed by Moses, Josh 13:32.
4. Field of, 1 Chron 1:46.

MOABITES Descendants of Lot through his son Moab, Gen 19:37. Called the people of Chemosh, Num 21:27–30. The territory east of Jordan, bounded on the north by the Arnon River, Num 21:13; Judg 11:18. Israelites commanded not to attack the Moabites, Deut 2:9. Refuse passage of Jephthah's army through their territory, Judg 11:17, 18. Balak was king of, Num 22:2, 3; calls for Balaam to curse Israel, Num 22–24; Josh 24:9; Mic 6:

5. Are a snare to the Israelites, Num 25:1–3; Ruth 1:4, 5; 1 Kgs 11:1; 1 Chron 8:8–10; Ezra 9:1, 2; Neh 13:23. Land of, not given to the Israelites as a possession, Deut 2:9, 29. David takes refuge among, from Saul, 1 Sam 22:3, 4. David conquers, 2 Sam 8:2; 23:20; 1 Chron 11:22; 18:2–11. Israelites had war with, 2 Kgs 3:5–27; 13:20, 21; 24:2; 2 Chron 20. Prophecies concerning judgments upon, Isa 15, 16; 25:10; Jer 48.

MOABITESS A title of Ruth, Ruth 4:10.

MOADIAH A priest, Neh 12:12–21.

MOB At Thessalonica, Acts 17:5; Jerusalem, Acts 21:26–32; Ephesus, Acts 19:29–40.

MOCKING Ishmael mocks Isaac, Gen 21:9. Elijah mocks the priests of Baal, 1 Kgs 18:27. Zedekiah mocks Micaiah, 1 Kgs 22:24. Children mock Elisha, 2 Kgs 2:23. The tormenters of Job mock, Job 15:12; 30:1. The persecutors of Jesus mock him, Mt 26:67, 68; 27:28–31, 39–44; Mk 10:34; 14:65; 15:16–20, 29–32; Lk 23:11; Jn 19:2, 3, 5; 1 Pet 2:23. The Ammonites mock God, Ezk 25:3. Tyre mocks Jerusalem, Ezk 26:2. The stubbornly wicked mock, Isa 28:15, 22; 2 Pet 3:3.

See *Scoffing.*

FIGURATIVE. Prov 1:26.

MODESTY Of women, Prov 11:22; 1 Tim 2:9, 10.

INSTANCES OF. Saul, 1 Sam 9:21. Vashti, Esther 1:11, 12. Elihu, Job 32:4–7.

See *Humility.*

MOLE Lev 11:29, 30; Isa 2:20.

MOLECH Called also *Moloch* and *Milcom.* A god of the Ammonites, worshiped by the wives of Solomon, and by Solomon, 1 Kgs 11:1–8. Children sacrificed to, 2 Kgs 23:10; Jer 32:35; 2 Kgs 16:3; 21:6; 2 Chron 28:3; 57:5; Jer 7:31; Ezk 16:20, 21; 20:26, 31; 23:37, 39; see Lev 18:21; 20:1–5. Worshiped by Judah, Zeph 1:5.

MOLDING Of idols, Ex 32:4, 8; Deut 9:12; pillars, 1 Kgs 7:15; tank, 1 Kgs 7:23; done in the plain of Jordan, 1 Kgs 7:41–46; 2 Chron 4:17, 18.

MONARCHY Described by Samuel, 1 Sam 8:11–18.

See *Government; King.*

MONEY The Biblical references to money are most difficult to relate to current usage because: (1) Biblical references are to both minted coins and units of measure based on weight, and (2) such a diversity of units cannot be accurately related to an exact standard. Certain relationships between units of money do provide a partial basis of determination, limited by fluctuations of currency today: A denarius equals one day's wage; 10 gerahs equal one beka; two bekas equal one shekel; 50 shekels equal one mina; 60 minas equal one talent. Because these units were based on weight, the values varied according to the metal used.

Silver used as, Gen 20:16; 23:14–16; 37:28; 42:23–35; 43:12–23; 44:1–8; 47:14–18; Ex 21:32; 22:7, 17, 25; 30:16; Lev 22:11; Num 3:48–51; 18:16; Deut 14:25, 26; 23:19; Judg 16:18; 17:4, 5; 1 Kgs 21:2; 2 Kgs 5:26; 12:4, 5, 7–16; 15:19, 20; 22:7; 23:35; 2 Chron 24:5, 11; 14; 34:9, 14, 17; Neh 5:2–4; Esther 4:7; Prov 7:20; Eccl 7:12; 10:19; Isa 52:3; 55:1, 2; Jer 32:9, 10, 25; Mic 3:11; Mt 25:18, 27; 28:12–15; Lk 9:3; 19:15, 23; Acts 8:20.

Gold used as, Gen 13:1, 2; 24:35; 44:8, with *v.* 1; 1 Chron 21:25; Ezra 8:25–27; Isa 13:17; 46:6; Ezk 7:19; 28:4; Mt 2:11; 10:9; Acts 3:6; 20:33; 1 Pet 1:18.

Weighed, Gen 23:16; 43:21; Jer 32:9, 10; Zech 11:12. Likeness on, Mt 22:20, 21. Conscience, Judg 17:2; Mt 27:3, 5. Atonement, Ex 30:11–16; Lev 5:15, 16. Sin, 2 Kgs 12:16. Value of, varied corruptly, Amos 8:5. Love, Mt 6:24; Lk 16:9, 13; the root of evil, 1 Tim 6:10.

See *Denarius; Gerah; Penny; Shekel; Silver; Talent.*

MONEY CHANGERS Mt 21:12; Mk 11:15; Jn 2:15.

MONOPOLY Job 15:7, 8. Of lands, Isa 5:8; Mic 2:2; by Pharaoh, Gen 47:19–26; of food, Prov 11:26.

MONTH See *Calendar.*

MONUMENT See *Pillar.*

MOON Created by God, Gen 1:16; Ps 8:3; 136:7–9. Its light, Job 31:26; Eccl 12:2; Song 6:10; Jer 31:35; 1 Cor 15:41. Its influences, Deut 33:14; Ps 121:6. Seasons of (months), Ps 104:19. Joseph's dream concerning, Gen 37:9. Stands still, Josh 10:12, 13. Worship of, forbidden, Deut 4:19; 17:2, 3. Worshiped, 2 Kgs 23:5; Job 31:26, 27; Jer 7:18; 8:2; 44:17–19, 25. No light of, in the new Jerusalem, Rev 21:23. Darkening of, Job 25:5; Isa 13:10; 24:23; Ezk 32:7; Joel 2:10, 31; 3:15; Hab 3:11; Mt 24:29; Mk 13:24; Lk 21:25; Acts 2:20; Rev 6:12; 8:12.

FIGURATIVE. Shining of, Isa 30:26; 60:19; Rev 21:23.

Symbolical. Rev 12:1.

FEAST OF THE NEW MOON. Num 10:10; 28:11–15; 1 Chron 23:31; 2 Chron 31:3; Ezra 3:5. Traffic at time of, prohibited, Amos 8:5.

MORAL AGENCY See *Contingencies.*

MORALITY See *Duty, of Man to Man; Honesty; Integrity; Neighbor.*

MORAL LAW See *Law.*

MORDECAI A Jewish captive in Persia, Esther 2:5, 6. Foster father of Esther, Esther 2:7. Informs Ahasuerus of a conspiracy against his life, and is rewarded, Esther 2:21–23; 6:1–11. Promoted in Haman's place, Esther 8:1, 2, 15; 10:1–3. Intercedes with Ahasuerus for the Jews; establishes the festival of Purim in commemoration of their deliverance, Esther 8; 9.

MOREH 1. A plain near Shechem and Gilgal, Gen 12:6; Deut 11:30.

2. A hill in the plain of Jezreel where the Midianites camped, Judg 7:1.

MORIAH The place where God directed Abraham to sacrifice Isaac, Gen 22:2–4; and the site where the Temple was built, 1 Chron 21:26, 22:1; 2 Chron 3:1; and probable site of rebuilt temples, 2 Thess 2:4; Mt 24:15; Rev 11:1, 2.

MORNING STAR Name of Christ, 2 Pet 1:19.

See *Stars, Figurative.*

MORTAR 1. A hollow vessel used for pulverizing grain or other substances, Num 11:8.

2. Any cement used in building, Ex 1:13, 14. Slime or bitumen used as, in building tower of Babel, Gen 11:3, 4. Used to plaster houses, Lev 14:42, 45. Trampled to make firm, Nah 3:14.

See *Clay; Whitewash.*

MORTGAGE On land, Neh 5:2–4.

See *Land.*

MORTIFICATION INSTANCES OF. David's ambassadors, sent to Hanun, 2 Sam 10:1–5. Judas, Mt 27:3–5.

See *Humility.*

MOSAIC LAW See *Law.*

MOSERA An encampment of the Israelites where Aaron died, Deut 10:6. Probably identical with *Moseroth,* below.

MOSEROTH A camping place of the Israelites, Num 33:15–37.

MOSES A Levite and son of Amram, Ex 2:1–4; 6:20; Acts 7:20; Heb 11:23. Hidden in a small boat, Ex 2:3. Discovered and adopted by the daughter of Pharaoh, Ex 2:5–10. Learned in all the wisdom of Egypt, Acts 7:22. His loyalty to his race, Heb 11:24–26. Takes the life of an Egyptian; flees from Egypt; finds safety among the Midianites, Ex 2:11–22; Acts 7:24–29. Joins himself to Jethro, priest of Midian; marries his daughter Zipporah; has two sons, Ex 2:15–22; 18:3, 4. Is herdman for Jethro in the desert of Horeb, Ex 3:1. Has the vision of the burning bush, Ex 3:2–6. God reveals to him his purpose to deliver the Israelites and bring them into the land of Canaan, Ex 3:7–10. Commissioned as leader of the Israelites, Ex 3:10–22; 6:13. His rod miraculously turned into a serpent, and his hand made leprous, and each restored, Ex 4:1–9, 28. With his wife and sons leaves Jethro to perform his mission, Ex 4:18–20. His controversy with his wife on account of circumcision, Ex 4:20–26. Meets Aaron in the wilderness, Ex 4:27, 28.

With Aaron assembles the leaders of Israel, Ex 4:29–31. With Aaron goes before Pharaoh, in the name of Jehovah demands the liberty of his people, Ex 5:1. Rejected by Pharaoh; hardships of the Israelites increased, Ex 5. People complain against Moses and Aaron, Ex 5:20, 21; 15:24; 16:2, 3; 17:2, 3; Num 14:2–4; 16:41; 20:2–5; 21:4–6; Deut 1:12, 26–28. See *Israel.* Receives comfort and assurance from the Lord, Ex 6:1–9. Unbelief of the people, Ex 6:8, 9. Renews his appeal to Pharaoh, Ex 6:11. Under divine direction brings plagues on the land of Egypt, Ex chapters 7–12. Secures the deliverance of the people and leads them out of Egypt, Ex 13. Crosses the Red Sea; Pharaoh and his army are destroyed, Ex 14. Composes a song for the children of Israel on their deliverance from Pharaoh, Ex 15. Joined by his family in the wilderness, Ex 18:1–12.

Institutes a system of government, Ex 18:13–26; Num 11:16–30; Deut 1:9–18. Receives the law and ordains various statutes, see *Law of Moses.* Face of, transfigured, Ex 34:29–35; 2 Cor 3:13. Sets up the tabernacle, see *Tabernacle.* Reproves Aaron for making the golden calf, Ex 32:22, 23; for irregularity in the offerings, Lev 10:16–20. Jealousy of Aaron and Miriam toward, Num 12. Rebellion of Korah, Dathan, and Abiram against, Num 16. Appoints Joshua as his successor, Num 27:22, 23; Deut 31:7, 8, 14, 23; 34:9.

Not permitted to enter Canaan, but views the land from Mount Abarim, Num 27:12–14; Deut 1:37; 3:23–29; 32:48–52; 34:1–8. Death and burial of, Num 31:1, 2; Deut 32:50; 34:1–6. Body of, disputed over, Jude 1:9. One hundred and twenty years old at death, Deut 31:2. Mourning for, 30 days in the plains of Moab, Deut 34:8. His virility, Deut 31:2; 34:7.

Author of the Pentateuch, Mt 8:4; 19:7, 8; Mk 7:10; 12:19, 26; Lk 2:22; 16:29, 31; 20:28, 37, 38; 24:27, 44; Jn 1:17, 45; 3:14; 5:45, 46; 7:19, 21–23.

Present with Jesus on the mount of transfiguration, Mt 17:3, 4; Mk 9:4; Lk 9:30.

Type of Christ, Deut 18:15–18; Acts 3:21, 22; 7:37.

BLESSINGS OF. On the people, Lev 9:23; Num 10:35, 36; Deut 1:11. Last blessing on the twelve tribes, Deut 33.

CHARACTER OF. Murmurings of, Ex 5:22, 23; Num 11:10–15. Impatience of, Ex 5:22, 23; 6:12; 32:19; Num 11:10–15; 16:15; 20:10; 31:14. Respected and feared, Ex 33:8. Faith of, Num 10:29; Deut 9:1–3; Heb 11:23–28. Called *the man of God,* Deut 33:1. God spoke to, as a man to his friend, Ex 33:11. Magnified of God, Ex 19:9; Num 14:12–19; Deut 9:13–29, with Ex 32:30. Magnanimity of, toward Eldad and Medad, Num 11:29. Meekness of, Ex 14:13, 14; 15:24, 25; 16:2, 3, 7–9; Num 12:3, 4; 16:4–12. Obedience of, Ex 7:6; 40:16, 19, 21. Unaspiring, Num 14:12–19; Deut 9:13–29, with Ex 32:30.

INTERCESSORY PRAYERS OF. See *Intercession, Exemplified, Additional Instances of, Solicited, Answered.*

MIRACLES OF. See *Miracles.*

PROPHECIES OF. Ex 3:10; 4:5, 11, 12; 6:13; 7:2; 17:15, 16; 19:2–9; 33:11; Num 11:17; 12:7, 8; 36:13; Deut 5:31; 18:15, 18; 34:10–12; Hos 12:13; Mk 7:9, 10; Acts 7:37, 38.

MOTH An insect, Job 4:18, 19; Ps 39:11. Destructive of garments, Job 13:27, 28; Isa 50:9; 51:8; Hos 5:12.

FIGURATIVE. Lk 12:33; Jas 5:2.

MOTHER Ex 20:12. Honor your father and mother, that you may have a long, good life in the land the Lord your God will give you. Deut 5:16; Mt 15:4; 19:19; Mk 7:10; 10:19; Lk 18:20; Eph 6:2.

Ex 21:15. Anyone who strikes his father or mother shall surely be put to death. [17]Anyone who reviles or curses his mother or father shall surely be put to death.

Lev 18:7. A girl may not marry her father; nor a son his mother.

Lev 19:2. You must respect your mothers and fathers, and obey my Sabbath law, for I am the Lord your God.

Lev 20:9. Anyone who curses his father or mother shall surely be put to death—for he has cursed his own flesh and blood.

1 Kgs 19:20. Elisha left the oxen standing there and ran after Elijah and said to him, "First let me

go and say good-bye to my father and mother, and then I'll go with you!"

Prov 1:8. Listen to your father and mother. What you learn from them will stand you in good stead.

Prov 6:20. Young man, obey your father and your mother.

Prov 10:1. Happy is the man with a level-headed son; sad the mother of a rebel.

Prov 15:20. A rebellious son saddens his mother.

Prov 19:26. A son who mistreats his father or mother is a public disgrace.

Prov 20:20. God puts out the light of the man who curses his father or mother.

Prov 23:22. Don't despise an old mother's experience. [23]Get the facts at any price, and hold on tightly to all the good sense you can get. [24, 25]The father of a godly man has cause for joy—what pleasure a wise son is! So give your parents joy!

Prov 28:24. A man who robs his parents and says, "What's wrong with that?" is no better than a murderer.

Prov 29:15. Scolding and spanking a child helps him to learn. Left to himself, he brings shame to his mother.

Prov 30:11. There are those who curse their father and mother. [17]A man who mocks his father and despises his mother shall have his eye plucked out by ravens and eaten by vultures.

Isa 66:13. I will comfort you there as a little one is comforted by its mother. Isa 49:15.

Ezk 16:3. Tell her, the Lord God says: You are no better than the people of Canaan—your father must have been an Amorite and your mother a Hittite! [44]"Like mother, like daughter"—that is what everyone will say of you.

Mt 2:11. Entering the house where the baby and Mary his mother were, they threw themselves down before him, worshiping.

Mt 10:37. If you love your father and mother more than you love me, you are not worthy of being mine.

Mt 12:50. Anyone who obeys my Father in heaven is my brother, sister and mother!

Mt 15:4. For instance, God's law is "Honor your father and mother; anyone who reviles his parents must die." [5, 6]But you say, "Even if your parents are in need, you may give their support money to the church instead." And so, by your man-made rule, you nullify the direct command of God to honor and care for your parents. Mk 7:10–13.

Mk 1:30. They found Simon's mother-in-law sick in bed with a high fever. They told Jesus about her right away.

Jn 2:1. Two days later Jesus' mother was a guest at a wedding in the village of Cana in Galilee.

Jn 19:25. Standing near the cross were Jesus' mother, Mary, his aunt, the wife of Cleopas, and Mary Magdalene. [26]When Jesus saw his mother standing there beside me, his close friend, he said to her, "He is your son." [27]And to me he said, "She is your mother!" And from then on I took her into my home.

Gal 4:26. But our mother-city is the heavenly Jerusalem, and she is not a slave to Jewish laws.

2 Tim 1:5. I know how much you trust the Lord, just as your mother Eunice and your grandmother Lois do; and I feel sure you are still trusting him as much as ever.

Rev 17:5. A mysterious caption was written on her forehead: "Babylon the Great, Mother of Prostitutes and of Idol Worship Everywhere around the World."

See *Children, Duty of; Parents.*

MOTHER-IN-LAW Mt 10:35. Not to be defiled, Lev 18:17; 20:14; Deut 27:23. Beloved by Ruth, Ruth 1:14–17. Peter's, healed by Jesus, Mk 1: 29–31.

MOTIVE Ascribed to God, Ps 106:8; Ezk 36: 21, 22, 32. Seen by God, Ps 7:9; 26:2; Prov 21:2; Jer 11:20; 17:10; Rom 2:16. Right, required, Mt 6:1–18; 1 Thess 2:3. Sinful, Prov 20:27; Eccl 4:4; Jas 2:4; illustrated by Cain, Gen 4:7; 1 Jn 3:12.

MISUNDERSTOOD. The tribes of Reuben and Gad, in asking inheritance east of Jordan, Num 32: 1–33; when they built the altar, Josh 22:9–34. David's by King Hanun, 2 Sam 10:2, 3; 1 Chron 19: 2–4. The king of Syria's, in sending presents to the king of Israel by Naaman, 2 Kgs 5:5–7. Job's in his righteousness, Job 1:9–11; 2:4, 5.

MOTTO See *Inscription.*

MOUNT Famous mounts of the Bible: Seir, Gen 36:6–8; Sinai, Ex 19:11; Horeb, Ex 17:5, 6; Hor, Num 20:21, 22; Hermon, Deut 3:8; Gerizim, Ebal, Deut 11:29; Nebo, Deut 32:49; Gaash, Judg 2:9; Lebanon, Judg 3:1–3; Tabor, Judg 4:6; Bethel, 1 Sam 13:2; Gilboa, 1 Sam 31:1; Carmel, 1 Kgs 18:19; Ephraim, 1 Chron 6:66–69; Moriah, 2 Chron 3:1; Zion, Isa 25:6; Gilead, Jer 50:19; of Olives, Zech 14: 4.

MOUNTAIN Quaked and melted, Ps 97:5; Deut 4:11; 5:23; Judg 5:5; Isa 64:1–3; Mic 1:4; Nah 1:5. Overturning and removing of, Job 9:5; 14:18, 19; 28:9; Ezk 38:20. Abraham offers Isaac on Mount Moriah, afterward the site of the temple, Gen 22: 2. Horeb appointed as a place for the Israelites to worship, Ex 3:1, 12. Used for idolatrous worship, Deut 12:2; 1 Sam 10:5, 1 Kgs 14:23; Jer 3:6; Hos 4: 13. Jesus tempted on, Mt 4:8; Lk 4:5. Jesus preaches from, Mt 5:1. Jesus goes to, for prayer, Mt 14:23, 24; Lk 6:12; 9:28; is transfigured on, Mt 17:1–9; Mk 9: 2–10; Lk 9:28–36; meets his disciples on, after his resurrection, Mt 28:16, 17. Signals from, Isa 18:3; 30:17. Moved by faith, Mt 17:20; 21:21; Mk 11:22, 23. Burning mountains, see *Volcano.*

MOURNING For the dead: Head uncovered, Lev 10:6; 21:10; lying on ground, 2 Sam 12:16; personal appearance neglected, 2 Sam 14:2, 3; cutting the flesh, Lev 19:28; 21:1–5; Deut 14:1; Jer 16:6, 7; 41:5; lamentations, Gen 50:10; Ex 12:30; 1 Sam 30: 4; Jer 22:18; Mt 2:17, 18; fasting, 1 Sam 31:13; 2 Sam 1:12; 3:35, 36. Priests prohibited, except for closest relatives, Lev 21:1–11. For Nadab and Abihu forbidden, Lev 10:6. Sexes separated in, Zech 12: 12–14.

Hired mourners, 2 Chron 35:24, 25; Eccl 12:5; Jer 9:17, 18; Mt 9:23.

Abraham mourned for Sarah, Gen 23:1, 2; Egyptians, for Jacob 70 days, Gen 50:1–3; Israelites, for Aaron 30 days, Num 20:29. David's lamentations over the death of Saul and his sons, 2 Sam 1:17–27; the death of Abner, 2 Sam 3:33, 34; the death of Absalom, 2 Sam 18:33.

Jeremiah and the Temple choirs lament for Josiah, 2 Chron 35:24, 25.

For calamities and other sorrows: Tearing the garments, Gen 37:29, 34; 44:13; Num 14:6; Judg 11:35; 2 Sam 1:1, 2, 11; 13:19, 31; 15:32; 2 Kgs 2:12; 6:30; 11:13, 14; 19:1; 22:11, 18, 19; Ezra 9:3; Job 1:20; 2:12; Isa 37:1; Jer 41:5; Mt 26:65, 66; Acts 14:14. Wearing mourning clothes, Gen 38:14; 2 Sam 14:2, 3. See *Sackcloth.* Cutting or plucking off the hair and beard, Ezra 9:3; Jer 7:29. See *Baldness.* Covering the head and face, 2 Sam 15:30; 19:4; Jer 14:3, 4; Ezk 24:17; Mic 3:7; and the upper lip, Lev 13:45. Putting aside jewelry, Ex 33:4, 6. Walking barefoot, 2 Sam 15:30; Isa 20:2. Laying the hands on the head, 2 Sam 13:19. Dust on the head, Josh 7:6; Ezk 27:30. Sitting on the ground, Isa 3:25, 26.

Caused ceremonial defilement, Num 19:11–16; 31:19; Lev 21:1. Prevented offerings from being accepted, Deut 26:14; Hos 9:4.

See *Elegy.*

MOUSE Forbidden as food, Lev 11:29, 30; used as food, Isa 66:17.

Models of, 1 Sam 6:4, 5, 11, 18.

MOWING Ps 90:5, 6; Amos 7:1.

MOZA 1. A son of Caleb, 1 Chron 2:46.

2. A Benjaminite, 1 Chron 8:36, 37; 9:42, 43.

MOZAH A city of Benjamin, Josh 18:21–28.

MUD Blind man's eyes anointed with, Jn 9:6. See *Clay.*

MULBERRY TREE 1 Chron 14:14, 15; Lk 17:6.

MULE Uses of: For royal riders, 2 Sam 13:29, 30; 18:9; 1 Kgs 1:33, 38; ridden by couriers, Esther 8:9, 10, 14; by saints in Isaiah's prophetic vision of the kingdom of Christ, Isa 66:20; as pack animals, 2 Kgs 5:17; 1 Chron 12:40. Tribute paid in, 1 Kgs 10:25. Used in barter, Ezk 27:14; by the captives in returning from Babylon, Ezra 2:66, 67; Neh 7:68, 69; in war, Zech 14:15.

MUPPIM Son of Benjamin, Gen 46:19–22.

MURDER See *Homicide.*

MURMURING Of Israelites against Moses, Ex 5:21; 15:24; 16:2, 3; Num 16:2, 3, 13, 14, 41; 20:2–4.

AGAINST GOD. Ex 5:22. Then Moses went back to the Lord. "Lord," he protested, "how can you mistreat your own people like this? Why did you ever send me, if you were going to do this to them? [23]Ever since I gave Pharaoh your message, he has only been more and more brutal to them, and you have not delivered them at all!"

Ex 16:8. He has heard your complaints against him (for you aren't really complaining against *us* —who are *we?*). The Lord will give you meat to eat in the evening, and bread in the morning. [12]"I have heard their complaints. Tell them, 'In the evening you will have meat and in the morning you will be stuffed with bread, and you shall know that I am Jehovah your God.' "

Num 14:26, 27. Then the Lord added to Moses and to Aaron, "How long will these wicked people complain about me? For I have heard all that they have been saying. [28]Tell them, 'The Lord vows to do to you what you feared: [29]You will all die here in this wilderness! Not a single one of you twenty years old and older, who has complained against me, [30]shall enter the Promised Land. Only Caleb (son of Jephunneh) and Joshua (son of Nun) are permitted to enter it. [31]You said your children would become slaves of the people of the land. Well, instead I will bring *them* safely into the land and they shall inherit what you have despised. [32]But as for you, your dead bodies shall fall in this wilderness. [33]You must wander in the desert like nomads for forty years. In this way you will pay for your faithlessness, until the last of you lies dead in the desert. [34,35]Since the spies were in the land for forty days, you must wander in the wilderness for forty years—a year for each day, bearing the burden of your sins. I will teach you what it means to reject me. I, Jehovah, have spoken. Every one of you who has conspired against me shall die here in this wilderness.' " [36,37]Then the ten spies who had incited the rebellion against Jehovah by striking fear into the hearts of the people were struck dead before the Lord. chapter 17:10, 11.

Job 15:11. Is God's comfort too little for you? Is his gentleness too rough? [12]What is this you are doing, getting carried away by your anger, with flashing eyes? [13]And you turn against God and say all these evil things against him.

Job 33:12. All right, here is my reply: In this very thing, you have sinned by speaking of God that way. For God is greater than man. [13]Why should you fight against him just because he does not give account to you of what he does?

Job 34:37. For now you have added rebellion, arrogance and blasphemy to your other sins.

Ps 44:9. And yet for a time, O Lord, you have tossed us aside in dishonor, and have not helped us in our battles. [10]You have actually fought against us and defeated us before our foes. Our enemies have invaded our land and pillaged the countryside. [11]You have treated us like sheep in a slaughter pen, and scattered us among the nations. [12]You sold us for a pittance. You valued us at nothing at all. [13]The neighboring nations laugh and mock at us because of all the evil you have sent. [14]You have made the word "Jew" a byword of contempt and shame among the nations, disliked by all. [15,16]I am constantly despised, mocked, taunted and cursed by my vengeful enemies. [17]And all this has happened, Lord, despite our loyalty to you. We have not violated your covenant. [18]Our hearts have not deserted you! We have not left your path by a single step. [19]If we had, we could understand your punishing us in the barren wilderness and sending us into darkness and death. [20]If we had turned away from worshiping our God, and were worshiping idols, [21]would God know it? Yes, he knows the secrets of every heart. [22]But that is not our case. For we are facing death threats constantly because of serving you! We are like sheep awaiting slaughter. [23]Waken! Rouse yourself! Don't sleep, O Lord! Are we cast off forever? [24]Why do you look the other way? Why do you ignore our sorrows and oppression? [25]We lie face downward in the dust. [26]Rise up, O Lord, and come and help us. Save us by your constant love.

Ps 73:13. Have I been wasting my time? Why take the trouble to be pure? [14]All I get out of it is trouble and woe—every day and all day long! [15]If I had really said that, I would have been a traitor to your people. [16]Yet it is so hard to explain it—this prosperity of those who hate the Lord. [17]Then one day I went into God's sanctuary to meditate, and thought about the future of these evil men. [18]What a slippery path they are on—suddenly God will send them sliding over the edge of the cliff and down to their destruction: [19]an instant end to all their happiness, an eternity of terror. [20]Their present life is only a dream! They will awaken to the truth as one awakens from a dream of things that never really were! [21]When I saw this, what turmoil filled my heart! [22]I saw myself so stupid and so ignorant; I must seem like an animal to you, O God.

Ps 78:17. Yet they kept on with their rebellion, sinning against the God who is above all gods. [18]They murmured and complained, demanding other food than God was giving them. [19,20]They even spoke against God himself. "Why can't he give us decent food as well as water?" they grumbled. [21]Jehovah heard them and was angry; the fire of his wrath burned against Israel.

Prov 19:3. A man may ruin his chances by his own foolishness and then blame it on the Lord!

Eccl 7:10. Don't long for "the good old days," for you don't know whether they were any better than these!

Jer 15:10. What sadness is mine, my mother; oh, that I had died at birth. For I am hated everywhere I go. I am neither a creditor soon to foreclose nor a debtor refusing to pay—yet they all curse me.

Lam 3:39. Why then should we, mere humans as we are, murmur and complain when punished for our sins?

Mal 3:14. Listen; you have said, "It is foolish to worship God and obey him. What good does it do to obey his laws, and to sorrow and mourn for our sins?"

Lk 10:40. But Martha was the jittery type, and was worrying over the big dinner she was preparing. She came to Jesus and said, "Sir, doesn't it seem unfair to you that my sister just sits here while I do all the work? Tell her to come and help me."

Rom 9:19. Well then, why does God blame them for not listening? Haven't they done what he made them do? [20]No, don't say that. Who are you to criticize God? Should the thing made say to the one who made it, "Why have you made me like this?"

1 Cor 10:10. And don't murmur against God and his dealings with you, as some of them did, for that is why God sent his Angel to destroy them.

Phil 2:14. In everything you do, stay away from complaining and arguing.

Jas 5:9. Don't grumble about each other, brothers. Are you yourselves above criticism? For see! The great Judge is coming.

Jude 1:16. These men are constant gripers, never satisfied, doing whatever evil they feel like.

INSTANCES OF. Cain, Gen 4:13, 14. Rachel, Gen 30:1. Moses, Ex 5:22, 23; Num 11:11–15. Israelites, Ex 5:21; 14:11, 12; 15:23, 24; 16:2, 3; 17:2, 3; Num 11:1–10, 33; 14; 16:41; 20:2–5; 21:5, 6; Deut 1:27, 28; Ps 106:24–26. Korah, Num 16:8–12; Job, Job chapters 3; 6; 7; 9; 10; 13; 19; 23; 30. David, 2 Sam 6:8; Ps 116:10, 11. Elijah, 1 Kgs 19:4, 10. Solomon, Eccl 2:17, 18. Hezekiah, Isa 38:10–18. Jeremiah, Jer 20:14–18; Lam 3. Jonah, Jon 4. Jews, against Jesus, Jn 6:41–43, 52.

See *Doubting; Envy; Ingratitude.* See also *Contentment; Resignation.*

MUSHI A son of Merari, Ex 6:19; 1 Chron 6: 19–21, 44–47.

MUSCLES Gen 32:32; Job 40:16; Ezk 37:6, 8.

MUSIC Music at the original creation, Job 38:6, 7. First recorded singing on earth, Ex 15:1. Refreshes, and drives away evil spirits, 1 Sam 16:23. Provides atmosphere for ministering the Word, 2 Kgs 3:15, 16. Fills house of God with glory, 2 Chron 5:13, 14. Brings defeat to the enemy, 2 Chron 20:21, 22. Brings men to God, Ps 40:1–3; Acts 16:25–31. Israel's lost song, Ps 137:1–4. Israel's song restored, Ezra 3:11. Secret of joyful song, Eph 5:18, 19; Col 3:16. Singing in heaven, Rev 5:9. Teachers of, 1 Chron 15:22; 25:6, 7; 2 Chron 23:12. Physical effect of, on man, 1 Sam 16:15, 16, 23. Accompanied the offering of sacrifices, 2 Chron 29:27, 28. Choirmaster, Neh 12:42; Hab 3:19. In heaven, Rev 5:8, 9; 14:2, 3; 15:2–4.

INSTRUMENTS OF. Invented by Jubal, Gen 4: 21; by David, 1 Chron 23:4, 5; 2 Chron 7:6; 29:26; Amos 6:5. Made by Solomon, 1 Kgs 10:12; 2 Chron 9:11; Eccl 2:8.

Cornet, Dan 3:5, 7, 10. See *Trumpet.*

Cymbal. See *Cymbal.*

Drums. See *Drums.*

Dulcimer, a double pipe, Dan 3:5, 7, 10.

Flute, Gen 4:21; Dan 3:5, 7, 10.

Harp. See *Harp.*

Horn, Ps 150:4.

Lute. See *Lute.*

Lyre. See *Lyre.*

Pipe. See *Pipe.*

Psaltery. See *Psaltery.*

Sackbut, a harp, Dan 3:5, 7, 10.

Tambourine. See *Tambourine.*

Timbrel, a tambourine. See *Timbrel.*

Trumpet. See *Trumpet.*

Zither. See *Zither.*

SYMBOLS USED IN.

Alamoth. Literally *virgins.* A musical term which appears in 1 Chron 15:20. It seems to indicate the rendering of the song by female voices, possibly soprano.

Higgaion. In Ps 9:16, combined with "Selah," it may have been intended to indicate a pause in the vocal music while the instruments rendered an interlude.

Selah. See *Higgaion,* above.

Sheminith. In 1 Chron 15:21, translated "eighth," probably indicates the measure, movement, or pitch.

Shigionoth. In Hab 3:1, is supposed to have been a musical term to guide in singing the song. At the close of the chapter the author refers the ode "to the choir director . . . to be accompanied by stringed instruments." The term may suggest the movement in interpreting the music set to it.

UNCLASSIFIED SCRIPTURES RELATING TO. Gen 31:27. Why didn't you give me a chance to have a farewell party, with singing and orchestra and harp?

Ex 15:1. Then Moses and the people of Israel sang this song to the Lord: I will sing to the Lord, for he has triumphed gloriously; he has thrown both horse and rider into the sea. [*vs.* 1–27.] [20]Then Miriam the prophetess, the sister of Aaron, took a timbrel and led the women in dances. [21]And Miriam sang this song: Sing to the Lord, for he has triumphed gloriously. The horse and rider have been drowned in the sea.

Num 21:17, 18. What happened is described in this song that the people sang: Spring up, O well! Sing of the water! This is a well the leaders dug. It was hollowed with their staves and shovels.

Judg 5:1. Then Deborah and Barak sang this song about the wonderful victory: [2]"Praise the Lord! Israel's leaders bravely led; the people gladly followed! Yes, bless the Lord! [3]Listen, O you kings and princes, for I shall sing about the Lord, the God of Israel." *vs.* 1–31.

Judg 11:34. When Jephthah returned home his daughter—his only child—ran out to meet him, playing on a tambourine and dancing for joy.

1 Sam 18:6. But something had happened when the victorious Israeli army was returning home after David had killed Goliath. Women came out from all the towns along the way to celebrate and to cheer for King Saul, and were singing and dancing for joy with tambourines and cymbals. [7]However, this was their song: "Saul has slain his thousands, and David his ten thousands!"

1 Kgs 1:40. Then they all returned with him to Jerusalem, making a joyous and noisy celebration all along the way.

1 Chron 6:31. King David appointed songleaders and choirs to praise God in the Tabernacle after he had placed the Ark in it. [32]Then, when Solomon built the Temple at Jerusalem, the choirs carried on their work there.

1 Chron 15:16. King David also ordered the Levite leaders to organize the singers into an orchestra, and they played loudly and joyously upon psaltries, harps, and cymbals. [17]Heman (son of Joel), Asaph (son of Berechiah), and Ethan (son of Kushaiah) from the clan of Merari were the heads of the musicians. [18]The following men were chosen as their assistants: Zechariah, Ja-aziel, Shemiramoth, Jehiel, Unni, Eliab, Benaiah, Ma-asseiah, Mattithiah, Eliphelehu, Mikneiah, Obed-edom and Je-iel, the door keepers. [19]Heman, Asaph, and Ethan were chosen to sound the bronze cymbals; [20]and Zechariah, Aziel, Shemiramoth, Jehiel, Unni, Eliab, Ma-aseiah, and Benaiah comprised an octet accompanied by harps. [21]Mattithiah, Eliphelehu, Mikneiah, Obed-edom, Je-iel, and Azaziah were the harpists. [22]The song leader was Chenaniah, the chief of the Levites, who was selected for his skill. [24]Shebaniah, Joshaphat, Nethanel, Amasai, Zechariah, Benaiah, and Eliezer—all of whom were priests—formed a bugle corps to march at the head of the procession. And Obededom and Jehiah guarded the Ark. [27]David, the Levites carrying the Ark, the singers, and Chenaniah the song leader were all dressed in linen robes. David also wore a linen ephod. [28]So the leaders of Israel took the Ark to Jerusalem with shouts of joy, the blowing of horns and trumpets, the crashing of cymbals, and loud playing on the harps and zithers.

1 Chron 16:4. He appointed certain of the Levites to minister before the Ark by giving constant praise and thanks to the Lord God of Israel and by asking for his blessings upon his people. . . . [5]Asaph, the leader of this detail, sounded the cymbals. His associates were Zechariah, Je-iel, Shemiramoth, Jehiel, Mattithiah, Eliab, Benaiah, Obededom, and Je-iel; they played the harps and zithers. [6]The priests Benaiah and Jahaziel played their trumpets regularly before the Ark. [7]At that time David began the custom of using choirs in the Tabernacle to sing thanksgiving to the Lord. Asaph was the director of this choral group of priests. [8]"Oh, give thanks to the Lord and pray to him," they sang. "Tell the peoples of the world about his mighty doings. [9]Sing to him; yes, sing his praises and tell of his marvelous works. [10]Glory in his holy name; let all rejoice who seek the Lord. [11]Seek the Lord; yes, seek his strength and seek his face untiringly. [12,13]O descendants of his servant Abraham, O chosen sons of Jacob, remember his mighty miracles and his marvelous miracles and his authority: [14]He is the Lord our God! His authority is seen throughout the earth. [15]Remember his covenant forever—the words he commanded to a thousand generations: [16]His agreement with Abraham, and his oath to Isaac, [17]and his confirmation to Jacob. He promised Israel with an everlasting promise: [18]'I will give you the land of Canaan as your inheritance.' [19]When Israel was few in number—oh, so few—and merely strangers in the Promised Land; [20]when they wandered from country to country, from one kingdom to another —[21]God didn't let anyone harm them. Even kings were killed who sought to hurt them. [22]'Don't harm my chosen people,' he declared. 'These are my prophets—touch them not.' [23]Sing to the Lord, O earth, declare each day that he is the one who

saves! [24]Show his glory to the nations! Tell everyone about his miracles. [25]For the Lord is great, and should be highly praised; he is to be held in awe above all gods. [26]The other so-called gods are demons, but the Lord made the heavens. [27]Majesty and honor march before him, strength and gladness walk beside him. [28]O people of all nations of the earth, ascribe great strength and glory to his name! [29]Yes, ascribe to the Lord the glory due his name! Bring an offering and come before him; worship the Lord when clothed with holiness! [30]Tremble before him, all the earth! The world stands unmoved. [31]Let the heavens be glad, the earth rejoice; let all the nations say, 'It is the Lord who reigns.' [32]Let the vast seas roar, let the countryside and everything in it rejoice! [33]Let the trees in the woods sing for joy before the Lord, for he comes to judge the earth. [34]Oh, give thanks to the Lord, for he is good; his love and his kindness go on forever. [35]Cry out to him, 'Oh, save us, God of our salvation; bring us safely back from among the nations. Then we will thank your holy name, and triumph in your praise.' [36]Blessed be Jehovah, God of Israel, forever and forevermore." And all the people shouted "Amen!" and praised the Lord. [37]David arranged for Asaph and his fellow Levites to minister regularly at the Tabernacle, doing each day whatever needed to be done. [38]This group included Obed-edom (the son of Jeduthun), Hosah and sixty-eight of their colleagues as guards. [39]Meanwhile the old Tabernacle of the Lord on the hill of Gibeon continued to be active. David left Zadok the priest and his fellow-priests to minister to the Lord there. [41]David also appointed Heman, Jeduthun, and several others who were chosen by name to give thanks to the Lord for his constant love and mercy. [42]They used their trumpets and cymbals to accompany the singers with loud praises to God.

1 Chron 23:3. At this time a census was taken of the men of the tribe of Levi who were thirty years or older. The total came to 38,000. [5]David instructed, ". . . Four thousand will be temple guards, and four thousand will praise the Lord with the musical instruments I have made." [6]Then David divided them into three main divisions named after the sons of Levi—the Gershom division, the Kohath division and the Merari division. [27](This census of the tribe of Levi was one of the last things David did before his death.) [30]Each morning and evening they stood before the Lord to sing thanks and praise to him.

1 Chron 25:1. David and the officials of the Tabernacle then appointed men to prophesy to the accompaniment of zithers, harps, and cymbals. These men were from the groups of Asaph, Heman, and Jeduthun. Here is a list of their names and their work: [*vs.* 2, 3.] [4,5]Under the direction of Heman, the king's private chaplain, were his sons. . . . (For God had honored him with fourteen sons and three daughters.) [6,7]Their music ministry included the playing of cymbals, harps, and zithers; all were under the direction of their father as they performed this ministry in the Tabernacle. Asaph, Jeduthun, and Heman reported directly to the king. They and their families were all trained in singing praises to the Lord; each one—288 of them in all—was a master musician. [8]The singers were appointed to their particular term of service by coin-toss, without regard to age or reputation. *vs.* 9–31.

2 Chron 5:12. The singers were Asaph, Heman, Jeduthun and all their sons and brothers, dressed in finespun linen robes and standing at the east side of the altar. The choir was accompanied by 120 priests who were trumpeters, while others played the cymbals, lyres, and harps. [13,14]The band and chorus united as one to praise and thank the Lord; their selections were interspersed with trumpet obbligatos, the clashing of cymbals, and the loud playing of other musical instruments—all praising and thanking the Lord. Their theme was "He is so good! His lovingkindness lasts forever!" And at that moment the glory of the Lord, coming as a bright cloud, filled the Temple.

2 Chron 20:19. Then the Levites of the Kohath clan and the Korah clan stood to praise the Lord God of Israel with songs of praise that rang out strong and clear. [21]After consultation with the leaders of the people, he determined that there should be a choir leading the march, clothed in sanctified garments and singing the song "His Lovingkindness Is Forever" as they walked along praising and thanking the Lord! [22]And at the moment they began to sing and to praise, the Lord caused the armies of Ammon, Moab, and Mount Seir to begin fighting among themselves, and they destroyed each other! [28]They marched into Jerusalem accompanied by a band of harps, lyres, and trumpets and proceeded to the Temple.

2 Chron 23:12. She rushed over to the Temple to see what was going on—and there stood the king by his pillar at the entrance, with the army officers and the trumpets surrounding him, and people from all over the land rejoicing and blowing trumpets, and the singers singing, accompanied by an orchestra leading the people in a great psalm of praise. Athaliah ripped her clothes and screamed, "Treason! Treason!" [18]Jehoiada now appointed the Levite priests as guards, and to sacrifice the burnt offering to the Lord as prescribed in the law of Moses. He made the identical assignments of the Levite clans that King David had. They sang with joy as they worked.

2 Chron 29:25, 26. He organized Levites at the Temple into an orchestral group, using cymbals, psalteries, and harps. This was in accordance with the directions of David and the prophets Gad and Nathan—who had received their instructions from the Lord. The priests formed a trumpet corps. [27]Then Hezekiah ordered the burnt offering to be placed upon the altar, and as the sacrifice began, the instruments of music began to play the songs of the Lord, accompanied by the trumpets. [28]Throughout the entire ceremony everyone worshiped the Lord as the singers sang and the trumpets blew.

2 Chron 31:2. Hezekiah now organized the priests and Levites into service corps to offer the burnt offerings and peace offerings, and to worship and give thanks and praise to the Lord.

2 Chron 35:15. The singers (the sons of Asaph) were in their places, following directions issued centuries earlier by King David, Asaph, Heman, and Jeduthun the king's prophet. The gatekeepers guarded the gates, and didn't need to leave their posts of duty, for their meals were brought to them by their Levite brothers. [25]And all Judah and Jerusalem, including even Jeremiah the prophet, mourned for him [Josiah], as did the Temple choirs. To this day they still sing sad songs about his death, for these songs of sorrow were recorded among the official lamentations.

Ezra 2:64. So a total of 42,360 persons returned to Judah; in addition to 7,337 slaves and 200 choir members, both men and women.

Ezra 3:10. When the builders completed the foundation of the Temple, the priests put on their priestly robes and blew their trumpets; and the descendants of Asaph crashed their cymbals to praise the Lord in the manner ordained by King David. [11]They sang rounds of praise and thanks to God, singing this song: "He is good, and his love and mercy toward Israel will last forever." Then all the people gave a great shout, praising God because the foundation of the Temple had been laid.

Neh 12:24. These were the chiefs of the Levites at that time: Hashabiah, Sherebiah, and Jeshua (son of Kadmi-el). Their fellow-clansmen helped them during the ceremonies of praise and thanksgiving just as commanded by David the man of God. [27]During the dedication of the new Jerusalem wall, all the Levites throughout the land came to Jerusalem to assist in the ceremonies and to take part in the joyous occasion with their thanksgiving, cymbals, psaltries, and harps. [28]The choir members also came to Jerusalem from the surrounding villages and from the villages of the Netophathites; [29]they also came from Beth-gilgal and the area of Geba and Azmaveth, for the singers had built their own villages as suburbs of Jerusalem. [30]The priests and Levites first dedicated themselves, then the people, the gates, and the wall. [31]I led the Judean leaders to the top of the wall and divided them into two long lines to walk in opposite directions along the top of the wall, giving thanks as they went. *vs.* 31–47.

Job 21:12. They spend their time singing and dancing.

Job 30:31. The voice of joy and gladness has turned to mourning.

Ps 33:1. Let all the joys of the godly well up in praise to the Lord, for it is right to praise him. [2]Play joyous melodies of praise upon the lyre and on the harp. [3]Compose new songs of praise to him, accompanied skillfully on the harp; sing joyfully. [4]For all God's words are right, and everything he does is worthy of our trust.

Ps 68:4. Sing praises to the Lord! Raise your voice in song to him who rides upon the clouds! Jehovah is his name—oh, rejoice in his presence. [25]Singers in front, musicians behind, girls playing the timbrels in between. [26]Let all the people of Israel praise the Lord, who is Israel's fountain. [32]Sing to the Lord, O kingdoms of the earth—sing praises to the Lord, [33]to him who rides upon the ancient heavens, whose mighty voice thunders from the sky. [34]Power belongs to God! His majesty shines down on Israel; his strength is mighty in the heavens. [35]What awe we feel, kneeling here before him in the sanctuary. The God of Israel gives strength and mighty power to his people. Blessed be God! *vs.* 1–35.

Ps 81:1. The Lord makes us strong! Sing praises! Sing to Israel's God! [2]Sing, accompanied by drums; pluck the sweet lyre and harp. [3]Sound the trumpet! Come to the joyous celebrations at full moon, new moon and all the other holidays.

Ps 87:7. And in the festivals they'll sing, "All my heart is in Jerusalem."

Ps 92:1. It is good to say, "Thank you" to the Lord, to sing praises to the God who is above all gods. [2]Every morning tell him, "Thank you for your kindness," and every evening rejoice in all his faithfulness. [3]Sing his praises, accompanied by music from the harp and lute and lyre.

Ps 98:1. Sing a new song to the Lord telling about his mighty deeds! For he has won a mighty victory by his power and holiness. [2,3]He has announced this victory and revealed it to every nation by fulfilling his promise to be kind to Israel. The whole earth has seen God's salvation of his people. [4]That is why the earth breaks out in praise to God and sings for utter joy! [5]Sing your praise accompanied by music from the harp. [6]Let the cornets and trumpets shout! Make a joyful symphony before the Lord the King! [7]Let the sea in all its vastness roar with praise! Let the earth and all those living on it shout, "Glory to the Lord." [8]Let the waves clap their hands in glee, and the hills sing out their songs of joy before the Lord.

Ps 104:33. I will sing to the Lord as long as I live. I will praise God to my last breath!

Ps 105:2. Sing his praises and tell everyone about his miracles.

Ps 135:1, 2. Hallelujah! Yes, let his people praise him as they stand in his Temple courts. [3]Praise the Lord because he is so good; sing to his wonderful name.

Ps 137:1. Weeping, we sat beside the rivers of Babylon thinking of Jerusalem. [2]We have put away our lyres, hanging them upon the branches of the willow trees, [3,4]for how can we sing? Yet our captors, our tormentors, demand that we sing for them the happy songs of Zion! [5,6]If I forget you, O Jerusalem, let my right hand forget its skill upon the harp. If I fail to love her more than my highest joy, let me never sing again.

Ps 144:9. I will sing you a new song, O God, with a ten-stringed harp.

Ps 149:1. Hallelujah! Yes, praise the Lord! Sing him a new song. Sing his praises, all his people. [2]O Israel, rejoice in your Maker. O people of Jerusalem, exult in your King. [3]Praise his name with dancing, accompanied by drums and lyre. [6]Adore him, O his people!

Ps 150:1. Hallelujah! Yes, praise the Lord! Praise him in his Temple, and in the heavens he made with mighty power. [2]Praise him for his mighty works. Praise his unequaled greatness. [3]Praise him with the trumpet and with lute and harp. [4]Praise him with the tambourines and processional. Praise him with stringed instruments and horns. [5]Praise him with the cymbals, yes, loud clanging cymbals. [6]Let everything alive give praises to the Lord! *You* praise him! Hallelujah!

Eccl 2:8. In the cultural arts, I organized men's and women's choirs and orchestras.

Isa 5:12. You furnish lovely music at your grand parties; the orchestras are superb! But for the Lord you have no thought or care.

Isa 14:11. Your might and power are gone; they are buried with you. All the pleasant music in your palace has ceased; now maggots are your sheet, worms your blanket!

Isa 16:10. Gone now is the gladness, gone the joy of harvest. The happy singing in the vineyards will be heard no more; the treading out of the grapes in the wine presses has ceased forever. I have ended all their harvest joys.

Isa 23:16. She will sing sweet songs as a harlot sings who, long absent from her lovers, walks the streets to look for them again and is remembered.

Isa 24:8. The melodious chords of the harp and timbrel are heard no more; the happy days are ended. [9]No more are the joys of wine and song; strong drink turns bitter in the mouth.

Isa 30:29. But the people of God will sing a song of solemn joy, like songs in the night when holy feasts are held; his people will have gladness of heart, as when a flutist leads a pilgrim band to Jerusalem to the Mountain of the Lord, the Rock of Israel. [32]And when the Lord smites them, his people will rejoice with music and song. Jer 31:4.

Ezk 26:13. I will stop the music of your songs. No more will there be the sound of harps among you.

Ezk 33:32. You are very entertaining to them, like someone who sings lovely songs with a beautiful voice or plays well on an instrument. They hear what you say but don't pay any attention to it!

Dan 3:4. A herald shouted out, "O people of all nations and languages, this is the king's command: [5]When the band strikes up, you are to fall flat on the ground to worship King Nebuchadnezzar's golden statue; [6]anyone who refuses to obey will immediately be thrown into a flaming furnace." [7]So when the band began to play, everyone—whatever his nation, language, or religion—fell to the ground and worshiped the statue. *vs.* 10–16.

Amos 6:5. You sing idle songs to the sound of the harp, and fancy yourselves to be as great musicians as King David was.

Amos 8:10. And I will turn your parties into times of mourning, and your songs of joy will be turned to cries of despair.

Mt 9:23. Jesus arrived at the rabbi's home and saw the noisy crowds and heard the funeral music.

Mt 11:17. We played wedding and you weren't happy, so we played funeral but you weren't sad.

Mk 14:26. Then they sang a hymn and went out to the Mount of Olives.

1 Cor 14:15. I will sing in unknown tongues and also in ordinary language, so that I can understand the praise I am giving.

Eph 5:19. Talk with each other much about the Lord, quoting psalms and hymns and singing sacred songs, making music in your hearts to the Lord.

Col 3:16. Remember what Christ taught and let his words enrich your lives and make you wise; teach them to each other and sing them out in psalms and hymns and spiritual songs, singing to the Lord with thankful hearts.

Heb 2:12. For he says in the book of Psalms, "I will talk to my brothers about God my Father, and together we will sing his praises."

Rev 14:2. And I heard a sound from heaven like the roaring of a great waterfall or the rolling of mighty thunder. It was the singing of a choir accompanied by harps. [3]This tremendous choir—144,000 strong—sang a wonderful new song in front of the throne of God and before the four Living Beings and the twenty-four Elders; and no one could sing this song except those 144,000 who had been redeemed from the earth.

Rev 18:22. Never again will the sound of music be there—no more pianos, saxophones, and trumpets. No industry of any kind will ever again exist there, and there will be no more milling of the grain.

See *Praise; Psalms.*

MUSTARD Mt 13:31, 32; 17:20; Mk 4:30–33; Lk 13:19; 17:6.

MUSTER Of troops, Josh 22:12; Judg 3:27; 1 Sam 14:17; 17:1; 28:1; 2 Sam 20:4; 1 Kgs 20:15, 26, 27; 2 Kgs 3:6–8; 6:24; 14:11; 25:19; Isa 13:4; Nah 2: 1.

See *Armies.*

MUTINY Israelites against Moses, Num 14:4. See *Conspiracy.*

MYRA A city of Lycia. Paul visits, Acts 27: 5.

MYRRH A fragrant gum. A product of the land of Canaan, Song 4:6, 13, 14; 5:1. One of the compounds in the holy anointing oil, Ex 30:22, 23. Used as a perfume, Esther 2:12–14; Ps 45:8; Prov 7: 16, 17; Song 1:13; 3:6; 5:13. Brought by wise men as a present to Jesus, Mt 2:11. Used for embalming, Jn 19:39. Traffic in, Gen 37:25; 43:11. Tribute paid in, 1 Kgs 10:25.

MYRTLE Neh 8:15; Isa 41:19; 55:13; Zech 1:8.

MYSIA A province of Asia Minor, Paul visits, Acts 16:7, 8.

MYSTERIES AND SECRETS Deut 29: 29. There are secrets the Lord your God has not revealed to us, but these words which he has revealed are for us and our children to obey forever.

Job 15:8. Have you heard the secret counsel of

God? Are you called into his counsel room? Do you have a monopoly on wisdom?

Ps 25:14. Friendship with God is reserved for those who reverence him. With them alone he shares the secrets of his promises.

Mt 11:25. And Jesus prayed this prayer: "O Father, Lord of heaven and earth, thank you for hiding the truth from those who think themselves so wise, and for revealing it to little children."

Mt 13:11. Then he explained to them that only they were permitted to understand about the Kingdom of Heaven, and others were not. [35]He never spoke to them without at least one illustration. For it had been prophesied, "I will talk in parables; I will explain mysteries hidden since the beginning of time."

Mk 4:11. He replied, "You are permitted to know some truths about the Kingdom of God that are hidden to those outside the Kingdom."

Lk 8:10. He replied, "God has granted you to know the meaning of these parables, for they tell a great deal about the Kingdom of God. But these crowds hear the words and do not understand, just as the ancient prophets predicted."

Jn 3:8. "Just as you can hear the wind but can't tell where it comes from or where it will go next, so it is with the Spirit. We do not know on whom he will next bestow this life from heaven." [9]"What do you mean?" Nicodemus asked. [10,11]Jesus replied, "You, a respected Jewish teacher, and yet you don't understand these things? I am telling you what I know and have seen—and yet you won't believe me. [12]But if you don't even believe me when I tell you about such things as these that happen here among men, how can you possibly believe if I tell you what is going on in heaven?"

Rom 16:25, 26. I commit you to God, who is able to make you strong and steady in the Lord, just as the Gospel says, and just as I have told you. This is God's plan of salvation for you Gentiles, kept secret from the beginning of time. But now as the prophets foretold and as God commands, this message is being preached everywhere, so that people all around the world will have faith in Christ and obey him.

1 Cor 2:7. Our words are wise because they are from God, telling of God's wise plan to bring us into the glories of heaven. This plan was hidden in former times, though it was made for our benefit before the world began. [8]But the great men of the world have not understood it; if they had, they never would have crucified the Lord of Glory. [9]That is what is meant by the Scriptures which say that no mere man has ever seen, heard or even imagined what wonderful things God has ready for those who love the Lord. [10]But we know about these things because God has sent his Spirit to tell us, and his Spirit searches out and shows us all of God's deepest secrets.

2 Cor 3:12. Since we know that this new glory will never go away, we can preach with great boldness, [13]and not as Moses did, who put a veil over his face so that the Israelis could not see the glory fade away. [14]Not only Moses' face was veiled, but his people's minds and understanding were veiled and blinded too. Even now when the Scripture is read it seems as though Jewish hearts and minds are covered by a thick veil, because they cannot see and understand the real meaning of the Scriptures. For this veil of misunderstanding can be removed only by believing in Christ. [15]Yes, even today when they read Moses' writings their hearts are blind and they think that obeying the Ten Commandments is the way to be saved. [16]But whenever anyone turns to the Lord from his sins, then the veil is taken away. [17]The Lord is the Spirit who gives them life, and where he is there is freedom (from trying to be saved by keeping the laws of God). [18]But we Christians have no veil over our faces; we can be mirrors that brightly reflect the glory of the Lord. And as the Spirit of the Lord works within us, we become more and more like him.

Eph 1:9. God has told us his secret reason for sending Christ, a plan he decided on in mercy long ago; [10]and this was his purpose: that when the time is ripe he will gather us all together from wherever we are—in heaven or on earth—to be with him in Christ, forever.

Eph 3:3. God himself showed me this secret plan of his, that the Gentiles, too, are included in his kindness. [4]I say this to explain to you how I know about these things. [5]In olden times God did not share this plan with his people, but now he has revealed it by the Holy Spirit to his apostles and prophets. [9]And to explain to everyone that God is the Savior of the Gentiles too, just as he who made all things had secretly planned from the very beginning. [18,19]And may you be able to feel and understand, as all God's children should, how long, how wide, how deep, and how high his love really is; and to experience this love for yourselves, though it is so great that you will never see the end of it or fully know or understand it. And so at last you will be filled up with God himself.

Eph 6:19. Pray for me, too, and ask God to give me the right words as I boldly tell others about the Lord, and as I explain to them that his salvation is for the Gentiles too.

Col 1:25. God has sent me to help his church and to tell his secret plan to you Gentiles. [26,27]He has kept this secret for centuries and generations past, but now at last it has pleased him to tell it to those who love him and live for him, and the riches and glory of his plan are for you Gentiles too. And this is the secret: *that Christ in your hearts is your only hope of glory.*

Col 2:2. This is what I have asked of God for you: that you will be encouraged and knit together by strong ties of love, and that you will have the rich experience of knowing Christ with real certainty and clear understanding. *For God's secret plan, now at last made known, is Christ himself.*

Col 4:3. Don't forget to pray for us too, that God will give us many chances to preach the Good News of Christ for which I am here in jail. [4]Pray that I will be bold enough to tell it freely and fully, and make it plain, as, of course, I should.

2 Thess 2:7. As for the work this man of rebellion and hell will do when he comes, it is already going on, but he himself will not come until the one who is holding him back steps out of the way.

1 Tim 3:9. They must be earnest, wholehearted followers of Christ who is the hidden Source of their faith. [16]It is quite true that the way to live a godly life is not an easy matter. But the answer lies in Christ, who came to earth as a man, was proved spotless and pure in his Spirit, was served by angels, was preached among the nations, was accepted by men everywhere and was received up again to his glory in heaven.

Heb 5:11. There is much more I would like to say along these lines, but you don't seem to listen, so it's hard to make you understand.

1 Pet 1:10. This salvation was something the prophets did not fully understand. Though they wrote about it, they had many questions as to what it all could mean. [11]They wondered what the Spirit of Christ within them was talking about, for he told them to write down the events which, since then, have happened to Christ: his suffering, and his great glory afterwards. And they wondered when and to whom all this would happen. [12]They were finally told that these things would not occur during their lifetime, but long years later, during yours. And now at last this Good News has been plainly announced to all of us. It was preached to us in the power of the same heaven-sent Holy Spirit who spoke to them; and it is all so strange and wonderful that even the angels in heaven would give a great deal to know more about it.

Rev 10:7. But that when the seventh angel blew his trumpet, then God's veiled plan—mysterious through the ages ever since it was announced by his servants the prophets—would be fulfilled.

See *Church, the True.*

MYTH See *Fable.*

N

NAAM Son of Caleb, 1 Chron 4:15.

NAAMAH 1. A wife of Solomon and mother of King Rehoboam, 1 Kgs 14:21, 31; 2 Chron 12:13.

2. A city of Judah, Josh 15:37–44.

NAAMAN 1. Descendant of Benjamin, Gen 46:19–22; Num 26:38–41; 1 Chron 8:3–5.

2. Son of Ehud, 1 Chron 8:6, 7.

3. A Syrian general, healed of leprosy by Elisha, 2 Kgs 5:1–23; Lk 4:27.

NAARAH 1. A wife of Ashhur, 1 Chron 4:5, 6.

2. A city on the southern boundary of Ephraim, Josh 16:7.

NAARAI Called also *Paarai.* One of David's heroes, 2 Sam 23:24–39; 1 Chron 11:26–47.

NAARAN A city in the eastern limits of Ephraim, 1 Chron 7:28.

NABAL Husband of Abigail. History of, 1 Sam 25:2–38.

NABOTH A Jezreelite. His vineyard forcibly taken by Ahab; stoned at the instigation of Jezebel, 1 Kgs 21:1–19. His murder avenged, 2 Kgs 9:21–36.

NACHON Called also *Chidon.* Uzzah killed at the threshing floor of, 2 Sam 6:6, 7; 1 Chron 13:9.

NADAB 1. Son of Aaron, Ex 6:23. Called to Mount Sinai with Moses and Aaron to worship, Ex 24:1, 9, 10. Consecrated to priesthood, Ex 28:1, 4, 40–43. Offers unholy fire to God, and is destroyed, Lev 10:1, 2; Num 3:4; 26:61. Is buried, Lev 10:4, 5. His father and brothers forbidden to mourn, Lev 10:6, 7.

2. Son and successor of Jeroboam, 1 Kgs 14:20. His wicked reign; murdered by Baasha, 1 Kgs 15: 25–31.

3. Great-grandson of Jerahmeel, 1 Chron 2: 28, 30.

4. A Benjaminite, 1 Chron 8:30–32; 9:35–37.

NAGGAI An ancestor of Jesus, Lk 3:23–38.

NAHALAL Called also *Nahalol.* A Levitical city, Josh 19:15, 16; 21:34, 35; Judg 1:30.

NAHALIEL A stopping place of the Israelites, Num 21:19.

NAHAM Brother of Hodiah's wife, 1 Chron 4:19.

NAHAMANI A Jewish exile, Neh 7:7.

NAHARAI Called also *Nahari.* One of David's heroes, 2 Sam 23:24–39; 1 Chron 11:26–47.

NAHASH 1. An Ammonite king. Defeated by Saul at Jabesh-gilead, 1 Sam 11:1–11. Kindness of, to David, and death, 2 Sam 10:1, 2; 1 Chron 19:1, 2.

2. Father of Abigail, 2 Sam 17:25.

NAHATH 1. Son of Reuel, Gen 36:13, 14, 17; 1 Chron 1:37.

2. Called also *Toah* and *Tohu.* A Levite, 1 Chron 6:25–27, 33–38; 1 Sam 1:1.

3. A Levite and overseer of the sacred supplies, 2 Chron 31:12, 13.

NAHBI A leader of Naphtali, and one of the 12 spies, Num 13:3–15.

NAHOR 1. Grandfather of Abraham, Gen 11: 22–26; 1 Chron 1:24–27. In the lineage of Christ, Lk 3:23–38.

2. Brother of Abraham, Gen 11:26; Josh 24:2. Marriage and descendants of, Gen 11:29; 22:20–24; 24:15, 16, 24.

NAHSHON Son of Amminadab, Ex 6:23; Num 1:2–15; 1 Chron 2:10. A leader of Judah, Num 2:3–31; 10:14; 1 Chron 2:10. Liberality of, Num 7: 12–17. In the lineage of Christ, Mt 1:4; Lk 3:23–38.

NAHUM One of the minor prophets. Prophesies against the Assyrians; declares the majesty of God and his care for his people, Nah 1. Foretells the destruction of Nineveh, Nah chapters 2; 3.

NAIL Jer 10:4. Made of bronze, Ex 38:20, 29; of iron, 1 Chron 22:3; of gold, 2 Chron 3:9. Jael kills Sisera with, Judg 4:21.

FIGURATIVE. Isa 22:23–25; Zech 10:4.

NAIN A city in Galilee. Jesus restores to life a widow's son in, Lk 7:11.

NAIOTH A place in Ramah, 1 Sam 19:18, 19, 22; 20:1.

NAME Value of a good, Prov 22:1; Eccl 7:1. A new name given to the people of Israel, Isa 61:6; 62: 2. To Abraham, Gen 17:5; Sarah, Gen 17:15; Jacob, Gen 32:28. For prayer in the name of the Lord Jesus Christ, see *Jesus Christ, Names and Titles of, In his Name.*

Symbolical. Hos 1:3–6, 9; 2:1.

NAMES OF GOD God, Gen 1:1, meaning *Elohim,* or *El,* "the strong one;" Lord, Gen 15:2, 3, meaning *Adonai,* "Master;" and Lord, or God, Gen 2:4, meaning *Jehovah,* or "the self-existent one;" Almighty, Gen 17:1, or *El Shaddai,* "Giver of strength;" God of Highest Heaven, Gen 14:18, or

El Elyon, "God the highest;" Eternal God, Gen 21:33, or *El Olam,* "the eternally existent One;" Mighty God, Isa 9:6, or *El Gibbor,* "the powerful One;" Lord God, Gen 2:4, or *Jehovah Elohim;* Lord Jehovah, Gen 15:2, 3, or *Adonai Jehovah;* and Lord of the heavens, 1 Sam 1:3, or *Jehovah Sabaoth* (with reference to the armies under his command, found primarily in prophecy). See *Jehovah.*

NAMES OF JESUS See *Jesus, Names and Titles of.*

NAOMI Wife of Elimelech; mother-in-law of Ruth; lived in Moab; returns to Bethlehem; relative of Boaz, Ruth chapters 1–4.

NAPHISH A son of Ishmael, Gen 25:12–15; 1 Chron 1:28–31.

NAPHTALI 1. Son of Jacob and Bilhah, Gen 30:7, 8; 35:25. Jacob blesses, Gen 49:21. Sons of, Gen 46:23–25; 1 Chron 7:13.

2. Tribe of. Census of, Num 1:20–46; 26:48–50. Position assigned to, in camp and march, Num 2:3–31; 10:25–27. Moses's blessing on, Deut 33:23. Inheritance of, Josh 19:32–39; Judg 1:33; Ezk 48:3.

Defeat Sisera, Judg 4:6, 10; 5:18. Follow Gideon, Judg 6:35; 7:23. Aid in conveying the ark to Jerusalem, Ps 68:27. Military operations of, 1 Chron 12:24–37, 40; against, 1 Kgs 15:20; 2 Kgs 15:29; 2 Chron 16:4.

Prophecies concerning, Isa 9:1, 2; Rev 7:4–8.

NAPHTUHIM The inhabitants of central Egypt, Gen 10:13, 14; 1 Chron 1:11, 12.

NARCISSUS HOUSE Believers at Rome, Rom 16:11.

NARD An aromatic plant, Song 4:13, 14. A fragrant oil from, used in anointing, Jn 12:30.

NATHAN 1. Son of David and Bathsheba, 2 Sam 5:14–16; 1 Chron 3:5; 14:4–7. He was one of the ancestors of Mary, mother of the Lord, Lk 3:23–38.

2. A prophet in the time of David. His message to David concerning the building of a temple, 2 Sam 7:1–17; 1 Chron 17:1–15. Reproves David for his adultery with Bath-sheba and his murder of Uriah, 2 Sam 12:1–15. Assists Bath-sheba in securing for Solomon, her son, succession to the throne, 1 Kgs 1:10–14, 22–27. Assists in anointing Solomon, 1 Kgs 1:32–45.

Wrote histories, 1 Chron 29:29; 2 Chron 9:29. Assists David in the organization of the Temple, 2 Chron 29:25, 26.

3. An inhabitant of Zobah in Syria; father of Igal, one of David's men, 2 Sam 23:24–39.

4. Father of Azariah and Zabud, 1 Kgs 4:1–6.

5. Son of Attai, father of Zabad, a descendant of Judah, 1 Chron 2:36.

6. A Jew sent by Ezra from the Ahava River to Casiphia, Ezra 8:16; perhaps the same as the Nathan of Ezra 10:34–42.

NATHANAEL Becomes a disciple of Jesus, Jn 1:45–49; 21:2.

NATHAN-MELECH An idolatrous eunuch, 2 Kgs 23:11.

NATIONS Sins of, Isa 30:1, 2. Punished, Isa 14:26, 27; Jer 5:29; 18:6–10; 25:12–33; Ezk 2:3–5; 39:23, 24; Dan 7:9–12; 9:3–16; Hos 7:12; Joel 1:1–20; Amos 9:9; Zeph 3:6, 8. Perish, Ps 9:17; Isa 60:12.

National adversity, prayer in, Judg 21:2–4; 2 Chron 7:13, 14; Ps 74; Joel 2:12; lamented, Ezra 9; Neh 1:4–11; Jer 6:14; 8:11, 20, 21; 9:1, 2. See *Sin, National.*

Prayer for, Ps 85:1–7; Lam 2:20–22; 5; Dan 9:3–21.

Involved in sins of rulers, Gen 20:4, 9, 10; 2 Sam 24:10–17; 1 Chron 21:7–17; of other individuals, as Achan, Josh 7:1, 11–26.

Peace of, Job 34:29, 30; Ps 33:12; 89:14–18. Promises of peace to, Lev 26:6; 1 Kgs 2:33; 2 Kgs 20:19; 1 Chron 22:9; Ps 29:11; 46:9; 72:3, 7; 128:6; Isa 2:4; 14:4–7; 60:17, 18; 65:25; Jer 30:10; 50:34; Ezk 34:25–28; Hos 2:18; Mic 4:3, 4; Zech 1:11; 3:10; 8:4, 5; 9:10; 14:11. Prayer for peace, Jer 29:7; 1 Tim 2:1, 2. Peace given by God, Josh 21:44; 1 Chron 22:18; 23:25; Ps 147:13, 14; Eccl 3:8; Isa 45:7. Instances of national peace, Josh 14:15; Judg 3:11, 30; 1 Kgs 4:24, 25. See *War.*

Godliness exalts, Prov 14:34.

Principles determining their destiny: Relationship to God, Ps 33:12; 9:17; Isa 60:12; Jer 49:17; Zeph 2:5. Relationship to the law, Prov 14:34; Gen 15:16; 19:13; Mt 24:12. God's purpose to save individuals, 2 Pet 3:9, 15, 16; Acts 15:14; Lk 24:47. Satan weakens and deceives nations, Rev 12:9; Isa 14:12; Dan 10:13, 20, 21. Relationship to Israel, Deut 32:8, 9; Gen 12:3; 26:4. Relationship to Jerusalem, Lk 21:24; cf. 21:10, 25.

Why God has withheld judgment: to save men, 1 Pet 3:8–10; to permit worldwide preaching, Lk 24:47; Acts 1:8; there is a predetermined time, 2 Cor 6:2; Gal 4:4; Rev 12:9.

Nations named in the end time, Ezk 38:1–6; Isa 19:17. All nations existing at that time, Jer 25:26.

Nations during the tribulation: Lose all their Christians, Jn 14:2, 3; 1 Thess 4:17. Lose the presence of the Holy Spirit, 2 Thess 2:7. Are governed by a world dictator, Rev 13:1–8. Distress and perplexity of, Lk 21:25. Demon control, Rev 16:14. Invade the land of Palestine, Zech 14:1, 2; Rev 16:14–16. Lose all their Jews, Ezk 36:24; 39:28. Many individuals saved, Rev 7:9, 13–17. Judged by the Lord, Joel 3:2, 11–14; Mt 25:31–46.

Nations during the kingdom: Ruled by Christ, Ps 22:28; Zech 14:9; Isa 2:4. Call Israel blessed, Mal 3:12; Ps 72:17. Worship and service, Rev 15:3, 4; Zech 2:11, 12; Mic 4:2. Missionary activity, Isa 66:19; 49:6; Ps 67:1, 2.

Nations in eternity: To continue forever, Rev 21:24, 26; 22:2; Isa 66:22, 23.

Remarkable place of prayer in prophecy concerning the nations: Ps 106:47; Isa 64:1, 2; Jer 10:25; Ps 9:19; Ps 2:8; Rev 22:20.

See *Gentiles; Heathen; Government; King; Ruler.*

NATURAL MAN The unsaved man, governed by his senses rather than by the Holy Spirit, 1 Cor 2:14; distinguished from spiritual and carnal Christians, 1 Cor 2:15; 3:1.

NATURALIZATION Acts 22:28; Eph 2:12, 19.

NATURAL RELIGION See *Religion, Natural.*

NAVIGATION Sounding in, Acts 27:28. See *Commerce; Navy; Sailor.*

NAVEL Song 7:2. Treatment of, at birth, Ezk 16:4.

NAVY Solomon's, 1 Kgs 9:26; Hiram's, 1 Kgs 10:11; Jehoshaphat's, 1 Kgs 22:48; of Cyprus, Dan 11:30, 31, 40.

See *Commerce; Navigation; Sailor.*

NAZARENE See *Nazareth.*

NAZARETH A village in Galilee. Joseph and Mary live in, Mt 2:23; Lk 1:26, 27; 2:4, 39, 51. Jesus from, Mt 21:11; Mk 1:24; 10:47; Lk 4:34; 18:37; 24:19. People of, reject Jesus, Lk 4:16–30. Its reputation questionable, Jn 1:46.

NAZIRITE Law concerning, Num 6:1–21; Judg 13:5. Character of, Lam 4:7; Amos 2:11, 12.

INSTANCES OF. Samson, Judg 13:5, 7; 16: 16, 17. Samuel, 1 Sam 1:11. Rechabites, Jer 35. John the Baptist, Mt 11:18; Lk 1:15; 7:33.

NEAH A city in Zebulun, Josh 19:13.

NEAPOLIS A seaport of Macedonia. Paul visits, Acts 16:11.

NEARIAH 1. Son of Shemaiah, 1 Chron 3: 21–23.

2. A Simeonite leader, 1 Chron 4:42.

NEBAIOTH Son of Ishmael, Gen 25:12–15; 28:9; 36:2, 3; 1 Chron 1:28–31. Prophecies concerning, Isa 60:7.

NEBALLAT A town occupied by the Benjaminites after the captivity, Neh 11:31–35.

NEBAT Father of Jeroboam, 1 Kgs 11:26; 2 Chron 9:29.

NEBO 1. A city allotted to Reuben, Num 32: 3, 4, 37, 38; 1 Chron 5:7, 8. Prophecies concerning, Isa 15:2; Jer 48:1, 22.

2. A mountain east of the Jordan. Moses views Canaan from, Deut 32:49, 50; dies on, Deut 34:1, 5.

3. A city in Judah, Ezra 2:3–35; Neh 7:8–38.

4. The ancestor of certain Jews, Ezra 10:43.

5. A Babylonian idol, Isa 46:1, 2.

NEBUCHADNEZZAR King of Babylon, Jer 21:1, 2. Empire of, see *Babylon.* His administration, Dan chapters 1–4. Conquests of: Of Jerusalem, 2 Kgs 25:4, 5; 1 Chron 6:4–15; 2 Chron 36:5–21; Ezra 1:7; Jer 39. Of Egypt, 2 Kgs 24:7; Jer 46:2. Of Tyre, Ezk 29:18. Became a believer, Dan 4:34–37. An instrument of God's judgments, Jer 27:8. Prophecies concerning, Jer 21:7, 10; 22:24, 25; 25:8, 9; 27:6–9; 32:28; 43:10; 46:13; 49:30–33; Ezk 26:7–12.

NEBUSHAZBAN Chief eunuch under Nebuchadnezzar, Jer 39:13.

NEBUZARADAN Captain of the guard of King Nebuchadnezzar. Commands the Assyrian army which besieged Jerusalem and took the inhabitants to Babylon, 2 Kgs 25:8–21; Jer 39:9, 10; 43:6; 52:12–30. Protects Jeremiah, Jer 39:11–14; 40: 1–5.

NECKLACE Ex 35:22; Num 31:50; Song 4:9; Isa 3:19; Ezk 16:11.

FIGURATIVE. Ps 73:6.

See *Chains.*

NECO King of Egypt, 2 Chron 35:20, 22; 36: 4. See *Pharaoh, 8.*

NECROMANCY Deut 18:11; 26:14; Isa 8:19; 29:4.

INSTANCE OF. The witch of En-dor, 1 Sam 28: 7–19.

See *Sorcery; Witchcraft.*

NEDABIAH Son of Jeconiah, 1 Chron 3:17, 18.

NEEDLE Mt 19:24; Mk 10:25; Lk 18:25.

NEEDLEWORK See *Embroidery.*

NEGEB A triangular desert region in southern Israel, also rendered "south," Gen 12:9; 13:1; Deut 33:23; Job 37:9; Ezk 20:46; Zech 14:4.

NEHEMIAH 1. Son of Hecaliah, Neh 1:1. Cupbearer of Ar-ta-xerxes, Neh 1:11; 2:1, 2. Is grieved over the desolation of his country, Neh 1. Is sent by the king to rebuild Jerusalem, Neh 2:1–8. List of the people whom he led from Babylon, Neh 7; and of the priests and Levites, Neh 12:1–22. Rebuilds Jerusalem, Neh chapters 2–6. His administration as ruler of the people, Neh chapters 5; 6; 8; 9; 10; 11; 13.

2. Two Jews who returned to Jerusalem from exile, Ezra 2:2; Neh 7:7; and Neh 3:16.

NEHUM A chief exile, Neh 7:7.

NEHUSHTA Wife of Jehoiakim, king of Judah, and mother of Jehoiachin, 2 Kgs 24:6, 8, 9.

NEIEL A landmark on the boundary of Asher, Josh 19:27.

NEIGHBOR Ex 20:17. You must not be envious of your neighbor's house, or want to sleep with his wife, or want to own his slaves, oxen, donkeys, or anything else he has.

Ex 23:4. If you come upon an enemy's ox or donkey that has strayed away, you must take it back to its owner. [5]If you see your enemy trying to get his donkey onto its feet beneath a heavy load, you must not go on by, but must help him.

Lev 6:2. If anyone sins against me by refusing to return a deposit on something borrowed or rented, or by refusing to return something entrusted to him, or by robbery, or by oppressing his neighbor, [3]or by finding a lost article and lying about it, swearing that he doesn't have it— [4, 5]on the day he is found guilty of any such sin, he shall restore what he took, adding a twenty percent fine, and give it to the one he has harmed; and on the same day he shall bring his guilt offering to the Tabernacle.

Lev 19:13. You shall not rob nor oppress anyone, and you shall pay your hired workers promptly. If something is due them, don't even keep it overnight. [16]Don't gossip. Don't falsely accuse your neighbor of some crime, for I am Jehovah. [17]Don't hate your brother. Rebuke anyone who sins; don't let him get away with it, or you will be equally guilty.

18. Don't seek vengeance. Don't bear a grudge; but love your neighbor as yourself, for I am Jehovah. Mt 19:19; 22:38, 39; Mk 12:31; Lk 10:27; Rom 13:9; Gal 5:14; Jas 2:8.

Deut 22:1. If you see someone's ox or sheep wandering away, don't pretend you didn't see it; take it back to its owner. [2]If you don't know who the owner is, take it to your farm and keep it there until the owner comes looking for it, and then give it to him. [3]The same applies to donkeys, clothing, or anything else you find. Keep it for its owner. [4]If you see someone trying to get an ox or donkey onto its feet when it has slipped beneath its load, don't look the other way. Go and help!

Ps 15:1. Lord, who may go and find refuge and shelter in your tabernacle up on your holy hill? [2]Anyone who leads a blameless life and is truly sincere. [3]Anyone who refuses to slander others, does not listen to gossip, never harms his neighbor.

Prov 3:29. Don't plot against your neighbor; he is trusting you.

Prov 11:12. To quarrel with a neighbor is foolish; a man with good sense holds his tongue. Prov 25: 8–10.

Prov 24:28, 29. Don't testify spitefully against an innocent neighbor. Why lie about him? Don't say, "Now I can pay him back for all his meanness to me!"

Isa 58:6. No, the kind of fast I want is that you stop oppressing those who work for you and treat them fairly and give them what they earn. [7]I want you to share your food with the hungry and bring right into your own homes those who are helpless, poor and destitute. Clothe those who are cold and don't hide from relatives who need your help. [8]If you do these things, God will shed his own glorious light upon you. He will heal you; your godliness will lead you forward, and goodness will be a shield before you, and the glory of the Lord will protect you from behind. [9]Then, when you call, the Lord will answer. "Yes, I am here," he will quickly reply. All you need to do is to stop oppressing the weak, and to stop making false accusations and spreading vicious rumors! [10]Feed the hungry! Help those in trouble! Then your light will shine out from the darkness, and the darkness around you shall be as bright as day. [11]And the Lord will guide you continually, and satisfy you with all good things, and keep you healthy too; and you will be like a well-watered garden, like an ever-flowing spring. [12]Your sons will rebuild the long-deserted ruins of your cities, and you will be known as "The People Who Rebuild Their Walls and Cities." [13]If you keep the Sabbath holy, not having your own fun and business on that day, but enjoying the Sabbath and speaking of it with delight as the Lord's holy day, and honoring the Lord in what you do, not following your own desires and pleasure, nor talking idly— [14]then the Lord will be your delight, and I will see to it that you ride high, and get your full share of the blessings I promised to Jacob, your father. The Lord has spoken.

Zech 8:16. "Here is your part: Tell the truth. Be fair. Live at peace with everyone. [17]Don't plot harm to others; don't swear that something is true when it isn't! How I hate all that sort of thing!" says the Lord.

Mt 7:12. Do for others what you want them to do for you. This is the teaching of the laws of Moses in a nutshell.

Mt 25:34. Then I, the King, shall say to those at my right, "Come, blessed of my Father, into the Kingdom prepared for you from the founding of the world. [35]For I was hungry and you fed me; I was thirsty and you gave me water; I was a stranger and you invited me into your homes; [36]naked and you clothed me; sick and in prison, and you visited me." [37]Then these righteous ones will reply, "Sir, when did we ever see you hungry and feed you? Or thirsty and give you anything to drink? [38]Or a stranger, and help you? Or naked, and clothe you? [39]When did we ever see you sick or in prison, and visit you?" [40]And I, the King, will tell them, "When you did it to these my brothers you were doing it to me!" [41]Then I will turn to those on my left and say, "Away with you, you cursed ones, into the eternal fire prepared for the devil and his demons. [42]For I was hungry and you wouldn't feed me; thirsty, and you wouldn't give me anything to drink; [43]a stranger, and you refused me hospitality; naked, and you wouldn't clothe me; sick, and in prison, and you didn't visit me." [44]Then they will reply, "Lord, when did we ever see you hungry or thirsty or a stranger or naked or sick or in prison, and not help you?" [45]And I will answer, "When you refused to help the least of these my brothers, you were refusing help to me." [46]And they shall go away into eternal punishment; but the righteous into everlasting life.

Lk 10:25. One day an expert on Moses' laws came to test Jesus' orthodoxy by asking him this question: "Teacher, what does a man need to do to live forever in heaven?" [26]Jesus replied, "What does Moses' law say about it?" [27]"It says," he replied, "that you must love the Lord your God with all your heart, and with all your soul, and with all your strength, and with all your mind. And you must love your neighbor just as much as you love yourself." [28]"Right!" Jesus told him. "*Do* this and *you* shall live!" [29]The man wanted to justify (his lack of love for some kinds of people), so he asked, "Which neighbors?" [30]Jesus replied with an illustration: "A Jew going on a trip from Jerusalem to Jericho was attacked by bandits. They stripped him of his clothes and money and beat him up and left him lying half dead beside the road. [31]By chance a Jewish priest came along; and when he saw the man lying there, he crossed to the other side of the road and passed him by. [32]A Jewish Temple-assistant walked over and looked at him lying there, but then went on. [33]But a despised Samaritan came along, and when he saw him, he felt deep pity. [34]Kneeling beside him the Samaritan soothed his wounds with medicine and bandaged them. Then he put the man on his donkey and walked along beside him till they came to an inn, where he nursed him through the night. [35]The next day he handed the innkeeper two twenty-dollar bills and told him to take care of the man. 'If his bill runs higher than that,' he said, 'I'll pay the difference the next time I am here.' [36]Now which of these three would you say was a neighbor to the bandits' victim?" [37]The man replied, "The one who showed him some pity." Then Jesus said, "Yes, now go and do the same."

Rom 13:10. Love does no wrong to anyone. That's why it fully satisfies all of God's requirements. It is the only law you need.

Rom 15:2. Let's please the other fellow, not ourselves, and do what is for his good and thus build him up in the Lord.

Gal 6:10. That's why whenever we can we should always be kind to everyone, and especially to our Christian brothers.

Heb 13:3. Don't forget about those in jail. Suffer with them as though you were there yourself. Share the sorrow of those being mistreated, for you know what they are going through.

Jas 2:8. Yes indeed, it is good when you truly obey our Lord's command, "You must love and help your neighbors just as much as you love and take care of yourself." [9]But you are breaking this law of our Lord's when you favor the rich and fawn over them; it is sin.

See *Duty; Man.*

NEKODA A name of two families of Jewish exiles, Ezra 2:43–54, 60; Neh 7:46–56, 62.

NEMUEL 1. A Reubenite, Num 26:5–11.

2. A son of Simeon, Num 26:12–14; 1 Chron 4:24.

NEOPHYTES Mk 4:33; Jn 16:4, 12; 1 Cor 3: 1, 2; 8:9.

NEPHEG 1. Son of Izhar, Ex 6:21.

2. A son of David, 2 Sam 5:14–16; 1 Chron 3:6–8; 14:4–7.

NEPHISHESIM A family of the Nethinim, Neh 7:46–56.

NEPHTOAH A spring between Judah and Benjamin, Josh 15:9; 18:15.

NEPOTISM Of Joseph, Gen 47:11, 12. Of Saul, 1 Sam 14:50, 51. Of David, 2 Sam 8:16; 19:13. Of Nehemiah, Neh 7:2.

NER Father of Abner, 1 Sam 14:50, 51; of Kish, 1 Chron 8:33; 9:39.

NEREUS A Christian at Rome, Rom 16:15.

NERGAL A Babylonian god, 2 Kgs 17:30.

NERGAL-SHAREZER The name of two Babylonian officials, Jer 39:3, 13.

NERI An ancestor of Jesus, Lk 3:23–38.

NERIAH Father of Baruch, Jer 32:12.

NEST Bird's, Num 24:21, 22; Ps 104:17; Isa 31: 4, 5; 60:8; Mt 8:20.

NET Hidden in a pit, Ps 35:7, 8. Set for wild animals, Isa 51:20. Fish caught in, Mt 4:18–21; 13: 47, 48; Lk 5:4; Jn 21:6–11.

See *Snare; Trap.*

FIGURATIVE. Job 19:6; Ps 35:8; 66:11; 140:5; Eccl 7:26; 9:12; Isa 19:8; Ezk 26:5, 14; 47:10; Hos 7: 12.

NETHANEL 1. The leader of Issachar, Num 2:3–31; 10:15. Numbers the tribe, Num 1:2–15. Liberality of, for the tabernacle, Num 7:18–23.

2. Son of Jesse, 1 Chron 2:14.

3. A priest and musician, 1 Chron 15:24.

4. A Levite, 1 Chron 24:6.

5. Son of Obed-edom, and temple guard, 1 Chron 26:4, 5.

6. An official sent by Jehoshaphat to teach the law in the cities of Judah, 2 Chron 17:7–9.

7. A Levite, 2 Chron 35:9.

8. A priest who divorced his Gentile wife, Ezra 10:22.

9. A priest, Neh 12:12–21.

10. A Levite and musician, Neh 12:35, 36.

NETHANIAH 1. Father of Ishmael, 2 Kgs 25:23; Jer 40:8, 13, 14; 41:1.

2. A singer, and a chief temple musician, 1 Chron 25:2, 9–31.

3. A Levite appointed by Jehoshaphat to accompany the officials who were to teach the law to Judah, 2 Chron 17:7–9.

4. Father of Jehudi, Jer 36:14, 15.

NETHINIM Assistants to the Levites, literally "those who are given," Ezra 8:20. Return from the captivity, 1 Chron 9:2; Ezra 2:43–54, 58, 70; 7: 7–9, 24; 8:17; Neh 3:26, 31; 7:46–56, 60, 73; 10:28; 11:3, 21.

NETOPHAH A city in Judah, Ezra 2:23–35; Neh 7:8–38.

NETTLE An obnoxious plant, Isa 34:13.

FIGURATIVE. Job 30:7; Zeph 2:9.

NEW CREATURE See *Regeneration.*

NEW MOON Feast of, Num 10:10; 28:11–15; 1 Chron 23:31; 2 Chron 31:3. Selling at time of, suspended, Amos 8:5.

NEZIAH One of the Nethinim, Ezra 2:43–54; Neh 7:46–56.

NEZIB A city in Judah, Josh 15:37–44.

NIBHAZ A Syrian god, 2 Kgs 17:31.

NIBSHAN A city of Judah, Josh 15:48–62.

NICANOR A deacon of the church at Jerusalem, Acts 6:5.

NICODEMUS A Jewish rabbi. Becomes a disciple of Jesus, Jn 3:1–10; 7:50–53; 19:39–42.

NICOLAITANS Greek form of Balaamites, Rev 2:6, 15.

NICOLAUS A proselyte of Antioch, and deacon of the church at Jerusalem, Acts 6:5, 6. Possible founder of Nicolaitan sect, which see.

NICOPOLIS A city of Thrace. Paul lives in, Tit 3:12.

NIGHT Gen 1:4, 5, 16, 18. Meditations in, Ps 19:2; 63:6; 77:6; 119:148; 139:11. Worship in, Ps 134: 1. Jesus prays all night, Lk 6:12. No night in the new Jerusalem, Rev 21:25; 22:5.

Divided into watches, Judg 7:19, 20; Isa 21:11, 12; Lk 12:38. Divided into hours. Acts 23:23, 24. Used figuratively. Isa 15:1: 21:11, 12; Jn 9:4; Rom 13:12, 13; 1 Thess 5:5.

NIGHTHAWK Forbidden as food, Lev 11: 13–19; Deut 14:11–18.

NILE RIVER Isa 19:5–10; 23:2, 3; Ezk 29:3; Amos 8:8.

NIMRAH A city in Gad, Num 32:3, 4.

NIMRIM Area on the borders of Gad and Moab, Isa 15:6; Jer 48:34.

NIMROD Son of Cush. "A mighty hunter, blessed of God," Gen 10:8, 9; 1 Chron 1:10. Founder of Babylon, see *Babylon.*

NIMSHI Ancester of Jehu, 2 Kgs 9:2, 14.

NINEVEH Capital of the Assyrian empire, Gen 10:11, 12. Contained a population of upwards of 120,000 when Jonah preached, Jon 4:11. Extent of, Jon 3:3. Sennacherib in, 2 Kgs 19:36, 37; Isa 37:37, 38. Jonah preaches to, Jon 1:1, 2, 3. Zephaniah foretells the desolation of, Zeph 2: 13–15.

NISROCH An Assyrian god, 2 Kgs 19:36, 37; Isa 37:37, 38.

NOADIAH 1. A Levite who assisted in weighing the silver, gold, and other valuables for the Temple brought back from Babylon, Ezra 8:33.

2. A false prophetess, Neh 6:14.

NOAH 1. Son of Lamech, Gen 5:28–31. Builds an ark and saves his family from the flood, Gen 6: 14–22; 7; 8; Mt 24:37, 38; Lk 17:27; Heb 11:7; 1 Pet 3:20. Builds an altar and offers sacrifices, Gen 8:20, 21. Receives the promise from God that no flood would again destroy the earth; the rainbow instituted as a sign of the promise, Gen 8:20, 22; 9: 9–17. Intoxication of, and his curse on Canaan, Gen 9:20–27. His blessing upon Shem and Japheth, Gen 9:26, 27. Dies at the age of 950 years, Gen 9: 28, 29.

2. A daughter of Zelophehad, special legislation in regard to the inheritance of, Num 26:28–37; 27: 1–7; 36; Josh 17:3–7.

NOB A city of Benjamin, Neh 11:31–35. Called "the city of the priests," 1 Sam 22:19. Home of Ahimelech, the priest, 1 Sam 21:1; 22:11, 12. Probable seat of the tabernacle in Saul's time, 1 Sam 21: 4, 6, 9. David flees to, and is aided by Ahimelech, 1 Sam 21:1–9; 22: 9, 10. Destroyed by Saul, 1 Sam 22: 19. Prophecy concerning, Isa 10:32.

NOBAH An Israelite, Num 32:42.

NOBLEMAN Lk 19:12–27.

NOD Cain lived in, Gen 4:16.

NOGAH Son of David, 1 Chron 3:6–8; 14:4–7.

NOHAH Son of Benjamin, 1 Chron 8:1, 2.

NOLLE PROSEQUI Of the complaint against Paul, Acts 18:12–17.

NONCONFORMITY See *Form; Formalism.*

NOPHAH A city of Moab, Num 21:27–30.

NOSE Jewels for, Prov 11:22; Ezk 16:12. Mutilated, Ezk 23:25.

NOVEMBER See *Calendar.*

NUMBERS See *Seven; Forty.*

NURSE Gen 24:59; 35:8; Ex 2:7; Ruth 4:16, 17; 2 Kgs 11:2, 3; 2 Chron 22:12; 1 Thess 2:7. Careless, 2 Sam 4:4.

NUT Gen 43:11; Song 6:11.

NYMPHAS A Christian of Laodicea. House of, used as a place of worship, Col 4:15.

O

OAK A tree. Grew in Palestine, Gen 35:4. Absalom hung in the branches of, 2 Sam 18:9, 14. Of weeping, Deborah buried under, Gen 35:8. Oars made of, Ezk 27:6.

FIGURATIVE. Amos 2:9.

OAR Ezk 27:6.

OATH A solemn qualification. Used in solemnizing covenants: Between Abraham and the king of Sodom, Gen 14:22, 23; and Abimelech, Gen 21:22, 23; between Isaac and Abimelech, Gen 26:26–29, 31. Abraham requires oath of his servant Eliezer, Gen 24:2, 3, 9. Esau confirms the sale of his birthright by, Gen 25:33. Jacob confirms the pact between him and Laban by, Gen 31:53; requires Joseph to swear that he would bury him with his ancestors, Gen 47:28–31. Joseph requires a like oath, Gen 50:25. Rahab requires an oath from the spies, Josh 2:12–14; 6:22. The Israelites confirm the covenant with the Gibeonites by, Josh 9:3–20. Moses covenants with Caleb by, Josh 14:9. The leaders of Gilead confirm their pledge to Jephthah by, Judg 11:10. The Israelites swear in Mizpah, Judg 21:5. Ruth swears to Naomi, Ruth 1:17. Boaz swears to Ruth, Ruth 3:13. Saul swears to Jonathan, 1 Sam 19:6. Jonathan and David confirm a covenant by, 1 Sam 20:3, 13–17. David swears to Saul, 1 Sam 24:21, 22; 2 Sam 21:7. Saul swears to the witch of Endor, 1 Sam 28:10. David swears not to eat until sundown, 2 Sam 3:35, 36. Joab confirms his word by, 2 Sam 19:7. David swears to Bathsheba that Solomon shall be king, 1 Kgs 1:28–30. Solomon confirms his word by, 1 Kgs 2:23, 24; so also does Shime-i, 1 Kgs 2:42. Elisha seals his vow to follow Elijah by, 2 Kgs 2:1, 2. King of Israel confirms his word with an, 2 Kgs 6:31. Jehoiada requires an oath from the rulers, 2 Kgs 11:4. Zedekiah violates, 2 Chron 36:13; Ezk 17:18. Ezra requires, of the priests and Levites, Ezra 10:5, 16–19; so also does Nehemiah, Neh 5:12, 13. Zedekiah swears to Jeremiah, Jer 38:16. Peter confirms his denial of Jesus by, Mk 14:71.

ATTRIBUTED TO GOD. Gen 22:16; Ps 89:35, 36; 95:11; 105:8, 9; 132:11; Isa 14:24; 45:23; Jer 11:5; 22:5; 49:13; 51:14; Lk 1:72, 73; Heb 3:11, 18; 4:3; 6:13, 14, 17; 7:21, 28; Rev 10:6.

UNCLASSIFIED SCRIPTURES RELATING TO. Ex 20:7. You shall not use the name of Jehovah your God irreverently, nor use it to swear to a falsehood. You will not escape punishment if you do. Deut 5:11.

Ex 22:10. If a man asks his neighbor to keep a donkey, ox, sheep, or any other animal for him, and it dies, or is hurt, or gets away, and there is no eyewitness to report just what happened to it, [11]then the neighbor must take an oath that he has not stolen it, and the owner must accept his word, and no restitution shall be made for it.

Ex 23:1. Do not pass along untrue reports. Do not cooperate with an evil man by affirming on the witness stand something you know is false.

Lev 6:2. If anyone sins against me by refusing to return a deposit on something borrowed or rented, or by refusing to return something entrusted to him, or by robbery, or by oppressing his neighbor, [3]or by finding a lost article and lying about it, swearing that he doesn't have it— [4, 5]on the day he is found guilty of any such sin, he shall restore what he took, adding a twenty percent fine, and give it to the one he has harmed; and on the same day he shall bring his guilt offering to the Tabernacle.

Lev 19:12. You must not swear to a falsehood, thus bringing reproach upon the name of your God, for I am Jehovah.

Num 5:19. He shall require her to swear that she is innocent, and then he shall say to her, "If no man has slept with you except your husband, be free from the effects of this bitter water that causes the curse. [20]But if you have committed adultery, [21, 22]then Jehovah shall make you a curse among your people, for he will make your thigh rot away and your body swell." And the woman shall be required to say, "Yes, let it be so." [23]Then the priest shall write these curses in a book and wash them off into the bitter water. [24](When he requires the woman to drink the water, it becomes bitter within her [if she is guilty].)

Deut 6:13. When you are full, don't forget to be reverent to him and to serve him and to use *his* name alone to endorse your promises.

1 Kgs 8:31. If a man is accused of doing something wrong and then, standing here before your altar, swears that he didn't do it, [32]hear him in heaven and do what is right; judge whether or not he did it.

Ps 15:1. Lord, who may go and find refuge and shelter in your tabernacle up on your holy hill? Anyone who leads a blameless life and is truly sincere. [4]Speaks out against sin, criticizes those committing it, commends the faithful followers of the Lord, keeps a promise even if it ruins him.

Eccl 8:2. Obey the king as you have vowed to do.

Isa 48:1. Hear me, my people: you swear allegiance to the Lord without meaning a word of it.

Jer 4:2. And if you will swear by me alone, the living God, and begin to live good, honest clean lives, then you will be a testimony to the nations of the world and they will come to me and glorify my name.

Jer 5:2. Even under oath, they lie.

Dan 9:11. All Israel has disobeyed; we have turned away from you and haven't listened to your voice. And so the awesome curse of God has crushed us—the curse written in the law of Moses your servant.

Dan 12:7. He replied, with both hands lifted to heaven, taking oath by him who lives forever, that they will not end until three and a half years after the power of God's people has been crushed.

Mt 5:33. Again, the law of Moses says, "You shall not break your vows to God, but must fulfill them all." [34]But I say: Don't make any vows! And even to say, "By heavens!" is a sacred vow to God, for the heavens are God's throne. [35]And if you say "By the earth!" it is a sacred vow, for the earth is his footstool. And don't swear "By Jerusalem!" for Jerusalem is the capital of the great King. [36]Don't swear "By my head!" for you can't turn one hair white or black. [37]Say just a simple "Yes, I will" or "No, I won't." Your word is enough. To strengthen your promise with a vow shows that something is wrong.

Mt 14:7. So he vowed to give her anything she wanted. [9]The king was grieved, but because of his oath, and because he didn't want to back down in front of his guests, he issued the necessary orders. *vs.* 3–12; Mk 6:26.

Mt 23:18. And you say that to take an oath "By the altar" can be broken, but to swear "By the gifts on the altar" is binding! [19]Blind! For which is greater, the gift on the altar, or the altar itself that sanctifies the gift? [20]When you swear "By the altar" you are swearing by it and everything on it, [21]and when you swear "By the Temple" you are swearing by it, and by God who lives in it. [22]And when you swear "By heavens" you are swearing by the Throne of God and by God himself.

Mt 26:63. But Jesus remained silent. Then the High Priest said to him, "I demand in the name of the living God that you tell us whether you claim to be the Messiah, the Son of God."

Acts 23:12, 13. The next morning some forty or more of the Jews got together and bound themselves by a curse neither to eat nor drink until they had killed Paul! [14]Then they went to the chief priests and elders and told them what they had done.

2 Cor 1:23. I call upon this God to witness against me if I am not telling the absolute truth: the reason I haven't come to visit you yet is that I don't want to sadden you with a severe rebuke.

Gal 1:20. Listen to what I am saying, for I am telling you this in the very presence of God. This is exactly what happened—I am not lying to you.

Heb 6:16. When a man takes an oath, he is calling upon someone greater than himself to force him to do what he has promised, or to punish him if he later refuses to do it; the oath ends all argument about it.

Jas 5:12. But most of all, dear brothers, do not swear either by heaven or earth or anything else; just say a simple yes or no, so that you will not sin and be condemned for it.

Rev 10:5. Then the mighty angel standing on the sea and land lifted his right hand to heaven, [6]and swore by him who lives forever and ever, who created heaven and everything in it and the earth and all that it contains and the sea and its inhabitants, that there should be no more delay.

See *Covenant; False witness; God, Name of, Not to be Profaned; Perjury.*

OBADIAH 1. The overseer of Ahab's house. Conceals in a cave 100 prophets persecuted by Jezebel, 1 Kgs 18:3, 4. Meets Elijah and receives a commission from him, 1 Kgs 18:3–16.

2. Descendant of David, 1 Chron 3:21, 22.

3. A descendant of Tola, 1 Chron 7:3.

4. Son of Azel, 1 Chron 8:38, 9:44.

5. A Levite, 1 Chron 9:15, 16.

6. A Gadite warrior who joined David at Ziklag, 1 Chron 12:8–13.

7. Father of Ishmaiah, 1 Chron 27:16–22.

8. A leader of Judah who instructed the people in the law, 2 Chron 17:7–9.

9. A Levite. One of the overseers in the repairing of the temple by Josiah, 2 Chron 34:12.

10. A descendant of Joab who returned from Babylon, Ezra 8:2–14.

11. A priest who sealed with Nehemiah a covenant to observe God's law, Neh 10:1–8.

12. A gatekeeper of Jerusalem, under Nehemiah, Neh 12:25.

13. A prophet who prophesied the destruction of Edom, Obd 1.

OBAL Called also *Ebal.* A son of Joktan, Gen 10:26–30; 1 Chron 1:20–23.

OBDURACY Hardheartedness. 2 Chron 36:15. Jehovah the God of their fathers sent his prophets again and again to warn them, for he had compassion on his people and on his Temple. [16]But the people mocked these messengers of God and despised their words, scoffing at the prophets until the anger of the Lord could no longer be restrained, and there was no longer any remedy.

Ps 95:8. Don't harden your hearts as Israel did in the wilderness at Meribah and Massah. [9]For there your fathers doubted me, though they had seen so many of my miracles before. My patience was severely tried by their complaints. [10]"For forty years I watched them in disgust," the Lord God says. They were a nation whose thoughts and heart were far away from me. They refused to accept my laws. [11]Therefore in mighty wrath I swore that they would never enter the Promised Land, the place of rest I planned for them." Heb 3:7, 8, 15; 4:7.

Prov 1:24. I have called you so often but still you won't come. I have pleaded, but all in vain. [25]For you have spurned my counsel and reproof. [26]Some day you'll be in trouble, and I'll laugh! Mock me, will you!—I'll mock you! [27]When a storm of terror surrounds you, and when you are engulfed by anguish and distress, [28]then I will not answer your cry for help. It will be too late though you search for me ever so anxiously. [29]For you closed your eyes to the facts and did not choose to reverence and trust the Lord, [30]and you turned your back on me, spurning my advice. [31]That is why you must eat the bitter fruit of having your own way, and experience the full terrors of the pathway you have chosen.

Prov 29:1. The man who is often reproved but refuses to accept criticism will suddenly be broken and never have another chance.

Rev 9:20. But the men left alive after these plagues *still refused to worship God!* They would not renounce their demon-worship, nor their idols made of gold and silver, brass, stone, and wood—which neither see nor hear nor walk! [21]Neither did they change their mind and attitude about all their murders and witchcraft, their immorality and theft.

See *Affliction, Impenitence in; Impenitence; Reprobate.*

INSTANCES OF. The antediluvians, Gen 6:3, 5, 7. Sodomites, Gen 19:9, 14. Pharaoh, Ex 7:14, 22, 23; 8:15, 19, 31, 32; 9:7, 12, 35; 10:20, 28. Israelites, Num 14:22. Sons of Eli, 1 Sam 2:22–25.

OBED 1. Son of Boaz and grandfather of David, Ruth 4:16–22; 1 Chron 2:12; Mt 1:5; Lk 3: 23–38.

2. Son of Ephlal and grandson of Zabad, 1 Chron 2:37, 38.

3. One of David's heroes, 1 Chron 11:26–47.

4. Son of Shemaiah. A gatekeeper of the Temple, 1 Chron 26:6, 7.

5. Father of Azariah, 2 Chron 23:1.

OBED-EDOM 1. A Levite who kept the Ark, 2 Sam 6:10; 1 Chron 13:13, 14. Ark removed from, 2 Sam 6:12; 1 Chron 15:25.

2. Guard of the Ark, 1 Chron 15:18, 24.

3. Appointed to minister before the Ark, 1 Chron 16:4, 5.

4. A guard of the Temple, 1 Chron 16:38.

5. A guardian of the Temple treasures in the time of Amaziah, 2 Chron 25:24.

OBEDIENCE Gen 18:19. And I have picked him out to have godly descendants and a godly household—men who are just and good—so that I can do for him all I have promised.

Ex 19:5. Now if you will obey me and keep your part of my contract with you, you shall be my own little flock from among all the nations of the earth; for all the earth is mine.

Ex 20:6. But I lavish my love upon thousands of those who love me and obey my commandments. Deut 5:9, 10.

Ex 24:7. And he read to the people the Book he had written—the Book of the Covenant—containing God's directions and laws. And the people said again, "We solemnly promise to obey every one of these rules." Josh 24:24.

Num 9:23. So it was that they camped or traveled at the commandment of the Lord; and whatever the Lord told Moses they should do, they did.

Num 14:24. But my servant Caleb is a different kind of man—he has obeyed me fully. I will bring him into the land he entered as a spy, and his descendants shall have their full share in it. Josh 14: 6–14.

Josh 22:2. And addressed them as follows: "You have done as the Lord's disciple Moses commanded you, and have obeyed every order I have given you."

1 Kgs 3:14. And I will give you a long life if you follow me and obey my laws as your father David did.

2 Kgs 18:6. For he [Hezekiah] followed the Lord in everything, and carefully obeyed all of God's commands to Moses.

2 Kgs 21:8. If the people of Israel will only follow the instructions I gave them through Moses, I will never again expel them from this land of their fathers.

Neh 1:5. "O Lord God," I cried out; "O great and awesome God who keeps his promises and is so loving and kind to those who love and obey him! Hear my prayer!"

Ps 1:2. But they delight in doing everything God wants them to, and day and night are always meditating on his laws and thinking about ways to follow him more closely.

Ps 18:44. Even those I didn't know before come now and bow before me. Foreigners who have never seen me submit instantly.

Ps 25:10. And when we obey him, every path he guides us on is fragrant with his lovingkindness and his truth.

Ps 99:7. He spoke to them from the pillar of cloud and they followed his instructions.

Ps 103:17, 18. But the lovingkindness of the Lord is from everlasting to everlasting, to those who reverence him; his salvation is to children's children of those who are faithful to his covenant and remember to obey him! [20]Bless the Lord, you mighty angels of his who carry out his orders, listening for each of his commands. [21]Yes, bless the Lord, you armies of his angels who serve him constantly.

Ps 111:10. How can men be wise? The only way to begin is by reverence for God. For growth in wisdom comes from obeying his laws.

Ps 112:1. Praise the Lord! For all who fear God and trust in him are blessed beyond expression. Yes, happy is the man who delights in doing his commands.

Ps 119:2. Happy are all who search for God, and always do his will. [4]You have given us your laws to obey— [5]oh, how I want to follow them consistently. [6]Then I will not be disgraced, for I will have a clean record. [8]I *will* obey! Oh, don't forsake me and let me slip back into sin again. [10]I have tried my best to find you—don't let me wander off from your instructions. [15]I will meditate upon them and give them my full respect. [16]I will delight in them and not forget them. [22]Don't let them scorn me for obeying you. [30]Help me, undeserving as I am, to obey your laws, for I have chosen to do right. [31]I cling to your commands and follow them as closely as I can. Lord, don't let me make a mess of things. [33]Just tell me what to do and I will do it, Lord. [44, 45]Therefore I will keep on obeying you forever and forever, free within the limits of your laws. [55]I obey them even at night and keep my thoughts, O Lord, on you. [56]What a blessing this has been to me —to constantly obey. [59, 60]I thought about the wrong direction in which I was headed, and turned around and came running back to you. [77]Surround me with your tender mercies, that I may live. For your law is my delight. [87]They had almost finished me off, yet I refused to yield and disobey your laws. [97]Oh, how I love them. I think about them all day long. [100]They make me even wiser than the aged. [101]I have refused to walk the paths of evil for I remain obedient to your Word. [102]No, I haven't turned away from what you taught me. [104]And since only your rules can give me wisdom and understanding, no wonder I hate every false teaching. [105]Your words are a flashlight to light the path ahead of me, and keep me from stumbling. [106]I've said it once and I'll say it again and again: I will obey these wonderful laws of yours. [109]My life hangs in the balance, but I will not give up obedience to your laws. [112]I am determined to obey you until I die. [129]Your laws are wonderful; no wonder I obey them. [166]I long for your salvation, Lord, and so I have obeyed your laws. [167]I have looked for your commandments and I love them very much; [168]yes, I have searched for them. You know this because everything I do is known to you.

Ps 143:10. Help me to do your will, for you are my God. Lead me in good paths, for your Spirit is good.

Prov 1:33. But all who listen to me shall live in peace and safety, unafraid.

Prov 19:16. Keep the commandments and keep your life; despising them means death.

Prov 28:7. Young men who are wise obey the law; a son who is a member of a lawless gang is a shame to his father.

Isa 1:19. If you will only let me help you, if you will only obey, then I will make you rich! Jer 7:23.

Ezk 18:19. "What?" you ask. "Doesn't the son pay for his father's sins?" No! For if the son does what is right and keeps my laws, he shall surely live.

Ezk 33:14. And when I tell the wicked he will die and then he turns from his sins and does what is fair and right— [15]if he gives back the borrower's pledge and returns what he has stolen and walks along the paths of right, not doing evil—he shall surely live. He shall not die. [16]None of his past sins shall be brought up against him, for he has turned to the good and shall surely live.

Dan 7:27. Then every nation under heaven, and all their power, shall be given to the people of God; they shall rule all things forever, and all rulers shall serve and obey them.

Mt 5:19. And so if anyone breaks the least commandment, and teaches others to, he shall be the least in the Kingdom of Heaven. But those who teach God's laws *and obey them* shall be great in the Kingdom of Heaven.

Mt 6:24. You cannot serve two masters: God and money. For you will hate one and love the other, or else the other way around.

Mt 9:9. As Jesus was going on down the road, he saw a tax collector, Matthew, sitting at a tax collection booth. "Come and be my disciple," Jesus said to him, and Matthew jumped up and went along with him. Mk 2:14.

Mt 12:50. Then he added, "Anyone who obeys my Father in heaven is my brother, sister and mother!"

Mt 13:23. The good ground represents the heart of a man who listens to the message and understands it and goes out and brings thirty, sixty, or even a hundred others into the Kingdom. *v.* 8; Mk 4:20; Lk 8:15.

Mt 25:20. The man to whom he had entrusted the $5,000 brought him $10,000. [21]His master praised him for good work. "You have been faithful in handling this small amount," he told him, "so now I will give you many more responsibilities. Begin the joyous tasks I have assigned to you." [22]Next came the man who had received the $2,000, with the report, "Sir, you gave me $2,000 to use, and I have doubled it." [23]"Good work," his master said. "You are a good and faithful servant. You have been faithful over this small amount, so now I will give you much more."

Mk 3:35. Anyone who does God's will is my brother, and my sister, and my mother.

Lk 1:6. Zacharias and Elizabeth were godly folk, careful to obey all of God's laws in spirit as well as in letter.

Lk 6:46. So why do you call me "Lord" when you won't obey me? [47, 48]But all those who come and listen and obey me are like a man who builds a house on a strong foundation laid upon the underlying rock. When the flood waters rise and break against the house, it stands firm, for it is strongly built.

Lk 8:21. He remarked, "My mother and my brothers are all those who hear the message of God and obey it."

Lk 11:28. He replied, "Yes, but even more blessed are all who hear the Word of God and put it into practice."

Lk 12:37. There will be great joy for those who are ready and waiting for his return. He himself will seat them and put on a waiter's uniform and serve them as they sit and eat! [38]He may come at nine o'clock at night—or even at midnight. But whenever he comes there will be joy for his servants who are ready!

Jn 8:28. So Jesus said, "When you have killed the Messiah, then you will realize that I am he and I have not been telling you my own ideas, but have spoken what the Father taught me. [51]With all the earnestness I have I tell you this—no one who obeys me shall ever die!"

Jn 9:4. All of us must quickly carry out the tasks assigned us by the one who sent me, for there is little time left before the night falls and all work comes to an end.

Jn 10:27. My sheep recognize my voice, and I know them, and they follow me.

Jn 14:15. "If you love me, obey me." [23]Jesus replied, "Because I will only reveal myself to those who love me and obey me. The Father will love them too, and we will come to them and live with them. [31]But I will freely do what the Father requires of me so that the world will know that I love the Father."

Jn 15:10. When you obey me you are living in my love, just as I obey my Father and live in his love. [14]And you are my friends if you obey me. [16]You didn't choose me! I chose you! I appointed you to go and produce lovely fruit always.

Acts 4:19. But Peter and John replied, "You decide whether God wants us to obey you instead of him!"

Acts 5:29. But Peter and the apostles replied, "We must obey God rather than men."

Rom 6:17. Thank God that though you once chose to be slaves of sin, now you have obeyed with all your heart the teaching to which God has committed you.

Eph 2:10. It is God himself who has made us what we are and given us new lives from Christ Jesus; and long ages ago he planned that we should spend these lives in helping others.

Phil 2:12. Dearest friends, when I was there with you, you were always so careful to follow my instructions. And now that I am away you must be even more careful to do the good things that result from being saved, obeying God with deep reverence, shrinking back from all that might displease him.

Heb 10:7. Then I said, "See, I have come to do your will, to lay down my life, just as the Scriptures said that I would."

Jas 2:10. And the person who keeps every law of God, but makes one little slip, is just as guilty as the person who has broken every law there is. [11]For the God who said you must not marry a woman who already has a husband also said you must not murder, so even though you have not broken the marriage laws by committing adultery, but have murdered someone, you have entirely broken God's laws and stand utterly guilty before him. [12]You will be judged on whether or not you are doing what Christ wants you to. So watch what you do and what you think.

1 Pet 1:2. Dear friends, God the Father chose you long ago and knew you would become his children. And the Holy Spirit has been at work in your hearts, cleansing you with the blood of Jesus Christ and making you to please him. May God bless you richly and grant you increasing freedom from all anxiety and fear. [14]Obey God because you are his children; don't slip back into your old ways—doing evil because you knew no better.

1 Jn 2:3. And how can we be sure that we belong to him? By looking within ourselves: are we really trying to do what he wants us to? [4]Someone may say, "I am a Christian; I am on my way to heaven; I belong to Christ." But if he doesn't do what Christ tells him to, he is a liar. [5]But those who do what Christ tells them to will learn to love God more and more. That is the way to know whether or not you are a Christian. [6]Anyone who says he is a Christian should live as Christ did. [17]And this world is fading away, and these evil, forbidden things will go with it, but whoever keeps doing the will of God will live forever.

1 Jn 3:22. And get whatever we ask for because we are obeying him and doing the things that please him. [24]Those who do what God says—they are living with God and he with them.

1 Jn 5:2. So you can find out how much you love God's children—your brothers and sisters in the Lord—by how much you love and obey God. [3]Loving God means doing what he tells us to do, and really, that isn't hard at all.

2 Jn 1:6. If we love God, we will do whatever he tells us to. And he has told us from the very first to love each other. [9]For if you wander beyond the teaching of Christ, you will leave God behind; while if you are loyal to Christ's teachings, you will have God too. Then you will have both the Father and the Son.

Rev 12:17. Then the furious Dragon set out to attack the rest of her children—all who were keeping God's commandments and confessing that they belong to Jesus.

Rev 22:6, 7. Then the angel said to me, "These words are trustworthy and true: 'I am coming soon!' God, who tells his prophets what the future holds, has sent his angel to tell you this will happen soon. Blessed are those who believe it and all else written in the scroll." Rev 1:3.

See *Blessing, Contingent on Obedience.*

COMMANDED. Gen 17:9. "Your part of the contract," God told him, "is to obey its terms."

Ex 23:22. But if you are careful to obey him, following all my instructions, then I will be an enemy to your enemies.

Lev 19:36. For I am Jehovah your God who brought you from the land of Egypt. [37]You must heed all of my commandments and ordinances, carefully obeying them. *v.* 19.

Lev 20:8. You must obey all of my commandments, for I am the Lord who sanctifies you. [22]You must obey all of my laws and ordinances so that I will not throw you out of your new land. Lev 22:31; Deut 5:1, 32.

Lev 26:3. If you obey all of my commandments, [4, 5]I will give you regular rains, and the land will yield bumper crops, and the trees will be loaded with fruit long after the normal time! And grapes will still be ripening when sowing time comes again. You shall eat your fill, and live safely in the land, 6for I will give you peace, and you will go to sleep without fear. I will chase away the dangerous animals. 7You will chase your enemies; they will die beneath your swords. 8Five of you will chase a hundred, and a hundred of you, ten thousand! You will defeat all of your enemies. 9I will look after you, and multiply you, and fulfill my covenant with you. 10You will have such a surplus of crops that you won't know what to do with them when the new harvest is ready! 11And I will live among you, and not despise you. 12I will walk among you and be your God, and you shall be my people. 13For I am the Lord your God who brought you out of the land of Egypt, with the intention that you be slaves no longer; I have broken your chains and will make you walk with dignity.

Num 15:38. Tell the people of Israel to make tassels for the hems of their clothes (this is a permanent regulation from generation to generation) and to attach the tassels to their clothes with a blue cord. 39The purpose of this regulation is to remind you, whenever you notice the tassels, of the commandments of the Lord, and that you are to obey his laws instead of following your own desires and going your own ways, as you used to do in serving other gods. 40It will remind you to be holy to your God.

Deut 4:1. And now, O Israel, listen carefully to these laws I teach you, and obey them if you want to live and enter into and possess the land given you by the Lord God of your ancestors. 2Do not add other laws or subtract from these; just obey them, for they are from the Lord your God. 5These are the laws for you to obey when you arrive in the land where you will live. They are from the Lord your God. He has given them to me to pass on to you. 6If you obey them they will give you a reputation for wisdom and intelligence. When the surrounding nations hear these laws they will exclaim, "What other nation is as wise and prudent as Israel!" 9But watch out! Be very careful never to forget what you have seen God doing for you. May his miracles have a deep and permanent effect upon your lives! Tell your children and your grandchildren about the glorious miracles he did. 10Tell them especially about the day you stood before the Lord at Mount Horeb, and he told me, "Summon the people before me and I will instruct them, so that they will learn always to reverence me, and so that they can teach my laws to their children." 39This is your wonderful thought for the day: Jehovah is God both in heaven and down here upon the earth; and there is no God other than him! 40You must obey these laws that I will tell you today, so that all will be well with you and your children, and so that you will live forever in the land the Lord your God is giving you. *vs.* 1–40; chapter 30:2, 3.

Deut 5:1. Moses continued speaking to the people of Israel and said, "Listen carefully now to all these laws God has given you; learn them, and be sure to obey them!" 32So Moses told the people, "You must obey all the commandments of the Lord your God, following his directions in every detail, going the whole way he has laid out for you; 33only then will you live long and prosperous lives in the land you are to enter and possess." *vs.* 1–33.

Deut 6:1. The Lord your God told me to give you all these commandments which you are to obey in the land you will soon be entering, where you will live. 2The purpose of these laws is to cause you, your sons, and your grandsons to reverence the Lord your God by obeying all of his instructions as long as you live; if you do, you will have long, prosperous years ahead of you. 3Therefore, O Israel, listen closely to each command and be careful to obey it, so that all will go well with you, and so that you will have many children. If you obey these commands you will become a great nation in a glorious land "flowing with milk and honey," even as the God of your fathers promised you. 4O Israel, listen: Jehovah is our God, Jehovah alone. 5You must love him with *all* your heart, soul, and might. 6And you must think constantly about these commandments I am giving you today. 7You must teach them to your children and talk about them when you are at home or out for a walk; at bedtime and the first thing in the morning. 8Tie them on your finger, wear them on your forehead, 9and write them on the doorposts of your house! *vs.* 1–25.

Deut 8:1. You must obey all the commandments I give you today. If you do, you will not only live, you will multiply and will go in and take over the land promised to your fathers by the Lord. 2Do you remember how the Lord led you through the wilderness for all those forty years, humbling you and testing you to find out how you would respond, and whether or not you would really obey him? 3Yes, he humbled you by letting you go hungry and then feeding you with manna, a food previously unknown to both you and your ancestors. He did it to help you realize that food isn't everything, and that real life comes by obeying every command of God. 4For all these forty years your clothes haven't grown old, and your feet haven't been blistered or swollen. 5So you should realize that, as a man punishes his son, the Lord punishes you to help you. 6Obey the laws of the Lord your God. Walk in his ways and fear him. 11But that is the time to be careful! Beware that in your plenty you don't forget the Lord your God and begin to disobey him. 12, 13For when you have become full and prosperous and have built fine homes to live in, and when your flocks and herds have become very large, and your silver and gold have multiplied, 14that is the time to watch out that you don't become proud, and forget the Lord your God who brought you out of your slavery in the land of Egypt. 16He fed you with manna in the wilderness (it was a kind of bread unknown before) so that you would become humble and so that your trust in him would grow, and he could do you good. 17He did it so that you would never feel that it was your own power and might that made you wealthy. [18]Always remember that it is the Lord your God who gives you power to become rich, and he does it to fulfill his promise to your ancestors. [19]But if you forget about the Lord your God and worship other gods instead, and follow evil ways, you shall certainly perish, [20]just as the Lord has caused other nations in the past to perish. That will be your fate, too, if you don't obey the Lord your God.

Deut 10:12, 13. And now, Israel, what does the Lord your God require of you except to listen carefully to all he says to you, and to obey for your own good the commandments I am giving you today, and to love him, and to worship him with all your hearts and souls?

Deut 11:1. You must love the Lord your God and obey every one of his commands. [2]Listen! I am not talking now to your children who have never experienced the Lord's punishments or seen his greatness and his awesome power. [3]They weren't there to see the miracles he did in Egypt against Pharaoh and all his land. [8]How carefully, then, you should obey these commandments I am going to give you today, so that you may have the strength to go in and possess the land you are about to enter. [9]If you obey the commandments, you will have a long and good life in the land the Lord promised to your ancestors and to you, their descendants—a wonderful land "flowing with milk and honey"! [13]And if you will carefully obey all of his commandments that I am going to give you today, and if you will love the Lord your God with all your hearts and souls, and will worship him, [14]then he will continue to send both the early and late rains that will produce wonderful crops of grain, grapes for your wine, and olive oil. [15]He will give you lush pastureland for your cattle to graze in, and you yourselves shall have plenty to eat and be fully content. [16]But beware that your hearts do not turn from God to worship other gods. [17]For if you do, the anger of the Lord will be hot against you, and he will shut the heavens—there will be no rain and no harvest, and you will quickly perish from the good land the Lord has given you. [18]So keep these commandments carefully in mind. Tie them to your hand to remind you to obey them, and tie them to your forehead between your eyes! [19]Teach them to your children. Talk about them when you are sitting at home, when you are out walking, at bedtime, and before breakfast! [20]Write them upon the doors of your houses and upon your gates, [21]so that as long as there is sky above the earth, you and your children will enjoy the good life awaiting you in the land the Lord has promised you. [22]If you carefully obey all the commandments I give you, loving the Lord your God, walking in all his ways, and clinging to him, [23]then the Lord will drive out all the nations in your land, no matter how much greater and stronger than you they might be. [24]Wherever you go, the land is yours. Your frontiers will stretch from the southern Negeb to Lebanon, and from the Euphrates River to the Mediterranean Sea. [25]No one will be able to stand against you, for the Lord your God will send fear and dread ahead of you wherever you go, just as he has promised. [26]I am giving you the choice today between God's blessing or God's curse! [27]There will be blessing if you obey the commandments of the Lord your God which I am giving you today, [28]and a curse if you refuse them and worship the gods of these other nations. [32]But you must obey all the laws I am giving you today.

Deut 13:4. You must *never* worship any God but Jehovah; obey only his commands and cling to him.

Deut 26:16. You must wholeheartedly obey all of these commandments and ordinances which the Lord your God is giving you today. [17]You have declared today that he is your God, and you have promised to obey and keep his laws and ordinances, and to heed all he tells you to do. [18]And the Lord has declared today that you are his very own people, just as he promised, and that you must obey all of his laws.

Deut 27:1. Then Moses and the elders of Israel gave the people these further instructions to obey: [2-4]"When you cross the Jordan River and go into the Promised Land—a land 'flowing with milk and honey'—take out boulders from the river bottom and immediately pile them into a monument on the other side, at Mount Ebal. Face the stones with a coating of lime and then write the laws of God in the lime. [5, 6]And build an altar there to the Lord your God. Use uncut boulders, and on the altar offer burnt offerings to the Lord your God. [7]Sacrifice peace offerings upon it also, and feast there with great joy before the Lord your God. [8]Write all of these laws plainly (upon the monument)." [9]Then Moses and the Levite-priests addressed all Israel as follows: "O Israel, listen! Today you have become the people of the Lord your God, [10]so today you must begin to obey all of these commandments I have given you."

Deut 28:1. If you fully obey all of these commandments of the Lord your God, the laws I am declaring to you today, God will transform you into the greatest nation in the world. [2-6]These are the blessings that will come upon you: Blessings in the city, blessings in the field; many children, ample crops, large flocks and herds; blessings of fruit and bread; blessings when you come in, blessings when you go out. [7]The Lord will defeat your enemies before you; they will march out together against you but scatter before you in seven directions! [8]The Lord will bless you with good crops and healthy cattle, and prosper everything you do when you arrive in the land the Lord your God is giving you. [9]He will change you into a holy people dedicated to himself; this he has promised to do if you will only obey him and walk in his ways. [10]All the nations in the world shall see that you belong to the Lord, and they will stand in awe. [11]The Lord will give you an abundance of good things in the land, just as he promised; many children, many cattle, and abundant crops. [12]He will open to you his wonderful treasury of rain in the heavens, to give you fine crops every season. He will bless everything you do; and you shall lend to many nations, but shall not borrow from them. 13If you will only listen and obey the commandments of the Lord your God that I am giving you today, he will make you the head and not the tail, and you shall always have the upper hand. 14But each of these blessings depends on your not turning aside in any way from the laws I have given you; and you must never worship other gods. 15-19If you won't listen to the Lord your God and won't obey these laws I am giving you today, then all of these curses shall come upon you: Curses in the city; Curses in the fields; curses on your fruit and bread; the curse of barren wombs; curses upon your crops; curses upon the fertility of your cattle and flocks; curses when you come in; curses when you go out. 20For the Lord himself will send his personal curse upon you. You will be confused and a failure in everything you do, until at last you are destroyed because of the sin of forsaking him. 21He will send disease among you until you are destroyed from the face of the land which you are about to enter and possess. 22He will send tuberculosis, fever, infections, plague, and war. He will blight your crops, covering them with mildew. All these devastations shall pursue you until you perish. 23The heavens above you will be as unyielding as bronze, and the earth beneath will be as iron. 24The land will become as dry as dust for lack of rain, and dust storms shall destroy you. 25The Lord will cause you to be defeated by your enemies. You will march out to battle gloriously, but flee before your enemies in utter confusion; and you will be tossed to and fro among all the nations of the earth. 26Your dead bodies will be food to the birds and wild animals, and no one will be there to chase them away. 27He will send upon you Egyptian boils, tumors, scurvy, and itch, for none of which will there be a remedy. 28He will send madness, blindness, fear, and panic upon you. 29You shall grope in the bright sunlight just as the blind man gropes in darkness. You shall not prosper in anything you do; you will be oppressed and robbed continually, and nothing will save you. 30Someone else will marry your fiancée; someone else will live in the house you build; someone else will eat the fruit of the vineyard you plant. 31Your oxen shall be butchered before your eyes, but you won't get a single bite of the meat. Your donkeys will be driven away as you watch, and will never return to you again. Your sheep will be given to your enemies. And there will be no one to protect you. 32You will watch as your sons and daughters are taken away as slaves. Your heart will break with longing for them, but you will not be able to help them. 33A foreign nation you have not even heard of will eat the crops you will have worked so hard to grow. You will always be oppressed and crushed. 34You will go mad because of all the tragedy you see around you. 35The Lord will cover you with boils from head to foot. 36He will exile you and the king you will choose, to a nation to whom neither you nor your ancestors gave a second thought; and while in exile you shall worship gods of wood and stone! 37You will become an object of horror, a proverb and a byword among all the nations, for the Lord will thrust you away. 38You will sow much but reap little, for the locusts will eat your crops. 39You will plant vineyards and care for them, but you won't eat the grapes or drink the wine, for worms will destroy the vines. 40Olive trees will be growing everywhere, but there won't be enough olive oil to anoint yourselves! For the trees will drop their fruit before it is matured. 41Your sons and daughters will be snatched away from you as slaves. 42The locusts shall destroy your trees and vines. 43Foreigners living among you shall become richer and richer while you become poorer and poorer. 44They shall lend to you, not you to them! They shall be the head and you shall be the tail! 45All these curses shall pursue and overtake you until you are destroyed—all because you refuse to listen to the Lord your God. 46These horrors shall befall you and your descendants as a warning: 47, 48You will become slaves to your enemies because of your failure to praise God for all that he has given you. The Lord will send your enemies against you, and you will be hungry, thirsty, naked, and in want of everything. A yoke of iron shall be placed around your neck until you are destroyed! 49The Lord will bring a distant nation against you, swooping down upon you like an eagle; a nation whose language you don't understand— 50a nation of fierce and angry men who will have no mercy upon young or old. 51They will eat you out of house and home until your cattle and crops are gone. Your grain, new wine, olive oil, calves, and lambs will all disappear. 52That nation will lay seige to your cities and knock down your highest walls—the walls you will trust to protect you. 53You will even eat the flesh of your own sons and daughters in the terrible days of siege that lie ahead. 54The most tenderhearted man among you will be utterly callous toward his own brother and his beloved wife and his children who are still alive. 55He will refuse to give them a share of the flesh he is devouring—the flesh of his own children—because he is starving in the midst of the siege of your cities. 56, 57The most tender and delicate woman among you—the one who would not so much as touch her feet to the ground—will refuse to share with her beloved husband, son and daughter. She will hide from them the afterbirth and the new baby she has borne, so that she herself can eat them: so terrible will be the hunger during the siege and the awful distress caused by your enemies at your gates. 58, 59If you refuse to obey all the laws written in this book, thus refusing reverence to the glorious and fearful name of Jehovah your God, then Jehovah will send perpetual plagues upon you and upon your children. 60He will bring upon you all the diseases of Egypt which you feared so much, and they shall plague the land. 61And that is not all! The Lord will bring upon you every sickness and plague there is, even those not mentioned in this book, until you are destroyed. [62]There will be few of you left, though before you were as numerous as stars. All this if you do not listen to the Lord your God. [63]Just as the Lord has rejoiced over you and has done such wonderful things for you and has multiplied you, so the Lord at that time will rejoice in destroying you; and you shall disappear from the land. [64]For the Lord will scatter you among all the nations from one end of the earth to the other. There you will worship heathen gods that neither you nor your ancestors have known, gods made of wood and stone! [65]There among those nations you shall find no rest, but the Lord will give you trembling hearts, darkness, and bodies wasted from sorrow and fear. [66]Your lives will hang in doubt. You will live night and day in fear, and will have no reason to believe that you will see the morning light. [67]In the morning you will say, "Oh, that night were here!" And in the evening you will say, "Oh, that morning were here!" You will say this because of the awesome horrors surrounding you. [68]Then the Lord will send you back to Egypt in ships, a journey I promised you would never need to make again; and there you will offer to sell yourselves to your enemies as slaves—but no one will even want to buy you.

Deut 32:46. Moses made these comments: "Meditate upon all the laws I have given you today, and pass them on to your children. [47]These laws are not mere words—they are your life! Through obeying them you will live long, plentiful lives."

Josh 22:5. Be sure to continue to obey all of the commandments Moses gave you. Love the Lord and follow his plan for your lives. Cling to him and serve him enthusiastically.

Josh 23:6. But be very sure to follow all the instructions written in the book of the laws of Moses; do not deviate from them the least little bit. [7]Be sure that you do not mix with the heathen people still remaining in the land; do not even mention the names of their gods, much less swear by them or worship them.

Josh 24:14. So revere Jehovah and serve him in sincerity and truth. Put away forever the idols which your ancestors worshiped. . . . Worship the Lord alone. [15]But if you are unwilling to obey the Lord, then decide today whom you will obey.

1 Sam 12:24. Trust the Lord and sincerely worship him; think of all the tremendous things he has done for you.

1 Sam 15:22. Samuel replied, "Has the Lord as much pleasure in your burnt offerings and sacrifices as in your obedience? Obedience is far better than sacrifice. He is much more interested in your listening to him than in your offering the fat of rams to him."

2 Kgs 17:37. The descendants of Jacob were to obey all of God's laws and *never* worship other gods. [38]For God had said, "*You must never forget the covenant I made with you; never worship other gods.*"

1 Chron 16:15. Remember his covenant forever—the words he commanded to a thousand generations.

1 Chron 28:9. "Solomon, my son, get to know the God of your fathers. Worship and serve him with a clean heart and a willing mind, for the Lord sees every heart and understands and knows every thought. If you seek him, you will find him; but if you forsake him, he will permanently throw you aside. [10]So be very careful, for the Lord has chosen you to build his holy temple. Be strong and do as he commands." [20]Then he continued, "Be strong and courageous and get to work. Don't be frightened by the size of the task, for the Lord my God is with you; he will not forsake you. He will see to it that everything is finished correctly."

Ezra 7:10. This was because Ezra had determined to study and obey the laws of the Lord and to become a Bible teacher, teaching those laws to the people of Israel. [23]"And whatever else the God of heaven demands for his Temple; for why should we risk God's wrath against the king and his sons?"

Ps 76:11. Fulfill all your vows that you have made to Jehovah your God. Let everyone bring him presents. He should be reverenced and feared.

Eccl 12:13. Here is my final conclusion: fear God and obey his commandments, for this is the entire duty of man.

Jer 26:13. But if you stop your sinning and begin obeying the Lord your God, he will cancel all the punishment he has announced against you.

Jer 38:20. Jeremiah replied, "You won't get into their hands if only you will obey the Lord; your life will be spared and all will go well for you."

Mal 4:4. Remember to obey the laws I gave all Israel through Moses my servant on Mount Horeb.

Mt 9:9. As Jesus was going on down the road, he saw a tax collector, Matthew, sitting at a tax collection booth. "Come and be my disciple," Jesus said to him, and Matthew jumped up and went along with him. Mk 2:14.

Mt 19:17. "When you call me good you are calling me God," Jesus replied, "for God alone is truly good. But to answer your question, you can get to heaven if you keep the commandments. [29]And anyone who gives up his home, brothers, sisters, father, mother, wife, children, or property, to follow me, shall receive a hundred times as much in return, and shall have eternal life."

Jn 12:26. If these Greeks want to be my disciples, tell them to come and follow me, for my servants must be where I am. And if they follow me, the Father will honor them.

Jn 13:17. You know these things—now do them! That is the path of blessing.

Jn 14:15. If you love me, obey me. [21]The one who obeys me is the one who loves me; and because he loves me, my Father will love him; and I will too, and I will reveal myself to him.

Gal 3:10. Yes, and those who depend on the Jewish laws to save them are under God's curse, for the Scriptures point out very clearly, "Cursed is everyone who at any time breaks a single one of these laws that are written in God's Book of the Law." [12]How different from this way of faith is the way of law which says that a man is saved by obeying every law of God, without one slip.

Gal 5:3. I'll say it again. Anyone trying to find favor with God by being circumcised must always obey every other Jewish law or perish.

Eph 4:1. I beg you—I, a prisoner here in jail for serving the Lord—to live and act in a way worthy of those who have been chosen for such wonderful blessings as these. [17]Live no longer as the unsaved do, for they are blinded and confused.

Eph 6:6, 7. Don't work hard only when your master is watching and then shirk when he isn't looking; work hard and with gladness all the time, as though working for Christ, doing the will of God with all your hearts. [8]Remember, the Lord will pay you for each good thing you do, whether you are slave or free.

Phil 2:12. Dearest friends, when I was there with you, you were always so careful to follow my instructions. And now that I am away you must be even more careful to do the good things that result from being saved, obeying God with deep reverence, shrinking back from all that might displease him.

1 Tim 6:14. That you fulfill all he has told you to do, so that no one can find fault with you from now until our Lord Jesus Christ returns. [18]Tell them to use their money to do good. They should be rich in good works and should give happily to those in need, always being ready to share with others whatever God has given them.

Heb 13:16. Don't forget to do good and to share what you have with those in need, for such sacrifices are very pleasing to him.

Jas 1:22. And remember, it is a message to obey, not just to listen to. So don't fool yourselves. [23]For if a person just listens and doesn't obey, he is like a man looking at his face in a mirror; [24]as soon as he walks away, he can't see himself anymore or remember what he looks like. [25]But if anyone keeps looking steadily into God's law for free men, he will not only remember it but he will do what it says, and God will greatly bless him in everything he does.

See *Commandments; Duty; Law.*

EXEMPLIFIED. Gen 6:9. He was the only truly righteous man living on the earth at that time. He tried always to conduct his affairs according to God's will.

Num 9:23. So it was that they camped or traveled at the commandment of the Lord; and whatever the Lord told Moses they should do, they did.

Num 14:24. But my servant Caleb is a different kind of man—he has obeyed me fully. I will bring him into the land he entered as a spy, and his descendants shall have their full share in it. Josh 14:6–14.

2 Kgs 18:6. For he followed the Lord in everything, and carefully obeyed all of God's commands to Moses.

2 Kgs 20:3. "O Lord," he pleaded, "remember how I've always tried to obey you and to please you in everything I do."

2 Chron 24:16. He was buried in the City of David among the kings, because he had done so much good for Israel, for God, and for the Temple.

2 Chron 31:20. In this way King Hezekiah handled the distribution throughout all Judah, doing what was just and fair in the sight of the Lord his God. [21]He worked very hard to encourage respect for the Temple, the law, and godly living, and was very successful.

Ezra 7:10. This was because Ezra had determined to study and obey the laws of the Lord and to become a Bible teacher, teaching those laws to the people of Israel.

Neh 7:2. I gave the responsibility of governing Jerusalem to my brother Hanani and to Hananiah, the commander of the fortress—a very faithful man who revered God more than most people do.

Job 1:8. Then the Lord asked Satan, "Have you noticed my servant Job? He is the finest man in all the earth—a good man who fears God and will have nothing to do with evil."

Ps 17:3. You have tested me and seen that I am good. You have come even in the night and found nothing amiss and know that I have told the truth.

Ps 26:3. For I have taken your lovingkindness and your truth as my ideals. [4]I do not have fellowship with tricky, two-faced men; they are false and hypocritical. [5]I hate the sinners' hangouts and refuse to enter them. [6]I wash my hands to prove my innocence and come before your altar.

Ps 99:7. He spoke to them from the pillar of cloud and they followed his instructions.

Ps 101:2. I will try to walk a blameless path, but how I need your help, especially in my own home, where I long to act as I should. [3]Help me to refuse the low and vulgar things; help me to abhor all crooked deals of every kind, to have no part in them.

Ps 106:30. And continued until Phineas executed those whose sins had caused the plague to start. [31](For this good deed Phineas will be remembered forever.)

Ps 119:30. For I have chosen to do right. [31]I cling to your commands and follow them as closely as I can. Lord, don't let me make a mess of things. [40]I long to obey them! Therefore in fairness renew my life. [44, 45]Therefore I will keep on obeying you forever and forever, free within the limits of your laws. [47]How I love your laws! How I enjoy your commands! [48]"Come, come to me," I call to them, for I love them and will let them fill my life. [51]Proud men hold me in contempt for obedience to God, but I stand unmoved. [54]For these laws of yours have been my source of joy and singing through all these years of my earthly pilgrimage. [55]I obey them even at night and keep my thoughts, O Lord, on you. [56]What a blessing this has been to me—to constantly obey. [59, 60]I thought about the wrong direction in which I was headed, and turned around and came running back to you. [67]I used to wander off until you punished me; now I closely follow all you say. [99]Proud men have made up lies about me, but the truth is that I obey your laws with all my heart. [100]They make me even wiser than the aged. [101]I have refused to walk the paths of evil for I will remain obedient to your Word. [102]No, I haven't turned away from what you taught me. [105]Your words are a flashlight to light the path ahead of me, and keep me from stumbling. [106]I've said it once and I'll say it again and again: I will obey these wonderful laws of yours. [110]The wicked have set their traps for me along your path, but I will not turn aside. [112]I am determined to obey you until I die. [166]I long for your salvation, Lord, and so I have obeyed your laws. [167]I have looked for your commandments and I love them very much; [168]yes, I have searched for them. You know this because everything I do is known to you.

Acts 23:1. Gazing intently at the Council, Paul began: "Brothers, I have always lived before God in all good conscience!"

Acts 24:16. Because of this I try with all my strength to always maintain a clear conscience before God and man.

Rom 6:17. Thank God that though you once chose to be slaves of sin, now you have obeyed with all your heart the teaching to which God has committed you.

2 Cor 1:12. We are so glad that we can say with utter honesty that in all our dealings we have been pure and sincere, quietly depending upon the Lord for his help, and not on our own skills. And that is even more true, if possible about the way we have acted toward you.

2 Cor 6:3. We try to live in such a way that no one will ever be offended or kept back from finding the Lord by the way we act, so that no one can find fault with us and blame it on the Lord.

Phil 3:7. But all these things that I once thought very worthwhile—now I've thrown them all away so that I can put my trust and hope in Christ alone. [8]Yes, everything else is worthless when compared with the priceless gain of knowing Christ Jesus my Lord. I have put aside all else, counting it worth less than nothing, in order that I can have Christ, [9]and become one with him, no longer counting on being saved by being good enough or by obeying God's laws, but by trusting Christ to save me; for God's way of making us right with himself depends on faith—counting on Christ alone. [10]Now I have given up everything else—I have found it to be the only way to really know Christ and to experience the mighty power that brought him back to life again, and to find out what it means to suffer and to die with him. [11]So, whatever it takes, I will be one who lives in the fresh newness of life of those who are alive from the dead. [12]I don't mean to say I am perfect. I haven't learned all I should even yet, but I keep working toward that day when I will finally be all that Christ saved me for and wants me to be. [13]No, dear brothers, I am still not all I should be but I am bringing all my energies to bear on this one thing: Forgetting the past and looking forward to what lies ahead, [14]I strain to reach the end of the race and receive the prize for which God is calling us up to heaven because of what Christ Jesus did for us.

1 Thess 1:9. For *they* keep telling *us* about the wonderful welcome you gave us, and how you turned away from your idols to God so that now the living and true God only is your Master.

1 Thess 2:10. You yourselves are our witnesses—as is God—that we have been pure and honest and faultless toward every one of you.

2 Tim 1:3. How I thank God for you, Timothy. I pray for you every day, and many times during the long nights I beg God to bless you richly. He is my fathers' God, and mine, and my only purpose in life is to please him.

Rev 2:19. I am aware of all your good deeds—your kindness to the poor, your gifts and service to them; also I know your love and faith and patience, and I can see your constant improvement in all these things.

Rev 3:4. Yet even there in Sardis some haven't soiled their garments with the world's filth; they shall walk with me in white, for they are worthy.

Rev 14:4. For they are spiritually undefiled, pure as virgins, following the Lamb wherever he goes. They have been purchased from among the men on the earth as a consecrated offering to God and the Lamb. [5]No falsehood can be charged against them; they are blameless.

See *Blessing, Contingent on Obedience; Commandments.*

FILIAL. See *Children.*

INSTANCES OF. Noah, Gen 6:9, 10, 22; 7:5; Heb 11:7. Abraham, Gen 12:1–4; 17:23; 21:4, 5; 22:12; Neh 9:8; Acts 7:3–8; Heb 11:8–17; Jas 2:21. Bethuel and Laban, Gen 24:50. Jacob, Gen 35:1, 7. Moses, Num 27:12–22; Heb 3:2, 3. Moses and Aaron, Ex 7:6; 40:16, 21, 23, 32. Israelites, Ex 12:28; 32:25–29; 39:42, 43; Num 9:20, 21; Deut 33:9; Judg 2:7–9; Ps 99:7. Under the preaching of Haggai, Hag 1:12.

Caleb, Deut 1:36. Joshua, Josh 10:40; 11:15. Reubenites, Josh 22:2, 3. Gideon, Judg 6:25–28. David, 1 Sam 18:14; 25:28; 1 Kgs 11:6, 34; 15:5; 2 Chron 29:2; Acts 13:22. Elisha, 1 Kgs 19:19–21. Hezekiah, 2 Kgs 18:6; 2 Chron 31:20, 21; Isa 38:3. Josiah, 2 Kgs 22:1, 2; 23:24, 25. Asa, 2 Chron 14:2. Jehoshaphat, 2 Chron 17:3–6; 20:32; 22:9. Jehoiada, 2 Chron 24:16. Uzziah, 2 Chron 26:4, 5. Jotham, 2 Chron 27:2. Levites, 2 Chron 29:34. Cyrus, 2 Chron 36:22, 23; Ezra 1:1–4. Ezra, Ezra 7:10. Hananiah, Neh 7:2. Job, Job 1:8. Daniel, Dan 6:10. Three Hebrews, Dan 3. Jonah, Jon 3:3. Ninevites, Jon 3:4–10.

Zacharias, Lk 1:6. Simeon, Lk 2:25. Joseph, Mt 1:24; 2:14. Mary, Lk 1:38.

Jesus, Mt 3:15; 26:39, 42; Lk 22:41, 42; Jn 4:32, 34; 5:30; 12:49, 50; 14:31; 17:4; Heb 3:2.

John the Baptist, Mt 3:15. John and James, Mk 1:19, 20. Matthew, Mt 9:9. Simon and Andrew, Mk 1:16–18. Levi, Mk 2:14. Nathanael, Jn 1:47. The rich young man, Mt 19:20; Mk 10:19, 20; Lk 18:21. The disciples, Jn 17:6. Cornelius, Acts 10:2. Paul, Acts 23:1; Acts 26:4, 5; 2 Tim 1:3.

TO CIVIL LAW. See *Citizens.*

OBIL An Ishmaelite. Camel keeper for David, 1 Chron 27:30.

OBJECT TEACHING See *Instruction.*

OBLATION See *Offerings.*

OBLIGATION A motive of obedience, Deut 4:32–40; chapters 6–11; 26:16; 32:6; 1 Sam 12:24; 1 Chron 16:12, 13; Rom 2:4; 2 Cor 5:15. Acknowledgement of, Ps 116:12–14, 17.

See *Duty.*

OBOTH A camping place of the Israelites in the 40 years' wandering, Num 21:10; 33:43.

OBSEQUIOUSNESS INSTANCES OF. Abigail, 1 Sam 25:23–31, 41. Mephibosheth, 2 Sam 9:8. The woman of Tekoa, 2 Sam 14:4–20.

OBSTETRICS Ezk 16:4.

See *Midwifery.*

OCCULT SCIENCE See *Sorcery.*

OCEAN See *Seas.*

OCHRAN An Asherite and the father of Pagiel who assisted in the census of Israel, Num 1:2–15; 2:3–31; 10:26.

OCTOBER See *Calendar.*

ODED 1. A prophet in Samaria, 2 Chron 28:9.

2. Father of the prophet Azariah, 2 Chron 15:1.

ODOR See *Incense; Perfume.*

OFFENSES See *Sin; Temptation.*

OFFERINGS Offered at the door of the Tabernacle, Lev 1:2, 3; 3:2; 17:3, 4, 8, 9; at the Temple, 2 Chron 7:12; 1 Kgs 8:62, 63; 12:27. All animal sacrifices must be eight days old or over, Lev 22:26, 27. Must be salted, Lev 2:13; Ezk 43:24; Mk 9:49; accompanied with leaven, Lev 7:13; without leaven, Ex 23:18; 34:25. Eaten, 1 Sam 9:12, 13. Ordinance relating to scapegoat, Lev 16:7–26. Atonement for sin made by, see *Atonement.*

FIGURATIVE. Ps 51:16, 17; Jer 33:10, 11; Rom 12:1; Phil 4:18; Heb 13:15.

ANIMAL SACRIFICES. A type of Christ, Ps 40:6–8, with Heb 10:1–14; Isa 53:11, 12, with Lev 16:21; Jn 1:29; 1 Cor 5:7; 2 Cor 5:21; Eph 5:2; Heb 9:19–28; 10:1, 11, 12; 13:11–13; Rev 5:6.

BURNT. Lev 9:2. Its purpose was to make an atonement for sin, Lev 1:4; 7. Ordinances concerning, Ex 29:15–18; Lev 1; 5:7–10; 6:9–13; 17:8, 9; 23:18, 26–37; Num 15:23–25; 19:9; 28:26–31; 29. Accompanied by other offerings, Num 15:3–16. Skins of, belonged to priests, Lev 7:8. Offered daily, morning and evening, Gen 15:17; Ex 29:38–42; Lev 6:19, 20; Num 28; 29:6; 1 Chron 16:40; 2 Chron 2:4; 13:11; Ezra 3:3; Ezk 46:13–15. Music with, Num 10:10.

DRINK. Libations of wine offered with the sacrifices, Gen 35:13, 14; Ex 29:40, 41; 30:9; Lev 23:13, 18; Num 6:17; 15:23, 24; 28:5–15, 24–31; 29:6–11, 18–40; 2 Kgs 16:13; 1 Chron 29:21; 2 Chron 29:35; Ezra 7:17.

OF FIRST FRUITS. See *First Fruits.*

FREE WILL. Must be perfect, Lev 22:17–25. To be eaten by priests, Lev 7:11–18. With meat and drink offerings, Num 15:1–16. Obligatory when promised in a vow, Deut 16:10; 23:23.

GRAIN. See *Offerings, Meal.*

GUILT. Ordinances concerning, Lev 5; 6:1–7; 7:1–7; 14:10–22; 15:15, 29, 30; 19:21, 22; Num 6:12; Ezra 10:19. To be eaten by the priests, Lev 7:6, 7; 14:13; Num 18:9, 10. Offered by idolaters, 1 Sam 6:3, 8, 17, 18. See *Offerings, Sin,* below.

HEAVE. Given to the priests' families as part of their compensation, Lev 10:14; Num 5:9, 10; 18:10–19, 24. Consecrated by being elevated by the priest, Lev 10:15. Consisted of the right thigh and breast, Ex 29:27, 28; Lev 7:12–14, 32–34; 10:15; spoils, including captives and other articles of war, Num 31:29–41. When offered, Lev 7:12–14; Num 6:20; 15:19–21. In certain instances this offering was brought to the Tabernacle, or Temple, Deut 12:6, 11, 17, 18. To be offered on taking possession of the land of Canaan, Num 15:17–21.

HUMAN SACRIFICES. Forbidden, Lev 18:21; 20:1–5; Deut 12:31. Offered by Abraham, Gen 22:1–19; Heb 11:17–19; by Canaanites, Deut 12:31; Moabites, 2 Kgs 3:27. Israelites, 2 Kgs 16:3; 2 Chron 28:3; 2 Kgs 23:10; Isa 57:5; Jer 7:31; 19:5; 32:35; Ezk 16:20, 21; 20:26, 31; 23:37, 39; by the Sepharites to idols, 2 Kgs 17:31. To demons, Ps 106:37, 38; and to Baal, Jer 19:5, 6.

IDOLS, OFFERINGS TO. Ex 32:6; Acts 7:41; 15:27–29; 21:25; 1 Cor 8:1, 4, 7, 10; 10:19, 28; cf. Rom 14:13–23.

INSUFFICIENCY OF. Heb 8:7. The old agreement didn't even work. If it had, there would have been no need for another to replace it. [8]But God himself found fault with the old one, for he said, "The day will come when I will make a new agreement with the people of Israel and the people of Judah. [9]This new agreement will not be like the old one I gave to their fathers on the day when I took them by the hand to lead them out of the land of Egypt; they did not keep their part in that agreement, so I had to cancel it. [10]But this is the new agreement I will make with the people of Israel, says the Lord: I will write my laws in their minds so that they will know what I want them to do without my even telling them, and these laws will be in their hearts so that they will want to obey them, and I will be their God and they shall be my people. [11]And no one then will need to speak to his friend or neighbor or brother, saying, 'You, too, should know the Lord,' because everyone, great and small, will know me already. [12]And I will be merciful to them in their wrongdoings, and I will remember their sins no more." [13]God speaks of these new promises, of this new agreement, as taking the place of the old one; for the old one is out of date now and has been put aside forever.

Heb 9:1, 2. Now in that first agreement between God and his people there were rules for worship and there was a sacred tent down here on earth. Inside this place of worship there were two rooms. The first one contained the golden candlestick and a table with special loaves of holy bread upon it; this part was called the Holy Place. [3]Then there was a curtain and behind the curtain was a room called the Holy of Holies. [4]In that room there were a golden incense-altar and the golden chest, called the ark of the covenant, completely covered on all

sides with pure gold. Inside the ark were the tablets
of stone with the Ten Commandments written on
them, and a golden jar with some manna in it, and
Aaron's wooden cane that budded. [5]Above the
golden chest were statues of angels called cherubim
—the guardians of God's glory—with their wings
stretched out over the ark's golden cover, called
the mercy seat. But enough of such details. [6]Well,
when all was ready the priests went in and out of
the first room whenever they wanted to, doing their
work. [7]But only the high priest went into the inner
room, and then only once a year, all alone, and
always with blood which he sprinkled on the mercy
seat as an offering to God to cover his own mistakes and sins, and the mistakes and sins of all the
people. [8]And the Holy Spirit uses all this to point
out to us that under the old system the common
people could not go into the Holy of Holies as long
as the outer room and the entire system it represents were still in use. [9]This has an important lesson for us today. For under the old system, gifts
and sacrifices were offered, but these failed to
cleanse the hearts of the people who brought them.
[10]For the old system dealt only with certain rituals
—what foods to eat and drink, rules for washing
themselves, and rules about this and that. The people had to keep these rules to tide them over until
Christ came with God's new and better way. [11]He
came as High Priest of this better system which we
now have. He went into that greater, perfect tabernacle in heaven, not made by men nor part of this
world, [12]and once for all took blood into that inner
room, the Holy of Holies, and sprinkled it on the
mercy seat; but it was not the blood of goats and
calves. No, he took his own blood, and with it he,
by himself, made sure of our eternal salvation.
[13]And if under the old system the blood of bulls and
goats and the ashes of young cows could cleanse
men's bodies from sin, [14]just think how much more
surely the blood of Christ will transform our lives
and hearts. His sacrifice frees us from the worry of
having to obey the old rules, and makes us want to
serve the living God. For by the help of the eternal
Holy Spirit, Christ willingly gave himself to God
to die for our sins—he being perfect, without a
single sin or fault. [15]Christ came with this new
agreement so that all who are invited may come
and have forever all the wonders God has promised them. For Christ died to rescue them from the
penalty of the sins they had committed while still
under that old system.

Heb 10:1. The old system of Jewish laws gave
only a dim foretaste of the good things Christ
would do for us. The sacrifices under the old system were repeated again and again, year after year,
but even so they could never save those who lived
under their rules. [2]If they could have, one offering
would have been enough; the worshipers would
have been cleansed once for all, and their feeling of
guilt would be gone. [3]But just the opposite happened: those yearly sacrifices reminded them of
their disobedience and guilt instead of relieving
their minds. [4]For it is not possible for the blood of
bulls and goats really to take away sins. [5]That is
why Christ said, as he came into the world, "O
God, the blood of bulls and goats cannot satisfy
you, so you have made ready this body of mine for
me to lay as a sacrifice upon your altar. [6]You were
not satisfied with the animal sacrifices, slain and
burnt before you as offerings for sin. [7]Then I said,
'See, I have come to do your will, to lay down my
life, just as the Scriptures said that I would.' "
[8]After Christ said this, about being satisfied with
the various sacrifices and offerings required under
the old system, [9]he then added, "Here I am. I have
come to give my life." He cancels the first system
in favor of a far better one. [10]Under this new plan
we have been forgiven and made clean by Christ's
dying for us once and for all. [11]Under the old agreement the priests stood before the altar day after day
offering sacrifices that could never take away our
sins. [12]But Christ gave himself to God for our sins
as one sacrifice for all time, and then sat down in
the place of highest honor at God's right hand.
[18]Now, when sins have once been forever forgiven
and forgotten, there is no need to offer more sacrifices to get rid of them. [19]And so, dear brothers,
now we may walk right into the very Holy of Holies where God is, because of the blood of Jesus.
[20]This is the fresh, new, life-giving way which
Christ has opened up for us by tearing the curtain
—his human body—to let us into the holy presence
of God.

See *Ordinances.*

MEAT, OR MEAL. Ordinances concerning, Ex 29:40, 41; 30:9; 40:29; Lev 2; 5:11, 12; 6:14–23; 7:9–13, 37; 9:17; 23:13, 15–17; Num 4:16; 5:15, 18, 25, 26; 8:8; 15:3–16, 23, 24; 18:9; 28:5, 9, 10, 12, 13, 20, 21, 26–31; 29:3, 4, 14. To be eaten in the holy place, Lev 10:13; Num 18:9, 10. Offered with the sacrifices, Num 15:3–16. Not mixed with leaven, Lev 2:4, 11; 6:14–18; 10:12, 13; Num 6:15, 17. Storerooms for, in the temple reconstructed by Ezra, Neh 12:44; 13:5, 6; provided for in the vision of Ezekiel, Ezk 42:13.

PEACE. Laws concerning, Ex 29:19–22, 31; Lev 7:11–15, 17, 18; 9:3, 4, 15–21; 23:19; Num 6:14; 10:10.

SIN. Ordinances concerning, Ex 29:10–14 with Heb 13:11–13; Lev 4; 5; 6:1–7, 26–30; 9:1–21; 12:6–8; 14:19, 22, 31; 15:30; 23:19; Num 6:10, 11, 14, 16; 8:8, 12; 15:27; 28:15, 22–24, 30; 29:5, 6, 11, 16–38. Temporary, Dan 11:30, 31; Heb 9; 10. See *Offerings, Guilt.*

SPECIAL SACRIFICES. In consecration of the altar, see *Altar;* of priests, see *Priest;* of the temple, see *Temple, Dedication of;* for leprosy, see *Leprosy;* for defilement, see *Defilement.*

THANK. Ordinances concerning, Lev 7:11–15; 22:29, 30; Deut 12:11, 12.

TRESPASS. See *Offering, Guilt; Offering, Sin; above.*

UNAVAILING WHEN NOT ACCOMPANIED BY PIETY. 1 Sam 15:22. Samuel replied, "Has the Lord as much pleasure in your burnt offerings and sacrifices as in your obedience? Obedience is far better than sacrifice. He is much more interested in your listening to him than in your offering the fat of rams to him."

Ps 40:6. It isn't sacrifices and offerings which you really want from your people. Burnt animals bring no special joy to your heart.

Ps 50:8. I have no complaint about the sacrifices you bring to my altar, for you bring them regularly. [9]But it isn't sacrificial bullocks and goats that I really want from you. [10, 11]For all the animals of field and forest are mine! The cattle on a thousand hills! And all the birds upon the mountains! [12]If I were hungry, I would not mention it to you—for all the world is mine, and everything in it. [13]No, I don't need your sacrifices of flesh and blood. [14]What I want from you is your true thanks; I want your promises fulfilled.

Ps 51:16. You don't want penance, if you did, how gladly I would do it! You aren't interested in offerings burned before you on the altar. [17]It is a broken spirit you want—remorse and penitence. A broken and a contrite heart, O God, you will not ignore.

Prov 21:3. God is more pleased when we are just and fair than when we give him gifts. [27]God loathes the gifts of evil men, especially if they are trying to bribe him!

Isa 1:11. I am sick of your sacrifices. Don't bring me any more of them. I don't want your fat rams; I don't want to see the blood from your offerings. [12, 13]Who wants your sacrifices when you have no sorrow for your sins? The incense you bring me is a stench in my nostrils. Your holy celebrations of the new moon and the Sabbath, and your special days for fasting—even your most pious meetings—all are frauds! I want nothing more to do with them. [14]I hate them all; I can't stand the sight of them.

Isa 40:16. All of Lebanon's forests do not contain sufficient fuel to consume a sacrifice large enough to honor him, nor are all its animals enough to offer to our God.

Isa 66:3. But those who choose their own ways, delighting in their sins, are cursed. God will not accept their offerings. When such men sacrifice an ox on the altar of God, it is no more acceptable to him than human sacrifice. If they sacrifice a lamb, or bring an offering of grain, it is as loathsome to God as putting a dog or the blood of a swine on his altar! When they burn incense to him, he counts it the same as though they blessed an idol.

Jer 6:20. There is no use now in burning sweet incense from Sheba before me! Keep your expensive perfumes! I cannot accept your offerings; they have no sweet fragrance for me.

Jer 7:21. The Lord of Hosts, the God of Israel says, Away with your offerings and sacrifices! [22]It wasn't offerings and sacrifices I wanted from your fathers when I led them out of Egypt. That was not the point of my command. [23]But what I told them was: *Obey* me and I will be your God and you shall be my people; only do as I say and all shall be well!

Hos 6:6. I don't want your sacrifices—I want your love; I don't want your offerings—I want you to know me.

Hos 8:13. Her people love the ritual of their sacrifice, but to me it is meaningless! I will call for an accounting of their sins and punish them; they shall return to Egypt.

Amos 5:21. I hate your show and pretense—your hypocrisy of "honoring" me with your religious feasts and solemn assemblies. [22]I will not accept your burnt offerings and thank offerings. I will not look at your offerings of peace. [23]Away with your hymns of praise—they are mere noise to my ears. I will not listen to your music, no matter how lovely it is. [24]I want to see a mighty flood of justice —a torrent of doing good.

Mic 6:6. "How can we make up to you for what we've done?" you ask. "Shall we bow before the Lord with offerings of yearling calves?" Oh, no! [7]For if you offered him thousands of rams and ten thousands of rivers of olive oil—would that please him? Would he be satisfied? If you sacrificed your oldest child, would that make him glad? Then would he forgive your sins? Of course not! [8]No, he has told you what he wants, and this is all it is: *to be fair and just and merciful, and to walk humbly with your God.*

Mk 12:33. And I know it is far more important to love him with all my heart and understanding and strength, and to love others as myself, than to offer all kinds of sacrifices on the altar of the Temple.

VOW. Lev 7:16–18; 22:17–25; Deut 23:21–23.

WAVE. Ordinances concerning, Ex 29:22, 26–28; Lev 7:29–34; 8:25–29; 9:19–21; 10:14, 15; 23:9–11, 17–20; Num 5:25; 6:19, 20. Belonged to the priests, Ex 29:26–28; Lev 7:31, 34; 8:29; 10:15; 23:20; Num 18:11, 18. To be eaten, Lev 10:14, 15; Num 18:11, 18, 19, 31.

WOOD. Fuel for the Temple, Neh 10:34; 13:31.

OFFICER CIVIL. Chosen by the people, Deut 1:13–16; appointed by kings, 2 Sam 8:16–18; 20:23–26; 1 Kgs 4:1–19; 9:22; Ezra 7:25.

See *Government; Judge; Ruler.*

ECCLESIASTICAL. See *Priest; Levites; Apostles; Deacon; Elder.*

MILITARY. Isa 3:3. Of the guard, 2 Kgs 11:15. Of Naphtali, 1 Chron 12:24–37. Of David, 2 Sam 23; 1 Chron 11; 12.

Roman, in charge of the soldiers who crucified Jesus, testifies, "Truly, this was the son of God!" Mt 27:54; Mk 15:39, 44, 45; Lk 23:47. See *Julius.* One whose servant was healed by Jesus, Mt 8:5–13.

See *Armies; Battalion Leader; Captain; Colonel; Commander; General; Lieutenant.*

OFFICIAL See *Officer.*

OFFSPRING See *Children.*

OG King of Bashan. A man of gigantic stature, Num 21:33; Deut 3:11; Josh 12:4; 13:12. Defeated and killed by Moses, Num 21:33–35; Deut 1:1–5; 3:1–7; 29:7; 31:4; Josh 2:10; 9:10; Ps 135:10, 11; 136:18–20. Land of, given to Gad, Reuben, and Manasseh, Num 32:33; Deut 3:8–17; 4:47–49; 29:7, 8; Josh 12:4–6; 13:12, 30, 31; Neh 9:22; Ps 136:20, 21.

OHAD Son of Simeon, Gen 46:8–14; Ex 6:15.

OHEL Son of Zerubbabel, 1 Chron 3:19, 20.

OHOLAH Name of an imaginary woman, typical of idolatry, Ezk 23:4, 5.

OHOLIAB A craftsman who assisted in building the Tabernacle, Ex 31:6; 35:34; 36:1, 2; 38:23.

OHOLIBAH An imaginary character, typical of idolatry, Ezk 23:4, 5.

OHOLIBAMAH 1. Wife of Esau, Gen 26:2, 3, 18, 19. She is probably identical with Judith, of Gen 26:34.

2. An Edomite prince, Gen 36:40–43.

OIL Sacred, Ex 30:22–25; 31:11; 35:5–19, 28; 37:29; 39:33–40; Num 4:16. Uses of, Ex 30:26–33. Compounded by Bezalel, Ex 37:1, 29. Punishment for profaning, Ex 30:31–33.

Used for idols, Ezk 23:41. Illuminating, for Tabernacle, Ex 25:1–7; 27:20; Lev 24:1–4. For domestic use, Mt 25:2–4. Used for food, Lev 2:4, 5; 14:10, 21; Deut 12:17; 1 Kgs 17:12–16. For the head, Ps 23:5; Lk 7:46. For anointing kings, 1 Sam 10:1; 16:1, 13; 1 Kgs 1:39. Commerce in, 2 Kgs 4:1–7.

Miracles of, 1 Kgs 17:12–15; 2 Kgs 4:1–7.

FIGURATIVE. Job 29:6; Isa 61:1; Zech 4:12; Mt 25:2–4.

See *Anointing; Ointment.*

OINTMENT 2 Chron 16:13, 14; Esther 2:12–14; Isa 38:21; Amos 6:6; Lk 23:56; 24:1; Jn 19:39; Rev 18:13.

See *Oil.*

OLD AGE Gen 15:15. But you will die in peace, at a ripe old age.

Gen 47:9. Jacob replied, "I have lived 130 long, hard years, and I am not nearly as old as many of my ancestors."

Lev 19:32. You shall give due honor and respect to the elderly, in the fear of God. 1 Tim 5:1.

Deut 34:7. Moses was 120 years old when he died, yet his eyesight was perfect and he was as strong as a young man.

2 Sam 19:34. "No," he replied, "I am far too old for that. [35]I am eighty years old today, and life has lost its excitement. Food and wine are no longer tasty, and entertainment is not much fun; I would only be a burden to my lord the king. [36]Just to go across the river with you is all the honor I need! [37]Then let me return again to die in my own city, where my father and mother are buried."

2 Chron 29:28. He died at an old age, wealthy and honored; and his son Solomon reigned in his place.

Job 5:26. You shall live a long, good life; like standing grain, you'll not be harvested until it's time!

Job 12:12. And as you say, older men like me are wise. They understand.

Job 32:4. Elihu had waited until now to speak because the others were older than he. [5]But when he saw that they had no further reply, he spoke out angrily, [6]and said, "I am young and you are old, so I held back and did not dare to tell you what I think, [7]for those who are older are said to be wiser; [8, 9]but it is not mere age that makes men wise. Rather, it is the spirit in a man, the breath of the Almighty which makes him intelligent."

Job 42:17. Then at last he died, an old, old man, after living a long, good life.

Ps 71:9. And now, in my old age, don't set me aside. Don't forsake me now when my strength is failing. [18]And now that I am old and gray, don't forsake me. Give me time to tell this new generation (and their children too) about all your mighty miracles.

Ps 90:10. Seventy years are given us! And some may even live to eighty. But even the best of these years are often emptiness and pain; soon they disappear, and we are gone.

Ps 92:14. Even in old age they will still produce fruit and be vital and green.

Ps 148:12. Young men and maidens, old men and children— [13]all praise the Lord together.

Prov 16:31. White hair is a crown of glory and is seen most among the godly.

Prov 23:22. Listen to your father's advice and don't despise an old mother's experience.

Eccl 6:3. Even if a man has a hundred sons and as many daughters and lives to be very old, but leaves so little money at his death that his children can't even give him a decent burial—I say that he would be better off born dead. [6]Though a man lives a thousand years twice over, but doesn't find contentment—well, what's the use?

Eccl 12:1. Don't let the excitement of being young cause you to forget about your Creator. Honor him in your youth before the evil years come—when you'll no longer enjoy living. [2]It will be too late then to try to remember him, when the sun and light and moon and stars are dim to your old eyes, and there is no silver lining left among your clouds. [3]For there will come a time when your limbs will tremble with age, and your strong legs will become weak, and your teeth will be too few to do their work, and there will be blindness, too. [4]Then let your lips be tightly closed while eating, when your teeth are gone! And you will waken at dawn with the first note of the birds; but you yourself will be deaf and tuneless, with quavering voice. [5]You will be afraid of heights and of falling—a white-haired, withered old man, dragging himself along: without sexual desire, standing at death's door, and nearing his everlasting home as the mourners go along the streets. [6]Yes, remember your Creator now while you are young, before the silver cord of life snaps, and the golden bowl is broken, and the pitcher is broken at the fountain, and the wheel is broken at the cistern; [7]and the dust returns to the earth as it was, and the spirit returns to God who gave it.

Isa 46:4. I will be your God through all your lifetime, yes, even when your hair is white with age. I made you and I will carry you along and be your Savior.

Lk 2:37. And [Anna] was very old, for she had been a widow for eighty-four years following seven years of marriage. She never left the Temple but stayed there night and day, worshiping God by praying and often fasting.

Tit 2:2. Teach the older men to be serious and unruffled; they must be sensible, knowing and believing the truth and doing everything with love and patience. [3]Teach the older women to be quiet and respectful in everything they do. They must not go around speaking evil of others and must not be heavy drinkers, but they should be teachers of goodness.

Philemon 1:9. But I love you and prefer just to ask you—I, Paul, an old man now, here in jail for the sake of Jesus Christ.

See *Longevity; Ailment.*

OLIVE A fruit tree. Leaf of, brought by the dove to Noah's ark, Gen 8:11. Common to the land of Canaan, Ex 23:11; Deut 6:10–12; 8:8; 28:40. Branches of, used for shelters, Neh 8:15. Bears flowers, Job 15:33. Precepts concerning gleaning the fruit of, Deut 24:20; Isa 17:6. Cherubim and doors made of the wood of, 1 Kgs 6:23–28, 31–33. Fable of, Judg 9:8.

FIGURATIVE. Of prosperity, Ps 128:3. The wild, a figure of the Gentiles; the cultivated, of the Jews, Rom 11:17–21, 24.

Symbolical. Zech 4:2–12; Rev 11:4.

FRUIT OF. Oil extracted from, used as illuminating oil in the Tabernacle, Lev 24:1, 2; Zech 4:12. See *Oil.*

OLIVES, MOUNT OF Called *Mount of Destruction,* 2 Kgs 23:13. East of Jerusalem. The highway to and from the east passed over it, 2 Sam 15:30. Jesus' triumphant entry into Jerusalem by way of, Mt 21:1; Mk 11:1; Lk 19:29, 36, 37. Jesus goes to, Mt 24:3; 26:30; Mk 13:3, 4; 14:26; Lk 21:37, 38; 22:39. Jesus makes his ascension from, Acts 1:12. Christ returns to, Zech 14:4.

OLYMPAS A believer at Rome, Rom 16:15.

OMAR Son of Eliphaz, grandson of Esau, Gen 36:10–12, 15, 16; 1 Chron 1:36.

OMEGA See *Alpha and Omega.*

OMER A dry measure, one-tenth of an ephah, approximately 2 quarts (2 liters), Ex 16:16–18, 36.

OMNIPOTENCE See *God, Omnipotent; Jesus, Omnipotence of.*

OMNIPRESENCE See *God, Omnipresent; Jesus, Omnipresence of.*

OMNISCIENCE See *God, Omniscient; Jesus, Omniscience of.*

OMRI 1. King of Israel. Was commander of the army of Israel, and was proclaimed king by the army upon news of assassination of King Elah, 1 Kgs 16:15, 16. Defeats his rival, Tibni, and establishes himself, 1 Kgs 16:17–22. Surrendered cities to king of Syria, 1 Kgs 10:34. Wicked reign and death of, 1 Kgs 16:23–28. Denounced by Micah, Mic 6:16.

2. A son of Becher, grandson of Benjamin, 1 Chron 7:8.

3. A descendant of Perez, 1 Chron 9:4.

4. Son of Michael, a ruler of tribe of Issachar in time of David, 1 Chron 27:16–22.

ON A leader of the Reubenites who rebelled against Moses, Num 16:1.

ONAM 1. A son of Shobal, Gen 36:23; 1 Chron 1:40.

2. Son of Jerahmeel, 1 Chron 2:26, 28.

ONAN Son of Judah. Killed for his refusal to consummate his marriage to his brother's widow, Gen 38:3–5, 8–10; 46:8–14; Num 26:19–22; 1 Chron 2:3.

ONESIMUS A fugitive slave and convert of Paul, Col 4:9; Philemon 1:10.

ONESIPHORUS A loyal Christian of Ephesus, 2 Tim 1:16, 17; 4:19.

ONION Num 11:4, 5.

ONO A town of Benjamin, 1 Chron 8:12; Neh 6:2; 11:31–35.

ONYCHA A component of the sacred ointment, made from the shells of a species of mussel, Ex 30:34.

ONYX Precious stone, Job 28:16; Ezk 28:13. Used in erecting the Temple, 1 Chron 29:2. Used in the ephod and chestpiece, Ex 28:9–12, 20; 39:6, 7, 13. Contributed by Israelites for the priests' garments, Ex 25:1–7; 35:5–9.

OPHEL The ancient name given to the hill on which Jebus or Jerusalem stood; after its capture by the Israelites it became the city of David, the stronghold of Zion, 2 Sam 5:6–9; 1 Chron 11:4–8. In the days of Nehemiah it was the home of the Nethinims, Neh 3:26, 27; 11:21. The word Ophel, meaning a hill or tower, was applied primarily to the southeastern hill, south of the temple and above the spring Gihon.

OPHIR 1. Son of Joktan, Gen 10:26–30; 1 Chron 1:20–23.

2. A country celebrated for its gold and other valuable merchandise. Products of, used by Solomon and Hiram, 1 Kgs 9:27, 28; 10:11; 2 Chron 8:17, 18; 9:10. Jehoshaphat sends ships to, which are wrecked, 1 Kgs 22:48. Gold of, proverbial for its fineness, 1 Chron 29:4; Job 28:16; Ps 45:9; Isa 13:12.

OPHNI A town of Benjamin, Josh 18:21–28.

OPHRAH 1. A city in Benjamin, Josh 18:21–28; 1 Sam 13:17. Possibly identical with *Ephron,* 2 Chron 13:18, 19; and *Ephraim,* Jn 11:54.

2. A city in Manasseh, home of Gideon, Judg 6:11, 24; 8:27, 32; 9:5.

3. Son of Meonothai, 1 Chron 4:14.

OPINION, PUBLIC Kings influenced by, see *Kings.* Jesus inquires about, Mt 16:13; Lk 9:18. Feared by Nicodemus, Jn 3:1, 2; Joseph of Arimathea, Jn 19:38; the parents of the man who was born blind, Jn 9:21–23; rulers, who believed in Jesus, but feared the Pharisees, Jn 12:42, 43; chief priests, who feared to answer the questions of Jesus, Mt 21:26; Mk 11:18, 32; 12:12; and to further persecute the disciples, Acts 4:21; 5:26, 27.

CONCESSIONS TO. By Paul, in circumcising Timothy, Acts 16:3. James and the Christian elders, who required Paul to observe certain rites, Acts 21:18–27. Disciples, who urged circumcision, Gal 6:12. Peter and Barnabas with others, Gal 2:11–14.

CORRUPT YIELDING TO. By Herod, in the case of John the Baptist, Mk 6:26; of Peter, Acts

12:3; by Peter, concerning Jesus, Mt 26:69–75; by Pilate, Mt 27:23–27; Mk 15:15; Lk 23:13–25; Jn 18: 38, 39; 19:4–16; by Felix and Festus, concerning Paul, Acts 24:27; 25:9.

OPPORTUNITY THE MEASURE OF RESPONSIBILITY. Prov 1:24. I have called you so often but still you won't come. I have pleaded, but all in vain. [25]For you have spurned my counsel and reproof. [26]Some day you'll be in trouble, and I'll laugh! Mock me, will you?—I'll mock you! [27]When a storm of terror surrounds you, and when you are engulfed by anguish and distress, [28]then I will not answer your cry for help. It will be too late though you search for me ever so anxiously. [29]For you closed your eyes to the facts and did not choose to reverence and trust the Lord, [30]and you turned your back on me, spurning my advice. [31]That is why you must eat the bitter fruit of having your own way, and experience the full terrors of the pathway you have chosen. [32]For you turned away from me—to death; your own complacency will kill you. Fools! [33]But all who listen to me shall live in peace and safety, unafraid.

Jer 8:20. The harvest is finished; the summer is over and we are not saved.

Ezk 3:19. But if you warn them and they keep on sinning, and refuse to repent, they will die in their sins, but you are blameless—you have done all you could. chapter 33:1–17.

Hos 5:6. Then at last, they will come with their flocks and herds to sacrifice to God, but it will be too late—they will not find him. He has withdrawn from them and they are left alone.

Mt 10:14. Any city or home that doesn't welcome you—shake off the dust of that place from your feet as you leave. [15]Truly, the wicked cities of Sodom and Gomorrah will be better off at Judgment Day than they.

Mt 11:20. Then he began to pour out his denunciations against the cities where he had done most of his miracles, because they hadn't turned to God. [21]"Woe to you, Chorazin, and woe to you, Bethsaida! For if the miracles I did in your streets had been done in wicked Tyre and Sidon their people would have repented in shame and humility. [22]Truly, Tyre and Sidon will be better off on the Judgment Day than you! [23]And Capernaum, though highly honored, shall go down to hell! For if the marvelous miracles I did in you had been done in Sodom, it would still be here today. [24]Truly, Sodom will be better off at the Judgment Day than you."

Mt 23:34. I will send you prophets, and wise men, and inspired writers, and you will kill some by crucifixion, and rip open the backs of others with whips in your synagogues, and hound them from city to city, [35]so that you will become guilty of all the blood of murdered godly men from righteous Abel to Zechariah (son of Barachiah), slain by you in the Temple between the altar and the sanctuary. [36]Yes, all the accumulated judgment of the centuries shall break upon the heads of this very generation. [37]O Jerusalem, Jerusalem, the city that kills the prophets, and stones all those God sends to her! How often I have wanted to gather your children together as a hen gathers her chicks beneath her wings, but you wouldn't let me. [38]And now your house is left to you, desolate.

Mt 25:1. The kingdom of Heaven can be illustrated by the story of ten bridesmaids who took their lamps and went to meet the bridegroom. [2-4]But only five of them were wise enough to fill their lamps with oil, while the other five were foolish and forgot. [5, 6]So, when the bridegroom was delayed, they lay down to rest until midnight, when they were roused by the shout, "The bridegroom is coming! Come out and welcome him!" [7, 8]All the girls jumped up and trimmed their lamps. Then the five who hadn't any oil begged the others to share with them, for their lamps were going out. [9]But the others replied, "We haven't enough. Go instead to the shops and buy some for yourselves." [10]But while they were gone, the bridegroom came, and those who were ready went in with him to the marriage feast, and the door was locked. [11]Later, when the other five returned, they stood outside, calling, "Sir, open the door for us!" [12]But he called back, "Go away! It is too late!" [13]So stay awake and be prepared, for you do not know the date or moment of my return. [14]Again, the Kingdom of Heaven can be illustrated by the story of a man going into another country, who called together his servants and loaned them money to invest for him while he was gone. [Luke 19:12–27] [15]He gave $5,000 to one, $2,000 to another, and $1,000 to the last—dividing it in proportion to their abilities—and then left on his trip. [16]The man who received the $5,000 began immediately to buy and sell with it and soon earned another $5,000. [17]The man with $2,000 went right to work, too, and earned another $2,000. [18]But the man who received the $1,000 dug a hole in the ground and hid the money for safekeeping. [19]After a long time their master returned from his trip and called them to him to account for his money. [20]The man to whom he had entrusted the $5,000 brought him $10,000. [21]His master praised him for good work. "You have been faithful in handling this small amount," he told him, "so now I will give you many more responsibilities. Begin the joyous tasks I have assigned to you." [22]Next came the man who had received the $2,000, with the report, "Sir, you gave me $2,000 to use, and I have doubled it." [23]"Good work," his master said. "You are a good and faithful servant. You have been faithful over this small amount, so now I will give you much more." [24, 25]Then the man with the $1,000 came and said, "Sir, I knew you were a hard man, and I was afraid you would rob me of what I earned, so I hid your money in the earth and here it is!" [26]But his master replied, "Wicked man! Lazy slave! Since you knew I would demand your profit, [27]you should at least have put my money into the bank so I could have some interest. [28]Take the money from this man and give it to the man with the $10,000. [29]For the man who uses well what he is given shall be given more, and he shall have abundance. But from the man who is unfaithful, even what little responsibility he has shall be taken from him. [30]And throw the useless servant out into outer darkness: there shall be weeping and gnashing of teeth." [31]But when I, the Messiah, shall come in my glory, and all the angels with me, then I shall sit upon my throne of glory. [32]And all the nations shall be gathered before me. And I will separate the people as a shepherd separates the sheep from the goats, [33]and place the sheep at my right hand, and the goats at my left. [34]Then I, the King, shall say to those at my right, "Come, blessed of my Father, into the Kingdom prepared for you from the founding of the world. [35]For I was hungry and you fed me; I was thirsty and you gave me water; I was a stranger and you invited me into your homes; [36]naked and you clothed me; sick and in prison, and you visited me." [37]Then these righteous ones will reply, "Sir, when did we ever see you hungry and feed you? Or thirsty and give you anything to drink? [38]Or a stranger, and help you? Or naked, and clothe you? [39]When did we ever see you sick or in prison, and visit you?" [40]And I, the King, will tell them, "When you did it to these my brothers you were doing it to me!" [41]Then I will turn to those on my left and say, "Away with you, you cursed ones, into the eternal fire prepared for the devil and his demons. [42]For I was hungry and you wouldn't feed me; thirsty and you wouldn't give me anything to drink; [43]a stranger, and you refused me hospitality; naked, and you wouldn't clothe me; sick, and in prison, and you didn't visit me" [44]Then they will reply, "Lord, when did we ever see you hungry or thirsty or a stranger or naked or sick or in prison, and not help you?" [45]And I will answer, "When you refused to help the least of these my brothers, you were refusing help to me." [46]And they shall go away into eternal punishment; but the righteous into everlasting life.

Lk 12:47. He will be severely punished, for though he knew his duty he refused to do it.

Lk 13:25. But when the head of the house has locked the door, it will be too late. Then if you stand outside knocking, and pleading, "Lord, open the door for us," he will reply, "I do not know you." [26]"But we ate with you, and you taught in our streets," you will say. [27]And he will reply, "I tell you, I don't know you. You can't come in here, guilty as you are. Go away." [28]And there will be great weeping and gnashing of teeth as you stand outside and see Abraham, Isaac, Jacob, and all the prophets within the Kingdom of God.

Lk 14:16. Jesus replies with this illustration: "A man prepared a great feast and sent out many invitations. [17]When all was ready, he sent his servants around to notify the guests that it was time for them to arrive. [18]But they all began making excuses. One said he had just bought a field and wanted to inspect it, and asked to be excused. [19]Another said he had just bought five pair of oxen and wanted to try them out. [20]Another had just been married and for that reason couldn't come. [21]The servant returned and reported to his master what they had said. His master was angry and told him to go quickly into the streets and alleys of the city and to invite the beggars, crippled, lame, and blind. [22]But even then, there was still room. [23]'Well, then,' said his master, 'go out into the country lanes and out behind the hedges and urge anyone you find to come, so that the house will be full. [24]For none of those I invited first will get even the smallest taste of what I had prepared for them.'"

See *Judgment of God, According to Opportunity; Responsibility.*

OPPRESSION God is a refuge from, Ps 9:9. Prayers against, Ps 17:9; 44:24; 119:121, 134; Isa 38:14. God's aid promised against, Ps 12:5; 72:4, 14; Jer 50:34. God will judge, Ps 103:6; Eccl 5:8; Isa 10; Jer 22:17; Ezk 22:7; Amos 4:1; Mic 2:2; Mal 3:5; Jas 5:4. National, God judges, Acts 7:7. National, relieved, Ex 3:9; Deut 26:6, 7; Judg 2:12–14; 6:6–8; 2 Kgs 13:5; Isa 52:4.

INSTANCES OF. Of Hagar, by Sarah, Gen 16:6. Of Israelites, by Egyptians, Ex 1:10–22; 5. Rehoboam resolves to oppress the Israelites, 1 Kgs 12:13, 14.

UNCLASSIFIED SCRIPTURES RELATING TO. Ex 22:21. You must not oppress a stranger in any way; remember, you yourselves were foreigners in the land of Egypt. [22]You must not exploit widows or orphans; [23]if you do so in any way, and they cry to me for my help, I will surely give it. [24]And my anger shall flame out against you, and I will kill you with enemy armies, so that your wives will be widows and your children fatherless.

Deut 23:15, 16. If a slave escapes from his master, you must not force him to return; let him live among you in whatever town he shall choose, and do not oppress him.

Deut 24:14, 15. Never oppress a poor hired man, whether a fellow Israelite or a foreigner living in your town. Pay him his wage each day before sunset, for since he is poor he needs it right away; otherwise he may cry out to the Lord against you and it would be counted as a sin against you.

Job 5:15. God saves the fatherless and the poor from the grasp of these oppressors.

Ps 9:9. All who are oppressed may come to him. He is a refuge for them in their times of trouble.

Ps 10:17. Lord, you know the hopes of humble people. Surely you will hear their cries and comfort their hearts by helping them. [18]You will be with the orphans and all who are oppressed, so that mere earthly man will terrify them no longer.

Ps 12:5. The Lord replies, "I will arise and defend the oppressed, the poor, the needy. I will rescue them as they have longed for me to do."

Ps 62:10, 11. Don't become rich by extortion and robbery. And don't let the rich men be proud.

Ps 74:21. O Lord, don't let your downtrodden people be constantly insulted. Give cause for these poor and needy ones to praise your name!

Ps 119:134. Rescue me from the oppression of evil men; then I can obey you.

Prov 14:31. Anyone who oppresses the poor is

insulting God who made them. To help the poor is to honor God.

Prov 22:16. He who gains by oppressing the poor or by bribing the rich shall end in poverty. [22]Don't rob the poor and sick!

Prov 28:3. When a poor man oppresses those even poorer, he is like an unexpected flood sweeping away their last hope. [16]Only a stupid prince will oppress his people.

Prov 30:14. They devour the poor with teeth as sharp as knives!

Eccl 4:1. Next I observed all the oppression and sadness throughout the earth—the tears of the oppressed, and no one helping them, while on the side of their oppressors were powerful allies.

Eccl 5:8. If you see some poor man being oppressed by the rich, with miscarriage of justice anywhere throughout the land, don't be surprised! For every official is under orders from higher up, and the higher officials look up to their superiors. And so the matter is lost in red tape and bureaucracy.

Isa 33:15. I will tell you who can live here: All who are honest and fair, who reject making profit by fraud, who hold back their hands from taking bribes, who refuse to listen to those who plot murder, who shut their eyes to all enticement to do wrong. [16]Such as these shall dwell on high. The rocks of the mountains will be their fortress of safety; food will be supplied to them and they will have all the water they need.

Isa 58:6. No, the kind of fast I want is that you stop oppressing those who work for you and treat them fairly and give them what they earn.

Jer 21:12. I am ready to judge you because of all the evil you are doing. Quick! Give justice to these you judge! Begin doing what is right before my burning fury flashes out upon you like a fire no man can quench.

Ezk 22:29. Even the common people oppress and rob the poor and needy and cruelly extort from aliens.

Ezk 45:9. For the Lord God says to the rulers: Quit robbing and cheating my people out of their land, and expelling them from their homes. Always be fair and honest.

Amos 5:11. You trample the poor and steal their smallest crumb by all your taxes, fines, and usury; therefore you will never live in the beautiful stone houses you are building nor drink the wine from the lush vineyards you are planting. [12]For many and great are your sins. I know them all so well. You are the enemies of everything good; you take bribes; you refuse justice to the poor.

Amos 8:4. Listen, you merchants who rob the poor, trampling on the needy; [5]you who long for the Sabbath to end and the religious holidays to be over, so you can get out and start cheating again—using your weighted scales and under-sized measures; [6]you who make slaves of the poor, buying them for their debt of a piece of silver or a pair of shoes, or selling them your moldy wheat.

Mic 2:1. Woe to you who lie awake at night, plotting wickedness; you rise at dawn to carry out your schemes; because you can, you do. [2]You want a certain piece of land, or someones else's house (though it is all he has); you take it by fraud and threats and violence. [3]But the Lord God says, I will reward your evil with evil; nothing can stop me; never again will you be proud and haughty after I am through with you. Isa 5:8.

Hab 2:5. What's more, these arrogant Chaldeans are betrayed by all their wine, for it is treacherous. In their greed they have collected many nations, but like death and hell, they are never satisfied. [6]The time is coming when all their captives will taunt them saying: "You robbers! At last justice has caught up with you! Now you will get your just deserts for your oppression and extortion!" [7]Suddenly your debtors will rise up in anger and turn on you and take all you have while you stand trembling and helpless. [8]You have ruined many nations; now they will ruin you. You murderers! You have filled the countryside with lawlessness and all the cities too. [9]Woe to you for getting rich by evil means, attempting to live beyond the reach of danger. [10]By the murders you commit, you have shamed your name and forfeited your lives. [11]The very stones in the walls of your homes cry out against you, and the beams in the ceilings echo what they say.

Zech 7:10. Tell them to stop oppressing widows and orphans, foreigners and poor people, and to stop plotting evil against each other.

Mt 23:2. You would think these Jewish leaders and these Pharisees were Moses, the way they keep making up so many laws! [3]And of course you should obey their every whim! It may be all right to do what they say, but above anything else, *don't follow their example.* For they don't do what they tell you to do. [4]They load you with impossible demands that they themselves don't even try to keep.

Jas 2:6. And yet, of the two strangers, you have despised the poor man. Don't you realize that it is usually the rich men who pick on you and drag you into court?

ORACLE Ex 28:15, 29, 30, 31.

ORATOR Job 12:20.

INSTANCES OF. Jonah, Jon 3:4–10. The apostles, Acts 2:1–41. Tertullus, Acts 24:1. Apollos, Acts 18:24–28.

ORCHESTRA Isa 38:20. Used in festivities, Isa 5:12.

See *Music.*

ORDAIN, ORDAINED These words are used in the sense of establishing, Num 28:6; Ezra 3:10; and in the sense of appointing or setting apart, Ex 29:35; 32:29; 1 Kgs 12:31–33; Acts 10:42.

See *Ordination.*

ORDINANCES Ex 28:43; Lev 18:26; 19:37; 20:22; 26:46; Num 29:6; 36:13; Deut 26:16, 17; 2 Chron 9:10; Ezk 20:19.

INSUFFICIENCY OF, FOR SALVATION. Isa 1:10. An apt comparison! Listen, you leaders of Israel, you men of Sodom and Gomorrah, as I call you now. Listen to the Lord. Hear what he is telling you! [11]I am sick of your sacrifices. Don't bring me any more of them. I don't want your fat rams; I don't want to see the blood from your offerings. [12, 13]Who wants your sacrifices when you have no sorrow for your sins? The incense you bring me is a stench in my nostrils. Your holy celebrations of the new moon and the Sabbath, and your special days for fasting—even your most pious meetings—all are frauds! I want nothing more to do with them. [14]I hate them all; I can't stand the sight of them. [15]From now on, when you pray with your hands stretched out to heaven, I won't look or listen. Even though you make many prayers, I will not hear, for your hands are those of murderers; they are covered with the blood of your innocent victims. [16]Oh, wash yourselves! Be clean! Let me no longer see you doing all these wicked things; quit your evil ways. [17]Learn to do good, to be fair and to help the poor, the fatherless, and widows.

Gal 5:6. And we to whom Christ has given eternal life don't need to worry about whether we have been circumcised or not, or whether we are obeying the Jewish ceremonies or not; for all we need is faith working through love.

Gal 6:15. It doesn't make any difference now whether we have been circumcised or not; what counts is whether we really have been changed into new and different people.

Eph 2:15. By his death he ended the angry resentment between us, caused by the Jewish laws which favored the Jews and excluded the Gentiles, for he died to annul that whole system of Jewish laws. Then he took the two groups that had been opposed to each other and made them parts of himself; thus he fused us together to become one new person, and at last there was peace.

Col 2:14. And blotted out the charges proved against you, the list of his commandments which you had not obeyed. He took this list of sins and destroyed it by nailing it to Christ's cross. [20]Since you died, as it were, with Christ and this has set you free from following the world's ideas of how to be saved—by doing good and obeying various rules—why do you keep right on following them anyway, still bound by such rules as [21]not eating, tasting, or even touching certain foods? [22]Such rules are mere human teachings, for food was made to be eaten and used up. [23]These rules may seem good, for rules of this kind require strong devotion and are humiliating and hard on the body, but they have no effect when it comes to conquering a person's evil thoughts and desires. They only make him proud.

Heb 9:1. Now in that first agreement between God and his people there were rules for worship and there was a sacred tent down here on earth. [8]And the Holy Spirit uses all this to point out to us that under the old system the common people could not go into the Holy of Holies as long as the outer room and the entire system it represents were still in use. [9]This has an important lesson for us today. For under the old system, gifts and sacrifices were offered, but these failed to cleanse the hearts of the people who brought them. [10]For the old system dealt only with certain rituals—what foods to eat and drink, rules for washing themselves, and rules about this and that. The people had to keep these rules to tide them over until Christ came with God's new and better way.

See *Commandments; Form; Formalism; Law.*

ORDINATION 1. In the Old Testament, Moses laid hands on Joshua in setting him apart as his successor, Num 27:18, 23; Deut 34:9. Priests and others were solemnly set apart to their ministry, 1 Chron 9:22; 2 Chron 11:15; Jeremiah was ordained or set apart by God, Jer 1:5.

2. In the New Testament, Christ ordained by appointing the disciples to their ministry or service, Mk 3:14, 15; Jn 15:16.

3. The disciples chose Matthias to take Judas' place through prayer and the use of the lot, Acts 1:21–26.

4. The apostles appointed the seven deacons with the laying on of hands, Acts 6:5, 6. Barnabas and Paul were set apart in the same way, Acts 13:1–4. Elders were ordained in a manner not described, Tit 1:5.

See *Minister, New Testament, Ordination of; Ordain.*

OREB 1. An officer of Midian, overcome by Gideon and killed by the Ephraimites, Judg 7:25; 8:2, 3; Ps 83:11.

2. A rock probably west of the Jordan, where Oreb was killed, Judg 7:25; Isa 10:26.

OREN Son of Jerahmeel, 1 Chron 2:25.

ORION The constellation of, Job 9:9; 38:31; Amos 5:8.

ORNAMENTS Ex 33:4, 5; Judg 8:21; 2 Sam 1:24; 1 Kgs 7:24; Isa 3:18; Ezk 16:11, 17.

FIGURATIVE. Ps 76:10; Isa 3:17; 49:18.

ORNAN A Jebusite, 1 Chron 21:15–25; 2 Chron 3:1. Called *Araunah,* 2 Sam 24:16–25.

ORPAH Daughter-in-law of Naomi, Ruth 1:4, 14.

ORPHAN Ex 22:22. You must not exploit widows and orphans; [23]if you do so in any way, and they cry to me for my help, I will surely give it. [24]And my anger shall flame out against you, and I will kill you with enemy armies, so that your wives will be widows and your children fatherless.

Deut 10:18. He gives justice to the fatherless and widows. He loves foreigners and gives them food and clothing.

Deut 14:28. Every third year you are to use your entire tithe for the local welfare programs: [29]Give it to the Levites who have no inheritance among you, or to foreigners, or to widows and orphans within your city, so that they can eat and be satisfied; and then Jehovah your God will bless you and your work.

Deut 16:11. It is a time to rejoice before the Lord with your family and household. And don't forget to include the local Levites, foreigners, widows, and orphans. Invite them to accompany you to the celebration at the sanctuary. [14]This will be a happy time of rejoicing together with your family and servants. And don't forget to include the Levites, foreigners, orphans, and widows of your town.

Deut 24:17. Justice must be given to migrants and orphans and you must never accept a widow's garment in pledge of her debt. [18]Always remember that you were slaves in Egypt, and that the Lord your God rescued you; that is why I have given you this command. [19]If, when reaping your harvest, you forget to bring in a sheaf from the field, don't go back after it. Leave it for the migrants, orphans, and widows; then the Lord your God will bless and prosper all you do. [20]When you beat the olives from your olive trees, don't go over the boughs twice; leave anything remaining for the migrants, orphans, and widows. [21]It is the same for the grapes in your vineyard; don't glean the vines after they are picked, but leave what's left for those in need. [22]Remember that you were slaves in the land of Egypt—that is why I am giving you this command.

Deut 26:12. Every third year is a year of special tithing. That year you are to give all your tithes to the Levites, migrants, orphans, and widows, so that they will be well fed. [13]Then you shall declare before the Lord your God, "I have given all of my tithes to the Levites, the migrants, the orphans, and the widows, just as you commanded me; I have not violated or forgotten any of your rules."

Deut 27:19. Cursed is he who is unjust to the foreigner, the orphan, and the widow.

Job 6:27. That would be like injuring a helpless orphan, or selling a friend.

Job 22:9. You sent widows away without helping them, and broke the arms of orphans.

Job 24:3. And even the donkeys of the poor and fatherless are taken. Poor widows must surrender the little they have as a pledge to get a loan. [9]The wicked snatch fatherless children from their mother's breasts, and take a poor man's baby as a pledge before they will loan him any money or grain.

Job 29:12. For I, as an honest judge, helped the poor in their need, and the fatherless who had no one to help them. [13]I helped those who were ready to perish and they blessed me. And I caused the widows' hearts to sing for joy.

Job 31:16. If I have hurt the poor or caused widows to weep, [17]or refused food to hungry orphans —[18](but we have always cared for orphans in our home, treating them as our own children). [21]Or if I have taken advantage of an orphan because I have thought I could get away with it.

Ps 10:14. You are known as the helper of the helpless. [17]Lord, you know the hopes of humble people. Surely you will hear their cries and comfort their hearts by helping them. [18]You will be with the orphans and all who are oppressed, so that mere earthly man will terrify them no longer.

Ps 27:10. For if my father and mother should abandon me, you would welcome and comfort me.

Ps 68:5. He is a father to the fatherless; he gives justice to the widows, for he is holy.

Ps 82:3. Give fair judgment to the poor man, the fatherless, the destitute.

Ps 94:6. They murder widows, immigrants, and orphans.

Ps 146:9. He protects the immigrants, and cares for the orphans and widows. But he turns topsy-turvy the plans of the wicked.

Prov 23:10, 11. Don't steal the land of defenseless orphans by moving their ancient boundary marks, for their Redeemer is strong; he himself will accuse you.

Isa 1:17. Learn to do good, to be fair and to help the poor, the fatherless, and widows. [23]Your leaders are rebels, companions of thieves; all of them take bribes and won't defend the widows and orphans.

Isa 10:1. Woe to unjust judges and to those who issue unfair law, says the Lord. [2]. . . Yes, it is true that they even rob the widows and fatherless children.

Jer 5:28. And well fed and well groomed, and there is no limit to their wicked deeds. They refuse justice to orphans and the rights of the poor.

Jer 7:6. And stop exploiting orphans, widows and foreigners. . . . [7]Then, and only then, will I let you stay in this land that I gave to your fathers to keep forever.

Jer 22:3. The Lord says: Be fairminded. Do what is right! Help those in need of justice! Quit your evil deeds! Protect the rights of aliens and immigrants, orphans and widows; stop murdering the innocent!

Jer 49:11. But I will preserve your fatherless children who remain, and let your widows depend on me.

Hos 14:3. Never again will we call the idols we have made "our gods"; for in you alone, O Lord, the fatherless find mercy.

Mal 3:5. I will move swiftly against . . . those who cheat their hired hands or oppress widows and orphans.

Jas 1:27. The Christian who is pure and without fault, from God the Father's point of view, is the one who takes care of orphans and widows, and who remains true to the Lord—not soiled and dirtied by his contacts with the world.

See *Adoption; Children; Widow.*

INSTANCES OF. Lot, Gen 11:27, 28. Daughters of Zelophehad, Num 27:1–5. Jotham, Judg 9:16–21. Mephibosheth, 2 Sam 9:3. Joash, 2 Kgs 11:1–12. Esther, Esther 2:7. A type of Jerusalem in affliction, Lam 5:3.

OSNAPPER A noble Assyrian prince, who colonized the cities of Samaria after the Israelites were taken captive to Assyria, Ezra 4:10.

OSPREY A carnivorous bird. Forbidden as food, Lev 11:13–19; Deut 14:11–18.

OSTENTATION In prayer and charity, Mt 6:1; Prov 25:14.

OSTRICH Job 30:28, 29; 39:13–18; Lam 4:3, 4; Isa 13:21; 34:13; 43:20; Jer 50:39. The cry of, Mic 1:8. Forbidden as food, Lev 11:13–19; Deut 14:11–18.

OTHNI Son of Shemaiah, 1 Chron 26:6, 7.

OTHNI-EL Son of Kenaz and nephew of

Caleb. Conquers Kiriath-sepher, and as a reward secures Caleb's daughter as his wife, Josh 15:16–20; Judg 1:12, 13. Becomes deliverer and judge of Israel, Judg 3:8–11. Death of, Judg 3:11. Descendants of, 1 Chron 4:13, 14.

OVEN For baking, Ex 8:3, 4; Lev 2:4; 11:35; 26:26.

See *Bread.*

FIGURATIVE. Hos 7:4.

OVERCOMING See *Perseverance.*

OVERSEER Acts 20:28.

See *Guardian; Pastor.*

OWL A carnivorous bird, Ps 102:6; Isa 34:11, 15; Zeph 2:14. Unclean, Lev 11:13–19; Deut 14:11–18.

OX See *Bull; Cattle.*

OZEM 1. Son of Jesse, 1 Chron 2:15.

2. Son of Jerahmeel, 1 Chron 2:25.

OZNI Son of Gad, Num 26:15–18.

P

PAARAI One of David's valiant men, 2 Sam 23:24–39. Called *Naarai* in 1 Chron 11:26–47.

PACK ANIMALS Used for transporting supplies, 1 Chron 12:40.

PACT See *Contract.*

PADDAN-ARAM A district of Mesopotamia, home of Rebekah, Gen 25:20 and of Laban, Gen 28:2–9. Called *Syria* in Hos 12:12.

See *Mesopotamia.*

PADON One of the Nethinim, Ezra 2:43–54; Neh 7:46–56.

PAGIEL Son of Ochran and leader of the tribe of Asher at the time of the exodus, Num 1:2–15; 2:3–31; 7:72–77; 10:26.

PAHATH-MOAB The ancestor of an influential family of Judah, which returned to Jerusalem from the captivity, Ezra 2:3–35; 10:30; Neh 3:11; 7:8–38.

PAI A city in Edom, 1 Chron 1:50. Called *Pau* in Gen 36:31–39.

PAIN Job 14:22. For him there is only sorrow and pain.

Job 30:17. My weary nights are filled with pain as though something were relentlessly gnawing at my bones. [18]All night long I toss and turn, and my garments bind about me.

Job 33:19. Or, God sends sickness and pain, even though no bone is broken.

Ps 6:6. I am worn out with pain; every night my pillow is wet with tears.

Ps 18:26. You give blessings to the pure but pain to those who leave your paths.

Ps 69:26. For they persecute the one you have smitten, and scoff at the pain of the one you have pierced. 1 Pet 4:1.

Lam 3:5. He has built forts against me and surrounded me with anguish and distress.

Mt 4:24. And whatever their illness and pain . . . he healed them all. Mt 8:5–7.

Rom 8:23. And even we Christians, although we have the Holy Spirit within us as a foretaste of future glory, also groan to be released from pain and suffering.

Rev 12:2. She was pregnant and screamed in the pain of her labor, awaiting her delivery. Gen 3:16; Isa 26:17; 1 Tim 2:15.

Rev 21:4. He will wipe away all tears from their eyes, and there shall be no more death, nor sorrow, nor crying, nor pain. All of that has gone forever.

See *Afflictions.*

PAINTING Around the eyes, 2 Kgs 9:30; Jer 4:30; Ezk 23:40. Of rooms, Jer 22:14. Of portraits, Ezk 23:14, 15.

See *Picture.*

PALACE For kings, 1 Kgs 21:1; 2 Kgs 15:25; Jer 27:18; 49:27; Hos 8:14; Amos 1:4; 2:5; Nah 2:6; Acts 23:35. For governors, Mk 15:16; Jn 18:28, 33; 19:9. Of David, 2 Sam 7:2. Of Solomon, 1 Kgs 7:1–12. At Babylon, Dan 4:29; 6:18. At Shushan, Neh 1:1; Esther 1:1–3; 7:7. Archives kept in, Ezra 6:2.

FIGURATIVE. Of a government, Amos 1:4; 2:2; Nah 2:6.

PALAL Son of Uzai. One of the workmen in rebuilding the walls of Jerusalem, Neh 3:25.

PALE HORSE Symbol of death, Rev 6:8.

PALESTINE See *Canaan.*

PALLU Son of Reuben, Gen 46:8–14; Ex 6:14; Num 26:5–11; 1 Chron 5:3.

PALM TREE Deborah judged Israel under, Judg 4:5. Temple decorated with carvings of, 1 Kgs 6:29, 32, 35; 2 Chron 3:5. In the Temple seen in the vision of Ezekiel, Ezk 40:16; 41:17, 18. Branches of, thrown in the way when Jesus made his triumphal entry into Jerusalem, Jn 12:13. Jericho was called the *City of Palm Trees,* Deut 34:3.

FIGURATIVE. Of the prosperity of the godly, Ps 92:12. Used as a symbol of victory, Rev 7:9.

PALSY See *Paralysis.*

PALTI 1. A chief Benjaminite and one of the twelve spies sent into Canaan, Num 13:3–15.

2. Son-in-law of Saul, 1 Sam 25:44; 2 Sam 3:15, 16.

PALTIEL A leader of Issachar and one of the committee of twelve appointed to divide Canaan among the tribes, Num 34:16–28.

PAMPHYLIA A province in Asia Minor. Men of, in Jerusalem, Acts 2:10. Paul goes to, Acts 13:13; 14:24. John Mark, in, Acts 13:13; 15:38.

PANIC In armies, Lev 26:17; Deut 32:30; Josh 23:10; Ps 35:5. From God, Gen 35:5; Ex 15:14–16; Judg 7:22; 1 Sam 14:15–20; 2 Kgs 7:6, 7; 2 Chron 20:22, 23.

See *Armies.*

PANTHER Song 4:8.

PANTOMIME By Isaiah, Isa 20:2, 3. By Ezekiel, Ezk 4:1–8, 12:18. Agabus, Acts 21:11.

PAPER Prov 26:21; Eccl 7:6; Jer 32:12–16; Lk 1:63.

See *Parchment.*

PAPHOS A city of Cyprus. Paul blinds a sorcerer in, Acts 13:6–13.

PAPRYUS Reeds, Moses' boat of, Ex 2:3.

FIGURATIVE. Isa 58:5.

PARABLE Of the trees, Judg 9:8–15. Of the lamb, 2 Sam 12:1–6. Of the woman of Tekoa, 2 Sam 14:5–12. Of the robe torn into pieces, 1 Kgs 11:30–32. Of the prisoner of war, 1 Kgs 20: 39–42. Of the thistle and cedar, 2 Kgs 14:9. Of a vine of Egypt, Ps 80:8–16. Of the vineyard, Isa 5: 1–7; 27:2, 3. Of the farmer, Isa 28:23–29. Of the jugs filled with wine, Jer 13:12–14. Of the vine, Ezk 15; 17:5–10; 19:10–14. Of the two eagles, Ezk 17. Of lions' cubs, Ezk 19:1–9. Of Oholah and Oholibah, Ezk 23. The boiling pot, Ezk 24:3–5. The vine, Jon 4:6, 7. The sheet let down from heaven in Peter's vision, Acts 10:9–16. The two covenants, Gal 4:22–31. The mercenary soldier, 2 Tim 2:3, 4. Farmers, 2 Tim 2: 6. Furnished house, 2 Tim 2:20, 21. The athlete, 2 Tim 2:5. Mirror, Jas 1:23–25.

See *Jesus, Parables of; Symbols; Types.*

PARADISE The name of the place to which Christ went after his crucifixion, Lk 23:43. Many students believe this was somewhere within Sheol or Hades, the unseen world of departed spirits, Ps 16:10; Acts 2:27, 31. Since Christ went to the heart of the earth, Mt 12:39, 40, and is said to have descended into the lowest parts of the earth before his ascension, Eph 4:8–10, it is thought that Paradise at that time was located in that region. For the reason that Paradise was in the third heaven when Paul went there later, 2 Cor 12:1–4, it is understood that its location was changed when Christ ascended to heaven. Other students hold this view to be unjustified by the Scriptures cited.

See *Hades; Heaven; Sheol.*

PARADOX Prov 13:7. Some rich people are poor, and some poor people have great wealth!

Mt 10:39. If you cling to your life, you will lose it; but if you give it up for me, you will save it. chapter 16:25; Mk 8:35; Lk 17:33.

Jn 12:25. If you love your life down here—you will lose it. If you despise your life down here—you will exchange it for eternal glory.

1 Cor 3:18. Stop fooling yourselves. If you count yourself above average in intelligence, as judged by this world's standards, you had better put this all aside and be a fool rather than let it hold you back from the true wisdom from above.

2 Cor 6:4. In fact, in everything we do we try to show that we are true ministers of God. We patiently endure suffering and hardship and trouble of every kind. [8]We stand true to the Lord whether others honor us or despise us, whether they criticize us or commend us. We are honest, but they call us liars. [9]The world ignores us, but we are known to God; we live close to death, but here we are, still very much alive. We have been injured but kept from death. [10]Our hearts ache, but at the same time we have the joy of the Lord. We are poor, but we give rich spiritual gifts to others. We own nothing, and yet we enjoy everything.

2 Cor 12:3. But anyway, there I was in paradise, [4]and heard things so astounding that they are beyond a man's power to describe or put in words (and anyway I am not allowed to tell them to others.) [10]Since I know it is all for Christ's good, I am quite happy about "the thorn," and about insults and hardships, persecutions and difficulties; for when I am weak, then I am strong—the less I have, the more I depend on him. [11]You have made me act like a fool—boasting like this—for you people ought to be writing about me and not making me write about myself. There isn't a single thing these other marvelous fellows have that I don't have too, even though I am really worth nothing at all.

Eph 3:17. And I pray that Christ will be more and more at home in your hearts, living within you as you trust in him. May your roots go down deep into the soil of God's marvelous love; [18, 19]and may you be able to feel and understand, as all God's children should, how long, how wide, how deep, and how high his love really is; and to experience this love for yourselves, though it is so great that you will never see the end of it or fully know or understand it. And so at last you will be filled up with God himself.

Phil 3:7. But all these things that I once thought very worthwhile—now I've thrown them all away so that I can put my trust and hope in Christ alone.

Rev 21:18. The city itself was pure, transparent gold like glass! [21]The twelve gates were made of pearls—each gate from a single pearl! And the main street was pure, transparent gold, like glass.

PARAH A city in Benjamin, Josh 18:21–28.

PARALYSIS Cured by Jesus, Mt 4:24; 8:5, 6, 13; 9:2, 5, 6; by Philip, Acts 8:7; Peter, Acts 9: 33, 34.

See *Lameness.*

PARAN Desert or wilderness of, Gen 21:20, 21; Num 10:12; 12:16; 13:26. Mountains of, Deut 33: 2; Hab 3:3. Israelites camp in, Num 12:16. David takes refuge in, 1 Sam 25:1. Hadad flees to, 1 Kgs 11:16–18.

PARCHMENT 2 Tim 4:13.

PARDON See *Sin, Forgiveness of.*

PARENTS God's promises to, conferred on children, Gen 6:18; Ex 20:5, 6; Ps 103:17, 18. Curses conferred, Ex 20:5; Lev 20:5; Isa 14:20; Jer 9:14; Lam 5:7; Ezk 16:44, 45. Involved in children's wickedness, 1 Sam 2:27–36; 4:10–22.

Partiality of: Isaac for Esau, Gen 25:28; Rebekah for Jacob, Gen 25:28; 27:6–17; Jacob for Joseph, Gen 33:2; 37:3; 48:22; for Benjamin, Gen 42:4. See *Partiality.*

Parental affection exemplified: By Hagar, Gen 21:14, 16; Rebekah's mother, Gen 24:55; Isaac and Rebekah, Gen 25:28; Jacob, Gen 37:3; 42:4, 38; 43: 13, 14; 45:26–28; 48:10, 11; Moses's mother, Ex 2; Naomi, Ruth 1:8, 9; Hannah, 1 Sam 2:19; David,

2 Sam 12:18–23; 13:37–39; 14:1, 33; 18:5, 12, 13, 33; 19:1–6; Rizpah, 2 Sam 21:10; the mother of the infant brought to Solomon by the harlots, 1 Kgs 3:22–28; Mary, Mt 12:46, 47; Lk 2:48; Jn 2:5; 19:25; Jairus, Mk 5:22, 23; father of demoniac, Mk 9:24; official, Jn 4:49.

Indulgent: Eli, 1 Sam 2:27–36; 3:13, 14; David, 1 Kgs 1:6.

Paternal blessings of: Of Noah, Gen 9:24–27; Abraham, Gen 17:18; Isaac, Gen 27:8–40; 28:2–4; Jacob, Gen 48:15–20; 49:1–28.

Prayers in behalf of children: Of Hannah, 1 Sam 1:27; David, 2 Sam 7:25–29; 12:16; 1 Chron 17:16–27; 22:12; 29:19; Job, Job 1:5.

Paternal reproaches, Gen 9:24, 25; 49:3–7.

INFLUENCE OF. See *Influence.*

UNCLASSIFIED SCRIPTURES RELATING TO. Gen 18:19. And I have picked him out to have godly descendants and a godly household—men who are just and good—so that I can do for him all I have promised.

Ex 10:2. What stories you can tell your children and grandchildren about the incredible things I am doing in Egypt! Tell them what fools I made of the Egyptians, and how I proved to you that I am Jehovah.

Ex 12:26. "And your children ask, 'What does all this mean? What is this ceremony about?' [27]You will reply, 'It is the celebration of Jehovah's passing over us, for he passed over the homes of the people of Israel, though he killed the Egyptians; he passed over our houses and did not come in to destroy us.' " And all the people bowed their heads and worshiped.

Ex 13:8. During those celebration days each year you must explain to your children why you are celebrating—it is a celebration of what the Lord did for you when you left Egypt. [14]And in the future, when your children ask you, "What is this all about?" you shall tell them, "With mighty miracles Jehovah brought us out of Egypt from our slavery."

Ex 20:5. You must never bow to an image or worship it in any way; for I, the Lord your God, am very possessive. I will not share your affection with any other god! And when I punish people for their sins, the punishment continues upon the children, grandchildren, and great-grandchildren of those who hate me. [Lam 5:7.] [10]But the seventh day is a day of Sabbath rest before the Lord your God. On that day you are to do no work of any kind, nor shall your son, daughter, or slaves—whether men or women—or your cattle or your house guests. Lev 23:3.

Ex 21:17. Anyone who reviles or curses his mother or father shall surely be put to death.

Lev 20:9. Anyone who curses his father or mother shall surely be put to death—for he has cursed his own flesh and blood.

Deut 4:9. But watch out! Be very careful never to forget what you have seen God doing for you. May his miracles have a deep and permanent effect upon your lives! Tell your children and your grandchildren about the glorious miracles he did. [10]Tell them especially about the day you stood before the Lord at Mount Horeb, and he told me, "Summon the people before me and I will instruct them, so that they will learn always to reverence me, and so that they can teach my laws to their children."

Deut 6:7. You must teach them to your children and talk about them when you are at home or out for a walk; at bedtime and the first thing in the morning. [20]In the years to come when your son asks you, "What is the purpose of these laws which the Lord our God has given us?" [21]you must tell him, "We were Pharaoh's slaves in Egypt, and the Lord brought us out of Egypt with great power [22]and mighty miracles—with terrible blows against Egypt and Pharaoh and all his people. We saw it all with our own eyes. [23]He brought us out of Egypt so that he could give us this land he had promised to our ancestors. [24]And he has commanded us to obey all of these laws and to reverence him so that he can preserve us alive as he has until now."

Deut 11:18. So keep these commandments carefully in mind. Tie them to your hand to remind you to obey them, and tie them to your forehead between your eyes! [19]Teach them to your children. Talk about them when you are sitting at home, when you are out walking, at bedtime, and before breakfast! [20]Write them upon the doors of your houses and upon your gates, [21]so that as long as there is sky above the earth, you and your children will enjoy the good life awaiting you in the land the Lord has promised you.

Deut 32:46. Moses made these commandments: "Meditate upon all the laws I have given you today, and pass them on to your children."

Ps 78:5. For he gave his laws to Israel, and commanded our fathers to teach them to their children, [6]so that they in turn could teach their children too. Thus his laws pass down from generation to generation.

Ps 103:13. He is like a father to us, tender and sympathetic to those who reverence him.

Prov 13:22. When a good man dies, he leaves an inheritance to his grandchildren; but when a sinner dies, his wealth is stored up for the godly. [24]If you refuse to discipline your son, it proves you don't love him; for if you love him you will be prompt to punish him.

Prov 19:18. Discipline your son in his early years while there is hope. If you don't you will ruin his life.

Prov 22:6. Teach a child to choose the right path, and when he is older he will remain upon it. [15]A youngster's heart is filled with rebellion, but punishment will drive it out of him.

Prov 23:13, 14. Don't fail to correct your children; discipline won't hurt them! They won't die if you use a stick on them! Punishment will keep them out of hell.

Prov 27:11. My son, how happy I will be if you turn out to be sensible! It will be a public honor to me.

Prov 29:15. Scolding and spanking a child helps him to learn. Left to himself, he brings shame to his mother. [17]Discipline your son and he will give you happiness and peace of mind.

Prov 31:28. Her children stand and bless her; so does her husband.

Isa 38:19. The living, only the living, can praise you as I do today. One generation makes known your faithfulness to the next.

Isa 49:15. Never! Can a mother forget her little child and not have love for her own son?

Isa 66:13. I will comfort you there as a little one is comforted by its mother.

Jer 31:1. At that time, says the Lord, all the families of Israel shall recognize me as the Lord; they shall act like my people.

Jer 49:11. But I will preserve your fatherless children who remain, and let your widows depend upon me.

Joel 1:3. In years to come, tell your children about it; pass the awful story down from generation to generation.

Mal 4:6. His preaching will bring fathers and children together again, to be of one mind and heart, for they will know that if they do not repent, I will come and utterly destroy their land.

Mt 10:37. If you love your father and mother more than you love me, you are not worthy of being mine; or if you love your son or daughter more than me, you are not worthy of being mine.

Lk 11:11. You men who are fathers—if your boy asks for bread, do you give him a stone? If he asks for fish, do you give him a snake? [12]If he asks for an egg, do you give him a scorpion? (Of course not!) [13]And if even sinful persons like yourselves give children what they need, don't you realize that your heavenly Father will do at least as much, and give the Holy Spirit to those who ask for him?

2 Cor 12:14. And little children don't pay for their father's and mother's food—it's the other way around; parents supply food for their children.

Eph 6:4. And now a word to you parents. Don't keep on scolding and nagging your children, making them angry and resentful. Rather, bring them up with the loving discipline the Lord himself approves, with suggestions and godly advice.

Col 3:21. Fathers, don't scold your children so much that they become discouraged and quit trying.

1 Thess 2:11. We talked to you as a father to his own children—don't you remember?

1 Tim 3:4. He must have a well-behaved family, with children who obey quickly and quietly. [5]For if a man can't make his own little family behave, how can he help the whole church? [12]Deacons should have only one wife and they should have happy, obedient families.

1 Tim 5:8. But anyone who won't care for his own relatives when they need help, especially those living in his own family, has no right to say he is a Christian. Such a person is worse than the heathen.

Tit 1:6. The men you choose must be well thought of for their good lives; they must have only one wife and their children must love the Lord and not have a reputation for being wild or disobedient to their parents.

Tit 2:4. These older women must train the younger women to live quietly, to love their husbands and their children.

Heb 12:7. Let God train you, for he is doing what any loving father does for his children. Whoever heard of a son who was never corrected?

See *Children; Instruction.*

PARMASHTA Son of Haman, Esther 9:7–10.

PARMENAS One of the disciples, Acts 6:5.

PARNACH Father of Elizaphan, Num 34:16–28.

PAROSH The ancestor of one of the families which returned to Jerusalem from captivity in Babylon, Ezra 2:3–35; 8:2–14; 10:25; Neh 7:8–38; 10:14–27.

PARRICIDE 2 Kgs 19:37; 2 Chron 32:21; Isa 37:38.

PARSHANDATHA Son of Haman, Esther 9:7–10.

PARSIMONY Of the Jews toward the temple, Hag 1:2, 4, 6, 8, 9; toward God, Mal 3:8, 9. Of the disciples, when the perfume was poured on Jesus, Mt 26:8, 9; Jn 12:4, 5. Punishment of, Hag 1:9–11.

See *Liberality.*

PARSIN Meaning "divided," Dan 5:24, 25, 28.

PARTHIANS The inhabitants of Parthia, a country northwest of Persia, Acts 2:9.

PARTIALITY Among Christians forbidden, 1 Tim 5:21. Of parents for particular children, see *Parents.* Its effect on other children, Gen 37:4.

PARTICEPS CRIMINIS Accomplice, 2 Jn 1:11.

See *Collusion.*

PARTNERSHIP With God, 1 Cor 3:7, 9; 2 Cor 6:1; Phil 2:13.

See *Providence.*

PARTRIDGE 1 Sam 26:20.

PARUAH Father of Jehoshaphat, 1 Kgs 4:8–19.

PARVAIM An unknown gold region, 2 Chron 3:6.

PASACH Son of Japhlet, 1 Chron 7:33.

PASCHAL LAMB See *Passover.*

PAS-DAMMIM A battle between David and the Philistines, fought at, 1 Chron 11:13. Called *Ephes-dammim* in 1 Sam 17:1.

PASEAH 1. A son of Eshton, 1 Chron 4:11, 12.

2. Ancestor of a family which returned to Jerusalem from captivity in Babylon, Ezra 2:43–54; Neh 3:6; 7:46–56.

3. Father of Joiada, probably identical with preceding, Neh 3:6.

PASHHUR 1. A priest, son of Malchiah, 1 Chron 9:12; Jer 21:1.

2. Ancestor of an influential family, Ezra 2:36–39; 10:22; Neh 7:39–42.

3. A priest who signed the covenant with Nehemiah, Neh 10:1–8.

4. Son of Immer and governor of the temple. Beats and imprisons Jeremiah, Jer 20:1–6.

5. Father of Gedaliah, who persecuted Jeremiah, Jer 38:1.

PASSION See *Jesus, Sufferings of.*

PASSOVER Institution of, Ex 12:3–49; 23:15–18; 34:18; Lev 23:4–8; Num 9:2–5, 13, 14; 28:16–25; Deut 16:1–8, 16; Ps 81:3, 5. Design of, Ex 12:21–28.

Special passover, for those who were defiled or on a trip, to be held in second month, Num 9:6–12; 2 Chron 30:2–4. Lamb killed by Levites, for those who were ceremonially unclean, 2 Chron 30:17–19; 35:3–11; Ezra 6:20. Strangers authorized to celebrate, Ex 12:48, 49; Num 9:14.

Observed at place designated by God, Deut 16:5–7; with unleavened bread, Ex 12:8, 15–20; 13:3, 7; 23:15; Lev 23:6; Num 9:11; 28:17; Deut 16:3, 4; Luke 22:7; 1 Cor 5:8. Penalty for neglecting to observe, Num 9:13.

Reinstituted, Ezk 45:21–24.

Observation of, renewed by the Israelites on entering Canaan, Josh 5:10–12; by Hezekiah, 2 Chron 30:1; by Josiah, 2 Kgs 23:22, 23; 2 Chron 35:1, 18; after return from captivity, Ezra 6:19, 20. Observed by Jesus, Mt 26:17–19; Lk 22:15; Jn 2:13, 23. Jesus in the temple at time of, Lk 2:41–50. Jesus crucified at time of, Mt 26:2; Mk 14:1, 2; Jn 18:28. The lamb of, a type of Christ, 1 Cor 5:7. Lord's supper ordained at, Mt 26:26–28; Mk 14:12–25; Lk 22:7–20.

Prisoner released at, by the Romans, Mt 27:15; Mk 15:6; Luke 23:16–18; Jn 18:39. Peter imprisoned at time of, Acts 12:3.

See *Feasts.*

PASSPORTS Given to Nehemiah, Neh 2:7–9.

PASTOR 1 Tim 3:1–7; Tit 1:5–9. The Old Testament Hebrew word and New Testament Greek word mean shepherd, and are usually so rendered. The work of pastors and teachers is "that God's people will be equipped to do better work for him, building up the church, the body of Christ, to a position of strength and maturity." Eph 4:12. The meaning of the word has given rise to the modern concept of the pastor as the shepherd of the flock, as has 1 Pet 5:2, with such qualifications as gentleness and love, 1 Thess 2:7, 8; steadiness, 2 Tim 4:5; a ministry of exhortation and comfort, 1 Thess 2:11, and the oversight of the congregation, 1 Pet 5:2.

See *Elder; Minister.*

PATARA A Lycian city in Asia Minor. Visited by Paul, Acts 21:1, 2.

PATHROS A part of Upper Egypt. Jewish captives in, Ezk 29:14. Prophecy against, Ezk 30:14.

PATHRUSIM Descendants of Mizraim, Gen 10:13, 14; 1 Chron 1:11, 12.

PATIENCE Ps 37:7. Rest in the Lord; wait patiently for him to act. Don't be envious of evil men who prosper. [8]Stop your anger! Turn off your wrath. Don't fret and worry—it only leads to harm. [9]For the wicked shall be destroyed, but those who trust the Lord shall be given every blessing.

Prov 15:18. A quick-tempered man starts fights; a cool-tempered man tries to stop them.

Eccl 7:8. Finishing is better than starting! Patience is better than pride! [9]Don't be quick-tempered—that is being a fool.

Lam 3:26. It is good both to hope and wait quietly for the salvation of the Lord. [27]It is good for a young man to be under discipline.

Lk 8:15. But the good soil represents honest, good-hearted people. They listen to God's words and cling to them and steadily spread them to others who also soon believe.

Lk 21:19. For if you stand firm, you will win your souls.

Rom 2:7. He will give eternal life to those who patiently do the will of God, seeking for the unseen glory and honor and eternal life that he offers.

Rom 5:3. We can rejoice, too, when we run into problems and trials for we know that they are good for us—they help us learn to be patient. [4]And patience develops strength of character in us and helps us trust God more each time we use it until finally our hope and faith are strong and steady.

Rom 8:25. But if we must keep trusting God for something that hasn't happened yet, it teaches us to wait patiently and confidently.

Rom 12:12. Be glad for all God is planning for you. Be patient in trouble, and prayerful always.

Rom 15:4. These things that were written in the Scriptures so long ago are to teach us patience and to encourage us, so that we will look forward expectantly to the time when God will conquer sin and death. [5]May God who gives patience, steadiness, and encouragement help you to live in complete harmony with each other—each with the attitude of Christ toward the other.

1 Cor 13:4. Love is very patient and kind, never jealous or envious, never boastful or proud, [5]never haughty or selfish or rude. Love does not demand its own way. It is not irritable or touchy. It does not hold grudges and will hardly even notice when others do it wrong.

2 Cor 6:4. In fact, in everything we do we try to show that we are true ministers of God. We patiently endure suffering and hardship and trouble of every kind. [5]We have been beaten, put in jail, faced angry mobs, worked to exhaustion, stayed awake through sleepless nights of watching, and gone without food. [6]We have proved ourselves to be what we claim by our wholesome lives and by our understanding of the Gospel and by our patience. We have been kind and truly loving and filled with the Holy Spirit.

Gal 5:22. But when the Holy Spirit controls our lives he will produce this kind of fruit in us: love, joy, peace, patience, kindness, goodness, faithfulness.

Gal 6:9. And let us not get tired of doing what is right, for after a while we will reap a harvest of blessing if we don't get discouraged and give up.

Eph 4:1. I beg you—I, a prisoner here in jail for serving the Lord—to live and act in a way worthy of those who have been chosen for such wonderful blessings as these. [2]Be humble and gentle. Be patient with each other, making allowance for each other's faults because of your love.

Col 3:12. Since you have been chosen by God who has given you this new kind of life, and because of his deep love and concern for you, you should practice tenderhearted mercy and kindness to others. Don't worry about making a good impression on them but be ready to suffer quietly and patiently. [13]Be gentle and ready to forgive; never hold grudges. Remember, the Lord forgave you, so you must forgive others.

1 Thess 1:3. We never forget your loving deeds as we talk to our God and Father about you, and your strong faith and steady looking forward to the return of our Lord Jesus Christ.

1 Thess 5:14. Dear brothers . . . be patient with everyone.

2 Thess 3:5. May the Lord bring you into an ever deeper understanding of the love of God and of the patience that comes from Christ.

1 Tim 1:16. But God had mercy on me so that Christ Jesus could use me as an example to show everyone how patient he is with even the worst sinners, so that others will realize that they, too, can have everlasting life.

1 Tim 6:11. Oh, Timothy, you are God's man. Run from all these evil things and work instead at what is right and good, learning to trust him and love others, and to be patient and gentle.

2 Tim 2:24. God's people must not be quarrelsome; they must be gentle, patient teachers of those who are wrong. [25]Be humble when you are trying to teach those who are mixed up concerning the truth. For if you talk meekly and courteously to them they are more likely, with God's help, to turn away from their wrong ideas and believe what is true. chapter 4:2.

Tit 2:1. But as for you, speak up for the right living that goes along with true Christianity. [2]Teach the older men to be serious and unruffled; they must be sensible, knowing and believing the truth and doing everything with love and patience. [9]Urge slaves to obey their masters and to try their best to satisfy them.

Heb 6:12. Then, knowing what lies ahead for you, you won't become bored with being a Christian, nor become spiritually dull and indifferent, but you will be anxious to follow the example of those who receive all that God has promised them because of their strong faith and patience. [15]Then Abraham waited patiently until finally God gave him a son, Isaac, just as he had promised.

Heb 10:36. You need to keep on patiently doing God's will if you want him to do for you all that he has promised.

Heb 12:1. Since we have such a huge crowd of men of faith watching us from the grandstands, let us strip off anything that slows us down or holds us back, and especially those sins that wrap themselves so tightly around our feet and trip us up; and let us run with patience the particular race that God has set before us.

Jas 1:3. For when the way is rough, your patience has a chance to grow. [4]So let it grow, and don't try to squirm out of your problems. For when your patience is finally in full bloom, then you will be ready for anything, strong in character, full and complete. [19]Dear brothers, don't ever forget that it is best to listen, speak little, and not become angry.

Jas 5:7. Now as for you, dear brothers who are waiting for the Lord's return, be patient, like a farmer who waits until the autumn for his precious harvest to ripen. [8]Yes, be patient. And take courage, for the coming of the Lord is near.

1 Pet 2:19. Praise the Lord if you are punished for doing right! [20]Of course, you get no credit for being patient if you are beaten for doing wrong; but if you do right and suffer for it, and are patient beneath the blows, God is well pleased. [21]This suffering is all part of the work God has given you. Christ, who suffered for you, is your example. Follow in his steps: [22]He never sinned, never told a lie, [23]never answered back when insulted; when he suffered he did not threaten to get even; he left his case in the hands of God who always judges fairly.

2 Pet 1:5. But to obtain these gifts, you need more than faith; you must also work hard to be good, and even that is not enough. For then you must learn to know God better and discover what he wants you to do. [6]Next, learn to put aside your own desires so that you will become patient and godly, gladly letting God have his way with you.

Rev 1:9. It is I, your brother John, a fellow sufferer for the Lord's sake, who am writing this letter to you. I, too, have shared the patience Jesus gives, and we shall share his kingdom!

Rev 3:10. Because you have patiently obeyed me despite the persecution, therefore I will protect you from the time of Great Tribulation and temptation, which will come upon the world to test everyone.

Rev 14:12. Let this encourage God's people to endure patiently every trial and persecution, for they are his saints who remain firm to the end in obedience to his commands and trust in Jesus.

See similar topics, *Endurance; Meekness.*

INSTANCES OF. Isaac toward the people of Gerar, Gen 26:15–22. Moses, Ex 16:7–9. Job, Job 1:21; Jas 5:11. David, Ps 40:1. Simeon, Lk 2:25. Paul, 2 Tim 3:10. Prophets, Jas 5:10. The Thessalonians, 2 Thess 1:4. The church at Ephesus, Rev 2:2, 3; and Thyatira, Rev 2:19. John, Rev 1:9.

PATMOS An island in the Aegean Sea. John an exile on, Rev 1:9.

PATRIARCH Head of a family, Acts 7:8.

PATRIARCHAL GOVERNMENT See *Government.*

PATRICIDE Of Sennacherib, 2 Kgs 19:37; Isa 37:38.

PATRIOTISM Deut 26:1. When you arrive in the land and have conquered it and are living there, [2, 3]you must present to the Lord at his sanctuary the first sample from each annual harvest. Bring it in a basket and hand it to the priest on duty and say to him "This gift is my acknowledgment that the Lord my God has brought me to the land he promised our ancestors." 4The priest will then take the basket from your hand and set it before the altar. 5You shall then say before the Lord your God, "My ancestors were migrant Arameans who went to Egypt for refuge. They were few in number, but in Egypt they became a mighty nation. 6, 7The Egyptians mistreated us and we cried to the Lord God. He heard us and saw our hardship, toil, and oppression, 8and brought us out of Egypt with mighty miracles and a powerful hand. He did great and awesome miracles before the Egyptians, 9and has brought us to this place and given us this land 'flowing with milk and honey!' 10And now, O Lord, see, I have brought you a token of the first of the crops from the ground you have given me." Then place the samples before the Lord your God, and worship him. 11Afterwards, go and feast on all the good things he has given you. Celebrate with your family and with any Levites or migrants living among you.

Judg 5:1. Then Deborah and Barak sang this song about the wonderful victory: 2"Praise the Lord! Israel's leaders bravely led; the people gladly followed! Yes, bless the Lord! 3Listen, O you kings and princes, for I shall sing about the Lord, the God of Israel. 4When you led us out from Seir, out across the fields of Edom, the earth trembled and the sky poured down its rain. 5Yes, even Mount Sinai quaked at the presence of the God of Israel! 6In the days of Shamgar and of Jael, the main roads were deserted. Travelers used the narrow, crooked side paths. 7Israel's population dwindled, until Deborah became a mother to Israel. 8When Israel chose new gods, everything collapsed. Our masters would not let us have a shield or spear. Among forty thousand men of Israel, not a weapon could be found! 9How I rejoice in the leaders of Israel who offered themselves so willingly! Praise the Lord! 10Let all Israel, rich and poor, join in his praises—those who ride on white donkeys and sit on rich carpets, and those who are poor and must walk. 11The village musicians gather at the village well to sing of the triumphs of the Lord. Again and again they sing the ballad of how the Lord saved Israel with an army of peasants! The people of the Lord marched through the gates! 12Awake, O Deborah, and sing! Arise, O Barak! O son of Abino-am, lead away your captives! 13, 14Down from Mount Tabor marched the noble remnant. The people of the Lord marched down against great odds. They came from Ephraim and Benjamin, from Machir and from Zebulun. 15Down into the valley went the princes of Issachar with Deborah and Barak. At God's command they rushed into the valley. (But the tribe of Reuben didn't go. 16Why did you sit at home among the sheepfolds, playing your shepherd pipes? Yes, the tribe of Reuben has an uneasy conscience. 17Why did Gilead remain across the Jordan, and why did Dan remain with his ships? And why did Asher sit unmoved upon the seashore, at ease beside his harbors?) 18But the tribes of Zebulun and Naphtali dared to die upon the fields of battle. 19The kings of Canaan fought in Taanach by Megiddo's springs, but did not win the victory. 20The very stars of heaven fought Sisera. 21The rushing Kishon River swept them away. March on, my soul, with strength! 22Hear the stamping of the horsehoofs of the enemy! See the prancing of his steeds! 23But the Angel of Jehovah put a curse on Meroz. 'Curse them bitterly,' he said, 'Because they did not come to help the Lord against his enemies.' 24Blessed be Jael, the wife of Heber the Kenite—yes, may she be blessed above all women who live in tents. 25He asked for water and she gave him milk in a beautiful cup! 26Then she took a tent pin and a workman's hammer and pierced Sisera's temples, crushing his head. She pounded the tent pin through his head, 27and he lay at her feet, dead. 28The mother of Sisera watched through the window for his return. 'Why is his chariot so long in coming? Why don't we hear the sound of the wheels?' 29But her ladies-in-waiting—and she herself—replied, 30'There is much loot to be divided, and it takes time. Each man receives a girl or two; and Sisera will get gorgeous robes, and he will bring home many gifts for me.' 31O Lord, may all your enemies perish as Sisera did, but may those who love the Lord shine as the sun!" After that there was peace in the land for forty years.

Ps 51:18. And Lord, don't punish Israel for my sins—help your people and protect Jerusalem.

Ps 85:1. Lord, you have poured out amazing blessings on this land! You have restored the fortunes of Israel, 2and forgiven the sins of your people—yes, covered over each one, 3so that all your wrath, your blazing anger, is now ended. 4Now bring us back to loving you, O Lord, so that your anger will never need rise against us again. 5(Or will you be always angry—on and on to distant generations?) 6Oh, revive us? Then your people can rejoice in you again. 7Pour out your love and kindness on us, Lord, and grant us your salvation. 8I am listening carefully to all the Lord is saying—for he speaks peace to his people, his saints, if they will only stop their sinning. 9Surely his salvation is near to those who reverence him; our land will be filled with his glory. 10Mercy and truth have met together. Grim justice and peace have kissed! 11Truth rises from the earth and righteousness smiles down from heaven. 12Yes, the Lord pours down his blessings on the land and it yields its bountiful crops. 13Justice goes before him to make a pathway for his steps.

Ps 122:6. Pray for the peace of Jerusalem. May all who love this city prosper. 7O Jerusalem, may there be peace within your walls and prosperity in your palaces.

Ps 128:5. May the Lord continually bless you with heaven's blessings as well as with human joys. 6May you live to enjoy your grandchildren! And may God bless Israel!

Ps 137:1. Weeping, we sat beside the rivers of Babylon thinking of Jerusalem. 2We have put away our lyres, hanging them upon the branches of the willow trees, [3], [4]for how can we sing? Yet our captors, our tormentors, demand that we sing for them the happy songs of Zion! [5], [6]If I forget you, O Jerusalem, let my right hand forget its skill upon the harp. If I fail to love her more than my highest joy, let me never sing again.

Isa 62:1. Because I love Zion, because my heart yearns for Jerusalem, I will not cease to pray for her or to cry out to God on her behalf until she shines forth in his righteousness and is glorious in his salvation.

Jer 8:11. They give useless medicine for my people's grievous wounds, for they assure them all is well when that isn't so at all! [21]I weep for the hurt of my people; I stand amazed, silent, dumb with grief. [22]Is there no medicine in Gilead? Is there no physician there? Why doesn't God do something? Why doesn't he help?

Jer 9:1. Oh, that my eyes were a fountain of tears; I would weep forever; I would sob day and night for the slain of my people! [2]Oh, that I could go away and forget them and live in some wayside shack in the desert, for they are all adulterous, treacherous men.

Lam 5:1. O Lord, remember all that has befallen us; see what sorrows we must bear! [2]Our homes, our nation, now are filled with foreigners. [3]We are orphans—our fathers dead, our mothers widowed. [4]We must even pay for water to drink; our fuel is sold to us at the highest of prices. [5]We bow our necks beneath the victors' feet; unending work is now our lot. [6]We beg for bread from Egypt, and Assyria too. [7]Our fathers sinned but died before the hand of judgment fell. We have borne the blow that they deserved! [8]Our former servants have become our masters; there is no one left to save us. [9]We went into the wilderness to hunt for food, risking death from enemies. [10]Our skin was black from famine. [11]They rape the women of Jerusalem and the girls of Judah's cities. [12]Our princes are hanged by their thumbs. Even aged men are treated with contempt. [13]They take away the young men to grind their grain and the little children stagger beneath their heavy loads. [14]The old men sit no longer in the city gates; the young no longer dance and sing. [15]The joy of our hearts has ended; our dance has turned to death. [16]Our glory is gone. The crown is fallen from our head. Woe upon us for our sins. [17]Our hearts are faint and weary; our eyes grow dim. [18]Jerusalem and the Temple of the Lord are desolate, deserted by all but wild animals lurking in the ruins. [19]O Lord, forever you remain the same! Your throne continues from generation to generation. [20]Why do you forget us forever? Why do you forsake us for so long? [21]Turn us around and bring us back to you again! That is our only hope! Give us back the joys we used to have! [22]*Or have you utterly rejected us? Are you angry with us still?*

See *Country, Love of.*

INSTANCES OF. Moses, Heb 11:24–26. Deborah, Judg 4; 5. The tribes of Zebulun and Naphtali, Judg 5:18–20. Eli, 1 Sam 4:17, 18. Phinehas' wife, 1 Sam 4:19–22. Joab, 2 Sam 10:12. Uriah, 2 Sam 11:11. Hadad, 1 Kgs 11:21, 22. The lepers of Samaria, 2 Kgs 7:9. Nehemiah, Neh 1:2, 4–11; 2:3.

LACKING IN. The tribes of Reuben, Asher, and Dan, Judg 5:15–17. Inhabitants of Meroz, Judg 5:23; of Succoth and Penuel, Judg 8:4–17.

PATROBAS A believer at Rome, Rom 16:14.

PATTERN Of the Tabernacle, Heb 8:5; 9:23. See *Tabernacle.*

PAU Called also *Pai.* A city of Edom, Gen 36:31–39; 1 Chron 1:50.

PAUL Called also *Saul,* Acts 7:58; 22:7, 13; 26:14. Of the tribe of Benjamin, Rom 11:1; Phil 3:5. Personal appearance of, 2 Cor 10:10; 11:6. Born in Tarsus, Acts 9:11; 21:39; 22:3. Educated at Jerusalem in the school of Gamaliel, Acts 22:3; 26:4. A zealous Pharisee, Acts 22:3; 23:6; 26:5; 2 Cor 11:22; Gal 1:14; Phil 3:5. A Roman, Acts 16:37; 22:25–28. Persecutes the Christians; present at, and gives consent to, the stoning of Stephen, Acts 7:58; 8:1, 3; 9:1; 22:4. Sent to Damascus with letters for the arrest and return to Jerusalem of Christians, Acts 9:1, 2. His vision and conversion, Acts 9:3–22; 22:4–19; 26:9–15; 1 Cor 9:1; 15:8; Gal 1:13; 1 Tim 1:12, 13. Is baptized, Acts 9:18; 22:16. Called to be a missionary and an apostle, Acts 22:14–21; 26:16–18; Rom 1:1; 1 Cor 1:1; 9:1, 2; 15:9; Gal 1:1; 15:16; Eph 1:1; Col 1:1; 1 Tim 1:1; 2:7; 2 Tim 1:1, 11; Tit 1:1. Preaches in Damascus, Acts 9:20, 22. Is persecuted by the Jews, Acts 9:23, 24. Escapes by being let down from the wall in a basket; goes to Arabia, Gal 1:17; Jerusalem, Acts 9:25, 26; Gal 1:18, 19. Received by the disciples in Jerusalem, Acts 9:26–29. Goes to Caesarea, Acts 9:30; 18:22. Sent to the Gentiles, Acts 13:2, 3, 47, 48; 22:17–21; Rom 11:13; 15:15, 16; Gal 1:15–24. Has Barnabas as his companion, Acts 11:25, 26. Teaches at Antioch one year, Acts 11:26. Conveys the contributions of the Christians in Antioch to the Christians in Jerusalem, Acts 11:27–30. Returns with John Mark to Antioch, Acts 12:25. Visits Seleucia, Acts 13:4; Cyprus, Acts 13:4. Preaches at Salamis, Acts 13:5; at Paphos, Acts 13:6, 7. Sergius Paulus, governor of the country, is a convert of, Acts 13:6–12. Contends with Elymas the sorcerer, Acts 13:6–12. Visits Perga in Pamphylia, Acts 13:13. John, a companion of, departs for Jerusalem, Acts 13:13. Visits Antioch in Pisidia, and preaches in the synagogue, Acts 13:14–41. His message received gladly by the Gentiles, Acts 13:42, 28. Persecuted and expelled, Acts 13:50, 51. Visits Iconium, and preaches to the Jews and Greeks; is persecuted; escapes to Lystra; goes to Derbe, Acts 14:1–6. Heals a crippled man, Acts 14:8–10. The people attempt to worship him, Acts 14:11–18. Is persecuted by certain Jews from Antioch and Iconium, and is stoned, Acts 14:19; 2 Cor 11:25; 2 Tim 3:11. Goes to Derbe, where he preaches the gospel, and returns to Lystra, and to Iconium, and to Antioch, encourages the believers, exhorts them to continue in the faith and ordains elders, Acts 14:19–23. Revisits Pisidia, Pamphylia, Perga, Attalia, and Antioch, in Syria, where he stayed, Acts 14:24–28. Contends with the Judaizing Christians against circumcision, Acts 15:1, 2. Refers the question as to circumcision to the apostles and elders at Jerusalem, Acts 15:2, 4. He and Barnabas declare to the apostles at Jerusalem the miracles and wonders God had done among the Gentiles through them, Acts 15:12. Returns to Antioch, accompanied by Barnabas, Judas, and Silas with letters to the Gentiles, Acts 15:22, 25.

Makes his second tour of the churches, Acts 15: 36. Chooses Silas as his companion and passes through Syria and Cilicia, encouraging the churches, Acts 15:36–41. Visits Lystra; circumcises Timothy, Acts 16:1–5. Goes through Phrygia and Galatia; is forbidden by the Holy Spirit to preach in Asia; visits Mysia; tries to go to Bithynia, but is restrained by the Spirit; goes to Troas, where he has a vision of a man saying, "Come over here [Macedonia], and help us"; immediately proceeds to Macedonia, Acts 16:6–10. Visits Samothrace and Neapolis; comes to Philippi, the chief city of Macedonia; visits a place of prayer at the river bank; preaches the word; the merchant, Lydia, of Thyatira, is converted and baptized, Acts 16:11–15. Causes the demon to come out of the fortune-teller, Acts 16:16–18. Persecuted, beaten and thrown into prison with Silas; sings songs of praise in the prison; an earthquake shakes the prison; he preaches to the alarmed jailer, who believes, and is baptized with his household, Acts 16:19–34. Is released by the civil authorities on the grounds of his Roman citizenship, Acts 16:35–39; 2 Cor 6:5; 11: 25; 1 Thess 2:2. Is received at the home of Lydia, Acts 16:40. Visits Amphipolis, and Apollonia, and Thessalonica, preaches in the synagogue, Acts 17: 1–4. Is persecuted, Acts 17:5–9; 2 Thess 1:1–4. Escapes to Beroea by night; preaches in the synagogue; many believe, Acts 17:10–12. Persecuted by the Jews who come from Thessalonica; is conducted by the believers to Athens, Acts 17:13–15. Disputes on Mars hill with Grecians, Acts 17:16–34. Visits Corinth; lives with Aquila and his wife, Priscilla, who are tentmakers; joins in their handicraft; reasons in the synagogue every Sabbath; is rejected by the Jews; turns to the Gentiles; makes his home with Justus; continues there one year and six months, teaching the word of God, Acts 18:1–11. Persecuted by Jews, brought before the governor, charged with false teaching; accusation dismissed; leaves after several days, and sails to Syria, accompanied by Aquila and Priscilla; Acts 18:12–18. Visits Ephesus, where he leaves Aquila and Priscilla; enters into a synagogue, where he reasons with the Jews; starts on his return journey to Jerusalem; visits Caesarea; goes through Galatia and Phrygia, encouraging the believers, Acts 18:18–23. Returns to Ephesus; baptizes in the name of the Lord Jesus, and lays his hands on the disciples, who are baptized with the Holy Spirit; preaches in the synagogue; remains in Ephesus for two years; heals the sick, Acts 19:1–12. Reproves the exorcists; casts a demon out of a man, and many believe, bringing their books of sorcery to be burned, Acts 19:13–20; 1 Cor 16:8, 9. Sends Timothy and Erastus to Greece, but remains himself in Asia for a while, Acts 19:21, 22. The spread of the gospel through his preaching interferes with the idol makers; he is persecuted, and a great uproar of the city is created; the mayor appeases the people; dismisses the accusation against Paul, and disperses the people, Acts 19:23–41; 2 Cor 1:8; 2 Tim 4:14. Proceeds to Greece after encouraging the churches along the way; stays three months; returns through Macedonia, accompanied by Sopater, Aristarchus, Secundus, Gaius, Timothy, Tychicus, and Trophimus, Acts 20:1–6. Visits Troas; preaches until break of day; restores to life the young man who fell from the window, Acts 20:6–12. Visits Assos, Mitylene, Chios, Samos, and Miletus, hurrying to Jerusalem, to be there at Pentecost, Acts 20:13–16. Sends for the elders of the church of Ephesus; tells them how he had preached in Turkey, and his temptations and afflictions testifying repentance toward God; declares he was drawn by the Holy Spirit to Jerusalem; exhorts them to take heed to themselves and the flock over whom the Holy Spirit had made them overseers; kneels down and prays and makes his departure, Acts 20:17–38. Visits Cos, Rhodes, Patara; takes ship for Tyre; stays at Tyre a week; is escorted by the disciples to the outskirts of the city; kneels down and prays; takes ship; comes to Ptolemais; greets the believers, and stays one day, Acts 21:1–7. Departs for Caesarea; enters the house of Philip, the evangelist; is admonished by Agabus not to go to Jerusalem, Acts 21: 8–15. Is received by the believers gladly; talks of the things that had been done among the Gentiles by his ministry; enters the Temple; the people are stirred against him by Jews from Turkey; an uproar is created; he is thrown out of the Temple; the commander of the garrison interposes and arrests him, Acts 21:17–33. His defense, Acts 21:33–40; 22: 1–21. Is confined, Acts 22:24–30. Is brought before the Council; his defense, Acts 22:30; 23:1–5. Is returned to the armory, Acts 23:10. Is cheered by a vision, promising him that he will witness in Rome, Acts 23:11. Jews conspire against his life, Acts 23: 12–15. Thwarted by his nephew, Acts 23:16–22. Is escorted to Caesarea by a military guard, Acts 23: 23–33. Is confined in Herod's palace in Caesarea, Acts 23:35. His trial before Felix, Acts 24. Remains in custody for two years, Acts 24:27. His trial before Festus, Acts 25:1–12. Appeals to Caesar, Acts 25:10–12. His examination before Agrippa, Acts 25: 13–27; 26. Is taken to Rome in custody of Julius, a centurion, and guard of soldiers; travels by ship, accompanied by other prisoners, and sails by way of the coasts of Asia; stops at Sidon, and at Myra, Acts 27:1–5. Transferred to a ship of Alexandria; sails by way of Cnidus, Salmone, Crete, and the Fair Havens, Acts 27:6–8. Predicts misfortune to the ship; his advice ignored, and the voyage resumed, Acts 27:9–13. The ship encounters a tempest; Paul encourages and comforts the officers and crew; the soldiers advise putting the prisoners to death; the centurion interferes, and all on board, consisting of two hundred and seventy-six souls, are saved, Acts 27:14–44. The ship is wrecked, and all on board take refuge on the island of Malta; kind treatment by the inhabitants of the island, Acts 27:14–44; 28:1, 2. Is bitten by a snake and miraculously saved, Acts 28:3–6. Heals the governor's father and others, Acts 28:7–10. Is delayed in Malta three months; proceeds on the voyage; stops at Syracuse; sails by Rhegium and Puteoli; meets believers who accompany him to Rome from Appian Forum; arrives at Rome; is delivered to the captain of the guard; is permitted to live by himself in custody of a soldier, Acts 28:11–16. Calls the Jewish leaders together; states his situation; is kindly received; expounds the gospel; testifies to the kingdom of God, Acts 28:17–29. Lives two years in his own rented house, preaching and teaching, Acts 28:30, 31.

Supports himself, Acts 18:2, 3; 20:33–35. Sickness of, in Asia, 2 Cor 1:8–11. His resolute determination to go to Jerusalem against the repeated admonition of the Holy Spirit, Acts 20:22, 23; 21:4, 10–14. Taken up to the third heaven, 2 Cor 12:1–4. Has "a thorn in my flesh," 2 Cor 12:7–9; Gal 4:13, 14. His independence of character, 1 Thess 2:9; 2 Thess 3:8. Persecutions of, 1 Thess 2:2; Heb 10:34. Persecutions endured by, see below. Zeal of, see *Zeal, of Paul.*

PERSECUTIONS ENDURED BY. Acts 9:16. "And I will show him how much he must suffer for me." [23]After a while the Jewish leaders determined to kill him. [24]But Paul was told about their plans, that they were watching the gates of the city day and night prepared to murder him. [25]So during the night some of his converts let him down in a basket through an opening in the city wall! [29]But then some Greek-speaking Jews with whom he had argued plotted to murder him.

Acts 16:19. Her masters' hopes of wealth were now shattered; they grabbed Paul and Silas and dragged them before the judges at the marketplace. [20, 21]"These Jews are corrupting our city," they shouted. "They are teaching the people to do things that are against the Roman laws." [22]A mob was quickly formed against Paul and Silas, and the judges ordered them stripped and beaten with wooden whips. [23]Again and again the rods slashed down across their bared backs; and afterwards they were thrown into prison. The jailer was threatened with death if they escaped, [24]so he took no chances, but put them into the inner dungeon and clamped their feet into the stocks.

Acts 20:22. And now I am going to Jerusalem, drawn there irresistibly by the Holy Spirit, not knowing what awaits me, [23]except that the Holy Spirit has told me in city after city that jail and suffering lie ahead. [24]But life is worth nothing unless I use it for doing the work assigned me by the Lord Jesus—the work of telling others the Good News about God's mighty kindness and love.

Acts 21:13. But he said, "Why all this weeping? You are breaking my heart! For I am ready not only to be jailed at Jerusalem, but also to die for the sake of the Lord Jesus." [27]The seven days were almost ended when some Jews from Turkey saw him in the Temple and roused a mob against him. They grabbed him, [28]yelling, "Men of Israel! Help! Help! This is the man who preaches against our people and tells everybody to disobey the Jewish laws. He even talks against the Temple and defiles it by bringing Gentiles in!" [29](For down in the city earlier that day, they had seen him with Trophimus, a Gentile from Ephesus in Turkey, and assumed that Paul had taken him into the Temple.) [30]The whole population of the city was electrified by these accusations and a great riot followed. Paul was dragged out of the Temple, and immediately the gates were closed behind him. [31]As they were killing him, word reached the commander of the Roman garrison that all Jerusalem was in an uproar. [32]He quickly ordered out his soldiers and officers and ran down among the crowd. When the mob saw the troops coming, they quit beating Paul. [33]The commander arrested him and ordered him bound with double chains. Then he asked the crowd who he was and what he had done.

Acts 22:22. The crowd listened until Paul came to that word, then with one voice they shouted, "Away with such a fellow! Kill him! He isn't fit to live!" [23]They yelled and threw their coats in the air and tossed up handfuls of dust. [24]So the commander brought him inside and ordered him lashed with whips to make him confess his crime. He wanted to find out why the crowd had become so furious!

Acts 23:10. The shouting grew louder and louder, and the men were tugging at Paul from both sides, pulling him this way and that. Finally the commander, fearing they would tear him apart, ordered his soldiers to take him away from them by force and bring him back to the armory. [12, 13]The next morning some forty or more of the Jews got together and bound themselves by a curse neither to eat nor drink until they had killed Paul! [14]Then they went to the chief priests and elders and told them what they had done. [15]"Ask the commander to bring Paul back to the Council again," they requested. "Pretend you want to ask a few more questions. We will kill him on the way."

Rom 8:35. Who then can ever keep Christ's love from us? When we have trouble or calamity, when we are hunted down or destroyed, is it because he doesn't love us anymore? And if we are hungry, or penniless, or in danger, or threatened with death, has God deserted us? [36]No, for the Scriptures tell us that for his sake we must be ready to face death at every moment of the day—we are like sheep awaiting slaughter; [37]but despite all this, overwhelming victory is ours through Christ who loved us enough to die for us.

1 Cor 4:9. Sometimes I think God has put us apostles at the very end of the line, like prisoners soon to be killed, put on display at the end of a victor's parade, to be stared at by men and angels alike. [11]To this very hour we have gone hungry and thirsty, without even enough clothes to keep us warm. We have been kicked around without homes

of our own. [12]We have worked wearily with our hands to earn our living. We have blessed those who cursed us. We have been patient with those who injured us. [13]We have replied quietly when evil things have been said about us. Yet right up to the present moment we are like dirt under foot, like garbage.

2 Cor 1:8. I think you ought to know, dear brothers, about the hard time we went through in Asia. We were really crushed and overwhelmed, and feared we would never live through it. [9]We felt we were doomed to die and saw how powerless we were to help ourselves; but that was good, for then we put everything into the hands of God, who alone could save us, for he can even raise the dead. [10]And he did help us, and saved us from a terrible death; yes, and we expect him to do it again and again.

2 Cor 4:8. We are pressed on every side by troubles, but not crushed and broken. We are perplexed because we don't know why things happen as they do, but we don't give up and quit. [9]We are hunted down, but God never abandons us. We get knocked down, but we get up again and keep going. [10]These bodies of ours are constantly facing death just as Jesus did; so it is clear to all that it is only the living Christ within (who keeps us safe). [11]Yes, we live under constant danger to our lives because we serve the Lord, but this gives us constant opportunities to show forth the power of Jesus Christ within our dying bodies. [12]Because of our preaching we face death, but it has resulted in eternal life for you.

2 Cor 6:4. In fact, in everything we do we try to show that we are true ministers of God. We patiently endure suffering and hardship and trouble of every kind. [5]We have been beaten, put in jail, faced angry mobs, worked to exhaustion, stayed awake through sleepless nights of watching, and gone without food. [8]We stand true to the Lord whether others honor us or despise us, whether they criticize us or commend us. We are honest, but they call us liars. [9]The world ignores us, but we are known to God; we live close to death, but here we are, still very much alive. We have been injured but kept from death. [10]Our hearts ache, but at the same time we have the joy of the Lord. We are poor, but we give rich spiritual gifts to others. We own nothing, and yet we enjoy everything.

2 Cor 11:23. They say they serve Christ? But I have served him far more! (Have I gone mad to boast like this?) I have worked harder, been put in jail oftener, been whipped times without number and faced death again and again and again. [24]Five different times the Jews gave me their terrible thirty-nine lashes. [25]Three times I was beaten with rods. Once I was stoned. Three times I was shipwrecked. Once I was in the open sea all night and the whole next day. [26]I have traveled many weary miles and have been often in great danger from flooded rivers, and from robbers, and from my own people, the Jews, as well as from the hands of the Gentiles. I have faced grave dangers from mobs in the cities and from death in the deserts and in the stormy seas and from men who claim to be brothers in Christ but are not. [27]I have lived with weariness and pain and sleepless nights. Often I have been hungry and thirsty and have gone without food; often I have shivered with cold, without enough clothing to keep me warm. [32]For instance, in Damascus the governor under King Aretas kept guards at the city gates to catch me; [33]but I was let down by rope and basket from a hole in the city wall, and so I got away! (What popularity!)

2 Cor 12:10. Since I know it is all for Christ's good, I am quite happy about "the thorn," and about insults and hardships, and persecutions and difficulties; for when I am weak, then I am strong —the less I have, the more I depend on him.

Gal 5:11. Some people even say that I myself am preaching that circumcision and Jewish laws are necessary to the plan of salvation. Well, if I preached that, I would be persecuted no more—for that message doesn't offend anyone. The fact that I am still persecuted proves that I am still preaching salvation through faith in the cross of Christ alone.

Gal 6:17. From now on please don't argue with me about these things, for I carry on my body the scars of the whippings and wounds from Jesus' enemies that mark me as his slave. 1 Thess 3:4.

Phil 1:30. We are in this fight together. You have seen me suffer for him in the past; and I am still in the midst of a great and terrible struggle now, as you know so well.

Phil 2:17. And if my lifeblood is, so to speak, to be poured out over your faith which I am offering up to God as a sacrifice—that is, if I am to die for you—even then I will be glad, and will share my joy with each of you. [18]For you should be happy about this, too, and rejoice with me for having this privilege of dying for you.

Col 1:24. But part of my work is to suffer for you; and I am glad, for I am helping to finish up the remainder of Christ's sufferings for his body, the church.

1 Thess 2:2. You know how badly we had been treated at Philippi just before we came to you, and how much we suffered there. Yet God gave us the courage to boldly repeat the same message to you, even though we were surrounded by enemies. [14]And then, dear brothers, you suffered what the churches in Judea did, persecution from your own countrymen, just as they suffered from their own people the Jews. [15]After they had killed their own prophets, they even executed the Lord Jesus; and now they have brutally persecuted us and driven us out.

2 Tim 1:12. That is why I am suffering here in jail and I am certainly not ashamed of it, for I know the one in whom I trust, and I am sure that he is able to safely guard all that I have given him until the day of his return.

2 Tim 2:9. It is because I have preached these great truths that I am in trouble here and have been put in jail like a criminal. But the Word of God is

not chained, even though I am. [10]I am more than willing to suffer if that will bring salvation and eternal glory in Christ Jesus to those God has chosen.

2 Tim 3:11. You know how many troubles I have had as a result of my preaching the Good News. You know about all that was done to me while I was visiting in Antioch, Iconium, and Lystra, but the Lord delivered me. [12]Yes, and those who decide to please Christ Jesus by living godly lives will suffer at the hands of those who hate him.

2 Tim 4:16. The first time I was brought before the judge no one was here to help me. Everyone had run away. I hope that they will not be blamed for it. [17]But the Lord stood with me and gave me the opportunity to boldly preach a whole sermon for all the world to hear. And he saved me from being thrown to the lions.

PAVILION See *Tabernacle.*

PAWN, OR PLEDGE Ex 22:26; Deut 24:10–13, 17; Job 24:3; Prov 22:26, 27; Ezk 18:5, 7, 12; 33:15; Amos 2:8.

See *Surety.*

PEACE Exemplified by Abraham, Gen 13:8, 9; Abimelech, Gen 26:29; Mordecai, Esther 10:3; David, Ps 120:7.

See *Charitableness; Nations, Peace of.*

SOCIAL. Gen 45:24. So he sent his brothers off. "Don't quarrel along the way!" was his parting shot!

Lev 26:6. For I will give you peace, and you will go to sleep without fear. I will chase away the dangerous animals.

Job 5:23. Dangerous animals will be at peace with you. [24]You need not worry about your home while you are gone; nothing shall be stolen from your barns.

Ps 34:14. Try to live in peace with everyone; work hard at it. 1 Pet 3:11.

Ps 120:6. I am tired of being here among these men who hate peace. [7]I am for peace, but they are for war, and my voice goes unheeded in their councils.

Ps 133:1. How wonderful it is, how pleasant, when brothers live in harmony!

Prov 12:20. Deceit fills hearts that are plotting for evil; joy fills hearts that are planning for good!

Prov 15:17. It is better to eat soup with someone you love than steak with someone you hate.

Prov 16:7. When a man is trying to please God, God makes even his worst enemies to be at peace with him.

Prov 17:1. A dry crust eaten in peace is better than steak every day along with argument and strife. [14]It is hard to stop a quarrel once it starts, so don't let it begin.

Prov 20:3. It is an honor for a man to stay out of a fight. Only fools insist on quarreling.

Isa 2:4. The Lord will settle international disputes; all the nations will convert their weapons of war into implements of peace. Then at the last all wars will stop and all military training will end.

Jer 29:7. And work for the peace and prosperity of Babylon. Pray for her, for if Babylon has peace, so will you.

Hos 2:18. At that time I will make a treaty between you and the wild animals, birds, and snakes, not to fear each other any more; and I will destroy all weapons, and all wars will end. Then you will lie down in peace and safety, unafraid.

Zech 8:19. Love truth and peace!

Mt 5:9. Happy are those who strive for peace—they shall be called the sons of God.

Mt 10:21. Brother shall betray brother to death, and fathers shall betray their own children. And children shall rise against their parents and cause their deaths. [22]Everyone shall hate you because you belong to me. But all of you who endure to the end shall be saved. [34]Don't imagine that I came to bring peace to the earth! No, rather, a sword. [35]I have come to set a man against his father, and a daughter against her mother, and a daughter-in-law against her mother-in-law—[36]A man's worst enemies will be right in his own home!

Mk 9:50. Live in peace with each other.

Lk 2:14. "Glory to God in the highest heaven," they sang, "and peace on earth for all those pleasing him."

Acts 7:26. The next day he visited them again and saw two men of Israel fighting. He tried to be a peacemaker. "Gentlemen," he said, "you are brothers and shouldn't be fighting like this! It is wrong!" [27]But the man in the wrong told Moses to mind his own business. "Who made *you* ruler and judge over us?" he asked. [28]"Are you going to kill me as you killed that Egyptian yesterday?" [29]At this, Moses fled the country, and lived in the land of Midian, where his two sons were born.

Acts 17:7. "And Jason has let them into his home. They are all guilty of treason, for they claim another king, Jesus, instead of Caesar." [8, 9]The people of the city, as well as the judges, were concerned at these reports and let them go only after they had posted bail.

Rom 12:18. Don't quarrel with anyone. Be at peace with everyone, just as much as possible.

Rom 14:19. In this way aim for harmony in the church and try to build each other up.

1 Cor 14:33. God is not one who likes things to be disorderly and upset. He likes harmony, and he finds it in all the other churches.

2 Cor 13:11. Be happy. Grow in Christ. Pay attention to what I have said. Live in harmony and peace.

Eph 4:3. Try always to be led along together by the Holy Spirit, and so be at peace with one another.

1 Thess 5:13. And remember, no quarreling among yourselves.

1 Tim 2:2. So that we can live in peace and quietness, spending our time in godly living and thinking much about the Lord.

2 Tim 2:22. Stay close to anything that makes you want to do right. Have faith and love, and enjoy the companionship of those who love the Lord and have pure hearts.

Heb 12:14. Try to stay out of all quarrels and seek to live a clean and holy life, for one who is not holy will not see the Lord.

Jas 3:17. But the wisdom that comes from heaven is first of all pure and full of quiet gentleness. Then it is peace-loving and courteous. It allows discussion and is willing to yield to others; it is full of mercy and good deeds. It is wholehearted and straightforward and sincere. [18]And those who are peacemakers will plant seeds of peace and reap a harvest of goodness.

1 Pet 3:10. If you want a happy, good life, keep control of your tongue, and guard your lips from telling lies. [11]Turn away from evil and do good. Try to live in peace even if you must run after it to catch and hold it!

SPIRITUAL. Job 22:21. Quit quarreling with God! Agree with him and you will have peace at last! His favor will surround you if you will only admit that you were wrong. [26]Then you will delight yourself in the Lord, and look up to God.

Ps 1:1. Oh, the joys of those who do not follow evil men's advice, who do not hang around with sinners, scoffing at the things of God: [2]But they delight in doing everything God wants them to, and day and night are always meditating on his laws and thinking about ways to follow him more closely.

Ps 4:8. I will lie down in peace and sleep, for though I am alone, O Lord, you will keep me safe.

Ps 17:15. But as for me, my contentment is not in wealth but in seeing you and knowing all is well between us. And when I awake in heaven, I will be fully satisfied, for I will see you face to face.

Ps 25:12. Where is the man who fears the Lord? God will teach him how to choose the best. [13]He shall live within God's circle of blessing.

Ps 29:11. He will give his people strength. He will bless them with peace.

Ps 37:4. Be delighted with the Lord. Then he will give you all your heart's desires. [11]But all who humble themselves before the Lord shall be given every blessing, and shall have wonderful peace. [37]But the good man—what a different story! For the good man—the blameless, the upright, the man of peace—he has a wonderful future ahead of him. For him there is a happy ending.

Ps 73:25. Whom have I in heaven but you? And I desire no one on earth as much as you! [26]My health fails; my spirits droop, yet God remains! He is the strength of my heart; he is mine forever!

Ps 85:8. I am listening carefully to all the Lord is saying—for he speaks peace to his people, his saints, if they will only stop their sinning.

Ps 119:165. Those who love your laws have great peace of heart and mind and do not stumble.

Ps 125:1. Those who trust in the Lord are steady as Mount Zion, unmoved by any circumstance. [5]And let Israel have quietness and peace.

Prov 3:16, 17. Wisdom gives: A long, good life, riches, honor, pleasure, peace. [24]With them on guard you can sleep without fear. *vs.* 13–18.

Isa 9:6. These will be his royal titles: "Wonderful," "Counselor," "The Mighty God," "The Everlasting Father," "The Prince of Peace."

Isa 11:6. In that day the wolf and the lamb will lie down together, and the leopard and goats will be at peace. Calves and fat cattle will be safe among lions, and a little child shall lead them all. [7]The cows will graze among bears; cubs and calves will lie down together, and lions will eat grass like cows. [8]Babies will crawl safely among poisonous snakes, and a little child who puts his hand in a nest of deadly adders will pull it out unharmed. [9]Nothing will hurt or destroy in all my holy mountain, for as the waters fill the sea, so shall the earth be full of the knowledge of the Lord. [13]Then, at last, the jealousy between Israel and Judah will end; they will not fight each other any more.

Isa 12:1. On that day you will say, "Praise the Lord! He was angry with me, but now he comforts me. [2]See, God has come to save me! I will trust and not be afraid, for the Lord is my strength and song; he is my salvation."

Isa 25:7. At that time he will remove the cloud of gloom, the pall of death that hangs over the earth; [8]he will swallow up death forever. The Lord God will wipe away all tears and take away forever all insults and mockery against his land and people. The Lord has spoken—he will surely do it!

Isa 26:3. He will keep in perfect peace all those who trust in him, whose thoughts turn often to the Lord! [12]Lord, grant us peace; for all we have and are has come from you.

Isa 27:5. If I find thorns and briars bothering her, I will burn them up unless these enemies of mine surrender and beg for peace and my protection.

Isa 28:12. They could have rest in their own land if they would obey him, if they were kind and good. He told them that, but they wouldn't listen to him.

Isa 30:26. The moon will be as bright as the sun, and the sunlight brighter than seven days! So it will be when the Lord begins to heal his people and to cure the wounds he gave them.

Isa 32:2. He will shelter Israel from the storm and wind. He will refresh her as a river in the desert and as the cooling shadow of a mighty rock within a hot and weary land. [17]And out of justice, peace. Quietness and confidence will reign forever more. [18]My people will live in safety, quietly at home.

Isa 48:18. Oh, that you had listened to my laws! Then you would have had peace flowing like a gentle river, and great waves of righteousness.

Isa 53:5. He was chastised that we might have peace; he was lashed—and we were healed!

Isa 54:1. Sing, O childless woman! Break out into loud song, Jerusalem, for she who was abandoned has more blessings now than she whose husband stayed! [10]For the mountains may depart and the hills disappear, but my kindness shall not leave you. My promise of peace for you will never be broken, says the Lord who has mercy upon you.

Isa 55:2. Why spend your money on foodstuffs that don't give you strength? Why pay for groceries that don't do you any good? Listen and I'll tell you where to get good food that fattens up the soul!

[12]You will live in joy and peace. The mountains and hills, the trees of the field—all the world around you—will rejoice.

Isa 57:1. The good men perish; the godly die before their time and no one seems to care or wonder why. No one seems to realize that God is taking them away from evil days ahead. [2]For the godly who die shall rest in peace. [19]Peace, peace to them, both near and far, for I will heal them all. Zech 9:10.

Isa 60:20. Your sun shall never set; the moon shall not go down—for the Lord will be your everlasting light; your days of mourning all will end.

Jer 33:6. Nevertheless the time will come when I will heal Jerusalem's damage and give her prosperity and peace.

Ezk 34:25. I will make a peace pact with them.

Hag 2:8, 9. "The future splendor of this Temple will be greater than the splendor of the first one! For I have plenty of silver and gold to do it! And here I will give peace," says the Lord.

Mal 2:5. The purpose of these laws was to give him life and peace.

Lk 1:79. To give light to those who sit in darkness and death's shadow, and to guide us to the path of peace.

Lk 2:14. "Glory to God in the highest heaven," they sang, "and peace on earth for all those pleasing him." [29]"Lord," he said, "now I die content!"

Jn 7:38. For the Scriptures declare that rivers of living water shall flow from the inmost being of anyone who believes in me.

Jn 14:27. I am leaving you with a gift—peace of mind and heart! And the peace I give isn't fragile like the peace the world gives. So don't be troubled or afraid.

Jn 16:33. I have told you all this so that you will have peace of heart and mind.

Acts 10:36. I'm sure you have heard about the Good News for the people of Israel—that there is peace with God through Jesus, the Messiah, who is Lord of all creation.

Rom 2:10. But there will be glory and honor and peace from God for all who obey him, whether they are Jews or Gentiles.

Rom 5:1. So now, since we have been made right in God's sight by faith in his promises, we can have real peace with him because of what Jesus Christ our Lord has done for us.

Rom 8:6. Following after the Holy Spirit leads to life and peace.

Rom 10:15. And how will anyone go and tell them unless someone sends him? That is what the Scriptures are talking about when they say, "How beautiful are the feet of those who preach the Gospel of peace with God and bring glad tidings of good things." In other words, how welcome are those who come preaching God's Good News!

Rom 14:17. For, after all, the important thing for us as Christians is not what we eat or drink but stirring up goodness and peace and joy from the Holy Spirit.

Rom 15:13. So I pray for you Gentiles that God who gives hope will keep you happy and full of peace as you believe in him. I pray that God will help you overflow with hope in him through the Holy Spirit's power within you. [33]And now may our God, who gives peace, be with you all. Amen.

Gal 1:3. May peace and blessing be yours from God the Father and from the Lord Jesus Christ. 1 Cor 1:3; 2 Cor 1:2; 1 Thess 1:1; 1 Tim 1:2; 2 Tim 1:2; Tit 1:4; Philemon 1:3; Rev 1:4.

Gal 5:22. But when the Holy Spirit controls our lives he will produce this kind of fruit in us: love, joy, peace.

Eph 2:14. For Christ himself is our way of peace. He has made peace between us Jews and you Gentiles by making us all one family, breaking down the wall of contempt that used to separate us. [15]By his death he ended the angry resentment between us, caused by the Jewish laws which favored the Jews and excluded the Gentiles, for he died to annul that whole system of Jewish laws. Then he took the two groups that had been opposed to each other and made them parts of himself; thus he fused us together to become one new person, and at last there was peace. [16]As parts of the same body, our anger against each other has disappeared, for both of us have been reconciled to God. And so the feud ended at last at the cross. [17]And he has brought this Good News of peace to you Gentiles who were very far away from him and to us Jews who were near.

Phil 4:7. If you do this you will experience God's peace, which is far more wonderful than the human mind can understand. His peace will keep your thoughts and your hearts quiet and at rest as you trust in Christ Jesus. [9]Keep putting into practice all you learned from me and saw me doing, and the God of peace will be with you.

Col 1:20. It was through what his Son did that God cleared a path for everything to come to him—all things in heaven and on earth—for Christ's death on the cross has made peace with God for all by his blood.

Col 3:15. Let the peace of heart which comes from Christ be always present in your hearts and lives, for this is your responsibility and privilege as members of his body. And always be thankful.

2 Thess 3:16. May the Lord of peace himself give you his peace no matter what happens.

See *Charitableness; Joy; Praise.*

PEACE OFFERINGS Ex 20:24; 24:5; Lev 7:11; 19:5. Offered by the leaders, Num 7:17; by Joshua, Josh 8:31; by David, 2 Sam 6:17; 24:25.

See *Offerings.*

PEACOCK 1 Kgs 10:22; 2 Chron 9:21; Prov 30:29–31.

PEARL Rev 17:4; 18:12, 16. "Pearl of great value," Mt 13:45, 46.

FIGURATIVE. Mt 7:6.

Symbolical. Rev 21:21.

PEAS Gen 25:34.

See *Lentils.*

PEDAHEL Leader of Naphtali, Num 34:16–28.

PEDAHZUR Father of Gamaliel, Num 2:2–15; 7:54–59; 10:23.

PEDAIAH 1. Grandfather of King Jehoiakim, 2 Kgs 23:36, 37.

2. Father of Zerubbabel, 1 Chron 3:17–20.

3. Father of Joel, 1 Chron 27:16–22.

4. Son of Parosh, Neh 3:25.

5. A Levite appointed as an administrator by Nehemiah, Neh 8:1–5; 13:13.

6. A Benjaminite, Neh 11:7–9.

PEG See *Nail.*

PEKAH Son of Remaliah. Commanding general of the army of Israel, 2 Kgs 15:25. Conspires against and assassinates King Pekahiah, 2 Kgs 15:25. Is made king of Israel, 2 Kgs 15:27. Victorious in war with Judah, 2 Chron 28:5, 6. Is plotted against and killed by Hoshea, 2 Kgs 15:30, 31. Prophecies against, Isa 7:1–16; 8:4–10.

PEKAHIAH Son of Menahem. King of Israel, 2 Kgs 15:22–26. Plotted against and killed by Pekah, 2 Kgs 15:25.

PEKOD An area of Babylonia, Jer 50:21; Ezk 23:23.

PELAIAH 1. Son of Eli-o-enai, 1 Chron 3:24.

2. A Levite who assisted Ezra in instructing the people in the law, Neh 8:7, 8; 10:9–13.

PELALIAH A priest, Neh 11:10–14.

PELATIAH 1. A son of Hananiah, of the family of David, 1 Chron 3:21, 22.

2. A Simeonite who was captain in an expedition against the Amalekites, 1 Chron 4:42, 43.

3. One of those who signed the covenant with Nehemiah, Neh 10:14–27.

4. An officer against whom Ezekiel prophesied, and who fell dead at the close of the prophecy, Ezk 11:1–13.

PELEG Son of Eber, Gen 10:25; 11:16–19; 1 Chron 1:19, 24–27.

PELET 1. Son of Jahdai, 1 Chron 2:47.

2. Son of Azmaveth, 1 Chron 12:3–7.

PELETH 1. A Reubenite, Num 16:1.

2. Son of Jonathan, 1 Chron 2:33.

PELETHITES A part of David's bodyguard, 2 Sam 8:18; 15:18; 20:23; 1 Chron 18:17.

PELICAN Lev 11:13–19; Deut 14:11–18.

PELON Home of two of David's warriors: Helez, 1 Chron 11:26–47; 27:10; and Ahijah, 1 Chron 11:26–47. Possibly in Ephraim.

PELUSIUM A city of Egypt, Ezk 30:15, 16.

PEN 2 Cor 3:3. Made of iron, Job 19:24; Jer 17:1.

PENALTY See *Judgments; Punishment; Sin, Punishment of; Wicked, Punishment of.*

PENIEL See *Penuel.*

PENINNAH One of Elkanah's wives, 1 Sam 1:2.

PENITENCE See *Repentance; Sin, Confession of.*

PENITENT PROMISES TO. Lev 26:40, 41. But at last they shall confess their sins and their fathers' sins of treachery against me. (Because they were against me, I was against them, and brought them into the land of their enemies.) When at last their evil hearts are humbled and they accept the punishment I send them for their sins, [42]then I will remember again my promises to Abraham, Isaac, and Jacob, and I will remember the land (and its desolation).

Num 5:6. Tell the people of Israel that when anyone, man or woman, betrays the Lord by betraying a trust, it is sin. [7]He must confess his sin and make full repayment for what he has stolen, adding twenty percent and returning it to the person he took it from.

Deut 4:29. But you will also begin to search again for Jehovah your God, and you shall find him when you search for him with all your hearts and souls. [30]When those bitter days have come upon you in the latter times, you will finally return to the Lord your God and listen to what he tells you. [31]For the Lord your God is merciful—he will not abandon you nor destroy you nor forget the promises he has made to your ancestors.

Deut 5:29. Oh, that they would always have such a heart for me, wanting to obey my commandments. Then all would go well with them in the future, and with their children throughout all generations!

Deut 30:1. When all these things have happened to you—the blessings and the curses I have listed—you will meditate upon them as you are living among the nations where the Lord your God will have driven you. [2]If at that time you want to return to the Lord your God, and you and your children have begun wholeheartedly to obey all of the commandments I have given you today, [3]then the Lord your God will rescue you from your captivity! He will have mercy upon you and come and gather you out of all the nations where he will have scattered you. [4]Though you are at the ends of the earth, he will go and find you and bring you back again [5]to the land of your ancestors. You shall possess the land again, and he will do you good and bless you even more than he did your ancestors! [6]He will cleanse your hearts and the hearts of your children and of your children's children so that you will love the Lord your God with all your hearts and souls, and Israel shall come alive again! [7, 8]If you return to the Lord and obey all the commandments that I command you today, the Lord your God will take his curses and turn them against your enemies—against those who hate you and persecute you. [9]The Lord your God will prosper everything you do and give you many children and much cattle and wonderful crops; for the Lord will again rejoice over you as he did over your fathers. [10]He will rejoice if you but obey the commandments written in this book of the law, and if you turn to the Lord your God with all your hearts and souls.

2 Kgs 22:18, 19. But because you were sorry and concerned and humbled yourself before the Lord when you read the book and its warnings that this land would be cursed and become desolate, and because you have torn your clothing and wept before me in contrition, I will listen to your plea.

1 Chron 28:9. Solomon, my son, get to know the

God of your fathers. Worship and serve him with a clean heart and a willing mind, for the Lord sees every heart and understands and knows every thought. If you seek him, you will find him; but if you forsake him, he will permanently throw you aside.

Job 22:23. If you return to God and put right all the wrong in your home, then you will be restored. [24]If you give up your lust for money, and throw your gold away, [25]then the Almighty himself shall be your treasure; he will be your precious silver! [26]Then you will delight yourself in the Lord, and look up to God. [27]You will pray to him, and he will hear you, and you will fulfill all your promises to him. [28]Whatever you wish will happen! And the light of heaven will shine upon the road ahead of you. [29]If you are attacked and knocked down, you will know that there is someone who will lift you up again. Yes, he will save the humble.

Job 23:6. Would he merely overpower me with his greatness? No, he would listen with sympathy.

Job 33:26. And when he prays to God, God will hear and answer and receive him with joy, and return him to his duties. [27]And he will declare to his friends, "I sinned, but God let me go. [28]He did not let me die. I will go on living in the realm of light."

Ps 6:8. Go, leave me now, you men of evil deeds, for the Lord has heard my weeping [9]and my pleading. He will answer all my prayers.

Ps 9:10. All those who know your mercy, Lord, will count on you for help. For you have never yet forsaken those who trust in you.

Ps 22:26. The poor shall eat and be satisfied; all who seek the Lord shall find him and shall praise his name. Their hearts shall rejoice with everlasting joy.

Ps 24:3. Who may climb the mountain of the Lord and enter where he lives? Who may stand before the Lord? [4]Only those with pure hands and hearts, who do not practice dishonesty and lying. [5]They will receive God's own goodness as their blessing from him, planted in their lives by God himself, their Savior. [6]These are the ones who are allowed to stand before the Lord and worship the God of Jacob.

Ps 32:5. Until I finally admitted all my sins to you and stopped trying to hide them. I said to myself, "I will confess them to the Lord." And you forgave me! All my guilt is gone. [6]Now I say that each believer should confess his sins to God when he is aware of them, while there is time to be forgiven. Judgment will not touch him if he does.

Ps 34:18. The Lord is close to those whose hearts are breaking; he rescues those who are humbly sorry for their sins.

Ps 51:17. It is a broken spirit you want—remorse and penitence. A broken and a contrite heart, O God, you will not ignore.

Ps 70:4. But fill the followers of God with joy. Let those who love your salvation exclaim, "What a wonderful God he is!"

Ps 90:14. Satisfy us in our earliest youth with your lovingkindness, giving us constant joy to the end of our lives. [15]Give us gladness in proportion to our former misery! Replace the evil years with good.

Ps 145:18. He is close to all who call on him sincerely. [19]He fulfills the desires of those who reverence and trust him; he hears their cries for help and rescues them.

Ps 147:3. He heals the brokenhearted, binding up their wounds.

Isa 27:5. I will burn them up, unless these enemies of mine surrender and beg for peace and my protection.

Ezk 18:21. But if a wicked person turns away from all his sins and begins to obey my laws and do what is just and right, he shall surely live and not die. [22]All his past sins will be forgotten, and he shall live because of his goodness. [23]Do you think I like to see the wicked die? asks the Lord. Of course not! I only want him to turn from his wicked ways and live. Ezk 33:10–16.

Mt 5:4. Those who mourn are fortunate! for they shall be comforted.

Mt 6:14, 15.Your heavenly Father will forgive you if you forgive those who sin against you; but if you refuse to forgive *them, he* will not forgive *you.*

Mt 7:7. Ask, and you will be given what you ask for. Seek, and you will find. Knock, and the door will be opened. [Lk 11:9–13.] [8]For everyone who asks, receives. Anyone who seeks, finds. If only you will knock, the door will open. [9]If a child asks his father for a loaf of bread, will he be given a stone instead? [10]If he asks for fish, will he be given a poisonous snake? Of course not! [11]And if you hard-hearted, sinful men know how to give good gifts to your children, won't your Father in heaven even more certainly give good gifts to those who ask him for them?

Mt 11:28. Come to me and I will give you rest—all of you who work so hard beneath a heavy yoke. [29, 30]Wear my yoke—for it fits perfectly—and let me teach you; for I am gentle and humble, and you shall find rest for your souls; for I give you only light burdens.

Mt 12:20. He does not crush the weak, or quench the smallest hope; he will end all conflict with his final victory. [31, 32]Even blasphemy against me or any other sin, can be forgiven—all except one: speaking against the Holy Spirit shall never be forgiven, either in this world or in the world to come. Lk 12:10.

Mt 18:11. And I, the Messiah, came to save the lost. Lk 19:9, 10.

Lk 4:18, 19. "The Spirit of the Lord is upon me; he has appointed me to preach Good News to the poor; he has sent me to heal the brokenhearted and to announce that captives shall be released and the blind shall see, that the downtrodden shall be freed from their oppressors, and that God is ready to give blessings to all who come to him.

Lk 6:37. Never criticize or condemn—or it will

all come back on you. Go easy on others; then they will do the same for you.

Lk 15:3, 4. So Jesus used this illustration: "If you had a hundred sheep and one of them strayed away and was lost in the wilderness, wouldn't you leave the ninety-nine others to go and search for the lost one until you found it? [5]And then you would joyfully carry it home on your shoulders. [6]When you arrived you would call together your friends and neighbors to rejoice with you because your lost sheep was found. [7]Well, in the same way heaven will be happier over one lost sinner who returns to God than over ninety-nine others who haven't strayed away! [Mt 18:12–14.] [8]Or take another illustration: A woman has ten valuable silver coins and loses one. Won't she light a lamp and look in every corner of the house and sweep every nook and cranny until she finds it? [9]And then won't she call in her friends and neighbors to rejoice with her? [10]In the same way there is joy in the presence of the angels of God when one sinner repents." To further illustrate the point, he told them this story: [11]"A man had two sons. [12]When the younger told his father, 'I want my share of your estate now, instead of waiting until you die!' his father agreed to divide his wealth between his sons. [13]A few days later this younger son packed all his belongings and took a trip to a distant land, and there wasted all his money on parties and prostitutes. [14]About the time his money was gone a great famine swept over the land, and he began to starve. [15]He persuaded a local farmer to hire him to feed his pigs. [16]The boy became so hungry that even the pods he was feeding the swine looked good to him. And no one gave him anything. [17]When he finally came to his senses, he said to himself, 'At home even the hired men have food enough and to spare, and here I am, dying of hunger! [18]I will go home to my father and say, "Father, I have sinned against both heaven and you, [19]and am no longer worthy of being called your son. Please take me on as a hired man." ' [20]So he returned home to his father. And while he was still a long distance away, his father saw him coming, and was filled with loving pity and ran and embraced him and kissed him. [21]His son said to him 'Father, I have sinned against heaven and you, and am not worthy of being called your son—' [22]But his father said to the slaves, 'Quick! Bring the finest robe in the house and put it on him. And a jeweled ring for his finger; and shoes! [23]And kill the calf we have in the fattening pen. We must celebrate with a feast, [24]for this son of mine was dead and has returned to life. He was lost and is found.' So the party began. [25]Meanwhile, the older son was in the fields working; when he returned home, he heard dance music coming from the house, [26]and he asked one of the servants what was going on. [27]'Your brother is back,' he was told, 'and your father has killed the calf we were fattening and has prepared a great feast to celebrate his coming home again unharmed.' [28]The older brother was angry and wouldn't go in. His father came out and begged him, [29]but he replied, 'All these years I've worked hard for you and never once refused to do a single thing you told me to; and in all that time you never gave me even one young goat for a feast with my friends. [30]Yet when this son of yours comes back after spending your money on prostitutes, you celebrate by killing the finest calf we have on the place.' [31]'Look, dear son,' his father said to him, 'you and I are very close, and everything I have is yours. [32]But it is right to celebrate. For he is your brother; and he was dead and has come back to life! He was lost and is found!' "

Lk 18:10. Two men went to the Temple to pray. One was a proud, self-righteous Pharisee, and the other a cheating tax collector. [11]The proud Pharisee "prayed" this prayer: "Thank God, I am not a sinner like everyone else, especially like that tax collector over there! For I never cheat, I don't commit adultery, [12]I go without food twice a week, and I give to God a tenth of everything I earn." [13]But the corrupt tax collector stood at a distance and dared not even lift his eyes to heaven as he prayed, but beat upon his chest in sorrow, exclaiming, "God, be merciful to me, a sinner." [14]I tell you, this sinner, not the Pharisee, returned home forgiven! For the proud shall be humbled, but the humble shall be honored.

Jn 6:37. But some will come to me—those the Father has given me—and I will never, never reject them.

Jn 10:9. Yes, I am the Gate. Those who come in by way of the Gate will be saved and will go in and out and find green pastures.

Acts 13:38. Brothers! Listen! In this man Jesus, there is forgiveness for your sins! [39]Everyone who trusts in him is freed from all guilt and declared righteous—something the Jewish law could never do.

Rom 10:9. For if you tell others with your own mouth that Jesus Christ is your Lord, and believe in your own heart that God has raised him from the dead, you will be saved. [10]For it is by believing in his heart that a man becomes right with God; and with his mouth he tells others of his faith, confirming his salvation. [11]For the Scriptures tell us that no one who believes in Christ will ever be disappointed. [12]Jew and Gentile are the same in this respect; they all have the same Lord who generously gives his riches to all those who ask him for them. [13]Anyone who calls upon the name of the Lord will be saved.

1 Jn 1:9. But if we confess our sins to him, he can be depended on to forgive us and to cleanse us from every wrong. (And it is perfectly proper for God to do this for us because Christ died to wash away our sins.)

See *Forgiveness; Repentance; Sin, Confession of.* See also *Obduracy; Reprobate.*

PENNY A unit of money equal to the smallest measure according to various systems of exchange found in the Bible. An inexact term, it is used for a number of Hebrew, Greek, and Roman monetary units which were used to convey the smallest sum, Gen 31:42; Ezra 8:29; Mt 5:26; 10:29; 22:19; 1 Cor 9:15.

See *Money; Denarius.*

PENSION Of Levites, 2 Chron 31:16–18.

PENTECOST Called *Festival of Weeks,* Ex 34:22; Deut 16:10; *Harvest Pilgrimage,* Ex 23:16; *Day of First-fruits,* Num 28:26; *Day of Pentecost,* Acts 2:1; 20:16; 1 Cor 16:8.

Institution of, Ex 23:16; 34:22; Lev 23:15–21; Num 28:26–31; Deut 16:9–12, 16.

Holy Spirit given to the apostles on the first day of, Acts 2.

See *Feasts.*

PENURIOUSNESS See *Parsimony.*

PENUEL 1. Called also *Peniel.* City built where Jacob wrestled with the angel, Gen 32:30; Judg 8:8, 9, 17; 1 Kgs 12:25.

2. Ancestor of Gedor, 1 Chron 4:3, 4.

3. A Benjaminite, 1 Chron 8:22–25.

PEOPLE Common. Heard Jesus gladly, Mt 7:28; 9:8, 33; 13:54.

PEOR 1. A mountain in Moab from which Balaam viewed the people of Israel, and where Balak built seven altars, Num 23:28–30.

2. See *Baal-peor.*

PERESH Son of Machir, 1 Chron 7:16.

PEREZ A twin son of Judah by Tamar, Gen 38:29; 1 Chron 2:4. Children of, Gen 46:8–14; Num 26:19–22; 1 Chron 2:5; 9:4; return from captivity, Neh 11:4–6. In the lineage of Jesus, Mt 1:3; Lk 3:23–38.

PERFECTION Ascribed to Noah, Gen 6:8–10; Jacob, Num 23:18–24; David, 2 Sam 22:24; 1 Kgs 11:4, 6; Asa, 1 Kgs 15:14; 2 Chron 15:17; Job, Job 1:1; Zacharias and Elizabeth, Lk 1:6; Nathanael, Jn 1:47.

UNCLASSIFIED SCRIPTURES RELATING TO. Gen 17:1. When Abram was ninety-nine years old, God appeared to him and told him, "I am the Almighty; obey me and live as you should."

Deut 5:32. So Moses told the people, "You must obey all the commandments of the Lord your God, following his directions in every detail, going the whole way he has laid out for you."

Deut 18:13. You must walk blamelessly before the Lord your God.

Josh 23:6. But be very sure to follow all the instructions written in the book of the laws of Moses; do not deviate from them the least little bit.

1 Kgs 8:61. O my People, may you live good and perfect lives before the Lord our God; may you always obey his laws and commandments, just as you are doing today.

1 Chron 28:9. Solomon, my son, get to know the God of your fathers. Worship and serve him with a clean heart and a willing mind, for the Lord sees every heart and understands and knows every thought. If you seek him, you will find him; but if you forsake him, he will permanently throw you aside. 1 Chron 29:19.

2 Chron 6:36. If they sin against you (and who has never sinned?) and you become angry.

2 Chron 16:9. For the eyes of the Lord search back and forth across the whole earth, looking for people whose hearts are perfect toward him, so that he can show his great power in helping them.

Job 9:20. But I? Am I righteous? My own mouth says no. Even if I were perfect, God would prove me wicked. [21]And even if I am utterly innocent, I dare not think of it. I despise what I am.

Ps 4:1. O God, you have declared me perfect in your eyes, you have always cared for me in my distress; now hear me as I call again.

Ps 37:31. He is just and fair and knows right from wrong. [37]The good man—what a different story! For the good man—the blameless, the upright, the man of peace—he has a wonderful future ahead of him. For him there is a happy ending.

Ps 101:2. I will try to walk a blameless path, but how I need your help, especially in my own home, where I long to act as I should.

Ps 106:3. Happiness comes to those who are fair to others and are always just and good.

Ps 119:1. Happy are all who perfectly follow all the laws of God. [2]Happy are all who search for God, and always do his will, [3]rejecting compromise with evil, and walking only in his paths. [6]Then I will not be disgraced, for I will have a clean record. [96]Nothing is perfect except your words. chapter 19: 7, 8.

Prov 2:21. For only good men enjoy life to the full.

Eccl 7:20. And there is not a single man in all the earth who is always good and never sins.

Mt 5:6. Happy are those who long to be just and good, for they shall be completely satisfied. [48]But you are to be perfect, even as your Father in heaven is perfect.

Mt 19:21. Jesus told him, "If you want to be perfect, go and sell everything you have and give the money to the poor, and you will have treasure in heaven; and come, follow me."

Lk 6:40. How can a student know more than his teacher? But if he works hard, he may learn much.

Rom 10:5. For Moses wrote that if a person could be perfectly good and hold out against temptation all his life and never sin once, only then could he be pardoned and saved.

1 Cor 13:10. But when we have been made perfect and complete, then the need for these inadequate special gifts will come to an end, and they will disappear.

2 Cor 7:1. Having such great promises as these, dear friends, let us turn away from everything wrong, whether of body or spirit, and purify ourselves, living in the wholesome fear of God, giving ourselves to him alone.

Eph 4:11. Some of us have been given special ability as apostles; to others he has given the gift of being able to preach well; some have special ability in winning people to Christ, helping them to trust him as their Savior; still others have a gift for caring for God's people as a shepherd does his sheep, leading and teaching them in the ways of God. [12]Why is it that he gives us these special abilities to do certain things best? It is that God's people will be equipped to do better work for him, building up the church, the body of Christ, to a position of strength and maturity; [13]until finally we all believe alike about our salvation and about our Savior, God's Son, and all become full-grown in the Lord—yes, to the point of being filled full with Christ.

Phil 1:10. For I want you always to see clearly the difference between right and wrong, and to be inwardly clean, no one being able to criticize you from now until our Lord returns.

Phil 2:15. So that no one can speak a word of blame against you. You are to live clean, innocent lives as children of God in a dark world full of people who are crooked and stubborn. Shine out among them like beacon lights.

Phil 3:12. I don't mean to say I am perfect. I haven't learned all I should even yet, but I keep working toward that day when I will finally be all Christ saved me for and wants me to be. [13]No, dear brothers, I am still not all I should be but I am bringing all my energies to bear on this one thing: Forgetting the past and looking forward to what lies ahead, [14]I strain to reach the end of the race and receive the prize for which God is calling us up to heaven because of what Christ Jesus did for us. [15]I hope all of you who are mature Christians will see eye-to-eye with me on these things, and if you disagree on some point, I believe that God will make it plain to you.

Col 1:21. This includes you who were once so far away from God. You were his enemies and hated him and were separated from him by your evil thoughts and actions, yet now he has brought you back as his friends. [22]He has done this through the death on the cross of his own human body, and now as a result Christ has brought you into the very presence of God, and you are standing there before him with nothing left against you—nothing left that he could even chide you for. [28]So everywhere we go we talk about Christ to all who will listen, warning them and teaching them as well as we know how. We want to be able to present each one to God, perfect because of what Christ has done for each of them.

Col 2:9. For in Christ there is all of God in a human body; [10]*so you have everything when you have Christ,* and you are filled with God through your union with Christ. He is the highest Ruler, with authority over every other power. [11]When you came to Christ he set you free from your evil desires, not by a bodily operation of circumcision but by a spiritual operation, the baptism of your souls.

Col 3:14. Most of all, let love guide your life, for then the whole church will stay together in perfect harmony.

Col 4:12. Epaphras, from your city, a servant of Christ Jesus, sends you his love. He is always earnestly praying for you, asking God to make you strong and perfect and to help you know his will in everything you do.

1 Thess 3:10. For night and day we pray on and on for you, asking God to let us see you again, to fill up any little cracks, there may yet be in your faith. [13]This will result in your hearts being made strong, sinless and holy by God our Father, so that you may stand before him guiltless on that day when our Lord Jesus Christ returns with all those who belong to him.

2 Tim 2:1. Oh, Timothy, my son, be strong with the strength Christ Jesus gives you.

Heb 6:1. Let us stop going over the same old ground again and again, always teaching those first lessons about Christ. Let us go on instead to other things and become mature in our understanding, as strong Christians ought to be.

Heb 10:14. For by that one offering he made forever perfect in the sight of God all those whom he is making holy.

Heb 13:20, 21. And now may the God of peace, who brought again from the dead our Lord Jesus, equip you with all you need for doing his will. May he who became the Shepherd of the sheep by an everlasting agreement between God and you, signed with his blood, produce in you through the power of Christ all that is pleasing to him. To him be glory forever and ever. Amen.

Jas 1:4. So let it grow, and don't try to squirm out of your problems. For when your patience is finally in full bloom, then you will be ready for anything, strong in character, full and complete. [25]But if anyone keeps looking steadily into God's law for free men, he will not only remember it but he will do what it says, and God will greatly bless him in everything he does.

Jas 3:2. If anyone can control his tongue, it proves that he has perfect control over himself in every other way.

1 Pet 5:10. After you have suffered a little while, our God, who is full of kindness through Christ, will give you his eternal glory. He personally will come and pick you up, and set you firmly in place, and make you stronger than ever.

1 Jn 2:5. But those who do what Christ tells them to will learn to love God more and more. That is the way to know whether or not you are a Christian.

1 Jn 3:6. So if we stay close to him, obedient to him, we won't be sinning either; but as for those who keep on sinning, they should realize this: They sin because they have never really known him or become his. [7]Oh, dear children, don't let anyone deceive you about this: if you are constantly doing what is good, it is because you *are* good, even as he is. [8]But if you keep on sinning, it shows that you belong to Satan, who since he first began to sin has kept steadily at it. But the Son of God came to destroy these works of the devil. [9]The person who has been born into God's family does not make a practice of sinning, because now God's life is in him; so he can't keep on sinning, for this new life has been born into him and controls him—he has been born again. [10]So now we can tell who is a child of God and who belongs to Satan. Whoever is living a life of sin and doesn't love his brother shows that he is not in God's family.

1 Jn 4:12. For though we have never yet seen God, when we love each other God lives in us and his love within us grows ever stronger.

1 Jn 5:18. No one who has become part of God's family makes a practice of sinning, for Christ, God's Son, holds him securely and the devil cannot get his hands on him.

Jude 1:24, 25. And now—all glory to God. . . . He is able to keep you from slipping and falling away, and to bring you, sinless and perfect, into his glorious presence.

See *God, Perfection of; Holiness; Jesus, Perfection of; Sanctification.*

PERFIDY See *Conspiracy; Hypocrisy; Treachery.*

PERFUME 2 Kgs 20:13; Prov 27:9; Eccl 7:1; 10:1; Song 1:3; 3:6; 4:10; Isa 3:20; 57:9; Mt 26:7; Mk 14:3–5; Jn 12:3–5. Used in the Tabernacle, Ex 30:7; 35:28. Beds perfumed with myrrh, Prov 7:16, 17.

FIGURATIVE. 2 Cor 2:14, 16; Eph 5:2.

See *Anointing.*

PERFUMER 1 Sam 8:13; Neh 3:8. Skills used in making oil and incense, Ex 30:25; 37:29.

PERGA The capital of Pamphylia. Paul preaches in, Acts 13:13, 14; 14:25.

PERGAMOS A city of Mysia. One of the "seven churches" in, Rev 1:11; 2:12–17.

PERIDA One of Solomon's officials. Descendants of, returned to Jerusalem from captivity in Babylon, Neh 7:57–59. Called *Peruda* in Ezra 2:55–57.

PERIZZITES One of the seven nations in the land of Canaan, Gen 13:7. Territory of, given to Abraham, Gen 15:19–21; Ex 3:8; 23:23. Doomed to destruction, Deut 20:17. Not all destroyed; Israelites intermarry with, Judg 3:5–7; Ezra 9:1, 2.

See *Canaanites.*

PERJURY Lev 6:2. If anyone sins against me by refusing to return a deposit on something borrowed or rented, or by refusing to return something entrusted to him, or by robbery, or by oppressing his neighbor, [3]or by finding a lost article and lying about it, swearing that he doesn't have it—[4, 5]on the day he is found guilty of any such sin, he shall restore what he took, adding a twenty percent fine, and give it to the one he has harmed; and on the same day he shall bring his guilt offering to the Tabernacle. [6]His guilt offering shall be a ram without defect, and must be worth whatever value you demand. He shall bring it to the priest, [7]and the priest shall make atonement for him before the Lord, and he shall be forgiven.

Lev 19:12. You must not swear to a falsehood, thus bringing reproach upon the name of your God, for I am Jehovah.

Isa 48:1. Hear me, my people: you swear allegiance to the Lord without meaning a word of it, when you boast of living in the Holy City and brag about depending on the God of Israel.

Jer 5:2. Even under oath, they lie.

Jer 7:9. Do you really think that you can steal, murder, commit adultery, lie, and worship Baal and all of those new gods of yours.

Hos 10:4. They make promises they don't intend to keep. Therefore punishment will spring up among them like poisonous weeds in the furrows of the field.

Zech 5:4. "I am sending this curse into the home of every thief and everyone who swears falsely by my name," says the Lord of Hosts. "And my curse shall remain upon his home and completely destroy it."

Zech 8:17. "Don't plot harm to others; don't swear that something is true when it isn't! How I hate all that sort of thing!" says the Lord.

Mal 3:5. At that time my punishments will be quick and certain; I will move swiftly against wicked men who trick the innocent, against adulterers, and liars.

Mt 5:33. Again, the law of Moses says, "You shall not break your vows to God, but must fulfill them all."

1 Tim 1:9. But they were not made for us, whom God has saved; they are for sinners who hate God, have rebellious hearts, curse and swear, attack their fathers and mothers, and murder. [10]Yes, these laws are made to identify as sinners all who are immoral and impure: homosexuals, kidnappers, liars, and all others who do things that contradict the glorious Good News of our blessed God, whose messenger I am.

See *False Witness; Lying; Oath.*

INSTANCES OF. Zedekiah, 2 Chron 36:13. Witnesses against Naboth, 1 Kgs 21:8–13; David, Ps 35:11; Jesus, Mt 26:59; Mk 14:56, 57; Stephen, Acts 6:11, 13, 14. Peter, when he denied Jesus with an oath, Mt 26:74; Mk 14:71.

PERSECUTION OF JESUS. Gen 3:15. From now on you and the woman will be enemies, as will all of your offspring and hers. And I will put the fear of you into the woman, and between your offspring and hers. He shall strike you on your head, while you will strike at his heel.

Ps 2:1. What fools the nations are to rage against the Lord! How strange that men should try to outwit God! [2]For a summit conference of the nations has been called to plot against the Lord and his Messiah, Christ the King. [3]"Come, let us break his chains," they say, "and free ourselves from all this slavery to God." [4]But God in heaven merely laughs! He is amused by all their puny plans. [5]And then in fierce fury he rebukes them and fills them with fear.

Ps 22:1. My God, my God, why have you forsaken me? Why do you refuse to help me or even to listen to my groans? [2]Day and night I keep on weeping, crying for your help, but there is no reply —[3, 4]for *you are holy.* The praises of our fathers surrounded your throne; they trusted you and you delivered them. [6]But I am a worm, not a man, scorned and despised by my own people and by all mankind. [7]Everyone who sees me mocks and sneers and shrugs. [8]"Is this the one who rolled his burden on the Lord?" they laugh. "Is this the one who claims the Lord delights in him? We'll believe it when we see God rescue him!" [11]Don't leave me now, for trouble is near and no one else can possibly help. [12]I am surrounded by fearsome enemies, strong as the giant bulls from Bashan. [13]They come at me with open jaws, like roaring lions attacking their prey. [14]My strength has drained away like water, and all my bones are out of joint. My heart melts like wax; [15]my strength has dried up like sun-baked clay; my tongue sticks to my mouth, for you have laid me in the dust of death. [16]The enemy, this gang of evil men, circles me like a pack of dogs; they have pierced my hands and feet. [17]I can count every bone in my body. See these men of evil gloat and stare; [18]they divide my clothes among themselves by a toss of the dice. [19]O Lord, don't stay away. O God my Strength, hurry to my aid. [20]Rescue me from death; spare my precious life from all these evil men. [21]Save me from these lions' jaws and from the horns of these wild oxen. Yes, God will answer me and rescue me.

Ps 69:7. Though I am mocked and cursed and shamed for your sake. [8]Even my own brothers pretend they don't know me! [9]My zeal for God and his work burns hot within me. And because I advocate your cause, your enemies insult me even as they insult you. [20]Their contempt has broken my heart; my spirit is heavy within me. If even one would show some pity, if even one would comfort me! [21]For food they gave me poison; for my awful thirst they offered me vinegar. [26]For they persecute the one you have smitten, and scoff at the pain of the one you have pierced. *vs.* 1–21.

Ps 109:25. I am a symbol of failure to all mankind; when they see me they shake their heads.

Isa 49:7. The Lord, the Redeemer and Holy One of Israel, says to the one who is despised, rejected by mankind, and kept beneath the heel of earthly rulers: "Kings shall stand at attention when you pass by; princes shall bow low because the Lord has chosen you; he, the faithful Lord, the Holy One of Israel, chooses you."

Isa 50:6. I give my back to the whip, and my cheeks to those who pull out the beard. I do not hide from shame—they spit in my face.

Isa 52:14. They shall see my Servant beaten and bloodied, so disfigured one would scarcely know it was a person standing there.

Isa 53:2. In God's eyes he was like a tender green shoot, sprouting from a root in dry and sterile ground. But in our eyes there was no attractiveness at all, nothing to make us want him. [3]We despised him and rejected him—a man of sorrows, acquainted with bitterest grief. We turned our backs on him and looked the other way when he went by. He was despised and we didn't care. [4]Yet it was *our* grief he bore, *our* sorrows that weighed him down. And we thought his troubles were a punishment from God, for his *own* sins! [5]But he was wounded and bruised for *our* sins. He was chastised that we might have peace; he was lashed—and we were healed! [7]He was oppressed and he was afflicted, yet he never said a word. He was brought as a lamb to the slaughter; and as a sheep before her shearers is dumb, so he stood silent before the ones condemning him. [8]From prison and trial they led him away to his death. But who among the people of that day realized it was their sins that he was dying for—that he was suffering their punishment? [9]He was buried like a criminal in a rich man's grave; but he had done no wrong, and had never spoken an evil word. [10]Yet it was the Lord's good plan to bruise him and fill him with grief.

Mic 5:1. With a rod they shall strike the Judge of Israel on the face.

Mt 2:13. After they were gone, an angel of the Lord appeared to Joseph in a dream. "Get up and flee to Egypt with the baby and his mother," the angel said, "and stay there until I tell you to return, for King Herod is going to try to kill the child."

Mt 12:14. Then the Pharisees called a meeting to plot Jesus' arrest and death. [24]But when the Pharisees heard about the miracle they said, "He can cast out demons because he is Satan, king of devils." Mk 3:22; Lk 6:11; 11:15.

Mt 16:1. One day the Pharisees and Sadducees came to test Jesus' claim of being the Messiah by asking him to show some great demonstrations in the skies.

Mt 26:3. At that very moment the chief priests and other Jewish officials were meeting at the residence of Caiaphas the High Priest, [4]to discuss ways of capturing Jesus quietly, and killing him. [14]Then Judas Iscariot, one of the twelve apostles, went to the chief priests, [15]and asked, "How much will you pay me to get Jesus into your hands?" And they gave him thirty silver coins. [16]From that time on, Judas watched for an opportunity to betray Jesus to them. [Mark 14:1, 48] [59]The chief priest and, in fact, the entire Jewish Supreme Court assembled there and looked for witnesses who would lie about Jesus, in order to build a case against him that would result in a death sentence.

Mt 27:25. And the mob yelled back, "His blood be on us and on our children!" [26]Then Pilate released Barabbas to them. And after he had whipped Jesus, he gave him to the Roman soldiers to take away and crucify. [27]But first they took him into the armory and called out the entire contingent. [28]They stripped him and put a scarlet robe on him, [29]and made a crown from long thorns and put it on his head, and placed a stick in his right hand as a scepter and knelt before him in mockery. "Hail, King of the Jews," they yelled. [30]And they spat on him and grabbed the stick and beat him on the head with it. [39]And the people passing by hurled abuse, shaking their heads at him and saying, [40]"So! You can destroy the Temple and build it again in three days, can you? Well, then, come on down from the cross if you are the Son of God!" [41-43]And the chief priests and Jewish leaders also mocked him. "He saved others," they scoffed, "but he can't save himself! So you are the King of Israel, are you? Come down from the cross and we'll believe you! He trusted God—let God show his approval by delivering him! Didn't he say, 'I am God's Son'?" [44]And the robbers also threw the same in his teeth. Mk 15; Jn 19.

Mk 3:6. At once the Pharisees went away and met with the Herodians to discuss plans for killing Jesus. [21]When his friends heard what was happening they came to try to take him home with them. "He's out of his mind," they said.

Mk 15:34. Then Jesus called out with a loud voice, "Eli, Eli, lama sabachthani?" ("My God, my God, why have you deserted me?") with chapters 16; 17.

Lk 4:28. These remarks stung them to fury; [29]and jumping up, they mobbed him and took him to the edge of the hill on which the city was built, to push him over the cliff.

Lk 7:34. But I eat my food and drink my wine, and you say, "What a glutton Jesus is! And he drinks! And has the lowest sort of friends!" Mt 11:19.

Lk 11:53, 54. The Pharisees and legal experts were furious; and from that time on they plied him fiercely with a host of questions, trying to trap him into saying something for which they could have him arrested.

Lk 12:50. There is a terrible baptism ahead of me, and how I am pent up until it is accomplished! Mt 20:22.

Lk 13:31. A few minutes later some Pharisees said to him, "Get out of here if you want to live, for King Herod is after you!"

Lk 19:14. But some of his people hated him and sent him their declaration of independence, stating that they had rebelled and would not acknowledge him as their king. [47]After that he taught daily in the Temple, but the chief priests and other religious leaders and the business community were trying to find some way to get rid of him. Mk 11:18.

Lk 20:20. Watching their opportunity, they sent secret agents pretending to be honest men. Mt 22:15; Mk 12:13.

Lk 22:2. The chief priests and other religious leaders were actively plotting Jesus' murder, trying to find a way to kill him without starting a riot—a possibility they greatly feared. [3]Then Satan entered into Judas Iscariot, who was one of the twelve disciples, [4]and he went over to the chief priests and captains of the Temple guards to discuss the best way to betray Jesus to them. [5]They were, of course, delighted to know that he was ready to help them and promised him a reward. [52]Then Jesus addressed the chief priests and captains of the Temple guards and the religious leaders who headed the mob. "Am I a robber," he asked, "that you have come armed with swords and clubs to get me? [53]Why didn't you arrest me in the Temple? I was there every day. But this is your moment—the time when Satan's power reigns supreme." [63, 64]Now the guards in charge of Jesus began mocking him. They blindfolded him and hit him with their fists and asked, "Who hit you that time, prophet?" [65]And they threw all sorts of other insults at him. Mt 26:67; Mk 14:65.

Lk 23:11. Now Herod and his soldiers began mocking and ridiculing Jesus; and putting a kingly robe on him, they sent him back to Pilate. [23]But they shouted louder and louder for Jesus' death, and their voices prevailed. Mk 15:14.

Jn 5:16. So they began harassing Jesus as a Sabbath breaker.

Jn 7:1. After this, Jesus went to Galilee, going from village to village, for he wanted to stay out of Judea where the Jewish leaders were plotting his death. [7]"For the world can't hate you; but it does hate me, because I accuse it of sin and evil. [19]None of *you* obeys the laws of Moses! So why pick on *me* for breaking them? Why kill *me* for this?" [20]The crowd replied, "You're out of your mind! Who's trying to kill you?" [30]Then the Jewish leaders sought to arrest him; but no hand was laid on him; for God's time had not yet come. [32]When the Pharisees heard that the crowds were in this mood, they and the chief priests sent officers to arrest Jesus.

Jn 8:37. "(Yes, I realize that you are descendants of Abraham!) And yet some of you are trying to kill me because my message does not find a home within your hearts. [40]But instead you are trying to kill me—and all because I told you the truth I heard from God. Abraham wouldn't do a thing like that!" [48]"You Samaritan! Foreigner! Devil!" the Jewish leaders snarled. "Didn't we say all along you were possessed by a demon?" [52]The leaders of the Jews said, "Now we know you are possessed by a demon. Even Abraham and the mightiest prophets died, and yet you say that obeying you will keep a man from dying!" [59]At that point the Jewish leaders picked up stones to kill him. But Jesus was hidden from them, and walked past them and left the Temple. Jn 10:31.

Jn 10:20. Some of them said, "He has a demon or else is crazy. Why listen to a man like that?" [39]Once again they started to arrest him. But he walked away and left them.

Jn 11:57. Meanwhile the chief priests and Pharisees had publicly announced that anyone seeing Jesus must report him immediately so that they could arrest him.

Jn 14:30. I don't have much more time to talk to you, for the evil prince of this world approaches. He has no power over me.

Jn 15:18. For you get enough hate from the world! But then, it hated me before it hated you. [20]Do you remember what I told you? "A slave isn't greater than his master!" So since they persecuted me, naturally they will persecute you. And if they had listened to me, they would listen to you! [21]The people of the world will persecute you because you belong to me, for they don't know God who sent me. [24]If I hadn't done such mighty miracles among them they would not be counted guilty. But as it is, they saw these miracles and yet they hated both of us—me and my Father. [25]This has fulfilled what the prophets said concerning the Messiah, "They hated me without reason."

Jn 18:22. One of the soldiers standing there struck Jesus with his fist. "Is that the way to answer the High Priest?" he demanded. [23]"If I lied, prove it," Jesus replied. "Should you hit a man for telling the truth?" [29]So Pilate, the governor, went out to them and asked, "What is your charge against this man? What are you accusing him of doing?" [30]"We wouldn't have arrested him if he weren't a criminal!" they retorted.

Jn 19:6. At the sight of him the chief priests and Jewish officials began yelling, "Crucify! Crucify!" "*You* crucify him," Pilate said. "I find him *not guilty.*" [15]"Away with him," they yelled. "Away with him—crucify him!"

Acts 2:23. But God, following his prearranged plan, let you use the Roman government to nail him to the cross and murder him.

Acts 3:13. For it is the God of Abraham, Isaac, Jacob and of all our ancestors who has brought glory to his servant Jesus by doing this. I refer to the Jesus whom you rejected before Pilate, despite Pilate's determination to release him. [14]You didn't want him freed—this holy, righteous one. Instead you demanded the release of a murderer. [15]And you killed the Author of Life; but God brought him back to life again. And John and I were witnesses of this fact, for after you killed him we saw him alive!

Acts 4:27. That is what is happening here in this city today! For Herod the king, and Pontius Pilate the governor, and all the Romans—as well as the people of Israel—are united against Jesus, your anointed Son, your holy servant.

Acts 7:52. Name one prophet your ancestors didn't persecute! They even killed the ones who predicted the coming of the Righteous One—the Messiah whom you betrayed and murdered.

Acts 13:27. The Jews in Jerusalem and their leaders fulfilled prophecy by killing Jesus; for they didn't recognize him, or realize that he is the one the prophets had written about, though they heard the prophets' words read every Sabbath. [28]They found no just cause to execute him, but asked Pilate to have him killed anyway. [29]When they had fulfilled all the prophecies concerning his death, he was taken from the cross and placed in a tomb.

Heb 12:2. Keep your eyes on Jesus, our leader and instructor. He was willing to die a shameful death on the cross because of the joy he knew would be his afterwards; and now he sits in the place of honor by the throne of God. [3]If you want to keep from becoming fainthearted and weary, think about his patience as sinful men did such terrible things to him.

1 Pet 4:1. Since Christ suffered and underwent pain, you must have the same attitude he did; you must be ready to suffer, too. For remember, when your body suffers, sin loses its power.

OF THE RIGHTEOUS. Gen 49:23. He has been severely injured by those who shot at him and persecuted him.

Job 1:8. Then the Lord asked Satan, "Have you noticed my servant Job? He is the finest man in all the earth—a good man who fears God and will have nothing to do with evil." [9]"Why shouldn't he, when you pay him so well?" Satan scoffed.

Job 2:4, 5. "Skin for skin," Satan replied. "A man will give anything to save his life. Touch his body with sickness and he will curse you to your face!"

Job 12:4. I, the man who begged God for help, and God answered him, have become a laughingstock to my neighbors. Yes, I, a righteous man, am now the man they scoff at. [5]Meanwhile the rich mock those in trouble and are quick to despise all those in need.

Ps 11:2. For the wicked have strung their bows, drawn their arrows tight against the bowstrings, and aimed from ambush at the people of God.

Ps 37:32. Evil men spy on the godly, waiting for an excuse to accuse them and then demanding their death.

Ps 38:20. They repay me evil for good and hate me for standing for the right.

Ps 42:3. Day and night I weep for his help, and all the while my enemies taunt me. "Where is this God of yours?" they scoff. [10]Their taunts pierce me like a fatal wound; again and again they scoff, "Where is that God of yours?"

Ps 44:15, 16. I am constantly despised, mocked, taunted and cursed by my vengeful enemies. [17]And all this has happened, Lord, despite our loyalty to you. We have not violated your covenant. [22]For we are facing death threats constantly because of serving you! We are like sheep awaiting slaughter. [18]Our hearts have not deserted you! We have not left your path by a single step.

Ps 56:5. They are always twisting what I say. All their thoughts are how to harm me.

Ps 69:10. How they scoff and mock me when I mourn and fast before the Lord! [11]How they talk about me when I wear sackcloth to show my humiliation and sorrow for my sins! [12]I am the talk of the town and the song of the drunkards.

Ps 74:7. And set the sanctuary on fire, and razed it to the ground—your sanctuary, Lord. [8]"Let's wipe out every trace of God," they said, and went through the entire country burning down the assembly places where we worshiped you.

Ps 94:5. See them oppressing your people, O Lord, afflicting those you love.

Ps 119:51. Proud men hold me in contempt for obedience to God, but I stand unmoved. [61]Evil men have tried to drag me into sin, but I am firmly anchored to your laws. [69]Proud men have made up lies about me, but the truth is that I obey your laws with all my heart. [78]Let the proud be disgraced, for they have cut me down with all their lies. But I will concentrate my thoughts upon your laws. [85, 86]These proud men who hate your truth and laws have dug deep pits for me to fall in. Their lies have brought me into deep trouble. Help me, for you love only truth. [87]They had almost finished me off, yet I refused to yield and disobey your laws. [95]Though the wicked hide along the way to kill me, I will quietly keep my mind upon your promises. [110]The wicked have set their traps for me along your path, but I will not turn aside. [157]My enemies are so many. They try to make me disobey, but I have not swerved from your will. [161]Great men have persecuted me, though they have no reason to, but I stand in awe of only your words.

Prov 29:10. The godly pray for those who long to kill them. [27]The good hate the badness of the wicked. The wicked hate the goodness of the good.

Isa 29:20. Bullies will vanish and scoffers will cease, and all those plotting evil will be killed—[21]the violent man who fights at the drop of a hat, the man who waits in hiding to beat up the judge who sentenced him, and the men who use any excuse to be unfair.

Isa 51:12. I, even I, am he who comforts you and gives you all this joy. So what right have you to fear mere mortal men, who wither like the grass and disappear? [13]And yet you have no fear of God, your Maker—you have forgotten him, the one who spread the stars throughout the skies and made the earth. Will you be in constant dread of men's oppression, and fear their anger all day long?

Isa 59:15. Yes, truth is gone, and anyone who tries a better life is soon attacked. The Lord saw all the evil and was displeased to find no steps taken against sin.

Jer 2:30. I have punished your children but it did them no good; they still will not obey. And you yourselves have killed my prophets as a lion kills its prey.

Jer 11:19. I had been as unsuspecting as a lamb or ox on the way to slaughter. I didn't know that they were planning to kill me! "Let's destroy this man and all his messages," they said. "Let's kill him so that his name will be forever forgotten."

Jer 15:10. Then Jeremiah said, "What sadness is mine, my mother; oh, that I had died at birth. For I am hated everywhere I go. I am neither a creditor soon to foreclose nor a debtor refusing to pay—yet they all curse me."

Jer 18:18. Then the people said, "Come, let's get rid of Jeremiah. . . . Let's silence him that he may speak no more against us, nor bother us again."

Jer 20:8. They scoff and mock and make my name a household joke. *v.* 7.

Jer 26:11. Then the priests and the false prophets presented their accusations to the officials and the people. "This man should die!" they said. "You have heard with your own ears what a traitor he is, for he has prophesied against this city." [12]Then Jeremiah spoke in his defense. "The Lord sent me," he said, "to prophesy against this Temple and this city. He gave me every word of all that I have spoken. [13]But if you stop your sinning and begin obeying the Lord your God, he will cancel all the punishment he has announced against you. [14]As for me, I am helpless and in your power—do with me as you think best."

Jer 50:7. All who found them devoured them.

Amos 5:10. How you hate honest judges! How you despise people who tell the truth!

Hab 1:13. We are wicked, but they far more! Will you, who cannot allow sin in any form stand idly by while they swallow us up? Should you be silent while the wicked destroy those who are better than they?

Mt 5:10. Happy are those who are persecuted because they are good, for the Kingdom of Heaven is theirs. [11]When you are reviled and persecuted and lied about because you are my followers—wonderful! [12]Be *happy* about it! Be *very glad!* For a *tremendous reward* awaits you up in heaven. And remember, the ancient prophets were persecuted too. [44]But I say: Love your *enemies!* Pray for those who *persecute* you! Lk 6:26, 27.

Mt 10:16. I am sending you out as sheep among wolves. Be as wary as serpents and harmless as doves. [17]But beware! For you will be arrested and tried, and whipped in the synagogues. [18]Yes, and you must stand trial before governors and kings for my sake. This will give you the opportunity to tell them about me, yes, to witness to the world. [21]Brother shall betray brother to death, and fathers shall betray their own children. And children shall rise against their parents and cause their deaths. [22]Everyone shall hate you because you belong to me. But all of you who endure to the end shall be saved. [23]When you are persecuted in one city, flee to the next! I will return before you have reached them all! [28]Don't be afraid of those who can kill only your bodies—but can't touch your souls! Fear only God who can destroy both soul and body in hell.

Mt 20:22. But Jesus told her, "You don't know what you are asking!" Then he turned to James and John and asked them, "Are you able to drink from the terrible cup I am about to drink from?" "Yes," they replied, "we are able!" [23]"You shall indeed drink from it," he told them.

Mt 23:34. I will send you prophets, and wise men, and inspired writers, and you will kill some by crucifixion, and rip open the backs of others with whips in your synagogues, and hound them from city to city, [35]so that you will become guilty of all the blood of murdered godly men from righteous Abel to Zechariah (son of Barachiah), slain by you in the Temple between the altar and the sanctuary.

Mt 24:8. But all this will be only the beginning of the horrors to come. [9]Then you will be tortured and killed and hated all over the world because you are mine, [10]and many of you shall fall back into sin and betray and hate each other.

Mk 8:35. If you insist on saving your life, you will lose it. Only those who throw away their lives for my sake and for the sake of the Good News will ever know what it means to really live. Lk 17:33.

Mk 9:42. But if someone causes one of these little ones who believe in me to lose faith—it would be better for that man if a huge millstone were tied around his neck and he were thrown into the sea.

Mk 13:9. But when these things begin to happen, watch out! For you will be in great danger. You will be dragged before the courts, and beaten in the synagogues, and accused before governors and kings of being my followers. This is your opportunity to tell them the Good News. [11]But when you are arrested and stand trial, don't worry about what to say in your defense. Just say what God tells you to. Then you will not be speaking, but the Holy Spirit will. [12]Brothers will betray each other to death, fathers will betray their own children, and children will betray their parents to be killed. [13]And everyone will hate you because you are mine. But all who endure to the end without renouncing me shall be saved.

Lk 6:22. What happiness it is when others hate you and exclude you and insult you and smear your name because you are mine! [23]When that happens, rejoice! Yes, leap for joy! For you will have a great reward awaiting you in heaven. And you will be in good company—the ancient prophets were treated that way too!

Lk 21:12. But before all this occurs, there will be a time of special persecution, and you will be dragged into synagogues and prisons and before kings and governors for my Name's sake. [13]But as a result, the Messiah will be widely known and honored. [14]Therefore, don't be concerned about how to answer the charges against you, [15]for I will give you the right words and such logic that none of your opponents will be able to reply! [16]Even those closest to you—your parents, brothers, relatives, and friends will betray you and have you arrested; and some of you will be killed. [17]And everyone will hate you because you are mine and are called by my Name. [18]But not a hair of your head will perish! [19]For if you stand firm, you will win your souls.

Jn 12:42. However, even many of the Jewish leaders believed him to be the Messiah but wouldn't admit it to anyone because of their fear that the Pharisees would excommunicate them from the synagogue.

Jn 15:18. For you get enough hate from the world! But then, it hated me before it hated you. [19]The world would love you if you belonged to it; but you don't—for I chose you to come out of the world, and so it hates you.

Jn 16:1. I have told you these things so that you won't be staggered (by all that lies ahead). [2]For you will be excommunicated from the synagogues, and indeed the time is coming when those who kill you will think they are doing God a service.

Jn 17:14. I have given them your commands. And the world hates them because they don't fit in with it, just as I don't.

Acts 4:16. "What shall we do with these men?" they asked each other. "We can't deny that they have done a tremendous miracle, and everybody in Jerusalem knows about it. [17]But perhaps we can stop them from spreading their propaganda. We'll tell them that if they do it again we'll really throw the book at them." [18]So they called them back in, and told them never again to speak about Jesus. [19]But Peter and John replied, "You decide whether God wants us to obey you instead of him! [20]We cannot stop telling about the wonderful things we saw Jesus do and heard him say."

Acts 5:29. But Peter and the apostles replied, "We must obey God rather than men." [40]The Council accepted his advice, called in the apostles, had them beaten, and then told them never again to speak in the name of Jesus, and finally let them go. [41]They left the Council chamber rejoicing that God had counted them worthy to suffer dishonor for his name. [42]And every day, in the Temple and in their home Bible classes, they continued to teach and preach that Jesus is the Messiah.

Acts 7:52. Name one prophet your ancestors didn't persecute! They even killed the ones who predicted the coming of the Righteous One—the Messiah whom you betrayed and murdered.

Acts 8:4. But the believers who had fled Jerusalem went everywhere preaching the Good News about Jesus!

Acts 28:22. But we want to hear what you believe, for the only thing we know about these Christians is that they are denounced everywhere!

Rom 8:17. And since we are his children, we will share his treasures—for all God gives to his Son Jesus is now ours too. But if we are to share his glory, we must also share his suffering. [35]Who then can ever keep Christ's love from us? When we have trouble or calamity, when we are hunted down or destroyed, is it because he doesn't love us anymore? And if we are hungry, or penniless, or in danger, or threatened with death, has God deserted us? [36]No, for the Scriptures tell us that for his sake we must be ready to face death at every moment of the day—we are like sheep awaiting slaughter; [37]but despite all this, overwhelming victory is ours through Christ who loved us enough to die for us.

1 Cor 4:9. Sometimes I think God has put us apostles at the very end of the line, like prisoners soon to be killed, put on display at the end of a victor's parade, to be stared at by men and angels alike. [10]Religion has made us foolish, you say, but of course you are all such wise and sensible Christians! We are weak but not you! You are well thought of, while we are laughed at. [11]To this very hour we have gone hungry and thirsty without even enough clothes to keep us warm. We have been kicked around without homes of our own. [12]We have worked wearily with our hands to earn our living. We have blessed those who cursed us. We have been patient with those who injured us. [13]We have replied quietly when evil things have been said about us. Yet right up to the present moment we are like dirt under foot, like garbage.

1 Cor 13:3. If I gave everything I have to poor people, and if I were burned alive for preaching the Gospel but didn't love others, it would be of no value whatever.

2 Cor 4:8. We are pressed on every side by trouble, but not crushed and broken. We are perplexed because we don't know why things happen as they do, but we don't give up and quit. [9]We are hunted down, but God never abandons us. We get knocked down, but we get up again and keep going. [10]These bodies of ours are constantly facing death just as Jesus did; so it is clear to all that it is only the living Christ within (who keeps us safe). [Jn 15:20.] [11]Yes, we live under constant danger to

our lives because we serve the Lord, but this gives us constant opportunities to show forth the power of Jesus Christ within our dying bodies. [12]Because of our preaching we face death, but it has resulted in eternal life for you.

2 Cor 6:4. In fact, in everything we do we try to show that we are true ministers of God. We patiently endure suffering and hardship and trouble of every kind. [5]We have been beaten, put in jail, faced angry mobs, worked to exhaustion, stayed awake through sleepless nights of watching, and gone without food. [8]We stand true to the Lord whether others honor us or despise us, whether they criticize us or commend us. We are honest, but they call us liars. [9]The world ignores us, but we are known to God; we live close to death, but here we are, still very much alive. We have been injured but kept from death. [10]Our hearts ache, but at the same time we have the joy of the Lord. We are poor, but we give rich spiritual gifts to others. We own nothing, and yet we enjoy everything.

2 Cor 11:23. They say they serve Christ? But I have served him far more! (Have I gone mad to boast like this?) I have worked harder, been put in jail oftener, been whipped times without number, and faced death again and again and again. [24]Five different times the Jews gave me their terrible thirty-nine lashes. [25]Three times I was beaten with rods. Once I was stoned. Three times I was shipwrecked. Once I was in the open sea all night and the whole next day. [26]I have traveled many weary miles and have been often in great danger from flooded rivers, and from robbers, and from my own people, the Jews, as well as from the hands of the Gentiles. I have faced grave dangers from mobs in the cities and from death in the deserts and in the stormy seas and from men who claim to be brothers in Christ but are not. [27]I have lived with weariness and pain and sleepless nights. Often I have been hungry and thirsty and have gone without food; often I have shivered with cold, without enough clothing to keep me warm.

2 Cor 12:10. Since I know it is all for Christ's good, I am quite happy about "the thorn," and about insults and hardships, persecutions and difficulties; for when I am weak, then I am strong—the less I have, the more I depend on him.

Gal 4:29. And so we who are born of the Holy Spirit are persecuted now by those who want us to keep the Jewish laws, just as Isaac the child of promise was persecuted by Ishmael the slave-wife's son.

Gal 6:12. Those teachers of yours who are trying to convince you to be circumcised are doing it for just one reason: so that they can be popular and avoid the persecution they would get if they admitted that the cross of Christ alone can save. [17]I carry on my body the scars of the whippings and wounds from Jesus' enemies that mark me as his slave.

Phil 1:12. And I want you to know this, dear brothers: Everything that has happened to me here has been a great boost in getting out the Good News concerning Christ. [13]For everyone around here, including all the soldiers over at the barracks, knows that I am in chains simply because I am a Christian. [14]And because of my imprisonment many of the Christians here seem to have lost their fear of chains! Somehow my patience has encouraged them and they have become more and more bold in telling others about Christ. [27]But whatever happens to me, remember always to live as Christians should . . . tell the Good News [28]fearlessly, no matter what your enemies may do. They will see this as a sign of their downfall, but for you it will be a clear sign from God that he is with you, and that he has given you eternal life with him. [29]For to you has been given the privilege not only of trusting him but also of suffering for him.

Col 1:24. But part of my work is to suffer for you; and I am glad, for I am helping to finish up the remainder of Christ's sufferings for his body, the church.

1 Thess 1:6. So you became our followers and the Lord's; for you received our message with joy from the Holy Spirit in spite of the trials and sorrows it brought you.

1 Thess 2:2. You know how badly we had been treated at Philippi just before we came to you and how much we suffered there. Yet God gave us the courage to boldly repeat same message to you, even though we were surrounded by enemies. [14]And then, dear brothers, you suffered what the churches in Judea did, persecution from your own countrymen, just as they suffered from their own people the Jews. [15]After they had killed their own prophets, they even executed the Lord Jesus; and now they have brutally persecuted us and driven us out. They are against both God and man.

2 Thess 1:4. We are happy to tell other churches about your patience and complete faith in God, in spite of all the crushing troubles and hardships you are going through.

2 Tim 1:8. If you will stir up this inner power, you will never be afraid to tell others about our Lord, or to let them know that I am your friend even though I am here in jail for Christ's sake. You will be ready to suffer with me for the Lord, for he will give you strength in suffering. [12]That is why I am suffering here in jail and I am certainly not ashamed of it, for I know the one in whom I trust, and I am sure that he is able to safely guard all that I have given him until the day of his return.

2 Tim 2:9. It is because I have preached these great truths that I am in trouble here and have been put in jail like a criminal. But the Word of God is not chained, even though I am. [10]I am more than willing to suffer if that will bring salvation and eternal glory in Christ Jesus to those God has chosen. [12]And if we think that our present service for him is hard, just remember that some day we are going to sit with him and rule with him. But if we give up when we suffer, and turn against Christ, then he must turn against us.

2 Tim 3:2. For people will love only themselves [3]. . . and sneer at those who try to be good. [12]Yes, and those who decide to please Christ Jesus by

living godly lives will suffer at the hands of those who hate him. Mk 10:30.

2 Tim 4:16. The first time I was brought before the judge no one was here to help me. Everyone had run away. I hope that they will not be blamed for it. [17]But the Lord stood with me and gave me the opportunity to boldly preach a whole sermon for all the world to hear. And he saved me from being thrown to the lions.

Heb 10:32. Don't ever forget those wonderful days when you first learned about Christ. Remember how you kept right on with the Lord even though it meant terrible suffering. [33]Sometimes you were laughed at and beaten, and sometimes you watched and sympathized with others suffering the same things. [34]You suffered with those thrown into jail, and you were actually joyful when all you owned was taken from you, knowing that better things were awaiting you in heaven, things that would be yours forever.

Heb 11:25. Chose to share ill-treatment with God's people instead of enjoying the fleeting pleasures of sin. [26]He thought that it was better to suffer for the promised Christ than to own all the treasures of Egypt, for he was looking forward to the great reward that God would give him. [27]And it was because he trusted God that he left the land of Egypt and wasn't afraid of the king's anger. Moses kept right on going; it seemed as though he could see God right there with him. [33]These people all trusted God and as a result won battles, overthrew kingdoms, ruled their people well, and received what God had promised them; they were kept from harm in a den of lions, [34]and in a fiery furnace. Some, through their faith, escaped death by the sword. Some were made strong again after they had been weak or sick. Others were given great power in battle; they made whole armies turn and run away. [35]And some women, through faith, received their loved ones back again from death. But others trusted God and were beaten to death, preferring to die rather than turn from God and be free—trusting that they would rise to a better life afterwards. [36]Some were laughed at and their backs cut open with whips, and others were chained in dungeons. [37, 38]Some died by stoning and some by being sawed in two; others were promised freedom if they would renounce their faith, then were killed with the sword. Some went about in skins of sheep and goats, wandering over deserts and mountains, hiding in dens and caves. They were hungry and sick and ill-treated—too good for this world.

Heb 12:3. If you want to keep from becoming fainthearted and weary, think about his patience as sinful men did such terrible things to him. [4]After all, you have never yet struggled against sin and temptation until you sweat great drops of blood.

Heb 13:13. So let us go out to him beyond the city walls (that is, outside the interests of this world, being willing to be despised) to suffer with him there, bearing his shame.

Jas 2:6. Don't you realize that it is usually the rich men who pick on you and drag you into court?

Jas 5:6. You have condemned and killed good men who had no power to defend themselves against you. [10]For examples of patience in suffering, look at the Lord's prophets.

1 Pet 3:14. But even if they should, you are to be envied, for God will reward you for it. [16]Do what is right; then if men speak against you, calling you evil names, they will become ashamed of themselves for falsely accusing you when you have only done what is good. [17]Remember, if God wants you to suffer, it is better to suffer for doing good than for doing wrong!

1 Pet 4:3. You have had enough in the past of the evil things the godless enjoy—sex sin, lust, getting drunk, wild parties, drinking bouts, and the worship of idols, and other terrible sins. [4]Of course, your former friends will be very surprised when you don't eagerly join them any more in the wicked things they do, and they will laugh at you in contempt and scorn. [12]Dear friends, don't be bewildered or surprised when you go through the fiery trials ahead, for this is no strange, unusual thing that is going to happen to you. [13]Instead, be really glad—because these trials will make you partners with Christ in his suffering, and afterwards you will have the wonderful joy of sharing his glory in that coming day when it will be displayed. [14]Be happy if you are cursed and insulted for being a Christian, for when that happens the Spirit of God will come upon you with great glory. [16]But it is no shame to suffer for being a Christian. Praise God for the privilege of being in Christ's family and being called by his wonderful name! [19]So if you are suffering according to God's will, keep on doing what is right and trust yourself to the God who made you, for he will never fail you.

1 Jn 3:1. See how very much our heavenly Father loves us, for he allows us to be called his children —think of it—and we really *are!* But since most people don't know God, naturally they don't understand that we are his children. [13]So don't be surprised, dear friends, if the world hates you.

Rev 2:3. You have patiently suffered for me without quitting. [10]Stop being afraid of what you are about to suffer—for the devil will soon throw some of you into prison to test you. You will be persecuted for "ten days." Remain faithful even when facing death and I will give you the crown of life—an unending, glorious future. [13]I am fully aware that you live in the city where Satan's throne is, at the center of satanic worship; and yet you have remained loyal to me, and refused to deny me, even when Antipas, my faithful witness, was martyred among you by Satan's devotees.

Rev 6:9. And when he broke open the fifth seal, I saw an altar, and underneath it all the souls of those who had been martyred for preaching the Word of God and for being faithful in their witnessing. [10]They called loudly to the Lord and said, "O Sovereign Lord, holy and true, how long will it be before you judge the people of the earth for what they've done to us? When will you avenge our blood against those living on the earth?" [11]White robes were given to each of them, and they were told to rest a little longer until their other brothers, fellow servants of Jesus, had been martyred on the earth and joined them.

Rev 7:13. Then one of the twenty-four Elders asked me, "Do you know who these are, who are clothed in white, and where they come from?" [14]"No, sir," I replied. "Please tell me." "These are the ones coming out of the Great Tribulation," he said; "they washed their robes and whitened them by the blood of the Lamb. [15]That is why they are here before the throne of God, serving him day and night in his temple. The one sitting on the throne will shelter them; [16]they will never be hungry again, nor thirsty, and they will be fully protected from the scorching noontime heat. [17]For the Lamb standing in front of the throne will feed them and be their Shepherd and lead them to the springs of the Water of Life. And God will wipe their tears away."

Rev 12:11. They defeated him by the blood of the Lamb, and by their testimony; for they did not love their lives but laid them down for him.

Rev 17:6. I could see that she was drunk—drunk with the blood of the martyrs of Jesus she had killed.

Rev 20:4. Then I saw thrones, and sitting on them were those who had been given the right to judge. And I saw the souls of those who had been beheaded for their testimony about Jesus, for proclaiming the Word of God, and who had not worshiped the Creature or his statue, nor accepted his mark on their foreheads or their hands. They had come to life again and now they reigned with Christ for a thousand years.

See *Paul.*

A vehicle for God's punishment, Lam 1:3. Diffuses the gospel, Acts 8:1, 4; 11:19–21; Phil 1:12–14.

Prayer for deliverance from, Ps 70:1–4; 83; 140: 1, 4; 142:6. Deliverance from, Ps 124; 129:1, 2.

Instances of. Of Abel, Gen 4:8; Mt 23:35; 1 Jn 3: 12. Of Lot, Gen 19:9. Of Moses, Ex 2:15; 17:4. Of David, Ps 31:13; 59:1, 2. Of prophets martyred by Jezebel, 1 Kgs 18:4. Of Gideon, Judg 6:28–32. Of Elijah, 1 Kgs 18:10; 19; 2 Kgs 1:9; 2:23. Of Micaiah, 1 Kgs 22:26; 2 Chron 18:26. Of Elisha, 2 Kgs 6:31. Of Hanani, 2 Chron 16:10. Of Zechariah, 2 Chron 24:21; Mt 23:35. Of Job, Job 13:4–13; 16:1–4; 17:2; 19: 1–5; 30:1–10. Of Jeremiah, Jer 15:10, 15; 17:15–18; 18: 18–23; 26; 32:2; 33:1; 36:26; 37; 38:1–6. Of Uriah, Jer 26:23. Of prophets, Mt 21:35, 36. Of the three Hebrew captives in Babylon, Dan 3:8–23. Of Daniel, Dan 6. Of the Jews, Ezra 4; Neh 4. Of John the Baptist, Mt 14:3–12. Of James, Acts 12:2. Of Simon, Mk 15:21. Of the disciples, Jn 9:22, 23, 34; 20:19. Of Lazarus, Jn 12:10. Of the apostles, Acts 4:3–18; 5: 18–42; 12:1–19; Rev 1:9. Of Stephen, Acts 6:9–15; 7. Of the church, Acts 8:1; 9:1–14; Gal 1:13. Of Timothy, Heb 13:23. Of John, Rev 1:9. Of Antipas, Rev 2:13. Of the church of Smyrna, Rev 2:8–10. See *Paul.*

PERSEVERANCE 1 Chron 16:11. Seek the Lord; yes, seek his strength and seek his face untiringly.

Job 17:9. The righteous shall move onward and forward; those with pure hearts shall become stronger and stronger.

Ps 37:24. If they fall it isn't fatal, for the Lord holds them with his hand. [28]For the Lord loves justice and fairness; he will never abandon his people. They will be kept safe forever; but all who love wickedness shall perish.

Ps 73:24. You will keep on guiding me all my life with your wisdom and counsel; and afterwards receive me into the glories of heaven.

Prov 4:18. But the good man walks along in the ever-brightening light of God's favor; the dawn gives way to morning splendor.

Jer 32:40. And I will make an everlasting covenant with them, promising never again to desert them, but only to do them good. I will put a desire into their hearts to worship me, and they shall never leave me.

Hos 12:6. Oh, come back to God. Live by the principles of love and justice, and always be expecting much from him, your God.

Mt 24:13. But those enduring to the end shall be saved. Mt 10:22; Mk 13:13.

Mk 4:3. Listen! A farmer decided to sow some grain. As he scattered it across the field, [4]some of it fell on a path, and the birds came and picked it off the hard ground and ate it. [5, 6]Some fell on thin soil with underlying rock. It grew up quickly enough, but soon wilted beneath the hot sun and died because the roots had no nourishment in the shallow soil. [7]Other seeds fell among thorns that shot up and crowded the young plants so that they produced no grain. [8]But some of the seeds fell into good soil and yielded thirty times as much as he had planted—some of it even sixty or a hundred times as much!

Lk 10:42. There is really only one thing worth being concerned about. Mary has discovered it—and I won't take it away from her!

Lk 22:31. Simon, Simon, Satan has asked to have you, to sift you like wheat, [32]but I have pleaded in prayer for you that your faith should not completely fail.

Jn 6:37. But some will come to me—those the Father has given me—and I will never, never reject them. [39]And this is the will of God, that I should not lose even one of those he has given me, but that I should raise them to eternal life at the Last Day. [40]For it is my Father's will that everyone who sees his Son and believes on him should have eternal life—that I should raise him at the Last Day.

Jn 8:31. Jesus said to them, "You are truly my disciples if you live as I tell you to, [32]and you will know the truth, and the truth will set you free."

Jn 10:28. I give them eternal life and they shall never perish. No one shall snatch them away from me, [29]for my Father has given them to me, and he is more powerful than anyone else, so no one can kidnap them from me.

Jn 15:4. Take care to live in me, and let me live in you. For a branch can't produce fruit when severed from the vine. Nor can you be fruitful apart from me. [5]Yes, I am the Vine; you are the branches. Whoever lives in me and I in him shall produce a large crop of fruit. For apart from me you can't do a thing. [7]But if you stay in me and obey my commands, you may ask any request you like, and it will be granted! [9]I have loved you even as the Father has loved me. Live within my love.

Acts 11:23. When he arrived and saw the wonderful things God was doing, he was filled with excitement and joy, and encouraged the believers to stay close to the Lord, whatever the cost.

Acts 13:43. And many Jews and godly Gentiles who worshiped at the synagogue followed Paul and Barnabas down the street as the two men urged them to accept the mercies God was offering.

Acts 14:21. After preaching this Good News there and making disciples, they returned again to Lystra, Iconium, and Antioch, [22]where they helped the believers to grow in love for God and each other. They encouraged them to continue in the faith in spite of all the persecution, reminding them that they must enter into the Kingdom of God through many tribulations.

Rom 2:6. He will give each one whatever his deeds deserve. [7]He will give eternal life to those who patiently do the will of God, seeking for the unseen glory and honor and eternal life that he offers.

Rom 8:30. And having chosen us, he called us to come to him; and when we came, he declared us "not guilty," filled us with Christ's goodness, gave us right standing with himself, and promised us his glory. [33]Who dares accuse us whom God has chosen for his own? Will God? No! He is the one who has forgiven us and given us right standing with himself. [34]Who then will condemn us? Will Christ? *No!* For he is the one who died for us and came back to life again for us and is sitting at the place of highest honor next to God, pleading for us there in heaven. [35]Who then can ever keep Christ's love from us? When we have trouble or calamity, when we are hunted down or destroyed, is it because he doesn't love us anymore? And if we are hungry, or penniless, or in danger, or threatened with death, has God deserted us? [37]But despite all this, overwhelming victory is ours through Christ who loved us enough to die for us. [38]For I am convinced that nothing can ever separate us from his love. Death can't, and life can't. The angels won't, and all the powers of hell itself cannot keep God's love away. Our fears for today, our worries about tomorrow, [39]or where we are—high above the sky, or in the deepest ocean—nothing will ever be able to separate us from the love of God demonstrated by our Lord Jesus Christ when he died for us.

Rom 11:29. For God's gifts and his call can never be withdrawn; he will never go back on his promises.

1 Cor 1:8. And he guarantees right up to the end that you will be counted free from all sin and guilt on that day when he returns. [9]God will surely do this for you, for he always does just what he says, and he is the one who invited you into this wonderful friendship with his Son, even Christ our Lord.

1 Cor 15:1. Now let me remind you, brothers, of what the Gospel really is, for it has not changed—it is the same Good News I preached to you before. You welcomed it then and still do now, for your faith is squarely built upon this wonderful message; [2]and it is this Good News that saves you if you still firmly believe it, unless of course you never really believed it in the first place. [58]So, my dear brothers, since future victory is sure, be strong and steady, always abounding in the Lord's work, for you know that nothing you do for the Lord is ever wasted as it would be if there were no resurrection.

1 Cor 16:13. Keep your eyes open for spiritual danger; stand true to the Lord; act like men; be strong.

2 Cor 1:21. It is this God who has made you and me into faithful Christians and commissioned us apostles to preach the Good News. [22]He has put his brand upon us—his mark of ownership—and given us his Holy Spirit in our hearts as guarantee that we belong to him, and as the first installment of all that he is going to give us.

2 Cor 5:9. So our aim is to please him always in everything we do, whether we are here in this body or away from this body and with him in heaven. [15]He died for all so that all who live—having received eternal life from him—might live no longer for themselves, to please themselves, but to spend their lives pleasing Christ who died and rose again for them.

Gal 5:1. So Christ has made us free. Now make sure that you stay free and don't get all tied up again in the chains of slavery to Jewish laws and ceremonies. [10]I am trusting the Lord to bring you back to believing as I do about these things. God will deal with that person, whoever he is, who has been troubling and confusing you.

Gal 6:9. And let us not get tired of doing what is right, for after a while we will reap a harvest of blessing if we don't get discouraged and give up.

Eph 4:14. Then we will no longer be like children, forever changing our minds about what we believe because someone has told us something different, or has cleverly lied to us and made the lie sound like the truth.

Eph 6:13. So use every piece of God's armor to resist the enemy whenever he attacks, and when it is all over, you will still be standing up. [18]Pray all the time. Ask God for anything in line with the Holy Spirit's wishes. Plead with him, reminding him of your needs, and keep praying earnestly for all Christians everywhere.

Phil 1:6. And I am sure that God who began the good work within you will keep right on helping you grow in his grace until his task within you is finally finished on that day when Jesus Christ returns. [27]But whatever happens to me, remember always to live as Christians should, so that, whether I ever see you again or not, I will keep on hearing good reports that you are standing side by side with one strong purpose—to tell the Good News.

Phil 3:16. Fully obey the truth you have.

Phil 4:1. Dear brother Christians, I love you and long to see you, for you are my joy and my reward for my work. My beloved friends, stay true to the Lord.

Col 1:10. And asking that the way you live will always please the Lord and honor him, so that you will always be doing good, kind things for others, while all the time you are learning to know God better and better. [22]He has done this through the death on the cross of his own human body, and now as a result Christ has brought you into the very presence of God, and you are standing there before him with nothing left against you—nothing left that he could even chide you for; [23]the only condition is that you fully believe the Truth, standing in it steadfast and firm, strong in the Lord, convinced of the Good News that Jesus died for you, and never shifting from trusting him to save you.

Col 2:7. Let your roots grow down into him and draw up nourishment from him. See that you go on growing in the Lord, and become strong and vigorous in the truth you were taught.

1 Thess 3:8. We can bear anything as long as we know that you remain strong in him. [13]This will result in your hearts being made strong, sinless and holy by God our Father.

1 Thess 5:21. But test everything that is said to be sure it is true, and if it is, then accept it.

2 Thess 2:15. With all these things in mind, dear brothers, stand firm and keep a strong grip on the truth that we taught you in our letters and during the time we were with you. [16]May our Lord Jesus Christ himself . . . [17]comfort your hearts with all comfort, and help you in every good thing you say and do.

2 Thess 3:13. And to the rest of you I say, dear brothers, never be tired of doing right.

2 Tim 1:12. That is why I am suffering here in jail and I am certainly not ashamed of it, for I know the one in whom I trust, and I am sure that he is able to safely guard all that I have given him until the day of his return. [13]Hold tightly to the pattern of truth I taught you, especially concerning the faith and love Christ Jesus offers you.

2 Tim 2:1. On, Timothy, my son, be strong with the strength Christ Jesus gives you. [3]Take your share of suffering as a good soldier of Jesus Christ, just as I do. [12]And if we think that our present service for him is hard, just remember that some day we are going to sit with him and rule with him. But if we give up when we suffer, and turn against Christ, then he must turn against us.

2 Tim 3:14. But you must keep on believing the things you have been taught. You know they are true for you know that you can trust those of us who have taught you.

2 Tim 4:18. Yes, and the Lord will always deliver me from all evil and will bring me into his heavenly kingdom.

Tit 1:9. Their belief in the truth which they have been taught must be strong and steadfast, so that they will be able to teach it to others and show those who disagree with them where they are wrong.

Heb 2:1. So we must listen very carefully to the truths we have heard, or we may drift away from them.

Heb 3:5. Well, Moses did a fine job working in God's house, but he was only a servant; and his work was mostly to illustrate and suggest those things that would happen later on. [6]But Christ, God's faithful Son, is in complete charge of God's house. And we Christians are God's house—he lives in us!—if we keep up our courage firm to the end, and our joy and our trust in the Lord. [14]For if we are faithful to the end, trusting God just as we did when we first became Christians, we will share in all that belongs to Christ.

Heb 4:14. But Jesus the Son of God is our great High Priest who has gone to heaven itself to help us; therefore let us never stop trusting him.

Heb 6:1. Let us stop going over the same old ground again and again, always teaching those first lessons about Christ. Let us go on instead to other things and become mature in our understanding, as strong Christians ought to be. [11]And we are anxious that you keep right on loving others as long as life lasts, so that you will get your full reward. [12]Then, knowing what lies ahead for you, you won't become bored with being a Christian, nor become spiritually dull and indifferent, but you will be anxious to follow the example of those who receive all that God has promised them because of their strong faith and patience. [15]Then Abraham waited patiently until finally God gave him a son, Isaac, just as he had promised. [17]God also bound himself with an oath, so that those he promised to help would be perfectly sure and never need to wonder whether he might change his plans. [18]He has given us both his promise and his oath, two things we can completely count on, for it is impossible for God to tell a lie. Now all those who flee to him to save them can take new courage when they hear such assurances from God; now they can know without doubt that he will give them the salvation he has promised them.

Heb 10:23. Now we can look forward to the salvation God has promised us. There is no longer any room for doubt, and we can tell others that salvation is ours, for there is no question that he will do what he says. [35]Do not let this happy trust in the Lord die away, no matter what happens. Remember your reward! [36]You need to keep on patiently doing God's will if you want him to do for you all that he has promised.

Heb 12:1. Since we have such a huge crowd of men of faith watching us from the grandstands, let us strip off anything that slows us down or holds us back, and especially those sins that wrap themselves so tightly around our feet and trip us up; and let us run with patience the particular race that God has set before us. [2]Keep your eyes on Jesus, our leader and instructor. He was willing to die a shameful death on the cross because of the joy he knew would be his afterwards; and now he sits in the place of honor by the throne of God. [3]If you want to keep from becoming fainthearted and weary, think about his patience as sinful men did such terrible things to him. [4]After all, you have never yet struggled against sin and temptation until you sweat great drops of blood. [5]And have you quite forgotten the encouraging words God spoke to you, his child? He said, "My son, don't be angry when the Lord punishes you. Don't be discouraged when he has to show you where you are wrong. [6]For when he punishes you, it proves that he loves you. When he whips you it proves you are really his child." [7]Let God train you, for he is doing what any loving father does for his children. Whoever heard of a son who was never corrected? [8]If God doesn't punish you when you need it, as other fathers punish their sons, then it means that you aren't really God's son at all—that you don't really belong in his family. [9]Since we respect our fathers here on earth, though they punish us, should we not all the more cheerfully submit to God's training so that we can begin really to live? [10]Our earthly fathers trained us for a few brief years, doing the best for us that they knew how, but God's correction is always right and for our best good, that we may share his holiness. [11]Being punished isn't enjoyable while it is happening—it hurts! But afterwards we can see the result, a quiet growth in grace and character. [12]So take a new grip with tired hands, stand firm on your shaky legs, [13]and mark out a straight, smooth path for your feet so that those who follow you, though weak and lame, will not fall and hurt themselves, but become strong. [15]Look after each other so that not one of you will fail to find God's best blessings. Watch out that no bitterness takes root among you, for as it springs up it causes deep trouble, hurting many in their spiritual lives.

Heb 13:9. So do not be attracted by strange, new ideas. Your spiritual strength comes as a gift from God. [13]So let us go out to him beyond the city walls (that is, outside the interests of this world, being willing to be despised) to suffer with him there, bearing his shame.

Jas 1:4. So let it grow, and don't try to squirm out of your problems. For when your patience is finally in full bloom, then you will be ready for anything, strong in character, full and complete. [12]Happy is the man who doesn't give in and do wrong when he is tempted, for afterwards he will get as his reward the crown of life that God has promised those who love him. [25]But if anyone keeps looking steadily into God's law for free men, he will not only remember it but he will do what it says, and God will greatly bless him in everything he does.

Jas 5:10. For examples of patience in suffering, look at the Lord's prophets. [11]We know how happy they are now because they suffered greatly for it. Job is an example of a man who continued to trust the Lord in sorrow; from his experiences we can see how the Lord's plan finally ended in good, for he is full of tenderness and mercy.

1 Pet 1:4. And God has reserved for his children the priceless gift of eternal life; it is kept in heaven for you, pure and undefiled, beyond the reach of change and decay. [5]And God, in his mighty power, will make sure that you get there safely to receive it, because you are trusting him. It will be yours in that coming last day for all to see. [6]So be truly glad! There is wonderful joy ahead, even though the going is rough for a while down here. [7]These trials are only to test your faith, to see whether or not it is strong and pure. It is being tested as fire tests gold and purifies it—and your faith is far more precious to God than mere gold; so if your faith remains strong after being tried in the test tube of fiery trials, it will bring you much praise and glory and honor on the day of his return.

1 Pet 5:8. Be careful—watch out for attacks from Satan, your great enemy. He prowls around like a hungry, roaring lion, looking for some victim to tear apart.

2 Pet 1:10. So, dear brothers, work hard to prove that you really are among those God has called and chosen, and then you will never stumble or fall away. [11]And God will open wide the gates of heaven for you to enter into the eternal kingdom of our Lord and Savior Jesus Christ.

2 Pet 3:17. I am warning you ahead of time, dear brothers, so that you can watch out and not be carried away by the mistakes of these wicked men, lest you yourselves become mixed up too. [18]But grow in spiritual strength and become better acquainted with our Lord and Savior Jesus Christ.

1 Jn 2:19. These "against-Christ" people used to be members of our churches, but they never really belonged with us or else they would have stayed. When they left us it proved that they were not of us at all. [27]But you have received the Holy Spirit and he lives within you, in your hearts, so that you don't need anyone to teach what is right. For he teaches you all things, and he is the Truth, and no liar; and so, just as he has said, you must live in Christ, never to depart from him.

Rev 2:7. Let this message sink into the ears of anyone who listens to what the Spirit is saying to the churches: To everyone who is victorious, I will give fruit from the Tree of Life in the Paradise of God. [10]Stop being afraid of what you are about to suffer—for the devil will soon throw some of you into prison to test you. You will be persecuted for "ten days." Remain faithful even when facing death and I will give you the crown of life—an unending, glorious future. [11]Let everyone who can hear, listen to what the Spirit is saying to the churches: He who is victorious shall not be hurt by the Second Death. [17]Let everyone who can hear, listen to what the Spirit is saying to the churches: Everyone who is victorious shall eat of the hidden manna, the secret nourishment from heaven; and I will give to each a white stone, and on the stone will be engraved a new name that no one else knows except the one receiving it. [25]Hold tightly to what you have until I come. [26]To everyone who overcomes—who to the very end keeps on doing things that please me—I will give power over the nations. [27]You will rule them with a rod of iron just as my Father gave me the authority to rule them; they will be shattered like a pot of clay that is broken into tiny pieces. [28]And I will give you the Morning Star!

Rev 3:5. Everyone who conquers will be clothed in white, and I will not erase his name from the Book of Life, but I will announce before my Father and his angels that he is mine. [11]Look, I am coming soon! Hold tightly to the little strength you have—so that no one will take away your crown. [12]As for the one who conquers, I will make him a pillar in the temple of my God; he will be secure, and will go out no more; and I will write my God's Name on him, and he will be citizen in the city of my God—the New Jerusalem, coming down from heaven from my God; and he will have my new Name inscribed upon him. [21]I will let every one who conquers sit beside me on my throne, just as I took my place with my Father on his throne when I had conquered.

Rev 13:10. The people of God who are destined for prison will be arrested and taken away; those destined for death will be killed. But do not be dismayed, for here is your opportunity for endurance and confidence.

Rev 14:12. Let this encourage God's people to endure patiently every trial and persecution, for they are his saints who remain firm to the end in obedience to his commands and trust in Jesus.

Rev 16:15. Take note: I will come as unexpectedly as a thief! Blessed are all who are awaiting me, who keep their robes in readiness and will not need to walk naked and ashamed.

Rev 21:7. Everyone who conquers will inherit all these blessings, and I will be his God and he will be my son. [8]But cowards who turn back from following me, and those who are unfaithful to me, and the corrupt, and murderers, and the immoral, and those conversing with demons, and idol worshipers and all liars—their doom is in the Lake that burns with fire and sulphur. This is the Second Death.

Rev 22:11. And when that time comes, all doing wrong will do it more and more; the vile will become more vile; good men will be better; those who are holy will continue on in greater holiness.

See *Character; Instability; Stability.*

INSTANCES OF. Jacob, in prayer, Gen 32:22–26. Caleb and Joshua, in depicting the land of promise, Num 14:24, 36–38.

PERSEVERANCE OF THE SAINTS A theological expression referring to the safety and security of the believer resulting from his faith in Christ, according to the Calvinistic view.

See *Security of the Believer.*

PERSIA An empire which extended from India to Ethiopia, comprising 127 provinces, Esther 1:1–3; Dan 6:1. Government of, restricted by constitutional limitations, Esther 8:8; Dan 6:8–12. Municipal governments in, provided with dual administrators, Neh 3:9, 12, 16–18. The governing officials advisory in matters of administration, Dan 6:1–7. Status of woman in, queen sat on a throne beside the king, Neh 2:6. Vashti divorced for refusing to appear before the king's courtiers, Esther 1:10–22; 2:4.

Israel captive in, 2 Chron 36:20; captivity foretold, Hos 13:16. Men of, in the Tyrian army, Ezk 27:10.

Rulers of: Ahasuerus, Esther 1:3. Darius, Dan 5:31; 6; 9:1. Artaxerxes I, Ezra 4:7–24. Artaxerxes II, Ezra 7; Neh 1:1; 2; 5:14. Cyrus, 2 Chron 36:22, 23; Ezra 1; 3:7; 4:3; 5:13, 14, 17; 6:3; Isa 41:2, 3; 44:28; 45:1–4, 13; 46:11; 48:14, 15. Officials of, Esther 1:13–15.

Systems of justice, Ezra 7:25. Prophecies concerning, Isa 13:17; 21:1–10; Jer 49:34–39; 51:11–64; Ezk 32:24, 25; 38:5; Dan 2:31–45; 5:28; 7; 8; 11:1–4.

See *Babylon; Chaldea.*

PERSIS A Christian woman in Rome, Rom 16:12.

PERSONAL CALL See *Call, Personal; Minister, Call of.*

PERSONIFICATION Of wisdom, Prov 1; 2:1–9; 8; 9. Many students see Christ and his bride, the true church, personified in the Song of Solomon.

See *Pantomime.*

PERUDA One of Solomon's officials. Descendants of, return to Jerusalem from captivity in Babylon, Ezra 2:55–57. Called *Perida* in Neh 7:57–59.

PESTILENCE Hab 3:5. Sent as a judgment on Israel, Lev 26:16, 25; Deut 28:21; 2 Chron 7:13; Jer 14:12; 21:6; 24:10. In prophecy, Ezk 38:22; Mt 24:7; Lk 21:11; Rev 6:7, 8. Sent on Egypt, see *Egypt; Plague.*

PETER Called also *Simon, son of Jonah,* Mt 16:16–19; Mk 3:16–19; Jn 1:42. A fisherman, Mt 4:18; Lk 5:1–7; Jn 21:3. Call of, Mt 4:18–20; Mk 1:16–18; Lk 5:1–11. His wife's mother healed, Mt 8:14; Mk 1:29, 30; Lk 4:38, 39. An apostle, Mt 10:2–4; 16:18, 19; Mk 3:16–19; Lk 6:14–16; Acts 1:13, 14. An evangelist, Mk 1:36, 37. Confesses Jesus as Christ, Mt 16:16–19; Mk 8:29; Lk 9:20; Jn 6:68, 69. His presumption in chiding Jesus, Mt 16:22, 23; Mk 8:32, 33; when the crowd was pressing Jesus and the woman with the hemorrhage touched him, Lk 8:45; in refusing to let Jesus wash his feet, Jn 13:6–11. Present at the healing of Jairus's daughter, Mk 5:37; Lk 8:51; at the transfiguration, Mt 17:1–4; Mk 9:2–6; Lk 9:28–33; 2 Pet 1:16–18; in Gethsemane, Mt 26:36–46; Mk 14:33–52; Lk 22:40–46. Seeks to understand the parable of the steward, Lk 12:41; the law of forgiveness, Mt 18:21; the law of defilement, Mt 15:15; the prophecy of Jesus concerning his second coming, Mk 13:3, 4. Walks on the water of the sea of Galilee, Mt 14:28–31. Sent with John to prepare the Passover, Lk 22:8. Calls attention to the withered fig tree, Mk 11:21. His denial foretold by Jesus, and his profession of fidelity, Mt 26:33–35; Mk 14:29–31; Lk 22:31–34; Jn 13:36–38. Cuts off the ear of Malchus, Mt 26:51; Mk 14:47; Lk 22:50. Follows Jesus to the high priest's residence, Mt 26:58; Mk 14:54; Lk 22:54; Jn 18:15. His denial of Jesus, and his repentance, Mt 26:69–75; Mk 14:66–72; Lk 22:55–62; Jn 18:17, 18, 25–27. Visits the tomb, Lk 24:12; Jn 20:2–6. Jesus sends message to, after the resurrection, Mk 16:7. Jesus appears to, Lk 24:33, 34; 1 Cor 15:4, 5. Present at the Sea of Galilee when Jesus appeared to his disciples; leaps into the water, and swims to shore when he recognizes Jesus, is commissioned to feed the flock of Christ, Jn 21:1–23. Lives in Jerusalem, Acts 1:14. His statement before the disciples concerning the death of Judas, and his recommendation that the vacancy among the disciples be filled, Acts 1:15–22. Preaches at Pentecost, Acts 2:14–40. Heals the lame man at the temple gate, Acts 3. Accused by the council; his defense, Acts 4:1–23. Foretells the death of Ananias and Sapphira, Acts 5:1–11. Imprisoned and beaten; his defense before the council, Acts 5:17–42. Goes to Samaria, Acts 8:14. Prays for the baptism of the Holy Spirit, Acts 8:15–18. Rebukes Simon, the sorcerer, who desires to purchase similar power, Acts 8:18–24. Returns to Jerusalem, Acts 8:25. Receives Paul, Gal 1:18; 2:7–9. Visits Lydda; heals Aeneas, Acts 9:32–34. Visits Joppa; lives with Simon, the tanner; raises Dorcas from the dead, Acts 9:36–43. Has a vision of a sheet containing forbidden food, Acts 10:9–16. Receives the servants of Cornelius; goes to Caesarea; preaches and baptizes Cornelius and his household, Acts 10. Advocates, in the council of the apostles and elders, the preaching of the gospel to the Gentiles, Acts 11:1–18; 15:7–11. Imprisoned; then rescued by an angel, Acts 12:3–19. Writes two epistles, 1 Pet 1:1; 2 Pet 1:1. Miracles of, see *Miracles.*

PETHAHIAH 1. A priest in the reign of David, 1 Chron 24:7–18.

2. A Levite who divorced his Gentile wife, Ezra 10:23. Probably identical with the one mentioned, Neh 9:5.

3. A counselor of Ar-ta-xerxes, Neh 11:24.

PETHOR A city in Mesopotamia. Home of the prophet Balaam, Num 22:5, 6; Deut 23:4.

PETHUEL Father of the prophet Joel, Joel 1:1.

PETITION Right of, recognized by Pharaoh, Ex 5:15–18; Israel, Num 27:1–5; 32:1–5; 36:1–5; Josh 17:4, 14, 16–18; 21:1, 2; David, 1 Kgs 1:15–21; Rehoboam, 1 Kgs 12:1–17; 2 Chron 10; Jehoram, 2 Kgs 8:3, 6; Ahasuerus, Esther 7:2.

A word used for prayer: Hannah, 1 Sam 1:17, 19, 20; Daniel, Dan 6:12; See also Hos 14:2; Jn 16:26.

PE-ULLETHAI A Temple guard, 1 Chron 26:4, 5.

PHARAOH A title used for the kings of Egypt, used alone or with an identifying second name. 1. Ruler of Egypt at the time of Abraham, Gen 12:14–20; Ps 105:14.

2. Ruler of Egypt at the time of the famine. See *Egypt; Israel; Joseph, 1.*

3. Ruler of Egypt at the time of the deliverance and exodus of the Israelites. See *Israel.*

4. Father-in-law of Mered, 1 Chron 4:17.

5. Ruler of Egypt at the time of David, 1 Kgs 11:16–22.

6. Father-in-law of Solomon, 1 Kgs 3:1; 9:16. Possibly the same as 5, above.

7. Ruler of Egypt at the time of Hezekiah, 2 Kgs 18:20, 21.

8. Pharaoh-neco. His invasion of Assyria, Josiah's death, 2 Kgs 23:29–35; 24:7; 2 Chron 35:20–23; 36:3, 4; Jer 46:2; 47:1.

9. Pharaoh-hophra, Jer 37:4–7; 44; Ezk 17:15–17. Prophecies, Jer 44:30; 46:25, 26; Ezk 29; 30:21–26.

PHARISEES A sect of the Jews, Acts 15:5. Doctrines of, Mt 15:9; concerning the resurrection, Acts 23:6, 8; association with tax collectors and sinners, Mt 9:11–13.

Traditions of, in regard to fasting, Mt 9:14; Lk 18:12; the washing of hands, Mt 15:1–3; Mk 7:1–15; the duties of children to parents, Mt 15:4–9; the Sabbath, Mt 12:2–8. Hypocrisy of, reproved by John, Mt 3:7–10; by Jesus, Mt 6:2–8, 16–18; 15:1–9; 16:1–12; 21:33–46; 23:2–33; Lk 11:14–54; 12:1; 15:1–9. Reject John, Lk 7:30; Christ, Mt 12:38–40; 15:12; Jn 7:48. Come to Jesus with questions, Mt 19:3; 22:15–22.

Minister to Jesus, Lk 7:36; 11:37, 38; 14:1. Become disciples of Jesus, Jn 3:1, 2; Acts 15:5; 22:3.

Paul, a Pharisee, Acts 23:6; 26:5.

See *Herodians; Sadducees.*

PHARPAR A river of Damascus. Referred to by Naaman, 2 Kgs 5:12.

PHICHOL Commander of the Philistine army, Gen 21:22, 32; 26:26.

PHILADELPHIA A city of Lydia. One of the "seven churches" at, Rev 1:11; 3:7–13.

PHILANTHROPHY Isa 58:6–12.

See *Benevolence; Charitableness; Charity; Liberality; Neighbor; Poor.*

PHILEMON A Christian in Colose. Paul's letter to, Philemon 1:1–25.

PHILETUS An heretical teacher at Rome, 2 Tim 2:17, 18.

PHILIP 1. Son of Herod the Great and Mariamne, and first husband of Herodias, Mt 14:3; Mk 6:17, 18; Lk 3:19, 20.

2. Son of Herod the Great and Cleopatra of Jerusalem. Granted tetrarchy of Iturea, Lk 3:1, 2. Rebuilder of Caesarea Philippi, Mt 16:13; Mk 8:27.

3. One of the seven deacons, Acts 6:5. Successfully preaches in Samaria, Acts 8:4–14. Expounds the scriptures to the Ethiopian eunuch whom he baptizes, Acts 8:27–38. Caught away by the Spirit to Azotus, preaches in the cities, and goes to Caesarea, and entertains Paul, Acts 21:8. Has four daughters, prophetesses, Acts 21:9.

4. One of the 12 disciples, Mt 10:2–4; Mk 3:16–19; Lk 6:14–16; Acts 1:14. Call of, Jn 1:43. Brings Nathanael to Jesus, Jn 1:45–50. Assists in caring for the crowd whom Jesus miraculously feeds, Jn 6:2–7. Brings certain Greeks to Jesus who desire to see him, Jn 12:20–22. Asks Jesus to show the Father, Jn 14:8–13.

PHILIPPI A city of Macedonia. Paul preaches in, Acts 16:12–40; 20:1–6; 1 Thess 2:1, 2. Contributes to Paul's support, Phil 4:10–18. Paul sends Epaphroditus to, Phil 2:25. Paul writes a letter to the Christians of, Phil 1:1.

PHILISTIA The sea coast west of Dan and Simeon, Judg 10:6; Ps 83:7; 87:4; Joel 3:4.

PHILISTINES Descendants of Mizraim, Gen 10:13, 14; 1 Chron 1:11, 12; Jer 47:4; Amos 9:7. Called *Cherethites,* 1 Sam 30:14–16; Ezk 25:16; Zeph 2:5; *Casluhim,* Gen 10:14; 1 Chron 1:11, 12. Territory of, Ex 13:17, 18; 23:31; Deut 2:23; Josh 13:2–7; 15:47; leaders of, Judg 16:5; 1 Sam 5:8, 11; 6:12; 7:7; 29:2, 6, 7.

Kings of: Abimelech I, Gen 20; Abimelech II, Gen 26; Achish, 1 Sam 21:10–15; 27:2–12; 28:1, 2; 29. Allowed to remain in Canaan, Judg 3:3, 4. Shamgar kills 600 with an ox goad, Judg 3:31. For their history during the leadership of Samson, see Judg chapters 13–16. Defeat the Israelites; take the ark; suffer plagues, and return the ark, 1 Sam chapters 4–6. Army of, 1 Sam 13:5. Defeated by Samuel, 1 Sam 7; by Saul and Jonathan, 1 Sam 9:16; 13; 14. Their champion, Goliath, killed by David, 1 Sam 17. David kills 200, 1 Sam 18:22–30. David finds refuge among, 1 Sam 27. Defeat the Israelites and kill Saul and his sons, 1 Sam 31; 1 Chron 10:1. Defeated by David, 2 Sam 5:17–25; 23:9–16; 1 Chron 14:8–16. Pay tribute to Jehoshaphat, 2 Chron 17:11. Defeated by Hezekiah, 2 Kgs 18:8. Prophecies against, Isa 9:11, 12; 14:29–31; Jer 25:17–20; 47; Ezk 25:15–17; Amos 1:6–8; Zeph 2:4–7; Zech 9:5–7.

PHILOLOGUS A disciple in Rome, Rom 16:15.

PHILOSOPHY The love of wisdom, the search for meaning in life, Eccl chapters 1–7. A philosophical discourse on wisdom, Job 28. Philosophical inductions and deductions relating to God and his providence, Job 5:8–20; 9; 10:2–21; 12:6–25; 33:12–30; 37. Reveals the mysteries of providence, Prov 25:2, 3; Rom 1:19, 20. Is not sufficient for an adequate knowledge of God, 1 Cor 1:21, 22; or of salvation through the atonement of Jesus Christ, 1 Cor 2:6–10. Use of, was not Paul's method of preaching the gospel, 1 Cor 1:17, 19, 21; 2:1–5, 13. Greek schools of, Acts 17:18. Rabbinical, Col 2:8, 16–19; 1 Tim 6:20.

See *Reasoning; also God, Unclassified Scriptures Relating to.*

PHINEHAS 1. High priest, Ex 6:25; 1 Chron 6:4–15, 50–53. Religious zeal of, Num 25: 7–15; Ps 106:30. Chief of the Korahite Levites, 1 Chron 9:19, 20. Sent to sound the trumpets in the battle with the Midianites, Num 31:6. A commissioner to the Israelites east of the Jordan, Josh 22: 13–32. Inheritance allotted to, Josh 24:33. Mediator in behalf of the people, Judg 20:28.

2. Son of Eli, 1 Sam 1:3. Wickedness of, 1 Sam 2: 12–17, 22–25, 34. Killed in battle, 1 Sam 4:4–11, 17, 19. Sons of, 1 Sam 14:3.

3. A priest, Ezra 8:33.

PHLEGON A disciple in Rome, Rom 16:14.

PHOEBE A deacon of the church at Cenchreae, Rom 16:1, 2.

PHOENICIA Judg 18:7. Inhabitants of, descended from Canaan, Gen 10:15–19. Called *Sidonians,* Ezk 32:30. Jews from, hear Jesus, Mk 3:7, 8. Paul visits the churches in, Acts 15:3; 21:2–4; 27:3.

PHOENIX A harbor of Crete, Acts 27:12.

PHRYGIA An inland province of Asia Minor. People from, in Jerusalem, Acts 2:10. Paul in, Acts 16:6; 18:23.

PHYGELLUS A Christian in Asia. Turns from Paul, 2 Tim 1:15.

PHYLACTERY A small box containing slips of parchment on which were written portions of the law, Deut 6:4–9; 11:18. Worn ostentatiously by the Jews, on the head and left arm, Mt 23:5.

PHYSICIAN 2 Chron 16:12; Mt 9:12; Mk 5: 25; Lk 8:43, 44. Proverbs about, Mk 2:17; Lk 4:23. Luke a physician, Col 4:14.

FIGURATIVE. Job 13:4; Jer 8:22; Lk 5:31.

PHYSIOGNOMY Character revealed in, Isa 3:9.

See *Face.*

PHYSIOLOGY Job 10:11; Ps 139:14–16.

See *Anatomy; Hygiene.*

FIGURATIVE. Eph 4:15, 16; Col 2:19.

PICTURE Isa 49:16; Ezk 4:1; 8:10, 11; 23:14–16; Mt 22:20; Mk 12:16.

PIECE OF SILVER See *Silver.*

PIETY See *Religion.*

PIG See *Swine.*

PIGEON Used as sacrifice, Gen 15:9; Lev 1:14; 5:7; 12:8; 14:22; Num 6:10; Lk 2:24.

See *Dove.*

PIHAHIROTH The place on the western shore of the Red Sea where Pharaoh overtook the Israelites, Ex 14:2, 3, 9; Num 33:7, 8.

PILATE, PONTIUS Roman governor of Judea, Mt 27:2; Lk 3:1, 2. Causes slaughter of certain Galileans, Lk 13:1. Tries Jesus and orders his crucifixion, Mt 27; Mk 15; Lk 23; Jn 18:28–40; 19; Acts 3:13; 4:27; 13:28; 1 Tim 6:13. Allows Joseph of Arimathea to take Jesus' body, Mt 27:57, 58; Mk 15:42–45; Lk 23:50–52; Jn 19:38.

PILDASH Son of Nahor, Gen 22:20–23.

PILHA One of those who signed the covenant with Nehemiah, Neh 10:14–27.

PILLAR Of Solomon's temple, 1 Kgs 7:13–22; 2 Kgs 25:17. Broken and taken to Babylon, 2 Kgs 25:13; Jer 52:17, 20, 21. Of Solomon's palaces, 1 Kgs 7:6.

Pillar of salt, Lot's wife turned to, Gen 19:26; Lk 17:32. Monuments erected to commemorate events: By Jacob, his vision of angels, Gen 28:18, with 31: 13; 35:13, 14; his covenant with Laban, Gen 31:45; by Moses, the covenant between Jehovah and Israel, Ex 24:4; by Joshua, the passing over Jordan, Josh 4:1–9, with Deut 27:2–6; Josh 8:20, 21; at Shechem, Josh 24:25–27, with Judg 9:6; by Samuel, the confusion of the Philistines, 1 Sam 7:12; by Absalom, to keep his name in remembrance, 2 Sam 18:18. As a boundary, Josh 15:6, with 18:17; a marker, 2 Sam 20:8–10; 1 Kgs 1:9. Prophecy of one in Egypt, Isa 19:19. Monuments of idolatry, to be destroyed, Deut 12:3.

See *Cloud, Pillar of.*

FIGURATIVE. Rev 3:12.

PILLOW A support for the head, Ps 6:6; Amos 3:12. Stones used for, Gen 28:11, 18. Made of goats' hair, 1 Sam 19:13. Jesus sleeps on, Mk 4:38.

PILOT Ezk 27:8, 27–29; Jas 3:4.

PILTAI A priest who returned to Jerusalem from captivity in Babylon, Neh 12:12–21.

PIN See *Nail.*

PINE A tree, Isa 41:19; 60:13.

PINON A leader of Edom, Gen 36:40–43; 1 Chron 1:51–54.

PIPE A wind instrument of music, Gen 4:21.

See *Flute; Music, Instruments of.*

PIRAM A king of the Amorites. Overcome and killed by Joshua, Josh 10:3, 16–18, 24–27.

PIRATHON A place in the land of Ephraim, Judg 12:15. Men of, Judg 12:13; 2 Sam 23:24–39; 1 Chron 11:26–47; 27:14.

PISGAH A ridge or mountain east of the Jordan, opposite to Jericho. The Israelites come to, Num 21:20. A boundary of the country assigned to the Reubenites and Gadites, Deut 3:17; 4:49; Josh 12:3; 13:20. Balaam prophesies on, Num 23:14–24. Moses views Palestine from, Deut 3:27; 34:1–4.

PISHON One of the rivers of Eden, Gen 2:11, 12.

PISIDIA A province in Asia Minor. Paul visits, Acts 13:14; 14:24.

PISPA An Asherite, 1 Chron 7:38.

PIT Three categories of the word are used in the Bible to designate distinct types of places, all below the surface of the earth.

1. The region of the dead in the Old Testament, Ezk 31:14–18; 32:18–32, distinguished from the land of the living, Ezk 26:20. The place of the wicked dead, a part of Sheol (which see), Job 33:30; Ps 55:23; 69:15; Isa 14:15; Ezk 26:20; 28:8; 32:25, 29, 30; Zech 9:11.

2. The great bottomless abyss which is destined to be the eternal dwelling of Satan, Lk 8:31; Rev 9:1, 11; 17:8; 20:1, 3.

3. Any of a variety of natural or excavated holes in the earth, Judg 6:1; 2 Sam 17:9; 23:20; 1 Chron 11:22; Isa 24:18; Jer 18:22; Hos 5:2; Mk 12:1; Lk 14:5.

See *Hades; Hell; Paradise; Sheol.*

PITCH An opaque mineral used as a plaster and cement, Isa 34:9.

See *Tar.*

PITCHER Lk 22:10. Golden, Ex 25:29.

FIGURATIVE. Eccl 12:6.

See *Jar; Pottery.*

PITHOM A store city in lower Egypt, Ex 1:11.

PITHON Son of Micah, 1 Chron 8:35; 9:41.

PITY Of God, Job 33:23, 24; Isa 63:9. Of Jesus, Mk 6:34; see *Jesus, Compassion of.*

Not to be shown offenders, Deut 7:16; 13:8; 19:13, 21; 25:11, 12.

See *Mercy.*

INSTANCES OF. The master of the poor servant, Mt 18:27.

PLAGUE As a judgment on the Egyptians, Ps 78:50; 135:8, 9; Acts 7:36. The plague of blood, Ex 7:14–25; frogs, Ex 8:1–15; lice, Ex 8:16–19; flies, Ex 8:20–24. On cattle, Ex 9:1–7. Of boils, Ex 9:8–12; hail, Ex 9:18–34; locusts, Ex 10:1–20; darkness, Ex 10:21–23. Death of the firstborn, Ex 11:4–7; 12:17, 29, 30.

On the Israelites: Because of idolatry, Ex 32:35; after eating quail, Num 11:33; after refusing to enter the promised land, Num 14:36–38; after murmuring because of the destruction of Korah, Num 16:41–50; of serpents, Num 21:6; for the sin of Peor, Josh 22:17, 18; because of David's sin, 2 Sam 24:10–25.

On the Philistines, 1 Sam 6:4, 5.

Pronounced as a judgment, Lev 26:21; Deut 28:58, 59; Hab 3:5. Foretold, Rev 11:6; 15:1, 6–8; 16; 22:18, 19.

See *Judgments; Pestilence.*

PLANE TREE Gen 30:37.

PLANET See *Astronomy; Stars.*

PLAN OF SALVATION See *Jesus, Mission of; Redemption; Salvation.*

PLANTS See *Botany.*

PLASTER Lev 14:42, 43, 48; Deut 27:2–4; Dan 5:5.

PLATTER dedicated to the Temple, Num 7:13, 84–86.

PLEADING Deut 17:8. Of the guilty, Josh 7:19–21. Jesus declined to plead, Mt 26:62. Prisoners required to plead, Acts 7:1.

See *Defense.*

PLEASURE WORLDLY. Job 20:12. He enjoyed the taste of his wickedness, letting it melt in his mouth, [13]sipping it slowly, lest it disappear. [14]But suddenly the food he has eaten turns sour within him. [15]He will vomit the plunder he gorged. God won't let him keep it down. [16]It is like poison and death to him.

Job 21:12, 13. They spend their time singing and dancing. They are wealthy and need deny themselves nothing; they are prosperous to the end.

Prov 9:17. Stolen melons are the sweetest; stolen apples taste the best!

Prov 15:21. If a man enjoys folly, something is wrong! The sensible stay on the pathways of right.

Prov 21:17. A man who loves pleasure becomes poor; wine and luxury are not the way to riches!

Eccl 2:1, 2. I said to myself, "Come now, be merry; enjoy yourself to the full." But I found that this, too, was futile. For it is silly to be laughing all the time; what good does it do? [3]So, after a lot of thinking, I decided to try the road of drink, while still holding steadily to my course of seeking wisdom. Next I changed my course again and followed the path of folly, so that I could experience the only happiness most men have throughout their lives. [4, 5] [6]Then I tried to find fulfillment by inaugurating a great public works program: homes, vineyards, gardens, parks and orchards for myself, and reservoirs to hold the water to irrigate my plantations. [7, 8]Next I bought slaves, both men and women, and others were born within my household. I also bred great herds and flocks, more than any of the kings before me. I collected silver and gold as taxes from many kings and provinces. In cultural arts, I organized men's and women's choirs and orchestras. And then there were my many beautiful concubines. [9]So I became greater than any of the kings in Jerusalem before me, and with it all I remained clear-eyed, so that I could evaluate all these things. [10]Anything I wanted, I took, and did not restrain myself from any joy. I even found great pleasure in hard work. This pleasure was, indeed, my only reward for all my labors. [11]But as I looked at everything I had tried, it was all so useless, a chasing of the wind, and there was nothing really worthwhile anywhere. [12]Now I began a study of the comparative virtues of wisdom and folly, and anyone else would come to the same conclusion I did— [13]that wisdom is of more value than foolishness, just as light is better than darkness.

Isa 5:11. Woe to you who get up early in the morning to go on long drinking bouts that last till late at night—woe to you drunken bums. [12]You furnish lovely music at your grand parties; the orchestras are superb! But for the Lord you have no thought or care.

Isa 22:12. The Lord God of Hosts called you to repent, to weep and mourn and shave your heads in sorrow for your sins, and to wear clothes made of sackcloth to show your remorse. [13]But instead, you sing and dance and play, and feast and drink. "Let us eat, drink, and be merry," you say: "What's the difference, for tomorrow we die."

Isa 47:8. O pleasure-mad kingdom, living at ease, bragging as the greatest in the world—listen to the sentence of my court upon your sins. You say, "I alone am God! I'll never be a widow; I'll never lose my children." [9]Well, those two things shall come upon you in one moment, in full measure in one day: widowhood and the loss of your children, despite all your witchcraft and magic.

Amos 6:1. Woe to those lounging in luxury at Jerusalem and Samaria, so famous and popular among the people of Israel.

Lk 8:14. The seed among the thorns represents those who listen and believe God's words but whose faith afterwards is choked out by worry and riches and the responsibilities and pleasures of life. And so they are never able to help anyone else to believe the Good News.

Rom 1:32. They were fully aware of God's death penalty for these crimes, yet they went right ahead and did them anyway, and encouraged others to do them, too.

2 Thess 2:12. And all of them will be justly judged for believing falsehood, refusing the Truth, and enjoying their sins.

1 Tim 5:6. But not if they are spending their time running around gossiping, seeking only pleasure and thus ruining their souls.

2 Tim 3:4. They will betray their friends; they will be hotheaded, puffed up with pride, and prefer good times to worshiping God.

Tit 3:3. Once we, too, were foolish and disobedient; we were misled by others and became slaves to many evil pleasures and wicked desires. Our lives were full of resentment and envy. We hated others and they hated us.

Heb 11:25. But chose to share ill-treatment with God's people instead of enjoying the fleeting pleasures of sin. [26]He thought that it was better to suffer for the promised Christ than to own all the treasures of Egypt, for he was looking forward to the great reward that God would give him.

2 Pet 2:13. That is the pay these teachers will have for their sin. For they live in evil pleasures day after day. They are a disgrace and a stain among you, deceiving you by living in foul sin on the side while they join your love feasts as though they were honest men.

See *Happiness; Joy; Worldliness.*

PLEDGE Gen 38:17–20. Creditor must not enter house of a debtor to take, Ex 22:26, 27; Deut 24:10–13.

See *Pawn; Surety.*

PLEIADES A constellation, Job 9:9; 38:31.

PLOW Points of, sharpened by the Philistine blacksmiths, 1 Sam 13:20, 21. Used by Elisha with 12 teams of oxen, 1 Kgs 19:19. By Job's servants, Job 1:14, 15.

Jerusalem plowed as a field, Jer 26:18; Mic 3:12. The plowing of the wicked in sin, Prov 21:4.

FIGURATIVE. Jer 4:3; Hos 10:12.

PLOWSHARE 1 Sam 13:20; Isa 2:4; Joel 3:10; Mic 4:3.

PLUMBLINE Amos 7:7, 8; Zech 4:10.

FIGURATIVE. Isa 28:17.

POCHERETH-HAZZEBAIM The ancestor of a family that returned to Jerusalem from captivity in Babylon, Ezra 2:55–57; Neh 7:57–59.

POET Greek, Acts 17:28; Tit 1:12.

See *Poetry; Psalms; Songs.*

POETRY A major literary form of the Old and, to a lesser extent, New Testaments, expressed in several major forms, many designated for musical accompaniment.

ACROSTIC. Poetry which uses the first letters of lines or stanzas to spell out a significant word or phrase. In the Hebrew Psalm 119, there are 22 8-line stanzas, and the first letters of each stanza correspond with the 22-letter Hebrew alphabet. See also Ps 25; 34; 37; 11; 112; Prov 31:10–31.

DIDACTIC. Poetry which is instructive, Deut 32; Job; Proverbs; Song of Solomon.

ELEGAIC. Poetry written as a memorial for one who has died, 2 Sam 1:19–27; 3:33, 34; 18:33. See *Elegy.*

EPIC. Poetry of a narrative nature, Ex 15:1–21; 1 Sam 2:1–10; Lk 1:42–55, 68–79.

HYMNAL. With musical instruments, called also psalm, Ps 3; 63; 95:2.

LAMENT. A special type of poem of 5-phrase units, Lam 1–5.

POLICY See *Diplomacy.*

POLITICS Statecraft.

CORRUPTION IN. Ps 12:8; in court of Ahasuerus, Esther 3; of Darius, Dan 6:4–15.

INSTANCES OF. Absalom, electioneering for the throne, 2 Sam 15:2–6. Pilate, condemning Jesus to gratify popular clamor, Mt 27:23–27; Mk 15:15; Lk 23:13–35; Jn 18:38, 39; 19:4–13.

MINISTERS IN. Zadok the priest, a partisan of David, 2 Sam 15:24–29. Nathan, the prophet, influences the selection of David's successor, 1 Kgs 1: 11–40.

WOMEN IN. The wise woman of Abel, who saved the city through diplomacy, 2 Sam 20:16–22. Bath-sheba, in securing the crown for Solomon, 1 Kgs 1:15–21. Herodias, in influencing the administration of Herod, Mt 14:3–11; Mk 6:17–28. Mother of Zebedee's children, in seeking favor for her sons, Mt 20:20–23.

For influence in, see *Influence, Political.*

See *Diplomacy; Government.*

POLL TAX See *Tax.*

POLYGAMY Forbidden, Lev 18:18; Deut 17: 17; Mal 2:14, 15; Mt 19:4–6; Mk 10:2–8; 1 Tim 3:2, 12; Tit 1:6. Authorized, 2 Sam 12:8.

Tolerated, Ex 21:10; 1 Sam 1:2; 2 Chron 24:3. Practiced, Job 27:15; by Lamech, Gen 4:19; Abraham, Gen 16; Esau, Gen 26:34; 28:9; Jacob, Gen 29:30; Asshur, 1 Chron 4:5; Gideon, Judg 8:30; Elkanah, 1 Sam 1:2; David, 1 Sam 25:39–44; 2 Sam 3:2–5; 5:13; 1 Chron 14:3; Solomon, 1 Kgs 11: 1–8; Rehoboam, 2 Chron 11:18–23; Abijah, 2 Chron 13:21; Jehoram, 2 Chron 21:14; Joash, 2 Chron 24:3; Ahab, 2 Kgs 10:1; Jehoiachin, 2 Kgs 24:15; Belshazzar, Dan 5:2–4; see 1 Chron 2–8; Hosea, Hos 3:1, 2. Mosaic law respecting the firstborn in, Deut 21:15–17.

Sought by women after the earth's population is decimated, Isa 4:1.

The evil effects of: Husband's favoritism in, Deut 21:15–17; Jacob's, Gen 29:30; 30:15; Elkanah's, 1 Sam 1:5; Rehoboam's, 2 Chron 11:21. Domestic unhappiness in Abraham's family, Gen 16; 21:8–16; Jacob's, Gen 29:30–34; 30:1–23; Elkanah's, 1 Sam 1: 4–7. On Solomon, 1 Kgs 11:4–8.

See *Concubinage; Marriage.*

POLYTHEISM Gen 31:21; 35:4; Josh 24:2, 23; Judg 2:12–14; 3:7; 10:16; 17:4, 5; Jer 2:28; 11:13; Dan 4:8; 1 Cor 8:5.

POMEGRANATE A fruit. Abounded in the land of Canaan, 1 Sam 14:2. Brought by the spies to show the fruitfulness of the land of Canaan, Num 13:23. Figures of, were embroidered on the ephod, Ex 28:33, 34; 39:24; carved on the pillars of the temple, 1 Kgs 7:16–22; 41–46; Jer 52:22, 23. Wine made of, Song 8:2.

PONTIUS See *Pilate.*

PONTUS A province of Asia Minor, Acts 2: 9; 1 Pet 1:1. Aquila lived in, Acts 18:2, 3.

POOL Of Samaria, 1 Kgs 22:38; of Jerusalem, upper pool, 2 Kgs 18:17; Isa 36:2; lower pool, Isa 22: 9–11; Siloam, Neh 3:15; Jn 9:7, 11; of Heshbon, Song 7:4.

POOR Atonement money of, uniform with that of the rich, Ex 30:15. Inexpensive offerings of, Lev 5:7; 12:8; 14:21, 22.

See *Benevolence; Charity; Liberality; Orphan; Poverty; Widow.* Also see *Rich; Riches.*

UNCLASSIFIED SCRIPTURES RELATING TO. Ex 23:3. Do not slant your testimony in favor of a man just because he is poor. [6]A man's poverty is no excuse for twisting justice against him.

Lev 19:15. Judges must always be just in their sentences, not noticing whether a person is poor or rich; they must always be perfectly fair.

1 Sam 2:7. Some he causes to be poor and others to be rich. He cuts one down and lifts another up.

Neh 8:10. "It is time to celebrate with a hearty meal, and to send presents to those in need, for the joy of the Lord is your strength. You must not be dejected and sad!" [12]So the people went away to eat a festive meal and to send presents; it was a time of great and joyful celebration because they could hear and understand God's words.

Job 29:11. All rejoiced in what I said. All who saw me spoke well of me. [12]For I, as an honest judge, helped the poor in their need, and the fatherless who had no one to help them. [13]I helped those who were ready to perish and they blessed me. And I caused the widows' hearts to sing for joy. [15]I served as eyes for the blind and feet for the lame. [16]I was as a father to the poor, and saw to it that even strangers received a fair trial.

Job 30:25. And did I not weep for those in trouble? Wasn't I deeply grieved for the needy?

Job 31:15. For God made me, and made my servant too. He created us both. [16]If I have hurt the poor or caused widows to weep, [17]or refused food to hungry orphans— [18](but we have always cared for orphans in our home, treating them as our own children)— [19, 20]or if I have seen anyone freezing and not given him clothing, or fleece from my sheep to keep him warm, [21]or if I have taken advantage of an orphan because I thought I could get away with it— [22]if I have done any of these things, then let my arm be torn from its socket! Let my shoulder be wrenched out of place!

Job 34:19. For he doesn't care how great a man may be, and doesn't pay any more attention to the rich than to the poor. He made them all. Prov 22:2.

Ps 37:16. It is better to have little and be godly than to own an evil man's wealth.

Ps 82:3. Give fair judgment to the poor man, the afflicted, the fatherless, the destitute. [4]Rescue the poor and needy from the grasp of evil men.

Ps 109:16. For he refused all kindness to others, and persecuted those in need, and hounded brokenhearted ones to death.

Prov 10:15. The rich man's wealth is his only strength. The poor man's poverty is his only curse.

Prov 13:7. Some rich people are poor, and some poor people have great wealth! [8]Being kidnapped and held for ransom never worries the poor man! [23]A poor man's farm may have good soil, but injustice robs him of its riches.

Prov 14:20. Even his own neighbors despise the poor man, while the rich have many "friends." [21]To despise the poor is to sin. Blessed are those who pity them. [31]Anyone who oppresses the poor is insulting God who made them. To help the poor is to honor God.

Prov 18:23. The poor man pleads and the rich man answers with insults.

Prov 19:1. Better be poor and honest than rich and dishonest. [4]A wealthy man has many "friends"; the poor man has none left. [7]A poor man's own brothers turn away from him in embarrassment; how much more his friends! He calls after them, but they are gone. [17]When you help the poor you are lending to the Lord—and he pays wonderful interest on your loan! [22]Kindness makes a man attractive. And it is better to be poor than dishonest.

Prov 20:13. If you love sleep, you will end in poverty. Stay awake, work hard, and there will be plenty to eat!

Prov 21:13. He who shuts his ears to the cries of the poor will be ignored in his own time of need.

Prov 22:2. The rich and the poor are alike before the Lord who made them all. [9]Happy is the generous man, the one who feeds the poor.

Prov 23:21. Don't carouse with drunkards and gluttons, for they are on their way to poverty. And remember that too much sleep clothes a man with rags.

Prov 28:6. Better to be poor and honest than rich and a cheater. [8]Income from exploiting the poor will end up in the hands of someone who pities them. [11]Rich men are conceited, but their real poverty is evident to the poor. [19]Hard work brings prosperity; playing around brings poverty.

Prov 29:14. A king who is fair to the poor shall have a long reign.

Eccl 4:5, 6. The fool won't work and almost starves, but feels that it is better to be lazy and barely get by, than to work hard when, in the long run, it is all so futile. [13]It is better to be a poor but wise youth than to be an old and foolish king who refuses all advice.

Eccl 6:7, 8. Wise men and fools alike spend their lives scratching for food, and never seem to get enough. Both have the same problem, yet the poor man who is wise lives a far better life.

Eccl 9:15. There was in the city a wise man, very poor, and he knew what to do to save the city, and so it was rescued. But afterwards no one thought any more about him. [16]Then I realized that though wisdom is better than strength, nevertheless, if the wise man is poor, he will be despised, and what he says will not be appreciated.

Jer 22:16. He saw to it that justice and help were given the poor and the needy and all went well for him. This is how a man lives close to God.

Ezk 16:49. Your sister Sodom's sins were pride and laziness and too much food, while the poor and needy suffered outside her door.

Mt 25:42. "For I was hungry and you wouldn't feed me; thirsty, and you wouldn't give me anything to drink." [45]And I will answer, "When you refused to help the least of these my brothers, you were refusing help to me."

Mt 26:11. You will always have the poor among you, but you won't always have me. Mk 14:7.

Mk 12:43, 44. He called his disciples to him and remarked, "That poor widow has given more than all those rich men put together! For they gave a little of their extra fat, while she gave up her last penny."

Lk 6:35. Love your *enemies!* Do good to *them!* Lend to *them!* And don't be concerned about the fact that they won't repay. Then your reward from heaven will be very great, and you will truly be acting as sons of God: for he is kind to the *unthankful* and to those who are *very wicked. vs.* 30–34.

Lk 16:20. One day Lazarus, a diseased beggar, was laid at his door. [21]As he lay there longing for scraps from the rich man's table, the dogs would come and lick open sores.

Jn 12:6. Not that he cared for the poor, but he was in charge of the disciples' funds and often dipped into them for his own use!

Jas 1:9. A Christian who doesn't amount to much in this world should be glad, for he is great in the Lord's sight. [10]But a rich man should be glad that his riches mean nothing to the Lord, for he will soon be gone.

DUTY TO. Ex 22:25. If you lend money to a needy fellow-Hebrew, you are not to handle the transaction in an ordinary way, with interest. [26]If you take his clothing as a pledge of his repayment, you must let him have it back at night. [27]For it is probably his only warmth; how can he sleep without it? If you don't return it, and he cries to me for help, I will hear and be very gracious to him (at your expense), for I am very compassionate.

Ex 23:11. But let the land rest and lie fallow during the seventh year, and let the poor among the people harvest any volunteer crop that may come up; leave the rest for the animals to enjoy. The same rule applies to your vineyards and your olive groves.

Lev 19:9. When you harvest your crops, don't reap the corners of your fields, and don't pick up stray grains of wheat from the ground. [10]It is the same with your grape crop—don't strip every last piece of fruit from the vines, and don't pick up the grapes that fall to the ground. Leave them for the poor and for those traveling through, for I am Jehovah your God. chapter 23:22.

Lev 25:25. If anyone becomes poor and sells some of his land, then his nearest relatives may redeem it. [26]If there is no one else to redeem it, and he himself gets together enough money, [27]then he may always buy it back at a price proportionate to the number of harvests until the Jubilee, and the owner must accept the money and return the land to him. [28]But if the original owner is not able to redeem it, then it shall belong to the new owner until the Year of Jubilee; but at the Jubilee year it must be returned again.

[35]If your brother becomes poor, you are responsible to help him; invite him to live with you as a guest in your home. [36]Fear your God and let your brother live with you; and don't charge him interest on the money you lend him. [37]Remember—no interest; and give him what he needs, at your cost: don't try to make a profit! [39]If a fellow Israelite becomes poor and sells himself to you, you must

not treat him as an ordinary slave, [40]but rather as a hired servant or as a guest; and he shall serve you only until the Year of Jubilee. [41]At that time he can leave with his children, and return to his own family and possessions. [42]For I brought you from the land of Egypt, and you are my servants; so you may not be sold as ordinary slaves, [43]or treated harshly; fear your God.

Deut 14:28. Every third year you are to use your entire tithe for local welfare programs: [29]Give it to the Levites who have no inheritance among you, or to foreigners, or to widows and orphans within your city, so that they can eat and be satisfied; and then Jehovah your God will bless you and your work.

Deut 15:2. Every creditor shall write "Paid in full" on any promissory note he holds against a fellow Israelite, for the Lord has released everyone from his obligation. [3](This release does not apply to foreigners.) [4, 5]No one will become poor because of this, for the Lord will greatly bless you in the land he is giving you if you obey this command. The only prerequisite for his blessing is that you carefully heed all the commands of the Lord your God that I am giving you today. [6]He will bless you as he has promised. You shall lend money to many nations but will never need to borrow! You shall rule many nations, but they shall not rule over you! [7]But if, when you arrive in the land the Lord will give you, there are any among you who are poor, you must not shut your heart or hand against them; [8]you must lend them as much as they need. [9]Beware! Don't refuse a loan because the year of debt cancellation is close at hand! If you refuse to make the loan and the needy man cries out to the Lord, it will be counted against you as a sin. [10]You must lend him what he needs, and don't moan about it either! For the Lord will prosper you in everything you do because of this! [11]There will always be some among you who are poor; that is why this commandment is necessary. You must lend to them liberally. [12]If you buy a Hebrew slave, whether a man or woman, you must free him at the end of the sixth year you have owned him, [13]and don't send him away empty-handed! [14]Give him a large farewell present from your flock, your olive press, and your wine press. Share with him in proportion as the Lord your God has blessed you.

Deut 24:12, 13. If the man is poor and gives you his cloak as security, you are not to sleep in it. Take it back to him at sundown so that he can use it through the night and bless you; and the Lord your God will count it as righteousness for you.

14, 15. Never oppress a poor hired man, whether a fellow Israelite or a foreigner living in your town. Pay him his wage each day before sunset, for since he is poor he needs it right away; otherwise he may cry out to the Lord against you and it would be counted as a sin against you. [16]Fathers shall not be put to death for the sins of their sons nor the sons for the sins of their fathers; every man worthy of death shall be executed for his own crime.

17. Justice must be given to migrants and orphans and you must never accept a widow's garment in pledge of her debt. [18]Always remember that you were slaves in Egypt, and that the Lord your God rescued you; that is why I have given you this command. [19]If, when reaping your harvest, you forget to bring in a sheaf from the field, don't go back after it. Leave it for the migrants, orphans, and widows; then the Lord your God will bless and prosper all you do. [20]When you beat the olives from your olive trees, don't go over the boughs twice; leave anything remaining for the migrants, orphans, and widows. [21]It is the same for the grapes in your vineyard; don't glean the vines after they are picked, but leave what is left for those in need.

Deut 26:12. Every third year is a year of special tithing. That year you are to give all your tithes to the Levites, migrants, orphans, and widows, so that they will be well fed. [13]Then you shall declare before the Lord your God, "I have given all of my tithes to the Levites, the migrants, the orphans, and widows, just as you commanded me; I have not violated or forgotten any of your rules."

Neh 8:10. It is a time to celebrate with a hearty meal, and to send presents to those in need, for the joy of the Lord is your strength. You must not be dejected and sad!

Ps 37:21. Evil men borrow and "cannot pay it back"! But the good man returns what he owes with some extra besides. [26]Instead, the godly are able to be generous with their gifts and loans to others, and their children are a blessing.

Ps 41:1. God blesses those who are kind to the poor. He helps them out of their troubles. [2]He protects them and keeps them alive; he publicly honors them and destroys the power of their enemies. [3]He nurses them when they are sick, and soothes their pains and worries.

Ps 112:4. When darkness overtakes him, light will come bursting in. He is kind and merciful—[5]and all goes well for the generous man who conducts his business fairly. [9]He gives generously to those in need. His deeds will never be forgotten. He shall have influence and honor.

Prov 28:27. If you give to the poor, your needs will be supplied! But a curse upon those who close their eyes to poverty.

Prov 29:7. The good man knows the poor man's rights; the godless don't care.

Prov 31:9. Yes, speak up for the poor and needy and see that they get justice. [19, 20]She sews for the poor, and generously gives to the needy.

Isa 1:17. Learn to do good, to be fair and to help the poor, the fatherless, and widows.

Isa 16:3. (The ambassadors, who accompany the gift to Jerusalem) plead for advice and help. "Give us sanctuary. Protect us. Do not turn us over to our foes. [4]Let our outcasts stay among you; hide them from our enemies! God will reward you for your kindness to us."

Isa 58:7. I want you to share your food with the hungry and bring right into your own homes those who are helpless, poor and destitute. Clothe those who are cold and don't hide from relatives who need your help. [10]Feed the hungry! Help those in trouble! Then your light will shine out from the darkness, and the darkness around you shall be as bright as day.

Ezk 18:7. And is a merciful creditor, not holding on to the items given to him in pledge by poor debtors, and is no robber, but gives food to the hungry and clothes to those in need. *vs.* 16, 17.

Dan 4:27. O King Nebuchadnezzar, listen to me —stop sinning; do what you know is right; be merciful to the poor. Perhaps even yet God will spare you.

Zech 7:10. Tell them to stop oppressing widows and orphans, foreigners and poor people, and to stop plotting evil against each other.

Mt 5:42. Give to those who ask and don't turn away from those who want to borrow. Lk 6:30.

Mt 19:21. Jesus told him, "If you want to be perfect, go and sell everything you have and give the money to the poor, and you will have treasure in heaven; and come, follow me."

Mt 25:35. For I was hungry and you fed me; I was thirsty and you gave me water; I was a stranger and you invited me into your homes; [36]naked and you clothed me; sick and in prison, and you visited me.

Mk 14:7. You always have the poor among you, and they badly need your help, and you can aid them whenever you want to; but I won't be here much longer. Jn 12:8.

Lk 3:11. "If you have two coats," he replied, "give one to the poor. If you have extra food, give it away to those who are hungry."

Lk 11:41. Purity is best demonstrated by generosity.

Lk 12:33. Sell what you have and give to those in need. This will fatten your purses in heaven! And the purses of heaven have no rips or holes in them. Your treasures there will never disappear; no thief can steal them; no moth can destroy them.

Lk 14:12. Then he turned to his host. "When you put on a dinner," he said, "don't invite friends, brothers, relatives, and rich neighbors! For they will return the invitation. [13]Instead, invite the poor, the crippled, the lame, and the blind. [14]Then at the resurrection of the godly, God will reward you for inviting those who can't repay you."

Lk 18:22. "There is still one thing you lack," Jesus said. "Sell all you have and give the money to the poor—it will become treasure for you in heaven—and come, follow me."

Lk 19:8. Meanwhile, Zacchaeus stood before the Lord and said, "Sir, from now on I will give half my wealth to the poor, and if I find I have overcharged anyone on his taxes, I will penalize myself by giving him back four times as much!"

Acts 20:35. And I was a constant example to you in helping the poor; for I remembered the words of the Lord Jesus, "It is more blessed to give than to receive."

Rom 12:8. If you are a preacher, see to it that your sermons are strong and helpful. If God has given you money, be generous in helping others with it. If God has given you administrative ability and put you in charge of the work of others, take the responsibility seriously. Those who offer comfort to the sorrowing should do so with Christian cheer. [13]When God's children are in need, you be the one to help them out. And get into the habit of inviting guests home for dinner or, if they need lodging, for the night. [20]Instead, feed your enemy if he is hungry. If he is thirsty give him something to drink and you will be "heaping coals of fire on his head." In other words, he will feel ashamed of himself for what he has done to you.

1 Cor 13:3. If I gave everything I have to poor people, and if I were burned alive for preaching the Gospel but didn't love others, it would be of no value whatever.

1 Cor 16:1. Now here are the directions about the money you are collecting to send to the Christians in Jerusalem; (and, by the way, these are the same directions I gave to the churches in Galatia). [2]On every Lord's Day each of you should put aside something from what you have earned during the week, and use it for this offering. The amount depends on how much the Lord has helped you earn. Don't wait until I get there and then try to collect it all at once.

2 Cor 6:10. Our hearts ache, but at the same time we have the joy of the Lord. We are poor, but we give rich spiritual gifts to others. We own nothing, and yet we enjoy everything.

2 Cor 9:5. So I have asked these other brothers to arrive ahead of me to see that the gift you promised is on hand and waiting. I want it to be a real gift and not look as if it were being given under pressure. [6]But remember this—if you give little, you will get little. A farmer who plants just a few seeds will get only a small crop, but if he plants much, he will reap much. [7]Every one must make up his own mind as to how much he should give. Don't force anyone to give more than he really wants to, for cheerful givers are the ones God prizes. *vs.* 1–15; 2 Cor 8:9.

Gal 2:10. The only thing they did suggest was that we must always remember to help the poor, and I, too, was eager for that.

Gal 6:10. That's why whenever we can we should always be kind to everyone, and especially to our Christian brothers.

Eph 4:28. If anyone is stealing he must stop it and begin using those hands of his for honest work so he can give to others in need.

1 Tim 5:9. A widow who wants to become one of the special church workers should be at least sixty years old and have been married only once. [10]She must be well thought of by everyone because of the good she has done. Has she brought up her children well? Has she been kind to strangers as well as to other Christians? Has she helped those who are sick and hurt? Is she always ready to show kindness? [16]Let me remind you again that a widow's relatives must take care of her, and not leave this to the church to do. Then the church can spend its money for the care of widows who are all

alone and have nowhere else to turn.

Heb 13:3. Don't forget about those in jail. Suffer with them as though you were there yourself. Share the sorrow of those being mistreated, for you know what they are going through.

Jas 1:27. The Christian who is pure and without fault, from God the Father's point of view, is the one who takes care of orphans and widows.

Jas 2:2. If a man comes into your church dressed in expensive clothes and with valuable gold rings on his fingers, and at the same moment another man comes in who is poor and dressed in threadbare clothes, [3]and you make a lot of fuss over the rich man and give him the best seat in the house and say to the poor man, "You can stand over there if you like, or else sit on the floor"—well, [4]judging a man by his wealth shows that you are guided by wrong motives. [5]Listen to me, dear brothers: God has chosen poor people to be rich in faith, and the Kingdom of Heaven is theirs, for that is the gift God has promised to all those who love him. [6]And yet, of the two strangers, you have despised the poor man. Don't you realize that it is usually the rich men who pick on you and drag you into court? [7]And all too often they are the ones who laugh at Jesus Christ, whose noble name you bear. [8]Yes indeed, it is good when you truly obey our Lord's command, "You must love and help your neighbors just as much as you love and take care of yourself." [9]But you are breaking this law of our Lord's when you favor the rich and fawn over them; it is sin. [15]If you have a friend who is in need of food and clothing, [16]and you say to him, "Well, good-bye and God bless you; stay warm and eat hearty," and then don't give him clothes or food, what good does that do?

Jas 5:4. For listen! Hear the cries of the field workers whom you have cheated of their pay. Their cries have reached the ears of the Lord of Hosts.

1 Jn 3:17. But if someone who is supposed to be a Christian has money enough to live well, and sees a brother in need, and won't help him—how can God's love be within *him?* [18]Little children, let us stop just *saying* we love people; let us *really* love them, and *show* it by our *actions.* [19]Then we will know for sure, by our actions, that we are on God's side, and our consciences will be clear, even when we stand before the Lord.

FIGURATIVE. Lk 6:20.

See *Creditor; Debtor; Employee; Employer; Servant; Wages.*

GOD'S CARE OF. 1 Sam 2:7. Some he causes to be poor and others to be rich. He cuts one down and lifts another up. [8]He lifts the poor from the dust—yes, from a pile of ashes—and treats them as princes sitting in the seats of honor. For all the earth is the Lord's and he has set the world in order.

Job 5:15. God saves the fatherless and the poor from the grasp of these oppressors. [16]And so at last the poor have hope, and the fangs of the wicked are broken.

Job 31:15. For God made me, and made my servant too. He created us both.

Job 34:18. Are you going to condemn this God who says to kings and nobles, "You are wicked and unjust"? [19]For he doesn't care how great a man may be, and doesn't pay any more attention to the rich than to the poor. He made them all. [28]Causing the cry of the poor to come to the attention of God. Yes, he hears the cries of those being oppressed.

Ps 9:18. For the needs of the needy shall not be ignored forever; the hopes of the poor shall not always be crushed.

Ps 10:14. Lord, you see what they are doing. You have noted each evil act. You know what trouble and grief they have caused. Now punish them. O Lord, the poor man trusts himself to you; you are known as the helper of the helpless.

Ps 12:5. The Lord replies, "I will arise and defend the oppressed, the poor, the needy. I will rescue them as they have longed for me to do."

Ps 14:6. He is the refuge of the poor and humble when evildoers are oppressing them.

Ps 22:26. The poor shall eat and be satisfied; all who seek the Lord shall find him and shall praise his name.

Ps 34:6. This poor man cried to the Lord—and the Lord heard him and saved him out of his troubles.

Ps 35:10. From the bottom of my heart praise rises to him. Where is his equal in all of heaven and earth? Who else protects the weak and helpless from the strong, and the poor and needy from those who would rob them?

Ps 68:10. There your people lived, for you gave them this home when they were destitute.

Ps 69:33. For Jehovah hears the cries of his needy ones, and does not look the other way.

Ps 72:2. Help him to give justice to your people, even to the poor. [4]Help him to defend the poor and needy and to crush their oppressors. [12]He will take care of the helpless and poor when they cry to him; for they have no one else to defend them. [13]He feels pity for the weak and needy, and will rescue them. [14]He will save them from oppression and from violence, for their lives are precious to him.

Ps 74:21. O Lord, don't let your downtrodden people be constantly insulted. Give cause for these poor and needy ones to praise your name!

Ps 102:17. He will listen to the prayers of the destitute, for he is never too busy to heed their requests.

Ps 107:9. For he satisfies the thirsty soul and fills the hungry soul with good. [36]He brings the hungry to settle there and build their cities. [41]For he rescues the poor who are godly and gives them many children and much prosperity.

Ps 109:31. For he stands beside the poor and hungry to save them from their enemies.

Ps 113:7. And lifts the poor from the dirt, and the hungry from the garbage dump, [8]and sets them among princes!

Ps 132:15. I will make this city prosperous and satisfy her poor with food.

Ps 140:12. But the Lord will surely help those they persecute; he will maintain the rights of the poor.

Ps 146:5. But happy is the man who has the God of Jacob as his helper, whose hope is in the Lord his God. 7And gives justice to the poor and oppressed, and food to the hungry.

Prov 22:2. The rich and the poor are alike before the Lord who made them all. 22, 23Don't rob the poor and sick! For the Lord is their defender. If you injure them he will punish you.

Prov 29:13. Rich and poor are alike in this: each depends on God for light.

Eccl 5:8. If you see some poor man being oppressed by the rich, with miscarriage of justice anywhere throughout the land, don't be surprised! For every official is under orders from higher up, and the higher officials look up to their superiors. And so the matter is lost in red tape and bureaucracy.

Isa 11:4. But will defend the poor and the exploited. He will rule against the wicked who oppress them.

Isa 14:30. I will shepherd the poor of my people; they shall graze in my pasture! The needy shall lie down in peace. But as for you—I will wipe you out with famine and the sword. 32What then shall we tell the reporters? Tell them that the Lord has founded Jerusalem and is determined that the poor of his people will find a refuge within her walls.

Isa 25:4. But to the poor, O Lord, you are a refuge from the storm, a shadow from the heat, a shelter from merciless men who are like a driving rain that melts down an earthen wall.

Isa 29:19. The meek will be filled with fresh joy from the Lord, and the poor shall exult in the Holy One of Israel.

Isa 41:17. When the poor and needy seek water and there is none and their tongues are parched from thirst, then I will answer when they cry to me. I, Israel's God, will not ever forsake them.

Jer 20:13. Therefore I will sing out in thanks to the Lord! Praise him! For he has delivered me, poor and needy, from my oppressors.

Zeph 3:12. Those who are left will be the poor and the humble, and they will trust in the name of the Lord.

Zech 11:7. And I fed the flock as I had been told to do.

Mt 11:5. The blind people I've healed, and the lame people now walking without help, and the cured lepers, and the deaf who hear, and the dead raised to life; and tell him about my preaching the Good News to the poor. Lk 7:20–22.

Lk 4:18. The Spirit of the Lord is upon me; he has appointed me to preach Good News to the poor.

Lk 16:22. Finally the beggar died and was carried by the angels to be with Abraham in the place of the righteous dead.

Jas 2:5. Listen to me, dear brothers: God has chosen poor people to be rich in faith, and the Kingdom of Heaven is theirs, for that is the gift God has promised to all those who love him.

See *God, Goodness of, Providence of.*

KINDNESS TO.

Instances of. To Ruth, Ruth 2:23; by Boaz, Ruth 2:14–16. To the widow of Zarephath, 1 Kgs 17:12–24. Prophet's widow, 2 Kgs 4:1–7. Jews, Esther 9:22. By Job, Job 29:11–16; 31:16–21, 38–40; the Temanites, Isa 21:14; Nebuzaradan, Jer 39:10; the good Samaritan, Lk 10:33–35; Zacchaeus, Lk 19:8; Christian churches, Acts 6:1; 11:29; Rom 15:25, 26; 2 Cor 8:1–4; Dorcas, Acts 9:36; Cornelius, Acts 10:2, 4; church at Antioch, Acts 11:29, 30; Paul, Rom 15:25; churches of Macedonia and Achaia, Rom 15:26; 2 Cor 8:1–5.

OPPRESSIONS OF. Neh 5:1. About this time there was a great outcry of protest from parents against some of the rich Jews who were profiteering on them. 2-4What was happening was that families who ran out of money for food had to sell their children or mortgage their fields, vineyards, and homes to these rich men; and some couldn't even do that, for they already had borrowed to the limit to pay their taxes. 5"We are their brothers, and our children are just like theirs," the people protested. "Yet we must sell our children into slavery to get enough money to live. We have already sold some of our daughters, and we are helpless to redeem them, for our fields, too, are mortgaged to these men." 6I was very angry when I heard this; 7so after thinking about it I spoke out against these rich government officials. "What is this you are doing?" I demanded. "How dare you demand a mortgage as a condition for helping another Israelite?" Then I called a public trial to deal with them. 8At the trial I shouted at them, "The rest of us are doing all we can to *help* our Jewish brothers who have returned from exile as slaves in distant lands, but you are forcing them right back into slavery again. How often must we redeem them?" And they had nothing to say in their own defense. 9Then I pressed further. "What you are doing is very evil," I exclaimed. "Should you not walk in the fear of our God? Don't we have enough enemies among the nations around us who are trying to destroy us? 10The rest of us are lending money and grain to our fellow-Jews without any interest. I beg you, gentlemen, stop this business of usury. 11Restore their fields, vineyards, oliveyards, and homes to them this very day and drop your claims against them." 12So they agreed to do it and said that they would assist their brothers without requiring them to mortgage their lands and sell them their children. Then I summoned the priests and made these men formally vow to carry out their promises. 13And I invoked the curse of God upon any of them who refused. "May God destroy your homes and livelihood if you fail to keep this promise," I declared. And all the people shouted, "Amen," and praised the Lord. And the rich men did as they had promised.

Job 20:19. For he has oppressed the poor and foreclosed their homes; he will never recover. 20Though he was always greedy, now he has nothing; of all the things he dreamed of—none remain.

[21]Because he stole at every opportunity, his prosperity shall not continue.

Job 22:6. For instance, you must have refused to loan money to needy friends unless they gave you all their clothing as a pledge—yes, you must have stripped them to the bone. [7]You must have refused water to the thirsty, and bread to the starving. [9]You sent widows away without helping them, and broke the arms of orphans. [10, 11]That is why you are now surrounded by traps and sudden fears, and darkness and waves of horror.

Job 24:4. The needy are kicked aside; they must get out of the way. [7]All night they lie naked in the cold, without clothing or covering. [8]They are wet with the showers of the mountains and live in caves for want of a home. [9]The wicked snatch fatherless children from their mother's breasts, and take a poor man's baby as a pledge before they will loan him any money or grain. [10]That is why they must go about naked, without clothing, and are forced to carry food while they are starving.

Ps 10:2. Come and deal with all these proud and wicked men who viciously persecute the poor. Pour upon these men the evil they planned for others! [8]They lurk in dark alleys of the city and murder passersby. [9]Like lions they crouch silently, waiting to pounce upon the poor. Like hunters they catch their victims in their traps. [10]The unfortunate are overwhelmed by their superior strength and fall beneath their blows.

Ps 37:14. Evil men take aim to slay the poor; they are ready to butcher those who do right.

Prov 14:20. Even his own neighbors despise the poor man, while the rich have many "friends."

Prov 17:5. Mocking the poor is mocking the God who made them. He will punish those who rejoice at others' misfortunes.

Prov 19:7. A poor man's own brothers turn away from him in embarrassment; how much more his friends! He calls after them, but they are gone.

Prov 22:7. Just as the rich rule the poor, so the borrower is servant to the lender. [16]He who gains by oppressing the poor or by bribing the rich shall end in poverty.

Prov 28:3. When a poor man oppresses those even poorer, he is like an unexpected flood sweeping away their last hope. [15]A wicked ruler is as dangerous to the poor as a lion or bear attacking them.

Prov 30:14. They devour the poor with teeth as sharp as knives!

Eccl 5:8. If you see some poor man being oppressed by the rich, with miscarriage of justice anywhere throughout the land, don't be surprised! For every official is under orders from higher up, and the higher officials look up to their superiors. And so the matter is lost in red tape and bureaucracy.

Isa 3:14. First to feel his wrath will be the elders and the princes, for they have defrauded the poor. They have filled their barns with grain extorted from the helpless peasants. [15]"How dare you grind my people in the dust like that?" the Lord of Hosts will demand of them.

Isa 10:1. Woe to unjust judges and to those who issue unfair laws, says the Lord, [2]so that there is no justice for the poor, the widows and orphans. Yes, it is true that they even rob the widows and fatherless children.

Isa 32:6. Everyone will recognize an evil man when he sees him, and hypocrites will fool no one at all. Their lies about God and their cheating of the hungry will be plain for all to see. [7]The smooth tricks of evil men will be exposed, as will all the lies they use to oppress the poor in the courts.

Ezk 18:12. And oppresses the poor and needy, and robs his debtors by refusing to let them redeem what they have given him in pledge, and loves idols and worships them.

Ezk 22:29. Even the common people oppress and rob the poor and needy and cruelly extort from aliens.

Amos 2:6. The Lord says, "The people of Israel have sinned again and again, and I will not forget it. I will not leave them unpunished any more. For they have perverted justice by accepting bribes, and sold into slavery the poor who can't repay their debts; they trade them for a pair of shoes. [7]They trample the poor in the dust and kick aside the meek. . . . [8]At their religious feasts they lounge in clothing stolen from their debtors, and in my own Temple they offer sacrifices of wine they purchased with stolen money."

Amos 4:1. Listen to me, you "fat cows" of Bashan living in Samaria—you women who encourage your husbands to rob the poor and crush the needy—you who never have enough to drink! [2]The Lord God has sworn by his holiness that the time will come when he will put hooks in your noses and lead you away like the cattle you are; they will drag the last of you away with fish-hooks!

Amos 5:11. You trample the poor and steal their smallest crumb by all your taxes, fines, and usury; therefore you will never live in the beautiful stone houses you are building, nor drink the wine from the lush vineyards you are planting. [12]For many and great are your sins. I know them all so well. You are the enemies of everything good; you take bribes; you refuse justice to the poor.

Amos 8:4. Listen, you merchants who rob the poor, trampling on the needy. [6]You who make slaves of the poor, buying them for their debt of a piece of silver or a pair of shoes, or selling them your moldy wheat.

Jas 2:6. You have despised the poor man.

See under sub-topic, *Poor, Duty to.*

Instances of. The widow's son, 2 Kgs 4:1–7.

See *Creditor; Debtor; Servant; Wages.*

POPLAR A tree, Gen 30:37; Hos 4:13.

POPULAR SINS Laws against, Ex 23:2, 3. See *Sin.*

POPULARITY INSTANCES OF. David, 2 Sam 3:35, 36. Absalom, 2 Sam 15:2–6, 13. Job, Job 29.

PORATHA Son of Haman, Esther 9:7–10.

PORCH See *Temple.*

PORCIUS See *Festus.*

PORCUPINE Isa 14:23; 34:11.

PORK See *Swine.*

POTIPHAR An officer of Pharaoh. Joseph's master, Gen 37:36; 39:1.

POTIPHERA A priest of Heliopolis. Joseph's father-in-law, Gen 41:45, 50; 46:19–22.

POTTERY Clay prepared for, by treading, Isa 41:25. Containers made of, Jer 18:3, 4; Lam 4:2. Place for manufacture of, outside the wall of Jerusalem, bought as a cemetery for foreigners, Mt 27:7–10.

FIGURATIVE. Isa 64:8; Rom 9:21. Of weakness, in the statue in Nebuchadnezzar's vision, Dan 2:41, 42.

POVERTY Prov 6:11. And as you sleep, poverty creeps upon you like a robber and destroys you; want attacks you in full armor.

Prov 10:15. The rich man's wealth is his only strength. The poor man's poverty is his only curse.

Prov 15:16. Better a little with reverence for God, than great treasure and trouble with it.

Prov 16:8. A little, gained honestly, is better than great wealth gotten by dishonest means. Eccl 4:5, 6.

Prov 20:13. If you love sleep, you will end in poverty. Stay awake, work hard, and there will be plenty to eat!

Prov 23:21. Drunkards and gluttons . . . are on their way to poverty. And remember that too much sleep clothes a man with rags.

Prov 24:33. "A little extra sleep, a little more slumber, a little folding of the hands to rest" [34]means that poverty will break in upon you suddenly like a robber, and violently like a bandit.

Prov 28:19. Hard work brings prosperity; playing around brings poverty.

Prov 30:8. Second, give me neither poverty nor riches! Give me just enough to satisfy my needs! [9]For if I grow rich, I may become content without God. And if I am too poor, I may steal, and thus insult God's holy name.

POWER OF CHRIST. As the Son of God, is the power of God, Jn 5:17–19; 10:28–30; as man, is from the Father, Acts 10:38.

Described as supreme, Eph 1:19–21; 1 Pet 3:22; unlimited, Mt 28:18; over all mankind, Jn 17:2; over all things, Jn 3:35; Eph 1:22; glorious, 2 Thess 1:9; everlasting, 1 Tim 6:16. Is able to conquer all things, Phil 3:21.

Exemplified in creation, Jn 1:3, 10; Col 1:16; upholding all things, Col 1:17; Heb 1:3; salvation, Isa 63:1; Heb 7:25; his teaching, Mt 7:28, 29; Lk 4:32; performing miracles, Mt 8:27; Lk 5:17; healing, Lk 6:19; 8:46; enabling others to perform miracles, Mt 10:1; Mk 16:17, 18; Lk 10:17; forgiving sins, Mt 9:5, 6; Acts 5:31; giving spiritual life, Jn 5:21, 25, 26; giving eternal life, Jn 17:2; raising the dead, Jn 5:28, 29; rising from the dead, Jn 2:19; 10:18; overcoming the world, Jn 16:33; overcoming Satan, Col 2:15; Heb 2:14; destroying the works of Satan, 1 Jn 3:8; ministers should explain, 2 Pet 1:16.

Believers made willing by, Ps 110:3; helped by, Heb 2:18; strengthened by, Phil 4:13; 2 Tim 4:17; preserved by, 2 Tim 1:12; 4:18; bodies of, shall be changed by, Phil 3:21; demonstrate, 2 Cor 12:9. Present in the church, 1 Cor 5:3, 4. Shall be exhibited at his second coming, Mk 13:26; 2 Pet 1:16. Shall subdue all enemies, 1 Cor 15:24. The wicked shall be destroyed by, Ps 2:9; Isa 11:4; 63:3; 2 Thess 1:9.

See *Jesus.*

OF GOD. One of his attributes, 1 Chron 29:11.

Expressed by the voice of God, Ps 29:3, 4; 68:33; finger of God, Ex 8:19; Ps 8:3; hand of God, Isa 48:13; arm of God, Isa 52:10; thunder of his power, Job 26:14.

Described as great, Ps 79:11; incredible, Nah 1:3; strong, Ps 89:13; glorious, Ex 15:6; Ps 89:13; mighty, Job 9:4; Ps 136:11, 12; Isa 63:12; everlasting, Isa 26:4; Rom 1:20; sovereign, Rom 9:21, 22; effectual, Isa 43:13; Eph 3:7; irresistible, Deut 32:39; Dan 4:35; incomparable, Ex 15:11, 12; Deut 3:23–25; Job 40:9; Ps 89:8; wonderful, Job 5:9; incredible, Job 9:10; incomprehensible, Job 26:14; Eccl 3:11.

All things possible to, Mt 19:26. Nothing too hard for, Gen 18:14; Jer 32:27. Can save by many or by few, 1 Sam 14:6. Is the source of all strength, 1 Chron 29:12; Ps 68:35.

Exemplified in the creation, Ps 102:25; Jer 10:12; in establishing and governing all things, Ps 65:6; 66:7; in the miracles of Christ, Lk 11:20; in the resurrection of Christ, 2 Cor 13:4; Col 2:12; in the resurrection of believers, 1 Cor 6:14; in making the gospel effectual, Rom 1:16; 1 Cor 1:18, 24; in saving his people, Ps 106:8; in the destruction of the wicked, Ex 9:16; Rom 9:22.

Saints long for exhibitions of, Ps 63:1, 2; have confidence in, Jer 20:11; receive more grace by, 2 Cor 9:8; strengthened by, Eph 6:10; Col 1:11; cared for by, Ps 37:17; Isa 41:10; supported in hardship by, 2 Cor 6:7; 2 Tim 1:8; rescued by, Neh 1:10; Dan 3:17; taught by, Job 36:22; kept by, for eternal life, 1 Pet 1:5. Exerted on behalf of the saints, 1 Chron 16:9. Works in and for believers, 2 Cor 13:4; Eph 1:19; 3:20. The faith of believers stands in, 1 Cor 2:4, 5.

Should be acknowledged, 1 Chron 29:11; Isa 33:13; pleaded in prayer, Ps 79:11; Mt 6:13; feared, Jer 5:22; Mt 10:28; celebrated, Ps 21:13; Jude 1:24, 25. Efficiency of ministers is through, 1 Cor 3:6–8; Gal 2:7–9; Eph 3:7. Is a reason for trust, Isa 26:4; Rom 4:21.

The wicked do not know, Mt 22:29; have against them, Ezra 8:22; will be destroyed by, Lk 12:5. The heavenly beings extolled, Rev 4:11; 5:13; 11:17.

See *God, Omnipotent, Power of.*

OF THE HOLY SPIRIT. Is the power of God, Mt 12:28, with Lk 11:20. Christ commenced his ministry in, Lk 4:14. Christ performed his miracles by, Mt 12:28.

Exemplified in creation, Gen 1:2; Job 26:13; Ps 104:30; the conception of Christ, Lk 1:35; raising Christ from the dead, 1 Pet 3:18; giving spiritual life, Ezk 37:11–14, with Rom 8:11; performing miracles, Rom 15:19; making the gospel effective,

1 Cor 2:4; 1 Thess 1:5; overcoming all difficulties, Zech 4:6, 7. Promised by the Father, Lk 24:49. Promised by Christ, Acts 1:8.

Believers upheld by, Ps 51:11; strengthened by, Eph 3:16; enabled to speak the truth boldly by, Mic 3:8; Acts 6:5, 10; 2 Tim 1:7, 8; helped in prayer by, Rom 8:26; overflow in hope through, Rom 15:13. Qualifies minister, Lk 24:49; Acts 1:8, 9. God's word the instrument of, Eph 6:17.

See *Holy Spirit.*

SPIRITUAL. Gen 32:28. "It isn't [Jacob] anymore!" the Man told him. "It is Israel—one who has power with God. Because you have been strong with God, you shall prevail with men."

Isa 40:29. He gives power to the tired and worn out, and strength to the weak. [30]Even the youths shall be exhausted, and the young men will all give up. [31]But they that wait upon the Lord shall renew their strength. They shall mount up with wings like eagles; they shall run and not be weary; they shall walk and not faint.

Mk 9:29. Jesus replied, "Cases like this require prayer."

Lk 1:17. He will be a man of rugged spirit and power like Elijah, the prophet of old; and he will precede the coming of the Messiah, preparing the people for his arrival. He will soften adult hearts to become like little children's, and will change disobedient minds to the wisdom of faith.

Lk 4:32. Here, too, the people were amazed at the things he said. For he spoke as one who knew the truth.

Lk 24:49. And now I will send the Holy Spirit upon you, just as my Father promised. Don't begin telling others yet—stay here in the city until the Holy Spirit comes and fills you with power from heaven.

Jn 7:38. "For the Scriptures declare that rivers of living water shall flow from the inmost being of anyone who believes in me." [39](He was speaking of the Holy Spirit, who would be given to everyone believing in him; but the Spirit had not yet been given, because Jesus had not yet returned to his glory in heaven.)

Acts 1:8. But when the Holy Spirit has come upon you, you will receive power to testify about me with great effect, to the people in Jerusalem, throughout Judea, in Samaria, and to the ends of the earth, about my death and resurrection.

Acts 2:2. Suddenly there was a sound like the roaring of a mighty windstorm in the skies above them and it filled the house where they were meeting. [3]Then, what looked like flames or tongues of fire appeared and settled on their heads. [4]And everyone present was filled with the Holy Spirit and began speaking in languages they didn't know, for the Holy Spirit gave them this ability.

Acts 6:8. Stephen, the man so full of faith and the Holy Spirit's power, did spectacular miracles among the people.

1 Cor 1:24. But God has opened the eyes of those called to salvation, both Jews and Gentiles, to see that Christ is the mighty power of God to save them; Christ himself is the center of God's wise plan for their salvation. [25]This so-called "foolish" plan of God is far wiser than the wisest plan of the wisest man, and God in his weakness—Christ dying on the cross—is far stronger than any man. [26]Notice among yourselves, dear brothers, that few of you who follow Christ have big names or power or wealth. [27]Instead, God has deliberately chosen to use ideas the world considers foolish and of little worth in order to shame those people considered by the world as wise and great. [28]He has chosen a plan despised by the world, counted as nothing at all, and used it to bring down to nothing those the world considers great.

1 Cor 4:19. But I will come, and soon, if the Lord will let me, and then I'll find out whether these proud men are just big talkers or whether they really have God's power. [20]The Kingdom of God is not just talking; it is living by God's power.

2 Cor 12:9. Each time he said, "No. But I am with you; that is all you need. My power shows up best in weak people." Now I am glad to be a living demonstration of Christ's power, instead of showing off my own power and abilities.

Eph 1:19. I pray that you will begin to understand how incredibly great his power is to help those who believe him. It is that same mighty power [20]that raised Christ from the dead and seated him in the place of honor at God's right hand in heaven.

1 Thess 1:5. For when we brought you the Good News, it was not just meaningless chatter to you; no, you listened with great interest. What we told you produced a powerful effect upon you, for the Holy Spirit gave you great and full assurance that what we said was true. And you know how our very lives were further proof to you of the truth of our message.

2 Tim 1:7. For the Holy Spirit, God's gift, does not want you to be afraid of people, but to be wise and strong, and to love them and enjoy being with them.

Heb 6:5. And know how good the Word of God is, and felt the mighty powers of the world to come.

See *Holy Spirit.*

PRAISE Song of Moses, after passing through the Red Sea, Ex 15:1–19. Of Miriam, Ex 15:21. Of Deborah, after defeating the Canaanites, Judg 5. Of Hannah, 1 Sam 2:1–10. Of David, celebrating his rescue from Saul, 2 Sam 22; on bringing the ark to Zion, 1 Chron 16:8–36; at the close of his reign, 1 Chron 29:10–19.

The chorus when Solomon brought the ark into the Temple, 2 Chron 5:13, 14.

Psalms of, for God's goodness to Israel, Psalms 46; 48; 65; 66; 68; 76; 81; 85; 98; 105; 124; 126; 129; 135; 136. See printed scriptures below. For God's goodness to righteous men, Psalms 23; 34; 36; 91; 100; 103; 107; 117; 121. See printed scriptures below. For God's goodness to individuals, Psalms 9; 18; 22; 30; 40; 75; 103; 108; 116; 118; 138; 144. For God's attributes, Psalms 8; 19; 22; 24; 29; 33; 47; 50; 65; 66; 76; 77; 92; 93; 95; 96; 97; 98; 99; 104;

111; 113; 114; 115; 134; 139; 147; 148; 150.

UNCLASSIFIED SCRIPTURES RELATING TO. Gen 14:20. The blessing of the supreme God, Creator of heaven and earth, be upon you, Abram: and blessed be God, who has delivered your enemies over to you.

Ex 15:1. Then Moses and the people of Israel sang this song to the Lord: I will sing to the Lord, for he has triumphed gloriously; he has thrown both horse and rider into the sea. [2]The Lord is my strength, my song, and my salvation. He is my God, and I will praise him. He is my father's God —I will exalt him.

Deut 10:21. He is your praise and he is your God, the one who has done mighty miracles you yourselves have seen.

Judg 5:3. Listen, O you kings and princes, for I shall sing about the Lord, the God of Israel.

2 Sam 22:4. I will call upon the Lord, who is worthy to be praised. Ps 18:3.

1 Chron 16:31. "Let the heavens be glad, the earth rejoice; let all the nations say, It is the Lord who reigns. [33]Let the trees in the wood sing for joy before the Lord, for he comes to judge the earth. [34]Oh, give thanks to the Lord, for he is good; his love and his kindness go on forever. [36]Blessed be Jehovah, God of Israel, forever and forevermore." And all the people shouted "Amen!" and praised the Lord.

1 Chron 23:30. Each morning and evening they stood before the Lord to sing thanks and praise to him.

2 Chron 7:3. All the people had been watching and now they fell flat on the pavement, and worshiped and thanked the Lord.

Neh 9:5. Then the Levite leaders called out to the people, "Stand up and praise the Lord your God, for he lives from everlasting to everlasting. Praise his glorious name! It is far greater than we can think or say." The leaders in this part of the service were Jeshua, Kadmi-el, Bani, Hashabneiah, Sherebiah, Hodiah, Shebaniah, and Pethaniah. [6]Then Ezra prayed, "You alone are God. You have made the skies and the heavens, the earth and the seas, and everything in them. You preserve it all; and all the angels of heaven worship you."

Job 36:24. Instead, glorify him for his mighty works for which he is so famous.

Ps 7:17. Oh, how grateful and thankful I am to the Lord because he is so good. I will sing praise to the name of the Lord who is above all lords.

Ps 8:2. You have taught the little children to praise you perfectly. May their example shame and silence your enemies!

Ps 9:11. Oh, sing out your praises to the God who lives in Jerusalem. Tell the world about his unforgettable deeds.

Ps 21:13. Accept our praise, O Lord, for all your glorious power. We will write songs to celebrate your mighty acts!

Ps 22:22. I will praise you to all my brothers; I will stand up before the congregation and testify of the wonderful things you have done. [23]"Praise the Lord, each one of you who fears him," I will say. "Each of you must fear and reverence his name. Let all Israel sing his praises." [25]Yes, I will stand and praise you before all the people. I will publicly fulfill my vows in the presence of all who reverence your name.

Ps 24:7. Open up, O ancient gates, and let the King of Glory in. [8]Who is this King of Glory? The Lord, strong and mighty, invincible in battle. [10]Who is this King of Glory? The Commander of all heaven's armies!

Ps 26:12. I publicly praise the Lord for keeping me from slipping and falling.

Ps 28:6. Oh, praise the Lord, for he has listened to my pleadings! [7]He is my strength, my shield from every danger. I trusted in him, and he helped me. Joy rises in my heart until I burst out in songs of praise to him.

Ps 30:4. Oh, sing to him you saints of his; give thanks to his holy name. Ps 97:12.

Ps 32:11. So rejoice in him, all those who are his, and shout for joy, all those who try to obey him.

Ps 33:1. Let all the joys of the godly well up in praise to the Lord, for it is right to praise him. [2]Play joyous melodies of praise upon the lyre and on the harp. [3]Compose new songs of praise to him, accompanied skillfully on the harp; sing joyfully.

Ps 34:1. I will praise the Lord no matter what happens. I will constantly speak of his glories and grace. [2]I will boast of all his kindness to me. Let all who are discouraged take heart. [3]Let us praise the Lord together, and exalt his name.

Ps 35:18. Save me, and I will thank you publicly before the entire congregation, before the largest crowd I can find. [28]And I will tell everyone how great and good you are; I will praise you all day long.

Ps 41:13. Bless the Lord, the God of Israel, who exists from everlasting ages past—and on into everlasting eternity ahead. Amen and amen!

Ps 42:4. Take courage, my soul! Do you remember those times (but how could you ever forget them!) when you led a great procession to the Temple on festival days, singing with joy, praising the Lord?

Ps 43:3. Oh, send out your light and your truth —let them lead me. Let them lead me to your Temple on your holy mountain, Zion. [4]There I will go to the altar of God my exceeding joy, and praise him with my harp. O God—my God!

Ps 47:1. Come, everyone, and clap for joy! Shout triumphant praises to the Lord! [6, 7]Sing out your praises to our God, our King. Yes, sing your highest praises to our King, the King of all the earth. Sing thoughtful praises!

Ps 48:1. How great is the Lord! How much we should praise him. He lives upon Mount Zion in Jerusalem.

Ps 50:23. But true praise is a worthy sacrifice; this really honors me. Those who walk my paths will receive salvation from the Lord.

Ps 51:15. For my lips will be unsealed—oh, how I will praise you.

Ps 52:9. O Lord, I will praise you forever and ever for your punishment. And I will wait for your mercies—for everyone knows what a merciful God you are.

Ps 56:10. I am trusting God—oh, praise his promises! [12]I will surely do what I have promised, Lord, and thank you for your help.

Ps 57:7. O God, my heart is quiet and confident. No wonder I can sing your praises! [8]Rouse yourself, my soul! Arise, O harp and lyre! Let us greet the dawn with song! [9]I will thank you publicly throughout the land. I will sing your praises among the nations. Ps 108:1–3.

Ps 61:8. And I will praise your name continually, fulfilling my vow of praising you each day.

Ps 63:3. For your love and kindness are better to me than life itself. How I praise you! [5]At last I shall be fully satisfied; I will praise you with great joy. [6]I lie awake at night thinking of you.

Ps 65:1. O God in Zion, we wait before you in silent praise, and thus fulfill our vow. And because you answer prayer, all mankind will come to you with their requests.

Ps 66:1. Sing to the Lord, all the earth! [2]Sing of his glorious name! Tell the world how wonderful he is. [4]All the earth shall worship you and sing of your glories. [8]Let everyone bless God and sing his praises.

Ps 67:3. How everyone throughout the earth will praise the Lord! [4]How glad the nations will be, singing for joy because you are their King and will give true justice to their people!

Ps 68:4. Sing praises to the Lord! Raise your voice in song to him who rides upon the clouds! Jehovah is his name—oh, rejoice in his presence. [26]Let all the people of Israel praise the Lord, who is Israel's fountain. [32]Sing to the Lord, O kingdoms of the earth—sing praises to the Lord, [33]to him who rides upon the ancient heavens, whose mighty voice thunders from the sky. [34]Power belongs to God! His majesty shines down on Israel; his strength is mighty in the heavens.

Ps 69:30. Then I will praise God with my singing! My thanks will be his praise. [34]Praise him, all heaven and earth! Praise him, all the seas and everything in them!

Ps 70:4. But fill the followers of God with joy. Let those who love your salvation exclaim, "What a wonderful God he is!"

Ps 71:8. All day long I'll praise and honor you, O God, for all that you have done for me. [14]I will keep on expecting you to help me. I praise you more and more. [22]I will praise you with music, telling of your faithfulness to all your promises, O Holy One of Israel.

Ps 75:1. How we thank you, Lord! Your mighty miracles give proof that you care.

Ps 79:13. Then we your people, the sheep of your pasture, will thank you forever and forever, praising your greatness from generation to generation.

Ps 81:1. The Lord makes us strong! Sing praises! Sing to Israel's God!

Ps 84:4. How happy are those who can live in your Temple, singing your praises.

Ps 86:12. With all my heart I will praise you. I will give glory to your name forever.

Ps 89:5. All heaven shall praise your miracles, O Lord; myriads of angels will praise you for your faithfulness. [52]And yet—blessed be the Lord forever! Amen and amen!

Ps 92:1. It is good to say, "Thank you" to the Lord, to sing praises to the God who is above all gods. [2]Every morning tell him, "Thank you for your kindness," and every evening rejoice in all his faithfulness. [3]Sing his praises, accompanied by music from the harp and lute and lyre.

Ps 95:1. Oh, come, let us sing to the Lord! Give a joyous shout in honor of the Rock of our salvation! [2]Come before him with thankful hearts. Let us sing him psalms of praise. [6]Come kneel before the Lord our Maker, [7]for he is our our God. We are his sheep and he is our Shepherd. Oh, that you would hear him calling you today and come to him!

Ps 96:1. Sing a new song to the Lord! Sing it everywhere around the world! [2]Sing out his praises! Bless his name. Each day tell someone that he saves. [3]Publish his glorious acts throughout the earth. Tell everyone about the amazing things he does. [4]For the Lord is great beyond description, and greatly to be praised. Worship only him among the gods! [7]O nations of the world, confess that God alone is glorious and strong. [8]Give him the glory he deserves! Bring your offering and come to worship him. [9]Worship the Lord with the beauty of holy lives. Let the earth tremble before him.

Ps 98:4. That is why the earth breaks out in praise to God and sings for utter joy! [5]Sing your praise accompanied by music from the harp. [6]Let the cornets and trumpets shout! Make a joyful symphony before the Lord, the King!

Ps 99:3. Let them reverence your great and holy name. [5]Exalt the Lord our holy God! Bow low before his feet. [9]Exalt the Lord our God, and worship at his holy mountain in Jerusalem, for he is holy.

Ps 100:1. Shout with joy before the Lord, O earth! [2]Obey him gladly; come before him, singing with joy. [3]Try to realize what this means—the Lord is God! He made us—we are his people, the sheep of his pasture. [4]Go through his open gates with great thanksgiving; enter his courts with praise. Give thanks to him and bless his name. [5]For the Lord is always good. He is always loving and kind, and his faithfulness goes on and on to each succeeding generation.

Ps 101.1. I will sing about your lovingkindness and your justice, Lord. I will sing your praises!

Ps 103:20. Bless the Lord, you mighty angels of his who carry out his orders, listening for each of his commands. [21]Yes, bless the Lord, you armies of his angels who serve him constantly. [22]Let everything everywhere bless the Lord. And how I bless him too!

Ps 104:33. I will sing to the Lord as long as I live. I will praise God to my last breath! [34]May he be pleased by all these thoughts about him, for he is the source of all my joy.

Ps 105:1. Thank the Lord for all the glorious things he does; proclaim them to the nations. [2]Sing his praises and tell everyone about his miracles. [3]Glory in the Lord; O worshipers of God, rejoice. [4]Search for him and for his strength, and keep on searching! [5]Think of the mighty deeds he did for us, his chosen ones.

Ps 106:1. Hallelujah! Thank you, Lord! How good you are! Your love for us continues on forever. [48]Blessed be the Lord, the God of Israel, from everlasting to everlasting. Let all the people say, "Amen!" Hallelujah!

Ps 107:8. Oh, that these men would praise the Lord for his lovingkindness, and for all of his wonderful deeds! [*vs.* 15, 21, 31.] [9]For he satisfies the thirsty soul and fills the hungry soul with good. [32]Let them praise him publicly before the congregation, and before the leaders of the nation.

Ps 109:30. But I will give repeated thanks to the Lord, praising him to everyone.

Ps 111:1. Hallelujah! I want to express publicly before his people my heartfelt thanks to God for his mighty miracles. All who are thankful should ponder them with me. [10]How can men be wise? The only way to begin is by reverence for God. For growth in wisdom comes from obeying his laws. Praise his name forever.

Ps 113:1. Hallelujah! O servants of Jehovah, praise his name. [2]Blessed is his name forever and forever.

Ps 115:18. We praise him forever! Hallelujah! Praise the Lord!

Ps 116:12. But now what can I offer Jehovah for all he has done for me? [13]I will bring him an offering of wine and praise his name for saving me. [14]I will publicly bring him the sacrifice I vowed I would. [17]I will worship you and offer you a sacrifice of thanksgiving. [18, 19]Here in the courts of the Temple in Jerusalem, before all the people, I will pay everything I vowed to the Lord. Praise the Lord.

Ps 117:1. Praise the Lord, all nations everywhere. Praise him, all the peoples of the earth. [2]For he loves us very dearly, and his truth endures. Praise the Lord.

Ps 118:15. Songs of joy at the news of our rescue are sung in the homes of the godly. [28]For you are my God, and I shall give you this thanks and this praise. [29]Oh, give thanks to the Lord, for he is so good! For his lovingkindness is forever.

Ps 119:7. After you have corrected me I will thank you by living as I should! [62]At midnight I will rise to give my thanks to you for our good laws. [108]Accept my grateful thanks and teach me your desires. [164]I will praise you seven times a day because of your wonderful laws. [171]I will praise you for letting me learn your laws. [172]I will sing about their wonder, for each of them is just. [175]If you will let me live, I will praise you; let your laws assist me.

Ps 134:1. Oh, bless the Lord, you who serve him as watchmen in the Temple every night. [2]Lift your hands in holiness and bless the Lord.

Ps 135:1, 2. Hallelujah! Yes, let his people praise him as they stand in his Temple courts. [3]Praise the Lord because he is so good; sing to his wonderful name. [19]O Israel, bless Jehovah! High priests of Aaron, bless his name. [20]O Levite priests, bless the Lord Jehovah! Oh, bless his name, all of you who trust and reverence him. [21]All people of Jerusalem, praise the Lord, for he lives here in Jerusalem. Hallelujah!

Ps 136:2. Oh, give thanks to the God of gods, for his lovingkindness continues forever. *vs.* 1–26.

Ps 138:1. Lord, with all my heart I thank you. I will sing your praises before the armies of angels in heaven. [2]I face your Temple as I worship, giving thanks to you for all your lovingkindness and your faithfulness, for your promises are backed by all the honor of your name.

Ps 140:13. Surely the godly are thanking you, for they shall live in your presence.

Ps 144:1. Bless the Lord who is my immovable Rock. He gives me strength and skill in battle. [2]He is always kind and loving to me; he is my fortress, my tower of strength and safety, my deliverer. He stands before me as a shield. He subdues my people under me. [9]I will sing you a new song, O God, with a ten-string harp.

Ps 145:1, 2. I will praise you, my God and King, and bless your name each day and forever. [3]Great is Jehovah! Greatly praise him! His greatness is beyond discovery! [4]Let each generation tell its children what glorious things he does. [5]I will meditate about your glory, splendor, majesty and miracles. [6]Your awe-inspiring deeds shall be on every tongue; I will proclaim your greatness. [7]Everyone will tell about how good you are, and sing about your righteousness. [8]Jehovah is kind and merciful, slow to get angry, full of love. [9]He is good to everyone, and his compassion is intertwined with everything he does. [10]All living things shall thank you, Lord, and your people will bless you. [11]They will talk together about the glory of your kingdom and mention examples of your power. [12]They will tell about your miracles and about the majesty and glory of your reign. [13]For your kingdom never ends. You rule generation after generation. [14]The Lord lifts the fallen and those bent beneath their loads. [15]The eyes of all mankind look up to you for help; you give them their food as they need it. [16]You constantly satisfy the hunger and thirst of every living thing. [17]The Lord is fair in everything he does, and full of kindness. [18]He is close to all who call on him sincerely. [19]He fulfills the desires of those who reverence and trust him; he hears their cries for help and rescues them. [20]He protects all those who love him, but destroys the wicked. [21]I will praise the Lord and call on all men everywhere to bless his holy name forever and forever.

Ps 146:1. Praise the Lord! Yes, really praise him! [2]I will praise him as long as I live, yes, even with my dying breath. [3]Don't look to men for help; their greatest leaders fail; [4]for every man must die. His breathing stops, life ends, and in a moment all he planned for himself is ended. [5]But happy is the man who has the God of Jacob as his helper, whose hope is in the Lord his God—[6]the God who made both earth and heaven, the seas and everything in them. He is the God who keeps every promise, [7]and gives justice to the poor and oppressed, and food to the hungry. He frees the prisoners, [8]and opens the eyes of the blind; he lifts the burdens from those bent down beneath their loads. For the Lord loves good men. [9]He protects the immigrants, and cares for the orphans and widows. But he turns topsy-turvy the plans of the wicked. [10]The Lord will reign forever. O Jerusalem, your God is King in every generation! Hallelujah! Praise the Lord!

Ps 147:1. Hallelujah! Yes, praise the Lord! How good it is to sing his praises! How delightful, and how right! [2]He is rebuilding Jerusalem and bringing back the exiles. [3]He heals the brokenhearted, binding up their wounds. [4]He counts the stars and calls them all by name. [5]How great he is! His power is absolute! His understanding is unlimited. [6]The Lord supports the humble, but brings the wicked into the dust. [7]Sing out your thanks to him; sing praises to our God, accompanied by harps. [8]He covers the heavens with clouds, sends down the showers and makes the green grass grow in mountain pastures. [9]He feeds the wild animals and the young ravens cry to him for food. [10]The speed of a horse is nothing to him. How puny in his sight is the strength of a man. [11]But his joy is in those who reverence him, those who expect him to be loving and kind. [12]Praise him, O Jerusalem! Praise your God, O Zion! [13]For he has fortified your gates against all enemies, and blessed your children. [14]He sends peace across your nation, and fills your barns with plenty of the finest wheat. [15]He sends his orders to the world. How swiftly his word flies. [16]He sends the snow in all its lovely whiteness, and scatters the frost upon the ground, [17]and hurls the hail upon the earth. Who can stand before his freezing cold? [18]But then he calls for warmer weather, and the spring winds blow and all the river ice is broken. [19]He has made known his laws and ceremonies of worship to Israel—[20]something he has not done with any other nation; they have not known his commands. Hallelujah! Yes, praise the Lord!

Ps 148:1. Praise the Lord, O heavens! Praise him from the skies! [2]Praise him, all his angels, all the armies of heaven. [3]Praise him, sun and moon, and all you twinkling stars. [4]Praise him, skies above. Praise him, vapors high above the clouds. [5]Let everything he has made give praise to him. For he issued his command, and they came into being; [6]he established them forever and forever. His orders will never be revoked. [7]And praise him down here on earth, you creatures of the ocean depths. [8]Let fire and hail, snow, rain, wind and weather, all obey. [9]Let the mountains and hills, the fruit trees and cedars, [10]the wild animals and cattle, the snakes and birds, [11]the kings and all the people, with their rulers and judges, [12]young men and maidens, old men and children—[13]all praise the Lord together. For he alone is worthy. His glory is far greater than all of earth and heaven. [Hab 3:3.] [14]He has made his people strong, honoring his godly ones—the people of Israel, the people closest to him. Hallelujah! Yes, praise the Lord!

Ps 149:1. Hallelujah! Yes, praise the Lord! Sing him a new song. Sing his praises, all his people. [2]O Israel, rejoice in your Maker. O people of Jerusalem, exult in your King. [3]Praise his name with dancing, accompanied by drums and lyre. [4, 5]For Jehovah enjoys his people; he will save the humble. Let his people rejoice in this honor. Let them sing for joy as they lie upon their beds. [6, 7]Adore him, O his people! And take a double-edged sword to execute his punishment upon the nations. [8]Bind their kings and leaders with iron chains, [9]and execute their sentences. He is the glory of his people. Hallelujah! Praise him!

Ps 150:1. Hallelujah! Yes, praise the Lord! Praise him in his Temple and in the heavens he made with mighty power. [2]Praise him for his mighty works. Praise his unequaled greatness. [3]Praise him with the trumpet and with lute and harp. [4]Praise him with the tambourines and processional. Praise him with stringed instruments and horns. [5]Praise him with the cymbals, yes, loud clanging cymbals. [6]Let everything alive give praises to the Lord! *You* praise him! Hallelujah!

Isa 12:1. On that day you will say, "Praise the Lord! He was angry with me, but now he comforts me. [2]See, God has come to save me! I will trust and not be afraid, for the Lord is my strength and song; he is my salvation. [3]Oh, the joy of drinking deeply from the Fountain of Salvation!" [4]In that wonderful day you will say, "Thank the Lord! Praise his name! Tell the world about his wondrous love. How mighty he is!" [5]Sing to the Lord, for he has done wonderful things. Make known his praise around the world. [6]Let all the people of Jerusalem shout his praise with joy. For great and mighty is the Holy One of Israel, who lives among you.

Isa 24:14. But all who are left will shout and sing for joy; those in the west will praise the majesty of God, [15, 16]and those in the east will respond with praise. Hear them singing to the Lord from the ends of the earth, singing glory to the Righteous One!

Isa 25:1. O Lord, I will honor and praise your name, for you are my God; you do such wonderful things! You planned them long ago, and now you have accomplished them, just as you said! Joel 2:26.

Isa 35:10. These, the ransomed of the Lord, will go home along that road to Zion, singing the songs of everlasting joy. For them all sorrow and all sighing will be gone forever; only joy and gladness will be there.

Isa 38:18. For dead men cannot praise you. They cannot be filled with hope and joy. [19]The living, only the living, can praise you as I do today. One generation makes known your faithfulness to the next.

Isa 42:10. Sing a new song to the Lord; sing his praises, all you who live in earth's remotest corners! Sing, O sea! Sing, all you who live in distant lands beyond the sea! [11]Join in the chorus, you desert cities —Kedar and Sela! And you, too, dwellers in the mountain tops. [12]Let the western coastlands glorify the Lord and sing his mighty power.

Isa 43:21. I have made Israel for myself, and these my people will some day honor me before the world.

Isa 49:13. Sing for joy, O heavens; shout, O earth. Break forth with song, O mountains, for the Lord has comforted his people, and will have compassion upon them in their sorrow.

Isa 51:3. And the Lord will bless Israel again, and make her deserts blossom; her barren wilderness will become as beautiful as the Garden of Eden. Joy and gladness will be found there, thanksgiving and lovely songs.

Isa 52:7. How beautiful upon the mountains are the feet of those who bring the happy news of peace and salvation, the news that the God of Israel reigns. [8]The watchmen shout and sing with joy, for right before their eyes they see the Lord God bring his people home again. [9]Let the ruins of Jerusalem break into joyous song, for the Lord has comforted his people; he has redeemed Jerusalem. [10]The Lord has bared his holy arm before the eyes of all the nations; the ends of the earth shall see the salvation of our God.

Isa 61:3. To all who mourn in Israel he will give: beauty for ashes; joy instead of mourning; praise instead of heaviness. For God has planted them like strong and graceful oaks for his own glory.

Jer 31:7. For the Lord says, Sing with joy for all that I will do for Israel, the greatest of the nations! Shout out with praise and joy: "The Lord has saved his people, the remnant of Israel."

Jer 33:10, 11. The Lord declares that the happy voices of bridegrooms and of brides, and the joyous song of those bringing thanksgiving offerings to the Lord will be heard again in this doomed Land. The people will sing: "Praise the Lord! For he is good and his mercy endures forever!" For I will make this land happier and more prosperous than it has ever been before.

Dan 2:20. Blessed be the name of God forever and ever, for he alone has all wisdom and all power. [23]I thank and praise you, O God of my fathers, for you have given me wisdom and glowing health, and now, even this vision of the king's dream, and the understanding of what it means.

Dan 4:37. Now, I, Nebuchadnezzar, praise and glorify and honor the King of Heaven, the Judge of all, whose every act is right and good; for he is able to take those who walk proudly and push them into the dust!

Jon 2:9. I will never worship anyone but you! For how can I thank you enough for all you have done? I will surely fulfill my promises. For my deliverance comes from the Lord alone.

Mt 26:30. And when they had sung a hymn, they went out to the Mount of Olives. Mk 14:26.

Lk 1:46. Mary responded, "Oh, how I praise the Lord. [47]How I rejoice in God my Savior! [48]For he took notice of his lowly servant girl, and now generation after generation forever shall call me blest of God. [49]For he, the mighty Holy One, has done great things to me. [50]His mercy goes on from generation to generation, to all who reverence him. [51]How powerful is his mighty arm! How he scatters the proud and haughty ones! [52]He has torn princes from their thrones and exalted the lowly. [53]He has satisfied the hungry hearts and sent the rich away with empty hands. [54]And how he has helped his servant Israel! He has not forgotten his promise to be merciful. [55]For he promised our fathers—Abraham and his children—to be merciful to them forever." [67]Then his father Zacharias was filled with the Holy Spirit and gave this prophecy: [68]"Praise the Lord, the God of Israel, for he has come to visit his people and has redeemed them. [69]He is sending us a Mighty Savior from the royal line of his servant David, [70]just as he promised through his holy prophets long ago— [71]someone to save us from our enemies, from all who hate us. [72, 73]He has been merciful to our ancestors, yes, to Abraham himself, by remembering his sacred promise to him, [74]and by granting us the privilege of serving God fearlessly, freed from our enemies, [75]and by making us holy and acceptable, ready to stand in his presence forever."

Lk 2:20. Then the shepherds went back again to their fields and flocks, praising God for the visit of the angels, and because they had seen the child, just as the angel had told them.

Lk 17:15. One of them came back to Jesus, shouting, "Glory to God, I'm healed!"

Lk 19:37. And as they reached the place where the road started down from the Mount of Olives, the whole procession began to shout and sing as they walked along, praising God for all the wonderful miracles Jesus had done. [38]"God has given us a King!" they exulted. "Long live the King! Let all heaven rejoice! Glory to God in the highest heavens!"

Lk 24:52. And they worshiped him, and returned to Jerusalem filled with mighty joy, [53]and were continually in the Temple, praising God.

Acts 2:46. They worshiped together regularly at the Temple each day, met in small groups in homes for Communion, and shared their meals with great joy and thankfulness, [47]praising God.

Acts 4:24. Then all the believers united in this prayer: "O Lord, Creator of heaven and earth and of the sea and everything in them."

Acts 16:25. Around midnight, as Paul and Silas were praying and singing hymns to the Lord—and the other prisoners were listening.

Rom 11:36. For everything comes from God alone. Everything lives by his power, and everything is for his glory. To him be glory evermore.

Rom 16:27. To God, who alone is wise, be the glory forever through Jesus Christ our Lord. Amen.

1 Cor 14:15. Well, then, what shall I do? I will do both. I will pray in unknown tongues and also in ordinary language that everyone understands. I will sing in unknown tongues and also in ordinary language, so that I can understand the praise I am giving.

1 Cor 15:57. How we thank God for all of this! It is he who makes us victorious through Jesus Christ our Lord!

Eph 1:3. How we priase God, the Father of our Lord Jesus Christ, who has blessed us with every blessing in heaven because we belong to Christ.

Eph 3:20. Now glory be to God who by his mighty power at work within us is able to do far more than we would ever dare to ask or even dream of—infinitely beyond our highest prayers, desires, thoughts, or hopes. [21]May he be given glory forever and ever through endless ages because of his master plan of salvation for the church through Jesus Christ.

Eph 5:19. Talk with each other much about the Lord, quoting psalms and hymns and singing sacred songs, making music in your hearts to the Lord.

Phil 4:20. Now unto God our Father be glory forever and ever. Amen.

1 Tim 1:17. Glory and honor to God forever and ever. He is the King of the ages, the unseen one who never dies; he alone is God, and full of wisdom. Amen.

Heb 2:12. For he says in the book of Psalms, "I will talk to my brothers about God my Father, and together we will sing his praises."

Heb 13:15. With Jesus' help we will continually offer our sacrifice of praise to God by telling others of the glory of his name.

Jas 5:13. Is anyone among you suffering? He should keep on praying about it. And those who have reason to be thankful should continually be singing praises to the Lord.

1 Pet 1:3. All honor to God, the God and Father of our Lord Jesus Christ; for it is his boundless mercy that has given us the privilege of being born again, so that we are now members of God's own family. Now we live in the hope of eternal life because Christ rose again from the dead.

1 Pet 2:9. But you are not like that, for you have been chosen by God himself—you are priests of the King, you are holy and pure, you are God's very own—all this so that you may show to others how God called you out of the darkness into his wonderful light.

1 Pet 4:11. Are you called to preach? Then preach as though God himself were speaking through you. Are you called to help others? Do it with all the strength and energy that God supplies, so that God will be glorified through Jesus Christ—to him be glory and power forever and ever. Amen.

1 Pet 5:11. To him be all power over all things, forever and ever. Amen.

2 Pet 3:18. But grow in spiritual strength and become better acquainted with our Lord and Savior Jesus Christ. To him be all glory and splendid honor, both now and forevermore. Good-bye.

Jude 1:24, 25. And now—all glory to him who alone is God, who saves us through Jesus Christ our Lord; yes, splendor and majesty, all power and authority are his from the beginning; his they are and his they evermore shall be. And he is able to keep you from slipping and falling away, and to bring you, sinless and perfect, into his glorious presence with mighty shouts of everlasting joy. Amen.

Rev 1:6. He has gathered us into his kingdom and made us priests of God his Father. Give to him everlasting glory! He rules forever! Amen!

Rev 14:7. "Fear God," he shouted, "and extol his greatness. For the time has come when he will sit as Judge. Worship him who made the heaven and the earth, the sea and all its sources."

IN HEAVEN. Neh 9:6. Then Ezra prayed, "You alone are God. You have made the skies and the heavens, the earth and the seas, and everything in them. You preserve it all; and all the angels of heaven worship you."

Job 38:7. As the morning stars sang together and all the angels shouted for joy?

Ps 103:20. Bless the Lord, you mighty angels of his who carry out orders, listening for each of his commands.

Ps 148:2. Praise him, all his angels, all the armies of heaven. [4]Praise him, skies above. Praise him, vapors high above the clouds.

Isa 6:3. In a great antiphonal chorus they sang, "Holy, holy, holy, is the Lord of Hosts; the whole earth is filled with his glory."

Ezk 3:12. Then the Spirit lifted me up and the glory of the Lord began to move away, accompanied by the sound of a great earthquake.

Lk 2:13. Suddenly the angel was joined by a vast host of others—the armies of heaven—praising God: [14]"Glory to God in the highest heaven," they sang, "and peace on earth for all those pleasing him."

Lk 15:10. In the same way there is joy in the presence of the angels of God when one sinner repents. *v.* 7.

Rev 1:6. He has gathered us into his kingdom and made us priests of God his Father. Give to him everlasting glory! He rules forever! Amen!

Rev 4:8. Each of these Living Beings had six wings, and the central sections of their wings were covered with eyes. Day after day and night after night they kept on saying, "Holy, holy, holy, Lord God Almighty—the one who was, and is, and is to come." [9]And when the Living Beings gave glory and honor and thanks to the one sitting on the throne, who lives forever and ever, [10]the twenty-four Elders fell down before him and worshiped him, the Eternal Living One, and cast their crowns before the throne, singing, [11]"O Lord, you are worthy to receive the glory and the honor and the power, for you have created all things. They were created and called into being by your act of will."

Rev 5:9. They were singing him a new song with these words: "You are worthy to take the scroll and break its seals and open it; for you were slain, and your blood has bought people from every nation as gifts for God. [10]And you have gathered them into a kingdom and made them priests of our God; they shall reign upon the earth." [11]Then in my vision I heard the singing of millions of angels surrounding the throne and the Living Beings and the Elders: [12]"The Lamb is worthy" (loudly they sang it!) "—the Lamb who was slain. He is worthy to receive the power, and the riches, and the wisdom, and the strength, and the honor, and the glory, and the blessing." [13]And then I heard everyone in heaven and earth, and from the dead beneath the earth and in the sea, exclaiming, "The blessing and the honor and the glory and the power belong to the one sitting on the throne, and to the Lamb forever and ever." [14]And the four Living Beings kept saying, "Amen!" And the twenty-four Elders fell down and worshiped him.

Rev 7:9. After this I saw a vast crowd, too great to count, from all nations and provinces and languages, standing in front of the throne and before the Lamb, clothed in white, with palm branches in their hands. [10]And they were shouting with a mighty shout, "Salvation comes from our God upon the throne, and from the Lamb." [11]And now all the angels were crowding around the throne and around the Elders and the four Living Beings, and falling face down before the throne and worshiping God. [12]"Amen!" they said, "Blessing, and glory, and wisdom, and thanksgiving, and honor, and power, and might, be to our God forever and forever. Amen!"

Rev 11:16. And the twenty-four Elders sitting on their thrones before God threw themselves down in worship, saying, [17]"We give thanks, Lord God Almighty, who is and was, for now you have assumed your great power and have begun to reign."

Rev 14:2. And I heard a sound from heaven like the roaring of a great waterfall or the rolling of mighty thunder. It was the singing of a choir accompanied by harps. [3]This tremendous choir—144,000 strong—sang a wonderful new song in front of the throne of God and before the four Living Beings and the twenty-four Elders; and no one could sing this song except those 144,000 who had been redeemed from the earth.

Rev 15:3, 4. And they were singing the song of Moses, the servant of God, and the song of the Lamb: "Great and marvelous are your doings, Lord God Almighty. Just and true are your ways, O King of Ages. Who shall not fear, O Lord, and glorify your Name? For you alone are holy. All nations will come and worship before you, for your righteous deeds have been disclosed."

Rev 19:1. After this I heard the shouting of a vast crowd in heaven, "Hallelujah! Praise the Lord! Salvation is from our God. Honor and authority belong to him alone; [2]for his judgments are just and true. He has punished the Great Prostitute who corrupted the earth with her sin; and he has avenged the murder of his servants." [3]Again and again their voices rang, "Praise the Lord! The smoke from her burning ascends forever and forever!" [4]Then the twenty-four Elders and four Living Beings fell down and worshiped God, who was sitting upon the throne, and said, "Amen! Hallelujah! Praise the Lord!" [5]And out of the throne came a voice that said, "Praise our God, all you his servants, small and great, who fear him." [6]Then I heard again what sounded like the shouting of a huge crowd, or like the waves of a hundred oceans crashing on the shore, or like the mighty rolling of great thunder, "Praise the Lord. For the Lord our God, the Almighty, reigns. [7]Let us be glad and rejoice and honor him; for the time has come for the wedding banquet of the Lamb, and his bride has prepared herself."

PRAYER *Miscellany of Minor Sub-Topics; Unclassified Scriptures Relating to; Answer to, Promised; Answered; Instances of Answered; Confession in; Importunity in; Instances of Importunity in; Intercessory; Of the Wicked Not Heard; Pleas Offered in; Thanksgiving before Taking Food.*

MISCELLANY OF MINOR SUB-TOPICS. Attitudes in, see *Worship.* Prayer test proposed by Elijah, 1 Kgs 18:24–39.

Daily in the morning, Ps 5:3; 88:13; 143:8; twice daily, Ps 88:1; thrice daily, Ps 55:17; Dan 6:10; all night, Lk 6:12; without stopping, 1 Thess 5:17.

Boldness in: Commanded, Heb 4:16. Exemplified by Abraham in his request concerning Sodom, Gen 18:22–32; by Moses, asking for assistance in delivering Israel, Ex 33:12, 18. Secret, Gen 24:63; Mt 6:6. Weeping in, Ezra 10:1. In loud voice, satirized by Elijah, 1 Kgs 18:27. Long: Of Pharisees, Mt 23:13, 14; scribes, Mk 12:40; Lk 20:47. Profuse, to be avoided, Eccl 5:1–3; Mt 6:7, 8. Vain repetitions of, to be avoided, Mt 6:7, 8.

Signs asked for, as assurance of answer: By Abraham's servant, Gen 24:14. Gideon asks for a sign of dew on a fleece, Judg 6:36–40.

Rebuked: Of Moses, at the Red Sea, Ex 14:15, when he prayed to see Canaan, Deut 3:23–27; of Joshua, Josh 7:10, 11.

Evils averted by, Jer 26:19.

Unbelief in, Job 21:15.

"Lord's Prayer," Mt 6:9–13; Lk 11:2–4.

Answer to, withheld: Of Balaam, Deut 23:5; Josh 24:10; of Job, Job 30:20, with 42:12; of the Israelites, when attacked by the Amorites, Deut 1:45. The prayer of Jesus, "Let this cup be taken away," Mt 26:39, 42, 44, with *vs.* 45–75 and chapter 27.

Answer to, delayed, Ps 22:1, 2; 40:1; 80:4; 88:14; Jer 42:7; Hab 1:2; Lk 18:7.

Answer to, exceeds request: Solomon asked wisdom; the answer included wisdom, riches, honor, and long life, 1 Kgs 3:7–14; 2 Chron 1:10–12. The disciples prayed for Peter; the answer included Peter's deliverance, Acts 12:15, with *v.* 5.

Answer to, different from the request: Moses asked to be permitted to cross Jordan; the answer was permission to view the Promised land, Deut 3:23–27. The Israelites lusted for the foods of Egypt; the answer gave them food, but also leanness of soul, Ps 106:14, 15. Martha and Mary asked Jesus to come and heal their brother Lazarus; Jesus delayed, but raised Lazarus from the dead, Jn 11. Paul asked that the thorn in the flesh be removed; the answer was a promise of strength to endure it, 2 Cor 12:8, 9.

In behalf of nations, see *Nations, Prayer for.*

Penitential: Of David, Ps 51:1–17; the tax collector, Lk 18:13. See *Prayer, Confession in,* below, and *Sin, Confession of.*

Imprecatory: Num 16:15; 22:5–11; 23:7–10; 24:3–10; Deut 11:29, 30; 27:11–13; 33:11; Josh 8:33, 34; Judg 16:28; 2 Sam 16:10–12; Neh 4:4, 5; 5:13; Job 3:1–10; 27:7; Ps 5:10; 6:10; 9:20; 10:2, 15; 25:3; 28:4; 31:17, 18; 35:4, 8, 26; 40:14, 15; 54:5; 55:9, 15; 56:7; 58:7; 59:5, 11, 14, 15; 68:1, 2; 69:23, 24, 27, 28; 70:2, 3; 71:13; 79:10, 12; 83:13–17; 94:1, 2; 109:7, 9–20, 28, 29; 119:78, 84; 129:5; 140:9, 10; 143:12; 144:6; Jer 11:20; 12:3; 15:15; 17:18; 18:21–23; 20:12; Lam 1:22; 3:64–66; Gal 1:8, 9; 2 Tim 4:14, 15.

Submission in: Exemplified by Jesus, Mt 26:39; Mk 14:36; Lk 22:41, 42; David, 2 Sam 12:22, 23; Job, Job 1:20, 21.

Private, commanded: Mt 6:6.

Exemplified: By Lot, Gen 19:18–20. Eliezer, Gen 15:2, 3; 24:12. Jacob, Gen 32:9–12. Gideon, Judg 6:22, 36, 39. Hannah, 1 Sam 1:10. David, 2 Sam 7:18–29. Hezekiah, 2 Kgs 20:2, 3. Isaiah, 2 Kgs 20:11. Manasseh, 2 Chron 33:18, 19. Ezra, Ezra 9:5, 6. Nehemiah, Neh 2:4. Jeremiah, Jer 32:16–25. Daniel, Dan 9:3, 19. Jonah, Jon 2:1. Habakkuk, Hab 1:2. Anna, Lk 2:36, 37. Jesus, Mt 14:23, 24; 26:36, 39; Mk 1:35; Lk 9:18, 29. Paul, Acts 9:11. Peter, Acts 9:40; 10:9, 10. Cornelius, Acts 10:30.

Family: By Abraham, Gen 12:5, 8. Jacob, Gen 35:3. Cornelius, Acts 10:2.

Social: Mt 18:19, 20; Acts 1:13, 14; 16:25; 20:36; 21:5. Held in private homes, Acts 1:13, 14; 12:12; in the Temple, Acts 2:46; 3:1.

Of Jesus: On a hill, Mt 14:23, 24; Mk 6:46; Lk 6:12; 9:28. In Gethsemane, Mt 26:36; Mk 14:32; Lk 22:39–45. The Lord's prayer, Mt 6:9; Lk 11:1. Before day, Mk 1:35. In distress, Jn 12:27; Heb 5:7. In the wilderness, Lk 5:16. In behalf of Peter, Lk 22:31, 32. For the Comforter, Jn 14:15, 16. After the supper, Jn 17.

Of the apostles: Acts 1:24, 25.

To idols, 1 Kgs 18:26–29.

UNCLASSIFIED SCRIPTURES RELATING TO. Gen 32:24. And was there alone; and a Man wrestled with him until dawn. [25]And when the Man saw that he couldn't win the match, he struck Jacob's hip, and knocked it out of joint at the socket. [26]Then the Man said, "Let me go, for it is dawn." But Jacob panted, "I will not let you go until you bless me." [27]"What is your name?" the Man asked. "Jacob," was the reply. [28]"It isn't anymore!" the Man told him. "It is Israel—one who has power with God. Because you have been strong with God, you shall prevail with men." Hos 12:4.

1 Chron 16:11. Seek the Lord; yes, seek his strength and seek his face untiringly. [35]Cry out to him, "Oh, save us, God of our salvation; bring us safely back from among the nations. Then we will thank your holy name, and triumph in your praise."

2 Chron 7:14. Then if my people will humble themselves and pray, and search for me, and turn from their wicked ways, I will hear them from heaven and forgive their sins and heal their land.

Neh 4:9. But we prayed to our God and guarded the city day and night to protect ourselves.

Ps 27:8. My heart has heard you say, "Come and talk with me, O my people." And my heart responds, "Lord, I am coming."

Ps 105:3. Glory in the Lord; O worshipers of God, rejoice.

Ps 145:18. He is close to all who call on him sincerely.

Prov 15:8. The Lord hates the gifts of the wicked, but delights in the prayers of his people.

Eccl 5:2. Don't be a fool who doesn't even realize it is sinful to make rash promises to God, for he is in heaven and you are only here on earth, so let your words be few.

Isa 55:6. Seek the Lord while you can find him. Call upon him now while he is near.

Lam 3:41. Let us lift our hearts and hands to him in heaven.

Zech 12:10. Then I will pour out the spirit of grace and prayer on all the people of Jerusalem, and they will look on him they pierced, and mourn for him as for an only son, and grieve bitterly for him as for an oldest child who died.

Mt 6:5. And now about prayer. When you pray, don't be like the hypocrites who pretend piety by praying publicly on street corners and in the synagogues where everyone can see them. Truly, that is all the reward they will ever get. [6]But when you pray, go away by yourself, all alone, and shut the door behind you and pray to your Father secretly, and your Father, who knows your secrets, will reward you. [7, 8]Don't recite the same prayer over and over as the heathen do, who think prayers are answered only by repeating them again and again. Remember, your Father knows exactly what you need even before you ask him! [9]Pray along these lines: "Our Father in heaven, we honor your holy name. [10]We ask that your kingdom will come now. May your will be done here on earth, just as it is in heaven. [11]Give us our food again today, as usual, [12]and forgive us our sins, just as we have forgiven those who have sinned against us. [13]Don't bring us into temptation, but deliver us from the Evil One. Amen."

Mt 7:7. Ask, and you will be given what you ask for. Seek, and you will find. Knock, and the door will be opened. [8]For everyone who asks, receives. Anyone who seeks, finds. If only you will knock, the door will open. Mt 21:22; Mk 11:24.

Mk 9:28. Afterwards, when Jesus was alone in the house with his disciples, they asked him, "Why couldn't we cast that demon out?" [29]Jesus replied, "Cases like this require prayer."

Lk 11:1. Once when Jesus had been out praying, one of his disciples came to him as he finished and said, "Lord, teach us a prayer to recite just as John taught one to his disciples." [2]And this is the prayer he taught them: "Father, may your name be honored for its holiness; send your Kingdom soon. [3]Give us our food day by day. [4]And forgive our sins—for we have forgiven those who sinned against us. And don't allow us to be tempted." [5, 6]Then teaching them more about prayer, he used this illustration: "Suppose you went to a friend's house at midnight, wanting to borrow three loaves of bread. You would shout up to him, 'A friend of mine has just arrived for a visit and I've nothing to give him to eat.' [7]He would call down from his bedroom, 'Please don't ask me to get up. The door is locked for the night and we are all in bed. I just can't help you this time.' [8]But I'll tell you this—though he won't do it as a friend, if you keep knocking long enough he will get up and give you everything you want—just because of your persistence. [9]And so it is with prayer—keep on asking and you will keep on getting; keep on looking and you will keep on finding; knock and the door will be opened. [10]Everyone who asks, receives; all who seek, find; and the door is opened to everyone who knocks. [11]You men who are fathers—if your boy asks for bread, do you give him a stone? If he asks for fish, do you give him a snake? [12]If he asks for an egg, do you give him a scorpion? (Of course not!) [13]And if even sinful persons like yourselves give children what they need, don't you realize that your heavenly Father will do at least as much, and give the Holy Spirit to those who ask for him?"

Lk 18:1. One day Jesus told his disciples a story to illustrate their need for constant prayer and to show them that they must keep praying until the answer comes.

Rom 8:26. And in the same way—by our faith—the Holy Spirit helps us with our daily problems and in our praying. For we don't even know what we should pray for, nor how to pray as we should; but the Holy Spirit prays for us with such feeling that it cannot be expressed in words.

1 Cor 14:15. Well, then, what shall I do? I will do both. I will pray in unknown tongues and also in ordinary language that everyone understands. I will sing in unknown tongues and also in ordinary language, so that I can understand the praise I am giving.

Eph 3:11. In just the way he had always planned it through Jesus Christ our Lord. [12]Now we can come fearlessly right into God's presence, assured of his glad welcome when we come with Christ and trust in him.

Eph 6:18. Pray all the time. Ask God for anything in line with the Holy Spirit's wishes. Plead with him, reminding him of your needs, and keep praying earnestly for all Christians everywhere. [19]Pray for me, too, and ask God to give me the right words as I boldly tell others about the Lord, and as I explain to them that his salvation is for the Gentiles too.

Phil 4:6. Don't worry about anything; instead, pray about everything; tell God your needs and don't forget to thank him for his answers.

Col 4:2. Don't be weary in prayer; keep at it; watch for God's answers and remember to be thankful when they come.

1 Thess 5:17. Always keep on praying. *v.* 25.

1 Tim 2:8. So I want men everywhere to pray with holy hands lifted up to God, free from sin and anger and resentment.

Heb 4:16. So let us come boldly to the very throne of God and stay there to receive his mercy and to find grace to help us in our times of need.

Jas 5:16. Admit your faults to one another and pray for each other so that you may be healed. The earnest prayer of a righteous man has great power and wonderful results.

Jude 1:20. But you, dear friends, must build up your lives ever more strongly upon the foundation of our holy faith, learning to pray in the power and strength of the Holy Spirit.

Rev 5:8. And as he took the scroll, the twenty-four Elders fell down before the Lamb, each with a harp and golden vials filled with incense—the prayers of God's people!

Rev 8:3. Then another angel with a golden censer came and stood at the altar; and a great quantity of incense was given to him to mix with the prayers of God's people, to offer upon the golden altar before the throne. [4]And the perfume of the incense mixed with prayers ascended up to God from the altar where the angel had poured them out.

ANSWER TO, PROMISED. Ex 6:5. And now I have heard the groanings of the people of Israel, in slavery now to the Egyptians, and I remember my promise. Acts 7:34.

Ex 22:23. If you do so in any way, and they cry to me for my help, I will surely give it. [27]For it is probably his only warmth; how can he sleep without it? If you don't return it, and he cries to me for help, I will hear and be very gracious to him (at your expense), for I am very compassionate.

Ex 33:17. And the Lord had replied to Moses, "Yes, I will do what you have asked, for you have certainly found favor with me, and you are my friend." [18]Then Moses asked to see God's glory. [19]The Lord replied, "I will make my goodness pass before you, and I will announce to you the meaning of my name Jehovah, the Lord. I show kindness and mercy to anyone I want to. [20]But you may not see the glory of my face, for man may not see me and live."

Deut 4:7. For what other nation, great or small, has God among them, as the Lord our God is here among us whenever we call upon him? [29]But you will also begin to search again for Jehovah your God, and you shall find him when you search for him with all your hearts and souls. [30]When those bitter days have come upon you in the latter times, you will finally return to the Lord your God and listen to what he tells you. [31]For the Lord your God is merciful—he will not abandon you nor destroy you nor forget the promises he has made to your ancestors.

1 Chron 28:9. Solomon, my son, get to know the God of your fathers. Worship and serve him with a clean heart and a willing mind, for the Lord sees every heart and understands and knows every thought. If you seek him, you will find him; but if you forsake him, he will permanently throw you aside.

2 Chron 7:13. If I shut up the heavens so that

there is no rain, or if I command the locust swarms to eat up all of your crops, or if I send an epidemic among you, [14]then if my people will humble themselves and pray, and search for me, and turn from their wicked ways, I will hear them from heaven and forgive their sins and heal their land. [15]I will listen, wide awake, to every prayer made in this place. 1 Kgs 8:22–53; 2 Chron 6.

Job 8:5. And you begged Almighty God for them—[6]if you were pure and good, he would hear your prayer, and answer you, and bless you with a happy home.

Job 12:4. I, the man who begged God for help, and God answered him, have become a laughingstock to my neighbors. Yes, I, a righteous man, am now the man they scoff at.

Job 22:27. You will pray to him, and he will hear you, and you will fulfill all your promises to him.

Job 33:26. And when he prays to God, God will hear and answer and receive him with joy, and return him to his duties.

Ps 9:10. All those who know your mercy, Lord, will count on you for help. For you have never yet forsaken those who trust in you. [12]He who avenges murder has an open ear to those who cry to him for justice. He does not ignore the prayers of men in trouble when they call to him for help.

Ps 10:17. Lord, you know the hopes of humble people. Surely you will hear their cries and comfort their hearts by helping them.

Ps 18:3. All I need to do is cry to him—oh, praise the Lord—and I am saved from all my enemies!

Ps 32:6. Now I say that each believer should confess his sins to God when he is aware of them, while there is time to be forgiven. Judgment will not touch him if he does.

Ps 34:15. For the eyes of the Lord are intently watching all who live good lives, and he gives attention when they cry to him. [17]Yes, the Lord hears the good man when he calls to him for help, and saves him out of all his troubles.

Ps 37:4. Be delighted with the Lord. Then he will give you all your heart's desires. [5]Commit everything you do to the Lord. Trust him to help you do it and he will.

Ps 38:15. For I am waiting for you, O Lord my God. Come and protect me.

Ps 50:14, 15. What I want from you is your true thanks; I want your promises fulfilled. *I want you to trust me in your times of trouble, so I can rescue you, and you can give me glory.*

Ps 55:16. But I will call upon the Lord to save me —and he will. [17]I will pray morning, noon, and night, pleading aloud with God; and he will hear and answer.

Ps 56:9. The very day I call for help, the tide of battle turns. My enemies flee! This one thing I *know: God is for me!*

Ps 65:2. And because you answer prayer, all mankind will come to you with their requests. [5]With dread deeds and awesome power you will defend us from our enemies, O God who saves us. You are the only hope of all mankind throughout the world and far away upon the sea.

Ps 69:33. For Jehovah hears the cries of his needy ones, and does not look the other way.

Ps 81:10. Open your mouth wide and see if I won't fill it.

Ps 86:5. O Lord, you are so good and kind, so ready to forgive; so full of mercy for all who ask your aid. [6]Listen closely to my prayer, O God. Hear my urgent cry. [7]I will call to you whenever trouble strikes, and you will help me.

Ps 91:15. When he calls on me I will answer; I will be with him in trouble, and rescue him and honor him.

Ps 102:17. He will listen to the prayers of the destitute, for he is never too busy to heed their requests. [18]I am recording this so that future generations will also praise the Lord for all that he has done. And a people that shall be created shall praise the Lord. [19]Tell them that God looked down from his temple in heaven, [20]and heard the groans of his people in slavery—they were children of death—and released them.

Ps 145:18. He is close to all who call on him sincerely. [19]He fulfills the desires of those who reverence and trust him; he hears their cries for help and rescues them.

Prov 2:3–5. Yes, if you want better insight and discernment, and are searching for them as you would for lost money or hidden treasure, then wisdom will be given you, and knowledge of God himself; you will soon learn the importance of reverence for the Lord and of trusting him.

Prov 3:6. In everything you do, put God first, and he will direct you and crown your efforts with success.

Prov 10:24. The wicked man's fears will all come true, and so will the good man's hopes.

Prov 15:8. The Lord hates the gifts of the wicked, but delights in the prayers of his people. [29]The Lord is far from the wicked, but he hears the prayers of the righteous.

Prov 16:1. We can make our plans, but the final outcome is in God's hands.

Isa 19:20. This will be for a sign of loyalty to the Lord of Hosts; then when they cry to the Lord for help against those who oppress them, he will send them a Savior—and he shall deliver them.

Isa 30:19. O my people in Jerusalem, you shall weep no more, for he will surely be gracious to you at the sound of your cry. He will answer you.

Isa 55:6. Seek the Lord while you can find him. Call upon him now while he is near.

Isa 58:9. Then, when you call, the Lord will answer. "Yes, I am here," he will quickly reply. All you need to do is to stop oppressing the weak, and to stop making false accusations and spreading vicious rumors!

Isa 65:24. I will answer them before they even call to me. While they are still talking to me about their needs, I will go ahead and answer their prayers!

Jer 29:12. In those days when you pray, I will

listen. [13]You will find me when you seek me, if you look for me in earnest.

Jer 31:9. Tears of joy will stream down their faces, and I will lead them home with great care. They shall walk beside the quiet streams and not stumble. For I am a Father to Israel, and Ephraim is my oldest child.

Jer 33:3. Ask me and I will tell you some remarkable secrets about what is going to happen here.

Lam 3:25. The Lord is wonderfully good to those who wait for him, to those who seek for him.

Ezk 36:37. The Lord God says: I am ready to hear Israel's prayers for these blessings, and to grant them their requests. Let them but ask and I will multiply them like the flocks that fill Jerusalem's streets at time of sacrifice.

Joel 2:18. Then the Lord will pity his people and be indignant for the honor of his land! [19]He will reply, "See, I am sending you much corn and wine and oil, to fully satisfy your need. No longer will I make you a laughingstock among the nations." [32]"Everyone who calls upon the name of the Lord will be saved; even in Jerusalem some will escape, just as the Lord has promised, for he has chosen some to survive."

Amos 5:4. The Lord says to the people of Israel, "Seek me—and live. [5]Don't seek the idols of Bethel, Gilgal, or Beer-sheba; for the people of Gilgal will be carried off to exile, and those of Bethel shall surely come to grief." [6]Seek the Lord and live, or else he will sweep like fire through Israel and consume her, and none of the idols in Bethel can put it out.

Zeph 2:3. Beg him to save you, all who are humble—all who have tried to obey. Walk humbly and do what is right; perhaps even yet the Lord will protect you from his wrath in that day of doom.

Zech 10:1. Ask the Lord for rain in the springtime, and he will answer with lightning and showers. Every field will become a lush pasture. [6]"I will strengthen Judah, yes, and Israel too; I will reestablish them because I love them. It will be as though I had never cast them all away for I, the Lord their God, will hear their cries."

Zech 13:9. I will bring the third that remain through the fire and make them pure, as gold and silver are refined and purified by fire. They will call upon my name and I will hear them; I will say, "These are my people," and they will say, "The Lord is our God."

Mt 6:5. And now about prayer. When you pray, don't be like the hypocrites who pretend piety by praying publicly on street corners and in the synagogues where everyone can see them. Truly, that is all the reward they will ever get. [6]But when you pray, go away by yourself, all alone, and shut the door behind you and pray to your Father secretly, and your Father, who knows your secrets, will reward you. [7, 8]Don't recite the same prayer over and over as the heathen do, who think prayers are answered only by repeating them again and again. Remember, your Father knows exactly what you need even before you ask him! [9]Pray along these lines: 'Our Father in heaven, we honor your holy name. *vs.* 9–13.

Mt 7:7. Ask, and you will be given what you ask for. Seek, and you will find. Knock, and the door will be opened. [8]For everyone who asks, receives. Anyone who seeks, finds. If only you will knock, the door will open. [9]If a child asks his father for a loaf of bread, will he be given a stone instead? [10]If he asks for fish, will he be given a poisonous snake? Of course not! [11]And if you hardhearted, sinful men know how to give good gifts to your children, won't your Father in heaven even more certainly give good gifts to those who ask him for them?

Mt 18:19. I also tell you this—if two of you agree down here on earth concerning anything you ask for, my Father in heaven will do it for you. [20]For where two or three gather together because they are mine, I will be right there among them.

Mt 21:22. You can get anything—*anything* you ask for in prayer—if you believe."

Mk 11:24. Listen to me! You can pray for *anything,* and *if you believe, you have it;* it's yours! [25]But when you are praying, first forgive anyone you are holding a grudge against, so that your Father in heaven will forgive you your sins too.

Lk 11:13. And if even sinful persons like yourselves give children what they need, don't you realize that your heavenly Father will do at least as much, and give the Holy Spirit to those who ask for him? *vs.* 5–12.

Lk 18:6. Then the Lord said, "If even an evil judge can be worn down like that, [7]don't you think that God will surely give justice to his people who plead with him day and night? [8]Yes! He will answer them quickly! But the question is, When I, the Messiah, return, how many will I find who have faith (and are praying)?" *vs.* 1–5.

Jn 4:10. He replied, "If you only knew what a wonderful gift God has for you, and who I am, you would ask me for some living water!" [23, 24]For it's not *where* we worship that counts, but *how* we worship—is our worship spiritual and real? Do we have the Holy Spirit's help? For God is Spirit, and we must have his help to worship as we should. The Father wants this kind of worship from us.

Jn 9:31. Well, God doesn't listen to evil men, but he has open ears to those who worship him and do his will.

Jn 14:13. You can ask him for *anything,* using my name, and I will do it, for this will bring praise to the Father because of what I, the Son, will do for you. [14]Yes, ask *anything,* using my name, and I will do it!

Jn 15:7. But if you stay in me and obey my commands, you may ask any request you like, and it will be granted! [16]You didn't choose me! I chose you! I appointed you to go and produce lovely fruit always, so that no matter what you ask for from the Father, using my name, he will give it to you.

Jn 16:23. At that time you won't need to ask me for anything, for you can go directly to the Father and ask him, and he will give you what you ask for because you use my name. [24]You haven't tried this before, (but begin now). Ask, using my name, and you will receive, and your cup of joy will overflow. [26]Then you will present your petitions over my signature! And I won't need to ask the Father to grant you these requests, [27]for the Father himself loves you dearly because you love me and believe that I came from the Father.

Acts 22:16. And now, why delay? Go and be baptized, and be cleansed from your sins, calling on the name of the Lord.

Rom 8:26. And in the same way—by our faith—the Holy Spirit helps us with our daily problems and in our praying. For we don't even know what we should pray for, now how to pray as we should; but the Holy Spirit prays for us with such feeling that it cannot be expressed in words.

Rom 10:12. Jew and Gentile are the same in this respect: they all have the same Lord who generously gives his riches to all those who ask him for them. [13]Anyone who calls upon the name of the Lord will be saved.

Eph 2:18. Now all of us, whether Jews or Gentiles, may come to God the Father with the Holy Spirit's help because of what Christ has done for us.

Eph 3:20. Now glory be to God who by his mighty power at work within us is able to do far more than we would ever dare to ask or even dream of—infinitely beyond our highest prayers, desires, thoughts, or hopes.

Heb 4:16. So let us come boldly to the very throne of God and stay there to receive his mercy and to find grace to help us in our times of need.

Heb 10:22. Let us go right in, to God himself, with true hearts fully trusting him to receive us, because we have been sprinkled with Christ's blood to make us clean, and because our bodies have been washed with pure water. [23]Now we can look forward to the salvation God has promised us. There is no longer any room for doubt, and we can tell others that salvation is ours, for there is no question that he will do what he says.

Heb 11:6. You can never please God without faith, without depending on him. Anyone who wants to come to God must believe that there is a God and that he rewards those who sincerely look for him.

Jas 1:5. If you want to know what God wants you to do, ask him, and he will gladly tell you, for he is always ready to give a bountiful supply of wisdom to all who ask him; he will not resent it. [6]But when you ask him, be sure that you really expect him to tell you, for a doubtful mind will be as unsettled as a wave of the sea that is driven and tossed by the wind; [7, 8]and every decision you then make will be uncertain, as you turn first this way, and then that. If you don't ask with faith, don't expect the Lord to give you any solid answer.

Jas 4:8. And when you draw close to God, God will draw close to you. Wash your hands, you sinners, and let your hearts be filled with God alone to make them pure and true to him. [10]Then when you realize your worthlessness before the Lord, he will lift you up, encourage and help you.

Jas 5:16. Admit your faults to one another and pray for each other so that you may be healed. The earnest prayer of a righteous man has great power and wonderful results.

1 Jn 3:22. And whatever we ask for because we are obeying him and doing the things that please him.

1 Jn 5:14. And we are sure of this, that he will listen to us whenever we ask him for anything in line with his will. [15]And if we really know he is listening when we talk to him and make our requests, then we can be sure that he will answer us.

ANSWERED. Job 34:28. Causing the cry of the poor to come to the attention of God. Yes, he hears the cries of those being oppressed.

Ps 3:4. I cried out to the Lord, and he heard me from his Temple in Jerusalem.

Ps 4:1. O God, you have declared me perfect in your eyes, you have always cared for me in my distress; now hear me as I call again. Have mercy on me. Hear my prayer.

Ps 6:8. Go, leave me now, you men of evil deeds, for the Lord has heard my weeping [9]and my pleading. He will answer all my prayers.

Ps 18:6. In my distress I screamed to the Lord for his help. And he heard me from heaven, my cry reached his ears. Ps 120:1.

Ps 21:2. For you have given him his heart's desire, everything he asks you for!

Ps 22:4. The praises of our fathers surrounded your throne; they trusted you and you delivered them. [5]You heard their cries for help and saved them; they were never disappointed when they sought your aid. [24]"For he has not despised my cries of deep despair; he has not turned and walked away. When I cried to him, he heard and came."

Ps 28:6. Oh, praise the Lord, for he has listened to my pleadings!

Ps 30:2. O Lord, my God, I pleaded with you, and you gave me my health again. [3]You brought me back from the brink of the grave, from death itself, and here I am alive!

Ps 31:22. I spoke too hastily when I said, "The Lord has deserted me," for you listened to my plea and answered me.

Ps 34:4. For I cried to him and he answered me! He freed me from all my fears. [5]Others too were radiant at what he did for them. Theirs was no downcast look of rejection! [6]This poor man cried to the Lord—and the Lord heard him and saved him out of his troubles.

Ps 40:1. I waited patiently for God to help me; then he listened and heard my cry.

Ps 66:19. But he listened! He heard my prayer! He paid attention to it! [20]Blessed be God who didn't turn away when I was praying, and didn't refuse me his kindness and love.

Ps 77:1. I cry to the Lord; I call and call to him. Oh, that he would listen. [2]I am in deep trouble and I need his help so badly. All night long I pray, lifting my hands to heaven, pleading. There can be no joy for me until he acts.

Ps 81:7. He said, "You cried to me in trouble and I saved you; I answered from Mount Sinai where the thunder hides. I tested your faith at Meribah, when you complained there was no water."

Ps 99:6. When Moses and Aaron and Samuel, his prophet, cried to him for help, he answered them. [7]He spoke to them from the pillar of cloud and they followed his instructions. [8]O Jehovah our God! You answered them and forgave their sins, yet punished them when they went wrong.

Ps 106:44. Yet, even so, he listened to their cries and heeded their distress.

Ps 107:6. "Lord, help!" they cried, and he did! [7]He led them straight to safety and a place to live. *vs.* 13–20.

Ps 116:1. I love the Lord because he hears my prayers and answers them. [2]Because he bends down and listens, I will pray as long as I breathe!

Ps 118:5. In my distress I prayed to the Lord and he answered me and rescued me. [21]O Lord, thank you so much for answering my prayer and saving me.

Ps 119:26. I told you my plans and you replied. Now give me your instructions.

Ps 138:3. When I pray, you answer me, and encourage me by giving me the strength I need.

Lam 3:57. Yes, you came at my despairing cry and told me not to fear. [58]O Lord, you are my lawyer! Plead my case! For you have redeemed my life.

Hos 12:4. Yes, he wrestled with the Angel and prevailed. He wept and pleaded for a blessing from him. He met God there at Bethel face to face. God spoke to him.

Jon 2:1. Then Jonah prayed to the Lord his God from inside the fish: [2]"In my great trouble I cried to the Lord and he answered me; from the depths of death I called, and Lord, you heard me! [7]When I had lost all hope, I turned my thoughts once more to the Lord. And my earnest prayer went to you in your holy Temple."

Lk 23:42. Then he said, "Jesus, remember me when you come into your Kingdom." [43]And Jesus replied, "Today you will be with me in Paradise. This is a solemn promise."

Acts 4:31. After this prayer, the building where they were meeting shook and they were all filled with the Holy Spirit and boldly preached God's message.

2 Cor 12:8. Three different times I begged God to make me well again. [9]Each time he said, "No. But I am with you; that is all you need. My power shows up best in weak people."

Jas 5:17. Elijah was as completely human as we are, and yet when he prayed earnestly that no rain would fall, none fell for the next three and one half years! [18]Then he prayed again, this time that it *would* rain, and down it poured and the grass turned green and the gardens began to grow again.

INSTANCES OF ANSWERED. Cain, Gen 4:13–15. Abraham, for a son, Gen 15; pleading for Sodom, Gen 18:23–33; for Ishmael, Gen 17:20; for Abimelech, Gen 20:17. Hagar, for deliverance, Gen 16:7–13. Abraham's servant, for guidance, Gen 24:12–52. Rebekah, concerning her pains in pregnancy, Gen 25:22, 23. Jacob, for deliverance from Esau, Gen 32:8–32; 33:1–17. Moses, for help at the Red Sea, Ex 14:15, 16; at the water of Marah, Ex 15:25; at Horeb, Ex 17:4–6; in the battle with the Amalekites, Ex 17:8–14; concerning the murmuring of the Israelites for meat, Num 11:11–35; in behalf of Miriam's leprosy, Num 12:13–15. Moses, Aaron, and Samuel, Ps 99:6.

Israelites: for deliverance from slavery, Ex 2:23–25; 3:7–10; Acts 7:34; from Pharaoh's army, Ex 14:10–30; from Cushan-rishathaim, Judg 3:9, 15; Sisera, Judg 4:2, 3, 23, 24; 1 Sam 12:9–11; Ammon, Judg 10:6–18; 11:1–33; for God's favor under the reproofs of Azariah, 2 Chron 15:1–15; from Babylonian slavery, Neh 9:27.

Gideon, asking the token of dew, Judg 6:36–40. Manoah, asking about Samson, Judg 13:8, 9. Samson, asking for strength, Judg 16:28–30. Hannah, asking for a child, 1 Sam 1:10–17, 19, 20. David, asking whether Keilah would surrender to him, 1 Sam 23:10–12; at Ziklag, 1 Sam 30:8; whether he should go into Judah after Saul's death, 2 Sam 2:1; whether he should go against the Philistines, 2 Sam 5:19–25. David, in adversity, Ps 118:5; 138:3. Solomon, asking wisdom, 1 Kgs 3:1–13; 9:2, 3. Elijah, raising the widow's son, 1 Kgs 17:22; asking fire on his sacrifice, 1 Kgs 18:36–38; rain, 1 Kgs 17:1; 18:1, 42–45; Jas 5:17. Elisha, leading the Syrian army, 2 Kgs 6:17–20. Jabez, asking for prosperity, 1 Chron 4:10. Abijah, for victory over Jeroboam, 2 Chron 13:13–17. Asa, for victory over Zerah, 2 Chron 14:11–15. The people of Judah, 2 Chron 15:15. Jehoshaphat, for victory over the Canaanites, 2 Chron 18:31; 20:6–27. Jehoahaz, for victory over Hazael, 2 Kgs 13:4. Priests and Levites, when blessing the people, 2 Chron 30:27. Hezekiah and Isaiah, for deliverance from Sennacherib, 2 Kgs 19:14–20; 2 Chron 32:20–23; to save Hezekiah's life, 2 Kgs 20:1–7, 11; 2 Chron 32:24. Manasseh, for deliverance from the king of Babylon, 2 Chron 33:13, 19. Reubenites, for deliverance from the Hagrites, 1 Chron 5:20. The Jews, returning from the captivity, Ezra 8:21, 23. Ezekiel, to have the baking of his bread of affliction changed, Ezk 4:12–15. Daniel, for the interpretation of Nebuchadnezzar's dream, Dan 2:19–23; interceding for the people, Dan 9:20–23; in a vision, Dan 10:12. Zacharias, for a son, Lk 1:13. The leper, for healing, Mt 8:2, 3; Mk 1:40–42; Lk 5:12, 13. Roman army captain, for his slave, Mt 8:5–13; Lk 7:3–10; Jn 4:50, 51. Peter, asking that Dorcas be restored, Acts 9:40. The disciples, for Peter, Acts 12:5–17. Paul, to be restored to health, 2 Cor 1:9–11.

CONFESSION IN. Lev 5:5. In any of these cases, he shall confess his sin.

Lev 26:40. But at last they shall confess their sins and their fathers' sins of treachery against me. (Because they were against me, I was against them, and brought them into the land of their enemies.)

Num 5:5, 6. Then the Lord said to Moses, "Tell the people of Israel that when anyone, man or woman, betrays the Lord by betraying a trust, it is sin. [7]He must confess his sin and make full repayment for what he has stolen, adding twenty percent and returning it to the person he took it from."

Judg 10:10. Finally the Israelis turned to Jehovah again and begged him to save them. "We have sinned against you and have forsaken you as our God and have worshiped idols," they confessed. [15]But they pleaded with him again and said, "We have sinned. Punish us in any way you think best, only save us once more from our enemies."

1 Sam 12:10. Then they cried to the Lord again and confessed that they had sinned by turning away from him and worshiping the Baal and Ashtaroth idols. And they pleaded, "We will worship you and you alone if you will only rescue us from our enemies."

1 Kgs 8:47. And they come to their senses and turn to you and cry to you saying, "We have sinned, we have done wrong."

Ezra 9:6. And cried out, "O my God, I am ashamed; I blush to lift up my face to you, for our sins are piled higher than our heads and our guilt is as boundless as the heavens. [15]O Lord God of Israel, you are a just God; what hope can we have if you give us justice as we stand here before you in our wickedness?"

Neh 1:6, 7. Listen carefully to what I say! Look down and see me praying night and day for your people Israel. I confess that we have sinned against you; yes, I and my people have committed the horrible sin of not obeying the commandments you gave us through your servant Moses.

Neh 9:2. And the Israelis separated themselves from all foreigners. [3]. . . They took turns confessing their own sins and those of their ancestors. [33]Every time you punished us you were being perfectly fair; we have sinned so greatly that you gave us only what we deserved. [34]Our kings, princes, priests, and ancestors didn't obey your laws or listen to your warnings. [35]They did not worship you despite the wonderful things you did for them and the great goodness you showered upon them. You gave them a large, fat land, but they refused to turn from their wickedness.

Job 7:20. Has my sin harmed you, O God, Watcher of mankind? Why have you made me your target, and made my life so heavy a burden to me?

Job 40:4. I am nothing—how could I ever find the answers? I lay my hand upon my mouth in silence. [5]I have said too much already.

Ps 31:10. I am pining away with grief; my years are shortened, drained away because of sadness. My sins have sapped my strength; I stoop with sorrow and with shame.

Ps 32:3. There was a time when I wouldn't admit what a sinner I was. But my dishonesty made me miserable and filled my days with frustration. [5]Until I finally admitted all my sins to you and stopped trying to hide them. I said to myself, "I will confess them to the Lord." And you forgave me! All my guilt is gone.

Ps 38:4. They are like a flood, higher than my head; they are a burden too heavy to bear. [5, 6]My wounds are festering and full of pus. Because of my sins I am bent and racked with pain. My days are filled with anguish. [7]My loins burn with inflammation and my whole body is diseased. [8]I am exhausted and crushed; I groan in despair. [10]My heart beats wildly, my strength fails, and I am going blind. [18]I confess my sins; I am sorry for what I have done.

Ps 40:12. For problems far too big for me to solve are piled higher than my head. Meanwhile my sins, too many to count, have all caught up with me and I am ashamed to look up. My heart quails within me.

Ps 51:3. For I admit my shameful deed—it haunts me day and night. [4]It is against you and you alone I sinned, and did this terrible thing. You saw it all, and your sentence against me is just.

Ps 69:5. O God, you know so well how stupid I am, and you know all my sins.

Ps 106:6. Both we and our fathers have sinned so much. [7]They weren't impressed by the wonder of your miracles in Egypt, and soon forgot your many acts of kindness to them. Instead they rebelled against you at the Red Sea.

Ps 119:176. I have wandered away like a lost sheep; come and find me for I have not turned away from your commandments.

Ps 130:3. Lord, if you keep in mind our sins then who can ever get an answer to his prayers?

Prov 28:13. A man who refuses to admit his mistakes can never be successful. But if he confesses and forsakes them, he gets another chance.

Isa 6:5. Then I said, "My doom is sealed, for I am a foul-mouthed sinner, a member of a sinful, foul-mouthed race; and I have looked upon the King, the Lord of heaven's armies."

Isa 59:12. For your sins keep piling up before the righteous God, and testify against you. Yes, we know what sinners we are. [13]We know our disobedience; we have denied the Lord our God. We know what rebels we are and how unfair we are, for we carefully plan our lies.

Jer 3:13. Only acknowledge your guilt; admit that you rebelled against the Lord your God and committed adultery against him by worshiping idols under every tree; confess that you refused to follow me. [25]We lie in shame and in dishonor, for we and our fathers have sinned from childhood against the Lord our God; we have not obeyed him.

Jer 14:7. O Lord, we have sinned against you grievously, yet help us for the sake of your own reputation! [20]O Lord, we confess our wickedness, and that of our fathers too.

Lam 1:18. And the Lord is right, for we rebelled. And yet, O people everywhere, behold and see my anguish and despair, for my sons and daughters are taken far away as slaves to distant lands.

Lam 3:42. For we have sinned; we have rebelled against the Lord, and he has not forgotten it.

Lam 5:16. Our glory is gone. The crown is fallen

from our head. Woe upon us for our sins.

Dan 9:5. But we have sinned so much; we have rebelled against you and scorned your commands. [6]We have refused to listen to your servants the prophets, whom you sent again and again down through the years, with your messages to our kings and princes and to all the people. [7]O Lord, you are righteous; but as for us, we are always shamefaced with sin, just as you see us now; yes, all of us—the men of Judah, the people of Jerusalem, and all Israel, scattered near and far wherever you have driven us because of our disloyalty to you. [8]O Lord, we and our kings and princes and fathers are weighted down with shame because of all our sins. [9]But the Lord our God is merciful, and pardons even those who have rebelled against him. [10]O Lord our God, we have disobeyed you; we have flouted all the laws you gave us through your servants, the prophets. [11]All Israel has disobeyed; we have turned away from you and haven't listened to your voice. And so the awesome curse of God has crushed us—the curse written in the law of Moses your servant. [12]And you have done exactly as you warned us you would do, for never in all history has there been a disaster like what happened at Jerusalem to us and our rulers. [13]Every curse against us written in the law of Moses has come true; all the evils he predicted—all have come. But even so we still refuse to satisfy the Lord our God by turning from our sins and doing right. [14]And so the Lord deliberately crushed us with the calamity he prepared; he is fair in everything he does, but we would not obey. [15]O Lord our God, you brought lasting honor to your name by removing your people from Egypt in a great display of power. Lord, do it again!

IMPORTUNITY IN. Gen 18:23. Then Abraham approached him and said, "Will you kill good and bad alike? [24]Suppose you find fifty godly people within the city—will you destroy it, and not spare it for their sakes? [25]That wouldn't be right! Surely you wouldn't do such a thing, to kill the godly with the wicked! Why, you would be treating godly and wicked exactly the same! Surely you wouldn't do that! Should not the Judge of all the earth be fair?" [26]And God replied, "If I find fifty godly people there, I will spare the entire city for their sake." [27]Then Abraham spoke again. "Since I have begun, let me go on and speak further to the Lord, though I am but dust and ashes. [28]*Suppose there are only forty-five?* Will you destroy the city for lack of five? And God said, "I will not destroy it if I find forty-five." [29]Then Abraham went further with his request. "*Suppose there are only forty?*" And God replied, "I won't destroy it if there are forty." [30]"Please don't be angry," Abraham pleaded. "Let me speak: *suppose only thirty are found there?*" And God replied, "I won't do it if there are thirty there." [31]Then Abraham said, "Since I have dared to speak to God, let me continue—*Suppose there are only twenty?*" And God said, "Then I won't destroy it for the sake of the twenty." [32]Finally, Abraham said, "Oh, let not the Lord be angry; I will speak but this once more! *Suppose only ten are found?*" And God said, "Then, for the sake of the ten, I won't destroy it."

Gen 32:24. Then returned again to the camp and was there alone; and a Man wrestled with him until dawn. [25]And when the Man saw that he couldn't win the match, he struck Jacob's hip, and knocked it out of joint at the socket. [26]Then the Man said, "Let me go, for it is dawn." But Jacob panted, "I will not let you go until you bless me." [27]"What is your name?" the Man asked. "Jacob," was the reply. [28]"It isn't anymore!" the Man told him. "It is Israel—one who has power with God. Because you have been strong with God, you shall prevail with men." [29]"What is *your* name?" Jacob asked him. "No, you mustn't ask," the Man told him. And he blessed him there.

Ex 32:32. Yet now if you will only forgive their sin—and if not, then blot *me* out of the book you have written.

Deut 9:25. That is why I fell down before him for forty days and nights when the Lord was ready to destroy you.

Judg 6:36. Then Gideon said to God, "If you are really going to use me to save Israel as you promised, [37]prove it to me in this way: I'll put some wool on the threshing floor tonight, and if, in the morning, the fleece is wet and the ground is dry, I will know you are going to help me!" [38]And it happened just that way! When he got up the next morning he pressed the fleece together and wrung out a whole bowlful of water! [39]Then Gideon said to the Lord, "Please don't be angry with me, but let me make one more test: this time let the fleece remain dry while the ground around it is wet!" [40]So the Lord did as he asked; that night the fleece stayed dry, but the ground was covered with dew!

Judg 16:28. Then Samson prayed to the Lord and said, "O Lord Jehovah, remember me again—please strengthen me one more time, so that I may pay back the Philistines for the loss of at least one of my eyes."

1 Sam 1:10. She was in deep anguish and was crying bitterly as she prayed to the Lord. [11]And she made this vow: "O Lord of heaven, if you will look down upon my sorrow and answer my prayer and give me a son, then I will give him back to you, and he'll be yours for his entire lifetime and his hair shall never be cut."

1 Sam 12:23. As for me, far be it from me that I should sin against the Lord by ending my prayers for you.

1 Kgs 8:22, 23. Then, as all the people watched, Solomon stood before the altar of the Lord with his hands spread out towards heaven and said, "O Lord God of Israel, there is no god like you in heaven or earth, for you are loving and kind and you keep your promises to your people if they do their best to do your will. [24]Today you have fulfilled your promise to my father David, who was your servant; [25]and now, O Lord God of Israel, fulfill your further promise to him: that if his descendants follow your ways and try to do your will as he

did, one of them shall always sit upon the throne of Israel. [26]Yes, O God of Israel, fulfill this promise too. [27]But is it possible that God would really live on earth? Why, even the skies and the highest heavens cannot contain you, much less this Temple I have built! [28]And yet, O Lord my God, you have heard and answered my request: [29]Please watch over this Temple night and day—this place you have promised to live in—and as I face toward the Temple and pray, whether by night or by day, please listen to me and answer my requests. [30]Listen to every plea of the people of Israel whenever they face this place to pray; yes, hear in heaven where you live, and when you hear, forgive."

Ezra 9:5. Finally I stood before the Lord in great embarrassment; then I fell to my knees and lifted my hands to the Lord, [6]and cried out, "O my God, I am ashamed; I blush to lift up my face to you, for our sins are piled higher than our heads and our guilt is as boundless as the heavens."

Neh 1:4. When I heard this, I sat down and cried. In fact, I refused to eat for several days, for I spent the time in prayer to the God of heaven. [5]"O Lord God," I cried out; "O great and awesome God who keeps his promises and is so loving and kind to those who love and obey him! Hear my prayer! [6]Listen carefully to what I say! Look down and see me praying night and day for your people Israel."

Ps 17:1. I am pleading for your help, O Lord; for I have been honest and have done what is right, and you must listen to my earnest cry! [6]Why am I praying like this? Because I know you will answer me, O God! Yes, listen as I pray.

Ps 22:1. My God, my God, why have you forsaken me? Why do you refuse to help me or even to listen to my groans? [2]Day and night I keep on weeping, crying for your help, but there is no reply. [19]O Lord, don't stay away. O God my Strength, hurry to my aid.

Ps 28:1. I plead with you to help me, Lord, for you are my Rock of safety. If you refuse to answer me, I might as well give up and die. [2]Lord, I lift my hands to heaven and implore your help. Oh, listen to my cry.

Ps 35:22. Lord, you know all about it. Don't stay silent! Don't desert me now! [23]Rise up, O Lord my God; vindicate me.

Ps 55:1. Listen to my prayer, O God; don't hide yourself when I cry to you. [2]Hear me, Lord! Listen to me! For I groan and weep beneath my burden of woe. [16]But I will call upon the Lord to save me —and he will. [17]I will pray morning, noon, and night, pleading aloud with God; and he will hear and answer.

Ps 57:2. I will cry to the God of heaven who does such wonders for me.

Ps 61:1. O God, listen to me! Hear my prayer! [2]For wherever I am, though far away at the ends of the earth, I will cry to you for help. When my heart is faint and overwhelmed, lead me to the mighty, towering Rock of safety.

Ps 70:5. But I am in deep trouble. Rush to my aid, for only you can help and save me. O Lord, don't delay.

Ps 86:3. Be merciful, O Lord, for I am looking up to you in constant hope. [6]Listen closely to my prayer, O God. Hear my urgent cry.

Ps 88:1. O Jehovah, God of my salvation, I have wept before you day and night. [2]Now hear my prayers, oh listen to my cry. [9]My eyes grow dim with weeping. Each day I beg your help; O Lord, I reach my pleading hands to you for mercy. [13]O Lord, I plead for my life and will keep on pleading day by day.

Ps 102:1. Lord, hear my prayer! Listen to my plea! [2]Don't turn away from me in this time of my distress. Bend down your ear and give me speedy answers.

Ps 119:58. With all my heart I want your blessings. Be merciful just as you promised. [145]I am praying with great earnestness; answer me, O Lord, and I will obey your laws. [146]"Save me," I cry, "for I am obeying." [147]Early in the morning, before the sun is up, I was praying and pointing out how much I trust in you.

Ps 130:1. O Lord, from the depths of despair I cry for your help: [2]"Hear me! Answer! Help me!"

Ps 141:1. Quick, Lord, answer me—for I have prayed. Listen when I cry to you for help! [2]Regard my prayer as my evening sacrifice and as incense wafting up to you.

Ps 142:1, 2. How I plead with God, how I implore his mercy, pouring out my troubles before him.

Isa 38:2. When Hezekiah heard this, he turned his face to the wall and prayed: [3]"O Lord, don't you remember how true I've been to you and how I've always tried to obey you in everything you said?" Then he broke down with great sobs.

Isa 62:7. Take no rest, all you who pray, and give God no rest until he establishes Jerusalem and makes her respected and admired throughout the earth.

Isa 64:12. After all of this, must you still refuse to help us, Lord? Will you stand silent and still punish us?

Dan 9:3. So I earnestly pleaded with the Lord God (to end our captivity and send us back to our own land). As I prayed, I fasted, and wore rough sackcloth, and sprinkled myself with ashes. [16]"Yet because of all your faithful mercies, Lord, please turn away your furious anger from Jerusalem, your own city, your holy mountain. For the heathen mock at you because your city lies in ruins for our sins. [17]O our God, hear your servant's prayer! Listen as I plead! Let your face shine again with peace and joy upon your desolate sanctuary—for your own glory, Lord. [18]O my God, bend down your ear and listen to my plea. Open your eyes and see our wretchedness, how your city lies in ruins—for everyone knows that it is yours. We don't ask because we merit help, but because you are so merciful despite our grievous sins. [19]O Lord, hear; O Lord, forgive. O Lord, listen to me and act! Don't delay —for your own sake, O my God, because your people and your city bear your name."

Jon 1:14. Then they shouted out a prayer to Jehovah, Jonah's God. "O Jehovah," they pleaded, "don't make us die for this man's sin, and don't hold us responsible for his death, for it is not our fault."

Hab 1:2. O Lord, how long must I call for help before you will listen? I shout to you in vain; there is no answer. "Help! Murder!" I cry, but no one comes to save.

Mt 15:22. A woman from Canaan who was living there came to him, pleading, "Have mercy on me, O Lord, King David's Son! For my daughter has a demon within her, and it torments her constantly." [23]But Jesus gave her no reply—not even a word. Then his disciples urged him to send her away. "Tell her to get going," they said, "for she is bothering us with all her begging." [24]Then he said to the woman, "I was sent to help the Jews—the lost sheep of Israel—not the Gentiles." [25]But she came and worshiped him and pled again, "Sir, help me!" [26]"It doesn't seem right to take bread from the children and throw it to the dogs," he said. [27]"Yes, it is!" she replied, "for even the puppies beneath the table are permitted to eat the crumbs that fall." [28]"Woman," Jesus told her, "your faith is large, and your request is granted." And her daughter was healed right then. Mk 7:25–29.

Lk 7:3. When the captain heard about Jesus, he sent some respected Jewish elders to ask him to come and heal his slave.

Lk 11:5, 6. Then, teaching them more about prayer, he used this illustration: "Suppose you went to a friend's house at midnight, wanting to borrow three loaves of bread. You would shout up to him, 'A friend of mine has just arrived for a visit and I've nothing to give him to eat.' [7]He would call down from his bedroom, 'Please don't ask me to get up. The door is locked for the night and we are all in bed. I just can't help you this time.' [8]But I tell you this—though he won't do it as a friend, if you keep knocking long enough he will get up and give you everything you want—just because of your persistence."

Lk 18:1. One day Jesus told his disciples a story to illustrate their need for constant prayer and to show them that they must keep praying until the answer comes. [2]"There was a city judge," he said, "a very godless man who had great contempt for everyone. [3]A widow of that city came to him frequently to appeal for justice against a man who had harmed her. [4, 5]The judge ignored her for a while, but eventually she got on his nerves. 'I fear neither God nor man,' he said to himself, 'but this woman bothers me. I'm going to see that she gets justice, for she is wearing me out with her constant coming!' " [6]Then the Lord said, "If even an evil judge can be worn down like that, [7]don't you think that God will surely give justice to his people who plead with him day and night?"

Lk 22:44. For he was in such agony of spirit that he broke into a sweat of blood, with great drops falling to the ground as he prayed more and more earnestly.

Rom 8:26. And in the same way—by our faith—the Holy Spirit helps us with our daily problems and in our praying. For we don't even know what we should pray for, nor how to pray as we should; but the Holy Spirit prays for us with such feeling that it cannot be expressed in words.

2 Cor 12:8. Three different times I begged God to make me well again.

Eph 6:18. Pray all the time. Ask God for anything in line with the Holy Spirit's wishes. Plead with him, reminding him of your needs, and keep praying earnestly for all Christians everywhere.

Heb 5:7. Yet while Christ was here on earth he pleaded with God, praying with tears and agony of soul to the only one who would save him from (premature) death. And God heard his prayers because of his strong desire to obey God at all times.

Instances of Importunity in. Jacob, Gen 32:22–30. See above. Moses, Ex 33:12–16; 34:9. Elijah, 1 Kgs 18:24–44. The two blind men of Jericho, Mt 20:30, 31; Mk 10:48; Lk 18:39. The Syrophoenician woman, Mt 15:22–28; Mk 7:25–30. The Roman army captain, Mt 8:5, 6; Lk 7:3, 4.

INTERCESSORY. See *Intercession; Jesus, Mediation of.*

OF THE WICKED NOT HEARD. See *Wicked, Prayer of.*

PLEAS OFFERED IN. Gen 32:9. Then Jacob prayed, "O God of Abraham my grandfather, and of my father Isaac—O Jehovah who told me to return to the land of my relatives, and said that you would do me good—[10]I am not worthy of the least of all your loving kindnesses shown me again and again just as you promised me. For when I left home I owned nothing except a walking stick! And now I am two armies! [11]O Lord, please deliver me from destruction at the hand of my brother Esau, for I am frightened—terribly afraid that he is coming to kill me and these mothers and my children. [12]But you promised to do me good, and to multiply my descendants until they become as the sands along the shores—too many to count."

Ex 32:11. But Moses begged God not to do it. "Lord," he pleaded, "why is your anger so hot against your own people whom you brought from the land of Egypt with such great power and mighty miracles? [12]Do you want the Egyptians to say, 'God tricked them into coming to the mountains so that he could slay them, destroying them from off the face of the earth'? Turn back from your fierce wrath. Turn away from this terrible evil you are planning against your people! [13]Remember your promise to your servants—to Abraham, Isaac, and Israel. For you swore by your own self, 'I will multiply your posterity as the stars of heaven, and I will give them all of this land I have promised to your descendants, and they shall inherit it forever.' "

Ex 33:13. Please, if this is really so, guide me clearly along the way you want me to travel so that I will understand you and walk acceptably before you. For don't forget that this nation is your people.

Num 14:13. "But what will the Egyptians think when they hear about it?" Moses pleaded with the Lord. "They know full well the power you displayed in rescuing your people. [14]They have told this to the inhabitants of this land, who are well aware that you are with Israel and that you talk with her face to face. They see the pillar of cloud and fire standing above us, and they know that you lead and protect us day and night. [15]Now if you kill all your people, the nations that have heard your fame will say, [16]'The Lord had to kill them because he wasn't able to take care of them in the wilderness. He wasn't strong enough to bring them into the land he swore he would give them.' [17, 18]Oh, please, show the great power (of your patience) by forgiving our sins and showing us your steadfast love. Forgive us, even though you have said that you don't let sin go unpunished, and that you punish the father's fault in the children to the third and fourth generation."

Num 16:22. But Moses and Aaron fell face downward to the ground before the Lord. "O God, the God of all mankind," they pleaded, "must you be angry with all the people when one man sins?"

Deut 3:24, 25. O Lord God, please let me cross over into the Promised Land—the good land beyond the Jordan River with its rolling hills—and Lebanon. I want to see the result of all the greatness and power you have been showing us; for what God in all of heaven or earth can do what you have done for us?

Deut 9:18. Then, for another forty days and nights I lay before the Lord, neither eating bread nor drinking water, for you had done what the Lord hated most, thus provoking him to great anger. [25]That is why I fell down before him for forty days and nights when the Lord was ready to destroy you. [26]I prayed to him, "O Lord God, don't destroy your own people. They are your inheritance saved from Egypt by your mighty power and glorious strength. [27]Don't notice the rebellion and stubbornness of these people, but remember instead your promises to your servants Abraham, Isaac, and Jacob. Oh, please overlook the awful wickedness and sin of these people. [28]For if you destroy them the Egyptians will say, 'It is because the Lord wasn't able to bring them to the land he promised them,' or 'He destroyed them because he hated them: he brought them into the wilderness to slay them.' [29]They are your people and your inheritance which you brought from Egypt by your great power and your mighty arm."

Josh 7:8. O Lord, what am I to do now that Israel has fled from her enemies! [9]For when the Canaanites and the other nearby nations hear about it, they will surround us and attack us and wipe us out. And then what will happen to the honor of your great name?

2 Sam 7:25. And now, Lord God, do as you have promised concerning me and my family. [26]And may you be eternally honored when you have established Israel as your people and have established my dynasty before you. [27]For you have revealed to me, O Lord of heaven, God of Israel, that I am the first of a dynasty which will rule your people forever; that is why I have been bold enough to pray this prayer of acceptance. [28]For you are indeed God, and your words are truth; and you have promised me these good things—[29]so do as you have promised! Bless me and my family forever! May our dynasty continue on and on before you; for you, Lord God, have promised it.

1 Kgs 8:25. And now, O Lord God of Israel, fulfill your further promise to him: that if his descendants follow your ways and try to do your will as he did, one of them shall always sit upon the throne of Israel. [26]Yes, O God of Israel, fulfill this promise too. [59]And may these words of my prayer be constantly before him day and night, so that he helps me and all of Israel in accordance with our daily needs. [60]May people all over the earth know that the Lord is God, and that there is no other god at all.

1 Kgs 18:36. At the customary time for offering the evening sacrifice, Elijah walked up to the altar and prayed, "O Lord God of Abraham, Isaac, and Israel, prove today that you are the God of Israel and that I am your servant; prove that I have done all this at your command. [37]O Lord, answer me! Answer me so these people will know that you are God and that you have brought them back to yourself."

2 Kgs 19:15. Then he prayed this prayer: "O Lord God of Israel, sitting on your throne high above the angels, you alone are the God of all the kingdoms of the earth. You created the heavens and the earth. [16]Bend low, O Lord, and listen. Open your eyes, O Lord, and see. Listen to this man's defiance of the living God. [17]Lord, it is true that the kings of Assyria have destroyed all those nations, [18]and have burned their idol-gods. But they weren't gods at all; they were destroyed because they were only things that men had made of wood and stone. [19]O Lord our God, we plead with you to save us from his power; then all the kingdoms of the earth will know that you alone are God." Isa 37:15–20.

2 Chron 14:11. "O Lord," he cried out to God, "no one else can help us! Here we are, powerless against this mighty army. Oh, help us, Lord our God! For we trust in you alone to rescue us, and in your name we attack this vast horde. Don't let mere men defeat you!"

Neh 1:8. Oh, please remember what you told Moses! You said, *"If you sin, I will scatter you among the nations; [9]but if you return to me and obey my laws, even though you are exiled to the farthest corners of the universe, I will bring you back to Jerusalem. For Jerusalem is the place in which I have chosen to live."*

Neh 9:32. And now, O great and awesome God, you who keep your promises of love and kindness —do not let all the hardships we have gone through become as nothing to you. Great trouble has come upon us and upon our kings and princes and priests and prophets and ancestors from the days when the kings of Assyria first triumphed over us until now.

Ps 4:1. O God, you have declared me perfect in your eyes; you have always cared for me in my distress; now hear me as I call again. Have mercy on me. Hear my prayer.

Ps 9:19. O Lord, arise and judge and punish the nations; don't let them conquer you! [20]Make them tremble in fear; put the nations in their place until at last they know they are but puny men.

Ps 25:6, 7. Overlook my youthful sins, O Lord! Look at me instead through eyes of mercy and forgiveness, through eyes of everlasting love and kindness.

Ps 27:9. Oh, do not hide yourself when I am trying to find you. Do not angrily reject your servant. You have been my help in all my trials before; don't leave me now. Don't forsake me, O God of my salvation.

Ps 31:3. Yes, you are my Rock and my fortress; honor your name by leading me out of this peril.

Ps 38:16. Put an end to their arrogance, these who gloat when I am cast down!

Ps 69:6. O Lord God of the armies of heaven, don't let me be a stumbling block to those who trust in you. O God of Israel, don't let me cause them to be confused. [13]But I keep right on praying to you, Lord. For now is the time—you are bending down to hear! You are ready with a plentiful supply of love and kindness. Now answer my prayer and rescue me as you promised. [16]O Jehovah, answer my prayers, for your lovingkindness is wonderful; your mercy is so plentiful, so tender and so kind.

Ps 71:18. And now that I am old and gray, don't forsake me. Give me time to tell this new generation (and their children too) about all your mighty miracles.

Ps 74:10. How long, O God, will you allow our enemies to dishonor your name? Will you let them get away with this forever? [11]Why do you delay? Why hold back your power? Unleash your fist and give them a final blow. [18]Lord, see how these enemies scoff at you. O Jehovah, an arrogant nation has blasphemed your name. [20]Remember your promise! For the land is full of darkness and cruel men. [21]O Lord, don't let your downtrodden people be constantly insulted. Give cause for these poor and needy ones to praise your name! [22]Arise, O God, and state your case against our enemies. Remember the insults these rebels have hurled against you all day long. [23]Don't overlook the cursing of these enemies of yours; it grows louder and louder.

Ps 79:10. Why should the heathen nations be allowed to scoff, "Where is their God?" Publicly avenge this slaughter of your people! [11]Listen to the sighing of the prisoners and those condemned to die. Demonstrate the greatness of your power by saving them. [12]O Lord, take sevenfold vengeance on these nations scorning you.

Ps 83:1. O God, don't sit idly by, silent and inactive when we pray. Answer us! Deliver us! [2]Don't you hear the tumult and commotion of your enemies? Don't you see what they are doing, these proud men who hate the Lord? [18]Until they learn that you alone, Jehovah, are the God above all gods in supreme charge of all the earth.

Ps 86:1. Bend down and hear my prayer, O Lord, and answer me, for I am deep in trouble. [2]Protect me from death, for I try to follow all your laws. Save me, for I am serving you and trusting you. [3]Be merciful, O Lord, for I am looking up to you in constant hope. [4]Give me happiness, O Lord, for I worship only you. [5]O Lord, you are so good and kind, so ready to forgive; so full of mercy for all who ask your aid. [17]Send me a sign of your favor. When those who hate me see it they will lose face because you help and comfort me.

Ps 89:49. Lord, where is the love you used to have for me? Where is your kindness that you promised to David with a faithful pledge? [50]Lord, see how all the people are despising me. [51]Your enemies joke about me, the one you anointed as their king.

Ps 106:47. O Lord God, save us! Regather us from the nations so we can thank your holy name and rejoice and praise you.

Ps 109:21. But as for me, O Lord, deal with me as your child, as one who bears your name! Because you are so kind, O Lord, deliver me. [22, 23]I am slipping down the hill to death; I am shaken off from life as easily as a man brushes a grasshopper from his arm. [24]My knees are weak from fasting and I am skin and bones. [25]I am a symbol of failure to all mankind; when they see me they shake their heads. [26]Help me, O Lord my God! Save me because you are loving and kind. [27]Do it publicly, so all will see that you yourself have done it.

Ps 115:1. Glorify your name, not ours, O Lord! Cause everyone to praise your lovingkindness and your truth. [2]Why let the nations say, "Their God is dead!"

Ps 119:38. Reassure me that your promises are for me, for I trust and revere you. [42]Then I will have an answer for those who taunt me, for I trust your promises. [43]May I never forget your words; for they are my only hope. [49]Never forget your promises to me your servant, for they are my only hope. [73]You made my body, Lord; now give me sense to heed your laws. [94]I am yours! Save me! For I have tried to live according to your desires. [116]Lord, you promised to let me live! Never let it be said that God failed me. [124]Lord, deal with me in lovingkindness, and teach me, your servant, to obey. [145]I am praying with great earnestness; answer me, O Lord, and I will obey your laws. [146]"Save me," I cry, "for I am obeying." [149]Because you are so loving and kind, listen to me and make me well again. [153]Look down upon my sorrows and rescue me, for I am obeying your commands. [173]Stand ready to help me because I have chosen to follow your will. [174]O Lord, I have longed for your salvation, and your law is my delight. [175]If you will let me live, I will praise you; let your laws assist me. [176]I Have wandered away like a lost sheep; come and find me for I have not turned away from your commandments.

Ps 143:11. Lord, saving me will bring glory to your name. Bring me out of all this trouble because you are true to your promises. [12]And because you are loving and kind to me, cut off all my enemies and destroy those who are trying to harm me; for I am your servant.

Isa 63:17. O Lord, why have you hardened our hearts and made us sin and turn against you? Return and help us, for we who belong to you need you so. [18]How briefly we possessed Jerusalem! And now our enemies have destroyed her. [19]O God, why do you treat us as though we weren't your people, as though we were a heathen nation that never called you "Lord"?

Jer 14:21. Do not hate us, Lord, for the sake of your own name. Do not disgrace yourself and the throne of your glory by forsaking your promise to bless us!

Jer 18:20. Should they repay evil for good? They have set a trap to kill me, yet I spoke well of them to you and tried to defend them from your anger. [21]Now, Lord, let their children starve to death and let the sword pour out their blood! Let their wives be widows and be bereft of all their children! Let their men die in epidemics and their youth die in battle!

Lam 3:56. And you heard me! You listened to my pleading; you heard my weeping! [57]Yes, you came at my despairing cry and told me not to fear. [58]O Lord, you are my lawyer! Plead my case! For you have redeemed my life. [59]You have seen the wrong they did to me; be my Judge, to prove me right. [60]You have seen the plots my foes have laid against me. [61]You have heard the vile names they have called me, [62]and all they say about me and their whispered plans. [63]See how they laugh and sing with glee, preparing my doom.

Joel 2:17. The priests, the ministers of God, will stand between the people and the altar weeping; and they will pray, "Spare your people, O our God; don't let the heathen rule them, for they belong to you. Don't let them be disgraced by the taunts of the heathen who say, 'Where is this God of theirs? How weak and helpless he must be!' "

THANKSGIVING AND, BEFORE TAKING FOOD. 1 Sam 9:12, 13. "Yes," they replied, "stay right on this road. He lives just inside the city gates. He has just arrived back from a trip to take part in a public sacrifice up on the hill. So hurry, because he'll probably be leaving about the time you get there; the guests can't eat until he arrives and blesses the food."

Mt 14:19. Then he told the people to sit down on the grass; and he took the five loaves and two fish, looked up into the sky and asked God's blessing on the meal, then broke the loaves apart and gave them to the disciples to place before the people. Mk 6:41; Lk 9:16; Jn 6:11.

Mt 26:26. As they were eating, Jesus took a small loaf of bread and blessed it and broke it apart and gave it to the disciples and said, "Take it and eat it, for this is my body." [27]And he took a cup of wine and gave thanks for it and gave it to them and said, "Each one drink from it." Mk 14:22, 23; Lk 22:19; 1 Cor 11:24.

Mk 8:6. So he told the crowd to sit down on the ground. Then he took the seven loaves, thanked God for them, broke them into pieces and passed them to his disciples; and the disciples placed them before the people. [7]A few small fish were found, too, so Jesus also blessed these and told the disciples to serve them. Mt 15:36.

Acts 27:35. Then he took some hardtack and gave thanks to God before them all, and broke off a piece and ate it.

Rom 14:6. So is the person who eats meat that has been offered to idols; he is thankful to the Lord for it; he is doing right. And the person who won't touch such meat, he, too, is anxious to please the Lord, and is thankful.

1 Cor 10:30. If I can thank God for the food and enjoy it, why let someone spoil everything just because he thinks I am wrong? [31]Well, I'll tell you why. It is because you must do everything for the glory of God, even your eating and drinking.

1 Tim 4:3. They will say it is wrong to be married and wrong to eat meat, even though God gave these things to well-taught Christians to enjoy and be thankful for. [4]For everything God made is good, and we may eat it gladly if we are thankful for it, [5]and if we ask God to bless it, for it is made good by the Word of God and prayer.

PRAYERFULNESS Ps 5:1, 2. O Lord, hear me praying; listen to my plea, O God my King, for I will never pray to anyone but you. [3]Each morning I will look to you in heaven and lay my requests before you, praying earnestly.

Ps 42:8. Yet day by day the Lord also pours out his steadfast love upon me, and through the night I sing his songs and pray to God who gives me life.

Ps 109:4. I love them, but even while I am praying for them, they are trying to destroy me.

Ps 116:2. Because he bends down and listens, I will pray as long as I breathe!

Dan 6:10. But though Daniel knew about it, he went home and knelt down as usual in his upstairs bedroom, with its windows open toward Jerusalem, and prayed three times a day, just as he always had, giving thanks to his God.

Lk 2:37. For she had been a widow for eighty-four years following seven years of marriage. She never left the Temple but stayed there night and day worshiping God by praying and often fasting.

Acts 6:4. Then we can spend our time in prayer, preaching, and teaching.

Acts 10:2. He was a godly man, deeply reverent, as was his entire household. He gave generously to charity and was a man of prayer. [9]The next day, as they were nearing the city, Peter went up on the flat roof of his house to pray.

Rom 1:9. God knows how often I pray for you. Day and night I bring you and your needs in prayer to the one I serve with all my might, telling others the Good News about his Son.

Rom 12:12. Be glad for all God is planning for you. Be patient in trouble, and prayerful always.

Eph 1:16. I have never stopped thanking God for you. I pray for you constantly.

Col 1:9. So ever since we first heard about you we have kept on praying and asking God to help you understand what he wants you to do; asking him to make you wise about spiritual things.

1 Thess 3:10. For night and day we pray on and on for you, asking God to let us see you again, to fill up any little cracks there may yet be in your faith.

1 Thess 5:17. Always keep on praying.

1 Tim 5:5. The church should care for widows who are poor and alone in the world, if they are looking to God for his help and spending much time in prayer.

2 Tim 1:3. How I thank God for you, Timothy. I pray for you every day, and many times during the long nights I beg my God to bless you richly. He is my fathers' God, and mine, and my only purpose in life is to please him.

See *Supplication.*

PRAYERLESSNESS Job 15:4. Have you no fear of God? No reverence for him?

Job 21:14. All this despite the fact that they ordered God away and wanted no part of him and his ways. [15]"Who is Almighty God?" they scoff. "Why should we obey him? What good will it do us?"

Job 27:10. For he does not delight himself in the Almighty or pay any attention to God except in times of crisis.

Ps 14:4. They eat my people like bread and wouldn't think of praying! Don't they really know any better? Ps 53:4.

Ps 79:6. Pour out your wrath upon the godless nations, not on us! And on kingdoms that refuse to pray, that will not call upon your name!

Isa 43:22. But O my people, you won't ask my help; you have grown tired of me!

Isa 64:7. Yet no one calls upon your name or pleads with you for mercy.

Jer 10:21. The shepherds of my people have lost their senses; they no longer follow God nor ask his will. Therefore they perish and their flocks are scattered. [25]Pour out your fury on the nations who don't obey the Lord.

Dan 9:13. Every curse against us written in the law of Moses has come true; all the evils he predicted—all have come. But even so we still refuse to satisfy the Lord our God by turning from our sins and doing right.

Hos 7:7. They kill their kings one after another, and none cries out to me for help.

Jon 1:6. So the captain went down after him. "What do you mean," he roared, "sleeping at a time like this? Get up and cry to your god, and see if he will have mercy on us and save us!"

Zeph 1:6. And I will destroy those who formerly worshiped the Lord, but no longer do, and those who never loved him and never wanted to.

PREACHING The act of exhorting, prophesying, reproving, teaching. Solomon called preacher, Eccl 1:1, 12–15. Noah, 2 Pet 2:5. Sitting while, Mt 5:1; Lk 4:20; 5:3. Moses, slow of speech, Ex 4: 10–12.

Repentance, the subject of John the Baptist's, Mt 3:2; Mk 1:4, 5; Lk 3:3; of Christ's, Mt 4:17; Mk 1:15; the apostles, Mk 6:12. "God's Good News" the subject of Christ's, Mk 1:14, 15; 2:2; Lk 8:1. Christ crucified and risen, the content of Paul's, Acts 17: 3.

Jonah told to preach, Jon 3:1. Preaching of the cross foolishness, 1 Cor 1:18. Apostolic preaching described, 1 Cor 15:1–4. Preaching Christ, Acts 8:4, 5; 9:20; 1 Cor 1:23; 2 Cor 4:5. Preaching the gospel, Acts 8:4, 25; 14:7, 21; 15:34–36; 16:10; Rom 1:15; 10: 15; 1 Cor 1:17; 9:14, 16; 2 Cor 10:14. Preaching the resurrection, Acts 4:2. The gospel preached everywhere in apostolic times, Acts 8:4; Rom 1:8; Col 1: 23. The gospel of the kingdom yet to be preached in all the world, Mt 24:14; 26:13; Mk 13:10; 14:9.

Effective: By Azariah, 2 Chron 15:1–15; by Jonah, Jon 3; Mt 12:41; Lk 11:32; by Peter and other apostles, Acts 2:14–41; by Philip, Acts 8:5–12, 27–38; by Paul, Acts 9:20; 13:16–43. See *Revival.*

Impenitence under: Of Asa, 2 Chron 16:7–10; Ahab, 2 Chron 18:6–26; the Jews, Acts 13:46.

See *Obduracy.* See also *Minister; Call, Personal.*

UNCLASSIFIED SCRIPTURES RELATING TO. Mt 11:25. And Jesus prayed this prayer: "O Father, Lord of heaven and earth, thank you for hiding the truth from those who think themselves so wise, and for revealing it to little children. [Ps 8:2.] [26]Yes, Father, for it pleased you to do it this way!" Lk 10: 21.

1 Cor 1:17. For Christ didn't send me to baptize, but to preach the Gospel; and even my preaching sounds poor, for I do not fill my sermons with profound words and high sounding ideas, for fear of diluting the mighty power there is in the simple message of the cross of Christ. [18]I know very well how foolish it sounds to those who are lost, when they hear that Jesus died to save them. But we who are saved recognize this message as the very power of God. [21]For God in his wisdom saw to it that the world would never find God through human brilliance, and then he stepped in and saved all those who believed his message, which the world calls foolish and silly. [23]So when we preach about Christ dying to save them, the Jews are offended and the Gentiles say it's all nonsense. [27]Instead, God has deliberately chosen to use ideas the world considers foolish and of little worth in order to shame those people considered by the world as wise and great. [28]He has chosen a plan despised by the world, counted as nothing at all, and used it to bring down to nothing those the world considers great, [29]so that no one anywhere can ever brag in the presence of God.

1 Cor 2:1. Dear brothers, even when I first came to you I didn't use lofty words and brilliant ideas to tell you God's message. [2]For I decided that I would speak only of Jesus Christ and his death on the cross. [3]I came to you in weakness—timid and trembling. [4]And my preaching was very plain, not

with a lot of oratory and human wisdom, but the Holy Spirit's power was in my words, proving to those who heard them that the message was from God. [5]I did this because I wanted your faith to stand firmly upon God, not on man's great ideas. [6]Yet when I am among mature Christians I do speak with words of great wisdom, but not the kind that comes from here on earth, and not the kind that appeals to the great men of this world, who are doomed to fall. [7]Our words are wise because they are from God, telling of God's wise plan to bring us into the glories of heaven. This plan was hidden in former times, though it was made for our benefit before the world began. [8]But the great men of the world have not understood it; if they had, they never would have crucified the Lord of Glory. [12]And God has actually given us his Spirit (not the world's spirit) to tell us about the wonderful free gifts of grace and blessing that God has given us. [13]In telling you about these gifts we have even used the very words given to us by the Holy Spirit, not words that we as men might choose. So we use the Holy Spirit's words to explain the Holy Spirit's facts.

1 Cor 14:1. Let love be your greatest aim; nevertheless, ask also for the special abilities the Holy Spirit gives, and especially the gift of prophecy, being able to preach the messages of God. [2]But if your gift is that of being able to "speak in tongues," that is, to speak in languages you haven't learned, you will be talking to God but not to others, since they won't be able to understand you. You will be speaking by the power of the Spirit but it will all be a secret. [3]But one who prophesies, preaching the messages of God, is helping others grow in the Lord, encouraging and comforting them. [4]So a person "speaking in tongues" helps himself grow spiritually, but one who prophesies, preaching messages from God, helps the entire church grow in holiness and happiness. [5]I wish you all had the gift of "speaking in tongues" but even more, I wish you were all able to prophesy, preaching God's messages, for that is a greater and more useful power than to speak in unknown languages—unless, of course, you can tell everyone afterwards what you were saying, so that they can get some good out of it too. [6]Dear friends, even if I myself should come to you talking in some language you don't understand, how would that help you? But if I speak plainly what God has revealed to me, and tell you the things I know, and what is going to happen, and the great truths of God's Word—that is what you need; that is what will help you. [7]Even musical instruments—the flute, for instance, or the harp—are examples of the need for speaking in plain, simple English rather than in unknown languages. For no one will recognize the tune the flute is playing unless each note is sounded clearly. [8]And if the army bugler doesn't play the right notes, how will the soldiers know that they are being called to battle? [9]In the same way, if you talk to a person in some language he doesn't understand, how will he know what you mean? You might as well be talking to an empty room. [10]I suppose that there are hundreds of different languages in the world, and all are excellent for those who understand them, [11]but to me they mean nothing. A person talking to me in one of these languages will be a stranger to me and I will be a stranger to him. [12]Since you are so anxious to have special gifts from the Holy Spirit, ask him for the very best, for those that will be of real help to the whole church. [13]If someone is given the gift of speaking in unknown tongues, he should pray also for the gift of knowing what he has said, so that he can tell people afterwards, plainly. [14]For if I pray in a language I don't understand, my spirit is praying but I don't know what I am saying. [15]Well, then, what shall I do? I will do both. I will pray in unknown tongues and also in ordinary language that everyone understands. I will sing in unknown tongues and also in ordinary language, so that I can understand the praise I am giving; [16]for if you praise and thank God with the spirit alone, speaking in another language, how can those who don't understand you be praising God along with you? How can they join you in giving thanks when they don't know what you are saying? [17]You will be giving thanks very nicely, no doubt, but the other people present won't be helped. [18]I thank God that I "speak in tongues" privately more than any of the rest of you. [19]But in public worship I would much rather speak five words that people can understand and be helped by, than ten thousand words while "speaking in tongues" in an unknown language. [20]Dear brothers, don't be childish in your understanding of these things. Be innocent babies when it comes to planning evil, but be men of intelligence in understanding matters of this kind. [24]But if you prophesy preaching God's Word, (even though such preaching is mostly for believers) and an unsaved person or a new Christian comes in who does not understand about these things, all these sermons will convince him of the fact that he is a sinner, and his conscience will be pricked by everything he hears. [25]As he listens, his secret thoughts will be laid bare and he will fall down on his knees and worship God, declaring that God is really there among you.

2 Cor 2:14. But thanks be to God! For through what Christ has done, he has triumphed over us so that now wherever we go he uses us to tell others about the Lord and to spread the Gospel like a sweet perfume. [15]As far as God is concerned there is a sweet, wholesome fragrance in our lives. It is the fragrance of Christ within us, an aroma to both the saved and the unsaved all around us. [16]To those who are not being saved, we seem a fearful smell of death and doom, while to those who know Christ we are a life-giving perfume. But who is adequate for such a task as this?

2 Cor 3:12. Since we know that this new glory will never go away, we can preach with great boldness, [13]and not as Moses did, who put a veil over his face so that the Israelis could not see the glory fade away.

Col 1:23. The only condition is that you fully

believe the Truth, standing in it steadfast and firm, strong in the Lord, convinced of the Good News that Jesus died for you, and never shifting from trusting him to save you. This is the wonderful news that came to each of you and is now spreading all over the world. And I, Paul, have the joy of telling it to others. [24]But part of my work is to suffer for you; and I am glad, for I am helping to finish up the remainder of Christ's sufferings for his body, the church. [25]God has sent me to help his church and to tell his secret plan to you Gentiles. [26, 27]He has kept this secret for centuries and generations past, but now at last it has pleased him to tell it to those who love him and live for him, and the riches and glory of his plan are for you Gentiles too. And this is the secret: *that Christ in your hearts is your only hope of glory.* [28]So everywhere we go we talk about Christ to all who will listen, warning them and teaching them as well as we know how. We want to be able to present each one to God, perfect because of what Christ has done for each of them. [29]This is my work, and I can do it only because Christ's mighty energy is at work within me.

1 Thess 1:5. For when we brought you the Good News, it was not just meaningless chatter to you; no, you listened with great interest. What we told you produced a powerful effect upon you, for the Holy Spirit gave you great and full assurance that what we said was true.

1 Thess 2:3. So you can see that we were not preaching with any false motives or evil purposes in mind; we were perfectly straightforward and sincere. [4]For we speak as messengers from God, trusted by him to tell the truth; we change his message not one bit to suit the taste of those who hear it; for we serve God alone, who examines our hearts' deepest thoughts. [5]Never once did we try to win you with flattery, as you very well know, and God knows we were not just pretending to be your friends so that you would give us money! [6]As for praise, we have never asked for it from you or anyone else, although as apostles of Christ we certainly had a right to some honor from you. [7]But we were as gentle among you as a mother feeding and caring for her own children. [8]We loved you dearly —so dearly that we gave you not only God's message, but our own lives too. [9]Don't you remember, dear brothers, how hard we worked among you? Night and day we toiled and sweated to earn enough to live on so that our expenses would not be a burden to anyone here, as we preached God's Good News among you. [10]You yourselves are our witnesses—as is God—that we have been pure and honest and faultless toward every one of you. [11]We talked to you as a father to his own children—don't you remember?—pleading with you, encouraging you and even demanding [12]that your daily lives should not embarrass God, but bring joy to him who invited you into his kingdom to share his glory.

1 Tim 6:20. Oh, Timothy, don't fail to do these things that God entrusted to you. Keep out of foolish arguments with those who boast of their "knowledge" and thus prove their lack of it. [21]Some of these people have missed the most important thing in life—they don't know God.

2 Tim 2:15. Work hard so God can say to you, "Well done." Be a good workman, one who does not need to be ashamed when God examines your work. Know what his Word says and means. [16]Steer clear of foolish discussions which lead people into the sin of anger with each other.

Tit 1:3. And now in his own good time he has revealed this Good News and permits me to tell it to everyone. By command of God our Savior I have been trusted to do this work for him.

Tit 3:8. These things I have told you are all true. Insist on them so that Christians will be careful to do good deeds all the time, for this is not only right, but it brings results. [9]Don't get involved in arguing over unanswerable questions and controversial theological ideas; keep out of arguments and quarrels about obedience to Jewish laws, for this kind of thing isn't worthwhile; it only does harm.

PRECEPTS See *Commandments; Law.*

PRECIOUS STONES See *Stones.*

PREDESTINATION OR FOREORDAINING Meaning literally "to anoint beforehand," predestination refers to the Biblical teaching that God in his perfect knowledge has determined those who would be saved by God.

The verses presented in this topic deal with the eternal plan, design or purpose of God for the people of the earth. For other references, see under *Chosen; Election.*

Gen 21:12. For Isaac is the son through whom my promise will be fulfilled. [13]And I will make a nation of the descendants of the slave-girl's son, too, because he also is yours.

Ex 9:15. I could have killed you all by now, [16]but I didn't, for I wanted to demonstrate my power to you and to all the earth.

Ex 33:19. The Lord replied, "I will make my goodness pass before you, and I will announce to you the meaning of my name Jehovah, the Lord. I show kindness and mercy to anyone I want to."

Deut 7:7. He didn't choose you and pour out his love upon you because you were a larger nation than any other, for you were the smallest of all! [8]It was just because he loves you, and because he kept his promise to your ancestors. That is why he brought you out of slavery in Egypt with such amazing power and mighty miracles.

Deut 10:15. And yet he rejoiced in your fathers and loved them so much that he chose you, their children, to be above every other nation, as is evident today. Deut 4:37.

Deut 32:8. When God divided up the world among the nations, he gave each of them a supervising angel!

Josh 11:20. For the Lord made the enemy kings want to fight the Israelis instead of asking for peace; so they were mercilessly killed, as the Lord had commanded Moses.

1 Sam 12:22. The Lord will not abandon his cho-

sen people, for that would dishonor his great name. He made you a special nation for himself—just because he wanted to!

1 Kgs 12:15. So the king refused the people's demands. (But the Lord's hand was in it—he caused the new king to do this in order to fulfill his promise to Jeroboam, made through Ahijah, the prophet from Shiloh.)

1 Kgs 20:42. Then the prophet told him, "The Lord says, 'Because you have spared the man I said must die, now you must die in his place, and your people shall perish instead of his.' "

2 Kgs 19:25. Why haven't you realized long before this that it is I, the Lord, who lets you do these things? I decreed your conquest of all those fortified cities!

2 Chron 6:6. But now I have chosen Jerusalem as that city, and David as that king.

Job 23:13. Nevertheless, his mind concerning me remains unchanged, and who can turn him from his purposes? Whatever he wants to do, he does. [14]So he will do to me all he has planned, and there is more ahead.

Ps 33:12. Blessed is the nation whose God is the Lord, whose people he has chosen as his own.

Ps 65:4. How greatly to be envied are those you have chosen to come and live with you within the holy tabernacle courts! What joys await us among all the good things there.

Ps 78:67. But he rejected Joseph's family, the tribe of Ephraim, [68]and chose the tribe of Judah—and Mount Zion which he loved. [70]He chose his servant David, taking him from feeding sheep, [71, 72]and from following the ewes with lambs; God presented David to his people as their shepherd and he cared for them with a true heart and skillful hands.

Ps 105:17. Then he sent Joseph as a slave to Egypt to save his people from starvation. [18]There in prison they hurt his feet with fetters, and placed his neck in an iron collar, [19]until God's time finally came—how God tested his patience! [20]Then the king sent for him and set him free. [21]He was put in charge of all the king's possessions. [22]At his pleasure he could imprison the king's aides and teach the king's advisors.

Ps 135:4. For the Lord has chosen Israel as his personal possession.

Prov 16:4. The Lord has made everything for his own purposes—even the wicked, for punishment.

Isa 44:1. Listen to me, O my servant Israel, O my chosen ones: [2]The Lord who made you, who will help you, says, O servant of mine, don't be afraid. O Jerusalem, my chosen ones, don't be afraid. [7]Who else can tell you what is going to happen in days ahead? Let them tell you if they can, and prove their power. Let them do as I have done since ancient times.

Jer 1:4. The Lord said to me, [5]"I knew you before you were formed within your mother's womb; before you were born I sanctified you and appointed you as my spokesman to the world."

Mal 1:2, 3. "I have loved you very deeply," says the Lord. But you retort, "Really? When was this?" And the Lord replies, "I showed my love for you by loving your father, Jacob. I didn't need to. I even rejected his very own brother, Esau, and destroyed Esau's mountains and inheritance, to give it to the jackals of the desert."

Mt 11:25. And Jesus prayed this prayer: "O Father, Lord of heaven and earth, thank you for hiding the truth from those who think themselves so wise, and for revealing it to little children. [26]Yes, Father, for it pleased you to do it this way!"

Mt 20:16. "And so it is that the last shall be first, and the first, last." [chapter 22:14.] [23]"You shall indeed drink from it," he told them. "But I have no right to say who will sit on the thrones next to mine. Those places are reserved for the persons my Father selects."

Mk 13:20. And unless the Lord shortens that time of calamity, not a soul in all the earth will survive. But for the sake of his chosen ones he will limit those days. [22]For there will be many false Messiahs and false prophets who will do wonderful miracles that would deceive, if possible, even God's own children.

Lk 4:25, 26. For example, remember how Elijah the prophet used a miracle to help the widow of Zarephath—a foreigner from the land of Sidon. There were many Jewish widows needing help in those days of famine, for there had been no rain for three and one-half years, and hunger stalked the land; yet Elijah was not sent to them. [27]Or think of the prophet Elisha, who healed Naaman, a Syrian, rather than the many Jewish lepers needing help.

Lk 8:10. He replied, "God has granted you to know the meaning of these parables, for they tell a great deal about the Kingdom of God. But these crowds hear the words and do not understand, just as the ancient prophets predicted."

Lk 10:20. However, the important thing is not that demons obey you, but that your names are registered as citizens of heaven.

Lk 22:22. I must die. It is part of God's plan. But, oh, the horror awaiting that man who betrays me. Mt 26:24; Mk 14:21.

Jn 6:37. But some will come to me—those the Father has given me—and I will never, never reject them. [39]And this is the will of God, that I should not lose even one of all those he has given me, but that I should raise them to eternal life at the Last Day. [44]For no one can come to me unless the Father who sent me draws him to me, and at the Last Day I will cause all such to rise again from the dead. [45]As it is written in the Scriptures, "They shall all be taught of God." Those the Father speaks to, who learn the truth from him, will be attracted to me.

Jn 15:16. You didn't choose me! I chose you! I appointed you to go and produce lovely fruit always, so that no matter what you ask for from the Father, using my name, he will give it to you. [19]The world would love you if you belonged to it; but you don't—for I chose you to come out of the world, and so it hates you.

Jn 17:2. For you have given him authority over every man and woman in all the earth. He gives eternal life to each one you have given him. [6]I have told these men all about you. They were in the world, but then you gave them to me. Actually, they were always yours, and you gave them to me; and they have obeyed you. [9]My plea is not for the world but for those you have given me because they belong to you.

Jn 21:23. So the rumor spread among the brotherhood that that disciple wouldn't die! But that isn't what Jesus said at all! He only said, "If I want him to live until I come, what is that to you?"

Acts 2:23. "But God, following his prearranged plan, let you use the Roman government to nail him to the cross and murder him. [39]For Christ promised him to each one of you who has been called by the Lord our God, and to your children and even to those in distant lands!" [47]And each day God added to them all who were being saved.

Acts 3:18. But God was fulfilling the prophecies that the Messiah must suffer all these things.

Acts 4:28. They won't stop at anything that you in your wise power will let them do.

Acts 17:26. He created all the people of the world from one man, Adam, and scattered the nations across the face of the earth. He decided beforehand which should rise and fall, and when. He determined their boundaries.

Acts 22:14. Then he told me, "The God of our fathers has chosen you to know his will and to see the Messiah and hear him speak."

Rom 1:6. And you, dear friends in Rome, are among those he dearly loves; you, too, are invited by Jesus Christ to be God's very own—yes, his holy people.

Rom 8:28. And we know that all that happens to us is working for our good if we love God and are fitting into his plans. [29]For from the very beginning God decided that those who came to him—and all along he knew who would—should become like his Son, so that his Son would be the First, with many brothers. [30]And having chosen us, he called us to come to him; and when we came, he declared us "not guilty," filled us with Christ's goodness, gave us right standing with himself, and promised us his glory. [33]Who dares accuse us whom God has chosen for his own? Will God? No! He is the one who has forgiven us and given us right standing with himself.

Rom 9:11–13. God told her that Esau, the child born first, would be a servant to Jacob, his twin brother. In the words of the Scripture, "I chose to bless Jacob, but not Esau." And God said this before the children were even born, before they had done anything either good or bad. This proves that God was doing what he had decided from the beginning; it was not because of what the children did but because of what God wanted and chose. [14]Was God being unfair? Of course not. [15]For God had said to Moses, "If I want to be kind to someone, I will. And I will take pity on anyone I want to." [16]And so God's blessings are not given just because someone decides to have them or works hard to get them. They are given because God takes pity on those he wants to. [17]Pharaoh, king of Egypt, was an example of this fact. For God told him he had given him the kingdom of Egypt for the very purpose of displaying the awesome power of God against him: so that all the world would hear about God's glorious name. [18]So you see, God is kind to some just because he wants to be, and he makes some refuse to listen. [*vs.* 7–33.] [23, 24]And he has a right to take others such as ourselves, who have been made for pouring the riches of his glory into, whether we are Jews or Gentiles, and to be kind to us so that everyone can see how very great his glory is. [27]Isaiah the prophet cried out concerning the Jews that though there would be millions of them, only a small number would ever be saved. [28]"For the Lord will execute his sentence upon the earth, quickly ending his dealings, justly cutting them short." [29]And Isaiah says in another place that except for God's mercy all the Jews would be destroyed—all of them—just as everyone in the cities of Sodom and Gomorrah perished.

Rom 11:5. It is the same today. Not all the Jews have turned away from God; there are a few being saved as a result of God's kindness in choosing them. [7]So this is the situation: Most of the Jews have not found the favor of God they are looking for. A few have—the ones God has picked out—but the eyes of the others have been blinded. [8]This is what our Scriptures refer to when they say that God has put them to sleep, shutting their eyes and ears so that they do not understand what we are talking about when we tell them of Christ. And so it is to this very day.

1 Cor 1:26. Notice among yourselves, dear brothers, that few of you who follow Christ have big names or power or wealth. [27]Instead, God has deliberately chosen to use ideas the world considers foolish and of little worth in order to shame those people considered by the world as wise and great. [28]He has chosen a plan despised by the world, counted as nothing at all, and used it to bring down to nothing those the world considers great, [29]so that no one anywhere can ever brag in the presence of God.

1 Cor 2:7. Our words are wise because they are from God, telling of God's wise plan to bring us into the glories of heaven. This plan was hidden in former times, though it was made for our benefit before the world began.

Gal 1:15. For even before I was born God had chosen me to be his, and called me—what kindness and grace.

Eph 1:4. Long ago, even before he made the world, God chose us to be his very own, through what Christ would do for us; he decided then to make us holy in his eyes, without a single fault—we who stand before him covered with his love. [5]His unchanging plan has always been to adopt us into his own family by sending Jesus Christ to die for us. And he did this because he wanted to! [9]God has told us his secret reason for sending Christ, a plan he decided on in mercy long ago; [10]and this was his purpose: that when the time is ripe he will gather us all together from wherever we are—in heaven or on earth—to be with him in Christ, forever. [11]Moreover, because of what Christ has done we have become gifts to God that he delights in, for as part of God's sovereign plan we were chosen from the beginning to be his, and all things happen just as he decided long ago.

Eph 2:10. It is God himself who has made us what we are and given us new lives from Christ Jesus; and long ages ago he planned that we should spend these lives in helping others.

Eph 3:11. In just the way he had always planned it through Jesus Christ our Lord.

Col 3:12. Since you have been chosen by God who has given you this new kind of life, and because of his deep love and concern for you, you should practice tenderhearted mercy and kindness to others. Don't worry about making a good impression on them but be ready to suffer quietly and patiently.

1 Thess 1:4. We know that God has chosen you, dear brothers, much beloved of God.

1 Thess 2:12. That your daily lives should not embarrass God, but bring joy to him who invited you into his kingdom to share his glory.

2 Thess 2:13. But we must forever give thanks to God for you, our brothers loved by the Lord, because God chose from the very first to give you salvation, cleansing you by the work of the Holy Spirit and by your trusting in the Truth.

2 Tim 1:9. It is he who saved us and chose us for his holy work, not because we deserved it but because that was his plan long before the world began.

Tit 1:1, 2. From: Paul, the slave of God and the messenger of Jesus Christ. I have been sent to bring faith to those God has chosen and to teach them to know God's truth—the kind of truth that changes lives—so that they can have eternal life, which God promised them before the world began —and he cannot lie.

Jas 1:18. And it was a happy day for him when he gave us our new lives, through the truth of his Word, and we became, as it were, the first children in his new family.

1 Pet 1:2. Dear friends, God the Father chose you long ago and knew you would become his children. And the Holy Spirit has been at work in your hearts, cleansing you with the blood of Jesus Christ and making you to please him. [20]God chose him for this purpose long before the world began, but only recently was he brought into public view, in these last days, as a blessing to you.

2 Pet 1:10. So, dear brothers, work hard to prove that you really are among those God has called and chosen, and then you will never stumble or fall away.

Jude 1:4. I say this because some godless teachers have wormed their way in among you, saying that after we become Christians we can do just as we like without fear of God's punishment. The fate of such people was written long ago, for they have turned against our only Master and Lord, Jesus Christ.

Rev 13:8. And all mankind—whose names were not written down before the founding of the world in the slain Lamb's Book of Life—worshiped the evil Creature.

PRESCIENCE See *God, Foreknowledge of.*

PRESENTS To Abraham, by Pharaoh, Gen 12:16; by Abimelech, Gen 20:14. To Rebekah, Gen 24:22. To Esau, Gen 32:13–15. To prophets, 1 Kgs 14:3; 2 Kgs 4:42. To those in adversity, Job 42:10, 11.

Betrothal, Gen 24:53. Marriage, Esther 2:18. Conciliatory, Gen 32:20; 33:8–11; 1 Sam 25:27–35; Prov 21:14. To confirm promises, Gen 21:28–30; 1 Sam 18:1–4. Rewards of service, Dan 5:7. Kings to kings, 2 Sam 8:10; 1 Kgs 10:10, 13; 15:18, 19.

To corrupt courts, forbidden, Ex 23:8; Deut 16:19; 27:25; Isa 5:23. See *Bribery.*

See *Liberality.*

PRESUMPTION Ex 5:2. "Is that so?" retorted Pharaoh. "And who is Jehovah, that I should listen to him, and let Israel go? I don't know Jehovah and I will not let Israel go."

Ex 14:11. And they turned against Moses, whining, "Have you brought us out here to die in the desert because there were not enough graves for us in Egypt? Why did you make us leave Egypt? [12]Isn't this what we told you, while we were slaves, to leave us alone? We said it would be better to be slaves to the Egyptians than dead in the wilderness."

Ex 17:7. Moses named the place Massah (meaning "tempting Jehovah to slay us"), and sometimes they referred to it as Meribah (meaning "argument" and "strife!")—for it was there that the people of Israel argued against God and tempted him to slay them by saying, "Is Jehovah going to take care of us or not?"

Num 15:30. But anyone who deliberately makes the "mistake," whether he is a native Israeli or a foreigner, is blaspheming Jehovah, and shall be cut off from among his people.

Num 16:41. But the very next morning all the people began muttering again against Moses and Aaron, saying, "You have killed the Lord's people."

Num 21:5. They began to murmur against God and to complain against Moses. "Why have you brought us out of Egypt to die here in the wilderness?" they whined. "There is nothing to eat here, and nothing to drink, and we hate this insipid manna."

Deut 29:19. Let no one blithely think, when he hears the warnings of this curse, "I shall prosper even though I walk in my own stubborn way!" [20]For the Lord will not pardon! His anger and jealousy will be hot against that man. And all the curses written in this book shall lie heavily upon him, and the Lord will blot out his name from under heaven.

1 Kgs 20:28. Then a prophet went to the king of

Israel with this message from the Lord: "Because the Syrians have declared, 'The Lord is a God of the hills and not of the plains,' I will help you defeat this vast army, and you shall know that I am indeed the Lord."

1 Kgs 22:24. Then Zedekiah (son of Chenaanah) walked over and slapped Micaiah on the face. "When did the Spirit of the Lord leave me and speak to you?" he demanded.

Job 15:25, 26. Armed with his tin shield, he clenches his fist against God, defying the Almighty, stubbornly assaulting him.

Ps 19:13. And keep me from deliberate wrongs; help me to stop doing them. Only then can I be free of guilt and innocent of some great crime.

Ps 131:1. Lord, I am not proud and haughty. I don't think myself better than others. I don't pretend to "know it all."

Prov 18:12. Pride ends in destruction; humility ends in honor. [13]What a shame—yes, how stupid! —to decide before knowing the facts!

Prov 25:6, 7. Don't demand an audience with the king as though you were some powerful prince. It is better to wait for an invitation rather than to be sent back to the end of the line, publicly disgraced!

Isa 5:18. Woe to those who drag their sins behind them like a bullock on a rope. [19]They even mock the Holy One of Israel and dare the Lord to punish them. "Hurry up and punish us, O Lord," they say. "We want to see what you can do!" [20]They say that what is right is wrong, and what is wrong is right; that black is white and white is black; bitter is sweet and sweet is bitter. [21]Woe to those who are wise and shrewd in their own eyes! [22]Woe to those who are "heroes" when it comes to drinking, and boast about the liquor they can hold. [23]They take bribes to pervert justice, letting the wicked go free and putting innocent men in jail. [24]Therefore God will deal with them and burn them. They will disappear like straw on fire. Their roots will rot and their flowers wither, for they have thrown away the laws of God and despised the Word of the Holy One of Israel. [25]That is why the anger of the Lord is hot against his people; that is why he has reached out his hand to smash them. The hills will tremble, and the rotting bodies of his people will be thrown as refuse in the streets. But even so, his anger is not ended; his hand is heavy on them still.

Isa 10:15. But the Lord says, "Shall the axe boast greater power than the man who uses it? Is the saw greater than the man who saws? Can a rod strike unless a hand is moving it? Can a cane walk by itself?"

Isa 14:13. For you said to yourself, "I will ascend to heaven and rule the angels. I will take the highest throne. I will preside on the Mount of Assembly far away in the north. [14]I will climb to the highest heavens and be like the Most High."

Isa 28:14. Therefore hear the word of the Lord, you scoffing rulers in Jerusalem: [15]You have struck a bargain with Death, you say, and sold yourselves to the devil in exchange for his protection against the Assyrians. "They can never touch us," you say, "for we are under the care of one who will deceive and fool them." [16]But the Lord God says, See, I am placing a Foundation Stone in Zion—a firm, tested, precious Cornerstone that is safe to build on. He who believes need never run away again. [17]I will take the line and plummet of justice to check the foundation wall you built; it looks so fine, but it is so weak a storm of hail will knock it down! The enemy will come like a flood and sweep it away, and you will be drowned. [18]I will cancel your agreement of compromise with Death and the devil, so when the terrible enemy floods in, you will be trampled into the ground. [22]So scoff no more, lest your punishment be made even greater, for the Lord God of Hosts has plainly told me that he is determined to crush you.

Isa 29:15. Woe to those who try to hide their plans from God, who try to keep him in the dark concerning what they do! "God can't see us," they say to themselves. "He doesn't know what is going on!" [16]How stupid can they be! Isn't he, the Potter, greater than you, the jars he makes? Will you say to him, "He didn't make us"? Does a machine call its inventor dumb? [20]Bullies will vanish and scoffers will cease, and all those plotting evil will be killed.

Isa 45:9. Woe to the man who fights with his Creator. Does the pot argue with its maker? Does the clay dispute with him who forms it, saying, "Stop, you're doing it wrong!" or the pot exclaim, "How clumsy can you be!"? [10]Woe to the baby just being born who squalls to his father and mother, "Why have you produced me? Can't you do anything right at all?"

Isa 58:3. "We have fasted before you," they say. "Why aren't you impressed? Why don't you see our sacrifices? Why don't you hear our prayers? We have done much penance, and you don't even notice it!" I'll tell you why! Because you are living in evil pleasure even while you are fasting, and you keep right on oppressing your workers.

Isa 65:5. Yet they say to one another, "Don't come too close, you'll defile me! For I am holier than you!"

Jer 23:24. And as for the false prophets and priests and people who joke about "today's sad news from God," I will punish them and their families for saying this.

Mt 4:5. Then Satan took him to Jerusalem to the roof of the Temple. [6]"Jump off," he said, "and prove you are the Son of God; for the Scriptures declare, 'God will send his angels to keep you from harm,' . . . they will prevent you from smashing on the rocks below." [Lk 4:9–11.] [7]Jesus retorted, "It also says not to put the Lord your God to a foolish test!" Deut 6:16.

Lk 12:18. And finally exclaimed, "I know—I'll tear down my barns and build bigger ones! Then I'll have room enough. [19]And I'll sit back and say to myself, 'Friend, you have enough stored away for years to come. Now take it easy! Wine, women, and song for you!' " [20]But God said to him, "Fool! Tonight you die. Then who will get it all?"

Lk 14:7. When he noticed that all who came to

the dinner were trying to sit near the head of the table, he gave them this advice: [8]"'If you are invited to a wedding feast, don't always head for the best seat. For if someone more respected than you shows up, [9]the host will bring him over to where you are sitting and say, 'Let this man sit here instead.' And you, embarrassed, will have to take whatever seat is left at the foot of the table! [10]Do this instead—start at the foot; and when your host sees you he will come and say, 'Friend, we have a better place than this for you!' Thus you will be honored in front of all the other guests. [11]For everyone who tries to honor himself shall be humbled; and he who humbles himself shall be honored."

Lk 18:11. The proud Pharisee "prayed" this prayer: "Thank God, I am not a sinner like everyone else, especially that tax collector over there! For I never cheat, I don't commit adultery, [12]I go without food twice a week, and I give to God a tenth of everything I earn."

Rom 1:32. They were fully aware of God's death penalty for these crimes, yet they went right ahead and did them anyway, and encouraged others to do them, too.

Rom 9:20. No, don't say that. Who are you to criticize God? Should the thing made say to the one who made it, "Why have you made me like this?" [21]When a man makes a jar out of clay, doesn't he have a right to use the same lump of clay to make one jar beautiful, to be used for holding flowers, and another to throw garbage into?

1 Cor 10:9. And don't try the Lord's patience—they did, and died from snake bites. [10]And don't murmur against God and his dealings with you, as some of them did, for that is why God sent his Angel to destroy them. [11]All these things happened to them as examples—as object lessons to us—to warn us against doing the same things; they were written down so that we could read about them and learn from them in these last days as the world nears its end. [12]So be careful. If you are thinking, "Oh, I would never behave like that"—let this be a warning to you. For you too may fall into sin.

2 Thess 2:3. And then the man of rebellion will come—the son of hell. [4]He will defy every god there is, and tear down every other object of adoration and worship. He will go in and sit as God in the temple of God, claiming that he himself is God.

Jas 4:13. Look here, you people who say, "Today or tomorrow we are going to such and such a town, stay there a year, and open up a profitable business." [14]How do you know what is going to happen tomorrow? For the length of your lives is as uncertain as the morning fog—now you see it; soon it is gone. [15]What you ought to say is, "If the Lord wants us to, we shall live and do this or that." [16]Otherwise you will be bragging about your own plans, and such self-confidence never pleases God.

2 Pet 2:10. He is especially hard on those who follow their own evil, lustful thoughts, and those who are proud and willful, daring even to scoff at the Glorious Ones without so much as trembling, [11]although the angels in heaven who stand in the very presence of the Lord, and are far greater in power and strength than these false teachers, never speak out disrespectfully against these evil Mighty Ones.

INSTANCES OF. Satan, when he said to Eve, "You'll not die!" Gen 3:1–5. Builders of Babel, Gen 11:3, 4. Abraham, in questioning about Sodom, Gen 18:22–32. Moses, in rebuking Jehovah, Num 11:11–15, 22. Nadab and Abihu, Lev 10:1, 2. Israelites, in going against the Amalekites, Num 14:44, 45; murmuring at Meribah, Ex 17:2, 7; in reviling God, Mal 1:6, 7, 12; 3:7, 8, 13. Korah, Dathan, and Abiram, Num 16:3. Saul, in sacrificing, 1 Sam 13:8–14; sparing the Amalekites, 1 Sam 15:3, 9–23. Men of Bethshemesh, 1 Sam 6:19. Uzzah, in steadying the ark, 2 Sam 6:6, 7. David's anger at Uzzah's death, 2 Sam 6:8. David, in counting the people of Israel, 2 Sam 24:1–17. Jeroboam, 1 Kgs 13:4. Ben-hadad, 1 Kgs 20:10. Uzziah, 2 Chron 26:16. Sennacherib, 2 Chron 32:13, 14. Job, in cursing the day of his birth, Job 3; reproved by Eliphaz, Job 4; 5. Jonah, Jon 4:1–8. Peter, in objecting to Jesus' statement that he must be killed, Mt 16:21–23; Mk 8:32; in reflecting on Jesus' knowledge when he asked, amid a crowd, who touched him, Lk 8:45; in objecting to Jesus washing his feet, Jn 13:8; in asking Jesus, "What about him, Lord? What sort of death will he die?" Jn 21:20–22. The disciples, in rebuking those who brought little children to Jesus, Mt 19:13; Mk 10:13, 14; Lk 18:15; in their indignation at the anointing of Jesus, Mt 26:8, 9; Mk 14:4, 5; Jn 12:5. Reproving Jesus, Jn 7:3–5. James and John, in desiring to call down fire on the Samaritans, Lk 9:54. Those who reviled Jesus, Mt 27:41–43; Mk 15:29–32. Theudas, Acts 5:36. Sons of Sceva, Acts 19:13, 14. Diotrephes, 3 Jn 1:9.

See *Blasphemy*, which is presumption; *Mocking; Pride.*

PRIDE Ex 18:10. "Bless the Lord," Jethro said. . . . [11]I know now that the Lord is greater than any other god because he delivered his people from the proud and cruel Egyptians."

Lev 26:19. I will break your proud power and make your heavens as iron, and your earth as bronze.

Deut 8:11. But that is the time to be careful! Beware that in your plenty you don't forget the Lord your God and begin to disobey him. [12, 13]For when you have become full and prosperous and have built fine homes to live in, and when your flocks and herds have become very large, and your silver and gold have multiplied, [14]that is the time to watch out that you don't become proud, and forget the Lord your God who brought you out of your slavery in the land of Egypt. [17]He did it so that you would never feel that it was your own power and might that made you wealthy. [18]Always remember that it is the Lord your God who gives you power to become rich, and he does it to fulfill his promise to your ancestors. [19]But if you forget about the Lord your God and worship other gods instead, and follow evil ways, you shall certainly perish, [20]just as the Lord has caused other nations in the past to perish. That will be your fate, too, if you don't obey the Lord your God.

Judg 9:14. Then all the trees finally turned to the thorn bush. "You be our king!" they exclaimed. [15]And the thorn bush replied, "If you really want me, come and humble yourselves beneath my shade! If you refuse, let fire flame forth from me and burn down the great cedars of Lebanon!"

1 Sam 2:3. Quit acting so proud and arrogant! The Lord knows what you have done, and he will judge your deeds. [4]Those who were mighty are mighty no more! Those who were weak are now strong. [5]Those who were well are now starving; those who were starving are fed.

1 Kgs 20:11. The king of Israel retorted, "Don't count your chickens before they hatch!"

2 Kgs 14:9. But King Joash replied, "The thistle of Lebanon demanded of the mighty cedar tree, 'Give your daughter to be a wife for my son.' But just then a wild animal passed by and stepped on the thistle and trod it into the ground! [10]You have destroyed Edom and are very proud about it; but my advice to you is, be content with your glory and stay home! Why provoke disaster for both yourself and Judah?" 2 Chron 25:18, 19.

Job 11:12. Mere man is as likely to be wise as a wild donkey's colt is likely to be born a man!

Job 12:2. Yes, I realize you know everything! All wisdom will die with you! [3]Well, I know a few things myself—you are no better than I am. And who doesn't know these things you've been saying?

Job 13:2. I know as much as you do. I'm not stupid. [5]Oh, please be quiet! That would be your highest wisdom.

Job 15:1. *The answer of Eliphaz the Temanite:* [2]"You are supposed to be a wise man, and yet you give us all this foolish talk. You are nothing but a windbag. [3]It isn't right to speak so foolishly. What good do such words do? [4, 5]Have you no fear of God? No reverence for him? Your sins are telling your mouth what to say! Your words are based on clever deception, [6]but why should I condemn you? Your own mouth does! [7, 8]Are you the wisest man alive? Were you born before the hills were made? Have you heard the secret counsel of God? Are you called into his counsel room? Do you have a monopoly on wisdom? [9]What do you know more than we do? What do you understand that we don't? [10]On our side are aged men much older than your father! [11]Is God's comfort too little for you? Is his gentleness too rough? [12]What is this you are doing, getting carried away by your anger, with flashing eyes? [13]And you turn against God and say all these evil things against him.

Job 18:3. Have we become like animals to you, stupid and dumb? [4]Just because you tear your clothes in anger, is this going to start an earthquake? Shall we all go and hide?

Job 21:30–32. The evil man is usually spared in the day of calamity, and allowed to escape. No one rebukes him openly. No one repays him for what he has done. And an honor guard keeps watch at his grave.

Job 32:8, 9. But it is not mere age that makes men wise. Rather, it is the spirit in a man, the breath of the Almighty which makes him intelligent. [10]So listen to me awhile and let me express my opinion. [11, 12]I have waited all this time, listening very carefully to your arguments, but not one of them has convinced Job that he is a sinner, or has proved that he is. [13]And don't give me that line about "only God can convince the sinner of his sin."

Job 37:24. No wonder men everywhere fear him! For he is not impressed by the world's wisest men!

Ps 9:20. Make them tremble in fear; put the nations in their place until at last they know they are but puny men.

Ps 10:2. Come and deal with all these proud and wicked men who viciously persecute the poor. Pour upon these men the evil they planned for others! [3]For these men brag of all their evil lusts; they revile God and congratulate those the Lord abhors, whose only goal in life is money. [4]These wicked men, so proud and haughty, seem to think that God is dead. They wouldn't think of looking for him! [5]Yet there is success in everything they do, and their enemies fall before them. They do not see your punishment awaiting them. [6]They boast that neither God nor man can ever keep them down—somehow they'll find a way! [11]"God isn't watching," they say to themselves; "he'll never know!"

Ps 12:3, 4. But the Lord will not deal gently with people who act like that; he will destroy those proud liars who say, "We will lie to our hearts' content. Our lips are our own; who can stop us?"

Ps 18:27. You deliver the humble but condemn the proud and haughty ones.

Ps 31:23. Oh, love the Lord, all of you who are his people; for the Lord protects those who are loyal to him, but harshly punishes all who haughtily reject him.

Ps 49:11. You name your estates after yourselves as though your lands could be forever yours, and you could live on them eternally.

Ps 52:7. See what happens to those who despise God and trust in their wealth, and become ever more bold in their wickedness.

Ps 73:6. So their pride sparkles like a jeweled necklace, and their clothing is woven of cruelty! [8]They scoff at God and threaten his people. How proudly they speak! [9]They boast against the very heavens, and their words strut through the earth.

Ps 75:4. I warned the proud to cease their arrogance! I told the wicked to lower their insolent gaze, [5]and to stop being stubborn and proud. [6]For promotion and power come from nowhere on earth.

Ps 101:5. I will not permit conceit and pride.

Ps 119:21. You rebuke those cursed proud ones who refuse your commands. [69]Proud men have made up lies about me, but the truth is that I obey your laws with all my heart. [70]Their minds are dull and stupid, but I have sense enough to follow you. [78]Let the proud be disgraced, for they have cut me down with all their lies.

Ps 138:6. Yet though he is so great, he respects the humble, but proud men must keep their distance.

Prov 3:34. The Lord mocks at mockers, but helps the humble.

Prov 6:16, 17. For there are six things the Lord hates—no, seven: Haughtiness. . . .

Prov 8:13. For wisdom hates pride, arrogance.

Prov 10:17. Anyone willing to be corrected is on the pathway to life. Anyone refusing has lost his chance.

Prov 11:2. Proud men end in shame, but the meek become wise.

Prov 12:9. It is better to get your hands dirty—and eat, than to be too proud to work—and starve. [15]A fool thinks he needs no advice.

Prov 13:10. Pride leads to arguments.

Prov 14:21. To despise the poor is to sin.

Prov 15:5. Only a fool despises his father's advice. [10]If they stop trying, the Lord will punish them; if they rebel against that punishment, they will die. [12]A mocker stays away from wise men because he hates to be scolded. [25]The Lord destroys the possessions of the proud. [32]But to reject criticism is to harm yourself and your own best interests.

Prov 16:5. Pride disgusts the Lord. Take my word for it—*proud men shall be punished.* [18]Pride goes before destruction and haughtiness before a fall. [19]Better poor and humble than proud and rich.

Prov 17:19. Sinners love to fight; boasting is looking for trouble.

Prov 18:11. The rich man thinks of his wealth as an impregnable defense, a high wall of safety. What a dreamer! [12]Pride ends in destruction; humility ends in honor.

Prov 20:6. Most people will tell you what loyal friends they are, but are they telling the truth?

Prov 21:4. Pride, lust, and evil actions are all sin. [24]Mockers are proud, haughty and arrogant.

Prov 25:14. One who doesn't give the gift he promised is like a cloud blowing over a desert without dropping any rain. [27]It is bad for men to think about all the honors they deserve!

Prov 26:5. Prick his conceit with silly replies! [12]There is one thing worse than a fool, and that is a man who is conceited. [16]Yet in his own opinion he is smarter than seven wise men.

Prov 27:2. Don't praise yourself; let others do it!

Prov 28:11. Rich men are conceited, but their real poverty is evident to the poor. [25]Greed causes fighting.

Prov 29:8. Fools start fights everywhere while wise men try to keep peace. [23]Pride ends in a fall, while humility brings honor.

Prov 30:11, 12. There are those who curse their father and mother, and feel themselves faultless despite their many sins. [13]They are proud beyond description, arrogant, disdainful.

Isa 2:11. For the day is coming when your proud looks will be brought low; the Lord alone will be exalted. [12]On that day the Lord of Hosts will move against the proud and haughty and bring them to the dust. [13]All the tall cedars of Lebanon and all the mighty oaks of Bashan shall bend low, [14]and all the high mountains and hills, [15]and every high tower and wall, [16]and all the proud ocean ships and trim harbor craft—*all* shall be crushed before the Lord that day. [17]All the glory of mankind will bow low; the pride of men will lie in the dust, and the Lord alone will be exalted.

Isa 3:16. Next, he will judge the haughty Jewish women, who mince along, noses in the air, tinkling bracelets on their ankles, with wanton eyes that rove among the crowds to catch the glances of the men. [17]The Lord will send a plague of scabs to ornament their heads! He will expose their nakedness for all to see. [18]No longer shall they tinkle with self-assurance as they walk. For the Lord will strip away their artful beauty and their ornaments, [19]their necklaces and bracelets and veils of shimmering gauze. [20]Gone shall be their scarves and ankle chains, headbands, earrings, and perfumes; [21]their rings and jewels, [22]and party clothes and negligees and capes and ornate combs and purses; [23]their mirrors, lovely lingerie, beautiful dresses and veils. [24]Instead of smelling of sweet perfume, they'll stink; for sashes they'll use ropes; their well-set hair will all fall out; they'll wear sacks instead of robes. All their beauty will be gone; all that will be left to them is shame and disgrace. [25, 26]Their husbands shall die in battle; the women, ravaged, shall sit crying on the ground.

Isa 5:8. You buy up property so others have no place to live. Your homes are built on great estates so you can be alone in the midst of the earth! [15]In that day the haughty shall be brought down to the dust; the proud shall be humbled.

Isa 9:8–10. The Lord has spoken out against that braggart Israel who says that though our land lies in ruins now, we will rebuild it better than before. The sycamore trees are cut down, but we will replace them with cedars!

Isa 10:5, 6. Assyria is the whip of my anger; his military strength is my weapon upon this godless nation, doomed and damned; he will enslave them and plunder them and trample them like dirt beneath his feet. [7]But the king of Assyria will not know that it is I who sent him. He will merely think he is attacking my people as part of his plan to conquer the world. [8]He will declare that every one of his princes will soon be a king, ruling a conquered land. [9]"We will destroy Calno just as we did Carchemish," he will say, "and Hamath will go down before us as Arpad did; and we will destroy Samaria just as we did Damascus. [10]Yes, we have finished off many a kingdom whose idols were far greater than those in Jerusalem and Samaria, [11]so when we have defeated Samaria and her idols we will destroy Jerusalem with hers." [12]After the Lord has used the king of Assyria to accomplish his purpose, then he will turn upon the Assyrians and punish them too—for they are proud and haughty men. [13]They boast, "We in our own power and wisdom have won these wars. We are great and wise. By our own strength we broke down the walls and destroyed the people and carried off their treasures. 14In our greatness we have robbed their nests of riches and gathered up kingdoms as a farmer gathers eggs, and no one can move a finger or open his mouth to peep against us!" 15But the Lord says, "Shall the axe boast greater power than the man who uses it? Is the saw greater than the man who saws? Can a rod strike unless a hand is moving it? Can a cane walk by itself?" 16Because of all your evil boasting, O king of Assyria, the Lord of Hosts will send a plague among your proud troops, and strike them down.

Isa 13:11. I will crush the arrogance of the proud man and the haughtiness of the rich.

Isa 14:12. How you are fallen from heaven, O Lucifer, son of the morning! How you are cut down to the ground—mighty though you were against the nations of the world. 13For you said to yourself, "I will ascend to heaven and rule the angels. I will take the highest throne. I will preside on the Mount of Assembly far away in the north. 14I will climb to the highest heavens and be like the Most High." 15But instead, you will be brought down to the pit of hell, down to its lowest depths. 16Everyone there will stare at you and ask, "Can this be the one who shook the earth and the kingdoms of the world?"

Isa 22:16. "And who do you think you are, building this beautiful sepulchre in the rock for yourself? 19Yes, I will drive you out of office," says the Lord, "and pull you down from your high position."

Isa 23:7. This silent ruin is all that's left of your once joyous land. What a history was yours! Think of all the colonists you sent to distant lands! 9The Commander of the armies of heaven has done it to destroy your pride and show his contempt for all the greatness of mankind.

Isa 24:21. On that day the Lord will punish the fallen angels in the heavens, and the proud rulers of the nations on earth.

Isa 26:5. He humbles the proud and brings the haughty city to the dust; its walls come crashing down.

Isa 28:3. The proud city of Samaria—yes, the joy and delight of the drunkards of Israel—will be hurled to the ground and trampled beneath the enemies' feet.

Isa 47:7. You thought your reign would never end, Queen Kingdom of the world. You didn't care a whit about my people or think about the fate of those who do them harm. 8O pleasure-mad kingdom, living at ease, bragging as the greatest in the world—listen to the sentence of my court upon your sins. You say, "I alone am God! I'll never be a widow; I'll never lose my children." 9Well, those two things shall come upon you in one moment, in full measure in one day: widowhood and the loss of your children, despite all your witchcraft and magic. 10You felt secure in all your wickedness. "No one sees me," you said. Your "wisdom" and "knowledge" have caused you to turn away from me and claim that you yourself are Jehovah.

Jer 9:23. The Lord says: Let not the wise man bask in his wisdom, nor the mighty man in his might, nor the rich man in his riches. 24Let them boast in this alone: That they truly know me, and understand that I am the Lord of justice and of righteousness whose love is steadfast; and that I love to be this way.

Jer 13:8, 9. Then the Lord said: This illustrates the way that I will rot the pride of Judah and Jerusalem. 15Oh, that you were not so proud and stubborn! Then you would listen to the Lord, for he has spoken. 17Do you still refuse to listen? Then in loneliness my breaking heart shall mourn because of your pride. My eyes will overflow with tears because the Lord's flock shall be carried away as slaves.

Jer 48:7. For you trusted in your wealth and skill; therefore you shall perish. Your god Chemosh, with his priests and princes, shall be taken away to distant lands! 14Do you remember that boast of yours: "We are heroes, mighty men of war"? 15But now Moab is to be destroyed; her destroyer is on the way; her choicest youth are doomed to slaughter, says the King, the Lord of Hosts. 29We have all heard of the pride of Moab, for it is very great. We know your loftiness, your arrogance and your haughty heart. Isa 16:6, 7.

Jer 49:4. You are proud of your fertile valleys, but they will soon be ruined. O wicked daughter, you trusted in your wealth and thought no one could ever harm you. 16You have been fooled by your fame and your pride, living there in the mountains of Petra, in the clefts of the rocks. But though you live among the peaks with the eagles, I will bring you down, says the Lord.

Jer 50:31. For see, I am against you, O people so proud; and now your day of reckoning has come. 32Land of pride, you will stumble and fall and no one will raise you up, for the Lord will light a fire in the cities of Babylon that will burn everything around them.

Ezk 16:56. In your proud days you held Sodom in unspeakable contempt.

Ezk 28:2, 3. Son of dust, say to the prince of Tyre: The Lord God says: You are so proud you think you are God, sitting on the throne of a god on your island home in the midst of the seas. But you are only a man, and not a god, though you boast yourself to be like God. You are wiser than Daniel, for no secret is hidden from you. 4You have used your wisdom and understanding to get great wealth—gold and silver and many treasures. 5Yes, your wisdom has made you very rich and very proud. 6Therefore the Lord God says: Because you claim that you are as wise as God, 7an enemy army, the terror of the nations, shall suddenly draw their swords against your marvelous wisdom and defile your splendor! 8They will bring you to the pit of hell and you shall die as those pierced with many wounds, there on your island in the heart of the seas. 9Then will you boast as a god? At least to these invaders you will be no god, but merely man! 17Your heart was filled with pride because of all your beauty; you corrupted your wisdom for the sake of your splendor. Therefore I have cast you down to the ground and exposed you helpless before the curious gaze of kings.

Ezk 30:6. For the Lord says: All Egypt's allies shall fall, and the pride of her power shall end.

Ezk 31:10. But Egypt has become proud and arrogant, the Lord God says. Therefore because she has set herself so high above the others, reaching to the clouds, [11]I will deliver her into the hands of a mighty nation. *vs.* 12–14.

Dan 4:37. Now, I, Nebuchadnezzar, praise and glorify and honor the King of Heaven, the Judge of all, whose every act is right and good; for he is able to take those who walk proudly and push them into the dust!

Dan 11:45. He will halt between Jerusalem and the sea, and there pitch his royal tents, but while he is there his time will suddenly run out and there will be no one to help him.

Hos 5:5. The very arrogance of Israel testifies against her in my court. She will stumble under her load of guilt, and Judah, too, shall fall. Hos 7:10.

Hos 10:11. Ephraim is accustomed to treading out the grain—an easy job she loves. I have never put her under a heavy yoke before; I have spared her tender neck. But now I will harness her to the plow and harrow. Her days of ease are gone.

Obd 1:3. You are proud because you live in those high, inaccessible cliffs. "Who can ever reach us way up here!" you boast. Don't fool yourselves! [4]Though you soar as high as eagles, and build your nest among the stars, I will bring you plummeting down, says the Lord.

Nah 3:19. There is no healing for your wound—it is far too deep to cure. All who hear your fate will clap their hands for joy, for where can one be found who has not suffered from your cruelty?

Hab 2:4. Note this: Wicked men trust themselves alone (as these Chaldeans do), and fail; but the righteous man trusts in me, and lives! [5]What's more, these arrogant Chaldeans are betrayed by all their wine, for it is treacherous. In their greed they have collected many nations, but like death and hell, they are never satisfied. [9]Woe to you for getting rich by evil means, attempting to live beyond the reach of danger.

Zeph 2:10. They will receive the wages of their pride, for they have scoffed at the people of the Lord of Hosts. [15]This is the fate of that vast, prosperous city that lived in such security, that said to herself, "In all the world there is no city as great as I." But now—see how she has become a place of utter ruins, a place for animals to live! Everyone passing that way will mock, or shake his head in disbelief.

Zeph 3:11. And then you will no longer need to be ashamed of yourselves, for you will no longer be rebels against me. I will remove all your proud and arrogant men from among you; there will be no pride or haughtiness on my holy mountain.

Mal 4:1. "Watch now," the Lord of Hosts declares, "the day of judgment is coming, burning like a furnace. The proud and wicked will be burned up like straw; like a tree, they will be consumed—roots and all."

Mt 23:6. And how they love to sit at the head table at banquets, and in the reserved pews in the synagogue! [7]How they enjoy the deference paid them on the streets, and to be called "Rabbi" and "Master"! [8]Don't ever let anyone call you that. For only God is your Rabbi and all of you are on the same level, as brothers. [10]And don't be called "Master," for only one is your master, even the Messiah. [11]The more lowly your service to others, the greater you are. To be the greatest, be a servant. [12]But those who think themselves great shall be disappointed and humbled. Mt 20:26, 27; Mk 10:43; Lk 9:46; 18:14.

Mk 7:21. For from within, out of men's hearts, come evil thoughts [22]. . . pride, and all other folly.

Mk 12:38. Beware of the teachers of religion! For they love to wear the robes of the rich and scholarly, and to have everyone bow to them as they walk through the markets. [39]They love to sit in the best seats in the synagogues, and at the places of honor at banquets. Lk 20:45–47.

Lk 1:51. How he scatters the proud and haughty ones! [52]He has torn princes from their thrones and exalted the lowly.

Lk 11:43. Woe to you Pharisees! For how you love the seats of honor in the synagogues and the respectful greetings from everyone as you walk through the markets!

Lk 14:8. If you are invited to a wedding feast, don't always head for the best seat. For if someone more respected than you shows up, [9]the host will bring him over to where you are sitting and say, "Let this man sit here instead." And you, embarrassed, will have to take whatever seat is left at the foot of the table!

Lk 20:46. Beware of these experts in religion, for they love to parade in dignified robes and to be bowed to by the people as they walk along the street. And how they love the seats of honor in the synagogues and at religious festivals! Mt 23:6, 7.

Rom 1:22. Claiming themselves to be wise without God, they became utter fools instead. [29]Their lives became full of every kind of wickedness and sin. [30]They were . . . proud braggarts.

Rom 11:17. But some of these branches from Abraham's tree, some of the Jews, have been broken off. And you Gentiles who were branches from, we might say, a wild olive tree, were grafted in. So now you, too, receive the blessing God has promised Abraham and his children, sharing in God's rich nourishment of his own special olive tree. [18]But you must be careful not to brag about being put in to replace the branches that were broken off. Remember that you are important only because you are now a part of God's tree; you are just a branch, not a root. [19]"Well," you may be saying, "those branches were broken off to make room for me so I must be pretty good." [20]Watch out! Remember that those branches, the Jews, were broken off because they didn't believe God, and you are there only because you do. Do not be proud; be humble and grateful—and careful. [21]For if God did not spare the branches he put there in the first place, he won't spare you either. [25]I want you to know about this truth from God, dear brothers, so that you will not feel proud and start bragging. Yes, it is true that some of the Jews have set themselves against the Gospel now, but this will last only until all of you Gentiles have come to Christ—those of you who will.

Rom 12:3. As God's messenger I give each of you God's warning: Be honest in your estimate of yourselves, measuring your value by how much faith God has given you. [16]Don't try to get into the good graces of important people, but enjoy the company of ordinary folks. And don't think you know it all!

1 Cor 1:29. So that no one anywhere can ever brag in the presence of God.

1 Cor 3:18. Stop fooling yourselves. If you count yourself above average in intelligence, as judged by this world's standards, you had better put this all aside and be a fool rather than let it hold you back from the true wisdom from above.

1 Cor 4:6. I have used Apollos and myself as examples to illustrate what I have been saying: that you must not have favorites. You must not be proud of one of God's teachers more than another. [7]What are you so puffed up about? What do you have that God hasn't given you? And if all you have is from God, why act as though you are so great, and as though you have accomplished something on your own? [8]. . . You are full and spiritually contented, rich kings on your thrones, leaving us far behind! I wish you really were already on your thrones, for when that time comes you can be sure that we will be there, too, reigning with you. [10]Religion has made us foolish, you say, but of course you are all such wise and sensible Christians! We are weak, but not you! You are well thought of, while we are laughed at.

1 Cor 5:2. And are you still so conceited, so "spiritual"? Why aren't you mourning in sorrow and shame, and seeing to it that this man is removed from your membership? [6]What a terrible thing it is that you are boasting about your purity, and yet you let this sort of thing go on. Don't you realize that if even one person is allowed to go on sinning, soon all will be affected?

1 Cor 8:1. But although being a "know-it-all" makes us feel important, what is really needed to build the church is love. [2]If anyone thinks he knows all the answers, he is just showing his ignorance.

1 Cor 10:12. So be careful. If you are thinking, "Oh, I would never behave like that"—let this be a warning to you. For you too may fall into sin.

1 Cor 13:4. Love is . . . never boastful or proud.

1 Cor 14:38. But if anyone still disagrees—well, we will leave him in his ignorance.

2 Cor 10:5. These weapons can break down every proud argument against God and every wall that can be built to keep men from finding him. With these weapons I can capture rebels and bring them back to God, and change them into men whose hearts' desire is obedience to Christ. [12]Oh, don't worry, I wouldn't dare say that I am as wonderful as these other men who tell you how good they are! Their trouble is that they are only comparing themselves with each other, and measuring themselves against their own little ideas. What stupidity! [18]When someone boasts about himself and how well he has done, it doesn't count for much. But when the Lord commends him, that's different!

2 Cor 12:7. I will say this: because these experiences I had were so tremendous, God was afraid I might be puffed up by them; so I was given a physical condition which has been a thorn in my flesh, a messenger from Satan to hurt and bother me, and prick my pride.

Gal 6:3. If anyone thinks he is too great to stoop to this, he is fooling himself. He is really a nobody.

Eph 4:17. Let me say this, then, speaking for the Lord: Live no longer as the unsaved do, for they are blinded and confused.

Phil 2:3. Don't be selfish; don't live to make a good impression on others. Be humble, thinking of others as better than yourself.

1 Tim 2:9, 10. And the women should be the same way, quiet and sensible in manner and clothing. Christian women should be noticed for being kind and good, not for the way they fix their hair or because of their jewels or fancy clothes.

1 Tim 3:6. The pastor must not be a new Christian, because he might be proud of being chosen so soon, and pride comes before a fall. (Satan's downfall is an example.)

1 Tim 6:3. Some may deny these things, but they are the sound, wholesome teachings of the Lord Jesus Christ. . . . [4]Anyone who says anything different is both proud and stupid. [17]Tell those who are rich not to be proud and not to trust in their money.

2 Tim 3:2. For people will love only themselves and their money; they will be proud and boastful. [4]They will betray their friends; they will be hotheaded, puffed up with pride.

Jas 3:1. Dear brothers, don't be too eager to tell others their faults, for we all make many mistakes; and when we teachers of religion, who should know better do wrong, our punishment will be greater than it would be for others.

Jas 4:6. As the Scripture says, God gives strength to the humble, but sets himself against the proud and haughty.

1 Pet 5:3. Don't be tyrants, but lead them by your good example. *v.* 5.

1 Jn 2:16. For all these worldly things, these evil desires—the craze for sex, the ambition to buy everything that appeals to you, and the pride that comes from wealth and importance—these are not from God. They are from this evil world itself.

Rev 3:17. You say, "I am rich, with everything I want; I don't need a thing!" And you don't realize that spiritually you are wretched and miserable and poor and blind and naked. [18]My advice to you is to buy pure gold from me, gold purified by fire

—only then will you truly be rich. And to purchase from me white garments, clean and pure, so you won't be naked and ashamed; and to get medicine from me to heal your eyes and give you back your sight.

Rev 18:7. She has lived in luxury and pleasure—match it now with torments and with sorrows. She boasts, "I am queen upon my throne. I am no helpless widow. I will not experience sorrow."
8Therefore the sorrows of death and mourning and famine shall overtake her in a single day, and she shall be utterly consumed by fire; for mighty is the Lord who judges her.

See *Rich, The.*

INSTANCES OF. Ahithophel, 2 Sam 17:23. Naaman, refusing to wash in the Jordan River, 2 Kgs 5:11–13. Hezekiah, in displaying his resources, 2 Kgs 20:13; 2 Chron 32:31; Isa 39:2. Uzziah, 2 Chron 26:16–19. Haman, Esther 3:5, 6; 5:11, 13; 6:6; 7:9, 10. Kings of Tyre, Ezk 28:2, 3. Nebuchadnezzar, Dan 4:30–34; 5:20.

See *Ambition.*

PRIEST ANTEMOSAIC. Melchizedek, Gen 14:18; Heb 5:6, 10; 6:20; 7:1–21. Jethro, Ex 2:16. Priests in Israel before the giving of the law, Ex 19:22, 24. Called messenger, Eccl 5:6, 7.

MOSAIC. Ex 28:1–4; 29:9, 44; Num 3:10; 18:7; 1 Chron 23:13. Hereditary descent of office, Ex 27:21; 28:43; 29:9. Consecration of, Ex 29:1–9, 19–35; 40:12–16; Lev 6:19–23; 8:6–35; Heb 7:21. Is holy, Lev 21:6, 7; 22:9, 16. Washing of, Ex 40:30–32; Lev 16:24; see *Consecration of,* above. Must be without defect, Lev 21:16–23. Garments of, Ex 28:2–43; 39:1–29; Lev 6:10, 11; 8:13; Ezk 44:17–19. Put on garments in Temple, Ezk 42:14; 44:19. Atonement for, Lev 16:6, 24; Ezk 44:27. Defilement and purification of, Ezk 44:25, 26. Marriage of, Lev 21:7–15; Ezk 44:22. Quarters for, in temple, Ezk 40:45, 46. Exempt from tax, Ezra 7:24. Armed and organized for war at the time of the discontent toward Saul, 1 Chron 12:24–37. Beard and hair of, Ezk 44:20.

Twenty-four groups of, 1 Chron 24:1–19; 28:13, 21; 2 Chron 8:14; 31:2; 35:4, 5; Ezra 2:36–39; Neh 13:30. Chosen by lot, Lk 1:8, 9, 23.

Usurpations of duties of, Num 3:10; 16; 18:7; 2 Chron 26:17, 18. Priests were appointed by Jeroboam who were not Levites, 1 Kgs 12:31; 13:33.

See *Levites; Minister, Old Testament.*

COMPENSATION FOR. No part of the land of Canaan allowed to, Num 18:20; Deut 10:9; 14:27; 18:1, 2; Josh 13:14, 33; 14:3, 4; 18:7; Ezk 44:28. Provided with cities and suburbs, Lev 25:32–34; Num 35:2–8; Josh 21:1–4, 9–19, 41, 42; 1 Chron 6:55–60; Neh 11:3, 20; Ezk 45:1–6; 48:8–20. Own lands devoted to the Lord, Lev 27:21. Tithes of the tithes, Num 18:8–18, 25–32; Neh 10:38. Part of the spoils of war, including captives, Num 31:25–29. Firstfruits, Lev 23:20; 24:9; Num 18:12, 13, 17, 18; Deut 18:3–5; Neh 10:36. Redemption money, Lev 27:23; of firstborn, Num 3:46–51; 18:14–16. Things devoted, Lev 27:21; Num 5:9, 10; 18:14, 15. Fines, Lev 5:16; 22:14; Num 5:8. Trespass money and other trespass offerings, Lev 5:15, 17, 18; Num 5:5–10; 18:9; 2 Kgs 12:16. The Bread of the Presence, Ex 25:30; Lev 24:5–9; 2 Chron 2:4; 13:11; Neh 10:33; Mt 12:4; Heb 9:2. Portions of sacrifices and offerings, Ex 29:27–34; Lev 2:2, 3, 9, 10; 5:12, 13, 16; 6:15–18, 26; 7:6–10, 31–34; 10:12–14; 14:12, 13; Num 6:19, 20; 18:8–19; Deut 18:3–5; 1 Sam 2:13, 14; Ezk 44:28–31; 45:1–4; 1 Cor 9:13; 10:18.

Regulations by Hezekiah concerning income, 2 Chron 31:4–19. Portion of land allotted to, in redistribution in Ezekiel's vision, Ezk 48:8–14. For support of their families, Lev 22:11–13; Num 18:11, 19.

DUTIES OF. To offer sacrifices, Lev 1:4–17; 2:2, 16; 3:3–16; 4:5–12, 17, 25, 26, 30–35; 1 Chron 16:40; 2 Chron 13:11; 29:34; 35:11–14; Ezra 6:20; Heb 10:11; see *Offerings.* To offer the first fruits, Lev 23:9–11; Deut 26:2–4. Pronounce blessings, Num 6:22–27; Deut 21:5; 2 Chron 30:27. Teach the law, Lev 10:11; Deut 24:8; 27:14; 31:9–13; 33:10; Mal 2:7. Light the lamps in the Tabernacle, Ex 27:20, 21; Lev 24:3, 4; 2 Chron 13:11. Keep the sacred fire always burning, Lev 6:12, 13. To furnish a quota of wood for the sanctuary, Neh 10:34. Responsible for the sanctuary, Num 4:5–15; 18:1, 5, 7. To act as scribes, Ezra 7:1–6; Neh 8:9. Be present at and supervise the tithing, Neh 10:38. Sound the trumpet in calling assemblies and in battle, Num 10:1–10; 31:6; Josh 6; 2 Chron 13:12. Examine lepers, see *Leprosy.* Purify the unclean, Lev 15:31; see *Defilement.* Value things offered, Lev 27:8, 12. Officiate in the Holy Place, Heb 9:1, 2, 6. Chiefs of Levites, Num 3:7–9, 31–35; 4:17–19, 28, 33; 1 Chron 9:20. To act as magistrates, Num 5:14–31; Deut 17:8–13; 19:17; 21:5; 2 Chron 19:8; Ezk 44:23, 24. To encourage the army before battle, Deut 20:2–4. Carry the ark through the Jordan, Josh 3; 4:15–18; in battle, 1 Sam 4:3–5.

FIGURATIVE. Ex 19:6; Isa 61:6; 1 Pet 2:9; Rev 1:6; 5:10; 20:6.

HIGH PRIEST. Moses did not designate Aaron chief or high priest. The function he served was superior to that of other priests. The title appears after the institution of the office, Lev 21:10–15; Num 3:31–35. For qualifications, consecration, etc., see under the general topic above, *Priest, Mosaic.*

Garments of, Ex 28:2–43; 29:1–31; Lev 8:7–9. Respect due to, Acts 23:5.

Duties of. Had charge of the sanctuary and altar, Num 18:2, 3, 5, 7. To offer sacrifices, 1 Chron 23:13; Heb 5:1–3; 8:3. To designate subordinate priests for duty, Num 4:17–19; 1 Sam 2:36. To officiate in dedication of Levites, Num 8:11–21. To have charge of the treasury, 2 Kgs 12:10; 22:3, 4; 2 Chron 24:6–14; 34:9. To light the lamps of Tabernacle, Ex 27:20, 21; 30:8; Lev 24:3, 4; Num 8:2, 3. To burn incense, Ex 30:7, 8; 1 Sam 2:28. To place holy bread on the table every Sabbath, Lev 24:5–8. To offer for his own unintentional sins, Lev 4:3–12.

On the Day of Atonement, Ex 30:10; Lev 16; Heb 5:1–3; 9:7, 22, 23.

Judicial, Num 5:15; Deut 17:8–13; 1 Sam 4:18; Hos 4:4; Mt 26:3, 57, 62; Acts 5:21–28; 23:1–5. To take the census, Num 1:2–15. Officiate at choice of ruler,

Num 27:18, 19, 21. Distribute spoils of war, Num 31: 26–29.

Compensations of: See *Priest, Compensations for,* above.

A second priest, under the high priest, Num 3: 32; 4:16; 31:6; 1 Chron 9:20; 2 Sam 15:24; 2 Kgs 25: 18; Lk 3:1, 2.

MISCELLANEOUS FACTS CONCERNING. Loyal to Rehoboam at the time of the revolt of the ten tribes, 2 Chron 11:13, 14. Zeal of, in purging the temple, 2 Chron 29:4–17. Wickedness of, 2 Chron 36:14. Taken with the other captives to Babylon, Jer 29:1. Return from captivity, Ezra 1:5; 2:36–39, 61, 70; 3:8; 7:7–9; 8:24–30; Neh 7:39–42, 63–73; 10:1–8; 12:1–7. Polluted by marrying idolatrous wives, Ezra 9:1, 2; 10:5, 16–19; Neh 10:28. Restore the altar, and offer sacrifices, Ezra 3:1–6. Supervise the building of the Temple, Ezra 3:8–13. Inquire of John the Baptist whether he were the Christ, Jn 1:19. Conspire to kill Jesus, Mt 26:3–5, 14, 15, 47, 51; Mk 14:10, 11, 43–47, 53–65; 15:1; Lk 22:1–6, 50, 54, 66–71; 23:1, 2; Jn 11:47; 19:15, 16, 18. Try and condemn Jesus, Mt 26:57–68; 27:1, 2; Mk 14:53–65; Lk 22:54–71; 23:13–24; Jn 18:15–32. Incite the people to ask that Barabbas be released and Jesus killed, Mt 27:20; Mk 15:11; Lk 23:17, 18. Persecute the disciples, Acts 22:5. Reprove and threaten Peter and John, Acts 4:6–21; 5:17–41. Try, condemn, and stone Stephen, Acts 6:12–15; 7. Paul brought before, Acts 22:30; 23:1–5. Many converts among, Acts 6:7.

Corrupt, Jer 23:11, 12; Ezk 22:26; Lk 10:31. Instances of: Eli's sons, 1 Sam 2:12–17, 22; of the captivity, Ezra 9:1, 2; 10:16–22; Neh 13:4–9, 13, 28, 29.

Zealous, 1 Chron 9:10–13. Priestly office performed by prophets, 1 Sam 16:5.

PRIESTHOOD NEW TESTAMENT. In contrast to the Old Testament with its family of priests within Israel, the New Testament teaches that the true church is a priesthood in the sense that every believer is a priest, 1 Pet 2:5, 9; Rev 1:6; 5:10; 20:6, offering spiritual sacrifices, 1 Pet 2:5; the sacrifice of praise, Heb 13:15, 16; the sacrifice of participating in the work of the gospel, Phil 4:18; and the presenting of the body as a living sacrifice, Rom 12:1, 2.

PRIMOGENITURE See *Firstborn; Birthright.*

PRINCE OF PEACE See *Jesus.*

PRINCESSES Taught in household duties, 2 Sam 13:8, 9.

PRISCILLA Wife of Aquila. A disciple at Corinth, Acts 18:1–3, 18, 25, 26; Rom 16:3, 4; 1 Cor 16:19; 2 Tim 4:19.

PRISON Gen 39:20; 42:16–19; Lev 24:12; Num 15:34; Ezra 7:26; Jer 33:1; 52:11; Lk 23:19; Acts 4:3; 12:4, 5. Public, Acts 5:18. Cells of, Acts 16:24. Dungeon in, see *Dungeon.*

FIGURATIVE. Of affliction, Deut 4:20.

See *Imprisonment; Prisoners.*

PRISONERS Joseph, Gen 39:20–23; 40; 41: 1–44. Jeremiah, Jer 38:6–28; 39:14. John the Baptist, Mt 11:2; 14:3–12; Mk 6:17, 18; Lk 3:19, 20. Jesus, Mt 26:47–75; 27; Mk 14:43–72; 15; Lk 22:47–71; 23; Jn 18:3–40; 19. Apostles, Acts 5:17–42. Peter, Acts 12: 3–19. Paul, Acts 16:19–40; 21:26–40; 22–28 inclusive. Silas, Acts 16:19–40.

Required to work, Judg 16:21. Fed bread and water, 1 Kgs 22:27. Kept in chains, Acts 12:6; in stocks, Jer 29:26; Acts 16:24.

Confined beneath the palace, Jer 32:2; house of the scribe, Jer 37:15, 16; in house of captain of the guard, Gen 40:3. Visited by friends, Mt 11:2; Acts 24:23. Chained to soldiers, Acts 12:6, 7.

Severe hardships of, mitigated, Jer 37:20, 21. Cruelty to, Jer 38:6; Lam 3:53, 54; see *Captive.* Guards responsible for, Acts 12:18, 19. Tortured to extort self-incriminating testimony, Acts 22:24. Scourged, Mt 27:26; Mk 15:15; Acts 16:23, 33; 2 Cor 6:5; 11:23, 24. Permitted to make a defense, Acts 24: 10; 25:8, 16; 26:1; 2 Tim 4:16. Kindness to: By the prison keeper to Jeremiah, Jer 38:7–28; by Philippian jailer to Paul, Acts 16:33; by Felix, Acts 24:23; by Julius, the soldier, Acts 27:1, 3; 28:16. To be visited and ministered to, Mt 25:35–46. Released at feasts, Mt 27:15–17; Mk 15:6; Lk 23:17, 18; Jn 18:39.

OF WAR. Put to death, Josh 10:16–27; 1 Sam 15: 33; 27:11; 2 Sam 12:31; 2 Kgs 25:7; 1 Chron 20:3; Lam 3:34–36; Hos 13:16; Amos 1:13; by divine command, Num 31:9–11, 17. Thumbs and toes cut off, Judg 1:4–6. Blinded, 2 Kgs 25:7. See *Captive.*

Consolations for, Ps 79:11; 102:19, 20; 146:7.

See *Captive; Imprisonment.*

FIGURATIVE. Isa 61:1; Lk 4:18, 19.

PRIVILEGE See *Judgment, According to Opportunity; Responsibility.*

PRIZE A reward of merit, 1 Cor 9:24.

FIGURATIVE. Phil 3:14.

PROBATION Adam on, Gen 2:15–17; 3:2, 3. Amorites, Gen 15:16. Solomon, 1 Kgs 3:14; 9:4–9, with chapter 11:9–13. Taught in parables of the investments, Mt 25:14–30; Lk 19:12–27; the fig tree, Lk 13:6–9; embezzling accountant, Lk 16:1–12. Taught by Paul, Heb 6.

None after death, Mt 12:31, 32; 25:10–13; 26:24. See *Perseverance.*

PROCHORUS An early Christian deacon, Acts 6:5.

PROCLAMATION Imperial, Gen 26:11; 2 Chron 30:1–10; Esther 1:22; 6:9; 8:9–14; Isa 40:3, 9; Dan 3:4–7; 4:1; 5:29. Emancipation, 2 Chron 36: 22, 23; Ezra 1:1–4.

PROCRASTINATION Ex 22:29. You must be prompt in giving me the tithe of your crops and your wine, and the redemption payment for your oldest son.

Ezk 12:22. Son of dust, what is that proverb they quote in Israel—"The days as they pass make liars out of every prophet." [27]Son of dust, the people of Israel say, "His visions won't come true for a long, long time." [28]Therefore say to them: "The Lord God says, All delay has ended! I will do it now!"

Mt 8:21. Another of his disciples said, "Sir, when my father is dead, then I will follow you." Lk 9:59, 61.

Mt 24:48. But if you are evil and say to yourself, "My Lord won't be coming for a while," [49]and begin oppressing your fellow servants, partying and getting drunk, [50]your Lord will arrive unannounced and unexpected, [51]and severely whip you and send you off to the judgment of the hypocrites; there will be weeping and gnashing of teeth.

Mt 25:2, 3, 4. But only five of them were wise enough to fill their lamps with oil, while the other five were foolish and forgot. [5, 6]So, when the bridegroom was delayed, they lay down to rest until midnight when they were roused by the shout, "The bridegroom is coming! Come out and welcome him!" [7, 8]All the girls jumped up and trimmed their lamps. Then the five who hadn't any oil begged the others to share with them, for their lamps were going out. [9]But the others replied, "We haven't enough. Go instead to the shops and buy some for yourselves." [10]But while they were gone, the bridegroom came, and those who were ready went in with him to the marriage feast, and the door was locked. [11]Later, when the other five returned, they stood outside, calling, "Sir, open the door for us!" [12]But he called back, "Go away! It is too late!" [13]So stay awake and be prepared, for you do not know the date or moment of my return.

Lk 9:59. Another time, when he invited a man to come with him and to be his disciple, the man agreed—but wanted to wait until his father's death. [60]Jesus replied, "Let those without eternal life concern themselves with things like that. Your duty is to come and preach the coming of the Kingdom of God to all the world." [61]Another said, "Yes, Lord, I will come, but first let me ask permission of those at home." [62]But Jesus told him, "Anyone who lets himself be distracted from the work I plan for him is not fit for the Kingdom of God."

Acts 24:25. And as he reasoned with them about righteousness and self-control and the judgment to come, Felix was terrified. "Go away for now," he replied, "and when I have a more convenient time, I'll call for you again."

1 Thess 5:2. For you know perfectly well that no one knows. That day of the Lord will come unexpectedly like a thief in the night. [3]When people are saying, "All is well, everything is quiet and peaceful"—then, all of a sudden, disaster will fall upon them as suddenly as a woman's birth pains begin when her child is born. And these people will not be able to get away anywhere—there will be no place to hide.

Heb 3:7, 8. And since Christ is so much superior, the Holy Spirit warns us to listen to him, to be careful to hear his voice today and not let our hearts become set against him, as the people of Israel did. They steeled themselves against his love and complained against him in the desert while he was testing them. [9]But God was patient with them forty years, though they tried his patience sorely; he kept right on doing his mighty miracles for them to see. [10]"But," God says, "I was very angry with them, for their hearts were always looking somewhere else instead of up to me, and they never found the paths I wanted them to follow." [11]Then God, full of this anger against them, bound himself with an oath that he would never let them come to his place of rest. [12]Beware then of your own hearts, dear brothers, lest you find that they, too, are evil and unbelieving and are leading you away from the living God. [13]Speak to each other about these things every day while there is still time, so that none of you will become hardened against God, being blinded by the glamor of sin. [14]For if we are faithful to the end, trusting God just as we did when we first became Christians, we will share in all that belongs to Christ. [15]But *now* is the time. Never forget the warning. "*Today* if you hear God's voice speaking to you, do not harden your hearts against him, as the people of Israel did when they rebelled against him in the desert." [16]And who were those people I speak of, who heard God's voice speaking to them but then rebelled against him? They were the ones who came out of Egypt with Moses their leader. [17]And who was it who made God angry for all those forty years? These same people who sinned and as a result died in the wilderness. [18]And to whom was God speaking when he swore with an oath that they could never go into the land he had promised his people? He was speaking to all those who disobeyed him. [19]And why couldn't they go in? Because they didn't trust him. chapter 4:1–7.

See *Excuses.*

INSTANCES OF. Pharaoh, Ex 8:10. Elisha, 1 Kgs 19:20, 21. Esther, Esther 5:7, 8.

PRODIGALITY See *Extravagance; Frugality; Industry.*

PRODIGAL SON Lk 15:11–32.

PROFANATION See *Profanity.*

PROFANITY See *Blasphemy; Oath.* Of the name of God, see *God,* under Miscellaneous Subtopics; of the Sabbath, see *Sabbath.*

PROFESSION False, Prov 20:6; Hos 8:2. Of faith in Jesus, see *Confession.*

See *Testimony, Religious.*

PROGNOSTICATION By astrologers, Isa 47:13.

See *Prophecy; Prophets.*

PROHIBITION Of the use of intoxicating liquors. To priests on duty, Lev 10:8, 9. To Nazirites, Num 6:3, 4.

See *Abstinence, Total; Commandments; Drunkenness.*

PROMISES To the afflicted, see *Afflictions, Comfort in.* To backsliders, see *Backslider.* To children, See *Children.* To orphans, see *Orphan.* To widows, see *Widow.* To penitents, see *Penitent.* To the righteous, see *Righteous.* To seekers, see *Seekers,* and other like subjects.

See also *Blessings, Spiritual; Covenant; God, Goodness of; Jesus, Compassion of, Love of; Vows.*

PROMOTION Ps 75:6, 7; 78:70–72; 113:7, 8. As a reward of merit, 1 Chron 11:5, 6.

INSTANCES OF. Abraham, Gen 12:2. Joseph, from imprisoned slave to prince, Gen 41:1–45. Moses, from exile to lawgiver, see *Moses.* Aaron, from slave to high priest, see *Aaron.* Saul, from obscurity to a scepter, see *Saul.* David, from shepherd to throne, see *David.* Jeroboam, from slave to throne, 1 Kgs 11:26–35. Baasha, "out of the dust" to throne, 1 Kgs 16:1, 2. Daniel, from captive to premier, Dan 2:48; see *Daniel.* Shadrach, Meshach, and Abednego, Dan 3:30.

PROOF Of God's intention, Ex 3:12. Circumcision, of the covenant of Abraham, Gen 17:11. Blood of the pascal lamb, Ex 12:13.

See *Sign; Token.*

PROPAGATION Of species, commanded, Gen 1:11, 12, 21–25, 28; 9:1, 7.

See *Barrenness.*

PROPERTY IN REAL ESTATE. Gen 23:17, 18; 26:20. Rights in, violated, Gen 21:25–33; 26:18–22. Dedicated, Lev 27:16–25. See *Land.*

Dwellings. Alienated for debt, Lev 25:29, 30; by absence, 2 Kgs 8:1–6; in villages, inalienable, Lev 25:31–33. Dedicated, Lev 27:14, 15.

Confiscation of (Naboth's vineyard), 1 Kgs 21:15, 16. Priests, exempt from taxes, Gen 47:22. Entail of, Num 27:1–11; 36:1–9. Inherited, Eccl 2:20–23. Boundary markers of, not to be moved, Deut 19:14; 27:17.

PERSONAL. Rights in, sacred, Ex 20:17; Deut 5:21. Laws concerning damage and violence to, Ex 21:28–36; 22:9; Deut 23:25. Strayed, to be returned to owner, Lev 6:3–5; Deut 22:1–3. Rented, Ex 22:14, 15; or loaned, Ex 22:10–15. Sold for debt, Prov 22:26–27; rights of redemption of, Jer 32:6, 7. Dedicated to God, redemption of, Lev 27:9–13, 26–33. In slaves, Ex 21:4.

PROPHECY Concerning Jesus, see *Jesus.*

Relating to various countries, nations, and cities, see under their respective titles. Respecting individuals, see under their names.

Inspired, Isa 28:22; Lk 1:70; 2 Tim 3:16; 2 Pet 1:20, 21. "The Lord said to," etc.: To Elijah, 1 Kgs 17:8, 9; 21:17, 28; Isaiah, Isa 2:1; 8:5; 13:1; 14:28; 38:4; Jeremiah, Jer 1:4; 7:1; 11:1; 13:8, 9; 16:1; 18:1; 25:1–3; 26:1; 27:1; 29:30; 30:1, 4; 32:1, 6, 7, 26; 33:1, 19, 23; 34:12; 35:12; 36:1; 37:6; 43:8; 44:1; 46:1; 49:34; 50:1; Ezekiel, Ezk 3:16; 6:1; 7:1; 11:14; 12;1, 8, 17, 21; 13:1; 14:12; 15:1; 16:1; 17:1, 11; 18:1; 20:45; 21:1, 8, 18; 22:1, 17, 23; 23:1; 24:1, 15, 20, 21; 25:1; 26:1; 27:1; 28:1, 11, 20; 29:1, 17; 30:1, 20; 31:1; 32:1, 17; 33:1, 23; 34:1; 36:16; 37:15; 38:1; Amos, Amos 7:14, 15; Jonah, Jon 3:1; Haggai, Hag 2:1, 10, 20; Zechariah, Zech 1:7; 4:8; 6:9; 7:1, 4, 8, 9; 8:1, 18.

Publicly proclaimed, Jer 11:6. Exemplified in pantomine, Ezk 4; 5:1–4; Acts 21:11. Written by a secretary, Jer 45:1; on a scroll, Jer 51:60.

Proof of God's foreknowledge, Isa 43:9. Sure fulfillment of, Ezk 12:22–25, 28; Hab 2:3; Mt 5:18; 24:35; Acts 13:27, 29. Cessation of, Lam 2:9.

Of apostasy, 1 Jn 2:18; Jude 1:17, 18; false teachers, 2 Pet 2:3. Tribulations of the righteous, Rev 2:10.

CONCERNING THE MESSIAH, AND THE FULFILLMENT.

Gen 12:3; 18:18; 22:18	Quoted in	Acts 3:25; Gal 3:8, 9.
Gen 17:7, 8, 19; 22:16, 17		Lk 1:55, 72–74.
Deut 18:15, 18		Acts 3:21–23.
Ps 2:1, 2		Acts 4:25, 26.
Ps 2:7		Acts 13:32, 33; Heb 1:5, 6; 5:5.
Ps 8:2		Mt 21:16.
Ps 8:4–6		Heb 2:6–8.
Ps 16:8–11		Acts 2:25–28, 31.
Ps 16:10		Acts 13:35.
Ps 22:1		Mt 27:46; Mk 15:34.
Ps 22:18		Mt 27:35; Mk 15:24; Lk 23:34; Jn 19:23, 24.
Ps 22:22		Heb 2:12.
Ps 31:5, 6		Lk 23:46.
Ps 41:9		Jn 13:18; Acts 1:16.
Ps 45:6, 7		Heb 1:8, 9.
Ps 68:18		Eph 4:8–10.
Ps 69:21		Mt 27:48; Mk 15:36; Lk 23:36; Jn 19:28, 29.
Ps 69:25; 109:8		Acts 1:20.
Ps 95:7–11		Heb 3:7–11; 4:3, 5–7.
Ps 102:25–27		Heb 1:10–12.
Ps 110:1		Mt 22:44; Mk 12:36; Lk 20:42, 43; Acts 2:34, 35; Heb 1:13.
Ps 110:4		Heb 5:6.
Ps 118:22, 23		Mt 21:42; Mk 12:10, 11; Lk 20:17; Acts 4:11.
Ps 118:25, 26		Mt 21:9; Mk 11:9; Jn 12:13.
Ps 132:11, 17		Lk 1:69; Acts 2:30.
Isa 7:14		Mt 1:23.
Isa 9:1, 2		Mt 4:15, 16.
Isa 9:7, with Dan 7:14, 27		Lk 1:32, 33.
Isa 11:10		Rom 15:12.
Isa 25:8		1 Cor 15:54.
Isa 28:16		Rom 9:33; 1 Pet 2:6.
Isa 40:3–5		Mt 3:3; Mk 1:3; Lk 3:4–6.
Isa 42:1–4		Mt 12:17–21.
Isa 49:6		Lk 2:32; Acts 13:47, 48; 26:23.
Isa 53:1		Jn 12:38; Rom 10:16.
Isa 53:3–6		Acts 26:22, 23.
Isa 53:4–6, 11		1 Pet 2:24, 25.
Isa 53:4		Mt 8:17.
Isa 53:9		1 Pet 2:22.
Isa 53:12		Mk 15:28; Lk 22:37.
Isa 54:13		Jn 6:45.
Isa 55:3		Acts 13:34.
Isa 59:20, 21		Rom 11:26, 27.
Jer 31:31–34		Heb 8:8–12; 10:16, 17.
Hos 1:10		Rom 9:26.
Hos 2:23		Rom 9:25; 1 Pet 2:10.
Joel 2:28–32		Acts 2:16–21.
Amos 9:11, 12		Acts 15:16, 17.
Mic 5:2		Mt 2:5, 6; Jn 7:41, 42.
Hab 1:5		Acts 13:40, 41.
Hag 2:6		Heb 12:26.
Zech 9:9		Mt 21:4, 5; Jn 12:14, 15.
Zech 11:13		Mt 27:9, 10.
Zech 12:10		Jn 19:37.
Zech 13:7		Mt 26:31, 56; Mk 14:27, 50.
Mal 3:1		Mt 11:10; Mk 1:2; Lk 7:27.
Mal 4:5, 6		Mt 11:13, 14; 17:10–13; Mk 9:11–13; Lk 1:16, 17.

See *Jesus, Prophecies Concerning; Prophetesses; Prophets.*

MISCELLANEOUS FULFILLED. The birth and zeal of Josiah, 1 Kgs 13:2; 2 Kgs 23:1–20. Death of the prophet of Judah, 1 Kgs 13:21, 22, 24–30. Extinction of Jeroboam's family, 1 Kgs 14:5–11; of Baasha's family, 1 Kgs 16:2, 3, 9–13. Concerning the rebuilding of Jericho, Josh 6:26; 1 Kgs 16:34. The drought, foretold by Elijah, 1 Kgs 17:14. Destruction of Ben-hadad's army, 1 Kgs 20:13–30. The death of a man who refused to kill a prophet, 1 Kgs 20:35, 36. The death of Ahab, 1 Kgs 20:42; 21:18–24; 22:31–38. The death of Ahaziah, 2 Kgs 1: 3–17. Elijah's translation, 2 Kgs 2:3–11. Cannibalism among the children of Israel, Lev 26:29; Deut 28:53; 2 Kgs 6:26–30; Jer 19:9; Lam 4:10. The death of the Samaritan king, 2 Kgs 7:2, 19, 20. The end of the famine in Samaria, 2 Kgs 7:1–18. Jezebel's tragic death, 1 Kgs 21:23; 2 Kgs 9:10, 33–36. The defeat of Syria by Joash, 2 Kgs 13:16–25. Conquests of Jeroboam, 2 Kgs 14:25–28. Four generations of Jehu to sit on the throne of Israel, 2 Kgs 10:30, with 2 Kgs 15:12. Destruction of Sennacherib's army, and his death, 2 Kgs 19:5–7, 20–37. The captivity of Judah, 2 Kgs 20:17, 18; 24:10–16; 25:11–21. Concerning Christ, see *Jesus, Prophecies Concerning.* Also see above. Concerning John, Mt 3:3. Rachel weeping for her children, Jer 31:15; Mt 2:17, 18. Deliverance of Jeremiah, Jer 39:15–18. Invasion of Judah by the Chaldeans, Hab 1:6–11; fulfilled, 2 Kgs 25; 2 Chron 36:17–21. Betrayal of Jesus by Judas, prophecy, Ps 41:9; fulfillment, Jn 13:18; 18: 1–9. Judas' self-destruction, Ps 69:25; Acts 1:16, 20; fulfilled, Mt 27:5; Acts 1:16–20. Outpouring of the Holy Spirit, Joel 2:28, 29; fulfilled, Acts 2:16–21. Spiritual blindness of the Jews, Isa 6:9; 29:13; fulfilled, Mk 7:6, 7; Acts 28:25–27. Mission of Jesus, Ps 68:18; fulfilled, Eph 4:8, 10; see *Jesus, Mission of.* Captivity of the Jews, Jer 25:11, 12; 29: 10, 14; 32:3–5; Dan 9:2, with 2 Kgs 25:1–8; Ezra 1. Of the destruction of the ship in which Paul sailed, Acts 27:10, 18–44.

PROPHETS Called *Seers,* 1 Sam 9:9–11, 19; 2 Chron 9:29; 12:15; Isa 29:10; 30:10, 11. Schools of, 1 Kgs 20:35; 2 Kgs 2:3–15; 4:1, 38; 9:1. Kept the chronicles, 1 Chron 29:29; 2 Chron 9:29; 12:15. Counsellors to kings, Isa 37:2, 3. Not honored in their own country, Mt 13:57; Lk 4:24–27; Jn 4:43, 44.

Inspired by angels, Zech 1:9, 13, 14, 19; Acts 7:53; Gal 3:19; Heb 2:2. Persecutions of, 2 Chron 36:16; Amos 2:12. Martyrs, Jer 2:30; Mt 23:37; Mk 12:5; Lk 13:34; 1 Thess 2:15; Heb 11:37, 38; Rev 16:6.

COMPENSATIONS OF. Presents, 1 Sam 9:7, 8; 1 Kgs 14:3; 2 Kgs 4:42; 8:8, 9; Ezk 13:19. Presents refused by, Num 22:18; 1 Kgs 13:7, 8; 2 Kgs 5:5, 16.

FALSE. 1 Kgs 13:18; Neh 6:12, 13; Jer 23:25–27, 30–32; Lam 2:14. Admonitions to, Deut 13:1–3. Denunciations against, Deut 18:20; Jer 14:15. Punishment of, Jer 13:13–16; 20:6; 28:16, 17; 29:32; Zech 13:3. In the end time, Mt 24:11, 24; Mk 13:22; 2 Pet 2:1; 1 Jn 4:1.

Instances of. No-adiah, Neh 6:14; four hundred in Samaria, 1 Kgs 22:6–12; 2 Chron 18:3–5.

See *Minister, False.*

INSPIRED WORDS OF. Gen 40:8. And they replied, "We both had dreams last night, but there is no one here to tell us what they mean." "Interpreting dreams is God's business," Joseph replied. "Tell me what you saw."

Gen 41:16. "I can't do it by myself," Joseph replied, "but God will tell you what it means!" [38]As they discussed who should be appointed for the job, Pharaoh said, "Who could do it better than Joseph? For he is a man who is obviously filled with the Spirit of God." [39]Turning to Joseph, Pharaoh said to him, "Since God has revealed the meaning of the dreams to you, you are the wisest man in the country!"

Ex 3:14. " 'The Sovereign God,' " was the reply. "Just say, 'I Am has sent me!' [15]Yes, tell them, 'Jehovah, the God of your ancestors Abraham, Isaac, and Jacob, has sent me to you.' (This is my eternal name, to be used throughout all generations.)"

Ex 4:12. "Now go ahead and do as I tell you, for I will help you to speak well, and I will tell you what to say. [15]So I will tell you what to tell him, and I will help both of you to speak well, and I will tell you what to do." [27]Now Jehovah said to Aaron, "Go into the wilderness to meet Moses."

Ex 6:13. Then the Lord ordered Moses and Aaron to return to the people of Israel and to Pharaoh, king of Egypt, demanding that the people be permitted to leave. [29]The Lord said, "I am Jehovah. Go in and give Pharaoh the message I have given you." Ex 7:2.

Ex 19:3. Moses climbed the rugged mountain to meet with God, and from somewhere in the mountain God called to him and said, "Give these instructions to the people of Israel." [9]Then he said to Moses, "I am going to come to you in the form of a dark cloud, so that the people themselves can hear me when I talk with you, and then they will always believe you." [19]As the trumpet blast grew louder and louder, Moses spoke and God thundered his reply.

Ex 24:16. And the glory of the Lord rested upon Mt. Sinai and the cloud covered it six days; the seventh day he called to Moses from the cloud.

Ex 25:22. And I will meet with you there and talk with you from above the place of mercy between the cherubim; and the Ark will contain the laws of my covenant. There I will tell you my commandments for the people of Israel.

Ex 33:11. The Lord spoke to Moses face to face, as a man speaks to his friend.

Num 7:89. When Moses went into the Tabernacle to speak with God, he heard the Voice speaking to him from above the place of mercy over the Ark, the spot between the two cherubim. Lev 1:1; Num 1:1.

Num 9:8. Moses said he would ask the Lord about it. *vs.* 9, 10.

Num 11:17. "I will come down and talk with you there and I will take of the Spirit which is on you and will put it upon them also; they shall bear the burden of the people along with you, so that you will not have the task alone." [25]And the Lord came down in the Cloud and talked with Moses, and the Lord took of the Spirit that was upon Moses and put it upon the seventy elders; and when the Spirit rested upon them, they prophesied for some time.

Num 12:6. And the Lord said to them, "Even with a prophet, I would communicate by visions and dreams; [7, 8]but that is not how I communicate with my servant Moses. He is completely at home in my house! With him I speak face to face! And he shall see the very form of God! Why then were you not afraid to criticize him?"

Num 16:28. And Moses said, "By this you shall know that Jehovah has sent me to do all these things that I have done—for I have not done them on my own. [29]If these men die a natural death or from some ordinary accident or disease, then Jehovah has not sent me."

Num 22:18. "If he were to give me a palace filled with silver and gold, I could do nothing contrary to the command of the Lord my God." [38]Balaam replied, "I have come, but I have no power to say anything except what God tells me to say; and that is what I shall speak."

Num 23:5. Then the Lord gave Balaam a message for King Balak. [12]But Balaam replied, "Can I say anything except what Jehovah tells me to? [20]Look! I have received a command to bless them, for God has blessed them, and I cannot reverse it!" [26]But Balaam replied, "Didn't I tell you that I must say whatever Jehovah tells me to?"

Num 24:1. He went at once and looked out toward the camp of Israel [2]which stretched away across the plains, divided by tribal areas. Then the Spirit of God came upon him, [3, 4]and he spoke this prophecy concerning them: "Balaam the son of Beor says that the man whose eyes are open says, 'I have listened to the word of God, I have seen what God Almighty showed me; I fell, and my eyes were opened.' " *vs.* 15, 16.

Deut 1:5. Here, then, is Moses' address to Israel, stating all the laws God had commanded him to pass on to them: [6]"It was forty years ago, at Mount Horeb, that Jehovah our God told us, 'You have stayed here long enough.' "

Deut 5:4. He spoke with you face to face from the center of the fire, there at the mountain. [5]I stood as an intermediary between you and Jehovah, for you were afraid of the fire and did not go up to him on the mountain. He spoke to me and I passed on his laws to you. This is what he said: [6]"I am Jehovah your God who rescued you from slavery in Egypt. [31]Then you come back and stand here beside me, and I will give you all my commandments, and you shall teach them to the people; and they will obey them in the land I am giving to them."

Deut 34:9. Joshua (son of Nun) was full of the spirit of wisdom, for Moses had laid his hands upon him; so the people of Israel obeyed him, and followed the commandments that the Lord had given to Moses. [10]There has never been another prophet like Moses, for the Lord talked to him face to face. [11]And at God's command he performed amazing miracles which have never been equaled. He did great and terrifying wonders before Pharaoh and his entire court in Egypt.

Josh 3:7. "Today," the Lord told Joshua, "I will give you great honor, so that all Israel will know that I am with you just as I was with Moses."

Judg 6:7. Then at last the people of Israel began to cry out to the Lord for help. [8]However, the Lord's reply through the prophet he sent to them was this: "The Lord God of Israel brought you out of slavery in Egypt, [9]and rescued you from the Egyptians and from all who were cruel to you, and drove out your enemies from before you, and gave you their land. [10]He told you that he is the Lord your God, and that you must not worship the gods of the Amorites who live around you on every side. But you have not listened to him." [34]Then the Spirit of the Lord came upon Gideon, and he blew a trumpet as a call to arms. Judg 11:29; 1 Chron 12: 18.

Judg 13:25. And the Spirit of the Lord began to excite him whenever he visited the parade grounds of the army of the tribe of Dan, located between the cities of Zorah and Eshta-ol. Judg 14:6, 19.

1 Sam 3:1. Meanwhile little Samuel was helping the Lord by assisting Eli. Messages from the Lord were very rare in those days. [7](Samuel had never had a message from Jehovah before.) [19]As Samuel grew, the Lord was with him and people listened carefully to his advice. [20]And all Israel from Dan to Beersheba knew that Samuel was going to be a prophet of the Lord. [21]Then the Lord began to give messages to him there at the Tabernacle in Shiloh. *vs.* 4–10.

1 Sam 9:6. "I've just thought of something! There is a prophet who lives here in this city; he is held in high honor by all the people because everything he says comes true." [15]The Lord had told Samuel the previous day, [16]"About this time tomorrow I will send you a man from the land of Benjamin." *vs.* 16–20.

1 Sam 10:6. "At that time the Spirit of the Lord will come mightily upon you, and you will prophesy with them and you will feel and act like a different person. [7]From that time on your decisions should be based on whatever seems best under the circumstances, for the Lord will guide you." [10]When Saul and the servant arrived at the Hill of God they saw the prophets coming toward them, and the Spirit of God came upon him, and he too began to prophesy.

1 Sam 16:13. And the Spirit of Jehovah came upon him and gave him great power from that day onward.

1 Sam 19:20. He sent soldiers to capture him; but when they arrived and saw Samuel and the other prophets prophesying, the Spirit of God came upon them and they also began to prophesy. [23]But on the way to Naioth the Spirit of God came upon Saul, and he too began to prophesy! *v.* 24.

2 Sam 7:4. But that night the Lord said to Nathan. *vs.* 3–7; 2 Sam 12:1.

2 Sam 23:2. The Spirit of the Lord spoke by me, and his word was on my tongue. [3]The Rock of Israel said to me: "One shall come who rules righteously, who rules in the fear of God." Acts 2:30.

1 Kgs 13:20. Then, suddenly, while they were sitting at the table, a message from the Lord came to the old man.

1 Kgs 14:5. But the Lord told him that the queen, pretending to be someone else, would come to ask about her son, for he was very sick. And the Lord told him what to tell her.

1 Kgs 17:1. Then Elijah, the prophet from Tishbe in Gilead, told King Ahab, "As surely as the Lord God of Israel lives—the God whom I worship and serve—there won't be any dew or rain for several years until I say the word!" [24]"Now I know for sure that you are a prophet," she told him afterward, "and that whatever you say is from the Lord!"

1 Kgs 18:36. Elijah walked up to the altar and prayed, "O Lord God . . . prove today that you are the God of Israel and that I am your servant; prove that I have done all this at your command." [46]And the Lord gave special strength to Elijah.

1 Kgs 19:9. But the Lord said to him, "What are you doing here, Elijah?"

1 Kgs 22:14. But Micaiah told him, "This I vow, that I will say only what the Lord tells me to! [28]If you return in peace," Micaiah replied, "it will prove that the Lord has not spoken through me." Then he turned to the people standing nearby and said, "Take note of what I've said." 2 Chron 18:27.

2 Kgs 1:12. Elijah replied, "If I am a man of God, let fire come down from heaven and destroy you and your fifty men." And again the fire from God burned them up.

2 Kgs 2:9. And Elisha replied, "Please grant me twice as much prophetic power as you have had." [15]When the young prophets of Jericho saw what had happened, they exclaimed, "The spirit of Elijah rests upon Elisha!"

2 Kgs 3:11. But Jehoshaphat, the king of Judah, asked, "Isn't there a prophet of the Lord with us? If so, we can find out what to do!" "Elisha is here," one of the king of Israel's officers replied. Then he added, "He was Elijah's assistant." [12]"Fine," Jehoshaphat said. "He's just the man we want." [15]And as the lute was played, the message of the Lord came to Elisha.

2 Kgs 4:27. But the prophet said, "Let her alone; something is deeply troubling her and the Lord hasn't told me what it is."

2 Kgs 5:8. But when Elisha the prophet heard about the king of Israel's plight, he sent this message to him: "Why are you so upset? Send Naaman to me, and he will learn that there is a true prophet of God here in Israel."

2 Kgs 6:8. Once when the king of Syria was at war with Israel, he said to his officers, "We will mobilize our forces at ______" (naming the place). [9]Immediately Elisha warned the king of Israel, "Don't go near ______" (naming the same place) "for the Syrians are planning to mobilize their troops there!" [10]The king sent a scout to see if Elisha was right, and sure enough, he had saved him from disaster. This happened several times. [11]The king of Syria was puzzled. He called together his officers and demanded, "Which of you is the traitor? Who has been informing the king of Israel about my plans?" [12]"It's not us, sir," one of the officers replied. "Elisha, the prophet, tells the king of Israel even the words you speak in the privacy of your bedroom!" [17]Then Elisha prayed, "Lord, open his eyes and let him see!" And the Lord opened the young man's eyes so that he could see horses of fire and chariots of fire everywhere upon the mountain! [32]Elisha was sitting in his house at a meeting with the elders of Israel when the king sent a messenger to summon him. But before the messenger arrived Elisha said to the elders, "This murderer has sent a man to kill me. When he arrives, shut the door and keep him out, for his master will soon follow him."

2 Kgs 10:10. The Lord has done that, for everything he says comes true. He declared through his servant Elijah that this would happen to Ahab's descendants.

1 Chron 21:18. Then the angel of the Lord told Gad to instruct David to build an altar to the Lord at the threshing-floor of Ornan the Jebusite.

1 Chron 28:12. For the Holy Spirit had given David all these plans. [19]"Every part of this blueprint," David told Solomon, "was given to me in writing from the hand of the Lord." Ex 25:9; 26:30; 2 Chron 8:14.

2 Chron 20:14. The Spirit of the Lord came upon one of the men standing there—Jehaziel. 2 Chron 15:1; 24:20.

2 Chron 26:5. While Zechariah was alive Uzziah was always eager to please God. Zechariah was a man who had special revelations from God.

2 Chron 33:18. The rest of Manasseh's deeds, and his prayer to God, and God's reply through the prophets. Ezra 5:1, 2.

2 Chron 36:12. For he refused to take the counsel of Jeremiah the prophet, who gave him messages from the Lord. *v.* 15.

Neh 9:30. You were patient with them for many years. You sent your prophets to warn them about their sins.

Job 32:8, 9. Rather, it is the spirit in a man, the breath of the Almighty which makes him intelligent.

Job 33:14. For God speaks again and again, [15]in dreams, in visions of the night when deep sleep falls on men as they lie on their beds. [16]He opens their ears in times like that, and gives them wisdom and instruction.

Ps 103:7. He revealed his will and nature to Moses and the people of Israel.

Isa 6:1. I saw the Lord! He was sitting on a lofty throne, and the Temple was filled with his glory. [8]Then I heard the Lord asking, "Whom shall I send as a messenger to my people? Who will go?" And I said, "Lord, I'll go! Send *me.*" [9]And he said,

"Yes, go. But tell my people this." *vs.* 1–7.

Isa 8:11. The Lord has said in strongest terms: Do not under any circumstances, go along with the plans of Judah.

Isa 44:26. But what my prophets say, I do; when they say Jerusalem will be delivered and the cities of Judah lived in once again—it shall be done!

Isa 63:11. Where is the God who sent his Holy Spirit to be among his people?

Jer 1:1, 2. These are God's messages to Jeremiah the priest (the son of Hilkiah) who lived in the town of Anathoth in the land of Benjamin. The first of these messages came to him in the thirteenth year of the reign of Amon's son Josiah, king of Judah. chapters 2:1; 7:1; 11:1; 13:1–3; 16:1; 18:1; 24:4, 5; 26:1, 12; 27:1, 2; 29:30; 33:1; 34:1; Obd 1:1; Jon 1:1; Mic 1:1; Zech 1:1, 7.

4. The Lord said to me, [5]"I knew you before you were formed within your mother's womb; before you were born I sanctified you and appointed you as my spokesman to the world." [6]"O Lord God," I said, "I can't do that! I'm far too young! I'm only a youth!" [7]"Don't say that," he replied, "for you will go wherever I send you and speak whatever I tell you to. [8]And don't be afraid of the people, for I, the Lord, will be with you and see you through." [9]Then he touched my mouth and said, "See, I have put my words in your mouth! [10]Today your work begins, to warn the nations and the kingdoms of the world. In accord with my words spoken through your mouth I will tear down some and destroy them, and plant others and nurture them and make them strong and great."

Jer 7:25. Ever since the day your fathers left Egypt until now, I have kept on sending them my prophets, day after day. Jer 25:2, 3.

Jer 11:18. Then the Lord told me all about their plans and showed me their evil plots.

Jer 20:9. And I can't quit! For if I say I'll never again mention the Lord—never more speak his name—then his word in my heart is like fire that burns in my bones, and I can't hold it in any longer.

Jer 23:9. My heart is broken for the false prophets, full of deceit. I awake with fear and stagger as a drunkard does from wine, because of the awful fate awaiting them, for God has decreed holy words of judgment against them.

Jer 26:2. Stand out in front of the Temple of the Lord and make an announcement to all the people who have come there to worship from many parts of Judah. Give them the entire message; don't leave out one word of all I have for them to hear.

Jer 42:4. "All right," Jeremiah replied. "I will ask him and I will tell you what he says. I will hide nothing from you." [7]Ten days later the Lord gave his reply to Jeremiah.

Ezk 1:1–3. The heavens were suddenly opened to me and I saw visions from God. [20, 21]For the spirit of the four living beings was in the wheels; so wherever their spirit went, the wheels and the living beings went there too.

Ezk 2:1. "I will talk to you." [2]And the Spirit entered into me as he spoke, and set me on my feet. [4]"But I am sending you to give them my messages—the messages of the Lord God. [5]And whether they listen or not . . . they will at least know they have had a prophet among them."

Ezk 3:10. Then he added: "Son of dust, let all my words sink deep into your own heart first; listen to them carefully for yourself. [11]Then, afterward, go to your people in exile, and whether or not they will listen, tell them: This is what the Lord God says!" [12]Then the Spirit lifted me up and the glory of the Lord began to move away, accompanied by the sound of a great earthquake. [14]The Spirit lifted me up and took me away. . . . I went in bitterness and anger, but the hand of the Lord was strong upon me. [16]At the end of the seven days, the Lord said to me: [17]"Son of dust, I have appointed you as a watchman for Israel; whenever I send my people a warning, pass it on to them at once." [22]I was helpless in the hand of God, and when he said to me, "Go out into the valley and I will talk to you there." [24]Then the Spirit entered into me and set me on my feet. He talked to me and said. [27]"But whenever I give you a message, then I will loosen your tongue and let you speak, and you shall say to them: The Lord God says."

Ezk 8:1. Then, late in August of the sixth year of King Jehoiachin's captivity, as I was talking with the elders of Judah in my home, the power of the Lord God fell upon me.

Ezk 11:1. Then the Spirit lifted me and brought me over to the east gate of the Temple. [4]"Therefore, son of dust, prophesy against them loudly and clearly." [5]Then the Spirit of the Lord came upon me and told me to say: "The Lord says to the people of Israel." [24]Afterwards the Spirit of God carried me back again to Babylon, to the Jews in exile there.

Ezk 33:22. Now the hand of the Lord had been upon me the previous evening, and he had healed me so that I could speak again by the time the man arrived.

Ezk 37:1. The power of the Lord was upon me and I was carried away by the Spirit of the Lord to a valley full of old, dry bones that were scattered everywhere across the ground.

Ezk 40:1. The hand of the Lord was upon me, [2]and in a vision he took me to the land of Israel.

Ezk 43:5. Then the Spirit took me up and brought me into the inner court; and the glory of the Lord filled the Temple.

Dan 1:17. God gave these four youths great ability to learn and they soon mastered all the literature and science of the time, and God gave to Daniel special ability in understanding the meanings of dreams and visions.

Dan 2:19. And that night in a vision God told Daniel what the king had dreamed.

Dan 7:16. So I approached one of those standing beside the throne and asked him the meaning of all these things, and he explained them to me.

Dan 8:16. And I heard a man's voice calling from

across the river, "Gabriel, tell Daniel the meaning of his dream."

Dan 9:2. In that first year of his reign, I, Daniel, learned from the book of Jeremiah the prophet, that Jerusalem must lie desolate for seventy years. [6]"We have refused to listen to your servants the prophets, whom you sent again and again down through the years, with your messages to our kings and princes and to all the people. [10]O Lord our God, we have disobeyed you; we have flouted all the laws you gave us through your servants, the prophets." [*vs.* 1–21.] [22]And he said to me, "Daniel, I am here to help you understand God's plans."

Dan 10:7. I, Daniel, alone saw this great vision; the men with me saw nothing, but they were suddenly filled with unreasoning terror and ran to hide, [8]and I was left alone. When I saw this frightening vision my strength left me, and I grew pale and weak with fright. [9]Then he spoke to me, and I fell to the ground face downward in a deep faint.

Hos 1:1. These are the messages from the Lord to Hosea. *v.* 2.

Hos 12:10. I sent my prophets to warn you with many a vision and many a parable and dream.

Joel 2:28. After I have poured out my rains again, I will pour out my Spirit upon all of you! Your sons and daughters will prophesy; your old men will dream dreams, and your young men see visions. [29]And I will pour out my Spirit even on your slaves, men and women alike.

Amos 3:7. "But always, first of all, I warn you through my prophets. This now I have done." [8]The Lion has roared—tremble in fear. The Lord God has sounded your doom—I dare not refuse to proclaim it.

Amos 7:7. Then he showed me this: The Lord was standing beside a wall built with a plumbline checking it with a plumbline to see if it was straight. [14]But Amos replied, "I am not really one of the prophets. I do not come from a family of prophets. I am just a herdsman and fruit picker. [15]But the Lord took me from caring for the flocks and told me, 'Go and prophesy to my people Israel.' "

Amos 9:1. I saw the Lord standing beside the altar, saying, "Smash the tops of the pillars and shake the Temple until the pillars crumble and the roof crashes down upon the people below. Though they run, they will not escape; they all will be killed."

Jon 3:1, 2. Then the Lord spoke to Jonah again: [2]"Go to that great city, Nineveh," he said, "and warn them of their doom, as I told you to before!"

Mic 3:8. But as for me, I am filled with power, with the Spirit of the Lord, fearlessly announcing God's punishment on Israel for her sins.

Hab 3:2. O Lord, now I have heard your report, and I worship you in awe for the fearful things you are going to do. [16]I tremble when I hear all this; my lips quiver with fear. My legs give way beneath me and I shake in terror. I will quietly wait for the day of trouble to come upon the people who invade us.

Hag 1:13. Then the Lord told them (again sending the message through Haggai, his messenger), "I am with you, I will bless you."

Zech 2:9. I will smash them with my fist and their slaves will be their rulers! *Then you will know it was the Lord of Hosts who sent me.*

Zech 7:12. They hardened their hearts like flint, afraid to hear the words that God, the Lord of Hosts, commanded them—the laws he had revealed to them by his Spirit through the early prophets. That is why such great wrath came down on them from God.

Mk 12:36. For David himself said—and the Holy Spirit was speaking through him when he said it—"God said to my Lord, sit at my right hand until I make your enemies your footstool."

Lk 1:15. And he will be filled with the Holy Spirit, even from before his birth! [41]Elizabeth was filled with the Holy Spirit. [67]Then his father Zacharias was filled with the Holy Spirit and gave this prophecy.

Lk 2:25. That day a man named Simeon, a Jerusalem resident, was in the Temple. He was a good man, very devout, filled with the Holy Spirit and constantly expecting the Messiah to come soon. [26]For the Holy Spirit had revealed to him that he would not die until he had seen him—God's anointed King. [27]The Holy Spirit had impelled him to go to the Temple that day.

Lk 3:2. A message came from God to John (the son of Zacharias), as he was living out in the deserts.

Jn 1:6. God sent John the Baptist as a witness.

Acts 2:2. Suddenly there was a sound like the roaring of a mighty windstorm in the skies above them and it filled the house where they were meeting. [3]Then, what looked like flames or tongues of fire appeared and settled on their heads. [4]And everyone present was filled with the Holy Spirit and began speaking in languages they didn't know, for the Holy Spirit gave them this ability.

Acts 3:18. But God was fulfilling the prophecies that the Messiah must suffer all these things.

Acts 7:55. But Stephen, full of the Holy Spirit, gazed steadily upward into heaven and saw the glory of God and Jesus standing at God's right hand. *v.* 56.

Acts 8:29. The Holy Spirit said to Philip, "Go over and walk along beside the chariot." [39]And when they came up out of the water, the Spirit of the Lord caught away Philip, and the eunuch never saw him again.

Acts 11:28. And one of them, named Agabus, stood up in one of the meetings to predict by the Spirit that a great famine was coming upon the land of Israel.

Acts 21:4. We went ashore, found the local believers and stayed with them a week. These disciples warned Paul—the Holy Spirit prophesying through them—not to go on to Jerusalem. [10]During our stay of several days, a man named Agabus, who also had the gift of prophecy, arrived from Judea [11]and visited us. He took Paul's belt, bound his own feet and hands with it and said, "The Holy

Spirit declares, 'So shall the owner of this belt be bound by the Jews in Jerusalem and turned over to the Romans.' "

Acts 28:25. But after they had argued back and forth among themselves, they left with this final word from Paul ringing in their ears: "The Holy Spirit was right when he said through Isaiah the prophet."

Rom 1:1. This letter is from Paul, Jesus Christ's slave, chosen to be a missionary, and sent out to preach God's Good News. [2]This Good News was promised long ago by God's prophets in the Old Testament.

1 Cor 12:7. The Holy Spirit displays God's power through each of us as a means of helping the entire church. [8]To one person the Spirit gives the ability to give wise advice; someone else may be especially good at studying and teaching, and this is his gift from the same Spirit. [9]He gives special faith to another, and to someone else the power to heal the sick. [10]He gives power for doing miracles to some, and to others power to prophesy and preach. He gives someone else the power to know whether evil spirits are speaking through those who claim to be giving God's messages—or whether it is really the Spirit of God who is speaking. Still another person is able to speak in languages he never learned; and others, who do not know the language either, are given power to understand what he is saying. [11]It is the same and only Holy Spirit who gives all these gifts and powers, deciding which each one of us should have.

1 Cor 14:32. Remember that a person who has a message from God has the power to stop himself or wait his turn.

Heb 1:1. Long ago God spoke in many different ways to our fathers through the prophets (in visions, dreams, and even face to face).

Heb 3:5. Well, Moses did a fine job working in God's house, but he was only a servant; and his work was mostly to illustrate and suggest those things that would happen later on.

1 Pet 1:10. This salvation was something the prophets did not fully understand. Though they wrote about it, they had many questions as to what it all could mean. [11]They wondered what the Spirit of Christ within them was talking about, for he told them to write down the events which, since then, have happened to Christ: his suffering, and his great glory afterwards. And they wondered when and to whom all this would happen.

2 Pet 1:20, 21. For no prophecy recorded in Scripture was ever thought up by the prophet himself. It was the Holy Spirit within these godly men who gave them true messages from God.

Jude 1:14. Enoch, who lived seven generations after Adam, knew about these men and said this about them: "See, the Lord is coming with millions of his holy ones."

Rev 2:7. Let this message sink into the ears of anyone who listens to what the Spirit is saying to the churches.

Rev 10:7. Then God's veiled plan—mysterious through the ages ever since it was announced by his servants the prophets.

Rev 14:13. And I heard a voice in the heavens above me saying, "Write this down: At last the time has come for his martyrs to enter into their full reward. Yes, says the Spirit, they are blest indeed, for now they shall rest from all their toils and trials."

Rev 22:6, 7. Then the angel said to me, "... God, who tells his prophets what the future holds, has sent his angel to tell you this will happen soon. Blessed are those who believe it and all else written in the scroll." [8]I, John, saw and heard all these things, and fell down to worship the angel who showed them to me.

See the prophetic books, Isaiah through Malachi.

See *Revelation; Word of God, Inspiration of.*

PROPHETESSES Ezk 13:17; Joel 2:28, 29. Miriam, Ex 15:20. Deborah, Judg 4:4. Huldah, 2 Kgs 22:14. No-adiah, Neh 6:14. Elizabeth, Lk 1: 41–45. Anna, Lk 2:36–38. Daughters of Philip, Acts 21:9. Jezebel, Rev 2:20.

See *Women.*

PROPITIATION Rom 3:25; 5:1, 10, 11; 2 Cor 5:18, 19; Col 1:20–22; 1 Jn 2:2; 3:10; Heb 9:5.

See *Atonement; Redemption.*

PROSPERITY From God, Gen 33:11; 49: 24–26; Ps 127:1; 128:1, 2. Design of, Eccl 7:14. Dangers of, Deut 8:10–18; 31:20; 32:15; Jer 5:7; Hos 13: 6. Evil effects of, Hos 4:7. Pride in, 2 Chron 32:25. Forgetfulnesses of God in, 2 Chron 12:1; 26:16. The prosperous despise the unfortunate, Job 12:5.

Promised to the righteous, Job 22:23–27.

Prudence in. Instances of: Joseph and Daniel, as deduced from their general conduct. See *Joseph; Daniel.*

See *Blessing, Temporal; Rich, The; Riches.*

PROSTITUTE Shamelessness of, Prov 2:16, 17; 7:11–27; 9:13. Devices of, Prov 7:10; 9:14–17; Isa 23:15, 16; Hos 2:13. To be shunned, Prov 5:3–20; 7: 25–27. Earnings of, not to be offered to the Lord, Deut 23:17, 18.

Rahab, Josh 2:3–6; 6:17, 23, 25; Heb 11:31.

See *Adultery; Prostitution.*

PROSTITUTION Forbidden, Lev 19:29; Deut 23:17, 18. Punishment of, Lev 21:9.

FIGURATIVE. Ezk 16; 23; Rev 17:1–6.

See *Adultery; Idolatry; Lasciviousness.*

PROUD See *Pride.*

PROVERBS Design of, Prov 1:1–4. Written by Solomon, Prov 1:1; 25:1.

MISCELLANY OF. 1 Sam 10:12. So that is the origin of the proverb, "Is Saul a prophet, too?"

1 Sam 24:13. As that old proverb says, "Wicked is as wicked does," but despite your wickedness, I'll not touch you. [14]And who is the king of Israel trying to catch anyway? Should he spend his time chasing one who is as worthless as a dead dog or a flea?

2 Sam 20:18. So she told him, "There used to be a saying, "If you want to settle an argument, ask advice at Abel.' "

1 Kgs 20:11. The king of Israel retorted, "Don't count your chickens before they hatch!"

Prov 1:17. When a bird sees a trap being set, it stays away.

Ezk 12:22. Son of dust, what is that proverb they quote in Israel—"The days as they pass make liars out of every prophet." [23]The Lord God says, I will put an end to this proverb and they will soon stop saying it. Give them this one instead: "The time has come for all these prophecies to be fulfilled."

Ezk 16:44. "Like mother, like daughter"—that is what everyone will say of you.

Ezk 18:2. Why do people use this proverb about the land of Israel: The children are punished for their fathers' sins? [3]As I live, says the Lord God, you will not use this proverb any more in Israel, [Jer 31:29.] [4]For all souls are mine to judge—fathers and sons alike—and my rule is this: It is for a man's own sins that he will die.

Hos 4:9. And thus it is: "Like priests, like people."

Mt 12:33. A tree is identified by its fruit. Lk 6:44.

Lk 4:23. Then he said, "Probably you will quote me that proverb, 'Physician, heal yourself.' "

Lk 14:34. What good is salt that has lost its saltiness?

Jn 1:46. "Nazareth!" exclaimed Nathanael. "Can anything good come from there?"

Gal 6:7. A man will always reap just the kind of crop he sows!

See *Riddle.*

PROVIDENCE, OF GOD See *God, Providence of, Overruling Intervention Showing.*

PROXY In priest's service, 2 Chron 30:17–19. See *Substitution; Suffering, Vicarious.*

PRUDENCE Job 34:3. We can choose the sounds we want to listen to; we can choose the taste we want in food, [4]and we should choose to follow what is right. But first of all we must define among ourselves what is good.

Ps 39:1. I said to myself, I'm going to quit complaining! I'll keep quiet, especially when the ungodly are around me.

Ps 112:5. And all goes well for the generous man who conducts his business fairly.

Prov 6:1. Son, if you endorse a note for someone you hardly know, guaranteeing his debt, you are in serious trouble. [2]You may have trapped yourself by your agreement.

Prov 8:12. Wisdom and good judgment live together, for wisdom knows where to discover knowledge and understanding.

Prov 11:13. A gossip goes around spreading rumors, while a trustworthy man tries to quiet them. [15]Be sure you know a person well before you vouch for his credit! Better refuse than suffer later. [29]The fool . . . will finally have nothing worthwhile left. He shall be the servant of a wiser man.

Prov 12:8. Everyone admires a man with good sense. [16]A fool is quick-tempered; a wise man stays cool when insulted. [23]A wise man doesn't display his knowledge, but a fool displays his foolishness.

Prov 13:16. A wise man thinks ahead; a fool doesn't, and even brags about it!

Prov 14:8. The wise man looks ahead. [15]Only a simpleton believes what he is told! A prudent man checks to see where he is going. [16]A wise man is cautious and avoids danger; a fool plunges ahead with great confidence. [18]The simpleton is crowned with folly; the wise man is crowned with knowledge.

Prov 15:5. Only a fool despises his father's advice; a wise son considers each suggestion. [22]Plans go wrong with too few counselors; many counselors bring success.

Prov 16:20. God blesses those who obey him; happy the man who puts his trust in the Lord. [21]The wise man is known by his common sense.

Prov 17:2. A wise slave will rule his master's wicked sons and share their estate. [18]It is poor judgment to countersign another's note, to become responsible for his debts.

Prov 18:15. The intelligent man is always open to new ideas. In fact, he looks for them. [16]A bribe does wonders; it will bring you before men of importance!

Prov 19:2. It is dangerous and sinful to rush into the unknown.

Prov 20:5. Though good advice lies deep within a counselor's heart, the wise man will draw it out. [16]It is risky to make loans to strangers! [18]Don't go ahead with your plans without the advice of others; don't go to war until they agree.

Prov 21:5. Steady plodding brings prosperity; hasty speculation brings poverty. [20]The wise man saves for the future, but the foolish man spends whatever he gets. [23]Keep your mouth closed and you'll stay out of trouble.

Prov 22:3. A prudent man foresees the difficulties ahead and prepares for them; the simpleton goes blindly on and suffers the consequences. [7]Just as the rich rule the poor, so the borrower is servant to the lender. [26, 27]Unless you have the extra cash on hand, don't countersign a note. Why risk everything you own? They'll even take your bed!

Prov 23:1–3. When dining with a rich man, be on your guard and don't stuff yourself, though it all tastes so good; for he is trying to bribe you, and no good is going to come of his invitation. [9]Don't waste your breath on a rebel. He will despise the wisest advice.

Prov 24:6. Don't go to war without wise guidance; there is safety in many counselors. [27]Develop your business first before building your house.

Prov 25:8, 9, 10. Don't be hot-headed and rush to court! You may start something you can't finish and go down before your neighbor in shameful defeat. So discuss the matter with him privately. Don't tell anyone else, lest he accuse you of slander and you can't withdraw what you said.

Prov 26:4, 5. When arguing with a rebel, don't use foolish arguments as he does, or you will become as foolish as he is! Prick his conceit with silly replies!

Prov 27:12. A sensible man watches for problems

ahead and prepares to meet them.

Prov 29:8. Fools start fights everywhere while wise men try to keep peace. [11]A rebel shouts in anger; a wise man holds his temper in and cools it.

Eccl 7:16, 17. So don't be too good or too wise! Why destroy yourself? On the other hand, don't be too wicked either—don't be a fool! Why should you die before your time?

Eccl 8:2, 3. Obey the king as you have vowed to do. Don't always be trying to get out of doing your duty, even when it's unpleasant. For the king punishes those who disobey.

Eccl 10:1. Dead flies will cause even a bottle of perfume to stink! Yes, a small mistake can outweigh much wisdom and honor. [10]A dull axe requires great strength; be wise and sharpen the blade.

Hos 14:9. Whoever is wise, let him understand these things. Whoever is intelligent, let him listen. For the paths of the Lord are true and right, and good men walk along them. But sinners trying it will fail.

Amos 5:13. Therefore those who are wise will not try to interfere with the Lord in the dread day of your punishment.

Mt 5:25. Come to terms quickly with your enemy before it is too late and he drags you into court and you are thrown into a debtor's cell, [26]for you will stay there until you have paid the last penny.

Mt 7:6. Don't give holy things to depraved men. Don't give pearls to swine! They will trample the pearls and turn and attack you.

Lk 14:28. But don't begin until you count the cost. For who would begin construction of a building without first getting estimates and then checking to see if he has enough money to pay the bills? [29]Otherwise he might complete only the foundation before running out of funds. And then how everyone would laugh! [30]"See that fellow there?" they would mock. "He started that building and ran out of money before it was finished!" [31]Or what king would ever dream of going to war without first sitting down with his counselors and discussing whether his army of 10,000 is strong enough to defeat the 20,000 men who are marching against him? [32]If the decision is negative, then while the enemy troops are still far away, he will send a truce team to discuss terms of peace.

Rom 14:16. Don't do anything that will cause criticism against yourself even though you know that what you do is right.

1 Cor 6:12. I can do anything I want to if Christ has not said no, but some of these things aren't good for me. Even if I am allowed to do them, I'll refuse to if I think they might get such a grip on me that I can't easily stop when I want to. chapter 10:23.

1 Cor 8:8. Just remember that God doesn't care whether we eat it or not. We are no worse off if we don't eat it, and no better off if we do. [9]But be careful not to use your freedom to eat it, lest you cause some Christian brother to sin whose conscience is weaker than yours. [10]You see, this is what may happen: Someone who thinks it is wrong to eat this food will see you eating at a temple restaurant, for you know there is no harm in it. Then he will become bold enough to do it too, although all the time he still feels it is wrong. [11]So because you "know it is all right to do it," you will be responsible for causing great spiritual damage to a brother with a tender conscience for whom Christ died. [12]And it is a sin against Christ to sin against your brother by encouraging him to do something he thinks is wrong. [13]So if eating meat offered to idols is going to make my brother sin, I'll not eat any of it as long as I live, because I don't want to do this to him.

1 Cor 10:25. Here's what you should do. Take any meat you want that is sold at the market. Don't ask whether or not it was offered to idols, lest the answer hurt your conscience. [26]For the earth and every good thing in it belongs to the Lord and is yours to enjoy. [27]If someone who isn't a Christian asks you out to dinner, go ahead; accept the invitation if you want to. Eat whatever is on the table and don't ask any questions about it. Then you won't know whether or not it has been used as a sacrifice to idols, and you won't risk having a bad conscience over eating it. [28]But if someone warns you that this meat has been offered to idols, then don't eat it for the sake of the man who told you, and of his conscience. [29]In this case his feeling about it is the important thing, not yours. But why, you may ask, must I be guided and limited by what someone else thinks? [30]If I can thank God for the food and enjoy it, why let someone spoil everything just because he thinks I am wrong? [31]Well, I'll tell you why. It is because you must do everything for the glory of God, even your eating and drinking. [32]So don't be a stumbling block to anyone, whether they are Jews or Gentiles or Christians. [33]That is the plan I follow, too. I try to please everyone in everything I do, not doing what I like or what is best for me, but what is best for them, so that they may be saved.

Col 4:5. Make the most of your chances to tell others the Good News. Be wise in all your contacts with them.

Jas 1:19. Dear brothers, don't ever forget that it is best to listen much, speak little, and not become angry.

See *Diplomacy; Gentleness; Wisdom.*

INSTANCES OF. Jacob, in his conduct toward Esau, Gen 32:3–21; toward his sons, after Dinah's assault, Gen 34:5, 30. Joseph, in the affairs of Egypt, Gen 41:33–57. Jethro's advice to Moses, Ex 18:17–23. The Israelites, in the threatened war with the two and one-half tribes, Josh 22:10–34. Saul, in not killing the Jabesh-gileadites, 1 Sam 11:13. David, in his conduct with Saul, 1 Sam 18:5–30; in overthrowing Ahithophel's counsel, 2 Sam 15:33–37. Abigail, in averting David's wrath, 1 Sam 25:18–31. Achish, in dismissing David, 1 Sam 29. Elijah, in his escape from Jezebel, 1 Kgs 19:3, 4. Rehoboam's counselors, 1 Kgs 12:7. Jehoram, in suspecting a

Syrian stratagem, 2 Kgs 7:12, 13. Nehemiah, in conduct of affairs at Jerusalem, Neh 2:11–16; 4:13–23. Daniel, Dan 1:8–14. Certain elders of Israel, Jer 26:17–23. Of Jesus, in charging those who were healed not to advertise his miracles, Mt 9:30; 16:20; Mk 3:12; 5:43; 7:36; 8:30; 9:9; going to the feast secretly, Jn 7:10; in stopping his public ministry, Jn 11:54; 12:36; in avoiding his enemies, Mt 12:14–16; Mk 3:7, 8; Jn 11:47–54. Joseph, in his conduct toward Mary, Mt 1:19. Peter, in escaping Herod, Acts 12:17. Paul in circumcising Timothy, Acts 16:3; in performing temple rites, Acts 21:20–27; in setting the Jewish sects on each other, Acts 23:6; avoiding suspicion in administering the gifts of the churches, 2 Cor 8:20; his lack of, in his persistence in going to Jerusalem despite the warnings of the Spirit and his friends, Acts 20:22–25, 37, 38; 21:10–14; Paul and Barnabas, in escaping persecution, Acts 14:5, 6; Paul and Silas, in escaping from Beroea, Acts 17:10–15. The mayor of Ephesus, in averting a riot, Acts 19:29–41.

See *Diplomacy.*

PRUNING Lev 25:3, 4; Isa 5:6; 18:5; Jn 15:2–6. Pruning hook, Isa 2:4; Joel 3:10; Mic 4:3.

PSALMS Of Moses, celebrating the deliverance at the Red Sea, Ex 15:1–19. Didactic songs composed by Moses, celebrating the providence, righteousness, and judgments of God, Deut 32:1–43; Ps 90. Song of Deborah, celebrating Israel's victory over Sisera, Judg 5. Of Hannah, in thankfulness for a son, 1 Sam 2:1–10. Of David, celebrating his rescue, 2 Sam 22; on the occasion of moving the ark, 1 Chron 16:7–36; at the close of his reign, 2 Sam 23:2–7; 1 Chron 29:10–19. Of Isaiah, Isa 12; 25; 26. Of Hezekiah, celebrating deliverance from death, Isa 38:9–20. Of Mary, Lk 1:46–55. Elizabeth, Lk 1:42–45. Zacharias, Lk 1:68–79.

In the book of Psalms itself, 73 out of the 150 are ascribed to David in the Hebrew titles; Ps 90 to Moses; 72 and 127 to Solomon; 88 to Heman; 89 to Ethan; 50, 73–83 to Asaph; 42, 44–49, 84, 85, 87, 88, to the sons of Korah; 49 are anonymous. Outstanding prophetic psalms are Ps 2, of Christ as Redeemer and King; 22, of his sufferings and death on the cross; 110, of his priesthood; 16, of his resurrection; 72, of his future kingdom. Topics touched upon in the Psalms are referred to throughout this volume.

See *Song.*

PSALTERY A harp, 1 Sam 10:5. Used in religious services, 1 Chron 15:16; 2 Chron 29:25, 26. At the dedication of the new wall when the captives returned, Neh 12:27. Used in idolatrous worship, Dan 3:5, 7, 10.

See *Music, Instruments of.*

PTOLEMAIS A seaport in Asher, formerly called *Acco,* which see. Paul visits, Acts 21:7.

PUAH 1. A Hebrew midwife, Ex 1:15, 16.

2. Father of Tola, Judg 10:1.

3. See *Puvah.*

PUBLICANS Roman tax collectors, Mt 18:17; Lk 7:29.

See *Tax, Collectors of.*

PUBLIUS Governor of the island of Malta. Father of, healed by Paul, Acts 28:7, 8.

PUDENS A Christian in Rome, 2 Tim 4:21.

PUL King of Assyria. Forced tribute from Menahem, king of Israel, 2 Kgs 15:19, 20; 1 Chron 5:26.

PULPIT Neh 8:1–5.

PUNISHMENT DEATH PENALTY. Shall not be pardoned, Num 35:31. In the Mosaic law the death penalty was inflicted for murder, Gen 9:5, 6; Lev 24:17; Num 35:16–21, 30–33; Deut 17:6; manslaughter, Ex 21:23; adultery, Lev 20:10; Deut 22:23, 24; incest, Lev 20:11, 12, 14; bestiality, Ex 22:19; Lev 20:15, 16; homosexuality, Lev 18:22; 20:13; incontinence, Deut 22:21–24; rape of a engaged virgin, Deut 22:23–27; perjury, Zech 5:4; kidnapping, Ex 21:16; Deut 24:7; fornication, committed by a priest's daughter, Lev 21:9; for witchcraft, Ex 22:18; offering human sacrifice, Lev 20:1–5; for striking or cursing father or mother, Ex 21:15, 17; Lev 20:9; disobedience to parents, Deut 21:18–21; theft, Zech 5:3, 4; blasphemy, Lev 24:11–16, 23; for Sabbath desecration, Ex 35:2; Num 15:32–36; for prophesying falsely, or propagating false doctrines, Deut 13:1–10; sacrificing to false gods, Ex 22:20; refusing to abide by the decision of court, Deut 17:12; for treason, 1 Kgs 2:25; Esther 2:23; sedition, Acts 5:36, 37.

Modes of Execution of Death Penalty. Burning, Gen 38:24; Lev 20:14; 21:9; Jer 29:22; Ezk 23:25; Dan 3:19–23; stoning, Lev 20:1, 2, 27; 24:13, 14; Num 14:10, 11; 15:33–36; Deut 13:10; 17:5; 22:21, 23, 24; Josh 7:25; hanging, Deut 21:22, 23; Josh 8:29; beheading, Mt 14:10; Mk 6:16, 27, 28; crucifixion, Mt 27:35, 38; Mk 15:25, 27; Lk 23:32, 33; the sword, Ex 32:27, 28; 1 Kgs 2:25; impaling, Gen 40:22.

Executed by the witnesses, Deut 13:9; 17:7; Acts 7:58; by the congregation, Num 15:35, 36; Deut 13:9.

Not inflicted on testimony of less than two witnesses, Num 35:30; Deut 17:6; 19:15.

MINOR OFFENSES. Punishable by scourging, Deut 22:17, 18; 25:1–3; Prov 17:10; Mt 27:26; Mk 15:15; Lk 23:16; Jn 19:1; Acts 22:24, 29; stocks, Job 33:11; Jer 20:2; 29:26; Acts 16:24; fines, Ex 22:1; Lev 5:15, 6:4, 5; Deut 22:19; Prov 6:31; imprisonment, Gen 39:20; 40; see *Prison.* Confinement within limits, 1 Kgs 2:26, 36–38. Enslavement, Gen 43:18; Ex 22:3; 2 Kgs 4:1; Mt 18:25.

IMPOSED. On children, Ex 34:7; Jer 31:29; Lam 5:7; Ezk 18:2, 3.

See *Afflictions, Design of; Chastisement; Fine; Judgments; Retaliation; Wicked, Punishment of.*

ACCORDING TO DEEDS. Job 34:11. Rather, he punishes the sinners.

Isa 3:11. But say to the wicked, "Your doom is sure. You too shall get your just deserts. Your well-earned punishment is on the way."

Isa 59:18. He will repay his enemies for their evil deeds—fury for his foes in distant lands.

Jer 17:10. Only the Lord knows! He searches all hearts and examines deepest motives so he can give to each person his right reward, according to his deeds—how he has lived.

Ezk 7:3. No hope remains, for I will loose my anger on you for your worshiping of idols. [27]For I will do to them the evil they have done, and give them all their just deserts. They shall learn that I am the Lord.

Ezk 16:59. For the Lord God says: I will repay you for your broken promises. You lightly broke your solemn vows to me.

Ezk 39:24. I turned my face away and punished them in proportion to the vileness of their sins.

Zech 1:6. "We have gotten what we deserved from God," they said. "He has done just what he warned us he would."

Mt 5:22. But I have added to that rule, and tell you that if you are only *angry,* even in your own home, you are in danger of judgment! If you call your friend an idiot, you are in danger of being brought before the court. And if you curse him, you are in danger of the fires of hell.

Mt 16:27. For I, the Son of Mankind, shall come with my angels in the glory of my Father and judge each person according to his deeds.

Mt 23:13, 14. Woe to you, Pharisees, and you other religious leaders. . . . You pretend to be holy, with all your long, public prayers in the streets, while you are evicting widows from their homes. Hypocrites! Lk 20:47.

Lk 12:47. He will be severely punished, for though he knew his duty he refused to do it. [48]But anyone who is not aware that he is doing wrong will be punished only lightly. Much is required from those to whom much is given, for their responsibility is greater. See Parable of vineyard, Isa 5:1–7; husbandman, Mt 21:33–41; of the investments, Mt 25:14–30.

See *Judgment, According to Opportunity and Works.*

DELAYED. Ps 50:21. I remained silent—you thought I didn't care—but now your time of punishment has come, and I list all the above charges against you.

Ps 55:19. God himself—God from everlasting ages past—will answer them! For they refuse to fear him or even honor his commands.

Prov 1:24. I have called you so often but still you won't come. I have pleaded, but all in vain. [25]For you have spurned my counsel and reproof. [26]Some day you'll be in trouble, and I'll laugh! Mock me, will you?—I'll mock you! [27]When a storm of terror surrounds you, and when you are engulfed by anguish and distress, [28]then I will not answer your cry for help. It will be too late though you search for me ever so anxiously. [29]For you closed your eyes to the facts and did not choose to reverence and trust the Lord, [30]and you turned your back on me, spurning my advice. [31]That is why you must eat the bitter fruit of having your own way, and experience the full terrors of the pathway you have chosen.

Eccl 8:11. Because God does not punish sinners instantly, people feel it is safe to do wrong. [12]But though a man sins a hundred times and still lives, I know very well that those who fear God will be better off, [13]unlike the wicked, who will not live long, good lives—their days shall pass away as quickly as shadows because they don't fear God.

Hab 1:2. O Lord, how long must I call for help before you will listen? I shout to you in vain; there is no answer. "Help! Murder!" I cry, but no one comes to save. [3]Must I forever see this sin and sadness all around me? Wherever I look there is oppression and bribery and men who love to argue and to fight. [4]The law is not enforced and there is no justice given in the courts, for the wicked far outnumber the righteous, and bribes and trickery prevail.

DESIGN OF.

To Secure Obedience. Gen 2:17. You may eat any fruit in the garden except fruit from the Tree of Conscience—for its fruit will open your eyes to make you aware of right and wrong, good and bad. If you eat its fruit, you will be doomed to die.

Ex 20:3. You may worship no other god than me. [4]You shall not make yourselves any idols: any images resembling animals, birds, or fish. [5]You must never bow to an image or worship it in any way; for I, the Lord your God, am very possessive. I will not share your affection with any other god! And when I punish people for their sins, the punishment continues upon the children, grandchildren, and great-grandchildren of those who hate me.

Lev 26:14. But if you will not listen to me or obey me, [15]but reject my laws, [16]this is what I will do to you: I will punish you with sudden terrors and panic, and with tuberculosis and burning fever; your eyes shall be consumed and your life shall ebb away; you will sow your crops in vain, for your enemies will eat them. [17]I will set my face against you and you will flee before your attackers; those who hate you will rule you; you will even run when no one is chasing you! [18]And if you still disobey me, I will punish you seven times more severely for your sins. [19]I will break your proud power and make your heavens as iron, and your earth as bronze. [20]Your strength shall be spent in vain; for your land shall not yield its crops, nor your trees their fruit. [21]And if even then you will not obey me and listen to me, I will send you seven times more plagues because of your sins. [22]I will send wild animals to kill your children and destroy your cattle and reduce your numbers so that your roads will be deserted. [23]And if even this will not reform you, but you continue to walk against my wishes, [24]then I will walk against your wishes, and I, even I, will personally smite you seven times for your sin. [25]I will revenge the breaking of my covenant by bringing war against you. You will flee to your cities, and I will send a plague among you there; and you will be conquered by your enemies. [26]I will destroy your food supply so that one oven will be large enough to bake all the bread available for ten entire families; and you will still be hungry after your pittance has been doled out to you. [27]And if you still won't listen to me or obey me, [28]then I will let loose my great anger and send you seven times greater punishment for your sins. [29]You shall eat your own sons and daughters, [30]and I will destroy the altars on the hills where you worship your idols, and I will cut down your incense altars, leaving your dead bodies to rot among your idols; and I will abhor you. [31]I will make your cities desolate, and destroy your places of worship, and will not respond to your incense offerings. [32]Yes, I will desolate your land; your enemies shall live in it, utterly amazed at what I have done to you. [33]I will scatter you out among the nations, destroying you with war as you go. Your land shall be desolate and your cities destroyed. [34, 35]Then at last the land will rest and make up for the many years you refused to let it lie idle; for it will lie desolate all the years that you are captives in enemy lands. Yes, then the land will rest and enjoy its Sabbaths! It will make up for the rest you didn't give it every seventh year when you lived upon it. [36]And for for those who are left alive, I will cause them to be dragged away to distant lands as prisoners of war, and slaves. There they will live in constant fear. The sound of a leaf driven in the wind will send them fleeing as though chased by a man with a sword; they shall fall when no one is pursuing them. [37]Yes, though none pursue they shall stumble over each other in flight, as though fleeing in battle, with no power to stand before their enemies. [38]You shall perish among the nations and be destroyed among your enemies. [39]Those left shall pine away in enemy lands because of their sins, the same sins as those of their fathers.

Deut 13:10. Stone him to death because he has tried to draw you away from the Lord your God who brought you from the land of Egypt, the place of slavery. [11]Then all Israel will hear about his evil deed, and will fear such wickedness as this among you.

Deut 21:21. Then the men of the city shall stone him to death. In this way you shall put away this evil from among you, and all the young men of Israel will hear about what happened and will be afraid. chapter 17:13; 19:20.

Prov 19:25. Punish a mocker and others will learn from his example. Reprove a wise man and he will be the wiser.

Prov 21:11. The wise man learns by listening; the simpleton can learn only by seeing scorners punished.

Prov 26:3. Guide a horse with a whip, a donkey with a bridle, and a rebel with a rod to his back!

See *Judgments, Design of.*

DIVINE.

No Escape from. Job 11:20. But the wicked shall find no way to escape; their only hope is death.

Prov 1:24. I have called you so often but still you won't come. I have pleaded, but all in vain. [25]For you have spurned my counsel and reproof. [26]Some day you'll be in trouble, and I'll laugh! Mock me, will you?—I'll mock you! [27]When a storm of terror surrounds you, and when you are engulfed by anguish and distress, [28]then I will not answer your cry for help. It will be too late though you search for me ever so anxiously. [29]For you closed your eyes to the facts and did not choose to reverence and trust the Lord, [30]and you turned your back on me, spurning my advice. [31]That is why you must eat the bitter fruit of having your own way, and experience the full terrors of the pathway you have chosen.

Prov 11:21. You can be very sure that the evil man will not go unpunished forever.

Prov 16:5. Pride disgusts the Lord. Take my word for it—*proud men shall be punished.*

Prov 29:1. The man who is often reproved but refuses to accept criticism will suddenly be broken and never have another chance.

Jer 11:11. Therefore, the Lord says, I am going to bring calamity down upon them and they shall not escape. Though they cry for mercy, I will not listen to their pleas.

Jer 15:1. Then the Lord said to me, Even if Moses and Samuel stood before me pleading for these people, even then I wouldn't help them—away with them! Get them out of my sight!

Jer 25:28. And if they refuse to accept the cup, tell them, "The Lord of Hosts says you *must* drink it! You cannot escape! [29]I have begun to punish my own people, so should you go free? No, you shall not evade punishment. I will call for war against all the peoples of the earth."

Amos 2:14. "Your swiftest warriors will stumble in flight. The strong will all be weak, and the great ones can no longer save themselves. [15]The archer's aim will fail, the swiftest runners won't be fast enough to flee, and even the best of horsemen can't outrun the danger then. [16]The most courageous of your mighty men will drop their weapons and run for their lives that day." The Lord God has spoken.

Zeph 1:18. Your silver and gold will be of no use to you in that day of the Lord's wrath. You cannot ransom yourselves with it. For the whole land will be devoured by the fire of his jealousy. He will make a speedy riddance of all the people of Judah. Ezk 7:19.

Mt 10:28. Don't be afraid of those who can kill only your bodies—but can't touch your souls! Fear only God who can destroy both soul and body in hell.

Mt 23:33. Snakes! Sons of vipers! How shall you escape the judgment of hell?

Rom 2:3. Do you think that God will judge and condemn others for doing them and overlook you when you do them, too?

Col 3:25. And if you don't do your best for him, he will pay you in a way that you won't like—for he has no special favorites who can get away with shirking.

Heb 2:3. What makes us think that we can escape if we are indifferent to this great salvation?

Heb 12:25. For if the people of Israel did not escape when they refused to listen to Moses, the earthly messenger, how terrible our danger if we refuse to listen to God who speaks to us from heaven!

ETERNAL. Isa 34:8. For it is the day of vengeance, the year of recompense for what Edom has done to Israel. [9]The streams of Edom will be filled with burning pitch, and the ground will be covered with fire. [10]This judgment on Edom will never end. Its smoke will rise up forever. The land will lie deserted from generation to generation; no one will live there anymore.

Dan 12:2. And many of those whose bodies lie dead and buried will rise up, some to everlasting life and some to shame and everlasting contempt.

Mt 3:12. He will separate the chaff from the grain, burning the chaff with never-ending fire, and storing away the grain.

Mt 10:28. Don't be afraid of those who can kill only your bodies—but can't touch your souls! Fear only God who can destroy both soul and body in hell.

Mt 18:8. So if your hand or foot causes you to sin, cut it off and throw it away. Better to enter heaven crippled than to be in hell with both of your hands and feet.

Mt 25:41. Then I will turn to those on my left and say, "Away with you, you cursed ones, into the eternal fire prepared for the devil and his demons." [46]And they shall go away into eternal punishment; but the righteous into everlasting life.

Mk 3:29. But blasphemy against the Holy Spirit can never be forgiven. It is an eternal sin.

Lk 3:17. He will separate chaff from grain, and burn up the chaff with eternal fire and store away the grain.

Jn 5:29. And shall rise again—those who have done good, to eternal life; and those who have continued in evil, to judgment.

Heb 6:2. You don't need further instruction about baptism and spiritual gifts and the resurrection of the dead and eternal judgment.

Heb 10:28. A man who refused to obey the laws given by Moses was killed without mercy if there were two or three witnesses to his sin. [29]Think how much more terrible the punishment will be for those who have trampled underfoot the Son of God and treated his cleansing blood as though it were common and unhallowed, and insulted and outraged the Holy Spirit who brings God's mercy to his people. [30]For we know him who said, "Justice belongs to me; I will repay them"; who also said, "The Lord himself will handle these cases." [31]It is a fearful thing to fall into the hands of the living God.

Rev 14:10. Must drink the wine of the anger of God; it is poured out undiluted into God's cup of wrath. And they will be tormented with fire and burning sulphur in the presence of the holy angels and the Lamb. [11]The smoke of their torture rises forever and ever, and they will have no relief day or night, for they have worshiped the Creature and his statue, and have been tattooed with the code of his name.

Rev 19:3. The smoke from her burning ascends forever and forever.

Rev 20:10. Then the devil who had betrayed them will again be thrown into the Lake of Fire burning with sulphur where the Creature and False Prophet are, and they will be tormented day and night forever and ever.

See *Wicked, Punishment of.*

PUNON A city of Edom. A camping ground of the Israelites, in their 40 years' wandering, Num 33:42.

PURAH A servant of Gideon, Judg 7:10, 11.

PURIFICATION Sanitary and symbolical. For women before marriage, Esther 2:12–14; after intercourse, Lev 15:18; after childbirth, Lev 12:6–8; Lk 2:22; after menstruation, Lev 15:19–33; 2 Sam 11:4. Of the Jews before the Passover, Jn 11:55. For those who have killed in battle, Num 31:19–24. Of Levites, see below. Of lepers, see *Leprosy.* By fire, for things that resist fire, Num 31:23. By blood, Ex 24:5–8; Lev 14:6, 7; Heb 9:12–14, 19–22. By abstaining from sexual intercourse, Ex 19:15. Washing in water parts of animal sacrifices, Lev 1:9, 13; 9:14; 2 Chron 4:6. Penalty to be imposed upon those who do not observe the ordinances concerning, Lev 7:20, 21; Num 19:13, 20.

Water of, Num 19:17–21; 31:23. Washing hands in water, symbolical of innocency, Deut 21:6; Ps 26:6; Mt 27:24. Traditions of the elders concerning, Mt 15:2; Mk 7:2–5, 8, 9; Lk 11:37, 38. Of Paul, to show his fidelity to the law, Acts 21:24, 26, 27.

FIGURATIVE. Ps 26:6; 51:7; Ezk 36:25; Heb 10:22.

See *Ablution; Defilement; Sanitation.*

SCRIPTURES RELATING TO. Gen 35:2. So Jacob instructed all those in his household . . . to wash themselves and to put on fresh clothing.

Ex 19:10. Go down now and see that the people are ready for my visit. Sanctify them today and tomorrow, and have them wash their clothes. [14]So Moses went down to the people and sanctified them and they washed their clothing.

Ex 29:4. Bathe Aaron and his sons there at the entrance.

Ex 30:18. Make a bronze basin with a bronze pedestal. Put it between the Tabernacle and the altar, and fill it with water. [19]Aaron and his sons shall wash their hands and feet there, [20]when they go into the Tabernacle to appear before the Lord, or when they approach the altar to burn offerings to the Lord. They must always wash before doing so, or they will die. [21]These are instructions to Aaron and his sons from generation to generation.

Ex 40:12. "Now bring Aaron and his sons to the entrance of the Tabernacle and wash them with water." [30]Next he placed the wash-basin between the tent and the altar, and filled it with water so that the priests could use it for washing. [31]Moses and Aaron and Aaron's sons washed their hands and feet there. [32]Whenever they walked past the altar to enter the Tabernacle, they stopped and washed, just as the Lord had commanded Moses.

Lev 8:6. Then he took Aaron and his sons and washed them with water.

Lev 14:8. Then the man who is cured shall wash his clothes, shave off all his hair, and bathe himself, and return to live inside the camp; however, he must stay outside his tent for seven days. [9]The seventh day he shall again shave all the hair from his head, beard, and eyebrows, and wash his clothes and bathe, and shall then be declared fully cured of his leprosy.

Lev 15:4. Any bed he lies on and anything he sits on is contaminated; [5]so anyone touching the man's bed is ceremonially defiled until evening, and must wash his clothes and bathe himself. [6]Anyone sitting on a seat the man has sat upon while defiled is himself ceremonially unclean until evening, and must wash his clothes and bathe himself. [7]The same instructions apply to anyone touching him. [8]Anyone he spits on is ceremonially unclean until evening, and must wash his clothes and bathe himself. [9]Any saddle he rides on is defiled. [10]Anyone touching or carrying anything else that was beneath him shall be defiled until evening, and must wash his clothes and bathe himself. [11]If the defiled man touches anyone without first rinsing his hands, that person must wash his clothes and bathe himself and be defiled until evening. [12]Any earthen pot touched by the defiled man must be broken, and every wooden utensil must be rinsed in water. [13]When the discharge stops, he shall begin a seven-day cleansing ceremony by washing his clothes and bathing in running water. [16]Whenever a man's semen goes out from him, he shall take a complete bath and be unclean until the evening. [17]Any clothing or bedding the semen spills on must be washed and remain ceremonially defiled until evening. [18]After sexual intercourse, the woman as well as the man must bathe, and they are ceremonially defiled until the next evening. [19]Whenever a woman menstruates, she shall be in a state of ceremonial defilement for seven days afterwards, and during that time anyone touching her shall be defiled until evening. [20]Anything she lies on or sits on during that time shall be defiled. [21-23]Anyone touching her bed or anything she sits upon shall wash his clothes and bathe himself and be ceremonially defiled until evening. [24]A man having sexual intercourse with her during this time is ceremonially defiled for seven days, and every bed he lies upon shall be defiled. [25]If the menstrual flow continues after the normal time, or at some irregular time during the month, the same rules apply as indicated above, [26]so that anything she lies upon during that time is defiled, just as it would be during her normal menstrual period, and everything she sits on is in a similar state of defilement. [27]Anyone touching her bed or anything she sits on shall be defiled, and shall wash his clothes and bathe and be defiled until evening.

Lev 16:4. He must bathe himself and put on the sacred linen coat, shorts, belt, and turban. [24]Then he shall bathe in a sacred place, put on his clothes again, and go out and sacrifice his own burnt offering and the burnt offering for the people, making atonement for himself and for them. [26](The man who took the goat out into the desert shall afterwards wash his clothes and bathe himself and then come back into the camp.) [28]Afterwards, the person doing the burning shall wash his clothes and bathe himself and then return to camp.

Lev 17:15. And anyone—native born or foreigner—who eats the dead body of an animal that dies of itself, or is torn by wild animals, must wash his clothes and bathe himself and be defiled until evening; after that he shall be declared cleansed.

Lev 22:3. From now on and forever, if a priest who is ceremonially defiled sacrifices the animals brought by the people or handles the gifts dedicated to Jehovah, he shall be discharged from the priesthood. For I am Jehovah!

Num 8:6. Now set apart the Levites from the other people of Israel. [7]Do this by sprinkling water of purification upon them, then having them shave their entire bodies and wash their clothing and themselves. [21]The Levites purified themselves and washed their clothes, and Aaron presented them to the Lord in a gesture of offering. He then performed the rite of atonement over them to purify them.

Num 19:7. Then he must wash his clothes, and bathe, and afterwards return to the camp and be ceremonially defiled until the evening. [8]And the one who burns the animal must wash his clothes, and bathe, and he too shall be defiled until evening. [19]This shall take place on the third and seventh days; then the defiled person must wash his clothes and bathe himself, and that evening he will be out from under the defilement.

2 Chron 4:6. He also constructed ten vats for water to wash the offerings, five to the right of the huge tank and five to the left. The priests used the tank, and not the vats, for their own washing.

Mk 7:2. And noticed that some of his disciples failed to follow the usual Jewish rituals before eating. [3](For the Jews, especially the Pharisees, will never eat until they have sprinkled their arms to the elbows, as required by their ancient traditions. [4]So when they come home from the market they must always sprinkle themselves in this way before touching any food. This is but one of many examples of laws and regulations they have clung to for centuries, and still follow, such as their ceremony of cleansing for pots, pans and dishes.) [5]So the religious leaders asked him, "Why don't your disciples follow our age-old customs? For they eat without first performing the washing ceremony." [6, 7]Jesus replied, "You bunch of hypocrites! Isaiah the prophet described you very well when he said, 'These people speak very prettily about the Lord but they have no love for him at all. Their worship is a farce, for they claim that God commands the people to obey their petty rules.' How right Isaiah was! [8]For you ignore God's specific orders and substitute your own traditions. [9]You are simply rejecting God's laws and trampling them under your feet for the sake of tradition. Mt 15:2.

Heb 9:10. For the old system dealt only with certain rituals—what foods to eat and drink, rules for washing themselves, and rules about this and that. The people had to keep these rules to tide them over until Christ came with God's new and better way.

PURIM A feast instituted to commemorate the deliverance of Jews from the plot of Haman, Esther 9:20–32.

PURITY OF HEART. Ps 18:24. And so the Lord has paid me with his blessings, for I have done what is right, and I am pure of heart. [26]You give blessings to the pure but pain to those who leave your paths.

Ps 24:3. Who may climb the mountain of the Lord and enter where he lives? Who may stand before the Lord? [4]Only those with pure hands and hearts, who do not practice dishonesty and lying. [5]They will receive God's own goodness as their blessing from him, planted in their lives by God himself, their Savior.

Ps 51:7. Sprinkle me with the cleansing blood and I shall be clean again. Wash me and I shall be whiter than snow.

Ps 65:3. Though sins fill our hearts, you forgive them all.

Ps 73:1. How good God is to Israel—to those whose hearts are pure.

Prov 20:9. Who can ever say, "I have cleansed my heart; I am sinless"?

Isa 1:18. No matter how deep the stain of your sins, I can take it out and make you as clean as freshly fallen snow. Even if you are stained as red as crimson, I can make you white as wool! [25]I myself will melt you in a smelting pot, and skim off your slag.

Isa 6:7. He touched my lips with it and said, "Now you are pronounced 'Not guilty' because this coal has touched your lips. Your sins are all forgiven."

Dan 11:35. And some who are most gifted in the things of God will stumble in those days and fall, but this will only refine and cleanse them and make them pure until the final end of all their trials, at God's appointed time.

Dan 12:10. Many shall be purified by great trials and persecutions. But the wicked shall continue in their wickedness, and none of them will understand. Only those who are willing to learn will know what it means.

Mal 3:2. But who can live when he appears? Who can endure his coming? For he is like a blazing fire refining precious metal and he can bleach the dirtiest garments! [3]Like a refiner of silver he will sit and closely watch as the dross is burned away. He will purify the Levites, the ministers of God, refining them like gold or silver, so that they will do their work for God with pure hearts.

Mt 5:8. Happy are those whose hearts are pure, for they shall see God.

Jn 15:2. He lops off every branch that doesn't produce. And he prunes those branches that bear fruit for even larger crops.

Eph 5:3. Let there be no sex sin, impurity or greed among you. Let no one be able to accuse you of any such things. *v.* 4; Col 3:5.

Phil 4:8. And now, brothers . . . fix your thoughts on what is true and good and right. Think about things that are pure and lovely, and dwell on the fine, good things in others. Think about all you can praise God for and be glad about.

1 Tim 1:5. What I am eager for is that all the Christians there will be filled with love that comes from pure hearts, and that their minds will be clean and their faith strong.

1 Tim 5:22. Be sure that you yourself stay away from all sin.

2 Tim 2:21. If you stay away from sin you will be like one of these dishes made of purest gold—the very best in the house—so that Christ himself can use you for his highest purposes. [22]Run from anything that gives you the evil thoughts that young men often have, but stay close to anything that makes you want to do right. Have faith and love, and enjoy the companionship of those who love the Lord and have pure hearts.

Tit 1:15. A person who is pure of heart sees goodness and purity in everything.

Heb 9:13. And if under the old system the blood of bulls and goats and the ashes of young cows could cleanse men's bodies from sin, [14]just think how much more surely the blood of Christ will transform our lives and hearts. His sacrifice frees us from the worry of having to obey the old rules, and makes us want to serve the living God. For by the help of the eternal Holy Spirit, Christ willingly gave himself to God to die for our sins—he being perfect, without a single sin or fault.

Heb 10:2. The worshipers would have been cleansed once for all, and their feeling of guilt would be gone.

Jas 4:8. Wash your hands, you sinners, and let your hearts be filled with God alone to make them pure and true to him.

1 Pet 1:22. Now you can have real love for everyone because your souls have been cleansed from selfishness and hatred when you trusted Christ to save you; so see to it that you really do love each other warmly, with all your hearts.

1 Jn 3:3. And everyone who really believes this will try to stay pure because Christ is pure.

For the symbolisms of purity, see *Ablution; Color, White; Defilement; Purification.*

PURSE Isa 3:22.

PURVEYOR For Solomon, 1 Kgs 4:7–19, 27.

PUT 1. Son of Ham, Gen 10:6; 1 Chron 1:5–9.

2. The descendants of Put, or the country inhabited by them, Jer 46:9; Ezk 27:10; 30:5; 38:5; Nah 3:9.

PUTEOLI A seaport of Italy. Paul stays a week at, Acts 28:13, 14.

PUTIEL The father-in-law of Eleazar the priest, Ex 6:25.

PUVAH Called also *Puah.* Son of Issachar, Gen 46:8–14; Num 26:23–25; 1 Chron 7:1. Descendants of, Num 26:23–25.

QUAIL Miracle of, in the wilderness of Sihn, Ex 16:13; at Kibroth-hattaavah, Num 11:31, 32; Ps 105:40.

QUARANTINE See *Sanitation, Quarantine.*

QUARRELING See *Strife.*

QUARRIES Judg 3:17–19, 26.

QUARTUS A Christian in Corinth, Rom 16: 23.

QUEEN The wife of a king, 1 Kgs 11:19. Crowned, Esther 1:11; 2:17. Divorced, Esther 1:10–22. Sits on a throne beside the king, Neh 2:5, 6. Gives parties for the women of the royal household, Esther 1:9. Exerts an evil influence in public affairs, see *Jezebel.* Counsels the king, Dan 5:10–12. Of Sheba visits Solomon, 1 Kgs 10:1–13. Candace, of Ethiopia, Acts 8:27.

The reigning sovereign, Athaliah, see *Athaliah.*

Mesopotamian goddess called Queen of Heaven, Jer 7:18; 44:7–19, 25. Worshiped, see *Idolatry.*

QUICKENING Or making alive. Of the church: By the Father, Ps 71:20; 80:18; Rom 4:17; 8:11; 1 Tim 6:13; by the Son, Jn 5:21; 1 Cor 15:45; by the Holy Spirit, Jn 6:63; Rom 8:11; 2 Cor 3:6; 1 Pet 3:18.

QUIRINIUS Governor of Syria, Lk 2:2.

QUIVER For arrows, Ps 127:5; Isa 49:2; Ezk 21:21.

QUOTATIONS AND ALLUSIONS IN THE NEW TESTAMENT FROM, AND TO, THE OLD TESTAMENT. Mt 1:23. *Listen! The virgin shall conceive a child!* She shall give birth to a Son, and he shall be called "Emmanuel" (meaning "God is with us"). Isa 7:14.

Mt 2:6. O little town of Bethlehem, you are not just an unimportant Judean village, for a Governor shall rise from you to rule my people Israel. Mic 5:2.

15. I have called my Son from Egypt. Hos 11:1.

18. Screams of anguish come from Ramah, weeping unrestrained; Rachel weeping for her children, uncomforted—for they are dead. Jer 31:15.

Mt 3:3. I hear a shout from the wilderness, "Prepare a road for the Lord—straighten out the path where he will walk." Isa 40:3.

Mt 4:4. For the Scriptures tell us that bread won't feed men's souls: obedience to every word of God is what we need. Deut 8:3; Lk 4:4.

6. "God will send his angels to keep you from harm," . . . they will prevent you from smashing on the rocks below. Ps 91:11, 12; Lk 4:9–11.

7. Jesus retorted, "It also says not to put the Lord your God to a foolish test!" Deut 6:16; Lk 4: 12.

10. Worship only the Lord God. Obey only him. Deut 6:13; 10:20; Lk 4:8.

15, 16. The land of Zebulun and the land of Naphtali, beside the Lake, and the countryside beyond the Jordan River, and Upper Galilee where so many foreigners live—there the people who sat in darkness have seen a great Light; they sat in the land of death, and the Light broke through upon them. Isa 9:1, 2; 42:7; Lk 2:32.

Mt 5:5. The meek and lowly are fortunate! for the whole wide world belongs to them. Ps 37:11.

21. If you kill, you must die. Ex 20:13; Deut 5:17.

27. You shall not commit adultery. Ex 20:14; Deut 5:18.

31. If anyone wants to be rid of his wife, he can divorce her merely by giving her a letter of dismissal. Deut 24:1; Mt 19:7; Mk 10:4.

33. You shall not break your vows to God, but must fulfill them all. Ex 20:7; Lev 19:12; Deut 5:11.

38. If a man gouges out another's eye, he must pay with his own eye. If a tooth gets knocked out, knock out the tooth of the one who did it. Ex 21:24.

43. Love your *friends* and hate your enemies. Lev 19:18; Mt 19:19; 22:38, 39; Mk 12:31; Lk 10:27; Rom 13:9; Gal 5:14; Jas 2:8.

Mt 7:23. Go away, for your deeds are evil. Ps 6:8.

Mt 8:17. He took our sicknesses and bore our diseases. Isa 53:4.

Mt 9:13. It isn't your sacrifices and your gifts I want—I want you to be merciful. Hos 6:6; Mt 12:7.

Mt 10:35. I have come to set a man against his father, and a daughter against her mother, and a daughter-in-law against her mother-in-law. Mic 7: 6; Mk 13:12; Lk 12:53.

Mt 11:10.—A messenger to precede me, to announce my coming, and prepare people to receive me. Mal 3:1; Mk 1:2; Lk 7:27.

Mt 12:18. Look at my Servant. See my Chosen One. He is my Beloved, in whom my soul delights. I will put my Spirit upon him, and he will judge the nations. [19]He does not fight nor shout; he does not raise his voice! [20]He does not crush the weak, or quench the smallest hope; he will end all conflict with his final victory, [21]and his name shall be the hope of all the world. Isa 42:1–4.

Mt 13:14. They hear, but don't understand; they look, but don't see! [15]For their hearts are fat and heavy, and their ears are dull, and they have closed their eyes in sleep, [16]so they won't see and hear and understand and turn to God again, and let me heal them. Isa 6:9, 10; Mk 4:11, 12; 8:18; Lk 8:10; Jn 12:40; Acts 28:26, 27.

35. I will talk in parables; I will explain mysteries hidden since the beginning of time. Ps 78:2, 3.

Mt 15:4. Honor your father and mother; [Ex 20:12.] anyone who reviles his parents must die. Ex 21:17.

8. These people say they honor me, but their hearts are far away. [9]Their worship is worthless, for they teach their manmade laws instead of those from God. Isa 29:13.

Mt 18:16. But if not, then take one or two others with you and go back to him again, proving everything you say by these witnesses. Deut 19:15; Jn 8:17; 2 Cor 13:1.

Mt 19:4. It is written that at the beginning God created man and woman. Gen 1:27.

5. And that a man should leave his father and mother, and be forever united to his wife. The two shall become one—no longer two, but one! Gen 2:24; Eph 5:31.

18. Don't kill, don't commit adultery, don't steal, don't lie, [19]honor your father and mother, and love your neighbor as yourself! Ex 20:12–17; Mt 22:39; Lk 18:20; Col 3:20.

Mt 21:5. Tell Jerusalem her King is coming to her, riding humbly on a donkey's colt! Zech 9:9; Jn 12:15.

9. God bless King David's Son! . . . God's Man is here! . . . Bless him, Lord! . . . Praise God in highest heaven! Ps 118:26; Mk 11:9; Jn 12:13.

13. "The Scriptures say my Temple is a place of prayer," he declared, "but you have turned it into a den of thieves." Isa 56:7; Jer 7:11; Mk 11:17; Lk 19:46.

16. Even little babies shall praise him! Ps 8:2.

33. A certain landowner planted a vineyard with a hedge around it. Isa 5:1, 2; Mk 12:1; Lk 20:9.

42. The stone rejected by the builders has been made the honored cornerstone; how remarkable! what an amazing thing the Lord has done. Ps 118:22, 23; Mk 12:10; Lk 20:17; Acts 4:11; 1 Pet 2:6, 7.

Mt 22:24. Sir, Moses said that if a man died without children, his brother should marry the widow and their children would get all the dead man's property. Deut 25:5; Mk 12:19; Lk 20:28.

32. I *am* the God of Abraham, Isaac, and Jacob? Ex 3:6; Mk 12:26; Lk 20:37, 38; Acts 7:32.

37. Love the Lord your God with all your heart, soul, and mind. Deut 6:5; Mk 12:29, 30; Lk 10:27.

39. Love your neighbor as much as you love yourself. Lev 19:18; Mk 12:31; Lk 10:27.

44. God said to my Lord, Sit at my right hand until I put your enemies beneath your feet. Ps 110:1; Mk 12:36; Lk 20:42, 43; Acts 2:34, 35; Heb 1:13.

Mt 23:39. You will never see me again until you are ready to welcome the one sent to you from God. Ps 118:26; Lk 13:35.

Mt 24:15. So, when you see the horrible thing (told about by Daniel the prophet) standing in a holy place. Dan 9:27; Mk 13:14; Lk 21:20.

Mt 26:31. God will smite the Shepherd, and the sheep of the flock will be scattered. Zech 13:7.

Mt 27:9. They took the thirty pieces of silver—the price at which he was valued by the people of Israel— [10]and purchased a field from the potters as the Lord directed me. Zech 11:12, 13.

35. After the crucifixion, the soldiers threw dice to divide up his clothes among themselves. Ps 22:18; Jn 19:24.

46. My God, my God, why have you forsaken me? Ps 22:1.

Mk 1:2. God announced that he would send his Son to earth, and that a special messenger would arrive first to prepare the world for his coming. Mal 3:1; Lk 7:27.

3. And will proclaim that everyone must straighten out his life to be ready for the Lord's arrival. Isa 40:3, 4.

Mk 7:6, 7. These people speak very prettily about the Lord but they have no love for him at all. Their worship is a farce, for they claim that God commands the people to obey their petty rules. Isa 29:13.

10. Honor your father and mother. . . . Anyone who speaks against his father or mother must die. Ex 20:12; 21:17; Deut 5:16.

Mk 9:48. Where the worm never dies, and the fire never goes out. Isa 66:24.

Mk 10:6, 7. For from the very first he made man and woman to be joined together permanently in marriage; therefore a man is to leave his father and mother, [8]and he and his wife are united so that they are no longer two, but one. Gen 1:27; 2:24.

19. Don't kill, don't commit adultery, don't steal, don't lie, don't cheat, respect your father and mother. Ex 20:12–17; Deut 5:16–20.

Mk 11:9. Hail to the King! Praise God for him who comes in the name of the Lord! Ps 118:26.

Mk 12:29. Hear, O Israel! The Lord our God is the one and only God. Deut 6:4.

30. And you must love him with all your heart and soul and mind and strength. Deut 6:5.

31. You must love others as much as yourself. No other commandments are greater than these. Lev 19:18.

Mk 14:27. I will kill the Shepherd, and the sheep will scatter. Zech 13:7.

Mk 15:28. He was counted among evil men. Isa 53:12.

34. Eli, Eli, lama sabachthani? (My God, my God, why have you deserted me?) Ps 22:1.

Lk 1:17. He will be a man of rugged spirit and power like Elijah, the prophet of old; and he will precede the coming of the Messiah, preparing the people for his arrival. He will soften adult hearts to become like little children's, and will change disobedient minds to the wisdom of faith. Mal 4:5, 6.

Mary's magnificat, Lk 1:46–55. Compare with 1 Sam 2:1–11; Ps 103:17; 113:7, 8; Isa 41:8–14.

Lk 2:23. If a woman's first child is a boy, he shall be dedicated to the Lord. Ex 13:1, 2, 12.

24. Either a pair of turtledoves or two young pigeons. Lev 12:8.

Lk 3:4. A voice shouting from the barren wilderness, "Prepare a road for the Lord to travel on! Widen the pathway before him! [5]Level the mountains! Fill up the valleys! Straighten the curves! Smooth out the ruts! [6]And then all mankind shall see the Savior sent from God." Isa 40:3–5.

Lk 4:18, 19. The Spirit of the Lord is upon me; he has appointed me to preach Good News to the poor; he has sent me to heal the brokenhearted and to announce that captives shall be released and the blind shall see, that the downtrodden shall be freed from their oppressors, and that God is ready to give blessings to all who come to him. Isa 61:1, 2.

Lk 8:10. But these crowds hear the words and do not understand, just as the ancient prophets predicted. Isa 6:9.

Lk 22:37. He will be condemned as a criminal! Isa 53:12.

Lk 23:30. Mankind will beg the mountains to fall on them and crush them, and the hills to bury them. Hos 10:8.

46. Then Jesus shouted, "Father, I commit my spirit to you." Ps 31:5.

Jn 1:23. I am a voice from the barren wilderness, shouting as Isaiah prophesied, "Get ready for the coming of the Lord!" Isa 40:3.

Jn 2:17. Concern for God's House will be my undoing. Ps 69:9.

Jn 6:31. Moses gave them bread from heaven. Ps 78:24.

45. They shall all be taught of God. Isa 54:13.

Jn 7:38. For the Scriptures declare that rivers of living water shall flow from the inmost being of anyone who believes in me. [Not identified.]

42. For the Scriptures clearly state that the Messiah will be born of the royal line of David, [Isa 11:1; Jer 23:5, 6; 33:15], in *Bethlehem,* the village where David was born. Mic 5:2.

Jn 10:34. In your own Law it says that men are gods! Ps 82:6.

Jn 12:38. Lord, who will believe us? Who will accept God's mighty miracles as proof? Isa 53:1; Rom 10:16.

40. God has blinded their eyes and hardened their hearts so that they can neither see nor understand nor turn to me to heal them. Isa 6:9, 10.

Jn 13:18. One who eats supper with me will betray me. Ps 41:9.

Jn 15:25. They hated me without reason. Ps 35:19; 69:4; 109:3; 119:161; Lam 3:52.

Jn 19:24. They divided my clothes among them, and cast lots for my robe. *v.* 29; Ps 22:18.

36. Not one of his bones shall be broken. Ex 12:46; Ps 34:20.

37. They shall look on him whom they pierced. Zech 12:10.

Acts 1:20. Let his home become desolate with no one living in it. . . . Let his work be given to someone else to do. Ps 69:25; 109:8.

Acts 2:17. "In the last days," God said, "I will pour out my Holy Spirit upon all mankind, and your sons and daughters shall prophesy, and your young men shall see visions, and your old men dream dreams. [18]Yes, the Holy Spirit shall come upon all my servants, men and women alike, and they shall prophesy. [19]And I will cause strange demonstrations in the heavens and on the earth—blood and fire and clouds of smoke; [20]the sun shall turn black and the moon blood-red before that awesome Day of the Lord arrives. [21]But anyone who asks for mercy from the Lord shall have it and shall be saved." Joel 2:28–32; Rom 10:13.

25. I know the Lord is always with me. He is helping me. God's mighty power supports me. [26]No wonder my heart is filled with joy and my tongue shouts his praises! For I know all will be well with me in death— [27]You will not leave my soul in hell or let the body of your Holy Son decay. [28]You will give me back my life, and give me wonderful joy in your presence. *v.* 31; Ps 16:8–11.

Acts 3:22. The Lord God will raise up a Prophet among you, who will resemble me! Listen carefully to everything he tells you. [23]Anyone who will not listen to him shall be utterly destroyed. Deut 18:15–19.

25. You are included in God's promise to your ancestors to bless the entire world through the Jewish race. Gen 12:3, 7; 22:18.

Acts 4:11. A stone discarded by the builders which became the capstone of the arch. Ps 118:22; Mt 21:42; Mk 12:10; Lk 20:17.

25, 26. Why do the heathen rage against the Lord, and the foolish nations plan their little plots against Almighty God? The kings of the earth unite to fight against him, and against the anointed Son of God! Ps 2:1, 2.

Acts 7:3. And told him to leave his native land, to say good-bye to his relatives and to start out for a country that God would direct him to. *v.* 5; Gen 12:1, 7; 13:15; 15:18.

6. But God also told him that these descendants of his would leave the land and live in a foreign country and there become slaves for 400 years. [7]"But I will punish the nation that enslaves them," God told him, "and afterwards my people will return to this land of Israel and worship me here." Gen 15:13, 14.

9. These men [the twelve patriarchs] were very jealous of Joseph and sold him to be a slave in Egypt. But God was with him, [10]and delivered him out of all of his anguish, and gave him favor before Pharaoh, king of Egypt. God also gave Joseph unusual wisdom. Gen 37:11, 28; 39:3; 41:40–42.

11. But a famine developed in Egypt and Canaan and there was great misery for our ancestors. Gen 42.

13. The second time they went, Joseph revealed

his identity to his brothers. . . . [14]Then Joseph sent for his father Jacob and all his brothers' families to come to Egypt, seventy-five persons in all. Gen 45:1, 16; 46:26, 27.

15. So Jacob came to Egypt, where he died, and all his sons. [16]All of them were taken to Shechem and buried in the tomb Abraham bought. Gen 49:29–33; 50:1–13.

17, 18. The Jewish people greatly multiplied in Egypt; but then a king was crowned who had no respect for Joseph's memory. [19]This king plotted against our race, forcing parents to abandon their children in the fields. Ex 1.

20. About that time Moses was born—a child of divine beauty. His parents hid him at home for three months, [21]and when at last they could no longer keep him hidden, and had to abandon him, Pharaoh's daughter found him and adopted him as her own son. Ex 2:1, 2, 5–10.

23. One day as he was nearing his fortieth birthday, it came into his mind to visit his brothers, the people of Israel. [24]During this visit he saw an Egyptian mistreating a man of Israel. So Moses killed the Egyptian. *vs.* 25–29; Ex 2:11–15.

26. The next day he visited them again and saw two men of Israel fighting. He tried to be a peacemaker. "Gentlemen," he said, "you are brothers and shouldn't be fighting like this! It is wrong!" [27]But the man in the wrong told Moses to mind his own business. "Who made *you* a ruler and judge over us?" he asked. [28]"Are you going to kill me as you killed that Egyptian yesterday?" *vs.* 23–25, 35; Ex 2:11–15.

30. Forty years later, in the desert near Mount Sinai, an Angel appeared to him in a flame of fire in a bush. Ex 3:2.

31. Moses saw it and wondered what it was, and as he ran to see, the voice of the Lord called out to him. *v.* 32; Ex 3:3–10; Mk 12:26.

33. Take off your shoes, for you are standing on holy ground. [34]I have seen the anguish of my people in Egypt and have heard their cries. I have come down to deliver them. Come, I will send you to Egypt. Ex 3:5–10.

36. And by means of many remarkable miracles he led them out of Egypt and through the Red Sea, and back and forth through the wilderness for forty years. Ex chapters 7–12.

37. God will raise up a Prophet much like me from among your brothers. Deut 18:15.

38. Moses was the go-between—the mediator between the people of Israel and the Angel who gave them the Law of God—the Living Word—on Mount Sinai. Ex 19.

39. But our fathers rejected Moses and wanted to return to Egypt. Num 20:1–11.

40. Make idols for us, so that we will have gods to lead us back; for we don't know what has become of this Moses, who brought us out of Egypt. Ex 32:1–6, 23.

42. Was it to me you were sacrificing during those forty years in the desert, Israel? [43]No, your real interest was in your heathen gods—Sakkuth, and the star god Kaiway, and in all the images you made. So I will send you into captivity far away beyond Babylon. Amos 5:25–27.

44. Our ancestors carried along with them a portable Temple, or Tabernacle, through the wilderness. Ex 25:40; 26:30; Heb 8:5.

46. God blessed David greatly, and David asked for the privilege of building a permanent Temple for the God of Jacob. [47]But it was Solomon who actually built it. 1 Kgs 8:17–20.

49. "The heaven is my throne," says the Lord through his prophets, "and earth is my footstool. What kind of home could you build?" asks the Lord. "Would I stay in it? [50]Didn't I make both heaven and earth?" Isa 66:1, 2.

Acts 8:32. He was led as a sheep to the slaughter, and as a lamb is silent before the shearers, so he opened not his mouth; [33]in his humiliation, justice was denied him; and who can express the wickedness of the people of his generation? For his life is taken from the earth. Isa 53:7, 8.

Acts 13:17. The God of this nation Israel chose our ancestors and honored them in Egypt by gloriously leading them out of their slavery. Ex chapters 7–14; Deut 7:19.

18. And he nursed them through forty years of wandering around in the wilderness. Books of Exodus, Leviticus, Numbers, Deuteronomy.

19. Then he destroyed seven nations in Canaan, and gave Israel their land as an inheritance. Book of Joshua.

22. David (son of Jesse) is a man after my own heart, for he will obey me. Ps 89:20; 1 Sam 13:14.

33. Today I have honored you as my son. Ps 2:7.

34. I will do for you the wonderful thing I promised David. Isa 55:3.

35. God will not let his Holy One decay. Ps 16:10.

41. Look and perish, you despisers (of the truth), for I am doing something in your day—something that you won't believe when you hear it announced. Hab 1:5.

47. I have made you a light to the Gentiles, to lead them from the farthest corners of the earth to my salvation. Isa 49:6.

Acts 15:16. Afterwards (says the Lord), I will return and renew the broken contract with David, [17]so that Gentiles, too, will find the Lord—all those marked with my name. Amos 9:11, 12.

Acts 23:5. Never speak evil of any of your rulers. Ex 22:28.

Rom 1:17. The man who finds life will find it through trusting God. Hab 2:4.

Rom 2:24. No wonder the Scriptures say that the world speaks evil of God because of you. Isa 52:5.

Rom 3:4. God's words will always prove true and right, no matter who questions them. Ps 51:4.

10. No one is good—no one in all the world is innocent. [11]No one has ever really followed God's paths, or even truly wanted to. [12]Every one has turned away; all have gone wrong. No one anywhere has kept on doing what is right; not one. Ps 14:1–3; Eccl 7:20.

13. Their talk is foul and filthy like the stench from an open grave. Their tongues are loaded with lies [Ps 5:9]. Everything they say has in it the sting and poison of deadly snakes. Ps 140:3.

14. Their mouths are full of cursing and bitterness. Ps 10:7.

15. They are quick to kill. . . . [16]Wherever they go they leave misery and trouble behind them, [17]and they have never known what it is to feel secure or enjoy God's blessing. Isa 59:7, 8.

18. They care nothing about God nor what he thinks of them. Ps 36:1.

Rom 4:3. Abraham *believed God,* and that is why God canceled his sins and declared him "not guilty." Gen 15:6.

7. Blessed, and to be envied, . . . are those whose sins are forgiven and put out of sight. [8]Yes, what joy there is for anyone whose sins are no longer counted against him by the Lord. Ps 32:1, 2.

17. God made Abraham the father of many nations. Gen 17:5.

18. God told Abraham that he would give him a son who would have many descendants and become a great nation. Gen 15:5.

Rom 7:7. It was the law that showed me my sin. I would never have known the sin in my heart—the evil desires that are hidden there—if the law had not said, "You must not have evil desires in your heart." Ex 20:17.

Rom 8:36. For his sake we must be ready to face death at every moment of the day—we are like sheep awaiting slaughter. Ps 44:22.

Rom 9:7. The Scriptures say that the promises apply only to Abraham's son Isaac and Isaac's descendants. Gen 21:12.

9. Next year I will give you and Sarah a son. Gen 18:10.

12. God told her that Esau, the child born first, would be a servant to Jacob, his twin brother. Gen 25:23.

13. I chose to bless Jacob, but not Esau. Mal 1:2, 3.

15. If I want to be kind to someone, I will. And I will take pity on anyone I want to. Ex 33:19.

17. For God told him he had given him the kingdom of Egypt for the very purpose of displaying the awesome power of God against him: so that all the world would hear about God's glorious name. Ex 9:16.

25. God says that he will find other children for himself (who are not from his Jewish family) and will love them, though no one had ever loved them before. Hos 2:23.

26. And the heathen, of whom it once was said, "You are not my people," shall be called "sons of the Living God." Hos 1:10.

27. Concerning the Jews . . . though there would be millions of them, only a small number would ever be saved. [28]"For the Lord will execute his sentence upon the earth, quickly ending his dealings, justly cutting them short." Isa 10:22, 23.

29. Except for God's mercy all the Jews would be destroyed—all of them—just as everyone in the cities of Sodom and Gomorrah perished. Isa 1:9.

33. I have put a Rock in the path of the Jews, and many will stumble over him (Jesus). Those who believe in him will never be disappointed. Ps 118:22; Isa 8:14, 15; 28:16; 1 Pet 2:6, 7.

Rom 10:5. If a person could be perfectly good and hold out against temptation all his life and never sin once, only then could he be pardoned and saved. Lev 18:4, 5.

6. "You don't need to search the heavens to find Christ and bring him down to help you," and [7]"You don't need to go among the dead to bring Christ back to life again." [8]For salvation . . . is already within easy reach of each of us; in fact, it is as near as our own hearts and mouths. Deut 30:12–14.

11. No one who believes in Christ will ever be disappointed. Isa 28:16.

13. Anyone who calls upon the name of the Lord will be saved. Joel 2:32.

15. How beautiful are the feet of those who preach the Gospel of peace with God and bring glad tidings of good things. Isa 52:7.

16. For Isaiah the prophet said, "Lord, who has believed me when I told them?" Isa 53:1.

18. Have they heard God's Word? Yes, for it has gone wherever they are; the Good News has been told to the ends of the earth. Ps 19:3, 4.

19. God had said that he would make his people jealous and try to wake them up by giving his salvation to the foolish heathen nations. Deut 32:21.

20. God would be found by people who weren't even looking for him. [21]In the meantime, he keeps on reaching out his hands to the Jews, but they keep arguing and refusing to come. Isa 65:2.

Rom 11:3. Elijah the prophet was complaining to God about the Jews, telling God how they had killed the prophets and torn down God's altars; Elijah claimed that he was the only one left in all the land who still loved God, and now they were trying to kill him too. 1 Kgs 19:14.

4. I have seven thousand others besides you who still love me and have not bowed down to idols! 1 Kgs 19:18.

8. God has put them to sleep, shutting their eyes and ears so that they do not understand what we are talking about. Isa 6:9, 10; 29:10; Ezk 12:2.

9. Let their good food and other blessings trap them into thinking all is well between themselves and God. Let these good things boomerang on them and fall back upon their heads to justly crush them. Ps 69:22.

10. Let their eyes be dim . . . so that they cannot see, and let them walk bent-backed forever with a heavy load. Ps 69:23.

26. There shall come out of Zion a Deliverer, and he shall turn the Jews from all ungodliness. [27]At that time I will take away their sins, just as I promised. Isa 59:20, 21; 27:9.

34. For who among us can know the mind of the Lord? Who knows enough to be his counselor and guide? Isa 40:13.

Rom 12:19. Never avenge yourselves. Leave that to God, for he has said that he will repay those who deserve it. Deut 32:35; Heb 10:30.

20. Instead, feed your enemy if he is hungry. If he is thirsty give him something to drink and you will be "heaping coals of fire on his head." Prov 25: 21, 22.

Rom 13:9. If you love your neighbor as much as you love yourself you will not want to harm or cheat him, or kill him or steal from him. And you won't sin with his wife or want what is his, or do anything else the Ten Commandments say is wrong. All ten are wrapped up in this one, to love your neighbor as you love yourself. Ex 20:13–17; Lev 19:18; Deut 5:16–21.

Rom 14:11. For it is written, "As I live," says the Lord, "every knee shall bow to me and every tongue confess to God." Isa 45:23.

Rom 15:3. He came for the very purpose of suffering under the insults of those who were against the Lord. Ps 69:9.

9. I will praise you among the Gentiles, and sing to your name. 2 Sam 22:50; Ps 18:49.

10. Be glad, O you Gentiles, along with his people the Jews. Deut 32:43.

11. Praise the Lord, O you Gentiles, let everyone praise him. Ps 117:1.

12. There shall be an Heir in the house of Jesse, and he will be King over the Gentiles; they will pin their hopes on him alone. Isa 11:1, 10.

21. Those who have never heard the name of Christ before will see and understand. Isa 52:14, 15.

1 Cor 1:19. I will destroy all human plans of salvation no matter how wise they seem to be, and ignore the best ideas of men, even the most brilliant of them. Isa 29:14.

31. If anyone is going to boast, let him boast only of what the Lord has done. Jer 9:24; 2 Cor 10:17.

1 Cor 2:9. No mere man has ever seen, heard or even imagined what wonderful things God has ready for those who love the Lord. Isa 64:4.

16. He has never been one to know the Lord's thoughts, or to discuss them with him. Rom 11:34.

1 Cor 3:19. God uses man's own brilliance to trap him; he stumbles over his own "wisdom" and falls. Job 5:13.

20. The Lord knows full well how the human mind reasons, and how foolish and futile it is. Ps 94:11.

1 Cor 6:16. And don't you know that if a man joins himself to a prostitute she becomes a part of him and he becomes a part of her? For God tells us in the Scripture that in his sight the two become one person. Gen 2:24.

1 Cor 9:9. You must not put a muzzle on an ox to keep it from eating when it is treading out the wheat. Deut 25:4.

1 Cor 10:7. The people sat down to eat and drink and then got up to dance. Ex 32:6.

20. Those who offer food to these idols are united together in sacrificing to demons, certainly not to God. Deut 32:17.

26. For the earth and every good thing in it belongs to the Lord and is yours to enjoy. Ps 24: 1; 50:12.

1 Cor 14:21. We are told . . . that God would send men from other lands to speak in foreign languages to his people, but even then they would not listen. Isa 28:11, 12.

1 Cor 15:25. For Christ will be King until he has defeated all his enemies. Ps 110:1.

27. For the rule and authority over all things has been given to Christ by his Father. Ps 8:6.

32. Let us eat, drink, and be merry. What's the difference? For tomorrow we die. Isa 22:13.

45. The first man, Adam, was given a natural, human body. Gen 2:7.

54. Death is swallowed up in victory. Isa 25:8.

55. O death, where then your victory? Where then your sting? Hos 13:14.

2 Cor 3:13. And not as Moses did, who put a veil over his face so that the Israelis could not see the glory fade away. Ex 34:33.

2 Cor 6:2. Your cry came to me at a favorable time, when the doors of welcome were wide open. I helped you on a day when salvation was being offered. Isa 49:8.

16. I will live in them and walk among them, and I will be their God and they shall be my people. Lev 26:11, 12; Ezk 37:27.

17. Leave them; separate yourselves from them; don't touch their filthy things, and I will welcome you. Isa 52:11, 12.

18. And be a Father to you, and you will be my sons and daughters. 2 Sam 7:14.

2 Cor 8:15. He that gathered much had nothing left over, and he that gathered little had enough. Ex 16:18.

2 Cor 9:9. The godly man gives generously to the poor. His good deeds will be an honor to him forever. Ps 112:9.

2 Cor 13:1. If two or three have seen a wrong, it must be punished. Deut 19:15.

Gal 3:6. God declared him [Abraham] fit for heaven only because he believed God's promises. Gen 15:6.

8. I will bless those in every nation who trust in me as you do. Gen 12:3; 18:18.

10. Cursed is everyone who at any time breaks a single one of these laws that are written in God's Book of the Law. Deut 27:26.

11. The man who finds life will find it through trusting God. Hab 2:4.

12. A man is saved by obeying every law of God, without one slip. Lev 18:5.

13. Anyone who is hanged on a tree is cursed. Deut 21:23.

Gal 4:27. Now you can rejoice, O childless woman; you can shout with joy though you never before had a child. For I am going to give you many children—more children than the slave-wife has. Isa 54:1.

30. God told Abraham to send away the slave-wife and her son. Gen 21:10.

Gal 5:14. Love others as you love yourself. Lev 19:18.

Eph 4:8. When Christ returned triumphantly to heaven after his resurrection and victory over Satan, he gave generous gifts to men. Ps 68:18.

25. Stop lying to each other; tell the truth, for we are parts of each other. Zech 8:16.

26. If you are angry, don't sin by nursing your grudge. Ps 4:4.

Eph 5:31. A man must leave his father and mother when he marries, so that he can be perfectly joined to his wife, and the two shall be one. Gen 2:24.

Eph 6:2. Honor your father and mother. . . . [3]If you honor your father and mother, yours will be a long life, full of blessing. Ex 20:12; Deut 5:16.

1 Tim 5:18. Never tie up the mouth of an ox when it is treading out the grain—let him eat as he goes along! [Deut 25:4.] . . . Those who work deserve their pay! Lev 19:13; Deut 24:14, 15.

2 Tim 2:19. The Lord knows those who are really his. Num 16:5.

Heb 1:5, 6. You are my Son, and today I have given you the honor that goes with that name. [Ps 2:7.] . . . I am his Father and he is my Son. [2 Sam 7:14.] . . . Let all the angels of God worship him. Ps 97:7.

7. God speaks of his angels as messengers swift as the wind and as servants made of flaming fire. Ps 104:4.

8. Your kingdom, O God, will last forever and ever; its commands are always just and right. [9]You love right and hate wrong; so God, even your God, has poured out more gladness upon you than on anyone else. Ps 45:6, 7.

10. Lord, in the beginning you made the earth, and the heavens are the work of your hands. [11]They will disappear into nothingness, but you will remain forever. They will become worn out like old clothes, [12]and some day you will fold them up and replace them. But you yourself will never change, and your years will never end. Ps 102:25–27.

13. Sit here beside me in honor until I crush all your enemies beneath your feet. Ps 110:1.

Heb 2:6. What is mere man that you are so concerned about him? And who is this Son of Man you honor so highly? [7]For though you made him lower than the angels for a little while, now you have crowned him with glory and honor. [8]And you have put him in complete charge of everything there is. Nothing is left out. Ps 8:4–6.

12. I will talk to my brothers about God my Father, and together we will sing his praises. Ps 22:22.

13. I will put my trust in God along with my brothers. . . . See, here am I and the children God gave me. Isa 8:17, 18.

Heb 3:2. Moses also faithfully served in God's house. Num 12:7, 8.

7, 8. Be careful to hear his voice today and not let our hearts become set against him as the people of Israel did. They steeled themselves against his love and complained against him in the desert while he was testing them. [9]But God was patient with them forty years, though they tried his patience sorely; he kept right on doing his mighty miracles for them to see. [10]"But," God says, "I was very angry with them, for their hearts were always looking somewhere else instead of up to me, and they never found the paths I wanted them to follow." Ps 95:7–11; Heb 4:7.

Heb 4:3. "I have sworn in my anger that those who don't believe me will never get in," even though he has been ready and waiting for them since the world began. Ps 95:11.

4. God rested on the seventh day of creation, having finished all that he had planned to make. Gen 2:2; Ex 20:11.

Heb 5:5. My Son, today I have honored you. Ps 2:7.

6. You have been chosen to be a priest forever, with the same rank as Melchizedek. Heb 6:20; 7:11, 17, 21; Ps 110:4.

Heb 6:14. That he would bless Abraham again and again, and give him a son and make him the father of a great nation of people. Gen 22:16, 17.

Heb 7:1. When Abraham was returning home . . . Melchizedek met him and blessed him. Gen 14:18–20.

Heb 8:5. God warned him to follow exactly the pattern of the heavenly tabernacle as shown to him on Mount Sinai. Ex 25:40; 26:30.

8. The day will come when I will make a new agreement with the people of Israel and the people of Judah. *vs.* 9–12; Jer 31:31–34.

Heb 9:20. This is the blood that marks the beginning of the agreement between you and God. Ex 24:8.

Heb 10:5. O God, the blood of bulls and goats cannot satisfy you, so you have made ready this body of mine for me to lay as a sacrifice upon your altar. [6]You were not satisfied with the animal sacrifices, slain and burnt before you as offerings for sin. [7]Then I said, "See, I have come to do your will, to lay down my life, just as the Scriptures said that I would." Ps 40:6–8.

13. Waiting for his enemies to be laid under his feet. Ps 110:1.

30. Justice belongs to me; I will repay them. . . . The Lord himself will handle these cases. Deut 32:35, 36.

38. And those whose faith has made them good in God's sight must live by faith. Hab 2:3, 4.

Heb 11:3. By faith—by believing God—we know that the world and the stars—in fact, all things—were made at God's command. Ps 33:6.

4. It was by faith that Abel obeyed God and brought an offering that pleased God more than Cain's offering did. Gen 4:4.

5. Enoch trusted God too, and that is why God took him away to heaven without dying. Gen 5:21–24.

7. Noah . . . built the ark and saved his family. Gen 6:22.

8. Abraham trusted God . . . and Abraham obeyed. Gen 12:1–5.

11. Sarah, too, had faith, and because of this she

was able to become a mother in spite of her old age. Gen 18:11, 12; 21:1, 2.

12. And so a whole nation came from Abraham . . . like the stars of the sky and the sand on the ocean shores, there is no way to count them. Gen 22:17.

17. Abraham . . . offered up his son Isaac. Gen 22:9, 10.

18. Even Isaac, through whom God had promised to give Abraham a whole nation of descendants! Gen 21:12.

20. By faith . . . Isaac knew God would give future blessings to his two sons, Jacob and Esau. Gen 27:26–29.

21. Jacob . . . blessed each of Joseph's two sons. Gen 48:15–20.

22. Joseph . . . made them promise to carry his bones with them when they left! Gen 50:25.

23. Moses' parents. . . . hid him for three months. Ex 2:2.

27. He left the land of Egypt. . . . Moses kept right on going. Ex 10:28, 29.

28. He commanded them to kill a lamb . . . and sprinkle the blood on the doorposts of their homes. Ex 12:21, 27, 28.

29. The people of Israel trusted God and went right through the Red Sea as though they were on dry ground. Ex 14:22.

30. It was faith that brought the walls of Jericho tumbling down after the people of Israel had walked around them seven days. Josh 6:20.

31. Rahab the harlot did not die. Josh 6:23, 25.

32. It would take too long to recount the stories of the faith of Gideon and Barak and Samson and Jephthah and David and Samuel and all the other prophets. Judg 4:10–17; 7; 11:32, 33; 16:28–30; 1 Sam 7:9–12; 19:8.

33. These people all trusted God . . . overthrew kingdoms . . . were kept from harm in a den of lions, [34]and in a fiery furnace. Dan 3:26; 6:22.

35. And some women, through faith, received their loved ones back again from death. 1 Kgs 17:17–23; 2 Kgs 4:32–37.

36. And others were chained in dungeons. Gen 39:20; Jer 20:1–3.

37. Some died by stoning. 1 Kgs 21:13.

38. Some went about . . . wandering over deserts and mountains, hiding in dens and caves. 1 Kgs 18:3, 4, 13.

Heb 12:5. My son, don't be angry when the Lord punishes you. Don't be discouraged when he has to show you where you are wrong. [6]For when he punishes you, it proves that he loves you. When he whips you it proves you are really his child. Prov 3:11, 12.

16. Esau . . . traded his rights as the oldest son for a single meal. Gen 25:29–33.

18. You have not had to stand face to face with terror, flaming fire, gloom, darkness and a terrible storm. . . . [19]For there was an awesome trumpet blast, and a voice with a message so terrible that the people begged God to stop speaking. Ex 19:16; Deut 4:11, 12.

20. If even an animal touched the mountain it must die. Ex 19:13.

21. Moses himself was so frightened at the sight that he shook with terrible fear. Deut 9:19.

26. "Next time," he says, "I will not only shake the earth, but the heavens too." Hag 2:6.

Heb 13:5. I will never, *never* fail you nor forsake you. Deut 31:6, 8; Josh 1:5.

6. The Lord is my Helper and I am not afraid of anything that mere man can do to me. Ps 118:6.

15. With Jesus' help we will continually offer our sacrifice of praise to God by telling others of the glory of his name. Hos 14:2.

Jas 2:8. You must love and help your neighbors just as much as you love and take care of yourself. Lev 19:18.

11. Even though you have not broken the marriage laws by committing adultery, but have murdered someone, you have entirely broken God's laws. Ex 20:13, 14; Deut 5:18.

23. Abraham trusted God, and the Lord declared him good in God's sight. Gen 15:6.

Jas 4:6. God gives strength to the humble, but sets himself against the proud and haughty. Prov 3:34.

1 Pet 1:16. You must be holy, for I am holy. Lev 11:44; 19:1, 2; 20:7.

24. Yes, our natural lives will fade as grass does when it becomes all brown and dry. All our greatness is like a flower that droops and falls; [25]but the Word of the Lord will last forever. Isa 40:6–8.

1 Pet 2:6. See, I am sending Christ to be the carefully chosen, precious Cornerstone of my church, and I will never disappoint those who trust in him. *vs.* 7, 8; Isa 28:16.

7. The same Stone that was rejected by the builders has become the Cornerstone. Ps 118:22; Isa 8:14, 15.

9. You are priests of the King, you are holy and pure. Ex 19:6; Deut 14:2; Mal 3:17.

22. He never sinned, never told a lie. Isa 53:9.

24. For his wounds have healed ours! Isa 53:4, 5.

1 Pet 3:10. If you want a happy, good life, keep control of your tongue, and guard your lips from telling lies. [11]Turn away from evil and do good. Try to live in peace even if you must run after it to catch and hold it! [12]For the Lord is watching his children, listening to their prayers; but the Lord's face is hard against those who do evil. Ps 34:12–16.

15. Quietly trust yourself to Christ your Lord. Isa 8:12, 13.

1 Pet 5:5. God gives special blessings to those who are humble, but sets himself against those who are proud. Prov 3:34.

2 Pet 2:22. A dog comes back to what he has vomited. Prov 26:11.

R

RAAMAH 1. Son of Cush, called also *Raama,* 1 Chron 1:5–9. Gen 10:7.

2. A place in Arabia, Ezk 27:22.

RA-AMIAH One of those who returned to Jerusalem from captivity in Babylon, Neh 7:7. Called *Re-el-aiah* in Ezra 2:2.

RA-AMSES See *Rameses.*

RABBAH 1. A city east of the Jordan, originally belonging to the Ammonites, Josh 13:25. Bedstead of the giant Og kept at, Deut 3:11. Taken by David, 2 Sam 11:1; 12:26–31; 1 Chron 20:1, 2. Prophesied against, Jer 49:2, 3; Ezk 21:19, 20; 25:5; Amos 1:14.

2. A city in Judah, Josh 15:48–62.

RABBI The title of a teacher, Mt 23:7, 8. Ostentatiously used by the Pharisees, Mt 9:18; 23:7. Used in addressing Jesus, Mt 26:25. Forbidden by Jesus as a title to his disciples, Mt 23:8.

RABBITH A city in Issachar, Josh 19:17–23.

RACAL A city in Judah, 1 Sam 30:27–31.

RACE 1. Human. Unity of, Gen 3:20; Mal 2:10; Acts 17:26.

2. Foot race.

FIGURATIVE: Ps 19:5; Eccl 9:11; 1 Cor 9:24; Heb 12:1.

RACHAL A city in Judah, 1 Sam 30:29.

RACHEL Daughter of Laban and wife of Jacob. Meets Jacob at the well, Gen 29:9–13. Jacob serves Laban 14 years to secure her for his wife, Gen 29:15–30. Sterility of, Gen 29:31. Her grief because of her sterility; gives her servant to Jacob in order to secure children for herself, Gen 30:1–8, 15, 22–34. Later fertility of; becomes the mother of Joseph, Gen 30:22–25; of Benjamin, Gen 35:16–18, 24. Steals the household gods of her father, Gen 31:4, 14–20, 33–35. Her death and burial, Gen 35:18–20; 48:7; 1 Sam 10:2.

RADDAI Son of Jesse, 1 Chron 2:14.

RAHAB 1. A woman of Jericho. Assists the spies of Israel, Josh 2. Is spared at the taking of Jericho, Josh 6:17–25. Ancestor of Joseph, Mt 1:5. Faith of, commended, Heb 11:31; Jas 2:25.

2. A symbolical name applied to Egypt, Ps 89:10; Isa 30:7; 51:9.

RAHAM Son of Shema, 1 Chron 2:44.

RAILING INSTANCES OF. 1 Sam 25:14.

See *Slander; Speaking, Evil.*

RAIN Forty days of, at the time of the flood, Gen 7:4, 10–12, 17–24. The plague of, on Egypt, Ex 9:22–26, 33, 34. Miraculously caused by Samuel, 1 Sam 12:16–19; by Elijah, 1 Kgs 18:41–45. North wind brings, Prov 25:23. From the clouds, Prov 3:20. Withheld as judgment, Deut 11:17; 28:24; 1 Kgs 8:35, 36; 2 Chron 7:13; Jer 3:3; Amos 4:7; Zech 14:17. The earth shall never again be destroyed by, Gen 9:8–17. Sent by God, Deut 11:13, 14; Job 37:6; Isa 30:23; Jer 5:23, 24; 14:22. Contingent upon obedience, Lev 26:3–5; Deut 11:13, 14. Prayer for, 1 Kgs 8:35, 36; 2 Chron 6:26, 27. Answer to prayer for, promised, 2 Chron 7:13, 14; Zech 10:1. Withheld, in answer to prayer, Jas 5:17, 18. Restored in the day of the Lord, Joel 2:23.

Rainy season in Palestine in December, Ezra 10:9, 13.

See *Meteorology.*

FIGURATIVE. Ps 72:6.

RAINBOW A sign that the earth shall never again be destroyed by flood, Gen 9:8–17; Ezk 1:27, 28. Symbolical, Rev 4:3; 10:1.

See *Meteorology.*

RAISIN Preserved grape. Given by Abigail to David, 1 Sam 25:18. Given to the famishing Egyptian to revive him, 1 Sam 30:11, 12. Given by Ziba to David, 2 Sam 16:1. Given to David at Ziklag, 1 Chron 12:40. Cakes of, 2 Sam 6:19.

RAISING From the dead. See *Dead; Resurrection.*

RAKEM A descendant of Machir, son of Manasseh, 1 Chron 7:16.

RAKKATH A city in Naphtali, Josh 19:35–39.

RAKKON A city in Dan, Josh 19:41–46.

RAM 1. Son of Hezron and an ancestor of Jesus, Ruth 4:18–22; 1 Chron 2:9, 10. Called *Aram,* Mt 1:3, 4; and *Arni,* Lk 3:33.

2. Son of Jerahmeel, 1 Chron 2:25, 27.

3. An ancestor, probably of Elihu, mentioned in Job 32:2.

4. A sheep. Skins of, used for the roof of the tabernacle, Ex 26:14; 39:33–40. Seen in Daniel's vision, Dan 8:3, 20. Used in sacrifice, see *Offerings.*

Trumpets made of the horns of, see *Trumpet.*

RAMAH 1. A city allotted to Benjamin, Josh 18:21–28; Judg 19:12, 13. Attempted fortification of, by King Baasha; destruction of, by Asa, 1 Kgs 15: 17–22; 2 Chron 16:1–6. People of, return from the Babylonian captivity, Ezra 2:3–35; Neh 7:8–38; 11: 31–35. Jeremiah imprisoned in, Jer 40:1. Prophecies concerning, Isa 10:28, 29; Jer 31:15; Hos 5:8; Mt 2: 18.

2. A city of Asher, Josh 19:29.

3. A city of Naphtali, Josh 19:35–39.

4. Called also *Ramathaim-Zophim.* A city in Ephraim, Judg 4:5; 1 Sam 1:1. Home of Elkanah, 1 Sam 1:1, 19, 20; 2:11; and of Samuel, 1 Sam 1:19, 20; 7:17; 8:4; 15:34; 16:13. David flees to, 1 Sam 19:18. Samuel dies and is buried in, 1 Sam 25:1; 28:3.

5. Called *Ramah-in-the-Negeb.* A city of Simeon, Josh 19:8; called also *South Ramoth,* 1 Sam 30:27–31.

RAMATHAIM-ZOPHIM See *Ramah, 4.*

RAMATH-MIZPEH A town in Gad, Josh 13:26.

RAMESES Called also *Ra-amses.* The district in Egypt inhabited by the Israelites, Gen 47: 11; Ex 1:11; 12:37; Num 33:3–6. City of, built by the Israelites as a store city for Pharaoh, Ex 1:11.

RAMIAH An Israelite in the time of Ezra. Had taken a heathen wife, Ezra 10:25.

RAMOTH 1. A city of Issachar, allotted to the Levites, 1 Chron 6:73.

2. Ramoth in Gilead. See *Ramoth-Gilead.*

3. South Ramoth. See *Ramah, 5.*

RAMOTH-GILEAD A city of Gad, and a city of refuge, Deut 4:43; Josh 20:8; 1 Chron 6:80. One of Solomon's commissaries at, 1 Kgs 4:8–19. In the possession of the Syrians, 1 Kgs 22:3. Besieged by Israel and Judah; Ahab killed at, 1 Kgs 22: 29–37; 2 Chron 18. Recovered by Joram; Joram wounded at, 2 Kgs 8:28, 29; 9:14, 15; 2 Chron 22: 5, 6. Elisha anoints Jehu king at, 2 Kgs 9:1–6.

RANSOM Of a man's life, Ex 21:30; 30:11, 12; Ps 49:7–9; Prov 6:35; 13:8; Hos 13:14.

FIGURATIVE. Job 33:23, 24; Isa 35:10; 51:10; Mt 20:28; 1 Tim 2:6.

See *Jesus, Savior; Redemption.*

RAPE Law imposes death penalty for, Deut 22:25–27. Captives afflicted with, Isa 13:16; Jer 13: 22; Lam 5:11; Zech 14:1, 2.

INSTANCES OF. Of the wife of a Levite, by Benjaminites; tribe of Benjamin nearly exterminated by the army of the other tribes, as punishment for, Judg 19:22–30; 20:35–39. Of Tamar by Amnon; avenged in the death of Amnon at the hand of Absalom, Tamar's brother, 2 Sam 13:6–33.

RAPHA, RAPHAH 1. Son of Benjamin, 1 Chron 8:1, 2.

2. Called also *Rephaiah.* A descendant of Jonathan, 1 Chron 8:37; 9:43.

RAPHU A Benjaminite, Num 13:3–15.

RAPTURE A popular term used with reference to the resurrection and translation of believers, Jn 14:2, 3; 1 Cor 15:51, 52; Phil 3:20,21; 1 Thess 3:13; 4:13–18. The word comes from a Latin verb meaning to seize or to snatch, and is a synonym for translation. Associated with the translation are exhortations to waiting, 1 Thess 1:10, watching, 1 Thess 5:6, looking forward to seeing his glory, 2 Tim 4:8, Tit 2:13, and exhorting one another as the day approaches, Heb 10:25. Song 2: 10–13 is often used by premillenialists in connection with the rapture.

See *Church, True.*

RASHNESS Lev 5:4. If anyone makes a rash vow, whether the vow is good or bad, when he realizes what a foolish vow he has taken, he is guilty.

Prov 14:29. A wise man controls his temper. He knows that anger causes mistakes.

Prov 19:2. It is dangerous and sinful to rush into the unknown.

Prov 20:25. It is foolish and rash to make a promise to the Lord before counting the cost.

Prov 21:5. Steady plodding brings prosperity; hasty speculation brings poverty.

Prov 25:8. Don't be hot-headed and rush to court! You may start something you can't finish and go down before your neighbor in shameful defeat.

Prov 29:20. There is more hope for a fool than for a man of quick temper.

Eccl 5:2. Don't be a fool who doesn't even realize it is sinful to make rash promises to God, for he is in heaven and you are only here on earth, so let your words be few.

Eccl 7:9. Don't be quick-tempered—that is being a fool.

INSTANCES OF. Moses, in killing the Egyptian, Ex 2:11, 12; Acts 7:24, 25. When he struck the rock, Num 20:10–12. Jephthah's vow, Judg 11:30–39. Israel's vow to destroy the Benjaminites, Judg 21: 1–23. Uzzah, in steadying the ark. 2 Sam 6:6, 7. David, in his generosity to Ziba, 2 Sam 16:4; with chap. 19:26–29. Rehoboam, in forsaking the counsel of the old men, 1 Kgs 12:8–15. Josiah, in fighting against Neco, 2 Chron 35:20–25. Naaman, in refusing to wash in Jordan, 2 Kgs 5:11, 12. James and John, in desiring to call down fire on the Samaritans, Lk 9:54. Paul, in persisting in going to Jerusalem, against the repeated admonitions of the Holy Spirit, Acts 21:4,10–15. The Roman officers, in rejecting Paul's counsel, Acts 27:11.

RAT See *Mouse.* Lev 11:29, 30.

RAVEN A black carnivorous bird, Prov 30: 17; Song 5:11. Forbidden as food, Lev 11:13–19; Deut 14:11–18. Preserved by Noah in the ark, Gen 8:7. Fed Elijah, 1 Kgs 17:4–6. Cared for by divine providence, Lk 12:24.

RAZOR Nazirite forbidden to use, Num 6:5.

FIGURATIVE. Isa 7:20; Ezk 5:1.

READING Taught, Deut 6:9; 11:20. Joshua reading the words of the law, Josh 8:34. Reading the laws of God, Neh 8:7, 8; 9:3; 13:1. Reading out of the Book of the Lord, Isa 34:16. Reading God's messages to the people, Jer 36:6–23. Anyone can read it . . . and rush to tell the others, Hab 2:2. Haven't you ever read? Mt 12:3,5; 19:4; 21:16, 42. Reading the prophet Daniel, Mt 24:15. The eunuch reading Isaiah, Acts 8:28–33. Reading the epistles, Col 4:16; 1 Thess 5:27. Read and explain the Scriptures, 1 Tim 4:13. Blessed is he that reads the prophecy, Rev 1:3. Reading the book in heaven, Rev 5:4.

REAIAH 1. A man of Judah, son of Shobal, 1 Chron 4:2. Apparently called *Haroeh,* 1 Chron 2:52.

2. Son of Micah, a Reubenite, 1 Chron 5:5.

3. Ancestor of a family which returned to Jerusalem from captivity in Babylon, Ezra 2:43–54; Neh 7:46–56.

REAPING Ps 129:6, 7. The ark of the Lord returned by the Philistines at the time of, 1 Sam 6:13. Laws concerning gleaning at the time of, see *Gleaning.* Sowing and reaping, Job 4:7, 8; Prov 22:8; Gal 6:7–9. Reaping sparingly and bountifully, 2 Cor 9:6. The farmer overtaking the reaper, Amos 9:13. Reaping the whirlwind, Hos 8:7. Reaping in the last days, Jas 5:4. Reaping the earth, Rev 14:15.

FIGURATIVE. Ps 126:6; Hos 10:12, 13.

REASONING With God, Job 13:3, 17–28. God reasons with men, Ex 4:11; 20:5, 11; Isa 1:18; 5:3, 4; 43:26; Hos 4:1; Mic 6:2.

Natural understanding, Dan 4:36. To be applied to religion, 1 Cor 10:15; 1 Pet 3:15. Not a sufficient guide in human affairs, Deut 12:8; Prov 3:4, 5; 14:12. Of the Pharisees, Lk 5:21, 22; 20:5. Of Paul from the Scriptures, Acts 17:2; 18:4, 19; 24:25. The gospel cannot be explained by, 1 Cor 1:18–28; 2:1–14.

See *Investigation; Philosophy.*

REBA A king of Midian. Killed by the Israelites, Num 31:8; Josh 13:21.

REBECCA See *Rebekah.*

REBEKAH Daughter of Bethuel, grandniece of Abraham, Gen 22:20–23. Becomes Isaac's wife, Gen 24:15–67; 25:20. Mother of Esau and Jacob, Gen 25:21–28. Passes as Isaac's sister, Gen 26:6–11. Displeased with Esau's wives, Gen 26:34, 35. Prompts Jacob to deceive Isaac, Gen 27:5–29. Sends Jacob to Laban, Gen 27:42–46. Burial place of, Gen 49:31. Called *Rebecca,* Rom 9:10.

REBEL Prov 10:1. Happy is the man with a level-headed son; sad the mother of a rebel.

Prov 14:9. The common bond of rebels is their guilt.

Prov 15:7. Only the good can give good advice. Rebels can't. [20]A rebellious son saddens his mother.

Prov 17:25. A rebellious son is a grief to his father and a bitter blow to his mother. Prov 19:13.

Prov 18:2. A rebel doesn't care about the facts. All he wants to do is yell.

Prov 26:3. Guide a horse with a whip, a donkey with a bridle, and a rebel with a rod to his back! [8]Honoring a rebel will backfire like a stone tied to a slingshot! [9]A rebel will misapply an illustration so that its point will no more be felt than a thorn in the hand of a drunkard. [10]The master may get better work from an untrained apprentice than from a skilled rebel!

Prov 29:11. A rebel shouts in anger; a wise man holds his temper in and cools it.

REBELLION Treasonable, Prov 17:11.

INSTANCES OF. Absalom, 2 Sam chapters 15–18. Sheba, 2 Sam 20. Revolt of the ten tribes, 1 Kgs 12:16–20; 2 Chron 10; 13:5–12. Rebellion of Satan, Isa 14:12–17; Ezk 28:12–19. See *Sin.*

REBUKE See *Reproof.*

RECAH A city of unknown location, 1 Chron 4:11, 12.

RECHAB 1. Son of Rimmon. Murders Ish-bosheth, son of Saul; put to death by David, 2 Sam 4:5–12.

2. Father of Jonadab, 2 Kgs 10:15, 23; 1 Chron 2:55; Jer 35:6, 16, 18, 19. Ancestor of the Rechabites, Jer 35.

3. Father of Malchijah, Neh 3:14.

RECHABITES A family of Kenites descended from Rechab, through Jonadab, 1 Chron 2:55; Jer 35:6. Commanded by Jonadab not to drink wine, Jer 35:6. Adhere to the injunction of abstinence; perpetuation of the family promised as a reward, Jer 35.

See *Abstinence, Total; Nazirites.*

RECIPROCITY Rom 15:27; 1 Cor 9:11; Gal 6:6.

RECONCILIATION Between man and man, Mt 5:23–26. Of Esau and Jacob, Gen 33:4, 11. Between Pilate and Herod, Lk 23:12.

BETWEEN GOD AND MAN. Lev 8:15. Moses killed it. He smeared some of the blood with his finger upon the four horns of the altar, and upon the altar itself, to sanctify it, and poured out the rest of the blood at the base of the altar; thus he sanctified the altar, making atonement for it.

Ezk 45:15. From each 200 sheep in all your flocks in Israel, give him one sheep. These are the meal offerings, burnt offerings and thank offerings to make atonement for those who bring them, says the Lord God. [16]All the people of Israel shall bring their offerings to the prince. [17]The prince shall be required to furnish the people with sacrifices for public worship . . . to make reconciliation for the people of Israel.

Dan 9:24. The Lord has commanded 490 years of further punishment upon Jerusalem and your people. Then at last they will learn to stay away from sin, and their guilt will be cleansed; then the kingdom of everlasting righteousness will begin, and the Most Holy Place (in the Temple) will be rededicated, as the prophets have declared.

Rom 5:1. So now, since we have been made right in God's sight by faith in his promises, we can have real peace with him because of what Jesus Christ our Lord has done for us. [10]And since, when we were his enemies, we were brought back to God by the death of his Son, what blessings he must have for us now that we are his friends, and he is living within us!

Rom 11:15. When God turned away from them it meant that he turned to the rest of the world to offer his salvation; and now it is even more wonderful when the Jews come to Christ. It will be like dead people coming back to life.

2 Cor 5:18. All these new things are from God who brought us back to himself through what Christ Jesus did. And God has given us the privilege of urging everyone to come into his favor and

be reconciled to him. [19]For God was in Christ, restoring the world to himself, no longer counting men's sins against them but blotting them out. This is the wonderful message he has given us to tell others. [20]We are Christ's ambassadors. God is using us to speak to you: we beg you, as though Christ himself were here pleading with you, receive the love he offers you—be reconciled to God. [21]For God took the sinless Christ and poured into him our sins. Then, in exchange, he poured God's goodness into us!

Eph 2:15. By his death he ended the angry resentment between us, caused by the Jewish laws which favored the Jews and excluded the Gentiles, for he died to annul that whole system of Jewish laws. Then he took the two groups that had been opposed to each other and made them parts of himself; thus he fused us together to become one new person, and at last there was peace. [16]As parts of the same body, our anger against each other has disappeared, for both of us have been reconciled to God. And so the feud ended at last at the cross. [17]And he has brought this Good News of peace to you Gentiles who were very far away from him, and to us Jews who were near. [18]Now all of us, whether Jews or Gentiles, may come to God the Father with the Holy Spirit's help because of what Christ has done for us.

Col 1:20. It was through what his Son did that God cleared a path for everything to come to him —all things in heaven and on earth—for Christ's death on the cross has made peace with God for all by his blood. [21]This includes you who were once so far away from God. You were his enemies and hated him and were separated from him by your evil thoughts and actions, yet now he has brought you back as his friends. [22]He has done this through the death on the cross of his own human body, and now as a result Christ has brought you into the very presence of God, and you are standing there before him with nothing left against you—nothing left that he could even chide you for.

Heb 2:17. And it was necessary for Jesus to be like us, his brothers, so that he could be our merciful and faithful High Priest before God, a Priest who would be both merciful to us and faithful to God in dealing with the sins of the people.

See *Atonement; Jesus, Mission of; Propitiation; Redemption.*

RECONNAISSANCE Of Jericho, Josh 2:1–24; Bethel, Judg 1:22, 23; Laish, Judg 18:2–10.

RECORD See *Book.*

RECORDER See *Scribe; Secretary.*

RECREATION Jesus takes, from the fatigues of his ministry, Mk 6:31, 32; 7:24. See *Rest.*

RED See *Color.*

REDEEMER Hebrew *goel,* the nearest kinsman, rendered kinsman or relative in Num 5:8; Ruth 2:20; 3:9, 12; 4:1, 3, and redeemer in Job 19:25; Ps 19:14; Prov 23:10, 11; Isa 41:14; 43:14; 44:6, 24; 47:4; 48:17; 49:7, 26; 54:5, 8; 59:20; 60:16; 63:16; Jer 50:34. Rendered redeem or redeemed, it appears in many other Old Testament passages.

The story of Ruth and Boaz illustrates the kinsman redeemer, able and willing to redeem a paternal estate lost because of poverty, Lev 25:25, or an Israelite who had sold himself, Lev 25:47–49; Ruth 2:1; 4:1–15.

Christ is the Redeemer, our Kinsman, who delivers all who were slaves to Satan, Heb 2:13–15, sold into sin, Rom 7:14, with his precious blood, 1 Pet 1:18–20. See Isa 49:24 and Job 19:25: I know that my Redeemer lives, and that he will stand upon the earth at last.

See *Redemption.*

REDEMPTION Of persons or property, Lev 25:25–34; 27:1–33; Ruth 4:3–10. Redemption money paid to priests, Num 3:46–51. Of firstborn, see *Firstborn;* of land, see *Jubilee.*

OF OUR SOULS. Ps 111:9. He has paid a full ransom for his people; now they are always free to come to Jehovah (what a holy, awe-inspiring name that is).

Ps 130:7. O Israel, hope in the Lord; for he is loving and kind, and comes to us with armloads of salvation.

Mt 20:28. For I, the Messiah, did not come to be served, but to serve, and to give my life as a ransom for many. Mk 10:45.

Acts 20:28. And now beware! Be sure that you feed and shepherd God's flock—his church, purchased with his blood—for the Holy Spirit is holding you responsible as overseers.

Rom 3:24. Yet now God declares us "not guilty" of offending him if we trust in Jesus Christ, who in his kindness freely takes away our sins. [25]For God sent Christ Jesus to take the punishment for our sins and to end all God's anger against us. He used Christ's blood and our faith as the means of saving us from his wrath. In this way he was being entirely fair, even though he did not punish those who sinned in former times. For he was looking forward to the time when Christ would come and take away those sins. [26]And now in these days also he can receive sinners in this same way, because Jesus took away their sins. But isn't this unfair for God to let criminals go free, and say that they are innocent? No, for he does it on the basis of their trust in Jesus who took away their sins.

1 Cor 1:30. For it is from God alone that you have your life through Christ Jesus. He showed us God's plan of salvation; he was the one who made us acceptable to God; he made us pure and holy and gave himself to purchase our salvation.

1 Cor 6:20. For God has bought you with a great price. So use every part of your body to give glory back to God, because he owns it.

1 Cor 7:23. You have been bought and paid for by Christ, so you belong to him—be free now from all these earthly prides and fears.

Gal 1:4. He died for our sins just as God our Father planned, and rescued us from this evil world in which we live.

Gal 2:20. I have been crucified with Christ: and I myself no longer live, but Christ lives in me. And the real life I now have within this body is a result of my trusting in the Son of God, who loved me and gave himself for me.

Gal 4:4. But when the right time came, the time God decided on, he sent his Son, born of a woman, born as a Jew, [5]to buy freedom for us who were slaves to the law so that he could adopt us as his very own sons.

Eph 1:7. So overflowing is his kindness towards us that he took away all our sins through the blood of his Son, by whom we are saved.

Eph 5:2. Be full of love for others, following the example of Christ who loved you and gave himself to God as a sacrifice to take away your sins. And God was pleased, for Christ's love for you was like sweet perfume to him.

Col 1:14. Who bought our freedom with his blood and forgave us all our sins. [20]It was through what his Son did that God cleared a path for everything to come to him—all things in heaven and on earth—for Christ's death on the cross has made peace with God for all by his blood. [21]This includes you who were once so far away from God. You were his enemies and hated him and were separated from him by your evil thoughts and actions, yet now he has brought you back as his friends. [22]He has done this through the death on the cross of his own human body, and now as a result Christ has brought you into the very presence of God, and you are standing there before him with nothing left against you—nothing left that he could even chide you for.

1 Tim 2:6. *By giving his life for all mankind.* This is the message which at the proper time God gave to the world.

Tit 2:14. He died under God's judgment against our sins, so that he could rescue us from constant falling into sin and make us his very own people, with cleansed hearts and real enthusiasm for doing kind things for others.

Heb 9:12. And once for all took blood into that inner room, the Holy of Holies, and sprinkled it on the mercy seat; but it was not the blood of goats and calves. No, he took his own blood, and with it he, by himself, made sure of our eternal salvation. [15]Christ came with this new agreement so that all who are invited may come and have forever all the wonders God has promised them. For Christ died to rescue them from the penalty of the sins they had committed while still under that old system.

1 Pet 1:18. God paid a ransom to save you from the impossible road to heaven which your fathers tried to take, and the ransom he paid was not mere gold or silver, as you very well know. [19]But he paid for you with the precious lifeblood of Christ, the sinless, spotless Lamb of God.

Rev 5:9. They were singing him a new song with these words: "You are worthy to take the scroll and break its seal and open it; for you were slain, and your blood has bought people from every nation as gifts for God. [10]And you have gathered them into a kingdom and made them priests of our God; they shall reign upon the earth."

See *Atonement; Ransom; Redeemer.*

RED HEIFER Of purification, Num 19.

RED SEA The locusts which devastated Egypt destroyed in, Ex 10:19. Israelites cross; Pharaoh and his army drowned in, Ex 14; 15:1, 4, 19; Num 33:8; Deut 11:4; Josh 2:10; 4:23; 24:6, 7; Judg 11:16; 2 Sam 22:16; Neh 9:9–11; Ps 66:6; 78:13, 53; 106:7–11, 21, 22; 136:13–15; Isa 43:16, 17; Acts 7:36; 1 Cor 10:1, 2; Heb 11:29. Israelites camp by, Ex 14: 2, 9; Num 14:25; 21:4; 33:10; Deut 1:40; 2:1. Boundary of the promised land, Ex 23:31. Solomon builds ships on, 1 Kgs 9:26.

Wilderness of, Ex 13:17, 18.

REED A water plant, Ex 2:3; Isa 19:6; 35:7.

FIGURATIVE. Isa 58:5. Of weakness, 1 Kgs 14: 15; Job 8:11–13; Isa 42:3;

RE-EL-AIAH A returned captive from Babylon, Ezra 2:2. Called *Ra-amiah,* Neh 7:7.

REFINING The process of eliminating by fire the dross of metals. Of gold, 1 Chron 28:18. Of silver, 1 Chron 29:4, 5. Of wine, Isa 25:6. Of the child of God, Job 23:10; Isa 43:2; Heb 12:29; Jas 1: 2, 3; 1 Pet 1:7; Rev 2:18.

FIGURATIVE. Of the corrective judgments of God, Isa 1:25; 48:10; Jer 9:7; Zech 13:9; Mal 3:2, 3. Of the purity of the word of God, Ps 12:6; 119:140.

REFUGE CITIES OF. From the avenger of blood, Ex 21:13, 14; Num 35:11–32; Deut 4:41–43; 19: 2–13; Josh 20:1–6. List of, Josh 20:7–9. Roads made to, Deut 19:2, 3.

REFUGEE SLAVES Laws concerning, Deut 23:15, 16.

See *Servant, Bond.*

REGEM Son of Jahdai, 1 Chron 2:47.

REGEM-MELECH A messenger sent from the Jews in Babylon to Jerusalem, Zech 7:2.

REGENCY 1 Kgs 22:47; 2 Kgs 15:5.

REGENERATION Deut 30:6. He will cleanse your hearts and the hearts of your children and of your children's children so that you will love the Lord your God with all your hearts and souls, and Israel shall come alive again! Deut 29:4.

1 Kgs 8:58. May he give us the desire to do his will in everything, and to obey all the commandments and instructions he has given our ancestors.

Ps 36:9. For you are the Fountain of life; our light is from your Light.

Ps 51:2. Oh, wash me, cleanse me from this guilt. Let me be pure again. [7]Sprinkle me with the cleansing blood and I shall be clean again. Wash me and I shall be whiter than snow. [10]Create in me a new, clean heart, O God, filled with clean thoughts and right desires.

Ps 65:3. Though sins fill our hearts, you forgive them all.

Ps 68:18. He ascends the heights, leading many captives in his train. He receives gifts for men, even those who once were rebels. God will live among us here.

Ps 87:4. Nowadays when I mention among my friends the names of Egypt and Babylonia, Philistia and Tyre, or even distant Ethiopia, someone boasts that he was born in one or another of those countries. [6]When he registers her citizens he will place a checkmark beside the names of those who were born here.

Ps 110:3. In that day of your power your people shall come to you willingly, dressed in holy altar robes. And your strength shall be renewed day by day like morning dew.

Prov 12:28. The path of the godly leads to life. So why fear death?

Prov 14:27. Reverence for the Lord is a fountain of life; its waters keep a man from death.

Isa 1:16. Oh, wash yourselves! Be clean! Let me no longer see you doing all these wicked things; quit your evil ways. [17]Learn to do good, to be fair and to help the poor, the fatherless, and widows. [25]I myself will melt you in a smelting pot, and skim off your slag.

Isa 4:2–4. Those whose names are written down to escape the destruction of Jerusalem will be washed and rinsed of all their moral filth by the horrors and the fire. They will be God's holy people. And the land will produce for them its lushest bounty and its richest fruit.

Isa 12:3. Oh, the joy of drinking deeply from the Fountain of Salvation!

Isa 26:12. Lord, grant us peace; for all we have and are has come from you.

Isa 29:23. For when they see the surging birth rate and the expanding economy, then they will fear and rejoice in my name, and praise the Holy One of Israel, and stand in awe of him.

Isa 32:3. Then at last the eyes of Israel will open wide to God; his people will listen to his voice. [4]Even the hotheads among them will be full of sense and understanding, and those who stammer in uncertainty will speak out plainly. [15]Until at last the Spirit is poured down on us from heaven. Then once again enormous crops will come. [17]And out of justice, peace. Quietness and confidence will reign forever more.

Isa 35:5. And when he comes, he will open the eyes of the blind, and unstop the ears of the deaf. [6]The lame man will leap up like a deer, and those who could not speak will shout and sing!

Isa 42:16. He will bring blind Israel along a path they have not seen before. He will make the darkness bright before them and smooth and straighten out the road ahead.

Isa 43:7. All who claim me as their God will come, for I have made them for my glory; I created them.

Isa 44:3. For I will give you abundant water for your thirst and for your parched fields. And I will pour out my Spirit and my blessings on your children. [4]They shall thrive like watered grass, like willows on a river bank. [5]"I am the Lord's," they'll proudly say, or, "I am a Jew," and tattoo upon their hands the name of God or the honored name of Israel.

Isa 49:9. Through you I am saying to the prisoners of darkness, "Come out! I am giving you your freedom!"

Isa 55:1. Say there! is anyone thirsty? Come and drink—even if you have no money! Come, take your choice of wine and milk—it's all free! [2]Why spend your money on foodstuffs that don't give you strength? Why pay for groceries that don't do you any good? Listen and I'll tell you where to get good food that fattens up the soul! [3]Come to me with your ears wide open. Listen, for the life of your soul is at stake.

Jer 13:23. Can the Ethiopian change the color of his skin? or a leopard take away his spots? Nor can you who are so used to doing evil now stand being good.

Jer 17:13. O Lord, the Hope of Israel, all who turn away from you shall be disgraced and shamed; they are registered for earth and not for glory, for they have forsaken the Lord, the Fountain of living waters. [14]Lord, you alone can heal me, you alone can save, and my praises are for you alone. Jer 31:18.

Jer 24:7. I will give them hearts that respond to me. They shall be my people and I will be their God, for they shall return to me with great joy.

Jer 31:3. For long ago the Lord had said to Israel: I have loved you, O my people, with an everlasting love; with lovingkindness I have drawn you to me. [33]I will inscribe my laws upon their hearts, so that they shall want to honor me; then they shall truly be my people and I will be their God. [34]At that time it will no longer be necessary to admonish one another to know the Lord. For everyone, both great and small, shall really know me then, says the Lord, and I will forgive and forget their sins. Heb 8:10,11.

Jer 32:38. And they shall be my people and I will be their God. [39]And I will give them one heart and mind to worship me forever, for their own good and for the good of all their descendants. [40]And I will make an everlasting covenant with them, promising never again to desert them, but only to do them good. I will put a desire into their hearts to worship me, and they shall never leave me.

Jer 33:6. Nevertheless the time will come when I will heal Jerusalem's damage and give her prosperity and peace.

Ezk 11:19. I will give you one heart and a new spirit; I will take from you your hearts of stone and give you tender hearts of love for God, [20]so that you can obey my laws and be my people, and I will be your God.

Ezk 16:9. Then, when the marriage had taken place, I gave you beautiful clothes of linens and silk, embroidered, and sandals made of dolphin hide.

Ezk 18:31. Put them behind you and receive a new heart and a new spirit. For why will you die, O Israel?

Ezk 36:26. And I will give you a new heart—I will give you new and right desires—and put a new spirit within you. I will take out your stony hearts of sin and give you new hearts of love. [Ezk 11:19.] [27]And I will put my Spirit within you so that you will obey my laws and do whatever I command. [29]I will cleanse away your sins.

Ezk 37:1, 2. The power of the Lord was upon me and I was carried away by the Spirit of the Lord to a valley full of old, dry bones that were scattered everywhere across the ground. He led me around among them, [3]and then he said to me: "Son of dust, can these bones become people again?" I replied, "Lord, you alone know the answer to that." [4]Then he told me to speak to the bones and say: "O dry bones, listen to the words of God, [5]for the Lord God says, See! I am going to make you live and breathe again! [6]I will replace the flesh and muscles on you and cover you with skin. I will put breath into you, and you shall live and know I am the Lord." [7]So I spoke these words from God, just as he told me to; and suddenly there was a rattling noise from all across the valley, and the bones of each body came together and attached to each other as they used to be. [8]Then, as I watched, the muscles and flesh formed over the bones, and skin covered them, but the bodies had no breath. [9]Then he told me to call to the wind and say: "The Lord God says: Come from the four winds, O Spirit, and breathe upon these slain bodies, that they may live again." [10]So I spoke to the winds as he commanded me and the bodies began breathing; they lived, and stood up—a very great army. [11]Then he told me what the vision meant: "These bones," he said, "represent all the people of Israel. They say: 'We have become a heap of dried-out bones—all hope is gone.' [12]But tell them, the Lord God says: My people, I will open your graves of exile and cause you to rise again and return to the land of Israel. [13]And, then at last, O my people, you will know I am the Lord. [14]I will put my Spirit into you, and you shall live and return home again to your own land. Then you will know that I, the Lord, have done just what I promised you."

Ezk 44:7. By letting the uncircumcised into my sanctuary—those who have no heart for God—when you offer me my food, the fat and the blood. Thus you have broken my covenant in addition to all your other sins. [9]The Lord God says: No foreigner of all the many among you shall enter my sanctuary if he has not been circumcised and does not love the Lord.

Zech 12:10. Then I will pour out the spirit of grace and prayer on all the people of Jerusalem, and they will look on him they pierced, and mourn for him as for an only son, and grieve bitterly for him as for an oldest child who died.

Mt 12:33. A tree is identified by its fruit. A tree from a select variety produces good fruit; poor varieties don't. [34]You brood of snakes! How could evil men like you speak what is good and right? For a man's heart determines his speech. [35]A good man's speech reveals the rich treasures within him. An evil-hearted man is filled with venom, and his speech reveals it. [43, 44]This evil nation is like a man possessed by a demon. For if the demon leaves, it goes into the deserts for a while, seeking rest but finding none. Then it says, "I will return to the man I came from." So it returns and finds the man's heart clean but empty!

Mt 13:23. The good ground represents the heart of a man who listens to the message and understands it and goes out and brings thirty, sixty, or even a hundred others into the Kingdom. [Mk 4:20.] [33]The Kingdom of Heaven can be compared to a woman making bread. She takes a measure of flour and mixes in the yeast until it permeates every part of the dough. Lk 13:20, 21.

Mt 18:3. Unless you turn to God from your sins and become as little children, you will never get into the Kingdom of Heaven. Mk 10:15; Lk 18:16, 17.

Mk 4:26. Here is another story illustrating what the Kingdom of God is like: "A farmer sowed his field, [27]and went away, and as the days went by, the seeds grew and grew without his help. [28]For the soil made the seeds grow. First a leaf-blade pushed through, and later the wheat-heads formed and finally the grain ripened, [29]and then the farmer came at once with his sickle and harvested it."

Lk 1:16. And he will persuade many a Jew to turn to the Lord his God. [17]He will be a man of rugged spirit and power like Elijah, the prophet of old; and he will precede the coming of the Messiah, preparing the people for his arrival. He will soften adult hearts to become like little children's, and will change disobedient minds to the wisdom of faith.

Lk 8:35. Soon a crowd came out to see for themselves what had happened and saw the man who had been demon-possessed sitting quietly at Jesus' feet, clothed and sane! And the whole crowd was badly frightened. [38]The man who had been demon-possessed begged to go too, but Jesus said no. [39]"Go back to your family," he told him, "and tell them what a wonderful thing God has done for you." So he went all through the city telling everyone about Jesus' mighty miracle. Mk 5:19, 20.

Jn 1:4. Eternal life is in him, and this life gives light to all mankind. [13]All those who believe this are reborn!—not a physical rebirth resulting from human passion or plan—but from the will of God. [16]We have all benefited from the rich blessings he brought to us—blessing upon blessing heaped upon us!

Jn 3:3. Jesus replied, "With all the earnestness I possess I tell you this: Unless you are born again, you can never get into the Kingdom of God." [4]"Born again!" exclaimed Nicodemus. "What do you mean? How can an old man go back into his mother's womb and be born again?" [5]Jesus replied, "What I am telling you so earnestly is this: Unless one is born of water and the Spirit, he cannot enter the Kingdom of God. [6]Men can only reproduce human life, but the Holy Spirit gives new life from heaven; [7]so don't be surprised at my statement that you must be born again! [8]Just as you can hear the wind but can't tell where it comes from or where it will go next, so it is with the Spirit. We do not know on whom he will next bestow his life from heaven."

Jn 4:10. He replied, "If you only knew what a wonderful gift God has for you, and who I am, you would ask me for some *living* water!" [14]"But the water I give them," he said, "becomes a perpetual spring within them, watering them forever with eternal life."

Jn 5:24. I say emphatically that anyone who listens to my message and believes in God who sent me has eternal life, and will never be damned for his sins, but has already passed out of death into life.

Jn 6:44. For no one can come to me unless the Father who sent me draws him to me, and at the Last Day I will cause all such to rise again from the dead. [45]As it is written in the Scriptures, 'They shall all be taught of God.' Those the Father speaks to, who learn the truth from him, will be attracted to me. [47]How earnestly I tell you this—anyone who believes in me already has eternal life! [50, 51]But the Bread from heaven gives eternal life to everyone who eats it. I am that Living Bread that came down out of heaven. Anyone eating this Bread shall live forever. [57]I live by the power of the living Father who sent me, and in the same way those who partake of me shall live because of me!

Jn 8:12. I am the Light of the world. So if you follow me, you won't be stumbling through the darkness, for living light will flood your path. [32]And you will know the truth, and the truth will set you free. [36]So if the Son sets you free, you will indeed be free.

Jn 10:9. Yes, I am the Gate. Those who come in by way of the Gate will be saved and will go in and out and find green pastures. [10]The thief's purpose is to steal, kill and destroy. My purpose is to give life in all its fullness.

Jn 13:8. "No," Peter protested, "you shall never wash my feet!" "But if I don't, you can't be my partner, Jesus replied.

Jn 15:1. I am the true Vine, and my Father is the Gardener. [3]He has already tended you by pruning you back for greater strength and usefulness by means of the commands I gave you.

Jn 17:2. For you have given him authority over every man and woman in all the earth. He gives eternal life to each one you have given him.

Acts 2:38. And Peter replied, "Each one of you must turn from sin, return to God, and be baptized in the name of Jesus Christ for the forgiveness of your sins; then you also shall receive this gift, the Holy Spirit." [47]Each day God added to them all who were being saved.

Acts 3:26. And as soon as God had brought his servant to life again, he sent him first of all to you men of Israel, to bless you by turning you back from your sins.

Acts 11:17. And since it was *God* who gave these Gentiles the same gift he gave us when we believed on the Lord Jesus Christ, who was I to argue? [21]And the Lord honored this effort so that large numbers of these Gentiles became believers.

Acts 15:9. He made no distinction between them and us, for he cleansed their lives through faith, just as he did ours.

Acts 16:14. One of them was Lydia. . . . the Lord opened her heart and she accepted all that Paul was saying.

Acts 21:19. After greetings were exchanged, Paul recounted the many things God had accomplished among the Gentiles through his work.

Acts 26:18. To open their eyes to their true condition so that they may repent and live in the light of God instead of in Satan's darkness, so that they may receive forgiveness for their sins and God's inheritance along with all people everywhere whose sins are cleansed away, who are set apart by faith in me.

Rom 2:28. For you are not real Jews just because you were born of Jewish parents or because you have gone through the Jewish initiation ceremony of circumcision. [29]No, a real Jew is anyone whose heart is right with God. For God is not looking for those who cut their bodies in actual body circumcision, but he is looking for those with changed hearts and minds. Whoever has that kind of change in his life will get his praise from God, even if not from you.

Rom 6:3. When we became Christians and were baptized to become a part of Jesus Christ; through his death the power of your sinful nature was shattered. [4]Your old sin-loving nature was buried with him by baptism when he died, and when God the Father, with glorious power, brought him back to life again, you were given his wonderful new life to enjoy. [5]For you have become a part of him, and so you died with him, so to speak, when he died; and now you share his new life, and shall rise as he did. [6]Your old evil desires were nailed to the cross with him; that part of you that loves to sin was crushed and fatally wounded, so that your sin-loving body is no longer under sin's control, no longer needs to be a slave to sin; [7]for when you are deadened to sin you are freed from all its allure and its power over you. [8]And since your old sin-loving nature "died" with Christ, we know that you will share his new life. [9]Christ rose from the dead and will never die again. Death no longer has any power over him. [10]He died once for all to end sin's power, but now he lives forever in unbroken fellowship with God. [11]So look upon your old sin nature as dead and unresponsive to sin, and instead be alive to God, alert to him, through Jesus Christ our Lord. [12]Do not let sin control your puny body any longer; do not give in to its sinful desires. [13]Do not let any part of your bodies become tools of wickedness, to be used for sinning; but give yourselves completely to God—every part of you—for you are back from death and you want to be tools in the hands of God, to be used for his good purposes. [14]Sin need never again be your master, for now you are no longer tied to the law where sin enslaves you, but you are free under God's favor and mercy. [15]Does this mean that now we can go ahead and sin and not worry about it? (For our salvation does not depend on keeping the law, but on receiving God's grace!) Of course not! [16]Don't you realize that you can choose your own master? You can choose sin (with death) or else obedience (with acquittal). The one to whom you offer yourself—he will take you and be your master and you will be his slave.

[17]Thank God that though you once chose to be slaves of sin, now you have obeyed with all your heart the teaching to which God has committed you. [18]And now you are free from your old master, sin; and you have become slaves to your new master, righteousness. [19]I speak this way, using the illustration of slaves and masters, because it is easy to understand: just as you used to be slaves to all kinds of sin, so now you must let yourselves be slaves to all that is right and holy. [20]In those days when you were slaves of sin you didn't bother much with goodness. [21]And what was the result? Evidently not good, since you are ashamed now even to think about those things you used to do, for all of them end in eternal doom. [22]But now you are free from the power of sin and are slaves of God, and his benefits to you include holiness and everlasting life. [23]For the wages of sin is death, but the free gift of God is eternal life through Jesus Christ our Lord.

Rom 7:6. But now you need no longer worry about the Jewish laws and customs because you "died" while in their captivity, and now you can really serve God; not in the old way, mechanically obeying a set of rules, but in the new way. [24, 25]Oh, what a terrible predicament I'm in! Who will free me from my slavery to this deadly lower nature? Thank God! It has been done by Jesus Christ our Lord. He has set me free.

Rom 8:2. For the power of the life-giving Spirit —and this power is mine through Christ Jesus— has freed me from the vicious circle of sin and death. [3]We aren't saved from sin's grasp by knowing the commandments of God, because we can't and don't keep them, but God put into effect a different plan to save us. He sent his own Son in a human body like ours—except that ours are sinful —and destroyed sin's control over us by giving himself as a sacrifice for our sins. [4]So now we can obey God's laws if we follow after the Holy Spirit and no longer obey the old evil nature within us. [5]Those who let themselves be controlled by their lower natures live only to please themselves, but those who follow after the Holy Spirit find themselves doing those things that please God. [6]Following after the Holy Spirit leads to life and peace, but following after the old nature leads to death. [9]But you are not like that. You are controlled by your new nature if you have the Spirit of God living in you. (And remember that if anyone doesn't have the Spirit of Christ living in him, he is not a Christian at all.) [13]For if you keep on following it you are lost and will perish, but if through the power of the Holy Spirit you crush it and its evil deeds, you shall live. [14]For all who are led by the Spirit of God are sons of God. [15]And so we should not be like cringing, fearful slaves, but we should behave like God's very own children, adopted into the bosom of his family, and calling to him, "Father, Father." [16]For his Holy Spirit speaks to us deep in our hearts, and tells us that we really are God's children.

Rom 12:2. Don't copy the behavior and customs of this world, but be a new and different person with a fresh newness in all you do and think. Then you will learn from your own experience how his ways will really satisfy you.

Rom 15:16. For I am, by God's grace, a special messenger from Jesus Christ to you Gentiles, bringing you the Gospel and offering you up as a fragrant sacrifice to God; for you have been made pure and pleasing to him by the Holy Spirit.

1 Cor 1:9. God will surely do this for you, for he always does just what he says, and he is the one who invited you into this wonderful friendship with his Son, even Christ our Lord. [24]But God has opened the eyes of those called to salvation, both Jews and Gentiles, to see that Christ is the mighty power of God to save them; Christ himself is the center of God's wise plan for their salvation. [30]For it is from God alone that you have your life through Christ Jesus. He showed us God's plan of salvation; he was the one who made us acceptable to God; he made us pure and holy and gave himself to purchase our salvation.

1 Cor 2:12. And God has actually given us his Spirit (not the world's spirit) to tell us about the wonderful free gifts of grace and blessing that God has given us. [14]But the man who isn't a Christian can't understand and can't accept these thoughts from God, which the Holy Spirit teaches us. They sound foolish to him, because only those who have the Holy Spirit within them can understand what the Holy Spirit means. Others just can't take it in. [15]But the spiritual man has insight into everything, and that bothers and baffles the man of the world, who can't understand him at all. [16]How could he? For certainly he has never been one to know the Lord's thoughts, or to discuss them with him, or to move the hands of God by prayer. But strange as it seems, we Christians actually do have within us a portion of the very thoughts and mind of Christ.

1 Cor 3:6. My work was to plant the seed in your hearts, and Apollos' work was to water it, but it was God, not we, who made the garden grow in your hearts. [7]The person who does the planting or watering isn't very important, but God is important because he is the one who makes things grow. [9]We are only God's co-workers. You are *God's* garden, not ours; you are *God's* building, not ours.

1 Cor 6:11. But now your sins are washed away, and you are set apart for God, and he has accepted you because of what the Lord Jesus Christ and the Spirit of our God have done for you.

1 Cor 12:6. There are many ways in which God works in our lives, but it is the same God who does the work in and through all of us who are his. [13]Each of us is a part of the one body of Christ. Some of us are Jews, some are Gentiles, some are slaves and some are free. But the Holy Spirit has fitted us all together into one body. We have been baptized into Christ's body by the one Spirit, and have all been given that same Holy Spirit.

1 Cor 15:10. But whatever I am now it is all because God poured out such kindness and grace upon me.

2 Cor 1:21. It is this God who has made you and me into faithful Christians and commissioned us apostles to preach the Good News. [22]He has put his brand upon us—his mark of ownership—and given us his Holy Spirit in our hearts as guarantee that we belong to him, and as the first installment of all that he is going to give us.

2 Cor 3:3. They can see that you are a letter from Christ, written by us. It is not a letter written with pen and ink, but by the Spirit of the living God; not one carved on stone, but in human hearts. [18]But we Christians have no veil over our faces; we can be mirrors that brightly reflect the glory of the Lord. And as the Spirit of the Lord works within us, we become more and more like him.

2 Cor 4:6. For God, who said, "Let there be light in the darkness," has made us understand that it is the brightness of his glory that is seen in the face of Jesus Christ.

2 Cor 5:5. This is what God has prepared for us and, as a guarantee, he has given us his Holy Spirit. [17]When someone becomes a Christian he becomes a brand new person inside. He is not the same any more. A new life has begun!

Gal 2:20. I have been crucified with Christ: and I myself no longer live, but Christ lives in me. And the real life I now have within this body is a result of my trusting in the Son of God, who loved me and gave himself for me.

Gal 4:29. And so we who are born of the Holy Spirit are persecuted now by those who want us to keep the Jewish laws, just as Isaac the child of promise was persecuted by Ishmael the slave-wife's son.

Gal 6:15. It doesn't make any difference now whether we have been circumcised or not; what counts is whether we really have been changed into new and different people.

Eph 2:1. Once you were under God's curse, doomed forever for your sins. [5]That even though we were spiritually dead and doomed by our sins, he gave us back our lives again when he raised Christ from the dead—only by his undeserved favor have we ever been saved— [6]and lifted us up from the grave into glory along with Christ, where we sit with him in the heavenly realms—all because of what Christ Jesus did. [8]Because of his kindness you have been saved through trusting Christ. And even trusting is not of yourselves; it too is a gift from God. [10]It is God himself who has made us what we are and given us new lives from Christ Jesus; and long ages ago he planned that we should spend these lives in helping others.

Eph 4:7. However, Christ has given each of us special abilities—whatever he wants us to have out of his rich storehouse of gifts. [8]The Psalmist tells about this, for he says that when Christ returned triumphantly to heaven after his resurrection and victory over Satan, he gave generous gifts to men. [16]Under his direction the whole body is fitted together perfectly, and each part in its own special way helps the other parts, so that the whole body is healthy and growing and full of love. [21]If you have really heard his voice and learned from him the truths concerning himself, [22]then throw off your old evil nature—the old you that was a partner in your evil ways—rotten through and through, full of lust and sham. [23]Now your attitudes and thoughts must all be constantly changing for the better. [24]Yes, you must be a new and different person, holy and good. Clothe yourself with this new nature.

Eph 5:14. Awake, O sleeper, and rise up from the dead; and Christ shall give you light.

Phil 1:6. And I am sure that God who began the good work within you will keep right on helping you grow in his grace until his task within you is finally finished on that day when Jesus Christ returns.

Col 2:11. When you came to Christ he set you free from your evil desires, not by a bodily operation of circumcision but by a spiritual operation, the baptism of your souls. [12]For in baptism you see how your old, evil nature died with him and was buried with him; and then you came up out of death with him into a new life because you trusted the Word of the mighty God who raised Christ from the dead. [13]You were dead in sins, and your sinful desires were not yet cut away. Then he gave you a share in the very life of Christ, for he forgave all your sins.

Col 3:9. Don't tell lies to each other; it was your old life with all its wickedness that did that sort of thing; now it is dead and gone. [10]You are living a brand new kind of life that is continually learning more and more of what is right, and trying constantly to be more and more like Christ who created this new life within you.

2 Thess 2:13. But we must forever give thanks to God for you, our brothers loved by the Lord, because God chose from the very first to give you salvation, cleansing you by the work of the Holy Spirit and by your trusting in the Truth.

Tit 3:5. Then he saved us—not because we were good enough to be saved, but because of his kindness and pity—by washing away our sins and giving us the new joy of the indwelling Holy Spirit. [6]whom he poured out upon us with wonderful fullness—and all because of what Jesus Christ our Savior did.

Heb 4:1. Although God's promise still stands—his promise that all may enter his place of rest—we ought to tremble with fear because some of you may be on the verge of failing to get there after all. [2]For this wonderful news—the message that God wants to save us—has been given to us just as it was to those who lived in the time of Moses. But it didn't do them any good because they didn't believe it. They didn't mix it with faith. [3]For only we who believe God can enter into his place of rest. He has said, "I have sworn in my anger that those who don't believe me will never get in," even though he has been ready and waiting for them since the world began. [4]We know he is ready and waiting because it is written that God rested on the seventh day of creation, having finished all that he had planned to make. [5]Even so they didn't get in, for God finally said, "They shall never enter my rest." [6]Yet the promise remains and some get in—but not those who had the first chance, for they disobeyed God and failed to enter. [7]But he has set another time for coming in, and that time is now. He announced this through King David long years after man's first failure to enter, saying in the words already quoted, "Today when you hear him calling, do not harden your hearts against him." [8]This new place of rest he is talking about does not mean the land of Israel that Joshua led them into. If that were what God meant, he would not have spoken long afterwards about "today" being the time to get in. [9]So there is a full complete rest *still waiting* for the people of God. [10]Christ has already entered there. He is resting from his work, just as God did after the creation. [11]Let us do our best to go into that place of rest, too, being careful not to disobey God as the children of Israel did, thus failing to get in. [12]For whatever God says to us is full of living power: it is sharper than the sharpest dagger, cutting swift and deep into our innermost thoughts and desires with all their parts, exposing us for what we really are.

Heb 10:16. "This is the agreement I will make with the people of Israel, though they broke their first agreement: I will write my laws into their minds so that they will always know my will, and I will put my laws into their hearts so that they will want to obey them." [17]And then he adds, "I will never again remember their sins and lawless deeds." [22]Let us go right in, to God himself, with true hearts fully trusting him to receive us, because we have been sprinkled with Christ's blood to make us clean, and because our bodies have been washed with pure water. . . . [23]There is no longer any room for doubt, and we can tell others that salvation is ours, for there is no question that he will do what he says.

Jas 1:18. And it was a happy day for him when he gave us our new lives, through the truth of his Word, and we became, as it were, the first children in his new family.

Jas 5:19. Dear brothers, if anyone has slipped away from God and no longer trusts the Lord, and someone helps him understand the Truth again, [20]that person who brings him back to God will have saved a wandering soul from death, bringing about the forgiveness of his many sins.

1 Pet 1:2. Dear friends, God the Father chose you long ago and knew you would become his children. And the Holy Spirit has been at work in your hearts, cleansing you with the blood of Jesus Christ and making you to please him. May God bless you richly and grant you increasing freedom from all anxiety and fear. [3]All honor to God, the God and Father of our Lord Jesus Christ; for it is his boundless mercy that has given us the privilege of being born again, so that we are now members of God's own family. Now we live in the hope of eternal life because Christ rose again from the dead. [22]Now you can have real love for everyone because your souls have been cleansed from selfishness and hatred when you trusted Christ to save you; so see to it that you really do love each other warmly, with all your hearts. [23]For you have a new life. It was not passed on to you from your parents, for the life they gave you will fade away. This new one will last forever, for it comes from Christ, God's ever-living Message to men.

1 Pet 2:9. But you are not like that, for you have been chosen by God himself—you are priests of the King, you are holy and pure, you are God's very own—all this so that you may show to others how God called you out of the darkness into his wonderful light.

2 Pet 1:3. For as you know him better, he will give you, through his great power, everything you need for living a truly good life: he even shares his own glory and his own goodness with us! [4]And by that same mighty power he has given us all the other rich and wonderful blessings he promised; for instance, the promise to save us from the lust and rottenness all around us, and to give us his own character.

1 Jn 2:27. But you have received the Holy Spirit and he lives within you, in your hearts, so that you don't need anyone to teach you what is right. For he teaches you all things, and he is the Truth, and no liar; and so, just as he has said, you must live in Christ, never to depart from him. [29]Since we know that God is always good and does only right, we may rightly assume that all those who do right are his children.

1 Jn 3:9. The person who has been born into God's family does not make a practice of sinning, because now God's life is in him; so he can't keep on sinning, for this new life has been born into him and controls him—he has been *born again.* [14]If we love other Christians it proves that we have been delivered from hell and given eternal life.

1 Jn 4:7. Dear friends, let us practice loving each other, for love comes from God and those who are loving and kind show that they are the children of God, and that they are getting to know him better.

1 Jn 5:1. If you believe that Jesus is the Christ—that he is God's Son and your Savior—then you are a child of God. And all who love the Father love his children too. [4]For every child of God can obey him, defeating sin and evil pleasure by trusting Christ to help him. [5]But who could possibly fight and win this battle except by believing that Jesus is truly the Son of God? [11]And what is it that God has said? That he has given us eternal life, and that this life is in his Son. [12]So whoever has God's Son has life; whoever does not have his Son, does not have life. [18]No one who has become part of God's family makes a practice of sinning, for Christ, God's Son, holds him securely and the devil cannot get his hands on him.

See *Atonement; Reconciliation; Redemption; Sanctification; Sin, Forgiveness of.*

INSTANCES OF. Jacob, Gen 32:29. Saul, 1 Sam 10:9. Saul of Tarsus, Acts 9:3–18. All righteous persons, see *Righteous.*

REGICIDE Of Eglon, Judg 3:16–23. Of Saul, 2 Sam 1:16. Of Ishbosheth, 2 Sam 4:5–8. Of Nadab, 1 Kgs 15:27–29. Of Elah, 1 Kgs 16:9–11. Of Joram, 2 Kgs 9:24. Of Ahaziah, 2 Kgs 9:27. Of Joash, 2 Kgs 12:20,21. Of Amaziah, 2 Kgs 14:19,20. Of Zechariah, 2 Kgs 15:10. Of Shallum, 2 Kgs 15:14. Of Pekahiah, 2 Kgs 15:25. Of Pekah, 2 Kgs 15:30. Of Sennacherib, 2 Kgs 19:36, 37; Isa 37:37, 38.
See *Homicide.*

REGISTRATION Of citizens, Isa 4:2–4.
See *Census.*

REHABIAH Son of Eliezer, 1 Chron 23:17; 24:21; 26:25.

REHOB 1. Father of Hadadezer, king of Zobah, 2 Sam 8:3, 11, 12.

2. A Levite who sealed the covenant with Nehemiah, Neh 10:9–13.

3. A town in northern Palestine. The limit of the investigation made by the twelve spies, Num 13:21. Possessed by the Syrians, 2 Sam 10:6–8. Called *Beth-rehob,* Judg 18:28.

4. An unlocated town of Asher, Josh 19:28.

5. A Levitical city of Asher, Josh 19:30; 21:30, 31; 1 Chron 6:75. Canaanites not expelled from, Judg 1:31, 32.

REHOBOAM Successor to Solomon as king, 1 Kgs 11:43; 2 Chron 9:31. Refuses to reform abuses, 1 Kgs 12:1–15; 2 Chron 10:1–15. Ten tribes, under leadership of Jeroboam, successfully revolt from, 1 Kgs 12:16–24; 2 Chron 10:16–19; 11:1–4. Builds fortified cities; is temporarily prosperous, 2 Chron 11:5–23. Invaded by king of Egypt and Jerusalem ransacked, 1 Kgs 14:25–28; 2 Chron 12:1–12. Death of, 1 Kgs 14:31; 2 Chron 12:16. Genealogy and descendants of, 1 Chron 3; Mt 1.

REHOBOTH 1. Called *Rehoboth-Ir.* A city built by Nimrod, Gen 10:11, 12.

2. A city of the Edomites, Gen 36:31–39; 1 Chron 1:48.

3. The name given to a well dug by Isaac, Gen 26:22.

REHUM 1. A captive who returned to Jerusalem from Babylon, Ezra 2:2. Called *Nehum,* Neh 7:7.

2. A governor who wrote a letter to Artaxerxes, influencing him against the Jews, Ezra 4:8, 9, 17, 23.

3. A Levite who repaired part of the wall of Jerusalem, Neh 3:17.

4. A Jew of the exile who signed the covenant with Nehemiah, Neh 10:14–27.

5. A priest who returned to Jerusalem from captivity in Babylon, Neh 12:1–7.

REI An Israelite loyal to David at the time of Adonijah's usurpation, 1 Kgs 1:8.

REJECTION Of God, see *God, Rejected.* Of Jesus, see *Jesus, Rejected.*

REJOICING See *Praise.*

REKEM 1. A king of the Midianites, killed by the Israelites, Num 31:8; Josh 13:21.

2. A son of Hebron, 1 Chron 2:43, 44.

3. A city in Benjamin, Josh 18:21–28.

RELATIVE Distant, Prov 27:10.
See *Brother.*

RELEASE YEAR OF. See *Jubilee, Year of.*

RELIGION FAMILY. See *Family.*

NATIONAL. Supported by taxes, Ex 30:11–16; 38:25, 26. Priests supported by the State, 1 Kgs 18:19; 2 Chron 11:13–15. Subverted by Jeroboam, 1 Kgs 12:26–33; 2 Chron 11:13–15. Established by Jeroboam, 1 Kgs 12:26–33.

NATURAL. Natural religion is a theological term referring to that which may be learned of God through nature, Rom 1:19, 20, or a consciousness of God. Job 12:7–9. Who doesn't know that the Lord does things like that? Ask the dumbest beast—he knows that it is so; ask the birds—they will tell you; or let the earth teach you, or the fish in the sea. [10]For the soul of every living thing is in the hand of God, and the breath of all mankind. [11]Just as my mouth can taste good food, so my mind tastes truth when I hear it. [12]And as you say, older men like me are wise. They understand. [13]But true wisdom and power are God's. He alone knows what we should do; he understands. [14]And how great is his might! What he destroys can't be rebuilt. When he closes in on a man, there is no escape. [15]He withholds the rain and the earth becomes a desert; he sends the storms, and floods the ground. [16]Yes, with him is strength and wisdom. Deceivers and deceived are both his slaves.

Job 35:10. Yet none of them cry to God, asking, "Where is God my Maker who gives songs in the night, [11]and makes us a little wiser than the animals and birds?" [12]But when anyone does cry out this question to him, he never replies by instant punishment of the tyrants.

Job 37:1. My heart trembles at this. [2]Listen, listen to the thunder of his voice. [3]It rolls across the heavens and his lightning flashes out in every direction. [4]Afterwards comes the roaring of the thunder —the tremendous voice of his majesty. [5]His voice is glorious in the thunder. We cannot comprehend the greatness of his power. [6]For he directs the snow, the showers, and storm to fall upon the earth. [7]Man's work stops at such a time, so that all men everywhere may recognize his power. [8]The wild animals hide in the rocks or in their dens. [9]From the south comes the rain; from the north, the cold. [10]God blows upon the rivers, and even the widest torrents freeze. [11]He loads the clouds with moisture and they send forth his lightning. [12]The lightning bolts are directed by his hand, and do whatever he commands throughout the earth. [13]He sends the storms as punishment, or, in his lovingkindness, to encourage. [14]Listen, O Job, stop and consider the wonderful miracles of God. [15]Do you know how God controls all nature, and causes the lightning to flash forth from the clouds? [16,17]Do you understand the balancing of the clouds with wonderful perfection and skill? Do you know why you become warm when the south wind is blowing and everything is still? [18]Can you spread out the gigantic mirror of the skies as he does? [19,20]You who think you know so much, teach the rest of us how we should approach God. For we are too dull to know! With your wisdom, would we then dare to approach him? Well, does a man wish to be swallowed alive? [21]For as we cannot look at the sun for its brightness when the winds have cleared away the clouds, [22]neither can we gaze at the terrible majesty of God breaking forth upon us from heaven, clothed in dazzling splendor. [23]We cannot imagine the power of the Almighty, and yet he is so just and merciful that he does not destroy us. [24]No wonder men everywhere fear him! For he is not impressed by the world's wisest men!

Ps 8:1. O Lord our God, the majesty and glory of your name fills all the earth and overflows the heavens. [2]You have taught the little children to praise you perfectly. May their example shame and silence your enemies! [3]When I look up into the night skies and see the work of your fingers—the moon and the stars you have made— [4]I cannot understand how you can bother with mere puny man, to pay any attention to him! [5]And yet you have made him only a little lower than the angels, and placed a crown of glory and honor upon his head. [6]You have put him in charge of everything you made; everything is put under his authority: [7]all sheep and oxen, and wild animals too, [8]the birds and fish, and all the life in the sea. [9]O Jehovah, our Lord, the majesty and glory of your name fills the earth.

Ps 19:1. The heavens are telling the glory of God; they are a marvelous display of his craftsmanship. [2]Day and night they keep on telling about God. [3,4]Without a sound or word, silent in the skies, their message reaches out to all the world. The sun lives in the heavens where God placed it [5]and moves out across the skies as radiant as a bridegroom going to his wedding, or as joyous as an athlete looking forward to a race! [6]The sun crosses the heavens from end to end, and nothing can hide from its heat. Ps 29.

Acts 14:17. But he never left himself without a witness; there were always his reminders—the kind things he did such as sending you rain and good crops and giving you food and gladness.

Acts 17:23. For as I was out walking I saw your many altars, and one of them had this inscription on it—"To the Unknown God." You have been worshiping him without knowing who he is, and now I wish to tell you about him. [24]He made the world and everything in it, and since he is Lord of heaven and earth, he doesn't live in manmade temples; [25]and human hands can't minister to his needs —for he has no needs! He himself gives life and breath to everything, and satisfies every need there is. [26]He created all the people of the world from one man, Adam, and scattered the nations across the face of the earth. He decided beforehand which should rise and fall, and when. He determined their boundaries. [27]His purpose in all of this is that they should seek after God, and perhaps feel their way toward him and find him—though he is not far from any one of us. [28]For in him we live and move and are! As one of your own poets says it, "We are the sons of God."

Rom 1:18. But God shows his anger from heaven against all sinful, evil men who push away the truth from them. [19]For the truth about God is known to them instinctively; God has put this knowledge in their hearts. [20]Since earliest times men have seen the earth and sky and all God made, and have known of his existence and great eternal power. So they will have no excuse (when they stand before God at Judgment Day).

Rom 10:16. But not everyone who hears the Good News has welcomed it, for Isaiah the prophet said, "Lord, who has believed me when I told them?" [17]Yet faith comes from listening to this Good News—the Good News about Christ. [18]But what about the Jews? Have they heard God's Word? Yes, for it has gone wherever they are; the Good News has been told to the ends of the earth.

See *Revival.*

TRUE. Mt 5:1, 2. One day as the crowds were gathering, he went up the hillside with his disciples and sat down and taught them there. [3]"Humble men are very fortunate!" he told them, "for the Kingdom of Heaven is given to them. [4]Those who mourn are fortunate! for they shall be comforted. [5]The meek and lowly are fortunate! for the whole wide world belongs to them. [6]Happy are those who long to be just and good, for they shall be completely satisfied. [7]Happy are the kind and merciful, for they shall be shown mercy. [8]Happy are those whose hearts are pure, for they shall see God. [9]Happy are those who strive for peace—they shall be called the sons of God. [10]Happy are those who are persecuted because they are good, for the Kingdom of Heaven is theirs. [11]When you are reviled and persecuted and lied about because you are my followers—wonderful! [12]Be *happy* about it! Be *very glad!* for a *tremendous reward* awaits you up in heaven. And remember, the ancient prophets were persecuted too. [13]You are the world's seasoning, to make it tolerable. If you lose your flavor, what will happen to the world? And you yourselves will be thrown out and trampled underfoot as worthless. [14]You are the world's light—a city on a hill, glowing in the night for all to see. [15, 16]Don't hide your light! Let it shine for all; let your good deeds glow for all to see, so that they will praise your heavenly Father. [17]Don't misunderstand why I have come—it isn't to cancel the laws of Moses and the warnings of the prophets. No, I came to fulfill them, and to make them all come true. [18]With all the earnestness I have I say: Every law in the Book will continue until its purpose is achieved. [19]And so if anyone breaks the least commandment, and teaches others to, he shall be the least in the Kingdom of Heaven. But those who teach God's laws *and obey them* shall be great in the Kingdom of Heaven. [20]But I warn you—unless your goodness is greater than that of the Pharisees and other Jewish leaders, you can't get into the Kingdom of Heaven at all! [21]Under the laws of Moses the rule was, 'If you kill, you must die.' [22]But I have added to that rule, and tell you that if you are only *angry,* even in your own home, you are in danger of judgment! If you call your friend an idiot, you are in danger of being brought before the court. And if you curse him, you are in danger of the fires of hell. 23So if you are standing before the altar in the Temple, offering a sacrifice to God, and suddenly remember that a friend has something against you, 24leave your sacrifice there beside the altar and go and apologize and be reconciled to him, and then come and offer your sacrifice to God. 25Come to terms quickly with your enemy before it is too late and he drags you into court and you are thrown into a debtor's cell, 26for you will stay there until you have paid the last penny. 27The laws of Moses said, 'You shall not commit adultery.' 28But I say: Anyone who even looks at a woman with lust in his eye has already committed adultery with her in his heart. 29So if your eye—even if it is your best eye!—causes you to lust, gouge it out and throw it away. Better for part of you to be destroyed than for all of you to be cast into hell. 30And if your hand—even your right hand—causes you to sin, cut it off and throw it away. Better that than find yourself in hell. 31The law of Moses says, 'If anyone wants to be rid of his wife, he can divorce her merely by giving her a letter of dismissal.' 32But I say that a man who divorces his wife, except for fornication, causes her to commit adultery if she marries again. And he who marries her commits adultery. 33Again, the law of Moses says, 'You shall not break your vows to God, but must fulfill them all.' 34But I say: Don't make any vows! And even to say, 'By heavens!' is a sacred vow to God, for the heavens are God's throne. 35And if you say 'By the earth!' it is a sacred vow, for the earth is his footstool. And don't swear 'By Jerusalem!' for Jerusalem is the capital of the great King. 36Don't even swear 'By my head!' for you can't turn one hair white or black. 37Say just a simple 'Yes, I will' or 'No, I won't.' Your word is enough. To strengthen your promise with a vow shows that something is wrong. 38The law of Moses says, 'If a man gouges out another's eye, he must pay with his own eye. If a tooth gets knocked out, knock out the tooth of the one who did it.' 39But I say: Don't resist violence! If you are slapped on one cheek, turn the other too. 40If you are ordered to court, and your shirt is taken from you, give your coat too. 41If the military demand that you carry their gear for a mile, carry it two. 42Give to those who ask, and don't turn away from those who want to borrow. 43There is a saying, 'Love your *friends* and hate your enemies.' 44But I say: Love your *enemies!* Pray for those who *persecute* you! 45In that way you will be acting as true sons of your Father in heaven. For he gives his sunlight to both the evil and the good, and sends rain on the just and on the unjust too. 46If you love only those who love you, what good is that? Even scoundrels do that much. 47If you are friendly only to your friends, how are you different from anyone else? Even the heathen do that. 48But you are to be perfect, even as your Father in heaven is perfect."

Mt 6:1. "Take care! don't do your good deeds publicly, to be admired, for then you will lose the reward from your Father in heaven. 2When you give a gift to a beggar, don't shout about it as the hypocrites do—blowing trumpets in the synagogues and streets to call attention to their acts of charity! I tell you in all earnestness, they have received all the reward they will ever get. 3But when you do a kindness to someone, do it secretly—don't tell your left hand what your right hand is doing. 4And your Father who knows all secrets will reward you. 5And now about prayer. When you pray, don't be like the hypocrites who pretend piety by praying publicly on street corners and in the synagogues where everyone can see them. Truly, that is all the reward they will ever get. 6But when you pray, go away by yourself, all alone, and shut the door behind you and pray to your Father secretly, and your Father, who knows your secrets, will reward you. 7, 8Don't recite the same prayer over and over as the heathen do, who think prayers are answered only by repeating them again and again. Remember, your Father knows exactly what you need even before you ask him! 9Pray along these lines: 'Our Father in heaven, we honor your holy name. 10We ask that your kingdom will come now. May your will be done here on earth, just as it is in heaven. 11Give us our food again today, as usual, 12and forgive us our sins, just as we have forgiven those who have sinned against us. 13Don't bring us into temptation, but deliver us from the Evil One. Amen.' 14, 15Your heavenly Father will forgive you if you forgive those who sin against you; but if *you* refuse to forgive *them, he* will not forgive *you.* 16And now about fasting. When you fast, declining your food for a spiritual purpose, don't do it publicly, as the hypocrites do, who try to look wan and disheveled so people will feel sorry for them. Truly, that is the only reward they will ever get. 17But when you fast, put on festive clothing, 18so that no one will suspect you are hungry, except your Father who knows every secret. And he will reward you. 19Don't store up treasures here on earth where they can erode away or may be stolen. 20Store them in heaven where they will never lose their value, and are safe from thieves. 21If your profits are in heaven your heart will be there too. 22If your eye is pure, there will be sunshine in your soul. 23But if your eye is clouded with evil thoughts and desires, you are in deep spiritual darkness. And oh, how deep that darkness can be! 24You cannot serve two masters: God and money. For you will hate one and love the other, or else the other way around. 25So my counsel is: Don't worry about *things*—food, drink, and clothes. For you already have life and a body—and they are far more important than what to eat and wear. 26Look at the birds! They don't worry about what to eat—they don't need to sow or reap or store up food—for your heavenly Father feeds them. And you are far more valuable to him than they are. 27Will all your worries add a single moment to your life? 28And why worry about your clothes? Look at the field lilies! They don't worry about theirs. 29Yet

King Solomon in all his glory was not clothed as beautifully as they. [30]And if God cares so wonderfully for flowers that are here today and gone tomorrow, won't he more surely care for you, O men of little faith? [31, 32]So don't worry at all about having enough food and clothing. Why be like the heathen? For they take pride in all these things and are deeply concerned about them. But your heavenly Fathen already knows perfectly well that you need them, [33]and he will give them to you if you give him first place in your life and live as he wants you to. [34]So don't be anxious about tomorrow. God will take care of your tomorrow too. Live one day at a time."

Mt 7:1. "Don't criticize, and then you won't be criticized. [2]For others will treat you as you treat them. [3]And why worry about a speck in the eye of a brother when you have a board in your own? [4]Should you say, 'Friend, let me help you get that speck out of your eye,' when you can't even see because of the board in your own? [5]Hypocrite! First get rid of the board. Then you can see to help your brother. [6]Don't give holy things to depraved men. Don't give pearls to swine! They will trample the pearls and turn and attack you. [7]Ask, and you will be given what you ask for. Seek, and you will find. Knock, and the door will be opened. [8]For everyone who asks, receives. Anyone who seeks, finds. If only you will knock, the door will open. [9]If a child asks his father for a loaf of bread, will he be given a stone instead? [10]If he asks for fish, will he be given a poisonous snake? Of course not! [11]And if you hardhearted, sinful men know how to give good gifts to your children, won't your Father in heaven even more certainly give good gifts to those who ask him for them? [12]Do for others what you want them to do for you. This is the teaching of the laws of Moses in a nutshell. [13]Heaven can be entered only through the narrow gate! The highway to hell is broad, and its gate is wide enough for all the multitudes who choose its easy way. [14]But the Gateway to Life is small, and the road is narrow, and only a few ever find it. [15]Beware of false teachers who come disguised as harmless sheep, but are wolves and will tear you apart. [16]You can detect them by the way they act, just as you can identify a tree by its fruit. You need never confuse grapevines with thorn bushes or figs with thistles. [17]Different kinds of fruit trees can quickly be identified by examining their fruit. [18]A variety that produces delicious fruit never produces an inedible kind. And a tree producing an inedible kind can't produce what is good. [19]So the trees having the inedible fruit are chopped down and thrown on the fire. [20]Yes, the way to identify a tree or a person is by the kind of fruit produced. [21]Not all who sound religious are really godly people. They may refer to me as 'Lord,' but still won't get to heaven. For the decisive question is whether they obey my Father in heaven. [22]At the Judgment many will tell me, Lord, Lord, we told others about you and used your name to cast out demons and to do many other great miracles.' [23]But I will reply, 'You have never been mine. Go away, for your deeds are evil.' [24]All who listen to my instructions and follow them are wise, like a man who builds his house on solid rock. [25]Though the rain comes in torrents, and the floods rise and the storm winds beat against his house, it won't collapse, for it is built on rock. [26]But those who hear my instructions and ignore them are foolish, like a man who builds his house on sand. [27]For when the rains and floods come, and storm winds beat against his house, it will fall with a mighty crash." [28]The crowds were amazed at Jesus' sermons, [29]for he taught as one who had great authority, and not as their Jewish leaders.

Mt 22:36. "Sir, which is the most important command in the laws of Moses?" [37]Jesus replied, " 'Love the Lord your God with all your heart, soul, and mind.' [38, 39]This is the first and greatest commandment. The second most important is similar: 'Love your neighbor as much as you love yourself.' [40]All the other commandments and all the demands of the prophets stem from these two laws and are fulfilled if you obey them. Keep only these and you will find that you are obeying all the others."

Acts 10:34. Then Peter replied, "I see very clearly that the Jews are not God's only favorites! [35]In every nation he has those who worship him and do good deeds and are acceptable to him."

Rom 8:1. So there is now no condemnation awaiting those who belong to Christ Jesus. [2]For the power of the life-giving Spirit—and this power is mine through Christ Jesus—has freed me from the vicious circle of sin and death. [3]We aren't saved from sin's grasp by knowing the commandments of God, because we can't and don't keep them, but God put into effect a different plan to save us. He sent his own Son in a human body like ours—except that ours are sinful—and destroyed sin's control over us by giving himself as a sacrifice for our sins. [4]So now we can obey God's laws if we follow after the Holy Spirit and no longer obey the old evil nature within us. [5]Those who let themselves be controlled by their lower natures live only to please themselves, but those who follow after the Holy Spirit find themselves doing those things that please God. [6]Following after the Holy Spirit leads to life and peace, but following after the old nature leads to death, [7]because the old sinful nature within us is against God. It never did obey God's laws and it never will. [8]That's why those who are still under the control of their old sinful selves, bent on following their old evil desires, can never please God. [9]But you are not like that. You are controlled by your new nature if you have the Spirit of God living in you. (And remember that if anyone doesn't have the Spirit of Christ living in him, he is not a Christian at all.) [10]Yet, even though Christ lives within you, your body will die because of sin; but your spirit will live, for Christ has pardoned it. [11]And if the Spirit of God, who raised up Jesus from the dead, lives in you, he will make your dying bodies live again after you die, by means of this same Holy Spirit living within you. [12]So, dear brothers, you have no obligations whatever to your old sinful nature to do what it begs you to do. [13]For if you keep on following it you are lost and will perish, but if through the power of the Holy Spirit you crush it and its evil deeds, you shall live. [14]For all who are led by the Spirit of God are sons of God. [15]And so we should not be like cringing, fearful slaves, but we should behave like God's very own children, adopted into the bosom of his family, and calling to him, "Father, Father." [16]For his Holy Spirit speaks to us deep in our hearts, and tells us that we really are God's children. [17]And since we are his children, we will share his treasures—for all God gives to his Son Jesus is now ours too. But if we are to share his glory, we must also share his suffering. [18]Yet what we suffer now is nothing compared to the glory he will give us later.

Rom 10:1. Dear brothers, the longing of my heart and my prayer is that the Jewish people might be saved. [2]I know what enthusiasm they have for the honor of God, but it is misdirected zeal. [3]For they don't understand that Christ has died to make them right with God. Instead they are trying to make themselves good enough to gain God's favor by keeping the Jewish laws and customs, but that is not God's way of salvation. [4]They don't understand that Christ gives to those who trust in him everything they are trying to get by keeping his laws. He ends all of that. [5]For Moses wrote that if a person could be perfectly good and hold out against temptation all his life and never sin once, only then could he be pardoned and saved. [6]But the salvation that comes through faith says, "You don't need to search the heavens to find Christ and bring him down to help you," and, [7]"You don't need to go among the dead to bring Christ back to life again." [8]For salvation that comes from trusting Christ—which is what we preach—is already within easy reach of each of us; in fact, it is as near as our own hearts and mouths. [9]For if you tell others with your own mouth that Jesus Christ is your Lord, and believe in your own heart that God has raised him from the dead, you will be saved. [10]For it is by believing in his heart that a man becomes right with God; and with his mouth he tells others of his faith, confirming his salvation. [11]For the Scriptures tell us that no one who believes in Christ will ever be disappointed. [12]Jew and Gentile are the same in this respect: they all have the same Lord who generously gives his riches to all those who ask him for them. [13]Anyone who calls upon the name of the Lord will be saved.

Rom 12:1. And so, dear brothers, I plead with you to give your bodies to God. Let them be a living sacrifice, holy—the kind he can accept. When you think of what he has done for you, is this too much to ask? [2]Don't copy the behavior and customs of this world, but be a new and different person with a fresh newness in all you do and think. Then you will learn from your own experience how his ways will really satisfy you. [3]As God's messenger I give each of you God's warning: Be honest in your estimate of yourselves, measuring your value by how much faith God has given you. [4, 5]Just as there are many parts to our bodies, so it is with Christ's body. We are all parts of it, and it takes every one of us to make it complete, for we each have different work to do. So we belong to each other, and each needs all the others. [6]God has given each of us the ability to do certain things well. So if God has given you the ability to prophesy, then prophesy whenever you can—as often as your faith is strong enough to receive a message from God. [7]If your gift is that of serving others, serve them well. If you are a teacher, do a good job of teaching. [8]If you are a preacher, see to it that your sermons are strong and helpful. If God has given you money, be generous in helping others with it. If God has given you administrative ability and put you in charge of the work of others, take the responsibility seriously. Those who offer comfort to the sorrowing should do so with Christian cheer. [9]Don't just pretend that you love others: really love them. Hate what is wrong. Stand on the side of the good. [10]Love each other with brotherly affection and take delight in honoring each other. [11]Never be lazy in your work but serve the Lord enthusiastically. [12]Be glad for all God is planning for you. Be patient in trouble, and prayerful always. [13]When God's children are in need, you be the one to help them out. And get into the habit of inviting guests home for dinner or, if they need lodging, for the night. [14]If someone mistreats you because you are a Christian, don't curse him; pray that God will bless him. [15]When others are happy, be happy with them. If they are sad, share their sorrow. [16]Work happily together. Don't try to act big. Don't try to get into the good graces of important people, but enjoy the company of ordinary folks. And don't think you know it all! [17]Never pay back evil for evil. Do things in such a way that everyone can see you are honest clear through. [18]Don't quarrel with anyone. Be at peace with everyone, just as much as possible. [19]Dear friends, never avenge yourselves. Leave that to God, for he has said that he will repay those who deserve it. (Don't take the law into your own hands.) [20]Instead, feed your enemy if he is hungry. If he is thirsty give him something to drink and you will be "heaping coals of fire on his head." In other words, he will feel ashamed of himself for what he has done to you. [21]Don't let evil get the upper hand but conquer evil by doing good.

1 Cor 13:1. If I had the gift of being able to speak in other languages without learning them, and could speak in every language there is in all of heaven and earth, but didn't love others, I would only be making noise. [2]If I had the gift of prophecy and knew all about what is going to happen in the future, knew everything about *everything,* but didn't love others, what good would it do? Even if I had the gift of faith so that I could speak to a mountain and make it move, I would still be worth nothing at all without love. [3]If I gave everything I have to poor people, and if I were burned alive for preaching the Gospel but didn't love others, it

would be of no value whatever. [4]Love is very patient and kind, never jealous or envious, never boastful or proud, [5]never haughty or selfish or rude. Love does not demand its own way. It is not irritable or touchy. It does not hold grudges and will hardly even notice when others do it wrong. [6]It is never glad about injustice, but rejoices whenever truth wins out. [7]If you love someone you will be loyal to him no matter what the cost. You will always believe in him, always expect the best of him, and always stand your ground in defending him. [8]All the special gifts and powers from God will someday come to an end, but love goes on forever. Someday prophecy, and speaking in unknown languages, and special knowledge—these gifts will disappear. [9]Now we know so little, even with our special gifts, and the preaching of those most gifted is still so poor. [10]But when we have been made perfect and complete, then the need for these inadequate special gifts will come to an end, and they will disappear. [11]It's like this: when I was a child I spoke and thought and reasoned as a child does. But when I became a man my thoughts grew far beyond those of my childhood, and now I have put away the childish things. [12]In the same way, we can see and understand only a little about God now, as if we were peering at his reflection in a poor mirror; but someday we are going to see him in his completeness, face to face. Now all that I know is hazy and blurred, but then I will see everything clearly, just as clearly as God sees into my heart right now. [13]There are three things that remain—faith, hope, and love—and the greatest of these is love.

Gal 5:22. But when the Holy Spirit controls our lives he will produce this kind of fruit in us: love, joy, peace, patience, kindness, goodness, faithfulness, [23]gentleness and self-control; and here there is no conflict with Jewish laws. [24]Those who belong to Christ have nailed their natural evil desires to his cross and crucified them there. [25]If we are living now by the Holy Spirit's power, let us follow the Holy Spirit's leading in every part of our lives.

1 Thess 5:15. See that no one pays back evil for evil, but always try to do good to each other and to everyone else. [16]Always be joyful. [17]Always keep on praying. [18]No matter what happens, always be thankful, for this is God's will for you who belong to Christ Jesus. [19]Do not smother the Holy Spirit. [20]Do not scoff at those who prophesy, [21]but test everything that is said to be sure it is true, and if it is, then accept it. [22]Keep away from every kind of evil. [23]May the God of peace himself make you entirely pure and devoted to God; and may your spirit and soul and body be kept strong and blameless until that day when our Lord Jesus Christ comes back again.

Jas 1:26. Anyone who says he is a Christian but doesn't control his sharp tongue is just fooling himself, and his religion isn't worth much. [27]The Christian who is pure and without fault, from God the Father's point of view, is the one who takes care of orphans and widows, and who remains true to the Lord—not soiled and dirtied by his contacts with the world.

Jas 2:8. Yes indeed, it is good when you truly obey your Lord's command, "You must love and help your neighbors just as much as you love and take care of yourself." [9]But you are breaking this law of our Lord's when you favor the rich and fawn over them; it is sin. [10]And the person who keeps every law of God, but makes one little slip, is just as guilty as the person who has broken every law there is. [11]For the God who said you must not marry a woman who already has a husband, also said you must not murder, so even though you have not broken the marriage laws by committing adultery, but have murdered someone, you have entirely broken God's laws and stand utterly guilty before him. [12]You will be judged on whether or not you are doing what Christ wants you to. So watch what you do and what you think; [13]for there will be no mercy to those who have shown no mercy. But if you have been merciful, then God's mercy toward you will win out over his judgment against you. [14]Dear brothers, what's the use of saying that you have faith and are Christians if you aren't proving it by helping others? Will *that* kind of faith save anyone? [15]If you have a friend who is in need of food and clothing, [16]and you say to him, "Well, good-bye and God bless you; stay warm and eat hearty," and then don't give him clothes or food, what good does that do? [17]So you see, it isn't enough just to have faith. You must also do good to prove that you have it. Faith that doesn't show itself by good works is no faith at all—it is dead and useless. [18]But someone may well argue, "You say the way to God is by faith alone, plus nothing; well, I say that good works are important too, for without good works you can't prove whether you have faith or not; but anyone can see that I have faith by the way I act." [19]Are there still some among you who hold that "only believing" is enough? Believing in one God? Well, remember that the demons believe this too—so strongly that they tremble in terror! [20]Fool! When will you ever learn that "believing" is useless without *doing* what God wants you to? Faith that does not result in good deeds is not real faith. [21]Don't you remember that even our father Abraham was declared good because of what he *did,* when he was willing to obey God, even if it meant offering his son Isaac to die on the altar? [22]You see, he was trusting God so much that he was willing to do whatever God told him to; his faith was made complete by what he did, by his actions, his good deeds. [23]And so it happened just as the Scriptures say, that Abraham trusted God, and the Lord declared him good in God's sight, and he was even called "the friend of God." [24]So you see, a man is saved by what he does, as well as by what he believes. [25]Rahab, the prostitute, is another example of this. She was saved because of what she did when she hid those messengers and sent them safely away by a different road. [26]Just as the body is dead when there is no spirit in it, so faith is dead if it is not the kind that results in good deeds.

2 Pet 1:5. But to obtain these gifts, you need more than faith; you must also work hard to be good, and even that is not enough. For then you must learn to know God better and discover what he wants you to do. [6]Next, learn to put aside your own desires so that you will become patient and godly, gladly letting God have his way with you. [7]This will make possible the next step, which is for you to enjoy other people and to like them, and finally you will grow to love them deeply. [8]The more you go on in this way, the more you will grow strong spiritually and become fruitful and useful to our Lord Jesus Christ. [9]But anyone who fails to go after these additions to faith is blind indeed, or at least very shortsighted, and has forgotten that God delivered him from the old life of sin so that now he can live a strong, good life for the Lord.

Jude 1:20. But you, dear friends, must build up your lives ever more strongly upon the foundation of our holy faith, learning to pray in the power and strength of the Holy Spirit. [21]Stay always within the boundaries where God's love can reach and bless you. Wait patiently for the eternal life that our Lord Jesus Christ in his mercy is going to give you.

See *Blessing, Spiritual; Commandments; Duty; Graces; Regeneration; Repentance; Sanctification; Sin, Forgiveness of.*

INSTANCES OF CONSPICUOUSLY RELIGIOUS PERSONS. Abel, Gen 4:4–8; Heb 11:4. Noah, Gen chapters 6–9. Abraham, Gen 12:1–8; 15; 17; 18:22–33. Jacob, Gen 28:10–22; 32:22–32. Moses, Ex 3:2–22; Deut 32; 33. Jethro, Ex 18:12. Joshua, Josh 1. Gideon, Judg 6; 7. Samuel, 1 Sam 3. David, see Psalms 34, 37, 40. Solomon, 1 Kgs 5: 2–5; 2 Chron 6. Hezekiah, 2 Kgs 18:1–7; 19:14–19. Jehoshaphat, 2 Chron 17:3–9; 19; 20. Jabez, 1 Chron 4:9, 10. Asa, 2 Chron 14; 15. Josiah, 2 Kgs 22; 23. Daniel, Dan 6:4–22. The three Hebrews, Dan 3. Zacharias, Lk 1:13, 67–79. Simeon, Lk 2:25–35. Anna, the prophetess, Lk 2:36, 37. The Roman army captain, Lk 7:1–10. Cornelius, Acts 10. Eunice and Lois, 2 Tim 1:5.

See, for additional instances, each of the apostles, disciples, and *John, Paul, Peter, Stephen;* also each of the prophets.

See *Idolatry; Intolerance; Teachers, False.*

REMALIAH Father of Pekah, king of Israel, 2 Kgs 15:25, 27; 16:1, 5; 2 Chron 28:6; Isa 7:1.

REMORSE Lev 23:32. For this is a Sabbath of solemn rest, and in it you shall humble your souls and be filled with remorse.

Ps 31:10. I am pining away with grief; my years are shortened, drained away because of sadness. My sins have sapped my strength; I stoop with sorrow and with shame.

Ps 38:2. Your arrows have struck deep; your blows are crushing me. [3, 4]Because of your anger my body is sick, my health is broken beneath my sins. They are like a flood, higher than my head; they are a burden too heavy to bear. [5, 6]My wounds are festering and full of pus. Because of my sins I am bent and racked with pain. My days are filled with anguish.

Ps 51:1. O loving and kind God, have mercy. Have pity upon me and take away the awful stain of my transgressions. [2]Oh, wash me, cleanse me from this guilt. Let me be pure again. [3]For I admit my shameful deed—it haunts me day and night. [4]It is against you and you alone I sinned, and did this terrible thing. You saw it all, and your sentence against me is just. [7]Sprinkle me with the cleansing blood and I shall be clean again. Wash me and I shall be whiter than snow. [8]And after you have punished me, give me back my joy again. [9]Don't keep looking at my sins—erase them from your sight. [10]Create in me a new, clean heart, O God, filled with clean thoughts and right desires. [11]Don't toss me aside, banished forever from your presence. Don't take your Holy Spirit from me. [12]Restore to me again the joy of your salvation, and make me willing to obey you. [13]Then I will teach your ways to other sinners, and they—guilty like me—will repent and return to you. [14, 15]Don't sentence me to death. O my God, you alone can rescue me. Then I will sing of your forgiveness, for my lips will be unsealed—oh, how I will praise you. [16]You don't want penance; if you did, how gladly I would do it! You aren't interested in offerings burned before you on the altar. [17]It is a broken spirit you want—remorse and penitence. A broken and a contrite heart, O God, you will not ignore.

Prov 1:25. For you have spurned my counsel and reproof. [26]Some day you'll be in trouble, and I'll laugh! Mock me, will you?—I'll mock you! [27]When a storm of terror surrounds you, and when you are engulfed by anguish and distress.

Prov 5:7. Young men, listen to me, and never forget what I'm about to say: [8]*Run from her! Don't go near her house,* [9]lest you fall to her temptation and lose your honor, and give the remainder of your life to the cruel and merciless; [10]lest strangers obtain your wealth, and you become a slave of foreigners. [11]Lest afterwards you groan in anguish and in shame, when syphilis consumes your body, [12]and you say, "Oh, if only I had listened! If only I had not demanded my own way! [13]Oh, why wouldn't I take advice? Why was I so stupid?"

Prov 28:1. The wicked flee when no one is chasing them!

Isa 2:19. When the Lord stands up from his throne to shake up the earth, his enemies will crawl with fear into the holes in the rocks and into the caves because of the glory of his majesty. *v.* 21.

Isa 6:5. Then I said, "My doom is sealed, for I am a foul-mouthed sinner, a member of a sinful, foul-mouthed race; and I have looked upon the King, the Lord of heaven's armies."

Isa 57:20. But those who still reject me are like the restless sea, which is never still, but always churns up mire and dirt. [21]There is no peace, says my God, for them! Isa 48:22.

Lam 1:20. *See, O Lord, my anguish;* my heart is broken and my soul despairs, for I have terribly rebelled.

Ezk 7:16. Any who escape will be lonely as mourning doves hiding on the mountains, each weeping for his sins. [17]All hands shall be feeble, and all knees as weak as water. [18]You shall clothe yourselves with sackcloth, and horror and shame shall cover you; you shall shave your heads in sorrow and remorse. [Isa 22:12.] [25]For the time has come for the cutting off of Israel. You will sue for peace, but you won't get it. [26]Calamity upon calamity will befall you; woe upon woe, disaster upon disaster! You will long for a prophet to guide you, but the priests and elders and the kings and princes will stand helpless, weeping in despair. Ezk 6:11.

Ezk 33:10. O people of Israel, you are saying: "Our sins are heavy upon us; we pine away with guilt. How can we live?"

Joel 2:13. Let your remorse tear at your hearts and not your garments.

Lk 13:28. And there will be great weeping and gnashing of teeth as you stand outside and see Abraham, Isaac, Jacob, and all the prophets within the Kingdom of God.

Acts 2:37. These words of Peter's moved them deeply, and they said to him and to the other apostles, "Brothers, what should we do?"

1 Jn 3:20. But if we have bad consciences and feel that we have done wrong, the Lord will surely feel it even more, for he knows everything we do.

INSTANCES OF. David, Ps 51. Peter, Mt 26:75. Judas, Mt 27:3–5.

See *Conviction, of Sin; Penitent; Repentance; Sin, Confession of.*

RENDING See *Tearing.*

RENTING Land, Mt 21:33–41; Lk 20:9–16. Houses, Acts 28:30.

REPENTANCE Attributed to God, Gen 6:6, 7; Ex 32:14; Deut 32:36; Judg 2:18; 1 Sam 15:11, 35; 2 Sam 24:16; 1 Chron 21:15; Ps 106:45; 110:4; 135:14; Jer 15:6; 18:8, 10; 26:3; 42:10; Joel 2:13; Amos 7:3, 6; Jon 3:9, 10. The theme of the preaching of John the Baptist, Mt 3; of Jesus, Mt 4:17; Mk 1:15. Exhortation to, Prov 1:23–33; Jer 7:3, 5; 26:3; Hos 14:1–3; Amos 5:4–6; Mt 3:2. Condition of God's favor, Lev 26:40–42; 2 Chron 7:14.

Unavailing to Israel, Num 14:39–45; to Esau, Heb 12:16, 17.

UNCLASSIFIED SCRIPTURES RELATING TO. Lev 26:40, 41. But at last they shall confess their sins and their fathers' sins of treachery against me. (Because they were against me, I was against them, and brought them into the land of their enemies.) When at last their evil hearts are humbled and they accept the punishment I send them for their sins, [42]then I will remember again my promises . . . and I will remember the land.

Deut 4:29. But you will also begin to search again for Jehovah your God, and you shall find him when you search for him with all your hearts and souls. [30]When those bitter days have come upon you in the latter times, you will finally return to the Lord your God and listen to what he tells you. [31]For the Lord your God is merciful—he will not abandon you nor destroy you nor forget the promises he has made to your ancestors.

Deut 30:1. "When all these things have happened to you—the blessings and the curses I have listed—you will meditate upon them as you are living among the nations where the Lord your God will have driven you. [2]If at that time you want to return to the Lord your God, and you and your children have begun wholeheartedly to obey all of the commandments I have given you today, [3]then the Lord your God will rescue you from your captivity! He will have mercy upon you and come and gather you out of all the nations where he will have scattered you. [7, 8]If you return to the Lord and obey all the commandments that I command you today, the Lord your God will take his curses and turn them against your enemies—against those who hate you and persecute you. [9]The Lord your God will prosper everything you do and give you many children and much cattle and wonderful crops; for the Lord will again rejoice over you as he did over your fathers. [10]He will rejoice if you but obey the commandments written in this book of the law, and if you turn to the Lord your God with all your hearts and souls.

Deut 32:29. Oh, that they were wise! Oh, that they could understand! Oh, that they would know what they are getting into!

1 Kgs 8:33, 34. And when your people sin and their enemies defeat them, hear them from heaven and forgive them if they turn to you again and confess that you are their God. Bring them back again to this land which you have given to their fathers. [35, 36]And when the skies are shut up and there is no rain because of their sin, hear them from heaven and forgive them when they pray toward this place and confess your name. And after you have punished them, help them to follow the good ways in which they should walk, and send rain upon the land which you have given your people. [37]If there is a famine in the land caused by plant disease or locusts or caterpillars, or if Israel's enemies besiege one of her cities, or if the people are struck by an epidemic or plague—or whatever the problem is— [38]then when the people realize their sin and pray toward this Temple, [39]hear them from heaven and forgive and answer all who have made an honest confession; for you know each heart. [40]In this way they will always learn to reverence you as they continue to live in this land which you have given their fathers. [41, 42]And when foreigners hear of your great name and come from distant lands to worship you (for they shall hear of your great name and mighty miracles) and pray toward this Temple, [43]hear them from heaven and answer their prayers. And all the nations of the earth will know and fear your name just as your own people Israel do; and all the earth will know that this is your Temple. [44]When you send your people out to battle against their enemies and they pray to you, looking toward your chosen city of Jerusalem and toward this Temple which I have built for your name, [45]hear their prayer and help them. [46]If they sin against you (and who doesn't?) and you become

angry with them and let their enemies lead them away as captives to some foreign land, whether far or near, [47]and they come to their senses and turn to you and cry to you saying, "We have sinned, we have done wrong"; [48]if they honestly return to you and pray toward this land which you have given their fathers, and toward this city of Jerusalem which you have chosen, and toward this Temple, which I have built for your name, [49]hear their prayers and pleadings from heaven where you live, and come to their assistance. [50]Forgive your people for all of their evil deeds, and make their captors merciful to them.

2 Chron 7:14. Then if my people will humble themselves and pray and search for me, and turn from their wicked ways, I will hear them from heaven and forgive their sins and heal their land. 2 Chron 6:36–39.

2 Chron 30:6. "Come back to the Lord God of Abraham, Isaac, and Israel," the king's letter said, "so that he will return to us who have escaped from the power of the kings of Assyria. [7]Do not be like your fathers and brothers who sinned against the Lord God of their fathers and were destroyed. [8]Do not be stubborn, as they were, but yield yourselves to the Lord and come to his Temple which he has sanctified forever, and worship the Lord your God so that his fierce anger will turn away from you. [9]For if you turn to the Lord again, your brothers and your children will be treated mercifully by their captors, and they will be able to return to this land. For the Lord your God is full of kindness and mercy and will not continue to turn away his face from you if you return to him."

Neh 1:9. But if you return to me and obey my laws, even though you are exiled to the farthest corners of the universe, I will bring you back to Jerusalem. For Jerusalem is the place in which I have chosen to live.

Job 11:13, 14. Before you turn to God and stretch out your hands to him, get rid of your sins and leave all iniquity behind you. [15]Only then, without the spots of sin to defile you, can you walk steadily forward to God without fear.

Job 22:23. If you return to God and put right all the wrong in your home, then you will be restored.

Job 33:26. And when he prays to God, God will hear and answer and receive him with joy, and return him to his duties. [27]And he will declare to his friends, "I sinned, but God let me go. [28]He did not let me die. I will go on living in the realm of light."

Job 34:31. Why don't people exclaim to their God, "We have sinned, but we will stop"? [32]Or, "We know not what evil we have done; only tell us, and we will cease at once."

Job 36:10. He helps them hear his instruction to turn away from their sin.

Ps 22:27. The whole earth shall see it and return to the Lord; the people of every nation shall worship him.

Ps 34:14. Turn from all known sin and spend your time in doing good. Try to live in peace with everyone; work hard at it. [18]The Lord is close to those whose hearts are breaking; he rescues those who are humbly sorry for their sins.

Ps 51:17. It is a broken spirit you want—remorse and penitence. A broken and a contrite heart, O God, you will not ignore.

Ps 95:7. Oh, that you would hear him calling you today and come to him! [8]Don't harden your hearts as Israel did in the wilderness at Meribah and Massah.

Ps 147:3. He heals the broken-hearted, binding up their wounds.

Prov 1:22. "You simpletons!" she cries. "How long will you go on being fools? How long will you scoff at wisdom and fight the facts? [23]Come here and listen to me! I'll pour out the spirit of wisdom upon you, and make you wise."

Prov 9:6. Leave behind your foolishness and begin to live; learn how to be wise.

Prov 28:13. A man who refuses to admit his mistakes can never be successful. But if he confesses and forsakes them, he gets another chance.

Isa 10:21. A remnant of them will return to the mighty God.

Isa 22:12. The Lord God of Hosts called you to repent, to weep and mourn and shave your heads in sorrow for your sins, and to wear clothes made of sackcloth to show your remorse.

Isa 31:6. Therefore, O my people, though you are such wicked rebels, come, return to God.

Isa 44:22. I've blotted out your sins; they are gone like morning mist at noon! Oh, return to me, for I have paid the price to set you free.

Isa 55:6. Seek the Lord while you can find him. Call upon him now while he is near. [7]Let men cast off their wicked deeds; let them banish from their minds the very thought of doing wrong! Let them turn to the Lord that he may have mercy upon them, and to our God, for he will abundantly pardon!

Isa 57:15. The high and lofty one who inhabits eternity, the Holy One, says this: I live in that high and holy place where those with contrite, humble spirits dwell; and I refresh the humble and give new courage to those with repentant hearts.

Isa 61:1. The Spirit of the Lord God is upon me. . . . He has sent me to comfort the broken-hearted, to announce liberty to captives and to open the eyes of the blind. [2]He has sent me to tell those who mourn that the time of God's favor to them has come, and the day of his wrath to their enemies.

Jer 3:4. And yet you say to me, "O Father, you have always been my Friend." [12]Therefore go and say to Israel, O Israel, my sinful people, come home to me again, for I am merciful; I will not be forever angry with you. [13]Only acknowledge your guilt; admit that you rebelled against the Lord your God and committed adultery against him by worshiping idols under every tree; confess that you refused to follow me. [14]O sinful children, come home, for I am your Master and I will bring you again to the land of Israel—one from here and two from there, wherever you are scattered. [19]And I thought how wonderful it would be for you to be here among my children. I planned to give you part of this beautiful land, the finest in the world. I looked forward to your calling me "Father," and thought that you would never turn away from me again.

Jer 4:1. O Israel, if you will truly return to me and absolutely discard your idols, [2]and if you will swear by me alone, the living God, and begin to live good, honest, clean lives, then you will be a testimony to the nations of the world and they will come to me and glorify my name. [3]The Lord is saying to the men of Judah and Jerusalem, Plow up the hardness of your hearts; otherwise the good seed will be wasted among the thorns. [4]Cleanse your minds and hearts, not just your bodies, or else my anger will burn you to a crisp because of all your sins. And no one will be able to put the fire out. [Deut 10:16.] [14]O Jerusalem, cleanse your hearts while there is time. You can yet be saved by casting out your evil thoughts.

Jer 6:8. This is your last warning, O Jerusalem. If you don't listen, I will empty the land. [16]Yet the Lord pleads with you still: Ask where the good road is, the godly paths you used to walk in, in the days of long ago. Travel there, and you will find rest for your souls.

Jer 7:5. If you stop your wicked thoughts and deeds, and are fair to others. [7]Then, and only then, will I let you stay in this land that I gave to your fathers to keep forever.

Jer 13:15. Oh, that you were not so proud and stubborn! Then you would listen to the Lord, for he has spoken. [16]Give glory to the Lord your God before it is too late, before he causes deep, impenetrable darkness to fall upon you so that you stumble and fall upon the dark mountains; then, when you look for light, you will find only terrible darkness.

Jer 18:8. Then if that nation renounces its evil ways, I will not destroy it as I had planned. [11]Therefore go and warn all Judah and Jerusalem, saying: Hear the word of the Lord. I am planning evil against you now instead of good; turn back from your evil paths and do what is right.

Jer 24:7. I will give them hearts that respond to me. They shall be my people and I will be their God, for they shall return to me with great joy.

Jer 25:5. Each time the message was this: Turn from the evil road you are traveling and from the evil things you are doing. Only then can you continue to live here in this land which the Lord gave to you and to your ancestors forever. Jer 35:15.

Jer 26:3. For perhaps they will listen and turn from their evil ways, and then I can withhold all the punishment I am ready to pour out upon them because of their evil deeds. [13]But if you stop your sinning and begin obeying the Lord your God, he will cancel all the punishment he has announced against you.

Jer 31:9. Tears of joy shall stream down their faces, and I will lead them home with great care. They shall walk beside the quiet streams and not stumble. For I am a Father to Israel, and Ephraim is my oldest child.

Jer 36:3. Perhaps when the people of Judah see in writing all the terrible things I will do to them, they will repent. And then I can forgive them. [7]Perhaps even yet they will turn from their evil ways and ask the Lord to forgive them before it is too late, even though these curses of God have been pronounced upon them.

Jer 50:4. Then the people of Israel and Judah shall join together, weeping and seeking the Lord their God. [5]They shall ask the way to Zion and start back home again. "Come," they will say, "let us be united to the Lord with an eternal pledge that will never be broken again."

Ezk 7:16. Any who escape will be lonely as mourning doves hiding on the mountains, each weeping for his sins.

Ezk 11:18. And when you return you will remove every trace of all this idol worship. [19]I will give you one heart and a new spirit; I will take from you your hearts of stone and give you tender hearts of love for God, [20]so that you can obey my laws and be my people, and I will be your God.

Ezk 12:3. For they are rebels. So now put on a demonstration, to show them what being exiled will be like. Pack whatever you can carry on your back and leave your home—go somewhere else. Go in the daylight so they can see, for perhaps even yet they will consider what this means, even though they are such rebels.

Ezk 14:6. Therefore warn them that the Lord God says: Repent and destroy your idols, and stop worshiping them in your hearts.

Ezk 16:61. And you will remember with shame all the evil you have done; and you will be overcome by my favor when I take your sisters, Samaria and Sodom, and make them your daughters, for you to rule over. You will know you don't deserve this gracious act, for you did not keep my covenant. [62]I will reaffirm my covenant with you, and you will know I am the Lord. [63]Despite all you have done, I will be kind to you again; you will cover your mouth in silence and in shame when I forgive you all that you have done, says the Lord God.

Ezk 18:21. But if a wicked person turns away from all his sins and begins to obey my laws and do what is just and right, he shall surely live and not die. [22]All his past sins will be forgotten, and he shall live because of his goodness. [23]Do you think I like to see the wicked die? asks the Lord. Of course not! I only want him to turn from his wicked ways and live. [27]And if a wicked person turns away from his wickedness and obeys the law, and does right, he shall save his soul, [28]for he has thought it over and decided to turn from his sins and live a good life. He shall surely live—he shall not die. [30]I will judge each of you, O Israel, and punish or reward each according to your own actions. Oh, turn from your sins while there is yet time. [31]Put them behind you and receive a new heart and a new spirit. For why will you die, O Israel? *v.* 32.

Ezk 20:43. Then you will look back at all your sins and loathe yourselves because of the evil you have done. Ezk 36:31.

Ezk 33:10. O people of Israel, you are saying: "Our sins are heavy upon us; we pine away with guilt. How can we live?" [11]Tell them: As I live, says the Lord God, I have no pleasure in the death of the wicked; *I desire that the wicked turn from his evil ways and live.* Turn, turn from your wickedness, for why will you die, O Israel? [12]For the good works of a righteous man will not save him if he turns to sin; and the sins of an evil man will not destroy him if he repents and turns from his sins. *vs.* 14–16, 19.

Ezk 37:23. They shall stop polluting themselves with idols and their other sins, for I will save them from all this foulness. Then they shall truly be my people and I their God.

Dan 4:27. O King Nebuchadnezzar, listen to me—stop sinning; do what you know is right; be merciful to the poor. Perhaps even yet God will spare you.

Hos 2:7. When she runs after her lovers she will not catch up with them. She will search for them but not find them. Then she will think, "I might as well return to my husband, for I was better off with him than I am now."

Hos 3:5. Afterward they will return to the Lord their God, and to the Messiah, their King, and they shall come trembling, submissive to the Lord and to his blessings, in the end times.

Hos 5:15. I will abandon them and return to my home until they admit their guilt and look to me for help again, for as soon as trouble comes, they will search for me.

Hos 10:12. Plant the good seeds of righteousness and you will reap a crop of my love; plow the hard ground of your hearts, for now is the time to seek the Lord, that he may come and shower salvation upon you.

Hos 12:6. Oh, come back to God. Live by the principles of love and justice, and always be expecting much from him, your God.

Hos 14:1. O Israel, return to the Lord, your God, for you have been crushed by your sins. [2]Bring your petition. Come to the Lord and say, "O Lord, take away our sins; be gracious to us and receive us, and we will offer you the sacrifice of praise."

Joel 1:14. Announce a fast; call a solemn meeting. Gather the elders and all the people into the Temple of the Lord your God, and weep before him there.

Joel 2:12. That is why the Lord says, "Turn to me now, while there is time. Give me all your hearts. Come with fasting, weeping, mourning. [13]Let your remorse tear at your hearts and not your garments." Return to the Lord your God, for he is gracious and merciful. He is not easily angered; he is full of kindness, and anxious not to punish you. [15]Sound the trumpet in Zion! Call a fast and gather all the people together for a solemn meeting. [16]Bring everyone—the elders, the children, and even the babies. Call the bridegroom from his quarters and the bride from her privacy. [17]The priests, the ministers of God, will stand between the people and the altar, weeping; and they will pray, "Spare your people, O our God; don't let the heathen rule them, for they belong to you. Don't let them be disgraced by the taunts of the heathen who say, 'Where is this God of theirs? How weak and helpless he must be!' " [18]Then the Lord will pity his people and be indignant for the honor of his land!

Amos 4:12. Therefore I will bring upon you all these further evils I have spoken of. Prepare to meet your God in judgment, Israel.

Amos 5:6. Seek the Lord and live. [15]Hate evil and love the good; remodel your courts into true halls of justice. Perhaps even yet the Lord God of Hosts will have mercy on his people who remain.

Jon 3:8. Everyone must wear sackcloth and cry mightily to God, and let everyone turn from his evil ways, from his violence and robbing. [9]Who can tell? Perhaps even yet God will decide to let us live, and will hold back his fierce anger from destroying us.

Hag 1:7. "Think it over," says the Lord of Hosts. "Consider how you have acted."

Zech 1:3. But he will turn again and favor you if only you return to him.

Zech 12:10. Then I will pour out the spirit of grace and prayer on all the people of Jerusalem, and they will look on him they pierced, and mourn for him as for an only son, and grieve bitterly for him as for an oldest child who died.

Mal 3:7. "Though you have scorned my laws from earliest time, yet you may still return to me," says the Lord of Hosts. "Come and I will forgive you."

Mt 3:2. "Turn from your sins . . . . turn to God . . . for the Kingdom of Heaven is coming soon." [7]"You sons of snakes!" he warned. "Who said that you could escape the coming wrath of God? [8]Before being baptized, prove that you have turned from sin by doing worthy deeds."

Mt 4:17. From then on, Jesus began to preach, "Turn from sin, and turn to God, for the Kingdom of heaven is near."

Mt 5:4. Those who mourn are fortunate! for they shall be comforted. Lk 6:21.

Mt 9:13. Then he added, "Now go away and learn the meaning of this verse of Scripture, 'It isn't your sacrifices and your gifts I want—I want you to be merciful.' For I have come to urge sinners, not the self-righteous back to God."

Mk 1:4. This messenger was John the Baptist. He lived in the wilderness and taught that all should be baptized as a public announcement of their decision to turn their backs on sin, so that God could forgive them. [15]"At last the time has come!" he announced. "God's Kingdom is near! Turn from your sins and act on this glorious news!" Lk 3:3.

Mk 2:17. When Jesus heard what they were saying, he told them, "Sick people need the doctor, not healthy ones! I haven't come to tell good people to repent, but the bad ones."

Mk 6:12. So the disciples went out, telling everyone they met to turn from sin.

Lk 5:32. My purpose is to invite sinners to turn from their sins, not to spend my time with those who think themselves already good enough.

Lk 10:13. What horrors await you, you cities of Chorazin and Bethsaida! For if the miracles I did for you had been done in the cities of Tyre and Sidon, their people would have sat in deep repentance long ago, clothed in sackcloth and throwing ashes on their heads to show their remorse.

Lk 13:1. About this time he was informed that Pilate had butchered some Jews from Galilee as they were sacrificing at the Temple in Jerusalem.
[2]"Do you think they were worse sinners than other men from Galilee?" he asked. "Is that why they suffered? [3]Not at all! And don't you realize that you also will perish unless you leave your evil ways and turn to God? [4]And what about the eighteen men who died when the Tower of Siloam fell on them? Were they the worst sinners in Jerusalem? [5]Not at all! And you, too, will perish unless you repent."

Lk 15:7. Well, in the same way heaven will be happier over one lost sinner who returns to God than over ninety-nine others who haven't strayed away! *vs.* 1–10.

Lk 18:13. But the corrupt tax collector stood at a distance and dared not even lift his eyes to heaven as he prayed, but beat upon his chest in sorrow, exclaiming, "God, be merciful to me, a sinner." [14]I tell you, this sinner, not the Pharisee, returned home forgiven! For the proud shall be humbled, but the humble shall be honored. *vs.* 10–14.

Lk 24:47. And that this message of salvation should be taken from Jerusalem to all the nations: *There is forgiveness of sins for all who turn to me.*

Acts 2:38. And Peter replied, "Each one of you must turn from sin, return to God, and be baptized in the name of Jesus Christ for the forgiveness of your sins; then you also shall receive this gift, the Holy Spirit." [40]Then Peter preached a long sermon, telling about Jesus and strongly urging all his listeners to save themselves from the evils of their nation.

Acts 3:19. Now change your mind and attitude to God and turn to him so he can cleanse away your sins and send you wonderful times of refreshment from the presence of the Lord.

Acts 5:31. Then, with mighty power, God exalted him to be a Prince and Savior, so that the people of Israel would have an opportunity for repentance, and for their sins to be forgiven.

Acts 8:22. Turn from this great wickedness and pray. Perhaps God will yet forgive your evil thoughts.

Acts 17:30. God tolerated man's past ignorance about these things, but now he commands everyone to put away idols and worship only him.

Acts 20:21. I have had one message for Jews and Gentiles alike—the necessity of turning from sin to God through faith in our Lord Jesus Christ.

Acts 26:20. I preached first to those in Damascus, then in Jerusalem and through Judea, and also to the Gentiles that all must forsake their sins and turn to God—and prove their repentance by doing good deeds.

Rom 2:4. Don't you realize how patient he is being with you? Or don't you care? Can't you see that he has been waiting all this time without punishing you, to give you time to turn from your sin? His kindness is meant to lead you to repentance.

Rom 11:23. On the other hand, if the Jews leave their unbelief behind them and come back to God, God will graft them back into the tree again. He has the power to do it.

Rom 14:11. For it is written, "As I live," says the Lord, "every knee shall bow to me and every tongue confess to God."

Eph 5:14. That is why God says in the Scriptures, "Awake, O sleeper, and rise up from the dead; and Christ shall give you light."

2 Tim 2:25. Be humble when you are trying to teach those who are mixed up concerning the truth. For if you talk meekly and courteously to them they are more likely, with God's help, to turn away from their wrong ideas and believe what is true.

Heb 6:1. Let us stop going over the same old ground again and again, always teaching those first lessons about Christ. Let us go on instead to other things and become mature in our understanding, as strong Christians ought to be. Surely we don't need to speak further about the foolishness of trying to be saved by being good, or about the necessity of faith in God.

Jas 4:8. And when you draw close to God, God will draw close to you. Wash your hands, you sinners, and let your hearts be filled with God alone to make them pure and true to him. [9]Let there be tears for the wrong things you have done. Let there be sorrow and sincere grief. Let there be sadness instead of laughter, and gloom instead of joy. [10]Then when you realize your worthlessness before the Lord, he will lift you up, encourage and help you.

1 Jn 1:9. But if we confess our sins to him, he can be depended on to forgive us and to cleanse us from every wrong.

Rev 2:5. Think about those times of your first love (how different now!) and turn back to me again and work as you did before; or else I will come and remove your candlestick from its place among the churches. [16]Change your mind and attitude, or else I will come to you suddenly and fight against them with the sword of my mouth.

Rev 3:2. Now wake up! Strengthen what little remains—for even what is left is at the point of death. Your deeds are far from right in the sight of God. [3]Go back to what you heard and believed at first; hold to it firmly and turn to me again. Unless you do, I will come suddenly upon you, unexpected as a thief, and punish you. [19]I continually discipline and punish everyone I love; so I must punish you, unless you turn from your indifference and become enthusiastic about the things of God.

See *Conviction; Penitent; Remorse; Sin, Confession of, Forgiveness of.*

INSTANCES OF. Joseph's brothers, of their maltreatment of Joseph, Gen 42:21; 50:16–18. Pharaoh, of his hardness of heart, Ex 9:27; 10:16, 17. Balaam, of his spiritual blindness, Num 22:34, with *vs.* 24–35. Israelites, of worshiping the golden calf, Ex 33: 3, 4; of their murmuring because of a lack of bread and water, when the plague of poisonous snakes came on them, Num 21:4–7; when rebuked by an angel for not expelling the Canaanites, Judg 2:1–5; of their idolatry, when tormented by the Philistines, Judg 10:6–16; 1 Sam 7:3–6; in asking for a king, 1 Sam 12:16–20; in the time of Asa, under the preaching of Azariah, 2 Chron 15:1–15; under the preaching of Oded, 2 Chron 28:9–15; under the influence of Hezekiah, 2 Chron 30:11. Achan, of his theft, Josh 7:20. Saul, when Samuel reproved him for not completely destroying the Amalekites, 1 Sam 15:24, with *vs.* 6–31. David, at the rebuke of Nathan, the prophet, of his sins of adultery and murder, 2 Sam 12:11, 13, with *vs.* 7–14. Rehoboam, when his kingdom was invaded, and Jerusalem besieged, 2 Chron 12:1–12. Hezekiah, at the time of his sickness, 2 Chron 32:26; when reproved by the prophet Micah, Jer 26:18, 19. Ahab, when reproved by Elijah for his idolatry, 1 Kgs 21:27, with *vs.* 17–29. Jehoahaz, 2 Kgs 13:4. Josiah, when he heard the law which had been discovered in the temple by Hilkiah, 2 Kgs 22:11–20. Manasseh, when he was taken captive to Babylon by the Assyrians, 2 Chron 33:12, 13. The Jews of the captivity, at the dedication of the temple, Ezra 6:21, 22; of their heathen marriages, Ezra 10; of their oppressive lending practices, Neh 5:1–13; after hearing the law expounded by Ezra, Neh 8:1–12; 9:1–3; under the preaching of Haggai, Hag 1. Jonah, after his punishment, Jon 2:2–9. The Ninevites, under the preaching of Jonah, Jon 3:4–9. The Jews, under the preaching of John the Baptist, Mt 3:6. The woman who anointed Jesus with perfume, Lk 7:37–48. The disobedient son, Mt 21:29. The prodigal son, Lk 15: 17–21. Peter, of his denial of Jesus, Mt 26:75; Mk 14:72; Lk 22:62. Judas, Mt 27:3–5; Acts 1:16, 18. The Ephesians, under the preaching of Paul, Acts 19:18, 19.

EXEMPLIFIED. Num 21:7. Then the people came to Moses and cried out, "We have sinned, for we have spoken against Jehovah and against you. Pray to him to take away the snakes." Moses prayed for the people.

2 Sam 24:10. But after he had taken the census, David's conscience began to bother him, and he said to the Lord, "What I did was very wrong. Please forgive this foolish wickedness of mine." [17]When David saw the angel, he said to the Lord, "Look, I am the one who has sinned! What have these sheep done? Let your anger be only against me and my family." 1 Chron 21:17.

2 Chron 29:6. For our fathers have committed a deep sin before the Lord our God; they abandoned the Lord and his Temple and turned their backs on it.

Ezra 9:4. Then many who feared the God of Israel because of this sin of his people came and sat with me until the evening burnt offering. [6]And cried out, "O my God, I am ashamed; I blush to lift up my face to you, for our sins are piled higher than our heads and our guilt is as boundless as the heavens. [10]And now, O God, what can we say after all of this? For once again we have abandoned you and broken your laws! [13]And now, even after our punishment in exile because of our wickedness (and we have been punished far less than we deserved), and even though you have let some of us return, [14]we have broken your commandments again and intermarried with people who do these awful things. Surely your anger will destroy us now until not even this little remnant escapes."

Neh 1:6, 7. Listen carefully to what I say! Look down and see me praying night and day for your people Israel. I confess that we have sinned against you; yes, I and my people have committed the horrible sin of not obeying the commandments you gave us through your servant Moses.

Neh 9:33. Every time you punished us you were being perfectly fair; we have sinned so greatly that you gave us only what we deserved. [34]Our kings, princes, priests, and ancestors didn't obey your laws or listen to your warnings. [35]They did not worship you despite the wonderful things you did for them and the great goodness you showered upon them. You gave them a large, fat land, but they refused to turn from their wickedness. *vs.* 16–37.

Job 7:20. Has my sin harmed you, O God, Watcher of mankind? Why have you made me your target, and made my life so heavy a burden to me?

Job 9:20. But I? Am I righteous? My own mouth says no. Even if I were perfect, God would prove me wicked.

Job 13:23. Tell me, what have I done wrong? Help me! Point out my sin to me.

Job 40:4. I am nothing—how could I ever find the answers? I lay my hand upon my mouth in silence.

Job 42:5. I had heard about you before, but now I have seen you, [6]and I loathe myself and repent in dust and ashes.

Ps 32:5. Until I finally admitted all my sins to you and stopped trying to hide them. I said to myself, "I will confess them to the Lord." And you forgave me! All my guilt is gone.

Ps 38:3, 4. Because of your anger my body is sick, my health is broken beneath my sins. They are like a flood, higher than my head; they are a burden too heavy to bear. [18]I confess my sins; I am sorry for what I have done.

Ps 40:12. For problems far too big for me to solve are piled higher than my head. Meanwhile my sins, too many to count, have all caught up with me and I am ashamed to look up. My heart quails within me.

Ps 41:4. "O Lord," I prayed, "be kind and heal me, for I have confessed my sins."

Ps 51:1. O loving and kind God, have mercy. Have pity upon me and take away the awful stain of my transgressions. [2]Oh, wash me, cleanse me from this guilt. Let me be pure again. [3]For I admit my shameful deed—it haunts me day and night. [4]It is against you and you alone I sinned, and did this terrible thing. You saw it all, and your sentence against me is just. [7]Sprinkle me with the cleansing blood and I shall be clean again. Wash me and I shall be whiter than snow. [8]And after you have punished me, give me back my joy again. [9]Don't keep looking at my sins—erase them from your sight. [10]Create in me a new, clean heart, O God, filled with clean thoughts and right desires. [11]Don't toss me aside, banished forever from your presence. Don't take your Holy Spirit from me. [12]Restore to me again the joy of your salvation, and make me willing to obey you. [13]Then I will teach your ways to other sinners, and they—guilty like me—will repent and return to you. [14, 15]Don't sentence me to death. O my God, you alone can rescue me. Then I will sing of your forgiveness, for my lips will be unsealed—oh, how I will praise you. [16]You don't want penance; if you did, how gladly I would do it! You aren't interested in offerings burned before you on the altar. [17]It is a broken spirit you want—remorse and penitence. A broken and a contrite heart, O God, you will not ignore.

Ps 69:5. O God, you know so well how stupid I am, and you know all my sins. [10]How they scoff and mock me when I mourn and fast before the Lord!

Ps 73:21. When I saw this, what turmoil filled my heart! [22]I saw myself so stupid and so ignorant; I must seem like an animal to you, O God.

Ps 106:6. Both we and our fathers have sinned so much.

Ps 119:59, 60. I thought about the wrong direction in which I was headed, and turned around and came running back to you. [176]I have wandered away like a lost sheep.

Ps 130:1. O Lord, from the depths of despair I cry for your help: [2]"Hear me! Answer! Help me!" [3]Lord, if you keep in mind our sins then who can ever get an answer to his prayers?

Isa 6:5. Then I said, "My doom is sealed, for I am a foul-mouthed sinner, a member of a sinful, foul-mouthed race; and I have looked upon the King, the Lord of heaven's armies."

Isa 38:15. But what can I say? For he himself has sent this sickness. All my sleep has fled because of my soul's bitterness. [17]Yes, now I see it all—it was good for me to undergo this bitterness, for you have lovingly delivered me from death; you have forgiven all my sins.

Isa 59:12. For your sins keep piling up before the righteous God, and testify against you. Yes, we know what sinners we are. *vs.* 13–15.

Isa 64:5. You welcome those who cheerfully do good, who follow godly ways. But we are not godly; we are constant sinners and have been all our lives. Therefore your wrath is heavy on us. How can such as we be saved? [6]We are all infected and impure with sin. When we put on our prized robes of righteousness we find they are but filthy rags. Like autumn leaves we fade, wither and fall. And our sins, like the wind, sweep us away. [7]Yet no one calls upon your name or pleads with you for mercy. Therefore you have turned away from us and turned us over to our sins.

Jer 3:21. I hear voices high upon the windswept mountains, crying, crying. It is the sons of Israel who have turned their backs on God and wandered far away. [22]O my rebellious children, come back to me again and I will heal you from your sins. And they reply, Yes, we will come, for you are the Lord our God. [25]We lie in shame and in dishonor, for we and our fathers have sinned from childhood against the Lord our God; we have not obeyed him.

Jer 8:14. Then the people will say, "Why should we wait here to die? Come, let us go to the walled cities and perish there. For the Lord our God has decreed our doom and given us a cup of poison to drink because of all our sins."

Jer 14:7. O Lord, we have sinned against you grievously, yet help us for the sake of your own reputation. [20]O Lord, we confess our wickedness, and that of our fathers too.

Jer 31:18. I have heard Ephraim's groans: "You have punished me greatly; but I needed it all, as a calf must be trained for the yoke. Turn me again to you and restore me, for you alone are the Lord, my God. [19]I turned away from God but I was sorry afterwards. I kicked myself for my stupidity. I was thoroughly ashamed of all I did in younger days."

Lam 3:40. Let us examine ourselves instead, and repent and turn again to the Lord. [41]Let us lift our hearts and hands to him in heaven.

Dan 9:5. But we have sinned so much; we have rebelled against you and scorned your commands. [6]We have refused to listen to your servants the prophets, whom you sent again and again down through the years, with your messages to our kings and princes and to all the people. [7]O Lord, you are righteous; but as for us, we are always shamefaced with sin, just as you see us now; yes, all of us—the men of Judah, the people of Jerusalem, and all Israel, scattered near and far wherever you have driven us because of our disloyalty to you.

Dan 10:12. Then he said, "Don't be frightened, Daniel, for your request has been heard in heaven and was answered the very first day you began to fast before the Lord and pray for understanding; that very day I was sent here to meet you."

Hos 6:1. Come, let us return to the Lord; it is he who has torn us—he will heal us. He has wounded —he will bind us up.

Hos 14:3. "Assyria cannot save us, nor can our strength in battle; never again will we call the idols we have made 'our gods'; for in you alone, O Lord, the fatherless find mercy." [8]O Ephraim! Stay away from idols! I am living and strong!

Jon 3:10. And when God saw that they had put a stop to their evil ways, he abandoned his plan to destroy them, and didn't carry it through.

Mic 7:9. I will be patient while the Lord

punishes me, for I have sinned against him; then he will defend me from my enemies, and punish them for all the evil they have done to me. God will bring me out of my darkness into the light, and I will see his goodness.

Lk 15:17. When he finally came to his senses, he said to himself, "At home even the hired men have food enough and to spare, and here I am, dying of hunger! [18]I will go home to my father and say, 'Father, I have sinned against both heaven and you, [19]and am no longer worthy of being called your son. Please take me on as a hired man.' " [20]So he returned home to his father.

1 Cor 15:9. For I am the least worthy of all the apostles, and I shouldn't even be called an apostle at all after the way I treated the church of God.

2 Cor 7:9. Now I am glad I sent it, not because it hurt you, but because the pain turned you to God. It was a good kind of sorrow you felt, the kind of sorrow God wants his people to have, so that I need not come to you with harshness. [10]For God sometimes uses sorrow in our lives to help us to turn away from sin and seek eternal life. We should never regret his sending it. But the sorrow of the man who is not a Christian is not the sorrow of true repentance and does not prevent eternal death. [11]Just see how much good this grief from the Lord did for you! You no longer shrugged your shoulders, but became earnest and sincere, and very anxious to get rid of the sin that I wrote you about. You became frightened about what had happened, and longed for me to come and help. You went right to work on the problem and cleared it up (punishing the man who sinned). You have done everything you could to make it right.

1 Pet 2:25. Like sheep you wandered away from God, but now you have returned to your Shepherd, the Guardian of your souls.

See *Sin, Confession of.*

REPETITION IN PRAYERS. See *Prayer.*

REPHA-EL A guard of the temple in the time of David, 1 Chron 26:7.

REPHAH A descendant of Ephraim, 1 Chron 7:25–27.

REPHAIAH 1. A descendant of David, 1 Chron 3:21, 22.

2. A Simeonite leader, 1 Chron 4:42.

3. Son of Tola, of the tribe of Issachar, 1 Chron 7:2.

4. A descendant of Jonathan, 1 Chron 9:43. Called *Raphah,* 1 Chron 8:37.

5. Mayor over half of Jerusalem in the time of Nehemiah, Neh 3:9.

REPHAIM The Hebrew word, from *rapha,* a terrible one, occurs as the name of an ancient people of gigantic stature in Gen 14:5, 6; 15:19–21; Deut 2:11, 20; 3:11, 13; Josh 12:4; 13:12; 17:15; and as the valley of Rephaim in Deut 15:8; 18:16; 2 Sam 5: 18, 22; 23:13; 1 Chron 11:15; 14:9; Isa 17:5. It is rendered giants in 2 Sam 21:16, 18, 20–22; 1 Chron 20: 4, 6–8. This race was called also *Anakim, Emim,* and *Zamzummim* by various tribes, Deut 2:11, 20, 21, and it is stated that the bedstead of Og, one of the Rephaim, was 13 1/2 feet long and 6 feet wide. They are believed to be a branch of the *Nephilim,* or fallen ones, the giants of Gen 6:4; Num 13:33.

The word Rephaim is rendered dead in Job 26: 5, 6; Prov 21:16; Isa 14:9. In these passages, it is thought to be derived from *rapheh,* shade or ghost.

See *Giants.*

REPHIDIM A camping place of Israel in the 40 years of wandering, Ex 17:1, 8; 19:2, 3; Num 33: 14.

REPORTS MAJORITY AND MINORITY. Of spies, Num 13:26–33; 14:6–11.

REPROBATE Rejected or condemned by God. Gen 6:5. When the Lord God saw the extent of human wickedness, and that the trend and direction of men's lives were only towards evil, [6]he was sorry he had made them. It broke his heart. [7]And he said, "I will blot out from the face of the earth all mankind that I created. Yes, and the animals too, and the reptiles and the birds. For I am sorry I made them."

Gen 19:13. For we will destroy the city completely. The stench of the place has reached to heaven and God has sent us to destroy it.

Deut 28:15–19. If you won't listen to the Lord your God and won't obey these laws I am giving you today, then all of these curses shall come upon you: Curses in the city; curses in the fields; curses on your fruit and bread; the curse of barren wombs; curses upon your crops; curses upon the fertility of your cattle and flocks; curses when you come in; curses when you go out. [20]For the Lord himself will send his personal curse upon you. You will be confused and a failure in everything you do, until at last you are destroyed because of the sin of forsaking him. [21]He will send disease among you until you are destroyed from the face of the land which you are about to enter and possess. [22]He will send tuberculosis, fever, infections, plague, and war. He will blight your crops, covering them with mildew. All these devastations shall pursue you until you perish. [23]The heavens above you will be as unyielding as bronze, and the earth beneath will be as iron. [24]The land will become as dry as dust for lack of rain, and dust storms shall destroy you. [25]The Lord will cause you to be defeated by your enemies. You will march out to battle gloriously, but flee before your enemies in utter confusion; and you will be tossed to and fro among all the nations of the earth. [26]Your dead bodies will be food to the birds and wild animals, and no one will be there to chase them away. [27]He will send upon you Egyptian boils, tumors, scurvy, and itch, for none of which will there be a remedy. [28]He will send madness, blindness, fear, and panic upon you. [29]You shall grope in the bright sunlight just as the blind man gropes in darkness. You shall not prosper in anything you do; you will be oppressed and robbed continually, and nothing will save you. [30]Someone else will marry your fiancée; someone else will live in the house you build; someone else will eat the fruit of the vineyard you plant. [31]Your oxen shall be butchered before your eyes, but you won't get a single bite of the meat. Your donkeys will be driven away as you watch, and will never return to you again. Your sheep will be given to your enemies. And there will be no one to protect you. [32]You will watch as your sons and daughters are taken away as slaves. Your heart will break with longing for them, but you will not be able to help them. [33]A foreign nation you have not even heard of will eat the crops you will have worked so hard to grow. You will always be oppressed and crushed. [34]You will go mad because of all the tragedy you see around you. [35]The Lord will cover you with boils from head to foot. [36]He will exile you and the king you choose, to a nation to whom neither you nor your ancestors gave a second thought; and while in exile you shall worship gods of wood and stone! [37]You will become an object of horror, a proverb and a byword among all the nations, for the Lord will thrust you away. [38]And you will sow much but reap little, for the locusts will eat your crops. [39]You will plant vineyards and care for them, but you won't eat the grapes or drink the wine, for worms will destroy the vines. [40]Olive trees will grow everywhere, but there won't be enough olive oil to anoint yourselves! For the trees will drop their fruit before it is matured. [41]Your sons and daughters will be snatched away from you as slaves. [42]The locusts shall destroy your trees and vines. [43]Foreigners living among you shall become richer and richer while you become poorer and poorer. [44]They shall lend to you, not you to them! They shall be the head and you shall be the tail! [45]All these curses shall pursue and overtake you until you are destroyed—all because you refuse to listen to the Lord your God. [46]These horrors shall befall you and your descendants as a warning: [47, 48]You will become slaves to your enemies because of your failure to praise God for all that he has given you. The Lord will send your enemies against you, and you will be hungry, thirsty, naked, and in want of everything. A yoke of iron shall be placed around your neck until you are destroyed! [49]The Lord will bring a distant nation against you, swooping down upon you like an eagle; a nation whose language you don't understand— [50]a nation of fierce and angry men who will have no mercy upon young or old. [51]They will eat you out of house and home until your cattle and crops are gone. Your grain, new wine, olive oil, calves, and lambs will all disappear. [52]That nation will lay siege to your cities and knock down your highest walls—the walls you will trust to protect you. [53]You will even eat the flesh of your own sons and daughters in the terrible days of siege that lie ahead. [54]The most tenderhearted man among you will be utterly callous toward his own brother and his beloved wife and his children who are still alive. [55]He will refuse to give them a share of the flesh he is devouring—the flesh of his own children—because he is starving in the midst of the siege of your cities. [56, 57]The most tender and delicate woman among you—the one who would not so much as touch her feet to the ground—will refuse to share with her beloved husband, son, and daughter. She will hide from them the afterbirth and the new baby she has borne, so that she herself can eat them: so terrible will be the hunger during the siege and the awful distress caused by your enemies at your gates. [58, 59]If you refuse to obey all the laws written in this book, thus refusing reverence to the glorious and fearful name of Jehovah your God, then Jehovah will send perpetual plagues upon you and upon your children. [60]He will bring upon you all the diseases of Egypt which you feared so much, and they shall plague the land. [61]And that is not all! The Lord will bring upon you every sickness and plague there is, even those not mentioned in this book, until you are destroyed. [62]There will be a few of you left, though before you were as numerous as stars. All this if you do not listen to the Lord your God. [63]Just as the Lord has rejoiced over you and has done such wonderful things for you and has multiplied you, so the Lord at that time will rejoice in destroying you; and you shall disappear from the land. [64]For the Lord will scatter you among all the nations from one end of the earth to the other. There you will worship heathen gods that neither you nor your ancestors have known, gods made of wood and stone! [65]There among those nations you shall find no rest, but the Lord will give you trembling hearts, darkness, and bodies wasted from sorrow and fear. [66]Your lives will hang in doubt. You will live night and day in fear, and will have no reason to believe that you will see the morning light. [67]In the morning you will say, "Oh, that night were here!" And in the evening you will say, "Oh, that morning were here!" You will say this because of the awesome horrors surrounding you. [68]Then the Lord will send you back to Egypt in ships, a journey I promised you would never need to make again; and there you will offer to sell yourselves to your enemies as slaves—but no one will even want to buy you.

Deut 31:17. Then my anger will flame out against them and I will abandon them, hiding my face from them, and they shall be destroyed. Terrible trouble will come upon them so that they will say, "God is no longer among us!" [18]I will turn away from them because of their sins in worshiping other gods.

Ps 81:11. But no, my people won't listen. Israel doesn't want me around. [12]So I am letting them go their blind and stubborn way, living according to their own desires.

Prov 1:24. I have called you so often but still you won't come. I have pleaded, but all in vain. [25]For you have spurned my counsel and reproof. [26]Some day you'll be in trouble, and I'll laugh! Mock me, will you?—I'll mock you! [27]When a storm of terror surrounds you, and when you are engulfed by anguish and distress, [28]then I will not answer your cry for help. It will be too late though you search for me ever so anxiously.

Isa 6:9. And he said, "Yes, go. But tell my people this: 'Though you hear my words repeatedly, you won't understand them. Though you watch and watch as I perform my miracles, still you won't know what they mean.' [10]Dull their understanding, close their ears and shut their eyes. I don't want them to see or to hear or to understand, or to turn to me to heal them."

Isa 22:12. The Lord God of Hosts called you to repent, to weep and mourn and shave your heads in sorrow for your sins, and to wear clothes made of sackcloth to show your remorse. [13]But instead, you sing and dance and play, and feast and drink. "Let us eat, drink, and be merry," you say: "What's the difference, for tomorrow we die." [14]The Lord of Hosts has revealed to me that this sin will never be forgiven you until the day you die.

Isa 28:13. So the Lord will spell it out for them again, repeating it over and over in simple words whenever he can; yet over this simple, straightforward message they will stumble and fall and be broken, trapped and captured.

Isa 29:9. You are amazed, incredulous? You don't believe it? Then go ahead and be blind if you must! You are stupid—and not from drinking, either! Stagger, and not from wine! [10]For the Lord has poured out upon you a spirit of deep sleep. He has closed the eyes of your prophets and seers, [11]so all of these future events are a sealed book to them. When you give it to one who can read, he says, "I can't for it's sealed." [12]When you give it to another, he says, "Sorry, I can't read."

Isa 65:12. Therefore I will "destine" you to the sword, and your "fate" shall be a dark one; for when I called, you didn't answer; when I spoke, you wouldn't listen. You deliberately sinned before my very eyes, choosing to do what you know I despise.

Jer 6:30. I must label them "Impure, Rejected Silver," and I have discarded them.

Jer 7:16. Pray no more for these people, Jeremiah. Neither weep for them nor pray nor beg that I should help them, for I will not listen.

Jer 15:1. Then the Lord said to me, Even if Moses and Samuel stood before me pleading for these people, even then I wouldn't help them—away with them! Get them out of my sight!

Hos 5:6. Then at last, they will come with their flocks and herds to sacrifice to God, but it will be too late—they will not find him. He has withdrawn from them and they are left alone.

Mt 13:14. This fulfills the prophecy of Isaiah: "They hear, but don't understand; they look, but don't see! [15]For their hearts are fat and heavy, and their ears are dull, and they have closed their eyes in sleep, [16]so they won't see and hear and understand and turn to God again, and let me heal them."

Mt 15:14. So ignore them. They are blind guides leading the blind, and both will fall into a ditch.

Mt 25:8. Then the five who hadn't any oil begged the others to share with them, for their lamps were going out. [9]But the others replied, "We haven't enough. Go instead to the shops and buy some for yourselves." [10]But while they were gone, the bridegroom came, and those who were ready went in with him to the marriage feast, and the door was locked. [11]Later, when the other five returned, they stood outside, calling, "Sir, open the door for us!" [12]But he called back, "Go away! It is too late!" [13]So stay awake and be prepared, for you do not know the date or moment of my return.

Mk 3:29. But blasphemy against the Holy Spirit can never be forgiven. It is an eternal sin.

Lk 13:24, 25. The door to heaven is narrow. Work hard to get in, for the truth is that many will try to enter but when the head of the house has locked the door, it will be too late. Then if you stand outside knocking, and pleading, "Lord, open the door for us," he will reply, "I do not know you." [26]"But we ate with you, and you taught in our streets," you will say. [27]And he will reply, "I tell you, I don't know you. You can't come in here, guilty as you are. Go away." [28]And there will be great weeping and gnashing of teeth as you stand outside and see Abraham, Isaac, Jacob, and all the prophets within the Kingdom of God.

Lk 14:24. For none of those I invited first will get even the smallest taste of what I had prepared for them.

Jn 10:26. But you don't believe me because you are not part of my flock.

Jn 17:12. During my time here I have kept safe within your family all of those you gave me. I guarded them so that not one perished, except the son of hell, as the Scriptures foretold.

Rom 9:21. When a man makes a jar out of clay, doesn't he have a right to use the same lump of clay to make one jar beautiful, to be used for holding flowers, and another to throw garbage into? [22]Does not God have a perfect right to show his fury and power against those who are fit only for destruction, those he has been patient with for all this time?

Rom 11:7. So this is the situation: Most of the Jews have not found the favor of God they are looking for. A few have—the ones God has picked out—but the eyes of the others have been blinded. [8]This is what our Scriptures refer to when they say that God has put them to sleep, shutting their eyes and ears so that they do not understand what we are talking about when we tell them of Christ. And so it is to this very day. [17]But some of these branches from Abraham's tree, some of the Jews, have been broken off. And you Gentiles who were branches from, we might say, a wild olive tree, were grafted in. So now you, too, receive the blessing God has promised Abraham and his children, sharing in God's rich nourishment of his own special olive tree. [18]But you must be careful not to brag about being put in to replace the branches that were broken off. Remember that you are important only because you are now a part of God's tree; you are just a branch, not a root. [19]"Well," you may be saying, "those branches were broken off to make room for me so I must be pretty good." [20]Watch out! Remember that those branches, the Jews, were broken off because they didn't believe God, and you are there only because you do. Do not be proud; be humble and grateful—and careful.

2 Cor 13:5. Check up on yourselves. Are you really Christians? Do you pass the test? Do you feel Christ's presence and power more and more within you? Or are you just pretending to be Christians when actually you aren't at all? [6]I hope you can agree that I have stood that test and truly belong to the Lord. [7]I pray that you will live good lives, not because that will be a feather in our caps, proving that what we teach is right; no, for we want you to do right even if we ourselves are despised.

2 Thess 2:7. As for the work this man of rebellion and hell will do when he comes, it is already going on, but he himself will not come until the one who is holding him back steps out of the way. [8]Then this wicked one will appear, whom the Lord Jesus will burn up with the breath of his mouth and destroy by his presence when he returns. [9]This man of sin will come as Satan's tool, full of satanic power, and will trick everyone with strange demonstrations, and will do great miracles. [10]He will completely fool those who are on their way to hell because they have said "no" to the Truth; they have refused to believe it and love it, and let it save them, [11]so God will allow them to believe lies with all their hearts, [12]and all of them will be justly judged for believing falsehood, refusing the Truth, and enjoying their sins.

2 Tim 3:8. And these teachers fight truth just as Jannes and Jambres fought against Moses. They have dirty minds, warped and twisted, and have turned against the Christian faith.

Heb 3:10. "But," God says, "I was very angry with them, for their hearts were always looking somewhere else instead of up to me, and they never found the paths I wanted them to follow." [11]Then God, full of this anger against them, bound himself with an oath that he would never let them come to his place of rest. [12]Beware then of your own hearts, dear brothers, lest you find that they, too, are evil and unbelieving and are leading you away from the living God. [17]And who was it who made God angry for all those forty years? These same people who sinned and as a result died in the wilderness. [18]And to whom was God speaking when he swore with an oath that they could never go into the land he had promised his people? He was speaking to all those who disobeyed him. [19]And why couldn't they go in? Because they didn't trust him.

Heb 6:4. There is no use trying to bring you back to the Lord again if you have once understood the Good News and tasted for yourself the good things of heaven and shared in the Holy Spirit, [5]and know how good the Word of God is, and felt the mighty powers of the world to come, [6]and then have turned against God. You cannot bring yourself to repent again if you have nailed the Son of God to the cross again by rejecting him, holding him up to mocking and to public shame. [7]When a farmer's land has had many showers upon it and good crops come up, that land has experienced God's blessing upon it. [8]But if it keeps on having crops of thistles and thorns, the land is considered no good and is ready for condemnation and burning off.

Heb 10:26. If anyone sins deliberately by rejecting the Savior after knowing the truth of forgiveness, this sin is not covered by Christ's death; there is no way to get rid of it. [27]There will be nothing to look forward to but the terrible punishment of God's awful anger which will consume all his enemies. [28]A man who refused to obey the laws given by Moses was killed without mercy if there were two or three witnesses to his sin. [29]Think how much more terrible the punishment will be for those who have trampled underfoot the Son of God and treated his cleansing blood as though it were common and unhallowed, and insulted and outraged the Holy Spirit who brings God's mercy to his people. [30]For we know him who said, "Justice belongs to me; I will repay them"; who also said, "The Lord himself will handle these cases." [31]It is a fearful thing to fall into the hands of the living God.

Heb 12:15. Look after each other so that not one of you will fail to find God's best blessings. Watch out that no bitterness takes root among you, for as it springs up it causes deep trouble, hurting many in their spiritual lives. [16]Watch out that no one becomes involved in sexual sin or becomes careless about God as Esau did: he traded his rights as the oldest son for a single meal. [17]And afterwards, when he wanted those rights back again, it was too late, even though he wept bitter tears of repentance. So remember, and be careful.

1 Jn 5:16. If you see a Christian sinning in a way that does not end in death, you should ask God to forgive him and God will give him life, unless he has sinned that one fatal sin. But there is that one sin which ends in death and if he has done that, there is no use praying for him.

Jude 1:4. I say this because some godless teachers have wormed their way in among you, saying that after we become Christians we can do just as we like without fear of God's punishment. The fate of such people was written long ago, for they have turned against our only Master and Lord, Jesus Christ. [5]My answer to them is: Remember this fact —which you know already—that the Lord saved a whole nation of people out of the land of Egypt, and then killed every one of them who did not trust and obey him. [6]And I remind you of those angels who were once pure and holy, but turned to a life of sin. Now God has them chained up in prisons of darkness, waiting for the judgment day. [7]And don't forget the cities of Sodom and Gomorrah and their neighboring towns, all full of lust of every kind including lust of men for other men. Those cities were destroyed by fire and continue to be a warning to us that there is a hell in which sinners are punished. [8]Yet these false teachers carelessly go right on living their evil, immoral lives, degrading their bodies and laughing at those in authority over them, even scoffing at the Glorious Ones. [9]Yet Michael, one of the mightiest of the angels, when he was arguing with Satan about Moses' body, did not dare to accuse even Satan, or jeer at him, but simply said, "The Lord rebuke you." [10]But these men mock and curse at anything they do not understand, and, like animals, they do whatever they feel like, thereby ruining their souls. [11]Woe upon them! For they follow the example of Cain who killed his brother; and, like Balaam, they will do anything for money; and like Korah, they have disobeyed God and will die under his curse. [12]When these men join you at the love feats of the church, they are evil smears among you, laughing and carrying on, gorging and stuffing themselves without a thought for others. They are like clouds blowing over dry land without giving rain, promising much, but producing nothing. They are like fruit trees without any fruit at picking time. They are not only dead, but doubly dead, for they have been pulled out, roots and all, to be burned. [13]All they leave behind them is shame and disgrace like the dirty foam left along the beach by the wild waves. They wander around looking as bright as stars, but ahead of them is the everlasting gloom and darkness that God has prepared for them.

Rev 22:11. And when that time comes, all doing wrong will do it more and more; the vile will become more vile; good men will be better; those who are holy will continue on in greater holiness.

See *Obduracy.*

INSTANCES OF. Israel, Num 14:26–45; Deut 1: 42, 43. Eli's family, 1 Sam 3:14. Saul, 1 Sam 15:23; 16:14; 18:11, 12; 28:15.

REPRODUCTION See *Propagation.*

REPROOF Lev 19:17. Rebuke anyone who sins; don't let him get away with it, or you will be equally guilty.

Ps 141:5. Let the godly smite me! It will be a kindness! If they reprove me, it is medicine! Don't let me refuse it.

Prov 9:7, 8. If you rebuke a mocker, you will only get a smart retort; yes, he will snarl at you. So don't bother with him; he will only hate you for trying to help him. But a wise man, when rebuked, will love you all the more.

Prov 10:17. Anyone willing to be corrected is on the pathway to life. Anyone refusing has lost his chance.

Prov 12:1. To learn, you must want to be taught. To refuse reproof is stupid.

Prov 13:18. If you refuse criticism you will end in poverty and disgrace; if you accept criticism you are on the road to fame.

Prov 15:5. Only a fool despises his father's advice; a wise son considers each suggestion. [10]If they stop trying [to be good], the Lord will punish them; if they rebel against that punishment, they will die. [12]A mocker stays away from wise men because he hates to be scolded. [31, 32]If you profit from constructive criticism you will be elected to the wise men's hall of fame. But to reject criticism is to harm yourself and your own best interests.

Prov 17:10. A rebuke to a man of common sense is more effective than a hundred lashes on the back of a rebel.

Prov 19:25. Punish a mocker and others will learn from his example. Reprove a wise man and he will be the wiser.

Prov 21:11. The wise man learns by listening; the simpleton can learn only by seeing scorners punished.

Prov 25:12. It is a badge of honor to accept valid criticism.

Prov 26:5. Prick his conceit with silly replies!

Prov 27:5. Open rebuke is better than hidden love! [6]Wounds from a friend are better than kisses from an enemy!

Prov 28:23. In the end, people appreciate frankness more than flattery.

Eccl 7:5. It is better to be criticized by a wise man than to be praised by a fool!

Amos 5:10. How you hate honest judges! How you despise people who tell the truth!

Mt 18:15. If a brother sins against you, go to him privately and confront him with his fault. If he listens and confesses it, you have won back a brother. [16]But if not, then take one or two others with you and go back to him again, proving everything you say by these witnesses. [17]If he still refuses to listen, then take your case to the church, and if the church's verdict favors you, but he won't accept it, then the church should excommunicate him.

Lk 17:3. Rebuke your brother if he sins, and forgive him if he is sorry. [4]Even if he wrongs you seven times a day and each time turns again and asks forgiveness, forgive him.

Jn 7:7. For the world can't hate you; but it does hate me, because I accuse it of sin and evil.

Gal 4:16. And now have I become your enemy because I tell you the truth?

Eph 4:15. Instead, we will lovingly follow the truth at all times—speaking truly, dealing truly, living truly—and so become more and more in every way like Christ who is the Head of his body, the church.

Eph 5:11. Take no part in the worthless pleasures of evil and darkness, but instead, rebuke and expose them. [13]But when you expose them, the light shines in upon their sin and shows it up, and when they see how wrong they really are, some of them may even become children of light!

Phil 3:1. Whatever happens, dear friends, be glad in the Lord. I never get tired of telling you this and it is good for you to hear it again and again.

1 Thess 5:14. Dear brothers, warn those who are lazy; comfort those who are frightened; take tender care of those who are weak; and be patient with everyone.

1 Tim 5:1. Never speak sharply to an older man, but plead with him respectfully just as though he were your own father. Talk to the younger men as you would to much loved brothers. [2]Treat the older women as mothers, and the girls as your sisters, thinking only pure thoughts about them. [20]If he has really sinned, then he should be rebuked in front of the whole church so that no one else will follow his example.

2 Tim 4:2. To preach the Word of God urgently

at all times, whenever you get the chance, in season and out, when it is convenient and when it is not. Correct and rebuke your people when they need it, encourage them to do right, and all the time be feeding them patiently with God's Word.

Tit 1:13. So speak to the Christians there as sternly as necessary to make them strong in the faith.

Heb 3:13. Speak to each other about these things every day while there is still time, so that none of you will become hardened against God, being blinded by the glamor of sin.

Rev 11:10. And there will be a worldwide holiday —people everywhere will rejoice and give presents to each other and throw parties to celebrate the death of the two prophets who had tormented them so much!

FAITHFULNESS IN.

Instances of. Moses, of Pharaoh, Ex 10:29; 11:8; of the Israelites, Ex 16:6–9; 32:19–30; Num 14:41; 20:10; 32:14; Deut 1:12, 26–43; 9:16–24; 29:2–4; 31: 27–29; 32:15–18; of Eleazar, Lev 10:16–18; of Korah, Num 16:8–12. Israelites, of the two and one-half tribes, Josh 22:15–20; of the tribe of Benjamin, Judg 20:12, 13. Samuel, of Saul, 1 Sam 15:14–35. Jonathan, of Saul, 1 Sam 19:4, 5. Nathan, of David, 2 Sam 12: 1–9. Joab, of David, 2 Sam 19:1–7; 24:3; 1 Chron 21: 3. The prophet Gad, of David, 2 Sam 24:13. Shemaiah, of Rehoboam, 2 Chron 12:5. A prophet of Judah, of Jeroboam, 1 Kgs 13:1–10; 2 Chron 13:8–11. Elijah, of Ahab, 1 Kgs 18:18–21; 21:20–24; of Ahaziah, 2 Kgs 1. Micaiah, of Ahab, 1 Kgs 22:14–28. Elisha, of Jehoram, 2 Kgs 3:13, 14; of Gehazi, 2 Kgs 5:26; of Hazael, 2 Kgs 8:11–13; of Jeroboam, 2 Kgs 13:19. Isaiah, of Hezekiah, 2 Kgs 20:17. Joash, of Jehoiada, 2 Kgs 12:7. Azariah, of Asa, 2 Chron 15:2; of Uzziah, 2 Chron 26:17, 18. Hanani, of Asa, 2 Chron 16:7–9. Jehu, of Jehoshaphat, 2 Chron 19:2. Zechariah, of the leaders of Judah, 2 Chron 24:20. Oded, of the people of Samaria, 2 Chron 28:9–11. Jeremiah, of the cities of Judah, Jer 26:7–11. Ezra, of the men of Judah and Benjamin, Ezra 10:10. Nehemiah, of the Jews, Neh 5: 6–13; of the contamination of the temple, and of the violation of the Sabbath, Neh 13. Daniel, of Nebuchadnezzar, Dan 4:27; of Belshazzar, Dan 5:17–23. Amos, of the Israelites, Amos 7:12–17. Jesus, of the Jews: when Pharisees and Sadducees came to him desiring a sign, Mt 16:1–4; Mk 8:11, 12; of the Jewish leaders and Pharisees, Mt 23; Lk 11:37–54; of the Pharisees, Lk 16; when they brought the woman to him who was caught in adultery, Jn 8:7. In his parables: Of the great feast, Lk 14:16–24; of the two sons, Mt 21:28–32; of the vineyard, Mt 21:33–46; Mk 12:1–12; Lk 20:9–20; of the fig tree, Lk 13:6–9; the withering of the fig tree, Mt 21:17–20; Mk 11: 12–14. John the Baptist, of the Jews, Mt 3:7–12; Lk 3:7–9; of Herod, Mt 14:3; Mk 6:17, 18; Lk 3:19, 20. Peter, of Simon, the sorcerer, Acts 8:20–23. Stephen, of the high priest, Acts 7:51–53. Paul, of Elymas, the sorcerer, Acts 13:9–11; of Ananias, the high priest, Acts 23:3. Paul and Silas, of the judges of Philippi, Acts 16:37–40.

DESPISED. By the Israelites, Num 14:9–11; Jer 26:11. By Ahab, 1 Kgs 18:17; 21:20; 22:8. By Asa, 2 Chron 16:10. By Herodias, Mk 6:17–19. By people of Nazareth, Lk 4:28, 29. Jews, Acts 5:33; 7:54.

See *Reprobate.*

REPUTATION, GOOD Prov 3:4, 5; 22:1; Eccl 7:1. Effect of a mistake on a good reputation, Eccl 10:1. Gamaliel's good, Acts 5:34. That of the Jerusalem leaders, Gal 2:2. Christ made himself of no reputation, Phil 2:7.

See *Character; Name.*

RESHEPH A descendant of Ephraim, 1 Chron 7:25–27.

RESIGNATION Job 5:17. How enviable the man whom God corrects! Oh, do not despise the chastening of the Lord when you sin.

Ps 4:4. Stand before the Lord in awe, and do not sin against him. Lie quietly upon your bed in silent meditation.

Ps 46:10. Stand silent! Know that I am God!

Prov 3:11. Young man, do not resent it when God chastens and corrects you, for his punishment is proof of his love.

Prov 18:14. A man's courage can sustain his broken body, but when courage dies, what hope is left?

Jer 51:50. Go, you who escaped the sword! Don't stand and watch—flee while you can! Remember the Lord and return to Jerusalem far away!

Lam 3:39. Why then should we, mere humans as we are, murmur and complain when punished for our sins?

Mic 6:9. The Lord's voice calls out to all Jerusalem—listen to the Lord if you are wise! The armies of destruction are coming; the Lord is sending them.

Mt 6:10. May your will be done here on earth, just as it is in heaven.

Lk 21:19. For if you stand firm, you will win your souls.

Rom 12:12. Be glad for all God is planning for you. Be patient in trouble, and prayerful always.

Phil 2:14. In everything you do, stay away from complaining and arguing.

Phil 4:11. Not that I was ever in need, for I have learned how to get along happily whether I have much or little. [12]I know how to live on almost nothing or with everything. I have learned the secret of contentment in every situation, whether it be a full stomach or hunger, plenty or want; [13]for I can do everything God asks me to with the help of Christ who gives me the strength and power.

Col 1:11. We are praying, too, that you will be filled with his mighty, glorious strength so that you can keep going no matter what happens—always full of the joy of the Lord.

1 Thess 3:3. And to keep you from becoming fainthearted in all the troubles you were going through. (But of course you know that such troubles are a part of God's plan for us Christians.)

2 Tim 2:3. Take your share of suffering as a good soldier of Jesus Christ, just as I do.

2 Tim 4:5. Stand steady, and don't be afraid of suffering for the Lord. Bring others to Christ.

Leave nothing undone that you ought to do.

Heb 10:34. You suffered with those thrown into jail, and you were actually joyful when all you owned was taken from you, knowing that better things were awaiting you in heaven, things that would be yours forever.

Heb 12:3. If you want to keep from becoming fainthearted and weary, think about his patience as sinful men did such terrible things to him. [4]After all, you have never yet struggled against sin and temptation until you sweat great drops of blood. [5]And have you quite forgotten the encouraging words God spoke to you, his child? He said, "My son, don't be angry when the Lord punishes you. Don't be discouraged when he has to show you where you are wrong." [9]Since we respect our fathers here on earth, though they punish us, should we not all the more cheerfully submit to God's training so that we can begin really to live? *vs.* 6–12.

Jas 1:9. A Christian who doesn't amount to much in this world should be glad, for he is great in the Lord's sight. [10]But a rich man should be glad that his riches mean nothing to the Lord, for he will soon be gone, like a flower that has lost its beauty and fades away.

Jas 4:7. So give yourselves humbly to God.

Jas 5:13. Is anyone among you suffering? He should keep on praying about it. And those who have reason to be thankful should continually be singing praises to the Lord.

1 Pet 1:6. So be truly glad! There is wonderful joy ahead, even though the going is rough for a while down here.

1 Pet 4:12. Dear friends, don't be bewildered or surprised when you go through the fiery trials ahead, for this is no strange, unusual thing that is going to happen to you. [13]Instead, be really glad—because these trials will make you partners with Christ in his suffering, and afterwards you will have the wonderful joy of sharing his glory in the coming day when it will be displayed. [19]So if you are suffering according to God's will, keep on doing what is right and trust yourself to the God who made you, for he will never fail you.

EXEMPLIFIED. Lev 10:1. But Nadab and Abihu, the sons of Aaron, placed unholy fire in their censers, laid incense on the fire, and offered the incense before the Lord—contrary to what the Lord had just commanded them! [2]So fire blazed forth from the presence of the Lord and destroyed them. [3]Then Moses said to Aaron, "This is what the Lord meant when he said, 'I will show myself holy among those who approach me, and I will be glorified before all the people.' " And Aaron was speechless.

Judg 10:15. But they pleaded with him again and said, "We have sinned. Punish us in any way you think best, only save us once more from our enemies."

1 Sam 3:18. So Samuel told him what the Lord had said. "It is the Lord's will," Eli replied; "let him do what he thinks best."

2 Sam 12:23. But why should I fast when he is dead? Can I bring him back again? I shall go to him, but he shall not return to me.

2 Sam 15:26. But if he is through with me, well, let him do what seems best to him.

2 Sam 16:10. "No!" the king said. "If the Lord has told him to curse me, who am I to say no? [11]My own son is trying to kill me, and this Benjaminite is merely cursing me. Let him alone, for no doubt the Lord has told him to do it."

2 Sam 24:14. "This is a hard decision," David replied, "but it is better to fall into the hand of the Lord (for his mercy is great) than into the hands of men."

2 Kgs 4:26. "Run and meet her and ask her what the trouble is. See if her husband is all right and if the child is well." "Yes," she told Gehazi, "everything is fine."

2 Kgs 20:19. "All right," Hezekiah replied, "if this is what the Lord wants, it is good." But he was really thinking, "At least there will be peace and security during the remainder of my own life!" Isa 39:8.

Neh 9:33. Every time you punished us you were being perfectly fair; we have sinned so greatly that you gave us only what we deserved.

Esther 4:16. Go and gather together all the Jews of Shushan and fast for me; do not eat or drink for three days, night or day; and I and my maids will do the same; and then, though it is strictly forbidden, I will go in to see the king; and if I perish, I perish.

Job 1:13. Not long afterwards when Job's sons and daughters were dining at the oldest brother's house, tragedy struck. [14, 15]A messenger rushed to Job's home with this news: "Your oxen were plowing, with the donkeys feeding beside them, when the Sabeans raided us, drove away the animals and killed all the farmhands except me. I am the only one left." [16]While this messenger was still speaking, another arrived with more bad news: "The fire of God has fallen from heaven and burned up your sheep and all the herdsmen, and I alone have escaped to tell you." [17]Before this man finished, still another messenger rushed in: "Three bands of Chaldeans have driven off your camels and killed your servants, and I alone have escaped to tell you." [18]As he was still speaking, another arrived to say, "Your sons and daughters were feasting in their oldest brother's home, [19]when suddenly a mighty wind swept in from the desert, and engulfed the house so that the roof fell in on them and all are dead; and I alone escaped to tell you." [20]Then Job stood up and tore his robe in grief and fell down upon the ground before God. [21]"I came naked from my mother's womb," he said, "and I shall have nothing when I die. The Lord gave me everything I had, and they were his to take away. Blessed be the name of the Lord." [22]In all of this, Job did not sin or revile God.

Job 2:9. His wife said to him, "Are you still trying to be godly when God has done all this to you? Curse him and die." [10]But he replied, "You talk like some heathen woman. What? Shall we receive only pleasant things from the hand of God and never anything unpleasant?" So in all this Job did nothing wrong.

Ps 39:9. Lord, I am speechless before you. I will not open my mouth to speak one word of complaint, for my punishment is from you.

Ps 103:10. He has not punished us as we deserve for all our sins.

Ps 119:75. I know, O Lord, that your decisions are right and that your punishment was right and did me good.

Jer 10:19. *Desperate is my wound. My grief is great. My sickness is incurable, but I must bear it.*

Lam 1:18. And the Lord is right, for we rebelled.

Dan 9:14. And so the Lord deliberately crushed us with the calamity he prepared; he is fair in everything he does, but we would not obey.

Mic 7:9. I will be patient while the Lord punishes me, for I have sinned against him; then he will defend me from my enemies, and punish them for all the evil they have done to me. God will bring me out of my darkness into the light, and I will see his goodness.

Mt 26:39. He went forward a little, and fell face downward on the ground, and prayed, "My Father! If it is possible, let this cup be taken away from me. But I want your will, not mine." Mk 14:36; Lk 22:41, 42.

Lk 23:40, 41. But the other criminal protested. "Don't you even fear God when you are dying? We deserve to die for our evil deeds, but this man hasn't done one thing wrong."

Jn 18:11. But Jesus said to Peter, "Put your sword away. Shall I not drink from the cup the Father has given me?"

Acts 7:59. And as the murderous stones came hurtling at him, Stephen prayed, "Lord Jesus, receive my spirit." [60]And he fell to his knees, shouting, "Lord, don't charge them with this sin!" and with that, he died.

Acts 21:14. When it was clear that he wouldn't be dissuaded, we gave up and said, "The will of the Lord be done."

Rom 5:3. We can rejoice, too, when we run into problems and trials for we know that they are good for us—they help us learn to be patient. [4]And patience develops strength of character in us and helps us trust God more each time we use it until finally our hope and faith are strong and steady. [5]Then, when that happens, we are able to hold our heads high no matter what happens and know that all is well, for we know how dearly God loves us, and we feel this warm love everywhere within us because God has given us the Holy Spirit to fill our hearts with his love.

2 Cor 6:9. The world ignores us, but we are known to God; we live close to death, but here we are, still very much alive. We have been injured but kept from death. [10]Our hearts ache, but at the same time we have the joy of the Lord. We are poor, but we give rich spiritual gifts to others. We own nothing, and yet we enjoy everything. *vs.* 3–11.

2 Cor 7:4. I have the highest confidence in you, and my pride in you is great. You have greatly encouraged me; you have made me so happy in spite of all my suffering.

Phil 1:20. For I live in eager expectation and hope that I will never do anything that will cause me to be ashamed of myself but that I will always be ready to speak out boldly for Christ while I am going through all these trials here, just as I have in the past; and that I will always be an honor to Christ, whether I live or whether I must die. [21]For to me, living means opportunities for Christ, and dying—well, that's better yet! [22]But if living will give me more opportunities to win people to Christ, then I really don't know which is better, to live or die! [23]Sometimes I want to live and at other times I don't, for I long to go and be with Christ. How much happier for *me* than being here! [24]But the fact is that I can be of more help to *you* by staying!

2 Thess 1:4. We are happy to tell other churches about your patience and complete faith in God, in spite of all the crushing troubles and hardships you are going through.

2 Tim 4:6. I say this because I won't be around to help you very much longer. My time has almost run out.

Jas 5:11. We know how happy they are now because they stayed true to him then, even though they suffered greatly for it. Job is an example of a man who continued to trust the Lord in sorrow; from his experiences we can see how the Lord's plan finally ended in good, for he is full of tenderness and mercy.

See *Affliction, Benefits of, Resignation in.*

RESPECT To the aged, Lev 19:32. To rulers, Prov 25:6, 7. To a host, Lk 14:10. To one another, Rom 12:10; Phil 2:3; 1 Pet 2:17.

RESPECT OF PERSONS Prov 24:23; 28:21; Jas 2:1–9. God does not have, Deut 10:17; 2 Chron 19:7; Job 31:13–15; 34:19; Acts 10:34; 15:9; Rom 2:11; 10:12; Eph 6:8, 9; Col 3:25; Jas 2:1–9; 1 Pet 1:17.

See *God, Judge; Justice.*

RESPONSIBILITY Attempts to shift: Adam, Gen 3:12, 13; Eve, Gen 3:13; Sarah, Gen 16:5, with *v.* 2, 3; Esau, Gen 27:36, with Gen 25:29–34; Aaron, Ex 32:22–24; Saul, 1 Sam 15:20, 21; Pilate, Mt 27:24. Assumed by the Jews for the death of Jesus, Mt 27:25.

Personal, Ezk 18:20, 30; Mt 12:37; Jn 9:41; 15:22–24; 1 Cor 3:8, 13–15; Gal 6:5; Rev 2:23.

ACCORDING TO PRIVILEGE. Ezk 18:1. Then the Lord's message came to me again. [2]"Why do people use this proverb about the land of Israel: The children are punished for their fathers' sins? [3]As I live, says the Lord God, you will not use this proverb any more in Israel, [4]for all souls are mine to judge—fathers and sons alike—and my rule is this: It is for a man's own sins that he will die. [5]But if a man is just and does what is lawful and right, [6]and has not gone out to the mountains to feast before the idols of Israel and worship them, and does not commit adultery, or lie with any woman during the time of her menstruation, [7]and is a merciful creditor, not holding on to the items given to him in pledge by poor debtors, and is no robber, but gives food to the hungry and clothes to those in need, [8]and grants loans without interest, and stays away from sin, and is honest and fair when judging others, [9]and obeys my laws—that man is just, says the Lord, and he shall surely live. [10]But if that man has a son who is a robber or murderer and who fulfills none of his responsibilities, [11]who refuses to obey the laws of God, but worships idols on the mountains and commits adultery, [12]and oppresses the poor and needy, and robs his debtors by refusing to let them redeem what they have given him in pledge, and loves idols and worships them, [13]and loans out his money at interest—shall that man live? No! He shall surely die and it is his own fault. [14]But if this sinful man has, in turn, a son who sees all his father's wickedness, so that he fears God and decides against that kind of life, [15]and doesn't go up on the mountains to feast before the idols and worship them, and does not commit adultery, [16]and is fair to those who borrow from him and doesn't rob them, but feeds the hungry and clothes the needy, [17]and helps the poor and does not loan money at interest, and obeys my laws —he shall not die because of his father's sins; he shall surely live. [18] But his father shall die for his own sins because he is cruel and robs and does wrong. [19]'What?' you ask. 'Doesn't the son pay for his father's sins?' No! For if the son does what is right and keeps my laws, he shall surely live. [20]The one who sins is the one who dies. The son shall not be punished for his father's sins, nor the father for his son's. The righteous person will be rewarded for his own goodness and the wicked person for his wickedness. [21]But if a wicked person turns away from all his sins and begins to obey my laws and do what is just and right, he shall surely live and not die. [22]All his past sins will be forgotten, and he shall live because of his goodness. [23]Do you think I like to see the wicked die? asks the Lord. Of course not! I only want him to turn from his wicked ways and live. [24]However, if a righteous person turns to sinning and acts like any other sinner, should he be allowed to live? No, of course not. All his previous goodness will be forgotten and he shall die for his sins. [25]Yet you say: 'The Lord isn't being fair!' Listen to me, O people of Israel. Am I the one who is unfair, or is it you? [26]When a good man turns away from being good and begins sinning and dies in his sins, he dies for the evil he has done. [27]And if a wicked person turns away from his wickedness and obeys the law, and does right, he shall save his soul, [28]for he has thought it over and decided to turn from his sins and live a good life. He shall surely live—he shall not die. [29]And yet the people of Israel keep saying: 'The Lord is unfair!' O people of Israel, it is you who are unfair, not I. [30]I will judge each of you, O Israel, and punish or reward each according to your own actions. Oh, turn from your sins while there is yet time.

Ezk 33:1. Once again a message came to me from the Lord. He said: [2]"Son of dust, tell your people: When I bring an army against a country, and the people of that land choose a watchman, [3]and when he sees the army coming, and blows the alarm to warn them, [4]then anyone who hears the alarm and refuses to heed it—well, if he dies the fault is his own. [5]For he heard the warning and wouldn't listen; the fault is his. If he had heeded the warning, he would have saved his life. [6]But if the watchman sees the enemy coming and doesn't sound the alarm and warn the people, he is responsible for their deaths. They will die in their sins, but I will charge the watchman with their deaths. [7]So with you, son of dust. I have appointed you as a watchman for the people of Israel; therefore listen to what I say and warn them for me. [8]When I say to the wicked, 'O wicked man, you will die!' and you don't tell him what I say, so that he does not repent —that wicked person will die in his sins, but I will hold you responsible for his death. [9]But if you warn him to repent and he doesn't, he will die in his sin, and you will not be responsible. [10]O people of Israel, you are saying: 'Our sins are heavy upon us; we pine away with guilt. How can we live?' [11]Tell them: As I live, says the Lord God, I have no pleasure in the death of the wicked; *I desire that the wicked turn from his evil ways and live.* Turn, turn from your wickedness, for why will you die, O Israel? [12]For the good works of a righteous man will not save him if he turns to sin; and the sins of an evil man will not destroy him if he repents and turns from his sins. [13]I have said the good man will live. But if he sins, expecting his past goodness to save him, then none of his good deeds will be remembered. I will destroy him for his sins. [14]And when I tell the wicked he will die and then he turns from his sins and does what is fair and right— [15]if he gives back the borrower's pledge and returns what he has stolen and walks along the paths of right, not doing evil—he shall surely live. He shall not die. [16]None of his past sins shall be brought up against him, for he has turned to the good and shall surely live. [17]And yet your people are saying the Lord isn't fair. The trouble is *they* aren't fair. [18]For again I say, when the good man turns to evil, he shall die. [19]But if the wicked turns from his wickedness and does what's fair and just, he shall live."

Mt 10:11. Whenever you enter a city or village, search for a godly man and stay in his home until you leave for the next town. [12]When you ask permission to stay, be friendly, [13]and if it turns out to be a godly home, give it your blessing; if not, keep the blessing. [14]Any city or home that doesn't welcome you—shake off the dust of that place from your feet as you leave. [15]Truly, the wicked cities of Sodom and Gomorrah will be better off at Judgment Day than they. Lk 9:5; 10:10–15.

Mt 11:20. Then he began to pour out his denunciations against the cities where he had done most of his miracles, because they hadn't turned to God. [21]"Woe to you, Chorazin, and woe to you, Bethsaida! For if the miracles I did in your streets had been done in wicked Tyre and Sidon their people would have repented long ago in shame and humility. [22]Truly, Tyre and Sidon will be better off on the Judgment Day than you! [23]And Capernaum, though highly honored, shall go down to hell! For if the marvelous miracles I did in you had been done in Sodom, it would still be here today. [24]Truly, Sodom will be better off at the Judgment Day than you."

Mt 12:41. The men of Nineveh shall arise against this nation at the judgment and condemn you. For when Jonah preached to them, they repented and turned to God from all their evil ways. And now a greater than Jonah is here—and you refuse to believe him. [42]The Queen of Sheba shall rise against this nation in the judgment, and condemn it; for she came from a distant land to hear the wisdom of Solomon; and now a greater than Solomon is here—and you refuse to believe him. Lk 11:31, 32.

Mt 23:31. In saying that, you are accusing yourselves of being the sons of wicked men. [32]And you are following in their steps, filling up the full measure of their evil. [33]Snakes! Sons of vipers! How shall you escape the judgment of hell? [34]I will send you prophets, and wise men, and inspired writers, and you will kill some by crucifixion, and rip open the backs of others with whips in your synagogues, and hound them from city to city, [35]so that you will become guilty of all the blood of murdered godly men from righteous Abel to Zechariah (son of Barachiah), slain by you in the Temple between the altar and the sanctuary. Lk 11:49–51.

Mt 25:14. Again, the Kingdom of Heaven can be illustrated by the story of a man going into another country, who called together his servants and loaned them money to invest for him while he was gone. [15]He gave $5,000 to one, $2,000 to another, and $1,000 to the last—dividing it in proportion to their abilities—and then left on his trip. [16]The man who received the $5,000 began immediately to buy and sell with it and soon earned another $5,000. [17]The man with $2,000 went right to work, too, and earned another $2,000. [18]But the man who received the $1,000 dug a hole in the ground and hid the money for safekeeping. [19]After a long time their master returned from his trip and called them to him to account for his money. [20]The man to whom he had entrusted the $5,000 brought him $10,000. [21]His master praised him for good work. "You have been faithful in handling this small amount," he told him, "so now I will give you many more responsibilities. Begin the joyous tasks I have assigned to you." [22]Next came the man who had received the $2,000, with the report, "Sir, you gave me $2,000 to use, and I have doubled it." [23]"Good work," his master said. "You are a good and faithful servant. You have been faithful over this small amount, so now I will give you much more." [24, 25]Then the man with the $1,000 came and said, "Sir, I knew you were a hard man, and I was afraid you would rob me of what I earned, so I hid your money in the earth and here it is!" [26]But his master replied, "Wicked man! Lazy slave! Since you knew I would demand your profit, [27]you should at least have put my money into the bank so I could have some interest. [28]Take the money from this man and give it to the man with the $10,000. [29]For the man who uses well what he is given shall be given more, and he shall have abundance. But from the man who is unfaithful, even what little responsibility he has shall be taken from him. [30]And throw the useless servant out into outer darkness: there shall be weeping and gnashing of teeth." Lk 19:12–27.

Mk 6:11. And whenever a village won't accept you or listen to you, shake off the dust from your feet as you leave; it is a sign that you have abandoned it to its fate.

Lk 13:6. Then he used this illustration: "A man planted a fig tree in his garden and came again and again to see if he could find any fruit on it, but he was always disappointed. [7]Finally he told his gardener to cut it down. 'I've waited three years and there hasn't been a single fig!' he said. 'Why bother with it any longer? It's taking up space we can use for something else.' [8]'Give it one more chance,' the gardener answered. 'Leave it another year, and I'll give it special attention and plenty of fertilizer. [9]If we get figs next year, fine; if not, I'll cut it down.' "

Lk 21:1. As he stood in the Temple, he was watching the rich tossing their gifts into the collection box. [2]Then a poor widow came by and dropped in two small copper coins. [3]"Really," he remarked, "this poor widow has given more than all the rest of them combined. [4]For they have given a little of what they didn't need, but she, poor as she is, has given everything she has."

Jn 3:18. There is no eternal doom awaiting those who trust him to save them. But those who don't trust him have already been tried and condemned for not believing in the only Son of God. [19]Their sentence is based on this fact: that the Light from heaven came into the world, but they loved the darkness more than the Light, for their deeds were evil.

Jn 12:48. But all who reject me and my message will be judged at the Day of Judgment by the truths I have spoken.

Jn 15:22. They would not be guilty if I had not come and spoken to them. But now they have no excuse for their sin. [24]If I hadn't done such mighty miracles among them they would not be counted guilty. But as it is, they saw these miracles and yet they hated both of us—me and my Father.

Acts 17:30. God tolerated man's past ignorance about these things, but now he commands everyone to put away idols and worship only him. [31]For he has set a day for justly judging the world by the man he has appointed, and has pointed him out by bringing him back to life again.

Rom 12:3. As God's messenger I give each of you God's warning: Be honest in your estimate of yourselves, measuring your value by how much faith God has given you. [6]God has given each of us the ability to do certain things well. So if God has given you the ability to prophesy, then prophesy whenever you can—as often as your faith is strong enough to receive a message from God. [7]If your gift is that of serving others, serve them well. If you are a teacher, do a good job of teaching. [8]If you are a preacher, see to it that your sermons are strong and helpful. If God has given you money, be generous in helping others with it. If God has given you administrative ability and put you in charge of the work of others, take the responsibility seriously. Those who offer comfort to the sorrowing should do so with Christian cheer.

Eph 4:7. However, Christ has given each of us special abilities—whatever he wants us to have out of his rich storehouse of gifts.

1 Tim 6:20. Oh, Timothy, don't fail to do these things that God entrusted to you. Keep out of foolish arguments with those who boast of their "knowledge" and thus prove their lack of it.

See *Judgment, According to Opportunity.*

RESPONSIVE RELIGIOUS SERVICE
Deut 27:14–26.

REST Divine institutions for, see *Sabbath.* Days of, Ex 23:12; 34:21. The annual feasts added rest days, Lev 23:7, 8, 21, 25, 28, 30, 31, 35, 36; Num 28:18, 25, 26; 29:1, 7, 12, 35. Recommended by Jesus, Mk 6:31, 32, with Mt 8:18, 24.

1. The rest of salvation, given by Christ, Mt 11:28.

2. The rest of service, found by the believer, Mt 11:29, 30.

3. Eternal rest, 2 Thess 1:7; Rev 14:13.

HEAVENLY. Thess 1:7.

SPIRITUAL. Jer 6:16; Mt 11:29, 30; Heb 4:1–11. See *Peace, Spiritual.*

RESTITUTION To be made for injury to life, limb, or property, Ex 21:30–36; Lev 24:18; for theft, Ex 22:1–4; Prov 6:30, 31; Ezk 33:15; for dishonesty, Lev 6:2–5; Num 5:7; Job 20:18; Ezk 33:15; Lk 19:8.

RESTORATION Of the Jews, see *Israel.* Of all things, Acts 3:21, 22; Rev 21:1–5.

RESURRECTION Job 14:12. So a man lies down for the last time, and does not rise again until the heavens are no more; he shall not awaken, nor be roused from his sleep. [13]Oh, that you would hide me with the dead, and forget me there until your anger ends; but mark your calendar to think of me again! [14]If a man dies, shall he live again? This thought gives me hope, so that in all my anguish I eagerly await sweet death! [15]You would call and I would come, and you would reward all I do.

Job 19:25. But as for me, I know that my Redeemer lives, and that he will stand upon the earth at last. [26]And I know that after this body has decayed, this body shall see God! [27]Then he will be on *my* side! Yes, I shall see him, not as a stranger, but as a friend! What a glorious hope!

Ps 16:9. Heart, body, and soul are filled with joy. [10]For you will not leave me among the dead; you will not allow your beloved one to rot in the grave.

Ps 17:15. But as for me, my contentment is not in wealth but in seeing you and knowing all is well between us. And when I awake in heaven, I will be fully satisfied, for I will see you face to face.

Ps 49:15. But as for me, God will redeem my soul from the power of death, for he will receive me.

Isa 25:8. He will swallow up death forever. The Lord God will wipe away all tears and take away forever all insults and mockery against his land and people. The Lord has spoken—he will surely do it!

Isa 26:19. Yet we have this assurance: Those who belong to God shall live again. Their bodies shall rise again! Those who dwell in the dust shall awake and sing for joy! For God's light of life will fall like dew upon them!

Ezk 37:1, 2. The power of the Lord was upon me and I was carried away by the Spirit of the Lord to a valley full of old, dry bones that were scattered everywhere across the ground. He led me around among them, [3]and then he said to me: "Son of dust, can these bones become people again?" I replied, "Lord, you alone know the answer to that." [4]Then he told me to speak to the bones and say: "O dry bones, listen to the words of God, [5]for the Lord God says, See! I am going to make you live and breathe again! [6]I will replace the flesh and muscles on you and cover you with skin. I will put breath into you, and you shall live and know I am the Lord." [7]So I spoke these words from God, just as he told me to; and suddenly there was a rattling noise from all across the valley, and the bones of each body came together and attached to each other as they used to be. [8]Then, as I watched, the muscles and flesh formed over the bones, and skin covered them, but the bodies had no breath. [9]Then he told me to call to the wind and say: "The Lord God says: Come from the four winds, O Spirit, and breathe upon these slain bodies, that they may live again." [10]So I spoke to the winds as he commanded me and the bodies began breathing; they lived, and stood up—a very great army. [11]Then he told me what the vision meant: "These bones," he said, "represent all the people of Israel. They say: 'We have become a heap of dried-out bones—all hope is gone.' [12]But tell them, the Lord God says: My people, I will open your graves of exile and cause you to rise again and return to the land of Israel. [13]And, then at last, O my people, you will know I am the Lord. [14]I will put my Spirit into you, and you shall live and return home again to your own land. Then you will know that I, the Lord, have done just what I promised you."

Dan 12:2. And many of those whose bodies lie dead and buried will rise up, some to everlasting life and some to shame and everlasting contempt. [3]And those who are wise—the people of God—shall shine as brightly as the sun's brilliance, and those who turn many to righteousness will glitter like stars forever. [13]But go on now to the end of your life and your rest; for you will rise again and have your full share of those last days.

Hos 13:14. Shall I ransom him from hell? Shall I redeem him from Death? O Death, bring forth your terrors for his tasting! O Grave, demonstrate your plagues! For I will not relent!

Mt 22:23. But that same day some of the Sadducees, who say there is no resurrection after death, came to him and asked, [24]"Sir, Moses said that if a man died without children, his brother should marry the widow and their children would get all the dead man's property. [25]Well, we had among us a family of seven brothers. The first of these men married and then died, without children, so his widow became the second brother's wife. [26]This brother also died without children, and the wife was passed to the next brother, and so on until she had been the wife of each of them. [27]And then she also died. [28]So whose wife will she be in the resurrection? For she was the wife of all seven of them!" [29]But Jesus said, "Your error is caused by your ignorance of the Scriptures and of God's power! [30]For in the resurrection there is no marriage; everyone is as the angels in heaven. [31]But now, as to whether there is a resurrection of the dead—don't you ever read the Scriptures? Don't you realize that God was speaking directly to you when he said, [32]'I *am* the God of Abraham, Isaac, and Jacob'? So God is not the God of the dead, but of the *living.*" Mk 12:18–27; Lk 20:27–38.

Mt 24:31. And I shall send forth my angels with the sound of a mighty trumpet blast, and they shall gather my chosen ones from the farthest ends of the earth and heaven.

Mt 25:1. The Kingdom of Heaven can be illustrated by the story of ten bridesmaids who took their lamps and went to meet the bridegroom. [2-4]But only five of them were wise enough to fill their lamps with oil, while the other five were foolish and forgot. [5, 6]So, when the bridegroom was delayed, they lay down to rest until midnight when they were roused by the shout, "The bridegroom is coming! Come out and welcome him!" [7, 8]All the girls jumped up and trimmed their lamps. Then the five who hadn't any oil begged the others to share with them, for their lamps were going out. [9]But the others replied, "We haven't enough. Go instead to the shops and buy some for yourselves." [10]But while they were gone, the bridegroom came, and those who were ready went in with him to the marriage feast, and the door was locked. [11]Later, when the other five returned, they stood outside, calling, "Sir, open the door for us!" [12]But he called back, "Go away! It is too late!" [13]So stay awake and be prepared, for you do not know the date or moment of my return.

Mt 27:52. And tombs opened, and many godly men and women who had died came back to life again. [53]After Jesus' resurrection, they left the cemetery and went into Jerusalem, and appeared to many people there.

Lk 14:14. Then at the resurrection of the godly, God will reward you for inviting those who can't repay you.

Lk 20:35. But when those who are counted worthy of being raised from the dead get to heaven, they do not marry. [36]And they never die again; in these respects they are like angels, and are sons of God, for they are raised up in new life from the dead. [37, 38]But as to your real question—whether or not there is a resurrection—why, even the writings of Moses himself prove this. For when he describes how God appeared to him in the burning bush, he speaks of God as "the God of Abraham, the God of Isaac, and the God of Jacob." To say that the Lord *is* some person's God means that person is *alive,* not dead! So from God's point of view, all men are living. Mt 22:30–32; Mk 12:25–27.

Jn 5:21. He will even raise from the dead anyone he wants to, just as the Father does. [25]And I solemnly declare that the time is coming, in fact, it is here, when the dead shall hear my voice—the voice of the Son of God—and those who listen shall live. [28]Don't be so surprised! Indeed the time is coming when all the dead in their graves shall hear the voice of God's Son, [29]and shall rise again—those who have done good, to eternal life; and those who have continued in evil, to judgment.

Jn 6:39. This is the will of God, that I should not lose even one of all those he has given me, but that I should raise them to eternal life at the Last Day. [40]For it is my Father's will that everyone who sees his Son and believes on him should have eternal life—that I should raise him at the Last Day. [44]For no one can come to me unless the Father who sent me draws him to me, and at the Last Day I will cause all such to rise again from the dead. [54]But anyone who does eat my flesh and drink my blood has eternal life, and I will raise him at the Last Day.

Jn 11:23. Jesus told her, "Your brother will come back to life again." [24]"Yes," Martha said, "when everyone else does, on Resurrection Day." [25]Jesus told her, "I am the one who raises the dead and gives them life again. Anyone who believes in me, even though he dies like anyone else, shall live again."

Jn 14:19. In just a little while I will be gone from the world, but I will still be present with you. For I will live again—and you will too.

Acts 2:26. "No wonder my heart is filled with joy and my tongue shouts his praises! For I know all will be well with me in death— [27]you will not leave my soul in hell or let the body of your Holy Son decay. [28]You will give me back my life, and give me wonderful joy in your presence." [29]Dear brothers, think! David wasn't referring to himself when he spoke these words I have quoted, for he died and was buried, and his tomb is still here among us. [30]But he was a prophet, and knew God had promised with an unbreakable oath that one of David's own descendants would (be the Messiah and) sit on David's throne. [31]David was looking far into the future and predicting the Messiah's resurrection, and saying that the Messiah's soul would not be left in hell and his body would not decay.

Acts 4:1. While they were talking to the people, the chief priests, the captain of the Temple police, and some of the Sadducees came over to them, [2]very disturbed that Peter and John were claiming that Jesus had risen from the dead.

Acts 17:18. Their reaction, when he told them about Jesus and his resurrection, was, "He's a dreamer," or, "He's pushing some foreign religion." [32]When they heard Paul speak of the resurrection of a person who had been dead, some laughed, but others said, "We want to hear more about this later."

Acts 23:6. Then Paul thought of something! Part of the Council were Sadducees, and part were Pharisees! So he shouted, "Brothers, I am a Pharisee, as were all my ancestors! And I am being tried here today because I believe in the resurrection of the dead!" [8]For the Sadducees say there is no resurrection or angels or even eternal spirit within us, but the Pharisees believe in all of these.

Acts 24:14. But one thing I do confess, that I believe in the way of salvation, which they refer to as a sect; I follow that system of serving the God of our ancestors; I firmly believe in the Jewish law and everything written in the books of prophecy; [15]and I believe, just as these men do, that there will be a resurrection of both the righteous and ungodly.

Acts 26:6. But the real reason behind their accusations is something else—it is because I am looking forward to the fulfillment of God's promise made to our ancestors. [7]The twelve tribes of Israel strive night and day to attain this same hope I have! Yet, O King, for me it is a crime they say! [8]But is it a crime to believe in the resurrection of the dead? Does it seem incredible to you that God can bring men back to life again?

Rom 4:16. So God's blessings are given to us by faith, as a free gift; we are certain to get them whether or not we follow Jewish customs if we have faith like Abraham's, for Abraham is the father of us all when it comes to these matters of faith. [17]That is what the Scriptures mean when they say that God made Abraham the father of many nations. God will accept all people in every nation who trust God as Abraham did. And this promise is from God himself, who makes the dead live again and speaks of future events with as much certainty as though they were already past. [18]So, when God told Abraham that he would give him a son who would have many descendants and become a great nation, Abraham believed God even though such a promise just couldn't come to pass! [19]And because his faith was strong, he didn't worry about the fact that he was too old to be a father, at the age of one hundred, and that Sarah his wife, at ninety, was also much too old to have a baby. [20]But Abraham never doubted. He believed God, for his faith and trust grew ever stronger, and he praised God for this blessing even before it happened. [21]He was completely sure that God was well able to do anything he promised.

Rom 8:10. Yet, even though Christ lives within you, your body will die because of sin; but your spirit will live, for Christ has pardoned it. [11]And if the Spirit of God, who raised up Jesus from the dead, lives in you, he will make your dying bodies live again after you die, by means of this same Holy Spirit living within you. [19]For all creation is waiting patiently and hopefully for that future day when God will resurrect his children. [21]And the world around us will share in the glorious freedom from sin which God's children enjoy. [22]For we know that even the things of nature, like animals and plants, suffer in sickness and death as they await this great event. [23]And even we Christians, although we have the Holy Spirit within us as a foretaste of future glory, also groan to be released from pain and suffering. We, too, wait anxiously for that day when God will give us our full rights as his children, including the new bodies he has promised us—bodies that will never be sick again and will never die.

1 Cor 6:14. And God is going to raise our bodies from the dead by his power just as he raised up the Lord Jesus Christ.

1 Cor 15:12. But tell me this! Since you believe that *Christ* rose from the dead, why are some of you saying that dead people will never come back to life again? [13]For if there is no resurrection of the dead, then Christ must still be dead. [14]And if he is still dead, then all our preaching is useless and your trust in God is empty, worthless, hopeless; [15]and we apostles are all liars because we have said that God raised Christ from the grave, and of course that isn't true if the dead do not come back to life again. [16]If they don't, then Christ is still dead, [17]and you are very foolish to keep on trusting God to save you, and you are still under condemnation for your sins; [18]in that case all Christians who have died are lost! [19]And if being a Christian is of value to us only now in this life, we are the most miserable of creatures. [20]But the fact is that Christ did actually rise from the dead, and has become the first of millions who will come back to life again some day. [21]Death came into the world because of what one man (Adam) did, and it is because of what this other man (Christ) has done that now there is the resurrection from the dead. [22]Everyone dies because all of us are related to Adam, being members of his sinful race, and wherever there is sin, death results. But all who are related to Christ will rise again. [23]Each, however, in his own turn: Christ rose first; then when Christ comes back, all his people will become alive again. [24]After that the end will come when he will turn the kingdom over to God the Father, having put down all enemies of every kind. [25]For Christ will be King until he has defeated all his enemies, [26]including the last enemy—death. This too must be defeated and ended. [27]For the rule and authority over all things has been given to Christ by his Father; except, of course, Christ does not rule over the Father himself, who gave him this power to rule. [28]When Christ has finally won the battle against all his enemies, then he, the Son of God, will put himself also under his Father's orders, so that God who has given him the victory over everything else will be utterly supreme. [29]If the dead will not come back to life again, then what point is there in people being baptized for those who are gone? Why do it unless you believe that the dead will some day rise again? [30]And why should we ourselves be continually risking our lives, facing death hour by hour? [31]For it is a fact

that I face death daily; that is as true as my pride in your growth in the Lord. 32And what value was there in fighting wild beasts—those men of Ephesus—if it was only for what I gain in this life down here? If we will never live again after we die, then we might as well go and have ourselves a good time: let us eat, drink, and be merry. What's the difference? For tomorrow we die, and that ends everything! 35But someone may ask, "How will the dead be brought back to life again? What kind of bodies will they have?" 36What a foolish question! You will find the answer in your own garden! When you put a seed into the ground it doesn't grow into a plant unless it "dies" first. 37And when the green shoot comes up out of the seed, it is very different from the seed you first planted. For all you put into the ground is a dry little seed of wheat, or whatever it is you are planting, 38then God gives it a beautiful new body—just the kind he wants it to have; a different kind of plant grows from each kind of seed. 39And just as there are different kinds of seeds and plants, so also there are different kinds of flesh. Humans, animals, fish, and birds are all different. 40The angels in heaven have bodies far different from ours, and the beauty and the glory of their bodies is different from the beauty and the glory of ours. 41The sun has one kind of glory while the moon and stars have another kind. And the stars differ from each other in their beauty and brightness. 42In the same way, our earthly bodies which die and decay are different from the bodies we shall have when we come back to life again, for they will never die. 43The bodies we have now embarrass us for they become sick and die; but they will be full of glory when we come back to life again. Yes, they are weak, dying bodies now, but when we live again they will be full of strength. 44They are just human bodies at death, but when they come back to life they will be superhuman bodies. For just as there are natural, human bodies, there are also supernatural, spiritual bodies. 45The Scriptures tell us that the first man, Adam, was given a natural, human body but Christ is more than that, for he was life-giving Spirit. 46First, then, we have these human bodies and later on God gives us spiritual, heavenly bodies. 47Adam was made from the dust of the earth, but Christ came from heaven above. 48Every human being has a body just like Adam's, made of dust, but all who become Christ's will have the same kind of body as his—a body from heaven. 49Just as each of us now has a body like Adam's, so we shall some day have a body like Christ's. 50I tell you this, my brothers: an earthly body made of flesh and blood cannot get into God's kingdom. These perishable bodies of ours are not the right kind to live forever. 51But I am telling you this strange and wonderful secret: we shall not all die, but we shall all be given new bodies! 52It will all happen in a moment, in the twinkling of an eye, when the last trumpet is blown. For there will be a trumpet blast from the sky and all the Christians who have died will suddenly become alive, with new bodies that will never, never die; and then we who are still alive shall suddenly have new bodies too. 53For our earthly bodies, the ones we have now that can die, must be transformed into heavenly bodies that cannot perish but will live forever. 54When this happens, then at last this Scripture will come true—"Death is swallowed up in victory." 55, 56O death, where then your victory? Where then your sting? For sin—the sting that causes death—will all be gone; and the law, which reveals our sins, will no longer be our judge. 57How we thank God for all of this! It is he who makes us victorious through Jesus Christ our Lord!

2 Cor 4:14. We know that the same God who brought the Lord Jesus back from death will also bring us back to life again with Jesus, and present us to him along with you.

2 Cor 5:1. For we know that when this tent we live in now is taken down—when we die and leave these bodies—we will have wonderful new bodies in heaven, homes that will be ours forevermore, made for us by God himself, and not by human hands. 2How weary we grow of our present bodies. That is why we look forward eagerly to the day when we shall have heavenly bodies which we shall put on like new clothes. 3For we shall not be merely spirits without bodies. 4These earthly bodies make us groan and sigh, but we wouldn't like to think of dying and having no bodies at all. We want to slip into our new bodies so that these dying bodies will, as it were, be swallowed up by everlasting life. 5This is what God has prepared for us and, as a guarantee, he has given us his Holy Spirit.

Phil 3:10. Now I have given up everything else—I have found it to be the only way to really know Christ and to experience the mighty power that brought him back to life again, and to find out what it means to suffer and to die with him. [Rom 6:5.] 11So, whatever it takes, I will be one who lives in the fresh newness of life of those who are alive from the dead. 21When he comes back he will take these dying bodies of ours and change them into glorious bodies like his own, using the same mighty power that he will use to conquer all else everywhere.

1 Thess 4:14. For since we believe that Jesus died and then came back to life again, we can also believe that when Jesus returns, God will bring back with him all the Christians who have died. 16For the Lord himself will come down from heaven with a mighty shout and with the soul-stirring cry of the archangel and the great trumpet-call of God. And the believers who are dead will be the first to rise to meet the Lord.

2 Tim 1:10. And now he has made all of this plain to us by the coming of our Savior Jesus Christ, who broke the power of death and showed us the way of everlasting life through trusting him.

2 Tim 2:18. They have left the path of truth, preaching the lie that the resurrection of the dead has already occurred; and they have weakened the faith of some who believe them.

Heb 6:2. You don't need further instruction

about baptism and spiritual gifts and the resurrection of the dead and eternal judgment.

Heb 11:19. He believed that if Isaac died God would bring him back to life again; and that is just about what happened, for as far as Abraham was concerned, Isaac was doomed to death, but he came back again alive! [35]And some women, through faith, received their loved ones back again from death. But others trusted God and were beaten to death, preferring to die rather than turn from God and be free—trusting that they would rise to a better life afterwards.

Rev 1:18. Though I am the First and Last, the Living One who died, who is now alive forevermore, who has the keys of hell and death—don't be afraid!

Rev 20:4. Then I saw thrones, and sitting on them were those who had been given the right to judge. And I saw the souls of those who had been beheaded for their testimony about Jesus, for proclaiming the Word of God, and who had not worshiped the Creature or his statue, nor accepted his mark on their foreheads or their hands. They had come to life again and now they reigned with Christ for a thousand years. [5]This is the First Resurrection. (The rest of the dead did not come back to life until the thousand years had ended.) [6]Blessed and holy are those who share in the First Resurrection. For them the Second Death holds no terrors, for they will be priests of God and of Christ, and shall reign with him a thousand years. [13]The oceans surrendered the bodies buried in them; and the earth and the underworld gave up the dead in them. Each was judged according to his deeds.

See *Dead, Raised; Resuscitation.*

OF JESUS. See *Jesus.*

FIGURATIVE. Of regeneration, Rom 6:4; Eph 2:1, 5, 6; Col 2:12; 3:1.

TYPIFIED. Isaac, Gen 22:13, with Heb 11:19. Jonah, Jon 2:10, with Mt 12:39, 40.

RESUSCITATION OR REVIVIFICATION The various individuals miraculously restored to life in the Bible are better spoken of as resuscitated than resurrected. In this category are: the widow's son in Zarephath, restored to life by Elijah, 1 Kgs 17:17–24; the Shunemmite's son, restored by Elisha, 2 Kgs 4:18–37; 2 Kgs 8:1–5; the man who was restored to life in the tomb of Elisha, 2 Kgs 13:21; the son of the widow of Nain, restored by Christ, Lk 7:11–16; Jairus' daughter, restored by Christ, Mt 9:18, 19, 23–26; Mk 5:22–24, 35–43; Lk 8:41, 42, 49–56; Lazarus, restored by Christ, Jn 11:1–45; Dorcas, restored by Peter, Acts 9:36–42; Eutychus, restored by Paul, Acts 20:9–12.

See *Resurrection.*

RETALIATION Ex 21:23. But if any harm comes to the woman and she dies, he shall be executed. [24]If her eye is injured, injure his; if her tooth is knocked out, knock out his; and so on—hand for hand, foot for foot, [25]burn for burn, wound for wound, lash for lash.

Lev 19:18. Don't seek vengeance. Don't bear a grudge; but love your neighbor as yourself, for I am Jehovah.

Lev 24:17. Also, all murderers must be executed. [18]Anyone who kills an animal (that isn't his) shall replace it. [19]The penalty for injuring anyone is to be injured in exactly the same way: [20]fracture for fracture, eye for eye, tooth for tooth. Whatever anyone does to another shall be done to him. [21]To repeat, whoever kills an animal must replace it, and whoever kills a man must die. [22]You shall have the same law for the foreigner as for the homeborn citizen, for I am Jehovah your God.

Deut 19:19. His penalty shall be the punishment he thought the other man would get. In this way you will purge out evil from among you. [20]Then those who hear about it will be afraid to tell lies on the witness stand. [21]You shall not show pity to a false witness. Life for life, eye for eye, tooth for tooth, hand for hand, foot for foot; this is your rule in such cases.

Ps 10:2. Come and deal with all these proud and wicked men who viciously persecute the poor. Pour upon these men the evil they planned for others!

Prov 20:22. Don't repay evil for evil. Wait for the Lord to handle the matter.

Prov 24:29. Don't say, "Now I can pay him back for all his meanness to me!"

Prov 26:27. The man who sets a trap for others will get caught in it himself. Roll a boulder down on someone, and it will roll back and crush you.

Isa 33:1. Woe to you, Assyrians, who have destroyed everything around you but have never felt destruction for yourselves. You expect others to respect their promises to you, while you betray them! Now you, too, will be betrayed and destroyed.

Mt 5:38. The law of Moses says, "If a man gouges out another's eye, he must pay with his own eye. If a tooth gets knocked out, knock out the tooth of the one who did it." [39]But I say: Don't resist violence! If you are slapped on one cheek, turn the other too. [40]If you are ordered to court, and your shirt is taken from you, give your coat too. [41]If the military demand that you carry their gear for a mile, carry it two. [42]Give to those who ask, and don't turn away from those who want to borrow. [43]There is a saying, "Love your *friends* and hate your enemies." [44]But I say: Love your *enemies!* Pray for those who *persecute* you!

Mt 7:1. Don't criticize, and then you won't be criticized. [2]For others will treat you as you treat them.

Lk 9:52. One day he sent messengers ahead to reserve rooms for them in a Samaritan village. [53]But they were turned away! The people of the village refused to have anything to do with them because they were headed for Jerusalem. [54]When word came back of what had happened, James and John said to Jesus, "Master, shall we order fire down from heaven to burn them up?" [55]But Jesus turned and rebuked them, [56]and they went on to another village.

Rom 12:17. Never pay back evil for evil. Do things in such a way that everyone can see you are honest clear through. [19]Dear friends, never avenge yourselves. Leave that to God, for he has said that he will repay those who deserve it. (Don't take the law into your own hands.)

1 Cor 6:7. To have such lawsuits at all is a real defeat for you as Christians. Why not just accept mistreatment and leave it at that? It would be far more honoring to the Lord to let yourselves be cheated. [8]But, instead, you yourselves are the ones who do wrong, cheating others, even your own brothers.

1 Thess 5:15. See that no one pays back evil for evil, but always try to do good to each other and to everyone else.

1 Pet 3:9. Don't repay evil for evil. Don't snap back at those who say unkind things about you. Instead, pray for God's help for them, for we are to be kind to others, and God will bless us for it.

See *Avenger; Hatred; Malice; Revenge.*

INSTANCES OF. Israelites on the Amalekites, Deut 25:17–19, with 1 Sam 15:1–9. Gideon on the leaders of Succoth, Judg 8:7, 13–16; kings of Midian, Judg 8:18–21; Penuel, Judg 8:8, 17. Joab on Abner, 2 Sam 3:27, 30. David upon Michal, 2 Sam 6:21–23; on Joab, 1 Kgs 2:5, 6; Shime-i, 1 Kgs 2:8, 9. Jews on the Persians, Esther 9.

RETRIBUTION See *Sin, Punishment of.*

REU Son of Peleg and ancestor of Abraham, Gen 11:18–21; 1 Chron 1:24–27. Ancestor of Jesus, Lk 3:23–38.

REUBEN Son of Jacob, Gen 29:32; 1 Chron 2:1. Brings mandrakes to his mother, Gen 30:14. Commits incest with one of his father's wives, and, as a result, forfeits the birthright, Gen 35:22; 49:4; 1 Chron 5:1. Adroitly seeks to save Joseph from the conspiracy of his brothers, Gen 37:21–30; 42:22. Offers to become surety for Benjamin, Gen 42:37. Jacob's prophetic benediction upon, Gen 49:3,4. His children, Gen 46:8–14; Ex 6:14; 1 Chron 5:3–6; Num 16:1.

REUBENITES The descendants of Reuben. Military enrollment of, at Sinai, Num 1:20–46; in Moab, Num 26:5–11. Place of, in camp and march, Num 2:3–31. Flag of, Num 10:18. Have their inheritance east of the Jordan, Num 32; Deut 3:1–20; Josh 13:15–23; 18:7. Assist the other tribes in conquest of the region west of the Jordan, Josh 1:12–18; 22:1–6. Unite with the tribes of Gad and Manasseh in building a monument to signify the unity of the tribes on the east of the Jordan with the tribes on the west of the river; monument misunderstood; the explanation and reconciliation, Josh 22:10–34. Reproached by Deborah, Judg 5:15, 16. Taken captive into Assyria, 2 Kgs 15:29; 1 Chron 5:26.

See *Israel.*

REUEL 1. Son of Esau, Gen 36:4,10,13,14,17; 1 Chron 1:35, 37.

2. Father-in-law of Moses, Ex 2:18; Num 10:29. Called also *Jethro,* see *Jethro.*

3. Father of Eliasaph, Num 2:3–31. Called *Deuel,* Num 1:14; 7:42–47; 10:20.

4. A Benjaminite, 1 Chron 9:7, 8.

REUMAH A concubine of Nahor, Gen 22:24.

REVELATION God reveals himself to Moses, Ex 3:1–6, 14; 6:1–3. The law is revealed, Ex chapters 20–35; Lev chapters 1–7; the design of the Temple, 1 Chron 28:11–19. The sonship of Jesus, Mt 3:17; 16:17; 17:5.

Revelation of the righteous judgment of God, Rom 2:5; of the mystery, Rom 16:25–27; of the Lord to Paul, 2 Cor 12:1,7; of the gospel to Paul, Gal 2:2; of who Christ is, Eph 1:17; the mystery shown to Paul by revelation, Eph 3:2,3; the future revelation of Jesus Christ, 1 Pet 1:13; the Revelation of Jesus Christ, Rev 1:1.

Those things which are revealed belong to us and to our children forever, Deut 29:29; the Lord revealed himself to Samuel, 1 Sam 3:21; truth revealed to Isaiah, Isa 22:14; the glory of the Lord shall be revealed, Isa 40:5; the power of the Lord revealed, Isa 53:1; secret revealed to Daniel, Dan 2:19,22, 28–30, by God, the Revealer of mysteries, Dan 2:47; a revelation to Daniel, Dan 10:1.

Everything secret to be revealed, Mt 10:26; God reveals the truth to children, Mt 11:25; revelation to Simeon that he would see Christ, Lk 2:26; the day when the Son of man is revealed, Lk 17:30; the righteousness of God revealed, Rom 1:17; the anger of God revealed, Rom 1:18; the glory to be revealed in us, Rom 8:18; God has revealed them to us by his Spirit, 1 Cor 2:10; every man's work revealed by fire, 1 Cor 3:13; the faith revealed, Gal 3:23; the mystery of Christ revealed, Eph 3:2–5; the Lord Jesus revealed from heaven, 2 Thess 1:7; the man of rebellion revealed, 2 Thess 2:3, 6, 8; salvation ready to be revealed, 1 Pet 5:1.

See *Prophecy; Prophet; Word of God, Inspiration of.*

REVENGE Forbidden, Lev 19:18; Prov 20:22; 24:28, 29; Rom 12:17, 19; 1 Thess 5:15; 1 Pet 3:9. Jesus an example of forbearing, 1 Pet 2:23. Rebuked by Jesus, Lk 9:54, 55. Inconsistent with a Christian spirit, Lk 9:55. Punishment for, Ezk 25:15–17; Amos 1:11, 12.

EXEMPLIFIED. By Simeon and Levi, Gen 34:25. By Samson, Judg 15:7, 8; 16:28–30. By Joab, 2 Sam 3:27. By Absalom, 2 Sam 13:21–28. By Jezebel, 1 Kgs 19:2. By Ahab, 1 Kgs 22:27. By Haman, Esther 3:8–15. By the Edomites, Ezk 25:12. By the Philistines, Ezk 25:15. By Herodias, Mk 6:19–24. By James and John, Lk 9:54. By the chief priests, Acts 5:33. By the Jews, Acts 7:54–59; 23:12, 13.

See *Retaliation; Vengeance.*

REVENUE Solomon's, 2 Chron 9:13, 14.

See *Tax.*

REVERENCE For God, Gen 17:2–4; Ex 3:5; 19:16–24; 34:29–35; Isa 45:9. See *Fear of God.* For God's house, Lev 19:30; 26:2. For ministers, 1 Sam 16:4; Acts 28:10; 1 Cor 16:18; Phil 2:29; 1 Thess 5:12, 13; 1 Tim 5:17; Heb 13:7, 17. See *Minister.* For kings and government, 1 Sam 24:6; 26:9, 11; 2 Sam 1:14; 16:21; Eccl 10:20; 1 Pet 2:17. See *Ruler.* For judges, Ex 22:28. See *Ruler.* For parents, Ex

20:12; Lev 19:1, 2; Isa 45:10. See *Parents*. For the aged, Lev 19:32; Job 32:4–7.

REVILING Of Jesus, Mt 27:39–44.

See *Mocking*.

REVIVAL RELIGIOUS. Zech 8:20–23. Prayer for, Hab 3:2. Prophecies concerning, Isa 32:15; Joel 2:28; Mic 4:1–8; Hab 3:2.

INSTANCES OF. Under Joshua, Josh 5:2–9; Samuel, 1 Sam 7:1–6; Elijah, 1 Kgs 18:17–40; Jehoash and Jehoiada, 2 Kgs chapters 11; 12; 2 Chron chapters 23; 24; Hezekiah, 2 Kgs 18:1–7; 2 Chron chapters 29–31; Josiah, 2 Kgs chapters 22; 23; 2 Chron chapters 34; 35; Asa, 2 Chron 14:2–5; 15:1–14; Manasseh, 2 Chron 33:12–19. In Nineveh, Jon 3:4–10. At Pentecost, and post-pentecostal times, Acts 2:1–42, 46, 47; 4:4; 5:15; 6:7; 9:35; 11:20, 21; 12:24; 14:1; 19:17–20.

See *Religion*.

REVOLT Of the ten tribes, 1 Kgs 12:1–24.

See *Rebellion*.

REWARD A MOTIVE FOR FAITHFULNESS. Ex 20:6. But I lavish my love upon thousands of those who love me and obey my commandments. [12]Honor your father and mother, that you may have a long, good life in the land the Lord your God will give you. Eph 6:1–3.

Lev 25:18. Obey my laws if you want to live safely in the land. [19]When you obey, the land will yield bumper crops and you can eat your fill in safety.

Lev 26:3. If you obey all of my commandments, [4, 5]I will give you regular rains, and the land will yield bumper crops, and the trees will be loaded with fruit long after the normal time! And grapes will still be ripening when sowing time comes again. You shall eat your fill, and live safely in the land, [6]for I will give you peace, and you will go to sleep without fear. I will chase away the dangerous animals. [7]You will chase your enemies; they will die beneath your swords. [8]Five of you will chase a hundred, and a hundred of you, ten thousand! You will defeat all of your enemies. [9]I will look after you, and multiply you, and fulfill my covenant with you. [10]You will have such a surplus of crops that you won't know what to do with them when the new harvest is ready! [11]And I will live among you, and not despise you. [12]I will walk among you and be your God, and you shall be my people. [13]For I am the Lord your God who brought you out of the land of Egypt, with the intention that you be slaves no longer; I have broken your chains and will make you walk with dignity. *vs.* 14–39.

40, 41. But at last they shall confess their sins and their fathers' sins of treachery against me. (Because they were against me, I was against them, and brought them into the land of their enemies.) When at last their evil hearts are humbled and they accept the punishment I send them for their sins, [42]then I will remember again my promises to Abraham, Isaac, and Jacob, and I will remember the land (and its desolation). [43]For the land shall enjoy its Sabbaths as it lies desolate. But then at last they shall accept their punishment for rejecting my laws and for despising my rule. [44]But despite all they have done, I will not utterly destroy them and my covenant with them, for I am Jehovah their God. [45]For their sakes I will remember my promises to their ancestors, to be their God. For I brought their forefathers out of Egypt as all the nations watched in wonder. I am Jehovah.

Deut 4:40. You must obey these laws that I will tell you today, so that all will be well with you and your children, and so that you will live forever in the land the Lord your God is giving you.

Deut 6:3. Therefore, O Israel, listen closely to each command and be careful to obey it, so that all will go well with you, and so that you will have many children. If you obey these commands you will become a great nation in a glorious land "flowing with milk and honey," even as the God of your fathers promised you. *v.* 18.

Deut 11:13. And if you will carefully obey all of his commandments that I am going to give you today, and if you will love the Lord your God with all your hearts and souls, and will worship him, [14]then he will continue to send both the early and late rains that will produce wonderful crops of grain, grapes for your wine, and olive oil. [15]He will give you lush pastureland for your cattle to graze in, and you yourselves shall have plenty to eat and be fully content. [16]But beware that your hearts do not turn from God to worship other gods. [18]So keep these commandments carefully in mind. Tie them to your hand to remind you to obey them, and tie them to your forehead between your eyes! [19]Teach them to your children. Talk about them when you are sitting at home, when you are out walking, at bed-time, and before breakfast! [20]Write them upon the doors of your houses and upon your gates, [21]so that as long as there is sky above the earth, you and your children will enjoy the good life awaiting you in the land the Lord has promised you. [26]I am giving you the choice today between God's blessing or God's curse! [27]There will be blessing if you obey the commandments of the Lord your God which I am giving you today, [28]and a curse if you refuse them and worship the gods of these other nations. [29]When the Lord your God brings you into the land to possess it, a blessing shall be proclaimed from Mount Gerizim, and a curse from Mount Ebal! chapter 27:12–26; Josh 8:33.

Deut 15:9. Beware! Don't refuse a loan because the year of debt cancellation is close at hand! If you refuse to make the loan and the needy man cries out to the Lord, it will be counted against you as a sin. [10]You must lend him what he needs, and don't moan about it either! For the Lord will prosper you in everything you do because of this! [11]There will always be some among you who are poor; that is why this commandment is necessary. You must lend to them liberally.

Deut 22:7. Let her go, and take only the young. The Lord will bless you for it.

Deut 24:19. If, when reaping your harvest, you forget to bring in a sheaf from the field, don't go back after it. Leave it for the migrants, orphans, and widows; then the Lord your God will bless and prosper all you do.

Deut 25:13–15. In all your transactions you must use accurate scales and honest measurements, so that you will have a long, good life in the land the Lord your God is giving you.

Isa 1:16. Oh, wash yourselves! Be clean! Let me no longer see you doing all these wicked things; quit your evil ways. [17]Learn to do good, to be fair and to help the poor, the fatherless, and widows. [18]Come, let's talk this over! says the Lord; no matter how deep the stain of your sins, I can take it out and make you as clean as freshly fallen snow. Even if you are stained as red as crimson, I can make you white as wool! [19]If you will only let me help you, if you will only obey, then I will make you rich! [20]But if you keep on turning your backs and refusing to listen to me, you will be killed by your enemies; I, the Lord, have spoken.

Isa 3:10. But all is well for the godly man. Tell him, "What a reward you are going to get!"

Isa 40:10. Yes, the Lord God is coming with mighty power; he will rule with awesome strength. See, his reward is with him, to each as he has done. [11]He will feed his flock like a shepherd; he will carry the lambs in his arms and gently lead the ewes with young.

Jer 22:3. The Lord says: Be fair-minded. Do what is right! Help those in need of justice! Quit your evil deeds! Protect the rights of aliens and immigrants, orphans and widows; stop murdering the innocent! [4]If you put an end to all these terrible deeds you are doing, then I will deliver this nation and once more give kings to sit on David's throne, and there shall be prosperity for all. chapter 17: 24–26.

Mt 10:32. If anyone publicly acknowledges me as his friend, I will openly acknowledge him as my friend before my Father in heaven. Lk 12:8.

Mt 16:24. Then Jesus said to the disciples, "If anyone wants to be a follower of mine, let him deny himself and take up his cross and follow me. [25]For anyone who keeps his life for himself shall lose it; and anyone who loses his life for me shall find it again. [26]What profit is there if you gain the whole world—and lose eternal life? What can be compared with the value of eternal life? [27]For I, the Son of Mankind, shall come with my angels in the glory of my Father and judge each person according to his deeds.

Mt 20:1. Here is another illustration of the Kingdom of Heaven. "The owner of an estate went out early one morning to hire workers for his harvest field. [2]He agreed to pay them $20 a day and sent them out to work. [3]A couple of hours later he was passing a hiring hall and saw some men standing around waiting for jobs, [4]so he sent them also into his fields, telling them he would pay them whatever was right at the end of the day. [5]At noon and again at three o'clock in the afternoon he did the same thing. [6]At five o'clock that evening he was in town again and saw some more men standing around and asked them, 'Why haven't you been working today?' [7]'Because no one hired us,' they replied. 'Then go on out and join the others in my fields,' he told them. [8]That evening he told the paymaster to call the men in and pay them, beginning with the last men first. [9]When the men hired at five o'clock were paid, each received $20. [10]So when the men hired earlier came to get theirs, they assumed they would receive much more. But they, too, were paid $20. [11, 12]They protested, 'Those fellows worked only one hour, and yet you've paid them just as much as those of us who worked all day in the scorching heat.' [13]'Friend,' he answered one of them, 'I did you no wrong! Didn't you agree to work all day for $20? [14]Take it and go. It is my desire to pay all the same; [15]is it against the law to give away my money if I want to? Should you be angry because I am kind?' [16]And so it is that the last shall be first, and the first, last."

Mt 25:34. Then I, the King, shall say to those at my right, "Come, blessed of my Father, into the Kingdom prepared for you from the founding of the world. [35]For I was hungry and you fed me; I was thirsty and you gave me water; I was a stranger and you invited me into your homes; [36]naked and you clothed me; sick and in prison, and you visited me." [37]Then these righteous ones will reply, "Sir, when did we ever see you hungry and feed you? Or thirsty and give you anything to drink? [38]Or a stranger, and help you? Or naked, and clothe you? [39]When did we ever see you sick or in prison, and visit you?" [40]And I, the King, will tell them, "When you did it to these my brothers you were doing it to me!" [41]Then I will turn to those on my left and say, "Away with you, you cursed ones, into the eternal fire prepared for the devil and his demons. [42]For I was hungry and you wouldn't feed me; thirsty, and you wouldn't give me anything to drink; [43]a stranger, and you refused me hospitality; naked, and you wouldn't clothe me; sick, and in prison, and you didn't visit me." [44]Then they will reply, "Lord, when did we ever see you hungry or thirsty or a stranger or naked or sick or in prison, and not help you?" [45]And I will answer, "When you refused to help the least of these my brothers, you were refusing help to me." [46]And they shall go away into eternal punishment; but the righteous into everlasting life.

Mk 10:21. Jesus felt genuine love for this man as he looked at him. "You lack only one thing," he told him; "go and sell all you have and give the money to the poor—and you shall have treasure in heaven—and come, follow me."

Mk 13:13. And everyone will hate you because you are mine. But all who endure to the end without renouncing me shall be saved.

Lk 6:22. What happiness it is when others hate you and exclude you and insult you and smear your name because you are mine! [23]When that happens, rejoice! Yes, leap for joy! For you will have a great reward awaiting you in heaven. And you will be in good company—the ancient prophets were treated that way too!

35. Love your *enemies!* Do good to *them!* Lend

to *them!* And don't be concerned about the fact that they won't repay. Then your reward from heaven will be very great, and you will truly be acting as sons of God: for he is kind to the *unthankful* and to those who are *very wicked.*

Acts 26:18. To open their eyes to their true condition so that they may repent and live in the light of God instead of in Satan's darkness, so that they may receive forgiveness for their sins and God's inheritance along with all people everywhere whose sins are cleansed away, who are set apart by faith in me.

Rom 2:10. But there will be glory and honor and peace from God for all who obey him, whether they are Jews or Gentiles.

1 Cor 3:8. Apollos and I are working as a team, with the same aim, though each of us will be rewarded for his own hard work.

Heb 10:34. You suffered with those thrown into jail, and you were actually joyful when all you owned was taken from you, knowing that better things were awaiting you in heaven, things that would be yours forever.

36. You need to keep on patiently doing God's will if you want him to do for you all that he has promised.

Heb 11:26. He thought that it was better to suffer for the promised Christ than to own all the treasures of Egypt, for he was looking forward to the great reward that God would give him.

Heb 12:1. Since we have such a huge crowd of men of faith watching us from the grandstands, let us strip off anything that slows us down or holds us back, and especially those sins that wrap themselves so tightly around our feet and trip us up; and let us run with patience the particular race that God has set before us. [2]Keep your eyes on Jesus, our leader and instructor. He was willing to die a shameful death on the cross because of the joy he knew would be his afterwards; and now he sits in the place of honor by the throne of God.

28. Since we have a kingdom nothing can destroy, let us please God by serving him with thankful hearts, and with holy fear and awe.

1 Pet 3:9. Don't repay evil for evil. Don't snap back at those who say unkind things about you. Instead, pray for God's help for them, for we are to be kind to others, and God will bless us for it. [10]If you want a happy, good life, keep control of your tongue, and guard your lips from telling lies. [11]Turn away from evil and do good. Try to live in peace even if you must run after it to catch and hold it! [12]For the Lord is watching his children, listening to their prayers; but the Lord's face is hard against those who do evil.

2 Pet 1:10. So, dear brothers, work hard to prove that you really are among those God has called and chosen, and then you will never stumble or fall away. [11]And God will open wide the gates of heaven for you to enter into the eternal kingdom of our Lord and Savior Jesus Christ.

Rev 2:10. Stop being afraid of what you are about to suffer. . . . You will be persecuted for "ten days." Remain faithful even when facing death and I will give you the crown of life—an unending, glorious future.

17. Let everyone who can hear, listen to what the Spirit is saying to the churches: Every one who is victorious shall eat of the hidden manna, the secret nourishment from heaven; and I will give to each a white stone, and on the stone will be engraved a new name that no one else knows except the one receiving it.

25. Only hold tightly to what you have until I come. [26]To every one who overcomes—who to the very end keeps on doing things that please me—I will give power over the nations. [27]You will rule them with a rod of iron just as my Father gave me the authority to rule them; they will be shattered like a pot of clay that is broken into tiny pieces. [28]And I will give you the Morning Star!

Rev 7:14. "These are the ones coming out of the Great Tribulation," he said; "they washed their robes and whitened them by the blood of the Lamb. [15]That is why they are here before the throne of God, serving him day and night in his temple. The one sitting on the throne will shelter them; [16]they will never be hungry again, nor thirsty, and they will be fully protected from the scorching noontime heat. [17]For the Lamb standing in front of the throne will feed them and be their Shepherd and lead them to the springs of the Water of Life. And God will wipe their tears away."

Rev. 22:12. See, I am coming soon, and my reward is with me, to repay everyone according to the deeds he has done.

See *Blessing, Contingent on Obedience; Punishment; Righteous, Promises to; Sin, Separates from God; Wicked, Punishment of.*

REZEPH A city destroyed by the Assyrians, 2 Kgs 19:12; Isa 37:12.

REZIN 1. A king of Syria who harassed the kingdom of Judah, 2 Kgs 15:37; 16:5–9. Prophecy against, Isa 7:1–9; 8:4–8; 9:11, 12.

2. A returned Babylonian captive, Ezra 2:43–54; Neh 7:46–56.

REZON King of Damascus. An adversary of Solomon, 1 Kgs 11:23–25.

RHEGIUM A city of Italy. Touched by Paul on the way to Rome, Acts 28:13.

RHESA An ancestor of Jesus, Lk 3:23–38.

RHODA A Christian girl in Jerusalem, Acts 12:13.

RHODES An island, Ezk 27:15. Visited by Paul, Acts 21:1.

RIBAI A Benjaminite. Father of Ittai, 2 Sam 23:24–39; 1 Chron 11:26–47.

RIBLAH A border town of Canaan, Num 34: 10, 11. King Jehoahaz jailed in, by Pharaoh, 2 Kgs 23:33. Headquarters of Nebuchadnezzar in siege of Jerusalem, 2 Kgs 25:6, 20, 21; Jer 39:5, 6; 52:9, 26.

RICH, THE Neh 5:1. About this time there was a great outcry of protest from parents against some of the rich Jews who were profiteering on them. [2-4]What was happening was that families who ran out of money for food had to sell their children or mortgage their fields, vineyards, and homes to these rich men; and some couldn't even do that, for they already had borrowed to the limit to pay their taxes. 5"We are their brothers, and our children are just like theirs," the people protested. "Yet we must sell our children into slavery to get enough money to live. We have already sold some of our daughters, and we are helpless to redeem them, for our fields, too, are mortgaged to these men." 6I was very angry when I heard this; 7so after thinking about it I spoke out against these rich government officials. "What is this you are doing?" I demanded. "How dare you demand a mortgage as a condition for helping another Israelite?" Then I called a public trial to deal with them. 8At the trial I shouted at them, "The rest of us are doing all we can to *help* our Jewish brothers who have returned from exile as slaves in distant lands, but you are forcing them right back into slavery again. How often must we redeem them?" And they had nothing to say in their own defense. 9Then I pressed further. "What you are doing is very evil," I exclaimed. "Should you not walk in the fear of our God? Don't we have enough enemies among the nations around us who are trying to destroy us? 10The rest of us are lending money and grain to our fellow-Jews without any interest. I beg you, gentlemen, stop this business of usury. 11Restore their fields, vineyards, oliveyards, and homes to them this very day and drop your claims against them." 12So they agreed to do it and said that they would assist their brothers without requiring them to mortgage their lands and sell them their children. Then I summoned the priests and made these men formally vow to carry out their promises. 13And I invoked the curse of God upon any of them who refused. "May God destroy your homes and livelihood if you fail to keep this promise," I declared. And all the people shouted, "Amen," and praised the Lord. And the rich men did as they had promised.

Job 21:7. The truth is that the wicked live on to a good old age, and become great and powerful. 8They live to see their children grow to maturity around them, and their grandchildren, too. 9Their homes are safe from every fear, and God does not punish them. 10Their cattle are productive, 11they have many happy children, 12, 13they spend their time singing and dancing. They are wealthy and need deny themselves nothing; they are prosperous to the end. 14All this despite the fact that they ordered God away and wanted no part of him and his ways. 15"Who is Almighty God?" they scoff. "Why should we obey him? What good will it do us?"

Job 27:13. This is the fate awaiting the wicked from the hand of the Almighty: 14If he has a multitude of children, it is so that they will die in war, or starve to death. 15Those who survive shall be brought down to the grave by disease and plague, with no one to mourn them, not even their wives. 16The evil man may accumulate money like dust, with closets jammed full of clothing— 17yes, he may order them made by his tailor, but the innocent shall wear that clothing, and shall divide his silver among them. 18Every house built by the wicked is as fragile as a spider web, as full of cracks as a leafy booth! 19He goes to bed rich, but wakes up to find that all his wealth is gone. 20Terror overwhelms him, and he is blown away in the storms of the night. 21The east wind carries him away, and he is gone. It sweeps him into eternity. 22For God shall hurl at him unsparingly. He longs to flee from God. 23Everyone will cheer at his death, and boo him into eternity.

Job 31:24. If I have put my trust in money, 25if my happiness depends on wealth. 28This, too, must be punished by the judges. For if I had done such things, it would mean that I denied the God of heaven.

Ps 49:16. So do not be dismayed when evil men grow rich and build their lovely homes. 17For when they die they carry nothing with them! Their honors will not follow them. 18Though a man calls himself happy all through his life.

Ps 52:1. You call yourself a *hero,* do you? You *boast* about this evil deed of yours against God's people. 2You are sharp as a tack in plotting your evil tricks. 3How you love wickedness—far more than good! And lying more than truth! 4You love to slander—you love to say anything that will do harm, O man with the lying tongue. 5But God will strike you down and pull you from your home, and drag you away from the land of the living. 6The followers of God will see it happen. They will watch in awe. Then they will laugh and say, 7"See what happens to those who despise God and trust in their wealth, and become ever more bold in their wickedness."

Ps 73:3. For I was envious of the prosperity of the proud and wicked. 4Yes, all through life their road is smooth! They grow sleek and fat. 5They aren't always in trouble and plagued with problems like everyone else, 6so their pride sparkles like a jeweled necklace, and their clothing is woven of cruelty! 7These fat cats have everything their hearts could ever wish for! 8They scoff at God and threaten his people. How proudly they speak! 9They boast against the very heavens, and their words strut through the earth. 10And so God's people are dismayed and confused, and drink it all in. 11"Does God realize what is going on?" they ask, 12"Look at these men of arrogance; they never have to lift a finger—theirs is a life of ease; and all the time their riches multiply." 13Have I been wasting my time? Why take the trouble to be pure? 14All I get out of it is trouble and woe—every day and all day long! 15If I had really said that, I would have been a traitor to your people. 16Yet it is so hard to explain it—this prosperity of those who hate the Lord. 17Then one day I went into God's sanctuary to meditate, and thought about the future of these evil men. 18What a slippery path they are on—suddenly God will send them sliding over the edge of the cliff and down to their destruction: 19an instant end to all their happiness, an eternity of terror. [20]Their present life is only a dream! They will awaken to the truth as one awakens from a dream of things that never really were! [21]When I saw this, what turmoil filled my heart! [22]I saw myself so stupid and so ignorant; I must seem like an animal to you, O God.

Prov 14:20. Even his own neighbors despise the poor man, while the rich have many "friends."

Prov 18:11. The rich man thinks of his wealth as an impregnable defense, a high wall of safety. What a dreamer! [23]The poor man pleads and the rich man answers with insults.

Prov 28:11. Rich men are conceited, but their real poverty is evident to the poor.

Eccl 5:13, 14. There is another serious problem I have seen everywhere—savings are put into risky investments that turn sour, and soon there is nothing left to pass on to one's son.

19, 20. And, of course, it is very good if a man has received wealth from the Lord and the good health to enjoy it. To enjoy your work and to accept your lot in life—that is indeed a gift from God. The person who does that will not need to look back with sorrow on his past, for God gives him joy.

Jer 5:7. How can I pardon you? For even your children have turned away, and worship gods that are not gods at all. I fed my people until they were fully satisfied, and their thanks was to commit adultery wholesale and to gang up at the city's brothels. [8]They are well-fed, lusty stallions, each neighing for his neighbor's mate. [9]Shall I not punish them for this? Shall I not send my vengeance on such a nation as this?

27. Like a coop full of chickens their homes are full of evil plots. And the result? Now they are great and rich, [28]and well fed and well groomed, and there is no limit to their wicked deeds. They refuse justice to orphans and the rights of the poor. [29]Should I sit back and act as though nothing is going on? the Lord God asks. Shouldn't I punish a nation such as this?

Jer 9:23. The Lord says: Let not the wise man bask in his wisdom, . . . nor the rich man in his riches.

Jer 17:11. Like a bird that fills her nest with young she has not hatched and which will soon desert her and fly away, so is the man who gets his wealth by unjust means. Sooner or later he will lose his riches and at the end of his life become a poor old fool.

Jer 22:13. And woe to you, King Jehoiakim, for you are building your great palace with forced labor. By not paying wages you are building injustice into its walls and oppression into its doorframes and ceilings. [14]You say, "I will build a magnificent palace with huge rooms and many windows, paneled throughout with fragrant cedar and painted a lovely red." [15]But a beautiful palace does not make a great king! Why did your father Josiah reign so long? Because he was just and fair in all his dealings. That is why God blessed him. [16]He saw to it that justice and help were given the poor and the needy and all went well for him. This is how a man lives close to God. [17]But you! You are full of selfish greed and all dishonesty! You murder the innocent, oppress the poor and reign with ruthlessness. [18]Therefore this is God's decree of punishment against King Jehoiakim, who succeeded his father Josiah on the throne: His family will not weep for him when he dies. His subjects will not even care that he is dead. [19]He shall be buried like a dead donkey—dragged out of Jerusalem and thrown on the garbage dump beyond the gate!

Ezk 7:19. Throw away your money! Toss it out like worthless rubbish, for it will have no value in that day of wrath. It will neither satisfy nor feed you, for your love of money is the reason for your sin. Zeph 1:18.

Ezk 28:5. Yes, your wisdom has made you very rich and very proud.

Amos 6:1. Woe to those lounging in luxury at Jerusalem and Samaria, so famous and popular among the people of Israel. [2]Go over to Calneh and see what happened there; then go to great Hamath and down to Gath in the Philistines' land. Once they were better and greater than you, but look at them now. [3]You push away all thought of punishment awaiting you, but by your deeds you bring the Day of Judgment near. [4]You lie on ivory beds surrounded with luxury, eating the meat of the tenderest lambs and the choicest calves. [5]You sing idle songs to the sound of the harp, and fancy yourselves to be as great musicians as King David was. [6]You drink wine by the bucketful and perfume yourselves with sweet ointments, caring nothing at all that your brothers need your help.

Mic 6:12. Your rich men are wealthy through extortion and violence; your citizens are so used to lying that their tongues can't tell the truth!

Zeph 1:18. Your silver and gold will be of no use to you in that day of the Lord's wrath.

Mt 19:24. I say it again—it is easier for a camel to go through the eye of a needle than for a rich man to enter the Kingdom of God! *v.* 23; Lk 18:24, 25.

Mk 10:17. As he was starting out on a trip, a man came running to him and knelt down and asked, "Good Teacher, what must I do to get to heaven?" [18]"Why do you call me good?" Jesus asked. "Only God is truly good! [19]But as for your question—you know the commandments: don't kill, don't commit adultery, don't steal, don't lie, don't cheat, respect your father and mother." [20]"Teacher," the man replied, "I've never once broken a single one of those laws." [21]Jesus felt genuine love for this man as he looked at him. "You lack only one thing," he told him; "go and sell all you have and give the money to the poor—and you shall have treasure in heaven—and come, follow me." [22]Then the man's face fell, and he went sadly away, for he was very rich. [Lk 18:22–26.] [23]Jesus watched him go, then turned around and said to his disciples. "It's almost impossible for the rich to get into the Kingdom of God!" [Mt 19:23.] [24]This amazed them. So Jesus said it again: "Dear children, how hard it is for those who trust in riches to enter the Kingdom of God. [25]It is easier for a camel to go through the eye of a needle than for a rich man to enter the Kingdom of God." [26]The disciples were incredulous! "Then who in the world can be saved, if not a rich man?" they asked. [27]Jesus looked at them intently, then said, "Without God, it is utterly impossible. But with God everything is possible."

Lk 6:24. But, oh, the sorrows that await the rich. For they have their only happiness down here. [25]They are fat and prosperous now, but a time of awful hunger is before them. Their careless laughter now means sorrow then.

Lk 12:15. "Beware! Don't always be wishing for what you don't have. For real life and real living are not related to how rich we are." [16]Then he gave an illustration: "A rich man had a fertile farm that produced fine crops. [17]In fact, his barns were full to overflowing—he couldn't get everything in. He thought about his problem, [18]and finally exclaimed, 'I know—I'll tear down my barns and build bigger ones! Then I'll have room enough. [19]And I'll sit back and say to myself, "Friend, you have enough stored away for years to come. Now take it easy! Wine, women, and song for you!" ' [20]But God said to him, 'Fool! Tonight you die. Then who will get it all?' [21]Yes, every man is a fool who gets rich on earth but not in heaven."

Lk 16:13. "For neither you nor anyone else can serve two masters. You will hate one and show loyalty to the other, or else the other way around—you will be enthusiastic about one and despise the other. You cannot serve both God and money." [14]The Pharisees, who dearly loved their money, naturally scoffed at all this. [19]"There was a certain rich man," Jesus said, "who was splendidly clothed and lived each day in mirth and luxury. [20]One day Lazarus, a diseased beggar, was laid at his door. [21]As he lay there longing for scraps from the rich man's table, the dogs would come and lick his open sores. [22]Finally the beggar died and was carried by the angels to be with Abraham in the place of the righteous dead. The rich man also died and was buried, [23]and his soul went into hell. There, in torment, he saw Lazarus in the far distance with Abraham. [24]'Father Abraham,' he shouted, 'have some pity! Send Lazarus over here if only to dip the tip of his finger in water and cool my tongue, for I am in anguish in these flames.' [25]But Abraham said to him, 'Son, remember that during your lifetime you had everything you wanted, and Lazarus had nothing. So now he is here being comforted and you are in anguish. [26]And besides, there is a great chasm separating us, and anyone wanting to come to you from here is stopped at its edge; and no one over there can cross to us.' "

1 Tim 6:17. Tell those who are rich not to be proud and not to trust in their money, which will soon be gone, but their pride and trust should be in the living God who always richly gives us all we need for our enjoyment. [18]Tell them to use their money to do good. They should be rich in good works and should give happily to those in need, always being ready to share with others whatever God has given them. [19]By doing this they will be storing up real treasure for themselves in heaven—it is the only safe investment for eternity! And they will be living a fruitful Christian life down here as well.

Jas 1:9. A Christian who doesn't amount to much in this world should be glad, for he is great in the Lord's sight. [10, 11]But a rich man should be glad that his riches mean nothing to the Lord, for he will soon be gone, like a flower that has lost its beauty and fades away, withered—killed by the scorching summer sun. So it is with rich men. They will soon die and leave behind all their busy activities.

Jas 5:1. Look here, you rich men, now is the time to cry and moan with anguished grief because of all the terrible troubles ahead of you. [2]Your wealth is even now rotting away, and your fine clothes are becoming mere moth-eaten rags. [3]The value of your gold and silver is dropping fast, yet it will stand as evidence against you, and eat your flesh like fire. That is what you have stored up for yourselves, to receive on that coming day of judgment.

See *Riches.*

INSTANCES OF. Abraham, Gen 13:1, 2; 24:35. Solomon, 1 Kgs 10:23. Hezekiah, 2 Kgs 20:12–18. Job, Job 1:2, 3. Joseph of Arimathea, Mt 27:57. Zacchaeus, Lk 19:1, 2.

RICHES Deut 6:10, 11, 12. When the Lord your God has brought you into the land he promised your ancestors, Abraham, Isaac, and Jacob, and when he has given you great cities full of good things—cities you didn't build, wells you didn't dig, and vineyards and olive trees you didn't plant—and when you have eaten until you can hold no more, then beware lest you forget the Lord who brought you out of the land of Egypt, the land of slavery.

Deut 8:10. When you have eaten your fill, bless the Lord your God for the good land he has given you. [11]But that is the time to be careful! Beware that in your plenty you don't forget the Lord your God and begin to disobey him. [12, 13]For when you have become full and prosperous and have built fine homes to live in, and when your flocks and herds have become very large, and your silver and gold have multiplied, [14]that is the time to watch out that you don't become proud, and forget the Lord your God who brought you out of your slavery in the land of Egypt. [15]Beware that you don't forget the God who led you through the great and terrible wilderness with the dangerous snakes and scorpions, where it was so hot and dry. He gave you water from the rock! [16]He fed you with manna in the wilderness (it was a kind of bread unknown before) so that you would become humble and so that your trust in him would grow, and he could do you good. [17]He did it so that you would never feel that it was your own power and might that made you wealthy. [18]Always remember that it is the Lord your God who gives you power to become rich, and he does it to fulfill his promise to your ancestors.

Deut 31:20. When I have brought them into the land I promised their ancestors—a land "flowing with milk and honey"—and when they have become fat and prosperous, and worship other gods and despise me and break my contract.

Deut 32:15. But Israel was soon overfed; yes, fat and bloated; then, in plenty, they forsook their God. They shrugged away the Rock of their salvation.

1 Sam 2:7. Some he causes to be poor and others to be rich. He cuts one down and lifts another up.

Ps 37:16. It is better to have little and be godly than to own an evil man's wealth.

Prov 10:2. Ill-gotten gain brings no lasting happiness; right living does. [22]The Lord's blessing is our greatest wealth. All our work adds nothing to it!

Prov 11:4. Your riches won't help you on Judgment Day; only righteousness counts then. [28]Trust in your money and down you go! Trust in God and flourish as a tree!

Prov 13:7. Some rich people are poor, and some poor people have great wealth! [8]Being kidnapped and held for ransom never worries the poor man!

Prov 15:6. There is treasure in being good, but trouble dogs the wicked. [16]Better a little with reverence for God, than great treasure and trouble with it. [17]It is better to eat soup with someone you love than steak with someone you hate.

Prov 16:8. A little, gained honestly, is better than great wealth gotten by dishonest means.

Prov 19:4. A wealthy man has many "friends"; the poor man has none left.

Prov 21:6. Dishonest gain will never last, so why take the risk?

Prov 23:4, 5. Don't weary yourself trying to get rich. Why waste your time? For riches can disappear as though they had the wings of a bird!

Prov 27:23, 24. Riches can disappear fast. And the king's crown doesn't stay in his family forever —so watch your business interests closely. Know the state of your flocks and your herds.

Prov 28:8. Income from exploiting the poor will end up in the hands of someone who pities them. [20]The man who wants to do right will get a rich reward. But the man who wants to get rich quick will quickly fail. [22]Trying to get rich quick is evil and leads to poverty.

Prov 30:8. First, help me never to tell a lie. Second, give me neither poverty nor riches! Give me just enough to satisfy my needs! [9]For if I grow rich, I may become content without God. And if I am too poor, I may steal, and thus insult God's holy name.

Eccl 5:9. And over them all is the king. Oh, for a king who is devoted to his country! Only he can bring order from this chaos. [10]He who loves money shall never have enough. The foolishness of thinking that wealth brings happiness! [11]The more you have, the more you spend, right up to the limits of your income, so what is the advantage of wealth—except perhaps to watch it as it runs through your fingers! [12]The man who works hard sleeps well whether he eats little or much, but the rich must worry and suffer insomnia. [13, 14]There is another serious problem I have seen everywhere—savings are put into risky investments that turn sour, and soon there is nothing left to pass on to one's son. [15]The man who speculates is soon back to where he began—with nothing. [16]This, as I said, is a very serious problem, for all his hard work has been for nothing; he has been working for the wind. It is all swept away. [17]All the rest of his life he is under a cloud—gloomy, discouraged, frustrated, and angry. [18]Well, one thing, at least, is good: it is for a man to eat well, drink a good glass of wine, accept his position in life, and enjoy his work whatever his job may be, for however long the Lord may let him live. [19, 20]And, of course, it is very good if a man has received wealth from the Lord, and the good health to enjoy it. To enjoy your work and to accept your lot in life—that is indeed a gift from God. The person who does that will not need to look back with sorrow on his past, for God gives him joy.

Eccl 6:1. Yes, there is a very serious evil which I have seen everywhere— [2]God has given to some men very great wealth and honor, so that they can have everything they want, but he doesn't give them the health to enjoy it, and they die and others get it all! This is absurd, a hollow mockery, and a serious fault.

Eccl 7:11. To be wise is as good as being rich; in fact, it is better. [12]You can get anything by either wisdom or money, but being wise has many advantages.

Eccl 10:19. A party gives laughter, and wine gives happiness, and money gives everything!

Isa 5:8. You buy up property so others have no place to live. Your homes are built on great estates so you can be alone in the midst of the earth!

Jer 48:36. Sad sings my heart for Moab and Kirheres, for all their wealth has disappeared.

Hos 12:8. Ephraim boasts, "I am so rich! I have gotten it all by myself! But riches can't make up for sin.

Mt 6:19. Don't store up treasures here on earth where they can erode away or may be stolen. [20]Store them in heaven where they will never lose their value, and are safe from thieves. [21]If your profits are in heaven your heart will be there too.

Mt 13:22. The ground covered with thistles represents a man who hears the message, but the cares of this life and his longing for money choke out God's Word, and he does less and less for God.

Mt 19:16. Someone came to Jesus with this question: "Good master, what must I do to have eternal life?" [17]"When you call me good you are calling me God," Jesus replied, "for God alone is truly good. But to answer your question, you can get to heaven if you keep the commandments." [18]"Which ones?" the man asked. And Jesus replied, "Don't kill, don't commit adultery, don't steal, don't lie, [19]honor your father and mother, and love your neighbor as yourself!" [20]"I've always obeyed every one of them," the youth replied. "What else must I do?" [21]Jesus told him, "If you want to be perfect, go and sell everything you have and give the money to the poor, and you will have treasure in heaven; and come, follow me." [22]But when the young man heard this, he went away sadly, for he was very rich. [23]Then Jesus said to his disciples, "It is almost impossible for a rich man to get into the Kingdom of Heaven. [24]I say it again—it is easier for a camel to go through the eye of a needle than for a rich man to enter the Kingdom of God!" [25]This remark confounded the disciples. "Then who in the world can be saved?" they asked. [26]Jesus looked at them intently and said, "Humanly speaking, no one. But with God, everything is possible." [27]Then Peter said to him, "We left everything to follow you. What will we get out of it?" [28]And Jesus replied, "When I, the Messiah, shall sit upon my glorious throne in the Kingdom, you my disciples shall certainly sit on twelve thrones judging the twelve tribes of Israel. [29]And anyone who gives up his home, brothers, sisters, father, mother, wife, children, or property, to follow me, shall receive a hundred times as much in return, and shall have eternal life." Mk 10:17–25; Lk 18:18–25.

Mk 4:19. But all too quickly the attractions of this world and the delights of wealth, and the search for success and lure of nice things come in and crowd out God's message from their hearts, so that no crop is produced.

Lk 12:15. Beware! Don't always be wishing for what you don't have. For real life and real living are not related to how rich we are.

1 Tim 6:4. Anyone who says anything different is both proud and stupid. . . . [5]These arguers . . . to them the Good News is just a means of making money. Keep away from them. [6]Do you want to be truly rich? You already are if you are happy and good. [7]After all, we didn't bring any money with us when we came into the world, and we can't carry away a single penny when we die. [8]So we should be well satisfied without money if we have enough food and clothing. [9]But people who long to be rich soon begin to do all kinds of wrong things to get money, things that hurt them and make them evil-minded and finally send them to hell itself. [10]For the love of money is the first step toward all kinds of sin. Some people have even turned away from God because of their love for it, and as a result have pierced themselves with many sorrows. [11]Oh, Timothy, you are God's man. Run from all these evil things and work instead at what is right and good, learning to trust him and love others, and to be patient and gentle. [17]Tell those who are rich not to be proud and not to trust in their money, which will soon be gone, but their pride and trust should be in the living God who always richly gives us all we need for our enjoyment. [18]Tell them to use their money to do good. They should be rich in good works and should give happily to those in need, always being ready to share with others whatever God has given them. [19]By doing this they will be storing up real treasure for themselves in heaven—it is the only safe investment for eternity! And they will be living a fruitful Christian life down here as well.

Jas 2:6. And yet. . . . don't you realize that it is usually the rich men who pick on you and drag you into court? [7]And all too often they are the ones who laugh at Jesus Christ, whose noble name you bear.

Jas 5:1. Look here, you rich men, now is the time to cry and groan with anguished grief because of all the terrible troubles ahead of you. [2]Your wealth is even now rotting away, and your fine clothes are becoming mere moth-eaten rags. [3]The value of your gold and silver is dropping fast, yet it will stand as evidence against you, and eat your flesh like fire. That is what you have stored up for yourselves, to receive on that coming day of judgment. [4]For listen! Hear the cries of the field workers whom you have cheated of their pay. Their cries have reached the ears of the Lord of Hosts. [5]You have spent your years here on earth having fun, satisfying your every whim, and now your fat hearts are ready for the slaughter.

1 Jn 3:17. But if someone who is supposed to be a Christian has money enough to live well, and sees a brother in need, and won't help him—how can God's love be within *him?*

FIGURATIVE. Rev 3:18.

See *Covetousness; Rich.*

RIDDLE Used as a test of wit at Samson's feast, Judg 14:12–18. By Agur, Prov 30:15, 16, 18–31.

See *Parable; Proverbs.*

RIGHTEOUS INDEX OF SUBTOPICS. *Miscellany of Minor Sub-Topics; Contrasted with the Wicked; Described; Promises to, Expressed or Implied; Unity of, with Christ.*

MISCELLANY OF MINOR SUB-TOPICS. Compared with: The sun, Judg 5:31; Mt 13:43; stars, Dan 12:3; lights, Mt 5:14; Phil 2:15; Mount Zion, Ps 125:1, 2; Lebanon, Hos 14:5–7; flock, Ex 19:5; jewels, Mal 3:17; gold, Job 23:10; Lam 4:2, dishes of gold and silver, 2 Tim 2:20; stones of a crown, Zech 9:16, 17; living stones, 1 Pet 2:5; babies, 1 Cor 14:20; 1 Pet 2:2; little children, Mt 11:25; 18:3, obedient children, 1 Pet 1:14; members of the body, 1 Cor 12:20, 27; soldiers, 2 Tim 2:3, 4; runners in a race, 1 Cor 9:24; Heb 12:1; athletes, 2 Tim 2:5; good servants, Mt 25:21; strangers and pilgrims, 1 Pet 2:11; sheep, Ps 78:52; Mt 25:33; Jn 10; lambs, Isa 40:11; Jn 21:15; calves, Mal 4:2; lions, Prov 28:1; Mic 5:8; eagles, Ps 103:5; Isa 40:31; doves, Ps 68:11–13; Isa 60:8; thirsting deer, Ps 42:1; good fish, Mt 13:47, 48; dew and showers, Mic 5:7; watered gardens, Isa 58:11; ever-flowing springs, Isa 58:11; vines, Song 6:11; Hos 14:7; branches of a vine, Jn 15:2, 4, 5; pomegranates, Song 4:13; good figs, Jer 24:2–7; lilies, Song 2:2; Hos 14:5; willows by the river bank, Isa 44:4; trees planted by rivers, Ps 1:3; cedars in Lebanon, Ps 92:12; palm trees, Ps 92:12; green olive trees, Ps 52:8; Hos 14:6; fruitful trees, Ps 1:3; Jer 17:8; wheat, Mt 3:12; 13:29, 30; salt, Mt 5:13.

Access of, to God, Ps 31:19, 20; Isa 12:6. Few, Mt 7:14; 22:14. Relation of, to God, Lev 20:24–26. Righteous and wicked, circumstances of, contrasted, Job 8; Ps 17:13–15. See below.

Judgment of, see *Judgment of God; Church, The True.* Fellowship of, see *Fellowship.* Hatred toward, see *Persecution.* Joy of, see *Joy.* Perseverance of, see *Perseverance.*

CONTRASTED WITH THE WICKED. See *Wicked, Described; Wicked, Contrasted with the Righteous.*

DESCRIBED. Ex 33:16. If you don't go with us, who will ever know that I and my people have found favor with you, and that we are different from any other people upon the face of the earth?

1 Sam 13:14. But now your dynasty must end; for the Lord wants a man who will obey him. And he has discovered the man he wants and has already appointed him as king over his people; for you have not obeyed the Lord's commandment.

Ezra 10:3. For we agree before our God to divorce our heathen wives and to send them away with our children; we will follow your commands, and the commands of the others who fear our God. We will obey the laws of God.

Ps 1:1. Oh, the joys of those who do not follow evil men's advice, who do not hang around with sinners, scoffing at the things of God: [2]But they delight in doing everything God wants them to, and day and night are always meditating on his laws and thinking about ways to follow him more closely. [3]They are like trees along a river bank bearing luscious fruit each season without fail. Their leaves shall never wither, and all they do shall prosper.

Ps 4:3. Mark this well: The Lord has set apart the redeemed for himself.

Ps 15:1. Lord, who may go and find refuge and shelter in your tabernacle up on your holy hill? [2]Anyone who leads a blameless life and is truly sincere. [3]Anyone who refuses to slander others, does not listen to gossip, never harms his neighbor, [4]speaks out against sin, criticizes those committing it, commends the faithful followers of the Lord, keeps a promise even if it ruins him, [5]does not crush his debtors with high interest rates, and refuses to testify against the innocent despite the bribes offered him—such a man shall stand firm forever.

Ps 24:3. Who may climb the mountain of the Lord and enter where he lives? Who may stand before the Lord? [4]Only those with pure hands and hearts, who do not practice dishonesty and lying. [5]They will receive God's own goodness as their blessing from him, planted in their lives by God himself, their Savior.

Ps 37:26. Instead, the godly are able to be generous with their gifts and loans to others, and their children are a blessing. [30, 31]The godly man is a good counselor because he is just and fair and knows right from wrong.

Ps 64:10. And the godly shall rejoice in the Lord, and trust and praise him.

Ps 84:7. They will grow constantly in strength and each of them is invited to meet with the Lord in Zion.

Ps 87:5. But someday the highest honor will be to be a native of Jerusalem! For the God above all gods will personally bless this city. [6]When he registers her citizens he will place a checkmark beside the names of those who were born here.

Ps 112:1. Praise the Lord! For all who fear God and trust in him are blessed beyond expression. Yes, happy is the man who delights in doing his commands. [2]His children shall be honored everywhere, for good men's sons have a special heritage. [3]He himself shall be wealthy, and his good deeds will never be forgotten. [4]When darkness overtakes him, light will come bursting in. He is kind and merciful— [5]and all goes well for the generous man who conducts his business fairly. [6]Such a man will not be overthrown by evil circumstances. God's constant care of him will make a deep impression on all who see it. [7]He does not fear bad news, nor live in dread of what may happen. For he is settled in his mind that Jehovah will take care of him. [8]That is why he is not afraid, but can calmly face his foes. [9]He gives generously to those in need. His deeds will never be forgotten. He shall have influence and honor. [10]Evil-minded men will be infuriated when they see all this; they will gnash their teeth in anger and slink away, their hopes thwarted.

Ps 119:1. Happy are all who perfectly follow the laws of God. [2]Happy are all who search for God, and always do his will, [3]rejecting compromise with evil, and walking only in his paths.

Prov 2:9. He shows how to distinguish right from wrong, how to find the right decision every time. [10]For wisdom and truth will enter the very center of your being, filling your life with joy. [11, 12]You will be given the sense to stay away from evil men who want you to be their partners in crime.

Prov 4:18. But the good man walks along in the ever-brightening light of God's favor; the dawn gives way to morning splendor.

Prov 13:5. A good man hates lies.

Prov 25:26. If a godly man compromises with the wicked, it is like polluting a fountain or muddying a spring.

Isa 33:15. I will tell you who can live here: All who are honest and fair, who reject making profit by fraud, who hold back their hands from taking bribes, who refuse to listen to those who plot murder, who shut their eyes to all enticement to do wrong. [16]Such as these shall dwell on high. The rocks of the mountains will be their fortress of safety; food will be supplied to them and they will have all the water they need.

Isa 51:1. Listen to me, all who hope for deliverance, who seek the Lord!

Isa 54:13. And all your citizens shall be taught by me, and their prosperity shall be great.

Isa 60:21. All your people will be good. They will possess their land forever, for I will plant them there with my own hands; this will bring me glory.

Isa 62:12. And they shall be called "The Holy People" and "The Lord's Redeemed," and Jerusalem shall be called "The Land of Desire" and "The City God Has Blessed."

Isa 63:8. He said, "They are my very own; surely they will not be false again." And he became their Savior.

Jer 31:12. They shall come home and sing songs of joy upon the hills of Zion, and shall be radiant over the goodness of the Lord—the good crops, the wheat and the wine and the oil, and the healthy flocks and herds. Their life shall be like a watered garden, and all their sorrows shall be gone. [13]The young girls will dance for joy, and men folk—old and young—will take their part in all the fun; for I will turn their mourning into joy and I will comfort them and make them rejoice, for their captivity with all its sorrows will be behind them. [14]I will feast the priests with the abundance of offerings brought to them at the Temple; I will satisfy my people with my bounty, says the Lord. [33]But this is the new contract I will make with them: I will inscribe my laws upon their hearts, so that they shall want to honor me; then they shall truly be my people and I will be their God. [34]At that time it will no longer be necessary to admonish one another to know the Lord. For everyone, both great and small, shall really know me then, says the Lord, and I will forgive and forget their sins.

Ezk 18:5. But if a man is just and does what is lawful and right, [6]and has not gone out to the mountains to feast before the idols of Israel and worship them, and does not commit adultery, nor lie with any woman during the time of her menstruation, [7]and is a merciful creditor, not holding on to the items given to him in pledge by poor debtors, and is no robber, but gives food to the hungry and clothes to those in need, [8]and grants loans without interest, and stays away from sin, and is honest and fair when judging others, [9]and obeys my laws—that man is just, says the Lord, and he shall surely live.

Ezk 44:9. The Lord God says: No foreigner of all the many among you shall enter my sanctuary if he has not been circumcised and does not love the Lord.

Zech 3:2. And the Lord said to Satan, "I reject your accusations, Satan; yes, I, the Lord, for I have decided to be merciful to Jerusalem—I rebuke you. I have decreed mercy to Joshua and his nation; they are like a burning stick pulled out of the fire." [7]"The Lord of Hosts declares: 'If you will follow the paths I set for you and do all I tell you to, then I will put you in charge of my Temple, to keep it holy; and I will let you walk in and out of my presence with these angels. [8]Listen to me, O Joshua the High Priest, and all you other priests, you are illustrations of the good things to come. Don't you see?—Joshua represents my servant The Branch whom I will send.'"

Mt 5:3. "Humble men are very fortunate!" he told them, "for the Kingdom of Heaven is given to them. [4]Those who mourn are fortunate! for they shall be comforted. [5]The meek and lowly are fortunate! for the whole wide world belongs to them. [6]Happy are those who long to be just and good, for they shall be completely satisfied. [7]Happy are the kind and merciful, for they shall be shown mercy. [8]Happy are those whose hearts are pure, for they shall see God. [9]Happy are those who strive for peace—they shall be called the sons of God. [10]Happy are those who are persecuted because they are good, for the Kingdom of Heaven is theirs. [13]You are the world's seasoning, to make it tolerable. If you lose your flavor, what will happen to the world? And you yourselves will be thrown out and trampled underfoot as worthless. [14]You are the world's light—a city on a hill, glowing in the night for all to see. [15, 16]Don't hide your light! Let it shine for all; let your good deeds glow for all to see, so that they will praise your heavenly Father."

Mt 7:16. You can detect them by the way they act, just as you can identify a tree by its fruit. You need never confuse grapevines with thorn bushes or figs with thistles. [17]Different kinds of fruit trees can quickly be identified by examining their fruit. [18]A variety that produces delicious fruit never produces an inedible kind. And a tree producing an inedible kind can't produce what is good. [19]So the trees having the inedible fruit are chopped down and thrown on the fire. [20]Yes, the way to identify a tree or a person is by the kind of fruit produced. [24]All who listen to my instructions and follow them are wise, like a man who builds his house on solid rock. [25]Though the rain comes in torrents, and the floods rise and the storm winds beat against his house, it won't collapse, for it is built on rock. [26]But those who hear my instructions and ignore them are foolish, like a man who builds his house on sand. [27]For when the rains and floods come, and storm winds beat against his house, it will fall with a mighty crash.

Mt 12:50. Then he added, "Anyone who obeys my Father in heaven is my brother, sister and mother!"

Mt 13:23. The good ground represents the heart of a man who listens to the message and understands it and goes out and brings thirty, sixty, or even a hundred others into the Kingdom. [38]The field is the world, and the seed represents the people of the Kingdom; the thistles are the people belonging to Satan.

Lk 6:45. A good man produces good deeds from a good heart. . . . Whatever is in the heart overflows into speech.

Lk 18:16, 17. Then Jesus called the children over to him and said to the disciples, "Let the little children come to me! Never send them away! For the Kingdom of God belongs to men who have hearts as trusting as these little children's. And anyone who doesn't have their kind of faith will never get within the Kingdom's gates." Mt 19:14; Mk 10:14, 15.

Jn 3:21. But those doing right come gladly to the Light to let everyone see that they are doing what God wants them to.

Jn 8:31. Jesus said to them, "You are truly my disciples if you live as I tell you to, [32]and you will know the truth, and the truth will set you free." [39]"Our father is Abraham," they declared. "No!" Jesus replied, "for if he were, you would follow his good example." [42]Jesus told them, "If that were so, then you would love me, for I have come to you from God. I am not here on my own, but he sent me. [47]Anyone whose Father is God listens gladly to the words of God. Since you don't, it proves you aren't his children."

Jn 10:4. He walks ahead of them; and they follow him, for they recognize his voice. [5]They won't follow a stranger but will run from him, for they don't recognize his voice. [27]My sheep recognize my voice, and I know them, and they follow me.

Jn 13:35. Your strong love for each other will prove to the world that you are my disciples.

Jn 15:14. And you are my friends if you obey me.

Acts 2:38. And Peter replied, "Each one of you must turn from sin, return to God, and be baptized in the name of Jesus Christ for the forgiveness of your sins; then you also shall receive this gift, the Holy Spirit." [47]The whole city was favorable to them, and each day God added to them all who were being saved.

Acts 8:36. And the eunuch said, "Look! Water! Why can't I be baptized?" [37]"You can," Philip answered, "if you believe with all your heart." And the eunuch replied, "I believe that Jesus Christ is the Son of God."

Acts 10:47. Peter asked, "Can anyone object to my baptizing them, now that they have received the Holy Spirit just as we did?"

Acts 11:23. When he arrived and saw the wonderful things God was doing, he was filled with excitement and joy, and encouraged the believers to stay close to the Lord, whatever the cost. [24]Barnabas was a kindly person, full of the Holy Spirit and strong in faith. As a result large numbers of people were added to the Lord.

Acts 18:7. After that he stayed with Titus Justus, a Gentile who worshiped God and lived next door to the synagogue. [8]However, Crispus, the leader of the synagogue, and all his household believed in the Lord and were baptized—as were many others in Corinth.

Rom 1:6, 7. And you, dear friends in Rome, are among those he dearly loves; you, too, are invited by Jesus Christ to be God's very own—yes, his holy people. May all God's mercies and peace be yours from God our Father and from Jesus Christ our Lord.

Rom 6:1. Well then, shall we keep on sinning so that God can keep on showing us more and more kindness and forgiveness? [2, 3]Of course not! Should we keep on sinning when we don't have to? For sin's power over us was broken when we became Christians and were baptized to become a part of Jesus Christ; through his death the power of your sinful nature was shattered. [4]Your old sin-loving nature was buried with him by baptism when he died, and when God the Father, with glorious power, brought him back to life again, you were given his wonderful new life to enjoy. [5]For you have become a part of him, and so you died with him, so to speak, when he died; and now you share his new life, and shall rise as he did. [6]Your old evil desires were nailed to the cross with him; that part of you that loves to sin was crushed and fatally wounded, so that your sin-loving body is no longer under sin's control, no longer needs to be a slave to sin; [7]for when you are deadened to sin you are freed from all its allure and its power over you. [8]And since your old sin-loving nature "died" with Christ, we know that you will share his new life. [9]Christ rose from the dead and will never die again. Death no longer has any power over him. [10]He died once for all to end sin's power, but now he lives forever in unbroken fellowship with God. [11]So look upon your old sin nature as dead and unresponsive to sin, and instead be alive to God, alert to him, through Jesus Christ our Lord. [12]Do not let sin control your puny body any longer; do not give in to its sinful desires. [13]Do not let any part of your bodies become tools of wickedness, to be used for sinning; but give yourselves completely to God—every part of you—for you are back from death and you want to be tools in the hands of God, to be used for his good purposes. [14]Sin need never again be your master, for now you are no longer tied to the law where sin enslaves you, but you are free under God's favor and mercy. [15]Does this mean that now we can go ahead and sin and not worry about it? (For our salvation does not depend on keeping the law, but on receiving God's grace!) Of course not! [16]Don't you realize that you can choose your own master? You can choose sin (with death) or else obedience (with acquittal). The one to whom you offer yourself—he will take you and be your master and you will be his slave. [17]Thank God that though you once chose to be slaves of sin, now you have obeyed with all your heart the teaching to which God has committed you. [18]And now you are free from your old master, sin; and you have become slaves to your new master, righteousness. [19]I speak this way, using the illustration of slaves and masters, because it is easy to understand: just as you used to be slaves to all kinds of sin, so now you must let yourselves be slaves to all that is right and holy. [20]In those days when you were slaves of sin you didn't bother much with goodness. [21]And what was the result? Evidently not good, since you are ashamed now even to think about those things you used to do, for all of them end in eternal doom. [22]But now you are free from the power of sin and are slaves of God, and his benefits to you include holiness and everlasting life. [23]For the wages of sin is death, but the free gift of God is eternal life through Jesus Christ our Lord.

Rom 8:5. Those who let themselves be controlled by their lower natures live only to please themselves, but those who follow after the Holy Spirit find themselves doing those things that please God. [6]Following after the Holy Spirit leads to life and peace, but following after the old nature leads to death. [9]But you are not like that. You are controlled by your new nature if you have the

Spirit of God living in you. (And remember that if anyone doesn't have the Spirit of Christ living in him, he is not a Christian at all.) [14]For all who are led by the Spirit of God are sons of God. [15]And so we should not be like cringing, fearful slaves, but we should behave like God's very own children, adopted into the bosom of his family, and calling to him, "Father, Father." [16]For his Holy Spirit speaks to us deep in our hearts, and tells us that we really are God's children. [29]For from the very beginning God decided that those who came to him —and all along he knew who would—should become like his Son, so that his Son would be the First, with many brothers. [35]Who then can ever keep Christ's love from us? When we have trouble or calamity, when we are hunted down or destroyed, is it because he doesn't love us anymore? And if we are hungry, or penniless, or in danger, or threatened with death, has God deserted us? [36]No, for the Scriptures tell us that for his sake we must be ready to face death at every moment of the day—we are like sheep awaiting slaughter; [37]but despite all this, overwhelming victory is ours through Christ who loved us enough to die for us. [38]For I am convinced that nothing can ever separate us from his love. Death can't, and life can't. The angels won't, and all the powers of hell itself cannot keep God's love away. Our fears for today, our worries about tomorrow, [39]or where we are—high above the sky, or in the deepest ocean—nothing will ever be able to separate us from the love of God demonstrated by our Lord Jesus Christ when he died for us.

Rom 9:8. This means that not all of Abraham's children are children of God, but only those who believe the promise of salvation which he made to Abraham.

Rom 15:14. I know that you are wise and good, my brothers, and that you know these things so well that you are able to teach others all about them.

Rom 16:19. But everyone knows that you stand loyal and true. This makes me very happy. I want you always to remain very clear about what is right, and to stay innocent of any wrong.

1 Cor 1:2. *To:* The Christians in Corinth, invited by God to be his people and made acceptable to him by Christ Jesus. *And to:* All Christians everywhere—whoever calls upon the name of Jesus Christ, our Lord and theirs. [26]Notice among yourselves, dear brothers, that few of you who follow Christ have big names or power or wealth. [27]Instead, God has deliberately chosen to use ideas the world considers foolish and of little worth in order to shame those people considered by the world as wise and great. [30]For it is from God alone that you have your life through Christ Jesus. He showed us God's plan of salvation; he was the one who made us acceptable to God; he made us pure and holy and gave himself to purchase our salvation.

1 Cor 2:12. And God has actually given us his Spirit (not the world's spirit) to tell us about the wonderful free gifts of grace and blessing that God has given us. [13]In telling you about these gifts we have even used the very words given to us by the Holy Spirit, not words that we as men might choose. So we use the Holy Spirit's words to explain the Holy Spirit's facts.

1 Cor 6:9, 10. Don't you know that those doing such things have no share in the Kingdom of God? Don't fool yourselves. Those who live immoral lives, who are idol worshipers, adulterers or homosexuals—will have no share in his kingdom. Neither will thieves or greedy people, drunkards, slanderers, or robbers. [11]There was a time when some of you were just like that but now your sins are washed away, and you are set apart for God, and he has accepted you because of what the Lord Jesus Christ and the Spirit of our God have done for you.

1 Cor 15:48. Every human being has a body just like Adam's, made of dust, but all who become Christ's will have the same kind of body as his—a body from heaven. [49]Just as each of us now has a body like Adam's, so we shall some day have a body like Christ's.

2 Cor 1:12. We are so glad that we can say with utter honesty that in all our dealings we have been pure and sincere, quietly depending upon the Lord for his help, and not on our own skills. And that is even more true, if possible, about the way we have acted toward you.

2 Cor 4:1. It is God himself, in his mercy, who has given us this wonderful work (of telling his Good News to others), and so we never give up. [2]We do not try to trick people into believing—we are not interested in fooling anyone. We never try to get anyone to believe that the Bible teaches what it doesn't. All such shameful methods we forego. We stand in the presence of God as we speak and so we tell the truth, as all who know us will agree.

2 Cor 5:17. When someone becomes a Christian he becomes a brand new person inside. He is not the same any more. A new life has begun! [21]For God took the sinless Christ and poured into him our sins. Then, in exchange, he poured God's goodness into us!

Gal 5:22. But when the Holy Spirit controls our lives he will produce this kind of fruit in us: love, joy, peace, patience, kindness, goodness, faithfulness, [23]gentleness and self-control; and here there is no conflict with Jewish laws. [24]Those who belong to Christ have nailed their natural evil desires to his cross and crucified them there. [25]If we are living now by the Holy Spirit's power, let us follow the Holy Spirit's leading in every part of our lives. [26]Then we won't need to look for honors and popularity, which lead to jealousy and hard feelings.

Eph 1:1. Dear Christian friends at Ephesus, ever loyal to the Lord: This is Paul writing to you, chosen by God to be Jesus Christ's messenger. [4]Long ago, even before he made the world, God chose us to be his very own, through what Christ would do for us; he decided then to make us holy in his eyes, without a single fault—we who stand before him covered with his love. [5]His unchanging plan has always been to adopt us into his own family by sending Jesus Christ to die for us. And he did this because he wanted to! [6]Now all praise to God for his wonderful kindness to us and his favor that he has poured out upon us, because we belong to his dearly loved Son. [7]So overflowing is his kindness towards us that he took away all our sins through the blood of his Son, by whom we are saved.

Eph 2:1. Once you were under God's curse, doomed forever for your sins. [4]But God is so rich in mercy; he loved us so much [5]that even though we were spiritually dead and doomed by our sins, he gave us back our lives again when he raised Christ from the dead—only by his undeserved favor have we ever been saved— [6]and lifted us up from the grave into glory along with Christ, where we sit with him in the heavenly realms—all because of what Christ Jesus did. [10]It is God himself who has made us what we are and given us new lives from Christ Jesus; and long ages ago he planned that we should spend these lives in helping others. [13]But now you belong to Christ Jesus, and though you once were far away from God, now you have been brought very near to him because of what Jesus Christ has done for you with his blood. [14]For Christ himself is our way of peace. He has made peace between us Jews and you Gentiles by making us all one family, breaking down the wall of contempt that used to separate us. [19]Now you are no longer strangers to God and foreigners to heaven, but you are members of God's very own family, citizens of God's country, and you belong in God's household with every other Christian. [20]What a foundation you stand on now: the apostles and the prophets; and the cornerstone of the building is Jesus Christ himself! [21]We who believe are carefully joined together with Christ as parts of a beautiful, constantly growing temple for God. [22]And you also are joined with him and with each other by the Spirit, and are part of this dwelling place of God.

Eph 3:17. And I pray that Christ will be more and more at home in your hearts, living within you as you trust in him. May your roots go down deep into the soil of God's marvelous love; [18, 19]and may you be able to feel and understand, as all God's children should, how long, how wide, how deep, and how high his love really is; and to experience this love for yourselves, though it is so great that you will never see the end of it or fully know or understand it. And so at last you will be filled up with God himself.

Eph 4:13. Until finally we all believe alike about our salvation and about our Savior, God's Son, and all become full-grown in the Lord—yes, to the point of being filled full with Christ. [14]Then we will no longer be like children, forever changing our minds about what we believe because someone has told us something different, or has cleverly lied to us and made the lie sound like the truth. [15, 16]Instead, we will lovingly follow the truth at all times—speaking truly, dealing truly, living truly—and so become more and more in every way like Christ who is the Head of his body, the church. Under his direction the whole body is fitted together perfectly, and each part in its own special way helps the other parts, so that the whole body is healthy and growing and full of love. [22]Then throw off your old evil nature—the old you that was a partner in your evil ways—rotten through and through, full of lust and sham. [23]Now your attitudes and thoughts must all be constantly changing for the better. [24]Yes, you must be a new and different person, holy and good. Clothe yourself with this new nature. [25]Stop lying to each other; tell the truth, for we are parts of each other and when we lie to each other we are hurting ourselves. [26]If you are angry, don't sin by nursing your grudge. Don't let the sun go down with you still angry—get over it quickly; [27]for when you are angry you give a mighty foothold to the devil. [28]If anyone is stealing he must stop it and begin using those hands of his for honest work so he can give to others in need. [29]Don't use bad language. Say only what is good and helpful to those you are talking to, and what will give them a blessing. [30]Don't cause the Holy Spirit sorrow by the way you live. Remember, he is the one who marks you to be present on that day when salvation from sin will be complete. [31]Stop being mean, bad-tempered and angry. Quarreling, harsh words, and dislike of others should have no place in your lives. [32]Instead, be kind to each other, tenderhearted, forgiving one another, just as God has forgiven you because you belong to Christ.

Eph 5:8. For though once your heart was full of darkness, now it is full of light from the Lord, and your behavior should show it!

Phil 2:15. So that no one can speak a word of blame against you. You are to live clean, innocent lives as children of God in a dark world full of people who are crooked and stubborn. Shine out among them like beacon lights.

Phil 3:3. For it isn't the *cutting of our bodies* that makes us children of God; it is *worshiping him with our spirits.* That is the only true "circumcision." We Christians glory in what Christ Jesus has done for us and realize that we are helpless to save ourselves. [7]But all these things that I once thought very worthwhile—now I've thrown them all away so that I can put my trust and hope in Christ alone. [8]Yes, everything else is worthless when compared with the priceless gain of knowing Christ Jesus my Lord. I have put aside all else, counting it worth less than nothing, in order that I can have Christ, [9]and become one with him, no longer counting on being saved by being good enough or by obeying God's laws, but by trusting Christ to save me; for God's way of making us right with himself depends on faith—counting on Christ alone. [10]Now I have given up everything else—I have found it to be the only way to really know Christ and to experience the mighty power that brought him back to life again, and find out what it means to suffer and to die with him. [11]So, whatever it takes, I will be one who lives in the fresh newness of life of those who are alive from the dead.

Phil 4:8. Fix your thoughts on what is true and good and right. Think about things that are pure and lovely, and dwell on the fine, good things in others. Think about all you can praise God for and be glad about.

Col 1:9. So ever since we first heard about you we have kept on praying and asking God to help you understand what he wants you to do; asking him to make you wise about spiritual things; [10]and asking that the way you live will always please the Lord and honor him, so that you will always be doing good, kind things for others, while all the time you are learning to know God better and better. [11]We are praying, too, that you will be filled with his mighty, glorious strength so that you can keep going no matter what happens—always full of the joy of the Lord, [12]and always thankful to the Father who has made us fit to share all the wonderful things that belong to those who live in the kingdom of light. [13]For he has rescued us out of the darkness and gloom of Satan's kingdom and brought us into the kingdom of his dear Son.

Col 2:7. Let your roots grow down into him and draw up nourishment from him. See that you go on growing in the Lord, and become strong and vigorous in the truth you were taught. Let your lives overflow with joy and thanksgiving for all he has done.

Col 3:3. You should have as little desire for this world as a dead person does. Your real life is in heaven with Christ and God.

1 Thess 1:3. We never forget your loving deeds as we talk to our God and Father about you, and your strong faith and steady looking forward to the return of our Lord Jesus Christ.

1 Thess 5:4. But, dear brothers, you are not in the dark about these things, and you won't be surprised as by a thief when that day of the Lord comes. [5]For you are all children of the light and of the day, and do not belong to darkness and night. [27]I command you in the name of the Lord to read this letter to all Christians.

2 Tim 2:19. A person who calls himself a Christian should not be doing things that are wrong. [21]If you stay away from sin you will be like one of these dishes made of purest gold—the very best in the house—so that Christ himself can use you for his highest purposes. [22]Run from anything that gives you the evil thoughts that young men often have, but stay close to anything that makes you want to do right. Have faith and love, and enjoy the companionship of those who love the Lord and have pure hearts. [23]Again I say, don't get involved in foolish arguments which only upset people and make them angry. [24]God's people must not be quarrelsome; they must be gentle, patient teachers of those who are wrong.

Philemon 1:5. Because I keep hearing of your love and trust in the Lord Jesus and in his people. [6]And I pray that as you share your faith with others it will grip their lives too, as they see the wealth of good things in you that come from Christ Jesus.

Heb 3:1. Therefore, dear brothers whom God has set apart for himself—you who are chosen for heaven. And we Christians are God's house—he lives in us!—if we keep up our courage firm to the end, and our joy and our trust in the Lord.

1 Pet 2:5. And now you have become living building-stones for God's use in building his house. What's more, you are his holy priests; so come to him—(you who are acceptable to him because of Jesus Christ). [9]For you have been chosen by God himself—you are priests of the King, you are holy and pure, you are God's very own—all this so that you may show to others how God called you out of the darkness into his wonderful light. [10]Once you were less than nothing; now you are God's own. Once you knew very little of God's kindness; now your very lives have been changed by it.

1 Pet 4:1. Since Christ suffered and underwent pain, you must be ready to suffer, too. For remember, when your body suffers, sin loses its power. [2]And you won't be spending the rest of your life chasing after evil desires, but will be anxious to do the will of God.

2 Pet 1:1. From: Simon Peter, a servant and missionary of Jesus Christ. *To:* All of you who have our kind of faith. The faith I speak of is the kind that Jesus Christ our God and Savior gives to us. How precious it is, and how just and good he is to give this same faith to each of us.

1 Jn 2:3. And how can we be sure that we belong to him? By looking within ourselves: are we really trying to do what he wants us to? [5]But those who do what Christ tells them to will learn to love God more and more. That is the way to know whether or not you are a Christian. [6]Anyone who says he is a Christian should live as Christ did. [12]I am writing these things to all of you, my little children, because your sins have been forgiven in the name of Jesus our Savior. [13]I am saying these things to you older men because you really know Christ, the one who has been alive from the beginning. And you young men, I am talking to you because you have won your battle with Satan. And I am writing to you younger boys and girls because you, too, have learned to know God our Father. [14]And so I say to you fathers who know the eternal God, and to you young men who are strong, with God's Word in your hearts, and have won your struggle against Satan: [15]Stop loving this evil world and all that it offers you.

1 Jn 3:2. Yes, dear friends, we are already God's children, right now, and we can't even imagine what it is going to be like later on. But we know this, that when he comes we will be like him, as a result of seeing him as he really is. [3]And everyone who really believes this will try to stay pure because Christ is pure. [6]So if we stay close to him, obedient to him, we won't be sinning either. . . . [7]Oh, dear children, don't let anyone deceive you about this: if you are constantly doing what is good, it is because you *are* good, even as he is. [9]The person who has been born into God's family does not make a practice of sinning, because now God's life is in him; so

he can't keep on sinning, for this new life has been born into him and controls him—he has been *born again.* [14]If we love other Christians it proves that we have been delivered from hell and given eternal life. But a person who doesn't have love for others is headed for eternal death. [18]Little children, let us stop just *saying* we love people; let us *really* love them, and *show it* by our *actions.* [19]Then we will know for sure, by our actions, that we are on God's side, and our consciences will be clear, even when we stand before the Lord.

1 Jn 4:7. Dear friends, let us practice loving each other, for love comes from God and those who are loving and kind show that they are the children of God, and that they are getting to know him better.

1 Jn 5:1. If you believe that Jesus is the Christ—that he is God's Son and your Savior—then you are a child of God. And all who love the Father love his children too.

2 Jn 1:9. While if you are loyal to Christ's teachings, you will have God too. Then you will have both the Father and the Son.

Rev 1:6. He has gathered us into his kingdom and made us priests of God his Father.

Rev 14:4. For they are spiritually undefiled, pure as virgins, following the Lamb wherever he goes. They have been purchased from among the men on the earth as a consecrated offering to God and the Lamb. [5]No falsehood can be charged against them; they are blameless.

Rev 17:14. For he is Lord over all lords, and King of kings, and his people are the called and chosen and faithful ones.

See *Wicked, Described.*

PROMISES TO, EXPRESSED OR IMPLIED. Gen 15:1. Afterwards Jehovah spoke to Abram in a vision, and this is what he told him: "Don't be fearful, Abram, for I will defend you. And I will give you great blessings."

Gen 22:17. I will bless you with incredible blessings and multiply your descendants into countless thousands and millions, like the stars above you in the sky, and like the sands along the seashore. These descendants of yours will conquer their enemies.

Ex 23:22. But if you are careful to obey him, following all my instructions, then I will be an enemy to your enemies.

Lev 26:4, 5. I will give you regular rains, and the land will yield bumper crops, and the trees will be loaded with fruit long after the normal time! And grapes will still be ripening when sowing time comes again. You shall eat your fill, and live safely in the land, [6]for I will give you peace, and you will go to sleep without fear. I will chase away the dangerous animals. [10]You will have such a surplus of crops that you won't know what to do with them when the new harvest is ready!

Deut 28:1. If you fully obey all these commandments of the Lord your God, the laws I am declaring to you today, God will transform you into the greatest nation in the world. [2-6]These are the blessings that will come upon you: Blessings in the city, blessings in the field; many children, ample crops, large flocks and herds; blessings of fruit and bread; blessings when you come in, blessings when you go out. [7]The Lord will defeat your enemies before you; they will march out together against you but scatter before you in seven directions! [8]The Lord will bless you with good crops and healthy cattle, and prosper everything you do when you arrive in the land the Lord your God is giving you. [9]He will change you into a holy people dedicated to himself; this he has promised to do if you will only obey him and walk in his ways. [10]All the nations in the world shall see that you belong to the Lord, and they will stand in awe. [11]The Lord will give you an abundance of good things in the land, just as he promised: many children, many cattle, and abundant crops. [12]He will open to you his wonderful treasury of rain in the heavens, to give you fine crops every season. He will bless everything you do; and you shall lend to many nations, but shall not borrow from them. [13]If you will only listen and obey the commandments of the Lord your God that I am giving you today, he will make you the head and not the tail, and you shall always have the upper hand.

Deut 33:27. The eternal God is your Refuge, and underneath are the everlasting arms. He thrusts out your enemies before you; it is he who cries, "Destroy them!"

1 Sam 2:9. He will protect his godly ones. Prov 2:7, 8.

2 Chron 16:9. For the eyes of the Lord search back and forth across the whole earth, looking for people whose hearts are perfect toward him, so that he can show his great power in helping them.

Ezra 8:22. After all, we had told the king that our God would protect all those who worshiped him, and that disaster could come only to those who had forsaken him!

Job 5:11. And gives prosperity to the poor and humble, and takes sufferers to safety. [12]He frustrates the plans of crafty men. [13]They are caught in their own traps; he thwarts their schemes. [14]They grope like blind men in the daylight; they see no better in the daytime than at night. [15]God saves the fatherless and the poor from the grasp of these oppressors. [16]And so at last the poor have hope, and the fangs of the wicked are broken. [17]How enviable the man whom God corrects! Oh, do not despise the chastening of the Lord when you sin. [18]For though he wounds, he binds and heals again. [19]He will deliver you again and again, so that no evil can touch you. [20]He will keep you from death in famine, and from the power of the sword in time of war. [21]You will be safe from slander; no need to fear the future. [22]You shall laugh at war and famine; wild animals will leave you alone. [23]Dangerous animals will be at peace with you. [24]You need not worry about your home while you are gone; nothing shall be stolen from your barns. [25]Your sons shall become important men; your descendants shall be as numerous as grass! [26]You shall live a long, good life; like standing grain, you'll not be harvested until it's time! [27]I have found from experience that all of this is true. For your own good, listen to my counsel.

Job 8:4. If your children sinned against him, and he punished them, [5]and you begged Almighty God for them— [6]If you were pure and good, he would hear your prayer, and answer you, and bless you with a happy home. [7]And though you started with little, you would end with much.

20. But look! God will not cast away a good man, nor prosper evildoers. [21]He will yet fill your mouth with laughter and your lips with shouts of joy.

Job 11:15. Only then, without the spots of sin to defile you, can you walk steadily forward to God without fear. [16]Only then can you forget your misery. It will all be in the past. [17]And your life will be cloudless; any darkness will be as bright as morning! [18]You will have courage because you will have hope. You will take your time, and rest in safety. [19]You will lie down unafraid and many will look to you for help. [20]But the wicked shall find no way to escape; their only hope is death.

Job 22:21. Quit quarreling with God! Agree with him and you will have peace at last! His favor will surround you if you will only admit that you were wrong. [22]Listen to his instructions and store them in your heart. [23]If you return to God and put right all the wrong in your home, then you will be restored. [24]If you give up your lust for money, and throw your gold away, [25]then the Almighty himself shall be your treasure; he will be your precious silver! [26]Then you will delight yourself in the Lord, and look up to God. [27]You will pray to him, and he will hear you, and you will fulfill all your promises to him. [28]Whatever you wish will happen! And the light of heaven will shine upon the road ahead of you. [29]If you are attacked and knocked down, you will know that there is someone who will lift you up again. Yes, he will save the humble, [30]And help even sinners by your pure hands.

Job 36:7. He does not ignore the good men but honors them by placing them upon eternal, kingly thrones. [8]If troubles come upon them, and they are enslaved and afflicted, [9]then he takes the trouble to point out to them the reason, what they have done that is wrong, or how they have behaved proudly. [10]He helps them hear his instruction to turn away from their sin. [11]If they listen and obey him, then they will be blessed with prosperity throughout their lives. [12]If they won't listen to him, they shall perish in battle and die because of their lack of good sense.

Ps. 4:3. Mark this well: The Lord has set apart the redeemed for himself. Therefore he will listen to me and answer when I call to him.

Ps 5:12. For you bless the godly man, O Lord; you protect him with your shield of love.

Ps 15:2. Anyone who leads a blameless life and is truly sincere. [3]Anyone who refuses to slander others, does not listen to gossip, never harms his neighbor, [4]speaks out against sin, criticizes those committing it, commends the faithful followers of the Lord, keeps a promise even if it ruins him, [5]does not crush his debtors with high interest rates, and refuses to testify against the innocent despite the bribes offered him—such a man shall stand firm forever.

Ps 23:6. Your goodness and unfailing kindness shall be with me all of my life, and afterward I will live with you forever in your home.

Ps 25:10. And when we obey him, every path he guides us on is fragrant with his lovingkindness and his truth. [11]But Lord, my sins! How many they are. Oh, pardon them for the honor of your name. [12]Where is the man who fears the Lord? God will teach him how to choose the best. [13]He shall live within God's circle of blessing, and his children shall inherit the earth. [14]Friendship with God is reserved for those who reverence him. With them alone he shares the secrets of his promises. Prov 3: 32.

Ps 28:8. The Lord protects his people and gives victory to his anointed king.

Ps 29:11. He will give his people strength. He will bless them with peace.

Ps 32:6. Now I say that each believer should confess his sins to God when he is aware of them, while there is time to be forgiven. Judgment will not touch him if he does. [7]You are my hiding place from every storm of life; you even keep me from getting into trouble! You surround me with songs of victory. [8]I will instruct you (says the Lord) and guide you along the best pathway for your life; I will advise you and watch your progress. [10]Many sorrows come to the wicked, but abiding love surrounds those who trust in the Lord.

Ps 33:18, 19. But the eyes of the Lord are watching over those who fear him, who rely upon his steady love. He will keep them from death even in times of famine!

Ps 34:9. If you belong to the Lord, reverence him; for everyone who does this has everything he needs. [10]Even strong young lions sometimes go hungry, but those of us who reverence the Lord will never lack any good thing. [15]For the eyes of the Lord are intently watching all who live good lives, and he gives attention when they cry to him. [17]Yes, the Lord hears the good man when he calls to him for help, and saves him out of all his troubles.

Ps 37:3. Trust in the Lord instead. Be kind and good to others; then you will live safely here in the land and prosper, feeding in safety.

4. Be delighted with the Lord. Then he will give you all your heart's desires.

5. Commit everything you do to the Lord. Trust him to help you do it and he will.

9. For the wicked shall be destroyed, but those who trust the Lord shall be given every blessing.

18. Day by day the Lord observes the good deeds done by godly men, and gives them eternal rewards.

23. The steps of good men are directed by the Lord. He delights in each step they take. [24]If they fall it isn't fatal, for the Lord holds them with his hand. [25]I have been young and now I am old. And

in all my years I have never seen the Lord forsake a man who loves him; nor have I seen the children of the godly go hungry. [26]Instead, the godly are able to be generous with their gifts and loans to others, and their children are a blessing.

27. So if you want an eternal home, leave your evil, lowdown ways and live good lives. [28]For the Lord loves justice and fairness; he will never abandon his people. They will be kept safe forever; but all who love wickedness shall perish. [29]The godly shall be firmly planted in the land, and live there forever. [34]Don't be impatient for the Lord to act! Keep traveling steadily along his pathway and in due season he will honor you with every blessing, and you will see the wicked destroyed.

Ps 41:1. God blesses those who are kind to the poor. He helps them out of their troubles. [2]He protects them and keeps them alive; he publicly honors them and destroys the power of their enemies.

Ps 50:15. *I want you to trust me in your times of trouble, so I can rescue you, and you can give me glory.*

Ps 55:22. Give your burdens to the Lord. He will carry them. He will not permit the godly to slip or fall.

Ps 58:11. Then at last everyone will know that good is rewarded, and that there is a God who judges justly here on earth.

Ps 62:8. O my people, trust him all the time. Pour out your longings before him, for he can help!

Ps 65:4. How greatly to be envied are those you have chosen to come and live with you within the holy tabernacle courts!

Ps 73:24. You will keep on guiding me all my life with your wisdom and counsel; and afterwards receive me into the glories of heaven!

Ps 81:10. For it was I, Jehovah your God, who brought you out of the land of Egypt. Only test me! Open your mouth wide and see if I won't fill it. You will receive every blessing you can use!

Ps 84:11. For Jehovah God is our Light and our Protector. He gives us grace and glory. No good thing will he withhold from those who walk along his paths.

Ps 85:9. Surely his salvation is near to those who reverence him; our land will be filled with his glory.

Ps 91:1. We live within the shadow of the Almighty, sheltered by the God who is above all gods.

3. For he rescues you from every trap, and protects you from the fatal plague. [4]He will shield you with his wings! They will shelter you. His faithful promises are your armor. [5]Now you don't need to be afraid of the dark any more, nor fear the dangers of the day; [6]nor dread the plagues of darkness, nor disasters in the morning. [7]Though a thousand fall at my side, though ten thousand are dying around me, the evil will not touch me. [9]For Jehovah is my refuge! I choose the God above all gods to shelter me. [10]How then can evil overtake me or any plague come near? [11]For he orders his angels to protect you wherever you go. [12]They will steady you with their hands to keep you from stumbling against the rocks on the trail.

Ps 94:17. I would have died unless the Lord had helped me. [18]I screamed, "I'm slipping, Lord!" and he was kind and saved me.

Ps 97:10. The Lord loves those who hate evil; he protects the lives of his people, and rescues them from the wicked. [11]Light is sown for the godly and joy for the good.

Ps 111:5. He gives food to those who trust him; he never forgets his promises.

Ps 112:6. Such a man will not be overthrown by evil circumstances. God's constant care of him will make a deep impression on all who see it.

Ps 121:3, 4. He will never let me stumble, slip or fall. For he is always watching, never sleeping. [5]Jehovah himself is caring for you! He is your defender. [6]He protects you day and night. [7]He keeps you from all evil, and preserves your life. [8]He keeps his eye upon you as you come and go, and always guards you.

Ps 125:1. Those who trust in the Lord are steady as Mount Zion, unmoved by any circumstance. [2]Just as the mountains surround and protect Jerusalem, so the Lord surrounds and protects his people. [3]For the wicked shall not rule the godly, lest the godly be forced to do wrong.

Ps 128:1. Blessings on all who reverence and trust the Lord—on all who obey him! [2]Their reward shall be prosperity and happiness. [3]Your wife shall be contented in your home. And look at all those children! There they sit around the dinner table as vigorous and healthy as young olive trees. [4]That is God's reward to those who reverence and trust him. [5]May the Lord continually bless you with heaven's blessings as well as with human joys. [6]May you live to enjoy your grandchildren! And may God bless Israel!

Ps 145:18. He is close to all who call on him sincerely. [19]He fulfills the desires of those who reverence and trust him; he hears their cries for help and rescues them. [20]He protects all those who love him, but destroys the wicked. [21]I will praise the Lord and call on all men everywhere to bless his holy name forever and forever.

Prov 1:33. But all who listen to me shall live in peace and safety unafraid.

Prov 2:21. For only good men enjoy life to the full.

Prov 3:1, 2. My son, never forget the things I've taught you. If you want a long and satisfying life, closely follow my instructions. [3]Never forget to be truthful and kind. Hold these virtues tightly. Write them deep within your heart. [4, 5]If you want favor with both God and man, and a reputation for good judgment and common sense, then trust the Lord completely; don't ever trust yourself. [6]In everything you do, put God first, and he will direct you and crown your efforts with success.

7, 8. Don't be conceited, sure of your own wisdom. Instead, trust and reverence the Lord, and turn your back on evil; when you do that, then you will be given renewed health and vitality. [9, 10]Honor the Lord by giving him the first part of all your income, and he will fill your barns with wheat and barley and overflow your wine vats with the finest wines.

25, 26. You need not be afraid of disaster or the plots of wicked men, for the Lord is with you; he protects you.

Prov 10:3. The Lord will not let a good man starve to death, nor will he let the wicked man's riches continue forever.

Prov 12:2. The Lord blesses good men and condemns the wicked.

Prov 14:26. His children have a place of refuge and security.

Prov 15:29. The Lord is far from the wicked, but he hears the prayers of the righteous.

Prov 16:7. When a man is trying to please God, God makes even his worst enemies to be at peace with him.

Prov 21:21. The man who tries to be good, loving and kind finds life, righteousness and honor.

Prov 28:25. Greed causes fighting; trusting God leads to prosperity.

Prov 29:25. Fear of man is a dangerous trap, but to trust in God means safety.

Eccl 7:18. Tackle every task that comes along, and if you fear God you can expect his blessing.

Eccl 8:5. Those who obey him will not be punished. The wise man will find a time and a way to do what he says.

Isa 4:5. Then the Lord will provide shade on all Jerusalem—over every home and all its public grounds—a canopy of smoke and cloud throughout the day, and clouds of fire at night, covering the Glorious Land, [6]protecting it from daytime heat and from rains and storms.

Isa 11:6. In that day the wolf and the lamb will lie down together, and the leopard and goats will be at peace. Calves and fat cattle will be safe among lions, and a little child shall lead them all. [7]The cows will graze among bears; cubs and calves will lie down together, and lions will eat grass like the cows. [8]Babies will crawl safely among poisonous snakes, and a little child who puts his hand in a nest of deadly adders will pull it out unharmed. [9]Nothing will hurt or destroy in all my holy mountain, for as the waters fill the sea, so shall the earth be full of the knowledge of the Lord.

Isa 25:8. He will swallow up death forever. The Lord God will wipe away all tears and take away forever all insults and mockery against his land and people. The Lord has spoken—he will surely do it!

Isa 26:3. He will keep in perfect peace all those who trust in him, whose thoughts turn often to the Lord!

Isa 33:16. Such as these shall dwell on high. The rocks of the mountains will be their fortress of safety; food will be supplied to them and they will have all the water they need. [21]The glorious Lord will be to us as a wide river of protection, and no enemy can cross. [22]For the Lord is our Judge, our Lawgiver and our King; he will care for us and save us. [24]The people of Israel will no longer say, "We are sick and helpless," for the Lord will forgive them their sins and bless them.

Isa 35:10. These, the ransomed of the Lord, will go home along that road to Zion, singing the songs of everlasting joy. For them all sorrow and all sighing will be gone forever; only joy and gladness will be there.

Isa 40:10. Yes, the Lord God is coming with mighty power; he will rule with awesome strength. See, his reward is with him, to each as he has done. [11]He will feed his flock like a shepherd; he will carry the lambs in his arms and gently lead the ewes with young. [29]He gives power to the tired and worn out, and strength to the weak. [31]But they that wait upon the Lord shall renew their strength. They shall mount up with wings like eagles; they shall run and not be weary; they shall walk and not faint.

Isa 41:10. Fear not, for I am with you. Do not be dismayed. I am your God. I will strengthen you; I will help you; I will uphold you with my victorious right hand. [11]See, all your angry enemies lie confused and shattered. Anyone opposing you will die. [13]I am holding you by your right hand—I, the Lord your God—and I say to you, Don't be afraid; I am here to help you.

Isa 43:2. When you go through deep waters and great trouble, I will be with you. When you go through rivers of difficulty, you will not drown! When you walk through the fire of oppression, you will not be burned up—the flames will not consume you.

Isa 44:2. The Lord who made you, who will help you, says, O servant of mine, don't be afraid. O Jerusalem, my chosen ones, don't be afraid. [3]For I will give you abundant water for your thirst and for your parched fields. And I will pour out my Spirit and my blessings on your children.

Isa 49:9. Through you I am saying to the prisoners of darkness, "Come out! I am giving you your freedom!" They will be my sheep, grazing in green pastures and on the grassy hills. [10]They shall neither hunger nor thirst; the searing sun and scorching desert winds will not reach them any more. For the Lord in his mercy will lead them beside the cool waters. [11]And I will make my mountains into level paths for them; the highways shall be raised above the valleys. [12]See, my people shall return from far away, from north and west and south.

Isa 50:7. Because the Lord God helps me, I will not be dismayed; therefore, I have set my face like flint to do his will, and I know that I will triumph. [8]He who gives me justice is near. Who will dare to fight against me now? Where are my enemies? Let them appear! [9]See, the Lord God is for me! Who shall declare me guilty? All my enemies shall be destroyed like old clothes eaten up by moths!

Isa 51:11. The time will come when God's redeemed will all come home again. They shall come with singing to Jerusalem, filled with joy and everlasting gladness; sorrow and mourning will all disappear.

Isa 54:14. You will live under a government that is just and fair. Your enemies will stay far away; you will live in peace. Terror shall not come near. [17]But in that coming day no weapon turned against you shall succeed, and you will have justice against every courtroom lie. This is the heritage of the servants of the Lord. This is the blessing I have given you, says the Lord. *vs.* 1–16.

Isa 56:2. Blessed is the man who refuses to work during my Sabbath days of rest, but honors them; and blessed is the man who checks himself from doing wrong. [3]And my blessings are for Gentiles, too, when they accept the Lord; don't let them think that I will make them second-class citizens. And this is for the eunuchs too. They can be as much mine as anyone. [4]For I say this to the eunuchs who keep his Sabbaths holy and choose the things that please him, and come to grips with his laws: [5]I will give them—in my house, within my walls—a name far greater than the honor they would receive from having sons and daughters. For the name that I will give them is an everlasting one; it will never disappear. [6]As for the Gentiles, the outsiders who join the people of the Lord and serve him and love his name, and are his servants and don't desecrate the Sabbath, and have accepted his covenant and promises, [7]I will bring them also to my holy mountain of Jerusalem, and make them full of joy within my House of Prayer. I will accept their sacrifices and offerings, for my Temple shall be called "A House of Prayer for All People"! [8]For the Lord God who brings back the outcasts of Israel says, I will bring others too besides my people Israel.

Isa 57:1. The good men perish; the godly die before their time and no one seems to care or wonder why. No one seems to realize that God is taking them away from evil days ahead. [2]For the godly who die shall rest in peace.

Isa 58:8. If you do these things, God will shed his own glorious light upon you. He will heal you; your godliness will lead you forward, and goodness will be a shield before you, and the glory of the Lord will protect you from behind. [9]Then, when you call, the Lord will answer. "Yes, I am here," he will quickly reply. All you need to do is to stop oppressing the weak, and to stop making false accusations and spreading vicious rumors! [10]Feed the hungry! Help those in trouble! Then your light will shine out from the darkness, and the darkness around you shall be as bright as day. [11]And the Lord will guide you continually, and satisfy you with all good things, and keep you healthy too; and you will be like a well-watered garden, like an ever-flowing spring. [12]Your sons will rebuild the long-deserted ruins of your cities, and you will be known as "The People Who Rebuild Their Walls and Cities." [13]If you keep the Sabbath holy, not having your own fun and business on that day, but enjoying the Sabbath and speaking of it with delight as the Lord's holy day, and honoring the Lord in what you do, not following your own desires and pleasure, nor talking idly— [14]then the Lord will be your delight, and I will see to it that you ride high, and get your full share of the blessings I promised to Jacob, your father. The Lord has spoken.

Isa 59:20. He will come as a Redeemer to those in Zion who have turned away from sin. [21]"As for me, this is my promise to them," says the Lord: "My Holy Spirit shall not leave them, and they shall want the good and hate the wrong—they and their children and their children's children forever."

Isa 64:4. For since the world began no one has seen or heard of such a God as ours, who works for those who wait for him!

Isa 65:13. Therefore the Lord God says, You shall starve, but my servants shall eat; you shall be thirsty while they drink; you shall be sad and ashamed, but they shall rejoice. [14]You shall cry in sorrow and vexation and despair, while they sing for joy.

17. For see, I am creating new heavens and a new earth—so wonderful that no one will even think about the old ones anymore. [18]Be glad; rejoice forever in my creation. Look! I will recreate Jerusalem as a place of happiness, and her people shall be a joy! [19]And I will rejoice in Jerusalem, and in my people; and the voice of weeping and crying shall not be heard there any more. [20]No longer will babies die when only a few days old; no longer will men be considered old at 100! Only sinners will die that young! [21, 22]In those days, when a man builds a house, he will keep on living in it—it will not be destroyed by invading armies as in the past. My people will plant vineyards and eat the fruit themselves—their enemies will not confiscate it. For my people will live as long as trees and will long enjoy their hard-won gains. [23]Their harvests will not be eaten by their enemies; their children will not be born to be cannon fodder. For they are the children of those the Lord has blessed; and their children, too, shall be blessed. [24]I will answer them before they even call to me. While they are still talking to me about their needs, I will go ahead and answer their prayers! [25]The wolf and lamb shall feed together, the lion shall eat straw as the ox does, and poisonous snakes shall strike no more! In those days nothing and no one shall be hurt or destroyed in all my Holy Mountain, says the Lord.

Isa 66:13. I will comfort you there as a little one is comforted by its mother. [14]When you see Jerusalem, your heart will rejoice; vigorous health will be yours. All the world will see the good hand of God upon his people, and his wrath upon his enemies.

Jer 17:7. But blessed is the man who trusts in the Lord and has made the Lord his hope and confidence. [8]He is like a tree planted along a riverbank, with its roots reaching deep into the water—a tree not bothered by the heat nor worried by long months of drought. Its leaves stay green and it goes right on producing all its luscious fruit.

Ezk 18:5. But if a man is just and does what is lawful and right, [6]and has not gone out to the mountains to feast before the idols of Israel and worship them, and does not commit adultery, nor lie with any woman during the time of her menstruation, [7]and is a merciful creditor, not holding on to the items given to him in pledge by poor debtors, and is no robber, but gives food to the hungry and clothes to those in need, [8]and grants loans without interest, and stays away from sin, and is honest and fair when judging others, [9]and obeys my laws—that man is just, says the Lord and he shall surely live. [19]"What?" you ask. "Doesn't the son pay for his father's sins?" No! For if the son does what is right and keeps my laws, he shall surely live. [20]The one who sins is the one who dies. The son shall not be punished for his father's sins, nor the father for his son's. The righteous person will be rewarded for his own goodness and the wicked person for his wickedness.

Ezk 34:11. For the Lord God says: I will search and find my sheep. [12]I will be like a shepherd looking for his flock. I will find my sheep and rescue them from all the places they were scattered in that dark and cloudy day. [13]And I will bring them back from among the people and nations where they were, back home to their own land of Israel, and I will feed them upon the mountains of Israel and by the rivers where the land is fertile and good. [14]Yes, I will give them good pasture on the high hills of Israel. There they will lie down in peace and feed in luscious mountain pastures. [15, 16]I myself will be the Shepherd of my sheep, and cause them to lie down in peace, the Lord God says. I will seek my lost ones, those who strayed away, and bring them safely home again. I will put splints and bandages upon their broken limbs and heal the sick. And I will destroy the powerful, fat shepherds; I will feed them, yes—feed them punishment! [17]And as for you, O my flock—my people—the Lord God says, I will distinguish lambs from kids and rams from billy goats! [22]So I myself will save my flock; no more will they be picked on and destroyed. And I will notice which is plump and which is thin, and why! [23]And I will set one Shepherd over all my people, even my Servant, David. He shall feed them and be a Shepherd to them. [24]And I, the Lord, will be their God, and my Servant David shall be a Prince among my people. I, the Lord, have spoken it. [25]I will make a peace pact with them, and drive away the dangerous animals from the land so that my people can safely camp in the wildest places and sleep safely in the woods. [26]I will make my people and their homes around my hill a blessing. And there shall be showers, showers of blessing, for I will not shut off the rains but send them in their seasons. [27]Their fruit trees and fields will yield bumper crops, and everyone will live in safety. When I have broken off their chains of slavery and delivered them from those who profiteered at their expense, they shall know I am the Lord. [28]No more will other nations conquer them nor wild animals attack. They shall live in safety and no one shall make them afraid. [29]And I will raise up a notable Vine (the Messiah), in Israel so that my people will never again go hungry nor be shamed by heathen conquest. [30]In this way they will know that I, the Lord their God, am with them, and that they, the people of Israel, are my people, says the Lord God. [31]You are my flock, the sheep of my pasture. You are my men and I am your God, so says the Lord.

Dan 12:1. At that time Michael, the mighty angelic prince who stands guard over your nation, will stand up (and fight for you in heaven against satanic forces), and there will be a time of anguish for the Jews greater than any previous suffering in Jewish history. And yet every one of your people whose names are written in the Book will endure it. [2]And many of those whose bodies lie dead and buried will rise up, some to everlasting life and some to shame and everlasting contempt. [3]And those who are wise—the people of God—shall shine as brightly as the sun's brilliance, and those who turn many to righteousness will glitter like stars forever.

Hos 6:3. Oh, that we might know the Lord! Let us press on to know him, and he will respond to us as surely as the coming of dawn or the rain of early spring.

Nah 1:7. The Lord is good. When trouble comes, he is the place to go! And he knows everyone who trusts in him.

Hag 1:13. Then the Lord told them (again sending the message through Haggai, his messenger), "I am with you; I will bless you."

Hag 2:4. But take courage, O Zerubbabel and Joshua and all the people; take courage and work, for "I am with you," says the Lord of Hosts. [5]"For I promised when you left Egypt that my Spirit would remain among you; so don't be afraid."

Zech 3:7. The Lord of Hosts declares: "If you will follow the paths I set for you and do all I tell you to, then I will put you in charge of my Temple, to keep it holy; and I will let you walk in and out of my presence with these angels."

Mal 3:16. Then those who feared and loved the Lord spoke often of him to each other. And he had a Book of Remembrance drawn up in which he recorded the names of those who feared him and loved to think about him. [17]"They shall be mine," says the Lord of Hosts, "in that day when I make up my jewels. And I will spare them as a man spares an obedient and dutiful son. [18]Then you will see the difference between God's treatment of good men and bad, between those who serve him and those who don't."

Mal 4:2. "But for you who fear my name, the Sun of Righteousness will rise with healing in his wings. And you will go free, leaping with joy like calves let out to pasture. [3]Then you will tread upon the wicked as ashes underfoot," says the Lord of Hosts.

Mt 5:3. Humble men are very fortunate . . . for the Kingdom of Heaven is given to them.

4. Those who mourn are fortunate! for they shall be comforted.

5. The meek and lowly are fortunate! for the whole wide world belongs to them.

6. Happy are those who long to be just and good, for they shall be completely satisfied.

7. Happy are the kind and merciful, for they shall be shown mercy.

8. Happy are those whose hearts are pure, for they shall see God.

9. Happy are those who strive for peace—they shall be called the sons of God.

10. Happy are those who are persecuted because they are good, for the Kingdom of Heaven is theirs.

11. When you are reviled and persecuted and lied about because you are my followers—wonderful!

12. Be *happy* about it! Be *very glad!* for a *tremendous reward* awaits you up in heaven. And remember, the ancient prophets were persecuted too.

Mt 7:7. Ask, and you will be given what you ask for. Seek, and you will find. Knock and the door will be opened. [8]For everyone who asks, receives. Anyone who seeks, finds. If only you will knock, the door will open. Lk 11:9, 10.

Mt 8:11. And I tell you this, that many Gentiles (like this Roman officer), shall come from all over the world and sit down in the Kingdom of Heaven with Abraham, Isaac, and Jacob.

Mt 10:28. Don't be afraid of those who can kill only your bodies—but can't touch your souls! Fear only God who can destroy both soul and body in hell. [29]Not one sparrow (What do they cost? Two for a penny?) can fall to the ground without your Father knowing it. [30]And the very hairs of your head are all numbered. [31]So don't worry! You are more valuable to him than many sparrows. [32]If anyone publicly acknowledges me as his friend, I will openly acknowledge him as my friend before my father in heaven.

Mt 13:43. Then the godly shall shine as the sun in their Father's Kingdom. Let those with ears, listen!

Mt 18:10. Beware that you don't look down upon a single one of these little children. For I tell you that in heaven their angels have constant access to my Father. [19]I also tell you this—if two of you agree down here on earth concerning anything you ask for, my Father in heaven will do it for you. [20]For where two or three gather together because they are mine, I will be right there among them.

Mt 24:21. For there will be persecution such as the world has never seen in all its history, and will never see again. [22]In fact, unless those days are shortened, all mankind will perish. But they will be shortened for the sake of God's chosen people.

Mt 25:21. His master praised him for good work. "You have been faithful in handling this small amount," he told him, "so now I will give you many more responsibilities. Begin the joyous tasks I have assigned to you." Lk 19:16–21.

33. And place the sheep on my right hand, and the goats at my left. [34]Then I, the King, shall say to those at my right, "Come, blessed of my Father, into the Kingdom prepared for you from the founding of the world."

46. And they shall go away into eternal punishment; but the righteous into everlasting life.

Mt 28:20. And be sure of this—that I am with you always, even to the end of the world.

Mk 3:35. Anyone who does God's will is my brother, and my sister, and my mother.

Mk 8:35. If you insist on saving your life, you will lose it. Only those who throw away their lives for my sake and for the sake of the Good News will ever know what it means to really live.

Mk 9:41. If anyone so much as gives you a cup of water because you are Christ's—I say this solemnly—he won't lose his reward.

Mk 10:21. Jesus felt genuine love for this man as he looked at him. "You lack only one thing," he told him; "go and sell all you have and give the money to the poor—and you shall have treasure in heaven—and come, follow me."

29. And Jesus replied, "Let me assure you that no one has ever given up anything—home, brothers, sisters, mother, father, children, or property—for love of me and to tell others the Good News, [Mt 19:29.] [30]who won't be given back, a hundred times over, homes, brothers, sisters, mothers, children, and land—with persecutions! All these will be his here on earth, and in the world to come he shall have eternal life.

Mk 11:23. You can say to this Mount of Olives, "Rise up and fall into the Mediterranean," and your command will be obeyed. All that's required is that you really believe and have no doubt! [24]Listen to me! You can pray for *anything,* and *if you believe, you have it;* it's yours!

Mk 13:13. And everyone will hate you because you are mine. But all who endure to the end without renouncing me shall be saved.

27. And I will send out the angels to gather together my chosen ones from all over the world—from the farthest bounds of earth and heaven.

Lk 3:17. He will separate chaff from grain, and burn up the chaff with eternal fire and store away the grain. Mt 3:12.

Lk 6:20. Then he turned to his disciples and said, "What happiness there is for you who are poor, for the Kingdom of God is yours! [21]What happiness there is for you who are now hungry, for you are going to be satisfied. What happiness there is for you who weep, for the time will come when you shall laugh with joy! [22]What happiness it is when others hate you and exclude you and insult you and smear your name because you are mine! [23]When that happens, rejoice! Yes, leap for joy! For you will have a great reward awaiting you in heaven. And you will be in good company—the ancient prophets were treated that way too! Mt 5:3–12.

Lk 10:20. However, the important thing is not that demons obey you, but that your names are registered as citizens of heaven.

Lk 12:7. And he knows the number of hairs on your head! Never fear, you are far more valuable to him than a whole flock of sparrows. [32]So don't be afraid, little flock. For it gives your Father great happiness to give you the Kingdom.

Lk 16:22. Finally the beggar died and was carried by the angels to be with Abraham in the place of the righteous dead. The rich man also died and was buried, [23]and his soul went into hell. There, in torment, he saw Lazarus in the far distance with Abraham. [24]"Father Abraham," he shouted, "have some pity! Send Lazarus over here if only to dip the tip of his finger in water and cool my tongue, for I am in anguish in these flames." [25]But Abraham said to him, "Son, remember that during your lifetime you had everything you wanted, and Lazarus had nothing. So now he is here being comforted and you are in anguish."

Lk 18:29. "Yes," Jesus replied, "and everyone who has done as you have, leaving home, wife, brothers, parents, or children for the sake of the Kingdom of God, [30]will be repaid many times over now, as well as receiving eternal life in the world to come."

Lk 20:35. But when those who are counted worthy of being raised from the dead get to heaven, they do not marry. [36]And they never die again; in these respects they are like angels, and are sons of God, for they are raised up in new life from the dead.

Lk 21:18. But not a hair of your head will perish!

27. Then the peoples of the earth shall see me, the Messiah, coming in a cloud with power and great glory. [28]So when all these things begin to happen, stand straight and look up! For your salvation is near.

Lk 22:29. And because my Father has granted me a Kingdom, I, here and now, grant you the right [30]to eat and drink at my table in that Kingdom; and you will sit on thrones judging the twelve tribes of of Israel.

Lk 23:43. And Jesus replied, "Today you will be with me in Paradise."

Jn 3:15. So that anyone who believes in me will have eternal life.

16. For God loved the world so much that he gave his only Son so that anyone who believes in him shall not perish but have eternal life. [17]God did not send his Son into the world to condemn it, but to save it.

18. There is no eternal doom awaiting those who trust him to save them. But those who don't trust him have already been tried and condemned for not believing in the only Son of God.

36. And all who trust him—God's Son—to save them have eternal life.

Jn 4:14. "But the water I give them," he said, "becomes a perpetual spring within them, watering them forever with eternal life."

Jn 5:24. I say emphatically that anyone who listens to my message and believes in God who sent me has eternal life, and will never be damned for his sins, but has already passed out of death into life.

29. And shall rise again—those who have done good, to eternal life; and those who have continued in evil, to judgment.

Jn 6:39. And this is the will of God, that I should not lose even one of all those he has given me, but that I should raise them to eternal life at the Last Day. [40]For it is my Father's will that everyone who sees his Son and believes on him should have eternal life—that I should raise him at the Last Day.

Jn 8:12. Later, in one of his talks, Jesus said to the people, "I am the Light of the world. So if you follow me, you won't be stumbling through the darkness, for living light will flood your path. [51]With all the earnestness I have I tell you this—no one who obeys me shall ever die!"

Jn 9:31. Well, God doesn't listen to evil men, but he has open ears to those who worship him and do his will.

Jn 10:27. My sheep recognize my voice, and I know them, and they follow me. [28]I give them eternal life and they shall never perish. No one shall snatch them away from me, [29]for my Father has given them to me, and he is more powerful than anyone else, so no one can kidnap them from me.

Jn 12:25. If you love your life down here—you will lose it. If you despise your life down here—you will exchange it for eternal glory. [26]If these Greeks want to be my disciples, tell them to come and follow me, for my servants must be where I am. And if they follow me, the Father will honor them.

Jn 13:36. And Jesus replied, "You can't go with me now; but you will follow me later."

Jn 14:1. Let not your heart be troubled. You are trusting God, now trust in me. [2, 3]There are many homes up there where my Father lives, and I am going to prepare them for your coming. When everything is ready, then I will come and get you, so that you can always be with me where I am. If this weren't so, I would tell you plainly.

12, 13. In solemn truth I tell you, anyone believing in me shall do the same miracles I have done, and even greater ones, because I am going to be with the Father. You can ask him for *anything*, using my name, and I will do it, for this will bring praise to the Father because of what I, the Son, will do for you. [14]Yes, ask *anything*, using my name, and I will do it!

15, 16. If you love me, obey me; and I will ask the Father and he will give you another Comforter, and he will never leave you. [17]He is the Holy Spirit, the Spirit who leads into all truth. The world at large cannot receive him, for it isn't looking for him and doesn't recognize him. But you do, for he lives with you now and some day shall be in you. [18]No, I will not abandon you or leave you as orphans in the storm—I will come to you. [19]In just a little while I will be gone from the world, but I will still be present with you. For I will live again—and you will too. [20]When I come back to life again, you will know that I am in my Father, and you in me, and I in you. [21]The one who obeys me is the one who loves me; and because he loves me, my Father will love him; and I will too, and I will reveal myself to him.

23. Jesus replied, "Because I will only reveal myself to those who love me and obey me. The Father will love them too, and we will come to them and live with them."

Jn 16:33. I have told you all this so that you will

have peace of heart and mind. Here on earth you will have many trials and sorrows; but cheer up, for I have overcome the world.

Jn 17:2. For you have given him authority over every man and woman in all the earth. He gives eternal life to each one you have given him. [22]I have given them the glory you gave me—the glorious unity of being one, as we are. [24]Father, I want them with me—these you've given me—so that they can see my glory. You gave me the glory because you loved me before the world began!

Acts 10:4. And the angel replied, "Your prayers and charities have not gone unnoticed by God!" [31]He told me, "Cornelius, your prayers are heard and your charities have been noticed by God!"

Acts 20:32. And now I entrust you to God and his care and to his wonderful words which are able to build your faith and give you all the inheritance of those who are set apart for himself.

Acts 26:18. To open their eyes to their true condition so that they may repent and live in the light of God instead of in Satan's darkness, so that they may receive forgiveness for their sins and God's inheritance along with all people everywhere whose sins are cleansed away, who are set apart by faith in me.

Rom 2:7. He will give eternal life to those who patiently do the will of God, seeking for the unseen glory and honor and eternal life that he offers. [10]But there will be glory and honor and peace from God for all who obey him, whether they are Jews or Gentiles.

Rom 5:9. And since by his blood he did all this for us as sinners, how much more will he do for us now that he has declared us not guilty? Now he will save us from all of God's wrath to come. [10]And since, when we were his enemies, we were brought back to God by the death of his Son, what blessings he must have for us now that we are his friends, and he is living within us! [11]Now we rejoice in our wonderful new relationship with God—all because of what our Lord Jesus Christ has done in dying for our sins—making us friends of God. [17]The sin of this one man, Adam, caused *death to be king over all,* but all who will take God's gift of forgiveness and acquittal are *kings of life* because of this one man, Jesus Christ.

Rom 6:22. But now you are free from the power of sin and are slaves of God, and his benefits to you include holiness and everlasting life. [23]For the wages of sin is death, but the free gift of God is eternal life through Jesus Christ our Lord.

Rom 8:14. For all who are led by the Spirit of God are sons of God. [15]And so we should not be like cringing, fearful slaves, but we should behave like God's very own children, adopted into the bosom of his family, and calling to him, "Father, Father." [16]For his Holy Spirit speaks to us deep in our hearts, and tells us that we really are God's children. [17]And since we are his children, we will share his treasures—for all God gives to his Son Jesus is now ours too. But if we are to share his glory, we must also share his suffering. [18]Yet what we suffer now is nothing compared to the glory he will give us later.

28. And we know that all that happens to us is working for our good if we love God and are fitting into his plans.

32. Since he did not spare even his own Son for us but gave him up for us all, won't he also surely give us everything else? [33]Who dares accuse us whom God has chosen for his own? Will God? No! He is the one who has forgiven us and given us right standing with himself. [34]Who then will condemn us? Will Christ? *No!* For he is the one who died for us and came back to life again for us and is sitting at the place of highest honor next to God, pleading for us there in heaven. [35]Who then can ever keep Christ's love from us? When we have trouble or calamity, when we are hunted down or destroyed, is it because he doesn't love us anymore? And if we are hungry, or penniless, or in danger, or threatened with death, has God deserted us? [36]No, for the Scriptures tell us that for his sake we must be ready to face death at every moment of the day—we are like sheep awaiting slaughter; [37]but despite all this, overwhelming victory is ours through Christ who loved us enough to die for us. [38]For I am convinced that nothing can ever separate us from his love. Death can't, and life can't. The angels won't, and all the powers of hell itself cannot keep God's love away. Our fears for today, our worries about tomorrow, [39]or where we are—high above the sky, or in the deepest ocean—nothing will ever be able to separate us from the love of God demonstrated by our Lord Jesus Christ when he died for us.

Rom 9:33. God . . . said, "I have put a Rock in the path of the Jews, and many will stumble over him (Jesus). Those who believe in him will never be disappointed."

Rom 10:9. For if you tell others with your own mouth that Jesus Christ is your Lord, and believe in your own heart that God has raised him from the dead, you will be saved. [11]For the Scriptures tell us that no one who believes in Christ will ever be disappointed. [12]Jew and Gentile are the same in this respect: they all have the same Lord who generously gives his riches to all those who ask him for them. [13]Anyone who calls upon the name of the Lord will be saved.

Rom 13:11. Another reason for right living is this: you know how late it is; time is running out. Wake up, for the coming of the Lord is nearer now than when we first believed.

1 Cor 1:8. And he guarantees right up to the end that you will be counted free from all sin and guilt on that day when he returns. [9]God will surely do this for you, for he always does just what he says, and he is the one who invited you into this wonderful friendship with his Son, even Christ our Lord.

1 Cor 2:9. That is what is meant by the Scriptures which say that no mere man has ever seen, heard or even imagined what wonderful things God has ready for those who love the Lord.

1 Cor 3:21. So don't be proud of following the

wise men of this world. For God has already given you everything you need. [22]He has given you Paul and Apollos and Peter as your helpers. He has given you the whole world to use, and life and even death are your servants. He has given you all of the present and all of the future. All are yours, [23]and you belong to Christ, and Christ is God's.

1 Cor 6:2. Don't you know that some day we Christians are going to judge and govern the world? So why can't you decide even these little things among yourselves? [3]Don't you realize that we Christians will judge and reward the very angels in heaven? So you should be able to decide your problems down here on earth easily enough.

1 Cor 8:3. But the person who truly loves God is the one who is open to God's knowledge.

1 Cor 13:10. But when we have been made perfect and complete, then the need for these inadequate special gifts will come to an end, and they will disappear. [11]It's like this: when I was a child I spoke and thought and reasoned as a child does. But when I became a man my thoughts grew far beyond those of my childhood, and now I have put away the childish things. [12]In the same way, we can see and understand only a little about God now, as if we were peering at his reflection in a poor mirror; but someday we are going to see him in his completeness, face to face. Now all that I know is hazy and blurred, but then I will see everything clearly, just as clearly as God sees into my heart right now.

1 Cor 15:48. Every human being has a body just like Adam's, made of dust, but all who become Christ's will have the same kind of body as his—a body from heaven. [49]Just as each of us now has a body like Adam's, so we shall some day have a body like Christ's. [50]I tell you this, my brothers: an earthly body made of flesh and blood cannot get into God's kingdom. These perishable bodies of ours are not the right kind to live forever. [51]But I am telling you this strange and wonderful secret: we shall not all die, but we shall all be given new bodies! [52]It will all happen in a moment, in the twinkling of an eye, when the last trumpet is blown. For there will be a trumpet blast from the sky and all the Christians who have died will suddenly become alive, with new bodies that will never, never die; and then we who are still alive shall suddenly have new bodies too. [53]For our earthly bodies, the ones we have now that can die, must be transformed into heavenly bodies that cannot perish but will live forever. [54]When this happens, then at last this Scripture will come true—"Death is swallowed up in victory." [55, 56]O death, where then your victory? Where then your sting? For sin—the sting that causes death—will all be gone; and the law, which reveals our sins, will no longer be our judge. [57]How we thank God for all of this! It is he who makes us victorious through Jesus Christ our Lord!

2 Cor 1:20. He carries out and fulfills all of God's promises, no matter how many of them there are; and we have told everyone how faithful he is, giving glory to his name. [21]It is this God who has made you and me into faithful Christians and commissioned us apostles to preach the Good News. [22]He has put his brand upon us—his mark of ownership—and given us his Holy Spirit in our hearts.

2 Cor 4:14. We know that the same God who brought the Lord Jesus back from death will also bring us back to life again with Jesus, and present us to him along with you. [15]These sufferings of ours are for your benefit. And the more of you who are won to Christ, the more there are to thank him for his great kindness, and the more the Lord is glorified. [17]These troubles and sufferings of ours are, after all, quite small and won't last very long. Yet this short time of distress will result in God's richest blessing upon us forever and ever!

2 Cor 7:1. Having such great promises as these, dear friends, let us turn away from everything wrong, whether of body or spirit, and purify ourselves, living in the wholesome fear of God, giving ourselves to him alone.

Gal 3:29. And now that we are Christ's we are the true descendants of Abraham, and all of God's promises to him belong to us.

Gal 6:8. If he sows to please his own wrong desires, he will be planting seeds of evil and he will surely reap a harvest of spiritual decay and death; but if he plants the good things of the Spirit, he will reap the everlasting life which the Holy Spirit gives him. [9]And let us not get tired of doing what is right, for after a while we will reap a harvest of blessing if we don't get discouraged and give up.

Eph 1:18. I pray that your hearts will be flooded with light so that you can see something of the future he has called you to share. I want you to realize that God has been made rich because we who are Christ's have been given to him!

Eph 2:7. And now God can always point to us as examples of how very, very rich his kindness is, as shown in all he has done for us through Jesus Christ.

Eph 6:8. Remember, the Lord will pay you for each good thing you do, whether you are slave or free.

Phil 4:7. If you do this you will experience God's peace, which is far more wonderful than the human mind can understand. His peace will keep your thoughts and your hearts quiet and at rest as you trust in Christ Jesus.

19. And it is he who will supply all your needs from his riches in glory, because of what Christ Jesus has done for us.

Col 1:5. And you are looking forward to the joys of heaven, and have been ever since the Gospel first was preached to you. [12]And always thankful to the Father who has made us fit to share all the wonderful things that belong to those who live in the kingdom of light.

Col 3:4. And when Christ who is our real life comes back again, you will shine with him and share in his glories. [24]Remembering that it is the Lord Christ who is going to pay you, giving you your full portion of all he owns. He is the one you are really working for.

1 Thess 2:12. That your daily lives should not embarrass God, but bring joy to him who invited you into his kingdom to share his glory.

1 Thess 3:12. And may the Lord make your love to grow and overflow to each other and to everyone else, just as our love does toward you. [13]This will result in your hearts being made strong, sinless and holy by God our Father, so that you may stand before him guiltless on that day when our Lord Jesus Christ returns with all those who belong to him.

1 Thess 4:15. I can tell you this directly from the Lord: that we who are still living when the Lord returns will not rise to meet him ahead of those who are in their graves. [16]For the Lord himself will come down from heaven with a mighty shout and with the soul-stirring cry of the archangel and the great trumpet-call of God. And the believers who are dead will be the first to rise to meet the Lord. [17]Then we who are still alive and remain on the earth will be caught up with them in the clouds to meet the Lord in the air and remain with him forever. [18]So comfort and encourage each other with this news.

1 Thess 5:9. For God has not chosen to pour out his anger upon us, but to save us through our Lord Jesus Christ; [10]he died for us so that we can live with him forever, whether we are dead or alive at the time of his return. [11]So encourage each other to build each other up, just as you are already doing.

2 Thess 1:5. This is only one example of the fair, just way God does things, for he is using your sufferings to make you ready for his kingdom, [6]while at the same time he is preparing judgment and punishment for those who are hurting you. [7]And so I would say to you who are suffering, God will give you rest along with us when the Lord Jesus appears suddenly from heaven in flaming fire with his mighty angels.

2 Thess 2:13. But we must forever give thanks to God for you, our brothers loved by the Lord, because God chose from the very first to give you salvation, cleansing you by the work of the Holy Spirit and by your trusting in the Truth. [14]Through us he told you the Good News. Through us he called you to share in the glory of our Lord Jesus Christ.

1 Tim 1:16. But God had mercy on me so that Christ Jesus could use me as an example to show everyone how patient he is with even the worst sinners, so that others will realize that they, too, can have everlasting life.

1 Tim 4:8. Bodily exercise is all right, but spiritual exercise is much more important and is a tonic for all you do. So exercise yourself spiritually and practice being a better Christian, because that will help you not only now in this life, but in the next life too.

2 Tim 1:12. That is why I am suffering here in jail and I am certainly not ashamed of it, for I know the one in whom I trust, and I am sure that he is able to safely guard all that I have given him until the day of his return.

2 Tim 2:10. I am more than willing to suffer if that will bring salvation and eternal glory in Christ Jesus to those God has chosen. [11]I am comforted by this truth, that when we suffer and die for Christ it only means that we will begin living with him in heaven. [12] . . . But if we give up when we suffer, and turn against Christ, then he must turn against us. [19]But God's truth stands firm like a great rock, and nothing can shake it. It is a foundation stone with these words written on it: "The Lord knows those who are really his," and "A person who calls himself a Christian should not be doing things that are wrong."

2 Tim 4:8. In heaven a crown is waiting for me which the Lord, the righteous Judge, will give me on that great day of his return. And not just to me, but to all those whose lives show that they are eagerly looking forward to his coming back again.

Tit 2:11. For the free gift of eternal salvation is now being offered to everyone; [12]and along with this gift comes the realization that God wants us to turn from godless living and sinful pleasures and to live good, God-fearing lives day after day, [13]looking forward to that wonderful time we've been expecting, when his glory shall be seen—the glory of our great God and Savior Jesus Christ. [14]He died under God's judgment against our sins, so that he could rescue us from constant falling into sin and make us his very own people with cleansed hearts and real enthusiasm for doing kind things for others.

Tit 3:7. So that he could declare us good in God's eyes—all because of his great kindness; and now we can share in the wealth of the eternal life he gives us, and we are eagerly looking forward to receiving it.

Heb 1:14. No, for the angels are only spirit-messengers sent out to help and care for those who are to receive his salvation.

Heb 2:10. And it was right and proper that God, who made everything for his own glory, should allow Jesus to suffer, for in doing this he was bringing vast multitudes of God's people to heaven; for his suffering made Jesus a perfect Leader, one fit to bring them into their salvation. [15]Only in that way could he deliver those who through fear of death have been living all their lives as slaves to constant dread.

Heb 4:9. So there is a full complete rest *still waiting* for the people of God. [15]This High Priest of ours understands our weaknesses, since he had the same temptations we do, though he never once gave way to them and sinned. [16]So let us come boldly to the very throne of God and stay there to receive his mercy and to find grace to help us in our times of need.

Heb 6:10. For God is not unfair. How can he forget your hard work for him, or forget the way you used to show your love for him—and still do—by helping his children? [16]When a man takes an oath, he is calling upon someone greater than himself to force him to do what he has promised, or to punish him if he later refuses to do it; the oath ends all argument about it. [17]God also bound himself with an oath, so that those he promised to help would be perfectly sure and never need to wonder whether he might change his plans. [18]He has given us both his promise and his oath, two things we can completely count on, for it is impossible for God to tell a lie. Now all those who flee to him to save them can take new courage when they hear such assurances from God; now they can know without doubt that he will give them the salvation he has promised them. [19]This certain hope of being saved is a strong and trustworthy anchor for our souls, connecting us with God himself behind the sacred curtains of heaven, [20]where Christ has gone ahead to plead for us from his position as our High Priest, with the honor and rank of Melchizedek.

Heb 9:15. Christ came with this new agreement so that all who are invited may come and have forever all the wonders God has promised them. For Christ died to rescue them from the penalty of the sins they had committed while still under that old system. [28]So also Christ died only once as an offering for the sins of many people; and he will come again, but not to deal again with our sins. This time he will come bringing salvation to all those who are eagerly and patiently waiting for him.

Heb 10:34. You suffered with those thrown into jail, and you were actually joyful when all you owned was taken from you, knowing that better things were awaiting you in heaven, things that would be yours forever. [35]Do not let this happy trust in the Lord die away, no matter what happens. Remember your reward! [36]You need to keep on patiently doing God's will if you want him to do for you all that he has promised.

Heb 11:16. But they didn't want to. They were living for heaven. And now God is not ashamed to be called their God, for he has made a heavenly city for them.

Heb 12:22. But you have come right up into Mount Zion, to the city of the living God, the heavenly Jerusalem, and to the gathering of countless happy angels; [23]and to the church, composed of all those registered in heaven; and to God who is Judge of all; and to the spirits of the redeemed in heaven, already made perfect. [28]Since we have a kingdom nothing can destroy, let us please God by serving him with thankful hearts, and with holy fear and awe.

Heb 13:5. Stay away from the love of money; be satisfied with what you have. For God has said, "I will never, *never* fail you nor forsake you." [6]That is why we can say without any doubt or fear, "The Lord is my Helper and I am not afraid of anything that mere man can do to me."

Jas 1:5. If you want to know what God wants you to do, ask him, and he will gladly tell you, for he is always ready to give a bountiful supply of wisdom to all who ask him; he will not resent it.

12. Happy is the man who doesn't give in and do wrong when he is tempted, for afterwards he will get as his reward the crown of life that God has promised those who love him.

25. But if anyone keeps looking steadily into God's law for free men, he will not only remember it but he will do what it says, and God will greatly bless him in everything he does.

Jas 2:5. Listen to me, dear brothers: God has chosen poor people to be rich in faith, and the Kingdom of Heaven is theirs, for that is the gift God has promised to all those who love him.

Jas 4:8. And when you draw close to God, God will draw close to you.

1 Pet 1:2. Dear friends, God the Father chose you long ago and knew you would become his children. And the Holy Spirit has been at work in your hearts, cleansing you with the blood of Jesus Christ and making you to please him. May God bless you richly and grant you increasing freedom from all anxiety and fear. [3]All honor to God, the God and Father of our Lord Jesus Christ; for it is his boundless mercy that has given us the privilege of being born again, so that we are now members of God's own family. Now we live in the hope of eternal life because Christ rose again from the dead. [4]And God has reserved for his children the priceless gift of eternal life; it is kept in heaven for you, pure and undefiled, beyond the reach of change and decay. [5]And God, in his mighty power, will make sure that you get there safely to receive it, because you are trusting him. It will be yours in that coming last day for all to see.

1 Pet 2:5. And now you have become living building-stones for God's use in building his house. What's more, you are his holy priests; so come to him—(you who are acceptable to him because of Jesus Christ)—and offer to God those things that please him. [6]As the Scriptures express it, "See, I am sending Christ to be the carefully chosen, precious Cornerstone of my church, and I will never disappoint those who trust in him." [9]But you are not like that, for you have been chosen by God himself—you are priests of the King, you are holy and pure, you are God's very own—all this so that you may show to others how God called you out of the darkness into his wonderful light. [10]Once you were less than nothing; now you are God's own. Once you knew very little of God's kindness; now your very lives have been changed by it.

1 Pet 3:9. Don't repay evil for evil. Don't snap back at those who say unkind things about you. Instead, pray for God's help for them, for we are to be kind to others, and God will bless us for it. [10]If you want a happy good life, keep control of your tongue, and guard your lips from telling lies. [11]Turn away from evil and do good. Try to live in peace even if you must run after it to catch and hold it! [12]For the Lord is watching his children, listening to their prayers; but the Lord's face is hard against those who do evil.

1 Pet 4:13. Instead, be really glad—because these trials will make you partners with Christ in his suffering, and afterwards you will have the wonderful joy of sharing his glory in that coming day when it will be displayed.

1 Pet 5:4. And when the Head Shepherd comes, your reward will be a never-ending share in his glory and honor. [6]If you will humble yourselves under the mighty hand of God, in his good time he will lift you up. [7]Let him have all your worries and cares, for he is always thinking about you and watching everything that concerns you. [10]After you have suffered a little while, our God, who is full of kindness through Christ, will give you his eternal glory. He personally will come and pick you up, and set you firmly in place, and make you stronger than ever.

2 Pet 1:4. And by that same mighty power he has given us all the other rich and wonderful blessings he promised; for instance, the promise to save us from the lust and rottenness all around us, and to give us his own character. [10]So, dear brothers, work hard to prove that you really are among those God has called and chosen, and then you will never stumble or fall away. [11]And God will open wide the gates of heaven for you to enter into the eternal kingdom of our Lord and Savior Jesus Christ.

2 Pet 2:9. So also the Lord can rescue you and me from the temptations that surround us, and continue to punish the ungodly until the day of final judgment comes.

1 Jn 1:7. But if we are living in the light of God's presence, just as Christ does, then we have wonderful fellowship and joy with each other, and the blood of Jesus his Son cleanses us from every sin. [9]But if we confess our sins to him, he can be depended on to forgive us and to cleanse us from every wrong. (And it is perfectly proper for God to do this for us because Christ died to wash away our sins.)

1 Jn 2:17. And this world is fading away, and these evil, forbidden things will go with it, but whoever keeps doing the will of God will live forever. [25]And he himself has promised us this: *eternal life.* [28]And now, my little children, stay in happy fellowship with the Lord so that when he comes you will be sure that all is well, and will not have to be ashamed and shrink back from meeting him.

1 Jn 3:2. Yes, dear friends, we are already God's children, right now, and we can't even imagine what it is going to be like later on. But we do know this, that when he comes we will be like him, as a result of seeing him as he really is. [22]And get whatever we ask for because we are obeying him and doing the things that please him.

1 Jn 5:13. I have written this to you who believe in the Son of God so that you may know you have eternal life.

Rev 1:6. He has gathered us into his kingdom and made us priests of God his Father. Give to him everlasting glory! He rules forever! Amen!

Rev 2:7. To everyone who is victorious, I will give fruit from the Tree of Life in the Paradise of God. [10]Stop being afraid of what you are about to suffer—for the devil will soon throw some of you into prison to test you. You will be persecuted for "ten days." Remain faithful even when facing death and I will give you the crown of life—an unending, glorious future. [11]Let everyone who can hear, listen to what the Spirit is saying to the churches: He who is victorious shall not be hurt by the Second Death. [17]Let everyone who can hear, listen to what the Spirit is saying to the churches: Every one who is victorious shall eat of the hidden manna, the secret nourishment from heaven; and I will give to each a white stone, and on the stone will be engraved a new name that no one else knows except the one receiving it. [26]To every one who overcomes—who to the very end keeps on doing things that please me—I will give power over the nations. [27]You will rule them with a rod of iron just as my Father gave me the authority to rule them; they will be shattered like a pot of clay that is broken into tiny pieces. [28]And I will give you the Morning Star!

Rev 3:4. Yet even there in Sardis some haven't soiled their garments with the world's filth; they shall walk with me in white, for they are worthy. [5]Everyone who conquers will be clothed in white, and I will not erase his name from the Book of Life, but I will announce before my Father and his angels that he is mine. [10]Because you have patiently obeyed me despite the persecution, therefore I will protect you from the time of Great Tribulation and temptation, which will come upon the world to test everyone alive. [12]As for the one who conquers, I will make him a pillar in the temple of my God; he will be secure, and will go out no more; and I will write my God's Name on him, and he will be a citizen in the city of my God—the New Jerusalem, coming down from heaven from my God; and he will have my new Name inscribed upon him. [21]I will let every one who conquers sit beside me on my throne, just as I took my place with my Father on his throne when I had conquered.

Rev 7:3. "Wait! Don't do anything yet—hurt neither earth nor sea nor trees—until we have placed the Seal of God upon the foreheads of his servants." [4]How many were given this mark? I heard the number—it was 144,000, out of all twelve tribes of Israel. [9]After this I saw a vast crowd, too great to count, from all nations and provinces and languages, standing in front of the throne and before the Lamb, clothed in white, with palm branches in their hands. [10]And they were shouting with a mighty shout, "Salvation comes from our God upon the throne, and from the Lamb." [11]And now all the angels were crowding around the throne and around the Elders and the four Living Beings, and falling face down before the throne and worshiping God. [12]"Amen!" they said. "Blessing, and glory, and wisdom, and thanksgiving, and honor, and power, and might, be to our God forever and forever. Amen!" [13]Then one of the twenty-four Elders asked me, "Do you know who these are, who are clothed in white, and where they come from?" [14]"No, sir," I replied. "Please tell me." "These are the ones coming out of the Great Tribulation," he said; "they washed their robes and whitened them by the blood of the Lamb.

[15]That is why they are here before the throne of God, serving him day and night in his temple. The one sitting on the throne will shelter them; [16]they will never be hungry again, nor thirsty, and they will be fully protected from the scorching noon-time heat. [17]For the Lamb standing in front of the throne will feed them and be their Shepherd and lead them to the springs of the Water of Life. And God will wipe their tears away."

Rev 11:12. Then a loud voice will shout from heaven, "Come up!" And they will rise to heaven in a cloud as their enemies watch. [18]"The nations were angry with you, but now it is your turn to be angry with them. It is time to judge the dead, and reward your servants—prophets and people alike, all who fear your Name, both great and small—and to destroy those who have caused destruction upon the earth."

Rev 14:1. Then I saw a Lamb standing on Mount Zion in Jerusalem, and with him were 144,000 who had his Name and his Father's Name written on their foreheads. [2]And I heard a sound from heaven like the roaring of a great waterfall or the rolling of mighty thunder. It was the singing of a choir accompanied by harps. [3]This tremendous choir—144,000 strong—sang a wonderful new song in front of the throne of God and before the four Living Beings and the twenty-four Elders; and no one could sing this song except those 144,000 who had been redeemed from the earth. [4]For they are spiritually undefiled, pure as virgins, following the Lamb wherever he goes. They have been purchased from among the men on the earth as a consecrated offering to God and the Lamb. [5]No falsehood can be charged against them; they are blameless. [13]And I heard a voice in the heavens above me saying, "Write this down: At last the time has come for his martyrs to enter into their full reward. Yes, says the Spirit, they are blest indeed, for now they shall rest from all their toils and trials; for their good deeds follow them to heaven!"

Rev 16:15. Take note: I will come as unexpectedly as a thief! Blessed are all who are awaiting me, who keep their robes in readiness and will not need to walk naked and ashamed.

Rev 20:4. Then I saw thrones, and sitting on them were those who had been given the right to judge. And I saw the souls of those who had been beheaded for their testimony about Jesus, for proclaiming the Word of God, and who had not worshiped the Creature or his statue, nor accepted his mark on their foreheads or their hands. They had come to life again and now they reigned with Christ for a thousand years. [5]This is the First Resurrection. (The rest of the dead did not come back to life until the thousand years had ended.) [6]Blessed and holy are those who share in the First Resurrection. For them the Second Death holds no terrors, for they will be priests of God and of Christ, and shall reign with him a thousand years.

Rev 21:3. I heard a loud shout from the throne saying, "Look, the home of God is now among men, and he will live with them and they will be his people; yes, God himself will be among them. [4]He will wipe away all tears from their eyes, and there shall be no more death, nor sorrow, nor crying, nor pain. All of that has gone forever." [5]And the one sitting on the throne said, "See, I am making all things new!" And then he said to me, "Write this down, for what I tell you is trustworthy and true: [6]It is finished! I am the A and the Z—the Beginning and the End. I will give to the thirsty the springs of the Water of Life—as a gift! [7]Everyone who conquers will inherit all these blessings, and I will be his God and he will be my son." [24]Its light will light the nations of the earth, and the rulers of the world will come and bring their glory to it.

Rev 22:4. And they shall see his face; and his name shall be written on their foreheads. [5]And there will be no night there—no need for lamps or sun—for the Lord God will be their light; and they shall reign forever and ever. [7]"I am coming soon!" . . . Blessed are those who believe it and all else written in the scroll. [12]"See, I am coming soon, and my reward is with me, to repay everyone according to the deeds he has done. [14]Blessed forever are all who are washing their robes, to have the right to enter in through the gates of the city, and to eat the fruit from the Tree of Life."

See *Adoption; Afflictions, Comfort in; God, Preserver; Providence of.*

For promises in particular, see *Backslider; Obedience; Penitent, Promises to,* etc., under such topics as may be desired.

UNITY OF, WITH CHRIST (IN N.T.). Jn 6:56. Everyone who eats my flesh and drinks my blood is in me, and I in him. *vs.* 48–57.

Jn 14:20. When I come back to life again, you will know that I am in my Father, and you in me, and I in you.

Jn 15:1. I am the true Vine, and my Father is the Gardener. [2]He lops off every branch that doesn't produce. And he prunes those branches that bear fruit for even larger crops. [3]He has already tended you by pruning you back for greater strength and usefulness by means of the commands I gave you. [4]Take care to live in me, and let me live in you. For a branch can't produce fruit when severed from the vine. Nor can you be fruitful apart from me. [5]Yes, I am the Vine; you are the branches. Whoever lives in me and I in him shall produce a large crop of fruit. For apart from me you can't do a thing. [6]If anyone separates from me, he is thrown away like a useless branch, withers, and is gathered into a pile with all the others and burned. [7]But if you stay in me and obey my commands, you may ask any request you like, and it will be granted! [8]My true disciples produce bountiful harvests. This brings great glory to my Father. [9]I have loved you even as the Father has loved me. Live within my love. [10]When you obey me you are living in my love, just as I obey my Father and live in his love. [11]I have told you this so that you will be filled with my joy. Yes, your cup of joy will overflow! [19]The world would love you if you belonged to it; but you don't

—for I chose you to come out of the world, and so it hates you.

Jn 17:21. My prayer for all of them is that they will be of one heart and mind, just as you and I are, Father—that just as you are in me and I am in you, so they will be in us, and the world will believe you sent me. [22]I have given them the glory you gave me —the glorious unity of being one, as we are— [23]I in them and you in me, all being perfected into one. [26]And I have revealed you to them, and will keep on revealing you so that the mighty love you have for me may be in them, and I in them.

Rom 8:1. So there is now no condemnation awaiting those who belong to Christ Jesus. [10]Yet, even though Christ lives within you, your body will die because of sin; but your spirit will live, for Christ has pardoned it.

Rom 12:4, 5. Just as there are many parts to our bodies, so it is with Christ's body. We are all parts of it, and it takes every one of us to make it complete.

1 Cor 6:13. But sexual sin is never right: our bodies were not made for that, but for the Lord, and the Lord wants to fill our bodies with himself. [14]And God is going to raise our bodies from the dead by his power just as he raised up the Lord Jesus Christ. [15]Don't you realize that your bodies are actually part and members of Christ? So should I take parts of Christ and join him to a prostitute? Never! [16]And don't you know that if a man joins himself to a prostitute she becomes a part of him and he becomes a part of her? For God tells us in the Scripture that in his sight the two become one person. [17]But if you give yourself to the Lord, you and Christ are joined together as one person. [18]That is why I say to run from sex sin. No other sin affects the body as this one does. When you sin this sin it is against your own body. [19]Haven't you yet learned that your body is the home of the Holy Spirit God gave you, and that he lives within you? Your own body does not belong to you. [20]For God has bought you with a great price. So use every part of your body to give glory back to God, because he owns it.

1 Cor 10:16. When we ask the Lord's blessing upon our drinking from the cup of wine at the Lord's Table, this means, doesn't it, that all who drink it are sharing together the blessing of Christ's blood? And when we break off pieces of the bread from the loaf to eat there together, this shows that we are sharing together in the benefits of his body. [17]No matter how many of us there are, we all eat from the same loaf, showing that we are all parts of the one body of Christ.

1 Cor 12:12. Our bodies have many parts, but the many parts make up only one body when they are all put together. So it is with the "body" of Christ. [13]Each of us is a part of the one body of Christ. Some of us are Jews, some are Gentiles, some are slaves and some are free. But the Holy Spirit has fitted us all together into one body. We have been baptized into Christ's body by the one Spirit, and have all been given that same Holy Spirit. [27]All of you together are the one body of Christ and each one of you is a separate and necessary part of it.

2 Cor 5:17. When someone becomes a Christian he becomes a brand new person inside. He is not the same any more. A new life has begun! [21]For God took the sinless Christ and poured into him our sins. Then, in exchange, he poured God's goodness into us!

2 Cor 11:2. Your love should be for Christ alone, just as a pure maiden saves her love for one man only, for the one who will be her husband.

2 Cor 13:5. Do you feel Christ's presence and power more and more within you? Or are you just pretending to be Christians when actually you aren't at all?

Gal 2:20. I have been crucified with Christ: and I myself no longer live, but Christ lives in me. And the real life I now have within this body is a result of my trusting in the Son of God, who loved me and gave himself for me.

Eph 5:30. Just as Christ cares for his body the church, of which we are parts. [32]I know this is hard to understand, but it is an illustration of the way we are parts of the body of Christ.

Col 1:27. Now at last it has pleased him to tell it to those who love him and live for him, and the riches and glory of his plan are for you Gentiles too. And this is the secret: *that Christ in your hearts is your only hope of glory.*

Col 2:6. And now just as you trusted Christ to save you, trust him, too, for each day's problems; live in vital union with him. [7]Let your roots grow down into him and draw up nourishment from him.

1 Pet 4:13. Instead, be really glad—because these trials will make you partners with Christ in his suffering, and afterwards you will have the wonderful joy of sharing his glory in that coming day when it will be displayed.

1 Jn 2:6. Anyone who says he is a Christian should live as Christ did. [24]So keep on believing what you have been taught from the beginning. If you do, you will always be in close fellowship with both God the Father and his Son. [28]And now, my little children, stay in happy fellowship with the Lord so that when he comes you will be sure that all is well, and will not have to be ashamed and shrink back from meeting him.

1 Jn 3:6. So if we stay close to him, obedient to him, we won't be sinning either. [24]Those who do what God says—they are living with God and he with them. We know this is true because the Holy Spirit he has given us tells us so.

1 Jn 4:13. And he has put his own Holy Spirit into our hearts as a proof to us that we are living with him and he with us.

1 Jn 5:12. So whoever has God's Son has life; whoever does not have his Son, does not have life. [20]And now we are in God because we are in Jesus Christ his Son, who is the only true God; and he is eternal life.

2 Jn 1:9. If you are loyal to Christ's teachings,

you will have God too. Then you will have both the Father and the Son.

Rev 19:7. For the time has come for the wedding banquet of the Lamb, and his bride has prepared herself. [8]She is permitted to wear the cleanest and whitest and finest of linens. (Fine linen represents the good deeds done by the people of God.) [9]And the angel dictated this sentence to me: "Blessed are those who are invited to the wedding feast of the Lamb."

Rev 21:9. Come with me and I will show you the bride, the Lamb's wife.

See *Adoption; Communion; Fellowship.*

RIGHTEOUSNESS By faith, Gen 15:6; Rom 4:3, 4, 5, 9, 11, 13, 20, 22, 24. Garment of, Job 29:14; Mt 22:11–14. Imputed on account of obedience, Deut 24:12, 13.

FRUITS OF. Deut 6:25. For it always goes well with us when we obey all the laws of the Lord our God.

Josh 22:31. Phinehas replied to them, "Today we know that the Lord is among us because you have not sinned against the Lord as we thought; instead, you have saved us from destruction!"

Ps 1:3. They are like trees along a river bank, bearing luscious fruit each season without fail. Their leaves shall never wither, and all they do shall prosper.

Ps 15:1. Lord, who may go and find refuge and shelter in your tabernacle up on your holy hill? [2]Anyone who leads a blameless life and is truly sincere. [3]Anyone who refuses to slander others, does not listen to gossip, never harms his neighbor, [4]speaks out against sin, criticizes those committing it, commends the faithful followers of the Lord, keeps a promise even if it ruins him, [5]does not crush his debtors with high interest rates, and refuses to testify against the innocent despite the bribes offered him—such a man shall stand firm forever.

Ps 24:3. Who may climb the mountain of the Lord and enter where he lives? Who may stand before the Lord? [4]Only those with pure hands and hearts, who do not practice dishonesty and lying. [5]They will receive God's own goodness as their blessing from him, planted in their lives by God himself, their Savior.

Ps 101:3. Help me to refuse the low and vulgar things; help me to abhor all crooked deals of every kind, to have no part in them. [4]I will reject all selfishness and stay away from every evil.

Ps 106:3. Happiness comes to those who are fair to others and are always just and good.

Ps 112:4. When darkness overtakes him, light will come bursting in. He is kind and merciful—[5]and all goes well for the generous man who conducts his business fairly. [6]Such a man will not be overthrown by evil circumstances. God's constant care of him will make a deep impression on all who see it. [7]He does not fear bad news, nor live in dread of what may happen. For he is settled in his mind that Jehovah will take care of him. [8]That is why he is not afraid, but can calmly face his foes.

Prov 2:5. Then wisdom will be given you, and knowledge of God himself; you will soon learn the importance of reverence for the Lord and of trusting him. [6]For the Lord grants wisdom! His every word is a treasure of knowledge and understanding. [7, 8]He grants good sense to the godly—his saints. He is their shield, protecting them and guarding their pathway. [9]He shows how to distinguish right from wrong, how to find the right decision every time. [10]For wisdom and truth will enter the very center of your being, filling your life with joy. [11-13]You will be given the sense to stay away from evil men who want you to be their partners in crime—men who turn from God's ways to walk down dark and evil paths, [14]and exult in doing wrong, for they thoroughly enjoy their sins. [15]Everything they do is crooked and wrong. [16, 17]Only wisdom from the Lord can save a man from the flattery of prostitutes; these girls have abandoned their husbands and flouted the laws of God. [18]Their houses lie along the road to death and hell. [19]The men who enter them are doomed. None of these men will ever be the same again. [20]Follow the steps of the godly instead, and stay on the right path.

Prov 10:2. Ill-gotten gain brings no lasting happiness; right living does.

Prov 11:4. Your riches won't help you on Judgment Day; only righteousness counts then. [5]The upright are directed by their honesty. . . . [6]The good man's goodness delivers him. [18]The evil man gets rich for the moment, but the good man's reward lasts forever. [19]The good man finds life; the evil man, death. [30]Godly men are growing a tree that bears life-giving fruit, and all who win souls are wise.

Prov 12:28. The path of the godly leads to life. So why fear death? Prov 10:16.

Prov 13:6. A man's goodness helps him all through life, while evil men are being destroyed by their wickedness.

Prov 14:34. Godliness exalts a nation, but sin is a reproach to any people.

Prov 21:3. God is more pleased when we are just and fair than when we give him gifts.

Prov 29:7. The good man knows the poor man's rights; the godless don't care.

Isa 28:17. I will take the line and plummet of justice to check the foundation wall you built; it looks so fine, but it is so weak a storm of hail will knock it down! The enemy will come like a flood and sweep it away, and you will be drowned.

Isa 32:16. Then justice will rule through all the land, [17]and out of justice, peace. Quietness and confidence will reign forever more. [18]My people will live in safety, quietly at home.

Isa 33:15. I will tell you who can live here: All who are honest and fair, who reject making profit by fraud, who hold back their hands from taking bribes, who refuse to listen to those who plot murder, who shut their eyes to all enticement to do wrong. [16]Such as these shall dwell on high. The rocks of the mountains will be their fortress of safety; food will be supplied to them and they will have all the water they need. [17]Your eyes will see the King in his beauty, and the highlands of heaven far away.

Isa 55:12. You will live in joy and peace. The mountains and hills, the trees of the field—all the world around you—will rejoice. [13]Where once were thorns, fir trees will grow; where briars grew, the myrtle trees will sprout up. This miracle will make the Lord's name very great and be an everlasting sign (of God's power and love).

Isa 58:6. No, the kind of fast I want is that you stop oppressing those who work for you and treat them fairly and give them what they earn. [7]I want you to share your food with the hungry and bring right into your own homes those who are helpless, poor and destitute. Clothe those who are cold and don't hide from relatives who need your help. [8]If you do these things, God will shed his own glorious light upon you. He will heal you; your godliness will lead you forward, and goodness will be a shield before you, and the glory of the Lord will protect you from behind. [9]Then, when you call, the Lord will answer. "Yes, I am here," he will quickly reply. All you need to do is to stop oppressing the weak, and to stop making false accusations and spreading vicious rumors! [10]Feed the hungry! Help those in trouble! Then your light will shine out from the darkness, and the darkness around you shall be as bright as day. [11]And the Lord will guide you continually, and satisfy you with all good things, and keep you healthy too; and you will be like a well-watered garden, like an ever-flowing spring. [12]Your sons will rebuild the long-deserted ruins of your cities, and you will be known as "The People Who Rebuild Their Walls and Cities." [13]If you keep the Sabbath holy, not having your own fun and business on that day, but enjoying the Sabbath and speaking of it with delight as the Lord's holy day, and honoring the Lord in what you do, not following your own desires and pleasure, nor talking idly— [14]then the Lord will be your delight, and I will see to it that you ride high, and get your full share of the blessings I promised to Jacob, your father. The Lord has spoken.

Isa 62:1. Because I love Zion, because my heart yearns for Jerusalem, I will not cease to pray for her or to cry out to God on her behalf until she shines forth in his righteousness and is glorious in his salvation.

Ezk 18:5. But if a man is just and does what is lawful and right, [6]and has not gone out to the mountains to feast before the idols of Israel and worship them, and does not commit adultery, nor lie with any woman during the time of her menstruation, [7]and is a merciful creditor, not holding on to the items given to him in pledge by poor debtors, and is no robber, but gives food to the hungry and clothes to those in need, [8]and grants loans without interest, and stays away from sin, and is honest and fair when judging others, [9]and obeys my laws—that man is just, says the Lord, and he shall surely live.

Ezk 33:15. If he gives back the borrower's pledge and returns what he has stolen and walks along the paths of right, not doing evil—he shall surely live. He shall not die.

Dan 12:3. And those who are wise—the people of God—shall shine as brightly as the sun's brilliance, and those who turn many to righteousness will glitter like stars forever.

Hos 10:12. Plant the good seeds of righteousness and you will reap a crop of my love; plow the hard ground of your hearts, for now is the time to seek the Lord, that he may come and shower salvation upon you.

Mal 3:3. Like a refiner of silver he will sit and closely watch as the dross is burned away. He will purify the Levites, the ministers of God, refining them like gold or silver, so that they will do their work for God with pure hearts.

Mal 4:2. But for you who fear my name, the Sun of Righteousness will rise with healing in his wings.

Mt 5:20. But I warn you—unless your goodness is greater than that of the Pharisees and other Jewish leaders, you can't get into the Kingdom of Heaven at all!

Mt 12:35. A good man's speech reveals the rich treasures within him. An evil-hearted man is filled with venom, and his speech reveals it.

Mk 3:33. He replied, "Who is my mother? Who are my brothers?" [34]Looking at those around him he said, "These are my mother and brothers! [35]Anyone who does God's will is my brother, and my sister, and my mother." Mt 12:50.

Lk 3:10. The crowd replied, "What do you want us to do?" [11]"If you have two coats," he replied, "give one to the poor. If you have extra food, give it away to those who are hungry." [12]Even tax collectors—notorious for their corruption—came to be baptized and asked, "How shall we prove to you that we have abandoned our sins?" [13]"By your honesty," he replied. "Make sure you collect no more taxes than the Roman government requires you to." [14]"And us," asked some soldiers, "what about us?" John replied, "Don't extort money by threats and violence; don't accuse anyone of what you know he didn't do; and be content with your pay!"

Lk 8:15. But the good soil represents honest, good-hearted people. They listen to God's words and cling to them and steadily spread them to others who also soon believe.

Jn 3:21. But those doing right come gladly to the Light to let everyone see that they are doing what God wants them to. [33]Those who believe him discover that God is a fountain of truth.

Jn 8:47. "Anyone whose Father is God listens gladly to the words of God." [49]Jesus said, "I have no demon in me. For I honor my Father—and you dishonor me."

Jn 13:35. Your strong love for each other will prove to the world that you are my disciples.

Jn 14:21. The one who obeys me is the one who loves me; and because he loves me, my Father will love him; and I will too, and I will reveal myself to him. [22]Judas (not Iscariot, but his other disciple with that name) said to him, "Sir, why are you going to reveal yourself only to us disciples and not to the world at large?" [23]Jesus replied, "Because I will only reveal myself to those who love me and obey me. The Father will love them too, and we will come to them and live with them. [24]Anyone who doesn't obey me doesn't love me.

Jn 15:4. Take care to live in me, and let me live in you. For a branch can't produce fruit when severed from the vine. Nor can you be fruitful apart from me. [5]Yes, I am the Vine; you are the branches. Whoever lives in me and I in him shall produce a large crop of fruit. For apart from me you can't do a thing. [8]My true disciples produce bountiful harvests. This brings great glory to my Father. [12]I demand that you love each other as much as I love you.

Acts 9:36. In the city of Joppa there was a woman named Dorcas ("Gazelle"), a believer who was always doing kind things for others, especially for the poor.

Acts 11:29. So the believers decided to send relief to the Christians in Judea, each giving as much as he could. [30]This they did, consigning their gifts to Barnabas and Paul to take to the elders of the church in Jerusalem.

Acts 19:18, 19. Many of the believers who had been practicing black magic confessed their deeds and brought their incantation books and charms and burned them at a public bonfire. (Someone estimated the value of the books at $10,000.)

Rom 5:1. So now, since we have been made right in God's sight by faith in his promises, we can have real peace with him because of what Jesus Christ our Lord has done for us. [2]For because of our faith, he has brought us into this place of highest privilege where we now stand, and we confidently and joyfully look forward to actually becoming all that God has had in mind for us to be. [3]We can rejoice, too, when we run into problems and trials for we know that they are good for us—they help us learn to be patient. [4]And patience develops strength of character in us and helps us trust God more each time we use it until finally our hope and faith are strong and steady. [5]Then, when that happens, we are able to hold our heads high no matter what happens and know that all is well, for we know how dearly God loves us, and we feel this warm love everywhere within us because God has given us the Holy Spirit to fill our hearts with his love.

Rom 6:18. And now you are free from your old master, sin; and you have become slaves to your new master, righteousness. [19]I speak this way, using the illustration of slaves and masters, because it is easy to understand: just as you used to be slaves to all kinds of sin, so now you must let yourselves be slaves to all that is right and holy. [20]In those days when you were slaves of sin you didn't bother much with goodness. [21]And what was the result? Evidently not good, since you are ashamed now even to think about those things you used to do, for all of them end in eternal doom. [22]But now you are free from the power of sin and are slaves of God, and his benefits to you include holiness and everlasting life.

Rom 7:4. But you "died," as it were, with Christ on the cross; and since you are "dead," you are no longer "married to the law." . . . And now you are "married," so to speak, to the one who rose from the dead, so that you can produce good fruit, that is, good deeds for God. [5]When your old nature was still active, sinful desires were at work within you, making you want to do whatever God said not to, and producing sinful deeds, the rotting fruit of death. [6]But now you need no longer worry about the Jewish laws and customs because you "died" while in their captivity, and now you can really serve God; not in the old way, mechanically obeying a set of rules, but in the new way, (with all of your hearts and minds).

Rom 8:4. So now we can obey God's laws if we follow after the Holy Spirit and no longer obey the old evil nature within us. [5]Those who let themselves be controlled by their lower natures live only to please themselves, but those who follow after the Holy Spirit find themselves doing those things that please God. [6]Following after the Holy Spirit leads to life and peace, but following after the old nature leads to death.

Rom 14:17. For, after all, the important thing for us as Christians is not what we eat or drink but stirring up goodness and peace and joy from the Holy Spirit. [18]If you let Christ be Lord in these affairs, God will be glad; and so will others. [19]In this way aim for harmony in the church and try to build each other up.

Rom 15:1, 2. For we must bear the "burden" of being considerate of the doubts and fears of others —of those who feel these things are wrong. Let's please the other fellow, not ourselves, and do what is for his good and thus build him up in the Lord. [3]Christ didn't please himself. As the Psalmist said, "He came for the very purpose of suffering under the insults of those who were against the Lord." [4]These things that were written in the Scriptures so long ago are to teach us patience and to encourage us, so that we will look forward expectantly to the time when God will conquer sin and death. [5]May God who gives patience, steadiness, and encouragement help you to live in complete harmony with each other—each with the attitude of Christ toward the other. [6]And then all of us can praise the Lord together with one voice, giving glory to God, the Father of our Lord Jesus Christ. [7]So, warmly welcome each other into the church, just as Christ has warmly welcomed you; then God will be glorified.

1 Cor 4:19. But I will come, and soon, if the Lord will let me, and then I'll find out whether these proud men are just big talkers or whether they really have God's power. [20]The Kingdom of God is not just talking; it is living by God's power.

1 Cor 12:3. No one can say, "Jesus is Lord," and really mean it, unless the Holy Spirit is helping him.

1 Cor 13:1. If I had the gift of being able to speak

in other languages without learning them, and could speak in every language there is in all of heaven and earth, but didn't love others, I would only be making noise. [2]If I had the gift of prophecy and knew all about what is going to happen in the future, knew everything about *everything,* but didn't love others, what good would it do? Even if I had the gift of faith so that I could speak to a mountain and make it move, I would still be worth nothing at all without love. [3]If I gave everything I have to poor people, and if I were burned alive for preaching the Gospel but didn't love others, it would be of no value whatever. [4]Love is very patient and kind, never jealous or envious, never boastful or proud, [5]never haughty or selfish or rude. Love does not demand its own way. It is not irritable or touchy. It does not hold grudges and will hardly even notice when others do it wrong. [6]It is never glad about injustice, but rejoices whenever truth wins out. [7]If you love someone you will be loyal to him no matter what the cost. You will always believe in him, always expect the best of him, and always stand your ground in defending him. [8]All the special gifts and powers from God will someday come to an end, but love goes on forever. Someday prophecy, and speaking in unknown languages, and special knowledge—these gifts will disappear. [9]Now we know so little, even with our special gifts, and the preaching of those most gifted is still so poor. [10]But when we have been made perfect and complete, then the need for these inadequate special gifts will come to an end, and they will disappear. [11]It's like this: when I was a child I spoke and thought and reasoned as a child does. But when I became a man my thoughts grew far beyond those of my childhood, and now I have put away the childish things. [12]In the same way, we can see and understand only a little about God now, as if we were peering at his reflection in a poor mirror; but someday we are going to see him in his completeness, face to face. Now all that I know is hazy and blurred, but then I will see everything clearly, just as clearly as God sees into my heart right now. [13]There are three things that remain—faith, hope, and love—and the greatest of these is love.

2 Cor 5:17. When someone becomes a Christian he becomes a brand new person inside. He is not the same any more. A new life has begun!

2 Cor 7:10. For God sometimes uses sorrow in our lives to help us turn away from sin and seek eternal life. We should never regret his sending it. But the sorrow of the man who is not a Christian is not the sorrow of true repentance and does not prevent eternal death. [11]Just see how much good this grief from the Lord did for you! You no longer shrugged your shoulders, but became earnest and sincere, and very anxious to get rid of the sin that I wrote you about. You became frightened about what had happened, and longed for me to come and help. You went right to work on the problem and cleared it up (punishing the man who sinned). You have done everything you could to make it right.

2 Cor 9:10. For God, who gives seed to the farmer to plant, and later on, good crops to harvest and eat, will give you more and more seed to plant and will make it grow so that you can give away more and more fruit from your harvest.

2 Cor 10:5. These weapons can break down every proud argument against God and every wall that can be built to keep men from finding him. With these weapons I can capture rebels and bring them back to God, and change them into men whose hearts' desire is obedience to Christ.

2 Cor 13:5. Check up on yourselves. Are you really Christians? Do you pass the test? Do you feel Christ's presence and power more and more within you? Or are you just pretending to be Christians when actually you aren't at all?

Gal 4:6. And because we are his sons God has sent the Spirit of his Son into our hearts, so now we can rightly speak of God as our dear Father.

Gal 5:22. But when the Holy Spirit controls our lives he will produce this kind of fruit in us: love, joy, peace, patience, kindness, goodness, faithfulness, [23]gentleness and self-control; and here there is no conflict with Jewish laws.

Gal 6:7. Don't be misled; remember that you can't ignore God and get away with it: a man will always reap just the kind of crop he sows! [8]If he sows to please his own wrong desires, he will be planting seeds of evil and he will surely reap a harvest of spiritual decay and death; but if he plants the good things of the Spirit, he will reap the everlasting life which the Holy Spirit gives him.

Eph 1:13. And because of what Christ did, all you others too, who heard the Good News about how to be saved, and trusted Christ, were marked as belonging to Christ by the Holy Spirit, who long ago had been promised to all of us Christians. [14]His presence within us is God's guarantee that he really will give us all that he promised; and the Spirit's seal upon us means that God has already purchased us and that he guarantees to bring us to himself. This is just one more reason for us to praise our glorious God.

Eph 5:9. Because of this light within you, you should do only what is good and right and true.

Phil 1:11. May you always be doing those good, kind things which show that you are a child of God, for this will bring much praise and glory to the Lord. [27]But whatever happens to me, remember always to live as Christians should, so that, whether I ever see you again or not, I will keep on hearing good reports that you are standing side by side with one strong purpose—to tell the Good News [28]fearlessly, no matter what your enemies may do. They will see this as a sign of their downfall, but for you it will be a clear sign from God that he is with you, and that he has given you eternal life with him. [29]For to you has been given the privilege not only of trusting him but also of suffering for him.

Phil 2:13. For God is at work within you, helping you want to obey him, and then helping you do what he wants.

Phil 3:12. I don't mean to say I am perfect. I haven't learned all I should even yet, but I keep working toward that day when I will finally be all that Christ saved me for and wants me to be. [13]No, dear brothers, I am still not all I should be but I am bringing all my energies to bear on this one thing: Forgetting the past and looking forward to what lies ahead, [14]I strain to reach the end of the race and receive the prize for which God is calling us up to heaven because of what Christ Jesus did for us.

Phil 4:11. Not that I was ever in need, for I have learned how to get along happily whether I have much or little. [12]I know how to live on almost nothing or with everything. I have learned the secret of contentment in every situation, whether it be a full stomach or hunger, plenty or want; [13]for I can do everything God asks me to with the help of Christ who gives me the strength and power.

Col 1:12. And always thankful to the Father who has made us fit to share all the wonderful things that belong to those who live in the kingdom of light. [13]For he has rescued us out of the darkness and gloom of Satan's kingdom and brought us into the kingdom of his dear Son.

Col 3:3. You should have as little desire for this world as a dead person does. Your real life is in heaven with Christ and God. [5]Away then with sinful, earthly things; deaden the evil desires lurking within you; have nothing to do with sexual sin, impurity, lust and shameful desires; don't worship the good things of life, for that is idolatry. [9]Don't tell lies to each other; it was your old life with all its wickedness that did that sort of thing; now it is dead and gone. [10]You are living a brand new kind of life that is continually learning more and more of what is right, and trying constantly to be more and more like Christ who created this new life within you. [11]In this new life one's nationality or race or education or social position is unimportant; such things mean nothing. Whether a person has Christ is what matters, and he is equally available to all. [12]Since you have been chosen by God who has given you this new kind of life, and because of his deep love and concern for you, you should practice tenderhearted mercy and kindness to others. Don't worry about making a good impression on them but be ready to suffer quietly and patiently. [13]Be gentle and ready to forgive; never hold grudges. Remember, the Lord forgave you, so you must forgive others. [14]Most of all, let love guide your life, for then the whole church will stay together in perfect harmony. [15]Let the peace of heart which comes from Christ be always present in your hearts and lives, for this is your responsibility and privilege as members of his body. And always be thankful. [16]Remember what Christ taught and let his words enrich your lives and make you wise; teach them to each other and sing them out in psalms and hymns and spiritual songs, singing to the Lord with thankful hearts. [17]And whatever you do or say, let it be as a representative of the Lord Jesus, and come with him into the presence of God the Father to give him your thanks.

1 Thess 1:3. We never forget your loving deeds as we talk to our God and Father about you, and your strong faith and steady looking forward to the return of our Lord Jesus Christ. [9]For *they* keep telling *us* about the wonderful welcome you gave us, and how you turned away from your idols to God so that now the living and true God only is your Master. [10]And they speak of how you are looking forward to the return of God's Son from heaven—Jesus, whom God brought back to life—and he is our only Savior from God's terrible anger against sin.

2 Thess 1:3. Dear brothers, giving thanks to God for you is not only the right thing to do, but it is our duty to God, because of the really wonderful way your faith has grown, and because of your growing love for each other. [4]We are happy to tell other churches about your patience and complete faith in God, in spite of all the crushing troubles and hardships you are going through. [5]This is only one example of the fair, just way God does things, for he is using your sufferings to make you ready for his kingdom.

1 Tim 2:9, 10. And the women should be the same way, quiet and sensible in manner and clothing. Christian women should be noticed for being kind and good, not for the way they fix their hair or because of their jewels or fancy clothes.

1 Tim 5:9. A widow who wants to become one of the special church workers should be at least sixty years old and have been married only once. [10]She must be well thought of by everyone because of the good she has done. Has she brought up her children well? Has she been kind to strangers as well as to other Christians? Has she helped those who are sick and hurt? Is she always ready to show kindness?

2 Tim 2:22. Run from anything that gives you the evil thoughts that young men often have, but stay close to anything that makes you want to do right. Have faith and love, and enjoy the companionship of those who love the Lord and have pure hearts.

2 Tim 4:6. I say this because I won't be around to help you very much longer. My time has almost run out. Very soon now I will be on my way to heaven. [7]I have fought long and hard for my Lord, and through it all I have kept true to him. And now the time has come for me to stop fighting and rest. [8]In heaven a crown is waiting for me which the Lord, the righteous Judge, will give me on that great day of his return. And not just to me, but to all those whose lives show that they are eagerly looking forward to his coming back again.

Tit 2:2. Teach the older men to be serious and unruffled; they must be sensible, knowing and believing the truth and doing everything with love and patience. [11]For the free gift of eternal salvation is now being offered to everyone; [12]and along with this gift comes the realization that God wants us to turn from godless living and sinful pleasures and to live good, God-fearing lives day after day.

Tit 3:14. For our people must learn to help all who need their assistance, that their lives will be fruitful.

Philemon 1:5. Because I keep hearing of your love and trust in the Lord Jesus and in his people. [6]And I pray that as you share your faith with others it will grip their lives too, as they see the wealth of good things in you that come from Christ Jesus.

Jas 1:27. The Christian who is pure and without fault, from God the Father's point of view, is the one who takes care of orphans and widows, and who remains true to the Lord—not soiled and dirtied by his contacts with the world.

Jas 2:14. Dear brothers, what's the use of saying that you have faith and are Christians if you aren't proving it by helping others? Will *that* kind of faith save anyone? [15]If you have a friend who is in need of food and clothing, [16]and you say to him, "Well, good-bye and God bless you; stay warm and eat hearty," and then don't give him clothes or food, what good does that do? [17]So you see, it isn't enough just to have faith. You must also do good to prove that you have it. Faith that doesn't show itself by good works is no faith at all—it is dead and useless. [18]But someone may well argue, "You say the way to God is by faith alone, plus nothing; well, I say that good works are important too, for without good works you can't prove whether you have faith or not; but anyone can see that I have faith by the way I act." [19]Are there still some among you who hold that "only believing" is enough? Believing in one God? Well, remember that the demons believe this too—so strongly that they tremble in terror! [20]Fool! When will you ever learn that "believing" is useless without *doing* what God wants you to? Faith that does not result in good deeds is not real faith. [21]Don't you remember that even our father Abraham was declared good because of what he *did,* when he was willing to obey God, even if it meant offering his son Isaac to die on the altar? [22]You see, he was trusting God so much that he was willing to do whatever God told him to; his faith was made complete by what he did, by his actions, his good deeds. [23]And so it happened just as the Scriptures say, that Abraham trusted God, and the Lord declared him good in God's sight, and he was even called "the friend of God." [24]So you see, a man is saved by what he does, as well as by what he believes. [25]Rahab, the prostitute, is another example of this. She was saved because of what she did when she hid those messengers and sent them safely away by a different road. [26]Just as the body is dead when there is no spirit in it, so faith is dead if it is not the kind that results in good deeds.

Jas 3:11. Does a spring of water bubble out first with fresh water and then with bitter water? [12]Can you pick olives from a fig tree, or figs from a grape vine? No, and you can't draw fresh water from a salty pool. [13]If you are wise, live a life of steady goodness, so that only good deeds will pour forth. And if you don't brag about them, then you will be truly wise! [14]And by all means don't brag about being wise and good if you are bitter and jealous and selfish; that is the worst sort of lie. [15]For jealousy and selfishness are not God's kind of wisdom. Such things are earthly, unspiritual, inspired by the devil. [16]For wherever there is jealousy or selfish ambition, there will be disorder and every other kind of evil. [17]But the wisdom that comes from heaven is first of all pure and full of quiet gentleness. Then it is peace-loving and courteous. It allows discussion and is willing to yield to others; it is full of mercy and good deeds. It is wholehearted and straightforward and sincere. [18]And those who are peacemakers will plant seeds of peace and reap a harvest of goodness.

1 Pet 3:1, 2. Wives, fit in with your husbands' plans; for then if they refuse to listen when you talk to them about the Lord, they will be won by your respectful, pure behavior. Your godly lives will speak to them better than any words. [3]Don't be concerned about the outward beauty that depends on jewelry, or beautiful clothes, or hair arrangement. [4]Be beautiful inside, in your hearts, with the lasting charm of a gentle and quiet spirit which is so precious to God. [5]That kind of deep beauty was seen in the saintly women of old, who trusted God and fitted in with their husbands' plans. [6]Sarah, for instance, obeyed her husband Abraham, honoring him as head of the house. And if you do the same, you will be following in her steps like good daughters and doing what is right; then you will not need to fear (offending your husbands). [7]You husbands must be careful of your wives, being thoughtful of their needs and honoring them as the weaker sex. Remember that you and your wife are partners in receiving God's blessings, and if you don't treat her as you should, your prayers will not get ready answers. [8]And now this word to all of you: You should be like one big happy family, full of sympathy toward each other, loving one another with tender hearts and humble minds. [9]Don't repay evil for evil. Don't snap back at those who say unkind things about you. Instead, pray for God's help for them, for we are to be kind to others, and God will bless us for it. [10]If you want a happy, good life, keep control of your tongue, and guard your lips from telling lies. [11]Turn away from evil and do good. Try to live in peace even if you must run after it to catch and hold it! [13]Usually no one will hurt you for wanting to do good. [14]But even if they should, you are to be envied, for God will reward you for it.

1 Pet 4:2. And you won't be spending the rest of your life chasing after evil desires, but will be anxious to do the will of God.

2 Pet 1:5. But to obtain these gifts, you need more than faith; you must also work hard to be good, and even that is not enough. For then you must learn to know God better and discover what he wants you to do. [6]Next, learn to put aside your own desires so that you will become patient and godly, gladly letting God have his way with you. [7]This will make possible the next step, which is for you to enjoy other people and to like them, and finally you will grow to love them deeply. [8]The more you

go on in this way, the more you will grow strong spiritually and become fruitful and useful to our Lord Jesus Christ. [9]But anyone who fails to go after these additions to faith is blind indeed, or at least very shortsighted, and has forgotten that God delivered him from the old life of sin so that now he can live a strong, good life for the Lord.

1 Jn 2:3. And how can we be sure that we belong to him? By looking within ourselves: are we really trying to do what he wants us to? [4]Someone may say, "I am a Christian; I am on my way to heaven; I belong to Christ." But if he doesn't do what Christ tells him to, he is a liar. [5]But those who do what Christ tells them to will learn to love God more and more. That is the way to know whether or not you are a Christian. [6]Anyone who says he is a Christian should live as Christ did. [10]But whoever loves his fellow man is "walking in the light" and can see his way without stumbling around in darkness and sin. [11]For he who dislikes his brother is wandering in spiritual darkness and doesn't know where he is going, for the darkness had made him blind so that he cannot see the way. [24]So keep on believing what you have been taught from the beginning. If you do, you will always be in close fellowship with both God the Father and his Son. [29]Since we know that God is always good and does only right, we may rightly assume that all those who do right are his children.

1 Jn 3:3. And everyone who really believes this will try to stay pure because Christ is pure. [6]So if we stay close to him, obedient to him, we won't be sinning either; but as for those who keep on sinning, they should realize this: They sin because they have never really known him or become his. [7]. . . If you are constantly doing what is good, it is because you *are* good, even as he is. [9]The person who has been born into God's family does not make a practice of sinning, because now God's life is in him; so he can't keep on sinning, for this new life has been born into him and controls him—he has been *born again.* [10]So now we can tell who is a child of God and who belongs to Satan. Whoever is living a life of sin and doesn't love his brother shows that he is not in God's family; [11]for the message to us from the beginning has been that we should love one another. [14]If we love other Christians it proves that we have been delivered from hell and given eternal life. But a person who doesn't have love for others is headed for eternal death. [17]But if someone who is supposed to be a Christian has money enough to live well, and sees a brother in need, and won't help him—how can God's love be within *him?* [18]Little children, let us stop just *saying* we love people; let us *really* love them, and *show it* by our *actions.* [19]Then we will know for sure, by our actions, that we are on God's side, and our consciences will be clear, even when we stand before the Lord. [20]But if we have bad consciences and feel that we have done wrong, the Lord will surely feel it even more, for he knows everything we do. [21]But, dearly loved friends, if our consciences are clear, we can come to the Lord with perfect assurance and trust, [22]and get whatever we ask for because we are obeying him and doing the things that please him. [23]And this is what God says we must do: Believe on the name of his Son Jesus Christ, and love one another. [24]Those who do what God says—they are living with God and he with them. We know this is true because the Holy Spirit he has given us tells us so.

1 Jn 4:4. Dear young friends, you belong to God and have already won your fight with those who are against Christ, because there is someone in your hearts who is stronger than any evil teacher in this wicked world. [5]These men belong to this world, so, quite naturally, they are concerned about worldly affairs and the world pays attention to them. [6]But we are children of God; that is why only those who have walked and talked with God will listen to us. Others won't. That is another way to know whether a message is really from God; for if it is, the world won't listen to it. [7]Dear friends, let us practice loving each other, for love comes from God and those who are loving and kind show that they are the children of God, and that they are getting to know him better. [8]But if a person isn't loving and kind, it shows that he doesn't know God—for God is love. [9]God showed how much he loved us by sending his only Son into this wicked world to bring to us eternal life through his death. [10]In this act we see what real love is: it is not our love for God, but his love for us when he sent his Son to satisfy God's anger against our sins. [11]Dear friends, since God loved us as much as that, we surely ought to love each other too. [12]For though we have never yet seen God, when we love each other God lives in us and his love within us grows ever stronger. [13]And he has put his own Holy Spirit into our hearts as a proof to us that we are living with him and he with us. [14]And furthermore, we have seen with our own eyes and now tell all the world that God sent his Son to be their Savior. [15]Anyone who believes and says that Jesus is the Son of God has God living in him, and he is living with God. [16]We know how much God loves us because we have felt his love and because we believe him when he tells us that he loves us dearly. God is love, and anyone who lives in love is living with God and God is living in him. [17]And as we live with Christ, our love grows more perfect and complete; so we will not be ashamed and embarrassed at the day of judgment, but can face him with confidence and joy, because he loves us and we love him too. [18]We need have no fear of someone who loves us perfectly; his perfect love for us eliminates all dread of what he might do to us. If we are afraid, it is for fear of what he might do to us, and shows that we are not fully convinced that he really loves us. [19]So you see, our love for him comes as a result of his loving us first. [20]If anyone says "I love God," but keeps on hating his brother, he is a liar; for if he doesn't love his brother who is right there in front of him, how can he love God whom he has never seen? [21]And God himself has said that one must love not only God, but his brother too.

1 Jn 5:1. If you believe that Jesus is the Christ—that he is God's Son and your Savior—then you are a child of God. And all who love the Father love his children too. [2]So you can find out how much you love God's children—your brothers and sisters in the Lord—by how much you love and obey God. [3]Loving God means doing what he tells us to do, and really, that isn't hard at all; [4]for every child of God can obey him, defeating sin and evil pleasure by trusting Christ to help him. [5]But who could possibly fight and win this battle except by believing that Jesus is truly the Son of God? [10]All who believe this know in their hearts that it is true. If anyone doesn't believe this, he is actually calling God a liar, because he doesn't believe what God has said about his Son. [13]I have written this to you who believe in the Son of God so that you may know you have eternal life. [18]No one who has become part of God's family makes a practice of sinning, for Christ, God's Son, holds him securely and the devil cannot get his hands on him.

2 Jn 1:9. For if you wander beyond the teaching of Christ, you will leave God behind; while if you are loyal to Christ's teachings, you will have God too. Then you will have both the Father and the Son.

3 Jn 1:11. Dear friend, don't let this bad example influence you. Follow only what is good. Remember that those who do what is right prove that they are God's children; and those who continue in evil prove that they are far from God.

Rev 2:2. I know how many good things you are doing. I have watched your hard work and your patience; I know you don't tolerate sin among your members, and you have carefully examined the claims of those who say they are apostles but aren't. You have found out how they lie. [3]You have patiently suffered for me without quitting. [19]I am aware of all your good deeds—your kindness to the poor, your gifts and service to them; also I know your love and faith and patience, and I can see your constant improvement in all these things.

SYMBOLIZED. Ezk 47:12; Rev 22:2.

See *Sin, Fruits of; Works, Good.*

RIMMON 1. Father of the murderers of Ish-bosheth, 2 Sam 4:2, 3, 5–9.

2. A city south of Jerusalem, Zech 14:10. Allotted to Judah, Josh 15:21–32; Neh 11:25–30; afterward to Simeon, Josh 19:2–7; 1 Chron 4:32, 33. Called *En-rimmon,* Josh 19:2–7; Neh 11:25–30.

3. A city of Zebulun, Josh 19:13. Called *Rimmono,* 1 Chron 6:77.

4. A rock in Benjamin, Judg 20:45–47; 21:13.

5. A Syrian idol, 2 Kgs 5:18.

RIMMONO See *Rimmon, 3.*

RIMMON-PAREZ A camping place of the Israelites, Num 33:15–37.

RING Of gold, Num 31:50. Worn as a token of authority, Gen 41:41, 42. Given as a token, Esther 3:10, 12; 8:2–10. Worn in the nose, Job 40:24; Prov 11:22; Ezk 16:12. Offerings of, to the tabernacle, Ex 35:22; Num 31:50.

RINNAH A son of Shimon, 1 Chron 4:20.

RIPHATH A son of Gomer, Gen 10:3. Called *Diphath,* 1 Chron 1:5–9.

RISING EARLY. Prov 31:15. For devotions, Ps 5:3; 59:16; Song 7:12. Practised by the wicked, Mic 2:1; Zeph 3:7; by drunkards, Isa 5:11. Illustrates spiritual diligence, Rom 13:11–13.

Instances of. Lot, Gen 19:23; Abraham, Gen 19:27; 21:14; 22:3. Issac, Gen 26:31. Abimelech, Gen 20:8. Jacob, Gen 28:18; 32:31. Laban, Gen 31:55. Moses, Ex 8:20; 9:13. Joshua, Josh 3:1; 6:12–15; 7:16. Gideon, Judg 6:38. Elkanah, 1 Sam 1:19, 20. Samuel, 1 Sam 15:12. David, 1 Sam 17:20. Mary Magdalene, Mk 16:1, 2; Lk 24:1. Apostles, Acts 5:21.

See *Industry.*

LATE. Consequences of, Prov 6:9–11; 24:32–34. See *Idleness; Laziness.*

RISSAH A camping place of the Israelites, Num 33:15–37.

RITHMAH A camping place of the Israelites, Num 33:15–37.

RIVER Of Eden, Gen 2:10; of Egypt, Gen 15:18, see *Egypt, River of; Nile; Moses* found in, Ex 2:1–10; plague of waters of, Ex 7:17–25; 8:3–11; Euphrates, Deut 1:7; Josh 1:4; Arnon, Deut 2:35, 36; Jabbok, Deut 3:16; Kishon, Judg 4:7; Chebar, Ezk 1:1; Jordan, Mk 1:5; Abana and Pharpar, 2 Kgs 5:12; rivers of Babylon, Ps 137:1.

Tree planted by, Ps 1:3; rivers of delight, Ps 36:8; prosperity like a river, Isa 66:12; rivers of living water, Jn 7:38; cf. Isa 32:2; river of Water of Life, Rev 22:1, 2.

Future river to flow from Jerusalem, Ps 46:4; Ezk 47:1–12; Joel 3:18; Zech 14:8.

RIZIA An Asherite, 1 Chron 7:39.

RIZPAH Concubine of Saul, 2 Sam 3:7. Guards the bodies of her sons hanged by command of David, 2 Sam 21:8–11.

ROADS Public highways, Deut 2:27. From Gibeon to Beth-horon, Josh 10:10. From Bethel to Shechem, Judg 21:19. From Judea to Galilee, by way of Samaria, Jn 4:3–5, 43, 44. To the house of God, Judg 20:31. To cities of refuge, Deut 19:2, 3. Built by rulers, Num 20:17; 21:22.

FIGURATIVE. See *Highways.*

ROBBERS Prov 1:11–16. Dens of, Jer 7:11. Bands of, Hos 6:9; 7:1. Those who came before Christ were thieves and robbers, Jn 10:8; Barabbas a robber, Jn 18:40; robbers of churches, Acts 19:37. Paul in danger from, 2 Cor 11:26.

FIGURATIVE. Prov 6:11.

See *Robbery; Theft.*

ROBBERY Forbidden, Lev 19:13; Isa 61:8. Punished with death, Ezk 18:10, 13. Forgiven, Ezk 33:15. Robbing a neighbor, Ex 22:10, 11; the poor, Prov 22:22, 23; the fatherless, Isa 10:2. Robbing God, Mal 3:8, 9. God hates robbery, Isa 61:8.

INSTANCES OF. Judg 9:25; Lk 10:30.

See *Robbers, Theft.*

ROBE Robe of the ephod, Ex 28:31; Jonathan's, 1 Sam 18:4; Saul's, 1 Sam 24:4, 11; David's, 1 Chron 15:27; the king of Nineveh's, Jon 3:6; the prodigal's, Lk 15:22. Torn as a sign of grief, Job 1:20; 2:12. Garments of salvation, Isa 61:10, cf.

2 Chron 6:41. Christ's seamless garment, Jn 19:23, 24. Scarlet or purple robe placed on Christ, Mt 27: 28, 31; Lk 23:11; Jn 19:2, 5. White robes, Rev 6:11; 7:9, 13, 14. The bride of the lamb clothed in a robe of righteousness, Rev 19:7, 8. Parable of the man who was dressed in a wedding robe, Mt 22:11. See *Dress.*

ROCK Two different Hebrew words for rock appear early in the Scriptures, providing the basis for much later revelation about Christ in the way they are used. They are *tsur,* a confined outcropping such as men may stumble over, Ex 17:5, 6; Deut 8:15; Isa 8:14, 15 (quoted in 1 Pet 2:8), and *sela,* a lofty elevated rock or stronghold, Num 20:7–12; Ps 78:16. The first one was to be struck, the second one, spoken to.

Cleft of a rock, Ex 33:21, 22; honey and oil out of, Deut 32:13; Rock of his salvation, Deut 32:15; the Rock that fathered you, Deut 32:18; the fire out of the rock, Judg 6:21; the rock of Etam, Judg 15: 8; the rock of Rimmon, Judg 20:45; Jehovah is my Rock, 2 Sam 22:2; Ps 18:2; the rock of my salvation, 2 Sam 22:47; Isa 8:14; the Rock of Israel, 2 Sam 23: 3; my rock and my fortress, Ps 31:3; set my feet upon a rock, Ps 27:5; lead me to the rock of safety, Ps 61:2; my rock, my rescuer, defense and fortress, Ps 62:2, 6; shadow of a mighty rock in a weary land, Isa 32:2; living in the clefts of the rocks, Jer 49:16; Obd 1:3; house built on solid rock, Mt 7:24; upon this rock I will build my church, Mt 16:18; seeds fall on, Lk 8:6; rock of offense, Rom 9:33; 1 Pet 2:8; that Rock was Christ, 1 Cor 10:3, 4.

FIGURATIVE. Gen 49:24; 2 Sam 22:32, 47; 23: 3; Ps 18:2; 31:2; Isa 17:10; 32:2; Ezk 3:9; Mt 16:18; 1 Cor 10:3, 4.

Symbolical. Of the kingdom of Christ, Dan 2:34, 35.

See *Stones.*

ROCK-BADGER Ps 104:18.

See *Cliff Badger; Coney.*

ROCK OF ESCAPE In the wilderness of Maon, 1 Sam 23:28.

ROD See *Scepter.*

ROE See *Deer.*

ROGELIM The home of Barzillai, 2 Sam 17: 27; 19:31, 32.

ROHGAH Son of Shomer, 1 Chron 7:24.

ROMAMTI-EZER Son of Heman, 1 Chron 25:4, 5, 9–31.

ROMAN EMPIRE Ruled by Augustus Caesar, Lk 2:1; Tiberius Caesar, Lk 3:1, 2; Claudius Caesar, Acts 18:2, 3. Citizenship in, by birth, Acts 22:28; by purchase, Acts 22:28. Rights of citizens, Acts 16:37; 22:25–29; of trial, Acts 25:16; of appeal, Acts 25:10, 11, 21.

ROME The capital of the Roman empire. Jews excluded from, by Claudius, Acts 18:2, 3. Paul's visit to, see *Paul.* Visited by Onesiphorus, 2 Tim 1:16, 17. Paul desires to preach in, Rom 1:15. Christians in, Rom 16:5–17; Phil 1:12–18; 4:22; 2 Tim 4:21.

Paul's letter to the Christians in, Rom 1:6, 7; preaches to them the gospel of Christ, Rom 1:16; the condemnation of the Gentiles, Rom 1:18; and the Jews, Rom 2; God's judgment against all sin, Rom 2:6; 3; justification by faith in Jesus Christ, Rom 3:24; 4; 5; the faith of Abraham, Rom 4; the fruits of faith, Rom 5–7; the works of the flesh and the Spirit, Rom 8; God's supreme power over all, Rom 9; 11; the righteousness of the law and of faith, Rom 10. Exhorted to humility, love, and good works, Rom 12; to obey the government, Rom 13; to mutual forbearance, Rom 14; 15; requested to greet various fellow Christians, Rom 16.

ROOF See *House, Roof of.*

ROOSTER See *Cock Crowing.*

ROPE Triple-braided, Eccl 4:12. Used in binding prisoners, Judg 15:13. Worn on the head as a sign of submission, 1 Kgs 20:31, 32.

FIGURATIVE. Of love, Hos 11:4. Of temptations, Ps 140:5; Prov 5:22.

Symbolic. Token of mourning, 1 Kgs 20:31–33. See *Cord.*

ROSE 1 Kgs 6:18; Song 2:1.

ROSH 1. Son of Benjamin, Gen 46:19–22.

2. A nation which is to be involved in the invasion of Israel in the last days, Isa 66:19, whose chief or head is Gog, Ezk 38:1, 2; 39:1. Some scholars believe Rosh to be a name for Assyria, while others see it as an ancient name for Russia.

RUBY Job 28:18; Prov 8:11; Lam 4:7; called also *Sardius.* In the chestpiece, Ex 28:17; 39:10. In the clothing of the king of Tyre, believed to be one of the names of Satan, Ezk 28:12–15. Seen in John's apocalyptic vision of the foundation of the New Jerusalem, Rev 21:18–20.

FIGURATIVE. Rev 4:3.

RUFUS 1. Son of Simon, Mk 15:21.

2. A Christian in Rome, Rom 16:13. Possibly the same as 1, above.

RUHAMAH A symbolic name of Israel, Hos 2:1, meaning "pitied."

RULER Christ ascended above, Eph 1:21. The church reveals the wisdom of God to, Eph 3:10. Believers fight against, in prayer, Eph 6:12. Christ created, Col 1:16. Christ the head over, Col 2:10. Believers to be subject to, Tit 3:1. Appointed and removed by God, see *Government, God in.* Chastised, Dan 4. See *Nations.*

Monarchial, see *King.*

Patriarchal, Gen 27:27–29, 37. Instances of: Nimrod, Gen 10:8–10. Abraham, Gen 14:13–24; 17: 6; 21:21–32. Melchizedek, Gen 14:18. Isaac, Gen 26: 26–31. Judah, Gen 38:24. Heads of families, Ex 6: 14. Ishmael, Gen 17:20. Esau, and the kings of Edom, Gen 36.

Theocratic, see *Government.*

QUALIFICATIONS OF RIGHTEOUS. Gen 41:33. My suggestion is that you find the wisest man in Egypt and put him in charge of administering a nation-wide farm program.

Ex 18:21. Find some capable, godly, honest men who hate bribes, and appoint them as judges, one judge for each 1000 people; he in turn will have ten judges under him, each in charge of a hundred; and under each of them will be two judges, each responsible for the affairs of fifty people; and each of these will have five judges beneath him, each counseling ten persons. [22]Let these men be responsible to serve the people with justice at all times. Anything that is too important or complicated can be brought to you. But the smaller matters they can take care of themselves. That way it will be easier for you because you will share the burden with them.

Ex 23:8. Take no bribes, for a bribe makes you unaware of what you clearly see! A bribe hurts the cause of the person who is right.

Deut 1:13. So choose some men from each tribe who are wise, experienced, and understanding, and I will appoint them as your leaders.

Deut 16:18. Appoint judges and administrative officials for all the cities the Lord your God is giving you. They will administer justice in every part of the land. [19]Never twist justice to benefit a rich man, and never accept bribes. For bribes blind the eyes of the wisest and corrupt their decisions. [20]Justice must prevail. That is the only way you will be successful in the land which the Lord your God is giving you.

Deut 27:19. "Cursed is he who is unjust to the foreigner, the orphan, and the widow." And all the people shall reply, 'Amen.'

2 Sam 23:3. The Rock of Israel said to me: "One shall come who rules righteously, who rules in the fear of God. [4]He shall be as the light of the morning; a cloudless sunrise when the tender grass springs forth upon the earth; as sunshine after rain."

Ezra 7:25. And you, Ezra, are to use the wisdom God has given you to select and appoint judges and other officials to govern all the people west of the Euphrates River; if they are not familiar with the laws of your God, you are to teach them.

Ps 2:10. O kings and rulers of the earth, listen while there is time. [11]Serve the Lord with reverent fear; rejoice with trembling.

Ps 72:1. O God, help the king to judge as you would, and help his son to walk in godliness. [2]Help him to give justice to your people, even to the poor. [3]May the mountains and hills flourish in prosperity because of his good reign. [4]Help him to defend the poor and needy and to crush their oppressors. [5]May the poor and needy revere you constantly, as long as sun and moon continue in the skies! Yes, forever! [6]May the reign of this son of mine be as gentle and fruitful as the springtime rains upon the grass—like showers that water the earth! [7]May all good men flourish in his reign, with abundance of peace to the end of time. [8]Let him reign from sea to sea, and from the Euphrates River to the ends of the earth. [9]The desert nomads shall bow before him; his enemies shall fall face downward in the dust. [10]Kings along the Mediterranean coast—the kings of Tarshish and the islands—and those from Sheba and from Seba—all will bring their gifts. [11]Yes, kings from everywhere! All will bow before him! All will serve him! [12]He will take care of the helpless and poor when they cry to him; for they have no one else to defend them. [13]He feels pity for the weak and needy, and will rescue them. [14]He will save them from oppression and from violence, for their lives are precious to him. [15]And he shall live; and to him will be given the gold of Sheba, and there will be constant praise for him. His people will bless him all day long. [16]Bless us with abundant crops throughout the land, even on the highland plains; may there be fruit like that of Lebanon; may the cities be as full of people as the fields are of grass. [17]His name will be honored forever; it will continue as the sun; and all will be blessed in him; all nations will praise him.

Prov 16:10. God will help the king to judge the people fairly; there need be no mistakes. [12]It is a horrible thing for a king to do evil. His right to rule depends upon his fairness. [13]The king rejoices when his people are truthful and fair.

Prov 17:7. Truth from a rebel or lies from a king are both unexpected.

Prov 19:12. The king's anger is as dangerous as a lion's. But his approval is as refreshing as the dew on grass.

Prov 20:8. A king sitting as judge weighs all the evidence carefully, distinguishing the true from false. [26]A wise king stamps out crime by severe punishment. [28]If a king is kind, honest and fair, his kingdom stands secure.

Prov 21:1. Just as water is turned into irrigation ditches, so the Lord directs the king's thoughts. He turns them wherever he wants to.

Prov 24:23. It is wrong to sentence the poor, and let the rich go free. [24]He who says to the wicked, "You are innocent," shall be cursed by many people of many nations; [25]but blessings shall be showered on those who rebuke sin fearlessly. [26]It is an honor to receive a frank reply.

Prov 25:2, 3. It is God's privilege to conceal things, and the king's privilege to discover and invent. You cannot understand the height of heaven, the size of the earth, or all that goes on in the king's mind! [5]When you remove corrupt men from the king's court, his reign will be just and fair.

Prov 28:2. When there is moral rot within a nation, its government topples easily; but with honest, sensible leaders there is stability. [16]Only a stupid prince will oppress his people, but a king will have a long reign if he hates dishonesty and bribes.

Prov 29:2. With good men in authority, the people rejoice; but with the wicked in power, they groan. [4]A just king gives stability to his nation, but one who demands bribes destroys it. [14]A king who is fair to the poor shall have a long reign.

Prov 31:4. And it is not for kings, O Lemuel, to drink wine and whiskey. [5]For if they drink they may forget their duties and be unable to give justice to those who are oppressed. [8]You should defend those who cannot help themselves. [9]Yes, speak up for the poor and needy and see that they get justice.

Eccl 8:4. The king's command is backed by great power, and no one can withstand it or question it.

Eccl 10:16, 17. Woe to the land whose king is a

child and whose leaders are already drunk in the morning. Happy the land whose king is a nobleman, and whose leaders work hard before they feast and drink, and then only to strengthen themselves for the tasks ahead!

Isa 5:22. Woe to those who are "heroes" when it comes to drinking, and boast about the liquor they can hold. [23]They take bribes to pervert justice, letting the wicked go free and putting innocent men in jail.

Isa 16:5. Then, when the terror is past, God will establish David's throne forever, and on that throne he will place a just and righteous King.

Isa 28:6. He will give a longing for justice to your judges and great courage to your soldiers who are battling to the last before your gates.

Isa 60:17. I will exchange your brass for gold, your iron for silver, your wood for brass, your stones for iron. Peace and righteousness shall be your taskmasters!

Jer 13:18. Say to the king and queen-mother, Come down from your thrones and sit in the dust, for your glorious crowns are removed from your heads. They are no longer yours.

Rom 12:8. If you are a preacher, see to it that your sermons are strong and helpful. If God has given you money, be generous in helping others with it. If God has given you administrative ability and put you in charge of the work of others, take the responsibility seriously. Those who offer comfort to the sorrowing should do so with Christian cheer.

Rom 13:1. Obey the government, for God is the one who has put it there. There is no government anywhere that God has not placed in power. [2]So those who refuse to obey the laws of the land are refusing to obey God, and punishment will follow. [3]For the policeman does not frighten people who are doing right; but those doing evil will always fear him. So if you don't want to be afraid, keep the laws and you will get along well. [4]The policeman is sent by God to help you. But if you are doing something wrong, of course you should be afraid, for he will have you punished. He is sent by God for that very purpose. [5]Obey the laws, then, for two reasons: first, to keep from being punished, and second, just because you know you should. [6]Pay your taxes too, for these same two reasons. For government workers need to be paid so that they can keep on doing God's work, serving you. [7]Pay everyone whatever he ought to have: pay your taxes and import duties gladly, obey those over you, and give honor and respect to all those to whom it is due.

1 Tim 2:1. Here are my directions: Pray much for others; plead for God's mercy upon them; give thanks for all he is going to do for them. [2]Pray in this way for kings and all others who are in authority over us, or are in places of high responsibility, so that we can live in peace and quietness, spending our time in godly living and thinking much about the Lord.

1 Pet 2:13. For the Lord's sake, obey every law of your government: those of the king as head of the state, [14]and those of the king's officers, for he has sent them to punish all who do wrong, and to honor those who do right.

DUTIES OF. Ex 18:15, 16. "Well, because the people come to me with their disputes, to ask for God's decisions," Moses told him. "I am their judge, deciding who is right and who is wrong, and instructing them in God's ways. I apply the laws of God to their particular disputes." [20]"You will tell them his decisions, teaching them God's laws, and showing them the principles of godly living. [21]Find some capable, godly, honest men who hate bribes, and appoint them as judges, one judge for each 1000 people; he in turn will have ten judges under him, each in charge of a hundred; and under each of them will be two judges, each responsible for the affairs of fifty people; and each of these will have five judges beneath him, each counseling ten persons."

Ex 23:3. Do not slant your testimony in favor of a man just because he is poor. [6]A man's poverty is no excuse for twisting justice against him. [7]Keep far away from falsely charging anyone with evil; never let an innocent person be put to death. I will not stand for this. [9]Do not oppress foreigners; you know what it's like to be a foreigner; remember your own experience in the land of Egypt.

Lev 19:15. Judges must always be just in their sentences, not noticing whether a person is poor or rich; they must always be perfectly fair.

Lev 24:22. You shall have the same law for the foreigner as for the home-born citizen, for I am Jehovah your God.

Num 27:16. O Jehovah, the God of the spirits of all mankind, (before I am taken away) please appoint a new leader for the people, [17]a man who will lead them into battle and care for them, so that the people of the Lord will not be as sheep without a shepherd.

Deut 1:16. I instructed them to be perfectly fair at all times, even to foreigners! [17]"When giving your decisions," I told them, "never favor a man because he is rich; be fair to great and small alike. Don't fear their displeasure, for you are judging in the place of God. Bring me any cases too difficult for you, and I will handle them."

Deut 16:18. Appoint judges and administrative officials for all the cities the Lord your God is giving you. They will administer justice in every part of the land. [19]Never twist justice to benefit a rich man, and never accept bribes. For bribes blind the eyes of the wisest and corrupt their decisions. [20]Justice must prevail. That is the only way you will be successful in the land which the Lord your God is giving you.

Deut 17:16. Be sure that he doesn't build up a large stable of horses for himself, nor send his men to Egypt to raise horses for him there, for the Lord has told you, "Never return to Egypt again." [17]He must not have too many wives, lest his heart be turned away from the Lord, neither shall he be excessively rich. [18]And when he has been crowned and sits upon his throne as king, then he must copy these laws from the book kept by the Levite-priests. [19]That copy of the law shall be his constant companion. He must read from it every day of his life so that he will learn to respect the Lord his God by obeying all of his commands. [20]This regular reading of God's laws will prevent him from feeling that he is better than his fellow citizens. It will also prevent him from turning away from God's laws in the slightest respect, and will ensure his having a long, good reign. His sons will then follow him upon the throne.

Deut 19:18. They must be closely questioned, and if the witness is lying, [19]his penalty shall be the punishment he thought the other man would get. In this way you will purge out evil from among you.

Deut 24:16. Fathers shall not be put to death for the sins of their sons nor the sons for the sins of their fathers; every man worthy of death shall be executed for his own crime.

Deut 25:1. If a man is guilty of a crime, and the penalty is a beating, the judge shall command him to lie down and be beaten in his presence with up to forty stripes in proportion to the seriousness of the crime.

Josh 1:7. You need only to be strong and courageous and to obey to the letter every law Moses gave you, for if you are careful to obey every one of them you will be successful in everything you do. [8]Constantly remind the people about these laws, and you yourself must think about them every day and every night so that you will be sure to obey all of them. For only then will you succeed.

2 Chron 9:8. Blessed be the Lord your God! How he must love Israel to give them a just king like you!

2 Chron 19:6. Watch your step—I have not appointed you—God has; and he will stand beside you and help you give justice in each case that comes before you. [7]Be very much afraid to give any other decision than what God tells you to. For there must be no injustice among God's judges, no partiality, no taking of bribes.

Ezra 7:25. And you, Ezra, are to use the wisdom God has given you to select and appoint judges and other officials to govern all the people west of the Euphrates River; if they are not familiar with the laws of your God, you are to teach them. [26]Anyone refusing to obey the law of your God and the law of the king shall be punished immediately by death, banishment, confiscation of goods, or imprisonment.

Ps 82:2. How long will you judges refuse to listen to the evidence? How long will you shower special favors on the wicked? [3]Give fair judgment to the poor man, the afflicted, the fatherless, the destitute. [4]Rescue the poor and needy from the grasp of evil men.

Ps 148:11. The kings and all the people, with their rulers and their judges . . . [13]all praise the Lord together.

Isa 58:6. No, the kind of fast I want is that you stop oppressing those who work for you and treat them fairly and give them what they earn.

Jer 22:1. Then the Lord said to me: Go over and speak directly to the king of Judah and say, [2]Listen to this message from God, O king of Judah, sitting on David's throne; and let your servants and your people listen too. [3]The Lord says: Be fair-minded. Do what is right! Help those in need of justice! Quit your evil deeds! Protect the rights of aliens and immigrants, orphans and widows; stop murdering the innocent! Jer 21:12.

Zech 7:8, 9. Then this message from the Lord came to Zechariah. "Tell them to be honest and fair—and not to take bribes—and to be merciful and kind to everyone. [10]Tell them to stop oppressing widows and orphans, foreigners and poor people, and to stop plotting evil against each other."

Zech 8:16. Here is your part: Tell the truth. Be fair. Live at peace with everyone.

Rom 13:3. For the policeman does not frighten people who are doing right; but those doing evil will always fear him.

1 Tim 2:2. Pray in this way for kings and all others who are in authority over us, or are in places of high responsibility, so that we can live in peace and quietness, spending our time in godly living and thinking much about the Lord.

1 Pet 2:14. And those of the king's officers, for he has sent them to punish all who do wrong, and to honor those who do right.

RIGHTEOUS.

Instances of. Pharaoh, in his treatment of Abraham, Gen 12:15–20. Abimelech, in his treatment of Abraham, Gen 20; of Isaac, Gen 26:6–11. Joseph, in his conduct of the affairs of Egypt, Gen 41:37–57. Pharaoh, in his treatment of Jacob and his family, Gen 47:5–10; 50:1–6. Moses, in his administration of the affairs of the children of Israel, Num 16:15. See *Government, Mosaic.* Samuel, in not taking bribes, 1 Sam 12:3, 4. Saul, after the defeat of the Ammonites, 1 Sam 11:12, 13. David, see *David.* Solomon, in his judgment between the two women who claimed the same child, 1 Kgs 3:16–28; according to the testimony of the Queen of Sheba, 1 Kgs 10:6–9. Asa, in abolishing sodomy and other abominations of idolatry, 1 Kgs 15:11–15; 2 Chron 14:2–5. Jehoshaphat, in obeying the Lord, 1 Kgs 22: 41–46; 2 Chron 17:3–10; 19; 20:3–30. Hezekiah, in his fear of the Lord, 2 Kgs 18:1–3; 20:1–11; 2 Chron 30; 31. Josiah, in repairing the temple and in other good works, 2 Kgs 22; 23; 2 Chron 34; 35. Cyrus, in emancipating the Jews, Ezra 1. Darius, advancing the rebuilding of the temple, Ezra 6: 1–12. Ar-ta-xerxes, in commissioning Ezra to restore the forms of worship at Jerusalem, Ezra 7; Neh 2; 5:14. Nehemiah, Neh chapters 4; 5. Daniel, see *Daniel.* King of Nineveh, in repenting and proclaiming a fast, Jon 3:6–9.

WICKED. Gen 15:13. Then Jehovah told Abram, "Your descendants will be oppressed as slaves in a foreign land for 400 years. [14]But I will punish the nation that enslaves them, and at the end they will come away with great wealth."

Ex 3:9. Yes, the wail of the people of Israel has risen to me in heaven, and I have seen the heavy tasks the Egyptians have oppressed them with.

Deut 27:19. "Cursed is he who is unjust to the foreigner, the orphan, and the widow." And all the people shall reply, "Amen."

1 Sam 8:10. So Samuel told the people what the Lord had said: [11]"If you insist on having a king, he will conscript your sons and make them run before his chariots; [12]some will be made to lead his troops into battle, while others will be slave laborers; they will be forced to plow in the royal fields, and harvest his crops without pay; and make his weapons and chariot equipment. [13]He will take your daughters from you and force them to cook and bake and make perfumes for him. [14]He will take away the best of your fields and vineyards and olive groves and give them to his friends. [15]He will take a tenth of your harvest and distribute it to his favorites. [16]He will demand your slaves and the finest of your youth and will use your animals for his personal gain. [17]He will demand a tenth of your flocks, and you shall be his slaves. [18]You will shed bitter tears because of this king you are demanding, but the Lord will not help you."

2 Chron 28:19. For the Lord brought Judah very low on account of the evil deeds of King Ahaz of Israel, for he had destroyed the spiritual fiber of Judah and had been faithless to the Lord.

Neh 5:7. So after thinking about it I spoke out against these rich government officials. "What is this you are doing?" I demanded. "How dare you demand a mortgage as a condition for helping another Israelite?" Then I called a public trial to deal with them. [8]At the trial I shouted at them, "The rest of us are doing all we can to *help* our Jewish brothers who have returned from exile as slaves in distant lands, but you are forcing them right back into slavery again. How often must we redeem them?" And they had nothing to say in their own defense. [9]Then I pressed further. "What you are doing is very evil," I exclaimed. "Should you not walk in the fear of our God? Don't we have enough enemies among the nations around us who are trying to destroy us?"

Neh 9:34. Our kings, princes, priests, and ancestors didn't obey your laws or listen to your warnings. [35]They did not worship you despite the wonderful things you did for them and the great goodness you showered upon them. You gave them a large, fat land, but they refused to turn from their wickedness. [36]So now we are slaves here in the land of plenty which you gave to our ancestors! Slaves among all this abundance! [37]The lush yield of this land passes into the hands of the kings whom you have allowed to conquer us because of our sins. They have power over our bodies and our cattle, and we serve them at their pleasure and are in great misery.

Job 24:22. Yet sometimes it seems as though God preserves the rich by his power, and restores them to life when anyone else would die. [24]But though they are very great now, yet in a moment they shall be gone like all others, cut off like heads of grain.

Job 35:9. The oppressed may shriek beneath their wrongs and groan beneath the power of the rich.

Ps 10:17. Lord, you know the hopes of humble people. Surely you will hear their cries and comfort their hearts by helping them. [18]You will be with the orphans and all who are oppressed, so that mere earthly man will terrify them no longer.

Ps 12:5. The Lord replies, "I will arise and defend the oppressed, the poor, the needy. I will rescue them as they have longed for me to do." [7]O Lord, we know that you will forever preserve your own from the reach of evil men, [8]Although they prowl on every side and vileness is praised throughout the land.

Ps 49:20. For man with all his pomp must die like any animal.

Ps 58:1, 2. Justice? You high and mighty politicians don't even know the meaning of the word! Fairness? Which of you has any left? Not one! All your dealings are crooked: you give "justice" in exchange for bribes.

Ps 82:2. How long will you judges refuse to listen to the evidence? How long will you shower special favors on the wicked?

Ps 94:20. Will you permit a corrupt government to rule under your protection—a government permitting wrong to defeat right? [21]Do you approve of those who condemn the innocent to death?

Ps 110:5. God stands beside you to protect you. He will strike down many kings in the day of his anger.

Prov 17:15. The Lord despises those who say that bad is good, and good is bad. [26]How short-sighted to fine the godly for being good! And to punish nobles for being honest!

Prov 28:15. A wicked ruler is as dangerous to the poor as a lion or bear attacking them. [16]Only a stupid prince will oppress his people, but a king will have a long reign if he hates dishonesty and bribes. [28]When the wicked prosper, good men go away; when the wicked meet disaster, good men return.

Prov 29:2. With good men in authority, the people rejoice; but with the wicked in power, they groan. [4]A just king gives stability to his nation, but one who demands bribes destroys it. [12]A wicked ruler will have wicked aides on his staff.

Prov 30:21, 22. There are three things that make the earth tremble—no, four it cannot stand: A slave who becomes a king. A rebel who prospers.

Eccl 3:16. Moreover, I notice that throughout the earth justice is giving way to crime and even the police courts are corrupt. [17]I said to myself, "In due season God will judge everything man does, both good and bad."

Eccl 4:1. Next I observed all the oppression and sadness throughout the earth—the tears of the oppressed, and no one helping them, while on the side of their oppressors were powerful allies. [13]It is better to be a poor but wise youth than to be an old and foolish king who refuses all advice. [14]Such a lad could come from prison and succeed. He might even become king, though born in poverty.

Eccl 5:8. If you see some poor man being oppressed by the rich, with miscarriage of justice anywhere throughout the land, don't be surprised! For every official is under orders from higher up, and the higher officials look up to their superiors. And so the matter is lost in red tape and bureaucracy.

Eccl 8:9. I have thought deeply about all that goes on here in the world, where people have the power of injuring each other.

Eccl 10:5. There is another evil I have seen as I have watched the world go by, a sad situation concerning kings and rulers: [6]For I have seen foolish men given great authority, and rich men not given their rightful place of dignity! [7]I have even seen servants riding, while princes walk like servants! [16, 17]Woe to the land whose king is a child and whose leaders are already drunk in the morning. Happy the land whose king is a nobleman, and whose leaders work hard before they feast and drink, and then only to strengthen themselves for the tasks ahead!

Isa 1:23. Your leaders are rebels, companions of thieves; all of them take bribes and won't defend the widows and orphans.

Isa 3:12. O my people! Can't you see what fools your rulers are? Weak as women! Foolish as little children playing king. True leaders? No, misleaders! Leading you down the garden path to destruction. [14]First to feel his wrath will be the elders and the princes, for they have defrauded the poor. They have filled their barns with grain extorted from the helpless peasants. [15]"How dare you grind my people in the dust like that?" the Lord of Hosts will demand of them.

Isa 5:7. I have given you the story of God's people. They are the vineyard that I spoke about. Israel and Judah are his pleasant acreage! He expected them to yield a crop of justice, but found bloodshed instead. He expected righteousness, but the cries of deep oppression met his ears.

Isa 10:1. Woe to unjust judges and to those who issue unfair laws, says the Lord, [2]so that there is no justice for the poor, the widows and orphans. Yes, it is true that they even rob the widows and fatherless children. [3]Oh, what will you do when I visit you in that day when I send desolation upon you from a distant land? To whom will you turn then for your help? Where will your treasures be safe?

Isa 14:5. "For the Lord has crushed your wicked power, and broken your evil rule." [6]You persecuted my people with unceasing blows of rage and held the nations in your angry grip. You were unrestrained in tyranny. [19]But your body is thrown out like a broken branch; it lies in an open grave, covered with the dead bodies of those slain in battle. It lies as a carcass in the road, trampled and mangled by horses' hoofs. [20]No monument will be given you, for you have destroyed your nation and slain your people. Your son will not succeed you as the king. *vs.* 4–20.

Isa 28:14. Therefore hear the word of the Lord, you scoffing rulers in Jerusalem: [15]You have struck a bargain with Death, you say, and sold yourselves to the devil in exchange for his protection against the Assyrians. "They can never touch us," you say, "for we are under the care of one who will deceive and fool them."

Isa 29:20. Bullies will vanish and scoffers will cease, and all those plotting evil will be killed—[21]the violent man who fights at the drop of a hat, the man who waits in hiding to beat up the judge who sentenced him, and the men who use any excuse to be unfair.

Isa 30:33. The funeral pyre has long been ready, prepared for Molech, the Assyrian god; it is piled high with wood. The breath of the Lord, like fire from a volcano, will set it all on fire.

Isa 33:1. Woe to you, Assyrians, who have destroyed everything around you but have never felt destruction for yourselves. You expect others to respect their promises to you, while you betray them! Now you, too, will be betrayed and destroyed.

Isa 40:23. He dooms the great men of the world and brings them all to naught.

Isa 52:5. And now, what is this? asks the Lord. Why are my people enslaved again, and oppressed without excuse? Those who rule them shout in exultation, and my name is constantly blasphemed, day by day.

Isa 59:14. Our courts oppose the righteous man; fairness is unknown. Truth falls dead in the streets, and justice is outlawed. [15]Yes, truth is gone, and anyone who tries a better life is soon attacked. The Lord saw all the evil and was displeased to find no steps taken against sin.

Jer 5:28. And well fed and well groomed, and there is no limit to their wicked deeds. They refuse justice to orphans and the rights of the poor. [29]Should I sit back and act as though nothing is going on? the Lord God asks. Shouldn't I punish a nation such as this?

Ezk 21:25. O King Zedekiah, evil prince of Israel, your final day of reckoning is here. [26]Take off your jeweled crown, the Lord God says.

Ezk 22:6. Every leader in Israel who lives within your walls is bent on murder. [27]Your leaders are like wolves, who tear apart their victims, and they destroy lives for profit.

Ezk 28:2. Son of dust, say to the Prince of Tyre: The Lord God says: You are so proud you think you are God, sitting on the throne of a god on your island home in the midst of the seas. But you are only a man, and not a god, though you boast yourself to be like God.

Ezk 34:2. Son of dust, prophesy against the shepherds, the leaders of Israel, and say to them: The Lord God says to you: Woe to the shepherds who feed themselves instead of their flocks. Shouldn't shepherds feed the sheep? [3]You eat the best food and wear the finest clothes, but you let your flocks starve. [4]You haven't taken care of the weak nor tended the sick nor bound up the broken bones nor gone looking for those who have wandered away and are lost. Instead you have ruled them with force and cruelty. [7]Therefore, O shepherds, hear the word of the Lord: [8]As I live, says the Lord God, you abandoned my flock, leaving them to be attacked and destroyed, and you were no real shepherds at all, for you didn't search for them. You fed yourselves and let them starve; [9, 10]therefore I am against the shepherds, and I will hold them responsible for what has happened to my flock. I will take away their right to feed the flock—and take away their right to eat. I will save my flock from being taken for their food.

Ezk 45:9. For the Lord God says to the rulers: Quit robbing and cheating my people out of their land, and expelling them from their homes. Always be fair and honest.

Hos 5:10. The leaders of Judah have become the lowest sort of thieves. Therefore, I will pour my anger down upon them like a waterfall.

Hos 7:3. The king is glad about their wickedness; the princes laugh about their lies.

Hos 10:7. As for Samaria, her king shall disappear like a chip of wood upon an ocean wave.

Amos 3:10. My people have forgotten what it means to do right, says the Lord. "Their beautiful homes are full of the loot from their thefts and banditry. [11]"Therefore," the Lord God says, "an enemy is coming! He is surrounding them and will shatter their forts and plunder those beautiful homes."

Amos 4:1. Listen to me, you "fat cows" of Bashan living in Samaria—you women who encourage your husbands to rob the poor and crush the needy—you who never have enough to drink! [2]The Lord God has sworn by his holiness that the time will come when he will put hooks in your noses and lead you away like the cattle you are; they will drag the last of you away with fish-hooks!

Amos 5:11. You trample the poor and steal their smallest crumb by all your taxes, fines, and usury; therefore you will never live in the beautiful stone houses you are building, nor drink the wine from the lush vineyards you are planting. [12]For many and great are your sins. I know them all so well. You are the enemies of everything good; you take bribes; you refuse justice to the poor.

Amos 6:12. Can horses run on rocks? Can oxen plow the sea? Stupid even to ask, but no more stupid than what you do when you make a mockery of justice, and corrupt and sour all that should be good and right. [13]And just as stupid is your rejoicing in how great you are, when you are less than nothing! And priding yourselves on your own tiny power!

Mic 3:1. Listen, you leaders of Israel—you are supposed to know right from wrong, [2]yet you are the very ones who hate good and love evil; you skin my people and strip them to the bone. [3]You devour them, flog them, break their bones, and chop them up like meat for the cooking pot. [9]Listen to me, you leaders of Israel who hate justice and love unfairness, [10]and fill Jerusalem with murder and sin of every kind—[11]you leaders who take bribes; you priests and prophets who won't preach and prophesy until you're paid. (And yet you fawn upon the Lord and say, "All is well—the Lord is here among us. No harm can come to us.")

Mic 7:3. They go at their evil deeds with both hands, and how skilled they are in using them! The governor and judge alike demand bribes. The rich man pays them off and tells them whom to ruin. Justice is twisted between them. [4]Even the best of them are prickly as briars; the straightest is more crooked than a hedge of thorns. But your judgment day is coming swiftly now; your time of punishment is almost here; confusion, destruction, and terror will be yours.

Hab 1:4. The law is not enforced and there is no justice given in the courts, for the wicked far outnumber the righteous, and bribes and trickery prevail.

Hab 2:12. Woe to you who build cities with money gained from murdering and robbery! *vs.* 5–13.

Zeph 1:8. On that Day of Judgment I will punish the leaders and princes of Judah, and all others wearing heathen clothing.

Zeph 3:3. Her leaders are like roaring lions hunting for their victims—out for everything that they can get. Her judges are like ravenous wolves at evening time, who by dawn have left no trace of their prey.

Acts 23:3. Paul said to him, "God shall slap you, you whitewashed pigpen. What kind of judge are you to break the law yourself by ordering me struck like that?"

Jas 2:6. Don't you realize that it is usually the rich men who pick on you and drag you into court? [9]But you are breaking this law of our Lord's when you favor the rich and fawn over them; it is sin.

Instances of. Potiphar, putting Joseph into prison, Gen 39:20, with 40:15. Pharaoh, oppressing the Israelites, Ex chapters 1–11. Adoni-bezek, torturing 70 kings, Judg 1:7. Abimelech, killing his 70 brothers, Judg 9:1–5. Eli's sons, desecrating the sacrifices, 1 Sam 2:12–17; debauching themselves and the worshipers, 1 Sam 2:22. Samuel's sons, taking bribes, 1 Sam 8:1–5. Saul, sparing Agag and the best of the booty, 1 Sam 15:8–35; in jealously plotting against David, 1 Sam 18:8–29; seeking to kill David, 1 Sam 19; slaying Ahimelech and the priests, 1 Sam 22:7–19. Hanun, maltreating David's ambassadors, 2 Sam 10:4; 1 Chron 19:2–5. David, counting Israel and Judah, 2 Sam 24:1–9; 1 Chron 21:1–7; 27:23, 24. Solomon, luxurious, and idolatrous, 1 Kgs 11:1–13; oppressing the people, 1 Kgs 12:2–4; 4:7–23. Rehoboam, making the burdens heavy, 1 Kgs 12:8–11; 2 Chron 10:1–15. Jeroboam, perverting the worship, 1 Kgs 12:26–33; 13: 1–5; 14:16; elevating common people to the priesthood, 1 Kgs 12:31; 13:33; 2 Kgs 17:32; 2 Chron 11: 13–15; Ezk 44:7, with Num 3:10. Abijam, following in the sins of Rehoboam, 1 Kgs 15:3. Nadab, worshiping idols, 1 Kgs 15:26. Baasha, walking in the ways of Jeroboam, 1 Kgs 15:32–34. Asa, imprisoning the prophet, and oppressing the people, 2 Chron 16:10. Zimri, walking in the ways of Jeroboam, 1 Kgs 16:19. Omri, walking in the ways of Jeroboam, 1 Kgs 16:25–29. Ahab, serving Baal, 1 Kgs 16:30–33; 21:21–26; confiscating Naboth's vineyard, 1 Kgs 21, with 1 Sam 8:14; 1 Kgs 22:38; 2 Kgs 9:26. Jehoram, clinging to the sins of Jeroboam, 2 Kgs 3:2, 3. Hazael, in his plundering, 2 Kgs 8:12; 10:32, 33; 12:17; 13:3–7. Jehoram, walking in the ways of the kings of Israel, 2 Kgs 8:18; 2 Chron 21:13. Jehu, not forsaking the sins of Jeroboam, 2 Kgs 10:29. Jehoahaz, in following the sins of Jeroboam, 2 Kgs 13:1, 2. Joash, following the evil example of Jeroboam, 2 Kgs 13:10, 11. Jeroboam II, not giving up the sins of Jeroboam, 2 Kgs 14:23, 24. Zechariah, Menahem, Pekahiah, and Pekah, following the sins of Jeroboam, 2 Kgs 15:9, 18, 24, 28; conspiring against and killing Pekahiah, 2 Kgs 15: 25. Hoshea, who conspired against Pekah, 2 Kgs 15:30, in permitting Baal worship, 2 Kgs 17:1, 2, 7–18. Ahaz, burning his children in idolatrous sacrifice, 2 Kgs 16:3; 2 Chron 28:2–4. Manasseh, who committed the abominations of the heathen, 2 Kgs 21:1–17; 2 Chron 33:2–7. Amon, who followed the evil example of Manasseh, 2 Kgs 21: 19–22. Jehoahaz, who followed in the ways of his predecessors, 2 Kgs 23:31, 32. Jehoiakim, in walking in the ways of his ancestors, 2 Kgs 23:36, 37; and Jehoiachin, 2 Kgs 24:8, 9. Zedekiah, following the evil example of Jehoiakim, 2 Kgs 24: 18, 19; 2 Chron 36:12, 13; and persecuting Jeremiah, Jer 38: 5, 6. Joash, killing Zechariah, 2 Chron 24:2, 17–25. Ahaziah, doing evil at the advice of Ahab's family, 2 Chron 22:1–9. Amaziah, worshiping the gods of Seir, 2 Chron 25:14. Uzziah, invading the priest's office, 2 Chron 26:16. Ahasuerus and Haman, decreeing the death of the Jews, Esther 3. Nebuchadnezzar, commanding to destroy the wise men, Dan 2:1–13; and sending the three Hebrews to the furnace, Dan 3:1–23. Belshazzar, in drunkenness and committing sacrilege, Dan 5:22, 23. Darius, in deifying himself, Dan 6:7, 9. The government officials, conspiring against Daniel, Dan 6:1–9. Herod the Great, killing the children in Bethlehem, Mt 2: 16–18. Herod Antipas, in beheading John the Baptist, Mt 14:1–11; in craftiness and tyranny, Lk 13:31, 32; 23:6–15. Herod Agrippa, persecuting the church, Acts 12:1–19. Pilate, delivering Jesus for crucifixion, Mt 27:11–26; Mk 15:15. Chief priests, elders, and all the council, seeking witnesses who would lie about Jesus, Mt 26:59. Ananias, commanding to slap Paul, Acts 23:2.

See *Government; Judges; King.*

RUMAH A city of unascertained location. Home of Jehoiakim's mother, 2 Kgs 23:36, 37. Possibly same as *Arumah,* Judg 9:41.

RUST Sent as a judgment, Hag 2:17.

RUTH The daughter-in-law of Naomi, Ruth 1:4, 5. Her devotion to Naomi, Ruth 1:16, 17, with verses 6–18. Goes to Bethlehem, Ruth 1:19, 22. Gleaned in the field of Boaz, Ruth 2:2, 3. Receives kindness from Boaz, Ruth 2:4–17; 3:15–18. Under Naomi's instructions claims from Boaz the duty of a close relative, Ruth 3:1–9. Marries Boaz, Ruth 4: 9–13. Becomes an ancestor of Jesus, Ruth 4:13, 18–22.

S

SABBATH Signifying a rest period, Gen 2:2, 3; Lev 23; 25; 26:34, 35. Preparations for, Ex 16:22; Mt 27:62; Mk 15:42, 43; Lk 23:54; Jn 19:31. Religious usages on, Gen 2:3; Mk 6:2, 3; Lk 6:6; 13:10; Acts 13:14. Sacrifices on, Num 28:9, 10; Ezk 46:4, 5.

UNCLASSIFIED SCRIPTURES RELATING TO. Gen 2:2. So on the seventh day, having finished his task, God ceased from this work he had been doing, [3]and God blessed the seventh day and declared it holy, because it was the day when he ceased this work of creation.

Ex 16:5. "Tell them to gather twice as much as usual on the sixth day of each week." [23]And he told them, "Because the Lord has appointed tomorrow as a day of seriousness and rest, a holy Sabbath to the Lord when we must refrain from doing our daily tasks. So cook as much as you want to today, and keep what is left overnight." [24]And the next morning the food was wholesome and good, without maggots or odor. [25]Moses said, "This is your food for today, for today is the Sabbath to Jehovah and there will be no food on the ground today. [26]Gather the food for six days, but the seventh is a Sabbath, and there will be none there for you on that day." [27]But some of the people went out anyway to gather food, even though it was the Sabbath, but there wasn't any. [28, 29]"How long will these people refuse to obey?" the Lord asked Moses. "Don't they realize that I am giving them twice as much on the sixth day, so that there will be enough for two days? For the Lord has given you the seventh day as a day of Sabbath rest; stay in your tents and don't go out to pick up food from the ground that day." [30]So the people rested on the seventh day.

Ex 20:8. Remember to observe the Sabbath as a holy day. [9]Six days a week are for your daily duties and your regular work, [10]but the seventh day is a day of Sabbath rest before the Lord your God. On that day you are to do no work of any kind, nor shall your son, daughter, or slaves—whether men or women—or your cattle or your house guests. [11]For in six days the Lord made the heaven, earth, and sea, and everything in them, and rested the seventh day; so he blessed the Sabbath day and set it aside for rest.

Ex 23:12. Work six days only, and rest the seventh; this is to give your oxen and donkeys a rest, as well as the people of your household—your slaves and visitors.

Ex 31:13. Tell the people of Israel to rest on my Sabbath day, for the Sabbath is a reminder of the covenant between me and you forever; it helps you to remember that I am Jehovah who makes you holy. [14, 15]Yes, rest on the Sabbath, for it is holy. Anyone who does not obey this command must die; anyone who does any work on that day shall be killed. [16]Work six days only, for the seventh day is a special day of solemn rest, holy to the Lord. This law is a perpetual covenant and obligation for the people of Israel. [17]It is an eternal symbol of the covenant between me and the people of Israel. For in six days the Lord made heaven and earth, and rested on the seventh day, and was refreshed.

Ex 34:21. Even during plowing and harvest times, work only six days, and rest on the seventh.

Ex 35:2. Work six days only; the seventh day is a day of solemn rest, a holy day to be used to worship Jehovah; anyone working on that day must die.

3. Don't even light the fires in your homes that day.

Lev 19:2. You must respect your mothers and fathers, and obey my Sabbath law, for I am the Lord your God. [30]Keep my Sabbath laws and reverence my Tabernacle, for I am the Lord.

Lev 23:1, 2. The Lord said to Moses, "Announce to the people of Israel that they are to celebrate several annual festivals of the Lord—times when all Israel will assemble and worship me. [3](These are in addition to your Sabbaths—the seventh day of every week—which are always days of solemn rest in every home, times for assembling to worship, and for resting from the normal business of the week.) [26, 27]*The Day of Atonement* follows nine days later: All the people are to come together before the Lord, saddened by their sin; and they shall offer sacrifices by fire to the Lord. [28]Don't do any work that day, for it is a special day for making atonement before the Lord your God. [29]Anyone who does not spend the day in repentance and sorrow for sin shall be excommunicated from his people. [30, 31]And I will put to death anyone who does any kind of work that day. This is a law of Israel from generation to generation. [32]For this is a Sabbath of solemn rest, and in it you shall humble your souls and be filled with remorse; this time for atonement begins on the previous evening and goes on until the next evening." Lev 16:29–31.

Lev 24:5–8. Every Sabbath. . . . This will be a memorial offering made by fire to the Lord, in memory of his everlasting covenant with the people of Israel. 1 Chron 9:32.

Lev 26:2. You must obey my Sabbath laws of rest, and reverence my Tabernacle, for I am the Lord. [34, 35]Then at last the land will rest and make up for the many years you refused to let it lie idle; for it will lie desolate all the years that you are captives in enemy lands. Yes, then the land will rest and enjoy its Sabbaths! It will make up for the rest you didn't give it every seventh year when you lived upon it.

Num 15:32. One day while the people of Israel were in the wilderness, one of them was caught gathering wood on the Sabbath day. [33]He was arrested and taken before Moses and Aaron and the other judges. [34]They jailed him until they could find out the Lord's mind concerning him. [35]Then the Lord said to Moses, "The man must die—all the people shall stone him to death outside the camp." [36]So they took him outside the camp and killed him as the Lord had commanded.

Num 28:9, 10. On the Sabbath day, sacrifice two yearling male lambs—both without defect—in addition to the regular offerings. They are to be accompanied by a grain offering of six quarts of fine flour mixed with oil, and the usual drink offering.

Deut 5:12. Keep the Sabbath day holy. This is my command. [13]Work the other six days, [14]but the seventh day is the Sabbath of the Lord your God; no work shall be done that day by you or by any of your household—your sons, daughters, servants, oxens, donkeys, or cattle; even foreigners living among you must obey this law. Everybody must rest as you do. [15]Why should you keep the Sabbath? It is because you were slaves in Egypt, and the Lord your God brought you out with a great display of miracles.

2 Chron 36:21. Thus the word of the Lord spoken through Jeremiah came true, that the land must rest for seventy years to make up for the years when the people refused to observe the Sabbath.

Neh 9:13. You came down upon Mount Sinai and spoke with them from heaven and gave them good laws and true commandments, [14]including the laws about the holy Sabbath.

Neh 10:31. We further agreed that if the heathen people in the land should bring any grain or other produce to be sold on the Sabbath or on any other holy day, we would refuse to buy it.

Neh 13:15. One day I was on a farm and saw some men treading winepresses on the Sabbath, hauling in sheaves, and loading their donkeys with wine, grapes, figs, and all sorts of produce which they took that day into Jerusalem. So I opposed them publicly. [16]There were also some men from Tyre bringing in fish and all sorts of wares and selling them on the Sabbath to the people of Jerusalem. [17]Then I asked the leaders of Judah, "Why are you profaning the Sabbath? [18]Wasn't it enough that your fathers did this sort of thing and brought the present evil days upon us and upon our city? And now you are bringing more wrath upon the people of Israel by permitting the Sabbath to be desecrated in this way." [19]So from then on I commanded that the gates of the city be shut as darkness fell on Friday evenings and not be opened until the Sabbath had ended; and I sent some of my servants to guard the gates so that no merchandise could be brought in on the Sabbath day. [20]The merchants and tradesmen camped outside Jerusalem once or twice, [21]but I spoke sharply to them and said, "What are you doing out here, camping around the wall? If you do this again, I will arrest you." And that was the last time they came on the Sabbath. [22]Then I commanded the Levites to purify themselves and to guard the gates in order to preserve the sanctity of the Sabbath.

Ps 92 [1]It is good to say, "Thank you" to the Lord, to sing praises to the God who is above all gods. [2]Every morning tell him, "Thank you for your kindness," and every evening rejoice in all his faithfulness. [3]Sing his praises, accompanied by music from the harp and lute and lyre. [4]You have done so much for me, O Lord. No wonder I am glad! I sing for joy. [5]O Lord, what miracles you do! And how deep are your thoughts! [6]Unthinking people do not understand them! No fool can comprehend this: [7]that although the wicked flourish like weeds, there is only eternal destruction ahead of them. [8]But the Lord continues forever, exalted in the heavens, [9]while his enemies—all evil-doers—shall be scattered. [10]But you have made me as strong as a wild bull. How refreshed I am by your blessings! [11]I have heard the doom of my enemies announced and seen them destroyed. [12]But the godly shall flourish like palm trees, and grow tall as the cedars of Lebanon. [13]For they are transplanted into the Lord's own garden, and are under his personal care. [14]Even in old age they will still produce fruit and be vital and green. [15]This honors the Lord, and exhibits his faithful care. He is my shelter. There is nothing but goodness in him!

Ps 118:24. This is the day the Lord has made. We will rejoice and be glad in it.

Isa 1:12, 13. Who wants your sacrifices when you have no sorrow for your sins? The incense you bring me is a stench in my nostrils. Your holy celebrations of the new moon and the Sabbath, and your special days for fasting—even your most pious meetings—all are frauds!

Isa 56:2. Blessed is the man who refuses to work during my Sabbath days of rest, but honors them; and blessed is the man who checks himself from doing wrong. [4]For I say this to the eunuchs who keep his Sabbaths holy and choose the things that please him, and come to grips with his laws: [5]I will give them—in my house, within my walls—a name far greater than the honor they would receive from having sons and daughters. For the name that I will give them is an everlasting one; it will never disappear. [6]As for the Gentiles, the outsiders who join the people of the Lord and serve him and love his name, and are his servants and don't desecrate the Sabbath, and have accepted his covenant and promises, [7]I will bring them also to my holy mountain of Jerusalem, and make them full of joy within my House of Prayer. I will accept their sacrifices and offerings, for my Temple shall be called "A House of Prayer for All People"!

Isa 58:13. If you keep the Sabbath holy, not having your own fun and business on that day, but enjoying the Sabbath and speaking of it with delight as the Lord's holy day, and honoring the Lord in what you do, not following your own desires and pleasure, nor talking idly— [14]then the Lord will be your delight, and I will see to it that you ride high, and get your full share of the blessings I promised to Jacob, your father. The Lord has spoken.

Isa 66:23. All mankind shall come to worship me from week to week and month to month.

Jer 17:21, 22. The Lord says: Take warning and live; do no unnecessary work on the Sabbath day but make it a holy day. I gave this commandment to your fathers, [24]but if you obey me, says the Lord, and refuse to work on the Sabbath day and keep it separate, special and holy, [25]then this nation shall continue forever. There shall always be descendants of David sitting on the throne here in Jerusalem. [27]But if you will not listen to me, if you refuse to keep the Sabbath holy, if on the Sabbath you bring in loads of merchandise through these gates of Jerusalem, just as on other days, then I will set fire to these gates. The fire shall spread to the palaces and utterly destroy them, and no one shall be able to put out the raging flames.

Lam 2:6. He has violently broken down his Temple as though it were a booth of leaves and branches in a garden! No longer can the people celebrate their holy feasts and Sabbaths. Kings and priests together fall before his wrath.

Ezk 20:12. And I gave them the Sabbath—a day of rest every seventh day—as a symbol between them and me, to remind them that it is I, the Lord, who sanctifies them, that they are truly my people. [13]But Israel rebelled against me. There in the wilderness they refused my laws. They would not obey my rules even though obeying them means life. And they misused my Sabbaths. Then I thought, I will pour out my fury upon them and utterly consume them in the desert. [16]Because they laughed at my laws, ignored my wishes, and violated my Sabbaths—their hearts were with their idols! *vs.* 20, 21, 23, 24.

Ezk 22:8. The things of God are all despised; my Sabbaths are ignored.

Ezk 23:38. On the same day they defiled my Temple and ignored my Sabbaths.

Ezk 44:24. They shall see to it that the Sabbath is kept a sacred day.

Ezk 46:1. The Lord God says, the inner wall's eastern entrance shall be closed during the six work days but open on the Sabbath. [3]The people shall worship the Lord in front of this passageway on the Sabbaths and on the days of the new moon celebrations.

Amos 8:5. You who long for the Sabbath to end and the religious holidays to be over, so you can get out and start cheating again—using your weighted scales and under-sized measures.

Mt 12:1. About that time, Jesus was walking one day through some grainfields with his disciples. It was on the Sabbath, the Jewish day of worship, and his disciples were hungry; so they began breaking off heads of wheat and eating the grain. [2]But some Pharisees saw them do it and protested, "Your disciples are breaking the law. They are harvesting on the Sabbath." [3]But Jesus said to them, "Haven't you ever read what King David did when he and his friends were hungry? [4]He went into the Temple and they ate the special bread permitted to the priests alone. That was breaking the law too. [5]And haven't you ever read in the law of Moses how the priests on duty in the Temple may work on the Sabbath? [6]And truly, one is here who is greater than the Temple! [7]But if you had known the meaning of this Scripture verse, 'I want you to be merciful more than I want your offerings,' you would not have condemned those who aren't guilty! [8]For I, the Messiah, am master even of the Sabbath." Mk 2:28.

10. And noticed there a man with a deformed hand. The Pharisees asked Jesus, "Is it legal to work by healing on the Sabbath day?" (They were, of course, hoping he would say "Yes," so they could arrest him!) [11]This was his answer: "If you had just one sheep, and it fell into a well on the Sabbath, would you work to rescue it that day? Of course you would. [12]And how much more valuable is a person than a sheep! Yes, it is right to do good on the Sabbath." [13]Then he said to the man, "Stretch out your arm." And as he did, his hand became normal, just like the other one! Lk 6:1–10.

Mt 24:20. And pray that your flight will not be in winter, or on the Sabbath.

Mk 2:27. But the Sabbath was made to benefit man, and not man to benefit the Sabbath. *v.* 28.

Mk 6:2. The next Sabbath he went to the synagogue to teach.

Mk 16:1. The next evening, when the Sabbath ended, Mary Magdalene and Salome and Mary the mother of James went out and purchased embalming spices.

Lk 6:6. On another Sabbath he was in the synagogue teaching.

Lk 13:10. One Sabbath as he was teaching in a synagogue, [11]he saw a seriously handicapped woman who had been bent double for eighteen years and was unable to straighten herself. [12]Calling her over to him Jesus said, "Woman, you are healed of your sickness!" [13]He touched her, and instantly she could stand straight. How she praised and thanked God! [14]But the local Jewish leader in charge of the synagogue was very angry about it because Jesus had healed her on the Sabbath day. "There are six days of the week to work," he shouted to the crowd. "Those are the days to come for healing, not on the Sabbath!" [15]But the Lord replied, "You hypocrite! You work on the Sabbath! Don't you untie your cattle from their stalls on the Sabbath and lead them out for water? [16]And is it wrong for me, just because it is the Sabbath day, to free this Jewish woman from the bondage in which Satan has held her for eighteen years?" [17]This shamed his enemies. And all the people rejoiced at the wonderful things he did.

Lk 14:1, 2. One Sabbath as he was in the home of a member of the Jewish Council, the Pharisees were watching him like hawks to see if he would heal a man who was present who was suffering from dropsy. [3]Jesus said to the Pharisees and legal experts standing around, "Well, is it within the Law to heal a man on the Sabbath day, or not?" [4]And when they refused to answer, Jesus took the sick man by the hand and healed him and sent him away. [5]Then he turned to them: "Which of you doesn't work on the Sabbath?" he asked. "If your cow falls into a pit don't you proceed at once to get it out?" [6]Again they had no answer.

Lk 23:54. This was done late on Friday afternoon, the day of preparation for the Sabbath. [56]Then they went home and prepared spices and ointments to embalm him; but by the time they were finished it was the Sabbath, so they rested all that day as required by the Jewish law.

Jn 5:5. One of the men lying there had been sick for thirty-eight years. [6]When Jesus saw him and knew how long he had been ill, he asked him, "Would you like to get well?" [7]"I can't," the sick man said, "for I have no one to help me into the pool at the movement of the water. While I am trying to get there, someone else always gets in ahead of me." [8]Jesus told him, "Stand up, roll up your sleeping mat and go on home!" [9]Instantly, the man was healed! He rolled up the mat and began walking! But it was on the Sabbath when this miracle was done. [10]So the Jewish leaders objected. They said to the man who was cured, "You can't work on the Sabbath! It's illegal to carry that sleeping mat!" [11]"The man who healed me told me to," was his reply. [12]"Who said such a thing as that?" they demanded. [13]The man didn't know, and Jesus had disappeared into the crowd. [14]But afterwards Jesus found him in the Temple and told him, "Now you are well; don't sin as you did before, or something even worse may happen to you."

Jn 7:21–23. Jesus replied, "I worked on the Sabbath by healing a man, and you were surprised. But you work on the Sabbath, too, whenever you obey Moses' law of circumcision (actually, however, this tradition of circumcision is older than the Mosaic law); for if the correct time for circumcising your children falls on the Sabbath, you go ahead and do it, as you should. So why should I be condemned for making a man completely well on the Sabbath? [24]Think this through and you will see that I am right." chapter 9:1–34.

Jn 19:31. The Jewish leaders didn't want the victims hanging there the next day, which was the Sabbath (and a very special Sabbath at that, for it was the Passover), so they asked Pilate to order the legs of the men broken to hasten death; then their bodies could be taken down.

Acts 13:14. But Barnabas and Paul went on to Antioch, a city in the province of Pisidia. On the Sabbath they went into the synagogue for the services. [27]The Jews in Jerusalem and their leaders fulfilled prophecy by killing Jesus; for they didn't recognize him, or realize that he is the one the prophets had written about, though they heard the prophets' words read every Sabbath. [42]As the people left the synagogue that day, they asked Paul to return and speak to them again the next week. [44]The following week almost the entire city turned out to hear them preach the Word of God.

Acts 15:21. For these things have been preached against in Jewish synagogues in every city on every Sabbath for many generations.

Acts 16:13. On the Sabbath, we went a little way outside the city to a river bank where we understood some people met for prayer; and we taught the Scriptures to some women who came.

Acts 17:2. As was Paul's custom, he went there to preach, and for three Sabbaths in a row he opened the Scriptures to the people.

Acts 18:4. Each Sabbath found Paul at the synagogue, trying to convince the Jews and Greeks alike.

Col 2:16. So don't let anyone criticize you for what you eat or drink, or for not celebrating Jewish holidays and feasts or new moon ceremonies or Sabbaths.

Heb 4:4. We know he is ready and waiting because it is written that God rested on the seventh day of creation, having finished all that he had planned to make. *v.* 9.

OBSERVANCE OF. By Moses, Num 15:32–34. By Nehemiah, Neh 13:15, 21. By the women preparing to embalm the body of Jesus, Lk 23:56. By Paul, Acts 13:14. By disciples, Acts 16:13.

STRIKING FACTS ABOUT. Given as a sign to Israel, Ex 16:28, 29; 31:12–15; Neh 9:13, 14; Ezk 20:12. To cease for a prolonged period, Hos 2:11; cf. 3:4, 5. To be restored by Israel in the last days, Deut 30:7, 8; Ezk 44:24; 45:17; 46:1, 3; Mt 24:20. Instructions to Christians regarding the Sabbath, Col 2:16: So don't let anyone criticize you for what you eat or drink, or for not celebrating Jewish holidays and feasts or new moon ceremonies or Sabbaths. [17]For these were only temporary rules that ended when Christ came. They were only shadows of the real thing—of Christ himself.

VIOLATIONS OF.

Instances of. Gathering manna, Ex 16:27. Gathering wood, Num 15:32. Men of Tyre, Neh 13:16. Inhabitants of Jerusalem, Jer 17:21–23.

"CHRISTIAN SABBATH." See *Lord's Day.*

SABBATICAL YEAR A rest recurring every seventh year. Called *Year of Release,* Deut 31:10, 11. Ordinances concerning, Ex 23:9–11; Lev 25. Hebrew slaves set free in, Ex 21:2; Deut 15:12; Jer 34:14. Creditors required to cancel debts in,

Deut 15:1–6, 12–18; Neh 10:31. Ordinances concerning instruction in the law during, Deut 31:10–13; Neh 8:18. Punishment to follow violation of the ordinances concerning, Lev 26:34, 35, with 32–41; Jer 34:12–22.

See *Jubilee.*

SABEANS A people who invaded the land of Uz, Job 1:14, 15; Isa 43:3. Prophecies concerning, Isa 43:3; 45:14; Joel 3:8.

See *Sheba,* their country.

SABTA Called also *Sabtah.* Son of Cush, Gen 10:7; 1 Chron 1:5–9.

SABTECA Son of Cush, Gen 10:7; 1 Chron 1:5–9.

SACAR A Korahite. Son of Obed-edom, 1 Chron 26:4, 5.

SACHER Father of Ahiam, 1 Chron 11:26–47. Called *Sharar,* 2 Sam 23:24–39.

SACHIA Son of Shaharaim, 1 Chron 8:8–10.

SACKBUT A stringed instrument of music, Dan 3:5, 7, 10.

See *Music, Instruments of.*

SACKCLOTH A symbol of mourning, 1 Kgs 20:31, 32; Job 16:15; Isa 15:3; Lam 2:10; Ezk 7:18; Dan 9:3. Worn by Jacob when it was reported to him that Joseph had been eaten by wild animals, Gen 37:34. Animals covered with, at time of national mourning, Jon 3:8.

See *Mourning.*

SACRAMENTS See *Baptism; Lord's Supper; Church, The Visible.*

SACRIFICES FIGURATIVE. Isa 34:6; Ezk 39:17; Zeph 1:7, 8; Rom 12:1; Phil 2:17; 4:18. Of self-denial, Phil 3:7, 8. Of thanksgiving, Ps 116:17; Jer 33:10, 11. Of praise, Hos 14:2; Heb 13:15.

See *Offerings.*

SACRILEGE Profaning holy things. Forbidden, Lev 19:8; 1 Cor 3:17; Tit 1:11.

INSTANCES OF. Esau sells his birthright, Gen 25:33. Nadab and Abihu offer unholy fire, Lev 10:1–7; Num 3:4. Of Uzzah, 2 Sam 6:6, 7. Of Uzziah, 2 Chron 26:16–21. Of Korah and his company, Num 16:40. Of the people of Beth-shemesh, 1 Sam 6:19. Of Ahaz, 2 Chron 28:24. Of money-changers in the Temple, Mt 21:12, 13; Lk 19:45; Jn 2:14–16. Of those who partook of the Lord's Supper in an unworthy manner, 1 Cor 11:29.

SADDUCEES A sect of the Jews. Denounced by John the Baptist, Mt 3:7–9; Lk 3:7–9. Reject the doctrine of the resurrection, Mt 22:23–35; Mk 12:18–27; Lk 20:27–40; Acts 23:7, 8. Jesus warns his disciples against, Mt 16:6–12. Persecute the apostles, Acts 4:1–3; 5:17–33; 23:6.

SAFFRON Song 4:13, 14.

SAILOR 1 Kgs 9:27, 28; 2 Chron 8:17, 18; Ezk 27:27. Perils of, Ps 107:23–30; Jon 1:5; Acts 27:17–44. Cowardice of, Acts 27:30.

See *Ship; Commerce.*

SAINTS In the Old Testament, the word describes godly Israelites and others, 2 Chron 6:41; Ps 30:4; 85:8; 132:16; Prov 2:7, 8.

The New Testament reveals that all believers during the present age are saints, Acts 26:10. The word means set apart (to God), 1 Thess 3:13; 2 Thess 1:10. No special class of people holier than others is found in such passages. During the last days, the evil one will be allowed to persecute the saints, Dan 7:25. Saints are found on earth after the church has been translated, Rev 14:12.

See *Christian; Church, the True; Righteous.*

SAKKUTH Possibly an idol, Acts 7:43.

SALAMIS A city of Cyprus. Paul and Barnabas preached in, Acts 13:4, 5.

SALECAH A city of Gad, Deut 3:10; Josh 12:5; 13:11; 1 Chron 5:11.

SALEM See *Jerusalem.*

SALIM A city near to Aenon, Jn 3:23, 24.

SALLAI 1. A Benjaminite living in Jerusalem, Neh 11:7–9.

2. A priestly family, Neh 12:12–21. Called *Sallu,* Neh 12:1–7.

SALLU 1. A Benjaminite living in Jerusalem, 1 Chron 9:7, 8; Neh 11:7–9.

2. See *Sallai,* 2.

SALMA Son of Caleb, 1 Chron 2:51, 54.

See *Salmon.*

SALMON Called also *Salman.* Father of Boaz, Ruth 4:18–22; 1 Chron 2:11. In the lineage of Joseph, Mt 1:4, 5; Lk 3:23–38.

SALMONE A promontory of Crete, Acts 27:7, 8.

SALOME Mother of James and John, Mt 27:56, with Mk 15:40; 16:1. Asks Jesus to promote her sons, Mt 20:20, 21. Present at the cross, Mk 15:40; at the tomb, Mk 16:1, 2.

SALT Lot's wife turned into a pillar of, Gen 19:26. The city of Salt, Josh 15:48–62. The Valley of Salt, 2 Sam 8:13; 2 Kgs 14:7. Salt Sea, Gen 14:3; Deut 3:17; Josh 3:15, 16; 12:3; 15:2–4. Salt pits, Zeph 2:9. All animal sacrifices were required to be seasoned with, Lev 2:13; Ezra 6:9; Ezk 43:24. Used in ratifying covenants, Num 18:19. Elisha throws, into the well of Jericho, to purify it, 2 Kgs 2:20, 21.

FIGURATIVE. Of the purifying or preserving presence of the disciples, Mt 5:13; Mk 9:49, 50; Lk 14:34.

SALUTATIONS See *Greetings.*

SALVATION The subject of salvation is very widely treated in the Scriptures; many texts embrace a number of aspects of the theme. Dividing the topic into sub-topics is therefore impracticable. The following selection of Scripture passages from the Old and New Testaments is only suggestive of a vast revelation.

Illustrated by. A helmet, Isa 59:17; Eph 6:17; a shield, 2 Sam 22:36; a cup, Ps 116:13; clothing, 2 Chron 6:41; Ps 132:16; Isa 61:10; fountain, Isa 12:3; walls, Isa 26:1; 60:18; chariots, Hab 3:8, 9; a victory, 1 Cor 15:57.

Typified by the bronze snake, Num 21:4–9, with Jn 3:14, 15.

See *Atonement.*

UNCLASSIFIED SCRIPTURES RELATING TO. Gen 12:1. After the death of Abram's father, God told him, "Leave your own country behind you, and your own people, and go to the land I will guide you to. [3]And the entire world will be blessed because of you."

Ex 15:2. The Lord is my strength, my song, and my salvation. He is my God, and I will praise him. He is my father's God—I will exalt him.

Deut 30:19. I call heaven and earth to witness against you that today I have set before you life or death, blessing or curse. Oh, that you would choose life; that you and your children might live! [20]Choose to love the Lord your God and to obey him and to cling to him, for he is your life and the length of your days.

Deut 32:15. But Israel was soon overfed; yes, fat and bloated; then, in plenty, they forsook their God. They shrugged away the Rock of their salvation. Ps 95:1.

2 Sam 14:14. All of us must die eventually; our lives are like water that is poured out on the ground—it can't be gathered again. But God will bless you with a longer life if you will find a way to bring your son back from his exile.

1 Kgs 8:41, 42. And when foreigners hear of your great name and come from distant lands to worship you (for they shall hear of your great name and mighty miracles) and pray toward this Temple, [43]hear them from heaven and answer their prayers. And all the nations of the earth will know and fear your name just as your own people Israel do.

1 Chron 16:35. Cry out to him, "Oh, save us, God of our salvation; Bring us safely back from among the nations. Then we will thank your holy name, and triumph in your praise."

2 Chron 6:41. Let your priests, O Lord God, be clothed with salvation, and let your saints rejoice in your kind deeds.

Ps 3:8. For salvation comes from God. Ps 37:39.

Ps 36:8. You feed them with blessings from your own table and let them drink from your rivers of delight. [9]For you are the Fountain of life; our light is from your Light.

Ps 46:4. There is a river of joy flowing through the City of our God—the sacred home of the God above all gods.

Ps 63:5. At last I shall be fully satisfied; I will praise you with great joy. [6]I lie awake at night thinking of you.

Ps 65:4. How greatly to be envied are those you have chosen to come and live with you within the holy tabernacle courts! What joys await us among all the good things there.

Ps 68:18. He ascends the heights, leading many captives in his train. He receives gifts for men, even those who once were rebels. God will live among us here. [19]What a glorious Lord! He who daily bears our burdens also gives us our salvation. [20]He frees us! He rescues us from death.

Ps 86:13. For you love me so much! You are constantly so kind! You have rescued me from deepest hell.

Ps 90:14. Satisfy us in our earliest youth with your loving-kindness, giving us constant joy to the end of our lives.

Ps 91:16. I will satisfy him with a full life and give him my salvation.

Ps 98:2, 3. He has announced this victory and revealed it to every nation by fulfilling his promise to be kind to Israel. The whole earth has seen God's salvation of his people.

Ps 106:8. Even so you saved them—to defend the honor of your name and demonstrate your power to all the world.

Ps 107:9. For he satisfies the thirsty soul and fills the hungry soul with good.

Ps 121:1. Shall I look to the mountain gods for help? [2]No! My help is from Jehovah who made the mountains! And the heavens too! [3, 4]He will never let me stumble, slip or fall. For he is always watching, never sleeping. [5]Jehovah himself is caring for you! He is your defender. [6]He protects you day and night. [7]He keeps you from all evil, and preserves your life. [8]He keeps his eye upon you as you come and go, and always guards you.

Ps 132:16. I will clothe her priests with salvation; her saints shall shout for joy.

Prov 1:20. Wisdom shouts in the streets for a hearing. [21]She calls out to the crowds along Main Street, and to the judges in their courts, and to everyone in all the land.

Prov 8:1–3. Can't you hear the voice of wisdom? She is standing at the city gates and at every fork in the road, and at the door of every house. Listen to what she says: [4, 5]"Listen, men!" she calls. "How foolish and naive you are! Let me give you understanding. O foolish ones, let me show you common sense!"

Prov 9:1. Wisdom has built a palace supported on seven pillars, [2]and has prepared a great banquet, and mixed the wines, [3]and sent out her maidens inviting all to come. She calls from the busiest intersection in the city, [4]"Come, you simple ones without good judgment; [5]come to wisdom's banquet and drink the wines that I have mixed. [6]Leave behind your foolishness and begin to live; learn how to be wise."

Isa 1:18. Come, let's talk this over! says the Lord; no matter how deep the stain of your sins, I can take it out and make you as clean as freshly fallen snow. Even if you are stained as red as crimson, I can make you white as wool!

Isa 2:5. O Israel, come, let us walk in the light of the Lord, and be obedient to his laws!

Isa 25:6. Here on Mount Zion in Jerusalem, the Lord of Hosts will spread a wondrous feast for everyone around the world—a delicious feast of good food, with clear, well-aged wine and choice beef. [7]At that time he will remove the cloud of gloom, the pall of death that hangs over the earth.

Isa 29:18. In that day the deaf will hear the words of a book, and out of their gloom and darkness the blind will see my plans. [19]The meek will be filled with fresh joy from the Lord, and the poor shall exult in the Holy One of Israel. [24]Those in error will believe the truth, and complainers will be willing to be taught!

Isa 32:1. Look, a righteous King is coming, with

honest princes! [2]He will shelter Israel from the storm and wind. He will refresh her as a river in the desert and as the cooling shadow of a mighty rock within a hot and weary land. [3]Then at last the eyes of Israel will open wide to God; his people will listen to his voice. [4]Even the hotheads among them will be full of sense and understanding, and those who stammer in uncertainty will speak out plainly.

Isa 35:8. And a main road will go through that once-deserted land; it will be named "The Holy Highway." No evil-hearted men may walk upon it. God will walk there with you; even the most stupid cannot miss the way.

Isa 44:3. For I will give you abundant water for your thirst and for your parched fields. And I will pour out my Spirit and my blessings on your children.

Isa 45:17. But Israel shall be saved by Jehovah with eternal salvation; they shall never be disappointed in their God through all eternity.

Isa 46:12. Listen to me, you stubborn, evil men! [13]For I am offering you deliverance; not in the distant future, but right now! I am ready to save you, and I will restore Jerusalem, and Israel, who is my glory.

Isa 49:10. They shall neither hunger nor thirst; the searing sun and scorching desert winds will not reach them any more. For the Lord in his mercy will lead them beside the cool waters. [11]And I will make my mountains into level paths for them; the highways shall be raised above the valleys.

Isa 50:10. Who among you fears the Lord and obeys his Servant? If such men walk in darkness, without one ray of light, let them trust the Lord, let them rely upon their God.

Isa 51:4. Listen to me, my people; listen, O Israel, for I will see that right prevails. [5]My mercy and justice are coming soon; your salvation is on the way. I will rule the nations; they shall wait for me and long for me to come.

Isa 52:10. The Lord has bared his holy arm before the eyes of all the nations; the ends of the earth shall see the salvation of our God. [15]They shall stand dumbfounded, speechless in his presence. For they shall see and understand what they had not been told before.

Isa 55:1. Say there! Is anyone thirsty? Come and drink—even if you have no money! Come, take your choice of wine and milk—it's all free! [2]Why spend your money on foodstuffs that don't give you strength? Why pay for groceries that don't do you any good? Listen and I'll tell you where to get good food that fattens up the soul! [3]Come to me with your ears wide open. Listen, for the life of your soul is at stake. I am ready to make an everlasting covenant with you, to give you all the unfailing mercies and love that I had for King David. [6]Seek the Lord while you can find him. Call upon him now while he is near. [7]Let men cast off their wicked deeds; let them banish from their minds the very thought of doing wrong! Let them turn to the Lord that he may have mercy upon them, and to our God, for he will abundantly pardon!

Isa 56:1. Be just and fair to all, the Lord God says. Do what's right and good, for I am coming soon to rescue you. [6]As for the Gentiles, the outsiders who join the people of the Lord and serve him and love his name, and are his servants and don't desecrate the Sabbath, and have accepted his covenant and promises, [7]I will bring them also to my holy mountain of Jerusalem, and make them full of joy within my House of Prayer. I will accept their sacrifices and offerings, for my Temple shall be called "A House of Prayer for All People"! [8]For the Lord God who brings back the outcasts of Israel says, I will bring others too besides my people Israel.

Isa 57:18. I have seen what they do, but I will heal them anyway! I will lead them and comfort them, helping them to mourn and to confess their sins. [19]Peace, peace to them, both near and far, for I will heal them all.

Isa 61:1. The Spirit of the Lord is upon me, because the Lord has anointed me to bring good news to the suffering and afflicted. He has sent me to comfort the broken-hearted, to announce liberty to captives and to open the eyes of the blind. [2]He has sent me to tell those who mourn that the time of God's favor to them has come, and the day of his wrath to their enemies. [3]To all who mourn in Israel he will give: beauty for ashes; joy instead of mourning; praise instead of heaviness. For God has planted them like strong and graceful oaks for his own glory.

Isa 63:9. In all their affliction he was afflicted, and he personally saved them. In his love and pity he redeemed them and lifted them up and carried them through all the years.

Jer 3:23. We are weary of worshiping idols on the hills and of having orgies on the mountains. It is all a farce. Only in the Lord our God can Israel ever find her help and her salvation.

Jer 21:8. Tell these people, the Lord says: Take your choice of life or death!

Ezk 18:32. I do not enjoy seeing you die, the Lord God says. Turn, turn and live!

Joel 2:32. Everyone who calls upon the name of the Lord will be saved; even in Jerusalem some will escape, just as the Lord has promised, for he has chosen some to survive.

Amos 5:4. The Lord says to the people of Israel, "Seek me—and live."

Zech 14:8. Life-giving waters will flow out from Jerusalem, half toward the Dead Sea and half toward the Mediterranean, flowing continuously both in winter and in summer.

Mal 4:2. But for you who fear my name, the Sun of Righteousness will rise with healing in his wings.

Mt 1:21. And she will have a Son, and you shall name him Jesus (meaning "Savior"), for he will save his people from their sins.

Mt 3:9. Don't try to get by as you are, thinking, "We are safe for we are Jews—descendants of Abraham." That proves nothing. God can change these stones here into Jews!

Mt 11:28. Come to me and I will give you rest—

all of you who work so hard beneath a heavy yoke. [29, 30]Wear my yoke—for it fits perfectly—and let me teach you; for I am gentle and humble, and you shall find rest for your souls; for I give you only light burdens.

Mt 18:14. Just so, it is not my Father's will that even one of these little ones should perish.

Mt 21:31. Then Jesus explained his meaning: "Surely evil men and prostitutes will get into the Kingdom before you do."

Mt 22:9. "Now go out to the street corners and invite everyone you see." [10]So the servants did, and brought in all they could find, good and bad alike; and the banquet hall was filled with guests. [14]For many are called, but few are chosen.

Mt 23:37. O Jerusalem, Jerusalem, the city that kills the prophets, and stones all those God sends to her! How often I have wanted to gather your children together as a hen gathers her chicks beneath her wings, but you wouldn't let me.

Mt 24:14. And the Good News about the Kingdom will be preached throughout the whole world, so that all nations will hear it, and then, finally, the end will come.

Mk 2:17. When Jesus heard what they were saying, he told them, "Sick people need the doctor, not healthy ones! I haven't come to tell good people to repent, but the bad ones." Lk 5:31, 32.

Mk 16:15. And then he told them, "You are to go into all the world and preach the Good News to everyone, everywhere. [16]Those who believe and are baptized will be saved." Mt 28:19.

Lk 2:10. But the angel reassured them. "Don't be afraid!" he said. "I bring you the most joyful news ever announced, and it is for everyone!" [31]"I have seen the Savior you have given to the world. [32]He is the Light that will shine upon the nations, and he will be the glory of your people Israel!"

Lk 3:6. And then all mankind shall see the Savior sent from God.

Lk 7:47. Therefore her sins—and they are many —are forgiven, for she loved me much.

Lk 13:29. For people will come from all over the world to take their places there. [30]And note this: some who are despised now will be greatly honored then; and some who are highly thought of now will be least important then.

Lk 14:16. Jesus replied with this illustration: "A man prepared a great feast and sent out many invitations. [17]When all was ready, he sent his servant around to notify the guests that it was time for them to arrive. [18]But they all began making excuses. One said he had just bought a field and wanted to inspect it, and asked to be excused. [19]Another said he had just bought five pair of oxen and wanted to try them out. [20]Another had just been married and for that reason couldn't come. [21]The servant returned and reported to his master what they had said. His master was angry and told him to go quickly into the streets and alleys of the city and to invite the beggars, crippled, lame, and blind. [22]But even then, there was still room. [23]'Well, then,' said his master, 'go out into the country lanes and out behind the hedges and urge anyone you find to come, so that the house will be full. [24]For none of those I invited first will get even the smallest taste of what I had prepared for them.' "

Lk 15:2. But this caused complaints from the Jewish religious leaders and the experts on Jewish law because he was associating with such despicable people—even eating with them! [3,4]So Jesus used this illustration: "If you had a hundred sheep and one of them strayed away and was lost in the wilderness, wouldn't you leave the ninety-nine others to go and search for the lost one until you found it? [5]And then you would joyfully carry it home on your shoulders. [6]When you arrived you would call together your friends and neighbors to rejoice with you because your lost sheep was found. [7]Well, in the same way heaven will be happier over one lost sinner who returns to God than over ninety-nine others who haven't strayed away! [8]Or take another illustration: A woman has ten valuable silver coins and loses one. Won't she light a lamp and look in every corner of the house and sweep every nook and cranny until she finds it? [9]And then won't she call in her friends and neighbors to rejoice with her? [10]In the same way there is joy in the presence of the angels of God when one sinner repents." To further illustrate the point, he told them this story: [11]"A man had two sons. [12]When the younger told his father, 'I want my share of your estate now, instead of waiting until you die!' his father agreed to divide his wealth between his sons. [13]A few days later this younger son packed all his belongings and took a trip to a distant land, and there wasted all his money on parties and prostitutes. [14]About the time his money was gone a great famine swept over the land, and he began to starve. [15]He persuaded a local farmer to hire him to feed his pigs. [16]The boy became so hungry that even the pods he was feeding the swine looked good to him. And no one gave him anything. [17]When he finally came to his senses, he said to himself, 'At home even the hired men have food enough and to spare, and here I am, dying of hunger! [18]I will go home to my father and say, "Father, I have sinned against both heaven and you, [19]and am no longer worthy of being called your son. Please take me on as a hired man." ' [20]So he returned home to his father. And while he was still a long distance away, his father saw him coming, and was filled with loving pity and ran and embraced him and kissed him. [21]His son said to him, 'Father, I have sinned against heaven and you, and am not worthy of being called your son—' [22]But his father said to the slaves, 'Quick! Bring the finest robe in the house and put it on him. And a jeweled ring for his finger; and shoes! [23]And kill the calf we have in the fattening pen. We must celebrate with a feast, [24]for this son of mine was dead and has returned to life. He was lost and is found.' So the party began. [25]Meanwhile, the older son was in the fields working; when he returned home, he heard dance music coming from the house, [26]and he asked one of the servants what was going on. [27]'Your brother is back,' he was told, 'and your father has killed the calf we were fattening and has prepared a great feast to celebrate his coming home again unharmed.' [28]The older brother was angry and wouldn't go in. His father came out and begged him, [29]but he replied, 'All these years I've worked hard for you and never once refused to do a single thing you told me to; and in all that time you never gave me even one young goat for a feast with my friends. [30]Yet when this son of yours comes back after spending your money on prostitutes, you celebrate by killing the finest calf we have on the place.' [31]'Look, dear son,' his father said to him, 'you and I are very close, and everything I have is yours. [32]But it is right to celebrate. For he is your brother; and he was dead and has come back to life! He was lost and is found!' "

Lk 19:10. And I, the Messiah, have come to search for and to save such souls as his.

Lk 24:47. And that this message of salvation should be taken from Jerusalem to all the nations: *There is forgiveness of sins for all who turn to me.*

Jn 1:6, 7. God sent John the Baptist as a witness to the fact that Jesus Christ is the true Light.

Jn 3:14. And as Moses in the wilderness lifted up the bronze image of a serpent on a pole, even so I must be lifted up upon a pole, [15]so that anyone who believes in me will have eternal life. [16]For God loved the world so much that he gave his only Son so that anyone who believes in him shall not perish but have eternal life. [17]God did not send his Son into the world to condemn it, but to save it.

Jn 4:14. "But the water I give them," he said, "becomes a perpetual spring within them, watering them forever with eternal life. [22]But you Samaritans know so little about him, worshiping blindly, while we Jews know all about him, for salvation comes to the world through the Jews."

Jn 5:40. Yet you won't come to me so that I can give you this life eternal!

Jn 6:35. Jesus replied, "I am the Bread of Life. No one coming to me will ever be hungry again. Those believing in me will never thirst. [37]But some will come to me—those the Father has given me—and I will never, never reject them."

Jn 7:37. On the last day, the climax of the holidays, Jesus shouted to the crowds, "If anyone is thirsty, let him come to me and drink. [38]For the Scriptures declare that rivers of living water shall flow from the inmost being of anyone who believes in me."

Jn 10:16. I have other sheep, too, in another fold. I must bring them also, and they will heed my voice; and there will be one flock with one Shepherd.

Jn 11:51. This prophecy that Jesus should die for the entire nation came from Caiaphas in his position as High Priest—he didn't think of it by himself, but was inspired to say it. [52]It was a prediction that Jesus' death would not be for Israel only, but for all the children of God scattered around the world.

Jn 12:32. And when I am lifted up (on the cross), I will draw everyone to me.

Jn 15:4. Take care to live in me, and let me live in you. For a branch can't produce fruit when severed from the vine. Nor can you be fruitful apart from me. [5]Yes, I am the Vine; you are the branches. Whoever lives in me and I in him shall produce a large crop of fruit. For apart from me you can't do a thing.

Acts 2:39. For Christ promised him to each one of you who has been called by the Lord our God, and to your children and even to those in distant lands!

Acts 4:12. There is salvation in no one else! Under all heaven there is no other name for men to call upon to save them.

Acts 5:20. Go over to the Temple and preach about this Life!

Acts 11:17. "And since it was *God* who gave these Gentiles the same gift he gave us when we believed on the Lord Jesus Christ, who was I to argue?" [18]When the others heard this, all their objections were answered and they began praising God! "Yes," they said. "God has given to the Gentiles, too, the privilege of turning to him and receiving eternal life!"

Acts 13:26. Brothers—you sons of Abraham, and also all of you Gentiles here who reverence God—this salvation is for all of us! [38]Brothers! Listen! In this man Jesus, there is forgiveness for your sins! [39]Everyone who trusts in him is freed from all guilt and declared righteous—something the Jewish law could never do. [47]For this is as the Lord commanded when he said, "I have made you a light to the Gentiles, to lead them from the farthest corners of the earth to my salvation."

Acts 15:7. At the meeting, after long discussion, Peter stood and addressed them as follows: "Brothers, you all know that God chose me from among you long ago to preach the Good News to the Gentiles, so that they also could believe. [8]God, who knows men's hearts, confirmed the fact that he accepts Gentiles by giving them the Holy Spirit, just as he gave him to us. [9]He made no distinction between them and us, for he cleansed their lives through faith, just as he did ours. [11]Don't you believe that all are saved the same way, by the free gift of the Lord Jesus?"

Acts 16:17. She followed along behind us shouting, "These men are servants of God and they have come to tell you how to have your sins forgiven." [30]He brought them out and begged them, "Sirs, what must I do to be saved?" [31]They replied, "Believe on the Lord Jesus and you will be saved, and your entire household."

Acts 20:21. I have had one message for Jews and Gentiles alike—the necessity of turning from sin to God through faith in our Lord Jesus Christ.

Acts 28:28, 29. So I want you to realize that this salvation from God is available to the Gentiles too, and they will accept it.

Rom 1:5. And now, through Christ, all the kindness of God has been poured out upon us undeserving sinners; and now he is sending us out around the world to tell all people everywhere the great things God has done for them, so that they, too, will believe and obey him. [14]For I owe a great debt to you and to everyone else, both to civilized people and uncivilized alike; yes, to the educated and uneducated alike. [16]For I am not ashamed of this Good News about Christ. It is God's powerful method of bringing all who believe it to heaven. This message was preached first to the Jews alone, but now everyone is invited to come to God in this same way. [17]This Good News tells us that God makes us ready for heaven—makes us right in God's sight—when we put our faith and trust in Christ to save us. This is accomplished from start to finish by faith. As the Scripture says it, "The man who finds life will find it through trusting God."

Rom 2:26. And if the heathen obey God's laws, won't God give them all the rights and honors he planned to give the Jews?

Rom 3:21, 22. But now God has shown us a different way to heaven—not by "being good enough" and trying to keep his laws, but by a new way (though not new, really, for the Scriptures told about it long ago). Now God says he will accept and acquit us—declare us "not guilty"—if we trust Jesus Christ to take away our sins. And we all can be saved in this same way, by coming to Christ, no matter who we are or what we have been like. [23]Yes, all have sinned; all fall short of God's glorious ideal; [24]yet now God declares us "not guilty" of offending him if we trust in Jesus Christ, who in his kindness freely takes away our sins. [25]For God sent Christ Jesus to take the punishment for our sins and to end all God's anger against us. He used Christ's blood and our faith as the means of saving us from his wrath. In this way he was being entirely fair, even though he did not punish those who sinned in former times. For he was looking forward to the time when Christ would come and take away those sins. [26]And now in these days also he can receive sinners in this same way, because Jesus took away their sins. But isn't this unfair for God to let criminals go free, and say that they are innocent? No, for he does it on the basis of their trust in Jesus who took away their sins. [28]So it is that we are saved by faith in Christ and not by the good things we do. [29]And does God save only the Jews in this way? No, the Gentiles, too, may come to him in this same manner. [30]God treats us all the same; all, whether Jews or Gentiles, are acquitted if they have faith.

Rom 4:1, 2. Abraham was, humanly speaking, the founder of our Jewish nation. What were his experiences concerning this question of being saved by faith? Was it because of his good deeds that God accepted him? If so, then he would have something to boast about. But from God's point of view Abraham had no basis at all for pride. [3]For the Scriptures tell us Abraham *believed God,* and that is why God canceled his sins and declared him "not guilty." [4, 5]But didn't he earn his right to heaven by all the good things he did? No, for being saved is a gift; if a person could earn it by being good, then it wouldn't be free—but it is! It is *given* to those who do *not* work for it. For God declares sinners to be good in his sight if they have faith in Christ to save them from God's wrath. [6]King David spoke of this, describing the happiness of an undeserving sinner who is declared "not guilty" by God. [7]"Blessed, and to be envied," he said, "are those whose sins are forgiven and put out of sight. [8]Yes, what joy there is for anyone whose sins are no longer counted against him by the Lord." [9]Now then, the question: Is this blessing given only to those who have faith in Christ but also keep the Jewish laws, or is the blessing also given to those who do not keep the Jewish rules, but only trust in Christ? Well, what about Abraham? We say that he received these blessings through his faith. Was it by faith alone? Or because he also kept the Jewish rules? [10]For the answer to that question, answer this one: *When* did God give this blessing to Abraham? It was *before he became a Jew*—before he went through the Jewish initiation ceremony of circumcision. [11]It wasn't until later on, *after* God had promised to bless him *because of his faith,* that he was circumcised. The circumcision ceremony was a sign that Abraham already had faith and that God had already accepted him and declared him just and good in his sight—before the ceremony took place. So Abraham is the spiritual father of those who believe and are saved without obeying Jewish laws. We see, then, that those who do not keep these rules are justified by God through faith. [12]And Abraham is also the spiritual father of those Jews who have been circumcised. They can see from his example that it is not this ceremony that saves them, for Abraham found favor with God by faith alone, *before he was circumcised.* [13]It is clear, then, that God's promise to give the whole earth to Abraham and his descendants was not because Abraham obeyed God's laws but because he trusted God to keep his promise. [14]So if you still claim that God's blessings go to those who are "good enough," then you are saying that God's promises to those who have faith are meaningless, and faith is foolish. [15]But the fact of the matter is this: when we try to gain God's blessing and salvation by keeping his laws we always end up under his anger, for we always fail to keep them. The only way we can keep from breaking laws is not to have any to break! [16]So God's blessings are given to us by faith, as a free gift; we are certain to get them whether or not we follow Jewish customs if we have faith like Abraham's, for Abraham is the father of us all when it comes to these matters of faith. [17]That is what the Scriptures mean when they say that God made Abraham the father of many nations. God will accept all people in every nation who trust God as Abraham did. And this promise is from God himself, who makes the dead live again and speaks of future events with as much certainty as though they were already past. [18]So, when God told Abraham that he would give him a son who would have many descendants and become a great nation, Abraham believed God even though such a promise just couldn't come to pass! [19]And because his faith was strong, he didn't worry about the fact that he was too old to be a father, at the age of one hundred, and that Sarah his wife, at ninety, was also much too old to have a baby. [20]But Abraham never doubted. He believed God, for his faith and trust grew ever stronger, and he praised God for this blessing even before it happened. [21]He was completely sure that God was well able to do anything he promised. [22]And because of Abraham's faith God forgave his sins and declared him "not guilty." [23]Now this wonderful statement —that he was accepted and approved through his faith—wasn't just for Abraham's benefit. [24]It was for us, too, assuring us that God will accept us in the same way he accepted Abraham—when we believe the promises of God who brought back Jesus our Lord from the dead. [25]He died for our sins and rose again to make us right with God, filling us with God's goodness.

Rom 5:1. So now, since we have been made right in God's sight by faith in his promises, we can have real peace with him because of what Jesus Christ our Lord has done for us. [2]For because of our faith, he has brought us into this place of highest privilege where we now stand, and we confidently and joyfully look forward to actually becoming all that God has had in mind for us to be. *vs.* 15–21.

Rom 7:24, 25. Oh, what a terrible predicament I'm in! Who will free me from my slavery to this deadly lower nature? Thank God! It has been done by Jesus Christ our Lord. He has set me free.

Rom 9:30. Well then, what shall we say about these things? Just this, that God has given the Gentiles the opportunity to be acquitted by faith, even though they had not been really seeking God. [31]But the Jews, who tried so hard to get right with God by keeping his laws, never succeeded. [32]Why not? Because they were trying to be saved by keeping the law and being good instead of by depending on faith. They have stumbled over the great stumbling stone. [33]God warned them of this in the Scriptures when he said, "I have put a Rock in the path of the Jews, and many will stumble over him (Jesus). Those who believe in him will never be disappointed."

Rom 10:4. They don't understand that Christ gives to those who trust in him everything they are trying to get by keeping his laws. He ends all of that. [8]For salvation that comes from trusting Christ—which is what we preach—is already within easy reach of each of us; in fact, it is as near as our own hearts and mouths. [9]For if you tell others with your own mouth that Jesus Christ is your Lord, and believe in your own heart that God has raised him from the dead, you will be saved. [10]For it is by believing in his heart that a man becomes right with God; and with his mouth he tells others of his faith, confirming his salvation. [11]For the Scriptures tell us that no one who believes in Christ will ever be disappointed. [12]Jew and Gentile are the same in this respect: they all have the same Lord who generously gives his riches to all those who ask him for them. [13]Anyone who calls upon the name of the Lord will be saved.

Rom 11:6. And if it is by God's kindness, then it is not by their being good enough. For in that case the free gift would no longer be free—it isn't free when it is earned. [11]Does this mean that God has rejected his Jewish people forever? Of course not! His purpose was to make his salvation available to the Gentiles, and then the Jews would be jealous and begin to want God's salvation for themselves. [12]Now if the whole world became rich as a result of God's offer of salvation, when the Jews stumbled over it and turned it down, think how much greater a blessing the world will share in later on when the Jews, too, come to Christ. *vs.* 1–36.

Rom 15:9. And remember that he came also that the Gentiles might be saved and give glory to God for his mercies to them. That is what the Psalmist meant when he wrote: "I will praise you among the Gentiles, and sing to your name." [16]For I am, by God's grace, a special messenger from Jesus Christ to you Gentiles, bringing you the Gospel and offering you up as a fragrant sacrifice to God; for you have been made pure and pleasing to him by the Holy Spirit.

1 Cor 1:18. I know very well how foolish it sounds to those who are lost, when they hear that Jesus died to save them. But we who are saved recognize this message as the very power of God.

1 Cor 6:11. There was a time when some of you were just like that but now your sins are washed away, and you are set apart for God, and he has accepted you because of what the Lord Jesus Christ and the Spirit of our God have done for you.

2 Cor 5:17. When someone becomes a Christian he becomes a brand new person inside. He is not the same any more. A new life has begun! [20]We are Christ's ambassadors. God is using us to speak to you: we beg you, as though Christ himself were here pleading with you, receive the love he offers you—be reconciled to God.

2 Cor 6:1. As God's partners we beg you not to toss aside this marvelous message of God's great kindness. [17]That is why the Lord has said, "Leave them; separate yourselves from them; don't touch their filthy things, and I will welcome you, [18]and be a Father to you, and you will be my sons and daughters."

2 Cor 7:10. For God sometimes uses sorrow in our lives to help us turn away from sin and seek eternal life. We should never regret his sending it. But the sorrow of the man who is not a Christian is not the sorrow of true repentance and does not prevent eternal death.

Gal 1:4. He died for our sins just as God our Father planned, and rescued us from this evil world in which we live.

Gal 2:16. And yet we Jewish Christians know very well that we cannot become right with God by obeying our Jewish laws, but only by faith in Jesus Christ to take away our sins. And so we, too, have trusted Jesus Christ, that we might be accepted by God because of faith—and not because we have obeyed the Jewish laws. For no one will ever be saved by obeying them.

Gal 3:8. What's more, the Scriptures looked forward to this time when God would save the Gentiles also, through their faith. God told Abraham about this long ago when he said, "I will bless those in every nation who trust in me as you do." [13]But Christ has bought us out from under the doom of that impossible system by taking the curse for our wrong-doing upon himself. For it is written in the Scripture, "Anyone who is hanged on a tree is cursed" (as Jesus was hung upon a wooden cross). [14]Now God can bless the Gentiles, too, with this same blessing he promised to Abraham; and all of us as Christians can have the promised Holy Spirit through this faith. [21]Well then, are God's laws and God's promises against each other? Of course not! If we could be saved by his laws, then God would not have had to give us a different way to get out of the grip of sin. [26]For now we are all children of God through faith in Jesus Christ, [27]and we who have been baptized into union with Christ are enveloped by him. [28]We are no longer Jews or Greeks or slaves or free men or merely men or women, but we are all the same—we are Christians; we are one in Christ Jesus. *vs.* 1–28.

Eph 1:9. God has told us his secret reason for sending Christ, a plan he decided on in mercy long ago; [10]and this was his purpose: that when the time is ripe he will gather us all together from wherever we are—in heaven or on earth—to be with him in Christ, forever. [13]And because of what Christ did, all you others too, who heard the Good News about how to be saved, and trusted Christ, were marked as belonging to Christ by the Holy Spirit, who long ago had been promised to all of us Christians.

Eph 2:1. Once you were under God's curse, doomed forever for your sins. [3]All of us used to be just as they are, our lives expressing the evil within us, doing every wicked thing that our passions or our evil thoughts might lead us into. We started out bad, being born with evil natures, and were under God's anger just like everyone else. [4]But God is so rich in mercy; he loved us so much [5]that even though we were spiritually dead and doomed by our sins, he gave us back our lives again when he raised Christ from the dead—only by his undeserved favor have we ever been saved. [8]Because of his kindness you have been saved through trusting Christ. And even trusting is not of yourselves; it too is a gift from God. [9]Salvation is not a reward for the good we have done, so none of us can take any credit for it. [14]For Christ himself is our way of peace. He has made peace between us Jews and you Gentiles by making us all one family, breaking down the wall of contempt that used to separate us. [15]By his death he ended the angry resentment between us, caused by the Jewish laws which favored the Jews and excluded the Gentiles, for he died to annul that whole system of Jewish laws. Then he took the two groups that had been opposed to each other and made them parts of himself; thus he fused us together to become one new person, and at last there was peace. [17]And he has brought this Good News of peace to you Gentiles who were very far away from him, and to us Jews who were near.

Eph 3:6. The Gentiles will have their full share with the Jews in all the riches inherited by God's sons; both are invited to belong to his church, and all of God's promises of mighty blessings through Christ apply to them both when they accept the Good News about Christ and what he has done for them. [9]And to explain to everyone that God is the Savior of the Gentiles too, just as he who made all things had secretly planned from the very beginning.

Eph 5:14. That is why God says in the Scriptures, "Awake, O sleeper, and rise up from the dead; and Christ shall give you light."

Phil 2:12. You must be even more careful to do the good things that result from being saved, obeying God with deep reverence, shrinking back from all that might displease him.

Phil 3:7. But all these things that I once thought very worthwhile—now I've thrown them all away so that I can put my trust and hope in Christ alone. [8]Yes, everything else is worthless when compared with the priceless gain of knowing Christ Jesus my Lord. I have put aside all else, counting it worth less than nothing, in order that I can have Christ, [9]and become one with him, no longer counting on being saved by being good enough or by obeying God's laws, but by trusting Christ to save me; for God's way of making us right with himself depends on faith—counting on Christ alone. [10]Now I have given up everything else—I have found it to be the only way to really know Christ and to experience the mighty power that brought him back to life again, and to find out what it means to suffer and to die with him. [11]So, whatever it takes, I will be one who lives in the fresh newness of life of those who are alive from the dead.

Col 1:6. The same Good News that came to you is going out all over the world. [20]It was through what his Son did that God cleared a path for everything to come to him—all things in heaven and on earth—for Christ's death on the cross has made peace with God for all by his blood. [21]This includes you who were once so far away from God. You were his enemies and hated him and were separated from him by your evil thoughts and actions, yet now he has brought you back as his friends. [22]He has done this through the death on the cross of his own human body, and now as a result Christ has brought you into the very presence of God, and you are standing there before him with nothing left against you—nothing left that he could even chide you for: [23]the only condition is that you fully believe the Truth, standing in it steadfast and firm, strong in the Lord, convinced of the Good News that Jesus died for you, and never shifting from trusting him to save you. This is the wonderful news that came to each of you and is now spreading all over the world. [26, 27]He has kept this secret for centuries and generations past, but now at last it has pleased him to tell it to those who love him and live for him, and the riches and glory of his plan are for you Gentiles too. And this is the secret: *that Christ in your hearts is your only hope of glory.*

Col 3:11. In this new life one's nationality or race or education or social position is unimportant; such things mean nothing. Whether a person has Christ is what matters, and he is equally available to all.

1 Thess 5:8. But let us who live in the light keep sober, protected by the armor of faith and love, and wearing as our helmet the happy hope of salvation.
[9]For God has not chosen to pour out his anger upon us, but to save us through our Lord Jesus
Christ; [10]he died for us so that we can live with him forever, whether we are dead or alive at the time of his return.

2 Thess 2:13. God chose from the very first to give you salvation, cleansing you by the work of the Holy Spirit and by your trusting in the Truth.
[14]Through us he called you to share in the glory of our Lord Jesus Christ.

1 Tim 1:13. I used to scoff at the name of Christ. I hunted down his people, harming them in every way I could. But God had mercy on me because I didn't know what I was doing, for I didn't know
Christ at that time. [15]How true it is, and how I long that everyone should know it, that Christ Jesus came into the world to save sinners—and I was the
greatest of them all. [16]But God had mercy on me so that Christ Jesus could use me as an example to show everyone how patient he is with even the worst sinners, so that others will realize that they, too, can have everlasting life.

1 Tim 2:3. This is good and pleases God our
Savior, [4]for he longs for all to be saved and to
understand this truth: [5]*That God is on one side and all the people on the other side, and Christ Jesus, himself man, is between them to bring them to-*
gether, [6]*by giving his life for all mankind.* This is the message which at the proper time God gave to the world.

1 Tim 4:10. We work hard and suffer much in order that people will believe it, for our hope is in the living God who died for all, and particularly for those who have accepted his salvation.

2 Tim 1:9. It is he who saved us and chose us for his holy work, not because we deserved it but because that was his plan long before the world began —to show his love and kindness to us through
Christ. [10]And now he has made all of this plain to us by the coming of our Savior Jesus Christ, who broke the power of death and showed us the way of everlasting life through trusting him.

2 Tim 2:10. I am more than willing to suffer if that will bring salvation and eternal glory in Christ Jesus to those God has chosen.

2 Tim 3:15. You know how, when you were a small child, you were taught the holy Scriptures; and it is these that make you wise to accept God's salvation by trusting in Christ Jesus.

Tit 2:11. For the free gift of eternal salvation is now being offered to everyone.

Tit 3:3. Once we, too, were foolish and disobedient; we were misled by others and became slaves to many evil pleasures and wicked desires. Our lives were full of resentment and envy. We hated others
and they hated us. [4]But when the time came for the kindness and love of God our Savior to appear,
[5]then he saved us—not because we were good enough to be saved, but because of his kindness and pity—by washing away our sins and giving us the
new joy of the indwelling Holy Spirit [6]whom he poured out upon us with wonderful fullness—and
all because of what Jesus Christ our Savior did [7]so
that he could declare us good in God's eyes—all because of his great kindness; and now we can share in the wealth of the eternal life he gives us, and we are eagerly looking forward to receiving it.

Heb 1:14. No, for the angels are only spirit-messengers sent out to help and care for those who are to receive his salvation.

Heb 2:3. What makes us think that we can escape if we are indifferent to this great salvation announced by the Lord Jesus himself, and passed
on to us by those who heard him speak? [10]And it was right and proper that God, who made everything for his own glory should allow Jesus to suffer, for in doing this he was bringing vast multitudes of God's people to heaven; for his suffering made Jesus a perfect Leader, one fit to bring them into their salvation.

Heb 4:1. Although God's promise still stands—his promise that all may enter his place of rest—we ought to tremble with fear because some of you may be on the verge of failing to get there after all.
[2]For this wonderful news—the message that God wants to save us—has been given to us just as it was to those who lived in the time of Moses. But it didn't do them any good because they didn't be-
lieve it. They didn't mix it with faith. [3]For only we who believe God can enter into his place of rest. He has said, "I have sworn in my anger that those who don't believe me will never get in," even though he has been ready and waiting for them since the
world began. [4]We know he is ready and waiting because it is written that God rested on the seventh day of creation, having finished all that he had
planned to make. [5]Even so they didn't get in, for God finally said, "They shall never enter my rest."
[6]Yet the promise remains and some get in—but not those who had the first chance, for they disobeyed
God and failed to enter. [7]But he has set another time for coming in, and that time is now. He announced this through King David long years after man's first failure to enter, saying in the words already quoted, "Today when you hear him calling, do not harden your hearts against him." [8]This new place of rest he is talking about does not mean the land of Israel that Joshua led them into. If that were what God meant, he would not have spoken long afterwards about "today" being the time to
get in. [9]So there is a full complete rest *still waiting*
for the people of God. [10]Christ has already entered there. He is resting from his work, just as God did after the creation.

Heb 5:9. It was after he had proved himself perfect in this experience that Jesus became the Giver of eternal salvation to all those who obey him.

Heb 7:25. He is able to save completely all who come to God through him. Since he will live forever, he will always be there to remind God that he has paid for their sins with his blood.

Jas 1:21. So get rid of all that is wrong in your life, both inside and outside, and humbly be glad for the wonderful message we have received, for it is able to save our souls as it takes hold of our hearts.

1 Pet 1:5. And God, in his mighty power, will make sure that you get there safely to receive it, because you are trusting him. It will be yours in that coming last day for all to see. [9]And your further reward for trusting him will be the salvation of your souls. [10]This salvation was something the prophets did not fully understand. Though they wrote about it, they had many questions as to what it all could mean.

2 Pet 3:9. He isn't really being slow about his promised return, even though it sometimes seems that way. But he is waiting, for the good reason that he is not willing that any should perish, and he is giving more time for sinners to repent. [15]And remember why he is waiting. He is giving us time to get his message of salvation out to others.

1 Jn 2:25. And he himself has promised us this: *eternal life.*

1 Jn 4:9. God showed how much he loved us by sending his only Son into this wicked world to bring to us eternal life through his death. [10]In this act we see what real love is: it is not our love for God, but his love for us when he sent his Son to satisfy God's anger against our sins.

1 Jn 5:11. And what is it that God has said? That he has given us eternal life, and that this life is in his Son.

Jude 1:3. Dearly loved friends, I had been planning to write you some thoughts about the salvation God has given us, but now I find I must write of something else instead, urging you to stoutly defend the truth which God gave, once for all, to his people to keep without change through the years.

Rev 3:17. You say, "I am rich, with everything I want; I don't need a thing!" And you don't realize that spiritually you are wretched and miserable and poor and blind and naked. [18]My advice to you is to buy pure gold from me, gold purified by fire —only then will you truly be rich. And to purchase from me white garments, clean and pure, so you won't be naked and ashamed; and to get medicine from me to heal your eyes and give you back your sight. [20]Look! I have been standing at the door and I am constantly knocking. If anyone hears me calling him and opens the door, I will come in and fellowship with him and he with me.

Rev 5:9. They were singing him a new song with these words: "You are worthy to take the scroll and break its seals and open it; for you were slain, and your blood has bought people from every nation as gifts for God."

Rev 7:9. After this I saw a vast crowd, too great to count, from all nations and provinces and languages, standing in front of the throne and before the Lamb, clothed in white, with palm branches in their hands. [10]And they were shouting with a mighty shout, "Salvation comes from our God upon the throne, and from the Lamb."

Rev 14:6. And I saw another angel flying through the heavens, carrying the everlasting Good News to preach to those on earth—to every nation, tribe, language and people.

Rev 21:6. I will give to the thirsty the springs of the Water of Life—as a gift!

Rev 22:17. The Spirit and the bride say, "Come," Let each one who hears them say the same, "Come." Let the thirsty one come—anyone who wants to; let him come and drink the Water of Life without charge.

See *Adoption; Redemption; Regeneration; Sanctification.*

CONDITIONS OF. Mt 3:2. Turn from your sins . . . turn to God . . . for the Kingdom of Heaven is coming soon.

Mt 18:3. And said, "Unless you turn to God from your sins and become as little children, you will never get into the Kingdom of Heaven."

Mt 19:16. Someone came to Jesus with this question: "Good master, what must I do to have eternal life?" [17]"When you call me good you are calling me God," Jesus replied, "for God alone is truly good. But to answer your question, you can get to heaven if you keep the commandments." [18]"Which ones?" the man asked. And Jesus replied, "Don't kill, don't commit adultery, don't steal, don't lie, [19]honor your father and mother, and love your neighbor as yourself!" [20]"I've always obeyed every one of them," the youth replied. "What else must I do?" [21]Jesus told him, "If you want to be perfect, go and sell everything you have and give the money to the poor, and you will have treasure in heaven; and come, follow me." Lk 18:18–26.

Mt 24:13. But those enduring to the end shall be saved.

Mk 1:4. This messenger was John the Baptist. He lived in the wilderness and taught that all should be baptized as a public announcement of their decision to turn their backs on sin, so that God could forgive them.

Lk 3:8. First go and prove by the way you live that you really have repented. And don't think you are safe because you are descendants of Abraham. That isn't enough. God can produce children of Abraham from these desert stones!

Lk 14:25. Great crowds were following him. He turned around and addressed them as follows: [26]"Anyone who wants to be my follower must love me far more than he does his own father, mother, wife, children, brothers, or sisters—yes, more than his own life—otherwise he cannot be my disciple. [27]And no one can be my disciple who does not carry his own cross and follow me. [28]But don't begin until you count the cost. For who would begin construction of a building without first getting estimates and then checking to see if he has enough money to pay the bills? [29]Otherwise he might complete only the foundation before running out of funds. And then how everyone would laugh! [30]"'See that fellow there?' they would mock. 'He started that building and ran out of money before it was finished!' [31]Or what king would ever dream of going to war without first sitting down with his counselors and discussing whether his army of 10,000 is strong enough to defeat the 20,000 men who are marching against him? [32]If the decision is negative, then while the enemy troops are still far away, he will send a truce team to discuss terms of peace. [33]So no one can become my disciple unless he first sits down and counts his blessings—and then renounces them all for me."

Jn 3:3. Jesus replied, "With all the earnestness I possess I tell you this: Unless you are born again, you can never get into the Kingdom of God." [4]"'Born again!" exclaimed Nicodemus. "What do you mean? How can an old man go back into his mother's womb and be born again?" [5]Jesus replied, "What I am telling you so earnestly is this: Unless one is born of water and the Spirit, he cannot enter the Kingdom of God. [6]Men can only reproduce human life, but the Holy Spirit gives new life from heaven; [7]so don't be surprised at my statement that you must be born again! [8]Just as you can hear the wind but can't tell where it comes from or where it will go next, so it is with the Spirit. We do not know on whom he will next bestow this life from heaven." [9]"What do you mean?" Nicodemus asked. [10, 11]Jesus replied, "You, a respected Jewish teacher, and yet you don't understand these things? I am telling you what I know and have seen —and yet you won't believe me. [12]But if you don't even believe me when I tell you about such things as these that happen here among men, how can you possibly believe if I tell you what is going on in heaven?"

14. "And as Moses in the wilderness lifted up the bronze image of a serpent on a pole, even so I must be lifted up upon a pole, [15]so that anyone who believes in me will have eternal life. [16]For God loved the world so much that he gave his only Son so that anyone who believes in him shall not perish but have eternal life. [17]God did not send his Son into the world to condemn it, but to save it. [18]There is no eternal doom awaiting those who trust him to save them. But those who don't trust him have already been tried and condemned for not believing in the only Son of God."

Jn 5:24. I say emphatically that anyone who listens to my message and believes in God who sent me has eternal life, and will never be damned for his sins, but has already passed out of death into life.

Jn 6:28. They replied, "What should we do to satisfy God?" [29]Jesus told them, "This is the will of God, that you believe in the one he has sent."

47. "How earnestly I tell you this—anyone who believes in me already has eternal life!"

Jn 9:35. When Jesus heard what had happened, he found the man and said, "Do you believe in the Messiah?"

Jn 11:25. Jesus told her, "I am the one who raises the dead and gives them life again. Anyone who believes in me, even though he dies like anyone else, shall live again. [26]He is given eternal life for believing in me and shall never perish. Do you believe this, Martha?"

Jn 12:36. Make use of the Light while there is still time; then you will become light bearers.

Jn 20:31. But these are recorded so that you will believe that he is the Messiah, the Son of God, and that believing in him you will have life.

Acts 2:38. And Peter replied, "Each one of you must turn from sin, return to God, and be baptized in the name of Jesus Christ for the forgiveness of your sins; then you also shall receive this gift, the Holy Spirit."

Acts 3:19. Now change your mind and attitude to God and turn to him so he can cleanse away your sins and send you wonderful times of refreshment from the presence of the Lord. [23]Anyone who will not listen to him shall be utterly destroyed.

Acts 16:30. He brought them out and begged them, "Sirs, what must I do to be saved?" [31]They replied, "Believe on the Lord Jesus and you will be saved, and your entire household."

See *Blessings, Contingent on Obedience; Faith; Obedience; Repentance; Perseverance.*

PLAN OF. Mk 4:11. He replied, "You are permitted to know some truths about the Kingdom of God that are hidden to those outside the Kingdom.

Jn 6:44. For no one can come to me unless the Father who sent me draws him to me, and at the Last Day I will cause all such to rise again from the dead. *vs.* 37, 65.

45. As it is written in the Scriptures, "They shall all be taught of God." Those the Father speaks to, who learn the truth from him, will be attracted to me.

Jn 17:4. I brought glory to you here on earth by doing everything you told me to.

Jn 18:11. But Jesus said to Peter, "Put your sword away. Shall I not drink from the cup the Father has given me?"

Jn 19:28. Jesus knew that everything was now finished, and to fulfill the Scriptures said, "I'm thirsty." [29]A jar of sour wine was sitting there, so a sponge was soaked in it and put on a hyssop branch and held up to his lips. [30]When Jesus had tasted it, he said, "It is finished," and bowed his head and dismissed his spirit.

Acts 3:18. But God was fulfilling the prophecies that the Messiah must suffer all these things.

Acts 17:3. Explaining the prophecies about the sufferings of the Messiah and his coming back to life, and proving that Jesus is the Messiah.

Rom 1:16. For I am not ashamed of this Good News about Christ. It is God's powerful method of bringing all who believe it to heaven. This message was preached first to the Jews alone, but now everyone is invited to come to God in this same way. [17]This Good News tells us that God makes us ready for heaven—makes us right in God's sight—when we put our faith and trust in Christ to save us. This is accomplished from start to finish by faith. As the Scripture says it, "The man who finds life will find it through trusting God."

Rom 10:3. For they don't understand that Christ has died to make them right with God. Instead they are trying to make themselves good enough to gain God's favor by keeping the Jewish laws and customs, but that is not God's way of salvation. [4]They don't understand that Christ gives to those who trust in him everything they are trying to get by keeping his laws. He ends all of that. [5]For Moses wrote that if a person could be perfectly good and hold out against temptation all his life and never sin once, only then could he be pardoned and saved. [6]But the salvation that comes through faith says, "You don't need to search the heavens to find Christ and bring him down to help you," and [7]"You don't need to go among the dead to bring Christ back to life again." [8]For salvation that comes from trusting Christ—which is what we preach—is already within easy reach of each of us; in fact, it is as near as our own hearts and mouths. [9]For if you tell others with your own mouth that Jesus Christ is your Lord, and believe in your own heart that God has raised him from the dead, you will be saved.

Rom 16:25, 26. I commit you to God, who is able to make you strong and steady in the Lord, just as the Gospel says, and just as I have told you. This is God's plan of salvation for you Gentiles, kept secret from the beginning of time. But now as the prophets foretold and as God commands, this message is being preached everywhere, so that people all around the world will have faith in Christ and obey him.

1 Cor 1:21. For God in his wisdom saw to it that the world would never find God through human brilliance, and then he stepped in and saved all those who believed his message, which the world calls foolish and silly. [22]It seems foolish to the Jews because they want a sign from heaven as proof that what is preached is true; and it is foolish to the Gentiles because they believe only what agrees with their philosophy and seems wise to them. [23]So when we preach about Christ dying to save them, the Jews are offended and the Gentiles say it's all nonsense. [24]But God has opened the eyes of those called to salvation, both Jews and Gentiles, to see that Christ is the mighty power of God to save them; Christ himself is the center of God's wise plan for their salvation. [25]This so-called "foolish" plan of God is far wiser than the wisest plan of the wisest man, and God in his weakness—Christ dying on the cross—is far stronger than any man.

1 Cor 2:7. Our words are wise because they are from God, telling of God's wise plan to bring us into the glories of heaven. This plan was hidden in former times, though it was made for our benefit before the world began. [8]But the great men of the world have not understood it; if they had, they never would have crucified the Lord of Glory. [9]That is what is meant by the Scriptures which say that no mere man has ever seen, heard or even imagined what wonderful things God has ready for those who love the Lord.

2 Cor 5:18. All these new things are from God who brought us back to himself through what Christ Jesus did. And God has given us the privilege of urging everyone to come into his favor and be reconciled to him. [19]For God was in Christ, restoring the world to himself, no longer counting men's sins against them but blotting them out. This is the wonderful message he has given us to tell others.

Gal 4:4. But when the right time came, the time God decided on, he sent his Son, born of a woman, born as a Jew, [5]to buy freedom for us who were slaves to the law so that he could adopt us as his very own sons.

Eph 1:3. How we praise God, the Father of our Lord Jesus Christ, who has blessed us with every blessing in heaven because we belong to Christ. [4]Long ago, even before he made the world, God chose us to be his very own, through what Christ would do for us; he decided then to make us holy in his eyes, without a single fault—we who stand before him covered with his love. [5]His unchanging plan has always been to adopt us into his own family by sending Jesus Christ to die for us. And he did this because he wanted to! [6]Now all praise to God for his wonderful kindness to us and his favor that he has poured out upon us, because we belong to his dearly loved Son. [7]So overflowing is his kindness towards us that he took away all our sins through the blood of his Son, by whom we are saved; [8]and he has showered down upon us the richness of his grace—for how well he understands us and knows what is best for us at all times. [9]God has told us his secret reason for sending Christ, a plan he decided on in mercy long ago; [10]and this was his purpose; that when the time is ripe he will gather us all together from wherever we are—in heaven or on earth—to be with him in Christ, forever. [11]Moreover, because of what Christ has done we have become gifts to God that he delights in, for as part of God's sovereign plan we were chosen from the beginning to be his, and all things happen just as he decided long ago. [12]God's purpose in this was that we should praise God and give glory to him for doing these mighty things for us, who were the first to trust in Christ. [13]And because of what Christ did, all you others too, who heard the Good News about how to be saved, and trusted Christ, were marked as belonging to Christ by the Holy Spirit, who long ago had been promised to all of us Christians. [14]His presence within us is God's guarantee that he really will give us all that he promised; and the Spirit's seal upon us means that God has already purchased us and that he guarantees to bring us to himself. This is just one more reason for us to praise our glorious God. [15]That is why, ever since I heard of your strong faith in the Lord Jesus and of the love you have for Christians everywhere, [16, 17]I have never stopped thanking

God for you. I pray for you constantly, asking God, the glorious Father of our Lord Jesus Christ, to give you wisdom to see clearly and really understand who Christ is and all that he has done for you. [18]I pray that your hearts will be flooded with light so that you can see something of the future he has called you to share. I want you to realize that God has been made rich because we who are Christ's have been given to him! [19]I pray that you will begin to understand how incredibly great his power is to help those who believe him. It is that same mighty power [20]that raised Christ from the dead and seated him in the place of honor at God's right hand in heaven, [21]far, far above any other king or ruler or dictator or leader. Yes, his honor is far more glorious than that of anyone else either in this world or in the world to come. [22]And God has put all things under his feet and made him the supreme Head of the church— [23]which is his body, filled with himself, the Author and Giver of everything everywhere.

Eph 2:4. But God is so rich in mercy; he loved us so much [5]that even though we were spiritually dead and doomed by our sins, he gave us back our lives again when he raised Christ from the dead—only by his undeserved favor have we ever been saved— [6]and lifted us up from the grave into glory along with Christ, where we sit with him in the heavenly realms—all because of what Christ Jesus did. [7]And now God can always point to us as examples of how very, very rich his kindness is, as shown in all he has done for us through Jesus Christ. [8]Because of his kindness you have been saved through trusting Christ. And even trusting is not of yourselves; it too is a gift from God. [9]Salvation is not a reward for the good we have done, so none of us can take any credit for it. [10]It is God himself who has made us what we are and given us new lives from Christ Jesus; and long ages ago he planned that we should spend these lives in helping others.

Eph 3:1. I Paul, the servant of Christ, am here in jail because of you—for preaching that you Gentiles are a part of God's house. [2, 3]No doubt you already know that God has given me this special work of showing God's favor to you Gentiles, as I briefly mentioned before in one of my letters. God himself showed me this secret plan of his, that the Gentiles, too, are included in his kindness. [4]I say this to explain to you how I know about these things. [5]In olden times God did not share this plan with his people, but now he has revealed it by the Holy Spirit to his apostles and prophets. [6]And this is the secret: that the Gentiles will have their full share with the Jews in all the riches inherited by God's sons; both are invited to belong to his church, and all of God's promises of mighty blessings through Christ apply to them both when they accept the Good News about Christ and what he has done for them. [7]God has given me the wonderful privilege of telling everyone about this plan of his; and he has given me his power and special ability to do it well. [8]Just think! Though I did nothing to deserve it, and though I am the most useless Christian there is, yet I was the one chosen for this special joy of telling the Gentiles the Glad News of the endless treasures available to them in Christ; [9]and to explain to everyone that God is the Savior of the Gentiles too, just as he who made all things had secretly planned from the very beginning. [10]And his reason? To show to all the rulers in heaven how perfectly wise he is when all of his family—Jews and Gentiles alike—are seen to be joined together in his church, [11]in just the way he had always planned it through Jesus Christ our Lord.

Eph 6:19. Pray for me, too, and ask God to give me the right words as I boldly tell others about the Lord, and as I explain to them that his salvation is for the Gentiles too.

Col 1:19. For God wanted all of himself to be in his Son. [20]It was through what this Son did that God cleared a path for everything to come to him—all things in heaven and on earth—for Christ's death on the cross has made peace with God for all by his blood. [21]This includes you who were once so far away from God. You were his enemies and hated him and were separated from him by your evil thoughts and actions, yet now he has brought you back as his friends. [22]He has done this through the death on the cross of his own human body, and now as a result Christ has brought you into the very presence of God, and you are standing there before him with nothing left against you—nothing left that he could even chide you for; [23]the only condition is that you fully believe the Truth, standing in it steadfast and firm, strong in the Lord, convinced of the Good News that Jesus died for you, and never shifting from trusting him to save you. This is the wonderful news that came to each of you and is now spreading all over the world. And I, Paul, have the joy of telling it to others. [26, 27]He has kept this secret for centuries and generations past, but now at last it has pleased him to tell it to those who love him and live for him, and the riches and glory of his plan are for you Gentiles too. And this is the secret: *that Christ in your hearts is your only hope of glory.*

2 Thess 2:13. But we must forever give thanks to God for you, our brothers loved by the Lord, because God chose from the very first to give you salvation, cleansing you by the work of the Holy Spirit and by your trusting in the Truth. [14]Through us he told you the Good News. Through us he called you to share in the glory of our Lord Jesus Christ.

1 Tim 3:16. It is quite true that the way to live a godly life is not an easy matter. But the answer lies in Christ, who came to earth as a man, was proved spotless and pure in his Spirit, was served by angels, was preached among the nations, was accepted by men everywhere and was received up again to his glory in heaven.

2 Tim 1:9. It is he who saved us and chose us for his holy work, not because we deserved it but because that was his plan long before the world began

—to show his love and kindness to us through Christ. [10]And now he has made all of this plain to us by the coming of our Savior Jesus Christ, who broke the power of death and showed us the way of everlasting life through trusting him.

Tit 3:5. Then he saved us—not because we were good enough to be saved, but because of his kindness and pity—by washing away our sins and giving us the new joy of the indwelling Holy Spirit [6]whom he poured out upon us with wonderful fullness—and all because of what Jesus Christ our Savior did [7]so that he could declare us good in God's eyes—all because of his great kindness; and now we can share in the wealth of the eternal life he gives us, and we are eagerly looking forward to receiving it.

Heb 2:9. But we do see Jesus—who for awhile was a little lower than the angels—crowned now by God with glory and honor because he suffered death for us. Yes, because of God's great kindness, Jesus tasted death for everyone in all the world. [10]And it was right and proper that God, who made everything for his own glory, should allow Jesus to suffer, for in doing this he was bringing vast multitudes of God's people to heaven; for his suffering made Jesus a perfect Leader, one fit to bring them into their salvation. [14]Since we, God's children, are human beings—made of flesh and blood—he became flesh and blood too by being born in human form; for only as a human being could he die and in dying break the power of the devil who had the power of death. [15]Only in that way could he deliver those who through fear of death have been living all their lives as slaves to constant dread. [16]We all know he did not come as an angel but as a human being—yes, a Jew. [17]And it was necessary for Jesus to be like us, his brothers, so that he could be our merciful and faithful High Priest before God, a Priest who would be both merciful to us and faithful to God in dealing with the sins of the people. [18]For since he himself has now been through suffering and temptation, he knows what it is like when we suffer and are tempted, and he is wonderfully able to help us.

Heb 6:17. God also bound himself with an oath, so that those he promised to help would be perfectly sure and never need to wonder whether he might change his plans. [18]He has given us both his promise and his oath, two things we can completely count on, for it is impossible for God to tell a lie. Now all those who flee to him to save them can take new courage when they hear such assurances from God; now they can know without doubt that he will give them the salvation he has promised them. [19]This certain hope of being saved is a strong and trustworthy anchor for our souls, connecting us with God himself behind the sacred curtains of heaven, [20]where Christ has gone ahead to plead for us from his position as our High Priest, with the honor and rank of Melchizedek.

1 Pet 1:23. For you have a new life. It was not passed on to you from your parents, for the life they gave you will fade away. This new one will last forever, for it comes from Christ, God's ever-living Message to men. [24]Yes, our natural lives will fade as grass does when it becomes all brown and dry. All our greatness is like a flower that droops and falls; [25]but the Word of the Lord will last forever. And his message is the Good News that was preached to you.

Rev 1:5. And from Jesus Christ who faithfully reveals all truth to us. He was the first to rise from death, to die no more. He is far greater than any king in all the earth. All praise to him who always loves us and who set us free from our sins by pouring out his lifeblood for us. [6]He has gathered us into his kingdom and made us priests of God his Father. Give to him everlasting glory! He rules forever! Amen!

See *Jesus, Mission of; Redemption; Regeneration; Sanctification; Sin, Forgiveness of.*

SAMARIA 1. City of, built by Omri, 1 Kgs 16:24. Capital of the kingdom of the ten tribes, 1 Kgs 22:51; 2 Kgs 13:9, 10. Beseiged by Ben-hadad, 1 Kgs 20; 2 Kgs 6:24–33; 7. The Syrian army is led into, by Elisha, who miraculously blinds them, 2 Kgs 6:8–23. Ahab ruled in, see *Ahab; Jezebel.* Besieged by Shalmaneser, king of Assyria, three years; taken; the people carried away to Halah and Habor, and the cities of the Medes, 2 Kgs 17:5, 6; 18:9–11. Idolatry of, 1 Kgs 16:32; 2 Kgs 13:6. Temple of, destroyed, 2 Kgs 10:17–28; 23:19. Paul and Barnabas preach in, Acts 15:3. Visited by Philip, Peter, and John, Acts 8:5–25.

2. Territory of, 1 Kgs 14:32. Foreign colonies distributed among the cities of, by the king of Assyria, 2 Kgs 17:24–41; Ezra 4:8–10. Roads through, from Judea into Galilee, Lk 17:11; Jn 4:3–8. Jesus travels through, Jn 4:1–42; heals lepers in, Lk 17:11–19. The good Samaritan from, Lk 10:33–35. No dealings between the Jews and the inhabitants of, Jn 4:9. Expect the Messiah, Jn 4:25. Disciples made from the inhabitants of, Jn 4:39–42; Acts 8:5–8, 14–17, 25. Jesus forbids the apostles to preach in the cities of, Mt 10:5.

SAMGAR-NEBO A Babylonian officer. At the siege of Jerusalem, Jer 39:3.

SAMLAH One of the ancient kings of Edom, Gen 36:31–39; 1 Chron 1:47, 48.

SAMOS An island in the Aegean Sea. Touched at by Paul, Acts 20:15.

SAMOTHRACE An island in the Aegean Sea. Touched at by Paul, Acts 16:11.

SAMSON A judge of Israel, Judg 16:31. A Danite, son of Manoah; miraculous birth of; a Nazirite from birth; his mother forbidden to drink wine, or to eat any unclean thing during gestation, Judg 13:2–7, 24, 25. Wants to marry a Philistine woman; kills a lion, Judg 14:1–7. His marriage celebration and the riddle propounded, Judg 14:8–19. Kills 30 Philistines, Judg 14:19. Wife of, estranged, Judg 14:20; 15:1, 2. Is avenged for the estrangement of his wife, Judg 15:3–8. His great strength, Judg 15:7–14; Heb 11:32. Kills 1,000 Philistines with the jawbone of an ass, Judg 15:12–17. Miraculously supplied with water, Judg 15:18, 19. Cohabits with Delilah, her schemes with the Philistines to overcome him, Judg 16:1–20. Is blinded by the Philistines and confined to hard labor in prison; pulls down the pillars of the temple, meets his death and kills many of his enemies, Judg 16:21–31; Heb 11:32.

SAMUEL Miraculous birth of, 1 Sam 1:7–20. Consecrated to God before his birth, 1 Sam 1:11, 21–28. His mother's song of thanksgiving, 1 Sam 2:1–10. Ministered in the house of God, 1 Sam 2:11, 18, 19. Blessed by God, 1 Sam 2:21; 3:19. His vision concerning the family of Eli, 1 Sam 3:1–18. A prophet of the Israelites, 1 Sam 3:20, 21. A judge of Israel, his court at Bethel, Gilgal, Mizpeh, and Ramah, 1 Sam 7:15–17. Organizes the tabernacle service, 1 Chron 9:22; 26:28; 2 Chron 35:18. Israelites repent under his reproofs and admonitions, 1 Sam 7:4–6. The Philistines defeated through his intercession and sacrifices, 1 Sam 7:7–14. Makes his corrupt sons judges in Israel, 1 Sam 8:1–3. People desire a king; he protests, 1 Sam 8:4–22. Anoints Saul king of Israel, 1 Sam 9; 10. Reconfirms the kingdom of Saul, 1 Sam 11:12–15. Reproves Saul; foretells that his dynasty will end, 1 Sam 13:11–15; 15. Anoints David to be king, 1 Sam 16. Shelters David when escaping from Saul, 1 Sam 19:18. Death of; the lament for him, 1 Sam 25:1. Called up by the witch of Endor, 1 Sam 28:3–20. His integrity as judge and ruler, 1 Sam 12:1–5; Ps 99:6; Jer 15:1; Heb 11:32. Chronicles of, 1 Chron 29:29. Sons of, 1 Chron 6:28, 33–38.

SANBALLAT An enemy of the Jews in rebuilding Jerusalem after the captivity, Neh 2:10, 19; 4:7; 13:28.

SANCTIFICATION Is the state of being set apart from the secular and sinful, for a sacred purpose. It is used not only of people, but of days, places, and things, Gen 2:3; Ex 13:1, 2; 29:43; 40:10–13. The Father sanctifies, 1 Thess 5:23; the Son sanctifies, Eph 5:26; Heb 2:11; 13:12; the Holy Spirit sanctifies, Rom 15:15, 16; 2 Thess 2:13; 1 Pet 1:2. As a position, believers are already sanctified, Acts 20:32; 1 Cor 1:2; 6:11; Heb 10:10; Jude 1:1. As to actual experience, they are to regard themselves as dead indeed to sin, Rom 6:1–11, to be holy, as God is holy, 1 Pet 1:15, 16. As to their destiny, they will be perfectly sanctified when Christ returns, Rom 8:29, 30; 1 Jn 3:1–3; Jude 1:24, 25. The words *sanctification, saint,* and *holy, holiness* come from the same Hebrew and Greek roots.

Firstborn of the Israelites sanctified, Ex 13:1, 2. All Israel sanctified, Ex 19:10, 14. Material things sanctified by anointing, Ex 40:9–11. The Lord the sanctifier, Ex 31:12, 13; Lev 20:8; 21:8, 23; 22:9, 16; Ezk 20:12. The altar sanctified the gift, Ex 29:37; 30:29. Tabernacle sanctified by God's presence, Ex 29:43, 44; 40:34, 35.

UNCLASSIFIED SCRIPTURES RELATING TO. Ex 31:13. Tell the people of Israel to rest on my Sabbath day, for the Sabbath is a reminder of the covenant between me and you forever; it helps you to remember that I am Jehovah who makes you holy.

Ex 33:16. If you don't go with us, who will ever know that I and my people have found favor with you, and that we are different from any other people upon the face of the earth?

Lev 21:1. The Lord said to Moses: "Tell the priests never to defile themselves by touching a dead person, [2, 3]unless it is a near relative—a mother, father, son, daughter, brother, or unmarried sister for whom he has special responsibility since she has no husband. [4]For the priest is a leader among his people and he may not ceremonially defile himself as an ordinary person can. [5]The priests shall not clip bald spots in their hair or beards, nor cut their flesh. [6]They shall be holy unto their God, and shall not dishonor and profane his name; otherwise they will be unfit to make food offerings by fire to the Lord their God. [7]A priest shall not marry a prostitute, nor a woman of another tribe, and he shall not marry a divorced woman, for he is a holy man of God. [8]The priest is set apart to offer the sacrifices of your God; he is holy, for I, the Lord who sanctifies you, am holy. [9]The daughter of any priest who becomes a prostitute, thus violating her father's holiness as well as her own, shall be burned alive. [10]The High Priest —anointed with the special anointing oil and wearing the special garments—must not let his hair hang loose in mourning, nor tear his clothing, [11]nor be in the presence of any dead person—not even his father or mother. [12]He shall not leave the sanctuary (when on duty), nor treat my Tabernacle like an ordinary house, for the consecration of the anointing oil of his God is upon him; I am Jehovah. [13]He must marry a virgin. [14, 15]He may not marry a widow, nor a woman who is divorced, nor a prostitute. She must be a virgin from his own tribe, for he must not be the father of children of mixed blood—half priestly and half ordinary." [16, 17]And the Lord said to Moses, "Tell Aaron that any of his descendants from generation to generation who have any bodily defect may not offer the sacrifices to God. [18]For instance, if a man is blind or lame, or has a broken nose or any extra fingers or toes, [19]or has a broken foot or hand, [20]or has a humped back or is a dwarf, or has a defect in his eye, or has pimples or scabby skin, or has imperfect testicles— [21]although he is a descendant of Aaron—he is not permitted to offer the fire sacrifices to the Lord because of his physical defect. [22]However, he shall be fed with the food of the priests from the offerings sacrificed to God, both from the holy and most holy offerings. [23]But he shall not go in behind the veil, nor come near the altar, because of the physical defect; this would defile my sanctuary, for it is Jehovah who sanctifies it."

Jer 1:5. I knew you before you were formed within your mother's womb; before you were born I sanctified you and appointed you as my spokesman to the world.

Ezk 37:28. And when my Temple remains among them, then the nations shall know that I, the Lord, have set Israel apart for special blessings.

Jn 17:17. Make them pure and holy through teaching them your words of truth. [19]And I consecrate myself to meet their need for growth in truth and holiness.

Acts 26:17. Yes, I am going to send you to the Gentiles [18]to open their eyes to their true condition so that they may repent and live in the light of God instead of in Satan's darkness, so that they may receive forgiveness for their sins and God's inheritance along with all people everywhere whose sins are cleansed away, who are set apart by faith in me.

Rom 15:16. For I am, by God's grace, a special messenger from Jesus Christ to you Gentiles, bringing you the Gospel and offering you up as a fragrant sacrifice to God; for you have been made pure and pleasing to him by the Holy Spirit.

1 Cor 1:2. *To:* The Christians in Corinth, invited by God to be his people and made acceptable to him by Christ Jesus. *And to:* All Christians everywhere—whoever calls upon the name of Jesus Christ, our Lord and theirs. [30]For it is from God alone that you have your life through Christ Jesus. He showed us God's plan of salvation; he was the one who made us acceptable to God; he made us pure and holy and gave himself to purchase our salvation.

1 Cor 6:11. There was a time when some of you were just like that but now your sins are washed away, and you are set apart for God, and he has accepted you because of what the Lord Jesus Christ and the Spirit of our God have done for you.

2 Cor 1:21. It is this God who has made you and me into faithful Christians and commissioned us apostles to preach the Good News. [22]He has put his brand upon us—his mark of ownership—and given us his Holy Spirit in our hearts as guarantee that we belong to him, and as the first installment of all that he is going to give us.

Gal 2:20. I have been crucified with Christ: and I myself no longer live, but Christ lives in me. And the real life I now have within this body is a result of my trusting in the Son of God, who loved me and gave himself for me.

Gal 6:14. As for me, God forbid that I should boast about anything except the cross of our Lord Jesus Christ. Because of that cross my interest in all the attractive things of the world was killed long ago, and the world's interest in me is also long dead.

Eph 1:3. How we praise God, the Father of our Lord Jesus Christ, who has blessed us with every blessing in heaven because we belong to Christ. [4]Long ago, even before he made the world, God chose us to be his very own, through what Christ would do for us; he decided then to make us holy in his eyes, without a single fault—we who stand before him covered with his love.

Eph 3:19. And to experience this love for yourselves, though it is so great that you will never see the end of it or fully know or understand it. And so at last you will be filled up with God himself.

Eph 4:7. However, Christ has given each of us special abilities—whatever he wants us to have out of his rich storehouse of gifts. [12]It is that God's people will be equipped to do better work for him, building up the church, the body of Christ, to a position of strength and maturity; [13]until finally we all believe alike about our salvation and about our Savior, God's Son, and all become full-grown in the Lord—yes, to the point of being filled full with Christ. [15, 16]Instead, we will lovingly follow the truth at all times—speaking truly, dealing truly, living truly—and so become more and more in every way like Christ who is the Head of his body, the Church. Under his direction the whole body is fitted together perfectly, and each part in its own special way helps the other parts, so that the whole body is healthy and growing and full of love.

Eph 5:25. And you husbands, show the same kind of love to your wives as Christ showed to the church when he died for her, [26]to make her holy and clean, washed by baptism and God's Word; [27]so that he could give her to himself as a glorious church without a single spot or wrinkle or any other blemish, being holy and without a single fault.

Col 2:11. When you came to Christ he set you free from your evil desires, not by a bodily operation of circumcision but by a spiritual operation, the baptism of your souls.

1 Thess 4:3, 4. For God wants you to be holy and pure, and to keep clear of all sexual sin so that each of you will marry in holiness and honor.

1 Thess 5:23. May the God of peace himself make you entirely pure and devoted to God; and may your spirit and soul and body be kept strong and blameless until that day when our Lord Jesus Christ comes back again.

2 Thess 2:13. God chose from the very first to give you salvation, cleansing you by the work of the Holy Spirit and by your trusting in the Truth. [14]Through us he told you the Good News. Through us he called you to share in the glory of our Lord Jesus Christ.

2 Tim 2:11. I am comforted by this truth, that when we suffer and die for Christ it only means that we will begin living with him in heaven. [21]If you stay away from sin you will be like one of these dishes made of purest gold—the very best in the house—so that Christ himself can use you for his highest purposes.

Heb 2:11. We who have been made holy by Jesus, now have the same Father he has. That is why Jesus is not ashamed to call us his brothers.

Heb 9:14. Just think how much more surely the blood of Christ will transform our lives and hearts. His sacrifice frees us from the worry of having to obey the old rules, and makes us want to serve the living God.

Heb 10:10. Under this new plan we have been forgiven and made clean by Christ's dying for us once and for all. [14]For by that one offering he made forever perfect in the sight of God all those whom he is making holy.

Heb 12:10. Our earthly fathers trained us for a few brief years, doing the best for us that they knew how, but God's correction is always right and for our best good, that we may share his holiness.

Heb 13:12. That is why Jesus suffered and died outside the city, where his blood washed our sins away. [21]May he who became the great Shepherd of the sheep by an everlasting agreement between God and you, signed with his blood, produce in you through the power of Christ all that is pleasing to him.

1 Pet 1:2. Dear friends, God the Father chose you long ago and knew you would become his children. And the Holy Spirit has been at work in your hearts, cleansing you with the blood of Jesus Christ and making you to please him. May God bless you richly and grant you increasing freedom from all anxiety and fear.

2 Pet 1:2. Do you want more and more of God's kindness and peace? Then learn to know him better and better. [3]For as you know him better, he will give you, through his great power, everything you need for living a truly good life: he even shares his own glory and his own goodness with us! [4]And by that same mighty power he has given us all the other rich and wonderful blessings he promised; for instance, the promise to save us from the lust and rottenness all around us, and to give us his own character.

1 Jn 1:9. But if we confess our sins to him, he can be depended on to forgive us and to cleanse us from every wrong. (And it is perfectly proper for God to do this for us because Christ died to wash away our sins.)

Jude 1:1. From: Jude, a servant of Jesus Christ, and a brother of James. *To:* Christians everywhere —beloved of God and chosen by him. [25]And he is able to keep you from slipping and falling away, and to bring you, sinless and perfect, into his glorious presence with mighty shouts of everlasting joy. Amen.

Rev 7:14. "These are the ones coming out of the Great Tribulation," he said; "they washed their robes and whitened them by the blood of the Lamb."

See *Holiness; Regeneration; Redemption; Salvation; Sin, Forgiveness of.*

SANCTUARY A holy place of worship. In the tabernacle, Lev 10:13. Divine dwelling place, Deut 12:11. Reverence for, Num 18:5–7. Responsibility of high priest, Ex 27:21; Lev 24:34; Num 18: 5–7 The holy place in the temple, 1 Kgs 6:20, 23–28.

FIGURATIVE. Ezk 11:16; Jn 2:19, 21.

See *Congregation; Tabernacle; Temple.*

SANDAL See *Shoe.*

SANHEDRIN The 70 Hebrews who formed the supreme court of justice in Israel. The word is rendered *court* or *Supreme Court* in Mt 5:22; 26: 59; Mk 14:55; 15:1; Lk 22:66; and *council* in Jn 11: 47; Acts 4:15; 6:12; 22:30; 23:1; 24:20. The Sanhedrin was made up of chief priests, scribes and elders of the people, Mt 26:3, including Pharisees and Sadducees. Caiaphas presided in Christ's day, Mt 26:3, Ananias in Paul's, Acts 23:2.

See *Government.*

SANITATION CARCASSES. Lev 5:2. Anyone touching anything ceremonially unclean—such as the dead body of an animal forbidden for food, wild or domesticated, or the dead body of some forbidden insect—is guilty, even though he wasn't aware of touching it.

Lev 10:4. Then Moses called for Misha-el and Elzaphon, Aaron's cousins, the sons of Uzziel, and told them, "Go and get the charred bodies from before the Tabernacle, and carry them outside the camp." [5]So they went over and got them, and carried them out in their coats as Moses had told them to.

Lev 11:24. Anyone touching their dead bodies shall be defiled until the evening, [25]and must wash his clothes immediately. He must also quarantine himself until nightfall, as being ceremonially defiled. [26]You are also defiled by touching any animal with only semi-parted hoofs, or any animal that does not chew the cud. [27]Any animal that walks on paws is forbidden to you as food. Anyone touching the dead body of such an animal shall be defiled until evening. [28]Anyone carrying away the carcass shall wash his clothes and be ceremonially defiled until evening; for it is forbidden to you. [31]Anyone touching their dead bodies shall be defiled until evening, [32]and anything upon which the carcass falls shall be defiled—any article of wood, or of clothing, a rug, or a sack; anything it touches must be put into water, and is defiled until evening. After that it may be used again. [33]If it falls into a pottery bowl, anything in the bowl is defiled, and you shall smash the bowl. [34]If the water used to cleanse the defiled article touches any food, all of it is defiled. Any drink which is in the defiled bowl is also contaminated. [35]If the dead body of such an animal touches any clay oven, it is defiled and must be smashed. [36]If the body falls into a spring or cistern where there is water, that water is not defiled; yet anyone who pulls out the carcass is defiled. [37]And if the carcass touches grain to be sown in the field, it is not contaminated; [38]but if the seeds are wet and the carcass falls upon it, the seed is defiled. [39]If an animal which you are permitted to eat dies of disease, anyone touching the carcass shall be defiled until evening. [40]Also, anyone eating its meat or carrying away its carcass shall wash his clothes and be defiled until evening.

Lev 22:4. And any priest who touches a dead person, . . . [6]that priest shall be defiled until evening, and shall not eat of the holy sacrifices until after he has bathed that evening.

Num 9:6. But as it happened, some of the men had just attended a funeral, and were ceremonially defiled by having touched the dead, so they couldn't eat the Passover lamb that night. [10]"If any of the people of Israel, now or in the generations to come, are defiled at Passover time because of touching a dead body, or if they are on a journey and cannot be present, they may still celebrate the Passover, but one month later."

Num 19:11. Anyone who touches a dead human body shall be defiled for seven days. [12]and must purify himself the third and seventh days with water (run through the ashes of the red heifer); then he will be purified; but if he does not do this on the third day, he will continue to be defiled even after the seventh day. [13]Anyone who touches a dead person and does not purify himself in the manner specified, has defiled the Tabernacle of the Lord, and shall be excommunicated from Israel. The cleansing water was not sprinkled upon him, so the defilement continues. [14]When a man dies in a tent, these are the various regulations: Everyone who enters the tent, and those who are in it at the time, shall be defiled seven days. [15]Any container in the tent without a lid over it is defiled. [16]If someone out in a field touches the corpse of someone who has been killed in battle, or who has died in any other way, or if he even touches a bone or a grave, he shall be defiled seven days.

Num 31:19. Now stay outside of the camp for seven days, all of you who have killed anyone or touched a dead body. Then purify yourselves and your captives on the third and seventh days.

Deut 21:22. If a man has committed a crime worthy of death, and is executed and then hanged on a tree, [23]his body shall not remain on the tree overnight. You must bury him the same day, for anyone hanging on a tree is cursed of God. Don't defile the land the Lord your God has given you.

CHILDBIRTH. Ezk 16:4. When you were born, no one cared for you. When I first saw you, your umbilical cord was uncut, and you had been neither washed nor rubbed with salt nor clothed.

CIRCUMCISION. See *Circumcision.*

CONTAGION. Lev 5:2. Anyone touching anything ceremonially unclean—such as the dead body of an animal forbidden for food, wild or domesticated, or the dead body of some forbidden insect—is guilty, even though he wasn't aware of touching it. [3]Or if he touches human discharge of any kind, he becomes guilty as soon as he realizes that he has touched it.

Lev 7:19. Any meat that comes into contact with anything that is ceremonially unclean shall not be eaten, but burned. [21]Anyone who touches anything that is ceremonially unclean, whether it is uncleanness from man or beast, and then eats the peace offering, shall be cut off from his people, for he has defiled what is holy.

Lev 11:24. Anyone touching their dead bodies shall be defiled until the evening, [25]and must wash his clothes immediately. He must also quarantine himself until nightfall, as being ceremonially defiled. [26]You are also defiled by touching any animal with only semi-parted hoofs, or any animal that does not chew the cud. [27]Any animal that walks on paws is forbidden to you as food. Anyone touching the dead body of such an animal shall be defiled until evening. [28]Anyone carrying away the carcass shall wash his clothes and be ceremonially defiled until evening; for it is forbidden to you. [31]Anyone touching their dead bodies shall be defiled until evening, [32]and anything upon which the carcass falls shall be defiled—any article of wood, or of clothing, a rug, or a sack; anything it touches must be put into water, and is defiled until evening. After that it may be used again. [33]If it falls into a pottery bowl, anything in the bowl is defiled, and you shall smash the bowl. [34]If the water used to cleanse the defiled article touches any food, all of it is defiled. Any drink which is in the defiled bowl is also contaminated. [35]If the dead body of such an animal touches any clay oven, it is defiled and must be smashed. [36]If the body falls into a spring or cistern where there is water, that water is not defiled; yet anyone who pulls out the carcass is defiled. [37]And if the carcass touches grain to be sown in the field, it is not contaminated; [38]but if the seeds are wet and the carcass falls upon it, the seed is defiled. [39]If an animal which you are permitted to eat dies of disease, anyone touching the carcass shall be defiled until evening. [40]Also, anyone eating its meat or carrying away its carcass shall wash his clothes and be defiled until evening.

Lev 13:2. If anyone notices a swelling in his skin, or a scab or boil or pimple with transparent skin, leprosy is to be suspected. He must be brought to Aaron the priest or to one of his sons [3]for the spot to be examined. If the hair in this spot turns white, and if the spot looks to be more than skin deep, it is leprosy, and the priest must declare him a leper. [45]Anyone who is discovered to have leprosy must tear his clothes and let his hair grow in wild disarray, and cover his upper lip and call out as he goes, "I am a leper, I am a leper." [46]As long as the disease lasts, he is defiled and must live outside the camp. [47, 48]If leprosy is suspected in a woolen or linen garment or fabric, or in a piece of leather or leather-work. [52]And he must burn the clothing, fabric, linen or woolen covering, or leather article, for it is contagious and must be destroyed by fire.

Lev 14:2. Regulations concerning a person whose leprosy disappears: [3]The priest shall go out of the camp to examine him. If the priest sees that the leprosy is gone. [8]Then the man who is cured shall wash his clothes, shave off all his hair, and bathe himself, and return to live inside the camp; however, he must stay outside his tent for seven days. [9]The seventh day he shall again shave all the hair from his head, beard, and eyebrows, and wash his clothes and bathe, and shall then be declared fully cured of his leprosy. [34]"When you arrive in the land of Canaan which I have given you, and I place leprosy in some house there, [35]then the owner of the house shall come and report to the priest, 'It seems to me that there may be leprosy in my house!' [36]The priest shall order the house to be emptied before he examines it, so that everything in the house will not be declared contaminated if he decides that there is leprosy there. [37]If he finds greenish or reddish streaks in the walls of the house which seem to be beneath the surface of the wall, [38]he shall close up the house for seven days, [39]and return the seventh day to look at it again. If the spots have spread in the wall, [40]then the priest shall order the removal of the spotted section of wall, and the material must be thrown into a defiled place outside the city. [41]Then he shall order the inside walls of the house scraped thoroughly, and the scrapings dumped in a defiled place outside the city. [42]Other stones shall be brought to replace those that have been removed, new mortar used, and the house replastered. [43]But if the spots appear again, [44]the priest shall come again and look, and if he sees that the spots have spread, it is leprosy, and the house is defiled. [45]Then he shall order the destruction of the house—all its stones, timbers, and mortar shall be carried out of the city to a defiled place."

Num 5:2. "Inform the people of Israel that they must expel all lepers from the camp, and all who have open sores, or who have been defiled by touching a dead person. [3]This applies to men and women alike. Remove them so that they will not defile the camp where I live among you." [4]These instructions were put into effect.

Num 9:6. But as it happened, some of the men had just attended a funeral, and were ceremonially defiled by having touched the dead, so they couldn't eat the Passover lamb that night. [10]"If any of the people of Israel, now or in the generations to come, are defiled at Passover time because of touching a dead body, or if they are on a journey and cannot be present, they may still celebrate the Passover, but one month later."

Num 19:11. Anyone who touches a dead human body shall be defiled for seven days, [12]and must purify himself the third and seventh days with water (run through the ashes of the red heifer); then he will be purified; but if he does not do this on the third day, he will continue to be defiled even after the seventh day. [13]Anyone who touches a dead person and does not purify himself in the manner specified, has defiled the Tabernacle of the Lord, and shall be excommunicated from Israel. The cleansing water was not sprinkled upon him, so the defilement continues. [14]When a man dies in a tent, these are the various regulations: Everyone who enters the tent, and those who are in it at the time, shall be defiled seven days. [15]Any container in the tent without a lid over it is defiled. [16]If someone out in a field touches the corpse of someone who has been killed in battle, or who has died in any other way, or if he even touches a bone or a grave, he shall be defiled seven days. [22]And anything a defiled person touches shall be defiled until evening.

Deut 23:10. Any man who becomes ceremonially defiled because of a seminal emission during the night must leave the camp, [11]and stay outside until the evening; then he shall bathe himself and return at sunset.

Deut 24:8. Be very careful to follow the instructions of the priest in cases of leprosy, for I have given him rules and guidelines you must obey to the letter.

DISINFECTION. Lev 2:13. Every offering must be seasoned with salt, because the salt is a reminder of God's covenant.

Lev 7:19. Any meat that comes into contact with anything that is ceremonially unclean shall not be eaten, but burned.

Lev 11:24. Anyone touching their dead bodies shall be defiled until the evening, [25]and must wash his clothes immediately. He must also quarantine himself until nightfall, as being ceremonially defiled. [26]You are also defiled by touching any animal with only semi-parted hoofs, or any animal that does not chew the cud. [27]Any animal that walks on paws is forbidden to you as food. Anyone touching the dead body of such an animal shall be defiled until evening. [28]Anyone carrying away the carcass shall wash his clothes and be ceremonially defiled until evening; for it is forbidden to you. [29, 30]These are the forbidden small animals which scurry about your feet or crawl upon the ground: The mole, the rat, the great lizard, the gecko, the mouse, the lizard, the snail, the chameleon. [31]Anyone touching their dead bodies shall be defiled until evening, [32]and anything upon which the carcass falls shall be defiled—any article of wood, or of clothing, a rug, or a sack; anything it touches must be put into water, and is defiled until evening. After that it may be used again. [33]If it falls into a pottery bowl, anything in the bowl is defiled, and you shall smash the bowl. [34]If the water used to cleanse the defiled article touches any food, all of it is defiled. Any drink which is in the defiled bowl is also contaminated. [35]If the dead body of such an animal touches any clay oven, it is defiled and must be smashed. [36]If the body falls into a spring or cistern where there is water, that water is not defiled; yet anyone who pulls out the carcass is defiled. [37]And if the carcass touches grain to be sown in the field, it is not contaminated; [38]but if the seeds are wet and the carcass falls upon it, the seed is defiled. [39]If an animal which you are permitted to eat dies of disease, anyone touching the carcass shall be defiled until evening. [40]Also, anyone eating its meat or carrying away its carcass shall wash his clothes and be defiled until evening.

Num 31:19. Now stay outside of the camp for seven days, all of you who have killed anyone or touched a dead body. Then purify yourselves and your captives on the third and seventh days. [20]Remember also to purify all your garments and everything made of leather, goat's hair, or wood. [22]Anything that will stand heat—such as gold, silver, bronze, iron, tin, or lead—[23]shall be passed through fire in order to be made ceremonially pure; it must then be further purified with the purification water. But anything that won't stand heat shall be purified by the water alone. [24]On the seventh day you must wash your clothes and be purified, and then you may come back into the camp.

See *Purification.*

FILTH, DISPOSITION OF. Ex 29:14. Then take the body, including the skin and the dung, outside the camp and burn it as a sin offering. [34]If any of the meat or bread remains until the morning, burn it; it shall not be eaten, for it is holy. Lev 7:17, 18; 19:6.

Lev 4:11, 12. But the remainder of the young bull—the skin, meat, head, legs, internal organs, and intestines—shall be carried to a ceremonially clean place outside the camp—a place where the ashes are brought from the altar—and burned there on a wood fire. *v.* 21.

Lev 7:19. Any meat that comes into contact with anything that is ceremonially unclean shall not be eaten, but burned.

Lev 8:17. The carcass of the young bull, with its hide and dung, was burned outside the camp, as the Lord had commanded Moses. [32]Anything left of the meat and bread must be burned.

Lev 9:11. But he burned the meat and hide outside the camp.

Lev 16:27. And the young bull and the goat used for the sin offering (their blood was taken into the Holy Place by Aaron, to make atonement) shall be carried outside the camp and burned, including the hides and internal organs. [28]Afterwards, the person doing the burning shall wash his clothes and bathe himself and then return to camp.

Deut 23:12. The toilet area shall be outside the camp. [13]Each man must have a spade as part of his equipment; after every bowel movement he must dig a hole with the spade and cover the excrement.

Heb 13:11. Under the system of Jewish laws the high priest brought the blood of the slain animals into the sanctuary as a sacrifice for sin, and then the bodies of the animals were burned outside the city. Lev 6:30.

FOOD. Lev 3:17. This is a permanent law throughout your land, that you shall eat neither fat nor blood.

Lev 7:15. After the animal has been sacrificed and presented to the Lord as a peace offering to show special appreciation and thanksgiving to him, its meat is to be eaten that same day, and none left to be eaten the next day. [16]However, if someone brings a sacrifice that is not for thanksgiving, but is because of a vow or is simply a voluntary offering to the Lord, any portion of the sacrifice that is not eaten the day it is sacrificed may be eaten the next day. [17, 18]But anything left over until the third day shall be burned. For if any of it is eaten on the third day, the Lord will not accept it; it will have no value as a sacrifice, and there will be no credit to the one who brought it to be offered; and the priest who eats it shall be guilty, for it is detestable to the Lord, and the person who eats it must answer for his sin. [19]Any meat that comes into contact with anything that is ceremonially unclean shall not be eaten, but burned; and as for the meat that may be eaten, it may be eaten only by a person who is ceremonially clean. [23]Tell the people of Israel never to eat fat, whether from oxen, sheep, or goats. [24]The fat of an animal that dies of disease, or is attacked and killed by wild animals, may be used for other purposes, but never eaten. [25]Anyone who eats fat from an offering sacrificed by fire to the Lord shall be outlawed from his people. [26, 27]Never eat blood, whether of birds or animals. Anyone who does shall be excommunicated from his people.

Lev 11:2, 3. Tell the people of Israel that the animals which may be used for food include any animals with cloven hooves which chews its cud. [4-7]This means that the following may *not* be eaten: The camel (it chews the cud but does not have cloven hooves); the coney, or rock badger (because although it chews the cud, it does not have cloven hooves); the hare (because although it chews the cud, it does not have cloven hooves); the swine (because although it has cloven hooves, it does not chew the cud). [8]You may not eat their meat or even touch their dead bodies; they are forbidden foods for you. [9]As to fish, you may eat whatever has fins and scales, whether taken from rivers or from the sea; [10]but all other water creatures are strictly forbidden to you. [11]You mustn't eat their meat or even touch their dead bodies. [12]I'll repeat it again—any water creature that does not have fins or scales is forbidden to you. [13-19]Among the birds, these are the ones you may *not* eat: The eagle, the metire, the osprey, the falcon (all kinds), the kite, the raven (all kinds), the ostrich, the nighthawk, the seagull, the hawk (all kinds), the owl, the cormorant, the ibis, the marsh hen, the pelican, the vulture, the stork, the heron (all kinds), the hoopoe, the bat. [20]Flying insects with four legs must not be eaten, [21, 22]with the exception of those that jump; locusts of all varieties—ordinary locusts, bald locusts, crickets, and grasshoppers—may be eaten. [23]All other things that fly and have four feet are forbidden to you. [26]You are also defiled by touching any animal with only semi-parted hoofs, or any animal that does not chew the cud. [27]Any animal that walks on paws is forbidden to you as food. Anyone touching the dead body of such an animal shall be defiled until evening. [29, 30]These are the forbidden small animals which scurry about your feet or crawl upon the ground: The mole, the rat, the great lizard, the gecko, the mouse, the lizard, the snail, the chameleon. [31]Anyone touching their dead bodies shall be defiled until evening, [32]and anything upon which the carcass falls shall be defiled—any article of wood, or of clothing, a rug, or a sack; anything it touches must be put into water, and is defiled until evening. After that it may be used again. [33]If it falls into a pottery bowl, anything in the bowl is defiled, and you shall smash the bowl. [34]If the water used to cleanse the defiled article touches any food, all of it is defiled. Any drink which is in the defiled bowl is also contaminated. [35]If the dead body of such an animal touches any clay oven, it is defiled and must be smashed. [36]If the body falls into a spring or cistern where there is water, that water is not defiled; yet anyone who pulls out the carcass is defiled. [37]And if the carcass touches grain to be sown in the field, it is not contaminated; [38]but if the seeds are wet and the carcass falls upon it, the seed is defiled. [39]If an animal which you are permitted to eat dies of disease, anyone touching the carcass shall be defiled until evening. [40]Also, anyone eating its meat or carrying away its carcass shall wash his clothes and be defiled until evening. [41, 42]Animals that crawl shall not be eaten. This includes all reptiles that slither along upon their bellies as well as those that have legs. No crawling thing with many feet may be eaten, for it is defiled. [43]Do not defile yourselves by touching it. [46]These are the laws concerning animals, birds, and whatever swims in the water or crawls upon the ground. [47]These are the distinctions between what is ceremonially clean and may be eaten, and what is ceremonially defiled and may not be eaten, among all animal life upon the earth.

Lev 17:10. And I will turn my face against anyone, whether an Israelite or a foreigner living among you, who eats blood in any form. I will excommunicate him from his people. [11]For the life of the flesh is in the blood, and I have given you the blood to sprinkle upon the altar as an atonement for your souls; it is the blood that makes atonement because it is the life. [12]That is the reasoning behind my decree to the people of Israel, that neither they, nor any foreigner living among them, may eat blood. [13]Anyone, whether an Israelite or a foreigner living among you, who goes hunting and kills an animal or bird of a kind permitted for food, must pour out the blood and cover it with dust, [14]for the blood is the life. That is why I told the people of Israel never to eat it, for the life of every bird and animal is its blood. Therefore, anyone who eats blood must be excommunicated. [15]And anyone—native born or foreigner—who eats the dead body of an animal that dies of itself, or is torn by wild animals, must wash his clothes and bathe himself and be defiled until evening; after that he shall be declared cleansed.

Lev 19:5. When you sacrifice a peace offering to the Lord, offer it correctly so that it will be accepted: [6]Eat it the same day you offer it, or the next day at the latest; any remaining until the third day must be burned. [7]For any of it eaten on the third day is repulsive to me, and will not be accepted. [8]If you eat it on the third day you are guilty, for you profane the holiness of Jehovah, and you shall be excommunicated from Jehovah's people. [26]You must not eat meat with undrained blood.

Lev 22:8. He may not eat any animal that dies of itself or is torn by wild animals, for this will defile him.

Deut 12:16. The only restriction is that you are not to eat the blood—pour it out on the ground, like water. [20-23]If, when the Lord enlarges your borders, the central altar is too far away from you, then your flocks and herds may be butchered on your own farms, just as you do now with gazelle and deer. And even persons who are ceremonially defiled may eat them. The only restriction is never to eat the blood, for the blood is the life, and you shall not eat the life with the meat. [24, 25]Instead, pour the blood out upon the earth. If you do, all will be well with you and your children. Deut 15: 22, 23.

Deut 14:3, 4, 5. You are not to eat any animal I have declared to be ceremonially defiled. These are the animals you may eat: The ox, the sheep, the goat, the deer, the gazelle, the roebuck, the wild goat, the ibex, the antelope, and the mountain sheep. [6]Any animal that has cloven hooves and chews the cud may be eaten, [7]but if the animal doesn't have both, it may not be eaten. So you may not eat the camel, the hare, or the coney. They chew the cud but do not have cloven hooves. [8]Pigs may not be eaten because, although they have cloven hooves, they don't chew the cud. You may not even touch the dead bodies of such animals. [9]Only sea animals with fins and scales may be eaten; [10]all other kinds are ceremonially defiled. [11-18]You may eat any bird except the following: The eagle, the buzzard, the falcon (any variety), the raven (any variety), the ostrich, the nighthawk, the sea gull, the hawk (any variety), the screech owl, the great owl, the horned owl, the pelican, the vulture, the cormorant, the stork, the heron (any variety), the hoopoe, the bat. [19, 20]With certain exceptions, winged insects are a defilement to you and may not be eaten. [21]Don't eat anything that has died a natural death. However, a foreigner among you may eat it. You may give it or sell it to him, but don't eat it yourself, for you are holy to the Lord your God. You must not boil a young goat in its mother's milk. [26]When you arrive, use the money to buy an ox, a sheep, some wine, or some strong drink, to feast there before the Lord your God, and to rejoice with your household.

GLUTTONY, DISEASE RESULTING FROM. Num 11:18. "And tell the people to purify themselves, for tomorrow they shall have meat to eat. Tell them, 'The Lord has heard your tearful complaints about all you left behind in Egypt, and he is going to give you meat. You shall eat it, [19, 20]not for just a day or two, or five or ten or even twenty! For one whole month you will have meat until you vomit it from your noses; for you have rejected the Lord who is here among you, and you have wept for Egypt.' " [31]The Lord sent a wind that brought quail from the sea, and let them fall into the camp and all around it! As far as one could walk in a day in any direction, there were quail flying three or four feet above the ground. [32]So the people caught and killed quail all that day and through the night and all the next day too! The least anyone gathered was 100 bushels! Quail were spread out all around the camp. [33]But as everyone began eating the meat, the anger of the Lord rose against the people and he killed large numbers of them with a plague.

PENALTIES CONCERNING. Deut 28:15. If you won't listen to the Lord your God and won't obey these laws I am giving you today, then all of these curses shall come upon you. [21]He will send disease among you until you are destroyed from the face of the land which you are about to enter and possess. [22]He will send tuberculosis, fever, infections, plague, and war. He will blight your crops, covering them with mildew. All these devastations shall pursue you until you perish. [27]He will send upon you Egyptian boils, tumors, scurvy, and itch, for none of which will there be a remedy. [35]The Lord will cover you with boils from head to foot. [45]All these curses shall pursue and overtake you until you are destroyed—all because you refuse to listen to the Lord your God. [59]Then Jehovah will send perpetual plagues upon you and upon your children. [60]He will bring upon you all the diseases of Egypt which you feared so much, and they shall plague the land. [61]And that is not all! The Lord will bring upon you every sickness and plague there is, even those not mentioned in this book, until you are destroyed. [62]There will be few of you left, though before you were as numerous as stars. All this if you do not listen to the Lord your God.

QUARANTINE. Lev 13:45. Anyone who is discovered to have leprosy must tear his clothes and let his hair grow in wild disarray, and cover his upper lip and call out as he goes, "I am a leper, I am a leper." [46]As long as the disease lasts, he is defiled and must live outside the camp.

Lev 14:2. Regulations concerning a person whose leprosy disappears: "[3]The priest shall go out of the camp to examine him. If the priest sees that the leprosy is gone. [8]Then the man who is cured shall wash his clothes, shave off all his hair, and bathe himself, and return to live inside the camp; however, he must stay outside his tent for seven days."

Lev 15:19. Whenever a woman menstruates, she shall be in a state of ceremonial defilement for seven days afterwards, and during that time anyone touching her shall be defiled until evening.

Num 5:2. Inform the people of Israel that they must expel all lepers from the camp, and all who have open sores, or who have been defiled by touching a dead person. [3]This applies to men and women alike. Remove them so that they will not defile the camp where I live among you.

Num 31:14. But Moses was very angry with the army officers and battalion leaders. [15]"Why have you let all the women live?" he demanded. [16]"These are the very ones who followed Balaam's advice and caused the people of Israel to worship idols on Mount Peor, and they are the cause of the plague that destroyed us. [17]Now kill all the boys and all the women who have had sexual intercourse."

Deut 23:10. Any man who becomes ceremonially defiled because of a seminal emission during the night must leave the camp, [11]and stay outside until the evening; then he shall bathe himself and return at sunset.

Instances of. Num 12:10. As the Cloud moved from above the Tabernacle, Miriam suddenly became white with leprosy. [14]And the Lord said to Moses, "If her father had but spit in her face she would be defiled seven days. Let her be confined outside the camp for seven days, and after that she can come back again." [15]So Miriam was excluded from the camp for seven days, and the people waited until she was brought back in before they traveled again.

2 Kgs 7:3. Now there were four lepers sitting outside the city gates.

2 Kgs 15:5. Because of this the Lord struck him with leprosy, which lasted until the day of his death; so he lived in a house by himself. 2 Chron 26:21.

Lk 17:12. And as they entered a village there, ten lepers stood at a distance.

VENEREAL DISEASE AND GENITAL HYGIENE. Lev 15:2. "Any man who has a genital discharge is ceremonially defiled. [3]This applies not only while the discharge is active, but also for a time after it heals. [4]Any bed he lies on and anything he sits on is contaminated; [5]so anyone touching the man's bed is ceremonially defiled until evening, and must wash his clothes and bathe himself. [6]Anyone sitting on a seat the man has sat upon while defiled is himself ceremonially unclean until evening, and must wash his clothes and bathe himself. [7]The same instructions apply to anyone touching him. [8]Anyone he spits on is ceremonially unclean until evening, and must wash his clothes and bathe himself. [9]Any saddle he rides on is defiled. [10]Anyone touching or carrying anything else that was beneath him shall be defiled until evening, and must wash his clothes and bathe himself. [11]If the defiled man touches anyone without first rinsing his hands, that person must wash his clothes and bathe himself and be defiled until evening. [12]Any earthen pot touched by the defiled man must be broken, and every wooden utensil must be rinsed in water. [13]When the discharge stops, he shall begin a seven-day cleansing ceremony by washing his clothes and bathing in running water. [16]Whenever a man's semen goes out from him, he shall take a complete bath and be unclean until the evening. [17]Any clothing or bedding the semen spills on must be washed and remain ceremonially defiled until evening. [18]After sexual intercourse, the woman as well as the man must bathe, and they are ceremonially defiled until the next evening. [19]Whenever a woman menstruates, she shall be in a state of ceremonial defilement for seven days afterwards, and during that time anyone touching her shall be defiled until evening. [20]Anything she lies on or sits on during that time shall be defiled. [21-23]Anyone touching her bed or anything she sits upon shall wash his clothes and bathe himself and be ceremonially defiled until evening. [24]A man having sexual intercourse with her during this time is ceremonially defiled for seven days, and every bed he lies upon shall be defiled. [Lev 20:18.] [25]If the menstrual flow continues after the normal time, or at some irregular time during the month, the same rules apply as indicated above, [26]so that anything she lies upon during that time is defiled, just as it would be during her normal menstrual period, and everything she sits on is in a similar state of defilement. [27]Anyone touching her bed or anything she sits on shall be defiled, and shall wash his clothes and bathe and be defiled until evening. [28]Seven days after the menstruating stops, she is no longer ceremonially defiled. [31]In this way you shall cleanse the people of Israel from their defilement, lest they die because of defiling my Tabernacle that is among them." [32]This, then, is the law for the man who is defiled by a genital disease or by a seminal emission; [33]and for a woman's menstrual period; and for anyone who has sexual intercourse with her while she is in her period of defilement afterwards.

Lev 22:4. No priest who is a leper or who has a running sore may eat the holy sacrifices until healed. And any priest who touches a dead person, or who is defiled by a seminal emission, [6]that priest shall be defiled until evening, and shall not eat of the holy sacrifices until after he has bathed that evening.

WOMEN IN CHILDBIRTH. Lev 12:2. When a baby boy is born, the mother shall be ceremonially defiled for seven days, and under the same restrictions as during her monthly periods. [4]Then, for the next thirty-three days, while she is recovering from her ceremonial impurity, she must not touch anything sacred, nor enter the Tabernacle. [5]When a baby girl is born, the mother's ceremonial impurity shall last two weeks, during which time she will be under the same restrictions as during menstruation. Then for a further sixty-six days she shall continue her recovery.

See *Ablution; Defilement; Leprosy; Purification; Uncleanness.*

SANSANNAH A city of Judah, Josh 15:21–32.

SAPH Called also *Sippai.* A Philistine giant, 2 Sam 21:18; 1 Chron 20:4.

SAPPHIRA Wife of Ananias. Falsehood and death of, Acts 5:1–10.

SAPPHIRE A precious stone, Job 28:6, 16; Isa 54:11; Ezk 28:13. Set in the chestpiece, Ex 28:18. The color of the sky, Ezk 1:26. Seen in the foundation of the New Jerusalem in John's apocalyptic vision, Rev 21:18–20. Not the modern sapphire; possibly lapis lazuli. See Bible dictionaries.

SARAH Called also *Sarai.* Wife of Abraham, Gen 11:29–31; 12:5. Half-sister to Abraham, Gen 12:10–20; 20:11, 12. Abraham represents her as his sister, and Abimelech, king of Gerar, takes her; she is restored to Abraham by means of a dream, Gen 20:1–14. Is sterile; gives her maid, Hagar, to Abraham as a wife, Gen 16:1–3. Her jealousy of Hagar, Gen 16:4–6; 21:9–14. Her miraculous conception of Isaac, Gen 17:15–21; 18:9–15. Name changed from Sarai to Sarah, Gen 17:15. Gives birth to Isaac, Gen 21:1–3, 6–8. Death and burial of, Gen 23; 25:9, 10. Character of, Heb 11:11; 1 Pet 3:5, 6.

SARAPH A descendent of Shelah, 1 Chron 4:21, 22.

SARCASM INSTANCES OF. Cain's self-justifying argument when God asked him where Abel was, Gen 4:9. Israelites reproaching Moses, Ex 14:11. God reproaching Israel, Num 11:19, 20; Judg 10:14. Balak reproaching Balaam, Num 24:11. Joshua to descendants of Joseph, Josh 17:15. By Jotham, Judg 9:7–19; Samson, Judg 14:18. The men of Jabesh to Nahash, 1 Sam 11:10. Eliab to David, 1 Sam 17:28. Elijah to the priests of Baal, 1 Kgs 18:27. David's reply to Michal's irony, 2 Sam 6:21. Ahab's reply to Ben-hadad, 1 Kgs 20:11. Joash to Amaziah, 2 Kgs 14:9, 10; 2 Chron 25:18, 19. Rabshakeh to Hezekiah, 2 Kgs 18:23, 24. Sanballat's address to the army of Samaria, Neh 4:1, 2. Zophar to Job, Job 11:12. Job to Zophar, Job 12:2, 3. The persecutors of Jesus, Mt 27:28, 29; Lk 23:11; Jn 19:2, 3, 5, 15. Paul, 1 Tim 4:7. Agrippa to Paul, Acts 26:28.

See *Irony; Satire.*

SARDIS A city in Asia. One of the seven churches in, Rev 1:11; 3:1–4.

SARDIUS See *Ruby.*

SARDONYX A precious stone.

FIGURATIVE. In the foundation of the heavenly city, Rev 21:18–20.

SARGON A king of Assyria, Isa 20:1.

SARID A city on the boundary of the tribe of Zebulun, Josh 19:10.

SARSECHIM An officer of Babylon. Present at the taking of Jerusalem, Jer 39:3.

SASH Worn by the high priest, Ex 28:4, 39; 39:29; Lev 8:7; 16:4; other priests, Ex 28:40; 29:9; Lev 8:13; women, Isa 3:24. Embroidered, Ex 28:8, 39.

See *Belt; Loincloth.*

SATAN Called Abaddon, Rev 9:11; Accuser of our brothers, Rev 12:10; Apollyon, Rev 9:11; Beelzebub, Mt 12:24; Lk 11:15; the Destroyer, Rev 9:11; the devil, Lk 4:6, 7; 2 Cor 6:15; Rev 20:2; Dragon, Rev 20:2; enemy, Mt 13:39; 1 Pet 5:8; the evil, Mt 13:19; father of liars, Jn 8:44; liar, Jn 8:44; Lucifer, son of the morning, Isa 14:12; king of demons, Mk 3:22; Lk 11:15; king of devils, Mt 12:24; king of Tyre, Ezk 28:12–15; murderer, Jn 8:44; old serpent, Rev 12:9; 20:2; prince of the bottomless pit, Rev 9:11; of this world, Jn 12:31; 14:30; 16:11; of the power of the air, Eph 2:2; red Dragon, Rev 12:3; Satan, 1 Chron 21:1; Job 1:6; Jn 13:27; Acts 5:3; 26:18; Rom 16:20; serpent, Gen 3:4, 14; Tempter, Mk 14:38; the god of this evil world, 2 Cor 4:4.

Against the nations, Isa 14:12; his willful sin, Isa 14:13, 14; his doom, Isa 14:15–17; his wisdom and beauty, Ezk 28:12; his glory when he was first created, Ezk 28:13; his original ministry, Ezk 28:14; sin found in him, Ezk 28:15; his final destruction, Ezk 28:16–19, Rev 20:10.

Kingdom of, to be destroyed, Mt 12:29; 13:30; Lk 11:21, 22; 1 Jn 3:8. Followers of, Rev 2:9; 3:9.

UNCLASSIFIED SCRIPTURES RELATING TO. Gen 3:1. The serpent was the craftiest of all the creatures the Lord God had made. So the serpent came to the woman. "Really?" he asked. "*None* of the fruit in the garden? God says you mustn't eat *any* of it?" [4]"That's a lie!" the serpent hissed. "You'll not die! [5]God knows very well that the instant you eat it you will become like him, for your eyes will be opened—you will be able to distinguish good from evil!" [14]So the Lord God said to the serpent, "This is your punishment: You are singled out from among all the domestic and wild animals of the whole earth—to be cursed. You shall grovel in the dust as long as you live, crawling along on your belly. [15]From now on you and the woman will be enemies, as will all of your offspring and hers. And I will put the fear of you into the woman, and between your offspring and hers. He shall strike you on your head, while you will strike at his heel."

1 Chron 21:1. Then Satan brought disaster upon Israel, for he made David decide to take a census.

Job 1:6. One day as the angels came to present themselves before the Lord, Satan, the Accuser came with them. 7"Where have you come from?" the Lord asked Satan. And Satan replied, "From patroling the earth." 8Then the Lord asked Satan, "Have you noticed my servant Job? He is the finest man in all the earth—a good man who fears God and will have nothing to do with evil." 9"Why shouldn't he, when you pay him so well?" Satan scoffed. 10"You have always protected him and his home and his property from all harm. You have prospered everything he does—look how rich he is! No wonder he 'worships' you! 11But just take away his wealth, and you'll see him curse you to your face!" 12And the Lord replied to Satan, "You may do anything you like with his wealth, but don't harm him physically." So Satan went away.

Job 2:3. "Well, have you noticed my servant Job?" the Lord asked. "He is the finest man in all the earth—a good man who fears God and turns away from all evil. And he has kept his faith in me despite the fact that you persuaded me to let you harm him without any cause." 4, 5"Skin for skin," Satan replied. "A man will give anything to save his life. Touch his body with sickness and he will curse you to your face." 6"Do with him as you please," the Lord replied; "only spare his life." 7So Satan went out from the presence of the Lord and struck Job with a terrible case of boils from head to foot.

Job 9:24. The whole earth is in the hands of the wicked. God blinds the eyes of the judges and lets them be unfair. If not he, then who?

Isa 14:12. How you are fallen from heaven, O Lucifer, son of the morning! How you are cut down to the ground—mighty though you were against the nations of the world. 13For you said to yourself, "I will ascend to heaven and rule the angels. I will take the highest throne. I will preside on the Mount of Assembly far away in the north. 14I will climb to the highest heavens and be like the Most High." 15But instead, you will be brought down to the pit of hell, down to its lowest depths. 16Everyone there will stare at you and ask, "Can this be the one who shook the earth and the kingdoms of the world? 17Can this be the one who destroyed the world and made it into a shambles and demolished its greatest cities and had no mercy on his prisoners?"

Ezk 28:12. "Son of dust, weep for the king of Tyre. Tell him, the Lord God says: You were the perfection of wisdom and beauty. 13You were in Eden, the garden of God; your clothing was bejeweled with every precious stone—ruby, topaz, diamond, chrysolite, onyx, jasper, sapphire, carbuncle, and emerald—all in beautiful settings of finest gold. They were given to you on the day you were created. 14I appointed you to be the anointed guardian cherub. You had access to the holy mountain of God. You walked among the stones of fire. 15You were perfect in all you did from the day you were created until that time when wrong was found in you. 16Your great wealth filled you with internal turmoil and you sinned. Therefore, I cast you out of the mountain of God like a common sinner. I destroyed you, O overshadowing cherub, from the midst of the stones of fire. 17Your heart was filled with pride because of all your beauty; you corrupted your wisdom for the sake of your splendor. Therefore I have cast you down to the ground and exposed you helpless before the curious gaze of kings. 18You defiled your holiness with lust for gain; therefore I brought forth fire from your own actions and let it burn you to ashes upon the earth in the sight of all those watching you. 19All who know you are appalled at your fate; you are an example of horror; you are destroyed forever."

Zech 3:1. Then the Angel showed me (in my vision) Joshua the High Priest standing before the Angel of the Lord; and Satan was there too, at the Angel's right hand, accusing Joshua of many things. 2And the Lord said to Satan, "I reject your accusations, Satan; yes, I, the Lord, for I have decided to be merciful to Jerusalem—I rebuke you. I have decreed mercy to Joshua and his nation; they are like a burning stick pulled out of the fire."

Mt 4:1. Then Jesus was led out into the wilderness by the Holy Spirit, to be tempted there by Satan. 2For forty days and forty nights he ate nothing and became very hungry. 3Then Satan tempted him to get food by changing stones into loaves of bread. "It will prove you are the Son of God," he said. 4But Jesus told him, "No! For the Scriptures tell us that bread won't feed men's souls: obedience to every word of God is what we need." 5Then Satan took him to Jerusalem to the roof of the Temple. 6"Jump off," he said, "and prove you are the Son of God; for the Scriptures declare, 'God will send his angels to keep you from harm,' . . . they will prevent you from smashing on the rocks below." 7Jesus retorted, "It also says not to put the Lord your God to a foolish test!" 8Next Satan took him to the peak of a very high mountain and showed him the nations of the world and all the glory. 9"I'll give it all to you," he said, "if you will only kneel and worship me." 10"Get out of here, Satan," Jesus told him. "The Scriptures say, 'Worship only the Lord God. Obey only him.' " 11Then Satan went away, and angels came and cared for Jesus. Mk 1:12, 13; Lk 4:1–13.

Mt 13:19. The hard path where some of the seeds fell represents the heart of a person who hears the Good News about the Kingdom and doesn't understand it; then Satan comes and snatches away the seeds from his heart. [Mk 4:15; Lk 8:12.] 38The field is the world, and the seed represents the people of the Kingdom; the thistles are the people belonging to Satan. [39]The enemy who sowed the thistles among the wheat is the devil; the harvest is the end of the world, and the reapers are the angels.

Mt 25:41. Then I will turn to those on my left and say, "Away with you, you cursed ones, into the eternal fire prepared for the devil and his demons."

Mk 3:22. But the Jewish teachers of religion who had arrived from Jerusalem said, "His trouble is that he's possessed by Satan, king of demons. That's why demons obey him." [23]Jesus summoned these men and asked them (using proverbs they all understood), "How can Satan cast out Satan? [24]A kingdom divided against itself will collapse. [25]A home filled with strife and division destroys itself. [26]And if Satan is fighting against himself, how can he accomplish anything? He would never survive." Mt 9:34; Lk 11:15, 18.

Lk 10:18. "Yes," he told them, "I saw Satan falling from heaven as a flash of lightning!"

Lk 13:16. And is it wrong for me, just because it is the Sabbath day, to free this Jewish woman from the bondage in which Satan has held her for eighteen years?

Lk 22:31. Simon, Simon, Satan has asked to have you, to sift you like wheat. [53]Why didn't you arrest me in the Temple? I was there every day. But this is your moment—the time when Satan's power reigns supreme.

Jn 8:38. I am telling you what I saw when I was with my Father. But you are following the advice of *your* father. [41]No, you are obeying your *real* father when you act that way. [44]For you are the children of your father the devil and you love to do the evil things he does. He was a murderer from the beginning and a hater of truth—there is not an iota of truth in him. When he lies, it is perfectly normal; for he is the father of liars.

Jn 12:31. The time of judgment for the world has come—and the time when Satan, the prince of this world, shall be cast out.

Jn 13:2. During supper the devil had already suggested to Judas Iscariot, Simon's son, that this was the night to carry out his plan to betray Jesus. [27]As soon as Judas had eaten it, Satan entered into him.

Jn 14:30. I don't have much more time to talk to you, for the evil prince of this world approaches. He has no power over me.

Jn 16:11. There is deliverance from judgment because the prince of this world has already been judged.

Acts 5:3. But Peter said, "Ananias, Satan has filled your heart. When you claimed this was the full price, you were lying to the Holy Spirit."

Acts 13:10. You son of the devil, full of every sort of trickery and villainy, enemy of all that is good, will you never end your opposition to the Lord?

Acts 26:18. To open their eyes to their true condition so that they may repent and live in the light of God instead of in Satan's darkness, so that they may receive forgiveness for their sins and God's inheritance along with all people everywhere whose sins are cleansed away, who are set apart by faith in me.

Rom 16:20. The God of peace will soon crush Satan under your feet.

1 Cor 7:5. So do not refuse these rights to each other. The only exception to this rule would be the agreement of both husband and wife to refrain from the rights of marriage for a limited time, so that they can give themselves more completely to prayer. Afterwards, they should come together again so that Satan won't be able to tempt them because of their lack of self-control.

2 Cor 2:11. A further reason for forgiveness is to keep from being outsmarted by Satan; for we know what he is trying to do.

2 Cor 4:4. Satan, who is the god of this evil world, has made him blind, unable to see the glorious light of the Gospel that is shining upon him.

2 Cor 11:3. But I am frightened, fearing that in some way you will be led away from your pure and simple devotion to our Lord, just as Eve was deceived by Satan in the Garden of Eden. [14]Yet I am not surprised! Satan can change himself into an angel of light, [15]so it is no wonder his servants can do it too, and seem like godly ministers. In the end they will get every bit of punishment their wicked deeds deserve.

2 Cor 12:7. So I was given a physical condition which has been a thorn in my flesh, a messenger from Satan to hurt and bother me, and prick my pride.

Eph 2:2. You went along with the crowd and were just like all the others, full of sin, obeying Satan, the mighty prince of the power of the air, who is at work right now in the hearts of those who are against the Lord.

Eph 4:27. For when you are angry you give a mighty foothold to the devil.

Eph 6:11. Put on all of God's armor so that you will be able to stand safe against all strategies and tricks of Satan. [12]For we are not fighting against people made of flesh and blood, but against persons without bodies—the evil rulers of the unseen world, those mighty satanic beings and great evil princes of darkness who rule this world; and against huge numbers of wicked spirits in the spirit world.

13. So use every piece of God's armor to resist the enemy whenever he attacks, and when it is all over, you will still be standing up. [14]But to do this, you will need the strong belt of truth and the breastplate of God's approval. [15]Wear shoes that are able to speed you on as you preach the Good News of peace with God. [16]In every battle you will need faith as your shield to stop the fiery arrows aimed at you by Satan.

Col 1:13. For he has rescued us out of the darkness and gloom of Satan's kingdom and brought us into the Kingdom of his dear Son.

Col 2:15. In this way God took away Satan's power to accuse you of sin, and God openly displayed to the whole world Christ's triumph at the cross where your sins were all taken away.

1 Thess 2:18. We wanted very much to come and I, Paul, tried again and again, but Satan stopped us.

1 Thess 3:5. As I was saying, when I could bear the suspense no longer I sent Timothy to find out whether your faith was still strong. I was afraid that perhaps Satan had gotten the best of you and that all our work had been useless.

2 Thess 2:9. This man of sin will come as Satan's tool, full of satanic power, and will trick everyone with strange demonstrations, and will do great miracles.

1 Tim 1:20. Hymenaeus and Alexander are two examples of this. I had to give them over to Satan to punish them until they could learn not to bring shame to the name of Christ.

1 Tim 3:6. The pastor must not be a new Christian, because he might be proud of being chosen so soon, and pride comes before a fall. (Satan's downfall is an example.) [7]Also, he must be well spoken of by people outside the church—those who aren't Christians—so that Satan can't trap him with many accusations.

1 Tim 5:15. For I am afraid that some of them have already turned away from the church and been led astray by Satan.

2 Tim 2:26. Then they will come to their senses and escape from Satan's trap of slavery to sin which he uses to catch them whenever he likes, and then they can begin doing the will of God.

Heb 2:14. Since we, God's children, are human beings—made of flesh and blood—he became flesh and blood too by being born in human form; for only as a human being could he die and in dying break the power of the devil who had the power of death.

Jas 4:7. Resist the devil and he will flee from you.

1 Pet 5:8. Be careful—watch out for attacks from Satan, your great enemy. He prowls around like a hungry, roaring lion, looking for some victim to tear apart. [9]Stand firm when he attacks. Trust the Lord; and remember that other Christians all around the world are going through these sufferings too.

2 Pet 2:4. For God did not spare even the angels who sinned but threw them into hell, chained in gloomy caves and darkness until the judgment day.

1 Jn 2:13. And you young men, I am talking to you because you have won your battle with Satan.

1 Jn 3:8. But if you keep on sinning, it shows that you belong to Satan, who since he first began to sin has kept steadily at it. But the Son of God came to destroy these works of the devil. [10]So now we can tell who is a child of God and who belongs to Satan. [12]We are not to be like Cain, who belonged to Satan and killed his brother. Why did he kill him? Because Cain had been doing wrong and he knew very well that his brother's life was better than his.

1 Jn 5:18. No one who has become part of God's family makes a practice of sinning, for Christ, God's Son, holds him securely and the devil cannot get his hands on him.

Jude 1:6. And I remind you of those angels who were once pure and holy, but turned to a life of sin. Now God has them chained up in prisons of darkness, waiting for the judgment day. [9]Yet Michael, one of the mightiest of the angels, when he was arguing with Satan about Moses' body, did not dare to accuse even Satan, or jeer at him, but simply said, "The Lord rebuke you."

Rev 2:9. I know how much you suffer for the Lord, and I know all about your poverty (but you have heavenly riches!) I know the slander of those opposing you, who say that they are Jews—the children of God—but they aren't, for they support the cause of Satan. [Rev 3:9.] [10]Stop being afraid of what you are about to suffer—for the devil will soon throw some of you into prison to test you. You will be persecuted for "ten days." Remain faithful even when facing death and I will give you the crown of life. [13]I am fully aware that you live in the city where Satan's throne is, at the center of satanic worship; and yet you have remained loyal to me, and refused to deny me, even when Antipas, my faithful witness, was martyred among you by Satan's devotees. [24]As for the rest of you in Thyatira who have not followed this false teaching ("deeper truths," as they call them—depths of Satan, really).

Rev 9:11. Their king is the Prince of the bottomless pit whose name in Hebrew is Abaddon, and in Greek, Apollyon (and in English, the Destroyer).

Rev 12:9. This great Dragon—the ancient serpent called the devil, or Satan, the one deceiving the whole world—was thrown down onto the earth with all his army. [10]Then I heard a loud voice shouting across the heavens, "It has happened at last! God's salvation and the power and the rule, and the authority of his Christ are finally here; for the Accuser of our brothers has been thrown down from heaven onto earth—he accused them day and night before our God. [11]They defeated him by the blood of the Lamb, and by their testimony; for they did not love their lives but laid them down for him. [12]Rejoice, O heavens! You citizens of heaven, rejoice! Be glad! But woe to you people of the world, for the devil has come down to you in great anger, knowing that he has little time."

Rev 20:1. Then I saw an angel come down from heaven with the key to the bottomless pit and a heavy chain in his hand. [2]He seized the Dragon—that old Serpent, the devil, Satan—and bound him in chains for 1,000 years, [3]and threw him into the bottomless pit, which he then shut and locked, so that he could not fool the nations any more until the thousand years were finished. Afterwards he would be released again for a little while. [7]When the thousand years end, Satan will be let out of his prison. [8]He will go out to deceive the nations of the world and gather them together, with Gog and Magog, for battle—a mighty host, numberless as sand along the shore. [10]Then the devil who had betrayed them will again be thrown into the Lake of Fire burning with sulphur where the Creature and False Prophet are, and they will be tormented day and night forever and ever.

See *Demons.*

SATIRE Hannah's song of exultation over Peninnah, 1 Sam 2:1–10, with chapter 1:5–10. Of Jesus against hypocrites, Mt 23:2–33; Mk 12:13–40; Lk 11:39–54.

SAUL 1. King of Israel. A Benjaminite, son of Kish, 1 Sam 9:1, 2. Sons of, 1 Chron 8:33. His personal appearance, 1 Sam 9:2; 10:23. Made king of Israel, 1 Sam 9; 10; 11:12–15; Hos 13:11. Camps at Gibe-ah, 1 Sam 14:2; 15:34; Isa 10:28, 29. Defeats the Philistines, 1 Sam 13; 14:46, 52. Destroys the Amalekites, 1 Sam 15. Is reproved by Samuel for usurping the priestly function, 1 Sam 13:11–14; for disobedience in not completely destroying the Amalekites; the loss of his kingdom foretold, 1 Sam 15. Dedicates the spoils of war, 1 Sam 15: 21–25; 1 Chron 26:28. Sends messengers to Jesse, asking that David be sent to him as musican and bodyguard, 1 Sam 16:17–23. Defeats the Philistines after Goliath is killed by David, 1 Sam 17. His jealousy of David; gives his daughter, Michal, to David to be his wife; becomes David's enemy, 1 Sam 18. Tries to kill David; Jonathan intercedes and incurs his father's displeasure; David's loyalty to him; Saul's repentance; prophecies, 1 Sam 19. Hears Doeg testify against Ahimelech, and kills the priest and his family, 1 Sam 22:9–19. Pursues David to the wilderness of Ziph; the Ziphites betray David to, 1 Sam 23. Pursues David to En-gedi, 1 Sam 24:1–6. His life saved by David, 1 Sam 24:5–8. Saul's contrition for his bad faith, 1 Sam 24:16–22. David is again betrayed to, by the Ziphites; Saul pursues him to Hachilah Hill; his life spared again by David; his confession, and his blessing upon David, 1 Sam 26. Kills the Gibeonites; crime avenged by the death of seven of his sons, 2 Sam 21:1–9. His kingdom invaded by Philistines; seeks counsel of the witch of Endor, who foretells his death, 1 Sam 28:3–25. Is defeated, and with his sons is killed, 1 Sam 31; their bodies exposed in Bethshan; rescued by the people of Jabesh and burned; bones of, buried under a tree at Jabesh, 1 Sam 31, with 2 Sam 1:1, 2; 1 Chron 10. His death a judgment because of his sins, 1 Chron 10:13.

2. Of Tarsus. See *Paul.*

SAVED The term is widely used in Scripture, as the translation of the various derivatives of the Hebrew and Greek words to save, to make safe, to deliver. With reference to man's salvation it is used in three tenses. Of the past; we have been delivered from the guilt and penalty of sin, Lk 7:50; 1 Cor 1: 18; 2 Cor 2:15; 2 Tim 1:9. Of the present, we are being saved from the power of sin, Jn 17:17; Rom 6:14; 8:2; Gal 5:16; Phil 2:12, 13. Of the future, we shall be saved from the very presence of sin, Rom 13:11; Eph 5:25–27; Phil 1:6; 1 Pet 1:3–5; 1 Jn 3:1, 2.

In one or more of these senses, the word appears in: Deut 33:29; Ps 80:3, 7, 19; Isa 30:15; 45:17, 22; 64:5; Jer 8:20; 17:14; Mt 10:22; 19:25; 24:13; Mk 10: 26; 13:13; 16:16; Lk 7:50; 8:12; 13:23; 18:26; Jn 3:17; 5: 34; 10:9; Acts 2:21 (cf Joel 2:32); Acts 2:47; 4:12; 11: 14; 15:1, 11; 16:30, 31; Rom 5:9, 10; 8:24; 10:1, 9, 13; 11: 26; 1 Cor 1:18; 3:15; 5:5; 10:33; 15:2; 2 Cor 2:15; Eph 2:5, 8; 1 Thess 2:16; 2 Thess 2:10; 1 Tim 2:4; 2 Tim 1:9; Tit 3:5; 1 Pet 4:18.

See *Salvation; Jesus Christ, Savior.*

SAVIOR See *Jesus Christ, Savior.*

SAW Used as an instrument of torture, 2 Sam 12:31; Heb 11:37, 38; for cutting stone, 2 Sam 12:31; 1 Chron 20:3.

FIGURATIVE. Isa 10:15.

SCAB Disease of the skin, Lev 13:1, 2, 6–8; 14: 56; 21:20; 22:22; Deut 28:27; Isa 3:17.

See *Disease; Sanitation; Scurvy.*

SCALES 1. FIGURATIVE. Fell from Paul's eyes, Acts 9:18.

2. Used for weighing, Isa 40:15. Must be just, Ezk 45:10. Dishonest scales used, Hos 12:7; Amos 8:5; Mic 6:10, 11; detestable, Prov 20:23.

FIGURATIVE. Ps 62:9; Isa 40:15.

SCAPEBIRD Lev 14:4–7, 53.

SCAPEGOAT Lev 16:7–10, 20–34. See *Azazel.*

SCARF Worn by women, Isa 3:20.

SCARLET See *Color.*

SCEPTER A wand used by kings to signify favor or disfavor to those who desired an audience, Esther 5:2; 8:4. A symbol of authority, Esther 4:11; Mt 27:29. Made of gold, Esther 4:11; of iron, Ps 2: 9; Rev 2:27.

FIGURATIVE. Gen 49:10; Ps 45:6; 108:8; Ezk 19: 11.

SCEVA A Jew of Ephesus, Acts 19:13–17.

SCHOOL Of the prophets, at Naioth, 1 Sam 19:20; Bethel, 2 Kgs 2:3; Jericho, 2 Kgs 2:5, 15; Gilgal, 2 Kgs 4:38; Jerusalem, probably, 2 Kgs 22: 14; 2 Chron 34:22. Crowded attendance at, 2 Kgs 6:1.

In the home, Deut 4:9, 10; 6:7, 9; 11:19, 20; Ps 78: 5–8. Bible school, Deut 31:10–13.

State, 2 Chron 17:7–9; Dan 1:3–21. Of Gamaliel, Acts 5:34; 22:3. Of Tyrannus, Acts 19:9. Schoolmaster, Gal 3:24, 25. Instruction concerning establishing, 2 Tim 2:2.

See *Instruction.*

SCIENCE Observations of, and deductions from, facts, Job 26:7–14; 28; Eccl 1:12–18. Of Babylon, Dan 1:17.

See *Geology; Astronomy; Philosophy.*

SCOFFING 2 Chron 30:6. "Come back to the Lord God of Abraham, Isaac, and Israel," the king's letter said, "so that he will return to us who have escaped from the power of the kings of Assyria. [7]Do not be like your fathers and brothers who sinned against the Lord God of their fathers and were destroyed. [8]Do not be stubborn, as they were, but yield yourselves to the Lord and come to his Temple which he has sanctified forever, and worship the Lord your God so that his fierce anger will turn away from you. [9]For if you turn to the Lord again, your brothers and your children will be treated mercifully by their captors, and they will be able to return to this land. For the Lord your God is full of kindness and mercy and will not continue to turn away his face from you if you return to him." [10]So the messengers went from city to city throughout Ephraim and Manasseh and as far as Zebulun. But for the most part they were received with laughter and scorn!

2 Chron 36:16. But the people mocked these messengers of God and despised their words, scoffing at the prophets until the anger of the Lord could no longer be restrained, and there was no longer any remedy.

Job 21:14. All this despite the fact that they ordered God away and wanted no part of him and his ways. [15]"Who is Almighty God?" they scoff. "Why should we obey him? What good will it do us?"

Job 34:7. Who else is as arrogant as Job?

Ps 1:1. Oh, the joys of those who do not follow evil men's advice, who do not hang around with sinners, scoffing at the things of God.

Ps 42:3. Day and night I weep for his help, and all the while my enemies taunt me. "Where is this God of yours?" they scoff. *v.* 10.

Ps 73:11. "Does God realize what is going on?" they ask.

Ps 78:19, 20. They even spoke against God himself. "Why can't he give us decent food as well as water?" they grumbled.

Ps 107:11. They rebelled against the Lord, scorning him who is the God above all gods. [12]That is why he broke them with hard labor; they fell and none could help them rise again.

Prov 1:22. "You simpletons!" she cries. "How long will you go on being fools? How long will you scoff at wisdom and fight the facts? [25]For you have spurned my counsel and reproof."

Prov 3:34. The Lord mocks at mockers, but helps the humble.

Prov 9:12. Wisdom is its own reward, and if you scorn her, you hurt only yourself.

Prov 13:1. A wise youth accepts his father's rebuke; a young mocker doesn't.

Prov 14:6. A mocker never finds the wisdom he claims he is looking for, yet it comes easily to the man with common sense. [9]The common bond of rebels is their guilt.

Prov 19:29. Mockers and rebels shall be severely punished.

Prov 21:11. The wise man learns by listening; the simpleton can learn only by seeing scorners punished. [24]Mockers are proud, haughty and arrogant.

Prov 22:10. Throw out the mocker, and you will be rid of tension, fighting and quarrels.

Prov 24:9. The rebel's schemes are sinful, and the mocker is the scourge of all mankind.

Isa 5:18. Woe to those. . . . [19]They even mock the Holy One of Israel and dare the Lord to punish them. "Hurry up and punish us, O Lord," they say. "We want to see what you can do!" [24]Therefore God will deal with them and burn them. They will disappear like straw on fire. Their roots will rot and their flowers wither, for they have thrown away the laws of God and despised the Word of the Holy One of Israel. [25]That is why the anger of the Lord is hot against his people; that is why he has reached out his hand to smash them. The hills will tremble, and the rotting bodies of his people will be thrown as refuse in the streets. But even so, his anger is not ended; his hand is heavy on them still.

Isa 10:15. But the Lord says, "Shall the axe boast greater power than the man who uses it? Is the saw greater than the man who saws? Can a rod strike unless a hand is moving it? Can a cane walk by itself?"

Isa 29:20. Bullies will vanish and scoffers will cease, and all those plotting evil will be killed.

Isa 57:4. Who is it you mock, making faces and sticking out your tongues?

Jer 17:15. Men scoff at me and say, "What is this word of the Lord you keep talking about? If these threats of yours are really from God, why don't they come true?"

Jer 43:2. And all the other proud men, said to Jeremiah, "You lie! The Lord our God hasn't told you to tell us not to go to Egypt!"

Lam 1:7. And now in the midst of all Jerusalem's sadness she remembers happy bygone days. She thinks of all the precious joys she had before her mocking enemy struck her down—and there was no one to give her aid.

Ezk 8:12. Then the Lord said to me: "Son of dust, have you seen what the elders of Israel are doing in their minds? For they say, 'The Lord doesn't see us; he has gone away!' "

Ezk 9:9. But he said to me, "The sins of the people of Israel and Judah are very great and all the land is full of murder and injustice, for they say, 'The Lord doesn't see it! He has gone away!' "

Ezk 11:2. Then the Spirit said to me, "Son of dust, these are the men who are responsible for all of the wicked counsel being given out in this city. [3]For they say to the people, 'It is time to rebuild Jerusalem, for our city is an iron shield and will protect us from all harm.' "

Ezk 12:22. Son of dust, what is that proverb they quote in Israel—"The days as they pass make liars out of every prophet."

Hos 7:5. On the king's birthday, the princes get him drunk; he makes a fool of himself and drinks with those who mock him.

Mt 12:24. But when the Pharisees heard about the miracle they said, "He can cast out demons because he is Satan, king of devils." Mk 3:22; Lk 11:15.

Lk 4:23. Then he said, "Probably you will quote me that proverb, 'Physician, heal yourself'—meaning, 'Why don't you do miracles here in your home town like those you did in Capernaum?' "

Lk 16:14. The Pharisees, who dearly loved their money, naturally scoffed at all this.

Acts 2:13. But others in the crowd were mocking. "They're drunk, that's all!" they said.

Acts 13:45. But when the Jewish leaders saw the crowds, they were jealous, and cursed and argued against whatever Paul said.

Acts 17:18. He also had an encounter with some of the Epicurean and Stoic philosophers. Their reaction, when he told them about Jesus and his resurrection, was, "He's a dreamer," or, "He's pushing some foreign religion." [32]When they heard Paul speak of the resurrection of a person who had been dead, some laughed, but others said, "We want to hear more about this later."

Heb 10:29. Think how much more terrible the punishment will be for those who have trampled underfoot the Son of God and treated his cleansing blood as though it were common and unhallowed, and insulted and outraged the Holy Spirit who brings God's mercy to his people.

2 Pet 3:3. First, I want to remind you that in the last days there will come scoffers who will do every wrong they can think of, and laugh at the truth. [4]This will be their line of argument: "So Jesus promised to come back, did he? Then where is he? He'll never come! Why, as far back as anyone can remember everything has remained exactly as it was since the first day of creation."

See *Hatred; Malice; Unbelief.*

INSTANCES OF. Ishmael, Gen 21:9. Children at Bethel, 2 Kgs 2:23. Ephraim and Manasseh, 2 Chron 30:10. Leaders of Judah, 2 Chron 36:16. Sanballat, Neh 4:1. Enemies of Job, Job 30:1, 9. Enemies of David, Ps 35:15, 16. Rulers of Israel, Isa 28:14. Ammonites, Ezk 25:3. Tyrians, Ezk 26:2. Heathen, Ezk 36:2, 3. Soldiers, Mt 27:28–30; Lk 23:36. Chief priests, Mt 27:41–43. Pharisees, Lk 16:14. The men who held Jesus, Lk 22:63, 64. Herod, Lk 23:11. Jewish leaders, Lk 23:35. Some of the crowd, Acts 2:13. Athenians, Acts 17:32.

SCORPION A venomous insect common in the wilderness through which the children of Israel travelled, Deut 8:15. Power over, given to the seventy, Lk 10:19. Unfit for food, Lk 11:12. Sting of, in the tail, Rev 9:10.

FIGURATIVE. Of enemies, Ezk 2:6. Of cruelty, 1 Kgs 12:11.

Symbolical. Rev 9:3, 5, 10.

SCORPION PASS See *Akrabbim.*

SCOURGING Corporal punishment by stripes. Prescribed by the Mosaic law for fornication, Deut 22:17, 18; for other offenses, Deut 25:1–3. Forty stripes the maximum limit, Deut 25:1–3. Of slaves avenged, Ex 21:20. Foretold by Jesus as a persecution of his followers, Mt 10:17.

Of children, see *Children, Correction of; Punishment.*

INSTANCES OF. Of Jesus, Mt 20:19; 27:26; Mk 15:15; Lk 23:16; 22; Jn 19:1; Of Paul and Silas, Acts 16:23. Of Paul, Acts 21:32; 22:24; 2 Cor 11:24, 25. Of Sosthenes, Acts 18:17.

FIGURATIVE. Of the oppressions of rulers, 1 Kgs 12:11; Ezk 32:24. See *Assault and Battery.*

SCRIBE A writer and transcriber of the law, 1 Chron 27:32; Ezra 4:8, 9, 17; Neh 13:13; Jer 36:12. King's secretary, Isa 36:3, 22; 37:2. Instructors in the law, Mt 7:29. See *Levites.* Hypocrisy of, reproved by Jesus, Mt 16:21.

See *Secretary.*

SCRIPTURES Fulfilled, Mk 15:28; Lk 4:21; Jn 19:23, 24, 28, 36, 37; must be fulfilled, Acts 1:16; cannot be untrue, Jn 10:14–36; concludes all are prisoners of sin, Gal 3:22; given by inspiration from God, 2 Tim 3:16; not of human origin, 2 Pet 1:20; expounded by Christ, Lk 24:27; explained by Christ, Lk 24:32, 45; search the Scriptures, Jn 5:39; Paul explained, Acts 17:2; searching daily, Acts 17:11; holy, 2 Tim 3:15; comfort of, Rom 15:4; gospel is according to, 1 Cor 15:3, 4; twisting, 2 Pet 3:15, 16.

See *Word of God.*

SCROLL Curses written in, 2 Chron 35:24. Prophecies written in, by Jeremiah, Jer 36:28; 51:60, 63. Made in a roll, Isa 34:4; Jer 36:2–4; Zech 5:1; Rev 6:14. Sometimes written on both sides, Ezk 2:9, 10; Rev 5:1. Eating of, Ezk 2:8–10; 3:1–3; Rev 10:2–10. Sealed, Rev 5:1–5.

See *Book.*

SCURVY Deut 28:27.

See *Scab.*

SEA Creation of, Gen 1:9, 10; Ps 95:5; 104:3. Boundaries of, established by God, Job 26:10; 38:8, 9; Ps 33:7; 104:9; Jer 5:22. Calmed by Jesus, Mt 8:24–26; Mk 4:37–39. Jesus walked on, Mt 14:25–31; Jn 6:18, 19. Dead, to be given up by, at the resurrection, Rev 20:13.

Symbolical. In Daniel's dream, Dan 7:2, 3. In John's apocalyptic vision, Rev 4:6; 8:8, 9; 10:2, 5, 6, 8; 13:1; 15:2; 16:3; 21:1.

See *Red Sea.*

SEAGULL Forbidden as food, Lev 11:13–19; Deut 14:15.

SEAL A stamp used for signing and authorizing documents. Given as a pledge, Gen 38:18. Engraved, Ex 28:11, 21, 36; 39:6, 7, 14. Decrees signed by, 1 Kgs 21:8; Esther 8:8. Documents sealed with: Ahab's letter, 1 Kgs 21:8; covenants, Isa 8:16; decrees, Esther 8:8; deeds, Jer 32:10. Treasures secured by, Deut 32:34. Lion's den made secure by, Dan 6:17; tomb of Jesus, Mt 27:66.

FIGURATIVE. Song 8:6. Of secrecy, Isa 29:11; Rev 5:1. Of certainty of divine approval, Eph 4:30; Rev 7:3.

SEAMEN See *Sailor.*

SEASONS Gen 1:14, 15; 8:22; Ps 104:19; Jer 33:20, 21; Mt 24:32; Mk 12:2.

SEAWEED Jon 2:5.

SEBA 1. Son of Cush, Gen 10:7; 1 Chron 1:5–9. 2. A region in Arabia, Ps 72:10; Isa 43:3.

SEBAM A city of Reuben, Num 32:3, 4. Apparently called also *Sibmah.*

See *Sibmah.*

SEBAT See *Calendar.*

SECOND DEATH Rev 20:14.

See *Wicked, Punishment of.*

SECRET Charity to be given in, Mt 6:4. Prayer to be offered in, Mt 6:6. Of others not to be divulged, Prov 25:8–10; Mt 18:15.

UNCLASSIFIED SCRIPTURES RELATING TO. Deut 29:29. There are secrets the Lord your God has not revealed to us, but these words which he has revealed are for us and our children to obey forever.

Deut 31:21. I know now, even before they enter the land, what these people are like.

1 Sam 16:7. But the Lord said to Samuel, "Don't judge by a man's face or height, for this is not the

one. I don't make decisions the way you do! Men judge by outward appearance, but I look at a man's thoughts and intentions."

2 Sam 7:20. What can I say? For you know what I am like!

2 Kgs 19:27. I know everything about you. I know all your plans and where you are going next.

Ps 25:14. Friendship with God is reserved for those who reverence him. With them alone he shares the secrets of his promises.

Ps 44:21. Would God not know it? Yes, he knows the secrets of every heart.

Ps 90:8. You spread out our sins before you—our secret sins—and see them all.

Eccl 12:14. For God will judge us for everything we do, including every hidden thing, good or bad.

Dan 2:28. But there is a God in heaven who reveals secrets.

47. "Truly, O Daniel," the king said, "your God is the God of gods, Ruler of kings, the Revealer of mysteries, because he has told you this secret."

Mt 10:26. For the time is coming when the truth will be revealed: their secret plots will become public information.

Mk 4:22. All that is now hidden will someday come to light.

Lk 8:16. (Another time he asked,) "Who ever heard of someone lighting a lamp and then covering it up to keep it from shining? No, lamps are mounted in the open where they can be seen. [17]This illustrates the fact that someday everything (in men's hearts) shall be brought to light and made plain to all. Lk 12:1–3.

Rom 2:16. The day will surely come when at God's command Jesus Christ will judge the secret lives of everyone, their inmost thoughts and motives; this is all part of God's great plan which I proclaim.

1 Cor 4:5. So be careful not to jump to conclusions before the Lord returns as to whether someone is a good servant or not. When the Lord comes, he will turn on the light so that everyone can see exactly what each one of us is really like, deep down in our hearts. Then everyone will know why we have been doing the Lord's work. At that time God will give to each one whatever praise is coming to him.

Heb 4:12. For whatever God says to us is full of living power: it is sharper than the sharpest dagger, cutting swift and deep into our innermost thoughts and desires with all their parts, exposing us for what we really are. [13]He knows about everyone, everywhere. Everything about us is bare and wide open to the all-seeing eyes of our living God; nothing can be hidden from him to whom we must explain all that we have done.

See *Mysteries and Secrets.*

SECRETARY 2 Sam 8:17; 20:25; 1 Kgs 4:1–6; 2 Kgs 12:10–12; 18:18, 37; 22:1–14; 1 Chron 24:6; Neh 13:13; Esther 3:12; 8:9, 10; Jer 36:4; 45:1; Acts 12:20. Military, 2 Chron 26:11. King's secretary, 2 Kgs 12:10–12; 22:1–14; Esther 3:12; 8:9, 10.

See *Scribe.*

SECUNDUS A Thessalonian Christian. Accompanies Paul from Corinth, Acts 20:4–6.

SECURITY FOR DEBT. See *Debt; Surety.*

FALSE. From the evils of sin. Promises peace and long life, Job 29:18. Is ignorant of God and truth, Ps 10:4; 50:21. Trusts in lies, Isa 28:15; Rev 3:17. Is inconsiderate and forgetful, Isa 47:7. Relies on pride and earthly possessions, Jer 49:4, 16. Is deceived by pride, Obd 1:3; Rev 18:7. Puts off the Judgment Day, Amos 6:3. Leads to increased wrongdoing, Eccl 8:11. Its refuges to be scattered, Isa 28:17. Ruin shall overtake it, Isa 47:9; Amos 9:10.

God is against it, Jer 21:13; Ezk 39:6; Amos 6:1.

See *Confidence, False; Self-Deception; Self-Delusion.*

SECURITY OF THE BELIEVER A theological expression used with reference to the safekeeping of believers, based on the literal interpretation of such passages as Jn 3:15, 16; 6:37; 10:28, 29; 17:11; Rom 8:29, 30, 34; Heb 9:24; 1 Jn 2:1. It is to be distinguished from *Assurance,* which see.

SEDITION Jerusalem a place of, Ezra 4:15, 19. Charged against Paul, Acts 24:5. How punished, Acts 5:36, 37.

SEDUCTION Prov 6:25; 7:21, 25; 2 Tim 3:6, 13; Rev 14:8. Laws concerning, Ex 22:16, 17; Lev 19:20; Deut 22:23–29.

See *Rape.*

INSTANCES OF. Of Dinah, Gen 34:2. Tamar, 2 Sam 13:1–14.

SEED Every herb, tree, and grass, produces its own, Gen 1:11, 12, 29. Each kind has its own body, 1 Cor 15:38. Not to be mixed in sowing, Lev 19:19; Deut 22:9.

Parables concerning, Mt 13; Lk 8.

Illustrative, Eccl 11:6; Hos 10:12; 2 Cor 9:6; Gal 6:7, 8.

Sowing of, type of burial of the body, 1 Cor 15:36–38.

SEEKER Deut 4:29. But you will also begin to search again for Jehovah your God, and you shall find him when you search for him with all your hearts and souls.

1 Chron 16:11. Seek the Lord; yes, seek his strength and seek his face untiringly.

1 Chron 22:19. Now try with every fiber of your being to obey the Lord your God, and you will soon be bringing the Ark and the other holy articles of worship into the Temple of the Lord!

1 Chron 28:9. Solomon, my son, get to know the God of your fathers. Worship and serve him with a clean heart and a willing mind, for the Lord sees every heart and understands and knows every thought. If you seek him, you will find him; but if you forsake him, he will permanently throw you aside.

2 Chron 15:2. "Listen to me, Asa! Listen, armies of Judah and Benjamin!" he shouted. "The Lord will stay with you as long as you stay with him! Whenever you look for him, you will find him. But if you forsake him, he will forsake you."

2 Chron 26:5. While Zechariah was alive Uzziah was always eager to please God. Zechariah was a man who had special revelations from God. And as long as the king followed the paths of God, he prospered, for God blessed him.

2 Chron 30:18, 19. The King Hezekiah prayed for them and they were permitted to eat the Passover anyway, even though this was contrary to God's rules. But Hezekiah said, "May the good Lord pardon everyone who determines to follow the Lord God of his fathers, even though he is not properly sanctified for the ceremony."

Job 5:8. My advice to you is this; Go to God and confess your sins to him.

Job 8:5. And you begged Almighty God for them—[6]If you were pure and good, he would hear your prayer, and answer you, and bless you with a happy home.

Job 23:8. I seek him here, I seek him there, and cannot find him. [9]I seek him in his workshop in the North, but cannot find him there; nor can I find him in the South; there, too, he hides himself.

Ps 14:2. The Lord looks down from heaven on all mankind to see if there are any who are wise, who want to please God.

Ps 17:1. I am pleading for your help, O Lord; for I have been honest and have done what is right, and you must listen to my earnest cry! [2]Publicly acquit me, Lord, for you are always fair.

Ps 22:26. All who seek the Lord shall find him and shall praise his name.

Ps 24:3. Who may climb the mountain of the Lord and enter where he lives? Who may stand before the Lord? [4]Only those with pure hands and hearts, who do not practice dishonesty and lying. [5]They will receive God's own goodness as their blessing from him, planted in their lives by God himself, their Savior. [6]These are the ones who are allowed to stand before the Lord and worship the God of Jacob.

Ps 25:5. Lead me; teach me; for you are the God who gives me salvation. I have no hope except in you. [15]My eyes are ever looking to the Lord for help, for he alone can rescue me.

Ps 27:4. The one thing I want from God, the thing I seek most of all, is the privilege of meditating in his Temple, living in his presence every day of my life, delighting in his incomparable perfections and glory. [8]My heart has heard you say, "Come and talk with me, O my people." And my heart responds, "Lord, I am coming." [14]Don't be impatient. Wait for the Lord, and he will come and save you! Be brave, stout-hearted and courageous. Yes, wait and he will help you.

Ps 33:20. We depend upon the Lord alone to save us. Only he can help us; he protects us like a shield.

Ps 34:4. For I cried to him and he answered me! He freed me from all my fears.

Ps 40:1. I waited patiently for God to help me; then he listened and heard my cry. [2]He lifted me out of the pit of despair, out from the bog and the mire, and set my feet on a hard, firm path and steadied me as I walked along. [3]He has given me a new song to sing, of praises to our God. Now many will hear of the glorious things he did for me, and stand in awe before the Lord, and put their trust in him. [4]Many blessings are given to those who trust the Lord, and have no confidence in those who are proud, or who trust in idols.

Ps 42:1. As the deer pants for water, so I long for you, O God. [2]I thirst for God, the living God. Where can I find him to come and stand before him? [3]Day and night I weep for his help, and all the while my enemies taunt me. "Where is this God of yours?" they scoff. [4]Take courage, my soul! Do you remember those times (but how could you ever forget them!) when you led a great procession to the Temple on festival days, singing with joy, praising the Lord?

Ps 53:2. God looks down from heaven, searching among all mankind to see if there is a single one who does right and really seeks for God.

Ps 63:1. O God, my God! How I search for you! How I thirst for you in this parched and weary land where there is no water. How I long to find you! [2]How I wish I could go into your sanctuary to see your strength and glory, [3]for your love and kindness are better to me than life itself. How I praise you! [4]I will bless you as long as I live, lifting up my hands to you in prayer. [5]At last I shall be fully satisfied; I will praise you with great joy. [6]I lie awake at night thinking of you—[7]of how much you have helped me—and how I rejoice through the night beneath the protecting shadow of your wings. [8]I follow close behind you, protected by your strong right arm.

Ps 69:32. The humble shall see their God at work for them. No wonder they will be so glad! All who seek for God shall live in joy.

Ps 70:4. But fill the followers of God with joy. Let those who love your salvation exclaim, "What a wonderful God he is!" [5]But I am in deep trouble. Rush to my aid, for only you can help and save me. O Lord, don't delay.

Ps 77:1. I cry to the Lord; I call and call to him. Oh, that he would listen. [2]I am in deep trouble and I need his help so badly. All night long I pray, lifting my hands to heaven, pleading. There can be no joy for me until he acts. [3]I think of God and moan, overwhelmed with longing for his help. [4]I cannot sleep until you act. I am too distressed even to pray! [5]I keep thinking of the good old days of the past, long since ended. [6]Then my nights were filled with joyous songs. I search my soul and meditate upon the difference now. [7]Has the Lord rejected me forever? Will he never again be favorable? [8]Is his lovingkindness gone forever? Has his promise failed? [9]Has he forgotten to be kind to one so undeserving? Has he slammed the door in anger on his love?

Ps 78:34. Then at last, when he had ruined them, they walked awhile behind him; how earnestly they turned around and followed him!

Ps 81:10. For it was I, Jehovah your God, who brought you out of the land of Egypt. Only test me!

Open your mouth wide and see if I won't fill it. You will receive every blessing you can use!

Ps 84:2. I long, yes, faint with longing to be able to enter your courtyard and come near to the Living God.

Ps 105:4. Search for him and for his strength, and keep on searching!

Ps 119:2. Happy are all who search for God, and always do his will. [10]I have tried my best to find you —don't let me wander off from your instructions.

Ps 130:5. That is why I wait expectantly, trusting God to help, for he has promised. [6]I long for him more than sentinels long for the dawn.

Ps 143:6. I reach out for you. I thirst for you as parched land thirsts for rain.

Ps 145:18. He is close to all who call on him sincerely. [19]He fulfills the desires of those who reverence and trust him; he hears their cries for help and rescues them.

Prov 2:3–5. Yes, if you want better insight and discernment, and are searching for them as you would for lost money or hidden treasure, then wisdom will be given you, and knowledge of God himself; you will soon learn the importance of reverence for the Lord and of trusting him.

Prov 8:17. I love all who love me. Those who search for me shall surely find me. [34]Happy is the man who is so anxious to be with me that he watches for me daily at my gates, or waits for me outside my home!

Prov 28:5. Evil men don't understand the importance of justice, but those who follow the Lord are much concerned about it.

Song 3:1. *The Girl:* "One night my lover was missing from my bed. I got up to look for him but couldn't find him. [2]I went out into the streets of the city and the roads to seek him, but I searched in vain. [3]The police stopped me and I said to them, 'Have you seen him anywhere, this one I love so much?' [4]It was only a little while afterwards that I found him and held him and would not let him go until I had brought him into my childhood home, into my mother's old bedroom."

Isa 8:19. Can the living find out the future from the dead? Why not ask your God?

Isa 21:11. "How much time is left?" [12]The watchman replies, "Your judgment day is dawning now. Turn again to God, so that I can give you better news. Seek for him, then come and ask again!"

Isa 26:9. All night long I search for you; earnestly I seek for God.

Isa 44:3. For I will give you abundant water for your thirst and for your parched fields. And I will pour out my Spirit and my blessings on your children. [4]They shall thrive like watered grass, like willows on a river bank.

Isa 45:19. I publicly proclaim bold promises; I do not whisper obscurities in some dark corner so that no one can know what I mean. And I didn't tell Israel to ask me for what I didn't plan to give! No, for I, Jehovah, speak only truth and righteousness. [22]Let all the world look to me for salvation! For I am God; there is no other.

Isa 49:9. Through you I am saying to the prisoners of darkness, "Come out! I am giving you your freedom!" They will be my sheep, grazing in green pastures and on the grassy hills. [10]They shall neither hunger nor thirst; the searing sun and scorching desert wind will not reach them any more. For the Lord in his mercy will lead them beside the cool waters. [11]And I will make my mountains into level paths for them; the highways shall be raised above the valleys. [12]See, my people shall return from far away, from north and west and south. [23]Those who wait for me shall never be ashamed.

Isa 51:1. Listen to me, all who hope for deliverance, who seek the Lord! Consider the quarry from which you were mined, the rock from which you were cut!

Isa 55:6. Seek the Lord while you can find him. Call upon him now while he is near. [7]Let men cast off their wicked deeds; let them banish from their minds the very thought of doing wrong! Let them turn to the Lord that he may have mercy upon them, and to our God, for he will abundantly pardon!

Isa 59:20. He will come as a Redeemer to those in Zion who have turned away from sin.

Isa 61:1. The Spirit of the Lord God is upon me, because the Lord has anointed me to bring good news to the suffering and afflicted. He has sent me to comfort the broken-hearted, to announce liberty to captives and to open the eyes of the blind. [2]He has sent me to tell those who mourn that the time of God's favor to them has come, and the day of his wrath to their enemies. [3]To all who mourn in Israel he will give: Beauty for ashes; joy instead of mourning; praise instead of heaviness. For God has planted them like strong and graceful oaks for his own glory.

Jer 29:13. You will find me when you seek me, if you look for me in earnest.

Jer 42:3. Beg the Lord your God to show us what to do and where to go.

Jer 50:4. Then the people of Israel and Judah shall join together, weeping and seeking the Lord their God.

Lam 3:25. The Lord is wonderfully good to those who wait for him, to those who seek for him. [26]It is good both to hope and wait quietly for the salvation of the Lord. [41]Let us lift our hearts and hands to him in heaven.

Ezk 18:21. But if a wicked person turns away from all his sins and begins to obey my laws and do what is just and right, he shall surely live and not die. [22]All his past sins will be forgotten, and he shall live because of his goodness. [23]Do you think I like to see the wicked die? asks the Lord. Of course not! I only want him to turn from his wicked ways and live.

Dan 9:3. So I earnestly pleaded with the Lord God (to end our captivity and send us back to our own land). As I prayed, I fasted, and wore rough sackcloth, and sprinkled myself with ashes.

Hos 3:5. Afterward they will return to the Lord their God, and to the Messiah, their King, and they shall come trembling, submissive to the Lord and to his blessings, in the end times.

Hos 5:15. I will abandon them and return to my home until they admit their guilt and look to me for help again, for as soon as trouble comes, they will search for me.

Hos 10:12. For now is the time to seek the Lord, that he may come and shower salvation upon you.

Joel 2:12. That is why the Lord says, "Turn to me now, while there is time. Give me all your hearts. Come with fasting, weeping, mourning. [13]Let your remorse tear at your hearts and not your garments." Return to the Lord your God, for he is gracious and merciful. He is not easily angered; he is full of kindness, and anxious not to punish you.

Amos 5:4. The Lord says to the people of Israel, "Seek me—and live. [5]Don't seek the idols of Bethel, Gilgal, or Beer-sheba; for the people of Gilgal will be carried off to exile, and those of Bethel shall surely come to grief." [6]Seek the Lord and live, or else he will sweep like fire through Israel and consume her, and none of the idols in Bethel can put it out. [8]Seek him who created the Seven Stars and the constellation Orion, who turns darkness into morning, and day into night, who calls forth the water from the ocean and pours it out as rain upon the land. The Lord, Jehovah, is his name. [14]Be good, flee evil—and live! Then the Lord God of Hosts will truly be your Helper, as you have claimed he is.

Amos 8:12. Men will wander everywhere from sea to sea, seeking the Word of the Lord, searching, running here and going there, but will not find it.

Zeph 2:3. Beg him to save you, all who are humble—all who have tried to obey. Walk humbly and do what is right; perhaps even yet the Lord will protect you from his wrath in that day of doom.

Zech 8:20, 21. People from around the world will come on pilgrimages and pour into Jerusalem from many foreign cities to attend these celebrations. People will write their friends in other cities and say, "Let's go to Jerusalem to ask the Lord to bless us, and be merciful to us. I'm going! Please come with me. Let's go *now!*" [22]Yes, many people, even strong nations, will come to the Lord of Hosts in Jerusalem to ask for his blessing and help. [23]In those days ten men from ten different nations will clutch at the coat sleeves of one Jew and say, "Please be my friend, for I know that God is with you."

Mt 5:6. Happy are those who long to be just and good, for they shall be completely satisfied.

Lk 6:21. What happiness there is for you who are now hungry, for you are going to be satisfied!

Lk 11:9. And so it is with prayer—keep on asking and you will keep on getting; keep on looking and you will keep on finding; knock and the door will be opened. [Mt 7:7–12.] [10]Everyone who asks, receives; all who seek, find; and the door is opened to everyone who knocks. [11]You men who are fathers—if your boy asks for bread, do you give him a stone? If he asks for fish, do you give him a snake? [12]If he asks for an egg, do you give him a scorpion? (Of course not!) [13]And if even sinful persons like yourselves give children what they need, don't you realize that your heavenly Father will do at least as much, and give the Holy Spirit to those who ask for him?

Lk 13:24. The door to heaven is narrow. Work hard to get in, for the truth is that many will try to enter but when the head of the house has locked the door, it will be too late.

Lk 14:26. Anyone who wants to be my follower must love me far more than he does his own father, mother, wife, children, brothers, or sisters—yes, more than his own life—otherwise he cannot be my disciple. [27]And no one can be my disciple who does not carry his own cross and follow me. [28]But don't begin until you count the cost. For who would begin construction of a building without first getting estimates and then checking to see if he has enough money to pay the bills? [29]Otherwise he might complete only the foundation before running out of funds. And then how everyone would laugh! [30]"See that fellow there?" they would mock. "He started that building and ran out of money before it was finished!" [31]Or what king would ever dream of going to war without first sitting down with his counselors and discussing whether his army of 10,000 is strong enough to defeat the 20,000 men who are marching against him? [32]If the decision is negative, then while the enemy troops are still far away, he will send a truce team to discuss terms of peace. [33]So no one can become my disciple unless he first sits down and counts his blessings—and then renounces them all for me.

Lk 16:16. Until John the Baptist began to preach, the laws of Moses and the messages of the prophets were your guides. But John introduced the Good News that the Kingdom of God would come soon. And now eager multitudes are pressing in.

Jn 6:37. But some will come to me—those the Father has given me—and I will never, never reject them.

Acts 2:21. But anyone who asks for mercy from the Lord shall have it and shall be saved.

Acts 17:27. His purpose in all of this is that they should seek after God, and perhaps feel their way toward him and find him—though he is not far from any one of us.

Rom 3:11. No one has ever really followed God's paths, or even truly wanted to.

Rom 10:13. Anyone who calls upon the name of the Lord will be saved.

Heb 7:25. He is able to save completely all who come to God through him. Since he will live forever, he will always be there to remind God that he has paid for their sins with his blood.

Heb 9:28. So also Christ died only once as an offering for the sins of many people; and he will come again, but not to deal again with our sins. This time he will come bringing salvation to all those who are eagerly and patiently waiting for him.

Heb 11:6. You can never please God without faith, without depending on him. Anyone who wants to come to God must believe that there is a God and that he rewards those who sincerely look for him.

Jas 4:8. And when you draw close to God, God will draw close to you.

Rev 3:20. Look! I have been standing at the door and I am constantly knocking. If anyone hears me calling him and opens the door, I will come in and fellowship with him and he with me.

Rev 21:6. I will give to the thirsty the springs of the Water of Life—as a gift!

Rev 22:17. The Spirit and the bride say, "Come." Let each one who hears them say the same, "Come." Let the thirsty one come—anyone who wants to; let him come and drink the Water of Life without charge.

See *Backslider; Penitent; Sin, Confession of, Forgiveness of.*

INSTANCES OF. Asa, 2 Chron 14:7. Jehoshaphat, 2 Chron 17:3, 4. Uzziah, 2 Chron 26:5. Hezekiah, 2 Chron 31:21. Josiah, 2 Chron 34:3. Ezra, Ezra 7:10. David, Ps 34:4. Daniel, Dan 9:3, 4. The Magi, Mt 2:1, 2.

See *Penitent; Zeal.*

SEER See *Prophet.*

SEGUB 1. Son of Hiel, the rebuilder of Jericho, 1 Kgs 16:34.

2. Great-grandson of Judah, 1 Chron 2:4, 5, 21, 22.

SEIR 1. A mountain range in Edom, Deut 1:1–5. Along the route from Horeb to Kadesh-barnea, Deut 1:1–5. Israelites journey by, Deut 1:1–5; 2:1; 33:2. Originally inhabited by Horites, Gen 14:5, 6; 36:20–30; Deut 2:12; and later by the descendants of Esau after they destroyed the Horites, Deut 2:12, 22, with Gen 32:3; 33:14, 16; 36:6–9; Num 24:15–19; Deut 2:4, 5. The southern boundary of the conquests of Joshua, Josh 11:15–18.

2. A Horite chief, Gen 36:20, 21.

SEIRAH A city of unknown location, Judg 3:26.

SELA A city in Edom, 2 Kgs 14:7; Isa 16:1. See *Jokthe-el.*

SELAH A term usually regarded as a pause during which the singers stopped, and only the instruments could be heard. Because the Septuagint renders it as a rest calling for meditation on the preceding words, some students understand the term to mean, "Stop and think," Ps 9:16.

SELED A descendant of Jerahmeel, 1 Chron 2:30.

SELEUCIA A city of Syria on the Mediterranean. Paul visits, Acts 13:4.

SELF-CONDEMNATION 2 Sam 24:17. When David saw the angel, he said to the Lord, "Look, I am the one who has sinned! What have these sheep done? Let your anger be only against me and my family."

Job 9:20. But I? Am I righteous? My own mouth says no. Even if I were perfect, God would prove me wicked.

Prov 5:12. And you say, "Oh, if only I had listened! If only I had not demanded my own way! [13]Oh, why wouldn't I take advice? Why was I so stupid?"

Mt 23:31. In saying that, you are accusing yourselves of being the sons of wicked men.

Mt 25:24, 25. Then the man with the $1,000 came and said, "Sir, I knew you were a hard man, [Lk 19:21, 22.] and I was afraid you would rob me of what I earned, so I hid your money in the earth and here it is!" [26]But his master replied, "Wicked man! Lazy slave! Since you knew I would demand your profit, [27]you should at least have put my money into the bank so I could have some interest."

Mk 12:1. Here are some story-illustrations Jesus gave to the people at that time: "A man planted a vineyard and built a wall around it and dug a pit for pressing out the grape juice, and built a watchman's tower. Then he leased the farm to tenant farmers and moved to another country. [2]At grape-picking time he sent one of his men to collect his share of the crop. [3]But the farmers beat up the man and sent him back empty-handed. [4]The owner then sent another of his men, who received the same treatment, only worse, for his head was seriously injured. [5]The next man he sent was killed; and later, others were either beaten or killed until [6]there was only one left—his only son. He finally sent him, thinking they would surely give him their full respect. [7]But when the farmers saw him coming they said, 'He will own the farm when his father dies. Come on, let's kill him—and then the farm will be ours!' [8]So they caught him and murdered him and threw his body out of the vineyard. [9]What do you suppose the owner will do when he hears what happened? He will come and kill them all, and lease the vineyard to others. [10]Don't you remember reading this verse in the Scriptures? 'The Rock the builders threw away became the cornerstone, the most honored stone in the building! [11]This is the Lord's doing and it is an amazing thing to see.' " [12]The Jewish leaders wanted to arrest him then and there for using this illustration, for they knew he was pointing at them—they were the wicked farmers in his story. But they were afraid to touch him for fear of a mob. So they left him and went away. Mt 21:33–41.

Jn 8:7. So he stood up again and said, "All right, hurl the stones at her until she dies. But only he who has never sinned may throw the first!" [9]And the Jewish leaders slipped away one by one, beginning with the eldest, until only Jesus was left in front of the crowd with the woman.

Acts 22:24. So the commander brought him inside and ordered him lashed with whips to make him confess his crime. He wanted to find out why the crowd had become so furious!

Rom 2:1. "Well," you may be saying, "what terrible people you have been talking about!" But wait a minute! You are just as bad. When you say they are wicked and should be punished, you are talking about yourselves, for you do these very same things.

See *Self-Incrimination; Remorse; Repentance.*

INSTANCES OF. Achan, Josh 7:19–25. David, 2 Sam 12:5–7. Ahab, 1 Kgs 20:39–42.

SELF-CONFIDENCE See *Confidence, False.*

SELF-CONTROL Of Saul, 1 Sam 10:27. Of David, 1 Sam 24:1–15; 26:1–20. Of Jesus, Mt 26:62, 63; 27:12–14.

See *Abstinence, Total; Graces, Christian; Patience; Tact;* also, *Rashness.*

SELF-DECEPTION Jas 1:26.

See *Confidence, False; Security, False.*

SELF-DEFENSE Accused heard in, Mt 27:11–14; Mk 15:2–5; Lk 23:3; Jn 7:51; Acts 2:37–40; 22; 23; 24:10–21; 26.

SELF-DELUSION A characteristic of the wicked, Ps 49:18. Prosperity frequently leads to, Ps 30:6, 7; Hos 12:8; Lk 12:17–19. Obstinate sinners often given up to, Ps 81:11, 12; Hos 4:17; 2 Thess 2:10, 11.

Exhibited in thinking that: Our own ways are right, Prov 14:12; we should continue in established evil practices, Jer 44:17; we are faultless, Prov 30:12; we are better than others, Lk 18:11; we are rich in spiritual things, Rev 3:17; we may have prosperity while in sin, Deut 29:19; we are above adversity, Ps 10:6; gifts entitle us to heaven, Mt 7:21, 22; position entitles us to heaven, Mt 3:9; Lk 13:24–26; God will not punish our sins, Jer 5:12; Christ will not come to judge, 2 Pet 3:4; our lives will be prolonged, Isa 56:12; Lk 12:19; Jas 4:13.

Frequently persevered in, to the last, Mt 7:22; 25:11, 12; Lk 13:24, 25. Fatal consequences of, Mt 7:23; 24:48–51; Lk 12:20; 1 Thess 5:3.

EXEMPLIFIED. Ahab, 1 Kgs 20:27, 34. Israelites, Hos 12:8. Jews, Jn 8:33, 41. Church of Laodicea, Rev 3:17.

See *Confidence, False; Security, False.*

SELF-DENIAL Gen 22:12. "Lay down the knife; don't hurt the lad in any way," the Angel said, "for I know that God is first in your life—you have not withheld even your beloved son from me." with *vs.* 1–12.

2 Sam 24:24. But the king said to Araunah, "No, I will not have it as a gift. I will buy it, for I don't want to offer to the Lord my God burnt offerings that have cost me nothing." So David paid him for the threshing floor and the oxen.

Ps 132:2–4. I couldn't rest, I couldn't sleep, thinking how I ought to build a permanent home for the Ark of the Lord, a Temple for the mighty one of Israel.

Prov 16:32. It is better to be slow-tempered than famous; it is better to have self-control than to control an army.

Prov 23:1, 2. When dining with a rich man, be on your guard and don't stuff yourself, though it all tastes so good; for he is trying to bribe you, and no good is going to come of his invitation.

Dan 10:3. All that time I tasted neither wine nor meat, and of course I went without desserts. I neither washed nor shaved nor combed my hair.

Mt 5:29. So if your eye—even if it is your best eye!—causes you to lust, gouge it out and throw it away. Better for part of you to be destroyed than for all of you to be cast into hell. [30]And if your hand —even your right hand—causes you to sin, cut it off and throw it away. Better that than find yourself in hell. Mk 9:43, 44.

Mt 8:19. Just then one of the Jewish religious teachers said to him, "Teacher, I will follow you no matter where you go!" [20]But Jesus said, "Foxes have dens and birds have nests, but I, the Messiah, have no home of my own—no place to lay my head." [Lk 9:57, 58.] [21]Another of his disciples said, "Sir, when my father is dead, then I will follow you." [22]But Jesus told him, "Follow me *now!* Let those who are spiritually dead care for their own dead." Lk 9:59, 60.

Mt 10:37. If you love your father and mother more than you love me, you are not worthy of being mine; or if you love your son or daughter more than me, you are not worthy of being mine. [38]If you refuse to take up your cross and follow me, you are not worthy of being mine. [39]If you cling to your life, you will lose it; but if you give it up for me, you will save it.

Mt 13:44. The Kingdom of Heaven is like a treasure a man discovered in a field. In his excitement, he sold everything he owned to get enough money to buy the field—and get the treasure, too! [45]Again, the Kingdom of Heaven is like a pearl merchant on the lookout for choice pearls. [46]He discovered a real bargain—a pearl of great value—and sold everything he owned to purchase it!

Mt 16:24. Then Jesus said to the disciples, "If anyone wants to be a follower of mine, let him deny himself and take up his cross and follow me. [25]For anyone who keeps his life for himself shall lose it; and anyone who loses his life for me shall find it again." Mk 8:34, 35; Lk 9:23, 24.

Mt 18:8. So if your hand or foot causes you to sin, cut it off and throw it away. Better to enter heaven crippled than to be in hell with both of your hands and feet. [9]And if your eye causes you to sin, gouge it out and throw it away. Better to enter heaven with one eye than to be in hell with two. Mk 9:43, 44.

Mt 19:12. "Some are born without the ability to marry, and some are disabled by men, and some refuse to marry for the sake of the Kingdom of Heaven. Let anyone who can, accept my statement." [21]Jesus told him, "If you want to be perfect, go and sell everything you have and give the money to the poor, and you will have treasure in heaven; and come, follow me." Lk 12:33.

Lk 5:11. And as soon as they landed, they left everything and went with him. [27]Later on as Jesus left the town he saw a tax collector—with the usual reputation for cheating—sitting at a tax collection booth. The man's name was Levi. Jesus said to him, "Come and be one of my disciples!" [28]So Levi left everything, sprang up and went with him. Mk 2:14.

Lk 14:26. Anyone who wants to be my follower must love me far more than he does his own father, mother, wife, children, brothers, or sisters—yes, more than his own life—otherwise he cannot be my disciple. [27]And no one can be my disciple who does not carry his own cross and follow me. [33]So no one can become my disciple unless he first sits down and counts his blessings—and then renounces them all for me. *vs.* 28–32.

Lk 18:27. He replied, "God can do what men can't!" [28]And Peter said, "We have left our homes and followed you." [29]"Yes," Jesus replied, "and everyone who has done as you have, leaving home, wife, brothers, parents, or children for the sake of the Kingdom of God, [Mk 10:29.] [30]will be repaid many times over now, as well as receiving eternal life in the world to come."

Lk 21:2. Then a poor widow came by and dropped in two small copper coins. [3]"Really," he remarked, "this poor widow has given more than all the rest of them combined. [4]For they have given a little of what they didn't need, but she, poor as she is, has given everything she has." Mk 12:43, 44.

Jn 12:25. If you love your life down here—you will lose it. If you despise your life down here—you will exchange it for eternal glory. Mt 16:25; Mk 8: 35.

Acts 20:22. And now I am going to Jerusalem, drawn there irresistibly by the Holy Spirit, not knowing what awaits me, [23]except that the Holy Spirit has told me in city after city that jail and suffering lie ahead. [24]But life is worth nothing unless I use it for doing the work assigned me by the Lord Jesus—the work of telling others the Good News about God's mighty kindness and love.

Acts 21:13. But he said, "Why all this weeping? You are breaking my heart! For I am ready not only to be jailed at Jerusalem, but also to die for the sake of the Lord Jesus."

Rom 6:6. Your old evil desires were nailed to the cross with him; that part of you that loves to sin was crushed and fatally wounded, so that your sin-loving body is no longer under sin's control, no longer needs to be a slave to sin.

Rom 8:12. So, dear brothers, you have no obligations whatever to your old sinful nature to do what it begs you to do. [13]For if you keep on following it you are lost and will perish, but if through the power of the Holy Spirit you crush it and its evil deeds, you shall live. [35]Who then can ever keep Christ's love from us? When we have trouble or calamity, when we are hunted down or destroyed, is it because he doesn't love us anymore? And if we are hungry, or penniless, or in danger, or threatened with death, has God deserted us? [36]No, for the Scriptures tell us that for his sake we must be ready to face death at every moment of the day—we are like sheep awaiting slaughter.

Rom 13:14. But ask the Lord Jesus Christ to help you live as you should, and don't make plans to enjoy evil.

Rom 14:1. Give a warm welcome to any brother who wants to join you, even though his faith is weak. Don't criticize him for having different ideas from yours about what is right and wrong. [2]For instance, don't argue with him about whether or not to eat meat that has been offered to idols. You may believe there is no harm in this, but the faith of others is weaker; they think it is wrong, and will go without any meat at all and eat vegetables rather than eat that kind of meat. [3]Those who think it is all right to eat such meat must not look down on those who won't. And if you are one of those who won't, don't find fault with those who do. For God has accepted them to be his children. [4]They are God's servants, not yours. They are responsible to him, not to you. Let him tell them whether they are right or wrong. And God is able to make them do as they should. [5]Some think that Christians should observe the Jewish holidays as special days to worship God, but others say it is wrong and foolish to go to all that trouble, for every day alike belongs to God. On questions of this kind everyone must decide for himself. [6]If you have special days for worshiping the Lord, you are trying to honor him; you are doing a good thing. So is the person who eats meat that has been offered to idols; he is thankful to the Lord for it; he is doing right. And the person who won't touch such meat, he, too, is anxious to please the Lord, and is thankful. [7]We are not our own bosses to live or die as we ourselves might choose. [8]Living or dying we follow the Lord. Either way we are his. [9]Christ died and rose again for this very purpose, so that he can be our Lord both while we live and when we die. [10]You have no right to criticize your brother or look down on him. Remember, each of us will stand personally before the Judgment Seat of God. [11]For it is written, "As I live," says the Lord, "every knee shall bow to me and every tongue confess to God." [12]Yes, each of us will give an account of himself to God. [13]So don't criticize each other any more. Try instead to live in such a way that you will never make your brother stumble by letting him see you doing something he thinks is wrong. [14]As for myself, I am perfectly sure on the authority of the Lord Jesus that there is nothing really wrong with eating meat that has been offered to idols. But if someone believes it is wrong, then he shouldn't do it because for him it is wrong. [15]And if your brother is bothered by what you eat, you are not acting in love if you go ahead and eat it. Don't let your eating ruin someone for whom Christ died. [16]Don't do anything that will cause criticism against yourself even though you know that what you do is right. [17]For, after all, the important thing for us as Christians is not what we eat or drink but stirring up goodness and peace and joy from the Holy Spirit. [18]If you let Christ be Lord in these affairs, God will be glad; and so will others. [19]In this way aim for harmony in the church and try to build each other up. [20]Don't undo the work of God for a chunk of meat. Remember, there is nothing wrong with the meat, but it is wrong to eat it if it makes another stumble. [21]The right thing to do is to quit eating meat or drinking wine or doing anything else that offends your brother or makes him sin. [22]You may know that there is nothing wrong with what you do, even from God's point of view, but keep it to yourself; don't flaunt your faith in front of others who might be hurt by it. In this situation, happy is the man who does not sin by doing what he knows is right.

Rom 15:1, 2. Even if we believe that it makes no difference to the Lord whether we do these things, still we cannot just go ahead and do them to please ourselves; for we must bear the "burden" of being considerate of the doubts and fears of others—of those who feel these things are wrong. Let's please the other fellow, not ourselves, and do what is for his good and thus build him up in the Lord. [3]Christ didn't please himself. As the Psalmist said, "He came for the very purpose of suffering under the insults of those who were against the Lord." [4]These things that were written in the Scriptures so long ago are to teach us patience and to encourage us, so that we will look forward expectantly to the time when God will conquer sin and death. [5]May God who gives patience, steadiness, and encouragement help you to live in complete harmony with each other—each with the attitude of Christ toward the other.

1 Cor 6:12. I can do anything I want to if Christ has not said no, but some of these things aren't good for me. Even if I am allowed to do them, I'll refuse to if I think they might get such a grip on me that I can't easily stop when I want to.

1 Cor 8:10. You see, this is what may happen: Someone who thinks it is wrong to eat this food will see you eating at a temple restaurant, for you know there is no harm in it. Then he will become bold enough to do it too, although all the time he still feels it is wrong. [11]So because you "know it is all right to do it," you will be responsible for causing great spiritual damage to a brother with a tender conscience for whom Christ died. [12]And it is a sin against Christ to sin against your brother by encouraging him to do something he thinks is wrong. [13]So if eating meat offered to idols is going to make my brother sin, I'll not eat any of it as long as I live, because I don't want to do this to him.

1 Cor 9:12. You give them to others who preach to you, and you should. But shouldn't we have an even greater right to them? Yet we have *never* used this right, but supply our own needs without your help. We have never demanded payment of any kind for fear that, if we did, you might be less interested in our message to you from Christ. [15]Yet I have never asked you for one penny. And I am not writing this to hint that I would like to start now. In fact, I would rather die of hunger than lose the satisfaction I get from preaching to you without charge. [18]Under this circumstance, what is my pay? It is the special joy I get from preaching the Good News without expense to anyone, never demanding my rights. [19]And this has a real advantage: I am not bound to obey anyone just because he pays my salary; yet I have freely and happily become a servant of any and all so that I can win them to Christ. [23]I do this to get the Gospel to them and also for the blessing I myself receive when I see them come to Christ. [25]To win the contest you must deny yourselves many things that would keep you from doing your best. An athlete goes to all this trouble just to win a blue ribbon or a silver cup, but we do it for a heavenly reward that never disappears. [26]So I run straight to the goal with purpose in every step. I fight to win. I'm not just shadow-boxing or playing around. [27]Like an athlete I punish my body, treating it roughly, training it to do what it should, not what it wants to. Otherwise I fear that after enlisting others for the race, I myself might be declared unfit and ordered to stand aside.

1 Cor 10:23. You are certainly free to eat food offered to idols if you want to; it's not against God's laws to eat such meat, but that doesn't mean that you should go ahead and do it. It may be perfectly legal, but it may not be best and helpful. [24]Don't think only of yourself. Try to think of the other fellow, too, and what is best for him.

2 Cor 6:3. We try to live in such a way that no one will ever be offended or kept back from finding the Lord by the way we act, so that no one can find fault with us and blame it on the Lord.

Gal 2:20. I have been crucified with Christ: and I myself no longer live, but Christ lives in me. And the real life I now have within this body is a result of my trusting in the Son of God, who loved me and gave himself for me.

Gal 5:16. I advise you to obey only the Holy Spirit's instructions. He will tell you where to go and what to do, and then you won't always be doing the wrong things your evil nature wants you to. [17]For we naturally love to do evil things that are just the opposite from the things that the Holy Spirit tells us to do; and the good things we want to do when the Spirit has his way with us are just the opposite of our natural desires. These two forces within us are constantly fighting each other to win control over us, and our wishes are never free from their pressures. [24]Those who belong to Christ have nailed their natural evil desires to his cross and crucified them there.

Gal 6:14. As for me, God forbid that I should boast about anything except the cross of our Lord Jesus Christ. Because of that cross my interest in all the attractive things of the world was killed long ago, and the world's interest in me is also long dead.

Phil 2:4. Don't just think about your own affairs, but be interested in others, too, and in what they are doing. *vs.* 5–8.

Phil 3:7. But all these things that I once thought very worthwhile—now I've thrown them all away so that I can put my trust and hope in Christ alone. [8]Yes, everything else is worthless when compared with the priceless gain of knowing Christ Jesus my Lord. I have put aside all else, counting it worth less than nothing, in order that I can have Christ, [9]and become one with him, no longer counting on being saved by being good enough or by obeying God's laws, but by trusting Christ to save me; for God's way of making us right with himself depends on faith—counting on Christ alone.

Col 3:5. Away then with sinful, earthly things;

deaden the evil desires lurking within you; have nothing to do with sexual sin, impurity, lust and shameful desires; don't worship the good things of life, for that is idolatry.

2 Tim 2:4. And as Christ's soldier do not let yourself become tied up in worldly affairs, for then you cannot satisfy the one who has enlisted you in his army.

Tit 2:12. And along with this gift comes the realization that God wants us to turn from godless living and sinful pleasures and to live good, God-fearing lives day after day.

Heb 13:13. So let us go out to him beyond the city walls (that is, outside the interests of this world, being willing to be despised) to suffer with him there, bearing his shame.

1 Pet 2:11. Dear brothers, you are only visitors here. Since your real home is in heaven I beg you to keep away from the evil pleasures of this world; they are not for you, for they fight against your very souls. [12]Be careful how you behave among your unsaved neighbors; for then, even if they are suspicious of you and talk against you, they will end up praising God for your good works when Christ returns. [13]For the Lord's sake, obey every law of your government: those of the king as head of the state, [14]and those of the king's officers, for he has sent them to punish all who do wrong, and to honor those who do right. [15]It is God's will that your good lives should silence those who foolishly condemn the Gospel without knowing what it can do for them, having never experienced its power. [16]You are free from the law, but that doesn't mean you are free to do wrong. Live as those who are free to do only God's will at all times.

1 Pet 4:1. Since Christ suffered and underwent pain, you must have the same attitude he did; you must be ready to suffer, too. For remember, when your body suffers, sin loses its power, [2]and you won't be spending the rest of your life chasing after evil desires, but will be anxious to do the will of God.

3 Jn 7. For they are traveling for the Lord, and take neither food, clothing, shelter, nor money from those who are not Christians, even though they have preached to them.

Rev 12:11. They defeated him by the blood of the Lamb, and by their testimony; for they did not love their lives but laid them down for him.

See *Cross; Humility.*

INSTANCES OF. Abraham, when he accorded to Lot, his junior, his choice of the land of Canaan, Gen 13:9, with 17:7, 8. Moses, in choosing rather to suffer ill-treatment with the people of God than enjoy the pleasures of sin, Heb 11:24, 25; in taking no compensation from the Israelites for his services, Num 16:15. Samuel, in his administration of justice, 1 Sam 12:3, 4. The widow of Zarephath, in sharing with Elijah the last of her food, 1 Kgs 17:12–15. Daniel, in his temperance, Dan 1:8; in refusing rewards from Belshazzar, Dan 5:16, 17. Esther, in risking her life for the deliverance of her people, Esther 4:16. The Rechabites, in refusing to drink wine, or even to plant vineyards, Jer 35:6, 7.

Peter and other apostles, in abandoning their vocations and following Jesus, Mt 4:20; 9:9; Mk 1:16–20; 2:14; Lk 5:11, 27, 28; in leaving all and following Jesus, Mt 19:27; Mk 10:28. The widow, who put her all into the treasury, Lk 21:4. The early Christians, in having everything in common, Acts 2:44, 45; 4:34, 35. Joseph, in selling his possessions, and giving to the apostles, Acts 4:36, 37. Paul, in counting his life worth nothing, Acts 20:24; Phil 3:7, 8; in not coveting any man's money or apparel, Acts 20:33; in working for his own support while he also taught, Acts 20:34, 35; 1 Cor 4:12; 10:33.

SELF-EXALTATION Job 12:3. Well, I know a few things myself—you are no better than I am. And who doesn't know these things you've been saying?

Ezk 31:10. But Egypt has become proud and arrogant, the Lord God says. Therefore because she has set herself so high above the others, reaching to the clouds, [11]I will deliver her into the hands of a mighty nation, to destroy her as her wickedness deserves. I, myself, will cut her down. [12]A foreign army (from Babylon)—the terror of the nations—will invade her land and cut her down and leave her fallen on the ground. Her branches will be scattered across the mountains and valleys and rivers of the land. All those who live beneath her shade will go away and leave her lying there. [13]The birds will pluck off her twigs and the wild animals will lie among her branches; [14]let no other nation exult with pride for its own prosperity, though it be higher than the clouds, for all are doomed and they will land in hell, along with all the proud men of the world.

Obd 1:3. You are proud because you live in those high, inaccessible cliffs. "Who can ever reach us way up here!" you boast. Don't fool yourselves! [4]Though you soar as high as eagles, and build your nest among the stars, I will bring you plummeting down, says the Lord.

Lk 14:7. When he noticed that all who came to the dinner were trying to sit near the head of the table, he gave them this advice: [8]"If you are invited to a wedding feast, don't always head for the best seat. For if someone more respected than you shows up, [9]the host will bring him over to where you are sitting and say, 'Let this man sit here instead.' And you, embarrassed, will have to take whatever seat is left at the foot of the table! [10]Do this instead—start at the foot; and when your host sees you he will come and say, 'Friend, we have a better place than this for you!' Thus you will be honored in front of all the other guests. [11]For everyone who tries to honor himself shall be humbled; and he who humbles himself shall be honored."

2 Cor 10:5. These weapons can break down every proud argument against God and every wall that can be built to keep men from finding him. With these weapons I can capture rebels and bring them back to God, and change them into men whose hearts' desire is obedience to Christ. [17]As the Scriptures say, "If anyone is going to boast, let him

boast about what the Lord has done and not about himself." [18]When someone boasts about himself and how well he has done, it doesn't count for much. But when the Lord commends him, that's different!

Gal 6:3. If anyone thinks he is too great to stoop to this, he is fooling himself. He is really a nobody.

2 Thess 2:4. He will defy every god there is, and tear down every other object of adoration and worship. He will go in and sit as God in the temple of God, claiming that he himself is God.

See *Pride; Selfishness; Self-Righteousness.*

INSTANCES OF. Pharaoh, Ex 9:17. Korah, Dathan, and Abiram, Num 16:1–3. Sennacherib, 2 Chron 32:9–19. Lucifer, Isa 14:12–15. Prince of Tyre, making himself God, Ezk 28:2, 3, 9. Nebuchadnezzar, Dan 4:30; 5:20. Belshazzar, Dan 5:23. Simon the sorcerer, Acts 8:9–11. Herod, when deified by the people, Acts 12:20–23.

SELF-EXAMINATION Lev 16:29. This is a permanent law: You must do no work on the twenty-fifth day of September, but spend the day in self-examination and humility.

Job 13:23. Tell me, what have I done wrong? Help me! Point out my sin to me.

Ps 4:4. Stand before the Lord in awe, and do not sin against him. Lie quietly upon your bed in silent meditation.

Ps 19:12. But how can I ever know what sins are lurking in my heart? Cleanse me from these hidden faults.

Ps 26:2. Cross-examine me, O Lord, and see that this is so; test my motives and affections too.

Ps 77:6. Then my nights were filled with joyous songs. I search my soul and meditate upon the difference now.

Ps 119:59, 60. I thought about the wrong direction in which I was headed, and turned around and came running back to you.

Ps 139:23. Search me, O God, and know my heart; test my thoughts. [24]Point out anything you find in me that makes you sad, and lead me along the path of everlasting life.

Jer 17:9. The heart is the most deceitful thing there is, and desperately wicked. No one can really know how bad it is!

Lam 3:40. Let us examine ourselves instead, and repent and turn again to the Lord.

Hag 1:7. "Think it over," says the Lord of Hosts. "Consider how you have acted, and what has happened as a result!"

Mt 26:22. Sorrow chilled their hearts, and each one asked, "Am I the one?" Mk 14:19.

1 Cor 11:27. So if anyone eats this bread and drinks from this cup of the Lord in an unworthy manner, he is guilty of sin against the body and the blood of the Lord. [28]That is why a man should examine himself carefully before eating the bread and drinking from the cup. [31]But if you carefully examine yourselves before eating you will not need to be judged and punished.

2 Cor 13:5. Check up on yourselves. Are you really Christians? Do you pass the test? Do you feel Christ's presence and power more and more within you? Or are you just pretending to be Christians when actually you aren't at all?

Gal 6:3. If anyone thinks he is too great to stoop to this, he is fooling himself. He is really a nobody. [4]Let everyone be sure that he is doing his very best, for then he will have the personal satisfaction of work well done, and won't need to compare himself with someone else. [5]Each of us must bear some faults and burdens of his own. For none of us is perfect!

See *Meditation; Repentance; Sin, Confession of.*

SELF-INCRIMINATION Num 5:11–27; 1 Kgs 8:31, 32; Acts 22:24. See *Self-Condemnation.*

INSTANCES OF. Achan, Josh 7:19–25.

SELF-INDULGENCE INSTANCES OF. Solomon, Eccl 2:10. The rich fool, Lk 12:16–20. Dives, the rich man, Lk 16:19.

See *Gluttony; Idleness; Laziness; also Self-Denial.*

SELFISHNESS Gen 4:9. But afterwards the Lord asked Cain, "Where is your brother? Where is Abel?" "How should I know?" Cain retorted. "Am I supposed to keep track of him wherever he goes?"

Num 32:6. "You mean you want to sit here while your brothers go across and do all the fighting?" Moses demanded.

Ps 38:11. My loved ones and friends stay away, fearing my disease. Even my own family stands at a distance.

Ps 101:4. I will reject all selfishness and stay away from every evil.

Prov 11:26. People curse the man who holds his grain for higher prices, but they bless the man who sells it to them in their time of need.

Prov 18:17. Any story sounds true until someone tells the other side and sets the record straight.

Prov 24:11, 12. Rescue those who are unjustly sentenced to death; don't stand back and let them die. Don't try to disclaim responsibility by saying you didn't know about it. For God, who knows all hearts, knows yours, and he knows you knew! And he will reward everyone according to his deeds.

Prov 28:27. If you give to the poor, your needs will be supplied! But a curse upon those who close their eyes to poverty.

Ezk 34:18. Is it a small thing to you, O evil shepherds, that you not only keep the best of the pastures for yourselves, but trample down the rest? That you take the best water for yourselves, and muddy the rest with your feet?

Mic 3:11. You leaders who take bribes; you priests and prophets who won't preach and prophesy until you're paid. (And yet you fawn upon the Lord and say, "All is well—the Lord is here among us. No harm can come to us.")

Hag 1:4. Is it then the right time for you to live in luxurious homes, when the Temple lies in ruins? [9]You hope for much but get so little. And when you bring it home, I blow it away—it doesn't last at all. Why? Because my Temple lies in ruins and you don't care. Your only concern is your own fine homes. [10]That is why I am holding back the rains from heaven and giving you such scant crops.

Zech 7:6. And even now in your holy feasts to God, you don't think of me, but only of the food and fellowship and fun.

Mal 1:10. Oh, to find one priest among you who would shut the doors and refuse this kind of sacrifice. I have no pleasure in you," says the Lord of Hosts, "and I will not accept your offerings."

Mt 19:21. Jesus told him, "If you want to be perfect, go and sell everything you have and give the money to the poor, and you will have treasure in heaven; and come, follow me." [22]But when the young man heard this, he went away sadly, for he was very rich.

Lk 6:32. Do you think you deserve credit for merely loving those who love you? Even the godless do that! [33]And if you do good only to those who do you good—is that so wonderful? Even sinners do that much! [34]And if you lend money only to those who can repay you, what good is that? Even the most wicked will lend to their own kind for full return!

Rom 14:15. And if your brother is bothered by what you eat, you are not acting in love if you go ahead and eat it. Don't let your eating ruin someone for whom Christ died.

Rom 15:1, 2. Even if we believe that it makes no difference to the Lord whether we do these things, still we cannot just go ahead and do them to please ourselves; for we must bear the "burden" of being considerate of the doubts and fears of others—of those who feel these things are wrong. Let's please the other fellow, not ourselves, and do what is for his good and thus build him up in the Lord. [3]Christ didn't please himself.

1 Cor 10:24. Don't think only of yourself. Try to think of the other fellow, too, and what is best for him.

2 Cor 5:15. He died for all so that all who live—having received eternal life from him—might live no longer for themselves, to please themselves, but to spend their lives pleasing Christ who died and rose again for them.

Gal 6:2. Share each other's troubles and problems, and so obey our Lord's command.

Phil 2:4. Don't just think about your own affairs, but be interested in others, too, and in what they are doing. [20]There is no one like Timothy for having a real interest in you; [21]everyone else seems to be worrying about his own plans and not those of Jesus Christ. 1 Cor 13:4, 5.

2 Tim 3:2. For people will love only themselves and their money; they will be proud and boastful, sneering at God, disobedient to their parents, ungrateful to them, and thoroughly bad. [3]They will be hardheaded and never give in to others; they will be constant liars and troublemakers and will think nothing of immorality. They will be rough and cruel, and sneer at those who try to be good. [4]They will betray their friends; they will be hotheaded, puffed up with pride, and prefer good times to worshiping God.

Jas 2:15. If you have a friend who is in need of food and clothing, [16]and you say to him, "Well, good-bye and God bless you; stay warm and eat hearty," and then don't give him clothes or food, what good does that do?

1 Jn 3:17. But if someone who is supposed to be a Christian has money enough to live well, and sees a brother in need, and won't help him—how can God's love be within *him?*

See *Liberality; Poor; Unselfishness.*

SELF-RIGHTEOUSNESS Num 16:3. They went to Moses and Aaron and said, "We have had enough of your presumption; you are no better than anyone else; everyone in Israel has been chosen of the Lord, and he is with all of us. What right do you have to put yourselves forward, claiming that we must obey you, and acting as though you were greater than anyone else among all these people of the Lord?"

Deut 9:4. Then, when the Lord has done this for you, don't say to yourselves, "The Lord has helped us because we are so good!" No, it is because of the wickedness of the other nations that he is doing it. [5]It is not at all because you are such fine, upright people that the Lord will drive them out from before you! I say it again, it is only because of the wickedness of the other nations, and because of his promises to your ancestors, Abraham, Isaac, and Jacob, that he will do it. [6]I say it yet again: *Jehovah your God is not giving you this good land because you are good, for you are not*—you are a wicked, stubborn people.

1 Sam 2:9. He will protect his godly ones, but the wicked shall be silenced in darkness. No one shall succeed by strength alone.

Job 11:4. You claim you are pure in the eyes of God! [5]Oh, that God would speak and tell you what he thinks! [6]Oh, that he would make you truly see yourself, for he knows everything you've done. Listen! God is doubtless punishing you far less than you deserve!

Job 12:2. Yes, I realize you know everything! All wisdom will die with you!

Job 13:3. Oh, how I long to speak directly to the Almighty. I want to talk this over with God himself. [13]Be silent now and let me alone, that I may speak—and I am willing to face the consequences. [15]God may kill me for saying this—in fact, I expect him to. Nevertheless I am going to argue my case with him. [18]This is my case: *I know that I am righteous.* [19]Who can argue with me over this? If you could prove me wrong I would stop defending myself and die.

Job 16:17. Yet I am innocent, and my prayer is pure. [18]O earth, do not conceal my blood. Let it protest on my behalf.

Job 18:2. Who are you trying to fool? Speak some sense if you want us to answer! [3]Have we become like animals to you, stupid and dumb? [4]Just because you tear your clothes in anger, is this going to start an earthquake? Shall we all go and hide?

Job 21:27. I know what you are going to say—[28]you will tell me of rich and wicked men who came to disaster because of their sins. [29]But I reply, Ask anyone who has been around and he can tell you the truth.

Job 22:2. Is mere man of any worth to God? Even the wisest is of value only to himself! [3]Is it any pleasure to the Almighty if you are righteous? Would it be any gain to him if you were perfect?

Job 32:1. The three men refused to reply further to Job because he kept insisting on his innocence. [2]Then Elihu (son of Barachel, the Buzite, of the Clan of Ram) became angry because Job refused to admit he had sinned and to acknowledge that God had just cause for punishing him.

Job 33:8. You have said it in my hearing, yes, you've said it again and again— [9]"I am pure, I am innocent; I have not sinned."

Job 35:2. Do you think it is right for you to claim, "I haven't sinned." [7]Or if you are good, is this some great gift to him? [8]Your sins may hurt another man, or your good deeds may profit him.

Ps 10:5. Yet there is success in everything they do, and their enemies fall before them. They do not see your punishment awaiting them. [6]They boast that neither God nor man can ever keep them down—somehow they'll find a way!

Prov 12:15. A fool thinks he needs no advice, but a wise man listens to others.

Prov 14:12. Before every man there lies a wide and pleasant road that seems right but ends in death.

Prov 16:2. We can always "prove" that we are right, but is the Lord convinced?

Prov 20:6. Most people will tell you what loyal friends they are, but are they telling the truth?

Prov 21:2. We can justify our every deed but God looks at our motives.

Prov 25:14. One who doesn't give the gift he promised is like a cloud blowing over a desert without dropping any rain. [27]Just as it is harmful to eat too much honey, so also it is bad for men to think about all the honors they deserve!

Prov 26:12. There is one thing worse than a fool, and that is a man who is conceited.

Prov 27:2. Don't praise yourself; let others do it! [21]The purity of silver and gold can be tested in a crucible, but a man is tested by his reaction to men's praise.

Prov 28:13. A man who refuses to admit his mistakes can never be successful. But if he confesses and forsakes them, he gets another chance. [26]A man is a fool to trust himself! But those who use God's wisdom are safe.

Prov 30:11, 12. There are those who curse their father and mother, and feel themselves faultless despite their many sins. [13]They are proud beyond description, arrogant, disdainful.

Isa 5:21. Woe to those who are wise and shrewd in their own eyes!

Isa 28:17. I will take the line and plummet of justice to check the foundation wall you built; it looks so fine, but it is so weak a storm of hail will knock it down! The enemy will come like a flood and sweep it away, and you will be drowned. [20]The bed you have made is far too short to lie on; the blankets are too narrow to cover you.

Isa 47:7. You thought your reign would never end, Queen Kingdom of the world. You didn't care a whit about my people or think about the fate of those who do them harm.

Isa 50:11. But see here, you who live in your own light, and warm yourselves from your own fires and not from God's; you will live among sorrows.

Isa 64:6. We are all infected and impure with sin. When we put on our prized robes of righteousness we find they are but filthy rags.

Isa 65:3. All day long they insult me to my face by worshiping idols in many gardens and burning incense on the rooftops of their homes. [4]At night they go out among the graves and caves to worship evil spirits, and they eat pork and other forbidden foods. [5]Yet they say to one another, "Don't come too close, you'll defile me! For I am holier than you!" They stifle me. Day in and day out they infuriate me.

Jer 2:13. For my people have done two evil things: They have forsaken me, the Fountain of Life-giving Water; and they have built for themselves broken cisterns that can't hold water! [22]No amount of soap or lye can make you clean. You are stained with guilt that cannot ever be washed away. I see it always before me, the Lord God says. [23]You say it isn't so, that you haven't worshiped idols? How can you say a thing like that? Go and look in any valley in the land! Face the awful sins that you have done, O restless female camel, seeking for a male! [34]Your clothing is stained with the blood of the innocent and the poor. Brazenly you murder without a cause. [35]And yet you say, "I haven't done a thing to anger God. I'm sure he isn't angry!" I will punish you severely because you say, "I haven't sinned!"

Jer 7:4. But don't be fooled by those who lie to you and say that since the Temple of the Lord is here, God will never let Jerusalem be destroyed.

Jer 8:8. How can you say, "We understand his laws," when your teachers have twisted them up to mean a thing I never said?

Jer 17:5. The Lord says: Cursed is the man who puts his trust in mortal man and turns his heart away from God.

Jer 49:4. You are proud of your fertile valleys, but they will soon be ruined. O wicked daughter, you trusted in your wealth and thought no one could ever harm you. [16]You have been fooled by your fame and your pride, living there in the mountains of Petra, in the clefts of the rocks. But though you live among the peaks with the eagles, I will bring you down, says the Lord.

Ezk 33:24. Son of dust, the scattered remnants of Judah living among the ruined cities keep saying, "Abraham was only one man and yet he got possession of the whole country! We are many, so we should certainly be able to get it back!" [25]But the Lord God says: You are powerless, for you do evil! You eat meat with the blood; you worship idols, and murder. Do you suppose I'll let you have the land? [26]Murderers! Idolators! Adulterers! Should you possess the land?

Hos 12:8. Ephraim boasts, "I am so rich! I have gotten it all by myself!" But riches can't make up for sin.

Amos 6:13. And just as stupid is your rejoicing in how great you are, when you are less than nothing! And priding yourselves on your own tiny power!

Hab 2:4. Note this: Wicked men trust themselves alone (as these Chaldeans do), and fail; but the righteous man trusts in me, and lives!

Zeph 3:11. And then you will no longer need to be ashamed of yourselves, for you will no longer be rebels against me. I will remove all your proud and arrogant men from among you; there will be no pride or haughtiness on my holy mountain.

Mt 7:22. At the Judgment many will tell me, "Lord, Lord, we told others about you and used your name to cast out demons and to do many other great miracles." [23]But I will reply, "You have never been mine. Go away, for your deeds are evil."

Mt 9:10. Later, as Jesus and his disciples were eating dinner (at Matthew's house), there were many notorious swindlers there as guests! [11]The Pharisees were indignant. "Why does your teacher associate with men like that?" [12]"Because people who are well don't need a doctor! It's the sick people who do!" was Jesus' reply. [13]Then he added, "Now go away and learn the meaning of this verse of Scripture, 'It isn't your sacrifices and your gifts I want—I want you to be merciful.' For I have come to urge sinners, not the self-righteous, back to God." Mk 2:16; Lk 5:30.

Mt 16:6. "Watch out!" Jesus warned them; "beware of the yeast of the Pharisees and Sadducees." Mk 8:15.

Mt 19:16. Someone came to Jesus with this question: "Good master, what must I do to have eternal life?" [17]"When you call me good you are calling me God," Jesus replied, "for God alone is truly good. But to answer your question, you can get to heaven if you keep the commandments." [18]"Which ones?" the man asked. And Jesus replied, "Don't kill, don't commit adultery, don't steal, don't lie, [19]honor your father and mother, and love your neighbor as yourself!" [20]"I've always obeyed every one of them," the youth replied. "What else must I do?" [21]Jesus told him, "If you want to be perfect, go and sell everything you have and give the money to the poor, and you will have treasure in heaven; and come, follow me." [22]But when the young man heard this, he went away sadly, for he was very rich. Mk 10:17–22; Lk 18:18–23.

Mt 22:12. "Friend," he asked, "how does it happen that you are here without a wedding robe?" And the man had no reply. [13]Then the king said to his aides, "Bind him hand and foot and throw him out into the outer darkness where there is weeping and gnashing of teeth."

Mt 23:29, 30. Yes, woe to you, Pharisees, and you religious leaders—hypocrites! For you build monuments to the prophets killed by your fathers and lay flowers on the graves of the godly men they destroyed, and say, "We certainly would never have acted as our fathers did." [31]In saying that, you are accusing yourselves of being the sons of wicked men.

Lk 7:36. One of the Pharisees asked Jesus to come to his home for lunch and Jesus accepted the invitation. As they sat down to eat, [37]a woman of the streets—a prostitute—heard he was there and brought an exquisite flask filled with expensive perfume. [38]Going in, she knelt behind him at his feet, weeping, with her tears falling down upon his feet; and she wiped them off with her hair and kissed them and poured the perfume on them. [39]When Jesus' host, a Pharisee, saw what was happening and who the woman was, he said to himself, "This proves that Jesus is no prophet, for if God had really sent him, he would know what kind of woman this one is!" [40]Then Jesus spoke up and answered his thoughts, "Simon," he said to the Pharisee, "I have something to say to you." "All right, Teacher," Simon replied, "go ahead." [41]Then Jesus told him this story: "A man loaned money to two people—$5,000 to one and $500 to the other. [42]But neither of them could pay him back, so he kindly forgave them both, letting them keep the money! Which do you suppose loved him most after that?" [43]"I suppose the one who had owed him the most," Simon answered. "Correct," Jesus agreed. [44]Then he turned to the woman and said to Simon, "Look! See this woman kneeling here! When I entered your home, you didn't bother to offer me water to wash the dust from my feet, but she has washed them with her tears and wiped them with her hair. [45]You refused me the customary kiss of greeting, but she has kissed my feet again and again from the time I first came in. [46]You neglected the usual courtesy of olive oil to anoint my head, but she has covered my feet with rare perfume. [47]Therefore her sins—and they are many—are forgiven, for she loved me much; but one who is forgiven little, shows little love." [48]And he said to her, "Your sins are forgiven." [49]Then the men at the table said to themselves, "Who does this man think he is, going around forgiving sins?" [50]And Jesus said to the woman, "Your faith has saved you; go in peace."

Lk 10:25. One day an expert on Moses' laws came to test Jesus' orthodoxy by asking him this question: "Teacher, what does a man need to do to live forever in heaven?" [26]Jesus replied, "What does Moses' law say about it?" [27]"It says," he replied, "that you must love the Lord your God with all your heart, and with all your soul, and with all your strength, and with all your mind. And you must love your neighbor just as much as you love yourself." [28]"Right!" Jesus told him. "*Do* this and *you* shall live!" [29]The man wanted to justify (his lack of love for some kinds of people), so he asked, "Which neighbors?" [30]Jesus replied with an illustration: "A Jew going on a trip from Jerusalem to Jericho was attacked by bandits. They stripped him of his clothes and money and beat him up and left him lying half dead beside the road. [31]By chance a Jewish priest came along; and when he saw the man lying there, he crossed to the other side of the road and passed him by. [32]A Jewish Temple-assistant walked over and looked at him lying there, but then went on. [33]But a despised Samaritan came along, and when he saw him, he felt deep pity. [34]Kneeling beside him the Samaritan soothed his wounds with medicine and bandaged them. Then he put the man on his donkey and walked along beside him till they came to an inn, where he nursed him through the night. [35]The next day he handed the innkeeper two twenty dollar bills and told him to take care of the man. "If his bill runs higher than that," he said, "I'll pay the difference the next time I am here." [36]Now which of these three would you say was a neighbor to the bandits' victim?" [37]The man replied, "The one who showed him some pity." Then Jesus said, "Yes, now go and do the same."

Lk 15:2. But this caused complaints from the Jewish religious leaders and the experts on Jewish law because he was associating with such despicable people—even eating with them! [25]Meanwhile, the older son was in the fields working; when he returned home, he heard dance music coming from the house, [26]and he asked one of the servants what was going on. [27]"Your brother is back," he was told, "and your father has killed the calf we were fattening and has prepared a great feast to celebrate his coming home again unharmed." [28]The older brother was angry and wouldn't go in. His father came out and begged him, [29]but he replied, "All these years I've worked hard for you and never once refused to do a single thing you told me to; and in all that time you never gave me even one young goat for a feast with my friends. [30]Yet when this son of yours comes back after spending your money on prostitutes, you celebrate by killing the finest calf we have on the place." [31]"Look, dear son," his father said to him, "you and I are very close, and everything I have is yours. [32]But it is right to celebrate. For he is your brother; and he was dead and has come back to life! He was lost and is found!"

Lk 16:14. The Pharisees, who dearly loved their money, naturally scoffed at all this. [15]Then he said to them, "You wear a noble, pious expression in public, but God knows your evil hearts. Your pretense brings you honor from the people, but it is an abomination in the sight of God."

Lk 18:9. Then he told this story to some who boasted of their virtue and scorned everyone else: [10]"Two men went to the Temple to pray. One was a proud, self-righteous Pharisee, and the other a cheating tax collector. [11]The proud Pharisee 'prayed' this prayer: 'Thank God, I am not a sinner like everyone else, especially like that tax collector over there! For I never cheat, I don't commit adultery, [12]I go without food twice a week, and I give to God a tenth of everything I earn.' [13]But the corrupt tax collector stood at a distance and dared not even lift his eyes to heaven as he prayed, but beat upon his chest in sorrow, exclaiming, 'God, be merciful to me, a sinner.' [14]I tell you, this sinner, not the Pharisee, returned home forgiven! For the proud shall be humbled, but the humble shall be honored."

Jn 9:34. "You illegitimate bastard, you!" they shouted. "Are you trying to teach *us?*" And they threw him out. [39]Then Jesus told him, "I have come into the world to give sight to those who are spiritually blind and to show those who think they see that they are blind." [40]The Pharisees who were standing there asked, "Are you saying we are blind?" [41]"If you were blind, you wouldn't be guilty," Jesus replied. "But your guilt remains because you claim to know what you are doing."

Rom 2:17. You Jews think all is well between yourselves and God because he gave his laws to you; you brag that you are his special friends. [18]Yes, you know what he wants; you know right from wrong and favor the right because you have been taught his laws from earliest youth. [19]You are so sure of the way to God that you could point it out to a blind man. You think of yourselves as beacon lights, directing men who are lost in darkness to God. [20]You think that you can guide the simple and teach even children the affairs of God, for you really know his laws, which are full of all knowledge and truth.

Rom 3:27. Then what can we boast about doing, to earn our salvation? Nothing at all. Why? Because our acquittal is not based on our good deeds; it is based on what Christ has done and our faith in him.

Rom 10:3. For they don't understand that Christ has died to make them right with God. Instead they are trying to make themselves good enough to gain God's favor by keeping the Jewish laws and customs, but that is not God's way of salvation.

Rom 11:19. "Well," you may be saying, "those branches were broken off to make room for me so I must be pretty good." [20]Watch out! Remember that those branches, the Jews, were broken off because they didn't believe God, and you are there only because you do. Do not be proud; be humble and grateful—and careful. [21]For if God did not spare the branches he put there in the first place, he won't spare you either.

2 Cor 1:9. We felt we were doomed to die and saw how powerless we were to help ourselves; but that was good, for then we put everything into the hands of God, who alone could save us, for he can even raise the dead.

2 Cor 10:17. As the Scriptures say, "If anyone is going to boast, let him boast about what the Lord has done and not about himself." [18]When someone boasts about himself and how well he has done, it doesn't count for much. But when the Lord commends him, that's different!

Gal 6:3. If anyone thinks he is too great to stoop to this, he is fooling himself. He is really a nobody.

Rev 3:17. You say, "I am rich, with everything I want; I don't need a thing!" And you don't realize that spiritually you are wretched and miserable and poor and blind and naked. [18]My advice to you is to buy pure gold from me, gold purified by fire—only then will you truly be rich. And to purchase from me white garments, clean and pure, so you won't be naked and ashamed; and to get medicine from me to heal your eyes and give you back your sight.

See *Hypocrisy; Self-Exaltation.*

INSTANCES OF. Saul, 1 Sam 15:13–31. Young man, see above. Lawyer, see above. Pharisees, Lk 11:33–54; Jn 8:33–59; 9:28–34. Israel, Rom 10:3. Church of Laodicea, Rev 3:17.

SELF-WILL Stubbornness, Forbidden, 2 Chron 30:8; Ps 75:5. Results from unbelief, 2 Kgs 17:14; pride, Neh 9:16, 29; evil thoughts, Jer 7:24. God knows, Isa 48:4. Exhibited in refusing to pay attention to God, Prov 1:24; refusing to pay attention to the messengers of God, 1 Sam 8:19; Jer 44:16; Zech 7:11; refusing to obey God, Neh 9:16, 17; Isa 42:24; Ps 78:10; refusing to obey parents, Deut 21:18, 19; refusing to be corrected, Deut 21:18; Jer 5:3; 7:28; rebelling against God, Deut 31:27; Ps 78:8; resisting the Holy Ghost, Acts 7:51; following evil thoughts, Jer 7:24; with Jer 23:17; going backward and not forward, Jer 7:24; heinousness of, 1 Sam 15:23.

Ministers should be without, Tit 1:7; warn their people against, Heb 3:7–12; pray that their people may be forgiven for, Ex 34:9; Deut 9:27. Characteristic of the wicked, Prov 7:11, 12; 2 Pet 2:10. The wicked cling to, Judg 2:19. Punishment for, Deut 21:21; Prov 29:1.

Illustrated: Ps 32:9; Jer 31:18.

EXEMPLIFIED. Simeon and Levi, Gen 49:6. Israelites, Ex 32:9; Deut 9:6, 13, 14. Saul, 1 Sam 25:19–23. David, 2 Sam 24:4. Josiah, 2 Chron 35:22. Zedekiah, 2 Chron 36:13.

See *Obduracy.*

SEMACHIAH Son of Shemaiah, 1 Chron 26:6, 7.

SEMEIN An ancestor of Jesus, Lk 3:23–38.

SENAAH A city of unknown location, Ezra 2:3–35; Neh 7:8–38.

SENATE The Sanhedrin, Acts 5:21.

See *Elder; Government; Sanhedrin.*

SENEH A rock protecting the garrison of the Philistines at Michmash, 1 Sam 14:4.

SENIR Amorite name of one peak of Mount Hermon, Deut 3:9; 1 Chron 5:23; Song 4:8; Ezk 27:5.

SENNACHERIB King of Assyria. Invades Judah; besieges to Jerusalem, but abandons the country and returns to Assyria, 2 Kgs 18:17–37; 19:8; 2 Chron 32:1–23; Isa 36; 37. Death of, 2 Kgs 19:35–37; Isa 37:36–38.

SENSUALITY Eccl 2:24. So I decided that there was nothing better for a man to do than to enjoy his food and drink, and his job. Then I realized that even this pleasure is from the hand of God.

Eccl 8:15. Then I decided to spend my time having fun, because I felt that there was nothing better in all the earth than that a man should eat, drink, and be merry, with the hope that this happiness would stick with him in all the hard work which God gives to mankind everywhere.

Eccl 11:9. Young man, it's wonderful to be young! Enjoy every minute of it! Do all you want to; take in everything, but realize that you must account to God for everything you do.

Isa 22:13. But instead, you sing and dance and play, and feast and drink. "Let us eat, drink, and be merry," you say: "What's the difference, for tomorrow we die."

Isa 56:12. "Come," they say. "We'll get some wine and have a party; let's all get drunk. This is really living; let it go on and on, and tomorrow will be better yet!"

Lk 12:19. "And I'll sit back and say to myself, 'Friend, you have enough stored away for years to come. Now take it easy! Wine, women, and song for you!' " [20]But God said to him, "Fool! Tonight you die. Then who will get it all?"

Lk 16:25. But Abraham said to him, "Son, remember that during your lifetime you had everything you wanted, and Lazarus had nothing. So now he is here being comforted and you are in anguish."

1 Cor 15:32. And what value was there in fighting wild beasts—those men of Ephesus—if it was only for what I gain in this life down here? If we will never live again after we die, then we might as well go and have ourselves a good time: let us eat, drink, and be merry. What's the difference? For tomorrow we die, and that ends everything! [33]Don't be fooled by those who say such things. If you listen to them you will start acting like them.

Jas 5:5. You have spent your years here on earth having fun, satisfying your every whim, and now your fat hearts are ready for the slaughter.

Jude 1:18. That in the last times there would come these scoffers whose whole purpose in life is to enjoy themselves in every evil way imaginable. [19]They stir up arguments; they love the evil things of the world; they do not have the Holy Spirit living in them.

See *Adultery; Drunkenness; Fornication; Gluttony; Lasciviousness; Self-Indulgence; Sodomy;* also *Abstinence, Total; Continence; Self-Denial; Temperance.*

SENTRY Ps 127:1; Jer 37:13.

See *Watchman.*

SE-ORIM A leader of a priestly group in the Temple, 1 Chron 24:7–18.

SEPARATION A term widely used with reference to the human side of sanctification. In the Old Testament, Israel was separate from other nations, Ex 33:16; Lev 20:24, 26; Num 16:8, 9; 23:7–10; Deut 14:2; Ezra 10:11; Isa 66:22. In the New Testament, the believer is positionally set apart to Christ, Jn 17:14, 17; Rom 6:1–11; Gal 6:14. In his experience he is to be set apart from evil, 2 Cor 6:14–18, and unholy associations, 2 Tim 2:21; 2 Jn 1:9–11.

See *Sanctification.*

SEPHAR A mountain in Arabia, Gen 10:26–30.

SEPHARVAIM An Assyrian city, from which the king of Assyria colonized Samaria, 2 Kgs 17:24; 18:34; 19:13; Isa 36:19; 37:13.

SEPTEMBER See *Calendar.*

SEPULCHER See *Burial.*

SERAH Daughter of Asher, Gen 46:16, 17; Num 26:44–47; 1 Chron 7:30.

SERAIAH 1. Called also *Sheva, Shisha,* and *Shavsha.* David's secretary, 2 Sam 8:17; 20:25; 1 Kgs 4:3; 1 Chron 18:16.

2. Chief priest at the time of the taking of Jerusalem, 2 Kgs 25:18. Father of Ezra, Ezra 7:1–5. Killed by Nebuchadnezzar, 2 Kgs 25:18–21; Jer 52:24–27.

3. An Israelite captain who surrendered to Gedaliah, 2 Kgs 25:23; Jer 40:8.

4. Son of Kenaz, 1 Chron 4:13, 14.

5. Son of Azariah, 1 Chron 6:4–15.

6. A priest who returned from the Babylonian captivity, Ezra 2:2. Called *Azariah* in Neh 7:7.

7. Another priest who returned from captivity, Neh 12:1–7, 12–21.

8. One who signed the covenant with Nehemiah, Neh 10:1–8. Possibly identical with 7, above.

9. A leader of the Temple after the captivity, Neh 11:10–14.

10. Son of Azri-el. Commanded by King Jehoiakim to seize Jeremiah, Jer 36:26.

11. A servant of Zedekiah, Jer 51:59–62.

SERAPHIM Celestial beings, Isa 6:2, 6.
See *Cherubim; Angel.*

SERED Son of Sebulun, Gen 46:8–14; Num 26:26, 27.

SEREDITES Family of, Num 26:26, 27.

SERGEANT 1 Chron 26:2, 3; Mt 27:54.
See *Officer, Roman.*

SERGIUS PAULUS A Roman governor and convert of Paul, Acts 13:6–12.

SERMON Of Jesus, "on the mount," Mt 5; 6; 7; by the sea, Mt 13:1–52; Mk 4:2–33.
See *Preaching; Minister.*

SERPENT Satan appears in the form of to Eve, Gen 3:1–15; 2 Cor 11:3. Subtlety of, Gen 3:1; Eccl 10:8, 9; Mt 10:16. Curse on, Gen 3:14, 15; 49:17. Feeds on the dust, Gen 3:14; Isa 65:25. Venom of, Deut 32:24, 33; Prov 23:31, 32. The rod of Moses transformed into, Ex 4:3; 7:15. Charming of, Eccl 10:11. Constriction of, Rev 9:19. Sea serpent, Amos 9:3. The seventy given power over, Lk 10:19.

FIGURATIVE. Gen 49:17; Isa 14:29; 65:25. Illustrates effect of wine, Deut 32:33; Prov 23:32.
See *Snake.*

SERPENT'S STONE A stone near En-Rogel, 1 Kgs 1:9.

SERUG An ancestor of Abraham, Gen 11:20–23; 1 Chron 1:24–27; Lk 3:23–38.

SERVANT Distinguished as bond servant, who was a slave, and hired servant.

BOND. Laws of Moses concerning, Ex 21:1–11, 20, 21, 26, 27, 32; Lev 19:20–22; 25:6, 7, 10, 35–55; Deut 15:12, 14, 18; 24:7. Kidnapping forbidden, Deut 21:10–14; 24:7; 1 Tim 1:10, 11; Rev 18:11–13. Fugitive, not to be returned to master, Deut 23:15, 16. David erroneously supposed to be a fugitive servant, 1 Sam 25:10. Instances of fugitive: Hagar, commanded by an angel to return to her mistress, Gen 16:9–12. Sought by Shime-i, 1 Kgs 2:39–41. Interceded for by Paul, Philemon 1:10–21.

Rights of those born to a master, Gen 14:14; 17:13, 24–27; Ex 21:4; Prov 29:21; Eccl 2:7, 8; Jer 2:14.

Bought and sold, Gen 17:13, 24–27; 37:28, 36; 39:17; Deut 28:68; Esther 7:4; Ezk 27:13; Joel 3:6; Amos 8:6; Rev 18:13. Captives of war made, Deut 20:14; 21:10–14; 2 Kgs 5:2; 2 Chron 28:8, 10; Lam 5:13; captive bond servants shared by priests and Levites, Num 31:28–47. Thieves punished by being made, Gen 43:18; Ex 22:3. Defaulting debtors made, Lev 25:39; Mt 18:25. Children of defaulting debtors sold for, Lev 25:39; 2 Kgs 4:1–7; Mt 18:25. Voluntary servitude of, Lev 25:47; Deut 15:16, 17; Josh 9:11–21. Given as dowry, Gen 29:24, 29. Owned by priests, Lev 22:11; Mk 14:66, 67. Servants owned servants, 2 Sam 9:10. The master might marry, or give in marriage, Ex 21:7–10; Deut 21:10–14; 1 Chron 2:34, 35. Taken in concubinage, Gen 16:1, 2, 3, 6; 30:3, 9. Used as soldiers by Abraham, Gen 14:14.

Must be circumcised, Gen 17:13, 24–27; Ex 12:44. Must enjoy religious privileges with the master's household, Deut 12:12; 16:11, 14; 29:10, 11. Must have rest on the sabbath, Ex 20:10; 23:12; Deut 5:14. Equal status of, with other disciples of Jesus, 1 Cor 7:21, 22; 12:13; Gal 3:28; Eph 6:8. Kindness to, commanded, Lev 25:43; Eph 6:9.

Bond service threatened, as a national punishment, for disobedience of Israel, Deut 28:68; Joel 3:7, 8. Degrading influences of bondage exemplified by cowardice, Ex 14:11, 12; Judg 5:16–18, 23.

Emancipation of, Ezra 1:1–4; Jer 34:8–22; 1 Cor 7:21. Freedmen, Acts 6:9.

Cruelty to: To Hagar, Gen 16:1–6; Gal 4:22–31; to the Israelites, Ex 1:8–22; 2:1–4; Acts 7:19, 34. Sick, abandoned, 1 Sam 30:13.

Kindness to, by the centurion, Mt 8:8–13; Lk 7:2–10; Paul, Philem 1–21.

Instances of. Joseph, Gen 37:26–28, 36. Israelites, Ex 1:10–22; 5:7–14; Deut 6:10–12, 21. Gibeonites, Josh 9:22–27. Canaanites, 1 Kgs 9:20, 21. Jews in Babylon, 2 Chron 36:20, Esther chapters 1–10. Emancipation of, 2 Chron 36:22, 23; Ezra 1:1–4.

Figurative. Lev 25:42, 55; Ps 116:16; Isa 52:3; Mt 24:45–51; Lk 12:35–48; 17:7–9; Jn 8:32–35; Rom 6:16–22; 1 Cor 4:1; 7:21–23; Gal 5:13; 1 Pet 2:16; 2 Pet 2:19; Rev 7:3.

Instances of Good. Joseph, Gen 39:2–20; 41:9–57; Acts 7:10; Elisha, 2 Kgs 2:1–7. Servants of Abraham, Gen 24; of Boaz, Ruth 2:4, 5; of Jonathan, 1 Sam 14:7; of Abigail, 1 Sam 25:14–17; of David, 2 Sam 12:18; 15:15, 21; of Ziba, 2 Sam 9; of Naaman, 2 Kgs 5:2, 3, 13; of Nehemiah, Neh 4:16, 23; of the Roman officer, Mt 8:8, 9; of Cornelius, Acts 10:7; Onesimus, Philemon 1:11. Servants in the parables of the investments and the nobleman's $20,000, Mt 25:14–23; Lk 19:12–19.

Wicked and Unfaithful. Jeroboam, 1 Kgs 11:26; Gehazi, 2 Kgs 5:20–27; Zimri, 1 Kgs 16:9, 10; 2 Kgs 9:31; Onesimus, Philemon 1:11.

Of Abraham and Lot, Gen 13:7. Of Abimelech, Gen 21:25. Of Ziba, 2 Sam 16:1–4, with 2 Sam 19: 26, 27. Of Absalom, 2 Sam 13:28–30; 14:30. Of Shime-i, 1 Kgs 2:39. Of Joash, 2 Kgs 12:19–21. Of Amon, 2 Kgs 21:23. Of Job, Job 19:15, 16. In the parables of the investments and the nobleman's $20,000, Mt 25:24–30; Lk 19:20–26. In the parable of the vineyard, Mt 21:33–41; Mk 12:1–9.

Conspiracy by. See *Conspiracy.*

Unclassified Scriptures Relating to. Gen 16:6. "You have my permission to punish the girl as you see fit," Abram replied. So Sarai beat her and she ran away. [7]The Angel of the Lord found her beside a desert spring along the road to Shur. [8]*The Angel:* "Hagar, Sarai's maid, where have you come from, and where are you going?" *Hagar:* "I am running away from my mistress." [9]*The Angel:* "Return to your mistress and act as you should."

Ex 20:10. But the seventh day is a day of Sabbath rest before the Lord your God. On that day you are to do no work of any kind, nor shall your son, daughter, or slaves—whether men or women—or your cattle or your house guests. Deut 5:14.

Neh 5:8. At the trial I shouted at them, "The rest of us are doing all we can to *help* our Jewish brothers who have returned from exile as slaves in distant lands, but you are forcing them right back into slavery again. How often must we redeem them?" And they had nothing to say in their own defense.

Job 19:15. Those living in my home, even my servants, regard me as a stranger. I am like a foreigner to them. [16]I call my servant, but he doesn't come; I even beg him!

Job 31:13. If I have been unfair to my servants, [14]how could I face God? What could I say when he questioned me about it?

Ps 123:2. We look to Jehovah our God for his mercy and kindness just as a servant keeps his eyes upon his master or a slave girl watches her mistress for the slightest signal.

Prov 13:17. An unreliable messenger can cause a lot of trouble. Reliable communication permits progress.

Prov 17:2. A wise slave will rule his master's wicked sons and share their estate.

Prov 19:10. It doesn't seem right for a fool to succeed or for a slave to rule over princes!

Prov 25:13. A faithful employee is as refreshing as a cool day in the hot summertime.

Prov 27:18. A workman may eat from the orchard he tends; anyone should be rewarded who protects another's interests.

Prov 29:19. Sometimes [for a servant] mere words are not enough—discipline is needed. For the words may not be heeded. [21]Pamper a servant from childhood, and he will expect you to treat him as a son!

Prov 30:10. Never falsely accuse a man to his employer, lest he curse you for your sin. [21-23]There are three things that make the earth tremble—no, four it cannot stand: A slave who becomes a king. A rebel who prospers. A bitter woman when she finally marries. A servant girl who marries her mistress' husband.

Eccl 7:21. Don't eavesdrop! You may hear your servant cursing you!

Eccl 10:7. I have even seen servants riding, while princes walk like servants!

Isa 52:3. For the Lord says, When I sold you into exile I asked no fee from your oppressors; now I can take you back again and owe them not a cent!

Jer 22:13. And woe to you, King Jehoiakim, for you are building your great palace with forced labor. By not paying wages you are building injustice into its walls and oppression into its doorframes and ceilings.

Jer 34:8. This is the message that came to Jeremiah from the Lord after King Zedekiah of Judah had freed all the slaves in Jerusalem—[9](for King Zedekiah had ordered everyone to free his Hebrew slaves, both men and women. He had said that no Jew should be the master of another Jew for all were brothers. [10]The princes and all the people had obeyed the king's command and freed their slaves, but the action was only temporary. [11]They changed their minds and made their servants slaves again. [12]That is why the Lord gave the following message to Jerusalem.) [13]The Lord, the God of Israel, says: I made a covenant with your fathers long ago when I brought them from their slavery in Egypt. [14]I told them that every Hebrew slave must be free after serving six years. But this was not done. [15]Recently you began doing what was right, as I commanded you, and freed your slaves. You had solemnly promised me in my Temple that you would do it. [16]But now you refuse and have defiled my name by shrugging off your oath and have made them slaves again. [17]Therefore, says the Lord, because you will not listen to me and release them, I will release you to the power of death by war and famine and disease. And I will scatter you over all the world as exiles.

Lam 5:8. Our former servants have become our masters; there is no one left to save us.

Zeph 1:9. Yes, I will punish those who follow heathen customs and who rob and kill to fill their masters' homes with evil gain of violence and fraud.

Mal 1:6. A son honors his father, a servant honors his master.

Mt 8:9. I know, because I am under the authority of my superior officers and I have authority over my soldiers, and I say to one, "Go," and he goes, and to another, "Come," and he comes, and to my slave boy, "Do this or that," and he does it.

Mt 24:45. Are you a wise and faithful servant of the Lord? Have I given you the task of managing my household, to feed my children day by day? [46]Blessings on you if I return and find you faithfully doing your work. [47]I will put such faithful ones in charge of everything I own! [48]But if you are evil and say to yourself, "My Lord won't be coming for a while," [49]and begin oppressing your fellow servants, partying and getting drunk, [50]your Lord will arrive unannounced and unexpected, [51]and severely whip you and send you off to the judgment of the hypocrites; there will be weeping and gnashing of teeth.

Lk 12:35. "Be prepared—all dressed and ready—[36]for your Lord's return from the wedding feast. Then you will be ready to open the door and let him in the moment he arrives and knocks. [37]There will be great joy for those who are ready and waiting for his return. He himself will seat them and put on a waiter's uniform and serve them as they sit and eat! [38]He may come at nine o'clock at night—or even at midnight. But whenever he comes there will be joy for his servants who are ready! [39]Everyone would be ready for him if they knew the exact hour of his return—just as they would be ready for a thief if they knew when he was coming. [40]So be ready all the time. For I, the Messiah, will come when least expected." [41]Peter asked, "Lord, are you talking just to us or to everyone?" [42-44]And the Lord replied, "I'm talking to any faithful, sensible man whose master gives him the responsibility of feeding the other servants. If his master returns and finds that he has done a good job, there will be a reward—his master will put him in charge of all he owns. [45]But if the man begins to think, 'My Lord won't be back for a long time,' and begins to whip the men and women he is supposed to protect, and to spend his time at drinking parties and in drunkenness— [46]well, his master will return without notice and remove him from his position of trust and assign him to the place of the unfaithful. [47]He will be severely punished, for though he knew his duty he refused to do it. [48]But anyone who is not aware that he is doing wrong will be punished only lightly. Much is required from those to whom much is given, for their responsibility is greater."

Lk 16:1. Jesus now told this story to his disciples: "A rich man hired an accountant to handle his affairs, but soon a rumor went around that the accountant was thoroughly dishonest. [2]So his employer called him in and said, 'What's this I hear about your stealing from me? Get your report in order, for you are to be dismissed.' [3]The accountant thought to himself, 'Now what? I'm through here, and I haven't the strength to go out and dig ditches, and I'm too proud to beg. [4]I know just the thing! And then I'll have plenty of friends to take care of me when I leave!' [5, 6]So he invited each one who owed money to his employer to come and discuss the situation. He asked the first one, 'How much do you owe him?' 'My debt is 850 gallons of olive oil,' the man replied. 'Yes, here is the contract you signed,' the accountant told him. 'Tear it up and write another one for half that much!' [7]"And how much do you owe him?' he asked the next man. 'A thousand bushels of wheat,' was the reply. 'Here,' the accountant said, 'take your note and replace it with one for only 800 bushels!' [8]The rich man had to admire the rascal for being so shrewd. And it is true that the citizens of this world are more clever (in dishonesty!) than the godly are. [9]But shall I tell *you* to act that way, to buy friendship through cheating? Will this ensure your entry into an everlasting home in heaven? [10]*No!* For unless you are honest in small matters, you won't be in large ones. If you cheat even a little, you won't be honest with greater responsibilities. [11]And if you are untrustworthy about worldly wealth, who will trust you with the true riches of heaven? [12]And if you are not faithful with other people's money, why should you be entrusted with money of your own? [13]For neither you nor anyone else can serve two masters. You will hate one and show loyalty to the other, or else the other way around—you will be enthusiastic about one and despise the other. You cannot serve both God and money."

Lk 17:7–9. When a servant comes in from plowing or taking care of sheep, he doesn't just sit down and eat, but first prepares his master's meal and serves him his supper before he eats his own. And he is not even thanked, for he is merely doing what he is supposed to do.

Lk 22:27. Out in the world the master sits at the table and is served by his servants. But not here! For I am your servant.

Jn 13:16. How true it is that a servant is not greater than his master. Nor is the messenger more important than the one who sends him. Mt 10:24, 25.

1 Cor 4:2. Now the most important thing about a servant is that he does just what his master tells him to.

1 Cor 7:21. Are you a slave? Don't let that worry you—but of course, if you get a chance to be free, take it. [22]If the Lord calls you, and you are a slave, remember that Christ has set you free from the awful power of sin; and if he has called you and you are free, remember that you are now a slave of Christ. [23]You have been bought and paid for by Christ, so you belong to him—be free now from all these earthly prides and fears. [24]So, dear brothers, whatever situation a person is in when he becomes a Christian, let him stay there, for now the Lord is there to help him.

Eph 6:5. Slaves, obey your masters; be eager to give them your very best. Serve them as you would Christ. [6,7]Don't work hard only when your master is watching and then shirk when he isn't looking; work hard and with gladness all the time, as though working for Christ, doing the will of God with all your hearts. [8]Remember, the Lord will pay you for each good thing you do, whether you are slave or free. [9]And you slave owners must treat your slaves right, just as I have told them to treat you. Don't keep threatening them; remember, you yourselves are slaves to Christ; you have the same Master they do, and he has no favorites.

Col 3:22. You slaves must always obey your earthly masters, not only trying to please them when they are watching you but all the time; obey them willingly because of your love for the Lord and because you want to please him. [23]Work hard and cheerfully at all you do, just as though you were working for the Lord and not merely for your masters, [24]remembering that it is the Lord Christ who is going to pay you, giving you your full portion of all he owns. He is the one you are really working for. [25]And if you don't do your best for him, he will pay you in a way that you won't like —for he has no special favorites who can get away with shirking.

1 Tim 6:1. Christian slaves should work hard for their owners and respect them; never let it be said that Christ's people are poor workers. Don't let the name of God or his teaching be laughed at because of this. [2]If their owner is a Christian, that is no excuse for slowing down; rather they should work all the harder because a brother in the faith is being helped by their efforts.

Tit 2:9. Urge slaves to obey their masters and to try their best to satisfy them. They must not talk back, [10]nor steal, but must show themselves to be entirely trustworthy. In this way they will make people want to believe in our Savior and God.

1 Pet 2:18. Servants, you must respect your masters and do whatever they tell you—not only if they are kind and reasonable, but even if they are tough and cruel. [19]Praise the Lord if you are punished for doing right! [20]Of course, you get no credit for being patient if you are beaten for doing wrong; but if you do right and suffer for it, and are patient beneath the blows, God is well pleased.

See *Employee; Employer; Master.*

HIRED. Jacob, Gen 29:15; 30:26; reemployed, Gen 30:27–34; 31:6, 7, 41. Parable of laborers for a vineyard, Mt 20:1–15; of the father of the prodigal son, Lk 15:17, 19. The prodigal, Lk 15:15–19.

Treatment of, more considerate than that accorded slaves, Lev 25:53. Await employment in hiring hall, Mt 20:1–3. Wages paid in livestock and food, Gen 30:31, 32; 2 Chron 2:10; in money, Mt 20: 2.

Unclassified Scriptures Relating to. Lev 19:13. You shall not rob nor oppress anyone, and you shall pay your hired workers promptly. If something is due them, don't even keep it overnight.

Lev 25:39. If a fellow Israelite becomes poor and sells himself to you, you must not treat him as an ordinary slave, [40]but rather as a hired servant or as a guest; and he shall serve you only until the Year of Jubilee. [41]At that time he can leave with his children, and return to his own family and possessions.

Deut 24:14, 15. Never oppress a poor hired man, whether a fellow Israelite or a foreigner living in your town. Pay him his wage each day before sunset, for since he is poor he needs it right away; otherwise he may cry out to the Lord against you and it would be counted as a sin against you.

Job 7:1. How mankind must struggle. A man's life is long and hard, like that of a slave. [2]How he longs for the day to end. How he grinds on to the end of the week and his wages.

Mal 3:5. "At that time my punishments will be quick and certain; I will move swiftly against wicked men who trick the innocent, against adulterers, and liars, against all those who cheat their hired hands, or oppress widows and orphans, or defraud strangers, and do not fear me," says the Lord of Hosts.

Mt 10:9. Don't take any money with you; [10]don't even carry a duffle bag with extra clothes and shoes, or even a walking stick; for those you help should feed and care for you. Lk 10:7.

Rom 4:4. But didn't he earn his right to heaven by all the good things he did? No, for being saved is a gift; if a person could earn it by being good, then it wouldn't be free—but it is!

Col 4:1. You slave owners must be just and fair to all your slaves. Always remember that you, too, have a Master in heaven who is closely watching you.

1 Tim 5:18. For the Scriptures say, "Never tie up the mouth of an ox when it is treading out the grain —let him eat as he goes along!" And in another place, "Those who work deserve their pay!"

Jas 5:4. For listen! Hear the cries of the field workers whom you have cheated of their pay. Their cries have reached the ears of the Lord of Hosts.

See *Master; Wages.*

SERVICE See *Altruism.*

SESSION, PRESENT A theological expression referring to the present ministry of Christ at the right hand of the father, Jn 14:2, 3; Eph 1: 20–23; Col 3:1; Heb 1:13; 7:25; 1 Jn 2:1; Rev 3:21.

See *Jesus Christ.*

SETH Son of Adam, Gen 4:25, 26; 5:3–8; 1 Chron 1:1–4; Lk 3:23–38.

SETHUR One of the 12 spies, Num 13:3–15.

SEVEN Interesting facts concerning the number.

DAYS. Week consists of, Gen 2:3; Ex 20:11; Deut 5:13, 14. Noah in the ark before the flood, Gen 7: 4, 10–12; remains in the ark after sending out the dove, Gen 8:10, 12. Mourning for Jacob lasted, Gen 50:10; of Job, Job 2:13. The plague of bloody waters in Egypt lasted, Ex 7:24, 25. The Israelites circled Jericho, Josh 6:3, 4. The passover lasted, Ex 12:15. Saul directed by Samuel to wait at Gilgal for his command, 1 Sam 10:8; 13:8. The elders of Jabesh-gilead ask for a truce of, 1 Sam 11:3. Dedication of the temple lasted two weeks, 1 Kgs 8:65. Ezekiel sits by the Chebar River, Ezk 3:14, 15. The Feast of Tabernacles lasted, Lev 23:33, 34, 42. Consecration of priests and altars lasted, Ex 29:30, 35; Ezk 43: 25, 26. Defilements lasted, Lev 12:2; 13:4. Fasts of, 1 Sam 31:13; 2 Sam 12:16, 18, 22. The firstborn of oxen and sheep shall remain with mother, before being offered, Ex 22:30. The feast of Ahasuerus continued, Esther 1:5. Paul stays at Tyre, Acts 21: 4; at Puteoli, Acts 28:14.

WEEKS. In Daniel's vision concerning the coming of the Messiah, Dan 9:24, 25.

MONTHS. Holy convocations in the seventh month, Lev 23:23–44; Num 29; Ezk 45:25.

YEARS. Jacob serves for each of his wives, Gen 29:15–30. Of plenty, Gen 41:1–32, 53. Famine lasted in Egypt, Gen 41:1–32, 54–57; in Canaan, 2 Sam 24: 13; 2 Kgs 8:1. Insanity of Nebuchadnezzar, Dan 4: 32. Seven times, the period between the jubilees, Lev 25:8.

MISCELLANY OF SEVENS. Of clean animals taken into the ark, Gen 7:2. Abraham gives Abimelech seven lambs, Gen 21:28, 29. Rams, lambs and bulls to the number of, required in sacrifices, Lev 23:18; Num 23:1; 29:32; 1 Chron 15:26; Ezk 45:23. Blood sprinkling seven times, Lev 4:6; 14:7; oil, 14: 16. Fourteen cows and 14 heads of grain in Pharaoh's vision, Gen 41:2–7. The Israelites circled Jericho seven times, on the seventh day sounding seven trumpets, Josh 6:4. Elisha's servant looked seven times for appearance of rain, 1 Kgs 18:43. Naaman required to wash in Jordan seven times, 2 Kgs 5: 10. Seven steps in the Temple seen in Ezekiel's vision, Ezk 40:22, 26. The heat of Nebuchadnezzar's furnace intensified seven times, Dan 3:19. The light of the sun intensified sevenfold, Isa 30:26. The threatened sevenfold punishment of Israel, Lev 26: 18–21. Silver purified seven times, Ps 12:6. Worshiping seven times a day, Ps 119:164. Seven eunuchs at the court of Ahasuerus, Esther 1:10; seven officials, Esther 1:14. Seven counsellors at the court of Artaxerxes, Ezra 7:14. Seven maids given to Esther, Esther 2:9. Symbolical of many sons, Ruth 4:15; 1 Sam 2:5; Jer 15:9; of generosity, Eccl 11:1, 2. Seven wise men, Prov 26:16. Seven women shall seek polygamous marriage, Isa 4:1. Seven shepherds to be watch over Israel, Mic 5:5, 6. Seven inscriptions, Zech 3:9. Seven lamps and tubes, Zech 4:2. Seven deacons in the apostolic church, Acts 6:3. Seven churches in Asia, Rev 1:4, 20. Seven seals, Rev 5: 1. Seven thunders, Rev 10:3. Seven heads and seven crowns, Rev 12:3; 13:1; 17:9. Seven kings, Rev 17:10. Seven Stars, Rev 1:16, 20; 3:1; Amos 5:8. Seven spirits, Rev 1:4; 3:1; 4:5; 5:6. Seven eyes of the Lord, Zech 4:10; Rev 5:6. Seven golden candlesticks, Rev 1:12. Seven angels with seven trumpets, Rev 8:2. Seven plagues, Rev 15:1. Seven horns and seven eyes, Rev 5:6. Seven angels with seven plagues, Rev 15:6. Seven golden flasks, Rev 15:6, 7. Scarlet colored beast having seven heads, Rev 17:3.

SEVENTY The senate of the Israelites composed of 70 elders, Ex 24:1, 9; Num 11:16, 24, 25. Seventy disciples sent out by Jesus, Lk 10:1–17. The Jews captive in Babylon 70 years, Jer 25:11, 12; 29: 10; Dan 9:2; Zech 1:12; 7:5. See *Israel*.

Seventy weeks in the vision of Daniel, Dan 9:24.

SEXUAL RELATIONS See *Copulation; Marriage*.

SHA-ALABBIN See *Sha-albim*.

SHA-ALBIM A city of Dan, Josh 19:41–46; Judg 1:35. One of Solomon's commissary cities, 1 Kgs 4:8–19. Called *Sha-alabbin*, Josh 19:41–46.

SHAALIM A district of unknown location, 1 Sam 9:4.

SHAAPH 1. Son of Jahdai, 1 Chron 2:47.

2. Son of Caleb, 1 Chron 2:48, 49.

SHAARAIM 1. A city of Judah, Josh 15:33–36; 1 Sam 17:52.

2. A city of Simeon, 1 Chron 4:31.

SHAASHGAZ A eunuch of Ahasuerus, Esther 2:12–14.

SHABBETHAI 1. A Levite, assistant to Ezra, Ezra 10:15. An expounder of the law, Neh 8: 7, 8.

2. A chief Levite, Neh 11:15–17.

SHACKLES Used for securing prisoners, Mk 5:3, 4.

See *Chains; Fetters; Handcuffs*.

SHADRACH Called also *Hananiah*. A Hebrew captive in Babylon, Dan 1; 2:17, 49; 3.

SHAGEE Father of Jonathan, one of David's guard, 1 Chron 11:26–47.

SHAHARAIM A Benjaminite, 1 Chron 8:8–10.

SHAHAZUMAH A city in Issachar, Josh 19:17–23.

SHALISHA A district bordering on Ephraim, 1 Sam 9:4.

SHALLECHETH One of the gates of the Temple, 1 Chron 26:16.

SHALLUM 1. King of Israel, 2 Kgs 15:10, 13–15.

2. Husband of Huldah, the prophetess, 2 Kgs 22:14; 2 Chron 34:22.

3. Son of Sismai, 1 Chron 2:40, 41.

4. See *Jehoahaz, 3*.

5. Grandson of Simeon, 1 Chron 4:25.

6. Son of Zadok, 1 Chron 6:4–15; Ezra 7:1–5. Called *Meshullam*, 1 Chron 9:10, 11; Neh 11:10–14.

7. See *Shillem*.

8. A gatekeeper of the Temple, 1 Chron 9:17–19, 31.

9. Father of Jehizkiah, 2 Chron 28:12.

10. The ancestor of a family of returned exiles, Ezra 2:40–42; Neh 7:43–45.

11. A gatekeeper who divorced his wife, Ezra 10: 24.

12. A son of Bani, who divorced his wife, Ezra 10:34–42.

13. A Jew who repaired a portion of the wall of Jerusalem, Neh 3:12.

14. A Jew who repaired a gate of Jerusalem, Neh 3:15.

15. Uncle of Jeremiah, Jer 32:6, 7.

16. Father of Ma-aseiah, Jer 35:4.

SHALMAI One of the Nethinim, Neh 7:46–56. Called *Shamlai*, Ezra 2:43–54.

SHALMAN Identified by some authorities with Salaman, Hos 10:14. Other authorities disagree, and leave his identity uncertain.

SHALMANESER King of Assyria. Overthrows the kingdom of Israel, 2 Kgs 17:3–6; 18:9–11.

SHAMA One of David's warriors, 1 Chron 11: 26–47.

SHAME Jesus ashamed of those who are ashamed of him, Mk 8:38; Lk 9:26. Of Adam and Eve, Gen 3:10. Lack of, by the Israelites when they worshiped the golden calf, Ex 32:25; the wicked, Zeph 3:5. Of the cross, Heb 12:2. Ashamed before Christ at his coming, 1 Jn 2:28.

SHAMGAR A judge and deliverer of Israel, Judg 3:31; 5:6.

SHAMHUTH One of David's commanders, 1 Chron 27:8.

SHAMIR 1. A city in the mountains of Judah, Josh 15:48–62.

2. A city in Ephraim. Home and burial place of Tola, the judge, Judg 10:1, 2.

3. Son of Micah, a Levite, 1 Chron 24:24, 25.

SHAMLAI See *Shalmai.*

SHAMMA Son of Zophah, an Asherite, 1 Chron 7:36, 37.

SHAMMAH 1. Son of Reuel, Gen 36:13, 14, 17; 1 Chron 1:37.

2. David's brother, 1 Sam 16:9; 17:13. Called *Shime-ah,* 2 Sam 13:3, 32, 33; *Shime-i,* 2 Sam 21:21; *Shimea,* 1 Chron 2:13; 20:7.

3. One of David's mighty men, son of Agee, 2 Sam 23:11, 12.

4. One of David's mighty men, 2 Sam 23:24–29. Called *Shammoth,* 1 Chron 11:26–47.

5. A Hararite, one of David's mighty men, 2 Sam 23:24–39.

SHAMMAI 1. Son of Onam, 1 Chron 2:28, 32.

2. Father of Maon, 1 Chron 2:44, 45.

3. Son of Mered, 1 Chron 4:17.

SHAMMOTH One of David's mighty men, 1 Chron 11:26–47. Called *Shammah,* 2 Sam 23:24–39.

SHAMMUA 1. The representative of Reuben among the 12 spies sent into Canaan, Num 13:3–15.

2. Son of David, 2 Sam 5:14–16; 1 Chron 14:4–7. Called *Shime-a,* 1 Chron 3:5.

3. A Levite, father of Abda, Neh 11:15–17. Called *Shemaiah,* 1 Chron 9:15, 16.

4. A priest, Neh 12:12–21.

SHAMSHERAI Son of Jeroham, 1 Chron 8: 26, 27.

SHANTY Isa 1:8.
See *Booth.*

SHAPHAM A leader of Gad, 1 Chron 5:12.

SHAPHAN 1. A secretary of King Josiah, 2 Kgs 22:3–14; 2 Chron 34:8–20. Father of Ahikam and grandfather of Gedaliah, 2 Kgs 22:12, 13; 25: 22; 2 Chron 34:20; Jer 26:24; 39:14. Father of Elasah, Jer 29:3; Gemariah, Jer 36:10–12.

2. Father of Ja-azaniah, Ezk 8:11.

SHAPHAT 1. The representative of Simeon among the spies sent into Canaan, Num 13:3–15.

2. Father of Elisha, 1 Kgs 19:16.

3. Son of Shemaiah, 1 Chron 3:21, 22.

4. A Gadite, 1 Chron 5:12.

5. Son of Adlai, 1 Chron 27:29.

SHAPIR A city prophesied against by Micah, Mic 1:11.

SHARAI A descendant of Bani, who divorced his Gentile wife, Ezra 10:34–42.

SHARAR Father of Ahiam, 2 Sam 23:24–39. Called *Sacher,* 1 Chron 11:26–47.

SHAREZER 1. Son of Sennacherib, 2 Kgs 19: 37; Isa 37:38.

2. A delegate to priests and prophets to consult as to fasting and mourning, Zech 7:2.

SHARON 1. The coastal plain of Palestine north of Joppa, Acts 9:35. David's herds in, 1 Chron 27:29. Roses and beauty of, Song 2:1; Isa 33:9; 35:2; 65:10.

2. A place of unascertained location, 1 Chron 5: 16.

SHARUHEN A city in Simeon, Josh 19:2–7.

SHASHAI A descendant of Bani, who divorced his Gentile wife, Ezra 10:34–42.

SHASHAK A Benjaminite, 1 Chron 8:14, 22–25.

SHAUL 1. Son of Simeon, Gen 46:8–14; Ex 6: 15; Num 26:12–14; 1 Chron 4:24.

2. An ancient king of Edom, Gen 36:37; 1 Chron 1:48, 49.

3. A Kohathite, 1 Chron 6:24.

SHAVEH A valley. Called also "King's Valley," Gen 14:17. Absalom's monument in, 2 Sam 18: 18.

SHAVING Forbidden to Nazirites, Num 6:5; Judg 13:5; to priests, Ezk 44:20.
See *Beard.*

SHAVSHA See *Seraiah, 1.*

SHEAL A descendant of Bani, who divorced his Gentile wife, Ezra 10:29.

SHEALTIEL Father of Zerubbabel and ancestor of Jesus, 1 Chron 3:17, 18; Ezra 3:1, 2, 8; 5:1, 2; Neh 12:1–7; Hag 1:1, 12; Mt 1:12; Lk 3:23–38.

SHEARIAH Son of Azel, 1 Chron 8:38; 9:44.

SHEAR-JASHUB The symbolic name of a son of Isaiah, Isa 7:3; 8:18.

SHEBA 1. Son of Raamah, Gen 10:7; 1 Chron 1:5–9.

2. Son of Joktan, Gen 10:26–30; 1 Chron 1:20–23.

3. Son of Jokshan, Gen 25:3; 1 Chron 1:32.

4. A Benjaminite who led an insurrection against David, 2 Sam 20.

5. A Gadite, 1 Chron 5:13.

6. A city of Simeon, Josh 19:2–7.

7. A country in Arabia. Queen of, visits Solomon, 1 Kgs 10:1–13; 2 Chron 9:1–12. Kings of, bring gifts to Solomon, Ps 72:10. Rich in gold, Ps 72:15; incense, Jer 6:20. Merchandise of, Ezk 27:22, 23; 38:13. Prophecies concerning the people of, coming into the kingdom of Messiah, Isa 60:6.
See *Sabeans.*

SHEBANIAH 1. A priest in the time of David, 1 Chron 15:24.

2. A Levite who joined Nehemiah in covenant, Neh 9:4, 5; 10:9–13.

3. A priest who joined Nehemiah in covenant, Neh 10:1–8; 12:12–21.

4. A Levite who joined Nehemiah in covenant, Neh 10:9–13.

SHEBAR A son of Caleb, 1 Chron 2:48, 49.

SHEBNA(H) A secretary of Hezekiah, 2 Kgs 18:18, 26, 37; 19:2; Isa 22:15–19; 36:3, 11, 22; 37:2.

SHEBUEL 1. Son of Gershom, 1 Chron 23:16; 26:23, 24. Called *Shuba-el,* 1 Chron 24:20.

2. A singer, son of Heman, 1 Chron 25:4, 5. Called *Shuba-el,* 1 Chron 25:9–31.

SHECANIAH 1. A descendant of David, 1 Chron 3:21, 22.

2. A priest of the time of David, 1 Chron 24:7–18.

3. A priest of the time of Hezekiah, 2 Chron 31:14, 15.

4. Two men whose descendants returned with Ezra from captivity in Babylon, Ezra 8:2–14.

5. A Jew who proposed to Ezra the divorce of Gentile wives, Ezra 10:2.

6. Father of Shemaiah, Neh 3:29.

7. Father-in-law of Tobiah, Neh 6:18.

8. A Levite who returned with Zerubbabel from captivity in Babylon, Neh 12:1–7.

SHECHEM 1. A city and district in the central part of the land of Canaan. Abraham stays in, Gen 12:6. Jacob buys a piece of ground in, and erects an altar, Gen 33:18–20. The flocks and herds of Jacob kept in, Gen 37:12–14. Joseph buried in, Josh 24:32. Jacob buried in, Acts 7:16, with Gen 50:12, 13. A city of refuge in Ephraim, Josh 20:7; 21:20–22; Judg 21:19. Joshua assembled the tribes of Israel at, with all their elders, officers, and judges, and presented them before the Lord, Josh 24:1–28. Abimelech made king at, Judg 8:31; 9. Rehoboam crowned at, 1 Kgs 12:1. Destroyed by Abimelech, Judg 9:45; rebuilt by Jeroboam, 1 Kgs 12:25. Men of, killed by Ishmael, Jer 41:5–7. Possibly the same as *Sychar;* Jesus visits; disciples made in, Jn 4:1–42.

2. Son of Hamor; seduces Jacob's daughter; killed by Jacob's sons, Gen 33:19; 34; Josh 24:32; Acts 7:16.

3. Ancestor of the Shechemites, Num 26:28–37; Josh 17:2.

4. Son of Shemida, 1 Chron 7:19.

SHECHEMITES Descendants of Shechem, Num 26:28–37.

SHEDEUR Father of Elizur, Num 1:2–15; 2:3–31; 7:30–35; 10:18.

SHEEP Offered in sacrifice, by Abel, Gen 4:4; by Noah, Gen 8:20; by Abraham, Gen 22:13. See *Offerings.* Required in the Mosaic offerings, see *Offerings.* The land of Bashan adapted to the raising of, Deut 32:14; Gilead, Num 32:1–4; Kedar, Ezk 27:21; Nabaioth, Isa 60:7; Sharon, Isa 65:10. Jacob's management of, Gen 30:31–40. Milk of, used for food, Deut 32:14. Shearing of, Gen 31:17–20; 38:12–17; Isa 53:7; feasting at the time of shearing, 1 Sam 25:11, 36; 2 Sam 13:21–24. First fleece of, belonging to priests and Levites, Deut 18:4. Tribute paid in, 2 Kgs 3:4; 1 Chron 5:21; 2 Chron 17:11. Mountain, Deut 14:3–5.

FIGURATIVE. 1 Chron 21:17; Ps 74:1; Jer 13:20. Of backsliders, Jer 50:6. Of lost sinners, Mt 9:36; 10:6. Of the righteous, Jer 50:17; Ezk 34; Mt 26:31; Mk 14:27; Jn 10:1–16. Of the defenselessness of ministers, Mt 10:16.

Parable of the lost, Mt 18:11–13; Lk 15:3–7.

SHEEP GATE An ancient gate of Jerusalem, Neh 3:1, 32; 12:39; Jn 5:2.

SHEERAH Daughter of Ephraim, 1 Chron 7:24.

SHEET Of Peter's vision, Acts 10:11.

SHEHARIAH A Benjaminite, 1 Chron 8:26, 27.

SHEKEL From the Hebrew word "to weigh," a unit of monetary reckoning based upon weight, the value of which varied according to the metal used. Probably equal to two fifths ounce (11.5 grams), 1/3000 of a talent, and 20 gerahs. Shekels appeared in nugget form rather than being struck into coins. Used to weigh gold, 1 Chron 21:25; cinnamon, Ex 30; 22, 23; myrrh, Ex 30:22, 23. Fines paid in, Deut 22:19, 28, 29. Sanctuary revenues paid in, Ex 30:13.

See *Money; Talent.*

SHEKINAH The visible sign of God's presence on the Ark of the Lord in the Holy of holies, Ex 25:22; Lev 16:1, 2; 2 Sam 6:1, 2; 2 Kgs 19:14, 15; Ps 80:1; Isa 37:16, 17; Ezk 9:3; 10:18; Heb 9:5.

SHELAH 1. Son of Judah, Gen 38:3–5, 11, 14, 26; 46:8–14; Num 26:19–22; 1 Chron 2:3; 4:21, 22.

2. Son of Arpachshad and ancestor of Joseph, Gen 10:24; 11:12–15; 1 Chron 1:18, 24–27; Lk 3:23–38.

SHELAMOTH See *Shelomith, 3.*

SHELANITES Descendants of Shelah, Num 26:19–22. Apparently called *Shilonites,* 1 Chron 9:5.

SHELEMIAH 1. A Temple gatekeeper, 1 Chron 26:14, 15.

2. Name of two descendants of Bani who divorced their Gentile wives, Ezra 10:34–42.

3. Father of Hananiah, Neh 3:30.

4. A priest appointed as an administrator by Nehemiah, Neh 13:13.

5. Son of Cushi, Jer 36:14, 15.

6. Son of Abdeel, commended to arrest Jeremiah, Jer 36:26.

7. Father of Jehucal, Jer 37:3; 38:1.

8. Father of Irijah, Jer 37:13.

SHELEPH Son of Joktan, Gen 10:26–30; 1 Chron 1:20–23.

SHELESH Son of Helem, 1 Chron 7:35.

SHELOMI Father of Ahihud, Num 34:16–28.

SHELOMITH 1. Mother of a blasphemer, Lev 24:11.

2. Daughter of Zerubbabel, 1 Chron 3:19, 20.

3. A son of Izhar, 1 Chron 23:18. Called *Shelamoth,* 1 Chron 24:22.

4. A son or daughter of Rehoboam, 2 Chron 11:20.

5. Ancestor of a family that returned with Ezra from captivity in Babylon, Ezra 8:2–14.

SHELOMOTH 1. Son of Shime-i, 1 Chron 23:8, 9.

2. A descendant of Eliezer, 1 Chron 26:25, 26, 28.

SHELTER See *Booth.*

SHELUMI-EL Son of Zuri-shaddai, and leader of Simeon in the time of Moses, Num 1:2–15; 2:3–31; 7:36–41; 10:19.

SHEM Son of Noah. Preserved in the ark, Gen 5:32; 6:9, 10; 7:13; 9:18; 1 Chron 1:1–4. His filial conduct, Gen 9:23–27. Descendants of, Gen 10:1, 21–31; 11:10–29; 1 Chron 1:17–54. Ancestor of Jesus, Lk 3:36.

SHEMA 1. A city of Judah, Josh 15:21–32.

2. A son of Hebron, 1 Chron 2:43, 44.

3. Son of Joel, 1 Chron 5:7, 8. Called *Shemaiah,* 1 Chron 5:4.

4. A Benjaminite, 1 Chron 8:13.

5. A man who stood at the right hand of Ezra when he read the law to the people, Neh 8:1–5.

SHEMAAH Father of two of David's mighty men, 1 Chron 12:3–7.

SHEMAIAH 1. A prophet in the time of Rehoboam. Prevents Rehoboam from war with Jeroboam, 1 Kgs 12:22–24; 2 Chron 11:2–4. Prophesies the punishment of Rehoboam by Shishak, king of Egypt, 2 Chron 12:5, 7. Writes histories, 2 Chron 12:15.

2. A descendant of David, 1 Chron 3:21, 22; Neh 3:29.

3. A Simeonite, 1 Chron 4:34–39.

4. Son of Joel, 1 Chron 5:4. Called *Shema,* 1 Chron 5:7, 8.

5. A Merarite, 1 Chron 9:14. In charge of the business of the Temple in time of Nehemiah, Neh 11:15–17.

6. Son of Galal, 1 Chron 9:15, 16. Called *Shammua,* Neh 11:17.

7. A chief Levite in time of David; assisted in moving the Ark from Obed-edom, 1 Chron 15:4–10, 11.

8. A Levite who assisted in the division of the priests, 1 Chron 24:6.

9. A Temple guard in the time of David, 1 Chron 26:4–7.

10. A Levite sent by Jehoshaphat to instruct the people in the law, 2 Chron 17:7–9.

11. A Levite, son of Jeduthun, 2 Chron 29:12–14.

12. A Levite, 2 Chron 31:14, 15.

13. A Levite who contributed largely for Passover sacrifices, 2 Chron 35:9.

14. A Jew who returned from Babylon with Ezra, Ezra 8:2–14.

15. A Levitical leader with Ezra, Ezra 8:16.

16. A priest who divorced his Gentile wife, Ezra 10:21.

17. An Israelite who divorced his Gentile wife, Ezra 10:31, 32.

18. A false prophet in the time of Nehemiah, Neh 6:10.

19. A priest with Zerubbabel, Neh 10:1–8; 12:1–7, 12–21.

20. A priest, son of Mattaniah, Neh 12:35, 36.

21. The name of three men who celebrated the dedication of the new wall of Jerusalem, Neh 12: 34–36, 42.

22. Father of the prophet Uriah, Jer 26:20.

23. A false prophet, Jer 29:24–32.

24. Father of Delaiah, Jer 36:12.

SHEMARIAH 1. One of David's mighty men, 1 Chron 12:3–7.

2. Son of Rehoboam, 2 Chron 11:19.

3. Name of two Israelites who divorced their Gentile wives, Ezra 10:31, 32, 34–42.

SHEMEBER King of Zeboiim, Gen 14:2.

SHEMER 1. Owner of the site on which Samaria was built, 1 Kgs 16:24.

2. A Levite, father of Bani, 1 Chron 6:44–47.

3. An Asherite, son of Heber, 1 Chron 7:24. Called *Shomer,* 1 Chron 7:32.

SHEMIDA Descendant of Gilead, Num 26: 28–37; Josh 17:2; 1 Chron 7:19.

SHEMINITH See *Music.*

SHEMIRAMOTH 1. A Levite musician, 1 Chron 15:18, 20; 16:5.

2. A Levite sent by Jehoshaphat to instruct the people in the law, 2 Chron 17:7–9.

SHEMUEL 1. A Simeonite appointed on the committee to divide the land of Canaan, Num 34: 16–28.

2. Head of a family of Issachar, 1 Chron 7:2.

SHENAZZAR Son of Jeconiah, 1 Chron 3: 17, 18.

SHEOL A Hebrew word used throughout the Old Testament with reference to the unseen world, the place beneath the earth where, before the cross, both the just and the unjust went after death. It is often rendered hell, the pit, and the grave. See *Hell; Pit.*

In the New Testament the exact equivalent of the Hebrew *sheol* is the Greek word *hades,* cf. Ps 16:10 with Acts 2:27. The remarkably uniform Old and New Testament revelations are here brought together.

Sheol is described as below the surface of the earth, Num 16:30–33; Amos 9:2; in the heart of the earth, Mt 12:40; Acts 2:27; the underworld, Isa 28: 15; the land of death, Jon 2:2–6. It is spoken of as cruel, Song 8:6; insatiable, Prov 27:20; Isa 5:14; with gates, Isa 38:10; with a mouth, Ps 141:6, 7; powerful, Mt 16:18; a prison, Jon 2:2–6.

The wicked went down into that part of Sheol called the pit (see *Pit*), including Pharaoh, Assyria, Elam, Meshech, Tubal, Edom, Sidon, with their multitudes, Ezk 31:16–18; 32:17–32; and all other wicked men, Ps 9:17. Korah and his company went there, Num 16:30–33, as did the rich man of Lk 16: 22, 23. Lucifer is to be "brought down to the pit of hell, down to its lowest depths," Isa 14:15. This region of Sheol is said to be a place of weakness, Isa 14:10; shame, Ezk 32:25, 30; poverty, Ps 49:14; torment, remorse, memory, and consciousness, Lk 16:23–28.

The region in Sheol where the righteous dead went prior to Calvary was separated by a great chasm from the lower region, Lk 16:26; Ps 86:13. It was "open to God's knowledge," Prov 15:11; who brought his people there, 1 Sam 2:6; Hos 13:14. It was a place of peace, Isa 57:1, 2; and comfort, Lk 16:25. Righteous persons inhabiting the higher region, called Abraham's bosom, Lk 16:22; and Paradise, Lk 23:43, included Abraham, Lk 16:22–25; the fathers, Gen 15:15; Jacob, Gen 37:33–35; Samuel, 1 Sam 28:13, 14; the thief on the cross, Lk 23: 43; the beggar Lazarus, Lk 16:23–25.

After his crucifixion Christ descended into Sheol, Ps 16:10; Acts 2:27; Eph 4:9. At his ascension he "leads many captives," Ps 68:18–20; Eph 4:8–10, generally understood to mean that he took the righteous occupants of Sheol with him to heaven (see *Paradise*), in accordance with the prophecies that he would at some time deliver his people from Sheol, 1 Sam 2:6; Hos 13:14; Ps 71:20. Therefore the powers of Sheol or Hades do not prevail against the righteous in the Old Testament, so that believers now go directly to heaven at death, Mt 16:18; Phil 1:23. See *Church, The True; Paradise.*

Christ has the keys to Sheol, Rev 1:18, which will ultimately give up its wicked dead for judgment, Rev 20:11–15. Sheol will then come to an end, and the lake of fire will take its place, Rev 20:10, 15.

See *Gehenna; Grave; Hades; Hell; Paradise; Pit; Tartarus.*

SHEPHAM A place on the eastern boundary of Canaan, Num 34:10, 11.

SHEPHATIAH 1. Son of David, 2 Sam 3:4; 1 Chron 3:3.

2. A Benjaminite, father of Meshullam, 1 Chron 9:7, 8.

3. A valiant man who joined David at Ziklag, 1 Chron 12:3–7.

4. A ruler of Simeon, 1 Chron 27:16–22.

5. Son of Jehoshaphat, 2 Chron 21:2.

6. The name of two men, ancestors of families which returned to Jerusalem from captivity in Babylon, Ezra 2:3–35; 8:2–14; Neh 7:8–38; and Ezra 2:55–57; Neh 7:57–59.

7. A descendant of Perez, Neh 11:4–6.

8. An enemy of Jeremiah, Jer 38:1–4.

SHEPHER A mountain camping place of the Israelites in the desert, Num 33:15–37.

SHEPHERD One who cares for flocks, Gen 31:38–40; Ps 78:52, 53; Jer 31:10; Amos 3:12; Lk 2:8. David the, defends his flock against a lion and a bear, 1 Sam 17:34, 35. Causes the flock to rest, Ps 23:2, 3; Song 1:7; Jer 33:12. Counts the flock, Lev 27:32; Jer 33:13. Knows his flocks by name, Jn 10:3–5. Keeps the sheep and goats apart, Mt 25:32. Waters the flocks, Gen 29:2–10. Keeps the flocks in sheepfolds, Num 32:16; 1 Sam 24:3; Jn 10:1. Watchtowers of, Mic 4:8. Dogs of, Job 30:1. Despised by the Egyptians, Gen 46:34. Angels appeared to, Lk 2:8–20.

INSTANCES OF. Abel, Gen 4:2. Rachel, Gen 29:9. Daughters of Jethro, Ex 2:16. Moses, Ex 3:1. David, 1 Sam 16:10, 11; 2 Sam 7:8; Ps 78:70.

FIGURATIVE. Gen 49:24. Of God's care, Ps 23; 78:52; 80:1. Of prophets, priests, Levites, and civil authorities, Ezk 34. Of Christ, Zech 13:7; Mt 26:31; Jn 10:1–16; Heb 13:20, 21; 1 Pet 2:25. Name given to Jesus, Isa 40:11; Mk 14:27; Jn 10:11; 1 Pet 2:25; 5:4. Name given to Cyrus, Isa 44:28. See *Pastor.*

SHEPHI See *Shepho.*

SHEPHO Son of Shobal, Gen 36:23. Called *Shephi,* 1 Chron 1:40.

SHEPHUPHAM Son of Benjamin, Num 26:38–41.

SHEPHUPHAN Son of Bela, 1 Chron 8:3–5.

SHEREBIAH A Levite assistant to Ezra, Ezra 8:18, 24.

2. A Levite who signed the covenant with Nehemiah, Neh 8:7, 8; 9:4, 5; 10:9–13.

3. A Levite who accompanied Zerubbabel, Neh 12:8, 24.

SHERESH Son of Machir, 1 Chron 7:16.

SHERIFF Dan 3:2.

SHESHAI A son of Anak, Num 13:22; Josh 15:14; Judg 1:10.

SHESHAN A descendant of Jerahmeel, 1 Chron 2:31, 34, 35.

SHESH-BAZZAR A name given, apparently, to Zerubbabel, Ezra 1:8, 11; 5:14, 16.

See *Zerubbabel.*

SHETH Another name for Moabites, Num 24:17.

SHETHAR An official of Persia, Esther 1:14.

SHETHAR-BOZENAI An official of Persia, Ezra 5:3, 6; 6:6, 13.

SHEVA 1. See *Seraiah, 1.*

2. Son of Caleb, 1 Chron 2:48, 49.

SHEWBREAD Mk 2:25, 26; Lk 6:4.

See *Bread of the Presence.*

SHIBAH "The Well of the Oath," a name given by Isaac to a well, Gen 26:33.

SHIBBOLETH A password, Judg 12:6.

SHIELD Defensive armor, Ps 35:2. Used by the Benjaminites, 2 Chron 14:8; 17:17. Uzziah equipped the children of Israel with, 2 Chron 26:14. Made of bronze, 1 Kgs 14:27; of gold, 2 Sam 8:7; 1 Kgs 10:16, 17; 2 Chron 9:15, 16; of wood, Ezk 39:9, 10; of tin, Job 15:26. Stored in armories, 1 Kgs 10:16, 17; 2 Chron 11:12; 32:5, 27; in the Temple, 2 Kgs 11:10; 2 Chron 23:9. Painted red, Nah 2:3.

See *Arms.*

FIGURATIVE. Of God's protection, Deut 33:29; 2 Sam 22:3, 36; Ps 5:12; 18:2, 35; 33:20; 59:11; 84:9. Of God's truth, Ps 91:4.

SHIGIONOTH Hab 3:1.

See *Music.*

SHIHOR A river of Egypt, given by some authorities as the Nile, 1 Chron 13:5.

SHIHOR-LIBNATH A place on the border of Asher, Josh 19:24–26.

SHIKKERON A city of Judah, Josh 15:10, 11.

SHILHI Grandfather of Jehoshaphat, 1 Kgs 22:42; 2 Chron 20:31.

SHILHIM A city of Judah, Josh 15:21–32.

SHILLEM Called also *Shallum.* Son of Naphtali, Gen 46:23–25; Num 26:48–50; 1 Chron 7:13.

SHILOAH A stream or pool, Isa 8:6. Probably identical with *Siloam,* which see.

SHILOH 1. A name of Jesus, Gen 49:10.

2. City of Ephraim, north of Bethel, and on the road from Bethel to Shechem, Judg 21:19. Tabernacle at, Josh 18:1, 8–10; Judg 18:31; 1 Sam 1:3, 9, 21, 22, 24; 2:13, 14; Ps 78:60; Jer 7:12. Seat of government during the time of Joshua, Josh 21:1, 2. The place of rendezvous for the tribes, Josh 22:9, 12; Judg 21:10–12. Eli lived at, 1 Sam 1:9; 4:12, 13; dies at, 1 Sam 4:18. Ahijah the prophet lives at, 1 Kgs 14:2. Devoted men from, killed by Ishmael, Jer 41:5–9.

SHILONITE 1. Ahijah, a prophet from Shiloh, 1 Kgs 11:29; 12:15; 15:29; 2 Chron 9:29; 10:15.

2. Used, apparently, to denote a descendant of Shilon, 1 Chron 9:5; Neh 11:4–6.

See *Shelanites.*

SHILSHAH Son of Zophah, 1 Chron 7:36, 37.

SHIMEA 1. See *Shammua, 2.*

2. See *Shammah, 2.*

3. A Merarite Levite, 1 Chron 6:29, 30.

4. Grandfather of Asaph, 1 Chron 6:39–43.

SHIMEAH 1. A Benjaminite, son of Mikloth, 1 Chron 8:30–32. Called *Shimeam,* 1 Chron 9:38.

2. See *Shammah, 2.*

SHIMEAM See *Shimeah, 1.*

SHIMEATH Mother of an assassin of King Joash, 2 Kgs 12:21; 2 Chron 24:26.

SHIMEATHITES A family of writers, 1 Chron 2:55.

SHIME-I 1. Son of Gershon, Ex 6:17; Num 3:16–24; 1 Chron 6:17; 23:7.

2. A Benjaminite. Curses David; David's magnanimity toward, 2 Sam 16:5–13; 19:16–23, with 1 Kgs 2:36–46.

3. Brother of David, 2 Sam 21:20, 21.

4. An officer of David, 1 Kgs 1:8.

5. One of Solomon's commissary officers, 1 Kgs 4:8–19. Possibly the same as 4, above.

6. Grandson of Jeconiah, 1 Chron 3:19.

7. Son of Zaccur, 1 Chron 4:26, 27.

8. A Reubenite. Son of Gog, 1 Chron 5:4.

9. A Merarite. Son of Libni, 1 Chron 6:29, 30.

10. A Gershonite. Son of Jahath, 1 Chron 6:39–43.

11. Father of a family in Benjamin, 1 Chron 8:19–21.

12. A Levite, 1 Chron 23:8, 9.

13. A Levite, son of Jeduthun, 1 Chron 25:3. A leader of singers in time of David, 1 Chron 25:9–31.

14. David's overseer of vineyards, 1 Chron 27:27.

15. A son of Heman, 2 Chron 29:12–14.

16. A Levite. Treasurer of tithes and offerings in the time of Hezekiah, 2 Chron 31:12, 13. Possibly the same as 15, above.

17. A Levite who divorced his Gentile wife, Ezra 10:23.

18. The name of two Israelites who divorced Gentile wives, Ezra 10:33, 34–42.

19. A Benjaminite. Grandfather of Mordecai, Esther 2:5.

SHIME-ON An Israelite who divorced his Gentile wife, Ezra 10:31, 32.

SHIMON A man of Judah, 1 Chron 4:20.

SHIMRATH Son of Shime-i, 1 Chron 8:19–21.

SHIMRI 1. Head of a family in Simeon, 1 Chron 4:34–39.

2. Father of Jedia-el, one of David's mighty men, 1 Chron 11:26–47.

3. A Merarite, 1 Chron 26:10.

4. A Levite in the time of Hezekiah, 2 Chron 29:12–14.

SHIMRITH A Moabitess, mother of Jehozabad, murderer of King Joash, 2 Chron 24:26. Called *Shomer,* 2 Kgs 12:21.

SHIMRON 1. Son of Issachar, Gen 46:8–14; Num 26:23–25; 1 Chron 7:1.

2. A city in Zebulun, Josh 11:1; 19:15, 16. See *Shimron-meron.*

SHIMRONITES The family of Shimron, Num 26:23–25.

SHIMRON-MERON A city conquered by Joshua, Josh 12:8–24. Probably identical with *Shimron, 2,* which see.

SHIMSHAI A scribe, Ezra 4:8, 9, 17, 23.

SHINAB King of Admah, Gen 14:2.

SHINAR Land of, See *Babylon.*

SHION A city in Issachar, Josh 19:17–23.

SHIP Built by Noah, Gen 6:12–22; by Solomon, 1 Kgs 9:26; 2 Chron 8:17, 18; by Jehoshaphat, 1 Kgs 22:48; 2 Chron 20:35, 36; of resinous wood, Gen 6:14; of fir wood, Ezk 27:5; sealed with tar, Gen 6:14. Equipped with helm, Jas 3:4; rudder, Acts 27:40; tackle, Isa 33:23; Acts 27:19; sails, Isa 33:23; Acts 27:17, 40; sails of linen, Ezk 27:7; masts, Isa 33:23; Ezk 27:5; oars, Jon 1:13; Mk 6:48; anchor, Acts 27:29, 30, 40; Heb 6:19; lifeboats, Acts 27:30, 32. Used in commerce, Acts 21:3; 27:10; in commerce with Tarshish, 1 Kgs 22:48; Isa 60:9; Jon 1:3; with Ophir, 1 Kgs 10:11; 2 Chron 8:17, 18; with Adramyttium, Acts 27:2; for passenger traffic, Isa 60:9; Jon 1:3; Acts 20:13; 27:2, 37; 28:11; for ferriage, 2 Sam 19:18. Repaired by calking, Ezk 27:9. Wrecked at Ezion-geber, 1 Kgs 22:48; 2 Chron 20:35–37; at Melita, Acts 27:14, 15, 44. Warships used by Cyprus, Num 24:23, 24; Dan 11:30, 31.

See *Ark, Noah's; Navy; Sailor.*

SHIPHI Father of Ziza, 1 Chron 4:34–39.

SHIPHRAH A Hebrew midwife, Ex 1:15, 16.

SHIPHTAN Father of Kemuel, the representative of Ephraim on the committee which divided the promised land among the Israelites, Num 34:16–28.

SHISHA See *Seriah, 1.*

SHISHAK King of Egypt. Gives asylum to Jeroboam, 1 Kgs 11:40. Conquers Jerusalem, 1 Kgs 14:25, 26; 2 Chron 12:2–9.

SHITRAI A chief herder of David, 1 Chron 27:29.

SHIZA A Reubenite. Father of Adina, one of David's mighty men, 1 Chron 11:26–47.

SHOA An unknown country or city, or a symbolical term, Ezk 23:23.

SHOBAB 1. Son of David, 2 Sam 5:14–16; 1 Chron 3:5; 14:4–7.

2. Son of Caleb, 1 Chron 2:18.

SHOBACH Commander of Hadadezer's forces. Killed by David's army, 2 Sam 10:15, 16, 18. Called *Shophach,* 1 Chron 19:16–18.

SHOBAI A gatekeeper, whose descendants returned to Jerusalem with Zerubbabel, Ezra 2:40–42.

SHOBAL 1. Descendant of Seir, Gen 36:20, 21, 23; 1 Chron 1:38–40.

2. Descendant of Caleb, 1 Chron 2:50, 52; of the tribe of Judah, 1 Chron 4:1, 2.

SHOBEK A Jew who signed the covenant with Nehemiah, Neh 10:14–27.

SHOBI Son of Nahash. Brought supplies to David in his escape from Absalom, 2 Sam 17:27.

SHOE Taken off on holy ground, Ex 3:5; Josh 5:15; Acts 7:33. Taken off in mourning, Ezk 24:17. Of the Israelites, did not wear out, Deut 29:5. Removed in token of refusal to observe the levirate marriage, Deut 25:9; to validate a business transaction, Ruth 4:7, 8. Poor sold for a pair of, Amos 2:6; 8:6. Made of dolphin hide, Ezk 16:9, 10; straps of, Isa 5:27; loosing of, a humble service, Mk 1:7; Lk 3:16.

SHOHAM A Merarite, 1 Chron 24:26, 27.

SHOMER 1. See *Shemer,* 3.

2. See *Shimrith.*

SHOPHACH See *Shobach.*

SHOUTING IN JOY AND PRAISE. 1 Chron 15:28. So the leaders of Israel took the Ark to Jerusalem with shouts of joy, the blowing of horns and trumpets, the crashing of cymbals, and loud playing on the harps and zithers.

2 Chron 15:12. Then they entered into a contract to worship only the Lord God of their fathers, [13]and agreed that anyone who refused to do this must die—whether old or young, man or woman. [14]They shouted out their oath of loyalty to God with trumpets blaring and horns sounding.

Ezra 3:11. They sang rounds of praise and thanks to God, singing this song: "He is good, and his love and mercy toward Israel will last forever." Then all the people gave a great shout, praising God because the foundation of the Temple had been laid. [12]But many of the priests and Levites and other leaders—the old men who remembered Solomon's beautiful Temple—wept aloud, while others were shouting for joy! [13]So the shouting and the weeping mingled together in a loud commotion that could be heard from far away!

Ps 5:11. But make everyone rejoice who puts his trust in you. Keep them shouting for joy because you are defending them. Fill all who love you with your happiness.

Ps 47:1. Come, everyone, and clap for joy! Shout triumphant praises to the Lord!

Isa 12:6. Let all the people of Jerusalem shout his praise with joy. For great and mighty is the Holy One of Israel, who lives among you.

Lk 17:15. One of them came back to Jesus, shouting, "Glory to God, I'm healed!"

Lk 19:37. And as they reached the place where the road started down from the Mount of Olives, the whole procession began to shout and sing as they walked along, praising God for all the wonderful miracles Jesus had done. [38]"God has given us a King!" they exulted. "Long live the King! Let all heaven rejoice! Glory to God in the highest heavens!" [39]But some of the Pharisees among the crowd said, "Sir, rebuke your followers for saying things like that!" [40]He replied, "If they keep quiet, the stones along the road will burst into cheers!" [41]But as they came closer to Jerusalem and he saw the city ahead, he began to cry.

Acts 3:8. So that he came up with a leap, stood there a moment and began walking! Then, walking, leaping, and praising God, he went into the Temple with them. [9]When the people inside saw him walking and heard him praising God.

Rev 5:12. "The Lamb is worthy" (loudly they sang it!) "—the Lamb who was slain. He is worthy to receive the power, and the riches, and the wisdom, and the strength, and the honor, and the glory, and the blessing." [13]And then I heard everyone in heaven and earth, and from the dead beneath the earth and in the sea, exclaiming, "The blessing and the honor and the glory and the power belong to the one sitting on the throne, and to the Lamb forever and ever." [14]And the four Living Beings kept saying, "Amen!" And the twenty-four Elders fell down and worshiped him.

SHOVEL A utensil in the Tabernacle, Ex 27:3; 38:3; Num 4:14; Temple, 1 Kgs 7:40; Jer 52:18.

SHRINE An idolatrous symbol of the Temple of Diana, Acts 19:24.

SHUA 1. A Canaanite and father-in-law of Judah, Gen 38:2; 1 Chron 2:3.

2. Daughter of Heber, 1 Chron 7:32.

SHUAH Son of Abraham by his wife, or concubine, Keturah, Gen 25:1, 2; 1 Chron 1:32.

SHUAL 1. Son of Zophah, 1 Chron 7:36, 37.

2. A region near Ophrah, possibly in Benjamin, 1 Sam 13:17.

SHUBAEL See *Shebuel, 1 and 2.*

SHUHAH Brother of Chelub, 1 Chron 4:11, 12.

SHUHAM Son of Dan, Num 26:42, 43. Called *Hushim,* Gen 46:23–25.

SHULAMITE Meaning peaceful, it is the title given to the young woman of Song 6:13.

SHUNAMMITE 1. A person from Shunem. Abishag, the girl who nursed David, 1 Kgs 1:3, 4; desired by Adonijah as his wife, 1 Kgs 2:13–25.

2. A woman who gave hospitality to Elisha, and whose son he raised to life, 2 Kgs 4:8–37.

SHUNEM A city allotted to the tribe of Issachar, Josh 19:17–23. Elisha stays at, with the Shunammite, 2 Kgs 4. A girl found in, to nurse David, 1 Kgs 1:3, 4.

SHUNI Son of Gad, Gen 46:16, 17; Num 26:15–18.

SHUPPIM 1. Son of Ir, 1 Chron 7:12, 15.

2. A Levite, 1 Chron 26:16.

SHUR A wilderness southwest of Palestine, Gen 16:7; 20:1; 25:18; Ex 15:22; 1 Sam 15:7; 27:8.

SHUSHAN Capital of the Medo-Persian empire, Esther 1:1–3; 3:15. King's palace at, Neh 1:1; Esther 1:1–3, 5; 2:5,8; 8:14.

SHUTHELAH 1. Son of Ephraim, Num 26:28–37; 1 Chron 7:20, 21.

2. Son of Zabad, 1 Chron 7:20, 21.

SIA See *Siaha.*

SIAHA Called also *Sia.* One of the Nethinim, Ezra 2:43–54; Neh 7:46–56.

SIBBECAI A captain in David's army, 2 Sam 21:18; 1 Chron 11:26–47; 20:4; 27:11.

SIBMAH A city of Reuben, Num 32:38; Josh

13:19; Isa 16:8, 9; Jer 48:32. Apparently called also *Sebam,* Num 32:3, 4.

SIBRAIM A city of Syria, Ezk 47:16.

SICK, THE Visiting, Ps 41:6. Visiting, a duty, Mt 25:36, 43.

FIGURATIVE. Isa 1:5, 6; Hos 5:13.

See *Afflicted; Afflictions; Disease.*

SICKLE An agricultural implement used for cutting grain, Deut 23:25; 1 Sam 13:20, 21; Mk 4:29.

FIGURATIVE. Of the judgments of God, Joel 3:13; Rev 14:14–19.

SICKNESS See *Afflictions; Disease.*

SIDDIM VALLEY A valley bordering the Dead Sea. Scene of the defeat of the king of Sodom, Gen 14:3, 8–10.

SIDON 1. Son of Canaan, Gen 10:15–19; 1 Chron 1:13–16.

2. A city on the northern boundary of the Canaanites, Gen 10:15–19. Designated by Jacob as the border of Zebulun, Gen 49:13. Was on the northern boundary of Asher, Josh 19:28; 2 Sam 24:6. Belonged to the land of Israel according to promise, Josh 13:2–7. Israelites failed to make conquest of, Judg 1:31, 32; 3:1–3. The inhabitants of, contributed cedar for the first and second temple, 1 Kgs 5:6; 1 Chron 22:4; Ezra 3:7. Solomon marries women of, 1 Kgs 11:1. Ahab marries a woman of, 1 Kgs 16:31. People of, come to hear Jesus, Mk 3:7, 8; Lk 6:17, 18. Inhabitants of, offend Herod, Acts 12:20–23.

Commerce of, Isa 23:2–4, 12. Sailors of, Ezk 27:8. Prophecies concerning, Jer 25:15–22; 27:3–11; 47:4; Ezk 28:21–23; 32:30; Joel 3:4–8, Zech 9:2. Jesus visits the region of, and heals the daughter of the Canaanite woman, Mt 15:21–28; Mk 7:24–31. Visited by Paul, Acts 27:3.

SIEGE Offer of a truce must be made to the city before beginning, Deut 20:10–12. Conducted by erecting embankments parallel to the walls of the besieged city, Deut 20:19, 20; Isa 29:3; 37:33. Battering rams used in, see *Battering rams.* Distress of the inhabitants during, 2 Kgs 6:24–30; 25:3; Isa 9:19, 20; 36:12; Jer 19:9. Cannibalism in, 2 Kgs 6:26–30.

INSTANCES OF. Of Jericho, Josh 6; Rabbah, 2 Sam 11:1; Abel, 2 Sam 20:15; Gibbethon, 1 Kgs 15:27; Tirzah, 1 Kgs 16:17. Jerusalem, by the people of Judah, Judg 1:8; by David, 2 Sam 5:6, 9; by Rezin, king of Syria, and Pekah, son of Remaliah, king of Israel, 2 Kgs 16:5; by Nebuchadnezzar, 2 Kgs 24:10, 11; Dan 1:1, 2; 2 Kgs 25:1–3; Jer 52; by Sennacherib, 2 Chron 32:1–23. Samaria, 1 Kgs 20:1; 2 Kgs 6:24; 17:5; 18:9–11.

SIEVE FIGURATIVE. Amos 9:9.

SIFTER FIGURATIVE. Isa 30:28; Jer 15:7; Lk 22:31; Heb 12:27.

SIGN 1. A miracle to confirm faith, Mt 16:4; 24:3, 30; Mk 8:11, 12; 13:3, 4; Jn 2:11. Asked for by, and given to, Abraham, Gen 15:8–17; Moses, Ex 4:1–9; Gideon, Judg 6:17, 36–40; Hezekiah, 2 Kgs 20:8; Zacharias, Lk 1:18. Given to Jeroboam, 1 Kgs 13:3–5.

The mark of Cain, Gen 4:15. Rainbow, that the world would never again be destroyed by a flood, Gen 9:12–17. Miracles of Moses, of the divine authority of his missions, Ex 4:1–9. Blood of the pascal lamb, Ex 12:13. The Passover, Ex 13:9. Consecration of the firstborn, Ex 13:14–16. The Sabbath, Ex 13:12, 13, 17. A fringe, Num 15:38–40. Cover of the altar, Num 16:38–40. Aaron's rod, Num 17:10. Scarlet rope, Josh 2:17, 18, 21. Monuments, Josh 4:2–9. Dew on Gideon's fleece, Judg 6:36–40.

Prayer for signs of mercy, Ps 86:17. A token of coming events, Mt 16:2–4; 24:3.

See *Miracles; Proof; Token.*

2. See *Superscription.*

SIGNAL Isa 5:26.

FIGURATIVE. Isa 49:22; Jer 4:6.

See *Armies; Banner; Flag; Trumpet.*

SIHN Desert of, a wilderness between Elim and Sinai. Israelites journey through, Ex 16:1; Num 33:11; murmur for bread in, Ex 16:2; manna and quail given in, Ex 16:4–36.

SIHON King of the Amorites. His seat of government at Heshbon, Num 21:25, 26. The proverbial chant celebrating the victory of Sihon over the Moabites, Num 21:27–30. Conquest of his kingdom by the Israelites, Num 21:21–26; Deut 2:24–37; 3:1, 2, 6, 8.

SILAS Called also *Silvanus.* Sent to Paul, in Antioch, from Jerusalem, Acts 15:22–33. Becomes Paul's companion, Acts 15:40, 41; 2 Cor 1:19; 1 Thess 1:1; 2 Thess 1:1. Imprisoned with Paul in Philippi, Acts 16:19–40. Driven, with Paul, from Thessalonica, Acts 17:4–10. Left by Paul at Beroea, Acts 17:14. Rejoins Paul at Corinth, Acts 17:15; 18:5. Carries Peter's epistle to Asia Minor, 1 Pet 5:12.

SILK Wearing apparel made of, Ezk 16:9, 10, 13. Merchandise of, Rev 18:12.

See *Cotton; Linen.*

SILIA A place of uncertain location, 2 Kgs 12:20.

SILOAM Called also *Shiloah.* A pool in Jerusalem, Neh 3:15; Isa 8:6. Jesus directs the blind man, whom he healed, to wash in, Jn 9:1–11.

2. Tower of, in the wall of Jerusalem, falls and kills 18 people, Lk 13:4.

SILVANUS See *Silas.*

SILVER From Tarshish, Ezk 27:12. Refining of, Prov 17:3; 25:4, 5; Jer 6:29, 30; Ezk 22:18–22; Zech 13:9; Mal 3:3. See *Refining.* Used for money, Gen 13:1, 2; 20:16; 23:13–16; Amos 8:6; Mt 26:15. See *Money.* For ornamentation of, and in the manufacture of, the utensils for the Tabernacle, Ex 26:18, 19; 27:17; 35:24; 36:24; 38:25, 26; Num 7:13, 84–86; of the Temple, 1 Chron 28:14; 29:2–5; Ezra 5:14; 6:5; 8:26, 27; Dan 5:2–4. Cups made of, Gen 44:2; trumpets, Num 10:2; cords, Eccl 12:6; chains, Isa 40:19; shrines, Acts 19:24; idols, Ex 20:23; Isa 30:22; Hos 13:2; baskets, Prov 25:11; beads, Song 1:11; see *Jewels;* battlement, Song 8:9.

Dishes and gifts of, Num 7:84–86; 2 Sam 8:10; 1 Kgs 10:25; 2 Kgs 12:13, 14; 1 Chron 18:10; 2 Chron 24:14; Ezra 5:14; 6:5; Dan 5:2–4; 11:8.

Abundance of, 1 Kgs 10:27; 1 Chron 22:14; 29:

2–7; 2 Chron 1:15; Eccl 2:7, 8; Isa 2:7. Dross from, Prov 25:4, 5. Reprobate, Jer 6:30. Workers in, 2 Chron 2:14; Acts 19:24. See *Smith.*

See *Money.*

SYMBOLICAL. Dan 2:32, 35.

SILVERSMITH Acts 19:24.

See *Smith.*

SIMEON 1. Son of Jacob, Gen 29:33; 35:23; Ex 1:1–4; 1 Chron 2:1, 2. With Levi avenges on the Shechemites the seduction of Dinah, Gen 34; 49: 5–7. Jacob's denunciation of, Gen 34:30; 49:5–7. Goes down into Egypt to buy grain; is bound by Joseph and detained, Gen 42:24, 36; 43:23. His descendants, Gen 46:8–14; Ex 6:15; Num 26:12–14; 1 Chron 4:24–33. See *Tribe of,* below.

2. Tribe of: Military enrollment of, at Sinai, Num 1:20–46; 2:3–31; in the plains of Moab, Num 26:12–14. Place of, in camp and march, Num 2: 3–31; 10:18, 19. Inheritance allotted to, Josh 19:1–9; Judg 1:3–17; 1 Chron 4:24–43. Stood on Mount Gerizim to bless at the time of the reading of the law, Deut 27:12. Joined with the people of Judah and Benjamin in the renewal of the passover, 2 Chron 15:9, with *vs.* 1–15. Idolatry of, 2 Chron 34: 6, with *vs.* 1–7.

See *Israel.*

3. A devout man in Jerusalem. Blesses Jesus in the temple, Lk 2:25–35.

4. An ancestor of Jesus, Lk 3:23–38.

SIMON 1. See *Peter.*

2. One of the twelve apostles, Mt 10:2–4; Mk 3: 16–19; Lk 6:14–16; Acts 1:14.

3. A brother of Jesus, Mt 13:55; Mk 6:2, 3.

4. A leper. Jesus dines with, Mt 26:6; Mk 14:3.

5. A man of Cyrene. Compelled to carry Jesus' cross, Mt 27:32; Mk 15:21; Lk 23:26.

6. A Pharisee. Jesus dines with, Lk 7:36–44.

7. The father of Judas Iscariot, Jn 6:71; 13:1–3, 26.

8. A sorcerer. Converted by Philip; rebuked by Peter, Acts 8:9–13, 18–24.

9. A tanner. Peter stays with, Acts 9:43; 10:5, 6, 32.

SIMONY Ecclesiastical corruption, Acts 8: 18, 19.

SIN INDEX OF SUB-TOPICS. *Miscellany of Minor Sub-topics; Unclassified Scripture Relating to, Defining and Illustrating; Confession of; Consequences of, Imposed on Children; Conviction of; Forgiveness of; Fruits of; Known to God; Love of; National, Punishment of, with Instances of; Punishment of; Repugnant to God; Repugnant to the Righteous; Separates from God.*

MISCELLANY OF MINOR SUB-TOPICS. Paul's discussion of the responsibility for, Rom chapters 2–9. Degrees in, Lk 7:41–47; 12:47, 48. Progressive, Deut 29:19; 1 Kgs 16:31; Ps 1:1; Isa 5:18; 30:1; Jer 9: 3; 16:11, 12; Hos 13:2; 2 Tim 3:13. Its progressiveness exemplified in Joseph's brothers, 1. Jealousy, Gen 37:4. 2. Conspiracy, Gen 37:18. 3. Murder, Gen 37: 19, 20.

Sinfulness of, Job 22:5; Ps 25:11; Isa 1:18; Rom 7: 13. Defiles, Ps 51:2, 7; Isa 1:18; 1 Jn 1:7. See *Defilement.*

To be hated, Deut 7:26; Ps 119:113. By the body, Eccl 5:6. The besetting, Heb 12:1. Little sins, Song 2:15.

Unpardonable, Mt 12:31, 32; Mk 3:29; Lk 12:10; 1 Jn 5:16, 17. Instances of unpardonable: Israel's, Num 14:26–45; of Eli's family, 1 Sam 3:14. See *Reprobate.* No escape from the consequences of, Gen 3:8–12; Isa 28:18–22; Amos 9:1–4; Mt 23:33; Heb 2: 3. See *Punishment, No Escape from.* Attempt to hide, vain, Isa 29:15; 59:6. Secret sins, Ps 19:12; 44: 21; 64:1, 2; 90:8; Eccl 12:14; Ezk 8:12; 11:5; Mt 10:26; Lk 8:17; 12:2, 3; Jn 3:20; Rom 2:16; Eph 5:12. Fools mock at, Prov 14:9.

Against knowledge, Prov 26:11; Lk 12:47, 48; Jn 9:41; 15:22; Rom 1:21, 32; 2:17–23; Heb 10:26; Jas 4: 17; 2 Pet 2:21, 22. See *Ignorance, Sins of.* Not imputed to the righteous, Ps 32:2; ignorant, Rom 5: 13; redeemed, 2 Cor 5:19.

Pleasures of, Job 20:12–16; 21:12, 13; Lk 8:14; Heb 11:24, 25. See *Pleasure, Worldly.*

In believers a reproach to the Lord, 2 Sam 12:14. None in heaven, Rev 22:3, 4.

UNCLASSIFIED SCRIPTURES RELATING TO, DEFINING AND ILLUSTRATING. Deut 29:18. The day that any of you—man or woman, family or tribe of Israel—begins to turn away from the Lord our God and desires to worship these gods of other nations, that day a root will be planted that will grow bitter and poisonous fruit.

2 Chron 12:14. But he was an evil king, for he never did decide really to please the Lord.

Job 14:4. How can you demand purity in one born impure?

Job 22:5. Not at all! It is because of your wickedness! Your sins are endless!

Ps 25:11. But Lord, my sins! How many they are. Oh, pardon them for the honor of your name.

Ps 95:10. "For forty years I watched them in disgust," the Lord God says. "They were a nation whose thoughts and heart were far away from me. They refused to accept my laws."

Prov 4:23. *Above all else, guard your affections.* For they influence everything else in your life.

Prov 24:8. To plan evil is as wrong as doing it. [9]The rebel's schemes are sinful, and the mocker is the scourge of all mankind.

Eccl 5:6. In that case, your mouth is making you sin. Don't try to defend yourself by telling the messenger from God that it was all a mistake (to make the vow). That would make God very angry; and he might destroy your prosperity.

Isa 1:6. From head to foot you are sick and weak and faint, covered with bruises and welts and infected wounds, unanointed and unbound. [18]Come, let's talk this over! says the Lord; no matter how keep the stain of your sins, I can take it out and make you clean as freshly fallen snow. Even if you are stained as red as crimson, I can make you white as wool!

Isa 44:20. The poor, deluded fool feeds on ashes; he is trusting what can never give him any help at all. Yet he cannot bring himself to ask, "Is this thing, this idol that I'm holding in my hand, a lie?"

Jer 7:24. But they wouldn't listen; they kept on doing whatever they wanted to, following their own stubborn, evil thoughts. They went backward instead of forward.

Jer 17:9. The heart is the most deceitful thing there is, and desperately wicked. No one can really know how bad it is!

Ezk 20:16. Because they laughed at my laws, ignored my wishes, and violated my Sabbaths—their hearts were with their idols!

Mt 5:28. But I say: Anyone who even looks at a woman with lust in his eye has already committed adultery with her in his heart.

Mt 12:31. Even blasphemy against me or any other sin can be forgiven—all except one: speaking against the Holy Spirit shall never be forgiven. [Mk 3:29; Lk 12:10; 1 Jn 5:16, 17.] [33]A tree is identified by its fruit. A tree from a select variety produces good fruit; poor varieties don't. [Mt 7:17, 18.] [34]You brood of snakes! How could evil men like you speak what is good and right? For a man's heart determines his speech. [35]A good man's speech reveals the rich treasures within him. An evil-hearted man is filled with venom, and his speech reveals it. Lk 6:45.

Mt 13:24. Here is another illustration Jesus used: "The Kingdom of Heaven is like a farmer sowing good seed in his field; [25]but one night as he slept, his enemy came and sowed thistles among the wheat. [38]The field is the world, and the seed represents the people of the Kingdom; the thistles are the people belonging to Satan. [39]The enemy who sowed the thistles among the wheat is the devil; the harvest is the end of the world, and the reapers are the angels."

Mt 15:2. "Why do your disciples disobey the ancient Jewish traditions?" they demanded. "For they ignore our ritual of ceremonial handwashing before they eat." [3]He replied, "And why do your traditions violate the direct commandments of God? [4]For instance, God's law is 'Honor your father and mother; anyone who reviles his parents must die.' [5, 6]But you say, 'Even if your parents are in need, you may give their support money to the church instead.' And so, by your man-made rule, you nullify the direct command of God to honor and care for your parents. [7]You hypocrites! Well did Isaiah prophesy of you, [8]'These people say they honor me, but their hearts are far away. [9]Their worship is worthless, for they teach their man-made laws instead of those from God.' " [10]Then Jesus called to the crowds and said, "Listen to what I say and try to understand: [11]You aren't made unholy by eating non-kosher food! It is what you *say* and *think* that makes you unclean." [12]Then the disciples came and told him, "You offended the Pharisees by that remark." [13, 14]Jesus replied, "Every plant not planted by my Father shall be rooted up, so ignore them. They are blind guides leading the blind, and both will fall into a ditch." [15]Then Peter asked Jesus to explain what he meant when he said that people are not defiled by non-kosher food. [16]"Don't you understand?" Jesus asked him. [17]"Don't you see that anything you eat passes through the digestive tract and out again? [18]But evil words come from an evil heart, and defile the man who says them. [19]For from the heart come evil thoughts, murder, adultery, fornication, theft, lying and slander. [20]These are what defile; but there is no spiritual defilement from eating without first going through the ritual of ceremonial handwashing!"

Jn 8:34. Jesus replied, "You are slaves of sin, every one of you. [44]For you are the children of your father the devil and you love to do the evil things he does. He was a murderer from the beginning and a hater of truth—there is not an iota of truth in him. When he lies, it is perfectly normal; for he is the father of liars."

Rom 5:12. When Adam sinned, sin entered the entire human race. His sin spread death throughout all the world, so everything began to grow old and die, for all sinned. [13](We know that it was Adam's sin that caused this) because although, of course, people were sinning from the time of Adam until Moses, God did not in those days judge them guilty of death for breaking his laws—because he had not yet given his laws to them, nor told them what he wanted them to do. [14]So when their bodies died it was not for their own sins since they themselves had never disobeyed God's special law against eating the forbidden fruit, as Adam had. What a contrast between Adam and Christ who was yet to come! [15]And what a difference between man's sin and God's forgiveness! For this one man, Adam, brought death to many through his *sin.* But this one man, Jesus Christ, brought forgiveness to many through God's *mercy.* [16]Adam's *one* sin brought the penalty of death to many, while Christ freely takes away *many* sins and gives glorious life instead. [17]The sin of this one man, Adam, caused *death to be king over all,* but all who will take God's gift of forgiveness and acquittal are *kings of life* because of this one man, Jesus Christ. [18]Yes, Adam's *sin* brought *punishment* to all, but Christ's *righteousness* makes men *right with God,* so that they can live. [19]Adam caused many to be sinners because he *disobeyed* God, and Christ caused many to be made acceptable to God because he *obeyed.* [20]The Ten Commandments were given so that all could see the extent of their failure to obey God's laws. But the more we see our sinfulness, the more we see God's abounding grace forgiving us. [21]Before, sin ruled over all men and brought them to death, but now God's kindness rules instead, giving us right standing with God and resulting in eternal life through Jesus Christ our Lord.

Rom 7:7. Well then, am I suggesting that these laws of God are evil? Of course not! No, the law is not sinful but it was the law that showed me my sin. I would never have known the sin in my heart—the evil desires that are hidden there—if the law had not said, "You must not have evil desires in your heart." [13]But how can that be? Didn't the law cause my doom? How then can it be good? No, it was sin, devilish stuff that it is, that used what was good to bring about my condemnation. So you can see how cunning and deadly and damnable it is. For it uses God's good laws for its own evil purposes.

Rom 14:23. But anyone who believes that something he wants to do is wrong shouldn't do it. He sins if he does, for he thinks it *is* wrong, and so for him it *is* wrong. Anything that is done apart from what he feels is right is sin.

1 Cor 5:6. What a terrible thing it is that you are boasting about your purity, and yet you let this sort of thing go on. Don't you realize that if even one person is allowed to go on sinning, soon all will be affected?

Eph 2:1. Once you were under God's curse, doomed forever for your sins. [2]You went along with the crowd and were just like all the others, full of sin, obeying Satan, the mighty prince of the power of the air, who is at work right now in the hearts of those who are against the Lord.

Heb 3:13. Speak to each other about these things every day while there is still time, so that none of you will become hardened against God, being blinded by the glamor of sin.

Heb 12:15. Look after each other so that not one of you will fail to find God's best blessings. Watch out that no bitterness takes root among you, for as it springs up it causes deep trouble, hurting many in their spiritual lives.

Jas 1:14. Temptation is the pull of man's own evil thoughts and wishes. [15]These evil thoughts lead to evil actions and afterwards to the death penalty from God.

Jas 2:10. And the person who keeps every law of God, but makes one little slip, is just as guilty as the person who has broken every law there is. [11]For the God who said you must not marry a woman who already has a husband, also said you must not murder, so even though you have not broken the marriage laws by committing adultery, but have murdered someone, you have entirely broken God's laws and stand utterly guilty before him.

Jas 4:1. What is causing the quarrels and fights among you? Isn't it because there is a whole army of evil desires within you? [2]You want what you don't have, so you kill to get it. You long for what others have, and can't afford it, so you start a fight to take it away from them. And yet the reason you don't have what you want is that you don't ask God for it. [3]And even when you do ask you don't get it because your whole aim is wrong—you want only what will give *you* pleasure. [17]Remember, too, that knowing what is right to do and then not doing it is sin.

2 Pet 1:4. And by that same mighty power he has given us all the other rich and wonderful blessings he promised; for instance, the promise to save us from the lust and rottenness all around us, and to give us his own character.

1 Jn 3:4. But those who keep on sinning are against God, for every sin is done against the will of God. [6]So if we stay close to him, obedient to him, we won't be sinning either; but as for those who keep on sinning, they should realize this: They sin because they have never really known him or become his. [8]But if you keep on sinning, it shows that you belong to Satan, who since he first began to sin has kept steadily at it. But the Son of God came to destroy these works of the devil. [9]The person who has been born into God's family does not make a practice of sinning, because now God's life is in him; so he can't keep on sinning, for this new life has been born into him and controls him—he has been *born again.* [10]So now we can tell who is a child of God and who belongs to Satan. Whoever is living a life of sin and doesn't love his brother shows that he is not in God's family. [15]Anyone who hates his Christian brother is really a murderer at heart; and you know that no one wanting to murder has eternal life within.

1 Jn 5:17. Every wrong is a sin, of course.

For various phases of, and those similar to, this topic, not found under this heading, see *Atonement; Conviction; Depravity; Regeneration; Repentance; Reprobate; Salvation; Sanctification; Wicked, Punishment of.*

CONFESSION OF. Lev 16:21. Laying both hands upon its head, confess over it all the sins of the people of Israel. He shall lay all their sins upon the head of the goat and send it into the desert, led by a man appointed for the task.

Num 14:40. They were up early the next morning, and started towards the Promised Land. "Here we are!" they said. "We realize that we have sinned, but now we are ready to go on into the land the Lord has promised us."

2 Sam 24:10. But after he had taken the census, David's conscience began to bother him and he said to the Lord, "What I did was very wrong. Please forgive this foolish wickedness of mine." [17]When David saw the angel, he said to the Lord, "Look, I am the one who has sinned! What have these sheep done? Let your anger be only against me and my family." 1 Chron 21:17.

2 Chron 29:6. For our fathers have committed a deep sin before the Lord our God; they abandoned the Lord and his Temple and turned their backs on it.

Ezra 9:4. Then many who feared the God of Israel because of this sin of his people came and sat with me until the time of the evening burnt offering. [5]Finally I stood before the Lord in great embarrassment; then I fell to my knees and lifted my hands to the Lord, [6]and cried out, "O my God, I am ashamed; I blush to lift up my face to you, for our sins are piled higher than our heads and our guilt is as boundless as the heavens. [7]Our whole history has been one of sin; that is why we and our kings and our priests were slain by the heathen kings—we were captured, robbed, and disgraced, just as we are today. [10]And now, O God, what can we say after all of this? For once again we have abandoned you and broken your laws! [11]The prophets warned us that the land we would possess was totally defiled by the horrible practices of the people living there. From one end to the other it is filled with corruption. [12]You told us not to let our daughters marry their sons, and not to let our sons marry their daughters, and not to help those nations in any way. You warned us that only if we followed this rule could we become a prosperous nation and forever leave that prosperity to our children as an inheritance. [13]And now, even after our punishment in exile because of our wickedness (and we have been punished far less than we deserved), and even though you have let some of us return, [14]we have broken your commandments again and intermarried with people who do these awful things. Surely your anger will destroy us now until not even this little remnant escapes. [15]O Lord God of Israel, you are a just God; what hope can we have if you give us justice as we stand here before you in our wickedness?"

Neh 1:6, 7. Listen carefully to what I say! Look down and see me praying night and day for your people Israel. I confess that we have sinned against you; yes, I and my people have committed the horrible sin of not obeying the commandments you gave us through your servant Moses. *vs.* 8, 9.

Neh 9:2. This time they fasted and clothed themselves with sackcloth and sprinkled dirt in their hair. And the Israelis separated themselves from all foreigners. [3]The laws of God were read aloud to them for two or three hours, and for several more hours they took turns confessing their own sins and those of their ancestors. And everyone worshiped the Lord their God. [33]Every time you punished us you were being perfectly fair; we have sinned so greatly that you gave us only what we deserved. [34]Our kings, princes, priests, and ancestors didn't obey your laws or listen to your warnings. [35]They did not worship you despite the wonderful things you did for them and the great goodness you showered upon them. You gave them a large, fat land, but they refused to turn from their wickedness. *vs.* 5–38.

Job 7:20. Has my sin harmed you, O God, Watcher of mankind? Why have you made me your target, and made my life so heavy a burden to me?

Job 9:20. But I? Am I righteous? My own mouth says no. Even if I were perfect, God would prove me wicked.

Job 13:23. Tell me, what have I done wrong? Help me! Point out my sin to me.

Job 40:4. I am nothing—how could I ever find the answers? I lay my hand upon my mouth in silence.

Job 42:5. (But now I say,) "I had heard about you before, but now I have seen you, [6]and I loathe myself and repent in dust and ashes."

Ps 32:5. Until I finally admitted all my sins to you and stopped trying to hide them. I said to myself, "I will confess them to the Lord." And you forgave me! All my guilt is gone.

Ps 38:3, 4. Because of your anger my body is sick, my health is broken beneath my sins. They are like a flood, higher than my head; they are a burden too heavy to bear. [18]I confess my sins; I am sorry for what I have done.

Ps 40:11. O Lord, don't hold back your tender mercies from me! My only hope is in your love and faithfulness. [12]Otherwise I perish, for problems far too big for me to solve are piled higher than my head. Meanwhile my sins, too many to count, have all caught up with me and I am ashamed to look up. My heart quails within me.

Ps 41:4. "O Lord," I prayed, "be kind and heal me, for I have confessed my sins."

Ps 51:2. Oh, wash me, cleanse me from this guilt. Let me be pure again. [3]For I admit my shameful deed—it haunts me day and night. [4]It is against you and you alone I sinned, and did this terrible thing. You saw it all, and your sentence against me is just. [5]But I was born a sinner, yes, from the moment my mother conceived me.

Ps 69:5. O God, you know so well how stupid I am, and you know all my sins.

Ps 73:21. When I saw this, what turmoil filled my heart! [22]I saw myself so stupid and so ignorant; I must seem like an animal to you, O God.

Ps 106:6. Both we and our fathers have sinned so much.

Ps 119:59, 60. I thought about the wrong direction in which I was headed, and turned around and came running back to you. [176]I have wandered away like a lost sheep; come and find me for I have not turned away from your commandments.

Ps 130:3. Lord, if you keep in mind our sins then who can ever get an answer to his prayers?

Isa 6:5. Then I said, "My doom is sealed, for I am a foul-mouthed sinner, a member of a sinful, foul-mouthed race; and I have looked upon the King, the Lord of heaven's armies."

Isa 26:13. O Lord our God, once we worshiped other gods; but now we worship you alone.

Isa 59:12. For your sins keep piling up before the righteous God, and testify against you. Yes, we know what sinners we are. [13]We know our disobedience; we have denied the Lord our God. We know what rebels we are and how unfair we are, for we carefully plan our lies. [14]Our courts oppose the righteous man; fairness is unknown. Truth falls dead in the streets, and justice is outlawed. [15]Yes, truth is gone, and anyone who tries a better life is soon attacked. The Lord saw all the evil and was displeased to find no steps taken against sin.

Isa 64:5. You welcome those who cheerfully do good, who follow godly ways. But we are not godly; we are constant sinners and have been all our lives. Therefore your wrath is heavy on us. How can such as we be saved? [6]We are all infected and impure with sin. When we put on our prized robes of righteousness we find they are but filthy rags. Like autumn leaves we fade, wither and fall. And our sins, like the wind, sweep us away. [7]Yet no one calls upon your name or pleads with you for mercy. Therefore you have turned away from us and turned us over to our sins.

Jer 3:21. I hear voices high upon the windswept

mountains, crying, crying. It is the sons of Israel who have turned their backs on God and wandered far away. [22]O my rebellious children, come back to me again and I will heal you from your sins. And they reply, Yes, we will come, for you are the Lord our God. [25]We lie in shame and in dishonor, for we and our fathers have sinned from childhood against the Lord our God; we have not obeyed him.

Jer 8:14. Then the people will say, "Why should we wait here to die? Come, let us go to the walled cities and perish there. For the Lord our God has decreed our doom and given us a cup of poison to drink because of all our sins. [15]We expected peace, but no peace came; we looked for health but there was only terror."

Jer 14:7. O Lord, we have sinned against you grievously, yet help us for the sake of your own reputation! [20]O Lord, we confess our wickedness, and that of our fathers too.

Jer 31:18. I have heard Ephraim's groans: "You have punished me greatly; but I needed it all, as a calf must be trained for the yoke. Turn me again to you and restore me, for you alone are the Lord, my God. [19]I turned away from God but I was sorry afterwards. I kicked myself for my stupidity. I was thoroughly ashamed of all I did in younger days."

Lam 1:18. And the Lord is right, for we rebelled. [20]*See, O Lord, my anguish;* my heart is broken and my soul despairs, for I have terribly rebelled.

Lam 3:40. Let us examine ourselves instead, and repent and turn again to the Lord. [41]Let us lift our hearts and hands to him in heaven, [42]for we have sinned; we have rebelled against the Lord, and he has not forgotten it.

Dan 9:5. But we have sinned so much; we have rebelled against you and scorned your commands. [6]We have refused to listen to your servants the prophets, whom you sent again and again down through the years, with your messages to our kings and princes and to all the people. [8]O Lord, we and our kings and princes and fathers are weighted down with shame because of all our sins. [9]But the Lord our God is merciful, and pardons even those who have rebelled against him. [10]O Lord our God, we have disobeyed you; we have flouted all the laws you gave us through your servants, the prophets. [11]All Israel has disobeyed; we have turned away from you and haven't listened to your voice. And so the awesome curse of God has crushed us—the curse written in the law of Moses your servant. [15]O Lord our God, you brought lasting honor to your name by removing your people from Egypt in a great display of power. Lord, do it again!

Lk 15:17. When he finally came to his senses, he said to himself, "At home even the hired men have food enough and to spare, and here I am, dying of hunger! [18]I will go home to my father and say, 'Father, I have sinned against both heaven and you, [19]and am no longer worthy of being called your son. Please take me on as a hired man.' " [20]So he returned home to his father. And while he was still a long distance away, his father saw him coming, and was filled with loving pity and ran and embraced him and kissed him. [21]His son said to him, "Father, I have sinned against heaven and you, and am not worthy of being called your son."

1 Cor 15:9. For I am the least worthy of all the apostles, and I shouldn't even be called an apostle at all after the way I treated the church of God.

Jas 5:16. Admit your faults to one another and pray for each other so that you may be healed.

1 Jn 1:8. If we say that we have no sin, we are only fooling ourselves, and refusing to accept the truth. [9]But if we confess our sins to him, he can be depended on to forgive us and to cleanse us from every wrong. (And it is perfectly proper for God to do this for us because Christ died to wash away our sins.) [10]If we claim we have not sinned, we are lying and calling God a liar, *for he says we have sinned.*

CONSEQUENCES OF, IMPOSED ON CHILDREN. Ex 20:5. For I, the Lord your God, am very possessive. I will not share your affection with any other god! And when I punish people for their sins, the punishment continues upon the children, grandchildren, and great-grandchildren of those who hate me. Ex 34:7.

Lev 26:39. Those left shall pine away in enemy lands because of their sins, the same sins as those of their fathers. *v.* 40, 41.

Num 14:33. You must wander in the desert like nomads for forty years. In this way you will pay for your faithlessness, until the last of you lies dead in the desert.

Job 5:4. Their children are cheated, with no one to defend them.

Job 18:19. He will have neither son nor grandson left, nor any other relatives.

Job 21:19. "Well," you say, "at least God will punish their children!" But I say that God should punish the man who sins, not his children! Let him feel the penalty himself.

Ps 21:10. The Lord will destroy them and their children.

Ps 109:9, 10. May his children become fatherless and his wife a widow; may they be evicted from the ruins of their home.

Isa 13:16. Their little children will be dashed to death against the pavement right before their eyes.

Isa 14:20. No monument will be given you, for you have destroyed your nation and slain your people. Your son will not succeed you as the king. [21]Slay the children of this sinner. Do not let them rise and conquer the land nor rebuild the cities of the world. [22]I, myself, have risen against him, says the Lord of heaven's armies, and will cut off his children and his children's children from ever sitting on his throne.

Jer 31:29. The people shall no longer quote this proverb—"Children pay for their fathers' sins." [30]For everyone shall die for his own sins—the person eating sour grapes is the one whose teeth are set on edge.

Jer 32:18. You are loving and kind to thousands, yet children suffer for their fathers' sins; you are the great and mighty God, the Lord of Hosts. Isa 65:7.

Lam 5:7. Our fathers sinned but died before the hand of judgment fell. We have borne the blow that they deserved!

Rom 5:12. When Adam sinned, sin entered the entire human race. His sin spread death throughout all the world, so everything began to grow old and die, for all sinned. [13][We know that it was Adam's sin that caused this] because although, of course, people were sinning from the time of Adam until Moses, God did not in those days judge them guilty of death for breaking his laws—because he had not yet given his laws to them, nor told them what he wanted them to do. [14]So when their bodies died it was not for their own sins since they themselves had never disobeyed God's special law against eating the forbidden fruit, as Adam had. What a contrast between Adam and Christ who was yet to come! [15]And what a difference between man's sin and God's forgiveness! For this one man, Adam, brought death to many through his *sin.* But this one man, Jesus Christ, brought forgiveness to many through God's *mercy.* [16]Adam's *one* sin brought the penalty of death to many, while Christ freely takes away *many* sins and gives glorious life instead. [17]The sin of this one man, Adam, caused *death to be king over all,* but all who will take God's gift of forgiveness and acquittal are *kings of life* because of this one man, Jesus Christ. [18]Yes, Adam's *sin* brought *punishment* to all, but Christ's *righteousness* makes men *right with God,* so that they can live. [19]Adam caused many to be sinners because he *disobeyed* God, and Christ caused many to be made acceptable to God because he *obeyed.* [20]The Ten Commandments were given so that all could see the extent of their failure to obey God's laws. But the more we see our sinfulness, the more we see God's abounding grace forgiving us. [21]Before, sin ruled over all men and brought them to death, but now God's kindness rules instead, giving us right standing with God and resulting in eternal life through Jesus Christ our Lord.

See *Wicked.*

CONVICTION OF. See *Conviction; Repentance, Instances of.*

FORGIVENESS OF. Ex 34:6. "I am Jehovah, the merciful and gracious God," he said, "slow to anger and rich in steadfast love and truth. [7]I, Jehovah, show this steadfast love to many thousands by forgiving their sins; or else I refuse to clear the guilty, and require that a father's sins be punished in the sons and grandsons, and even later generations." Num 14:17, 18.

Lev 4:20. He shall follow the same procedure as for a sin offering; in this way the priest shall make atonement for the nation, and everyone will be forgiven. [26]All the fat shall be burned upon the altar, just as if it were the fat of the sacrifice of a thank-offering; thus the priest shall make atonement for the leader concerning his sin, and he shall be forgiven. *vs.* 31, 35; Lev 5:10–13; Num 15:25.

Lev 5:4. If anyone makes a rash vow, whether the vow is good or bad, when he realizes what a foolish vow he has taken, he is guilty. [5]In any of these cases, he shall confess his sin [6]and bring his guilt offering to the Lord, a female lamb or goat, and the priest shall make atonement for him, and he shall be freed from his sin, and need not fulfill the vow. [7]If he is too poor to bring a lamb to the Lord, then he shall bring two turtledoves or two young pigeons as his guilt offering; one of the birds shall be his sin offering and the other his burnt offering. [8]The priest shall offer as the sin sacrifice whichever bird is handed to him first, wringing its neck, but not severing its head from its body. [9]Then he shall sprinkle some of the blood at the side of the altar and the rest shall be drained out at the base of the altar; this is the sin offering. [10]He shall offer the second bird as a burnt offering, following the customary procedures that have been set forth; so the priest shall make atonement for him concerning his sin and he shall be forgiven.

Num 14:20. Then the Lord said, "All right, I will pardon them as you have requested."

2 Sam 12:13. "I have sinned against the Lord," David confessed to Nathan. Then Nathan replied, "Yes, but the Lord has forgiven you, and you won't die for this sin."

1 Kgs 8:33, 34. And when your people sin and their enemies defeat them, hear them from heaven and forgive them if they turn to you again and confess that you are their God. Bring them back again to this land which you have given to their fathers. *vs.* 22–50.

Job 10:13, 14. Yet all the time your real motive in making me was to destroy me if I sinned; and to refuse to forgive my iniquity.

Ps 19:12. But how can I ever know what sins are lurking in my heart? Cleanse me from these hidden faults.

Ps 25:7. Overlook my youthful sins, O Lord! Look at me instead through eyes of mercy and forgiveness, through eyes of everlasting love and kindness. [11]But Lord, my sins! How many they are. Oh, pardon them for the honor of your name. [18]See my sorrows; feel my pain; forgive my sins.

Ps 32:1, 2. What happiness for those whose guilt has been forgiven! What joys when sins are covered over! What relief for those who have confessed their sins and God has cleared their record. [5]Until I finally admitted all my sins to you and stopped trying to hide them. I said to myself, "I will confess them to the Lord." And you forgave me! All my guilt is gone.

Ps 51:9. Don't keep looking at my sins—erase them from your sight.

Ps 65:3. Though sins fill our hearts, you forgive them all.

Ps 79:9. Help us, God of our salvation! Help us for the honor of your name. Oh, save us and forgive our sins.

Ps 85:2. And forgiven the sins of your people—yes, covered over each one, [3]so that all your wrath, your blazing anger, is now ended.

Ps 99:8. O Jehovah our God! You answered

them and forgave their sins, yet punished them when they went wrong.

Ps 103:12. He has removed our sins as far away from us as the east is from the west.

Ps 130:4. But you forgive! What an awesome thing this is!

Isa 1:18. Come, let's talk this over! says the Lord; no matter how deep the stain of your sins, I can take it out and make you as clean as freshly fallen snow. Even if you are stained as red as crimson, I can make you white as wool!

Isa 6:6. Then one of the seraphs flew over to the altar and with a pair of tongs picked out a burning coal. [7]He touched my lips with it and said, "Now you are pronounced 'Not guilty' because this coal has touched your lips. Your sins are all forgiven."

Isa 43:25. I, yes, I alone am he who blots away your sins for my own sake and will never think of them again. [26]Oh, remind me of this promise of forgiveness, for we must talk about your sins. Plead your case for my forgiving you.

Isa 44:21. Pay attention, Israel, for you are my servant; I made you, and I will not forget to help you. [22]I've blotted out your sins; they are gone like morning mist at noon! Oh, return to me, for I have paid the price to set you free.

Isa 55:6. Seek the Lord while you can find him. Call upon him now while he is near. [7]Let men cast off their wicked deeds; let them banish from their minds the very thought of doing wrong! Let them turn to the Lord that he may have mercy upon them, and to our God, for he will abundantly pardon!

Jer 2:22. No amount of soap or lye can make you clean. You are stained with guilt that cannot ever be washed away. I see it always before me, the Lord God says.

Jer 5:1. Run up and down through every street in all Jerusalem: search high and low and see if you can find one fair and honest man! Search every square, and if you find just one, I'll not destroy the city! [7]How can I pardon you? For even your children have turned away, and worship gods that are not gods at all. I fed my people until they were fully satisfied, and their thanks was to commit adultery wholesale and to gang up at the city's brothels.

Jer 31:34. At that time it will no longer be necessary to admonish one another to know the Lord. For everyone, both great and small, shall really know me then, says the Lord, and I will forgive and forget their sins.

Jer 33:8. And I will cleanse away all their sins against me, and pardon them.

Ezk 33:14. And when I tell the wicked he will die and then he turns from his sins and does what is fair and right— [15]if he gives back the borrower's pledge and returns what he has stolen and walks along the paths of right, not doing evil—he shall surely live. He shall not die. [chapter 18:21, 22.] [16]None of his past sins shall be brought up against him, for he has turned to the good and shall surely live.

Mt 1:21. And she will have a Son, and you shall name him Jesus (meaning "Savior"), for he will save his people from their sins.

Mt 6:12. And forgive us our sins, just as we have forgiven those who have sinned against us. [14, 15]Your heavenly Father will forgive you if you forgive those who sin against you; but if *you* refuse to forgive *them, he* will not forgive *you.*

Mt 18:23. The Kingdom of Heaven can be compared to a king who decided to bring his accounts up to date. [24]In the process, one of his debtors was brought in who owed him $10,000,000! [25]He couldn't pay, so the king ordered him sold for the debt, also his wife and children and everything he had. [26]But the man fell down before the king, his face in the dust, and said, "Oh, sir, be patient with me and I will pay it all." [27]Then the king was filled with pity for him and released him and forgave his debt.

Mt 26:28. For this is my blood, sealing the New Covenant. It is poured out to forgive the sins of multitudes.

Mk 2:5. When Jesus saw how strongly they believed that he would help, Jesus said to the sick man, "Son, your sins are forgiven!" [7]"What? This is blasphemy! Does he think he is God? For only God can forgive sins." Mt 9:2, 5, 6; Lk 5:21, 23, 24.

Mk 3:28. I solemnly declare that any sin of man can be forgiven, even blasphemy against me.

Lk 3:3. Then John went from place to place on both sides of the Jordan River, preaching that people should be baptized to show that they had turned to God and away from their sins, in order to be forgiven. Mt 3:6.

Lk 24:47. And that this message of salvation should be taken from Jerusalem to all the nations: *There is forgiveness of sins for all who turn to me.*

Jn 8:10. Then Jesus stood up again and said to her, "Where are your accusers? Didn't even one of them condemn you?" [11]"No, sir," she said. And Jesus said, "Neither do I. Go and sin no more."

Jn 20:23. If you forgive anyone's sins, they are forgiven. If you refuse to forgive them, they are unforgiven.

Acts 2:38. And Peter replied, "Each one of you must turn from sin, return to God, and be baptized in the name of Jesus Christ for the forgiveness of your sins; then you also shall receive this gift, the Holy Spirit."

Acts 10:36. I'm sure you have heard about the Good News for the people of Israel—that there is peace with God through Jesus, the Messiah, who is Lord of all creation. [43]And all the prophets have written about him, saying that everyone who believes in him will have their sins forgiven through his name.

Acts 13:38. Brothers! Listen! In this man Jesus, there is forgiveness for your sins! [39]Everyone who trusts in him is freed from all guilt and declared righteous—something the Jewish law could never do.

Acts 26:16. Now stand up! For I have appeared to you to appoint you as my servant and my witness. You are to tell the world about this experience and about the many other occasions when I shall appear to you. [17]And I will protect you from both your own people and the Gentiles. Yes, I am going to send you to the Gentiles [18]to open their eyes to their true condition so that they may repent and live in the light of God instead of in Satan's darkness, so that they may receive forgiveness for their sins and God's inheritance along with all people everywhere whose sins are cleansed away, who are set apart by faith in me.

Rom 4:7. "Blessed, and to be envied," he said, "are those whose sins are forgiven and put out of sight. [8]Yes, what joy there is for anyone whose sins are no longer counted against him by the Lord."

Eph 4:32. Instead, be kind to each other, tenderhearted, forgiving one another, just as God has forgiven you because you belong to Christ.

Col 2:13. You were dead in sins, and your sinful desires were not yet cut away. Then he gave you a share in the very life of Christ, for he forgave all your sins.

Heb 8:12. And I will be merciful to them in their wrongdoings, and I will remember their sins no more.

Heb 9:22. In fact we can say that under the old agreement almost everything was cleansed by sprinkling it with blood, and without the shedding of blood there is no forgiveness of sins.

Heb 10:2. If they could have, one offering would have been enough; the worshipers would have been cleansed once for all, and their feeling of guilt would be gone. [17]And then he adds, "I will never again remember their sins and lawless deeds." [18]Now, when sins have once been forever forgiven and forgotten, there is no need to offer more sacrifices to get rid of them.

Jas 5:15. And their prayer, if offered in faith, will heal him, for the Lord will make him well; and if his sickness was caused by some sin, the Lord will forgive him. [20]That person who brings him back to God will have saved a wandering soul from death, bringing about the forgiveness of his many sins.

1 Jn 1:7. But if we are living in the light of God's presence, just as Christ does, then we have wonderful fellowship and joy with each other, and the blood of Jesus his Son cleanses us from every sin. [9]But if we confess our sins to him, he can be depended on to forgive us and to cleanse us from every wrong. (And it is perfectly proper for God to do this for us because Christ died to wash away our sins.)

1 Jn 2:1. But if you sin, there is someone to plead for you before the Father. His name is Jesus Christ, the one who is all that is good and who pleases God completely. [2]He is the one who took God's wrath against our sins upon himself, and brought us into fellowship with God; and he is the forgiveness for our sins, and not only ours but all the world's. [12]I am writing these things to all of you, my little children, because your sins have been forgiven in the name of Jesus our Savior.

1 Jn 5:16. If you see a Christian sinning in a way that does not end in death, you should ask God to forgive him and God will give him life, unless he has sinned that one fatal sin. But there is that one sin which ends in death and if he has done that, there is no use praying for him. Mt 12:31, 32; Lk 12: 10.

Rev 1:5. And from Jesus Christ who faithfully reveals all truth to us. He was the first to rise from death, to die no more. He is far greater than any king in all the earth. All praise to him who always loves us and who set us free from our sins by pouring out his lifeblood for us.

See *Atonement; Conviction; Offerings; Repentance.*

FRUITS OF. Gen 3:7. And as they ate it, suddenly they became aware of their nakedness, and were embarrassed. So they strung fig leaves together to cover themselves around the hips. [8]That evening they heard the sound of the Lord God walking in the garden; and they hid themselves among the trees. [9]The Lord God called to Adam, "Why are you hiding?" [10]And Adam replied, "I heard you coming and didn't want you to see me naked. So I hid." [11]"Who told you you were naked?" the Lord God asked. "Have you eaten fruit from the tree I warned you about?" [12]"Yes," Adam admitted, "But it was the woman you gave me who brought me some, and I ate it." [13]Then the Lord God asked the woman, "How could you do such a thing?" "The serpent tricked me," she replied. [14]So the Lord God said to the serpent, "This is your punishment: You are singled out from among all the domestic and wild animals of the whole earth—to be cursed. You shall grovel in the dust as long as you live, crawling along on your belly. [15]From now on you and the woman will be enemies, as will all of your offspring and hers. And I will put the fear of you into the woman, and between your offspring and hers. He shall strike you on your head, while you will strike at his heel." [16]Then God said to the woman, "You shall bear children in intense pain and suffering; yet even so, you shall welcome your husband's affections, and he shall be your master." [17]And to Adam, God said, "Because you listened to your wife and ate the fruit when I told you not to, I have placed a curse upon the soil. All your life you will struggle to extract a living from it. [18]It will grow thorns and thistles for you, and you shall eat its grasses. [19]All your life you will sweat to master it, until your dying day. Then you will return to the ground from which you came. For you were made from the ground, and to the ground you will return." [20]The man named his wife Eve (meaning "The life-giving one"), for he said, "She shall become the mother of all mankind"; [21]and the Lord God clothed Adam and his wife with garments made from skins of animals. [22]Then the Lord said, "Now that the man has become as we are, knowing good from bad, what if he eats the fruit of the Tree of Life and lives forever?" [23]So the Lord God banished him forever from the Garden of Eden, and sent him out to farm the ground from which he had been taken. [24]Thus God expelled him, and placed mighty angels at the east of the garden of Eden, with a flaming sword to guard the entrance to the Tree of Life.

Gen 4:9. But afterwards the Lord asked Cain, "Where is your brother? Where is Abel?" "How should I know?" Cain retorted. "Am I supposed to keep track of him wherever he goes?" [10]But the Lord said, "Your brother's blood calls to me from the ground. What have you done? [11]You are hereby banished from this ground which you have defiled with your brother's blood. [12]No longer will it yield crops for you, even if you toil on it forever! From now on you will be a fugitive and a tramp upon the earth, wandering from place to place." [13]Cain replied to the Lord, "My punishment is greater than I can bear. [14]For you have banished me from my farm and from you, and made me a fugitive and a tramp; and everyone who sees me will try to kill me."

Gen 6:5. When the Lord God saw the extent of human wickedness, and that the trend and direction of men's lives were only towards evil, [6]he was sorry he had made them. It broke his heart. [7]And he said, "I will blot out from the face of the earth all mankind that I created. Yes, and the animals too, and the reptiles and the birds. For I am sorry I made them."

Deut 29:18. The day that any of you—man or woman, family or tribe of Israel—begins to turn away from the Lord our God and desires to worship these gods of other nations, that day a root will be planted that will grow bitter and poisonous fruit.

1 Kgs 13:33. Despite the prophet's warning, Jeroboam did not turn away from his evil ways; instead, he made more priests than ever from the common people, to offer sacrifices to idols in the shrines on the hills. Anyone who wanted to could be a priest. [34]This was a great sin, and resulted in the destruction of Jeroboam's kingdom and the death of all of his family.

Job 4:8. Experience teaches that it is those who sow sin and trouble who harvest the same.

Job 5:2. They die in helpless frustration, overcome by their own anger. [3]Those who turn from God may be successful for the moment, but then comes sudden disaster.

Job 13:26. You write bitter things against me and bring up all the follies of my youth.

Job 20:11. Though still a young man, his bones shall lie in the dust.

Ps 5:10. O God, hold them responsible. Catch them in their own traps; let them fall beneath the weight of their own transgressions, for they rebel against you.

Ps 9:15. The nations fall into the pitfalls they have dug for others; the trap they set has snapped on them. [16]The Lord is famous for the way he punishes the wicked in their own snares!

Ps 10:2. Come and deal with all these proud and wicked men who viciously persecute the poor. Pour upon these men the evil they planned for others!

Ps 94:23. God has made the sins of evil men to boomerang upon them! He will destroy them by their own plans. Jehovah our God will cut them off.

Ps 141:10. Let them fall into their own snares, while I escape.

Prov 1:31. That is why you must eat the bitter fruit of having your own way, and experience the full terrors of the pathway you have chosen.

Prov 3:35. The wise are promoted to honor, but fools are promoted to shame!

Prov 5:22. The wicked man is doomed by his own sins; they are ropes that catch and hold him. [23]He shall die because he will not listen to the truth; he has let himself be led away into incredible folly.

Prov 8:36. But the one who misses me has injured himself irreparably. Those who refuse me show that they love death.

Prov 10:24. The wicked man's fears will all come true, and so will the good man's hopes. [29]God protects the upright but destroys the wicked. [30]The good shall never lose God's blessings, but the wicked shall lose everything. [31]The good man gives wise advice, but the liar's counsel is shunned.

Prov 11:5. The upright are directed by their honesty; the wicked shall fall beneath their load of sins. [6]The good man's goodness delivers him; the evil man's treachery is his undoing. [7]When an evil man dies, his hopes all perish, for they are based upon this earthly life. [18]The evil man gets rich for the moment, but the good man's reward lasts forever. [19]The good man finds life; the evil man, death. [27]If you search for good you will find God's favor; if you search for evil you will find his curse. [29]The fool who provokes his family to anger and resentment will finally have nothing worthwhile left. He shall be the servant of a wiser man.

Prov 12:13. Lies will get any man into trouble, but honesty is its own defense. [14]Telling the truth gives a man great satisfaction, and hard work returns many blessings to him. [21]No real harm befalls the good, but there is constant trouble for the wicked. [26]The good man asks advice from friends; the wicked plunge ahead—and fall.

Prov 13:5. A good man hates lies; wicked men lie constantly and come to shame. [6]A man's goodness helps him all through life, while evil men are being destroyed by their wickedness. [15]A man with good sense is appreciated. A treacherous man must walk a rocky road.

Prov 22:8. The unjust tyrant will reap disaster and his reign of terror shall end.

Prov 27:8. A man who strays from home is like a bird that wanders from its nest.

Prov 28:1. The wicked flee when no one is chasing them! But the godly are bold as lions!

Prov 29:5, 6. Flattery is a trap; evil men are caught in it, but good men stay away and sing for joy.

Prov 30:20. There is another thing too: how a prostitute can sin and then say, "What's wrong with that?"

Isa 3:9. The very look on their faces gives them

away and shows their guilt. And they boast that their sin is equal to the sin of Sodom; they are not even ashamed. What a catastrophe! They have doomed themselves. [11]But say to the wicked, "Your doom is sure. You too shall get your just deserts. Your well-earned punishment is on the way."

Isa 9:18. He will burn up all this wickedness, these thorns and briars; and the flames will consume the forests, too, and send a vast cloud of smoke billowing up from their burning.

Isa 14:21. Slay the children of this sinner. Do not let them rise and conquer the land nor rebuild the cities of the world.

Isa 50:11. But see here, you who live in your own light, and warm yourselves from your own fires and not from God's; you will live among sorrows.

Isa 57:20. But those who still reject me are like the restless sea, which is never still, but always churns up mire and dirt. [21]There is no peace, says my God, for them!

Jer 2:17. And you have brought this on yourselves by rebelling against the Lord your God when he wanted to lead you and show you the way! [19]Your own wickedness will punish you. You will see what an evil, bitter thing it is to rebel against the Lord your God, fearlessly forsaking him, says the Lord, the God of Hosts.

Jer 4:18. Your ways have brought this down upon you; it is a bitter dose of your own medicine, striking deep within your hearts.

Jer 5:25. And so I have taken away these wondrous blessings from them. This sin has robbed them of all of these good things.

Jer 7:19. Am I the one that they are hurting? asks the Lord. Most of all they hurt themselves, to their own shame.

Jer 14:16. And the people to whom they prophesy—their bodies shall be thrown out into the streets of Jerusalem, victims of famine and war; there shall be no one to bury them. Husbands, wives, sons and daughters—all will be gone. For I will pour out terrible punishment upon them for their sins.

Jer 21:14. And I myself will destroy you for your sinfulness, says the Lord. I will light a fire in the forests that will burn up everything in its path.

Ezk 11:21. "But as for those now in Jerusalem, who long for idols, I will repay them fully for their sins," the Lord God says. Ezk 22:31.

Ezk 23:31. You have followed in your sister's footsteps, so I will punish you with the same terrors that destroyed her. [32]Yes, the terrors that fell upon her will fall upon you—and the cup from which she drank was full and large. And all the world will mock you for your woe. [33]You will reel like a drunkard beneath the awful blows of sorrow and distress, just as your sister Samaria did. [34]In deep anguish you will drain that cup of terror to the very bottom and will lick the inside to get every drop. For I have spoken, says the Lord. [35]Because you have forgotten me and turned your backs upon me, therefore you must bear the consequence of all your sin.

Hos 8:7. They have sown the wind and they will reap the whirlwind. Their cornstalks stand there barren, withered, sickly, with no grain; if it has any, foreigners will eat it.

Hos 10:13. But you have cultivated wickedness and raised a thriving crop of sins. You have earned the full reward of trusting in a lie—believing that military might and great armies can make a nation safe!

Hos 12:14. But Ephraim has bitterly provoked the Lord. The Lord will sentence him to death as payment for his sins.

Hos 13:9. O Israel, if I destroy you, who can save you?

Mic 7:13. But first comes terrible destruction to Israel for the great wickedness of her people.

Mk 7:21. For from within, out of men's hearts, come evil thoughts of lust, theft, murder, adultery, [22]wanting what belongs to others, wickedness, deceit, lewdness, envy, slander, pride, and all other folly. [23]All these vile things come from within; they are what pollute you and make you unfit for God.

Rom 5:12. When Adam sinned, sin entered the entire human race. His sin spread death throughout all the world, so everything began to grow old and die, for all sinned. [13](We know that it was Adam's sin that caused this) because although, of course, people were sinning from the time of Adam until Moses, God did not in those days judge them guilty of death for breaking his laws—because he had not yet given his laws to them, nor told them what he wanted them to do. [14]So when their bodies died it was not for their own sins since they themselves had never disobeyed God's special law against eating the forbidden fruit, as Adam had. What a contrast between Adam and Christ who was yet to come! [15]And what a difference between man's sin and God's forgiveness! For this one man, Adam, brought death to many through his *sin.* But this one man, Jesus Christ, brought forgiveness to many through God's *mercy.* [16]Adam's *one* sin brought the penalty of death to many, while Christ freely takes away *many* sins and gives glorious life instead. [17]The sin of this one man, Adam, caused *death to be king over all,* but all who will take God's gift of forgiveness and acquittal are *kings of life* because of this one man, Jesus Christ. [18]Yes, Adam's *sin* brought *punishment* to all, but Christ's *righteousness* makes men *right with God,* so that they can live. [19]Adam caused many to be sinners because he *disobeyed* God, and Christ caused many to be made acceptable to God because he *obeyed.* [20]The Ten Commandments were given so that all could see the extent of their failure to obey God's laws. But the more we see our sinfulness, the more we see God's abounding grace forgiving us. [21]Before, sin ruled over all men and brought them to death, but now God's kindness rules instead, giving us right standing with God and resulting in eternal life through Jesus Christ our Lord.

Rom 7:5. When your old nature was still active, sinful desires were at work within you, making you want to do whatever God said not to, and producing sinful deeds, the rotting fruit of death.

1 Cor 3:3. For you are still only baby Christians, controlled by your own desires, not God's. When you are jealous of one another and divide up into quarreling groups, doesn't that prove you are still babies, wanting your own way?

1 Cor 6:9, 10. Don't you know that those doing such things have no share in the Kingdom of God? Don't fool yourselves. Those who live immoral lives, who are idol worshipers, adulterers or homosexuals—will have no share in his kingdom. Neither will thieves or greedy people, drunkards, slanderers, or robbers. [11]There was a time when some of you were just like that but now your sins are washed away, and you are set apart for God, and he has accepted you because of what the Lord Jesus Christ and the Spirit of our God have done for you.

Gal 5:19. But when you follow your own wrong inclinations your lives will produce these evil results: impure thoughts, eagerness for lustful pleasure, [20]idolatry, spiritism (that is, encouraging the activity of demons), hatred and fighting, jealousy and anger, constant effort to get the best for yourself, complaints and criticisms, the feeling that everyone else is wrong except those in your own little group—and there will be wrong doctrine, [21]envy, murder, drunkenness, wild parties, and all that sort of thing. Let me tell you again as I have before, that anyone living that sort of life will not inherit the kingdom of God.

Gal 6:7. Don't be misled; remember that you can't ignore God and get away with it: a man will always reap just the kind of crop he sows! [8]If he sows to please his own wrong desires, he will be planting seeds of evil and he will surely reap a harvest of spiritual decay and death; but if he plants the good things of the Spirit, he will reap the everlasting life which the Holy Spirit gives him.

1 Pet 4:3. You have had enough in the past of the evil things the godless enjoy—sex sin, lust, getting drunk, wild parties, drinking bouts, and the worship of idols, and other terrible sins.

KNOWN TO GOD. Gen 3:11. "Who told you you were naked?" the Lord God asked. "Have you eaten fruit from the tree I warned you about?"

Gen 4:10. But the Lord said, "Your brother's blood calls to me from the ground. What have you done?"

Gen 18:13. Then God said to Abraham, "Why did Sarah laugh? Why did she say 'Can an old woman like me have a baby?' "

Ex 16:8, 9. For he has heard your complaints against him (for you aren't really complaining against *us*—who are *we?*) The Lord will give you meat to eat in the evening, and bread in the morning. Come now before Jehovah, and hear his reply to your complaints. *vs.* 11, 12.

Num 12:2. And they said, "Has the Lord spoken only through Moses? Hasn't he spoken through us, too?" But the Lord heard them.

Num 14:26, 27. Then the Lord added to Moses and to Aaron, "How long will these wicked people complain about me? For I have heard all that they have been saying."

Deut 1:34. Well, the Lord heard their complaining and was very angry.

Deut 31:21. And great disasters come upon them, then this song will remind them of the reason for their woes. (For this song will live from generation to generation.) I know now, even before they enter the land, what these people are like.

Deut 32:34. But Israel is my special people, sealed as jewels within my treasury.

Job 10:13, 14. Yet all the time your real motive in making me was to destroy me if I sinned; and to refuse to forgive my iniquity. Josh 7:10–15.

Job 11:11. For he knows perfectly all the faults and sins of mankind; he sees all sin without searching.

Job 14:16. But now, instead, you give me so few steps upon the stage of life, and notice every mistake I make. [17]You bundle them all together as evidence against me.

Job 20:27. The heavens will reveal his sins, and the earth will give testimony against him.

Job 34:21. For God carefully watches the goings on of all mankind; he sees them all. [22]No darkness is thick enough to hide evil men from his eyes. [25]He watches what they do and in a single night he overturns them, destroying them, Job 24:22, 23.

Ps 44:20. If we had turned away from worshiping our God, and were worshiping idols, [21]would God not know it? Yes, he knows the secrets of every heart.

Ps 69:5. O God, you know so well how stupid I am, and you know all my sins.

Ps 90:8. You spread out our sins before you—our secret sins—and see them all.

Ps 94:11. The Lord is fully aware of how limited and futile the thoughts of mankind are.

Isa 29:15. Woe to those who try to hide their plans from God, who try to keep him in the dark concerning what they do! "God can't see us," they say to themselves. "He doesn't know what is going on!"

Jer 2:22. No amount of soap or lye can make you clean. You are stained with guilt that cannot ever be washed away. I see it always before me, the Lord God says.

Jer 16:17. For I am closely watching you and I see every sin. You cannot hope to hide from me.

Jer 29:23. For these men have done a terrible thing among my people. They have committed adultery with their neighbors' wives and have lied in my name. I know, for I have seen everything they do, says the Lord.

Ezk 21:24. The Lord God says: Again and again your guilt cries out against you, for your sins are open and unashamed. Wherever you go, whatever you do, all is filled with sin. And now the time of punishment has come.

Hos 5:3. I have seen your evil deeds: Isreal, you have left me as a prostitute leaves her husband; you are utterly defiled.

Hos 7:2. Her people never seem to recognize that

I am watching them. Their sinful deeds give them away on every side; I see them all.

Amos 5:12. For many and great are your sins. I know them all so well. You are the enemies of everything good; you take bribes; you refuse justice to the poor.

Amos 9:1. I saw the Lord standing beside the altar, saying, "Smash the tops of the pillars and shake the Temple until the pillars crumble and the roof crashes down upon the people below. Though they run, they will not escape; they all will be killed. [2]Though they dig down to Sheol, I will reach down and pull them up; though they climb into the heavens, I will bring them down. [3]Though they hide among the rocks at the top of Carmel, I will search them out and capture them. Though they hide at the bottom of the ocean, I will send the sea-serpent after them to bite and destroy them. [4]Though they volunteer for exile, I will command the sword to kill them there. I will see to it that they receive evil and not good. [8]The eyes of the Lord God are watching Israel, that sinful nation, and I will root her up and scatter her across the world. *Yet I have promised that this rooting out will not be permanent.*"

Hab 2:11. The very stones in the walls of your homes cry out against you, and the beams in the ceilings echo what they say.

Mal 2:14. "Why has God abandoned us?" you cry. I'll tell you why; it is because the Lord has seen your treachery in divorcing your wives who have been faithful to you through the years, the companions you promised to care for and keep.

Mt 10:26. But don't be afraid of those who threaten you. For the time is coming when the truth will be revealed: their secret plots will become public information.

Mt 22:18. But Jesus saw what they were after. "You hypocrites!" he exclaimed. "Who are you trying to fool with your trick questions?"

Mt 26:46. Up! Let's be going! Look! Here comes the man who is betraying me!

Lk 6:8. How well he knew their thoughts! But he said to the man with the deformed hand, "Come and stand here where everyone can see." So he did.

Jn 4:17, 18. "But I'm not married," the woman replied. "All too true!" Jesus said. "For you have had five husbands, and you aren't even married to the man you're living with now." [19]"Sir," the woman said, "you must be a prophet."

Jn 5:42. For as I know so well, you don't have God's love within you.

Jn 6:64. "But some of you don't believe me." (For Jesus knew from the beginning who didn't believe and knew the one who would betray him.)

Jn 13:11. For Jesus knew who would betray him. That is what he meant when he said, "Not all of you are clean."

Rev 2:23. And I will strike her children dead. And all the churches shall know that I am he who searches deep within men's hearts, and minds; I will give to each of you whatever you deserve.

See *God, Omniscient; Jesus, Omniscience of.*

LOVE OF. Job 15:16. How much less someone like you, who is corrupt and sinful, drinking in sin as a sponge soaks up water!

Job 20:12. He enjoyed the taste of his wickedness, letting it melt in his mouth, [13]sipping it slowly, lest it disappear.

Prov 2:14. And exult in doing wrong, for they thoroughly enjoy their sins.

Prov 4:17. They eat and drink wickedness and violence!

Prov 10:23. A fool's fun is being bad; a wise man's fun is being wise!

Prov 16:30. The wicked man stares into space with pursed lips, deep in thought, planning his evil deeds.

Prov 26:11. As a dog returns to his vomit, so a fool repeats his folly.

Jer 14:10. But the Lord replies: You have loved to wander far from me and have not tried to follow in my paths. Now I will no longer accept you as my people; now I will remember all the evil you have done, and punish your sins.

Ezk 20:16. Because they laughed at my laws, ignored my wishes, and violated my Sabbaths—their hearts were with their idols!

Hos 4:8. The priests rejoice in the sins of the people; they lap it up and lick their lips for more!

Hos 9:10. O Isreal, how well I remember those first delightful days when I led you through the wilderness! How refreshing was your love! How satisfying, like the early figs of summer in their first season! But then you deserted me for Baal-peor, to give yourselves to other gods, and soon you were as foul as they.

Mic 7:3. They go at their evil deeds with both hands, and how skilled they are in using them! The governor and judge alike demand bribes. The rich man pays them off and tells them whom to ruin. Justice is twisted between them.

Jn 3:19. Their sentence is based on this fact: that the Light from heaven came into the world, but they loved the darkness more than the Light, for their deeds were evil. [20]They hated the heavenly Light because they wanted to sin in the darkness. They stayed away from that Light for fear their sins would be exposed and they would be punished.

Jn 12:43. For they loved the praise of men more than the praise of God.

1 Pet 3:19. And it was in the spirit that he visited the spirits in prison, and preached to them— [20]spirits of those who, long before in the days of Noah, had refused to listen to God, though he waited patiently for them while Noah was building the ark. Yet only eight persons were saved from drowning in that terrible flood.

2 Pet 2:22. There is an old saying that "A dog comes back to what he has vomited, and a pig is washed only to come back and wallow in the mud again." That is the way it is with those who turn again to their sin.

See *Reprobate; Wicked, Described.*

NATIONAL, PUNISHMENT OF. Gen 6:5. When the Lord God saw the extent of human wickedness, and that the trend and direction of men's lives were only towards evil, [6]he was sorry he had made them. It broke his heart. [7]And he said, "I will blot out from the face of the earth all mankind that I created. Yes, and the animals too, and the reptiles and the birds. For I am sorry I made them."

Gen 7:21. And all living things upon the earth perished—birds, domestic and wild animals, and reptiles and all mankind— [22]everything that breathed and lived upon dry land.

Lev 26:14. But if you will not listen to me or obey me, [15]but reject my laws, [16]this is what I will do to you: I will punish you with sudden terrors and panic, and with tuberculosis and burning fever; your eyes shall be consumed and your life shall ebb away; you will sow your crops in vain, for your enemies will eat them. [17]I will set my face against you and you will flee before your attackers; those who hate you will rule you; you will even run when no one is chasing you! [18]And if you still disobey me, I will punish you seven times more severely for your sins. [19]I will break your proud power and make your heavens as iron, and your earth as bronze. [20]Your strength shall be spent in vain; for your land shall not yield its crops, nor your trees their fruit. [21]And if even then you will not obey me and listen to me, I will send you seven times more plagues because of your sins. [22]I will send wild animals to kill your children and destroy your cattle and reduce your numbers so that your roads will be deserted. [23]And if even this will not reform you, but you continue to walk against my wishes, [24]then I will walk against your wishes, and I, even I, will personally smite you seven times for your sin. [25]And I will revenge the breaking of my covenant by bringing war against you. You will flee to your cities, and I will send a plague among you there; and you will be conquered by your enemies. [26]I will destroy your food supply so that one oven will be large enough to bake all the bread available for ten entire families; and you will still be hungry after your pittance has been doled out to you. [27]And if you still won't listen to me or obey me, [28]then I will let loose my great anger and send you seven times greater punishment for your sins. [29]You shall eat your own sons and daughters, [30]and I will destroy the altars on the hills where you worship your idols, and I will cut down your incense altars, leaving your dead bodies to rot among your idols; and I will abhor you. [31]I will make your cities desolate, and destroy your places of worship, and will not respond to your incense offerings. [32]Yes, I will desolate your land; your enemies shall live in it, utterly amazed at what I have done to you. [33]I will scatter you out among the nations, destroying you with war as you go. Your land shall be desolate and your cities destroyed. [34, 35]Then at last the land will rest and make up for the many years you refused to let it lie idle; for it will lie desolate all the years that you refused to let it lie idle; for it will lie desolate all the years that you are captives in enemy lands. Yes, then the land will rest and enjoy its Sabbaths! It will make up for the rest you didn't give it every seventh year when you lived upon it. [36]And for those who are left alive, I will cause them to be dragged away to distant lands as prisoners of war, and slaves. There they will live in constant fear. The sound of a leaf driven in the wind will send them fleeing as though chased by a man with a sword; they shall fall when no one is pursuing them. [37]Yes, though none pursue they shall stumble over each other in flight, as though fleeing in battle, with no power to stand before their enemies. [38]You shall perish among the nations and be destroyed among your enemies.

Deut 9:5. It is not at all because you are such fine, upright people that the Lord will drive them out from before you! I say it again, it is only because of the wickedness of the other nations, and because of his promises to your ancestors, Abraham, Isaac, and Jacob, that he will do it.

Job 34:29, 30. Yet when he chooses not to speak, who can criticize? Again, he may prevent a vile man from ruling, thus saving a nation from ruin, and he can depose an entire nation just as easily.

Isa 19:4. I will hand over Egypt to a hard, cruel master, to a vicious king, says the Lord of Hosts.

Jer 12:17. But any nation refusing to obey me will be expelled again and finished, says the Lord.

Jer 25:31. That cry of judgment will reach the farthest ends of the earth, for the Lord has a case against all the nations—all mankind. He will slaughter all the wicked. [32]See, declares the Lord of Hosts, the punishment shall go from nation to nation—a great whirlwind of wrath shall rise against the farthest corners of the earth. [33]On that day those the Lord has slain shall fill the earth from one end to the other. No one shall mourn for them nor gather up the bodies to bury them; they shall fertilize the earth. [34]Weep and moan, O evil shepherds; let the leaders of mankind beat their heads upon the stones, for their time has come to be slaughtered and scattered; they shall fall like fragile women. [35]And you will find no place to hide, no way to escape. [36]Listen to the frantic cries of the shepherds and to the leaders shouting in despair, for the Lord has spoiled their pastures. [37]People now living undisturbed will be cut down by the fierceness of the anger of the Lord. [38]He has left his lair like a lion seeking prey; their land has been laid waste by warring armies—because of the fierce anger of the Lord.

Jer 46:28. Fear not, O Jacob, my servant, says the Lord, for I am with you. I will destroy all the nations to which I have exiled you, but I will not destroy you. I will punish you, but only enough to correct you.

Ezk 16:49. Your sister Sodom's sins were pride and laziness and too much food, while the poor and needy suffered outside her door. [50]She insolently worshiped many idols as I watched. Therefore I crushed her.

Jon 1:2. Go to the great city of Nineveh, and give them this announcement from the Lord: "I am going to destroy you, for your wickedness rises before me; it smells to highest heaven."

See *Government; Nations.*

Instances of. The Sodomites, Gen 18:20. Egyptians, Ex chapters 7–14; see *Egypt.* Isrealites, Lev 26:14–39; Deut 32:30; 2 Sam 21:1; 24:1; 2 Kgs 24:3, 4, 20; 2 Chron 36:21; Ezra 9; Neh 9:36, 37; Isa 1: 21–23; 3:4, 8; 5; 59:1–15; Jer 2:4, 5; 6:9; 23; 30:11–15; Lam 1:3, 8, 14; 4:6; Ezk 2; 7; 22; 24:6–14; 28:18; 33: 25, 26; 36:16–20; 39:23, 24; 44:4–15; Hos 4:1–11; 6: 8–10; 7:1–7; 13; Amos chapters 2; 5; Mic 6; 7:1–6. Babylon, Jer 50:45, 46; 51; see *Babylon.*

See also prophecies cited in the topics *Assyria; Damascus; Edom; Elam; Ethiopia; Philistines; Syria.*

PUNISHMENT OF. Gen 2:17. You may eat any fruit in the garden except fruit from the Tree of Conscience—for its fruit will open your eyes to make you aware of right and wrong, good and bad. If you eat its fruit, you will be doomed to die.

Gen 3:16. Then God said to the woman, "You shall bear children in intense pain and suffering; yet even so, you shall welcome your husband's affections, and he shall be your master." [17]And to Adam, God said, "Because you listened to your wife and ate the fruit when I told you not to, I have placed a curse upon the soil. All your life you will struggle to extract a living from it. [18]It will grow thorns and thistles for you, and you shall eat its grasses. [19]All your life you will sweat to master it, until your dying day. Then you will return to the ground from which you came. For you were made from the ground, and to the ground you will return."

Gen 4:7. It can be bright with joy if you will do what you should! But if you refuse to obey, watch out. Sin is waiting to attack you, longing to destroy you. But you can conquer it!

Gen 6:3. Then Jehovah said, "My Spirit must not forever be disgraced in man, wholly evil as he is. I will give him 120 years to mend his ways." [5]When the Lord God saw the extent of human wickedness, and that the trend and direction of men's lives were only towards evil, [6]he was sorry he had made them. It broke his heart. [7]And he said, "I will blot out from the face of the earth all mankind that I created. Yes, and the animals too, and the reptiles and the birds. For I am sorry I made them."

Gen 18:20. So the Lord told Abraham, "I have heard that the people of Sodom and Gomorrah are utterly evil, and that everything they do is wicked."

Gen 19:13. For we will destroy the city completely. The stench of the place has reached to heaven and God has sent us to destroy it.

Ex 32:33. And the Lord replied to Moses, "Whoever has sinned against me will be blotted out of my book. [34]And now go, lead the people to the place I told you about, and I assure you that my Angel shall travel on ahead of you; however, when I come to visit these people, I will punish them for their sins."

Ex 34:7. I, Jehovah, show this steadfast love to many thousands by forgiving their sins; or else I refuse to clear the guilty, and require that a father's sins be punished in the sons and grandsons, and even later generations.

Lev 26:14. But if you will not listen to me or obey me, [15]but reject my laws, [16]this is what I will do to you: I will punish you with sudden terrors and panic, and with tuberculosis and burning fever; your eyes shall be consumed and your life shall ebb away; you will sow your crops in vain, for your enemies will eat them. [17]I will set my face against you and you will flee before your attackers; those who hate you will rule you; you will even run when no one is chasing you! [18]And if you still disobey me, I will punish you seven times more severely for your sins. [19]I will break your proud power and make your heavens as iron, and your earth as bronze. [20]Your strength shall be spent in vain; for your land shall not yield its crops, nor your trees their fruit. [21]And if even then you will not obey me and listen to me, I will send you seven times more plagues because of your sins.

Num 15:30. But anyone who deliberately makes the "mistake," whether he is a native Israeli or a foreigner, is blaspheming Jehovah, and shall be cut off from among his people. [31]For he has despised the commandment of the Lord and deliberately failed to obey his law; he must be executed, and die in his sin.

Num 32:23. But if you don't do as you have said, then you will have sinned against the Lord, and you may be sure that your sin will catch up with you.

Job 21:17. Yet the wicked get away with it every time. They never have trouble, and God skips them when he distributes his sorrows and anger.

Ps 95:10. "For forty years I watched them in disgust," the Lord God says. "They were a nation whose thoughts and heart were far away from me. They refused to accept my laws. [11]Therefore in mighty wrath I swore that they would never enter the Promised Land, the place of rest I planned for them."

Jer 44:2, 3. The Lord of Hosts, the God of Israel, says: You saw what I did to Jerusalem and to all the cities of Judah. Because of all their wickedness they lie in heaps and ashes, without a living soul. For my anger rose high against them for worshiping other gods—"gods" that neither they nor you nor any of your fathers have ever known. [5]But they wouldn't listen and wouldn't turn back from their wicked ways; they have kept right on with their sacrifices to these "gods." [6]And so my fury and anger boiled forth and fell as fire upon the cities of Judah and into the streets of Jerusalem, and there is desolation until this day.

See *Punishment; Wicked, Punishment of.*

REPUGNANT TO GOD. Gen 6:6. He was sorry he had made them. It broke his heart. [7]And he said, "I will blot out from the face of the earth all mankind that I created. Yes, and the animals too, and the reptiles and the birds. For I am sorry I made them."

Num 22:32. "Why did you beat your donkey those three times?" the angel demanded. "I have come to stop you because you are headed for destruction."

Deut 25:16. All who cheat with unjust weights and measurements are detestable to the Lord your God.

Deut 32:19. God saw what they were doing, and detested them! His sons and daughters were insulting him.

2 Sam 11:27. Then, when the period of mourning was over, David sent for her and brought her to the palace and she became one of his wives; and she gave birth to his son. But the Lord was very displeased with what David had done.

1 Kgs 14:22. During his reign the people of Judah, like those in Israel, did wrong and angered the Lord with their sin, for it was even worse than that of their ancestors.

Ps 5:4. I know you get no pleasure from wickedness and cannot tolerate the slightest sin. [5]Therefore proud sinners will not survive your searching gaze, for how you hate their evil deeds. [6]You will destroy them for their lies; how you abhor all murder and deception.

Ps 10:3. For these men brag of all their evil lusts; they revile God and congratulate those the Lord abhors, whose only goal in life is money.

Ps 11:5. He puts the righteous and the wicked to the test; he hates those loving violence.

Ps 78:59. When God saw their deeds, his wrath was strong and he despised his people.

Ps 95:10. "For forty years I watched them in disgust," the Lord God says. "They were a nation whose thoughts and heart were far away from me. They refused to accept my laws."

Ps 106:40. That is why Jehovah's anger burned against his people, and he abhorred them.

Prov 3:32. For such men are an abomination to the Lord, but he gives his friendship to the godly. Prov 11:20.

Prov 6:16–19. For there are six things the Lord hates—no, seven: Haughtiness, lying, murdering, plotting evil, eagerness to do wrong, a false witness, sowing discord among brothers.

Prov 15:8. The Lord hates the gifts of the wicked, but delights in the prayers of his people. [9]The Lord despises the deeds of the wicked, but loves those who try to be good. [26]The Lord hates the thoughts of the wicked but delights in kind words.

Prov 21:27. God loathes the gifts of evil men, especially if they are trying to bribe him!

Isa 43:24. You have brought me no sweet-smelling incense nor pleased me with the sacrificial fat. No, you have presented me only with sins, and wearied me with all your faults.

Jer 25:7. But you won't listen; you have gone ahead and made me furious with your idols. So you have brought upon yourselves all the evil that has come your way.

Jer 44:4. I sent my servants, the prophets, to protest over and over again and to plead with them not to do this horrible thing I hate. [21]"Do you think the Lord didn't know that you and your fathers and your king and princes and all the people were burning incense to idols in the cities of Judah and in the streets of Jerusalem? [22]It was because he could no longer bear all the evil things you were doing that he made your land desolate, an incredible ruin, cursed, without an inhabitant, as it is today."

Hab 1:13. We are wicked, but they far more! Will you, who cannot allow sin in any form stand idly by while they swallow us up? Should you be silent while the wicked destroy those who are better than they?

Zech 8:17. "Don't plot harm to others; don't swear that something is true when it isn't! How I hate all that sort of thing!" says the Lord.

Lk 16:15. Then he said to them, "You wear a noble, pious expression in public, but God knows your evil hearts. Your pretense brings you honor from the people, but it is an abomination in the sight of God."

Rev 2:6. But there is this about you that is good: You hate the deeds of the licentious Nicolaitans, just as I do.

See *God, Holiness of; Holiness.*

REPUGNANT TO THE RIGHTEOUS. Gen 39:7. One day at about this time Potiphar's wife began making eyes at Joseph, and suggested that he come and sleep with her. [8]Joseph refused. "Look," he told her, "my master trusts me with everything in the entire household; [9]he himself has no more authority here than I have! He has held back nothing from me except you yourself because you are his wife. How can I do such a wicked thing as this? It would be a great sin against God."

Deut 7:26. Do not bring an idol into your home and worship it, for then your doom is sealed. Utterly detest it, for it is a cursed thing.

Job 1:1. There lived in the land of Uz a man named Job—a good man who feared God and stayed away from evil.

Job 21:16. Look, everything the wicked touch has turned to gold! But I refuse even to deal with people like that.

Ps 26:5. I hate the sinners' hangouts and refuse to enter them. [9, 10]Don't treat me as a common sinner or murderer who plots against the innocent and demands bribes.

Ps 84:10. I would rather be a doorman of the Temple of my God than live in palaces of wickedness.

Ps 101:3. Help me to refuse the low and vulgar things; help me to abhor all crooked deals of every kind, to have no part in them. [4]I will reject all selfishness and stay away from every evil. [7]But I will not allow those who deceive and lie to stay in my house.

Ps 119:104. And since only your rules can give me wisdom and understanding, no wonder I hate every false teaching. [v. 128.] [113]I hate those who are undecided whether or not to obey you; but my choice is clear—I love your law. [163]How I hate all falsehood but how I love your laws.

Ps 120:2. Deliver me, O Lord, from liars. [5, 6]My troubles pile high among these haters of the Lord, these men of Meshech and Kedar. I am tired of being here among these men who hate peace. [7]I am for peace, but they are for war, and my voice goes unheeded in their councils.

Ps 139:19. Surely you will slay the wicked, Lord! Away, bloodthirsty men! Begone! [20]They blaspheme your name and stand in arrogance against you—how silly can they be? [21]O Lord, shouldn't I hate those who hate you? Shouldn't I be grieved with them? [22]Yes, I hate them, for your enemies are my enemies too.

Prov 8:13. If anyone respects and fears God, he will hate evil. For wisdom hates pride, arrogance, corruption and deceit of every kind.

Prov 29:27. The good hate the badness of the wicked. The wicked hate the goodness of the good.

Jer 9:2. Oh, that I could go away and forget them and live in some wayside shack in the desert, for they are all adulterous, treacherous men.

Rom 7:15. I don't understand myself at all, for I really want to do what is right, but I can't. I do what I don't want to—what I hate. [19]When I want to do good, I don't; and when I try not to do wrong, I do it anyway. [23, 24]But there is something else deep within me, in my lower nature, that is at war with my mind and wins the fight and makes me a slave to the sin that is still within me. In my mind I want to be God's willing servant but instead I find myself still enslaved to sin. So you see how it is: my new life tells me to do right, but the old nature that is still inside me loves to sin. Oh, what a terrible predicament I'm in! Who will free me from my slavery to this deadly lower nature?

2 Pet 2:7, 8. But at the same time the Lord rescued Lot out of Sodom because he was a good man, sick of the terrible wickedness he saw everywhere around him day after day.

Jude 1:23. And as for others, help them to find the Lord by being kind to them, but be careful that you yourselves aren't pulled along into their sins. Hate every trace of their sin while being merciful to them as sinners.

Rev 2:2. I know how many good things you are doing. I have watched your hard work and your patience; I know you don't tolerate sin among your members, and you have carefully examined the claims of those who say they are apostles but aren't. You have found out how they lie.

See *Holiness.*

SEPARATES FROM GOD. Deut 31:17. Then my anger will flame out against them and I will abandon them, hiding my face from them, and they shall be destroyed. Terrible trouble will come upon them, so that they will say, "God is no longer among us!" [18]I will turn away from them because of their sins in worshiping other gods.

Josh 7:12. That is why the people of Israel are being defeated. That is why your men are running from their enemies—for they are cursed. I will not stay with you any longer unless you completely rid yourselves of this sin.

2 Chron 24:20. Then the Spirit of God came upon Zechariah, Jehoiada's son. He called a meeting of all the people. Standing before them upon a platform, he said to them, "God wants to know why you are disobeying his commandments. For when you do, everything you try fails. You have forsaken the Lord, and now he has forsaken you."

Job 13:24. Why do you turn away from me? Why hand me over to my enemy?

Job 23:3. Oh, that I knew where to find God—that I could go to his throne and talk with him there. [8]But I search in vain. I seek him here, I seek him there, and cannot find him. [9]I seek him in his workshop in the North, but cannot find him there; nor can I find him in the South; there, too, he hides himself.

Ps 78:59. When God saw their deeds, his wrath was strong and he despised his people. [60]Then he abandoned his Tabernacle at Shiloh, where he had lived among mankind, [61]and allowed his Ark to be captured; he surrendered his glory into enemy hands.

Isa 59:1. Listen now! The Lord isn't too weak to save you. And he isn't getting deaf! He can hear you when you call! [2]But the trouble is that your sins have cut you off from God. Because of sin he has turned his face away from you and will not listen anymore.

Isa 64:7. Yet no one calls upon your name or pleads with you for mercy. Therefore you have turned away from us and turned us over to our sins.

Ezk 23:18. And I despised her just as I despised her sister, because she flaunted herself before them and gave herself to their lust.

Hos 9:12. And if your children grow, I will take them from you; all are doomed. Yes, it will be a sad day when I turn away and leave you alone.

Amos 3:2. Of all the peoples of the earth, I have chosen you alone. That is why I must punish you the more for all your sins. [3]For how can we walk together with your sins between us?

Mic 3:4. And then you plead with the Lord for his help in times of trouble! Do you really expect him to listen? He will look the other way!

Lk 13:27. And he will reply, "I tell you, I don't know you. You can't come in here, guilty as you are. Go away." Mt 7:23; 25:41.

Rom 8:7. Because the old sinful nature within us is against God. It never did obey God's laws and it never will.

Heb 12:14. Try to stay out of all quarrels and seek to live a clean and holy life, for one who is not holy will not see the Lord.

See *God, Holiness of; Wicked, Punishment of.*

SINAI 1. A mountain in the peninsula east of Red Sea. Called also *Horeb.* Israelites arrive at, in their wanderings in the wilderness, Ex 16:1; 19:2, 3; Deut 1:1–5. The law delivered to Moses on, Ex 19:2–25; 20; 24:12–18; 32:15, 16; 34:2–4; Lev 7:38; 25:1; 26:46; 27:34; Num 3:1; Deut 4:15; 29:1; 33:2; Neh 9:13; Ps 68:8, 17; Mal 4:4; Acts 7:30, 38.

FIGURATIVE. Gal 4:24, 25.

See *Horeb; Israel.*

2. Wilderness of. Israelites journeyed in, Num

10:12; kept the Passover in, Num 9:1–5; counted in, Num 26:64, 65.

SINCERITY Does not exempt from guilt, Gen 20. See *Ignorance, Sins of.* Forgiveness of enemies must be sincere, Mt 18:35. Servants must render honest service, Eph 6:5–7. Whatever is done must be in, 1 Cor 10:31. Jesus was an example of, 1 Pet 2:22. Ministers should be examples of, Tit 2:7. Opposed to human wisdom, 2 Cor 1:12.

Should characterize our love to God, 2 Cor 8:8, 24; our love to Jesus, Eph 6:24; our service to God, Josh 24:14; our faith, 1 Tim 1:5; our love to one another, Rom 12:9; 1 Pet 1:22; 1 Jn 3:18; our whole conduct, 2 Cor 1:12; the preaching of the gospel, 2 Cor 2:17; 1 Thess 2:3–5.

A characteristic of the doctrines of the gospel, 1 Pet 2:2, 3. The gospel sometimes preached without, Phil 1:16, 17. The wicked devoid of, Ps 5:9; 55:21. Exhortations to, 1 Cor 5:8; 1 Pet 2:1. Prayer for, on behalf of others, Phil 1:10. Blessedness of, Ps 32:1, 2.

EXEMPLIFIED. By men of Zebulun, 1 Chron 12:24–37. By Hezekiah, Isa 38:3. By Nathanael, Jn 1:47. By Paul, 2 Cor 1:12. By Timothy, 2 Tim 1:5. By Lois and Eunice, 2 Tim 1:5.

SINEWS Job 10:11; 40:17; Col 2:19.

SINGERS See *Music.*

SINGING See *Music.*

SINITES A tribe of Canaanites, Gen 10:15–19; 1 Chron 1:13–16.

SINLESSNESS Ps 119:3. Rejecting compromise with evil, and walking only in his paths.

Acts 24:16. Because of this I try with all my strength to always maintain a clear conscience before God and man.

2 Cor 5:21. For God took the sinless Christ and poured into him our sins. Then, in exchange, he poured God's goodness into us!

Phil 1:9. My prayer for you is . . . [10]I want you always to see clearly the difference between right and wrong, and to be inwardly clean, no one being able to criticize you from now until our Lord returns. [11]May you always be doing those good, kind things which show that you are a child of God, for this will bring much praise and glory to the Lord.

1 Thess 3:13. This will result in your hearts being made strong, sinless and holy by God our Father, so that you may stand before him guiltless on that day when our Lord Jesus Christ returns with all those who belong to him.

1 Thess 5:23. May the God of peace himself make you entirely pure and devoted to God; and may your spirit and soul and body be kept strong and blameless until that day when our Lord Jesus Christ comes back again.

1 Pet 2:22. He never sinned, never told a lie.

1 Pet 4:1. Since Christ suffered and underwent pain, you must have the same attitude he did; you must be ready to suffer, too. For remember, when your body suffers, sin loses its power, [2]and you won't be spending the rest of your life chasing after evil desires, but will be anxious to do the will of God.

1 Jn 1:8. If we say that we have no sin, we are only fooling ourselves, and refusing to accept the truth. [10]If we claim we have not sinned, we are lying and calling God a liar, *for he says we have sinned.*

1 Jn 3:5. And you know that he became a man so that he could take away our sins, and that there is no sin in him, no missing of God's will at any time in any way.

1 Jn 3:6. So if we stay close to him, obedient to him, we won't be sinning either; but as for those who keep on sinning, they should realize this: They sin because they have never really known him or become his. [9]The person who has been born into God's family does not make a practice of sinning, because now God's life is in him; so he can't keep on sinning, for this new life has been born into him and controls him—he has been *born again.*

SINNER See *Wicked.*

SIN OFFERING 2 Kgs 12:16.

See *Conscience Money.*

SIPHMOTH A city of Judah, 1 Sam 30:27–31.

SIPPAI A Philistine giant, 1 Chron 20:4. Called *Saph,* 2 Sam 21:18.

SIRAH The name of a well, 2 Sam 3:26.

SIRION Sidonian name of Mount Hermon, Deut 3:9; 4:48; Ps 29:5, 6.

SISERA 1. Commander of a Canaanite army, defeated by Barak, killed by Jael, Judg 4; 5:20–31; 1 Sam 12:9; Ps 83:9.

2. One of the Nethinim, Ezra 2:43–54; Neh 7:46–56.

SISMAI Son of Eleasah, 1 Chron 2:40.

SITHRI A son of Uzziel, Ex 6:22.

SITNAH A name given by Isaac to a well, Gen 26:21.

SIVAN See *Calendar.*

SKEPTICISM Job 21:15; 22:17; Ps 14:1; 53:1; Zeph 1:12; Mal 3:14, 15. Of Pharaoh, Ex 5:2. Of Thomas, Jn 20:25–28.

See *Unbelief.*

SKIN Clothes of, Gen 3:21. For covering the Tabernacle, Ex 25:1–7; Num 4:8–14. Diseases of, Lev 13:38, 39; Deut 28:27; Job 7:5.

See *Boil; Leprosy.*

SKIRT See *Dress.*

SLANDER Comes from the evil heart, Lk 6:45. Often arises from hatred, Ps 109:2, 3. Idleness leads to, 1 Tim 5:13. By a neighbor, Prov 11:9. A characteristic of the devil, Rev 12:10. The wicked love, Ps 52:4. They who indulge in, are fools, Prov 10:18. Women warned against, Tit 2:3. Ministers' wives should avoid, 1 Tim 3:11. Christ was exposed to, Ps 35:11; Mt 26:60, 61. Ministers exposed to, Rom 3:8; 2 Cor 6:8. The nearest relatives exposed to, Ps 50:20. Believers exposed to, Ps 38:12; 109:2; 1 Pet 4:4.

Saints should keep from, Ps 34:13–15, with 1 Pet 3:10; should put aside, Eph 4:31; should be warned against, Tit 3:1, 2; should give no occasion for, 1 Pet 2:12; 3:16; should return good for, 1 Cor 4:13; happy in enduring, Mt 5:11; characterized as avoiding, Ps 15:1, 3; will be safe from, Job 5:21.

Should not be listened to, 1 Sam 24:9, 10; causes anger, Prov 25:23.

Effects of: Separating friends, Prov 16:28; 17:9; relished by hearers, Prov 18:8; 26:22; tension, Prov 26:20; discord among brothers, Prov 6:16–19; murder, Ps 31:13; Ezk 22:9.

The tongue of, is poisonous, Ps 140:3; Eccl 10:11; is destructive, Prov 11:9. End of, is madness, Eccl 10:12, 13. Men shall give account for, Mt 12:36. Punishment for, Deut 19:16–21.

UNCLASSIFIED SCRIPTURES RELATING TO. Ex 23:1. Do not pass along untrue reports. Do not cooperate with an evil man by affirming on the witness stand something you know is false.

Deut 22:13, 14. If a man marries a girl, then after sleeping with her accuses her of having had premarital intercourse with another man, saying, "She was not a virgin when I married her," [15]then the girl's father and mother shall bring the proof of her virginity to the city judges. [16]Her father shall tell them, "I gave my daughter to this man to be his wife, and now he despises her, [17, 18]and has accused her of shameful things, claiming that she was not a virgin when she married; yet here is the proof." And they shall spread the garment before the judges. The judges shall sentence the man to be whipped, [19]and fine him one hundred dollars to be given to the girl's father, for he has falsely accused a virgin of Israel. She shall remain his wife and he may never divorce her.

Job 5:21. You will be safe from slander; no need to fear the future.

Ps 41:6. They act so friendly when they come to visit me while I am sick; but all the time they hate me and are glad that I am lying there upon my bed of pain. And when they leave, they laugh and mock. [7]They whisper together about what they will do when I am dead. [8]"It's fatal, whatever it is," they say. "He'll never get out of that bed!" [9]Even my best friend has turned against me—a man I completely trusted; how often we ate together.

Ps 50:20. You slander your own brother.

Ps 101:5. I will not tolerate anyone who secretly slanders his neighbors; I will not permit conceit and pride.

Prov 10:18. To hate is to be a liar; to slander is to be a fool.

Prov 25:23. As surely as a wind from the north brings cold, just as surely a retort causes anger.

Jer 6:28. Are they not the worst of rebels, full of evil talk against the Lord? They are insolent as brass, hard and cruel as iron.

Jer 9:4. Beware of your neighbor! Beware of your brother! All take advantage of one another and spread their slanderous lies.

Rom 1:29. Their lives became full of every kind of wickedness and sin, of greed and hate, envy, murder, fighting, lying, bitterness, and gossip. [30]They were backbiters.

1 Cor 4:13. We have replied quietly when evil things have been said about us. Yet right up to the present moment we are like dirt under foot, like garbage.

1 Cor 6:10. Those who live immoral lives . . . will have no share in his kingdom. Neither will thieves or greedy people, drunkards, slanderers, or robbers.

2 Cor 12:20. For I am afraid that when I come to visit you I won't like what I find, and then you won't like the way I will have to act. I am afraid that I will find you quarreling, and envying each other, and being angry with each other, and acting big, and saying wicked things about each other and whispering behind each other's backs, filled with conceit and disunity.

Jas 4:11. Don't criticize and speak evil about each other, dear brothers. If you do, you will be fighting against God's law of loving one another, declaring it is wrong. But your job is not to decide whether this law is right or wrong, but to obey it.

1 Pet 2:1. So get rid of your feelings of hatred. Don't just pretend to be good! Be done with dishonesty and jealousy and talking about others behind their backs.

2 Pet 2:10. And those who are proud and willful, daring even to scoff at the Glorious Ones without so much as trembling.

INSTANCES OF. Joseph, by Potiphar's wife, Gen 39:14–18. Land of Canaan misrepresented by the spies, Num 14:34–38. Of Mephibosheth, by Ziba, 2 Sam 16:3; 19:24–30. Of David, by his enemies, Ps 31:13; 35:21; 41:5; 64:3; 140:3. Of Naboth, by Jezebel, 1 Kgs 21:9–14. Of Jeremiah, by the Jews, Jer 18:18. Of Jesus, by the Jews falsely that he was a glutton, Mt 11:19; that he blasphemed, Mk 14:63, 64; Jn 5:18; that he was possessed by a demon, Jn 8:48, 52; 10:20; that he was seditious, Lk 23:5; that he was a king, Lk 23:2; Jn 18:37, with 19:1–5. Of Paul, see *Paul.*

See *Accusation, False; False Witness; Gossip; Lying; Speaking, Evil.*

SLAVERY Of Israelites, in Egypt, Ex 1:13, 14; 2:23; 6:6; in Persia, Ezra 9:9.

FIGURATIVE. Rom 7:23; 2 Tim 2:26.

See *Servant, Bond.*

SLEEP From God, Ps 127:2. Of the lazy, Prov 6:9, 10. Of Jesus, Mt 8:24; Mk 4:38; Lk 8:23. A symbol of death, Job 14:11, 12; Jn 11:11–13. Mistaken for death, Mt 9:24; Mk 5:39; Lk 8:52.

See *Death.*

SLIME Ps 58:8.

SLING Used for throwing stones, 1 Sam 25:29; Prov 26:8. David kills Goliath with, 1 Sam 17:40–51. Expert use of, 1 Chron 12:2. Used in war, 1 Chron 26:14.

See *Armies; Arms.*

SLUGGARD See *Idleness; Laziness.*

SMITH A worker in metals. Tubal-cain, Gen 4:22. Bezalel, Ex 31:1–11. The Philistines, 1 Sam 13:19. Jewish, carried captive to Babylon, 2 Kgs 24:14; Jer 24:1. Helped to build the Temple, 1 Chron 22:16. The manufacturers of idols, Isa 41:7; 44:12. Genius of, from God, Ex 31:3–5; 35:30–35; Isa 54:16.

FIGURATIVE. Zech 1:20.

SMITING See *Assault and Battery.*

SMOKE FIGURATIVE. Ps 68:2; Isa 6:4; Hos 13:3.

SMYRNA A city of Asia. One of the "seven churches" in, Rev 1:11; 2:8.

SNAIL A crustacean. Forbidden as food, Lev 11:29, 30. Perishable, Ps 58:8.

SNAKE 1 Kgs 4:33; Ps 58:4, 5; 91:13; 148:10; Eccl 10:8, 9; Isa 11:8; Amos 5:19. Poisonous, sent as a plague on the Israelites, Num 21:6–9; Deut 8:15; 1 Cor 10:9. Wound of, miraculously healed by looking at the bronze, set up by Moses, Num 21:8, 9. Venom of, Ps 58:4, 5; Acts 28:5, 6; illustrates speech of the wicked, Ps 140:31; Rom 3:13. Mentioned in Solomon's riddle, Prov 30:19. Charming of, Jer 8:17. Unfit for food, Lev 11:41, 42; Mt 7:10; Lk 11:11; Acts 10:12. Apostles given power over, Mk 16:18; Acts 28:5. Fastens on Paul's hand, Acts 28: 3. Idols of, Rom 1:23.

FIGURATIVE. Isa 14:29; 30:6; 65:25; Jer 8:17; Mic 7:17; Mt 3:7; 12:34; Lk 3:7.

See *Serpent.*

SNARE Eccl 9:12.

FIGURATIVE. Of idolatry, Deut 7:25. Of the evils in life of the wicked, Ps 9:16; 141:10; Eccl 7:26; Jer 48:44. Of the devices of the wicked to deceive the righteous, Josh 23:13; Ps 124:7; Prov 7:23; Lam 4:20. Of punishment, Ezk 17:20.

See *Ambush; Conspiracy; Net; Pit; Trap.*

SNOW Ps 147:16; 148:8; Prov 26:1; Isa 55:10. In Palestine, 2 Sam 23:20; 1 Chron 11:22. In Uz, Job 6:15–18; 37:6; 38:22, 23. On Lebanon mountains, Jer 18:14.

FIGURATIVE. Of purity, Ps 51:7; Isa 1:18; Lam 4: 7; Dan 7:9; Rev 1:14. Of disease, 2 Kgs 5:27.

SNUFFERS In the Tabernacle, Ex 25:38. Provided for the lamps in the Temple, 1 Kgs 7:50; 2 Kgs 12:13, 14; 25:14, 15; Jer 52:18.

SO King of Egypt, 2 Kgs 17:4.

SOAP Jer 2:22.

SOBRIETY Commanded, 1 Pet 1:13; 5:8. The gospel designed to teach, Tit 2:12. With watchfulness, 1 Thess 5:6. With prayer, 1 Pet 4:7. Required in ministers, 1 Tim 3:2, 3; Tit 1:8; wives of ministers, 1 Tim 3:11; older men, Tit 2:2; young men, Tit 2:6; young women, Tit 2:4; all believers, 1 Thess 5:6, 8. Women should exhibit in manner and clothing, 1 Tim 2:9, 10. We should estimate our character and talents with, Rom 12:3. We should live in, Tit 2:12. Motive for, 1 Pet 4:7; 5:8.

See *Temperance; Drunkenness.*

SOCO 1. Son of Heber, 1 Chron 4:18.

2. See *Socoh, 1.*

SOCOH 1. Called also *Soco.* A city of Judah, Josh 15:35; 1 Sam 17:1. Rebuilt and fortified by Rehoboam, 2 Chron 11:5–10. Taken by Philistines, 2 Chron 28:17, 18.

2. A town in Sharon. One of Solomon's commissaries in, 1 Kgs 4:8–19.

3. A city in the mountains of Judah, Josh 15: 48–62.

SODA Prov 25:20.

SODI A man of Zebulun, Num 13:3–15.

SODOM Situated in the plains of the Jordan, Gen 13:10. The southeastern limit of the Canaanites, Gen 10:15–19. Lot settles in, Gen 13:12. King of, joins other kings of the nations resisting the invasion of Chedorlaomer, Gen 14:1–12. Wickedness of the inhabitants of, Gen 13:13; 19:4–13; Deut 32:32; Isa 3:9; Jer 23:14; Lam 4:6; Ezk 16:46, 48, 49; Jude 1:7. Abraham's intercession for, Gen 18:16–33. Destroyed because of the wickedness of the people, Gen 19:1–29; Deut 29:23; Isa 13:19; Jer 49:18; 50:40; Lam 4:6; Amos 4:11; Zeph 2:9; Mt 10:15; Lk 17:29; Rom 9:29; 2 Pet 2:6.

FIGURATIVE. Of wickedness, Deut 32:32; Isa 1: 10; Ezk 16:46–56.

SODOMITES Inhabitants of Sodom. Wickedness of, Gen 19:4–14. Destroyed by fire as a judgment, Gen 19:24, 25. To be judged according to opportunity, Mt 11:24; Lk 10:12.

SODOMY See *Bestiality; Homosexuality; Sodomites.*

SOIL See *Ground.*

SOLDERING Isa 41:7.

SOLDIERS Military enrollment of Israel in the wilderness of Sinai, Num 1; 2; in the plain of Moab, Num 26. Levies of, in the ratio of one man to ten subject to duty, Judg 20:10. Dress in scarlet, Nah 2:3. Cowards excused from duty as, Deut 20: 8; Judg 7:3. Others exempt from service, Deut 20: 5–9; 24:5. Come to John, Lk 3:14. Mock Jesus, Mt 27:27–31; Mk 15:16–20; Lk 23:11, 36, 37. Officers concerned in the betrayal of Jesus, Lk 22:4. Crucified Jesus, Mt 27:26, 31–37; Mk 15:16–24; Jn 19:23, 24. Guard the tomb, Mt 27:65; 28:11–15. Guard prisoners, Acts 12:4–6; 28:16. Maintain the peace, Acts 21:31–35. Their duty as sentinels, Acts 12:19. Perform escort duty, Acts 21:31–33, 35; 22:24–28; 23:23, 24, 31–33; 27:1, 31, 42, 43; 28:16.

FIGURATIVE. Of divine protection, Isa 59:16, 17. Of the Christian, Eph 6:11–17; 2 Tim 2:3.

See *Armies.*

SOLOMON Son of David by Bath-sheba, 2 Sam 12:24; 1 Kgs 1:13, 17, 21. Nick-named Jedidiah, 2 Sam 12:25. Ancestor of Joseph, Mt 1:6. Succeeds David to the throne of Israel, 1 Kgs 1: 11–48; 2:12; 1 Chron 23:1; 28; Eccl 1:12–15. Anointed king a second time, 1 Chron 29:22. His prayer for wisdom, and his dream, 1 Kgs 3:5–14; 2 Chron 1: 7–12. Covenant renewed in a vision after the dedication of the temple, 1 Kgs 9:1–9; 2 Chron 7:12–22. His rigorous reign, 1 Kgs 2.

Builds the temple, 1 Kgs 5; 6; 9:10; 2 Chron 2; 3; 4; 6:10; 7:11; Jer 52:20; Acts 7:45–47. Dedicates the temple, 1 Kgs 8; 2 Chron 6. Renews the corps of the priests and Levites, and the forms of service according to the commandment of Moses and the regulations of David, 2 Chron 8:12–16; 35:4, 5; Neh 12:45.

Builds his palace, 1 Kgs 3:1; 7:1, 8; 9:10; 2 Chron 7:11; 8:1; Eccl 2:4–6; his Hall of the Forest of Lebanon, 1 Kgs 7:2–5; for Pharaoh's daughter, 1 Kgs 7:8–12; 9:24; 2 Chron 8:11. Throne room of, 1 Kgs 7:7; 10:18–20. Builds Millo, the wall of Jerusalem, the cities of Hazor, Megiddo, Gezer, Beth-horon, Baalath, Tamar, store cities, and cities for chariots, and for cavalry, 1 Kgs 9:15–19; 2 Chron 9:25. Provides an armory, 1 Kgs 10:16, 17. Plants vineyards and orchards of all kinds of fruit trees; makes reservoirs, Eccl 2:4–6; imports apes and peacocks, 1 Kgs 10:22. Drinking cups in his palace, 1 Kgs 10:21; 2 Chron 9:20. Musicians and musical instruments of his court, 1 Kgs 10:12; 2 Chron 9:11; Eccl 2:7, 8. The splendor of his court, 1 Kgs 10:5–9, 12; 2 Chron 9:3–8; Eccl 2:9; Mt 6:29; Lk 12:27.

Commerce of, 1 Kgs 9:27, 28; 10:11, 12, 22, 28, 29; 2 Chron 1:16, 17; 8:17,18; 9:13–22, 28. Presents received by, 1 Kgs 10:10; 2 Chron 9:9, 23, 24. Is visited by the queen of Sheba, 1 Kgs 10:1–13; 2 Chron 9:1–12. Wealth of, 1 Kgs 9; 10:10, 14, 15, 23, 27; 2 Chron 1:15; 9:1, 9, 13, 14, 24, 27. Has 700 wives and 300 concubines, 1 Kgs 11:3, with Deut 17:17; their influence over him, 1 Kgs 11:3, 4. Marries one of Pharaoh's daughters, 1 Kgs 3:1. Builds idolatrous temples, 1 Kgs 11:1–8; 2 Kgs 23:13. His idolatry, 1 Kgs 3:3, 4; 2 Kgs 23:13; Neh 13:26.

Extent of his dominions, 1 Kgs 4:21, 24; 2 Chron 7:8; 9:26. Receives tribute, 1 Kgs 4:21; 9:20, 21; 2 Chron 8:7, 8. Officers of, 1 Kgs 2:35; 4:1–19; 2 Chron 8:9, 10. His purveyors, 1 Kgs 4:7–19. Divides his kingdom into subsistence departments: the daily subsistence rate for his court, 1 Kgs 4:7–23, 27, 28.

Military equipment of, 1 Kgs 4:26, 28; 10:16, 17, 26, 28; 2 Chron 1:14; 9:25, with Deut 17:15, 16. Cedes certain cities to Hiram, 1 Kgs 9:10–13. Wisdom and fame of, 1 Kgs 4:29–34; 10:3, 4, 8, 23, 24; 1 Chron 29:24, 25; 2 Chron 9:2–7, 22, 23; Eccl 1:16–18; Mt 12:42. Piety of, 1 Kgs 3:5–15; 4:29; 8. Beloved of God, 2 Sam 12:24. Justice of, illustrated in his judgment of the two prostitutes, 1 Kgs 3:16–28. Oppressions of, 1 Kgs 12:2–4; 2 Chron 10:4.

Reigns 40 years, 2 Chron 9:30. Death of, 2 Chron 9:29–31.

Prophecies concerning, 2 Sam 7:12–16; 1 Kgs 11:9–13; 1 Chron 17:11–14; 28:6, 7; Ps 132:11.

A type of Christ, Ps 45:2–17; 72.

SOLOMON'S HALL A part of the outer court of the Temple, Jn 10:22, 23; Acts 3:11; 5:12.

SON FIGURATIVE. Of man's relation to God, Ex 4:22.

See *Adoption; God, Fatherhood of; Jesus, Son of God, Son of Man.*

SON-IN-LAW Unjust, Jacob, Gen 30:37–42. Faithful, Peter, Mk 1:29, 30; Lk 4:38.

SONG Sung at the passover, Mt 26:30; Mk 14:26. Didactic, Deut 32. Impersonation of the church, Song chapters 1–8. Of Moses and the Lamb, Rev 15:3, 4. New, Ps 33:3; 40:3; 96:1; Rev 5:9. Sacred, singing of, commanded, Eph 5:19; Col 3:16. Of praise, see *Praise; Thankfulness.* Of redemption, Rev 5:9, 10. Of the redeemed, Rev 14:2, 3–5. Of thanksgiving, see *Thankfulness.* War, Ex 15:1–21; Num 21:27–30; Judg 5; 2 Sam 1:19–27; 22. Solomon wrote 1005, 1 Kgs 4:32.

See *Poetry; Praise.*

SONSHIP OF BELIEVERS See *Adoption.*

SOOTHSAYER See *Sorcery.*

SOPATER A Christian of Beroea, Acts 20:4.

SOPHERETH A servant of Solomon, whose descendants returned from captivity to Jerusalem, Neh 7:57–59. Also called *Hassophereth,* Ezra 2:55–57.

SORCERY Divination by an alleged assistance of evil spirits. Forbidden, Lev 19:26–28, 31; 20:6; Deut 18:9–14. Denounced, Isa 8:19.

Practiced: By the Egyptians, Isa 19:3, 11, 12; by the magicians, Ex 7:11, 22; 8:7, 18; by Balaam, Num 22:5, 6; 23:18–24, with chapters 22, 23; by Jezebel, 2 Kgs 9:22; by the Ninevites, Nah 3:4, 5; by the Babylonians, Isa 47:9–13; Ezk 21:21, 22; Dan 2:1–3, 10, 27; by Belshazzar, Dan 5:7, 15; by Simon Magus, Acts 8:9–11; by Elymas, Acts 13:8; by the slave girl at Philippi, Acts 16:16; by vagabond Jews, Acts 19:13; by sons of Sceva, Acts 19:14, 15; by astrologers, Jer 10:2, 3; Mic 3:6, 7; by false prophets, Jer 14:14; 27:9; 29:8, 9; Ezk 13:6–9; 22:28; Mt 24:24.

To end, Ezk 12:23, 24; 13:23; Mic 5:12.

Messages of, false, Ezk 21:29; Zech 10:2; 2 Thess 2:9. False prophets shall be shamed, Mic 3:7. Result of our old, evil nature, Gal 5:20. Wickedness of, 1 Sam 15:23. Vainness of, Isa 44:25. Punishment for, Ex 22:18; Lev 20:27; Deut 13:5. Divining by familiar spirits, 1 Chron 10:13; 2 Chron 33:6; Isa 8:19; 19:3; 29:4; by entrails, Ezk 21:21; by idols, 2 Kgs 23:24; Ezk 21:21; by rods, Hos 4:12.

Saul consulted the medium of Endor, 1 Sam 28:7–25.

Books of, destroyed, Acts 19:18, 19.

SOREK Valley of, Judg 16:4.

SORROW God takes notice of Hagar's, Gen 21:17–21; Israelites, Ex 3:7–10.

For sin, 2 Cor 7:10, 11. See *Repentance; Sin, Confession of.*

No sorrow in heaven, Rev 21:4. "All sorrow and all sighing will be gone forever," Isa 35:10.

Of Hannah, 1 Sam 1:15, 16. Of David for Absalom, 2 Sam 18:33; 19:1–10. Jeremiah, Lam 1:12. Of Mary and Martha, Jn 11:19–40. Jesus, Isa 53:11; Mt 26:37–44; Mk 14:34–42; Lk 22:41–44.

From bereavement: Of Jacob for Joseph, Gen 37:34, 35; for Benjamin, Gen 43:14.

Of the lost, Mt 8:12; 13:42, 50; 22:13; 24:51; 25:30; Lk 13:28; 16:23. See *Wicked, Punishment of.*

See *Afflictions, Benefits of, Consolation in, Design of, Resignation in; Suffering.*

SOSIPATER Relative of Paul, Rom 16:21.

SOSTHENES Leader of the synagogue in Corinth, Acts 18:17, and a Christian with whom Paul wrote the first letter to the Corinthians, 1 Cor 1:1.

SOTAI A servant of Solomon whose descendants returned from captivity to Jerusalem, Ezra 2:55–57; Neh 7:57–59.

SOUL A term used for a variety of related terms in the Old Testament Hebrew and New Testament Greek. The categories of use are inexact, although the major Greek and Hebrew words used are closely related. The difficulty stems from the differences of understanding of "person" in the two testaments. The Hebrew viewed man as body (physical) and soul (non-physical) while New Testament writers believed in a more complex being consisting of body (physical), soul (non-physical), and spirit (distinct from the soul). It is clear that man has a soul, Gen 12:11–13; Deut 4:9; Ps 6:3; 103:1; Mt 26:38; Acts 2:27; just as he has a spirit, Mk 8:12; Acts 19:21; Rom 1:9; Jas 2:26, and a body, Mk 5:29; Lk 22:19; Rom 6:12.

1. Used of the whole person, Lev 16:17; 2 Kgs 7:10; Neh 2:11, 12; Ps 49:8, 9; Ezk 29:11; Acts 23:22; 1 Cor 15:45.

2. Used of the whole non-physical part of man, which is eternal, Deut 6:5; Job 12:10; 24:5; 27:2; Ps 42:4, 5; 49:15; 55:15; 77:6; Jer 44:2, 3; Lam 3:20; Ezk 18:27.

3. Used of the non-physical part of man but distinguished from the spirit, Mt 10:28; 26:38; Mk 7:15, 16; Lk 12:4; Acts 2:27, 31; 1 Thess 5:23; Heb 4:12, and which is the seat of the will, affections and personality, Acts 15:24ff; Rom 1:27; 1 Tim 5:6; Heb 5:7; 3 Jn 1:2. The spirit touched by God can take control of the soul, 1 Cor 15:44–46.

See *Body; Immortality; Man, A Spirit; Spirit.*

SOUNDING In navigation, Acts 27:28.

SOVEREIGNTY Of God, see *God, Sovereign.* Of man, see *Man, Dominion of.*

SOWER Parable of the, Mt 13:2–8; Mk 4:3–20; Lk 8:5–8. Sowing, Eccl 11:4; Isa 28:25.

FIGURATIVE. Ps 126:5; Isa 32:20; Hos 8:7; 10:12; Gal 6:7, 8.

SPAIN Paul plans to visit, Rom 15:24, 28.

SPARROW Ps 102:7; Prov 26:2. Nests of, Ps 84:3. Two, sold for a penny, Mt 10:29; Lk 12:6.

SPEAKING EVIL. Ex 22:28. You shall not blaspheme God, nor curse government officials—your judges and your rulers.

Job 19:18. Even young children despise me. When I stand to speak, they mock.

Ps 10:7. Their mouths are full of profanity and lies and fraud. They are always boasting of their evil plans. [8]They lurk in dark alleys of the city and murder passersby.

Ps 12:3, 4. But the Lord will not deal gently with people who act like that; he will destroy those proud liars who say, "We will lie to our hearts' content. Our lips are our own; who can stop us?"

Ps 34:13. Then watch your tongue! Keep your lips from lying.

Ps 35:21. They shout that they have seen *me* doing wrong! "Aha!" they say. "With our own eyes we saw him do it."

Ps 41:5. But my enemies say, "May he soon die and be forgotten!" [6]They act so friendly when they come to visit me while I am sick; but all the time they hate me and are glad that I am lying there upon my bed of pain. And when they leave, they laugh and mock. [7]They whisper together about what they will do when I am dead. [8]"It's fatal, whatever it is," they say. "He'll never get out of that bed!" [9]Even my best friend has turned against me—a man I completely trusted; how often we ate together.

Ps 52:2. You are sharp as a tack in plotting your evil tricks. [3]How you love wickedness—far more than good! And lying more than truth! [4]You love to slander—you love to say anything that will do harm, O man with the lying tongue.

Ps 59:12. They are proud, cursing liars. Angrily destroy them. Wipe them out.

Ps 64:2. Oh, preserve my life from the conspiracy of these wicked men, these gangs of criminals. [3]They cut me down with sharpened tongues; they aim their bitter words like arrows straight at my heart. [4]They shoot from ambush at the innocent. Suddenly the deed is done, yet they are not afraid. [5]They encourage each other to do evil. They meet in secret to set their traps. "He will never notice them here," they say.

Ps 69:12. I am the talk of the town and the song of the drunkards. [26]For they persecute the one you have smitten, and scoff at the pain of the one you have pierced.

Ps 70:3. Confuse them! Shame them! Stop them! Don't let them keep on mocking me!

Ps 102:8. My enemies taunt me day after day and curse at me.

Ps 106:33. For he became angry and spoke foolishly.

Ps 119:23. For even princes sit and talk against me, but I will continue in your plans.

Ps 120:1. In my troubles I pled with God to help me and he did! [2]Deliver me, O Lord, from liars. [3]O lying tongue, what shall be your fate? [4]You shall be pierced with sharp arrows and burned with glowing coals. [5], [6]My troubles pile high among these haters of the Lord, these men of Meshech and Kedar. I am tired of being here among these men who hate peace. [7]I am for peace, but they are for war, and my voice goes unheeded in their councils.

Ps 140:3. Their words sting like poisonous snakes. [11]Don't let liars prosper here in our land; quickly punish them.

Prov 6:16–19. For there are six things the Lord hates—no, seven: Haughtiness, lying, murdering, plotting evil, eagerness to do wrong, a false witness, sowing discord among brothers.

Prov 10:11. There is living truth in what a good man says, but the mouth of the evil man is filled with curses. [19]Don't talk so much. You keep putting your foot in your mouth. Be sensible and turn off the flow! [31]The good man gives wise advice, but the liar's counsel is shunned. [32]The upright speak what is helpful; the wicked speak rebellion.

Prov 12:5. A good man's mind is filled with honest thoughts; an evil man's mind is crammed with lies. [6]The wicked accuse; the godly defend. [13]Lies will get any man into trouble, but honesty is its own defense. [17]A good man is known by his truthfulness; a false man by deceit and lies. [18]Some people like to make cutting remarks, but the words of the wise soothe and heal. [19]Truth stands the test of time; lies are soon exposed.

Prov 13:3. Self-control means controlling the tongue! A quick retort can ruin everything.

Prov 14:25. A witness who tells the truth saves

good men from being sentenced to death, but a false witness is a traitor.

Prov 15:1. A soft answer turns away wrath, but harsh words cause quarrels. [4]Gentle words cause life and health; griping brings discouragement. [28]A good man thinks before he speaks; the evil man pours out his evil words without a thought.

Prov 16:27. Idle hands are the devil's workshop; idle lips are his mouthpiece. [28]An evil man sows strife; gossip separates the best of friends.

Prov 17:4. The wicked enjoy fellowship with others who are wicked; liars enjoy liars. [9]Love forgets mistakes; nagging about them parts the best of friends.

Prov 18:8. What dainty morsels rumors are. They are eaten with great relish! [21]Those who love to talk will suffer the consequences. Men have died for saying the wrong thing! [23]The poor man pleads and the rich man answers with insults.

Prov 19:1. Better be poor and honest than rich and dishonest. [22]Kindness makes a man attractive. And it is better to be poor than dishonest. [28]A worthless witness cares nothing for truth—he enjoys his sinning too much.

Prov 25:23. As surely as a wind from the north brings cold, just as surely a retort causes anger!

Prov 26:20. Fire goes out for lack of fuel, and tensions disappear when gossip stops. [21]A quarrelsome man starts fights as easily as a match sets fire to paper. [22]Gossip is a dainty morsel eaten with great relish. [23]Pretty words may hide a wicked heart, just as a pretty glaze covers a common clay pot. [28]Flattery is a form of hatred and wounds cruelly.

Eccl 7:22. For you know how often you yourself curse others!

Eccl 10:20. Never curse the king, not even in your thoughts; nor the rich man, either; for a little bird will tell them what you've said.

Isa 6:5. Then I said, "My doom is sealed, for I am a foul-mouthed sinner, a member of a sinful, foul-mouthed race; and I have looked upon the King, the Lord of heaven's armies."

Isa 32:6. Everyone will recognize an evil man when he sees him, and hypocrites will fool no one at all. Their lies about God and their cheating of the hungry will be plain for all to see. [7]The smooth tricks of evil men will be exposed, as will all the lies they use to oppress the poor in the courts.

Jer 20:10. Yet on every side I hear their whispered threats, and am afraid. "We will report you," they say. Even those who were my friends are watching me, waiting for a fatal slip. "He will trap himself," they say, "and then we will get our revenge on him."

Mt 5:22. But I have added to that rule, and tell you that if you are only *angry,* even in your own home, you are in danger of judgment! If you call your friend an idiot, you are in danger of being brought before the court. And if you curse him, you are in danger of the fires of hell. [37]Say just a simple "Yes, I will" or "No, I won't." Your word is enough. To strengthen your promise with a vow shows that something is wrong.

Mt 12:34. You brood of snakes! How could evil men like you speak what is good and right? For a man's heart determines his speech. [35]A good man's speech reveals the rich treasures within him. An evil-hearted man is filled with venom, and his speech reveals it. [Lk 6:45.] [36]And I tell you this, that you must give account on Judgment Day for every idle word you speak. [37]Your words now reflect your fate then: either you will be justified by them or you will be condemned.

Acts 23:5. "I didn't realize he was the High Priest, brothers," Paul replied, "for the Scriptures say, 'Never speak evil of any of your rulers.' "

Rom 1:29. Their lives became full of every kind of wickedness and sin, of greed and hate, envy, murder, fighting, lying, bitterness, and gossip. [30]They were backbiters, haters of God, insolent, proud braggarts.

Rom 3:13. Their talk is foul and filthy like the stench from an open grave. Their tongues are loaded with lies. Everything they say has in it the sting and poison of deadly snakes. [14]Their mouths are full of cursing and bitterness.

1 Cor 6:10. Those who live immoral lives . . . will have no share in his kingdom. Neither will thieves or greedy people, drunkards, slanderers, or robbers.

Eph 4:25. Stop lying to each other; tell the truth, for we are parts of each other and when we lie to each other we are hurting ourselves. [29]Don't use bad language. Say only what is good and helpful to those you are talking to, and what will give them a blessing. [31]Stop being mean, bad-tempered and angry. Quarreling, harsh words, and dislike of others should have no place in your lives.

Eph 5:4. Dirty stories, foul talk and coarse jokes —these are not for you. Instead, remind each other of God's goodness and be thankful.

Tit 1:10. For there are many who refuse to obey; this is especially true among those who say that all Christians must obey the Jewish laws. But this is foolish talk; it blinds people to the truth, [11]and it must be stopped. Already whole families have been turned away from the grace of God. Such teachers are only after your money.

Tit 3:2. They must not speak evil of anyone, nor quarrel, but be gentle and truly courteous to all.

Jas 1:26. Anyone who says he is a Christian but doesn't control his sharp tongue is just fooling himself, and his religion isn't worth much. *v.* 19.

Jas 3:5. So also the tongue is a small thing, but what enormous damage it can do. A great forest can be set on fire by one tiny spark. [6]And the tongue is a flame of fire. It is full of wickedness, and poisons every part of the body. And the tongue is set on fire by hell itself, and can turn our whole lives into a blazing flame of destruction and disaster. [8]But no human being can tame the tongue. It is always ready to pour out its deadly poison. [9]Sometimes it praises our heavenly Father, and sometimes it breaks out into curses against men who are made like God. [10]And so blessing and cursing come pouring out of the same mouth. Dear brothers, surely this is not right!

Jas 4:11. Don't criticize and speak evil about each other, dear brothers. If you do, you will be fighting against God's law of loving one another, declaring it is wrong. But your job is not to decide whether this law is right or wrong, but to obey it.

1 Pet 2:1. So get rid of your feelings of hatred. Don't just pretend to be good! Be done with dishonesty and jealousy and talking about others behind their backs.

1 Pet 3:9. Don't repay evil for evil. Don't snap back at those who say unkind things about you. Instead, pray for God's help for them, for we are to be kind to others, and God will bless us for it. [10]If you want a happy, good life, keep control of your tongue, and guard your lips from telling lies.

2 Pet 2:7, 8. But at the same time the Lord rescued Lot out of Sodom because he was a good man, sick of the terrible wickedness he saw everywhere around him day after day. [10]He is especially hard on those who follow their own evil, lustful thoughts, and those who are proud and willful, daring even to scoff at the Glorious Ones without so much as trembling.

Jude 1:8. Yet these false teachers carelessly go right on living their evil, immoral lives, degrading their bodies and laughing at those in authority over them, even scoffing at the Glorious Ones. [10]But these men mock and curse at anything they do not understand.

See *Accusation, False; Blasphemy; Busybody; Flattery; Gossip; Lying; Slander; Uncharitableness.*

FOLLY IN. Job 13:5. Oh, please be quiet! That would be your highest wisdom.

Job 16:3. Won't you ever stop your flow of foolish words? What have I said that makes you speak so endlessly? [4]But perhaps I'd sermonize the same as you—if you were I and I were you. I would spout off my criticisms against you and shake my head at you.

Job 42:3. I was talking about things I knew nothing about and did not understand, things far too wonderful for me.

Prov 10:14. A wise man holds his tongue. Only a fool blurts out everything he knows; that only leads to sorrow and trouble.

Prov 12:23. A wise man doesn't display his knowledge, but a fool displays his foolishness.

Prov 13:3. Self-control means controlling the tongue! A quick retort can ruin everything.

Prov 14:3. A rebel's foolish talk should prick his own pride! But the wise man's speech is respected.

Prov 15:2. A wise teacher makes learning a joy; a rebellious teacher spouts foolishness. [7]Only the good can give good advice. Rebels can't. [14]A wise man is hungry for truth, while the mocker feeds on trash.

Prov 18:6, 7. A fool gets into constant fights. His mouth is his undoing! His words endanger him. [13]What a shame—yes, how stupid!—to decide before knowing the facts!

Prov 26:4. When arguing with a rebel, don't use foolish arguments as he does, or you will become as foolish as he is! [7]In the mouth of a fool a proverb becomes as useless as a paralyzed leg. [9]A rebel will misapply an illustration so that its point will no more be felt than a thorn in the hand of a drunkard.

Prov 29:11. A rebel shouts in anger; a wise man holds his temper in and cools it. [20]There is more hope for a fool than for a man of quick temper.

Prov 30:10. Never falsely accuse a man to his employer, lest he curse you for your sin.

Eccl. 5:3. Just as being too busy gives you nightmares, so being a fool makes you a blabbermouth. [7]Dreaming instead of doing is foolishness, and there is ruin in a flood of empty words; fear God instead.

Eccl 10:12, 13. It is pleasant to listen to wise words, but a fool's speech brings him to ruin. Since he begins with a foolish premise, his conclusion is sheer madness. [14]A fool knows all about the future and tells everyone in detail! But who can really know what is going to happen?

Mt 12:36. And I tell you this, that you must give account on Judgment Day for every idle word you speak. [37]Your words now reflect your fate then: either you will be justified by them or you will be condemned.

Eph 5:4. Dirty stories, foul talk and coarse jokes —these are not for you. Instead, remind each other of God's goodness and be thankful.

See *Fool.*

WISDOM IN. Job 16:5. But no! I would speak in such a way that it would help you. I would try to take away your grief.

Job 27:4. My lips shall speak no evil, my tongue shall speak no lies.

Ps 15:1. Lord, who may go and find refuge and shelter in your tabernacle up on your holy hill? [2]Anyone who leads a blameless life and is truly sincere. [3]Anyone who refuses to slander others, does not listen to gossip, never harms his neighbor.

Ps 39:1. I said to myself, I'm going to quit complaining! I'll keep quiet, especially when the ungodly are around me.

Ps 50:23. But true praise is a worthy sacrifice; this really honors me. Those who walk my paths will receive salvation from the Lord.

Ps 119:13. I have recited your laws. [27]Make me understand what you want; for then I shall see your miracles. [46]I will speak to kings about their value, and they will listen with interest and respect. [54]For these laws of yours have been my source of joy and singing through all these years of my earthly pilgrimage. [172]I will sing about their wonder, for each of them is just.

Ps 141:3. Help me, Lord, to keep my mouth shut and my lips sealed.

Ps 145:5. I will meditate about your glory, splendor, majesty and miracles. [6]Your awe-inspiring deeds shall be on every tongue; I will proclaim your greatness. [7]Everyone will tell about how good you are, and sing about your righteousness. [11]They will talk together about the glory of your kingdom and mention examples of your power. [12]They will tell about your miracles and about the majesty and glory of your reign.

Prov 10:11. There is living truth in what a good man says, but the mouth of the evil man is filled with curses. [13]Men with common sense are admired as counselors; those without it are beaten as servants. [19]Don't talk so much. You keep putting your foot in your mouth. Be sensible and turn off the flow! [20]When a good man speaks, he is worth listening to, but the words of fools are a dime a dozen. [21]A godly man gives good advice, but a rebel is destroyed by lack of common sense. [31]The good man gives wise advice, but the liar's counsel is shunned. [32]The upright speak what is helpful; the wicked speak rebellion.

Prov 11:12. To quarrel with a neighbor is foolish; a man with good sense holds his tongue. [13]A gossip goes around spreading rumors, while a trustworthy man tries to quiet them. [14]Without wise leadership, a nation is in trouble; but with good counselors there is safety.

Prov 12:6. The wicked accuse; the godly defend. [14]Telling the truth gives a man great satisfaction, and hard work returns many blessings to him. [16]A fool is quick-tempered; a wise man stays cool when insulted. [17]A good man is known by his truthfulness; a false man by deceit and lies. [18]Some people like to make cutting remarks, but the words of the wise soothe and heal. [19]Truth stands the test of time; lies are soon exposed. [20]Deceit fills hearts that are plotting for evil; joy fills hearts that are planning for good! [23]A wise man doesn't display his knowledge, but a fool displays his foolishness.

Prov 13:2. The good man wins his case by careful argument; the evil-minded only wants to fight. [3]Self-control means controlling the tongue! A quick retort can ruin everything.

Prov 14:3. A rebel's foolish talk should prick his own pride! But the wise man's speech is respected.

Prov 15:1. A soft answer turns away wrath, but harsh words cause quarrels. [2]A wise teacher makes learning a joy; a rebellious teacher spouts foolishness. [4]Gentle words cause life and health; griping brings discouragement. [7]Only the good can give good advice. Rebels can't. [23]Everyone enjoys giving good advice, and how wonderful it is to be able to say the right thing at the right time! [26]The Lord hates the thoughts of the wicked but delights in kind words. [28]A good man thinks before he speaks; the evil man pours out his evil words without a thought.

Prov 16:21. The wise man is known by his common sense, and a pleasant teacher is the best. [23]From a wise mind comes careful and persuasive speech. [24]Kind words are like honey—enjoyable and healthful.

Prov 17:7. Truth from a rebel or lies from a king are both unexpected. [27, 28]The man of few words and settled mind is wise; therefore, even a fool is thought to be wise when he is silent. It pays him to keep his mouth shut.

Prov 18:4. A wise man's words express deep streams of thought. [20]Ability to give wise advice satisfies like a good meal.

Prov 21:23. Keep your mouth closed and you'll stay out of trouble.

Prov 24:6. Don't go to war without wise guidance; there is safety in many counselors.

Prov 25:11. Timely advice is as lovely as golden apples in a silver basket. [15]Be patient and you will finally win, for a soft tongue can break hard bones.

Prov 29:11. A rebel shouts in anger; a wise man holds his temper in and cools it.

Prov 31:26. When she speaks, her words are wise, and kindness is the rule for everything she says.

Eccl 3:7. A time to tear; a time to repair; a time to be quiet; a time to speak up.

Eccl 7:5. It is better to be criticized by a wise man than to be praised by a fool!

Eccl 9:17. But even so, the quiet words of a wise man are better than the shout of a king of fools.

Eccl 10:12. It is pleasant to listen to wise words, but a fool's speech brings him to ruin.

Eccl 12:9. But then, because the Preacher was wise, he went on teaching the people all he knew; and he collected proverbs and classified them. [10]For the Preacher was not only a wise man, but a good teacher; he not only taught what he knew to the people but taught them in an interesting manner. [11]The wise man's words are like goads that spur to action. They nail down important truths. Students are wise who master what their teachers tell them.

Amos 5:13. Therefore those who are wise will not try to interfere with the Lord in the dread day of your punishment.

Zeph 3:13. They will not be sinners, full of lies and deceit. They will live quietly, in peace, and lie down in safety, and no one will make them afraid.

Zech 8:16. Here is your part: Tell the truth. Be fair. Live at peace with everyone.

Mt 12:37. Your words now reflect your fate then: either you will be justified by them or you will be condemned.

Lk 6:45. A good man produces good deeds from a good heart. And an evil man produces evil deeds from his hidden wickedness. Whatever is in the heart overflows into speech. Mt 12:35.

Eph 4:22. Then throw off your old evil nature—the old you that was a partner in your evil ways—rotten through and through, full of lust and sham. [25]Stop lying to each other; tell the truth, for we are parts of each other and when we lie to each other we are hurting ourselves. [29]Don't use bad language. Say only what is good and helpful to those you are talking to, and what will give them a blessing.

Phil 1:27. I will keep on hearing good reports that you are standing side by side with one strong purpose—to tell the Good News.

Col 4:6. Let your conversation be gracious as well as sensible, for then you will have the right answer for everyone.

Jas 1:19. Dear brothers, don't ever forget that it

is best to listen much, speak little, and not become angry. [26]Anyone who says he is a Christian but doesn't control his sharp tongue is just fooling himself, and his religion isn't worth much.

Jas 3:2. If anyone can control his tongue, it proves that he has perfect control over himself in every other way. [13]If you are wise, live a life of steady goodness, so that only good deeds will pour forth. And if you don't brag about them, then you will be truly wise!

1 Pet 2:12. Be careful how you behave among your unsaved neighbors; for then, even if they are suspicious of you and talk against you, they will end up praising God for your good works when Christ returns.

1 Pet 3:15. Quietly trust yourself to Christ your Lord and if anybody asks why you believe as you do, be ready to tell him, and do it in a gentle and respectful way. [16]Do what is right; then if men speak against you, calling you evil names, they will become ashamed of themselves for falsely accusing you when you have only done what is good.

Rev 14:5. No falsehood can be charged against them; they are blameless.

See *Wisdom.*

SPEAR An implement of war. Spears and javelins differed in weight and size, but had similar uses. Goliath's, 1 Sam 17:4–7. Saul's, 1 Sam 18:10–12. Stored in the Temple, 2 Chron 23:9. Changed into pruning hooks, Isa 2:4; Mic 4:3. Pruning hooks beat into, Joel 3:10. Pierced Jesus' side, Jn 19:34; Zech 12:10; Rev 1:7.

SPELT A kind of wheat. Used in bread, Ezk 4:9.

SPICES In the formula for the anointing oil, Ex 25:1–7; 35:5–9. Stores of, 2 Kgs 20:13. Used in the Temple, 1 Chron 9:29. Exported from Gilead, Gen 37:25. Sent as a present by Jacob to Joseph, Gen 43:11. Presented by the Queen of Sheba to Solomon, 1 Kgs 10:2, 10. Sold in the markets of Tyre, Ezk 27:22. Mountains of (Bether), Song 2:17. Used in the embalming of Asa, 2 Chron 16:13, 14. Prepared for embalming the body of Jesus, Mk 16:1; Lk 23:56; Jn 19:39, 40.

SPIDER Web of, figurative of the hope of the sinner, Job 8:14; 27:18.

SPIES Gen 42:8, 9. Sent to investigate Canaan, Num 13; 14; Deut 1:22; Jazer, Num 21:31, 32; Jericho, Josh 2:1. Used by David, 1 Sam 26:3, 4; at the court of Absalom, 2 Sam 15:10; 17:1–17. Pharisees acted as, Lk 20:20. In the church of Galatia, Gal 2:4.

SPINNING By hand, Ex 35:25, 26; Lk 12:27.

SPIRIT That in the immaterial part of man which is related to worship, communion with God, and divine influence. It is distinguished from the body and soul, 1 Thess 5:23; but in some passages spirit seems to be used interchangeably with soul, Mt 11:29, 30. We are to win souls, (not spirits), Prov 11:30; the Spirit speaks to our spirit, (not our soul), Rom 8:16.

The spirit of Jacob revived, Gen 45:27; Samson's spirit revived, Judg 15:19; the Lord stirred up the spirit of Cyrus, 2 Chron 36:22, 23; a troubled spirit, Job 21:4; a cheerful spirit, Job 29:24; there is a spirit in man, Job 32:8, 9; the spirit urges, Job 32:18; into your hand I commit my spirit, Ps 31:5; Lk 23:46; a broken spirit, Ps 51:17; Prov 17:22; the spirit of man is the Lord's searchlight, Prov 20:27; humble spirit, Isa 57:15; a willing spirit, Mt 26:41; worship in the spirit, Jn 4:21–24. See *Man.*

SPIRITUAL BLESSINGS See *Blessing, Spiritual; Holy Spirit; Sanctification.*

SPIRITUAL BLINDNESS See *Blindness, Spiritual.*

SPIRITUAL DILIGENCE See *Zeal.*

SPIRITUALISM See *Necromancy; Sorcery.*

SPIRITUALITY Described as the only thing worthy of concern, Lk 10:42; as love and devotion to God, Deut 6:5; Josh 22:5; 1 Kgs 8:22, 23; Ps 1:2; 51:6.

Brings peace, Isa 26:3; Jer 33:6; Rom 8:6; 14:17; indifference to worldly benefits, 1 Cor 7:29–31; Col 3:1–3; thirst for heavenly blessings, Mt 5:6; Jn 6:27; discernment, 1 Cor 2:15.

Is produced by the indwelling of the Holy Spirit, Jn 14:15–17; Rom 8:4.

SPIRITUAL GIFTS See *Gifts from God.*

SPIRITUAL PEACE See *Joy; Peace.*

SPITTING In the face, as an indignity, Num 12:14; Deut 25:9; Job 30:10; Mt 26:67; 27:30. Jesus used spittle in healing, Mk 7:33; 8:23. Prophecy that Jesus would be spat upon, Isa 50:6; Lk 18:32.

SPOILS Of war, Gen 14:11, 12; Num 31:9–11; Deut 2:35, 36. Divided between the combatants and non-combatants of the Israelites, including priests and Levites, Num 31:25–54; 1 Sam 30:24. Dedicated to the Lord, 1 Sam 15:15; 1 Chron 26:27; 2 Chron 15:11.

SPONGE Job 15:16; Mt 27:48; Mk 15:36; Jn 19:29.

SPOONS Of the Tabernacle, Ex 25:29; Num 4:7. Of the Temple, 1 Kgs 7:50; 2 Chron 4:22.

SPRING 1. Season of, promised annual return of, Gen 8:22. Described, Prov 27:25–27; Song 2:11–13.

2. Of water. Hot, Gen 36:24. Gushing, Deut 8:7. "The Spring of the Man Who Prayed," miraculously supplied to Samson, Judg 15:19. The Spring of Gihon, 2 Chron 32:30; 33:14. He placed springs into the valleys, Ps 104:10. A private spring, Song 4:12. Springs in the desert, Isa 35:7; 41:18.

FIGURATIVE. Corrupt, Prov 25:26; Jas 3:11.

See *Well.*

SPRINKLING Of blood, Lev 14:7, 51, 52; 16:14; Heb 9:13, 19, 21; 11:28; 12:24. See *Blood.* Of water, Num 8:7; Ezk 36:25; Heb 9:19; 10:22.

STABILITY OF CHARACTER. Ps 57:7. O God, my heart is quiet and confident. No wonder I can sing your praises! Ps 108:1; 112:7.

Mt 10:22. Everyone shall hate you because you belong to me. But all of you who endure to the end shall be saved. Mt 24:13.

Mk 4:20. But the good soil represents the hearts of those who truly accept God's message and produce a plentiful harvest for God—thirty, sixty, or even a hundred times as much as was planted in their hearts.

1 Cor 7:20. Usually a person should keep on with the work he was doing when God called him.

1 Cor 15:58. So, my dear brothers, since future victory is sure, be strong and steady, always abounding in the Lord's work, for you know that nothing you do for the Lord is ever wasted as it would be if there were no resurrection.

2 Thess 2:15. With all these things in mind, dear brothers, stand firm and keep a strong grip on the truth that we taught you in our letters and during the time we were with you.

2 Thess 3:3. But the Lord is faithful; he will make you strong and guard you from satanic attacks of every kind.

Heb 10:23. Now we can look forward to the salvation God has promised us. There is no longer any room for doubt, and we can tell others that salvation is ours, for there is no question that he will do what he says.

Heb 13:9. So do not be attracted by strange, new ideas. Your spiritual strength comes as a gift from God, not from ceremonial rules about eating certain foods—a method which, by the way, hasn't helped those who have tried it!

Jas 1:23. For if a person just listens and doesn't obey, he is like a man looking at his face in a mirror; [24]as soon as he walks away, he can't see himself anymore or remember what he looks like. [25]But if anyone keeps looking steadily into God's law for free men, he will not only remember it but he will do what it says, and God will greatly bless him in everything he does.

Rev 22:11. And when that time comes, all doing wrong will do it more and more; the vile will become more vile; good men will be better; those who are holy will continue on in greater holiness.

See *Character; Decision; Perseverance.*

STABLE Prov 14:4.

STACHYS A Christian in Rome, Rom 16:9.

STACTE An unknown spice used in compounding the holy incense, Ex 30:34. It was possibly myrrh in the form of drops.

STAIRS Of David, Neh 3:15; 12:37.

STALL For cattle, Lk 13:15; for horses, 2 Chron 9:25.

STAMMERING Isa 32:4; Mk 7:37. Of Moses, Ex 4:10.

STANDING A theological term used to describe a believer's position, based on the perfect work of Christ, in contrast with the believer's state, or the actual condition of his soul from day to day. The believer is a child of God, Jn 1:11, 12; is made right by faith, Rom 5:1; has access to God, Rom 5:2; is an heir of God and a joint heir with Christ, Rom 8:17; is the home of the Holy Spirit, 1 Cor 6:19; is baptized into the body of Christ, 1 Cor 12:13; is blessed with all spiritual blessings, Eph 1:3; belongs to Christ, Eph 1:6; is sealed with the Holy Spirit, Eph 1:13; is born to an inheritance which is reserved in heaven, 1 Pet 1:3–5.

See *State, the Believer's.*

STARS Created by God, Gen 1:16; Ps 8:3; 33:6; 136:7, 9; Amos 5:8. Differ in splendor, 1 Cor 15:41. Worship of, forbidden, Deut 4:19. Worshiped, 2 Kgs 17:16; 21:3–5; 23:5; Jer 19:13; Amos 5:25–27; Zeph 1:5; Acts 7:42, 43. Constellations of, Orion, Job 9:9; Amos 5:8; serpent, Job 26:13. Planets, 2 Kgs 23:5; the morning star, Job 38:6, 7; Rev 2:28; 22:16. Darkening of, Job 9:7; Eccl 12:2; Isa 13:10; 34:4; Joel 2:10; 3:15; Rev 8:11, 12. Comets, Jude 13. Falling of, Dan 8:10; Mt 24:29; Mk 13:25; Rev 6:13; 8:10; 9:1; 12:4. Guides the wise men, Mt 2:2, 7, 9, 10.

FIGURATIVE. Of the deliverer, Num 24:15–19. Seven stars of the seven churches, Rev 1:16, 20. Crown of twelve stars, Rev 12:1. Of Jesus, Rev 22:16.

STATE See *Government.*

STATE, THE BELIEVER'S A theological term which describes a believer's actual spiritual condition as it compares with his standing, or perfect position, in Christ. It may be illustrated by comparing 1 Cor 1:2–9 with 1 Cor 1:11; 3:1–4; 4:18. The first passage describes the Corinthian believers as saints, called unto the fellowship of Christ. The other passages describe these same believers as having arguments among themselves, as carnal, and proud; their actual state as unspiritual.

See *Standing.*

STATESMANSHIP Wisdom in, Prov 28:2. School in, Dan 1:3–5. Skilled in, instances of: Joseph, Gen 47:15–26; Samuel, 1 Sam 11:12–15; Nathan, 1 Kgs 1:11–14; Jeroboam, 1 Kgs 12:26–33; Daniel, see *Daniel.*

See *Diplomacy; Government; King; Ruler.*

STAVES Used as weapons, Mt 26:47; Mk 14:43.

Symbolical. Zech 11:7–14.

STEADFASTNESS See *Decision; Perseverance; Stability.*

STEALING See *Theft.*

STEPHANAS A Christian in Corinth, whose family Paul baptized, 1 Cor 1:16; 16:15, 17.

STEPHEN A Christian martyr. Appointed one of the committee of seven to oversee the daily distribution, Acts 6:3, 5, 6. Faith and power of, Acts 6:5, 8–10. False charges against, Acts 6:11–15. Defense of, Acts 7. Stoned, Acts 7:54–60; 8:1, 22:20. Burial of, Acts 8:2. Gentle and forgiving spirit of, Acts 7:59, 60.

STERILITY Of women. See *Barrenness.*

STEW 2 Kgs 4:38.

See *Broth.*

STEWARD Gen 15:2; 43:19; 1 Chron 28:1; 2 Chron 9:4; Lk 8:3.

FIGURATIVE. The faithful steward described, Lk 12:35–38, 42–44. The unfaithful, described, Lk 16:1–8. See parable of the nobleman and $20,000, Lk 19:12–27; of the investments, Mt 25:14–30. Must be faithful, 1 Cor 4:1, 2; Tit 1:7; 1 Pet 4:10.

See *Cupbearer.*

STEWARDSHIP The Christian use of time, talents, and possessions in accordance with New Testament principles. Related Scriptures: You cannot serve God and money, Mt 6:24. Give, and you will get, Lk 6:38. Parable of the rich fool, Lk 12:16–21. Making friends through cheating, Lk 16: 9–13. The rich young ruler; the rich entering the kingdom of God, Lk 18:18–30. More blessed to give than to receive, Acts 20:35. Giving with generosity, Rom 12:8. Distributing to needy believers, Rom 12: 13. Doing all for the glory of God, 1 Cor 10:31. Putting aside from earnings, for offering, 1 Cor 16: 2. Christ freely gave, became poor, 2 Cor 8:9. Reaping bountifully, 2 Cor 9:6. God loves a cheerful giver, 2 Cor 9:7. Giving to those in need, Eph 4:28. The danger of riches, the love of money is the first step to sin, 1 Tim 6:6–11. God will not forget what we do, Heb 6:10. With such sacrifices God is well pleased, Heb 13:16. Warning to the rich in the last days, Jas 5:1–5. Compassion to the needy, 1 Jn 3:17.

Central passage dealing with, 2 Cor 8; 9. Stewardship includes providing a worthy income to pastors and missionaries, Lk 10:7; 1 Cor 9:7–14.

See *Giving; Liberality; Tithe.*

STICKS Used as symbols, Ezk 37:16.

STIFF-NECKED See *Impenitent; Obduracy.*

STOCKS Feet fastened in, as a punishment, Job 33:11; Jer 20:2; 29:6. In prisons, Acts 16:24.

STOICISM A Grecian philosophy, inculcating doctrines of severe morality, self-denials, and inconvenient services. Scripture analogies to: John the Baptist wears camel's hair and subsists on locusts and wild honey, Mt 3:4; doesn't drink wine and fasts often, Mt 11:18; Lk 7:33. Jesus requires self-denials and "crosses," Mt 10:38, 39; 16:24; Mk 8:34, 35; Lk 9:23–26; 14:27; the subordination of family ties, Mt 10:37; Lk 14:26. Paul teaches that the mind as at war with the lower nature, Rom 7: 23–25, with *vs.* 14–22; that the body must be kept under, 1 Cor 9:27; advises celibacy, 1 Cor 7:1–9, 25, 26, 32, 33, 39, 40.

School of, at Athens, Acts 17:18.

See *Asceticism.*

STOICS See *Stoicism; Asceticism.*

STONES Commandments engraved on, Ex 24:12; 31:18; 34:1–4; Deut 4:13; 5:22; 9:9–11; 10:1–3. The law of Moses written on, Josh 8:32. Houses built of, Amos 5:11. Temple built of, 1 Kgs 5:17, 18; 7:9–12; Mt 24:3; Lk 19:44; 21:5, 6. Prepared in the quarries, 1 Kgs 6:7. Hewn, Ex 34:1; Deut 10:1; 1 Kgs 5:17; 6:36; 7:9; 2 Kgs 12:11, 12; 22:5, 6; 1 Chron 22:2; 2 Chron 34:10, 11; Lam 3:9. Stonemasons, 1 Kgs 5:18; 2 Kgs 12:11, 12; 1 Chron 22:15.

City walls built of, Neh 4:1, 2. Monuments of, Gen 28:18–22; 31:45–52; Josh 4:2–9, 20–24; 24:26; 1 Sam 7:12. Large, as landmarks, at Beth-shemesh, 1 Sam 6:18; Serpent's, 1 Kgs 1:9.

Thrown on cursed ground, 2 Kgs 3:19, 25. Used in building altars, Josh 8:31; for closing tombs, Mt 27:60; Mk 15:46; 16:3. Tombs hewn in, Mt 27:60; Mk 15:46. Idols made of, Deut 4:28; 28:36, 64; 29: 17; 2 Kgs 19:18; Isa 37:19; Ezk 20:32.

Large, in Solomon's Temple, 1 Kgs 5:17, 18; 7: 9–12. Magnificent, in Herod's, Mk 13:1. Skill in throwing, 1 Chron 12:2. See *Sling.*

See *Chalcedony; Marble; Onyx; Pillar.* See also *Precious,* below.

FIGURATIVE. Zech 3:9. Of temptation, "Stone of stumbling," 1 Pet 2:8. Of Christ, "a Foundation Stone," "a precious Cornerstone," Isa 28:16; of Christ's rejection, the rejected cornerstone, Ps 118: 22; Mt 21:42–44; Mk 12:10; Lk 20:17, 18; Acts 4:11; the true foundation, Isa 28:16; 1 Cor 3:11; Eph 2:20; Rev 21:14. Of the impenitent heart, Ezk 36:26. Of the witness of the Spirit, the white stone, Rev 2:17. Believers as stones, 1 Pet 2:5.

See *Rock.*

PRECIOUS. In the chestpiece and ephod, Ex 28: 9–21; 39:6–14. Voluntary offerings of, by the Israelites for the chestpiece and ephod, Ex 35:27. Exported from Sheba, 1 Kgs 10:2, 10; 2 Chron 9:9, 10; Ezk 27:22; Ophir, 1 Kgs 10:11. Partial list of, Ezk 28: 13. Seen in the foundation of the New Jerusalem in John's apocalyptic vision, Rev 21:18–20.

In kings' crowns, 2 Sam 12:29, 20; 1 Chron 20: 2.

FIGURATIVE. Isa 54:11, 12. Merchandise of, Rev 18:12, 16.

See *Agate; Amber; Amethyst; Beryl; Carbuncle; Chrysolite; Chrysoprase; Coral; Crystal; Diamond; Emerald; Jacinth; Jasper; Ruby; Sapphire; Sardius; Sardonyx; Topaz.* See also *Jewels.*

STONING Capital punishment by, Ex 19:13; Deut 13:10; 17:5; 22:21; Heb 11:37, 38. Instances of stoning: Sabbath breaker, Num 15:32–36; Achan, Josh 7:25; Naboth, 1 Kgs 21:13; Stephen, Acts 7:59; Paul, Acts 14:19; 2 Cor 11:25.

See *Witness.*

STOOL See Footstool.

STORE CITIES Built for the storage of the king's supplies, Ex 1:11; 1 Kgs 9:19; 2 Chron 8:4, 6.

STOREHOUSE See *Treasury.*

STORK Forbidden as food, Lev 11:13–19; Deut 14:11–18. Nests of, in fir trees, Ps 104:17. Migratory, Jer 8:7.

FIGURATIVE. Zech 5:9.

STRAIGHT Name of a street in Damascus, Acts 9:11.

FIGURATIVE. Of righteousness, "straight paths," Isa 40:3, 4; Mt 3:3; Heb 12:13.

STRANGERS Mosaic law relating to: Authorized bondservice of, Lev 25:44, 45; usury of, Deut 15:3; 23:20; sale to, of flesh of animals that had died, Deut 14:21; forbid their being made kings over Israel, Deut 17:15; their eating the Passover, Ex 12:43, 48; their eating things offered in sacrifice, Ex 29:33; Lev 22:10, 12, 25; their blaspheming, Lev 24:15, 16; their touching the Tabernacle, Num 1:51; their eating blood, Lev 17:10; injustice to, Ex 12:49; Lev 24:22; Num 9:14; Deut 1:16; Jer 22:3; oppression of, forbidden, Ex 22:21; Lev 19:33, 34; Deut 24: 14, 15, 17; 27:19; Jer 22:3. Instances of oppression of, Ezk 22:29; Mal 3:5.

Required to observe the Sabbath, Ex 20:10; 23: 12. Might offer sacrifices, Lev 17:8, 9; 22:17–19. Were buried in separate cemeteries, Mt 27:7.

Kindness to, required, Lev 19:33, 34. Love of,

commanded, Deut 10:18, 19. Disdain of, forbidden, Deut 23:7. Marriage with, forbidden, Deut 25:5. Hospitality to, see *Hospitality.* Of a different language, 1 Cor 14:11.

See *Aliens; Charity; Gentiles; Heathen.*

STRANGLED Things dying by strangulation, forbidden as food, Acts 15:20, 27–29; 21:25.

STRATEGY In war, Gen 14:14, 15; 32:7, 8; Josh 8:3–25; Judg 7:16–23; 20:29–43; 2 Sam 15:32–34, with 17:7–14; Neh 6; Isa 15:1; Jer 6:5.

See *Ambush; Armies.*

STRAW Used for provender, Gen 24:32; Isa 65:25; for brick, Ex 5:7, 8.

FIGURATIVE. Of the wicked, Ex 15:7; Job 21:8; Isa 5:24; 40:24; Nah 1:10; Mal 4:1. Of the believer's works, 1 Cor 3:12.

See *Chaff; Grass.*

STRAY Animals straying to be returned, Ex 23:4; Deut 22:1–3. Instances of animals straying, Kish's, 1 Sam 9.

STRENGTH A title given to Jehovah, Ps 22:19. Spiritual, see *Power, Spiritual.*

STRIFE Gen 13:8. Then Abram talked it over with Lot. "This fighting between our men has got to stop," he said. "We can't afford to let a rift develop between our clans. Close relatives such as we must present a united front!"

Gen 45:24. So he sent his brothers off. "Don't quarrel along the way!" was his parting shot!

Ex 17:7. Moses named the place Massah (meaning "tempting Jehovah to slay us"), and sometimes they referred to it as Meribah (meaning "argument" and "strife!")—for it was there that the people of Israel argued against God and tempted him to slay them by saying, "Is Jehovah going to take care of us or not?" Num 27:14.

Deut 1:12. But what can one man do to settle all your quarrels and problems?

Ps 55:9. O Lord, make these enemies begin to quarrel among themselves—destroy them with their own violence and strife.

Prov 3:30. Don't get into needless fights.

Prov 6:12, 13. Let me describe for you a worthless and a wicked man; first, he is a constant liar; he signals his true intentions to his friends with eyes and feet and fingers. [14]Next, his heart is full of rebellion. And he spends his time thinking of all the evil he can do, and stirring up discontent. [16-19]For there are six things the Lord hates—no, seven: Haughtiness, lying, murdering, plotting evil, eagerness to do wrong, a false witness, sowing discord among brothers.

Prov 10:12. Hatred stirs old quarrels, but love overlooks insults.

Prov 13:10. Pride leads to arguments; be humble, take advice and become wise.

Prov 15:18. A quick-tempered man starts fights; a cool-tempered man tries to stop them.

Prov 16:28. An evil man sows strife; gossip separates the best of friends.

Prov 17:1. A dry crust eaten in peace is better than steak every day along with argument and strife. [14]It is hard to stop a quarrel once it starts, so don't let it begin. [19]Sinners love to fight; boasting is looking for trouble.

Prov 18:6. A fool gets into constant fights. His mouth is his undoing! His words endanger him. [19]It is harder to win back the friendship of an offended brother than to capture a fortified city. His anger shuts you out like iron bars.

Prov 19:13. A rebellious son is a calamity to his father, and a nagging wife annoys like constant dripping.

Prov 20:3. It is an honor for a man to stay out of a fight. Only fools insist on quarreling.

Prov 21:19. Better to live in the desert than with a quarrelsome, complaining woman.

Prov 22:10. Throw out the mocker, and you will be rid of tension, fighting and quarrels.

Prov 23:29, 30. Whose heart is filled with anguish and sorrow? Who is always fighting and quarreling? Who is the man with bloodshot eyes and many wounds? It is the one who spends long hours in the taverns, trying out new mixtures.

Prov 25:8. Don't be hot-headed and rush to court! You may start something you can't finish and go down before your neighbor in shameful defeat. [24]It is better to live in a corner of an attic than in a beautiful home with a cranky, quarrelsome woman.

Prov 26:17. Yanking a dog's ears is no more foolish than interfering in an argument that isn't any of your business. [20]Fire goes out for lack of fuel, and tensions disappear when gossip stops. [21]A quarrelsome man starts fights as easily as a match sets fire to paper.

Prov 28:25. Greed causes fighting; trusting God leads to prosperity.

Prov 29:22. A hot-tempered man starts fights and gets into all kinds of trouble.

Prov 30:33. As the churning of cream yields butter, and a blow to the nose causes bleeding, so anger causes quarrels.

Isa 41:11. See, all your angry enemies lie confused and shattered. Anyone opposing you will die. [12]You will look for them in vain—they will all be gone.

Isa 58:4. Look, what good is fasting when you keep on fighting and quarreling? This kind of fasting will never get you anywhere with me.

Hab 1:3. Must I forever see this sin and sadness all around me? Wherever I look there is oppression and bribery and men who love to argue and to fight.

Mt 5:25. Come to terms quickly with your enemy before it is too late and he drags you into court and you are thrown into a debtor's cell. [39]But I say: Don't resist violence! If you are slapped on one cheek, turn the other too. [40]If you are ordered to court, and your shirt is taken from you, give your coat too. [41]If the military demand that you carry their gear for a mile, carry it two.

Mt 10:34. Don't imagine that I came to bring peace to the earth! No, rather, a sword. [35]I have come to set a man against his father, and a daughter against her mother, and a daughter-in-law against her mother-in-law— [36]a man's worst enemies will be right in his own home!

Mt 12:25. Jesus knew their thoughts and replied, "A divided kingdom ends in ruin. A city or home divided against itself cannot stand."

Mt 18:15. If a brother sins against you, go to him privately and confront him with his fault. If he listens and confesses it, you have won back a brother. [16]But if not, then take one or two others with you and go back to him again, proving everything you say by these witnesses. [17]If he still refuses to listen, then take your case to the church, and if the church verdict favors you, but he won't accept it, then the church should excommunicate him.

Mk 3:24. A kingdom divided against itself will collapse. [Lk 11:17.] [25]A home filled with strife and division destroys itself.

Lk 12:51. Do you think I have come to give peace to the earth? *No!* Rather, strife and division! [52]From now on families will be split apart, three in favor of me, and two against—or perhaps the other way around. [53]A father will decide one way about me; his son, the other; mother and daughter will disagree; and the decision of an honored mother-in-law will be spurned by her daughter-in-law. [58]If you meet your accuser on the way to court, try to settle the matter before it reaches the judge, lest he sentence you to jail; [59]for if that happens you won't be free again until the last penny is paid in full.

Rom 2:8. But he will terribly punish those who fight against the truth of God and walk in evil ways —God's anger will be poured out upon them.

Rom 12:18. Don't quarrel with anyone. Be at peace with everyone, just as much as possible.

Rom 13:13. And put on the armor of right living, as we who live in the daylight should! . . . Don't spend your time in . . . fighting, or jealousy.

Rom 14:1. Give a warm welcome to any brother who wants to join you, even though his faith is weak. Don't criticize him for having different ideas from yours about what is right and wrong. [19]In this way aim for harmony in the church and try to build each other up. [21]The right thing to do is to quit eating meat or drinking wine or doing anything else that offends your brother or makes him sin.

Rom 16:17. And now there is one more thing to say before I end this letter. Stay away from those who cause divisions and are upsetting people's faith, teaching things about Christ that are contrary to what you have been taught. [18]Such teachers are not working for our Lord Jesus, but only want gain for themselves. They are good speakers, and simple-minded people are often fooled by them.

1 Cor 1:10. But, dear brothers, I beg you in the name of the Lord Jesus Christ to stop arguing among yourselves. Let there be real harmony so that there won't be splits in the church. I plead with you to be of one mind, united in thought and purpose. [11]For some of those who live at Chloe's house have told me of your arguments and quarrels, dear brothers. [12]Some of you are saying, "I am a follower of Paul"; and others say that they are for Apollos or for Peter; and some that they alone are the true followers of Christ. [13]And so, in effect, you have broken Christ into many pieces. But did I, Paul, die for your sins? Were any of you baptized in my name?

1 Cor 3:1. Dear brothers, I have been talking to you as though you were still just babies in the Christian life, who are not following the Lord, but your own desires; I cannot talk to you as I would to healthy Christians, who are filled with the Spirit. [3]For you are still only baby Christians, controlled by your own desires, not God's. When you are jealous of one another and divide up into quarreling groups, doesn't that prove you are still babies, wanting your own way? In fact, you are acting like people who don't belong to the Lord at all. [4]There you are, quarreling about whether I am greater than Apollos, and dividing the church. Doesn't this show how little you have grown in the Lord?

1 Cor 4:6. I have used Apollos and myself as examples to illustrate what I have been saying: that you must not have favorites. You must not be proud of one of God's teachers more than another. [7]What are you so puffed up about? What do you have that God hasn't given you? And if all you have is from God, why act as though you are so great, and as though you have accomplished something on your own?

1 Cor 6:1. How is it that when you have something against another Christian, you "go to law" and ask a heathen court to decide the matter instead of taking it to other Christians to decide which of you is right? [2]Don't you know that some day we Christians are going to judge and govern the world? So why can't you decide even these little things among yourselves? [3]Don't you realize that we Christians will judge and reward the very angels in heaven? So you should be able to decide your problems down here on earth easily enough. [4]Why then go to outside judges who are not even Christians? [5]I am trying to make you ashamed. Isn't there anyone in all the church who is wise enough to decide these arguments? [6]But, instead, one Christian sues another and accuses his Christian brother in front of unbelievers. [7]To have such lawsuits at all is a real defeat for you as Christians. Why not just accept mistreatment and leave it at that? It would be far more honoring to the Lord to let yourselves be cheated.

1 Cor 11:17. Next on my list of items to write you about is something else I cannot agree with. For it sounds as if more harm than good is done when you meet together for your communion services. [18]Everyone keeps telling me about the arguing that goes on in these meetings, and the divisions developing among you, and I can just about believe it. [19]But I suppose you feel this is necessary so that you who are always right will become known and recognized!

2 Cor 12:20. For I am afraid that when I come to visit you I won't like what I find, and then you won't like the way I will have to act. I am afraid

that I will find you quarreling, and envying each other, and being angry with each other, and acting big, and saying wicked things about each other and whispering behind each other's backs, filled with conceit and disunity.

Gal 5:10. I am trusting the Lord to bring you back to believing as I do about these things. God will deal with that person, whoever he is, who has been troubling and confusing you. [15]But if instead of showing love among yourselves you are always critical and catty, watch out! Beware of ruining each other. [19]But when you follow your own wrong inclinations your lives will produce these evil results: . . . [20]idolatry, spiritism (that is, encouraging the activity of demons), hatred and fighting, jealousy and anger, constant effort to get the best for yourself, complaints and criticisms, the feeling that everyone else is wrong except those in your own little group—and there will be wrong doctrine, [21]envy, murder, drunkenness, wild parties, and all that sort of thing. Let me tell you again as I have before, that anyone living that sort of life will not inherit the kingdom of God.

Phil 1:15. Some, of course, are preaching the Good News because they are jealous of the way God has used me. They want reputations as fearless preachers! [17]And some preach to make me jealous, thinking that their success will add to my sorrows here in jail!

Phil 2:3. Don't be selfish; don't live to make a good impression on others. Be humble, thinking of others as better than yourself. [14]In everything you do, stay away from complaining and arguing, [15]so that no one can speak a word of blame against you. You are to live clean, innocent lives as children of God in a dark world full of people who are crooked and stubborn. Shine out among them like beacon lights.

1 Tim 1:5. What I am eager for is that all the Christians there will be filled with love that comes from pure hearts, and that their minds will be clean and their faith strong. [6]But these teachers have missed this whole idea and spend their time arguing and talking foolishness. [7]They want to become famous as teachers of the laws of Moses when they haven't the slightest idea what those laws really show us.

1 Tim 2:8. So I want men everywhere to pray with holy hands lifted up to God, free from sin and anger and resentment.

1 Tim 3:2. For a pastor must be a good man whose life cannot be spoken against. . . . [3]He must not be a drinker or quarrelsome, but he must be gentle and kind, and not be one who loves money.

1 Tim 6:3. Some may deny these things, but they are the sound, wholesome teachings of the Lord Jesus Christ and are the foundation for a godly life. [4]Anyone who says anything different is both proud and stupid. He is quibbling over the meaning of Christ's words and stirring up arguments ending in jealousy and anger, which only lead to name-calling, accusations, and evil suspicions. [5]These arguers—their minds warped by sin—don't know how to tell the truth; to them the Good News is just a means of making money. Keep away from them. [20]Oh, Timothy, don't fail to do these things that God entrusted to you. Keep out of foolish arguments with those who boast of their "knowledge" and thus prove their lack of it. [21]Some of these people have missed the most important thing in life —they don't know God. May God's mercy be upon you.

2 Tim 2:14. Remind your people of these great facts, and command them in the name of the Lord not to argue over unimportant things. Such arguments are confusing and useless, and even harmful. [23]Again I say, don't get involved in foolish arguments which only upset people and make them angry. [24]God's people must not be quarrelsome; they must be gentle, patient teachers of those who are wrong. [25]Be humble when you are trying to teach those who are mixed up concerning the truth.

Tit 3:1. Remind your people. . . . [2]They must not speak evil of anyone, nor quarrel, but be gentle and truly courteous to all. [3]Once we, too, were foolish and disobedient; we were misled by others and became slaves to many evil pleasures and wicked desires. Our lives were full of resentment and envy. We hated others and they hated us. [9]Don't get involved in arguing over unanswerable questions and controversial theological ideas; keep out of arguments and quarrels about obedience to Jewish laws, for this kind of thing isn't worthwhile; it only does harm.

Jas 3:14. And by all means don't brag about being wise and good if you are bitter and jealous and selfish; that is the worst sort of lie. [15]For jealousy and selfishness are not God's kind of wisdom. Such things are earthly, unspiritual, inspired by the devil. [16]For wherever there is jealousy or selfish ambition, there will be disorder and every other kind of evil.

Jas 4:1. What is causing the quarrels and fights among you? Isn't it because there is a whole army of evil desires within you? [2]You want what you don't have, so you kill to get it. You long for what others have, and can't afford it, so you start a fight to take it away from them. And yet the reason you don't have what you want is that you don't ask God for it.

See *Anger; Envy; Jealousy; Malice.*

INSTANCES OF. Between Abraham and Lot's herdsmen, Gen 13:6, 7; Abimelech's, Gen 21:25; Isaac's and those of Gerar, Gen 26:20–22. Laban and Jacob, Gen 31:36, 37. Israelites, Deut 1:12. Jephthah and his brothers, Judg 11:2; and Ephraimites, Judg 12:1–6. Israel and Judah, about David, 2 Sam 19:41–43. Disciples, over who might be the greatest, Mk 9:34; Lk 22:24. Jews, concerning Jesus, Jn 10:19. Christians at Antioch, about circumcision, Acts 15:2. Paul and Barnabas, about Mark, Acts 15:38, 39. Pharisees and Sadducees, concerning the resurrection, Acts 23:7–10. Corinthians, 1 Cor 1:11, 12; 6:6.

STRIPES Forty stripes, Deut 25:1–3. With

his stripes we are healed, Isa 53:5; 1 Pet 2:24. Paul and Silas beaten, their stripes washed, Acts 16:23, 33.

See *Beating; Scourging; Whipping.*

STUBBORNNESS See *Impenitence; Obduracy; Self-Will.*

STUDENTS Poverty of, 2 Kgs 4:1. In state school, Dan 1. In schools of the prophets, 1 Sam 19:20; 1 Kgs 20:35; 2 Kgs 2:3, 5–7, 15; 4:1.

See *Instruction; School.*

STUMBLING FIGURATIVE. Ps 119:165. Causes of, Ps 69:6; Rom 14:13. Stone of, Rom 9:32; 1 Pet 2:8. Stumbling block, Ps 69:6; 1 Cor 10:32.

See *Temptation.*

SUAH An Asherite. Son of Zophah, 1 Chron 7:36, 37.

SUBJECT See *Citizen; Government; Patriotism; Ruler.*

SUBMISSION To authority: Jesus an example of, Mt 26:39, 42; Mk 14:36; Lk 22:41, 42; Heb 5:8.

Of Paul, 1 Cor 16:7.

See *Obedience.*

SUBSTITUTION Ex 28:37, 38. The offering for the offerer, Lev 1:4; 16:21, 22. Levites for the firstborn of the Israelites, Num 3:11, 12, 41, 45; 8:18. The life of Ahab for that of Ben-hadad, 1 Kgs 20:42.

See *Suffering, Vicarious.*

SUBURBS Num 35:3–5; Josh 14:3, 4; 2 Kgs 18:8; 1 Chron 6:55–57; 2 Chron 13:18, 19; Neh 12:29; Ezk 26:8; Jon 3:3; Zech 7:7; Acts 5:16.

SUCCESSION Of priests, irregularity in, Heb 7:1–28. See *Priests.* Of kings, see *Kings.*

SUCCOTH 1. A city probably east of the Jordan. Jacob builds a camp in, Gen 33:17. Allotted to Gad, Josh 13:27, 28. People of, punished by Gideon, Judg 8:5–8, 14–16. Located near the Jordan, 1 Kgs 7:41–46; 2 Chron 4:17, 18; Ps 60:6, 7; 108:7.

2. First camping place of the Israelites on leaving Rameses, Ex 12:37; 13:20; Num 33:5, 6.

SUFFERING FOR CHRIST. Acts 9:16. And I will show him how much he must suffer for me.

Rom 8:17. And since we are his children, we will share his treasures—for all God gives to his Son Jesus is now ours too. But if we are to share his glory, we must also share his suffering. [18]Yet what we suffer now is nothing compared to the glory he will give us later. [19]For all creation is waiting patiently and hopefully for that future day when God will resurrect his children. [20,21]For on that day thorns and thistles, sin, death, and decay—the things that overcame the world against its will at God's command—will all disappear, and the world around us will share in the glorious freedom from sin which God's children enjoy. [22]For we know that even the things of nature, like animals and plants, suffer in sickness and death as they await this great event. [23]And even we Christians, although we have the Holy Spirit within us as a foretaste of future glory, also groan to be released from pain and suffering. We, too, wait anxiously for that day when God will give us our full rights as his children, including the new bodies he has promised us—bodies that will never be sick again and will never die. [26]And in the same way—by our faith—the Holy Spirit helps us with our daily problems and in our praying. For we don't even know what we should pray for, nor how to pray as we should; but the Holy Spirit prays for us with such feeling that it cannot be expressed in words.

1 Cor 4:12. We have worked wearily with our hands to earn our living. We have blessed those who cursed us. We have been patient with those who injured us. [13]We have replied quietly when evil things have been said about us. Yet right up to the present moment we are like dirt under foot, like garbage.

2 Cor 1:7. God will tenderly comfort you when you undergo these same sufferings. He will give you the strength to endure.

2 Cor 4:11. Yes, we live under constant danger to our lives because we serve the Lord, but this gives us constant opportunities to show forth the power of Jesus Christ within our dying bodies. [12]Because of our preaching we face death, but it has resulted in eternal life for you. [13]We boldly say what we believe (trusting God to care for us), just as the Psalm writer did when he said, "I believe and therefore I speak." [14]We know that the same God who brought the Lord Jesus back from death will also bring us back to life again with Jesus, and present us to him along with you. [15]These sufferings of ours are for your benefit. And the more of you who are won to Christ, the more there are to thank him for his great kindness, and the more the Lord is glorified. [16]That is why we never give up. Though our bodies are dying, our inner strength in the Lord is growing every day. [17]These troubles and sufferings of ours are, after all, quite small and won't last very long. Yet this short time of distress will result in God's richest blessing upon us forever and ever! [18]So we do not look at what we can see right now, the troubles all around us, but we look forward to the joys in heaven which we have not yet seen. The troubles will soon be over, but the joys to come will last forever.

Phil 1:29. For to you has been given the privilege not only of trusting him but also of suffering for him.

Phil 2:27. And he surely was; in fact, he almost died. But God had mercy on him, and on me too, not allowing me to have this sorrow on top of everything else. [28]So I am all the more anxious to get him back to you again, for I know how thankful you will be to see him, and that will make me happy and lighten all my cares. [29]Welcome him in the Lord with great joy, and show your appreciation, [30]for he risked his life for the work of Christ and was at the point of death while trying to do for me the things you couldn't do because you were far away.

Phil 3:10. Now I have given up everything else —I have found it to be the only way to really know Christ and to experience the mighty power that brought him back to life again, and to find out what it means to suffer and to die with him.

Col 1:24. But part of my work is to suffer for you; and I am glad, for I am helping to finish up the remainder of Christ's sufferings for his body, the church.

2 Thess 1:4. We are happy to tell other churches about your patience and complete faith in God, in spite of all the crushing troubles and hardships you are going through. [5]This is only one example of the fair, just way God does things, for he is using your sufferings to make you ready for his kingdom.

2 Tim 2:12. And if we think that our present service for him is hard, just remember that some day we are going to sit with him and rule with him. But if we give up when we suffer, and turn against Christ, then he must turn against us.

Jas 5:10. For examples of patience in suffering, look at the Lord's prophets.

1 Pet 4:13. Instead, be really glad—because these trials will make you partners with Christ in his suffering, and afterwards you will have the wonderful joy of sharing his glory in that coming day when it will be displayed. [14]Be happy if you are cursed and insulted for being a Christian, for when that happens the Spirit of God will come upon you with great glory.

1 Pet 5:10. After you have suffered a little while, our God, who is full of kindness through Christ, will give you his eternal glory. He personally will come and pick you up, and set you firmly in place, and make you stronger than ever.

See *Afflictions; Persecution.*

OF CHRIST. Lk 24:46. And he said, "Yes, it was written long ago that the Messiah must suffer and die and rise again from the dead on the third day, [47]and that this message of salvation should be taken from Jerusalem to all the nations: *There is forgiveness of sins for all who turn to me." v.* 26.

Jn 6:51. I am that Living Bread that came down out of heaven. Anyone eating this Bread shall live forever; this Bread is my flesh given to redeem humanity.

Jn 10:11. I am the Good Shepherd. The Good Shepherd lays down his life for the sheep. [15]Just as my Father knows me and I know the Father; and I lay down my life for the sheep.

Jn 11:50. "Let this one man die for the people—why should the whole nation perish?" [51]This prophecy that Jesus should die for the entire nation came from Caiaphas in his position as High Priest—he didn't think of it by himself, but was inspired to say it. [52]It was a prediction that Jesus' death would not be for Israel only, but for all the children of God scattered around the world.

Rom 4:25. He died for our sins and rose again to make us right with God, filling us with God's goodness.

Rom 5:6. When we were utterly helpless with no way of escape, Christ came at just the right time and died for us sinners who had no use for him. [7]Even if we were good, we really wouldn't expect anyone to die for us, though, of course, that might be barely possible. [8]But God showed his great love for us by sending Christ to die for us while we were still sinners.

Rom 14:15. And if your brother is bothered by what you eat, you are not acting in love if you go ahead and eat it. Don't let your eating ruin someone for whom Christ died.

1 Cor 1:17. For Christ didn't send me to baptize, but to preach the Gospel; and even my preaching sounds poor, for I do not fill my sermons with profound words and high sounding ideas, for fear of diluting the mighty power there is in the simple message of the cross of Christ. [18]I know very well how foolish it sounds to those who are lost, when they hear that Jesus died to save them. But we who are saved recognize this message as the very power of God. [23]So when we preach about Christ dying to save them, the Jews are offended and the Gentiles say it's all nonsense. [24]But God has opened the eyes of those called to salvation, both Jews and Gentiles, to see that Christ is the mighty power of God to save them; Christ himself is the center of God's wise plan for their salvation.

1 Cor 8:11. So because you "know it is all right to do it," you will be responsible for causing great spiritual damage to a brother with a tender conscience for whom Christ died.

1 Cor 15:3. I passed on to you right from the first what had been told to me, that Christ died for our sins just as the Scriptures said he would.

2 Cor 5:14. Whatever we do, it is certainly not for our own profit, but because Christ's love controls us now. Since we believe that Christ died for all of us, we should also believe that we have died to the old life we used to live. [15]He died for all so that all who live—having received eternal life from him—might live no longer for themselves, to please themselves, but to spend their lives pleasing Christ who died and rose again for them.

Gal 1:4. He died for our sins just as God our Father planned, and rescued us from this evil world in which we live.

Gal 2:20. I have been crucified with Christ: and I myself no longer live, but Christ lives in me. And the real life I now have within this body is a result of my trusting in the Son of God, who loved me and gave himself for me. [21]I am not one of those who treats Christ's death as meaningless. For if we could be saved by keeping Jewish laws, then there was no need for Christ to die.

Eph 5:2. Be full of love for others, following the example of Christ who loved you and gave himself to God as a sacrifice to take away your sins. And God was pleased, for Christ's love for you was like sweet perfume to him. [25]And you husbands, show the same kind of love to your wives as Christ showed to the church when he died for her.

1 Thess 5:9. For God has not chosen to pour out his anger upon us, but to save us through our Lord Jesus Christ; [10]he died for us so that we can live with him forever, whether we are dead or alive at the time of his return.

Heb 2:9. But we do see Jesus—who for awhile

was a little lower than the angels—crowned now by God with glory and honor because he suffered death for us. Yes, because of God's great kindness, Jesus tasted death for everyone in all the world. [10]And it was right and proper that God, who made everything for his own glory, should allow Jesus to suffer, for in doing this he was bringing vast multitudes of God's people to heaven; for his suffering made Jesus a perfect Leader, one fit to bring them into their salvation. [14]Since we, God's children, are human beings—made of flesh and blood—he became flesh and blood too by being born in human form; for only as a human being could he die and in dying break the power of the devil who had the power of death. [18]For since he himself has now been through suffering and temptation, he knows what it is like when we suffer and are tempted, and he is wonderfully able to help us.

Heb 5:8. And even though Jesus was God's Son, he had to learn from experience what it was like to obey, when obeying meant suffering. [9]It was after he had proved himself perfect in this experience that Jesus became the Giver of eternal salvation to all those who obey him.

Heb 9:15. Christ came with this new agreement so that all who are invited may come and have forever all the wonders God has promised them. For Christ died to rescue them from the penalty of the sins they had committed while still under that old system. [16]Now, if someone dies and leaves a will —a list of things to be given away to certain people when he dies—no one gets anything until it is proved that the person who wrote the will is dead. [28]So also Christ died only once as an offering for the sins of many people; and he will come again, but not to deal again with our sins. This time he will come bringing salvation to all those who are eagerly and patiently waiting for him.

Heb 10:10. Under this new plan we have been forgiven and made clean by Christ's dying for us once and for all. [18]Now, when sins have once been forever forgiven and forgotten, there is no need to offer more sacrifices to get rid of them. [19]And so, dear brothers, now we may walk right into the very Holy of Holies where God is, because of the blood of Jesus. [20]This is the fresh, new, life-giving way which Christ has opened up for us by tearing the curtain—his human body—to let us into the holy presence of God.

1 Pet 2:21. This suffering is all part of the work God has given you. Christ, who suffered for you, is your example. Follow in his steps. [24]He personally carried the load of our sins in his own body when he died on the cross, so that we can be finished with sin and live a good life from now on. For his wounds have healed ours!

1 Pet 3:18. Christ also suffered. He died once for the sins of all us guilty sinners, although he himself was innocent of any sin at any time, that he might bring us safely home to God. But though his body died, his spirit lived on.

1 Pet 4:1. Since Christ suffered and underwent pain, you must have the same attitude he did; you must be ready to suffer, too. For remember, when your body suffers, sin loses its power.

1 Jn 3:16. We know what real love is from Christ's example in dying for us. And so we also ought to lay down our lives for our Christian brothers.

See *Atonement; Jesus, Death of, Design of his Death, Sufferings of.*

VICARIOUS. Ex 9:13. Then the Lord said to Moses, "Get up early in the morning and stand before Pharaoh and tell him, 'Jehovah the God of the Hebrews says, "Let my people go to worship me. [14]This time I am going to send a plague that will really speak to you and to your servants and to all the Egyptian people, and prove to you there is no other God in all the earth. [15]I could have killed you all by now, [16]but I didn't, for I wanted to demonstrate my power to you and to all the earth." ' "

Jn 15:13. And here is how to measure it—the greatest love is shown when a person lays down his life for his friends.

Rom 9:1–3. Oh, Israel, my people! Oh, my Jewish brothers! . . . . I would be willing to be forever damned if that would save you.

1 Pet 2:21. This suffering is all part of the work God has given you. Christ, who suffered for you, is your example. Follow in his steps.

1 Jn 3:16. We know what real love is from Christ's example in dying for us. And so we also ought to lay down our lives for our Christian brothers.

See above, *Suffering, of Christ.*

SUICIDE Amos 9:2; Rev 9:6. Temptation to, of Jesus, Mt 4:5, 6; Lk 4:9–11. Of the Philippian jailer, Acts 16:27.

See *Death, Desired.*

INSTANCES OF. Samson, Judg 16:29, 30. Saul and his armor-bearer, 1 Sam 31:3–5; 1 Chron 10:4, 5. Ahithophel, 2 Sam 17:23. Zimri, 1 Kgs 16:18. Judas, Mt 27:5; Acts 1:18.

SUING Mt 5:40. See *Creditor; Debtor.*

SUKKIIMS An African (?) race. Invaded Judah with Shishak, 2 Chron 12:3.

SULPHUR Flaming, Rev 9:17, 18; 14:10; 19:20; 21:8.

See *Brimstone.*

SUMMER Season of, promised while the earth remains, Gen 8:22. Cool rooms for, Judg 3:20. Homes, Amos 3:15. Fruits of, 2 Sam 16:1, 2; Isa 16:9; 28:4; Jer 40:10, 12; 48:32; Amos 8:1, 2; Mic 7:1. Drought of, Ps 32:4. Given by God, Ps 74:17. The time for labor and harvest, Prov 6:6–8; 10:5; 30:24–28; Jer 8:20. Snow in, Prov 26:1. Approach of, Mt 24:32; Mk 13:28; Lk 21:30.

FIGURATIVE. Jer 8:20.

SUN Created, Gen 1:14–18; Ps 74:16; 136:7; Jer 31:35; Rising and setting of, Eccl 1:3–7. Daily motion of, Ps 19:4, 6. Worship of, forbidden, Deut 4:19; 17:2, 3. Worshiped, Job 31:26–28; Jer 8:2; Ezk 8:16. Kings of Judah dedicated horses to, 2 Kgs 23:11.

Miracles concerning: Darkening of, Ex 10:21–23;

Isa 5:30; 24:23; Ezk 32:7; Joel 2:10, 31; 3:15; Amos 8:9; Mic 3:6; Hab 3:11; Mt 24:29; 27:45; Mk 13:24; 15:33; Lk 21:25; 23:44, 45; Acts 2:20; Rev 6:12; 8:12; 9:2; 16:8. Stands still, Josh 10:12, 13. Shadow of, goes back on Ahaz's sun dial, 2 Kgs 20:11; Isa 38:8.

Does not shine in the new Jerusalem, Rev 21:23.

FIGURATIVE. Mal 4:2; Judg 5:31; Isa 30:26; 60:20; Jer 15:9; Rev 1:16; 12:1; 19:17.

SUNDAY See *Lord's Day.*

SUN DIAL 2 Kgs 20:11; Isa 38:8.

SUNSTROKE 2 Kgs 4:19.

SUPEREROGATION The doctrine of excessive and meritorious righteousness, Ezk 33:12, 13; Lk 17:10.

SUPERSCRIPTION On the cross, Mt 27:37; Mk 15:26; Lk 23:38; Jn 19:19.

SUPERSTITION INSTANCES OF. Israelites, supposing that their defeat in battle with the Philistines was due to their not having brought with them the Ark of the Covenant, 1 Sam 4:3, with *vs.* 10, 11. Philistines, refusing to walk on the threshold of the temple of Dagon after the image of Dagon had repeatedly fallen, 1 Sam 5:5.

The belief of the Syrians concerning the help of the gods, 1 Kgs 20:23. Jews, attributing their troubles to having ceased offering sacrifices to the Queen of Heaven, Jer 44:17–19. Nebuchadnezzar, supposing that the spirit of the gods was in Daniel, Dan 4:8, 9. The sailors who threw Jonah into the sea, Jon 1:4–16. The disciples, supposing they saw a ghost when Jesus came walking on the sea, Mt 14:26; Mk 6:49, 50. Herod, imagining that John the Baptist had returned from the dead, Mk 6:14, 16.

The Gadarenes, because of Jesus casting out demons, Mt 8:34. The disciples who were frightened at the appearance of Peter, Acts 12:14, 15. The Ephesians, in their sorceries, Acts 19:13–19. The people of the island of Malta, in imagining Paul to be a god, Acts 28:6.

See *Idolatry; Sorcery.*

SUPPER See *Feasts; Lord's Supper.*

SUPPLICATION That form of intensified prayer by which a believer implores God's aid in a time of special need, 1 Kgs 8:33, 34, 47, 59; 2 Sam 24:25; 2 Chron 6:24; Esther 4:8; Job 8:5; 9:15; Ps 28:2, 6; 30:8; 142:1; Dan 6:11; Hos 12:4; Lk 1:13; 2:36, 37; 5:33; Acts 1:13; Rom 10:1; 2 Cor 1:11; 9:14; Eph 6:18; Phil 1:4, 19; 4:6; 1 Tim 2:1; 5:5; 2 Tim 1:3; Heb 5:7; Jas 5:16; 1 Pet 3:12.

See *Prayer.*

SURETY Gen 44:32; Ex 22:26, 27; Deut 24:10–13; Prov 6:1–5; 11:15; 17:18; 20:16; 22:26, 27; 27:13; Ezk 18:7, 12; 33:15; Amos 2:8.

SURFEITING See *Drunkenness; Gluttony.*

SUSA Capital of the Persian province of Elam, Dan 8:2. Residents of, relocated in Israel, Ezra 4:8–10.

SUSANNA A woman who contributed to the support of Jesus, Lk 8:3.

SUSI A Manassite, Num 13:3–15.

SUSPICION See *Accusation, False.*

SWADDLE Wrapping of children, Lk 2:7, 12.

SWALLOW Prov 26:2. Builds its nest in the sanctuary, Ps 84:3. Chattering of, figurative of the moaning of the afflicted, Isa 38:14. Migration of, Jer 8:7.

SWEARING See *Blasphemy; God, Name of not to be Profaned; Oath.*

SWEAT Gen 3:19; Ex 5:9; 1 Thess 2:9. An offense in the sanctuary, Ezk 44:18. Of blood, Lk 22:44; Heb 5:7; 12:4.

SWEET INCENSE Isa 43:24; Jer 6:20. Made of spices, Ex 25:6.

See *Incense.*

SWINE Forbidden as food, Lev 11:4–7; Deut 14:8. Used for food, Isa 65:4; 66:17; for sacrifice, Isa 66:3. Wild boar, Ps 80:13. Jewelry in the nose of, Prov 11:22. Viciousness of, Mt 7:6. Jesus sends devils into, Mt 8:28–32; Mk 5:11–14; Lk 8:32, 33. Feeding of, Lk 15:15, 16. Pig returns to its wallow, 2 Pet 2:22.

SWORD Used by Goliath, 1 Sam 21:9; Peter, Mt 26:51; Jn 18:10. To be beaten into plowshares, Isa 2:4; Mic 4:3. Made of plowshares, Joel 3:10. Double-bladed, Rev 1:16; 2:12.

FIGURATIVE. Of war, Gen 27:39, 40. Of judgments, Deut 32:40, 41; Zech 13:7. Of the malicious tongue, Ps 57:4; Prov 25:18. Of the Word, Eph 6:17.

Symbolical. Gen 3:24; Josh 5:13; Rev 1:16.

SWORD FIELD A battleground, 2 Sam 2:16.

SYCAMORE A tree. Abundant in the land of Canaan, 1 Kgs 10:27; 2 Chron 1:15; 9:27; Isa 9:8–10. Groves of, cared for, 1 Chron 27:28. Destroyed by hail, Ps 78:47. Zacchaeus climbs into, Lk 19:4.

SYCHAR See *Shechem, 1.*

SYENE A city in Egypt, Ezk 29:10; 30:6.

SYMBOLS AND SIMILITUDES Trees, of life and knowledge, Gen 2:9, 16, 17; 3:2, 3, 24; Rev 22:2. Rainbow, Gen 9:12, 13. Circumcision, of the covenant of Abraham, Gen 17:11; Rom 4:11. Passover, of the sparing of the firstborn, and of the atonement made by Christ, Ex 12:3–28; 1 Cor 5:7. Of the Lord's presence, the pillar of cloud, Ex 13:21, 22; 14:19, 20; 19:9, 16; thunder on Mount Sinai, Ex 19:9, 16. Darkness, of God's inscrutability, Ex 20:21; Lev 16:2; 1 Kgs 8:12, 13; Ps 18:11; 97:2; Heb 12:18, 19. The smitten rock, of Christ, Ex 17:5, 6; 1 Cor 10:3, 4. The sprinkled blood, of the covenant, Ex 24:8. Wine, of the atoning blood, Mt 26:27–29; Mk 14:23–25; Lk 22:17, 18, 20. The bronze snake, of Christ, Num 21:8, 9; Jn 3:14.

Sacrificial animals, Gen 15:8–11; Jn 1:29, 36. Waving the offering, Ex 29:24–28; Lev 8:27–29; 9:21. The whole system of Mosaic rites, Heb 9:9, 10, 18–23. Tabernacle, Ps 15:1; Heb 8:2, 5; 9:1–12, 23, 24. Sanctuary, Ps 20:2.

Salt, Num 18:19. Offering water to drink, Gen 24:13–16, 42–44. Lapping water, Judg 7:4–7. Invitation to approach, 1 Sam 14:8–12. Bowshot, by Jonathan, 1 Sam 20:21–37; by Joash, 2 Kgs 13:15–19. Men meeting Saul, 1 Sam 10:2–7. Rain and thunder, 1 Sam 12:16–18. Cracked altar, 1 Kgs 13:3, 5. Splitting of the veil, Mt 27:51; Mk 15:38; Lk 23:45. Wounding, 1 Kgs 20:35–40. Praying toward the Temple, 1 Kgs 8:29; Dan 6:10. Harvest, 2 Kgs 19: 29. Isaiah's children, Isa 8:18. Nakedness, Isa 20: 2–4. Almond rod, Jer 1:11. Sticks and staffs, Ezk 37: 16, 17; Zech 11:7, 10, 11, 14. Food, 2 Kgs 19:29; Isa 37: 30. Shadow on Ahaz's dial, 2 Kgs 20:8–11; Isa 38: 7, 8. Cooking, Jer 1:13; Ezk 4:9–15; 24:3–5. Belt, Jer 13:1–7; Acts 21:11. Jars, Jer 13:12; 19:1, 2, 10. Breaking of potter's jar, Jer 19. Good and bad figs, Jer 24. Basket of fruit, Jer 24:1–3; Amos 8:1, 2. Wine, Jer 25:15–17; Mt 26:27; Mk 14:23, Lk 22:17. Yokes, Jer 27:2, 3; 28:10. Jeremiah's deeds of land, Jer 32:1–16. Scroll thrown into Euphrates, Jer 51:63. Muteness, Ezk 3:26, 27; 29:21; 33:22; Lk 1:20–22, 62–64. Siege, Ezk 4:1–3. Posture, Ezk 4:4–8. Unclean food, Ezk 4:9–17. Ezekiel's beard, Ezk 5:1–4. Change of residence, Ezk 12:3–11. Eating food with carefulness, Ezk 12:17–20. Eating and drinking in fear, Ezk 12: 18. Vine, Ezk 15:2; 19:10–14. Death, Ezk 24:16–19. Boiling pot, Ezk 24:1–5. Mourning forbidden, Ezk 24:15–18. Two sticks, Ezk 37:15–28. Handwriting on the wall, Dan 5:5, 6, 16–28. Plumbline, Amos 7: 7, 8. Marrying a prostitute, Hos 1:2–9; 3:1–4. Scroll, Zech 5:2–4. Basket, Zech 5:6–11. Jonah, Mt 16:4; Lk 11:29, 30. Star in the east, Mt 2:2. Bread, Mt 26:26; Mk 14:22; Lk 22:19. Childhood, Mt 18:3; Mk 10:14, 15; Lk 18:16, 17. Manna, Jn 6:31–58.

OF THE HOLY SPIRIT. Water, Jn 3:5; 7:38, 39; cleansing by, Ezk 36:25; Eph 5:26; Heb 10:22; life-giving, Ps 1:3; Isa 27:3, 6; 44:3, 4; 58:11.

Fire, Mt 3:11; purifying, Isa 4:2–4; Mal 3:2, 3; illuminating, Ex 13:21; Ps 78:14; searching, Zeph 1: 12, with 1 Cor 2:10.

Wind, Song 4:16; incomprehensible, Jn 3:8; powerful, 1 Kgs 19:11, with Acts 2:2; sensible in its effect, Jn 3:8; reviving, Ezk 37:9, 10, 14.

Oil, healing, Isa 1:5, 6; Rev 18:13; comforting, Ps 23:5; illuminating, Zech 4:2, 3, 11–13; Mt 25:2–4; consecrating, Ex 29:7; 30:30; Isa 61:1.

Rain and dew, Ps 72:6; fertilizing, Ezk 34:26, 27; Hos 6:3; 10:12; 14:5; refreshing, Ps 68:9, 10; abundant, Ps 133:3.

A dove, Mt 3:16.

A voice, speaking, Mt 10:20; guiding, Isa 30:21, with Jn 16:13; warning, Heb 3:7–11.

A seal, Rev 7:2; earnest, Eph 1:13, 14; 4:30; 2 Cor 1:22.

Different languages, Acts 2:3, 6, 11.

Ablutions a symbol of purity, see *Ablution; Purification.* For symbolisms of color, see *Color.* See also *Allegory; Instruction, by Symbols, of Children, in Religion.*

SYMEON A disciple, Acts 13:1.

SYMPATHY Job 2:11. When three of Job's friends heard of all the tragedy that had befallen him, they got in touch with each other and traveled from their homes to comfort and console him. Their names were Eliphaz the Temanite, Bildad the Shuhite, and Zophar the Naamathite. [12]Job was so changed that they could scarcely recognize him. Wailing loudly in despair, they tore their robes and threw dust into the air and put earth on their heads to demonstrate their sorrow. [13]Then they sat upon the ground with him silently for seven days and nights, no one speaking a word; for they saw that his suffering was too great for words.

Job 6:14. One should be kind to a fainting friend, but you have accused me without the slightest fear of God.

Job 22:29. If you are attacked and knocked down, you will know that there is someone who will lift you up again. Yes, he will save the humble.

Eccl 7:2. It is better to spend your time at funerals than at festivals. For you are going to die and it is a good thing to think about it while there is still time.

2 Cor 1:4. When others are troubled, needing our sympathy and encouragement, we can pass on to them this same help and comfort God has given us.

Phil 2:1. Is there any such thing as Christians cheering each other up? Do you love me enough to want to help me? Does it mean anything to you that we are brothers in the Lord, sharing the same Spirit? Are your hearts tender and sympathetic at all? [2]Then make me truly happy by loving each other and agreeing wholeheartedly with each other, working together with one heart and mind and purpose.

Jas 1:27. The Christian who is pure and without fault, from God the Father's point of view, is the one who takes care of orphans and widows, and who remains true to the Lord—not soiled and dirtied by his contacts with the world.

1 Pet 3:8. You should be . . . full of sympathy toward each other.

See *Afflicted; Afflictions; Jesus, Compassion of; Pity.*

SYNAGOGUE 1. Primarily an assembly, Acts 13:43. Constitutes a court of justice, Lk 12:11; Acts 9:2. Had powers of criminal courts, Mt 10:17; 23:34; Acts 22:19; 26:11; of ecclesiatical courts, Jn 9: 22, 34; 12:42; 16:2.

2. Place of assembly. Scriptures read and expounded in, Neh 8:1–8; 9:3, 5; Mt 4:23; 9:35; 13:53, 54; Mk 1:39; Lk 4:15–33; 13:10; Jn 6:59; 18:20; Acts 9:20; 13:5–44; 14:1; 15:21; 17:1, 10; 18:4, 19, 25, 26.

In Jerusalem, Acts 6:9; Damascus, Acts 9:2, 20; other cities, Acts 14:1; 17:1, 10; 18:4. Built by the Roman captain, Lk 7:5. Jesus performed healing in, Mt 12:9–13; Lk 13:10–14. Charity given in, Mt 6: 2.

SYNTYCHE A Christian woman in Philippi, Phil 4:2.

SYRACUSE A city of Sicily, Paul visits, Acts 28:12.

SYRIA Highlands lying between the Euphrates River and the Mediterranean Sea. Called *Aram,* from the son of Shem, Gen 10:22, 23; Num 23:7–10; 1 Chron 1:17; 2:23. In the time of Abraham it seems to have embraced the region between the Tigris and Euphrates rivers, Gen 24:10, with chapter 25: 20, including Paddam-aram, Gen 25:20; 28:5. See *Mesopotamia.*

Minor kingdoms within the region: Zobah, 1 Sam 14:47; 2 Sam 8:3; 10:6–8; 1 Kgs 11:23;

1 Chron 18:5, 9; 19:6; Geshur, 2 Sam 15:7, 8; Rehob, 2 Sam 10:6–8; Damascus, 2 Sam 8:5, 6; 1 Chron 18: 5, 6; Hamath, 2 Sam 8:9, 10.

Conquest of: By David, 2 Sam 8:3–13; by Jeroboam, 2 Kgs 14:25, 28; by Tiglath-pileser, king of Assyria, 2 Kgs 16:7–9; 18:33, 34. People of, colonized in Samaria by the king of Assyria, 2 Kgs 17: 24. Confederate with Nebuchadnezzar, 2 Kgs 24: 2; Jer 39:5.

The Roman province of, included the land of Canaan, Lk 2:2, 3; and Pheonicia, Mk 7:26; Acts 21:3. The fame of Jesus extended over, Mt 4:24.

Paul goes to, with letters to apprehend the Christians; is converted and begins his evangelistic ministry, Acts 9:1–31. See *Paul.*

Paul preaches in, Acts 15:40, 41; 18:18; 21:3; Gal 1:21. Damascus, the capital of, see *Damascus.*

Wars between, and the kingdom of Judah and Israel, see *Israel.* Prophecies concerning, Isa 7:8–16; 8:4–8; 17:1–3; Jer 1:15; 49:23–27; Amos 1:3–5; Zech 9:1.

SYROPHOENICIAN The nationality of a woman whose daughter was cured by Jesus, Mt 15: 21–28; Mk 7:24–30.

T

TAANACH A city conquered by Joshua, Josh 12:8–24. Allotted to Manasseh, Josh 17:11; 1 Chron 7:29; Canaanites not driven from, Josh 17:12; Judg 1:27. Assigned to the Levites, Josh 21:25. The scene of Barak's victory, Judg 5:19. One of Solomon's commissaries at, 1 Kgs 4:8–19.

TAANATH-SHILOH A city of Ephraim, Josh 16:5, 6.

TABBAOTH One of the Nethinim, Ezra 2:43–54; Neh 7:46–56.

TABBATH A place to which the Midianites fled, Judg 7:22.

TABEEL 1. A Persian official in Samaria, Ezra 4:7.

2. Father of one whom the kings of Syria and Israel sought to make king in Judah instead of Ahaz, Isa 7:6.

TABERAH A place in the wilderness where the Israelites were punished for their complaining, Num 11:3; Deut 9:22.

TABERNACLE One existed before Moses received the pattern authorized on Mount Sinai, Ex 33:7–11. The one instituted by Moses was called *Sacred Temple,* Ex 25:8; *Tabernacle,* Ex 27:20; *Tent for Meeting with God,* Ex 33:7; *Sanctuary,* Lev 10:17.

Plan of, revealed to Moses, Ex 25:9; 26:30; 39:32, 42, 43; Acts 7:44; Heb 8:5. Materials for, voluntarily offered, Ex 25:1–8; 35:4–29: 36:3–7. Value of the materials contributed for, Ex 38:24–31. Workmen who constructed it were inspired, Ex 31:1–11; 35:30–35.

Description of: Frame, Ex 26:15–37; 36:20–38. Outer covering, Ex 25:1–7; 26:7–14; 36:14–19. Second covering, Ex 26:14; 35:5–9, 23; 36:19; 39:33–40. Curtains of, Ex 26:1–14, 31–37; 27:9–16; 35:10–19; 36:8–19, 35, 37. Court of, Ex 27:9–17; 38:9–16, 18; 40:8, 33.

Holy Place of, Ex 26:31–37; 40:22–26; Heb 9:1–6, 8. The Most Holy Place, Ex 26:33–35; 40:20, 21; Heb 9:3–5, 7, 8.

Furniture of, Ex 25:10–40; 27:1–8, 19; 37; 38:1–8. See *Altar; Ark; Candlestick; Cherubim; Laver; Mercy Seat; Shewbread.*

Completed, Ex 39:32. Dedicated, Num 7. Sanctified, Ex 29:43; 40:9–16; Num 7:1. Anointed with holy oil, Ex 30:25–27; Lev 8:10; Num 7:1. Sprinkled with blood, Lev 16:15–20; Heb 9:21, 23. Filled with the cloud of glory, Ex 40:34–38.

How prepared for removal during the travels of the Israelites, Num 1:51; 4:5–15. How and by whom carried, Num 4:5–33; 7:6–9. Strangers forbidden to touch, Num 1:51. Duties of the Levites concerning, see *Levites.* Defilement of, punished, Lev 15:31; Num 19:13, 20; Ezk 5:11; 23:38. Duties of the priests in relation to, see *Priests.* Israelites worship at, Num 10:3; 16:19, 42–44; 20:6; 25:6; 1 Sam 2:22; Ps 27:4. Offerings brought to, Lev 17:3, 4; Num 31:54; Deut 12:4–6, 11–14.

Tribes camped around, while in the wilderness, Num 2. All males required to appear before, three times each year, Ex 23:17. Tabernacle tax, Ex 30:11–16.

Carried in front of the Israelites in the line of march, Num 10:33–36; Josh 3:2–6. The Lord reveals himself at, Lev 1:1; Num 1:1; 7:89; 12:3–10; Deut 31:14, 15.

Pitched at Gilgal, Josh 4:18, 19; at Shiloh, Josh 18:1; 19:51; Judg 18:31; 21:19; 1 Sam 2:13, 14; 4:3, 4; Jer 7:12–14; at Bethel, Judg 20:18, 26–28; at Nob, 1 Sam 21:1–6; at Gibeon, 1 Chron 21:29. Rebuilt by David, and pitched on Mount Zion, 1 Chron 15:1; 16:1, 2; 2 Chron 1:4. Solomon offers sacrifice at, 2 Chron 1:2–6. Ark brought from the Tabernacle to the Temple by Solomon, 2 Chron 5:4, 5, with 1 Kgs 8:1–5.

Symbol of spiritual things, Ps 15:1; Heb 8:2, 5; 9:1–12, 24.

See *Levites; Priests; Temple.*

TABERNACLES, FEAST OF Called also *Feast of Ingathering, Festival of Shelters,* and the *Harvest Festival.* Instituted, Ex 23:16; 34:22; Lev 23:33–43; Num 29:12–40; Deut 16:13–16. Design of, Lev 23:42, 43. The law read in connection with, every seventh year, Deut 31:10–12; Neh 8:18.

Observance of, after the captivity, Ezra 3:4; Neh 8:14–18; by Jesus, Jn 7:2, 14. Observance of, omitted, Neh 8:17. Penalty for not observing, Zech 14:16–19.

Jeroboam institutes an idolatrous feast to correspond to, 1 Kgs 12:32, 33.

TABITHA A Christian woman in Joppa, called also *Dorcas.* Restored to life by Peter, Acts 9:36–41.

TABLE 1. An article of furniture, Judg 1:7;

1 Sam 20:34; 2 Kgs 4:10; Jn 2:15. Made of gold and silver, 1 Chron 28:16.

FIGURATIVE. Of the Lord's supper, 1 Cor 10:21; of idolatrous feasts, 1 Cor 10:21.

2. Of shewbread, see *Bread of the Presence, Table of.*

TABLET Ex 31:18; 32:15; 34:29. The commandments engraved upon, Ex 20:3–17; 24:12; Deut 4:13; 5:4–22; 9:10, 11; broken, Ex 24:12; 31:18; 32:15–19; Deut 4:13; 9:9–11, 17. A second set engraved, Ex 34:1; Deut 10:1–4. Placed in the ark, Deut 10:5; 1 Kgs 8:9; Heb 9:4.

FIGURATIVE. 2 Cor 3:3.

TABOR 1. A mountain on the border of Issachar, Josh 19:17–23; Judg 8:18; Ps 89:12; Jer 46:18; Hos 5:1. Assembling place of Barak's army, Judg 4:6, 12, 14.

2. A plain of unknown location, 1 Sam 10:3.

3. A Levitical city in Zebulun, 1 Chron 6:77.

See *Chisloth-tabor.*

TACT Prov 15:1; 25:15. In preaching, 1 Cor 9:19–22; 2 Cor 12:6. Of Gideon, Judg 8:1–3. Of Saul, in managing malcontents, 1 Sam 10:27; 11:7, 12–15. Nabal's wife, 1 Sam 25:18–38. In David's popular methods: in mourning for Abner, 2 Sam 3:28–37; in organizing temple music, 1 Chron 15:16–24; in securing popular consent to bringing the ark to Jerusalem, 1 Chron 13:1–4. Joab's trick in obtaining David's consent to the return of Absalom, 2 Sam 14:1–22. The wise woman of Abel, 2 Sam 20:16–22. Solomon, in arbitrating between the prostitutes, 1 Kgs 3:24–28.

Mordecai, in concealing Esther's nationality, Esther 2:10. Esther in placating the king, Esther chapters 5–7. Paul, in circumcising Timothy, Acts 16:3; in exposing jealous preachers, Phil 1:10–22; in stimulating benevolent giving, 2 Cor 8:1–8; 9:1–5; in aligning the two religious factions of the Jews against each other when he was in trouble, Acts 23:6–10. The mayor of Ephesus, Acts 19:35–41. The church council at Jerusalem, Acts 21:20–25.

TACTICS See *Armies; Strategy.*

TADMOR A city built in the desert by Solomon, 2 Chron 8:4; called *Tamar,* 1 Kgs 9:17, 18.

TAHAN 1. Son of Ephraim, Num 26:28–37.

2. A descendant of Ephraim, 1 Chron 7:25–27.

TAHASH Son of Nahor, Gen 22:24.

TAHATH 1. A camping place of the Israelites, Num 33:15–37.

2. A Kohathite, 1 Chron 6:22–24, 33–38.

3. The name of two Ephraimites, 1 Chron 7:20, 21.

TAHPANHES Called also *Tehaphnenes.* A city in Egypt, Jer 2:16; 43:7–9; 44:1; 46:14; Ezk 30:18.

TAHPENES A queen of Egypt, 1 Kgs 11:19, 20.

TAHRE-A Son of Micah, 1 Chron 9:41. Called *Tarea,* 1 Chron 8:35.

TAHTIM-HODSHI An unknown place, 2 Sam 24:6.

TAILORING Ex 31:10; 39:1.

TALENT A unit of monetary reckoning based upon weight, the value of which varied according to the metal used, and perhaps equal to 75 pounds (34 kilograms) and 3000 shekels. Of silver, Ex 38:25–27; 1 Chron 19:6; 22:14; of gold, Ex 25:39; 1 Chron 22:14. Parable of, Mt 18:24.

See *Money; Shekel.*

TALKING With God, see *Communion.*

TALMAI 1. A son of Anak, Num 13:22; Josh 15:14; Judg 1:10.

2. King of Geshur, 2 Sam 3:3; 13:37–39; 1 Chron 3:2.

TALMON A Temple gatekeeper, 1 Chron 9:17, 18. Family of, return from captivity with Zerubbabel, Ezra 2:40–42; Neh 11:19; 12:25.

TAMAR 1. Wife of the sons of Judah, Gen 38:6–24; Ruth 4:12; 1 Chron 2:4; Mt 1:3.

2. Daughter of David, 2 Sam 13:1–31; 1 Chron 3:9.

3. Daughter of Absalom, 2 Sam 14:27.

4. A city of unknown location, Ezk 47:19; 48:27, 28.

5. See *Tadmor.*

TAMBOURINE 1 Sam 18:6. Used by Jephthah's daughter, Judg 11:34. Used in worship, 2 Sam 6:5; 1 Chron 13:8; Ps 150:4.

See *Timbrel.*

TAMMUZ 1. An ancient Babylonian god, husband and brother of Ishtar, goddess of procreation. Counterpart of the Greek Adonis and the Egyptian Osiris. Hebrew women weeping for, Ezk 8:14.

2. See *Calendar.*

TANHUMETH Father of Seraiah, 2 Kgs 25:23; Jer 40:8.

TANIS See *Zoan.*

TANNING Acts 9:43; 10:5, 6.

TANTALIZING 1 Sam 1:6, 7; 1 Kgs 18:27.

TAPE Use of: measuring ground, 2 Sam 8:2.

See *Cord.*

TAPESTRY Prov 31:22. Of the Tabernacle, Ex 26:1–14, 31–37; 27:9–17; 36:8–18. Gold thread woven in, Ex 39:3.

See *Curtains; Embroidery.*

TAPHATH Daughter of Solomon, 1 Kgs 4:8–19.

TAPPUAH 1. A city of Judah, Josh 12:8–24; 15:33–36.

2. A city in Ephraim, Josh 16:8; 17:8.

3. Son of Hebron, 1 Chron 2:43.

4. See *Tiphsah.*

TAR Flaming, Gen 19:24. Used by Noah in the ark, Gen 6:14. Used in making the boat in which Moses was hidden, Ex 2:3.

See *Bitumen; Brimstone; Pitch.*

TARAIAH A city in Benjamin, Josh 18:21–28.

TAREA A son of Micah, 1 Chron 8:35. Called *Tahre-a,* 1 Chron 9:41.

TARE See *Thistle.*

TARIFF See *Duty.*

TARSHISH 1. Son of Javan, Gen 10:4; 1 Chron 1:5–9.

2. Probably Spain, Gen 10:4, 5; Ps 72:10; Isa 66:19. Solomon makes valuable imports from, 2 Chron 9:21. Commerce and wealth of, 2 Chron

9:21; 20:36; Isa 23:1–14; 60:9; Jer 10:9; Ezk 27:12, 25; 38:13. Jonah would escape to, Jon 1:3; 4:2. Prophecies concerning, Ps 72:10; Isa 23:1–14; 60:9; 66:19.

3. Son of Bilhan and descendant of Benjamin, 1 Chron 7:10.

4. A Persian official, Esther 1:13–15.

TARSUS Capital of Cilicia, in Asia Minor. Paul's birthplace, Acts 9:11; 21:39; 22:3. Paul sent to, from Jerusalem, to avoid assassination, Acts 9: 30. Paul brought from, by Barnabas, Acts 11:25, 26.

TARTAK An Assyrian idol, 2 Kgs 17:31.

TARTARUS The Greek word rendered *hell* in 2 Pet 2:4. Refers to pits of darkness, a region in the unseen world, into which God cast the angels who sinned. The word occurs nowhere else in the Bible. See Jude 1:6.

TASKMASTERS Ex 1:11; 3:7; 5:6–16.

FIGURATIVE. Isa 60:17.

See *Master; Oppression; Servant.*

TASSELS Prescribed for clothing worn by Israelites, Num 15:38–41; Deut 22:12.

See *Fringes.*

TASTE The taste of manna, Ex 16:31; Num 11: 8. Taste of the white of an egg, Job 6:5–7. The taste of the Word is sweet, Ps 119:102, 103. Taste not, Col 2:21. Christ tasted death for every man, Heb 2:9. Tasted of the heavenly gift and the Word, Heb 6: 4, 5. You have tasted the Lord's goodness, 1 Pet 2: 3.

TATTENAI A Persian governor in Samaria, Ezra 5:3, 6; 6:6, 13.

TATTLER See *Gossip.*

TATTOOING Forbidden, Lev 19:28. The mark of the Creature, Rev 13:16; 14:11.

FIGURATIVE. Isa 44:5; 49:16.

TAVERNS See *Three Taverns.*

TAX Poll, Ex 30:11–16; 38:26; Neh 10:32. Jesus pays, Mt 17:25–27.

Land, Gen 41:34, 35, 48; 2 Kgs 23:35. Land mortgaged for, Neh 5:2–4. Priests exempted from, Gen 47:26; Ezra 7:24. Paid in grain, Amos 7:1; in provisions, 1 Kgs 4:7–28.

Personal, 1 Kgs 9:15; 2 Kgs 15:19, 20; 23:35. Resisted by Israelites, 1 Kgs 12:18; 2 Chron 10:18.

COLLECTORS OF, 1 Kgs 4:6; Isa 33:18; Dan 11: 20; unpopular, Mt 9:9–11; Lk 18:11; stoned, 2 Chron 10:18; repent under the preaching of John the Baptist, Lk 3:12; 7:29. Matthew, the collector of Capernaum, becomes a disciple, Mt 9:9; 10:2–4; Mk 2:14; Lk 5:27. Zacchaeus, chief among, Lk 19: 2–10. Parable concerning, Lk 18:9–14.

TEACHERS Samuel, head of school of prophets, 1 Sam 19:20. Elisha, head of, at Gilgal, 2 Kgs 4:38. Wiser than my teachers, Ps 119:99. Of the law, Mt 8:19; Lk 2:46; 5:17; Acts 5:34; 1 Tim 1: 7. Placed by God in the church, 1 Cor 12:28. Jesus called, Mt 8:19; Mk 9:5; 11:21; Jn 13:14. Given by Christ, Eph 4:11. Paul a teacher of the Gentiles, 2 Tim 1:11.

See *Instruction; Jesus, Teacher; Minister, Duties of.*

FALSE. Admonition against, Deut 13:1–3; Mt 5: 19; 7:15; 15:2–20; 23:2–33; Lk 11:37–52. False teachers of the last days, 2 Tim 4:3; 2 Pet 2:1; cf. Acts 20:29.

See *Minister, False.*

TEACHING See *Instruction; Minister, Duties of.*

TEARING Of clothing, a sign of anguish, Gen 37:29, 34; 44:13; Num 14:6; Judg 11:35; 2 Sam 1:1, 2, 11; 13:19, 21; 15:32; 2 Kgs 2:12; 6:30; 11: 13, 14; 19:1; 22:11, 18, 19; Ezra 9:3; Job 1:20; 2:12; Isa 36:22; 37:1; Jer 41:5; Mt 26:65, 66; Acts 14:14.

FIGURATIVE. Joel 2:13. Symbol of tearing of a kingdom, 1 Sam 15:27, 28.

TEARS Ps 6:6; 39:12. Observed by God, Ps 56:8; Isa 38:3–5. Wiped away, Rev 7:17. None in heaven, Rev 21:4.

FIGURATIVE. Ps 80:5.

TEBALIAH Son of Hosah, 1 Chron 26:11.

TEBETH See *Calendar.*

TECHNICALITIES Legal, Mt 12:2, 10; Lk 6:2, 7.

TEETH Prov 10:26. Gnashing of, Ps 112:10; Lam 2:16; Mt 13:42, 50; 22:13; 24:51; 25:30; Mk 9: 18; Lk 13:28.

TEHAPHNEHES See *Tahpanhes.*

TEHINNAH Son of Eshton, 1 Chron 4:11, 12.

TEKEL Dan 5:24, 25, 27.

TEKOA 1. Son of Ashhur, 1 Chron 2:24; 4:5. Some authorities interpret these passages to mean that Ashhur colonized the town of Tekoa.

2. A city in Judah, 2 Chron 11:5–10. Home of the woman who interceded for Absalom, 2 Sam 14:2, 3. Fortified by Rehoboam, 2 Chron 11:5–10. People of, work on the new wall of Jerusalem, Neh 3:5, 27. Prophecy concerning, Jer 6:1. Home of Amos, Amos 1:1.

3. Wilderness of, 2 Chron 20:20.

TELABIB Colony of Jewish captives in Babylonia, Ezk 3:14, 15.

TELAH An Ephraimite, 1 Chron 7:25.

TELAIM A city of Judah, 1 Sam 15:4. Possibly the same as *Telem, 1.*

TELASSAR A city or district conquered by the Assyrians, 2 Kgs 19:12; Isa 37:12.

TELEM 1. A city of Judah, Josh 15:21–32. See *Telaim.*

2. A gatekeeper who divorced his Gentile wife, Ezra 10:24.

TEL-HARSHA A place in Babylonia, Ezra 2:59; Neh 7:61.

TEL-MELAH A place in Babylonia, Ezra 2: 59; Neh 7:61.

TEMA 1. Son of Ishmael, Gen 25:12–15; 1 Chron 1:28–31.

2. A people of Arabia, probably descendant from Tema, Ishmael's son, Job 6:19; Isa 21:14; Jer 25:23.

TEMAH One of the Nethinim, Ezra 2:43–54; Neh 7:46–56.

TEMAN 1. Son of Eliphaz, Gen 36:10–12, 15, 16, 40–43; 1 Chron 1:36, 51–54.

2. Called also *Temanites.* A people supposed to be descended from Teman, son of Eliphaz. Gen 36: 31–39; Job 2:11. Prophecies concerning, Jer 49:7; Ezk 25:13; Amos 1:12; Obd 1:9; Hab 3:3.

TEMANITE See *Teman, 2.*

TEMENI Son of Ashhur, 1 Chron 4:6.

TEMPER See *Anger; Malice; Self-Control.*

TEMPERANCE Esther 1:7. Drinks were served in golden goblets of many designs, and there was an abundance of royal wine, for the king was feeling very generous. [8]The only restriction on the drinking was that no one should be compelled to take more than he wanted, but those who wished could have as much as they pleased. For the king had instructed his officers to let everyone decide this matter for himself.

Prov 23:1–3. When dining with a rich man, be on your guard and don't stuff yourself, though it all tastes so good; for he is trying to bribe you, and no good is going to come of his invitation.

Prov 25:16. Do you like honey? Don't eat too much of it, or it will make you sick!

Dan 1:8. But Daniel made up his mind not to eat the food and wine given to them by the king. He asked the superintendent for permission to eat other things instead. [12]And suggested a ten-day diet of only vegetables and water; [13]then, at the end of this trial period the steward could see how they looked in comparison with the other fellows who ate the king's rich food, and decide whether or not to let them continue their diet. [14]The steward finally agreed to the test. [15]Well, at the end of the ten days, Daniel and his three friends looked healthier and better nourished than the youths who had been eating the food supplied by the king! [16]So after that the steward fed them only vegetables and water, without the rich foods and wines!

Rom 13:14. But ask the Lord Jesus Christ to help you live as you should, and don't make plans to enjoy evil.

1 Cor 9:25. To win the contest you must deny yourselves many things that would keep you from doing your best. An athlete goes to all this trouble just to win a blue ribbon or a silver cup, but we do it for a heavenly reward that never disappears. [27]Like an athlete I punish my body, treating it roughly, training it to do what it should, not what it wants to. Otherwise I fear that after enlisting others for the race, I myself might be declared unfit and ordered to stand aside.

1 Thess 5:6. So be on your guard, not asleep like the others. Watch for his return and stay sober. [7]Night is the time for sleep and the time when people get drunk. [8]But let us who live in the light keep sober, protected by the armor of faith and love, and wearing as our helmet the happy hope of salvation.

1 Tim 3:2. For a pastor must be a good man whose life cannot be spoken against. He must have only one wife, and he must be hard working and thoughtful, orderly, and full of good deeds. He must enjoy having guests in his home, and must be a good Bible teacher. [3]He must not be a drinker or quarrelsome. [Tit 1:7, 8.] [8]The deacons must be the same sort of good, steady men as the pastors. They must not be heavy drinkers and must not be greedy for money.

Tit 2:2. Teach the older men to be serious and unruffled; they must be sensible, knowing and believing the truth and doing everything with love and patience. [3]Teach the older women to be quiet and respectful in everything they do. They must not go around speaking evil of others and must not be heavy drinkers, but they should be teachers of goodness. [12]And along with this gift comes the realization that God wants us to turn from godless living and sinful pleasures and to live good, God-fearing lives day after day.

See *Abstinence; Drunkenness; Wine.*

TEMPLE SOLOMON'S. Called also *God's Temple,* Ezra 8:30; *Holy Temple,* 1 Chron 28:10; Ps 11:4; *Glorious Temple,* Isa 60:7; *House of Prayer,* Isa 56:7; *Holy, Beautiful Temple,* Isa 64:11; *Holy Mountain,* Isa 27:13; *Lord's Temple,* 2 Chron 8:1; *Temple of God,* 1 Chron 29:3; *Temple of the God of Israel,* Isa 2:3; *Temple of the God of their ancestors,* 1 Chron 24:17, 18; *Temple of the Lord,* 1 Chron 22:5; *Temple of the great God of Judah,* Ezra 5:8; *Temple of the Lord of Hosts,* Zech 14:21.

Greatness of, 2 Chron 2:5, 6. Beauty of, Isa 64:11. Holiness of, 1 Kgs 8:10; 9:2, 3; Lam 1:10; Jn 2:14–16.

David undertakes the building of, 2 Sam 7:2, 3; 1 Chron 22:7; 28:2; Ps 132:2–5; Acts 7:46; forbidden by God because he was a man of war, 2 Sam 7:4–12; 1 Kgs 5:3; 1 Chron 22:8; 28:3. Not asked for by God, 2 Sam 7:7. The building of, committed to Solomon, 2 Sam 7:13. David makes preparation for, 1 Chron 22; 28:14–18; 29:1–5; 2 Chron 3:1; 5:1. Built by Solomon, Acts 7:47. Solomon drafts men for the building of, 1 Kgs 5:13–16; 2 Chron 2:2, 17, 18.

Materials of, furnished by Hiram, 1 Kgs 5:8–18. Design and building of, 1 Kgs 6; 7:13–51; 1 Chron 28:11–19; 2 Chron 3; 4. Time when begun, 1 Kgs 6:1, 37; 2 Chron 3:2; finished, 1 Kgs 6:38. Site of, 1 Chron 21:28–30; 22:1; 2 Chron 3:1; where Abraham offered Isaac, Gen 22:2, 4.

Materials prepared for, 1 Kgs 5:17, 18. No tools used at the building site, 1 Kgs 6:7. Foundations of, 1 Kgs 5:17, 18.

Apartments and furnishings of: Holy of Holies, in 1 Kgs 6:19, 20; 8:6; 2 Chron 3:8. Called *Inner Sanctuary,* 1 Kgs 6:23–28. Description of, 1 Kgs 6:16, 19–35; 2 Chron 3:8–14; 4:22. Gold used in, 2 Chron 3:8–10. Contents of the Holy of Holies: Ark, 1 Kgs 6:19; 8:6; 2 Chron 5:2–10; see *Ark;* cherubims, 1 Kgs 6:23–28; 2 Chron 3:10–13; 5:7, 8. See *Ark; Cherubim; Veil; Mercy Seat.*

Holy Place, 1 Kgs 8:8, 10. Description of, 1 Kgs 6:15–18; 2 Chron 3:3, 5–7, 14–17. Contents of the Holy Place: The table of the Bread of the Presence, 1 Kgs 7:48; 2 Chron 29:18. See *Bread of the Presence, Table of.* Other tables of gold and silver, 1 Chron 28:16; 2 Chron 4:19. Lampstands and their utensils, 1 Kgs 7:49, 50; 1 Chron 28:15; 2 Chron 4:7, 20–22. See *Candlestick, Lampstand.* Altar of incense and its furniture, 1 Kgs 6:20; 7:48, 50; 1 Chron 28:17, 18; 2 Chron 4:19, 22. See *Altar, of Incense.*

Porch of, dimensions, 1 Kgs 6:3; 2 Chron 3:4. Doors of, 2 Chron 29:7. Overlaid with gold,

2 Chron 3:4. Pillars of, 1 Kgs 7:15–22; 2 Kgs 11:13, 14; 23:3; 25:17; 2 Chron 3:15–17; 4:12–16.

Rooms of, 1 Kgs 6:5–10; 2 Kgs 11:2, 3. Offerings brought to, Neh 10:37–40. Treasuries in, see *Treasury.*

Courts of: Of the priests, 2 Chron 4:9; inner, 1 Kgs 6:36; surrounded by rows of stones and cedar beams, 1 Kgs 6:36; 7:12. Contents of the courts: Altar of burnt offering, 2 Chron 15:8; see *Altar;* the bronze tank, 1 Kgs 7:23–37, 44, 46; 2 Chron 4:2–5, 10; ten vats, 1 Kgs 7:38–46; 2 Chron 4:6. Public court of, 2 Chron 4:9. Passageway for the Sabbath and king's entry, 2 Kgs 16:18.

Gates of: Upper gate, 2 Kgs 15:34, 35; New Gate, Jer 36:10; Beautiful Gate, Acts 3:2; eastern gate, closed on working days, open on the Sabbath, Ezk 46:1, 12. Gifts received at, 2 Chron 24:8–11.

Uses of the Temple: A home of the Lord, 1 Kgs 8:10–13; 9:2, 3; 2 Kgs 21:7; 1 Chron 29:1; 2 Chron 5:13, 14; 7:1–3, 16; Ezk 10:3, 4; Mic 1:2; to contain the ark of the covenant, 1 Kgs 8:21; for the offering of sweet incense, 2 Chron 2:4; for the Bread of the Presence and the burnt offerings, 2 Chron 2:4; for prayer and worship, 1 Kgs 8; 2 Kgs 19:14, 15; 2 Chron 30:27; Isa 27:13; 56:7; Jer 7:2; 26:2; Ezk 46:2, 3, 9; Zech 7:2, 3; 8:21, 22; prayer made toward, 1 Kgs 8:38; Dan 6:10; for an armory, 2 Kgs 11:10; 2 Chron 23:9, 10; for refuge, 2 Kgs 11: 15; Neh 6:10, 11.

Facts about: Dedication of, 1 Kgs 8; 2 Chron 5; 6; 7; services in, organized by David, 1 Chron 15: 16; 23:24. Pillaged by Shishak, 1 Kgs 14:25, 26; by Joash, king of Israel, 2 Kgs 14:14. Repaired: by Joash, king of Judah, 2 Kgs 12:4–14; 2 Chron 24: 7–14; by Josiah, 2 Kgs 22:3–7; 2 Chron 34:8–13. Ahaz changes the design of the altar in, 2 Kgs 16: 10–17. Purified by Hezekiah, 2 Chron 29:15–19. Converted into an idolatrous shrine by Manasseh, 2 Kgs 21:3–7; 2 Chron 33:4–7. Treasures of, used in the purchase of peace: By Asa, from Ben-hadad, 1 Kgs 15:18; by Joash, king of Judah, from Hazael, 2 Kgs 12:18; by Hezekiah, from the king of Assyria, 2 Kgs 18:15, 16. Ezekiel's vision concerning, Ezk 8: 16.

Destroyed by Nebuchadnezzar, and the valuable contents carried to Babylon, 2 Kgs 24:13; 25:9–17; 2 Chron 36:7, 19; Ezra 1:7; Ps 79:1; Isa 64:11; Jer 27: 16, 19–22; 28:3; 52:13, 17–23; Lam 2:7; 4:1. Cups of, used by Belshazzar, Dan 5:2–4.

Destruction of, foretold, Isa 66:6; Jer 27:18–22; Ezk 7:22, 25.

Restoration of, ordered by Cyrus, Ezra 1:7–11.

THE SECOND. Restored by Zerubbabel, Ezra 1; 2:68, 69; 3; 4; 5; 6:3–5; Neh 7:70–72; Isa 44:28; Hag 2:3. Building of, suspended, Ezra 4; resumed, Ezra 4:24; 5; 6; Hag 1:2–9; 2:14, 15; Zech 8:9; finished, Ezra 6:14, 15; dedicated, Ezra 6:15–18. Ar-ta-xerxes' favorable action toward, Ezra 7:11–28; 8:25–34.

Prophecies of its restoration, Isa 44:28; Hag 1; 2; Zech 1:16; 4:8–10; 6:12–15; 8:9–15; Mal 3:1.

EZEKIEL'S VISION OF. Ezk 37:26, 28; chapters 40–48.

HEROD'S. Forty-six years in building, Jn 2:20. Beautiful stonework of, Mk 13:1; Lk 21:5. Beautiful Gate of, Acts 3:10. Solomon's Hall, Jn 10:22, 23; Acts 3:11; 5:12. Treasury of, Mk 12:41–44. Zacharias, officiating priest in, has a vision of an angel; receives promise of a son, Lk 1:5–23, with *vs.* 57–64. Jesus brought to, according to the law and custom, Lk 2:21–39. Simeon blesses Jesus in, Lk 2:25–35; Anna, the prophetess, lives in, Lk 2: 36, 37. Jesus in, when a youth, Lk 2:46, 47; taken to the roof of, in his temptation, Mt 4:5–7; Lk 4: 9–12; teaches in, Mk 11:26–33; 12:35–44; 14:49; Jn 5: 14–47; 7:14–28; 8; 10:22–38; 18:20; performs miracles in, Mt 21:14, 15; drives money changers from, Mt 21: 12, 13; Mk 11:15–17; Lk 19:45, 46; Jn 2:15, 16.

Captains of, Lk 22:52; Acts 4:1; 5:24, 26, 27. Judas throws down money in, Mt 27:5.

Curtain of, split apart at the time of the crucifixion, Mt 27:51. The disciples worship in, after the resurrection, Lk 24:53; Acts 2:46; 3:1. Peter heals the lame man at the gate of, Acts 3:1–16. Disciples preach in, Acts 5:20, 21, 42. Paul's vision in, Acts 22:17–21. Paul observes the rites of, Acts 21:26–30; is apprehended in, Acts 21:33.

Prophecies concerning its destruction, by Daniel, Dan 8:11–15; 11:30, 31. Jesus foretells the destruction of, Mt 24:2; Mk 13:2; Lk 21:6.

A TEMPLE IN THE LAST DAYS. Mt 24:15; 2 Thess 2:4; Rev 11:1, 2; cf. Dan 9:27; 11:30, 31; 12:11.

FIGURATIVE. Of the body of Jesus, Mt 26:60, 61; 27:40; Jn 2:19. Of the indwelling of God, 1 Cor 3:16, 17; 2 Cor 6:16. Of the Church, Eph 2:21; 2 Thess 2:4; Rev 3:12.

IDOLATROUS. Of Dagon, at Ashdod, 1 Sam 5: 2; of the calves, at Beth-el, 1 Kgs 12:31–33; of Rimmon, at Damascus, 2 Kgs 5:18; of Baal, at Samaria, 2 Kgs 10:20, 21; at Babylon, 2 Chron 36:7; Dan 1: 1, 2; of Diana, at Ephesus, Acts 19:27.

Trophies stored in, 1 Sam 31:10; 1 Chron 10:9, 10; Dan 1:1, 2.

See *Tabernacle.*

TEMPORAL BLESSINGS See *Blessing.*

TEMPTATION Gen 3:1. The serpent was the craftiest of all the creatures the Lord God had made. So the serpent came to the woman. "Really?" he asked. "*None* of the fruit in the garden? God says you mustn't eat *any* of it?" [2,3]"Of course we may eat it." the woman told him. "It's only the fruit from the tree at the *center* of the garden that we are not to eat. God says we mustn't eat it or even touch it, or we will die." [4]"That's a lie!" the serpent hissed. "You'll not die! [5]God knows very well that the instant you eat it you will become like him, for your eyes will be opened—you will be able to distinguish good from evil!" [6]The woman was convinced. How lovely and fresh looking it was! And it would make her so wise! So she ate some of the fruit and gave some to her husband, and he ate it too. [7]And as they ate it, suddenly they became aware of their nakedness, and were embarrassed. So they strung fig leaves together to cover themselves around the hips. [8]That evening they heard the sound of the Lord God walking in the garden; and they hid themselves among the trees. [9]The

Lord God called to Adam, "Why are you hiding?" [10]And Adam replied, "I heard you coming and didn't want you to see me naked. So I hid." [11]"Who told you you were naked?" the Lord God asked. "Have you eaten fruit from the tree I warned you about?" [12]"Yes," Adam admitted, "but it was the woman you gave me who brought me some, and I ate it." [13]Then the Lord God asked the woman, "How could you do such a thing?" "The serpent tricked me," she replied.

Gen 20:6. "Yes, I know," the Lord replied. "That is why I held you back from sinning against me; that is why I didn't let you touch her."

Ex 34:12. Be very, very careful never to compromise with the people there in the land where you are going, for if you do, you will soon be following their evil ways. *vs.* 13–16.

Deut 7:25. Burn their idols and do not touch the silver or gold they are made of. Do not take it or it will be a snare to you, for it is horrible to the Lord your God.

Deut 8:11. But that is the time to be careful! Beware that in your plenty you don't forget the Lord your God and begin to disobey him. [12, 13]For when you have become full and prosperous and have built fine homes to live in, and when your flocks and herds have become very large, and your silver and gold have multiplied, [14]that is the time to watch out that you don't become proud, and forget the Lord your God who brought you out of your slavery in the land of Egypt. [17]He did it so that you would never feel that it was your own power and might that made you wealthy. [18]Always remember that it is the Lord your God who gives you power to become rich, and he does it to fulfill his promise to your ancestors.

Deut 13:3. Don't listen to him. For the Lord is testing you to find out whether or not you really love him with all your heart and soul.

1 Chron 21:1. Then Satan brought disaster upon Israel, for he made David decide to take a census.

2 Chron 32:30. He [Hezekiah] prospered in everything he did. [31]However, when ambassadors arrived from Babylon to find out about the miracle of his being healed, God left him to himself in order to test him and to see what he was really like.

Ps 119:165. Those who love your laws have great peace of heart and mind and do not stumble.

Prov 1:10. If young toughs tell you, "Come and join us"—turn your back on them! [11]"We'll hide and rob and kill," they say. [12]"Good or bad, we'll treat them all alike. [13]And the loot we'll get! All kinds of stuff! [14]Come on, throw in your lot with us; we'll split with you in equal shares." [15]Don't do it, son! Stay far from men like that, [16]for crime is their way of life, and murder is their specialty. [17]When a bird sees a trap being set, it stays away.

Prov 2:10. For wisdom and truth will enter the very center of your being, filling your life with joy. [11, 12]You will be given the sense to stay away from evil men who want you to be their partners in crime. [16]Only wisdom from the Lord can save a man from the flattery of prostitutes.

Prov 4:14. Don't do as the wicked do. [15]Avoid their haunts—turn away, go somewhere else.

Prov 5:6. For she does not know the path to life. She staggers down a crooked trail, and doesn't even realize where it leads. [7]Young men, listen to me, and never forget what I'm about to say: [8]*Run from her! Don't go near her house,* [9]lest you fall to her temptation and lose your honor, and give the remainder of your life to the cruel and merciless; [10]lest strangers obtain your wealth, and you become a slave of foreigners. [11]Lest afterwards you groan in anguish and in shame when syphilis consumes your body, [12]and you say, "Oh, if only I had listened! If only I had not demanded my own way! [13]Oh, why wouldn't I take advice? Why was I so stupid? [14]For now I must face public disgrace." [15]Drink from your own well, my son—be faithful and true to your wife. [16]Why should you beget children with women of the street? [17]Why share your children with those outside your home? [18]Let your manhood be a blessing; rejoice in the wife of your youth. [19]Let her charms and tender embrace satisfy you. Let her love alone fill you with delight. [20]Why delight yourself with prostitutes, embracing what isn't yours? [21]*For God is closely watching you,* and he weighs carefully everything you do.

Prov 6:27. Can a man hold fire against his chest and not be burned? [28]Can he walk on hot coals and not blister his feet?

Prov 7:7. And saw a simple-minded lad, a young man lacking common sense, [8, 9]walking at twilight down the street to the house of this wayward girl, a prostitute. [10]She approached him, saucy and pert, and dressed seductively. [11, 12]She was the brash, coarse type, seen often in the streets and markets, soliciting at every corner for men to be her lovers. [13]She put her arms around him and kissed him, and with a saucy look she said, [14]"I've decided to forget our quarrel! [15]I was just coming to look for you and here you are! [16, 17]My bed is spread with lovely, colored sheets of finest linen imported from Egypt, perfumed with myrrh, aloes and cinnamon. [18]Come on, let's take our fill of love until morning, [19]for my husband is away on a long trip. [20]He has taken a wallet full of money with him, and won't return for several days." [21]So she seduced him with her pretty speech, her coaxing and her wheedling, until he yielded to her. He couldn't resist her flattery. [22]He followed her as an ox going to the butcher, or as a stag that is trapped, [23]waiting to be killed with an arrow through its heart. He was as a bird flying into a snare, not knowing the fate awaiting it there.

Prov 9:15. Whispering to men going by, and to those minding their own business. [16]"Come home with me," she urges simpletons. [17]"Stolen melons are the sweetest; stolen apples taste the best!"

Prov 12:26. The good man asks advice from friends; the wicked plunge ahead—and fall.

Prov 14:27. Reverence for the Lord is a fountain of life; its waters keep a man from death. Prov 13:14.

Prov 16:29. Wickedness loves company—and leads others into sin.

Prov 19:27. Stop listening to teaching that contradicts what you know is right.

Prov 28:10. A curse on those who lead astray the godly. But men who encourage the upright to do good shall be given a worthwhile reward.

Eccl 7:26. A prostitute is more bitter than death. May it please God that you escape from her, but sinners don't evade her snares.

Isa 33:15. I will tell you who can live here: All who are honest and fair, who reject making profit by fraud, who hold back their hands from taking bribes, who refuse to listen to those who plot murder, who shut their eyes to all enticement to do wrong. [16]Such as these shall dwell on high. The rocks of the mountains will be their fortress of safety; food will be supplied to them and they will have all the water they need.

Jer 2:24. You are a wild donkey, sniffing the wind at mating time. (Who can restrain your lust?) Any jack wanting you need not search, for you come running to him! [25]Why don't you turn from all this weary running after other gods? But you say, "Don't waste your breath. I've fallen in love with these strangers and I can't stop loving them now!"

Jer 35:5. I set cups and jugs of wine before them and invited them to have a drink, [6]but they refused. "No," they said. "We don't drink, for Jonadab our father (son of Rechab) commanded that none of us should ever drink, neither we nor our children forever. [7]He also told us not to build houses or plant crops or vineyards and not to own farms, but always to live in tents; and that if we obeyed we would live long, good lives in our own land.

Hos 7:5. On the king's birthday, the princes get him drunk; he makes a fool of himself and drinks with those who mock him.

Amos 2:12. But you caused the Nazirites to sin by urging them to drink your wine, and you silenced my prophets, telling them, "Shut up!"

Mt 4:1. Then Jesus was led out into the wilderness by the Holy Spirit, to be tempted there by Satan. [2]For forty days and forty nights he ate nothing and became very hungry. [3]Then Satan tempted him to get food by changing stones into loaves of bread. "It will prove you are the Son of God," he said. [4]But Jesus told him, "No! For the Scriptures tell us that bread won't feed men's souls: obedience to every word of God is what we need." [5]Then Satan took him to Jerusalem to the roof of the Temple. [6]"Jump off," he said, "and prove you are the Son of God; for the Scriptures declare, 'God will send his angels to keep you from harm,' . . . they will prevent you from smashing on the rocks below." [7]Jesus retorted, "It also says not to put the Lord your God to a foolish test!" [8]Next Satan took him to the peak of a very high mountain and showed him the mountains of the world and all their glory. [9]"I'll give it all to you," he said, "if you will only kneel and worship me." [10]"Get out of here, Satan," Jesus told him. "The Scriptures say, 'Worship only the Lord God. Obey only him.' " [11]Then Satan went away, and angels came and cared for Jesus. Lk 4:1–13.

Mt 5:19. And so if anyone breaks the least commandment, and teaches others to, he shall be the least in the Kingdom of Heaven.

Mt 12:45. Then the demon finds seven other spirits more evil than itself, and all enter the man and live in him. And so he is worse off than before.

Mt 13:22. The ground covered with thistles represents a man who hears the message, but the cares of this life and his longing for money choke out God's Word, and he does less and less for God. Lk 8:13, 14.

Mt 18:6. But if any of you causes one of these little ones who trusts in me to lose his faith, it would be better for you to have a rock tied to your neck and be thrown into the sea. [7]Woe upon the world for all its evils. Temptation to do wrong is inevitable, but woe to the man who does the tempting. [8]So if your hand or foot causes you to sin, cut it off and throw it away. Better to enter heaven crippled than to be in hell with both of your hands and feet. [9]And if your eye causes you to sin, gouge it out and throw it away. Better to enter heaven with one eye than to be in hell with two.

Mt 26:31. Then Jesus said to them, "Tonight you will all desert me. For it is written in the Scriptures that God will smite the Shepherd, and the sheep of the flock will be scattered. [41]Keep alert and pray. Otherwise temptation will overpower you. For the spirit indeed is willing, but how weak the body is!" Lk 22:40.

Mk 4:15. The hard pathway, where some of the seed fell, represents the hard hearts of some of those who hear God's message; Satan comes at once to try to make them forget it. [17]Their roots don't go very deep, and though at first they get along fine, as soon as persecution begins, they wilt.

Mk 10:21. Jesus felt genuine love for this man as he looked at him. "You lack only one thing," he told him; "go and sell all you have and give the money to the poor—and you shall have treasure in heaven—and come, follow me." [22]Then the man's face fell, and he went sadly away, for he was very rich. [23]Jesus watched him go, then turned around and said to his disciples, "It's almost impossible for the rich to get into the Kingdom of God!" [24]This amazed them. So Jesus said it again: "Dear children, how hard it is for those who trust in riches to enter the Kingdom of God. [25]It is easier for a camel to go through the eye of a needle than for a rich man to enter the Kingdom of God."

Mk 13:21. And then if anyone tells you, "This is the Messiah," or, "That one is," don't pay any attention. [22]For there will be many false Messiahs and false prophets who will do wonderful miracles that would deceive, if possible, even God's own children.

Lk 11:4. And forgive our sins—for we have forgiven those who sinned against us. And don't allow us to be tempted.

Lk 22:3. Then Satan entered into Judas Iscariot, who was one of the twelve disciples. [31]"Simon,

Simon, Satan has asked to have you, to sift you like wheat, [32]but I have pleaded in prayer for you that your faith should not completely fail. So when you have repented and turned to me again, strengthen and build up the faith of your brothers. [46]"Asleep!" he said. "Get up! Pray God that you will not fall when you are tempted." Mk 14:38.

Jn 16:1. I have told you these things so that you won't be staggered (by all that lies ahead). [2]For you will be excommunicated from the synagogues, and indeed the time is coming when those who kill you will think they are doing God a service.

Rom 6:12. Do not let sin control your puny body any longer; do not give in to its sinful desires. [13]Do not let any part of your bodies become tools of wickedness, to be used for sinning; but give yourselves completely to God—every part of you—for you are back from death and you want to be tools in the hands of God, to be used for his good purposes. [14]Sin need never again be your master, for now you are no longer tied to the law where sin enslaves you, but you are free under God's favor and mercy.

Rom 7:5. When your old nature was still active, sinful desires were at work within you, making you want to do whatever God said not to, and producing sinful deeds, the rotting fruit of death.

Rom 8:35. Who then can ever keep Christ's love from us? When we have trouble or calamity, when we are hunted down or destroyed, is it because he doesn't love us anymore? And if we are hungry, or penniless, or in danger, or threatened with death, has God deserted us? [36]No, for the Scriptures tell us that for his sake we must be ready to face death at every moment of the day—we are like sheep awaiting slaughter; [37]but despite all this, overwhelming victory is ours through Christ who loved us enough to die for us. [38]For I am convinced that nothing can ever separate us from his love. Death can't, and life can't. The angels won't, and all the powers of hell itself cannot keep God's love away. Our fears for today, our worries about tomorrow, [39]or where we are—high above the sky, or in the deepest ocean—nothing will ever be able to separate us from the love of God demonstrated by our Lord Jesus Christ when he died for us.

Rom 12:21. Don't let evil get the upper hand but conquer evil by doing good.

Rom 14:13. So don't criticize each other any more. Try instead to live in such a way that you will never make your brother stumble by letting him see you doing something he thinks is wrong. [15]And if your brother is bothered by what you eat, you are not acting in love if you go ahead and eat it. Don't let your eating ruin someone for whom Christ died. [21]The right thing to do is to quit eating meat or drinking wine or doing anything else that offends your brother or makes him sin.

1 Cor 7:5. So do not refuse these rights to each other. The only exception to this rule would be the agreement of both husband and wife to refrain from the rights of marriage for a limited time, so that they can give themselves more completely to prayer. Afterwards, they should come together again so that Satan won't be able to tempt them because of their lack of self-control.

1 Cor 8:9. But be careful not to use your freedom to eat it, lest you cause some Christian brother to sin whose conscience is weaker than yours. [10]You see, this is what may happen: Someone who thinks it is wrong to eat this food will see you eating at a temple restaurant, for you know there is no harm in it. Then he will become bold enough to do it too, although all the time he still feels it is wrong. [11]So because you "know it is all right to do it," you will be responsible for causing great spiritual damage to a brother with a tender conscience for whom Christ died. [12]And it is a sin against Christ to sin against your brother by encouraging him to do something he thinks is wrong. [13]So if eating meat offered to idols is going to make my brother sin, I'll not eat any of it as long as I live, because I don't want to do this to him.

1 Cor 10:13. But remember this—the wrong desires that come into your life aren't anything new and different. Many others have faced exactly the same problems before you. And no temptation is irresistible. You can trust God to keep the temptation from becoming so strong that you can't stand up against it, for he has promised this and will do what he says. He will show you how to escape temptation's power so that you can bear up patiently against it.

28. But if someone warns you that this meat has been offered to idols, then don't eat it for the sake of the man who told you, and of his conscience. [29]In this case *his* feeling about it is the important thing, not yours. But why, you may ask, must I be guided and limited by what someone else thinks? [30]If I can thank God for the food and enjoy it, why let someone spoil everything just because he thinks I am wrong? [31]Well, I'll tell you why. It is because you must do everything for the glory of God, even your eating and drinking. [32]So don't be a stumbling block to anyone, whether they are Jews or Gentiles or Christians.

2 Cor 2:11. A further reason for forgiveness is to keep from being outsmarted by Satan; for we know what he is trying to do.

2 Cor 11:3. But I am frightened, fearing that in some way you will be led away from your pure and simple devotion to our Lord, just as Eve was deceived by Satan in the Garden of Eden. [14]Yet I am not surprised! Satan can change himself into an angel of light, [15]so it is no wonder his servants can do it too, and seem like godly ministers. In the end they will get every bit of punishment their wicked deeds deserve.

2 Cor 12:7. I will say this: because these experiences I had were so tremendous, God was afraid I might be puffed up by them; so I was given a physical condition which has been a thorn in my flesh, a messenger from Satan to hurt and bother me, and prick my pride. Gal 4:14.

Gal 5:17. For we naturally love to do evil things that are just the opposite from the things that the

Holy Spirit tells us to do; and the good things we want to do when the Spirit has his way with us are just the opposite of our natural desires. These two forces within us are constantly fighting each other to win control over us, and our wishes are never free from their pressures.

Eph 4:27. For when you are angry you give a mighty foothold to the devil.

Eph 6:11. Put on all of God's armor so that you will be able to stand safe against all strategies and tricks of Satan. [13]So use every piece of God's armor to resist the enemy whenever he attacks, and when it is all over, you will still be standing up. [14]But to do this, you will need the strong belt of truth and the breastplate of God's approval. [15]Wear shoes that are able to speed you on as you preach the Good News of peace with God. [16]In every battle you will need faith as your shield to stop the fiery arrows aimed at you by Satan. [17]And you will need the helmet of salvation and the sword of the Spirit —which is the Word of God.

1 Thess 3:5. As I was saying, when I could bear the suspense no longer I sent Timothy to find out whether your faith was still strong. I was afraid that perhaps Satan had gotten the best of you and that all our work had been useless.

1 Tim 5:15. For I am afraid that some of them have already turned away from the church and been led astray by Satan.

1 Tim 6:9. But people who long to be rich soon begin to do all kinds of wrong things to get money, things that hurt them and make them evil-minded and finally send them to hell itself. [10]For the love of money is the first step toward all kinds of sin. Some people have even turned away from God because of their love for it, and as a result have pierced themselves with many sorrows.

2 Tim 3:13. In fact, evil men and false teachers will become worse and worse, deceiving many, they themselves having been deceived by Satan.

Heb 2:18. For since he himself has now been through suffering and temptation, he knows what it is like when we suffer and are tempted, and he is wonderfully able to help us.

Heb 4:15. This High Priest of ours understands our weaknesses, since he had the same temptations we do, though he never once gave way to them and sinned.

Heb 12:3. If you want to keep from becoming fainthearted and weary, think about his patience as sinful men did such terrible things to him. [4]After all, you have never yet struggled against sin and temptation until you sweat great drops of blood.

Jas 1:2. Dear brothers, is your life full of difficulties and temptations? Then be happy, [3]for when the way is rough, your patience has a chance to grow. [4]So let it grow, and don't try to squirm out of your problems. For when your patience is finally in full bloom, then you will be ready for anything, strong in character, full and complete. [12]Happy is the man who doesn't give in and do wrong when he is tempted, for afterwards he will get as his reward the crown of life that God has promised those who love him. [13]And remember, when someone wants to do wrong it is never God who is tempting him, for God never wants to do wrong and never tempts anyone else to do it. [14]Temptation is the pull of man's own evil thoughts and wishes. [15]These evil thoughts lead to evil actions and afterwards to the death penalty from God. [16]So don't be misled, dear brothers.

Jas 4:7. Resist the devil and he will flee from you.

1 Pet 1:6. So be truly glad! There is wonderful joy ahead, even though the going is rough for a while down here. [7]These trials are only to test your faith, to see whether or not it is strong and pure. It is being tested as fire tests gold and purifies it—and your faith is far more precious to God than mere gold; so if your faith remains strong after being tried in the test tube of fiery trials, it will bring you much praise and glory and honor on the day of his return.

1 Pet 4:12. Dear friends, don't be bewildered or surprised when you go through the fiery trials ahead, for this is no strange, unusual thing that is going to happen to you.

1 Pet 5:8. Be careful—watch out for attacks from Satan, your great enemy. He prowls around like a hungry, roaring lion, looking for some victim to tear apart. [9]Stand firm when he attacks. Trust the Lord; and remember that other Christians all around the world are going through these sufferings too.

2 Pet 2:9. So also the Lord can rescue you and me from the temptations that surround us, and continue to punish the ungodly until the day of final judgment comes.

18. They proudly boast about their sins and conquests, and, using lust as their bait, they lure back into sin those who have just escaped from such wicked living.

2 Pet 3:17. I am warning you ahead of time, dear brothers, so that you can watch out and not be carried away by the mistakes of these wicked men, lest you yourselves become mixed up too.

1 Jn 2:16. For all these worldly things, these evil desires—the craze for sex, the ambition to buy everything that appeals to you, and the pride that comes from wealth and importance—these are not from God. They are from this evil world itself. [26]These remarks of mine about the Antichrist are pointed at those who would dearly love to blindfold you and lead you astray.

1 Jn 4:4. Dear young friends, you belong to God and have already won your fight with those who are against Christ, because there is someone in your hearts who is stronger than any evil teacher in this wicked world.

Rev 3:10. Because you have patiently obeyed me despite the persecution, therefore I will protect you from the time of Great Tribulation and temptation, which will come upon the world to test everyone alive.

Rev 12:10. Then I heard a loud voice shouting across the heavens, "It has happened at last! God's salvation and the power and the rule, and the authority of his Christ are finally here; for the Accuser of our brothers has been thrown down from heaven onto earth—he accused them day and night before our God. [11]They defeated him by the blood of the Lamb, and by their testimony; for they did not love their lives but laid them down for him." [17]Then the furious Dragon set out to attack the rest of her children—all who were keeping God's commandments and confessing that they belong to Jesus. He stood waiting on an ocean beach.

See *Demons; Faith, Trial of; Satan.*

A TEST. Gen 22:1. Later on, God tested Abraham's (faith and obedience). "Abraham!" God called. "Yes, Lord?" he replied. *vs.* 2–14; Heb 11:17.

Deut 8:2. Do you remember how the Lord led you through the wilderness for all those forty years, humbling you and testing you to find out how you would respond, and whether or not you would really obey him? [5]So you should realize that, as a man punishes his son, the Lord punishes you to help you.

Deut 13:1. If there is a prophet among you, or one who claims to foretell the future by dreams, [2]and if his predictions come true but he says, "Come, let us worship the gods of the other nations," [3]don't listen to him. For the Lord is testing you to find out whether or not you really love him with all your heart and soul.

2 Chron 32:31. However, when ambassadors arrived from Babylon to find out about the miracle of his being healed, God left him to himself in order to test him and to see what he was really like.

Job 1:8. Then the Lord asked Satan, "Have you noticed my servant Job? He is the finest man in all the earth—a good man who fears God and will have nothing to do with evil." [9]"Why shouldn't he, when you pay him so well?" Satan scoffed. [10]"You have always protected him and his home and his property from all harm. You have prospered everything he does—look how rich he is! No wonder he 'worships' you! [11]But just take away his wealth, and you'll see him curse you to your face!" [12, 13]And the Lord replied to Satan, "You may do anything you like with his wealth, but don't harm him physically." So Satan went away; and sure enough, not long afterwards when Job's sons and daughters were dining at the oldest brother's house, tragedy struck. [14, 15]A messenger rushed to Job's home with this news: "Your oxen were plowing, with the donkeys feeding beside them, when the Sabeans raided us, drove away the animals and killed all the farmhands except me. I am the only one left." [16]While this messenger was still speaking, another arrived with more bad news: "The fire of God has fallen from heaven and burned up your sheep and all the herdsmen, and I alone have escaped to tell you." [17]Before this man finished, still another messenger rushed in: "Three bands of Chaldeans have driven off your camels and killed your servants, and I alone have escaped to tell you." [18]As he was still speaking, another arrived to say, "Your sons and daughters were feasting in their oldest brother's home, [19]when suddenly a mighty wind swept in from the desert, and engulfed the house so that the roof fell in on them and all are dead; and I alone escaped to tell you." [20]Then Job stood up and tore his robe in grief and fell down upon the ground before God. [21]"I came naked from my mother's womb," he said, "and I shall have nothing when I die. The Lord gave me everything I had, and they were his to take away. Blessed be the name of the Lord." [22]In all of this, Job did not sin or revile God.

Job 2:3. "Well, have you noticed my servant Job?" the Lord asked. "He is the finest man in all the earth—a good man who fears God and turns away from all evil. And he has kept his faith in me despite the fact that you persuaded me to let you harm him without any cause." [4, 5]"Skin for skin," Satan replied. "A man will give anything to save his life. Touch his body with sickness and he will curse you to your face!" [6]"Do with him as you please," the Lord replied; "only spare his life." [7]So Satan went out from the presence of the Lord and struck Job with a terrible case of boils from head to foot. [8]Then Job took a broken piece of pottery to scrape himself, and sat among the ashes. [9]His wife said to him, "Are you still trying to be godly when God has done all this to you? Curse him and die." [10]But he replied, "You talk like some heathen woman. What? Shall we receive only pleasant things from the hand of God and never anything unpleasant?" So in all this Job said nothing wrong.

Ps 66:10. You have purified us with fire, O Lord, like silver in a crucible. [11]You captured us in your net and laid great burdens on our backs. [12]You sent troops to ride across our broken bodies. We went through fire and flood. But in the end, you brought us into wealth and great abundance. [13]Now I have come to your Temple with burnt-offerings to pay my vows.

Dan 12:10. Many shall be purified by great trials and persecutions. But the wicked shall continue in their wickedness, and none of them will understand. Only those who are willing to learn will know what it means.

Zech 13:9. I will bring the third that remain through the fire and make them pure, as gold and silver are refined and purified by fire.

Jas 1:2. Dear brothers, is your life full of difficulties and temptations? Then be happy, [3]for when the way is rough, your patience has a chance to grow. [12]Happy is the man who doesn't give in and do wrong when he is tempted, for afterwards he will get as his reward the crown of life that God has promised those who love him.

1 Pet 1:6. So be truly glad! There is wonderful joy ahead, even though the going is rough for a while down here. [7]These trials are only to test your faith, to see whether or not it is strong and pure. It is being tested as fire tests gold and purifies it—and your faith is far more precious to God than mere gold; so if your faith remains strong after being tried in the test tube of fiery trials, it will bring you much praise and glory and honor on the day of his return.

See *Affliction, Design of; Faith, Trial of.*

LEADING INTO. Prayer against being led into, Mt 6:13; Lk 22:40.

Instances of. Abraham leads Pharaoh, Gen 12:18, 19; Abimelech, Gen 20:9, 10. Balak tempts Balaam, Num 22; 23; 24. The old prophet of Bethel, the prophet of Judah, 1 Kgs 13:15–19. Gideon leads Israel into sin, Judg 8:27. Jeroboam leads Israel into, 1 Kgs 15:30.

See *Temptation, Resistance to, Yielding to,* below.

RESISTANCE TO. Gen 39:7. One day at about this time Potiphar's wife began making eyes at Joseph, and suggested that he come and sleep with her. [8]Joseph refused. "Look," he told her, "my master trusts me with everything in the entire household; [9]he himself has no more authority here than I have! He has held back nothing from me except you yourself because you are his wife. How can I do such a wicked thing as this? It would be a great sin against God." [10]But she kept on with her suggestions day after day, even though he refused to listen, and kept out of her way as much as possible.

Neh 4:9. But we prayed to our God and guarded the city day and night to protect ourselves.

Job 31:1. I made a covenant with my eyes not to look with lust upon a girl. [5]If I have lied and deceived— [6]but God knows that I am innocent— [7, 8]or if I have stepped off God's pathway, or if my heart has lusted for what my eyes have seen, or if I am guilty of any other sin, then let someone else reap the crops I have sown and let all that I have planted be rooted out. [9]Or if I have longed for another man's wife, [10]then may I die, and may my wife be in another man's home, and someone else become her husband. [11]For lust is a shameful sin, a crime that should be punished. [12]It is a devastating fire that destroys to hell, and would root out all I have planted. [13]If I have been unfair to my servants, [14]how could I face God! What could I say when he questioned me about it? [15]For God made me, and made my servant too. He created us both. [16]If I have hurt the poor or caused widows to weep, [17]or refused food to hungry orphans. [19, 20]or if I have seen anyone freezing and not given him clothing, or fleece from my sheep to keep him warm, [21]or if I have taken advantage of an orphan because I thought I could get away with it— [22]if I have done any of these things, then let my arm be torn from its socket! Let my shoulder be wrenched out of place! [23]Rather that than face the judgment sent by God; that I dread more than anything else. For if the majesty of God opposes me, what hope is there? [24]If I have put my trust in money, [25]if my happiness depends on wealth, [26]or if I have looked at the sun shining in the skies, or the moon walking down her silver pathway, [27]and my heart has been secretly enticed, and I have worshiped them by kissing my hand to them, [28]this, too, must be punished by the judges. For if I had done such things, it would mean that I denied the God of heaven. [29]If I have rejoiced at harm to an enemy— [30](but actually I have never cursed anyone nor asked for revenge)— [31]or if any of my servants have ever gone hungry— [32](actually I have never turned away even a stranger but have opened my doors to all) — [33]or if, like Adam, I have tried to hide my sins, [34]fearing the crowd and its contempt, so that I refused to acknowledge my sin and do not go out of my way to help others. [38, 39]Or if my land accuses me because I stole the fruit it bears, or if I have murdered its owners to get their land for myself, [40]then let thistles grow on that land instead of wheat, and weeds instead of barley.

Ps 17:4. I have followed your commands and have not gone along with cruel and evil men.

Ps 73:2. But as for me, I came *so* close to the edge of the cliff! My feet were slipping and I was almost gone. [3]For I was envious of the prosperity of the proud and wicked. [4]Yes, all through life their road is smooth! They grow sleek and fat. [5]They aren't always in trouble and plagued with problems like everyone else, [6]so their pride sparkled like a jeweled necklace, and their clothing is woven of cruelty! [7]These fat cats have everything their hearts could ever wish for! [8]They scoff at God and threaten his people. How proudly they speak! [9]They boast against the very heavens, and their words strut through the earth. [10]And so God's people are dismayed and confused, and drink it all in. [11]"Does God realize what is going on?" they ask. [12]"Look at these men of arrogance; they never have to lift a finger—theirs is a life of ease; and all the time their riches multiply." [13]Have I been wasting my time? Why take the trouble to be pure? [14]All I get out of it is trouble and woe—every day and all day long! [15]If I had really said that, I would have been a traitor to your people. [16]Yet it is so hard to explain it—this prosperity of those who hate the Lord. [17]Then one day I went into God's sanctuary to meditate, and thought about the future of these evil men. [18]What a slippery path they are on—suddenly God will send them sliding over the edge of the cliff and down to their destruction: [19]an instant end to all their happiness, an eternity of terror. [20]Their present life is only a dream! They will awaken to the truth as one awakens from a dream of things that never really were! [21]When I saw this, what turmoil filled my heart! [22]I saw myself so stupid and so ignorant; I must seem like an animal to you, O God. [23]But even so, you love me! You are holding my right hand! [24]You will keep on guiding me all my life with your wisdom and counsel; and afterwards receive me into the glories of heaven! [25]Whom have I in heaven but you? And I desire no one on earth as much as you! [26]My health fails; my spirits droop, yet God remains! He is the strength of my heart; he is mine forever!

Ps 94:17. I would have died unless the Lord had helped me. [18]I screamed. "I'm slipping, Lord!" and he was kind and saved me.

Ps 119:101. I have refused to walk the paths of evil for I will remain obedient to your Word. [110]The wicked have set their traps for me along your path, but I will not turn aside.

Amos 4:12. Therefore I will bring upon you all these further evils I have spoken of. Prepare to meet your God in judgment, Israel.

Mt 4:1. Then Jesus was led out into the wilderness by the Holy Spirit, to be tempted there by Satan. [2]For forty days and forty nights he ate nothing and became very hungry. [3]Then Satan tempted him to get food by changing stones into loaves of bread. "It will prove you are the Son of God," he said. [4]But Jesus told him, "No! For the Scriptures tell us that bread won't feed men's souls: obedience to every word of God is what we need." [5]Then Satan took him to Jerusalem to the roof of the Temple. [6]"Jump off," he said, "and prove you are the Son of God; for the Scriptures declare, 'God will send his angels to keep you from harm,' . . . they will prevent you from smashing on the rocks below." [7]Jesus retorted, "It also says not to put the Lord your God to a foolish test!" [8]Next Satan took him to the peak of a very high mountain and showed him the nations of the world and all their glory. [9]"I'll give it all to you," he said, "if you will only kneel and worship me." [10]"Get out of here, Satan," Jesus told him. "The Scriptures say, 'Worship only the Lord God. Obey only him.' " [11]Then Satan went away, and angels came and cared for Jesus. Luke 4:1–13.

Mt 24:42. So be prepared, for you don't know what day your Lord is coming. [43]Just as a man can prevent trouble from thieves by keeping watch for them, [44]so you can avoid trouble by always being ready for my unannounced return.

Mt 25:13. So stay awake and be prepared, for you do not know the date or moment of my return.

Mt 26:38. Then he told them, "My soul is crushed with horror and sadness to the point of death . . . stay here . . . stay awake with me." [39]He went forward a little, and fell face downward on the ground, and prayed, "My Father! If it is possible, let this cup be taken away from me. But I want your will, not mine." [40]Then he returned to the three disciples and found them asleep. "Peter," he called, "couldn't you even stay awake with me one hour? [41]Keep alert and pray. Otherwise temptation will overpower you. For the spirit indeed is willing, but how weak the body is!" [42]Again he left them and prayed, "My Father! If this cup cannot go away until I drink it all, your will be done."

Mk 13:33. And since you don't know when it will happen, stay alert. Be on the watch (for my return). [34]My coming can be compared with that of a man who went on a trip to another country. He laid out his employees' work for them to do while he was gone, and told the gatekeeper to watch for his return. [35-37]Keep a sharp lookout! For you do not know when I will come, at evening, at midnight, early dawn or late daybreak. Don't let me find you sleeping. *Watch for my return!* This is my message to you and to everyone else.

Mk 14:37. Then he returned to the three disciples and found them asleep. "Simon!" he said. "Asleep? Couldn't you watch with me even one hour? [38]Watch with me and pray lest the Tempter overpower you. For though the spirit is willing enough, the body is weak."

Lk 12:35. Be prepared—all dressed and ready—[36]for your Lord's return from the wedding feast. Then you will be ready to open the door and let him in the moment he arrives and knocks. [37]There will be great joy for those who are ready and waiting for his return. He himself will seat them and put on a waiter's uniform and serve them as they sit and eat! [38]He may come at nine o'clock at night —or even at midnight. But whenever he comes there will be joy for his servants who are ready!

Lk 21:33. And though all heaven and earth shall pass away, yet my words remain forever true. [34, 35]Watch out! Don't let my sudden coming catch you unawares; don't let me find you living in careless ease, carousing and drinking, and occupied with the problems of this life, like all the rest of the world. [36]Keep a constant watch. And pray that if possible you may arrive in my presence without having to experience these horrors.

1 Cor 16:13. Keep your eyes open for spiritual danger; stand true to the Lord; act like men; be strong.

Jas 4:7. So give yourselves humbly to God. Resist the devil and he will flee from you.

1 Pet 4:7. The end of the world is coming soon. Therefore be earnest, thoughtful men of prayer.

1 Pet 5:8. Be careful—watch out for attacks from Satan, your great enemy. He prowls around like a hungry, roaring lion, looking for some victim to tear apart. [9]Stand firm when he attacks. Trust the Lord; and remember that other Christians all around the world are going through these sufferings too.

Rev 3:2. Now wake up! Strengthen what little remains—for even what is left is at the point of death. Your deeds are far from right in the sight of God. [3]Go back to what you heard and believed at first; hold to it firmly and turn to me again. Unless you do, I will come suddenly upon you, unexpected as a thief, and punish you.

Instances of. Joseph resists the temptation to commit adultery. Gen 39:7–12. Balaam, in refusing to curse the children of Israel, Num 22:7–18; 24:12, 13. The prophet of Judah, 1 Kgs 13:7–9. Micaiah, 1 Kgs 22:13–28. Job, Job 1:6–21; 2:4–10. Rechabites, Jer 35. David, to injure Saul, 1 Sam 26:5–25. The people of Jerusalem, not to trust the Lord, 2 Kgs 18:30–36. Jesus, Mt 4:1–11.

YIELDING TO.

Instances of. Adam and Eve, Gen 3:1–19. Sarah, to lie, Gen 12:11–13; 18:13–15; 20:13. Isaac, to lie, Gen 26:7. Jacob, to defraud Esau, Gen 27:6–13. Balaam, Num 22:15–23; 2 Pet 2:15. Achan, Josh 7:21. David, to commit adultery, 2 Sam 11:2–5; to take a census, 1 Chron 21. Solomon, to become an idolater through the influences of his wives, 1 Kgs 11:4; Neh 13:26. The prophet of Judah, 1 Kgs 13:11–19. Hezekiah, 2 Kgs 20:12–20; Isa 39:1–4, 6, 7; Peter, Mt 26:69–74; Mk 14:66–71; Lk 22:55–60.

TEN Used for an indefinite number, Lev 26:26; Num 14:22; Zech 8:23.

TEN COMMANDMENTS Written by God, Ex 24:12; 31:18; 32:16; Deut 5:22; 9:10; Hos 8:12. Divine authority of, Ex 20:1, 2; 34:27, 28; Deut 5:4–22. Called *Covenant,* Ex 34:28; *Contract,* Deut 9:9–11.

See *Commandments.*

Ex 20:1. Then God issued this edict: [2]"I am Jehovah your God who liberated you from your slavery in Egypt. [3]You may worship no other god than me. [4]You shall not make yourselves any idols: any images resembling animals, birds, or fish. [5]You must never bow to an image or worship it in any way; for I, the Lord your God, am very possessive. I will not share your affection with any other god! And when I punish people for their sins, the punishment continues upon the children, grandchildren, and great-grandchildren of those who hate me; [6]but I lavish my love upon thousands of those who love me and obey my commandments. [7]You shall not use the name of Jehovah your God irreverently, nor use it to swear to a falsehood. You will not escape punishment if you do. [8]Remember to observe the Sabbath as a holy day. [9]Six days a week are for your daily duties and your regular work, [10]but the seventh day is a day of Sabbath rest before the Lord your God. On that day you are to do no work of any kind, nor shall your son, daughter, or slaves—whether men or women—or your cattle or your house guests. [11]For in six days the Lord made the heaven, earth, and sea, and everything in them, and rested the seventh day; so he blessed the Sabbath day and set it aside for rest. [12]Honor your father and mother, that you may have a long, good life in the land the Lord your God will give you. [13]You must not murder. [14]You must not commit adultery. [15]You must not steal. [16]You must not lie. [17]You must not be envious of your neighbor's house, or want to sleep with his wife, or want to own his slaves, oxen, donkeys, or anything else he has."

Deut 5:7. Never worship any god but me. [8]Never make idols; don't worship images, whether of birds, animals, or fish. [9, 10]You shall not bow down to any images nor worship them in any way, for I am the Lord your God. I am a jealous God, and I will bring the curse of a father's sins upon even the third and fourth generation of the children of those who hate me; but I will show kindness to a thousand generations of those who love me and keep my commandments. You must never use my name to make a vow you don't intend to keep. I will not overlook that. [12]Keep the Sabbath day holy. This is my command. [13]Work the other six days, [14]but the seventh day is the Sabbath of the Lord your God; no work shall be done that day by you or by any of your household—your sons, daughters, servants, oxen, donkeys, or cattle; even foreigners living among you must obey this law. Everybody must rest as you do. [15]Why should you keep the Sabbath? It is because you were slaves in Egypt, and the Lord your God brought you out with a great display of miracles. [16]Honor your father and mother (remember, this is a commandment of the Lord your God); if you do so, you shall have a long, prosperous life in the land he is giving you. [17]You must not murder. [18]You must not commit adultery. [19]You must not steal. [20]You must not tell lies. [21]You must not burn with desire for another man's wife, nor envy him for his home, land, servants, oxen, donkeys, nor anything else he owns.

Mt 19:18. "Which ones?" the man asked. And Jesus replied, "Don't kill, don't commit adultery, don't steal, don't lie, [19]honor your father and mother, and love your neighbor as yourself!"

Mt 22:34, 35. When they [Pharisees] heard that he had routed the Sadducees with his reply, they thought up a fresh question of their own to ask him. One of them, a lawyer, spoke up: [36]"Sir, which is the most important command in the laws of Moses?" [37]Jesus replied, " 'Love the Lord your God with all your heart, soul, and mind.' [38, 39]This is the first and greatest commandment. The second most important is similar: 'Love your neighbor as much as you love yourself.' [40]All the other commandments and all the demands of the prophets stem from these two laws and are fulfilled if you obey them. Keep only these and you will find that you are obeying all the others."

Lk 10:25. One day an expert on Moses' laws came to test Jesus' orthodoxy by asking him this question: "Teacher, what does a man need to do to live forever in heaven?" [26]Jesus replied, "What does Moses' law say about it?" [27]"It says," he replied, "that you must love the Lord your God with all your heart, and with all your soul, and with all your strength, and with all your mind. And you must love your neighbor just as much as you love yourself." [28]"Right!" Jesus told him. "Do this and you shall live!"

Rom 13:8. Pay all your debts except the debt of love for others—never finish paying that! For if you love them, you will be obeying all of God's laws, fulfilling all his requirements. [9]If you love your neighbor as much as you love yourself you will not want to harm or cheat him, or kill him or steal from him. And you won't sin with his wife or want what is his, or do anything else the Ten Commandments say is wrong. All ten are wrapped up in this one, to love your neighbor as you love yourself. [10]Love does no wrong to anyone. That's why it fully satisfies all of God's requirements. It is the only law you need.

Gal 3:10. Yes, and those who depend on the Jewish laws to save them are under God's curse, for the Scriptures point out very clearly, "Cursed is everyone who at any time breaks a single one of these laws that are written in God's Book of the Law." [19]Well then, why were these laws given? They were added after the promise was given, to show men how guilty they are of breaking God's laws. But this system of law was to last only until the coming of Christ, the Child to whom God's promise was made. (And there is this further difference. God gave his laws to angels to give to Moses, who then gave them to the people; [20]but when God gave his promise to Abraham, he did it by himself alone, without angels or Moses as go-betweens.) [21]If we could be saved by his laws, then God would not have had to give us a different way to get out of the grip of sin—for the Scriptures insist we are all its prisoners. [24]The Jewish laws were our teacher and guide until Christ came to give us right standing with God through our faith.

1 Tim 1:8. Those laws are good when used as God intended. [9]But they were not made for us, whom God has saved; they are for sinners who hate God, have rebellious hearts, curse and swear, attack their fathers and mothers and murder.

Jas 2:10. And the person who keeps every law of God, but makes one little slip, is just as guilty as the person who has broken every law there is. [11]For the God who said you must not marry a woman who already has a husband, also said you must not murder, so even though you have not broken the marriage laws by committing adultery, but have murdered someone, you have entirely broken God's laws and stand utterly guilty before him.

TENANTS Evicted, Mt 21:41; Mk 12:9; Lk 20:16.

TENT Used for homes, Gen 4:20; by Noah, Gen 9:20, 21; by Abraham, Gen 12:8; 13:18; 18:1; by Lot, Gen 13:5; by Jacob, Gen 31:33; by Moses, Ex 18:7; by Arabians, Isa 13:20; by shepherds, Isa 38:12; Jer 6:3. Women had tents apart from men, Gen 24:67; 31:33. Used for cattle, 2 Chron 14:15. Shakeable, Isa 24:20. Manufacture of, Acts 18:2, 3. Used as a place of worship, see *Tabernacle.*

TERAH 1. Father of Abraham, Gen 11:24–32; Lk 3:34. Was an idolater, Josh 24:2.

2. A camping place of the Israelites, Num 33:15–37.

TERAPHIM Household idols. Used by Laban, stolen by Rachel, Gen 31:17–20, 30–35; by Micah, stolen by the Danites, Judg 17:4, 5; 18:14, 17–20. Condemned and disposed of by Jacob, Gen 35:2–4, with Gen 31:35–39. Destroyed by Josiah, see *Idol.*

TEREBINTH A tree, Hos 4:13.

TERESH A Persian eunuch. Plotted against Ahasuerus, Esther 2:21–23; 6:1, 2.

TERTIUS Paul's secretary in writing the book of Romans, Rom 16:22.

TERTULLUS Accuser of Paul before Felix, Acts 24:1, 2, 9.

TESTAMENT A will, Heb 9:16–18. The new covenant, Mt 26:28; Mk 14:24; Lk 22:20; 1 Cor 11:25.

See *Covenant.*

TESTIMONY LEGAL. See *Evidence; Witness.*

ARK OF. See *Ark.*

RELIGIOUS. 1 Chron 16:8. "Oh, give thanks to the Lord and pray to him," they sang. "Tell the peoples of the world about his mighty doings. [9]Sing to him; yes, sing his praises and tell of his marvelous works."

Ps 9:11. Oh, sing out your praises to the God who lives in Jerusalem. Tell the world about his unforgettable deeds.

Ps 18:49. For this, O Lord, I will praise you among the nations.

Ps 26:6. I wash my hands to prove my innocence and come before your altar, [7]singing a song of thanksgiving and telling about your miracles.

Ps 107:2. Has the Lord redeemed you? Then speak out! Tell others he has saved you from your enemies.

Ps 119:27. Make me understand what you want; for then I shall see your miracles. [172]I will sing about their wonder, for each of them is just.

Ps 145:11. They will talk together about the glory of your kingdom and mention examples of your power. [12]They will tell about your miracles and about the majesty and glory of your reign.

Isa 12:4. In that wonderful day you will say, "Thank the Lord! Praise his name! Tell the world about his wondrous love. How mighty he is!" [5]Sing to the Lord, for he has done wonderful things. Make known his praise around the world. [6]Let all the people of Jerusalem shout his praise with joy. For great and mighty is the Holy One of Israel, who lives among you.

Isa 32:4. Even the hotheads among them will be full of sense and understanding, and those who stammer in uncertainty will speak out plainly.

Isa 43:10. But I have witnesses, O Israel, says the Lord! You are my witnesses and my servants, chosen to know and to believe me and to understand that I alone am God. There is no other God; there never was and never will be. chapter 44:8.

Isa 45:24. "In Jehovah is all my righteousness and strength," the people shall declare. And all who were angry with him shall come to him and be ashamed.

Jer 51:10. The Lord has vindicated us. Come, let us declare in Jerusalem all the Lord our God has done.

Mk 4:21. Then he asked them, "When someone lights a lamp, does he put a box over it to shut out the light? Of course not! The light couldn't be seen or used. A lamp is placed on a stand to shine and be useful." Mt 5:15, 16; Lk 8:16.

Mk 5:16. Those who saw what happened were telling everyone about it. [19]But Jesus said no. "Go home to your friends," he told him, "and tell them what wonderful things God has done for you; and how merciful he has been." [20]So the man started off to visit the Ten Towns of that region and began to tell everyone about the great things Jesus had done for him; and they were awestruck by his story.

Lk 8:38. The man who had been demon-possessed begged to go too, but Jesus said no. [39]"Go back to your family," he told him, "and tell them what a wonderful thing God has done for you." So he went all through the city telling everyone about Jesus' mighty miracle.

Lk 12:8. And I assure you of this: I, the Messiah, will publicly honor you in the presence of God's angels if you publicly acknowledge me here on earth as your Friend. [9]But I will deny before the angels those who deny me here among men. Mt 10: 32.

Lk 24:48. You have seen these prophecies come true.

Jn 4:28, 29. Then the woman left her waterpot beside the well and went back to the village and told everyone, "Come and meet a man who told me everything I ever did! Can this be the Messiah?" [30]So the people came streaming from the village to see him. [39]Many from the Samaritan village believed he was the Messiah because of the woman's report: "He told me everything I ever did!" [40, 41]When they came out to see him at the well, they begged him to stay at their village; and he did, for two days, long enough for many of them to believe in him after hearing him. [42]Then they said to the woman, "Now we believe because we have heard him ourselves, not just because of what you told us. He is indeed the Savior of the world."

Jn 15:27. And you also must tell everyone about me, because you have been with me from the beginning.

Acts 1:8. But when the Holy Spirit has come upon you, you will receive power to testify about me with great effect, to the people in Jerusalem, throughout Judea, in Samaria, and to the ends of the earth, about my death and resurrection. [22]Let us select someone who has been with us constantly from our first association with the Lord—from the time he was baptized by John until the day he was taken from us into heaven.

Rom 10:9. For if you tell others with your own mouth that Jesus Christ is your Lord, and believe in your own heart that God has raised him from the dead, you will be saved. [10]For it is by believing in his heart that a man becomes right with God; and with his mouth he tells others of his faith, confirming his salvation.

1 Cor 1:5. He has enriched your whole life. He has helped you speak out for him and has given you a full understanding of the truth; [6]what I told you Christ could do for you has happened!

1 Cor 12:3. No one speaking by the power of the Spirit of God can curse Jesus, and no one can say, "Jesus is Lord," and really mean it, unless the Holy Spirit is helping him.

1 Cor 13:1. If I had the gift of being able to speak in other languages without learning them, and could speak in every language there is in all of heaven and earth, but didn't love others, I would only be making noise.

Eph 5:19. Talk with each other much about the Lord, quoting psalms and hymns and singing sacred songs, making music in your hearts to the Lord.

Phil 3:7. But all these things that I once thought very worthwhile—now I've thrown them all away so that I can put my trust and hope in Christ alone. [8]Yes, everything else is worthless when compared with the priceless gain of knowing Christ Jesus my Lord. I have put aside all else, counting it worth less than nothing, in order that I can have Christ, [9]and become one with him, no longer counting on being saved by being good enough or by obeying God's laws, but by trusting Christ to save me; for God's way of making us right with himself depends on faith—counting on Christ alone. [10]Now I have given up everything else—I have found it to be the only way to really know Christ and to experience the mighty power that brought him back to life again, and to find out what it means to suffer and to die with him. [11]So, whatever it takes, I will be one who lives in the fresh newness of life of those who are alive from the dead. [12]I don't mean to say I am perfect. I haven't learned all I should even yet, but I keep working toward that day when I will finally be all that Christ saved me for and wants me to be. [13]No, dear brothers, I am still not all I should be but I am bringing all my energies to bear on this one thing: Forgetting the past and looking forward to what lies ahead, [14]I strain to reach the end of the race and receive the prize for which God is calling us up to heaven because of what Christ Jesus did for us.

1 Tim 6:12. Fight on for God. Hold tightly to the eternal life which God has given you, and which you have confessed with such a ringing confession before many witnesses. [13]I command you before God who gives life to all, and before Christ Jesus who gave a fearless testimony before Pontius Pilate.

2 Tim 1:8. If you will stir up this inner power, you will never be afraid to tell others about our Lord, or to let them know that I am your friend even though I am here in jail for Christ's sake. You will be ready to suffer with me for the Lord, for he will give you strength in suffering.

Heb 2:3. What makes us think that we can escape if we are indifferent to this great salvation announced by the Lord Jesus himself, and passed on to us by those who heard him speak? [12]For he says in the book of Psalms, "I will talk to my brothers about God my Father, and together we will sing his praises."

1 Pet 3:15. Quietly trust yourself to Christ your Lord and if anybody asks why you believe as you do, be ready to tell him, and do it in a gentle and respectful way.

1 Pet 5:1. And now, a word to you elders of the church. I, too, am an elder; with my own eyes I saw Christ dying on the cross; and I, too, will share his glory and his honor when he returns.

Rev 12:11. They defeated him by the blood of the Lamb, and by their testimony; for they did not love their lives but laid them down for him.

See *Confession.*

Religious, Exemplified. Job 19:25. But as for me, I know that my Redeemer lives, and that he will stand upon the earth at last. [26]And I know that after this body has decayed, this body shall see God! [27]Then he will be on *my* side! Yes, I shall see him, not as a stranger, but as a friend! What a glorious hope!

Ps 16:5. The Lord himself is my inheritance, my prize. He is my food and drink, my highest joy! He guards all that is mine. [6]He sees that I am given pleasant brooks and meadows as my share! What a wonderful inheritance! [7]I will bless the Lord who counsels me; he gives me wisdom in the night. He tells me what to do. [8]I am always thinking of the Lord; and because he is so near, I never need to stumble or to fall. [9]Heart, body, and soul are filled with joy.

Ps 18:2. The Lord is my fort where I can enter and be safe; no one can follow me in and slay me. He is a rugged mountain where I hide; he is my Savior, a rock where none can reach me, and a tower of safety. He is my shield. He is like the strong horn of a mighty fighting bull. [3]All I need to do is cry to him—oh, praise the Lord—and I am saved from all my enemies!

35. You have given me your salvation as my shield. Your right hand, O Lord, supports me; your gentleness has made me great. [36]You have made wide steps beneath my feet so that I need never slip.

Ps 22:22. I will praise you to all my brothers; I will stand up before the congregation and testify of the wonderful things you have done.

Ps 23:1. Because the Lord is my Shepherd, I have everything I need! [2, 3]He lets me rest in the meadow grass and leads me beside the quiet streams. He restores my failing health. He helps me do what honors him the most. [4]Even when walking through the dark valley of death I will not be afraid, for you are close beside me, guarding, guiding all the way. [5]You provide delicious food for me in the presence of my enemies. You have welcomed me as your guest; blessings overflow! [6]Your goodness and unfailing kindness shall be with me all of my life, and afterwards I will live with you forever in your home.

Ps 26:12. I publicly praise the Lord for keeping me from slipping and falling.

Ps 27:1. The Lord is my light and my salvation; whom shall I fear? [2]When evil men come to destroy me, they will stumble and fall! [3]Yes, though a mighty army marches against me, my heart shall know no fear! I am confident that God will save me. [4]The one thing I want from God, the thing I seek most of all, is the privilege of meditating in his Temple, living in his presence every day of my life, delighting in his incomparable perfections and glory. [5]There I'll be when troubles come. He will hide me. He will set me on a high rock [6]out of reach of all my enemies. Then I will bring him sacrifices and sing his praises with much joy. [13]I am expecting the Lord to rescue me again, so that once again I will see his goodness to me here in the land of the living.

Ps 28:6. Oh, praise the Lord, for he has listened to my pleadings! [7]He is my strength, my shield from every danger. I trusted in him, and he helped me. Joy rises in my heart until I burst out in songs of praise to him. [8]The Lord protects his people and gives victory to his anointed king.

Ps 30:1. I will praise you, Lord, for you have saved me from my enemies. You refuse to let them triumph over me. [2]O Lord my God, I pleaded with you, and you gave me my health again. [3]You brought me back from the brink of the grave, from death itself, and here I am alive! [4]Oh, sing to him you saints of his; give thanks to his holy name. [5]His anger lasts a moment; his favor lasts for life! Weeping may go on all night, but in the morning there is joy. [6]In my prosperity I said, "This is forever; nothing can stop me now! The Lord has shown me his favor. He has made me steady as a mountain."

Ps 34:1. I will praise the Lord no matter what happens. I will constantly speak of his glories and grace. [2]I will boast of all his kindness to me. Let all who are discouraged take heart. [3]Let us praise the Lord together, and exalt his name. [4]For I cried to him and he answered me! He freed me from all my fears. [8]Oh, put God to the test and see how kind he is! See for yourself the way his mercies shower down on all who trust in him. [9]If you belong to the Lord, reverence him; for everyone who does this has everything he needs.

Ps 35:28. And I will tell everyone how great and good you are; I will praise you all day long.

Ps 40:1. I waited patiently for God to help me; then he listened and heard my cry. [2]He lifted me out of the pit of despair, out from the bog and the mire, and set my feet on a hard, firm path and steadied me as I walked along. [3]He has given me a new song to sing, of praises to our God. Now many will hear of the glorious things he did for me, and stand in awe before the Lord, and put their trust in him. [9]I have told everyone the Good News that you forgive men's sins. I have not been timid about it, as you well know, O Lord.

Psa 54:7. God has rescued me from all my trouble.

Ps 57:7. O God, my heart is quiet and confident. No wonder I can sing your praises! [8]Rouse yourself, my soul! Arise, O harp and lyre! Let us greet the dawn with song! [9]I will thank you publicly throughout the land. I will sing your praises among the nations.

Ps 62:1. I stand silently before the Lord, waiting for him to rescue me. For salvation comes from him alone. [2]Yes, he alone is my Rock, my rescuer, defense and fortress. Why then should I be tense with fear when troubles come?

Ps 66:16. Come and hear, all of you who reverence the Lord, and I will tell you what he did for me: [17]For I cried to him for help, with praises ready on my tongue. [18]He would not have listened if I had not confessed my sins. [19]But he listened! He heard my prayer! He paid attention to it! [20]Blessed be God who didn't turn away when I was praying, and didn't refuse me his kindness and love.

Ps 71:15. I cannot count the times when you have faithfully rescued me from danger. I will tell everyone how good you are, and of your constant daily care. [16]I walk in the strength of the Lord God. I tell everyone that you alone are just and good. [17]O God, you have helped me from my earliest childhood—and I have constantly testified to others of the wonderful things you do. [18]And now that I am old and gray, don't forsake me. Give me time to tell this new generation (and their children too) about all your mighty miracles. [24]I will talk to others all day long about your justice and your goodness. For all who tried to hurt me have been disgraced and dishonored.

Ps 73:23. But even so, you love me! You are holding my right hand! [24]You will keep on guiding me all my life with your wisdom and counsel; and afterwards receive me into the glories of heaven! [25]Whom have I in heaven but you? And I desire no one on earth as much as you! [26]My health fails; my spirits droop, yet God remains! He is the strength of my heart; he is mine forever! [28]But as for me, I get as close to him as I can! I have chosen him and I will tell everyone about the wonderful ways he rescues me.

Ps 77:12. Those wonderful deeds are constantly in my thoughts. I cannot stop thinking about them.

Ps 89:1. Forever and ever I will sing about the tender kindness of the Lord! Young and old shall hear about your blessings.

Ps 91:2. This I declare, that he alone is my refuge, my place of safety; he is my God, and I am trusting him. [3]For he rescues you from every trap, and protects you from the fatal plague. [4]He will shield you with his wings! They will shelter you. His faithful promises are your armor. [5]Now you don't need to be afraid of the dark any more, nor fear the dangers of the day; [6]nor dread the plagues of darkness, nor disasters in the morning. [7]Though a thousand fall at my side, though ten thousand are dying around me, the evil will not touch me. [8]I will see how the wicked are punished but I will not share it. [9]For Jehovah is my refuge! I choose the God above all gods to shelter me. [10]How then can evil overtake me or any plague come near? [11]For he orders his angels to protect you wherever you go. [12]They will steady you with their hands to keep you from stumbling against the rocks on the trail. [13]You can safely meet a lion or step on poisonous snakes, yes, even trample them beneath your feet!

Ps 116:1. I love the Lord because he hears my prayers and answers them. [2]Because he bends down and listens, I will pray as long as I breathe! [3]Death stared me in the face—I was frightened and sad. [4]Then I cried, "Lord, save me!" [5]How kind he is! How good he is! So merciful, this God of ours! [6]The Lord protects the simple and the childlike; I was facing death and then he saved me. [7]Now I can relax. For the Lord has done this wonderful miracle for me. [8]He has saved me from death, my eyes from tears, my feet from stumbling. [9]I shall live! Yes, in his presence—here on earth! [10, 11]In my discouragement I thought, "They are lying when they say I will recover." [12]But now what can I offer Jehovah for all he has done for me? [13]I will bring him an offering of wine and praise his name for saving me. [14]I will publicly bring him the sacrifice I vowed I would.

Ps 119:13. I have recited your laws. [26]I told you my plans and you replied. Now give me your instructions. [27]Make me understand what you want; for then I shall see your miracles. [44-46]Therefore I will keep on obeying you forever and forever, free within the limits of your laws. I will speak to kings about their value, and they will listen with interest and respect. [67]I used to wander off until you punished me; now I closely follow all you say. [71]The punishment you gave me was the best thing that could have happened to me, for it taught me to pay attention to your laws.

Ps 145:4. Let each generation tell its children what glorious things he does. [5]I will meditate about your glory, splendor, majesty and miracles. [6]Your awe-inspiring deeds shall be on every tongue; I will proclaim your greatness. [7]Everyone will tell about how good you are, and sing about your righteousness. [10]All living things shall thank you, Lord, and your people will bless you. [11]They will talk together about the glory of your kingdom and mention examples of your power. [12]They will tell about your miracles and about the majesty and glory of your reign.

Dan 4:1. This is the proclamation of Nebuchadnezzar the king, which he sent to people of every language in every nation of the world: Greetings: [2]I want you all to know about the strange thing that the Most High God did to me. [3]It was incredible—a mighty miracle! And now I know for sure that his kingdom is everlasting; he reigns forever and ever.

34. At the end of seven years I, Nebuchadnezzar, looked up to heaven, and my sanity returned, and I praised and worshiped the Most High God and honored him who lives forever, whose rule is everlasting, his kingdom evermore. [35]All the people of the earth are nothing when compared to him; he does whatever he thinks best among the hosts of heaven, as well as here among the inhabitants of earth. No one can stop him or challenge him, saying, 'What do you mean by doing these things?' [36]When my mind returned to me, so did my honor and glory and kingdom. My counselors and officers came back to me and I was reestablished as head of my kingdom, with even greater honor than before. [37]Now, I, Nebuchadnezzar, praise and glorify and honor the King of Heaven, the Judge of all, whose every act is right and good; for he is able to take those who walk proudly and push them into the dust! *vs.* 1–37.

Jn 9:17. Then the Pharisees turned on the man who had been blind and demanded, "This man who opened you eyes—who do you say he is?" "I think he must be a prophet sent from God," the man replied. [30]"Why, that's very strange!" the man replied. "He can heal blind men, and yet you don't know anything about him! [31]Well, God doesn't listen to evil men, but he has open ears to those who worship him and do his will. [32]Since the world began there has never been anyone who could open the eyes of someone born blind. [33]If this man were not from God, he couldn't do it."

Acts 2:4. And everyone present was filled with the Holy Spirit and began speaking in languages they didn't know, for the Holy Spirit gave them this ability. [5]Many godly Jews were in Jerusalem that day for the religious celebrations, having arrived from many nations. [6]And when they heard the roaring in the sky above the house, crowds came running to see what it was all about, and were stunned to hear their own languages being spoken by the disciples. [7]"How can this be?" they exclaimed. "For these men are all from Galilee, [8]and yet we hear them speaking all the native languages of the lands where we were born! [9]Here we are—Parthians, Medes, Elamites, men from Mesopotamia, Judea, Cappadocia, Pontus, Ausia, [10]Phrygia, Pamphylia, Egypt, the Cyrene language areas of Libya, visitors from Rome—both Jews and Jewish converts— [11]Cretans, and Arabians. And we all hear these men telling in our own languages about the mighty miracles of God!"

Acts 3:15. And you killed the Author of Life; but God brought him back to life again. And John and I are witnesses of this fact, for after you killed him we saw him alive!

Acts 4:18. So they called them back in, and told them never again to speak about Jesus. [19]But Peter and John replied, "You decide whether God wants us to obey you instead of him! [20]We cannot stop telling about the wonderful things we saw Jesus do and heard him say."

Acts 5:31. Then, with mighty power, God exalted him to be a prince and Savior, so that the people of Israel would have an opportunity for repentance, and for their sins to be forgiven. [32]And we are witnesses of these things, and so is the Holy Spirit, who is given by God to all who obey him.

Acts 13:31. And he was seen many times during the next few days by the men who had accompanied him to Jerusalem from Galilee—these men have constantly testified to this in public witness.

Acts 26:12. I was on such a mission to Damascus, armed with the authority and commission of the chief priests, [13]when one day about noon, sir, a light from heaven brighter than the sun shone down on me and my companions. [14]We all fell down, and I heard a voice speaking to me in Hebrew, "Saul, Saul, why are you persecuting me? You are only hurting yourself." [15]"Who are you, sir?" I asked. And the Lord replied, "I am Jesus, the one you are persecuting. [16]Now stand up! For I have appeared to you to appoint you as my servant and my witness. You are to tell the world about this experience and about the many other occasions when I shall appear to you. [17]And I will protect you from both your own people and the Gentiles. Yes, I am going to send you to the Gentiles [18]to open their eyes to their true condition so that they may repent and live in the light of God instead of in Satan's darkness, so that they may receive forgiveness for their sins and God's inheritance along with all people everywhere whose sins are cleansed away, who are set apart by faith in me." [19]And so, O King Agrippa, I was not disobedient to that vision from heaven! [20]I preached first to those in Damascus, then in Jerusalem and through Judea, and also to the Gentiles that all must forsake their sins and turn to God—and prove their repentance by doing good deeds. [21]The Jews arrested me in the Temple for preaching this, and tried to kill me, [22]but God protected me so that I am still alive today to tell these facts to everyone, both great and small. I teach nothing except what the prophets and Moses said — [23]that the Messiah would suffer, and be the First to rise from the dead, to bring light to Jews and Gentiles alike. Acts 22.

1 Cor 15:15. And we apostles are all liars because we have said that God raised Christ from the grave, and of course that isn't true if the dead do not come back to life again.

2 Cor 4:13. We boldly say what we believe (trusting God to care for us), just as the Psalm writer did when he said, "I believe and therefore I speak." [14]We know that the same God who brought the Lord Jesus back from death will also bring us back to life again with Jesus, and present us to him along with you.

2 Cor 5:1. For we know that when this tent we live in now is taken down—when we die and leave these bodies—we will have wonderful new bodies in heaven, homes that will be ours forevermore, made for us by God himself, and not by human hands.

Gal 2:20. I have been crucified with Christ: and I myself no longer live, but Christ lives in me. And the real life I now have within this body is a result of my trusting in the Son of God, who loved me and gave himself for me.

Phil 3:4. Yet if anyone ever had reason to hope that he could save himself, it would be I. If others could be saved by what they are, certainly I could! [5]For I went through the Jewish initiation ceremony when I was eight days old, having been born into a pure-blooded Jewish home that was a branch of the old original Benjamin family. So I was a real Jew if there ever was one! What's more, I was a member of the Pharisees who demand the strictest obedience to every Jewish law and custom. [6]And sincere? Yes, so much so that I greatly persecuted the church; and I tried to obey every Jewish rule and regulation right down to the very last point. [7]But all these things that I once thought very worthwhile—now I've thrown them all away so that I can put my trust and hope in Christ alone. [8]Yes, everything else is worthless when compared with the priceless gain of knowing Christ Jesus my Lord. I have put aside all else, counting it worth less than nothing, in order that I can have Christ, [9]and become one with him, no longer counting on being saved by being good enough or by obeying God's laws, but by trusting Christ to save me; for God's way of making us right with himself depends on faith—counting on Christ alone. [10]Now I have given up everything else—I have found it to be the only way to really know Christ and to experience the mighty power that brought him back to life again, and to find out what it means to suffer and to die with him. [11]So, whatever it takes, I will be one who lives in the fresh newness of life of those who are alive from the dead. [12]I don't mean to say

I am perfect. I haven't learned all I should even yet, but I keep working toward that day when I will finally be all that Christ saved me for and wants me to be. [13]No, dear brothers, I am still not all I should be but I am bringing all my energies to bear on this one thing: Forgetting the past and looking forward to what lies ahead, [14]I strain to reach the end of the race and receive the prize for which God is calling us up to heaven because of what Christ Jesus did for us.

2 Tim 1:12. That is why I am suffering here in jail and I am certainly not ashamed of it, for I know the one in whom I trust, and I am sure that he is able to safely guard all that I have given him until the day of his return.

2 Tim 4:7. I have fought long and hard for my Lord, and through it all I have kept true to him. And now the time has come for me to stop fighting and rest. [8]In heaven a crown is waiting for me which the Lord, the righteous Judge, will give me on that great day of his return. And not just to me, but to all those whose lives show that they are eagerly looking forward to his coming back again.

Tit 1:1, 2. From: Paul, the slave of God and the messenger of Jesus Christ. I have been sent to bring faith to those God has chosen and to teach them to know God's truth—the kind of truth that changes lives—so that they can have eternal life, which God promised them before the world began—and he cannot lie.

Tit 3:3. Once we, too, were foolish and disobedient; we were misled by others and became slaves to many evil pleasures and wicked desires. Our lives were full of resentment and envy. We hated others and they hated us. [4]But when the time came for the kindness and love of God our Savior to appear, [5]then he saved us—not because we were good enough to be saved, but because of his kindness and pity—by washing away our sins and giving us the new joy of the indwelling Holy Spirit [6]whom he poured out upon us with wonderful fullness—and all because of what Jesus Christ our Savior did [7]so that he could declare us good in God's eyes—all because of his great kindness; and now we can share in the wealth of the eternal life he gives us, and we are eagerly looking forward to receiving it.

1 Pet 5:12. I hope I have encouraged you by this letter for I have given you a true statement of the way God blesses. What I have told you here should help you to stand firmly in his love.

2 Pet 1:16. For we have not been telling you fairy tales when we explained to you the power of our Lord Jesus Christ and his coming again. My own eyes have seen his splendor and his glory.

1 Jn 1:1. Christ was alive when the world began, yet I myself have seen him with my own eyes and listened to him speak. I have touched him with my own hands. He is God's message of Life. [2]This one who is Life from God has been shown to us and we guarantee that we have seen him; I am speaking of Christ, who is eternal Life. He was with the Father and then was shown to us. [3]Again I say, we are telling you about what we ourselves have actually seen and heard, so that you may share the fellowship and the joys we have with the Father and with Jesus Christ his Son. [4]And if you do as I say in this letter, then you, too, will be full of joy, and so will we.

FALSE. See *False Witness*.

TETRARCH A Roman ruler, Mt 14:1; Lk 9:7.

THADDAEUS One of the twelve apostles, Mt 10:2–4; Mk 3:16–19.

THANKFULNESS Jesus set an example of, Mt 11:25; 26:27; Jn 11:41. The heavenly beings engage in, Rev 4:9; 7:11, 12; 11:16, 17. Commanded, Ps 50:14, 15.

Should be offered to God, Ps 50:14, 15; to Christ, 1 Tim 1:12; through Christ, Rom 1:8; Col 3:17; Heb 13:15; in the name of Christ, Eph 5:20; in behalf of ministers, 2 Cor 1:11; in private worship, Dan 6:10; in public worship, Ps 35:18; in everything, 1 Thess 5:18; upon the completion of great undertakings, Neh 12:31, 32; before eating, Jn 6:11; Acts 27:35; always, Eph 1:16, 17; 5:20; 1 Thess 1:2; as the remembrance of God's holiness, Ps 30:4; 97:12; for the goodness, love and mercy of God, Ps 106:1; 107:1; 136:1–3; for the gift of Christ, 2 Cor 9:15; for Christ's power and reign, Rev 11:17; for the reception and effectual working of the word of God in others, 1 Thess 2:13; for deliverance through Christ, from sinful old nature, Rom 7:23–25; for victory over death and the grave, 1 Cor 15:54–57; for wisdom and health, Dan 2:23; for the triumph of the gospel, 2 Cor 2:14; for the conversion of others, Rom 6:17; for faith exhibited by others, Rom 1:8; 2 Thess 1:3; for love exhibited by others, 2 Thess 1:3; for the grace bestowed on others, 1 Cor 1:4; Phil 1:3–6; for the zeal exhibited by others, 2 Cor 8:16; for nearness of God's presence, Ps 75:1; for appointment to the ministry, 1 Tim 1:12; for willingness to offer our property for God's service, 1 Chron 29:6–14; for the supply of our physical needs, Rom 14:6, 7; 1 Tim 4:3, 4; for all men, 1 Tim 2:1; for all things, 2 Cor 9:11; Eph 5:20.

Should be accompanied by intercession for others, 1 Tim 2:1; 2 Tim 1:3; Philemon 1:4. Should always accompany prayer, Neh 11:15–17; Phil 4:6; Col 4:2. Should always accompany praise, Ps 92:1; Heb 13:15. Expressed in songs, 1 Chron 16:7. Ministers appointed to offer, in public, 1 Chron 16:4, 7; 23:30; 2 Chron 31:2.

Believers exhorted to, Ps 105:1; Col 3:15; resolve to offer, Ps 18:49; 30:12; habitually offer, Dan 6:10; offer sacrifices of, Ps 116:17; overflow with joy and, Col 2:7; praise God by, Ps 69:30; come before God with, Ps 95:2; should enter God's gates with, Ps 100:4. Of hypocrites, full of boasting, Lk 18:11. The wicked averse to, Rom 1:21.

EXEMPLIFIED. David, 1 Chron 29:13. Levites, 2 Chron 5:11–14. Daniel, Dan 2:23. Jonah, Jon 2:9. Simeon, Lk 2:28. Anna, Lk 2:38. Paul, Acts 28:15.

COMMANDED. Gen 35:1. "Move on to Bethel now, and settle there," God said to Jacob, "and build an altar to worship the God who appeared to you when you fled from your brother Esau."

Ex 12:14. You shall celebrate this event each year (this is a permanent law) to remind you of this fatal night. [17]This annual "Celebration with Unleavened Bread" will cause you always to remember today as the day when I brought you out of the land of Egypt; so it is a law that you must celebrate this day annually, generation after generation. [42]This night was selected by the Lord to bring his people out from the land of Egypt; so the same night was selected as the date of the annual celebration of God's deliverance.

Ex 13:3. Then Moses said to the people, "This is a day to remember forever—the day of leaving Egypt and your slavery; for the Lord has brought you out with mighty miracles. Now remember, during the annual celebration of this event you are to use no yeast; don't even have any in your homes. [8]During those celebration days each year you must explain to your children why you are celebrating—it is a celebration of what the Lord did for you when you left Egypt. [9]This annual memorial week will brand you as his own unique people, just as though he had branded his mark of ownership upon your hands or your forehead. [10]So celebrate the event annually in late March. [14]And in the future, when your children ask you, 'What is this all about?' you shall tell them, 'With mighty miracles Jehovah brought us out of Egypt from our slavery. [15]Pharaoh wouldn't let us go, so Jehovah killed all the firstborn males throughout the land of Egypt, both of men and animals; that is why we now give all the firstborn males to the Lord—except that all the eldest sons are always bought back.' [16]Again I say, this celebration shall identify you as God's people, just as much as if his brand of ownership were placed upon your foreheads. It is a reminder that the Lord brought us out of Egypt with great power."

Ex 16:32. Then Moses gave them this further instruction from the Lord: they were to take three quarts of it to be kept as a museum specimen forever, so that later generations could see the bread the Lord had fed them with in the wilderness, when he brought them from Egypt.

Ex 34:26. And you must bring the best of the first of each year's crop to the Tabernacle of the Lord your God.

Lev 19:24. And the fourth year the entire crop shall be devoted to the Lord, and shall be given to the Lord in praise to him.

Lev 23:14. Until this is done you must not eat any of the harvest for yourselves—neither fresh kernels nor bread nor parched grain. This is a permanent law throughout your nation.

Deut 12:18. All these must be brought to the central altar where you, your children, and the Levites shall eat them before the Lord your God. He will tell you where this altar must be located. Rejoice before the Lord your God in everything you do.

Deut 16:9. Seven weeks after the harvest begins, [10]there shall be another festival before the Lord your God called the Festival of Weeks. At that time bring to him a free-will offering proportionate in size to his blessing upon you as judged by the amount of your harvest. [11]It is a time to rejoice before the Lord with your family and household. And don't forget to include the local Levites, foreigners, widows, and orphans. Invite them to accompany you to the celebration at the sanctuary. [12]Remember! You were a slave in Egypt, so be sure to carry out this command. [13]Another celebration, the Festival of Shelters, must be observed for seven days at the end of the harvest season, after the grain is threshed and the grapes have been pressed. [14]This will be a happy time of rejoicing together with your family and servants. And don't forget to include the Levites, foreigners, orphans, and widows of your town. [15]This feast will be held at the sanctuary, which will be located at the place the Lord will designate. It is a time of deep thanksgiving to the Lord for blessing you with a good harvest and in so many other ways; it shall be a time of great joy.

Deut 26:10. "And now, O Lord, see, I have brought you a token of the first of the crops from the ground you have given me." Then place the samples before the Lord your God, and worship him.

Judg 5:11. The village musicians gather at the village well to sing of the triumphs of the Lord. Again and again they sing the ballad of how the Lord saved Israel with an army of peasants! The people of the Lord marched through the gates!

Ps 48:11. O Jerusalem, rejoice! O people of Judah, rejoice! For God will see to it that you are finally treated fairly.

Ps 50:14, 15. What I want from you is your true thanks; I want your promises fulfilled. *I want you to trust me in your times of trouble, so I can rescue you, and you can give me glory.*

Ps 98:1. Sing a new song to the Lord telling about his mighty deeds! For he has won a mighty victory by his power and holiness.

Ps 105:1. Thank the Lord for all the glorious things he does; proclaim them to the nations. [5]Think of the mighty deeds he did for us, his chosen ones. [42]For he remembered his sacred promises to Abraham his servant. [43]So he brought his chosen ones singing into the Promised Land. [44]He gave them the lands of the Gentiles, complete with their growing crops; they ate what others planted. [45]This was done to make them faithful and obedient to his laws. Hallelujah! *vs.* 1–45.

Ps 106:1. Hallelujah! Thank you, Lord! How good you are! Your love for us continues on forever.

Ps 107:1. Say "Thank you" to the Lord for being so good, for always being so loving and kind. [2]Has the Lord redeemed you? Then speak out! Tell others he has saved you from your enemies. [15]Oh, that these men would praise the Lord for his loving-kindness and for all of his wonderful deeds! [22]Let them tell him "Thank you" as their sacrifice, and sing about his glorious deeds. [42]Good men everywhere will see it and be glad, while evil men are stricken silent. [43]Listen, if you are wise, to what I am saying. Think about the lovingkindness of the Lord!

Ps 118:1. Oh, thank the Lord, for he's so good! His lovingkindness is forever. [4]Let the Gentile converts chant, "His lovingkindness is forever."

Prov 3:9, 10. Honor the Lord by giving him the first part of all your income, and he will fill your barns with wheat and barley and overflow your wine vats with the finest wines.

Eccl 7:14. Enjoy prosperity whenever you can, and when hard times strike, realize that God gives one as well as the other—so that everyone will realize that nothing is certain in this life.

Isa 48:20. Yet even now, be free from your captivity! Leave Babylon, singing as you go; shout to the ends of the earth that the Lord has redeemed his servants, the Jews.

Joel 2:26. Once again you will have all the food you want. Praise the Lord, who does these miracles for you. Never again will my people experience disaster such as this.

Rom 2:4. Don't you realize how patient he is being with you? Or don't you care? Can't you see that he has been waiting all this time without punishing you, to give you time to turn from your sin? His kindness is meant to lead you to repentance.

Rom 15:27. Because the news about Christ came to these Gentiles from the church in Jerusalem. And since they received this wonderful spiritual gift of the Gospel from there, they feel that the least they can do in return is to give some material aid.

Eph 5:4. Dirty stories, foul talk and coarse jokes —these are not for you. Instead, remind each other of God's goodness and be thankful. [19]Talk with each other much about the Lord, quoting psalms and hymns and singing sacred songs, making music in your hearts to the the Lord. [20]Always give thanks for everything to our God and Father in the name of our Lord Jesus Christ.

Phil 4:6. Don't worry about anything; instead, pray about everything; tell God your needs and don't forget to thank him for his answers.

Col 1:12. And always thankful to the Father who has made us fit to share all the wonderful things that belong to those who live in the kingdom of light.

Col 2:7. Let your roots grow down into him and draw up nourishment from him. See that you go on growing in the Lord, and become strong and vigorous in the truth you were taught. Let your lives overflow with joy and thanksgiving for all he has done.

Col 3:15. Let the peace of heart which comes from Christ be always present in your hearts and lives, for this is your responsibility and privilege as members of his body. And always be thankful. [16]Remember what Christ taught and let his words enrich your lives and make you wise; teach them to each other and sing them out in psalms and hymns and spiritual songs, singing to the Lord with thankful hearts. [17]And whatever you do or say, let it be as a representative of the Lord Jesus, and come with him into the presence of God the Father to give him your thanks.

Col 4:2. Don't be weary in prayer; keep at it; watch for God's answers and remember to be thankful when they come.

1 Thess 5:18. No matter what happens, always be thankful, for this is God's will for you who belong to Christ Jesus.

1 Tim 2:1. Here are my directions: Pray much for others; plead for God's mercy upon them; give thanks for all he is going to do for them.

1 Tim 4:3. They will say it is wrong to be married and wrong to eat meat, even though God gave these things to well-taught Christians to enjoy and be thankful for. [4]For everything God made is good, and we may eat it gladly if we are thankful for it, [5]and if we ask God to bless it, for it is made good by the Word of God and prayer.

Heb 13:15. With Jesus' help we will continually offer our sacrifice of praise to God by telling others of the glory of his name.

Jas 1:9. A Christian who doesn't amount to much in this world should be glad, for he is great in the Lord's sight.

See *Joy; Praise; Psalms.*

EXEMPLIFIED. Gen 32:10. I am not worthy of the least of all your loving kindnesses shown me again and again just as you promised me. For when I left home I owned nothing except a walking stick! And now I am two armies!

Gen 48:11. And Israel said to Joseph, "I never thought that I would see you again, but now God has let me see your children too." [15]Then he blessed Joseph with this blessing: "May God, the God of my fathers Abraham and Isaac, the God who has shepherded me all my life, wonderfully bless these boys. [16]He is the Angel who has kept me from all harm. May these boys be an honor to my name and to the names of my fathers Abraham and Isaac; and may they become a mighty nation."

Ex 15:1. Then Moses and the people of Israel sang this song to the Lord: I will sing to the Lord, for he has triumphed gloriously; He has thrown both horse and rider into the sea. [2]The Lord is my strength, my song, and my salvation. He is my God, and I will praise him. He is my father's God —I will exalt him. [3]The Lord is a warrior—yes, Jehovah is his name. [4]He has overthrown Pharaoh's chariots and armies, drowning them in the sea. The famous Egyptian captains are dead beneath the waves. [5]The water covers them. They went down into the depths like a stone. [6]Your right hand, O Lord, is glorious in power; it dashes the enemy to pieces. [7]In the greatness of your majesty you overthrew all those who rose against you. You sent forth your anger, and it consumed them as fire consumes straw. [8]At the blast of your breath the waters divided! They stood as solid walls to hold the seas apart. [9]The enemy said, "I will chase after them, catch up with them, destroy them. I will cut them apart with my sword and divide the captured booty." [10]But God blew with his wind, and the sea covered them. They sank as lead in the mighty waters. [11]Who else is like the Lord among the gods? Who is glorious in holiness like him? Who is so awesome in splendor, a wonder-working God? [12]You reached out your hand and the earth swallowed them. [13]You have led the people you redeemed. But in your lovingkindness you have guided them wonderfully to your holy land. [14]The nations heard what happened, and they trembled. Fear has gripped the people of Philistia. [15]The leaders of Edom are appalled, the mighty men of Moab tremble; all the people of Canaan melt with fear. [16]Terror and dread have overcome them. O Lord, because of your great power they won't attack us! Your people whom you purchased will pass by them in safety. [17]You will bring them in and plant them on your mountain, your own homeland, Lord—the sanctuary you made for them to live in. [18]Jehovah shall reign forever and forever. [19]The horses of Pharaoh, his horsemen, and his chariots tried to follow through the sea; but the Lord let down the walls of water on them while the people of Israel walked through on dry land. [20]Then Miriam the prophetess, the sister of Aaron, took a timbrel and led the women in dances. [21]And Miriam sang this song: Sing to the Lord, for he has triumphed gloriously. The horse and rider have been drowned in the sea.

Num 21:17, 18. What happened is described in this song that the people sang: Spring up, O well! Sing of the water! This is a well the leaders dug. It was hollowed with their staves and shovels.

1 Kgs 8:56. Blessed be the Lord who has fulfilled his promise and given rest to his people Israel; not one word has failed of all the wonderful promises proclaimed by his servant Moses.

1 Chron 29:14. But who am I and who are my people that we should be permitted to give anything to you? Everything we have has come from you, and we only give you what is yours already!

Ezra 7:27. Well, praise the Lord God of our ancestors, who made the king want to beautify the Temple of the Lord in Jerusalem!

Ps 9:1. O Lord, I will praise you with all my heart, and tell everyone about the marvelous things you do. [2]I will be glad, yes, filled with joy because of you. I will sing your praises, O Lord God above all gods. [4]You have vindicated me; you have endorsed my work, declaring from your throne that it is good.

Ps 13:6. I will sing to the Lord because he has blessed me so richly.

Ps 22:23. "Praise the Lord, each one of you who fears him," I will say. "Each of you must fear and reverence his name. Let all Israel sing his praises, [24]for he has not despised my cries of deep despair; he has not turned and walked away. When I cried to him, he heard and came." [25]Yes, I will stand and praise you before all the people. I will publicly fulfill my vows in the presence of all who reverence your name.

Ps 26:7. Singing a song of thanksgiving and telling about your miracles.

Ps 28:7. He is my strength, my shield from every danger. I trusted in him, and he helped me. Joy rises in my heart until I burst out in songs of praise to him.

Ps 30:1. I will praise you, Lord, for you have saved me from my enemies. You refuse to let them triumph over me. [3]You brought me back from the brink of the grave, from death itself, and here I am alive! [11]Then he turned my sorrow into joy! He took away my clothes of mourning and gave me gay and festive garments to rejoice in [12]so that I might sing glad praises to the Lord instead of lying in silence in the grave. O Lord my God, I will keep on thanking you forever!

Ps 31:7. I am radiant with joy because of your mercy, for you have listened to my troubles and have seen the crisis in my soul. [21]Blessed is the Lord, for he has shown me that his never-failing love protects me like the walls of a fort!

Ps 35:9. But I will rejoice in the Lord. He shall rescue me! [10]From the bottom of my heart praise rises to him. Where is his equal in all of heaven and earth? Who else protects the weak and helpless from the strong, and the poor and needy from those who would rob them? [18]Save me, and I will thank you publicly before the entire congregation, before the largest crowd I can find.

Ps 40:2. He lifted me out of the pit of despair, out from the bog and the mire, and set my feet on a hard, firm path and steadied me as I walked along. [3]He has given me a new song to sing, of praises to our God. Now many will hear of the glorious things he did for me, and stand in awe before the Lord, and put their trust in him. [5]O Lord my God, many and many a time you have done great miracles for us, and we are ever in your thoughts. Who else can do such glorious things? No one else can be compared with you. There isn't time to tell of all your wonderful deeds.

Ps 41:11. I know you are pleased with me because you haven't let my enemies triumph over me. [12]You have preserved me because I was honest; you have admitted me forever to your presence.

Ps 44:7. Only you can give us the victory over those who hate us. [8]My constant boast is God. I can never thank you enough!

Ps 54:6. Gladly I bring my sacrifices to you; I will praise your name, O Lord, for it is good. [7]God has rescued me from all my trouble, and triumphed over my enemies.

Ps 56:12. I will surely do what I have promised, Lord, and thank you for your help. [13]For you have saved me from death and my feet from slipping, so that I can walk before the Lord in the land of the living.

Ps 59:16. But as for me, I will sing each morning about your power and mercy. For you have been my high tower of refuge, a place of safety in the day of my distress. [17]O my Strength, to you I sing my praises; for you are my high tower of safety, my God of mercy.

Ps 66:8. Let everyone bless God and sing his praises, [9]for he holds our lives in his hands. And he holds our feet to the path. [12]You sent troops to ride across our broken bodies. We went through fire and flood. But in the end, you brought us into wealth and great abundance. [13]Now I have come to your Temple with burnt-offerings to pay my vows. [14]For when I was in trouble I promised you many offerings. [15]That is why I am bringing you these fat he-goats, rams and calves. The smoke of their sacrifice shall rise before you. [16]Come and hear, all of you who reverence the Lord, and I will tell you what he did for me. [20]Blessed be God who didn't turn away when I was praying, and didn't refuse me his kindness and love.

Ps 68:19. What a glorious Lord! He who daily bears our burdens also gives us our salvation.

Ps 71:15. I cannot count the times when you have faithfully rescued me from danger. I will tell everyone how good you are, and of your constant, daily care. [23]I will shout and sing your praises for redeeming me. [24]I will talk to others all day long about your justice and your goodness. For all who tried to hurt me have been disgraced and dishonored.

Ps 79:13. Then we your people, the sheep of your pasture, will thank you forever and forever, praising your greatness from generation to generation.

Ps 89:1. Forever and ever I will sing about the tender kindness of the Lord! Young and old shall hear about your blessings.

Ps 92:1. It is good to say, "Thank you" to the Lord, to sing praises to the God who is above all gods. [2]Every morning tell him, "Thank you for your kindness," and every evening rejoice in all his faithfulness. [4]You have done so much for me, O Lord. No wonder I am glad! I sing for joy.

Ps 98:1. Sing a new song to the Lord telling about his mighty deeds! For he has won a mighty victory by his power and holiness.

Ps 100:4. Go through his open gates with great thanksgiving; enter his courts with praise. Give thanks to him and bless his name.

Ps 102:18. I am recording this so that future generations will also praise the Lord for all that he has done. And a people that shall be created shall praise the Lord. [19]Tell them that God looked down from his temple in heaven, [20]and heard the groans of his people in slavery—they were children of death—and released them.

Ps 104:1. I bless the Lord: O Lord my God, how great you are! You are robed with honor and with majesty and light! You stretched out the starry curtain of the heavens.

Ps 116:12. But now what can I offer Jehovah for all he has done for me? [13]I will bring him an offering of wine and praise his name for saving me. [14]I will publicly bring him the sacrifice I vowed I would. [17]I will worship you and offer you a sacrifice of thanksgiving.

Ps 119:65. Lord, I am overflowing with your blessings, just as you promised. [108]Accept my grateful thanks and teach me your desires.

Ps 136:1. Oh, give thanks to the Lord, for he is good; his lovingkindness continues forever. [2]Give thanks to the God of gods, for his lovingkindness continues forever. [3]Give thanks to the Lord of lords, for his lovingkindness continues forever. [4]Praise him who alone does mighty miracles, for his lovingkindness continues forever. [5]Praise him who made the heavens, for his lovingkindness continues forever. [6]Praise him who planted the water within the earth, for his lovingkindness continues forever. [7]Praise him who made the heavenly lights, for his lovingkindness continues forever: [8]the sun to rule the day, for his lovingkindness continues forever; [9]and the moon and stars at night, for his lovingkindness continues forever. [10]Praise the God who smote the firstborn of Egypt, for his lovingkindness to Israel continues forever. [11, 12]He brought them out with mighty power and upraised fist to strike their enemies, for his lovingkindness to Israel continues forever. [13]Praise the Lord who opened the Red Sea to make a path before them, for his lovingkindness continues forever, [14]and led them safely through, for his lovingkindness continues forever—[15]But drowned Pharaoh's army in the sea, for his lovingkindness to Israel continues forever. [16]Praise him who led his people through the wilderness, for his lovingkindness continues forever. [17]Praise him who saved his people from the power of mighty kings, for his lovingkindness continues forever, [18]and killed famous kings who were their enemies, for his lovingkindness to Israel continues forever: [19]Sihon, king of Amorites—for God's lovingkindness to Israel continues forever—[20]and Og, king of Bashan—for his lovingkindness to Israel continues forever. [21]God gave the land of these kings to Israel as a gift forever, for his lovingkindness to Israel continues forever; [22]yes, a permanent gift to his servant Israel, for his lovingkindness continues forever. [23]He remembered our utter weakness, for his lovingkindness continues forever. [24]And saved us from our foes, for his lovingkindness continues forever. [25]He gives food to every living thing, for his lovingkindness continues forever. [26]Oh, give thanks to the God of heaven, for his lovingkindness continues forever.

Isa 63:7. I will tell of the lovingkindnesses of God. I will praise him for all he has done; I will rejoice in his great goodness to Israel, which he has granted in accordance with his mercy and love.

Dan 2:23. I thank and praise you, O God of my fathers, for you have given me wisdom and glowing health, and now, even this vision of the king's dream, and the understanding of what it means.

Dan 4:2. I want you all to know about the strange thing that the Most High God did to me. [34]At the end of seven years I, Nebuchadnezzar, looked up to heaven, and my sanity returned, and I praised and worshiped the Most High God and honored him who lives forever, whose rule is everlasting, his kingdom evermore.

Dan 6:22. "My God has sent his angel," he said, "to shut the lions' mouths so that they can't touch me."

Acts 2:46. They worshiped together regularly at the Temple each day, met in small groups in homes for Communion, and shared their meals with great joy and thankfulness, [47]praising God. The whole city was favorable to them.

Acts 28:15. The brothers in Rome had heard we were coming and came to meet us at the Forum on the Appian Way. Others joined us at The Three Taverns. When Paul saw them, he thanked God and took courage.

Rom 14:6. So is the person who eats meat that has been offered to idols; he is thankful to the Lord for it; he is doing right. And the person who won't touch such meat, he, too, is anxious to please the Lord, and is thankful.

Col 1:3. Whenever we pray for you we always begin by giving thanks to God the Father of our Lord Jesus Christ.

1 Tim 1:12. How thankful I am to Christ Jesus our Lord for choosing me as one of his messengers, and giving me the strength to be faithful to him.

See *Joy; Praise.*

OF MAN TO MAN. The Israelites, to Joshua, Josh 19:49, 50. The spies, to Rahab, Josh 6:22–25. Saul, to the Kenites, 1 Sam 15:6. Naomi, to Boaz, Ruth 2:19, 20. David, to the men of Jabesh-gilead, 2 Sam 2:5–7; to Hanun, 2 Sam 10:2; to Barzillai, 1 Kgs 2:7. Paul, to Phoebe, Rom 16:1–4; to Onesiphorus, 2 Tim 1:16–18. The people of Malta, to Paul, Acts 28:10.

TO GOD.

Instances of. Of Eve, Gen 4:1, 25. Of Noah, Gen 8:20. Of Melchizedek, Gen 14:19, 20. Of Lot, Gen 19:18–20. Of Sarah, Gen 21:6, 7. Of Abraham, Gen 12:7; 13:3, 4. Of Abraham's servant, Gen 24:27, 35. Of Isaac, Gen 26:22. Of Leah, Gen 29:32–35. Of Rachel, Gen 30:6. Of Jacob, Gen 31:42; 35:3, 7. Of Joseph, Gen 41:51, 52. Of Moses, Ex 15:1–19. Of Miriam, Ex 15:20–22. Of Jethro, Ex 18:10. Of Israel, Ex 4:31; Num 21:17, 18; 31:48–54; 1 Chron 29:22. Of Deborah, Judg 5. Of Hannah, 1 Sam 1:27, 28. Of Samuel, 1 Sam 7:12. Of David, 2 Sam 6:21. See *Psalms,* above. Of the Queen of Sheba, 1 Kgs 10:9. Of Hiram, 2 Chron 2:12. Of Jehoshaphat's army, 2 Chron 20:27, 28. Of the Levites, Neh 9:4–38. Of the Jews, Neh 12:43. Of the sailors, Jon 1:16. Of the shepherds, Lk 2:20. Those whom Jesus healed: The paralyzed man, Lk 5:25; the healed demoniac, Lk 8:39; the woman bent double, Lk 13:13; one of the ten lepers whom Jesus healed, Lk 17:15, 16; blind Bartimaeus, Lk 18:43; Mk 10:46–52; the government official for his son, Jn 4:53. The lame man healed by Peter, Acts 3:7, 8. Before eating, by Jesus, Mt 14:19; Mk 8:6, 7; Jn 6:11; Paul, Acts 27:35.

See *Praise; Prayer, Before Taking Food.*

THANK OFFERINGS See *Offerings.*

THANKSGIVING See *Praise; Thankfulness.*

THEATER Acts 19:29, 31.

THEBES A city on the Nile, Jer 46:25; Ezk 30:14–16; Nah 3:8.

THEBEZ A city of Manasseh, in besieging which Abimelech was killed, Judg 9:50–57; 2 Sam 11:19–21.

THEFT AND THIEVES Ex 20:15. You must not steal. Deut 5:19; Mt 19:18; Lk 18:20; Rom 13:9.

Ex 21:16. A kidnapper must be killed, whether he is caught in possession of his victim or has already sold him as a slave. Deut 24:7.

Ex 22:1. If a man steals an ox or sheep and then kills or sells it, he shall pay a fine of five to one—five oxen shall be returned for each stolen ox. For sheep, the fine shall be four to one—four sheep returned for each sheep stolen. [2]If a thief is caught in the act of breaking into a house and is killed, the one who killed him is not guilty. [3]But if it happens in the daylight, it must be presumed to be murder and the man who kills him is guilty. If a thief is captured, he must make full restitution; if he can't, then he must be sold as a slave for his debt. [4]If he is caught in the act of stealing a live ox or donkey or sheep or whatever it is, he shall pay double value as his fine. [10]If a man asks his neighbor to keep a donkey, ox, sheep, or any other animal for him, and it dies, or is hurt, or gets away, and there is no eye-witness to report just what happened to it, [11]then the neighbor must take an oath that he has not stolen it, and the owner must accept his word, and no restitution shall be made for it. [12]But if the animal or property has been stolen, the neighbor caring for it must repay the owner. [13]If it was attacked by some wild animal, he shall bring the torn carcass to confirm the fact, and shall not be required to make restitution. [14]If a man borrows an animal (or anything else) from a neighbor, and it is injured or killed, and the owner is not there at the time, then the man who borrowed it must pay for it. [15]But if the owner is there, he need not pay; and if it was rented, then he need not pay, because this possibility was included in the original rental fee.

Lev 6:2. If anyone sins against me by refusing to return a deposit on something borrowed or rented, or by refusing to return something entrusted to him, or by robbery, or by oppressing his neighbor, [3]or by finding a lost article and lying about it, swearing that he doesn't have it—[4, 5]on the day he is found guilty of any such sin, he shall restore what he took, adding a twenty percent fine, and give it to the one he has harmed; and on the same day he shall bring his guilt offering to the Tabernacle. [6]His guilt offering shall be a ram without defect, and must be worth whatever value you demand. He shall bring it to the priest, [7]and the priest shall make atonement for him before the Lord, and he shall be forgiven.

Lev 19:11. You must not steal nor lie nor defraud. [13]You shall not rob nor oppress anyone, and you shall pay your hired workers promptly. If something is due them, don't even keep it overnight.

Deut 23:24. You may eat your fill of the grapes from another man's vineyard, but do not take any away in a container. [25]It is the same with someone else's grain—you may eat a few handfuls of it, but don't use a sickle.

Ps 50:18. You see a thief and help him. Prov 29:24.

Ps 62:10. Don't become rich by extortion and robbery.

Prov 6:30. Excuses might even be found for a thief, if he steals when he is starving! [31]But even so, he is fined seven times as much as he stole, though it may mean selling everything in his house to pay it back.

Prov 21:6. Dishonest gain will never last, so why take the risk?

Isa 61:8. For I, the Lord, love justice; I hate robbery and wrong.

Jer 2:26. Like a thief, the only shame that Israel knows is getting caught.

Jer 7:9. Do you really think that you can steal, murder, commit adultery, lie, and worship Baal and all of those new gods of yours, [10]and then come here and stand before me in my Temple and chant, "We are saved!"—only to go right back to all these evil things again?

Ezk 22:29. Even the common people oppress and rob the poor and needy and cruelly extort from aliens.

Hos 4:1. Hear the word of the Lord, O people of Israel. The Lord has filed a lawsuit against you listing the following charges: There is no faithfulness, no kindness, no knowledge of God in your land. [2]You swear and lie and kill and steal and commit adultery. There is violence everywhere, with one murder after another. Hos 7:1; Amos 3:10.

Nah 3:1. Woe to Nineveh, City of Blood, full of lies, crammed with plunder.

Zech 5:3. "This scroll," he told me, "represents the words of God's curse going out over the entire land. It says that all who steal and lie have been judged and sentenced to death." *v.* 4.

Mt 6:19. Don't store up treasures here on earth where they can erode away or may be stolen. [20]Store them in heaven where they will never lose their value, and are safe from thieves. Lk 12:33.

Mt 15:19. For from the heart come evil thoughts, murder, adultery, fornication, theft, lying and slander. Mk 7:21, 22.

Mk 11:17. He told them, "It is written in the Scriptures, 'My Temple is to be a place of prayer for all nations,' but you have turned it into a den of robbers." Mt 21:13; Lk 19:45, 46.

Mk 15:27. Two robbers were also crucified that morning, their crosses on either side of his. Mt 27: 38, 44.

Jn 10:1. Anyone refusing to walk through the gate into a sheepfold, who sneaks over the wall, must surely be a thief! *v.* 10.

Rom 2:21. Yes, you teach others—then why don't you teach yourselves? You tell others not to steal—do *you* steal?

1 Cor 6:8. But, instead, you yourselves are the ones who do wrong, cheating others, even your own brothers. [10]Those who live immoral lives . . . will have no share in his kingdom. Neither will thieves or greedy people . . . or robbers.

Eph 4:28. If anyone is stealing he must stop it and begin using those hands of his for honest work so he can give to others in need.

Tit 2:10. Nor steal, but must show themselves to be entirely trustworthy. In this way they will make people want to believe in our Savior and God.

1 Pet 4:15. Don't let me hear of your suffering for murdering or stealing or making trouble or being a busybody and prying into other people's affairs.

Rev 3:3. I will come suddenly upon you, unexpected as a thief, and punish you. Lk 12:39; 1 Thess 5:2, 4; 2 Pet 3:10.

Rev 9:21. Neither did they change their mind and attitude about all their murders and witchcraft, their immorality and theft.

See *Dishonesty.*

FIGURATIVE. Jer 49:9, 10; Obd 1:5.

INSTANCES OF. By Rachel, of the household gods, Gen 31:21, 34, 35. Achan, Josh 7:10, 11. Micah, Judg 17:2. The spies of Laish, Judg 18:14–27. Judas, Jn 12:6.

THEOCRACY Established, Ex 19:8; 24:3, 7; Deut 5:25–29; 33:2–5; Judg 8:23, 24; 1 Sam 12:12. Rejected by Israel, 1 Sam 8:7, 19; 10:18, 19; 2 Chron 13:8.

See *God, Sovereign; Government.*

THEOLOGY Theology is the study or science of God, in which all facts concerning him and all his works are arranged, compared, and defended. For the source material found in the Bible, see under *God.*

THEOPHILUS A Christian to whom Luke addressed the books Luke and Acts, Lk 1:1; Acts 1:1.

THESSALONIANS See *Thessalonica.*

THESSALONICA A city of Macedonia. Paul visits, Acts 17:1; Phil 4:16. People of, presecute Paul, Acts 17:5–9, 11, 13. Men of, accompany Paul, Acts 20:4; 27:2. Paul writes to Christians in, 1 Thess 1:1. Demas goes to, 2 Tim 4:10.

THEUDAS A Jewish insurrectionist, Acts 5: 36.

THIRST Figurative of the ardent desire of the devout mind, Ps 22:15; 42:1–3; 63:1; 107:4–9; 143: 6; Isa 55:1; Amos 8:11–13; Jn 4:14, 15; 6:35; 7:37; Rev 21:6; 22:17.

See *Desire, Spiritual; Diligence; Hunger, Spiritual; Zeal.*

THISTLE A noxious plant, Gen 3:18; Job 31: 40; Hos 10:8. Parables of, 2 Kgs 14:9; 2 Chron 25: 18; Mt 7:16; 13:24–30, 38–42.

FIGURATIVE. Hos 9:6.

See *Nettle.*

THOMAS Called *The Twin.* One of the 12 apostles, Mt 10:2–4; Mk 3:16–19; Lk 6:14–16. Present at the raising of Lazarus, Jn 11:16. Asks Jesus the way to the Father's house, Jn 14:5. Absent when Jesus first appeared to the disciples after the resurrection, Jn 20:24. Skepticism of, Jn 20:25. Sees Jesus after the resurrection, Jn 20:26–29; 21: 1, 2. Lives with the other apostles in Jerusalem, Acts 1:13, 14. Loyalty of, to Jesus, Jn 11:16; 20:28.

THORN The ground cursed with, Gen 3:18. Used for fuel, Ps 58:9. Hedges formed of, Hos 2: 6; Mic 7:4. Crown of, mockingly put on Jesus' head, Mt 27:29; Mk 15:16, 17; Jn 19:2, 5. Thorns finally to be removed, Isa 55:13. Land bearing thorns and thistles is condemned, Heb 6:8.

See *Bramble.*

FIGURATIVE. Bush, allegory of, Judg 9:14, 15. Of afflictions, Num 33:55; 2 Cor 12:7. Of the adversities of the wicked, Prov 22:5. Of the evils that spring from the heart to choke the truth, Mt 13:7, 22. Paul's thorn in the flesh, 2 Cor 12:7.

THREAD Judg 16:9. See *Flax.*

THREE TAVERNS A town in Italy. Roman Christians meet Paul in, Acts 28:15.

THRESHING By beating, Ruth 2:17; by treading, Deut 25:4; Hos 10:11; 1 Cor 9:9; 1 Tim 5:18. With instruments of wood, 2 Sam 24:22; of iron, Amos 1:3; with a wheel, Isa 28:27, 28. Floors for, Gen 50:10, 11; Judg 6:37; Ruth 3:2–14; 1 Sam 23:1; 2 Sam 6:6; Job 39:12; Hos 9:1; Joel 2:24. Floor of Araunah bought by David for a place of sacrifice, 2 Sam 24:16–25.

THRONE Of Pharaoh, Ex 11:5. Of David, 1 Kgs 2:24; 1 Chron 29:23; Ps 132:11, 12; Isa 9:7; Jer 13:13; 17:25; Lk 1:32. Of Solomon, 1 Kgs 2:19; 2 Chron 9:17–19. Of ivory, 1 Kgs 10:18–20. Of Herod, Acts 12:21. Of Israel, 1 Kgs 10:9.

Abdicated by David, 1 Kgs 1:32–40.

Of Christ, Mt 19:28; 25:31; Acts 2:30; Rev 3:21; 7:17; 22:3.

Of Satan, Rev 2:13.

Of grace and mercy, Heb 4:16.

FIGURATIVE. Ps 62:3, 4. Anthropomorphic use of: Of God, 2 Chron 18:18; Ps 9:4, 7, 8; 47:8; 89:14, 15; 97:2; 103:19; Isa 6:1; 66:1; Mt 5:34; 23:22; Heb 12:2; Rev 14:3.

THUMB Blood put on, in consecration, Ex 29:19, 20; Lev 8:23; in purification, Lev 14:14, 25. Oil put on, Lev 14:17, 28. Of prisoners cut off, Judg 1:4–6. See *Hand.*

THUMMIM See *Urim and Thummim.*

THUNDER Sent as a plague upon the Egyptians, Ex 9:23–34; the Philistines, in battle with the Israelites, 1 Sam 7:10. Sent as a judgment, Isa 29:6. On Sinai, Ex 19:16; Ps 77:18. A token of God's anger, 1 Sam 12:17, 18. A manifestation of God's power, Job 26:14; Ps 77:18. Sons of Zebedee called sons of, Mk 3:17. Sound of, from heaven, Jn 12:29. In the book of Revelation, 4:5; 6:1; 10:3, 4; 11:19; 14:2; 16:18; 19:6.

THYATIRA Home of Lydia, a convert of Paul, Acts 16:14. John given a message for, Rev 1:11; 2:18, 24, 25.

TIBERIAS 1. A city on the Sea of Galilee, Jn 6:22, 23.

2. Sea of, a name given to the Sea of Galilee, Jn 6:1.

See *Galilee, 2.*

TIBERIUS CAESAR Emperor of Rome, Lk 3:1.

TIBHATH A city conquered by David, 1 Chron 18:8.

TIBNI Chosen by half of Israel to be king; death of, 1 Kgs 16:21, 22.

TIDAL King of Goiim, Gen 14:1.

TIGLATH-PILESER Called also *Tilgath-pilneser,* king of Assyria. Invades Israel; takes part of the people captive to Assyria, 2 Kgs 15:29; 1 Chron 5:6, 26. Forms an alliance with Ahaz; captures Damascus, 2 Kgs 16:7–10; 2 Chron 28:19–21.

TIKVAH 1. Called also *Tokhath,* father of Shallum, 2 Kgs 22:14; 2 Chron 34:22.

2. Father of Jahzeiah, Ezra 10:15.

TILE Lk 5:19.

TILGATH-PILNESER See *Tiglath-pileser.*

TILON Son of Shimon, 1 Chron 4:20.

TIMAEUS Father of Bartimaeus, the blind man cured by Jesus, Mk 10:46.

TIMBREL An instrument of music of the tambourine sort, 1 Sam 10:5; Isa 24:8. Used by Miriam, Ex 15:20. Used in religious service, Ps 68:25; Used in dances, Jer 31:4. See *Drums; Music, Instruments of; Tambourine.*

TIME Beginning of, Gen 1:1, 14, 15. Mysteries hidden since the beginning of, Mt 13:34, 35. Epochs of: Before the flood, Josh 24:2. The exodus, Ex 19:1; 40:17; 1 Kgs 6:1. Daniel's reckoning of time, and times, and half times, Dan 7:25; 12:7.

Indicated by a sundial, 2 Kgs 20:9–11; Isa 38:8. Division of, into days and hours, Ex 14:24; 1 Sam 11:11; Mt 14:25; Mk 6:48.

One day as a thousand years, 2 Pet 3:8. At the right time, Gal 4:4; Eph 1:10. End of, Job 26:10; Rev 10:6.

Time periods in prophecy: Israel to be in Egypt 400 years, Gen 15:13, 14; Israel to be in Babylon 70 years, Jer 25:11; 29:10; Dan 9:2; 7 sevens plus 62 sevens (of years) from the issuing of the commandment to rebuild Jerusalem until Messiah and his death, Dan 9:25; covenant of the coming king with Israel to be for seven years, Dan 9:27; 1290 days, Dan 12:11; 1335 days, Dan 12:12; Satan to be bound 1000 years, Rev 20:2, 3; resurrected martyrs to reign with Christ 1000 years, Rev 20:4–6.

TIMNA 1. Daughter of Seir, Gen 36:22; 1 Chron 1:38, 39. Concubine of Eliphaz, Gen 36:10–12.

2. A king of Edom, Gen 36:40–43; 1 Chron 1:36, 51–54.

TIMNAH 1. A city in Judah, Josh 15:10, 11; 19:43; 2 Chron 28:17, 18.

2. A city in the hill country of Judah, Josh 15:48–62.

3. A city given by some authorities as identical with *Timnah, 1,* Gen 38:12–14.

4. Home of Samson's wife, Judg 14:1, 2, 5. Believed by some authorities to be identical with the preceding.

TIMNATH-HERES See *Timnath-serah.*

TIMNATH-SERAH A city, called also *Timnath-heres.* Given to Joshua, Josh 19:50. Joshua buried in, Josh 24:30; Judg 2:7–9.

TIMON A member of the committee of seven appointed to supervise the daily distribution, Acts 6:5.

TIMOTHY The companion of Paul. Parentage of, Acts 16:1. Reputation and Christian faith of, Acts 16:2; 1 Cor 4:17; 16:10; 2 Tim 1:5; 3:15. Circumcised; becomes Paul's companion, Acts 16:3; 1 Thess 3:2, 3. Left by Paul at Beroea, Acts 17:14. Rejoins Paul at Corinth, Acts 17:15; 18:5. Sent to Greece, Acts 19:22. Rejoined by Paul; accompanies Paul to Asia, Acts 20:1–4. Sends greetings to the Romans, Rom 16:21. Sent to the Corinthians, 1 Cor 4:17; 16:10, 11. Preaches to the Corinthians, 2 Cor 1: 19. Sent to the Philippians, Phil 2:19, 23. Sent to the Thessalonians, 1 Thess 3:2, 3, 6. Left by Paul in Ephesus, 1 Tim 1:3, 2–4. Imprisoned with Paul in Rome, Phil 2:19–23; Philemon 1:1; Heb 13:23.

Joins Paul in the Epistle to the Philippians, Phil 1:1; to the Colossians, Col 1:1, 2; to the Thessalonians, 1 Thess 1:1; 2 Thess 1:1; to Philemon, Philemon 1:1, 2.

Zeal of, Phil 2:19–22; 1 Tim 6:12. Power of, 1 Tim 4:14; 2 Tim 1:6. Paul's love for, 1 Cor 4:17; Phil 2:22; 1 Tim 1:2, 18; 2 Tim 1:2–4. Paul writes to, 1 Tim 1:1, 2; 2 Tim 1:1, 2.

TIN Num 31:22; Job 15:25, 26; Ezk 22:18–20; 27:12.

TIPHSAH A city on the Euphrates, 1 Kgs 4: 24; possibly the same as *Tappuah* in 2 Kgs 15:16.

TIRAS Son of Japheth, Gen 10:2; 1 Chron 1: 5–9.

TIRHAKAH A king of Ethiopia, 2 Kgs 19:9; Isa 37:8, 9.

TIRHANAH Son of Caleb, 1 Chron 2:48, 49.

TIRI-A Son of Jehallelel, 1 Chron 4:16.

TIRZAH 1. A daughter of Zelophehad, Num 26:28–37; 36:11, 12; Josh 17:3. Special legislation in regard to the inheritance of, Num 27:1–11; 36; Josh 17:3, 4.

2. A city of Canaan. Captured by Joshua, Josh 12:8–24. Becomes the residence of the kings of Israel, 1 Kgs 14:17; 15:21, 28; 16:17, 23. Royal residence moved from, 1 Kgs 16:23, 24. Base of military operations of Menahem, 2 Kgs 15:14, 16. Beauty of, Song 6:4.

TITHE Paid by Abraham to Melchizedek, Gen 14:19, 20; Heb 7:2–6. Jacob vows a tenth of all his property to God, Gen 28:22.

Mosaic laws instituting, Lev 27:30–33; Num 18: 21–24; Deut 12:6, 7, 17, 19; 14:22–29; 26:12–15. Customs relating to, Neh 10:37, 38; Amos 4:4; Heb 7: 5–9. Tenth of tithes for priests, Num 18:25, 26; Neh 10:38. Stored in the temple, Neh 10:38–40; 12:44; 13: 5, 12; 2 Chron 31:11–13; Mal 3:10.

Payment of, resumed in Hezekiah's reign, 2 Chron 31:5–10. Under Nehemiah, Neh 13:12. Withheld, Neh 13:10; Mal 3:8.

Customary in later times, Mt 23:23; Lk 11:42; 18: 12. Observed by idolaters, Amos 4:4, 5.

See *Benevolence; Charity; Giving; Liberality; Tax.*

TITLE To real estate. See *Land.*

TITUS A Greek companion of Paul. Paul's love for, 2 Cor 2:13; 7:6, 7, 13, 14; 8:23; Tit 1:4. With Paul in Macedonia, 2 Cor 7:5, 6. Affection of, for the Corinthians, 2 Cor 7:13–15. Sent to Corinth, 2 Cor 8:6, 16–22; 12:17, 18. Character of, 2 Cor 12: 18. Accompanies Paul to Jerusalem, Gal 2:1–3. Compare Acts 15:1–29. Left by Paul in Crete, Tit 1:5; to rejoin him in Nicopolis, Tit 3:12. Paul writes to, Tit 1:1–4. With Paul in Rome, 2 Tim 4:10. Goes to Dalmatia, 2 Tim 4:10.

TOAH See *Nahath, 2.*

TOB A district in Syria, Judg 11:3; 2 Sam 10: 6–8.

TOBADONIJAH A Levite sent by Jehoshaphat to instruct the people in the law, 2 Chron 17:7–9.

TOBIAH 1. Ancestor of a family of Babylonian captives, Ezra 2:60; Neh 7:62.

2. An enemy of the Jews in the time of Nehemiah. Opposes the rebuilding of the wall of Jerusalem, Neh 2:10, 19; 4:3, 7, 8. Conspires to injure and intimidate Nehemiah, Neh 6:1–14, 19. Subverts leaders of Judah, Neh 6:17, 18. Allies himself with Eliashib, the priest, Neh 13:4–9.

TOBIJAH 1. A Levite sent by Jehoshaphat to instruct the people in the law, 2 Chron 17:7–9.

2. A captive in Babylon, Zech 6:10, 11, 14.

TOCHEN A city in Simeon, 1 Chron 4:32, 33.

TOE Anointed in consecration, Ex 29:19, 20; Lev 8:23, 24; in purification, Lev 14:14, 17, 25, 28. Of prisoners of war cut off, Judg 1:4–6. Six, on each foot, 2 Sam 21:20, 21; 1 Chron 20:6, 7.

TOGARMAH Son of Gomer, Gen 10:3; 1 Chron 1:5–9. Descendants of, Ezk 27:14; 38:6.

TOHU See *Nahath, 2.*

TOI Called also *Tou.* King of Hamath, 2 Sam 8:9, 10; 1 Chron 18:9, 10.

TOKEN Of authority, Gen 41:41, 42. Of harvest, Deut 26:10. Of alliance, Isa 16:1. Of surrender, Isa 36:16. Christ a, Isa 49:8, 9. Of forgiveness, Joel 2:23. Of God's agreement, Lk 22:20.

See *Miracles; Proof; Sign.*

TOKHATH See *Tikvah, 1.*

TOLA 1. Son of Issachar, Gen 46:8–14; Num 26:23–25; 1 Chron 7:1, 2.

2. A judge of Israel, Judg 10:1, 2.

TOLAD See *Eltolad.*

TOLERATION Religious, Mic 4:4, 5; Mk 9: 38–40; Lk 9:49, 50; Acts 17:11, 28, 31; Rom 14; 1 Cor 10:28–32.

See *Intolerance.*

TOLL See *Tribute; Tax.*

TOMB See *Burial.*

TOMBSTONE At Rachel's grave, Gen 35: 20.

See *Pillar.*

TONGS 1 Kgs 7:49; 2 Chron 4:21; Isa 6:6.

TONGUE Language, Ps 114:1; Ezk 3:6. Gift of, Acts 2:1–18, 33; 10:46, 47; 19:6; 1 Cor 12:10, 28, 30; 14.

Loquacious, Prov 10:19. Restrained by wisdom, Prov 17:27, 28; 21:23; Eccl 3:7. Hasty, Prov 29:20.

See *Language.*

An evil, see *Slander; Speaking, Evil.*

TONGUES The miraculous gift of the early Christians, 1 Cor 12:10, 28, 30; 13:8; 14:2–19, 21–28, 39. Principles governing the use of, 1 Cor 14:26–40.

TOOLS See *Agriculture, Implements of; Art.*

TOPAZ A precious stone, Song 5:14; Ezk 28:13; Rev 21:18–20. In the chestpiece, Ex 28:17;

39:10. Ethiopian, celebrated, Job 28:19.

TOPHEL A place in the wilderness of Sinai, Deut 1:1.

TOPHETH An altar in the Valley of the Sons of Hinnom, 2 Kgs 23:10. Jewish children sacrificed to Molech in, 2 Kgs 23:10; Jer 7:31 32; 19:6, 11–14; 32:35. See also 2 Chron 28:3; 33:6. Destroyed by Josiah, 2 Kgs 23:10. Horror of, Isa 30:33.

TOPOGRAPHY Of Canaan, Josh 13:15–33; 15; 18:9.

TORCH Miraculously appeared at Abram's sacrifice, Gen 15:17. Used by Samson, Judg 15:4.

TORMENTS Of the wicked, Lk 16:23–28; Rev 14:10, 11.

See *Wicked, Punishment of.*

TOTAL ABSTINENCE See *Abstinence.*

TOU See *Toi.*

TOWEL Jn 13:4, 5.

TOWER Of Babel, Gen 11:1–9. Of Eder, Gen 35:21. Of Penuel, Judg 8:8, 9, 17. Of the Hundred, Neh 3:1; 12:39. Of Hananel, Neh 3:1; 12:39; Jer 31: 38, 39; Zech 14:10. Of David, Song 4:4. Of Siloam, Lk 13:4. In the walls of Jerusalem, 2 Chron 26:9; Neh 12:38, 39. Of other cities, 2 Chron 14:7. For watchmen or sentinels, 2 Kgs 9:17; 18:8.

Parable of, Lk 14:28, 29.

See *Forts.*

FIGURATIVE. Of divine protection, 2 Sam 22:3; Ps 18:2; 61:3; 144:2.

TOWN See *Cities.*

TRACHONITIS A part of the tetrarchy of Philip, Lk 3:1, 2.

TRADE 1. Occupation. See under name of each trade.

2. Commerce. See *Commerce.*

TRADITION The body of precepts, largely ritual, held by the Jews to have been orally given by Moses and handed down to succeeding generations, and respected as equal to the written Word, but called by Christ man-made rules, Mt 12:1–8; 15: 2–6; Mk 7:3–9; Lk 6:1–11; Col 2:8; 1 Pet 1:18. Not authoritative, Mt 15:3–20; 1 Tim 1:3, 4; 4:7. In 2 Thess 2:15; 3:6; 1 Cor 11:2; it refers to Paul's teaching, whether oral or written. "The traditional rules of my religion," Gal 1:14, were precepts received from the fathers, oral or written.

TRAFFIC Suspended on the Sabbath, Neh 13: 15–22.

TRAIN Retinue or procession, 1 Kgs 10:2; Ps 68:18.

TRAITOR Judas, Mt 26:14–16, 46–50; Mk 14: 10, 11, 43–45; Lk 22:3–6, 21–23, 47, 48; Jn 12:2, 27–30; 18:2–8, 13.

See *Treason.*

TRAMP Gen 4:12, 14.

TRANCE Of Balaam, Num 24:14–19. Of Peter, Acts 10: 9, 10. Of Paul, Acts 22:17, 18.

TRANSFIGURATION Of Moses, Ex 34: 29–35. Of Jesus, Mt 17:2–9; Mk 9:2–10; Lk 9:29–36; 2 Pet 1:16–18. Of Stephen, Acts 6:15.

TRANSLATION Transporting to heaven. Of Enoch, Gen 5:21–24; Heb 11:5. Of Elijah, 2 Kgs 2:1–12. Of Jesus, Mk 16:19; Lk 24:51; Acts 1:9–11. Desired by Paul, 2 Cor 5:4. Of all believers when Christ returns for them, Jn 14:2, 3; 1 Thess 4:16, 17.

See *Rapture.*

TRAP Josh 23:13; Job 18:10; Jer 5:26; Amos 3: 5. Set for birds, Prov 1:17.

FIGURATIVE. Ps 9:15; 10:9; 31:4; 57:6; Prov 29: 5. Of the evils in the life of the wicked, Job 18:8–10. Of the devices of the wicked to deceive the righteous, Ps 91:3; Jer 5:26.

See *Net; Snare.*

TRAY Ex 25:38; Num 4:9. John the Baptist's head carried on, Mt 14:8, 11.

TREACHERY Jer 9:8. Of Rahab to her people, Josh 2. Of the man of Bethel, Judg 1:24, 25. Of Jael, Judg 4:18–21. Of Shechemites, Judg 9:22, 23. Of Joab, 2 Sam 3:26, 27. Of Baanah and Rechab, 2 Sam 4:6, 7. Of David to Uriah, 2 Sam 11. Of Joab to Amasa, 2 Sam 20:8–10. Of Jehu, 2 Kgs 10:18–28. Of the enemies of Nehemiah, Neh 6.

See *Conspiracy; Treason.*

TREASON INSTANCES OF. Of Aaron and Miriam against Moses, Num 12:1–11. Of Korah, Dathan, and Abiram against Moses and Aaron, Num 16:1–33. Of Rahab against Jericho, Josh 2. Of the betrayer of Bethel, Judg 1:24, 25. Of the Shechemites against Abimelech, Judg 9:22–25. Of the Ephraimites against Jephthah, Judg 12:1–4. Of the Israelites against Saul, 1 Sam 10:27; against Rehoboam, 1 Kgs 12:16–19. Of the Egyptian servant against the Amalekites, 1 Sam 30:15, 16. Of Abner against Ish-bosheth, 2 Sam 3:6–21. Of Jehoiada against Athaliah, 2 Kgs 11:13–16. Of Absalom against his father, see *Absalom.*

Death penalty for, Esther 2:23.

Jesus falsely accused of, Mt 27:11, 29, 20; Lk 23: 2, 3, 38; Jn 19:12, 14, 15, 19. Paul falsely accused of, Acts 17:7.

David's amnesty of the traitors, 2 Sam 19:16–23; to Amasa, 2 Sam 19:13.

See *Conspiracy; Treachery.*

TREASURE A thing of highly estimated value. Money, Gen 42:25, 27, 28, 35; 43:23, with *vs.* 18, 21, 22. Jewelry, 1 Chron 29:8.

Jesus forbids the hoarding of, Mt 6:19; 19:21; Lk 12:33. Hidden, Mt 13:44.

See *Riches.*

FIGURATIVE. Of the graces of the spirit, Prov 21:20; Isa 33:6. Of spiritual understanding, Mt 13: 52; Col 2:3. Of the object of the affections, Mt 6: 19–21; Lk 12:34. Of spiritual calling, 2 Cor 4:6, 7.

The believer's knowledge of the glory of God called treasure, 2 Cor 4:7. Parable of, Mt 13:44.

TREASURER 2 Chron 34:8; Ezra 1:8; Jn 13: 29; Acts 8:27; Rom 16:23.

TREASURY Of kings, 2 Kgs 20:13; 1 Chron 27:25; 2 Chron 32:27–29; Ezra 1:7, 8; Esther 3:9. Treasurers in charge of, Ezra 7:20, 21.

Heathen temples used for, Dan 1:1, 2.

Tabernacle used for, Num 31:54; Josh 6:19, 24. Solomon's Temple used for, 1 Kgs 7:51; 2 Kgs 12: 4–14, 18; 22:3–6; 1 Chron 28:11, 12; Mt 27:6; Mk 12: 41, 43, 44; Lk 21:1; Jn 8:20. Under the charge of the Levites, 1 Chron 26:20–22. Storage areas provided in the temple for various kinds of offerings, Neh 10:38–40; 13:5, 9, 12; Mal 3:10. Priests and Levites in charge of, 1 Chron 9:26; 26:20–28; Neh 12:44; 13:13.

See *Archives.*

TREATY Between nations: Israelites and Gibeonites, Josh 9:3–15; Judah and Syria, 1 Kgs 15:19. Cession of territory by, 1 Kgs 9:10–14; 20:34. Sacredness of, Josh 9:16–21, with chapter 2:8–21; cf. Dan 9:27.

Reciprocity, 1 Kgs 5:1–12. With idolatrous nations forbidden, Ex 34:12, 15.

TREE Of life, Gen 2:9; 3:22, 24; Rev 22:14. Of conscience, Gen 2:9, 16, 17; 3:2–6, 11, 12, 17. Laws concerning, Lev 19:23; Deut 20:19.

FIGURATIVE. Ps 1:3; Song 2:3; Jer 17:8; Mt 12:33. Parable of, Judg 9:8–15.

Symbolical. Dan 4:10–12.

TRESPASS 2 Chron 26:17, 18. Of an ox, Ex 21:28–36. Of a brother, Mt 18:15–18; Lk 17:2–4. Creditor shall not enter debtor's house to take security, Deut 24:10.

Trespass offering, see *Offerings, Sin, Guilt.*

TRIAL Before court, Lev 24:10–14. Right of, Jn 7:51; Acts 16:37–39; 22:25–30. Of Jesus, see *Jesus, History of.* See also *Peter; John, the Apostle; Stephen; Paul.*

See *Court; Justice; Prisoners.*

OF FAITH. See *Faith; Temptation.*

TRIBULATION Acts 14:22.

See *Afflictions; Persecution; Suffering.*

TRIBULATION, THE GREAT The expression appears in Rev 7:14. It describes the largest theme of prophecy except for the kingdom.

CALLED. A time of anguish, greater than any previous suffering, Dan 12:1; the time of Jacob's trouble, Jer 30:7; a destruction from the Almighty, Joel 1:15; the day of the Lord's wrath, Zeph 1:18; persecution, such as the world has never before seen in all its history, and will never see again, Mt 24:21; days of horror as have never been since the beginning of God's creation, nor will ever be again, Mk 13:19; the time . . . which will come upon the world to test everyone alive, Rev 3:10, the anger of the Lamb; the great day of their anger, Rev 6:16, 17; the Great Tribulation, Rev 7:14.

CHARACTER OF. Primarily the outpouring of the wrath of God upon the earth, prior to the manifestation of his wrath as he sits in judgment. It is the day of the Lord, cruel both with wrath and fierce anger, Isa 13:9, 13; the day of the Lord's wrath, Zeph 1:18; when God will pour out his fury, Ezk 7:8, 9; the day of wrath, Ezk 7:19; the anger of the Lamb, Rev 6:16, 17; the wine of the anger of God, poured out undiluted, Rev 14:10; the great winepress of God's wrath, Rev 14:19; the outpouring of the flasks of the wrath of God, Rev 15:1, 7; 16:1–21; the winepress of the fierceness of the wrath of Almighty God, Rev 19:15.

The time of the anger of Satan, and his angels, Rev 9:1–11, 14, 15; 12:7–12; 16:13, 14. The time of the wrath of men, Mt 24:12; Gal 5:20; Lk 17:26; Gen 6:11.

REASONS FOR. To refine Israel in preparation for the kingdom, Ezk 20:37, 38; Zech 13:9; to test and to punish, Isa 13:11; Dan 2:44; Rev 3:10; Rev 7:9, 14; Mt 25:31–46; to prepare the earth for the kingdom, Isa 30:26; Ps 72:16; Ezk 36:34, 35; Isa 24:21; Rev 12:9; 20:1–3.

PROMINENT PERSONAGES IN. The two witnesses, Rev 11:3–13; the beast, or Creature, Rev 13:1–10; cf. Dan 7:8; 9:26; 11:36; 2 Thess 2:3, 8; the false prophet, Rev 13:11–18.

WHEN IT TAKES PLACE. In the latter days, Deut 4:27–31; when some Jews have returned to their land in unbelief, Joel 2:1–27; Ezk 38:8, 15, 16; 39:22; Zech 12:2, 3, 10; 14:1–3; before the second coming of Christ to the earth and his regathering Israel, his elect, Mt 24:27–31; Deut 30:3.

EVENTS INCLUDED. Trouble so terrible that the days are shortened, Mt 24:21, 22; the devil and his angels thrown down onto the earth, Rev 12:9; infernal locusts come out of the smoke of the pit, Rev 9:1–6; evil spirits gather the nations to Armageddon, Rev 16:13, 14; the seals broken, Rev 5, 6; the trumpets blown, Rev 8, 9; the flasks of wrath poured out, Rev 16:1–21; the apostate world religion destroyed, Rev 17:16; Palestine invaded by the armies of the nations, Zech 14:1–3.

To begin after the abomination of desolation is seen in the holy place, Mt 24:15–21; to last seven years, Dan 9:24–27; divided into two equal parts, cf. half that time, Dan 9:27; time, times and half a time, Rev 12:14; 42 months, Rev 11:2; 13:5; 1,260 days, Rev 11:3; 12:6. The latter half is more properly the great tribulation. Christ returns immediately afterward, Mt 24:29, 30.

TRIBUTE From conquered nations, Josh 16:10; Judg 1:30–33; 2 Kgs 15:19, 20; 23:35; Mt 17:24–27; 22:15–22; Lk 2:1–5. By Arabians to Solomon, 2 Chron 9:13, 14; to Jehoshaphat, 2 Chron 17:11.

See *Duty; Tax.*

TRINITY THE HOLY. Gen 1:26. Then God said, "Let us make a man—someone like ourselves. . . ."

Gen 3:22. Then the Lord said, "Now that the man has become as we are, knowing good from bad. . . ."

Isa 11:2. And the Spirit of the Lord shall rest upon him . . . . [3]His delight will be obedience to the Lord.

Isa 42:1. See my Servant, whom I uphold; my Chosen One, in whom I delight. I have put my Spirit upon him. Mt 12:18.

Isa 48:16. Come closer and listen. I have always told you plainly what would happen, so that you could clearly understand. And now the Lord God and his Spirit have sent me (with this message).

Isa 61:1. The Spirit of the Lord God is upon me, because the Lord has anointed me to bring good news to the suffering and afflicted. He has sent me to comfort the broken-hearted, to announce liberty to captives and to open the eyes of the blind. [Lk 4:18, 19.] [2]He has sent me to tell those who mourn that the time of God's favor to them has come, and the day of his wrath to their enemies. [3]To all who mourn in Israel he will give: Beauty for ashes; joy instead of mourning; praise instead of heaviness. For God has planted them like strong and graceful oaks for his own glory.

Isa 63:9. In all their affliction he was afflicted, and he personally saved them. . . . [10]But they rebelled against him and grieved his Holy Spirit. Dan 2:47.

Mt 1:18. These are the facts concerning the birth of Jesus Christ: His mother, Mary, was engaged to be married to Joseph. But while she was still a virgin she became pregnant by the Holy Spirit. [20]He fell into a dream, and saw an angel standing beside him. "Joseph, son of David," the angel said, "don't hesitate to take Mary as your wife! For the child within her has been conceived by the Holy Spirit."

Mt 3:11. But someone else is coming, far greater than I am, so great that I am not worthy to carry his shoes! He shall baptize you with the Holy Spirit and with fire. Mk 1:8; Lk 3:16.

Mt 12:28. But if I am casting out demons by the Spirit of God, then the Kingdom of God has arrived among you.

Mt 28:19. Therefore go and make disciples in all the nations, baptizing them into the name of the Father and of the Son and of the Holy Spirit.

Lk 1:35. The angel replied, "The Holy Spirit shall come upon you, and the power of God shall overshadow you; so the baby born to you will be utterly holy—the Son of God."

Lk 3:22. And the Holy Spirit in the form of a dove settled upon him, and a voice from heaven said, "You are my much loved Son, yes, my delight." Mt 3:16.

Lk 4:1. Then Jesus, full of the Holy Spirit, left the Jordan River, being urged by the Spirit out into the barren wastelands of Judea. [14]Then Jesus returned to Galilee, full of the Holy Spirit's power.

Jn 1:32. Then John told about seeing the Holy Spirit in the form of a dove descending from heaven and resting upon Jesus. [33]"I didn't know he was the one," John said again, "but at the time God sent me to baptize he told me, 'When you see the Holy Spirit descending and resting upon someone—he is the one you are looking for. He is the one who baptizes with the Holy Spirit.' "

Jn 3:34. For this one—sent by God—speaks God's words, for God's Spirit is upon him without measure or limit. [35]The Father loves this man because he is his Son, and God has given him everything there is.

Jn 7:39. He was speaking of the Holy Spirit, who would be given to everyone believing in him; but the Spirit had not yet been given, because Jesus had not yet returned to his glory in heaven.

Jn 14:16. And I will ask the Father and he will give you another Comforter, and he will never leave you. [17]He is the Holy Spirit, the Spirit who leads into all truth. The world at large cannot receive him, for it isn't looking for him and doesn't recognize him. But you do, for he lives with you now and some day shall be in you. [26]But when the Father sends the Comforter instead of me—and by the Comforter I mean the Holy Spirit—he will teach you much, as well as remind you of everything I myself have told you.

Jn 15:26. But I will send you the Comforter—the Holy Spirit, the source of all truth. He will come to you from the Father and will tell you all about me.

Jn 16:7. But the fact of the matter is that it is best for you that I go away, for if I don't, the Comforter won't come. If I do, he will—for I will send him to you. [13]When the Holy Spirit, who is truth, comes, he shall guide you into all truth, for he will not be presenting his own ideas, but will be passing on to you what he has heard. He will tell you about the future. [14]He shall praise me and bring me great honor by showing you my glory. [15]All the Father's glory is mine; this is what I mean when I say that he will show you my glory.

Jn 20:22. Then he breathed on them and told them, "Receive the Holy Spirit."

Acts 1:2. He returned to heaven after giving his chosen apostles further instructions from the Holy Spirit. [4]In one of these meetings he told them not to leave Jerusalem until the Holy Spirit came upon them in fulfillment of the Father's promise, a matter he had previously discussed with them. [5]"John baptized you with water," he reminded them, "but you shall be baptized with the Holy Spirit in just a few days."

Acts 2:33. And now he sits on the throne of highest honor in heaven, next to God. And just as promised, the Father gave him the authority to send the Holy Spirit—with the results you are seeing and hearing today.

Acts 10:36, 37. I'm sure you have heard about the Good News for the people of Israel—that there is peace with God through Jesus, the Messiah, who is Lord of all creation. This message has spread all through Judea, beginning with John the Baptist in Galilee. [38]And you no doubt know that Jesus of Nazareth was anointed by God with the Holy Spirit and with power, and he went around doing good and healing all who were possessed by demons, for God was with him.

Rom 1:3. It is the Good News about his Son, Jesus Christ our Lord, who came as a human baby, born into King David's royal family line; [4]and by being raised from the dead he was proved to be the mighty Son of God, with the holy nature of God himself.

Rom 8:9. But you are not like that. You are controlled by your new nature if you have the Spirit of God living in you. (And remember that if anyone doesn't have the Spirit of Christ living in him, he is not a Christian at all.) [10]Yet, even though Christ lives within you, your body will die because of sin; but your spirit will live, for Christ has pardoned it. [11]And if the Spirit of God, who raised up Jesus from the dead, lives in you, he will make your dying bodies live again after you die, by means of this same Holy Spirit living within you. [26]And in the same way—by our faith

—the Holy Spirit helps us with our daily problems and in our praying. For we don't even know what we should pray for, nor how to pray as we should; but the Holy Spirit prays for us with such feeling that it cannot be expressed in words. [27]And the Father who knows all hearts knows, of course, what the Spirit is saying as he pleads for us in harmony with God's own will.

1 Cor 2:10. But we know about these things because God has sent his Spirit to tell us, and his Spirit searches out and shows us all of God's deepest secrets. [11]No one can really know what anyone else is thinking, or what he is really like, except that person himself. And no one can know God's thoughts except God's own Spirit.

1 Cor 6:19. Haven't you yet learned that your body is the home of the Holy Spirit God gave you, and that he lives within you? Your own body does not belong to you.

1 Cor 8:6. But we know that there is only one God, the Father, who created all things and made us to be his own; and one Lord Jesus Christ, who made everything and gives us life.

1 Cor 12:3. No one speaking by the power of the Spirit of God can curse Jesus, and no one can say "Jesus is Lord," and really mean it, unless the Holy Spirit is helping him. [4]Now God gives us many kinds of special abilities, but it is the same Holy Spirit who is the source of them all. [5]There are different kinds of service to God, but it is the same Lord we are serving. [6]There are many ways in which God works in our lives, but it is the same God who does the work in and through all of us who are his.

2 Cor 1:21. It is this God who has made you and me into faithful Christians and commissioned us apostles to preach the Good News. [22]He has put his brand upon us—his mark of ownership—and given us his Holy Spirit in our hearts as guarantee that we belong to him, and as the first installment of all that he is going to give us. 2 Cor 5:5.

2 Cor 3:17. The Lord is the Spirit who gives them life, and where he is there is freedom.

2 Cor 13:14. May the grace of our Lord Jesus Christ be with you all. May God's love and the Holy Spirit's friendship be yours.

Gal 4:4. But when the right time came, the time God decided on, he sent his Son, born of a woman, born as a Jew. [6]And because we are his sons God has sent the Spirit of his Son into our hearts, so now we can rightly speak of God as our dear Father.

Phil 1:19. I am going to keep on being glad, for I know that as you pray for me, and as the Holy Spirit helps me, this is all going to turn out for my good.

Col 2:2. That you will be encouraged and knit together by strong ties of love, and that you will have the rich experience of knowing Christ with real certainty and clear understanding. *For God's secret plan, now at last made known, is Christ himself.*

2 Thess 2:13. But we must forever give thanks to God for you, our brothers loved by the Lord, because God chose from the very first to give you salvation, cleansing you by the work of the Holy Spirit and by your trusting in the Truth. [14]Through us he told you the Good News. Through us he called you to share in the glory of our Lord Jesus Christ. [16]May our Lord Jesus Christ himself and God our Father, who has loved us and given us everlasting comfort and hope which we don't deserve.

1 Tim 3:16. But the answer lies in Christ, who came to earth as a man, was proved spotless and pure in his Spirit, was served by angels, was preached among the nations, was accepted by men everywhere and was received up again to his glory in heaven.

Tit 3:4. But when the time came for the kindness and love of God our Savior to appear, [5]then he saved us—not because we were good enough to be saved, but because of his kindness and pity—by washing away our sins and giving us the new joy of the indwelling Holy Spirit [6]whom he poured out upon us with wonderful fullness—and all because of what Jesus Christ our Savior did.

Heb 9:14. Just think how much more surely the blood of Christ will transform our lives and hearts. His sacrifice frees us from the worry of having to obey the old rules, and makes us want to serve the living God.

1 Pet 1:2. Dear friends, God the Father chose you long ago and knew you would become his children. And the Holy Spirit has been at work in your hearts, cleansing you with the blood of Jesus Christ.

1 Pet 3:18. Christ also suffered. He died once for the sins of all us guilty sinners, although he himself was innocent of any sin at any time, that he might bring us safely home to God. But though his body died, his spirit lived on.

1 Jn 5:6. God said so with a voice from heaven when Jesus was baptized, and again as he was facing death. . . . And the Holy Spirit, forever truthful, says it too. So we have these three witnesses: the voice of the Holy Spirit in our hearts, the voice from heaven at Christ's baptism, and the voice before he died. And they all say the same thing: that Jesus Christ is the Son of God.

Rev 4:8. Each of these Living Beings had six wings, and the central sections of their wings were covered with eyes. Day after day and night after night they kept on saying, "Holy, holy, holy, Lord God Almighty—the one who was and is, and is to come."

See *God; Holy Spirit; Jesus Christ.*

TROAS A seaport of Mysia, in Asia Minor. Paul visits, Acts 16:8, 11; 20:5, 6; 2 Cor 2:12; 2 Tim 4:13.

TROPHIES Goliath's head and armor, 1 Sam 17:54; 21:9; Saul's, 1 Sam 31:8–10. Placed in temples, see *Temple.*

TROPHIMUS An Ephesian companion of Paul. Accompanies Paul from Greece to Asia, Acts 20:4. With Paul in Jerusalem; made the occasion of an attack on Paul, Acts 21:27–30. Left ill at Miletus, 2 Tim 4:20.

TROUBLE BORROWING. Mt 6:25. So my counsel is: Don't worry about *things*—food, drink, and clothes. For you already have life and a body —and they are far more important than what to eat and wear. [26]Look at the birds! They don't worry about what to eat—they don't need to sow or reap or store up food—for your heavenly Father feeds them. And you are far more valuable to him than they are. [27]Will all your worries add a single moment to your life? [28]And why worry about your clothes? Look at the field lilies! They don't worry about theirs. [29]Yet King Solomon in all his glory was not clothed as beautifully as they. [30]And if God cares so wonderfully for flowers that are here today and gone tomorrow, won't he more surely care for you, O men of little faith? [31, 32]So don't worry at all about having enough food and clothing. Why be like the heathen? For they take pride in all these things and are deeply concerned about them. But your heavenly Father already knows perfectly well that you need them, [33]and he will give them to you if you give him first place in your life and live as he wants you to. [34]"So don't be anxious about tomorrow. God will take care of your tomorrow too. Live one day at a time.

Mk 5:35. While he was still talking to her, messengers arrived from Jairus' home with the news that it was too late—his daughter was dead and there was no point in Jesus' coming now. [36]But Jesus ignored their comments and said to Jairus, "Don't be afraid. Just trust me."

Jn 14:1. Let not your heart be troubled. You are trusting God, now trust in me.

Jn 16:6. Instead you are only filled with sorrow. [7]But the fact of the matter is that it is best for you that I go away, for if I don't, the Comforter won't come. If I do, he will—for I will send him to you.

Phil 4:6. Don't worry about anything.

1 Pet 5:7. Let him have all your worries and cares, for he is always thinking about you and watching everything that concerns you.

See *Afflictions; Suffering.*

INSTANCES OF. Israelites at the Red Sea, Ex 14: 10–12; about water, Ex 15:23–25; 17:2, 3; Num 20: 1–13; food, Ex 16:2, 3; Num 11:4–33. When Moses lingered in the mountain, Ex 32:1. When the spies brought their adverse report, Num 13:28, 29, 31–33; 14:1–4, with *vs.* 4–12. Elijah, under the broom bush and in the cave, 1 Kgs 19:4–15. The disciples as to how the crowd could be fed, Mt 14:15; Mk 6:37; in the storm, when Jesus was asleep in the boat, Mt 8:23–26; Mk 4:36–39; Lk 8:22–24; when Jesus was crucified, Lk 24:4–9, 24–31, 36–40. Mary at the sepulchre, Jn 20:11–17. The people in the shipwreck, Acts 27:22–25, 30–36.

TRUCE In battle, 2 Sam 2:26–31.

TRUMPET Made of ram's horn, Josh 6:3–8, 12–14; of silver, Num 10:1, 2. Uses of, prescribed by Moses, Num 10:1–10. Used in war, Job 39:24, 25; Jer 4:19; 6:1, 17; Ezk 7:14; Amos 2:2; 3:6; Zeph 1:16; 1 Cor 14:8. To summon soldiers, by Phinehas, Num 31:6; by Ehud, Judg 3:27; by Gideon, Judg 6:34; by Saul, 1 Sam 13:3, 4; by Joab, 2 Sam 2:28; 18:16; 20: 22; by Absalom, 2 Sam 15:10; by Sheba, 2 Sam 20: 1; by Nehemiah, Neh 4:18, 19. By Gideon's soldiers, Judg 7:8–22. In war, of Abijah, 2 Chron 13:12–14. In the siege of Jericho, Josh 6:3–20.

Sounded in time of danger, Ezk 33:3–6; Joel 2:1.

Used at Sinai, Ex 19:13–19; 20:18; Heb 12:19; on the great day of atonement, Isa 27:13; at the jubilee, Lev 25:9; at the bringing of the Ark to Jerusalem, 2 Sam 6:5, 15; 1 Chron 13:8; 15:28; the anointing of kings, 1 Kgs 1:34, 39; 2 Kgs 9:13; 11:13, 14; dedication of Solomon's Temple, 2 Chron 5:11–14; 7:6; in worship, 1 Chron 15:24; 16:42; Ps 81:3, 4; at Jehoshaphat's triumph, 2 Chron 20:28; at the foundation of the second Temple, Ezra 3:10, 11; at the dedication of the wall, Neh 12:35, 36, 40, 41.

IN PROPHECY. Mt 24:31; 1 Cor 15:52; 1 Thess 4: 16; Rev 1:10; 4:1; 8; 9:1–14; 10:7; 11:15.

FIGURATIVE. Isa 27:13; Ezk 33:3; Joel 2:1; Zech 9:14; Mt 6:2.

See *Music, Instruments of.*

TRUMPETS, FEAST OF When and how observed, Lev 23:23–25; Num 29:1–6. Celebrated after the captivity with joy, Neh 8:9–12.

See *Feasts.*

TRUST See *Faith; Waiting.*

TRUSTEE Mosaic law concerning, Ex 22:7–13; Lev 6:2–7. The parable of the investments, Mt 25:14–28; of the nobleman, Lk 19:12–27.

See *Steward.*

TRUTH Believers should worship God in, Jn 4:21–24, with Ps 145:18; serve God in, Josh 24:14; 1 Sam 12:24; walk before God in, 1 Kgs 2:4; 2 Kgs 20:3; keep religious feast with, 1 Cor 5:8; esteem, as inestimable, Prov 23:23; love, Zech 8:19; rejoice in, 1 Cor 13:6; speak, to one another, Zech 8:16; Eph 4:25; execute judgment with, Zech 8:16; meditate upon, Phil 4:8; hold on to, Prov 3:3; write, within the heart, Prov 3:3.

The fruit of the Spirit is in, Eph 5:9.

Ministers should speak, 2 Cor 12:6; Gal 4:16; teach in, 1 Tim 2:7; Prove themselves by, 2 Cor 6: 7, 8.

Judges should be men of, Ex 18:21.

Kings are preserved by, Prov 20:28.

Good men are known by, Prov 12:17; are the delight of God, Prov 12:22.

The wicked are without, Hos 4:1, 2; do not speak, Jer 9:5; do not uphold, Isa 59:14, 15; do not care for, Isa 59:4; Jer 9:3; are punished for want of, Jer 9:5, 9; Hos 4:1, 3.

Is in Christ, 1 Tim 2:7. John bare witness to, Jn 5:33. Changes lives, Tit 1:1. Is sanctifying, Jn 17:17, 19. Is purifying, 1 Pet 1:22. Is part of the Christian armor, Eph 6:14. Abides continually with believers, 2 Jn 1:2. Should be acknowledged, 2 Tim 2:25. Should be believed, 2 Thess 2:12, 13. Should be obeyed, Rom 2:8; Gal 3:1. Should be loved, 2 Thess 2:10. Should be manifested, 2 Cor 4:2. Should be understood, 2 Tim 2:15. The wicked ignore, 2 Tim 4:4. The wicked fight, 2 Tim 3:8. The wicked destitute of, 1 Tim 6:5. The Church contains and promotes, 1 Tim 3:15. The devil is devoid of, Jn 8:44.

OF GOD. Is one of his attributes, Isa 65:16; he keeps, forever, Ps 146:6; abundant, Ex 34:5, 6; inviolable, Num 23:18–24; Tit 1:2. Exhibited in his ways, Rev 15:3, 4; works, Ps 33:4; 111:7; Dan 4:37; judicial statutes, Ps 19:9; word, Ps 119:160; Jn 17:17; fulfillment of promises in Christ, 2 Cor 1:20; fulfillment of his covenant, Mic 7:20; dealings with believers, Ps 25:10; deliverance of believers, Ps 57:3; punishment of the wicked, Rev 16:7. Is a shield and armor to believers, Ps 91:4. We should confide in, Ps 31:5, 6; Tit 1:1, 2. Plead in prayer, Ps 89:49. Pray for its manifestation to ourselves, 2 Chron 6:17. Pray for its exhibition to others, 2 Sam 2:6. Make known, to others, Isa 38:19. Praise, Ps 71:22; 138:2. Is denied by the devil, Gen 3:4, 5; the self-righteous, 1 Jn 1:10; unbelievers, 1 Jn 5:10.

UNCLASSIFIED SCRIPTURES RELATING TO. Ex 34:6. And passed in front of him and announced the meaning of his name. "I am Jehovah, the merciful and gracious God," he said, "slow to anger and rich in steadfast love and truth."

2 Sam 7:28. For you indeed are God, and your words are truth.

Ps 12:6. The Lord's promise is sure. He speaks no careless word; all he says is purest truth, like silver seven times refined.

Ps 25:10. And when we obey him, every path he guides us on is fragrant with his lovingkindness and his truth.

Ps 31:5. You have rescued me, O God who keeps his promises.

Ps 40:10. I have not kept this Good News hidden in my heart, but have proclaimed your lovingkindness and truth to all the congregation.

Ps 51:6. You deserve honesty from the heart; yes, utter sincerity and truthfulness.

Ps 85:10. Mercy and truth have met together. Grim justice and peace have kissed! [11]Truth rises from the earth and righteousness smiles down from heaven.

Ps 86:15. But you are merciful and gentle, Lord, slow in getting angry, full of constant lovingkindness and of truth.

Ps 89:14. Your throne is founded on two strong pillars—the one is Justice and the other Righteousness. Mercy and Truth walk before you as your attendants.

Ps 96:13. For the Lord is coming to judge the earth; he will judge the nations fairly and with truth!

Ps 117:2. For he loves us very dearly, and his truth endures.

Prov 12:19. Truth stands the test of time; lies are soon exposed.

Prov 16:13. The king rejoices when his people are truthful and fair.

Isa 25:1. O Lord, I will honor and praise your name, for you are my God; you do such wonderful things! You planned them long ago, and now you have accomplished them, just as you said!

Isa 45:19. I, Jehovah, speak only truth and righteousness.

Isa 59:14. Truth falls dead in the streets, and justice is outlawed. [15]Yes, truth is gone.

Isa 65:16. And yet, the days will come when all who invoke a blessing or take an oath shall swear by the God of Truth.

Jer 5:3. O Lord, you will take naught but truth.

Mic 7:20. You will bless us as you promised Jacob long ago. You will set your love upon us, as you promised our father Abraham!

Mt 21:44. All who stumble on this rock of truth shall be broken, but those it falls on will be scattered as dust.

Jn 1:14. And Christ became a human being and lived here on earth among us and was full of loving forgiveness and truth.

Jn 3:33. Those who believe him discover that God is a fountain of truth.

Jn 8:31. Jesus said to them, "You are truly my disciples if you live as I tell you to, [32]and you will know the truth, and the truth will set you free."

Jn 14:6. Jesus told him, "I am the Way—yes, and the Truth and the Life. [17]He is the Holy Spirit, the Spirit who leads into all truth."

Jn 16:13. When the Holy Spirit, who is truth, comes, he shall guide you into all truth.

Jn 17:17. Make them pure and holy through teaching them your words of truth. [19]And I consecrate myself to meet their need for growth in truth and holiness.

Jn 18:37. Pilate replied, "But you are a king then?" "Yes," Jesus said. "I was born for that purpose. And I came to bring truth to the world. All who love the truth are my followers." [38]"What is truth?" Pilate exclaimed. Then he went out again to the people and told them, "He is not guilty of any crime."

TRYPHAENA A Christian woman in Rome, Rom 16:12.

TRYPHOSA A Christian woman in Rome, Rom 16:12.

TUBAL Son of Japheth, Gen 10:2; 1 Chron 1: 5–9. Descendants of, become a nation, Isa 66:19; Ezk 27:13; 32:26; 38:2, 3; 39:1.

TUBAL-CAIN Instructor of those who worked in brass and iron, Gen 4:22.

TUBERCULOSIS Lev 26:16; Deut 28:22.

TUMOR 1 Sam 5:6, 9, 12; 6:4, 5, 11, 17.

See *Boil.*

TURBAN Worn by priests, Ex 28:40; 29:9; 39:28; Lev 8:13; Ezk 44:18.

See *Crown; Dress.*

TURKEY 1. See *Ararat.*

2. See *Asia.*

3. See *Mesopotamia.*

TURTLEDOVE See *Dove.*

TUTOR 2 Kgs 10:1; 1 Chron 27:32; Acts 22:3; Gal 4:1, 2.

TWIN BROTHERS, THE A ship of Alexandria, Acts 28:11.

TWINS Jacob and Esau, Gen 25:24–26. Perez and Zerah, Gen 38:27–30.

TYCHICUS An Asian companion of Paul. Accompanies Paul from Greece to Asia, Acts 20:

4. With Paul in Nicopolis, Tit 3:12. With Paul in Rome, Eph 6:21, 22; Col 4:7, 8. Sent to Ephesus, Eph 6:21, 22; 2 Tim 4:12. Sent to Colosse, Col 4:7, 8.

TYPES MISCELLANEOUS. Bride, a type of the Church, Rev 21:2, 9; 22:17. The Tabernacle a type of the heavenly sanctuary, Ex 40; Heb 8:2, 5; 9:1–12. The saving of Noah and his family, of the salvation through the gospel, 1 Pet 3:20, 21.

Defilement a type of sin, see *Defilement; Purification.* Leaven a type of sin, see *Yeast.* Ablutions were, see *Ablution.*

See *Allegory; Parable; Symbols.*

OF THE SAVIOR. Col 2:17; Heb 9:7–15, 18–28; 10:1–10. High priest, typical of the mediatorship, Ex 28:1, 12, 29, 30, 31, 37, 38; Lev 16:15; Zech 6:12, 13, with Heb 5; 8:2; 10:21. The institutions ordained by Moses, Mt 26:54; Lk 24:25–27, 44–47; Col 2:14–17; Heb 10:1–14. The sacrifices, Lev 4:2, 3, 11, 12; Heb 9:7–15, 18–25; 10:1–22, 29; 13:11–13; 1 Pet 1:19; Rev 5:6. The morning and evening sacrifice, Jn 1:29, 36. The red heifer, Num 19:1–6, with Heb 9:13, 14. The paschal lamb, 1 Cor 5:7. The bronze altar, Ex 27:1, 2, with Heb 13:10. The basin of brass, Ex 30:17–20, with Zech 13:1; Eph 5:26, 27. Mercy seat, Ex 25:17–22, with Heb 4:16. The veil, Ex 40:21; 2 Chron 3:14, with Heb 10:20. Bread, Jn 6:32–35; 1 Cor 10:3, 4. Cities of refuge, Num 35:6, with Heb 6:18. Bronze serpent, Num 21:9; Jn 3:14, 15. Tree of life, Gen 2:9, with Jn 1:4; Rev 22:2.

Adam, Rom 5:14; 1 Cor 15:45. Abel, Gen 4:8, 10, with Heb 12:24. Noah, Gen 5:28–31, with 2 Cor 1:5. Melchizedek, Heb 7:1–17. Moses, Deut 18:15, 18; Acts 3:20–22; 7:37; Heb 3:2–6. David, 2 Sam 8:15; Ps 89:19, 20; Ezk 37:24; Phil 2:9. Eliakim, Isa 22:20–22; Rev 3:7. Jonah, Jon 1:17, with Mt 12:40.

TYRANNUS An Ephesian. Paul taught in the school of, for two years, Acts 19:9, 10.

TYRANNY See *Government, Tyrannical.*

TYRE 1. Kingdom of. Hiram, king of, 1 Kgs 5:1; 2 Chron 2:3. Sends material to David for his palace, 2 Chron 2:3. Men and materials sent from, to Solomon, for the erection of the temple and his houses, 1 Kgs 5:1–11; 9:10–12; 2 Chron 2:3–16.

See *Hiram.*

2. City of. Situated on the shore of the Mediterranean. On the northern boundary of Asher, Josh 19:29. Fortified, Josh 19:29; 2 Sam 24:7. Commerce of, 1 Kgs 9:26–28; 10:11; Isa 23; Ezk 27; 28:1–19; Zech 9:2; Acts 21:3. Merchants of, Isa 23:8. Antiquity of, Isa 23:7. Riches of, Isa 23:8; Zech 9:3. Besieged by Nebuchadnezzar, Ezk 26:7; 29:18.

Jesus goes to the coasts of, Mt 15:21. Heals the daughter of the Syrophoenician woman near, Mt 15:21–28; Mk 7:24–31. Crowds from, come to hear Jesus, and to be healed of their diseases, Mk 3:7, 8; Lk 6:17, 18. Herod's hostility toward, Acts 12:20–23. Paul visits, Acts 21:3–7.

To be judged according to its opportunity and privileges, Mt 11:21, 22; Lk 10:13, 14.

Prophecies relating to, Ps 45:12; 87:4; Isa 23; Jer 25:22; 27:1–11; 47:4; Ezk chapters 26–28; Joel 3:4–8; Amos 1:9, 10; Zech 9:2–4.

U

UCAL A man mentioned only in Prov 30:1.

UEL An Israelite who divorced his Gentile wife, Ezra 10:34.

ULAI A river of Persia, Dan 8:2, 16.

ULAM 1. Son of Sheresh, 1 Chron 7:16, 17. 2. Son of Eshek, 1 Chron 8:39, 40.

ULLA An Asherite, 1 Chron 7:39.

UMMAH A city of Asher, Josh 19:30, 31.

UNBELIEF Ex 4:1. But Moses said, "They won't believe me! They won't do what I tell them to. They'll say, 'Jehovah never appeared to you!' "

Num 11:21. But Moses said, "There are 600,000 men alone (besides all the women and children), and yet you promise them meat for a whole month! [22]If we butcher all our flocks and herds it won't be enough! We would have to catch every fish in the ocean to fulfill your promise!" [23]Then the Lord said to Moses, "When did I become weak? Now you shall see whether my word comes true or not!"

Num 20:12. But the Lord said to Moses and Aaron, "Because you did not believe me and did not sanctify me in the eyes of the people of Israel, you shall not bring them into the land I have promised them!" [13]This place was named Meribah (meaning "Rebel Waters"), because it was where the people of Israel fought against Jehovah, and where he showed himself to be holy before them.

Ps 78:19, 20. They even spoke against God himself. "Why can't he give us decent food as well as water?" they grumbled. [21]Jehovah heard them and was angry; the fire of his wrath burned against Israel, [22]because they didn't believe in God or trust in him to care for them.

32. Yet even so the people kept on sinning and refused to believe in miracles.

Ps 95:8. Don't harden your heart as Israel did in the wilderness at Meribah and Massah. [9]For there your father doubted me, though they had seen so many of my miracles before. My patience was severely tried by their complaints. [10]"For forty years I watched them in disgust," the Lord God says. "They were a nation whose thoughts and heart were far away from me. They refused to accept my laws. [11]Therefore in mighty wrath I swore that they would never enter the Promised Land, the place of rest I planned for them."

Ps 106:7. They weren't impressed by the wonder of your miracles in Egypt, and soon forgot your many acts of kindness to them. Instead they rebelled against you at the Red Sea. [24]They refused to enter the Promised Land, for they wouldn't believe his solemn oath to care for them.

Isa 7:9. You don't believe me? If you want me to protect you, you must learn to believe what I say.

Isa 53:1. But, oh, how few believe it! Who will listen? To whom will God reveal his saving power? [Jn 12:38.] [2]In God's eyes he was like a tender green shoot, sprouting from a root in dry and sterile ground. But in our eyes there was no attractiveness at all, nothing to make us want him. [3]We despised him and rejected him—a man of sorrows, acquainted with bitterest grief. We turned our backs on him and looked the other way when he went by. He was despised and we didn't care.

Isa 58:3. "We have fasted before you," they say. "Why aren't you impressed? Why don't you see our sacrifices? Why don't you hear our prayers? We have done much penance, and you don't even notice it!" I'll tell you why! Because you are living in evil pleasure even while you are fasting, and you keep right on oppressing your workers.

Jer 5:12. They have lied and said, "He won't bother us! No evil will come upon us! There will be neither famine nor war! [13]God's prophets," they say, "are windbags full of words with no divine authority. Their claims of doom will fall upon themselves, not us!" [14]Therefore this is what the Lord God of Hosts says to his prophets: Because of talk like this I'll take your words and prophecies and turn them into raging fire and burn up these people like kindling wood.

Mal 1:2. "I have loved you very deeply," says the Lord. But you retort, "Really? When was this?" [7]"You offer polluted sacrifices on my altar." "Polluted sacrifices? When have we ever done a thing like that?" "Every time you say, 'Don't bother bringing anything very valuable to offer to God!' "

Mt 10:14. Any city or home that doesn't welcome you—shake off the dust of that place from your feet as you leave. [15]Truly, the wicked cities of Sodom and Gomorrah will be better off at Judgment Day than they.

Mt 11:16. What shall I say about this nation?

These people are like children playing, who say to their little friends, [17]"We played wedding and you weren't happy, so we played funeral but you weren't sad." [18]For John the Baptist doesn't even drink wine and often goes without food, and you say, "He's crazy." [19]And I, the Messiah, feast and drink, and you complain that I am "a glutton and a drinking man, and hang around with the worst sort of sinners!" But brilliant men like you can justify your every inconsistency! Lk 7:31–35.

Mt 13:13. "That is why I use these illustrations, so people will hear and see but not understand. [14]This fulfills the prophecy of Isaiah: 'They hear, but don't understand; they look, but don't see! [15]For their hearts are fat and heavy, and their ears are dull, and they have closed their eyes in sleep, [16]so they won't see and hear and understand and turn to God again, and let me heal them.' " [Isa 6:9, 10.] [58]And so he did only a few great miracles there, because of their unbelief.

Mt 17:17. Jesus replied, "Oh, you stubborn, faithless people! How long shall I bear with you? Bring him here to me." [19]Afterwards the disciples asked Jesus privately, "Why couldn't we cast that demon out?" [20]"Because of your little faith," Jesus told them. "For if you had faith even as small as a tiny mustard seed you could say to this mountain, 'Move!' and it would go far away. Nothing would be impossible."

Mt 21:32. For John the Baptist told you to repent and turn to God, and you wouldn't, while very evil men and prostitutes did. And even when you saw this happening, you refused to repent, and so you couldn't believe.

Mk 6:2, 3. The next Sabbath he went to the synagogue to teach, and the people were astonished at his wisdom and his miracles because he was just a local man like themselves. "He's no better than we are," they said. "He's just a carpenter, Mary's boy, and a brother of James and Joseph, Judas and Simon. And his sisters live right here among us." And they were offended! [4]Then Jesus told them, "A prophet is honored everywhere except in his home town and among his relatives and by his own family." [5]And because of their unbelief he couldn't do any mighty miracles among them except to place his hands on a few sick people and heal them. [6]And he could hardly accept the fact that they wouldn't believe in him.

Mk 8:38. And anyone who is ashamed of me and my message in these days of unbelief and sin, I, the Messiah, will be ashamed of him when I return in the glory of my father, with the holy angels.

Mk 9:24. The father instantly replied, "I *do* have faith; oh, help me to have *more!*"

Mk 16:14. Still later he appeared to the eleven disciples as they were eating together. He rebuked them for their unbelief—their stubborn refusal to believe those who had seen him alive from the dead. [16]Those who believe and are baptized will be saved. But those who refuse to believe will be condemned.

Lk 8:12. The hard path where some seed fell represents the hard hearts of those who hear the words of God, but then the devil comes and steals the words away and prevents people from believing and being saved. [2 Cor 4:4.] [18]So be careful how you listen; for whoever has, to him shall be given more; and whoever does not have, even what he thinks he has shall be taken away from him. Mk 4:24, 25.

Lk 10:16. Those who welcome you are welcoming me. And those who reject you are rejecting me. And those who reject me are rejecting God who sent me.

Lk 12:46. Well, his master will return without notice and remove him from his position of trust and assign him to the place of the unfaithful.

Lk 13:34. O Jerusalem, Jerusalem! The city that murders the prophets. The city that stones those sent to help her. How often I have wanted to gather your children together even as a hen protects her brood under her wings, but you wouldn't let me.

Lk 14:16. Jesus replied with this illustration: "A man prepared a great feast and sent out many invitations. [17]When all was ready, he sent his servant around to notify the guests that it was time for them to arrive. [18]But they all began making excuses. One said he had just bought a field and wanted to inspect it, and asked to be excused. [19]Another said he had just bought five pair of oxen and wanted to try them out. [20]Another had just been married and for that reason couldn't come. [21]The servant returned and reported to his master what they had said. His master was angry and told him to go quickly into the streets and alleys of the city and to invite the beggars, crippled, lame, and blind. [22]But even then, there was still room. [23]'Well, then,' said his master, 'go out into the country lanes and out behind the hedges and urge anyone you find to come, so that the house will be full. [24]For none of those I invited first will get even the smallest taste of what I had prepared for them.' "

Lk 16:31. But Abraham said, "If they won't listen to Moses and the prophets, they won't listen even though someone rises from the dead."

Lk 18:8. When I, the Messiah, return, how many will I find who have faith (and are praying)?

Lk 19:41. But as they came closer to Jerusalem and he saw the city ahead, he began to cry. [42]"Eternal peace was within your reach and you turned it down," he wept, "and now it is too late."

Lk 22:67, 68. And instructed to state whether or not he claimed to be the Messiah. But he replied, "If I tell you, you won't believe me or let me present my case."

Lk 24:11. But the story sounded like a fairy tale to the men—they didn't believe it. [21]We had thought he was the glorious Messiah and that he had come to rescue Israel. [25]Then Jesus said to them, "You are such foolish, foolish people! You find it so hard to believe all that the prophets wrote in the Scriptures! [26]Wasn't it clearly predicted by the prophets that the Messiah would have to suffer all these things before entering his time of glory?"

Lk 24:36. And just as they were telling about it,

Jesus himself was suddenly standing there among them, and greeted them. [37]But the whole group was terribly frightened, thinking they were seeing a ghost! [38]"Why are you frightened?" he asked. "Why do you doubt that it is really I? [39]Look at my hands! Look at my feet! You can see that it is I, myself! Touch me and make sure that I am not a ghost! For ghosts don't have bodies, as you see that I do!" [40]As he spoke, he held out his hands for them to see (the marks of the nails), and showed them (the wounds in) his feet. [41]Still they stood there undecided, filled with joy and doubt. Then he asked them, "Do you have anything here to eat?" [42]They gave him a piece of broiled fish, [43]and he ate it as they watched! [44]Then he said, "When I was with you before, don't you remember my telling you that everything written about me by Moses and the prophets and in the Psalms must all come true?" [45]Then he opened their minds to understand at last these many Scriptures!

Jn 1:10. But although he made the world, the world didn't recognize him when he came. [11]Even in his own land and among his own people, the Jews, he was not accepted.

Jn 3:7. "So don't be surprised at my statement that you must be born again! [11]I am telling you what I know and have seen—and yet you won't believe me. [12]But if you don't even believe me when I tell you about such things as these that happen here among men, how can you possibly believe if I tell you what is going on in heaven? [18]There is no eternal doom awaiting those who trust him to save them. But those who don't trust him have already been tried and condemned for not believing in the only Son of God." [32]He tells what he has seen and heard, but how few believe what he tells them! [36]And all who trust him—God's Son—to save them have eternal life; those who don't believe and obey him shall never see heaven, but the wrath of God remains upon them.

Jn 4:48. Jesus asked, "Won't any of you believe in me unless I do more and more miracles?"

Jn 5:38. But you are not listening to him, for you refuse to believe me—the one sent to you with God's message. [40]Yet you won't come to me so that I can give you this life eternal! [43]I know, because I have come to you representing my Father and you refuse to welcome me, though you readily enough receive those who aren't sent from him, but represent only themselves! [44]No wonder you can't believe! For you gladly honor each other, but you don't care about the honor that comes from the only God! [46]For you have refused to believe Moses. He wrote about me, but you refuse to believe him, so you refuse to believe in me. [47]And since you don't believe what he wrote, no wonder you don't believe me either.

Jn 6:36. "But the trouble is, as I have told you before, you haven't believed even though you have seen me." [60]Even his disciples said, "This is very hard to understand. Who can tell what he means?" [61]Jesus knew within himself that his disciples were complaining and said to them, "Does *this* offend you? [62]Then what will you think if you see me, the Messiah, return to heaven again? [64]But some of you don't believe me." (For Jesus knew from the beginning who didn't believe and knew the one who would betray him.) [66]At this point many of his disciples turned away and deserted him. [70]Then Jesus said, "I chose the twelve of you, and one is a devil." [71]He was speaking of Judas, son of Simon Iscariot, one of the Twelve, who would betray him.

Jn 8:24. "That is why I said that you will die in your sins; for unless you believe that I am the Messiah, the Son of God, you will die in your sins. [45]And so when I tell the truth, you just naturally don't believe it! [46]Which of you can truthfully accuse me of one single sin? (No one!) And since I am telling you the truth, why don't you believe me? [47]Anyone whose Father is God listens gladly to the words of God. Since you don't, it proves you aren't his children." [52]The leaders of the Jews said, "Now we know you are possessed by a demon. Even Abraham and the mightiest prophets died, and yet you say that obeying you will keep a man from dying! [53]So you are greater than our father Abraham, who died? And greater than the prophets, who died? Who do you think you are?"

Jn 10:25. "I have already told you, and you don't believe me," Jesus replied, "The proof is in the miracles I do in the name of my Father. [26]But you don't believe me because you are not part of my flock. [37]Don't believe me unless I do miracles of God. [38]But if I do, believe them even if you don't believe me. Then you will become convinced that the Father is in me, and I in the Father."

Jn 12:37. But despite all the miracles he had done, most of the people would not believe he was the Messiah. [39]But they couldn't believe, for as Isaiah also said: [40]"God has blinded their eyes and hardened their hearts so that they can neither see nor understand nor turn to me to heal them." [47]If anyone hears me and doesn't obey me, I am not his judge—for I have come to save the world and not to judge it. [48]But all who reject me and my message will be judged at the Day of Judgment by the truths I have spoken.

Jn 14:17. He is the Holy Spirit, the Spirit who leads into all truth. The world at large cannot receive him, for it isn't looking for him and doesn't recognize him. But you do, for he lives with you now and some day shall be in you.

Jn 16:8. And when he has come he will convince the world of its sin. [9]The world's sin is unbelief in me.

Jn 20:27. Then he said to Thomas, "Put your finger into my hands. Put your hand into my side. Don't be faithless any longer. Believe!"

Acts 13:40. Oh, be careful! Don't let the prophets' words apply to you. For they said, [41]"Look and perish, you despisers (of the truth), for I am doing something in your day—something that you won't believe when you hear it announced."

Acts 19:9. But some rejected his message and publicly spoke against Christ, so he left, refusing to preach to them again.

Acts 22:18. And saw a vision of God saying to me, "Hurry! Leave Jerusalem, for the people here won't believe you when you give them my message."

Acts 28:24. Some believed, and some didn't.

Rom 1:18. But God shows his anger from heaven against all sinful, evil men who push away the truth from them.

Rom 3:3. True, some of them were unfaithful, but just because they broke their promises to God, does that mean God will break his promises?

Rom 4:20. But Abraham never doubted. He believed God, for his faith and trust grew ever stronger, and he praised God for this blessing even before it happened.

Rom 9:31. But the Jews, who tried so hard to get right with God by keeping his laws, never succeeded. [32]Why not? Because they were trying to be saved by keeping the law and being good instead of by depending on faith.

Rom 10:6. But the salvation that comes through faith says, "You don't need to search the heavens to find Christ and bring him down to help you," and, [7]"You don't need to go among the dead to bring Christ back to life again." [14]But how shall they ask him to save them unless they believe in him? And how can they believe in him if they have never heard about him? And how can they hear about him unless someone tells them? [16]But not everyone who heard the Good News has welcomed it, for Isaiah the prophet said, "Lord, who has believed me when I told them?" [21]In the meantime, he keeps on reaching out his hands to the Jews, but they keep arguing and refusing to come.

Rom 11:20. Watch out! Remember that those branches, the Jews, were broken off because they didn't believe God, and you are there only because you do. Do not be proud; be humble and grateful —and careful. [30]Once you were rebels against God, but when the Jews refused his gifts God was merciful to you instead. [31]And now the Jews are the rebels, but some day they, too, will share in God's mercy upon you. [32]For God has given them all up to sin so that he could have mercy upon all alike.

Rom 14:23. But anyone who believes that something he wants to do is wrong shouldn't do it. He sins if he does, for he thinks it is wrong, and so for him it *is* wrong. Anything that is done apart from what he feels is right is sin.

1 Cor 1:18. I know very well how foolish it sounds to those who are lost, when they hear that Jesus died to save them. But we who are saved recognize this message as the very power of God. [22]It seems foolish to the Jews because they want a sign from heaven as proof that what is preached is true; and it is foolish to the Gentiles because they believe only what agrees with their philosophy and seems wise to them. [23]So when we preach about Christ dying to save them, the Jews are offended and the Gentiles say it's all nonsense.

1 Cor 2:14. But the man who isn't a Christian can't understand and can't accept these thoughts from God, which the Holy Spirit teaches us. They sound foolish to him, because only those who have the Holy Spirit within them can understand what the Holy Spirit means. Others just can't take it in.

1 Cor 14:22. So you see that being able to "speak in tongues" is not a sign to God's children concerning his power, but is a sign to the unsaved. However, prophecy (preaching the deep truths of God) is what the Christians need, and unbelievers aren't yet ready for it.

2 Cor 6:14. Don't be teamed with those who do not love the Lord, for what do the people of God have in common with the people of sin? How can light live with darkness? [15]And what harmony can there be between Christ and the devil? How can a Christian be a partner with one who doesn't believe? [16]And what union can there be between God's temple and idols? For you are God's temple, the home of the living God, and God has said of you, "I will live in them and walk among them, and I will be their God and they shall be my people."

2 Thess 2:11. So God will allow them to believe lies with all their hearts, [12]and all of them will be justly judged for believing falsehood, refusing the Truth, and enjoying their sins.

2 Thess 3:2. Pray too that we will be saved out of the clutches of evil men, for not everyone loves the Lord.

1 Tim 1:13. Even though I used to scoff at the name of Christ. I hunted down his people, harming them in every way I could. But God had mercy on me because I didn't know what I was doing, for I didn't know Christ at that time.

2 Tim 2:13. Even when we are too weak to have any faith left, he remains faithful to us and will help us, for he cannot disown us who are part of himself.

Tit 1:15. A person who is pure of heart sees goodness and purity in everything; but a person whose own heart is evil and untrusting finds evil in everything, for his dirty mind and rebellious heart color all he sees and hears.

Heb 3:12. Beware then of your own hearts, dear brothers, lest you find that they, too, are evil and unbelieving and are leading you away from the living God. [16]And who were those people I speak of, who heard God's voice speaking to them but then rebelled against him? They were the ones who came out of Egypt with Moses their leader. [17]And who was it who made God angry for all those forty years? These same people who sinned and as a result died in the wilderness. [18]And to whom was God speaking when he swore with an oath that they could never go into the land he had promised his people? He was speaking to all those who disobeyed him. [19]And why couldn't they go in? Because they didn't trust him.

Heb 4:1. Although God's promise still stands—his promise that all may enter his place of rest—we ought to tremble with fear because some of you may be on the verge of failing to get there after all. [2]For this wonderful news—the message that God wants to save us—has been given to us just as it was to those who lived in the time of Moses. But it didn't do them any good because they didn't believe it. They didn't mix it with faith. [3]For only we who believe God can enter into his place of rest. He has said, "I have sworn in my anger that those who don't believe me will never get in," even though he has been ready and waiting for them since the world began. [6]Yet the promise remains and some get in—but not those who had the first chance, for they disobeyed God and failed to enter. [11]Let us do our best to go into that place of rest, too, being careful not to disobey God as the children of Israel did, thus failing to get in.

Heb 11:6. You can never please God without faith, without depending on him. Anyone who wants to come to God must believe that there is a God and that he rewards those who sincerely look for him. [31]By faith—because she believed in God and his power—Rahab the harlot did not die with all the others in her city when they refused to obey God, for she gave a friendly welcome to the spies.

Heb 12:25. So see to it that you obey him who is speaking to you. For if the people of Israel did not escape when they refused to listen to Moses, the earthly messenger, how terrible our danger if we refuse to listen to God who speaks to us from heaven!

Jas 1:6. But when you ask him, be sure that you really expect him to tell you, for a doubtful mind will be as unsettled as a wave of the sea that is driven and tossed by the wind; [7, 8]. . . If you don't ask with faith, don't expect the Lord to give you any solid answer.

1 Pet 2:7. Yes, he is very precious to you who believe; and to those who reject him, well—"The same Stone that was rejected by the builders has become the Cornerstone, the most honored and important part of the building." [8]And the Scriptures also say, "He is the Stone that some will stumble over, and the Rock that will make them fall." They will stumble because they will not listen to God's Word, nor obey it, and so this punishment must follow—that they will fall.

2 Pet 3:4. This will be their line of argument: "So Jesus promised to come back, did he? Then where is he? He'll never come! Why, as far back as anyone can remember everything has remained exactly as it was since the first day of creation."

1 Jn 2:22. And who is the greatest liar? The one who says that Jesus is not Christ. Such a person is antichrist, for he does not believe in God the Father and in his Son. [23]For a person who doesn't believe in Christ, God's Son, can't have God the Father either.

1 Jn 4:3. If not, the message is not from God but from one who is against Christ, like the "Antichrist" you have heard about who is going to come, and his attitude of enmity against Christ is already abroad in the world.

1 Jn 5:10. All who believe this know in their hearts that it is true. If anyone doesn't believe this, he is actually calling God a liar, because he doesn't believe what God has said about his Son. [12]So whoever has God's Son has life; whoever does not have his Son, does not have life.

Jude 1:5. Remember this fact—which you know already—that the Lord saved a whole nation of people out of the land of Egypt, and then killed every one of them who did not trust and obey him.

INSTANCES OF. Eve, Gen 3:4–6. Moses and Aaron, Num 20:12. Israelites, Deut 9:23; 2 Kgs 17:14; Ps 78. Naaman, 2 Kgs 5:12. Samaritan officer, 2 Kgs 7:2. Zacharias, Lk 1:20. Chief priests, Lk 22:67, 68. The Jews, Mk 1:45; 2:6–11; 8:11, 12; 15:29–32; Jn 5:38, 40, 43, 46, 47. Disciples, Mt 17:17, 20; Mk 4:38, 40; Lk 24:11, 25, 41–45. Brothers of Christ, Jn 7:5. Thomas, Jn 20:25. Jews of Iconium, Acts 14:2. Thessalonian Jews, Acts 17:5. Jews in Jerusalem, Rom 15:31. Ephesians, Acts 19:9. Saul, 1 Tim 1:13. People of Jericho, Heb 11:31.

UNCHARITABLENESS Isa 29:20. Bullies will vanish and scoffers will cease, and all those plotting evil will be killed—[21]the violent man who fights at the drop of a hat, the man who waits in hiding to beat up the judge who sentenced him, and the men who use any excuse to be unfair.

Mt 7:1. Don't criticize, and then you won't be criticized. [2]For others will treat you as you treat them. [3]And why worry about a speck in the eye of a brother when you have a board in your own? [4]Should you say, "Friend, let me help you get that speck out of your eye," when you can't even see because of the board in your own? [5]Hypocrite! First get rid of the board. Then you can see to help your brother. Lk 6:37–42.

Jn 8:7. They kept demanding an answer, so he stood up again and said, "All right, hurl the stones at her until she dies. But only he who never sinned may throw the first!"

Rom 2:1. But wait a minute! You are just as bad. When you say they are wicked and should be punished, you are talking about yourselves, for you do these very same things.

Rom 14:1. Give a warm welcome to any brother who wants to join you, even though his faith is weak. Don't criticize him for having different ideas from yours about what is right and wrong. [2]For instance, don't argue with him about whether or not to eat meat that has been offered to idols. You may believe there is no harm in this, but the faith of others is weaker; they think it is wrong, and will go without any meat at all and eat vegetables rather than eat that kind of meat. [3]Those who think it is all right to eat such meat must not look down on those who won't. And if you are one of those who won't, don't find fault with those who do. For God has accepted them to be his children. [4]They are God's servants, not yours. They are responsible to him, not to you. Let him tell them whether they are right or wrong. And God is able to make them do as they should. [5]Some think that Christians should observe the Jewish holidays as special days to worship God, but others say it is wrong and foolish to go to all that trouble, for every day alike belongs to God. On questions of this kind everyone must decide for himself. [6]If you have special days for worshiping the Lord, you are trying to honor him; you are doing a good thing. So is the person who eats meat that has been offered to idols; he is thankful to the Lord for it; he is doing right. And the person who won't touch such meat, he, too, is anxious to please the Lord, and is thankful. [7]We are not our own bosses to live or die as we ourselves might choose. [8]Living or dying we follow the Lord. Either way we are his. [9]Christ died and rose again for this very purpose, so that he can be our Lord both while we live and when we die. [10]You have no right to criticize your brother or look down on him. Remember, each of us will stand personally before the Judgment Seat of God. [11]For it is written, "As I live," says the Lord, "every knee shall bow to me and every tongue confess to God." [12]Yes, each of us will give an account of himself to God. [13]So don't criticize each other any more. Try instead to live in such a way that you will never make your brother stumble by letting him see you doing something he thinks is wrong. [14]As for myself, I am perfectly sure on the authority of the Lord Jesus that there is nothing really wrong with eating meat that has been offered to idols. But if someone believes it is wrong, then he shouldn't do it because for him it is wrong. [15]And if your brother is bothered by what you eat, you are not acting in love if you go ahead and eat it. Don't let your eating ruin someone for whom Christ died.

1 Cor 4:3. What about me? Have I been a good servant? Well, I don't worry over what you think about this, or what anyone else thinks. I don't even trust my own judgment on this point. [4]My conscience is clear, but even that isn't final proof. It is the Lord himself who must examine me and decide. [5]So be careful not to jump to conclusions before the Lord returns as to whether someone is a good servant or not. When the Lord comes, he will turn on the light so that everyone can see exactly what each one of us is really like, deep down in our hearts. Then everyone will know why we have been doing the Lord's work. At that time God will give to each one whatever praise is coming to him. [7]What are you so puffed up about? What do you have that God hasn't given you? And if all you have is from God, why act as though you have accomplished something on your own?

1 Cor 13:1. If I had the gift of being able to speak in other languages without learning them, and could speak in every language there is in all of heaven and earth, but didn't love others, I would only be making noise. [2]If I had the gift of prophecy and knew all about what is going to happen in the future, knew everything about *everything,* but didn't love others, what good would it do? Even if I had the gift of faith so that I could speak to a mountain and make it move, I would still be worth nothing at all without love. [3]If I gave everything I have to poor people, and if I were burned alive for preaching the Gospel but didn't love others, it would be of no value whatever. [4]Love is very patient and kind, never jealous or envious, never boastful or proud, [5]never haughty or selfish or rude. Love does not demand its own way. It is not irritable or touchy. It does not hold grudges and will hardly even notice when others do it wrong. [6]It is never glad about injustice, but rejoices whenever truth wins out.

Jas 4:11. Don't criticize and speak evil about each other, dear brothers. If you do, you will be fighting against God's law of loving one another, declaring it is wrong. But your job is not to decide whether this law is right or wrong, but to obey it. [12]Only he who made the law can rightly judge among us. He alone decides to save us or destroy. So what right do you have to judge or criticize others?

See *Accusation, False; Charitableness; Gossip; Slander; Speaking, Evil.*

INSTANCES OF. The Israelites toward Moses, charging him with having made them abhorred by the Egyptians, Ex 5:21; charging him with bringing them out of Egypt to die, Ex 14:11, 12; in murmuring against Moses, see *Murmuring, Instances of.*

The tribes west of Jordan toward the two and a half tribes, Num 32:1–33; Josh 22:11–31. Of Eli toward Hannah, 1 Sam 1:14–17.

Eliab toward David, charging him with presumption, when he offered to fight Goliath, 1 Sam 17:28. Officers of Ammon toward David, when he sent ambassadors to convey his sympathy to Hanun, 2 Sam 10:3. Bildad toward Job, Job 8. Eliphaz toward Job, Job 15; 22; 42:7, 8. Zophar toward Job, Job 11:1–6; 20. Nathanael, when he said, "Can anything good come from [Nazareth]?" Jn 1:46. The Jews, charging Paul with teaching contrary to the law and against the Temple, Acts 21:28.

UNCIRCUMCISION Lev 19:23. Uncircumcised heart, Ezk 44:7, 9.

UNCLEAN Creatures designated as such, Lev 11; Deut 14.

See *Uncleanness.*

UNCLEANNESS Lev 5:2, 3; 7:20, 21; 17:15; 21:1–15; 22:1–8; Num 5:1–3; 9:6–11; 19; 31:19; Deut 23:9–11.

See *Ablution; Defilement; Purification; Sanitation.*

SPIRITUAL. Eph 2:11.

UNCTION See *Anointing.*

UNFAITHFULNESS Prov 24:11, 12. Rescue those who are unjustly sentenced to death; don't stand back and let them die. Don't try to disclaim responsibility by saying you didn't know about it. For God, who knows all hearts, knows yours, and he knows you knew! And he will reward everyone according to his deeds.

Isa 5:1. Now I will sing a song about his vineyard to the one I love. *My Beloved has a vineyard on a very fertile hill.* [2]*He plowed it and took out all the rocks and planted his vineyard with the choicest vines. He built a watchtower and cut a winepress in the rocks. Then he waited for the harvest, but the grapes that grew were wild and sour and not at all the sweet ones he expected.* [3]Now, men of Jerusalem and Judah, you have heard the case! You be the judges! [4]What more could I have done? Why did my vineyard give me wild grapes instead of sweet? [5]I will tear down the fences and let my vineyard go to pasture to be trampled by cattle and sheep. [6]I won't prune it or hoe it, but let it be overgrown with briars and thorns. I will command the clouds not to rain on it any more. [7]I have given you the story of God's people. They are the vineyard that I spoke about. Israel and Judah are his pleasant acreage! He expected them to yield a crop of justice, but found bloodshed instead. He expected righteousness, but the cries of deep oppression met his ears.

Hos 10:1. How prosperous Israel is—a luxuriant vine all filled with fruit! But the more wealth I give her, the more she pours it on the altars of her heathen gods; the richer the harvests I give her, the more beautiful the statues and idols she erects. [2]The hearts of her people are false toward God. They are guilty and must be punished. God will break down their heathen altars and smash their idols.

Mt 3:10. And even now the axe of God's judgment is poised to chop down every unproductive tree. They will be chopped and burned.

Mt 13:12. "For to him who has will more be given," he told them, "and he will have great plenty; but from him who has not, even the little he has will be taken away."

Mt 21:19. And noticed a fig tree beside the road. He went over to see if there were any figs, but there were only leaves. Then he said to it, "Never bear fruit again!" And soon the fig tree withered up. [20]The disciples were utterly amazed and asked, "How did the fig tree wither so quickly?" Mk 11:13, 14.

33. "Now listen to this story: A certain landowner planted a vineyard with a hedge around it, and built a platform for the watchman, then leased the vineyard to some farmers on a sharecrop basis, and went away to live in another country. [34]At the time of the grape harvest he sent his agents to the farmers to collect his share. [35]But the farmers attacked his men, beat one, killed one and stoned another. [36]Then he sent a larger group of his men to collect for him, but the results were the same. [37]Finally the owner sent his son, thinking they would surely respect him. [38]But when these farmers saw the son coming they said among themselves, 'Here comes the heir to this estate; come on, let's kill him and get it for ourselves!' [39]So they dragged him out of the vineyard and killed him. [40]When the owner returns, what do you think he will do to those farmers?" [41]The Jewish leaders replied, "He will put the wicked men to a horrible death, and lease the vineyard to others who will pay him promptly." [42]Then Jesus asked them, "Didn't you ever read in the Scriptures: 'The stone rejected by the builders has been made the honored cornerstone; how remarkable! what an amazing thing the Lord has done'? [43]What I mean is that the Kingdom of God shall be taken away from you, and given to a nation that will give God his share of the crop." Mk 12:1–9.

Mt 25:8. Then the five who hadn't any oil begged the others to share with them, for their lamps were going out. [9]But the others replied, "We haven't enough. Go instead to the shops and buy some for yourselves." [10]But while they were gone, the bridegroom came, and those who were ready went in with him to the marriage feast, and the door was locked. [11]Later, when the other five returned, they stood outside, calling, "Sir, open the door for us!" [12]But he called back, "Go away! It is too late!" [13]So stay awake and be prepared, for you do not know the date or moment of my return. *vs.* 1–13.

24, 25. Then the man with the $1,000 came and said, "Sir, I knew you were a hard man, and I was afraid you would rob me of what I earned, so I hid your money in the earth and here it is!" [26]But his master replied, "Wicked man! Lazy slave! Since you knew I would demand your profit, [27]you should at least have put my money into the bank so I could have some interest. [28]Take the money from this man and give it to the man with the $10, 000. [29]For the man who uses well what he is given shall be given more, and he shall have abundance. But from the man who is unfaithful, even what little responsibility he has shall be taken from him. [30]And throw the useless servant out into outer darkness: there shall be weeping and gnashing of teeth." *vs.* 14–30; Lk 19:12–27.

41. Then I will turn to those on my left and say, "Away with you, you cursed ones, into the eternal fire prepared for the devil and his demons. [42]For I was hungry and you wouldn't feed me; thirsty, and you wouldn't give me anything to drink; [43]a stranger, and you refused me hospitality; naked, and you wouldn't clothe me; sick, and in prison, and you didn't visit me." [44]Then they will reply, "Lord, when did we ever see you hungry or thirsty or a stranger or naked or sick or in prison, and not help you?" [45]And I will answer, "When you refused to help the least of these my brothers, you were refusing help to me." [46]And they shall go away into eternal punishment; but the righteous into everlasting life. *vs.* 31–46.

Lk 13:6. Then he used this illustration: "A man planted a fig tree in his garden and came again and again to see if he could find any fruit on it, but he was always disappointed. [7]Finally he told his gardener to cut it down. 'I've waited three years and there hasn't been a single fig!' he said. 'Why bother with it any longer? It's taking up space we can use for something else.' [8]'Give it one more chance,' the gardener answered. 'Leave it another year, and I'll give it special attention and plenty of fertilizer. [9]If we get figs next year, fine; if not, I'll cut it down.' "

Jn 15:2. He lops off every branch that doesn't produce. And he prunes those branches that bear fruit for even larger crops.

2 Pet 1:8. The more you go on in this way, the more you will grow strong spiritually and become fruitful and useful to our Lord Jesus Christ. [9]But anyone who fails to go after these additions to faith is blind indeed, or at least very shortsighted, and has forgotten that God delivered him from the old

life of sin so that now he can live a strong, good life for the Lord.

See *Sin, Fruits of; Unfruitfulness.* See also *Righteousness, Fruits of.*

OF FRIENDS. See *Friends, False.*

UNFRUITFULNESS Isa 5:2. He plowed it and took out all the rocks and planted his vineyard with the choicest vines. He built a watchtower and cut a winepress in the rocks. Then he waited for the harvest, but the grapes that grew were wild and sour and not at all the sweet ones he expected.

Mt 3:10. And even now the axe of God's judgment is poised to chop down every unproductive tree. They will be chopped and burned. Lk 3:9.

Mt 7:19. So the trees having the inedible fruit are chopped down and thrown on the fire.

Mt 13:4. As he scattered the seed across the ground, some fell beside a path, and the birds came and ate it. [5]And some fell on rocky soil where there was little depth of earth; the plants sprang up quickly enough in the shallow soil, [6]but the hot sun soon scorched them and they withered and died, for they had so little root. [7]Other seeds fell among thorns, and the thorns choked out the tender blades.

Mt 21:19. And noticed a fig tree beside the road. He went over to see if there were any figs, but there were only leaves. Then he said to it, "Never bear fruit again!" And soon the fig tree withered up. [20]The disciples were utterly amazed and asked, "How did the fig tree wither so quickly?" Mk 11:13.

Lk 13:6. Then he used this illustration: "A man planted a fig tree in his garden and came again and again to see if he could find any fruit on it, but he was always disappointed. [7]Finally he told his gardener to cut it down. 'I've waited three years and there hasn't been a single fig!' he said. 'Why bother with it any longer? It's taking up space we can use for something else.' [8]'Give it one more chance,' the gardener answered. 'Leave it another year, and I'll give it special attention and plenty of fertilizer. [9]If we get figs next year, fine; if not, I'll cut it down.' "

Jn 15:2. He lops off every branch that doesn't produce. And he prunes those branches that bear fruit for even larger crops. [4]Take care to live in me, and let me live in you. For a branch can't produce fruit when severed from the vine. Nor can you be fruitful apart from me. [6]If anyone separates from me, he is thrown away like a useless branch, withers, and is gathered into a pile with all the others and burned.

See *Sin, Fruits of; Unfaithfulness.* See also *Righteousness, Fruits of.*

UNIFORM FIGURATIVE. Isa 22:21.

UNION Advantages of, Prov 15:22; Eccl 4: 9–12.

OF THE RIGHTEOUS. See *Unity, of the Righteous;* of the righteous with Christ, see *Righteous, Unity of, with Christ.*

UNITY OF THE GODHEAD. See *God, Unity of.*

OF THE RIGHTEOUS. Ps 133:1. How wonderful it is, how pleasant, when brothers live in harmony!

Isa 52:8. The watchmen shout and sing with joy, for right before their eyes they see the Lord God bring his people home again.

Mt 23:8. Don't ever let anyone call you that. For only God is your Rabbi and all of you are on the same level, as brothers.

Acts 4:32. All the believers were of one heart and mind, and no one felt that what he owned was his own; everyone was sharing.

Rom 12:16. Work happily together.

Rom 14:19. In this way aim for harmony in the church and try to build each other up.

Rom 15:5. May God who gives patience, steadiness, and encouragement help you to live in complete harmony with each other—each with the attitude of Christ toward the other. [6]And then all of us can praise the Lord together with one voice, giving glory to God, the Father of our Lord Jesus Christ.

1 Cor 1:10. But, dear brothers, I beg you in the name of the Lord Jesus Christ to stop arguing among yourselves. Let there be real harmony so that there won't be splits in the church. I plead with you to be of one mind, united in thought and purpose.

2 Cor 13:11. Be happy. Grow in Christ. Pay attention to what I have said. Live in harmony and peace. And may the God of love and peace be with you.

Eph 4:3. Try always to be led along together by the Holy Spirit, and so be at peace with one another.

Phil 1:27. But whatever happens to me, remember always to live as Christians should, so that, whether I ever see you again or not, I will keep on hearing good reports that you are standing side by side with one strong purpose—to tell the Good News.

Phil 2:2. Then make me truly happy by loving each other and agreeing wholeheartedly with each other, working together with one heart and mind and purpose.

Phil 3:17. Dear brothers, pattern your lives after mine and notice who else lives up to my example.

1 Pet 3:8. And now this word to all of you: You should be like one big happy family, full of sympathy toward each other, loving one another with tender hearts and humble minds.

See *Communion; Fellowship.*

UNKNOWN TONGUE See *Tongues.*

UNLEAVENED BREAD See *Bread; Passover.*

UNNI A musician in the time of David, 1 Chron 15:18, 20.

UNNO A Levite in the time of Nehemiah, Neh 12:9.

UNPARDONABLE SIN 2 Kgs 24:3, 4; Mt 12:31, 32; Lk 12:10; Heb 6:4–6; 1 Jn 5:16. In every age there is a great crime, Ps 19:13.

See *Obduracy; Reprobate.*

INSTANCES OF. Israel, Num 14:26–45. Eli's family, 1 Sam 3:14.

UNSELFISHNESS Rom 12:10. Love each other with brotherly affection and take delight in honoring each other.

Rom 15:1, 2. Even if we believe that it makes no difference to the Lord whether we do these things, still we cannot just go ahead and do them to please ourselves; for we must bear the "burden" of being considerate of the doubts and fears of others—of those who feel these things are wrong. Let's please the other fellow, not ourselves, and do what is for his good and thus build him up in the Lord. [3]Christ didn't please himself. As the Psalmist said, "He came for the very purpose of suffering under the insults of those who were against the Lord."

1 Cor 9:19. And this has a real advantage: I am not bound to obey anyone just because he pays my salary; yet I have freely and happily become a servant of any and all so that I can win them to Christ. [20]When I am with the Jews I seem as one of them so that they will listen to the Gospel and I can win them to Christ. When I am with Gentiles who follow Jewish customs and ceremonies I don't argue, even though I don't agree, because I want to help them. [21]When with the heathen I agree with them as much as I can, except of course that I must always do what is right as a Christian. And so, by agreeing, I can win their confidence and help them too. [22]When I am with those whose consciences bother them easily, I don't act as though I know it all and don't say they are foolish; the result is that they are willing to let me help them. Yes, whatever a person is like, I try to find common ground with him so that he will let me tell him about Christ and let Christ save him. [23]I do this to get the Gospel to them and also for the blessing I myself receive when I see them come to Christ.

1 Cor 10:24. Don't think only of yourself. Try to think of the other fellow, too, and what is best for him. [33]That is the plan I follow, too. I try to please everyone in everything I do, not doing what I like or what is best for me, but what is best for them, so that they may be saved.

1 Cor 13:4. Love is very patient and kind, never jealous or envious, never boastful or proud, [5]never haughty or selfish or rude. Love does not demand its own way. It is not irritable or touchy. It does not hold grudges and will hardly even notice when others do it wrong.

2 Cor 5:14. But because Christ's love controls us now. Since we believe that Christ died for all of us, we should also believe that we have died to the old life we used to live. [15]He died for all so that all who live—having received eternal life from him—might live no longer for themselves, to please themselves, but to spend their lives pleasing Christ who died and rose again for them.

2 Cor 8:9. You know how full of love and kindness our Lord Jesus was: though he was so very rich, yet to help you he became so very poor, so that by being poor he could make you rich.

Phil 2:3. Don't be selfish; don't live to make a good impression on others. Be humble, thinking of others as better than yourself. [4]Don't just think about your own affairs, but be interested in others, too, and in what they are doing.

Phil 4:5. Let everyone see that you are unselfish and considerate in all you do. Remember that the Lord is coming soon.

Jas 2:8. Yes indeed, it is good when you truly obey our Lord's command, "You must love and help your neighbors just as much as you love and take care of yourself."

INSTANCES OF. Abraham, Gen 13:9; 14:23, 24. King of Sodom, Gen 14:21. Men of Heth, Gen 23: 5, 6, 11. Judah, Gen 44:33, 34. Moses, Num 11:29; 14:12–19. Gideon, Judg 8:22–24. Saul, 1 Sam 11:12, 13. Jonathan, 1 Sam 23:17, 18. David, 1 Sam 24:17; 2 Sam 15:19, 20; 23:16, 17; 1 Chron 21:17; Ps 69:6. Araunah, 2 Sam 24:22–24. Nehemiah, Neh 5:14–18. Jews, Esther 9:15. Daniel, Dan 5:17. Jonah, Jon 1: 12, 13. Joseph, Mt 1:19. The disciples, Acts 4:34, 35. Priscilla and Aquilla, Rom 16:3, 4. Paul, 1 Cor 10: 33; Phil 1:18; 4:17; 2 Thess 3:8. Philemon, Philemon 1:13, 14.

See *Charitableness; Fellowship; Fraternity; Selfishness.*

UPHAZ A country famous for gold, Jer 10:9.

UPRIGHTNESS See *Righteousness.*

UR 1. Abraham's native place, Gen 11:27, 28. Abraham leaves, Gen 11:31; 15:7; Neh 9:7.

2. Father of Eliphal, one of David's mighty men, 1 Chron 11:26–47.

URBANUS A Christian in Rome, Rom 16:9.

URI 1. Son of Hur, and father of Bezalel, Ex 31:1; 35:30, 31; 38:22; 1 Chron 2:20; 2 Chron 1:5, 6.

2. Father of Geber, one of Solomon's officials, 1 Kgs 4:8–19.

3. A Levite who divorced his heathen wife, Ezra 10:24.

URIAH 1. One of David's mighty men, 2 Sam 23:24–39; 1 Chron 11:26–47. David's adultery with the wife of, 2 Sam 11:2–5; 1 Kgs 15:5. Summoned from battle by David, 2 Sam 11:6–13. Noble spirit of, 2 Sam 11:11. David arranges the death of, 2 Sam 11:14–25. David marries the widow of, 2 Sam 11:26, 27; Mt 1:6.

2. A priest in the time of Ahaz. Builds a new altar for Ahaz, 2 Kgs 16:10–16. Probably identical with 5, below.

3. A priest. The father of Meremoth, Ezra 8:33; Neh 3:4, 21.

4. A priest. Assistant to Ezra, Neh 8:1–5.

5. A priest. Witness to one of Isaiah's prophecies, Isa 8:2. Probably identical with 2, above.

6. A prophet in the time of Jehoiakim. Prophesies against Judah, Jer 26:20. Fled to Egypt; taken; killed by Jehoiakim, Jer 26:21–23.

URIEL 1. A Levite. Son of Tahath, 1 Chron 6: 22–24. Possibly same as 2, below.

2. A Levite. Assisted in moving the ark, 1 Chron 15:4–12.

3. Grandfather of King Abijah, 2 Chron 13:1, 2.

URIM AND THUMMIM Objects possibly used in sacred oracle to determine God's will. In the breastplate, Ex 28:30, 31; Lev 8:8. Eleazar to ask counsel for Joshua, after the judgment of, Num 27:21. Only priests might interpret, Deut 33:8; Ezra 2:62, 63; Neh 7:64, 65. Israelites consult, Judg 1:1; 20:18, 22–24. Withheld answer from King Saul, 1 Sam 28:5, 6.

USURPATION OF POLITICAL FUNCTIONS. By Absalom, 2 Sam 15:1–12. By Adonijah, 1 Kgs 1:5–9. By Baasha, 1 Kgs 15:27, 28. By Zimri, 1 Kgs 16:9, 10. By Jehu, 2 Kgs 9:11–37. By Athaliah, 2 Kgs 11:1–16. By Shallum, 2 Kgs 15:10.

IN ECCLESIASTICAL AFFAIRS. By Saul, in assuming priestly functions, 1 Sam 13:8–14. By Solomon, in forcing Abiathar out of the priesthood, 1 Kgs 2:26, 27. By Uzziah, in assuming priestly offices, 2 Chron 26:16–21. By Ahaz, 2 Kgs 16:11–13.

See *Government, Ecclesiastical.*

OF EXECUTIVE POWER. In ordering Naboth's death and confiscation of his vineyard, 1 Kgs 21: 7–19. In the scheme of Joseph to dispossess the Egyptians of their real and personal property, Gen 47:13–26. Of Pharaoh, making slaves of the Israelites, Ex 1:9–22. Moses accused of, Num 16:3.

USURY Interest, not necessarily unreasonable exaction, but all income from loans. Forbidden, Ex 22:25; Lev 25:35–37; Deut 23:19; Ps 15:5; Prov 28:8; Jer 15:10; Ezk 18:8, 13, 17; 22:12. Exaction of, rebuked, Neh 5:1–13. Authorized, of foreigners, Deut 23:20. Exacted by Jews, Ezk 22:12; Amos 5: 11.

Just men do not require, Ezk 18:8.

See *Interest; Money.*

UTHAI 1. Son of Ammihud, 1 Chron 9:4.

2. Son of Bigvai. Returned from Babylon with Ezra, Ezra 8:2–14.

UZ 1. Son of Aram, Gen 10:23; 1 Chron 1:17.

2. Son of Nahor, Gen 22:20–23.

3. Son of Dishan, Gen 36:28–30; 1 Chron 1:42.

4. A country of unknown location. Home of Job, Job 1:1. Prophecies concerning, Jer 25:19, 20; Lam 4:21.

UZAI Father of Palal, Neh 3:25.

UZAL Descendant of Joktan, Gen 10:26–30; 1 Chron 1:20–23.

UZZA 1. See *Uzzah, 1.*

2. Proprietor of the burial place of kings Manasseh and Amon, 2 Kgs 21:18, 26.

3. Descendant of Ehud, 1 Chron 8:6, 7.

4. One of the Nethinim, Ezra 2:43–54; Neh 7: 46–56.

UZZAH 1. Called also *Uzza,* son of Abinadab. Driver of the cart in moving the ark, 2 Sam 6:3; 1 Chron 13:7. Stricken dead for touching the ark, 2 Sam 6:6–8; 1 Chron 13:9–11.

2. Son of Merari, 1 Chron 6:29, 30.

UZZEN-SHEERAH A village built by Sheerah, 1 Chron 7:24.

UZZI 1. A priest. Son of Bukki, 1 Chron 6: 4–15, 50–53; Ezra 7:1–5.

2. Grandson of Issachar, 1 Chron 7:2, 3.

3. Grandson of Benjamin, 1 Chron 7:7.

4. Son of Michri, 1 Chron 9:7, 8.

5. An overseer of the Levites, Neh 11:22, 23.

6. Priests in the time of Nehemiah, Neh 12:19, 42.

UZZIA One of David's mighty men, 1 Chron 11:26–47.

UZZIAH 1. Called *Azariah.* King of Judah, 2 Kgs 14:21; 15:1, 2; 2 Chron 26:1, 3. Rebuilds Elath, 2 Kgs 14:22; 2 Chron 26:2. Reigns righteously, 2 Kgs 15:3; 2 Chron 26:4, 5. Defeats the Philistines, 2 Chron 26:6, 7. Takes tribute from the Ammonites; strengthens the kingdom, 2 Chron 26:8, 9. Promotes cattle raising and agriculture, 2 Chron 26:10. Military establishment of, 2 Chron 26:11–15. Is presumptuous in burning incense; stricken with leprosy; quarantined, 2 Chron 26:16–21; 2 Kgs 15: 5. Jotham regent during quarantine of, 2 Kgs 15:5; 2 Chron 26:21. Death of, 2 Kgs 15:7; 2 Chron 26: 23. History of, written by Isaiah, 2 Chron 26:22; Isa 1:1. Earthquake in the reign of, Amos 1:2; Zech 14:5.

2. Descendant of Kohath, 1 Chron 6:22–24.

3. Father of Jonathan, 1 Chron 27:25.

4. A priest. Divorces his Gentile wife, Ezra 10: 21.

5. Father of Athaiah, Neh 11:4–6.

UZZIEL 1. A son of Kohath, Ex 6:18, 22; Lev 10:4.

2. A Simeonite leader, 1 Chron 4:42.

3. Son of Bela, 1 Chron 7:7.

4. One of David's musicians, 1 Chron 25:4, 5.

5. A Levite. Descendant of Jeduthun, 2 Chron 29:12–14.

6. A goldsmith. Aided in repairing the walls of Jerusalem, Neh 3:8.

V

VAIZATHA Son of Haman, Esther 9:7–10.

VALLEY Of Eschol, Num 32:9; Deut 1:24; Achor, Josh 7:24, 26; 15:7; called "Valley of Troubles," Hos 2:15; Aijalon, Josh 10:12; of the giants, or Rephaim, Josh 15:8; 18:16; 2 Sam 5:18, 22; 1 Chron 11:15; 14:9; Jezreel, Judg 6:33; Sorek, Judg 16:4; Elah, 1 Sam 17:2, 19; 21:9; of Salt, 2 Sam 8:13; 2 Kgs 14:7; 1 Chron 18:12; full of trenches, 2 Kgs 3:16; Hinnom, 2 Kgs 23:10; 2 Chron 28:3; 33:6; of Blessing, 2 Chron 20:26; Megiddo, 2 Chron 35:22; of death, Ps 23:4; of Weeping, Ps 84:6; of vision, Isa 22:1; to be filled, Isa 40:4; of Gog's Army, Ezk 39:11; Jehoshaphat, Joel 3:2, 12; judgment, Joel 3:14; in prophecy, Zech 14:4, 5; Lk 3:5.

VALOR See *Courage.*

VANIAH An Israelite. Divorces his Gentile wife, Ezra 10:34–42.

VANITY Pride or futility. A consequence of the fall, Rom 8:20. Every man is, Ps 39:11. All men are, Ps 62:9. Man at his best is, Ps 39:5, 6. Man is like to, Ps 144:4. The thoughts of man are, Ps 94:11. The days of man are, Job 7:16; Eccl 6:12. Childhood and youth are, Eccl 11:10. The beauty of man is, Ps 39:11; Prov 31:30. The help of man is, Ps 60:11; Lam 4:17. Man's own righteousness is, Isa 57:12. Worldly wisdom is, Eccl 2:15, 20–23; 1 Cor 3:20. Worldly pleasure is, Eccl 2:1. Worldly anxiety is, Ps 39:5, 6; 127:2. Worldly labor is, Eccl 2:11; 4:4. Wordly enjoyment is, Eccl 2:3, 10, 11. Worldly possessions are, Eccl 2:4–11. Ill-gotten gain is, Prov 10:2. Gaining wealth is, Eccl 2:24–26; 4:8. Love of wealth is, Eccl 5:10. Unblessed riches are, Eccl 6:2. Riches gotten by dishonesty are, Prov 21:6. All earthly things are, Eccl 1:2. Foolish arguments are, 1 Tim 1:6, 7; 6:20; 2 Tim 2:14, 16; Tit 3:9. The conduct of the ungodly is, 1 Pet 1:18. The religion of hypocrites is, Jas 1:26. The worship of the heathen is, Isa 1:12, 13; Mt 6:7, 8. False teaching is but, Jer 23:32. Mere external religion is, 1 Tim 4:8; Heb 13:9. Charity without love is, 1 Cor 13:3. Faith without works is, Jas 2:14. Idolatry is, 2 Kgs 17:15; Ps 31:5, 6; Isa 44:9, 10; Jer 10:8; 18:15. Wealth gotten by, disappears, Prov 13:11.

Saints hate the thoughts of, Ps 119:113; pray to be kept from, Prov 30:8; avoid, Ps 24:4; avoid those given to, Ps 26:4.

The wicked, though full of, affect to be wise, Job 11:12; meditate on, Ps 2:1; Acts 4:25, 26; Rom 1:21; devise, Ps 36:4; speak, Ps 10:7; 12:2; 41:6; count God's service as, Job 21:15; Mal 3:14, 15; allure others by words of, 2 Pet 2:18; follow after, Jer 2:5; Eph 4:17; inherit, Jer 16:19; reap, Jer 12:13; judicially given up to, Isa 57:13.

Fools follow those given to, Prov 12:11. Following those given to, leads to poverty, Prov 28:19. All should know and acknowledge, Deut 4:35.

See *Pride.*

VASHTI Wife of King Ahasuerus. Put away for refusing to appear at a royal banquet, Esther 1:9–22; 2:1, 4, 17.

VEDAN A place whose merchants traded with Tyre, Ezk 27:19.

VEGETARIANS Persons who eat no meat, Rom 14:2.

VEGETATION Created the third day, Gen 1:11, 12; 2:5. For food, Gen 1:29, 30.

VEIL 1. Hangings used in the Tabernacle to divide the Holy of Holies from the Holy Place, Heb 6:19; 9:3. Ordinances prescribing, Ex 26:31–33. Made by Bezalel and Oholiab, Ex 36:35, 36. A covering for the ark, Ex 35:10–19; 40:21; Num 4:5.

2. Of the Temple, 2 Chron 3:14. Split at the time of the crucifixion of Jesus, Mt 27:51; Mk 15:38; Lk 23:45.

FIGURATIVE. Heb 10:20.

3. Worn by Rebekah, Gen 24:65; by Tamar, Gen 38:14; by Moses, to screen his face when he came down from Mount Sinai, Ex 34:33, 35; 2 Cor 3:13–16; cf. Israel, vs. 15, 16.

See *Dress; Tapestry.*

VENERATION For parents, Gen 48:15, 16.

See *Old Age; Parents; Reverence.*

VENGEANCE Belongs to God, Deut 32:35; Ps 94:1; Rom 12:19; Heb 10:30.

INSTANCES OF. Sons of Jacob on Hamor and Shechem, Gen 34:20–31.

See *Judgments; Revenge; Retaliation.*

VENTRILOQUISM Isa 29:4.

VERDICT Against Jesus, Mt 26:65, 66; 27:24–26; Mk 15:15; Lk 23:24; Jn 19:16.

See *Court.*

VESTMENTS Of priests, see *Priests.*

VIAL Of oil, 2 Kgs 9:1–3.

VICARIOUS DEATH. The ram for Isaac,

Gen 22:13. Jesus for sinners, see *Jesus, Death of, Mission of, Sufferings of.*

See *Atonement; Sufferings, Vicarious; Jesus, Savior.*

VICEREGENCY Position as deputy or representative. Of Elisha, in miraculously rewarding the Shunemmite, 2 Kgs 4:15–17; in cursing Gehazi, 2 Kgs 5:27.

VIGILANCE INSTANCE OF. King of Jericho, Josh 2:1–3.

See *Watchman.*

VICTORIES In battle, from God, Ps 55:18; 76:5, 6. Celebrated in song, Judg 5; 2 Sam 22; by women, 1 Sam 18:6, 7.

See *Armies; War, God in.*

VINE Degeneracy of, Jer 2:21. Fable of, Judg 9:12, 13. Pruned, Isa 5:6; Jn 15:1–5. Parables of, Ps 80:8–14; Ezk 17:6–10; 19:10–14.

A title of Christ, Jer 33:15.

Jonah used to make a shelter, Jon 4:6–10.

Symbolical. Jn 15:1–5.

See *Vineyard.*

VINEGAR A sour wine. Forbidden to Nazirites, Num 6:3, 4. Used with food, Ps 69:21; Prov 10:26; 25:20. Offered to Christ on the cross, Mt 27:34, 38; Jn 19:29, with Mk 15:23.

VINEYARD Of Noah, Gen 9:20, 21. Of Naboth, 1 Kgs 21:1. Towers in, Isa 5:2; Mt 21:33; Mk 12:1. Winepress in, Isa 5:2. Leased, Song 8:11, 12; Mt 21:33–39. Of kings, 1 Chron 27:26–28. Neglected, Prov 24:30, 31; Isa 7:23. Meadow, Judg 11:33.

Parables of, Isa 5:1–7; 27:2, 3; Jer 12:10; Mt 20:1–16; 21:28–31, 33–41; Lk 20:9–16. Laws concerning, Ex 23:11; Lev 19:10; 25:3; Deut 20:6.

See *Vine; Wine.* See also *Abstinence.*

VIOLENCE Earth filled with, Gen 6:11–13; violence and strife in the city, Ps 55:9; he will disappear, Isa 60:18; Jerusalem is full of, Ezk 7:23; land filled with, Ezk 8:17; 28:16; against your brother Israel, Obd 1:10; don't resist, Mt 5:39; kingdom of heaven suffers violence, Mt 11:12; Babylon overthrown with, Rev 18:21.

VIPER FIGURATIVE. Mt 23:33.

VIRGIN Proofs of, Deut 22:13–31. Dowry of, Ex 22:17. Character of, to be protected, Deut 22:17–24. Betrothal of, a quasi marriage, Deut 22:23, 24. Distinguishing clothing of, 2 Sam 13:18. Priests may marry none but, Lev 21:14. Mourn in the Temple, Lam 1:4; 2:10. Virginity of, bewailed, Judg 11:37–39. Parables of the wise and the foolish, Mt 25:1–13. Mother of Jesus a, Isa 7:14; Mt 1:23; Lk 1:27. Advised by Paul not to marry, 1 Cor 7.

Parable of, Mt 25:1–13.

FIGURATIVE. Of the church, Isa 62:5; Jer 31:4; 2 Cor 11:2. Of personal purity, 1 Cor 7:25, 37; Rev 14:4.

VIRGINITY See *Virgin.*

VIRTUE Isa 55:5; Lk 18:9; Phil 4:8; 2 Pet 1:5.

See *Chastity; Continence; Courage.*

VISION A mode of revelation, Num 12:6; 1 Sam 3:1; 2 Chron 26:5; Job 33:15; Ps 89:19; Jer 14:14; Dan 1:17; Hos 12:10; Joel 2:28; Obd 1:1; Hab 2:2; Acts 2:17; 10:1–18.

Of Abraham, concerning his descendants, Gen 15:1–17. Of Jacob, of the ladder with ascending and descending angels, Gen 28:12; at Beer-sheba, Gen 46:2. Of Joshua, of the commander of the Lord's army, Josh 5:13–15. Of Moses, of the burning bush, Ex 3:2; of the glory of God, Ex 24:9–11; 33:18–23. Of Pharaoh, of the cattle, Gen 41:1–7.

Of the Israelites, of the manifestation of the glory of God, Ex 24:10, 17; Heb 12:18–21. Of Balaam, in a trance, see *Balaam.* Of Elisha, at the translation of Elijah, 2 Kgs 2:11. Of Elisha's servant, of the chariots of the Lord, 2 Kgs 6:17. Of Micaiah, of the defeat of the Israelites; of the Lord on his throne; and of a lying spirit, 1 Kgs 22:17–23; 2 Chron 18:16–22. Of David, of the angel of the Lord by the threshing floor of Ornan, 1 Chron 21:15–18. Of Job, of a spirit, Job 4:12–16. Of Isaiah, of the Lord and his glory in the Temple, Isa 6; of the Valley of Vision, Isa 22. Of Jeremiah, of an almond rod, Jer 1:11; of the boiling pot, Jer 1:13.

Of Ezekiel, of the glory of God, Ezk 1:3, 12–14; 23; of the scroll, Ezk 2:9, 10; of the man of fire, Ezk 8; 9; of the coals of fire, Ezk 10:1–7; of the dry bones, Ezk 37:1–14; of the city and Temple, Ezk chapters 40–48; of the rivers, Ezk 47:1–12.

Of Daniel, of the four beasts, Dan 7; of the Ancient of Days, Dan 7:9–27; of the ram and the buck goat, Dan 8; of the angel, Dan 10.

Of Amos, of locusts, Amos 7:1, 2; of fire, Amos 7:4; of a plumbline, Amos 7:7, 8; of ripe fruit, Amos 8:1, 2; of the Temple, Amos 9:1.

Of Zechariah, of horses, Zech 1:8–11; of horns and blacksmiths, Zech 1:18–21; of the High Priest, Zech 3:1–4; of the golden lampstand, Zech 4; of the flying scroll, Zech 5:1–4; of the mountains and chariots, Zech 6:1–8.

Of Zacharias, in the Temple, Lk 1:13–22. Of John the Baptist, at the baptism of Jesus, Mt 3:16; Mk 1:10; Lk 3:22; Jn 1:32–34. Peter, James, and John, of the transfiguration of Jesus and the appearance of Moses and Elijah, Mt 17:1–9; Lk 9:28–36. Of the people, of the tongues of fire at Pentecost, Acts 2:2, 3. Of Stephen, of Christ, Acts 7:55, 56. Of Paul, of Christ, on the way to Damascus, Acts 9:3–6; 1 Cor 9:1; of Ananias, Acts 9:12; of a man of Macedonia, saying, "Come over here and help us," Acts 16:9; in Corinth, Acts 18:9, 10; in a trance, Acts 22:17–21; of paradise, 2 Cor 12:1–4. Of Ananias, of Christ, Acts 9:10–12. Of Cornelius, of an angel, Acts 10:3. Of Peter, of the sheet let down from heaven, Acts 10:9–18.

Of John on the island of Patmos, the Book of Revelation, including: Christ, and the golden candlesticks, Rev 1:10–20; the open door, Rev 4:1; a rainbow and throne, Rev 4:2, 3; 24 elders, Rev 4:4; seven lamps, Rev 4:5; crystal sea, Rev 4:6; four living beings, Rev 4:6–8; scroll with seven seals, Rev 5:1–5; golden vials, Rev 5:8; of the six seals, Rev 6; four horses, Rev 6:2–8; earthquake and celestial phenomena, Rev 6:12–14; four angels, Rev 7:1; sealing of the 144,000, Rev 7:2–8; of the seventh seal and seven angels, Rev chapters 8–11; of the censer, Rev 8:5; hail and fire, Rev 8:7; mountain thrown into the sea, Rev 8:8, 9; falling star, Rev 8:10, 11; 9:1; the third part of sun and moon and stars darkened, Rev 8:12; bottomless pit, Rev 9:2; locusts, Rev 9:3–11; four demons loosed from the Euphrates, Rev 9:14; army of horsemen, Rev 9:16–19; angel with a scroll, Rev 10:1–10; seven thunders, Rev 10:3, 4; measurement of the temple, Rev 11:1, 2; two witnesses, Rev 11:3–12; court of the Gentiles, Rev 11:2; two olive trees and two candlesticks, Rev 11:4; the beast out of the bottomless pit, Rev 11:7; fall of the city, Rev 11:13; second and third woes, Rev 11:14; a woman clothed with the sun; birth of the male child, Rev 12; a red Dragon, Rev 12:3–17; war in heaven, Rev 12:7–9; the Creature rising out of the sea, Rev 13:1–10; the animal coming out of the earth, Rev 13:11–18; the Lamb on Mount Zion, Rev 14:1–5; the angel having the everlasting gospel, Rev 14:6, 7; the angel proclaiming the fall of Babylon, Rev 14:8–13; the Son of Man with a sickle, Rev 14:14–16; angel reaping the harvest, Rev 14:15–20; angel coming out of the temple, Rev 14:17–19; an angel having power over fire, Rev 14:18; the vine and the winepress, Rev 14:18–20; angels with the seven last plagues, Rev 15; ocean of glass, Rev 15:2; temple opened, Rev 15:5; the plague upon the men who had the mark of the Creature, Rev 16:2; oceans turned into blood, Rev 16:3; the seven angels with the seven flasks of the wrath of God, Rev 16; 17; destruction of Babylon, Rev 18; of the crowd praising, Rev 19:1–9; of him who is faithful and true riding a white horse, Rev 19:11–16; angel in the sun, Rev 19:17–21; Satan bound a thousand years, Rev 20:1–3; thrones of judgment, and the Resurrection, and the freeing of Satan, Rev 20:1–10; great white throne, Rev 20:11; opening of the Book of Life, Rev 20:12; death and hell, Rev 20:14; New Jerusalem, Rev 21; river of the Water of Life, Rev 22:1; tree of life, Rev 22:2.

See *Dream*.

VISITATION By God, Isa 10:3; 1 Pet 2:12; with punishment, Jer 8:12; 51:18.

VISITOR See *Guest*.

VOICE OF GOD. Ezk 1:24, 27, 28; 10:5; Jn 12:28–30; Acts 7:31; 9:4, 7; 26:14, 15.

See *Anthropomorphisms*.

VOLCANO Deut 4:11; 5:23; Ps 97:5; 104:32; 144:5; Isa 34:9, 10; 64:1–3; Jer 51:25; Mic 1:4; Nah 1:5, 6.

FIGURATIVE. Isa 30:33.

See *Brimstone; Earthquake; Mountain*.

VOLUNTARY OFFERINGS See *Free-Will Offerings*.

VOLUPTUOUSNESS See *Lasciviousness; Sensuality*.

VOPHSI Father of Nahbi, Num 13:3–15.

VOWS Mosaic laws concerning, Lev 23:37, 38; Num 29:39. Must be voluntary, see below. Must be performed, see below. Estimation of the value of things offered in vows, to be made by the priest, according to age and sex of the person making the offering, Lev 27:1–13. The value of the offering of real estate, to be decided by the priest, Lev 27:14, 15; of a field, Lev 27:16–25.

Edible things offered in, to be eaten the same day they were offered, or the next day, Lev 7:16–18. Things offered in, to be brought to the tabernacle or temple, Deut 12:6, 11, 17, 18, 26, 27; belonged to the priests, Num 18:14, 15.

Rash: By Jephthah, in consecration of his daughter as a sacrifice, if his campaign against the Ammonites were successful, Judg 11:29–40; the Israelites, to destroy the Benjaminites, Judg 21:5, 6, with chapters 20; 21.

UNCLASSIFIED SCRIPTURES RELATING TO. Gen 28:20. And Jacob vowed this vow to God: "If God will help and protect me on this journey and give me food and clothes, [21]and will bring me back safely to my father, then I will choose Jehovah as my God!" Gen 31:13.

Lev 5:4. If anyone makes a rash vow, whether the vow is good or bad, when he realizes what a foolish vow he has taken, he is guilty. [5]In any of these cases he shall confess his sin [6]and bring his guilt offering to the Lord, a female lamb or goat, and the priest shall make atonement for him, and he shall be freed from his sin, and need not fulfill the vow. [7]If he is too poor to bring a lamb to the Lord, then he shall bring two turtledoves or two young pigeons as his guilt offering; one of the birds shall be his sin offering and the other his burnt offering. [8]The priest shall offer as the sin sacrifice whichever bird is handed to him first, wringing its neck, but not severing its head from its body. [9]Then he shall sprinkle some of the blood at the side of the altar and the rest shall be drained out at the base of the altar; this is the sin offering. [10]He shall offer the second bird as a burnt offering, following the customary procedures that have been set forth so the priest shall make atonement for him concerning his sin and he shall be forgiven. [11]If he is too poor to bring turtledoves or young pigeons as his sin offering, then he shall bring a tenth of a bushel of fine flour. He must not mix it with olive oil or put any incense on it, because it is a sin offering. [12]He shall bring it to the priest and the priest shall take out a handful as a representative portion, and burn it on the altar just as any other offering to Jehovah made by fire; this shall be his sin offering. [13]In this way the priest shall make atonement for him for any sin of this kind, and he shall be forgiven. The rest of the flour shall belong to the priest, just as was the case with the grain offering.

Lev 22:18. Tell Aaron and his sons and all the people of Israel that if an Israelite or other person living among you offers a burnt offering sacrifice to the Lord—whether it is to fulfill a promise or is a spontaneous free will offering— [19]it will only be acceptable to the Lord if it is a male animal without defect; it must be a young bull or a sheep or a goat. [20]Anything that has a defect must not be offered, for it will not be accepted. [21]Anyone sacrificing a peace offering to the Lord from the herd or flock, whether to fulfill a vow or as a voluntary offering, must sacrifice an animal that has no defect, or it will not be accepted: [22]An animal that is blind or disabled or mutilated, or which has sores or itch or any other skin disease, must not be offered to the Lord; it is not a fit burnt offering for the altar of the Lord. [23]If the young bull or lamb presented to the Lord has anything superfluous or lacking in its body parts, it may be offered as a free will offering, but not for a vow. [24]An animal that has injured genitals—crushed or castrated—shall not be offered to the Lord at any time. [25]This restriction applies to the sacrifices made by foreigners among you as well as those made by yourselves, for no defective animal is acceptable for this sacrifice.

Num 15:2. When your children finally live in the land I am going to give them, [3, 4]and they want to please the Lord with a burnt offering or any other offering by fire, their sacrifice must be an animal from their flocks of sheep and goats, or from their herds of cattle. Each sacrifice—whether an ordinary one, or a sacrifice to fulfill a vow, or a free-will offering, or a special sacrifice at any of the annual festivals—must be accompanied by a grain offering. If a lamb is being sacrificed, use three quarts of fine flour mixed with three pints of oil, [5]accompanied by three pints of wine for a drink offering. [6]If the sacrifice is a ram, use six quarts of fine flour mixed with four pints of oil, [7]and four pints of wine for a drink offering. This will be a sacrifice that is a pleasing fragrance to the Lord. [8, 9]If the sacrifice is a young bull, then the grain offering accompanying it must consist of nine quarts of fine flour mixed with three quarts of oil, [10]plus three quarts of wine for the drink offering. This shall be offered by fire as a pleasing fragrance to the Lord. [11, 12]These are the instructions for what is to accompany each sacrificial bull, ram, lamb, or young goat. [13, 14]These instructions apply both to native-born Israelis and to foreigners living among you who want to please the Lord with sacrifices offered by fire; [15, 16]For there is the same law for all, native-born or foreigner, and this shall be true forever from generation to generation; all are equal before the Lord. Yes, one law for all!

Num 30:2. "The Lord has commanded that when anyone makes a promise to the Lord, either to do something or to quit doing something, that vow must not be broken: the person making the vow must do exactly as he has promised. [3]If a woman promises the Lord to do or not do something, and she is still a girl at home in her father's home, [4]and her father hears that she has made a vow with penalties, but says nothing, then her vow shall stand. [5]But if her father refuses to let her make the vow, or feels that the penalties she has agreed to are too harsh, then her promise will automatically become invalid. Her father must state his disagreement on the first day he hears about it; and then Jehovah will forgive her because her father would not let her do it. [6]If she takes a vow or makes a foolish pledge, and later marries, [7]and her husband learns of her vow and says nothing on the day he hears of it, her vow shall stand. [8]But if her husband refuses to accept her vow or foolish pledge, his disagreement makes it void, and Jehovah will forgive her. [9]But if the woman is a widow or is divorced, she must fulfill her vow. [10]If she is married and living in her husband's home when she makes the vow, [11]and her husband hears of it and does nothing, the vow shall stand; [12]but if he refuses to allow it on the first day he hears of it, her vow is void and Jehovah will forgive her. [13]So her husband may either confirm or nullify her vow, [14]but if he says nothing for a day, then he has already agreed to it. [15]If he waits more than a day and then refuses to permit the vow, whatever penalties to which she agreed shall come upon him—he shall be responsible." [16]These, then, are the commandments the Lord gave Moses concerning relationships between a man and his wife and between a father and his daughter who is living at home. *v.* 1.

Deut 23:21. When you make a vow to the Lord, be prompt in doing whatever it is you promised him, for the Lord demands that you promptly fulfill your vows; it is a sin if you don't. [22](But it is not a sin if you refrain from vowing!) [23]Once you make the vow, you must be careful to do as you have said, for it was your own choice, and you have vowed to the Lord your God.

Job 22:27. You will pray to him, and he will hear you, and you will fulfill all your promises to him.

Ps 22:25. Yes, I will stand and praise you before all the people. I will publicly fulfill my vows in the presence of all who reverence your name.

Ps 50:14, 15. What I want from you is your true thanks; I want your promises fulfilled. *I want you to trust me in your times of trouble, so I can rescue you, and you can give me glory.*

Ps 56:12. I will surely do what I have promised, Lord, and thank you for your help.

Ps 61:5. For you have heard my vows, O God. [8]And I will praise your name continually, fulfilling my vow of praising you each day.

Ps 65:1. O God in Zion, we wait before you in silent praise, and thus fulfill our vow.

Ps 66:13. Now I have come to your Temple with burnt-offerings to pay my vows. [14]For when I was in trouble I promised you many offerings.

Ps 76:11. Fulfill all your vows that you have made to Jehovah your God. Let everyone bring him presents. He should be reverenced and feared.

Ps 116:14. I will publicly bring him the sacrifice I vowed I would. [15]His loved ones are very precious to him and he does not lightly let them die. [16]O Lord, you have freed me from my bonds and I will serve you forever. [17]I will worship you and offer you a sacrifice of thanksgiving. [18, 19]Here in the courts of the Temple in Jerusalem, before all the people, I will pay everything I vowed to the Lord. Praise the Lord.

Prov 20:25. It is foolish and rash to make a promise to the Lord before counting the cost.

Eccl 5:4. So when you talk to God and vow to him that you will do something, don't delay in doing it, for God has no pleasure in fools. Keep your promise to him. [5]It is far better not to say you'll do something than to say you will and then not do it. [6]In that case, your mouth is making you sin. Don't try to defend yourself by telling the messenger from God that it was all a mistake (to make the vow). That would make God very angry; and he might destroy your prosperity.

Jon 2:9. I will never worship anyone but you! For how can I thank you enough for all you have done? I will surely fulfill my promises. For my deliverance comes from the Lord alone.

Nah 1:15. See, the messengers come running down the mountains with glad news: "The invaders have been wiped out and we are safe!" O Judah, proclaim a day of thanksgiving, and worship only the Lord, as you have vowed. For this enemy from Nineveh will never come again. He is cut off forever; he will never be seen again.

See *Contract; Covenant.*

INSTANCES OF. Of Jacob, see above, Gen 28: 20–22. Of the mother of Micah, in the dedication of silver for the making of an idol, Judg 17:2, 3. Of Hannah, to consecrate to the Lord the child for which she prayed, 1 Sam 1:11, with *vs.* 27, 28. Of Absalom, 2 Sam 15:7, 8. Of Job, not to entertain lustful thoughts, Job 31:1. Of David, Ps 132:2–5. Of Ananias and Sapphira, in the dedication of the proceeds of the sale of their land, Acts 5:1–11. Of the Jews, to kill Paul, Acts 23:12–15. Of Jephthah, and of the Israelites, see *Rash Vows,* above.

See *Nazirite.*

VULTURE A carnivorous bird, Jer 49:22; Zeph 2:14; forbidden as food, Lev 11:13–19; Deut 14: 11–18.

FIGURATIVE. Ps 102:6; Jer 48:40; Hos 8:1.

See *Cormorant; Falcon; Kite.*

W

WAFER Ex 29:2, 23; Lev 2:4; 7:12; 8:26; Num 6:15, 19; 1 Chron 23:29.

WAGES Of Jacob, Gen 29:15–30; 30:28–34; 31:7, 41. Parable concerning, Mt 20:1–15.

See *Master; Servant.*

UNCLASSIFIED SCRIPTURES RELATING TO. Lev 19:13. You shall not rob nor oppress anyone, and you shall pay your hired workers promptly. If something is due them, don't even keep it overnight.

Deut 24:14, 15. Never oppress a poor hired man, whether a fellow Israelite or a foreigner living in your town. Pay him his wage each day before sunset, for since he is poor he needs it right away; otherwise he may cry out to the Lord against you and it would be counted as a sin against you.

Deut 25:4. Don't muzzle an ox as it treads out the grain.

Jer 22:13. And woe to you, King Jehoiakim, for you are building your great palace with forced labor. By not paying wages you are building injustice into its walls and oppression into its doorframes and ceilings.

Hag 1:6. You plant much but harvest little. You have scarcely enough to eat or drink, and not enough clothes to keep you warm. Your income disappears, as though you were putting it into pockets filled with holes!

Mal 3:5. "At that time my punishments will be quick and certain; I will move swiftly . . . against all those who cheat their hired hands, or oppress widows and orphans, or defraud strangers, and do not fear me," says the Lord of Hosts.

Lk 3:14. "And us," asked some soldiers, "what about us?" John replied, ". . . be content with your pay!"

Lk 10:7. For the workman is worthy of his wages! Mt 10:10.

Rom 4:4. But didn't he earn his right to heaven by all the good things he did? No, for being saved is a gift.

Rom 6:23. For the wages of sin is death, but the free gift of God is eternal life through Jesus Christ our Lord.

Col 4:1. You slave owners must be just and fair to all your slaves. Always remember that you, too, have a Master in heaven who is closely watching you.

Jas 5:4. For listen! Hear the cries of the field workers whom you have cheated of their pay. Their cries have reached the ears of the Lord of Hosts.

WAGON Gen 45:19, 27; Num 7:3–9; Ezk 23:24.

See *Cart.*

WAITING On God: As the God of providence, Jer 14:22; as the God of salvation, Ps 25:5; as the giver of all temporal provisions, Ps 104:27, 28; 145:15, 16.

For mercy, Ps 52:9; 123:2; pardon, Ps 39:7, 8; the Consolation of Israel, Lk 2:25; salvation, Gen 49:18; Ps 62:1, 2; guidance and teaching, Ps 25:5; protection, Ps 33:20; 59:9, 10; the fulfillment of his word, Hab 2:3; the fulfillment of his promises, Acts 1:4; hope of righteousness by faith, Gal 5:5; return of Christ, 1 Cor 1:7; 1 Thess 1:10. God calls us to, Zeph 3:8. Exhortations and encouragements to, Ps 27:14; 37:7; Hos 12:6.

Should be with the soul, Ps 62:1, 5; with earnest desire, Ps 130:6; with patience, Ps 37:7; 40:1; quietly, Lam 3:26; with hope in his promises, Ps 130:5; with full confidence, Mic 7:7; continually, Hos 12:6; specially in adversity, Ps 59:1–9; Isa 8:17. Believers resolve to, Ps 52:9. Believers have expectation from, Ps 62:5. Believers plead, in prayer, Ps 25:21; Isa 33:2. The patience of believers often tried in, Ps 69:3.

They who engage in, wait on him only, Ps 62:5; Prov 20:22; are heard, Ps 40:1; are blessed, Ps 37:9; Isa 30:18; Dan 12:12; experience his goodness, Lam 3:25; shall not be disgraced, Ps 25:3; Isa 49:23; shall renew their strength, Isa 40:31; shall be saved, Isa 25:9; shall rejoice in salvation, Isa 25:9; shall receive the glorious things prepared by God for them, Isa 64:4. Illustrated, Ps 123:2; Lk 12:36; Jas 5:7.

EXEMPLIFIED. David, Ps 40:1; Isaiah, Isa 8:17; Micah, Mic 7:7; Joseph, Mk 15:42, 43.

WALKING With God: According to his commands, Ps 1; in his ways, Deut 8:6; 28:9; 1 Kgs 8:35, 36; 11:38; Ps 50:23; in the old paths, Jer 6:16; a steady tread, 2 Sam 22:34; as taught by him, 1 Kgs 8:35, 36; Isa 30:21; uprightly, Ps 26:11; Prov

2:7; humbly, Mic 6:8; not after our old nature, but after the Spirit, Gal 5:16; in the fear of the Lord, Acts 9:31; in the light, 1 Jn 2:9, 10; in white clothing, Rev 3:4.

INSTANCES OF. Enoch, Gen 5:24; Noah, Gen 6:9.

WALLS Of the cities: Of Bashan, destroyed by the Israelites, Deut 3:5, 6; of Jericho, Josh 2:15; 6; of Jerusalem, see *Jerusalem;* of Babylon, Jer 51:44; wide, Jer 51:58; of Beth-shan, 1 Sam 31:10; of Rabbah, Amos 1:14; of Abel, 2 Sam 20:15.

Houses built on, Josh 2:15. Double, 2 Kgs 25:4, 5. Sentinels on, see *Watchman.* Vineyard, Num 22:24. Broken, Prov 24:30, 31; Eccl 10:8, 9.

FIGURATIVE. Isa 26:1. Of the new Jerusalem, Rev 21:12, 14, 17–21. Of righteousness, Ezk 22:30.

WAR Divine approval of, 2 Sam 22:35. Civil, Judg 12:1–6; 20; 2 Sam 2:12–31; 3:1; 20; 1 Kgs 14:30; 16:21; Isa 19:2; forbidden, 2 Chron 11:4; averted, Josh 22:11–34. Enemy harangued by leader of opposing side, 2 Kgs 18:19–36; 2 Chron 13:4–12. Of extermination, Num 31:7–17; Deut 2:33, 34; 3:6; 20:13–18; Josh 6:21, 24; 8:24, 25; 10:2–40; 11:11–23; 1 Sam 15:3–9; 27:8–11.

God in, Ex 14:13, 14; Deut 1:30; 3:21, 22; 7:17–24; 20:1, 4; 31:6–8, 23; 32:29, 30; Josh 1:1, 5–7, 9; Judg 1:2; 6:16; 7:8, 9; 11:29; 1 Sam 17:45–47; 19:5; 30:7, 8; 2 Sam 5:22–24; 22:18; 1 Kgs 20:28; Ps 18:34; 76:3; Jer 46:15; Amos 5:8, 9; Zech 10:5. God uses, as a judgment, Ex 23:24; Lev 26:17, 31–39; Deut 28:25–68; 32:30; Judg 2:12–14; 2 Kgs 15:37; 1 Chron 5:22, 26; 21:12; 2 Chron 12:1–12; 15:6; 24:23, 24; 33:11; 36; Job 19:29; Ps 44:9–16; 60:1–3; 105:25; Isa 5:1–8, 25–30; 9:8–12; 13:3, 4, 9; 19:2; 34:2–6; 43:28; 45:7; Jer 12:7, 12; 46:15–17, 20, 21; 47:6, 7; 48:10; 49:5; 50:25; Ezk 23:22–25; Amos 3:6; 4:11; Zeph 1:7–18; Zech 8:10; 14:1, 2.

Repugnant to God, 1 Chron 22:8, 9; Ps 68:30; 120:5–7; Rev 13:10. God sends panic in, Ex 15:14–16; threatens defeat in, Deut 32:25; 1 Sam 2:10; 2 Chron 18:12–16; Isa 30:15–17; Ezk 15:5–8; 21:9–17; inflicts defeat in, Josh 7:12, 13; 2 Chron 12:5–8; 24:23, 24; Ps 76:3; 78:66; 79:10; Isa 5:25; Jer 46:15, 16.

Counsels of, Josh 22:10–34; Judg 7:10, 11; 2 Sam 16:20; 17:1–15; Ps 48:4–7; Prov 11:14; 20:18. Wisdom required in, Prov 21:22; 24:6; Eccl 9:14–18; Lk 14:31, 32.

Tumult of, Amos 2:2. Victims, neglected, Isa 14:19; 18:6. Evils of, 2 Sam 2:26; Ps 46:8; 79:1–3; 137:9; Isa 3:5, 25, 26; 5:29, 30; 6:11, 12; 9:5, 19–21; 13:15, 16; 15; 16:9, 10; 18:6; 19:2–16; 32:13, 14; 33:8, 9; 34:7–15; Jer 4:19–31; 5:16, 17; 6:24–26; 7:33, 34; 8:16, 17; 9:10–21; 10:20; 13:14; 14:18; 15:8, 9; 19:7–9; 25:33; 46:3–12; 47:3; 48:28, 33; 51:30–58; Lam chapters 1–5; Ezk 33:27; 39:17–19; Hos 10:14; 13:16; Joel 2:2–10; Amos 1:13; 6:9, 10; 8:3; Nah 2:10; 3:3, 10; Zech 14:1, 2; Lk 21:20–26; Rev 19:17, 18.

To end, Ps 46:9; Isa 2:4; Mic 4:3.

Wars and signs of, Mt 24:6; Mk 13:7; Lk 21:9.

See *Armies; Arms; Fort; Soldiers; Strategy; Tower; Watchman.*

FIGURATIVE. Warfare of believers: Is not by human means, 2 Cor 10:3. Is a good warfare, 1 Tim 1:18, 19. Is for God, 1 Tim 6:12.

Is against the devil, Gen 3:15; 2 Cor 2:11; Eph 6:12; Jas 4:7; 1 Pet 5:8; Rev 12:17; our lower nature, Rom 7:23–25; 1 Cor 9:25–27; 2 Cor 12:7; Gal 5:17; 1 Pet 2:11; enemies, Ps 38:19; 56:1, 2; 59:3; the world, Jn 16:33; 1 Jn 5:4, 5; death, 1 Cor 15:26, with Heb 2:14, 15.

Often arises from the opposition of friends or relatives, Mic 7:6; Mt 10:35, 36. To be carried on under Christ, as our Leader, Heb 2:10; under the Lord's banner, Ps 60:4, 5; with faith, 1 Tim 1:18, 19; with steadfastness in the faith, 1 Cor 16:13; 1 Pet 5:9, with Heb 10:23; with earnestness, Jude 1:3; with watchfulness, 1 Cor 16:13; 1 Pet 5:8; with sobriety, 1 Thess 5:6; with endurance of suffering, 2 Tim 2:3, 10; with self-denial, 1 Cor 9:25–27; with confidence in God, Ps 27:1–3; with prayer, Ps 35:1–3; Eph 6:18; without earthly entanglements, 2 Tim 2:4.

Believers are all engaged in, Phil 1:30; must stand firm in, Eph 6:13, 14; exhorted to diligence in, 1 Tim 6:12; Jude 1:3; encouraged in, Isa 41:11, 12; 51:12; Mic 7:8; 1 Jn 4:4; helped by God in, Ps 140:6–8; comforted by God in, 2 Cor 7:5, 6; strengthened by God in, Ps 20:2; 27:14; Isa 41:10; strengthened by Christ in, 2 Cor 12:9; 2 Tim 4:17; delivered by Christ in, 2 Tim 4:18; thank God for victory in, Rom 7:23–25; 1 Cor 15:57.

Armor for: a belt of truth, Eph 6:14; the breastplate of God's approval, Eph 6:14; shoes of speed to preach the gospel, Eph 6:15; shield of faith, Eph 6:16; helmet of salvation, Eph 6:17; 1 Thess 5:8; sword of the Spirit, Eph 6:17; called God's armor, Eph 6:11; called godly man's arsenal, 2 Cor 6:7; called armor of right living, Rom 13:12, 13; not made by man, 2 Cor 10:4; mighty through God, 2 Cor 10:4, 5; every piece is required, Eph 6:13; must be put on, Rom 13:12, 13; Eph 6:11; includes weapons of defense and attack, 2 Cor 6:7.

Victory in, is from God, 1 Cor 15:57; 2 Cor 2:14; through Christ, Rom 7:23–25; 1 Cor 15:57; 2 Cor 12:9; Rev 12:11; by faith, Heb 11:33–38; 1 Jn 5:4, 5; over the devil, Rom 16:20; 1 Jn 2:14; over our old nature, Rom 7:23–25; Gal 5:24; over the world, 1 Jn 5:4, 5; over all that exalts itself, 2 Cor 10:5; over death and the grave, Isa 25:8; 26:19; Hos 13:14; 1 Cor 15:54–56; triumphant, Rom 8:37; 2 Cor 10:5.

They who overcome in, shall eat of the hidden manna, Rev 2:17; eat of the Tree of Life, Rev 2:7; be clothed in white raiment, Rev 3:5; be pillars in the temple of God, Rev 3:12; sit with Christ on his throne, Rev 3:21; have a white stone, and on it a new name engraved, Rev 2:17; have power over the nations, Rev 2:26; have the name of God written on them by Christ, Rev 3:12; have God as their God, Rev 21:7; have the Morning Star, Rev 2:28; inherit all things, Rev 21:7; be confessed by Christ before God the Father, Rev 3:5; be sons of God, Rev 21:7; not be hurt by the Second Death, Rev 2:11; not have their names erased from the Book of Life, Rev 3:5.

Symbolized by a red horse, Rev 6:4.

IN HEAVEN.

Symbolical. Rev 12:7.

WARFARE See *War.* Spiritual, see *Figurative,* under *War.*

WARNING See *Wicked, Warned.*

WASHING Of hands, a token of innocency, Deut 21:6, 7; Ps 26:6; Mt 27:24. Of feet, Gen 18:4; 24:32; Lk 7:38.

See *Ablutions; Purification.*

FIGURATIVE. Of regeneration, Ps 51:7; Isa 1:16; 4:2–4; Zech 13:1; 1 Cor 6:11; Eph 5:26; Tit 3:5.

WATCH A division of time, see *Night; Time.*

WATCHFULNESS Ex 23:13. Be sure to obey all of these instructions; and remember—never mention the name of any other god.

Ex 34:12. Be very, very careful never to compromise with the people there in the land where you are going, for if you do, you will soon be following their evil ways.

Deut 4:9. But watch out! Be very careful never to forget what you have seen God doing for you. May his miracles have a deep and permanent effect upon your lives! Tell your children and grandchildren about the glorious miracles he did. [23]Beware lest you break the contract the Lord your God has made with you! You will break it if you make any idols, for the Lord your God has utterly forbidden this.

Deut 11:16. But beware that your hearts do not turn from God to worship other gods.

Deut 27:9. Then Moses and the Levite-priests addressed all Israel as follows: "O Israel, listen! Today you have become the people of the Lord your God."

Josh 22:5. Be sure to continue to obey all of the commandments Moses gave you. Love the Lord and follow his plan for your lives. Cling to him and serve him enthusiastically. Deut 6:17.

Josh 23:11. So be very careful to keep on loving him.

1 Kgs 2:3. Obey the laws of God and follow all his ways; keep each of his commands written in the law of Moses so that you will prosper in everything you do, wherever you turn.

1 Kgs 8:25. And now, O Lord God of Israel, fulfill your further promise to him: that if his descendants follow your ways and try to do your will as he did, one of them shall always sit upon the throne of Israel. 1 Kgs 2:4.

2 Chron 19:7. Be very much afraid to give any other decision than what God tells you to. For there must be no injustice among God's judges, no partiality, no taking of bribes.

Neh 4:9. But we prayed to our God and guarded the city day and night to protect ourselves.

Job 36:18. Watch out! Don't let your anger at others lead you into scoffing at God! Don't let your suffering embitter you at the only one who can deliver you. [19]Do you really think that if you shout loudly enough against God, he will be ashamed and repent? Will this put an end to your chastisement? [20]Do not desire the night-time, with its opportunities for crime. [21]Turn back from evil, for it was to prevent you from getting into a life of evil that God sent this suffering.

Ps 39:1. I said to myself, I'm going to quit complaining! I'll keep quiet, especially when the ungodly are around me.

Ps 102:7 I lie awake, lonely as a solitary sparrow on the roof.

Ps 119:9. How can a young man stay pure? By reading your Word and following its rules.

Ps 141:3. Help me, Lord, to keep my mouth shut and my lips sealed.

Prov 4:23. *Above all else, guard your affections.* For they influence everything else in your life. [25]Look straight ahead; don't even turn your head to look. [26]Watch your step. Stick to the path and be safe.

Prov 8:34. Happy is the man who is so anxious to be with me that he watches for me daily at my gates, or waits for me outside my home!

Prov 16:17. The path of the godly leads away from evil; he who follows that path is safe.

Prov 28:26. A man is a fool to trust himself! But those who use God's wisdom are safe.

Nah 2:1. Nineveh, you are finished! You are already surrounded by enemy armies! Sound the alarm! Man the ramparts! Muster your defenses, full force, and keep a sharp watch for the enemy attack to begin!

Hab 2:1. I will climb my watchtower now, and wait to see what answer God will give to my complaint.

Mal 2:15. Therefore guard your passions! Keep faith with the wife of your youth.

Mt 6:1. Take care! don't do your good deeds publicly, to be admired, for then you will lose the reward from your Father in heaven.

Mt 16:6. "Watch out!" Jesus warned them; "beware of the yeast of the Pharisees and Sadducees."

Mt 18:10. Beware that you don't look down upon a single one of these little children. For I tell you that in heaven their angels have constant access to my Father.

Mt 24:4. Jesus told them, "Don't let anyone fool you."

Mt 25:13. So stay awake and be prepared, for you do not know the date or moment of my return.

Mt 26:40. Then he returned to the three disciples and found them asleep. "Peter," he called, "couldn't you even stay awake with me one hour? [41]Keep alert and pray. Otherwise temptation will overpower you. For the spirit indeed is willing, but how weak the body is!"

Mk 4:24. And be sure to put into practice what you hear. The more you do this, the more you will understand what I tell you. Lk 8:18.

Mk 13:9. But when these things begin to happen, watch out! For you will be in great danger. You will be dragged before the courts, and beaten in the synagogues, and accused before governors and kings of being my followers. This is your opportunity to tell them the Good News. [*vs.* 10–20.] [21]And then if anyone tells you, "This is the Messiah," or, "That one is," don't pay any attention. [22]For there will be many false Messiahs and false prophets who will do wonderful miracles that would deceive, if possible, even God's own children. [23]Take care! I have warned you! [32]However, no one, not even the angels in heaven, nor I myself, knows the day or hour when these things will happen; only the Father knows. [33]And since you don't know when it will happen, stay alert. Be on the watch (for my return). [34]My coming can be compared with that of a man who went on a trip to another country. He laid out his employees' work for them to do while he was gone, and told the gatekeeper to watch for his return. [35-37]Keep a sharp lookout! For you do not know when I will come, at evening, at midnight, early dawn or late daybreak. Don't let me find you sleeping. *Watch for my return!* This is my message to you and to everyone else. Mt 24:42–51; Lk 21:8–36.

Lk 11:35. So watch out that the sunshine isn't blotted out.

Lk 12:15. Beware! Don't always be wishing for what you don't have. For real life and real living are not related to how rich we are. [35]Be prepared —all dressed and ready—[36]for your Lord's return from the wedding feast. Then you will be ready to open the door and let him in the moment he arrives and knocks. [37]There will be great joy for those who are ready and waiting for his return. He himself will seat them and put on a waiter's uniform and serve them as they sit and eat! [38]He may come at nine o'clock at night—or even at midnight. But whenever he comes there will be joy for his servants who are ready! [39]Everyone would be ready for him if they knew the exact hour of his return —just as they would be ready for a thief if they knew when he was coming. [40]So be ready all the time. For I, the Messiah, will come when least expected. Mt 24:42–47; Mk 13:33–37.

Acts 20:28. And now beware! Be sure that you feed and shepherd God's flock—his church, purchased with his blood—for the Holy Spirit is holding you responsible as overseers. [29]I know full well that after I leave you, false teachers, like vicious wolves, will appear among you, not sparing the flock. [30]Some of you yourselves will distort the truth in order to draw a following. [31]Watch out! Remember the three years I was with you—my constant watchcare over you night and day and my many tears for you.

Rom 11:21. For if God did not spare the branches he put there in the first place, he won't spare you either.

Rom 13:11. Another reason for right living is this: you know how late it is; time is running out. Wake up, for the coming of the Lord is nearer now than when we first believed.

1 Cor 7:29. The important thing to remember is that our remaining time is very short, (and so are our opportunities for doing the Lord's work). For that reason those who have wives should stay as free as possible for the Lord; [30]happiness or sadness or wealth should not keep anyone from doing God's work. [31]Those in frequent contact with the exciting things the world offers should make good use of their opportunities without stopping to enjoy them; for the world in its present form will soon be gone.

1 Cor 9:27. Like an athlete I punish my body, treating it roughly, training it to do what it should, not what it wants to. Otherwise I fear that after enlisting others for the race, I myself might be declared unfit and ordered to stand aside.

1 Cor 10:12. So be careful. If you are thinking, "Oh, I would never behave like that"—let this be a warning to you. For you too may fall into sin.

1 Cor 11:28. That is why a man should examine himself carefully before eating the bread and drinking from the cup.

1 Cor 16:13. Keep your eyes open for spiritual danger; stand true to the Lord; act like men; be strong.

Gal 6:1. Dear brothers, if a Christian is overcome by some sin, you who are godly should gently and humbly help him back onto the right path, remembering that next time it might be one of you who is in the wrong.

Eph 5:15. So be careful how you act; these are difficult days. Don't be fools; be wise.

Eph 6:18. Pray all the time. Ask God for anything in line with the Holy Spirit's wishes. Plead with him, reminding him of your needs, and keep praying earnestly for all Christians everywhere.

Phil 3:2. Watch out for those wicked men—dangerous dogs, I call them—who say you must be circumcised to be saved.

Phil 4:5. Remember that the Lord is coming soon.

Col 4:2. Don't be weary in prayer; keep at it; watch for God's answers and remember to be thankful when they come. [17]Be sure that you do all the Lord has told you to.

1 Thess 5:4. But, dear brothers, you are not in the dark about these things, and you won't be surprised as by a thief when that day of the Lord comes. [6]So be on your guard, not asleep like the others. Watch for his return and stay sober. [21]But test everything that is said to be sure it is true, and if it is, then accept it.

1 Tim 4:16. Keep a close watch on all you do and think. Stay true to what is right and God will bless you and use you to help others.

2 Tim 4:5. Stand steady, and don't be afraid of suffering for the Lord. Bring others to Christ. Leave nothing undone that you ought to do.

Heb 2:1. So we must listen very carefully to the truths we have heard, or we may drift away from them.

Heb 3:12. Beware then of your own hearts, dear brothers, lest you find that they, too, are evil and unbelieving and are leading you away from the living God.

Heb 12:15. Look after each other so that not one of you will fail to find God's best blessings. Watch out that no bitterness takes root among you, for as it springs up it causes deep trouble, hurting many in their spiritual lives.

1 Pet 1:13. So now you can look forward soberly and intelligently to more of God's kindness to you

when Jesus Christ returns. [17]And remember that your heavenly Father to whom you pray has no favorites when he judges. He will judge you with perfect justice for everything you do; so act in reverent fear of him from now on until you get to heaven.

1 Pet 4:7. The end of the world is coming soon. Therefore be earnest, thoughtful men of prayer.

1 Pet 5:8. Be careful—watch out for attacks from Satan, your great enemy. He prowls around like a hungry, roaring lion, looking for some victim to tear apart.

2 Pet 1:19. So we have seen and proved that what the prophets said came true. You will do well to pay close attention to everything they have written, for, like lights shining into dark corners, their words help us to understand many things that otherwise would be dark and difficult. But when you consider the wonderful truth of the prophets' words, then the light will dawn in your souls and Christ the Morning Star will shine in your hearts.

2 Pet 3:17. I am warning you ahead of time, dear brothers, so that you can watch out and not be carried away by the mistakes of these wicked men, lest you yourselves become mixed up too.

1 Jn 5:18. No one who has become part of God's family makes a practice of sinning, for Christ, God's Son, holds him securely and the devil cannot get his hands on him.

2 Jn 1:8. Beware of being like them, and losing the prize that you and I have been working so hard to get. See to it that you win your full reward from the Lord.

Jude 1:20. But you, dear friends, must build up your lives ever more strongly upon the foundation of our holy faith, learning to pray in the power and strength of the Holy Spirit. [21]Stay always within the boundaries where God's love can reach and bless you. Wait patiently for the eternal life that our Lord Jesus Christ in his mercy is going to give you.

Rev 3:2. Now wake up! Strengthen what little remains—for even what is left is at the point of death. Your deeds are far from right in the sight of God. [3]Go back to what you heard and believed at first; hold to it firmly and turn to me again. Unless you do, I will come suddenly upon you, unexpected as a thief, and punish you. [11]Look, I am coming soon! Hold tightly to the little strength you have—so that no one will take away your crown.

Rev 16:15. Take note: I will come as unexpectedly as a thief! Blessed are all who are awaiting me, who keep their robes in readiness and will not need to walk naked and ashamed.

See *Temptation.*

WATCHMAN A sentinel. On the walls of cities, Song 5:7; of Jerusalem, 2 Sam 13:34; 18:24, 25; Neh 4:9; 7:3; Isa 52:8; 62:6, 7; of Babylon, Isa 21:5–12; Jer 51:12. On towers, 2 Kgs 9:17; 2 Chron 20:24; Jer 31:6. At the gates of the temple, 2 Kgs 11:6–8. Alarm, sounded by, Ezk 33:2–6. Unfaithfulness in the discharge of duty of, punished by death, Ezk 33:6; Acts 12:19.

WATER Creation of, Ps 148:4, 5. Covered the whole earth, Gen 1:9, 10. Daily allowance of, Ezk 4:11. City waterworks, 2 Kgs 20:20. Vision of, by Ezekiel, Ezk 47:1–5. Of separation, Num 19:1–22. Libation of, 1 Sam 7:6. Irrigation with, see *Irrigation.* Miraculously supplied to the Israelites, Ex 17: 1, 5, 6; Num 20:11; to Samson, Judg 15:19; to Jehoshaphat's army, 2 Kgs 3:16–20. Purified by Elisha, 2 Kgs 2:19–22; Red Sea divided, Ex 14:21, 22; the Jordan River, Josh 3:13–17; 2 Kgs 2:6–8, 13, 14. Jesus walks on, Mt 14:25. Changed to wine, Jn 2: 1–11; to blood, Rev 16:3–5.

FIGURATIVE. Water of life, Jn 4:14; 7:37–39; Rev 21:6; 22:17. Of affliction, 2 Sam 22:17; Ps 69:1; Isa 30:20; 43:2. Of salvation, Isa 12:3; 49:10; 55:1; Ezk 36:25; Jn 4:10; 7:38. Domestic love, Prov 5:15.

Symbolical. Isa 8:7, 8; Rev 8:11; 12:15; 16:4; 17:1, 15.

WAVE OFFERING See *Offerings, Wave.*

WAX Ps 22:14; 68:2; 97:5; Mic 1:4.

WAY FIGURATIVE. Of holiness, Isa 35:8, 9; Jer 6:16; Hos 14:9. Of righteousness, narrow, Mt 7: 14. Of sin, broad, Mt 7:13. Jesus the, Jn 14:6; Heb 10:20. Doctrines taught by Christ, Acts 24:14.

WEALTH See *Riches.*

WEAPONS See *Armor; Arms.*

WEATHER Signs of, Mt 16:2, 3. Sayings concerning, Job 37:9, 16, 17, 22.

See *Meteorology.*

WEAVING Isa 19:9; 38:12. Bezalel skilled in, Ex 35:35. Wrought by women, 2 Kgs 23:7. Of the ephod, Ex 28:32; 39:22. Of robes, Ex 39:27.

Weaver's loom, Judg 16:14; beam; 2 Sam 21:19; 1 Chron 11:23; 20:5.

WEDDING See *Marriage.*

WEEDING Mt 13:28.

WEEPING Job 30:25. In perdition, Mt 8:12; 22:13; 24:51; 25:30. None in heaven, Rev 7:17. Penitential, Jer 50:4; Joel 2:12. Instances of penitential: The Israelites, Judg 2:4, 5. Peter, Mt 26:75; Mk 14: 72; Lk 22:62. While doing good, Ps 126:5, 6. For others, Jer 9:1. Because of tribulation, Ps 42:3; Jer 22:10; Amos 5:16, 17. Succeeded by joy, Ps 30:5. Valley of, Ps 84:6.

INSTANCES OF. Of Abraham for Sarah, Gen 23:1, 2. Of Esau, Gen 27:38. Of Jacob and Esau, Gen 33:4. Of Jacob, Gen 37:35. Of Joseph, Gen 42: 24; 43:30; 45:2, 14; 46:29; 50:1, 16, 17. Of Hannah, 1 Sam 1:7. Of Jonathan and David, 1 Sam 20:41. Of David, 2 Sam 3:32; 13:36; 15:23, 30; 18:33. Of Hezekiah, 2 Kgs 20:3; Isa 38:3. Of Jesus, over Jerusalem, Lk 19:41; at the grave of Lazarus, Jn 11:35; before his death, Heb 5:7. Of Mary, when she washed the feet of Jesus, Lk 7:38; Jn 11:1, 2, 33. Of Mary Magdalene, Jn 20:11. Of Paul, Acts 20:19; Phil 3:18.

WEIGHTS Must be just, Lev 19:35, 36; Deut 25:13–15; Prov 11:1; 16:11; 20:10, 23; Mic 6:10, 11.

See *Measure; Money.*

WELL The occasion of feuds: Between Abraham and Abimelech, Gen 21:25–30; between Isaac and Abimelech, Gen 26:15–22, 32, 33. Of Jacob, Jn 4:6. Of Solomon, Eccl 2:6. Of Uzziah, 2 Chron 26:10. Of Hezekiah, see *Gihon, 2.* At Haran, Gen 24:16. Elisha purifies, 2 Kgs 2:21, 22.

FIGURATIVE. Prov 5:15. Of salvation, Isa 12:3; Jn 4:14. Without water, Jer 15:18; 2 Pet 2:17.

See *Spring.*

WELL OF ANGER, THE See *Sitnah.*

WHALE Ps 104:26. Created, Gen 1:21, 22.

WHEAT Rev 6:6. Grown in Palestine, 1 Kgs 5:11; Ps 147:14; Ezk 27:17. Offerings of, Num 18:12. Prophecy of the sale of a measure of, Rev 6:6.

Parables of, Mt 13:25; Lk 16:7. Winnowing of, Mt 3:12; Lk 3:17. Chaff of, Jer 23:28; Mt 3:12; Lk 3: 17. Growth of, figurative of vicarious death, Jn 12: 23, 24.

FIGURATIVE. Of God's mercy, Ps 147:14. Of self-righteousness, Jer 12:13. Of Christ, Jn 12:23, 24.

See *Grain.*

WHEEL Potter's, Jer 18:3.

FIGURATIVE. Eccl 12:6.

Symbolical. Ezk 1:15–21; 3:13; 10:9–19; 11:22.

WHIP 1 Kgs 12:11; Prov 26:3; Nah 3:2.

WHIPPING Suffered by Paul, 2 Cor 11:23.

See *Scourging.*

WHIRLWIND Ps 77:18; Amos 1:14. Destructive, Isa 29:6; 41:16; Dan 11:40. From the Negeb, Isa 21:1; in the land of Canaan, Zech 9:14. Elijah taken to heaven in, 2 Kgs 2:1, 2, 11. God answered Job in, Job 38:1; 40:6.

See *Meteorology.*

FIGURATIVE. Of the judgment of God, Job 30: 22; Jer 23:19; 25:32; 30:23; Zech 7:14. Of enemies, Jer 4:13; Hab 3:14. Of the fruits of unrighteousness, Hos 8:7; 12:1.

WHISPER See *Busybody; Gossip; Slander.*

WHISPERER A slanderer, 2 Cor 12:20.

See *Slander; Speaking, Evil.*

WHITE See *Color.*

WHITEWASH Ezk 13:10–15; 22:28.

See *Mortar.*

WHORE Hos 4:18.

See *Harlot; Prostitute.*

WICKED Compared with: Animals, Ps 49:12; 2 Pet 2:12; ashes underfoot, Mal 4:3; bad fish, Mt 13:47, 48; baker's oven, Hos 7:4; bees, Ps 118:12; blighted grain, 2 Kgs 19:26; the blind, Zeph 1:17; Mt 15:13, 14; brass and iron, Jer 6:28; Ezk 22:18–20; briars and thorns, Isa 55:13; broken branches, Isa 14:19; bulls of Bashan, Ps 22:12; carcasses trampled underfoot, Isa 14:19; cedars of Lebanon, Ps 37:35, 36; chaff, Ps 1:4; Mt 3:12; clay pots, Prov 26:23; clouds without rain, Jude 1:12; deaf cobras, Ps 58: 4, 5; dew that quickly dries, Hos 13:3; dogs, Prov 26:11; 2 Pet 2:22; dreams, Job 20:8; dross, Ezk 22: 18–20; flame, Ps 118:12; fools building on sand, Mt 7:26; fuel for fire, Isa 9:19, 20; garden without water, Isa 1:30; goats, Mt 25:32; grass, 2 Kgs 19:26; Ps 37:2; horses rushing into the battle, Jer 8:6; impure silver, Jer 6:30; inferior trees, Lk 6:43; lions greedy for prey, Ps 17:12; mausoleums, Mt 23:27; melting wax, Ps 68:2; morning mist, Hos 13:3; motheaten garments, Isa 50:9; 51:8; restless sea, Isa 57:20; rocky soil, Mt 13:5; rotten figs, Jer 24:8; scorpions, Ezk 2:6; scum, Ps 119:119; shrub in the desert, Jer 17:6; smoke, Hos 13:3; snakes, Ps 58:4; Mt 23:33; springs without water, 2 Pet 2:17; straw, Job 21:18; Mal 4:1; swine, Mt 7:6; 2 Pet 2:22; thistles, Mt 13:38; wandering stars, Jude 1:13; wayward children, Mt 11:16; weeds, Ps 92:7; whirlwinds, Prov 10:25; wild waves of the sea, Jude 1:13; withered tree, Isa 1:30.

God is angry with, Ps 5:5, 6; 7:11; Rom 9:13; 1 Cor 10:5. Spirit of God withdrawn from, Gen 6: 3; Hos 4:17–19; Rom 1:24, 26, 28. Hate believers, Mt 5:11, 12; Lk 6:22, 23. Worship of, offensive to God, Ps 50:16, 17; Isa 1:10–15.

Present and future state of the wicked and righteous contrasted, Job 8, Ps 49. See below.

Prosperity of, Job 5:3–5; 12:6; 15:27, 28; 20:5, 22; 21:7–13; Ps 37:1, 35, 36; 49:10–15; 73:3–22; 92:6, 7; Jer 12:1, 2; Hab 1:3, 4, 13–17; Mal 3:14, 15. Hate reproof, 1 Kgs 22:8; 2 Chron 18:7. God's mercy to, Job 33:14–30; love for, Deut 5:29; 32:29; Mt 18: 11–14; Jn 3:16, 17; Rom 5:8; 1 Jn 3:16; 4:9, 10. Dread God, Job 18:11. Eliphaz's exhortation to, Job 22: 21–30. Punishment of, Job 27:13–23; 15:20–35; 18: 5–21; 20:5–29; 21:7–33; 24:2–24; Jer 5:25; Ezk 11:10; 12:19, 20; Zech 14:17–19. False hope of, Job 8:13–18.

Gospel invitation to, illustrated by the parables of the estate owner, Mt 20:1–16; and wedding feast, Mt 22:1–14.

Warned, Jer 7:13–15, 23–25; 25:4–6; 26:2–6, 12, 13; 29:16–19; Ezk 33:8; Dan 4:4–27; 5:5–29; Zeph 2: 1, 2; Lk 3:7–9; 1 Cor 10:11; Jude 1:4–7; Rev 3:1–3, 16–19. Terrors of, at the judgment, Rev 1:7. Death of, Ps 49:14.

See *Impenitence; Obduracy; Penitence; Reprobate; Seeker; Sin, Confession of.*

CONTRASTED WITH THE RIGHTEOUS. Ps 1:1. Oh, the joys of those who do not follow evil men's advice, who do not hang around with sinners, scoffing at the things of God: [2]But they delight in doing everything God wants them to, and day and night are always meditating on his laws and thinking about ways to follow him more closely. [3]They are like trees along a river bank bearing luscious fruit each season without fail. Their leaves shall never wither, and all they do shall prosper. [4]But for sinners, what a different story! They blow away like chaff before the wind. [5]They are not safe on Judgment Day; they shall not stand among the godly. [6]For the Lord watches over all the plans and paths of godly men, but the paths of the godless lead to doom. Prov 4:14–19.

Ps 11:5. He puts the righteous and the wicked to the test; he hates those loving violence.

Ps 17:14. Come and save me from these men of the world whose only concern is earthly gain—these men whom you have filled with your treasures so that their children and grandchildren are rich and prosperous. [15]But as for me, my contentment is not in wealth but in seeing you and knowing all is well between us. And when I awake in heaven, I will be fully satisfied, for I will see you face to face.

Ps 32:10. Many sorrows come to the wicked, but abiding love surrounds those who trust in the Lord.

Ps 37:17. For the strength of evil men shall be

broken, but the Lord takes care of those he has forgiven. [18]Day by day the Lord observes the good deeds done by godly men, and gives them eternal rewards. [19]He cares for them when times are hard; even in famine, they will have enough. [20]But evil men shall perish. These enemies of God will wither like grass, and disappear like smoke. [21]Evil men borrow and "cannot pay it back"! But the good man returns what he owes with some extra besides. [22]Those blessed by the Lord shall inherit the earth, but those cursed by him shall die. [37]But the good man—what a different story! For the good man—the blameless, the upright, the man of peace—he has a wonderful future ahead of him. For him there is a happy ending. [38]But evil men shall be destroyed, and their posterity shall be cut off.

Ps 68:6. He gives families to the lonely, and releases prisoners from jail, singing with joy! But for rebels there is famine and distress.

Ps 73:1. How good God is to Israel—to those whose hearts are pure. [2]But as for me, I came so close to the edge of the cliff! My feet were slipping and I was almost gone. [3]For I was envious of the prosperity of the proud and wicked. [4]Yes, all through life their road is smooth! They grow sleek and fat. [5]They aren't always in trouble and plagued with problems like everyone else, [6]so their pride sparkles like a jeweled necklace, and their clothing is woven of cruelty! [7]These fat cats have everything their hearts could ever wish for! [8]They scoff at God and threaten his people. How proudly they speak! [9]They boast against the very heavens, and their words strut through the earth. [10]And so God's people are dismayed and confused, and drink it all in. [11]"Does God realize what is going on?" they ask. [12]"Look at these men of arrogance; they never have to lift a finger—theirs is a life of ease; and all the time their riches multiply." [13]Have I been wasting my time? Why take the trouble to be pure? [14]All I get out of it is trouble and woe—every day and all day long! [15]If I had really said that, I would have been a traitor to your people. [16]Yet it is so hard to explain it—this prosperity of those who hate the Lord. [17]Then one day I went into God's sanctuary to meditate, and thought about the future of these evil men. [18]What a slippery path they are on—suddenly God will send them sliding over the edge of the cliff and down to their destruction: [19]an instant end to all their happiness, an eternity of terror. [20]Their present life is only a dream! They will awaken to the truth as one awakens from the dream of things that never really were! [21]When I saw this, what turmoil filled my heart! [22]I saw myself so stupid and so ignorant; I must seem like an animal to you, O God. [23]But even so, you love me! You are holding my right hand! [24]You will keep on guiding me all my life with your wisdom and counsel; and afterwards receive me into the glories of heaven! [25]Whom have I in heaven but you? And I desire no one on earth as much as you! [26]My health fails; my spirits droop, yet God remains! He is the strength of my heart; he is mine forever! [27]But those refusing to worship God will perish, for he destroys those serving other gods. [28]But as for me, I get as close to him as I can! I have chosen him and I will tell everyone about the wonderful ways he rescues me.

Ps 75:10. "I will cut off the strength of evil men," says the Lord, "and increase the power of good men in their place."

Ps 91:7. Though a thousand fall at my side, though ten thousand are dying around me, the evil will not touch me. [8]I will see how the wicked are punished but I will not share it.

Ps 107:33. He dries up rivers, [34]and turns the good land of the wicked into deserts of salt. [35]Again, he turns deserts into fertile, watered valleys. [36]He brings the hungry to settle there and build their cities, [37]to sow their fields and plant their vineyards, and reap their bumper crops! [38]How he blesses them! They raise big families there, and many cattle.

Ps 125:5. But lead evil men to execution. And let Israel have quietness and peace.

Prov 10:6. The good man is covered with blessings from head to foot, but an evil man inwardly curses his luck. [9]A good man has firm footing, but a crook will slip and fall. [21]A godly man gives good advice, but a rebel is destroyed by lack of common sense. [23]A fool's fun is being bad; a wise man's fun is being wise. [24]The wicked man's fears will all come true, and so will the good man's hopes. [25]Disaster strikes like a cyclone and the wicked are whirled away. But the good man has a strong anchor. [28]The hope of good men is eternal happiness; the hopes of evil men are all in vain. [29]God protects the upright but destroys the wicked. [30]The good shall never lose God's blessings, but the wicked shall lose everything. [32]The upright speak what is helpful; the wicked speak rebellion.

Prov 11:3. A good man is guided by his honesty; the evil man is destroyed by his dishonesty. [5]The upright are directed by their honesty; the wicked shall fall beneath their load of sins. [6]The good man's goodness delivers him; the evil man's treachery is his undoing. [8]God rescues good men from danger while letting the wicked fall into it. [10]The whole city celebrates a good man's success—and also the godless man's death. [11]The good influence of godly citizens causes a city to prosper, but the moral decay of the wicked drives it downhill. [18]The evil man gets rich for the moment, but the good man's reward lasts forever. [19]The good man finds life; the evil man, death. [20]The Lord hates the stubborn but delights in those who are good. [21]You can be very sure that the evil man will not go unpunished forever. And you can also be very sure that God will rescue the children of the godly. [23]The good man can look forward to happiness, while the wicked can expect only wrath. [31]Even the godly shall be rewarded here on earth; how much more the wicked!

Prov 12:3. Wickedness never brings real success; only the godly have that. [5]A good man's mind is filled with honest thoughts; an evil man's mind is crammed with lies. [6]The wicked accuse; the godly defend. 7The wicked shall perish; the godly shall stand. 13Lies will get any man into trouble, but honesty is its own defense. 21No real harm befalls the good, but there is constant trouble for the wicked. 26The good man asks advice from friends; the wicked plunge ahead—and fall.

Prov 13:6. A man's goodness helps him all through life, while evil men are being destroyed by their wickedness. 13Despise God's Word and find yourself in trouble. Obey it and succeed. 17An unreliable messenger can cause a lot of trouble. Reliable communication permits progress. 21Curses chase sinners, while blessings chase the righteous!

Prov 14:19. Evil men shall bow before the godly. 22Those who plot evil shall wander away and be lost, but those who plan good shall be granted mercy and quietness. 32The godly have a refuge when they die, but the wicked are crushed by their sins.

Prov 15:6. There is treasure in being good, but trouble dogs the wicked.

Prov 21:18. The wicked will finally lose; the righteous will finally win. 26He is greedy to get, while the godly love to give!

Prov 22:5. The rebel walks a thorny, treacherous road; the man who values his soul will stay away.

Prov 28:1. The wicked flee when no one is chasing them! But the godly are bold as lions! 4To complain about the law is to praise wickedness. To obey the law is to fight evil. 5Evil men don't understand the importance of justice, but those who follow the Lord are much concerned about it. 13A man who refuses to admit his mistakes can never be successful. But if he confesses and forsakes them, he gets another chance. 14Blessed is the man who reveres God, but the man who doesn't care is headed for serious trouble. 18Good men will be rescued from harm, but cheaters will be destroyed.

Isa 32:1. Look, a righteous King is coming, with honest princes! 2He will shelter Israel from the storm and wind. He will refresh her as a river in the desert and as the cooling shadow of a mighty rock within a hot and weary land. 3Then at last the eyes of Israel will open wide to God; his people will listen to his voice. 4Even the hotheads among them will be full of sense and understanding, and those who stammer in uncertainty will speak out plainly. 5In those days the ungodly, the atheists, will not be heroes! Wealthy cheaters will not be spoken of as generous, understanding men! 6Everyone will recognize an evil man when he sees him, and hypocrites will fool no one at all. Their lies about God and their cheating of the hungry will be plain for all to see. 7The smooth tricks of evil men will be exposed, as will all the lies they use to oppress the poor in the courts. 8But good men will be generous to others and will be blessed of God for all they do.

Isa 65:13. Therefore the Lord God says, You shall starve, but my servants shall eat; you shall be thirsty while they drink; you shall be sad and ashamed, but they shall rejoice. 14You shall cry in sorrow and vexation and despair, while they sing for joy.

Mal 3:18. Then you will see the difference between God's treatment of good men and bad, between those who serve him and those who don't.

Rom 2:7. He will give eternal life to those who patiently do the will of God, seeking for the unseen glory and honor and eternal life that he offers. 8But he will terribly punish those who fight against the truth of God and walk in evil ways—God's anger will be poured out upon them. 9There will be sorrow and suffering for Jews and Gentiles alike who keep on sinning. 10But there will be glory and honor and peace from God for all who obey him, whether they are Jews or Gentiles.

Eph 2:12. Remember that in those days you were living utterly apart from Christ; you were enemies of God's children and he had promised you no help. You were lost, without God, without hope. 13But now you belong to Christ Jesus, and though you once were far away from God, now you have been brought very near to him because of what Jesus Christ has done for you with his blood. 14For Christ himself is our way of peace. He has made peace between us Jews and you Gentiles by making us all one family, breaking down the wall of contempt that used to separate us.

Phil 2:15. You are to live clean, innocent lives as children of God in a dark world full of people who are crooked and stubborn. Shine out among them like beacon lights.

1 Thess 5:5. For you are all children of the light and of the day, and do not belong to darkness and night. 6So be on your guard, not asleep like the others. Watch for his return and stay sober. 7Night is the time for sleep and the time when people get drunk. 8But let us who live in the light keep sober, protected by the armor of faith and love, and wearing as our helmet the happy hope of salvation.

Tit 1:15. A person who is pure of heart sees goodness and purity in everything; but a person whose own heart is evil and untrusting finds evil in everything, for his dirty mind and rebellious heart color all he sees and hears.

1 Pet 4:17. For the time has come for judgment, and it must begin first among God's own children. And if even we who are Christians must be judged, what terrible fate awaits those who have never believed in the Lord? 18If the righteous are barely saved, what chance will the godless have?

1 Jn 1:6. So if we say we are his friends, but go on living in spiritual darkness and sin, we are lying. 7But if we are living in the light of God's presence, just as Christ does, then we have wonderful fellowship and joy with each other, and the blood of Jesus his Son cleanses us from every sin.

1 Jn 3:3. And everyone who really believes this will try to stay pure because Christ is pure. 4But those who keep on sinning are against God, for every sin is done against the will of God. 5And you know that he became a man so that he could take away our sins, and that there is no sin in him, no missing of God's will at any time in any way. 6So if we stay close to him, obedient to him, we won't be sinning either; but as for those who keep on

sinning, they should realize this: They sin because they have never really known him or become his. [7]Oh, dear children, don't let anyone deceive you about this: if you are constantly doing what is good, it is because you *are* good, even as he is. [8]But if you keep on sinning, it shows that you belong to Satan, who since he first began to sin has kept steadily at it. But the Son of God came to destroy these works of the devil. [9]The person who has been born into God's family does not make a practice of sinning, because now God's life is in him; so he can't keep on sinning, for this new life has been born into him and controls him—he has been *born again.* [10]So now we can tell who is a child of God and who belongs to Satan. Whoever is living a life of sin and doesn't love his brother shows that he is not in God's family; [11]for the message to us from the beginning has been that we should love one another. [12]We are not to be like Cain, who belonged to Satan and killed his brother. Why did he kill him? Because Cain had been doing wrong and he knew very well that his brother's life was better than his. [13]So don't be surprised, dear friends, if the world hates you. [14]If we love other Christians it proves that we have been delivered from hell and given eternal life. But a person who doesn't have love for others is headed for eternal death. [15]Anyone who hates his Christian brother is really a murderer at heart; and you know that no one wanting to murder has eternal life within. [16]We know what real love is from Christ's example in dying for us. And so we also ought to lay down our lives for our Christian brothers. [17]But if someone who is supposed to be a Christian has money enough to live well, and sees a brother in need, and won't help him—how can God's love be within *him?*

DESCRIBED. Gen 13:13. The men of this area were unusually wicked, and sinned greatly against Jehovah.

Gen 18:20. So the Lord told Abraham, "I have heard that the people of Sodom and Gomorrah are utterly evil, and that everything they do is wicked."

Lev 18:25. That entire country is defiled with this kind of activity; that is why I am punishing the people living there, and will throw them out of the land.

Deut 9:13. "Let me alone that I may destroy this evil, stubborn people!" the Lord told me. [24]Yes, you have been rebellious against the Lord from the first day I knew you.

Deut 32:10. God protected them in the howling wilderness as though they were the apple of his eye. [32]They act like men of Sodom and Gomorrah: Their deeds are bitter with poison; [33]they drink the wine of serpent venom.

1 Sam 24:13. As that old proverb says, "Wicked is as wicked does," but despite your wickedness, I'll not touch you.

1 Kgs 21:20. "So my enemy has found me!" Ahab exclaimed to Elijah. "Yes," Elijah answered, "I have come to place God's curse upon you because you have sold yourself to the devil."

2 Chron 28:10. And now are you going to make slaves of these people from Judah and Jerusalem? What about your own sins against the Lord your God? [22]In this time of deep trial, King Ahaz collapsed spiritually.

Ezra 9:11. The prophets warned us that the land we would possess was totally defiled by the horrible practices of the people living there. From one end to the other it is filled with corruption.

Job 14:4. How can you demand purity in one born impure?

Job 15:16. How much less someone like you, who is corrupt and sinful, drinking in sin as a sponge soaks up water! [20]A wicked man is always in trouble throughout his life. [21]He is surrounded by terrors, and if there are good days they will soon be gone. [22]He dares not go out into the darkness, lest he be murdered. [23, 24]He wanders around begging for food. He lives in fear, distress, and anguish. His enemies conquer him as a king defeats his foes. [25, 26]Armed with his tin shield, he clenches his fist against God, defying the Almighty, stubbornly assaulting him. [27, 28]This wicked man is fat and rich, and has lived in conquered cities after killing off their citizens. [29]But he will not continue to be rich, or to extend his possessions. [30]No, darkness shall overtake him forever; the breath of God shall destroy him; the flames shall burn up all he has. [31]Let him no longer trust in foolish riches; let him no longer deceive himself, for the money he trusts in will be his only reward. [32]Before he dies, all this futility will become evident to him. For all he counted on will disappear, [33]and fall to the ground like a withered grape. How little will come of his hopes! [34]For the godless are barren: they can produce nothing truly good. God's fire consumes them with all their possessions. [35]They only thing they can "conceive" is sin, and their hearts give birth only to wickedness.

Job 20:12. He enjoyed the taste of his wickedness, letting it melt in his mouth, [13]sipping it slowly, lest it disappear.

Job 22:5. Not at all! It is because of your wickedness! Your sins are endless!

Job 24:2. For a crime wave has engulfed us—landmarks are moved, flocks of sheep are stolen, [3]and even the donkeys of the poor and fatherless are taken. Poor widows must surrender the little they have as a pledge to get a loan. [4]The needy are kicked aside; they must get out of the way. [5]Like the wild donkeys in the desert, the poor must spend all their time just getting barely enough to keep soul and body together. They are sent into the desert to search for food for their children. [6]They eat what they find that grows wild, and must even glean the vineyards of the wicked. [7]All night they lie naked in the cold, without clothing or covering. [8]They are wet with the showers of the mountains and live in caves for want of a home. [9]The wicked snatch fatherless children from their mother's breasts, and take a poor man's baby as a pledge before they will loan him any money or grain. [10]That is why they must go about naked, without clothing, and are forced to carry food while they are starving. [11]They are forced to press out the olive oil without tasting it, and to tread out the grape juice as they suffer from thirst. [12]The bones of the dying cry from the city; the wounded cry for help; yet God does not respond to their moaning. [13]The wicked rebel against the light and are not acquainted with the right and the good. [14, 15]They are murderers who rise in the early dawn to kill the poor and needy; at night they are thieves and adulterers, waiting for the twilight, "when no one will see me," they say. They mask their faces so no one will know them. [16]They break into houses at night and sleep in the daytime—they are not acquainted with the light. [17]The black night is their morning; they ally themselves with the terrors of the darkness. [18]But how quickly they disappear from the face of the earth. Everything they own is cursed. They leave no property for their children. [19]Death consumes sinners as drought and heat consume snow. [20]Even the sinner's own mother shall forget him. Worms shall feed sweetly on him. No one will remember him any more. For wicked men are broken like a tree in the storm. [21]For they have taken advantage of the childless who have no protecting sons. They refuse to help the needy widows. [22, 23]Yet sometimes it seems as though God preserves the rich by his power, and restores them to life when anyone else would die. God gives them confidence and strength, and helps them in many ways. [24]But though they are very great now, yet in a moment they shall be gone like all others, cut off like heads of grain.

Ps 5:9. For they cannot speak one truthful word. Their hearts are filled to the brim with wickedness. Their suggestions are full of the stench of sin and death. Their tongues are filled with flatteries to gain their wicked ends.

Ps 7:14. The wicked man conceives an evil plot, labors with its dark details, and brings to birth his treachery and lies; [15]let him fall into his own trap. [16]May the violence he plans for others boomerang upon himself; let him die.

Ps 10:4. These wicked men, so proud and haughty, seem to think that God is dead. They wouldn't think of looking for him! [5]Yet there is success in everything they do, and their enemies fall before them. They do not see your punishment awaiting them. [6]They boast that neither God nor man can ever keep them down—somehow they'll find a way! [7]Their mouths are full of profanity and lies and fraud. They are always boasting of their evil plans. [8]They lurk in dark alleys of the city and murder passersby. [9]Like lions they crouch silently, waiting to pounce upon the poor. Like hunters they catch their victims in their traps. [10]The unfortunate are overwhelmed by their superior strength and fall beneath their blows. [11]"God isn't watching," they say to themselves; "he'll never know!"

Ps 36:1. Sin lurks deep in the hearts of the wicked, forever urging them on to evil deeds. They have no fear of God to hold them back. [2]Instead, in their conceit, they think they can hide their evil deeds and not get caught. [3]Everything they say is crooked and deceitful; they are no longer wise and good. [4]They lie awake at night to hatch their evil plots, instead of planning how to keep away from wrong.

Ps 37:12. The Lord is laughing at those who plot against the godly.

Ps 49:20. For man with all his pomp must die like any animal.

Ps 50:17. For you have refused my discipline, disregarding my laws. [18]You see a thief and help him, and spend your time with evil and immoral men. [19]You curse and lie, and vile language streams from your mouths. [20]You slander your own brother.

Ps 52:1. You call yourself a *hero,* do you? You *boast* about this evil deed of yours against God's people. [2]You are sharp as a tack in plotting your evil tricks. [3]How you love wickedness—far more than good! And lying more than truth! [4]You love to slander—you love to say anything that will do harm, O man with the lying tongue.

Ps 53:1. Only a fool would say to himself, "There is no God." And why does he say it? Because of his wicked heart, his dark and evil deeds. His life is corroded with sin. [2]God looks down from heaven, searching among all mankind to see if there is a single one who does right and really seeks for God. [3]But all have turned their backs on him; they are filthy with sin—corrupt and rotten through and through. Not one is good, not one! [4]How can this be? Can't they understand anything? For they devour my people like bread and refuse to come to God. [5]But soon unheard-of terror will fall on them. God will scatter the bones of these, your enemies. They are doomed, for God has rejected them.

Ps 58:3. These men are born sinners, lying from their earliest words! [4, 5]They are poisonous as deadly snakes, cobras that close their ears to the most expert of charmers.

Ps 59:6. At evening they come to spy, slinking around like dogs that prowl the city. [7]I hear them shouting insults and cursing God, for "No one will hear us," they think.

Ps 64:3. They cut me down with sharpened tongues; they aim their bitter words like arrows straight at my heart. [4]They shoot from ambush at the innocent. Suddenly the deed is done, yet they are not afraid. [5]They encourage each other to do evil. They meet in secret to set their traps. "He will never notice them here," they say. [6]They keep a sharp lookout for opportunities of crime. They spend long hours with all their endless evil thoughts and plans.

Ps 73:4. Yes, all through life their road is smooth! They grow sleek and fat. [5]They aren't always in trouble and plagued with problems like everyone else, [6]so their pride sparkles like a jeweled necklace, and their clothing is woven of cruelty! [7]These fat cats have everything their hearts could ever wish for! [8]They scoff at God and threaten his people. How proudly they speak! [9]They boast against the very heavens, and their words strut through the earth. [10]And so God's people are dismayed and confused, and drink it all in. [11]"Does God realize what is going on?" they ask. [12]"Look at these men of arrogance; they never have to lift a finger—theirs is a life of ease; and all the time their riches multiply."

Ps 94:3. Lord, how long shall the wicked be allowed to triumph and exult? [4]Hear their insolence! See their arrogance! How these men of evil boast! [5]See them oppressing your people, O Lord, afflicting those you love. [6, 7]They murder widows, immigrants, and orphans, for "The Lord isn't looking," they say, "and besides, he doesn't care." [8]Fools!

Ps 119:155. The wicked are far from salvation for they do not care for your laws.

Prov 1:29. For you closed your eyes to the facts and did not choose to reverence and trust the Lord, [30]and you turned your back on me, spurning my advice.

Prov 2:12, 13. Stay away from evil men who want you to be their partners in crime—men who turn from God's ways to walk down dark and evil paths, [14]and exult in doing wrong, for they thoroughly enjoy their sins. [15]Everything they do is crooked and wrong. [16, 17]Only wisdom from the Lord can save a man from the flattery of prostitutes; these girls have abandoned their husbands and flouted the laws of God. [18]Their houses lie along the road to death and hell. [19]The men who enter them are doomed. None of these men will ever be the same again.

Prov 4:16. For evil men don't sleep until they've done their evil deed for the day. They can't rest unless they cause someone to stumble and fall.

Prov 6:12, 13. Let me describe for you a worthless and a wicked man; first, he is a constant liar; he signals his true intentions to his friends with eyes and feet and fingers. [14]Next, his heart is full of rebellion. And he spends his time thinking of all the evil he can do, and stirring up discontent. [15]But he will be destroyed suddenly, broken beyond hope of healing.

Prov 10:23. A fool's fun is being bad; a wise man's fun is being wise!

Prov 13:19. It is pleasant to see plans develop. That is why fools refuse to give them up even when they are wrong.

Prov 14:9. The common bond of rebels is their guilt.

Prov 15:9, 10. The Lord despises the deeds of the wicked, but loves those who try to be good. If they stop trying, the Lord will punish them; if they rebel against that punishment, they will die.

Prov 27:22. You can't separate a rebel from his foolishness though you crush him to powder.

Prov 28:4. To complain about the law is to praise wickedness. To obey the law is to fight evil.

Eccl 3:18. And then I realized that God is letting the world go on its sinful way so that he can test mankind, and so that men themselves will see that they are no better than beasts.

Eccl 8:11. Because God does not punish sinners instantly, people feel it is safe to do wrong.

Isa 1:4. Oh, what a sinful nation they are! They walk bent-backed beneath their load of guilt. Their fathers before them were evil too. Born to be bad, they have turned their backs upon the Lord, and have despised the Holy One of Israel. They have cut themselves off from my help. [5, 6]Oh, my people, haven't you had enough of punishment? Why will you force me to whip you again and again? Must you forever rebel? From head to foot you are sick and weak and faint, covered with bruises and welts and infected wounds, unanointed and unbound.

Isa 3:9. The very look on their faces gives them away and shows their guilt. And they boast that their sin is equal to the sin of Sodom; they are not even ashamed.

Isa 5:11. Woe to you who get up early in the morning to go on long drinking bouts that last till late at night—woe to you drunken bums. [12]You furnish lovely music at your grand parties; the orchestras are superb! But for the Lord you have no thought or care. [18]Woe to those who drag their sins behind them like a bullock on a rope. [19]They even mock the Holy One of Israel and dare the Lord to punish them. "Hurry up and punish us, O Lord," they say. "We want to see what you can do!" [20]They say that what is right is wrong, and what is wrong is right; that black is white and white is black; bitter is sweet and sweet is bitter. [21]Woe to those who are wise and shrewd in their own eyes! [22]Woe to those who are "heroes" when it comes to drinking, and boast about the liquor they can hold. [23]They take bribes to pervert justice, letting the wicked go free and putting innocent men in jail. [24]Therefore God will deal with them and burn them. They will disappear like straw on fire. Their roots will rot and their flowers wither, for they have thrown away the laws of God and despised the Word of the Holy One of Israel. [25]That is why the anger of the Lord is hot against his people; that is why he has reached out his hand to smash them. The hills will tremble, and the rotting bodies of his people will be thrown as refuse in the streets. But even so, his anger is not ended; his hand is heavy on them still.

Isa 26:10. Your kindness to the wicked doesn't make them good; they keep on doing wrong and take no notice of your majesty. [11]They do not listen when you threaten; they will not look to see your upraised fist. Show them how much you love your people. Perhaps then they will be ashamed! Yes, let them be burned up by the fire reserved for your enemies.

Isa 30:1. Woe to my rebellious children, says the Lord; you ask advice from everyone but me, and decide to do what I don't want you to do. You yoke yourselves with unbelievers, thus piling up your sins. [9]For if you don't write it, they will claim I never warned them. "Oh, no," they'll say, "you never told us that!" For they are stubborn rebels. [10, 11]They tell my prophets, "Shut up—we don't want any more of your reports!" Or they say, "Don't tell us the truth; tell us nice things; tell us lies. Forget all this gloom; we've heard more than enough about your 'Holy One of Israel' and all he says."

Isa 32:6. Everyone will recognize an evil man when he sees him, and hypocrites will fool no one at all. Their lies about God and their cheating of the hungry will be plain for all to see. [7]The smooth tricks of evil men will be exposed, as will all the lies they use to oppress the poor in the courts.

Isa 57:20. But those who still reject me are like the restless sea, which is never still, but always churns up mire and dirt. [21]There is no peace, says my God, for them!

Isa 59:2. But the trouble is that your sins have cut you off from God. Because of sin he has turned his face away from you and will not listen anymore. [3]For your hands are those of murderers and your fingers are filthy with sin. You lie and grumble and oppose the good. [4]No one cares about being fair and true. Your lawsuits are based on lies; you spend your time plotting evil deeds and doing them. [5]You spend your time and energy in spinning evil plans which end up in deadly actions. [6]You cheat and shortchange everyone. Everything you do is filled with sin; violence is your trademark. [7]Your feet run to do evil and rush to murder; your thoughts are only of sinning, and wherever you go you leave behind a trail of misery and death. [8]You don't know what true peace is, nor what it means to be just and good; you continually do wrong and those who follow you won't experience any peace, either.

Isa 63:19. O God, why do you treat us as though we weren't your people, as though we were a heathen nation that never called you "Lord"?

Jer 2:22. No amount of soap or lye can make you clean. You are stained with guilt that cannot ever be washed away. I see it always before me, the Lord God says. [23]You say it isn't so, that you haven't worshiped idols? How can you say a thing like that? Go and look in any valley in the land! Face the awful sins that you have done, O restless female camel, seeking for a male! [24]You are a wild donkey, sniffing the wind at mating time. (Who can restrain your lust?) Any jack wanting you need not search, for you come running to him! [25]Why don't you turn from all this weary running after other gods? But you say, "Don't waste your breath. I've fallen in love with these strangers and I can't stop loving them now!"

Jer 3:5. So you talk, and keep right on doing all the evil that you can.

Jer 4:22. Until my people leave their foolishness, for they refuse to listen to me; they are dull, retarded children who have no understanding. They are smart enough at doing wrong, but for doing right they have no talent, none at all.

Jer 5:4. Then I said, "But what can we expect from the poor and ignorant? They don't know the ways of God. How can they obey him?" [5]I will go now to their leaders, the men of importance, and speak to them, for they know the ways of the Lord and the judgment that follows sin. But they too had utterly rejected their God. [26]Among my people are wicked men who lurk for victims like a hunter hiding in a blind. They set their traps for men. [27]Like a coop full of chickens their homes are full of evil plots. And the result? Now they are great and rich, [28]and well fed and well groomed, and there is no limit to their wicked deeds. They refuse justice to orphans and the rights of the poor.

Jer 6:7. She spouts evil like a fountain! Her streets echo with the sounds of violence; her sickness and wounds are ever before me. [15]Were my people ashamed when they worshiped idols? No, not at all—they didn't even blush. Therefore they shall lie among the slain. They shall die beneath my anger. Jer 8:12.

Jer 8:6. I listen to their conversation and what do I hear? Is anyone sorry for sin? Does anyone say, "What a terrible thing I have done?" No, all are rushing pell-mell down the path of sin as swiftly as a horse rushing to the battle!

Jer 9:3. "They bend their tongues like bows to shoot their arrows of untruth. They care nothing for right and go from bad to worse; they care nothing for me," says the Lord. [4]Beware of your neighbor! Beware of your brother! All take advantage of one another and spread their slanderous lies. [5]With practiced tongues they fool and defraud each other; they wear themselves out with all their sinning. [6]"They pile evil upon evil, lie upon lie, and utterly refuse to come to me," says the Lord.

Jer 11:8. But your fathers didn't do it. They wouldn't even listen. Each followed his own stubborn will and his proud heart. [15]What right do my beloved people have to come any more to my Temple? For you have been unfaithful and worshiped other gods. Can promises and sacrifices now avert your doom and give you life and joy again?

Jer 13:10. This evil nation refuses to listen to me, and follows its own evil desires and worships idols; therefore it shall become as this loincloth—good for nothing.

Jer 14:10. But the Lord replies: You have loved to wander far from me and have not tried to follow in my paths. Now I will no longer accept you as my people; now I will remember all the evil you have done, and punish your sins.

Jer 17:1. My people sin as though commanded to, as though their evil were laws chiseled with an iron pen or diamond point upon their stony hearts or on the corners of their altars.

Jer 30:12. For your sin is an incurable bruise, a terrible wound. [13]There is no one to help you or to bind up your wound and no medicine does any good. [14]All your lovers have left you and don't care anything about you any more; for I have wounded you cruelly, as though I were your enemy; mercilessly, as though I were an implacable foe; for your sins are so many, your guilt is so great. [15]Why do you protest your punishment? Your sin is so scandalous that your sorrow should never end! It is because your guilt is great that I have had to punish you so much.

Ezk 3:7. I am sending you to the people of Israel,

and they won't listen to you any more than they listened to me! For the whole lot of them are hard, impudent and stubborn.

Ezk 11:12. And you will know I am the Lord—you who have not obeyed me, but rather have copied the nations all around you.

Ezk 16:47. You have not merely sinned as they do—no, that was nothing to you; in a very short time you far surpassed them.

Ezk 20:16. Because they laughed at my laws, ignored my wishes, and violated my Sabbaths—their hearts were with their idols!

Hos 4:8. The priests rejoice in the sins of the people; they lap it up and lick their lips for more!

Hos 7:3. The king is glad about their wickedness; the princes laugh about their lies. [9]Worshiping foreign gods has sapped their strength, but they don't know it. Ephraim's hair is turning gray, and he doesn't even realize how weak and old he is.

Hos 9:10. O Israel, how well I remember those first delightful days when I led you through the wilderness! How refreshing was your love! How satisfying, like the early figs of summer in their first season! But then you deserted me for Baal-peor, to give yourselves to other gods, and soon you were as foul as they.

Hos 13:12. Ephraim's sins are harvested and stored away for punishment.

Amos 5:10. How you hate honest judges! How you despise people who tell the truth!

Mic 3:1. Listen, you leaders of Israel—you are supposed to know right from wrong, [2]yet you are the very ones who hate good and love evil.

Mic 7:2. The good men have disappeared from the earth; not one fairminded man is left. They are all murderers, turning against even their own brothers. [3]They go at their evil deeds with both hands, and how skilled they are in using them! The governor and judge alike demand bribes. The rich man pays them off and tells them whom to ruin. Justice is twisted between them. [4]Even the best of them are prickly as briars; the straightest is more crooked than a hedge of thorns.

Zeph 3:5. The wicked know no shame. [7]I thought, "Surely they will listen to me now—surely they will heed my warnings, so that I'll not need to strike again." But no; however much I punish them, they continue all their evil ways from dawn to dusk and dusk to dawn.

Hag 2:14. "You people," he said (speaking for the Lord), "were contaminating your sacrifices by living with selfish attitudes and evil hearts—and not only your sacrifices, but everything else that you did as a 'service' to me."

Mt 4:16. There the people who sat in darkness have seen a great Light; they sat in the land of death, and the Light broke through upon them.

Mt 6:23. But if your eye is clouded with evil thoughts and desires, you are in deep spiritual darkness. And oh, how deep that darkness can be!

Mt 18:11. And I, the Messiah, came to save the lost.

Mk 4:11. He replied, "You are permitted to know some truths about the Kingdom of God that are hidden to those outside the Kingdom."

Lk 1:79. To give light to those who sit in darkness and death's shadow.

Lk 19:10. This man was one of the lost sons of Abraham, and I, the Messiah, have come to search for and to save such souls as his.

Jn 3:18. But those who don't trust him have already been tried and condemned for not believing in the only Son of God. [19]Their sentence is based on this fact: that the Light from heaven came into the world, but they loved the darkness more than the Light, for their deeds were evil. [20]They hated the heavenly Light because they wanted to sin in the darkness. They stayed away from that Light for fear their sins would be exposed and they would be punished.

Jn 5:42. For as I know so well, you don't have God's love within you.

Jn 8:34. Jesus replied, "You are slaves of sin, every one of you. [44]For you are the children of your father the devil and you love to do the evil things he does."

Acts 8:21. You can have no part in this, for your heart is not right before God. [23]For I can see that there is jealousy and sin in your heart.

Acts 13:10. You son of the devil, full of every sort of trickery and villainy, enemy of all that is good, will you never end your opposition to the Lord?

Rom 1:20. So they will have no excuse (when they stand before God at Judgment Day). [21]Yes, they knew about him all right, but they wouldn't admit it or worship him or even thank him for all his daily care. And after awhile they began to think up silly ideas of what God was like and what he wanted them to do. The result was that their foolish minds became dark and confused. [22]Claiming themselves to be wise without God, they became utter fools instead. [23]And then, instead of worshiping the glorious, everliving God, they took wood and stone and made idols for themselves, carving them to look like mere birds and animals and snakes and puny men. [24]So God let them go ahead into every sort of sex sin, and do whatever they wanted to—yes, vile and sinful things with each other's bodies. [25]Instead of believing what they knew was the truth about God, they deliberately chose to believe lies. So they prayed to the things God made, but wouldn't obey the blessed God who made these things. [26]That is why God let go of them and let them do all these evil things, so that even their women turned against God's natural plan for them and indulged in sex sin with each other. [27]And the men, instead of having a normal sex relationship with women, burned with lust for each other, men doing shameful things with other men and, as a result, getting paid within their own souls with the penalty they so richly deserved. [28]So it was that when they gave God up and would not even acknowledge him, God gave them up to doing everything their evil minds could think of. [29]Their lives became full of every kind of wickedness and sin, of greed and hate, envy, murder, fighting, lying, bitterness, and gossip. [30]They were backbiters, haters of God, insolent, proud braggarts, always thinking of new ways of sinning and continually being disobedient to their parents. [31]They tried to misunderstand, broke their promises, and were heartless—without pity. [32]They were fully aware of God's death penalty for these crimes, yet they went right ahead and did them anyway, and encouraged others to do them, too.

Rom 2:8. But he will terribly punish those who fight against the truth of God and walk in evil ways.

Rom 3:10. As the Scriptures say, "No one is good—no one in all the world is innocent." [11]No one has ever really followed God's paths, or even truly wanted to. [12]Every one has turned away; all have gone wrong. No one anywhere has kept on doing what is right; not one. [13]Their talk is foul and filthy like the stench from an open grave. Their tongues are loaded with lies. Everything they say has in it the sting and poison of deadly snakes. [14]Their mouths are full of cursing and bitterness. [15]They are quick to kill, hating anyone who disagrees with them. [16]Wherever they go they leave misery and trouble behind them, [17]and they have never known what it is to feel secure or enjoy God's blessing. [18]They care nothing about God nor what he thinks of them.

Rom 8:5. Those who let themselves be controlled by their lower natures live only to please themselves. [7]Because the old sinful nature within us is against God. It never did obey God's laws and it never will. [8]That's why those who are still under the control of their old sinful selves, bent on following their old evil desires, can never please God.

Rom 9:8. This means that not all of Abraham's children are children of God.

Eph 2:1. Once you were under God's curse, doomed forever for your sins. [2]You went along with the crowd and were just like all the others, full of sin, obeying Satan, the mighty prince of the power of the air, who is at work right now in the hearts of those who are against the Lord. [3]All of us used to be just as they are, our lives expressing the evil within us, doing every wicked thing that our passions or our evil thoughts might lead us into. We started out bad, being born with evil natures, and were under God's anger just like everyone else. [12]Remember that in those days you were living utterly apart from Christ; you were enemies of God's children and he had promised you no help. You were lost, without God, without hope.

Eph 4:17, 18. Let me say this, then, speaking for the Lord: Live no longer as the unsaved do, for they are blinded and confused. Their closed hearts are full of darkness; they are far away from the life of God because they have shut their minds against him, and they cannot understand his ways. [19]They don't care anymore about right and wrong and have given themselves over to impure ways. They stop at nothing, being driven by their evil minds and reckless lusts.

Eph 5:11. Take no part in the worthless pleasures of evil and darkness, but instead, rebuke and expose them. [12]It would be shameful even to mention here those pleasures of darkness which the ungodly do.

Phil 2:15. You are to live clean, innocent lives as children of God in a dark world full of people who are crooked and stubborn. Shine out among them like beacon lights.

Col 1:21. And were separated from him by your evil thoughts and actions.

1 Thess 5:7. Night is the time for sleep and the time when people get drunk.

2 Thess 1:8. Those who do not wish to know God, and who refuse to accept his plan to save them through our Lord Jesus Christ.

1 Tim 1:9. But they were not made for us, whom God has saved; they are for sinners who hate God, have rebellious hearts, curse and swear, attack their fathers and mothers, and murder. [10]Yes, these laws are made to identify as sinners all who are immoral and impure: homosexuals, kidnappers, liars, and all others who do things that contradict the glorious Good News.

2 Tim 3:2. For people will love only themselves and their money; they will be proud and boastful, sneering at God, disobedient to their parents, ungrateful to them, and thoroughly bad. [3]They will be hardheaded and never give in to others; they will be constant liars and troublemakers and will think nothing of immorality. They will be rough and cruel, and sneer at those who try to be good. [4]They will betray their friends; they will be hotheaded, puffed up with pride, and prefer good times to worshiping God. [5]They will go to church, yes, but they won't really believe anything they hear. Don't be taken in by people like that. [6]They are the kind who craftily sneak into other people's homes and make friendships with silly, sin-burdened women and teach them their new doctrines. [7]Women of that kind are forever following new teachers, but they never understand the truth. [8]And these teachers fight truth just as Jannes and Jambres fought against Moses. They have dirty minds, warped and twisted, and have turned against the Christian faith. [9]But they won't get away with all this forever. Some day their deceit will be well known to everyone, as was the sin of Jannes and Jambres. [10]But you know from watching me that I am not that kind of person. You know what I believe and the way I live and what I want. You know my faith in Christ and how I have suffered. You know my love for you, and my patience. [11]You know how many troubles I have had as a result of my preaching the Good News. You know about all that was done to me while I was visiting in Antioch, Iconium and Lystra, but the Lord delivered me. [12]Yes, and those who decide to please Christ Jesus by living godly lives will suffer at the hands of those who hate him. [13]In fact, evil men and false teachers will become worse and worse, deceiving many, they themselves having been deceived by Satan.

Tit 1:15. A person who is pure of heart sees goodness and purity in everything; but a person whose own heart is evil and untrusting finds evil in everything, for his dirty mind and rebellious heart color all he sees and hears. [16]Such persons claim they know God, but from seeing the way they act, one knows they don't. They are rotten and disobedient, worthless so far as doing anything good is concerned.

Tit 3:3. Once we, too, were foolish and disobedient; we were misled by others and became slaves to many evil pleasures and wicked desires. Our lives were full of resentment and envy. We hated others and they hated us.

2 Pet 2:10. He is especially hard on those who follow their own evil, lustful thoughts, and those who are proud and willful, daring even to scoff at the Glorious Ones without so much as trembling. [12]But false teachers are fools—no better than animals. They do whatever they feel like; born only to be caught and killed, they laugh at the terrifying powers of the underworld which they know so little about; and they will be destroyed along with all the demons and powers of hell. [13]That is the pay these teachers will have for their sin. For they live in evil pleasures day after day. They are a disgrace and a stain among you, deceiving you by living in foul sin on the side while they join your love feasts as though they were honest men. [14]No woman can escape their sinful stare, and of adultery they never have enough. They make a game of luring unstable women. They train themselves to be greedy; and are doomed and cursed. [15]They have gone off the road and become lost like Balaam, the son of Beor, who fell in love with the money he could make by doing wrong; [16]but Balaam was stopped from his mad course when his donkey spoke to him with a human voice, scolding and rebuking him. [17]These men are as useless as dried-up springs of water, promising much and delivering nothing; they are as unstable as clouds driven by the storm winds. They are doomed to the eternal pits of darkness. [18]They proudly boast about their sins and conquests, and, using lust as their bait, they lure back into sin those who have just escaped from such wicked living. [19]"You aren't saved by being good," they say, "so you might as well be bad. Do what you like, be free." But these very teachers who offer this "freedom" from law are themselves slaves to sin and destruction. For a man is a slave to whatever controls him.

1 Jn 3:8. But if you keep on sinning, it shows that you belong to Satan, who since he first began to sin has kept steadily at it. But the Son of God came to destroy these works of the devil. [10]So now we can tell who is a child of God and who belongs to Satan. Whoever is living a life of sin and doesn't love his brother shows that he is not in God's family. [14]If we love other Christians it proves that we have been delivered from hell and given eternal life. But a person who doesn't have love for others is headed for eternal death. [15]Anyone who hates his Christian brother is really a murderer at heart; and you know that no one wanting to murder has eternal life within.

Jude 1:12. When these men join you at the love feasts of the church, they are evil smears among you, laughing and carrying on, gorging and stuffing themselves without a thought for others. They are like clouds blowing over dry land without giving rain, promising much, but producing nothing. They are like fruit trees without any fruit at picking time. They are not only dead, but doubly dead, for they have been pulled out, roots and all, to be burned. [13]All they leave behind them is shame and disgrace like the dirty foam left along the beach by the wild waves. They wander around looking as bright as stars, but ahead of them is the everlasting gloom and darkness that God has prepared for them.

Rev 3:17. You say, "I am rich, with everything I want; I don't need a thing!" And you don't realize that spiritually you are wretched and miserable and poor and blind and naked. [18]My advice to you is to buy pure gold from me, gold purified by fire —only then will you truly be rich. And to purchase from me white garments, clean and pure, so you won't be naked and ashamed; and to get medicine from me to heal your eyes and give you back your sight.

PRAYER OF. Deut 1:45. Then they returned and wept before the Lord, but he wouldn't listen.

Deut 3:26. But the Lord was angry with me because of you, and would not let me cross over. "Speak of it no more," he ordered.

2 Sam 22:42. They looked in vain for help; they cried to God, but he refused to answer.

Job 27:9. Will God listen to his cry when trouble comes upon him?

Job 35:12. But when anyone does cry out this question to him, he never replies by instant punishment of the tyrants. [13]But it is false to say he doesn't hear those cries.

Ps 18:41. They shouted for help but no one dared to rescue them; they cried to the Lord, but he refused to answer them.

Ps 66:18. He would not have listened if I had not confessed my sins.

Prov 1:24. I have called you so often but still you won't come. I have pleaded, but all in vain. [25]For you have spurned my counsel and reproof. [26]Some day you'll be in trouble, and I'll laugh! Mock me, will you?—I'll mock you! [27]When a storm of terror surrounds you, and when you are engulfed by anguish and distress, [28]then I will not answer your cry for help. It will be too late though you search for me ever so anxiously.

Prov 15:8. The Lord hates the gifts of the wicked, but delights in the prayers of his people. [29]The Lord is far from the wicked, but he hears the prayers of the righteous.

Prov 21:13. He who shuts his ears to the cries of the poor will be ignored in his own time of need. [27]God loathes the gifts of evil men, especially if they are trying to bribe him!

Prov 28:9. God doesn't listen to the prayers of men who flout the law.

Isa 1:15. From now on, when you pray with your

hands stretched out to heaven, I won't look or listen. Even though you make many prayers, I will not hear, for your hands are those of murderers; they are covered with the blood of your innocent victims.

Isa 45:19. And I didn't tell Israel to ask me for what I didn't plan to give!

Isa 59:2. But the trouble is that your sins have cut you off from God. Because of sin he has turned his face away from you and will not listen anymore.

Jer 11:11. Therefore, the Lord says, I am going to bring calamity down upon them and they shall not escape. Though they cry for mercy, I will not listen to their pleas.

Jer 14:12. When they fast, I will not pay any attention; when they present their offerings and sacrifices to me, I will not accept them. What I will give them in return is war and famine and disease.

Jer 15:1. Then the Lord said to me, Even if Moses and Samuel stood before me pleading for these people, even then I wouldn't help them—away with them! Get them out of my sight!

Jer 18:17. I will scatter my people before their enemies as the east wind scatters dust; and in all their trouble I will turn my back on them and refuse to notice their distress.

Lam 3:8. And though I cry and shout, he will not hear my prayers! [44]You have veiled yourself as with a cloud so that our prayers do not reach through.

Ezk 8:18. Therefore I will deal with them in fury. I will neither pity nor spare. And though they scream for mercy, I will not listen.

Ezk 20:3. Son of dust, say to the elders of Israel: The Lord God says: How dare you come to ask my help? I swear that I will tell you nothing. [31]For when you offer gifts to them and give your little sons to be burned to ashes as you do even today, shall I listen to you or help you, Israel? As I live, the Lord God says, I will not give you any message, though you have come to me to ask.

Hos 5:6. Then at last, they will come with their flocks and herds to sacrifice to God, but it will be too late—they will not find him. He has withdrawn from them and they are left alone.

Mic 3:4. And then you plead with the Lord for his help in times of trouble! Do you really expect him to listen? He will look the other way!

Zech 7:12. They hardened their hearts like flint, afraid to hear the words that God, the Lord of Hosts, commanded them—the laws he had revealed to them by his Spirit through the early prophets. That is why such great wrath came down on them from God. [13]I called but they refused to listen, so when they cried to me, I turned away.

Mal 1:9. "God have mercy on us," you recite; "God be gracious to us!" But when you bring that kind of gift, why should he show you any favor at all?

Mal 2:11. In Judah, in Israel, and in Jerusalem, there is treachery, for the men of Judah have defiled God's holy and beloved Temple by marrying heathen women who worship idols. [12]May the Lord cut off from his covenant every last man, whether priest or layman, who has done this thing! [13]Yet you cover the altar with your tears because the Lord doesn't pay attention to your offerings anymore, and you receive no blessing from him.

Jn 9:31. Well, God doesn't listen to evil men, but he has open ears to those who worship him and do his will.

Jas 1:6. But when you ask him, be sure that you really expect him to tell you, for a doubtful mind will be as unsettled as a wave of the sea that is driven and tossed by the wind. [7, 8]. . . If you don't ask with faith, don't expect the Lord to give you any solid answer.

Jas 4:3. And even when you do ask you don't get it because your whole aim is wrong—you want only what will give *you* pleasure.

1 Pet 3:7. You husbands must be careful of your wives, being thoughtful of their needs and honoring them as the weaker sex. Remember that you and your wife are partners in receiving God's blessings, and if you don't treat her as you should, your prayers will not get ready answers.

PUNISHMENT OF. Gen 2:16, 17. But the Lord God gave the man this warning: "You may eat any fruit in the garden except fruit from the Tree of Conscience—for its fruit will open your eyes to make you aware of right and wrong, good and bad. If you eat its fruit, you will be doomed to die."

Gen 3:16. Then God said to the woman, "You shall bear children in intense pain and suffering; yet even so, you shall welcome your husband's affections, and he shall be your master." [17]And to Adam, God said, "Because you listened to your wife and ate the fruit when I told you not to, I have placed a curse upon the soil. All your life you will struggle to extract a living from it. [18]It will grow thorns and thistles for you, and you shall eat its grasses. [19]All your life you will sweat to master it, until your dying day. Then you will return to the ground from which you came. For you were made from the ground, and to the ground you will return."

Gen 4:7. It can be bright with joy if you will do what you should! But if you refuse to obey, watch out. Sin is waiting to attack you, longing to destroy you.

Gen 6:3. Then Jehovah said, "My Spirit must not forever be disgraced in man, wholly evil as he is." [7]And he said, "I will blot out from the face of the earth all mankind that I created. Yes, and the animals too, and the reptiles and the birds. For I am sorry I made them." [12, 13]As God observed how bad it was, and saw that all mankind was vicious and depraved, he said to Noah, "I have decided to destroy all mankind; for the earth is filled with crime because of man. Yes, I will destroy mankind from the earth."

Ex 20:5. You must never bow to an image or worship it in any way; for I, the Lord your God, am very possessive. I will not share your affection with any other god! And when I punish people for their sins, the punishment continues upon the children, grandchildren, and great-grandchildren of those who hate me. Ex 34:7.

Ex 32:33. And the Lord replied to Moses, "Whoever has sinned against me will be blotted out of my book. [34]And now go, lead the people to the place I told you about, and I assure you that my Angel shall travel on ahead of you; however, when I come to visit these people, I will punish them for their sins." [35]And the Lord sent a great plague upon the people because they had worshiped Aaron's calf.

Lev 26:14. But if you will not listen to me or obey me, [15]but reject my laws, [16]this is what I will do to you: I will punish you with sudden terrors and panic, and with tuberculosis and burning fever; your eyes shall be consumed and your life shall ebb away; you will sow your crops in vain, for your enemies will eat them. [17]I will set my face against you and you will flee before your attackers; those who hate you will rule you; you will even run when no one is chasing you! [18]And if you still disobey me, I will punish you seven times more severely for your sins. *vs.* 18–39.

Num 15:31. For he has despised the commandment of the Lord and deliberately failed to obey his law; he must be executed, and die in his sin.

Num 32:23. But if you don't do as you have said, then you will have sinned against the Lord, and you may be sure that your sin will catch up with you.

Deut 7:9. Understand, therefore, that the Lord your God is the faithful God . . . [10]But those who hate him shall be punished publicly and destroyed. He will deal with them personally.

Deut 11:26. I am giving you the choice today between God's blessing or God's curse! [28]And a curse if you refuse them and worship the gods of these other nations.

Deut 28:20. For the Lord himself will send his personal curse upon you. You will be confused and a failure in everything you do, until at last you are destroyed because of the sin of forsaking him. *vs.* 15–68.

Deut 30:15. Look, today I have set before you life and death, depending on whether you obey or disobey. [19]I call heaven and earth to witness against you that today I have set before you life or death, blessing or curse. Oh, that you would choose life; that you and your children might live!

Deut 31:29. I know that after my death you will utterly defile yourselves and turn away from God and his commands; and in the days to come evil will crush you for you will do what the Lord says is evil, making him very angry.

1 Sam 3:11. Then the Lord said to Samuel, "I am going to do a shocking thing in Israel. [12]I am going to do all of the dreadful things I warned Eli about. [13]I have continually threatened him and his entire family with punishment because his sons are blaspheming God, and he doesn't stop them. [14]So I have vowed that the sins of Eli and of his sons shall never be forgiven by sacrifices and offerings."

1 Sam 12:25. But if you continue to sin, you and your king will be destroyed.

2 Sam 3:39. And even though I am God's chosen king, I can do nothing with these two sons of Zeruiah. May the Lord repay wicked men for their wicked deeds.

2 Sam 7:14. If he sins, I will use other nations to punish him,

2 Sam 22:27. To those who are pure, you show yourself pure; but you destroy those who are evil. [28]You will save those in trouble, but you bring down the haughty; for you watch their every move. Ps 18:26, 27.

2 Sam 23:6. But the godless are as thorns to be thrown away, for they tear the hand that touches them. [7]One must be armed to chop them down; they shall be burned.

1 Kgs 21:20. "So my enemy has found me!" Ahab exclaimed to Elijah. "Yes," Elijah answered, "I have come to place God's curse upon you because you have sold yourself to the devil. [21]The Lord is going to bring great harm to you and sweep you away; he will not let a single one of your male descendants survive!"

1 Chron 10:13. Saul died for his disobedience to the Lord and because he had consulted a medium, [14]and did not ask the Lord for guidance. So the Lord killed him and gave the kingdom to David, the son of Jesse.

1 Chron 15:13. The Lord destroyed us before because we handled the matter improperly—you were not carrying it.

1 Chron 28:9. But if you forsake him, he will permanently throw you aside.

2 Chron 15:2. The Lord will stay with you as long as you stay with him! Whenever you look for him, you will find him. But if you forsake him, he will forsake you.

Job 4:8. Experience teaches that it is those who sow sin and trouble who harvest the same. [9]They die beneath the hand of God.

Job 5:3. Those who turn from God may be successful for the moment, but then comes sudden disaster. [14]They grope like blind men in the daylight; they see no better in the daytime than at night.

Job 8:20. But look! God will not cast away a good man, nor prosper evildoers. [22]Those who hate you shall be clothed with shame, and the wicked destroyed.

Job 10:13, 14. Yet all the time your real motive in making me was to destroy me if I sinned; and to refuse to forgive my iniquity. [15]Just the slightest wickedness, and I am done for.

Job 11:20. But the wicked shall find no way to escape; their only hope is death.

Job 15:20. A wicked man is always in trouble throughout his life. [21]He is surrounded by terrors, and if there are good days they will soon be gone. [22]He dares not go out into the darkness, lest he be murdered. [23, 24]He wanders around begging for food. He lives in fear, distress, and anguish. His enemies conquer him as a king defeats his foes. *vs.* 27–30.

Job 18:5. The truth remains that if you do not

prosper, it is because you are wicked. And your bright flame shall be put out. 6There will be darkness in every home where there is wickedness. 7The confident stride of the wicked man will be shortened; he will realize his failing strength. 8, 9He walks into traps, and robbers will ambush him. 10There is a booby-trap in every path he takes. 11He has good cause for fear—his enemy is close behind him! 12His vigor is depleted by hunger; calamity stands ready to pounce upon him! 13His skin is eaten by disease. Death shall devour him. 14The wealth he trusted in shall reject him, and he shall be brought down to the King of Terrors. 15His home shall disappear beneath a fiery barrage of brimstone. 16He shall die from the roots up, and all his branches will be lopped off. 17All memory of his existence will perish from the earth; no one will remember him. 18He will be driven out from the kingdom of light into darkness, and chased out of the world. 19He will have neither son nor grandson left, nor any other relatives. 20Old and young alike will be horrified by his fate. 21Yes, that is what happens to sinners, to those rejecting God.

Job 19:29. I warn you, you yourselves are in danger of punishment for your attitude.

Job 20:5. The triumph of the wicked has been short-lived, and the joy of the godless but for a moment? 6Though the godless be proud as the heavens, and walk with his nose in the air, 7yet he shall perish forever, cast away like his own dung. Those who knew him will wonder where he is gone. 8He will fade like a dream. 9Neither his friends nor his family will ever see him again. 10His children shall beg from the poor, their hard labor shall repay his debts. 11Though still a young man, his bones shall lie in the dust. 12He enjoyed the taste of his wickedness, letting it melt in his mouth, 13sipping it slowly, lest it disappear. 14But suddenly the food he has eaten turns sour within him. 15He will vomit the plunder he gorged. God won't let him keep it down. 16It is like poison and death to him. 17He shall not enjoy the goods he stole; they will not be butter and honey to him after all. 18His labors shall not be rewarded; wealth will give him no joy. 19For he has oppressed the poor and foreclosed their homes; he will never recover. 20Though he was always greedy, now he has nothing; of all the things he dreamed of—none remain. 21Because he stole at every opportunity, his prosperity shall not continue. 22He shall run into trouble at the peak of his powers; all the wicked shall destroy him. 23Just as he is about to fill his belly, God will rain down wrath upon him. 24He will be chased and struck down. 25The arrow is pulled from his body —and the glittering point comes out from his gall. The terrors of death are upon him. 26His treasures will be lost in deepest darkness. A raging fire will devour his goods, consuming all he has left. 27The heavens will reveal his sins, and the earth will give testimony against him. 28His wealth will disappear beneath the wrath of God. 29This is what awaits the wicked man, for God prepares it for him.

Job 21:7. The truth is that the wicked live on to a good old age, and become great and powerful. 8They live to see their children grow to maturity around them, and their grandchildren, too. 9Their homes are safe from every fear, and God does not punish them. 10Their cattle are productive, 11they have many happy children, 12, 13they spend their time singing and dancing. They are wealthy and need deny themselves nothing; they are prosperous to the end. 14All this despite the fact that they ordered God away and wanted no part of him and his ways. 15"Who is Almighty God?" they scoff. "Why should we obey him? What good will it do us?" 16Look, everything the wicked touch has turned to gold! But I refuse even to deal with people like that. 17Yet the wicked get away with it every time. They never have trouble, and God skips them when he distributes his sorrows and anger. 18Are they driven before the wind like straw? Are they carried away by the storm? Not at all! 19"Well," you say, "at least God will punish their children!" But I say that God should punish the man who sins, not his children! Let him feel the penalty himself. 20Yes, let him be destroyed for his iniquity. Let him drink deeply of the anger of the Almighty. 21For when he is dead, then he will never again be able to enjoy his family. 22But who can rebuke God, the supreme Judge? 23, 24He destroys those who are healthy, wealthy, fat, and prosperous; 25God also destroys those in deep and grinding poverty who have never known anything good. 26Both alike are buried in the same dust, both eaten by the same worms. 27I know what you are going to say—28you will tell me of rich and wicked men who came to disaster because of their sins. 29But I reply, Ask anyone who has been around and he can tell you the truth, 30-32that the evil man is usually spared in the day of calamity, and allowed to escape. No one rebukes him openly. No one repays him for what he has done. And an honor guard keeps watch at his grave. 33A great funeral procession precedes and follows him as the soft earth covers him.

Job 27:8. But what hope has the godless when God cuts him off and takes away his life? 9Will God listen to his cry when trouble comes upon him? 10For he does not delight himself in the Almighty or pay any attention to God except in times of crisis. 11I will teach you about God—12but really, I don't need to, for you yourselves know as much about him as I do; yet you are saying all these useless things to me. 13This is the fate awaiting the wicked from the hand of the Almighty: 14If he has a multitude of children, it is so that they will die in war, or starve to death. 15Those who survive shall be brought down to the grave by disease and plague, with no one to mourn them, not even their wives. 16The evil man may accumulate money like dust, with closets jammed full of clothing—17yes, he may order them made by his tailor, but the innocent shall wear that clothing, and shall divide his silver among them. 18Every house built by the wicked is as fragile as a spider web, as full of cracks as a leafy booth! 19He goes to bed rich, but wakes up to find that all his wealth is gone. [20]Terror overwhelms him, and he is blown away in the storms of the night. [21]The east wind carries him away, and he is gone. It sweeps him into eternity. [22]For God shall hurl at him unsparingly. He longs to flee from God. [23]Everyone will cheer at his death, and boo him into eternity.

Job 31:1. I made a covenant with my eyes not to look with lust upon a girl. [2, 3]I know full well that Almighty God above sends calamity on those who do.

Job 34:22. No darkness is thick enough to hide evil men from his eyes.

Job 36:12. If they won't listen to him, they shall perish in battle and die because of their lack of good sense. [17]But you are too preoccupied with your imagined grievances against others.

Ps 1:4. But for sinners, what a different story! They blow away like chaff before the wind. [5]They are not safe on Judgment Day; they shall not stand among the godly. [6]For the Lord watches over all the plans and paths of godly men, but the paths of the godless lead to doom.

Ps 2:4. But God in heaven merely laughs! He is amused by all their puny plans. [5]And then in fierce fury he rebukes them and fills them with fear. [9]Rule them with an iron rod; smash them like clay pots!

Ps 3:7. I will cry to him, "Arise, O Lord! Save me, O my God!" And he will slap them in the face, insulting them and breaking off their teeth.

Ps 5:5. Therefore proud sinners will not survive your searching gaze, for how you hate their evil deeds.

Ps 7:11. God is a judge who is perfectly fair, and he is angry with the wicked every day. [12]Unless they repent, he will sharpen his sword and slay them. He has bent and strung his bow [13]and fitted it with deadly arrows made from shafts of fire.

Ps 9:5. You have rebuked the nations and destroyed the wicked, blotting out their names forever and ever. [17]The wicked shall be sent away to hell; this is the fate of all the nations forgetting the Lord.

Ps 10:15. Break the arms of these wicked men. Go after them until the last of them is destroyed.

Ps 11:6. He will rain down fire and brimstone on the wicked and scorch them with his burning wind.

Ps 18:14. He flashed his fearful arrows of lightning and routed all my enemies. See how they run!

Ps 21:9, 10. When you appear, they will be destroyed in the fierce fire of your presence. The Lord will destroy them and their children.

Ps 28:4. Give them the punishment they so richly deserve! Measure it out to them in proportion to their wickedness; pay them back for all their evil deeds. [5]They care nothing for God or what he has done or what he has made; therefore God will dismantle them like old buildings, never to be rebuilt again.

Ps 32:10. Many sorrows come to the wicked.

Ps 34:16. But the Lord has made up his mind to wipe out even the memory of evil men from the earth. [21]Calamity will surely overtake the wicked; heavy penalties are meted out to those who hate the good.

Ps 36:12. Look! They have fallen. They are thrown down and will not rise again.

Ps 37:1. Never envy the wicked! [2]Soon they fade away like grass and disappear. [9]For the wicked shall be destroyed, but those who trust the Lord shall be given every blessing. [10]Only a little while and the wicked shall disappear. You will look for them in vain. [17]For the strength of evil men shall be broken, but the Lord takes care of those he has forgiven. [20]But evil men shall perish. These enemies of God will wither like grass, and disappear like smoke. [22]Those blessed by the Lord shall inherit the earth, but those cursed by him shall die. [34]Don't be impatient for the Lord to act! Keep traveling steadily along his pathway and in due season he will honor you with every blessing, and you will see the wicked destroyed. [35, 36]I myself have seen it happen: a proud and evil man, towering like a cedar of Lebanon, but when I looked again, he was gone! I searched but could not find him! [37]But the good man—what a different story! For the good man—the blameless, the upright, the man of peace—he has a wonderful future ahead of him. For him there is a happy ending. [38]But evil men shall be destroyed, and their posterity shall be cut off. *vs.* 12–22.

Ps 39:11. When you punish a man for his sins, he is destroyed, for he is as fragile as a moth-infested cloth; yes, man is frail as breath.

Ps 50:22. This is the last chance for all of you who have forgotten God, before I tear you apart—and no one can help you then.

Ps 52:5. But God will strike you down and pull you from your home, and drag you away from the land of the living.

Ps 55:19. God himself—God from everlasting ages past—will answer them! [23]He will send my enemies to the pit of destruction. Murderers and liars will not live out half their days. But I am trusting you to save me.

Ps 56:7. They expect to get away with it. Don't let them, Lord. In anger cast them to the ground.

Ps 58:6. O God, break off their fangs. Tear out the teeth of these young lions, Lord. [7]Let them disappear like water into thirsty ground. Make their weapons useless in their hands. [8]Let them be as snails that dissolve into slime; and as those who die at birth, who never see the sun. [9]God will sweep away both old and young. He will destroy them more quickly than a cooking pot can feel the blazing fire of thorns beneath it.

Ps 59:5. (And O Jehovah, God of heaven's armies, God of Israel, arise and punish the heathen nations surrounding us.) Do not spare these evil, treacherous men. [8]Lord, laugh at them! (And scoff at these surrounding nations too.)

Ps 64:7. But God himself will shoot them down. Suddenly his arrow will pierce them. [8]They will stagger backward, destroyed by those they spoke against. All who see it happening will scoff at them.

Ps 68:1. Arise, O God, and scatter all your enemies! Chase them away! [2]Drive them off like smoke before the wind; melt them like wax in fire! So let the wicked perish at the presence of God. [6]He gives families to the lonely, and releases prisoners from jail, singing with joy! But for rebels there is famine and distress. [21]But he will crush his enemies, for they refuse to leave their guilty, stubborn ways.

Ps 73:2. But as for me, I came so close to the edge of the cliff! My feet were slipping and I was almost gone. [3]For I was envious of the prosperity of the proud and wicked. [4]Yes, all through life their road is smooth! They grow sleek and fat. [5]They aren't always in trouble and plagued with problems like everyone else, [6]so their pride sparkles like a jeweled necklace, and their clothing is woven of cruelty! [7]These fat cats have everything their hearts could ever wish for! [8]They scoff at God and threaten his people. How proudly they speak! [9]They boast against the very heavens, and their words strut through the earth. [10]And so God's people are dismayed and confused, and drink it all in. [11]"Does God realize what is going on?" they ask. [12]"Look at these men of arrogance; they never have to lift a finger—theirs is a life of ease; and all the time their riches multiply." [13]Have I been wasting my time? Why take the trouble to be pure? [14]All I get out of it is trouble and woe—every day and all day long! [15]If I had really said that, I would have been a traitor to your people. [16]Yet it is so hard to explain it—this prosperity of those who hate the Lord. [17]Then one day I went into God's sanctuary to meditate, and thought about the future of these evil men. [18]What a slippery path they are on—suddenly God will send them sliding over the edge of the cliff and down to their destruction: [19]an instant end to all their happiness, an eternity of terror. [20]Their present life is only a dream! They will awaken to the truth as one awakens from a dream of things that never really were! [21]When I saw this, what turmoil filled my heart! [27]But those refusing to worship God will perish, for he destroys those serving other gods.

Ps 75:8. In Jehovah's hand there is a cup of pale and sparkling wine. It is his judgment, poured out upon the wicked of the earth. They must drain that cup to the dregs. [10]"I will cut off the strength of evil men," says the Lord, "and increase the power of good men in their place."

Ps 78:49. He loosed on them the fierceness of his anger, sending sorrow and trouble. He dispatched against them a band of destroying angels. [50]He gave free course to his anger and did not spare the Egyptians' lives, but handed them over to plagues and sickness. *vs.* 1–67.

Ps 89:10. You have cut haughty Egypt to pieces. Your enemies are scattered by your awesome power. [30-32]If his children forsake my laws and don't obey them, then I will punish them.

Ps 91:8. I will see how the wicked are punished but I will not share it.

Ps 92:7. That although the wicked flourish like weeds, there is only eternal destruction ahead of them. [8]But the Lord continues forever, exalted in the heavens, [9]while his enemies—all evil-doers—shall be scattered.

Ps 94:13. And gives us respite from our enemies while God traps them and destroys them. [23]God has made the sins of evil men to boomerang upon them! He will destroy them by their own plans. Jehovah our God will cut them off.

Ps 97:3. Fire goes forth before him and burns up all his foes.

Ps 101:8. My daily task will be to ferret out criminals and free the city of God from their grip.

Ps 104:35. Let all sinners perish—all who refuse to praise him.

Ps 106:18. And fire fell from heaven to consume these wicked men. [43]Again and again he delivered them from their slavery, but they continued to rebel against him, and were finally destroyed by their sin.

Ps 107:17. Others, the fools, were ill because of their sinful ways. [33]He dries up rivers, [34]and turns the good land of the wicked into deserts of salt.

Ps 109:6. Show him how it feels! Let lies be told about him, and bring him to court before an unfair judge. [7]When his case is called for judgment, let him be pronounced guilty. Count his prayers as sins. [8]Let his years be few and brief; let others step forward to replace him. [9, 10]May his children become fatherless and his wife a widow; may they be evicted from the ruins of their home. [11]May creditors seize his entire estate and strangers take all he has earned. [12, 13]Let no one be kind to him; let no one pity his fatherless children. May they die. May his family name be blotted out in a single generation. [14]Punish the sins of his father and mother. Don't overlook them. [15]Think constantly about the evil things he has done, and cut off his name from the memory of man. [16]For he refused all kindness to others, and persecuted those in need, and hounded brokenhearted ones to death. [17]He loved to curse others; now you curse him. He never blessed others; now don't you bless him. [18]Cursing is as much a part of him as his clothing, or as the water he drinks, or the rich food he eats. [19]Now may those curses return and cling to him like his clothing or his belt.

Ps 119:21. You rebuke those cursed proud ones who refuse your commands. [118]But you have rejected all who reject your laws. They are only fooling themselves. [119]The wicked are the scum you skim off and throw away. [155]The wicked are far from salvation for they do not care for your laws.

Ps 129:4. The Lord is good. For he has snapped the chains that evil men had bound me with.

Ps 139:19. Surely you will slay the wicked, Lord! Away, blood-thirsty men! Begone!

Ps 145:20. He protects all those who love him, but destroys the wicked.

Ps 146:9. He protects the immigrants, and cares for the orphans and widows. But he turns topsy-turvy the plans of the wicked.

Ps 147:6. The Lord supports the humble, but brings the wicked into the dust.

Prov 2:22. Evil men lose the good things they might have had, and they themselves shall be destroyed.

Prov 3:33. The curse of God is on the wicked.

Prov 6:12, 13. Let me describe for you a worthless and a wicked man; first, he is a constant liar; he signals his true intentions to his friends with eyes and feet and fingers. [14]Next, his heart is full of rebellion. And he spends his time thinking of all the evil he can do, and stirring up discontent. [15]But he will be destroyed suddenly, broken beyond hope of healing.

Prov 10:3. The Lord will not let a good man starve to death, nor will he let the wicked man's riches continue forever. [6]The good man is covered with blessings from head to foot, but an evil man inwardly curses his luck. [7]We all have happy memories of good men gone to their reward, but the names of wicked men stink after them. [8]The wise man is glad to be instructed, but a self-sufficient fool falls flat on his face. [14]A wise man holds his tongue. Only a fool blurts out everything he knows; that only leads to sorrow and trouble. [24]The wicked man's fears will all come true, and so will the good man's hopes. [25]Disaster strikes like a cyclone and the wicked are whirled away. But the good man has a strong anchor. [27]Reverence for God adds hours to each day; so how can the wicked expect a long, good life? [28]The hope of good men is eternal happiness; the hopes of evil men are all in vain. [29]God protects the upright but destroys the wicked. [30]The good shall never lose God's blessings, but the wicked shall lose everything. [31]The good man gives wise advice, but the liar's counsel is shunned.

Prov 11:3. A good man is guided by his honesty; the evil man is destroyed by his dishonesty. [5]The upright are directed by their honesty; the wicked shall fall beneath their load of sins. [6]The good man's goodness delivers him; the evil man's treachery is his undoing. [7]When an evil man dies, his hopes all perish, for they are based upon this earthly life. [8]God rescues good men from danger while letting the wicked fall into it. [19]The good man finds life; the evil man, death. [21]You can be very sure that the evil man will not go unpunished forever. And you can also be very sure that God will rescue the children of the godly. [23]The good man can look forward to happiness, while the wicked can expect only wrath.

Prov 12:2. The Lord blesses good men and condemns the wicked. [3]Wickedness never brings real success; only the godly have that. [7]The wicked shall perish; the godly shall stand.

Prov 13:2. The good man wins his case by careful argument; the evil-minded only wants to fight. [5]A good man hates lies; wicked men lie constantly and come to shame. [6]A man's goodness helps him all through life, while evil men are being destroyed by their wickedness. [9]The good man's life is full of light. The sinner's road is dark and gloomy. [21]Curses chase sinners, while blessings chase the righteous! [25]The good man eats to live, while the evil man lives to eat.

Prov 14:12. Before every man there lies a wide and pleasant road that seems right but ends in death. [Prov 16:25.] [19]Evil men shall bow before the godly. [32]The wicked are crushed by their sins.

Prov 16:4. The Lord has made everything for his own purposes—even the wicked, for punishment. [5]Pride disgusts the Lord. Take my word for it—*proud men shall be punished.*

Prov 18:3. Sin brings disgrace.

Prov 19:16. Keep the commandments and keep your life; despising them means death.

Prov 21:12. The godly learn by watching ruin overtake the wicked. [15]A good man loves justice, but it is a calamity to evil-doers. [16]The man who strays away from common sense will end up dead!

Prov 22:5. The rebel walks a thorny, treacherous road; the man who values his soul will stay away. [22, 23]Don't rob the poor and sick! For the Lord is their defender. If you injure them he will punish you.

Prov 24:20. For the evil man has no future; his light will be snuffed out. [22]For you will go down with them to sudden disaster, and who knows where it all will end?

Prov 28:14. Blessed is the man who reveres God, but the man who doesn't care is headed for serious trouble. [18]Good men will be rescued from harm, but cheaters will be destroyed.

Prov 29:1. The man who is often reproved but refuses to accept criticism will suddenly be broken and never have another chance. [16]When rulers are wicked, their people are too; but good men will live to see the tyrant's downfall.

Eccl 2:26. For God gives those who please him wisdom, knowledge, and joy; but if a sinner becomes wealthy, God takes the wealth away from him and gives it to those who please him.

Eccl 7:17. Don't be too wicked either—don't be a fool! Why should you die before your time?

Eccl 8:12. But though a man sins a hundred times and still lives, I know very well that those who fear God will be better off, [13]unlike the wicked, who will not live long, good lives—their days shall pass away as quickly as shadows because they don't fear God.

Isa 3:11. But say to the wicked, "Your doom is sure. You too shall get your just deserts. Your well-earned punishment is on the way."

Isa 5:11. Woe to you who get up early in the morning to go on long drinking bouts that last till late at night—woe to you drunken bums. [12]You furnish lovely music at your grand parties; the orchestras are superb! But for the Lord you have no thought or care. [13]Therefore I will send you into exile far away because you neither know nor care that I have done so much for you. Your great and honored men will starve, and the common people will die of thirst. [14]Hell is licking its chops in anticipation of this delicious morsel, Jerusalem. Her great and small shall be swallowed up, and all her drunken throngs. [24]Therefore God will deal with them and burn them. They will disappear like straw on fire. Their roots will rot and their flowers wither, for they have thrown away the laws of God and despised the Word of the Holy One of Israel.

Isa 9:18. He will burn up all this wickedness, these thorns and briars; and the flames will consume the forests, too, and send a vast cloud of smoke billowing up from their burning.

Isa 10:3. Oh, what will you do when I visit you in that day when I send desolation upon you from a distant land? To whom will you turn then for your help? Where will your treasures be safe?

Isa 11:4. But will defend the poor and the exploited. He will rule against the wicked who oppress them.

Isa 13:9. For see, the day of the Lord is coming, the terrible day of his wrath and fierce anger. The land shall be destroyed, and all the sinners with it. [11]And I will punish the world for its evil, the wicked for their sin; I will crush the arrogance of the proud man and the haughtiness of the rich.

Isa 24:17. Terror and the captivity of hell are still your lot, O men of the world. [18]When you flee in terror you will fall into a pit, and if you escape from the pit you will step into a trap, for destruction falls from the heavens upon you; the world is shaken beneath you.

Isa 26:21. Look! The Lord is coming from the heavens to punish the people of the earth for their sins. The earth will no longer hide the murderers. The guilty will be found.

Isa 28:18. I will cancel your agreement of compromise with Death and the devil, so when the terrible enemy floods in, you will be trampled into the ground. [19]Again and again that flood will come and carry you off, until at last the unmixed horror of the truth of my warnings will finally dawn on you. [20]The bed you have made is far too short to lie on; the blankets are too narrow to cover you. [21]The Lord will come suddenly and in anger, as at Mount Perazim and Gibeon, to do a strange, unusual thing—to destroy his own people! [22]So scoff no more, lest your punishment be made even greater, for the Lord God of Hosts has plainly told me that he is determined to crush you.

Isa 33:11. You Assyrians will gain nothing by all your efforts. Your own breath will turn to fire and kill you. [12]Your armies will be burned to lime, like thorns cut down and tossed in the fire. [14]The sinners among my people shake with fear. "Which one of us," they cry, "can live here in the presence of this all-consuming, Everlasting Fire?"

Isa 40:2. Speak tenderly to Jerusalem and tell her that her sad days are gone. Her sins are pardoned, and the Lord will give her twice as many blessings as he gave her punishment before. Jer 16: 18.

Isa 48:22. But there is no peace, says the Lord, for the wicked.

Isa 50:11. But see here, you who live in your own light, and warm yourselves from your own fires and not from God's; you will live among sorrows.

Isa 57:20. But those who still reject me are like the restless sea, which is never still, but always churns up mire and dirt. [21]There is no peace, says my God, for them!

Isa 64:5. But we are not godly; we are constant sinners and have been all our lives. Therefore your wrath is heavy on us. How can such as we be saved? [6]We are all infected and impure with sin. When we put on our prized robes of righteousness we find they are but filthy rags. Like autumn leaves we fade, wither and fall. And our sins, like the wind, sweep us away. [7]Yet no one calls upon your name or pleads with you for mercy. Therefore you have turned away from us and turned us over to our sins.

Isa 65:12. Therefore I will "destine" you to the sword, and your "fate" shall be a dark one; for when I called, you didn't answer; when I spoke, you wouldn't listen. You deliberately sinned before my very eyes, choosing to do what you know I despise. [13]Therefore the Lord God says, You shall starve, but my servants shall eat; you shall be thirsty while they drink; you shall be sad and ashamed, but they shall rejoice. [14]You shall cry in sorrow and vexation and despair, while they sing for joy.

Jer 8:12. Are they ashamed because they worship idols? No, not in the least; they don't even know how to blush! That is why I will see to it that they lie among the fallen. I will visit them with death. [13]Their figs and grapes will disappear, their fruit trees will die, and all the good things I prepared for them will soon be gone. [14]Then the people will say, "Why should we wait here to die? Come, let us go to the walled cities and perish there. For the Lord our God has decreed our doom and given us a cup of poison to drink because of all our sins." [20]"The harvest is finished; the summer is over and we are not saved." [21]I weep for the hurt of my people; I stand amazed, silent, dumb with grief. [22]Is there no medicine in Gilead? Is there no physician there? Why doesn't God do something? Why doesn't he help?

Jer 9:1. Oh, that my eyes were a fountain of tears; I would weep forever; I would sob day and night for the slain of my people!

Jer 13:14. And I will smash fathers and sons against each other, says the Lord. I will not let pity nor mercy spare them from utter destruction. [16]Give glory to the Lord your God before it is too late, before he causes deep, impenetrable darkness to fall upon you so that you stumble and fall upon the dark mountains; then, when you look for light, you will find only terrible darkness. [22]And if you ask yourself, Why is all this happening to me? it is because of the grossness of your sins; that is why you have been raped and destroyed by the invading army.

Jer 14:10. But the Lord replies: You have loved to wander far from me and have not tried to follow in my paths. Now I will no longer accept you as my people; now I will remember all the evil you have done, and punish your sins. [12]When they fast, I will not pay any attention; when they present their offerings and sacrifices to me, I will not accept them. What I will give them in return is war and famine and disease.

Jer 21:14. And I myself will destroy you for your sinfulness, says the Lord. I will light a fire in the forests that will burn up everything in its path.

Jer 25:31. That cry of judgment will reach the farthest ends of the earth, for the Lord has a case against all the nations—all mankind. He will slaughter all the wicked.

Jer 36:31. And I will punish him and his family and his officials because of their sins. I will pour out upon them all the evil I promised—upon them and upon all the people of Judah and Jerusalem, for they wouldn't listen to my warnings.

Jer 44:23. The very reason all these terrible things have befallen you is because you have burned incense and sinned against the Lord and refused to obey him.

Jer 49:12. The Lord says to Edom: If the innocent must suffer, how much more must you! You must not go unpunished! You must drink this cup of judgment!

Lam 3:39. Why then should we, mere humans as we are, murmur and complain when punished for our sins?

Lam 4:22. Israel's exile for her sins will end at last, but Edom's never.

Lam 5:16. Our glory is gone. The crown is fallen from our head. Woe upon us for our sins. [17]Our hearts are faint and weary; our eyes grow dim.

Ezk 3:18. If you refuse to warn the wicked when I want you to tell them, you are under the penalty of death, therefore repent and save your life—they will die in their sins, but I will punish you. I will demand your blood for theirs. [19]But if you warn them and they keep on sinning, and refuse to repent, they will die in their sins, but you are blameless—you have done all you could. [20]And if a good man becomes bad, and you refuse to warn him of the consequences, and the Lord destroys him, his previous good deeds won't help him—he shall die in his sin. But I will hold you responsible for his death, and punish you.

Ezk 5:4. Then take a few hairs out and throw them into the fire, for a fire shall come from this remnant and destroy all Israel. [8]Therefore the Lord God says, I, even I, am against you and will punish you publicly while all the nations watch. [9]Because of the terrible sins you have committed, I will punish you more terribly than I have ever done before or will ever do again. [10]Fathers will eat their own sons, and sons will eat their fathers; and those who survive will be scattered into all the world. [11]For I promise you: Because you have defiled my Temple with idols and evil sacrifices, therefore I will not spare you nor pity you at all. [12]One-third of you will die from famine and disease; one third will be slaughtered by the enemy; and one-third I will scatter to the winds, sending the sword of the enemy chasing after you. [13]Then at last my anger will be appeased. And all Israel will know that what I threaten, I do. [14]So I will make a public example of you before all the surrounding nations and before everyone traveling past the ruins of your land. [15]You will become a laughingstock to the world and an awesome example to everyone, for all to see what happens when the Lord turns against an entire nation in furious rebuke. I, the Lord, have spoken it! [16]I will shower you with deadly arrows of famine to destroy you. The famine will become more and more serious until every bit of bread is gone. [17]And not only famine will come, but wild animals will attack you and kill you and your families; disease and war will stalk your land, and the sword of the enemy will slay you; I, the Lord, have spoken it!

Ezk 7:4. "I will turn my eyes away and show no pity; I will repay you in full, and you shall know I am the Lord." [5, 6]The Lord God says: "With one blow after another I will finish you. The end has come; your final doom is waiting."

Ezk 9:5. Then I heard the Lord tell the other men: "Follow him through the city and kill everyone whose forehead isn't marked. Spare not nor pity them—[6]kill them all—old and young, girls, women and little children; but don't touch anyone with the mark. And begin right here at the Temple." And so they began by killing the seventy elders. [7]And he said, "Defile the Temple! Fill its courts with the bodies of those you kill! God!" And they went out through the city and did as they were told. [10]"And so I will not spare them nor have any pity on them, and I will fully repay them for all that they have done."

Ezk 11:21. "But as for those now in Jerusalem, who long for idols, I will repay them fully for their sins," the Lord God says.

Ezk 18:1. Then the Lord's message came to me again. [2]"Why do people use this proverb about the land of Israel: The children are punished for their fathers' sins? [3]As I live, says the Lord God, you will not use this proverb any more in Israel, [4]for all souls are mine to judge—fathers and sons alike—and my rule is this: It is for a man's own sins that he will die. [5]But if a man is just and does what is lawful and right, [6]and has not gone out to the mountains to feast before the idols of Israel and worship them, and does not commit adultery, nor lie with any woman during the time of her menstruation, [7]and is a merciful creditor, not holding on to the items given to him in pledge by poor debtors, and is no robber, but gives food to the hungry and clothes to those in need, [8]and grants loans without interest, and stays away from sin, and is honest and fair when judging others, [9]and obeys my laws—that man is just, says the Lord, and he shall surely live. [10]But if that man has a son who is a robber or murderer and who fulfills none of his responsibilities, [11]who refuses to obey the laws of God, but worships idols on the mountains and commits adultery, [12]and oppresses the poor and needy, and robs his debtors by refusing to let them redeem what they have given him in pledge, and loves idols and worships them, [13]and loans out his money at interest—shall that man live? No! He shall surely die and it is his own fault. 14But if this sinful man has, in turn, a son who sees all his father's wickedness, so that he fears God and decides against that kind of life, 15and doesn't go up on the mountains to feast before the idols and worship them, and does not commit adultery, 16and is fair to those who borrow from him and doesn't rob them, but feeds the hungry and clothes the needy, 17and helps the poor and does not loan money at interest, and obeys my laws—he shall not die because of his father's sins; he shall surely live. 18But his father shall die for his own sins because he is cruel and robs and does wrong. 19'What?' you ask. 'Doesn't the son pay for his father's sins?' No! For if the son does what is right and keeps my laws, he shall surely live. 20The one who sins is the one who dies. The son shall not be punished for his father's sins, nor the father for his son's. The righteous person will be rewarded for his own goodness and the wicked person for his wickedness. 21But if a wicked person turns away from all his sins and begins to obey my laws and do what is just and right, he shall surely live and not die. 22All his past sins will be forgotten, and he shall live because of his goodness. 23Do you think I like to see the wicked die? asks the Lord. Of course not! I only want him to turn from his wicked ways and live. 24However, if a righteous person turns to sinning and acts like any other sinner, should he be allowed to live? No, of course not. All his previous goodness will be forgotten and he shall die for his sins. 25Yet you say: 'The Lord isn't being fair!' Listen to me, O people of Israel. Am I the one who is unfair, or is it you? 26When a good man turns away from being good and begins sinning and dies in his sins, he dies for the evil he has done. 27And if a wicked person turns away from his wickedness and obeys the law, and does right, he shall save his soul, 28for he has thought it over and decided to turn from his sins and live a good life. He shall surely live—he shall not die. 29And yet the people of Israel keep saying: 'The Lord is unfair!' O people of Israel, it is you who are unfair, not I. 30I will judge each of you, O Israel, and punish or reward each according to your own actions. Oh, turn from your sins while there is yet time. 31Put them behind you and receive a new heart and a new spirit. For why will you die, O Israel? 32I do not enjoy seeing you die, the Lord God says. Turn, turn and live!"

Ezk 20:8. But they rebelled against me and would not listen. They didn't get rid of their idols, nor forsake the gods of Egypt. Then I thought, I will pour out my fury upon them and fulfill my anger against them while they are still in Egypt.

Ezk 22:14. How strong and courageous will you be then, in my day of reckoning? For I, the Lord, have spoken, and I will do all that I have said. 20Therefore the Lord God says: Because you are worthless dross, I will bring you to my crucible in Jerusalem, to smelt you with the heat of my wrath. 21I will blow the fire of my wrath upon you. 31And so the Lord God says: I will pour out my anger upon you; I will consume you with the fire of my wrath. I have heaped upon you the full penalty for all your sins.

Ezk 24:13. It is the rust and corruption of your filthy lewdness, of worshiping your idols. And now, because I wanted to cleanse you and you refused, remain filthy until my fury has accomplished all its terrors upon you! 14I, the Lord, have spoken it; it shall come to pass and I will do it.

Ezk 25:7. Therefore I will lay my hand heavily upon you, delivering you to many nations for devastation. I will cut you off from being a nation any more. I will destroy you; then you shall know I am the Lord.

Ezk 33:7. So with you, son of dust. I have appointed you as a watchman for the people of Israel; therefore listen to what I say and warn them for me. 8When I say to the wicked, "O wicked man, you will die!" and you don't tell him what I say, so that he does not repent—that wicked person will die in his sins, but I will hold you responsible for his death. 9But if you warn him to repent and he doesn't, he will die in his sin, and you will not be responsible. 10O people of Israel, you are saying: "Our sins are heavy upon us; we pine away with guilt. How can we live?" 11Tell them: As I live, says the Lord God, I have no pleasure in the death of the wicked; *I desire that the wicked turn from his evil ways and live.* Turn, turn from your wickedness, for why will you die, O Israel? 12For the good works of a righteous man will not save him if he turns to sin; and the sins of an evil man will not destroy him if he repents and turns from his sins. 13I have said the good man will live. But if he sins, expecting his past goodness to save him, then none of his good deeds will be remembered. I will destroy him for his sins. 14And when I tell the wicked he will die and then he turns from his sins and does what is fair and right—15if he gives back the borrower's pledge and returns what he has stolen and walks along the paths of right, not doing evil—he shall surely live. He shall not die. 16None of his past sins shall be brought up against him, for he has turned to the good and shall surely live. 17And yet your people are saying the Lord isn't fair. The trouble is *they* aren't fair. 18For again I say, when the good man turns to evil, he shall die. 19But if the wicked turns from his wickedness and does what's fair and just, he shall live. 20Yet you are saying the Lord isn't fair. But I will judge each of you in accordance with his deeds.

Dan 12:2. And many of those whose bodies lie dead and buried will rise up, some to everlasting life and some to shame and everlasting contempt.

Hos 2:9. But now I will take back the wine and ripened corn I constantly supplied, and the clothes I gave her to cover her nakedness—I will no longer give her rich harvests of grain in its season, or wine at the time of the grape harvest. 10Now I will expose her nakedness in public for all her lovers to see, and no one will be able to rescue her from my hand. 11I will put an end to all her joys, her parties, holidays, and feasts. 12I will destroy her vineyards and her orchards—gifts she claims her lovers gave her—and let them grow into a jungle; wild animals will eat their fruit. [13]For all the incense that she burned to Baal her idol and for the times when she put on her earrings and jewels and went out looking for her lovers, and deserted me: for all these things I will punish her, says the Lord.

Hos 5:4. Your deeds won't let you come to God again, for the spirit of adultery is deep within you, and you cannot know the Lord. [5]The very arrogance of Israel testifies against her in my court. She will stumble under her load of guilt, and Judah, too, shall fall. [6]Then at last, they will come with their flocks and herds to sacrifice to God, but it will be too late—they will not find him. He has withdrawn from them and they are left alone. [9]Hear this announcement, Israel: When your day of punishment comes, you will become a heap of rubble.

Hos 7:12. But as she flies, I throw my net over her and bring her down like a bird from the sky; I will punish her for all her evil ways. [13]Woe to my people for deserting me; let them perish, for they have sinned against me. I wanted to redeem them but their hard hearts would not accept the truth.

Hos 9:7. The time of Israel's punishment has come; the day of recompense is almost here and soon Israel will know it all too well. "The prophets are crazy"; "The inspired men are mad." Yes, so they mock, for the nation is weighted with sin, and shows only hatred for those who love God. [9]The things my people do are as depraved as what they did in Gibeah long ago. The Lord does not forget. He will surely punish them. [15]All their wickedness began at Gilgal; there I began to hate them. I will drive them from my land because of their idolatry. I will love them no more, for all their leaders are rebels.

Hos 10:8. And the idol altars of Aven at Bethel where Israel sinned will crumble. Thorns and thistles will grow up to surround them. And the people will cry to the mountains and hills to fall upon them and crush them. Lk 23:30; Rev 6:16; 9:6.

Hos 12:2. But the Lord is bringing a lawsuit against Judah, too. Judah also will be justly punished for his ways. [14]But Ephraim has bitterly provoked the Lord. The Lord will sentence him to death as payment for his sins.

Hos 13:1. It used to be when Israel spoke, the nations shook with fear, for he was a mighty prince; but he worshiped Baal and sealed his doom. [3]They shall disappear like morning mist, like dew that quickly dries away, like chaff blown by the wind, like a cloud of smoke.

Hos 14:9. Whoever is wise, let him understand these things. Whoever is intelligent, let him listen. For the paths of the Lord are true and right, and good men walk along them. But sinners trying it will fail.

Joel 2:1. Sound the alarm in Jerusalem! Let the blast of the warning trumpet be heard upon my holy mountain! Let everyone tremble in fear, for the day of the Lord's judgment approaches. [2]It is a day of darkness and gloom, of black clouds and thick darkness. What a mighty army! It covers the mountains like night! How great, how powerful these "people" are! The likes of them have not been seen before, and never will again throughout the generations of the world!

Joel 3:13. Now let the sickle do its work; the harvest is ripe and waiting. Tread the winepress, for it is full to overflowing with the wickedness of these men. [14]Multitudes, multitudes waiting in the valley for the verdict of their doom! For the Day of the Lord is near, in the Valley of Judgment. [15]The sun and moon will be darkened and the stars withdraw their light. [16]The Lord shouts from his Temple in Jerusalem and the earth and sky begin to shake. But to his people Israel, the Lord will be very gentle. He is their Refuge and Strength.

Amos 3:2. Of all the peoples of the earth, I have chosen you alone. That is why I must punish you the more for all your sins.

Amos 5:18. You say, "If only the Day of the Lord were here, for then God would deliver us from all our foes." But you have no idea what you ask. For that day will *not* be light or prosperity, but darkness and doom! How terrible the darkness will be for you; not a ray of joy or hope will shine. [19]In that day you will be as a man who is chased by a lion—and met by a bear, or a man in a dark room who leans against a wall—and puts his hand on a snake. [20]Yes, that will be a dark and hopeless day for you.

Amos 8:14. And those who worship the idols of Samaria, Dan, and Beersheba shall fall and never rise again.

Amos 9:1. I saw the Lord standing beside the altar, saying, "Smash the tops of the pillars and shake the Temple until the pillars crumble and the roof crashes down upon the people below. Though they run, they will not escape; they all will be killed. [2]Though they dig down to Sheol, I will reach down and pull them up; though they climb into the heavens, I will bring them down. [3]Though they hide among the rocks at the top of Carmel, I will search them out and capture them. Though they hide at the bottom of the ocean, I will send the sea-serpent after them to bite and destroy them. [4]Though they volunteer for exile, I will command the sword to kill them there. I will see to it that they receive evil and not good." [5]The Lord God of Hosts touches the land and it melts, and all its people mourn. It rises like the river Nile in Egypt, and then sinks again. [10]"But all these sinners who say, 'God will not touch us,' will die by the sword."

Jon 3:9. Who can tell? Perhaps even yet God will decide to let us live, and will hold back his fierce anger from destroying us.

Mic 2:3. But the Lord God says, I will reward your evil with evil; nothing can stop me; never again will you be proud and haughty after I am through with you.

Mic 6:13. Therefore I will wound you! I will make your hearts miserable for all your sins.

Nah 1:2. God is jealous over those he loves; that is why he takes vengeance on those who hurt them. He furiously destroys their enemies. [8]But he sweeps away his enemies with an overwhelming flood; he pursues them all night long. [9]What are you thinking of, Nineveh, to defy the Lord? He will stop you with one blow; he won't need to strike again. [10]He tosses his enemies into the fire like a tangled mass of thorns. They burst into flames like straw.

Zeph 1:12. I will search with lanterns in Jerusalem's darkest corners to find and punish those who sit contented in their sins, indifferent to God, thinking he will let them alone. [13]They are the very ones whose property will be plundered by the enemy, whose homes will be ransacked; they will never have a chance to live in the new homes they have built. They will never drink wine from the vineyards they have planted. [14]That terrible day is near. Swiftly it comes—a day when strong men will weep bitterly. [15]It is a day of the wrath of God poured out; it is a day of terrible distress and anguish, a day of ruin and desolation, of darkness, gloom, clouds, blackness. [16]Trumpet calls and battle cries; down go the walled cities and strongest battlements! [17]I will make you as helpless as a blind man searching for a path, because you have sinned against the Lord; therefore your blood will be poured out into the dust and your bodies will lie there rotting on the ground. [18]Your silver and gold will be of no use to you in that day of the Lord's wrath. You cannot ransom yourselves with it. For the whole land will be devoured by the fire of his jealousy. He will make a speedy riddance of all the people of Judah.

Zech 5:2. "What do you see?" he asked. "A flying scroll!" I replied. "It appears to be about thirty feet long and fifteen feet wide!" [3]"This scroll," he told me, "represents the words of God's curse going out over the entire land. It says that all who steal and lie have been judged and sentenced to death. [4]I am sending this curse into the home of every thief and everyone who swears falsely by my name," says the Lord of Hosts. "And my curse shall remain upon his home and completely destroy it."

Mal 3:17. "They shall be mine," says the Lord of Hosts, "in that day when I make up my jewels. And I will spare them as a man spares an obedient and dutiful son. [18]Then you will see the difference between God's treatment of good men and bad, between those who serve him and those who don't."

Mal 4:1. "Watch now," the Lord of Hosts declares, "the day of judgment is coming, burning like a furnace. The proud and wicked will be burned up like straw; like a tree, they will be consumed—roots and all."

Mt 3:7. But when he saw many Pharisees and Sadducees coming to be baptized, he denounced them. "You sons of snakes!" he warned. "Who said that you could escape the coming wrath of God? [Lk 3:7.] [10]And even now the axe of God's judgment is poised to chop down every unproductive tree. They will be chopped and burned. [Mt 7:19; Lk 13:7, 9.] [12]He will separate the chaff from the grain, burning the chaff with never-ending fire, and storing away the grain." Lk 3:17.

Mt 5:19. And so if anyone breaks the least commandment, and teaches others to, he shall be the least in the Kingdom of Heaven. *vs.* 20–30.

Mt 7:13. Heaven can be entered only through the narrow gate! The highway to hell is broad, and its gate is wide enough for all the multitudes who choose its easy way. [Lk 13:24, 25.] [26]But those who hear my instructions and ignore them are foolish, like a man who builds his house on sand. [27]For when the rains and floods come, and storm winds beat against his house, it will fall with a mighty crash. Lk 6:49.

Mt 8:12. And many an Israelite—those for whom the Kingdom was prepared—shall be cast into outer darkness, into the place of weeping and torment.

Mt 10:28. Don't be afraid of those who can kill only your bodies—but can't touch your souls! Fear only God who can destroy both soul and body in hell. [Lk 12:4, 5.] [33]But if anyone publicly denies me, I will openly deny him before my Father in heaven. Mk 8:38; Lk 9:26.

Mt 11:23. And Capernaum, though highly honored, shall go down to hell!

Mt 13:12, 13. "For to him who has will more be given," he told them, "and he will have great plenty; but from him who has not, even the little he has will be taken away. That is why I use these illustrations, so people will hear and see but not understand. [Mk 4:25; Lk 8:18; 19:26.] [14]This fulfills the prophecy of Isaiah: 'They hear, but don't understand; they look, but don't see! [15]For their hearts are fat and heavy, and their ears are dull, and they have closed their eyes in sleep, [16]so they won't see and hear and understand and turn to God again, and let me heal them.' [Mk 4:11, 12; Jn 12:40.] [30]Let both grow together until the harvest, and I will tell the reapers to sort out the thistles and burn them, and put the wheat in the barn. [38]The field is the world, and the seed represents the people of the Kingdom; the thistles are the people belonging to Satan. [39]The enemy who sowed the thistles among the wheat is the devil; the harvest is the end of the world, and the reapers are the angels. [40]Just as in this story the thistles are separated and burned, so shall it be at the end of the world: [41]I will send my angels and they will separate out of the Kingdom every temptation and all who are evil, [42]and throw them into the furnace and burn them. There shall be weeping and gnashing of teeth. [49]That is the way it will be at the end of the world—the angels will come and separate the wicked people from the godly, [50]casting the wicked into the fire; there shall be weeping and gnashing of teeth."

Mt 15:13. Jesus replied, "Every plant not planted by my Father shall be rooted up." Jn 15:2.

Mt 18:7. Woe upon the world for all its evils. Temptation to do wrong is inevitable, but woe to the man who does the tempting. [8]So if your hand or foot causes you to sin, cut if off and throw it away. Better to enter heaven crippled than to be in hell with both of your hands and feet. [9]And if your eye causes you to sin, gouge it out and throw it away. Better to enter heaven with one eye than to be in hell with two. [Mk 9:43, 44.] [34]Then the angry king sent the man to the torture chamber until he had paid every last penny due. [35]So shall my heavenly Father do to you if you refuse to truly forgive your brothers. Mk 11:26–28.

Mt 21:41. The Jewish leaders replied, "He will put the wicked men to a horrible death, and lease the vineyard to others who will pay him promptly." [Mk 12:1–9.] [44]"All who stumble on this rock of truth shall be broken, but those it falls on will be scattered as dust." Lk 20:18.

Mt 22:13. Then the king said to his aides, "Bind him hand and foot and throw him out into the outer darkness where there is weeping and gnashing of teeth." Mt 8:12.

Mt 23:33. Snakes! Sons of vipers! How shall you escape the judgment of hell? Mt 12:34.

Mt 24:50. Your Lord will arrive unannounced and unexpected, [51]and severely whip you and send you off to the judgment of the hypocrites; there will be weeping and gnashing of teeth. Lk 12:46, 47.

Mt 25:30. "And throw the useless servant out into outer darkness: there shall be weeping and gnashing of teeth." [32]And all the nations shall be gathered before me. And I will separate the people as a shepherd separates the sheep from the goats, [33]and place the sheep at my right hand, and the goats at my left. [41]Then I will turn to those on my left and say, "Away with you, you cursed ones, into the eternal fire prepared for the devil and his demons." [46]And they shall go away into eternal punishment; but the righteous into everlasting life.

Mt 26:24. For I must die just as was prophesied, but woe to the man by whom I am betrayed. Far better for that one if he had never been born. Mk 14:21; Lk 22:22.

Mk 12:40. But they shamelessly cheat widows out of their homes and then, to cover up the kind of men they really are, they pretend to be pious by praying long prayers in public. Because of this, their punishment will be the greater.

Mk 16:16. But those who refuse to believe will be condemned.

Lk 9:24. Whoever loses his life for my sake will save it, but whoever insists on keeping his life will lose it; [25]and what profit is there in gaining the whole world when it means forfeiting one's self? Mt 16:26; Mk 8:36.

Lk 13:3. "And don't you realize that you also will perish unless you leave your evil ways and turn to God?" [*v.* 5.] [6]Then he used this illustration: "A man planted a fig tree in his garden and came again and again to see if he could find any fruit on it, but he was always disappointed. [7]Finally he told his gardener to cut it down. 'I've waited three years and there hasn't been a single fig!' he said. 'Why bother with it any longer? It's taking up space we can use for something else.' [Mt 21:19.] [27]And he will reply, 'I tell you, I don't know you. You can't come in here, guilty as you are. Go away.' [28]And there will be great weeping and gnashing of teeth as you stand outside and see Abraham, Isaac, Jacob, and all the prophets within the Kingdom of God." Mt 7:23.

Lk 16:22. Finally the beggar died and was carried by the angels to be with Abraham in the place of the righteous dead. The rich man also died and was buried, [23]and his soul went into hell. There, in torment, he saw Lazarus in the far distance with Abraham. [24]"Father Abraham," he shouted, "have some pity! Send Lazarus over here if only to dip the tip of his finger in water and cool my tongue, for I am in anguish in these flames." [25]But Abraham said to him, "Son, remember that during your lifetime you had everything you wanted, and Lazarus had nothing. So now he is here being comforted and you are in anguish. [26]And besides, there is a great chasm separating us, and anyone wanting to come to you from here is stopped at its edge; and no one over there can cross to us." [27]Then the rich man said, "O Father Abraham, then please send him to my father's home—[28]for I have five brothers—to warn them about this place of torment lest they come here when they die."

Lk 17:1. "There will always be temptations to sin," Jesus said one day to his disciples, "but woe to the man who does the tempting. [2]If he were thrown into the sea with a huge rock tied to his neck, he would be far better off than facing the punishment in store for those who harm these little children's souls."

Lk 19:27. And now about these enemies of mine who revolted—bring them in and execute them before me.

Lk 23:30. Mankind will beg the mountains to fall on them and crush them, and the hills to bury them. [Isa 2:19.] [31]For if such things as this are done to me, the Living Tree, what will they do to you?

Jn 3:15. So that anyone who believes in me will have eternal life. [16]For God loved the world so much that he gave his only Son so that anyone who believes in him shall not perish but have eternal life. [18]There is no eternal doom awaiting those who trust him to save them. But those who don't trust him have already been tried and condemned for not believing in the only Son of God. [36]And all who trust him—God's Son—to save them have eternal life; those who don't believe and obey him shall never see heaven, but the wrath of God remains upon them.

Jn 5:14. But afterwards Jesus found him in the Temple and told him, "Now you are well; don't sin as you did before, or something even worse may happen to you. [29]And shall rise again—those who have done good, to eternal life; and those who have continued in evil, to judgment."

Jn 7:34. You will search for me but not find me. And you won't be able to come where I am! Jn 8:21.

Jn 17:12. During my time here I have kept safe within your family all of these you gave me. I guarded them so that not one perished, except the son of hell, as the Scriptures foretold.

Acts 1:18. He bought a field with the money he received for his treachery and falling headlong there, he burst open, spilling out his bowels. [25]"Show us which of these men you have chosen as an apostle to replace Judas the traitor, who has gone on to his proper place."

Acts 3:23. Anyone who will not listen to him [the Prophet] shall be utterly destroyed.

Rom 1:18. But God shows his anger from heaven against all sinful, evil men who push away the truth from them.

Rom 2:5. But no, you won't listen; and so you are saving up terrible punishment for yourselves because of your stubbornness in refusing to turn from your sin; for there is going to come a day of wrath when God will be the just Judge of all the world. [8]But he will terribly punish those who fight against the truth of God and walk in evil ways—God's anger will be poured out upon them. [9]There will be sorrow and suffering for Jews and Gentiles alike who keep on sinning. [12-15]He will punish sin wherever it is found. He will punish the heathen when they sin, even though they never had God's written laws, for down in their hearts they know right from wrong. . . . And God will punish the Jews for sinning because they have his written laws but don't obey them.

Rom 5:12. When Adam sinned, sin entered the entire human race. His sin spread death throughout all the world, so everything began to grow old and die, for all sinned. [21]Before, sin ruled over all men and brought them to death, but now God's kindness rules instead, giving us right standing with God and resulting in eternal life through Jesus Christ our Lord.

Rom 6:16. Don't you realize that you can choose your own master? You can choose sin (with death) or else obedience (with acquittal). [21]And what was the result? Evidently not good, since you are ashamed now even to think about those things you used to do, for all of them end in eternal doom.

Rom 8:2. For the power of the life-giving Spirit —and this power is mine through Christ Jesus— has freed me from the vicious circle of sin and death. [6]Following after the Holy Spirit leads to life and peace, but following after the old nature leads to death, [7]because the old sinful nature within us is against God. It never did obey God's laws and it never will. [13]For if you keep on following it you are lost and will perish, but if through the power of the Holy Spirit you crush it and its evil deeds, you shall live.

Rom 9:22. Does not God have a perfect right to show his fury and power against those who are fit only for destruction, those he has been patient with for all this time?

Rom 11:22. Notice how God is both kind and severe. He is very hard on those who disobey.

Rom 14:23. But anyone who believes that something he wants to do is wrong shouldn't do it. He sins if he does, for he thinks it is wrong, and so for him it *is* wrong. Anything that is done apart from what he feels is right is sin.

1 Cor 3:17. If anyone defiles and spoils God's home, God will destroy him. For God's home is holy and clean, and you are that home.

1 Cor 5:5. And cast out this man from the fellowship of the church and into Satan's hands, to punish him, in the hope that his soul will be saved when our Lord Jesus Christ returns. [13]God alone is the Judge of those on the outside. But you yourselves must deal with this man and put him out of your church.

1 Cor 6:9, 10. Don't you know that those doing such things have no share in the Kingdom of God? Don't fool yourselves. Those who live immoral lives, who are idol worshipers, adulterers or homosexuals—will have no share in his kingdom. Neither will thieves or greedy people, drunkards, slanderers, or robbers.

1 Cor 9:27. Like an athlete I punish my body, treating it roughly, training it to do what it should, not what it wants to. Otherwise I fear that after enlisting others for the race, I myself might be declared unfit and ordered to stand aside.

1 Cor 10:5. Yet after all this most of them did not obey God, and he destroyed them in the wilderness. [6]From this lesson we are warned that we must not desire evil things as they did, [7]nor worship idols as they did. (The Scriptures tell us, "The people sat down to eat and drink and then got up to dance" in worship of the golden calf.) [8]Another lesson for us is what happened when some of them sinned with other men's wives, and 23,000 fell dead in one day. [9]And don't try the Lord's patience—they did, and died from snake bites. [10]And don't murmur against God and his dealings with you, as some of them did, for that is why God sent his Angel to destroy them. [11]All these things happened to them as examples—as object lessons to us—to warn us against doing the same things; they were written down so that we could read about them and learn from them in these last days as the world nears its end.

1 Cor 15:21. Death came into the world because of what one man (Adam) did, and it is because of what this other man (Christ) has done that now there is the resurrection from the dead. [22]Everyone died because all of us are related to Adam, being members of his sinful race, and wherever there is sin, death results. But all who are related to Christ will rise again.

2 Cor 7:10. But the sorrow of the man who is not a Christian is not the sorrow of true repentance and does not prevent eternal death.

Gal 3:10. Yes, and those who depend on the Jewish laws to save them are under God's curse, for the Scriptures point out very clearly, "Cursed is everyone who at any time breaks a single one of these laws that are written in God's Book of the Law."

Gal 5:19. But when you follow your own wrong inclinations your lives will produce these evil results: impure thoughts, eagerness for lustful pleasure, [20]idolatry, spiritism (that is, encouraging the activity of demons), hatred and fighting, jealousy and anger, constant effort to get the best for yourself, complaints and criticisms, the feeling that everyone else is wrong except those in your own little group—and there will be wrong doctrine, [21]envy, murder, drunkenness, wild parties, and all that sort of thing. Let me tell you again as I have before, that anyone living that sort of life will not inherit the kingdom of God.

Gal 6:8. If he sows to please his own wrong desires, he will be planting seeds of evil and he will surely reap a harvest of spiritual decay and death.

Eph 5:5. You can be sure of this: The kingdom of Christ and of God will never belong to anyone who is impure or greedy, for a greedy person is really an idol worshiper—he loves and worships the good things of this life more than God. [6]Don't be fooled by those who try to excuse these sins, for the terrible wrath of God is upon all those who do them.

Phil 3:18. For I have told you often before, and I say it again now with tears in my eyes, there are many who walk along the Christian road who are really enemies of the cross of Christ. [19]Their future is eternal loss, for their god is their appetite: they are proud of what they should be ashamed of; and all they think about is this life here on earth.

Col 3:25. And if you don't do your best for him, he will pay you in a way that you won't like—for he has no special favorites who can get away with shirking.

1 Thess 1:10. And they speak of how you are looking forward to the return of God's Son from heaven—Jesus, whom God brought back to life—and he is our only Savior from God's terrible anger against sin.

1 Thess 5:3. When people are saying, "All is well, everything is quiet and peaceful"—then, all of a sudden, disaster will fall upon them as suddenly as a woman's birth pains begin when her child is born. And these people will not be able to get away anywhere—there will be no place to hide. Isa 13:8.

2 Thess 1:5. This is only one example of the fair, just way God does things, for he is using your sufferings to make you ready for his kingdom, [6]while at the same time he is preparing judgment and punishment for those who are hurting you. [7]And so I would say to you who are suffering, God will give you rest along with us when the Lord Jesus appears suddenly from heaven in flaming fire with his mighty angels, [8]bringing judgment on those who do not wish to know God, and who refuse to accept his plan to save them through our Lord Jesus Christ. [9]They will be punished in everlasting hell, forever separated from the Lord, never to see the glory of his power.

2 Thess 2:8. Then this wicked one will appear, whom the Lord Jesus will burn up with the breath of his mouth and destroy by his presence when he returns. [9]This man of sin will come as Satan's tool, full of satanic power, and will trick everyone with strange demonstrations, and will do great miracles. [10]He will completely fool those who are on their way to hell because they have said "no" to the Truth; they have refused to believe it and love it, and let it save them.

1 Tim 1:20. Hymenaeus and Alexander are two examples of this. I had to give them over to Satan to punish them until they could learn not to bring shame to the name of Christ.

1 Tim 5:24. Remember that some men, even pastors, lead sinful lives and everyone knows it. In such situations you can do something about it. But in other cases only the judgment day will reveal the terrible truth.

2 Tim 2:12. And if we think that our present service for him is hard, just remember that some day we are going to sit with him and rule with him. But if we give up when we suffer, and turn against Christ, then he must turn against us. [13]Even when we are too weak to have any faith left, he remains faithful to us and will help us, for he cannot disown us who are part of himself.

Heb 2:2. For since the messages from angels have always proved true and people have always been punished for disobeying them, [3]what makes us think that we can escape if we are indifferent to this great salvation announced by the Lord Jesus himself?

Heb 6:8. But if it keeps on having crops of thistles and thorns, the land is considered no good and is ready for condemnation and burning off.

Heb 10:27. There will be nothing to look forward to but the terrible punishment of God's awful anger which will consume all his enemies. [28]A man who refused to obey the laws given by Moses was killed without mercy if there were two or three witnesses to his sin. [29]Think how much more terrible the punishment will be for those who have trampled underfoot the Son of God and treated his cleansing blood as though it were common and unhallowed, and insulted and outraged the Holy Spirit who brings God's mercy to his people. [30]For we know him who said, "Justice belongs to me; I will repay them"; who also said, "The Lord himself will handle these cases." [31]It is a fearful thing to fall into the hands of the living God.

Jas 1:14. Temptation is the pull of man's own evil thoughts and wishes. [15]These evil thoughts lead to evil actions and afterwards to the death penalty from God.

Jas 5:1. Look here, you rich men, now is the time to cry and groan with anguished grief because of all the terrible troubles ahead of you. [2]Your wealth is even now rotting away, and your fine clothes are becoming mere moth-eaten rags. [3]The value of your gold and silver is dropping fast, yet it will stand as evidence against you, and eat your flesh like fire. That is what you have stored up for yourselves, to receive on that coming day of judgment. [20]That person who brings him back to God will have saved a wandering soul from death, bringing about the forgiveness of his many sins.

1 Pet 3:12. But the Lord's face is hard against those who do evil.

1 Pet 4:17. For the time has come for judgment, and it must begin first among God's own children.

And if even we who are Christians must be judged, what terrible fate awaits those who have never believed in the Lord? [18]If the righteous are barely saved, what chance will the godless have?

2 Pet 2:3. These teachers in their greed will tell you anything to get hold of your money. But God condemned them long ago and their destruction is on the way. [4]For God did not spare even the angels who sinned, but threw them into hell, chained in gloomy caves and darkness until the judgment day. [5]And he did not spare any of the people who lived in ancient times before the flood except Noah, the one man who spoke up for God, and his family of seven. At that time God completely destroyed the whole world of ungodly men with the vast flood. [6]Later, he turned the cities of Sodom and Gomorrah into heaps of ashes and blotted them off the face of the earth, making them an example for all the ungodly in the future to look back upon and fear. [7, 8]But at the same time the Lord rescued Lot out of Sodom because he was a good man, sick of the terrible wickedness he saw everywhere around him day after day. [9]So also the Lord can rescue you and me from the temptations that surround us, and continue to punish the ungodly until the day of final judgment comes. [12]But false teachers are fools—no better than animals. They do whatever they feel like; born only to be caught and killed, they laugh at the terrifying powers of the underworld which they know so little about; and they will be destroyed along with all the demons and powers of hell. [13]That is the pay these teachers will have for their sin. For they live in evil pleasures day after day. They are a disgrace and a stain among you, deceiving you by living in foul sin on the side while they join your love feasts as though they were honest men. [14]No woman can escape their sinful stare, and of adultery they never have enough. They make a game of luring unstable women. They train themselves to be greedy; and are doomed and cursed. [15]They have gone off the road and become lost like Balaam, the son of Beor, who fell in love with the money he could make by doing wrong; [16]but Balaam was stopped from his mad course when his donkey spoke to him with a human voice, scolding and rebuking him. [17]These men are as useless as dried-up springs of water, promising much and delivering nothing; they are as unstable as clouds driven by the storm winds. They are doomed to the eternal pits of darkness.

1 Jn 3:14. If we love other Christians it proves that we have been delivered from hell and given eternal life. But a person who doesn't have love for others is headed for eternal death. [15]Anyone who hates his Christian brother is really a murderer at heart; and you know that no one wanting to murder has eternal life within.

Jude 1:5. My answer to them is: Remember this fact—which you know already—that the Lord saved a whole nation of people out of the land of Egypt, and then killed every one of them who did not trust and obey him. [6]And I remind you of those angels who were once pure and holy, but turned to a life of sin. Now God has them chained up in prisons of darkness, waiting for the judgment day. [7]And don't forget the cities of Sodom and Gomorrah and their neighboring towns, all full of lust of every kind including lust of men for other men. Those cities were destroyed by fire and continue to be a warning to us that there is a hell in which sinners are punished. [11]Woe upon them! For they follow the example of Cain who killed his brother; and, like Balaam, they will do anything for money; and like Korah, they have disobeyed God and will die under his curse. [12]When these men join you at the love feasts of the church, they are evil smears among you, laughing and carrying on, gorging and stuffing themselves without a thought for others. They are like clouds blowing over dry land without giving rain, promising much, but producing nothing. They are like fruit trees without any fruit at picking time. They are not only dead, but doubly dead, for they have been pulled out, roots and all, to be burned. [13]All they leave behind them is shame and disgrace like the dirty foam left along the beach by the wild waves. They wander around looking as bright as stars, but ahead of them is the everlasting gloom and darkness that God has prepared for them. [14]Enoch, who lived seven generations after Adam, knew about these men and said this about them: "See, the Lord is coming with millions of his holy ones. [15]He will bring the people of the world before him in judgment, to receive just punishment, and to prove the terrible things they have done in rebellion against God, revealing all they have said against him."

Rev 2:22. Pay attention now to what I am saying: I will lay her upon a sickbed of intense affliction, along with all her immoral followers, unless they turn again to me, repenting of their sin with her; [23]and I will strike her children dead. And all the churches shall know that I am he who searches deep within men's hearts, and minds; I will give to each of you whatever you deserve.

Rev 3:3. Go back to what you heard and believed at first; hold on to it firmly and turn to me again. Unless you do, I will come suddenly upon you, unexpected as a thief, and punish you.

Rev 6:15. The kings of the earth, and world leaders and rich men, and high-ranking military officers, and all men great and small, slave and free, hid themselves in the caves and rocks of the mountains, [16]and cried to the mountains to crush them. "Fall on us," they pleaded, "and hide us from the face of the one sitting on the throne, and from the anger of the Lamb, [17]because the great day of their anger has come, and who can survive it?"

Rev 9:4. They were told not to hurt the grass or plants or trees, but to attack those people who did not have the mark of God on their foreheads. [5]They were not to kill them, but to torture them for five months with agony like the pain of scorpion stings. [6]In those days men will try to kill themselves but won't be able to—death will not come. They will long to die—but death will flee away! [15]They had been kept in readiness for that year and month and day and hour, and now they were turned loose to kill a third of all mankind. [18]The horses' heads looked much like lions', and smoke and fire and flaming sulphur billowed from their mouths, killing one-third of all mankind.

Rev 11:18. The nations were angry with you, but now it is your turn to be angry with them. It is time to judge the dead, and reward your servants—prophets and people alike, all who fear your Name, both great and small—and to destroy those who have caused destruction upon the earth.

Rev 14:9. Then a third angel followed them shouting, "Anyone worshiping the Creature from the sea and his statue and accepting his mark on the forehead or the hand, [10]must drink the wine of the anger of God; it is poured out undiluted into God's cup of wrath. And they will be tormented with fire and burning sulphur in the presence of the holy angels and the Lamb. [11]The smoke of their torture rises forever and ever, and they will have no relief day or night, for they have worshiped the Creature and his statue, and have been tattooed with the code of his name.

Rev 16:2. So the first angel left the temple and poured out his flask over the earth, and horrible, malignant sores broke out on everyone who had the mark of the Creature and was worshiping his statue. [3]The second angel poured out his flask upon the oceans, and they became like the watery blood of a dead man; and everything in all the oceans died. [4]The third angel poured his flask upon the rivers and springs and they became blood. [5]And I heard this angel of the waters declaring, "You are just in sending this judgment, O Holy One, who is and was, [6]for your saints and prophets have been martyred and their blood poured out upon the earth; and now, in turn, you have poured out the blood of those who murdered them; it is their just reward." [7]And I heard the angel of the altar say, "Yes, Lord God Almighty, your punishments are just and true." [8]Then the fourth angel poured out his flask upon the sun, causing it to scorch all men with its fire. [9]Everyone was burned by this blast of heat, and they cursed the name of God who sent the plagues—they did not change their mind and attitude to give him glory. [10]Then the fifth angel poured out his flask upon the throne of the Creature from the sea, and his kingdom was plunged into darkness. And his subjects gnawed their tongues in anguish, [11]and cursed the God of heaven for their pains and sores, but they refused to repent of all their evil deeds. [12]The sixth angel poured out his flask upon the great River Euphrates and it dried up so that the kings from the east could march their armies westward without hindrance. [13]And I saw three evil spirits disguised as frogs leap from the mouth of the Dragon, the Creature, and his False Prophet. [14]These miracle-working demons conferred with all the rulers of the world to gather them for battle against the Lord on that great coming Judgment Day of God Almighty. [15]"Take note: I will come as unexpectedly as a thief! Blessed are all who are awaiting me, who keep their robes in readiness and will not need to walk naked and ashamed." [16]And they gathered all the armies of the world near a place called, in Hebrew, Armageddon—the Mountain of Megiddo. [17]Then the seventh angel poured out his flask into the air; and a mighty shout came from the throne of the temple in heaven, saying, "It is finished!" [18]Then the thunder crashed and rolled, and lightning flashed; and there was a great earthquake of a magnitude unprecedented in human history. [19]The great city of "Babylon" split into three sections, and cities around the world fell in heaps of rubble; and so all of "Babylon's" sins were remembered in God's thoughts, and she was punished to the last drop of anger in the cup of the wine of the fierceness of his wrath. [20]And islands vanished, and mountains flattened out, [21]and there was an incredible hailstorm from heaven; hailstones weighing a hundred pounds fell from the sky onto the people below, and they cursed God because of the terrible hail.

Rev 18:5. For her sins are piled as high as heaven and God is ready to judge her for her crimes.

Rev 19:15. In his mouth he held a sharp sword to strike down the nations; he ruled them with an iron grip; and he trod the winepress of the fierceness of the wrath of Almighty God. [17]Then I saw an angel standing in the sunshine, shouting loudly to the birds, "Come! Gather together for the supper of the Great God! [18]Come and eat the flesh of kings, and captains, and great generals; of horses and riders; and of all humanity, both great and small, slave and free." [19]Then I saw the Evil Creature gathering the governments of the earth and their armies to fight against the one sitting on the horse and his army. [20]And the Evil Creature was captured, and with him the False Prophet, who could do mighty miracles when the Evil Creature was present—miracles that deceived all who had accepted the Evil Creature's mark, and who worshiped his statue. Both of them—the Evil Creature and his False Prophet—were thrown alive into the Lake of Fire that burns with sulphur. [21]And their entire army was killed with the sharp sword in the mouth of the one riding the white horse, and all the birds of heaven were gorged with their flesh.

Rev 20:10. Then the devil who had betrayed them will again be thrown into the Lake of Fire burning with sulphur where the Creature and False Prophet are, and they will be tormented day and night forever and ever. [15]And if anyone's name was not found recorded in the Book of Life, he was thrown into the Lake of Fire.

Rev 21:8. "But cowards who turn back from following me, and those who are unfaithful to me, and the corrupt, and murderers, and the immoral, and those conversing with demons, and idol worshipers and all liars—their doom is in the Lake that burns with fire and sulphur. This is the Second Death." [27]Nothing evil will be permitted in it [new Jerusalem]—no one immoral or dishonest.

Rev 22:19. And if anyone subtracts any part of these prophecies, God shall take away his share in the Tree of Life, and in the Holy City just described.

See *Judgments; Hell; Punishment.*

WIDOW Vows of, binding, Num 30:9. When daughters of priests, to be supported by their fathers, Lev 22:13. Priests forbidden to marry, Lev 21: 14, 15. Marriage of, authorized, Rom 7:3; 1 Cor 7: 39. Widows' dower, see *Dowry.*

UNCLASSIFIED SCRIPTURES RELATING TO. Ex 22:22. You must not exploit widows or orphans; [23]if you do so in any way, and they cry to me for my help, I will surely give it. [24]And my anger shall flame out against you, and I will kill you with enemy armies, so that your wives will be widows and your children fatherless.

Deut 10:18. He gives justice to the fatherless and widows. He loves foreigners and gives them food and clothing.

Deut 14:28. Every third year you are to use your entire tithe for local welfare programs: [29]Give it to the Levites who have no inheritance among you, or to foreigners, or to widows and orphans within your city, so that they can eat and be satisfied; and then Jehovah your God will bless you and your work.

Deut 16:11. It is a time to rejoice before the Lord with your family and household. And don't forget to include the local Levites, foreigners, widows, and orphans. Invite them to accompany you to the celebration at the sanctuary. [12]Remember! You were a slave in Egypt, so be sure to carry out this command. [13]Another celebration, the Festival of Shelters, must be observed for seven days at the end of the harvest season, after the grain is threshed and the grapes have been pressed. [14]This will be a happy time of rejoicing together with your family and servants. And don't forget to include the Levites, foreigners, orphans, and widows of your town.

Deut 24:17. Justice must be given to migrants and orphans and you must never accept a widow's garment in pledge of her debt. [19]If, when reaping your harvest, you forget to bring in a sheaf from the field, don't go back after it. Leave it for the migrants, orphans, and widows; then the Lord your God will bless and prosper all you do. [20]When you beat the olives from your olive trees, don't go over the boughs twice; leave anything remaining for the migrants, orphans, and widows. [21]It is the same for the grapes in your vineyard; don't glean the vines after they are picked, but leave what's left for those in need.

Deut 25:5. If a man's brother dies without a son, his widow must not marry outside the family; instead, her husband's brother must marry her and sleep with her. [6]The first son she bears to him shall be counted as the son of the dead brother, so that his name will not be forgotten. [7]But if the dead man's brother refuses to do his duty in this matter, refusing to marry the widow, then she shall go to the city elders and say to them, "My husband's brother refuses to let his brother's name continue —he refuses to marry me." [8]The elders of the city will then summon him and talk it over with him, and if he still refuses, [9]the widow shall walk over to him in the presence of the elders, pull his sandal from his foot and spit in his face. She shall then say, "This is what happens to a man who refuses to build his brother's house." [10]And ever afterwards his house shall be referred to as "the home of the man who had his sandal pulled off!"

Deut 27:19. Cursed is he who is unjust to the foreigner, the orphan, and the widow.

Job 22:5. Not at all! It is because of your wickedness! Your sins are endless! [9]You sent widows away without helping them.

Job 24:3. Poor widows must surrender the little they have as a pledge to get a loan. [21]For they have taken advantage of the childless who have no protecting sons. They refuse to help the needy widows.

Job 29:13. And I caused the widows' hearts to sing for joy.

Job 31:16. If I have hurt the poor or caused widows to weep. [22]If I have done any of these things, then let my arm be torn from its socket! Let my shoulder be wrenched out of place!

Ps 68:5. He is a father to the fatherless; he gives justice to the widows, for he is holy.

Ps 94:6. They murder widows, immigrants, and orphans.

Ps 146:9. He protects the immigrants, and cares for the orphans and widows.

Prov 15:25. The Lord . . . cares for widows.

Isa 1:17. Learn to do good, to be fair and to help . . . widows. [23]Your leaders are rebels, companions of thieves; all of them take bribes and won't defend the widows and orphans. Ezk 22:7.

Isa 10:1. Woe to unjust judges and to those who issue unfair laws, says the Lord, [2]so that there is no justice for the poor, the widows and orphans. Yes, it is true that they even rob the widows and fatherless children.

Jer 7:6. And stop exploiting orphans, widows and foreigners. . . . [7]Then, and only then, will I let you stay in this land that I gave to your fathers to keep forever.

Jer 22:3. Do what is right! . . . Protect the rights of aliens and immigrants, orphans and widows.

Jer 49:11. And let your widows depend upon me.

Zech 7:10. Tell them to stop oppressing widows and orphans.

Mal 3:5. I will move swiftly against . . . all those who cheat their hired hands or oppress widows.

Mt 23:14. Woe to you, Pharisees, and you other religious leaders. Hypocrites! . . . You are evicting widows from their homes. Mic 2:9; Mk 12:40; Lk 20:47.

Acts 6:1. There were rumblings of discontent. Those who spoke only Greek complained that their widows were being discriminated against, that they were not being given as much food, in the daily distribution, as the widows who spoke Hebrew.

1 Tim 5:3. The church should take loving care of women whose husbands have died, if they don't have anyone else to help them. [4]But if they have

children or grandchildren, these are the ones who should take the responsibility, for kindness should begin at home, supporting needy parents. This is something that pleases God very much. [5]The church should care for widows who are poor and alone in the world, if they are looking to God for his help and spending much time in prayer; [6]but not if they are spending their time running around gossiping, seeking only pleasure and thus ruining their souls. [9]A widow who wants to become one of the special church workers should be at least sixty years old and have been married only once. [10]She must be well thought of by everyone because of the good she has done. Has she brought up her children well? Has she been kind to strangers as well as to other Christians? Has she helped those who are sick and hurt? Is she always ready to show kindness? [11]The younger widows should not become members of this special group because after awhile they are likely to disregard their vow to Christ and marry again. [12]And so they will stand condemned because they broke their first promise. [16]Let me remind you again that a widow's relatives must take care of her, and not leave this to the church to do. Then the church can spend its money for the care of widows who are all alone and have nowhere else to turn.

Jas 1:27. The Christian who is pure and without fault, from God the Father's point of view, is the one who takes care of orphans and widows, and who remains true to the Lord—not soiled and dirtied by his contacts with the world.

INSTANCES OF. Naomi, Ruth 1:3. Ruth, Ruth chapters 1–4. The widow of Zarephath, who fed Elijah during a famine, 1 Kgs 17. The woman whose sons Elisha saved from being sold for debt, 2 Kgs 4:1–7. Anna, Lk 2:36, 37. The woman who gave two coins in the Temple, Mk 12:41–44; Lk 21:2; of Nain, whose only son Jesus raised from the dead, Lk 7:11–15.

FIGURATIVE. Isa 47:8; 54:4; Lam 1:1.

See *Woman; Marriage, Levirate.*

WIFE Called Lovely, Ezk 24:16; Helper, Gen 2:18–20. The judgment pronounced against Eve, Gen 3:16. Relation of, to husband, Gen 2:18, 23, 24; 1 Cor 11:3–12. Domestic duties of, Gen 18:6; Prov 31:13–27. Beloved, by Isaac, Gen 24:67; by Jacob, Gen 29:30. Slighted, Gen 29:31–33. Loyal, Gen 31:14–16. Unfaithful, Num 5:11–31; Potiphar's, Gen 39:7; Bathsheba, 2 Sam 11:2–5. Contentious, Zipporah, Ex 4:25. See *Unclassified Scriptures,* below. Idolatrous, Solomon's wives, 1 Kgs 11:4–8; Neh 13:26; Jezebel, 1 Kgs 21; 2 Kgs 9:30–37. Stubborn, Vashti, Esther 1:10–22. Tactful, Abigail, 1 Sam 25:3, 14–42.

Bought, Gen 29; Ex 21:7–11; Ruth 4:10. Obtained by violence, Judg 21. Procured, Gen 24; 34:4–10; 38:6.

Vows of, Num 30:6–16.

See *Divorce; Marriage; Virgin.*

UNCLASSIFIED SCRIPTURES RELATING TO. Gen 2:18. And the Lord God said, "It isn't good for man to be alone; I will make a companion for him, a helper suited to his needs." [23]"This is it!" Adam exclaimed. "She is part of my own bone and flesh! Her name is 'woman' because she was taken out of a man." [24]This explains why a man leaves his father and mother and is joined to his wife in such a way that the two become one person.

Gen 3:16. Then God said to the woman, "You shall bear children in intense pain and suffering; yet even so, you shall welcome your husband's affections, and he shall be your master."

Esther 1:20. "When this decree is published throughout your great kingdom, husbands everywhere, whatever their rank, will be respected by their wives!" [21]The king and all his aides thought this made good sense, so he followed Memucan's counsel, [22]and sent letters to all of his provinces, in all the local languages, stressing that every man should rule his home, and should assert his authority.

Ps 128:3. Your wife shall be contented in your home. And look at all those children! There they sit around the dinner table as vigorous and healthy as young olive trees. [4]That is God's reward to those who reverence and trust him.

Prov 12:4. A worthy wife is her husband's joy and crown; the other kind corrodes his strength and tears down everything he does.

Prov 14:1. A wise woman builds her house, while a foolish woman tears hers down by her own efforts.

Prov 18:22. The man who finds a wife finds a good thing; she is a blessing to him from the Lord.

Prov 19:13. A nagging wife annoys like constant dripping. [14]A father can give his sons homes and riches, but only the Lord can give them understanding wives.

Prov 25:24. It is better to live in a corner of an attic than in a beautiful home with a cranky, quarrelsome woman. Prov 21:9, 19.

Prov 30:21, 22, 23. There are three things that make the earth tremble—no, four it cannot stand: A slave who becomes a king. A rebel who prospers. A bitter woman when she finally marries. A servant girl who marries her mistress' husband.

Prov 31:10. If you can find a truly good wife, she is worth more than precious gems! [11]Her husband can trust her, and she will richly satisfy his needs. [12]She will not hinder him but help him all her life. [13]She finds wool and flax and busily spins it. [14]She buys imported foods, brought by ship from distant ports. [15]She gets up before dawn to prepare breakfast for her household, and plans the day's work for her servant girls. [16]She goes out to inspect a field, and buys it; with her own hands she plants a vineyard. [17]She is energetic, a hard worker, [18]and watches for bargains. She works far into the night! [19, 20]She sews for the poor, and generously gives to the needy. [21]She has no fear of winter for her household, for she has made warm clothes for all of them. [22]She also upholsters with finest tapestry; her own clothing is beautifully made—a purple gown of pure linen. [23]Her husband is well known, for he sits in the council chamber with the other civic leaders. [24]She makes belted linen garments to sell to the merchants. 25She is a woman of strength and dignity, and has no fear of old age. 26When she speaks, her words are wise, and kindness is the rule for everything she says. 27She watches carefully all that goes on throughout her household, and is never lazy. 28Her children stand and bless her; so does her husband. He praises her with these words: 29"There are many fine women in the world, but you are the best of them all!" 30Charm can be deceptive and beauty doesn't last, but a woman who fears and reverences God shall be greatly praised. 31Praise her for the many fine things she does. These good deeds of hers shall bring her honor and recognition from even the leaders of the nations.

1 Cor 7:2. But usually it is best to be married, each man having his own wife, and each woman having her own husband, because otherwise you might fall back into sin. 3The man should give his wife all that is her right as a married woman, and the wife should do the same for her husband: 4for a girl who marries no longer has full right to her own body, for her husband then has his rights to it, too; and in the same way the husband no longer has full right to his own body, for it belongs also to his wife. 5So do not refuse these rights to each other. The only exception to this rule would be the agreement of both husband and wife to refrain from the rights of marriage for a limited time, so that they can give themselves more completely to prayer. Afterwards, they should come together again so that Satan won't be able to tempt them because of their lack of self-control. 6I'm not saying you *must* marry; but you certainly *may* if you wish. 10Now, for those who are married I have a command, not just a suggestion. And it is not a command from me, for this what the Lord himself has said: A wife must not leave her husband. 11But if she is separated from him, let her remain single or else go back to him. And the husband must not divorce his wife. 12Here I want to add some suggestions of my own. These are not direct commands from the Lord, but they seem right to me: If a Christian has a wife who is not a Christian, but she wants to stay with him anyway, he must not leave her or divorce her. 13And if a Christian woman has a husband who isn't a Christian, and he wants her to stay with him, she must not leave him. 14For perhaps the husband who isn't a Christian may become a Christian with the help of his Christian wife. And the wife who isn't a Christian may become a Christian with the help of her Christian husband. Otherwise, if the family separates, the children might never come to know the Lord; whereas a united family may, in God's plan, result in the children's salvation. 16For, after all, there is no assurance to you wives that your husbands will be converted if they stay; and the same may be said to you husbands concerning your wives. 27Of course, if you already are married, don't separate because of this. But if you aren't, don't rush into it at this time. 28But if you men decide to go ahead anyway and get married now, it is all right; and if a girl gets married in times like these, it is no sin. However, marriage will bring extra problems that I wish you didn't have to face right now. 29The important thing to remember is that our remaining time is very short, (and so are our opportunities for doing the Lord's work). For that reason those who have wives should stay as free as possible for the Lord. 32In all you do, I want you to be free from worry. An unmarried man can spend his time doing the Lord's work and thinking how to please him. 33But a married man can't do that so well; he has to think about his earthly responsibilities and how to please his wife. 34His interests are divided. It is the same with a girl who marries. She faces the same problem. A girl who is not married is anxious to please the Lord in all she is and does. But a married woman must consider other things such as housekeeping and the likes and dislikes of her husband. 38So the person who marries does well, and the person who doesn't marry does even better. 39The wife is part of her husband as long as he lives; if her husband dies, then she may marry again, but only if she marries a Christian. 40But in my opinion she will be happier if she doesn't marry again; and I think I am giving you counsel from God's Spirit when I say this.

1 Cor 11:3. But there is one matter I want to remind you about: that a wife is responsible to her husband. 7Man's glory is the woman. 8The first man didn't come from woman, but the first woman came out of man. 9And Adam, the first man, was not made for Eve's benefit, but Eve was made for Adam. 11But remember that in God's plan men and women need each other. 12For although the first woman came out of man, all men have been born from women ever since, and both men and women come from God their Creator.

1 Cor 14:34. Women should be silent during the church meetings. They are not to take part in the discussion, for they are subordinate to men as the Scriptures also declare. 35If they have any questions to ask, let them ask their husbands at home, for it is improper for women to express their opinions in church meetings.

Eph 5:22. You wives must submit to your husbands' leadership in the same way you submit to the Lord. 23For a husband is in charge of his wife in the same way Christ is in charge of his body the church. (He gave his very life to take care of it and be its Savior!) 24So you wives must willingly obey your husbands in everything, just as the church obeys Christ. 25And you husbands, show the same kind of love to your wives as Christ showed to the church when he died for her. 28That is how husbands should treat their wives, loving them as parts of themselves. For since a man and his wife are now one, a man is really doing himself a favor and loving himself when he loves his wife! 31"A man must leave his father and mother when he marries, so that he can be perfectly joined to his wife, and the two shall be one." 33So again I say, a man must love his wife as a part of himself; and the wife must see to it that she deeply respects her husband—obeying, praising and honoring him.

Col 3:18. You wives, submit yourselves to your husbands, for that is what the Lord has planned for you. [19]And you husbands must be loving and kind to your wives and not bitter against them, nor harsh.

1 Tim 3:11. Their wives must be thoughtful, not heavy drinkers, not gossipers, but faithful in everything they do.

1 Tim 5:9. A widow who wants to become one of the special church workers should be at least sixty years old and have been married only once. [10]She must be well thought of by everyone because of the good she has done. Has she brought up her children well? Has she been kind to strangers as well as to other Christians? Has she helped those who are sick and hurt? Is she always ready to show kindness? [14]So I think it is better for these younger widows to marry again and have children, and take care of their own homes; then no one will be able to say anything against them.

Tit 2:3. Teach the older women to be quiet and respectful in everything they do. They must not go around speaking evil of others and must not be heavy drinkers, but they should be teachers of goodness. [4]These older women must train the younger women to live quietly, to love their husbands and their children, [5]and to be sensible and clean minded, spending their time in their own homes, being kind and obedient to their husbands, so that the Christian faith can't be spoken against by those who know them.

1 Pet 3:1, 2. Wives, fit in with your husbands' plans; for then if they refuse to listen when you talk to them about the Lord, they will be won by your respectful, pure behavior. Your godly lives will speak to them better than any words. [3]Don't be concerned about the outward beauty that depends on jewelry, or beautiful clothes, or hair arrangement. [4]Be beautiful inside, in your hearts, with the lasting charm of a gentle and quiet spirit which is so precious to God. [5]That kind of deep beauty was seen in the saintly women of old, who trusted God and fitted in with their husbands' plans. [6]Sarah, for instance, obeyed her husband Abraham, honoring him as head of the house. And if you do the same, you will be following in her steps like good daughters and doing what is right; then you will not need to fear (offending your husbands). [7]You husbands must be careful of your wives, being thoughtful of their needs and honoring them as the weaker sex. Remember that you and your wife are partners in receiving God's blessings, and if you don't treat her as you should, your prayers will not get ready answers.

See *Bride; Husband; Parents; Widow; Women.*

WILD BULL See *Wild Ox.*

WILD OX Intractable, Job 39:9–12. Horned, Deut 33:17; Ps 22:21. Great strength of, Num 23:18–24; 24:3–9; Job 39:9–12; Ps 92:10.

WILDERNESS Wandering of Israelites in, see *Israel.* Pastures in, Ps 65:11, 12. A voice shouting in, Isa 40:3; Mt 3:3; Lk 3:4; Jn 1:23. Jesus tempted in, Mt 4:1; Mk 1:12, 13; Lk 4:1. Serpent lifted up in, Jn 3:14. Manna in, Jn 6:48–51. Israel to flee to, Rev 12:6, 14. John's vision in, Rev 17:3.

See *Desert.*

WILL THE MENTAL FACULTY. Freedom of, recognized by God, Gen 4:6–10; Deut 5:29; 1 Kgs 20:42; Isa 1:18–20; 43:26; Jer 36:3, 7; Jn 7:17.

See *Blessing, Contingent on Obedience; Choice; Contingency.*

OF GOD, THE SUPREME RULE OF DUTY. Mt 6:10. May your will be done here on earth, just as it is in heaven. Lk 11:2.

Mt 12:50. Anyone who obeys my Father in heaven is my brother, sister and mother! Mk 3:35.

Mt 26:39. He went forward a little, and fell face downward on the ground, and prayed, "My Father! If it is possible, let this cup be taken away from me. But I want your will, not mine." [Mk 14:36; Lk 22:41, 42.] [42]Again he left them and prayed, "My Father! If this cup cannot go away until I drink it all, your will be done." Acts 21:14.

Jn 4:34. Then Jesus explained: "My nourishment comes from doing the will of God who sent me, and from finishing his work."

Jn 5:30. But I pass no judgment without consulting the Father. I judge as I am told. And my judgment is absolutely fair and just, for it is according to the will of God who sent me and is not merely my own.

Jn 6:38. For I have come here from heaven to do the will of God who sent me, not to have my own way. [39]And this is the will of God, that I should not lose even one of all those he has given me, but that I should raise them to eternal life at the Last Day. [40]For it is my Father's will that everyone who sees his Son and believes on him should have eternal life —that I should raise him at the Last Day.

Acts 18:21. "I must by all means be at Jerusalem for the holiday," he said. But he promised to return to Ephesus later if God permitted.

Rom 12:2. Don't copy the behavior and customs of this world, but be a new and different person with a fresh newness in all you do and think. Then you will learn from your own experience how his ways will really satisfy you.

Rom 15:32. Then I will be able to come to you with a happy heart by the will of God, and we can refresh each other.

1 Cor 4:19. But I will come, and soon, if the Lord will let me, and then I'll find out whether these proud men are just big talkers or whether they really have God's power.

1 Cor 16:7. This time I don't want to make just a passing visit and then go right on; I want to come and stay awhile, if the Lord will let me.

Heb 6:3. The Lord willing, we will go on now to other things.

Jas 4:15. What you ought to say is, "If the Lord wants us to, we shall live and do this or that." Rom 1:10.

See *Agency.*

A TESTAMENT. Of Abraham, Gen 25:5, 6. Jacob, Gen 48; 49. David, 1 Kgs 2:1–9. Jehoshaphat, 2 Chron 21:3, 4. May not be annulled, Gal 3:

15. In force after death only, Heb 9:16, 17.

See *Testament.*

WILLFULNESS See *Obduracy; Self-will.*

WILLOW Lev 23:40; Job 40:22; Ps 137:2; Isa 15:7; Ezk 17:5.

FIGURATIVE. Isa 44:4.

WIND Strong, Ex 14:21.

East: Hot and blasting in Egypt, Gen 41:6; in the valley of the Euphrates, Ezk 19:12; in Canaan, Hos 13:15; at Nineveh, Jon 4:8; tempestuous, in Uz, Job 27:21.

West: Took away the plague of locusts from the land of Egypt, Ex 10:19.

North: Brings humidity, Prov 25:23.

South: Lk 12:55; Soothing, Job 37:16, 17; purifying, Job 37:21.

FIGURATIVE. Hos 4:19. Of the judgments of God, Jer 22:22; Hos 13:15; Mt 7:25. Of the Spirit, Jn 3:8.

WINDOW Gen 6:16; 26:8; Josh 2:15, 21; 1 Kgs 6:4; Ezk 40:16–36; Acts 20:9.

WINE Made from grapes, Gen 40:11; 49:11; Isa 25:6; Jer 40:10, 12; from pomegranates, Song 8:2. Kept in jars, Jer 13:12; 48:12; in skins, Josh 9:3–5, 13; Ps 119:83; Mt 9:17; Mk 2:22; Lk 5:37, 38; in casks, Job 32:19. Cellars for, 1 Chron 27:27. New, Lk 5:38. Old, Lk 5:39.

Medicinal use of, Prov 31:6, 7; recommended by Paul to Timothy, 1 Tim 5:23. Used at meals, Mt 26:27–29; Mk 14:23. Made by Jesus at the marriage feast in Cana, Jn 2:9, 10. Sacramental use of, Mt 26:27–29; Lk 22:17–20.

Forbidden to priests while on duty, Lev 10:8, 9; Ezk 44:21; to Nazirites, Num 6:1–4; see *Nazirite.* Abstinence from, of Daniel, Dan 1:5, 8, 16; 10:3; of servants of Ahasuerus, Esther 1:8; of Timothy, 1 Tim 5:23. Samson's mother forbidden to drink, Judg 13:4, 5. Forbidden to kings, Prov 31:4. Denied to the Israelites in the wilderness, that they might know that the Lord was their God, Deut 29:6. Offered with sacrifices, Ex 29:40; Lev 23:13; Num 15:5, 10; 28:7, 14. Given by Melchizedek to Abraham, Gen 14:18. Fermented, Lev 10:8, 9; Num 6:3, 4; 28:7; Deut 14:26; 29:6; Prov 23:31, 32; Mk 2:22. Refined, Isa 25:6; Jer 48:11. Commerce in, Rev 18:13. Banquets of, Esther 5:6. Given to Jesus at the crucifixion, Mt 27:48; Mk 15:23; Lk 23:36; Jn 19:29. Intoxication from the use of, Ps 104:15.

INSTANCES OF INTOXICATION FROM. Noah, Gen 9:20, 21; Lot, Gen 19:32; Joseph and his brothers, Gen 43:34; Nabal, 1 Sam 25:36; Amnon, 2 Sam 13:28; Ahasuerus, Esther 1:10; kings of Israel, Hos 7:5; falsely charged against the disciples, Acts 2:13.

FIGURATIVE. Of the divine judgments, Ps 75:8; Jer 51:7. Of the joy of wisdom, Prov 9:2, 5. Of the joys of religion, Isa 25:6; 55:1; Joel 2:19. Of sin, Rev 14:8. Of God's wrath, Rev 16:19.

Symbolical. Of the blood of Jesus, Mt 26:28; Mk 14:23, 24; Lk 22:20; Jn 6:53–56.

UNCLASSIFIED SCRIPTURES RELATING TO. Deut 14:26. When you arrive, use the money to buy an ox, a sheep, some wine, or some strong drink, to feast there before the Lord your God, and to rejoice with your household.

Deut 33:28. So Israel dwells safely, prospering in a land of corn and wine, while the gentle rains descend from heaven.

2 Kgs 18:32. Until I take you to another land just like this one—with plentiful crops, grain, wine, olive trees, and honey. All of this instead of death! Don't listen to King Hezekiah when he tries to persuade you that the Lord will deliver you.

2 Chron 32:28. He also built many storehouses for his grain, new wine, and olive oil, with many stalls for his animals, and folds for the great flocks of sheep and goats he purchased.

Neh 10:39, 40. The people and the Levites were required by law to bring these offerings of grain, new wine, and olive oil to the Temple and place them in the sacred containers for use by the ministering priests, the gatekeepers, and the choir singers. So we agreed together not to neglect the Temple of our God.

Ps 104:14. The tender grass grows up at his command to feed the cattle, and there are fruit trees, vegetables and grain for man to cultivate, [15]and wine to make him glad, and olive oil as lotion for his skin, and bread to give him strength.

Prov 31:6, 7. Hard liquor is for sick men at the brink of death, and wine for those in deep depression. Let them drink to forget their poverty and misery.

Eccl 2:3. So, after a lot of thinking, I decided to try the road of drink, while still holding steadily to my course of seeking wisdom. Next I changed my course again and followed the path of folly, so that I could experience the only happiness most men have throughout their lives. [11]But as I looked at everything I had tried, it was all so useless, a chasing of the wind, and there was nothing really worthwhile anywhere.

Isa 56:12. "Come," they say. "We'll get some wine and have a party; let's all get drunk. This is really living; let it go on and on, and tomorrow will be better yet!"

Jer 31:12. They shall come home and sing songs of joy upon the hills of Zion, and shall be radiant over the goodness of the Lord—the good crops, the wheat and the wine and the oil, and the healthy flocks and herds.

Hos 2:8. She doesn't realize that all she has, has come from me. It was I who gave her all the gold and silver that she used in worshiping Baal, her god! [9]But now I will take back the wine and ripened corn I constantly supplied. [22]Then the earth can answer the parched cry of the grain, the grapes, and the olive trees for moisture and for dew—and the whole grand chorus shall sing together that "God sows!"

Joel 1:5. Wake up and weep, you drunkards, for all the grapes are ruined and all your wine is gone!

Joel 2:24. The threshing floors will pile high again with wheat, and the presses overflow with olive oil and wine.

Joel 3:3. They divided up my people as their

slaves; they traded a young lad for a prostitute, and a little girl for wine enough to get drunk.

Amos 6:6. You drink wine by the bucketful and perfume yourselves with sweet ointments, caring nothing at all that your brothers need your help.

Mic 2:11. "I'll preach to you the joys of wine and drink"—that is the kind of drunken, lying prophet that you like!

Hab 2:5. What's more, these arrogant Chaldeans are betrayed by all their wine, for it is treacherous. In their greed they have collected many nations, but like death and hell, they are never satisfied.

Zech 9:17. How wonderful and beautiful all shall be! The abundance of grain and wine will make the young men and girls flourish.

Zech 10:7. They shall be like mighty warriors. They shall be happy as with wine.

1 Tim 5:23. By the way, this doesn't mean you should completely give up drinking wine. You ought to take a little sometimes as medicine for your stomach because you are sick so often.

See *Vine; Vineyard.*

ADMONITIONS AGAINST THE USE OF. Lev 10:8, 9. Never drink wine or strong drink when you go into the Tabernacle, lest you die; and this rule applies to your sons and to all your descendants from generation to generation.

Num 6:3. He must not thereafter, during the entire period of his special consecration to the Lord, taste strong drink or wine or even fresh wine, grape juice, grapes, or raisins!

Judg 13:4. Don't drink any wine or beer, and don't eat any food that isn't kosher.

Prov 20:1. Wine gives false courage; hard liquor leads to brawls; what fools men are to let it master them, making them reel drunkenly down the street!

Prov 21:17. A man who loves pleasure becomes poor; wine and luxury are not the way to riches!

Prov 23:29, 30. Whose heart is filled with anguish and sorrow? Who is always fighting and quarreling? Who is the man with bloodshot eyes and many wounds? It is the one who spends long hours in the taverns, trying out new mixtures. [31]Don't let the sparkle and the smooth taste of strong wine deceive you. [32]For in the end it bites like a poisonous serpent; it stings like an adder.

Prov 31:4. And it is not for kings, O Lemuel, to drink wine and whiskey. [5]For if they drink they may forget their duties and be unable to give justice to those who are oppressed.

Isa 5:11. Woe to you who get up early in the morning to go on long drinking bouts that last till late at night—woe to you drunken bums. [22]Woe to those who are "heroes" when it comes to drinking, and boast about the liquor they can hold.

Isa 24:9. No more are the joys of wine and song; strong drink turns bitter in the mouth.

Isa 28:1. Woe to the city of Samaria, surrounded by her rich valley—Samaria, the pride and delight of the drunkards of Israel! Woe to her fading beauty, the crowning glory of a nation of men lying drunk in the streets! [3]The proud city of Samaria—yes, the joy and delight of the drunkards of Israel—will be hurled to the ground and trampled beneath the enemies' feet. [7]But Jerusalem is now led by drunks! Her priests and prophets reel and stagger, making stupid errors and mistakes.

Jer 23:9. My heart is broken for the false prophets, full of deceit. I awake with fear and stagger as a drunkard does from wine, because of the awful fate awaiting them, for God has decreed holy words of judgment against them.

Jer 35:2. Go to the settlement where the families of the Rechabites live and invite them to the Temple. Take them into one of the inner rooms and offer them a drink of wine. [3]So I went over to see Jaazaniah (son of Jeremiah, who was the son of Habazziniah), and brought him and all his brothers and sons—representing all the Rechab families—[4]to the Temple, into the room assigned for the use of the sons of Hanan the prophet (the son of Igdaliah). This room was located next to the one used by the palace official, directly above the room of Ma-aseiah (son of Shallum), who was the temple doorman. [5]I set cups and jugs of wine before them and invited them to have a drink, [6]but they refused. "No," they said. "We don't drink, for Jonadab our father (son of Rechab) commanded that none of us should ever drink, neither we nor our children forever. [7]He also told us not to build houses or plant crops or vineyards and not to own farms, but always to live in tents; and that if we obeyed we would live long, good lives in our own land. [8]And we have obeyed him in all these things. We have never had a drink of wine since then, nor our wives or our sons or daughters either. [9]We haven't built houses or owned farms or planted crops. [10]We have lived in tents and have fully obeyed everything that Jonadab our father commanded us." [14]They don't drink, because their father told them not to. But I have spoken to you again and again and you won't listen or obey. [18, 19]Then Jeremiah turned to the Rechabites and said: "The Lord of Hosts, the God of Israel, says that because you have obeyed your father in every respect, he shall always have descendants who will worship me."

Ezk 44:21. No priest may drink wine before coming to the inner court.

Hos 4:11. Wine, women, and song have robbed my people of their brains.

Lk 1:15. For he will be one of the Lord's great men. He must never touch wine or hard liquor—and he will be filled with the Holy Spirit, even from before his birth!

Rom 14:21. The right thing to do is to quit eating meat or drinking wine or doing anything else that offends your brother or makes him sin.

Eph 5:18. Don't drink too much wine, for many evils lie along that path; be filled instead with the Holy Spirit, and controlled by him.

Tit 2:3. Teach the older women to be quiet and respectful in everything they do. They must not go around speaking evil of others and must not be heavy drinkers, but they should be teachers of goodness.

See *Abstinence; Drunkenness.*

WINEBIBBER Jesus falsely accused of being a, Mt 11:19; Lk 7:34.

WINE PRESS Num 18:27, 30; Deut 15:14; Judg 6:11. In vineyards, Isa 5:2; Mk 12:1. Trodden with joy and shouting, Jer 48:33.

FIGURATIVE. Treading the, of the day of vengeance, Isa 63:2, 3; of the judgments of God, Lam 1:15; Rev 14:19, 20.

WINE TASTER Pharaoh's, imprisoned and released, Gen 40.

See *Cupbearer.*

WINGS Of the cherubim, Ex 25:20; 37:9; 1 Kgs 8:6. Of the seraphim, Isa 6:2.

FIGURATIVE. Israel carried on eagles' wings, Ex 19:4. God's care of Israel likened to eagles' wings, Deut 32:9–12. Of the wind, 2 Sam 22:11; Ps 104:3. Hide me in the shadow of your wings, Ps 17: 8. Take refuge in the shadow of your wings, Ps 36: 7. I will hide beneath the shadow of your wings, Ps 57:1. How I rejoice beneath the shadow of your wings, Ps 63:7. He will shield you with his wings, Ps 91:4. Riches disappear as though they had wings, Prov 23:5. Mounting up with wings like eagles, Isa 40:31. Wings of the living beings, Ezk 1: 6–12, 23–25; 10:5–21. A Lion with eagle's wings, Dan 7:4. Rise with healing in his wings, Mal 4:2. As a hen gathers her chicks under her wings, Mt 23:37. Wings of the living beings, Rev 4:8. Wings of the locusts, Rev 9:9.

WINNOWING Of grain, Ruth 3:2; Isa 30: 24; Jer 51:2; Mt 3:12.

FIGURATIVE. Of Babylon, Isa 21:10.

WINTER Annual return of, shall never stop, Gen 8:22. Plowing in, in Canaan, Prov 20:4. Rainy season in, in Canaan, Song 2:11. Shipping suspended in, on the Mediterranean Sea, Acts 27:12; 28:11. Paul remains one, at Nicopolis, Tit 3:12. Summer and winter houses, Jer 36:22; Amos 3:15.

See *Meteorology.*

WISDOM Of Joseph, Gen 41:16, 25–39; Acts 7:10. Of Moses, Acts 7:22. Of Solomon, 1 Kgs 3:12, 16–28; 4:29–34; 5:12; 10:23, 24. Of Ethan, Heman, Calcol, and Darda, 1 Kgs 4:31. Of the leaders of Issachar, 1 Chron 12:24–37. Of Ezra, Ezra 7:25. Of Daniel, Dan 1:17; 5:14. Of the Magi, Mt 2:1–12. Of Paul, 2 Pet 3:15, 16.

Special skills: Of Bezalel, Ex 31:3–5; 35:30–35; 36:1, 2. Of Oholiab, Ex 31:6; 35:34, 35; 36:1, 2; of other skilled artisans, Ex 36:1, 2; of women, Ex 35: 26. Of Hiram, 1 Kgs 7:13, 14; 2 Chron 2:13, 14.

SPIRITUAL.

Unclassified Scriptures Relating to. Deut 32:29. Oh, that they were wise! Oh, that they could understand! Oh, that they would know what they are getting into!

Job 5:27. I have found from experience that all of this is true. For your own good, listen to my counsel.

Job 8:8. Read the history books and see. [10]But the wisdom of the past will teach you. The experience of others will speak to you.

Job 12:2. Yes, I realize you know everything! All wisdom will die with you! [3]Well, I know a few things myself—you are no better than I am. And who doesn't know these things you've been saying? [7-9]Who doesn't know that the Lord does things like that? Ask the dumbest beast—he knows that it is so: ask the birds—they will tell you; or let the earth teach you, or the fish of the sea. [10]For the soul of every living thing is in the hand of God, and the breath of all mankind. [11]Just as my mouth can taste good food, so my mind tastes truth when I hear it. [12]And as you say, older men like me are wise. They understand. [13]But true wisdom and power are God's. He alone knows what we should do; he understands. [16]Yes, with him is strength and wisdom. Deceivers and deceived are both his slaves. [17]He makes fools of counselors and judges. [22]He floods the darkness with light, even the dark shadow of death.

Job 28:12. But though men can do all these things, they don't know where to find wisdom and understanding. [13]They not only don't know how to get it, but, in fact, it is not to be found among the living. [14]"It's not here," the oceans say; and the seas reply, "Nor is it here." [15]It cannot be bought for gold or silver, [16]nor for all the gold of Ophir or precious onyx stones or sapphires. [17]Wisdom is far more valuable than gold and glass. It cannot be bought for jewels mounted in fine gold. [18]Coral or crystal is worthless in trying to get it; its price is far above rubies. [19]Topaz from Ethiopia cannot purchase it, nor even the purest gold. [20]Then where can we get it? Where can it be found? [21]For it is hid from the eyes of all mankind; even the sharp-eyed birds in the sky cannot discover it. [22]But Destruction and Death speak of knowing something about it! [23, 24]And God surely knows where it is to be found, for he looks throughout the whole earth, under all the heavens. [25]He makes the winds blow and sets the boundaries of the oceans. [26]He makes the laws of the rain and a path for the lightning. [27]He knows where wisdom is and declares it to all who will listen. He established it and examined it thoroughly. [28]And this is what he says to all mankind: "Look, to fear the Lord is true wisdom; to forsake evil is real understanding."

Job 32:7. For those who are older are said to be wiser; [8, 9]but it is not mere age that makes men wise. Rather, it is the spirit in a man, the breath of the Almighty which makes him intelligent.

Job 42:5. I had heard about you before, but now I have seen you.

Ps 73:24. You will keep guiding me all my life with your wisdom and counsel; and afterwards receive me into the glories of heaven.

Ps 107:43. Listen, if you are wise, to what I am saying. Think about the lovingkindness of the Lord!

Ps 111:10. How can men be wise? The only way to begin is by reverence for God. For growth in wisdom comes from obeying his laws.

Prov 1:5. I want those already wise to become the wiser and become leaders. [7]How does a man become wise? The first step is to trust and reverence the Lord! Only fools refuse to be taught. [20]Wisdom shouts in the streets for a hearing. 21She calls out to the crowds along Main Street, and to the judges in their courts, and to everyone in all the land: 22"You simpletons!" she cries. "How long will you scoff at wisdom and fight the facts? 23Come here and listen to me! I'll pour out the spirit of wisdom upon you, and make you wise. 24I have called you so often but still you won't come. I have pleaded, but all in vain. 25For you have spurned my counsel and reproof. 26Some day you'll be in trouble, and I'll laugh! Mock me, will you?—I'll mock you! 27When a storm of terror surrounds you, and when you are engulfed by anguish and distress, 28then I will not answer your cry for help. It will be too late though you search for me ever so anxiously. 29For you closed your eyes to the facts and did not choose to reverence and trust the Lord, 30and you turned your back on me, spurning my advice. 31That is why you must eat the bitter fruit of having your own way, and experience the full terrors of the pathway you have chosen. 32For you turned away from me—to death; your own complacency will kill you. Fools! 33But all who listen to me shall live in peace and safety, unafraid."

Prov 2:1, 2. Every young man who listens to me and obeys my instructions will be given wisdom and good sense. 3-5Yes, if you want better insight and discernment, and are searching for them as you would for lost money or hidden treasure, then wisdom will be given you, and knowledge of God himself; you will soon learn the importance of reverence for the Lord and of trusting him. 6For the Lord grants wisdom! His every word is a treasure of knowledge and understanding. 7, 8He grants good sense to the godly—his saints. He is their shield, protecting them and guarding their pathway. 9He shows how to distinguish right from wrong, how to find the right decision every time. 10For wisdom and truth will enter the very center of your being, filling your life with joy. 11-13You will be given the sense to stay away from evil men who want you to be their partners in crime—men who turn from God's ways to walk down dark and evil paths, 14and exult in doing wrong, for they thoroughly enjoy their sins. 15Everything they do is crooked and wrong. 16, 17Only wisdom from the Lord can save a man from the flattery of prostitutes; these girls have abandoned their husbands and flouted the laws of God. 18Their houses lie along the road to death and hell. 19The men who enter them are doomed. None of these men will ever be the same again. 20Follow the steps of the godly instead, and stay on the right path.

Prov 3:13–15. The man who knows right from wrong and has good judgment and common sense is happier than the man who is immensely rich! For such wisdom is far more valuable than precious jewels. Nothing else compares with it. 16, 17Wisdom gives: A long, good life, riches, honor, pleasure, peace. 18Wisdom is a tree of life to those who eat her fruit; happy is the man who keeps on eating it. 19The Lord's wisdom founded the earth; his understanding established all the universe and space. 20The deep fountains of the earth were broken open by his knowledge, and the skies poured down rain. 21Have two goals: wisdom—that is, knowing and doing right—and common sense. Don't let them slip away, 22for they fill you with living energy, and are a feather in your cap. 23They keep you safe from defeat and disaster and from stumbling off the trail. 24-26With them on guard you can sleep without fear; you need not be afraid of disaster or the plots of wicked men, for the Lord is with you; he protects you. 34The Lord mocks at mockers, but helps the humble. 35The wise are promoted to honor, but fools are promoted to shame!

Prov 4:4. He told me never to forget his words. "If you follow them," he said, "you will have a long and happy life. 5*Learn to be wise,*" he said, "*and develop good judgment and common sense! I cannot overemphasize this point.*" 6Cling to wisdom—she will protect you. Love her—she will guard you. 7Determination to be wise is the first step toward becoming wise! And with your wisdom, develop common sense and good judgment. 8, 9If you exalt wisdom, she will exalt you. Hold her fast and she will lead you to great honor; she will place a beautiful crown upon your head. 10My son, listen to me and do as I say, and you will have a long, good life. 11I would have you learn this great fact: that a life of doing right is the wisest life there is. 12If you live that kind of life, you'll not limp or stumble as you run. 13Carry out my instructions; don't forget them, for they will lead you to real living. 18But the good man walks along in the ever-brightening light of God's favor; the dawn gives way to morning splendor, 19while the evil man gropes and stumbles in the dark. 20Listen, son of mine, to what I say. Listen carefully. 21Keep these thoughts ever in mind; let them penetrate deep within your heart, 22for they will mean real life for you, and radiant health.

Prov 7:2. Obey me and live! Guard my words as your most precious possession. 3Write them down, and also keep them deep within your heart. 4Love wisdom like a sweetheart; make her a beloved member of your family.

Prov 8:1–30. Can't you hear the voice of wisdom? She is standing at the city gates and at every fork in the road, and at the door of every house. Listen to what she says: 4, 5"Listen, men!" she calls. "How foolish and naive you are! Let me give you understanding. O foolish ones, let me show you common sense! 6, 7Listen to me! For I have important information for you. Everything I say is right and true, for I hate lies and every kind of deception. 8My advice is wholesome and good. There is nothing of evil in it. 9My words are plain and clear to anyone with half a mind—if it is only open! 10My instruction is far more valuable than silver or gold." 11For the value of wisdom is far above rubies; nothing can be compared with it. [Eccl 7:11.] 12Wisdom and good judgment live together, for wisdom knows where to discover knowledge and understanding. 13If anyone respects and fears God, he will hate evil. For wisdom hates pride, arrogance, corruption and deceit of every kind. [14, 15]"I, Wisdom, give good advice and common sense. Because of my strength, kings reign in power. I show the judges who is right and who is wrong. [16]Rulers rule well with my help. [17]I love all who love me. Those who search for me shall surely find me. [18]Unending riches, honor, justice and righteousness are mine to distribute. [19]My gifts are better than the purest gold or sterling silver! [20]My paths are those of justice and right. [21]Those who love and follow me are indeed wealthy. I fill their treasuries. [22]The Lord formed me in the beginning, before he created anything else. [23]From ages past, I am. I existed before the earth began. [24]I lived before the oceans were created, before the springs bubbled forth their waters onto the earth; [25]before the mountains and the hills were made. [26]Yes, I was born before God made the earth and fields, and high plateaus. [27-29]I was there when he established the heavens and formed the great springs in the depths of the oceans. I was there when he set the limits of the seas and gave them his instructions not to spread beyond their boundaries. I was there when he made the blueprint for the earth and oceans. [30]I was always at his side like a little child. I was his constant delight, laughing and playing in his presence. [31]And how happy I was with what he created—his wide world and all his family of mankind! [32]And so, young men, listen to me, for how happy are all who follow my instructions. [33]Listen to my counsel—oh, don't refuse it—and be wise. [34]Happy is the man who is so anxious to be with me that he watches for me daily at my gates, or waits for me outside my home! [35]For whoever finds me finds life and wins approval from the Lord. [36]But the one who misses me has injured himself irreparably. Those who refuse me show that they love death."

Prov 9:1. Wisdom has built a palace supported on seven pillars, [2]and has prepared a great banquet, and mixed the wines, [3]and sent out her maidens inviting all to come. She calls from the busiest intersections in the city, [4]"Come, you simple ones without good judgment; [5]come to wisdom's banquet and drink the wines that I have mixed. [6]Leave behind your foolishness and begin to live; learn how to be wise." [9]Teach a wise man, and he will be the wiser; teach a good man, and he will learn more. [10]*For the reverence and fear of God are basic to all wisdom. Knowing God results in every other kind of understanding.* [11]"I, Wisdom, will make the hours of your day more profitable and the years of your life more fruitful." [12]Wisdom is its own reward, and if you scorn her, you hurt only yourself.

Prov 10:8. The wise man is glad to be instructed, but a self-sufficient fool falls flat on his face. [13]Men with common sense are admired as counselors; those without it are beaten as servants. [14]A wise man holds his tongue. Only a fool blurts out everything he knows; that only leads to sorrow and trouble. [21]A godly man gives good advice, but a rebel is destroyed by lack of common sense. [23]A fool's fun is being bad; a wise man's fun is being wise!

Prov 11:12. To quarrel with a neighbor is foolish; a man with good sense holds his tongue. *v.* 9.

Prov 12:1. To learn, you must want to be taught. To refuse reproof is stupid. [8]Everyone admires a man with good sense, but a man with a warped mind is despised. [15]A fool thinks he needs no advice, but a wise man listens to others.

Prov 13:14. The advice of a wise man refreshes like water from a mountain spring. Those accepting it become aware of the pitfalls on ahead. [15]A man with good sense is appreciated. A treacherous man must walk a rocky road. [16]A wise man thinks ahead; a fool doesn't, and even brags about it! Prov 14:18.

Prov 14:6. A mocker never finds the wisdom he claims he is looking for, yet it comes easily to the man with common sense. [7]If you are looking for advice, stay away from fools. [8]The wise man looks ahead. The fool attempts to fool himself and won't face facts. [16]A wise man is cautious and avoids danger; a fool plunges ahead with great confidence. [29]A wise man controls his temper. He knows that anger causes mistakes. [Prov 29:11.] [33]Wisdom is enshrined in the hearts of men of common sense, but it must shout loudly before fools will hear it.

Prov 15:7. Only the good can give good advice. Rebels can't. [*v.* 2] [14]A wise man is hungry for truth, while the mocker feeds on trash. [33]Humility and reverence for the Lord will make you both wise and honored.

Prov 16:16. How much better is wisdom than gold, and understanding than silver! [20]God blesses those who obey him; happy the man who puts his trust in the Lord. [21]The wise man is known by his common sense, and a pleasant teacher is the best. [22]Wisdom is a fountain of life to those possessing it, but a fool's burden is his folly. [23]From a wise mind comes careful and persuasive speech. [24]Kind words are like honey—enjoyable and healthful.

Prov 17:10. A rebuke to a man of common sense is more effective than a hundred lashes on the back of a rebel. [24]Wisdom is the main pursuit of sensible men, but a fool's goals are at the ends of the earth!

Prov 18:15. The intelligent man is always open to new ideas. In fact, he looks for them.

Prov 19:8. He who loves wisdom loves his own best interest and will be a success. [20]Get all the advice you can and be wise the rest of your life.

Prov 21:11. The wise man learns by listening; the simpleton can learn only by seeing scorners punished.

Prov 22:17–19. Listen to this wise advice; follow it closely, for it will do you good, and you can pass it on to others: *Trust in the Lord.* [20, 21]In the past, haven't I been right? Then believe what I am telling you now, and share it with others.

Prov 23:12. Don't refuse to accept criticism; get all the help you can. [19]O my son, be wise and stay in God's paths. [23]Get the facts at any price, and hold on tightly to all the good sense you can get.

Prov 24:13,14. My son, honey whets the appetite, and so does wisdom! When you enjoy becoming wise, there is hope for you. A bright future lies ahead!

Prov 28:5. Evil men don't understand the importance of justice, but those who follow the Lord are much concerned about it. [7]Young men who are wise obey the law; a son who is a member of a lawless gang is a shame to his father. Prov 29:3.

Eccl 87:1. How wonderful to be wise, to understand things, to be able to analyze them and interpret them. Wisdom lights up a man's face, softening its hardness. [5]Those who obey him will not be punished. The wise man will find a time and a way to do what he says.

Eccl 9:13. Here is another thing that has made a deep impression on me as I have watched human affairs: [14]There was a small city with only a few people living in it, and a great king came with his army and besieged it. [15]There was in the city a wise man, very poor, and he knew what to do to save the city, and so it was rescued. But afterwards no one thought any more about him. [16]Then I realized that though wisdom is better than strength, nevertheless, if the wise man is poor, he will be despised, and what he says will not be appreciated. [17]But even so, the quiet words of a wise man are better than the shout of a king of fools. [18]Wisdom is better than weapons of war, but one rotten apple can spoil a barrelful.

Eccl 10:12. It is pleasant to listen to wise words, but a fool's speech brings him to ruin.

Eccl 12:11. The wise man's words are like goads that spur to action. They nail down important truths. Students are wise who master what their teachers tell them.

Isa 2:3. "Come," everyone will say, "let us go up the mountain of the Lord, to the Temple of the God of Israel; there he will teach us his laws, and we will obey them." For in those days the world will be ruled from Jerusalem.

Isa 11:9. Nothing will hurt or destroy in all my holy mountain, for as the waters fill the sea, so shall the earth be full of the knowledge of the Lord.

Isa 29:24. Those in error will believe the truth, and complainers will be willing to be taught!

Isa 33:6. An abundance of salvation is stored up for Judah in a safe place, along with wisdom and knowledge and reverence for God.

Jer 9:23. The Lord says: Let not the wise man bask in his wisdom, nor the mighty man in his might, nor the rich man in his riches. [24]Let them boast in this alone: That they truly know me, and understand that I am the Lord of justice and of righteousness whose love is steadfast; and that I love to be this way.

Jer 31:34. At that time it will no longer be necessary to admonish one another to know the Lord. For everyone, both great and small, shall really know me then, says the Lord, and I will forgive and forget their sins.

Dan 11:32. He will flatter those who hate the things of God, and win them over to his side. But the people who know their God shall be strong and do great things. [33]Those with spiritual understanding will have a wide ministry of teaching in those days.

Dan 12:3. And those who are wise—the people of God—shall shine as brightly as the sun's brilliance, and those who turn many to righteousness will glitter like stars forever. [4]But Daniel, keep this prophecy a secret; seal it up so that it will not be understood until the end times, when travel and education shall be vastly increased! [10]Many shall be purified by great trials and persecutions. But the wicked shall continue in their wickedness, and none of them will understand. Only those who are willing to learn will know what it means.

Hos 6:3. "Oh, that we might know the Lord! Let us press on to know him, and he will respond to us as surely as the coming of dawn or the rain of early spring." [6]I don't want your sacrifices—I want your love; I don't want your offerings—I want you to know me.

Hos 14:9. Whoever is wise, let him understand these things. Whoever is intelligent, let him listen. For the paths of the Lord are true and right, and good men walk along them.

Mt 6:22. If your eye is pure, there will be sunshine in your soul. [23]But if your eye is clouded with evil thoughts and desires, you are in deep spiritual darkness. And oh, how deep that darkness can be! Lk 11:34–36.

Mt 7:24. All who listen to my instructions and follow them are wise, like a man who builds his house on solid rock. [25]Though the rain comes in torrents, and the floods rise and the storm winds beat against his house, it won't collapse, for it is built on rock.

Mt 11:19. But brilliant men like you can justify your every inconsistency! Lk 7:35.

Mt 25:1. The Kingdom of Heaven can be illustrated by the story of ten bridesmaids who took their lamps and went to meet the bridegroom. [2-4]But only five of them were wise enough to fill their lamps with oil, while the other five were foolish and forgot. [5, 6]So, when the bridegroom was delayed, they lay down to rest until midnight, when they were roused by the shout, "The bridegroom is coming! Come out and welcome him!" [7, 8]All the girls jumped up and trimmed their lamps. Then the five who hadn't any oil begged the others to share with them, for their lamps were going out. [9]But the others replied, "We haven't enough. Go instead to the shops and buy some for yourselves." [10]But while they were gone, the bridegroom came, and those who were ready went in with him to the marriage feast, and the door was locked. [11]Later, when the other five returned, they stood outside, calling, "Sir, open the door for us!" [12]But he called back, "Go away! It is too late!" [13]So stay awake and be prepared, for you do not know the date or moment of my return.

Mk 12:32. The teacher of religion replied, "Sir, you have spoken a true word in saying that there is only one God and no other. [33]And I know it is far more important to love him with all my heart and understanding and strength, and to love others as myself, than to offer all kinds of sacrifices on the altar of the Temple." [34]Realizing this man's understanding, Jesus said to him, "You are not far from the Kingdom of God." After that, no one dared ask him any more questions.

Lk 1:17. He will be a man of rugged spirit and power like Elijah, the prophet of old; and he will precede the coming of the Messiah, preparing the people for his arrival. He will soften adult hearts to become like little children's, and will change disobedient minds to the wisdom of faith.

Jn 7:17. If any of you really determines to do God's will, then you will certainly know whether my teaching is from God or is merely my own.

Jn 8:32. And you will know the truth, and the truth will set you free.

Jn 10:4. He walks ahead of them; and they follow him, for they recognize his voice. [14]I am the Good Shepherd and know my own sheep, and they know me.

Jn 17:3. And this is the way to have eternal life —by knowing you, the only true God, and Jesus Christ, the one you sent to earth! [7]Now they know that everything I have is a gift from you, [8]for I have passed on to them the commands you gave me; and they accepted them and know of a certainty that I came down to earth from you, and they believe you sent me. [25]O righteous Father, the world doesn't know you, but I do; and these disciples know you sent me.

Acts 6:10. But none of them were able to stand against Stephen's wisdom and spirit.

Rom 15:14. I know that you are wise and good, my brothers, and that you know these things so well that you are able to teach others all about them.

Rom 16:19. But everyone knows that you stand loyal and true. This makes me very happy. I want you always to remain very clear about what is right, and to stay innocent of any wrong.

1 Cor 2:6. Yet when I am among mature Christians I do speak with words of great wisdom, but not the kind that comes from here on earth, and not the kind that appeals to the great men of this world, who are doomed to fall. [7]Our words are wise because they are from God, telling of God's wise plan to bring us into the glories of heaven. This plan was hidden in former times, though it was made for our benefit before the world began. [8]But the great men of the world have not understood it; if they had, they never would have crucified the Lord of Glory. [9]That is what is meant by the Scriptures which say that no mere man has ever seen, heard or even imagined what wonderful things God has ready for those who love the Lord. [10]But we know about these things because God has sent his Spirit to tell us, and his Spirit searches out and shows us all of God's deepest secrets. [11]No one can really know what anyone else is thinking, or what he is really like, except that person himself. And no one can know God's thoughts except God's own Spirit. [12]And God has actually given us his Spirit (not the world's spirit) to tell us about the wonderful free gifts of grace and blessing that God has given us. [13]In telling you about these gifts we have even used the very words given to us by the Holy Spirit, not words that we as men might choose. So we use the Holy Spirit's words to explain the Holy Spirit's facts. [14]But the man who isn't a Christian can't understand and can't accept these thoughts from God, which the Holy Spirit teaches us. They sound foolish to him, because only those who have the Holy Spirit within them can understand what the Holy Spirit means. Others just can't take it in. [15]But the spiritual man has insight into everything, and that bothers and baffles the man of the world, who can't understand him at all. [16]How could he? For certainly he has never been one to know the Lord's thoughts, or to discuss them with him, or to move the hands of God by prayer. But, strange as it seems, we Christians actually do have within us a portion of the very thoughts and mind of Christ.

1 Cor 3:18. Stop fooling yourselves. If you count yourself above average in intelligence, as judged by this world's standards, you had better put this all aside and be a fool rather than let it hold you back from the true wisdom from above.

1 Cor 8:3. But the person who truly loves God is the one who is open to God's knowledge.

1 Cor 13:11. It's like this: when I was a child I spoke and thought and reasoned as a child does. But when I became a man my thoughts grew far beyond those of my childhood, and now I have put away the childish things.

1 Cor 14:20. Dear brothers, don't be childish in your understanding of these things. Be innocent babies when it comes to planning evil, but be men of intelligence in understanding matters of this kind.

2 Cor 2:11. A further reason for forgiveness is to keep from being outsmarted by Satan; for we know what he is trying to do.

2 Cor 8:7. You people there are leaders in so many ways—you have so much faith, so many good preachers, so much learning, so much enthusiasm, so much love for us. Now I want you to be leaders also in the spirit of cheerful giving.

Gal 4:9. And now that you have found God (or I should say, now that God has found you) how can it be that you want to go back again and become slaves once more . . . ?

Eph 4:11. Some of us have been given special ability as apostles; to others he has given the gift of being able to preach well; some have special ability in winning people to Christ, helping them to trust him as their Savior; still others have a gift for caring for God's people as a shepherd does his sheep, leading and teaching them in the ways of God. [12]Why is it that he gives us these special abilities to do certain things best? It is that God's people will be equipped to do better work for him, building up the church, the body of Christ, to a position of strength and maturity; [13]until finally we all believe alike about our salvation and about our Savior, God's Son, and all become full-grown in the Lord—yes, to the point of being filled full with Christ.

Eph 5:15, 16. So be careful how you act; these are difficult days. Don't be fools; be wise: make the most of every opportunity you have for doing good. [17]Don't act thoughtlessly, but try to find out and do whatever the Lord wants you to.

Phil 3:7. But all these things that I once thought very worthwhile—now I've thrown them all away so that I can put my trust and hope in Christ alone. [8]Yes, everything else is worthless when compared with the priceless gain of knowing Christ Jesus my Lord. I have put aside all else, counting it worth less than nothing, in order that I can have Christ. [10]I have found it to be the only way to really know Christ and to experience the mighty power that brought him back to life again, and to find out what it means to suffer and to die with him.

Col 3:10. You are living a brand new kind of life that is continually learning more and more of what is right, and trying constantly to be more and more like Christ who created this new life within you. [16]Remember what Christ taught and let his words enrich your lives and make you wise; teach them to each other and sing them out in psalms and hymns and spiritual songs, singing to the Lord with thankful hearts.

1 Thess 5:4. But, dear brothers, you are not in the dark about these things, and won't be surprised as by a thief when that day of the Lord comes. [5]For you are all children of the light and of the day, and do not belong to darkness and night.

1 Tim 2:4. For he longs for all to be saved and to understand this truth.

2 Tim 3:15. You know how, when you were a small child, you were taught the holy Scriptures; and it is these that make you wise to accept God's salvation by trusting in Christ Jesus.

Jas 3:13. If you are wise, live a life of steady goodness, so that only good deeds will pour forth. And if you don't brag about them, then you will be truly wise!

1 Jn 4:6. But we are children of God; that is why only those who have walked and talked with God will listen to us. Others won't. That is another way to know whether a message is really from God; for if it is, the world won't listen to it.

See *Knowledge; Speaking, Wisdom in.*

Spiritual, from God. Ex 4:11. "Who makes mouths?" Jehovah asked him. "Isn't it I, the Lord? Who makes a man so that he can speak or not speak, see or not see, hear or not hear? [12]Now go ahead and do as I tell you, for I will help you to speak well, and I will tell you what to say."

Ex 8:9. "Be so kind as to tell me when you want them to go," Moses said, "and I will pray that the frogs will die at the time you specify, everywhere except in the river." [10]"Do it tomorrow," Pharaoh said. "All right," Moses replied, "it shall be as you have said; then you will know that there is no one like the Lord our God."

Deut 4:5. These are the laws for you to obey when you arrive in the land where you will live. They are from the Lord our God. He has given them to me to pass on to you. [6]If you obey them they will give you a reputation for wisdom and intelligence. When the surrounding nations hear these laws they will exclaim, "What other nation is as wise and prudent as Israel!" [35]He did these things so you would realize that Jehovah is God, and that there is no one else like him. [36]He let you hear his voice instructing you from heaven, and he let you see his great pillar of fire upon the earth; you even heard his words from the center of the fire.

Deut 29:4. But even yet the Lord hasn't given you hearts that understand or eyes that see or ears that hear!

1 Chron 22:12. And may the Lord give you the good judgment to follow all his laws when he makes you king of Israel.

Neh 9:20. You sent your good Spirit to instruct them, and you did not stop giving them bread from heaven or water for their thirst.

Job 11:5. Oh, that God would speak and tell you what he thinks! [6]Oh, that he would make you truly see yourself, for he knows everything you've done. Listen! God is doubtless punishing you far less than you deserve!

Job 22:21. Quit quarreling with God! Agree with him and you will have peace at last! His favor will surround you if you will only admit that you were wrong. [22]Listen to his instructions and store them in your heart.

Job 32:7. For those who are older are said to be wiser; [8, 9]but it is not mere age that makes men wise. Rather, it is the spirit in a man, the breath of the Almighty which makes him intelligent.

Job 33:16. He opens their ears in times like that, and gives them wisdom and instruction.

Job 35:10. Yet none of them cry to God, asking, "Where is God my Maker who gives songs in the night, [11]and makes us a little wiser than the animals and birds?"

Job 36:22. Look, God is all-powerful. Who is a teacher like him?

Job 38:36. Who gives intuition and instinct? [37]Who is wise enough to number all the clouds? Who can tilt the water jars of heaven . . . ?

Ps 16:7. I will bless the Lord who counsels me; he gives me wisdom in the night. He tells me what to do.

Ps 19:1. The heavens are telling the glory of God; they are a marvelous display of his craftsmanship. [2]Day and night they keep on telling about God.

Ps 25:8. The Lord is good and glad to teach the proper path to all who go astray; [9]he will teach the ways that are right and best to those who humbly turn to him. [12]Where is the man who fears the Lord? God will teach him how to choose the best. [14]Friendship with God is reserved for those who reverence him. With them alone he shares the secrets of his promises.

Ps 32:8. I will instruct you (says the Lord) and guide you along the best pathway for your life; I will advise you and watch your progress.

Ps 36:9. For you are the Fountain of life; our light is from your Light.

Ps 51:6. You deserve honesty from the heart; yes,

utter sincerity and truthfulness. Oh, give me this wisdom.

Ps 71:17. O God, you have helped me from my earliest childhood—and I have constantly testified to others of the wonderful things you do.

Ps 94:12. So he helps us by punishing us. This makes us follow his paths.

Ps 112:4. When darkness overtakes him, light will come bursting in. He is kind and merciful.

Ps 119:130. As your plan unfolds, even the simple can understand it.

Prov 1:23. Come here and listen to me! I'll pour out the spirit of wisdom upon you, and make you wise.

Prov 2:6. For the Lord grants wisdom! His every word is a treasure of knowledge and understanding. [7]He grants good sense to the godly—his saints.

Prov 3:5. Trust the Lord completely; don't ever trust yourself. [6]In everything you do, put God first, and he will direct you and crown your efforts with success.

Eccl 2:26. For God gives those who please him wisdom, knowledge, and joy.

Isa 11:1. The royal line of David will be cut off, chopped down like a tree; but from the stump will grow a Shoot—yes, a new Branch from the old root. [2]And the Spirit of the Lord shall rest upon him, the Spirit of wisdom, understanding, counsel and might; the Spirit of knowledge and of the fear of the Lord. [3]His delight will be obedience to the Lord. He will not judge by appearance, false evidence, or hearsay.

Isa 30:21. And if you leave God's paths and go astray, you will hear a Voice behind you say, "No, this is the way; walk here."

Isa 42:6. "I the Lord have called you to demonstrate my righteousness. I will guard and support you, for I have given you to my people as the personal confirmation of my covenant with them. You shall also be a light to guide the nations unto me. [7]You will open the eyes of the blind, and release those who sit in prison darkness and despair." [16]He will bring blind Israel along a path they have not seen before. He will make the darkness bright before them and smooth and straighten out the road ahead. He will not forsake them.

Isa 48:17. The Lord, your Redeemer, the Holy One of Israel, says, I am the Lord your God, who punishes you for your own good and leads you along the paths that you should follow.

Isa 54:13. And all your citizens shall be taught by me, and their prosperity shall be great.

Jer 24:7. I will give them hearts that respond to me. They shall be my people and I will be their God, for they shall return to me with great joy.

Dan 1:17. God gave these four youths great ability to learn and they soon mastered all the literature and science of the time, and God gave to Daniel special ability in understanding the meanings of dreams and visions.

Dan 2:20. Saying, "Blessed be the name of God forever and ever, for he alone has all wisdom and all power. [21]World events are under his control. He removes kings and sets others on their thrones. He gives wise men their wisdom, and scholars their intelligence. [22]He reveals profound mysteries beyond man's understanding. He knows all hidden things, for he is light, and darkness is no obstacle to him. [23]I thank and praise you, O God of my fathers, for you have given me wisdom and glowing health, and now, even this vision of the king's dream, and the understanding of what it means."

Mt 11:25. And Jesus prayed this prayer: "O Father, Lord of heaven and earth, thank you for hiding the truth from those who think themselves so wise, and for revealing it to little children. [26]Yes, Father, for it pleased you to do it this way! . . . [27]Everything has been entrusted to me by my Father. Only the Father knows the Son, and the Father is known only by the Son and by those to whom the Son reveals him."

Mt 13:11. Then he explained to them that only they were permitted to understand about the Kingdom of Heaven, and others were not.

Mt 16:16. Simon Peter answered, "The Christ, the Messiah, the Son of the living God." [17]"God has blessed you, Simon, son of Jonah," Jesus said, "for my Father in heaven has personally revealed this to you—this is not from any human source."

Lk 1:76. And you, my little son, shall be called the prophet of the glorious God, for you will prepare the way for the Messiah. [77]You will tell his people how to find salvation through forgiveness of their sins. [78]All this will be because the mercy of our God is very tender, and heaven's dawn is about to break upon us, [79]to give light to those who sit in darkness and death's shadow, and to guide us to the path of peace.

Lk 12:11. And when you are brought to trial before these Jewish rulers and authorities in the synagogues, don't be concerned about what to say in your defense, [12]for the Holy Spirit will give you the right words even as you are standing there.

Lk 21:15. For I will give you the right words and such logic that none of your opponents will be able to reply!

Lk 24:32. They began telling each other how their hearts had felt strangely warm as he talked with them and explained the Scriptures during the walk down the road. [45]Then he opened their minds to understand at last these many Scriptures!

Jn 1:1, 2. Before anything else existed, there was Christ, with God. He has always been alive and is himself God. [4]Eternal life is in him, and this life gives light to all mankind. [5]His life is the light that shines through the darkness—and the darkness can never extinguish it. [6, 7]God sent John the Baptist as a witness to the fact that Jesus Christ is the true Light. [8]John himself was not the Light; he was only a witness to identify it. [9]Later on, the one who is the true Light arrived to shine on everyone coming into the world. [17]For Moses gave us only the Law with its rigid demands and merciless justice, while Jesus Christ brought us loving forgiveness as well.

Jn 6:45. As it is written in the Scriptures, "They

shall all be taught of God." Those the Father speaks to, who learn the truth from him, will be attracted to me.

Jn 8:12. Later, in one of his talks, Jesus said to the people, "I am the Light of the world. So if you follow me, you won't be stumbling through the darkness, for living light will flood your path."
[31]Jesus said to them, "You are truly my disciples if you live as I tell you to, [32]and you will know the truth, and the truth will set you free."

Jn 9:5. "But while I am still here in the world, I give it my light." [39]Then Jesus told him, "I have come into the world to give sight to those who are spiritually blind and to show those who think they see that they are blind."

Jn 12:46. I have come as a Light to shine in this dark world, so that all who put their trust in me will no longer wander in the darkness.

Jn 14:7. If you had known who I am, then you would have known who my Father is. From now on you know him—and have seen him!

Jn 16:13. When the Holy Spirit, who is truth, comes, he shall guide you into all truth, for he will not be presenting his own ideas, but will be passing on to you what he has heard. He will tell you about the future. [14]He shall praise me and bring me great honor by showing you my glory.

Jn 17:6. I have told these men all about you. They were in the world, but then you gave them to me. Actually, they were always yours, and you gave them to me; and they have obeyed you. [26]And I have revealed you to them, and will keep on revealing you so that the mighty love you have for me may be in them, and I in them.

Jn 18:37. I was born for that purpose. And I came to bring truth to the world. All who love the truth are my followers.

Rom 1:19. For the truth about God is known to them instinctively; God has put this knowledge in their hearts. [20]Since earliest times men have seen the earth and sky and all God made, and have known of his existence and great eternal power.

1 Cor 1:30. For it is from God alone that you have your life through Christ Jesus. He showed us God's plan of salvation; he was the one who made us acceptable to God; he made us pure and holy and gave himself to purchase our salvation.

1 Cor 2:9. That is what is meant by the Scriptures which say that no mere man has ever seen, heard or even imagined what wonderful things God has ready for those who love the Lord. [10]But we know about these things because God has sent his Spirit to tell us, and his Spirit searches out and shows us all of God's deepest secrets. [11]No one can really know what anyone else is thinking, or what he is really like, except that person himself. And no one can know God's thoughts except God's own Spirit.
[12]And God has actually given us his Spirit (not the world's spirit) to tell us about the wonderful free gifts of grace and blessing that God has given us.
[13]In telling you about these gifts we have even used the very words given to us by the Holy Spirit, not words that we as men might choose. So we use the Holy Spirit's words to explain the Holy Spirit's facts. [14]But the man who isn't a Christian can't understand and can't accept these thoughts from God, which the Holy Spirit teaches us. They sound foolish to him, because only those who have the Holy Spirit within them can understand what the Holy Spirit means. Others just can't take it in.

1 Cor 12:8. To one person the Spirit gives the ability to give wise advice; someone else may be especially good at studying and teaching, and this is his gift from the same Spirit.

2 Cor 4:6. For God, who said, "Let there be light in the darkness," has made us understand that it is the brightness of his glory that is seen in the face of Jesus Christ.

Phil 3:15. I hope all of you who are mature Christians will see eye-to-eye with me on these things, and if you disagree on some point, I believe that God will make it plain to you.

Col 1:26, 27. He has kept this secret for centuries and generations past, but now at last it has pleased him to tell it to those who love him and live for him, and the riches and glory of his plan are for you Gentiles too. And this is the secret: *that Christ in your hearts is your only hope of glory.* [28]So everywhere we go we talk about Christ to all who will listen, warning them and teaching them as well as we know how.

2 Tim 1:7. For the Holy Spirit, God's gift, does not want you to be afraid of people, but to be wise and strong, and to love them and enjoy being with them.

Jas 3:17. But the wisdom that comes from heaven is first of all pure and full of quiet gentleness. Then it is peace-loving and courteous. It allows discussion and is willing to yield to others; it is wholehearted and straightforward and sincere.

2 Pet 1:2. Do you want more and more of God's kindness and peace? Then learn to know him better and better. [3]For as you know him better, he will give you, through his great power, everything you need for living a truly good life: he even shares his own glory and his own goodness with us! [4]And by that same mighty power he has given us all the other rich and wonderful blessings he promised; for instance, the promise to save us from the lust and rottenness all around us, and to give us his own character. [5]But to obtain these gifts, you need more than faith; you must also work hard to be good, and even that is not enough. For then you must learn to know God better and discover what he wants you to do. [8]The more you go on in this way, the more you will grow strong spiritually and become fruitful and useful to our Lord Jesus Christ.
[12]I plan to keep on reminding you of these things even though you already know them and are really getting along quite well!

2 Pet 3:18. But grow in spiritual strength and become better acquainted with our Lord and Savior Jesus Christ.

1 Jn 2:20. But you are not like that, for the Holy Spirit has come upon you, and you know the truth.
[27]But you have received the Holy Spirit and he lives

within you, in your hearts, so that you don't need anyone to teach you what is right. For he teaches you all things, and he is the Truth, and no liar; and so, just as he has said, you must live in Christ, never to depart from him.

1 Jn 5:20. And we know that Christ, God's Son, has come to help us understand and find the true God. And now we are in God because we are in Jesus Christ his Son.

See *God, Wisdom of.*

Prayer for Spiritual. Num 27:21. He shall be the one to consult with Eleazar the priest in order to get directions from the Lord. The Lord will speak to Eleazar through the use of the Urim, and Eleazar will pass on these instructions to Joshua and the people. In this way the Lord will continue to give them guidance.

Judg 20:18. Before the battle the Israeli army went to Bethel first to ask counsel from God.

1 Kgs 3:7. O Lord my God, now you have made me the king instead of my father David, but I am as a little child who doesn't know his way around. [9]Give me an understanding mind so that I can govern your people well and know the difference between what is right and what is wrong. For who by himself is able to carry such a heavy responsibility? 2 Chron 1:10.

1 Kgs 8:36. Hear them from heaven and forgive them when they pray toward this place and confess your name. And after you have punished them, help them to follow the good ways in which they should walk.

Job 34:32. Or, "We know not what evil we have done; only tell us, and we will cease at once."

Ps 5:8. Lord, lead me as you promised me you would; otherwise my enemies will conquer me. Tell me clearly what to do, which way to turn.

Ps 25:4. Show me the path where I should go, O Lord; point out the right road for me to walk. [5]Lead me; teach me; for you are the God who gives me salvation. I have no hope except in you.

Ps 27:11. Tell me what to do, O Lord, and make it plain because I am surrounded by waiting enemies.

Ps 31:3. Yes, you are my Rock and my fortress; honor your name by leading me out of this peril.

Ps 39:4. Lord, help me to realize how brief my time on earth will be. Help me to know that I am here for but a moment more.

Ps 43:3. Oh, send out your light and your truth —let them lead me. Let them lead me to your Temple on your holy mountain, Zion.

Ps 86:11. Tell me where you want me to go and I will go there. May every fiber of my being unite in reverence to your name.

Ps 90:12. Teach us to number our days and recognize how few they are; help us to spend them as we should.

Ps 119:12. Blessed Lord, teach me your rules. [18]Open my eyes to see wonderful things in your Word. [19]I am a pilgrim here on earth: how I need a map—and your commands are my chart and guide. [26]I told you my plans and you replied. Now give me your instructions. [27]Make me understand what you want; for then I shall see your miracles. [33, 34]Just tell me what to do and I will do it, Lord. As long as I live I'll wholeheartedly obey. [66]Now teach me good judgment as well as knowledge. For your laws are my guide. [68]You are good and do only good; make me follow your lead. [73]You made my body, Lord; now give me sense to heed your laws. [80]Help me to love your every wish; then I will never have to be ashamed of myself. [124]Lord, deal with me in lovingkindness, and teach me, your servant, to obey; [125]for I am your servant; therefore give me common sense to apply your rules to everything I do. [135]Look down in love upon me and teach me all your laws. [144]Your laws are always fair; help me to understand them and I shall live. [169]O Lord, listen to my prayers; give me the common sense you promised. [171]I praise you for letting me learn your laws.

Ps 139:24. Point out anything you find in me that makes you sad, and lead me along the path of everlasting life.

Eph 1:16, 17. I have never stopped thanking God for you. I pray for you constantly, asking God, the glorious Father of our Lord Jesus Christ, to give you wisdom to see clearly and really understand who Christ is and all that he has done for you. [18]I pray that your hearts will be flooded with light so that you can see something of the future he has called you to share. I want you to realize that God has been made rich because we who are Christ's have been given to him! [19]I pray that you will begin to understand how incredibly great his power is to help those who believe him. It is that same mighty power [20]that raised Christ from the dead.

Eph 3:14, 15. When I think of the wisdom and scope of his plan I fall down on my knees and pray to the Father of all the great family of God—some of them already in heaven and some down here on earth—[16]that out of his glorious, unlimited resources he will give you the mighty inner strengthening of his Holy Spirit. [17]And I pray that Christ will be more and more at home in your hearts, living within you as you trust in him. May your roots go down deep into the soil of God's marvelous love; [18, 19]and may you be able to feel and understand, as all God's children should, how long, how wide, how deep, and how high his love really is; and to experience this love for yourselves, though it is so great that you will never see the end of it or fully know or understand it. And so at last you will be filled up with God himself.

Eph 6:18. Pray all the time. Ask God for anything in line with the Holy Spirit's wishes. Plead with him, reminding him of your needs, and keep praying earnestly for all Christians everywhere. [19]Pray for me, too, and ask God to give me the right words as I boldly tell others about the Lord, and as I explain to them that his salvation is for the Gentiles too. [20]I am in chains now for preaching this message from God. But pray that I will keep on speaking out boldly for him even here in prison, as I should.

Phil 1:9. My prayer for you is that you will overflow more and more with love for others, and at the same time keep on growing in spiritual knowledge and insight, [10]for I want you always to see clearly the difference between right and wrong, and to be inwardly clean, no one being able to criticize you from now until our Lord returns.

Col 1:9. So ever since we first heard about you we have kept on praying and asking God to help you understand what he wants you to do; asking him to make you wise about spiritual things; [10]and asking that the way you live will always please the Lord and honor him, so that you will always be doing good, kind things for others, while all the time you are learning to know God better and better.

Col 2:1. I wish you could know how much I have struggled in prayer for you and for the church in Laodicea, and for my many other friends who have never known me personally. [2]This is what I have asked of God for you: that you will be encouraged and knit together by strong ties of love, and that you will have the rich experience of knowing Christ with real certainty and clear understanding. *For God's secret plan, now at last made known, is Christ himself.* [3]In him lie hidden all the mighty, untapped treasures of wisdom and knowledge.

Col 4:2. Don't be weary in prayer; keep at it; watch for God's answers and remember to be thankful when they come. [3]Don't forget to pray for us too, that God will give us many chances to preach the Good News of Christ for which I am here in jail. [4]Pray that I will be bold enough to tell it freely and fully, and make it plain, as, of course, I should.

2 Tim 2:7. Think over these three illustrations, and may the Lord help you to understand how they apply to you.

Jas 1:5. If you want to know what God wants you to do, ask him, and he will gladly tell you, for he is always ready to give a bountiful supply of wisdom to all who ask him; he will not resent it.

See *Desire, Spiritual.*

WORLDLY. Gen 3:6. The woman was convinced. How lovely and fresh looking it was! And it would make her so wise! So she ate some of the fruit and gave some to her husband, and he ate it too. [7]And as they ate it, suddenly they became aware of their nakedness, and were embarrassed. So they strung fig leaves together to cover themselves around the hips.

Job 4:18, 19. If God cannot trust his own messengers (for even angels make mistakes), how much less men made of dust, who are crushed to death as easily as moths! [20]They are alive in the morning, but by evening they are dead, gone forever with hardly a thought from anyone. [21]Their candle of life is snuffed out. They die and no one cares.

Job 5:12. He frustrates the plans of crafty men. [13]They are caught in their own traps; he thwarts their schemes.

Job 11:2. Shouldn't someone stem this torrent of words? Is a man proved right by all this talk? [12]Mere man is as likely to be wise as a wild donkey's colt is likely to be born a man!

Job 37:24. No wonder men everywhere fear him! For he is not impressed by the world's wisest men!

Prov 3:7. Don't be conceited, sure of your own wisdom. Instead, trust and reverence the Lord, and turn your back on evil.

Prov 15:21. If a man enjoys folly, something is wrong! The sensible stay on the pathways of right. [22]Plans go wrong with too few counselors; many counselors bring success.

Prov 16:25. Before every man there lies a wide and pleasant road he thinks is right, but it ends in death.

Prov 17:2. A wise slave will rule his master's wicked sons and share their estate. [10]A rebuke to a man of common sense is more effective than a hundred lashes on the back of a rebel.

Prov 20:18. Don't go ahead with your plans without the advice of others; don't go to war until they agree.

Prov 21:20. The wise man saves for the future, but the foolish man spends whatever he gets. [22]The wise man conquers the strong man and levels his defenses. [30]No one, regardless of how shrewd or well-advised he is, can stand against the Lord.

Prov 24:3, 4. Any enterprise is built by wise planning, becomes strong through common sense, and profits wonderfully by keeping abreast of the facts. [5]A wise man is mightier than a strong man. Wisdom is mightier than strength. [6]Don't go to war without wise guidance; there is safety in many counselors. [7]Wisdom is too much for a rebel. He'll not be chosen as a counselor!

Eccl 1:18. For the more my wisdom, the more my grief; to increase knowledge only increases distress.

Eccl 2:1. I said to myself, "Come now, be merry; enjoy yourself to the full." But I found that this, too, was futile. For it is silly to be laughing all the time; what good does it do? [3]So, after a lot of thinking, I decided to try the road of drink, while still holding steadily to my course of seeking wisdom. Next I changed my course again and followed the path of folly, so that I could experience the only happiness most men have throughout their lives. [4-6]Then I tried to find fulfillment by inaugurating a great public works program: homes, vineyards, gardens, parks and orchards for myself, and reservoirs to hold the water to irrigate my plantations. [7, 8]Next I bought slaves, both men and women, and others were born within my household. I also bred great herds and flocks, more than any of the kings before me. I collected silver and gold as taxes from many kings and provinces. In the cultural arts, I organized men's and women's choirs and orchestras. And then there were my many beautiful concubines. [9]So I became greater than any of the kings in Jerusalem before me, and with it all I remained clear-eyed, so that I could evaluate all these things. [10]Anything I wanted, I took, and did not restrain myself from any joy. I even found great pleasure in hard work.

This pleasure was, indeed, my only reward for all my labors. [11]But as I looked at everything I had tried, it was all so useless, a chasing of the wind, and there was nothing really worthwhile anywhere. [12]Now I began a study of the comparative virtues of wisdom and folly, and anyone else would come to the same conclusion I did—[13, 14]that wisdom is of more value than foolishness, just as light is better than darkness; for the wise man sees, while the fool is blind. And yet I noticed that there was one thing that happened to wise and foolish alike —[15]just as the fool will die, so will I. So of what value is all my wisdom? Then I realized that even wisdom is futile. [16]For the wise and fool both die, and in the days to come both will be long forgotten. [17]So now I hate life because it is all so irrational; all is foolishness, chasing the wind. [18]And I am disgusted about this, that I must leave the fruits of all my hard work to others. [19]And who can tell whether my son will be a wise man or a fool? And yet all I have will be given to him—how discouraging! [20-23]So I turned in despair from hard work as the answer to my search for satisfaction. For though I spend my life searching for wisdom, knowledge, and skill, I must leave all of it to someone who hasn't done a day's work in his life; he inherits all my efforts, free of charge. This is not only foolish, but unfair. So what does a man get for all his hard work? Days full of sorrow and grief, and restless, bitter nights. It is all utterly ridiculous. [24-26]So I decided that there was nothing better for a man to do than to enjoy his food and drink, and his job. Then I realized that even this pleasure is from the hand of God. For who can eat or enjoy apart from him? For God gives those who please him wisdom, knowledge, and joy; but if a sinner becomes wealthy, God takes the wealth away from him and gives it to those who please him. So here, too, we see an example of foolishly chasing the wind.

Eccl 7:11. To be wise is as good as being rich; in fact, it is better. [12]You can get anything by either wisdom or money, but being wise has many advantages. [13]See the way God does things and fall into line. Don't fight the facts of nature. [16, 17]So don't be too good or too wise! Why destroy yourself? On the other hand, don't be too wicked either—don't be a fool! Why should you die before your time? [18]Tackle every task that comes along, and if you fear God you can expect his blessing. [19]A wise man is stronger than the mayors of ten big cities! [20]And there is not a single man in all the earth who is always good and never sins. [21, 22]Don't eavesdrop! You may hear your servant cursing you! For you know how often you yourself curse others! [23]I have tried my best to be wise. I declared, "I *will* be wise," but it didn't work. [24]Wisdom is far away, and very difficult to find. [25]I searched everywhere, determined to find wisdom and the reason for things, and to prove to myself the wickedness of folly, and that foolishness is madness.

Eccl 8:1. How wonderful to be wise, to understand things, to be able to analyze them and interpret them. Wisdom lights up a man's face, softening its hardness. [16, 17]In my search for wisdom I observed all that was going on everywhere across the earth—ceaseless activity day and night. (Of course, only God can see everything, and even the wisest man who says he knows everything doesn't!)

Eccl 10:2. A wise man's heart leads him to do right, and a fool's heart leads him to do evil. [3]You can identify a fool just by the way he walks down the street! [10]A dull axe requires great strength; be wise and sharpen the blade.

Isa 5:21. Woe to those who are wise and shrewd in their own eyes!

Isa 28:24. Does a farmer always plow and never sow? Is he forever harrowing the soil and never planting it? [25]Does he not finally plant his many kinds of grain, each in its own section of his land? [26]He knows just what to do, for God has made him see and understand. [27]He doesn't thresh all grains the same. A sledge is never used on dill, but it is beaten with a stick. A threshing wheel is never rolled on cummin, but it is beaten softly with a flail. [28]Bread grain is easily crushed, so he doesn't keep on pounding it. [29]The Lord of Hosts is a wonderful teacher and gives the farmer wisdom.

Isa 29:14. "Therefore I will take awesome vengeance on these hypocrites, and make their wisest counselors as fools." [15]Woe to those who try to hide their plans from God, who try to keep him in the dark concerning what they do! "God can't see us," they say to themselves. "He doesn't know what is going on!" [16]How stupid can they be! Isn't he, the Potter, greater than you, the jars he makes? Will you say to him, "He didn't make us"? Does a machine call its inventor dumb?

Isa 47:10. You felt secure in all your wickedness. "No one sees me," you said. Your "wisdom" and "knowledge" have caused you to turn away from me and claim that you yourself are Jehovah. [11]That is why disaster shall overtake you suddenly.

Jer 8:7. The stork knows the time of her migration, as does the turtledove, and the crane, and the swallow. They all return at God's appointed time each year; but not my people! They don't accept the laws of God. [8]How can you say, "We understand his laws," when your teachers have twisted them up to mean a thing I never said? [9]These wise teachers of yours will be shamed by exile for this sin, for they have rejected the word of the Lord. Are they then so wise?

Jer 9:23. The Lord says: Let not the wise man bask in his wisdom, nor the mighty man in his might, nor the rich man in his riches. [24]Let them boast in this alone: That they truly know me, and understand that I am the Lord of justice and of righteousness whose love is steadfast; and that I love to be this way.

Jer 49:7. The Lord of Hosts says: Where are all your wise men of days gone by? Is there not one left in all of Teman?

Ezk 28:2, 3. Son of dust, say to the prince of Tyre: The Lord God says: You are so proud you think you are God. . . . But you are only a man, and not a god, though you boast yourself to be like God. You are wiser than Daniel, for no secret is hidden from you. [4]You have used your wisdom and understanding to get great wealth—gold and silver and many treasures. [5]Yes, your wisdom has made you very rich and very proud. [6]Therefore the Lord God says: Because you claim you are as wise as God, [7]an enemy army, the terror of the nations, shall suddenly draw their swords against your marvelous wisdom and defile your splendor! *vs.* 12, 17.

Mt 7:24. All who listen to my instructions and follow them are wise, like a man who builds his house on solid rock. [25]Though the rain comes in torrents, and the floods rise and the storm winds beat against his house, it won't collapse, for it is built on rock. [26]But those who hear my instructions and ignore them are foolish, like a man who builds his house on sand. [27]For when the rains and floods come, and storm winds beat against his house, it will fall with a mighty crash.

Mt 11:25. And Jesus prayed this prayer: "O Father, Lord of heaven and earth, thank you for hiding the truth from those who think themselves so wise, and for revealing it to little children." Lk 10: 21.

Lk 16:8. The rich man had to admire the rascal for being so shrewd. And it is true that the citizens of this world are more clever (in dishonesty!) than the godly are.

Rom 1:21. Yes, they knew about him all right, but they wouldn't admit it or worship him or even thank him for all his daily care. And after awhile they began to think up silly ideas of what God was like and what he wanted them to do. The result was that their foolish minds became dark and confused. [22]Claiming themselves to be wise without God, they became utter fools instead. [23]And then, instead of worshiping the glorious, ever-living God, they took wood and stone and made idols for themselves, carving them to look like mere birds and animals and snakes and puny men.

1 Cor 1:17. For Christ didn't send me to baptize, but to preach the Gospel; and even my preaching sounds poor, for I do not fill my sermons with profound words and high sounding ideas, for fear of diluting the mighty power there is in the simple message of the cross of Christ. [18]I know very well how foolish it sounds to those who are lost, when they hear that Jesus died to save them. But we who are saved recognize this message as the very power of God. [19]For God says, "I will destroy all human plans of salvation no matter how wise they seem to be, and ignore the best ideas of men, even the most brilliant of them." [20]So what about these wise men, these scholars, these brilliant debaters of this world's great affairs? God has made them all look foolish, and shown their wisdom to be useless nonsense. [Isa 44:25.] [21]For God in his wisdom saw to it that the world would never find God through human brilliance, and then he stepped in and saved all those who believed his message, which the world calls foolish and silly. [22]It seems foolish to the Jews because they want a sign from heaven as proof that what is preached is true; and it is foolish to the Gentiles because they believe only what agrees with their philosophy and seems wise to them. [23]So when we preach about Christ dying to save them, the Jews are offended and the Gentiles say it's all nonsense. [24]But God has opened the eyes of those called to salvation, both Jews and Gentiles, to see that Christ is the mighty power of God to save them; Christ himself is the center of God's wisest plan for their salvation. [25]This so-called "foolish" plan of God is far wiser than the wisest plan of the wisest man, and God in his weakness —Christ dying on the cross—is far stronger than any man. [26]Notice among yourselves, dear brothers, that few of you who follow Christ have big names or power or wealth. [27]Instead, God has deliberately chosen to use ideas the world considers foolish and of little worth in order to shame those people considered by the world as wise and great.

1 Cor 2:1. Dear brothers, even when I first came to you I didn't use lofty words and brilliant ideas to tell you God's message. [2]For I decided that I would speak only of Jesus Christ and his death on the cross. [3]I came to you in weakness—timid and trembling. [4]And my preaching was very plain, not with a lot of oratory and human wisdom, but the Holy Spirit's power was in my words, proving to those who heard them that the message was from God. [5]I did this because I wanted your faith to stand firmly upon God, not on man's great ideas. [6]Yet when I am among mature Christians I do speak with words of great wisdom, but not the kind that comes from here on earth, and not the kind that appeals to the great men of this world, who are doomed to fall. [7]Our words are wise because they are from God, telling of God's wise plan to bring us into the glories of heaven. This plan was hidden in former times, though it was made for our benefit before the world began. [8]But the great men of the world have not understood it; if they had, they never would have crucified the Lord of Glory. [9]That is what is meant by the Scriptures which say that no mere man has ever seen, heard or even imagined what wonderful things God has ready for those who love the Lord. [10]But we know about these things because God has sent his Spirit to tell us, and his Spirit searches out and shows us all of God's deepest secrets. [11]No one can really know what anyone else is thinking, or what he is really like, except that person himself. And no one can know God's thoughts except God's own Spirit. [12]And God has actually given us his Spirit (not the world's spirit) to tell us about the wonderful free gifts of grace and blessing that God has given us. [13]In telling you about these gifts we have even used the very words given to us by the Holy Spirit, not words that we as men might choose. So we use the Holy Spirit's words to explain the Holy Spirit's facts. [14]But the man who isn't a Christian can't understand and can't accept these thoughts from God, which the Holy Spirit teaches us. They sound foolish to him, because only those who have the

Holy Spirit within them can understand what the Holy Spirit means.

1 Cor 3:18. Stop fooling yourselves. If you count yourself above average in intelligence, as judged by this world's standards, you had better put this all aside and be a fool rather than let it hold you back from the true wisdom from above. [19]For the wisdom of this world is foolishness to God. As it says in the book of Job, God uses man's own brilliance to trap him; he stumbles over his own "wisdom" and falls. [20]And again, in the book of Psalms, we are told that the Lord knows full well how the human mind reasons, and how foolish and futile it is.

1 Cor 8:1. But although being a "know-it-all" makes us feel important, what is really needed to build a church is love. [2]If anyone thinks he knows all the answers, he is just showing his ignorance.

2 Cor 1:12. We are so glad that we can say with utter honesty that in all our dealings we have been pure and sincere, quietly depending upon the Lord for his help, and not on our own skills. And that is even more true, if possible, about the way we have acted toward you.

Col 2:8. Don't let others spoil your faith and joy with their philosophies, their wrong and shallow answers built on men's thoughts and ideas, instead of on what Christ has said.

1 Tim 6:20. Oh, Timothy, don't fail to do these things that God entrusted to you. Keep out of foolish arguments with those who boast of their "knowledge" and thus prove their lack of it. [21]Some of these people have missed the most important thing in life—they don't know God.

Jas 3:15. For jealousy and selfishness are not God's kind of wisdom. Such things are earthly, unspiritual, inspired by the devil.

See *Knowledge.*

WISE MEN Of Egypt, Gen 41:8, 24. Solomon, 1 Kgs 4:29–34. Of Babylon, Dan 4:18. Of the East, Mt 2:1–12. All who win souls are wise, Prov 11:30.

See *Wisdom.*

WITCHCRAFT Law concerning, Ex 22:18; Lev 19:31; 20:6, 27. Witch of Endor, 1 Sam 28:7–25. Witches destroyed, 1 Sam 28:3, 9.

See *Sorcery.*

WITNESS Lev 5:1; Prov 18:17. Qualified by oath, Ex 22:11; Num 5:19, 21, 22; 1 Kgs 8:31, 32; by laying hands on the accused, Lev 24:13, 14. Two necessary to establish a fact, Num 35:30; Deut 17:6; 19:15; Mt 18:16; Jn 8:17; 2 Cor 13:1; 1 Tim 5:19; Heb 10:28. Required to throw the first stone in executing sentence, Deut 13:9; 17:5–7; Acts 7:58.

To the transfer of land, Gen 21:25–30; 23:11, 16–18; Ruth 4:1–9; Jer 32:9–12, 24, 44. To marriage, Ruth 4:10, 11; Isa 8:2, 3. Incorruptible, Ps 15:4. Corrupted by money, Mt 28:11–15; Acts 6:11, 13.

FIGURATIVE. Of instruction in righteousness, Rev 11:3.

See *Courts; Evidence; False Witness; Holy Spirit; Lying; Testimony; Testimony, Religious.*

WITNESS, ALTAR OF Built by the people of Reuben and God, Josh 22:34.

WIZARD See *Sorcery; Witchcraft.*

WOLF Ravenous, Gen 49:27; Jer 5:6; Ezk 22:27; Hab 1:8; Zeph 3:3; Jn 10:12.

FIGURATIVE. Of the enemies of the righteous, Mt 7:15; 10:16; Jn 10:12; Acts 20:29. Of the reconciling power of the gospel, Isa 11:6; 65:25.

WOMEN Creation of, Gen 1:27; 2:21, 22. Named, Gen 2:23. Fall of, and curse upon, Gen 3:1–16; 2 Cor 11:3; 1 Tim 2:14. Promise to, Gen 3:15.

Had separate apartments in dwelling, Gen 24:67; 31:33; Esther 2:9, 11. Veiled the face, Gen 24:65; see *Veil.*

Vows of, Num 30:3–16. When jealously charged with infidelity, guilt or innocence to be determined by trial, Num 5:11–31.

Took part in ancient worship, Ex 15:20, 21; 38:8; 1 Sam 2:22; in choir, Ezra 2:65; Neh 7:67. Assisted at the Tabernacle, Ex 38:8; 1 Sam 2:22. Donated jewelry to the Tabernacle, Ex 35:22; mirrors, Ex 38:8. Required to attend reading of the law, Deut 31:12; Josh 8:35.

Purifications of: After menstruation, Lev 15:19–33; 2 Sam 11:4; childbirth, Lev 12; Lk 2:22. Difference in ceremonies made between male and female children, Lev 12.

Religious privileges of, among early Christians, Acts 1:14; 12:12, 13; 1 Cor 11:5; 14:34; 1 Tim 2:11.

Domestic duties of, Gen 18:6; Prov 31:15–20; Mt 24:41. Cooked, Gen 18:6; spun, Ex 35:25, 26; embroidered, Prov 31:22. Made garments, 1 Sam 2:19; Prov 31:19–24; Acts 9:39. Gleaned, Ruth 2:8, 9. Kept vineyards, Song 1:6. Tended flocks and herds, Gen 24:11, 13, 14, 19, 20; 29:9; Ex 2:16. Were gatekeepers, Jn 18:16, 17; Acts 12:13, 14.

Forbidden to wear men's clothing, Deut 22:5. Wore hair long, 1 Cor 11:5–15. Rules for dress of Christian, 1 Tim 2:9, 10; 1 Pet 3:3, 4. Ornaments of, Isa 3:16–23.

Weaker than men, 1 Pet 3:7. Are timid, Isa 19:16; Jer 50:37; 51:30; Nah 3:13; affectionate, 2 Sam 1:26; tender to her offspring, Isa 49:15; Lam 4:10; joyful, Judg 11:34; 21:21; Jer 31:13; Zech 9:16, 17; courteous to strangers, Gen 24:17. Could not marry without consent of parents, Gen 24:3, 4; 34:6, 7; Ex 22:17. Not to be married considered a calamity, Judg 11:37; Ps 78:63; Isa 4:1. Taken captive, Num 31:9–11, 15, 17, 18, 32–35; Lam 1:18; Ezk 30:17, 18. Shrewd, 2 Sam 20:16–22.

Punishment to be inflicted on men for seducing, when engaged, Deut 22:23–27. Punishment for seducing, when not engaged, Ex 22:16, 17; Deut 22:28, 29. Treated with cruelty in war, Deut 32:25; Lam 2:21; 5:11.

Virtuous, held high in estimation, Ruth 3:11; Prov 31:10–30.

Fond of self-indulgence, Isa 32:9–11; of ornaments, Jer 2:32. Subtle and deceitful, Prov 6:24–29, 32–35; 7:6–27; Eccl 7:26. Silly, and easily led into error, 2 Tim 3:6. Zealous in promoting superstition and idolatry, Num 31:15, 16; Neh 13:26; Jer 7:18; Ezk 13:17, 23. Active in instigating iniquity, 1 Kgs 21:25. Guilty of sodomy, Rom 1:26.

As rulers: Deborah, Judg 4:4; Athaliah, 2 Kgs 11: 1–16; 2 Chron 22:2, 3, 10–12; Queen of Sheba, 1 Kgs 10:1–13; Candace, Acts 8:27; Persian queen sat beside the king, Neh 2:5, 6. Patriotic: Miriam, Ex 15:20; Deborah, Judg 5; women of Israel, 1 Sam 18:6; of the Philistines, 2 Sam 1:20. Aid in defensive operations, Judg 9:53.

As poets: Miriam, Ex 15:21; Deborah, Judg 5; Hannah, 1 Sam 2:1–10; Elizabeth, Lk 1:42–45; Mary, Lk 1:46–55.

As prophets: Miriam, Ex 15:20, 21; Mic 6:4; Deborah, Judg 4:4, 5; Huldah, 2 Kgs 22:14–20; 2 Chron 34:22–28; No-adiah, Neh 6:14; Anna, Lk 2:36–38; Philip's daughter's, Acts 21:9. False prophets, Ezk 13:17–23.

In business, Prov 31:14–18, 24. Property rights of: In inheritance, Num 27:1–11; 36; Josh 17:3–6; Job 42:15; to sell real estate, Ruth 4:3–9.

Sold for husband's debts, Mt 18:25.

First to sin, Gen 3:6. Present at the cross, Mt 27: 55, 56; Mk 15:40, 41. First at the sepulcher, Mk 15: 46, 47; 16:1–6; Lk 23:27, 28, 49, 55, 56; 24:1–10. First to whom the risen Lord appeared, Mk 16:9; Jn 20: 14–18.

Converted by preaching of Paul, Acts 16:14, 15; 17:4, 12, 34.

Social status of: In Persia, Esther 1:10–22; Dan 5: 1–12; in Roman customs, Acts 24:24; 25:13, 23; 26: 30.

UNCLASSIFIED SCRIPTURES RELATING TO. Gen 2:18. And the Lord God said, "It isn't good for man to be alone; I will make a companion for him, a helper suited to his needs." [21]Then the Lord God caused the man to fall into a deep sleep, and took one of his ribs and closed up the place from which he had removed it, [22]and made the rib into a woman, and brought her to the man. [23]"This is it!" Adam exclaimed. "She is part of my own bone and flesh! Her name is 'woman' because she was taken out of a man." [24]This explains why a man leaves his father and mother and is joined to his wife in such a way that the two become one person.

Gen 3:16. Then God said to the woman, "You shall bear children in intense pain and suffering; yet even so, you shall welcome your husband's affections, and he shall be your master."

Esther 1:20. "When this decree is published throughout your great kingdom, husbands everywhere, whatever their rank, will be respected by their wives!" [21]The king and all his aides thought this made good sense, so he followed Memucan's counsel, [22]and sent letters to all of his provinces, in all the local languages, stressing that every man should rule his home, and should assert his authority.

Ps 68:11. The Lord speaks. The enemy flees. The women at home cry out the happy news.

Prov 11:16. Honor goes to kind and gracious women. [22]A beautiful woman lacking discretion and modesty is like a fine gold ring in a pig's snout.

Prov 12:4. A worthy wife is her husband's joy and crown; the other kind corrodes his strength and tears down everything he does.

Prov 14:1. A wise woman builds her house, while a foolish woman tears hers down by her own efforts.

Prov 18:22. The man who finds a wife finds a good thing; she is a blessing to him from the Lord.

Prov 19:13. A nagging wife annoys like constant dripping. [14]A father can give his sons homes and riches, but only the Lord can give them understanding wives.

Prov 21:9. It is better to live in the corner of an attic than with a crabby woman in a lovely home. [19]Better to live in the desert than with a quarrelsome, complaining woman. Prov 25:24.

Prov 27:15. A constant dripping on a rainy day and a cranky woman are much alike! [16]You can no more stop her complaints than you can stop the wind or hold onto anything with oil-slick hands.

Prov 30:21, 22, 23. There are three things that make the earth tremble—no, four it cannot stand: A slave who becomes a king. A rebel who prospers. A bitter woman when she finally marries. A servant girl who marries her mistress' husband.

Prov 31:10. If you can find a truly good wife, she is worth more than precious gems! [11]Her husband can trust her, and she will richly satisfy his needs. [12]She will not hinder him, but help him all her life. [13]She finds wool and flax and busily spins it. [14]She buys imported foods, brought by ship from distant ports. [15]She gets up before dawn to prepare breakfast for her household, and plans the day's work for her servant girls. [16]She goes out to inspect a field, and buys it; with her own hands she plants a vineyard. [17]She is energetic, a hard worker, [18]and watches for bargains. She works far into the night! [19, 20]She sews for the poor, and generously gives to the needy. [21]She has no fear of winter for her household, for she has made warm clothes for all of them. [22]She also upholsters with finest tapestry; her own clothing is beautifully made—a purple gown of pure linen. [23]Her husband is well known, for he sits in the council chamber with the other civic leaders. [24]She makes belted linen garments to sell to the merchants. [25]She is a woman of strength and dignity, and has no fear of old age. [26]When she speaks, her words are wise, and kindness is the rule for everything she says. [27]She watches carefully all that goes on throughout her household, and is never lazy. [28]Her children stand and bless her; so does her husband. He praises her with these words: [29]"There are many fine women in the world, but you are the best of them all!" [30]Charm can be deceptive and beauty doesn't last, but a woman who fears and reverences God shall be greatly praised. [31]Praise her for the many fine things she does. These good deeds of hers shall bring her honor and recognition from even the leaders of the nations.

Eccl 7:26. A prostitute is more bitter than death. May it please God that you escape from her, but sinners don't evade her snares. [27, 28]This is my conclusion, says the Preacher. Step by step I came to this result after researching in every direction: One tenth of one percent of the men I interviewed could be said to be wise, but not one woman!

Isa 3:16. Next, he will judge the haughty Jewish women, who mince along, noses in the air, tinkling bracelets on their ankles, with wanton eyes that rove among the crowds to catch the glances of the men. [17]The Lord will send a plague of scabs to ornament their heads! He will expose their nakedness for all to see. [18]No longer shall they tinkle with self-assurance as they walk. For the Lord will strip away their artful beauty and their ornaments, [19]their necklaces and bracelets and veils of shimmering gauze. [20]Gone shall be their scarves and ankle chains, headbands, earrings, and perfumes; [21]their rings and jewels, [22]and party clothes and negligees and capes and ornate combs and purses; [23]their mirrors, lovely lingerie, beautiful dresses and veils. [24]Instead of smelling of sweet perfume, they'll stink; for sashes they'll use ropes; their well-set hair will all fall out; they'll wear sacks instead of robes. All their beauty will be gone; all that will be left to them is shame and disgrace.

Isa 32:9. Listen, you women who loll around in lazy ease; listen to me and I will tell you your reward: [10]In a short time—in just a little more than a year—suddenly you'll care, O careless ones. For the crops of fruit will fail; the harvest will not take place. [11]Tremble, O women of ease; throw off your unconcern. Strip off your pretty clothes—wear sackcloth for your grief. [12]Beat your breasts in sorrow for those bountiful farms of yours that will soon be gone, and for those fruitful vines of other years.

Ezk 13:17. Son of dust, speak out against the women prophets too who pretend the Lord has given them his messages. [18]Tell them the Lord God says: Woe to these women who are damning the souls of my people, of both young and old alike, by tying magic charms on their wrists and furnishing them with magic veils and selling them indulgences. They refuse to even offer help unless they get a profit from it. [19]For the sake of a few paltry handfuls of barley or a piece of bread will you turn away my people from me? You have led those to death who should not die! And you have promised life to those who should not live, by lying to my people—and how they love it! [20]And so the Lord says: I will crush you because you hunt my people's souls with all your magic charms. I will tear off the charms and set my people free like birds from cages. [21]I will tear off the magic veils and save my people from you; they will no longer be your victims, and you shall know I am the Lord. [22]Your lies have discouraged the righteous, when I didn't want it so. And you have encouraged the wicked by promising life, though they continue in their sins. [23]But you will lie no more; no longer will you talk of seeing "visions" that you never saw, nor practice your magic, for I will deliver my people out of your hands by destroying you, and you shall know I am the Lord.

1 Cor 11:3. But there is one matter I want to remind you about: that a wife is responsible to her husband, her husband is responsible to Christ, and Christ is responsible to God. [4]That is why, if a man refuses to remove his hat while praying or preaching, he dishonors Christ. [5]And that is why a woman who publicly prays or prophesies without a covering on her head dishonors her husband (for her covering is a sign of her subjection to him). [6]Yes, if she refuses to wear a head covering, then she should cut off all her hair. And if it is shameful for a woman to have her head shaved, then she should wear a covering. [7]But a man should not wear anything on his head (when worshiping, for his hat is a sign of subjection to men). God's glory is man made in his image, and man's glory is the woman. [8]The first man didn't come from woman, but the first woman came out of man. [9]And Adam, the first man, was not made for Eve's benefit, but Eve was made for Adam. [10]So a woman should wear a covering on her head as a sign that she is under man's authority, a fact for all the angels to notice and rejoice in. [11]But remember that in God's plan men and women need each other. [12]For although the first woman came out of man, all men have been born from women ever since, and both men and women come from God their Creator. [13]What do you yourselves really think about this? Is it right for a woman to pray in public without covering her head? [14, 15]Doesn't even instinct itself teach us that women's heads should be covered? For women are proud of their long hair, while a man with long hair tends to be ashamed.

1 Cor 14:34. Women should be silent during the church meetings. They are not to take part in the discussion, for they are subordinate to men as the Scriptures also declare. [35]If they have any questions to ask, let them ask their husbands at home, for it is improper for women to express their opinions in church meetings.

1 Tim 2:9, 10. And the women should be the same way, quiet and sensible in manner and clothing. Christian women should be noticed for being kind and good, not for the way they fix their hair or because of their jewels or fancy clothes. [11]Women should listen and learn quietly and humbly. [12]I never let women teach men or lord it over them. Let them be silent in your church meetings. [13]Why? Because God made Adam first, and afterwards he made Eve. [14]And it was not Adam who was fooled by Satan, but Eve, and sin was the result. [15]So God sent pain and suffering to women when their children are born, but he will save their souls if they trust in him, living quiet, good, and loving lives. Ps 68:11.

1 Tim 3:11. Their wives must be thoughtful, not heavy drinkers, not gossipers, but faithful in everything they do.

1 Tim 5:1. Never speak sharply to an older man, but plead with him respectfully just as though he were your own father. Talk to the younger men as you would to much loved brothers. [2]Treat the older women as mothers, and the girls as your sisters, thinking only pure thoughts about them. [3]The church should take loving care of women whose husbands have died, if they don't have anyone else to help them. [4]But if they have children or grand-

children, these are the ones who should take the responsibility, for kindness should begin at home, supporting needy parents. This is something that pleases God very much. [5]The church should care for widows who are poor and alone in the world, if they are looking to God for his help and spending much time in prayer; [6]but not if they are spending their time running around gossiping, seeking only pleasure and thus ruining their souls. [7]This should be your church rule so that the Christians will know and do what is right. [8]But anyone who won't care for his own relatives when they need help, especially those living in his own family, has no right to say he is a Christian. Such a person is worse than the heathen. [9]A widow who wants to become one of the special church workers should be at least sixty years old and have been married only once. [10]She must be well thought of by everyone because of the good she has done. Has she brought up her children well? Has she been kind to strangers as well as to other Christians? Has she helped those who are sick and hurt? Is she always ready to show kindness? [11]The younger widows should not become members of this special group because after awhile they are likely to disregard their vow to Christ and marry again. [12]And so they will stand condemned because they broke their first promise. [13]Besides, they are likely to be lazy and spend their time gossiping around from house to house, getting into other people's business. [14]So I think it is better for these younger widows to marry again and have children, and take care of their own homes; then no one will be able to say anything against them. [15]For I am afraid that some of them have already turned away from the church and been led astray by Satan. [16]Let me remind you again that a widow's relatives must take care of her, and not leave this to the church to do. Then the church can spend its money for the care of widows who are all alone and have nowhere else to turn.

2 Tim 3:6. They are the kind who craftily sneak into other people's homes and make friendships with silly, sin-burdened women and teach them their new doctrines. [7]Women of that kind are forever following new teachers, but they never understand the truth.

Tit 2:3. Teach the older women to be quiet and respectful in everything they do. They must not go around speaking evil of others and must not be heavy drinkers, but they should be teachers of goodness. [4]These older women must train the younger women to live quietly, to love their husbands and their children, [5]and to be sensible and clean minded, spending their time in their own homes, being kind and obedient to their husbands, so that the Christian faith can't be spoken against by those who know them.

See *Widow; Wife*.

See also *Husband; Parents*.

GOOD.

Instances of. Deborah, a judge, prophetess, and military leader, Judg 4; 5. Mother of Samson, Judg 13:23. Naomi, Ruth 1; 2; 3:1. Ruth, Ruth 1:4, 5, 14–22, and chapters 2–4. Hannah, the mother of Samuel, 1 Sam 1:9–18, 24–28. Widow of Zarephath, who fed Elijah during the famine, 1 Kgs 17:8–24. The Shunemmite, who gave hospitality to Elisha, 2 Kgs 4:8–38. Vashti, Esther 1:11, 12. Esther, Esther 4:15–17. Mary, Lk 1:26–38. Elizabeth, Lk 1:6, 41–45. Anna, Lk 2:36, 37. The widow who dropped her pennies into the collection boxes, Mk 12:41–44; Lk 21:2–4. Mary and Martha, Mk 14:3–9; Lk 10:42; Jn 11:5. Mary Magdelene, Mk 16:1; Lk 8:2; Jn 20:1, 2, 11–16. Pilate's wife, Mt 27:19. Dorcas, Acts 9:36. Lydia, Acts 16:14. Priscilla, Acts 18:25, 26. Phoebe, Rom 16:1, 2. Julia, Rom 16:15. Mary, Rom 16:6. Philippians, Phil 4:3. Lois and Eunice, 2 Tim 1:5. Rahab, Heb 11:31.

Figurative. Of the church of Christ, Gal 4:26; Rev 12:1. Of believers, Mt 25:1–4; 2 Cor 11:2; Rev 14: 4.

WICKED. 2 Kgs 9:30–37; 23:7; Jer 44:15–19, 25; Ezk 8:14; Rom 1:26. Zeal of, in licentious practices of idolatry, 2 Kgs 23:7; Hos 4:13, 14. Cunning and licentious, Prov 2:16–19; 5:3–20; 6:24–29, 32–35; 7: 6–27; Eccl 7:26; Ezk 16:32. Commits forgery, 1 Kgs 21:8. Silly and gullible, 2 Tim 3:6.

Instances of. Eve, in yielding to temptation and seducing her husband, Gen 3:6; 1 Tim 2:14. Sarah, in her jealousy and malice toward Hagar, Gen 21: 9–11, with *vs.* 12–21. Lot's wife, in her rebellion against her situation, and against the destruction of Sodom, Gen 19:26; Lk 17:32. The daughters of Lot, in their incestuous lust, Gen 19:31–38. Rebekah, in her partiality for Jacob, and her plan to secure for him Isaac's blessing, Gen 27:11–17. Rachel, in her jealousy of Leah, Gen 30:1; in stealing idols, 31:21, 34. Leah, in her imitation of Rachel in the matter of children, Gen 30:9–18. Tamar, in her adultery, Gen 38:14–24. Potiphar's wife, in her lust for and slander against Joseph, Gen 39:7–20. Zipporah, in her persecution of Moses on account of his religious obligations, Ex 4:25, 26. Miriam, in her sedition with Aaron against Moses, Num 12. Delilah, in her conspiracy against Samson, Judg 16:4–20. Peninnah, the wife of Elkanah, in her jealous taunting of Hannah, 1 Sam 1:4–8. The Midianite woman in the camp of Israel, taken in adultery, Num 25:6–8. Michal, in her derision of David's religious zeal, 2 Sam 6:16, 20–23. Bath-sheba, in her adultery, in becoming the wife of her husband's murderer, 2 Sam 11:4, 5, 27; 12:9, 10. Solomon's wives, in their idolatrous and wicked influence over Solomon, 1 Kgs 11:1–11; Neh 13:26. Jezebel, in her persecution and destruction of the prophets of the Lord, 1 Kgs 18:3, 4, 13; in her persecution of Elijah, 1 Kgs 19:2; in her conspiracy against Naboth, to take his vineyard, 1 Kgs 21:1–16; in her evil counsels to, and influence over, Ahab, 1 Kgs 21:25, with *vs.* 17–27, and 2 Kgs 9:30–37. The cannibal mothers of Samaria, 2 Kgs 6:26–30. Athaliah, in destroying the royal household and usurping the throne, 2 Kgs 11:1–16; 2 Chron 22:10, 12; 23:12–14. No-adiah, a false prophetess, in troubling the Jews when they were restoring Jerusalem, Neh 6:14. Haman's wife, in counseling him to hang Mordecai, Esther 5:14; 6:13. Job's wife, in counseling him to curse God, Job 2:9; 19:17. The idolatrous wife of Hosea, Hos 1: 2, 3; 3:1. Herodias, in her incestuous marriage with Herod, Mt 14:3, 4; Mk 6:17–19; Lk 3:19, 20; scheming the death of John the Baptist, Mt 14:6–11; Mk 6:24–28. The daughter of Herodias, in her complicity with her mother in securing the death of John the Baptist, Mt 14:8; Mk 6:17–28. Sapphira, in her blasphemous falsehood, Acts 5:1–10. The woman caught in adultery and brought to Jesus in the Temple, Jn 8:1–11.

FIGURATIVE. Of backsliding, Jer 6:2; Rev 17:4, 18. Of the wicked, Isa 32:9, 11; Mt 25:1–13.

Symbolical. Of wickedness, Zech 5:7, 8; Rev 17; 19:2.

See *Wife.*

WONDERFUL A name of Messiah, Isa 9:6. See Judg 13:18.

See *Jesus, Names and Titles of.*

WOOD Aromatic, Rev 18:12.

WOODCARVER See *Carpentry; Carving.*

WOOL Used for clothing, Lev 13:47–52; Prov 31:13; 44:17. Prohibited in the priest's Temple clothing, Ezk 44:17. Mixing of, with other fabrics forbidden, Lev 19:19; Deut 22:11. Fleece of, Judg 6:37. First fleece of, belonged to the priests, Deut 18:4.

WORD A title of Jesus, Jn 1:1, 14; Rev 19:13. See *Jesus, Names and Titles of.*

WORD OF GOD Called *Book,* Mt 5:18; *Book of the Future,* Dan 10:20, 21; *Book of the Law,* Deut 30:10; Gal 3:10; *Book of the Law of the Lord,* 2 Chron 17:7–9; *Book of the Lord,* Isa 34:16; *Gospel,* 1 Cor 15:1; *Holy Scriptures,* 2 Tim 3:15; *Law of God,* Neh 8:1–3; *Scriptures,* 1 Cor 15:3; *Sword of the Spirit,* Eph 6:17; *The Word,* Ps 119:9; 2 Tim 2:15; *Word of God,* Lk 11:28; Gal 6:6; *Word of Life,* Phil 2:16; *Word of the Lord,* 1 Thess 1:8.

Likened to seed, Mt 13:2–8, 18–23, 37, 38; Mk 4: 3–20, 26–32; Lk 8:5–15; to a sharp dagger, Heb 4: 12.

To be read publicly, Deut 31:10–13; Josh 8:33–35; 2 Kgs 23:1, 2; 2 Chron 17:7–9; Neh 8:1–8, 13, 18; Jer 36:6; Acts 13:15, 27; Col 4:16; 1 Thess 5:27. The people stood and responded by saying "Amen," Neh 8:6; Ex 24:7; Deut 27:12–26. Expounded, Neh 8:7, 8; by Jesus, Lk 4:16–27; 24:27, 45. Searched, Acts 17:11. Searching of, enjoined, Jn 5:39; 7:52. Texts of, to be written on doorposts, Deut 6:9; 11: 20. Not to be added to, or subtracted from, Deut 4:2; 12:32; Prov 30:6; Rev 22:18, 19. Conviction of sin from reading, 2 Kgs 22:9–13; 2 Chron 17:7–10; 34.

Fulfilled by Jesus, Mt 5:17; Lk 24:27; Jn 19:23, 24. Testify of Jesus, Jn 5:39; Acts 10:43; 18:28; 1 Cor 15: 3. See *Jesus, Prophecies Concerning.* Taught by the apostles, Acts 2; 3; 8:32, 35; 13:27; 17:2; 18:24; 28:23. The standard for judgment, Jn 12:48; Rom 2:16. Not to be handled deceitfully, 2 Cor 4:2.

UNCLASSIFIED SCRIPTURES RELATING TO. Ex 19:9. Then he said to Moses, "I am going to come to you in the form of a dark cloud, so that the people themselves can hear me when I talk with you, and then they will always believe you."

Ex 24:3. Then Moses announced to the people all the laws and regulations God had given him; and the people answered in unison, "We will obey them all." [4]Moses wrote down the laws.

Deut 4:2. Do not add other laws or subtract from these; just obey them, for they are from the Lord your God. [Deut 12:32.] [5]These are the laws for you to obey when you arrive in the land where you will live. They are from the Lord our God. He has given them to me to pass on to you. [6]If you obey them they will give you a reputation for wisdom and intelligence. When the surrounding nations hear these laws they will exclaim, "What other nation is as wise and prudent as Israel!" [8]And what nation, no matter how great, has laws as fair as these I am giving you today? [10]Tell them especially about the day you stood before the Lord at Mount Horeb, and he told me, "Summon the people before me and I will instruct them, so that they will learn always to reverence me, and so that they can teach my laws to their children." [14]Yes, it was at that time that the Lord commanded me to issue the laws you must obey when you arrive in the Promised Land.

Deut 6:6. And you must think constantly about these commandments I am giving you today. [7]You must teach them to your children and talk about them when you are at home or out for a walk; at bedtime and the first thing in the morning. [8]Tie them on your finger, wear them on your forehead, [9]and write them on the doorposts of your house! Deut 11:18–21.

Deut 8:3. Yes, he humbled you by letting you go hungry and then feeding you with manna, a food previously unknown to both you and your ancestors. He did it to help you realize that food isn't everything, and that real life comes by obeying every command of God. Mt 4:4.

Deut 17:18. And when he has been crowned and sits upon his throne as king, then he must copy these laws from the book kept by the Levite-priests. [19]That copy of the law shall be his constant companion. He must read from it every day of his life so that he will learn to respect the Lord his God by obeying all of his commands.

Deut 27:2–4. When you cross the Jordan River and go into the Promised Land—a land 'flowing with milk and honey'—take out boulders from the river bottom and immediately pile them into a monument on the other side, at Mount Ebal. Face the stones with a coating of lime and then write the laws of God in the lime. [8]Write all of these laws plainly.

Deut 29:29. There are secrets the Lord your God has not revealed to us, but these words which he has revealed are for us and our children to obey forever.

Deut 30:11. Obeying these commandments is not something beyond your strength and reach; [12]for these laws are not in the far heavens, so distant that you can't hear and obey them, and with no one to bring them down to you; [13]nor are they beyond the ocean, so far that no one can bring you their message; [14]but they are very close at hand—in your hearts and on your lips—so that you can obey them.

Deut 31:9. Then Moses wrote out the laws he had already delivered to the people and gave them to the priests, the sons of Levi, who carried the Ark containing the Ten Commandments of the Lord. Moses also gave copies of the laws to the elders of Israel. [10, 11]The Lord commanded that these laws be read to all the people at the end of every seventh year—the Year of Release—at the Festival of Tabernacles, when all Israel would assemble before the Lord at the sanctuary. [12]"Call them all together," the Lord instructed, "—men, women, children, and foreigners living among you—to hear the laws of God and to learn his will, so that you will reverence the Lord your God and obey his laws. [13]Do this so that your little children who have not known these laws will hear them and learn how to revere the Lord your God as long as you live in the Promised Land."

19. "Now write down the words of this song, and teach it to the people of Israel as my warning to them. [21]And great disasters come upon them, then this song will remind them of the reason for their woes. (For this song will live from generation to generation.) I know now, even before they enter the land, what these people are like."

26. To put this book of the law beside the Ark, as a solemn warning to the people of Israel.

Josh 1:8. Constantly remind the people about these laws, and you yourself must think about them every day and every night so that you will be sure to obey all of them. For only then will you succeed.

Josh 3:9. Then Joshua summoned all the people and told them, "Come and listen to what the Lord your God has said."

Josh 8:32. And as the people of Israel watched, Joshua carved upon the stones of the altar each of the Ten Commandments. [33]Then all the people of Israel—including the elders, officers, judges, and the foreigners living among them—divided into two groups, half of them standing at the foot of Mount Gerizim and half at the foot of Mount Ebal. Between them stood the priests with the Ark, ready to pronounce their blessing. (This was all done in accordance with the instructions given long before by Moses.) [34]Joshua then read to them all of the statements of blessing and curses that Moses had written in the book of God's laws. [35]Every commandment Moses had ever given was read before the entire assembly, including the women and children and the foreigners who lived among the Israelis.

2 Sam 22:31. As for God, his way is perfect; the word of the Lord is true. Ps 18:30.

1 Chron 16:15. Remember his covenant forever—the words he commanded to a thousand generations.

2 Chron 15:3. For a long time now, over in Israel, the people haven't worshiped the true God, and have not had a true priest to teach them. They have lived without God's laws.

Job 22:22. Listen to his instructions and store them in your heart.

Job 23:12. I have not refused his commandments but have enjoyed them more than my daily food.

Ps 1:2. But they delight in doing everything God wants them to, and day and night are always meditating on his laws and thinking about ways to follow him more closely.

Ps 12:6. The Lord's promise is sure. He speaks no careless word; all he says is purest truth, like silver seven times refined.

Ps 17:4. I have followed your commands and have not gone along with cruel and evil men.

Ps 19:7, 8. God's laws are perfect. They protect us, make us wise, and give us joy and light. [9]God's laws are pure, eternal, just. [10]They are more desirable than gold. They are sweeter than honey dripping from a honeycomb. [11]For they warn us away from harm and give success to those who obey them.

Ps 33:4. For all God's words are right. [6]He merely spoke, and the heavens were formed, and all the galaxies of stars.

Ps 40:8. And I delight to do your will, my God, for your law is written upon my heart! *v.* 7.

Ps 43:3. Oh, send out your light and your truth—let them lead me. Let them lead me to your Temple on your holy mountain, Zion.

Ps 56:4. Yes, I will trust the promises of God. And since I am trusting him, what can mere man do to me?

Ps 78:1. O my people, listen to my teaching. Open your ears to what I am saying. [7]In this way each generation has been able to obey his laws and to set its hope anew on God and not forget his glorious miracles. [8]Thus they did not need to be as their fathers were—stubborn, rebellious, unfaithful, refusing to give their hearts to God.

Ps 85:8. I am listening carefully to all the Lord is saying—for he speaks peace to his people, his saints, if they will only stop their sinning.

Ps 93:5. Your royal decrees cannot be changed. Holiness is forever the keynote of your reign.

Ps 102:18. I am recording this so that future generations will also praise the Lord for all that he has done. And a people that shall be created shall praise the Lord.

Ps 107:19. Then they cried to the Lord in their troubles, and he helped them and delivered them. [20]He spoke, and they were healed—snatched from the door of death.

Ps 111:7. All he does is just and good, and all his laws are right, [8]for they are formed from truth and goodness, and stand firm forever.

Ps 119:9. How can a young man stay pure? By reading your Word and following its rules. [11]I have thought much about your words, and stored them in my heart so that they would hold me back from sin. [12]Blessed Lord, teach me your rules. [13]I have recited your laws, [14]and rejoiced in them more than in riches. [15]I will meditate upon them and give them my full respect. [16]I will delight in them and not forget them. [18]Open my eyes to see wonderful things in your Word. [19]I am but a pilgrim here on earth: how I need a map—and your commands are my chart and guide. [20]I long for your instructions more than I can tell. [*vs.* 40–42.] [23]For even princes sit and talk against me, but I will continue in your plans. [24]Your laws are both my light and my counselors. [25]I am completely discouraged—I lie in the dust. Revive me by your Word. [28]I weep with grief; my heart is heavy with sorrow; encourage and cheer me with your words. [30]Help me, undeserving as I am, to obey your laws, for I have chosen to do right. [31]I cling to your commands and follow them as closely as I can. Lord, don't let me make a mess of things. [33, 34]Just tell me what to do and I will do it, Lord. As long as I live I'll wholeheartedly obey. [35]Make me walk along the right paths for I know how delightful they really are. [41]Therefore in fairness renew my life, for this was your promise—yes, Lord, to save me! [44-46]Therefore I will keep on obeying you forever and forever, free within the limits of your laws. I will speak to kings about their value, and they will listen with interest and respect. [47]How I love your laws! How I enjoy your commands! [48]"Come, come to me," I call to them, for I love them and will let them fill my life. [49, 50]Never forget your promises to me your servant, for they are my only hope. They give me strength in all my troubles; how they refresh and revive me! [51]Proud men hold me in contempt for obedience to God, but I stand unmoved. [52]From my earliest youth I have tried to obey you; your Word has been my comfort. [54]For these laws of yours have been my source of joy and singing through all these years of my earthly pilgrimage. [61]Evil men have tried to drag me into sin, but I am firmly anchored to your laws. [66]Now teach me good judgment as well as knowledge. For your laws are my guide. [67]I used to wander off until you punished me; now I closely follow all you say. [70]Their minds are dull and stupid, but I have sense enough to follow you. [72]They [your laws] are more valuable to me than millions in silver and gold! [74]All those who fear and trust in you will welcome me because I too am trusting in your Word. [*v.* 147.] [76, 77]Now let your lovingkindness comfort me, just as you promised. Surround me with your tender mercies, that I may live. For your law is my delight. [78]Let the proud be disgraced, for they have cut me down with all their lies. But I will concentrate my thoughts upon your laws. [81]I faint for your salvation; but I expect your help, for you have promised it. [*v.* 147.] [82]My eyes are straining to see your promises come true. When will you comfort me with your help? [83]I am shriveled like a wineskin in the smoke, exhausted with waiting. But still I cling to your laws and obey them. [86]Their lies have brought me into deep trouble. Help me, for you love only truth. [89]Forever, O Lord, your Word stands firm in heaven. [92]I would have despaired and perished unless your laws had been my deepest delight. [93]I will never lay aside your laws, for you have used them to restore my joy and health. [96]Nothing is perfect except your words. [97]Oh, how I love them. I think about them all day long. [98]They make me wiser than my enemies, because they are my constant guide. [99]Yes, wiser than my teachers, for I am ever thinking of your rules. [100]They make me even wiser than the aged. [103]Your words are sweeter than honey. [104]And since only your rules can give me wisdom and understanding, no wonder I hate every false teaching. [105]Your words are a flashlight to light the path ahead of me, and keep me from stumbling. [109]My life hangs in the balance, but I will not give up obedience to your laws. [111]Your laws are my joyous treasure forever. [113]I hate those who are undecided whether or not to obey you; but my choice is clear —I love your law. [115]Begone, you evil-minded men. Don't try to stop me from obeying God's commands. [119]The wicked are the scum you skim off and throw away; no wonder I love to obey your laws! [127]While I love your commandments more than the finest gold. [128]Every law of God is right, whatever it concerns. I hate every other way. [129]Your laws are wonderful; no wonder I obey them. [130]As your plan unfolds, even the simple can understand it. [131]No wonder I wait expectantly for each of your commands. [133]Guide me with your law so that I will not be overcome by evil. [138]Your demands are just and right. [140]I have thoroughly tested your promises and that is why I love them so much. [141]I am worthless and despised, but I don't despise your laws. [142]Your justice is eternal for your laws are perfectly fair. [143]In my distress and anguish, your commandments comfort me. [144]Your laws are always fair; help me to understand them and I shall live. [148]I stay awake through the night to think about your promises. [151]But you are near, O Lord; all your commandments are based on truth. [152]I have known from earliest days that your will never changes. [153]Look down upon my sorrows and rescue me, for I am obeying your commands. [157]My enemies are so many. They try to make me disobey, but I have not swerved from your will. [158]I loathed these traitors because they care nothing for your laws. [159]Lord, see how much I really love your demands. Now give me back my life and health because you are so kind. [160]There is utter truth in all your laws; your decrees are eternal. [161]Great men have persecuted me, though they have no reason to, but I stand in awe of only your words. [162]I rejoice in your laws like one who finds a great treasure. [163]How I hate all falsehood but how I love your laws. [165]Those who love your laws have great peace of heart and mind and do not stumble. [167]I have looked for your commandments and I love them very much. [171]I praise you for letting me learn your laws. [172]I will sing about their wonder, for each of them is just. [173]Stand ready to help me because I have chosen to follow your will. [174]O Lord, I have longed for your salvation, and your law is my delight.

Ps 138:2. I face your Temple as I worship, giving thanks to you for all your lovingkindness and your faithfulness, for your promises are backed by all the honor of your name.

Ps 147:15. He sends his orders to the world. How swiftly his word flies. [19]He has made known his laws and ceremonies of worship to Israel. *v.* 20.

Prov 6:20. Young man, obey your father and your mother. [21]Tie their instructions around your finger so you won't forget. Take to heart all of their advice. [22]Every day and all night long their counsel will lead you and save you from harm; when you wake up in the morning, let their instructions guide you into the new day. [23]For their advice is a beam of light directed into the dark corners of your mind to warn you of danger and to give you a good life.

Prov 22:20, 21. In the past, haven't I been right? Then believe what I am telling you now, and share it with others.

Prov 30:5. Every word of God proves true. He defends all who come to him for protection. [6]Do not add to his words, lest he rebuke you, and you be found a liar.

Eccl 5:1. As you enter the Temple, keep your ears open and your mouth shut!

Eccl 12:10. For the Preacher was not only a wise man, but a good teacher; he not only taught what he knew to the people, but taught them in an interesting manner. [11]The wise man's words are like goads that spur to action. They nail down important truths. Students are wise who master what their teachers tell them.

Isa 2:3. "Come," everyone will say, "let us go up the mountain of the Lord, to the Temple of the God of Israel; there he will teach us his laws, and we will obey them." For in those days the world will be ruled from Jerusalem.

Isa 8:16. Write down all these things I am going to do, says the Lord, and seal it up for the future. Entrust it to some godly man to pass on down to godly men of future generations. [20]"Check these witches' words against the Word of God!" he says. "If their messages are different than mine, it is because I have not sent them; for they have no light or truth in them."

Isa 28:13. So the Lord will spell it out for them again, repeating it over and over in simple words whenever he can; yet over this simple, straightforward message they will stumble and fall and be broken, trapped and captured.

Isa 30:21. And if you leave God's paths and go astray, you will hear a Voice behind you say, "No, this is the way; walk here."

Isa 34:16. Search the Book of the Lord and see all that he will do; not one detail will he miss; not one kite will be there without a mate, for the Lord has said it, and his Spirit will make it all come true.

Isa 40:8. The grass withers, the flowers fade, but the Word of our God shall stand forever.

Isa 51:7. Listen to me, you who know the right from wrong and cherish my laws in your hearts.

Isa 55:10. As the rain and snow come down from heaven and stay upon the ground to water the earth, and cause the grain to grow and to produce seed for the farmer and bread for the hungry, [11]so also is my Word. I send it out and it always produces fruit. It shall accomplish all I want it to, and prosper everywhere I send it.

Jer 8:9. These wise teachers of yours will be shamed by exile for this sin, for they have rejected the word of the Lord. Are they then so wise?

Jer 13:15. Oh, that you were not so proud and stubborn! Then you would listen to the Lord, for he has spoken.

Jer 15:16. Your words are what sustain me; they are food to my hungry soul. They bring joy to my sorrowing heart and delight me. How proud I am to bear your name, O Lord.

Jer 22:29. O earth, earth, earth! Hear the word of the Lord!

Jer 23:28. Let these false prophets tell their dreams and let my true messengers faithfully proclaim my every word. There is a difference between chaff and wheat! [29]Does not my word burn like fire? asks the Lord. Is it not like a mighty hammer that smashed the rock to pieces? [36]But stop using this term, "God's sad news." For what is sad is you and your lying. You are twisting my words and inventing "messages from God" that I didn't speak.

Ezk 3:3. "Eat it all," he said. And when I ate it, it tasted sweet as honey. [10]Then he added: "Son of dust, let all my words sink deep into your own heart first; listen to them carefully for yourself."

Ezk 44:5. And the Lord said to me: "Son of dust, notice carefully; use your eyes and ears. Listen to all I tell you about the laws and rules of the Temple of the Lord."

Dan 10:21. I am here to tell you what is written in the "Book of the Future."

Dan 12:4. "But Daniel, keep this prophecy a secret; seal it up so that it will not be understood until the end times, when travel and education shall be vastly increased!" [Dan 8:26.] [9]But he said, "Go now Daniel, for what I have said is not to be understood until the time of the end."

Hos 6:5. I sent my prophets to warn you of your doom; I have slain you with the words of my mouth, threatening you with death. Suddenly, without warning, my judgment will strike you as surely as day follows night.

Amos 8:11. "The time is surely coming," says the Lord God, "when I will send a famine on the land —not a famine of bread or water, but of hearing the words of the Lord. [12]Men will wander everywhere from sea to sea, seeking the Word of the Lord, searching, running here and going there, but will not find it. [13]Beautiful girls and fine young men alike will grow faint and weary, thirsting for the Word of God."

Mic 2:7. Is that the right reply for you to make, O House of Jacob? Do you think the Spirit of the Lord likes to talk to you so roughly? No! His threats are for your good, to get you on the path again.

Hab 2:2. And the Lord said to me, "Write my answer on a billboard, large and clear, so that anyone can read it at a glance and rush to tell the others."

Zech 1:4. Don't be like your fathers were! The earlier prophets pled in vain with them to turn from all their evil ways. "Come, return to me," the Lord God said. But no, they wouldn't listen; they paid no attention at all.

Mt 5:17. Don't misunderstand why I have come —it isn't to cancel the laws of Moses and the warnings of the prophets. No, I came to fulfill them, and to make them all come true.

Mt 7:24. All who listen to my instructions and follow them are wise, like a man who builds his house on solid rock. [25]Though the rain comes in torrents, and the floods rise and the storm winds beat against his house, it won't collapse, for it is built on rock. Lk 6:47, 48.

Mt 11:13. For all the laws and prophets looked forward (to the Messiah). Then John appeared. [15]If ever you were willing to listen, listen now!

Mt 13:23. The good ground represents the heart of a man who listens to the message and understands it and goes out and brings thirty, sixty, or even a hundred others into the Kingdom. Mk 4:20; Lk 8:15.

33. He also used this example: "The Kingdom of Heaven can be compared to a woman making bread. She takes a measure of flour and mixes in the yeast until it permeates every part of the dough." Lk 13:20, 21.

Mt 15:3. He replied, "And why do your traditions violate the direct commandments of God? [9]Their worship is worthless, for they teach their man-made laws instead of those from God."

Mt 22:29. But Jesus said, "Your error is caused by your ignorance of the Scriptures and of God's power."

Mk 1:15. "At last the time has come!" he announced. "God's Kingdom is near! Turn from your sins and act on this glorious news!"

Mk 7:9. You are simply rejecting God's laws and trampling them under your feet for the sake of tradition. [12]And so you break the law of God in order to protect your man-made tradition.

Mk 13:31. Heaven and earth shall disappear, but my words stand sure forever.

Lk 1:37. For every promise from God shall surely come true.

Lk 4:22. All who were there spoke well of him and were amazed by the beautiful words that fell from his lips.

Lk 8:11. This is its meaning: The seed is God's message to men. [12]The hard path where some seed fell represents the hard hearts of those who hear the words of God, but then the devil comes and steals the words away and prevents people from believing and being saved. [13]The stony ground represents those who enjoy listening to sermons, but somehow the message never really gets through to them and doesn't take root and grow. They know the message is true, and sort of believe for awhile; but when the hot winds of persecution blow, they lose interest. [14]The seed among the thorns represents those who listen and believe God's words but whose faith afterwards is choked out by worry and riches and the responsibilities and pleasures of life. And so they are never able to help anyone else to believe the Good News. [15]But the good soil represents honest, good-hearted people. They listen to God's words and cling to them and steadily spread them to others who also soon believe.

Lk 11:28. He replied, "Yes, but even more blessed are all who hear the Word of God and put it into practice."

Lk 16:17. But that doesn't mean that the Law has lost its force in even the smallest point. It is as strong and unshakable as heaven and earth. [29]But Abraham said, "The Scriptures have warned them again and again. Your brothers can read them any time they want to." [31]But Abraham said, "If they won't listen to Moses and the prophets, they won't listen even though someone rises from the dead."

Lk 24:32. They began telling each other how their hearts had felt strangely warm as he talked with them and explained the Scriptures during the walk down the road. [45]Then he opened their minds to understand at last these many Scriptures!

Jn 2:22. After he came back to life again, the disciples remembered his saying this and realized that what he had quoted from the Scriptures really did refer to him, and had all come true!

Jn 5:24. But I say emphatically that anyone who listens to my message and believes in God who sent me has eternal life, and will never be damned for his sins, but has already passed out of death into life. [39]You search the Scriptures, for you believe they give you eternal life. And the Scriptures point to me!

Jn 6:63. Only the Holy Spirit gives eternal life. Those born only once, with physical birth, will never receive this gift. But now I have told you how to get this true spiritual life.

Jn 8:30, 31. Then many of the Jewish leaders who heard him say these things began believing him to be the Messiah. Jesus said to them, "You are truly my disciples if you live as I tell you to, [32]and you will know the truth, and the truth will set you free."

Jn 10:35, 36. So if the Scripture, which cannot be untrue, speaks of those as gods to whom the message of God came, do you call it blasphemy when the one sanctified and sent into the world by the Father says, "I am the Son of God"?

Jn 15:3. He has already tended you by pruning you back for greater strength and usefulness by means of the commands I gave you.

Jn 17:8. For I have passed on to them the commands you gave me; and they accepted them and know of a certainty that I came down to earth from you, and they believe you sent me. [*v.* 14.] [17]Make them pure and holy through teaching them your words of truth. [20]I am not praying for these alone but also for the future believers who will come to me because of the testimony of these.

Jn 20:31. But these are recorded so that you will believe that he is the Messiah, the Son of God, and that believing in him you will have life.

Acts 10:15. The voice spoke again, "Don't contradict God! If he says something is kosher, then it is."

Acts 17:11. But the people of Beroea were more open minded than those in Thessalonica, and gladly listened to the message. They searched the Scriptures day by day to check up on Paul and Silas' statements to see if they were really so.

Acts 20:32. And now I entrust you to God and his care and to his wonderful words which are able to build your faith and give you all the inheritance of those who are set apart for himself.

Acts 26:18. To open their eyes to their true condition so that they may repent and live in the light of God instead of in Satan's darkness, so that they may receive forgiveness for their sins and God's inheritance along with all people everywhere whose sins are cleansed away, who are set apart by faith in me. [22]But God protected me so that I am still alive today to tell these facts to everyone, both great and small. I teach nothing except what the prophets and Moses said.

Rom 3:1. Then what's the use of being a Jew? Are there any special benefits for them from God? Is there any value in the Jewish circumcision ceremony? [2]Yes, being a Jew has many advantages. First of all, God trusted them with his laws (so that they could know and do his will).

Rom 4:23. Now this wonderful statement—that he was accepted and approved through his faith—wasn't just for Abraham's benefit. [24]It was for us, too, assuring us that God will accept us in the same way he accepted Abraham—when we believe the promises of God who brought back Jesus our Lord from the dead.

Rom 6:17. Thank God that though you once chose to be slaves of sin, now you have obeyed with all your heart the teaching to which God has committed you.

Rom 9:4. God has given you so much, but still you will not listen to him. He took you as his own special, chosen people and led you along with a bright cloud of glory and told you how very much he wanted to bless you. He gave you his rules for daily life so you would know what he wanted you to do. He let you worship him, and gave you mighty promises. [6]Well then, has God failed to fulfill his promises to the Jews? No!

Rom 10:17. Yet faith comes from listening to this Good News—the Good News about Christ.

Rom 12:2. Don't copy the behavior and customs of this world, but be a new and different person with a fresh newness in all you do and think. Then you will learn from your own experience how his ways will really satisfy you.

Rom 15:4. These things that were written in the Scriptures so long ago are to teach us patience and to encourage us.

Rom 16:26. But now as the prophets foretold and as God commands, this message is being preached everywhere, so that people all around the world will have faith in Christ and obey him.

1 Cor 2:13. In telling you about these gifts we have even used the very words given to us by the Holy Spirit, not words that we as men might choose. So we use the Holy Spirit's words to explain the Holy Spirit's facts.

1 Cor 7:6. I'm not saying you *must* marry; but you certainly *may* if you wish. [10]Now, for those who are married I have a command, not just a suggestion. And it is not a command from me, for this is what the Lord himself has said: A wife must not leave her husband. [12]Here I want to add some suggestions of my own. These are not direct commands from the Lord. 2 Cor 8:10.

1 Cor 9:10. Wasn't he also thinking about us? Of course he was. He said this to show us that Christian workers should be paid by those they help. Those who do the plowing and threshing should expect some share of the harvest. *v.* 9.

1 Cor 10:11. All these things happened to them as examples—as object lessons to us—to warn us against doing the same things; they were written down so that we could read about them and learn from them in these last days as the world nears its end.

1 Cor 11:2. I am so glad, dear brothers, that you have been remembering and doing everything I taught you.

1 Cor 15:3. I passed on to you right from the first what had been told to me, that Christ died for our sins just as the Scriptures said he would.

2 Cor 2:17. Only those who, like ourselves, are men of integrity, sent by God, speaking with Christ's power, with God's eye upon us. We are not like those hucksters—and there are many of them—whose idea in getting out the Gospel is to make a good living out of it.

2 Cor 3:6. He is the one who has helped us tell others about his new agreement to save them. We do not tell them that they must obey every law of God or die; but we tell them there is life for them from the Holy Spirit. The old way, trying to be saved by keeping the Ten Commandments, ends in death; in the new way, the Holy Spirit gives them life.

Gal 1:8. Let God's curses fall on anyone, including myself, who preaches any other way to be saved than the one we told you about; yes, if an angel comes from heaven and preaches any other message, let him be forever cursed. [*v.* 9.] [11]Dear friends, I solemnly swear that the way to heaven which I preach is not based on some mere human whim or dream. [12]For my message comes from no less a person than Jesus Christ himself, who told me what to say. No one else has taught me.

Eph 1:12. God's purpose in this was that we should praise God and give glory to him for doing these mighty things for us, who were the first to trust in Christ. [13]And because of what Christ did, all you others too, who heard the Good News about how to be saved, and trusted Christ, were marked as belonging to Christ by the Holy Spirit.

Eph 3:3. God himself showed me this secret plan of his . . . [4]I say this to explain to you how I know about these things. [5]In olden times God did not share this plan with his people, but now he has revealed it by the Holy Spirit to his apostles and prophets.

Eph 5:26. To make her holy and clean, washed by baptism and God's Word.

Eph 6:17. And you will need the helmet of salvation and the sword of the Spirit—which is the Word of God.

Phil 2:16. Holding out to them the Word of Life.

Col 1:5. And you are looking forward to the joys of heaven, and have been ever since the Gospel first was preached to you.

Col 3:16. Remember what Christ taught and let his words enrich your lives and make you wise; teach them to each other and sing them out in psalms and hymns and spiritual songs, singing to the Lord with thankful hearts.

1 Thess 1:5. For when we brought you the Good News, it was not just meaningless chatter to you; no, you listened with great interest. What we told you produced a powerful effect upon you, for the Holy Spirit gave you great and full assurance that what we said was true. [8]And now the Word of the Lord has spread out from you to others everywhere, far beyond your boundaries.

1 Thess 2:13. And we will never stop thanking God for this: that when we preached to you, you didn't think of the words we spoke as being just our own, but you accepted what we said as the very Word of God—which of course, it was—and it changed your lives when you believed it.

1 Thess 4:1, 2. Let me add this, dear brothers: You already know how to please God in your daily living, for you know the commands we gave you from the Lord Jesus himself. Now we beg you—yes, we demand of you in the name of the Lord Jesus—that you live more and more closely to that ideal.

1 Thess 5:20. Do not scoff at those who prophesy.

2 Thess 2:14. Through us he told you the Good News. Through us he called you to share in the glory of our Lord Jesus Christ. [15]With all these things in mind, dear brothers, stand firm and keep a strong grip on the truth that we taught you in our letters and during the time we were with you.

1 Tim 4:5. And if we ask God to bless it, for it is made good by the Word of God and prayer. [6]If you explain this to the others you will be doing your duty as a worthy pastor who is fed by faith and by the true teaching you have followed.

1 Tim 6:3. Some may deny these things, but they are the sound, wholesome teachings of the Lord Jesus Christ and are the foundation for a godly life. [4]Anyone who says anything different is both proud and stupid. He is quibbling over the meaning of Christ's words and stirring up arguments ending in jealousy and anger, which only lead to name-calling, accusations, and evil suspicions.

2 Tim 1:13. Hold tightly to the pattern of truth I taught you, especially concerning the faith and love Christ Jesus offers you.

2 Tim 2:8. Don't ever forget the wonderful fact that Jesus Christ was a Man, born into King David's family; and that he was God, as shown by the fact that he rose again from the dead. [9]It is because I have preached these great truths that I am in trouble here and have been put in jail like a criminal. But the Word of God is not chained, even though I am. [15]Work hard so God can say to you, "Well done." Be a good workman, one who does not need to be ashamed when God examines your work. Know what his Word says and means.

2 Tim 3:15. You know how, when you were a small child, you were taught the holy Scriptures; and it is these that make you wise to accept God's salvation by trusting in Christ Jesus. [16]The whole Bible was given to us by inspiration from God and is useful to teach us what is true and to make us realize what is wrong in our lives; it straightens us out and helps us do what is right. [17]It is God's way of making us well prepared at every point, fully equipped to do good to everyone.

Heb 1:1. Long ago God spoke in many different ways to our fathers through the prophets (in visions, dreams, and even face to face), telling them little by little about his plans. [2]But now in these days he has spoken to us through his Son to whom he has given everything, and through whom he made the world and everything there is.

Heb 2:1. So we must listen very carefully to the truths we have heard, or we may drift away from them. [2]For since the messages from angels have always proved true and people have always been punished for disobeying them, [3]what makes us think that we can escape if we are indifferent to this great salvation announced by the Lord Jesus himself, and passed on to us by those who heard him speak?

Heb 4:2. For this wonderful news—the message that God wants to save us—has been given to us just as it was to those who lived in the time of Moses. But it didn't do them any good because they didn't believe it. They didn't mix it with faith. [12]For whatever God says to us is full of living power: it is sharper than the sharpest dagger, cutting swift and deep into our innermost thoughts and desires with all their parts, exposing us for what we really are.

Heb 6:5. And know how good the Word of God is, and felt the mighty powers of the world to come.

Heb 10:7. Then I said, "See, I have come to do your will, to lay down my life, just as the Scriptures said that I would."

Heb 10:28. A man who refused to obey the laws given by Moses was killed without mercy if there were two or three witnesses to his sin.

Heb 11:3. By faith—by believing God—we know that the world and the stars—in fact, all things—were made at God's command; and that they were all made from things that can't be seen.

Jas 1:18. And it was a happy day for him when he gave us our new lives, through the truth of his Word, and we became, as it were, the first children in his new family. [19]Dear brothers, don't ever forget that it is best to listen much, speak little, and not become angry. [21]So get rid of all that is wrong in your life, both inside and outside, and humbly be glad for the wonderful message we have received, for it is able to save our souls as it takes hold of our hearts. [22]And remember, it is a message to obey, not just to listen to. So don't fool yourselves. [23]For if a person just listens and doesn't obey, he is like a man looking at his face in a mirror; [24]as soon as he walks away, he can't see himself anymore or remember what he looks like. [25]But if anyone keeps looking steadily into God's law for free men, he will not only remember it but he will do what it says, and God will greatly bless him in everything he does.

1 Pet 1:23. For you have a new life. It was not passed on to you from your parents, for the life they gave you will fade away. This new one will last forever, for it comes from Christ, God's ever-living Message to men. [24]Yes, our natural lives will fade as grass does when it becomes all brown and dry. All our greatness is like a flower that droops and falls; [25]but the Word of the Lord will last forever. And his message is the Good News that was preached to you.

2 Pet 1:4. And by that same mighty power he has given us all the other rich and wonderful blessings he promised; for instance, the promise to save us from the lust and rottenness all around us, and to give us his own character. [19]So we have seen and proved that what the prophets said came true. You will do well to pay close attention to everything they have written, for, like lights shining into dark corners, their words help us to understand many things that otherwise would be dark and difficult. But when you consider the wonderful truth of the prophets' words, then the light will dawn in your souls and Christ the Morning Star will shine in your hearts. [20, 21]For no prophecy recorded in Scripture was ever thought up by the prophet himself. It was the Holy Spirit within these godly men who gave them true messages from God.

2 Pet 3:1, 2. This is my second letter to you, dear brothers, and in both of them I have tried to remind you—if you will let me—about facts you already know: facts you learned from the holy prophets and from us apostles who brought you the words of our Lord and Savior. [15, 16]And remember why he is waiting. He is giving us time to get his message of salvation out to others. Our wise and beloved brother Paul has talked about these same things in many of his letters. Some of his comments are not easy to understand, and there are people who are deliberately stupid, and always demand some unusual interpretation—they have twisted his letters around to mean something quite different from what he meant, just as they do the other parts of the Scripture—and the result is disaster for them.

1 Jn 1:4. And if you do as I say in this letter, then you, too, will be full of joy, and so will we. [5]This is the message God has given us to pass on to you: that God is Light and in him is no darkness at all.

1 Jn 2:7. Dear brothers, I am not writing out a new rule for you to obey, for it is an old one you have always had, right from the start. You have heard it all before. [8]Yet it is always new, and works for you just as it did for Christ; and as we obey this commandment, *to love one another,* the darkness in our lives disappears and the new light of life in Christ shines in. [12]I am writing these things to all of you, my little children, because your sins have been forgiven in the name of Jesus our Savior. [14]And so I say to you fathers who know the eternal God, and to you young men who are strong, with God's Word in your hearts, and have won your struggle against Satan. [21]So I am not writing to you as to those who need to know the truth, but I warn you as those who can discern the difference between true and false.

1 Jn 5:11. And what is it that God has said? That he has given us eternal life, and that this life is in his Son. [13]I have written this to you who believe in the Son of God so that you may know you have eternal life.

Jude 1:3. Dearly loved friends, I have been planning to write you some thoughts about the salvation God has given us, but now I find I must write of something else instead, urging you to stoutly defend the truth which God gave, once for all, to his people to keep without change through the years.

Rev 1:2. John wrote it all down—the words of God and Jesus Christ and everything he heard and saw. [3]If you read this prophecy aloud to the church, you will receive a special blessing from the Lord. Those who listen to it being read and do what it says will also be blessed. For the time is near when these things will all come true.

Rev 22:18. And I solemnly declare to everyone who reads this book: If anyone adds anything to what is written here, God shall add to him the plagues described in this book. [19]And if anyone subtracts any part of these prophecies, God shall take away his share in the Tree of Life, and in the Holy City just described.

See *Commandments.*

INSPIRATION OF. Ex 19:7. Moses returned from the mountain and called together the leaders of the people and told them what the Lord had said.

Ex 20:1. Then God issued this edict.

Ex 24:4. Moses wrote down the laws. [12]And the Lord said to Moses, "Come up to me into the mountain, and remain until I give you the laws and commandments I have written on tablets of stone, so that you can teach the people from them."

Ex 25:21. Install the lid upon the Ark, and place within the Ark the tablets of stone I shall give you.

Ex 31:18. Then, as God finished speaking with Moses on Mount Sinai, he gave him the two tablets of stone on which the Ten Commandments were written with the finger of God.

Ex 32:16. God himself had written the commandments on the tablets.

Ex 34:27. And the Lord said to Moses, "Write down these laws that I have given you, for they represent the terms of my covenant with you and with Israel." [32]Afterwards, all the people came to him, and he gave them the commandments the Lord had given him upon the mountain.

Lev 26:46. These were the laws, ordinances, and instructions that Jehovah gave to the people of Israel, through Moses on Mount Sinai.

Deut 4:5. These are the laws for you to obey when you arrive in the land where you will live. They are from the Lord our God. He has given them to me to pass on to you. *v.* 14.

Deut 11:18. So keep these commandments carefully in mind. Tie them to your hand to remind you to obey them, and tie them to your forehead between your eyes!

Deut 31:19. Now write down the words of this song, and teach it to the people of Israel as my warning to them. [22]So, on that very day, Moses wrote down the words of the song and taught it to the Israelites.

2 Kgs 17:13. Again and again the Lord had sent prophets to warn both Israel and Judah to turn from their evil ways; he had warned them to obey his commandments which he had given to their ancestors through these prophets.

2 Chron 33:18. The rest of Manasseh's deeds, and his prayer to God, and God's reply through the prophets—this is all written in *The Annals of the Kings of Israel.*

Job 23:12. I have not refused his commandments but have enjoyed them more than my daily food.

Ps 78:5. For he gave his laws to Israel, and commanded our fathers to teach them to their children.

Ps 99:7. He spoke to them from the pillar of cloud and they followed his instructions.

Ps 147:19. He has made known his laws and ceremonies of worship to Israel.

Eccl 12:11. The wise man's words are like goads that spur to action. They nail down important truths. Students are wise who master what their teachers tell them.

Isa 30:12. This is the reply of the Holy One of Israel: Because you despise what I tell you and trust instead in frauds and lies and won't repent, [13]therefore calamity will come upon you suddenly, as upon a bulging wall that bursts and falls; in one moment it comes crashing down.

Isa 34:16. Search the Book of the Lord and see all that he will do; not one detail will he miss; not one kite will be there without a mate, for the Lord has said it, and his Spirit will make it all come true.

Jer 30:2. The Lord God of Israel says, Write down for the record all that I have said to you.

Jer 36:1. In the fourth year of the reign of King Jehoiakim of Judah (son of Josiah) the Lord gave this message to Jeremiah: [2]"Get a scroll and write down all my messages against Israel, Judah and the other nations. Begin with the first message back in the days of Josiah, and write down every one of them." [27]After the king had burned the scroll, the Lord said to Jeremiah: [28]Get another scroll and write everything again just as you did before. [32]Then Jeremiah took another scroll and dictated again to Baruch all he had written before, only this time the Lord added a lot more! Jer 51:59–64.

Ezk 11:25. And I told the exiles everything the Lord had shown me.

Dan 10:21. I am here to tell you what is written in the "Book of the Future."

Hos 8:12. Even if I gave her ten thousand laws, she'd say they weren't for her—that they applied to someone far away.

Zech 7:12. They hardened their hearts like flint, afraid to hear the words that God, the Lord of Hosts, commanded them—the laws he had revealed to them by his Spirit through the early prophets. That is why such great wrath came down on them from God.

Mt 22:31. But now, as to whether there is a resurrection of the dead—don't you ever read the Scriptures? Don't you realize that God was speaking directly to you when he said, [32]"I *am* the God of Abraham, Isaac, and Jacob"?

Lk 1:1, 2. Dear friend who loves God: Several biographies of Christ have already been written using as their source material the reports circulating among us from the early disciples and other eyewitnesses. [3]However, it occurred to me that it would be well to recheck all these accounts from first to last and after thorough investigation to pass this summary on to you, [4]to reassure you of the truth of all you were taught. [68]"Praise the Lord, the God of Israel, for he has come to visit his people and has redeemed them. [69]He is sending us a Mighty Savior from the royal line of his servant David, [70]just as he promised through his holy prophets long ago—[71]someone to save us from our enemies, from all who hate us. [72, 73]He has been merciful to our ancestors, yes, to Abraham himself, by remembering his sacred promise to him."

Acts 1:16. Brothers, it was necessary for the Scriptures to come true concerning Judas, who betrayed Jesus by guiding the mob to him, for this was predicted long ago by the Holy Spirit, speaking through King David.

Acts 28:25. But after they had argued back and forth among themselves, they left with this final word from Paul ringing in their ears: "The Holy Spirit was right when he said through Isaiah the prophet."

Rom 3:1. Then what's the use of being a Jew? Are there any special benefits for them from God? Is there any value in the Jewish circumcision ceremony? [2]Yes, being a Jew has many advantages. First of all, God trusted them with his laws. Heb 5:12, 13.

1 Cor 2:12. And God has actually given us his Spirit (not the world's spirit) to tell us about the wonderful free gifts of grace and blessing that God has given us. [13]In telling you about these gifts we have even used the very words given to us by the Holy Spirit, not words that we as men might choose. So we use the Holy Spirit's words to explain the Holy Spirit's facts.

1 Cor 7:10. Now, for those who are married I have a command, not just a suggestion. And it is not a command from me, for this is what the Lord

himself has said: A wife must not leave her husband.

1 Cor 14:37. You who claim to have the gift of prophecy or any other special ability from the Holy Spirit should be the first to realize that what I am saying is a commandment from the Lord himself.

Eph 6:17. And you will need the helmet of salvation and the sword of the Spirit—which is the Word of God.

Col 3:16. Remember what Christ taught and let his words enrich your lives and make you wise; teach them to each other and sing them out in psalms and hymns and spiritual songs, singing to the Lord with thankful hearts.

1 Thess 2:13. And we will never stop thanking God for this: that when we preached to you, you didn't think of the words we spoke as being just our own, but you accepted what we said as the very Word of God—which, of course, it was—and it changed your lives when you believed it.

1 Thess 4:1, 2. Let me add this, dear brothers: You already know how to please God in your daily living, for you know the commands we gave you from the Lord Jesus himself. Now we beg you—yes, we demand of you in the name of the Lord Jesus—that you live more and more closely to that ideal. [3]For God wants you to be holy and pure, and to keep clear of all sexual sin.

1 Tim 6:3. Some may deny these things, but they are the sound, wholesome teachings of the Lord Jesus Christ and are the foundation for a godly life. [4]Anyone who says anything different is both proud and stupid. He is quibbling over the meaning of Christ's words and stirring up arguments ending in jealousy and anger, which only lead to name-calling, accusations, and evil suspicions. [5]These arguers—their minds warped by sin—don't know how to tell the truth; to them the Good News is just a means of making money. Keep away from them.

2 Tim 3:16. The whole Bible was given to us by inspiration from God and is useful to teach us what is true and to make us realize what is wrong in our lives; it straightens us out and helps us do what is right. [17]It is God's way of making us well prepared at every point, fully equipped to do good to everyone.

Heb 1:1. Long ago God spoke in many different ways to our fathers through the prophets (in visions, dreams, and even face to face), telling them little by little about his plans. [2]But now in these days he has spoken to us through his Son to whom he has given everything, and through whom he made the world and everything there is.

Heb 3:7, 8. And since Christ is so much superior, the Holy Spirit warns us to listen to him, to be careful to hear his voice today and not let our hearts become set against him, as the people of Israel did. They steeled themselves against his love and complained against him in the desert while he was testing them.

Heb 4:12. For whatever God says to us is full of living power: it is sharper than the sharpest dagger, cutting swift and deep into our innermost thoughts and desires with all their parts, exposing us for what we really are.

1 Pet 1:11. They wondered what the Spirit of Christ within them was talking about, for he told them to write down the events which, since then, have happened to Christ: his suffering, and his great glory afterwards. And they wondered when and to whom all this would happen. [12]They were finally told that these things would not occur during their lifetime, but long years later, during yours. And now at last this Good News has been plainly announced to all of us. It was preached to us in the power of the same heaven-sent Holy Spirit who spoke to them; and it is all so strange and wonderful that even the angels in heaven would give a great deal to know more about it.

2 Pet 1:20, 21. For no prophecy recorded in Scripture was ever thought up by the prophet himself. It was the Holy Spirit within these godly men who gave them true messages from God.

2 Pet 3:2. I have tried to remind you—if you will let me—about facts you already know: facts you learned from the holy prophets and from us apostles who brought you the words of our Lord and Savior. [15]And remember why he is waiting. He is giving us time to get his message of salvation out to others. Our wise and beloved brother Paul has talked about these same things in many of his letters.

1 Jn 1:1. Christ was alive when the world began, yet I myself have seen him with my own eyes and listened to him speak. I have touched him with my own hands. He is God's message of Life. [2]This one who is Life from God has been shown to us and we guarantee that we have seen him; I am speaking of Christ, who is eternal Life. He was with the Father and then was shown to us. [3]Again I say, we are telling you about what we ourselves have actually seen and heard, so that you may share the fellowship and the joys we have with the Father and with Jesus Christ his Son. [4]And if you do as I say in this letter, then you, too, will be full of joy, and so will we. [5]This is the message God has given us to pass on to you: that God is Light and in him is no darkness at all.

Rev 1:1. This book unveils some of the future activities soon to occur in the life of Jesus Christ. God permitted him to reveal these things to his servant John in a vision; and then an angel was sent from heaven to explain the vision's meaning. [2]John wrote it down—the words of God and Jesus Christ and everything he heard and saw. [11]Saying, "I am A and Z, the First and Last!" And then I heard him say, "Write down everything you see, and send your letter to the seven churches in Turkey." [17, 18]When I saw him, I fell at his feet as dead; but he laid his right hand on me and said, "Don't be afraid! Though I am the First and Last, the Living One who died, who is now alive forevermore, who has the keys of hell and death—don't be afraid! [19]Write down what you have just seen, and what will soon be shown to you."

Rev 2:7. Let this message sink into the ears of

anyone who listens to what the Spirit is saying to the churches.

Rev 19:10. Then I fell down at his feet to worship him, but he said, "No! Don't! For I am a servant of God just as you are, and as your brother Christians are, who testify of their faith in Jesus. The purpose of all prophecy and of all I have shown you is to tell about Jesus."

Rev 22:6, 7. Then the angel said to me, "These words are trustworthy and true: 'I am coming soon!' God, who tells his prophets what the future holds, has sent his angel to tell you this will happen soon. Blessed are those who believe it and all else written in the scroll." [8]I, John, saw and heard all these things.

UNBELIEF IN. Ps 50:16. But God says to evil men: Recite my laws no longer, and stop claiming my promises, [17]for you have refused my discipline, disregarding my laws.

Prov 1:29. For you closed your eyes to the facts and did not choose to reverence and trust the Lord, [30]and you turned your back on me, spurning my advice.

Prov 13:13. Despise God's Word and find yourself in trouble. Obey it and succeed.

Isa 5:24. Therefore God will deal with them and burn them. They will disappear like straw on fire. Their roots will rot and their flowers wither, for they have thrown away the laws of God and despised the Word of the Holy One of Israel.

Isa 28:9. "Who does Isaiah think he is," the people say, "to speak to us like this! Are we little children, barely old enough to talk? [10]He tells us everything over and over again, a line at a time and in such simple words!" [11]But they won't listen; the only language they can understand is punishment! So God will punish them by sending against them foreigners who speak strange gibberish! Only then will they listen to him! [12]They could have rest in their own land if they would obey him, if they were kind and good. He told them that, but they wouldn't listen to him. [13]So the Lord will spell it out for them again, repeating it over and over in simple words whenever he can; yet over this simple, straightforward message they will stumble and fall and be broken, trapped and captured. [14]Therefore hear the word of the Lord, you scoffing rulers in Jerusalem.

Isa 30:9. For if you don't write it, they will claim I never warned them. "Oh, no," they'll say, "you never told us that!" For they are stubborn rebels. [10, 11]They tell my prophets, "Shut up—we don't want any more of your reports!" Or they say, "Don't tell us the truth; tell us nice things; tell us lies. Forget all this gloom; we've heard more than enough about your 'Holy One of Israel' and all he says."

Isa 53:1. But, oh, how few believe it! Who will listen? To whom will God reveal his saving power?

Jer 6:10. But who will listen when I warn them? Their ears are closed and they refuse to hear. The word of God has angered them; they don't want it at all.

Jer 8:9. These wise teachers of yours will be shamed by exile for this sin, for they have rejected the word of the Lord. Are they then so wise?

Hos 8:12. Even if I gave her ten thousand laws, she'd say they weren't for her—that they applied to someone far away.

Amos 2:12. But you caused the Nazirites to sin by urging them to drink your wine, and you silenced my prophets, telling them, "Shut up!"

Mic 2:6. "Don't say such things," the people say. "Don't harp on things like that. It's disgraceful, that sort of talk. Such evils surely will not come our way."

Lk 16:31. But Abraham said, "If they won't listen to Moses and the prophets, they won't listen even though someone rises from the dead."

Lk 24:25. Then Jesus said to them, "You are such foolish, foolish people! You find it so hard to believe all that the prophets wrote in the Scriptures!"

Jn 3:20. They hated the heavenly Light because they wanted to sin in the darkness. They stayed away from that Light for fear their sins would be exposed and they would be punished.

Jn 5:46. For you have refused to believe Moses. He wrote about me, but you refuse to believe him, so you refuse to believe in me. [47]And since you don't believe what he wrote, no wonder you don't believe me either.

Jn 8:37. (Yes, I realize that you are descendants of Abraham!) And yet some of you are trying to kill me because my message does not find a home within your hearts. [45]And so when I tell you the truth, you just naturally don't believe it!

1 Cor 1:18. I know very well how foolish it sounds to those who are lost, when they hear that Jesus died to save them. But we who are saved recognize this message as the very power of God. [22]It seems foolish to the Jews because they want a sign from heaven as proof that what is preached is true; and it is foolish to the Gentiles because they believe only what agrees with their philosophy and seems wise to them. [23]So when we preach about Christ dying to save them, the Jews are offended and the Gentiles say it's all nonsense.

2 Tim 3:8. And these teachers fight truth just as Jannes and Jambres fought against Moses. They have dirty minds, warped and twisted, and have turned against the Christian faith.

2 Tim 4:3. For there is going to come a time when people won't listen to the truth, but will go around looking for teachers who will tell them just what they want to hear. [4]They won't listen to what the Bible says but will blithely follow their own misguided ideas.

1 Pet 2:8. And the Scriptures also say, "He is the Stone that some will stumble over, and the Rock that will make them fall." They will stumble because they will not listen to God's Word, nor obey it, and so this punishment must follow—that they will fall.

2 Pet 3:15, 16. And remember why he is waiting. He is giving us time to get his message of salvation

out to others. Our wise and beloved brother Paul has talked about these same things in many of his letters. Some of his comments are not easy to understand, and there are people who are deliberately stupid, and always demand some unusual interpretation—they have twisted his letter around to mean something quite different from what he meant, just as they do the other parts of the Scripture—and the result is disaster for them.

Rev 22:19. And if anyone subtracts any part of these prophecies, God shall take away his share in the Tree of Life, and in the Holy City just described.

WORDS Of Jesus: Gracious, Lk 4:22; spirit and life, Jn 6:63; eternal life, Jn 6:68; shall judge, Jn 12:47, 48. Of the wise: As goads, and nails, Eccl 12:11; pleasant, Eccl 10:12, 13. Spoken at the proper time, Prov 15:23; Isa 50:4. Properly spoken, like apples of gold in a silver basket, Prov 25:11. Of the perfect man, controlled, Jas 3:1, 2.

Should be pleasing to God, Ps 19:14.

Of the teacher, should be plain, 1 Cor 14:9, 19. Unprofitable, to be avoided, 2 Tim 2:14. Unspeakable, heard by Paul in paradise, 2 Cor 12:4. Vain, to be disregarded, Eph 5:4; like a wind, Job 8:2. Idle, account must be given for on Judgment Day, Mt 12:36, 37. In a large number of, is sin, Prov 10:19. Fool known by many, Eccl 5:1–3; will ruin him, Prov 18:6–8; Eccl 10:12–14. Seditious, deceive the simple, Rom 16:18. Of the hypocrite, smooth as oil, Ps 55:21.

See *Busybody; Gossip; Slander; Speaking, Evil.*

WORK See *Industry; Labor.*

WORKS GOOD. Jesus an example of, Jn 10:32; Acts 10:38. Christian women should perform, 1 Tim 2:9, 10; 5:10. God remembers, Neh 13:14, with Heb 6:9, 10. Shall be judged, Eccl 12:14, with 2 Cor 5:10. In the judgment, will be an evidence of faith, Mt 25:34–40, with Jas 2:14–20. Ministers should be examples of, Tit 2:7. Ministers should exhort to, 1 Tim 6:17, 18; Tit 3:1, 8, 14. God is glorified by, Jn 15:8. Designed to lead others to glorify God, Mt 5:15, 16; 1 Pet 2:12. A blessing accompanies, Jas 1:25. Of the righteous, are perceived, 1 Tim 5:25.

Parables relating to: The investments, Mt 25:14–29; the nobleman, Lk 19:12–27; the workers in the field, Mt 20:11–15; the two sons, Mt 21:28–31; the barren fig tree, Lk 13:6–9.

UNCLASSIFIED SCRIPTURES RELATING TO. Deut 6:25. For it always goes well with us when we obey all the laws of the Lord our God.

Deut 24:12, 13. If the man is poor and gives you his cloak as security, you are not to sleep in it. Take it back to him at sundown so that he can use it through the night and bless you; and the Lord your God will count it as righteousness for you.

Neh 13:14. O my God, remember this good deed and do not forget all that I have done for the Temple. chapter 5:19.

Job 30:25. And did I not weep for those in trouble? Wasn't I deeply grieved for the needy?

Ps 37:3. Trust in the Lord instead. Be kind and good to others; then you will live safely here in the land and prosper, feeding in safety.

Ps 106:30. Phineas executed those whose sins had caused the plague to start. [31](For this good deed Phineas will be remembered forever.)

Jer 22:15. But a beautiful palace does not make a great king! Why did your father Josiah reign so long? Because he was just and fair in all his dealings. That is why God blessed him. [16]He saw to it that justice and help were given the poor and the needy and all went well for him. This is how a man lives close to God.

Ezk 14:14. If Noah, Daniel and Job were here today, they alone would be saved by their righteousness, and I would destroy the remainder of Israel, says the Lord God. *v.* 20.

Ezk 18:5. But if a man is just and does what is lawful and right, [6]and has not gone out to the mountains to feast before the idols of Israel and worship them, and does not commit adultery, nor lie with any woman during the time of her menstruation, [7]and is a merciful creditor, not holding on to the items given to him in pledge by poor debtors, and is no robber, but gives food to the hungry and clothes to those in need, [8]and grants loans without interest, and stays away from sin, and is honest and fair when judging others, [9]and obeys my laws—that man is just, says the Lord, and he shall surely live.

Mt 3:8. Before being baptized, prove that you have turned from sin by doing worthy deeds.

Mt 6:1. Take care! don't do your good deeds publicly, to be admired, for then you will lose the reward from your Father in heaven. [2]When you give a gift to a beggar, don't shout about it as the hypocrites do—blowing trumpets in the synagogues and streets to call attention to their acts of charity! I tell you in all earnestness, they have received all the reward they will ever get. [3]But when you do a kindness to someone, do it secretly—don't tell your left hand what your right hand is doing. [4]And your Father who knows all secrets will reward you.

Mt 10:42. And if, as my representatives, you give even a cup of cold water to a little child, you will surely be rewarded. Mk 9:41.

Mt 18:5. And any of you who welcomes a little child like this because you are mine, is welcoming me and caring for me.

Mt 19:16. Someone came to Jesus with this question: "Good master, what must I do to have eternal life?" [17]"When you call me good you are calling me God," Jesus replied, "for God alone is truly good. But to answer your question, you can get to heaven if you keep the commandments." [Mk 10:17; Lk 10:25.] [18]"Which ones?" the man asked. And Jesus replied, "Don't kill, don't commit adultery, don't steal, don't lie, [19]honor your father and mother, and love your neighbor as yourself!" [20]"I've always obeyed every one of them," the youth replied. "What else must I do?" [21]Jesus told him, "If you want to be perfect, go and sell everything you have and give the money to the poor, and you will have treasure in heaven; and come, follow me."

Mt 25:34. Then I, the King, shall say to those at my right, "Come, blessed of my Father, into the Kingdom prepared for you from the founding of the world. [35]For I was hungry and you fed me; I was thirsty and you gave me water; I was a stranger and you invited me into your homes; [36]naked and you clothed me; sick and in prison, and you visited me." [37]Then these righteous ones will reply, "Sir, when did we ever see you hungry and feed you? Or thirsty and give you anything to drink? [38]Or a stranger, and help you? Or naked, and clothe you? [39]When did we ever see you sick or in prison, and visit you?" [40]And I, the King, will tell them, "When you did it to these my brothers you were doing it to me!" [41]Then I will turn to those on my left and say, "Away with you, you cursed ones, into the eternal fire prepared for the devil and his demons. [42]For I was hungry and you wouldn't feed me; thirsty, and you wouldn't give me anything to drink; [43]a stranger, and you refused me hospitality; naked, and you wouldn't clothe me; sick, and in prison, and you didn't visit me." [44]Then they will reply, "Lord, when did we ever see you hungry or thirsty or a stranger or naked or sick or in prison, and not help you?" [45]And I will answer, "When you refused to help the least of these my brothers, you were refusing help to me." [46]And they shall go away into eternal punishment; but the righteous into everlasting life.

Jn 3:21. But those doing right come gladly to the Light to let everyone see that they are doing what God wants them to.

Jn 15:2. He lops off every branch that doesn't produce. And he prunes those branches that bear fruit for even larger crops. [3]He has already tended you by pruning you back for greater strength and usefulness by means of the commands I gave you. [4]Take care to live in me, and let me live in you. For a branch can't produce fruit when severed from the vine. Nor can you be fruitful apart from me. [5]Yes, I am the Vine; you are the branches. Whoever lives in me and I in him shall produce a large crop of fruit. For apart from me you can't do a thing. [6]If anyone separates from me, he is thrown away like a useless branch, withers, and is gathered into a pile with all the others and burned. [7]But if you stay in me and obey my commands, you may ask any request you like, and it will be granted! [8]My true disciples produce bountiful harvests. This brings great glory to my Father. [14]And you are my friends if you obey me.

Acts 10:4. Cornelius stared at him in terror. "What do you want, sir?" he asked the angel. And the angel replied, "Your prayers and charities have not gone unnoticed by God!" [38]"And you no doubt know that Jesus of Nazareth was anointed by God with the Holy Spirit and with power, and he went around doing good and healing all who were possessed by demons, for God was with him."

Rom 2:13. After all, salvation is not given to those who know what to do, unless they do it.

1 Cor 3:6. My work was to plant the seed in your hearts, and Apollos' work was to water it, but it was God, not we, who made the garden grow in your hearts. [7]The person who does the planting or watering isn't very important, but God is important because he is the one who makes things grow. [8]Apollos and I are working as a team, with the same aim, though each of us will be rewarded for his own hard work. [9]We are only God's co-workers. You are *God's* garden, not ours; you are *God's* building, not ours.

2 Cor 9:8. God is able to make it up to you by giving you everything you need and more, so that there will not only be enough for your own needs, but plenty left over to give joyfully to others.

Gal 6:4. Let everyone be sure that he is doing his very best, for then he will have the personal satisfaction of work well done, and won't need to compare himself with someone else.

Eph 2:10. It is God himself who has made us what we are and given us new lives from Christ Jesus; and long ages ago he planned that we should spend these lives in helping others.

Phil 1:11. May you always be doing those good, kind things which show that you are a child of God, for this will bring much praise and glory to the Lord.

Phil 2:13. For God is at work within you, helping you want to obey him, and then helping you do what he wants.

Col 1:10. And asking that the way you live will always please the Lord and honor him, so that you will always be doing good, kind things for others, while all the time you are learning to know God better and better.

Col 3:12. Since you have been chosen by God who has given you this new kind of life, and because of his deep love and concern for you, you should practice tenderhearted mercy and kindness to others. Don't worry about making a good impression on them but be ready to suffer quietly and patiently. [13]Be gentle and ready to forgive; never hold grudges. Remember, the Lord forgave you, so you must forgive others. [14]Most of all, let love guide your life, for then the whole church will stay together in perfect harmony. [17]And whatever you do or say, let it be as a representative of the Lord Jesus, and come with him into the presence of God the Father to give him your thanks.

1 Thess 1:3. We never forget your loving deeds as we talk to our God and Father about you, and your strong faith and steady looking forward to the return of our Lord Jesus Christ. [7]Then you yourselves became an example to all the other Christians in Greece. [8]And now the Word of the Lord has spread out from you to others everywhere, far beyond your boundaries, for wherever we go we find people telling us about your remarkable faith in God. We don't need to tell *them* about it.

2 Thess 2:17. Comfort your hearts with all comfort, and help you in every good thing you say and do.

1 Tim 2:10. Christian women should be noticed for being kind and good.

1 Tim 5:9. A widow who wants to become one of the special church workers should be at least sixty years old and have been married only once. [10]She must be well thought of by everyone because of the good she has done. Has she brought up her children well? Has she been kind to strangers as well as to other Christians? Has she helped those who are sick and hurt? Is she always ready to show kindness?

1 Tim 6:18. Tell them to use their money to do good. They should be rich in good works and should give happily to those in need, always being ready to share with others whatever God has given them. [19]By doing this they will be storing up real treasure for themselves in heaven—it is the only safe investment for eternity!

2 Tim 2:21. If you stay away from sin you will be like one of these dishes made of purest gold—the very best in the house—so that Christ himself can use you for his highest purposes.

2 Tim 3:16. The whole Bible was given to us by inspiration from God and is useful to teach us what is true and to make us realize what is wrong in our lives; it straightens us out and helps us do what is right. [17]It is God's way of making us well prepared at every point, fully equipped to do good to everyone.

Tit 2:14. He died under God's judgment against our sins, so that he could rescue us from constant falling into sin and make us his very own people, with cleansed hearts and real enthusiasm for doing kind things for others.

Tit 3:1. Remind your people to obey the government and its officers, and always to be obedient and ready for any honest work. [2]They must not speak evil of anyone, nor quarrel, but be gentle and truly courteous to all. [8]These things I have told you are all true. Insist on them so that Christians will be careful to do good deeds all the time, for this is not only right, but it brings results. [14]For our people must learn to help all who need their assistance, that their lives will be fruitful.

Heb 6:10. For God is not unfair. How can he forget your hard work for him, or forget the way you used to show your love for him—and still do—by helping his children?

Heb 10:24. In response to all he has done for us, let us outdo each other in being helpful and kind to each other and in doing good.

Heb 13:21. May he who became the great Shepherd of the sheep by an everlasting agreement between God and you, produce in you through the power of Christ all that is pleasing to him. To him be glory forever and ever. Amen.

Jas 1:22. And remember, it is a message to obey, not just to listen to. So don't fool yourselves. [23]For if a person just listens and doesn't obey, he is like a man looking at his face in a mirror; [24]as soon as he walks away, he can't see himself anymore or remember what he looks like. [25]But if anyone keeps looking steadily into God's law for free men, he will not only remember it but he will do what it says, and God will greatly bless him in everything he does. [26]Anyone who says he is a Christian but doesn't control his sharp tongue is just fooling himself, and his religion isn't worth much. [27]The Christian who is pure and without fault, from God the Father's point of view, is the one who takes care of orphans and widows, and who remains true to the Lord—not soiled and dirtied by his contacts with the world.

Jas 2:17. So you see, it isn't enough just to have faith. You must also do good to prove that you have it. Faith that doesn't show itself by good works is no faith at all—it is dead and useless.

Jas 3:13. If you are wise, live a life of steady goodness, so that only good deeds will pour forth. And if you don't brag about them, then you will be truly wise! [17]But the wisdom that comes from heaven is first of all pure and full of quiet gentleness. Then it is peace-loving and courteous. It allows discussion and is willing to yield to others; it is full of mercy and good deeds. It is wholehearted and straightforward and sincere. [18]And those who are peacemakers will plant seeds of peace and reap a harvest of goodness.

1 Pet 2:12. Be careful how you behave among your unsaved neighbors; for then, even if they are suspicious of you and talk against you, they will end up praising God for your good works when Christ returns.

Rev 14:13. And I heard a voice in the heavens above me saying, "Write this down: At last the time has come for his martyrs to enter into their full reward. Yes, says the Spirit, they are blest indeed, for now they shall rest from all their toils and trials; for their good deeds follow them to heaven!"

INSUFFICIENCY OF, FOR SALVATION. Ps 127:1. Unless the Lord builds a house, the builders' work is useless. Unless the Lord protects a city, sentries do no good. [2]It is senseless for you to work so hard from early morning until late at night, fearing you will starve to death; for God wants his loved ones to get their proper rest.

Eccl 1:14. And I applied myself to search for understanding about everything in the universe. I discovered that the lot of man, which God has dealt to him, is not a happy one. It is all foolishness, chasing the wind.

Isa 57:12. And then there is your "righteousness" and your "good works"—none of which will save you.

Isa 64:6. We are all infected and impure with sin. When we put on our prized robes of righteousness we find they are but filthy rags. Like autumn leaves we fade, wither and fall. And our sins, like the wind, sweep us away.

Ezk 33:12. For the good works of a righteous man will not save him if he turns to sin; and the sins of an evil man will not destroy him if he repents and turns from his sins. [13]I have said the good man will live. But if he sins, expecting his past goodness to save him, then none of his good deeds will be remembered. I will destroy him for his sins. [14]And when I tell the wicked he will die and then he turns from his sins and does what is fair and right—[15]if he gives back the borrower's pledge and returns what he has stolen and walks along the paths of right, not doing evil—he shall surely live. He shall not die. [16]None of his past sins shall be brought up against him, for he has turned to the good and shall surely live. [17]And yet your people are saying the Lord isn't fair. The trouble is *they* aren't fair. [18]For again I say, when the good man turns to evil, he shall die. [19]But if the wicked turns from his wickedness and does what's fair and just, he shall live.

Dan 9:18. O my God, bend down your ear and listen to my plea. Open your eyes and see our wretchedness, how your city lies in ruins—for everyone knows that it is yours. We don't ask because we merit help, but because you are so merciful despite our grievous sins.

Mt 5:20. But I warn you—unless your goodness is greater than that of the Pharisees and other Jewish leaders, you can't get into the Kingdom of Heaven at all!

Lk 17:7, 8, 9. When a servant comes in from plowing or taking care of sheep, he doesn't just sit down and eat, but first prepares his master's meal and serves him his supper before he eats his own. And he is not even thanked, for he is merely doing what he is supposed to do. [10]Just so, if you merely obey me, you should not consider yourselves worthy of praise. For you have simply done your duty!

Lk 18:9. Then he told this story to some who boasted of their virtue and scorned everyone else: [10]"Two men went to the Temple to pray. One was a proud, self-righteous Pharisee, and the other a cheating tax collector. [11]The proud Pharisee 'prayed' this prayer: 'Thank God, I am not a sinner like everyone else, especially like that tax collector over there! For I never cheat, I don't commit adultery, [12]I go without food twice a week, and I give to God a tenth of everything I earn.' [13]But the corrupt tax collector stood at a distance and dared not even lift his eyes to heaven as he prayed, but beat upon his chest in sorrow, exclaiming, 'God, be merciful to me, a sinner.' [14]I tell you, this sinner, not the Pharisee, returned home forgiven! For the proud shall be humbled, but the humble shall be honored."

Acts 13:39. Everyone who trusts in him is freed from all guilt and declared righteous—something the Jewish law could never do.

Rom 3:20. Now do you see it? No one can ever be made right in God's sight by doing what the law commands. For the more we know of God's laws, the clearer it becomes that we aren't obeying them; his laws serve only to make us see that we are sinners. [21, 22]But now God has shown us a different way to heaven—not by "being good enough" and trying to keep his laws, but by a new way (though not new, really, for the Scriptures told about it long ago). Now God says he will accept and acquit us —declare us "not guilty"—if we trust Jesus Christ to take away our sins. And we all can be saved in this same way, by coming to Christ, no matter who we are or what we have been like. [23]Yes, all have sinned; all fall short of God's glorious ideal; [24]yet now God declares us "not guilty" of offending him if we trust in Jesus Christ, who in his kindness freely takes away our sins. [25]For God sent Christ Jesus to take the punishment for our sins and to end all God's anger against us. He used Christ's blood and our faith as the means of saving us from his wrath. In this way he was being entirely fair, even though he did not punish those who sinned in former times. For he was looking forward to the time when Christ would come and take away those sins. [26]And now in these days also he can receive sinners in this same way, because Jesus took away their sins. But isn't this unfair for God to let criminals go free, and say that they are innocent? No, for he does it on the basis of their trust in Jesus who took away their sins. [27]Then what can we boast about doing, to earn our salvation? Nothing at all. Why? Because our acquittal is not based on our good deeds; it is based on what Christ has done and our faith in him. [28]So it is that we are saved by faith in Christ and not by the good things we do. [29]And does God save only the Jews in this way? No, the Gentiles, too, may come to him in this same manner. [30]God treats us all the same; all, whether Jews or Gentiles, are acquitted if they have faith. [31]Well then, if we are saved by faith, does this mean that we no longer need obey God's laws? Just the opposite! In fact, only when we trust Jesus can we truly obey him.

Rom 4:1, 2. Abraham was, humanly speaking, the founder of our Jewish nation. What were his experiences concerning this question of being saved by faith? Was it because of his good deeds that God accepted him? If so, then he would have something to boast about. But from God's point of view Abraham had no basis at all for pride. [3]For the Scriptures tell us Abraham *believed God,* and that is why God canceled his sins and declared him "not guilty." [4, 5]But didn't he earn his right to heaven by all the good things he did? No, for being saved is a gift; if a person could earn it by being good, then it wouldn't be free—but it is! It is *given* to those who do *not* work for it. For God declares sinners to be good in his sight if they have faith in Christ to save them from God's wrath. [6]King David spoke of this, describing the happiness of an undeserving sinner who is declared "not guilty" by God. [7]"Blessed, and to be envied," he said, "are those whose sins are forgiven and put out of sight. [8]Yes, what joy there is for anyone whose sins are no longer counted against him by the Lord." *vs.* 9–22.

Rom 8:3. We aren't saved from sin's grasp by knowing the commandments of God, because we can't and don't keep them, but God put into effect a different plan to save us. He sent his own Son in a human body like ours—except that ours are sinful—and destroyed sin's control over us by giving himself as a sacrifice for our sins.

Rom 9:16. And so God's blessings are not given just because someone decides to have them or works hard to get them. They are given because God takes pity on those he wants to. [31]But the Jews, who tried so hard to get right with God by keeping his laws, never succeeded. [32]Why not? Because they were trying to be saved by keeping the law and being good instead of by depending on faith. They have stumbled over the great stumbling stone.

Rom 11:6. And if it is by God's kindness, then it is not by their being good enough. For in that case the free gift would no longer be free—it isn't free when it is earned.

1 Cor 13:1. If I had the gift of being able to speak in other languages without learning them, and could speak in every language there is in all of heaven and earth, but didn't love others, I would only be making noise. [2]If I had the gift of prophecy and knew all about what is going to happen in the future, knew everything about *everything,* but didn't love others, what good would it do? Even if I had the gift of faith so that I could speak to a mountain and make it move, I would still be worth nothing at all without love. [3]If I gave everything I have to poor people, and if I were burned alive for preaching the Gospel but didn't love others, it would be of no value whatever.

Gal 2:16. And yet we Jewish Christians know very well that we cannot become right with God by obeying our Jewish laws, but only by faith in Jesus Christ to take away our sins. And so we, too, have trusted Jesus Christ, that we might be accepted by God because of faith—and not because we have obeyed the Jewish laws. For no one will ever be saved by obeying them. [19]For it was through reading the Scripture that I came to realize that I could never find God's favor by trying—and failing—to obey the laws. I came to realize that acceptance with God comes by believing in Christ. [21]I am not one of those who treats Christ's death as meaningless. For if we could be saved by keeping Jewish laws, then there was no need for Christ to die.

Gal 3:10. Yes, and those who depend on the Jewish laws to save them are under God's curse, for the Scriptures point out very clearly, "Cursed is everyone who at any time breaks a single one of these laws that are written in God's Book of the Law." [11]Consequently, it is clear that no one can ever win God's favor by trying to keep the Jewish laws, because God has said that the only way we can be right in his sight is by faith. As the prophet Habakkuk says it, "The man who finds life will find it through trusting God." [12]How different from this way of faith is the way of law which says that a man is saved by obeying every law of God, without one slip. [21]Well then, are God's laws and God's promises against each other? Of course not! If we could be saved by his laws, then God would not have had to give us a different way to get out of the grip of sin—for the Scriptures insist we are all its prisoners. *vs.* 1–29.

Gal 4:9. And now that you have found God (or I should say, now that God has found you) how can it be that you want to go back again and become slaves once more to another poor, weak, useless religion of trying to get to heaven by obeying God's laws? [10]You are trying to find favor with God by what you do or don't do on certain days or months or seasons or years. [11]I fear for you. I am afraid that all my hard work for you was worth nothing.

Gal 5:2. Listen to me, for this is serious: *if you are counting on circumcision and keeping the Jewish laws to make you right with God, then Christ cannot save you.* [4]Christ is useless to you if you are counting on clearing your debt to God by keeping those laws; you are lost from God's grace. [6]And we to whom Christ has given eternal life don't need to worry about whether we have been circumcised or not, or whether we are obeying the Jewish ceremonies or not; for all we need is faith working through love. [18]When you are guided by the Holy Spirit you need no longer force yourself to obey Jewish laws.

Gal 6:15. It doesn't make any difference now whether we have been circumcised or not; what counts is whether we really have been changed into new and different people.

Eph 2:8. Because of his kindness you have been saved through trusting Christ. And even trusting is not of yourselves; it too is a gift from God. [9]Salvation is not a reward for the good we have done, so none of us can take any credit for it.

Phil 3:3. For it isn't the *cutting of our bodies* that makes us children of God; it is *worshiping him with our spirits.* That is the only true "circumcision." We Christians glory in what Christ Jesus has done for us and realize that we are helpless to save ourselves. [4]Yet if anyone ever had reason to hope that he could save himself, it would be I. If others could be saved by what they are, certainly I could! [5]For I went through the Jewish initiation ceremony when I was eight days old, having been born into a pure-blooded Jewish home that was a branch of the old original Benjamin family. So I was a real Jew if there ever was one! What's more, I was a member of the Pharisees who demand the strictest obedience to every Jewish law and custom. [6]And sincere? Yes, so much so that I greatly persecuted the church; and I tried to obey every Jewish rule and regulation right down to the very last point. [7]But all these things that I once thought very worthwhile—now I've thrown them all away so that I can put my trust and hope in Christ alone. [8]Yes, everything else is worthless when compared with the priceless gain of knowing Christ Jesus my Lord. I have put aside all else, counting it worth less than nothing, in order that I can have Christ, [9]and become one with him, no longer counting on being saved by being good enough or by obeying God's laws, but by trusting Christ to save me; for God's way of making us right with himself depends on faith—counting on Christ alone.

Col 2:20. Since you died, as it were, with Christ and this has set you free from following the world's ideas of how to be saved—by doing good and obeying various rules—why do you keep right on following them anyway, still bound by such rules as

[21]not eating, tasting, or even touching certain foods? [22]Such rules are mere human teachings, for food was made to be eaten and used up. [23]These rules may seem good, for rules of this kind require strong devotion and are humiliating and hard on the body, but they have no effect when it comes to conquering a person's evil thoughts and desires. They only make him proud.

2 Tim 1:9. It is he who saved us and chose us for his holy work, not because we deserved it but because that was his plan long before the world began —to show his love and kindness to us through Christ.

Tit 3:4. But when the time came for the kindness and love of God our Savior to appear, [5]then he saved us—not because we were good enough to be saved, but because of his kindness and pity—by washing away our sins and giving us the new joy of the indwelling Holy Spirit.

Heb 4:3. For only we who believe God can enter into his place of rest. He has said, "I have sworn in my anger that those who don't believe me will never get in," even though he has been ready and waiting for them since the world began. [4]We know he is ready and waiting because it is written that God rested on the seventh day of creation, having finished all that he had planned to make. [5]Even so they didn't get in, for God finally said, "They shall never enter my rest." [6]Yet the promise remains and some get in—but not those who had the first chance, for they disobeyed God and failed to enter. [7]But he has set another time for coming in, and that time is now. He announced this through King David long years after man's first failure to enter, saying in the words already quoted, "Today when you hear him calling, do not harden your hearts against him." [8]This new place of rest he is talking about does not mean the land of Israel that Joshua led them into. If that were what God meant, he would not have spoken long afterwards about "today" being the time to get in. [9]So there is a full complete rest *still waiting* for the people of God. [10]Christ has already entered there. He is resting from his work, just as God did after the creation.

Heb 6:1. Let us stop going over the same old ground again and again, always teaching those first lessons about Christ. Let us go on instead to other things and become mature in our understanding, as strong Christians ought to be. Surely we don't need to speak further about the foolishness of trying to be saved by being good, or about the necessity of faith in God; [2]you don't need further instruction about baptism and spiritual gifts and the resurrection of the dead and eternal judgment.

Heb 9:1, 2. Now in that first agreement between God and his people there were rules for worship and there was a sacred tent down here on earth. Inside this place of worship there were two rooms. The first one contained the golden candlestick and a table with special loaves of holy bread upon it; this part was called the Holy Place. [3]Then there was a curtain and behind the curtain was a room called the Holy of Holies. [4]In that room there were a golden incense-altar and the golden chest, called the ark of the covenant, completely covered on all sides with pure gold. Inside the ark were the tablets of stone with the Ten Commandments written on them, and a golden jar with some manna in it, and Aaron's wooden cane that budded. [5]Above the golden chest were statues of angels called the cherubim—the guardians of God's glory—with their wings stretched out over the ark's golden cover, called the mercy seat. But enough of such details. [6]Well, when all was ready the priests went in and out of the first room whenever they wanted to, doing their work. [7]But only the high priest went into the inner room, and then only once a year, all alone, and always with blood which he sprinkled on the mercy seat as an offering to God to cover his own mistakes and sins, and the mistakes and sins of all the people. [8]And the Holy Spirit uses all this to point out to us that under the old system the common people could not go into the Holy of Holies as long as the outer room and the entire system it represents were still in use. [9]This has an important lesson for us today. For under the old system, gifts and sacrifices were offered, but these failed to cleanse the hearts of the people who brought them. [10]For the old system dealt only with certain rituals —what foods to eat and drink, rules for washing themselves, and rules about this and that. The people had to keep these rules to tide them over until Christ came with God's new and better way. [11]He came as High Priest of this better system which we now have. He went into that greater, perfect tabernacle in heaven, not made by men nor part of this world, [12]and once for all took blood into that inner room, the Holy of Holies, and sprinkled it on the mercy seat; but it was not the blood of goats and calves. No, he took his own blood, and with it he, by himself, made sure of our eternal salvation. [13]And if under the old system the blood of bulls and goats and the ashes of young cows could cleanse men's bodies from sin, [14]just think how much more surely the blood of Christ will transform our lives and hearts. His sacrifice frees us from the worry of having to obey the old rules, and makes us want to serve the living God. For by the help of the eternal Holy Spirit, Christ willingly gave himself to God to die for our sins—he being perfect, without a single sin or fault.

Jas 2:10. And the person who keeps every law of God, but makes one little slip, is just as guilty as the person who has broken every law there is. [11]For the God who said you must not marry a woman who already has a husband, also said you must not murder, so even though you have not broken the marriage laws by committing adultery, but have murdered someone, you have entirely broken God's laws and stand utterly guilty before him.

OF GOD. See *God, Creator, Works of.*

WORLD See *Earth.*

WORLDLINESS 1 Sam 8:19. But the people refused to listen to Samuel's warning. "Even so, we still want a king," they said, [20]"For we want to be like the nations around us."

Job 20:4. Don't you realize that ever since man was first placed upon the earth, [5]the triumph of the wicked has been short-lived, and the joy of the godless but for a moment? [6]Though the godless be proud as the heavens, and walk with his nose in the air, [7]yet he shall perish forever, cast away like his own dung. Those who knew him will wonder where he is gone. [8]He will fade like a dream. [9]Neither his friends nor his family will ever see him again. [10]His children shall beg from the poor, their hard labor shall repay his debts. [11]Though still a young man, his bones shall lie in the dust. [12]He enjoyed the taste of his wickedness, letting it melt in his mouth, [13]sipping it slowly, lest it disappear. [14]But suddenly the food he has eaten turns sour within him. [15]He will vomit the plunder he gorged. God won't let him keep it down. [16]It is like poison and death to him. [17]He shall not enjoy the goods he stole; they will not be butter and honey to him after all. [18]His labors shall not be rewarded; wealth will give him no joy. [19]For he has oppressed the poor and foreclosed their homes; he will never recover. [20]Though he was always greedy, now he has nothing; of all the things he dreamed of—none remain. [21]Because he stole at every opportunity, his prosperity shall not continue. [22]He shall run into trouble at the peak of his powers; all the wicked shall destroy him. [23]Just as he is about to fill his belly, God will rain down wrath upon him. [24]He will be chased and struck down. [25]The arrow is pulled from his body—and the glittering point comes out from his gall. The terrors of death are upon him. [26]His treasures will be lost in deepest darkness. A raging fire will devour his goods, consuming all he has left. [27]The heavens will reveal his sins, and the earth will give testimony against him. [28]His wealth will disappear beneath the wrath of God. [29]This is what awaits the wicked man, for God prepares it for him.

Job 21:11. They have many happy children, [12, 13]they spend their time singing and dancing. They are wealthy and need deny themselves nothing; they are prosperous to the end. [14]All this despite the fact that they ordered God away and wanted no part of him and his ways. [15]'Who is Almighty God?' they scoff. 'Why should we obey him? What good will it do us?'

Ps 49:16. So do not be dismayed when evil men grow rich and build their lovely homes. [17]For when they die they carry nothing with them! Their honors will not follow them. [18]Though a man calls himself happy all through life—and the world loudly applauds success.

Ps 73:2. But as for me, I came so close to the edge of the cliff! My feet were slipping and I was almost gone. [3]For I was envious of the prosperity of the proud and wicked. [4]Yes, all through life their road is smooth! They grow sleek and fat. [5]They aren't always in trouble and plagued with problems like everyone else, [6]so their pride sparkles like a jeweled necklace, and their clothing is woven of cruelty! [7]These fat cats have everything their hearts could ever wish for! [8]They scoff at God and threaten his people. How proudly they speak! [9]They boast against the very heavens, and their words strut through the earth. [10]And so God's people are dismayed and confused, and drink it all in. [11]"Does God realize what is going on?" they ask. [12]"Look at these men of arrogance; they never have to lift a finger—theirs is a life of ease; and all the time their riches multiply." [13]Have I been wasting my time? Why take the trouble to be pure? [14]All I get out of it is trouble and woe—every day and all day long! [15]If I had really said that, I would have been a traitor to your people. [16]Yet it is so hard to explain it—this prosperity of those who hate the Lord. [17]Then one day I went into God's sanctuary to meditate, and thought about the future of these evil men. [18]What a slippery path they are on—suddenly God will send them sliding over the edge of the cliff and down to their destruction: [19]an instant end to all their happiness, an eternity of terror. [20]Their present life is only a dream! They will awaken to the truth as one awakens from a dream of things that never really were! [21]When I saw this, what turmoil filled my heart! [22]I saw myself so stupid and so ignorant; I must seem like an animal to you, O God.

Prov 14:12. Before every man there lies a wide and pleasant road that seems right but ends in death. [13]Laughter cannot mask a heavy heart. When the laughter ends, the grief remains.

Prov 15:21. If a man enjoys folly, something is wrong! The sensible stay on the pathways of right.

Prov 21:17. A man who loves pleasure becomes poor; wine and luxury are not the way to riches!

Prov 23:20, 21. Don't carouse with drunkards and gluttons, for they are on their way to poverty. And remember that too much sleep clothes a man with rags.

Prov 27:1. Don't brag about your plans for tomorrow—wait and see what happens. [7]Even honey seems tasteless to a man who is full; but if he is hungry, he'll eat anything!

Eccl 1:8. Everything is unutterably weary and tiresome. No matter how much we see, we are never satisfied; no matter how much we hear, we are not content.

Eccl 2:1. I said to myself, "Come now, be merry; enjoy yourself to the full." But I found that this, too, was futile. For it is silly to be laughing all the time; what good does it do? [3]So, after a lot of thinking, I decided to try the road of drink, while still holding steadily to my course of seeking wisdom. Next I changed my course again and followed the path of folly, so that I could experience the only happiness most men have throughout their lives. [4, 5, 6]Then I tried to find fulfillment by inaugurating a great public works program: homes, vineyards, gardens, parks and orchards for myself, and reservoirs to hold the water to irrigate my plantations. [7, 8]Next I bought slaves, both men and women, and others were born within my household, I also bred great herds and flocks, more than any of the kings before me. I collected silver and gold as taxes from many kings and provinces.

In the cultural arts, I organized men's and women's choirs and orchestras. And then there were my many beautiful concubines. [9]So I became greater than any of the kings in Jerusalem before me, and with it all I remained clear-eyed, so that I could evaluate all these things. [10]Anything I wanted, I took, and did not restrain myself from any joy. I even found great pleasure in hard work. This pleasure was, indeed, my only reward for all my labors. [11]But as I looked at everything I had tried, it was all so useless, a chasing of the wind, and there was nothing really worthwhile anywhere. [12]Now I began a study of the comparative virtues of wisdom and folly, and anyone else would come to the same conclusion I did.

Eccl 6:11. The more words you speak, the less they mean, so why bother to speak at all? [12]In these few days of our empty lifetimes, who can say how one's days can best be spent? Who can know what will prove best for the future after he is gone? For who knows the future?

Eccl 8:15. Then I decided to spend my time having fun, because I felt that there was nothing better in all the earth than that a man should eat, drink, and be merry, with the hope that this happiness would stick with him in all the hard work which God gives to mankind everywhere. [16, 17]In my search for wisdom I observed all that was going on everywhere across the earth—ceaseless activity day and night. (Of course, only God can see everything, and even the wisest man who says he knows everything doesn't!)

Eccl 10:19. A party gives laughter, and wine gives happiness, and money gives everything!

Eccl 11:9. Young man, it's wonderful to be young! Enjoy every minute of it! Do all you want to; take in everything, but realize that you must account to God for everything you do. [10]So banish grief and pain, but remember that youth, with a whole life before it, can make serious mistakes.

Isa 22:12. The Lord God of Hosts called you to repent, to weep and mourn and shave your heads in sorrow for your sins, and to wear clothes made of sackcloth to show your remorse. [13]But instead, you sing and dance and play, and feast and drink. "Let us eat, drink, and be merry," you say: "What's the difference, for tomorrow we die."

Isa 24:7. All the joys of life will go: the grape harvest will fail, the wine will be gone, the merrymakers will sigh and mourn. [8]The melodious chords of the harp and timbrel are heard no more; the happy days are ended. [9]No more are the joys of wine and song; strong drink turns bitter in the mouth. [10]The city lies in chaos; every home and shop is locked up tight to keep out looters. [11]Mobs form in the streets, crying for wine; joy has reached its lowest ebb; gladness has been banished from the land.

Isa 28:4. Once glorious, her fading beauty surrounded by a fertile valley will suddenly be gone, greedily snatched away as an early fig is hungrily snatched and gobbled up!

Isa 32:9. Listen, you women who loll around in lazy ease; listen to me and I will tell you your reward: [10]In a short time—in just a little more than a year—suddenly you'll care, O careless ones. For the crops of fruit will fail; the harvest will not take place. [11]Tremble, O women of ease; throw off your unconcern. Strip off your pretty clothes—wear sackcloth for your grief.

Isa 47:7. You thought your reign would never end, Queen Kingdom of the world. You didn't care a whit about my people or think about the fate of those who do them harm. [8]O pleasure-mad kingdom, living at ease, bragging as the greatest in the world—listen to the sentence of my court upon your sins. You say, "I alone am God! I'll never be a widow; I'll never lose my children." [9]Well, those two things shall come upon you in one moment, in full measure in one day: widowhood and the loss of your children, despite all your witchcraft and magic.

Hos 9:1. O Israel, rejoice no more as others do, for you have deserted your God and sacrificed to other gods on every threshing floor. [11]The glory of Israel flies away like a bird, for your children will die at birth, or perish in the womb, or never even be conceived. [13]In my vision I have seen the sons of Israel doomed. The fathers are forced to lead their sons to slaughter.

Amos 6:3. You push away all thought of punishment awaiting you, but by your deeds you bring the Day of Judgment near. [4]You lie on ivory beds surrounded with luxury, eating the meat of the tenderest lambs and the choicest calves. [5]You sing idle songs to the sound of the harp, and fancy yourselves to be as great musicians as King David was. [6]You drink wine by the bucketful and perfume yourselves with sweet ointments, caring nothing at all that your brothers need your help. [7]Therefore you will be the first to be taken as slaves; suddenly your revelry will end.

Amos 8:10. And I will turn your parties into times of mourning, and your songs of joy will be turned to cries of despair. You will wear funeral clothes and shave your heads as signs of sorrow, as if your only son had died; bitter, bitter will be that day.

Mic 2:10. Up! Begone! This is no more your land and home, for you have filled it with sin and it will vomit you out.

Mic 6:14. You will eat but never have enough; hunger pangs and emptiness will still remain. And though you try and try to save your money, it will come to nothing at the end, and what little you succeed in storing up I'll give to those who conquer you!

Hag 1:6. You plant much but harvest little. You have scarcely enough to eat or drink, and not enough clothes to keep you warm. Your income disappears, as though you were putting it into pockets filled with holes!

Mt 6:25. So my counsel is: Don't worry about *things*—food, drink, and clothes. For you already have life and a body—and they are far more important than what to eat and wear. [26]Look at the birds!

They don't worry about what to eat—they don't need to sow or reap or store up food—for your heavenly Father feeds them. And you are far more valuable to him than they are. [27]Will all your worries add a single moment to your life? [28]And why worry about your clothes? Look at the field lilies! They don't worry about theirs. [29]Yet King Solomon in all his glory was not clothed as beautifully as they. [30]And if God cares so wonderfully for flowers that are here today and gone tomorrow, won't he more surely care for you, O men of little faith? [31, 32]So don't worry at all about having enough food and clothing. Why be like the heathen? For they take pride in all these things and are deeply concerned about them. But your heavenly Father already knows perfectly well that you need them, [33]and he will give them to you if you give him first place in your life and live as he wants you to. [34]So don't be anxious about tomorrow. God will take care of your tomorrow too. Live one day at a time.

Mt 10:39. If you cling to your life you will lose it; but if you give it up for me, you will save it. Mt 16:25; Mk 8:35; Lk 17:33; Jn 12:25.

Mt 16:26. What profit is there if you gain the whole world—and lose eternal life? What can be compared with the value of eternal life? Mk 8:36, 37.

Mt 18:1. About that time the disciples came to Jesus to ask which of them would be greatest in the Kingdom of Heaven! [2]Jesus called a small child over to him and set the little fellow down among them, [3]and said, "Unless you turn to God from your sins and become as little children, you will never get into the Kingdom of Heaven. [4]Therefore anyone who humbles himself as this little child, is the greatest in the Kingdom of Heaven." Lk 9:46–48; Mk 9:33–35.

Mt 24:37, 38. The world will be at ease—banquets and parties and weddings—just as it was in Noah's time before the sudden coming of the flood; [39]people wouldn't believe what was going to happen until the flood actually arrived and took them all away. So shall my coming be. Lk 17:26–29.

Lk 8:14. The seed among the thorns represents those who listen and believe God's words but whose faith afterwards is choked out by worry and riches and the responsibilities and pleasures of life. And so they are never able to help anyone else to believe the Good News. Mt 13:22; Mk 4:19.

Lk 12:19. And I'll sit back and say to myself, "Friend, you have enough stored away for years to come. Now take it easy! Wine, women, and song for you!"

Lk 14:17. When all was ready, he sent his servant around to notify the guests that it was time for them to arrive. [18]But they all began making excuses. One said he had just bought a field and wanted to inspect it, and asked to be excused. [19]Another said he had just bought five pair of oxen and wanted to try them out. [20]Another had just been married and for that reason couldn't come. [21]The servant returned and reported to his master what they had said. His master was angry and told him to go quickly into the streets and alleys of the city and to invite the beggars, crippled, lame, and blind. [22]But even then, there was still room. [23]"Well, then," said his master, "go out into the country lanes and out behind the hedges and urge anyone you find to come, so that the house will be full. [24]For none of those I invited first will get even the smallest taste of what I had prepared for them." Mt 22:1–6.

Lk 16:1. Jesus now told this story to his disciples: "A rich man hired an accountant to handle his affairs, but soon a rumor went around that the accountant was thoroughly dishonest. [2]So his employer called him in and said, 'What's this I hear about your stealing from me? Get your report in order, for you are to be dismissed.' [3]The accountant thought to himself, 'Now what? I'm through here, and I haven't the strength to go out and dig ditches, and I'm too proud to beg. [4]I know just the thing! And then I'll have plenty of friends to take care of me when I leave!' [5, 6]So he invited each one who owed money to his employer to come and discuss the situation. He asked the first one, 'How much do you owe him?' 'My debt is 850 gallons of olive oil,' the man replied. 'Yes, here is the contract you signed,' the accountant told him. 'Tear it up and write another one for half that much!' [7]'And how much do you owe him?' he asked the next man. 'A thousand bushels of wheat,' was the reply. 'Here,' the accountant said, 'take your note and replace it with one for only 800 bushels!' [8]The rich man had to admire the rascal for being so shrewd. And it is true that the citizens of this world are more clever (in dishonesty!) than the godly are. [9]But shall I tell *you* to act that way, to buy friendship through cheating? Will this ensure your entry into an everlasting home in heaven? [10]*No!* For unless you are honest in small matters, you won't be in large ones. If you cheat even a little, you won't be honest with greater responsibilities. [11]And if you are untrustworthy about worldly wealth, who will trust you with the true riches of heaven? [12]And if you are not faithful with other people's money, why should you be entrusted with money of your own? [13]For neither you nor anyone else can serve two masters. You will hate one and show loyalty to the other, or else the other way around—you will be enthusiastic about one and despise the other. You cannot serve both God and money." [19]"There was a certain rich man," Jesus said, "who was splendidly clothed and lived each day in mirth and luxury. [20]One day Lazarus, a diseased beggar, was laid at his door. [21]As he lay there longing for scraps from the rich man's table, the dogs would come and lick his open sores. [22]Finally the beggar died and was carried by the angels to be with Abraham in the place of the righteous dead. The rich man also died and was buried, [23]and his soul went into hell. There, in torment, he saw Lazarus in the far distance with Abraham. [24]'Father Abraham,' he shouted, 'have some pity! Send Lazarus over here if only to dip the tip of his finger in water and cool my tongue, for I am in anguish in these flames.' [25]But Abraham said to him, 'Son, remember that during your lifetime you had everything you wanted, and Lazarus had nothing. So now he is here being comforted and you are in anguish.' "

Lk 21:34, 35. Watch out! Don't let my sudden coming catch you unawares; don't let me find you living in careless ease, carousing and drinking, and occupied with the problems of this life, like all the rest of the world.

Jn 5:44. No wonder you can't believe! For you gladly honor each other, but you don't care about the honor that comes from the only God!

Jn 12:43. For they loved the praise of men more than the praise of God.

Jn 15:19. The world would love you if you belonged to it; but you don't—for I chose you to come out of the world, and so it hates you.

Rom 12:2. Don't copy the behavior and customs of this world, but be a new and different person with a fresh newness in all you do and think. Then you will learn from your own experience how his ways will really satisfy you.

1 Cor 7:29. The important thing to remember is that our remaining time is very short, (and so are our opportunities for doing the Lord's work). For that reason those who have wives should stay as free as possible for the Lord; [30]happiness or sadness or wealth should not keep anyone from doing God's work. [31]Those in frequent contact with the exciting things the world offers should make good use of their opportunities without stopping to enjoy them; for the world in its present form will soon be gone.

1 Cor 10:6. From this lesson we are warned that we must not desire evil things as they did.

1 Cor 15:32. And what value was there in fighting wild beasts—those men of Ephesus—if it was only for what I gain in this life down here? If we will never live again after we die, then we might as well go and have ourselves a good time; let us eat, drink, and be merry. What's the difference? For tomorrow we die, and that ends everything!

Phil 3:18. For I have told you often before, and I say it again now with tears in my eyes, there are many who walk along the Christian road who are really enemies of the cross of Christ. [19]Their future is eternal loss, for their god is their appetite: they are proud of what they should be ashamed of; and all they think about is this life here on earth.

Col 3:2. Let heaven fill your thoughts; don't spend your time worrying about things down here. [5]Away then with sinful, earthly things; deaden the evil desires lurking within you; have nothing to do with sexual sin, impurity, lust and shameful desires; don't worship the good things of life, for that is idolatry.

1 Tim 5:5. The church should care for widows who are poor and alone in the world, if they are looking to God for his help and spending much time in prayer; [6]but not if they are spending their time running around gossiping, seeking only pleasure and thus ruining their souls.

2 Tim 2:4. And as Christ's soldier do not let yourself become tied up in worldly affairs, for then you cannot satisfy the one who has enlisted you in his army. [22]Run from anything that gives you the evil thoughts that young men often have, but stay close to anything that makes you want to do right. Have faith and love, and enjoy the companionship of those who love the Lord and have pure hearts.

2 Tim 3:2. For people will love only themselves and their money; they will be proud and boastful, sneering at God, disobedient to their parents, ungrateful to them, and thoroughly bad. [3]They will be hardheaded and never give in to others; they will be constant liars and troublemakers and will think nothing of immorality. They will be rough and cruel, and sneer at those who try to be good. [4]They will betray their friends; they will be hotheaded, puffed up with pride, and prefer good times to worshiping God. [5]They will go to church, yes, but they won't really believe anything they hear. Don't be taken in by people like that. [6]They are the kind who craftily sneak into other people's homes and make friendships with silly, sin-burdened women and teach them their new doctrines. [7]Women of that kind are forever following new teachers, but they never understand the truth.

Tit 2:12. And along with this gift comes the realization that God wants us to turn from godless living and sinful pleasures and to live good, God-fearing lives day after day.

Tit 3:3. Once we, too, were foolish and disobedient; we were misled by others and became slaves to many evil pleasures and wicked desires. Our lives were full of resentment and envy. We hated others and they hated us.

Heb 11:24, 25. It was by faith that Moses, when he grew up, refused to be treated as the grandson of the king, but chose to share ill-treatment with God's people instead of enjoying the fleeting pleasures of sin. [26]He thought that it was better to suffer for the promised Christ than to own all the treasures of Egypt, for he was looking forward to the great reward that God would give him.

Jas 2:1. Dear brothers, how can you claim that you belong to the Lord Jesus Christ, the Lord of glory, if you show favoritism to rich people and look down on poor people? [2]If a man comes into your church dressed in expensive clothes and with valuable gold rings on his fingers, and at the same moment another man comes in who is poor and dressed in threadbare clothes, [3]and you make a lot of fuss over the rich man and give him the best seat in the house and say to the poor man, "You can stand over there if you like, or else sit on the floor" —well, [4]judging a man by his wealth shows that you are guided by wrong motives.

Jas 4:4. You are like an unfaithful wife who loves her husband's enemies. Don't you realize that making friends with God's enemies—the evil pleasures of this world—makes you an enemy of God? I say it again, that if your aim is to enjoy the evil pleasure of the unsaved world, you cannot also be a friend of God. [9]Let there be tears for the wrong things you have done. Let there be sorrow and sincere grief. Let there be sadness instead of laughter, and gloom instead of joy.

Jas 5:5. You have spent your years here on earth having fun, satisfying your every whim, and now your fat hearts are ready for the slaughter.

1 Pet 1:14. Obey God because you are his children; don't slip back into your old ways—doing evil because you knew no better. [24]Yes, our natural lives will fade as grass does when it becomes all brown and dry. All our greatness is like a flower that droops and falls.

1 Pet 2:11. Dear brothers, you are only visitors here. Since your real home is in heaven I beg you to keep away from the evil pleasures of this world; they are not for you, for they fight against your very souls.

1 Pet 4:3. You have had enough in the past of the evil things the godless enjoy—sex sin, lust, getting drunk, wild parties, drinking bouts, and the worship of idols, and other terrible sins. [4]Of course, your former friends will be very surprised when you don't eagerly join them any more in the wicked things they do, and they will laugh at you in contempt and scorn.

2 Pet 2:12. But false teachers are fools—no better than animals. They do whatever they feel like; born only to be caught and killed, they laugh at the terrifying powers of the underworld which they know so little about; and they will be destroyed along with all the demons and powers of hell. [13]That is the pay these teachers will have for their sin. For they live in evil pleasures day after day. They are a disgrace and a stain among you, deceiving you by living in foul sin on the side while they join your love feasts as though they were honest men. [14]No woman can escape their sinful stare, and of adultery they never have enough. They make a game of luring unstable women. They train themselves to be greedy; and are doomed and cursed. [15]They have gone off the road and become lost like Balaam, the son of Beor, who fell in love with the money he could make by doing wrong. [18]They proudly boast about their sins and conquests, and, using lust as their bait, they lure back into sin those who have just escaped from such wicked living.

1 Jn 2:15. Stop loving this evil world and all that it offers you, for when you love these things you show that you do not really love God; [16]for all these worldly things, these evil desires—the craze for sex, the ambition to buy everything that appeals to you, and the pride that comes from wealth and importance—these are not from God. They are from this evil world itself. [17]And this world is fading away, and these evil, forbidden things will go with it, but whoever keeps doing the will of God will live forever.

Jude 1:11. Woe upon them! For they follow the example of Cain who killed his brother; and, like Balaam, they will do anything for money; and like Korah, they have disobeyed God and will die under his curse. [12]When these men join you at the love feasts of the church, they are evil smears among you, gorging and stuffing themselves without a thought for others. They are like clouds blowing over dry land without giving rain, promising much, but producing nothing. They are like fruit trees without any fruit at picking time. They are not only dead, but doubly dead, for they have been pulled out, roots and all, to be burned. [13]All they leave behind them is shame and disgrace like the dirty foam left along the beach by the wild waves. They wander around looking as bright as stars, but ahead of them is the everlasting gloom and darkness that God has prepared for them. [16]These men are constant gripers, never satisfied, doing whatever evil they feel like; they are loud-mouthed "show-offs," and when they show respect for others, it is only to get something from them in return. [19]They stir up arguments; they love the evil things of the world; they do not have the Holy Spirit living in them.

See *Covetousness; Pleasures; Riches.*

INSTANCES OF. Esau, Gen 25:30–34; Heb 12:16. Jacob, Gen 25:31–34; 27:36; 30:37–43. Judah, Gen 37:26, 27. Israelites, Num 11:33, 34; Ps 78:18, 29–31. Balaam, 2 Pet 2:15; Jude 1:11, with Num 22; 23; 24. Eli's sons, 1 Sam 2:12–17. Gehazi, 2 Kgs 5:21–27. Herod, Mt 14:6, 7. Cretans, Tit 1:12.

WORM Ex 16:20, 24; Jon 4:7; to destroy this body, Job 21:26; Isa 51:8; shall cover them, Isa 14:11. I am a worm, not a man, Ps 22:6. Herod filled with, Acts 12:23.

FIGURATIVE. Job 25:6; Isa 66:24. Of remorse, Mk 9:44, 46, 48.

WORMWOOD A bitter plant, Prov 5:4.

FIGURATIVE. Prov 5:4.

Symbolical. Rev 8:11.

WORSHIP To be rendered to God only, Ex 20:3; Deut 5:7; 6:13; Mt 4:10; Lk 4:8; Acts 10:26; 14:15; Col 2:18; Rev 19:10; 22:8, 9.

Of Jesus, see *Jesus, Worship of.*

Acceptable to God, Gen 4:4; 8:21. Of the wicked rejected, Gen 4:5, 7. See *Prayer, of the Wicked.* "Guilt connected with errors regarding the offerings," Ex 28:38. Public, in the Temple, Jer 26:2; Lk 18:10; 24:53. David's ordinances for, 1 Chron chapters 23–26. Family, Deut 16:11, 14; of Abraham, Gen 12:7, 8; 13:3, 4, 18; of Jacob, Gen 35:2, 3; of Job, Job 1:5; of the Philippian jailer, Acts 16:34. In private homes, Acts 1:13, 14; 5:42; 12:12; 20:7–9; Rom 16:5; 1 Cor 16:19; Col 4:15; Philemon 1:1, 2. In the night, Isa 30:29; Acts 16:25. Jesus prays a whole night, Lk 6:12.

Attitudes in: Bowing, Ex 34:8; 2 Chron 29:29. Prostration, Gen 17:2–4; 2 Chron 20:18. Mk 3:11.

Prayer in, see *Prayer.*

God's presence in, Lev 19:30; Ps 84:4; Isa 56:7; Heb 10:25.

Loved by his people, Ps 27:4; 84:1–3, 10; Zech 8:20, 21.

Benedictions pronounced, see *Benedictions.*

The whole nation required to assemble for, including, men, women, children, servants, and strangers, Deut 16:11; 31:10–13; in Mount Gerizim and Mount Ebal, Josh 8:32–35. The word of God read in public assemblies, Ex 24:7; Deut 27:12–26; 31:10–13; Josh 8:33–35; 2 Kgs 23:1–3; Neh 8:1–8, 13–18; Mt 21:23; Lk 4:16, 17.

Of angels, forbidden, Col 2:18; Rev 19:10; 22:8, 9.

See *Afflictions, Prayer in; Blasphemy; Children; Church; Consecration; Dedication; Idolatry; Instruction, in Religion; Levites; Minister; Music; Offerings; Praise; Prayer; Preaching; Priest; Religion; Sacrilege; Servant; Stranger; Tabernacle; Temple; Thanksgiving; Women; Word of God; Young Men.*

UNCLASSIFIED SCRIPTURES RELATING TO. Gen 35:2. So Jacob instructed all those in his household to destroy the idols they had brought with them, and to wash themselves and to put on fresh clothing. [3]"For we are going to Bethel," he told them, "and I will build an altar there to the God who answered my prayers in the day of my distress, and was with me on my journey."

Ex 3:5. "Don't come any closer," God told him. "Take off your shoes, for you are standing on holy ground. [Josh 5:15.] [6]I am the God of your fathers —the God of Abraham, Isaac, and Jacob." (Moses covered his face with his hands, for he was afraid to look at God.)

Ex 5:1. After this presentation to the elders, Moses and Aaron went to see Pharaoh. They told him, "We bring you a message from Jehovah, the God of Israel. He says, 'Let my people go, for they must make a holy pilgrimage out into the wilderness, for a religious feast, to worship me there.' "

Ex 15:2. The Lord is my strength, my song, and my salvation. He is my God, and I will praise him. He is my father's God—I will exalt him.

Ex 19:10. "Go down now and see that the people are ready for my visit. Sanctify them today and tomorrow, and have them wash their clothes. [11]Then, the day after tomorrow, I will come down upon Mt. Sinai as all the people watch. [12]Set boundary lines the people may not pass, and tell them, 'Beware! Do not go up into the mountain or even touch its boundaries; whoever does shall die —[13]no hand shall touch him, but he shall be stoned or shot to death with arrows, whether man or animal.' Stay away from the mountain entirely until you hear a ram's horn sounding one long blast; then gather at the foot of the mountain!" [21]But the Lord told Moses, "Go back down and warn the people not to cross the boundaries. They must not come up here to see God, for they will die. [22]Even the priests on duty must sanctify themselves, lest Jehovah destroy them." [23]"But the people won't come up into the mountain!" Moses protested. "You told them not to! You told me to set boundaries around the mountain, and to declare it off limits because it is reserved for God." [24]But Jehovah said, "Go on down, and bring Aaron back with you, and don't let the priests and the people break across the boundaries to try to come up here, or I will destroy them."

Ex 20:24. The altars you make for me must be simple altars of earth. Offer upon them your sacrifices to me—your burnt offerings and peace offerings of sheep and oxen. Build altars only where I tell you to, and I will come and bless you there. [25]You may also build altars from stone, but if you do, then use only uncut stones and boulders. Don't chip or shape the stones with a tool, for that would make them unfit for my altar. [26]And don't make steps for the altar, or someone might look up beneath the skirts of your clothing and see your nakedness.

Ex 24:1. The Lord now instructed Moses, "Come up here with Aaron, Nadab, Abihu, and seventy of the elders of Israel. All of you except Moses are to worship at a distance. [2]Moses alone shall come near to the Lord; and remember, none of the ordinary people are permitted to come up into the mountain at all."

Ex 25:8. For I want the people of Israel to make me a sacred Temple where I can live among them. [22]And I will meet with you from above the place of mercy between the cherubim; and the Ark will contain the laws of my covenant. There I will tell you my commandments for the people of Israel. Num 17:4.

Ex 28:33, 34. The bottom edge of the ephod shall be embroidered with blue, purple, and scarlet pomegranates, alternated with gold bells. [35]Aaron shall wear the ephod whenever he goes in to minister to the Lord; the bells will tinkle as he goes in and out of the presence of the Lord in the Holy Place, so that he will not die.

Ex 29:43. And I will meet with the people of Israel there, and the Tabernacle shall be sanctified by my glory. Ex 40:34, 35.

Ex 30:19. Aaron and his sons shall wash their hands and feet there, [20]when they go into the Tabernacle to appear before the Lord, or when they approach the altar to burn offerings to the Lord. They must always wash before doing so, or they will die. [21]These are instructions to Aaron and his sons from generation to generation.

Ex 34:8. Moses fell down before the Lord and worshiped.

Lev 10:3. Then Moses said to Aaron, "This is what the Lord meant when he said, 'I will show myself holy among those who approach me, and I will be glorified before all the people.' " And Aaron was speechless.

Lev 16:2. The Lord said to Moses, "Warn your brother Aaron not to enter into the Holy Place behind the veil, where the Ark and the place of mercy are, just whenever he chooses. The penalty for intrusion is death. For I myself am present in the cloud above the place of mercy."

2 Kgs 17:36. They were to worship only the Lord who had brought them out of the land of Egypt with such tremendous miracles and power.

1 Chron 16:29. Yes, ascribe to the Lord the glory due his name! Bring an offering and come before him; worship the Lord when clothed with holiness! Ps 29:2.

2 Chron 5:13, 14. The band and chorus united as one to praise and thank the Lord; their selections were interspersed with trumpet obbligatos, the

clashing of cymbals, and the loud playing of other musical instruments—all praising and thanking the Lord. Their theme was "He is so good! His lovingkindness lasts forever!" And at that moment the glory of the Lord, coming as a bright cloud, filled the Temple so that the priests could not continue their work. 1 Kgs 8:3–11.

2 Chron 7:1. As Solomon finished praying, fire flashed down from heaven and burned up the sacrifices! And the glory of the Lord filled the Temple.

2 Chron 30:27. Then the priests and Levites stood and blessed the people, and the Lord heard their prayers from his holy temple in heaven.

Ezra 3:10. When the builders completed the foundation of the Temple, the priests put on their priestly robes and blew their trumpets; and the descendants of Asaph crashed their cymbals to praise the Lord in the manner ordained by King
David. [11]They sang rounds of praise and thanks to
God, singing this song: "He is good, and his love and mercy toward Israel will last forever." Then all the people gave a great shout, praising God because the foundation of the Temple had been laid.
[12]But many of the priests and Levites and other
leaders—the old men who remembered Solomon's beautiful Temple—wept aloud, while others were
shouting for joy! [13]So the shouting and the weeping
mingled together in a loud commotion that could be heard from far away!

Neh 10:39, 40. The people and the Levites were required by law to bring these offerings of grain, new wine, and olive oil to the Temple and place them in the sacred containers for use by the ministering priests, the gatekeepers, and the choir singers. So we agreed together not to neglect the Temple of our God.

Ps 5:7. But as for me, I will come into your Temple protected by your mercy and your love; I will worship you with deepest awe.

Ps 22:22. I will praise you to all my brothers; I will stand up before the congregation and testify of the wonderful things you have done.

Ps 24:3. Who may climb the mountain of the Lord and enter where he lives? Who may stand
before the Lord? [4]Only those with pure hands and
hearts, who do not practice dishonesty and lying.
[5]They will receive God's own goodness as their
blessing from him, planted in their lives by God
himself, their Savior. [6]These are the ones who are
allowed to stand before the Lord and worship the God of Jacob.

Ps 26:6. I wash my hands to prove my innocence
and come before your altar, [7]singing a song of
thanksgiving and telling about your miracles.
[8]Lord, I love your home, this shrine where the
brilliant, dazzling splendor of your presence lives.

Ps 27:4. The one thing I want from God, the thing I seek most of all, is the privilege of meditating in his Temple, living in his presence every day of my life, delighting in his incomparable perfections and glory.

Ps 29:2. Praise him for his majestic glory, the glory of his name. Come before him clothed in sacred garments.

Ps 35:18. Save me, and I will thank you publicly before the entire congregation, before the largest crowd I can find.

Ps 36:8. You feed them with blessings from your own table and let them drink from your rivers of delight.

Ps 42:4. Take courage, my soul! Do you remember those times (but how could you ever forget them!) when you led a great procession to the Temple on festival days, singing with joy, praising the Lord?

Ps 48:9. Lord, here in your Temple we meditate upon your kindness and your love.

Ps 51:19. And when my heart is right, then you will rejoice in the good that I do and in the bullocks I bring to sacrifice upon your altar.

Ps 55:14. What fellowship we had, what wonderful discussions as we walked together to the Temple of the Lord on holy days.

Ps 63:1. O God, my God! How I search for you! How I thirst for you in this parched and weary land where there is no water. How I long to find
you! [2]How I wish I could go into your sanctuary
to see your strength and glory.

Ps 65:4. How greatly to be envied are those you have chosen to come and live with you within the holy tabernacle courts! What joys await us among all the good things there.

Ps 66:4. All the earth shall worship you and sing
of your glories. [13]Now I have come to your Temple
with burnt-offerings to pay my vows. [14]For when I
was in trouble I promised you many offerings.

Ps 77:13. O God, your ways are holy. Where is there any other as mighty as you?

Ps 84:1. How lovely is your Temple, O Lord of
the armies of heaven. [2]I long, yes, faint with longing to be able to enter your courtyard and come
near to the Living God. [3]Even the sparrows and
swallows are welcome to come and nest among your altars and there have their young, O Lord of
heaven's armies, my King and my God! [4]How
happy are those who can live in your Temple, singing your praises. [10]A single day spent in your Tem-
ple is better than a thousand anywhere else! I would rather be a doorman of the Temple of my God than live in palaces of wickedness.

Ps 89:7. The highest of angelic powers stand in dread and awe of him. Who is as revered as he by those surrounding him?

Ps 93:5. Your royal decrees cannot be changed. Holiness is forever the keynote of your reign.

Ps 95:6. Come, kneel before the Lord our Maker.

Ps 98:2, 3. He has announced this victory and revealed it to every nation by fulfilling his promise to be kind to Israel. The whole earth has seen God's salvation of his people.

Ps 100:1. Shout with joy before the Lord, O earth!
[2]Obey him gladly; come before him, singing with
joy. [3]Try to realize what this means—the Lord is
God! He made us—we are his people, the sheep of
his pasture. [4]Go through his open gates with great

thanksgiving; enter his courts with praise. Give thanks to him and bless his name.

Ps 103:1. I bless the holy name of God with all my heart. [2]Yes, I will bless the Lord and not forget the glorious things he does for me. [3]He forgives all my sins. He heals me. [4]He ransoms me from hell. He surrounds me with lovingkindness and tender mercies.

Ps 107:6. "Lord, help!" they cried, and he did! [7]He led them straight to safety and a place to live. [8]Oh, that these men would praise the Lord for his lovingkindness, and for all of his wonderful deeds! [32]Let them praise him publicly before the congregation, and before the leaders of the nation.

Ps 116:12. But now what can I offer Jehovah for all he has done for me? [13]I will bring him an offering of wine and praise his name for saving me. [14]I will publicly bring him the sacrifice I vowed I would. [17]I will worship you and offer you a sacrifice of thanksgiving.

Ps 118:18. The Lord has punished me, but not handed me over to death. [19]Open the gates of the Temple—I will go in and give him my thanks.

Ps 119:108. Accept my grateful thanks and teach me your desires.

Ps 122:1. I was glad for the suggestion of going to Jerusalem, to the Temple of the Lord.

Ps 126:1. When Jehovah brought back his exiles to Jerusalem, it was like a dream! [2]How we laughed and sang for joy. And the other nations said, "What amazing things the Lord has done for them." [3]Yes, glorious things! What wonder! What joy!

Ps 132:7. But now it will be settled in the Temple, in God's permanent home here on earth. That is where we will go to worship him. [13]O Lord, you have chosen Jerusalem as your home: [14]"This is my permanent home where I shall live," you said, "for I have always wanted it this way."

Ps 138:2. I face your Temple as I worship, giving thanks to you for all your lovingkindness and your faithfulness, for your promises are backed by all the honor of your name.

Ps 149:1. Hallelujah! Yes, praise the Lord! Sing him a new song. Sing his praises, all his people.

Eccl 5:1, 2. As you enter the Temple, keep your ears open and your mouth shut! Don't be a fool who doesn't even realize it is sinful to make rash promises to God, for he is in heaven and you are only here on earth, so let your words be few.

Isa 1:11. I am sick of your sacrifices. Don't bring me any more of them. I don't want your fat rams; I don't want to see the blood from your offerings. [12, 13]Who wants your sacrifices when you have no sorrow for your sins? The incense you bring me is a stench in my nostrils. Your holy celebrations of the new moon and the Sabbath, and your special days for fasting—even your most pious meetings—all are frauds! I want nothing more to do with them. [14]I hate them all; I can't stand the sight of them. [15]From now on, when you pray with your hands stretched out to heaven, I won't look or listen. Even though you make many prayers, I will not hear, for your hands are those of murderers; they are covered with the blood of your innocent victims.

Isa 2:3. "Come," everyone will say, "let us go up the mountain of the Lord, to the Temple of the God of Israel; there he will teach us his laws, and we will obey them." For in those days the world will be ruled from Jerusalem. Mic 4:2.

Isa 4:5. Then the Lord will provide shade on all Jerusalem—over every home and all its public grounds—a canopy of smoke and cloud throughout the day, and clouds of fire at night, covering the Glorious Land.

Isa 12:5. Sing to the Lord, for he has done wonderful things. Make known his praise around the world. [6]Let all the people of Jerusalem shout his praise with joy. For great and mighty is the Holy One of Israel, who lives among you.

Isa 25:9. In that day the people will proclaim, "This is our God, in whom we trust, for whom we waited. Now at last he is here." What a day of rejoicing!

Isa 29:13. And so the Lord says, "Since these people say they are mine but they do not obey me, and since their worship amounts to mere words learned by rote, [14]therefore I will take awesome vengeance on these hypocrites, and make their wisest counselors as fools." [15]Woe to those who try to hide their plans from God, who try to keep him in the dark concerning what they do! "God can't see us," they say to themselves. "He doesn't know what is going on!" [16]How stupid can they be! Isn't he, the Potter, greater than you, the jars he makes? Will you say to him, "He didn't make us"? Does a machine call its inventor dumb?

Isa 30:29. But the people of God will sing a song of solemn joy, like songs in the night when holy feasts are held; his people will have gladness of heart, as when a flutist leads a pilgrim band to Jerusalem to the Mountain of the Lord, the Rock of Israel.

Isa 38:20. Think of it! The Lord healed me! Every day of my life from now on I will sing my songs of praise in the Temple, accompanied by the orchestra.

Isa 40:31. But they that wait upon the Lord shall renew their strength. They shall mount up with wings like eagles; they shall run and not be weary; they shall walk and not faint.

Isa 43:22. But O my people, you won't ask my help; you have grown tired of me! [23]You have not brought me the lambs for burnt offerings; you have not honored me with sacrifices. Yet my requests for offerings and incense have been very few! I have not treated you as slaves. [24]You have brought me no sweet-smelling incense nor pleased me with the sacrificial fat. No, you have presented me only with sins, and wearied me with all your faults.

Isa 49:13. Sing for joy, O heavens; shout, O earth. Break forth with song, O mountains, for the Lord has comforted his people, and will have compassion upon them in their sorrow.

Isa 52:9. Let the ruins of Jerusalem break into

joyous song, for the Lord has comforted his people; he has redeemed Jerusalem.

Isa 56:6. As for the Gentiles, the outsiders who join the people of the Lord and serve him and love his name, and are his servants and don't desecrate the Sabbath, and have accepted his covenant and promises, [7]I will bring them also to my holy mountain of Jerusalem, and make them full of joy within my House of Prayer.

Isa 66:1. Heaven is my throne and the earth is my footstool: What Temple can you build for me as good as that? [2]My hand has made both earth and skies, and they are mine. Yet I will look with pity on the man who has a humble and a contrite heart, who trembles at my word.

Jer 31:11. He will save Israel from those who are too strong for them! [12]They shall come home and sing songs of joy upon the hills of Zion, and shall be radiant over the goodness of the Lord—the good crops, the wheat and the wine and the oil, and the healthy flocks and herds. Their life shall be like a watered garden, and all their sorrows shall be gone.

Ezk 22:8. The things of God are all despised; my Sabbaths are ignored.

Hos 6:6. I don't want your sacrifices—I want your love; I don't want your offerings—I want you to know me.

Amos 5:21. I hate your show and pretense—your hypocrisy of "honoring" me with your religious feasts and solemn assemblies. [22]I will not accept your burnt offerings and thank offerings. I will not look at your offerings of peace. [23]Away with your hymns of praise—they are mere noise to my ears. I will not listen to your music, no matter how lovely it is. [24]I want to see a mighty flood of justice —a torrent of doing good.

Hab 2:20. But the Lord is in his holy Temple; let all the earth be silent before him.

Zech 8:21. People will write their friends in other cities and say, "Let's go to Jerusalem to ask the Lord to bless us, and be merciful to us. I'm going! Please come with me. Let's go *now!*" [22]Yes, many people, even strong nations, will come to the Lord of Hosts in Jerusalem to ask for his blessing and help.

Mal 3:3. Like a refiner of silver he will sit and closely watch as the dross is burned away. He will purify the Levites, the ministers of God, refining them like gold or silver, so that they will do their work for God with pure hearts. [4]Then once more the Lord will enjoy the offering brought to him by the people of Judah and Jerusalem, as he did before.

Mt 18:19. I also tell you this—if two of you agree down here on earth concerning anything you ask for, my Father in heaven will do it for you. [20]For where two or three gather together because they are mine, I will be right there among them.

Lk 4:8. Jesus replied, "We must worship God, and him alone. So it is written in the Scriptures."

Jn 4:23, 24. For it's not *where* we worship that counts, but *how* we worship—is our worship spiritual and real? Do we have the Holy Spirit's help? For God is Spirit, and we must have his help to worship as we should.

Acts 2:1. Seven weeks had gone by since Jesus' death and resurrection, and the Day of Pentecost had now arrived. As the believers met together that day, [2]suddenly there was a sound like the roaring of a mighty windstorm in the skies above them and it filled the house where they were meeting. [3]Then, what looked like flames or tongues of fire appeared and settled on their heads. [4]And everyone present was filled with the Holy Spirit and began speaking in languages they didn't know, for the Holy Spirit gave them this ability.

Acts 17:24. He made the world and everything in it, and since he is Lord of heaven and earth, he doesn't live in man-made temples; [25]and human hands can't minister to his needs—for he has no needs! He himself gives life and breath to everything, and satisfies every need there is.

1 Cor 11:13. What do you yourselves really think about this? Is it right for a woman to pray in public without covering her head? [20]When you come together to eat, it isn't the Lord's Supper you are eating, [21]but your own. For I am told that everyone hastily gobbles all the food he can without waiting to share with the others, so the one doesn't get enough and goes hungry while another has too much to drink and gets drunk. [22]What? Is this really true? Can't you do your eating and drinking at home, to avoid disgracing the church and shaming those who are poor and can bring no food? What am I supposed to say about these things? Do you want me to praise you? Well, I certainly do not!

1 Cor 14:15. Well, then, what shall I do? I will do both. I will pray in unknown tongues and also in ordinary language that everyone understands. I will sing in unknown tongues and also in ordinary language, so that I can understand the praise I am giving; [16]for if you praise and thank God with the spirit alone, speaking in another language, how can those who don't understand you be praising God along with you? How can they join you in giving thanks when they don't know what you are saying? [17]You will be giving thanks very nicely, no doubt, but the other people present won't be helped.

Phil 3:3. For it isn't the *cutting of our bodies* that makes us children of God; it is *worshiping him with our spirits.* That is the only true "circumcision." We Christians glory in what Christ Jesus has done for us and realize that we are helpless to save ourselves.

1 Tim 2:8. So I want men everywhere to pray with holy hands lifted up to God, free from sin and anger and resentment.

Heb 10:25. Let us not neglect our church meetings, as some people do, but encourage and warn each other, especially now that the day of his coming back again is drawing near.

Heb 12:28. Since we have a kingdom nothing can destroy, let us please God by serving him with thankful hearts, and with holy fear and awe.

1 Pet 2:5. And now you have become living building-stones for God's use in building his house. What's more, you are his holy priests; so come to him—(you who are acceptable to him because of Jesus Christ)—and offer to God those things that please him.

Rev 11:1. Now I was given a measuring stick and told to go and measure the temple of God, including the inner court where the altar stands, and to count the number of worshipers.

Rev 14:6. And I saw another angel flying through the heavens, carrying the everlasting Good News to preach to those on earth—to every nation, tribe, language and people. [7]"Fear God," he shouted, "and extol his greatness. For the time has come when he will sit as Judge. Worship him who made the heaven and the earth, the sea and all its sources."

Rev 15:4. Who shall not fear, O Lord, and glorify your Name? For you alone are holy. All nations will come and worship before you, for your righteous deeds have been disclosed.

See *Praise; Prayer; Thankfulness.*

COMMANDED. Gen 35:1. "Move on to Bethel now, and settle there," God said to Jacob, "and build an altar to worship the God who appeared to you when you fled from your brother Esau."

Ex 23:17. At these three times each year, every man in Israel shall appear before the Lord God. [Ex 34:23.] [18]No sacrificial blood shall be offered with leavened bread; no sacrificial fat shall be left unoffered until the next morning.

Deut 12:5. Rather, you must build a sanctuary for him at a place he himself will select as his home. [6]There you shall bring to the Lord your burnt offerings and other sacrifices—your tithes, your offerings presented by the gesture of waving before the altar, your offerings to fulfill your vows, your freewill offerings, and your offerings of the firstborn animals of your flocks and herds. [7]There you and your families shall feast before the Lord your God, and shall rejoice in all he has done for you. [11]Then you must bring all your burnt sacrifices and other offerings to his sanctuary, the place he will choose as his home. [12]You shall rejoice there before the Lord with your sons and daughters and servants; and remember to invite the Levites to feast with you, for they have no land of their own.

Deut 16:6. It must be eaten at the place the Lord shall choose as his sanctuary. Sacrifice it there on the anniversary evening just as the sun goes down. [7]Roast the lamb and eat it, then start back to your homes the next morning. [8]For the following six days you shall eat no bread made with yeast. On the seventh day there shall be a quiet gathering of the people of each city before the Lord your God. Don't do any work that day.

Deut 31:10, 11. The Lord commanded that these laws be read to all the people at the end of every seventh year—the Year of Release—at the Festival of Tabernacles, when all Israel would assemble before the Lord at the sanctuary. [12]"Call them all together," the Lord instructed, "—men, women, children, and foreigners living among you—to hear the laws of God and to learn his will, so that you will reverence the Lord your God and obey his laws. [13]Do this so that your little children who have not known these laws will hear them and learn how to revere the Lord your God as long as you live in the Promised Land."

Deut 33:19. They shall summon the people to celebrate their sacrifices with them. Lo, they taste the riches of the sea and the treasures of the sand.

2 Kgs 17:36. They were to worship only the Lord who had brought them out of the land of Egypt with such tremendous miracles and power.

Ps 45:11. Your royal husband delights in your beauty. Reverence him, for he is your Lord.

Ps 76:11. Fulfill all your vows that you have made to Jehovah your God. Let everyone bring him presents. He should be reverenced and feared.

Ps 96:8. Give him the glory he deserves! Bring your offering and come to worship him. [9]Worship the Lord with the beauty of holy lives. Let the earth tremble before him.

Ps 97:7. Let those who worship idols be disgraced—all who brag about their worthless gods—for every god must bow to him!

Ps 99:5. Exalt the Lord our holy God! Bow low before his feet.

Joel 1:14. Announce a fast; call a solemn meeting. Gather the elders and all the people into the Temple of the Lord your God, and weep before him there. [15]Alas, this terrible day of punishment is on the way. Destruction from the Almighty is almost here!

Joel 2:15. Sound the trumpet in Zion! Call a fast and gather all the people together for a solemn meeting. [16]Bring everyone—the elders, the children, and even the babies. Call the bridegroom from his quarters and the bride from her privacy. [17]The priests, the ministers of God, will stand between the people and the altar weeping; and they will pray, "Spare your people, O our God; don't let the heathen rule them, for they belong to you. Don't let them be disgraced by the taunts of the heathen who say, 'Where is this God of theirs? How weak and helpless he must be!' "

Nah 1:15. See, the messengers come running down the mountains with glad news: "The invaders have been wiped out and we are safe!" O Judah, proclaim a day of thanksgiving, and worship only the Lord, as you have vowed. For this enemy from Nineveh will never come again. He is cut off forever; he will never be seen again.

Hag 1:8. "Then go up into the mountains and bring down timber, and rebuild my Temple, and I will be pleased with it and appear there in my glory," says the Lord.

Zech 14:16. In the end, those who survive the plague will go up to Jerusalem each year to worship the King, the Lord of Hosts, to celebrate a time of thanksgiving. [17]And any nation anywhere in all the world that refuses to come to Jerusalem to worship the King, the Lord of Hosts, will have no rain. [18]But if Egypt refuses to come, God will punish her with some other plague.

Mt 8:4. Then Jesus says to him, "Don't stop to talk to anyone; go right over to the priest to be examined; and take with you the offering required by Moses' law for lepers who are healed—a public testimony of your cure." Mk 1:43, 44; Lk 5:14.

Heb 10:25. Let us not neglect our church meetings, as some people do, but encourage and warn each other, especially now that the day of his coming back again is drawing near. chapter 13:15.

Rev 14:7. "Fear God," he shouted, "and extol his greatness. For the time has come when he will sit as Judge. Worship him who made the heaven and the earth, the sea and all its sources."

Rev 19:10. Then I fell down at his feet to worship him, but he said, "No! Don't! For I am a servant of God just as you are, and as your brother Christians are, who testify of their faith in Jesus. The purpose of all prophecy and of all I have shown you is to tell about Jesus."

WOUNDS Treatment of, Isa 1:5, 6; Lk 10:34. cf Ps 38:5, 6; 147:3; Prov 23:29, 30; 27:6; Jer 30:17; Zech 13:6.

WRATH See *Anger; God, Anger of.*

WRESTLING Gen 32:22–25; Hos 12:4.

FIGURATIVE. Gen 30:8.

WRITING Copyists were called scribes. See *Scribes.*

See *Book; Engraving; Ink; Letters; Pen; Tablet.*

Y

YARDSTICK Used for measuring ground, Zech 2:1.

See *Cord.*

YARN Ezk 27:19.

See *Weaving.*

YEAR Gen 1:14, 15. Divided into months, Ex 12:2; Num 10:10; 28:11.

See *Calendar; Months.*

Annual feasts, Lev 25:5. See *Feasts.*

Redemption of houses sold, limited to one, Lev 25:29, 30. Land to rest one, in seven, Lev 25:5. Of debt cancellation, Deut 15:9.

Age computed by: Of Abraham, Gen 25:7, 8; of Jacob, Gen 47:9. See *Longevity.*

A thousand, with the Lord as one day, Ps 90:4; 2 Pet 3:8. Satan to be bound a thousand, Rev 20:2–4, 7. Christ reigns, Rev 20:6.

See *Jubilee, Year of; Millennium; Time.*

YEAST Or leaven. For bread, Ex 12:34, 39; Hos 7:4; Mt 13:33. Leavened bread used with peace offering, Lev 7:13; with wave offering, Lev 23:15–17. Leavened bread forbidden with meat offerings, Ex 23:18; 34:25; Lev 2:11; 6:17; 10:12; at the Passover, Ex 12:19, 20; 13:3, 6, 7; 23:15; with blood, Ex 23:18.

FIGURATIVE. Of the Pharisees, hypocrisy or religious externalism, Mt 16:6–12; Lk 12:1; of the Sadducees, disbelief in the resurrection, Mt 16:6–12; Mk 12:18; of Herod, worldliness and compromise, Mk 8:15; Mt 22:15–21. Parable of, Mt 13:33; Lk 13:20, 21.

YIRON A city of Naphtali, Josh 19:38.

YOKE FIGURATIVE. Isa 10:27; Jer 2:20; 28:2, 4, 10; 30:8; Lam 1:14; Mt 11:29, 30; Acts 15:10.

YOUNG MEN Ex 24:3. Then Moses announced to the people all the laws and regulations God had given him; and the people answered in unison, "We will obey them all." [4]Moses wrote down the laws; and early the next morning he built an altar at the foot of the mountain, with twelve pillars around the altar because there were twelve tribes of Israel. [5]Then he sent some of the young men to sacrifice the burnt offerings and peace offerings to the Lord.

1 Kgs 12:6. Rehoboam talked it over with the old men who had counseled his father Solomon. "What do you think I should do?" he asked them. [7]And they replied, "If you give them a pleasant reply and agree to be good to them and serve them well, you can be their king for forever." [8]But Rehoboam refused the old men's counsel and called in the young men with whom he had grown up. [9]"What do you think I should do?" he asked them. [10]And the young men replied, "Tell them, 'If you think my father was hard on you, well, I'll be harder! [11]Yes, my father was harsh, but I'll be even harsher! My father used whips on you, but I'll use scorpions!'" [12]So when Jeroboam and the people returned three days later, [13, 14]the new king answered them roughly. He ignored the old men's advice and followed that of the young men; [15]so the king refused the people's demands. (But the Lord's hand was in it—he caused the new king to do this in order to fulfill his promise to Jeroboam, made through Ahijah, the prophet from Shiloh.) 2 Chron 10:8, 9.

Ps 119:9. How can a young man stay pure? By reading your Word and following its rules.

Ps 148:12. Young men and maidens, old men and children—[13]all praise the Lord together. For he alone is worthy. His glory is far greater than all of earth and heaven.

Prov 1:1. These are the proverbs of King Solomon of Israel, David's son: [2]He wrote them to teach his people how to live—how to act in every circumstance, [3]for he wanted them to be understanding, just and fair in everything they did. [4]"I want to make the simple-minded wise!" he said. "I want to warn young men about some problems they will face. [5, 6]I want those already wise to become the wiser and become leaders by exploring the depths of meaning in these nuggets of truth." [7-9]How does a man become wise? The first step is to trust and reverence the Lord! Only fools refuse to be taught. Listen to your father and mother. What you learn from them will stand you in good stead; it will gain you many honors. [10]If young toughs tell you, "Come and join us"—turn your back on them! [11]"We'll hide and rob and kill," they say. [12]"Good or bad, we'll treat them all alike. [13]And the loot we'll get! All kinds of stuff! [14]Come on, throw in your lot with us; we'll split with you in equal shares." [15]Don't do it, son! Stay far from men like that, [16]for crime is their way of life, and murder is their specialty. [17]When a bird sees a trap being set, it stays away, [18]but not these men; they trap themselves! They lay a booby trap for their own lives. [19]Such is the fate of all who live by violence and murder. They will die a violent death. [20]Wisdom shouts in the streets for a hearing. [21]She calls out to the crowds along Main Street, and to the judges in their courts, and to everyone in all the land: [22]"You simpletons!" she cries. "How long will you go on being fools? How long will you scoff at wisdom and fight the facts? [23]Come here and listen to me! I'll pour out the spirit of wisdom upon you, and make you wise. [24]I have called you so often but still you won't come. I have pleaded, but all in vain. [25]For you have spurned my counsel and reproof. [26]Some day you'll be in trouble, and I'll laugh! Mock me, will you?—I'll mock you! [27]When a storm of terror surrounds you, and when you are engulfed by anguish and distress, [28]then I will not answer your cry for help. It will be too late though you search for me ever so anxiously. [29]For you closed your eyes to the facts and did not choose to reverence and trust the Lord, [30]and you turned your back on me, spurning my advice. [31]That is why you must eat the bitter fruit of having your own way, and experience the full terrors of the pathway you have chosen. [32]For you turned away from me—to death; your own complacency will kill you. Fools! [33]But all who listen to me shall live in peace and safety, unafraid."

Prov 2:1. Every young man who listens to me and obeys my instructions will be given wisdom and good sense. [3-5]Yes, if you want better insight and discernment, and are searching for them as you would for lost money or hidden treasure, then wisdom will be given you, and knowledge of God himself; you will soon learn the importance of reverence for the Lord and of trusting him. [6]For the Lord grants wisdom! His every word is a treasure of knowledge and understanding. [7, 8]He grants good sense to the godly—his saints. He is their shield, protecting them and guarding their pathway. [9]He shows how to distinguish right from wrong, how to find the right decision every time. [10]For wisdom and truth will enter the very center of your being, filling your life with joy. [11-13]You will be given the sense to stay away from evil men who want you to be their partners in crime—men who turn from God's ways to walk down dark and evil paths, [14]and exult in doing wrong, for they thoroughly enjoy their sins. [15]Everything they do is crooked and wrong. [16, 17]Only wisdom from the Lord can save a man from the flattery of prostitutes; these girls have abandoned their husbands and flouted the laws of God. [18]Their houses lie along the road to death and hell. [19]The men who enter them are doomed. None of these men will ever be the same again. [20]Follow the steps of the godly instead, and stay on the right path, [21]for only good men enjoy life to the full; [22]evil men lose the good things they might have had, and they themselves shall be destroyed.

Prov 3:1, 2. My son, never forget the things I've taught you. If you want a long and satisfying life, closely follow my instructions. [3]Never forget to be truthful and kind. Hold these virtues tightly. Write them deep within your heart. [4, 5]If you want favor with both God and man, and a reputation for good judgment and common sense, then trust the Lord completely; don't ever trust yourself. [6]In everything you do, put God first, and he will direct you and crown your efforts with success. [7, 8]Don't be conceited, sure of your own wisdom. Instead, trust and reverence the Lord, and turn your back on evil; when you do that, then you will be given renewed health and vitality. [9, 10]Honor the Lord by giving him the first part of all your income, and he will fill your barns with wheat and barley and overflow your wine vats with the finest wines. [11, 12]Young man, do not resent it when God chastens and corrects you, for his punishment is proof of his love. Just as a father punishes a son he delights in to make him better, so the Lord corrects you. [13-15]The man who knows right from wrong and has good judgment and common sense is happier than the man who is immensely rich! For such wisdom is far more valuable than precious jewels. Nothing else compares with it. [16, 17]Wisdom gives: A long, good life, riches, honor, pleasure, peace. [18]Wisdom is a tree of life to those who eat her fruit; happy is the man who keeps on eating it. [19]The Lord's wisdom founded the earth; his understanding established all the universe and space. [20]The deep fountains of the earth were broken open by his knowledge, and the skies poured down rain. [21]Have two goals: wisdom—that is, knowing and doing right—and common sense. Don't let them slip away, [22]for they fill you with living energy, and are a feather in your cap. [23]They keep you safe from defeat and disaster and from stumbling off the trail. [24-26]With them on guard you can sleep without fear; you need not be afraid of disaster or the plots of wicked men, for the Lord is with you; he protects you. [27, 28]Don't withhold repayment of your debts. Don't pay "some other time," if you can pay now. [29]Don't plot against your neighbor; he is trusting you. [30]Don't get into needless fights. [31]Don't envy violent men. Don't copy their ways. [32]For such men are an abomination to the Lord, but he gives his friendship to the godly. [33]The curse of God is on the wicked, but his blessing is on the upright. [34]The Lord mocks at mockers, but helps the humble. [35]The wise are promoted to honor, but fools are promoted to shame!

Prov 4:1, 2. Young men, listen to me as you would to your father. Listen, and grow wise, for I speak the truth—don't turn away. [3]For I, too, was once a son, tenderly loved by my mother as an only child, and the companion of my father. [4]He told me never to forget his words. "If you follow them," he said, "you will have a long and happy life. [5]*Learn to be wise,*" he said, "*and develop good judgment and common sense! I cannot overemphasize this point.*" [6]Cling to wisdom—she will protect you. Love her—she will guard you. [7]Determination to be wise is the first step toward becoming wise! And with your wisdom, develop common sense and good judgment. [8, 9]If you exalt wisdom, she will exalt you. Hold her fast and she will lead you to great honor; she will place a beautiful crown upon your head. [10]My son, listen to me and do as I say, and you will have a long, good life. [11]I would have you learn this great fact: that a life of doing right is the wisest life there is. [12]If you live that kind of life, you'll not limp or stumble as you run. [13]Carry out my instructions; don't forget them, for they will lead you to real living. [14]Don't do as the wicked do. [15]Avoid their haunts—turn away, go somewhere else, [16]for evil men don't sleep until they've done their evil for the day. They can't rest unless they cause someone to stumble and fall. [17]They eat and drink wickedness and violence! [18]But the good man walks along in the ever-brightening light of God's favor; the dawn gives way to morning splendor, [19]while the evil man gropes and stumbles in the dark. [20]Listen, son of mine, to what I say. Listen carefully. [21]Keep these thoughts ever in mind; let them penetrate deep within your heart, [22]for they will mean real life for you, and radiant health. [23]*Above all else, guard your affections.* For they influence everything else in your life. [24]Spurn the careless kiss of a prostitute. Stay far from her. [25]Look straight ahead; don't even turn your head to look. [26]Watch your step. Stick to the path and be safe. [27]Don't sidetrack; pull back your foot from danger.

Prov 5:1. Listen to me, my son! I know what I am saying; *listen!* [2]Watch yourself, lest you be indiscreet and betray some vital information. [3]For the lips of a prostitute are as sweet as honey, and smooth flattery is her stock in trade. [4]But afterwards only a bitter conscience is left to you, sharp as a double-edged sword. [5]She leads you down to death and hell. For she does not know the path to life. She staggers down a crooked trail, and doesn't even realize where it leads. [7]Young men, listen to me, and never forget what I'm about to say: [8]*Run from her! Don't go near her house,* [9]lest you fall to her temptation and lose your honor, and give the remainder of your life to the cruel and merciless; [10]lest strangers obtain your wealth, and you become a slave of foreigners. [11]Lest afterwards you groan in anguish and in shame, when syphilis consumes your body, [12]and you say, "Oh, if only I had listened! If only I had not demanded my own way! [13]Oh, why wouldn't I take advice? Why was I so stupid? [14]For now I must face public disgrace." [15]Drink from your own well, my son—be faithful and true to your wife. [16]Why should you beget children with women of the street? [17]Why share your children with those outside your home? [18]Let your manhood be a blessing; rejoice in the wife of your youth. [19]Let her charms and tender embrace satisfy you. Let her love alone fill you with delight. [20]Why delight yourself with prostitutes, embracing what isn't yours? [21]*For God is closely watching you,* and he weighs carefully everything you do. [22]The wicked man is doomed by his own sins; they are ropes that catch and hold him. [23]He shall die because he will not listen to the truth; he has let himself be led away into incredible folly. Prov 31: 1–3.

Prov 6:1. Son, if you endorse a note for someone you hardly know, guaranteeing his debt, you are in serious trouble. [2]You may have trapped yourself by your agreement. [3]Quick! Get out of it if you possibly can! Swallow your pride; don't let embarrassment stand in the way. Go and beg to have your name erased. [4]Don't put it off. Do it now. Don't rest until you do. [5]If you can get out of this trap you have saved yourself like a deer that escapes from a hunter, or a bird from the net. [6]Take a lesson from the ants, you lazy fellow. Learn from their ways and be wise! [7]For though they have no king to make them work, [8]yet they labor hard all summer, gathering food for the winter. [9]But you—all you do is sleep. When will you wake up? [10]"Let me sleep a little longer!" Sure, just a little more! [11]And as you sleep, poverty creeps upon you like a robber and destroys you; want attacks you in full armor. [12, 13]Let me describe for you a worthless and a wicked man; first, he is a constant liar; he signals his true intentions to his friends with eyes and feet and fingers. [14]Next, his heart is full of rebellion. And he spends his time thinking of all the evil he can do, and stirring up discontent. [15]But he will be destroyed suddenly, broken beyond hope of healing. [16-19]For there are six things the Lord hates—no seven: Haughtiness, lying, murdering, plotting evil, eagerness to do wrong, a false witness, sowing discord among brothers. [20]Young man, obey your father and your mother. [21]Tie their instructions around your finger so you won't forget. Take to heart all of their advice. [22]Every day and all night long their counsel will lead you and save you from harm; when you wake up in the morning, let their instructions guide you into the new day. [23]For their advice is a beam of light directed into the dark corners of your mind to warn you of danger and to give you a good life. [24]Their counsel will keep you far away from prostitutes with all their flatteries. [25]Don't lust for their beauty. Don't let their coyness seduce you. [26]For a prostitute will bring a man to poverty, and an adulteress may cost him his very life. [27]Can a man hold fire against his chest and not be burned? [28]Can he walk on hot coals and not blister his feet? [29]So it is with the man who commits adultery with another's wife. He shall not go unpunished for this sin. [30]Excuses might even be found for a thief, if he steals when he is starving! [31]But even so, he is fined seven times as much as he stole, though it may mean selling everything in his house to pay it back. [32]But the man who commits adultery is an utter fool, for he destroys his own soul. [33]Wounds and constant disgrace are his lot, [34]for the woman's husband will be furious in his jealousy, and he will have no mercy on you in his day of vengeance. [35]You won't be able to buy him off no matter what you offer.

Prov 7:1. Follow my advice, my son; always keep it in mind and stick to it. [2]Obey me and live! Guard my words as your most precious possession. [3]Write them down, and also keep them deep within your heart. 4 Love wisdom like a sweetheart; make her a beloved member of your family. 5 Let her hold you back from visiting a prostitute, from listening to her flattery. 6 I was looking out the window of my house one day, 7 and saw a simple-minded lad, a young man lacking common sense, 8, 9 walking at twilight down the street to the house of this wayward girl, a prostitute. 10 She approached him, saucy and pert, and dressed seductively. 11, 12 She was the brash, coarse type, seen often in the streets and markets, soliciting at every corner for men to be her lovers. 13 She put her arms around him and kissed him, and with a saucy look she said, 14 "I've decided to forget our quarrel! 15 I was just coming to look for you and here you are! 16, 17 My bed is spread with lovely, colored sheets of finest linen imported from Egypt, perfumed with myrrh, aloes and cinnamon. 18 Come on, let's take our fill of love until morning, 19 for my husband is away on a long trip. 20 He has taken a wallet full of money with him, and won't return for several days." 21 So she seduced him with her pretty speech, her coaxing and her wheedling, until he yielded to her. He couldn't resist her flattery. 22 He followed her as an ox going to the butcher, or as a stag that is trapped, 23 waiting to be killed with an arrow through its heart. He was as a bird flying into a snare, not knowing the fate awaiting it there. 24 Listen to me, young men, and not only listen but obey; 25 don't let your desires get out of hand; don't let yourself think about her. Don't go near her; stay away from where she walks, lest she tempt you and seduce you. 26 For she has been the ruin of multitudes—a vast host of men have been her victims. 27 If you want to find the road to hell, look for her house.

Prov 10:1. Happy is the man with a level-headed son; sad the mother of a rebel.

Prov 13:1. A wise youth accepts his father's rebuke; a young mocker doesn't.

Prov 15:5. Only a fool despises his father's advice; a wise son considers each suggestion. 20 A sensible son gladdens his father. A rebellious son saddens his mother.

Prov 17:2. A wise slave will rule his master's wicked sons and share their estate. 25 A rebellious son is a grief to his father and a bitter blow to his mother.

Prov 19:13. A rebellious son is a calamity to his father. 26 A son who mistreats his father or mother is a public disgrace. 27 Stop listening to teaching that contradicts what you know is right.

Prov 20:29. The glory of young men is their strength; of old men, their experience.

Prov 23:15, 16. My son, how I will rejoice if you become a man of common sense. Yes, my heart will thrill to your thoughtful wise words. 17, 18 Don't envy evil men but continue to reverence the Lord all the time, for surely you have a wonderful future ahead of you. There is hope for you yet! 19-21 O my son, be wise and stay in God's paths; don't carouse with drunkards and gluttons, for they are on their way to poverty. And remember that too much sleep clothes a man with rags. 22 Listen to your father's advice and don't despise an old mother's experience. 23 Get the facts at any price, and hold on tightly to all the good sense you can get. 24, 25 The father of a godly man has cause for joy—what pleasure a wise son is! So give your parents joy! 26-28 O my son, trust my advice—stay away from prostitutes. For a prostitute is a deep and narrow grave. Like a robber, she waits for her victims as one after another become unfaithful to their wives. 29, 30 Whose heart is filled with anguish and sorrow? Who is always fighting and quarreling? Who is the man with bloodshot eyes and many wounds? It is the one who spends long hours in the taverns, trying out new mixtures. 31 Don't let the sparkle and the smooth taste of strong wine deceive you. 32 For in the end it bites like a poisonous serpent; it stings like an adder. 33 You will see hallucinations and have delirium tremens, and you will say foolish, silly things that would embarrass you no end when sober. 34 You will stagger like a sailor tossed at sea, clinging to a swaying mast. 35 And afterwards you will say, "I didn't even know it when they beat me up . . . Let's go and have another drink!"

Prov 24:1. Don't envy godless men; don't even enjoy their company. 2 For they spend their days plotting violence and cheating. 3, 4 Any enterprise is built by wise planning, becomes strong through common sense, and profits wonderfully by keeping abreast of the facts. 5 A wise man is mightier than a strong man. Wisdom is mightier than strength. 6 Don't go to war without wise guidance; there is safety in many counselors. 7 Wisdom is too much for a rebel. He'll not be chosen as a counselor! 8 To plan evil is as wrong as doing it. 9 The rebel's schemes are sinful, and the mocker is the scourge of all mankind. 10 You are a poor specimen if you can't stand the pressure of adversity. 11, 12 Rescue those who are unjustly sentenced to death; don't stand back and let them die. Don't try to disclaim responsibility by saying you didn't know about it. For God, who knows all hearts, knows yours, and he knows you knew! And he will reward everyone according to his deeds. 13, 14 My son, honey whets the appetite, and so does wisdom! When you enjoy becoming wise, there is hope for you! A bright future lies ahead! 15, 16 O evil man, leave the upright man alone, and quit trying to cheat him out of his rights. Don't you know that this good man, though you trip him up seven times, will each time rise again? But one calamity is enough to lay you low. 17 Do not rejoice when your enemy meets trouble. Let there be no gladness when he falls—18 for the Lord may be displeased with you and stop punishing him! 19, 20 Don't envy the wicked. Don't covet his riches. For the evil man has no future; his light will be snuffed out. 21, 22 My son, watch your step before the Lord and the king, and don't associate with radicals. For you will go down with them to sudden disaster, and who knows where it all will end? *Here are some additional proverbs:* 23 It is wrong to sentence the poor, and let the rich go free. 24 He who says to the wicked, "You are innocent," shall be cursed by many people of many nations;

[25]but blessings shall be showered on those who rebuke sin fearlessly. [26]It is an honor to receive a frank reply. [27]Develop your business first before building your house. [28, 29]Don't testify spitefully against an innocent neighbor. Why lie about him? Don't say, "Now I can pay him back for all his meanness to me!" [30, 31]I walked by the field of a certain lazy fellow and saw that it was overgrown with thorns, and covered with weeds; and its walls were broken down. [32, 33]Then, as I looked, I learned this lesson: "A little extra sleep, a little more slumber, a little folding of the hands to rest" [34]means that poverty will break in upon you suddenly like a robber, and violently like a bandit.

Prov 27:11. My son, how happy I will be if you turn out to be sensible! It will be a public honor to me.

Prov 28:7. Young men who are wise obey the law; a son who is a member of a lawless gang is a shame to his father.

Prov 29:3. A wise son makes his father happy, but a lad who hangs around with prostitutes disgraces him.

Jer 22:18. Therefore this is God's decree of punishment against King Jehoiakim, who succeeded his father Josiah on the throne: His family will not weep for him when he dies. His subjects will not even care that he is dead. [19]He shall be buried like a dead donkey—dragged out of Jerusalem and thrown on the garbage dump beyond the gate! [20]Weep, for your allies are gone. Search for them in Lebanon; shout for them at Bashan; seek them at the fording points of Jordan. See, they are all destroyed. Not one is left to help you! [21]When you were prosperous I warned you, but you replied, "Don't bother me." Since childhood you have been that way—you just won't listen!

Mt 19:16. Someone came to Jesus with this question: "Good master, what must I do to have eternal life?" [17]"When you call me good you are calling me God," Jesus replied, "for God alone is truly good. But to answer your question, you can get to heaven if you keep the commandments." [18]"Which ones?" the man asked. And Jesus replied, "Don't kill, don't commit adultery, don't steal, don't lie, [19]honor your father and mother, and love your neighbor as yourself!" [20]"I've always obeyed every one of them," the youth replied. "What else must I do?" [21]Jesus told him, "If you want to be perfect, go and sell everything you have and give the money to the poor, and you will have treasure in heaven; and come, follow me." [22]But when the young man heard this, he went away sadly, for he was very rich. Mk 10:17–22; Lk 18:18–23.

Lk 15:11. A man had two sons. [12]When the younger told his father, "I want my share of your estate now, instead of waiting until you die!" his father agreed to divide his wealth between his sons. [13]A few days later this younger son packed all his belongings and took a trip to a distant land, and there wasted all his money on parties and prostitutes. [14]About the time his money was gone a great famine swept over the land, and he began to starve. [15]He persuaded a local farmer to hire him to feed his pigs. [16]The boy became so hungry that even the pods he was feeding the swine looked good to him. And no one gave him anything. [17]When he finally came to his senses, he said to himself, "At home even the hired men have food enough and to spare, and here I am, dying of hunger! [18]I will go home to my father and say, 'Father, I have sinned against both heaven and you, [19]and am no longer worthy of being called your son. Please take me on as a hired man.' " [20]So he returned home to his father. And while he was still a long distance away, his father saw him coming, and was filled with loving pity and ran and embraced him and kissed him. [21]His son said to him, "Father, I have sinned against heaven and you, and am not worthy of being called your son—" [22]But his father said to the slaves, "Quick! Bring the finest robe in the house and put it on him. And a jeweled ring for his finger; and shoes! [23]And kill the calf we have in the fattening pen. We must celebrate with a feast, [24]for this son of mine was dead and has returned to life. He was lost and is found." So the party began. [25]Meanwhile, the older son was in the fields working; when he returned home, he heard dance music coming from the house, [26]and he asked one of the servants what was going on. [27]"Your brother is back," he was told, "and your father has killed the calf we were fattening and has prepared a great feast to celebrate his coming home again unharmed." [28]The older brother was angry and wouldn't go in. His father came out and begged him, [29]but he replied, "All these years I've worked hard for you and never once refused to do a single thing you told me to; and in all that time you never gave me even one young goat for a feast with my friends. [30]Yet when this son of yours comes back after spending your money on prostitutes, you celebrate by killing the finest calf we have on the place." [31]"Look, dear son," his father said to him, "you and I are very close, and everything I have is yours. [32]But it is right to celebrate. For he is your brother; and he was dead and has come back to life! He was lost and is found!"

1 Tim 4:12. Don't let anyone think little of you because you are young. Be their ideal; let them follow the way you teach and live; be a pattern for them in your love, your faith, and your clean thoughts.

2 Tim 2:22. Run from anything that gives you the evil thoughts that young men often have, but stay close to anything that makes you want do to right. Have faith and love, and enjoy the companionship of those who love the Lord and have pure hearts. [23]Again I say, don't get involved in foolish arguments which only upset people and make them angry.

Tit 2:6. In the same way, urge the young men to behave carefully, taking life seriously.

Heb 11:24, 25. It was by faith that Moses, when he grew up, refused to be treated as the grandson of the king, but chose to share ill-treatment with God's people instead of enjoying the fleeting pleasures of sin. [26]He thought that it was better to suffer for the promised Christ than to own all the treasures of Egypt, for he was looking forward to the great reward that God would give him.

1 Jn 2:13. And you young men, I am talking to you because you have won your battle with Satan. And I am writing to you younger boys and girls because you, too, have learned to know God our Father. [14]And so I say to you fathers who know the eternal God, and to you young men who are strong, with God's Word in your hearts, and have won your struggle against Satan: [15]Stop loving this evil world and all that it offers you, for when you love these things you show that you do not really love God; [16]for all these worldly things, these evil desires—the craze for sex, the ambition to buy everything that appeals to you, and the pride that comes from wealth and importance—these are not from God. They are from this evil world itself. [17]And this world is fading away, and these evil, forbidden things will go with it, but whoever keeps doing the will of God will live forever.

INSTANCES OF RELIGIOUS. See *Joseph; Joshua; Josiah; Samuel, David, Solomon, Uriah.* The rich young man, Mt 19:16–22; Mk 10:17–22; Lk 18:18–23.

See *Children; Parents.*

Z

ZAANAN Called also *Zenan.* A place of uncertain location, Josh 15:37–44; Mic 1:11.

ZAANANNIM A plain near Kedesh, Josh 19:33; Judg 4:11.

ZAAVAN A son of Ezer, Gen 36:27; 1 Chron 1:42.

ZABAD 1. Son of Nathan, 1 Chron 2:36, 37.

2. An Ephraimite, 1 Chron 7:20, 21.

3. One of David's valiant men, 1 Chron 11:26–47.

4. An assassin of King Joash, 2 Chron 24:26; 25:3, 4. Called *Jozachar* in 2 Kgs 12:21.

5. Three Israelites who divorced their Gentile wives, Ezra 10:27, 33, 43.

ZABBAI 1. Son of Bebai, Ezra 10:28.

2. Father of Baruch, Neh 3:20.

ZABDI 1. Father of Carmi, and grandfather of Achan, Josh 7:1, 17, 18. Called *Zimri* in 1 Chron 2:6.

2. A Benjaminite, 1 Chron 8:19–21.

3. One of David's overseers, 1 Chron 27:27.

4. Son of Asaph, Neh 11:15–17. Called *Zichri* in 1 Chron 9:15, 16.

ZABDIEL An overseer of 128 mighty men who lived in Jerusalem, Neh 11:10–14.

ZABUD A friend and officer of Solomon, 1 Kgs 4:1–6.

ZACCAI A Jew whose descendants returned from exile, Ezra 2:3–35; Neh 7:8–38.

ZACCHAEUS A tax collector in Jericho. Entertains Jesus, Lk 19:1–10.

ZACCUR 1. A Reubenite, Num 13:3–15.

2. A Simeonite, 1 Chron 4:26.

3. A Merarite, 1 Chron 24:26, 27.

4. Son of Asaph, 1 Chron 25:2, 9–31; Neh 12:35, 36.

5. A returned exile, Ezra 8:2–14.

6. Son of Imri, Neh 3:2.

7. A Levite who signed the covenant with Nehemiah, Neh 10:9–13.

8. Father of Hanan, Neh 13:13.

ZACHARIAS Father of John the Baptist, Lk 1:5–80; 3:1, 2. See *Elizabeth; John the Baptist.*

ZADOK 1. High priest in the time of David's reign, 2 Sam 19:11, 12; 20:25; 1 Chron 15:11; 16:39. Removes the Ark from Jerusalem at the time of Absalom's usurpation; returns with it at David's command, 2 Sam 15:24–36; 17:15, 17–21. Remains loyal to David at the time of Adonijah's attempted usurpation, 1 Kgs 1:8, 26. Summoned by David to anoint Solomon, 1 Kgs 1:32–40, 44, 45. Performs the function of high priest after Abiathar was deposed by Solomon, 1 Kgs 2:35; 1 Chron 29:22.

2. Father of Jerusha, 2 Kgs 15:33; 2 Chron 27:1.

3. A descendant of 1, above, 1 Chron 6:4–15; 9:10, 11; Neh 11:10–14.

4. A man of courage, 1 Chron 12:24–37.

5. Son of Baana, Neh 3:4.

6. A priest, Neh 3:29.

7. A returned exile, Neh 10:14–27.

8. A treasurer of the Temple, Neh 13:13.

9. An ancestor of Jesus, Mt 1:14.

ZAHAM Grandson of Solomon, 2 Chron 11:19.

ZAIR A city of Edom, 2 Kgs 8:21.

ZALAPH Father of Hanun, Neh 3:30.

ZALMON 1. A mountain in Samaria, Judg 9:47, 48; Ps 68:14.

2. One of David's warriors, 2 Sam 23:24–39.

ZALMONAH One of the camping places of Israel, Num 33:41.

ZALMUNNA King of Midian, Judg 8:5–21; Ps 83:11.

ZANZUMMIM Called also *Zuzim.* A race of giants, Gen 14:5, 6; Deut 2:20, 21.

ZANOAH 1. A city of western Judah, Josh 15:33–36; 1 Chron 4:18; Neh 3:13; 11:25–30.

2. A city of eastern Judah, Josh 15:48–62.

ZAPHON A city of Gad, Josh 13:27, 28.

ZARED Called also *Zered.* A brook, Num 21:12; Deut 2:13–15.

ZAREPHATH A city between Tyre and Sidon, Elijah performs two miracles in, 1 Kgs 17:8–24; Lk 4:25, 26.

ZARETHAN A city of uncertain location, Josh 3:15, 16; 1 Kgs 4:8–19; 7:41–46.

ZATTU 1. One whose descendants returned with Zerubbabel, Ezra 2:3–35; 10:27; Neh 7:8–38.

2. Probably identical with Nehemiah, Neh 10:14–27.

ZAZA Son of Jonathan, 1 Chron 2:33.

ZEAL, RELIGIOUS Josh 24:15. "But if you are unwilling to obey the Lord, then decide today whom you will obey. Will it be the gods of your ancestors beyond the Euphrates or the gods of the Amorites here in this land? But as for me and my family, we will serve the Lord." [16]And the people replied, "We would never forsake the Lord and worship other gods!"

2 Sam 24:24. But the king said to Araunah, "No, I will not have it as a gift. I will buy it, for I don't want to offer to the Lord my God burnt offerings that have cost me nothing." So David paid him for the threshing floor and the oxen. [25]And David built an altar there to the Lord and offered burnt offerings and peace offerings.

1 Kgs 9:4. And if you live in honesty and truth as your father David did, always obeying me.

1 Chron 29:17. I know, my God, that you test men to see if they are good; for you enjoy good men. I have done all this with good motives, and I have watched your people offer their gifts willingly and joyously.

2 Chron 15:15. All were happy for this covenant with God, for they had entered into it with all their hearts and wills, and wanted him above everything else, and they found him! And he gave them peace throughout the nation.

2 Chron 19:3. But there are some good things about you, in that you got rid of the shame-idols throughout the land, and you have tried to be faithful to God.

Job 16:19. Yet even now the Witness to my innocence is there in heaven; my Advocate is there on high.

Ps 42:1. As the deer pants for water, so I long for you, O God. [2]I thirst for God, the living God. Where can I find him to come and stand before him?

Ps 60:4. But you have given us a banner to rally to; all who love truth will rally to it.

Ps 96:2. Sing out his praises! Bless his name. Each day tell someone that he saves. [3]Publish his glorious acts throughout the earth. Tell everyone about the amazing things he does. [10]Tell the nations that Jehovah reigns!

Ps 119:139. I am indignant and angry because of the way my enemies have disregarded your laws.

Prov 11:30. Godly men are growing a tree that bears life-giving fruit, and all who win souls are wise.

Eccl 9:10. Whatever you do, do well, for in death, where you are going, there is no working or planning, or knowing, or understanding.

Isa 58:12. Your sons will rebuild the long-deserted ruins of your cities, and you will be known as "The People Who Rebuild Their Walls and Cities."

Isa 60:1. Arise, my people! Let your light shine for all the nations to see! For the glory of the Lord is streaming from you.

Isa 62:6, 7. O Jerusalem, I have set intercessors on your walls who shall cry to God all day and all night for the fulfillment of his promises. Take no rest, all you who pray, and give God no rest until he establishes Jerusalem and makes her respected and admired throughout the earth.

Dan 12:3. And those who are wise—the people of God—shall shine as brightly as the sun's brilliance, and those who turn many to righteousness will glitter like stars forever.

Mic 5:7. Then the nation of Israel will refresh the world like a gentle dew or the welcome showers of rain.

Hab 2:2. And the Lord said to me, "Write my answer on a billboard, large and clear, so that anyone can read it at a glance and rush to tell the others."

Hag 2:4. But take courage, O Zerubbabel and Joshua and all the people; take courage and work, for "I am with you," says the Lord of Hosts. [5]"For I promised when you left Egypt that my Spirit would remain among you; so don't be afraid."

Zech 14:20. In that day the bells on the horses will have written on them, "These Are Holy Property"; and the trash can in the Temple of the Lord will be as sacred as the bowls beside the altar. [21]In fact, every container in Jerusalem and Judah shall be sacred to the Lord of Hosts; all who come to worship may use any of them free of charge to boil their sacrifices in; there will be no more grasping traders in the Temple of the Lord of Hosts.

Mt 5:13. You are the world's seasoning, to make it tolerable. If you lose your flavor, what will happen to the world? And you yourselves will be thrown out and trampled underfoot as worthless. [14]You are the world's light—a city on a hill, glowing in the night for all to see. [15, 16]Don't hide your light. Let it shine for all; let your good deeds glow for all to see, so that they will praise your heavenly Father. Mk 4:21, 22; Lk 8:16, 17.

Lk 22:32. "But I have pleaded in prayer for you that your faith should not completely fail. So when you have repented and turned to me again, strengthen and build up the faith of your brothers." [33]Simon said, "Lord, I am ready to go to jail with you, and even to die with you."

Jn 6:27. But you shouldn't be so concerned about perishable things like food. No, spend your energy seeking the eternal life that I, the Messiah, can give you. For God the Father has sent me for this very purpose.

Jn 9:4. All of us must quickly carry out the tasks assigned us by the one who sent me, for there is little time left before the night falls and all work comes to an end.

Acts 10:42. And he sent us to preach the Good News everywhere and to testify that Jesus is ordained of God to be the Judge of all—living and dead.

Acts 26:29. And Paul replied, "Would to God that whether my arguments are trivial or strong, both you and everyone here in this audience might become the same as I am, except for these chains."

Rom 1:8. Let me say first of all that wherever I go I hear you being talked about! For your faith in God is becoming known around the world. How I thank God through Jesus Christ for this good report, and for each one of you. [9]God knows how often I pray for you. Day and night I bring you and your needs in prayer to the one I serve with all my might, telling others the Good News about his Son.

Rom 7:22. I love to do God's will so far as my new nature is concerned.

Rom 12:11. Never be lazy in your work but serve the Lord enthusiastically.

1 Cor 5:8. So let us feast upon him and grow strong in the Christian life, leaving entirely behind us the cancerous old life with all its hatreds and wickedness. Let us feast instead upon the pure bread of honor and sincerity and truth.

1 Cor 7:29. The important thing to remember is that our remaining time is very short, (and so are our opportunities for doing the Lord's work). For that reason those who have wives should stay as free as possible for the Lord; [30]happiness or sadness or wealth should not keep anyone from doing God's work. [31]Those in frequent contact with the exciting things the world offers should make good use of their opportunities without stopping to enjoy them; for the world in its present form will soon be gone. [32]In all you do, I want you to be free from worry. An unmarried man can spend his time doing the Lord's work and thinking how to please him. [33]But a married man can't do that so well; he has to think about his earthly responsibilities and how to please his wife. [34]His interests are divided. It is the same with a girl who marries. She faces the same problem. A girl who is not married is anxious to please the Lord in all she is and does. But a married woman must consider other things such as housekeeping and the likes and dislikes of her husband.

1 Cor 13:3. If I gave everything I have to poor people, and if I were burned alive for preaching the Gospel but didn't love others, it would be of no value whatever.

1 Cor 14:12. Since you are so anxious to have special gifts from the Holy Spirit, ask him for the very best, for those that will be of real help to the whole church.

1 Cor 15:58. So, my dear brothers, since future victory is sure, be strong and steady, always abounding in the Lord's work, for you know that nothing you do for the Lord is ever wasted as it would be if there were no resurrection.

2 Cor 4:8. We are pressed on every side by troubles, but not crushed and broken. We are perplexed because we don't know why things happen as they do, but we don't give up and quit. [9]We are hunted down, but God never abandons us. We get knocked down, but we get up again and keep going. [10]These bodies of ours are constantly facing death just as Jesus did; so it is clear to all that it is only the living Christ within (who keeps us safe). [13]We boldly say what we believe (trusting God to care for us), just as the Psalm writer did when he said, "I believe and therefore I speak." [16]That is why we never give up. Though our bodies are dying, our inner strength in the Lord is growing every day. [17]These troubles and sufferings of ours are, after all, quite small and won't last very long. Yet this short time of distress will result in God's richest blessing upon us forever and ever! [18]So we do not look at what we can see right now, the troubles all around us, but we look forward to the joys in heaven which we have not yet seen. The troubles will soon be over, but the joys to come will last forever.

2 Cor 7:11. Just see how much good this grief from the Lord did for you! You no longer shrugged your shoulders, but became earnest and sincere, and very anxious to get rid of the sin that I wrote you about. You became frightened about what had happened, and longed for me to come and help. You went right to work on the problem and cleared it up (punishing the man who sinned). You have done everything you could to make it right.

2 Cor 9:2. For I know how eager you are to do it, and I have boasted to the friends in Macedonia that you were ready to send an offering a year ago. In fact, it was this enthusiasm of yours that stirred up many of them to begin helping.

Gal 4:18. It is a fine thing when people are nice to you with good motives and sincere hearts.

Gal 6:9. And let us not get tired of doing what is right, for after a while we will reap a harvest of blessing if we don't get discouraged and give up. 2 Thess 3:13.

Eph 5:15, 16. So be careful how you act; these are difficult days. Don't be fools; be wise: make the most of every opportunity you have for doing good.

Eph 6:14. But to do this, you will need the strong belt of truth and the breastplate of God's approval. [15]Wear shoes that are able to speed you on as you preach the Good News of peace with God. [16]In every battle you will need faith as your shield to stop the fiery arrows aimed at you by Satan. [17]And you will need the helmet of salvation and the sword of the Spirit—which is the Word of God. [18]Pray all the time. Ask God for anything in line with the Holy Spirit's wishes. Plead with him, reminding him of your needs, and keep praying earnestly for all Christians everywhere. [19]Pray for me, too, and ask God to give me the right words as I boldly tell others about the Lord, and as I explain to them that his salvation is for the Gentiles too. [20]I am in chains now for preaching this message from God. But pray that I will keep on speaking out boldly for him even here in prison, as I should.

Phil 1:27. But whatever happens to me, remember always to live as Christians should, so that, whether I ever see you again or not, I will keep on hearing good reports that you are standing side by side with one strong purpose—to tell the Good News [28]fearlessly, no matter what your enemies may do. They will see this as a sign of their downfall, but for you it will be a clear sign from God that he is with you, and that he has given you eternal life with him.

Phil 2:15. So that no one can speak a word of blame against you. You are to live clean, innocent lives as children of God in a dark world full of people who are crooked and stubborn. Shine out among them like beacon lights.

Phil 3:4. Yet if anyone ever had reason to hope

that he could save himself, it would be I. If others could be saved by what they are, certainly I could! [5]For I went through the Jewish initiation ceremony when I was eight days old, having been born into a pure-blooded Jewish home that was a branch of the old original Benjamin family. So I was a real Jew if there ever was one! What's more, I was a member of the Pharisees who demand the strictest obedience to every Jewish law and custom. [6]And sincere? Yes, so much so that I greatly persecuted the church; and I tried to obey every Jewish rule and regulation right down to the very last point. [7]But all these things that I once thought very worthwhile—now I've thrown them all away so that I can put my trust and hope in Christ alone. [8]Yes, everything else is worthless when compared with the priceless gain of knowing Christ Jesus my Lord. I have put aside all else, counting it worth less than nothing, in order that I can have Christ, [9]and become one with him, no longer counting on being saved by being good enough or by obeying God's laws, but by trusting Christ to save me; for God's way of making us right with himself depends on faith—counting on Christ alone. [10]Now I have given up everything else—I have found it to be the only way to really know Christ and to experience the mighty power that brought him back to life again, and to find out what it means to suffer and to die with him. [11]So, whatever it takes, I will be one who lives in the fresh newness of life of those who are alive from the dead. [12]I don't mean to say I am perfect. I haven't learned all I should even yet, but I keep working toward that day I will finally be all that Christ saved me for and wants me to be. [13]No, dear brothers, I am still not all I should be but I am bringing all my energies to bear on this one thing: Forgetting the past and looking forward to what lies ahead, [14]I strain to reach the end of the race and receive the prize for which God is calling us up to heaven because of what Christ Jesus did for us. [20]But our homeland is in heaven, where our Savior the Lord Jesus Christ is.

Col 4:5. Make the most of your chances to tell others the Good News. Be wise in all your contacts with them.

Tit 2:14. He died under God's judgment against our sins, so that he could rescue us from constant falling into sin and make us his very own people, with cleansed hearts and real enthusiasm for doing kind things for others.

Tit 3:1. Remind your people to obey the government and its officers, and always to be obedient and ready for any honest work.

Heb 10:34. You suffered with those thrown into jail, and you were actually joyful when all you owned was taken from you, knowing that better things were awaiting you in heaven, things that would be yours forever.

Heb 11:15. If they had wanted to, they could have gone back to the good things of this world. [16]But they didn't want to. They were living for heaven. And now God is not ashamed to be called their God, for he has made a heavenly city for them.

[24, 25]It was by faith that Moses, when he grew up, refused to be treated as the grandson of the king, but chose to share ill-treatment with God's people instead of enjoying the fleeting pleasures of sin. [26]He thought that it was better to suffer for the promised Christ than to own all the treasures of Egypt, for he was looking forward to the great reward that God would give him. [27]And it was because he trusted God that he left the land of Egypt and wasn't afraid of the king's anger. Moses kept right on going; it seemed as though he could see God right there with him.

Heb 13:13. So let us go out to him beyond the city walls (that is, outside the interest of this world, being willing to be despised) to suffer with him there, bearing his shame. [14]For this world is not our home; we are looking forward to our everlasting home in heaven. [15]With Jesus' help we will continually offer our sacrifice of praise to God by telling others of the glory of his name.

Jas 5:19. Dear brothers, if anyone has slipped away from God and no longer trusts the Lord, and someone helps him understand the Truth again, [20]that person who brings him back to God will have saved a wandering soul from death, bringing about the forgiveness of his many sins.

1 Pet 2:2. Long to grow up into the fullness of your salvation; cry for this as a baby cries for his milk.

2 Pet 3:14. Dear friends, while you are waiting for these things to happen and for him to come, try hard to live without sinning; and be at peace with everyone so that he will be pleased with you when he returns. 2 Pet 1:10, 11.

Jude 1:3. Dearly loved friends, I had been planning to write you some thoughts about the salvation God has given us, but now I find I must write of something else instead, urging you to stoutly defend the truth which God gave, once for all, to his people to keep without change through the years. [22]Try to help those who argue against you. Be merciful to those who doubt. [23]Save some by snatching them as from the very flames of hell itself. And as for others, help them to find the Lord by being kind to them, but be careful that you yourselves aren't pulled along into their sins. Hate every trace of their sin while being merciful to them as sinners.

Rev 3:19. I continually discipline and punish everyone I love; so I must punish you, unless you turn from your indifference and become enthusiastic about the things of God.

Rev 5:4. Then I wept with disappointment because no one anywhere was worthy; no one could tell us what it said. [5]But one of the twenty-four Elders said to me, "Stop crying, for look! The Lion of the tribe of Judah, the Root of David, has conquered, and proved himself worthy to open the scroll and to break its seven seals."

Rev 22:17. The Spirit and the bride say, "Come." Let each one who hears them say the same, "Come."

EXEMPLIFIED. Ex 32:31. So Moses returned to

the Lord and said, "Oh, these people have sinned a great sin, and have made themselves gods of gold. [32]Yet now if you will only forgive their sin—and if not, then blot *me* out of the book you have written."

Num 10:29. At last we are on our way to the Promised Land. Come with us and we will do you good; for the Lord has given wonderful promises to Israel!

Num 11:29. Are you jealous for my sake? I only wish that all of the Lord's people were prophets, and that the Lord would put his Spirit upon them all!

Deut 9:18. Then, for another forty days and nights I lay before the Lord, neither eating bread nor drinking water, for you had done what the Lord hated most, thus provoking him to great anger. *v.* 19.

Josh 24:14. "So revere Jehovah and serve him in sincerity and truth. Put away forever the idols which your ancestors worshiped when they lived beyond the Euphrates River and in Egypt. Worship the Lord alone. [15]But if you are unwilling to obey the Lord, then decide today whom you will obey. Will it be the gods of your ancestors beyond the Euphrates or the gods of the Amorites here in this land? But as for me and my family, we will serve the Lord." [16]And the people replied, "We would never forsake the Lord and worship other gods!"

1 Sam 17:26. David talked to some others standing there to verify the report. "What will a man get for killing this Philistine and ending his insults to Israel?" he asked them. "Who is this heathen Philistine, anyway, that he is allowed to defy the armies of the living God?"

1 Kgs 8:43. Hear them from heaven and answer their prayers. And all the nations of the earth will know and fear your name just as your own people Israel do; and all the earth will know that this is your Temple. *v.* 41, 42; 2 Chron 6:33.

1 Kgs 22:14. But Micaiah told him, "This I vow, that I will say only what the Lord tells me to!"

Job 6:10. I have not denied the words of the holy God.

Ps 40:7. Then I said, "See, I have come, just as all the prophets foretold. [8]And I delight to do your will, my God, for your law is written upon my heart!" [9]I have told everyone the Good News that you forgive men's sins. I have not been timid about it, as you well know, O Lord. [10]I have not kept this Good News hidden in my heart, but have proclaimed your lovingkindness and truth to all the congregation.

Ps 51:13. Then I will teach your ways to other sinners, and they—guilty like me—will repent and return to you.

Ps 69:7. Though I am mocked and cursed and shamed for your sake. [8]Even my own brothers pretend they don't know me! [9]My zeal for God and his work burns hot within me. And because I advocate your cause, your enemies insult me even as they insult you.

Ps 71:17. O God, you have helped me from my earliest childhood—and I have constantly testified to others of the wonderful things you do. [18]And now that I am old and gray, don't forsake me. Give me time to tell this new generation (and their children too) about all your mighty miracles.

Ps 94:16. Who will protect me from the wicked? Who will be my shield?

Ps 101:8. My daily task will be to ferret out criminals and free the city of God from their grip.

Ps 119:53. I am very angry with those who spurn your commands. [126]Lord, it is time for you to act. For these evil men have violated your laws. [136]I weep because your laws are disobeyed. [139]I am indignant and angry because of the way my enemies have disregarded your laws. [158]I loathed these traitors because they care nothing for your laws. Ps 9:19, 20; 74:9, 10, 18–23; 115:1, 2.

Prov 28:4. To complain about the law is to praise wickedness. To obey the law is to fight evil.

Eccl 12:9. But then, because the Preacher was wise, he went on teaching the people all he knew; and he collected proverbs and classified them. [10]For the Preacher was not only a wise man, but a good teacher; he not only taught what he knew to the people, but taught them in an interesting manner.

Isa 2:3. "Come," everyone will say, "let us go up the mountain of the Lord, to the Temple of the God of Israel; then he will teach us his laws, and we will obey them." For in those days the world will be ruled from Jerusalem. [5]O Israel, come, let us walk in the light of the Lord, and be obedient to his laws!

Isa 6:8. Then I heard the Lord asking, "Whom shall I send as a messenger to my people? Who will go?" And I said, "Lord, I'll go! Send *me.*"

Isa 59:17. He put on righteousness as armor, and the helmet of salvation on his head. He clothed himself with robes of vengeance and of godly fury.

Isa 62:1. Because I love Zion, because my heart yearns for Jerusalem, I will not cease to pray for her or to cry out to God on her behalf until she shines forth in his righteousness and is glorious in his salvation.

Jer 9:1. Oh, that my eyes were a fountain of tears; I would weep forever; I would sob day and night for the slain of my people! [2]Oh, that I could go away and forget them and live in some wayside shack in the desert, for they are all adulterous, treacherous men. [3]"They bend their tongues like bows to shoot their arrows of untruth. They care nothing for right and go from bad to worse; they care nothing for me," says the Lord.

Jer 13:17. Do you still refuse to listen? Then in loneliness my breaking heart shall mourn because of your pride. My eyes will overflow with tears because the Lord's flock shall be carried away as slaves.

Jer 17:16. Lord, I don't want the people crushed by terrible calamity. The plan is yours, not mine. It is *your* message I've given them, not my own. *I* don't want them doomed!

Jer 18:20. Should they repay evil for good? They have set a trap to kill me, yet I spoke well of them to you and tried to defend them from your anger.

Jer 20:9. And I can't quit! For if I say I'll never again mention the Lord—never more speak in his name—then his word in my heart is like fire that burns in my bones, and I can't hold it in any longer. Jer 26:12–15.

Ezk 9:4. And said to him, "Walk through the streets of Jerusalem and put a mark on the foreheads of the men who weep and sigh because of all the sins they see around them."

Ezk 44:15. However, the sons of Zadok, of the tribe of Levi, continued as my priests in the Temple when Israel abandoned me for idols. These men shall be my ministers; they shall stand before me to offer the fat and blood of the sacrifices, says the Lord God.

Dan 3:17. If we are thrown into the flaming furnace, our God is able to deliver us; and he will deliver us out of your hand, Your Majesty. [18]But if he doesn't, please understand, sir, that even then we will never under any circumstance serve your gods or worship the golden statue you have erected.

Mic 3:8. But as for me, I am filled with power, with the Spirit of the Lord, fearlessly announcing God's punishment on Israel for her sins.

Mic 7:1, 2. Woe is me! It is as hard to find an honest man as grapes and figs when harvest days are over. Not a cluster to eat, not a single early fig, however much I long for it! The good men have disappeared from the earth; not one fair-minded man is left. They are all murderers, turning against even their own brothers.

Hab 1:2. O Lord, how long must I call for help before you will listen? I shout to you in vain; there is no answer. "Help! Murder!" I cry, but no one comes to save. *vs.* 3, 4.

Mk 5:20. So the man started off to visit the Ten Towns of that region and began to tell everyone about the great things Jesus had done for him; and they were awestruck by his story. *v.* 19.

Mk 6:6. And he could hardly accept the fact that they wouldn't believe in him. Then he went out among the villages, teaching.

Mk 14:29. Peter said to him, "I will never desert you no matter what the others do!" [30]"Peter," Jesus said, "before the cock crows a second time tomorrow morning you will deny me three times." [31]"No!" Peter exploded. "Not even if I have to die with you! I'll *never* deny you!" And all the others vowed the same.

Mk 16:20. And the disciples went everywhere preaching, and the Lord was with them and confirmed what they said by the miracles that followed their messages.

Lk 1:16. And he will persuade many a Jew to turn to the Lord his God. [17]He will be a man of rugged spirit and power like Elijah, the prophet of old; and he will precede the coming of the Messiah, preparing the people for his arrival. He will soften adult hearts to become like little children's, and will change disobedient minds to the wisdom of faith. *v.* 15.

Lk 19:41. But as they came closer to Jerusalem and he saw the city ahead, he began to cry. *v.* 42; Mt 23:37.

Jn 1:40. (One of these men was Andrew, Simon Peter's brother.) [41]Andrew then went to find his brother Peter and told him, "We have found the Messiah!" [42]And he brought Peter to meet Jesus. [45]Philip now went off to look for Nathanael and told him, "We have found the Messiah!—the very person Moses and the prophets told about! His name is Jesus, the son of Joseph from Nazareth!" [46]"Nazareth!" exclaimed Nathanael. "Can anything good come from there?" "Just come and see for yourself," Philip declared.

Jn 4:34. Then Jesus explained: "My nourishment comes from doing the will of God who sent me, and from finishing his work. [35]Do you think the work of harvesting will not begin until the summer ends four months from now? Look around you! Vast fields of human souls are ripening all around us, and are ready now for reaping."

Acts 4:13. When the Council saw the boldness of Peter and John, and could see that they were obviously uneducated non-professionals, they were amazed and realized what being with Jesus had done for them! [18]So they called them back in, and told them never again to speak about Jesus. [19]But Peter and John replied, "You decide whether God wants us to obey you instead of him! [20]We cannot stop telling about the wonderful things we saw Jesus do and heard him say." [31]After this prayer, the building where they were meeting shook and they were all filled with the Holy Spirit and boldly preached God's message. [33]And the apostles preached powerful sermons about the resurrection of the Lord Jesus, and there was warm fellowship among all the believers. *vs.* 2, 8–12.

Acts 5:42. And every day, in the Temple and in their home Bible classes, they continued to teach and preach that Jesus is the Messiah. *vs.* 21, 25, 29–32.

Acts 6:4. "Then we can spend our time in prayer, preaching, and teaching." [10]But none of them were able to stand against Stephen's wisdom and spirit.

Acts 8:4. But the believers who had fled Jerusalem went everywhere preaching the Good News about Jesus! [35]So Philip began with this same Scripture and then used many others to tell him about Jesus. *vs.* 12, 25, 30, 40; Acts 11:19, 20, 24, 26.

Acts 18:25, 26. While he was in Egypt, someone had told him about John the Baptist and what John had said about Jesus, but that is all he knew. He had never heard the rest of the story! So he was preaching boldly and enthusiastically in the synagogue, "The Messiah is coming! Get ready to receive him!" Priscilla and Aquila were there and heard him—and it was a powerful sermon. Afterwards they met with him and explained what had happened to Jesus since the time of John, and all that it meant! [27]Apollos had been thinking about going to Greece, and the believers encouraged him in this. They wrote to their fellow-believers there, telling them to welcome him. And upon his arrival in Greece, he was greatly used of God to strengthen the church, [28]for he powerfully refuted all the Jewish arguments in public debate, showing by the Scriptures that Jesus is indeed the Messiah. *v.* 24.

Rom 1:11. For I long to visit you so that I can impart to you the faith that will help your church grow strong in the Lord.

Rom 9:1–3. Oh, Israel, my people! Oh, my Jewish brothers! How I long for you to come to Christ. My heart is heavy within me and I grieve bitterly day and night because of you. Christ knows and the Holy Spirit knows that it is no mere pretense when I say that I would be willing to be forever damned if that would save you.

Rom 10:1. Dear brothers, the longing of my heart and my prayer is that the Jewish people might be saved.

Rom 15:18. I dare not judge how effectively he has used others, but I know this: he has used me to win the Gentiles to God. [19]I have won them by my message and by the good way I have lived before them, and by the miracles done through me as signs from God—all by the Holy Spirit's power. In this way I have preached the full Gospel of Christ all the way from Jerusalem clear over into Illyricum. [20]But all the while my ambition has been to go still farther, preaching where the name of Christ has never yet been heard, rather than where a church has already been started by someone else. [21]I have been following the plan spoken of in the Scriptures where Isaiah says that those who have never heard the name of Christ before will see and understand.

2 Cor 5:9. So our aim is to please him always in everything we do, whether we are here in this body or away from this body and with him in heaven.

2 Cor 6:11. Oh, my dear Corinthian friends! I have told you all my feelings; I love you with all my heart.

2 Cor 8:1. Now I want to tell you what God in his grace has done for the churches in Macedonia. [2]Though they have been going through much trouble and hard times, they have mixed their wonderful joy with their deep poverty, and the result has been an overflow of giving to others. [3]They gave not only what they could afford, but far more; and I can testify that they did it because they wanted to, and not because of nagging on my part. [4]They begged us to take the money so that they could share in the joy of helping the Christians in Jerusalem. [5]Best of all, they went beyond our highest hopes, for their first action was to dedicate themselves to the Lord and to us, for whatever directions God might give to them through us. [16]I am thankful to God that he has given Titus the same real concern for you that I have. [17]He is glad to follow my suggestion that he visit you again—but I think he would have come anyway, for he is very eager to see you! [18]I am sending another well-known brother with him, who is highly praised as a preacher of the Good News in all the churches.

2 Cor 12:20. For I am afraid that when I come to visit you I won't like what I find, and then you won't like the way I will have to act. . . . [21]Yes, I am afraid that when I come God will humble me before you and I will be sad and mourn because many of you who have sinned became sinners and don't even care about the wicked, impure things you have done.

Eph 4:26. If you are angry, don't sin by nursing your grudge. Don't let the sun go down with you still angry—get over it quickly.

Phil 1:14. And because of my imprisonment many of the Christians here seem to have lost their fear of chains! Somehow my patience has encouraged them and they have become more and more bold in telling others about Christ. *vs.* 12–18.

Phil 2:22. But you know Timothy. He has been just like a son to me in helping me preach the Good News. [26]Now I am sending him home again, for he has been homesick for all of you and upset because you heard that he was ill. [30]For he risked his life for the work of Christ and was at the point of death while trying to do for me the things you couldn't do because you were far away. 1 Cor 16:10.

Phil 4:3. And I ask you, my true teammate, to help these women, for they worked side by side with me in telling the Good News to others; and they worked with Clement, too, and the rest of my fellow workers whose names are written in the Book of Life.

Col 4:7. Tychicus, our much loved brother, will tell you how I am getting along. He is a hard worker and serves the Lord with me. [8]I have sent him on this special trip just to see how you are, and to comfort and encourage you. [9]I am also sending Onesimus, a faithful and much loved brother, one of your own people. He and Tychicus will give you all the latest news. [10]Aristarchus, who is with me here as a prisoner, sends you his love, and so does Mark, a relative of Barnabas. And as I said before, give Mark a hearty welcome if he comes your way. [11]Jesus Justus also sends his love. These are the only Jewish Christians working with me here, and what a comfort they have been! Col 1:7; Eph 6:21.

1 Thess 1:2. We always thank God for you and pray for you constantly. [3]We never forget your loving deeds as we talk to our God and Father about you, and your strong faith and steady looking forward to the return of our Lord Jesus Christ. [4]We know that God has chosen you, dear brothers, much beloved of God. [5]For when we brought you the Good News, it was not just meaningless chatter to you; no, you listened with great interest. What we told you produced a powerful effect upon you, for the Holy Spirit gave you great and full assurance that what we said was true. And you know how our very lives were further proof to you of the truth of our message. [6]So you became our followers and the Lord's; for you received our message with joy from the Holy Spirit in spite of the trials and sorrows it brought you. [7]Then you yourselves be-

came an example to all the other Christians in Greece. [8]And now the Word of the Lord has spread out from you to others everywhere, far beyond your boundaries, for wherever we go we find people telling us about your remarkable faith in God.

1 Thess 3:1. Finally, when I could stand it no longer, I decided to stay alone in Athens [2]and send Timothy, our brother and fellow worker, God's minister, to visit you to strengthen your faith and encourage you.

2 Pet 1:12. I plan to keep on reminding you of these things even though you already know them and are really getting along quite well! [13, 14]. . . . As long as I am still here I intend to keep sending these reminders to you, [15]hoping to impress them so clearly upon you that you will remember them long after I have gone.

2 Pet 2:4. For God did not spare even the angels who sinned, but threw them into hell, chained in gloomy caves and darkness until the judgment day. [5]And he did not spare any of the people who lived in ancient times before the flood except Noah, the one man who spoke up for God, and his family of seven. At that time God completely destroyed the whole world of ungodly men with the vast flood.

3 Jn 4. I have no greater joy than to hear such things about my children. [5]Dear friend, you are doing a good work for God in taking care of the traveling teachers and missionaries who are passing through. [6]They have told the church here of your friendship and your loving deeds. I am glad when you send them on their way with a generous gift. [7]For they are traveling for the Lord, and take neither food, clothing, shelter, nor money from those who are not Christians, even though they have preached to them.

Jude 1:3. Dearly loved friends, I had been planning to write you some thoughts about the salvation God has given us, but now I find I must write of something else instead, urging you to stoutly defend the truth which God gave, once for all, to his people to keep without change through the years.

Rev 3:19. I continually discipline and punish everyone I love; so I must punish you, unless you turn from your indifference and become enthusiastic about the things of God.

INSTANCES OF. Moses, Ex 2:12; 11:8; 32:19, 20. Phinehas, Num 25:7–13; Ps 106:30. Joshua, Num 11:27–29; Josh 7:6; 8:28, 29. Gideon, Judg 6:11–32. Jephthah, Judg 11:30, 31, 34–39. Samuel, 1 Sam 12:23; 15:11, 35; 16:1. Saul, 1 Sam 14:38–44. David, 2 Sam 6; 7:2; 8:11, 12. Elijah, 1 Kgs 19:10. Obadiah, 1 Kgs 18:3, 4. Joash, 2 Kgs 12:2–16. Jehu, 2 Kgs 9; 10. Jehoiada, 2 Kgs 11:4–17; 2 Chron 23:1–17. Asa, 1 Kgs 15:11–15; 2 Chron 14:1–5, 15. Jehoshaphat, 2 Chron 17:3–10; 19. Hezekiah, 2 Chron 30; 31; Isa 37:1. Josiah, 2 Kgs 22; 23; 2 Chron 34:3–7, 29–33. Priests, 1 Chron 9:13; Ezra 8:17, 18. Ezra, Ezra 7:10; 9; 10. Nehemiah, Neh 4; 5; 8; 13:7–9, 15–28. Jeremiah, Jer 25:2–4. Shepherds, Lk 2:17, 18. Anna, Lk 2:38. Andrew and Philip, Jn 1:41–46. Two blind men proclaiming the miracle of healing, contrary to the warning of Jesus, Mt 9:30, 31. The restored leper, Mk 1:43–45. The healed deaf mute, Mk 7:36. Peter rebuking Jesus, Mt 16:22. Samaritan woman, Jn 4:28–30, 39. Peter, Acts 2:14–40; 3:12–26. John, see *John the Baptist.* Paul and Barnabas, Acts 11:22–26; 14:14, 15. Phoebe, Rom 16:1, 2. Ephesians, Rev 2:2, 3, 6.

See *Jesus, Zeal of;* also *Zeal, Exemplified by Paul,* below.

EXEMPLIFIED BY PAUL. Acts 9:20. And went at once to the synagogue to tell everyone there the Good News about Jesus—that he is indeed the Son of God! *vs.* 20–29.

Acts 14:22. Where they helped the believers to grow in love for God and each other. They encouraged them to continue in the faith in spite of all the persecution, reminding them that they must enter into the Kingdom of God through many tribulations. *vs.* 1–28.

Acts 15:40, 41. Paul chose Silas and, with the blessing of the believers, left for Syria and Cilicia, to encourage the churches there. *vs.* 30–36.

Acts 16:31. They replied, "Believe on the Lord Jesus and you will be saved, and your entire household." [32]Then they told him and all his household the Good News from the Lord. *vs.* 10, 13, 17.

Acts 17:2. As was Paul's custom, he went there to preach, and for three Sabbaths in a row he opened the Scriptures to the people, [3]explaining the prophecies about the sufferings of the Messiah and his coming back to life, and proving that Jesus is the Messiah. [16]While Paul was waiting for them in Athens, he was deeply troubled by all the idols he saw everywhere throughout the city. [17]He went to the synagogue for discussions with the Jews and the devout Gentiles, and spoke daily in the public square to all who happened to be there. *vs.* 22–31.

Acts 18:5. Paul spent his full time preaching and testifying to the Jews that Jesus is the Messiah. [6]But when the Jews opposed him and blasphemed, hurling abuse at Jesus, Paul shook off the dust from his robe and said, "Your blood be upon your own heads—I am innocent—from now on I will preach to the Gentiles." *vs.* 4, 19, 23; Acts 13:16–52.

Acts 20:18. . . . You men know that from the day I set foot in Turkey until now [19]I have done the Lord's work humbly—yes, and with tears—and have faced grave danger from the plots of the Jews against my life. [20]Yet I never shrank from telling you the truth, either publicly or in your homes. [21]I have had one message for Jews and Gentiles alike—the necessity of turning from sin to God through faith in our Lord Jesus Christ. [22]And now I am going to Jerusalem, drawn there irresistibly by the Holy Spirit, not knowing what awaits me, [23]except that the Holy Spirit has told me in city after city that jail and suffering lie ahead. [24]But life is worth nothing unless I use it for doing the work assigned me by the Lord Jesus—the work of telling others the Good News about God's mighty kindness and love. [26]Let me say plainly that no man's blood can be laid at my door, [27]for I didn't shrink from declaring all God's message to you. [31]Watch out! Remember the three years I was with you—my constant watchcare over you night and day and my many tears for you. [33]I have never been hungry for money or fine clothing—[34]you know that these hands of mine worked to pay my own way and even to supply the needs of those who were with me. *vs.* 7, 25; Acts 19:8–10, 21; 21:13.

Acts 24:25. And as he reasoned with them about righteousness and self-control and the judgment to come. *vs.* 14–25.

Acts 26:19. "I was not disobedient to that vision from heaven! [20]I preached first to those in Damascus, then in Jerusalem and through Judea, and also to the Gentiles that all must forsake their sins and turn to God—and prove their repentance by doing good deeds. [22]But God protected me so that I am still alive today to tell these facts to everyone, both great and small. I teach nothing except what the prophets and Moses said—[23]that the Messiah would suffer, and be the First to rise from the dead, to bring light to Jews and Gentiles alike." [29]And Paul replied, "Would to God that whether my arguments are trivial or strong, both you and everyone here in this audience might become the same as I am, except for these chains." *vs.* 1–29.

Acts 28:23. So a time was set and on that day large numbers came to his house. He told them about the Kingdom of God and taught them about Jesus from the Scriptures—from the five books of Moses and the books of prophecy. He began lecturing in the morning and went on into the evening! [30]Paul lived for the next two years in his rented house and welcomed all who visited him, [31]telling them with all boldness about the Kingdom of God and about the Lord Jesus Christ; and no one tried to stop him. *vs.* 24–28.

Rom 1:1. This letter is from Paul, Jesus Christ's slave, chosen to be a missionary, and sent out to preach God's Good News. [14]For I owe a great debt to you and to everyone else, both to civilized people and uncivilized alike; yes, to the educated and uneducated alike. [15]So, to the fullest extent of my ability, I am ready to come also to you in Rome to preach God's Good News. *vs.* 9–13.

Rom 9:1, 2, 3. Oh, Israel, my people! Oh, my Jewish brothers! How I long for you to come to Christ. My heart is heavy within me and I grieve bitterly day and night because of you. Christ knows and the Holy Spirit knows that it is no mere pretense when I say that I would be willing to be forever damned if that would save you.

Rom 10:1. Dear brothers, the longing of my heart and my prayer is that the Jewish people might be saved. Rom 11:13, 14.

Rom 15:19. In this way I have preached the full Gospel of Christ all the way from Jerusalem clear over into Illyricum. [20]But all the while my ambition has been to go still farther, preaching where the name of Christ has never yet been heard, rather than where a church has already been started by someone else. *vs.* 15–32; 2 Cor 10:14–16.

1 Cor 1:17. For Christ didn't send me to baptize, but to preach the Gospel; and even my preaching sounds poor, for I do not fill my sermons with profound words and high sounding ideas, for fear of diluting the mighty power there is in the simple message of the cross of Christ. [23]So when we preach about Christ dying to save them, the Jews are offended and the Gentiles say it's all nonsense.

1 Cor 2:1. Dear brothers, even when I first came to you I didn't use lofty words and brilliant ideas to tell you God's message. [2]For I decided that I would speak only of Jesus Christ and his death on the cross. [3]I came to you in weakness—timid and trembling. [4]And my preaching was very plain, not with a lot of oratory and human wisdom, but the Holy Spirit's power was in my words, proving to those who heard them that the message was from God. [13]In telling you about these gifts we have even used the very words given to us by the Holy Spirit, not words that we as men might choose. So we use the Holy Spirit's words to explain the Holy Spirit's facts. *vs.* 6, 7.

1 Cor 3:1. Dear brothers, I have been talking to you as though you were still just babies in the Christian life, who are not following the Lord, but your own desires; I cannot talk to you as I would to healthy Christians, who are filled with the Spirit. [2]I have had to feed you with milk and not with solid food, because you couldn't digest anything stronger. And even now you still have to be fed on milk. *vs.* 5–7.

1 Cor 4:12. We have worked wearily with our hands to earn our living. We have blessed those who cursed us. We have been patient with those who injured us. [13]We have replied quietly when evil things have been said about us. Yet right up to the present moment we are like dirt under foot, like garbage. *vs.* 1–21.

1 Cor 9:16. For just preaching the Gospel isn't any special credit to me—I couldn't keep from preaching it if I wanted to. I would be utterly miserable. Woe unto me if I don't. [18]Under this circumstance, what is my pay? It is the special joy I get from preaching the Good News without expense to anyone, never demanding my rights. [19]And this has a real advantage: I am not bound to obey anyone just because he pays my salary; yet I have freely and happily become a servant of any and all so that I can win them to Christ. [23]I do this to get the Gospel to them. [27]Like an athlete I punish my body, treating it roughly, training it to do what it should, not what it wants to. Otherwise I fear that after enlisting others for the race, I myself might be declared unfit and ordered to stand aside. *vs.* 12, 15, 17, 20, 21.

1 Cor 10:33. I try to please everyone in everything I do, not doing what I like or what is best for me, but what is best for them, so that they may be saved.

1 Cor 11:1. And you should follow my example, just as I follow Christ's.

1 Cor 13:1. If I had the gift of being able to speak in other languages without learning them, and could speak in every language there is in all of

heaven and earth, but didn't love others, I would only be making noise.

1 Cor 15:3. I passed on to you right from the first what had been told to me, that Christ died for our sins just as the Scriptures said he would. [10]But whatever I am now it is all because God poured out such kindness and grace upon me—and not without results: for I have worked harder than all the other apostles, yet actually I wasn't doing it, but God working in me, to bless me. [11]It makes no difference who worked the hardest, I or they; the important thing is that we preached the Gospel to you, and you believed it. [31]For it is a fact that I face death daily; that is as true as my pride in your growth in the Lord. *vs.* 1–32.

2 Cor 1:12. We are so glad that we can say with utter honesty that in all our dealings we have been pure and sincere, quietly depending upon the Lord for his help, and not on our own skills. And that is even more true, if possible, about the way we have acted toward you. *vs.* 15–19, 24.

2 Cor 2:17. Only those who, like ourselves, are men of integrity, sent by God, speaking with Christ's power, with God's eye upon us. We are not like those hucksters—and there are many of them—whose idea in getting out the Gospel is to make a good living out of it. *vs.* 12–16.

2 Cor 3:6. He is the one who has helped us tell others about his new agreement to save them. We do not tell them that they must obey every law of God or die; but we tell them there is life for them from the Holy Spirit. The old way, trying to be saved by keeping the Ten Commandments, ends in death; in the new way, the Holy Spirit gives them life. [12]Since we know that this new glory will never go away, we can preach with great boldness.

2 Cor 4:1. It is God himself, in his mercy, who has given us this wonderful work (of telling his Good News to others), and so we never give up. [2]We do not try to trick people into believing—we are not interested in fooling anyone. We never try to get anyone to believe that the Bible teaches what it doesn't. All such shameful methods we forego. We stand in the presence of God as we speak and so we tell the truth, as all who know us will agree. [5]We don't go around preaching about ourselves, but about Christ Jesus as Lord. All we say of ourselves is that we are your slaves because of what Jesus has done for us. [13]We boldly say what we believe (trusting God to care for us), just as the Psalm writer did when he said, "I believe and therefore I speak." *vs.* 8–15.

2 Cor 5:11. It is because of this solemn fear of the Lord, which is ever present in our minds, that we work so hard to win others. God knows our hearts, that they are pure in this matter, and I hope that, deep within, you really know it too. [13, 14]Are we insane (to say such things about ourselves)? If so, it is to bring glory to God. And if we are in our right minds, it is for your benefit. Whatever we do, it is certainly not for our own profit, but because Christ's love controls us now. Since we believe that Christ died for all of us, we should also believe that we have died to the old life we used to live. [20]We are Christ's ambassadors. God is using us to speak to you: we beg you, as though Christ himself were here pleading with you, receive the love he offers you—be reconciled to God. *v.* 18.

2 Cor 6:3. We try to live in such a way that no one will ever be offended or kept back from finding the Lord by the way we act, so that no one can find fault with us and blame it on the Lord. [4]In fact, in everything we do we try to show that we are true ministers of God. We patiently endure suffering and hardship and trouble of every kind. [5]We have been beaten, put in jail, faced angry mobs, worked to exhaustion, stayed awake through sleepless nights of watching, and gone without food. [6]We have proved ourselves to be what we claim by our wholesome lives and by our understanding of the Gospel and by our patience. We have been kind and truly loving and filled with the Holy Spirit. [7]We have been truthful, with God's power helping us in all we do. All of the godly man's arsenal—weapons of defense, and weapons of attack—have been ours. *vs.* 8–10.

2 Cor 7:2. Please open your hearts to us again, for not one of you has suffered any wrong from us. Not one of you was led astray. We have cheated no one nor taken advantage of anyone.

2 Cor 10:3. It is true that I am an ordinary, weak human being, but I don't use human plans and methods to win my battles.

2 Cor 11:9. And when that was gone and I was getting hungry I still didn't ask you for anything, for the Christians from Macedonia brought me another gift. I have never yet asked you for one cent, and I never will. *vs.* 7, 12.

[22]They brag that they are Hebrews, do they? Well, so am I. And they say that they are Israelites, God's chosen people? So am I. And they are descendants of Abraham? Well, I am too. [23]They say they serve Christ? But I have served him far more! (Have I gone mad to boast like this?) I have worked harder, been put in jail oftener, been whipped times without number, and faced death again and again and again. [24]Five different times the Jews gave me their terrible thirty-nine lashes. [25]Three times I was beaten with rods. Once I was stoned. Three times I was shipwrecked. Once I was in the open sea all night and the whole next day. [26]I have traveled many weary miles and have been often in great danger from flooded rivers, and from robbers, and from my own people, the Jews, as well as from the hands of the Gentiles. I have faced grave dangers from mobs in the cities and from death in the deserts and in the stormy seas and from men who claim to be brothers in Christ but are not. [27]I have lived with weariness and pain and sleepless nights. Often I have been hungry and thirsty and have gone without food; often I have shivered with cold, without enough clothing to keep me warm. [28]Then, besides all this, I have the constant worry of how the churches are getting along: [29]Who makes a mistake and I do not feel his sadness? Who falls without my longing to help

him? Who is spiritually hurt without my fury rising against the one who hurt him? [30]But if I must brag, I would rather brag about the things that show how weak I am. [31]God, the Father of our Lord Jesus Christ, who is to be praised forever and ever, knows I tell the truth. [32]For instance, in Damascus the governor under King Aretas kept guards at the city gates to catch me; [33]but I was let down by rope and basket from a hole in the city wall, and so I got away! (What popularity!)

2 Cor 12:10. Since I know it is all for Christ's good, I am quite happy about "the thorn," and about insults and hardships, persecutions and difficulties; for when I am weak, then I am strong—the less I have, the more I depend on him. [14]And it is still not going to cost you anything, for I don't want your money. I want *you!* . . . . [15]I am glad to give you myself and all I have for your spiritual good, even though it seems that the more I love you, the less you love me. [21]Yes, I am afraid that when I come God will humble me before you and I will be sad and mourn because many of you who have sinned became sinners and don't even care about the wicked, impure things you have done. *vs.* 17–19.

2 Cor 13:8. Our responsibility is to encourage the right at all times, not to hope for evil. *vs.* 6–9.

Gal 1:10. You can see that I am not trying to please you by sweet talk and flattery; no, I am trying to please God. If I were still trying to please men I could not be Christ's servant. [15]For even before I was born God had chosen me to be his, and called me—what kindness and grace—[16]to reveal his Son within me so that I could go to the Gentiles and show them the Good News about Jesus. When all this happened to me I didn't go at once and talk it over with anyone else.

Gal 2:2. I went there with definite orders from God to confer with the brothers there about the message I was preaching to the Gentiles. I talked privately to the leaders of the church so that they would all understand just what I had been teaching and, I hoped, agree that it was right. Gal 3:1.

Gal 4:19. Oh, my children, how you are hurting me! I am once again suffering for you the pains of a mother waiting for her child to be born—longing for the time when you will finally be filled with Christ. *v.* 11.

Gal 5:11. Some people even say that I myself am preaching that circumcision and Jewish laws are necessary to the plan of salvation. Well, if I preached that, I would be persecuted no more—for that message doesn't offend anyone.

Eph 6:20. I am in chains now for preaching this message from God. But pray that I will keep on speaking out boldly for him even here in prison, as I should. *v.* 17. Phil 1:16, 17; 4:11, 12, 17.

Phil 1:18. But whatever their motive for doing it, the fact remains that the Good News about Christ is being preached and I am glad. [20]For I live in eager expectation and hope that I will never do anything that will cause me to be ashamed of myself but that I will always be ready to speak out boldly for Christ while I am going through all these trials here, just as I have in the past; and that I will always be an honor to Christ, whether I live or whether I must die. [24]But the fact is that I can be of more help to you by staying! [25]Yes, I am still needed down here and so I feel certain I will be staying on earth a little longer, to help you grow and become happy in your faith. [27]But whatever happens to me, remember always to live as Christians should, so that, whether I ever see you again or not, I will keep on hearing good reports that you are standing side by side with one strong purpose—to tell the Good News. *vs.* 22, 23; Phil 2:16, 17.

Phil 3:4. Yet if anyone ever had reason to hope that he could save himself, it would be I. If others could be saved by what they are, certainly I could! [5]For I went through the Jewish initiation ceremony when I was eight days old, having been born into a pure-blooded Jewish home that was a branch of the old original Benjamin family. So I was a real Jew if there ever was one! What's more, I was a member of the Pharisees who demand the strictest obedience to every Jewish law and custom. [6]And sincere? Yes, so much so that I greatly persecuted the church; and I tried to obey every Jewish rule and regulation right down to the very last point. [7]But all these things that I once thought very worthwhile—now I've thrown them all away so that I can put my trust and hope in Christ alone. [8]Yes, everything else is worthless when compared with the priceless gain of knowing Christ Jesus my Lord. I have put aside all else, counting it worth less than nothing, in order that I can have Christ, [9]and become one with him, no longer counting on being saved by being good enough or by obeying God's laws, but by trusting Christ to save me; for God's way of making us right with himself depends on faith—counting on Christ alone. [10]Now I have given up everything else—I have found it to be the only way to really know Christ and to experience the mighty power that brought him back to life again, and to find out what it means to suffer and to die with him. [11]So, whatever it takes, I will be one who lives in the fresh newness of life of those who are alive from the dead. [12]I don't mean to say I am perfect. I haven't learned all I should even yet, but I keep working toward that day when I will finally be all that Christ saved me for and wants me to be. [13]No, dear brothers, I am still not all I should be but I am bringing all my energies to bear on this one thing: Forgetting the past and looking forward to what lies ahead, [14]I strain to reach the end of the race and receive the prize for which God is calling us up to heaven because of what Christ Jesus did for us. [15]I hope all of you who are mature Christians will see eye-to-eye with me on these things, and if you disagree on some point, I believe that God will make it plain to you—[16]if you fully obey the truth you have.

Col 1:28. So everywhere we go we talk about Christ to all who will listen, warning them and teaching them as well as we know how. We want to be able to present each one to God, perfect because of what Christ has done for each of them. [29]This is my work, and I can do it only because Christ's mighty energy is at work within me. *v.* 24.

Col 2:1. I wish you could know how much I have struggled in prayer for you and for the church in Laodicea, and for my many other friends who have never known me personally.

1 Thess 1:5. And you know how our very lives were further proof to you of the truth of our message. [6]So you became our followers and the Lord's.

1 Thess 2:2. You know how badly we had been treated at Philippi just before we came to you, and how much we suffered there. Yet God gave us the courage to boldly repeat the same message to you, even though we were surrounded by enemies. [3]So you can see that we were not preaching with any false motives or evil purposes in mind; we were perfectly straightforward and sincere. [4]For we speak as messengers from God, trusted by him to tell the truth; we change his message not one bit to suit the taste of those who hear it; for we serve God alone, who examines our hearts' deepest thoughts. [5]Never once did we try to win you with flattery, as you very well know, and God knows we were not just pretending to be your friends so that you would give us money! [6]As for praise, we have never asked for it from you or anyone else, although as apostles of Christ we certainly had a right to some honor from you. [8]We loved you dearly—so dearly that we gave you not only God's message, but our own lives too. [9]Don't you remember, dear brothers, how hard we worked among you? Night and day we toiled and sweated to earn enough to live on so that our expenses would not be a burden to anyone there, as we preached God's Good News among you. [10]You yourselves are our witnesses—as is God—that we have been pure and honest and faultless toward every one of you. [11]We talked to you as a father to his own children—don't you remember?—pleading with you, encouraging you. 2 Tim 1:3, 7, 11–13.

2 Thess 3:7. For you well know that you ought to follow our example: you never saw us loafing; [8]we never accepted food from anyone without buying it; we worked hard day and night for the money we needed to live on, in order that we would not be a burden to any of you. [9]It wasn't that we didn't have the right to ask you to feed us, but we wanted to show you, firsthand, how you should work for your living. Phil 3:17.

1 Tim 4:10. We work hard and suffer much in order that people will believe it, for our hope is in the living God who died for all. 2 Tim 2:9, 10.

2 Tim 3:10. You know what I believe and the way I live and what I want. You know my faith in Christ and how I have suffered. You know my love for you, and my patience. [11]You know how many troubles I have had as a result of my preaching the Good News. You know about all that was done to me while I was visiting in Antioch, Iconium and Lystra, but the Lord delivered me.

Heb 13:18. Pray for us, for our conscience is clear and we want to keep it that way.

WITHOUT KNOWLEDGE. Eccl 7:16. So don't be too good or too wise! Why destroy yourself?

Mt 8:19. Just then one of the Jewish religious teachers said to him, "Teacher, I will follow you no matter where you go!" [20]But Jesus said, "Foxes have dens and birds have nests, but I, the Messiah, have no home of my own—no place to lay my head." Lk 9:57, 58.

Jn 16:2. For you will be excommunicated from the synagogues, and indeed the time is coming when those who kill you will think they are doing God a service.

Acts 21:20. They praised God but then said, "You know, dear brother, how many thousands of Jews have also believed, and they are all very insistent that Jewish believers must continue to follow the Jewish traditions and customs."

Rom 10:2. I know what enthusiasm they have for the honor of God, but it is misdirected zeal. [3]For they don't understand that Christ has died to make them right with God. Instead they are trying to make themselves good enough to gain God's favor by keeping the Jewish laws and customs.

Gal 1:13. You know what I was like when I followed the Jewish religion—how I went after the Christians mercilessly, hunting them down and doing my best to get rid of them all. [14]I was one of the most religious Jews of my own age in the whole country, and tried as hard as I possibly could to follow all the old, traditional rules of my religion.

Gal 4:17. Those false teachers who are so anxious to win your favor are not doing it for your good. What they are trying to do is to shut you off from me so that you will pay more attention to them.

Phil 1:15. Some, of course, are preaching the Good News because they are jealous of the way God has used me. They want reputations as fearless preachers! But others have purer motives, [16, 17]preaching because they love me, for they know that the Lord has brought me here to use me to defend the Truth. And some preach to make me jealous, thinking that their success will add to my sorrows here in jail! [18]But whatever their motive for doing it, the fact remains that the Good News about Christ is being preached and I am glad.

IN PUNISHING THE WICKED. Moses and Levites, Ex 32:20, 26–29; Phinehas, Num 25:10–13; Ps 106:30, 31. Israelites, Josh 22:11–20; Judg 20. Samuel, 1 Sam 15:33. David, 2 Sam 1:14; 4:9–12. Elijah, 1 Kgs 18:40. Jehu, 2 Kgs 10:15–28. Jehoiada, 2 Kgs 11:18. Josiah, 2 Kgs 23:20.

IN REPROVING INIQUITY. See *Reproof, Faithfulness in.*

ZEALOT See *Simon, 2.*

ZEBADIAH 1. Two Benjaminites, 1 Chron 8:15–18.

2. An Israelite who joined David at Ziklag, 1 Chron 12:3–7.

3. A Korahite Temple guard, 1 Chron 26:2, 3.

4. Son of Asahel, 1 Chron 27:7.

5. An itinerant Levite teacher, 2 Chron 17:7–9.

6. Son of Ishmael and counselor of the king, 2 Chron 19:11.

7. Descendant of Shephatiah, Ezra 8:2–14.

8. A priest who defiled himself by marrying a heathen woman, Ezra 10:20.

ZEBAH King of Midian, Judg 8:5–21; Ps 83: 11.

ZEBEDEE Father of James and John, Mt 4: 21; 20:20; 27:56; Mk 1:20.

ZEBIDAH Wife of Josiah, king of Judah, 2 Kgs 23:36, 37.

ZEBINA Son of Nebo, Ezra 10:43.

ZEBOIIM One of the cities in the valley of Siddim, Gen 10:15–19; 14:2, 3, 9; Deut 29:23; Hos 11: 8.

ZEBOIM A city and valley in Benjamin, 1 Sam 13:18; Neh 11:31–35.

ZEBUL An officer of Abimelech, Judg 9:28–41.

ZEBULUN 1. Son of Jacob and Leah, Gen 30:20; 35:23; 46:8–14; 49:13; Ex 1:1–3; 1 Chron 2:1. Descendants of, Gen 46:8–14; Num 26:26, 27.

2. Tribe of. Place of, in march and camp, Num 2:3–31; 10:14, 16. Territory awarded to, Gen 49:13; Josh 19:10–16; Mt 4:12, 13. Indigenous inhabitants of the territory of, not expelled, Judg 1:30. Levitical cities of, Josh 21:34, 35; 1 Chron 6:77. Moses' blessing on, Deut 33:18, 19. Loyalty of, in resisting the enemies of Israel: with Barak against Sisera, Judg 4:6, 10; 5:13, 14, 18; with Gideon against the Midianites, Judg 6:35; with David when made king over Israel, 1 Chron 12:24–40. Joins with Hezekiah in renewing the Passover, 2 Chron 30:11, 17–19. Conquest of, by Tiglath-pileser; taken captive to Assyria, 2 Kgs 15:29; Isa 9:1. Jesus stayed in the land of, Mt 4:12–16. Twelve thousand sealed, Rev 7:8. See *Israel*.

ZECHARIAH 1. King of Israel, son of Jeroboam, and last of the house of Jehu, 2 Kgs 14:29; 15:8–12.

2. Grandfather of Hezekiah, 2 Kgs 18:1–3; 2 Chron 29:1.

3. A Reubenite, 1 Chron 5:7, 8.

4. Three Levites in the days of David, 1 Chron 9:21; 15:18, 20, 24; 16:5; 26:2, 3, 14, 15.

5. A Benjaminite, 1 Chron 9:35–37. Called *Zecher* in 1 Chron 8:30–32.

6. Two Kohathites, 1 Chron 24:24, 25; 2 Chron 34:12.

7. Temple guard, 1 Chron 26:11.

8. Father of Iddo, 1 Chron 27:16–22.

9. A government official sent by Jehoshaphat along with priests and Levites to teach in the cities, 2 Chron 17:7–9.

10. A Levite, and father of Jahaziel, 2 Chron 20: 14.

11. Son of Jehoshaphat, 2 Chron 21:2.

12. High priest, and son of Jehoiada. Put to death for prophesying against Jerusalem, 2 Chron 24: 20–22, 25; Mt 23:35; Lk 11:51.

13. A prophet in the reign of Uzziah, 2 Chron 26: 5.

14. A Levite in the reign of Hezekiah, 2 Chron 29:12–14.

15. A ruler of the Temple, 2 Chron 35:8.

16. The prophet. Son of Berechiah, Zech 1:1. Prophesied in the reign of Darius, Ezra 4:24; 5:1, 2; 6:14; Zech 1:1, 7; 7:1. Probably the priest mentioned in Neh 12:12–21.

17. Two or possibly three leaders who returned with Ezra, Ezra 8:3, 11, 16.

18. Name of five different Jews after the captivity, Ezra 10:26; Neh 8:1–5; 11:4–6, 10–14.

19. Two priests who played the trumpet at the dedication of the wall, Neh 12:35, 36, 40, 41.

20. Perhaps identical with 13, above, Isa 8:2.

ZEDAD A place on the northern boundary of Palestine, Num 34:7–9; Ezk 47:15.

ZEDEKIAH 1. Made king of Judah by Nebuchadnezzar, 2 Kgs 24:17–19; 1 Chron 3:15; 2 Chron 36:10; Jer 37:1. Rebels against Nebuchadnezzar, 2 Kgs 24:20; 2 Chron 36:13; Jer 52:3; Ezk 17:12–21. Forms an alliance with the king of Egypt, Ezk 17:11–18. The allegiance denounced by Jeremiah, 2 Chron 36:12; Jer 21; 24:8–10; 27:12–22; 32:3–5; 34; 37:7–10, 17; 38:14–28; by Ezekiel, Ezk 12: 10–16; 17:12–21. Imprisons Jeremiah because of his prophecies, Jer 32:2, 3; 37:15–21; 38:5–28. Seeks the intercession of Jeremiah with God in his behalf, Jer 21:1, 2; 37:3; 38:14–27. Evil reign of, 2 Kgs 24:18–20; 2 Chron 36:12, 13; Jer 37:2; 38:5, 19, 24–26; 52:2. Nebuchadnezzar destroys the city and Temple, takes him captive to Babylon, blinds his eyes, kills his sons, 2 Kgs 25:1–10; 2 Chron 36:17–20; Jer 1:3; 32:1, 2; 39:1–10; 51:59; 52:4–30.

2. Son of Jehoiakim, 1 Chron 3:16.

3. A priest and leader of the exiles who returned to Jerusalem, Neh 10:1–8.

4. A false prophet, Jer 29:21–23.

5. A leader of Judah, Jer 36:12.

6. A false prophet. Prophesies to Ahab victory over the Syrians, instead of defeat, 1 Kgs 22:11; 2 Chron 18:10. Slaps Micaiah, the true prophet, 1 Kgs 22:24; 2 Chron 18:23.

ZEEB A general of the army of Midian, Judg 7:25; 8:2, 3; Ps 83:11.

ZELAH A city in Benjamin, Josh 18:21–28.

ZELEK An Ammonite, 2 Sam 23:24–39; 1 Chron 11:26–47.

ZELOPHEHAD Grandson of Gilead. His daughters petition for his inheritance, Num 27:1–11; 36; Josh 17:3–6; 1 Chron 7:15.

ZELZAH A city of Benjamin, 1 Sam 10:2.

ZEMARAIM A mountain in Ephraim, 2 Chron 13:4.

ZEMARITES A tribe descended from Canaan, Gen 10:15–19; 1 Chron 1:13–16.

ZEMER A place located north of Lebanon, Ezk 27:8.

ZEMIRAH A son of Becher, 1 Chron 7:8.

ZENAN A city of Judah, Josh 15:37–44.

ZENAS A Christian believer and lawyer, Tit 3:13.

ZEPHANIAH 1. A priest in the reign of Zedekiah, king of Judah. Sent by the king to Jeremiah with a message soliciting the prophet's intercession and prayers, Jer 21:1, 2. Shows Jeremiah the false prophet's letter, Jer 29:25–29. Taken to Rib-

lah and killed, 2 Kgs 25:18–21; Jer 52:24–27.
2. A Kohathite, 1 Chron 6:33–38.
3. A prophet during the reign of Josiah, Zeph 1:1.
4. Father of Josiah, Zech 6:10, 11.

ZEPHATH A Canaanite city, Judg 1:17. See *Hormah.*

ZEPHATHAH A valley west of Judah, 2 Chron 14:9, 10.

ZEPHI See *Zepho.*

ZEPHO Called also *Zephi.* Son of Eliphaz, Gen 36:10–12, 15, 16; 1 Chron 1:36.

ZEPHON Son of Gad, Num 26:15–18.

ZER A city of Naphtali, Josh 19:35–39.

ZERAH 1. Son of Reuel, Gen 36:13, 14, 17; 1 Chron 1:37.
2. Father of Jobab, Gen 36:31–39; 1 Chron 1:44.
3. Son of Judah and Tamar, Gen 38:30; 46:8–14; Num 26:19–22; 1 Chron 2:4, 6; Neh 11:24; Mt 1:3.
4. Son of Simeon, Num 26:12–14; 1 Chron 4:24.
5. A Levite, 1 Chron 6:19–21, 39–43.
6. Commander of the Ethiopian army, 2 Chron 14:9–15.

ZERAHIAH 1. An ancestor of Ezra, 1 Chron 6:4–15, 50–53; Ezra 7:1–5.
2. Father of Eli-e-ho-enai, Ezra 8:2–14.

ZERED See *Zared.*

ZEREDAH 1. A city of Ephraim, 1 Kgs 11:26.
2. A city in Manasseh, 2 Chron 4:17, 18.

ZERERAH A district of uncertain location, Judg 7:22.

ZERESH Wife of Haman, Esther 5:10–14; 6:13.

ZERETH Son of Ashhur, 1 Chron 4:7.

ZERETH-SHAHAR A city in Reuben, Josh 13:19.

ZERI Son of Jeduthun, 1 Chron 25:3.

ZEROR Father of Abiel, 1 Sam 9:1.

ZERUAH Mother of Jeroboam, 1 Kgs 11:26.

ZERUBBABEL Called also *Shesh-bazzar.* Directs the rebuilding of the altar and Temple after his return from captivity in Babylon, Ezra 3:1–8; 4:2, 3; 5:1, 2, 14–16; Hag 1:12–15. Leads the emancipated Jews back from Babylon, Ezra 1:8–11; 2; Neh 12. Appoints the Levites to inaugurate the rebuilding of the Temple, Ezra 3:1–8. Prophecies relating to, Hag 2:2; Zech 4:6–10. An ancestor of Jesus, Mt 1:12; Lk 3:23–38.

ZERUIAH Sister, or stepsister, of David, 2 Sam 17:25; 1 Chron 2:16. Mother of three of David's great soldiers, 1 Chron 2:16; 2 Sam 2:18; 3:39; 16:9–11; 17:25.

ZETHAM Descendant of Ladan and son of Jehieli, 1 Chron 23:8, 9; 26:20–22.

ZETHAN Son of Bilhan, 1 Chron 7:10.

ZETHAR One of the seven eunuchs serving the king of Persia, Esther 1:10.

ZIA A Gadite, 1 Chron 5:13.

ZIBA Saul's servant. His loyalty to Mephibosheth, 2 Sam 9; To David, 2 Sam 16:1–4; 19:17, 26–29.

ZIBEON Son of Seir and a Hivite, Gen 36:2, 3, 20, 21, 24; 1 Chron 1:38–40.

ZIBIA A Benjaminite, 1 Chron 8:8–10.

ZIBIAH Wife of Ahaziah, 2 Kgs 12:1; 2 Chron 24:1.

ZICHRI 1. Son of Izhar, Ex 6:21.
2. Three Benjaminites, 1 Chron 8:19–21, 22–25, 26, 27.
3. A Levite, 1 Chron 9:15, 16.
4. A Levite, and father of Shelomoth, 1 Chron 26:25.
5. A Reubenite, 1 Chron 27:16–22.
6. Father of Amasiah, 2 Chron 17:16.
7. Father of Elishaphat, 2 Chron 23:1.
8. An Ephraimite, 2 Chron 28:7.
9. Father of Joel, Neh 11:7–9.
10. A priest, Neh 12:12–21.

ZIDDIM A city of Naphtali, Josh 19:35–39.

ZIDON See *Sidon.*

ZIF See *Calendar.*

ZIHA 1. One of the Nethinim, Ezra 2:43–54; Neh 7:46–56.
2. A leader of the Nethinim, Neh 11:21.

ZIKLAG A city within the territory allotted to the tribe of Judah, Josh 15:21–32. Reallotted to the tribe of Simeon, Josh 19:2–7. David lives at, 1 Sam 27:5, 6; 2 Sam 1:1; 1 Chron 12:1. Amalekites destroy, 1 Sam 30. Inhabited by the returned exiles of Judah, Neh 11:25–30.

ZILIAH Wife of Lamech, Gen 4:19, 22, 23.

ZILLETHAI 1. A Benjaminite, 1 Chron 8:19–21.
2. An officer of Manasseh, 1 Chron 12:20.

ZILPAH Leah's servant girl, Gen 29:24. Mother of Gad and Asher by Jacob, Gen 30:9–13; 35:26; 37:2; 46:18.

ZIMARAIM A city of Benjamin, Josh 18:21–28.

ZIMMAH A Gershonite Levite, 1 Chron 6:19–21, 39–43; 2 Chron 29:12–14.

ZIMRAN Son of Abraham, Gen 25:1, 2; 1 Chron 1:32.

ZIMRI 1. A leader of Simeon, Num 25:6–8, 14.
2. King of Israel, 1 Kgs 16:9–20; 2 Kgs 9:31.
3. Son of Zerah, 1 Chron 2:6.
4. A Benjaminite, 1 Chron 8:36; 9:42.
5. An unknown place, Jer 25:25.

ZIN, WILDERNESS OF A desert south of Judah, Num 13:21; 20:1; 27:14; 33:15–37; 34:3, 4; Deut 32:51; Josh 15:1–4.

ZINA See *Zizah.*

ZION Stronghold of Jerusalem. Taken from the Jebusites by David, 2 Sam 5:6–9; 1 Chron 11:5–7. Called thereafter "the city of David," 2 Sam 5:7, 9; 6:12; 1 Kgs 8:1; 1 Chron 11:5–7; 2 Chron 5:2. Ark of the Covenant placed in, 2 Sam 6:12, 16; 1 Kgs 8:1; 1 Chron 15:1, 29; 2 Chron 5:2. Removed from, to Solomon's Temple on Mount Moriah, 1 Kgs 8:1; 2 Chron 5:2; with 2 Chron 3:1.

The equivalent of Jerusalem, in such expressions as "daughter of Zion," which is used of the people of the city, Isa 52:2; 2 Kgs 19:21. Name of, applied to Jerusalem, Ps 9:11; 48:2, 11; 74:2; 87:1, 2; 132:13; Song 3:11; Isa 35:10; 52:1, 2; 62:1; Jer 31:6; 50:5; Lam 1:4; Joel 2:15; Rom 11:26. Called the city of God, Ps

87:2, 3; the City of the Lord; Isa 60:14. Restoration of, promised, Isa 52:1, 2; 59:20; Zeph 3:14, 16; Zech 2:6, 7. Name of, applied to the city of the redeemed, Heb 12:22; Rev 14:1.

See *Jerusalem.*

ZIOR a city in Judah, Josh 15:48–62.

ZIPH 1. Two cities of Judah: Josh 15:21–32; and Josh 15:48–62; 1 Sam 23:14, 15, 24, 25; 26:1; 2 Chron 11:5–10.

2. Grandson of Caleb, 1 Chron 2:42.

3. Son of Jehallelel, 1 Chron 4:16.

ZIPHAH A son of Jehallelel, 1 Chron 4:16.

ZIPHION A son of Gad, Gen 46:16, 17. Called *Zephon* in Num 26:15–18.

ZIPHRON A place in the north of Palestine, Num 34:7–9.

ZIPPOR Father of Balak, Num 22:2, 3; 23: 18–24.

ZIPPORAH Wife of Moses, Ex 2:16–22. Reproaches Moses, Ex 4:25, 26. Separates from Moses, is returned again to him by her father, Ex 18:2–6.

ZITHER A stringed musical instrument. Used in religious services, 1 Chron 13:8; 15:28; 16:5; 25:1–7.

ZIZ A pass in Judah, 2 Chron 20:16.

ZIZA 1. A Simeonite, 1 Chron 4:34–39.

2. Son of Rehoboam, 2 Chron 11:20.

ZIZAH A Gershonite, 1 Chron 23:10, 11. Called also *Zina.*

ZOAN A city in Egypt. Built seven years after Hebron in the land of Canaan, Num 13:22. Prophecies concerning, Ezk 30:14. Wise men from, were counselors of Pharaoh, Isa 19:11, 13. Rulers of, Isa 30:4.

ZOAR A city of the Moabites, near the Jordan, Gen 13:10. Territory of, Deut 34:3; Isa 15:5; Jer 48:34. King of, fought against Ched-or-laomer, Gen 14:2, 8, 9. Not destroyed with Sodom and Gomorrah, Gen 19:18–23, 30.

ZOBA See *Zobah.*

ZOBAH Called also *Zoba; Hamath-zobah.* A kingdom in the north of Palestine, 1 Sam 14:47. Conquest of, by David, 2 Sam 8:3–8, 11, 12; 1 Kgs 11:23, 24; 1 Chron 18:2–9. Its inhabitants, hired as mercenaries by the Ammonites against David, 2 Sam 10:6–19; 1 Chron 19:6–19. David writes a psalm after the conquest of, see title of Ps 60. Invaded by Solomon, 2 Chron 8:3.

ZOBEBAH A Judahite, 1 Chron 4:8.

ZODIAC Signs of, Job 9:9; 38:32.

ZOHAR 1. Father of Ephron, Gen 23:8; 25:9, 10.

2. Son of Simeon, Gen 46:8–14; Ex 6:15.

ZOHETH Son of Ishi, 1 Chron 4:20.

ZOPHAH Son of Helem, 1 Chron 7:35–37.

ZOPHAI Son of Elkanah, 1 Chron 6:25–27.

ZOPHAR One of Job's three friends, Job 2: 11; 11; 20; 42:7–9.

ZOPHIM A place on the top of Pisgah, Num 23:14.

ZORAH A city of Dan or Judah, Josh 15: 33–36; 19:41–46. The city of Samson, Judg 13:2, 3, 24, 25; 16:31. Representatives of the tribe of Dan sent from, to spy out the land they planned to conquer, Judg 18. Fortified by Rehoboam, 2 Chron 11:5–10. Resettled after the captivity, Neh 11:29.

ZUAR Father of Nethanel, Num 1:2–15; 2:3–31; 7:18–23; 10:15.

ZUPH 1. A Kohathite, 1 Sam 1:1; 1 Chron 6: 33–38.

2. A district northwest of Jerusalem, 1 Sam 9:5.

ZUR 1. A ruler of Midian, Num 25:15; 31:8; Josh 13:21.

2. A Benjaminite, 1 Chron 8:30–32; 9:35–37.

ZURIEL A Merarite, Num 3:31–35.

ZURI-SHADDAI Father of Shelumi-el, Num 1:2–15; 2:3–31; 7:36–41; 10:19.

ZUZIM See *Zamzummim.*